SCOTT®

2004 STANDARD POSTAGE STAMP CATALOGUE

ONE HUNDRED AND SIXTIETH EDITION IN SIX VOLUMES

VOLUME 1

UNITED STATES
and Affiliated Territories
UNITED NATIONS
COUNTRIES OF THE WORLD

A-B

EDITOR	James E. Kloetzel
ASSOCIATE EDITOR	William A. Jones
ASSISTANT EDITOR /NEW ISSUES & VALUING	Martin J. Frankevicz
VALUING ANALYST	Leonard J. Gellman
DESIGN MANAGER	Teresa M. Wenrick
IMAGE COORDINATOR	Nancy S. Martin
ELECTRONIC MEDIA MANAGER	Mark Kaufman
MARKETING/SALES DIRECTOR	William Fay
ADVERTISING	Renee Davis
CIRCULATION/PRODUCT PROMOTION MANAGER	Tim Wagner
EDITORIAL DIRECTOR/AMOS PRESS INC.	Michael Laurence

Released April 2003
Includes New Stamp Listings through the March, 2003 *Scott Stamp Monthly* Catalogue Update

Scott Publishing Co.

911 Vandemark Road, Sidney, OH 45365-0828
A division of AMOS PRESS, INC., publishers of *Linn's Stamp News, Coin World* and *Cars & Parts* magazine.

Table of Contents

See Volumes 2 through 6 for Countries of the World, C-Z

Volume 2: C-F
Volume 3: G-I
Volume 4: J-O
Volume 5: P-Sl
Volume 6: So-Z

Scott Publishing Mission Statement

The Scott Publishing Team exists to serve the recreational, educational and commercial hobby needs of stamp collectors and dealers.

We strive to set the industry standard for philatelic information and products by developing and providing goods that help collectors identify, value, organize and present their collections.

Quality customer service is, and will continue to be, our highest priority. We aspire toward achieving total customer satisfaction.

ISBN 0-89487-311-3

Library of Congress Card No. 2-3301

Scott Publishing Co.

SCOTT 911 VANDEMARK ROAD, SIDNEY, OHIO 45365 937-498-0802

Dear Scott Catalogue User:

An important new Scott product.

Volume 1 of the *2004 Scott Standard Postage Stamp Catalogue* ushers in a new valuing product: the Scott enhanced Valuing Supplement for important U.S. stamps. This new product will appear twice each year at the same times as Volume 1 and the U.S. Specialized catalogs, which are issued in April and October, respectively. The Valuing Supplements may be purchased either separately from, or together with, the Volume 1 and U.S. Specialized catalogs.

The 2004 Volume 1 Valuing Supplement, now available, values sound stamps in six different grades: Very Good, Fine, Fine-Very Fine, Very Fine, Extremely Fine and Superb. Each stamp is listed in the conditions noted in the Volume 1 and U.S. Specialized catalogs, starting with used, then unused without gum, unused with original gum, and mint never hinged. In all cases, the values for Very Fine stamps (or other grades, where applicable) match those in the Volume 1 listings, as they also will match the updated values in the U.S. Specialized when the second edition is published in October to coincide with that catalog.

The stamps that are valued in six different grades in the new Valuing Supplement include Scott 1-715, including booklet panes and coils (as singles, pairs and line pairs), C1-C31, E1-E14, F1, J1-J87, K1-K18, O1-O126, PR1-PR125, Q1-Q12, JQ1-JQ5, QE1-QE4a and RW1-RW69A. It's amazing how such a thin volume can contain so much information, reflecting a tremendous amount of research to establish the thousands of values contained therein, but we know that there are many collectors who will appreciate this specialized valuing information.

What about the value changes in the 2004 Volume 1?

Almost 13,500 value changes occur in this year's Volume 1. The stamps of the United States and its possessions lead the way with more than 2,300 value changes, many being in the back-of-the-book material.

Value changes for the United States are centered mostly in the rarer items, and most value changes are increases. There are many increases in the 1845-47 St. Louis "Bears" Postmaster Provisionals, Scott 11X1-11X8. However, the popular 1847 5¢ red brown Franklin, Scott 1, drops slightly to $550 used from $575 in the 2003 U.S. Specialized catalog. The 1856 12¢ red brown, Scott 12, also slips slightly, to $950 used from $1,000 last year. Otherwise, most value changes for early used or unused stamps with original gum are increases. There are some large value increases for more classic, seldom-seen errors such as double impressions and other varieties that found their way to the market in 2002.

The leader in increases for the 2004 Volume 1 U.S. listings undoubtedly is the unused coil pair of the 1908 2¢ carmine perf 12 horizontally, Scott 321. With only four expertized pairs recorded, one of the two finest sold in late 2002 for $360,000, which becomes the new catalog value for the pair, now valued in the grade of fine-very fine (as no higher grade is known).

Postal Stationery cut squares show considerable activity. Value increases include lower- and medium-valued items as well as the high-priced numbers. Positive activity also occurs in some of the higher-valued Revenue stamps.

Where's the action in the A-B countries?

For the countries of the world A-B, Australia leads the way with almost 1,600 changes, followed by Austria (almost 1,100), Albania (more than 750), and the United Nations with almost 700 value changes. All told, half of the A-B countries listed in Volume 1 have had more than 100 values changed.

Value changes for the stamps of Australia are divided between the Australian States (60 percent) and Australia proper (40 percent). New South Wales, with more than 400 changes, leads the way for the Australian States. The general trend appears to be upward; however, the changes are usually small. There are exceptions, and some stamps have moved up quite a bit, with the stamps of early Victoria from 1850-60 being an example. The 1-penny dull red imperf, Scott 1, picturing a seated Queen Victoria, climbs to $1,150 unused and $110 used in the 2004 catalogue, from $700 unused and $75 used last year.

Because of the increased use of self-adhesive Australian stamps and the corresponding decrease in the use of stamps with water-activated gum, used values for the latter are rising. A number of used stamps issued in the 1990s have had their values increased to the point where they are now the same as the mint, never-hinged values.

After Australia, other countries of the British Commonwealth with more than 200 value changes are Antigua, Barbados, Aitutaki, Barbuda, Burma and Ascension. Collectors of these and other Commonwealth countries need to check their particular countries of interest for details. However, particular note should be paid to Barbuda where startling value increases have occurred in stamps issued between 1984-86. One example is the 8-stamp Antigua set overprinted "Barbuda Mail," Scott 678-685, picturing 20th Century World Leaders. This set soars to $24 both mint, never hinged and used in the 2004 catalog, from $4.80 both ways last year.

This year, Scott valuers have carefully examined the regular stamps of Austria from 1850 to 1971, and the back-of-the-book material up to 1945. This has resulted in almost 1,100 value changes. The stamps issued prior to 1920 show a very strong upward trend. However, stamps issued between 1945-70 show a value trend that is mostly downward. We do, however, see increases in some used material issued just after WWII. The values for all mint, never-hinged military stamps are strongly higher. Many notes pertaining to imperforate stamps now show values, and most existing notes that did contain values now show increases.

Where are the editorial enhancements?

The new U.S. major numbers for the compound perf 12x10 and 10x12 issues of 1914, first introduced in the 2003 U.S. Specialized catalog, have been brought into Volume 1 of the Standard catalog. These are Scott 423A-423E, formerly Scott minor numbers 424a, 424b, 425c, 425d and 428a. In addition, the 17 perf 10 on one side error varieties, Scott 498g through 568c, have been added to Volume 1 for the first time.

U.S. color-omitted and color-missing errors are now differentiated as to cause. This new feature also was introduced in the 2003 U.S. Specialized, and is now brought forward into Volume 1. See the new section on page 31A of the introduction for an explanation of the new terminology.

In Albania, a new set has been added, Scott 1327A-1327E. This 5-stamp set issued in 1970-71 pictures industrial plants.

For Australia, the official stamp with an inverted "O.S." on the 5-pence King George V, Scott O10a, has been delisted because it is now thought to be a forgery. Three new minor double-impression varieties have been added to the stamps of Tasmania, Scott13d, 23c and 48a.

For Austria, three minors have been added to the 1919-20 issue, Scott 219-226, to identify additional perf 11.5 varieties. Two new varieties that have been added to the 2004 catalog are Scott 196b and 323b, a vertical pair imperforate between and a pair imperforate between, respectively. The definitive set issued from 1993-95 picturing scenes from monasteries has been closed and reordered to eliminate gaps in the numbering.

In Belgium, Scott Q487 has been changed to Scott 1848A because it is not a parcel post issue. Two recently issued sets from Benin, Scott 1183-1189 and 1211-1217, have been deleted because it has been determined that they were both illegal issues.

Listings for never-hinged stamps have been added after unused hinged sets throughout Volume 1, and footnotes throughout the catalog have been added or modified. See the Volume 1 Number Additions, Deletions & Changes listing on page 1090 for other additions.

Happy collecting,

James E. Kloetzel

James E. Kloetzel/Catalogue Editor

Acknowledgments

Our appreciation and gratitude go to the following individuals who have assisted us in preparing information included in the 2004 Scott Catalogues. Some helpers prefer anonymity. These individuals have generously shared their stamp knowledge with others through the medium of the Scott Catalogue.

Those who follow provided information that is in addition to the hundreds of dealer price lists and advertisements and scores of auction catalogues and realizations that were used in producing the catalogue values. It is from those noted here that we have been able to obtain information on items not normally seen in published lists and advertisements. Support from these people goes beyond data leading to catalogue values, for they also are key to editorial changes.

A special acknowledgment to Liane and Sergio Sismondo of The Classic Collector for their extraordinary assistance and knowledge sharing that has aided in the preparation of this year's Standard and Classic Specialized Catalogues.

Dr. Karl Agre
Donald R. Alexander (China Stamp Society)
A. R. Allison (Orange Free State Study Circle)
B. J. Ammel (The Nile Post)
Robert Ausubel (Great Britain Collectors Club)
Dr. H.U. Bantz
John Barone (Stamptracks)
Jack Hagop Barsoumian (International Stamp Co.)
Tim Bartshe (Philatelic Society for Greater Southern Africa)
William Batty-Smith (Sarawak Specialists' Society)
Jules K. Beck (Latin American Philatelic Society)
Roger S. Brody
Keith & Margie Brown
Mike Bush (Joseph V. Bush, Inc.)
Lawrence A. Bustillo (Suburban Stamp Inc.)
A. Bryan Camarda (University Stamp Co.)
Richard A. Champagne
Henry Chlanda
Bob Coale
Laurie Conrad
Frank D. Correl
Andrew Cronin (Canadian Society of Russian Philately)
William T. Crowe (The Philatelic Foundation)
Tony L. Crumbley (Carolina Coin & Stamp, Inc.)
Norman S. Davis
Tony Davis
Tom Derbyshire (University Stamp Co.)
John DeStefanis
Kenneth E. Diehl
Bob Dumaine (Sam Houston Duck Co.)
William S. Dunn
Esi Ebrani
Paul G. Eckman
Peter R. Feltus
Leon Finik (Loral Stamps)
Henry Fisher
Geoffrey Flack
Joseph E. Foley (Eire Philatelic Association)
Jeffrey M. Forster
Bob Genisol (Sultan Stamp Center)
Daniel E. Grau
Fred F. Gregory
Michael H. Grollnek
Harry Hagendorf
Calvet M. Hahn
Joe Hahn (Paraguay Collectors Club)
Erich E. Hamm (Philactica)
Alan Hanks
ohn B. Head
uce Hecht (Bruce L. Hecht Co.)
Robert R. Hegland
Lee H. Hill, Jr.
Harold Hite
Armen Hovsepian (ArmenStamp)
Jack R. Hughes (Fellowship of Samoa Specialists)
Philip J. Hughes (Croatian Philatelic Society)
Wilson Hulme
Kalman V. Illyefalvi (Society for Hungarian Philately)
Eric Jackson
Michael Jaffe (Michael Jaffe Stamps, Inc.)
Peter C. Jeannopoulos
Richard A. Johnson
Allan Katz (Ventura Stamp Company)
Stanford M. Katz
Lewis Kaufman
Dr. James W. Kerr
Charles F. Kezbers
Juri Kirsimagi (Estonian Philatelic Society)
Janet Klug
William V. Kriebel
John R. Lewis (The William Henry Stamp Co.)
Ulf Lindahl (Ethiopian Philatelic Society)
William A. Litle
Gary B. Little (Luxembourg Collectors Club)
Pedro Llach (Filatelia Llach, S.L.)
B. Lucas (Iran Philatelic Study Circle)
Dennis Lynch
Nick Markov (Italia Stamp Co.)
Marilyn R. Mattke
William K. McDaniel
Mark S. Miller
Allen Mintz (United Postal Stationery Society)
Chuck Q. Moo
William E. Mooz
David Mordant (Postmark and Postal History Society of Southern Africa)
Gary M. Morris (Pacific Midwest Co.)
Bruce M. Moyer (Moyer Stamps & Collectibles)
Richard H. Muller (Richard's Stamps)
James Natale
Victor Ostolaza
Dr. Everett L. Parker (St. Helena, Ascension & Tristan da Cunha Philatelic Society)
John E. Pearson (Pittwater Philatelic Service)
John Pedneault
Donald J. Peterson (International Philippine Philatelic Society)
Stanley M. Piller (Stanley M. Piller & Associates)
Todor Drumev Popov
Peter W. W. Powell
Bob Prager (Gary Posner, Inc.)
Stephen Radin (Albany Stamp Co.)
Ghassan D. Riachi
Ron Rice
Omar Rodriguez
Michael Rogers (Michael Rogers, Inc.)
Jon W. Rose
Michael Ruggiero
Frans H.A. Rummens (American Society for Netherlands Philately)
Christopher Rupp (Rupp Brothers Rare Stamps)
Mehrdad Sadri (Persiphila)
Richard H. Salz
Jacques C. Schiff, Jr. (Jacques C. Schiff, Jr., Inc.)
Bernard Seckler (Fine Arts Philatelists)
F. Burton Sellers
Charles F. Shreve (Shreves Philatelic Galleries, Inc.)
Jeff Siddiqui (Pakistan Philatelic Study Circle)
Sergio & Liane Sismondo (The Classic Collector)
Jack Solens (Armstrong Philatelics)
Christopher Smith
Ekrem Spahich (Croatian Philatelic Society)
Frits Staal
Richard Stambaugh
Frank J. Stanley, III
Richard Stark
Philip & Henry Stevens (postalstationery.com)
Mark Stucker
James F. Taff
Peter Thy (Philatelic Society for Greater Southern Africa)
Glenn Tjia (Quality Philatelics)
Scott R. Trepel (Siegel Auction Galleries, Inc.)
A. J. Ultee
Xavier Verbeck (American Belgian Philatelic Society)
Philip T. Wall
Daniel C. Warren
Richard A. Washburn
Giana Wayman (Asociacion Filatélica de Costa Rica)
William R. Weiss, Jr. (Weiss Philatelics)
Ed Wener (Indigo)
Don White (Dunedin Stamp Centre)
Kirk Wolford (Kirk's Stamp Company)
Robert F. Yacano (K-Line Philippines)
Ralph Yorio
John P. Zuckerman (Siegel Auction Galleries, Inc.)
Alfonso G. Zulueta, Jr.

Addresses, Telephone Numbers, Web Sites, E-Mail Addresses of General & Specialized Philatelic Societies

Collectors can contact the following groups for information about the philately of the areas within the scope of these societies, or inquire about membership in these groups. Aside from the general societies, we limit this list to groups that specialize in particular fields of philately, particular areas covered by the Scott Standard Postage Stamp Catalogue, and topical groups. Many more specialized philatelic societies exist than those listed below. These addresses were compiled in January 2002, and are, to the best of our knowledge, correct and current. Groups should inform the editors of address changes whenever they occur. The editors also want to hear from other such specialized groups not listed.

Unless otherwise noted all website addresses begin with http://

American Philatelic Society
PO Box 8000
State College PA 16803
Ph: (814) 237-3803
www.stamps.org
E-mail: relamb@stamps.org

American Stamp Dealers' Association
Joseph Savarese
3 School St.
Glen Cove NY 11542
Ph: (516) 759-7000
www.asdaonline.com
E-mail: asda@erols.com

International Society of Worldwide Stamp Collectors
Anthony Zollo
PO Box 150407
Lufkin TX 75915-0407
www.iswsc.org
E-mail: stamptmf@frontiernet.net

Junior Philatelists of America
Jennifer Arnold
PO Box 2625
Albany OR 97321
www.jpastamps.org
E-mail: exec.sec@jpastamps.org

Royal Philatelic Society
41 Devonshire Place
London, United Kingdom W1G 6JY

Royal Philatelic Society of Canada
PO Box 929, Station Q
Toronto, ON, Canada M4T 2P1
Ph: (888) 285-4143
www.rpsc.org
E-mail: info@rpsc.org

Groups focusing on fields or aspects found in world-wide philately (some may cover U.S. area only)

American Air Mail Society
Stephen Reinhard
PO Box 110
Mineola NY 11501
ourworld.compuserve.com/homepages/aams/
E-mail: sr1501@aol.com

American First Day Cover Society
Douglas Kelsey
PO Box 65960
Tucson AZ 85728-5960
Ph: (520) 321-0880
www.afdcs.org
E-mail: afdcs@aol.com

American Revenue Association
Eric Jackson
PO Box 728
Leesport PA 19533-0728
Ph: (610) 926-6200
www.revenuer.org
E-mail: eric@revenuer.com

American Topical Association
Paul E. Tyler
PO Box 50820
Albuquerque NM 87181-0820
Ph: (505) 323-8595
home.prcn.org/~pauld/ata/
E-mail: ATAStamps@juno.com

Errors, Freaks and Oddities Collectors Club
Jim McDevitt
PO Box 1126
Kingsland GA 31548
Ph: (912) 729-1573
E-mail: cwouscg@aol.com

Fakes and Forgeries Study Group
Anthony Torres
107 Hoover Rd.
Rochester NY 14617-3611
E-mail: ajtorres@rochester.rr.com

First Issues Collectors Club
Kurt Streepy
608 Whitethorn Way
Bloomington IN 47403
Ph: (812) 339-6229
E-mail: kstreepy@msn.com

International Philatelic Society of Joint Stamp Issues Collectors
Richard Zimmermann
124, Avenue Guy de Coubertin
Saint Remy Les Chevreuse, France
F-78470
perso.clubinternet.fr/rzimmerm/index.htm
E-mail: rzimmerm@club-internet.fr

National Duck Stamp Collectors Society
Anthony J. Monico
PO Box 43
Harleysville PA 19438-0043
www.hwcn.org/link/ndscs
E-mail: ndscs@hwcn.org

No Value Identified Club
Albert Sauvanet
Le Clos Royal B, Boulevard des Pas Enchantes
St. Sebastien-sur Loire, France 44230
E-mail: alain.vailly@irin.univ_nantes.fr

The Perfins Club
Bob Szymanski
10 Clarridge Circle
Milford MA 01757
E-mail: perfinman@attbi.com

Post Mark Collectors Club
David Proulx
7629 Homestead Drive
Baldwinsville NY 13027
E-mail: stampdance@baldcom.net

Postal History Society
Kalman V. Illyefalvi
8207 Daren Court
Pikesville MD 21208-2211
Ph: (410) 653-0665

Precancel Stamp Society
176 Bent Pine Hill
North Wales PA 19454
Ph: (215) 368-6082
E-mail: abentpine1@aol.com

United Postal Stationery Society
Cora Collins
PO Box 1792
Norfolk VA 23501-1792
Ph: (757) 420-3487
www.upss.org
E-mail: poststat@juno.com

Groups focusing on U.S. area philately as covered in the Standard Catalogue

Canal Zone Study Group
Richard H. Salz
60 27th Ave.
San Francisco CA 94121

Carriers and Locals Society
John D. Bowman
PO Box 382436
Birmingham AL 35238-2436
Ph: (205) 967-6200
www.pennypost.org
E-mail: jdbowman@premierhome.net

Confederate Stamp Alliance
Richard L. Calhoun
PO Box 581
Mt. Prospect IL 60056-0581

Hawaiian Philatelic Society
Kay H. Hoke
PO Box 10115
Honolulu HI 96816-0115
Ph: (808) 521-5721
E-mail: bannan@pixi.com

Plate Number Coil Collectors Club
Gene C. Trinks
3603 Bellows Court
Troy MI 48083
www.pnc3.org
E-mail: gctrinks@sprynet.com

United Nations Philatelists
Blanton Clement, Jr.
292 Springdale Terrace
Yardley PA 19067-3421
www.unpi.com
E-mail: bclemjr@aol.com

United States Stamp Society
Executive Secretary
PO Box 6634
Katy TX 77491-6631
www.usstamps.org

U.S. Cancellation Club
Roger Rhoads
3 Ruthana Way
Hockessin DE 19707
www.geocities.com/athens/2088/uscchome.htm
E-mail: rrrhoads@aol.com

U.S. Philatelic Classics Society
Mark D. Rogers
PO Box 80708
Austin TX 78708-0708
www.uspcs.org
E-mail: mrogers23@austin.rr.com

Groups focusing on philately of foreign countries or regions

Aden & Somaliland Study Group
Gary Brown
PO Box 106
Briar Hill, Victoria, Australia 3088
E-mail: garyjohn951@optushome.com.au

Albania Study Circle
Paul Eckman
PO Box 39880
Los Angeles CA 90039
members.netscapeonline.co.uk/johnsphipps/index.html
E-mail: peckman797@earthlink.net

American Society of Polar Philatelists (Antarctic areas)
Alan Warren
PO Box 39
Exton PA 19341-0039
south-pole.com/aspp.htm
E-mail: alanwar@att.net

Andorran Philatelic Study Circle
D. Hope
17 Hawthorn Dr.
Stalybridge, Cheshire, United Kingdom
SK15 1UE
www.chy-an-piran.demon.co.uk/
E-mail: apsc@chy-an-piran.demon.co.uk

Arabian Philatelic Association International
R. J. Thoden
4125 Windover Way
Melbourne FL 32934-8514
www.arabian-philatelic.com
E-mail: thodenr@aol.com

Australian States Study Circle
Ben Palmer
GPO 1751
Sydney, N.S.W., Australia 1043

Austria Philatelic Society
Ralph Schneider
PO Box 23049
Belleville IL 62223
Ph: (618) 277-6152
www.apsus.esmartweb.com
E-mail: rsstamps@aol.com

American Belgian Philatelic Society
Kenneth L. Costilow
621 Virginius Dr.
Virginia Beach VA 23452-4417
Ph: (757) 463-6081
groups.hamptonroads.com/ABPS
E-mail: kcos32@home.com

Bechuanalands and Botswana Society
Neville Midwood
69 Porlock Lane
Furzton, Milton Keynes, United Kingdom MK4 1JY
www.netcomuk.co.uk/~midsoft/bbsoc.html
E-mail: runnerpo@netcomuk.co.uk

Bermuda Collectors Society
Thomas J. McMahon
PO Box 1949
Stuart FL 34995

Brazil Philatelic Association
Kurt Ottenheimer
462 West Walnut St.
Long Beach NY 11561
Ph: (516) 431-3412
E-mail: oak462@juno.com

British Caribbean Philatelic Study Group
Dr. Reuben A. Ramkissoon
3011 White Oak Lane
Oak Brook IL 60523-2513

British North America Philatelic Society (Canada & Provinces)
H. P. Jacobi
5295 Moncton St.
Richmond, B.C., Canada V7E 3B2
www.bnaps.org
E-mail: beaver@telus.net

British West Indies Study Circle
W. Clary Holt
PO Drawer 59
Burlington NC 27216
Ph: (336) 227-7461

Burma Philatelic Study Circle
A. Meech
7208 91st Ave.
Edmonton, AB, Canada T6B 0R8
E-mail: ameech@telusplanet.net

Ceylon Study Group
R. W. P. Frost
42 Lonsdale Road, Cannington
Bridgewater, Somerset, United Kingdom TA5 2JS

China Stamp Society
Paul H. Gault
PO Box 20711
Columbus OH 43220
www.chinastampsociety.org
E-mail: secretary@chinastampsociety.org

Colombia/Panama Philatelic Study Group
PO Box 2245
El Cajon CA 92021
E-mail: jimacross@juno.com

Society for Costa Rica Collectors
Dr. Hector R. Mena
PO Box 14831
Baton Rouge LA 70808
www.socorico.org
E-mail: hrmena@aol.com

Croatian Philatelic Society (Croatia & other Balkan areas)
Ekrem Spahich
502 Romero, PO Box 696
Fritch TX 79036-0696
Ph: (806) 857-0129
www.croatianmall.com/cps/
E-mail: ou812@arn.net

Cuban Philatelic Society of America
Ernesto Cuesta
PO Box 34434
Bethesda MD 20827
www.philat.com/cpsa

Cyprus Study Circle
Jim Wigmore
19 Riversmeet, Appledore
Bideford, N. Devon, United Kingdom EX39 1RE
www.geocities.com/cyprusstudycircle
E-mail: istug@aol.com

Society for Czechoslovak Philately
Robert T. Cossaboom
PO Box 25332
Scott AFB IL 62225-0332
www.czechoslovakphilately.com
E-mail: klfck1@aol.com

Danish West Indies Study Unit of the Scandinavian Collectors Club
John L. Dubois
Thermalogic Corp.
22 Kane Industrial Drive
Hudson MA 01749
Ph: (800) 343-4492
dwi.thlogic.com
E-mail: jld@thlogic.com

East Africa Study Circle
Ken Hewitt
16 Ashleigh Road
Solihull, United Kingdom B91 1AE
E-mail: 106602.2410@compuserve.com

Egypt Study Circle
Mike Murphy
109 Chadwick Road
London, United Kingdom SE15 4PY
E-mail: egyptstudycircle@hotmail.com

Estonian Philatelic Society
Juri Kirsimagi
29 Clifford Ave.
Pelham NY 10803

Ethiopian Philatelic Society
Ulf Lindahl
640 S. Pine Creek Rd.
Fairfield CT 06430
Ph: (203) 255-8005
members.home.net/fbheiser/ethiopia5.htm
E-mail: ulindahl@optonline.net

Falkland Islands Philatelic Study Group
Carl J. Faulkner
Williams Inn, On-the-Green
Williamstown MA 01267-2620
Ph: (413) 458-9371

Faroe Islands Study Circle
Norman Hudson
28 Enfield Road
Ellesmere Port, Cheshire, United Kingdom CH65 8BY
www.pherber.com/fisc/fisc.html
E-mail: jntropics@hotmail.com

Former French Colonies Specialist Society
BP 628
75367 Paris Cedex 08, France
www.ifrance.com/colfra
E-mail: clubcolfra@aol.com

France & Colonies Philatelic Society
Walter Parshall
103 Spruce St.
Bloomfield NJ 07003-3514

Germany Philatelic Society
PO Box 779
Arnold MD 21012-4779
www.gps.nu
E-mail: germanyphilatelic@starpower.net

German Democratic Republic Study Group of the German Philatelic Society
Ken Lawrence
PO Box 8040
State College PA 16803-8040
Ph: (814) 237-3803
E-mail: apsken@aol.com

Gibraltar Study Circle
D. Brook
80 Farm Road
Weston Super Mare, Avon, United Kingdom BS22 8BD
www.abel.co.uk/~stirrups/GSC.HTM
E-mail: drstirrups@dundee.ac.uk

Great Britain Collectors Club
Parker A. Bailey, Jr.
PO Box 773
Merrimack NH 03054-0773
www.gbstamps.com/gbcc
E-mail: pbaileyjr@worldnet.att.net

Hellenic Philatelic Society of America (Greece and related areas)
Dr. Nicholas Asimakopulos
541 Cedar Hill Ave.
Wyckoff NJ 07481
Ph: (201) 447-6262

International Society of Guatemala Collectors
Mrs. Mae Vignola
105 22nd Ave.
San Francisco CA 94121

Haiti Philatelic Society
Ubaldo Del Toro
5709 Marble Archway
Alexandria VA 22315
E-mail: u007ubi@aol.com

Honduras Collectors Club
Jeff Brasor
PO Box 143383
Irving TX 75014

Hong Kong Stamp Society
Dr. An-Min Chung
3300 Darby Rd. Cottage 503
Haverford PA 19041-1064

Society for Hungarian Philately
Robert Morgan
2201 Roscomare Rd.
Los Angeles CA 90077-2222
www.hungarianphilately.org
E-mail: h.alanhoover@lycosemail.com

India Study Circle
John Warren
PO Box 7326
Washington DC 20044
Ph: (202) 564-6876
E-mail: warren.john@epa.gov

Indian Ocean Study Circle
K. B. Fitton
50 Firlands
Weybridge, Surrey, United Kingdom KT13 0HR
www.stampdomain.com/iosc
E-mail: keithfitton@intonet.co.uk

Society of Indo-China Philatelists
Norman S. Davis
PO Box 290406
Brooklyn NY 11229

Iran Philatelic Study Circle
Darrell R. Hill
1410 Broadway
Bethlehem PA 18015-4025
www.iranphilatelic.org
E-mail: d.r.hill@att.net

Eire Philatelic Association (Ireland)
Myron G. Hill III
PO Box 1210
College Park MD 20741-1210
eirephilatelicassoc.org
E-mail: mhill@radix.net

Society of Israel Philatelists
Paul S. Aufrichtig
300 East 42nd St.
New York NY 10017

Italy and Colonies Study Circle
Andrew D'Anneo
1085 Dunweal Lane
Calistoga CA 94515
E-mail: audanneo@napanet.net

International Society for Japanese Philately
Kenneth Kamholz
PO Box 1283
Haddonfield NJ 08033
www.isjp.org
E-mail: isjp@home.com

Korea Stamp Society
John E. Talmage
PO Box 6889
Oak Ridge TN 37831
www.pennfamily.org/KSS-USA
E-mail: jtalmage@usit.net

Latin American Philatelic Society
Piet Steen
197 Pembina Ave.
Hinton, AB, Canada T7V 2B2

Latvian Philatelic Society
Aris Birze
569 Rougemount Dr.
Pickering, ON, Canada L1W 2C1

Liberian Philatelic Society
William Thomas Lockard
PO Box 106
Wellston OH 45692
Ph: (740) 384-2020
E-mail: tlockard@zoomnet.net

Liechtenstudy USA (Liechtenstein)
Ralph Schneider
PO Box 23049
Belleville IL 62223
Ph: (618) 277-6152
www.rschneiderstamps.com/Liechtenstudy.htm
E-mail: rsstamps@aol.com

Lithuania Philatelic Society
John Variakojis
3715 W. 68th St.
Chicago IL 60629
Ph: (773) 585-8649
www.filatelija.lt/lps/
E-mail: variakojis@earthlink.net

Luxembourg Collectors Club
Gary B. Little
3304 Plateau Dr.
Belmont CA 94002-1312
www.luxcentral.com/stamps/LCC
E-mail: lcc@luxcentral.com

Malaya Study Group
Joe Robertson
12 Lisa Court
Downsland Road
Basingstoke, Hampshire, United Kingdom RG21 8TU
home.freeuk.net/johnmorgan/msg.htm

Malta Study Circle
Alec Webster
50 Worcester Road
Sutton, Surrey, United Kingdom SM2 6QB
E-mail: alecwebster50@hotmail.com

Mexico-Elmhurst Philatelic Society International
David Pietsch
PO Box 50997
Irvine CA 92619-0997
E-mail: mepsi@msn.com

Society for Moroccan and Tunisian Philately
206, bld. Pereire
75017 Paris, France
members.aol.com/Jhaik5814
E-mail: jhaik5814@aol.com

Nepal & Tibet Philatelic Study Group
Roger D. Skinner
1020 Covington Road
Los Altos CA 94024-5003
Ph: (650) 968-4163
fuchs-online.com/ntpsc/

American Society of Netherlands Philately
Jan Enthoven
221 Coachlite Ct. S.
Onalaska WI 54650
Ph: (608) 781-8612
www.cs.cornell.edu/Info/People/aswin/NL/neth
E-mail: jenthoven@centurytel.net

New Zealand Society of Great Britain
Keith C. Collins
13 Briton Crescent
Sanderstead, Surrey, United Kingdom CR2 0JN
www.cs.stir.ac.uk/~rgc/nzsgb
E-mail: rgc@cs.stir.ac.uk

Nicaragua Study Group
Erick Rodriguez
11817 S.W. 11th St.
Miami FL 33184-2501
clubs.yahoo.com/clubs/nicaraguastudygroup
E-mail: nsgsec@yahoo.com

Society of Australasian Specialists/ Oceania
Henry Bateman
PO Box 4862
Monroe LA 71211-4862
Ph: (800) 571-0293
members.aol.com/stampsho/saso.html
E-mail: hbateman@jam.rr.com

Orange Free State Study Circle
J. R. Stroud
28 Oxford St.
Burnham-on-sea, Somerset, United Kingdom TA8 1LQ
www.ofssc.org
E-mail: jrstroud@classicfm.net

Pacific Islands Study Group
John Ray
24 Woodvale Avenue
London, United Kingdom SE25 4AE
www.pisc.org.uk
E-mail: john.ray@bigfoot.com

Pakistan Philatelic Study Circle
Jeff Siddiqui
PO Box 7002
Lynnwood WA 98046
E-mail: jeffsiddiqui@msn.com

Centro de Filatelistas Independientes de Panama
Vladimir Berrio-Lemm
Apartado 0835-348
Panama, 10, Panama
E-mail: filatelia@cwpanama.net

Papuan Philatelic Society
Steven Zirinsky
PO Box 49, Ansonia Station
New York NY 10023
E-mail: szirinsky@compuserve.com

International Philippine Philatelic Society
Robert F. Yacano
PO Box 100
Toast NC 27049
Ph: (336) 783-0768
E-mail: yacano@advi.net

Pitcairn Islands Study Group
Nelson A. L. Weller
2940 Wesleyan Lane
Winston-Salem NC 27106
Ph: (336) 724-6384
E-mail: nalweller@aol.com

Plebiscite-Memel-Saar Study Group of the German Philatelic Society
Clay Wallace
100 Lark Court
Alamo CA 94507
E-mail: wallacec@earthlink.net

Polonus Philatelic Society (Poland)
Arkadius Walinski
7414 Lincoln Ave. - D
Skokie IL 60076-3898
Ph: (847) 674-4286

International Society for Portuguese Philately
Clyde Homen
1491 Bonnie View Rd.
Hollister CA 95023-5117
www.portugalstamps.com
E-mail: cjh@hollinet.com

Rhodesian Study Circle
William R. Wallace
PO Box 16381
San Francisco CA 94116
www.rhodesianstudycircle.org.uk
E-mail: bwall8rscr@earthlink.net

Canadian Society of Russian Philately
Andrew Cronin
PO Box 5722, Station A
Toronto, ON, Canada M5W 1P2
Ph: (905) 764-8968
www3.sympatico.ca/postrider/postrider
E-mail: postrider@sympatico.ca

Rossica Society of Russian Philately
Gerald D. Seiflow
27 N. Wacker Drive #167
Chicago IL 60606-3203
www.rossica.org
E-mail: ged.seiflow@rossica.org

Ryukyu Philatelic Specialist Society
Carmine J. DiVincenzo
PO Box 381
Clayton CA 94517-0381

St. Helena, Ascension & Tristan Da Cunha Philatelic Society
Dr. Everett L. Parker
HC 76, Box 32
Greenville ME 04441-9727
Ph: (207) 695-3163
ourworld.compuserve.com/homepages/ ST_HELENA_ASCEN_TDC
E-mail: eparker@prexar.com

St. Pierre & Miquelon Philatelic Society
David Salovey
320 Knights Corner
Stony Point NY 10980
E-mail: jamestaylor@wavehome.com

Associated Collectors of El Salvador
Jeff Brasor
PO Box 143383
Irving TX 75014

Fellowship of Samoa Specialists
Jack R. Hughes
PO Box 1260
Boston MA 02117-1260
members.aol.com/tongaJan/foss.html

Sarawak Specialists' Society
Stu Leven
4031 Samson Way
San Jose CA 95124-3733
Ph: (408) 978-0193
www.britborneostamps.org.uk
E-mail: stulev@ix.netcom.com

Scandinavian Collectors Club
Donald B. Brent
PO Box 13196
El Cajon CA 92020
www.scc-online.org
E-mail: dbrent47@sprynet.com

Slovakia Stamp Society
Jack Benchik
PO Box 555
Notre Dame IN 46556

Philatelic Society for Greater Southern Africa
William C. Brooks VI
PO Box 4158
Cucamonga CA 91729-4158
Ph: (909) 484-2806
www.homestead.com/psgsa/index.html
E-mail: bbrooks@hss.co.sbcounty.gov

Spanish Philatelic Society
Robert H. Penn
1108 Walnut Drive
Danielsville PA 18038
Ph: (610) 767-6793

Sudan Study Group
Charles Hass
PO Box 3435
Nashua NH 03061-3435
Ph: (603) 888-4160
E-mail: hassstamps@aol.com

American Helvetia Philatelic Society (Switzerland, Liechtenstein)
Richard T. Hall
PO Box 15053
Asheville NC 28813-0053
www.swiss-stamps.org
E-mail: secretary@swiss-stamps.org

Tannu Tuva Collectors Society
Ken Simon
513 Sixth Ave. So.
Lake Worth FL 33460-4507
Ph: (561) 588-5954
www.seflin.org/tuva
E-mail: p003115b@pb.seflin.org

Society for Thai Philately
H. R. Blakeney
PO Box 25644
Oklahoma City OK 73125
E-mail: HRBlakeney@aol.com

Transvaal Study Circle
J. Woolgar
132 Dale Street
Chatham, Kent ME4 6QH, United Kingdom
www.transvaalsc.org

Ottoman and Near East Philatelic Society (Turkey and related areas)
Bob Stuchell
193 Valley Stream Lane
Wayne PA 19087
E-mail: president@oneps.org

Ukrainian Philatelic & Numismatic Society
George Slusarczuk
PO Box 303
Southfields NY 10975-0303
www.upns.org
E-mail: Yurko@warwick.net

Vatican Philatelic Society
Sal Quinonez
2 Aldersgate, Apt. 119
Riverhead NY 11901
Ph: (516) 727-6426

British Virgin Islands Philatelic Society
Roger Downing
PO Box 11156
St. Thomas VI 00801-1156
Ph: (284) 494-2762
www.islandsun.com/FEATURES/bviphil9198.html
E-mail: issun@candwbvi.net

West Africa Study Circle
Dr. Peter Newroth
33-520 Marsett Place
Victoria, BC, Canada V8Z 7J1
ourworld.compuserve.com/homepages/FrankWalton

Western Australia Study Group
Brian Pope
PO Box 423
Claremont, Western Australia, Australia 6910

Yugoslavia Study Group of the Croatian Philatelic Society
Michael Lenard
1514 North 3rd Ave.
Wausau WI 54401
Ph: (715) 675-2833
E-mail: mjlenard@aol.com

Topical Groups

Americana Unit
Dennis Dengel
17 Peckham Rd.
Poughkeepsie NY 12603-2018
www.americanaunit.org
E-mail: info@americanaunit.org

Astronomy Study Unit
George Young
PO Box 632
Tewksbury MA 01876-0632
Ph: (978) 851-8283
www.fandm.edu/departments/astronomy/miscell/astunit.html
E-mail: george-young@msn.com

Bicycle Stamp Club
Norman Batho
358 Iverson Place
East Windsor NJ 08520
Ph: (609) 448-9547
members.tripod.com/~bicyclestamps
E-mail: normbatho@worldnet.att.net

Biology Unit
Alan Hanks
34 Seaton Dr.
Aurora, ON, Canada L4G 2K1
Ph: (905) 727-6993

Bird Stamp Society
G. P. Horsman
9 Cowley Drive, Worthy Down
Winchester, Hants., United Kingdom
SO21 2OW

Canadiana Study Unit
John Peebles
PO Box 3262, Station "A"
London, ON, Canada N6A 4K3
E-mail: john.peebles@odyssey.on.ca

Captain Cook Study Unit
Brian P. Sandford
173 Minuteman Dr.
Concord MA 01742-1923
www.captaincookstudyunit.com/
E-mail: USagent@captaincookstudyunit.com/

Casey Jones Railroad Unit
Oliver C. Atchison
PO Box 31631
San Francisco CA 94131-0631
Ph: (415) 648-8057
www.uqp.de/cjr/index.htm
E-mail: cjrrunit@aol.com

Cats on Stamps Study Unit
Mary Ann Brown
3006 Wade Rd.
Durham NC 27705

Chemistry & Physics on Stamps Study Unit
Dr. Roland Hirsch
20458 Water Point Lane
Germantown MD 20874
www.cpossu.org
E-mail: rfhirsch@cpossu.org

Chess on Stamps Study Unit
Anne Kasonic
7625 County Road #153
Interlaken NY 14847
www.iglobal.net/home/reott/stamps1.htm#cossu
E-mail: akasonic@epix.net

Christmas Philatelic Club
Linda Lawrence
312 Northwood Drive
Lexington KY 40505
Ph: (606) 293-0151
www.hwcn.org/link/cpc
E-mail: stamplinda@aol.com

Christopher Columbus Philatelic Society
Donald R. Ager
PO Box 71
Hillsboro NH 03244-0071
Ph: (603) 464-5379
E-mail: meganddon@conknet.com

Collectors of Religion on Stamps
Verna Shackleton
425 North Linwood Avenue #110
Appleton WI 54914
Ph: (920) 734-2417
www.powernetonline.com/~corosec/coros1.htm
E-mail: corosec@powernetonline.com

Dogs on Stamps Study Unit
Morris Raskin
202A Newport Rd.
Monroe Township NJ 08831
Ph: (609) 655-7411
www.dossu.org
E-mail: mraskin@nerc.com

Earth's Physical Features Study Group
Fred Klein
515 Magdalena Ave.
Los Altos CA 94024
www.philately.com/society_news/earths _physical.htm

Ebony Society of Philatelic Events and Reflections (African-American topicals)
Sanford L. Byrd
PO Box 8888
Corpus Christi, TX 78468-8888
www.slsabyrd.com/esper.htm
E-mail: esper@str.rr.com

Embroidery, Stitchery, Textile Unit
Helen N. Cushman
1001 Genter St., Apt. 9H
La Jolla CA 92037
Ph: (619) 459-1194

Europa Study Unit
Hank Klos
PO Box 611
Bensenville IL 60106
E-mail: eunity@aol.com or klosh@clearnet.org

Fine & Performing Arts
Ruth Richards
10393 Derby Dr.
Laurel MD 20723
www.philately.com/society_news/fap.htm
E-mail: bersec@aol.com

Fire Service in Philately
Brian R. Engler, Sr.
726 1/2 W. Tilghman St.
Allentown PA 18102-2324
Ph: (610) 433-2782
E-mail: brenglersr@enter.net

Gay & Lesbian History on Stamps Club
Joe Petronie
PO Box 190842
Dallas TX 75219-0842
www.glhsc.org
E-mail: glhsc@aol.com

Gems, Minerals & Jewelry Study Group
George Young
PO Box 632
Tewksbury MA 01876-0632
Ph: (978) 851-8283
www.rockhounds.com/rockshop/gmjsuapp.txt
E-mail: george-young@msn.com

Graphics Philately Association
Mark Winnegrad
PO Box 380
Bronx NY 10462-0380

Journalists, Authors & Poets on Stamps
Sol Baltimore
28742 Blackstone Dr.
Lathrup Village MI 48076

Lighthouse Stamp Society
Dalene Thomas
8612 West Warren Lane
Lakewood CO 80227-2352
Ph: (303) 986-6620
www.lighthousestampsociety.org
E-mail: dalene1@wideopenwest.com

Lions International Stamp Club
John Bargus
304-2777 Barry Rd. RR 2
Mill Bay, BC, Canada V0R 2P0
Ph: (250) 743-5782

Mahatma Gandhi On Stamps Study Circle
Pramod Shivagunde
Pratik Clinic, Akluj
Solapur, Maharashtra, India 413101
E-mail: drnanda@bom6.vsnl.net.in

Mask Study Unit
Carolyn Weber
1220 Johnson Drive, Villa 104
Ventura CA 93003-0540
www.home.prcn.org/~pauld/ata/units/masks.htm
E-mail: kencar@venturalink.net

Masonic Study Unit
Stanley R. Longenecker
930 Wood St.
Mount Joy PA 17552-1926
E-mail: natsco@usa.net

Mathematical Study Unit
Estelle Buccino
5615 Glenwood Rd.
Bethesda MD 20817-6727
Ph: (301) 718-8898
www.math.ttu.edu/msu/
E-mail: m.strauss@ttu.edu

Medical Subjects Unit
Dr. Frederick C. Skvara
PO Box 6228
Bridgewater NJ 08807
E-mail: fcskvara@bellatlantic.net

Mesoamerican Archeology Study Unit
Chris Moser
PO Box 1442
Riverside CA 92502
www.masu.homestead.com/info.html
E-mail:cmoser@ci.riverside.ca.us

Napoleonic Age Philatelists
Ken Berry
7513 Clayton Dr.
Oklahoma City OK 73132-5636
Ph: (405) 721-0044
E-mail: krb2@earthlink.net

Old World Archeological Study Unit
Eileen Meier
PO Box 369
Palmyra VA 22963

Parachute Study Group
Bill Wickert
3348 Clubhouse Road
Virginia Beach VA 23452-5339
Ph: (757) 486-3614
E-mail: bw47psg@worldnet.att.net

Petroleum Philatelic Society International
Linda W. Corwin
5427 Pine Springs Court
Conroe TX 77304
Ph: (936) 441-0216
E-mail: corwin@pdq.net

Philatelic Computing Study Group
Robert de Violini
PO Box 5025
Oxnard CA 93031-5025
www.pcsg.org
E-mail: dviolini@west.net

Philatelic Lepidopterists' Association
Alan Hanks
34 Seaton Dr.
Aurora, ON, Canada L4G 2K1
Ph: (905) 727-6933

Philatelic Music Circle
Cathleen Osborne
PO Box 1781
Sequim WA 98382
Ph: (360) 683-6373
www.stampshows.com/pmc.html

Rainbow Study Unit
Shirley Sutton
PO Box 37
Lone Pine, AB, Canada T0G 1M0
Ph: (780) 584-2268
E-mail: george-young@msn.com

Rotary on Stamps Unit
Donald Fiery
PO Box 333
Hanover PA 17331
Ph: (717) 632-8921

Scouts on Stamps Society International
Carl Schauer
PO Box 526
Belen NM 87002
Ph: (505) 864-0098
www.sossi.org
E-mail: rfrank@sossi.org

Ships on Stamps Unit
Robert Stuckert
2750 Highway 21 East
Paint Lick KY 40461
Ph: (859) 925-4901
www.shipsonstamps.org

Space Unit
Carmine Torrisi
PO Box 780241
Maspeth NY 11378
Ph: (718) 386-7882
stargate.1usa.com/stamps/
E-mail: ctorrisi1@juno.com

Sports Philatelists International
Margaret Jones
5310 Lindenwood Ave.
St. Louis MO 63109-1758
www.geocities.com/colosseum/track/6279

Stamps on Stamps Collectors Club
William Critzer
1360 Trinity Drive
Menlo Park CA 94025
Ph: (650) 234-1136
www.stampsonstamps.org
E-mail: wllmcritz@aol.com

Windmill Study Unit
Walter J. Hollien
PO Box 346
Long Valley NJ 07853-0346

Wine on Stamps Study Unit
James D. Crum
816 Kingsbury Ct.
Arroyo Grande CA 93420-4517
Ph: (805) 489-3559
E-mail: jdakcrum@aol.com

Women on Stamps Study Unit
Hugh Gottfried
2232 26th St.
Santa Monica CA 90405-1902
Ph: (310) 452-1442
E-mail: hgottfri@lausd.k12.ca.us

Zeppelin Collectors Club
Cheryl Ganz
PO Box A3843
Chicago IL 60690-3843

Expertizing Services

The following organizations will, for a fee, provide expert opinions about stamps submitted to them. Collectors should contact these organizations to find out about their fees and requirements before submitting philatelic material to them. The listing of these groups here is not intended as an endorsement by Scott Publishing Co.

General Expertizing Services

American Philatelic Expertizing Service (a service of the American Philatelic Society)
PO Box 8000
State College PA 16803
Ph: (814) 237-3803
Fax: (814) 237-6128
www.stamps.org
E-mail: ambristo@stamps.org
Areas of Expertise: Worldwide

B. P. A. Expertising, Ltd.
PO Box 137
Leatherhead, Surrey, United Kingdom KT22 0RG
E-mail: sec.bpa@tcom.co.uk
Areas of Expertise: British Commonwealth, Great Britain, Classics of Europe, South America and the Far East

Philatelic Foundation
501 Fifth Ave., Rm. 1901
New York NY 10017
Areas of Expertise: U.S. & Worldwide

Professional Stamp Experts
PO Box 6170
Newport Beach CA 92658
Ph: (877) STAMP-88
Fax: (949) 833-7955
www.collectors.com/pse
E-mail: pseinfo@collectors.com
Areas of Expertise: Stamps and covers of U.S., U.S. Possessions, British Commonwealth

Royal Philatelic Society Expert Committee
41 Devonshire Place
London, United Kingdom W1N 1PE
www.rpsl.org.uk/experts.html
E-mail: experts@rpsl.org.uk
Areas of Expertise: All

Expertizing Services Covering Specific Fields Or Countries

Canadian Society of Russian Philately Expertizing Service
PO Box 5722, Station A
Toronto, ON, Canada M5W 1P2
Fax: (416)932-0853
Areas of Expertise: Russian areas

China Stamp Society Expertizing Service
1050 West Blue Ridge Blvd
Kansas City MO 64145
Ph: (816) 942-6300
E-mail: hjmesq@aol.com
Areas of Expertise: China

Confederate Stamp Alliance Authentication Service
c/o Patricia A. Kaufmann
10194 N. Old State Road
Lincoln DE 19960-9797
Ph: (302) 422-2656
Fax: (302) 424-1990
www.webuystamps.com/csaauth.htm
E-mail: trish@ce.net
Areas of Expertise: Confederate stamps and postal history

Croatian Philatelic Society Expertizing Service
PO Box 696
Fritch TX 79036-0696
Ph: (806) 857-0129
E-mail: ou812@arn.net
Areas of Expertise: Croatia and other Balkan areas

Errors, Freaks and Oddities Collectors Club Expertizing Service
138 East Lakemont Dr.
Kingsland GA 31548
Ph: (912) 729-1573
Areas of Expertise: U.S. errors, freaks and oddities

Estonian Philatelic Society Expertizing Service
39 Clafford Lane
Melville NY 11747
Ph: (516) 421-2078
E-mail: esto4@aol.com
Areas of Expertise: Estonia

Hawaiian Philatelic Society Expertizing Service
PO Box 10115
Honolulu HI 96816-0115
Areas of Expertise: Hawaii

Hong Kong Stamp Society Expertizing Service
PO Box 206
Glenside PA 19038
Fax: (215) 576-6850
Areas of Expertise: Hong Kong

International Association of Philatelics Experts
United States Associate members:
Paul Buchsbayew
119 W. 57th St.
New York NY 10019
Ph: (212) 977-7734
Fax: (212) 977-8653
Areas of Expertise: Russia, Soviet Union

William T. Crowe
(see Philatelic Foundation)

John Lievsay
(see American Philatelic Expertizing Service and Philatelic Foundation)
Areas of Expertise: France

Robert W. Lyman
P.O. Box 348
Irvington on Hudson NY 10533
Ph and Fax: (914) 591-6937
Areas of Expertise: British North America, New Zealand

Robert Odenweller
P.O. Box 401
Bernardsville, NJ 07924-0401
Ph and Fax: (908) 766-5460
Areas of Expertise: New Zealand, Samoa to 1900

Alex Rendon
P.O. Box 323
Massapequa NY 11762
Ph and Fax: (516) 795-0464
Areas of Expertise: Bolivia, Colombia, Colombian States

Sergio Sismondo
10035 Carousel Center Dr.
Syracuse NY 13290-0001
Ph: (315) 422-2331
Fax: (315) 422-2956
Areas of Expertise: Cape of Good Hope, Canada, British North America

International Society for Japanese Philately Expertizing Committee
32 King James Court
Staten Island NY 10308-2910
Ph: (718) 227-5229
Areas of Expertise: Japan and related areas, except WWII Japanese Occupation issues

International Society for Portuguese Philately Expertizing Service
PO Box 43146
Philadelphia PA 19129-3146
Ph: (215) 843-2106
Fax: (215) 843-2106
E-mail: s.s.washburne@worldnet.att.net
Areas of Expertise: Portugal and colonies

Mexico-Elmhurst Philatelic Society International Expert Committee
PO Box 1133
West Covina CA 91793
Areas of Expertise: Mexico

Philatelic Society for Greater Southern Africa Expert Panel
13955 W. 30th Ave.
Golden CO 80401
Areas of expertise: Entire South and South West Africa area, Bechuanalands, Basutoland, Swaziland

Ryukyu Philatelic Specialist Society Expertizing Service
1710 Buena Vista Ave.
Spring Valley CA 91977-4458
Ph: (619) 697-3205
Areas of Expertise: Ryukyu Islands

Ukrainian Philatelic & Numismatic Society Expertizing Service
30552 Dell Lane
Warren MI 48092-1862
Ph: (810) 751-5754
Areas of Expertise: Ukraine, Western Ukraine

V. G. Greene Philatelic Research Foundation
Box 100, First Canadian Place
Toronto, ON, Canada M5X 1B2
Ph: (416) 863-4593
Fax: (416) 863-4592
Areas of Expertise: British North America

Information on Catalogue Values, Grade and Condition

Catalogue Value

The Scott Catalogue value is a retail value; that is, an amount you could expect to pay for a stamp in the grade of Very Fine with no faults. Any exceptions to the grade valued will be noted in the text. The general introduction on the following pages and the individual section introductions further explain the type of material that is valued. The value listed for any given stamp is a reference that reflects recent actual dealer selling prices for that item.

Dealer retail price lists, public auction results, published prices in advertising and individual solicitation of retail prices from dealers, collectors and specialty organizations have been used in establishing the values found in this catalogue. Scott Publishing Co. values stamps, but Scott is not a company engaged in the business of buying and selling stamps as a dealer.

Use this catalogue as a guide for buying and selling. The actual price you pay for a stamp may be higher or lower than the catalogue value because of many different factors, including the amount of personal service a dealer offers, or increased or decreased interest in the country or topic represented by a stamp or set. An item may occasionally be offered at a lower price as a "loss leader," or as part of a special sale. You also may obtain an item inexpensively at public auction because of little interest at that time or as part of a large lot.

Stamps that are of a lesser grade than Very Fine, or those with condition problems, generally trade at lower prices than those given in this catalogue. Stamps of exceptional quality in both grade and condition often command higher prices than those listed.

Values for pre-1900 unused issues are for stamps with approximately half or more of their original gum. Stamps with most or all of their original gum may be expected to sell for more, and stamps with less than half of their original gum may be expected to sell for somewhat less than the values listed. On rarer stamps, it may be expected that the original gum will be somewhat more disturbed than it will be on more common issues. Post-1900 unused issues are assumed to have full original gum. From breakpoints in most countries' listings, stamps are valued as never hinged, due to the wide availability of stamps in that condition. These notations are prominently placed in the listings and in the country information preceding the listings. Some countries also feature listings with dual values for hinged and never-hinged stamps.

Grade

A stamp's grade and condition are crucial to its value. The accompanying illustrations show examples of Very Fine stamps from different time periods, along with examples of stamps in Fine to Very Fine and Extremely Fine grades as points of reference.

FINE stamps (illustrations not shown) have designs that are noticeably off center on two sides. Imperforate stamps may have small margins, and earlier issues may show the design touching one edge of the stamp design. For perforated stamps, perfs may barely clear the design on one side, and very early issues normally will have the perforations slightly cutting into the design. Used stamps may have heavier than usual cancellations.

FINE-VERY FINE stamps may be somewhat off center on one side, or slightly off center on two sides. Imperforate stamps will have two margins of at least normal size, and the design will not touch any edge. For perforated stamps, the perfs are well clear of the design, but are still noticeably off center. *However, early issues of a country may be printed in such a way that the design naturally is very close to the edges. In these cases, the perforations may cut into the design very slightly.* Used stamps will not have a cancellation that detracts from the design.

VERY FINE stamps may be slightly off center on one side, but the design will be well clear of the edge. The stamp will present a nice, balanced appearance. Imperforate stamps will have three normal-sized margins. *However, early issues of many countries may be printed in such a way that the perforations may touch the design on one or more sides. Where this is the case, a boxed note will be found defining the centering and margins of the stamps being valued.* Used stamps will have light or otherwise neat cancellations. This is the grade used to establish Scott Catalogue values.

EXTREMELY FINE stamps are close to being perfectly centered. Imperforate stamps will have even margins that are larger than normal. Even the earliest perforated issues will have perforations clear of the design on all sides.

Scott Publishing Co. recognizes that there is no formally enforced grading scheme for postage stamps, and that the final price you pay or obtain for a stamp will be determined by individual agreement at the time of transaction.

Condition

Grade addresses only centering and (for used stamps) cancellation. *Condition* refers to factors other than grade that affect a stamp's desirability.

Factors that can increase the value of a stamp include exceptionally wide margins, particularly fresh color, the presence of selvage, and plate or die varieties. Unusual cancels on used stamps (particularly those of the 19th century) can greatly enhance their value as well.

Factors other than faults that decrease the value of a stamp include loss of original gum, regumming, a hinge remnant or foreign object adhering to the gum, natural inclusions, straight edges, and markings or notations applied by collectors or dealers.

Faults include missing pieces, tears, pin or other holes, surface scuffs, thin spots, creases, toning, short or pulled perforations, clipped perforations, oxidation or other forms of color changelings, soiling, stains, and such man-made changes as reperforations or the chemical removal or lightening of a cancellation.

Grading Illustrations

On the following two pages are illustrations of various stamps from countries appearing in this volume. These stamps are arranged by country, and they represent early or important issues that are often found in widely different grades in the marketplace. The editors believe the illustrations will prove useful in showing the margin size and centering that will be seen on the various issues.

In addition to the matters of margin size and centering, collectors are reminded that the very fine stamps valued in the Scott catalogues also will possess fresh color and intact perforations, and they will be free from defects.

Most examples shown are computer-manipulated images made from single digitized master illustrations.

Stamp Illustrations Used in the Catalogue

It is important to note that the stamp images used for identification purposes in this catlaogue may not be indicative of the grade of stamp being valued. Refer to the written discussion of grades on this page and to the grading illustrations on the following two pages for grading information.

Fine-Very Fine

SCOTT CATALOGUES VALUE STAMPS IN THIS GRADE

Very Fine

Extremely Fine

Fine-Very Fine

SCOTT CATALOGUES VALUE STAMPS IN THIS GRADE

Very Fine

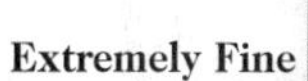

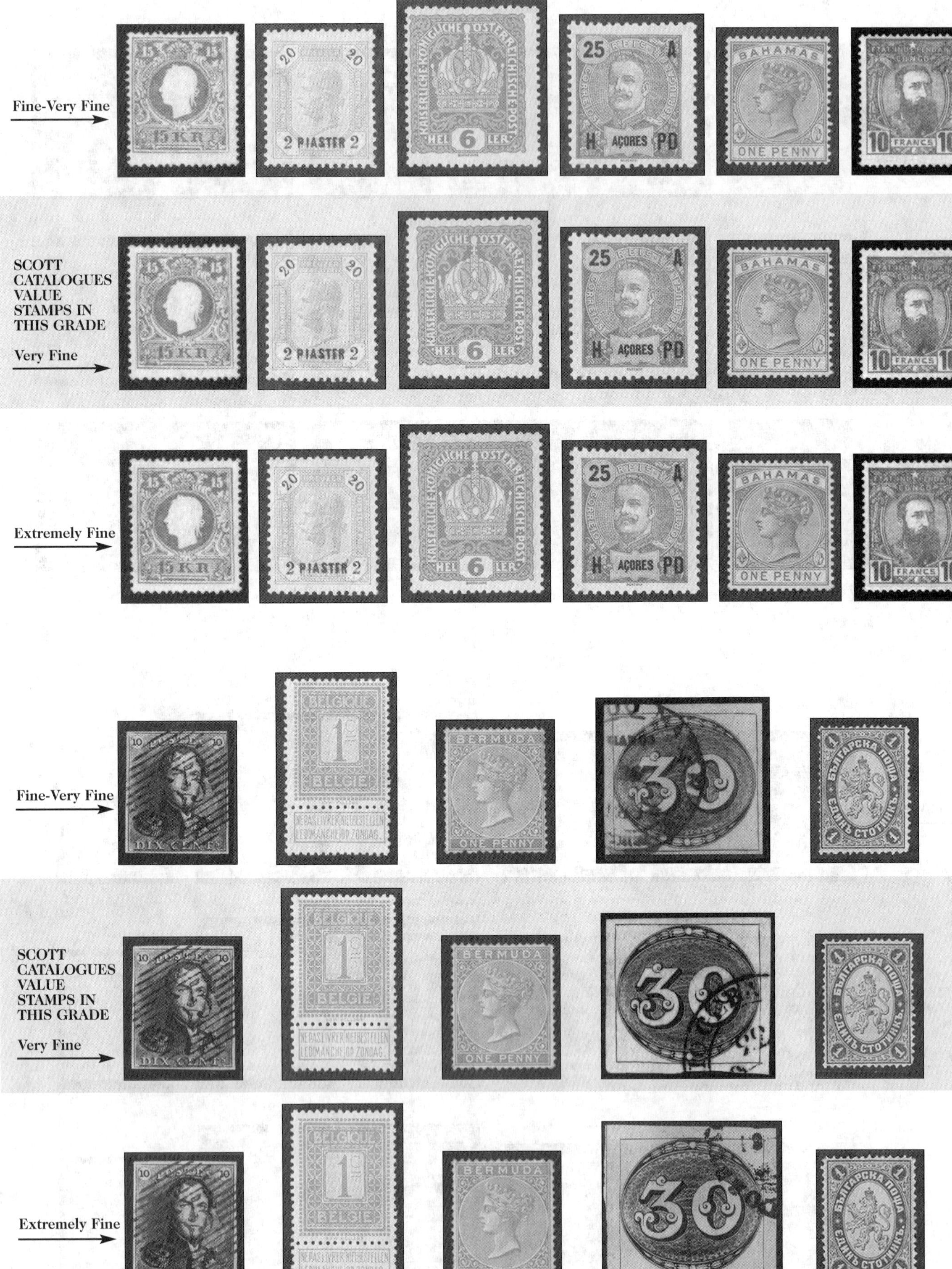
Fine-Very Fine
SCOTT CATALOGUES VALUE STAMPS IN THIS GRADE
Very Fine
Extremely Fine
Fine-Very Fine
SCOTT CATALOGUES VALUE STAMPS IN THIS GRADE
Very Fine
Extremely Fine

For purposes of helping to determine the gum condition and value of an unused stamp, Scott Publishing Co. presents the following chart which details different gum conditions and indicates how the conditions correlate with the Scott values for unused stamps. Used together, the Illustrated Grading Chart on the previous pages and this Illustrated Gum Chart should allow catalogue users to better understand the grade and gum condition of stamps valued in the Scott catalogues.

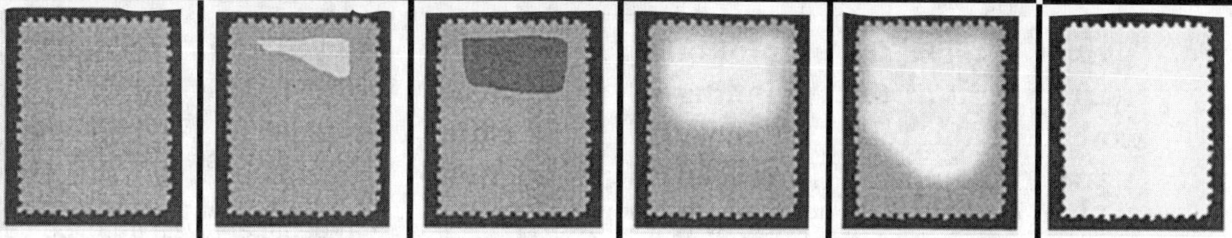

Gum Categories:	MINT N.H.	ORIGINAL GUM (O.G.)				NO GUM
	Mint Never Hinged *Free from any disturbance*	**Lightly Hinged** *Faint impression of a removed hinge over a small area*	**Hinge Mark or Remnant** *Prominent hinged spot with part or all of the hinge remaining*	**Large part o.g.** *Approximately half or more of the gum intact*	**Small part o.g.** *Approximately less than half of the gum intact*	**No gum** *Only if issued with gum*
Commonly Used Symbol:	★★	★	★	★	★	(★)
Pre-1900 Issues (Pre-1890 for U.S.)	*Very fine pre-1900 stamps in these categories trade at a premium over Scott value*			Scott Value for "Unused"		Scott "No Gum" listings for selected unused classic stamps
From 1900 to breakpoints for listings of never-hinged stamps	Scott "Never Hinged" listings for selected unused stamps	Scott Value for "Unused" (Actual value will be affected by the degree of hinging of the full o.g.)				
From breakpoints noted for many countries	Scott Value for "Unused"					

Never Hinged (NH; ★★): A never-hinged stamp will have full original gum that will have no hinge mark or disturbance. The presence of an expertizer's mark does not disqualify a stamp from this designation.

Original Gum (OG; ★): Pre-1900 stamps should have approximately half or more of their original gum. On rarer stamps, it may be expected that the original gum will be somewhat more disturbed that it will be on more common issues. Post-1900 stamps should have full original gum. Original gum will show some disturbance caused by a previous hinge(s) which may be present or entirely removed. The actual value of a post-1900 stamp will be affected by the degree of hinging of the full original gum.

Disturbed Original Gum: Gum showing noticeable effects of humidity, climate or hinging over more than half of the gum. The significance of gum disturbance in valuing a stamp in any of the Original Gum categories depends on the degree of disturbance, the rarity and normal gum condition of the issue and other variables affecting quality.

Regummed (RG; (★)): A regummed stamp is a stamp without gum that has had some type of gum privately applied at a time after it was issued. This normally is done to deceive collectors and/or dealers into thinking that the stamp has original gum and therefore has a higher value. A regummed stamp is considered the same as a stamp with none of its original gum for purposes of grading.

www.linns.com

Linn's Stamp News

WORLD'S LARGEST WEEKLY STAMP NEWS AND MARKETPLACE — $2.00 U.S. — FEBRUARY 5, 2001

34¢ Liberty, Flag, Four Flowers to be issued Feb. 7 in New York; no ceremony planned

Five semipostals for 2002-10; public will propose subjects

United Nations continues Endangered Species series

CONTENTS: PAGE 3

Catalogue Listing Policy

It is the intent of Scott Publishing Co. to list all postage stamps of the world in the *Scott Standard Postage Stamp Catalogue.* The only strict criteria for listing is that stamps be decreed legal for postage by the issuing country and that the issuing country actually have an operating postal system. Whether the primary intent of issuing a given stamp or set was for sale to postal patrons or to stamp collectors is not part of our listing criteria. Scott's role is to provide basic comprehensive postage stamp information. It is up to each stamp collector to choose which items to include in a collection.

It is Scott's objective to seek reasons why a stamp should be listed, rather than why it should not. Nevertheless, there are certain types of items that will not be listed. These include the following:

1. Unissued items that are not officially distributed or released by the issuing postal authority. Even if such a stamp is "accidentally" distributed to the philatelic or even postal market, it remains unissued. If such items are officially issued at a later date by the country, they will be listed. Unissued items consist of those that have been printed and then held from sale for reasons such as change in government, errors found on stamps or something deemed objectionable about a stamp subject or design.
2. Stamps "issued" by non-existent postal entities or fantasy countries, such as Nagaland, Occusi-Ambeno, Staffa, Sedang, Torres Straits and others.
3. Semi-official or unofficial items not required for postage. Examples include items issued by private agencies for their own express services. When such items are required for delivery, or are valid as prepayment of postage, they are listed.
4. Local stamps issued for local use only. Postage stamps issued by governments specifically for "domestic" use, such as Haiti Scott 219-228, or the United States non-denominated stamps, are not considered to be locals, since they are valid for postage throughout the country of origin.
5. Items not valid for postal use. For example, a few countries have issued souvenir sheets that are not valid for postage. This area also includes a number of worldwide charity labels (some denominated) that do not pay postage.
6. Intentional varieties, such as imperforate stamps that look like their perforated counterparts and are issued in very small quantities. These are often controlled issues intended for speculation.
7. Items distributed by the issuing government only to a limited group, such as a stamp club, philatelic exhibition or a single stamp dealer, and later brought to market at inflated prices. These items normally will be included in a footnote.

The fact that a stamp has been used successfully as postage, even on international mail, is not in itself sufficient proof that it was legitimately issued. Numerous examples of so-called stamps from non-existent countries are known to have been used to post letters that have successfully passed through the international mail system.

There are certain items that are subject to interpretation. When a stamp falls outside our specifications, it may be listed along with a cautionary footnote.

A number of factors are considered in our approach to analyzing how a stamp is listed. The following list of factors is presented to share with you, the catalogue user, the complexity of the listing process.

Additional printings — "Additional printings" of a previously issued stamp may range from an item that is totally different to cases where it is impossible to differentiate from the original. At least a minor number (a small-letter suffix) is assigned if there is a distinct change in stamp shade, noticeably redrawn design, or a significantly different perforation measurement. A major number (numeral or numeral and capital-letter combination) is assigned if the editors feel the "additional printing" is sufficiently different from the original that it constitutes a different issue.

Commemoratives — Where practical, commemoratives with the same theme are placed in a set. For example, the U.S. Civil War Centennial set of 1961-65 and the Constitution Bicentennial series of 1989-90 appear as sets. Countries such as Japan and Korea issue such material on a regular basis, with an announced, or at least predictable, number of stamps known in advance. Occasionally, however, stamp sets that were released over a period of years have been separated. Appropriately placed footnotes will guide you to each set's continuation.

Definitive sets — Blocks of numbers generally have been reserved for definitive sets, based on previous experience with any given country. If a few more stamps were issued in a set than originally expected, they often have been inserted into the original set with a capital-letter suffix, such as U.S. Scott 1059A. If it appears that many more stamps than the originally allotted block will be released before the set is completed, a new block of numbers will be reserved, with the original one being closed off. In some cases, such as the British Machin Head series or the U.S. Transportation and Great Americans series, several blocks of numbers exist. Appropriately placed footnotes will guide you to each set's continuation.

New country — Membership in the Universal Postal Union is not a consideration for listing status or order of placement within the catalogue. The index will tell you in what volume or page number the listings begin.

"No release date" items — The amount of information available for any given stamp issue varies greatly from country to country and even from time to time. Extremely comprehensive information about new stamps is available from some countries well before the stamps are released. By contrast some countries do not provide information about stamps or release dates. Most countries, however, fall between these extremes. A country may provide denominations or subjects of stamps from upcoming issues that are not issued as planned. Sometimes, philatelic agencies, those private firms hired to represent countries, add these later-issued items to sets well after the formal release date. This time period can range from weeks to years. If these items were officially released by the country, they will be added to the appropriate spot in the set. In many cases, the specific release date of a stamp or set of stamps may never be known.

Overprints — The color of an overprint is always noted if it is other than black. Where more than one color of ink has been used on overprints of a single set, the color used is noted. Early overprint and surcharge illustrations were altered to prevent their use by forgers.

Se-tenants — Connected stamps of differing features (se-tenants) will be listed in the format most commonly collected. This includes pairs, blocks or larger multiples. Se-tenant units are not always symmetrical. An example is Australia Scott 508, which is a block of seven stamps. If the stamps are primarily collected as a unit, the major number may be assigned to the multiple, with minors going to each component stamp. In cases where continuous-design or other unit se-tenants will receive significant postal use, each stamp is given a major Scott number listing. This includes issues from the United States, Canada, Germany and Great Britain, for example.

Understanding the Listings

On the opposite page is an enlarged "typical" listing from this catalogue. Below are detailed explanations of each of the highlighted parts of the listing.

A Scott number — Scott catalogue numbers are used to identify specific items when buying, selling or trading stamps. Each listed postage stamp from every country has a unique Scott catalogue number. Therefore, Germany Scott 99, for example, can only refer to a single stamp. Although the Scott catalogue usually lists stamps in chronological order by date of issue, there are exceptions. When a country has issued a set of stamps over a period of time, those stamps within the set are kept together without regard to date of issue. This follows the normal collecting approach of keeping stamps in their natural sets.

When a country issues a set of stamps over a period of time, a group of consecutive catalogue numbers is reserved for the stamps in that set, as issued. If that group of numbers proves to be too few, capital-letter suffixes, such as "A" or "B," may be added to existing numbers to create enough catalogue numbers to cover all items in the set. A capital-letter suffix indicates a major Scott catalogue number listing. Scott uses a suffix letter only once. Therefore, a catalogue number listing with a capital-letter suffix will not also be found with the same letter (lower case) used as a minor-letter listing. If there is a Scott 16A in a set, for example, there will not also be a Scott 16a. However, a minor-letter "a" listing may be added to a major number containing an "A" suffix (Scott 16Aa, for example).

Suffix letters are cumulative. A minor "b" variety of Scott 16A would be Scott 16Ab, not Scott 16b.

There are times when a reserved block of Scott catalogue numbers is too large for a set, leaving some numbers unused. Such gaps in the numbering sequence also occur when the catalogue editors move an item's listing elsewhere or have removed it entirely from the catalogue. Scott does not attempt to account for every possible number, but rather attempts to assure that each stamp is assigned its own number.

Scott numbers designating regular postage normally are only numerals. Scott numbers for other types of stamps, such as air post, semi-postal, postal tax, postage due, occupation and others have a prefix consisting of one or more capital letters or a combination of numerals and capital letters.

B Illustration number — Illustration or design-type numbers are used to identify each catalogue illustration. For most sets, the lowest face-value stamp is shown. It then serves as an example of the basic design approach for other stamps not illustrated. Where more than one stamp use the same illustration number, but have differences in design, the design paragraph or the description line clearly indicates the design on each stamp not illustrated. Where there are both vertical and horizontal designs in a set, a single illustration may be used, with the exceptions noted in the design paragraph or description line.

When an illustration is followed by a lower-case letter in parentheses, such as "A2(b)," the trailing letter indicates which overprint or surcharge illustration applies.

Illustrations normally are 70 percent of the original size of the stamp. An effort has been made to note all illustrations not illustrated at that percentage. Virtually all souvenir sheet illustrations are reduced even more. Overprints and surcharges are shown at 100 percent of their original size if shown alone, but are 70 percent of original size if shown on stamps. In some cases, the illustration will be placed above the set, between listings or omitted completely. Overprint and surcharge illustrations are not placed in this catalogue for purposes of expertizing stamps.

C Paper color — The color of a stamp's paper is noted in italic type when the paper used is not white.

D Listing styles — There are two principal types of catalogue listings: major and minor.

Major listings are in a larger type style than minor listings. The catalogue number is a numeral that can be found with or without a capital-letter suffix, and with or without a prefix.

Minor listings are in a smaller type style and have a small-letter suffix or (if the listing immediately follows that of the major number) may show only the letter. These listings identify a variety of the major item. Examples include perforation, color, watermark or printing method differences, multiples (some souvenir sheets, booklet panes and se-tenant combinations), and singles of multiples.

Examples of major number listings include 16, 28A, B97, C13A, 10N5, and 10N6A. Examples of minor numbers are 16a and C13Ab.

E Basic information about a stamp or set — Introducing each stamp issue is a small section (usually a line listing) of basic information about a stamp or set. This section normally includes the date of issue, method of printing, perforation, watermark and, sometimes, some additional information of note. *Printing method, perforation and watermark apply to the following sets until a change is noted.* Stamps created by overprinting or surcharging previous issues are assumed to have the same perforation, watermark and printing method as the original. Dates of issue are as precise as Scott is able to confirm and often reflect the dates on first-day covers, rather than the actual date of release.

F Denomination — This normally refers to the face value of the stamp; that is, the cost of the unused stamp at the post office at the time of issue. When a denomination is shown in parentheses, it does not appear on the stamp. This includes the non-denominated stamps of the United States, Brazil and Great Britain, for example.

G Color or other description — This area provides information to solidify identification of a stamp. In many recent cases, a description of the stamp design appears in this space, rather than a listing of colors.

H Year of issue — In stamp sets that have been released in a period that spans more than a year, the number shown in parentheses is the year that stamp first appeared. Stamps without a date appeared during the first year of the issue. Dates are not always given for minor varieties.

I Value unused and Value used — The Scott catalogue values are based on stamps that are in a grade of Very Fine unless stated otherwise. Unused values refer to items that have not seen postal, revenue or any other duty for which they were intended. Pre-1900 unused stamps that were issued with gum must have at least most of their original gum. Later issues are assumed to have full original gum. From breakpoints specified in most countries' listings, stamps are valued as never hinged. Stamps issued without gum are noted. Modern issues with PVA or other synthetic adhesives may appear ungummed. Self-adhesive stamps are valued as appearing undisturbed on their original backing paper. For a more detailed explanation of these values, please see the "Catalogue Value," "Condition" and "Understanding Valuing Notations" sections elsewhere in this introduction.

In some cases, where used stamps are more valuable than unused stamps, the value is for an example with a contemporaneous cancel, rather than a modern cancel or a smudge or other unclear marking. For those stamps that were released for postal and fiscal purposes, the used value represents a postally used stamp. Stamps with revenue cancels generally sell for less. Scott values for used self-adhesive stamps are for examples either on piece or off piece.

J Changes in basic set information — Bold type is used to show any changes in the basic data given for a set of stamps. This includes perforation differences from one stamp to the next or a different paper, printing method or watermark.

K Total value of a set — The total value of sets of three or more stamps issued after 1900 are shown. The set line also notes the range of Scott numbers and total number of stamps included in the grouping. The actual value of a set consisting predominantly of stamps having the minimum value of twenty cents may be less than the total value shown. Similary, the actual value or catalogue value of se-tenant pairs or of blocks consisting of stamps having the minimum value of twenty cents may be less than the catalogue values of the component parts.

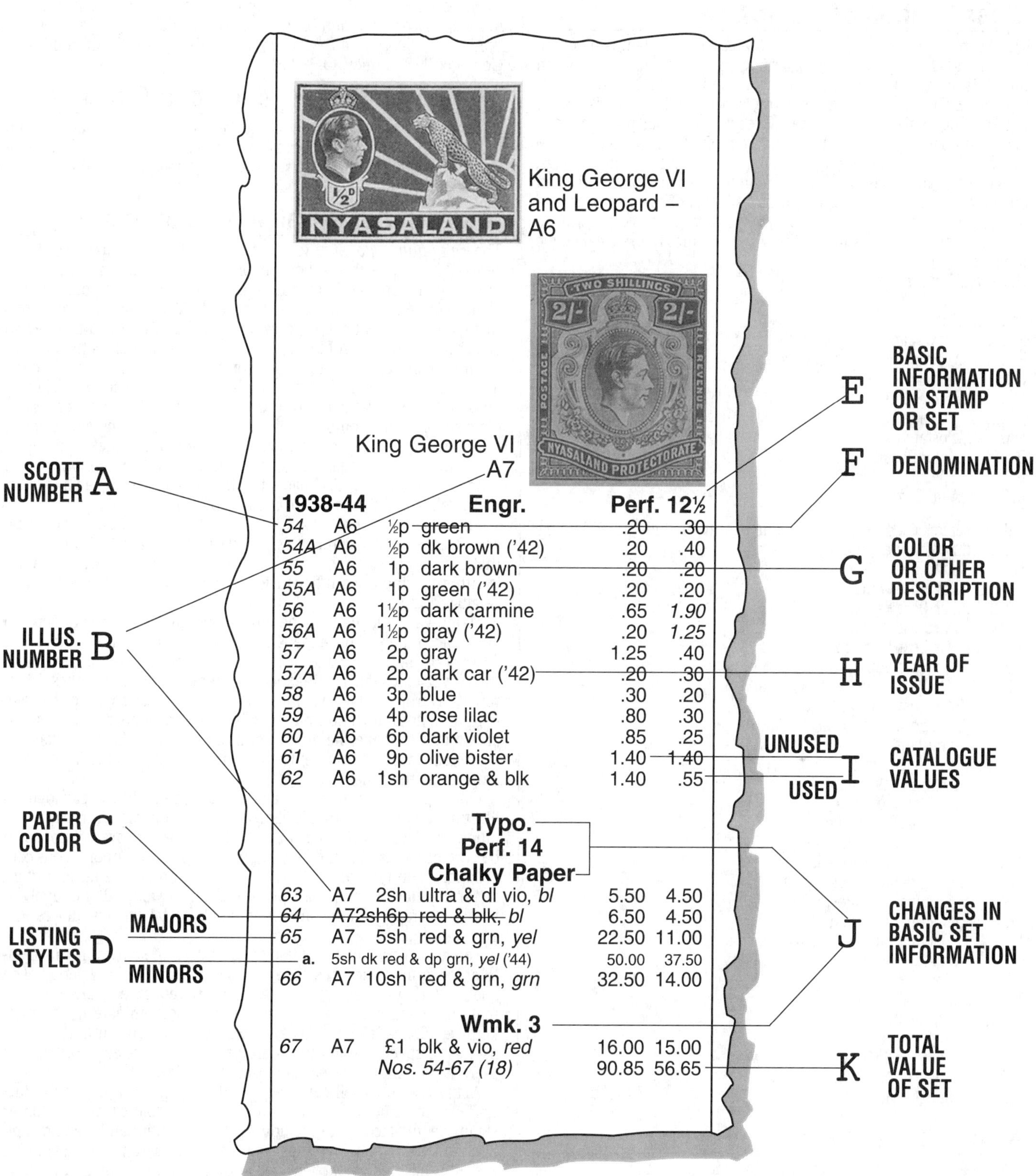

NYASALAND
King George VI and Leopard – A6
TWO SHILLINGS
2/-
POSTAGE
REVENUE
NYASALAND PROTECTORATE
King George VI A7
SCOTT NUMBER A
ILLUS. NUMBER B
PAPER COLOR C
LISTING STYLES D
MAJORS
MINORS
E BASIC INFORMATION ON STAMP OR SET
F DENOMINATION
G COLOR OR OTHER DESCRIPTION
H YEAR OF ISSUE
UNUSED
USED
I CATALOGUE VALUES
J CHANGES IN BASIC SET INFORMATION
K TOTAL VALUE OF SET
1938-44 Engr. Perf. 12½
54 A6 ½p green .20 .30
54A A6 ½p dk brown ('42) .20 .40
55 A6 1p dark brown .20 .20
55A A6 1p green ('42) .20 .20
56 A6 1½p dark carmine .65 1.90
56A A6 1½p gray ('42) .20 1.25
57 A6 2p gray 1.25 .40
57A A6 2p dark car ('42) .20 .30
58 A6 3p blue .30 .20
59 A6 4p rose lilac .80 .30
60 A6 6p dark violet .85 .25
61 A6 9p olive bister 1.40 1.40
62 A6 1sh orange & blk 1.40 .55
Typo.
Perf. 14
Chalky Paper
63 A7 2sh ultra & dl vio, bl 5.50 4.50
64 A7 2sh6p red & blk, bl 6.50 4.50
65 A7 5sh red & grn, yel 22.50 11.00
a. 5sh dk red & dp grn, yel ('44) 50.00 37.50
66 A7 10sh red & grn, grn 32.50 14.00
Wmk. 3
67 A7 £1 blk & vio, red 16.00 15.00
Nos. 54-67 (18) 90.85 56.65

Special Notices

Classification of stamps

The *Scott Standard Postage Stamp Catalogue* lists stamps by country of issue. The next level of organization is a listing by section on the basis of the function of the stamps. The principal sections cover regular postage, semi-postal, air post, special delivery, registration, postage due and other categories. Except for regular postage, catalogue numbers for all sections include a prefix letter (or number-letter combination) denoting the class to which a given stamp belongs. When some countries issue sets containing stamps from more than one category, the catalogue will at times list all of the stamps in one category (such as air post stamps listed as part of a postage set).

The following is a listing of the most commonly used catalogue prefixes.

Prefix...Category
C ....Air Post
M...........Military
P............Newspaper
N ....Occupation - Regular Issues
O...........Official
Q...........Parcel Post
J.............Postage Due
RA ....Postal Tax
B............Semi-Postal
E............Special Delivery
MR ....War Tax

Other prefixes used by more than one country include the following:
H ....Acknowledgment of Receipt
I.............Late Fee
CO.........Air Post Official
CQ.........Air Post Parcel Post
RAC.......Air Post Postal Tax
CF..........Air Post Registration
CB ....Air Post Semi-Postal
CBO.......Air Post Semi-Postal Official
CE ....Air Post Special Delivery
EY..........Authorized Delivery
S ....Franchise
G ....Insured Letter
GY ....Marine Insurance
MC ....Military Air Post
MQ........Military Parcel Post
NC.........Occupation - Air Post
NO.........Occupation - Official
NJ ....Occupation - Postage Due
NRA.......Occupation - Postal Tax
NB ....Occupation - Semi-Postal
NE ....Occupation - Special Delivery
QY ....Parcel Post Authorized Delivery
AR ....Postal-fiscal
RAJ ....Postal Tax Due
RAB ....Postal Tax Semi-Postal
F ....Registration
EB..........Semi-Postal Special Delivery
EO ....Special Delivery Official
QE ....Special Handling

New issue listings

Updates to this catalogue appear each month in the *Scott Stamp Monthly* magazine. Included in this update are additions to the listings of countries found in the *Scott Standard Postage Stamp Catalogue* and the *Specialized Catalogue of United States Stamps*, as well as corrections and updates to current editions of this catalogue.

From time to time there will be changes in the final listings of stamps from the *Scott Stamp Monthly* to the next edition of the catalogue. This occurs as more information about certain stamps or sets becomes available.

The catalogue update section of the *Scott Stamp Monthly* is the most timely presentation of this material available. Annual subscriptions to the *Scott Stamp Monthly* are available from Scott Publishing Co., Box 828, Sidney, OH 45365-0828.

Number additions, deletions & changes

A listing of catalogue number additions, deletions and changes from the previous edition of the catalogue appears in each volume. See Catalogue Number Additions, Deletions & Changes in the table of contents for the location of this list.

Understanding valuing notations

The *minimum catalogue value* of an individual stamp or set is 20 cents. This represents a portion of the cost incurred by a dealer when he prepares an individual stamp for resale. As a point of philatelic-economic fact, the lower the value shown for an item in this catalogue, the greater the percentage of that value is attributed to dealer mark up and profit margin. In many cases, such as the 20-cent minimum value, that price does not cover the labor or other costs involved with stocking it as an individual stamp. The sum of minimum values in a set does not properly represent the value of a complete set primarily composed of a number of minimum-value stamps, nor does the sum represent the actual value of a packet made up of minimum-value stamps. Thus a packet of 1,000 different common stamps — each of which has a catalogue value of 20-cents — normally sells for considerably less than 200 dollars!

The *absence of a retail value* for a stamp does not necessarily suggest that a stamp is scarce or rare. A dash in the value column means that the stamp is known in a stated form or variety, but information is either lacking or insufficient for purposes of establishing a usable catalogue value.

Stamp values in *italics* generally refer to items that are difficult to value accurately. For expensive items, such as those priced at $1,000 or higher, a value in italics indicates that the affected item trades very seldom. For inexpensive items, a value in italics represents a warning. One example is a "blocked" issue where the issuing postal administration may have controlled one stamp in a set in an attempt to make the whole set more valuable. Another example is an item that sold at an extreme multiple of face value in the marketplace at the time of its issue.

One type of warning to collectors that appears in the catalogue is illustrated by a stamp that is valued considerably higher in used condition than it is as unused. In this case, collectors are cautioned to be certain the used version has a genuine and contemporaneous cancellation. The type of cancellation on a stamp can be an important factor in determining its sale price. Catalogue values do not apply to fiscal, telegraph or non-contemporaneous postal cancels, unless otherwise noted.

Some countries have released back issues of stamps in canceled-to-order form, sometimes covering as much as a 10-year period. The Scott Catalogue values for used stamps reflect canceled-to-order material when such stamps are found to predominate in the marketplace for the issue involved. Notes frequently appear in the stamp listings to specify which items are valued as canceled-to-order, or if there is a premium for postally used examples.

Many countries sell canceled-to-order stamps at a marked reduction of face value. Countries that sell or have sold canceled-to-order stamps at *full* face value include Australia, Netherlands, France and Switzerland. It may be almost impossible to identify such stamps if the gum has been removed, because official government canceling devices are used. Postally used copies of these items on cover, however, are usually worth more than the canceled-to-order stamps with original gum.

Abbreviations

Scott Publishing Co. uses a consistent set of abbreviations throughout this catalogue to conserve space, while still providing necessary information.

COLOR ABBREVIATIONS

amb.....amber
anil.....aniline
ap.......apple
aqua.....aquamarine
az.......azure
bis.......bister
bl.........blue
bld.......blood
blk.......black
bril.......brilliant
brn.......brown
brnsh...brownish
brnz.....bronze
brt.......bright
brnt.....burnt
car.......carmine
cer.......cerise
chlky....chalky
cham...chamois
chnt.....chestnut
choc.....chocolate
chr.......chrome
cit........citron
cl.........claret
cob......cobalt
cop......copper
crim.....crimson
cr.........cream
dk........dark
dl.........dull
dp........deep
db........drab
emer....emerald
gldn.....golden
grysh....grayish
grn.......green
grnsh...greenish
hel.......heliotrope
hn........henna
ind.......indigo
int........intense
lav.......lavender
lem......lemon
lil.........lilac
lt..........light
mag.....magenta
man.....manila
mar......maroon
mv.......mauve
multi....multicolored
mlky....milky
myr......myrtle
ol.........olive
olvn.....olivine
org.......orange
pck......peacock
pnksh...pinkish
Prus.....Prussian
pur.......purple
redsh...reddish
res.......reseda
ros.......rosine
ryl........royal
sal........salmon
saph.....sapphire
scar......scarlet
sep.......sepia
sien......sienna
sil........silver
sl.........slate
stl........steel
turq.....turquoise
ultra.....ultramarine
Ven......Venetian
ver.......vermilion
vio.......violet
yel.......yellow
yelsh....yellowish

When no color is given for an overprint or surcharge, black is the color used. Abbreviations for colors used for overprints and surcharges include: "(B)" or "(Blk)," black; "(Bl)," blue; "(R)," red; and "(G)," green.

Additional abbreviations in this catalogue are shown below:

Adm...............Administration
AFL.................American Federation of Labor
Anniv..............Anniversary
APS.................American Philatelic Society
Assoc..............Association
ASSR..............Autonomous Soviet Socialist Republic
b.....................Born
BEP.................Bureau of Engraving and Printing
Bicent.............Bicentennial
Bklt.................Booklet
Brit.................British
btwn...............Between
Bur..................Bureau
c. or ca...........Circa
Cat.................Catalogue
Cent...............Centennial, century, centenary
CIO.................Congress of Industrial Organizations
Conf...............Conference
Cong...............Congress
Cpl.................Corporal
CTO................Canceled to order
d.....................Died
Dbl.................Double
EKU.................Earliest known use
Engr................Engraved
Exhib..............Exhibition
Expo...............Exposition
Fed.................Federation
GB...................Great Britain
Gen................General
GPO................General post office
Horiz..............Horizontal
Imperf.............Imperforate
Impt...............Imprint
Intl.................International
Invtd...............Inverted
L......................Left
Lieut., lt..........Lieutenant
Litho...............Lithographed
LL....................Lower left
LR...................Lower right
mm..................Millimeter
Ms...................Manuscript
Natl.................National
No...................Number
NY...................New York
NYC................New York City
Ovpt...............Overprint
Ovptd.............Overprinted
P......................Plate number
Perf.................Perforated, perforation
Phil.................Philatelic
Photo..............Photogravure
PO..................Post office
Pr....................Pair
P.R..................Puerto Rico
Prec................Precancel, precanceled
Pres................President
PTT.................Post, Telephone and Telegraph
Rio...................Rio de Janeiro
Sgt...................Sergeant
Soc.................Society
Souv...............Souvenir
SSR.................Soviet Socialist Republic, see ASSR
St.....................Saint, street
Surch..............Surcharge
Typo...............Typographed
UL..................Upper left
Unwmkd.........Unwatermarked
UPU................Universal Postal Union
UR...................Upper Right
US..................United States
USPOD...........United States Post Office Department
USSR..............Union of Soviet Socialist Republics
Vert................Vertical
VP...................Vice president
Wmk...............Watermark
Wmkd.............Watermarked
WWI..............World War I
WWII.............World War II

Examination

Scott Publishing Co. will not comment upon the genuineness, grade or condition of stamps, because of the time and responsibility involved. Rather, there are several expertizing groups that undertake this work for both collectors and dealers. Neither will Scott Publishing Co. appraise or identify philatelic material. The company cannot take responsibility for unsolicited stamps or covers sent by individuals.

How to order from your dealer

When ordering stamps from a dealer, it is not necessary to write the full description of a stamp as listed in this catalogue. All you need is the name of the country, the Scott catalogue number and whether the desired item is unused or used. For example, "Japan Scott 422 unused" is sufficient to identify the unused stamp of Japan listed as "422 A206 5y brown."

Basic Stamp Information

A stamp collector's knowledge of the combined elements that make a given stamp issue unique determines his or her ability to identify stamps. These elements include paper, watermark, method of separation, printing, design and gum. On the following pages each of these important areas is briefly described.

Paper

Paper is an organic material composed of a compacted weave of cellulose fibers and generally formed into sheets. Paper used to print stamps may be manufactured in sheets, or it may have been part of a large roll (called a web) before being cut to size. The fibers most often used to create paper on which stamps are printed include bark, wood, straw and certain grasses. In many cases, linen or cotton rags have been added for greater strength and durability. Grinding, bleaching, cooking and rinsing these raw fibers reduces them to a slushy pulp, referred to by paper makers as "stuff." Sizing and, sometimes, coloring matter is added to the pulp to make different types of finished paper.

After the stuff is prepared, it is poured onto sieve-like frames that allow the water to run off, while retaining the matted pulp. As fibers fall onto the screen and are held by gravity, they form a natural weave that will later hold the paper together. If the screen has metal bits that are formed into letters or images attached, it leaves slightly thinned areas on the paper. These are called watermarks.

When the stuff is almost dry, it is passed under pressure through smooth or engraved rollers - dandy rolls - or placed between cloth in a press to be flattened and dried.

Stamp paper falls broadly into two types: wove and laid. The nature of the surface of the frame onto which the pulp is first deposited causes the differences in appearance between the two. If the surface is smooth and even, the paper will be of fairly uniform texture throughout. This is known as *wove paper.* Early papermaking machines poured the pulp onto a continuously circulating web of felt, but modern machines feed the pulp onto a cloth-like screen made of closely interwoven fine wires. This paper, when held to a light, will show little dots or points very close together. The proper name for this is "wire wove," but the type is still considered wove. Any U.S. or British stamp printed after 1880 will serve as an example of wire wove paper.

Closely spaced parallel wires, with cross wires at wider intervals, make up the frames used for what is known as *laid paper.* A greater thickness of the pulp will settle between the wires. The paper, when held to a light, will show alternate light and dark lines. The spacing and the thickness of the lines may vary, but on any one sheet of paper they are all alike. See Russia Scott 31-38 for examples of laid paper.

Batonne, from the French word meaning "a staff," is a term used if the lines in the paper are spaced quite far apart, like the printed ruling on a writing tablet. Batonne paper may be either wove or laid. If laid, fine laid lines can be seen between the batons. The laid lines, which are a form of watermark, may be geometrical figures such as squares, diamonds, rectangles or wavy lines.

Quadrille is the term used when the lines in the paper form little squares. *Oblong quadrille* is the term used when rectangles, rather than squares, are formed. See Mexico-Guadalajara Scott 35-37 for examples of oblong quadrille paper.

Paper also is classified as thick or thin, hard or soft, and by color if dye is added during manufacture. Such colors may include yellowish, greenish, bluish and reddish.

Brief explanations of other types of paper used for printing stamps, as well as examples, follow.

Pelure — Pelure paper is a very thin, hard and often brittle paper that is sometimes bluish or grayish in appearance. See Serbia Scott 169-170.

Native — This is a term applied to handmade papers used to produce some of the early stamps of the Indian states. Stamps printed on native paper may be expected to display various natural inclusions that are normal and do not negatively affect value. Japanese paper, originally made of mulberry fibers and rice flour, is part of this group. See Japan Scott 1-18.

Manila — This type of paper is often used to make stamped envelopes and wrappers. It is a coarse-textured stock, usually smooth on one side and rough on the other. A variety of colors of manila paper exist, but the most common range is yellowish-brown.

Silk — Introduced by the British in 1847 as a safeguard against counterfeiting, silk paper contains bits of colored silk thread scattered throughout. The density of these fibers varies greatly and can include as few as one fiber per stamp or hundreds. U.S. revenue Scott R152 is a good example of an easy-to-identify silk paper stamp.

Silk-thread paper has uninterrupted threads of colored silk arranged so that one or more threads run through the stamp or postal stationery. See Great Britain Scott 5-6 and Switzerland Scott 14-19.

Granite — Filled with minute cloth or colored paper fibers of various colors and lengths, granite paper should not be confused with either type of silk paper. Austria Scott 172-175 and a number of Swiss stamps are examples of granite paper.

Chalky — A chalk-like substance coats the surface of chalky paper to discourage the cleaning and reuse of canceled stamps, as well as to provide a smoother, more acceptable printing surface. Because the designs of stamps printed on chalky paper are imprinted on what is often a water-soluble coating, any attempt to remove a cancellation will destroy the stamp. *Do not soak these stamps in any fluid.* To remove a stamp printed on chalky paper from an envelope, wet the paper from underneath the stamp until the gum dissolves enough to release the stamp from the paper. See St. Kitts-Nevis Scott 89-90 for examples of stamps printed on this type of chalky paper.

India — Another name for this paper, originally introduced from China about 1750, is "China Paper." It is a thin, opaque paper often used for plate and die proofs by many countries.

Double — In philately, the term double paper has two distinct meanings. The first is a two-ply paper, usually a combination of a thick and a thin sheet, joined during manufacture. This type was used experimentally as a means to discourage the reuse of stamps.

The design is printed on the thin paper. Any attempt to remove a cancellation would destroy the design. U.S. Scott 158 and other Banknote-era stamps exist on this form of double paper.

The second type of double paper occurs on a rotary press, when the end of one paper roll, or web, is affixed to the next roll to save time feeding the paper through the press. Stamp designs are printed over the joined paper and, if overlooked by inspectors, may get into post office stocks.

Goldbeater's Skin — This type of paper was used for the 1866 issue of Prussia, and was a tough, translucent paper. The design was printed in reverse on the back of the stamp, and the gum applied over the printing. It is impossible to remove stamps printed on this type of paper from the paper to which they are affixed without destroying the design.

Ribbed — Ribbed paper has an uneven, corrugated surface made by passing the paper through ridged rollers. This type exists on some copies of U.S. Scott 156-165.

Various other substances, or substrates, have been used for stamp manufacture, including wood, aluminum, copper, silver and gold foil, plastic, and silk and cotton fabrics.

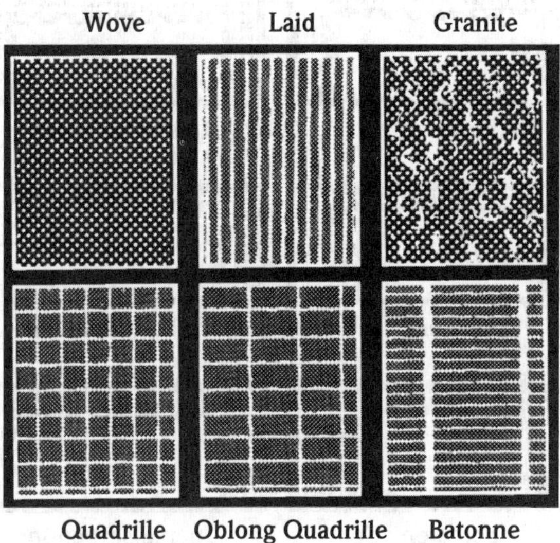

Watermarks

Watermarks are an integral part of some papers. They are formed in the process of paper manufacture. Watermarks consist of small designs, formed of wire or cut from metal and soldered to the surface of the mold or, sometimes, on the dandy roll. The designs may be in the form of crowns, stars, anchors, letters or other characters or symbols. These pieces of metal - known in the paper-making industry as "bits" - impress a design into the paper. The design sometimes may be seen by holding the stamp to the light. Some are more easily seen with a watermark detector. This important tool is a small black tray into which a stamp is placed face down and dampened with a fast-evaporating watermark detection fluid that brings up the watermark image in the form of dark lines against a lighter background. These dark lines are the thinner areas of the paper known as the watermark. Some watermarks are extremely difficult to locate, due to either a faint impression, watermark location or the color of the stamp. There also are electric watermark detectors that come with plastic filter disks of various colors. The disks neutralize the color of the stamp, permitting the watermark to be seen more easily.

Multiple watermarks of Crown Agents and Burma

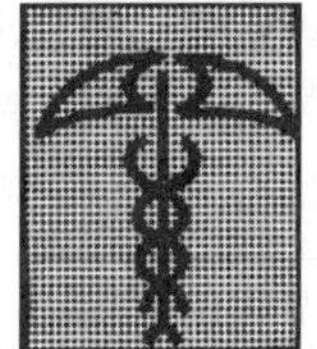

Watermarks of Uruguay, Vatican City and Jamaica

WARNING: Some inks used in the photogravure process dissolve in watermark fluids (Please see the section on Soluble Printing Inks). Also, see "chalky paper."

Watermarks may be found normal, reversed, inverted, reversed and inverted, sideways or diagonal, as seen from the back of the stamp. The relationship of watermark to stamp design depends on the position of the printing plates or how paper is fed through the press. On machine-made paper, watermarks normally are read from right to left. The design is repeated closely throughout the sheet in a "multiple-watermark design." In a "sheet watermark," the design appears only once on the sheet, but extends over many stamps. Individual stamps may carry only a small fraction or none of the watermark.

"Marginal watermarks" occur in the margins of sheets or panes of stamps. They occur on the outside border of paper (ostensibly outside the area where stamps are to be printed). A large row of letters may spell the name of the country or the manufacturer of the paper, or a border of lines may appear. Careless press feeding may cause parts of these letters and/or lines to show on stamps of the outer row of a pane.

Soluble Printing Inks

WARNING: Most stamp colors are permanent; that is, they are not seriously affected by short-term exposure to light or water. Many colors, especially of modern inks, fade from excessive exposure to light. There are stamps printed with inks that dissolve easily in water or in fluids used to detect watermarks. Use of these inks was intentional to prevent the removal of cancellations. Water affects all aniline inks, those on so-called safety paper and some photogravure printings - all such inks are known as *fugitive colors. Removal from paper of such stamps requires care and alternatives to traditional soaking.*

Separation

"Separation" is the general term used to describe methods used to separate stamps. The three standard forms currently in use are perforating, rouletting and die-cutting. These methods are done during the stamp production process, after printing. Sometimes these methods are done on-press or sometimes as a separate step. The earliest issues, such as the 1840 Penny Black of Great Britain (Scott 1), did not have any means provided for separation. It was expected the stamps would be cut apart with scissors or folded and torn. These are examples of imperforate stamps. Many stamps were first issued in imperforate formats and were later issued with perforations. Therefore, care must be observed in buying single imperforate stamps to be certain they were issued imperforate and are not perforated copies that have been altered by having the perforations trimmed away. Stamps issued imperforate usually are valued as singles. However, imperforate varieties of normally perforated stamps should be collected in pairs or larger pieces as indisputable evidence of their imperforate character.

PERFORATION

The chief style of separation of stamps, and the one that is in almost universal use today, is perforating. By this process, paper between the stamps is cut away in a line of holes, usually round, leaving little bridges of paper between the stamps to hold them together. Some types of perforation, such as hyphen-hole perfs, can be confused with roulettes, but a close visual inspection reveals that paper has been removed. The little perforation bridges, which project from the stamp when it is torn from the pane, are called the teeth of the perforation.

As the size of the perforation is sometimes the only way to differentiate between two otherwise identical stamps, it is necessary to be able to accurately measure and describe them. This is done with a perforation gauge, usually a ruler-like device that has dots or graduated lines to show how many perforations may be counted in the space of two centimeters. Two centimeters is the space universally adopted in which to measure perforations.

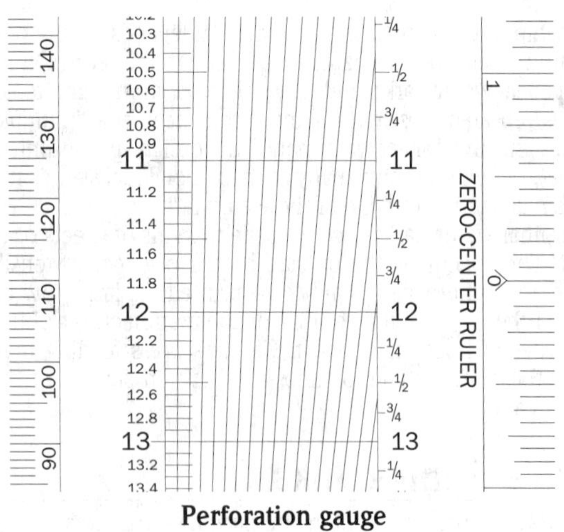
Perforation gauge

To measure a stamp, run it along the gauge until the dots on it fit exactly into the perforations of the stamp. If you are using a graduated-line perforation gauge, simply slide the stamp along the surface until the lines on the gauge perfectly project from the center of the bridges or holes. The number to the side of the line of dots or lines that fit the stamp's perforation is the measurement. For example, an "11" means that 11 perforations fit between two centimeters. The description of the stamp therefore is "perf. 11." If the gauge of the perforations on the top and bottom of a stamp differs from that on the sides, the result is what is known as *compound perforations.* In measuring compound perforations, the gauge at top and bottom is always given first, then the sides. Thus, a stamp that measures 11 at top and bottom and 10 1/2 at the sides is "perf. 11 x 10 1/2." See U.S. Scott 632-642 for examples of compound perforations.

Stamps also are known with perforations different on three or all four sides. Descriptions of such items are clockwise, beginning with the top of the stamp.

A perforation with small holes and teeth close together is a "fine perforation." One with large holes and teeth far apart is a "coarse perforation." Holes that are jagged, rather than clean-cut, are "rough perforations." *Blind perforations* are the slight impressions left by the perforating pins if they fail to puncture the paper. Multiples of stamps showing blind perforations may command a slight premium over normally perforated stamps.

The term *syncopated perfs* describes intentional irregularities in the perforations. The earliest form was used by the Netherlands from 1925-33, where holes were omitted to create distinctive patterns. Beginning in 1992, Great Britain has used an oval perforation to help prevent counterfeiting. Several other countries have started using the oval perfs or other syncopated perf patterns.

A new type of perforation, still primarily used for postal stationery, is known as microperfs. Microperfs are tiny perforations (in some cases hundreds of holes per two centimeters) that allows items to be intentionally separated very easily, while not accidentally breaking apart as easily as standard perforations. These are not currently measured or differentiated by size, as are standard perforations.

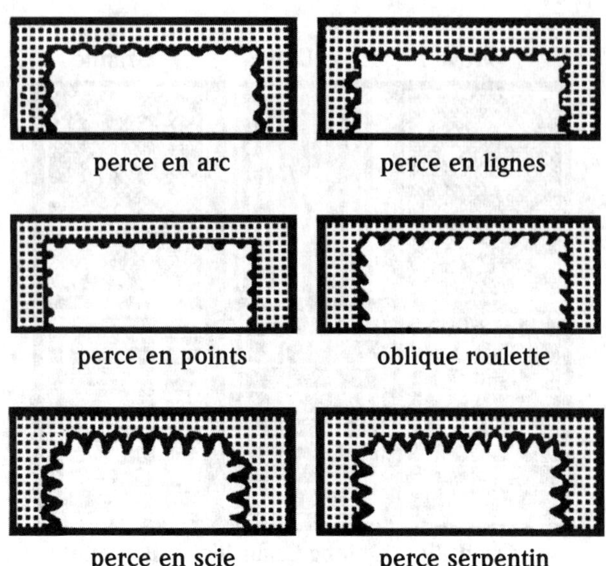

ROULETTING

In rouletting, the stamp paper is cut partly or wholly through, with no paper removed. In perforating, some paper is removed. Rouletting derives its name from the French roulette, a spur-like wheel. As the wheel is rolled over the paper, each point makes a small cut. The number of cuts made in a two-centimeter space determines the gauge of the roulette, just as the number of perforations in two centimeters determines the gauge of the perforation.

The shape and arrangement of the teeth on the wheels varies. Various roulette types generally carry French names:

Perce en lignes - rouletted in lines. The paper receives short, straight cuts in lines. This is the most common type of rouletting. See Mexico Scott 500.

Perce en points - pin-rouletted. This differs from a small perforation because no paper is removed, although round, equidistant holes are pricked through the paper. See Mexico Scott 242-256.

Perce en arc and *perce en scie* - pierced in an arc or saw-toothed designs, forming half circles or small triangles. See Hanover (German States) Scott 25-29.

Perce en serpentin - serpentine roulettes. The cuts form a serpentine or wavy line. See Brunswick (German States) Scott 13-18.

Once again, no paper is removed by these processes, leaving the stamps easily separated, but closely attached.

DIE-CUTTING

The third major form of stamp separation is die-cutting. This is a method where a die in the pattern of separation is created that later cuts the stamp paper in a stroke motion. Although some standard stamps bear die-cut perforations, this process is primarily used for self-adhesive postage stamps. Die-cutting can appear in straight lines, such as U.S. Scott 2522, shapes, such as U.S. Scott 1551, or imitating the appearance of perforations, such as New Zealand Scott 935A and 935B.

Printing Processes

ENGRAVING (Intaglio, Line-engraving, Etching)

Master die — The initial operation in the process of line engraving is making the master die. The die is a small, flat block of softened steel upon which the stamp design is recess engraved in reverse.

Master die

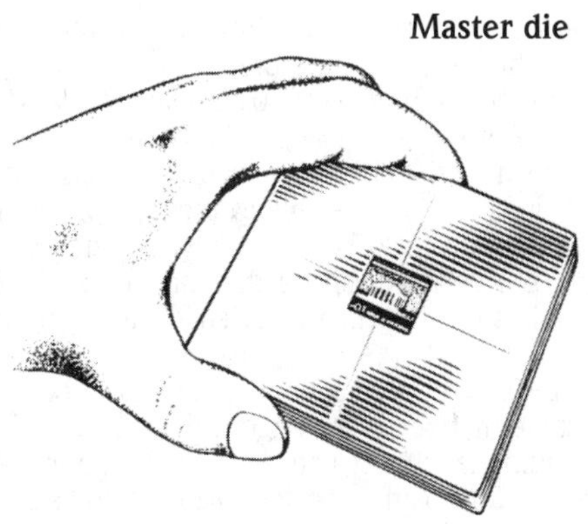

Photographic reduction of the original art is made to the appropriate size. It then serves as a tracing guide for the initial outline of the design. The engraver lightly traces the design on the steel with his graver, then slowly works the design until it is completed. At various points during the engraving process, the engraver hand-inks the die and makes an impression to check his progress. These are known as progressive die proofs. After completion of the engraving, the die is hardened to withstand the stress and pressures of later transfer operations.

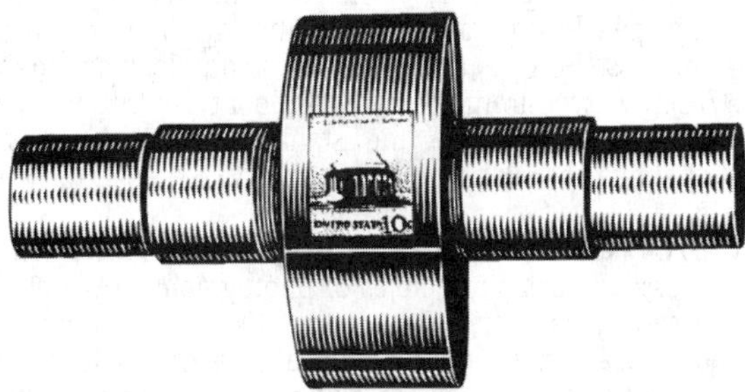

Transfer roll

Transfer roll — Next is production of the transfer roll that, as the name implies, is the medium used to transfer the subject from the master die to the printing plate. A blank roll of soft steel, mounted on a mandrel, is placed under the bearers of the transfer press to allow it to roll freely on its axis. The hardened die is placed on the bed of the press and the face of the transfer roll is applied to the die, under pressure. The bed or the roll is then rocked back and forth under increasing pressure, until the soft steel of the roll is forced into every engraved line of the die. The resulting impression on the roll is known as a "relief" or a "relief transfer." The engraved image is now positive in appearance and stands out from the steel. After the required number of reliefs are "rocked in," the soft steel transfer roll is hardened.

Different flaws may occur during the relief process. A defective relief may occur during the rocking in process because of a minute piece of foreign material lodging on the die, or some other cause. Imperfections in the steel of the transfer roll may result in a breaking away of parts of the design. This is known as a relief break, which will show up on finished stamps as small, unprinted areas. If a damaged relief remains in use, it will transfer a repeating defect to the plate. Deliberate alterations of reliefs sometimes occur. "Altered reliefs" designate these changed conditions.

Plate — The final step in pre-printing production is the making of the printing plate. A flat piece of soft steel replaces the die on the bed of the transfer press. One of the reliefs on the transfer roll is positioned over this soft steel. Position, or layout, dots determine the correct position on the plate. The dots have been lightly marked on the plate in advance. After the correct position of the relief is determined, the design is rocked in by following the same method used in making the transfer roll. The difference is that this time the image is being transferred from the transfer roll, rather than to it. Once the design is entered on the plate, it appears in reverse and is recessed. There are as many transfers entered on the plate as there are subjects printed on the sheet of stamps. It is during this process that double and shifted transfers occur, as well as re-entries. These are the result of improperly entered images that have not been properly burnished out prior to rocking in a new image.

Modern siderography processes, such as those used by the U.S. Bureau of Engraving and Printing, involve an automated form of rocking designs in on preformed cylindrical printing sleeves. The same process also allows for easier removal and re-entry of worn images right on the sleeve.

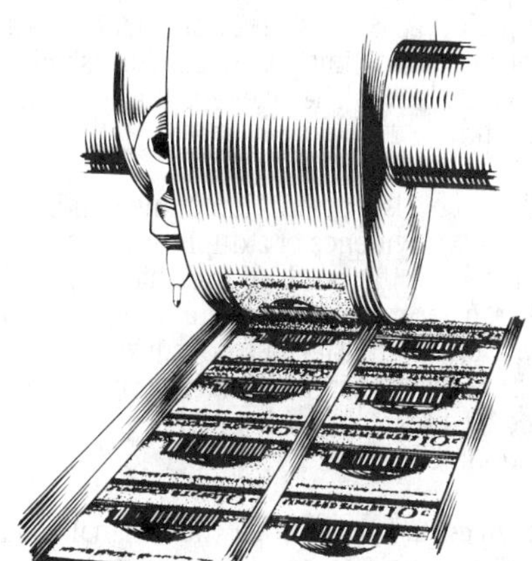

Transferring the design to the plate

Following the entering of the required transfers on the plate, the position dots, layout dots and lines, scratches and other markings generally are burnished out. Added at this time by the siderographer are any required *guide lines, plate numbers* or other *marginal markings.* The plate is then hand-inked and a proof impression is taken. This is known as a plate proof. If the impression is approved, the plate is machined for fitting onto the press, is hardened and sent to the plate vault ready for use.

On press, the plate is inked and the surface is automatically wiped clean, leaving ink only in the recessed lines. Paper is then forced under pressure into the engraved recessed lines, thereby receiving the ink. Thus, the ink lines on engraved stamps are slightly raised, and slight depressions (debossing) occur on the back of the stamp. Prior to the advent of modern high-speed presses and more advanced ink formulations, paper had to be dampened before receiving the ink. This sometimes led to uneven shrinkage by the time the stamps were perforated, resulting in improperly perforated stamps, or misperfs. Newer presses use drier paper, thus both *wet* and *dry printings* exist on some stamps.

Rotary Press — Until 1914, only flat plates were used to print engraved stamps. Rotary press printing was introduced in 1914, and slowly spread. Some countries still use flat-plate printing.

After approval of the plate proof, older *rotary press plates* require additional machining. They are curved to fit the press cylinder. "Gripper slots" are cut into the back of each plate to receive the "grippers," which hold the plate securely on the press. The plate is then hardened. Stamps printed from these bent rotary press plates are longer or wider than the same stamps printed from flat-plate presses. The stretching of the plate during the curving process is what causes this distortion.

Re-entry — To execute a re-entry on a flat plate, the transfer roll is re-applied to the plate, often at some time after its first use on the press. Worn-out designs can be resharpened by carefully burnishing out the original image and re-entering it from the transfer roll. If the original impression has not been sufficiently removed and the transfer roll is not precisely in line with the remaining impression, the resulting double transfer will make the re-entry obvious. If the registration is true, a re-entry may be difficult or impossible to distinguish. Sometimes a stamp printed from a successful re-entry is identified by having a much sharper and clearer impression than its neighbors. With the advent of rotary presses, post-press re-entries were not possible. After a plate was curved for the rotary press, it was impossible to make a re-entry. This is because the plate had already been bent once (with the design distorted).

However, with the introduction of the previously mentioned modern-style siderography machines, entries are made to the preformed cylindrical printing sleeve. Such sleeves are dechromed and softened. This allows individual images to be burnished out and re-entered on the curved sleeve. The sleeve is then rechromed, resulting in longer press life.

Double Transfer — This is a description of the condition of a transfer on a plate that shows evidence of a duplication of all, or a portion of the design. It usually is the result of the changing of the registration between the transfer roll and the plate during the rocking in of the original entry. Double transfers also occur when only a portion of the design has been rocked in and improper positioning is noted. If the worker elected not to burnish out the partial or completed design, a strong double transfer will occur for part or all of the design.

It sometimes is necessary to remove the original transfer from a plate and repeat the process a second time. If the finished re-worked image shows traces of the original impression, attributable to incomplete burnishing, the result is a partial double transfer.

With the modern automatic machines mentioned previously, double transfers are all but impossible to create. Those partially doubled images on stamps printed from such sleeves are more than likely re-entries, rather than true double transfers.

Re-engraved — Alterations to a stamp design are sometimes necessary after some stamps have been printed. In some cases, either the original die or the actual printing plate may have its "temper" drawn (softened), and the design will be re-cut. The resulting impressions from such a re-engraved die or plate may differ slightly from the original issue, and are known as "re-engraved." If the alteration was made to the master die, all future printings will be consistently different from the original. If alterations were made to the printing plate, each altered stamp on the plate will be slightly different from each other, allowing specialists to reconstruct a complete printing plate.

Dropped Transfers — If an impression from the transfer roll has not been properly placed, a dropped transfer may occur. The final stamp image will appear obviously out of line with its neighbors.

Short Transfer — Sometimes a transfer roll is not rocked its entire length when entering a transfer onto a plate. As a result, the finished transfer on the plate fails to show the complete design, and the finished stamp will have an incomplete design printed. This is known as a "short transfer." U.S. Scott No. 8 is a good example of a short transfer.

TYPOGRAPHY (Letterpress, Surface Printing, Flexography, Dry Offset, High Etch)

Although the word "Typography" is obsolete as a term describing a printing method, it was the accepted term throughout the first century of postage stamps. Therefore, appropriate Scott listings in this catalogue refer to typographed stamps. The current term for this form of printing, however, is "letterpress."

As it relates to the production of postage stamps, letterpress printing is the reverse of engraving. Rather than having recessed areas trap the ink and deposit it on paper, only the raised areas of the design are inked. This is comparable to the type of printing seen by inking and using an ordinary rubber stamp. Letterpress includes all printing where the design is above the surface area, whether it is wood, metal or, in some instances, hardened rubber or polymer plastic.

For most letterpress-printed stamps, the engraved master is made in much the same manner as for engraved stamps. In this instance, however, an additional step is needed. The design is transferred to another surface before being transferred to the transfer roll. In this way, the transfer roll has a recessed stamp design, rather than one done in relief. This makes the printing areas on the final plate raised, or relief areas.

For less-detailed stamps of the 19th century, the area on the die not used as a printing surface was cut away, leaving the surface area raised. The original die was then reproduced by stereotyping or electrotyping. The resulting electrotypes were assembled in the required number and format of the desired sheet of stamps. The plate used in printing the stamps was an electroplate of these assembled electrotypes.

Once the final letterpress plates are created, ink is applied to the raised surface and the pressure of the press transfers the ink impression to the paper. In contrast to engraving, the fine lines of letterpress are impressed on the surface of the stamp, leaving a debossed surface. When viewed from the back (as on a typewritten page), the corresponding line work on the stamp will be raised slightly (embossed) above the surface.

PHOTOGRAVURE (Gravure, Rotogravure, Heliogravure)

In this process, the basic principles of photography are applied to a chemically sensitized metal plate, rather than photographic paper. The design is transferred photographically to the plate through a halftone, or dot-matrix screen, breaking the reproduction into tiny dots. The plate is treated chemically and the dots form depressions, called cells, of varying depths and diameters, depending on the degrees of shade in the design. Then, like engraving, ink is applied to the plate and the surface is wiped clean. This leaves ink in the tiny cells that is lifted out and deposited on the paper when it is pressed against the plate.

Gravure is most often used for multicolored stamps, generally using the three primary colors (red, yellow and blue) and black. By varying the dot matrix pattern and density of these colors, virtually any color can be reproduced. A typical full-color gravure stamp will be created from four printing cylinders (one for each color). The original multicolored image will have been photographically separated into its component colors.

Modern gravure printing may use computer-generated dot-matrix screens, and modern plates may be of various types including metal-coated plastic. The catalogue designation of Photogravure (or "Photo") covers any of these older and more modern gravure methods of printing.

For examples of the first photogravure stamps printed (1914), see Bavaria Scott 94-114.

LITHOGRAPHY (Offset Lithography, Stone Lithography, Dilitho, Planography, Collotype)

The principle that oil and water do not mix is the basis for lithography. The stamp design is drawn by hand or transferred from engraving to the surface of a lithographic stone or metal plate in a greasy (oily) substance. This oily substance holds the ink, which will later be transferred to the paper. The stone (or plate) is wet with an acid fluid, causing it to repel the printing ink in all areas not covered by the greasy substance.

Transfer paper is used to transfer the design from the original stone or plate. A series of duplicate transfers are grouped and, in turn, transferred to the final printing plate.

Photolithography — The application of photographic processes to lithography. This process allows greater flexibility of design, related to use of halftone screens combined with line work. Unlike photogravure or engraving, this process can allow large, solid areas to be printed.

Offset — A refinement of the lithographic process. A rubber-covered blanket cylinder takes the impression from the inked lithographic plate. From the "blanket" the impression is *offset* or transferred to the paper. Greater flexibility and speed are the principal reasons offset printing has largely displaced lithography. The term "lithography" covers both processes, and results are almost identical.

EMBOSSED (Relief) Printing

Embossing, not considered one of the four main printing types, is a method in which the design first is sunk into the metal of the die. Printing is done against a yielding platen, such as leather or linoleum. The platen is forced into the depression of the die, thus forming the design on the paper in relief. This process is often used for metallic inks.

Embossing may be done without color (see Sardinia Scott 4-6); with color printed around the embossed area (see Great Britain Scott 5 and most U.S. envelopes); and with color in exact registration with the embossed subject (see Canada Scott 656-657).

HOLOGRAMS

For objects to appear as holograms on stamps, a model exactly the same size as it is to appear on the hologram must be created. Rather than using photographic film to capture the image, holography records an image on a photoresist material. In processing, chemicals eat away at certain exposed areas, leaving a pattern of constructive and destructive interference. When the phororesist is developed, the result is a pattern of uneven ridges that acts as a mold. This mold is then coated with metal, and the resulting form is used to press copies in much the same way phonograph records are produced.

A typical reflective hologram used for stamps consists of a reproduction of the uneven patterns on a plastic film that is applied to a reflective background, usually a silver or gold foil. Light is reflected off the background through the film, making the pattern present on the film visible. Because of the uneven pattern of the film, the viewer will perceive the objects in their proper three-dimensional relationships with appropriate brightness.

The first hologram on a stamp was produced by Austria in 1988 (Scott 1441).

FOIL APPLICATION

A modern tecnique of applying color to stamps involves the application of metallic foil to the stamp paper. A pattern of foil is applied to the stamp paper by use of a stamping die. The foil usually is flat, but it may be textured. Canada Scott 1735 has three different foil applications in pearl, bronze and gold. The gold foil was textured using a chemical-etch copper embossing die. The printing of this stamp also involved two-color offset lithography plus embossing.

COMBINATION PRINTINGS

Sometimes two or even three printing methods are combined in producing stamps. In these cases, such as Austria Scott 933 or Canada 1735 (described in the preceding paragraph), the multiple-printing technique can be determined by studing the individual characteristics of each printing type. A few stamps, such as Singapore Scott 684-684A, combine as many as three of the four major printing types (lithography, engraving and typography). When this is done it often indicates the incorporation of security devices against counterfeiting.

INK COLORS

Inks or colored papers used in stamp printing often are of mineral origin, although there are numerous examples of organic-based pigments. As a general rule, organic-based pigments are far more subject to varieties and change than those of mineral-based origin.

The appearance of any given color on a stamp may be affected by many aspects, including printing variations, light, color of paper, aging and chemical alterations.

Numerous printing variations may be observed. Heavier pressure or inking will cause a more intense color, while slight interruptions in the ink feed or lighter impressions will cause a lighter appearance. Stamps printed in the same color by water-based and solvent-based inks can differ significantly in appearance. This affects several stamps in the U.S. Prominent Americans series. Hand-mixed ink formulas (primarily from the 19th century) produced under different conditions (humidity and temperature) account for notable color variations in early printings of the same stamp (see U.S. Scott 248-250, 279B, for example). Different sources of pigment can also result in significant differences in color.

Light exposure and aging are closely related in the way they affect stamp color. Both eventually break down the ink and fade colors, so that a carefully kept stamp may differ significantly in color from an identical copy that has been exposed to light. If stamps are exposed to light either intentionally or accidentally, their colors can be faded or completely changed in some cases.

Papers of different quality and consistency used for the same stamp printing may affect color appearance. Most pelure papers, for example, show a richer color when compared with wove or laid papers. See Russia Scott 181a, for an example of this effect.

The very nature of the printing processes can cause a variety of differences in shades or hues of the same stamp. Some of these shades are scarcer than others, and are of particular interest to the advanced collector.

Luminescence

All forms of tagged stamps fall under the general category of luminescence. Within this broad category is fluorescence, dealing with forms of tagging visible under longwave ultraviolet light, and phosphorescence, which deals with tagging visible only under shortwave light. Phosphorescence leaves an afterglow and fluorescence does not. These treated stamps show up in a range of different colors when exposed to UV light. The differing wavelengths of the light activates the tagging material, making it glow in various colors that usually serve different mail processing purposes.

Intentional tagging is a post-World War II phenomenon, brought about by the increased literacy rate and rapidly growing mail volume. It was one of several answers to the problem of the need for more automated mail processes. Early tagged stamps served the purpose of triggering machines to separate different types of mail. A natural outgrowth was to also use the signal to trigger machines that faced all envelopes the same way and canceled them.

Tagged stamps come in many different forms. Some tagged stamps have luminescent shapes or images imprinted on them as a form of security device. Others have blocks (United States), stripes, frames (South Africa and Canada), overall coatings (United States), bars (Great Britain and Canada) and many other types. Some types of tagging are even mixed in with the pigmented printing ink (Australia Scott 366, Netherlands Scott 478 and U.S. Scott 1359 and 2443).

The means of applying taggant to stamps differs as much as the intended purposes for the stamps. The most common form of tagging is a coating applied to the surface of the printed stamp. Since the taggant ink is frequently invisible except under UV light, it does not interfere with the appearance of the stamp. Another common application is the use of phosphored papers. In this case the paper itself either has a coating of taggant applied before the stamp is printed, has taggant applied during the papermaking process (incorporating it into the fibers), or has the taggant mixed into the coating of the paper. The latter method, among others, is currently in use in the United States.

Many countries now use tagging in various forms to either expedite mail handling or to serve as a printing security device against counterfeiting. Following the introduction of tagged stamps for public use in 1959 by Great Britain, other countries have steadily joined the parade. Among those are Germany (1961); Canada and Denmark (1962); United States, Australia, France and Switzerland (1963); Belgium and Japan (1966); Sweden and Norway (1967); Italy (1968); and Russia (1969). Since then, many other countries have begun using forms of tagging, including Brazil, China, Czechoslovakia, Hong Kong, Guatemala, Indonesia, Israel, Lithuania, Luxembourg, Netherlands, Penrhyn Islands, Portugal, St. Vincent, Singapore, South Africa, Spain and Sweden to name a few.

In some cases, including United States, Canada, Great Britain and Switzerland, stamps were released both with and without tagging. Many of these were released during each country's experimental period. Tagged and untagged versions are listed for the aforementioned countries and are noted in some other countries' listings. For at least a few stamps, the experimentally tagged version is worth far more than its untagged counterpart, such as the 1963 experimental tagged version of France Scott 1024.

In some cases, luminescent varieties of stamps were inadvertently created. Several Russian stamps, for example, sport highly fluorescent ink that was not intended as a form of tagging. Older stamps, such as early U.S. postage dues, can be positively identified by the use of UV light, since the organic ink used has become slightly fluorescent over time. Other stamps, such as Austria Scott 70a-82a (varnish bars) and Obock Scott 46-64 (printed quadrille lines), have become fluorescent over time.

Various fluorescent substances have been added to paper to make it appear brighter. These optical brightners, as they are known, greatly affect the appearance of the stamp under UV light. The brightest of these is known as Hi-Brite paper. These paper varieties are beyond the scope of the Scott Catalogue.

Shortwave UV light also is used extensively in expertizing, since each form of paper has its own fluorescent characteristics that are impossible to perfectly match. It is therefore a simple matter to detect filled thins, added perforation teeth and other alterations that involve the addition of paper. UV light also is used to examine stamps that have had cancels chemically removed and for other purposes as well.

Gum

The Illustrated Gum Chart in the first part of this introduction shows and defines various types of gum condition. Because gum condition has an important impact on the value of unused stamps, we recommend studying this chart and the accompanying text carefully.

The gum on the back of a stamp may be shiny, dull, smooth, rough, dark, white, colored or tinted. Most stamp gumming adhesives use gum arabic or dextrine as a base. Certain polymers such as polyvinyl alcohol (PVA) have been used extensively since World War II.

The *Scott Standard Postage Stamp Catalogue* does not list items by types of gum. The *Scott Specialized Catalogue of United States Stamps* does differentiate among some types of gum for certain issues.

Reprints of stamps may have gum differing from the original issues. In addition, some countries have used different gum formulas for different seasons. These adhesives have different properties that may become more apparent over time.

Many stamps have been issued without gum, and the catalogue will note this fact. See, for example, United States Scott 40-47. Sometimes, gum may have been removed to preserve the stamp. Germany Scott B68, for example, has a highly acidic gum that eventually destroys the stamps. This item is valued in the catalogue with gum removed.

Reprints and Reissues

These are impressions of stamps (usually obsolete) made from the original plates or stones. If they are valid for postage and reproduce obsolete issues (such as U.S. Scott 102-111), the stamps are *reissues.* If they are from current issues, they are designated as *second, third,* etc., *printing.* If designated for a particular purpose, they are called *special printings.*

When special printings are not valid for postage, but are made from original dies and plates by authorized persons, they are *official reprints. Private reprints* are made from the original plates and dies by private hands. An example of a private reprint is that of the 1871-1932 reprints made from the original die of the 1845 New Haven, Conn., postmaster's provisional. *Official reproductions* or imitations are made from new dies and plates by government authorization. Scott will list those reissues that are valid for postage if they differ significantly from the original printing.

The U.S. government made special printings of its first postage stamps in 1875. Produced were official imitations of the first two stamps (listed as Scott 3-4), reprints of the demonetized pre-1861 issues (Scott 40-47) and reissues of the 1861 stamps, the 1869 stamps and the then-current 1875 denominations. Even though the official imitations and the reprints were not valid for postage, Scott lists all of these U.S. special printings.

Most reprints or reissues differ slightly from the original stamp in some characteristic, such as gum, paper, perforation, color or watermark. Sometimes the details are followed so meticulously that only a student of that specific stamp is able to distinguish the reprint or reissue from the original.

Remainders and Canceled to Order

Some countries sell their stock of old stamps when a new issue replaces them. To avoid postal use, the *remainders* usually are canceled with a punch hole, a heavy line or bar, or a more-or-less regular-looking cancellation. The most famous merchant of remainders was Nicholas F. Seebeck. In the 1880s and 1890s, he arranged printing contracts between the Hamilton Bank Note Co., of which he was a director, and several Central and South American countries. The contracts provided that the plates and all remainders of the yearly issues became the property of Hamilton. Seebeck saw to it that ample stock remained. The "Seebecks," both remainders and reprints, were standard packet fillers for decades.

Some countries also issue stamps *canceled-to-order (CTO),* either in sheets with original gum or stuck onto pieces of paper or envelopes and canceled. Such CTO items generally are worth less than postally used stamps. In cases where the CTO material is far more prevalent in the marketplace than postally used examples, the catalogue value relates to the CTO examples, with postally used examples noted as premium items. Most CTOs can be detected by the presence of gum. However, as the CTO practice goes back at least to 1885, the gum inevitably has been soaked off some stamps so they could pass as postally used. The normally applied postmarks usually differ slightly from standard postmarks, and specialists are able to tell the difference. When applied individually to envelopes by philatelically minded persons, CTO material is known as *favor canceled* and generally sells at large discounts.

Cinderellas and Facsimiles

Cinderella is a catch-all term used by stamp collectors to describe phantoms, fantasies, bogus items, municipal issues, exhibition seals, local revenues, transportation stamps, labels, poster stamps and many other types of items. Some cinderella collectors include in their collections local postage issues, telegraph stamps, essays and proofs, forgeries and counterfeits.

A *fantasy* is an adhesive created for a nonexistent stamp-issuing authority. Fantasy items range from imaginary countries (Occusi-Ambeno, Kingdom of Sedang, Principality of Trinidad or Torres Straits), to non-existent locals (Winans City Post), or nonexistent transportation lines (McRobish & Co.'s Acapulco-San Francisco Line).

On the other hand, if the entity exists and could have issued stamps (but did not) or was known to have issued other stamps, the items are considered *bogus* stamps. These would include the Mormon postage stamps of Utah, S. Allan Taylor's Guatemala and Paraguay inventions, the propaganda issues for the South Moluccas and the adhesives of the Page & Keyes local post of Boston.

Phantoms is another term for both fantasy and bogus issues.

Facsimiles are copies or imitations made to represent original stamps, but which do not pretend to be originals. A catalogue illustration is such a facsimile. Illustrations from the Moens catalogue of the last century were occasionally colored and passed off as stamps. Since the beginning of stamp collecting, facsimiles have been made for collectors as space fillers or for reference. They often carry the word "facsimile," "falsch" (German), "sanko" or "mozo" (Japanese), or "faux" (French) overprinted on the face or stamped on the back. Unfortunately, over the years a number of these items have had fake cancels applied over the facsimile notation and have been passed off as genuine.

Forgeries and Counterfeits

Forgeries and counterfeits have been with philately virtually from the beginning of stamp production. Over time, the terminology for the two has been used interchangeably. Although both forgeries and counterfeits are reproductions of stamps, the purposes behind their creation differ considerably.

Among specialists there is an increasing movement to more specifically define such items. Although there is no universally accepted terminology, we feel the following definitions most closely mirror the items and their purposes as they are currently defined.

Forgeries (also often referred to as *Counterfeits*) are reproductions of genuine stamps that have been created to defraud collectors. Such spurious items first appeared on the market around 1860, and most old-time collections contain one or more. Many are crude and easily spotted, but some can deceive experts.

An important supplier of these early philatelic forgeries was the Hamburg printer Gebruder Spiro. Many others with reputations in this craft included S. Allan Taylor, George Hussey, James Chute, George Forune, Benjamin & Sarpy, Julius Goldner, E. Oneglia and L.H. Mercier. Among the noted 20th-century forgers were Francois Fournier, Jean Sperati and the prolific Raoul DeThuin.

Forgeries may be complete replications, or they may be genuine stamps altered to resemble a scarcer (and more valuable) type. Most forgeries, particularly those of rare stamps, are worth only a small fraction of the value of a genuine example, but a few types, created by some of the most notable forgers, such as Sperati, can be worth as much or more than the genuine. Fraudulently produced copies are known of most classic rarities and many medium-priced stamps.

In addition to rare stamps, large numbers of common 19th- and early 20th-century stamps were forged to supply stamps to the early packet trade. Many can still be easily found. Few new philatelic forgeries have appeared in recent decades. Successful imitation of well-engraved work is virtually impossible. It has proven far easier to produce a fake by altering a genuine stamp than to duplicate a stamp completely.

Counterfeit (also often referred to as *Postal Counterfeit* or *Postal Forgery*) is the term generally applied to reproductions of stamps that have been created to defraud the government of revenue. Such items usually are created at the time a stamp is current and, in some cases, are hard to detect. Because most counterfeits are seized when the perpetrator is captured, postal counterfeits, particularly used on cover, are usually worth much more than a genuine example to specialists. The first postal counterfeit was of Spain's 4-cuarto carmine of 1854 (the real one is Scott 25). Apparently, the counterfeiters were not satisfied with their first version, which is now very scarce, and they soon created an engraved counterfeit, which is common. Postal counterfeits quickly followed in Austria, Naples, Sardinia and the Roman States. They have since been created in many other countries as well, including the United States.

An infamous counterfeit to defraud the government is the 1-shilling Great Britain "Stock Exchange" forgery of 1872, used on telegraph forms at the exchange that year. The stamp escaped detection until a stamp dealer noticed it in 1898.

Fakes

Fakes are genuine stamps altered in some way to make them more desirable. One student of this part of stamp collecting has estimated that by the 1950s more than 30,000 varieties of fakes were known. That number has grown greatly since then. The widespread existence of fakes makes it important for stamp collectors to study their philatelic holdings and use relevant literature. Likewise, collectors should buy from reputable dealers who guarantee their stamps and make full and prompt refunds should a purchased item be declared faked or altered by some mutually agreed-upon authority. Because fakes always have some genuine characteristics, it is not always possible to obtain unanimous agreement among experts regarding specific items. These students may change their opinions as philatelic knowledge increases. More than 80 percent of all fakes on the philatelic market today are regummed, reperforated (or perforated for the first time), or bear forged overprints, surcharges or cancellations.

Stamps can be chemically treated to alter or eliminate colors. For example, a pale rose stamp can be re-colored to resemble a blue shade of high market value. In other cases, treated stamps can be made to resemble missing color varieties. Designs may be changed by painting, or a stroke or a dot added or bleached out to turn an ordinary variety into a seemingly scarcer stamp. Part of a stamp can be bleached and reprinted in a different version, achieving an inverted center or frame. Margins can be added or repairs done so deceptively that the stamps move from the "repaired" into the "fake" category.

Fakers have not left the backs of the stamps untouched either. They may create false watermarks, add fake grills or press out genuine grills. A thin India paper proof may be glued onto a thicker backing to create the appearance an issued stamp, or a proof printed on cardboard may be shaved down and perforated to resemble a stamp. Silk threads are impressed into paper and stamps have been split so that a rare paper variety is added to an otherwise inexpensive stamp. The most common treatment to the back of a stamp, however, is regumming.

Some in the business of faking stamps have openly advertised foolproof application of "original gum" to stamps that lack it, although most publications now ban such ads from their pages. It is believed that very few early stamps have survived without being hinged. The large number of never-hinged examples of such earlier material offered for sale thus suggests the widespread extent of regumming activity. Regumming also may be used to hide repairs or thin spots. Dipping the stamp into watermark fluid, or examining it under longwave ultraviolet light often will reveal these flaws.

Fakers also tamper with separations. Ingenious ways to add margins are known. Perforated wide-margin stamps may be falsely represented as imperforate when trimmed. Reperforating is commonly done to create scarce coil or perforation varieties, and to eliminate the naturally occurring straight-edge stamps found in sheet margin positions of many earlier issues. Custom has made straight-edged stamps less desirable. Fakers have obliged by perforating straight-edged stamps so that many are now uncommon, if not rare.

Another fertile field for the faker is that of overprints, surcharges and cancellations. The forging of rare surcharges or overprints began in the 1880s or 1890s. These forgeries are sometimes difficult to detect, but experts have identified almost all. Occasionally, overprints or cancellations are removed to create non-overprinted stamps or seemingly unused items. This is most commonly done by removing a manuscript cancel to make a stamp resemble an unused example. "SPECIMEN" overprints may be removed by scraping and repainting to create non-overprinted varieties. Fakers use inexpensive revenues or pen-canceled stamps to generate unused stamps for further faking by adding other markings. The quartz lamp or UV lamp and a high-powered magnifying glass help to easily detect removed cancellations.

The bigger problem, however, is the addition of overprints, surcharges or cancellations - many with such precision that they are very difficult to ascertain. Plating of the stamps or the overprint can be an important method of detection.

Fake postmarks may range from many spurious fancy cancellations to a host of markings applied to transatlantic covers, to adding normally appearing postmarks to definitives of some countries with stamps that are valued far higher used than unused. With the increased popularity of cover collecting, and the widespread interest in postal history, a fertile new field for fakers has come about. Some have tried to create entire covers. Others specialize in adding stamps, tied by fake cancellations, to genuine stampless covers, or replacing less expensive or damaged stamps with more valuable ones. Detailed study of postal rates in effect at the time a cover in question was mailed, including the analysis of each handstamp used during the period, ink analysis and similar techniques, usually will unmask the fraud.

Restoration and Repairs

Scott Publishing Co. bases its catalogue values on stamps that are free of defects and otherwise meet the standards set forth earlier in this introduction. Most stamp collectors desire to have the finest copy of an item possible. Even within given grading categories there are variances. This leads to a controversial practice that is not defined in any universal manner: stamp *restoration.*

There are broad differences of opinion about what is permissible when it comes to restoration. Carefully applying a soft eraser to a stamp or cover to remove light soiling is one form of restoration, as is washing a stamp in mild soap and water to clean it. These are fairly accepted forms of restoration. More severe forms of restoration include pressing out creases or removing stains caused by tape. To what degree each of these is acceptable is dependent upon the individual situation. Further along the spectrum is the freshening of a stamp's color by removing oxide build-up or the effects of wax paper left next to stamps shipped to the tropics.

At some point in this spectrum the concept of *repair* replaces that of restoration. Repairs include filling thin spots, mending tears by reweaving or adding a missing perforation tooth. Regumming stamps may have been acceptable as a restoration or repair technique many decades ago, but today it is considered a form of fakery.

Restored stamps may or may not sell at a discount, and it is possible that the value of individual restored items may be enhanced over that of their pre-restoration state. Specific situations dictate the resultant value of such an item. Repaired stamps sell at substantial discounts from the value of sound stamps.

Terminology

Booklets — Many countries have issued stamps in small booklets for the convenience of users. This idea continues to become increasingly popular in many countries. Booklets have been issued in many sizes and forms, often with advertising on the covers, the panes of stamps or on the interleaving.

The panes used in booklets may be printed from special plates or made from regular sheets. All panes from booklets issued by the United States and many from those of other countries contain stamps that are straight edged on the sides, but perforated between. Others are distinguished by orientation of watermark or other identifying features. Any stamp-like unit in the pane, either printed or blank, that is not a postage stamp, is considered to be a *label* in the catalogue listings.

Scott lists and values booklet panes only. Complete booklets are listed and valued in only a few cases, such as Grenada Scott 1055 and some forms of British prestige booklets. Individual booklet panes are listed only when they are not fashioned from existing sheet stamps and, therefore, are identifiable from their sheet stamp counterparts.

Panes usually do not have a used value assigned to them because there is little market activity for used booklet panes, even though many exist used and there is some demand for them.

Cancellations — The marks or obliterations put on stamps by postal authorities to show that they have performed service and to prevent their reuse are known as cancellations. If the marking is made with a pen, it is considered a "pen cancel." When the location of the post office appears in the marking, it is a "town cancellation." A "postmark" is technically any postal marking, but in practice the term generally is applied to a town cancellation with a date. When calling attention to a cause or celebration, the marking is known as a "slogan cancellation." Many other types and styles of cancellations exist, such as duplex, numerals, targets, fancy and others. See also "precancels," below.

Coil Stamps — These are stamps that are issued in rolls for use in dispensers, affixing and vending machines. Those coils of the United States, Canada, Sweden and some other countries are perforated horizontally or vertically only, with the outer edges imperforate. Coil stamps of some countries, such as Great Britain and Germany, are perforated on all four sides and may in some cases be distinguished from their sheet stamp counterparts by watermarks, counting numbers on the reverse or other means.

Covers — Entire envelopes, with or without adhesive postage stamps, that have passed through the mail and bear postal or other markings of philatelic interest are known as covers. Before the introduction of envelopes in about 1840, people folded letters and wrote the address on the outside. Some people covered their letters with an extra sheet of paper on the outside for the address, producing the term "cover." Used airletter sheets, stamped envelopes and other items of postal stationery also are considered covers.

Errors — Stamps that have some major, consistent, unintentional deviation from the normal are considered errors. Errors include, but are not limited to, missing or wrong colors, wrong paper, wrong watermarks, inverted centers or frames on multicolor printing, inverted or missing surcharges or overprints, double impressions, missing perforations and others. Factually wrong or misspelled information, if it appears on all examples of a stamp, are not considered errors in the true sense of the word. They are errors of design. Inconsistent or randomly appearing items, such as misperfs or color shifts, are classified as freaks.

Color-Omitted Errors — This term refers to stamps where a missing color is caused by the complete failure of the printing plate to deliver ink to the stamp paper or any other paper. Generally, this is caused by the printing plate not being engaged on the press or the ink station running dry of ink during printing.

Color-Missing Errors — This term refers to stamps where a color or colors were printed somewhere but do not appear on the finished stamp. There are four different classes of color-missing errors, and the catalog indicates with a two-letter code appended to each such listing what caused the color to be missing:

FO = A *foldover* of the stamp sheet during printing may block ink from appearing on a stamp. Instead, the color will appear on the back of the foldover (where it might fall on the back of the selvage or perhaps on the back of another stamp).

EP = A piece of *extraneous paper* falling across the plate or stamp paper will receive the printed ink. When the extraneous paper is removed, an unprinted portion of stamp paper remains and shows partially or totally missing colors.

CM = A misregistration of the printing plates during printing will result in a *color misregistration*, and such a misregistration may result in a color not appearing on the finished stamp.

PS = A *perforation shift* after printing may remove a color from the finished stamp. Normally, this will occur on a row of stamps at the edge of the stamp pane.

Overprints and Surcharges — Overprinting involves applying wording or design elements over an already existing stamp. Overprints can be used to alter the place of use (such as "Canal Zone" on U.S. stamps), to adapt them for a special purpose ("Porto" on Denmark's 1913-20 regular issues for use as postage due stamps, Scott J1-J7) or to commemorate a special occasion (United States Scott 647-648).

A *surcharge* is a form of overprint that changes or restates the face value of a stamp or piece of postal stationery.

Surcharges and overprints may be handstamped, typeset or, occasionally, lithographed or engraved. A few hand-written overprints and surcharges are known.

Precancels — Stamps that are canceled before they are placed in the mail are known as precancels. Precanceling usually is done to expedite the handling of large mailings and generally allow the affected mail pieces to skip certain phases of mail handling.

In the United States, precancellations generally identified the point of origin; that is, the city and state. This information appeared across the face of the stamp, usually centered between parallel lines. More recently, bureau precancels retained the parallel lines, but the city and state designations were dropped. Recent coils have a service inscription that is present on the original printing plate. These show the mail service paid for by the stamp. Since these stamps are not intended to receive further cancellations when used as intended, they are considered precancels. Such items often do not have parallel lines as part of the precancellation.

In France, the abbreviation *Affranchts* in a semicircle together with the word *Postes* is the general form of precancel in use. Belgian precancellations usually appear in a box in which the name of the city appears. Netherlands precancels have the name of the city enclosed between concentric circles, sometimes called a "lifesaver." Precancellations of other countries usually follow these patterns, but may be any arrangement of bars, boxes and city names.

Precancels are listed in the Scott catalogues only if the precancel changes the denomination (Belgium Scott 477-478); if the precanceled stamp is different from the non-precanceled version (such as untagged U.S. precancels); or if the stamp exists only precanceled (France Scott 1096-1099, U.S. Scott 2265).

Proofs and Essays — Proofs are impressions taken from an approved die, plate or stone in which the design and color are the same as the stamp issued to the public. Trial color proofs are impressions taken from approved dies, plates or stones in colors that vary from the final version. An essay is the impression of a design that differs in some way from the issued stamp. "Progressive die proofs" generally are considered to be essays.

Provisionals — These are stamps that are issued on short notice and intended for temporary use pending the arrival of regular issues. They usually are issued to meet such contingencies as changes in government or currency, shortage of necessary postage values or military occupation.

During the 1840s, postmasters in certain American cities issued stamps that were valid only at specific post offices. In 1861, postmasters of the Confederate States also issued stamps with limited validity. Both of these examples are known as "postmaster's provisionals."

Se-tenant — This term refers to an unsevered pair, strip or block of stamps that differ in design, denomination or overprint.

Unless the se-tenant item has a continuous design (see U.S. Scott 1451a, 1694a) the stamps do not have to be in the same order as shown in the catalogue (see U.S. Scott 2158a).

Specimens — The Universal Postal Union required member nations to send samples of all stamps they released into service to the International Bureau in Switzerland. Member nations of the UPU received these specimens as samples of what stamps were valid for postage. Many are overprinted, handstamped or initial-perforated "Specimen," "Canceled" or "Muestra." Some are marked with bars across the denominations (China-Taiwan), punched holes (Czechoslovakia) or back inscriptions (Mongolia).

Stamps distributed to government officials or for publicity purposes, and stamps submitted by private security printers for official approval, also may receive such defacements.

The previously described defacement markings prevent postal use, and all such items generally are known as "specimens."

Tete Beche — This term describes a pair of stamps in which one is upside down in relation to the other. Some of these are the result of intentional sheet arrangements, such as Morocco Scott B10-B11. Others occurred when one or more electrotypes accidentally were placed upside down on the plate, such as Colombia Scott 57a. Separation of the tete-beche stamps, of course, destroys the tete beche variety.

Currency Conversion

Country	Dollar	Pound	S Franc	Yen	HK Dollar	Euro	Cdn Dollar	Aus Dollar
Australia	1.7702	2.8134	1.2256	0.0147	0.2269	1.8108	1.1342	-----
Canada	1.5608	2.4806	0.0807	0.0129	0.2001	1.5966	-----	0.8817
European Union	0.9776	1.5537	0.6769	0.0081	0.1253	-----	0.6263	0.5523
Hong Kong	7.8003	12.397	5.4007	0.0647	-----	7.9790	4.9976	4.4065
Japan	120.57	191.62	83.480	-----	15.457	123.33	77.249	68.111
Switzerland	1.4443	2.2954	-----	0.0120	0.1852	1.4774	0.9254	0.8159
United Kingdom	0.6292	-----	0.4356	0.0052	0.0807	0.6436	0.4031	0.3554
United States	-----	1.5893	0.6924	0.0083	0.1282	1.0229	0.6407	0.5649

Country	Currency	U.S. $ Equiv.
Afghanistan	afghani	.0002
Aitutaki	New Zealand dollar	.5144
Albania	lek	.0074
Algeria	dinar	.0127
Andorra (French)	euro	1.0229
Andorra (Spanish)	euro	1.0229
Angola	kwanza	.0175
Anguilla	East Caribbean dollar	.3745
Antigua	East Caribbean dollar	.3745
Argentina	peso	.2845
Armenia	dram	.0018
Aruba	guilder	.5587
Ascension	British pound	1.5893
Australia	dollar	.5649
Australian Antarctic Territory	dollar	.5649
Austria	euro	1.0229
Azerbaijan	manat	.0002
Bahamas	dollar	1.00
Bahrain	dinar	2.653
Bangladesh	taka	.0173
Barbados	dollar	.5025
Barbuda	East Caribbean dollar	.3745
Belarus	ruble	.0006
Belgium	euro	1.0229
Belize	dollar	.5076
Benin	Community of French Africa (CFA) franc	.00156
Bermuda	dollar	1.00
Bhutan	ngultrum	.0208
Bolivia	boliviano	.1339
Bosnia & Herzegovina	convertible mark	.5193
Botswana	pula	.1801
Brazil	real	.2681
British Antarctic Territory	British pound	1.5893
British Indian Ocean Territory	British pound	1.5893
Brunei	dollar	.5714
Bulgaria	lev	.5245
Burkina Faso	CFA franc	.00156
Burma	kyat	.1577
Burundi	franc	.0010
United Nations-New York	U.S. dollar	1.00
United Nations-Geneva	Swiss franc	.6924
United Nations-Vienna	euro	1.0229
United States	dollar	1.00

Source: ***Wall Street Journal*** *Dec. 16, 2002. Figures reflect values as of Dec. 13, 2002.*

COMMON DESIGN TYPES

Pictured in this section are issues where one illustration has been used for a number of countries in the Catalogue. Not included in this section are overprinted stamps or those issues which are illustrated in each country.

EUROPA

Europa, 1956

The design symbolizing the cooperation among the six countries comprising the Coal and Steel Community is illustrated in each country.

Belgium	496-497
France	805-806
Germany	748-749
Italy	715-716
Luxembourg	318-320
Netherlands	368-369

Europa, 1958

"E" and Dove — CD1

European Postal Union at the service of European integration.

1958, Sept. 13

Belgium	527-528
France	889-890
Germany	790-791
Italy	750-751
Luxembourg	341-343
Netherlands	375-376
Saar	317-318

Europa, 1959

6-Link Enless Chain — CD2

1959, Sept. 19

Belgium	536-537
France	929-930
Germany	805-806
Italy	791-792
Luxembourg	354-355
Netherlands	379-380

Europa, 1960

19-Spoke Wheel CD3

First anniverary of the establishment of C.E.P.T. (Conference Europeenne des Administrations des Postes et des Telecommunications.) The spokes symbolize the 19 founding members of the Conference.

1960, Sept.

Belgium	553-554
Denmark	379
Finland	376-377
France	970-971
Germany	818-820
Great Britain	377-378
Greece	688
Iceland	327-328
Ireland	175-176
Italy	809-810
Luxembourg	374-375
Netherlands	385-386
Norway	387
Portugal	866-867
Spain	941-942
Sweden	562-563
Switzerland	400-401
Turkey	1493-1494

Europa, 1961

19 Doves Flying as One — CD4

The 19 doves represent the 19 members of the Conference of European Postal and Telecommunications Administrations C.E.P.T.

1961-62

Belgium	572-573
Cyprus	201-203
France	1005-1006
Germany	844-845
Great Britain	383-384
Greece	718-719
Iceland	340-341
Italy	845-846
Luxembourg	382-383
Netherlands	387-388
Spain	1010-1011
Switzerland	410-411
Turkey	1518-1520

Europa, 1962

Young Tree with 19 Leaves CD5

The 19 leaves represent the 19 original members of C.E.P.T.

1962-63

Belgium	582-583
Cyprus	219-221
France	1045-1046
Germany	852-853
Greece	739-740
Iceland	348-349
Ireland	184-185
Italy	860-861
Luxembourg	386-387
Netherlands	394-395
Norway	414-415
Switzerland	416-417
Turkey	1553-1555

Europa, 1963

Stylized Links, Symbolizing Unity — CD6

1963, Sept.

Belgium	598-599
Cyprus	229-231
Finland	419
France	1074-1075
Germany	867-868
Greece	768-769
Iceland	357-358
Ireland	188-189
Italy	880-881
Luxembourg	403-404
Netherlands	416-417
Norway	441-442
Switzerland	429
Turkey	1602-1603

Europa, 1964

Symbolic Daisy — CD7

5th anniversary of the establishment of C.E.P.T. The 22 petals of the flower symbolize the 22 members of the Conference.

1964, Sept.

Austria	738
Belgium	614-615
Cyprus	244-246
France	1109-1110
Germany	897-898
Greece	801-802
Iceland	367-368
Ireland	196-197
Italy	894-895
Luxembourg	411-412
Monaco	590-591
Netherlands	428-429
Norway	458
Portugal	931-933
Spain	1262-1263
Switzerland	438-439
Turkey	1628-1629

Europa, 1965

Leaves and "Fruit" CD8

1965

Belgium	636-637
Cyprus	262-264
Finland	437
France	1131-1132
Germany	934-935
Greece	833-834
Iceland	375-376
Ireland	204-205
Italy	915-916
Luxembourg	432-433
Monaco	616-617
Netherlands	438-439
Norway	475-476
Portugal	958-960
Switzerland	469
Turkey	1665-1666

Europa, 1966

Symbolic Sailboat — CD9

1966, Sept.

Andorra, French	172
Belgium	675-676
Cyprus	275-277
France	1163-1164
Germany	963-964
Greece	862-863
Iceland	384-385
Ireland	216-217
Italy	942-943
Liechtenstein	415
Luxembourg	440-441
Monaco	639-640
Netherlands	441-442
Norway	496-497
Portugal	980-982
Switzerland	477-478
Turkey	1718-1719

Europa, 1967

Cogwheels CD10

1967

Andorra, French	174-175
Belgium	688-689
Cyprus	297-299
France	1178-1179
Germany	969-970
Greece	891-892
Iceland	389-390
Ireland	232-233
Italy	951-952
Liechtenstein	420
Luxembourg	449-450
Monaco	669-670
Netherlands	444-447
Norway	504-505
Portugal	994-996
Spain	1465-1466
Switzerland	482
Turkey	B120-B121

Europa, 1968

Golden Key with C.E.P.T. Emblem CD11

1968

Andorra, French	182-183
Belgium	705-706
Cyprus	314-316
France	1209-1210
Germany	983-984
Greece	916-917
Iceland	395-396
Ireland	242-243
Italy	979-980
Liechtenstein	442
Luxembourg	466-467
Monaco	689-691
Netherlands	452-453
Portugal	1019-1021
San Marino	687
Spain	1526
Turkey	1775-1776

Europa, 1969

"EUROPA" and "CEPT" CD12

Tenth anniversary of C.E.P.T.

1969

Andorra, French	188-189
Austria	837
Belgium	718-719
Cyprus	326-328
Denmark	458
Finland	483
France	1245-1246
Germany	996-997
Great Britain	585
Greece	947-948
Iceland	406-407
Ireland	270-271
Italy	1000-1001
Liechtenstein	453
Luxembourg	474-475
Monaco	722-724
Netherlands	475-476
Norway	533-534
Portugal	1038-1040
San Marino	701-702
Spain	1567
Sweden	814-816

Switzerland 500-501
Turkey 1799-1800
Vatican 470-472
Yugoslavia 1003-1004

Europa, 1970

Interwoven Threads CD13

1970

Andorra, French 196-197
Belgium 741-742
Cyprus 340-342
France 1271-1272
Germany 1018-1019
Greece 985, 987
Iceland 420-421
Ireland 279-281
Italy 1013-1014
Liechtenstein 470
Luxembourg 489-490
Monaco 768-770
Netherlands 483-484
Portugal 1060-1062
San Marino 729-730
Spain 1607
Switzerland 515-516
Turkey 1848-1849
Yugoslavia 1024-1025

Europa, 1971

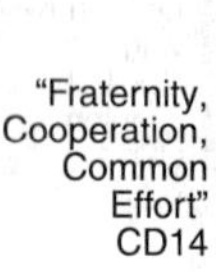

"Fraternity, Cooperation, Common Effort" CD14

1971

Andorra, French 205-206
Belgium 803-804
Cyprus 365-367
Finland 504
France 1304
Germany 1064-1065
Greece 1029-1030
Iceland 429-430
Ireland 305-306
Italy 1038-1039
Liechtenstein 485
Luxembourg 500-501
Malta 425-427
Monaco 797-799
Netherlands 488-489
Portugal 1094-1096
San Marino 749-750
Spain 1675-1676
Switzerland 531-532
Turkey 1876-1877
Yugoslavia 1052-1053

Europa, 1972

Sparkles, Symbolic of Communications CD15

1972

Andorra, French 210-211
Andorra, Spanish 62
Belgium 825-826
Cyprus 380-382
Finland 512-513
France 1341
Germany 1089-1090
Greece 1049-1050
Iceland 439-440
Ireland 316-317
Italy 1065-1066
Liechtenstein 504
Luxembourg 512-513
Malta 450-453
Monaco 831-832
Netherlands 494-495
Portugal 1141-1143
San Marino 771-772
Spain 1718
Switzerland 544-545
Turkey 1907-1908
Yugoslavia 1100-1101

Europa, 1973

Post Horn and Arrows CD16

1973

Andorra, French 319-320
Andorra, Spanish 76
Belgium 839-840
Cyprus 396-398
Finland 526
France 1367
Germany 1114-1115
Greece 1090-1092
Iceland 447-448
Ireland 329-330
Italy 1108-1109
Liechtenstein 528-529
Luxembourg 523-524
Malta 469-471
Monaco 866-867
Netherlands 504-505
Norway 604-605
Portugal 1170-1172
San Marino 802-803
Spain 1753
Switzerland 580-581
Turkey 1935-1936
Yugoslavia 1138-1139

Europa, 2000

CD17

2000

Albania 2621-2622
Andorra, French 522
Andorra, Spanish 262
Armenia 610-611
Austria 1814
Azerbaijan 698-699
Belarus 350
Belgium 1818
Bosnia & Herzegovina (Moslem) 358
Bosnia & Herzegovina (Serb) 111-112
Croatia 428-429
Cyprus 959
Czech Republic 3120
Denmark 1189
Estonia 394
Faroe Islands 376
Finland 1129
Aland Islands 166
France 2771
Georgia 228-229
Germany 2086-2087
Gibraltar 837-840
Great Britain (Guernsey) 805-809
Great Britain (Jersey) 935-936
Great Britain (Isle of Man) 883
Greece 1959
Greenland 363
Hungary 3699-3700
Iceland 910
Ireland 1230-1231
Italy 2349
Latvia 504
Liechtenstein 1178
Lithuania 668
Luxembourg 1035
Macedonia 187
Malta 1011-1012
Moldova 355
Monaco 2161-2162
Poland 3519
Portugal 2358
Portugal (Azores) 455
Portugal (Madeira) 208
Romania 4370
Russia 6589
San Marino 1480
Slovakia 355
Slovenia 424
Spain 3036
Sweden 2394
Switzerland 1074
Turkey 2762
Turkish Rep. of Northern Cyprus 500
Ukraine 379
Vatican City 115

The Gibraltar stamps are similar to the stamp illustrated, but none have the design shown above. All other sets listed above include at least one stamp with the design shown, but some include stamps with entirely different designs. Bulgaria Nos. 4131-4132 are Europa stamps with completely different designs.

PORTUGAL & COLONIES

Vasco da Gama

Fleet Departing CD20

Fleet Arriving at Calicut — CD21

Embarking at Rastello CD22

Muse of History CD23

San Gabriel, da Gama and Camoens CD24

Archangel Gabriel, the Patron Saint CD25

Flagship San Gabriel — CD26

Vasco da Gama — CD27

Fourth centenary of Vasco da Gama's discovery of the route to India.

1898

Azores 93-100
Macao 67-74
Madeira 37-44
Portugal 147-154
Port. Africa 1-8
Port. Congo 75-98
Port. India 189-196
St. Thomas & Prince Islands 170-193
Timor 45-52

Pombal
POSTAL TAX
POSTAL TAX DUES

Marquis de Pombal — CD28

Planning Reconstruction of Lisbon, 1755 — CD29

Pombal Monument, Lisbon — CD30

Sebastiao Jose de Carvalho e Mello, Marquis de Pombal (1699-1782), statesman, rebuilt Lisbon after earthquake of 1755. Tax was for the erection of Pombal monument. Obligatory on all mail on certain days throughout the year. Postal Tax Dues are inscribed "Multa."

1925

Angola RA1-RA3, RAJ1-RAJ3
Azores RA9-RA11, RAJ2-RAJ4
Cape Verde RA1-RA3, RAJ1-RAJ3
Macao RA1-RA3, RAJ1-RAJ3
Madeira RA1-RA3, RAJ1-RAJ3
Mozambique RA1-RA3, RAJ1-RAJ3
Nyassa RA1-RA3, RAJ1-RAJ3
Portugal RA11-RA13, RAJ2-RAJ4
Port. Guinea RA1-RA3, RAJ1-RAJ3
Port. India RA1-RA3, RAJ1-RAJ3
St. Thomas & Prince Islands RA1-RA3, RAJ1-RAJ3
Timor RA1-RA3, RAJ1-RAJ3

Vasco da Gama CD34

Mousinho de Albuquerque CD35

Dam CD36

Prince Henry the Navigator CD37

Affonso de Albuquerque CD38

Plane over Globe CD39

1938-39

Angola 274-291, C1-C9
Cape Verde 234-251, C1-C9
Macao 289-305, C7-C15
Mozambique 270-287, C1-C9

Port. Guinea 233-250, C1-C9
Port. India 439-453, C1-C8
St. Thomas & Prince
  Islands ... 302-319, 323-340, C1-C18
Timor 223-239, C1-C9

Lady of Fatima

Our Lady of the Rosary, Fatima, Portugal — CD40

1948-49

Angola 315-318
Cape Verde 266
Macao 336
Mozambique 325-328
Port. Guinea 271
Port. India 480
St. Thomas & Prince Islands 351
Timor 254

A souvenir sheet of 9 stamps was issued in 1951 to mark the extension of the 1950 Holy Year. The sheet contains: Angola No. 316, Cape Verde No. 266, Macao No. 336, Mozambique No. 325, Portuguese Guinea No. 271, Portuguese India Nos. 480, 485, St. Thomas & Prince Islands No. 351, Timor No. 254. The sheet also contains a portrait of Pope Pius XII and is inscribed "Encerramento do Ano Santo, Fatima 1951." It was sold for 11 escudos.

Holy Year

Church Bells and Dove CD41

Angel Holding Candelabra CD42

Holy Year, 1950.

1950-51

Angola 331-332
Cape Verde 268-269
Macao 339-340
Mozambique 330-331
Port. Guinea 273-274
Port. India 490-491, 496-503
St. Thomas & Prince Islands ... 353-354
Timor 258-259

A souvenir sheet of 8 stamps was issued in 1951 to mark the extension of the Holy Year. The sheet contains: Angola No. 331, Cape Verde No. 269, Macao No. 340, Mozambique No. 331, Portuguese Guinea No. 275, Portuguese India No. 490, St. Thomas & Prince Islands No. 354, Timor No. 258, some with colors changed. The sheet contains doves and is inscribed 'Encerramento do Ano Santo, Fatima 1951.' It was sold for 17 escudos.

Holy Year Conclusion

Our Lady of Fatima — CD43

Conclusion of Holy Year. Sheets contain alternate vertical rows of stamps and labels bearing quotation from Pope Pius XII, different for each colony.

1951

Angola 357
Cape Verde 270
Macao 352
Mozambique 356
Port. Guinea 275
Port. India 506
St. Thomas & Prince Islands 355
Timor 270

Medical Congress

CD44

First National Congress of Tropical Medicine, Lisbon, 1952. Each stamp has a different design.

1952

Angola 358
Cape Verde 287
Macao 364
Mozambique 359
Port. Guinea 276
Port. India 516
St. Thomas & Prince Islands 356
Timor 271

Postage Due Stamps

CD45

1952

Angola J37-J42
Cape Verde J31-J36
Macao J53-J58
Mozambique J51-J56
Port. Guinea J40-J45
Port. India J47-J52
St. Thomas & Prince Islands ... J52-J57
Timor J31-J36

Sao Paulo

Father Manuel de Nobrege and View of Sao Paulo — CD46

Founding of Sao Paulo, Brazil, 400th anniv.

1954

Angola 385
Cape Verde 297
Macao 382
Mozambique 395
Port. Guinea 291
Port. India 530
St. Thomas & Prince Islands 369
Timor 279

Tropical Medicine Congress

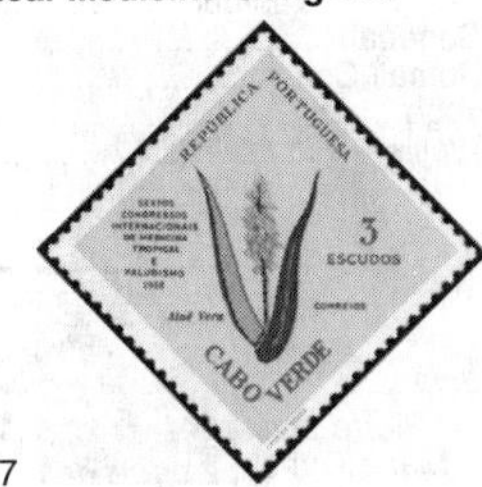

CD47

Sixth International Congress for Tropical Medicine and Malaria, Lisbon, Sept. 1958. Each stamp shows a different plant.

1958

Angola 409
Cape Verde 303
Macao 392
Mozambique 404
Port. Guinea 295
Port. India 569
St. Thomas & Prince Islands 371
Timor 289

Sports

CD48

Each stamp shows a different sport.

1962

Angola 433-438
Cape Verde 320-325
Macao 394-399
Mozambique 424-429
Port. Guinea 299-304
St. Thomas & Prince Islands ... 374-379
Timor 313-318

Anti-Malaria

Anopheles Funestus and Malaria Eradication Symbol — CD49

World Health Organization drive to eradicate malaria.

1962

Angola 439
Cape Verde 326
Macao 400
Mozambique 430
Port. Guinea 305
St. Thomas & Prince Islands 380
Timor 319

Airline Anniversary

Map of Africa, Super Constellation and Jet Liner — CD50

Tenth anniversary of Transportes Aereos Portugueses (TAP).

1963

Angola 490
Cape Verde 327
Mozambique 434
Port. Guinea 318
St. Thomas & Prince Islands 381

National Overseas Bank

Antonio Teixeira de Sousa — CD51

Centenary of the National Overseas Bank of Portugal.

1964, May 16

Angola 509
Cape Verde 328
Port. Guinea 319
St. Thomas & Prince Islands 382
Timor 320

ITU

ITU Emblem and the Archangel Gabriel — CD52

International Communications Union, Cent.

1965, May 17

Angola 511
Cape Verde 329
Macao 402
Mozambique 464
Port. Guinea 320
St. Thomas & Prince Islands 383
Timor 321

National Revolution

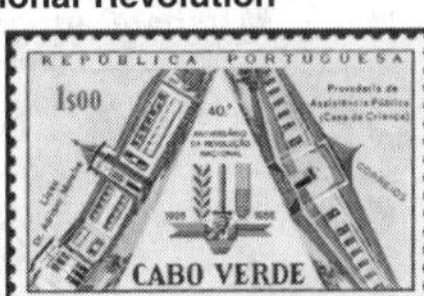

CD53

40th anniv. of the National Revolution. Different buildings on each stamp.

1966, May 28

Angola 525
Cape Verde 338
Macao 403
Mozambique 465
Port. Guinea 329
St. Thomas & Prince Islands 392
Timor 322

Navy Club

CD54

Centenary of Portugal's Navy Club. Each stamp has a different design.

1967, Jan. 31

Angola 527-528
Cape Verde 339-340
Macao 412-413
Mozambique 478-479
Port. Guinea 330-331
St. Thomas & Prince Islands ... 393-394
Timor 323-324

Admiral Coutinho

CD55

Centenary of the birth of Admiral Carlos Viegas Gago Coutinho (1869-1959), explorer and aviation pioneer. Each stamp has a different design.

1969, Feb. 17

Angola 547
Cape Verde 355
Macao 417
Mozambique 484
Port. Guinea 335
St. Thomas & Prince Islands 397
Timor 335

Administration Reform

Luiz Augusto Rebello da Silva — CD56

Centenary of the administration reforms of the overseas territories.

1969, Sept. 25

Angola 549
Cape Verde 357
Macao 419
Mozambique 491
Port. Guinea 337
St. Thomas & Prince Islands 399
Timor 338

Marshal Carmona

CD57

Birth centenary of Marshal Antonio Oscar Carmona de Fragoso (1869-1951), President of Portugal. Each stamp has a different design.

1970, Nov. 15

Angola 563
Cape Verde 359
Macao 422
Mozambique 493
Port. Guinea 340
St. Thomas & Prince Islands 403
Timor 341

Olympic Games

CD59

20th Olympic Games, Munich, Aug. 26-Sept. 11. Each stamp shows a different sport.

1972, June 20

Angola 569
Cape Verde 361
Macao 426
Mozambique 504
Port. Guinea 342
St. Thomas & Prince Islands 408
Timor 343

Lisbon-Rio de Janeiro Flight

CD60

50th anniversary of the Lisbon to Rio de Janeiro flight by Arturo de Sacadura and Coutinho, March 30-June 5, 1922. Each stamp shows a different stage of the flight.

1972, Sept. 20

Angola 570
Cape Verde 362
Macao 427
Mozambique 505
Port. Guinea 343
St. Thomas & Prince Islands 409
Timor 344

WMO Centenary

WMO Emblem — CD61

Centenary of international meterological cooperation.

1973, Dec. 15

Angola 571
Cape Verde 363
Macao 429
Mozambique 509
Port. Guinea 344
St. Thomas & Prince Islands 410
Timor 345

FRENCH COMMUNITY

Upper Volta can be found under Burkina Faso in Vol. 1
Madagascar can be found under Malagasy in Vol. 3

Colonial Exposition

People of French Empire CD70

Women's Heads CD71

France Showing Way to Civilization CD72

"Colonial Commerce" CD73

International Colonial Exposition, Paris.

1931

Cameroun 213-216
Chad 60-63
Dahomey 97-100
Fr. Guiana 152-155
Fr. Guinea 116-119
Fr. India 100-103
Fr. Polynesia 76-79
Fr. Sudan 102-105
Gabon 120-123
Guadeloupe 138-141
Indo-China 140-142
Ivory Coast 92-95
Madagascar 169-172
Martinique 129-132
Mauritania 65-68
Middle Congo 61-64
New Caledonia 176-179
Niger 73-76
Reunion 122-125
St. Pierre & Miquelon 132-135
Senegal 138-141
Somali Coast 135-138
Togo 254-257
Ubangi-Shari 82-85
Upper Volta 66-69
Wallis & Futuna Isls. 85-88

Paris International Exposition
Colonial Arts Exposition

"Colonial Resources" CD74 CD77

Overseas Commerce CD75

Exposition Building and Women CD76

"France and the Empire" CD78

Cultural Treasures of the Colonies CD79

Souvenir sheets contain one imperf. stamp.

1937

Cameroun 217-222A
Dahomey 101-107
Fr. Equatorial Africa 27-32, 73
Fr. Guiana 162-168
Fr. Guinea 120-126
Fr. India 104-110
Fr. Polynesia 117-123
Fr. Sudan 106-112
Guadeloupe 148-154
Indo-China 193-199
Inini 41
Ivory Coast 152-158
Kwangchowan 132
Madagascar 191-197
Martinique 179-185
Mauritania 69-75
New Caledonia 208-214
Niger 72-83
Reunion 167-173
St. Pierre & Miquelon 165-171
Senegal 172-178
Somali Coast 139-145
Togo 258-264
Wallis & Futuna Isls. 89

Curie

Pierre and Marie Curie CD80

40th anniversary of the discovery of radium. The surtax was for the benefit of the Intl. Union for the Control of Cancer.

1938

Cameroun B1
Cuba B1-B2
Dahomey B2
France B76
Fr. Equatorial Africa B1
Fr. Guiana B3
Fr. Guinea B2
Fr. India B6
Fr. Polynesia B5
Fr. Sudan B1
Guadeloupe B3
Indo-China B14
Ivory Coast B2
Madagascar B2
Martinique B2
Mauritania B3
New Caledonia B4
Niger B1
Reunion B4
St. Pierre & Miquelon B3
Senegal B3
Somali Coast B2
Togo B1

Caillie

Rene Caille and Map of Northwestern Africa — CD81

Death centenary of Rene Caillie (1799-1838), French explorer. All three denominations exist with colony name omitted.

1939

Dahomey 108-110
Fr. Guinea 161-163
Fr. Sudan 113-115
Ivory Coast 160-162
Mauritania 109-111
Niger 84-86
Senegal 188-190
Togo 265-267

New York World's Fair

Natives and New York Skyline CD82

1939

Cameroun 223-224
Dahomey 111-112
Fr. Equatorial Africa 78-79
Fr. Guiana 169-170
Fr. Guinea 164-165
Fr. India 111-112
Fr. Polynesia 124-125
Fr. Sudan 116-117
Guadeloupe 155-156
Indo-China 203-204
Inini 42-43
Ivory Coast 163-164
Kwangchowan 121-122
Madagascar 209-210
Martinique 186-187
Mauritania 112-113
New Caledonia 215-216
Niger 87-88
Reunion 174-175
St. Pierre & Miquelon 205-206
Senegal 191-192
Somali Coast 179-180
Togo 268-269
Wallis & Futuna Isls. 90-91

French Revolution

Storming of the Bastille CD83

French Revolution, 150th anniv. The surtax was for the defense of the colonies.

1939

Cameroun B2-B6
Dahomey B3-B7
Fr. Equatorial Africa B4-B8, CB1
Fr. Guiana B4-B8, CB1
Fr. Guinea B3-B7
Fr. India B7-B11
Fr. Polynesia B6-B10, CB1
Fr. Sudan B2-B6
Guadeloupe B4-B8
Indo-China B15-B19, CB1
Inini B1-B5
Ivory Coast B3-B7

Kwangchowan B1-B5
Madagascar B3-B7, CB1
Martinique B3-B7
Mauritania B4-B8
New Caledonia B5-B9, CB1
Niger B2-B6
Reunion B5-B9, CB1
St. Pierre & Miquelon B4-B8
Senegal B4-B8, CB1
Somali Coast B3-B7
Togo B2-B6
Wallis & Futuna Isls. B1-B5

Plane over Coastal Area CD85

All five denominations exist with colony name omitted.

1940

Dahomey C1-C5
Fr. Guinea C1-C5
Fr. Sudan C1-C5
Ivory Coast C1-C5
Mauritania C1-C5
Niger C1-C5
Senegal C12-C16
Togo C1-C5

Defense of the Empire

Colonial Infantryman — CD86

1941

Cameroun B13B
Dahomey B13
Fr. Equatorial Africa B8B
Fr. Guiana B10
Fr. Guinea B13
Fr. India B13
Fr. Polynesia B12
Fr. Sudan B12
Guadeloupe B10
Indo-China B19B
Inini B7
Ivory Coast B13
Kwangchowan B7
Madagascar B9
Martinique B9
Mauritania B14
New Caledonia B11
Niger B12
Reunion B11
St. Pierre & Miquelon B8B
Senegal B14
Somali Coast B9
Togo B10B
Wallis & Futuna Isls. B7

Colonial Education Fund

CD86a

1942

Cameroun CB3
Dahomey CB4
Fr. Equatorial Africa CB5
Fr. Guiana CB4
Fr. Guinea CB4
Fr. India CB3
Fr. Polynesia CB4
Fr. Sudan CB4
Kwangchowan CB4

Cross of Lorraine & Four-motor Plane CD87

1941-5

Cameroun C1-C7
Fr. Equatorial Africa C17-C23
Fr. Guiana C9-C10
Fr. India C1-C6
Fr. Polynesia C3-C9
Fr. West Africa C1-C3
Guadeloupe C1-C2
Madagascar C37-C43
Martinique C1-C2
New Caledonia C7-C13
Reunion C18-C24
St. Pierre & Miquelon C1-C7
Somali Coast C1-C7

Transport Plane CD88

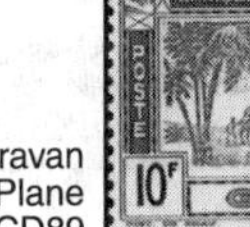
Caravan and Plane CD89

1942

Dahomey C6-C13
Fr. Guinea C6-C13
Fr. Sudan C6-C13
Ivory Coast C6-C13
Mauritania C6-C13
Niger C6-C13
Senegal C17-C25
Togo C6-C13

Red Cross

Marianne CD90

The surtax was for the French Red Cross and national relief.

1944

Cameroun B28
Fr. Equatorial Africa B38
Fr. Guiana B12
Fr. India B14
Fr. Polynesia B13
Fr. West Africa B1
Guadeloupe B12
Madagascar B15
Martinique B11
New Caledonia B13
Reunion B15
St. Pierre & Miquelon B13
Somali Coast B13
Wallis & Futuna Isls. B9

Eboue

CD91

Felix Eboue, first French colonial administrator to proclaim resistance to Germany after French surrender in World War II.

1945

Cameroun 296-297
Fr. Equatorial Africa 156-157
Fr. Guiana 171-172
Fr. India 210-211
Fr. Polynesia 150-151
Fr. West Africa 15-16
Guadeloupe 187-188
Madagascar 259-260
Martinique 196-197
New Caledonia 274-275
Reunion 238-239
St. Pierre & Miquelon 322-323
Somali Coast 238-239

Victory

Victory — CD92

European victory of the Allied Nations in World War II.

1946, May 8

Cameroun C8
Fr. Equatorial Africa C24
Fr. Guiana C11
Fr. India C7
Fr. Polynesia C10
Fr. West Africa C4
Guadeloupe C3
Indo-China C19
Madagascar C44
Martinique C3
New Caledonia C14
Reunion C25
St. Pierre & Miquelon C8
Somali Coast C8
Wallis & Futuna Isls. C1

Chad to Rhine

Leclerc's Departure from Chad — CD93

Battle at Cufra Oasis — CD94

Tanks in Action, Mareth — CD95

Normandy Invasion — CD96

Entering Paris — CD97

Liberation of Strasbourg — CD98

"Chad to the Rhine" march, 1942-44, by Gen. Jacques Leclerc's column, later French 2nd Armored Division.

1946, June 6

Cameroun C9-C14
Fr. Equatorial Africa C25-C30
Fr. Guiana C12-C17
Fr. India C8-C13
Fr. Polynesia C11-C16
Fr. West Africa C5-C10
Guadeloupe C4-C9
Indo-China C20-C25
Madagascar C45-C50
Martinique C4-C9
New Caledonia C15-C20
Reunion C26-C31
St. Pierre & Miquelon C9-C14
Somali Coast C9-C14
Wallis & Futuna Isls. C2-C7

UPU

French Colonials, Globe and Plane — CD99

Universal Postal Union, 75th anniv.

1949, July 4

Cameroun C29
Fr. Equatorial Africa C34
Fr. India C17
Fr. Polynesia C20
Fr. West Africa C15
Indo-China C26
Madagascar C55
New Caledonia C24
St. Pierre & Miquelon C18
Somali Coast C18
Togo C18
Wallis & Futuna Isls. C10

Tropical Medicine

Doctor Treating Infant CD100

The surtax was for charitable work.

1950

Cameroun B29
Fr. Equatorial Africa B39
Fr. India B15
Fr. Polynesia B14
Fr. West Africa B3
Madagascar B17
New Caledonia B14
St. Pierre & Miquelon B14
Somali Coast B14
Togo B11

Military Medal

Medal, Early Marine and Colonial Soldier — CD101

Centenary of the creation of the French Military Medal.

1952

Cameroun........332
Comoro Isls........39
Fr. Equatorial Africa........186
Fr. India........233
Fr. Polynesia........179
Fr. West Africa........57
Madagascar........286
New Caledonia........295
St. Pierre & Miquelon........345
Somali Coast........267
Togo........327
Wallis & Futuna Isls........149

Liberation

Allied Landing, Victory Sign and Cross of Lorraine — CD102

Liberation of France, 10th anniv.

1954, June 6

Cameroun........C32
Comoro Isls........C4
Fr. Equatorial Africa........C38
Fr. India........C18
Fr. Polynesia........C22
Fr. West Africa........C17
Madagascar........C57
New Caledonia........C25
St. Pierre & Miquelon........C19
Somali Coast........C19
Togo........C19
Wallis & Futuna Isls........C11

FIDES

Plowmen CD103

Efforts of FIDES, the Economic and Social Development Fund for Overseas Possessions (Fonds d' Investissement pour le Developpement Economique et Social). Each stamp has a different design.

1956

Cameroun........326-329
Comoro Isls........43
Fr. Polynesia........181
Fr. West Africa........65-72
Madagascar........292-295
New Caledonia........303
Somali Coast........268
Togo........331

Flower

CD104

Each stamp shows a different flower.

1958-9

Cameroun........333
Comoro Isls........45
Fr. Equatorial Africa........200-201
Fr. Polynesia........192
Fr. So. & Antarctic Terr........11
Fr. West Africa........79-83
Madagascar........301-302
New Caledonia........304-305
St. Pierre & Miquelon........357
Somali Coast........270
Togo........348-349
Wallis & Futuna Isls........152

Human Rights

Sun, Dove and U.N. Emblem CD105

10th anniversary of the signing of the Universal Declaration of Human Rights.

1958

Comoro Isls........44
Fr. Equatorial Africa........202
Fr. Polynesia........191
Fr. West Africa........85
Madagascar........300
New Caledonia........306
St. Pierre & Miquelon........356
Somali Coast........274
Wallis & Futuna Isls........153

C.C.T.A.

CD106

Commission for Technical Cooperation in Africa south of the Sahara, 10th anniv.

1960

Cameroun........335
Cent. Africa........3
Chad........66
Congo, P.R........90
Dahomey........138
Gabon........150
Ivory Coast........180
Madagascar........317
Mali........9
Mauritania........117
Niger........104
Upper Volta........89

Air Afrique, 1961

Modern and Ancient Africa, Map and Planes — CD107

Founding of Air Afrique (African Airlines).

1961-62

Cameroun........C37
Cent. Africa........C5
Chad........C7
Congo, P.R........C5
Dahomey........C17
Gabon........C5
Ivory Coast........C18
Mauritania........C17
Niger........C22
Senegal........C31
Upper Volta........C4

Anti-Malaria

CD108

World Health Organization drive to eradicate malaria.

1962, Apr. 7

Cameroun........B36
Cent. Africa........B1
Chad........B1
Comoro Isls........B1
Congo, P.R........B3
Dahomey........B15
Gabon........B4
Ivory Coast........B15
Madagascar........B19
Mali........B1
Mauritania........B16
Niger........B14
Senegal........B16
Somali Coast........B15
Upper Volta........B1

Abidjan Games

CD109

Abidjan Games, Ivory Coast, Dec. 24-31, 1961. Each stamp shows a different sport.

1962

Chad........83-84
Cent. Africa........19-20
Congo, P.R........103-104
Gabon........163-164, C6
Niger........109-111
Upper Volta........103-105

African and Malagasy Union

Flag of Union CD110

First anniversary of the Union.

1962, Sept. 8

Cameroun........373
Cent. Africa........21
Chad........85
Congo, P.R........105
Dahomey........155
Gabon........165
Ivory Coast........198
Madagascar........332
Mauritania........170
Niger........112
Senegal........211
Upper Volta........106

Telstar

Telstar and Globe Showing Andover and Pleumeur-Bodou — CD111

First television connection of the United States and Europe through the Telstar satellite, July 11-12, 1962.

1962-63

Andorra, French........154
Comoro Isls........C7
Fr. Polynesia........C29
Fr. So. & Antarctic Terr........C5
New Caledonia........C33
Somali Coast........C31
St. Pierre & Miquelon........C26
Wallis & Futuna Isls........C17

Freedom From Hunger

World Map and Wheat Emblem CD112

U.N. Food and Agriculture Organization's "Freedom from Hunger" campaign.

1963, Mar. 21

Cameroun........B37-B38
Cent. Africa........B2
Chad........B2
Congo, P.R........B4
Dahomey........B16
Gabon........B5
Ivory Coast........B16
Madagascar........B21
Mauritania........B17
Niger........B15
Senegal........B17
Upper Volta........B2

Red Cross Centenary

CD113

Centenary of the International Red Cross.

1963, Sept. 2

Comoro Isls........55
Fr. Polynesia........205
New Caledonia........328
St. Pierre & Miquelon........367
Somali Coast........297
Wallis & Futuna Isls........165

African Postal Union, 1963

UAMPT Emblem, Radio Masts, Plane and Mail CD114

Establishment of the African and Malagasy Posts and Telecommunications Union.

1963, Sept. 8

Cameroun........C47
Cent. Africa........C10
Chad........C9
Congo, P.R........C13
Dahomey........C19
Gabon........C13
Ivory Coast........C25
Madagascar........C75
Mauritania........C22
Niger........C27
Rwanda........36
Senegal........C32
Upper Volta........C9

Air Afrique, 1963

Symbols of Flight — CD115

First anniversary of Air Afrique and inauguration of DC-8 service.

1963, Nov. 19

Cameroun C48
Chad C10
Congo, P.R. C14
Gabon C18
Ivory Coast C26
Mauritania C26
Niger C35
Senegal C33

Europafrica

Europe and Africa Linked — CD116

Signing of an economic agreement between the European Economic Community and the African and Malagasy Union, Yaounde, Cameroun, July 20, 1963.

1963-64

Cameroun 402
Chad C11
Cent. Africa C12
Congo, P.R. C16
Gabon C19
Ivory Coast 217
Niger C43
Upper Volta C11

Human Rights

Scales of Justice and Globe CD117

15th anniversary of the Universal Declaration of Human Rights.

1963, Dec. 10

Comoro Isls. 58
Fr. Polynesia 206
New Caledonia 329
St. Pierre & Miquelon 368
Somali Coast 300
Wallis & Futuna Isls. 166

PHILATEC

Stamp Album, Champs Elysees Palace and Horses of Marly CD118

Intl. Philatelic and Postal Techniques Exhibition, Paris, June 5-21, 1964.

1963-64

Comoro Isls. 60
France 1078
Fr. Polynesia 207
New Caledonia 341
St. Pierre & Miquelon 369
Somali Coast 301
Wallis & Futuna Isls. 167

Cooperation

CD119

Cooperation between France and the French-speaking countries of Africa and Madagascar.

1964

Cameroun 409-410
Cent. Africa 39
Chad 103
Congo, P.R. 121
Dahomey 193
France 1111
Gabon 175
Ivory Coast 221
Madagascar 360
Mauritania 181
Niger 143
Senegal 236
Togo 495

ITU

Telegraph, Syncom Satellite and ITU Emblem CD120

Intl. Telecommunication Union, Cent.

1965, May 17

Comoro Isls. C14
Fr. Polynesia C33
Fr. So. & Antarctic Terr. C8
New Caledonia C40
New Hebrides 124-125
St. Pierre & Miquelon C29
Somali Coast C36
Wallis & Futuna Isls. C20

French Satellite A-1

Diamant Rocket and Launching Installation — CD121

Launching of France's first satellite, Nov. 26, 1965.

1965-66

Comoro Isls. C15-C16
France 1137-1138
Fr. Polynesia C40-C41
Fr. So. & Antarctic Terr. C9-C10
New Caledonia C44-C45
St. Pierre & Miquelon C30-C31
Somali Coast C39-C40
Wallis & Futuna Isls. C22-C23

French Satellite D-1

D-1 Satellite in Orbit — CD122

Launching of the D-1 satellite at Hammaguir, Algeria, Feb. 17, 1966.

1966

Comoro Isls. C17
France 1148
Fr. Polynesia C42
Fr. So. & Antarctic Terr. C11
New Caledonia C46
St. Pierre & Miquelon C32
Somali Coast C49
Wallis & Futuna Isls. C24

Air Afrique, 1966

Planes and Air Afrique Emblem — CD123

Introduction of DC-8F planes by Air Afrique.

1966

Cameroun C79
Cent. Africa C35
Chad C26
Congo, P.R. C42
Dahomey C42
Gabon C47
Ivory Coast C32
Mauritania C57
Niger C63
Senegal C47
Togo C54
Upper Volta C31

African Postal Union, 1967

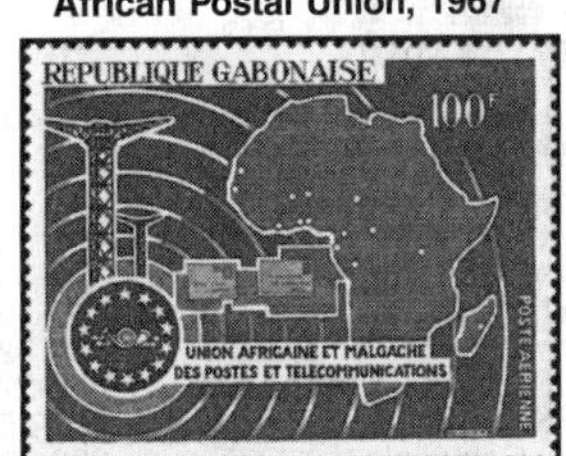

Telecommunications Symbols and Map of Africa — CD124

Fifth anniversary of the establishment of the African and Malagasy Union of Posts and Telecommunications, UAMPT.

1967

Cameroun C90
Cent. Africa C46
Chad C37
Congo, P.R. C57
Dahomey C61
Gabon C58
Ivory Coast C34
Madagascar C85
Mauritania C65
Niger C75
Rwanda C1-C3
Senegal C60
Togo C81
Upper Volta C50

Monetary Union

Gold Token of the Ashantis, 17-18th Centuries — CD125

West African Monetary Union, 5th anniv.

1967, Nov. 4

Dahomey 244
Ivory Coast 259
Mauritania 238
Niger 204
Senegal 294
Togo 623
Upper Volta 181

WHO Anniversary

Sun, Flowers and WHO Emblem CD126

World Health Organization, 20th anniv.

1968, May 4

Afars & Issas 317
Comoro Isls. 73
Fr. Polynesia 241-242
Fr. So. & Antarctic Terr. 31
New Caledonia 367
St. Pierre & Miquelon 377
Wallis & Futuna Isls. 169

Human Rights Year

Human Rights Flame — CD127

1968, Aug. 10

Afars & Issas 322-323
Comoro Isls. 76
Fr. Polynesia 243-244
Fr. So. & Antarctic Terr. 32
New Caledonia 369
St. Pierre & Miquelon 382
Wallis & Futuna Isls. 170

2nd PHILEXAFRIQUE

CD128

Opening of PHILEXAFRIQUE, Abidjan, Feb. 14. Each stamp shows a local scene and stamp.

1969, Feb. 14

Cameroun C118
Cent. Africa C65
Chad C48
Congo, P.R. C77
Dahomey C94
Gabon C82
Ivory Coast C38-C40
Madagascar C92
Mali C65

Mauritania C80
Niger C104
Senegal C68
Togo C104
Upper Volta C62

Concorde

Concorde in Flight CD129

First flight of the prototype Concorde supersonic plane at Toulouse, Mar. 1, 1969.

1969

Afars & Issas C56
Comoro Isls. C29
France C42
Fr. Polynesia C50
Fr. So. & Antarctic Terr. C18
New Caledonia C63
St. Pierre & Miquelon C40
Wallis & Futuna Isls. C30

Development Bank

Bank Emblem — CD130

African Development Bank, fifth anniv.

1969

Cameroun 499
Chad 217
Congo, P.R. 181-182
Ivory Coast 281
Mali 127-128
Mauritania 267
Niger 220
Senegal 317-318
Upper Volta 201

ILO

ILO Headquarters, Geneva, and Emblem — CD131

Intl. Labor Organization, 50th anniv.

1969-70

Afars & Issas 337
Comoro Isls. 83
Fr. Polynesia 251-252
Fr. So. & Antarctic Terr. 35
New Caledonia 379
St. Pierre & Miquelon 396
Wallis & Futuna Isls. 172

ASECNA

Map of Africa, Plane and Airport CD132

10th anniversary of the Agency for the Security of Aerial Navigation in Africa and Madagascar (ASECNA, Agence pour la Securite de la Navigation Aerienne en Afrique et a Madagascar).

1969-70

Cameroun 500
Cent. Africa 119
Chad 222
Congo, P.R. 197
Dahomey 269
Gabon 260
Ivory Coast 287
Mali 130
Niger 221
Senegal 321
Upper Volta 204

U.P.U. Headquarters

CD133

New Universal Postal Union headquarters, Bern, Switzerland.

1970

Afars & Issas 342
Algeria 443
Cameroun 503-504
Cent. Africa 125
Chad 225
Comoro Isls. 84
Congo, P.R. 216
Fr. Polynesia 261-262
Fr. So. & Antarctic Terr. 36
Gabon 258
Ivory Coast 295
Madagascar 444
Mali 134-135
Mauritania 283
New Caledonia 382
Niger 231-232
St. Pierre & Miquelon 397-398
Senegal 328-329
Tunisia 535
Wallis & Futuna Isls. 173

De Gaulle

CD134

First anniversary of the death of Charles de Gaulle, (1890-1970), President of France.

1971-72

Afars & Issas 356-357
Comoro Isls. 104-105
France 1322-1325
Fr. Polynesia 270-271
Fr. So. & Antarctic Terr. 52-53
New Caledonia 393-394
Reunion 377, 380
St. Pierre & Miquelon 417-418
Wallis & Futuna Isls. 177-178

African Postal Union, 1971

UAMPT Building, Brazzaville, Congo — CD135

10th anniversary of the establishment of the African and Malagasy Posts and Telecommunications Union, UAMPT. Each stamp has a different native design.

1971, Nov. 13

Cameroun C177
Cent. Africa C89
Chad C94
Congo, P.R. C136
Dahomey C146
Gabon C120
Ivory Coast C47
Mauritania C113
Niger C164
Rwanda C8
Senegal C105
Togo C166
Upper Volta C97

West African Monetary Union

African Couple, City, Village and Commemorative Coin — CD136

West African Monetary Union, 10th anniv.

1972, Nov. 2

Dahomey 300
Ivory Coast 331
Mauritania 299
Niger 258
Senegal 374
Togo 825
Upper Volta 280

African Postal Union, 1973

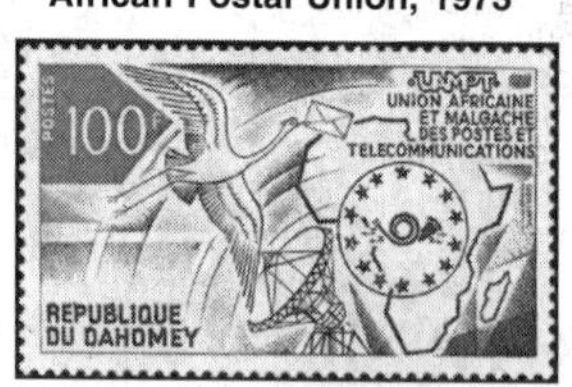

Telecommunications Symbols and Map of Africa — CD137

11th anniversary of the African and Malagasy Posts and Telecommunications Union (UAMPT).

1973, Sept. 12

Cameroun 574
Cent. Africa 194
Chad 294
Congo, P.R. 289
Dahomey 311
Gabon 320
Ivory Coast 361
Madagascar 500
Mauritania 304
Niger 287
Rwanda 540
Senegal 393
Togo 849
Upper Volta 297

Philexafrique II — Essen

CD138

CD139

Designs: Indigenous fauna, local and German stamps. Types CD138-CD139 printed horizontally and vertically se-tenant in sheets of 10 (2x5). Label between horizontal pairs alternately commemoratives Philexafrique II, Libreville, Gabon, June 1978, and 2nd International Stamp Fair, Essen, Germany, Nov. 1-5.

1978-1979

Benin C285-C286
Central Africa C200-C201
Chad C238-C239
Congo Republic C245-C246
Djibouti C121-C122
Gabon C215-C216
Ivory Coast C64-C65
Mali C356-C357
Mauritania C185-C186
Niger C291-C292
Rwanda C12-C13
Senegal C146-C147

BRITISH COMMONWEALTH OF NATIONS

The listings follow established trade practices when these issues are offered as units by dealers. The Peace issue, for example, includes only one stamp from the Indian state of Hyderabad. The U.P.U. issue includes the Egypt set. Pairs are included for those varieties issues with bilingual designs se-tenant.

Silver Jubilee

Windsor Castle and King George V CD301

Reign of King George V, 25th anniv.

1935

Antigua 77-80
Ascension 33-36
Bahamas 92-95
Barbados 186-189
Basutoland 11-14
Bechuanaland Protectorate 117-120
Bermuda 100-103
British Guiana 223-226
British Honduras 108-111
Cayman Islands 81-84
Ceylon 260-263
Cyprus 136-139
Dominica 90-93
Falkland Islands 77-80
Fiji 110-113
Gambia 125-128
Gibraltar 100-103
Gilbert & Ellice Islands 33-36
Gold Coast 108-111
Grenada 124-127
Hong Kong 147-150
Jamaica 109-112
Kenya, Uganda, Tanganyika 42-45
Leeward Islands 96-99
Malta 184-187
Mauritius 204-207
Montserrat 85-88
Newfoundland 226-229
Nigeria 34-37
Northern Rhodesia 18-21
Nyasaland Protectorate 47-50
St. Helena 111-114
St. Kitts-Nevis 72-75
St. Lucia 91-94
St. Vincent 134-137
Seychelles 118-121
Sierra Leone 166-169
Solomon Islands 60-63
Somaliland Protectorate 77-80
Straits Settlements 213-216
Swaziland 20-23
Trinidad & Tobago 43-46
Turks & Caicos Islands 71-74
Virgin Islands 69-72

The following have different designs but are included in the omnibus set:

Great Britain 226-229
Offices in Morocco 67-70, 226-229, 422-425, 508-510
Australia 152-154
Canada 211-216
Cook Islands 98-100
India 142-148
Nauru 31-34
New Guinea 46-47
New Zealand 199-201
Niue 67-69

Papua ... 114-117
Samoa ... 163-165
South Africa ... 68-71
Southern Rhodesia ... 33-36
South-West Africa ... 121-124

249 stamps

Coronation

Queen Elizabeth and King George VI CD302

1937

Aden ... 13-15
Antigua ... 81-83
Ascension ... 37-39
Bahamas ... 97-99
Barbados ... 190-192
Basutoland ... 15-17
Bechuanaland Protectorate ... 121-123
Bermuda ... 115-117
British Guiana ... 227-229
British Honduras ... 112-114
Cayman Islands ... 97-99
Ceylon ... 275-277
Cyprus ... 140-142
Dominica ... 94-96
Falkland Islands ... 81-83
Fiji ... 114-116
Gambia ... 129-131
Gibraltar ... 104-106
Gilbert & Ellice Islands ... 37-39
Gold Coast ... 112-114
Grenada ... 128-130
Hong Kong ... 151-153
Jamaica ... 113-115
Kenya, Uganda, Tanganyika ... 60-62
Leeward Islands ... 100-102
Malta ... 188-190
Mauritius ... 208-210
Montserrat ... 89-91
Newfoundland ... 230-232
Nigeria ... 50-52
Northern Rhodesia ... 22-24
Nyasaland Protectorate ... 51-53
St. Helena ... 115-117
St. Kitts-Nevis ... 76-78
St. Lucia ... 107-109
St. Vincent ... 138-140
Seychelles ... 122-124
Sierra Leone ... 170-172
Solomon Islands ... 64-66
Somaliland Protectorate ... 81-83
Straits Settlements ... 235-237
Swaziland ... 24-26
Trinidad & Tobago ... 47-49
Turks & Caicos Islands ... 75-77
Virgin Islands ... 73-75

The following have different designs but are included in the omnibus set:

Great Britain ... 234
Offices in Morocco ... 82, 439, 514
Canada ... 237
Cook Islands ... 109-111
Nauru ... 35-38
Newfoundland ... 233-243
New Guinea ... 48-51
New Zealand ... 223-225
Niue ... 70-72
Papua ... 118-121
South Africa ... 74-78
Southern Rhodesia ... 38-41
South-West Africa ... 125-132

202 stamps

Peace

King George VI and Parliament Buildings, London CD303

Return to peace at the close of World War II.

1945-46

Aden ... 28-29
Antigua ... 96-97
Ascension ... 50-51
Bahamas ... 130-131
Barbados ... 207-208
Bermuda ... 131-132
British Guiana ... 242-243
British Honduras ... 127-128
Cayman Islands ... 112-113
Ceylon ... 293-294
Cyprus ... 156-157
Dominica ... 112-113
Falkland Islands ... 97-98
Falkland Islands Dep. ... 1L9-1L10
Fiji ... 137-138
Gambia ... 144-145
Gibraltar ... 119-120
Gilbert & Ellice Islands ... 52-53
Gold Coast ... 128-129
Grenada ... 143-144
Jamaica ... 136-137
Kenya, Uganda, Tanganyika ... 90-91
Leeward Islands ... 116-117
Malta ... 206-207
Mauritius ... 223-224
Montserrat ... 104-105
Nigeria ... 71-72
Northern Rhodesia ... 46-47
Nyasaland Protectorate ... 82-83
Pitcairn Island ... 9-10
St. Helena ... 128-129
St. Kitts-Nevis ... 91-92
St. Lucia ... 127-128
St. Vincent ... 152-153
Seychelles ... 149-150
Sierra Leone ... 186-187
Solomon Islands ... 80-81
Somaliland Protectorate ... 108-109
Trinidad & Tobago ... 62-63
Turks & Caicos Islands ... 90-91
Virgin Islands ... 88-89

The following have different designs but are included in the omnibus set:

Great Britain ... 264-265
Offices in Morocco ... 523-524
Aden
Kathiri State of Seiyun ... 12-13
Qu'aiti State of Shihr and Mukalla ... 12-13
Australia ... 200-202
Basutoland ... 29-31
Bechuanaland Protectorate ... 137-139
Burma ... 66-69
Cook Islands ... 127-130
Hong Kong ... 174-175
India ... 195-198
Hyderabad ... 51
New Zealand ... 247-257
Niue ... 90-93
Pakistan-Bahawalpur ... O16
Samoa ... 191-194
South Africa ... 100-102
Southern Rhodesia ... 67-70
South-West Africa ... 153-155
Swaziland ... 38-40
Zanzibar ... 222-223

164 stamps

Silver Wedding

King George VI and Queen Elizabeth

CD304 CD305

1948-49

Aden ... 30-31
Kathiri State of Seiyun ... 14-15
Qu'aiti State of Shihr and Mukalla ... 14-15
Antigua ... 98-99
Ascension ... 52-53
Bahamas ... 148-149
Barbados ... 210-211
Basutoland ... 39-40
Bechuanaland Protectorate ... 147-148
Bermuda ... 133-134
British Guiana ... 244-245
British Honduras ... 129-130
Cayman Islands ... 116-117
Cyprus ... 158-159
Dominica ... 114-115
Falkland Islands ... 99-100
Falkland Islands Dep. ... 1L11-1L12
Fiji ... 139-140
Gambia ... 146-147
Gibraltar ... 121-122
Gilbert & Ellice Islands ... 54-55
Gold Coast ... 142-143
Grenada ... 145-146
Hong Kong ... 178-179
Jamaica ... 138-139
Kenya, Uganda, Tanganyika ... 92-93
Leeward Islands ... 118-119
Malaya
Johore ... 128-129
Kedah ... 55-56
Kelantan ... 44-45
Malacca ... 1-2
Negri Sembilan ... 36-37
Pahang ... 44-45
Penang ... 1-2
Perak ... 99-100
Perlis ... 1-2
Selangor ... 74-75
Trengganu ... 47-48
Malta ... 223-224
Mauritius ... 229-230
Montserrat ... 106-107
Nigeria ... 73-74
North Borneo ... 238-239
Northern Rhodesia ... 48-49
Nyasaland Protectorate ... 85-86
Pitcairn Island ... 11-12
St. Helena ... 130-131
St. Kitts-Nevis ... 93-94
St. Lucia ... 129-130
St. Vincent ... 154-155
Sarawak ... 174-175
Seychelles ... 151-152
Sierra Leone ... 188-189
Singapore ... 21-22
Solomon Islands ... 82-83
Somaliland Protectorate ... 110-111
Swaziland ... 48-49
Trinidad & Tobago ... 64-65
Turks & Caicos Islands ... 92-93
Virgin Islands ... 90-91
Zanzibar ... 224-225

The following have different designs but are included in the omnibus set:

Great Britain ... 267-268
Offices in Morocco ... 93-94, 525-526
Bahrain ... 62-63
Kuwait ... 82-83
Oman ... 25-26
South Africa ... 106
South-West Africa ... 159

138 stamps

U.P.U.

Mercury and Symbols of Communications — CD306

Plane, Ship and Hemispheres — CD307

Mercury Scattering Letters over Globe CD308

U.P.U. Monument, Bern CD309

Universal Postal Union, 75th anniversary.

1949

Aden ... 32-35
Kathiri State of Seiyun ... 16-19
Qu'aiti State of Shihr and Mukalla ... 16-19
Antigua ... 100-103
Ascension ... 57-60
Bahamas ... 150-153
Barbados ... 212-215
Basutoland ... 41-44
Bechuanaland Protectorate ... 149-152
Bermuda ... 138-141
British Guiana ... 246-249
British Honduras ... 137-140
Brunei ... 79-82
Cayman Islands ... 118-121
Cyprus ... 160-163
Dominica ... 116-119
Falkland Islands ... 103-106
Falkland Islands Dep. ... 1L14-1L17
Fiji ... 141-144
Gambia ... 148-151
Gibraltar ... 123-126
Gilbert & Ellice Islands ... 56-59
Gold Coast ... 144-147
Grenada ... 147-150
Hong Kong ... 180-183
Jamaica ... 142-145
Kenya, Uganda, Tanganyika ... 94-97
Leeward Islands ... 126-129
Malaya
Johore ... 151-154
Kedah ... 57-60
Kelantan ... 46-49
Malacca ... 18-21
Negri Sembilan ... 59-62
Pahang ... 46-49
Penang ... 23-26
Perak ... 101-104
Perlis ... 3-6
Selangor ... 76-79
Trengganu ... 49-52
Malta ... 225-228
Mauritius ... 231-234
Montserrat ... 108-111
New Hebrides, British ... 62-65
New Hebrides, French ... 79-82
Nigeria ... 75-78
North Borneo ... 240-243
Northern Rhodesia ... 50-53
Nyasaland Protectorate ... 87-90
Pitcairn Islands ... 13-16
St. Helena ... 132-135
St. Kitts-Nevis ... 95-98
St. Lucia ... 131-134
St. Vincent ... 170-173
Sarawak ... 176-179
Seychelles ... 153-156
Sierra Leone ... 190-193
Singapore ... 23-26
Solomon Islands ... 84-87
Somaliland Protectorate ... 112-115
Southern Rhodesia ... 71-72
Swaziland ... 50-53
Tonga ... 87-90
Trinidad & Tobago ... 66-69
Turks & Caicos Islands ... 101-104
Virgin Islands ... 92-95
Zanzibar ... 226-229

The following have different designs but are included in the omnibus set:

Great Britain ... 276-279
Offices in Morocco ... 546-549
Australia ... 223
Bahrain ... 68-71
Burma ... 116-121
Ceylon ... 304-306
Egypt ... 281-283
India ... 223-226
Kuwait ... 89-92
Oman ... 31-34
Pakistan-Bahawalpur 26-29, O25-O28
South Africa ... 109-111
South-West Africa ... 160-162

319 stamps

University

Arms of University College CD310

Alice, Princess of Athlone CD311

1948 opening of University College of the West Indies at Jamaica.

1951

- Antigua 104-105
- Barbados 228-229
- British Guiana 250-251
- British Honduras 141-142
- Dominica 120-121
- Grenada 164-165
- Jamaica 146-147
- Leeward Islands 130-131
- Montserrat 112-113
- St. Kitts-Nevis 105-106
- St. Lucia 149-150
- St. Vincent 174-175
- Trinidad & Tobago 70-71
- Virgin Islands 96-97

28 stamps

Coronation

Queen Elizabeth II — CD312

1953

- Aden 47
  - Kathiri State of Seiyun 28
  - Qu'aiti State of Shihr and Mukalla 28
- Antigua 106
- Ascension 61
- Bahamas 157
- Barbados 234
- Basutoland 45
- Bechuanaland Protectorate 153
- Bermuda 142
- British Guiana 252
- British Honduras 143
- Cayman Islands 150
- Cyprus 167
- Dominica 141
- Falkland Islands 121
- Falkland Islands Dependencies 1L18
- Fiji 145
- Gambia 152
- Gibraltar 131
- Gilbert & Ellice Islands 60
- Gold Coast 160
- Grenada 170
- Hong Kong 184
- Jamaica 153
- Kenya, Uganda, Tanganyika 101
- Leeward Islands 132
- Malaya
  - Johore 155
  - Kedah 82
  - Kelantan 71
  - Malacca 27
  - Negri Sembilan 63
  - Pahang 71
  - Penang 27
  - Perak 126
  - Perlis 28
  - Selangor 101
  - Trengganu 74
- Malta 241
- Mauritius 250
- Montserrat 127
- New Hebrides, British 77
- Nigeria 79
- North Borneo 260
- Northern Rhodesia 60
- Nyasaland Protectorate 96
- Pitcairn 19
- St. Helena 139
- St. Kitts-Nevis 119
- St. Lucia 156
- St. Vincent 185
- Sarawak 196
- Seychelles 172
- Sierra Leone 194
- Singapore 27
- Solomon Islands 88
- Somaliland Protectorate 127
- Swaziland 54
- Trinidad & Tobago 84
- Tristan da Cunha 13
- Turks & Caicos Islands 118
- Virgin Islands 114

The following have different designs but are included in the omnibus set:

- Great Britain 313-316
  - Offices in Morocco 579-582
- Australia 259-261
- Bahrain 92-95
- Canada 330
- Ceylon 317
- Cook Islands 145-146
- Kuwait 113-116
- New Zealand 280-284
- Niue 104-105
- Oman 52-55
- Samoa 214-215
- South Africa 192
- Southern Rhodesia 80
- South-West Africa 244-248
- Tokelau Islands 4

106 stamps

Royal Visit 1953

Separate designs for each country for the visit of Queen Elizabeth II and the Duke of Edinburgh.

1953

- Aden 62
- Australia 267-269
- Bermuda 163
- Ceylon 318
- Fiji 146
- Gibraltar 146
- Jamaica 154
- Kenya, Uganda, Tanganyika 102
- Malta 242
- New Zealand 286-287

13 stamps

West Indies Federation

Map of the Caribbean CD313

Federation of the West Indies, April 22, 1958.

1958

- Antigua 122-124
- Barbados 248-250
- Dominica 161-163
- Grenada 184-186
- Jamaica 175-177
- Montserrat 143-145
- St. Kitts-Nevis 136-138
- St. Lucia 170-172
- St. Vincent 198-200
- Trinidad & Tobago 86-88

30 stamps

Freedom from Hunger

Protein Food CD314

U.N. Food and Agricultural Organization's "Freedom from Hunger" campaign.

1963

- Aden 65
- Antigua 133
- Ascension 89
- Bahamas 180
- Basutoland 83
- Bechuanaland Protectorate 194
- Bermuda 192
- British Guiana 271
- British Honduras 179
- Brunei 100
- Cayman Islands 168
- Dominica 181
- Falkland Islands 146
- Fiji 198
- Gambia 172
- Gibraltar 161
- Gilbert & Ellice Islands 76
- Grenada 190
- Hong Kong 218
- Malta 291
- Mauritius 270
- Montserrat 150
- New Hebrides, British 93
- North Borneo 296
- Pitcairn 35
- St. Helena 173
- St. Lucia 179
- St. Vincent 201
- Sarawak 212
- Seychelles 213
- Solomon Islands 109
- Swaziland 108
- Tonga 127
- Tristan da Cunha 68
- Turks & Caicos Islands 138
- Virgin Islands 140
- Zanzibar 280

37 stamps

Red Cross Centenary

Red Cross and Elizabeth II CD315

1963

- Antigua 134-135
- Ascension 90-91
- Bahamas 183-184
- Basutoland 84-85
- Bechuanaland Protectorate 195-196
- Bermuda 193-194
- British Guiana 272-273
- British Honduras 180-181
- Cayman Islands 169-170
- Dominica 182-183
- Falkland Islands 147-148
- Fiji 203-204
- Gambia 173-174
- Gibraltar 162-163
- Gilbert & Ellice Islands 77-78
- Grenada 191-192
- Hong Kong 219-220
- Jamaica 203-204
- Malta 292-293
- Mauritius 271-272
- Montserrat 151-152
- New Hebrides, British 94-95
- Pitcairn Islands 36-37
- St. Helena 174-175
- St. Kitts-Nevis 143-144
- St. Lucia 180-181
- St. Vincent 202-203
- Seychelles 214-215
- Solomon Islands 110-111
- South Arabia 1-2
- Swaziland 109-110
- Tonga 134-135
- Tristan da Cunha 69-70
- Turks & Caicos Islands 139-140
- Virgin Islands 141-142

70 stamps

Shakespeare

Shakespeare Memorial Theatre, Stratford-on-Avon — CD316

400th anniversary of the birth of William Shakespeare.

1964

- Antigua 151
- Bahamas 201
- Bechuanaland Protectorate 197
- Cayman Islands 171
- Dominica 184
- Falkland Islands 149
- Gambia 192
- Gibraltar 164
- Montserrat 153
- St. Lucia 196
- Turks & Caicos Islands 141
- Virgin Islands 143

12 stamps

ITU

ITU Emblem CD317

Intl. Telecommunication Union, cent.

1965

- Antigua 153-154
- Ascension 92-93
- Bahamas 219-220
- Barbados 265-266
- Basutoland 101-102
- Bechuanaland Protectorate 202-203
- Bermuda 196-197
- British Guiana 293-294
- British Honduras 187-188
- Brunei 116-117
- Cayman Islands 172-173
- Dominica 185-186
- Falkland Islands 154-155
- Fiji 211-212
- Gibraltar 167-168
- Gilbert & Ellice Islands 87-88
- Grenada 205-206
- Hong Kong 221-222
- Mauritius 291-292
- Montserrat 157-158
- New Hebrides, British 108-109
- Pitcairn Islands 52-53
- St. Helena 180-181
- St. Kitts-Nevis 163-164
- St. Lucia 197-198
- St. Vincent 224-225
- Seychelles 218-219
- Solomon Islands 126-127
- Swaziland 115-116
- Tristan da Cunha 85-86
- Turks & Caicos Islands 142-143
- Virgin Islands 159-160

64 stamps

Intl. Cooperation Year

ICY Emblem CD318

1965

- Antigua 155-156
- Ascension 94-95
- Bahamas 222-223
- Basutoland 103-104
- Bechuanaland Protectorate 204-205
- Bermuda 199-200
- British Guiana 295-296
- British Honduras 189-190
- Brunei 118-119
- Cayman Islands 174-175
- Dominica 187-188
- Falkland Islands 156-157
- Fiji 213-214
- Gibraltar 169-170
- Gilbert & Ellice Islands 104-105
- Grenada 207-208
- Hong Kong 223-224
- Mauritius 293-294
- Montserrat 176-177
- New Hebrides, British 110-111
- New Hebrides, French 126-127
- Pitcairn Islands 54-55

St. Helena 182-183
St. Kitts-Nevis 165-166
St. Lucia 199-200
Seychelles 220-221
Solomon Islands 143-144
South Arabia 17-18
Swaziland 117-118
Tristan da Cunha 87-88
Turks & Caicos Islands 144-145
Virgin Islands 161-162

64 stamps

Churchill Memorial

Winston Churchill and St. Paul's, London, During Air Attack CD319

1966

Antigua 157-160
Ascension 96-99
Bahamas 224-227
Barbados 281-284
Basutoland 105-108
Bechuanaland Protectorate 206-209
Bermuda 201-204
British Antarctic Territory 16-19
British Honduras 191-194
Brunei 120-123
Cayman Islands 176-179
Dominica 189-192
Falkland Islands 158-161
Fiji 215-218
Gibraltar 171-174
Gilbert & Ellice Islands 106-109
Grenada 209-212
Hong Kong 225-228
Mauritius 295-298
Montserrat 178-181
New Hebrides, British 112-115
New Hebrides, French 128-131
Pitcairn Islands 56-59
St. Helena 184-187
St. Kitts-Nevis 167-170
St. Lucia 201-204
St. Vincent 241-244
Seychelles 222-225
Solomon Islands 145-148
South Arabia 19-22
Swaziland 119-122
Tristan da Cunha 89-92
Turks & Caicos Islands 146-149
Virgin Islands 163-166

136 stamps

Royal Visit, 1966

Queen Elizabeth II and Prince Philip CD320

Caribbean visit, Feb. 4 - Mar. 6, 1966.

1966

Antigua 161-162
Bahamas 228-229
Barbados 285-286
British Guiana 299-300
Cayman Islands 180-181
Dominica 193-194
Grenada 213-214
Montserrat 182-183
St. Kitts-Nevis 171-172
St. Lucia 205-206
St. Vincent 245-246
Turks & Caicos Islands 150-151
Virgin Islands 167-168

26 stamps

World Cup Soccer

Soccer Player and Jules Rimet Cup CD321

World Cup Soccer Championship, Wembley, England, July 11-30.

1966

Antigua 163-164
Ascension 100-101
Bahamas 245-246
Bermuda 205-206
Brunei 124-125
Cayman Islands 182-183
Dominica 195-196
Fiji 219-220
Gibraltar 175-176
Gilbert & Ellice Islands 125-126
Grenada 230-231
New Hebrides, British 116-117
New Hebrides, French 132-133
Pitcairn Islands 60-61
St. Helena 188-189
St. Kitts-Nevis 173-174
St. Lucia 207-208
Seychelles 226-227
Solomon Islands 167-168
South Arabia 23-24
Tristan da Cunha 93-94

42 stamps

WHO Headquarters

World Health Organization Headquarters, Geneva — CD322

1966

Antigua 165-166
Ascension 102-103
Bahamas 247-248
Brunei 126-127
Cayman Islands 184-185
Dominica 197-198
Fiji 224-225
Gibraltar 180-181
Gilbert & Ellice Islands 127-128
Grenada 232-233
Hong Kong 229-230
Montserrat 184-185
New Hebrides, British 118-119
New Hebrides, French 134-135
Pitcairn Islands 62-63
St. Helena 190-191
St. Kitts-Nevis 177-178
St. Lucia 209-210
St. Vincent 247-248
Seychelles 228-229
Solomon Islands 169-170
South Arabia 25-26
Tristan da Cunha 99-100

46 stamps

UNESCO Anniversary

"Education" — CD323

"Science" (Wheat ears & flask enclosing globe). "Culture" (lyre & columns). 20th anniversary of the UNESCO.

1966-67

Antigua 183-185
Ascension 108-110
Bahamas 249-251
Barbados 287-289
Bermuda 207-209
Brunei 128-130
Cayman Islands 186-188
Dominica 199-201
Gibraltar 183-185
Gilbert & Ellice Islands 129-131
Grenada 234-236
Hong Kong 231-233
Mauritius 299-301
Montserrat 186-188
New Hebrides, British 120-122
New Hebrides, French 136-138
Pitcairn Islands 64-66
St. Helena 192-194
St. Kitts-Nevis 179-181
St. Lucia 211-213
St. Vincent 249-251
Seychelles 230-232
Solomon Islands 171-173
South Arabia 27-29
Swaziland 123-125
Tristan da Cunha 101-103
Turks & Caicos Islands 155-157
Virgin Islands 176-178

84 stamps

Silver Wedding, 1972

Queen Elizabeth II and Prince Philip — CD324

Designs: borders differ for each country.

1972

Anguilla 161-162
Antigua 295-296
Ascension 164-165
Bahamas 344-345
Bermuda 296-297
British Antarctic Territory 43-44
British Honduras 306-307
British Indian Ocean Territory 48-49
Brunei 186-187
Cayman Islands 304-305
Dominica 352-353
Falkland Islands 223-224
Fiji 328-329
Gibraltar 292-293
Gilbert & Ellice Islands 206-207
Grenada 466-467
Hong Kong 271-272
Montserrat 286-287
New Hebrides, British 169-170
Pitcairn Islands 127-128
St. Helena 271-272
St. Kitts-Nevis 257-258
St. Lucia 328-329
St.Vincent 344-345
Seychelles 309-310
Solomon Islands 248-249
South Georgia 35-36
Tristan da Cunha 178-179
Turks & Caicos Islands 257-258
Virgin Islands 241-242

60 stamps

Princess Anne's Wedding

Princess Anne and Mark Phillips — CD325

Wedding of Princess Anne and Mark Phillips, Nov. 14, 1973.

1973

Anguilla 179-180
Ascension 177-178
Belize 325-326
Bermuda 302-303
British Antarctic Territory 60-61
Cayman Islands 320-321
Falkland Islands 225-226
Gibraltar 305-306
Gilbert & Ellice Islands 216-217
Hong Kong 289-290
Montserrat 300-301
Pitcairn Island 135-136
St. Helena 277-278
St. Kitts-Nevis 274-275
St. Lucia 349-350
St. Vincent 358-359
St. Vincent Grenadines 1-2
Seychelles 311-312
Solomon Islands 259-260
South Georgia 37-38
Tristan da Cunha 189-190
Turks & Caicos Islands 286-287
Virgin Islands 260-261

44 stamps

Elizabeth II Coronation Anniv.

CD326

CD327

CD328

Designs: Royal and local beasts in heraldic form and simulated stonework. Portrait of Elizabeth II by Peter Grugeon. 25th anniversary of coronation of Queen Elizabeth II.

1978

Ascension 229
Barbados 474
Belize 397
British Antarctic Territory 71
Cayman Islands 404
Christmas Island 87
Falkland Islands 275
Fiji 384
Gambia 380
Gilbert Islands 312
Mauritius 464
New Hebrides, British 258
St. Helena 317
St. Kitts-Nevis 354
Samoa 472
Solomon Islands 368
South Georgia 51
Swaziland 302
Tristan da Cunha 238
Virgin Islands 337

20 sheets

Queen Mother Elizabeth's 80th Birthday

CD330

Designs: Photographs of Queen Mother Elizabeth. Falkland Islands issued in sheets of 50; others in sheets of 9.

1980

Ascension 261
Bermuda 401
Cayman Islands 443
Falkland Islands 305
Gambia 412
Gibraltar 393
Hong Kong 364
Pitcairn Islands 193
St. Helena 341
Samoa 532
Solomon Islands 426
Tristan da Cunha 277

12 stamps

Royal Wedding, 1981

Prince Charles and Lady Diana — CD331

Wedding of Charles, Prince of Wales, and Lady Diana Spencer, St. Paul's Cathedral, London, July 29, 1981.

1981

Antigua 623-625
Ascension 294-296
Barbados 547-549
Barbuda 497-499
Bermuda 412-414
Brunei 268-270
Cayman Islands 471-473
Dominica 701-703
Falkland Islands 324-326
Falkland Islands Dep. 1L59-1L61
Fiji 442-444
Gambia 426-428
Ghana 759-761
Grenada 1051-1053
Grenada Grenadines 440-443
Hong Kong 373-375
Jamaica 500-503
Lesotho 335-337
Maldive Islands 906-908
Mauritius 520-522
Norfolk Island 280-282
Pitcairn Islands 206-208
St. Helena 353-355
St. Lucia 543-545
Samoa 558-560
Sierra Leone 509-517
Solomon Islands 450-452
Swaziland 382-384
Tristan da Cunha 294-296
Turks & Caicos Islands 486-488
Caicos Island 8-10
Uganda 314-316
Vanuatu 308-310
Virgin Islands 406-408

Princess Diana

CD332

CD333

Designs: Photographs and portrait of Princess Diana, wedding or honeymoon photographs, royal residences, arms of issuing country. Portrait photograph by Clive Friend. Souvenir sheet margins show family tree, various people related to the princess. 21st birthday of Princess Diana of Wales, July 1.

1982

Antigua 663-666
Ascension 313-316
Bahamas 510-513
Barbados 585-588
Barbuda 544-546
British Antarctic Territory 92-95
Cayman Islands 486-489
Dominica 773-776
Falkland Islands 348-351
Falkland Islands Dep. 1L72-1L75
Fiji 470-473
Gambia 447-450
Grenada 1101A-1105
Grenada Grenadines 485-491
Lesotho 372-375
Maldive Islands 952-955
Mauritius 548-551
Pitcairn Islands 213-216
St. Helena 372-375
St. Lucia 591-594
Sierra Leone 531-534
Solomon Islands 471-474
Swaziland 406-409
Tristan da Cunha 310-313
Turks and Caicos Islands 530A-534
Virgin Islands 430-433

250th anniv. of first edition of Lloyd's List (shipping news publication) & of Lloyd's marine insurance.

CD335

Designs: First page of early edition of the list; historical ships, modern transportation or harbor scenes.

1984

Ascension 351-354
Bahamas 555-558
Barbados 627-630
Cayes of Belize 10-13
Cayman Islands 522-525
Falkland Islands 404-407
Fiji 509-512
Gambia 519-522
Mauritius 587-590
Nauru 280-283
St. Helena 412-415
Samoa 624-627
Seychelles 538-541
Solomon Islands 521-524
Vanuatu 368-371
Virgin Islands 466-469

Queen Mother 85th Birthday

CD336

Designs: Photographs tracing the life of the Queen Mother, Elizabeth. The high value in each set pictures the same photograph taken of the Queen Mother holding the infant Prince Henry.

1985

Ascension 372-376
Bahamas 580-584
Barbados 660-664
Bermuda 469-473
Falkland Islands 420-424
Falkland Islands Dep. 1L92-1L96
Fiji 531-535
Hong Kong 447-450
Jamaica 599-603
Mauritius 604-608
Norfolk Island 364-368
Pitcairn Islands 253-257
St. Helena 428-432
Samoa 649-653
Seychelles 567-571
Solomon Islands 543-547
Swaziland 476-480
Tristan da Cunha 372-376
Vanuatu 392-396
Zil Elwannyen Sesel 101-105

Queen Elizabeth II, 60th Birthday

CD337

1986, April 21

Ascension 389-393
Bahamas 592-596
Barbados 675-679
Bermuda 499-503
Cayman Islands 555-559
Falkland Islands 441-445
Fiji 544-548
Hong Kong 465-469
Jamaica 620-624
Kiribati 470-474
Mauritius 629-633
Papua New Guinea 640-644
Pitcairn Islands 270-274
St. Helena 451-455
Samoa 670-674
Seychelles 592-596
Solomon Islands 562-566
South Georgia 101-105
Swaziland 490-494
Tristan da Cunha 388-392
Vanuatu 414-418
Zambia 343-347
Zil Elwannyen Sesel 114-118

Royal Wedding

Marriage of Prince Andrew and Sarah Ferguson CD338

1986, July 23

Ascension 399-400
Bahamas 602-603
Barbados 687-688
Cayman Islands 560-561
Jamaica 629-630
Pitcairn Islands 275-276
St. Helena 460-461
St. Kitts 181-182
Seychelles 602-603
Solomon Islands 567-568
Tristan da Cunha 397-398
Zambia 348-349
Zil Elwannyen Sesel 119-120

Queen Elizabeth II, 60th Birthday

Queen Elizabeth II & Prince Philip, 1947 Wedding Portrait — CD339

Designs: Photographs tracing the life of Queen Elizabeth II.

1986

Anguilla 674-677
Antigua 925-928
Barbuda 783-786
Dominica 950-953
Gambia 611-614
Grenada 1371-1374
Grenada Grenadines 749-752
Lesotho 531-534
Maldive Islands 1172-1175
Sierra Leone 760-763
Uganda 495-498

Royal Wedding, 1986

CD340

Designs: Photographs of Prince Andrew and Sarah Ferguson during courtship, engagement and marriage.

1986

Antigua 939-942
Barbuda 809-812
Dominica 970-973
Gambia 635-638
Grenada 1385-1388
Grenada Grenadines 758-761
Lesotho 545-548
Maldive Islands 1181-1184
Sierra Leone 769-772
Uganda 510-513

Lloyds of London, 300th Anniv.

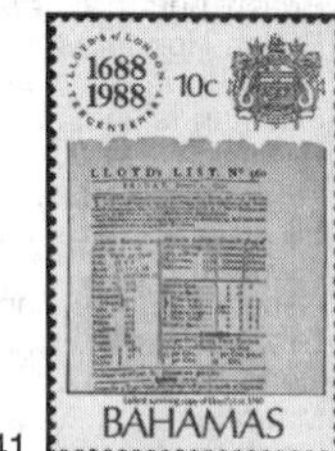

CD341

Designs: 17th century aspects of Lloyds, representations of each country's individual connections with Lloyds and publicized disasters insured by the organization.

1986

Ascension 454-457
Bahamas 655-658
Barbados 731-734
Bermuda 541-544
Falkland Islands 481-484
Liberia 1101-1104
Malawi 534-537
Nevis 571-574
St. Helena 501-504
St. Lucia 923-926
Seychelles 649-652
Solomon Islands 627-630
South Georgia 131-134
Trinidad & Tobago 484-487
Tristan da Cunha 439-442
Vanuatu 485-488
Zil Elwannyen Sesel 146-149

Moon Landing, 20th Anniv.

CD342

Designs: Equipment, crew photographs, spacecraft, official emblems and report profiles created for the Apollo Missions. Two stamps in each set are square in format rather than like the stamp shown; see individual country listings for more information.

1989

Ascension Is. 468-472
Bahamas 674-678
Belize 916-920
Kiribati 517-521
Liberia 1125-1129
Nevis 586-590
St. Kitts 248-252

British Commonwealth of Nations

Dominions, Colonies, Territories, Offices and Independent Members

Comprising stamps of the British Commonwealth and associated nations.

A strict observance of technicalities would bar some or all of the stamps listed under Burma, Ireland, Kuwait, Nepal, New Republic, Orange Free State, Samoa, South Africa, South-West Africa, Stellaland, Sudan, Swaziland, the two Transvaal Republics and others but these are included for the convenience of collectors.

1. Great Britain

Great Britain: Including England, Scotland, Wales and Northern Ireland.

2. The Dominions, Present and Past

AUSTRALIA

The Commonwealth of Australia was proclaimed on January 1, 1901. It consists of six former colonies as follows:

New South Wales
Queensland
South Australia
Victoria
Tasmania
Western Australia

Territories belonging to, or administered by Australia: Australian Antarctic Territory, Christmas Island, Cocos (Keeling) Islands, Nauru, New Guinea, Norfolk Island, Papua New Guinea.

CANADA

The Dominion of Canada was created by the British North America Act in 1867. The following provinces were former separate colonies and issued postage stamps:

British Columbia and Vancouver Island
New Brunswick
Newfoundland
Nova Scotia
Prince Edward Island

FIJI

The colony of Fiji became an independent nation with dominion status on Oct. 10, 1970.

GHANA

This state came into existence Mar. 6, 1957, with dominion status. It consists of the former colony of the Gold Coast and the Trusteeship Territory of Togoland. Ghana became a republic July 1, 1960.

INDIA

The Republic of India was inaugurated on January 26, 1950. It succeeded the Dominion of India which was proclaimed August 15, 1947, when the former Empire of India was divided into Pakistan and the Union of India. The Republic is composed of about 40 predominantly Hindu states of three classes: governor's provinces, chief commissioner's provinces and princely states. India also has various territories, such as the Andaman and Nicobar Islands.

The old Empire of India was a federation of British India and the native states. The more important princely states were autonomous. Of the more than 700 Indian states, these 43 are familiar names to philatelists because of their postage stamps.

CONVENTION STATES

Chamba
Faridkot
Gwalior
Jhind
Nabha
Patiala

NATIVE FEUDATORY STATES

Alwar
Bahawalpur
Bamra
Barwani
Bhopal
Bhor
Bijawar
Bundi
Bussahir
Charkhari
Cochin
Dhar
Duttia
Faridkot (1879-85)
Hyderabad
Idar
Indore
Jaipur
Jammu
Jammu and Kashmir
Jasdan
Jhalawar
Jhind (1875-76)
Kashmir
Kishangarh
Las Bela
Morvi
Nandgaon
Nowanuggur
Orchha
Poonch
Rajpeepla
Sirmur
Soruth
Travancore
Wadhwan

NEW ZEALAND

Became a dominion on September 26, 1907. The following islands and territories are, or have been, administered by New Zealand:

Aitutaki
Cook Islands (Rarotonga)
Niue
Penrhyn
Ross Dependency
Samoa (Western Samoa)
Tokelau Islands

PAKISTAN

The Republic of Pakistan was proclaimed March 23, 1956. It succeeded the Dominion which was proclaimed August 15, 1947. It is made up of all or part of several Moslem provinces and various districts of the former Empire of India, including Bahawalpur and Las Bela. Pakistan withdrew from the Commonwealth in 1972.

SOUTH AFRICA

Under the terms of the South African Act (1909) the self-governing colonies of Cape of Good Hope, Natal, Orange River Colony and Transvaal united on May 31, 1910, to form the Union of South Africa. It became an independent republic May 3, 1961.

Under the terms of the Treaty of Versailles, South-West Africa, formerly German South-West Africa, was mandated to the Union of South Africa.

SRI LANKA (CEYLON)

The Dominion of Ceylon was proclaimed February 4, 1948. The island had been a Crown Colony from 1802 until then. On May 22, 1972, Ceylon became the Republic of Sri Lanka.

3. Colonies, Past and Present; ControlledTerritory and Independent Members of the Commonwealth

Aden
Aitutaki
Antigua
Ascension
Bahamas
Bahrain
Bangladesh
Barbados
Barbuda
Basutoland
Batum
Bechuanaland
Bechuanaland Prot.
Belize
Bermuda
Botswana
British Antarctic Territory
British Central Africa
British Columbia and Vancouver Island
British East Africa
British Guiana

British Honduras
British Indian Ocean Territory
British New Guinea
British Solomon Islands
British Somaliland
Brunei
Burma
Bushire
Cameroons
Cape of Good Hope
Cayman Islands
Christmas Island
Cocos (Keeling) Islands
Cook Islands
Crete,
 British Administration
Cyprus
Dominica
East Africa & Uganda
 Protectorates
Egypt
Falkland Islands
Fiji
Gambia
German East Africa
Gibraltar
Gilbert Islands
Gilbert & Ellice Islands
Gold Coast
Grenada
Griqualand West
Guernsey
Guyana
Heligoland
Hong Kong
Indian Native States
 (see India)
Ionian Islands
Jamaica
Jersey
Kenya
Kenya, Uganda & Tanzania
Kuwait
Labuan
Lagos
Leeward Islands
Lesotho
Madagascar
Malawi
Malaya
 Federated Malay States
 Johore
 Kedah
 Kelantan
 Malacca
 Negri Sembilan
 Pahang
 Penang
 Perak
 Perlis
 Selangor
 Singapore
 Sungei Ujong
 Trengganu
Malaysia
Maldive Islands
Malta
Man, Isle of
Mauritius
Mesopotamia
Montserrat
Muscat
Namibia
Natal
Nauru
Nevis
New Britain
New Brunswick
Newfoundland
New Guinea
New Hebrides
New Republic
New South Wales
Niger Coast Protectorate
Nigeria
Niue
Norfolk Island
North Borneo
Northern Nigeria
Northern Rhodesia
North West Pacific Islands
Nova Scotia
Nyasaland Protectorate
Oman
Orange River Colony
Palestine
Papua New Guinea
Penrhyn Island
Pitcairn Islands
Prince Edward Island
Queensland
Rhodesia
Rhodesia & Nyasaland
Ross Dependency
Sabah
St. Christopher
St. Helena
St. Kitts
St. Kitts-Nevis-Anguilla
St. Lucia
St. Vincent
Samoa
Sarawak
Seychelles
Sierra Leone
Solomon Islands
Somaliland Protectorate
South Arabia
South Australia
South Georgia
Southern Nigeria
Southern Rhodesia
South-West Africa
Stellaland
Straits Settlements
Sudan
Swaziland
Tanganyika
Tanzania
Tasmania
Tobago
Togo
Tokelau Islands
Tonga
Transvaal
Trinidad
Trinidad and Tobago
Tristan da Cunha
Trucial States
Turks and Caicos
Turks Islands
Tuvalu
Uganda
United Arab Emirates
Victoria
Virgin Islands
Western Australia
Zambia
Zanzibar
Zululand

POST OFFICES IN FOREIGN COUNTRIES

Africa
 East Africa Forces
 Middle East Forces
Bangkok
China
Morocco
Turkish Empire

Colonies, Former Colonies, Offices, Territories Controlled by Parent States

Belgium

Belgian Congo
Ruanda-Urundi

Denmark

Danish West Indies
Faroe Islands
Greenland
Iceland

Finland

Aland Islands

France

COLONIES PAST AND PRESENT, CONTROLLED TERRITORIES

Afars & Issas, Territory of
Alaouites
Alexandretta
Algeria
Alsace & Lorraine
Anjouan
Annam & Tonkin
Benin
Cambodia (Khmer)
Cameroun
Castellorizo
Chad
Cilicia
Cochin China
Comoro Islands
Dahomey
Diego Suarez
Djibouti (Somali Coast)
Fezzan
French Congo
French Equatorial Africa
French Guiana
French Guinea
French India
French Morocco
French Polynesia (Oceania)
French Southern & Antarctic Territories
French Sudan
French West Africa
Gabon
Germany
Ghadames
Grand Comoro
Guadeloupe
Indo-China
Inini
Ivory Coast
Laos
Latakia
Lebanon
Madagascar
Martinique
Mauritania
Mayotte
Memel
Middle Congo
Moheli
New Caledonia
New Hebrides
Niger Territory
Nossi-Be
Obock
Reunion
Rouad, Ile
Ste.-Marie de Madagascar
St. Pierre & Miquelon
Senegal
Senegambia & Niger
Somali Coast
Syria
Tahiti
Togo
Tunisia
Ubangi-Shari
Upper Senegal & Niger
Upper Volta
Viet Nam
Wallis & Futuna Islands

POST OFFICES IN FOREIGN COUNTRIES

China
Crete
Egypt
Turkish Empire
Zanzibar

Germany

EARLY STATES

Baden
Bavaria
Bergedorf
Bremen
Brunswick
Hamburg
Hanover
Lubeck
Mecklenburg-Schwerin
Mecklenburg-Strelitz
Oldenburg
Prussia
Saxony
Schleswig-Holstein
Wurttemberg

FORMER COLONIES

Cameroun (Kamerun)
Caroline Islands
German East Africa
German New Guinea
German South-West Africa
Kiauchau
Mariana Islands
Marshall Islands
Samoa
Togo

Italy

EARLY STATES

Modena
Parma
Romagna
Roman States
Sardinia
Tuscany
Two Sicilies
  Naples
  Neapolitan Provinces
  Sicily

FORMER COLONIES, CONTROLLED TERRITORIES, OCCUPATION AREAS

Aegean Islands
  Calimno (Calino)
  Caso
  Cos (Coo)
  Karki (Carchi)
  Leros (Lero)
  Lipso
  Nisiros (Nisiro)
  Patmos (Patmo)
  Piscopi
  Rodi (Rhodes)
  Scarpanto
  Simi
  Stampalia
Castellorizo
Corfu
Cyrenaica
Eritrea
Ethiopia (Abyssinia)
Fiume
Ionian Islands
  Cephalonia
  Ithaca
  Paxos
Italian East Africa
Libya
Oltre Giuba
Saseno
Somalia (Italian Somaliland)
Tripolitania

POST OFFICES IN FOREIGN COUNTRIES

"ESTERO"*
Austria
China
  Peking
  Tientsin
Crete
Tripoli
Turkish Empire
  Constantinople
  Durazzo
  Janina
Jerusalem
Salonika
Scutari
Smyrna
Valona

*Stamps overprinted "ESTERO" were used in various parts of the world.

Netherlands

Aruba
Netherlands Antilles (Curacao)
Netherlands Indies
Netherlands New Guinea
Surinam (Dutch Guiana)

Portugal

COLONIES PAST AND PRESENT, CONTROLLED TERRITORIES

Angola
Angra
Azores
Cape Verde
Funchal
Horta
Inhambane
Kionga
Lourenco Marques
Macao
Madeira
Mozambique
Mozambique Co.
Nyassa
Ponta Delgada
Portuguese Africa
Portuguese Congo
Portuguese Guinea
Portuguese India
Quelimane
St. Thomas & Prince Islands
Tete
Timor
Zambezia

Russia

ALLIED TERRITORIES AND REPUBLICS, OCCUPATION AREAS

Armenia
Aunus (Olonets)
Azerbaijan
Batum
Estonia
Far Eastern Republic
Georgia
Karelia
Latvia
Lithuania
North Ingermanland
Ostland
Russian Turkestan
Siberia
South Russia
Tannu Tuva
Transcaucasian Fed. Republics
Ukraine
Wenden (Livonia)
Western Ukraine

Spain

COLONIES PAST AND PRESENT, CONTROLLED TERRITORIES

Aguera, La
Cape Juby
Cuba
Elobey, Annobon & Corisco
Fernando Po
Ifni
Mariana Islands
Philippines
Puerto Rico
Rio de Oro
Rio Muni
Spanish Guinea
Spanish Morocco
Spanish Sahara
Spanish West Africa

POST OFFICES IN FOREIGN COUNTRIES

Morocco
Tangier
Tetuan

Dies of British Colonial Stamps

DIE A

DIE B

DIE A:
1. The lines in the groundwork vary in thickness and are not uniformly straight.
2. The seventh and eighth lines from the top, in the groundwork, converge where they meet the head.
3. There is a small dash in the upper part of the second jewel in the band of the crown.
4. The vertical color line in front of the throat stops at the sixth line of shading on the neck.

DIE B:
1. The lines in the groundwork are all thin and straight.
2. All the lines of the background are parallel.
3. There is no dash in the upper part of the second jewel in the band of the crown.
4. The vertical color line in front of the throat stops at the eighth line of shading on the neck.

DIE I

DIE II

DIE I:
1. The base of the crown is well below the level of the inner white line around the vignette.
2. The labels inscribed "POSTAGE" and "REVENUE" are cut square at the top.
3. There is a white "bud" on the outer side of the main stem of the curved ornaments in each lower corner.
4. The second (thick) line below the country name has the ends next to the crown cut diagonally.

DIE Ia.	DIE Ib.
1 as die II.	1 and 3 as die II.
2 and 3 as die I.	2 as die I.

DIE II:
1. The base of the crown is aligned with the underside of the white line around the vignette.
2. The labels curve inward at the top inner corners.
3. The "bud" has been removed from the outer curve of the ornaments in each corner.
4. The second line below the country name has the ends next to the crown cut vertically.

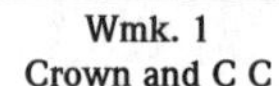
Wmk. 1
Crown and C C

Wmk. 2
Crown and C A

Wmk. 3
Multiple Crown and C A

Wmk. 4
Multiple Crown and Script C A

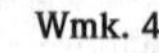
Wmk. 4a

Wmk. 314
St. Edward's Crown and C A Multiple

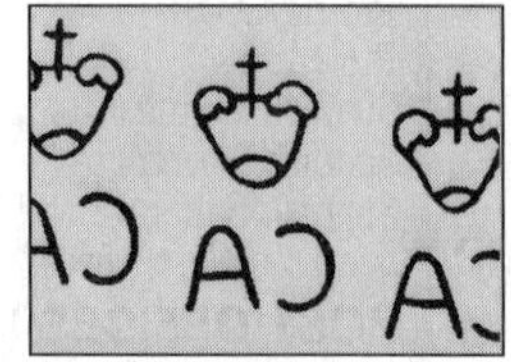

Wmk. 373

Wmk. 384

British Colonial and Crown Agents Watermarks

Watermarks 1 to 4, 314, 373, and 384, common to many British territories, are illustrated here to avoid duplication.

The letters "CC" of Wmk. 1 identify the paper as having been made for the use of the Crown Colonies, while the letters "CA" of the others stand for "Crown Agents." Both Wmks. 1 and 2 were used on stamps printed by De La Rue & Co.

Wmk. 3 was adopted in 1904; Wmk. 4 in 1921; Wmk. 314 in 1957; Wmk. 373 in 1974; and Wmk. 384 in 1985.

In Wmk. 4a, a non-matching crown of the general St. Edwards type (bulging on both sides at top) was substituted for one of the Wmk. 4 crowns which fell off the dandy roll. The non-matching crown occurs in 1950-52 printings in a horizontal row of crowns on certain regular stamps of Johore and Seychelles, and on various postage due stamps of Barbados, Basutoland, British Guiana, Gold Coast, Grenada, Northern Rhodesia, St. Lucia, Swaziland and Trinidad and Tobago. A variation of Wmk. 4a, with the non-matching crown in a horizontal row of crown-CA-crown, occurs on regular stamps of Bahamas, St. Kitts-Nevis and Singapore.

Wmk. 314 was intentionally used sideways, starting in 1966. When a stamp was issued with Wmk. 314 both upright and sideways, the sideways varieties usually are listed also – with minor numbers. In many of the later issues, Wmk. 314 is slightly visible.

Wmk. 373 is usually only faintly visible.

UNITED STATES

yu-ˌnī-təd ˈstāts

GOVT. — Republic
AREA — 3,615,211 sq. mi.
POP. — 281,421,906 (2000)
CAPITAL — Washington, DC

In addition to the 50 States and the District of Columbia, the Republic includes Guam, the Commonwealth of Puerto Rico, the Virgin Islands, American Samoa, Wake, Midway, and a number of small islands in the Pacific Ocean, all of which use stamps of the United States.

100 Cents = 1 Dollar

Catalogue values for unused stamps in this country are for Never Hinged items, beginning with Scott 772 in the regular postage section, Scott C19 in the air post section, Scott E17 in the special delivery section, Scott FA1 in the certified mail section, Scott O127 in officials section, Scott J88 in the postage due section, Scott RW1 in the hunting permit stamps section.

Watermarks

Wmk. 190—"USPS" in Single-lined Capitals

Wmk. 191—Double-lined "USPS" in Capitals

Watermark 191 has 9 letters for each horizontal row of 10 stamps. Watermark 190 has 8 to 9 letters for each horizontal row. Each watermark has 9 letters for each vertical row of 10 stamps This results in a number of stamps in each pane showing only a small portion of 1 or more watermark letters. This is especialy true of watermark 190.

Wmk. 190PI - PIPS, used in the Philippines
Wmk. 191PI - PIPS, used in the Philippines
Wmk. 191C - US-C, used for Cuba
Wmk. 191R - USIR

PROVISIONAL ISSUES BY POSTMASTERS

Values for Envelopes are for entires.

ALEXANDRIA, VA.

A1

Type I - 40 asterisks in circle.
Type II - 39 asterisks in circle.

1846 Typeset *Imperf.*

1X1 A1 5c black, *buff*, Type I —
- **a.** 5c black, *buff*, Type II 75,000.

1X2 A1 5c black, *blue*, Type I, on cover —

All known copies of Nos. 1X1-1X2 are cut to shape.

ANNAPOLIS, MD.

ENVELOPE

E1

1846

2XU1 E1 5c carmine red 225,000.

Handstamped impressions of the circular design with "2" in blue or red exist on envelopes and letter sheets. Values: blue $3,000, red $5,000.

A letter sheet exists with circular design and "5" handstamped in red. Values: blue $3,500, red $5,000.

A similar circular design in blue was used as a postmark.

BALTIMORE, MD.

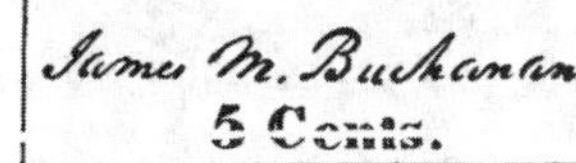

Signature of Postmaster—A1

1845 Engr. *Imperf.*

3X1 A1 5c black 5,250.
3X2 A1 10c black, on cover 50,000.
3X3 A1 5c black, *bluish* 65,000. 5,250.
3X4 A1 10c black, *bluish* 60,000.

Nos. 3X1-3X4 were printed from a plate of 12 (2x6) containing nine 5c and three 10c.

Envelopes

James M. Buchanan.
PAID

E1

The color given is that of the "PAID 5" and oval. "James M. Buchanan" is handstamped in black, blue or red. The paper is manila, buff, white, salmon or grayish.

1845 Handstamped
Various Papers

3XU1 E1 5c blue 6,500.
3XU2 E1 5c red 9,000.
3XU3 E1 10c blue 16,000.
3XU4 E1 10c red 19,000.

On the formerly listed "5+5" envelopes, the second "5" in oval is believed not to be part of the basic prepaid marking.

BOSCAWEN, N. H.

PAID
5
CENTS

A1

1846(?) Typeset *Imperf.*

4X1 A1 5c dull blue, *yellowish*, on cover 225,000.

BRATTLEBORO, VT.

Initials of Postmaster (FNP)—A1

Plate of 10 (5x2).

1846 Engr. *Imperf.*

5X1 A1 5c black, *buff* 10,000.

LOCKPORT, N. Y.

A1

Handstamped, "5" in Black Ms

1846

6X1 A1 5c red, *buff*, on cover 225,000.

MILLBURY, Mass.

George Washington—A1

Printed from a Woodcut

1846 *Imperf.*

7X1 A1 5c blue, *bluish* 130,000. 20,000.

NEW HAVEN, CONN.

Envelopes

E1

1845 Handstamped
Signed in Blue, Black, or Magenta

8XU1 E1 5c red (Bl or M) 80,000.
8XU2 E1 5c red, *light bluish* (Bk) 110,000.
8XU3 E1 5c dull blue, *buff* (Bl) 110,000.
8XU4 E1 5c dull blue (Bl) 110,000.

Values of Nos. 8XU1-8XU4 are a guide to value. They are based on auction realizations and retail sales and take condition into consideration. All New Haven envelopes are of almost equal rarity. An entire of No. 8XU2 is the finest example known. The other envelopes are valued according to condition as much as rarity.

Reprints were made at various times between 1871 and 1932. They can be distinguished from the originals, primarily due to differences in paper.

NEW YORK, N. Y.

George Washington—A1

Plate of 40 (5x8). Nos. 9X1-9X3 and varieties unused are valued without gum. Examples with original gum are extremely scarce and will command higher prices.

1845-46 Engr. *Imperf.*
Bluish Wove Paper

9X1 A1 5c blk, signed ACM, connected ('46) 1,400. 500.
- **a.** Signed ACM, AC connected 1,750. 550.
- **b.** Signed A.C.M. *3,750.* 700.
- **c.** Signed MMJr *9,000.*
- **d.** Signed RHM *13,000. 3,250.*
- **e.** Without signature 3,250. 750.

These stamps were usually initialed "ACM" in magenta ink, as a control, before being sold or passed through the mails.

A plate of 9 (3x3) was made from which proofs were printed in black on white and deep blue papers; also in blue, green, brown and red on white bond paper.

1847 Engr. *Imperf.*
Blue Wove Paper

9X2 A1 5c blk, signed ACM, connected *6,500.* 3,500.
- **a.** Signed RHM —
- **d.** Without signature *11,000. 7,250.*

On the listing example of No. 9X2a the "R" is illegible and does not match those of the other "RHM" signatures.

1847 Engr. *Imperf.*
Gray Wove Paper

9X3 A1 5c blk, signed ACM, connected 5,250. 2,100.
- **a.** Signed RHM *7,000.*
- **b.** Without signature *7,000.*

PROVIDENCE, R. I.

A1

A2

1846 Engr. *Imperf.*

10X1 A1 5c gray black 350. *1,750.*
10X2 A2 10c gray black 1,100. *15,000.*
- **a.** Pair, #10X1-10X2 1,750.

Plate of 12 (3x4) contains 11-5c and 1-10c.

Reprints were made in 1898. Each stamp bears one of the following letters on the back: B. O. G. E. R. T. D. U. R. B. I. N. Value of 5c, $50; 10c, $125; sheet, $725.

Reprint singles or sheets without back print sell for more.

ST. LOUIS, MO.

A1 A2 A3
Missouri Coat of Arms

Unused are valued without gum.

1845-46 Engr. *Imperf.*
Greenish Wove Paper

11X1 A1 5c black 7,000. 4,500.
11X2 A2 10c black 7,000. 4,000.
11X3 A3 20c black *30,000.*

Three varieties of 5c, 3 of 10c, 2 of 20c.

1846
Gray Lilac Paper

11X4 A1 5c black — 5,500.
11X5 A2 10c black 5,500. 3,000.
11X6 A3 20c black *22,500.*

One variety of 5c, 3 of 10c, 2 of 20c.

1847
Pelure Paper

11X7 A1 5c black *bluish* — 6,500.
11X8 A2 10c blk, *bluish* 6,500.
- **a.** Impression of 5c on back —

Three varieties of 5c, 3 of 10c.

Values of Nos. 11X7-11X8 reflect the usual poor condition of these stamps, which were printed on fragile pelure paper. Attractive copies with minor defects sell for considerably more.

Used values are for pen-canceled copies.

For Tuscumbia, Alabama, formerly listed as United States postmasters' provisional No. 12XU1, see the "3c 1861 Postmasters' Provisionals" section before the Confederate States of America Postmasters' Provisionals.

Please Note:

Stamps are valued in the grade of very fine unless otherwise indicated.

Values for early and valuable stamps are for examples with certificates of authenticity from acknowledged expert committees, or examples sold with the buyer having the right of certification. This applies to examples with original gum as well as examples without gum.

Beware of stamps offered "as is," as the gum on some unused stamps offered with "original gum" may be fraudulent, and stamps offered as unused without gum may in some cases be altered or faintly canceled used stamps.

Cancels on Used Stamps

Manuscript (pen) cancels reduce the value of used stamps by about 50%. See the Scott U.S. Specialized Catalogue for individual valuations.

GENERAL ISSUES

All Issues from 1847 to 1894 are Unwatermarked.

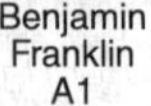

Benjamin Franklin A1

George Washington A2

1847, July 1 — Engr. — *Imperf.*

1	A1	5c red brn, *bluish*	6,250.	550.
		No gum	2,500.	
a.		5c dark brown, *bluish*	7,250.	625.
		No gum	3,100.	
b.		5c orange brown, *bluish*	8,000.	850.
		No gum	3,500.	
c.		5c red orange, *bluish*	*12,500.*	*6,000.*
		No gum	7,000.	
d.		Double impression		—
		Pen cancel		300.

The only known double impression shows part of the design doubled.

2	A2	10c black, *bluish*	*27,500.*	1,350.
		No gum	*12,500.*	
a.		Diagonal half used as 5c on cover		*13,000.*
b.		Vertical half used as 5c on cover		*35,000.*
c.		Horizontal half used as 5c on cover		—
		Pen cancel		750.

REPRODUCTIONS

Actually, official imitations made from new plates by order of the Post Office Department.

A3

A4

1875 — *Imperf.*

Bluish Paper Without Gum

3	A3	5c red brown	725.
4	A4	10c black	900.

Reproductions. The letters R. W. H. & E. at the bottom of each stamp are less distinct on the reproductions than on the originals.

5c. On the originals the left side of the white shirt frill touches the oval on a level with the top of the "F" of "Five." On the reproductions it touches the oval about on a level with the top of the figure "5." On the originals the bottom of the right leg of the "N" in "CENTS" is blunt. On the reproductions the "N" comes to a point at the bottom.

10c. On the reproductions, line of coat at left points to right tip of "X" and line of coat at right points to center of "S" of CENTS. On the originals, line of coat points to "T" of TEN and between "T" and "S" of CENTS. The bottom of the right leg of the "N" of "CENTS" shows the same difference as on the 5c originals and reproductions. On the reproductions the eyes have a sleepy look, the line of the mouth is straighter, and in the curl of hair near the left cheek is a strong black dot, while the originals have only a faint one.

Franklin — A5

ONE CENT

Type I. Has complete curved lines outside the labels with "U.S. Postage" and "One Cent." The scrolls below the lower label are turned under, forming little balls. The ornaments at top are substantially complete.

Values for type I are for stamps showing the marked characteristics plainly. Copies of type I showing the balls indistinctly sell for much lower prices.

Type Ib. Same as I but balls below the bottom label are not so clear. The plume-like scrolls at bottom are not complete.

A6

Type Ia. Same as I at bottom but top ornaments and outer line at top are partly cut away.

Type Ic. Same as Ia, but bottom right plume and ball ornament incomplete. Bottom left plume complete or nearly complete.

A7

Type II. The little balls of the bottom scrolls and the bottoms of the lower plume ornaments are missing. The side ornaments are substantially complete.

A8

Type III. The top and bottom curved lines outside the labels are broken in the middle. The side ornaments are complete.

Type IIIa. Similar to type III with the outer line broken at top or bottom but not both.

A9

Type IV. Similar to type II, but with the curved lines outside the labels recut at top or bottom or both.

Washington — A10

THREE CENTS

Type I. There is an outer frame line on all four sides.

Thomas Jefferson — A11

FIVE CENTS

Type I. There are projections on all four sides.

Washington — A12

TEN CENTS

Type I. The "shells" at the lower corners are practically complete. The outer line below the label is very nearly complete. The outer lines are broken above the middle of the top label and the "X" in each upper corner.

A13

Type II. The design is complete at the top. The outer line at the bottom is broken in the middle. The shells are partly cut away.

A14

Type III. The outer lines are broken above the top label and the "X" numerals. The outer line at the bottom and the shells are partly cut away, similar to Type II.

A15

Type IV. The outer lines have been recut at top or bottom or both.

Types I, II, III and IV have complete ornaments at the sides of the stamps and three pearls at each outer edge of the bottom panel.

Washington — A16

In Nos. 5-17, the 1c, 3c, and 12c have very small margins between the stamps. The 5c and 10c have moderate size margins. The values of these stamps take the margin size into consideration.

Values for No. 5A, 6b and 19b are for the less distinct positions. Best examples sell for more.

Values for No. 16 are for outer line recut at top. Other recuts sell for more.

1851-57 — *Imperf.*

5	A5	1c blue, I	*200,000.*	*45,000.*

Values for No. 5 are for copies with margins touching or slightly cutting into the design. Value unused is for an example with no gum.

5A	A5	1c blue, Ib	*16,500.*	*6,750.*
		No gum	*2,500.*	
6	A6	1c blue, Ia ('57)	*37,500.*	*10,000.*
		No gum	*20,000.*	
b.		Type Ic	*6,250.*	*1,600.*
		No gum	*2,750.*	
7	A7	1c blue, II	1,200.	160.
		No gum	525.	
8	A8	1c blue, III	*13,500.*	3,000.
		No gum	*6,000.*	

Values for type III are for at least a 2mm break in each outer line. Examples of type III with wider breaks in outer lines command higher prices; those with smaller breaks sell for less.

8A	A8	1c blue, IIIa	*4,600.*	1,050.
		No gum	2,100.	

Stamps of type IIIa with bottom line broken command higher prices than those with top line broken. See note after No. 8 on width of break of outer lines.

9	A9	1c bl, IV ('52)	750.	125.
		No gum	300.	
a.		Printed on both sides, reverse inverted		—

10 A10 3c org brown, I 3,250. 110.
No gum 1,500.
a. Printed on both sides 12,000.
11 A10 3c dull red, I 250. 11.
No gum 100.
c. Vertical half used as 1c on cover 5,000.
d. Diagonal half used as 1c on cover 5,000.
e. Double impression 5,000.
12 A11 5c red brown, I ('56) 19,000. 950.
No gum 9,250.
13 A12 10c grn, I ('55) 15,000. 800.
No gum 7,000.
14 A13 10c grn, II ('55) 4,500. 200.
No gum 2,000.
15 A14 10c grn, III ('55) 4,500. 200.
No gum 2,000.
16 A15 10c grn, IV ('55) 27,500. 1,600.
No gum 14,000.
17 A16 12c black 5,250. 325.
No gum 2,200.
a. Diagonal half used as 6c on cover 2,500.
b. Vertical half used as 6c on cover 8,500.
c. Printed on both sides 10,000.

Same Designs as 1851-56 Issues

Franklin—A20

ONE CENT

Type V. Similar to type III of 1851-57 but with side ornaments partly cut away.

Washington—A21

THREE CENTS

Type II. The outer frame line has been removed at top and bottom. The side frame lines were recut so as to be continuous from the top to the bottom of the plate. Stamps from the top or bottom rows show the ends of the side frame lines and may be mistaken for type IIa.

Type IIa. The side frame lines extend only to the top and bottom of the stamp design.

Jefferson — A22

FIVE CENTS

Type II. The projections at top and bottom are partly cut away.

Washington (Two typical examples) — A23

TEN CENTS

Type V. The side ornaments are slightly cut away. Usually only one pearl remains at each end of the lower label but some copies show two or three pearls at the right side.

At the bottom the outer line is complete and the shells nearly so. The outer lines at top are complete except over the right "X."

Washington A17

Franklin A18

Washington — A19

TWELVE CENTS

Plate I. Outer frame lines complete.

Plate III. Outer frame lines noticeably uneven or broken, sometimes partly missing.

Nos. 18-39 have small or very small margins. The values take into account the margin size.

1857-61 ***Perf. 15½***

18 A5 1c blue, I ('61) 2,000. 600.
No gum 900.
19 A6 1c blue, Ia 25,000. 6,500.
No gum 10,000.
b. Type Ic 2,900. 1,500.
No gum 1,300.
20 A7 1c blue, II 1,100. 250.
No gum 475.
21 A8 1c blue, III 12,500. 2,200.
No gum 6,000.
a. Horiz. pair, imperf. btwn. 16,000.
22 A8 1c blue, IIIa 2,000. 500.
No gum 900.
b. Horiz. pair, imperf. btwn. 5,000.

One pair of No. 22b has been reported. Beware of pairs with blind perforations.

23 A9 1c blue, IV 8,500. 700.
No gum 3,900.
24 A20 1c blue, V 175. 40.
No gum 80.
b. Laid paper —
25 A10 3c rose, I 2,500. 90.
No gum 1,150.
b. Vert. pair, imperf. horiz. 10,000.
26 A21 3c dull red, II 75. 7.50
No gum 27.50
a. 3c dull red, IIa 225. 60.
No gum 95.
b. Horiz. pair, imperf. vert., II 4,000. —
c. Vert. pair, imperf. horiz., II 10,000.
d. Horiz. pair, imperf. btwn., II —
e. Dbl. impression, II 2,500.
f. Horiz. strip of 3, imperf. vert., IIa, on cover 8,250.
27 A11 5c brick red, I ('58) 30,000. 1,400.
No gum 12,500.
28 A11 5c red brn, I 5,000. 800.
No gum 2,250.
b. 5c bright red brown 5,750. 1,000.
No gum 2,500.
28A A11 5c Indian red, I ('58) 32,500. 3,000.
No gum 17,000.
29 A11 5c brn, I ('59) 2,500. 350.
No gum 1,100.
30 A22 5c org brn, II ('61) 1,200. 1,100.
No gum 525.
30A A22 5c brn, II ('60) 2,000. 300.
No gum 900.
b. Printed on both sides 4,400. 4,650.
31 A12 10c green, I 17,500. 900.
No gum 8,250.
32 A13 10c green, II 5,250. 275.
No gum 2,500.
33 A14 10c green, III 5,250. 275.
No gum 2,500.
34 A15 10c green, IV 32,500. 2,250.
No gum 17,000.
35 A23 10c grn, V ('59) 275. 65.
No gum 110.
36 A16 12c black, plate I 1,450. 275.
No gum 650.
a. Diagonal half used as 6c on cover (I) 17,500.
b. 12c black, plate III ('59) 775. 180.
No gum 340.
c. Horizontal pair, imperf. between (I) 12,500.
37 A17 24c gray lil ('60) 1,600. 350.
a. 24c gray 1,600. 350.
No gum 675.
38 A18 30c orange ('60) 1,900. 450.
No gum 850.
39 A19 90c blue ('60) 2,900. 7,000.
No gum 1,300.
Pen cancel 2,000.

See Die and Plate proofs in the Scott United States Specialized Catalogue for imperfs. of the 12c, 24c, 30c, 90c.

Genuine cancellations on the 90c are rare. Used examples must be accompanied by certificates of authenticity issued by recognized expertizing committees.

REPRINTS OF 1857-60 ISSUE

White Paper

Without Gum

1875 ***Perf. 12***

40 A5 1c bright blue 625.
41 A10 3c scarlet 3,500.
42 A22 5c orange brown 1,250.
43 A12 10c blue green 3,250.
44 A16 12c greenish blk 3,500.
45 A17 24c black violet 3,500.
46 A18 30c yellow orange 3,500.
47 A19 90c deep blue 4,500.

Nos. 41-46 are valued in the grade of fine.

Nos. 40-47 exist imperf., value, set $25,000.

Essays-Trial Color Proofs

The paper of former Nos. 55-62 (Nos. 63E11e, 65-E15h, 67-E9e, 69-E6e, 72-E7h, Essay section, Nos. 70eTC, 71bTC, Trial Color Proof section, Scott U.S. Specialized) is thin and semitransparent.

That of the postage issues is thicker and more opaque, except Nos. 62B, 70c and 70d.

Franklin — A24

1c: There is a dash under the tip of the ornament at right of the numeral in upper left corner.

There is no dash on the essay.

Washington — A25

3c: Ornaments at corners are large and end in a small ball.

The ornaments are smaller and there is no ball on the essay.

Jefferson — A26

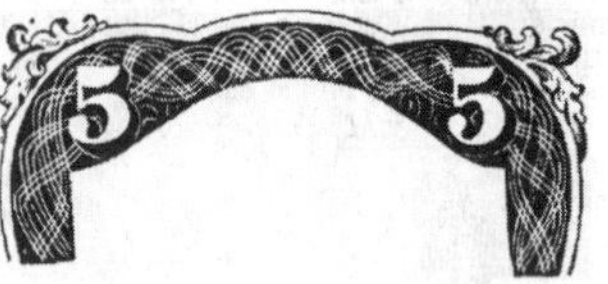

5c: Leaflets appear at each corner. These do not appear on the essay.

Washington — A27

A27

A27a

10c: On A27 a heavy curved line appears below the stars and an outer line above them which does not appear on A27a.

Washington — A28

12c: Ovals and scrolls appear at each corners.

These do not appear on the essay.

Washington
A29

Franklin
A30

Washington — A31

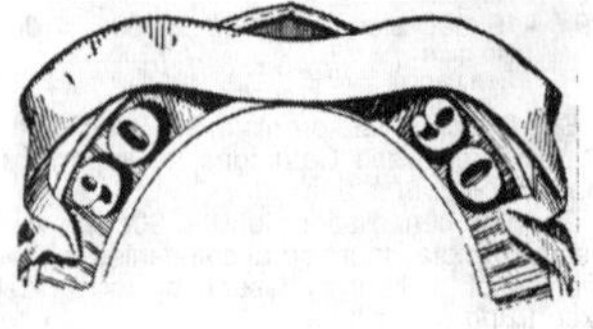

90c: Two pairs of parallel lines form an angle above the ribbon with "U. S. Postage". Between these lines is a row of dashes, and there is a point of color to the apex of the lower pair.

These do not appear on the essay.

1861 ***Perf. 12***

No.	Design	Description	Unused	Used
62B	A27a	10c dark green	*7,250.*	1,050.
		No gum	*3,250.*	

1861-62 ***Perf. 12***

No.	Design	Description	Unused	Used
63	A24	1c blue	325.00	32.50
		No gum	130.00	
a.		1c ultramarine	800.00	275.00
		No gum	325.00	
b.		1c dark blue	675.00	90.00
		No gum	275.00	
c.		Laid paper	—	*1,500.*
d.		Vert. pair, imperf. horiz.		—
e.		Printed on both sides	—	*2,500.*
64	A25	3c pink	9,000.	800.00
		No gum	*3,750.*	
a.		3c pigeon blood pink	*19,000.*	*3,500.*
		No gum	*9,000.*	
b.		3c rose pink	575.00	150.00
		No gum	260.00	
65	A25	3c rose	130.00	2.50
		No gum	52.50	
b.		Laid paper	—	—
d.		Vert. pair, imperf. horiz.	*3,500.*	*750.00*
e.		Printed on both sides	*3,250.*	*2,750.*
f.		Double impression		*7,500.*

The 3c lake can be found under No. 66 in the Trial Color Proofs section of the Scott U.S. Specialized Catalogue.

The imperf 3c lake under No. 66P in the same section.

The imperf 3c rose can be found in the Die and Plate Proofs section of the Specialized.

No.	Design	Description	Unused	Used
67	A26	5c buff	*21,000.*	800.00
a.		5c brown yellow	*21,000.*	850.00
		No gum	*9,500.*	
b.		5c olive yellow	—	1,250.

Values for Nos. 67, 67a, 67b reflect the normal small margins.

No.	Design	Description	Unused	Used
68	A27	10c yellow green	900.00	50.00
		No gum	400.00	
a.		10c dark green	950.00	62.50
		No gum	425.00	
b.		Vert. pair, imperf. horiz.		*3,500.*
69	A28	12c black	1,500.	100.00
		No gum	600.00	
70	A29	24c red lilac ('62)	2,500.	200.00
		No gum	1,000.	
a.		24c brown lilac	1,800.	150.00
		No gum	800.00	
b.		24c steel blue	*9,000.*	725.00
		No gum	*4,250.*	
c.		24c violet, thin paper	*10,000.*	1,300.
		No gum	*5,000.*	
d.		24c pale gray violet, thin paper	4,250.	1,500.
		No gum	1,900.	
71	A30	30c orange	1,750.	160.00
		No gum	800.00	
a.		Printed on both sides		—

Values for No. 71 are for copies with small margins, especially at sides. Large margined examples sell for much more.

No.	Design	Description	Unused	Used
72	A31	90c blue	3,250.	425.00
		No gum	1,400.	
a.		90c pale blue	3,000.	425.00
		No gum	1,350.	
b.		90c dark blue	3,250.	600.00
		No gum	1,500.	

Nos. 70c, 70d are on a thinner, harder and more transparent paper than Nos. 70, 70a, 70b, or the later Nos. 78, 78a, 78b and 78c.

Please Note:
Stamps are valued in the grade of very fine unless otherwise indicated.
Values for early and valuable stamps are for examples with certificates of authenticity from acknowledged expert committees, or examples sold with the buyer having the right of certification.
This applies to examples with original gum as well as examples without gum.
Beware of stamps offered "as is," as the gum on some unused stamps offered with "original gum" may be fraudulent, and stamps offered as unused without gum may in some cases be altered or faintly canceled used stamps.

Designs as 1861 Issue

Andrew
Jackson
A32

Abraham
Lincoln
A33

1861-66 ***Perf. 12***

No.	Design	Description	Unused	Used
73	A32	2c black ('63)	375.00	50.00
		No gum	140.00	
a.		Diag. half used as 1c as part of 3c rate on cover		1,150.
b.		Diagonal half used alone as 1c on cover		*3,000.*
c.		Horiz. half used as 1c as part of 3c rate on cover		*3,500.*
d.		Vert. half used as 1c as part of 3c rate on cover		1,250.
e.		Vert. half used alone as 1c on cover		—
f.		Printed on both sides		*5,000.*
g		Laid paper	—	—

The 3c scarlet can be found under No. 74 in the Scott U.S. Specialized Catalogue Trial Color Proofs section.

No.	Design	Description	Unused	Used
75	A26	5c red brown ('62)	4,750.	475.00
		No gum	2,100.	
76	A26	5c brown ('63)	1,350.	120.00
		No gum	550.00	
a.		5c black brown	1,600.	200.00
		No gum	650.00	
b.		Laid paper		—
77	A33	15c black ('66)	2,500.	160.00
		No gum	1,000.	
78	A29	24c lilac ('63)	1,400.	125.00
a.		24c grayish lilac	1,400.	125.00
b.		24c gray	1,400.	120.00
		No gum	575.00	
c.		24c blackish violet	*30,000.*	*2,750.*
		No gum	*20,000.*	
d.		Printed on both sides		—

Values for Nos. 75, 76, 76a reflect the normal small margins.

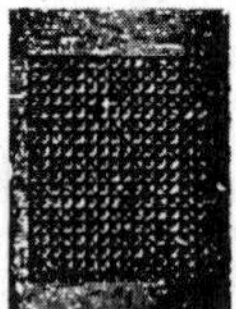

Grill

Same as 1861-66 Issues
Embossed with grills of various sizes

Grill with Points Up

Grills A and C were made by a roller covered with ridges shaped like an inverted V. Pressing the ridges into the stamp paper forced the paper into the pyramidal pits between the ridges, causing irregular breaks in the paper.

Grill B was made by a roller with raised bosses.

A. Grill covering the entire stamp

1867 ***Perf. 12***

No.	Design	Description	Unused	Used
79	A25	3c rose	5,250.	1,350.
		No gum	2,400.	
b.		Printed on both sides		—
80	A26	5c brown	—	*130,000.*
a.		5c dark brown		*130,000.*
81	A30	30c orange		*70,000.*

Nos. 79, 79b, are valued for fine-very fine centering but with minor perforation faults.

An essay which is often mistaken for No. 79 (#79-E15) shows the points of the grill as small squares faintly impressed in the paper, but not cutting through it.

On No. 79 the grill breaks through the paper. Copies free from defects are rare.

Eight copies of Nos. 80 and 80a (four unused, four used), and eight copies of No. 81 (one in a museum and not available to collectors) are known. All are more or less faulty and/or off-center.

Values are for off-center examples with small perforation faults.

The imperf. of the 3c rose can be found in the Scott U.S. Specialized Catalogue, Die and Plate Proofs section.

B. Grill about 18x15mm (22 by 18 points)

No.	Design	Description	Unused	Used
82	A25	3c rose		*185,000.*

The four known copies of No. 82 are fine.

C. Grill about 13x16mm (16 to 17 by 18 to 21 points)

No.	Design	Description	Unused	Used
83	A25	3c rose	5,250.	1,000.
		No gum	2,250.	

The grilled area on each of four C grills in the sheet may total about 18x15mm when a normal C grill adjoins a fainter grill extending to the right or left edge of the stamp.

This is caused by a partial erasure on the grill roller when it was changed to produce C grills instead of the all-over A grill.

The imperf. can be found in the *Scott U.S. Specialized Catalogue* Die and Plate Proofs section.

Grill with Points Down

The grills were produced by rollers with the surface covered by pyramidal bosses. On the Z grill the tips of the pyramids are very short horizontal ridges. On the D, E and F grills the ridges are vertical.

D. Grill about 12x14mm (15 by 17 to 18 points)

No.	Design	Description	Unused	Used
84	A32	2c black	*15,000.*	3,500.
		No gum	7,500.	

No. 84 is valued in the grade of fine.

No.	Design	Description	Unused	Used
85	A25	3c rose	6,500.	1,000.
		No gum	3,000.	

Z. Grill about 11x14mm (13 to 14 by 17 to 18 points)

No.	Design	Description	Unused	Used
85A	A24	1c blue		*935,000.*
85B	A32	2c black	7,500.	1,200.
		No gum	3,500.	
85C	A25	3c rose	*12,500.*	3,500.
		No gum	*6,000.*	
85D	A27	10c green		*95,000.*
85E	A28	12c black	*12,500.*	1,600.
		No gum	*5,250.*	
85F	A33	15c black		*240,000.*

Two copies of No. 85A are known. One is contained in the New York Public Library collection. Value represents 1998 auction sale price of the single example available to collectors.

Six copies of No. 85D are known. One is in the New York Public Library collection. Value is for a well-centered example with small faults.

Two copies of No. 85F are known. Value is for the much finer example.

E. Grill about 11x13mm (14 by 15 to 17 points)

No.	Design	Description	Unused	Used
86	A24	1c blue	3,000.	450.
		No gum	1,350.	
a.		1c dull blue	3,000.	425.
		No gum	1,350.	
87	A32	2c black	1,550.	160.
		No gum	675.	
a.		Diagonal half used as 1c on cover		*2,000.*
b.		Vertical half used as 1c on cover		*2,000.*
88	A25	3c rose	900.	22.50
		No gum	375.	
a.		3c lake red	950.	25.00
		No gum	425.	
89	A27	10c green	5,000.	300.
		No gum	2,200.	
90	A28	12c black	4,850.	350.
		No gum	2,100.	
91	A33	15c black	9,500.	625.
		No gum	4,500.	

F. Grill about 9x13mm (11 to 12 by 15 to 17 points)

No.	Design	Description	Unused	Used
92	A24	1c blue	1,250.	250.
a.		1c pale blue	1,250.	250.
		No gum	475.	
93	A32	2c black	500.	50.00
		No gum	200.	
a.		Vertical half used as 1c as part of 3c rate on cover		*1,250.*
b.		Diagonal half used as 1c as part of 3c rate on cover		*1,250.*
c.		Horizontal half used alone as 1c on cover		*2,500.*
d.		Diagonal half used alone as 1c on cover		*2,500.*
94	A25	3c red	375.	7.50
a.		3c rose	375.	7.50
		No gum	150.	
c.		Vert. pair, imperf. horiz.	*1,100.*	
d.		Printed on both sides	*2,250.*	

The imperf. 3c can be found in the Scott U.S. Specialized Catalogue Die and Plate Proofs section.

No.	Type	Description	Unused	Used
95	A26	5c brown	3,500.	800.
		No gum	1,300.	
a.		5c black brown	3,750.	1,000.
		No gum	1,500.	

Values for Nos. 95, 95a reflect the normal small margins.

No.	Type	Description	Unused	Used
96	A27	10c yel green	3,000.	210.
a.		10c dark green	3,000.	210.
		No gum	1,150.	
97	A28	12c black	3,000.	225.
		No gum	1,250.	
98	A33	15c black	3,500.	300.
		No gum	1,400.	
99	A29	24c gray lilac	6,250.	950.
		No gum	2,750.	
100	A30	30c orange	6,250.	800.
		No gum	2,750.	

Values for No. 100 are for copies with small margins, especially at sides. Large-margined examples sell for much more.

No.	Type	Description	Unused	Used
101	A31	90c blue	11,500.	1,500.
		No gum	5,250.	

Some authorities believe that more than one size of grill probably existed on one of the grill rolls.

Re-issue of 1861-66 Issues
Without Grill
Hard White Paper
White Crackly Gum

1875 ***Perf. 12***

No.	Type	Description	Unused	Used
102	A24	1c blue	*800.*	*1,100.*
		No gum	*425.*	
103	A32	2c black	*3,750.*	*5,500.*
		No gum	*2,000.*	
104	A25	3c brown red	*3,750.*	*6,500.*
		No gum	*2,200.*	
105	A26	5c brown	*3,000.*	*2,900.*
		No gum	*1,750.*	
106	A27	10c green	*3,250.*	*12,500.*
		No gum	*1,900.*	
107	A28	12c black	*4,500.*	*6,750.*
		No gum	*2,600.*	
108	A33	15c black	*4,500.*	*9,000.*
		No gum	*2,500.*	
109	A29	24c deep violet	*5,500.*	*10,000.*
		No gum	*3,250.*	
110	A30	30c brownish org	*5,500.*	*12,500.*
		No gum	*3,250.*	
111	A31	90c blue	*6,500.*	*50,000.*
		No gum	*3,900.*	

These stamps can be distinguished from the 1861-66 issues by the shades and the paper which is hard and very white instead of yellowish. The gum is white and crackly.

Franklin — A34

Post Horse and Rider — A35

Locomotive A36

Washington A37

Shield and Eagle — A38

S. S. Adriatic — A39

Landing of Columbus — A40

FIFTEEN CENTS
Type I. Picture unframed.

A40a

Type II. Picture framed.
Type III. Same as type I but without fringe of brown shading lines around central vignette.

Declaration of Independence A41

Shield, Eagle and Flags A42

Lincoln — A43

G. Grill measuring 9½x9mm (12 by 11 to 11½ points)

1869 ***Perf. 12***

No.	Type	Description	Unused	Used
112	A34	1c buff	825.00	160.00
		No gum	350.00	
b.		Without grill	*6,000.*	
113	A35	2c brown	750.00	75.00
		No gum	325.00	
b.		Without grill	*2,750.*	
c.		Half used as 1c on cover, diagonal, vert. or horiz.		*3,000.*
d.		Printed on both sides		*9,000.*
114	A36	3c ultramarine	300.00	18.00
		No gum	125.00	
a.		Without grill	*1,100.*	
b.		Vertical one third used as 1c on cover		—
c.		Vertical two thirds used as 2c on cover		*4,000.*
e.		Printed on both sides		—
115	A37	6c ultramarine	3,100.	210.00
		No gum	1,350.	
b.		Vertical half used as 3c on cover		—
116	A38	10c yellow	2,500.	140.
		No gum	1,000.	
117	A39	12c green	2,600.	150.
		No gum	1,100.	
118	A40	15c brn & bl, I	8,250.	650.
		No gum	3,750.	
a.		Without grill	*10,000.*	
119	A40a	15c brn & bl, II	3,750.	250.
		No gum	1,650.	
b.		Center inverted	*275,000.*	*17,000.*
c.		Center dbl., one invtd.		*60,000.*
120	A41	24c green & vio	7,750.	750.
		No gum	3,600.	
a.		Without grill	*9,500.*	
b.		Center inverted	*275,000.*	*18,000.*
121	A42	30c ultra & car	7,500.	550.
		No gum	3,600.	
a.		Without grill	*11,000.*	
b.		Flags inverted	*210,000.*	*70,000.*
122	A43	90c car & black	10,000.	2,350.
		No gum	4,900.	
a.		Without grill	*16,000.*	

Values of varieties of Nos. 112-122 without grill are for copies with original gum.

Most copies of Nos. 119b, 120b are faulty. Values are for fine centered copies with only minimal faults.

Re-issues of the 1869 Issue
Without Grill
Hard White Paper
White Crackly Gum

1875 ***Perf. 12***

No.	Type	Description	Unused	Used
123	A34	1c buff	500.	325.
		No gum	250.	
124	A35	2c brown	700.	500.
		No gum	350.	
125	A36	3c blue	*5,500.*	*20,000.*
		No gum	3,150.	

Used value for No. 125 is for an attractive copy with minimal faults.

No.	Type	Description	Unused	Used
126	A37	6c blue	*1,900.*	*2,100.*
		No gum	1,050.	
127	A38	10c yellow	2,100.	1,750.
		No gum	1,100.	
128	A39	12c green	2,750.	*2,750.*
		No gum	1,550.	
129	A40	15c brn & bl, III	2,000.	1,150.
		No gum	1,100.	
a.		Imperf. horiz., single	*4,000.*	*7,000*
		No gum	3,000.	

Type III is same as type I but without fringe of brown shading lines around central vignette.

No.	Type	Description	Unused	Used
130	A41	24c green & violet	2,250.	1,600.
		No gum	1,200.	
131	A42	30c ultra & car	3,100.	2,500.
		No gum	1,650.	
132	A43	90c car & blk	5,000.	*5,500.*
		No gum	2,750.	

1880-81

Soft Porous Paper

No.	Type	Description	Unused	Used
133	A34	1c buff	325.	200.
		No gum	150.	
a.		1c brown orange ('81)	240.	175.

No. 133 was issued with gum, No. 133a without gum.

Printed by the National Bank Note Company

Franklin — A44

A44

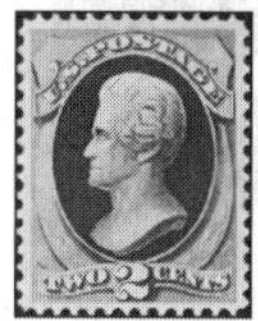

Jackson — A45

A45

Washington — A46

A46

Lincoln — A47

A47

Edwin M. Stanton — A48

A48

Jefferson — A49

A49

Henry Clay — A50

A50

Daniel Webster — A51

A51

Gen. Winfield Scott A52

Alexander Hamilton A53

Commodore O. H. Perry — A54

Two varieties of grill are known on this issue.

H. Grill about 10x12mm
(11 to 13 by 14 to 16 points)
On all values, 1c to 90c
I. Grill about 8½x10mm
(10 to 11 by 10 to 13 points)
On 1, 2, 3, 6, 7, 10 and 15c

On the 1870-71 stamps the grill impressions are usually faint or incomplete. This is especially true of the H grill, which often shows only a few points.

Values for 1c-7c are for stamps showing well-defined grills.

White Wove Paper

1870-71 ***Perf. 12***

134 A44 1c ultramarine 2,200. 150.00
No gum 900.00
135 A45 2c red brown 1,250. 70.00
No gum 525.00
a. Diagonal half used as 1c on cover —
b. Vertical half used as 1c on cover —
136 A46 3c green 725.00 20.00
No gum 325.00

The imperf. 3c can be found in the Scott U.S. Specialized Catalogue Die and Plate Proofs section.

137 A47 6c carmine 4,750. 525.
No gum 2,000.
138 A48 7c ver ('71) 3,500. 425.
No gum 1,450.
139 A49 10c brown 5,000. 675.
No gum 2,250.
140 A50 12c dull violet *22,500.* 3,000.
No gum *11,000.*
141 A51 15c orange 5,750. 1,200.
No gum 2,650.
142 A52 24c purple — *6,500.*
143 A53 30c black 15,000. 2,600.
No gum 7,000.
144 A54 90c carmine 15,000. 1,800.
No gum 6,750.

Without Grill
White Wove Paper

1870-71 ***Perf. 12***

145 A44 1c ultramarine 525.00 15.00
No gum 200.00
146 A45 2c red brown 325.00 9.00
No gum 130.00
a. Diagonal half used as 1c on cover *650.00*
b. Vertical half used as 1c on cover *750.00*
c. Horiz. half used as 1c on cover *750.00*
d. Double impression —
147 A46 3c green 300.00 1.50
No gum 120.00
a. Printed on both sides *1,750.*
b. Double impression *1,250.*

The imperf. 3c can be found in the Scott U.S. Specialized Catalogue Die and Plate Proofs section.

148 A47 6c carmine 800.00 25.00
No gum 325.00
a. Vert. half used as 3c on cover —
b. Double impression *1,500.*
149 A48 7c vermilion ('71) 950.00 90.00
No gum 400.00
150 A49 10c brown 1,000. 22.50
No gum 400.00
151 A50 12c dull violet 2,000. 160.00
No gum 875.00
152 A51 15c bright orange 2,200. 160.00
No gum 950.00
a. Double impression *1,650.*
153 A52 24c purple 1,600. 140.00
No gum 725.00
154 A53 30c black 5,750. 190.00
No gum 2,500.
155 A54 90c carmine 4,250. 300.00
No gum 1,900.

Printed by the Continental Bank Note Co.

Designs of the 1870-71 Issue with secret marks on the values from 1c to 15c as described and illustrated below.

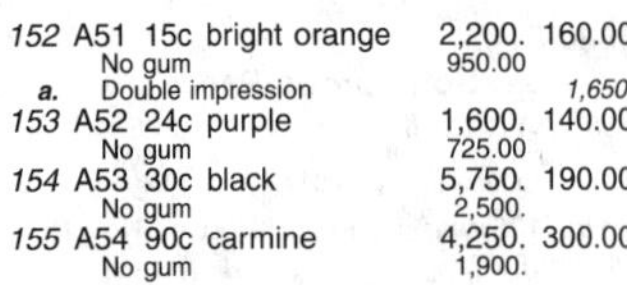

Franklin — A44a

1c. In pearl at left of numeral "1" is a small crescent.

Jackson — A45a

2c. Under the scroll at the left of "U. S." there is a small diagonal line. This mark seldom shows clearly. The stamp, No. 157, can be distinguished by its color.

Washington — A46a

3c. The under part of the upper tail of the left ribbon is heavily shaded.

Lincoln — A47a

6c. The first four vertical lines of the shading in the lower part of the left ribbon have been strengthened.

Stanton — A48a

7c. Two small semi-circles are drawn around the ends of the lines that outline the ball in the lower right hand corner.

Jefferson — A49a

10c. There is a small semi-circle in the scroll at the right end of the upper label.

Clay — A50a

12c. The balls of the figure "2" are crescent shaped.

Webster — A51a

15c. In the lower part of the triangle in the upper left corner two lines have been made heavier forming a "V."

This mark can be found on some of the Continental and American (1879) printings, but not all stamps show it.

Secret marks were added to the dies of the 24c, 30c and 90c but new plates were not made from them.

The various printings of these stamps can be distinguished only by the shades and paper.

White Wove Paper, thin to thick
Without Grill*

1873 ***Perf. 12***

156 A44a 1c ultramarine 250.00 3.75
No gum 105.00
e. With grill *2,000.*
f. Imperf., pair — *550.00*
157 A45a 2c brown 375.00 17.50
No gum 160.00
c. With grill *1,850.* *750.00*
d. Double impression — *5,000.*
e. Vertical half used as 1c on cover —
158 A46a 3c green 130.00 .60
No gum 47.50
e. With grill *500.00*
h. Horiz. pair, imperf. vert. —
i. Horiz. pair, imperf. btwn. *1,300.*
j. Double impression *3,250.*
k. Printed on both sides —

The imperf 3c, with and without grill, can be found in the Scott U.S. Specialized Catalogue Die and Plate Proofs section.

159 A47a 6c dull pink 425.00 17.50
No gum 190.00
b. With grill *1,800.*
160 A48a 7c orange ver 1,300. 80.00
No gum 575.00
a. With grill *3,250.*
161 A49a 10c brown 750.00 18.00
No gum 325.00
c. With grill *3,500.*
d. Horiz. pair, imperf. btwn. *2,500.*
162 A50a 12c black violet 2,250. 100.00
No gum 950.00
a. With grill *5,250.*
163 A51a 15c yellow orange 2,250. 110.00
No gum 950.00
a. With grill *5,250.*
164 A52 24c purple —
165 A53 30c gray black 2,750. 100.00
No gum 1,275.
c. With grill *22,500.*
166 A54 90c rose carmine 2,750. 250.00
No gum 1,250.

The Philatelic Foundation has certified as genuine a 24c on vertically ribbed paper, and that is the unique stamp listed as No. 164. Specialists believe that only Continental used ribbed paper. It is not known for sure whether or not Continental also printed the 24c value on regular paper; if it did, specialists currently are not able to distinguish these from No. 153.

* All values except 24c, 90c exist with experimental (J) grill, about 7x9½mm.

Special Printing of the 1873 Issue
Hard, White Wove Paper
Without Gum

1875 ***Perf. 12***

167 A44a 1c ultramarine *12,500.*
168 A45a 2c dark brown *5,750.*
169 A46a 3c blue green *15,000.* —
170 A47a 6c dull rose *14,500.*
171 A48a 7c redsh ver *3,250.*
172 A49a 10c pale brown *14,500.*
173 A50a 12c dark violet *4,750.*
174 A51a 15c bright orange *14,500.*
175 A52 24c dull purple *3,500.* *5,000.*
176 A53 30c greenish black *12,000.*
177 A54 90c violet car *14,000.*

Although perforated, these stamps were usually cut apart with scissors. As a result, the perforations are often much mutilated and the design is frequently damaged.

These can be distinguished from the 1873 issue by the shades, also by the paper, which is very white instead of yellowish.

These and the subsequent issues listed under this heading are special printings of stamps then in current use which, together with the reprints and reissues, were made for sale to collectors.

They were available for postage except for the Officials and demonetized issues.

Zachary Taylor — A55

Yellowish Wove Paper

1875, June 21 ***Perf. 12***

178 A45a 2c vermilion 400.00 10.00
No gum 175.00
b. Half used as 1c on cover —
c. With grill 750.00

The imperf 2c can be found in the Scott U.S. Specialized Catalogue Die and Plate Proofs section.

179 A55 5c blue 575.00 20.00
No gum 250.00
c. With grill 3,000.

Almost all of the stamps of the Continental Bank Note Co. printing including the Department stamps and some of the Newspaper stamps may be found upon a paper that shows more or less of the characteristics of a ribbed paper.

Special Printing of the 1875 Issue
Hard, White Wove Paper
Without Gum

1875

180 A45a 2c carmine ver *35,000.*
181 A55 5c bright blue *95,000.*

Please Note:

Stamps are valued in the grade of very fine unless otherwise indicated.

Values for early and valuable stamps are for examples with certificates of authenticity from acknowledged expert committees, or examples sold with the buyer having the right of certification.

This applies to examples with original gum as well as examples without gum.

Beware of stamps offered "as is," as the gum on some unused stamps offered with "original gum" may be fraudulent, and stamps offered as unused without gum may in some cases be altered or faintly canceled used stamps.

Printed by the American Bank Note Company
Same as 1870-75 Issues
Soft Porous Paper
Varying from Thin to Thick

1879 ***Perf. 12***

182 A44a 1c dark ultra 300.00 3.50
No gum 110.00
183 A45a 2c vermilion 130.00 3.00
No gum 55.00
a. Double impression — *5,000.*
184 A46a 3c green 100.00 .60
No gum 37.50
b. Double impression —

The imperf 3c can be found in the Scott U.S. Specialized Catalogue Die and Plate Proofs section.

185 A55 5c blue 525.00 12.00
No gum 225.00
186 A47a 6c pink 1,000. 22.50
No gum 425.00
187 A49 10c brn (without secret mark) 3,000. 25.00
No gum 1,200.
188 A49a 10c brown (with secret mark) 2,000. 25.00
No gum 875.00
189 A51a 15c red orange 350.00 22.50
No gum 140.00
190 A53 30c full black 1,100. 55.00
No gum 450.00
191 A54 90c carmine 2,250. 275.00
No gum 1,050.

The ABN Co. used many Continental plates to print the postage, Departmental and Newspaper stamps. Therefore, stamps bearing the Continental imprint were not always its product.

The ABN Co. also used the National 90c plate and possibly the 30c plate.

Early printings of No. 188 were from Continental plates 302 and 303 which contained the normal secret mark of 1873. After those plates were re-entered by the ABN Co. in 1880, pairs or multiple pieces contained combinations of normal, hairline or missing marks. The pairs or other multiples usually found contain at least one hairline mark which tended to disappear as the plate wore.

ABN Co. plates 377 and 378 were made in 1881 from the National transfer roll of 1870. No. 187 from those plates has no secret mark.

Perf 12 Trial Color Proofs on gummed stamp paper exist, as does a 15c without the blue "SAMPLE" overprint.

The imperf. 90c can be found in the Scott U.S. Specialized Catalogue Die and Plate Proofs section.

Special Printing of the 1879 Issue

Soft Porous Paper
Without Gum

1880 ***Perf. 12***

192	A44a	1c	dark ultra	*27,500.*
193	A45a	2c	black brown	*15,000.*
194	A46a	3c	blue green	*50,000.*
195	A47a	6c	dull rose	*25,000.*
196	A48a	7c	scar vermilion	*5,000.*
197	A49a	10c	deep brown	*28,500.*
198	A50a	12c	black purple	*8,000.*
199	A51a	15c	orange	*27,500.*
200	A52	24c	dark violet	*7,500.*
201	A53	30c	grnsh black	*18,000.*
202	A54	90c	dull carmine	*25,000.*
203	A45a	2c	scar vermilion	*55,000.*
204	A55	5c	deep blue	*85,000.*

Nos. 192 and 194 are valued in the grade of fine.

No. 197 was printed from Continental plate 302 (or 303) after plate was re-entered, therefore stamp may show normal, hairline or missing secret mark.

IMPORTANT INFORMATION REGARDING VALUES FOR NEVER-HINGED STAMPS

Collectors should be aware that the values given for never-hinged stamps from No. 205 on are for stamps in the grade of very fine, just as the value of all stamps in the catalogue are for very fine stamps unless indicated otherwise. The never-hinged premium as a percentage of value will be larger for stamps in extremely fine or superb grades, and the premium will be smaller for fine-very fine, fine or poor examples. This is particularly true of the issues of the late-19th and early-20th centuries. For example, in the grade of very fine, an unused stamp from this time period may be valued at $100 hinged and $180 never hinged. The never-hinged premium is thus 80%. But in a grade of extremely fine, this same stamp will not only sell for more hinged, but the never-hinged premium will increase, perhaps to 100%-300% or more over the higher extremely fine value.

In a grade of superb, a hinged copy will sell for much more than a very fine copy, and additionally the never-hinged premium will be much larger, perhaps as large as 300%-400% or more. On the other hand, the same stamp in a grade of fine or fine-very fine not only will sell for less than a very fine stamp in hinged condition, but additionally the never-hinged premium will be smaller than the never-hinged premium on a very fine stamp, perhaps as small as 15%-30%.

Please note that the above statements and percentages are NOT a formula for arriving at the values of stamps in hinged or never-hinged condition in the grades of fine, fine to very fine, extremely fine or superb. The percentages given apply only to the size of the premium for never-hinged condition that might be added to the stamp value for hinged condition.

The marketplace will determine what this value will be for grades other than very fine. Further, the percentages given are only generalized estimates. Some stamps or grades may have percentages for never-hinged condition that are higher or lower than the ranges given.

VALUES FOR NEVER-HINGED STAMPS PRIOR TO SCOTT 205

This catalogue does not value pre-1882 stamps in never-hinged condition.

Premiums for never-hinged condition in the classic era invariably are even larger than those premiums listed for the post-1882 issues.

Generally speaking, the earlier the stamp is listed in the catalogue, the larger will be the never-hinged premium. On some early classics, the premium will be several multiples of the unused, hinged values given in the catalogue.

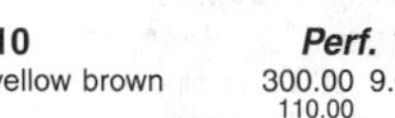

James A. Garfield — A56

1882, Apr. 10 ***Perf. 12***

205	A56	5c	yellow brown	300.00	9.00
			No gum	110.00	

Special Printing

Soft Porous Paper
Without Gum

1882

205C	A56	5c	gray brown	*40,000.*

See No. 216

Designs of 1873 Re-engraved

Franklin — A44b

1c. The vertical lines in the upper part of the stamp have been so deepened that the background often appears to be solid.

Lines of shading have been added to the upper arabesques.

Washington — A46b

3c. The shading at the sides of the central oval appears only about one-half the previous width.

A short horizontal dash has been cut about 1mm below the "TS" of "CENTS."

Lincoln — A47b

6c. On the original stamps four vertical lines can be counted from the edge of the panel to the outside of the stamp.

On the re-engraved stamps there are but three lines in the same place.

Jefferson — A49b

10c. On the original stamps there are five vertical lines between the left side of the oval and the edge of the shield. There are only four lines on the re-engraved stamps.

In the lower part of the latter, also, the horizontal lines of the background have been strengthened.

1881-82 ***Perf. 12***

206	A44b	1c	gray blue	85.00	.90
			No gum	30.00	
207	A46b	3c	blue green	85.00	.55
			No gum	30.00	
c.			Double impression		—
208	A47b	6c	rose ('82)	625.00	85.00
			No gum	225.00	
a.			6c deep brown red	550.00	120.00
			No gum	190.00	
209	A49b	10c	brown ('82)	170.00	6.00
			No gum	55.00	
b.			10c black brown	1,200.	150.00
			No gum	425.00	
c.			Double impression		—
			Nos. 206-209 (4)	965.00	92.45

Specimen stamps (usually overprinted "Sample") without overprint exist in a brown shade that differs from No. 209. The unoverprinted brown specimen is cheaper than No. 209. Expertization is recommended.

Washington
A57

Jackson
A58

1883, Oct. 1 ***Perf. 12***

210	A57	2c	red brown	50.00	.60
			No gum	17.50	
211	A58	4c	blue green	300.00	17.50
			No gum	115.00	

Imperfs can be found in the Scott U.S. Specialized Catalogue Die and Plate Proofs section.

Special Printing

Soft Porous Paper

1883-85

211B	A57	2c	pale red brown	450.	—
			Never hinged	725.	
			No gum	175.	
c.			Horiz. pair, imperf. btwn.	*2,000.*	
211D	A58	4c	deep blue grn	*35,000.*	

No. 211D is without gum.

Franklin — A59

1887 ***Perf. 12***

212	A59	1c	ultramarine	110.00	2.00
			No gum	37.50	
213	A57	2c	green	50.00	.40
			No gum	17.50	
b.			Printed on both sides		—
214	A46b	3c	vermilion	80.00	60.00
			No gum	27.50	
			Nos. 212-214 (3)	240.00	62.40

Imperf 1c, 2c can be found in the Scott U.S. Specialized Catalogue Die and Plate Proofs section.

1888 ***Perf. 12***

215	A58	4c	carmine	225.00	20.00
			No gum	85.00	
216	A56	5c	indigo	250.00	14.00
			No gum	100.00	
217	A53	30c	orange brown	450.00	110.00
			No gum	170.00	
218	A54	90c	purple	1,250.	250.00
			No gum	500.00	
			Nos. 215-218 (4)	2,175.	394.00

Imperfs can be found in the Scott U.S. Specialized Catalogue Die and Plate Proofs section.

Franklin
A60

Washington
A61

Jackson
A62

Lincoln
A63

Ulysses S. Grant
A64

Garfield
A65

William T. Sherman
A66

Daniel Webster
A67

Henry Clay
A68

Jefferson
A69

Perry — A70

1890-93 ***Perf. 12***

219	A60	1c	dull blue	30.00	.60
			Never hinged	65.00	
219D	A61	2c	lake	250.00	1.10
			Never hinged	550.00	
220	A61	2c	carmine	25.00	.55
			Never hinged	55.00	
a.			Cap on left "2"	140.00	2.75
			Never hinged	300.00	
c.			Cap on both "2's"	550.00	20.00
			Never hinged	1,150.	
221	A62	3c	purple	85.00	7.50
			Never hinged	190.00	
222	A63	4c	dark brown	95.00	3.00
			Never hinged	210.00	
223	A64	5c	chocolate	85.00	3.00
			Never hinged	190.00	
224	A65	6c	brown red	85.00	20.00
			Never hinged	190.00	
225	A66	8c	lilac ('93)	65.00	14.00
			Never hinged	150.00	
226	A67	10c	green	190.00	3.75
			Never hinged	425.00	
227	A68	15c	indigo	260.00	22.50
			Never hinged	575.00	
228	A69	30c	black	400.00	32.50
			Never hinged	900.00	
229	A70	90c	orange	600.00	130.00
			Never hinged	1,350.	
			Nos. 219-229 (12)	2,170.	238.50

The "cap on right 2" variety is due to imperfect inking, not a plate defect.

Imperfs. can be found in the Scott U.S. Specialized Catalogue Die and Plate Proofs section.

Columbian Exposition Issue

Columbus in Sight of Land — A71

Landing of Columbus
A72

Flagship of Columbus
A73

Fleet of Columbus
A74

Columbus Soliciting Aid from Isabella
A75

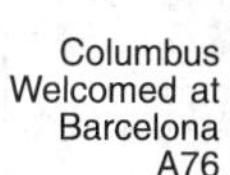

Columbus Welcomed at Barcelona
A76

Columbus Restored to Favor — A77

Columbus Presenting Natives A78

Columbus Announcing his Discovery A79

Columbus at La Rábida A80

Recall of Columbus A81

Isabella Pledging her Jewels A82

Columbus in Chains A83

Columbus Describing his Third Voyage A84

Isabella & Columbus A85

Columbus A86

1893			*Perf. 12*
230	A71 1c deep blue	22.50	.40
	Never hinged	45.00	
231	A72 2c brown violet	21.00	.30
	Never hinged	42.50	
232	A73 3c green	60.00	15.00
	Never hinged	120.00	
233	A74 4c ultra	87.50	7.50
	Never hinged	175.00	
a.	4c blue (error)	*19,000.*	*15,000.*
	Never hinged	32,500.	
234	A75 5c chocolate	95.00	8.00
	Never hinged	190.00	
235	A76 6c purple	85.00	22.50
	Never hinged	170.00	
a.	6c red violet	85.00	22.50
	Never hinged	170.00	
236	A77 8c magenta	75.00	11.00
	Never hinged	150.00	
237	A78 10c black brown	140.00	8.00
	Never hinged	280.00	
238	A79 15c dark green	240.00	70.00
	Never hinged	500.00	
239	A80 30c orange brn	300.00	90.00
	Never hinged	675.00	
240	A81 50c slate blue	600.00	160.00
	Never hinged	1,400.	
241	A82 $1 salmon	1,250.	625.00
	Never hinged	3,250.	
	No gum	650.00	
242	A83 $2 brown red	1,300.	600.00
	Never hinged	3,500.	
	No gum	675.00	
243	A84 $3 yellow green	2,000.	1,050.
	Never hinged	5,500.	
	No gum	1,100.	
a.	$3 olive green	2,000.	1,050.
	Never hinged	5,500.	
	No gum	1,100.	
244	A85 $4 crimson lake	2,750.	1,300.
	Never hinged	7,500.	
	No gum	1,400.	
a.	$4 rose carmine	2,750.	1,300.
	Never hinged	7,500.	
	No gum	1,400.	
245	A86 $5 black	3,100.	1,600.
	Never hinged	8,500.	
	No gum	1,650.	

World's Columbian Expo., Chicago, May 1-Oct. 30, 1893.

Nos. 230-245 are known imperf, but were not regularly issued.

See Scott U. S. Specialized Catalogue Die and Plate Proofs for the 2c.

Never-Hinged Stamps

See note after No. 218 regarding premiums for never-hinged stamps.

Bureau Issues

Starting in 1894, the Bureau of Engraving and Printing at Washington produced most U.S. postage stamps.

Until 1965 Bureau-printed stamps were engraved except Nos. 525-536, which are offset.

The combination of lithography and engraving (see #1253) was first used in 1964, and photogravure (see #1426) in 1971.

Franklin A87

Washington A88

Jackson A89

Lincoln A90

Grant A91

Garfield A92

Sherman A93

Webster A94

Clay A95

Jefferson A96

Perry A97

James Madison A98

John Marshall — A99

TWO CENTS

Triangle A (Type I)

Triangle B (Type II)

Type I. The horizontal lines of the ground work run across the triangle and are of the same thickness within it as without.

Type II. The horizontal lines cross the triangle but are thinner within it than without.

Triangle C (Types III and IV)

Type III. The horizontal lines do not cross the double frame lines of the triangle.

The lines within the triangle are thin, as in type II. Otherwise, design as type II.

Type IV

Type IV. Same triangle C as type III.

But other design differences include: (1) re-cutting and lengthening of hairline, (2) shaded toga button, (3) strengthening of lines on sleeve, (4) additional dots on ear, (5) "T" of "TWO" straight at right, (6) background lines extend into white oval opposite "U" of "UNITED." Many other differences exist.

ONE DOLLAR

Type I

Type I. The circles enclosing "$1" are broken where they meet the curved line below "One Dollar." The 15 left vert. rows of impressions from plate 76 are Type I, the balance Type II.

Type II

Type II. The circles are complete.

1894	**Unwmk.**		*Perf. 12*
246	A87 1c ultramarine	32.50	4.50
	Never hinged	75.00	
247	A87 1c blue	70.00	2.25
	Never hinged	160.00	
248	A88 2c pink, Type I	27.50	4.00
	Never hinged	62.50	
a.	Vert. pair, imperf horiz.	*5,500.*	
249	A88 2c car lake, I	150.00	3.50
	Never hinged	350.00	
250	A88 2c car, I	30.00	1.20
	Never hinged	65.00	
a.	2c rose, I	30.00	2.75
	Never hinged	65.00	
b.	2c scarlet, I ('95)	30.00	.75
	Never hinged	65.00	
d.	Horiz, pair, imperf. btwn.	*2,000.*	
251	A88 2c car, II	300.00	7.00
	Never hinged	650.00	
a.	2c scarlet, II	300.00	5.00
	Never hinged	650.00	
252	A88 2c car, III	120.00	7.00
	Never hinged	260.00	
a.	2c scarlet, III	120.00	7.00
	Never hinged	260.00	
b.	Horiz. pair, imperf. vert.	*1,500.*	
c.	Horiz. pair, imperf. btwn.	*1,750.*	
253	A89 3c purple	115.00	10.00
	Never hinged	250.00	
254	A90 4c dark brown	150.00	6.00
	Never hinged	350.00	
255	A91 5c chocolate	110.00	7.00
	Never hinged	240.00	
c.	Vert. pair, imperf. horiz.	*2,500.*	
256	A92 6c dull brown	175.00	22.50
	Never hinged	400.00	
a.	Vert. pair, imperf. horiz.	*1,600.*	
257	A93 8c vio brn ('95)	140.00	17.50
	Never hinged	300.00	
258	A94 10c dark green	300.00	12.50
	Never hinged	650.00	
259	A95 15c dark blue	300.00	60.00
	Never hinged	650.00	
260	A96 50c orange	575.00	130.00
	Never hinged	1,300.	
261	A97 $1 black, I	1,000.	350.00
	Never hinged	2,300.	
	No gum	350.	
261A	A97 $1 black, II	2,300.	750.00
	Never hinged	5,250.	
	No gum	750.	
262	A98 $2 bright blue	3,100.	1,100.
	Never hinged	7,000.	
	No gum	1,200.	
263	A99 $5 dark green	5,000.	2,250.
	Never hinged	12,000.	
	No gum	2,600.	

For imperfs. and the 2c pink, vert. pair, imperf. horiz., see Scott U. S. Specialized Catalogue Die and Plate Proofs.

Same as 1894 Issue

1895	**Wmk. 191**		*Perf. 12*
264	A87 1c blue	6.50	.50
	Never hinged	14.00	

265	A88	2c car, I	30.00	1.75
		Never hinged	65.00	
266	A88	2c car, II	30.00	3.75
		Never hinged	65.00	
267	A88	2c car, III	5.50	.25
		Never hinged	12.00	
a.		2c pink, III ('97	7.00	.65
		Never hinged	16.00	
b.		2c vermilion, III ('99)	30.00	3.00
c.		2c rose car, III ('99)	—	2.00

The three left vertical rows from plate 170 are type II, the balance being type III.

268	A89	3c purple	37.50	1.75
		Never hinged	80.00	
269	A90	4c dark brown	40.00	2.50
		Never hinged	87.50	
270	A91	5c chocolate	37.50	2.50
		Never hinged	80.00	
271	A92	6c dull brown	110.00	5.75
		Never hinged	240.00	
a.		Wmkd. USIR	9,000.	5,000.
272	A93	8c violet brown	65.00	1.90
		Never hinged	145.00	
a.		Wmkd. USIR	3,250.	600.00
273	A94	10c dark green	100.00	1.75
		Never hinged	225.00	
274	A95	15c dark blue	225.00	12.00
		Never hinged	500.00	
275	A96	50c orange	300.00	25.00
		Never hinged	650.00	
a.		50c red orange	325.00	32.50
		Never hinged	700.00	
276	A97	$1 blk, I	650.00	85.00
		Never hinged	1,500.	
		No gum	190.00	
276A	A97	$1 blk, II	1,300.	175.00
		Never hinged	3,000.	
		No gum	400.00	
277	A98	$2 bright blue	1,100.	350.00
		Never hinged	2,500.	
		No gum	400.00	
a.		$2 dark blue	1,100.	350.00
		Never hinged	2,500.	
		No gum	400.00	
278	A99	$5 dark green	2,300.	500.00
		Never hinged	5,500.	
		No gum	900.	

For imperfs. and the 1c horiz. pair, imperf. vert., see Scott U. S. Specialized Catalogue Die and Plate Proofs.

For "I.R." overprints see Nos. R155, R156-R158.

TEN CENTS

Type I

Type I. Tips of foliate ornaments do not impinge on white curved line below "TEN CENTS."

Type II

Type II. Tips of ornaments break curved line below "E" of "TEN" and "T" of "CENTS."

1897-1903 Wmk. 191 *Perf. 12*

279	A87	1c dp grn ('98)	9.00	.40
		Never hinged	20.00	
279B	A88	2c red, IV ('99)	9.00	.40
		Never hinged	20.00	
c.		2c rose car, IV ('99)	250.00	125.00
		Never hinged	550.00	
d.		2c org red, IV ('00)	10.00	.50
		Never hinged	22.50	
e.		Booklet pane of 6 ('00)	425.00	1,000.
		Never hinged	750.00	
f.		2c carmine, IV	10.00	.40
		Never hinged	22.00	
g.		2c pink, IV	12.50	.75
		Never hinged	27.50	
h.		2c ver, IV ('99)	11.00	.40
		Never hinged	24.00	
i.		2c brn org, IV ('99)	100.00	8.00
		Never hinged	220.00	
280	A90	4c rose brn ('98)	30.00	1.40
		Never hinged	65.00	
a.		4c lilac brown	30.00	1.40
		Never hinged	65.00	
b.		4c orange brown	30.00	1.40
		Never hinged	65.00	
281	A91	5c dk bl ('98)	35.00	1.10
		Never hinged	75.00	
282	A92	6c lake ('98)	45.00	4.00
		Never hinged	100.00	
a.		6c purple lake	60.00	7.50
		Never hinged	150.00	
282C	A94	10c brn, I ('98)	180.00	3.50
		Never hinged	400.00	
283	A94	10c org brn, II	125.00	3.00
		Never hinged	275.00	
284	A95	15c ol grn ('98)	160.00	10.00
		Never hinged	375.00	
		Nos. 279-284 (8)	593.00	23.80

For "I.R." overprints see Nos. R153-R154, R155A.

VALUES FOR VERY FINE STAMPS
Please note: Stamps are valued in the grade of very fine unless otherwise indicated.

Trans-Mississippi Exposition Issue

Marquette on the Mississippi A100

Farming in the West — A101

Indian Hunting Buffalo A102

Frémont on the Rocky Mountains A103

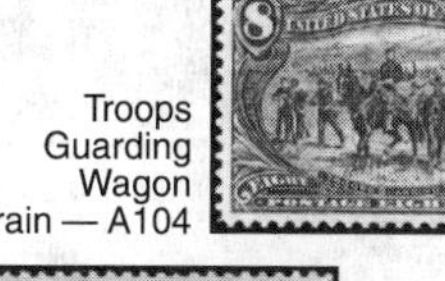

Troops Guarding Wagon Train — A104

Hardships of Emigration A105

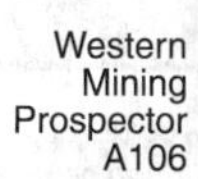

Western Mining Prospector A106

Western Cattle in Storm A107

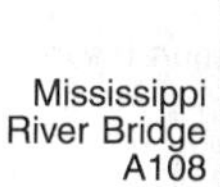

Mississippi River Bridge A108

1898, June 17 Wmk. 191 *Perf. 12*

285	A100	1c dk yel green	30.00	6.50
		Never hinged	65.00	
286	A101	2c copper red	27.50	1.75
		Never hinged	60.00	
287	A102	4c orange	140.00	24.00
		Never hinged	325.00	
288	A103	5c dull blue	140.00	21.00
		Never hinged	325.00	
289	A104	8c violet brown	180.00	42.50
		Never hinged	400.00	
a.		Vert. pair, imperf. horiz.	22,500.	
290	A105	10c gray violet	180.00	27.50
		Never hinged	400.00	
291	A106	50c sage green	700.00	190.00
		Never hinged	1,600.	
292	A107	$1 black	1,250.	600.00
		Never hinged	3,000.	
		No gum	650.	
293	A108	$2 orange brown	2,100.	1,000.
		Never hinged	5,000.	
		No gum	1,050.	
		Nos. 285-293 (9)	4,747.	1,913.

Trans-Mississippi Exposition, Omaha, Neb., June 1 to Nov. 1, 1898.

For "I.R." overprints see #R158A-R158B.

Never-Hinged Stamps
See note after No. 218 regarding premiums for never-hinged stamps.

Pan-American Exposition Issue

Fast Lake Navigation A109

"Empire State" Express — A110

Electric Automobile A111

Bridge at Niagara Falls — A112

Canal Locks at Sault Ste. Marie — A113

Fast Ocean Navigation A114

1901, May 1 Wmk. 191 *Perf. 12*

294	A109	1c green & black	18.50	3.00
		Never hinged	37.50	
a.		Center inverted	9,500.	8,500.
		Never hinged	17,000.	
295	A110	2c car & black	17.50	1.00
		Never hinged	35.00	
a.		Center inverted	42,500.	17,500.
296	A111	4c dp red brn & black	85.00	15.00
		Never hinged	170.00	
a.		Center inverted	30,000.	
297	A112	5c ultra & black	95.00	14.00
		Never hinged	190.00	
298	A113	8c brn vio & blk	120.00	50.00
		Never hinged	240.00	
299	A114	10c yel brn & blk	160.00	25.00
		Never hinged	325.00	
		Nos. 294-299 (6)	496.00	108.00
		Nos. 294-299, never hinged	938.50	

Buffalo, NY, May 1-Nov. 1, 1901.

No. 296a was a special printing.

Almost all unused copies of Nos. 295a and 296a have partial or disturbed gum. Values are for examples with full original gum that is slightly disturbed.

Franklin A115

Washington A116

Jackson
A117

Grant
A118

Lincoln
A119

Garfield
A120

Martha
Washington
A121

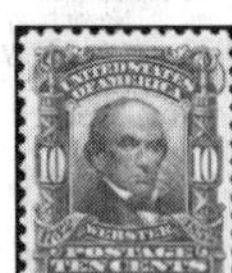
Webster
A122

Benjamin
Harrison
A123

Clay
A124

Jefferson
A125

David G.
Farragut
A126

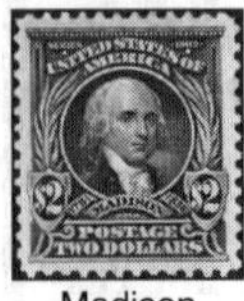
Madison
A127

Marshall
A128

1902-03 Wmk. 191 *Perf. 12*

300 A115 1c blue grn ('03) 12.00 .25
Never hinged 24.00
b. Booklet pane of 6 *600.00* —
Never hinged 1,100.
301 A116 2c carmine ('03) 16.00 .25
Never hinged 32.50
c. Booklet pane of 6 *500.00* —
Never hinged 900.00
302 A117 3c brt violet ('03) 55.00 3.00
Never hinged 110.00
303 A118 4c brown ('03) 60.00 1.60
Never hinged 120.00
304 A119 5c blue ('03) 60.00 1.75
Never hinged 120.00
305 A120 6c claret ('03) 72.50 3.00
Never hinged 150.00
306 A121 8c violet black 45.00 2.25
Never hinged 90.00
307 A122 10c pale red brn ('03) 70.00 1.90
Never hinged 140.00
308 A123 13c purple black 50.00 8.00
Never hinged 100.00
309 A124 15c ol grn ('03) 170.00 6.00
Never hinged 375.00
310 A125 50c orange ('03) 475.00 25.00
Never hinged 1,100.
311 A126 $1 black ('03) 750.00 65.00
Never hinged 1,900.
No gum 180.00
312 A127 $2 dk bl ('03) 1,200. 200.00
Never hinged 2,900.
No gum 300.
313 A128 $5 dk grn ('03) 2,900. 750.00
Never hinged *6,750.*
No gum 850.
Nos. 300-313 (14) 5,935. 1,068.

For listings of designs A127 and A128 with Perf. 10, see Nos. 479 and 480.

1906-08 *Imperf.*

314 A115 1c blue green 18.00 15.00
Never hinged 35.00
314A A118 4c brown ('08) *65,000. 40,000.*
Never hinged —
315 A119 5c blue ('08) 240.00 *850.00*
Never hinged 425.00

No. 314A was issued imperforate but all copies were privately perforated with large oblong perforations at the sides (Schermack type III).

Beware of copies of No. 303 with trimmed perforations and fake private perfs added.

Used copies of Nos. 314 & 315 must have contemporaneous cancels.

Coil Stamps

Imperforate stamps are known fraudulently perforated to resemble coil stamps and part perforate varieties.

1908 *Perf. 12 Horizontally*

316 A115 1c bl grn, pair *120,000.* —
317 A119 5c blue, pair *15,000.* 6,000.
Never hinged *25,000.*

Perf. 12 Vertically

318 A115 1c bl grn, pair *14,000.* —

Coil stamps for use in vending and affixing machines are perforated on two sides only, either horizontally or vertically.

They were first issued in 1908, using perf. 12. This was changed to 8½ in 1910, and to 10 in 1914.

Imperforate sheets of certain denominations were sold to the vending machine companies which applied a variety of private perforations and separations.

Several values of the 1902 and later issues are found on an apparently coarse ribbed paper caused by worn blankets on the printing press and are not true paper varieties.

All examples of Nos. 316-318 must be accompanied by certificates of authenticity issued by recognized expertizing committees.

Washington — A129

Type I

Type II

Type I. Leaf next to left "2" penetrates the border.

Type II. Strong line forming border left of leaf.

1903, Nov. 12 Wmk. 191 *Perf. 12*

319 A129 2c carmine, I 6.00 .25
Never hinged 12.00
a. 2c lake, I — —
b. 2c carmine rose, I 7.50 .40
Never hinged 15.00
c. 2c scarlet, I 6.00 .30
Never hinged 12.00
d. Vert. pair, imperf. horiz. *7,500.*
e. Vert. pair, imperf. btwn. *1,750.*
f. 2c lake, II 7.50 .25
Never hinged 15.00
g. Booklet pane of 6, car, I 125.00 —
Never hinged 240.00
h. As "g", II 675.00
Never hinged 475.00
i. 2c carmine, II 75.00 *50.00*
Never hinged 150.00
j. 2c carmine rose, II 50.00 1.75
Never hinged 100.00
k. 2c scarlet, II 50.00 .65
Never hinged 100.00
m. As "g," lake, I —
n. As "g," car rose, I 180.00 *300.00*
Never hinged 300.00
p. As "g," scarlet, I 170.00 *275.00*
Never hinged 275.00
q. As "g," lake, II 225.00 —
Never hinged 425.00

1906, Oct. 2 *Imperf.*

320 A129 2c carmine, I 17.50 17.50
Never hinged 35.00
a. 2c lake, II 45.00 40.00
Never hinged 90.00
b. 2c scarlet, I 17.50 12.50
Never hinged 35.00
c. 2c carmine rose, I 50.00 40.00
Never hinged 100.00
d. 2c carmine, II — —
Never hinged —

No. 320d was issued imperforate, but all copies were privately perforated with large oblong perforations at the sides (Schermack Type III).

Coil Stamps

1908 *Perf. 12 Horizontally*

321 A129 2c car, pair, I *360,000. 170,000.*

Four authenticated unused pairs are known. Value of the unused pair represents 2002 auction sale price of a fresh, lightly hinged, fine-very fine pair. The value for an unused pair is for a fine-very fine example, which is the highest grade known.

The used value is for a single on cover, of which two authenticated examples are known, both used from Indianapolis in 1908. Numerous counterfeits exist.

All examples of Nos. 321-322 must be accompanied by certificates of authenticity issued by recognized expertizing committees.

Perf. 12 Vertically

322 A129 2c car, pair, II *12,000.* —
Never hinged 9,500.

Louisiana Purchase Exposition

St. Louis, Mo., Apr. 30 - Dec. 1, 1904

Robert R.
Livingston
A130

Thomas
Jefferson
A131

James Monroe
A132

William
McKinley
A133

Map of
Louisiana
Purchase
A134

1904, Apr. 30 Wmk. 191 *Perf. 12*

323 A130 1c green 30.00 4.00
Never hinged 60.00
324 A131 2c carmine 27.50 1.75
Never hinged 55.00
a. Vert. pair, imperf. horiz. *10,000.*
325 A132 3c violet 90.00 30.00
Never hinged 180.00
326 A133 5c dark blue 95.00 25.00
Never hinged 190.00
327 A134 10c red brown 175.00 30.00
Never hinged 350.00
Nos. 323-327 (5) 417.50 90.75
Nos. 323-327, never hinged 775.00

Jamestown Exposition Issue

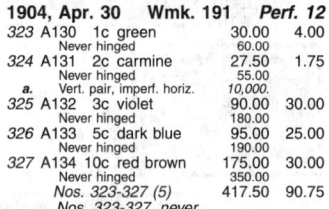

Captain John
Smith — A135

Founding of
Jamestown
A136

Pocahontas
A137

1907 Wmk. 191 *Perf. 12*

328 A135 1c green 30.00 4.00
Never hinged 60.00
329 A136 2c carmine 35.00 3.50
Never hinged 70.00
330 A137 5c blue 150.00 27.50
Never hinged 300.00
Nos. 328-330 (3) 215.00 35.00
Nos. 328-330, never hinged 370.00

Jamestown Expo., Hampton Roads, Va., Apr. 26 to Dec. 1.

Franklin
A138

Washington
A139

Washington — A140

There are several types of some of the 2c and 3c stamps of this and succeeding issues.

These types are described under the dates when they first appeared.

Illustrations of Types I-VII of the 2c (A140) and Types I-IV of the 3c (A140) are reproduced by permission of H. L. Lindquist.

Type I

THREE CENTS

Type I. Top line of the toga rope is weak and the rope shading lines are thin.

The fifth line from the left is missing.

The line between the lips is thin.

Used on both flat plate and rotary press printings.

1908-09 Wmk. 191 *Perf. 12*

331 A138 1c green 7.25 .25
Never hinged 14.50
a. Booklet pane of 6 160.00 *140.00*
Never hinged 250.00
332 A139 2c carmine 6.75 .25
Never hinged 13.50
a. Booklet pane of 6 135.00 *125.00*
Never hinged 210.00
333 A140 3c deep vio, I 35.00 2.50
Never hinged 70.00
334 A140 4c orange brown 42.50 1.00
Never hinged 85.00
335 A140 5c blue 55.00 2.00
Never hinged 125.00
336 A140 6c red orange 65.00 5.00
Never hinged 130.00
337 A140 8c olive green 50.00 2.50
Never hinged 100.00
338 A140 10c yellow ('09) 70.00 1.40
Never hinged 140.00
339 A140 13c bl grn ('09) 42.50 19.00
Never hinged 85.00
340 A140 15c pale ultra ('09) 70.00 5.50
Never hinged 140.00
341 A140 50c violet ('09) 350.00 20.00
Never hinged 725.00
342 A140 $1 vio brn ('09) 525.00 100.00
Never hinged 1,100.
Nos. 331-342 (12) 1,319. 159.40

For listings of China Clay papers see the Scott U.S. Specialized Catalogue.

For listing of other perforated sheet stamps of designs A138, A139 and A140 see

#357-366	Bluish Paper	
#374-382, 405-407	Single line wmk.	Perf. 12
#423A-423C	Single line wmk.	Perf. 12x10

#423D-423E	Single line wmk.	Perf. 10x12
#424-430	Single line wmk.	Perf. 10
#461	Single line wmk.	Perf. 11
#462-469	Unwmkd.	Perf. 10
#498-507	Unwmkd.	Perf. 11
#519	Double line wmk.	Perf. 11
#525-530, 536	Offset printing	
#538-546	Rotary press printing	

Imperf

343 A138 1c green 5.00 4.50
Never hinged 9.50
344 A139 2c carmine 6.00 3.00
Never hinged 11.50
345 A140 3c dp violet, I 11.50 *20.00*
Never hinged 22.00
346 A140 4c org brn ('09) 19.00 22.50
Never hinged 37.50
347 A140 5c blue ('09) 36.00 35.00
Never hinged 70.00
Nos. 343-347 (5) 77.50 85.00

For listings of other imperforate stamps of designs A138, A139 and A140, see #383-384, 408-409, 459 (single line wmk.), #481-485 (unwmkd.), #531-535 (offset printing).

Coil Stamps

1908-10 ***Perf. 12 Horizontally***

348 A138 1c green 37.50 25.00
Never hinged 75.00
349 A139 2c carmine ('09) 80.00 17.50
Never hinged 160.00
350 A140 4c org brn ('10) 160.00 140.00
Never hinged 325.00
351 A140 5c blue ('09) 175.00 175.00
Never hinged 350.00
Nos. 348-351 (4) 452.50 357.50

1909 ***Perf. 12 Vertically***

352 A138 1c green 95.00 55.00
Never hinged 180.00
353 A139 2c carmine 95.00 15.00
Never hinged 190.00
354 A140 4c orange brown 220.00 120.00
Never hinged 450.00
355 A140 5c blue 230.00 150.00
Never hinged 475.00
356 A140 10c yellow 2,750. 1,500.
Never hinged 5,500.

Beware of stamps offered as No. 356 which may be examples of No. 338 with perforations trimmed at top and/or bottom.

Beware also of plentiful fakes in the market-place of Nos. 348-355.

Authentication of all these coil stamps is advised.

For listings of other coil stamps of designs A138, A139 and A140, see #385-396, 410-413, 441-458 (single line wmk.), #486-496 (unwatermarked).

Bluish Paper

This was made with 35 percent rag stock instead of all wood pulp.

The grayish blue color goes through the paper showing clearly on the back as well as on the face.

1909 ***Perf. 12***

357 A138 1c green 90.00 *100.00*
Never hinged 180.00
358 A139 2c carmine 85.00 *100.00*
Never hinged 175.00
359 A140 3c dp violet, I 2,000. *2,600.*
Never hinged 4,000.
360 A140 4c org brn *24,000.*
Never hinged 37,500.
361 A140 5c blue 5,000. *12,500.*
Never hinged *10,000.*
362 A140 6c red orange 1,500. *5,000.*
Never hinged 3,000.
363 A140 8c olive green *26,000.*
Never hinged *40,000.*
364 A140 10c yellow 1,850. *5,500.*
Never hinged 3,750.
365 A140 13c blue green 3,000. *2,250.*
Never hinged 6,000.
366 A140 15c pale ultra 1,450. *11,000.*
Never hinged 2,900.

Nos. 360, 363 not regularly issued.

Lincoln Centenary of Birth Issue

Lincoln — A141

1909, Feb. 12 Wmk. 191 ***Perf. 12***

367 A141 2c carmine 5.50 1.75
Never hinged 9.50

Imperf

368 A141 2c carmine 19.00 20.00
Never hinged 35.00

1909 Bluish Paper ***Perf. 12***

369 A141 2c carmine 210.00 *275.00*
Never hinged 380.00

Alaska-Yukon-Pacific Exposition Issue

William H. Seward — A142

1909, June 1 Wmk. 191 ***Perf. 12***

370 A142 2c carmine 8.75 2.00
Never hinged 15.00

1909 ***Imperf.***

371 A142 2c carmine 22.50 22.50
Never hinged 40.00

Seattle, Wash., June 1 to Oct. 16.

Hudson-Fulton Celebration Issue

"Half Moon" and Steamship A143

1909, Sept. 25 Wmk. 191 ***Perf. 12***

372 A143 2c carmine 12.50 4.50
Never hinged 22.00

Imperf

373 A143 2c carmine 25.00 25.00
Never hinged 47.50

Tercentenary of the discovery of the Hudson River and Centenary of Robert Fulton's steamship.

Designs of 1908-09 Issue

1910-11 Wmk. 190 ***Perf. 12***

374 A138 1c green 7.00 .25
Never hinged 14.00
a. Booklet pane of 6 *175.00* *125.00*
Never hinged 280.00
375 A139 2c carmine 7.00 .25
Never hinged 14.00
a. Booklet pane of 6 100.00 *95.00*
Never hinged 175.00
b. 2c lake *475.00*
Never hinged *950.00*
c. Double impression *500.00*
Never hinged *1,000.*
376 A140 3c dp vio, I ('11) 20.00 1.75
Never hinged 42.50
377 A140 4c brown ('11) 32.50 .75
Never hinged 65.00
378 A140 5c blue ('11) 32.50 .50
Never hinged 67.50
379 A140 6c red org ('11) 37.50 .70
Never hinged 80.00
380 A140 8c ol grn ('11) 115.00 12.50
Never hinged 240.00
381 A140 10c yellow ('11) 105.00 4.50
Never hinged 210.00
382 A140 15c pale ultra ('11) 275.00 17.50
Never hinged 575.00
Nos. 374-382 (9) 631.50 38.70

1910 ***Imperf.***

383 A138 1c green 2.25 2.00
Never hinged 4.25
384 A139 2c carmine 3.75 2.50
Never hinged 7.00

Coil Stamps

1910 ***Perf. 12 Horizontally***

385 A138 1c green 40.00 20.00
Never hinged 80.00
386 A139 2c carmine 75.00 27.50
Never hinged 150.00

1910-11 ***Perf. 12 Vertically***

387 A138 1c green 200.00 75.00
Never hinged 400.00
388 A139 2c carmine 1,050. 500.00
Never hinged 2,000.
389 A140 3c dp vio, I ('11) *65,000.* *12,000.*
Never hinged *100,000.*

Stamps sold as Scott 388 frequently are privately perforated examples of No. 384, or examples of No. 375 with top and/or bottom perfs trimmed.

Stamps offered as No. 389 sometimes are examples of No. 376 with top and/or bottom perfs trimmed.

Expertization by competent authorities is recommended.

1910 ***Perf. 8½ Horizontally***

390 A138 1c green 5.00 *6.50*
Never hinged 9.50
391 A139 2c carmine 40.00 15.00
Never hinged 75.00

1910-13 ***Perf. 8½ Vertically***

392 A138 1c green 25.00 25.00
Never hinged 50.00
393 A139 2c carmine 47.50 10.00
Never hinged 95.00
394 A140 3c dp vio, I ('11) 57.50 55.00
Never hinged 115.00
395 A140 4c brown ('12) 60.00 52.50
Never hinged 120.00
396 A140 5c blue ('13) 57.50 50.00
Never hinged 115.00
Nos. 392-396 (5) 247.50 192.50

Panama-Pacific Exposition Issue

Vasco Nunez de Balboa — A144

Pedro Miguel Locks, Panama Canal — A145

Golden Gate — A146

Discovery of San Francisco Bay — A147

1913 Wmk. 190 ***Perf. 12***

397 A144 1c green 17.50 1.50
Never hinged 35.00
398 A145 2c carmine 20.00 .50
Never hinged 40.00
a. 2c carmine lake *1,100.*
Never hinged *1,800.*
399 A146 5c blue 80.00 9.50
Never hinged 160.00
400 A147 10c orange yel 135.00 20.00
Never hinged 275.00
400A A147 10c orange 210.00 16.00
Never hinged 425.00
Nos. 397-400A (5) 462.50 47.50
Nos. 397-400A, never hinged 852.50

1914-15 ***Perf. 10***

401 A144 1c green 27.50 5.50
Never hinged 55.00
402 A145 2c carmine ('15) 75.00 1.50
Never hinged 150.00
403 A146 5c blue ('15) 175.00 15.00
Never hinged 350.00
404 A147 10c orange ('15) 875.00 62.50
Never hinged 1,750.
Nos. 401-404 (4) 1,152. 84.50
Nos. 401-404, never hinged 2,140.

San Francisco, Cal., Feb. 20 to Dec. 4.

Type I

TWO CENTS

Type I. One shading line in the first curve of the ribbon above the left "2". One in the second curve of the ribbon above the right "2."

Button of the toga has a faint outline.

Top line of the toga rope, from the button to the front of the throat, very faint.

Shading lines at face terminate in front of the ear with little or no joining, forming a lock of hair.

Used on both flat and rotary press printings.

1912-14 Wmk. 190 *Perf. 12*

405 A140 1c green 7.00 .20
Never hinged 14.00
a. Vert. pair, imperf. horiz. *1,500.* —
b. Booklet pane of 6 60.00 *50.00*
Never hinged 100.00
406 A140 2c carmine, I 7.00 .20
Never hinged 14.00
a. Booklet pane of 6 60.00 *60.00*
Never hinged 100.00
b. Double impression —
c. 2c lake, type II *1,500.* —
407 A140 7c black ('14) 80.00 11.00
Never hinged 160.00
Nos. 405-407 (3) 94.00 11.40

1912 *Imperf.*

408 A140 1c green 1.10 .65
Never hinged 2.00
409 A140 2c carmine, I 1.30 .65
Never hinged 2.30

Coil Stamps

1912 *Perf. 8½ Horizontally*

410 A140 1c green 6.00 4.25
Never hinged 11.50
411 A140 2c carmine, I 10.00 4.00
Never hinged 19.00

Perf. 8½ Vertically

412 A140 1c green 25.00 5.50
Never hinged 47.50
413 A140 2c carmine, I 50.00 2.00
Never hinged 95.00
Nos. 410-413 (4) 91.00 15.75

Franklin — A148

1912-14 Wmk. 190 *Perf. 12*

414 A148 8c pale olive grn 45.00 1.25
Never hinged 95.00
415 A148 9c sal red ('14) 55.00 12.50
Never hinged 110.00
416 A148 10c orange yellow 45.00 .40
Never hinged 95.00
a. 10c brown yellow *1,000.* —
Never hinged *1,800.*
417 A148 12c claret brn ('14) 50.00 4.25
Never hinged 100.00
418 A148 15c gray 85.00 3.50
Never hinged 175.00
419 A148 20c ultra ('14) 200.00 15.00
Never hinged 400.00
420 A148 30c org red ('14) 125.00 15.00
Never hinged 250.00
421 A148 50c violet ('14) 425.00 22.50
Never hinged 900.00
Nos. 414-421 (8) 1,030. 74.40

No. 421 almost always has an offset of the frame lines on the back under the gum.

No. 422 does not have this offset.

VALUES FOR VERY FINE STAMPS

Please note: Stamps are valued in the grade of Very Fine unless otherwise indicated.

1912, Feb. 12 Wmk. 191 *Perf. 12*

422 A148 50c violet 250.00 17.50
Never hinged 525.00
423 A148 $1 violet brown 525.00 75.00
Never hinged 1,100.

Perforated sheet stamps of type A148: #431-440 (single line wmk., perf. 10), #460 (double line wmk. perf. 10), #470-478 (unwmkd., perf. 10), #508-518 (unwmkd., perf. 11).

1914 Wmk. 190 *Perf. 12x10*

423A A140 1c green *7,500.* *5,000.*
423B A140 2c rose red, I *30,000.* *10,000.*
423C A140 5c blue *12,500.*

Nos. 423A-423C formerly were Nos. 424a, 425d and 428a, respectively.

No. 423A unused is valued in the grade of fine. Values for 423A used and 423B-423C are for fine-very fine copies.

1914 Wmk. 190 *Perf. 10x12*

423D A140 1c green *7,500.*
423E A140 2c rose red, I —

Nos. 423D and 423E formerly were Nos. 424b and 425c, respectively. Only one example is recorded of No. 423E.

No. 423D is valued in the grade of fine-very fine.

1914-15 Wmk. 190 *Perf. 10*

424 A140 1c green 2.50 .20
Never hinged 5.00
c. Vert. pair, imperf. horiz. *2,000.* *1,750.*
Never hinged *3,000.*
d. Booklet pane of 6 5.25 *3.25*
Never hinged 8.50
e. As "d," imperf. *1,600.*
f. Vert. pair, imperf. btwn., straight edge at top *9,000.*

All known examples of No. 424e are without gum.

425 A140 2c rose red, I 2.30 .20
Never hinged 4.75
e. Booklet pane of 6 17.50 *15.00*
Never hinged 28.00
426 A140 3c dp vio, I 15.00 1.25
Never hinged 30.00
427 A140 4c brown 35.00 .50
Never hinged 70.00
428 A140 5c blue 35.00 .50
Never hinged 70.00
429 A140 6c red orange 50.00 1.40
Never hinged 100.00
430 A140 7c black 90.00 4.00
Never hinged 180.00
431 A148 8c pale ol grn 37.50 2.00
Never hinged 75.00
432 A148 9c salmon red 50.00 8.00
Never hinged 100.00
433 A148 10c orange yellow 47.50 .50
Never hinged 95.00
434 A148 11c dk grn ('15) 25.00 8.00
Never hinged 50.00
435 A148 12c claret brown 27.50 4.00
Never hinged 60.00
a. 12c copper red 30.00 6.00
Never hinged 70.00
437 A148 15c gray 135.00 9.00
Never hinged 280.00
438 A148 20c ultra 220.00 4.00
Never hinged 450.00
439 A148 30c orange red 260.00 18.00
Never hinged 550.00
440 A148 50c violet ('15) 575.00 18.00
Never hinged 1,250.
Nos. 424-440 (16) 1,607. 79.55

Coil Stamps

1914 *Perf. 10 Horizontally*

441 A140 1c green 1.00 1.00
Never hinged 1.90
442 A140 2c carmine, I 10.00 6.00
Never hinged 19.00

1914 *Perf. 10 Vertically*

443 A140 1c green 25.00 7.50
Never hinged 47.50
444 A140 2c carmine, I 40.00 3.00
Never hinged 80.00
a. 2c lake *1,250.*
445 A140 3c violet, I 225.00 125.00
Never hinged 450.00
446 A140 4c brown 125.00 50.00
Never hinged 240.00
447 A140 5c blue 45.00 27.50
Never hinged 85.00
Nos. 443-447 (5) 460.00 213.00

Type II

TWO CENTS

Type II. Shading lines in ribbons as on type I.

The toga button, rope, and shading lines are heavy.

The shading lines of the face at the lock of hair end in a strong vertical curved line.

Used on rotary press printings only.

Type III

TWO CENTS

Type III. Two lines of shading in the curves of the ribbons.

Other characteristics similar to type II.

Used on rotary press printings only.

Fraudulently altered copies of type III (Nos. 455, 488, 492 and 540) have had one line of shading scraped off to make them resemble type II (Nos. 454, 487, 491 and 539).

ROTARY PRESS STAMPS

The Rotary Press stamps are printed from plates that are curved to fit around a cylinder. This curvature produces stamps that are slightly larger, either horizontally or vertically, than those printed from flat plates.

Stamps from flat plates measure about 18½-19mm wide by 22mm high.

When the impressions are placed sideways on the curved plates the stamps are 19½-20mm wide; when they are placed vertically the stamps are 23mm high.

Coil Stamps

Rotary Press Printing

1915-16 *Perf. 10 Horizontally*

448 A140 1c green 6.00 3.25
Never hinged 11.50
449 A140 2c red, I 2,600. 600.00
Never hinged 5,250.
450 A140 2c car, III ('16) 10.00 4.50
Never hinged 19.00

1914-16 *Perf. 10 Vertically*

452 A140 1c green 10.00 2.00
Never hinged 19.00
453 A140 2c car rose, I 150.00 5.00
Never hinged 290.00
454 A140 2c red, II 82.50 10.00
Never hinged 160.00
455 A140 2c carmine, III 8.50 1.00
Never hinged 16.00
456 A140 3c vio, I ('16) 240.00 95.00
Never hinged 475.00
457 A140 4c brown ('16) 25.00 17.50
Never hinged 47.50
458 A140 5c blue ('16) 30.00 17.50
Never hinged 57.50
Nos. 452-458 (7) 546.00 148.00

1914, June 30 *Imperf.*

459 A140 2c car, I 240.00 *1,100.*
Never hinged 350.00

No. 459 is a horizontal coil.

The used value is for a copy with an authenticated contemporaneous cancel.

Flat Plate Printings

1915, Feb. 8 Wmk. 191 *Perf. 10*

460 A148 $1 violet black 850.00 100.00
Never hinged 1,850.

1915, June 17 Wmk. 190 *Perf. 11*

461 A140 2c pale carmine red, I 150.00 *300.00*
Never hinged 300.00

Fraudulently perforated copies of No. 409 are offered as No. 461.

The used value is for a copy with a contemporaneous cancel.

Unwatermarked

From 1916 onward all postage stamps except Nos. 519 and 832b are on unwatermarked paper.

1916-17 Unwmk. *Perf. 10*

462 A140 1c green 7.00 .35
Never hinged 13.00
a. Booklet pane of 6 9.50 *5.00*
Never hinged 15.00
463 A140 2c carmine, I 4.50 .25
Never hinged 8.50
a. Booklet pane of 6 95.00 *65.00*
Never hinged 150.00
464 A140 3c violet, I 75.00 14.00
Never hinged 160.00
465 A140 4c org brn 45.00 1.90
Never hinged 90.00
466 A140 5c blue 75.00 1.90
Never hinged 150.00
467 A140 5c car (error in plate of 2c, '17) 550.00 *750.00*
Never hinged 1,100.
468 A140 6c red orange 95.00 8.50
Never hinged 200.00
469 A140 7c black 130.00 14.00
Never hinged 275.00
470 A148 8c olive green 60.00 7.00
Never hinged 120.00
471 A148 9c salmon red 60.00 18.00
Never hinged 125.00
472 A148 10c orange yel 110.00 1.90
Never hinged 225.00
473 A148 11c dark green 40.00 18.00
Never hinged 80.00
474 A148 12c claret brown 55.00 6.50
Never hinged 120.00
475 A148 15c gray 200.00 14.00
Never hinged 400.00
476 A148 20c lt ultra 250.00 15.00
Never hinged 500.00
476A A148 30c orange red *3,450.* —
Never hinged *5,750.*
477 A148 50c lt violet ('17) 1,100. 80.00
Never hinged 2,350.
478 A148 $1 violet black 800.00 22.50
Never hinged 1,700.
Nos. 462-466,468-476,477-478 (16) 3,106. 223.80

No. 476A is valued in the grade of fine.

Types of 1903 Issue

1917, Mar. 22 *Perf. 10*

479 A127 $2 dark blue 275.00 40.00
Never hinged 550.00
480 A128 $5 light green 225.00 40.00
Never hinged 450.00

Type Ia

TWO CENTS

Type Ia. Design characteristics similar to type I except that all lines of design are stronger.

The toga button, toga rope and rope shading lines are heavy.

The latter characteristics are those of type II, which, however, occur only on impressions from rotary plates.

Used only on flat plates 10208 and 10209.

Type II

THREE CENTS

Type II. The top line of the toga rope is strong and the rope shading lines are heavy and complete.

The line between the lips is heavy.

Used on both flat plate and rotary press printings.

1916-17 ***Imperf.***

481 A140 1c green 1.00 .65
Never hinged 1.90
482 A140 2c carmine, I 1.40 1.25
Never hinged 2.60
482A A140 2c dp rose, Ia *50,000.*

No. 482A was issued imperforate but all copies were privately perforated with large oblong perforations at the sides (Schermack type III).

No. 500 exists with imperforate top sheet margin. Copies have been altered by trimming perforations. Some also have faked Schermack perfs.

483 A140 3c vio, I ('17) 13.00 7.50
Never hinged 24.00
484 A140 3c violet, II 10.00 5.00
Never hinged 19.00
485 A140 5c car (error in plate of 2c) ('17) *12,000.*
Never hinged *18,000.*

Although #485 is valued as a single stamp, such examples are seldom seen in the marketplace.

#485 usually is seen as the center stamp in a block of 9 with 8 #482 (value with #485 never hinged, $17,000) or as two center stamps in a block of 12 (value with both #485 never hinged, $25,000).

Coil Stamps

Rotary Press Printing

1916-19 ***Perf. 10 Horizontally***

486 A140 1c green ('18) .90 .40
Never hinged 1.70
487 A140 2c car, II 13.50 4.00
Never hinged 26.00
488 A140 2c car, III ('19) 2.50 1.75
Never hinged 4.75
489 A140 3c violet, I ('17) 5.00 1.50
Never hinged 9.50
Nos. 486-489 (4) 21.90 7.65

1916-22 ***Perf. 10 Vertically***

490 A140 1c green .55 .25
Never hinged 1.05
491 A140 2c car, II 2,200. 750.00
Never hinged 4,250.
492 A140 2c car, III 9.50 .40
Never hinged 18.00
493 A140 3c vio, I ('17) 16.00 3.00
Never hinged 30.00
494 A140 3c vio, II ('18) 10.00 1.10
Never hinged 19.00
495 A140 4c org brn ('17) 10.00 4.00
Never hinged 19.00
496 A140 5c blue ('19) 3.50 1.00
Never hinged 6.75
497 A148 10c org yel ('22) 20.00 14.00
Never hinged 38.00
Nos. 490,492-497 (7) 69.55 23.75

See note above #448 regarding #487, 491.

Blind Perfs.

Listings of imperforate-between varieties are for examples which show no trace of "blind perfs.," traces of impressions from the perforating pins which do not cut into the paper.

Types of 1912-14 Issue

Flat Plate Printings

1917-19 ***Perf. 11***

498 A140 1c green .35 .25
Never hinged .60
a. Vert. pair, imperf. horiz. 600.00
b. Horiz. pair, imperf. btwn. *325.00*
Never hinged *600.00*
c. Vert. pair, imperf. btwn. *450.00* —
d. Double impression 250.00 *750.00*
e. Booklet pane of 6 2.50 *1.00*
Never hinged 4.00
f. Booklet pane of 30 *1,000.*
Never hinged *1,600.*
g. Perf 10 at top or bottom *5,000.* —
Never hinged *7,500.*
499 A140 2c rose, I .35 .25
Never hinged .60
a. Vert. pair, imperf. horiz. 175.00
Never hinged 300.00
b. Horiz. pair, imperf. vert. *300.00* *225.00*
Never hinged *500.00*
c. Vert. pair, imperf. btwn. *650.00* *225.00*
e. Booklet pane of 6 4.00 *1.25*
Never hinged 6.50
f. Booklet pane of 30 *28,000.*
Never hinged *38,000.*
g. Double impression 175.00 —

No. 499b is valued in the grade of fine.

500 A140 2c dp rose, Ia 275.00 240.00
Never hinged 575.00
501 A140 3c lt violet, I 11.00 .25
Never hinged 22.50
b. Booklet pane of 6 75.00 *50.00*
Never hinged 120.00
c. Vert. pair, imperf. horiz. *750.00*
d. Double impression *2,500.* *2,500.*
Never hinged —
502 A140 3c dk violet, II 14.00 .75
Never hinged 30.00
b. Booklet pane of 6 60.00 *50.00*
Never hinged 95.00
c. Vert. pair, imperf. horiz. *450.00* —
Never hinged *800.00*
d. Double impression 500.00 300.00
Never hinged 850.00
e. Perf 10 at top or bottom *6,000.*
Never hinged *13,500.*
503 A140 4c brown 10.00 .30
Never hinged 20.00
b. Double impression —
504 A140 5c blue 9.00 .25
Never hinged 18.00
a. Horiz. pair, imperf. btwn. *2,500.* —
b. Double impression *900.00*
505 A140 5c rose (error in plate of 2c) 350.00 *550.00*
Never hinged 625.00
506 A140 6c red orange 12.50 .30
Never hinged 25.00
a. Perf 10 at top or bottom *3,500.* *3,250.*
Never hinged *13,500.*
507 A140 7c black 27.50 1.25
Never hinged 55.00
a. Perf 10 at top *7,500.*
508 A148 8c olive bister 12.00 .50
Never hinged 24.00
b. Vert. pair, imperf. btwn. — —
c. Perf 10 at top or bottom *4,500.*
509 A148 9c salmon red 14.00 1.75
Never hinged 27.50
a. Perf 10 at top or bottom *4,000.* *6,000.*
Never hinged *6,500.*
510 A148 10c orange yellow 17.00 .20
Never hinged 35.00
a. 10c brown yellow *900.00*
Never hinged *1,600.*
511 A148 11c lt green 9.00 2.50
Never hinged 18.00
a. Perf 10 at top or bottom *4,000.* *2,750.*
Never hinged *6,000.*
512 A148 12c claret brown 9.00 .35
Never hinged 18.00
a. 12c brown carmine 10.00 .40
Never hinged 20.00
b. Perf 10 at top or bottom — *3,250.*
513 A148 13c apple grn ('19) 11.00 6.00
Never hinged 22.50
514 A148 15c gray 37.50 1.00
Never hinged 75.00
a. Perf 10 at bottom *7,500.*
Never hinged *13,500.*
515 A148 20c light ultra 45.00 .40
Never hinged 90.00
b. Vert. pair, imperf. btwn. *1,500.*
c. Double impression *1,250.*
d. Perf 10 at top or bottom — *10,000.*

No. 515b is valued in the grade of fine. Beware of pairs with blind perforations inside the design of the top stamp that are offered as No. 515b.

516 A148 30c orange red 37.50 1.00
Never hinged 75.00
a. Perf 10 at top or bottom *5,000.* —
Never hinged *7,000.*
b. Double impression —
517 A148 50c red violet 65.00 .60
Never hinged 130.00
b. Vert. pair, imperf. btwn. & at bottom — *6,000.*
Never hinged 67.50
c. Perf 10 at top or bottom — *10,000.*
518 A148 $1 violet brown 50.00 1.50
Never hinged 100.00
b. $1 deep brown *1,800.* *1,050.*
Never hinged *3,000.*
Nos. 498-504,506-518 (20) 666.70 259.40

No. 517b is valued in average condition and may be a unique used pair. The editors would like to see authenticated evidence of an unused pair.

No. 518b is valued in the grade of fine to very fine.

Type of 1908-09 Issue

1917, Oct. 10 Wmk. 191 ***Perf. 11***

519 A139 2c carmine 450.00 *1,100.*
Never hinged 800.00

Fraudulently perforated copies of No. 344 are offered as No. 519.

The used value is for a stamp with an authenticated contemporaneous cancel.

Franklin — A149

1918, Aug. 19 Unwmk. ***Perf. 11***

523 A149 $2 org red & blk 625.00 240.00
Never hinged 1,250.
524 A149 $5 dp grn & blk 200.00 35.00
Never hinged 400.00

See No. 547 for $2 carmine & black.

Types of 1912-14 Issue

Type IV

TWO CENTS

Type IV. Top line of toga rope is broken. Shading lines in toga button are so arranged that the curving of the first and last form a "D (reversed) ID."

Line of color in left "2" is very thin and usually broken.

Used on offset printings only.

Type V

TWO CENTS

Type V. Top line of toga is complete.

Five vertical shading lines in toga button.

Line of color in left "2" is very thin and usually broken.

Shading dots on the nose and lip are as indicated on the diagram.

Used on offset printings only.

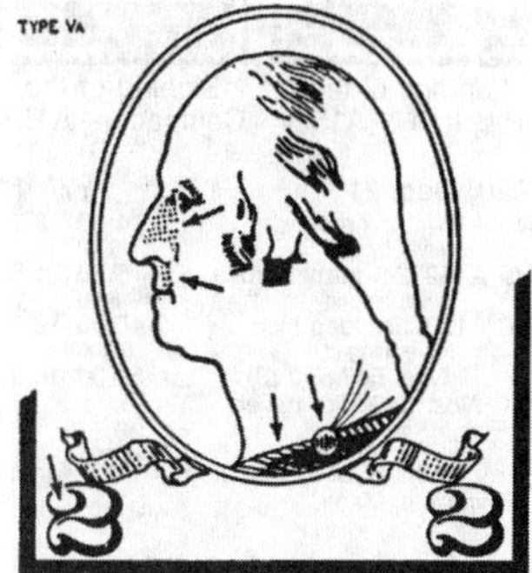

Type Va

TWO CENTS

Type Va. Characteristics same as type V, except in shading dots of nose. Third row from bottom has 4 dots instead of 6. Overall height of type Va is ⅓mm less than type V.

Used on offset printings only.

Type VI

TWO CENTS

Type VI. General characteristics same as type V, except that line of color in left "2" is very heavy.

Used on offset printings only.

Type VII

TWO CENTS

Type VII. Line of color in left "2" is invariably continuous, clearly defined, and heavier than in type V or Va, but not as heavy as in type VI.

Additional vertical row of dots has been added to the upper lip.

Numerous additional dots have been added to hair on top of head.

Used on offset printings only.

Type III

THREE CENTS

Type III. The top line of the toga rope is strong but the fifth shading line is missing as in type I.

Center shading line of the toga button consists of two dashes with a central dot.

The "P" and "O" of "POSTAGE" are separated by a line of color.

The frame line at the bottom of the vignette is complete.

Used on offset printings only.

Type IV

THREE CENTS

Type IV. Shading lines of toga rope are complete.

Second and fourth shading lines in toga button are broken in the middle and the third line is continuous with a dot in the center.

"P" and "O" of "POSTAGE" are joined.

Frame line at bottom of vignette is broken.

Used on offset printings only.

1918-20 Offset Printing *Perf. 11*

525 A140 1c gray green 2.50 .90
Never hinged 4.50
a. 1c dark green 6.00 1.75
Never hinged 11.00
c. Horiz. pair, imperf. btwn. 100.00
d. Double impression 40.00 30.00
Never hinged 72.50
526 A140 2c car, Type IV ('20) 27.50 4.00
Never hinged 50.00
527 A140 2c car, Type V ('20) 20.00 1.25
Never hinged 36.00
a. Double impression 65.00 10.00
Never hinged 120.00
b. Vert. pair, imperf. horiz. *600.00*
c. Horiz. pair, imperf. vert. *1,000.* —
528 A140 2c car, Type Va ('20) 9.50 .40
Never hinged 17.00
c. Double impression 27.50
g. Vert. pair, imperf. btwn. *3,500.*
528A A140 2c car, Type VI ('20) 52.50 1.75
Never hinged 110.00
d. Double impression 160.00 —
Never hinged 290.00
f. Vert. pair, imperf. horiz. —
h. Vert. pair, imperf. btwn. *1,000.*
528B A140 2c car, Type VII ('20) 22.50 .75
Never hinged 45.00
e. Double impression 70.00
529 A140 3c vio, Type III 3.50 .40
Never hinged 7.00
a. Double impression 40.00 —
b. Printed on both sides *1,500.*
530 A140 3c pur, Type IV 1.80 .30
Never hinged 3.25
a. Double impression 30.00 7.00
b. Printed on both sides *350.00*
Nos. 525-530 (8) 139.80 9.75

1918-20 ***Imperf.***

531 A140 1c green ('19) 9.50 8.00
Never hinged 17.00
532 A140 2c car rose, Type IV ('20) 40.00 27.50
Never hinged 72.50
533 A140 2c car, Type V ('20) 110.00 80.00
Never hinged 210.00
534 A140 2c car, Type Va ('20) 11.00 7.00
Never hinged 20.00
534A A140 2c car, Type VI ('20) 45.00 25.00
Never hinged 85.00
534B A140 2c car, Type VII ('20) 2,100. 1,250.
Never hinged 3,600.
535 A140 3c vio, Type IV 9.00 5.00
Never hinged 16.00
a. Double impression 100.00 —
Nos. 531-534A,535 (6) 224.50 152.50

1919, Aug. 15 ***Perf. 12½***

536 A140 1c gray green 22.50 20.00
Never hinged 40.00
a. Horiz. pair, imperf. vert. *900.00*

Victory Issue

"Victory" and Flags of the Allies — A150

Flat Plate Printing

1919, Mar. 3 Engr. ***Perf. 11***

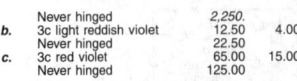

537 A150 3c violet 9.00 3.25
Never hinged 16.00
a. 3c deep red violet *1,400.* *2,000.*
Never hinged *2,250.*
b. 3c light reddish violet 12.50 4.00
Never hinged 22.50
c. 3c red violet 65.00 15.00
Never hinged 125.00

Victory of Allies in World War I.
No. 537a is valued in the grade of fine.

Rotary Press Printings

1919 ***Perf. 11x10***

Size: 19½ to 20mm wide by 22 to 22¼mm high

538 A140 1c green 11.00 8.50
Never hinged 20.00
a. Vert. pair, imperf. horiz. 50.00 *100.00*
Never hinged 87.50
539 A140 2c car rose, II 2,750. *5,250.*
Never hinged 4,000.
540 A140 2c car rose, III 13.00 8.50
Never hinged 23.50
a. Vert. pair, imperf. horiz. 50.00 *100.00*
Never hinged 87.50
b. Horiz. pair, imperf. vert. *1,250.*
541 A140 3c vio, II 45.00 30.00
Never hinged 85.00

The part perforate varieties of Nos. 538a and 540a were issued in sheets and may be had in blocks; similar part perforate varieties, Nos. 490 and 492, are from coils and are found only in strips.

See note over No. 448 regarding No. 539.
No. 539 is valued in the grade of fine.

Size: 19x22½-22¾mm

1920, May 26 ***Perf. 10x11***

542 A140 1c green 14.00 1.10
Never hinged 27.50

Size: 19x22½mm

1921 ***Perf. 10***

543 A140 1c green .50 .30
Never hinged .90
a. Horiz. pair, imperf. btwn. *1,750.*

Size: 19x22½mm

1922 ***Perf. 11***

544 A140 1c green *18,000.* *3,250.*
Never hinged *30,000.*

No. 544 is valued in the grade of fine.

Size: 19½-20x22mm

1921 ***Perf. 11***

545 A140 1c green 200.00 175.00
Never hinged 400.00
546 A140 2c car rose, III 125.00 *160.00*
Never hinged 240.00

Flat Plate Printing

1920, Nov. 1 ***Perf. 11***

547 A149 $2 carmine & black 175.00 40.00
Never hinged 325.00

Pilgrim Tercentenary Issue

"Mayflower" A151

Landing of the Pilgrims — A152

Signing of the Compact — A153

1920, Dec. 21 ***Perf. 11***

548 A151 1c green 4.50 2.25
Never hinged 9.00
549 A152 2c carmine rose 6.50 1.60
Never hinged 13.00
550 A153 5c deep blue 40.00 12.50
Never hinged 80.00
Nos. 548-550 (3) 51.00 16.35
Nos. 548-550, never hinged 90.25

Tercentenary of the landing of the Pilgrims at Plymouth, Mass.

Nathan Hale A154

Franklin A155

Harding A156

Washington A157

Lincoln A158

Martha Washington A159

Theodore Roosevelt A160

Garfield A161

McKinley A162

Grant A163

Jefferson A164

Monroe A165

Rutherford B. Hayes A166

Grover Cleveland A167

American Indian A168

Statue of Liberty A169

Golden Gate — A170

Niagara Falls — A171

American Buffalo A172

Arlington Amphitheater A173

Lincoln Memorial A174

US Capitol A175

Head of Freedom Statue, Capitol Dome — A176

1922-25 ***Perf. 11***

551 A154 ½c olive brn ('25) .30 .20
Never hinged .50
552 A155 1c dp green ('23) 1.50 .20
Never hinged 2.75
a. Booklet pane of 6 6.00 *2.00*
Never hinged 9.75
553 A156 1½c yel brn ('25) 2.50 .20
Never hinged 4.50
554 A157 2c carmine ('23) 1.30 .20
Never hinged 2.40
a. Horiz. pair, imperf. vert. *300.00*
b. Vert. pair, imperf. horiz. *4,000.*
Never hinged —
c. Booklet pane of 6 6.75 *2.00*
Never hinged 11.00
d. Perf 10 at top or bottom *7,000.* *5,000.*
555 A158 3c violet ('23) 17.50 1.25
Never hinged 31.00
556 A159 4c yel brn ('23) 19.00 .35
Never hinged 37.50
a. Vert. pair, imperf. horiz. *10,500.*
b. Perf 10 at top or bottom *3,000.* *10,000.*
557 A160 5c dark blue 19.00 .25
Never hinged 37.50
a. Imperf., pair *1,500.*
Never hinged *2,350.*
b. Horiz. pair, imperf. vert. —
c. Perf 10 at top or bottom — *7,500.*
558 A161 6c red orange 35.00 .85
Never hinged 75.00
559 A162 7c black ('23) 9.00 .65
Never hinged 16.00
560 A163 8c olive grn ('23) 50.00 .75
Never hinged 90.00
561 A164 9c rose ('23) 14.00 1.10
Never hinged 25.00
562 A165 10c orange ('23) 17.50 .30
Never hinged 35.00
a. Vert. pair, imperf. horiz. *1,500.*
Never hinged *2,350.*
b. Imperf., pair *1,500.*
c. Perf 10 at top or bottom *5,000.*
563 A166 11c light blue 1.40 .50
Never hinged 2.50
d. Imperf., pair *17,500.*
564 A167 12c brn vio ('23) 6.00 .30
Never hinged 10.50
a. Horiz. pair, imperf. vert. *1,750.*
565 A168 14c blue ('23) 4.00 .85
Never hinged 8.00
566 A169 15c gray 21.00 .25
Never hinged 37.50
567 A170 20c car rose ('23) 20.00 .25
Never hinged 37.50
a. Horiz. pair, imperf. vert. *1,500.*
Never hinged *2,400.*
568 A171 25c yellow green 18.00 .60
Never hinged 35.00
b. Vert. pair, imperf. horiz. *2,000.*
d. Perf 10 at top or bottom *5,000.* *11,000.*
569 A172 30c olive brn ('23) 30.00 .50
Never hinged 57.50
570 A173 50c lilac 50.00 .30
Never hinged 95.00
571 A174 $1 vio black ('23) 40.00 .55
Never hinged 77.50
572 A175 $2 dp bl ('23) 80.00 9.00
Never hinged 155.00
573 A176 $5 car & bl ('23) 125.00 15.00
Never hinged 225.00
a. $5 car lake & dark bl 200.00 17.50
Never hinged 375.00
Nos. 551-573 (23) 582.00 34.40
Nos. 551-573, never hinged 1,020.

No. 556a is unique. No. 568b is valued in the grade of fine.

For listings of other perforated stamps of designs A154 to A176 see

#578-579	Perf. 11x10
#581-591	Perf. 10
#594-595	Perf. 11
#632-642, 653, 692-696	Perf. 11x10½
#697-701	Perf. 10½x11

This series includes Nos. 622-623 (perf. 11).

1923-25 ***Imperf.***

575 A155 1c green 7.00 5.00
Never hinged 12.50
576 A156 1½c yel brn ('25) 1.40 1.50
Never hinged 2.50

577 A157 2c carmine 1.50 1.25
Never hinged 2.70
Nos. 575-577 (3) 9.90 7.75
Nos. 555-577, never hinged 16.50

The 1½c A156 rotary press imperforate is listed as No. 631.

Rotary Press Printings

Perf. 11x10

578 A155 1c green 95.00 *160.00*
Never hinged 175.00
579 A157 2c carmine 85.00 *140.00*
Never hinged 160.00

Nos. 578-579 were made from coil waste of Nos. 597, 599 and measure approximately 19¾x22¼mm.

1923-26 ***Perf. 10***

581 A155 1c green 11.00 .65
Never hinged 18.00
582 A156 1½c brown ('25) 5.50 .60
Never hinged 9.00
583 A157 2c car ('24) 3.00 .25
Never hinged 5.00
a. Booklet pane of 6 90.00 *50.00*
Never hinged 160.00
584 A158 3c violet ('25) 32.50 2.75
Never hinged 55.00
585 A159 4c yel brn ('25) 19.00 .55
Never hinged 32.50
586 A160 5c blue ('25) 19.00 .30
Never hinged 32.50
a. Horiz. pair, imperf. btwn. *8,500.*
587 A161 6c red org ('25) 9.25 .50
Never hinged 19.00
588 A162 7c black ('26) 13.50 6.25
Never hinged 22.50
589 A163 8c ol grn ('26) 30.00 4.00
Never hinged 50.00
590 A164 9c rose ('26) 6.00 2.25
Never hinged 10.00
591 A165 10c orange ('25) 72.50 .40
Never hinged 120.00
Nos. 581-591 (11) 221.25 18.50
Nos. 581-591, never hinged 352.00

Perf. 11

594 A155 1c green *16,000.* 6,750.
595 A157 2c carmine 300. *350.*
Never hinged 500.

Nos. 594-595 were made from coil waste of Nos. 597 and 599, and measure approximately 19¾x22¼mm.

No. 594 unused is valued without gum; both unused and used are valued with perforations just touching frameline on one side.

Perf. 11

596 A155 1c green *120,000.*
Precanceled *100,000.*

No. 596 was made from rotary press sheet waste and measures approximately 19¼x22½mm. A majority of the copies carry the Bureau precancel "Kansas City, Mo." No. 596 is valued in the grade of fine.

ROTARY PRESS DOUBLE PAPER

The web of paper used on rotary presses must be continuous, therefore any break in the paper must be lapped and pasted, causing the "double paper" varieties. These are no longer listed since they may occur on any rotary press stamp.

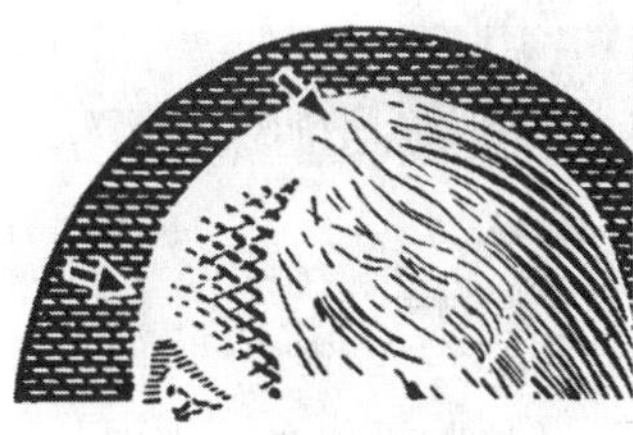

Type I

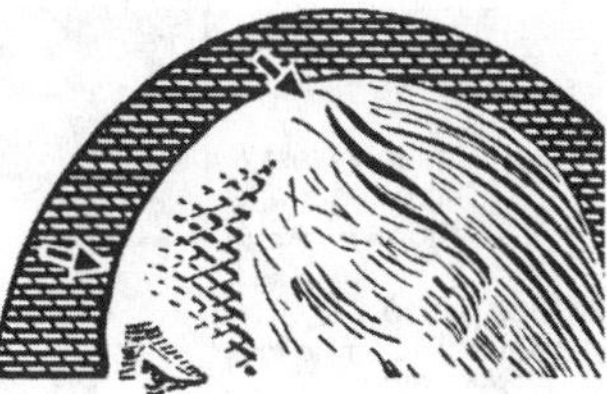

Type II

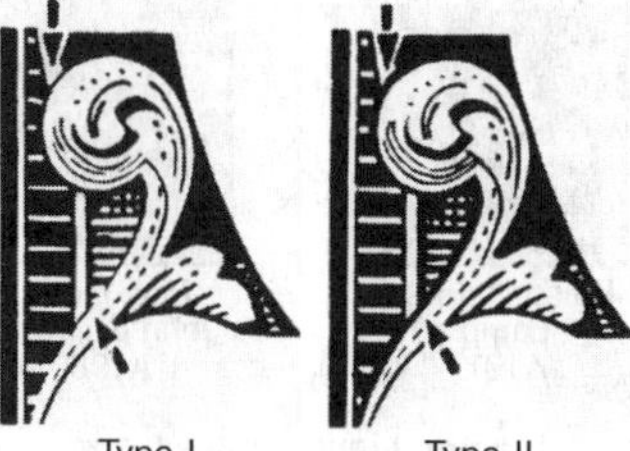

Type I Type II

Type I. No heavy hair lines at top center of head. Outline of left acanthus scroll generally faint at top and toward base at left side.

Type II. The heavy hair lines at top center of head; two being outstanding in the white area. Outline of left acanthus scroll very strong and clearly defined at top (under left edge of lettered panel) and at lower curve (above and to left of numeral oval). Type II is found only on Nos. 599A and 634A.

Coil Stamps

Rotary Press Printing

1923-29 ***Perf. 10 Vertically***

597 A155 1c green .30 .20
Never hinged .50
598 A156 1½c brown ('25) 1.00 .20
Never hinged 1.60
599 A157 2c car, I ('23) .40 .20
Never hinged .65
599A A157 2c car, II ('29) 125.00 11.00
Never hinged 200.00
600 A158 3c violet ('24) 7.25 .20
Never hinged 11.50
601 A159 4c yellow brown 4.50 .35
Never hinged 7.25
602 A160 5c dk bl ('24) 1.75 .20
Never hinged 2.80
603 A165 10c orange ('24) 4.00 .20
Never hinged 6.50

Perf. 10 Horizontally

604 A155 1c green ('24) .35 .20
Never hinged .55
605 A156 1½c yel brn ('25) .35 .20
Never hinged .55
606 A157 2c carmine .35 .20
Never hinged .55
Nos. 597-599,600-606 (10) 20.25 2.15
Nos. 597-599, 600-606, never hinged 32.45

Harding Memorial Issue

Warren G. Harding — A177

Flat Plate Printing
(19¼x22¼mm)

1923, Sept. 1 ***Perf. 11***

610 A177 2c black .65 .25
Never hinged 1.05
a. Horiz. pair, imperf. vert. *2,000.*

1923, Nov. 15 ***Imperf.***

611 A177 2c black 5.75 4.00
Never hinged 10.00

Rotary Press Printing
(19¼x22½mm)

1923, Sept. 12 ***Perf. 10***

612 A177 2c black 17.50 1.75
Never hinged 28.00

1923 ***Perf. 11***

613 A177 2c black *42,500.*

Tribute to President Warren G. Harding, who died August 2, 1923.

Nos. 610a, 613 valued in the grade of fine.

Huguenot-Walloon Tercentenary Issue

"New Netherland" A178

Landing at Fort Orange A179

Monument to Jan Ribault at Duvall County, Fla. — A180

Flat Plate Printings

1924, May 1 ***Perf. 11***

614 A178 1c dark green 2.75 3.25
Never hinged 4.25
615 A179 2c carmine rose 5.00 2.25
Never hinged 8.75
616 A180 5c dark blue 22.50 13.00
Never hinged 35.00
Nos. 614-616 (3) 30.25 18.50
Nos. 614-616, never hinged 48.00

Tercentenary of the settling of the Walloons and in honor of the Huguenots.

Lexington-Concord Issue

Washington at Cambridge A181

"Birth of Liberty," by Henry Sandham A182

The Minute Man, by Daniel Chester French A183

1925, Apr. 4 ***Perf. 11***

617 A181 1c deep green 2.50 2.50
Never hinged 4.00
618 A182 2c carmine rose 5.00 4.00
Never hinged 8.00
619 A183 5c dark blue 20.00 13.00
Never hinged 32.50
Nos. 617-619 (3) 27.50 19.50
Nos. 617-619, never hinged 44.50

150th anniv. of the Battle of Lexington-Concord.

Norse-American Issue

A184 A185

1925, May 18 ***Perf. 11***

620 A184 2c "Restaurationen" 4.00 3.00
Never hinged 6.50
621 A185 5c Viking Ship 12.50 11.00
Never hinged 24.00

100th anniv. of the arrival in NY on Oct. 9, 1825, of the sloop "Restaurationen" with the first group of immigrants from Norway to the US.

Benjamin Harrison A186

Woodrow Wilson A187

1925-26 ***Perf. 11***

622 A186 13c green ('26) 12.50 .55
Never hinged 21.00
623 A187 17c black 14.00 .25
Never hinged 24.00

Sesquicentennial Exposition Issue

Liberty Bell A188

1926, May 10 ***Perf. 11***

627 A188 2c carmine rose 3.00 .50
Never hinged 4.50

150th anniv. of the Declaration of Independence, Philadelphia, June 1-Dec. 1.

Statue of John Ericsson A189

Alexander Hamilton's Battery A190

Ericsson Memorial Issue

1926, May 29 ***Perf. 11***

628 A189 5c gray lilac 6.50 3.25
Never hinged 9.50

John Ericsson, builder of the "Monitor."

Battle of White Plains Issue

1926, Oct. 18 ***Perf. 11***

629 A190 2c carmine rose 2.25 1.70
Never hinged 3.25
a. Vertical pair, imperf. btwn. —

Battle of White Plains, NY, 150th anniv.

International Philatelic Exhibition

Souvenir Sheet

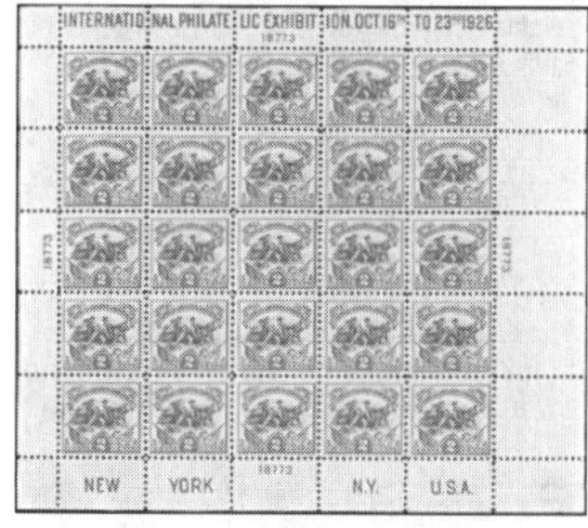

A190a

1926, Oct. 18 ***Perf. 11***

630 A190a 2c carmine rose, sheet of 25 375.00 450.00
Never hinged 575.00

Intl. Phil. Exhib. in NYC, Oct. 16-23. Size: 158-160¼x136-146½mm.

Condition Valued:

Centering: Overall centering will average very fine, but individual stamps may be better or worse.

Perforations: No folds along rows of perforations.

Gum: There may be some light gum bends but no gum creases.

Hinging: There may be hinge marks in the selvage and on up to two or three stamps, but no heavy hingling or hinge remnants (except in the ungummed portion of the wide selvage).

Margins: Top panes should have about ½ inch bottom margin and 1 inch top margin.

Bottom panes should have about ½ inch top margin and just under ¾ inch bottom margin. Both will have one wide side (usually 1½ inches plus) and one narrow (½ inch) side margin. The wide margin corner will have a small diagonal notch on top panes.

Types of 1922-26

Rotary Press Printings

1926, Aug. 27 ***Imperf.***

631 A156 1½c yellow brown 1.90 1.70
Never hinged 2.75

1926-34 ***Perf. 11x10½***

632 A155 1c green ('27) .20 .20
Never hinged .20
a. Booklet pane of 6 5.00 *2.25*
Never hinged 7.50

b. Vert. pair, imperf. btwn. 3,500. *125.00*
Never hinged 5,500.
c. Horiz. pair, imperf. btwn. *7,500.*

No. 632c is valued in the grade of fine.

633 A156 1½c yel brn ('27) 1.90 .20
Never hinged 2.60
634 A157 2c car, I .20 .20
Never hinged .20
b. 2c carmine lake — —
c. Horiz. pair, imperf. btwn. *7,000.*
d. Booklet pane of 6 1.50 *1.10*
Never hinged 2.50

No. 634c is valued in the grade of fine.

634A A157 2c car, II ('28) 350.00 13.50
Never hinged 575.00
635 A158 3c violet ('27) .40 .20
Never hinged .55
a. 3c bright violet ('34) .20 .20
Never hinged .30
636 A159 4c yel brn ('27) 2.10 .20
Never hinged 3.00
637 A160 5c dk bl ('27) 2.10 .20
Never hinged 3.00
638 A161 6c red org ('27) 2.10 .20
Never hinged 3.00
639 A162 7c black ('27) 2.10 .20
Never hinged 3.00
a. Vert. pair, imperf. btwn. 325.00 100.00
Never hinged *500.00*
640 A163 8c ol grn ('27) 2.10 .20
Never hinged 3.00
641 A164 9c rose ('27) 2.10 .20
Never hinged 3.00
642 A165 10c org ('27) 3.50 .20
Never hinged 5.00
Nos. 632-634,635-642 (11) 18.80 2.20
Nos. 632-634, 635-642 never hinged 26.55

The 1½c, 2c, 4c, 5c, 6c, 8c imperf. (dry print) are printer's waste.
For ½c, 11c-50c see Nos. 653, 692-701.

Vermont Sesquicentennial Issue

Green Mountain Boy — A191

Flat Plate Printing

1927, Aug. 3 ***Perf. 11***
643 A191 2c carmine rose 1.40 .80
Never hinged 2.00

Battle of Bennington, Vt., and independence of the State of Vermont, 150th anniv.

"The Surrender of General Burgoyne at Saratoga," by John Trumbull
A192

Washington at Prayer — A193

Burgoyne Campaign Issue

1927, Aug. 3 ***Perf. 11***
644 A192 2c carmine rose 3.75 2.10
Never hinged 5.50

Battles of Bennington, Oriskany, Fort Stanwix and Saratoga.

Valley Forge Issue

1928, May 26 ***Perf. 11***
645 A193 2c carmine rose 1.05 .50
Never hinged 1.45
a. 2c lake —
Never hinged —

150th anniv. of Washington's encampment at Valley Forge, Pa.

Battle of Monmouth Issue

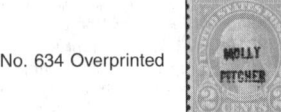

No. 634 Overprinted

Rotary Press Printing

1928, Oct. 20 ***Perf. 11x10½***
646 A157 2c carmine 1.10 1.10
Never hinged 1.50
a. "Pitcher" only *750.00*

The normal space between a vertical pair of the overprints is 18mm, but pairs are known with the space measuring 28mm.
150th anniv. of the Battle of Monmouth, NJ, as a memorial to "Molly Pitcher" (Mary Ludwig Hays), the heroine of the battle.
No. 646a is valued in the grade of fine.

Hawaii Sesquicentennial Issue

Nos. 634 and 637 Overprinted

Rotary Press Printing

1928, Aug. 13 ***Perf. 11x10½***
647 A157 2c carmine 4.50 4.50
Never hinged 7.00
648 A160 5c dark blue 12.50 13.50
Never hinged 20.00

150th anniv. of the discovery of the Hawaiian Islands by Captain Cook.
These stamps were on sale at post offices in the Hawaiian Islands and at the Postal Agency in Washington, DC.
They were not on sale at post offices in the Continental US, though they were valid for postage there.
Normally the overprints were placed 18mm apart vertically, but pairs exist with a space of 28mm between the overprints.

Aeronautics Conference Issue

Wright Airplane A194

Globe and Airplane A195

Flat Plate Printing

1928, Dec. 12 ***Perf. 11***
649 A194 2c carmine rose 1.25 .80
Never hinged 1.75
650 A195 5c blue 5.00 3.25
Never hinged 7.25

Intl. Civil Aeronautics Conf. at Washington, DC, Dec. 12-14, 1928, and of the 25th anniv. of the 1st airplane flight by the Wright brothers, Dec. 17, 1903.

George Rogers Clark Issue

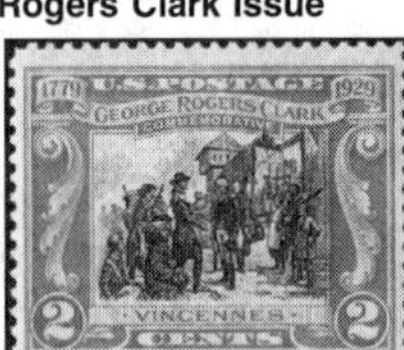

Surrender of Fort Sackville A196

1929, Feb. 25 ***Perf. 11***
651 A196 2c carmine & black .65 .50
Never hinged .90

150th anniv. of the surrender of Fort Sackville, the present site of Vincennes, Ind., to George Rogers Clark.

Type of 1925

Rotary Press Printing

1929, May 25 ***Perf. 11x10½***
653 A154 ½c olive brown .20 .20
Never hinged .20

Edison's First Lamp A197

Maj. Gen. John Sullivan A198

Electric Light Jubilee Issue

1929 Flat Plate Printing ***Perf. 11***
654 A197 2c carmine rose .70 .70
Never hinged 1.00

Rotary Press Printing

Perf. 11x10½

655 A197 2c carmine rose .65 .20
Never hinged .90

Coil Stamp (Rotary Press)

Perf. 10 Vertically

656 A197 2c carmine rose 14.00 1.75
Never hinged 21.00
Nos. 654-656 (3) 15.35 2.65

50th anniv. of invention of the incandescent lamp by Thomas Alva Edison, Oct. 21, 1879. Issued: #654, June 5; #655-656, June 11.

Sullivan Expedition Issue

Flat Plate Printing

1929, June 17 ***Perf. 11***
657 A198 2c carmine rose .70 .60
Never hinged 1.00
a. 2c lake 350.00 —
Never hinged 550.00

150th anniv. of the Sullivan Expedition in NY State during the Revolutionary War.

Nos. 632-634, 635-642 Overprinted

Rotary Press Printing

1929 ***Perf. 11x10½***
658 A155 1c green 2.50 2.00
Never hinged 4.00
a. Vert. pair, one without ovpt. *325.00*
659 A156 1½c brown 4.00 2.90
Never hinged 6.25
a. Vert. pair, one without ovpt. *350.00*
660 A157 2c carmine 4.50 1.00
Never hinged 7.00
661 A158 3c violet 22.50 15.00
Never hinged 35.00
a. Vert. pair, one without ovpt. *450.00*
Never hinged *675.00*
662 A159 4c yellow brown 22.50 9.00
Never hinged 35.00
a. Vert. pair, one without ovpt. *425.00*
663 A160 5c deep blue 14.00 9.75
Never hinged 22.00
664 A161 6c red orange 32.50 18.00
Never hinged 52.50
665 A162 7c black 30.00 27.50
Never hinged 47.50
a. Vert. pair, one without ovpt. —
666 A163 8c olive green 105.00 70.00
Never hinged 170.00
667 A164 9c light rose 16.00 11.25
Never hinged 25.00
668 A165 10c orange yel 25.00 12.00
Never hinged 39.00
Nos. 658-668 (11) 278.50 178.40
Nos. 658-668, never hinged 427.00

The existence of No. 665a has been questioned by specialists. The editors would like to see authenticated evidence of such a pair.
See note following No. 679.

Overprinted

669 A155 1c green 4.00 2.25
Never hinged 6.25
a. Vert. pair, one without ovpt. —
b. No period after "Nebr." (19338, 19339 UR 26, 36) 50.00
670 A156 1½c brown 3.75 2.50
Never hinged 5.75
671 A157 2c carmine 3.75 1.30
Never hinged 5.75
672 A158 3c violet 15.00 12.00
Never hinged 24.00
a. Vert. pair, one without ovpt. *425.00*
673 A159 4c yellow brown 21.00 15.00
Never hinged 35.00
674 A160 5c deep blue 20.00 15.00
Never hinged 31.00
675 A161 6c red orange 47.50 24.00
Never hinged 75.00
676 A162 7c black 25.00 18.00
Never hinged 42.50
677 A163 8c olive green 35.00 25.00
Never hinged 60.00
678 A164 9c light rose 42.50 27.50
Never hinged 67.50
a. Vert. pair, one without ovpt. *650.00*
679 A165 10c orange yel 125.00 22.50
Never hinged 210.00
Nos. 669-679 (11) 342.50 165.05
Nos. 669-679, never hinged 539.50

Nos. 658-660, 669-673, 677 and 678 are known with the overprints on vertical pairs spaced 32mm apart instead of the normal 22mm.
The existence of No. 669a has been questioned by specialists. The editors would like to see authenticated evidence of such a pair.
Important: Nos. 658-679 with original gum have either one horizontal gum breaker ridge per stamp or portions of two at the extreme top and bottom of the stamps, 21mm apart.
Multiple complete gum breaker ridges indicate a fake overprint. Absence of the gum breaker ridges indicates either regumming or regumming and a fake overprint.

Gen. Anthony Wayne Memorial A199

Lock No. 5, Monongahela River A200

Battle of Fallen Timbers Issue

Flat Plate Printing

1929, Sept. 14 ***Perf. 11***
680 A199 2c carmine rose .80 .80
Never hinged 1.10

General Anthony Wayne memorial and 135th anniv. of the Battle of Fallen Timbers, Ohio.

Ohio River Canalization Issue

1929, Oct. 19 ***Perf. 11***
681 A200 2c carmine rose .70 .65
Never hinged .95

Completion of the Ohio River Canalization Project between Cairo, Ill. and Pittsburgh.

Massachusetts Bay Colony Issue

Mass. Bay Colony Seal — A201

1930, Apr. 8 ***Perf. 11***
682 A201 2c carmine rose .60 .50
Never hinged .85

300th anniv. Massachusetts Bay Colony.

Carolina-Charleston Issue

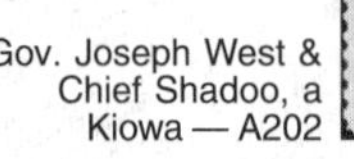

Gov. Joseph West & Chief Shadoo, a Kiowa — A202

1930, Apr. 10 ***Perf. 11***
683 A202 2c carmine rose 1.20 1.20
Never hinged 1.65

260th anniv. of the Province of Carolina founding, and the 250th anniv. of the City of Charleston, SC.

Warren G. Harding A203

William H. Taft A204

Type of 1922-26 Issue

Rotary Press Printing

1930 ***Perf. 11x10½***

684 A203 1½c brown .35 .20
Never hinged .50
685 A204 4c brown .90 .20
Never hinged 1.25

Coil Stamps

Perf. 10 Vert.

686 A203 1½c brown 1.80 .20
Never hinged 2.50
687 A204 4c brown 3.25 .45
Never hinged 4.50

Braddock's Field Issue

Statue of Col. George Washington — A205

Flat Plate Printing

1930, July 9 ***Perf. 11***

688 A205 2c carmine rose 1.00 .85
Never hinged 1.40

175th anniv. of the Battle of Braddock's Field, otherwise the Battle of Monongahela.

General von Steuben A206

General Casimir Pulaski A207

Von Steuben Issue

1930, Sept. 17 ***Perf. 11***

689 A206 2c carmine rose .55 .55
Never hinged .75
a. Imperf., pair 2,750.
Never hinged 3,500.

Gen. Baron Friedrich Wilhelm von Steuben (1730-1794), German soldier who served with distinction in American Revolution.

Pulaski Issue

1931, Jan. 16 ***Perf. 11***

690 A207 2c carmine rose .30 .25
Never hinged .40

150th anniv. (in 1929) of the death of Gen. Count Casimir Pulaski (1748-1779), Polish patriot and hero of American Revolution.

Types of 1922-26

Rotary Press Printing

1931 ***Perf. 11x10½***

692 A166 11c light blue 2.60 .20
Never hinged 3.70
693 A167 12c brown violet 5.50 .20
Never hinged 7.75
694 A186 13c yellow green 2.00 .20
Never hinged 2.80
695 A168 14c dark blue 3.75 .25
Never hinged 5.25
696 A169 15c gray 8.00 .20
Never hinged 11.25

Perf. 10½x11

697 A187 17c black 4.50 .20
Never hinged 6.25
698 A170 20c carmine rose 8.25 .20
Never hinged 11.50
699 A171 25c blue green 8.50 .20
Never hinged 12.00
700 A172 30c brown 15.00 .20
Never hinged 22.50
701 A173 50c lilac 37.50 .20
Never hinged 52.50
Nos. 692-701 (10) 95.60 2.05
Nos. 692-701, never hinged 135.50

"The Greatest Mother" — A208

Count de Rochambeau, Washington, Count de Grasse — A209

Red Cross Issue

Flat Plate Printing

1931, May 21 ***Perf. 11***

702 A208 2c black & red .25 .20
Never hinged .30
a. Red cross missing (FO) 40,000.

50th anniv. of the American Red Cross Society founding.

Yorktown Issue

1931, Oct. 19 ***Perf. 11***

703 A209 2c car rose & blk .40 .25
Never hinged .50
a. 2c lake & black 4.50 .75
Never hinged 6.25
b. 2c dark lake & black 450.00
Never hinged 700.00
c. Horiz. pair, imperf. vert. 5,000.
Never hinged 6,250.

Surrender of Yorktown, sesquicentennial.

Washington Bicentennial Issue

Various Portraits of George Washington

A210

A211

A212

A213

A214

A215

A216

A217

A218

A219

A220

A221

Rotary Press Printings

1932, Jan. 1 ***Perf. 11x10½***

704 A210 ½c olive brown .20 .20
Never hinged .20
705 A211 1c green .20 .20
Never hinged .20
706 A212 1½c brown .40 .20
Never hinged .55
707 A213 2c carmine rose .20 .20
Never hinged .20
708 A214 3c deep violet .55 .20
Never hinged .80
709 A215 4c light brown .25 .20
Never hinged .35
710 A216 5c blue 1.60 .20
Never hinged 2.25
711 A217 6c red orange 3.25 .20
Never hinged 4.50
712 A218 7c black .25 .20
Never hinged .35
713 A219 8c olive bister 2.75 .50
Never hinged 3.75
714 A220 9c pale red 2.40 .20
Never hinged 3.25
715 A221 10c orange yellow 10.00 .20
Never hinged 14.00
Nos. 704-715 (12) 22.05 2.70
Nos. 704-715, never hinged 30.40

200th anniv. of the birth of Washington.

Skier — A222

Boy and Girl Planting Tree — A223

Olympic Winter Games Issue

Flat Plate Printing

1932, Jan. 25 ***Perf. 11***

716 A222 2c carmine rose .40 .20
Never hinged .50

Olympic Winter Games, Lake Placid, NY, Feb. 4-13.

Arbor Day Issue

Rotary Press Printing

1932, Apr. 22 ***Perf. 11x10½***

717 A223 2c carmine rose .20 .20
Never hinged .20

60th anniv. of the 1st observance of Arbor Day in Nebr., April, 1872.

Birth centenary of Julius Sterling Morton, who conceived the plan and the name "Arbor Day," while a member of the Nebr. State Board of Agriculture.

10th Olympic Games Issue

Runner at Starting Mark A224

Myron's Discobolus A225

1932, June 15 ***Perf. 11x10½***

718 A224 3c violet 1.40 .20
Never hinged 1.75
719 A225 5c blue 2.20 .20
Never hinged 2.75

Los Angeles, Cal., July 30-Aug. 14.

Washington — A226

1932, June 16 ***Perf. 11x10½***

720 A226 3c deep violet .20 .20
Never hinged .20
b. Booklet pane of 6 37.50 7.50
Never hinged 60.00
c. Vert. pair, imperf. btwn. 1,250. 1,250.
Never hinged 1,650.

Coil Stamps

Rotary Press Printing

1932, June 24 ***Perf. 10 Vertically***

721 A226 3c deep violet 2.75 .20
Never hinged 3.50

1932, Oct. 12 ***Perf. 10 Horizontally***

722 A226 3c deep violet 1.50 .35
Never hinged 2.00

Garfield Type of 1922-26 Issue

1932, Aug. 18 ***Perf. 10 Vertically***

723 A161 6c deep orange 11.00 .30
Never hinged 15.00

William Penn A227

Daniel Webster A228

William Penn Issue

Flat Plate Printing

1932, Oct. 24 ***Perf. 11***

724 A227 3c violet .35 .20
Never hinged .45
a. Vert. pair, imperf. horiz. —

250th anniv. of the arrival in America of William Penn (1644-1718), English Quaker and founder of Pennsylvania.

Daniel Webster Issue

1932, Oct. 24 ***Perf. 11***

725 A228 3c violet .40 .25
Never hinged .50

Daniel Webster (1782-1852), statesman.

Georgia Bicentennial Issue

Gen. James Edward Oglethorpe — A229

1933, Feb. 12 ***Perf. 11***

726 A229 3c violet .35 .20
Never hinged .45

200th anniv. of the Colony of Georgia founding and James Edward Oglethorpe, who landed from England, Feb. 12th, 1733, and personally supervised the establishing of the colony.

Peace of 1783 Issue

Washington's Headquarters, Newburgh, NY — A230

Rotary Press Printing

1933, Apr. 19 ***Perf. 10½x11***

727 A230 3c violet .20 .20
Never hinged .20

150th anniv. of the Proclamation of Peace between the U.S. and Great Britain at the end of the Revolutionary War.

See No. 752.

Century of Progress Issue

Restoration of Fort Dearborn A231

Federal Building at Chicago, 1933 A232

1933, May 25 ***Perf. 10½x11***

728 A231 1c yellow green .20 .20
Never hinged .20
729 A232 3c violet .20 .20
Never hinged .20

"Century of Progress" Intl. Phil. Exhib., Chicago, 1933 and 100th anniv. of the incorporation of Chicago as a city.

American Philatelic Society Issue

Souvenir Sheets
Without Gum

Flat Plate Printing

1933, Aug. 25 ***Imperf.***

730 Sheet of 25 27.50 27.50
a. A231 1c deep yellow green .75 .50
731 Sheet of 25 25.00 25.00
a. A232 3c deep violet .65 .50

Sheet measures 134x120mm.
See Nos. 766-767.

National Recovery Act Issue

Group of Workers — A233

Rotary Press Printing

1933, Aug. 15 ***Perf. 10½x11***

732 A233 3c violet .20 .20
Never hinged .20

Issued to direct attention to and arouse support of the Nation for the NRA.

Byrd Antarctic Issue

World Map on van der Grinten's Projection — A234

Flat Plate Printing

1933, Oct. 9 ***Perf. 11***

733 A234 3c dark blue .50 .50
Never hinged .60

Second Antarctic expedition of Rear Admiral Richard E. Byrd.

In addition to the 3 cents postage, letters sent by the ships of the expedition to be canceled in Little America were subject to a service charge of 50 cents each.

See Nos. 735, 753.

Kosciuszko Issue

Statue of Gen. Tadeusz Kosciuszko — A235

1933, Oct. 13 ***Perf. 11***

734 A235 5c blue .55 .25
Never hinged .65
a. Horiz. pair, imperf. vert. *2,250.*
Never hinged *2,800.*

Gen. Tadeusz Kosciuszko (1746-1807), Polish soldier and statesman who served in American Revolution. 150th anniv. of grant of American citizenship.

National Stamp Exhibition Issue

Souvenir Sheet
Without Gum

1934, Feb. 10 ***Imperf.***

735 Sheet of 6 12.50 10.00
a. A234 3c dark blue 2.00 1.65

Sheet measures 87x93mm. See #768.

Maryland Tercentenary Issue

"The Ark" and "The Dove" — A236

1934, Mar. 23 ***Perf. 11***

736 A236 3c carmine rose .20 .20
Never hinged .20

300th anniv. of the founding of Maryland.

Mothers of America Issue

Adaptation of Whistler's Portrait of his Mother A237

Rotary Press Printing

1934, May 2 ***Perf. 11x10½***

737 A237 3c deep violet .20 .20
Never hinged .20

Flat Plate Printing

Perf. 11

738 A237 3c deep violet .20 .20
Never hinged .20

Mother's Day. See No. 754.

Wisconsin Tercentenary Issue

Nicolet's Landing A238

1934, July 7 ***Perf. 11***

739 A238 3c deep violet .20 .20
Never hinged .20
a. Vert. pair, imperf. horiz. *350.00*
Never hinged *600.00*
b. Horiz. pair, imperf. vert. *525.00*
Never hinged *900.00*

Tercentenary of the arrival of French explorer Jean Nicolet at Green Bay, Wis.
See No. 755.

National Parks Issue

El Capitan, Yosemite (California) A239

Old Faithful, Yellowstone (Wyoming) A243

Grand Canyon (Arizona) A240

Mt. Rainier and Mirror Lake (Washington) — A241

Mesa Verde (Colorado) A242

Crater Lake (Oregon) A244

Great Head, Acadia Park (Maine) A245

Great White Throne, Zion Park (Utah) A246

Great Smoky Mts. (North Carolina) A248

Mt. Rockwell (Mt. Sinopah) and Two Medicine Lake, Glacier Natl. Park (Montana) A247

1934 Flat Plate Printing ***Perf. 11***

740 A239 1c green .20 .20
Never hinged .20
a. Vert. pair, imperf. horiz., with gum *1,300.*
Never hinged *1,800.*
741 A240 2c red .20 .20
Never hinged .20
a. Vert. pair, imperf. horiz., with gum *475.00*
Never hinged *800.00*
b. Horiz. pair, imperf. vert., with gum *600.00*
Never hinged *1,000.*
742 A241 3c deep violet .20 .20
Never hinged .20
a. Vert. pair, imperf. horiz., with gum *700.00*
Never hinged *1,200.*
743 A242 4c brown .35 .40
Never hinged .45
a. Vert. pair, imperf. horiz., with gum *1,000.*
Never hinged *1,700.*
744 A243 5c blue .70 .65
Never hinged .95
a. Horiz. pair, imperf. vert., with gum *600.00*
Never hinged *1,000.*
745 A244 6c dark blue 1.10 .85
Never hinged 1.50
746 A245 7c black .60 .75
Never hinged .85
a. Horiz. pair, imperf. vert., with gum *725.00*
Never hinged *1,250.*
747 A246 8c sage green 1.60 1.50
Never hinged 2.20
748 A247 9c red orange 1.50 .65
Never hinged 2.10
749 A248 10c gray black 3.00 1.25
Never hinged 4.25
Nos. 740-749 (10) 9.45 6.65
Nos. 740-749, never hinged 12.90

National Parks Year.
See Nos. 750-751, 756-765, 769-770, 797.

American Philatelic Society Issue

Souvenir Sheet

1934, Aug. 28 ***Imperf.***

750 Sheet of 6 30.00 27.50
Never hinged 37.50
a. A241 3c deep violet 3.50 3.25
Never hinged 4.50

Sheet measures approximately 98x93mm.
See #770.

Trans-Mississippi Philatelic Exposition Issue

Souvenir Sheet

1934, Oct. 10 ***Imperf.***

751 Sheet of 6 12.50 12.50
Never hinged 16.00
a. A239 1c green 1.40 1.60
Never hinged 1.85

Sheet measures approximately 92x99mm.
See #769.

Special Printing (Nos. 752-771)

"Issued for a limited time in full sheets as printed, and in blocks thereof, to meet the requirements of collectors and others who may be interested" - From Postal Bulletin, No. 16614.

Issuance of the following 20 stamps in complete sheets resulted from the protest of collectors and others at the practice of presenting, to certain government officials, complete sheets of unsevered panes, imperforate (except Nos. 752 and 753) and generally ungummed.

Without Gum

Note: In 1940, the P.O. Department offered to and did gum full sheets of Nos. 756 to 765 and 769-770 sent in by owners. No other Special Printings were accepted for gumming.

Type of Peace Issue

Issued in sheets of 400

Rotary Press Printing

1935, Mar. 15 ***Perf. 10½x11***

752 A230 3c violet .20 .20

Type of Byrd Issue

Issued in sheets of 200

Flat Plate Printing

Perf. 11

753 A234 3c dark blue .50 .45

No. 753 is similar to No. 733. Positive identification is by pairs or blocks showing a guide line between stamps. These lines are found only on No. 753.

Type of Mothers of America Issue

Issued in sheets of 200

Imperf

754 A237 3c deep violet .60 .60

Type of Wisconsin Issue

Issued in sheets of 200

Imperf

755 A238 3c deep violet .60 .60

Types of National Parks Issue

Issued in sheets of 200

Imperf

756 A239 1c green .20 .20
757 A240 2c red .25 .25
758 A241 3c deep violet .50 .45
759 A242 4c brown .95 .95
760 A243 5c blue 1.50 1.40
761 A244 6c dark blue 2.40 2.25
762 A245 7c black 1.50 1.40
763 A246 8c sage green 1.60 1.50
764 A247 9c red orange 1.90 1.75
765 A248 10c gray black 3.75 3.50
Nos. 756-765 (10) 14.55 13.65

Souvenir Sheets

Type of Century of Progress Issue

Issued in sheets of 9 panes of 25 stamps each

Note: Single items from these sheets are identical with other varieties, 766 & 730, 766a & 730a, 767 & 731, 767a & 731a, 768 & 735, 768a & 735a, 769 & 756, 770 & 758.

Positive identification is by blocks or pairs showing wide gutters between stamps. These wide gutters occur only on Nos. 766-770 and measure, horiz., 13mm on Nos. 766-767; 16mm on No. 768, and 23mm on Nos. 769-770.

Imperf

766 Pane of 25 25.00 25.00
a. A231 1c yellow green .70 .50
767 Pane of 25 23.50 23.50
a. A232 3c violet .60 .50

National Exhibition Issue

Type of Byrd Issue

Issued in sheets of 25 panes of 6 stamps each

Imperf

768 Pane of 6 20.00 15.00
a. A234 3c dark blue 2.80 2.40

Types of National Parks Issue

Issued in sheets of 20 panes of 6 stamps each

Imperf

769 Pane of 6 12.50 11.00
a. A239 1c green 1.85 1.80
770 Pane of 6 30.00 24.00
a. A241 3c deep violet 3.25 3.10

Type of Air Post Special Delivery Issued in sheets of 200

Imperf

771 APSD1 16c dark blue 2.40 2.40

Catalogue values for unused stamps in this section, from this point to the end of the section, are for Never Hinged items.

VALUES FOR HINGED STAMPS AFTER NO. 771

This catalogue does not value unused stamps after No. 771 in hinged condition. Hinged unused stamps from No. 772 to the present are worth considerably less than the values given for unused stamps, which are for never-hinged examples.

Connecticut Tercentenary Issue

Charter Oak A249

Rotary Press Printing

1935, Apr. 26 ***Perf. 11x10½***

772 A249 3c violet .20 .20

300th anniv. of the settlement of Conn. See No. 778a.

California-Pacific Exposition Issue

View of San Diego Exposition A250

1935, May 29 ***Perf. 11x10½***

773 A250 3c purple .20 .20

California-Pacific Expo., San Diego. See No. 778b.

Boulder Dam Issue

Boulder Dam — A251

Flat Plate Printing

1935, Sept. 30 ***Perf. 11***

774 A251 3c purple .20 .20

Dedication of Boulder Dam.

Michigan Centenary Issue

Michigan State Seal A252

Rotary Press Printing

1935, Nov. 1 ***Perf. 11x10½***

775 A252 3c purple .20 .20

Advance celebration of Michigan statehood centenary. Michigan was admitted to Union Jan. 26, 1837. See No. 778c.

Texas Centennial Issue

Sam Houston, Stephen F. Austin and the Alamo A253

1936, Mar. 2 ***Perf. 11x10½***

776 A253 3c purple .20 .20

Centennial of Texas independence. See No. 778d.

Rhode Island Tercentenary Issue

Statue of Roger Williams — A254

1936, May 4 ***Perf. 10½x11***

777 A254 3c purple .20 .20

Settlement of Rhode Island, 1636.

Third International Philatelic Exhibition Issue

Souvenir Sheet

A254a

Flat Plate Printing

1936, May 9 ***Imperf.***

778	A254a Sheet of 4	1.75	1.75
a.	A249 3c violet	.40	.35
b.	A250 3c violet	.40	.35
c.	A252 3c violet	.40	.35
d.	A253 3c violet	.40	.35

Sheet measures 98x66mm.

Arkansas Centennial Issue

Arkansas Post, Old and New State Houses A255

Rotary Press Printing

1936, June 15 ***Perf. 11x10½***

782 A255 3c purple .25 .20

Centennial of Arkansas statehood.

Map of Oregon Territory A256

Susan B. Anthony — A257

Oregon Territory Issue

1936, July 14 ***Perf. 11x10½***

783 A256 3c purple .20 .20

Centenary of Oregon Territory opening.

Susan B. Anthony Issue

1936, Aug. 26 ***Perf. 11x10½***

784 A257 3c dark violet .20 .20

Susan Brownell Anthony (1820-1906), woman suffrage advocate, honored on 16th anniv. of ratification of 19th Amendment granting American women the right to vote.

Army Issue

George Washington, Nathanael Greene and Mount Vernon — A258

Andrew Jackson, Winfield Scott and the Hermitage A259

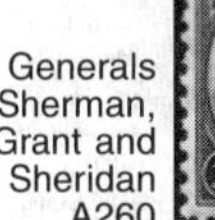

Generals Sherman, Grant and Sheridan A260

Generals Robert E. Lee, "Stonewall" Jackson and Stratford Hall — A261

US Military Academy, West Point A262

1936-37 ***Perf. 11x10½***

785	A258 1c green	.20	.20
786	A259 2c carmine ('37)	.20	.20
787	A260 3c purple ('37)	.20	.20
788	A261 4c gray ('37)	.30	.20
789	A262 5c ultra ('37)	.60	.25
	Nos. 785-789 (5)	1.50	1.05

Issued in honor of the United States Army.

Navy Issue

John Paul Jones and John Barry A263

Stephen Decatur and Thomas MacDonough — A264

Admirals David G. Farragut and David D. Porter A265

Admirals William T. Sampson, George Dewey and Winfield S. Schley A266

Seal of US Naval Academy and Naval Cadets A267

1936-37 ***Perf. 11x10½***

790	A263 1c green	.20	.20
791	A264 2c carmine ('37)	.20	.20
792	A265 3c purple ('37)	.20	.20
793	A266 4c gray ('37)	.30	.20
794	A267 5c ultra ('37)	.60	.25
	Nos. 790-794 (5)	1.50	1.05

Issued in honor of the United States Navy.

Northwest Ordinance Sesquicentennial Issue

Manasseh Cutler, Rufus Putnam and Map of Northwest Territory A268

1937, July 13 ***Perf. 11x10½***

795 A268 3c red violet .20 .20

150th anniv. of the adoption of the Ordinance of 1787 and the creation of the Northwest Territory.

Virginia Dare Issue

Virginia Dare and Parents — A269

Flat Plate Printing

1937, Aug. 18 ***Perf. 11***

796 A269 5c gray blue .20 .20

350th anniv. of the birth of Virginia Dare and the settlement at Roanoke Island. Virginia was the first child born in America of English parents (Aug. 18, 1587).

Society of Philatelic Americans

Souvenir Sheet

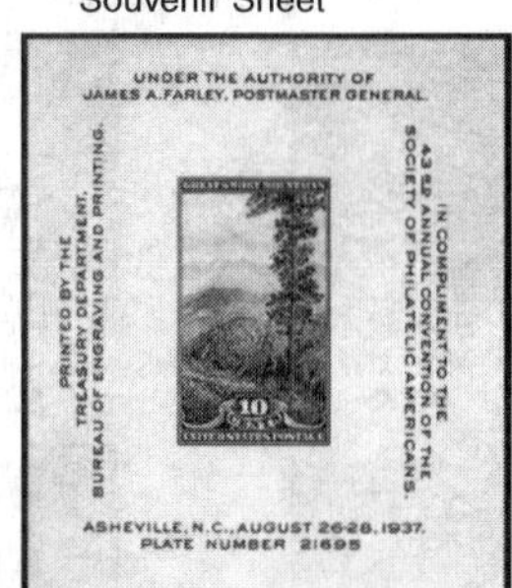

A269a

1937, Aug. 26 ***Imperf.***

797 A269a 10c blue green .60 .40

Sheet measures 67x78mm.

Constitution Sesquicentennial Issue

Signing of the Constitution A270

Rotary Press Printing

1937, Sept. 17 ***Perf. 11x10½***

798 A270 3c bright red violet .20 .20

Sesquicentennial of the Signing of the Constitution, Sept. 17, 1787.

Territorial Issues
Hawaii

Statue of Kamehameha I, Honolulu — A271

1937, Oct. 18 *Perf. 10½x11*

799	A271	3c violet	.20	.20

Alaska

Landscape with Mt. McKinley A272

1937, Nov. 12 *Perf. 11x10½*

800	A272	3c violet	.20	.20

Puerto Rico

La Fortaleza, San Juan A273

1937, Nov. 25 *Perf. 11x10½*

801	A273	3c bright violet	.20	.20

Virgin Islands

Charlotte Amalie A274

1937, Dec. 15 *Perf. 11x10½*

802	A274	3c light violet	.20	.20

Presidential Issue

Benjamin Franklin A275

George Washington A276

Martha Washington A277

John Adams A278

Thomas Jefferson A279

James Madison A280

White House A281

James Monroe A282

John Q. Adams A283

Andrew Jackson A284

Martin Van Buren A285

William H. Harrison A286

John Tyler — A287

James K. Polk — A288

Zachary Taylor A289

Millard Fillmore A290

Franklin Pierce A291

James Buchanan A292

Abraham Lincoln A293

Andrew Johnson A294

Ulysses S. Grant A295

Rutherford B. Hayes A296

James A. Garfield A297

Chester A. Arthur A298

Grover Cleveland A299

Benjamin Harrison A300

William McKinley A301

Theodore Roosevelt A302

William Howard Taft A303

Woodrow Wilson A304

Warren G. Harding A305

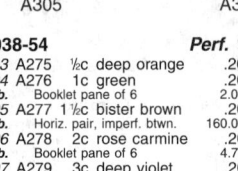

Calvin Coolidge A306

1938-54 *Perf. 11x10½*

803	A275	½c	deep orange	.20	.20
804	A276	1c	green	.20	.20
b.			Booklet pane of 6	2.00	*.50*
805	A277	1½c	bister brown	.20	.20
b.			Horiz. pair, imperf. btwn.	160.00	25.00
806	A278	2c	rose carmine	.20	.20
b.			Booklet pane of 6	4.75	*.85*
807	A279	3c	deep violet	.20	.20
a.			Booklet pane of 6	8.50	*2.00*
b.			Horiz. pair, imperf. btwn.	*1,500.*	—
c.			Imperf., pair	*2,500.*	
808	A280	4c	red violet	.75	.20
809	A281	4½c	dark gray	.20	.20
810	A282	5c	bright blue	.20	.20
811	A283	6c	red orange	.20	.20
812	A284	7c	sepia	.25	.20
813	A285	8c	olive green	.30	.20
814	A286	9c	rose pink	.30	.20
815	A287	10c	brown red	.25	.20
816	A288	11c	ultra	.65	.20
817	A289	12c	bright violet	.90	.20
818	A290	13c	blue green	1.25	.20
819	A291	14c	blue	.90	.20
820	A292	15c	blue gray	.40	.20
821	A293	16c	black	.90	.25
822	A294	17c	rose red	.85	.20
823	A295	18c	brown car	1.75	.20
824	A296	19c	bright violet	1.25	.35
825	A297	20c	brt blue grn	.70	.20
826	A298	21c	dull blue	1.25	.20
827	A299	22c	vermilion	1.00	.40
828	A300	24c	gray black	3.50	.20
829	A301	25c	deep red lil	.60	.20
830	A302	30c	deep ultra	3.50	.20
831	A303	50c	lt red violet	5.00	.20

Flat Plate Printing

Perf. 11

832	A304	$1	pur & black	6.50	.20
a.			Vert. pair, imperf. horiz.	*1,600.*	
b.			Wmkd. USIR ('51)	210.00	65.00
c.			$1 red violet & black ('54)	6.00	.20
d.			As "c," vert. pair, imperf. horiz.	*1,500.*	
e.			Vert. pair, imperf. btwn.	*2,750.*	
f.			As "c," vert. pair, imperf. btwn.	*8,500.*	
833	A305	$2	yel grn & blk	18.00	3.75
834	A306	$5	car & black	90.00	3.00
a.			$5 red brown & black	*2,000.*	*7,000.*
			Hinged	*3,000.*	
			Nos. 803-834 (32)	142.35	13.15

No. 805b used is always Bureau precanceled St. Louis Mo., and is generally with gum. Value is for gummed pair.

No. 832c is printed on thick white paper with smooth, colorless gum.

No. 834 can be chemically altered to resemble No. 834a. No. 834a should be purchased only with competent expert certification.

See Nos. 839-851.

Constitution Ratification Issue

Old Court House, Williamsburg, Va. — A307

Rotary Press Printing

1938, June 21 *Perf. 11x10½*

835	A307	3c deep violet	.25	.20

150th anniv. of the ratification of the U.S. Constitution.

Landing of the Swedes and Finns — A308

Statue Symbolizing Colonization of the West — A309

Swedish-Finnish Tercentenary Issue

Flat Plate Printing

1938, June 27 *Perf. 11*

836	A308	3c red violet	.20	.20

Tercentenary of the Swedish and Finnish settlement at Wilmington, Del.

Northwest Territory Issue

Rotary Press Printing

1938, July 15 *Perf. 11x10½*

837	A309	3c bright violet	.20	.20

Sesquicentennial of the settlement of the Northwest Territory.

Iowa Territory Centennial Issue

Old Capitol, Iowa City A310

1938, Aug. 24 *Perf. 11x10½*

838	A310	3c violet	.20	.20

Centenary of Iowa Territory.

Presidential Types of 1938

Coil Stamps

Rotary Press Printing

1939 *Perf. 10 Vertically*

839	A276	1c	green	.30	.20
840	A277	1½c	bister brown	.30	.20
841	A278	2c	rose carmine	.40	.20
842	A279	3c	deep violet	.50	.20
843	A280	4c	red violet	7.50	.40
844	A281	4½c	dark gray	.70	.40
845	A282	5c	bright blue	5.00	.35
846	A283	6c	red orange	1.10	.20
847	A287	10c	brown red	11.00	.50

Perf. 10 Horizontally

848	A276	1c	green	.85	.20
849	A277	1½c	bister brown	1.25	.30
850	A278	2c	rose carmine	2.50	.40
851	A279	3c	deep violet	2.25	.35
			Nos. 839-851 (13)	33.65	3.90

"Tower of the Sun" A311

Trylon and Perisphere A312

Golden Gate International Exposition Issue

Rotary Press Printing

1939, Feb. 18 ***Perf. 10½x11***

852 A311 3c bright purple .20 .20

Golden Gate Intl. Expo., San Francisco.

New York World's Fair Issue

1939, Apr. 1 ***Perf. 10½x11***

853 A312 3c deep purple .20 .20

Washington Inauguration Issue

George Washington Taking Oath of Office — A313

Flat Plate Printing

1939, Apr. 30 ***Perf. 11***

854 A313 3c bright red violet .40 .20

Sesquicentennial of George Washington's inauguration as 1st president.

Baseball Centennial Issue

Sand-lot Baseball Game A314

Rotary Press Printing

1939, June 12 ***Perf. 11x10½***

855 A314 3c violet 1.75 .20

Centennial of baseball.

Panama Canal Issue

Theodore Roosevelt, Gen. George W. Goethals and Gaillard Cut — A315

Flat Plate Printing

1939, Aug. 15 ***Perf. 11***

856 A315 3c deep red violet .25 .20

25th anniv. of the Panama Canal opening.

Printing Tercentenary Issue

Stephen Daye Press — A316

Rotary Press Printing

1939, Sept. 25 ***Perf. 10½x11***

857 A316 3c violet .20 .20

300th anniv. of printing in Colonial America.

50th Anniversary of Statehood Issue

Map of North and South Dakota, Montana and Washington A317

1939, Nov. 2 ***Perf. 11x10½***

858 A317 3c rose violet .20 .20

50th anniv. of admission to Statehood of North Dakota, South Dakota, Montana and Washington.

Famous Americans Issues

Authors

Washington Irving — A318

James Fenimore Cooper — A319

Ralph Waldo Emerson A320

Louisa May Alcott A321

Samuel L. Clemens (Mark Twain) — A322

1940 ***Perf. 10½x11***

859	A318	1c bright blue green	.20	.20
860	A319	2c rose carmine	.20	.20
861	A320	3c bright red violet	.20	.20
862	A321	5c ultra	.30	.20
863	A322	10c dark brown	1.65	1.20
		Nos. 859-863 (5)	2.55	2.00

Poets

Henry W. Longfellow A323

John Greenleaf Whittier A324

James Russell Lowell A325

Walt Whitman A326

James Whitcomb Riley — A327

1940 ***Perf. 10½x11***

864	A323	1c bright blue green	.20	.20
865	A324	2c rose carmine	.20	.20
866	A325	3c bright red violet	.20	.20
867	A326	5c ultra	.35	.20
868	A327	10c dark brown	1.75	1.25
		Nos. 864-868 (5)	2.70	2.05

Educators

Horace Mann A328

Mark Hopkins A329

Charles W. Eliot — A330

Frances E. Willard — A331

Booker T. Washington — A332

1940 ***Perf. 10½x11***

869	A328	1c bright blue green	.20	.20
870	A329	2c rose carmine	.20	.20
871	A330	3c bright red violet	.20	.20
872	A331	5c ultra	.40	.20
873	A332	10c dark brown	1.25	1.10
		Nos. 869-873 (5)	2.25	1.90

Scientists

John James Audubon A333

Dr. Crawford W. Long A334

Luther Burbank A335

Dr. Walter Reed A336

Jane Addams — A337

1940 ***Perf. 10½x11***

874	A333	1c bright blue green	.20	.20
875	A334	2c rose carmine	.20	.20
876	A335	3c bright red violet	.20	.20
877	A336	5c ultra	.25	.20
878	A337	10c dark brown	1.10	.85
		Nos. 874-878 (5)	1.95	1.65

Composers

Stephen Collins Foster — A338

John Philip Sousa — A339

Victor Herbert A340

Edward MacDowell A341

Ethelbert Nevin — A342

1940 ***Perf. 10½x11***

879	A338	1c bright blue green	.20	.20
880	A339	2c rose carmine	.20	.20
881	A340	3c bright red violet	.20	.20
882	A341	5c ultra	.40	.20
883	A342	10c dark brown	3.75	1.20
		Nos. 879-883 (5)	4.75	2.00

Artists

Gilbert Charles Stuart A343

James A. McNeill Whistler A344

Augustus Saint-Gaudens A345

Daniel Chester French A346

Frederic Remington — A347

1940 ***Perf. 10½x11***

884	A343	1c bright blue green	.20	.20
885	A344	2c rose carmine	.20	.20
886	A345	3c bright red violet	.20	.20
887	A346	5c ultra	.50	.20
888	A347	10c dark brown	1.75	1.25
		Nos. 884-888 (5)	2.85	2.05

Inventors

Eli Whitney — A348

Samuel F. B. Morse — A349

Cyrus Hall McCormick A350

Elias Howe A351

Alexander Graham Bell — A352

1940 ***Perf. 10½x11***

889 A348 1c brt blue green .20 .20
890 A349 2c rose carmine .20 .20
891 A350 3c bright red violet .25 .20
892 A351 5c ultra 1.10 .30
893 A352 10c dark brown 11.00 2.00
Nos. 889-893 (5) 12.75 2.90
Nos. 859-893 (35) 29.80 14.55

Pony Express Issue

Pony Express Rider A353

1940, Apr. 3 ***Perf. 11x10½***

894 A353 3c henna brown .25 .20

80th anniv. of the Pony Express.

Pan American Union Issue

The Three Graces from Botticelli's "Spring" — A354

1940, Apr. 14 ***Perf. 10½x11***

895 A354 3c light violet .20 .20

Pan American Union founding, 50th anniv.

Idaho Statehood Issue

Idaho Capitol, Boise A355

1940, July 3 ***Perf. 11x10½***

896 A355 3c bright violet .20 .20

Idaho statehood, 50th anniv.

Wyoming Statehood Issue

Wyoming State Seal — A356

1940, July 10 ***Perf. 10½x11***

897 A356 3c brown violet .20 .20

Wyoming statehood, 50th anniv.

Coronado Expedition Issue

"Coronado and His Captains," painted by Gerald Cassidy A357

1940, Sept. 7 ***Perf. 11x10½***

898 A357 3c violet .20 .20

400th anniv. of the Coronado Expedition.

National Defense Issue

Statue of Liberty — A358

90-millimeter Anti-aircraft Gun — A359

Torch of Enlightenment — A360

1940, Oct. 16 ***Perf. 11x10½***

899 A358 1c bright blue green .20 .20
a. Vert. pair, imperf. btwn. *650.00* —
b. Horiz. pair, imperf. btwn. 35.00 —
900 A359 2c rose carmine .20 .20
a. Horiz. pair, imperf. btwn. 40.00 —
901 A360 3c bright violet .20 .20
a. Horiz. pair, imperf. btwn. 27.50 —
Nos. 899-901 (3) .60 .60

Thirteenth Amendment Issue

"Emancipation," Statue of Lincoln and Slave, by Thomas Ball — A361

1940, Oct. 20 ***Perf. 10½x11***

902 A361 3c deep violet .20 .20

75th anniv. of the 13th Amendment to the Constitution.

Vermont Statehood Issue

Vermont Capitol, Montpelier A362

1941, Mar. 4 ***Perf. 11x10½***

903 A362 3c light violet .20 .20

Vermont statehood, 150th anniv.

Kentucky Statehood Issue

Daniel Boone and Three Frontiersmen, from mural by Gilbert White — A363

1942, June 1 ***Perf. 11x10½***

904 A363 3c violet .20 .20

Kentucky statehood, 150th anniv.

American Eagle — A364

Lincoln, Sun Yat-sen & Map A365

Win the War Issue

1942, July 4 ***Perf. 11x10½***

905 A364 3c violet .20 .20
b. 3c purple — —

Chinese Resistance Issue

1942, July 7 ***Perf. 11x10½***

906 A365 5c bright blue .85 .20

Five years' resistance of the Chinese people to Japanese aggression.

Allegory of Victory — A366

Allied Nations Issue

1943, Jan. 14 ***Perf. 11x10½***

907 A366 2c rose carmine .20 .20

Four Freedoms Issue

A367

1943, Feb. 12 ***Perf. 11x10½***

908 A367 1c Liberty Holding Torch of Freedom & Enlightenment .20 .20

Overrun Countries Issue

Flag of Poland A368

Frames Engraved, Centers Offset Letterpress

Rotary Press Printing

1943-44 **Unwmk.** ***Perf. 12***

909 A368 5c Poland .20 .20
910 A368 5c Czechoslovakia .20 .20
a. Double impression of "Czechoslovakia" —
911 A368 5c Norway .20 .20
a. Double impression of "Norway" —
912 A368 5c Luxembourg .20 .20
a. Double impression of "Luxembourg" —
913 A368 5c Netherlands .20 .20
914 A368 5c Belgium .20 .20
a. Double impression of "Belgium" —
915 A368 5c France .20 .20
916 A368 5c Greece .35 .25
917 A368 5c Yugoslavia .25 .20
a. Reverse printing of flag colors (blue and dark rose over black) —
918 A368 5c Albania .20 .20
a. Double impression of "Albania" —
919 A368 5c Austria .20 .20
a. Double impression of "Austria" —
920 A368 5c Denmark .20 .20
921 A368 5c Korea ('44) .20 .20
a. Double impression of "Korea" —
Nos. 909-921 (13) 2.80 2.65

Transcontinental Railroad Issue

"Golden Spike Ceremony" Painting by John McQuarrie A369

Engraved; Rotary Press Printing

1944, May 10 ***Perf. 11x10½***

922 A369 3c violet .20 .20

75th anniv. of the completion of the first transcontinental railroad.

Steamship Issue

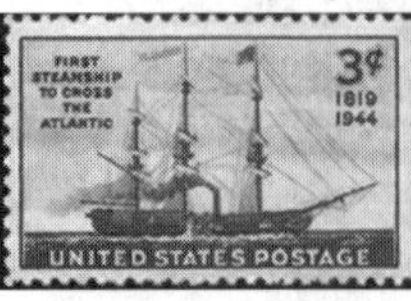

"Savannah" A370

1944, May 22 ***Perf. 11x10½***

923 A370 3c violet .20 .20

125th anniv. of the first steamship to cross the Atlantic Ocean.

Telegraph Issue

Telegraph Wires & the First Transmitted Words "What Hath God Wrought" A371

1944, May 24 ***Perf. 11x10½***

924 A371 3c bright red violet .20 .20

100th anniv. of the 1st message transmitted by telegraph.

Philippines Issue

View of Corregidor A372

1944, Sept. 27 ***Perf. 11x10½***

925 A372 3c deep violet .20 .20

Final resistance of the US and Philippine defenders on Corregidor.

Motion Pictures, 50th Anniv.

Motion Picture Showing for the Armed Forces in South Pacific A373

1944, Oct. 31 ***Perf. 11x10½***

926 A373 3c deep violet .20 .20

Florida Statehood Centenary

Old Florida Seal, St. Augustine Gates and State Capitol A374

1945, Mar. 3 ***Perf. 11x10½***

927 A374 3c bright red violet .20 .20

United Nations Conference Issue

A375

1945, Apr. 25 ***Perf. 11x10½***

928 A375 5c ultramarine .20 .20

United Nations conference, San Francisco.

Iwo Jima (Marines) Issue

Marines Raising the Flag on Mt. Suribachi, Iwo Jima — A376

1945, July 11 *Perf. 10½x11*
929 A376 3c yellow green .20 .20

Achievements of the US Marines in WWII.

Franklin D. Roosevelt Issue

Roosevelt and Hyde Park Home A377

Roosevelt and "Little White House," Warm Springs, Georgia A378

Roosevelt and White House A379

Roosevelt, Globe and Four Freedoms A380

1945-46 *Perf. 11x10½*
930 A377 1c blue green .20 .20
931 A378 2c carmine rose .20 .20
932 A379 3c purple .20 .20
933 A380 5c bright blue ('46) .20 .20
Nos. 930-933 (4) .80 .80

Franklin Delano Roosevelt (1882-1945).

Army Issue

US Troops Passing Arch of Triumph, Paris A381

1945, Sept. 28 *Perf. 11x10½*
934 A381 3c olive .20 .20

Achievements of the US Army in WWII.

Navy Issue

US Sailors A382

1945, Oct. 27 *Perf. 11x10½*
935 A382 3c blue .20 .20

Achievements of the US Navy in WWII.

Coast Guard Issue

Coast Guard Landing Craft and Supply Ship A383

1945, Nov. 10 *Perf. 11x10½*
936 A383 3c bright blue green .20 .20

Achievements of the US Coast Guard in WWII.

Alfred E. Smith — A384

US and Texas State Flags A385

Alfred E. Smith Issue

1945, Nov. 26 *Perf. 11x10½*
937 A384 3c purple .20 .20

Smith (1873-1944), governor of NY.

Texas Statehood Centenary

1945, Dec. 29 *Perf. 11x10½*
938 A385 3c dark blue .20 .20

Liberty Ship Unloading Cargo A386

Honorable Discharge Emblem — A387

Merchant Marine Issue

1946, Feb. 26 *Perf. 11x10½*
939 A386 3c blue green .20 .20

Achievements of the US Merchant Marine in WWII.

Veterans of World War II Issue

1946, May 9 *Perf. 11x10½*
940 A387 3c dark violet .20 .20

Issued to honor all veterans of WWII.

Tennessee Statehood, 150th Anniv.

Andrew Jackson, John Sevier & Tennessee Capitol A388

1946, June 1 *Perf. 11x10½*
941 A388 3c dark violet .20 .20

Iowa Statehood Centenary

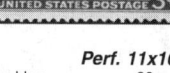

Iowa State Flag & Map A389

1946, Aug. 3 *Perf. 11x10½*
942 A389 3c deep blue .20 .20

Smithsonian Institution Issue

Smithsonian Institution — A390

1946, Aug. 10 *Perf. 11x10½*
943 A390 3c violet brown .20 .20

Centenary of the establishment of the Smithsonian Institution, Washington, DC.

Kearny Expedition Issue

"Capture of Santa Fe" by Kenneth M. Chapman A391

1946, Oct. 16 *Perf. 11x10½*
944 A391 3c brown violet .20 .20

Centenary of the entry of General Stephen Watts Kearny into Santa Fe.

Thomas Alva Edison Issue

Thomas A. Edison, Birth Centenary — A392

1947, Feb. 11 *Perf. 10½x11*
945 A392 3c bright red violet .20 .20

Joseph Pulitzer Birth Centenary

Joseph Pulitzer & Statue of Liberty A393

1947, Apr. 10 *Perf. 11x10½*
946 A393 3c purple .20 .20

U.S. Postage Stamp Centenary

Washington & Franklin; Early and Modern Mail-carrying Vehicles — A394

1947, May 17 *Perf. 11x10½*
947 A394 3c deep blue .20 .20

Centenary International Philatelic Exhibition (CIPEX)

A395

Flat Plate Printing

1947, May 19 *Imperf.*
948 A395 Souvenir sheet of 2 .55 .45
a. A1 5c blue .20 .20
b. A2 10c brown orange .25 .25

Sheet size varies: 96-98x66-68mm

Doctors Issue

"The Doctor," by Sir Luke Fildes A396

Rotary Press Printing

1947, June 9 *Perf. 11x10½*
949 A396 3c brown violet .20 .20

Issued to honor the physicians of America.

Utah Settlement Centenary

Pioneers Entering the Valley of Great Salt Lake A397

1947, July 24 *Perf. 11x10½*
950 A397 3c dark violet .20 .20

US Frigate Constitution Issue

Naval Architect's Drawing of Frigate Constitution A398

1947, Oct. 21 *Perf. 11x10½*
951 A398 3c blue green .20 .20

150th anniv. of the launching of the US Frigate Constitution ("Old Ironsides").

Everglades National Park Issue

Great White Heron and Map of Florida — A399

1947, Dec. 5 *Perf. 10½x11*
952 A399 3c bright green .20 .20

Dedication of Everglades Natl. Park, Florida, Dec. 6, 1947.

Dr. George Washington Carver Issue

Dr. George Washington Carver — A400

1948, Jan. 5 *Perf. 10½x11*
953 A400 3c bright red violet .20 .20

5th anniv. of the death of Dr. George Washington Carver, scientist.

California Gold Centennial Issue

Sutter's Mill, Coloma, California A401

1948, Jan. 24 *Perf. 11x10½*
954 A401 3c dark violet .20 .20

Discovery of gold in California, centenary.

Mississippi Territory, 150th Anniv.

Map, Seal and Gov. Winthrop Sargent A402

1948, Apr. 7 ***Perf. 11x10½***
955 A402 3c brown violet .20 .20

Four Chaplains Issue

Four Chaplains and Sinking S.S. Dorchester A403

1948, May 28 ***Perf. 11x10½***
956 A403 3c gray black .20 .20

George L. Fox, Clark V. Poling, John P. Washington and Alexander D. Goode, the four chaplains who sacrificed their lives in the sinking of the S.S. Dorchester, Feb. 3, 1943.

Wisconsin Statehood Centenary

Map on Scroll & State Capitol A404

1948, May 29 ***Perf. 11x10½***
957 A404 3c dark violet .20 .20

Swedish Pioneer Issue

Swedish Pioneer with Covered Wagon Moving Westward - A405

1948, June 4 ***Perf. 11x10½***
958 A405 5c deep blue .20 .20

Centenary of the coming of the Swedish pioneers to the Middle West.

Progress of Women Issue

Elizabeth Stanton, Carrie C. Catt & Lucretia Mott A406

1948, July 19 ***Perf. 11x10½***
959 A406 3c dark violet .20 .20

Century of progress of American women.

William Allen White Issue

William Allen White, Editor and Author — A407

1948, July 31 ***Perf. 10½x11***
960 A407 3c bright red violet .20 .20

U.S.-Canada Friendship Centenary

Niagara Railway Suspension Bridge A408

1948, Aug. 2 ***Perf. 11x10½***
961 A408 3c blue .20 .20

Francis Scott Key Issue

Key and American Flags of 1814 and 1948 A409

1948, Aug. 9 ***Perf. 11x10½***
962 A409 3c rose pink .20 .20

Key (1779-1843), Maryland lawyer and author of "The Star-Spangled Banner" (1813).

Salute to Youth Issue

Girl and Boy Carrying Books A410

1948, Aug. 11 ***Perf. 11x10½***
963 A410 3c deep blue .20 .20

Youth of America and "Youth Month," Sept. 1948.

Oregon Territory Issue

John McLoughlin, Jason Lee & Wagon on Oregon Trail — A411

1948, Aug. 14 ***Perf. 11x10½***
964 A411 3c brown red .20 .20

Centenary of the establishment of Ore. Terr.

Harlan Fiske Stone Issue

Chief Justice Harlan Fiske Stone — A412

1948, Aug. 25 ***Perf. 10½x11***
965 A412 3c bright red violet .20 .20

Palomar Mountain Observatory Issue

Observatory, Palomar Mt., Cal. — A413

1948, Aug. 30 ***Perf. 10½x11***
966 A413 3c blue .20 .20
a. Vert. pair, imperf btwn. *525.00*

Clara Barton, 1821-1912

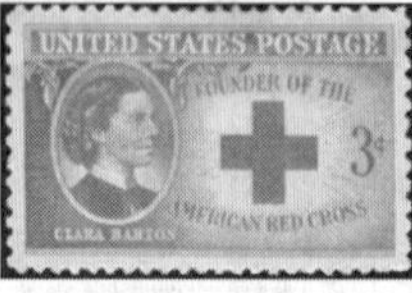

Founder of the American Red Cross (1882) A414

1948, Sept. 7 ***Perf. 11x10½***
967 A414 3c rose pink .20 .20

Poultry Industry Issue

Light Brahma Rooster A415

1948, Sept. 9 ***Perf. 11x10½***
968 A415 3c sepia .20 .20

Centenary of the establishment of the American poultry industry.

Gold Star Mothers Issue

Star and Palm Frond — A416

1948, Sept. 21 ***Perf. 10½x11***
969 A416 3c orange yellow .20 .20

Honoring mothers of deceased members of the U.S. armed forces.

Fort Kearny Issue

Fort Kearny and Pioneer Group A417

1948, Sept. 22 ***Perf. 11x10½***
970 A417 3c violet .20 .20

Establishment of Fort Kearny, Nebr., cent.

Volunteer Firemen Issue

Peter Stuyvesant; Early and Modern Fire Engines A418

1948, Oct. 4 ***Perf. 11x10½***
971 A418 3c bright rose carmine .20 .20

300th anniv. of the organization of the 1st volunteer firemen in America by Peter Stuyvesant (1592-1672), Dutch colonial gov. of New Netherland.

Indian Centennial Issue

Map of Indian Territory & Seals of Five Tribes A419

1948, Oct. 15 ***Perf. 11x10½***
972 A419 3c dark brown .20 .20

Cent. of the arrival in Indian Territory, later Okla., of the Five Civilized Indian Tribes.

Rough Riders Issue

Statue of Capt. William O. (Bucky) O'Neill A420

1948, Oct. 27 ***Perf. 11x10½***
973 A420 3c violet brown .20 .20

50th anniv. of the organization of the Rough Riders of the Spanish-American War.

Low and Girl Scout Emblem A421

Will Rogers — A422

Juliette Low Issue

1948, Oct. 29 ***Perf. 11x10½***
974 A421 3c blue green .20 .20

Juliette Gordon Low (1860-1927), organizer of the Girl Scouts of America.

Will Rogers Issue

1948, Nov. 4 ***Perf. 10½x11***
975 A422 3c bright red violet .20 .20

Will Rogers, 1879-1935, humorist and political commentator.

Fort Bliss and Rocket — A423

Moina Michael and Poppy Plant A424

Fort Bliss Centennial Issue

1948, Nov. 5 ***Perf. 10½x11***
976 A423 3c henna brown .20 .20

Centenary of Fort Bliss, Texas.

Moina Michael Issue

1948, Nov. 9 ***Perf. 11x10½***
977 A424 3c rose pink .20 .20

Michael (1870-1944), educator who originated (1918) Flanders Field Poppy Day idea as memorial to war dead.

Gettysburg Address Issue

Lincoln and Quotation from Gettysburg Address A425

1948, Nov. 19 ***Perf. 11x10½***
978 A425 3c bright blue .20 .20

85th anniv. of Abraham Lincoln's address at Gettysburg, Pa.

Torch and American Turners' Emblem A426

Joel Chandler Harris A427

American Turners Issue

1948, Nov. 20 ***Perf. 10½x11***
979 A426 3c carmine .20 .20

Centenary of the formation of the American Turners Society.

Joel Chandler Harris Issue

1948, Dec. 9 ***Perf. 10½x11***
980 A427 3c bright red violet .20 .20

Harris (1848-1908), editor and author.

Minnesota Territory Issue

Pioneer and Red River Oxcart A428

1949, Mar. 3 ***Perf. 11x10½***
981 A428 3c blue green .20 .20

Cent. of the establishment of Minn. Terr.

Washington and Lee University Issue

George Washington, Robert E. Lee and University Building — A429

1949, Apr. 12 ***Perf. 11x10½***
982 A429 3c ultramarine .20 .20

200th anniv. of the founding of Washington and Lee Univ.

Puerto Rico Election Issue

Puerto Rican Farmer Holding Cogwheel and Ballot Box A430

1949, Apr. 27 ***Perf. 11x10½***
983 A430 3c green .20 .20

1st gubernatorial election in the Territory of P.R., Nov. 2, 1948.

Annapolis Tercentenary Issue

Stoddert's 1718 Map of Regions about Annapolis, Redrawn A431

1949, May 23 ***Perf. 11x10½***
984 A431 3c aquamarine .20 .20

Founding of Annapolis, Md., 300th anniv

Union Soldier and GAR Veteran of 1949 A432

Edgar Allan Poe — A433

GAR Issue

1949, Aug. 29 ***Perf. 11x10½***
985 A432 3c bright rose carmine .20 .20

Final encampment of the Grand Army of the Republic, Indianapolis, Aug. 28 to Sept. 1.

Edgar Allan Poe Issue

1949, Oct. 7 ***Perf. 10½x11***
986 A433 3c bright red violet .20 .20

Poe (1809-1849), writer and poet.

Coin, Symbolizing Fields of Banking Service — A434

Samuel Gompers — A435

Bankers Issue

1950, Jan. 3 ***Perf. 11x10½***
987 A434 3c yellow green .20 .20

75th anniv. of the formation of the American Bankers Assoc.

Samuel Gompers Issue

1950, Jan. 27 ***Perf. 10½x11***
988 A435 3c bright red violet .20 .20

Gompers (1850-1924), labor leader.

National Capital Sesquicentennial Issue

Statue of Freedom on Capitol Dome — A436

Executive Mansion A437

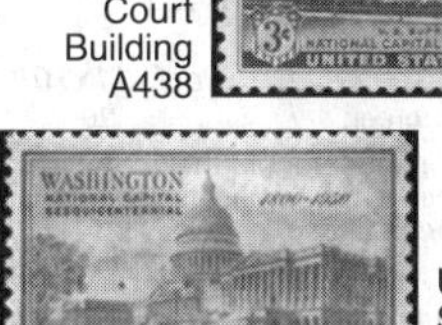

Supreme Court Building A438

United States Capitol A439

1950 ***Perf. 10½x11, 11x10½***
989 A436 3c bright blue .20 .20
990 A437 3c deep green .20 .20
991 A438 3c light violet .20 .20
992 A439 3c bright red violet .20 .20
Nos. 989-992 (4) .80 .80

150th anniv. of the establishment of the National Capital, Washington, DC.
Issued: Apr. 20; June 12; Aug. 2; Nov. 22.

Railroad Engineers Issue

"Casey" Jones and Locomotives of 1900 and 1950 — A440

1950, Apr. 29 ***Perf. 11x10½***
993 A440 3c violet brown .20 .20

Kansas City, Missouri, Issue

Kansas City Skyline, 1950 and Westport Landing, 1850 A441

1950, June 3 ***Perf. 11x10½***
994 A441 3c violet .20 .20

Incorporation of Kansas City, Mo., cent.

Boy Scouts Issue

Three Boys, Statue of Liberty and Scout Badge A442

1950, June 30 ***Perf. 11x10½***
995 A442 3c sepia .20 .20

Honoring the BSA on the occasion of the 2nd Natl. Jamboree, held at Valley Forge, Pa.

Indiana Territory Issue

Gov. William Henry Harrison & First Indiana Capitol, Vincennes A443

1950, July 4 ***Perf. 11x10½***
996 A443 3c bright blue .20 .20

150th anniv. establishment of Ind. Terr.

California Statehood Centenary

Gold Miner, Pioneers and S.S. Oregon A444

1950, Sept. 9 ***Perf. 11x10½***
997 A444 3c yellow orange .20 .20

United Confederate Veterans Final Reunion Issue

Confederate Soldier & United Confederate Veteran A445

1951, May 30 ***Perf. 11x10½***
998 A445 3c gray .20 .20

Final reunion of the United Confederate Veterans, Norfolk, Va, May 30, 1951.

Nevada Settlement Centennial

Carson Valley, c. 1851 A446

1951, July 14 ***Perf. 11x10½***
999 A446 3c light olive green .20 .20

Landing of Cadillac Issue

Detroit Skyline and Cadillac Landing A447

1951, July 24 ***Perf. 11x10½***
1000 A447 3c blue .20 .20

250th anniv. of the landing of Antoine de la Mothe Cadillac at Detroit.

Colorado Statehood Issue

Colorado Capitol and Mount of the Holy Cross A448

1951, Aug. 1 ***Perf. 11x10½***
1001 A448 3c blue violet .20 .20

Colorado statehood, 75th anniv. Design includes columbine and statue, "The Bronco Buster," by A. Phimister Proctor.

American Chemical Society Issue

A.C.S. Emblem and Symbols of Chemistry A449

1951, Sept. 4 ***Perf. 11x10½***
1002 A449 3c violet brown .20 .20

American Chemical Soc., 75th anniv.

Battle of Brooklyn Issue

Gen. George Washington Evacuating Army A450

1951, Dec. 10 ***Perf. 11x10½***
1003 A450 3c violet .20 .20

175th anniv. of the Battle of Brooklyn. Design includes Fulton Ferry House.

Betsy Ross Issue

Betsy Ross Showing Flag to Gen. George Washington, Robert Morris & George Ross — A451

1952, Jan. 2 ***Perf. 11x10½***
1004 A451 3c carmine rose .20 .20

200th anniv. of the birth of Betsy Ross, maker of the 1st American flag.

4-H Club Issue

Farm, Club Emblem, Boy and Girl A452

1952, Jan. 15 ***Perf. 11x10½***
1005 A452 3c blue green .20 .20

B. & O. Railroad Issue

Charter and Three Stages of Rail Transportation — A453

1952, Feb. 28 ***Perf. 11x10½***
1006 A453 3c bright blue .20 .20

125th anniv. of the granting of a charter to the Baltimore and Ohio Railroad Company by the Maryland Legislature.

A. A. A., 50th Anniv.

School Girls and Safety Patrolman, Automobiles of 1902 and 1952 — A454

1952, Mar. 4 ***Perf. 11x10½***
1007 A454 3c deep blue .20 .20

Torch of Liberty and Globe — A455

Spillway, Grand Coulee Dam A456

NATO Issue

1952, Apr. 4 ***Perf. 11x10½***
1008 A455 3c deep violet .20 .20

3rd anniv. of the signing of the North Atlantic Treaty.

Grand Coulee Dam Issue

1952, May 15 ***Perf. 11x10½***
1009 A456 3c blue green .20 .20

50 years of federal cooperation in developing the resources of rivers and streams in the West.

Lafayette Issue

Marquis de Lafayette, Flags, Cannon and Landing Party A457

1952, June 13 ***Perf. 11x10½***
1010 A457 3c bright blue .20 .20

Arrival of Lafayette in America, 175th anniv.

Mt. Rushmore Memorial Issue

Sculptured Heads on Mt. Rushmore — A458

1952, Aug. 11 ***Perf. 10½x11***
1011 A458 3c blue green .20 .20

25th anniv. of the dedication of the Mt. Rushmore Natl. Memorial.

Engineering Centennial Issue

George Washington Bridge & Covered Bridge of 1850s — A459

1952, Sept. 6 ***Perf. 11x10½***
1012 A459 3c violet blue .20 .20

Centenary of the founding of the American Soc. of Civil Engineers.

Service Women Issue

Women of the Marine Corps, Army, Navy and Air Force A460

1952, Sept. 11 ***Perf. 11x10½***
1013 A460 3c deep blue .20 .20

Honoring the women in the US Armed Services.

Gutenberg Bible Issue

Gutenberg Showing Proof to the Elector of Mainz A461

1952, Sept. 30 ***Perf. 11x10½***
1014 A461 3c violet .20 .20

500th anniv. of the printing of the 1st book, the Holy Bible, from movable type, by Johann Gutenberg.

Newspaper Boys Issue

Newspaper Boy, Torch and Group of Homes A462

1952, Oct. 4 ***Perf. 11x10½***
1015 A462 3c violet .20 .20

Red Cross Issue

Globe, Sun and Cross A463

Perf. 11x10½
1952, Nov. 21 **Cross Typo.**
1016 A463 3c deep blue & car .20 .20

National Guard Issue

National Guardsman and Amphibious Landing A464

1953, Feb. 23 ***Perf. 11x10½***
1017 A464 3c bright blue .20 .20

Ohio Statehood Sesquicentennial

Map and Ohio State Seal — A465

1953, Mar. 2 ***Perf. 11x10½***
1018 A465 3c chocolate .20 .20

Washington Territory Issue

Medallion, Pioneers and Washington Scene A466

1953, Mar. 2 ***Perf. 11x10½***
1019 A466 3c green .20 .20

Centenary of the organization of Washington Territory.

Louisiana Purchase, 150th Anniv.

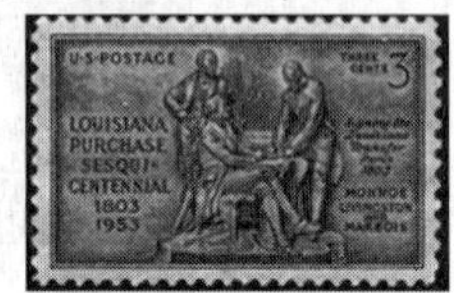

Monroe, Livingston and Barbé-Marbois — A467

1953, Apr. 30 ***Perf. 11x10½***
1020 A467 3c violet brown .20 .20

Opening of Japan Centennial Issue

Commodore Perry and 1st Anchorage off Tokyo Bay — A468

1953, July 14 ***Perf. 11x10½***
1021 A468 5c green .20 .20

Cent. of Commodore Matthew Calbraith Perry's negotiations with Japan, which opened her doors to foreign trade.

American Bar Association, 75th Anniv.

Section of Frieze, Supreme Court Room A469

1953, Aug. 24 ***Perf. 11x10½***
1022 A469 3c rose violet .20 .20

Sagamore Hill Issue

Home of Theodore Roosevelt A470

1953, Sept. 14 ***Perf. 11x10½***
1023 A470 3c yellow green .20 .20

Opening of Sagamore Hill, Theodore Roosevelt's home, as a national shrine.

Future Farmers Issue

Agricultural Scene and Future Farmer A471

1953, Oct. 13 ***Perf. 11x10½***
1024 A471 3c deep blue .20 .20

25th anniv. of the organization of Future Farmers of America.

Trucking Industry Issue

Truck, Farm and Distant City A472

1953, Oct. 27 ***Perf. 11x10½***
1025 A472 3c violet .20 .20

Trucking Industry in the US, 50th anniv.

General Patton Issue

Gen. George S. Patton, Jr., and Tank in Action A473

1953, Nov. 11 ***Perf. 11x10½***
1026 A473 3c blue violet .20 .20

Honoring Patton and the armored forces of the US army.

New York City, 300th Anniv.

Dutch Ship in New Amsterdam Harbor A474

1953, Nov. 20 ***Perf. 11x10½***
1027 A474 3c bright red violet .20 .20

Gadsden Purchase Issue

Map and Pioneer Group A475

1953, Dec. 30 ***Perf. 11x10½***
1028 A475 3c copper brown .20 .20

Centenary of James Gadsden's purchase of territory from Mexico, to adjust US-Mexico boundary.

Columbia University, 200th Anniv.

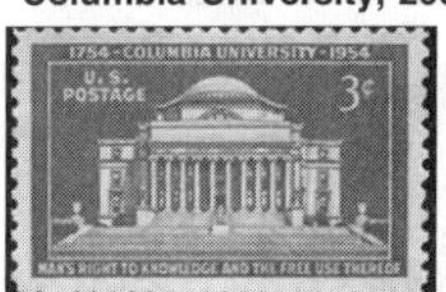

Low Memorial Library A476

1954, Jan. 4 ***Perf. 11x10½***
1029 A476 3c blue .20 .20

Wet and Dry Printings

In 1953 the Bureau of Engraving and Printing began experiments in printing on "dry" paper (moisture content 5-10 per cent). In previous "wet" printings the paper had a moisture content of 13-35 per cent.

The new process required a thicker, stiffer paper, special types of inks and greater pressure to force the paper into the recessed plates. The "dry" printings show whiter paper, a higher sheen on the surface, feel thicker and stiffer, and the designs stand out more clearly than on the "wet" printings.

Nos. 832c and 1041 (flat plate) were the first "dry" printings to be issued of flat-plate, regular-issue stamps. No. 1063 was the first rotary-press stamp to be produced entirely by "dry" printing.

All postage stamps have been printed by the "dry" process since the late 1950's.

See the Scott Specialized Catalogue of United States Stamps for listings of the wet and dry printings and for No. 1033 on Silkote paper.

Liberty Issue

Franklin A477

Washington A478

Palace of the Governors, Santa Fe — A478a

Mount Vernon — A479

Thomas Jefferson A480

Bunker Hill Monument, Mass. Flag, 1776 A481

Statue of Liberty A482

Abraham Lincoln A483

The Hermitage A484

James Monroe A485

Theodore Roosevelt A486

Woodrow Wilson A487

Statue of Liberty A488 A489

John J. Pershing A489a

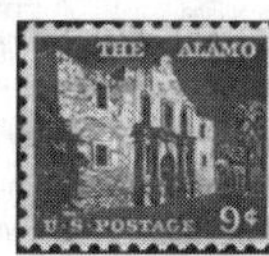

The Alamo A490

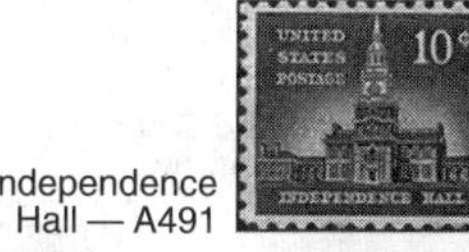

Independence Hall — A491

Statue of Liberty A491a

Benjamin Harrison A492

John Jay A493

Monticello A494

Paul Revere A495

Robert E. Lee A496

John Marshall A497

Susan B. Anthony A498

Patrick Henry A499

Alexander Hamilton A500

Perf. 11x10½, 10½x11

1954-68 **Rotary Press Printing**

1030 A477 ½c red org ('55) .20 .20
1031 A478 1c dark grn .20 .20
1031A A478a 1¼c turq ('60) .20 .20
1032 A479 1½c brn car ('56) .20 .20
1033 A480 2c car rose .20 .20
1034 A481 2½c gray bl ('59) .20 .20
1035 A482 3c deep vio .20 .20
a. Booklet pane of 6 4.00 *1.25*
b. Tagged ('66) .30 .25
c. Imperf., pair *2,000.*
d. Horiz. pair, imperf btwn. —
g. As "a," vert. imperf btwn. *5,000.*

No. 1057a measures about 19½x22mm; No. 1035c, about 18¾x22½mm.

1036 A483 4c red violet .20 .20
a. Booklet pane of 6 ('58) 2.75 *1.25*
b. Tagged ('63) .60 .40
d. As "a," imperf. horiz. —
1037 A484 4½c bl grn ('59) .20 .20
1038 A485 5c deep blue .20 .20
1039 A486 6c car ('55) .25 .20
b. Imperf., pair *11,000.*
1040 A487 7c rose car ('56) .20 .20
a. 7c dark rose carmine .20 .20

Flat Plate Printing

Perf. 11

Size: 22.7mm high

1041 A488 8c dk vio blue & car .25 .20
a. Double impression of carmine *650.00*

Rotary Press Printing

Size: 22.9mm high

1041B A488 8c dk vio blue & car .40 .20

Giori Press Printing

Redrawn Design

1042 A489 8c dk vio bl & car rose ('58) .20 .20

Rotary Press Printing

Perf. 11x10½, 10½x11

1042A A489a 8c brown ('61) .20 .20
1043 A490 9c rose lil ('56) .30 .20
a. 9c dark rose lilac .30 .20
1044 A491 10c rose lake ('56) .30 .20
b. 10c dark rose lake .25 .20
d. Tagged ('66) 2.00 1.00

Giori Press Printing

Perf. 11

1044A A491a 11c car & dk vio blue ('61) .30 .20
c. Tagged ('67) 2.00 1.60

Rotary Press Printing

Perf. 11x10½, 10½x11

1045 A492 12c red ('59) .35 .20
a. Tagged ('68) .35 .20
1046 A493 15c rose lake ('58) .60 .20
a. Tagged ('66) 1.10 .50
1047 A494 20c ultra ('56) .40 .20
a. 20c deep bright ultra .40 .20
1048 A495 25c green ('58) 1.10 .20
1049 A496 30c black ('55) .70 .20
b. 30c intense black .70 .20
1050 A497 40c brn red ('55) 1.50 .20
1051 A498 50c brt pur ('55) 1.50 .20
1052 A499 $1 purple ('55) 4.50 .20

Flat Plate Printing

Perf. 11

1053 A500 $5 black ('56) 60.00 6.75
Nos. 1030-1053 (28) 75.05 12.15

Luminescence

During 1963 quantities of certain issues (Nos. C64a, 1213b, 1213c and 1229a) were overprinted with phosphorescent coating, "tagged," for use in testing automated facing and canceling machines. Listings for tagged varieties of stamps previously issued without tagging start with Nos. 1035b and C59a.

The entire printings of Nos. 1238, 1278, 1280-1281, 1283B, 1286-1288, 1298-1305, 1323-1340, 1342-1362, 1364, and C69-C75 and all following listings, unless otherwise noted, were tagged.

Stamps tagged with zinc orthosilicate glow yellow green. Airmail stamps with calcium silicate overprint glow orange red. Both tagging overprints are activated only by shortwave ultraviolet light.

Coil Stamps

Perf. 10 Vert., Horiz. (1¼c, 4½c)

1954-73

1054 A478 1c dark grn .20 .20
b. Imperf., pair *2,500.* —
1054A A478a 1¼c turq ('60) .20 .20
1055 A480 2c rose car .35 .20
a. Tagged ('68) .20 .20
b. Imperf., pair (Bureau precanceled) *550.00*
c. As "a," imperf. pair *600.00*
1056 A481 2½c gray blue ('59) .25 .25
1057 A482 3c dp violet .35 .20
a. Imperf., pair *1,750.* —
b. Tagged ('66) 1.00 .50

No. 1057a measures about 19½x22mm; No. 1035c, about 18¾x22½mm.

1058 A483 4c red vio ('58) .20 .20
a. Imperf., pair 120.00 120.00
1059 A484 4½c blue grn ('59) 1.50 1.20
1059A A495 25c grn ('65) .50 .30
b. Tagged ('73) .80 .20
c. Imperf., pair 55.00
Nos. 1054-1059A (8) 3.55 2.75

Value for No. 1059Ac is for fine centering.

Nebraska Territory Issue

Mitchell Pass, Scotts Bluff & "The Sower," by Lee Lawrie A507

1954, May 7 ***Perf. 11x10½***
1060 A507 3c violet .20 .20

Establishment of the Nebraska Terr., cent.

Kansas Territory Issue

Wheat Field and Pioneer Wagon Train A508

1954, May 31 ***Perf. 11x10½***
1061 A508 3c brown orange .20 .20

Establishment of the Kansas Terr., cent.

George Eastman Issue

George Eastman (1854-1932), Inventor & Philanthropist — A509

1954, July 12 ***Perf. 10½x11***
1062 A509 3c violet brown .20 .20

Lewis and Clark Expedition Sesquicentennial

Landing of Lewis and Clark A510

1954, July 28 ***Perf. 11x10½***
1063 A510 3c violet brown .20 .20

Pennsylvania Academy of the Fine Arts

Charles Willson Peale in his Museum, Self-portrait — A511

1955, Jan. 15 ***Perf. 10½x11***
1064 A511 3c violet brown .20 .20

150th anniv. of the founding of the Pa. Acad. of the Fine Arts, Philadelphia.

Land Grant Colleges Issue

Open Book and Symbols of Subjects Taught A512

1955, Feb. 12 ***Perf. 11x10½***
1065 A512 3c green .20 .20

Cent. of the founding of Mich. State College and Penn. State Univ., 1st of the land-grant institutions.

Rotary International, 50th Anniv.

Torch, Globe and Rotary Emblem A513

1955, Feb. 23 ***Perf. 11x10½***
1066 A513 8c deep blue .20 .20

Armed Forces Reserve Issue

Marine, Coast Guard, Army, Navy, & Air Force Personnel A514

1955, May 21 ***Perf. 11x10½***
1067 A514 3c purple .20 .20

New Hampshire Issue

Great Stone Face — A515

1955, June 21 ***Perf. 10½x11***
1068 A515 3c green .20 .20

Honor NH on the occasion of the sesquicentennial of the discovery of the "Old Man of the Mountains."

Soo Locks Opening, Centenary

Map of Great Lakes and Two Steamers A516

1955, June 28 ***Perf. 11x10½***
1069 A516 3c blue .20 .20

Atoms for Peace Policy

Atomic Energy Encircling the Hemispheres — A517

1955, July 28 ***Perf. 11x10½***
1070 A517 3c deep blue .20 .20

Fort Ticonderoga Bicentenary

Map of the Fort, Ethan Allen and Artillery A518

1955, Sept. 18 ***Perf. 11x10½***
1071 A518 3c light brown .20 .20

Andrew W. Mellon Issue

Andrew W. Mellon — A519

1955, Dec. 20 ***Perf. 10½x11***
1072 A519 3c rose carmine .20 .20

Mellon, U.S. Sec. of the Treasury (1921-32), financier and art collector.

Benjamin Franklin Issue

"Franklin Taking Electricity from the Sky," by Benjamin West — A520

1956, Jan. 17 ***Perf. 10½x11***
1073 A520 3c bright carmine .20 .20

250th anniv. of the birth of Franklin.

Booker T. Washington Issue

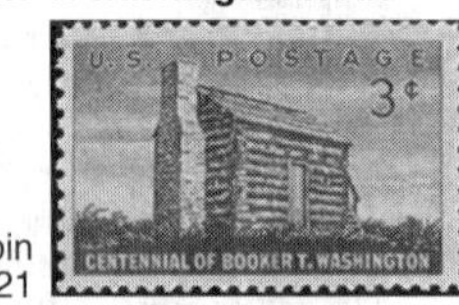

Log Cabin A521

1956, Apr. 5 ***Perf. 11x10½***
1074 A521 3c deep blue .20 .20

Washington (1856-1915), black educator.

5th International Philatelic Exhibition Issue

A522

Flat Plate Printing

1956, Apr. 28 ***Imperf.***
1075 A522 Souvenir sheet of 2 2.00 2.00
a. A482 3c deep violet .80 .80
b. A488 8c dk vio bl & carmine 1.00 1.00

No. 1075 measures 108x73mm; Nos. 1075a and 1075b measure 24x28mm.

New York Coliseum & Columbus Monument A523

Rotary Press Printing

1956, Apr. 30 ***Perf. 11x10½***
1076 A523 3c deep violet .20 .20

FIPEX, New York City, Apr. 28-May 6.

Wildlife Conservation Issue

Wild Turkey A524

Pronghorn Antelope A525

King Salmon A526

1956 ***Perf. 11x10½***
1077 A524 3c rose lake .20 .20
1078 A525 3c brown .20 .20
1079 A526 3c blue green .20 .20
Nos. 1077-1079 (3) .60 .60

Emphasizing the importance of Wildlife conservation in America.
Issued: May 5, June 22, Nov. 9.
See Nos. 1098, 1392.

Pure Food and Drug Laws, 50th Anniv.

Harvey W. Wiley — A527

1956, June 27 ***Perf. 10½x11***
1080 A527 3c dark blue green .20 .20

Wheatland Issue

President Buchanan's Home, "Wheatland," Lancaster, PA — A528

1956, Aug. 5 ***Perf. 11x10½***
1081 A528 3c black brown .20 .20

Labor Day Issue

Mosaic, AFL-CIO Headquarters A529

1956, Sept. 3 ***Perf. 10½x11***
1082 A529 3c deep blue .20 .20

Nassau Hall Issue

Nassau Hall, Princeton, NJ — A530

1956, Sept. 22 ***Perf. 11x10½***
1083 A530 3c black, *orange* .20 .20

200th anniv. of Nassau Hall, Princeton University.

Devils Tower Issue

Devils Tower — A531

1956, Sept. 24 ***Perf. 10½x11***
1084 A531 3c violet .20 .20

50th anniv. of the Federal law providing for protection of American natural antiquities.
Devils Tower Natl. Monument, Wyoming, is an outstanding example.

Children's Issue

Children of the World A532

1956, Dec. 15 ***Perf. 11x10½***
1085 A532 3c dark blue .20 .20

Promoting friendship among the world's children.

Alexander Hamilton Issue

Alexander Hamilton (1757-1804) and Federal Hall A533

1957, Jan. 11 ***Perf. 11x10½***
1086 A533 3c rose red .20 .20

Polio Issue

Allegory — A534

1957, Jan. 15 ***Perf. 10½x11***
1087 A534 3c red lilac .20 .20

Honoring "those who helped fight polio," and 20th anniv. of the Natl. Foundation for Infantile Paralysis and the March of Dimes.

Coast and Geodetic Survey Issue

Flag of Coast and Geodetic Survey and Ships at Sea A535

1957, Feb. 11 ***Perf. 11x10½***
1088 A535 3c dark blue .20 .20

150th anniv. of the establishment of the Coast and Geodetic Survey.

Architects Issue

Corinthian Capital and Mushroom Type Head & Shaft A536

1957, Feb. 23 ***Perf. 11x10½***
1089 A536 3c red lilac .20 .20

Centenary of the American Institute of Architects.

Steel Industry Centenary

American Eagle and Pouring Ladle — A537

1957, May 22 ***Perf. 10½x11***
1090 A537 3c bright ultra .20 .20

International Naval Review Issue

Aircraft Carrier and Jamestown Festival Emblem A538

1957, June 10 ***Perf. 11x10½***
1091 A538 3c blue green .20 .20

Intl. Naval Review and Jamestown Festival.

Oklahoma Statehood, 50th Anniv.

Map of Oklahoma, Arrow and Atom Diagram A539

1957, June 14 ***Perf. 11x10½***
1092 A539 3c dark blue .20 .20

School Teachers Issue

Teacher and Pupils A540

1957, July 1 ***Perf. 11x10½***
1093 A540 3c rose lake .20 .20

Honoring the school teachers of America.

Flag Issue

"Old Glory" (48 Stars) A541

Giori Press Printing

1957, July 4 ***Perf. 11***
1094 A541 4c dk blue & dp car .20 .20

Shipbuilding Issue

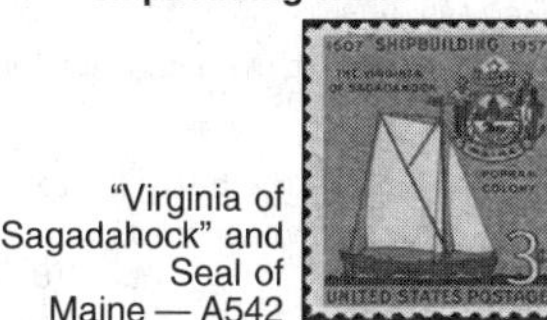

"Virginia of Sagadahock" and Seal of Maine — A542

Rotary Press Printing

1957, Aug. 15 ***Perf. 10½x11***
1095 A542 3c deep violet .20 .20

350th anniv. of shipbuilding in America.

Champion of Liberty Issue

Ramon Magsaysay, (1907-1957), Philippines President — A543

Giori Press Printing

1957, Aug. 31 ***Perf. 11***
1096 A543 8c car, ultra & ocher .20 .20

For other Champion of Liberty issues, see Nos. 1110-1111, 1117-1118, 1125-1126, 1136-1137, 1147-1148, 1159-1160, 1165-1166, 1168-1169, 1174-1175.

Marquis de Lafayette A544

Whooping Cranes A545

Lafayette Bicentenary Issue

Rotary Press Printing

1957, Sept. 6 ***Perf. 10½x11***
1097 A544 3c rose lake .20 .20

Bicentenary of the birth of Lafayette.

Wildlife Conservation Issue

Giori Press Printing

1957, Nov. 22 ***Perf. 11***
1098 A545 3c blue, ocher & grn .20 .20

Emphasizing the importance of Wildlife Conservation in America.

Bible, Hat and Quill Pen — A546

"Bountiful Earth" — A547

Religious Freedom Issue

Rotary Press Printing

1957, Dec. 27 ***Perf. 10½x11***
1099 A546 3c black .20 .20

Flushing Remonstrance, 300th anniv.

Gardening-Horticulture Issue

1958, Mar. 15
1100 A547 3c green .20 .20

Garden clubs of America and cent. of the birth of Liberty Hyde Bailey, horticulturist.

Brussels Fair Issue

US Pavilion at Brussels A551

Rotary Press Printing

1958, Apr. 17 ***Perf. 11x10½***
1104 A551 3c deep claret .20 .20

Opening of the Universal and Intl. Exhib., Brussels, Apr. 17.

James Monroe Issue

James Monroe, by Gilbert Stuart — A552

1958, Apr. 28 ***Perf. 11x10½***
1105 A552 3c purple .20 .20

Monroe (1758-1831), 5th pres. of the US.

Minnesota Statehood Centenary

Minnesota Lakes and Pines A553

Rotary Press Printing

1958, May 11
1106 A553 3c green .20 .20

Geophysical Year (IGY, 1957-58)

Solar Disc and Hands from Michelangelo's "Creation of Adam" — A554

Giori Press Printing

1958, May 31 ***Perf. 11***
1107 A554 3c black & red orange .20 .20

Gunston Hall Issue

Gunston Hall, Virginia A555

Rotary Press Printing

1958, June 12 ***Perf. 11x10½***
1108 A555 3c light green .20 .20

Bicent. of Gunston Hall and honoring George Mason, author of the Constitution of Va. and the Va. Bill of Rights.

Mackinac Bridge — A556

Simon Bolivar — A557

Mackinac Bridge Issue

1958, June 25 ***Perf. 10½x11***
1109 A556 3c bright greenish bl .20 .20

Dedication of Mackinac Bridge, Mich.

Champion of Liberty Issue

Rotary Press Printing

1958, July 24 ***Perf. 10½x11***
1110 A557 4c olive bister .20 .20

Giori Press Printing

Perf. 11

1111 A557 8c car, ultra & ocher .20 .20

Simon Bolivar, So. American freedom fighter.

Atlantic Cable Centennial Issue

Neptune, Globe and Mermaid A558

Rotary Press Printing

1958, Aug. 15 ***Perf. 11x10½***
1112 A558 4c reddish purple .20 .20

Centenary of the Atlantic Cable, linking the Eastern and Western hemispheres.

Lincoln Sesquicentennial Issue

Lincoln, by George Healy A559

Lincoln, by Gutzon Borglum A560

Abraham Lincoln and Stephen A. Douglas Debating A561

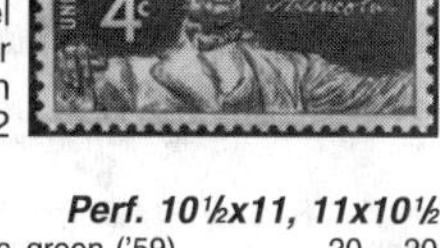

Lincoln, by Daniel Chester French A562

1958-59 ***Perf. 10½x11, 11x10½***

1113 A559 1c green ('59) .20 .20
1114 A560 3c purple ('59) .20 .20
1115 A561 4c sepia .20 .20
1116 A562 4c dark blue ('59) .20 .20
Nos. 1113-1116 (4) .80 .80

No. 1114 also for the founding of Cooper Union cent., NYC. No. 1115 also for the Lincoln-Douglas debates, cent.

Issue dates: Nos. 1113, 1114, 1116, Feb. 12, Feb. 27 and May 30. No. 1115, Aug. 27.

Lajos Kossuth, (1802-1892) A563

Early Press and Hand Holding Quill A564

Champion of Liberty Issue

Rotary Press Printing

1958, Sept. 19 ***Perf. 10½x11***
1117 A563 4c green .20 .20

Giori Press Printing

Perf. 11

1118 A563 8c car, ultra & ocher .20 .20

Kossuth, Hungarian freedom fighter.

Freedom of Press Issue

Rotary Press Printing

1958, Sept. 22 ***Perf. 10½x11***
1119 A564 4c black .20 .20

Honoring journalism and freedom of the press in connection with the 50th anniv. of the 1st School of Journalism at the Univ. of Mo.

Overland Mail Centenary

Mail Coach and Map of Southwest US — A565

1958, Oct. 10 ***Perf. 11x10½***
1120 A565 4c crimson rose .20 .20

Noah Webster A566

Forest Scene A567

Noah Webster Issue

1958, Oct. 16 ***Perf. 10½x11***
1121 A566 4c dark carmine rose .20 .20

Webster (1758-1843), lexicographer.

Forest Conservation Issue
Giori Press Printing

1958, Oct. 27 ***Perf. 11***
1122 A567 4c green, yel & brown .20 .20

Publicizing forest conservation and the protection of natural resources and honoring Theodore Roosevelt, a leading forest conservationist, on the cent. of his birth.

Fort Duquesne Issue

Occupation of Fort Duquesne A568

Rotary Press Printing

1958, Nov. 25 ***Perf. 11x10½***
1123 A568 4c blue .20 .20

Bicentennial of Fort Duquesne (Fort Pitt).

Oregon Statehood Centenary

Covered Wagon and Mt. Hood A569

1959, Feb. 14 ***Perf. 11x10½***
1124 A569 4c blue green .20 .20

José de San Martin — A570

NATO Emblem — A571

Champion of Liberty Issue
Rotary Press Printing

1959, Feb. 25 ***Perf. 10½x11***
1125 A570 4c blue .20 .20
a. Horiz. pair, imperf. btwn. *1,500.*

Giori Press Printing
Perf. 11

1126 A570 8c car, ultra & ocher .20 .20

San Martin, South American soldier and statesman.

NATO Issue
Rotary Press Printing

1959, Apr. 1 ***Perf. 10½x11***
1127 A571 4c blue .20 .20

North Atlantic Treaty Organ., 10th anniv.

Arctic Explorations Issue

North Pole, Dog Sled and "Nautilus" A572

1959, Apr. 6 ***Perf. 11x10½***
1128 A572 4c brt greenish blue .20 .20

Conquest of the Arctic by land by Rear Admiral Robert Edwin Peary in 1909 and by sea by the submarine "Nautilus" in 1958.

World Peace Through World Trade Issue

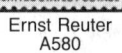

Globe and Laurel A573

1959, Apr. 20 ***Perf. 11x10½***
1129 A573 8c rose lake .20 .20

Issued in conjunction with the 17th Cong. of the Intl. Chamber of Commerce, Washington, DC, Apr. 19-25.

Silver Centennial Issue

Henry Comstock at Mount Davidson Site A574

1959, June 8 ***Perf. 11x10½***
1130 A574 4c black .20 .20

Cent. of the discovery of silver at the Comstock Lode, Nev.

St. Lawrence Seaway Issue

Great Lakes, Maple Leaf and Eagle Emblems A575

Giori Press Printing

1959, June 26 ***Perf. 11***
1131 A575 4c red & dark blue .20 .20

Opening of the St. Lawrence Seaway, June 26, 1959. See Canada No. 387.

49-Star Flag Issue

US Flag, 1959 A576

1959, July 4 ***Perf. 11***
1132 A576 4c ocher, dk blue & dp car .20 .20

Soil Conservation Issue

Modern Farm A577

1959, Aug. 26
1133 A577 4c bl, grn & ocher .20 .20

Tribute to farmers and ranchers who use soil and water conservation measures.

Petroleum Industry Issue

Oil Derrick — A578

Rotary Press Printing

1959, Aug. 27 ***Perf. 10½x11***
1134 A578 4c brown .20 .20

Cent. of the completion of the nation's 1st oil well at Titusville, Pa.

Dental Health Issue

Children A579

1959, Sept. 14 ***Perf. 11x10½***
1135 A579 4c green .20 .20

Publicizing dental health and cent. of the American Dental Assoc.

Ernst Reuter A580

Dr. Ephraim McDowell A581

Champion of Liberty Issue
Rotary Press Printing

1959, Sept. 29 ***Perf. 10½x11***
1136 A580 4c gray .20 .20

Giori Press Printing
Perf. 11

1137 A580 8c car, ultra & ocher .20 .20
a. Ocher missing (EP) *3,750.*
b. Ultramarine missing (EP) *3,750.*
c. Ocher & ultramarine missing (EP) *4,000.*
d. All colors missing (EP) *2,500.*

Ernst Reuter, mayor of Berlin 1948-53.

Dr. Ephraim McDowell Issue
Rotary Press Printing

1959, Dec. 3 ***Perf. 10½x11***
1138 A581 4c rose lake .20 .20
a. Vert. pair, imperf. btwn. *450.00*
b. Vert. pair, imperf. horiz. *350.00*

Honoring McDowell on the 150th anniv. of the 1st successful ovarian operation performed in the US.

American Credo Issue

Quotation from Washington's Farewell Address, 1796 — A582

Benjamin Franklin Quotation A583

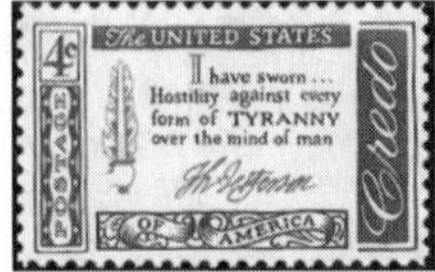

Thomas Jefferson Quotation A584

Francis Scott Key Quotation A585

Abraham Lincoln Quotation A586

Patrick Henry Quotation A587

Giori Press Printing

1960-61 ***Perf. 11***
1139 A582 4c dk vio blue & car .20 .20
1140 A583 4c olive bister & grn .20 .20
1141 A584 4c gray & vermilion .20 .20
1142 A585 4c car & dark blue .20 .20
1143 A586 4c magenta & green .20 .20
1144 A587 4c green & brown .20 .20
Nos. 1139-1144 (6) 1.20 1.20

Re-emphasizing the ideals upon which America was founded and honoring those great Americans who wrote or uttered the credos.

Issued: 1/20; 3/31; 5/8; 9/14; 11/19; 1/11/61.

Boy Scout Jubilee Issue

Boy Scout Giving Scout Sign A588

Giori Press Printing

1960, Feb. 8 ***Perf. 11***
1145 A588 4c red, dk bl & dk bis .20 .20

Boy Scouts of America, 50th anniv.

Olympic Rings and Snowflake A589

Thomas G. Masaryk A590

Olympic Winter Games Issue
Rotary Press Printing

1960, Feb. 18 ***Perf. 10½x11***
1146 A589 4c dull blue .20 .20

Opening of the 8th Olympic Winter Games, Squaw Valley, Feb. 18-29.

Champion of Liberty Issue
Rotary Press Printing

1960, Mar. 7 ***Perf. 10½x11***
1147 A590 4c blue .20 .20
a. Vert. pair, imperf. btwn. *3,250.*

Giori Press Printing
Perf. 11

1148 A590 8c car, ultra & ocher .20 .20
a. Horiz. pair, imperf. btwn. —

Masaryk, founder and pres. of Czechoslovakia (1918-35), 110th birth anniv.

World Refugee Year Issue

Refugee Family Walking Toward New Life A591

Rotary Press Printing

1960, Apr. 7 ***Perf. 11x10½***
1149 A591 4c gray black .20 .20

WRY, July 1, 1959-June 30, 1960.

Water Conservation Issue

Water, from Watershed to Consumer A592

Giori Press Printing

1960, Apr. 18 ***Perf. 11***
1150 A592 4c dk blue, brn org & green .20 .20
a. Brown orange missing (EP) *4,000.*

Stressing the importance of water conservation, and 7th Watershed Cong., Washington, DC.

SEATO Issue

SEATO Emblem — A593

Rotary Press Printing

1960, May 31 ***Perf. 10½x11***
1151 A593 4c blue .20 .20
a. Vert. pair, imperf. btwn. *150.00*

South-East Asia Treaty Org. and the SEATO Conf., Washington, DC, May 31-June 3.

American Woman Issue

Mother and Daughter A594

1960, June 2 ***Perf. 11x10½***
1152 A594 4c deep violet .20 .20

A tribute to American women and their accomplishments in civic affairs, education, arts and industry.

50-Star Flag Issue

US Flag, 1960 — A595

Giori Press Printing

1960, July 4 ***Perf. 11***
1153 A595 4c dark blue & red .20 .20

Pony Express Centennial Issue

Pony Express Rider A596

Rotary Press Printing

1960, July 19 ***Perf. 11x10½***
1154 A596 4c sepia .20 .20

Man in Wheelchair Operating Drill Press — A597

5th World Forestry Congress Seal — A598

Employ the Handicapped Issue

1960, Aug. 28 ***Perf. 10½x11***
1155 A597 4c dark blue .20 .20

Promoting employment of the physically handicapped and publicizing the 8th World Cong. of the Intl. Soc. for the Welfare of Cripples, NYC.

World Forestry Congress Issue

1960, Aug. 29
1156 A598 4c green .20 .20

5th World Forestry Cong., Seattle, Wash., Aug. 29-Sept. 10.

A599

A600

Mexican Independence Issue
Giori Press Printing

1960, Sept. 16 ***Perf. 11***
1157 A599 4c Independence Bell .20 .20

150th anniv. of Mexican independence. See Mexico No. 910.

US-Japan Treaty Issue

1960, Sept. 28 ***Perf. 11***

Washington Monument and Cherry Blossoms

1158 A600 4c blue & pink .20 .20

Cent. of the US-Japan Treaty of Amity and Commerce.

Ignacy Jan Paderewski A601

Robert A. Taft A602

Champion of Liberty Issue
Rotary Press Printing

1960, Oct. 8 ***Perf. 10½x11***
1159 A601 4c blue .20 .20

Giori Press Printing
Perf. 11

1160 A601 8c car, ultra & ocher .20 .20

Paderewski (1866-1941), Polish statesman and musician.

Senator Taft Memorial Issue
Rotary Press Printing

1960, Oct. 10 ***Perf. 10½x11***
1161 A602 4c dull violet .20 .20

Senator Taft (1889-1953), of Ohio.

Wheels of Freedom Issue

Globe and Steering Wheel with Tractor, Car and Truck A603

1960, Oct. 15 ***Perf. 11x10½***
1162 A603 4c dark blue .20 .20

Honoring the automotive industry and in connection with the National Automobile Show, Detroit, Oct. 15-23.

Boys' Clubs of America Issue

Profile of a Boy — A604

Giori Press Printing

1960, Oct. 18 ***Perf. 11***
1163 A604 4c ind, sl & rose red .20 .20

Boys' Clubs of America movement, cent.

Automated Post Office Issue

Architect's Sketch of New Post Office, Providence, RI — A605

1960, Oct. 20 ***Perf. 11***
1164 A605 4c dk blue & carmine .20 .20

Opening of the 1st automated PO in the US.

Baron Gustaf Emil Mannerheim A606

Camp Fire Girls Emblem A607

Champion of Liberty Issue
Rotary Press Printing

1960, Oct. 26 ***Perf. 10½x11***
1165 A606 4c blue .20 .20

Giori Press Printing
Perf. 11

1166 A606 8c car, ultra & ocher .20 .20

Mannerheim (1867-1951), marshal and pres. of Finland.

Camp Fire Girls Issue
Giori Press Printing

1960, Nov. 1 ***Perf. 11***
1167 A607 4c dk blue & brt red .20 .20

50th anniv. of the Camp Fire Girls' movement and with their Golden Jubilee Convention celebration.

Giuseppe Garibaldi (1807-1882) A608

Walter F. George (1878-1957) A609

Champion of Liberty Issue
Rotary Press Printing

1960, Nov. 2 ***Perf. 10½x11***
1168 A608 4c green .20 .20

Giori Press Printing
Perf. 11

1169 A608 8c car, ultra & ocher .20 .20

Garibaldi, Italian patriot and freedom fighter.

Senator George Memorial Issue
Rotary Press Printing

1960, Nov. 5 ***Perf. 10½x11***
1170 A609 4c dull violet .20 .20

Senator Walter F. George of Georgia.

Andrew Carnegie A610

John Foster Dulles A611

Andrew Carnegie Issue

1960, Nov. 25
1171 A610 4c deep claret .20 .20

Carnegie (1835-1919), industrialist and philanthropist.

John Foster Dulles Memorial Issue

1960, Dec. 6 ***Perf. 10½x11***
1172 A611 4c dull violet .20 .20

Dulles (1888-1959), Sec. of State (1953-59).

Echo I—Communications for Peace Issue

Radio Waves Connecting Echo I and Earth A612

1960, Dec. 15 ***Perf. 11x10½***
1173 A612 4c deep violet .20 .20

World's 1st communications satellite, Echo I, placed in orbit by NASA, Aug. 12, 1960.

Champion of Liberty Issue

Mahatma Gandhi — A613

Rotary Press Printing

1961, Jan. 26 ***Perf. 10½x11***
1174 A613 4c red orange .20 .20

Giori Press Printing
Perf. 11

1175 A613 8c car, ultra & ocher .20 .20

Mohandas K. Gandhi, leader in India's struggle for independence.

Range Conservation Issue

The Trail Boss and Modern Range A614

Giori Press Printing

1961, Feb. 2 ***Perf. 11***
1176 A614 4c bl, sl & brn org .20 .20

Importance of range conservation and meeting of the American Soc. of Range Management, Washington, DC. "The Trail Boss" from a drawing by Charles M. Russell is the Society's emblem.

Horace Greeley Issue

Horace Greeley (1811-1872), Publisher and Editor — A615

Rotary Press Printing

1961, Feb. 3 ***Perf. 10½x11***

1177 A615 4c dull violet .20 .20

Civil War Centennial Issue

Sea Coast Gun of 1861 A616

Rifleman at Shiloh, 1862 A617

Blue and Gray at Gettysburg, 1863 A618

Battle of the Wilderness, 1864 A619

Appomattox, 1865 — A620

1961-65 ***Perf. 11x10½***

1178 A616 4c light green .25 .20

1179 A617 4c blk, *peach blossom* .20 .20

Giori Press Printing

Perf. 11

1180 A618 5c gray & blue .20 .20

1181 A619 5c dark red & black .20 .20

1182 A620 5c Prus bl & blk .30 .20

a. Horiz. pair, imperf. vert. 4,500.

Nos. 1178-1182 (5) 1.15 1.00

Cent. of the firing on Fort Sumter, No. 1178; cent. of the Battle of Shiloh, No. 1179; cent. of the Battle of Gettysburg, No. 1180; cent. of the Battle of the Wilderness, No. 1181; cent. of the surrender of Gen. Robert E. Lee to Lt. Gen. Ulysses S. Grant at Appomattox Court House, No. 1182.

Issued: #1178-1182, 4/12; 4/7/62; 7/1/63; 5/5/64; 4/9/65.

Kansas Statehood Centenary

Sunflower, Pioneer Couple and Stockade A621

Giori Press Printing

1961, May 10 ***Perf. 11***

1183 A621 4c brn, dk red & grn, *yellow* .20 .20

Senator George W. Norris Issue

Norris and Norris Dam, Tenn. A622

Rotary Press Printing

1961, July 11 ***Perf. 11x10½***

1184 A622 4c blue green .20 .20

Norris (1861-1944) of Nebraska.

Naval Aviation, 50th Anniv.

Navy's First Plane (Curtiss A-1 of 1911) and Naval Air Wings A623

1961, Aug. 20

1185 A623 4c blue .20 .20

Workmen's Compensation Issue

Scales of Justice, Factory, Worker and Family — A624

1961, Sept. 4 ***Perf. 10½x11***

1186 A624 4c ultra, *grayish* .20 .20

50th anniv. of the 1st successful Workmen's Compensation Law, enacted by the Wis. legislature.

Frederic Remington Issue

Remington's "Smoke Signal" — A625

Giori Press Printing

1961, Oct. 4 ***Perf. 11***

1187 A625 4c multicolored .20 .20

Frederic Remington (1861-1909), artist of the West. The design is from an oil painting, Amon Carter Museum of Western Art, Fort Worth, Texas.

Sun Yat-sen A626

Basketball A627

Republic of China, 50th Anniv.

Rotary Press Printing

1961, Oct. 10 ***Perf. 10½x11***

1188 A626 4c blue .20 .20

Naismith-Basketball Issue

1961, Nov. 6 ***Perf. 10½x11***

1189 A627 4c brown .20 .20

Honoring basketball and James Naismith (1861-1939), who invented the game in 1891.

Nursing Issue

Student Nurse Lighting Candle — A628

Giori Press Printing

1961, Dec. 28 ***Perf. 11***

1190 A628 4c bl, grn, org & blk .20 .20

New Mexico Statehood, 50th Anniv.

Shiprock A629

1962, Jan. 6 ***Perf. 11***

1191 A629 4c lt bl, mar & bis .20 .20

Arizona Statehood, 50th Anniv.

Giant Saguaro Cactus — A630

1962 Feb. 14 ***Perf. 11***

1192 A630 4c car, vio bl & grn .20 .20

Project Mercury Issue

"Friendship 7" Capsule and Globe A631

1962, Feb. 20 ***Perf. 11***

1193 A631 4c dark blue & yellow .20 .20

First orbital flight of a US astronaut, Lt. Col. John H. Glenn, Jr., Feb. 20, 1962. Imperfs. are printers waste.

Malaria Eradication Issue

Great Seal of US and WHO Symbol A632

1962, Mar. 30 ***Perf. 11***

1194 A632 4c blue & bister .20 .20

WHO drive to eradicate malaria.

Charles Evans Hughes A633

Space Needle and Monorail A634

Charles Evans Hughes Issue

Rotary Press Printing

1962, Apr. 11 ***Perf. 10½x11***

1195 A633 4c black, *buff* .20 .20

Hughes (1862-1948), Gov. of NY, Chief Justice of the US.

Seattle World's Fair Issue

Giori Press Printing

1962, Apr. 25 ***Perf. 11***

1196 A634 4c red & dark blue .20 .20

"Century 21" Intl. Expo., Seattle, Wash., Apr. 21-Oct. 21.

Louisiana Statehood Sesquicentennial

Riverboat on the Mississippi A635

1962, Apr. 30 ***Perf. 11***

1197 A635 4c bl, dk sl grn & red .20 .20

Homestead Act Centenary

Sod Hut and Settlers A636

Rotary Press Printing

1962, May 20 ***Perf. 11x10½***

1198 A636 4c slate .20 .20

Girl Scout of America, 50th Anniv.

Senior Girl Scout & Flag A637

1962, July 24 ***Perf. 11x10½***

1199 A637 4c rose red .20 .20

Senator Brien McMahon Issue

Brien McMahon & Atomic Diagram A638

1962, July 28 ***Perf. 11x10½***

1200 A638 4c violet .20 .20

Honoring Sen. McMahon, Conn., for his role in opening the way to peaceful uses of atomic energy.

Apprenticeship Issue

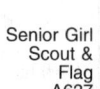

Machinist Handing Micrometer to Apprentice A639

1962, Aug. 31 ***Perf. 11x10½***

1201 A639 4c black, *yellow bister* .20 .20

Natl. Apprenticeship Program and 25th anniv. of the Natl. Apprenticeship Act.

Sam Rayburn Issue

Sam Rayburn and Capitol — A640

Giori Press Printing

1962, Sept. 16 *Perf. 11*
1202 A640 4c dk bl & red brn .20 .20

Sam Rayburn (1882-1961), Speaker of the House of Representatives.

Dag Hammarskjold Issue

UN Headquarters & Dag Hammarskjold — A641

Giori Press Printing

1962, Oct. 23 *Perf. 11*
1203 A641 4c black, brn & yel .20 .20

Hammarskjold, UN Sec. Gen., 1953-61.

Hammarskjold Special Printing

1962, Nov. 16
1204 A641 4c blk, brn & yel (inverted) .20 .20

No. 1204 was issued following discovery of No. 1203 with yellow background inverted.

Wreath and Candles — A642

Map of US and Lamp A643

Christmas Issue

Giori Press Printing

1962, Nov. 1 *Perf. 11*
1205 A642 4c green & red .20 .20

Higher Education Issue

1962, Nov. 14 *Perf. 11*
1206 A643 4c blue green & black .20 .20

Higher education's role in American cultural and industrial development in connection with the centenary celebrations of the signing of the law creating land-grant colleges and universities.

Winslow Homer Issue

"Breezing Up" — A644

1962, Dec. 15 *Perf. 11*
1207 A644 4c multicolored .20 .20
a. Horiz. pair, imperf. btwn. & at right *6,750.*

Winslow Homer (1836-1910), painter (showing his oil which hangs in the Natl. Gallery, Washington, DC).

Flag Issue

Flag over White House — A645

1963-66 *Perf. 11*
1208 A645 5c blue & red .20 .20
a. Tagged ('66) .20 .20
b. Horiz. pair, imperf. btwn. *1,500.*

Issued: #1208, Jan. 9; #1208a, Aug. 25.

Beware of pairs with faint blind perforations between offered as No. 1208b.

Regular Issue

Andrew Jackson A646

George Washington A650

Rotary Press Printing

1962-66 *Perf. 11x10½*
1209 A646 1c green ('63) .20 .20
a. Tagged ('66) .20 .20
1213 A650 5c dark blue gray .20 .20
a. Booklet pane 5 + label 3.00 *2.00*
b. Tagged ('63) .50 .20
c. As "a," tagged ('63) 2.00 *1.50*
d. Horiz. pair, imperf. btwn. *2,000.*

See Luminescence note after No. 1053.

Three different messages are found on the label in No. 1213a, and two messages on that of No. 1213c.

No. 1213d resulted from a paper foldover after perforating and before cutting into panes.

Unused catalogue numbers were left vacant for additional denominations.

Coil Stamps

Rotary Press

1962-66 *Perf. 10 Vert.*
1225 A646 1c green ('63) .20 .20
a. Tagged ('66) .20 .20
1229 A650 5c dk blue gray 1.10 .20
a. Tagged ('63) 1.40 .20
b. Imperf., pair *450.00*

Carolina Charter Issue

First Page of Carolina Charter A662

Giori Press Printing

1963, Apr. 6 *Perf. 11*
1230 A662 5c dk car & brown .20 .20

Carolina Charter, 1663, granting to 8 Englishmen lands, extending coast-to-coast roughly along the present border of Va. to the north and Fla. to the south. Original charter on display at Raleigh.

Food for Peace-Freedom from Hunger

Wheat — A663

1963, June 4 *Perf. 11*
1231 A663 5c green, buff & red .20 .20

American "Food for Peace" program and FAO "Freedom from Hunger" campaign.

West Virginia Statehood Centenary

Map of West Virginia & State Capitol A664

1963, June 20
1232 A664 5c green, red & blk .20 .20

Emancipation Proclamation Issue

Severed Chain A665

1963, Aug. 16 *Perf. 11*
1233 A665 5c dk bl, blk & red .20 .20

Cent. of Lincoln's Emancipation Proclamation, freeing about 3,000,000 slaves in 10 southern states.

Alliance for Progress Issue

Alliance Emblem A666

1963, Aug. 17
1234 A666 5c ultra & green .20 .20

2nd anniv. of the Alliance for Progress, which aims to stimulate economic growth & raise living standards in Latin America.

Cordell Hull Issue

Cordell Hull (1871-1955), Sec. of State (1933-44) — A667

Rotary Press Printing

1963, Oct. 5 *Perf. 10½x11*
1235 A667 5c blue green .20 .20

Eleanor Roosevelt Issue

Mrs. Franklin D. Roosevelt (1884-1962) — A668

1963, Oct. 11 *Perf. 11x10½*
1236 A668 5c bright purple .20 .20

Science Issue

"The Universe" A669

Giori Press Printing

1963, Oct. 14 *Perf. 11*
1237 A669 5c Prus blue & black .20 .20

Honoring the sciences and cent. of the Natl. Academy of Science.

Free City Mail Delivery Centenary

Letter Carrier, 1863 — A670

1963, Oct. 26 **Tagged** *Perf. 11*
1238 A670 5c gray, dk bl & red .20 .20

International Red Cross Centenary

A671

Design features Cuban Refugees on S.S. Morning Light & Red Cross Flag

1963, Oct. 29 *Perf. 11*
1239 A671 5c bluish black & red .20 .20

Christmas Issue

Natl. Christmas Tree & White House — A672

1963, Nov. 1 *Perf. 11*
1240 A672 5c dk blue, bluish black & red .20 .20
a. Tagged .65 .40

See Luminescence note after No. 1053.

Columbia Jays A673

Sam Houston A674

John J. Audubon Issue

1963, Dec. 7 *Perf. 11*
1241 A673 5c dark blue & multi .20 .20

John James Audubon (1785-1851), ornithologist and artist. The birds pictured are actually Collie's magpie jays.

Sam Houston Issue

Rotary Press Printing

1964, Jan. 10 *Perf. 10½x11*
1242 A674 5c black .20 .20

Sam Houston (1793-1863), soldier, pres. of Texas, US senator.

Charles M. Russell Issue

"Jerked Down" A675

Giori Press Printing

1964, Mar. 19 *Perf. 11*
1243 A675 5c ind, red brn & ol .20 .20

Russell (1864-1926), painter. The design is from a painting, Thomas Gilcrease Inst. of American History and Art, Tulsa, Okla.

New York World's Fair (1964-65)

Mall with Unisphere & "Rocket Thrower," by Donald De Lue A676

Rotary Press Printing

1964, Apr. 22 *Perf. 11x10½*

1244 A676 5c blue green .20 .20

John Muir Issue

John Muir (1838-1914), naturalist and conservationist and Redwood Forest — A677

Giori Press Printing

1964, Apr. 29 *Perf. 11*

1245 A677 5c brn, grn, yel grn & ol .20 .20

Kennedy Memorial Issue

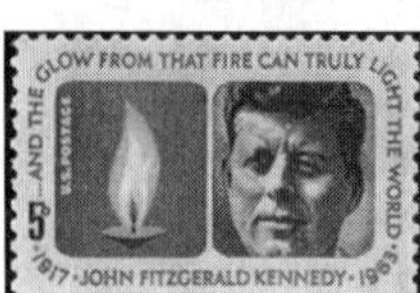

Pres. John F. Kennedy (1917-63) and Eternal Flame A678

Rotary Press Printing

1964, May 29 *Perf. 11x10½*

1246 A678 5c blue gray .20 .20

New Jersey Tercentenary Issue

Philip Carteret Landing at Elizabethtown & Map of New Jersey — A679

1964, June 15 *Perf. 10½x11*

1247 A679 5c bright ultra .20 .20

300th anniv. of English colonization of NJ. The design is from a mural by Howard Pyle in the Essex County Courthouse, Newark.

Nevada Statehood Centenary

Virginia City and Map of Nevada A680

Giori Press Printing

1964, July 22 *Perf. 11*

1248 A680 5c red, yellow & blue .20 .20

Flag A681

William Shakespeare A682

Register and Vote Issue

Giori Press Printing

1964, Aug. 1 *Perf. 11*

1249 A681 5c dark blue & red .20 .20

Campaign to draw more voters to the polls.

Shakespeare Issue

Rotary Press Printing

1964, Aug. 14 *Perf. 10½x11*

1250 A682 5c black brown, *tan* .20 .20

400th anniv. of the birth of Shakespeare (1564-1616).

Doctors Mayo Issue

Drs. William and Charles Mayo — A683

1964, Sept. 11 *Perf. 10½x11*

1251 A683 5c green .20 .20

William (1861-1939) and his brother, Charles (1865-1939), surgeons who founded the Mayo Foundation for Medical Education and Research in affiliation with the Univ. of Minn. at Rochester. From a sculpture by James Earle Fraser.

American Music Issue

Lute, Horn, Laurel, Oak and Music Score A684

Giori Press Printing

1964, Oct. 15 *Perf. 11*

Gray Paper with Blue Threads

1252 A684 5c red, black & blue .20 .20
- ***a.*** Blue omitted *1,000.*
- ***b.*** Blue missing (PS) —

50th anniv. of the founding of ASCAP (American Soc. of Composers, Authors and Publishers).

Beware of copies offered as No. 1252a which have traces of blue.

Homemakers Issue

Farm Scene Sampler A685

Lithographed, Engraved (Giori)

1964, Oct. 26 *Perf. 11*

1253 A685 5c multicolored .20 .20

Honoring American women as homemakers and 50th anniv. of the passage of the Smith-Lever Act. By providing economic experts under an extension service of the US Dept. of Agriculture, this legislation helped to improve homelife.

Christmas Issue

Holly A686 — Mistletoe A687

Poinsettia A688 — Sprig of Conifer A689

Giori Press Printing

1964, Nov. 9 *Perf. 11*

1254 A686 5c green, car & black .25 .20
- ***a.*** Tagged .60 .50
- ***b.*** Printed on gummed side —

1255 A687 5c car, green & black .25 .20
- ***a.*** Tagged .60 .50

1256 A688 5c car, green & black .25 .20
- ***a.*** Tagged .60 .50

1257 A689 5c black, green & car .25 .20
- ***a.*** Tagged .60 .50
- ***b.*** Block of 4, #1254-1257 1.10 1.00
- ***c.*** Block of 4, #1254a-1257a 2.50 2.25

Tagged stamps issued Nov. 10.

No. 1254b resulted from a paper foldover before printing and perforating.

Verrazano-Narrows Bridge Issue

Verrazano-Narrows Bridge and Map of NY Bay — A690

Rotary Press Printing

1964, Nov. 21 *Perf. 10½x11*

1258 A690 5c blue green .20 .20

Opening of the Verrazano-Narrows Bridge connecting Staten Island and Brooklyn, NY.

Fine Arts Issue

Abstract Design by Stuart Davis A691

Giori Press Printing

1964, Dec. 2 *Perf. 11*

1259 A691 5c ultra, blk & dull red .20 .20

Amateur Radio Issue

Radio Waves and Dial — A692

Rotary Press Printing

1964, Dec. 15 *Perf. 10½x11*

1260 A692 5c red lilac .20 .20

Honoring radio amateurs on the 50th anniv. of the American Radio Relay League.

Battle of New Orleans Issue

General Andrew Jackson and Sesquicentennial Medal — A693

Giori Press Printing

1965, Jan. 8 *Perf. 11*

1261 A693 5c dp car, vio bl & gray .20 .20

Battle of New Orleans, Chalmette Plantation, Jan. 8-18, 1815, which established 150 years of peace and friendship between the US and Great Britain.

Discus Thrower A694

Microscope and Stethoscope A695

Physical Fitness-Sokol Issue

1965, Feb. 15 *Perf. 11*

1262 A694 5c maroon & black .20 .20

Importance of physical fitness and cent. of the founding of the Sokol (athletic) org. in America.

Crusade Against Cancer Issue

1965, Apr. 1 *Perf. 11*

1263 A695 5c blk, pur & red org .20 .20

"Crusade Against Cancer" and stressing the importance of early diagnosis.

Churchill Memorial Issue

Winston Churchill — A696

Rotary Press Printing

1965, May 13 *Perf. 10½x11*

1264 A696 5c black .20 .20

Sir Winston Spencer Churchill (1874-1965), British statesman and WWII leader.

Magna Carta Issue

Procession of Barons and King John's Crown A697

Giori Press Printing

1965, June 15 *Perf. 11*

1265 A697 5c blk, yel ocher & red lilac .20 .20

750th anniv. of the Magna Carta, the basis of English and American common law.

International Cooperation Year Issue

ICY Emblem A698

1965, June 26 ***Perf. 11***
1266 A698 5c dull blue & black .20 .20

ICY, 1965, and 20th anniv. of the UN.

A699

A700

Salvation Army Issue

1965, July 2 ***Perf. 11***
1267 A699 5c red, blk & dark bl .20 .20

Cent. of the founding of the Salvation Army in London by William Booth.

Dante Alighieri Issue
Rotary Press Printing

1965, July 17 ***Perf. 10½x11***
1268 A700 5c maroon, *tan* .20 .20

Dante Alighieri (1265-1321), Italian poet. Design after a 16th cent. painting.

Herbert Hoover Issue

Pres. Herbert Clark Hoover (1874-1964) — A701

1965, Aug. 10 ***Perf. 10½x11***
1269 A701 5c rose red .20 .20

Robert Fulton Issue

Robert Fulton & Clermont A702

Giori Press Printing

1965, Aug. 19 ***Perf. 11***
1270 A702 5c black & blue .20 .20

Fulton (1765-1815), inventor of the 1st commercial steamship.

Settlement of Florida Issue

Spanish Explorer, Royal Flag of Spain and Ships — A703

Giori Press Printing

1965, Aug. 28
1271 A703 5c red, yel & blk .20 .20
a. Yellow omitted *350.00*

400th anniv. of the settlement of Fla., and the 1st permanent European settlement in the continental US, St. Augustine, Fla.
See Spain #1312.

Traffic Safety Issue

Traffic Signal A704

1965, Sept. 3 ***Perf. 11***
1272 A704 5c emer, blk & red .20 .20

Traffic safety and the prevention of traffic accidents.

John Copley Issue

Elizabeth Clarke Copley — A705

1965, Sept. 17
1273 A705 5c blk, brn & olive .20 .20

John Singleton Copley (1738-1815), painter. The portrait of the artist's daughter is from the oil painting "The Copley Family," which hangs in the Natl. Gallery of Art, Washington, DC.

International Telecommunication Union Centenary

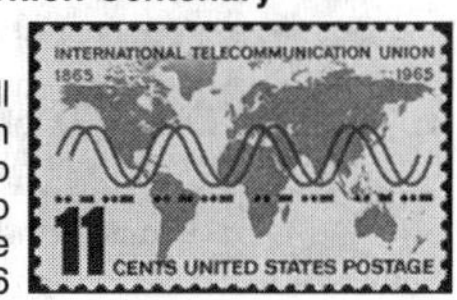

Gall Projection World Map & Radio Sine Wave A706

1965, Oct. 6 ***Perf. 11***
1274 A706 11c black, car & bis .35 .20

Adlai E. Stevenson A707

Angel with Trumpet A708

Adlai E. Stevenson Issue

1965, Oct. 23 **Litho., Engr. (Giori)**
1275 A707 5c pale blue, blk, car & vio blue .20 .20

Stevenson (1900-65), gov. of Ill., US ambassador to the UN.

Christmas Issue

Design features 1840 Weather Vane.

Giori Press Printing

1965, Nov. 2 ***Perf. 11***
1276 A708 5c car, dk ol grn & bis .20 .20
a. Tagged .75 .25

Prominent Americans Issue

Thomas Jefferson A710

Albert Gallatin A711

Frank Lloyd Wright & Guggenheim Museum A712

Francis Parkman A713

Lincoln A714

Washington A715

Washington (Redrawn)—A715a

Franklin D. Roosevelt A716

Albert Einstein A717

Andrew Jackson A718

Henry Ford, 1909 Model T A718a

John F. Kennedy A719

Oliver Wendell Holmes A720

George Catlett Marshall A721

Frederick Douglass A722

John Dewey A723

Thomas Paine A724

Lucy Stone A725

Eugene O'Neill A726

John Bassett Moore — A727

Perf. 11x10½, 10½x11

1965-78 **Rotary Press Printing**

1278	A710	1c green, tagged	.20	.20
a.		Booklet pane of 8	1.00	*.75*
b.		Bklt. pane of 4 + 2 labels	.80	*.60*
c.		Untagged (Bureau precanceled)		.20
1279	A711	1¼c lt green	.20	.20
1280	A712	2c dk blue gray, tagged	.20	.20
a.		Booklet pane of 5 + label	1.25	*.80*
b.		Untagged (Bureau precanceled)		.20
c.		Booklet pane of 6	1.00	*.75*
1281	A713	3c vio, tagged	.20	.20
a.		Untagged (Bureau precanceled)		.20
1282	A714	4c black	.20	.20
a.		Tagged	.20	.20
1283	A715	5c blue	.20	.20
a.		Tagged	.20	.20
1283B	A715a	5c blue, tagged	.20	.20
d.		Untagged (Bureau precanceled)		.20
1284	A716	6c gray brown	.20	.20
a.		Tagged	.20	.20
b.		Booklet pane of 8	1.50	*1.00*
c.		Booklet pane of 5 + label	1.50	*1.00*
d.		Horiz. pair, imperf. btwn.	—	
1285	A717	8c violet	.20	.20
a.		Tagged	.20	.20
1286	A718	10c lilac, tagged	.20	.20
b.		Untagged (Bureau precanceled)		.20
1286A	A718a	12c black, tagged	.25	.20
c.		Untagged (Bureau precanceled)		.25
1287	A719	13c brn, tagged	.30	.20
a.		Untagged (Bureau precanceled)		.35
1288	A720	15c mag, tagged	.30	.20
a.		Untagged (Bureau precanceled)		.30
d.		Type II	.55	.20

Type II: necktie does not touch coat at bottom.

Perf. 10

1288B	A720	15c mag, from bklt. pane	.35	.20
c.		Booklet pane of 8	2.80	*1.75*
e.		As "c," vert. imperf. btwn.	—	

Perf. 11x10½, 10½x11

1289	A721	20c deep olive	.40	.20
a.		Tagged	.40	.20
1290	A722	25c rose lake	.55	.20
a.		Tagged	.45	.20
b.		25c magenta	*25.00*	—
1291	A723	30c red lilac	.65	.20
a.		Tagged	.50	.20
1292	A724	40c blue black	.85	.20
a.		Tagged	.65	.20
1293	A725	50c rose magenta	1.00	.20
a.		Tagged	.80	.20
1294	A726	$1 dull purple	2.25	.20
a.		Tagged	1.65	.20
1295	A727	$5 gray black	10.00	2.25
a.		Tagged	8.50	2.00
		Nos. 1278-1295 (21)	18.90	6.25

On No. 1283B the highlights and shadows have been softened.

No. 1288B issued in booklets only. All stamps have one or two straight edges.

Issued (without tagging)—1965: 4c, 11/19.
1966: 5c, 2/22; 6c, 1/29; 8c, 3/14; $5, 12/3.
1967: 1¼c, 1/30; 20c, 10/24; 25c, 2/14; $1, 10/16.
1968: 30c, 10/21; 40c, 1/29; 50c, 8/13.
Dates for tagged: 1965: 4c, 12/1.
1966: 2c, 6/8; 5c, 2/23; 6c, 12/29; 8c, 7/6.
1967: 3c, 9/16; #1283B, 11/17; #1284b, 12/28; 10c, 3/15; 13c, 5/29.
1968: 1c, #1284c, 1/12; #1280a, 1/8; 12c, 7/30; 15c, 3/8.
1973: 20c, 25c, 30c, 40c, 50c, $1, $5, 4/3.
1978: No. 1288B, 6/14.

Franklin D. Roosevelt — A727a

Coil Stamps

Rotary Press Printing

1966-81 **Tagged** ***Perf. 10 Horiz.***

1297	A713	3c violet	.20	.20
a.		Imperf., pair	*30.00*	
b.		Untagged (Bureau precanceled)		.20
c.		As "b," imperf. pair		6.00

1298 A716 6c gray brn .20 .20
a. Imperf., pair *2,000.*

Perf. 10 Vertically

1299 A710 1c green .20 .20
a. Untagged (Bureau precanceled) .20
b. Imperf., pair *30.00* —
1303 A714 4c black .20 .20
a. Untagged (Bureau precanceled) .20
b. Imperf., pair *750.00*
1304 A715 5c blue .20 .20
a. Untagged (Bureau precanceled) .20
b. Imperf., pair *175.00*
e. As "a," imperf. pair *375.00*

No. 1304b is valued in the grade of fine.

1304C A715a 5c blue .20 .20
d. Imperf., pair *750.00*
1305 A727a 6c gray brn .20 .20
a. Imperf., pair *75.00*
b. Untagged (Bureau precanceled) .20
1305E A720 15c magenta .25 .20
f. Untagged (Bureau precanceled) .30
g. Imperf., pair *30.00*
h. Pair, imperf. between *200.00*
i. Type II .60 .20
j. Imperf., pair, type II *85.00*
1305C A726 $1 dull pur 2.00 .40
d. Imperf., pair *2,250.*
Nos. 1297-1305C (9) 3.65 2.00

Issued: 1c, 1/12/68; 3c, 11/4/75; 4c, 5/28/66; #1304, 9/8/66; 6c, #1298, 12/28/67; #1305, 2/28/68; $1, 1/12/73; 15c, 6/14/78.

See Nos. 1393-1395, 1397-1402 for more Prominent Americans.

Migratory Bird Treaty Issue

Migratory Birds over Canada-U.S. Border — A728

Giori Press Printing

1966, Mar. 16 ***Perf. 11***
1306 A728 5c blk, crim & dk blue .20 .20

50th anniv. of the Migratory Bird Treaty between the U.S. and Canada.

Humane Treatment of Animals Issue

Mongrel A729

Lithographed, Engraved (Giori)

1966, Apr. 9 ***Perf. 11***
1307 A729 5c org brown & black .20 .20

Humane treatment of all animals and cent. of the ASPCA.

Indiana Statehood Sesquicentennial

Sesquicentennial Seal — A730

Giori Press Printing

1966, Apr. 16
1308 A730 5c yel, ocher & vio bl .20 .20

Design features Sesquicentennial Seal; Map of Indiana with 19 Stars & Old Capitol at Corydon

American Circus Issue

Clown — A731

1966, May 2 ***Perf. 11***
1309 A731 5c multicolored .20 .20

Honoring the American circus on the cent. of the birth of John Ringling.

6th Intl. Phil. Exhib. Issues

Stamped Cover A732

A733

Lithographed, Engraved (Giori)

1966, May ***Perf. 11***
1310 A732 5c multicolored .20 .20

Souvenir Sheet

Imperf

1311 A733 5c multicolored .20 .20

SIPEX, Washington, DC, May 21-30. No. 1311 measures 108x74mm.
Issue dates: #1310, 21st; #1311, 23rd.

"Freedom" Checking "Tyranny" A734

Polish Eagle and Cross A735

Bill of Rights, 175th Anniv.

Giori Press Printing

1966, July 1 ***Perf. 11***
1312 A734 5c car, dk & lt blue .20 .20

Polish Millennium Issue

Rotary Press Printing

1966, July 30 ***Perf. 10½x11***
1313 A735 5c red .20 .20

1000th anniv. of the adoption of Christianity in Poland.

Tagging Extended

During 1966 experimental use of tagged stamps was extended to the Cincinnati Postal Region covering offices in Indiana, Kentucky and Ohio. To supply these offices about 12 percent of the following nine issues (Nos. 1314-1322) were tagged.

National Park Service Issue

National Park Service Emblem A736

Lithographed, Engraved (Giori)

1966, Aug. 25 ***Perf. 11***
1314 A736 5c yel, black & green .20 .20
a. Tagged .30 .25

50th anniv. of the Natl. Park Service of the Interior Dept. The design "Parkscape U.S.A." identifies Natl. Park Service facilities. No. 1314a was issued Aug. 26.

Marine Corps Reserve Issue

A737

Lithographed, Engraved (Giori)

1966, Aug. 29 ***Perf. 11***
1315 A737 5c blk, bis, red & ultra .20 .20
a. Tagged .30 .20
b. Blk & bis (engr.) missing (EP) *16,000.*

50th anniv. of the founding of the U.S. Marine Corps Reserve. Design includes Combat Marine, 1966; Frogman; WW II Flier; WW I "Devil Dog" & Marine, 1775.

General Federation of Women's Clubs

Women of 1890 and 1966 A738

Giori Press Printing

1966, Sept. 12 ***Perf. 11***
1316 A738 5c black, pink & blue .20 .20
a. Tagged .30 .20

75 years of service by the Gen. Fed. of Women's Clubs. No. 1316a was issued 9/13.

American Folklore Issue

Johnny Appleseed — A739

1966, Sept. 24 ***Perf. 11***
1317 A739 5c green, red & black .20 .20
a. Tagged .30 .20

Johnny Appleseed, (John Chapman, 1774-1845), who wandered over 100,000 square miles planting apple trees, and who gave away and sold seedlings to Midwest pioneers. No. 1317a issued Sept. 26.

Beautification of America Issue

Jefferson Memorial A740

1966, Oct. 5 ***Perf. 11***
1318 A740 5c emer, pink & blk .20 .20
a. Tagged .30 .20

Pres. Johnson's "Plant for a more beautiful America" campaign. Design features Jefferson Memorial, Tidal Basin & Cherry Blossoms.

Central U.S. Map With Great River Road — A741

Statue of Liberty & "Old Glory" — A742

Great River Road Issue

Lithographed, Engraved (Giori)

1966, Oct. 21 ***Perf. 11***
1319 A741 5c ver, yel, bl & grn .20 .20
a. Tagged .30 .20

5,600-mile Great River Road connecting New Orleans with Kenora, Ontario, following the Mississippi most of the way. No. 1319a issued Oct. 22.

Savings Bond-Servicemen Issue

1966, Oct. 26
1320 A742 5c red, dk & lt bl, blk .20 .20
a. Tagged .30 .20
b. Red, dark bl & blk missing (EP) *4,250.*
c. Dark blue (engr.) missing (EP) *8,500.*

25th anniv. of US Savings Bonds, and to honor American servicemen. No. 1320a issued Oct. 27.

Christmas Issue

Madonna and Child — A743

Lithographed, Engraved (Giori)

1966, Nov. 1 ***Perf. 11***
1321 A743 5c multicolored .20 .20
a. Tagged .30 .20

The design is from "Madonna and Child with Angels," by the Flemish artist Hans Memling (c. 1430-1494), National Gallery of Art, Washington, DC. No. 1321a was issued Nov. 2. See No. 1336.

Mary Cassatt Issue

"The Boating Party" A744

Giori Press Printing

1966, Nov. 17 ***Perf. 11***
1322 A744 5c multicolored .20 .20
a. Tagged .30 .25

Cassatt (1844-1926), painter. The original painting is in the Natl. Gallery of Art, Washington, DC.

National Grange Issue

Grange Poster, 1870 — A745

1967, Apr. 17 **Tagged** ***Perf. 11***
1323 A745 5c multicolored .20 .20

Cent. of the founding of the National Grange, American farmers' organization.

Phosphor Tagging

From No. 1323 onward, all postage issues are tagged, unless otherwise noted.

Tagging Omitted

Inadvertent omissions of tagging occurred on Nos. 1238, 1278, 1281, 1298 and 1305. In addition most tagged issues from 1967 on exist with tagging unintentionally omitted.

Canada Centenary Issue

Canadian Landscape A746

Giori Press Printing

1967, May 25 *Perf. 11*

1324 A746 5c multicolored .20 .20

Cent. of Canada's emergence as a nation.

Erie Canal Issue

Stern of Early Canal Boat A747

Lithographed, Engraved (Giori)

1967, July 4 *Perf. 11*

1325 A747 5c multicolored .20 .20

150th anniv. of the Erie Canal ground-breaking ceremony. The canal links Lake Erie and NYC.

"Peace"—Lions Issue

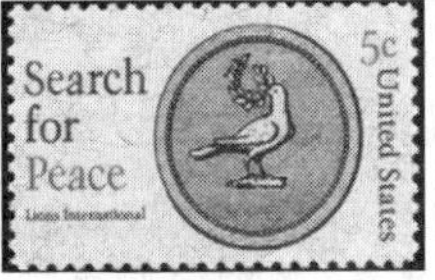

Peace Dove A748

Giori Press Printing

1967, July 5 *Perf. 11*

Gray Paper with Blue Threads

1326 A748 5c blue, red & black .20 .20

Publicizing the Search for Peace. This was the theme of an essay contest for young men and women sponsored by Lions Intl. on its 50th anniv.

Henry David Thoreau Issue

Henry David Thoreau (1817-1862), Writer — A749

1967, July 12

1327 A749 5c red, black & green .20 .20

Nebraska Statehood Centenary

Hereford Steer and Corn A750

Lithographed, Engraved (Giori)

1967, July 29 *Perf. 11*

1328 A750 5c dk red brn, lem & yel .20 .20

Voice of America Issue

Radio Transmission Tower and Waves — A751

1967, Aug. 1 **Giori Press Printing**

1329 A751 5c red, bl, blk & car .20 .20

25th anniv. of the radio branch of the US Information Agency (USIA).

American Folklore Issue

Davy Crockett & Scrub Pines A752

Lithographed, Engraved (Giori)

1967, Aug. 17 *Perf. 11*

1330 A752 5c grn, blk & yel .20 .20
- *a.* Vert. pair, imperf. btwn. *6,000.*
- *b.* Green (engr.) missing (FO) —
- *c.* Blk & grn (engr.) missing (FO) —

Crockett (1786-1836), frontiersman and congressman, died in defense of the Alamo.

A foldover on a pane of No. 1330 resulted in one example each of Nos. 1330b-1330c. Part of the colors appear on the back of the selvage and one freak stamp.

An engraved black-and-green-only impression appears on the gummed side of one almost-complete "stamp."

Space Accomplishments Issue

Space-Walking Astronaut — A753

Gemini 4 Capsule and Earth A754

Lithographed, Engraved (Giori)

1967, Sept. 29 *Perf. 11*

1331 A753 5c multicolored .50 .20

1332 A754 5c multicolored .50 .20
- *b.* Pair, #1331-1332 1.10 *1.25*

US accomplishments in space.

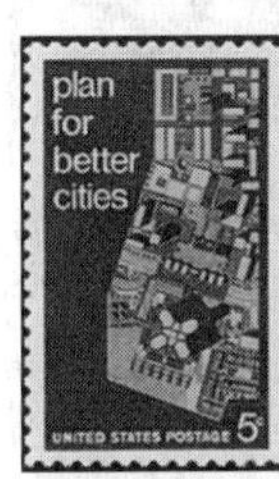

View of Model City — A755

Finnish Coat of Arms — A756

Urban Planning Issue

Lithographed, Engraved (Giori)

1967, Oct. 2 *Perf. 11*

1333 A755 5c dk & lt blue, black .20 .20

Importance of Urban Planning and the Intl. Conf. of the American Inst. of Planners, Washington, DC, Oct. 1-6.

Finnish Independence, 50th Anniv.

Engraved (Giori)

1967, Oct. 6 *Perf. 11*

1334 A756 5c blue .20 .20

Thomas Eakins Issue

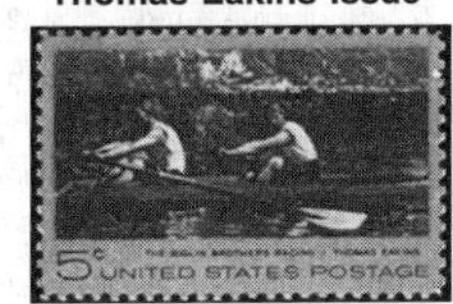

"The Biglin Brothers Racing" (Sculling on Schuylkill River, Philadelphia) — A757

1967, Nov. 2 **Photo.** *Perf. 12*

1335 A757 5c gold & multi .20 .20

Eakins (1844-1916), painter and sculptor. The painting is in the Natl. Gallery of Art, Washington, DC.

Christmas Issue

Madonna and Child, by Hans Memling — A758

Lithographed, Engraved (Giori)

1967, Nov. 6 *Perf. 11*

1336 A758 5c multicolored .20 .20

See note after No. 1321.

Magnolia A759

Flag and White House — A760

Mississippi Statehood, 150th Anniv.

Giori Press Printing

1967, Dec. 11 *Perf. 11*

1337 A759 5c brt grnsh bl, grn & red brn .20 .20

Flag Issue

Giori Press Printing

1968-71 *Perf. 11*

Size: 19x22mm

1338 A760 6c dk bl, red & grn .20 .20
- *k.* Vert. pair, imperf. btwn. *500.00*
- *s.* Red missing (FO) —

Vert. pairs have been offered as imperf. horiz. Some have had the gum washed off to make it difficult or impossible to detect blind perfs.

Coil Stamp

Multicolor Huck Press

Perf. 10 Vert.

Size: 18¼x21mm

1338A A760 6c dk blue, red & green ('69) .20 .20
- *b.* Imperf., pair *500.00*

Multicolor Huck Press

Perf. 11x10½

Size: 18¼x21mm

1338D A760 6c dk blue, red & green ('70) .20 .20
- *e.* Horiz. pair, imperf. btwn. *175.00*

1338F A760 8c multi ('71) .20 .20
- *i.* Vert. pair, imperf. 45.00
- *j.* Horiz. pair, imperf. btwn. 55.00
- *p.* Slate green omitted *400.00*
- *t.* Horiz. pair, imperf. vert. —

Issued: #1338, 1/24/68; #1338A, 5/30/69; #1338D, 8/7/70; 8c, 5/10/71.

Coil Stamp

1971, May 10 *Perf. 10 Vert.*

Size: 18¼x21mm

1338G A760 8c multi ('71) .20 .20
- *h.* Imperf., pair *55.00*

Farm House & Fields of Ripening Grain A761

Map of North & South America A762

Illinois Statehood, 150th Anniv.

Lithographed, Engraved (Giori)

1968, Feb. 12 *Perf. 11*

1339 A761 6c multicolored .20 .20

HemisFair '68 Issue

1968, Mar. 30 *Perf. 11*

1340 A762 6c blue, rose red & white .20 .20
- *a.* White omitted *1,250.*

HemisFair '68 exhib. at San Antonio, Tex., 4/6-10/6, for the 250th anniv. of San Antonio.

Airlift Issue

Eagle Holding Pennant A763

Lithographed, Engraved (Giori)

1968, Apr. 4 **Untagged** *Perf. 11*

1341 A763 $1 sep, dk blue, ocher & brn red 2.00 1.25

Issued to pay for airlift of parcels from and to US ports to servicemen overseas and in Alaska, Hawaii and P.R. Valid for all regular postage.

On Apr. 26, 1969, the POD ruled that henceforth No. 1341 "may be used toward paying the postage or fees for special services on airmail articles."

Support Our Youth Issue

Girls & Boys A764

Lithographed, Engraved (Giori)

1968, May 1 *Perf. 11*

1342 A764 6c ultra & orange red .20 .20

Support Our Youth program, and honoring the Benevolent and Protective Order of Elks, which extended its youth service program in observance of its centennial year.

Policeman and Small Boy — A765

Eagle Weather Vane — A766

Law and Order Issue

Giori Press Printing

1968, May 17 *Perf. 11*

1343 A765 6c chlky bl, blk & red .20 .20

The police as protector and friend and respect for law and order.

Register and Vote Issue

Lithographed, Engraved (Giori)

1968, June 27 ***Perf. 11***

1344 A766 6c blk, yel & org .20 .20

Campaign to draw more voters to the polls. The weather vane is from an old house in the Russian Hill section of San Francisco.

Historic Flag Series

Ft. Moultrie, 1776 A767

Ft. McHenry, 1795-1818 A768

Washington's Cruisers, 1775 — A769

Bennington, 1777 A770

Rhode Island, 1775 A771

First Stars and Stripes, 1777 A772

Bunker Hill, 1775 A773

Grand Union, 1776 A774

Philadelphia Light Horse, 1775 — A775

First Navy Jack, 1775 A776

Engraved (Giori) (#1345-1348, 1350): Engr. & Litho. (#1349, 1351-1354)

1968, July 4 ***Perf. 11***

1345 A767 6c dark blue .40 .25
1346 A768 6c dk blue & red .30 .25
1347 A769 6c dk blue & ol green .25 .25
1348 A770 6c dk blue & red .25 .25
1349 A771 6c dk blue, yel & red .25 .25
1350 A772 6c dk blue & red .25 .25
1351 A773 6c dk bl, ol grn & red .25 .25
1352 A774 6c dk blue & red .25 .25
1353 A775 6c dk blue, yel & red .25 .25
1354 A776 6c dk blue, red & yel .25 .25
a. Strip of 10, Nos. 1345-1354 2.75 3.25

Flags carried by American colonists and by citizens of the new United States. The flag sequence on the upper panes is as listed. On the lower panes the sequence is reversed with the Navy Jack in the 1st row and the Fort Moultrie flag in the 10th.

Walt Disney Issue

Disney and Children of the World — A777

1968, Sept. 11 **Photo.** ***Perf. 12***

1355 A777 6c multicolored .30 .20
a. Ocher (Walt Disney, 6c, etc.) omitted *600.* —
b. Vert. pair, imperf. horiz. *700.*
c. Imperf., pair *600.*
d. Black omitted *1,500.*
e. Horiz. pair, imperf. btwn. *4,750.*
f. Blue omitted *1,750.*

Disney (1901-1966), cartoonist, film producer, creator of Mickey Mouse.

Father Marquette Issue

Father Marquette and Louis Jolliet Exploring the Mississippi A778

Giori Press Printing

1968, Sept. 20 ***Perf. 11***

1356 A778 6c black, apple green & org brn .20 .20

Father Jacques Marquette (1637-1675). French Jesuit missionary, who with Louis Jolliet explored the Mississippi and its tributaries.

American Folklore Issue

Daniel Boone (1734-1820)

Pennsylvania Rifle, Powder Horn, Tomahawk Pipe & Knife — A779

Lithographed, Engraved (Giori)

1968, Sept. 26 ***Perf. 11***

1357 A779 6c yel, dp yel, mar & blk .20 .20

Daniel Boone, frontiersman and trapper.

Arkansas River Navigation Issue

Ship's Wheel, Power Transmission Tower & Barge — A780

1968, Oct. 1 ***Perf. 11***

1358 A780 6c brt bl, dk bl & blk .20 .20

Opening of the Arkansas River to commercial navigation.

Leif Erikson Issue

Leif Erikson, by Stirling Calder — A781

1968, Oct. 9 **Litho., Engr.** ***Perf. 11***

1359 A781 6c lt gray brn & blk brn .20 .20

Erikson, 11th cent. Norse explorer, was the 1st European to set foot on the American continent, at a place he called Vinland. The statue by an American sculptor is in Reykjavik, Iceland.

The light gray brown ink carries the tagging element.

Cherokee Strip Issue

Homesteaders Racing to Cherokee Strip — A782

Rotary Press Printing

1968, Oct. 15 ***Perf. 11x10½***

1360 A782 6c brown .20 .20

75th anniv. of the opening of the Cherokee Strip to settlers, Sept. 16, 1893.

John Trumbull Issue

Detail from "The Battle of Bunker's Hill" — A783

Lithographed, Engraved

1968, Oct. 18 ***Perf. 11***

1361 A783 6c multicolored .20 .20
b. Blk (engr.) missing (FO) *11,000.*

Trumbull (1756-1843), painter. The stamp shows Lt. Thomas Grosvenor and his attendant, Peter Salem. The painting is at Yale Univ., New Haven, CT.

Waterfowl Conservation Issue

Wood Ducks A784

Lithographed, Engraved (Giori)

1968, Oct. 24 ***Perf. 11***

1362 A784 6c black & multi .20 .20
a. Vert. pair, imperf. btwn. *550.* —
b. Red & dark blue omitted *900.*
c. Red omitted *1,750.*

Gabriel, from van Eyck's Annunciation A785

Chief Joseph, by Cyrenius Hall A786

Christmas Issue

Engraved (Multicolor Huck)

1968, Nov. 1 **Tagged** ***Perf. 11***

1363 A785 6c multicolored .20 .20
a. Untagged .20 .20
b. Imperf., pair, tagged *225.00*
c. Light yellow omitted *65.00* —
d. Imperf., pair, untagged *300.00*

"The Annunciation" by the 15th cent. Flemish artist Jan van Eyck is in the Natl. Gallery of Art, Washington, DC. No. 1363a was issued Nov. 2.

Luminescence

No. 1364 and all following postage stamps are tagged, unless otherwise noted.

American Indian Issue

Lithographed, Engraved (Giori)

1968, Nov. 4 ***Perf. 11***

1364 A786 6c black & multi .20 .20

Honoring American Indians and the opening of the Natl. Portrait Gallery, Oct. 5, 1968. Chief Joseph (Indian name Thunder Traveling over the Mountains) a leader of the Nez Percé tribe, was born c. 1840 in eastern Oregon and died at the Colesville Reservation in Washington in 1904.

Beautification of America Issue

Capitol, Azaleas and Tulips A787

Washington Monument, Potomac River and Daffodils — A788

Poppies and Lupines along Highway A789

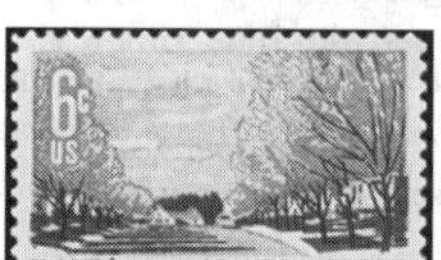

Blooming Crabapples along Street A790

Lithographed, Engraved (Giori)

1969, Jan. 16 ***Perf. 11***

1365 A787 6c multicolored .25 .20
1366 A788 6c multicolored .25 .20
1367 A789 6c multicolored .25 .20
1368 A790 6c multicolored .25 .20
a. Block of 4, #1365-1368 1.00 *1.75*

Natural Beauty Campaign for more beautiful cities, parks, highways and streets.

Eagle from Great Seal of US — A791

July Fourth, by Grandma Moses — A792

American Legion, 50th Anniv.

Lithographed, Engraved (Giori)

1969, Mar. 15 ***Perf. 11***

1369 A791 6c red, blue & black .20 .20

American Folklore Issue

Grandma Moses

Lithographed, Engraved (Giori)

1969, May 1 *Perf. 11*

1370 A792 6c multicolored .20 .20
a. Horiz. pair, imperf. btwn. *225.00* —
b. Black and Prus blue omitted *800.00*

Grandma Moses (Anna Mary Robertson Moses, 1860-1961), primitive painter of American life.

Beware of pairs with blind perfs. being offered as No. 1370a. No. 1370b often comes with mottled or disturbed gum. Such stamps sell for about two-thirds as much as copies with perfect gum.

Apollo 8 Issue

Moon Surface and Earth — A793

Giori Press Printing

1969, May 5 *Perf. 11*

1371 A793 6c blk, bl & ocher .20 .20

Apollo 8 mission, which put the 1st men into orbit around the moon, Dec. 21-27, 1968.

Imperfs. exist from printer's waste.

William Christopher Handy Issue

W. C. Handy (1873-1958), Jazz Musician and Composer — A794

Lithographed, Engraved (Giori)

1969, May 17 *Perf. 11*

1372 A794 6c multicolored .20 .20

California Settlement, 200th Anniv.

Carmel Mission Belfry — A795

1969, July 16 *Perf. 11*

1373 A795 6c multicolored .20 .20
b. Red (engr.) missing (CM) —

John Wesley Powell Issue

Powell Exploring Colorado River A796

1969, Aug. 1 *Perf. 11*

1374 A796 6c multicolored .20 .20

Powell (1834-1902), geologist and explorer of the Green and Colorado Rivers, 1869-1875.

Alabama Statehood, 150th Anniv.

Camellia & Yellow-shafted Flicker — A797

1969, Aug. 2 *Perf. 11*

1375 A797 6c multicolored .20 .20

Botanical Congress Issue

Douglas Fir (Northwest) A798

Lady's-slipper (Northeast) — A799

Ocotillo (Southwest) A800

Franklinia (Southeast) A801

Lithographed, Engraved (Giori)

1969, Aug. 23 *Perf. 11*

1376 A798 6c multicolored .35 .20
1377 A799 6c multicolored .35 .20
1378 A800 6c multicolored .35 .20
1379 A801 6c multicolored .35 .20
a. Block of 4, #1376-1379 1.50 *2.50*

11th Intl. Botanical Cong., Seattle, Wash., Aug. 24-Sept. 2.

Dartmouth College Case Issue

Daniel Webster & Dartmouth Hall — A802

Rotary Press Printing

1969, Sept. 22 *Perf. 10½x11*

1380 A802 6c green .20 .20

Sesquicentennial of the Dartmouth College case, argued by Daniel Webster before the Supreme Court, which reasserted the sanctity of contracts.

Professional Baseball Centenary

Batter A803

Lithographed, Engraved (Giori)

1969, Sept. 24 *Perf. 11*

1381 A803 6c yel, red, blk & grn .65 .20
a. Black (1869-1969, United States, 6c, Professional Baseball) omitted *1,100.*

Intercollegiate Football Centenary

Football Player & Coach A804

1969, Sept. 26 *Perf. 11*

1382 A804 6c red & green .20 .20

Dwight D. Eisenhower Issue

Dwight D. Eisenhower A805

Giori Press Printing

1969, Oct. 14 *Perf. 11*

1383 A805 6c blue, black & red .20 .20
b. Blue ("U.S. 6c Postage") missing (PS) —

Gen. Eisenhower, 34th Pres. (1890-1969).

Christmas Issue

Winter Sunday in Norway, Maine A806

Engraved (Multicolor Huck)

1969, Nov. 3 *Perf. 11x10½*

1384 A806 6c dk green & multi .20 .20
Precanceled .50 .20
b. Imperf., pair *1,000.*
c. Light green omitted *22.50*
d. Lt grn, red & yel omitted *950.00* —
e. Yellow omitted *2,250.*
g. Red & yellow omitted *3,000.*
h. Lt grn & yellow omitted —

The precancel value applies to the experimental precancel printed in four cities with the names between lines 4½mm apart: in black or green "ATLANTA, GA" and in green only "BALTIMORE, MD," "MEMPHIS, TN" and "NEW HAVEN, CT."

They were sold freely to the public and could be used on any class of mail at all post offices during the experimental program and thereafter.

Most examples of No. 1384c show orange where the offset green was.

Value is for this variety. Copies without orange sell for a premium.

Cured Child — A807

"Old Models" — A808

Hope for Crippled Issue

Lithographed, Engraved (Giori)

1969, Nov. 20 *Perf. 11*

1385 A807 6c multicolored .20 .20

Issued to encourage the rehabilitation of crippled children and adults, and to honor the Natl. Soc. for Crippled Children and Adults (Easter Seal Soc.) on its 50th anniv.

William M. Harnett Issue

1969, Dec. 3 *Perf. 11*

1386 A808 6c multicolored .20 .20

Harnett (1848-1892), painter. The painting is in the Museum of Fine Arts, Boston.

Natural History Issue

American Bald Eagle — A809

African Elephant Herd — A810

Tlingit Chief in Haida Ceremonial Canoe — A811

Brontosaurus, Stegosaurus & Allosaurus — A812

Lithographed, Engraved (Giori)

1970, May 6 *Perf. 11*

1387 A809 6c multicolored .20 .20
1388 A810 6c multicolored .20 .20
1389 A811 6c multicolored .20 .20
1390 A812 6c multicolored .20 .20
a. Block of 4, #1387-1390 .55 *.80*

1969-1970 celebration of the cent. of the American Museum of Natural History in NYC.

The design of No. 1390 is a detail from a mural by Rudolph Zallinger in Yale's Peabody Museum.

Maine Statehood Issue

Lighthouse at Two Lights, Maine A813

Lithographed, Engraved (Giori)

1970, July 9 *Perf. 11*

1391 A813 6c black & multi .20 .20

Sesquicentennial of Maine statehood. The painting by Edward Hopper (1882-1967) hangs in the Metropolitan Museum of Art, NYC.

Wildlife Conservation Issue

American Buffalo A814

Rotary Press Printing

1970, July 20 *Perf. 10½x11*

1392 A814 6c black, *light brown* .20 .20

Regular Issue

Dwight David Eisenhower

A815 — Dot between "R" and "U"

A815a — No dot between "R" and "U"

Benjamin Franklin A816

USPS Emblem A817

Fiorello H. LaGuardia A817a

Ernest Taylor Pyle A818

Dr. Elizabeth Blackwell A818a

Amadeo P. Giannini A818b

Rotary (6c, 7c, 14c, 16c, 18c, 21c, #1395); Giori (#1394); Photo. (#1396)

Perf. 11x10½, 10½x11; 11 (#1394)

1970-74

1393 A815 6c dark blue gray .20 .20
- *a.* Booklet pane of 8 1.50 *.75*
- *b.* Booklet pane of 5 + label 1.50 *.75*
- *c.* Untagged (Bureau precanceled) .20

1393D A816 7c brt blue ('72) .20 .20
- *e.* Untagged (Bureau precanceled) .20

1394 A815a 8c blk, red & bl gray ('71) .20 .20
- *b.* Red missing (PS) —
- *c.* Red and blue missing (PS) —

1395 A815 8c dp claret ('71) .20 .20
- *a.* Booklet pane of 8 1.80 *1.25*
- *b.* Booklet pane of 6 1.25 *1.10*
- *c.* Booklet pane of 4 + 2 labels ('72) 1.65 *1.00*
- *d.* Bklt. pane of 7 + label ('72) 1.90 *1.10*
- *e.* Vert. pair, imperf. btwn. 600.00

1396 A817 8c multi ('71) .20 .20
1397 A817a 14c gray brn ('72) .25 .20
- *a.* Untagged (Bureau precanceled) .25

1398 A818 16c brown ('71) .30 .20
- *a.* Untagged (Bureau precanceled) .35

1399 A818a 18c violet ('74) .35 .20
1400 A818b 21c green ('73) .40 .20
Nos. 1393-1400 (9) 2.30 1.80

No. 1395 was issued in booklets only. All stamps have one or two straight edges.

No. 1395e resulted from a paper foldover after perforating and before cutting into panes. At least 4 pairs are recorded from 3 panes (one No. 1395a and two No. 1395d) with different foldover patterns.

Issued: 6c, 8/6/70; 7c, 10/20/72; #1394-1395, 5/10/71; #1396, 7/1/71; 14c, 4/24/72; 16c, 5/7/71; 18c, 1/23/74; 21c, 6/27/73.

Coil Stamps

Rotary Press

1970-71 ***Perf. 10 Vert.***

1401 A815 6c dark blue gray .20 .20
- *a.* Untagged (Bureau precanceled) .20
- *b.* Imperf., pair 2,000.

1402 A815 8c deep claret .20 .20
- *a.* Imperf., pair 45.00
- *b.* Untagged (Bureau precanceled) .20
- *c.* Pair, imperf. btwn. 6,250.

Issue dates: 6c, Aug. 6; 8c, May 10, 1971.

Edgar Lee Masters Issue

A819

Lithographed, Engraved (Giori)

1970, Aug. 22 ***Perf. 11***

1405 A819 6c black & olive bister .20 .20

Edgar Lee Masters (1869-1950), Poet

Woman Suffrage Issue

Suffragettes, 1920 & Woman Voter, 1970 — A820

Giori Press Printing

1970, Aug. 26 ***Perf. 11***

1406 A820 6c blue .20 .20

50th anniv. of the 19th Amendment, which gave women the vote.

South Carolina Issue

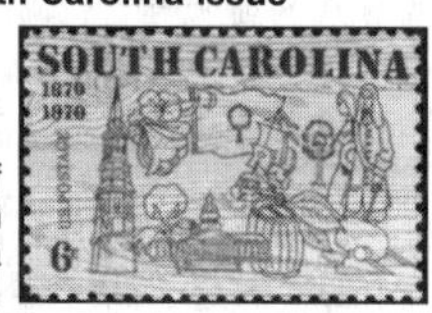

Symbols of South Carolina A821

Lithographed, Engraved (Giori)

1970, Sept. 12 ***Perf. 11***

1407 A821 6c bister, black & red .20 .20

300th anniv. of the founding of Charles Town (Charleston), the 1st permanent settlement of SC.

Against a background of pine wood the line drawings of the design represent the economic and historic development of SC: The spire of St. Phillip's Church, Capitol, state flag, a ship, 17th cent. man and woman, a Fort Sumter cannon, barrels, cotton, tobacco and yellow jessamine.

Stone Mountain Memorial Issue

A822

Giori Press Printing

1970, Sept. 19 ***Perf. 11***

1408 A822 6c gray .20 .20

Dedication of the Stone Mountain Confederate Memorial, featuring Robert E. Lee, Jefferson Davis & "Stonewall" Jackson, GA, May 9, 1970.

Fort Snelling Issue

Fort Snelling, Keelboat & Tepees A823

Lithographed, Engraved (Giori)

1970, Oct. 17 ***Perf. 11***

1409 A823 6c yellow & multi .20 .20

150th anniv. of Fort Snelling, MN, which was an important outpost for the opening of the Northwest.

Anti-Pollution Issue

Globe and Wheat A824

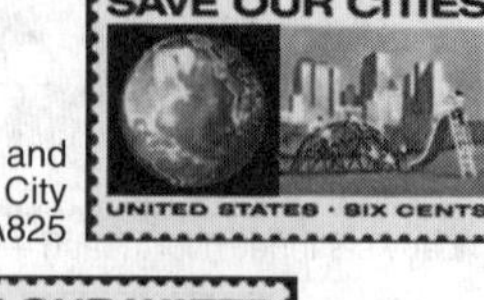

Globe and City A825

Globe and Bluegill A826

Globe and Seagull A827

1970, Oct. 28 Photo. ***Perf. 11x10½***

1410 A824 6c multicolored .25 .20
1411 A825 6c multicolored .25 .20
1412 A826 6c multicolored .25 .20
1413 A827 6c multicolored .25 .20
- *a.* Block of 4, #1410-1413 1.10 *1.50*

Christmas Issue

Nativity — A828

Tin and Cast-iron Locomotive A829

Toy Horse on Wheels A830

Mechanical Tricycle A831

Doll Carriage A832

1970, Nov. 5 Photo. ***Perf. 10½x11***

1414 A828 6c multicolored .20 .20
- *a.* Precanceled .20 .20
- *b.* Black omitted 550.00
- *c.* As "a," blue omitted 1,500.

Perf. 11x10½

1415 A829 6c multicolored .30 .20
- *a.* Precanceled .75 .20
- *b.* Black omitted 2,500.

1416 A830 6c multicolored .30 .20
- *a.* Precanceled .75 .20
- *b.* Black omitted 2,500.
- *c.* Imperf., pair (#1416, 1418) 4,000.

1417 A831 6c multicolored .30 .20
- *a.* Precanceled .75 .20
- *b.* Black omitted 2,500.

1418 A832 6c multicolored .30 .20
- *a.* Precanceled .75 .20
- *b.* Block of 4, #1415-1418 1.25 *1.75*
- *c.* As "b," precanceled 3.25 *3.75*
- *d.* Black omitted 2,500.
- *e.* As "b," black omitted 10,000.
- *f.* As "b," black omitted on #1417 & 1418 —

Nos. 1414-1418 (5) 1.40 1.00

No. 1414, Nativity, by Lorenzo Lotto (1480-1556). Nos. 1415-1418 are antique Christmas toys.

The precanceled stamps, Nos. 1414a-1418a, were furnished to 68 cities. The plates include two straight (No. 1414a) or two wavy (Nos. 1415a-1418a) black lines that make up the precancellation.

Unused values are for copies with gum and used values are for copies with an additional cancellation or without gum.

United Nations, 25th Anniv.

"UN" & UN Emblem A833

Lithographed, Engraved (Giori)

1970, Nov. 20 ***Perf. 11***

1419 A833 6c black, ver & ultra .20 .20

Landing of the Pilgrims Issue

Mayflower & Pilgrims — A834

Lithographed, Engraved (Giori)

1970, Nov. 21 ***Perf. 11***

1420 A834 6c blk, org, yel, brn, mag & bl .20 .20
- *a.* Orange & yellow omitted 900.00

Mayflower landing, 350th anniv.

Disabled Veterans & Servicemen Issue

A835

A836

Lithographed, Engraved (Giori)

1970, Nov. 24 ***Perf. 11***

1421 A835 6c multicolored .20 .20

Engr.

1422 A836 6c dk bl, blk & red .20 .20
- *a.* Pair, #1421-1422 .30 .30

50th anniv. of the Disabled Veterans of America Organization (No. 1421).

Honoring the contribution of servicemen, particularly those who were prisoners of war or missing in action (No. 1422).

Ewe and Lamb A837

Douglas MacArthur A838

American Wool Industry Issue
Lithographed, Engraved (Giori)

1971, Jan. 19 ***Perf. 11***

1423 A837 6c multicolored .20 .20
 b. Teal blue ("United States") missing (CM) —

450th anniv. of the introduction of sheep to the No. American continent and the beginning of the American wool industry.

Gen. Douglas MacArthur Issue
Giori Press Printing

1971, Jan. 26

1424 A838 6c blk, red & dk bl .20 .20
 a. Red missing (PS) —
 c. Blue missing (PS) —

MacArthur (1880-1964), Chief of Staff, Supreme Commander for the Allied Powers in the Pacific Area during WW II and Supreme Commander in Japan after the war.

Blood Donor Issue

Giving Blood Saves Lives A839

1971, Mar. 12 ***Perf. 11***

1425 A839 6c lt blue, scar & ind .20 .20

Salute to blood donors and spur to participation in the blood donor program.

Missouri Sesquicentennial Issue

"Independence and the Opening of the West" — A840

1971, May 8 Photo. ***Perf. 11x10½***

1426 A840 8c multicolored .20 .20

Detail, by Thomas Hart Benton. The stamp design shows a Pawnee facing a hunter-trapper and a group of settlers.

Wildlife Conservation Issue

Trout A841

Alligator — A842

Polar Bear, Cubs A843

California Condor — A844

Lithographed, Engraved (Giori)

1971, June 12 ***Perf. 11***

1427 A841 8c multicolored .20 .20
 a. Red omitted 1,250.
 b. Green (engr.) omitted —
1428 A842 8c multicolored .20 .20
1429 A843 8c multicolored .20 .20
1430 A844 8c multicolored .20 .20
 a. Block of 4, #1427-1430 .80 1.00
 b. As "a," lt grn & dk grn omitted from #1427-1428 4,500.
 c. As "a," red omitted from #1427, 1429-1430 7,500.

Antarctic Treaty Issue

Map of Antarctica A845

Giori Press Printing

1971, June 23

1431 A845 8c red & dark blue .20 .20
 b. Both colors missing (EP) 500.00

10th anniv. of the Antarctic Treaty pledging peaceful uses of and scientific cooperation in Antarctica.

No. 1431b should be collected se-tenant with a normal stamp and/or a partially printed stamp.

American Revolution Bicentennial

Bicentennial Commission Emblem — A846

Lithographed, Engraved (Giori)

1971, July 4 ***Perf. 11***

1432 A846 8c red, blue, gray & black .20 .20
 a. Gray & black missing (EP) 500.00
 b. Gray ("U.S. Postage 8c") missing (EP) 900.00

John Sloan Issue

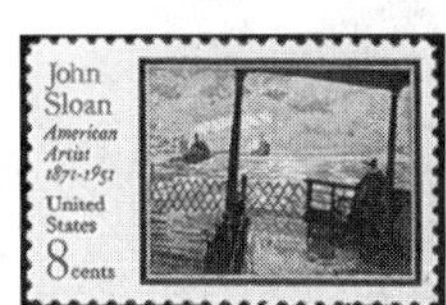

The Wake of the Ferry A847

1971, Aug. 2 ***Perf. 11***

1433 A847 8c multicolored .20 .20
 b. Red engr. ("John Sloan" and "8") missing (CM) —

Sloan (1871-1951), painter.

Space Achievement Decade Issue

Earth, Sun, Landing Craft on Moon A848

Lunar Rover A849

Lithographed, Engraved (Giori)

1971, Aug. 2 ***Perf. 11***

1434 A848 8c blk, bl, yel & red .20 .20
1435 A849 8c blk, bl, yel & red .20 .20
 b. Pair, #1434-1435 .40 .45
 d. As "b," bl & red (litho.) omitted 1,500.

Apollo 15 moon exploration mission July 26-Aug. 7.

Emily Elizabeth Dickinson A850

Sentry Box, Morro Castle, San Juan A851

Emily Dickinson Issue
Lithographed, Engraved (Giori)

1971, Aug. 28 ***Perf. 11***

1436 A850 8c multi, *greenish* .20 .20
 a. Black & olive (engr.) omitted 750.
 b. Pale rose omitted 7,500.
 c. Red omitted —

Dickinson (1830-1886), poet.

San Juan, PR, 450th Anniv.

1971, Sept. 12

1437 A851 8c multicolored .20 .20

VALUES FOR HINGED STAMPS AFTER NO. 771

This catalogue does not value unused stamps after No. 771 in hinged condition. Hinged unused stamps from No. 772 to the present are worth considerably less than the values given for unused stamps, which are for never-hinged examples.

Young Woman Drug Addict — A852

Hands Reaching for CARE — A853

Prevent Drug Abuse Issue

1971, Oct. 4 Photo. ***Perf. 10½x11***

1438 A852 8c bl, dp bl & blk .20 .20

Drug Abuse Prevention Week, Oct. 3-9.

CARE Issue

1971, Oct. 27

1439 A853 8c multicolored .20 .20
 a. Black omitted 4,750.

25th anniv. of CARE, a US-Canadian Cooperative for American Relief Everywhere.

Historic Preservation Issue

Decatur House, Washington, DC — A854

Whaling Ship Charles W. Morgan, Mystic, Conn. — A855

Cable Car, San Francisco — A856

San Xavier del Bac Mission, Tucson, Ariz. — A857

Lithographed, Engraved (Giori)

1971, Oct. 29 Buff Paper ***Perf. 11***

1440 A854 8c blk brn & ocher .20 .20
1441 A855 8c blk brn & ocher .20 .20
1442 A856 8c blk brn & ocher .20 .20
1443 A857 8c blk brn & ocher .20 .20
 a. Block of 4, #1440-1443 .75 1.00
 b. As "a," black brown omitted 2,250.
 c. As "a," ocher omitted —

Christmas Issue

Adoration of the Shepherds, by Giorgione A858

Partridge in a Pear Tree, by Jamie Wyeth A859

1971, Nov. 10 Photo. ***Perf. 10½x11***

1444 A858 8c gold & multi .20 .20
 a. Gold omitted 525.00
1445 A859 8c multicolored .20 .20

Sidney Lanier (1842-1881) A860

Peace Corps Poster, by David Battle A861

Sidney Lanier Issue
Giori Press Printing

1972, Feb. 3 ***Perf. 11***

1446 A860 8c blk, brn & lt bl .20 .20

Lanier, poet, musician, lawyer, educator.

Peace Corps Issue

1972, Feb. 11 Photo. ***Perf. 10½x11***

1447 A861 8c dk bl, lt bl & red .20 .20

National Parks Centennial Issue

Hulk of Ship A862 — Cape Hatteras Lighthouse A863

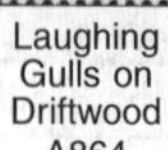

Laughing Gulls on Driftwood A864 — Laughing Gulls and Dune A865

Wolf Trap Farm, Vienna, Va. — A866

Old Faithful, Yellowstone — A867

Mt. McKinley, Alaska A868

Lithographed, Engraved (Giori)

1972 ***Perf. 11***

1448 A862 2c black & multi .20 .20
1449 A863 2c black & multi .20 .20
1450 A864 2c black & multi .20 .20
1451 A865 2c black & multi .20 .20
  a. Block of 4, #1448-1451 .25 *.45*
  b. As "a," black (litho.) omitted *2,250.*
1452 A866 6c black & multi .20 .20
1453 A867 8c blk, blue, brn & multi .20 .20
1454 A868 15c black & multi .30 .20
  b. Yellow omitted —

Cent. of Yellowstone Natl. Park, the 1st Natl. Park, and of the Natl. Park System. The four 2c stamps were issued for Cape Hatteras, NC, Natl. Seashore.

Issued: 2c, 4/5; 6c, 6/26; 8c, 3/1; 15c, 7/28.

See No. C84.

Family Planning Issue

Family — A869

1972, Mar. 18

1455 A869 8c black & multi .20 .20
  a. Yellow omitted *1,250.*
  c. Dark brown missing (FO) *9,500*

American Bicentennial
Colonial American Craftsmen

Glassmaker A870

Silversmith A871

Wigmaker A872

Hatter A873

1972, July 4 Engr. *Perf. 11x10½*
Dull Yellow Paper

1456 A870 8c deep brown .20 .20
1457 A871 8c deep brown .20 .20
1458 A872 8c deep brown .20 .20
1459 A873 8c deep brown .20 .20
  a. Block of 4, #1456-1459 .65 *.90*

Olympic Games Issue

Bicycling and Olympic Rings A874

Bobsledding A875

Running A876

1972, Aug. 17 Photo. *Perf. 11x10½*

1460 A874 6c multicolored .20 .20
1461 A875 8c multicolored .20 .20
1462 A876 15c multicolored .30 .20
  Nos. 1460-1462 (3) .70 .60

11th Winter Olympic Games, Sapporo, Japan, Feb. 3-13, and 20th Summer Olympic Games, Munich, Germany, Aug. 26-Sept. 11.

See No. C85.

Parent Teacher Association, 75th Anniv.

Blackboard A877

1972, Sept. 15 Photo. *Perf. 11x10½*

1463 A877 8c yellow & black .20 .20

Wildlife Conservation Issue

Fur Seals — A878

Cardinal — A879

Brown Pelican — A880

Bighorn Sheep — A881

Lithographed, Engraved

1972, Sept. 20 ***Perf. 11***

1464 A878 8c multicolored .20 .20
1465 A879 8c multicolored .20 .20
1466 A880 8c multicolored .20 .20
1467 A881 8c multicolored .20 .20
  a. Block of 4, #1464-1467 .65 *.90*
  b. As "a," brown omitted *4,000.*
  c. As "a," green & blue omitted *4,500.*
  d. As "a," red & brown omitted *3,000.*

Mail Order Issue

Rural Post Office Store A882

1972, Sept. 27 Photo. *Perf. 11x10½*

1468 A882 8c multicolored .20 .20

Cent. of mail order business, originated by Aaron Montgomery Ward, Chicago.

Osteopathic Medicine Issue

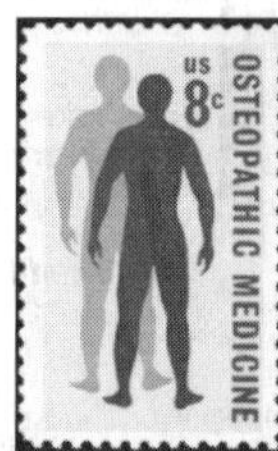

Man's Quest for Health — A883

1972, Oct. 9 Photo. *Perf. 10½x11*

1469 A883 8c yel, org & dk brn .20 .20

75th anniv. of the American Osteopathic Assoc., founded by Dr. Andrew T. Still.

American Folklore Issue

Tom Sawyer, by Norman Rockwell — A884

Lithographed, Engraved (Giori)

1972, Oct. 13 ***Perf. 11***

1470 A884 8c black & multi .20 .20
  a. Horiz. pair, imperf. btwn. *4,500.*
  b. Red & black (engr.) omitted *1,700.*
  c. Yellow & tan (litho.) omitted *2,400.*

Tom Sawyer, hero of "The Adventures of Tom Sawyer," by Mark Twain.

Angel from "Mary, Queen of Heaven" A885

Santa Claus A886

1972, Nov. 9 Photo. *Perf. 10½x11*

1471 A885 8c multicolored .20 .20
  a. Pink omitted *140.00*
  b. Black omitted *4,000.*
1472 A886 8c multicolored .20 .20

Design of No. 1471 shows detail from a painting by the Master of the St. Lucy Legend.

Pharmacy Issue

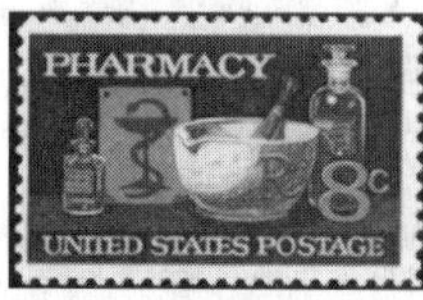

Mortar & Pestle, Bowl of Hygeia, 19th Century Medicine Bottles A887

Lithographed, Engraved (Giori)

1972, Nov. 10 ***Perf. 11***

1473 A887 8c black & multi .20 .20
  a. Blue & orange omitted *800.00*
  b. Blue omitted *2,100.*
  c. Orange omitted *2,100.*

Honoring American druggists, and 120th anniv. of the American Pharmaceutical Assoc.

Stamp Collecting Issue

U.S. No. 1 Under Magnifying Glass A888

1972, Nov. 17 ***Perf. 11***

1474 A888 8c dark blue green, black & brown .20 .20
  a. Black (litho.) omitted *600.00*

Love Issue

"Love," by Robert Indiana A889

1973, Jan. 26 Photo. *Perf. 11x10½*

1475 A889 8c red, emer & vio bl .20 .20

American Bicentennial
Communications in Colonial Times

Printer and Patriots Examining Pamphlet A890

Posting a Broadside A891

Postrider
A892

Drummer
A893

1973 Giori Press Printing ***Perf. 11***
1476 A890 8c ultra, grnsh blk & red .20 .20
1477 A891 8c black, ver & ultra .20 .20

Lithographed, Engraved (Giori)
1478 A892 8c multicolored .20 .20
a. Red missing (CM) —
1479 A893 8c multicolored .20 .20
Nos. 1476-1479 (4) .80 .80

Issued: No. 1476, Feb. 16; No. 1477, Apr. 13; No. 1478, June 22; No. 1479, Sept. 28.

Boston Tea Party

British Merchantman — A894

British Three-master — A895

Boats and Ship's Hull
A896

Boat and Dock
A897

Lithographed, Engraved (Giori)
1973, July 4 ***Perf. 11***
1480 A894 8c black & multi .20 .20
1481 A895 8c black & multi .20 .20
1482 A896 8c black & multi .20 .20
1483 A897 8c black & multi .20 .20
a. Block of 4, #1480-1483 .65 *.90*
b. As "a," black (engr.) omitted *1,500.*
c. As "a," black (litho.) omitted *1,200.*

American Arts Issue

Gershwin, Sportin' Life, Porgy & Bess
A898

Robinson Jeffers, Man & Children of Carmel with Burro
A899

Henry Ossawa Tanner, Palette & Rainbow
A900

Willa Cather, Pioneer Family & Covered Wagon
A901

1973 Photo. ***Perf. 11***
1484 A898 8c dp grn & multi .20 .20
a. Vert. pair, imperf. horiz. *240.00*
1485 A899 8c Prus bl & multi .20 .20
a. Vert. pair, imperf. horiz. *250.00*
1486 A900 8c yel brn & multi .20 .20
1487 A901 8c dp brn & multi .20 .20
a. Vert. pair, imperf. horiz. *275.00*
Nos. 1484-1487 (4) .80 .80

Honoring: No. 1484, George Gershwin (1898-1937), composer. No. 1485, Robinson Jeffers (1887-1962), poet. No. 1486, Henry Ossawa Tanner (1859-1937), black painter (portrait by Thomas Eakins). No. 1487, Willa Sibert Cather (1873-1947), novelist.
Issued: No. 1484, Feb. 28; No. 1485, Aug. 13; No. 1486, Sept. 10; No. 1487, Sept. 20.

Copernicus Issue

Nicolaus Copernicus (1473-1543), Polish Astronomer — A902

Lithographed, Engraved (Giori)
1973, Apr. 23 ***Perf. 11***
1488 A902 8c black & orange .20 .20
a. Orange omitted *1,000.*
b. Black (engraved) omitted *900.00*

The orange color can be chemically removed.
Expertization of No. 1488a is required.

Postal Service Employees' Issue

Stamp Counter
A903

Mail Collection
A904

Letter Facing on Conveyor Belt — A905

Parcel Post Sorting — A906

Mail Canceling
A907

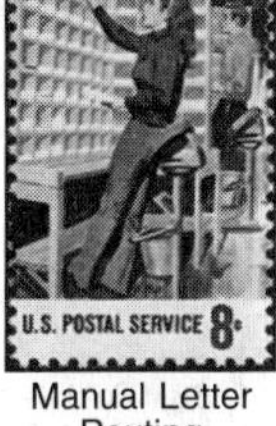

Manual Letter Routing
A908

Electronic Letter Routing — A909

Loading Mail on Truck — A910

Mailman
A911

Rural Mail Delivery
A912

1973, Apr. 30 Photo. ***Perf. 10½x11***
1489 A903 8c multicolored .20 .20
1490 A904 8c multicolored .20 .20
1491 A905 8c multicolored .20 .20
1492 A906 8c multicolored .20 .20
1493 A907 8c multicolored .20 .20
1494 A908 8c multicolored .20 .20
1495 A909 8c multicolored .20 .20
1496 A910 8c multicolored .20 .20
1497 A911 8c multicolored .20 .20
1498 A912 8c multicolored .20 .20
a. Strip of 10, Nos. 1489-1498 1.75 *2.00*

A tribute to USPS employees. Emerald inscription on back, printed beneath gum in water-soluble ink, includes the USPS emblem, "People Serving You" and a statement, differing for each of the 10 stamps, about some aspect of postal service.
Each stamp in top or bottom row has a tab with blue inscription enumerating various jobs in postal service.

Harry S Truman Issue

Harry S Truman, 33rd President (1884-1972)
A913

Giori Press Printing
1973, May 8 ***Perf. 11***
1499 A913 8c car rose, blk & bl .20 .20

Electronics Progress Issue

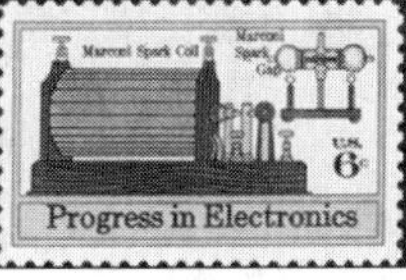

Marconi's Spark Coil and Gap
A914

Transistors and Printed Circuit Board
A915

Microphone, Speaker, Vacuum Tube, TV Camera Tube — A916

Lithographed, Engraved (Giori)
1973, July 10 ***Perf. 11***
1500 A914 6c lilac & multi .20 .20
1501 A915 8c tan & multi .20 .20
a. Black (inscriptions & "U.S. 8c") omitted *450.00*
b. Tan (background) & lilac omitted *1,250.*
1502 A916 15c gray green & multi .30 20
a. Black (inscriptions & "U.S. 15c") omitted *1,350.*
Nos. 1500-1502 (3) .70 .60

No. 1501b hinged is ½ unhinged value.
See No. C86.

Lyndon B. Johnson Issue

Lyndon B. Johnson (1908-1973), 36th President — A917

1973, Aug. 27 Photo. ***Perf. 11***
1503 A917 8c black & multi .20 .20
a. Horiz. pair, imperf. vert. *350.00*

Rural America Issue

Angus and Longhorn Cattle
A918

Chautauqua Tent and Buggies — A919

Wheat Fields and Train
A920

Lithographed, Engraved (Giori)
1973-74 ***Perf. 11***
1504 A918 8c multicolored .20 .20
a. Green & red brown omitted *950.00*
b. Vert. pair, imperf. between —
1505 A919 10c multicolored .20 .20
a. Black (litho.) omitted *2,000.*
1506 A920 10c multicolored .20 .20
a. Black & blue (engr.) omitted *700.00*
Nos. 1504-1506 (3) .60 .60

Cent. of introduction of Aberdeen Angus cattle to US (No. 1504); of Chautauqua Institution (No. 1505); of introduction of hard winter wheat into Kansas by Mennonite immigrants (No. 1506).
Issue dates: No. 1504, Oct. 5, 1973; No. 1505, Aug. 6, 1974; No. 1506, Aug. 16, 1974.

Christmas Issue

Small Cowper Madonna, by Raphael A921

Christmas Tree in Needlepoint A922

1973, Nov. 7 Photo. *Perf. 10½x11*

1507 A921 8c tan & multi .20 .20
1508 A922 8c green & multi .20 .20
a. Vert. pair, imperf. btwn. *300.00*

50-Star & 13-Star Flags A923

Jefferson Memorial & Signature A924

Mail Transport A925

Liberty Bell A926

Multicolor Huck Press

1973-74 Tagged *Perf. 11x10½*

1509	A923 10c red & blue	.20	.20
a.	Horiz. pair, imperf. btwn.	*50.*	—
b.	Blue omitted	*175.*	—
c.	Vert. pair, imperf.	*850.*	—
d.	Horiz. pair, imperf. vert.	*1,000.*	

Rotary Press Printing

1510	A924 10c blue	.20	.20
a.	Untagged (Bureau precanceled)		.20
b.	Booklet pane of 5 + label	1.65	*.90*
c.	Booklet pane of 8	1.65	*1.00*
d.	Booklet pane of 6 ('74)	5.25	*1.75*
e.	Vert. pair, imperf. horiz.	*525.00*	
f.	Vert. pair, imperf. btwn.	700.00	
1511	A925 10c multi, photo	.20	.20
a.	Yellow omitted	*65.00*	

The yellow can be chemically removed.

Coil Stamps

Perf. 10 Vert.

Rotary Press Printing

1518	A926 6.3c brick red	.20	.20
a.	Untagged (Bureau precanceled)		.20
b.	Imperf., pair	*210.00*	
c.	As "a," imperf. pair		*100.00*

Multicolor Huck Press

1519	A923 10c red & blue	.20	.20
a.	Imperf., pair	37.50	

Rotary Press Printing

1520	A924 10c blue	.25	.20
a.	Untagged (Bureau precanceled)		.25
b.	Imperf., pair	40.00	

Issued: #1509, 1519, 12/8/73; #1510, 1520, 12/14/73; #1511, 1/4/74; #1518, 10/1/74.

Veterans of Foreign Wars Issue

V.F.W. Emblem A928

Giori Press Printing

1974, Mar. 11 *Perf. 11*

1525 A928 10c red & dark blue .20 .20
b. Blue missing (PS) —

75th anniv. of Veterans of Spanish American and other Foreign Wars.

Robert Frost Issue

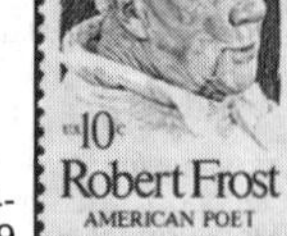
Robert Frost (1874-1963), Poet — A929

Rotary Press Printing

1974, Mar. 26 *Perf. 10½x11*

1526 A929 10c black .20 .20

EXPO '74 Issue

"Cosmic Jumper" A930

1974, Apr. 18 Photo. *Perf. 11*

1527 A930 10c multicolored .20 .20

EXPO '74, Spokane, Wash., May 4-Nov. 4. Theme, "Preserve the Environment."

Horse Racing Issue

Horses Rounding Turn A931

1974, May 4 Photo. *Perf. 11x10½*

1528 A931 10c yellow & multi .25 .20
a. Bl ("Horse Racing") omitted *875.00*
b. Red ("U.S. postage 10 cents") omitted —

Beware of stamps offered as No. 1528b that have traces of red.

Skylab Issue

Skylab A932

Lithographed, Engraved (Giori)

1974, May 14 *Perf. 11*

1529 A932 10c multicolored .20 .20
a. Vert. pair, imperf. btwn. —

1st anniv. of the launching of Skylab and to honor all who participated in the Skylab projects.

Centenary of UPU Issue

Michelangelo, from School of Athens — A933

Five Feminine Virtues — A934

Old Time Letter Rack — A935

Mlle. La Vergne — A936

Lady Writing Letter — A937

Inkwell and Quill — A938

Mrs. John Douglas — A939

Don Antonio Noreiga — A940

1974, June 6 Photo. *Perf. 11*

1530	A933 10c by Raphael	.20	.20
1531	A934 10c by Hokusai	.20	.20
1532	A935 10c by Peto	.20	.20
1533	A936 10c by Liotard	.20	.20
1534	A937 10c by Terborch	.20	.20
1535	A938 10c by Chardin	.20	.20
1536	A939 10c by Gainsborough	.20	.20
1537	A940 10c by Goya	.20	.20
a.	Block or strip, #1530-1537	1.75	1.60
b.	As "a" (block), imperf. vert.	*7,000.*	

Mineral Heritage Issue

Petrified Wood A941

Tourmaline — A942

Amethyst A943

Rhodochrosite — A944

Lithographed, Engraved (Giori)

1974, June 13 *Perf. 11*

1538	A941 10c lt blue & multi	.20	.20
a.	Light blue & yellow omitted	—	
1539	A942 10c lt blue & multi	.20	.20
a.	Light blue omitted	—	
b.	Black & purple omitted	—	
1540	A943 10c lt blue & multi	.20	.20
a.	Light blue & yellow omitted	—	
1541	A944 10c lt blue & multi	.20	.20
a.	Block or strip, #1538-1541	.80	.90
b.	As "a," lt bl & yel omitted	*1,900.*	
c.	Light blue omitted	—	
d.	Black & red omitted	—	

Kentucky Settlement Issue

Fort Harrod — A945

Lithographed, Engraved (Giori)

1974, June 15 *Perf. 11*

1542 A945 10c green & multi .20 .20
- *a.* Dull black (litho.) omitted 750.00
- *b.* Grn (engr. & litho.), blk (engr. & litho.), bl missing (EP) 3,000.
- *c.* Green (engr.) missing (EP) —
- *d.* Grn (engr.), blk (litho.) missing (EP) —
- *f.* Blue (litho.) omitted —

American Bicentennial
First Continental Congress

Carpenters' Hall A946

A947

A948

Independence Hall — A949

Giori Press Printing

1974, July 4 *Perf. 11*

1543 A946 10c dark blue & red .20 .20
1544 A947 10c gray, dk bl & red .20 .20
1545 A948 10c gray, dk bl & red .20 .20
1546 A949 10c red & dark blue .20 .20
- *a.* Block of 4, #1543-1546 .80 .90

Energy Conservation Issue

A950

Lithographed, Engraved (Giori)

1974, Sept. 23 *Perf. 11*

1547 A950 10c multicolored .20 .20
- *a.* Blue & orange omitted 850.00
- *b.* Orange & green omitted 600.00
- *c.* Green omitted 825.

Design features molecules and drops of gasoline & oil to publicize the importance of conserving all forms of energy.

American Folklore Issue

Legend of Sleepy Hollow A951

Lithographed, Engraved (Giori)

1974, Oct. 10 *Perf. 11*

1548 A951 10c dk bl, blk, org & yel .20 .20

Legend of Sleepy Hollow, by Washington Irving.

Design features Headless Horseman pursuing Ichabod Crane.

Retarded Children Issue

Retarded Child — A952

Giori Press Printing

1974, Oct. 12 *Perf. 11*

1549 A952 10c brn red & dk brn .20 .20

Natl. Assoc. of Retarded Citizens.

Christmas Issue

Angel, from Perussis Altarpiece, 1480 — A953

"The Road-Winter," by Currier & Ives — A954

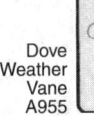

Dove Weather Vane A955

1974 **Photo.** *Perf. 10½x11*

1550 A953 10c multicolored .20 .20

Perf. 11x10½

1551 A954 10c multicolored .20 .20
- *a.* Buff omitted 35.00

No. 1551a is difficult to identify. Competent expertization is necessary.

Die Cut, Paper Backing Rouletted
Self-adhesive
Inscribed "Precanceled"
Untagged

1552 A955 10c multicolored .20 .20

Unused value of No. 1552 is for copy on rouletted paper backing as issued. Used value is for copy on piece, with or without postmark.

Most copies are becoming discolored, probably from the adhesive. Unused and used values are for discolored copies.

Die cutting includes crossed slashes through dove, applied to prevent removal and re-use of stamp. The stamp will separate into layers if soaked.

Issued: #1550-1551, 10/23; #1552, 11/15.

American Arts Issue

Benjamin West — A956

Paul Laurence Dunbar — A957

D. W. Griffith & Projector A958

1975 **Photo.** *Perf. 10½x11*

1553 A956 10c multicolored .20 .20

Perf. 11

1554 A957 10c multicolored .20 .20
- *a.* Imperf., pair 1,300.

Litho., Engr. (Giori)

1555 A958 10c multicolored .20 .20
- *a.* Brown (engr.) omitted 625.
- *Nos. 1553-1555 (3)* .60 .60

Honoring: West (1738-1820), painter (#1553). Dunbar (1872-1906), poet (#1554). David Lewelyn Wark Griffith (1875-1948), motion picture producer (#1555).

Issued: #1553, 2/10; #1554, 5/1; #1555, 5/27.

Space Issue

Pioneer 10 Passing Jupiter A959

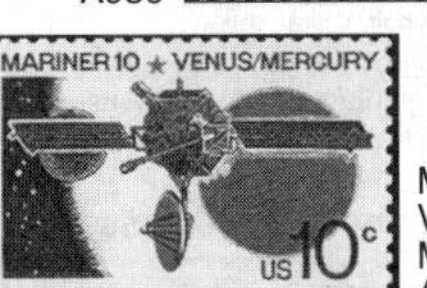

Mariner 10, Venus & Mercury A960

Lithographed, Engraved (Giori)

1975 *Perf. 11*

1556 A959 10c lt yel, dk yel, red, blue, & 2 dk blues .20 .20
- *a.* Red & dk yel omitted 1,400.
- *b.* Dk blues (engr.) omitted 950.
- *d.* Dark yellow omitted —

Imperfs. exist from printer's waste.

1557 A960 10c blk, red, ultra & bis .20 .20
- *a.* Red omitted 450.00 —
- *b.* Ultra & bister omitted 2,000.
- *d.* Red missing (PS) —

U.S. unmanned accomplishments in space. Pioneer 10 passed within 81,000 miles of Jupiter, Dec. 3, 1973. Mariner 10 explored Venus and Mercury in 1974, and Mercury again in Mar. 1975.

Issue dates: #1556, Feb. 28; #1557, Apr. 4.

Collective Bargaining Issue

"Labor and Management" — A961

1975, Mar. 13 **Photo.** *Perf. 11*

1558 A961 10c multicolored .20 .20

Collective Bargaining Law, enacted 1935 with Wagner Act. Imperfs. are printers waste.

American Bicentennial Contributors to the Cause

Sybil Ludington A962

Salem Poor A963

Haym Salomon A964

Peter Francisco A965

1975, Mar. 25 **Photo.** *Perf. 11x10½*

1559 A962 8c multicolored .20 .20
- *a.* Back inscription omitted 210.00

1560 A963 10c multicolored .20 .20
- *a.* Back inscription omitted 210.00

1561 A964 10c multicolored .20 .20
- *a.* Back inscription omitted 210.00
- *b.* Red omitted 250.00

1562 A965 18c multicolored .35 .20
- *Nos. 1559-1562 (4)* .95 .80

Ludington, age 16, rallied militia Apr. 26, 1777.

Poor, black freeman, fought in Battle of Bunker Hill.

Salomon, Jewish immigrant, raised money to finance Revolutionary War.

Francisco, Portuguese-French immigrant, joined Continental Army at 15.

An emerald inscription on back, printed beneath gum in water-soluble ink, gives a thumbnail sketch of the portrayed contributor.

Lexington-Concord Battle, 200th Anniv.

"Birth of Liberty," by Henry Sandham A966

1975, Apr. 19 **Photo.** *Perf. 11*

1563 A966 10c multicolored .20 .20
- *a.* Vert. pair, imperf. horiz. 425.00

Battle of Bunker Hill, 200th Anniv.

Battle of Bunker Hill, by John Trumbull — A967

1975, June 17 *Perf. 11*

1564 A967 10c multicolored .20 .20

Military Uniforms

Soldier with Flintlock Musket, Uniform Button — A968

Sailor with Grappling Hook, First Navy Jack, 1775 — A969

Marine with Musket, Full-rigged Ship — A970

Militiaman with Musket, Powder Horn — A971

1975, July 4 ***Perf. 11***

1565 A968 10c multicolored .20 .20
1566 A969 10c multicolored .20 .20
1567 A970 10c multicolored .20 .20
1568 A971 10c multicolored .20 .20
a. Block of 4, #1565-1568 .85 .90

Bicentenary of US Military Services.

Apollo Soyuz Space Issue

Apollo & Soyuz After Docking, Earth — A972

Spacecraft Before Docking, Earth & Project Emblem — A973

1975, July 15 **Photo.** ***Perf. 11***

1569 A972 10c multicolored .20 .20
1570 A973 10c multicolored .20 .20
a. Pair, #1569-1570 .45 .40
c. As "a," vert. pair, imperf. horiz. 1,750.
d. As "a," yellow omitted —

Apollo Soyuz space test project (Russo-American cooperation); launching, July 15; link-up, July 17.

Nos. 1569-1570 totally imperf are from printer's waste.

See Russia Nos. 4339-4340.

International Women's Year Issue

Worldwide Equality for Women A974

1975, Aug. 26 **Photo.** ***Perf. 11x10½***

1571 A974 10c bl, org & dk bl .20 .20

Postal Service Bicentennial Issue

Stagecoach and Trailer Truck A975

Old and New Locomotives — A976

Early Mail Plane and Jet — A977

Satellite for Transmission of Mailgrams — A978

1975, Sept. 3 **Photo.** ***Perf. 11x10½***

1572 A975 10c multicolored .20 .20
1573 A976 10c multicolored .20 .20
1574 A977 10c multicolored .20 .20
1575 A978 10c multicolored .20 .20
a. Block of 4, #1572-1575 .85 .90
b. As "a," red ("10c") omitted 9,500.

World Peace Through Law Issue

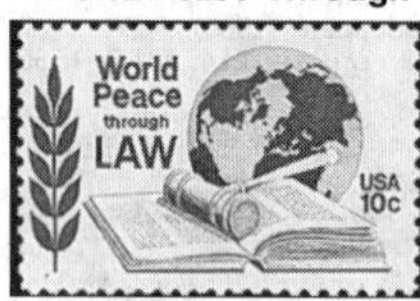

Law Book, Olive Branch and Globe A979

Giori Press Printing

1975, Sept. 29 ***Perf. 11***

1576 A979 10c green, Prus blue & rose brown .20 .20
b. Horiz. pair, imperf. vert. —

A prelude to 7th World Conf. of the World Peace Through Law Center at Washington, DC, Oct. 12-17.

Banking and Commerce Issue

Engine Turning, Indian Head Penny & Morgan Silver Dollar A980

Seated Liberty Quarter, $20 Gold (Double Eagle), Engine Turning A981

Lithographed, Engraved (Giori)

1975, Oct. 6 ***Perf. 11***

1577 A980 10c multicolored .25 .20
1578 A981 10c multicolored .25 .20
a. Pair, #1577-1578 .50 .40
b. As "a," brown & blue (litho.) omitted 2,000.
c. As "a," brown, blue & yellow (litho.) omitted 2,500.

Banking and commerce in the US and for the Centennial Convention of the American Bankers Association.

Christmas Issue

Madonna, by Domenico Ghirlandaio A982

Christmas Card, by Louis Prang, 1878 A983

1975, Oct. 14 **Photo.** ***Perf. 11***

1579 A982 (10c) multicolored .20 .20
a. Imperf., pair 90.00

Perf. 11.2

1580 A983 (10c) multicolored .20 .20
a. Imperf., pair 90.00
c. Perf. 10.9 .25 .20

Perf. 10.5x11.3

1580B A983 (10c) multicolored .65 .20

Americana Issue

Inkwell and Quill A984

Speaker's Stand A985

Early Ballot Box A987

Books, Bookmark, Eyeglasses A988

Dome of Capitol A994

Contemplation of Justice A995

Early American Printing Press A996

Torch A997

Liberty Bell A998

Eagle and Shield A999

Fort McHenry Flag A1001

Head, Statue of Liberty A1002

Old North Church, Boston A1003

Fort Nisqually A1004

Sandy Hook Lighthouse, NJ — A1005

Morris Township School No. 2, Devils Lake, ND — A1006

Iron "Betty" Lamp, 17th-18th Cent. A1007

Rush Lamp and Candle Holder A1008

Kerosene Table Lamp A1009

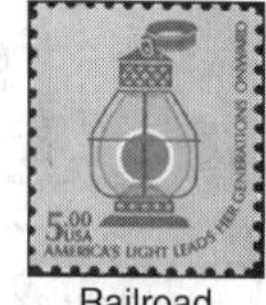

Railroad Conductor's Lantern, c. 1850 A1010

1975-81 **Engr.** ***Perf. 11x10½***

1581 A984 1c dk bl, *grnsh* .20 .20
a. Untagged (Bureau precanceled) .20
1582 A985 2c red brown, *grnsh* .20 .20
a. Untagged (Bureau precanceled) .20
b. Cream paper ('81) .20 .20
1584 A987 3c olive, *grnsh* .20 .20
a. Untagged (Bureau precanceled) .20
1585 A988 4c rose mag, *cr* .20 .20
a. Untagged (Bureau precanceled) 1.25

Size: 17½x20½mm

1590 A994 9c slate green .45 .20

From bklt. pane #1623a.

Perf. 10x9¾

1590A A994 9c slate green 22.50 15.00

From bklt. pane #1623Bc.

Size: 18½x22½mm

Perf. 11x10½

1591 A994 9c sl grn, *gray* .20 .20
a. Untagged (Bureau precanceled) .20
1592 A995 10c violet, *gray* .20 .20
a. Untagged (Bureau precanceled) .25
1593 A996 11c orange, *gray* .20 .20
1594 A997 12c brown red, *beige* .25 .20
1595 A998 13c brown .30 .20
a. Booklet pane of 6 2.25 1.00
b. Booklet pane of 7 + label 2.25 1.00
c. Booklet pane of 8 2.25 1.00
d. Bklt. pane of 5 + label ('76) 1.75 .75
e. Vert. pair, imperf btwn. 800.00

No. 1595e resulted from a paper foldover after perforating and before cutting into panes. Beware of printer's waste consisting of complete panes with perfs around all outside edges.

Photo.

Perf. 11

1596 A999 13c multicolored .25 .20
a. Imperf., pair 50.00 —
b. Yellow omitted 160.00

Engr.

1597 A1001 15c gray, dk blue & red .30 .20
- *a.* Vert. pair, imperf. *20.00*
- *b.* Gray omitted *600.00*
- *c.* Vert. strip of 3, imperf. btwn. & at top or bottom —

Perf. 11x10½

1598 A1001 15c gray, dk blue & red .40 .20
- *a.* Booklet pane of 8 4.25 *.80*

1599 A1002 16c blue .35 .20
1603 A1003 24c red, *blue* .50 .20
1604 A1004 28c brown, *blue* .55 .20
1605 A1005 29c blue, *blue* .60 .20
1606 A1006 30c green, *blue* .55 .20

Engr. & Litho.

Perf. 11

1608 A1007 50c tan, black & org .85 .20
- *a.* Black omitted *300.00*
- *b.* Vert. pair, imperf. horiz. *1,750.*

Beware of copies offered as No. 1608b that have blind perfs.

1610 A1008 $1 tan, brn, org & yel 2.00 .20
- *a.* Brn (engraved) omitted *225.*
- *b.* Tan, org & yel omitted *275.*
- *c.* Brown inverted *13,000.*

1611 A1009 $2 tan, dk grn, org & yel 3.75 .75
1612 A1010 $5 tan, red brn, yel & org 8.50 1.75
Nos. 1581-1612 (23) 43.50 21.50

Nos. 1590, 1590a, 1595, 1598 issued in booklets only. All stamps have one or two straight edges.

Years of issue: #1591, 1595-1596, 11c, 24c, 1975. #1590, 1c-4c, 10c, 1977. #1597-1598, 16c, 28c, 29c, $2, 1978. 30c-$1, $5, 1979. 12c, 1981.

Guitar A1011

Saxhorns A1012

Drum A1013

Piano A1014

Coil Stamps

Engr.

Perf. 10 Vertically

1613 A1011 3.1c brown, *yel* .20 .20
- *a.* Untagged (Bureau precanceled) .50
- *b.* Imperf., pair *1,400.*

1614 A1012 7.7c brown, *brt yel* .20 .20
- *a.* Untagged (Bureau precanceled) .35
- *b.* As "a," imperf., pair *1,600.*

1615 A1013 7.9c carmine, *yel* .20 .20
- *a.* Untagged (Bureau precanceled) .20
- *b.* Imperf., pair *600.00*

1615C A1014 8.4c dk blue, *yel* .20 .20
- *d.* Untagged (Bureau precanceled) .30 .30
- *e.* As "d," pair, imperf. btwn. 60.00
- *f.* As "d," imperf., pair 17.50

1616 A994 9c sl green, *gray* .20 .20
- *a.* Imperf., pair *160.00*
- *b.* Untagged (Bureau precanceled) .35
- *c.* As "b," imperf., pair *700.00*

1617 A995 10c violet, *gray* .20 .20
- *a.* Untagged (Bureau precanceled) .25
- *b.* Imperf., pair *60.00*

1618 A998 13c brown .25 .20
- *a.* Untagged (Bureau precanceled) .45
- *b.* Imperf., pair 25.00
- *g.* Vert. pair, imperf btwn. —
- *h.* As "a," imperf., pair —

1618C A1001 15c gray, dk blue & red .40 .20
- *d.* Imperf., pair 25.00
- *e.* Pair, imperf. between *150.00*
- *f.* Gray omitted *40.00*

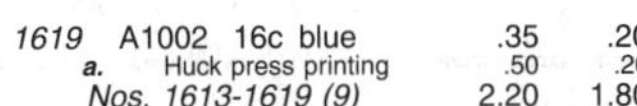

1619 A1002 16c blue .35 .20
- *a.* Huck press printing .50 .20

Nos. 1613-1619 (9) 2.20 1.80

The 16c was printed on two different presses. Huck press printings have white background without bluish tinge, are a fraction of a millimeter smaller than the Cottrell press printing (No. 1619), and have no joint lines.

Years of issue: 9c, 13c, 1975. 7.7c, 7.9c, 1976. 10c, 1977. 8.4c, 15c, 16c, 1978. 3.1c, 1979.

See Nos. 1811, 1813, 1816.

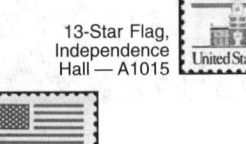

13-Star Flag, Independence Hall — A1015

Flag over Capitol — A1016

Multicolor Huck Press

1975-81 ***Perf. 11x10¾***

1622 A1015 13c dk bl, red & brn red .25 .20
- *a.* Horiz. pair, imperf. btwn. 50.00
- *b.* Vert. pair, imperf. *1,100.*
- *e.* Horiz. pair, imperf. vert. —

No. 1622 has large block tagging and nearly vertical multiple gum ridges.

Combination Press

Perf. 11¼

1622C A1015 13c dark blue & red ('81) 1.00 .25
- *d.* Vertical pair, imperf *150.00*

No. 1622C has small block tagging and flat gum.

Booklet Stamps

Perf. 11x10½ on 2 or 3 Sides

1623 A1016 13c blue & red ('77) .25 .20
- *a.* Bklt. pane, #1590, 7 #1623) 2.25 *1.25*
- *d.* Pair pair, #1590 & 1623 .70 *1.00*

Perf. 10x9¾ on 2 or 3 Sides

1623B A1016 13c blue & red .80 .80
- *c.* Booklet pane, #1590A, 7 #1623B 29.00 —
- *e.* Pair, #1590A & #1623B 24.00 22.50

Coil Stamp

Perf. 10 Vertically

1625 A1015 13c dk bl, red & brn red .25 .20
- *a.* Imperf, pair 25.00

American Bicentennial — Spirit of '76

Drummer Boy A1019

Old Drummer A1020

Fifer — A1021

Designed after painting "The Spirit of '76," by Archibald M. Willard.

1976, Jan. 1 **Photo.** ***Perf. 11***

1629 A1019 13c multicolored .25 .20
- *a.* Imperf., vert. pair —

1630 A1020 13c multicolored .25 .20
1631 A1021 13c multicolored .25 .20
- *a.* Strip of 3, #1629-1631 .75 .65
- *b.* As "a," imperf. *1,050.*
- *c.* Imperf., vert. pair #1631 *800.*

Interphil Issue

"Interphil 76" A1022

Lithographed, Engraved (Giori)

1976, Jan. 17 ***Perf. 11***

1632 A1022 13c dk blue & red (engr.), ultra & red (litho.) .20 .20
- *a.* Dark blue & red (engr.) missing (CM) —
- *c.* Red (engr.) missing (CM) —

Interphil 76 Intl. Phil. Exhib., Philadelphia, Pa., May 29-June 6.

State Flags A1023

1976, Feb. 23 **Photo.** ***Perf. 11***

1633 A1023 13c Delaware .25 .20
1634 A1024 13c Pennsylvania .25 .20
1635 A1025 13c New Jersey .25 .20
1636 A1026 13c Georgia .25 .20
1637 A1027 13c Connecticut .25 .20
1638 A1028 13c Massachusetts .25 .20
1639 A1029 13c Maryland .25 .20
1640 A1030 13c South Carolina .25 .20
1641 A1031 13c New Hampshire .25 .20
1642 A1032 13c Virginia .25 .20
1643 A1033 13c New York .25 .20
1644 A1034 13c North Carolina .25 .20
1645 A1035 13c Rhode Island .25 .20
1646 A1036 13c Vermont .25 .20
1647 A1037 13c Kentucky .25 .20
1648 A1038 13c Tennessee .25 .20
1649 A1039 13c Ohio .25 .20
1650 A1040 13c Louisiana .25 .20
1651 A1041 13c Indiana .25 .20
1652 A1042 13c Mississippi .25 .20
1653 A1043 13c Illinois .25 .20
1654 A1044 13c Alabama .25 .20
1655 A1045 13c Maine .25 .20
1656 A1046 13c Missouri .25 .20
1657 A1047 13c Arkansas .25 .20
1658 A1048 13c Michigan .25 .20
1659 A1049 13c Florida .25 .20
1660 A1050 13c Texas .25 .20
1661 A1051 13c Iowa .25 .20
1662 A1052 13c Wisconsin .25 .20
1663 A1053 13c California .25 .20
1664 A1054 13c Minnesota .25 .20
1665 A1055 13c Oregon .25 .20
1666 A1056 13c Kansas .25 .20
1667 A1057 13c West Virginia .25 .20
1668 A1058 13c Nevada .25 .20
1669 A1059 13c Nebraska .25 .20
1670 A1060 13c Colorado .25 .20
1671 A1061 13c North Dakota .25 .20
1672 A1062 13c South Dakota .25 .20
1673 A1063 13c Montana .25 .20
1674 A1064 13c Washington .25 .20
1675 A1065 13c Idaho .25 .20
1676 A1066 13c Wyoming .25 .20
1677 A1067 13c Utah .25 .20
1678 A1068 13c Oklahoma .25 .20
1679 A1069 13c New Mexico .25 .20
1680 A1070 13c Arizona .25 .20
1681 A1071 13c Alaska .25 .20
1682 A1072 13c Hawaii .25 .20
- *a.* Pane of 50 15.00 —

Telephone Centenary Issue

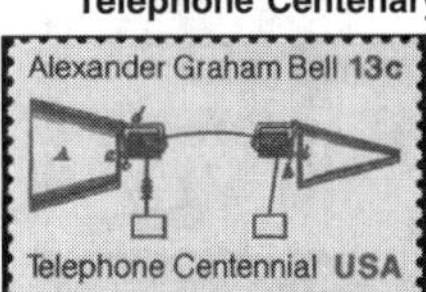

Bell's Telephone Patent Application A1073

Engraved (Giori)

1976, Mar. 10 ***Perf. 11***

1683 A1073 13c blk, pur & red, *tan* .25 .20
- *a.* Black & purple missing (EP) *500.00*
- *b.* Red missing (EP) —
- *c.* All colors missing (EP) —

1st telephone call by Alexander Graham Bell, Mar. 10, 1876.

On No. 1683a, the errors have only tiny traces of red present, so are best collected as a horiz. strip of 5 with 2 or 3 error stamps. No. 1683c also must be collected as a transitional strip.

Commercial Aviation Issue

A1074

1976, Mar. 19 **Photo.** ***Perf. 11***

1684 A1074 13c blue & multi .25 .20

50th anniv. of 1st contract airmail flights: Dearborn, MI to Cleveland, OH, 2/15/26; and Pasco, WA to Elko, NV, 4/6/26. Design features Ford-Pullman Monoplane & Laird Swallow Biplane.

Chemistry Issue

A1075

1976, Apr. 6 **Photo.** ***Perf. 11***

1685 A1075 13c multicolored .25 .20

Cent. of the American Chemical Society.

Design features Various Flasks, Separatory Funnel, Computer Tape, honoring American chemists.

AMERICAN BICENTENNIAL ISSUES

SOUVENIR SHEETS

See illustrations on page 48.

Designs, from Left to Right:

No. 1686, Surrender of Cornwallis at Yorktown, by John Trumbull:

a, Two British officers. b, Gen. Benjamin Lincoln. c, George Washington. d, John Trumbull, Col. Cobb, von Steuben, Lafayette, Thomas Nelson, Alexander Hamilton, John Laurens, Walter Stewart, all vert.

No. 1687, Declaration of Independence, by John Trumbull:

a, John Adams, Roger Sherman, Robert R. Livingston. b, Jefferson, Franklin. c, Thomas Nelson, Jr., Francis Lewis, John Witherspoon, Samuel Huntington. d, John Hancock, Charles Thomson. e, George Read, John Dickinson, Edward Rutledge

1687a, d, vert., b, c, e, horiz.

No. 1688, Washington Crossing the Delaware, by Emanuel Leutze/Eastman Johnson: a, Boatsman. b, Washington. c, Flag bearer. d, Men in boat. e, Men on shore

1688a, d, horiz., b, c, e, vert.

No. 1689, Washington Reviewing Army at Valley Forge, by William T. Trego:

a, Two officers. b, Washington. c, Officer, black horse. d, Officer, white horse. e, Three soldiers.

1689a, c, e, horiz., b, d, vert.

1976, May 29 **Litho.** ***Perf. 11***

1686 A1076 Sheet of 5 3.25 —
- *a.-e.* 13c multi, any single .45 .40
- *f.* USA 13c omitted on "b," "c" & "d," imperf., tagging omitted — *2,250.*
- *g.* USA 13c omitted on "a" & "e" *450.* —
- *h.* Imperf., tagging omitted *2,250.*
- *i.* USA 13c omitted on "b," "c" & "d" *450.*
- *j.* USA 13c double on "b" —
- *k.* USA 13c omitted on "c" & "d" *750.*
- *l.* USA 13c omitted on "e" *500.*
- *m.* USA 13c omitted, imperf., tagging omitted — —
- *n.* As "g," imperf., tagging omitted —

1687 A1077 Sheet of 5 4.25 —
- *a.-e.* 18c multi, any single .55 .55
- *f.* Design & marginal inscriptions omitted *3,000.*
- *g.* USA 18c omitted on "a" & "c" *750.*
- *h.* USA 18c omitted on "b," "d" & "e" *450.*
- *i.* USA 18c omitted on "d" *500.* *500.*
- *j.* Black omitted in design *2,000.*
- *k.* USA 18c omitted, imperf., tagging omitted *2,750.*
- *m.* USA 18c omitted on "b" & "e" *500.*
- *n.* USA 18c omitted on "b" & "d" —
- *p.* Imperf., tagged —
- *q.* USA 18c omitted on "c" —

1688 A1078 Sheet of 5 5.25 —
- *a.-e.* 24c multi, any single .70 .70
- *f.* USA 24c omitted, imperf., tagging omitted *3,500.*
- *g.* USA 24c omitted on "d" & "e" *450.* *450.*

A1076

A1077

A1078

A1079

h.		Design & marginal inscriptions omitted	*3,250.*	
i.		USA 24c omitted on "a," "b" & "c"	*500.*	—
j.		Imperf., tagging omitted	*3,000.*	
k.		USA 24c of "d" & "e" inverted	—	
l.		As "i," imperf., tagging omitted	*3,500.*	
n.		As No. 1688, perfs inverted	—	
1689	A1079	Sheet of 5	6.25	—
a.-e.		31c multi, any single	.85	.85
f.		USA 31c omitted, imperf.	*2,750.*	
g.		USA 31c omitted on "a" & "c"	*400.*	
h.		USA 31c omitted on "b," "d" & "e"	*450.*	—
i.		USA 31c omitted on "e"	*450.*	
j.		Black omitted in design	*2,000.*	
k.		Imperf., tagging omitted		*2,250.*
l.		USA 31c omitted on "b" & "d"	—	
m.		USA 31c omitted on "a" "c" & "e"	—	
n.		As "m," imperf., tagging omitted	—	
p.		As "h," imperf., tagging omitted		*2,500.*
q.		As "g," imperf., tagging omitted	*2,750.*	
r.		USA 31c omitted on "d" & "e"	—	
s.		As "f," tagging omitted	2,250.	
t.		"USA/31c" omitted on "d"	—	
v		As No. 1689, perfs inverted	—	
		Nos. 1686-1689 (4)	19.00	

Nos. 1688-1689 exist with inverted perfs.

Size of sheets: 203x152mm; stamps: 25x39½mm, 39½x25mm.

Issued in connection with Interphil 76 Intl. Phil. Exhib., Philadelphia, Pa, May 29-June 6.

Benjamin Franklin Issue

Franklin & Map of North America, 1776 A1080

Lithographed, Engraved (Giori)

1976, June 1 **_Perf. 11_**

1690	A1080 13c ultra & multi		.25	.20
a.	Light blue omitted		*225.00*	

American Bicentennial; Franklin (1706-1790), deputy postmaster general for the colonies (1753-1774) and statesman.

See Canada No. 691.

1976, July 4 **Photo.** **_Perf. 11_**

1691	A1081 13c multicolored	.30	.20
1692	A1082 13c multicolored	.30	.20
1693	A1083 13c multicolored	.30	.20
1694	A1084 13c multicolored	.30	.20
a.	Strip of 4, #1691-1694	1.20	1.10

Olympic Games Issue

Diving A1085 — Skiing A1086

Running A1087 — Skating A1088

1976, July 16 **Photo.** **_Perf. 11_**

1695	A1085 13c multicolored	.25	.20
1696	A1086 13c multicolored	.25	.20
1697	A1087 13c multicolored	.25	.20
1698	A1088 13c multicolored	.25	.20
a.	Block of 4, #1695-1698	1.10	*1.40*
b.	As "a," imperf.	*650.00*	

12th Winter Olympic Games, Innsbruck, Austria, Feb. 4-15, and 21st Summer Olympic Games, Montreal, Canada, July 17-Aug. 1.

Clara Maass Issue

Clara Maass, Newark German Hospital Pin — A1089

1976, Aug. 18 **Photo.** **_Perf. 11_**

1699	A1089 13c multicolored	.25	.20
a.	Horiz. pair, imperf. vert.	*450.00*	

Clara Maass (1876-1901), volunteer in fight against yellow fever, birth centenary.

Adolph S. Ochs Issue

Adolph S. Ochs, Publisher of the NY Times, 1896-1935 A1090

Giori Press Printing

1976, Sept. 18 **_Perf. 11_**

1700	A1090 13c black & gray	.25	.20

American Bicentennial Issue

American Bicentennial Issue

Declaration of Independence, by John Trumbull

A1081 A1082 A1083 A1084

Christmas Issue

Nativity, by John Singleton Copley A1091

Winter Pastime, by Nathaniel Currier A1092

1976, Oct. 27 Photo. *Perf. 11*

1701 A1091 13c multicolored	.25	.20
a. Imperf., pair	*100.00*	
1702 A1092 13c multicolored	.25	.20
a. Imperf., pair	*100.00*	
1703 A1092 13c multicolored	.25	.20
a. Imperf., pair	*110.00*	
b. Vert. pair, imperf. btwn.	—	
d. Red omitted	—	
e. Yellow omitted	—	
Nos. 1701-1703 (3)	.75	.60

No. 1702 has overall tagging. Lettering at base is black and usually ½mm below design. As a rule, no "snowflaking" in sky or pond. Pane of 50 has margins on 4 sides with slogans.

No. 1703 has block tagging the size of printed area. Lettering at base is gray black and usually ¾mm below design. "Snowflaking" generally in sky and pond. Pane has margin only at right or left, and no slogans.

Copies are known with various amounts of red or yellow missing. Nos. 1703d and 1703e have the color totally omitted. Expertization is recommended.

American Bicentennial Issue
Washington at Princeton

Washington, Nassau Hall, Hessians, 13-Star Flag — A1093

1977, Jan. 3 Photo. *Perf. 11*

1704 A1093 13c by Charles Willson Peale	.25	.20
a. Horiz. pair, imperf. vert.	*550.00*	

Washington's victory at Princeton over Lord Cornwallis, bicentennial.

Sound Recording Issue

Tin Foil Phonograph — A1094

Lithographed, Engraved (Giori)
1977, Mar. 23 *Perf. 11*

1705 A1094 13c black & multi	.25	.20

Centenary of invention of the phonograph by Thomas Alva Edison, and development of sophisticated recording industry.

American Folk Art Series
Pueblo Pottery

Zia — A1095

San Ildefonso A1096

Hopi — A1097

Acoma — A1098

1977, Apr. 13 Photo. *Perf. 11*

1706 A1095 13c multicolored	.25	.20
1707 A1096 13c multicolored	.25	.20
1708 A1097 13c multicolored	.25	.20
1709 A1098 13c multicolored	.25	.20
a. Block or strip of 4	1.00	1.00
b. As "a," imperf. vert.	*2,500.*	

Pueblo art, 1880-1920, from museums in NM, AZ and CO.

Lindbergh Flight Issue

Spirit of St. Louis A1099

1977, May 20 Photo. *Perf. 11*

1710 A1099 13c multicolored	.25	.20
a. Imperf., pair	*1,050.*	

Charles A. Lindbergh's solo transatlantic flight from NY to Paris, 50th anniv.

Colorado Statehood Issue

Columbine & Rocky Mountains — A1100

1977, May 21 Photo. *Perf. 11*

1711 A1100 13c multicolored	.25	.20
a. Horiz. pair, imperf. btwn.	*600.00*	
b. Horiz. pair, imperf. vert.	*900.00*	

Colorado became a state in 1876.

Butterfly Issue

Swallowtail A1101

Checkerspot — A1102

Dogface A1103

Orange Tip A1104

1977, June 6 Photo. *Perf. 11*

1712 A1101 13c tan & multi	.25	.20
1713 A1102 13c tan & multi	.25	.20
1714 A1103 13c tan & multi	.25	.20
1715 A1104 13c tan & multi	.25	.20
a. Block of 4, #1712-1715	1.00	1.00
b. As "a," imperf. horiz.	*15,000.*	

American Bicentennial Issues
Lafayette

Marquis de Lafayette A1105

1977, June 13 Engr. *Perf. 11*

1716 A1105 13c bl, blk & red	.25	.20
a. Red missing (PS)	—	

200th anniv. of Lafayette's landing on the coast of SC, north of Charleston.

Skilled Hands for Independence

Seamstress A1106

Blacksmith A1107

Wheelwright — A1108

Leatherworker — A1109

1977, July 4 Photo. *Perf. 11*

1717 A1106 13c multicolored	.25	.20
1718 A1107 13c multicolored	.25	.20
1719 A1108 13c multicolored	.25	.20
1720 A1109 13c multicolored	.25	.20
a. Block of 4, #1717-1720	1.00	1.00

Peace Bridge Issue

Peace Bridge & Dove A1110

1977, Aug. 4 Engr. *Perf. 11x10½*

1721 A1110 13c blue	.25	.20

50th anniv. of the Peace Bridge, connecting Buffalo, NY with Fort Erie, Ontario.

American Bicentennial Issue
Battle of Oriskany

Herkimer at Oriskany, by Yohn A1111

1977, Aug. 6 Photo. *Perf. 11*

1722 A1111 13c multicolored	.25	.20

200th anniv. of Battle of Oriskany, American Militia led by Brig. Gen. Nicholas Herkimer (1728-1777).

Energy Issue
Energy Conservation
A1112

Energy Development
A1113

1977, Oct. 20 Photo. *Perf. 11*

1723 A1112 13c multicolored	.25	.20
1724 A1113 13c multicolored	.25	.20
a. Pair, #1723-1724	.50	.50

Conservation and development of nation's energy resources.

Alta California Issue

Farm Houses A1114

Litho. & Engraved (Giori)
1977, Sept. 9 *Perf. 11*

1725 A1114 13c black & multi	.25	.20

El Pueblo de San José de Guadalupe, 1st civil settlement in Alta California, 200th anniv.

American Bicentennial Issue
Articles of Confederation

Members of Continental Congress in Conference A1115

Engraved (Giori)

1977, Sept. 30 *Perf. 11*

1726 A1115 13c red & brn, *cream* .25 .20
b. Red omitted *600.00*
c. Red & brown omitted *400.00*

200th anniv. of drafting the Articles of Confederation, York Town, Pa.

No. 1726b also has most of the brown color omitted. No. 1726c must be collected as a transition multiple, certainly with No. 1726b and preferably also with No. 1726.

Talking Picture, 50th Anniv. Issue

Movie Projector and Phonograph — A1116

Litho. & Engraved (Giori)

1977, Oct. 6 *Perf. 11*

1727 A1116 13c multicolored .25 .20

American Bicentennial Issue

Surrender at Saratoga

Surrender of Burgoyne, by John Trumbull A1117

1977, Oct. 7 **Photo.** *Perf. 11*

1728 A1117 13c multicolored .25 .20

200th anniv. of Gen. John Burgoyne's surrender at Saratoga.

Christmas Issue

Washington at Valley Forge A1118

Rural Mailbox A1119

1977, Oct. 21 **Photo.** *Perf. 11*

1729 A1118 13c multicolored .25 .20
a. Imperf., pair *75.00*
1730 A1119 13c multicolored .25 .20
a. Imperf., pair *300.00*

Carl Sandburg Issue

Carl Sandburg, by William A. Smith, 1952 — A1120

Engraved (Giori)

1978, Jan. 6 *Perf. 11*

1731 A1120 13c black & brown .25 .20
a. Brown omitted —

Sandburg (1878-1967), poet, biographer and collector of American folk songs.

Captain Cook Issue

Capt. Cook, by Nathaniel Dance, 1776 — A1121

"Resolution" and "Discovery," by John Webber — A1122

Giori Press Printing

1978, Jan. 20 *Perf. 11*

1732 A1121 13c dark blue .25 .20
1733 A1122 13c green .25 .20
a. Vert. pair, imperf. horiz. —
b. Pair, #1732-1733 .50 .50
c. As "b," imperf. between *4,500.*

Capt. James Cook, 200th anniv. of his arrival in Hawaii, at Waimea, Kauai, Jan. 20, 1778, and of his anchorage in Cook Inlet, near Anchorage, Alaska, June 1, 1778. Nos. 1732-1733 issued in panes of 50, containing 25 each of Nos. 1732-1733 including 5 No. 1732a. Design of No. 1733 is after etching "A View of Karakekooa in Owyhee."

Indian Head Penny, 1877 A1123

Eagle A1124

Roses — A1126

Engraved (Giori)

1978, Jan. 11 *Perf. 11*

1734 A1123 13c brown & blue green, *bister* .25 .20
a. Horiz. pair, imperf. vert. *300.00*

1978, May 22 **Photo.** *Perf. 11*

1735 A1124 (15c) orange .25 .20
a. Imperf., pair *90.00*
b. Vert. pair, imperf. horiz. *700.00*

Engr. *Perf. 11x10½*

1736 A1124 (15c) orange .25 .20
a. Booklet pane of 8 2.25 *1.25*
c. Vert. pair, imperf between —

See No. 1743

1978, July 11 **Engr.** *Perf. 10*

1737 A1126 15c multicolored .25 .20
a. Booklet pane of 8 2.25 *1.25*
b. As "a," imperf. —

Nos. 1736, 1737 issued in booklets only. All stamps have 1 or 2 straight edges.

Robertson Windmill, Williamsburg A1127

Old Windmill, Portsmouth A1128

Cape Cod Windmill, Eastham A1129

Dutch Mill, Batavia A1130

Southwestern Windmill — A1131

1980, Feb. 7 **Engr.** *Perf. 11*

Booklet Stamps

1738 A1127 15c sepia, *yellow* .30 .20
1739 A1128 15c sepia, *yellow* .30 .20
1740 A1129 15c sepia, *yellow* .30 .20
1741 A1130 15c sepia, *yellow* .30 .20
1742 A1131 15c sepia, *yellow* .30 .20
a. Bklt. pane, 2 ea #1738-1742 3.50 *3.00*
b. Strip of 5, #1738-1742 1.50 1.40

Coil Stamp

1978, May 22 **Engr.** ***Perf. 10 Vert.***

1743 A1124 (15c) orange .25 .20
a. Imperf., pair 90.00

No. 1743a is valued in the grade of fine.

Black Heritage Series

Harriet Tubman (1820-1913), Cart Carrying Slaves — A1133

1978, Feb. 1 **Photo.** *Perf. 10½x11*

1744 A1133 13c multicolored .25 .20

Tubman, born a slave, helped more than 300 slaves escape to freedom.

American Folk Art Series

American Quilts, Basket Design

A1134

A1135

A1136

A1137

1978, Mar. 8 **Photo.** *Perf. 11*

1745 A1134 13c multicolored .25 .20
1746 A1135 13c multicolored .25 .20
1747 A1136 13c multicolored .25 .20
1748 A1137 13c multicolored .25 .20
a. Block of 4, #1745-1748 1.00 1.00

American Dance Issue

Ballet A1138

Theater A1139

Folk Dance A1140

Modern Dance A1141

1978, Apr. 26 **Photo.** *Perf. 11*

1749 A1138 13c multicolored .25 .20
1750 A1139 13c multicolored .25 .20
1751 A1140 13c multicolored .25 .20
1752 A1141 13c multicolored .25 .20
a. Block of 4, #1749-1752 1.00 1.00

American Bicentennial Issue

French Alliance

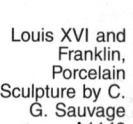

Louis XVI and Franklin, Porcelain Sculpture by C. G. Sauvage A1142

Giori Press Printing

1978, May 4 *Perf. 11*

1753 A1142 13c bl, blk & red .25 .20

Bicent. of French Alliance, signed in Paris, Feb. 6, 1778, and ratified by Continental Cong., May 4.

Early Cancer Detection Issue

Dr. George Papanicolaou (1883-1962) A1143

1978, May 18 **Engr.** *Perf. 10½x11*

1754 A1143 13c brown .25 .20

Papanicolaou, developer of Pap Test, early cancer detection in women.

Performing Arts Series

Jimmie Rodgers and Locomotive A1144

George M. Cohan, "Yankee Doodle Dandy" and Stars A1145

1978 **Photo.** ***Perf. 11***

1755 A1144 13c multicolored	.25	.20
1756 A1145 15c multicolored	.30	.20

Rodgers (1897-1933), the "Singing Brakeman, Father of Country Music," and Cohan (1878-1942), actor and playwright.

Issue dates: #1755, May 24; #1756, July 3.

CAPEX Issue

Wildlife from Canadian-US Border — A1146

Litho. & Engr. (Giori)

1978, June 10 ***Perf. 11***

1757 A1146 Block of 8	2.00	2.00
a. 13c Cardinal	.25	.20
b. 13c Mallard	.25	.20
c. 13c Canada goose	.25	.20
d. 13c Blue jay	.25	.20
e. 13c Moose	.25	.20
f. 13c Chipmunk	.25	.20
g. 13c Red fox	.25	.20
h. 13c Raccoon	.25	.20
i. As No. 1757, yellow, green, red, brown, blue, black (litho.) omitted	*7,000.*	
j. Strip of 4 (a-d), imperf. vert.	*7,000.*	
k. Strip of 4 (e-h), imperf. vert.	*4,750.*	
l. As No. 1757, "d" and "h" with black (engr.) omitted	—	

CAPEX, Canadian Intl. Phil. Exhib., Toronto, Ont., June 9-18.

Photography Issue

Photographic Equipment A1147

1978, June 26 **Photo.** ***Perf. 11***

1758 A1147 15c multicolored	.30	.20

Viking Missions to Mars Issue

Viking 1 Lander Scooping Up Soil on Mars A1148

1978, July 20 **Litho. & Engr.**

1759 A1148 15c multicolored	.30	.20

2nd anniv. of landing of Viking 1 on Mars.

American Owls Issue

Great Gray Owl A1149 — Saw-whet Owl A1150

Barred Owl A1151 — Great Horned Owl A1152

Litho. & Engr.

1978, Aug. 26 ***Perf. 11***

1760 A1149 15c multicolored	.30	.20
1761 A1150 15c multicolored	.30	.20
1762 A1151 15c multicolored	.30	.20
1763 A1152 15c multicolored	.30	.20
a. Block of 4, #1760-1763	1.25	1.25

American Trees Issue

Giant Sequoia A1153

White Pine A1154

White Oak A1155

Gray Birch A1156

1978, Oct. 9 **Photo.** ***Perf. 11***

1764 A1153 15c multicolored	.30	.20
1765 A1154 15c multicolored	.30	.20
1766 A1155 15c multicolored	.30	.20
1767 A1156 15c multicolored	.30	.20
a. Block of 4, #1764-1767	1.25	1.25
b. As "a," imperf. horiz.	*15,000.*	

Christmas Issue

Madonna and Child with Cherubim, by Andrea della Robbia A1157

Child on Hobby-horse and Christmas Trees A1158

1978, Oct. 18 **Photo.** ***Perf. 11***

1768 A1157 15c blue & multi	.30	.20
a. Imperf., pair	*90.00*	
1769 A1158 15c red & multi	.30	.20
a. Imperf., pair	*100.00*	
b. Vert. pair, imperf. horiz.	*2,000.*	

Value for #1768a is for an uncreased pair.

Robert F. Kennedy Issue

Robert F. Kennedy (1925-68), US Attorney General A1159

1979, Jan. 12 **Engr.** ***Perf. 11***

1770 A1159 15c blue	.35	.20

Black Heritage Series

Dr. Martin Luther King, Jr. (1929-68), and Civil Rights Marchers — A1160

1979, Jan. 13 **Photo.** ***Perf. 11***

1771 A1160 15c multicolored	.30	.20
a. Imperf., pair	—	

Civil rights leader.

Year of the Child Issue

Children A1161

1979, Feb. 15 **Engr.** ***Perf. 11***

1772 A1161 15c orange red	.30	.20

International Year of the Child.

John Steinbeck A1162

Albert Einstein A1163

John Steinbeck Issue

1979, Feb. 27 **Engr.** ***Perf. 10½x11***

1773 A1162 15c dark blue	.30	.20

John Ernst Steinbeck (1902-68), novelist.

Albert Einstein Issue

1979, Mar. 4 **Engr.** ***Perf. 10½x11***

1774 A1163 15c chocolate	.35	.20

Einstein (1879-1955), theoretical physicist.

American Folk Art Series

Pennsylvania Toleware

Coffeepot A1164

Tea Caddy — A1165

Sugar Bowl — A1166

Coffeepot A1167

1979, Apr. 19 **Photo.** ***Perf. 11***

1775 A1164 15c multicolored	.30	.20
1776 A1165 15c multicolored	.30	.20
1777 A1166 15c multicolored	.30	.20
1778 A1167 15c multicolored	.30	.20
a. Block of 4, #1775-1778	1.25	1.25
b. As "a," imperf. horiz.	*4,250.*	

American Architecture Series

Virginia Rotunda, by Thomas Jefferson A1168

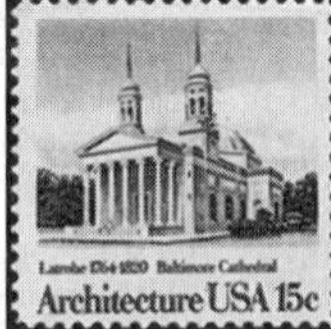

Baltimore Cathedral, by Benjamin Latrobe A1169

Boston State House, by Charles Bulfinch A1170

Philadelphia Exchange, by William Strickland A1171

1979, June 4 Engr. *Perf. 11*

1779 A1168 15c blk & brick red .30 .20
1780 A1169 15c blk & brick red .30 .20
1781 A1170 15c blk & brick red .30 .20
1782 A1171 15c blk & brick red .30 .20
a. Block of 4, #1779-1782 1.25 *1.50*

Endangered Flora Issue

Persistent Trillium A1172 — Hawaiian Wild Broadbean A1173

Contra Costa Wallflower A1174 — Antioch Dunes Evening Primrose A1175

1979, June 7 Photo. *Perf. 11*

1783 A1172 15c multicolored .30 .20
1784 A1173 15c multicolored .30 .20
1785 A1174 15c multicolored .30 .20
1786 A1175 15c multicolored .30 .20
a. Block of 4, #1783-1786 1.25 1.25
b. As "a," imperf. *600.00*

Seeing Eye Dogs Issue

German Shepherd Leading Man — A1176

1979, June 15

1787 A1176 15c multicolored .30 .20
a. Imperf., pair *425.00*

Special Olympics Issue

Child Holding Winner's Medal — A1177

1979, Aug. 9 *Perf. 11*

1788 A1177 15c multicolored .30 .20

Special Olympics for special children, Brockport, NY, Aug. 8-13.

John Paul Jones Issue

John Paul Jones, by Charles Willson Peale — A1178

1979, Sept. 23 Photo. *Perf. 11x12*

1789 A1178 15c multi .30 .20
c. Vert. pair, imperf. horiz. *175.*

Perf. 11

1789A A1178 15c multi .55 .20
d. Vert. pair, imperf. horiz. *150.*

Perf. 12

1789B A1178 15c multi *2,400. 1,000.*

John Paul Jones (1747-1792), Naval Commander, American Revolution.

Imperfs, perf or imperf gutter pairs and blocks exist from printer's waste.

Olympic Games Issue

Javelin — A1179

Running A1180

Swimming A1181

Rowing A1182

Equestrian A1183

1979 Photo. *Perf. 11*

1790 A1179 10c multicolored .20 .20
1791 A1180 15c multicolored .30 .20
1792 A1181 15c multicolored .30 .20
1793 A1182 15c multicolored .30 .20
1794 A1183 15c multicolored .30 .20
a. Block of 4, #1791-1794 1.25 *1.50*
b. As "a," imperf. *1,500.*

22nd Summer Olympic Games, Moscow, July 19-Aug. 3, 1980.

Issue dates: 10c, Sept. 5; 15c, Sept. 28.

Winter Olympic Games Issue

Speed Skating A1184

Downhill Skiing A1185

Ski Jump A1186

Ice Hockey A1187

1980, Feb. 1 Photo. *Perf. 11¼x10½*

1795 A1184 15c multicolored .35 .20
1796 A1185 15c multicolored .35 .20
1797 A1186 15c multicolored .35 .20
1798 A1187 15c multicolored .35 .20
b. Block of 4, #1795-1798 1.50 1.40

Perf. 11

1795A A1184 15c multicolored 1.05 .60
1796A A1185 15c multicolored 1.05 .60
1797A A1186 15c multicolored 1.05 .60
1798A A1187 15c multicolored 1.05 .60
c. Block of 4, #1795A-1798A 4.25 3.50

13th Winter Olympic Games, Lake Placid, NY, Feb. 12-24.

Christmas Issue

Virgin and Child, by Gerard David A1188

Santa Claus, Christmas Tree Ornament A1189

1979, Oct. 18 Photo. *Perf. 11*

1799 A1188 15c multicolored .30 .20
a. Imperf., pair *90.*
b. Vert. pair, imperf. horiz. *700.*
c. Vert. pair, imperf. btwn. *2,250.*
1800 A1189 15c multicolored .30 .20
a. Green & yellow omitted *625.*
b. Grn, yel & tan omitted *700.*

Nos. 1800a, 1800b always have the remaining colors misaligned.

No. 1800b is valued in the grade of fine.

Performing Arts Issue

Will Rogers (1879-1935), Actor and Humorist — A1190

1979, Nov. 4 Photo. *Perf. 11*

1801 A1190 15c multicolored .30 .20
a. Imperf., pair *225.00*

Viet Nam Veterans Issue

Ribbon for Viet Nam Service Medal A1191

1979, Nov. 11 Photo. *Perf. 11*

1802 A1191 15c multicolored .30 .20

A tribute to veterans of the Viet Nam War.

Performing Arts Series

W.C. Fields (1880-1946), actor and comedian — A1192

1980, Jan. 29 Photo. *Perf. 11*

1803 A1192 15c multicolored .30 .20
a. Imperf., pair —

Black Heritage Series

Benjamin Banneker (1731-1806), Astronomer and Mathematician, Transverse — A1193

1980, Feb. 15 Photo. *Perf. 11*

1804 A1193 15c multicolored .35 .20
a. Horiz. pair, imperf. vert. *800.00*

Imperf. printer's waste has been fraudulently perforated to simulate No. 1804a. Legitimate examples of No. 1804a do not have colors misregistered.

Letter Writing

Letters Preserve Memories A1194

P.S. Write Soon A1195

Letters Lift Spirits A1196

Letters Shape Opinions A1197

1980, Feb. 25

1805 A1194 15c multicolored .30 .20
1806 A1195 15c purple & multi .30 .20
1807 A1196 15c multicolored .30 .20
1808 A1195 15c green & multi .30 .20
1809 A1197 15c multicolored .30 .20
1810 A1195 15c red & multi .30 .20
a. Vert. strip of 6 #1805-1810 1.85 *2.25*
Nos. 1805-1810 (6) 1.80 1.20

Natl. Letter Writing Week, Feb. 24-Mar. 1.

Americana Type

Weaver Violins — A1199

Coil Stamps

1980-81 Engr. *Perf. 10 Vert.*

1811 A984 1c dk blue, *grnsh* .20 .20
a. Imperf., pair *175.00*
1813 A1199 3.5c purple, *yel* .20 .20
a. Untagged (Bureau precanceled, lines only) .20
b. Imperf., pair *225.00*
1816 A997 12c brown red, *beige* ('81) .25 .20
a. Untagged (Bureau precanceled) .25
b. Imperf., pair *200.00*
c. As "a," brownish red, *reddish beige* .25

A1207

1981, Mar. 15 Photo. *Perf. 11x10½*

1818 A1207 (18c) violet .35 .20

Engr. ***Perf. 10***

Booklet Stamp

1819 A1207 (18c) violet .40 .20
a. Booklet pane of 8 3.75 *2.25*

Coil Stamp

Perf. 10 Vert.

1820 A1207 (18c) violet .40 .20
a. Imperf., pair *100.00*
Nos. 1818-1820 (3) 1.15 .60

Frances Perkins

Frances Perkins (1882-1965), Sec. of Labor, 1933-45 (1st Woman Cabinet Member) — A1208

1980, Apr. 10 ***Perf. 10½x11***

1821 A1208 15c Prus blue .30 .20

Dolley Madison

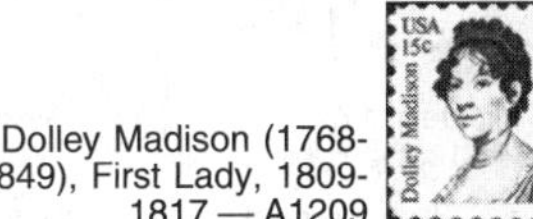

Dolley Madison (1768-1849), First Lady, 1809-1817 — A1209

1980, May 20 ***Perf. 11***

1822 A1209 15c red bwn & sepia .30 .20
a. Red brown missing (PS) —

Emily Bissell

Emily Bissell (1861-1948), Social Worker; Introduced Christmas seals in US — A1210

1980, May 31

1823 A1210 15c black & red .35 .20
a. Vert. pair, imperf. horiz. *400.00*
b. All colors missing (EP) —

Helen Keller

Helen Keller and Anne Sullivan — A1211

Litho. & Engr.

1980, June 27 ***Perf. 11***

1824 A1211 15c multicolored .30 .20

Keller (1880-1968), blind and deaf writer and lecturer taught by Sullivan (1867-1936).

Veterans Administration Emblem A1212

Gen. Bernardo de Galvez A1213

Veterans Administration

1980, July 21 **Photo.**

1825 A1212 15c car & vio bl .30 .20
a. Horiz. pair, imperf. vert. *450.00*

General Bernardo de Galvez

1980, July 23 **Engr.** ***Perf. 11***

1826 A1213 15c multicolored .30 .20
a. Red, brn & bl (engr.) omitted *800.*
b. Red, brn, bl (engr.), bl & yel (litho.) omitted *1,400.*

Galvez (1746-1786), helped defeat British in Battle of Mobile, 1780.

Coral Reefs

Brain Coral, Beaugregory Fish A1214

Elkhorn Coral, Porkfish A1215

Chalice Coral, Moorish Idol Fish A1216

Finger Coral, Sabertooth Blenny Fish A1217

1980, Aug. 26 **Photo.** ***Perf. 11***

1827 A1214 15c multicolored .30 .20
1828 A1215 15c multicolored .30 .20
1829 A1216 15c multicolored .30 .20
1830 A1217 15c multicolored .30 .20
a. Block of 4, #1827-1830 1.25 1.10
b. As "a," imperf. *1,000.*
c. As "a," vert. imperf. btwn. —
d. As "a," imperf. vert. *3,000.*

American Bald Eagle A1218

Edith Wharton A1219

Organized Labor

1980, Sept. 1 **Photo.** ***Perf. 11***

1831 A1218 15c multicolored .30 .20
a. Imperf., pair *375.00*

Edith Wharton

1980, Sept. 5 **Engr.** ***Perf. 10½x11***

1832 A1219 15c purple .30 .20

Edith Wharton (1862-1937), writer.

American Education

"Homage to the Square: Glow," by Josef Albers — A1220

1980, Sept. 12 **Photo.** ***Perf. 11***

1833 A1220 15c multicolored .30 .20
a. Horiz. pair, imperf. btwn. *240.00*

American Folk Art Series

Pacific Northwest Indian Masks

Heiltsuk, Bella Bella Tribe — A1221

Chilkat Tlingit Tribe — A1222

Tlingit Tribe — A1223

Bella Coola Tribe — A1224

1980, Sept. 25

1834 A1221 15c multicolored .30 .20
1835 A1222 15c multicolored .30 .20
1836 A1223 15c multicolored .30 .20
1837 A1224 15c multicolored .30 .20
a. Block of 4, #1834-1837 1.25 1.25

American Architecture Series

Smithsonian Institution, by James Renwick A1225

Trinity Church, Boston, by Henry Hobson Richardson A1226

Pennsylvania Academy of Fine Arts, by Frank Furness — A1227

Lyndhurst, Tarrytown, NY, by Alexander Jackson Davis A1228

1980, Oct. 9 **Engr.** ***Perf. 11***

1838 A1225 15c black & brick red .30 .20
1839 A1226 15c black & brick red .30 .20
1840 A1227 15c black & brick red .30 .20
1841 A1228 15c black & brick red .30 .20
a. Block of 4, #1838-1841 1.25 *1.50*
b. As "a," red missing on Nos. 1838 and 1839 (PS) *400.00*

Christmas

Madonna and Child A1229

Wreath, Toys on Windowsill A1230

1980, Oct. 31 **Photo.** ***Perf. 11***

1842 A1229 15c multicolored .30 .20
a. Imperf., pair *70.00*
1843 A1230 15c multicolored .30 .20
a. Imperf., pair *70.00*
b. Buff omitted 25.00
c. Vert. pair, imperf. horiz. —
d. Horiz. pair, imperf. between 4,000.

No. 1843b is difficult to identify and should have a competent certificate.

Great Americans

A1231

A1232

A1233

A1234

A1235

A1236

A1237

A1238

A1239

A1240

A1241 A1242

A1243 A1244

A1245 A1246

A1247 A1248

A1249 A1250

A1251 A1252

A1253 A1254

A1255 A1256

Perf. 11x10½, 11 (1, 6-11, 14, #1862, 22, 30, 39, 40, 50c)

1980-85 **Engr.**

1844 A1231 1c black .20 .20
a. Imperf. pair *300.*
b. Vert. pair, imperf. btwn. and at bottom *3,000.*
e. Vert. pair, imperf. horiz. —
1845 A1232 2c brown black .20 .20
1846 A1233 3c olive green .20 .20
1847 A1234 4c violet .20 .20
1848 A1235 5c henna brown .20 .20
1849 A1236 6c orange ver .20 .20
a. Vert. pair, imperf. btwn. and at bottom *2,000.*
1850 A1237 7c brt carmine .20 .20
1851 A1238 8c olive black .20 .20
1852 A1239 9c dark green .20 .20
1853 A1240 10c Prus blue .25 .20
b. Vert. pair, imperf. btwn. 900.
c. Horiz. pair, imperf. btwn. *2,250.*

Completely imperforate tagged or untagged stamps are from printer's waste.

1854 A1241 11c dark blue .30 .20
1855 A1242 13c lt maroon .30 .20

1856 A1243 14c slate green .30 .20
b. Vert. pair, imperf. horiz. *125.*
c. Horiz. pair, imperf. btwn. 9.00
d. Vert. pair, imperf. btwn. *1,900.*
e. All color omitted —

No. 1856e comes from a partially printed pane and should be collected as a vertical strip of 10, one stamp normal, one stamp transitional and 8 stamps with color omitted.

1857 A1244 17c green .35 .20
1858 A1245 18c dark blue .35 .20
1859 A1246 19c brown .40 .20
1860 A1247 20c claret .40 .20
1861 A1248 20c green .50 .20
1862 A1249 20c black .40 .20
1863 A1250 22c dk chalky bl .75 .20
d. Vert. pair, imperf. horiz. *2,500.*
e. Vert. pair, imperf. btwn. —
f. Horiz. pair, imperf. btwn. *2,500.*
1864 A1251 30c olive gray .60 .20
1865 A1252 35c gray .75 .20
1866 A1253 37c blue .80 .20
1867 A1254 39c rose lilac .90 .20
a. Vert. pair, imperf. horiz. *600.*
b. Vert. pair, imperf. btwn. *2,000.*
1868 A1255 40c dark green .90 .20
1869 A1256 50c brown .95 .20
Nos. 1844-1869 (26) 11.00 5.20

Years of issue: 19c, 1980. 17c, 18c, 35c, 1981. No. 1860, 2c, 13c, 37c, 1982. No. 1861, 1c, 3c-5c, 1983. No. 1862, 10c, 30c, 40c, 1984. 6c-9c, 11c, 14c, 22c, 39c, 50c, 1985.

A1261

A1262

Everett Dirksen

1981, Jan. 4 ***Perf. 11***

1874 A1261 15c gray .30 .20
a. All color omitted *500.00*

Everett Dirksen (1896-1969), Senate Minority Leader, 1960-69.

No. 1874a comes from a parially printed pane and may be collected as either a vertical strip of 3 or 5 (1 or 3 stamps normal, one stamp transitional and one stamp with color omitted) or as a pair with one partially printed stamp.

Black Heritage Series

1981, Jan. 30 **Photo.** ***Perf. 11***

1875 A1262 15c multicolored .35 .20

Whitney Moore Young (1921-71), civil rights leader.

Flowers

A1263

A1264

A1265

A1266

1981, Apr. 23 ***Perf. 11***

1876 A1263 18c multicolored .35 .20
1877 A1264 18c multicolored .35 .20
1878 A1265 18c multicolored .35 .20
1879 A1266 18c multicolored .35 .20
a. Block of 4, #1876-1879 1.40 1.25

A1267 A1268

A1269 A1270

A1271 A1272

A1273 A1274

A1275 A1276

1981, May 14 **Engr.** ***Perf. 11***

Booklet Stamps

1880 A1267 18c Bighorn .55 .20
1881 A1268 18c Puma .55 .20
1882 A1269 18c Harbor seal .55 .20
1883 A1270 18c American Buffalo .55 .20
1884 A1271 18c Brown bear .55 .20
1885 A1272 18c Polar bear .55 .20
1886 A1273 18c Elk (wapiti) .55 .20
1887 A1274 18c Moose .55 .20
1888 A1275 18c White-tailed deer .55 .20
1889 A1276 18c Pronghorn .55 .20
a. Bklt. pane of 10, #1880-1889 8.50 *7.00*
Nos. 1880-1889 (10) 5.50 2.00

See No. 1949.

A1277 A1278

A1279 A1280

Multicolor Huck Press

1981, Apr. 24 ***Perf. 11***

1890 A1277 18c multicolored .35 .20
a. Imperf., pair 110.00
b. Vert. pair, imperf. horiz. *850.00*

Coil Stamp

Perf. 10 Vert.

1891 A1278 18c multicolored .35 .20
a. Imperf., pair 30.00
b. Pair, imperf. btwn. —

Beware of pairs offered as imperf. between that have faint blind perfs.

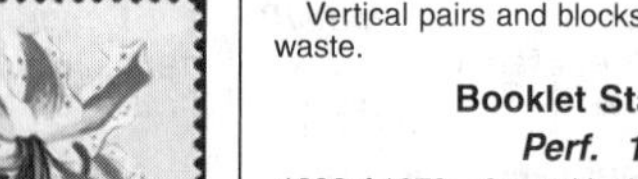

Vertical pairs and blocks exist from printer's waste.

Booklet Stamps

Perf. 11

1892 A1279 6c multicolored .50 .20
1893 A1280 18c multicolored .30 .20
a. Bklt. pane, 2 #1892, 6 #1893 3.00 *2.50*
b. As "a," vert. imperf. btwn. *75.00*
c. Pair, #1892, 1893 .90 *1.00*

Bureau Precanceled Coils

Starting with No. 1895b, Bureau precanceled coil stamps are valued unused as well as used. The coils issued with dull gum may be difficult to distinguish. When used normally these stamps do not receive any postal markings so that used stamps with an additional postal cancellation of any kind are worth considerably less than the values shown here.

A1281

1981, Dec. 17 ***Perf. 11***

1894 A1281 20c blk, dk blue & red .40 .20
a. Vert. pair, imperf. 35.00
b. Vert. pair, imperf. horiz. *550.00*
c. Dark blue omitted *85.00*
d. Black omitted *325.00*

Coil Stamp

Perf. 10 Vertical

1895 A1281 20c blk, dk blue & red .40 .20
b. Untagged (Bureau precanceled) .50 .50
d. Imperf., pair 10.00
e. Pair, imperf. btwn. *1,250.*
f. Black omitted 50.00
g. Dark blue omitted *1,500.*

Booklet Stamp

Perf. 11x10½

1896 A1281 20c blk, dk blue & red .40 .20
a. Booklet pane of 6 2.50 *2.25*
b. Booklet pane of 10 4.25 *3.25*

Transportation Coils

A1283 A1284

A1284A A1285

A1286 A1287

A1288 A1289

A1290

A1291

A1292

A1293

A1294

A1295

1981-84 Engr. *Perf. 10 Vert.*

1897 A1283 1c violet .20 .20
  b. Imperf., pair 675.00
1897A A1284 2c black .20 .20
  e. Imperf., pair 52.50

For similar designs to the 1c and 2c, see Nos. 2225-2226.

1898 A1284A 3c dk green .20 .20
1898A A1285 4c redsh brn .20 .20
  b. Untagged (Bureau precanceled) .20 .20
  c. As "b," imperf., pair 750.00
  d. No. 1898A, imperf., pair 850.00 —
1899 A1286 5c gray green .20 .20
  a. Imperf., pair 2,750.
1900 A1287 5.2c carmine .20 .20
  a. Untagged (Bureau precanceled) .20 .20
1901 A1288 5.9c blue .25 .20
  a. Untagged (Bureau precanceled, lines only) .20 .20
  b. As "a," imperf., pair 200.00
1902 A1289 7.4c brown .20 .20
  a. Untagged (Bureau precanceled) .20 .20
1903 A1290 9.3c car rose .30 .20
  a. Untagged (Bureau precanceled, lines only) .25 .25
  b. As "a," imperf., pair 120.00
1904 A1291 10.9c purple .30 .20
  a. Untagged (Bureau precanceled, lines only) .30 .25
  b. As "a," imperf., pair 140.00
1905 A1292 11c red .30 .20
  a. Untagged .25 .20
1906 A1293 17c ultra .35 .20
  a. Untagged (Bureau precanceled, Presorted First Class) .35 .35
  b. Imperf., pair 165.00
  c. As "a," imperf., pair 650.00
1907 A1294 18c dk brn .35 .20
  a. Imperf., pair 140.00
1908 A1295 20c vermilion .35 .20
  a. Imperf., pair 110.00
Nos. 1897-1908 (14) 3.60 2.80

Years of issue: 9.3c, 17c-20c, 1981. 2c, 4c, 5.9c, 10.9c, 1982. 1c, 3c, 5c, 5.2c, 1983. 7.4, 11c, 1984.

See Nos. 2123-2136, 2225-2231, 2252-2266, 2451-2468.

A1296

Perf. 10 Vert. on 1 or 2 Sides

1983, Aug. 12 Photo.

1909 A1296 $9.35 multi 21.00 15.00
  a. Booklet pane of 3 65.00 —

A1297

A1298

American Red Cross Centennial

1981, May 1 *Perf. 10½x11*

1910 A1297 18c multicolored .35 .20

Savings & Loan Sesquicentennial

1981, May 8 *Perf. 11*

1911 A1298 18c multicolored .35 .20

Space Achievement

A1299

A1303

A1300

A1304

A1301

A1302

A1306

A1305

1981, May 21 *Perf. 11*

1912 A1299 18c multicolored .40 .20
1913 A1300 18c multicolored .40 .20
1914 A1301 18c multicolored .40 .20
1915 A1302 18c multicolored .40 .20
1916 A1303 18c multicolored .40 .20
1917 A1304 18c multicolored .40 .20
1918 A1305 18c multicolored .40 .20
1919 A1306 18c multicolored .40 .20
  a. Block of 8, #1912-1919 3.25 3.00
  b. As "a," imperf. 8,000.

Professional Management

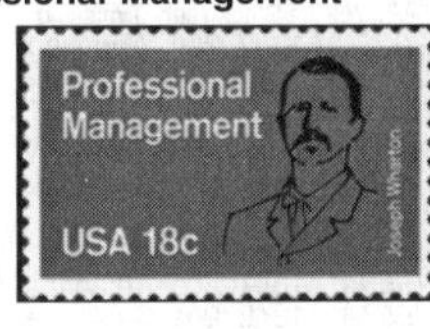

Joseph Wharton A1307

1981, June 18

1920 A1307 18c blue & black .35 .20

Preservation of Wildlife Habitats

A1308 A1309

A1310 A1311

1981, June 26

1921 A1308 18c multicolored .35 .20
1922 A1309 18c multicolored .35 .20
1923 A1310 18c multicolored .35 .20
1924 A1311 18c multicolored .35 .20
  a. Block of 4, #1921-1924 1.50 1.25

International Year of the Disabled

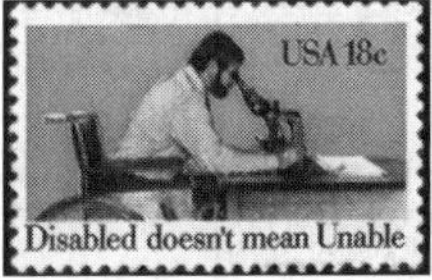

Man Looking through Microscope A1312

1981, June 29 Photo. *Perf. 11*

1925 A1312 18c multicolored .35 .20
  a. Vert. pair, imperf. horiz. 2,600.

Edna St. Vincent Millay, 1892-1950

A1313

Litho. & Engr.

1981, July 10 *Perf. 11*

1926 A1313 18c multicolored .35 .20
  a. Black (engr., inscriptions) omitted 300.00 —

Alcoholism

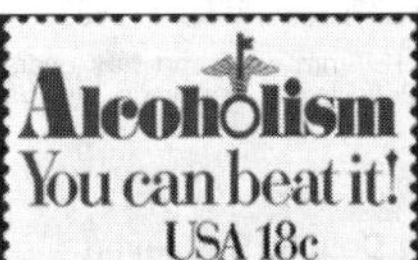

A1314

1981, Aug. 19 Engr. *Perf. 11*

1927 A1314 18c blue & black .40 .20
  a. Imperf., pair 400.
  b. Vert. pair, imperf. horiz. 2,500.

American Architecture Series

New York University Library by Sanford White A1315

Biltmore House by Richard Morris Hunt A1316

Palace of the Arts by Bernard Maybeck A1317

National Farmer's Bank by Louis Sullivan A1318

1981, Aug. 28 Engr. *Perf. 11*

1928 A1315 18c black & red .40 .20
1929 A1316 18c black & red .40 .20
1930 A1317 18c black & red .40 .20
1931 A1318 18c black & red .40 .20
  a. Block of 4, #1928-1931 1.65 1.75

Athletes

Mildred Didrikson Zaharias A1319

Robert Tyre Jones A1320

1981, Sept. 22 Engr. *Perf. 10½x11*

1932 A1319 18c purple .40 .20
1933 A1320 18c green .40 .20

Frederic Remington, 1861-1909

Coming Through the Rye A1321

1981, Oct. 9 *Perf. 11*

1934 A1321 18c gray, grn & brn .35 .20
  a. Vert. pair, imperf. btwn. 275.00
  b. Brown omitted 450.00

James Hoban, 1762?-1831

Irish-American Architect of White House — A1322

1981, Oct. 13 Photo. *Perf. 11*

1935 A1322 18c multicolored .35 .20
1936 A1322 20c multicolored .35 .20

See Ireland No. 504.

American Bicentennial

Battle of Yorktown A1323

Battle of Virginia Capes A1324

Litho. & Engr.

1981, Oct. 16 *Perf. 11*

1937 A1323 18c multicolored .35 .20
1938 A1324 18c multicolored .35 .20
a. Pair, #1937-1938 .90 .75
b. As "a," black (engr., inscriptions) omitted 400.00

Christmas

Madonna and Child, Botticelli — A1325

Felt Bear on Sled A1326

1981, Oct. 28 **Photo.** *Perf. 11*

1939 A1325 (20c) multicolored .40 .20
a. Imperf., pair 125.
b. Vert. pair, imperf. horiz. 1,650.
1940 A1326 (20c) multicolored .40 .20
a. Imperf., pair 275.
b. Vert. pair, imperf. horiz. 2,500.

John Hanson, 1721-1783

First President of Continental Congress — A1327

1981, Nov. 5 **Photo.** *Perf. 11*

1941 A1327 20c multicolored .40 .20

Desert Plants

Barrel Cactus — A1328

Saguaro — A1331

Agave — A1329

Beavertail Cactus — A1330

1981, Dec. 11 **Litho. & Engr.**

1942 A1328 20c multicolored .35 .20
1943 A1329 20c multicolored .35 .20
1944 A1330 20c multicolored .35 .20
1945 A1331 20c multicolored .35 .20
a. Block of 4, #1942-1945 1.50 1.25
b. As "a," deep brown omitted 6,500.
c. No. 1945 imperf., vert. pair 5,250.

A1332

A1333

1981, Oct. 11 **Photo.** *Perf. 11x10½*

1946 A1332 (20c) brown .40 .20
b. All color omitted —

No. 1946b comes from a partially printed pane with most stamps normal. It must be collected as a vertical pair or strip with normal or partially printed stamps attached.

Coil Stamp

Perf. 10 Vert.

1947 A1332 (20c) brown .60 .20
a. Imperf., pair 1,400.

Booklet Stamp

Perf. 11

1948 A1333 (20c) brown .40 .20
a. Booklet pane of 10 4.50 3.25

A1334

1982, Jan. 8 **Engr.** *Perf. 11*

1949 A1334 20c dk blue (from bklt. pane) .55 .20
a. Booklet pane of 10 5.50 2.50
b. As "a," vert. imperf. btwn. 110.00
c. Type II .55 .20
d. As "c," booklet pane of 10 11.00 —

No. 1949 is 18¾mm wide and has overall tagging. No. 1949c is 18½mm wide and has block tagging.

See No. 1880.

Franklin Delano Roosevelt

A1335

1982, Jan. 30 **Engr.** *Perf. 11*

1950 A1335 20c blue .40 .20

A1336

1982, Feb. 1 **Photo.** *Perf. 11¼*

1951 A1336 20c multicolored .40 .20
b. Imperf., pair 275.00
c. Blue omitted 225.00
d. Yellow omitted 1,000.
e. Purple omitted —

No. 1951c is valued in the grade of fine.

Perf. 11¼x10½

1951A A1336 20c multicolored .75 .25

A1337

A1338

George Washington

1982, Feb. 22 **Photo.** *Perf. 11*

1952 A1337 20c multicolored .40 .20

State Birds & Flowers

Perf. 10½x11¼

1982, Apr. 14 **Photo.**

1953 A1338 20c Alabama .50 .25
1954 A1339 20c Alaska .50 .25
1955 A1340 20c Arizona .50 .25
1956 A1341 20c Arkansas .50 .25
1957 A1342 20c California .50 .25
1958 A1343 20c Colorado .50 .25
1959 A1344 20c Connecticut .50 .25
1960 A1345 20c Delaware .50 .25
1961 A1346 20c Florida .50 .25
1962 A1347 20c Georgia .50 .25
1963 A1348 20c Hawaii .50 .25
1964 A1349 20c Idaho .50 .25
1965 A1350 20c Illinois .50 .25
1966 A1351 20c Indiana .50 .25
1967 A1352 20c Iowa .50 .25
1968 A1353 20c Kansas .50 .25
1969 A1354 20c Kentucky .50 .25
1970 A1355 20c Louisiana .50 .25
1971 A1356 20c Maine .50 .25
1972 A1357 20c Maryland .50 .25
1973 A1358 20c Massachusetts .50 .25
1974 A1359 20c Michigan .50 .25
1975 A1360 20c Minnesota .50 .25
1976 A1361 20c Mississippi .50 .25
1977 A1362 20c Missouri .50 .25
1978 A1363 20c Montana .50 .25
1979 A1364 20c Nebraska .50 .25
1980 A1365 20c Nevada .50 .25
1981 A1366 20c New Hampshire .50 .25
b. Black (engr.) missing (EP) 6,000.
1982 A1367 20c New Jersey .50 .25
1983 A1368 20c New Mexico .50 .25
1984 A1369 20c New York .50 .25
1985 A1370 20c North Carolina .50 .25
1986 A1371 20c North Dakota .50 .25
1987 A1372 20c Ohio .50 .25
1988 A1373 20c Oklahoma .50 .25
1989 A1374 20c Oregon .50 .25
1990 A1375 20c Pennsylvania .50 .25
1991 A1376 20c Rhode Island .50 .25
b. Black (engr.) missing (EP) 6,000.
1992 A1377 20c South Carolina .50 .25
1993 A1378 20c South Dakota .50 .25
1994 A1379 20c Tennessee .50 .25
1995 A1380 20c Texas .50 .25
1996 A1381 20c Utah .50 .25
1997 A1382 20c Vermont .50 .25
1998 A1383 20c Virginia .50 .25
1999 A1384 20c Washington .50 .25
2000 A1385 20c West Virginia .50 .25
2001 A1386 20c Wisconsin .50 .25
b. Black (engr.) missing (EP) —
2002 A1387 20c Wyoming .50 .25
b. Pane of 50, #1953-2002 25.00 —
d. Pane of 50, imperf. 27,500.

Perf. 11¼x11

1953A A1338 20c Alabama .55 .30
1954A A1339 20c Alaska .55 .30
1955A A1340 20c Arizona .55 .30
1956A A1341 20c Arkansas .55 .30
1957A A1342 20c California .55 .30
1958A A1343 20c Colorado .55 .30
1959A A1344 20c Connecticut .55 .30
1960A A1345 20c Delaware .55 .30
1961A A1346 20c Florida .55 .30
1962A A1347 20c Georgia .55 .30
1963A A1348 20c Hawaii .55 .30
1964A A1349 20c Idaho .55 .30
1965A A1350 20c Illinois .55 .30
1966A A1351 20c Indiana .55 .30
1967A A1352 20c Iowa .55 .30
1968A A1353 20c Kansas .55 .30
1969A A1354 20c Kentucky .55 .30
1970A A1355 20c Louisiana .55 .30
1971A A1356 20c Maine .55 .30
1972A A1357 20c Maryland .55 .30
1973A A1358 20c Massachusetts .55 .30
1974A A1359 20c Michigan .55 .30
1975A A1360 20c Minnesota .55 .30
1976A A1360 20c Mississippi .55 .30
1977A A1361 20c Missouri .55 .30
1978A A1362 20c Montana .55 .30
1979A A1363 20c Nebraska .55 .30
1980A A1364 20c Nevada .55 .30
1981A A1364 20c New Hampshire .55 .30
1982A A1365 20c New Jersey .55 .30
1983A A1366 20c New Mexico .55 .30
1984A A1369 20c New York .55 .30
1985A A1370 20c North Carolina .55 .30
1986A A1371 20c North Dakota .55 .30
1987A A1372 20c Ohio .55 .30
1988A A1373 20c Oklahoma .55 .30
1989A A1374 20c Oregon .55 .30
1990A A1375 20c Pennsylvania .55 .30
1991A A1376 20c Rhode Island .55 .30
1992A A1377 20c South Carolina .55 .30
1993A A1378 20c South Dakota .55 .30
1994A A1379 20c Tennessee .55 .30
1995A A1380 20c Texas .55 .30
1996A A1381 20c Utah .55 .30
1997A A1382 20c Vermont .55 .30
1998A A1383 20c Virginia .55 .30
1999A A1384 20c Washington .55 .30
2000A A1385 20c West Virginia .55 .30
2001A A1386 20c Wisconsin .55 .30
2002A A1387 20c Wyoming .55 .30
c. Pane of 50, Nos. 1953A-2002A 27.50 —

US-Netherlands

200th Anniv. of Diplomatic Recognition by the Netherlands — A1388

1982, Apr. 20 **Photo.** *Perf. 11*

2003 A1388 20c ver, brt blue & gray black .40 .20
a. Imperf., pair 325.00

See Netherlands Nos. 640-641.

Library of Congress

A1389

1982, Apr. 21 **Engr.** *Perf. 11*

2004 A1389 20c red & black .40 .20
a. All color missing —

No. 2004a must be collected se-tenant with transitional and normal stamps.

Consumer Education

A1390

Coil Stamp

1982, Apr. 27 **Engr.** *Perf. 10 Vert.*

2005 A1390 20c sky blue .55 .20
a. Imperf., pair 100.00

Knoxville World's Fair

A1391

A1392

A1393

A1394

1982, Apr. 29 Photo. *Perf. 11*

2006 A1391 20c multicolored	.40	.20
2007 A1392 20c multicolored	.40	.20
2008 A1393 20c multicolored	.40	.20
2009 A1394 20c multicolored	.40	.20
a. Block of 4, #2006-2009	1.65	1.50

American Author, 1832-1899

Frontispiece from "Ragged Dick" — A1395

1982, Apr. 30 Engr. *Perf. 11*

2010 A1395 20c red & black, *tan*	.40	.20
a. Red & Black omitted	—	

The Philatelic Foundation has issued a certificate for a pane of 50 with red and black colors omitted. Recognition of this error is by the paper and by a tiny residue of red ink from the tagging roller. The engraved plates did not strike the paper.

Aging Together

A1396

1982, May 21 *Perf. 11*

2011 A1396 20c brown	.40	.20

A1397

A1398

Performing Arts Series

Actors John, Ethel & Lionel Barrymore.

1982, June 8 Photo. *Perf. 11*

2012 A1397 20c multicolored	.40	.20

Dr. Mary E. Walker, 1832-1919

1982, June 10 Photo. *Perf. 11*

2013 A1398 20c multicolored	.40	.20

International Peace Garden

A1399

1982, June 30 Photo. *Perf. 11*

2014 A1399 20c multicolored	.40	.20
a. Blk (engr.) omitted	*260.00*	

A1400

A1401

America's Libraries

1982, July 13 Engr. *Perf. 11*

2015 A1400 20c red & black	.40	.20
a. Vert. pair, imperf. horiz.	*300.00*	
c. All colors missing (EP)	—	

Black Heritage Series

1982, Aug. 2 Photo. *Perf. 10½x11*

2016 A1401 20c multicolored	1.25	.20

Jackie Robinson (1919-72), baseball player.

Touro Synagogue

A1402

Photogravure, Engraved

1982, Aug. 22 *Perf. 11*

2017 A1402 20c multicolored	.40	.20
a. Imperf., pair	*2,500.*	

Wolf Trap Farm Park

A1403

1982, Sept. 1 Photo. *Perf. 11*

2018 A1403 20c multicolored	.40	.20

American Architecture Series

Fallingwater, Mill Run, Pa., by Frank Lloyd Wright — A1404

Illinois Institute of Technology by Ludwig Mies van der Rohe A1405

Gropius House, Lincoln, Mass., by Walter Gropius A1406

Dulles Airport, by Eero Saarinen A1407

1982, Sept. 30 Engr. *Perf. 11*

2019 A1404 20c black & brown	.45	.20
b. Red missing (PS)	—	
2020 A1405 20c black & brown	.45	.20
a. Red missing (PS)	—	
2021 A1406 20c black & brown	.45	.20
2022 A1407 20c black & brown	.45	.20
a. Block of 4, #2019-2022	2.00	1.75

St. Francis of Assisi, 1182-1226

A1408

1982, Oct. 7 Photo. *Perf. 11*

2023 A1408 20c multicolored	.40	.20

Ponce de Leon, 1527-1591

A1409

1982, Oct. 12 Photo. *Perf. 11*

2024 A1409 20c multicolored	.40	.20
a. Imperf., pair	*500.00*	
b. Vert. pair, Imperf. btwn. and at top	—	

Christmas

A1410

A1411

A1412

A1413

A1414

A1415

1982, Nov. 3 Photo. *Perf. 11*

2025 A1410 13c multicolored	.25	.20
a. Imperf., pair	*650.00*	

1982, Oct. 28

2026 A1411 20c multicolored	.40	.20
a. Imperf., pair	*150.00*	
b. Horiz. pair, imperf. vert.	—	
c. Vert. pair, imperf. horiz.	—	
2027 A1412 20c multicolored	.50	.20
2028 A1413 20c multicolored	.50	.20
2029 A1414 20c multicolored	.50	.20
2030 A1415 20c multicolored	.50	.20
a. Block of 4, #2027-2030	2.10	1.50
b. As "a," imperf.	*2,750.*	
c. As "a," imperf. horiz.	*750.*	
Nos. 2025-2030 (6)	2.65	1.20

Science & Industry

A1416

Litho. & Engr.

1983, Jan. 19 *Perf. 11*

2031 A1416 20c multicolored	.40	.20
a. Black (engr.) omitted	*1,400.*	

Balloons

A1417

A1420

A1418

A1419

1983, Mar. 31 Photo. *Perf. 11*

2032 A1417 20c multicolored	.40	.20
2033 A1418 20c multicolored	.40	.20
2034 A1419 20c multicolored	.40	.20
2035 A1420 20c multicolored	.40	.20
a. Block of 4, #2032-2035	1.65	1.50
b. As "a," imperf.	*4,250.*	
c. As "a," right stamp perf., otherwise imperf.	*4,500.*	

US-Sweden

A1421

1983, Mar. 24 Engr. *Perf. 11*

2036 A1421 20c multicolored	.40	.20

See Sweden No. 1453.

Civilian Conservation Corps

A1422

1983, Apr. 5 Photo. *Perf. 11*
2037 A1422 20c multicolored .40 .20
a. Imperf., pair *2,900.*
b. Vert. pair, imperf. horiz. —

Joseph Priestley, 1733-1804

A1423

1983, Apr. 13 Photo. *Perf. 11*
2038 A1423 20c multicolored .40 .20

Voluntarism

A1424

1983, Apr. 20 Engr. *Perf. 11*
2039 A1424 20c red & black .40 .20
a. Imperf., pair *750.00*

US-Germany

Concord, 1683
A1425

1983, Apr. 29 *Perf. 11*
2040 A1425 20c brown .40 .20

See Germany No. 1397.

Brooklyn Bridge

A1426

1983, May 17 Engr. *Perf. 11*
2041 A1426 20c blue .40 .20
b. All color missing (EP) —

T.V.A.

A1427

Photo. & Engr.
1983, May 18 *Perf. 11*
2042 A1427 20c multicolored .40 .20

Physical Fitness

A1428

1983, May 14 Photo. *Perf. 11*
2043 A1428 20c multicolored .40 .20

Black Heritage Series

A1429

1983, June 9 Photo.
2044 A1429 20c multicolored .40 .20
a. Imperf., pair *475.00*

Scott Joplin (1868-1917), ragtime composer.

Medal of Honor

A1430

Litho. & Engr.
1983, June 7 *Perf. 11*
2045 A1430 20c multicolored .40 .20
a. Red omitted *240.00*

A1431

A1432

George Herman Ruth, 1895-1948

1983, July 6 Engr. *Perf. 10½x11*
2046 A1431 20c blue 1.40 .20

Nathaniel Hawthorne, 1804-1864

1983, July 8 Photo. *Perf. 11*
2047 A1432 20c multicolored .45 .20

1984 Summer Olympics

Discus
A1433

High Jump
A1434

Archery
A1435

Boxing
A1436

1983, July 28 Photo. *Perf. 11*
2048 A1433 13c multicolored .35 .20
2049 A1434 13c multicolored .35 .20
2050 A1435 13c multicolored .35 .20
2051 A1436 13c multicolored .35 .20
a. Block of 4, #2048-2051 1.50 1.25

Signing of Treaty of Paris

John Adams, Franklin, John Jay, David Hartley
A1437

1983, Sept. 2 Photo. *Perf. 11*
2052 A1437 20c multicolored .40 .20

Civil Service

A1438

1983, Sept. 9 Photo. & Engr.
2053 A1438 20c buff, blue & red .40 .20

Metropolitan Opera

A1439

1983, Sept. 14 Litho. & Engr.
2054 A1439 20c yel & mar .40 .20

American Inventors

A1440

A1441

A1442

A1443

1983, Sept. 21 Litho. & Engr
2055 A1440 20c multicolored .45 .20
2056 A1441 20c multicolored .45 .20
2057 A1442 20c multicolored .45 .20
2058 A1443 20c multicolored .45 .20
a. Block of 4, #2055-2058 1.80 1.25
b. As "a," black omitted *375.00*

Streetcars

A1444

A1445

A1446

A1447

1983, Oct. 8 Photo. & Engr.
2059 A1444 20c multicolored .45 .20
2060 A1445 20c multicolored .45 .20
2061 A1446 20c multicolored .45 .20
2062 A1447 20c multicolored .45 .20
a. Block of 4, #2059-2062 1.80 1.40
b. As "a," black omitted *375.00*
c. As "a," black omitted on #2059, 2061 —

Christmas

A1448

A1449

1983, Oct. 28 Photo. *Perf. 11*
2063 A1448 20c multicolored .40 .20
2064 A1449 20c multicolored .40 .20
a. Imperf., pair *175.00*

A1450

Caribou and Alaska Pipeline — A1451

Martin Luther, 1483-1546

1983, Nov. 11 Photo. *Perf. 11*
2065 A1450 20c multicolored .40 .20

25th Anniv. of Alaska Statehood

1984, Jan. 3 Photo. *Perf. 11*
2066 A1451 20c multicolored .40 .20

Winter Olympic Games

Ice Dancing A1452 — Downhill Skiing A1453

Cross-country Skiing A1454 — Hockey A1455

1984, Jan. 6 ***Perf. 10½x11***

2067 A1452 20c multicolored .50 .20
2068 A1453 20c multicolored .50 .20
2069 A1454 20c multicolored .50 .20
2070 A1455 20c multicolored .50 .20
a. Block of 4, #2067-2070 2.10 1.50

14th Winter Olympic Games, Sarajevo, Yugoslavia, Feb. 8-19.

A1456 — A1457

Federal Deposit Insurance Corp., 50th Anniv.

1984, Jan. 12 ***Perf. 11***

2071 A1456 20c multicolored .40 .20

Love

1984, Jan. 31 **Photo. & Engr.**

2072 A1457 20c multicolored .40 .20
a. Horiz. pair, imperf. vert. *175.00*

Carter G. Woodson (1875-1950), Writer — A1458

Black Heritage Series

1984, Feb. 1 **Photo.**

2073 A1458 20c multicolored .40 .20
a. Horiz. pair, imperf. vert. *1,600.*

A1459

Dollar Sign, Coin — A1460

Soil and Water Conservation

1984, Feb. 6

2074 A1459 20c multicolored .40 .20

50th Anniv. of Credit Union Act

1984, Feb. 10 **Photo.** ***Perf. 11***

2075 A1460 20c multicolored .40 .20

Orchids

A1461

A1462

A1463

A1464

1984, Mar. 5

2076 A1461 20c Wild pink .50 .20
2077 A1462 20c Yellow lady's-slipper .50 .20
2078 A1463 20c Spreading pogonia .50 .20
2079 A1464 20c Pacific calypso .50 .20
a. Block of 4, #2076-2079 2.00 1.50

25th Anniv. of Hawaii Statehood

Eastern Polynesian Canoe, Golden Plover, Mauna Loa Volcano A1465

1984, Mar. 12 **Photo.** ***Perf. 11***

2080 A1465 20c multicolored .40 .20

National Archives

Abraham Lincoln, George Washington — A1466

1984, Apr. 16 **Photo.** ***Perf. 11***

2081 A1466 20c multicolored .40 .20

1984 Los Angeles Olympics

Diving A1467 — Long Jump A1468

Wrestling A1469 — Kayak A1470

1984, May 4 ***Perf. 11***

2082 A1467 20c multicolored .55 .20
2083 A1468 20c multicolored .55 .20
2084 A1469 20c multicolored .55 .20
2085 A1470 20c multicolored .55 .20
a. Block of 4, #2082-2085 2.40 1.90
b. As "a," imperf. btwn. vert. —

New Orleans World Exposition

River Wildlife A1471

1984, May 11 ***Perf. 11***

2086 A1471 20c multicolored .40 .20

Health Research

Lab Equipment A1472

1984, May 17 ***Perf. 11***

2087 A1472 20c multicolored .40 .20

A1473 — A1474

Performing Arts

Actor Douglas Fairbanks (1883-1939)

1984, May 23 **Photo. & Engr.**

2088 A1473 20c multicolored .40 .20
b. Horiz. pair, imperf btwn. —

Jim Thorpe, 1888-1953

1984, May 24 **Engr.** ***Perf. 11***

2089 A1474 20c dark brown .40 .20

Performing Arts

Tenor John McCormack (1884-1945) A1475

1984, June 6 **Photo.** ***Perf. 11***

2090 A1475 20c multicolored .40 .20

See Ireland No. 594.

25th Anniv. of St. Lawrence Seaway

Aerial View of Seaway, Freighters A1476

1984, June 26 **Photo.** ***Perf. 11***

2091 A1476 20c multicolored .40 .20

50th Anniv. of Waterfowl Preservation Act

"Mallards Dropping In," by Jay N. Darling A1477

1984, July 2 **Engr.** ***Perf. 11***

2092 A1477 20c blue .50 .20
a. Horiz. pair, imperf. vert. *400.00*

See No. RW1.

A1478 — Author — A1479

Roanoke Voyages

1984, July 13 **Photo.** ***Perf. 11***

2093 A1478 20c multicolored .40 .20

Herman Melville (1819-1891)

1984, Aug. 1 **Engr.** ***Perf. 11***

2094 A1479 20c sage green .40 .20

Horace Moses (1862-1947)

Junior Achievement Founder — A1480

1984, Aug. 6 **Engr.**

2095 A1480 20c org & dk brn .45 .20

Smokey Bear — A1481

Clemente, Puerto Rican Flag — A1482

1984, Aug. 13 **Litho. & Engr.**

2096 A1481 20c multicolored .40 .20
- *a.* Horiz. pair, imperf. btwn. *300.*
- *b.* Vert. pair, imperf. btwn. *240.*
- *c.* Block of 4, imperf. btwn, vert. and horiz. *5,500.*
- *d.* Horiz. pair, imperf. vert. *1,750.*

Roberto Clemente (1934-1972)

1984, Aug. 17 **Photo.** ***Perf. 11***

2097 A1482 20c multicolored 1.75 .20
- *a.* Horiz. pair, imperf. vert. *2,000.*

Dogs

Beagle, Boston Terrier A1483

Chesapeake Bay Retriever, Cocker Spaniel — A1484

Alaskan Malamute, Collie A1485

Black & Tan Coonhound, American Foxhound — A1486

1984, Sept. 7 **Photo.** ***Perf. 11***

2098 A1483 20c multicolored .45 .20
2099 A1484 20c multicolored .45 .20
2100 A1485 20c multicolored .45 .20
2101 A1486 20c multicolored .45 .20
- *a.* Block of 4, #2098-2101 1.90 1.90

Crime Prevention

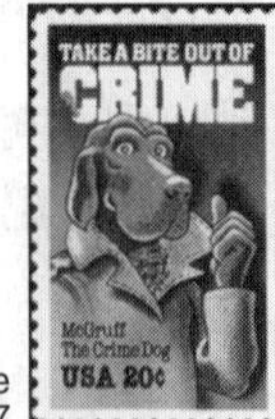

McGruff, The Crime Dog — A1487

1984, Sept. 26 **Photo.** ***Perf. 11***

2102 A1487 20c multicolored .40 .20

Hispanic Americans

A1488

1984, Oct. 31 **Photo.** ***Perf. 11***

2103 A1488 20c multicolored .40 .20
- *a.* Vert. pair, imperf. horiz. *2,250.*

A1489

A1490

Family Unity

1984, Oct. 1 **Photo. & Engr.**

2104 A1489 20c multicolored .40 .20
- *a.* Horiz. pair, imperf. vert. *550.00*
- *c.* Vert. pair, imperf. btwn. and at bottom —
- *d.* Horiz. pair, imperf. between —

Eleanor Roosevelt

1984, Oct. 11 **Engr.** ***Perf. 11***

2105 A1490 20c deep blue .40 .20

Nation of Readers

Lincoln, Son Tad — A1491

1984, Oct. 16 **Engr.** ***Perf. 11***

2106 A1491 20c brown & mar .40 .20

Christmas

Madonna and Child by Fra Filippo Lippi — A1492

Santa Claus — A1493

1984, Oct. 30 **Photo.** ***Perf. 11***

2107 A1492 20c multicolored .40 .20
2108 A1493 20c multicolored .40 .20
- *a.* Horiz. pair, imperf. vert. *950.00*

No. 2108a is valued in the grade of fine.

Vietnam Veterans Memorial

Memorial Wall — A1494

1984, Nov. 10 **Engr.** ***Perf. 11***

2109 A1494 20c multicolored .40 .20

Performing Arts

Composer Jerome Kern (1885-1945) A1495

1985, Jan. 23 **Photo.** ***Perf. 11***

2110 A1495 22c multicolored .40 .20

A1496

A1497

1985, Feb. 1 **Photo.** ***Perf. 11***

2111 A1496 (22c) green .55 .20
- *a.* Vert. pair, imperf. *35.*
- *b.* Vert. pair, imperf. horiz. *1,350.*

Coil Stamp

Perf. 10 Vert.

2112 A1496 (22c) green .60 .20
- *a.* Imperf., pair 45.00

Booklet Stamp

Perf. 11

2113 A1497 (22c) green .80 .20
- *a.* Booklet pane of 10 8.50 *3.00*
- *b.* As "a," imperf. btwn. horiz. —

A1498

Flag over Capitol Dome A1499

1985, Mar. 29 **Engr.** ***Perf. 11***

2114 A1498 22c bl, red & blk .40 .20

Coil Stamp

Perf. 10 Vert.

2115 A1498 22c bl, red & blk .40 .20
- *b.* Inscribed "T" at bottom ('87) .50 .40
- *c.* Black field of stars — —
- *e.* Imperf., pair 12.50

Booklet Stamp

Perf. 10 Horiz. on 1 or 2 Sides

2116 A1499 22c bl, red & blk .50 .20
- *a.* Booklet pane of 5 2.50 *1.25*

Seashells

Frilled Dogwinkle A1500

Reticulated Helmet A1501

New England Neptune A1502

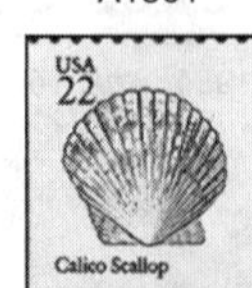

Calico Scallop A1503

Lightning Whelk — A1504

1985, Apr. 4 **Engr.** ***Perf. 10***

Booklet Stamps

2117 A1500 22c black & brn .40 .20
2118 A1501 22c multicolored .40 .20
2119 A1502 22c black & brn .40 .20
2120 A1503 22c black & violet .40 .20
2121 A1504 22c multicolored .40 .20
- *a.* Bklt. pane, 2 ea #2117-2121 4.00 *3.00*
- *b.* As "a," violet omitted *800.00*
- *c.* As "a," vert. imperf. btwn. *600.00*
- *d.* As "a," imperf. —
- *e.* Strip of 5, #2117-2121 2.00 —

Eagle and Half Moon — A1505

Type I. Washed out, dull appearance most evident in the black of the body of the eagle, and the red in the background between the eagle's shoulder and the moon. "$10.75" appears splotchy or grainy (P# 11111).

Type II. Brighter, more intense colors most evident in the black on the eagle's body, and red in the background. "$10.75" appears smoother, brighter, and less grainy (P# 22222).

Perf. 10 Vert. on 1 or 2 Sides

1985, Apr. 29 **Photo.** **Untagged**

2122 A1505 $10.75 multi, type I 19.00 7.50
- *a.* Booklet pane of 3 60.00 —
- *b.* Type II 22.50 —
- *c.* As "b," booklet pane of 3 70.00 —

Issued in booklets only.

Transportation Coils

A1506

A1507

A1508

A1509

A1510

A1511

A1512

A1513

A1514

A1515

A1516

Iceboat 1880s USA 14
A1517

A1518

A1519

1985-87 Engr. *Perf. 10 Vert.*

2123 A1506 3.4c dk bluish green .20 .20
a. Untagged (Bureau precanceled) .20 .20
2124 A1507 4.9c brn blk .20 .20
a. Untagged (Bureau precanceled) .20 .20
2125 A1508 5.5c dp mag .20 .20
a. Untagged (Bureau precanceled) .20 .20
2126 A1509 6c red brn .20 .20
a. Untagged (Bureau precanceled) .20 .20
b. As "a," imperf., pair 200.00
2127 A1510 7.1c lake .20 .20
a. Untagged (Bureau precanceled) .20 .20
2128 A1511 8.3c green .20 .20
a. Untagged (Bureau precanceled) .20 .20

For similar stamp see No. 2231.

2129 A1512 8.5c dk Prus green .20 .20
a. Untagged (Bureau precanceled) .20 .20
2130 A1513 10.1c slate blue .25 .20
a. Untagged (Bureau precanceled) .25 .25
b. As "a," imperf., pair (red precancel) 15.00
As "b," black precancel *95.00*
2131 A1514 11c dk green .25 .20
2132 A1515 12c dk bl, I .25 .20
a. Untagged (Bureau precanceled) .25 .25
b. Type II, untagged (Bureau precanceled) .40 .30

Type II has "Stanley Steamer 1909" ½mm shorter (17½mm) than No. 2132 (18mm).

2133 A1516 12.5c ol grn .25 .20
a. Untagged (Bureau precanceled) .25 .25
b. As "a," imperf., pair 50.00
2134 A1517 14c sky bl, I .30 .20
a. Imperf., pair 100.00
b. Type II .30 .20

Type II design is ¼mm narrower (17¼mm) than No. 2134 (17½mm) and has block tagging. No. 2134 has overall tagging.

2135 A1518 17c sky blue .30 .20
a. Imperf., pair *450.00*
2136 A1519 25c org brn .45 .20
a. Imperf., pair 10.00
b. Pair, imperf. between *750.00*
Nos. 2123-2136 (14) 3.45 2.80

Years of issue: 3.4c, 4.9c, 6c, 8.3c, 10.1c-14c, 1985. 5.5c, 17c, 25c, 1986. 7.1c, 8.5c, 1987.

See Nos. 1897-1908, 2225-2231, 2252-2266, 2451-2468.

Black Heritage Series

Mary McLeod Bethune (1875-1955), Educator — A1520

1985, Mar. 5 Photo. *Perf. 11*

2137 A1520 22c multicolored .40 .20

American Folk Art Series

Duck Decoys

Broadbill A1521

Mallard A1522

Canvasback A1523

Redhead A1524

1985, Mar. 22 Photo. *Perf. 11*

2138 A1521 22c multicolored .65 .20
2139 A1522 22c multicolored .65 .20
2140 A1523 22c multicolored .65 .20
2141 A1524 22c multicolored .65 .20
a. Block of 4, #2138-2141 4.00 2.75

Winter Special Olympics

Ice Skater, Emblem, Skier A1525

1985, Mar. 25 Photo. *Perf. 11*

2142 A1525 22c multicolored .40 .20
a. Vert. pair, imperf. horiz. *550.00*

Love

A1526

1985, Apr. 17 Photo.

2143 A1526 22c multicolored .40 .20
a. Imperf., pair *1,500.*

Rural Electrification Administration

Electrified Farm A1527

1985, May 11 Photo. & Engr.

2144 A1527 22c multicolored .45 .20
a. Vert. pair, imperf. btwn. —

AMERIPEX '86

US No. 134 — A1528

1985, May 25 Litho. & Engr.

2145 A1528 22c multicolored .40 .20
a. Red, black & blue omitted *200.*
b. Red & black omitted *1,250.*
c. Red omitted —
d. Black missing (PS) —

US First Lady

Abigail Adams (1744-1818) A1529

1985, June 14 Photo. *Perf. 11*

2146 A1529 22c multicolored .40 .20
a. Imperf., pair *275.00*

Architect, Sculptor

Frederic Auguste Bartholdi (1834-1904), Statue of Liberty — A1530

1985, July 18 Litho. & Engr.

2147 A1530 22c multicolored .40 .20

Examples exist with most, but not all, of the engraved black omitted.

George Washington, Washington Monument A1532

Envelopes A1533

COIL STAMPS

1985 Photo. *Perf. 10 Vert.*

2149 A1532 18c multicolored .35 .20
a. Untagged (Bureau precanceled) .35 .35
b. Imperf., pair *950.00*
c. As "a," imperf., pair *800.00*
2150 A1533 21.1c multicolored .40 .20
a. Untagged (Bureau precanceled) .40 .40

Issue dates: 18c, Nov. 6; 21.1c, Oct. 22.

Precancellations on Nos. 2149a ("PRESORTED FIRST CLASS"), 2150a ("ZIP+4") do not have lines.

Korean War Veterans

American Troops in Korea A1535

1985, July 26 Engr. *Perf. 11*

2152 A1535 22c gray grn & rose red .40 .20

Social Security Act, 50th Anniv.

Men, Women, Children, Corinthian Columns A1536

1985, Aug. 14 Photo. *Perf. 11*

2153 A1536 22c dp bl & lt bl .40 .20

World War I Veterans

The Battle of Marne, France, by Harvey Dunn A1537

1985, Aug. 26 Engr. *Perf. 11*

2154 A1537 22c gray grn & rose red .40 .20
a. Red missing (PS) —

Horses

Quarter Horse A1538

Morgan A1539

Saddlebred A1540

Appaloosa A1541

1985, Sept. 25 Photo. *Perf. 11*

2155 A1538 22c multicolored 1.00 .20
2156 A1539 22c multicolored 1.00 .20
2157 A1540 22c multicolored 1.00 .20
2158 A1541 22c multicolored 1.00 .20
a. Block of 4, #2155-2158 6.00 5.00

Public Education in America

Quill Pen, Apple, Spectacles, Penmanship Quiz — A1542

1985, Oct. 1 Photo. *Perf. 11*

2159 A1542 22c multicolored .45 .20

International Youth Year

YMCA Youth Camping, Cent. A1543

Boy Scouts, 75th Anniv. A1544

Big Brothers/Big Sisters Fed., 40th Anniv. — A1545

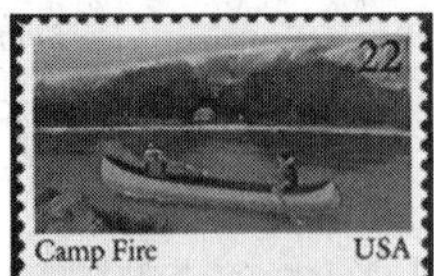

Camp Fire, Inc., 75th Anniv. A1546

1985, Oct. 7 Photo. *Perf. 11*

2160 A1543 22c multicolored .65 .20
2161 A1544 22c multicolored .65 .20
2162 A1545 22c multicolored .65 .20
2163 A1546 22c multicolored .65 .20
a. Block of 4, #2160-2163 3.00 2.25

Help End Hunger

Youths and the Elderly Suffering from Malnutrition A1547

1985, Oct. 15 Photo.

2164 A1547 22c multicolored .45 .20

Christmas

Genoa Madonna, Enameled Terra-Cotta by Luca Della Robbia (1400-1482) A1548

Poinsettia Plants A1549

1985, Oct. 30 Photo.

2165 A1548 22c multicolored .40 .20
a. Imperf., pair *100.00*
2166 A1549 22c multicolored .40 .20
a. Imperf., pair *130.00*

Arkansas Statehood, 150th Anniv.

Old State House, Little Rock A1550

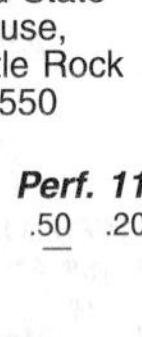

1986, Jan. 3 Photo. *Perf. 11*

2167 A1550 22c multicolored .50 .20
a. Vert. pair, imperf. horiz. —

Great Americans

A1551

A1552

A1553

A1554

A1555

A1556

A1557

A1558

A1559

A1560

A1561

A1562

A1563

A1564

A1565

A1566

A1567

A1568

A1569

A1570

A1571

A1572

A1573

A1574

A1575

A1576

A1577

A1578

Perf. 11, 11½x11 (#2185), 11.1x11 (#2179)

1986-94 Engr.

2168 A1551 1c brnsh ver .20 .20
2169 A1552 2c bright blue .20 .20
a. Untagged .20 .20
2170 A1553 3c bright blue .20 .20
a. Untagged .20 .20
2171 A1554 4c blue violet .20 .20
a. 4c grayish violet, untagged .20 .20
b. 4c deep grayish blue, untagged .20 .20
2172 A1555 5c dk ol grn .20 .20
2173 A1556 5c carmine .20 .20
a. Untagged .20 .20
2175 A1557 10c lake .20 .20
e. 10c carmine .25 .20
f. All color omitted —
2176 A1558 14c crimson .25 .20
2177 A1559 15c claret .35 .20
d. All color omitted —
2178 A1560 17c dull bl grn .35 .20
2179 A1561 20c red brown .40 .20
a. 20c orange brown .40 .20
2180 A1562 21c blue vio .40 .20
2181 A1563 23c purple .45 .20
2182 A1564 25c blue .45 .20
a. Booklet pane of 10 ('88) 4.50 *3.75*
d. Horiz. pair, imperf btwn. —
2183 A1565 28c myrtle grn .50 .20
2184 A1566 29c blue .55 .20
2185 A1567 29c indigo .50 .20
2186 A1568 35c black .65 .20
2187 A1569 40c dark blue .70 .20
2188 A1570 45c bright blue .85 .20
a. 45c blue 1.65 —
2189 A1571 52c purple 1.10 .20
2190 A1572 56c scarlet 1.10 .20
2191 A1573 65c dark blue 1.20 .20
2192 A1574 75c dp magenta 1.30 .20
2193 A1575 $1 dk Prus grn 2.50 .50
2194 A1576 $1 intense deep blue 1.75 .50
b. $1 deep blue 1.75 .50
d. $1 dark blue 1.75 .50
e. $1 blue 1.75 .60
2195 A1577 $2 brt violet 3.50 .50
2196 A1578 $5 copper red 8.00 1.00
Nos. 2168-2196 (28) 28.25 7.30

Booklet Stamp

Perf. 10 on 2 or 3 sides

2197 A1564 25c blue .45 .20
a. Booklet pane of 6 3.00 2.25

No. 2175f must be collected se-tenant with a partially printed stamp or longer vertical strip.

No. 2177d must be collected se-tenant with a partially printed stamp or longer horizontal strip.

The intense deep blue of No. 2194 is much deeper than the deep blue and dark blue of the other $1 varieties.

Issued: #2182, 1/11/86; #2172, 2/27/86; $2, 3/19/86; 17c, 6/18/86; 1c, 6/30/86; 4c, 7/14/86; 56c, 9/3/86; 3c, 9/15/86; #2193, 9/23/86; 14c, 2/12/87; 2c, 2/28/87; 10c, 8/15/87; $5, 8/25/87; #2183a, 2197, 5/3/88; 15c, 6/6/88; 45c, 6/17/88; 21c, 10/21/88; 23c, 11/4/88; 65c, 11/5/88; # 2197, 1988; #2194, 6/7/89; 28c, 9/14/89; #2173, 2/18/90; 40c, 9/6/90; #2188a, 2194b, 1990; 35c, 4/3/91; 52c, 6/3/91; 75c, 2/16/92; #2184, 3/9/92; #2194d, 1992; #2185, 4/13/93; #2171b, 2194e, 1993; 20c, 10/24/94; #2170a, 1994.

Stamp Collecting

Handstamped Cover, No. 213, Philatelic Memorabilia — A1581

Boy Examining Stamp Collection A1582

No. 836 Under Magnifying Glass, Sweden Nos. 268, 271 — A1583

1986 Presidents Miniature Sheet A1584

Perf. 10 Vert. on 1 or 2 Sides

1986, Jan. 23 Litho. & Engr.

Booklet Stamps

2198 A1581 22c multicolored .45 .20
2199 A1582 22c multicolored .45 .20
2200 A1583 22c multicolored .45 .20
2201 A1584 22c multicolored .45 .20
a. Bklt. pane of 4, #2198-2201 2.00 1.75
b. As "a," black omitted on #2198, 2201 50.00
c. As "a," blue (litho.) omitted on #2198-2200 *2,500.*
d. As "a," buff (litho.) omitted —

See Sweden Nos. 1585-1588.

A1585

A1586

Love

1986, Jan. 30 Photo. *Perf. 11*

2202 A1585 22c Puppy .40 .20

Black Heritage Series

1986, Feb. 4 Photo. *Perf. 11*

2203 A1586 22c multicolored .40 .20

Sojourner Truth (c. 1797-1883), abolitionist.

Republic of Texas, 150th Anniv.

Texas State Flag and Silver Spur — A1587

1986, Mar. 2 Photo.

2204 A1587 22c dk bl, dk red & grysh blk .40 .20
a. Horiz. pair, imperf. vert. *1,100.*
b. Dark red omitted *2,750.*
c. Dark blue omitted *7,500.*

Fish

Muskellunge — A1588

Atlantic Cod A1589

Largemouth Bass — A1590

Bluefin Tuna A1591

Catfish A1592

Perf. 10 Horiz. on 1 or 2 Sides

1986, Mar. 21 **Photo.**

Booklet Stamps

2205	A1588 22c multicolored	.60	.20
2206	A1589 22c multicolored	.60	.20
2207	A1590 22c multicolored	.60	.20
2208	A1591 22c multicolored	.60	.20
2209	A1592 22c multicolored	.60	.20
a.	Bklt. pane of 5, #2205-2209	5.50	*2.75*
b.	As "a," red omitted	—	

Public Hospitals

A1593

1986, Apr. 11 **Photo.** ***Perf. 11***

2210	A1593 22c multicolored	.40	.20
a.	Vert. pair, imperf. horiz.	*325.*	
b.	Horiz. pair, imperf. vert.	*1,350.*	

Performing Arts

Edward Kennedy "Duke" Ellington (1899-1974), Jazz Composer — A1594

1986, Apr. 29 **Photo.** ***Perf. 11***

2211	A1594 22c multicolored	.40	.20
a.	Vert. pair, imperf. horiz.	*1,000.*	—

Miniature Sheets

35 Presidents — A1599a

No. 2216: a, Washington. b, John Adams. c, Jefferson. d, Madison. e, Monroe. f, John Quincy Adams. g, Jackson. h, Van Buren. i, Harrison.

No. 2217; a, Tyler. b, Polk. c, Taylor. d, Fillmore. e, Pierce. f, Buchanan. g, Lincoln. h, Andrew Johnson. i, Grant.

No. 2218: a, Hayes. b, Garfield. c, Arthur. d, Cleveland. e, Harrison. f, McKinley. g, Theodore Roosevelt. h, Taft. i, Wilson.

No. 2219: a, Harding. b, Coolidge. c, Hoover. d, Franklin Delano Roosevelt. e, White House. f, Truman. g, Eisenhower. h, Kennedy. i, Lyndon B. Johnson.

1986, May 22 **Litho. & Engr.**

2216	A1599a Sheet of 9	4.25	—
a.-i.	22c any single	.45	.25
j.	Blue omitted	*3,250.*	
k.	Black inscription omitted	*2,000.*	
l.	Imperf.	*10,500.*	
2217	A1599b Sheet of 9	4.25	—
a.-i.	22c any single	.45	.25
j.	Black inscription omitted	*3,750.*	
2218	A1599c Sheet of 9	4.25	—
a.-i.	22c any single	.45	.25
j.	Brown omitted	—	
k.	Black inscription omitted	*2,900.*	
2219	A1599d Sheet of 9	4.25	—
a.-i.	22c any single	.45	.25
j.	Blackish blue (engr.) inscription omitted on a.-b., d.-e., g.-h.	—	
l.	Blackish blue (engr.) omitted	—	
	Nos. 2216-2219 (4)	17.00	

Issued at AMERIPEX '86 Intl. Phil. Exhib., Chicago, IL, May 22-June 1.

Arctic Explorers

Elisha Kent Kane A1600

Adolphus W. Greely A1601

Vilhjalmur Stefansson A1602

Robert E. Peary and Matthew Alexander Henson A1603

1986, May 28 **Photo.** ***Perf. 11***

2220	A1600 22c multicolored	.65	.20
2221	A1601 22c multicolored	.65	.20
2222	A1602 22c multicolored	.65	.20
2223	A1603 22c multicolored	.65	.20
a.	Block of 4, #2220-2223	2.75	2.25
b.	As "a," blk (engr.) omitted	*8,500.*	
c.	As "a," #2220 & 2221 black (engr.) omitted	—	

Statue of Liberty, Cent. — A1604

1986, July 4 **Engr.** ***Perf. 11***

2224	A1604 22c scar & dk bl	.40	.20
a.	Scarlet omitted	—	

See France No. 2014.

Transportation Coils

Types of 1982-85 and

A1604a

A1604b

1986-87 **Engr.** ***Perf. 10 Vert.***

2225	A1604a	1c violet	.20	.20
b.		Untagged	.20	.20
c.		Imperf., pair	*2,000.*	
2226	A1604b	2c black ('87)	.20	.20
a.		Untagged	.20	.20
2228	A1285	4c reddish brown	.20	.20
b.		Imperf., pair	*300.00*	
2231	A1511	8.3c grn (Bureau precancel)	.20	.20
		Nos. 2225-2231 (4)	.80	.80

Issued: 1c, 11/26; 2c, 3/6. Earliest known usage of 4c, 8/15/86; 8.3c, 8/29.

On No. 2228 "Stagecoach 1890s" is 17¾mm long, on No. 1898A 19¾mm long. On No. 2231 "Ambulance 1860s" is 18mm long, on No. 2128 18½mm long.

No. 2226 inscribed "2 USA;" No. 1897A inscribed "USA 2c."

America Folk Art Series

Navajo Art

A1605 A1606

A1607 A1608

Blankets in the Museum of the American Indian and Lowe Art Museum.

Litho. & Engr.

1986, Sept. 4 ***Perf. 11***

2235	A1605 22c multicolored	.50	.20
2236	A1606 22c multicolored	.50	.20
2237	A1607 22c multicolored	.50	.20
2238	A1608 22c multicolored	.50	.20
a.	Block of 4, #2235-2238	2.50	2.25
b.	As "a," blk (engr.) omitted	*350.00*	

Literary Arts

T. S. Eliot (1888-1965), Poet — A1609

1986, Sept. 26 **Engr.** ***Perf. 11***

2239	A1609 22c copper red	.40	.20

American Folk Art Series

Woodcarved Figurines

Highlander Figure A1610 Ship Figurehead A1611

Nautical Figure A1612 Cigar Store Figure A1613

1986, Oct. 1 **Photo.** ***Perf. 11***

2240	A1610 22c multicolored	.40	.20
2241	A1611 22c multicolored	.40	.20
2242	A1612 22c multicolored	.40	.20
2243	A1613 22c multicolored	.40	.20
a.	Block of 4, #2240-2243	1.75	*2.00*
b.	As "a," imperf. vert.	*1,250.*	

Christmas

Madonna, by Perugino (c. 1450-1523) A1614

Village Scene A1615

1986, Oct. 24 ***Perf. 11***

2244	A1614 22c multicolored	.40	.20
a.	Imperf., pair	*800.00*	
2245	A1615 22c multicolored	.40	.20

Michigan Statehood Sesquicent.

White Pine — A1616

1987, Jan. 26 **Photo.** ***Perf. 11***

2246	A1616 22c multicolored	.40	.20

Pan American Games, Indianapolis, August 7-25

Runner in Full Stride A1617

1987, Jan. 29 ***Perf. 11***

2247 A1617 22c multicolored .40 .20
a. Silver omitted *1,500.*

No. 2247a is valued in the grade of fine.

A1618

A1619

Love

1987, Jan. 30 Photo. *Perf. 11½x11*

2248 A1618 22c multicolored .40 .20

Black Heritage Series

1987, Feb. 20 Photo. *Perf. 11*

2249 A1619 22c multicolored .40 .20

Jean Baptiste Pointe du Sable (c. 1750-1818), pioneer trader, founder of Chicago

A1620

A1621

Performing Arts Series

Photo. & Engr.

1987, Feb. 27 ***Perf. 11***

2250 A1620 22c multicolored .40 .20
a. Black (engr.) omitted *5,000.*

Enrico Caruso (1873-1921), Opera Tenor.

Girl Scouts, 75th Anniv.

Litho. & Engr.

1987, Mar. 12 ***Perf. 11***

2251 A1621 22c 14 Achievement Badges .40 .20
a. All litho. colors omitted *2,500*
b. Red & black (engr.) omitted *2,000.*

All known examples of No. 2251a have been expertized, and certificate must accompany purchase.

The unique pane of No. 2251b has been expertized, and a certificate exists for the pane of 50.

Transportation Coils

A1622

A1623

A1624

A1625

A1626

A1627

A1628

A1629

A1630

A1631

A1632

A1633

A1634

A1635

A1636

1987-88 Engr. ***Perf. 10 Vert.***

2252 A1622 3c claret .20 .20
a. Untagged .20 .20
2253 A1623 5c black .20 .20
2254 A1624 5.3c blk (Bureau precancel in scarlet) .20 .20
2255 A1625 7.6c brn (Bureau precancel in scarlet) .20 .20
2256 A1626 8.4c dp clar (Bureau precancel in red) .20 .20
a. Imperf., pair *700.00*
2257 A1627 10c blue .20 .20
e. Imperf., pair —
2258 A1628 13c blk (Bureau precancel in red) .25 .25
2259 A1629 13.2c slate grn (Bureau precancel in red) .25 .25
a. Imperf., pair *100.00*
2260 A1630 15c violet .25 .20
c. Imperf., pair *800.00*
2261 A1631 16.7c rose (Bureau precancel in black) .30 .30
a. Imperf., pair *225.00*

All known copies of No. 2261a are miscut top to bottom.

2262 A1632 17.5c dark violet .30 .20
a. Untagged (Bureau precancel) .35 .30
b. Imperf., pair *1,750.*
2263 A1633 20c blue vio .35 .20
a. Imperf., pair *65.00*
2264 A1634 20.5c rose (Bureau precancel in black) .40 .40
2265 A1635 21c olive grn (Bureau precancel in red) .40 .40
a. Imperf., pair *55.00*
2266 A1636 24.1c deep ultra (Bureau precancel) .45 .45
Nos. 2252-2266 (15) 4.15 3.85

The 5.3c, 7.6c, 8.4c, 13c, 13.2c, 16.7c, 20.5c, 21c and 24.1c are only available precanceled and are untagged.

Years of issue: 5c, 10c, 17.5c, 1987; others, 1988.

See Nos. 1897-1908, 2123-2136, 2225-2231, 2451-2468.

Special Occasions

A1637

A1638

A1639

A1640

A1641

A1642

A1643

A1644

Perf. 10 on 1, 2, or 3 sides

1987, Apr. 20 Photo.

Booklet Stamps

2267 A1637 22c multicolored .65 .20
2268 A1638 22c multicolored .80 .20
2269 A1639 22c multicolored .80 .20
2270 A1640 22c multicolored .80 .20
2271 A1641 22c multicolored .80 .20
2272 A1642 22c multicolored .65 .20
2273 A1643 22c multicolored 1.25 .20
2274 A1644 22c multicolored .80 .20
a. Bklt. pane of 10, #2268-2271, 2273-2274, 2 each #2267, 2272 10.00 *5.00*
Nos. 2267-2274 (8) 6.55 1.60

United Way Centenary

Six Profiles A1645

Litho. & Engr.

1987, Apr. 28 ***Perf. 11***

2275 A1645 22c multicolored .40 .20

A1646

A1647

A1648

A1649

Pheasant A1649a

Grosbeak A1649b

Owl A1649c

Honeybee A1649d

Photo., Engr. (No. 2280), Litho. & Engr. (No. 2281)

1987-88 ***Perf. 11***

2276 A1646 22c multi .40 .20
a. Booklet pane of 20 8.50 —
b. As "a." vert. pair, imperf. btwn. —
2277 A1647 (25c) multi ('88) .45 .20
2278 A1648 25c multi ('88) .40 .20
Nos. 2276-2278 (3) 1.25 .60

Coil Stamps

Perf. 10 Vertical

2279 A1647 (25c) multi ('88) .45 .20
a. Imperf., pair *85.00* —
2280 A1649 25c Green trees ('88) .45 .20
c. Imperf., pair *14.00*
e. Black trees *100.00* —
f. Pair, imperf. btwn. *800.00*
2281 A1649d 25c multi ('88) .45 .20
a. Imperf., pair *50.00*
b. Black (engr.) omitted *60.00* —
c. Black (litho.) omitted *400.00*
d. Pair, imperf. between *1,000.*
e. Yellow (litho.) omitted *1,200.*
Nos. 2279-2281 (3) 1.35 .60

Beware of copies with traces of the litho. black that are offered as No. 2281c. Vertical pairs or blocks of No. 2281 and imperfs. with the engr. black missing are from printer's waste.

No. 2280c is on prephosphored paper (mottled tagging). Imperfs are also known with large block tagging, value, unused pair, $35.

No. 2281a has small block tagging. Imperfs are also known with large block tagging; value the same.

Booklet Stamps

Perf. 10 on 2 or 3 Sides, 11 on 2 or 3 sides (#2283)

2282 A1647 (25c) multi ('88) .50 .20
a. Booklet pane of 10 6.50 *3.50*

Vert. pairs, imperf between, are printer's waste. Other "varieties" probably exist.

2283 A1649a 25c multi ('88) .50 .20
a. Booklet pane of 10 6.00 *3.50*
b. 25c multi, red removed from sky 6.25 .20
c. As "b," booklet pane of 10 *67.50* —
d. As "a," horiz. imperf. between *2,250.*

Imperfs. are printer's waste.

2284 A1649b 25c multi ('88) .50 .20
2285 A1649c 25c multi ('88) .50 .20
b. Bklt. pane of 10, 5 each Nos. 2284-2285 5.00 *3.50*
d. Pair, Nos. 2284-2285 1.10 .25
2285A A1648 25c multi ('88) .50 .20
c. Booklet pane of 6 3.00 *2.00*
Nos. 2282-2285A (5) 2.50 1.00

Issued: #2276, 5/9; #2277, 2279, 2282, 3/22; #2278, 5/6; #2280, 5/20; #2281, 9/2; #2283, 4/29; #2284-2285, 5/28; #2285A, 7/5.

North American Wildlife — A1650

1987, June 13 Photo. *Perf. 11*

No.	Type	Value	Description	Unused	Used
2286	A1650	22c	Barn swallow	.85	.20
2287	A1651	22c	Monarch butterfly	.85	.20
2288	A1652	22c	Bighorn sheep	.85	.20
2289	A1653	22c	Broad-tailed hummingbird	.85	.20
2290	A1654	22c	Cottontail	.85	.20
2291	A1655	22c	Osprey	.85	.20
2292	A1656	22c	Mountain lion	.85	.20
2293	A1657	22c	Luna moth	.85	.20
2294	A1658	22c	Mule deer	.85	.20
2295	A1659	22c	Gray squirrel	.85	.20
2296	A1660	22c	Armadillo	.85	.20
2297	A1661	22c	Eastern chipmunk	.85	.20
2298	A1662	22c	Moose	.85	.20
2299	A1663	22c	Black bear	.85	.20
2300	A1664	22c	Tiger swallowtail	.85	.20
2301	A1665	22c	Bobwhite	.85	.20
2302	A1666	22c	Ringtail	.85	.20
2303	A1667	22c	Red-winged blackbird	.85	.20
2304	A1668	22c	American lobster	.85	.20
2305	A1669	22c	Black-tailed jack rabbit	.85	.20
2306	A1670	22c	Scarlet tanager	.85	.20
2307	A1671	22c	Woodchuck	.85	.20
2308	A1672	22c	Roseate spoonbill	.85	.20
2309	A1673	22c	Bald eagle	.85	.20
2310	A1674	22c	Alaskan brown bear	.85	.20
2311	A1675	22c	Iiwi	.85	.20
2312	A1676	22c	Badger	.85	.20
2313	A1677	22c	Pronghorn	.85	.20
2314	A1678	22c	River otter	.85	.20
2315	A1679	22c	Ladybug	.85	.20
2316	A1680	22c	Beaver	.85	.20
2317	A1681	22c	White-tailed deer	.85	.20
2318	A1682	22c	Blue jay	.85	.20
2319	A1683	22c	Pika	.85	.20
2320	A1684	22c	American Buffalo	.85	.20
2321	A1685	22c	Snowy egret	.85	.20
2322	A1686	22c	Gray wolf	.85	.20
2323	A1687	22c	Mountain goat	.85	.20
2324	A1688	22c	Deer mouse	.85	.20
2325	A1689	22c	Black-tailed prairie dog	.85	.20
2326	A1690	22c	Box turtle	.85	.20
2327	A1691	22c	Wolverine	.85	.20
2328	A1692	22c	American elk	.85	.20
2329	A1693	22c	California sea lion	.85	.20
2330	A1694	22c	Mockingbird	.85	.20
2331	A1695	22c	Raccoon	.85	.20
2332	A1696	22c	Bobcat	.85	.20
2333	A1697	22c	Black-footed ferret	.85	.20
2334	A1698	22c	Canada goose	.85	.20
2335	A1699	22c	Red fox	.85	.20
a.			Pane of 50, #2286-2335	47.50	
b.			2286b-2335b, any single, red omitted	—	

Ratification of the Constitution

A1700

A1701

A1702

A1703

A1704

A1705

A1706

A1707

A1708

A1709

A1710

A1711

A1712

Litho. & Engr., Photo. (#2337, 2343-2344, 2347)

1987-90 *Perf. 11*

No.	Type	Value	Description	Unused	Used
2336	A1700	22c	multi	.60	.20
2337	A1701	22c	multi	.60	.20
2338	A1702	22c	multi	.60	.20
a.			Black (engr.) omitted	*5,500.*	
2339	A1703	22c	multi ('88)	.60	.20
2340	A1704	22c	multi ('88)	.60	.20
2341	A1705	22c	dk blue & dk red ('88)	.60	.20
2342	A1706	22c	multi ('88)	.60	.20
2343	A1707	25c	multi ('88)	.60	.20
a.			Strip of 3, vert. imperf. btwn.	—	
b.			Red missing (PS)	—	
2344	A1708	25c	multi ('88)	.60	.20
2345	A1709	25c	multi ('88)	.60	.20
2346	A1710	25c	multi ('88)	.60	.20
2347	A1711	25c	multi ('89)	.60	.20
2348	A1712	25c	multi ('90)	.60	.20
			Nos. 2336-2348 (13)	7.80	2.60

Issued: #2336, 7/4; #2337, 8/26; #2238, 9/11; #2339, 1/6; #2340, 1/9; #2341, 2/6; 32342, 2/15; #2343, 5/23; #2344, 6/21; #2345, 6/25; #2346, 7/26; # 2347, 8/22; #2348, 5/29.

US-Morocco Diplomatic Relations Bicentennial

Arabesque, Dar Batha Palace, Fez — A1713

Litho. & Engr.

1987, July 18 *Perf. 11*

No.	Type	Value	Description	Unused	Used
2349	A1713	22c	scar & blk	.40	.20
a.			Black (engr.) omitted	*275.00*	

See Morocco No. 642.

Literary Arts Series

William Cuthbert Faulkner (1897-1962), Novelist — A1714

1987, Aug. 3 Engr. *Perf. 11*

No.	Type	Value	Description	Unused	Used
2350	A1714	22c	bright green	.40	.20

Imperfs. are from printer's waste.

American Folk Art Series

Lacemaking

A1715

A1716

A1717

A1718

Litho. & Engr.

1987, Aug. 14 *Perf. 11*

No.	Type	Value	Description	Unused	Used
2351	A1715	22c	ultra & white	.45	.20
2352	A1716	22c	ultra & white	.45	.20
2353	A1717	22c	ultra & white	.45	.20
2354	A1718	22c	ultra & white	.45	.20
a.			Block of 4, #2351-2354	1.90	1.90
b.			As "a," white omitted	*950.00*	

Drafting of the Constitution Bicentennial

A1719

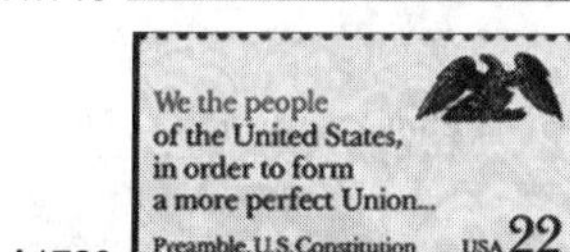

A1720

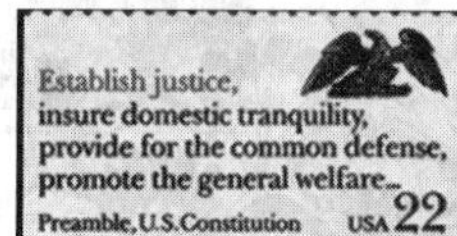

A1721

A1722

A1723

Perf. 10 Horiz. on 1 or 2 Sides

1987, Aug. 28 Photo.

Booklet Stamps

No.	Type	Value	Description	Unused	Used
2355	A1719	22c	multicolored	.55	.20
a.			Grayish grn (background) omitted	—	
2356	A1720	22c	multicolored	.55	.20
a.			Grayish grn (background) omitted	—	
2357	A1721	22c	multicolored	.55	.20
a.			Grayish grn (background) omitted	—	
2358	A1722	22c	multicolored	.55	.20
a.			Grayish grn (background) omitted	—	
2359	A1723	22c	multicolored	.55	.20
a.			Bklt. pane of 5, #2355-2359	2.75	*2.25*
b.			Grayish grn (background) omitted	—	

A1724

A1725

Signing of the Constitution

Litho. & Engr.

1987, Sept. 17 *Perf. 11*

No.	Type	Value	Description	Unused	Used
2360	A1724	22c	multicolored	.45	.20

Certified Public Accounting

1987, Sept. 21 Litho. & Engr.

No.	Type	Value	Description	Unused	Used
2361	A1725	22c	multicolored	1.50	.20
a.			Black (engr.) omitted	*725.00*	

Locomotives

Stourbridge Lion, 1829 — A1726

Best Friend of Charleston, 1830 — A1727

John Bull, 1831 A1728

Brother Jonathan, 1832 — A1729

Gowan & Marx, 1839 A1730

Perf. 10 Horiz. on 1 or 2 Sides

1987, Oct. 1

Booklet Stamps

2362 A1726 22c multicolored .55 .20
2363 A1727 22c multicolored .55 .20
2364 A1728 22c multicolored .55 .20
2365 A1729 22c multicolored .55 .20
a. Red omitted —
2366 A1730 22c multicolored .55 .20
a. Bklt. pane of 5, #2362-2366 2.75 *2.50*
b. As No. 2366, black (engr.) omitted (single) —
c. As No. 2366, blue omitted (single) —

Christmas

Moroni Madonna A1731

Christmas Ornaments A1732

1987, Oct. 23 Photo. *Perf. 11*

2367 A1731 22c multicolored .40 .20
2368 A1732 22c multicolored .40 .20

1988 Winter Olympics, Calgary

Skiing — A1733

1988, Jan. 10 Photo. *Perf. 11*

2369 A1733 22c multicolored .40 .20

Australia Bicentennial

Caricature of Australian Koala & American Bald Eagle — A1734

1988, Jan. 10 Photo. *Perf. 11*

2370 A1734 22c multicolored .40 .20

See Australia No. 1052.

Black Heritage Series

James Weldon Johnson, Author, Lyricist — A1735

1988, Feb. 2 Photo. *Perf. 11*

2371 A1735 22c multicolored .40 .20

Siamese, Exotic Shorthair A1736

Abyssinian, Himalayan A1737

Maine Coon, Burmese A1738

American Shorthair, Persian A1739

1988, Feb. 5 *Perf. 11*

2372 A1736 22c multicolored .45 .20
2373 A1737 22c multicolored .45 .20
2374 A1738 22c multicolored .45 .20
2375 A1739 22c multicolored .45 .20
a. Block of 4, #2372-2375 1.90 1.90

American Sports Issues

A1740

A1741

1988, Mar. 9 Litho. & Engr.

2376 A1740 22c multicolored .40 .20

Knute Kenneth Rockne (1888-1931), Notre Dame football coach.

1988, June 13 Photo. *Perf. 11*

2377 A1741 25c multicolored .45 .20

Francis Ouimet (1893-1967), 1st amateur golfer to win the US Open Championship.

Love Issue

Rose — A1742

A1743

1988 Photo. *Perf. 11*

2378 A1742 25c multicolored .45 .20
a. Imperf., pair *3,250.*
2379 A1743 45c multicolored .65 .20

Issue dates: 25c, July 4; 45c, Aug. 8.

1988 Summer Olympics, Seoul

Gymnastic Rings A1744

1988, Aug. 19 Photo. *Perf. 11*

2380 A1744 25c multicolored .45 .20

Classic Automobiles

1928 Locomobile — A1745

1929 Pierce-Arrow A1746

1931 Cord A1747

1932 Packard A1748

1935 Duesenberg — A1749

Perf. 10 Horiz. on 1 or 2 Sides

1988, Aug. 25 Litho. & Engr.

Booklet Stamps

2381 A1745 25c multicolored .60 .20
2382 A1746 25c multicolored .60 .20
2383 A1747 25c multicolored .60 .20
2384 A1748 25c multicolored .60 .20
2385 A1749 25c multicolored .60 .20
a. Bklt. pane of 5, #2381-2385 6.00 *2.25*
Nos. 2381-2385 (5) 3.00 1.00

Antarctic Explorers

Nathaniel Palmer (1799-1877) — A1750

Lt. Charles Wilkes (1798-1877) — A1751

Richard E. Byrd (1888-1957) — A1752

Lincoln Ellsworth (1880-1951) — A1753

1988, Sept. 14 Photo. *Perf. 11*

2386 A1750 25c multicolored .65 .20
2387 A1751 25c multicolored .65 .20
2388 A1752 25c multicolored .65 .20
2389 A1753 25c multicolored .65 .20
a. Block of 4, #2386-2389 2.75 2.00
b. Black (engr.) omitted *1,400.*
c. As "a," imperf. horiz. *3,000.*

Folk Art Series

Carousel Animals

Deer — A1754

Horse — A1755

Camel — A1756

Goat — A1757

1988, Oct. 1 Litho. & Engr. *Perf. 11*

2390 A1754 25c multicolored .65 .20
2391 A1755 25c multicolored .65 .20
2392 A1756 25c multicolored .65 .20
2393 A1757 25c multicolored .65 .20
a. Block of 4, #2390-2393 3.00 2.00

Express Mail Rate

Eagle in Flight — A1758

1988, Oct. 4 Litho. & Engr. *Perf. 11*

2394 A1758 $8.75 multi 13.50 8.00

Special Occasions

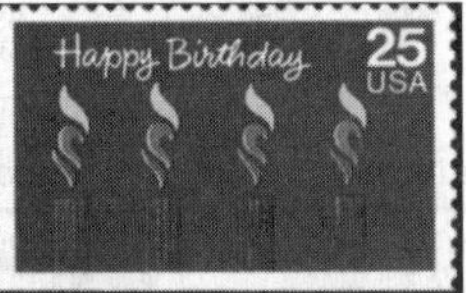

Happy Birthday — A1759

Best Wishes — A1760

Thinking of You — A1761

Love You — A1762

Perf. 11 on 2 or 3 sides

1988, Oct. 22 Photo.

Booklet Stamps

2395 A1759 25c multicolored .50 .20
2396 A1760 25c multicolored .50 .20
a. Bklt. pane of 6, 3 #2395 + 3 #2396 with gutter btwn. 3.50 *3.25*

2397 A1761 25c multicolored .50 .20
2398 A1762 25c multicolored .50 .20
a. Bklt. pane of 6, 3 #2397 + 3 #2398 with gutter btwn. 3.50 *3.25*
b. As "a," imperf. horiz. —
Nos. 2395-2398 (4) 2.00 .80

Madonna and Child, by Botticelli A1763

One-horse Open Sleigh & Village Scene A1764

Litho. & Engr., Photo. (No. 2400)
1988, Oct. 20 ***Perf. 11½***
2399 A1763 25c multicolored .45 .20
a. Gold omitted 30.00
2400 A1764 25c multicolored .45 .20

Montana Statehood Centennial

C.M. Russell and Friends, by Charles M. Russell (1865-1926) — A1765

Litho. & Engr.
1989, Jan. 15 ***Perf. 11***
2401 A1765 25c multicolored .45 .20

Imperfs without gum exist from printer's waste.

Black Heritage Series

Asa Philip Randolph (1889-1979), Labor & Civil Rights Leader — A1766

1989, Feb. 3 **Photo.** ***Perf. 11***
2402 A1766 25c multicolored .45 .20

North Dakota Statehood Centennial

A1767

1989, Feb. 21 ***Perf. 11***
2403 A1767 25c multicolored .45 .20

Washington Statehood Centennial

A1768

1989, Feb. 22 ***Perf. 11***
2404 A1768 25c multicolored .45 .20

Steamboats

Experiment, 1788-1790 — A1769

Phoenix, 1809 — A1770

New Orleans, 1812 — A1771

Washington, 1816 — A1772

Walk in the Water, 1818 — A1773

Perf. 10 Horiz. on 1 or 2 sides
1989, Mar. 3 **Litho. & Engr.**
Booklet Stamps
2405 A1769 25c multicolored .45 .20
2406 A1770 25c multicolored .45 .20
2407 A1771 25c multicolored .45 .20
2408 A1772 25c multicolored .45 .20
2409 A1773 25c multicolored .45 .20
a. Bklt. pane of 5, #2405-2409 2.25 1.75

A1774

A1775

World Stamp Expo '89
Nov. 17-Dec. 3, Washington, DC
Litho. & Engr.
1989, Mar. 16 ***Perf. 11***
2410 A1774 25c No. 122 .45 .20

Performing Arts
Arturo Toscanini (1867-1975), Italian Conductor
1989, Mar. 25 **Photo.** ***Perf. 11***
2411 A1775 25c multicolored .45 .20

Constitution Bicentennial

House of Representatives A1776

Senate A1777

Executive Branch A1778

Supreme Court A1779

1989-90 **Litho. & Engr.** ***Perf. 11***
2412 A1776 25c multicolored .50 .20
2413 A1777 25c multicolored .50 .20
2414 A1778 25c multicolored .50 .20
2415 A1779 25c multicolored .50 .20
Nos. 2412-2415 (4) 2.00 .80

Issue dates: #2412, Apr. 4; #2413, Apr. 6; #2414, Apr. 16; #2415, Feb. 2, 1990.

South Dakota State Centenary

State Flower, Pioneer Woman & Sod House on Grasslands A1780

1989, May 3 **Photo.** ***Perf. 11***
2416 A1780 25c multicolored .45 .20

American Sports

Henry Louis "Lou" Gehrig (1903-1941), Baseball Player for the New York Yankees — A1781

1989, June 10 **Photo.** ***Perf. 11***
2417 A1781 25c multicolored .50 .20

Literary Arts

Ernest Hemingway (1899-1961), Nobel Prize-winner for Literature, 1954 — A1782

1989, July 17 **Photo.** ***Perf. 11***
2418 A1782 25c multicolored .45 .20
a. Vert. pair, imperf. horiz. —

Moon Landing, 20th Anniv.

Raising the Flag on Lunar Surface, July 20, 1969 A1783

Litho. & Engr.
1989, July 20 ***Perf. 11x11½***
2419 A1783 $2.40 multicolored 4.00 2.00
a. Black (engr.) omitted *2,500.*
b. Imperf., pair *750.00*
c. Black (litho.) omitted *3,250.*

Natl. Assoc. of Letter Carriers, Cent.

Letter Carriers A1784

1989, Aug. 30 **Photo.** ***Perf. 11***
2420 A1784 25c multicolored .45 .20

Constitution Bicentennial

Bill of Rights — A1785

Litho. & Engr.
1989, Sept. 25 ***Perf. 11***
2421 A1785 25c multicolored .45 .20
a. Black (engr.) omitted *325.00*

Prehistoric Animals

Tyrannosaurus Rex — A1786

Pteranodon A1787

Stegosaurus A1788

Brontosaurus A1789

1989, Oct. 1 **Litho. & Engr.** ***Perf. 11***
2422 A1786 25c multicolored .65 .20
2423 A1787 25c multicolored .65 .20
2424 A1788 25c multicolored .65 .20
2425 A1789 25c multicolored .65 .20
a. Block of 4, #2422-2425 3.00 2.00
b. As "a," blk (engr.) omitted *750.00*

The correct name for "Brontosaurus" is "Apatosaurus."
No. 2425b is valued in the grade of fine.

Pre-Columbian America Issue

Southwest Carved Figure, A. D. 1150-1350 — A1790

Emblem of the Postal Union of the Americas and Spain (UPAE) and Southwestern Wood-carved Ritual Figure, Mogollon Culture, Mimbres Period, a Forerunner of the Hopi Indian Kachina Doll, A.D. 1150-1350.

1989, Oct. 12 Photo. *Perf. 11*
2426 A1790 25c multicolored .45 .20

Discovery of America, 500th anniv. (in 1992). See No. C121.

Christmas

Madonna and Child, by Caracci A1791

Sleigh Full of Presents A1792

Litho. & Engr.

1989, Oct. 19 *Perf. 11½*
2427 A1791 25c multicolored .45 .20
- *a.* Booklet pane of 10 4.75 *3.50*
- *b.* Red (litho.) omitted *750.00*
- *c.* As "a," imperf. —

Photo.

Perf. 11

2428 A1792 25c multicolored .45 .20
- *a.* Vert. pair, imperf. horiz. *2,000.*

Booklet Stamp

Perf. 11½ on 2 or 3 sides

2429 A1792 25c multicolored .45 .20
- *a.* Booklet pane of 10 4.75 *3.50*
- *b.* As "a," imperf. horiz. —
- *c.* Vert. pair, imperf. horiz. —
- *d.* As "a," red omitted —
- *e.* Imperf., pair —

Marked differences exist between Nos. 2428 and 2429: The runners on the sleigh in No. 2429 are twice as thick as those in No. 2428; in No. 2429 the package at upper left in the sleigh has a red bow, whereas the same package in No. 2428 has a red and black bow; and the ribbon on the upper right package in No. 2429 is green, whereas the same ribbon in No. 2428 is black.

Eagle and Shield — A1793

1989, Nov. 10 Photo. *Die Cut*

Self-Adhesive

2431 A1793 25c multicolored .50 .20
- *a.* Booklet pane of 18 11.00
- *b.* Vert. pair, no die cutting between *500.00*
- *c.* Pair, no die cutting —

Issued unfolded in panes of 18; peelable paper backing is booklet cover. Sold for $5.

Also available in strips of 18 with stamps spaced for use in affixing machines to service first day covers. Sold for $5.

Sold in 15 test cities and through the philatelic agency only.

Souvenir Sheet

World Stamp Expo, Washington, DC, Nov. 17-Dec. 3 — A1794

Litho. & Engr.

1989, Nov. 17 *Imperf.*
2433 A1794 Sheet of 4 14.00 9.00
- *a.* 90c like No. 122 2.00 1.75
- *b.* 90c like No. 132TC (blue frame, brown center) 2.00 1.75
- *c.* 90c like No. 132TC (green frame, blue center) 2.00 1.75
- *d.* 90c like No. 132TC (scarlet frame, blue center) 2.00 1.75

Traditional Mail Delivery

Stagecoach, c. 1850 — A1795

Paddlewheel Steamer A1796

Biplane — A1797

Depot-hack Type Automobile A1798

Litho. & Engr.

1989, Nov. 19 *Perf. 11*
2434 A1795 25c multicolored .45 .20
2435 A1796 25c multicolored .45 .20
2436 A1797 25c multicolored .45 .20
2437 A1798 25c multicolored .45 .20
- *a.* Block of 4, #2434-2437 2.00 1.75
- *b.* As "a," dark blue (engr.) omitted *600.00*

No. 2437b is valued in the grade of fine. Very fine blocks exist and sell for somewhat more.

1989, Nov. 28 *Imperf.*
2438 Sheet of 4 4.00 1.75
- *a.* A1795 25c multicolored .65 .25
- *b.* A1796 25c multicolored .65 .25
- *c.* A1797 25c multicolored .65 .25
- *d.* A1798 25c multicolored .65 .25
- *e.* Dark blue & gray (engr.) omitted *5,500.*

20th Universal Postal Union Congress.

VALUES FOR HINGED STAMPS AFTER NO. 771

This catalogue does not value unused stamps after No. 771 in hinged condition. Hinged unused stamps from No. 772 to the present are worth considerably less than the values given for unused stamps, which are for never-hinged examples.

Idaho State Centenary

Mountain Bluebird, Sawtooth Mountains — A1799

1990, Jan. 6 Photo. *Perf. 11*
2439 A1799 25c multicolored .45 .20

Love Issue

A1800

1990, Jan. 18 Photo. *Perf. 12½x13*
2440 A1800 25c black, brt bl, dk pink & emer grn .45 .20
- *a.* Imperf., pair *800.00*

Booklet Stamp

Perf. 11½ on 2 or 3 sides

2441 A1800 25c black, ultra, brt pink & dk grn .45 .20
- *a.* Booklet pane of 10 4.75 *3.50*
- *b.* As "a," bright pink omitted *1,700.*
- *c.* As "b," single stamp *160.*

No. 2441c may be obtained from booklet panes containing both normal and color-omitted stamps.

Black Heritage Series

Ida B. Wells (1862-1931), Journalist — A1801

1990, Feb. 1 Photo. *Perf. 11*
2442 A1801 25c multicolored .45 .20

Beach Umbrella — A1802

1990, Feb. 3 Photo. *Perf. 11*

Booklet Stamp

2443 A1802 15c multicolored .30 .20
- *a.* Booklet pane of 10 3.00 2.00
- *b.* As "a," blue omitted *1,400.*
- *c.* As No. 2443, blue omitted *140.*

Wyoming State Centenary

High Mountain Meadows, by Conrad Schwiering A1803

Litho. & Engr.

1990, Feb. 23 *Perf. 11*
2444 A1803 25c multicolored .45 .20
- *a.* Black (engr.) omitted *2,100.* —

Classic Films

The Wizard of Oz — A1804

Gone With the Wind — A1805

Beau Geste — A1806

Stagecoach A1807

1990, Mar. 23 Photo. *Perf. 11*
2445 A1804 25c multicolored 1.00 .20
2446 A1805 25c multicolored 1.00 .20
2447 A1806 25c multicolored 1.00 .20
2448 A1807 25c multicolored 1.00 .20
- *a.* Block of 4, #2445-2448 4.50 3.50

Literary Arts Series

Marianne Craig Moore (1887-1972), Poet — A1808

1990, Apr. 18 Photo. *Perf. 11*
2449 A1808 25c multicolored .45 .20
- *a.* All colors missing (EP) —

No. 2449a must be collected se-tenant with a partially printed stamp or in a larger horizontal strip.

TRANSPORTATION ISSUE

A1810

A1811

A1811a

A1812

A1816

A1822

A1823

A1825

A1827

Engr., Photo. (#2452B, 2452D, 2454, 2458)

1990-95 Coil Stamps *Perf. 9.8 Vert.*

Untagged: #2452B, 2452D, 2453, 2454, & 10c

2451 A1810 4c claret .20 .20
- *a.* Imperf., pair *700.00*
- *b.* Untagged .20 .20

2452 A1811 5c carmine .20 .20
- *a.* Untagged .20 .20
- *c.* Imperf., pair *700.00*

2452B A1811 5c carmine .20 .20
2452D A1811a 5c carmine .20 .20
- *e.* Imperf., pair —

2453 A1812 5c brn (Bureau precancel in gray) .20 .20
a. Imperf., pair 350.00
b. Gray omitted —
2454 A1812 5c red (Bureau precancel in gray) .20 .20
2457 A1816 10c grn (Bureau precancel in gray) .20 .20
a. Imperf., pair 250.00
b. All color omitted —
2458 A1816 10c grn (Bureau precancel in black) .20 .20
2463 A1822 20c green .40 .20
a. Imperf., pair 125.00
2464 A1823 23c dark blue .45 .20
b. Imperf., pair 150.00
2466 A1825 32c blue .60 .20
a. Imperf., pair 600.00
b. 32c bright blue 6.00 4.50
2468 A1827 $1 bl & scar 1.75 .50
a. Imperf., pair 2,750. —
Nos. 2451-2468 (12) 4.80 2.70

Issued: $1, 4/20; #2452, 8/31; 4c, 1/25/91; #2453, 2457, 5/25/91; #2454, 10/22/91; 23c, 4/12/91; #2452B, 12/8/92; #2458, 5/25/94; #2452D, 3/20/95; 32c, 6/2/95; #2463, 6/9/95

No. 2457b must be collected as part of a transitional strip with normal stamps having freak perfs.

Some pairs of No. 2468 appear to be imperf but have some blind perfs on the gum. Beware of copies with the gum removed.

Lighthouses

Admiralty Head, WA — A1829

Cape Hatteras, NC — A1830

West Quoddy Head, ME — A1831

American Shoals, FL — A1832

Sandy Hook, NJ — A1833

Perf. 10 Vert. on 1 or 2 Sides

1990, Apr. 26 Litho. & Engr.

Booklet Stamps

2470 A1829 25c multicolored 1.00 .20
2471 A1830 25c multicolored 1.00 .20
2472 A1831 25c multicolored 1.00 .20
2473 A1832 25c multicolored 1.00 .20
2474 A1833 25c multicolored 1.00 .20
a. Bklt. pane, #2470-2474 5.50 2.00
b. As "a," white (USA 25) omitted 80.00

Flag

A1834

1990, May 18 Photo. *Die Cut*

Self-adhesive

2475 A1834 25c dk red & dk bl .50 .25
a. Pane of 12 6.00

Sold only in panes of 12; peelable plastic backing inscribed in light ultramarine. Available for a test period of six months at 22 First National Bank automatic teller machines in Seattle.

Flora and Fauna Series

American Kestrel
A1840 A1841

Eastern Bluebird A1842

Fawn A1843

Cardinal A1844

Pumpkinseed Sunfish A1845

Bobcat A1846

Perf. 11, 11.2 (#2477)

1990-95 Litho. Untagged

2476 A1840 1c multicolored .20 .20
2477 A1841 1c multicolored .20 .20
2478 A1842 3c multicolored .20 .20
a. Vert. pair, imperf horiz. —
b. Double impression of all colors except yellow —

Photo.

Perf. 11½x11

2479 A1843 19c multicolored .35 .20
b. Red omitted 850.00

On No. 2479b other colors are shifted.

2480 A1844 30c multicolored .50 .20

Litho. & Engr.

Perf. 11

2481 A1845 45c multicolored .80 .20
a. Black (engr.) omitted 450.00 —
2482 A1846 $2 multicolored 3.00 1.25
a. Black (engr.) omitted 300.00
Nos. 2476-2482 (7) 5.25 2.45

Issued: $2, 6/1/90; 19c, 3/11/91; 3c, 30c, #2476, 6/22/91; 45c, 12/2/92; #2477, 5/10/95.

See Nos. 3031, 3044. Compare design A1842 with A2336.

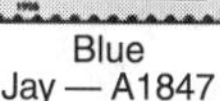

Blue Jay — A1847

Wood Duck — A1848

African Violets A1849

Peach A1850

Pear A1851

Red Squirrel A1852

Rose A1853

Pine Cone A1854

Booklet Stamps

1991-95 *Perf. 10.9x9.8*

2483 A1847 20c multicolored .50 .20
a. Booklet pane of 10 5.25 2.25
b. As "a," imperf —

See No. 3053.

Perf. 10 on 2 or 3 Sides

2484 A1848 29c blk & multi .50 .20
a. Booklet pane of 10 5.50 3.75
b. Vert. pair, imperf. between 200.00

Perf. 11 on 2 or 3 Sides

2485 A1848 29c red & multi .50 .20
a. Booklet pane of 10 5.50 4.00
b. Vert. pair, imperf btwn. —
c. Imperf, pair —

Perf. 10x11 on 2 or 3 Sides

2486 A1849 29c multicolored .50 .20
a. Booklet pane of 10 5.50 4.00

Perf. 11x10 on 2 or 3 Sides

2487 A1850 32c multicolored .60 .20
2488 A1851 32c multicolored .60 .20
a. Bklt. pane, 5 #2488b 6.00 4.25
b. Pair, #2487-2488 1.25 .30

Issued: #2484-2485, 4/12/91; #2486, 10/8/93; 20c, 6/15/95; 32c 7/8/95.

Booklet Stamps

1993-95 Photo.

Self-Adhesive *Serpentine Die Cut*

2489 A1852 29c multicolored .50 .20
a. Booklet pane of 18 10.00
b. As "a," die cutting omitted —
2490 A1853 29c red, green & black .50 .20
a. Booklet pane of 18 10.00
2491 A1854 29c multicolored .50 .20
a. Booklet pane of 18 11.00
b. Horiz. pair, no die cutting between 250.00
c. Coil with plate #B1 — 5.00

Serpentine Die Cut 11¼x11¾ on 2, 3 or 4 sides

2492 A1853 32c pk, grn & blk ('95) .60 .20
a. Booklet pane of 20+label 12.00
b. Bklt. pane of 15+label ('96) 8.75
c. Horiz. pair, no die cutting between —
d. As "a," 2 stamps and parts of 7 others printed on backing liner —
e. Booklet pane of 14 21.00
f. Booklet pane of 16 21.00
g. Coil with plate #S111 — 3.00
h. Vert. pair, no die cutting between —

Serpentine Die Cut 8.8 on 2, 3 or 4 sides

2493 A1850 32c multi ('95) .60 .20
2494 A1851 32c multi ('95) .60 .20
a. Booklet pane, 10 each #2493-2494+label 12.50
b. Pair, #2493-2494 1.20

Coil Stamps

Serpentine Die Cut 8.8 Vert.

2495 A1850 32c multi ('95) .60 .20
2495A A1851 32c multi ('95) .60 .20
b. Pair, #2495-2495A 1.20

Except for #2491c and 2492g with plate numbers, coil stamps of these issues are indistinguishable from booklet stamps once they are removed from the backing paper.

Issued: #2489, 6/25; #2490, 8/19; #2491, 11/5.

See Nos. 3048-3049, 3053-3054.

Scott values for used self-adhesive stamps are for examples either on piece or off piece.

Olympians

Jesse Owens, 1936 A1855

Ray Ewry, 1900-08 A1856

Hazel Wightman, 1924 A1857

Eddie Eagan, 1920, 1932 A1858

Helene Madison, 1932 A1859

1990, July 6 Photo. *Perf. 11*

2496 A1855 25c multicolored .60 .20
2497 A1856 25c multicolored .60 .20
2498 A1857 25c multicolored .60 .20
2499 A1858 25c multicolored .60 .20
2500 A1859 25c multicolored .60 .20
a. Strip of 5, #2496-2500 3.25 2.50
b. As "a," blue omitted —

Indian Headdresses

Assiniboin A1860

Cheyenne A1861

Comanche A1862

Flathead A1863

Shoshone
A1864

Perf. 11 on 2 or 3 sides

1990, Aug. 17 Litho. & Engr.

Booklet Stamps

2501 A1860 25c multicolored .55 .20
2502 A1861 25c multicolored .55 .20
2503 A1862 25c multicolored .55 .20
2504 A1863 25c multicolored .55 .20
2505 A1864 25c multicolored .55 .20
a. Bklt. pane, 2 ea #2501-2505 5.50 *3.50*
b. As "a," blk (engr.) omitted *3,250.*
c. Strip of 5, #2501-2505 2.75 1.00
d. As "a," horiz. imperf. btwn. —

Micronesia, Marshall Islands

Canoe & Federated States of Micronesia Flag
A1865

Stick Chart, Canoe & Republic of the Marshall Islands Flag
A1866

1990, Sept. 28 ***Perf. 11***

2506 A1865 25c multicolored .45 .20
2507 A1866 25c multicolored .45 .20
a. Pair, #2506-2507 .90 .60
b. As "a," blk (engr.) omitted *2,750.*

See Micronesia Nos. 124-126 and Marshall Islands No. 381.

Sea Creatures

Killer Whales
A1867

Northern Sea Lions
A1868

Sea Otter
A1869

Common Dolphin
A1870

1990, Oct. 3 Litho. & Engr. ***Perf. 11***

2508 A1867 25c multicolored .45 .20
2509 A1868 25c multicolored .45 .20
2510 A1869 25c multicolored .45 .20
2511 A1870 25c multicolored .45 .20
a. Block of 4, #2508-2511 1.90 1.90
b. As "a," blk (engr.) omitted *700.00*

See Russia Nos. 5933-5936.

Pre-Columbian America Issue

Grand Canyon
A1871

1990, Oct. 12 Photo. ***Perf. 11***

2512 A1871 25c multicolored .45 .20

Dwight David Eisenhower

A1872

1990, Oct. 13 Photo. ***Perf. 11***

2513 A1872 25c multicolored .60 .20
a. Imperf., pair *2,250.*

Christmas

Madonna and Child by Antonello da Messina
A1873

Christmas Tree
A1874

Litho. & Engr.

1990, Oct. 18 ***Perf. 11½***

2514 A1873 25c multicolored .45 .20
b. Booklet pane of 10 5.00 *3.25*

Photo.

Perf. 11

2515 A1874 25c multicolored .45 .20
a. Vert. pair, imperf horiz. *1,100.*
b. All colors missing (EP) —

Perf. 11½x11 on 2 or 3 Sides

2516 A1874 25c multicolored .45 .20
a. Booklet pane of 10 5.00 *3.25*
Nos. 2514-2516 (3) 1.35 .60

Marked differences exist between Nos. 2515 and 2516. The background red on No. 2515 is even while that on No. 2516 is splotchy. The bands across the tree and "GREETINGS" are blue green on No. 2515 and yellow green on No. 2516.

No. 2515b must be collected se-tenant with normal and/or partially printed stamp(s).

A1875

A1876

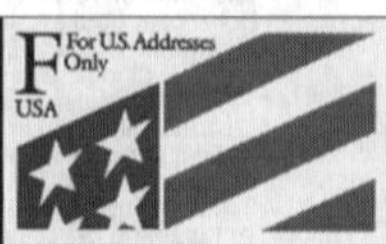

A1877

1991, Jan. 22 Photo. ***Perf. 13***

2517 A1875 (29c) yel, blk, red & yel grn .55 .20
a. Imperf., pair *700.00*
b. Horiz. pair, imperf. vert. *1,250.*

Do not confuse No. 2517a with No. 2518a. See note after No. 2518.

Coil Stamp

Perf. 10 Vert.

2518 A1875 (29c) yel, blk, dull red & dk yel grn .55 .20
a. Imperf., pair *37.50*

"For U.S. addresses only" is 17½mm long on No. 2517, 16½mm long on No. 2518. Design of No. 2517 measures 21½x17½mm, No. 2518, 21x18mm.

Booklet Stamps

Perf. 11 on 2 or 3 Sides

2519 A1875 (29c) yel, blk, dull red & dk grn .55 .20
a. Booklet pane of 10 6.50 *4.50*
2520 A1875 (29c) pale yel, blk, red & brt grn .55 .20
a. Booklet pane of 10 18.00 *4.50*
b. As "a," imperf horiz. —

No. 2519 has bullseye perforations that measure approximately 11.2. No. 2520 has less pronounced black lines in the leaf, which is a much brighter green than on No. 2519.

Litho.

Perf. 11

2521 A1876 (4c) bister & car .20 .20
a. Vert. pair, imperf. horiz. *110.00*
b. Imperf., pair *75.00*

Photo.

Imperf., Die Cut

Self-Adhesive

2522 A1877 (29c) blk, dk blue & red .55 .25
a. Pane of 12 7.00

No. 2522 sold only in panes of 12; peelable plastic backing inscribed in light ultramarine. Available during a test period at 22 First National Bank automatic teller machines in Seattle.

Flag Over Mt. Rushmore
A1878

Flower
A1879

1991, Mar. 29 Engr. ***Perf. 10 Vert.***

Coil Stamps

2523 A1878 29c bl, red & cl .55 .20
b. Imperf., pair *25.00*
c. Blue, red & brown 5.00 —

Photo.

2523A A1878 29c bl, red & brn .55 .20

On No. 2523A, USA and 29 are not outlined in white and appear farther from edge of design.

Issued: #2523, Mar. 29; #2523A, July 4.

1991-92 Photo. ***Perf. 11***

2524 A1879 29c dull yel, blk, red & pale yel grn .55 .20

Perf. 13x12¾

2524A A1879 29c dull yel, blk, red & yel grn .75 .20

Coil Stamps

Roulette 10 Vert.

2525 A1879 29c pale yel, blk, red & yel grn .55 .20

Perf. 10 Vert.

2526 A1879 29c pale yel, blk, red & yel grn .55 .20

Perf. 11 on 2 or 3 Sides

Booklet Stamp

2527 A1879 29c pale yel, blk, red & brt grn .55 .20
a. Booklet pane of 10 5.50 *3.50*
b. As "a," imperf. vert. 1,500.
c. Horiz. pair, imperf. vert. *250.*
d. As "a," imperf horiz. *2,500.*

Flower on Nos. 2524-2524A has grainy appearance, inscriptions look rougher.

Issue dates: #2524, 2524A, 2527, Apr. 5; #2525, Aug. 16; #2526, Mar. 3, 1992.

Flag, Olympic Rings — A1880

Perf. 11 on 2 or 3 Sides

1991, Apr. 21 Photo.

Booklet Stamp

2528 A1880 29c multicolored .55 .20
a. Booklet pane of 10 5.50 *3.50*
b. As "a," horiz. imperf btwn., perfed at top and bottom —
c. Vert. pair, imperf btwn, perfed at top and bottom —
d. Vert. strip of 3, top or bottom pair imperf between —
e. Vert. pair, imperf horiz. *2,000.*

No. 2528c comes from the misperfed booklet pane of No. 2528b. No. 2528d resulted from paper foldovers after normal perforating and before cutting into panes. Two No. 2528d are known.

No. 2528e is valued in the grade of fine.

Fishing Boat
A1881

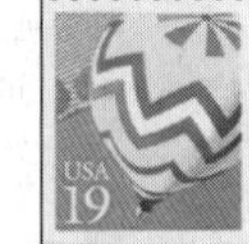

Balloon
A1882

1991-94 Photo. ***Perf. 9.8 Vert.***

Coil Stamps

2529 A1881 19c multicolored .35 .20
a. Type II ('93) .35 .20
b. As "a," untagged ('93) 1.00 .40
2529C A1881 19c multicolored .50 .20

Design of Type II stamps is created by a finer dot pattern. The vertical sides of "1" are smooth on Type II and jagged on Type I stamps.

No. 2529C has one loop of rope tying boat to piling, numerals and USA are taller and thinner.

Issued: #2529, 8/8/91; #2529C, 6/25/94.

Perf. 10 on 2 or 3 Sides

1991, May 17 Photo.

Booklet Stamp

2530 A1882 19c multicolored .35 .20
a. Booklet pane of 10 3.50 *2.75*

Flags on Parade
A1883

Liberty Torch
A1884

1991, May 30 Photo. ***Perf. 11***

2531 A1883 29c multicolored .55 .20

1991, June 25 Photo. ***Die Cut***

Booklet Pane

Self-Adhesive

2531A A1884 29c blk, gold & grn .55 .25
b. Booklet pane of 18 10.50
c. Pair, imperf —

Switzerland, 700th Anniv.

A1887

1991, Feb. 22 Photo. ***Perf. 11***

2532 A1887 50c multicolored 1.00 .25
a. Vert. pair, imperf horiz. *2,250.*

Imperfs exist from printers' waste.

See Switzerland No. 888.

A1888

A1889

Vermont Statehood Bicentennial

1991, Mar. 1 ***Perf. 11***

2533 A1888 29c multicolored .60 .20

Savings Bonds, 50th Anniv.

1991, Apr. 30 Photo. *Perf. 11*

2534 A1889 29c multicolored .55 .20

Love

A1890

A1891

1991, May 9 Photo. *Perf. 12½x13*

2535 A1890 29c multicolored .55 .20
  b. Imperf., pair —

Perf. 11

2535A A1890 29c multicolored .75 .20

Perf. 11 on 2 or 3 Sides

Booklet Stamp

2536 A1890 29c multicolored .55 .20
  a. Booklet pane of 10 5.50 *3.50*

"29" is closer to edge of design on No. 2536 than on No. 2535.

Perf. 11

2537 A1891 52c multicolored .90 .20

Literary Arts Series

William Saroyan A1892

1991, May 22 Photo. *Perf. 11*

2538 A1892 29c multicolored .55 .20

See Russia No. 6002.

Eagle, Olympic Rings — A1893

1991, Sept. 29 Photo. *Perf. 11*

2539 A1893 $1 gold & multi 1.75 .50
  a. Black omitted —

A1894

A1895

A1896

1991 Litho. & Engr. *Perf. 11*

Untagged (#2541-2542)

2540 A1894 $2.90 Priority 6.00 2.50
  a. Vert. pair, imperf horiz. —
2541 A1895 $9.95 Domestic express 20.00 7.50
  a. Imperf., pair —
2542 A1896 $14 Intl. express 25.00 10.00
  a. Red (engr. inscriptions) omitted *1,500.*
  Nos. 2540-2542 (3) 51.00 20.00

Both Nos. 2540 and 2541 exist imperf and with color missing from printer's waste.

Issued: $2.90, 7/7; $9.95, 6/16; $14, 8/31.

Priority Mail Rate

Futuristic Space Shuttle A1897

Space Shuttle Challenger A1898

Litho. & Engr.

1993, June 3 *Perf. 11x10½*

2543 A1897 $2.90 multicolored 5.00 2.25

Litho. & Engr.

1995, June 22 *Perf. 11.2*

2544 A1898 $3 dated "1995" 5.25 2.25
  b. Dated "1996" 5.25 2.25
  c. As "b,} horiz. pair, imperf between —
  d. As "b," imperf., pair *2,000.*

Express Mail Rate

Space Shuttle Endeavour A1898a

Litho. & Engr.

1995, Aug. 4 *Perf. 11*

2544A A1898a $10.75 multi 19.00 7.50

Fishing Flies

Royal Wulff A1899

Jock Scott A1900

Apte Tarpon Fly A1901

Lefty's Deceiver A1902

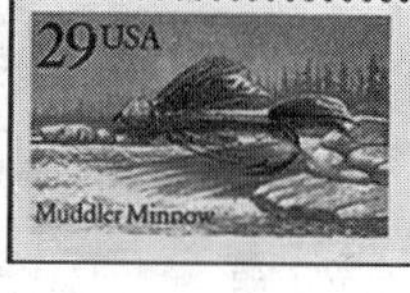

Muddler Minnow A1903

Perf. 11 Horiz. on 1 or 2 Sides

1991, May 31 Photo.

Booklet Stamps

2545 A1899 29c multicolored 1.00 .20
  a. Black omitted —
2546 A1900 29c multicolored 1.00 .20
  a. Black omitted —
2547 A1901 29c multicolored 1.00 .20
  a. Black omitted —
2548 A1902 29c multicolored 1.00 .20
2549 A1903 29c multicolored 1.00 .20
  a. Bklt. pane of 5, #2545-2549 5.50 *2.50*

Horiz. pairs, imperf. vert., exist from printers' waste.

A1904

A1905

Performing Arts

Cole Porter (1891-1964), Composer

1991, June 8 Photo. *Perf. 11*

2550 A1904 29c multicolored .55 .20
  a. Vert. pair, imperf. horiz. *650.00*

Operations Desert Shield & Desert Storm

1991, July 2 Photo. *Perf. 11*

2551 A1905 29c Southwest Asia service medal .55 .20
  a. Vert. pair, imperf horiz. *1,500.*

No. 2551 is 21mm wide.

Perf. 11 Vert. on 1 or 2 Sides

Booklet Stamp

2552 A1905 29c multicolored .55 .20
  a. Booklet pane of 5 2.75 *2.25*

No. 2552 is 20½mm wide. Inscriptions are shorter than on No. 2551.

No. 2552 vert. pairs, imperf horiz., are from printer's waste.

Summer Olympics

Pole Vault A1907

Discus A1908

Women's Sprints A1909

Javelin A1910

Women's Hurdles A1911

1991, July 12 Photo. *Perf. 11*

2553 A1907 29c multicolored .55 .20
2554 A1908 29c multicolored .55 .20
2555 A1909 29c multicolored .55 .20
2556 A1910 29c multicolored .55 .20
2557 A1911 29c multicolored .55 .20
  a. Strip of 5, #2553-2557 2.75 2.25

Numismatics

1858 Flying Eagle Cent, 1907 Standing Liberty Double Eagle, Series 1875 $1 Note, Series 1902 $10 National Currency Note — A1912

Litho. & Engr.

1991, Aug. 13 *Perf. 11*

2558 A1912 29c multicolored .55 .20

World War II

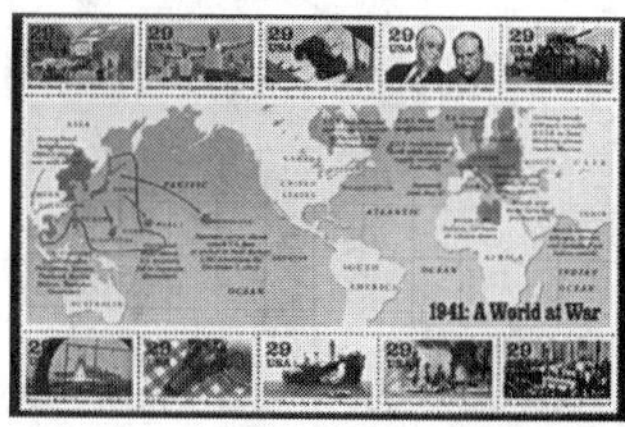

A1913

Designs and events of 1941: a, Military vehicles (Burma Road, 717-mile lifeline to China). b, Recruits (America's 1st peacetime draft). c, Shipments for allies (US supports allies with Lend-Lease Act). d, Roosevelt, Churchill (Atlantic Charter sets war aims of allies). e, Tank (America becomes the "arsenal of democracy"). f, Sinking of Destroyer Reuben James, Oct. 31. g, Gas mask, helmet (Civil defense mobilizes Americans at home). h, Liberty Ship, sea gull (1st Liberty ship delivered Dec. 30). i, Sinking ships (Japanese bomb Pearl Harbor, Dec. 7). j, Congress in session (US declares war on Japan, Dec. 8). Central label is the size of 15 stamps and shows world map, extent of Axis control.

Illustration reduced.

Litho. & Engr.

1991, Sept. 3 *Perf. 11*

2559 A1913 Block of 10 5.50 5.00
  a.-j. 29c any single .55 .30
  k. Black (engr.) omitted *10,000.*

No. 2559 has selvage at left and right and either top or bottom.

Basketball, 100th Anniversary

Basketball, Hoop, Players' Arms — A1914

1991, Aug. 28 Photo. *Perf. 11*

2560 A1914 29c multicolored .55 .20

District of Columbia Bicentennial

Capitol Building from Pennsylvania Avenue, Circa 1903 — A1915

Litho. & Engr.

1991, Sept. 7 *Perf. 11*

2561 A1915 29c multicolored	.55	.20
a. Black (engr.) omitted	*110.00*	

Comedians

Stan Laurel and Oliver Hardy A1916

Edgar Bergen and Charlie McCarthy A1917

Jack Benny A1918

Fanny Brice A1919

Bud Abbott and Lou Costello A1920

Perf. 11 on 2 or 3 Sides

1991, Aug. 29 **Litho. & Engr.**

Booklet Stamps

2562 A1916 29c multicolored	.55	.20
2563 A1917 29c multicolored	.55	.20
2564 A1918 29c multicolored	.55	.20
2565 A1919 29c multicolored	.55	.20
2566 A1920 29c multicolored	.55	.20
a. Bklt. pane, 2 ea #2562-2566	6.00	*3.50*
b. As "a," scarlet & bright violet (engr.) omitted	*700.00*	
c. Strip of 5, #2562-2566	2.75	—

Black Heritage Series

Jan E. Matzeliger (1852-1889), Inventor — A1921

1991, Sept. 15 **Photo.** *Perf. 11*

2567 A1921 29c multicolored	.55	.20
a. Horiz. pair, imperf. vert.	*1,250.*	
b. Vert. pair, imperf. horiz.	*1,250.*	
c. Imperf, pair	*750.00*	

Space Exploration

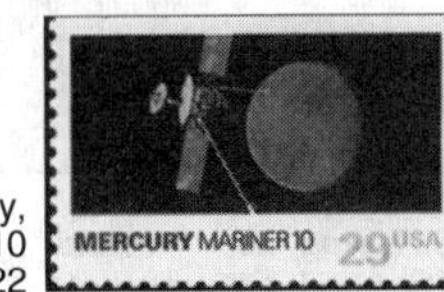

Mercury, Mariner 10 A1922

Venus, Mariner 2 A1923

Earth, Landsat A1924

Moon, Lunar Orbiter A1925

Mars, Viking Orbiter A1926

Jupiter, Pioneer 11 A1927

Saturn, Voyager 2 A1928

Uranus, Voyager 2 A1929

Neptune, Voyager 2 A1930

Pluto A1931

Perf. 11 on 2 or 3 Sides

1991, Oct. 1 **Photo.**

Booklet Stamps

2568 A1922 29c multicolored	.85	.20
2569 A1923 29c multicolored	.85	.20
2570 A1924 29c multicolored	.85	.20
2571 A1925 29c multicolored	.85	.20
2572 A1926 29c multicolored	.85	.20
2573 A1927 29c multicolored	.85	.20
2574 A1928 29c multicolored	.85	.20
2575 A1929 29c multicolored	.85	.20
2576 A1930 29c multicolored	.85	.20
2577 A1931 29c multicolored	.85	.20
a. Bklt. pane of 10, #2568-2577	9.00	*3.50*

Christmas

Madonna and Child by Antoniazzo Romano A1933

Santa Claus in Chimney A1934

Santa Checking List — A1935

Santa with Present — A1936

Santa at Fireplace — A1937

Santa and Sleigh — A1938

Litho. & Engr.

1991, Oct. 17 *Perf. 11*

2578 A1933 (29c) multicolored	.55	.20
a. Booklet pane of 10	5.75	*3.25*
b. As "a," single, red & black (engr.) omitted	*3,500.*	

Photo.

2579 A1934 (29c) multicolored	.55	.20
a. Horiz. pair, imperf. vert.	*300.00*	
b. Vert. pair, imperf. horiz.	*500.00*	

Booklet Stamps

Size: 25x18½mm

Perf. 11 on 2 or 3 Sides

2580 A1934 (29c) Type I	1.75	.20
2581 A1934 (29c) Type II	1.75	.20
a. Pair, #2580, 2581	3.50	.25
b. Bklt. pane, 2 each #2580, 2581	9.00	1.25
2582 A1935 (29c) multicolored	.55	.20
a. Booklet pane of 4	2.25	*1.25*
2583 A1936 (29c) multicolored	.55	.20
a. Booklet pane of 4	2.25	*1.25*
2584 A1937 (29c) multicolored	.55	.20
a. Booklet pane of 4	2.25	*1.25*
2585 A1938 (29c) multicolored	.55	.20
a. Booklet pane of 4	2.25	*1.25*
Nos. 2578-2585 (8)	6.80	1.60

The extreme left brick in top row of chimney is missing from Type II, No. 2581.

A1939

A1942

A1944

James K. Polk (1795-1849)

1995, Nov. 2 **Engr.** *Perf. 11.2*

2587 A1939 32c red brown	.60	.20

Surrender of Gen. John Burgoyne

1994, May 5 **Engr.** *Perf. 11.5*

2590 A1942 $1 blue	1.90	.50

Washington and Jackson

1994, Aug. 19 **Engr.** *Perf. 11.5*

2592 A1944 $5 slate green	8.00	2.50

Pledge of Allegiance A1946

Eagle and Shield A1947

A1950

Statue of Liberty — A1951

Perf. 10 on 2 or 3 sides

1992-93 **Photo.**

Booklet Stamps

2593 A1946 29c blk & multi	.55	.20
a. Booklet pane of 10	5.50	*4.25*

Perf. 11x10 on 2 or 3 Sides

2593B A1946 29c black & multi	1.25	.50
c. Bklt. pane of 10	12.50	*6.00*
2594 A1946 29c red & multi	.55	.20
a. Booklet pane of 10	5.50	*4.25*
b. Imperf., pair	*900.00*	

Denomination is red on #2594 and black on #2593.

Issued: #2593, 2593B, Sept. 8; #2594, 1993.

1992-94 **Litho. & Engr.** *Die Cut*

Self-Adhesive

2595 A1947 29c brown & multi	.55	.25
a. Bklt. pane of 17 + label	13.00	
b. Pair, no die cutting	*175.00*	
c. Brown (engr.) omitted	*450.00*	
d. As "a," no die cutting	*1,500.*	

Photo.

2596 A1947 29c green & multi	.55	.25
a. Bklt. pane of 17 + label	12.00	
2597 A1947 29c red & multi	.55	.25
a. Bklt. pane of 17 + label	10.00	
2598 A1950 29c red, cream & blue	.55	.20
a. Booklet pane of 18	10.00	
b. Coil with plate #111	—	3.75
2599 A1951 29c multicolored	.55	.20
a. Booklet pane of 18	10.00	
b. Coil with plate #D111	—	4.00

Plate No. and inscription reads down on No. 2595a and up on Nos. 2596a-2597a. Design is sharper and more finely detailed on Nos. 2595, 2597.

Except for #2598b and 2599b with plate numbers, coil stamps of these issues are indistinguishable from booklet stamps once they are removed from the backing paper.

Issued unfolded in panes of 17 + label; peelable paper backing is booklet cover. Sold for $5.

Issue dates: No. 2598, Feb. 4, 1994; No. 2599, June 24, 1994; others, Sept. 25, 1992.

See Nos. 3122, 3122E.

A1956

A1957

A1959

A1960

Flag Over White House — A1961

Perf. 10 Vert.

1991-93 Photo. Untagged

Coil Stamps

2602 A1956 (10c) multi .20 .20
a. Imperf., pair —
2603 A1957 (10c) orange yel & multi .20 .20
a. Imperf., pair *30.00*
b. Tagged 2.00 1.50
2604 A1957 (10c) gold & multi .20 .20
2605 A1959 23c multi (Bureau precancel in blue) .40 .40
2606 A1960 23c multi (Bureau Precanceled) .40 .40
2607 A1960 23c multi (Bureau precanceled) .40 .40
c. Imperf., pair *90.00*
2608 A1960 23c vio blue, red & blk (Bureau Precanceled) .40 .40
a. Imperf., pair —

"First Class" is 9½mm long on No. 2606, 9mm long on No. 2607, and 8½mm long on No. 2608

Engr.

2609 A1961 29c blue & red .55 .20
a. Imperf., pair *20.00*
b. Pair, imperf between *100.00*
Nos. 2602-2609 (8) 2.75 2.40

Issued: #2602, 12/13/91; #2603-2604, 5/29/93; #2605, 9/27/91; #2606, 7/21/92; #2607, 10/9/92; #2608, 5/14/93; 29c, 4/23/92.

See Nos. 2907, 3270-3271.

Winter Olympics

Hockey A1963

Figure Skating A1964

Speed Skating A1965

Skiing A1966

Bobsledding A1967

1992, Jan. 11 Photo. *Perf. 11*

2611 A1963 29c multicolored .55 .20
2612 A1964 29c multicolored .55 .20
2613 A1965 29c multicolored .55 .20
2614 A1966 29c multicolored .55 .20
2615 A1967 29c multicolored .55 .20
a. Strip of 5, #2611-2615 2.75 2.50

A1968

A1969

World Columbian Stamp Expo

1992, Jan. 24 Litho. & Engr.

2616 A1968 29c Detail from #129 .55 .20

Black Heritage Series

Litho. & Engr.

1992, Jan. 31 *Perf. 11*

2617 A1969 29c multicolored .55 .20

W.E.B. Du Bois (1868-1963), writer and civil rights leader.

Love

A1970

1992, Feb. 6 Photo. *Perf. 11*

2618 A1970 29c multicolored .55 .20
a. Horiz. pair, imperf vert. *700.00*
b. As "a," green omitted on right stamp —

Olympic Baseball

A1971

1992, Apr. 3 Photo. *Perf. 11*

2619 A1971 29c multicolored .55 .20

Voyages of Columbus

Seeking Queen Isabella's Support A1972

Crossing the Atlantic A1973

Approaching Land — A1974

Coming Ashore A1975

Litho. & Engr.

1992, Apr. 24 *Perf. 11*

2620 A1972 29c multicolored .55 .20
2621 A1973 29c multicolored .55 .20
2622 A1974 29c multicolored .55 .20
2623 A1975 29c multicolored .55 .20
a. Block of 4, #2620-2623 2.25 2.00

See Italy Nos. 1877-1880.

Voyages of Columbus

Souvenir Sheets

A1976

A1977

A1978

A1979

A1980

A1981

Illustrations reduced.

Margins on Nos. 2624-2628 are lithographed. Nos. 2624a-2628c, 2629 are similar in design to Nos. 230-245 but are dated 1492-1992.

Litho. & Engr.

1992, May 22 *Perf. 10½*

2624 A1976 Sheet of 3 1.90 —
a. A71 1c deep blue .20 .20
b. A74 4c ultramarine .20 .20
c. A82 $1 salmon 1.75 1.00
2625 A1977 Sheet of 3 7.25 —
a. A72 2c brown violet .20 .20
b. A73 3c green .20 .20
c. A85 $4 crimson lake 7.00 4.00
2626 A1978 Sheet of 3 1.50 —
a. A75 5c chocolate .20 .20
b. A80 30c orange brown .55 .30
c. A81 50c slate blue .85 .50
2627 A1979 Sheet of 3 5.25 —
a. A76 6c purple .20 .20
b. A77 8c magenta .20 .20
c. A84 $3 yellow green 5.00 3.00
2628 A1980 Sheet of 3 4.00 —
a. A78 10c black brown .20 .20
b. A79 15c dark green .30 .20
c. A83 $2 brown red 3.50 2.00
2629 A1981 Sheet of 1 8.75 —
a. A86 $5 black, single stamp 8.50 5.00
Nos. 2624-2629 (6) 28.65

See Italy Nos. 1883-1888, Portugal Nos. 1918-1923 and Spain Nos. 2677-2682.

Imperforate examples are known of all the Columbus souvenir sheets, but these are not listed in this catalogue. Their appearance several years after the issue date, in substantial quantities of all six sheets at the same time and, evidently, from a single source, with many small faults such as wrinkles and light creases that are not normally seen on these sheets, raises serious concerns about the legitimacy of these imperforate sheets as issued errors.

These circumstances have led the Scott editors to adopt the position that these imperforate sheets are indeed almost certainly printer's waste rather than issued errors. While it is possible that actual imperforate errors of one or more of the sheets may exist that were legitimately sold by the USPS, it is not possible to separate these (should they exist) from the many more numerous examples that apparently are printer's waste.

New York Stock Exchange Bicentennial

A1982

Litho. & Engr.

1992, May 17 *Perf. 11*

2630 A1982 29c grn, red & blk .55 .20
a. Black missing (EP) —
b. Black missing (CM) —
c. Center (black engr.) inverted —

No. 2630a must be collected se-tenant with a normal stamp or with a stamp with half of black engraving missing, or se-tenant with a normal stamp and an additional 2630a.

No. 2630b may be collected alone or se-tenant with No. 2630c.

The unique pane containing 28 No. 2630c and 12 No. 2630b sold at a 2002 auction for $488,750. The unique pane containing 4 No. 2630a, one stamp with half of black center missing and 35 normal stamps sold at the same auction for $18,400.

Space Accomplishments

Cosmonaut, US Space Shuttle
A1983

Astronaut, Russian Space Station
A1984

Sputnik, Vostok, Apollo Command & Lunar Modules
A1985

Soyuz, Mercury and Gemini Spacecraft
A1986

1992, May 29 Photo. *Perf. 11*

2631 A1983 29c multicolored .55 .20
2632 A1984 29c multicolored .55 .20
2633 A1985 29c multicolored .55 .20
2634 A1986 29c multicolored .55 .20
a. Block of 4, #2631-2634 2.25 1.90

See Russia Nos. 6080-6083.

Alaska Highway, 50th Anniversary

A1987

Litho. & Engr.

1992, May 30 *Perf. 11*

2635 A1987 29c multicolored .55 .20
a. Black (engr.) omitted *500.00*

Most known examples of No. 2635a have poor to fine centering. It is valued in the grade of fine. Very fine examples sell for much more.

Kentucky Statehood Bicentennial

A1988

1992, June 1 Photo. *Perf. 11*

2636 A1988 29c multicolored .55 .20
a. Dark blue missing (EP) —
b. Dark blue and red missing (EP) —
c. All colors missing (EP) —

Nos. 2636a-2636c must be collected se-tenant with normal stamps.

Summer Olympics

Soccer
A1989

Gymnastics
A1990

Volleyball
A1991

Boxing
A1992

Swimming
A1993

1992, June 11 Photo. *Perf. 11*

2637 A1989 29c multicolored .55 .20
2638 A1990 29c multicolored .55 .20
2639 A1991 29c multicolored .55 .20
2640 A1992 29c multicolored .55 .20
2641 A1993 29c multicolored .55 .20
a. Strip of 5, #2637-2641 2.75 2.50

Hummingbirds

Ruby-throated
A1994

Broad-billed
A1995

Costa's
A1996

Rufous
A1997

Calliope — A1998

Perf. 11 Vert. on 1 or 2 sides

1992, June 15 Photo.

Booklet Stamps

2642 A1994 29c multicolored .55 .20
2643 A1995 29c multicolored .55 .20
2644 A1996 29c multicolored .55 .20
2645 A1997 29c multicolored .55 .20
2646 A1998 29c multicolored .55 .20
a. Bklt. pane of 5, #2642-2646 2.75 *2.50*

Wildflowers

A1999

1992, July 24 Litho. *Perf. 11*

2647 A1999 29c Indian paintbrush .55 .20
2648 A2000 29c Fragrant water lily .55 .20
2649 A2001 29c Meadow beauty .55 .20
2650 A2002 29c Jack-in-the-pulpit .55 .20
2651 A2003 29c California poppy .55 .20
2652 A2004 29c Large-flowered trillium .55 .20
2653 A2005 29c Tickseed .55 .20
2654 A2006 29c Shooting star .55 .20
2655 A2007 29c Stream violet .55 .20
2656 A2008 29c Bluets .55 .20
2657 A2009 29c Herb Robert .55 .20
2658 A2010 29c Marsh marigold .55 .20
2659 A2011 29c Sweet white violet .55 .20
2660 A2012 29c Claret cup cactus .55 .20
2661 A2013 29c White mountain avens .55 .20
2662 A2014 29c Sessile bellwort .55 .20
2663 A2015 29c Blue flag .55 .20
2664 A2016 29c Harlequin lupine .55 .20
2665 A2017 29c Twinflower .55 .20
2666 A2018 29c Common sunflower .55 .20
2667 A2019 29c Sego lily .55 .20
2668 A2020 29c Virginia bluebells .55 .20
2669 A2021 29c Ohi'a lehua .55 .20
2670 A2022 29c Rosebud orchid .55 .20
2671 A2023 29c Showy evening primrose .55 .20
2672 A2024 29c Fringed gentian .55 .20
2673 A2025 29c Yellow lady's slipper .55 .20
2674 A2026 29c Passionflower .55 .20
2675 A2027 29c Bunchberry .55 .20
2676 A2028 29c Pasqueflower .55 .20
2677 A2029 29c Round-lobed hepatica .55 .20
2678 A2030 29c Wild columbine .55 .20
2679 A2031 29c Fireweed .55 .20
2680 A2032 29c Indian pond lily .55 .20
2681 A2033 29c Turk's cap lily .55 .20
2682 A2034 29c Dutchman's breeches .55 .20
2683 A2035 29c Trumpet honeysuckle .55 .20
2684 A2036 29c Jacob's ladder .55 .20
2685 A2037 29c Plains prickly pear .55 .20
2686 A2038 29c Moss campion .55 .20
2687 A2039 29c Bearberry .55 .20
2688 A2040 29c Mexican hat .55 .20
2689 A2041 29c Harebell .55 .20
2690 A2042 29c Desert five spot .55 .20
2691 A2043 29c Smooth Solomon's seal .55 .20
2692 A2044 29c Red maids .55 .20
2693 A2045 29c Yellow skunk cabbage .55 .20
2694 A2046 29c Rue anemone .55 .20
2695 A2047 29c Standing cypress .55 .20
2696 A2048 29c Wild flax .55 .20
a. Pane of 50, #2647-2696 27.50 —

World War II

A2049

Designs and events of 1942:

a, B-25's take off to raid Tokyo, Apr. 18. b, Ration coupons (food and other commodities rationed). c, Divebomber and deck crewman (U.S. wins Battle of the Coral Sea, May). d, Prisoners of war (Corregidor falls to Japanese, May 6). e, Dutch Harbor buildings on fire (Japan invades Aleutian Islands, June). f, Headphones, coded message (Allies decipher secret enemy codes). g, Yorktown lost, U.S. wins at Midway. h, Woman with drill (millions of women join war effort). i, Marines land on Guadalcanal, Aug. 7. j, Tank in desert (Allies land in North Africa, Nov.).

Central label is the size of 15 stamps and shows world map, extent of axis control.

Illustration reduced.

Litho. & Engr.

1992, Aug. 17 *Perf. 11*

2697 A2049 Block of 10 5.50 5.00
a.-j. 29c any single .55 .30
k. Red (litho.) omitted *8,000.*

No. 2697 has selvage at left and right and either top or bottom.

A2050

A2051

Literary Arts Series

Dorothy Parker

1992, Aug. 22 Photo. *Perf. 11*

2698 A2050 29c multicolored .55 .20

Dr. Theodore von Karman

1992, Aug. 31 Photo. *Perf. 11*

2699 A2051 29c multicolored .55 .20

Von Karman (1881-1963), rocket scientist.

Minerals

Azurite — A2052

Copper — A2053

Variscite
A2054

Wulfenite
A2055

Litho. & Engr.

1992, Sept. 17 *Perf. 11*

2700 A2052 29c multicolored .55 .20
2701 A2053 29c multicolored .55 .20
2702 A2054 29c multicolored .55 .20
2703 A2055 29c multicolored .55 .20
a. Block or strip, #2700-2703 2.25 2.00
b. As "a," silver (litho.) omitted *8,500.*

c. As "a," red (litho.) omitted —
d. As "a," silver omitted on two stamps —

Juan Rodriguez Cabrillo

Cabrillo, Ship, Map of San Diego Bay Area — A2056

Litho. & Engr.

1992, Sept. 28 ***Perf. 11***

2704 A2056 29c multicolored	.55	.20
a. Black (engr.) omitted	3,000.	

Wild Animals

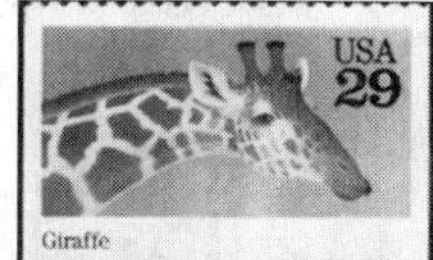

Giraffe A2057

Giant Panda A2058

Flamingo A2059

King Penguins A2060

White Bengal Tiger A2061

Perf. 11 Horiz. on 1 or 2 sides

1992, Oct. 1 **Photo.**

Booklet Stamps

2705 A2057 29c multicolored	.55	.20
2706 A2058 29c multicolored	.55	.20
2707 A2059 29c multicolored	.55	.20
2708 A2060 29c multicolored	.55	.20
2709 A2061 29c multicolored	.55	.20
a. Booklet pane, #2705-2709	2.75	*2.25*
b. As "a," imperforate	3,000.	

Christmas

Madonna and Child, by Giovanni Bellini — A2062

A2063

A2064

A2065

A2066

1992 **Litho. & Engr.** ***Perf. 11.2***

2710 A2062 29c multicolored	.55	.20
a. Booklet pane of 10	5.50	*3.50*

Litho.

Perf. 11½x11

2711 A2063 29c multicolored	.55	.20
2712 A2064 29c multicolored	.55	.20
2713 A2065 29c multicolored	.55	.20
2714 A2066 29c multicolored	.55	.20
a. Block of 4, #2711-2714	2.25	1.10

Booklet Stamps

Photo.

Perf. 11 on 2 or 3 Sides

2715 A2063 29c multicolored	.85	.20
2716 A2064 29c multicolored	.85	.20
2717 A2065 29c multicolored	.85	.20
2718 A2066 29c multicolored	.85	.20
a. Bklt. pane of 4, #2715-2718	3.50	*1.25*
b. As "a," imperf horiz.	—	
c. As "a," imperf	—	

Self-Adhesive

Die Cut

2719 A2064 29c multicolored	.60	.20
a. Booklet pane of 18	11.00	

"Greetings" is 27mm long on Nos. 2711-2714, 25mm long on Nos. 2715-2718 and 21½mm long on No. 2719. Nos. 2715-2719 differ in color from Nos. 2711-2714.

Issued: #2710-2718, 10/22; #2719, 10/28.

Chinese New Year

Year of the Rooster A2067

Litho. & Engr.

1992, Dec. 30 ***Perf. 11***

2720 A2067 29c multicolored	.55	.20

American Music Series

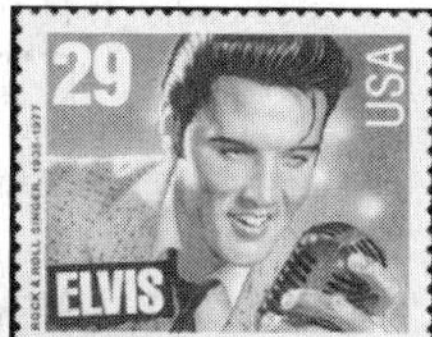

Elvis Presley A2068

Oklahoma! A2069

Hank Williams A2070

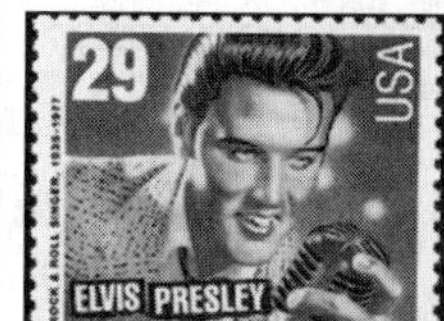

Elvis Presley A2071

Bill Haley A2072

Clyde McPhatter A2073

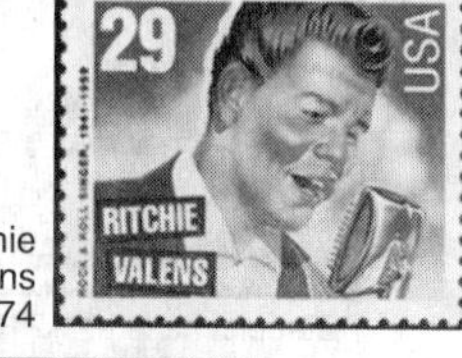

Ritchie Valens A2074

Otis Redding A2075

Buddy Holly A2076

Dinah Washington A2077

1993, Jan. 8 **Photo.** ***Perf. 11***

2721 A2068 29c multicolored	.55	.20
a. Imperf, pair	—	

1993, Mar. 30 **Photo.** ***Perf. 10***

2722 A2069 29c multicolored	.55	.20

1993, June 9

2723 A2070 29c multicolored	.55	.20

Perf. 11.2x11.5

2723A A2070 29c multicolored	*22.50*	*10.00*

1993, June 16

2724 A2071 29c multicolored	.60	.20
2725 A2072 29c multicolored	.60	.20
2726 A2073 29c multicolored	.60	.20
2727 A2074 29c multicolored	.60	.20
2728 A2075 29c multicolored	.60	.20
2729 A2076 29c multicolored	.60	.20
2730 A2077 29c multicolored	.60	.20
a. Vert. strip, #2724-2730	4.25	—

Booklet Stamps

Perf. 11 Horiz.

2731 A2071 29c multicolored	.55	.20
2732 A2072 29c multicolored	.55	.20
2733 A2073 29c multicolored	.55	.20
2734 A2074 29c multicolored	.55	.20
2735 A2075 29c multicolored	.55	.20
2736 A2076 29c multicolored	.55	.20
2737 A2077 29c multicolored	.55	.20
a. Booklet pane, 2 #2731, 1 each #2732-2737	5.00	*2.25*
b. Booklet pane of 4, #2731, 2735-2737 + tab	2.25	*1.50*

See Nos. 2769, 2771, 2775 and designs A2112-A2117.

Space Fantasy

A2086

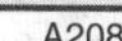

A2087

A2088

A2089

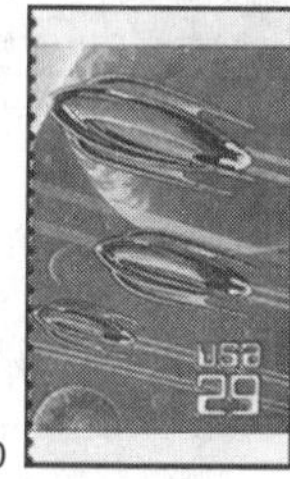

A2090

Perf. 11 Vert. on 1 or 2 Sides

1993, Jan. 25 **Photo.**

Booklet Stamps

2741 A2086 29c multicolored	.55	.20
2742 A2087 29c multicolored	.55	.20
2743 A2088 29c multicolored	.55	.20
2744 A2089 29c multicolored	.55	.20
2745 A2090 29c multicolored	.55	.20
a. Bklt. pane of 5, #2741-2745	2.75	*2.25*

Black Heritage Series

Percy Lavon Julian (1899-1975), Chemist — A2091

Litho. & Engr.

1993, Jan. 29 ***Perf. 11***

2746 A2091 29c multicolored	.55	.20

Oregon Trail

A2092

Litho. & Engr.

1993, Feb. 12 ***Perf. 11***

2747 A2092 29c multicolored	.55	.20

World University Games

A2093

1993, Feb. 25 **Photo.** ***Perf. 11***

2748 A2093 29c multicolored	.55	.20

Grace Kelly (1929-1982)

Actress, Princess of Monaco — A2094

1993, Mar. 24 Engr. *Perf. 11*

2749 A2094 29c blue .55 .20

See Monaco No. 1851.

Circus

Clown — A2095

Ringmaster A2096

Trapeze Artist — A2097

Elephant A2098

Illustrations reduced.

1993, Apr. 6 Litho. *Perf. 11*

2750 A2095 29c multicolored .55 .20
2751 A2096 29c multicolored .55 .20
2752 A2097 29c multicolored .55 .20
2753 A2098 29c multicolored .55 .20
a. Block of 4, #2750-2753 2.25 1.75

Cherokee Strip Land Run, Centennial

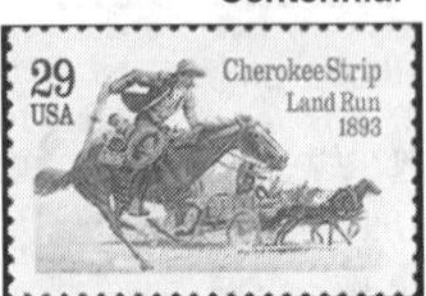

A2099

Litho. & Engr.

1993, Apr. 17 *Perf. 11*

2754 A2099 29c multicolored .55 .20

Dean Acheson (1893-1971)

Secretary of State — A2100

1993, Apr. 21 Engr. *Perf. 11*

2755 A2100 29c greenish gray .55 .20

Sporting Horses

Steeplechase — A2101

Thoroughbred Racing — A2102

Harness Racing A2103

Polo A2104

Litho. & Engr.

1993, May 1 *Perf. 11x11½*

2756 A2101 29c multicolored .55 .20
2757 A2102 29c multicolored .55 .20
2758 A2103 29c multicolored .55 .20
2759 A2104 29c multicolored .55 .20
a. Block of 4, #2756-2759 2.25 2.00
b. As "a," black (engr.) omitted *1,250.*

Garden Flowers

Hyacinth A2105

Daffodil A2106

Tulip — A2107

Iris — A2108

Lilac — A2109

Litho. & Engr.

1993, May 15 *Perf. 11 Vert.*

2760 A2105 29c multicolored .55 .20
2761 A2106 29c multicolored .55 .20
2762 A2107 29c multicolored .55 .20
2763 A2108 29c multicolored .55 .20
2764 A2109 29c multicolored .55 .20
a. Booklet pane, #2760-2764 2.75 *2.25*
b. As "a," blk (engr.) omitted *240.00*
c. As "a," imperf *2,250.*

World War II

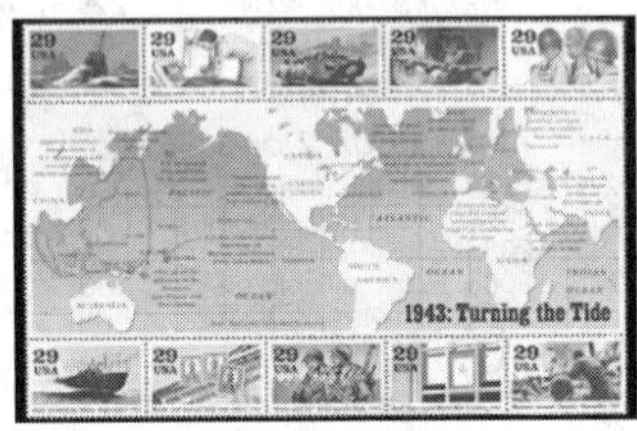

A2110

Designs and events of 1943:
a, Destroyers (Allied forces battle German U-boats). b, Military medics treat the wounded. c, Amphibious landing craft on beach (Sicily attacked by Allied forces, July). d, B-24s hit Ploesti refineries, August. e, V-mail delivers letters from home. f, PT boat (Italy invaded by Allies, Sept.). g, Nos. WS7, WS8, savings bonds (Bonds and stamps help war effort). h, "Willie and Joe" keep spirits high. i, Banner in window (Gold Stars mark World War II losses). j, Marines assault Tarawa, Nov.

Central label is the size of 15 stamps and shows world map with extent of Axis control and Allied operations.

Illustration reduced.

Litho. & Engr.

1993, May 31 *Perf. 11*

2765 A2110 Block of 10 + label 5.50 5.00
a.-j. 29c any single .55 .30

No. 2765 has selvage at left and right and either top or bottom.

Joe Louis (1914-1981)

A2111

Litho. & Engr.

1993, June 22 *Perf. 11*

2766 A2111 29c multicolored .55 .20

American Music Series

Oklahoma! Type and

Show Boat A2112

Porgy & Bess A2113

My Fair Lady A2114

Perf. 11 Horiz. on 1 or 2 Sides

1993, July 14 Photo.

Booklet Stamps

2767 A2112 29c multicolored .55 .20
2768 A2113 29c multicolored .55 .20
2769 A2069 29c multicolored .55 .20
2770 A2114 29c multicolored .55 .20
a. Booklet pane, #2767-2770 2.75 *2.25*

No. 2769 has smaller design size, brighter colors and shorter inscription than No. 2722, as well as a frameline around the design and other subtle design differences.

Hank Williams Type and

Patsy Cline A2115

The Carter Family A2116

Bob Wills A2117

1993, Sept. 25 Photo. *Perf. 10*

2771 A2070 29c multicolored .55 .20
2772 A2115 29c multicolored .55 .20
2773 A2116 29c multicolored .55 .20
2774 A2117 29c multicolored .55 .20
a. Block or horiz. strip of 4, #2771-2774 2.25 1.75

Booklet Stamps

Perf. 11 Horiz.

With Black Frameline

2775 A2070 29c multicolored .55 .20
2776 A2116 29c multicolored .55 .20
2777 A2115 29c multicolored .55 .20
2778 A2117 29c multicolored .55 .20
a. Booklet pane, #2775-2778 2.50 *2.00*
b. As "a," imperf *1,000.*

Inscription at left measures 27mm on No. 2771, 27½mm on No. 2723 and 22mm on No. 2775. No. 2723 shows only two tuning keys on guitar, while No. 2771 shows those two and parts of two others.

National Postal Museum

Independence Hall, Benjamin Franklin, Printing Press, Colonial Post Rider — A2118

Pony Express Rider, Civil War Soldier, Concord Stagecoach A2119

JN-4H Biplane, Charles Lindbergh, Railway Mail Car, 1931 Model A Ford Mail Truck
A2120

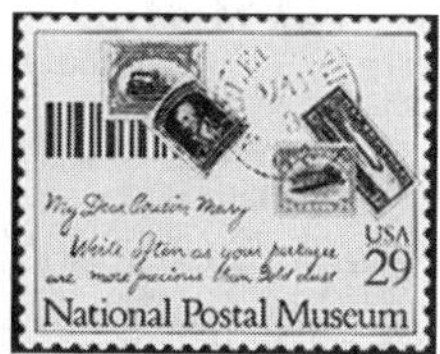

California Gold Rush Miner's Letter, Nos. 39, 295, C3a, C13, Barcode & Circular Date Stamp
A2121

Litho. & Engr.

1993, July 30 *Perf. 11*

2779 A2118 29c multicolored .55 .20
2780 A2119 29c multicolored .55 .20
2781 A2120 29c multicolored .55 .20
2782 A2121 29c multicolored .55 .20
a. Block or strip of 4, #2779-2782 2.25 2.00
b. As "a," engr. maroon (USA/29) & black ("My Dear...") omitted —
c. As "a," imperf *3,500.*

American Sign Language

A2122

A2123

1993, Sept. 20 **Photo.** *Perf. 11½*

2783 A2122 29c multicolored .55 .20
2784 A2123 29c multicolored .55 .20
a. Pair, #2783-2784 1.10 .75

Classic Books

A2124

A2125

A2126

A2127

Designs: No. 2785, Rebecca of Sunnybrook Farm, by Kate Douglas Wiggin. No. 2786, Little House on the Prairie, by Laura Ingalls Wilder. No. 2787, The Adventures of Huckleberry Finn, by Mark Twain. No. 2788, Little Women, by Louisa May Alcott.

Litho. & Engr.

1993, Oct. 23 *Perf. 11*

2785 A2124 29c multicolored .55 .20
2786 A2125 29c multicolored .55 .20
2787 A2126 29c multicolored .55 .20
2788 A2127 29c multicolored .55 .20
a. Block or horiz. strip of 4, #2785-2788 2.25 2.00
b. As "a," imperf *3,000.*

Christmas

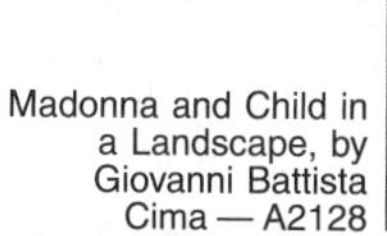

Madonna and Child in a Landscape, by Giovanni Battista Cima — A2128

Jack-in-the-Box
A2129

Red-Nosed Reindeer
A2130

Snowman
A2131

Toy Soldier Blowing Horn
A2132

Litho. & Engr.

1993, Oct. 21 *Perf. 11*

2789 A2128 29c multicolored .55 .20

Booklet Stamp

Size: 18x25mm

Perf. 11½x11 on 2 or 3 Sides

2790 A2128 29c multicolored .55 .20
a. Booklet pane of 4 2.25 *1.75*
b. Imperf pair —
c. As "a," imperf —

No. 2790 has darker colors and smaller inscriptions than No. 2789.

1993 **Photo.** *Perf. 11½*

2791 A2129 29c multicolored .55 .20
2792 A2130 29c multicolored .55 .20
2793 A2131 29c multicolored .55 .20
2794 A2132 29c multicolored .55 .20
a. Block or strip, #2791-2794 2.25 2.00

Booklet Stamps

Size: 18x21mm

Perf. 11x10 on 2 or 3 Sides

2795 A2132 29c multicolored .85 .20
2796 A2131 29c multicolored .85 .20
2797 A2130 29c multicolored .85 .20
2798 A2129 29c multicolored .85 .20
a. Booklet pane, 3 each #2795-2796, 2 each #2797-2798 8.50 *4.00*
b. Booklet pane, 3 each #2797-2798, 2 each #2795-2796 8.50 *4.00*
c. Block of 4, #2795-2798 3.40 1.75

Self-Adhesive

Size: 19½x26½mm

Die Cut

2799 A2131 29c multicolored .55 .20
a. Coil with plate #V1111111 — 3.50
2800 A2132 29c multicolored .55 .20
2801 A2129 29c multicolored .55 .20
2802 A2130 29c multicolored .55 .20
a. Bklt. pane, 3 ea #2799-2802 7.00
b. Block of 4, #2799-2802 2.00

Size: 17x20mm

2803 A2131 29c multicolored .55 .20
a. Booklet pane of 18 10.00

Except for #2799a with plate number, coil stamps are indistinguishable from booklet stamps once they are removed from the backing paper.

Snowman on Nos. 2793, 2799 has three buttons and seven snowflakes beneath nose (placement differs on both stamps). No. 2796 has two buttons and five snowflakes beneath nose. No. 2803 has two orange buttons and four snowflakes beneath nose.

Issued: #2791-2798, 10/21; #2799-2803, 10/28.

Mariana Islands

A2133

Litho. & Engr.

1993, Nov. 4 *Perf. 11*

2804 A2133 29c multicolored .55 .20

Columbus' Landing in Puerto Rico, 500th Anniv.

A2134

1993, Nov. 19 **Photo.** *Perf. 11.2*

2805 A2134 29c multicolored .55 .20

AIDS Awareness

A2135

1993, Dec. 1 **Photo.** *Perf. 11.2*

2806 A2135 29c black & red .55 .20
a. Perf. 11 vert. on 1 or 2 sides, from bklt. pane .55 .20
b. As "a," booklet pane of 5 2.75 *2.00*

Winter Olympics

Slalom
A2136

Luge
A2137

Ice Dancing
A2138

Cross-Country Skiing
A2139

Ice Hockey — A2140

1994, Jan. 6 **Litho.** *Perf. 11.2*

2807 A2136 29c multicolored .55 .20
2808 A2137 29c multicolored .55 .20
2809 A2138 29c multicolored .55 .20
2810 A2139 29c multicolored .55 .20
2811 A2140 29c multicolored .55 .20
a. Strip of 5, #2807-2811 2.75 2.50

Edward R. Murrow, Journalist (1908-65)

A2141

1994, Jan. 21 **Engr.** *Perf. 11.2*

2812 A2141 29c brown .55 .20

Love

A2142

A2143

A2144

1994 **Litho. & Engr.** *Die Cut*

Self-Adhesive (No. 2813)

2813 A2142 29c multicolored .55 .20
a. Booklet pane of 18 11.00
b. Coil with plate #B1 — 3.75

Photo.

Perf. 10.9x11.1 on 2 or 3 Sides

2814 A2143 29c multicolored .55 .20
a. Booklet pane of 10 5.50 *3.50*
b. As "a," imperf —
e. Horiz. pair, imperf btwn. —

Litho. & Engr.

Perf. 11.1

2814C A2143 29c multicolored .55 .20

Photo. & Engr.

Perf. 11.2

2815 A2144 52c multicolored 1.00 .20

Size of No. 2814C is 20x28mm. No. 2814 is 18x24½mm.

Except for #2813b with plate number, coil stamps are indistinguishable from booklet stamps once they are removed from the backing paper.

Issued: No. 2813, Jan. 27; Nos. 2814-2815, Feb. 14; No. 2814C, June 11.

No. 2814 was issued in booklets only.

Black Heritage Series

Dr. Allison Davis (1902-83), Social Anthropologist, Educator — A2145

1994, Feb. 1 Engr. *Perf. 11.2*

2816 A2145 29c red brn & brn .55 .20

Chinese New Year

Year of the Dog A2146

1994, Feb. 5 Photo. *Perf. 11.2*

2817 A2146 29c multicolored .55 .20

Buffalo Soldiers

A2147

Perf. 11.5x11.2

1994, Apr. 22 Litho. & Engr.

2818 A2147 29c multicolored .55 .20
 a. Double impression (second impression light) of red brown (engr. inscriptions) —

Silent Screen Stars

Rudolph Valentino (1895-1926) A2148

Clara Bow (1905-65) A2149

Charlie Chaplin (1889-1977) A2150

Lon Chaney (1883-1930) A2151

John Gilbert (1895-1936) A2152

Zasu Pitts (1898-1963) A2153

Harold Lloyd (1894-1971) A2154

Keystone Cops A2155

Theda Bara (1885-1955) A2156

Buster Keaton (1895-1966) A2157

Litho. & Engr.

1994, Apr. 27 *Perf. 11.2*

Red, Blk & Brt Vio

2819 A2148 29c .55 .20
2820 A2149 29c .55 .20
2821 A2150 29c .55 .20
2822 A2151 29c .55 .20
2823 A2152 29c .55 .20
2824 A2153 29c .55 .20
2825 A2154 29c .55 .20
2826 A2155 29c .55 .20
2827 A2156 29c .55 .20
2828 A2157 29c .55 .20
 a. Block of 10, #2819-2828 5.50 4.00
 b. As "a," black (litho.) omitted —
 c. As "a," black, red & brt vio (litho.) omitted —

Garden Flowers

Lily — A2158

Zinnia — A2159

Gladiola A2160

Marigold A2161

Rose — A2162

Perf. 10.9 Vert.

1994, Apr. 28 Litho. & Engr.

Booklet Stamps

2829 A2158 29c multicolored .55 .20
2830 A2159 29c multicolored .55 .20
2831 A2160 29c multicolored .55 .20
2832 A2161 29c multicolored .55 .20
2833 A2162 29c multicolored .55 .20
 a. Bklt. pane, #2829-2833 2.75 —
 b. As "a," imperf 2,250.
 c. As "a," blk (engr.) omitted 250.00

1994 World Cup Soccer Championships

A2163

A2164

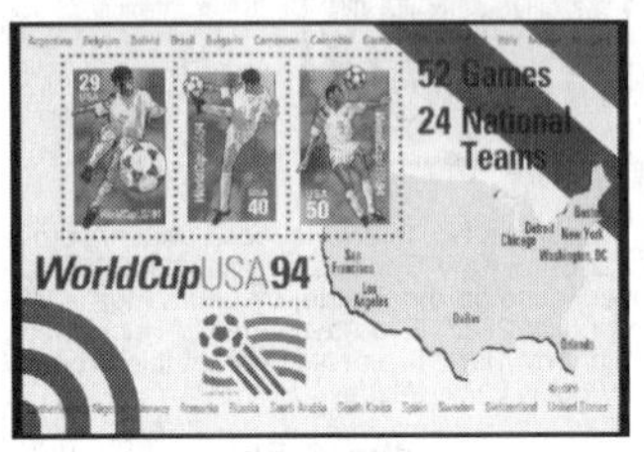

A2165

Design: 40c, Soccer player, diff.

1994, May 26 Photo. *Perf. 11.1*

2834 A2163 29c multicolored .55 .20
2835 A2163 40c multicolored .80 .20
2836 A2164 50c multicolored 1.00 .20
 Nos. 2834-2836 (3) 2.35 .60

Souvenir Sheet of 3

2837 A2165 #a.-c. 2.50 2.00

Nos. 2834-2836 are printed on phosphor-coated paper, while Nos. 2837a (29c), 2837b (40c), 2837c (50c) are block tagged. No. 2837c has a portion of the yellow map in the LR corner.

World War II

A2166

Designs and events of 1944:

a, Allied forces retake New Guinea. b, P-51s escort B-17s on bombing raids. c, Troops running from landing craft (Allies in Normandy, D-Day, June 6). d, Airborne units spearhead attacks. e, Officer at periscope (Submarines shorten war in Pacific). f, Parade (Allies free Rome, June 4; Paris, Aug. 25). g, Soldier firing flamethrower (US troops clear Saipan bunkers). h, Red Ball Express speeds vital supplies. i, Battleship firing main battery (Battle for Leyte Gulf, Oct. 23-26). j, Soldiers in snow (Bastogne and Battle of the Bulge, Dec.).

Central label is size of 15 stamps and shows world map with extent of Axis control and Allied operations.

Illustration reduced.

Litho. & Engr.

1994, June 6 *Perf. 10.9*

2838 A2166 Block of 10 + label 6.00 5.50
 a.-j. 29c any single .60 .30

No. 2838 has stamp selvage at left and right and either top or bottom.

Norman Rockwell

A2167

A2168

Perf. 10.9x11.1

1994, July 1 Litho. & Engr.

2839 A2167 29c multicolored .55 .20

Souvenir Sheet

Litho.

2840 A2168 Sheet of 4 4.00 2.75
 a. 50c Freedom from Want 1.00 .65
 b. 50c Freedom from Fear 1.00 .65
 c. 50c Freedom of Speech 1.00 .65
 d. 50c Freedom of Worship 1.00 .65

Moon Landing, 25th Anniv.

A2169

A2170

1994, July 20 Litho. *Perf. 11.2x11.1*

Miniature Sheet

2841 A2169 Sheet of 12 7.50 —
 a. 29c Single stamp .60 .60

Litho. & Engr.

Perf. 10.7x11.1

2842 A2170 $9.95 multicolored 17.50 7.50

Locomotives

Hudson's General A2171

McQueen's Jupiter A2172

Eddy's No. 242 A2173

Ely's No. 10 A2174

Buchanan's No. 999 A2175

Perf. 11 Horiz.

1994, July 28 Photo.

Booklet Stamps

2843	A2171	29c multicolored	.55	.20
2844	A2172	29c multicolored	.55	.20
2845	A2173	29c multicolored	.55	.20
2846	A2174	29c multicolored	.55	.20
2847	A2175	29c multicolored	.55	.20
a.		Booklet pane, #2843-2847	2.75	*2.00*
b.		As "a," imperf	—	

George Meany, Labor Leader (1894-1980)

A2176

1994, Aug. 16 Engr. *Perf. 11.1x11*

2848 A2176 29c blue .55 .20

American Music Series

Al Jolson (1886-1950) — A2177

Bing Crosby (1904-77) A2178

Ethel Waters (1896-1977) — A2179

Nat "King" Cole (1919-65) A2180

Ethel Merman (1908-84) A2181

Bessie Smith (1894-1937) — A2182

Muddy Waters (1915-83) A2183

Billie Holiday (1915-59) A2184

Robert Johnson (1911-38) A2185

Jimmy Rushing (1902-72) A2186

"Ma" Rainey (1886-1939) — A2187

Mildred Bailey (1907-51) A2188

Howlin' Wolf (1910-76) A2189

1994 Photo. *Perf. 10.1x10.2*

2849	A2177	29c multicolored	.60	.20
2850	A2178	29c multicolored	.60	.20
2851	A2179	29c multicolored	.60	.20
2852	A2180	29c multicolored	.60	.20
2853	A2181	29c multicolored	.60	.20
a.		Vert. strip of 5, #2849-2853	3.00	2.00

Perf. 11x10.8

Litho.

2854	A2182	29c multicolored	.60	.20
2855	A2183	29c multicolored	.60	.20
2856	A2184	29c multicolored	.60	.20
2857	A2185	29c multicolored	.60	.20
2858	A2186	29c multicolored	.50	.20
2859	A2187	29c multicolored	.60	.20
2860	A2188	29c multicolored	.60	.20
2861	A2189	29c multicolored	.60	.20
a.		Block of 9, #2854-2861 +1 additional stamp	5.50	4.50

Issued: Nos. 2849-2853, 9/1/94; Nos. 2854-2861, 9/17/94.

Literary Arts Series

James Thurber (1894-1961) A2190

Litho. & Engr.

1994, Sept. 10 *Perf. 11*

2862 A2190 29c multicolored .55 .20

Wonders Of The Sea

Diver, Motorboat A2191

Diver, Ship A2192

Diver, Ship's Wheel A2193

Diver, Coral A2194

1994, Oct. 3 Litho. *Perf. 11x10.9*

2863	A2191	29c multicolored	.55	.20
2864	A2192	29c multicolored	.55	.20
2865	A2193	29c multicolored	.55	.20
2866	A2194	29c multicolored	.55	.20
a.		Block of 4, #2863-2866	2.25	1.50
b.		As "a," imperf	*1,600.*	

Cranes

Black-Necked A2195

Whooping A2196

Litho. & Engr.

1994, Oct. 9 *Perf. 10.8x11*

2867	A2195	29c multicolored	.55	.20
2868	A2196	29c multicolored	.55	.20
a.		Pair, #2867-2868	1.10	.75
b.		Blk & mag (engr.) omitted	*2,000.*	
c.		As "a," dble. impression of engr. blk (Birds' names, "USA") & mag ("29")	*5,000.*	
d.		As "a," dble. impression of engr. blk ("USA") & mag ("29")	—	

See People's Republic of China Nos. 2528-2529.

Legends Of The West

Miniature Pane

A2197

g. Bill Pickett (1870-1932) (Revised)

Designs: a, Home on the Range. b, Buffalo Bill Cody (1846-1917), c, Jim Bridger (1804-81). d, Annie Oakley (1860-1926). e, Native American Culture. f, Chief Joseph (c. 1840-1904). h, Bat Masterson (1853-1921). i, John C. Fremont (1813-90). j, Wyatt Earp (1848-1929). k, Nellie Cashman (c. 1849-1925). l, Charles Goodnight (1826-1929). m, Geronimo (1823-1909). n, Kit Carson (1809-68). o, Wild Bill Hickok (1837-76). p, Western Wildlife. q, Jim Beckwourth (c. 1798-1866). r, Bill Tilghman (1854-1924). s, Sacagawea (c. 1787-1812). t, Overland Mail.

1994, Oct. 18 Photo. *Perf. 10.1x10*

2869	A2197	Pane of 20	12.00	—
a.-t.		29c any single	.60	.20
u.		As No. 2869, a.-e. imperf, f.-j. part perf.	—	

Legends Of The West (Recalled)

Miniature Pane

g. Bill Pickett (Recalled)

Nos. 2870b-2870d, 2870f-2870o, 2870q-2870s have a frameline around the vignette that is half the width of the frameline on similar stamps in No. 2869. Other design differences may exist.

1994 Photo. *Perf. 10.1x10*

2870 A2197 29c Pane of 20 190.00 —

150,000 panes were made available through a drawing. Panes were delivered in an envelope. Value is for pane without envelope.

Christmas

Madonna and Child, by Elisabetta Sirani A2200

Stocking A2201

Santa Claus
A2202

Cardinal in Snow
A2203

Litho. & Engr.

1994, Oct. 20 ***Perf. 11¼***

2871 A2200 29c multicolored .55 .20

Booklet Stamp

Perf. 9¾x11

2871A A2200 29c multicolored .60 .20
- *b.* Booklet pane of 10 6.25 *3.50*
- *c.* As "b," imperf. 2,000.

Perf. 11¼

Litho.

2872 A2201 29c multicolored .55 .20
- *a.* Booklet pane of 20 10.50 *3.00*
- *b.* Imperf., pair —
- *c.* As "a," imperf. horiz. —
- *d.* Quadruple impression of black, triple impression of blue, double impressions of red and yellow, green normal —
- *e* Vert. pair, imperf between —

Booklet Stamps

Photo.

Die Cut

Self-Adhesive

2873 A2202 29c multicolored .55 .20
- *a.* Booklet pane of 12 6.75
- *b.* Coil with plate #V1111 — 3.75

2874 A2203 29c multicolored .55 .20
- *a.* Booklet pane of 18 10.00

Except for #2873b with plate number, coil stamps are indistinguishable from booklet stamps once they are removed from the backing paper.

Bureau Of Engraving & Printing

Souvenir Sheet

A2204

Litho. & Engr.

1994, Nov. 3 ***Perf. 11***

2875 A2204 Sheet of 4 15.00 —
- *a.* $2 Single stamp 3.00 1.25

Chinese New Year

Year of the Boar
A2205

Perf. 11.2x11.1

1994, Dec. 30 **Photo.**

2876 A2205 29c multicolored .55 .20

A2206

A2207

A2208

A2208a

A2209

A2210

1994, Dec. 13 **Litho.** ***Perf. 11x10.8***

Untagged

2877 A2206 (3c) tan, bright blue & red .20 .20
- *a.* Imperf, pair *200.00*
- *b.* Double impression of red —

Perf. 10.8x10.9

2878 A2206 (3c) tan, dark blue & red .20 .20

Inscriptions on #2877 are in a thin typeface. Those on #2878 are in heavy, bold type.

No. 2877 imperf and with blue omitted is known from printer's waste.

Photo.

Perf. 11.2x11.1

Tagged

2879 A2207 (20c) black "G," yel & multi .40 .20
- *a.* Imperf, pair —

Perf. 11x10.9

2880 A2207 (20c) red "G," yellow & multi .50 .20

Perf. 11.2x11.1

2881 A2208 (32c) black "G" & multi .75 .20
- *a.* Booklet pane of 10 6.00 *3.75*

Perf. 11x10.9

2882 A2208 (32c) red "G" & multi .60 .20

Distance on #2882 from bottom of red G to top of flag immediately above is 13¾mm. Illustration A2208a shows #2885 superimposed over #2882.

Booklet Stamps

Perf. 10x9.9 on 2 or 3 Sides

2883 A2208 (32c) black "G" & multi .60 .20
- *a.* Booklet pane of 10 6.25 *3.75*

Perf. 10.9 on 2 or 3 Sides

2884 A2208 (32c) blue "G" & multi .60 .20
- *a.* Booklet pane of 10 6.00 *3.75*
- *b.* As "a," imperf —

Perf. 11x10.9 on 2 or 3 Sides

2885 A2208a (32c) red "G" & multi .65 .20
- *a.* Booklet pane of 10 6.50 *3.75*
- *b.* Pair, imperf vert. —
- *c.* Pair, imperf between —

Distance on #2885 from bottom of red G to top of flag immediately above is 13½mm. See note below #2882.

No. 2885c resulted from a paper foldover after perforating and before cutting into panes.

A2208b

A2208c

Die Cut

Self-Adhesive

2886 A2208b (32c) gray, blue, lt bl, red & blk .60 .20
- *a.* Booklet pane of 18 11.00
- *b.* Coil with plate #V11111 — 3.25

No. 2886 is printed on pre-phosphored paper and has only a small number of blue shading dots in the white stripes immediately below the flag's blue field.

Except for #2886b with plate number, coil stamps are indistinguishable from booklet stamps once they are removed from the backing paper.

2887 A2208c (32c) blk, bl & red .60 .20
- *a.* Booklet pane of 18 11.00

No. 2887 has noticeable blue shading in the white stripes immediately below the blue field and has overall tagging.

COIL STAMPS

1994-95 ***Perf. 9.8 Vert.***

2888 A2209 (25c) black "G" .50 .20

2889 A2208 (32c) black "G" .75 .20
- *a.* Imperf., pair *325.00*

2890 A2208 (32c) blue "G" .60 .20

2891 A2208 (32c) red "G" .75 .20

Rouletted 9.8 Vert.

2892 A2208 (32c) red "G" .60 .20

Perf. 9.8 Vert.

2893 A2210 (5c) grn & multi .20 .20

Nos. 2888-2892 issued 12/13/94. No. 2893 was only available through the Philatelic Fullfillment Center after its announcement 1/12/95.

Eagle and Shield Type of 1993 and:

Flag Over Porch
A2212

Butte
A2217

Mountain
A2218

Auto
A2220

Auto Tail Fin — A2223

Juke Box — A2225

Flag Over Field — A2230

1995-97 **Photo.** ***Perf. 10.4***

2897 A2212 32c multi .60 .20
- *a.* Imperf., vert. pair *80.00*

COIL STAMPS

Self-Adhesive

(#2902B, 2904A-2904B, 2906-2907, 2910, 2912A-2912B, 2915-2915D, 2919-2921)

Photo.

Perf. 9.8 Vert.

2902 A2217 (5c) yel, red & bl .20 .20
- *a.* Imperf., pair 750.00

Serpentine Die Cut 11.5 Vert.

2902B A2217 (5c) yel, red & bl .20 .20

Perf. 9.8 Vert.

2903 A2218 (5c) purple & multi .20 .20

Letters of inscription "USA NONPROFIT ORG." outlined in purple on #2903.

2904 A2218 (5c) bl & multi .20 .20
- *c.* Imperf., pair 500.00

Letters of inscription have no outline on #2904.

Serpentine Die Cut 11.2 Vert.

2904A A2218 (5c) purple & multi .20 .20

Serpentine Die Cut 9.8 Vert.

2904B A2218 (5c) purple & multi .20 .20

Letters of inscription outlined in purple on #2904B, not outlined on No. 2904A.

Perf. Perf. 9.8 Vert.

2905 A2220 (10c) blk, red brn & brn .20 .20

Serpentine Die Cut 11.5 Vert.

2906 A2220 (10c) blk, brn & red brn .20 .20

2907 A1957 (10c) gold & multi .20 .20

Perf. 9.8 Vert.

2908 A2223 (15c) dk org yel & multi .30 .30

No. 2908 has dark, bold colors, heavy shading lines and heavily shaded chrome.

2909 A2223 (15c) buff & multi .30 .30

No. 2909 has shinier chrome, more subdued colors and finer details than No. 2908.

Serpentine Die Cut 11.5 Vert.

2910 A2223 (15c) buff & multi .30 .30

Perf. 9.8 Vert.

2911 A2225 (25c) dk red, dk yel grn & multi .50 .50
- *a.* Imperf., pair —

No. 2911 has dark, saturated colors and dark blue lines in the music selection board.

2912 A2225 (25c) brt org red, brt yel grn & multi .50 .50

No. 2912 has bright colors, less shading and light blue lines in the music selection board.

Serpentine Die Cut 11.5 Vert.

2912A A2225 (25c) brt org red, brt yel grn & multi .50 .50

Serpentine Die Cut 9.8 Vert.

2912B A2225 (25c) dk red, dk yel grn & multi .50 .50

See No. 3132.

Perf. 9.8 Vert.

2913 A2212 32c bl, tan, brn, red & lt bl .60 .20
- *a.* Imperf., pair *45.00*

No. 2913 has pronounced light blue shading in the flag and red "1995" at left bottom. See No. 3133.

2914 A2212 32c bl, yel brn, red & gray .60 .20

No. 2914 has pale gray shading in the flag and blue "1995" at left bottom.

Serpentine Die Cut 8.7 Vert.

2915 A2212 32c multi .60 .30

Serpentine Die Cut 9.8 Vert.

2915A A2212 32c dk bl, tan, brn, red & lt bl .60 .20
- *h.* Imperf., pair —
- *i.* Tan omitted *2,000.*
- *j.* Double die cutting 30.00 —

On No. 2915Ai, all other colors except brown are severely shifted.

Serpentine Die Cut 11.5 Vert.

2915B A2212 32c As #2915A .60 .60

Serpentine Die Cut 10.9 Vert.

2915C A2212 32c As #2915A 1.00 .40

Serpentine Die Cut 9.8 Vert.

2915D A2212 32c dk bl, tan, brn, red & lt bl .60 .60

Die cutting on No. 2915A shows either 10 serpentine "peaks" on each side, 11 peaks on the left side and 10 peaks on the right side, or 10 peaks on the left side and 11 peaks on the right side. The last configuration is considered by specialists to be an error, and it is rare.

Stamps on multiples of No. 2915A touch, and are on a peelable backing the same size as the stamps, while those of No. 2915D are separated on the peelable backing, which is larger than the stamps.

No. 2915D has red "1997" at left bottom; No. 2915A has red "1996" at left bottom.

Sky on No. 3133 shows color gradation at lower right not on No. 2915D, and it has blue "1996" at left bottom.

Booklet Stamps

Perf. 10.8x9.8 on 2 or 3 Adjacent Sides

2916 A2212 32c bl, tan, brn, red & lt bl .65 .20
- *a.* Booklet pane of 10 6.50
- *b.* As "a," imperf —

Die Cut

2919 A2230 32c multi .60 .20
- *a.* Booklet pane of 18 11.00
- *b.* Vert. pair, no die cutting btwn. —

Serpentine Die Cut 8.7 on 2, 3 or 4 Adjacent Sides

2920 A2212 32c Large blue "1995" date .60 .20
- *a.* Booklet pane of 20+label 12.00
- *b.* Small blue "1995" date 4.50 .35
- *c.* As "b," booklet pane of 20+label 110.00
- *f.* As #2920, pane of 15+label *9.00* —
- *g.* As "a," partial pane of 10, 3 stamps and parts of 7 stamps printed on backing liner —
- *h.* As #2920, bklt. pane of 15 *35.00*
- *i.* As No. 2920, imperf pair —

Serpentine Die Cut 11.3 on 3 sides

2920D A2212 32c Dated blue "1996" .70 .25
- *e.* Booklet pane of 10 7.50

#2920D is dated "1996." Date on #2920 is nearly twice as large as date on #2920b. #2920f comes in various configurations.

No. 2920h is a pane of 16 with one stamp removed. The missing stamp is the lower right stamp in the pane or (more rarely) the upper left stamp. No. 2920h cannot be made from No. 2920f, a pane of 15 + label. The label is located in the sixth row of the pane and is die cut. If the label is removed, an impression of the die cutting appears on the backing paper.

Serpentine Die Cut 9.8 on 2 or 3 Adjacent Sides

2921 A2212 32c dk bl, tan, brn, red & lt bl, red "1996" date .75 .20
- *a.* Booklet pane of 10, red "1996" date 7.50
- *b.* As #2921, red "1997" date .75 .20
- *c.* As "a," red "1997" date 7.50
- *d.* Booklet pane of 5 + label, red "1997" date 3.75
- *e.* As "a," imperf *300.00*

Issued: #2902, 2905, 3/10/95; #2908-2909, 2911-2912, 2919, 3/17/95; #2915, 2920, 4/18/95; #2897, 2913-2914, 2916, 5/19/95; #2920d, 1/20/96; #2904B, 2912B, 2915D, 2921d, 1/24/97; #2903-2904, 3/16/96; #2915A, 5/21/97; #2907, 2921, 5/21/96; #2902B, 2904A, 2906, 2910, 2912A, 2915B, 6/15/96; #2915C, 5/21/96.

See Nos. 3132-3133.

Scott values for used self-adhesive stamps are for examples either on piece or off piece.

Great Americans Issue

A2248 A2249

A2250 A2251

A2253 A2255

A2256 A2257

A2258

Perf. 11.2, Serpentine Die Cut 11.7x11.5 (#2941-2942)

1995-99 **Engr.**

Self-Adhesive (#2941-2942)

2933	A2248 32c brown	.60	.20
2934	A2249 32c green	.60	.20
2935	A2250 32c lake	.60	.20
2936	A2251 32c blue	.60	.20
2938	A2253 46c carmine	.90	.20
2940	A2255 55c green	1.10	.20
a.	Imperf., pair	—	
2941	A2256 55c black	1.10	.20
2942	A2257 77c blue	1.50	.20
2943	A2258 78c bright violet	1.60	.20
a.	78c dull violet	1.60	.20
b.	78c pale violet	1.75	.30
	Nos. 2933-2943 (9)	8.60	1.80

Issued: #2933, 9/13; 46c, 10/20; 55c, 7/11; 78c, 8/18; #2934, 5/26/96; #2935, 4/3/98; #2936, 7/16/98; #2942, 11/9/98; #2941, 7/17/99.

Love

Cherub from Sistine Madonna, by Raphael

A2263 A2264

Litho. & Engr.

1995, Feb. 1 ***Perf. 11.2***

2948 A2263 (32c) multicolored .60 .20

Self-Adhesive

Die Cut

2949 A2264 (32c) multicolored .60 .20
- *a.* Booklet pane of 20 + label 12.00
- *b.* As No. 2949, red (engr.) omitted *450.00*
- *c.* As "a," red (engr.) omitted *9,000.*
- *d.* Red (engr.) missing (CM) —

No. 2949d must be collected se-tenant with a normal stamp.

Florida Statehood, 150th Anniv.

A2265

1995, Mar. 3 **Litho.** ***Perf. 11.1***

2950 A2265 32c multicolored .60 .20

Earth Day

Earth Clean-Up A2266

Solar Energy A2267

Tree Planting A2268

Beach Clean-Up A2269

1995, Apr. 20 **Litho.** ***Perf. 11.1x11***

2951	A2266 32c multicolored	.60	.20
2952	A2267 32c multicolored	.60	.20
2953	A2268 32c multicolored	.60	.20
2954	A2269 32c multicolored	.60	.20
a.	Block of 4, #2951-2954	2.40	1.75

Richard M. Nixon

Richard M. Nixon, 37th President (1913-94) — A2270

Litho. & Engr.

1995, Apr. 26 ***Perf. 11.2***

2955 A2270 32c multicolored .60 .20
- *a.* Red (engr.) missing (CM) *1,250.*

No. 2955 is known with red (engr. "Richard Nixon") inverted, and with red (engr.) omitted but only half of Nixon portrait present, both from printer's waste.

No. 2955a shows a complete Nixon portrait.

Black Heritage Series

Bessie Coleman, Aviator — A2271

1995, Apr. 27 **Engr.** ***Perf. 11.2***

2956 A2271 32c red & black .60 .20

Love

A2272

A2273

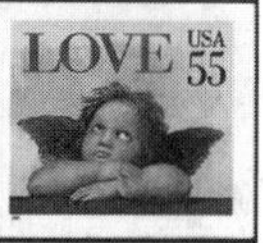

A2274

Cherubs from Sistine Madonna, by Raphael

Litho. & Engr.

1995, May 12 ***Perf. 11.2***

2957 A2272 32c multicolored .60 .20

2958 A2273 55c multicolored 1.10 .20

BOOKLET STAMPS

Perf. 9.8x10.8

2959 A2272 32c multicolored .60 .20
- *a.* Booklet pane of 10 6.00 *3.25*
- *b.* As "a," imperf —

Self-Adhesive

Die Cut

2960 A2274 55c multicolored 1.10 .20
- *a.* Booklet pane of 20 + label 22.50

Recreational Sports

Volleyball A2275

Softball A2276

Bowling A2277

Tennis A2278

Golf A2279

1995, May 20 **Litho.** ***Perf. 11.2***

2961	A2275 32c multicolored	.60	.20
2962	A2276 32c multicolored	.60	.20
2963	A2277 32c multicolored	.60	.20
2964	A2278 32c multicolored	.60	.20
2965	A2279 32c multicolored	.60	.20
a.	Vert. strip of 5, #2961-2965	3.00	2.00
b.	As "a," imperf	*2,500.*	
c.	As "a," yellow omitted	*2,500.*	
d.	As "a," yel, bl & mag omitted	*2,500.*	

Prisoners of War & Missing in Action

A2280

1995, May 29 ***Perf. 11.2***

2966 A2280 32c multicolored .60 .20

Legends of Hollywood

Marilyn Monroe (1926-62) — A2281

1995, June 1 **Photo.** ***Perf. 11.1***

2967 A2281 32c multicolored .60 .20
- *a.* Imperf., pair *500.00*

Texas Statehood

A2282

1995, June 16 **Litho.** ***Perf. 11.2***

2968 A2282 32c multicolored .60 .20

Great Lakes Lighthouses

Split Rock, Lake Superior A2283

St. Joseph, Lake Michigan A2284

Spectacle Reef, Lake Huron — A2285

Marblehead, Lake Erie — A2286

Thirty Mile Point, Lake Ontario — A2287

Perf. 11.2 Vert.

1995, June 17 Photo.

Booklet Stamps

2969	A2283	32c multicolored	.60	.20
2970	A2284	32c multicolored	.60	.20
2971	A2285	32c multicolored	.60	.20
2972	A2286	32c multicolored	.60	.20
2973	A2287	32c multicolored	.60	.20
a.		Booklet pane, #2969-2973	3.00	*2.75*

U.N., 50th Anniv.

A2288

1995, June 26 Engr. *Perf. 11.2*

2974	A2288	32c blue	.60	.20

Civil War

A2289

Designs: a, Monitor and Virginia. b, Robert E. Lee. c, Clara Barton. d, Ulysses S. Grant. e, Battle of Shiloh. f, Jefferson Davis. g, David Farragut. h, Frederick Douglass. i, Raphael Semmes. j, Abraham Lincoln. k, Harriet Tubman. l, Stand Watie. m, Joseph E. Johnston. n, Winfield Hancock. o, Mary Chesnut. p, Battle of Chancellorsville. q, William T. Sherman. r, Phoebe Pember. s, "Stonewall" Jackson. t, Battle of Gettysburg.

1995, June 29 Photo. *Perf. 10.1*

2975	A2289	Pane of 20	12.00	—
a.-t.		32c any single	.60	.20
u.		As "No. 2975," a.-e. imperf, f.-j. part perf	—	
v.		As "No. 2975," k.-t. imperf, f.-j. part perf	—	
w.		As "No. 2975," imperf	*1,500.*	
x.		Block of 9 (f.-h., k.-m., p.-r.), k.-l., p.-q. imperf vert.	—	

American Folk Art Series

Carousel Horses

A2290

A2291

A2292

A2293

1995, July 21 Litho. *Perf. 11*

2976	A2290	32c multicolored	.60	.20
2977	A2291	32c multicolored	.60	.20
2978	A2292	32c multicolored	.60	.20
2979	A2293	32c multicolored	.60	.20
a.		Block of 4, #2976-2979	2.40	2.00

Woman Suffrage

A2294

Litho. & Engr.

1995, Aug. 26 *Perf. 11.1x11*

2980	A2294	32c multicolored	.60	.20
a.		Black (engr.) omitted	425.00	
b.		Imperf, pair	*1,500.*	

No. 2980a is valued in the grade of fine. Very fine examples sell for much more.

World War II

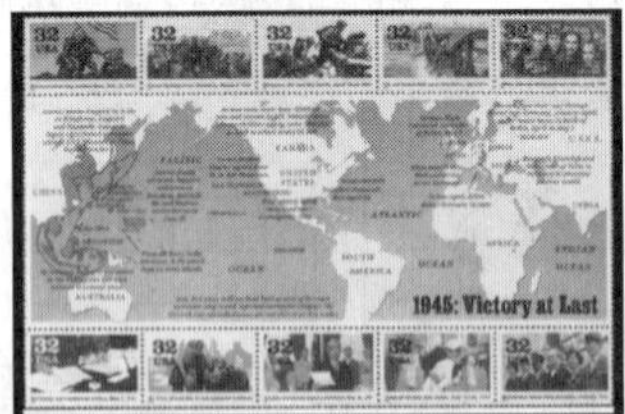

A2295

Designs and events of 1945:

a, Marines raise flag on Iwo Jima. b, Fierce fighting frees Manila by March 3, 1945. c, Soldiers advancing (Okinawa, the last big battle). d, Destroyed bridge (U.S. and Soviets link up at Elbe River). e, Allies liberate Holocaust survivors. f, Germany surrenders at Reims. g, Refugees (by 1945, World War II has uprooted millions). h, Truman announces Japan's surrender. i, Sailor kissing nurse (news of victory hits home). j, Hometowns honor their returning veterans.

Central label is size of 15 stamps and shows world map with extent of Axis control and Allied operations.

Illustration reduced.

Litho. & Engr.

1995, Sept. 2 *Perf. 11.1*

2981	A2295	Block of 10 + label	6.00	5.50
a.-j.		32c any single	.60	.30

No. 2981 has selvage at left and right and either top or bottom.

American Music Series

Louis Armstrong A2296

Coleman Hawkins A2297

James P. Johnson A2298

Jelly Roll Morton A2299

Charlie Parker A2300

Eubie Blake A2301

Charles Mingus A2302

Thelonious Monk A2303

John Coltrane A2304

Erroll Garner A2305

1995 Litho. *Perf. 11.1x11*

2982	A2296	32c white "32c"	.60	.20
2983	A2297	32c multicolored	.80	.20
2984	A2296	32c black "32c"	.80	.20
2985	A2298	32c multicolored	.80	.20
2986	A2299	32c multicolored	.80	.20
2987	A2300	32c multicolored	.80	.20
2988	A2301	32c multicolored	.80	.20
2989	A2302	32c multicolored	.80	.20
2990	A2303	32c multicolored	.80	.20
2991	A2304	32c multicolored	.80	.20
2992	A2305	32c multicolored	.80	.20
a.		Vert. block of 10, #2983-2992, top selvage	8.00	—
b.		Pane of 20, dark blue (inscriptions) omitted	—	

Issued: No. 2982, 9/1/95; others, 9/16/95.

Garden Flowers

A2306

A2307

A2308

A2309

A2310

Perf. 10.9 Vert.

1995, Sept. 19 Litho. & Engr.

Booklet Stamps

2993	A2306	32c Aster	.60	.20
2994	A2307	32c Chrysanthemum	.60	.20
2995	A2308	32c Dahlia	.60	.20
2996	A2309	32c Hydrangea	.60	.20
2997	A2310	32c Rudbeckia	.60	.20
a.		Booklet pane, #2993-2997	3.00	*2.25*

Eddie Rickenbacker Issue

A2311

1995, Sept. 25 Photo. *Perf. 11¼*

2998	A2311	60c Small "1995"	1.25	.25
a.		Large "1995"	1.25	.25

Eddie Rickenbacker (1890-1973), Aviator.

Date on No. 2998 is 1mm long, on No. 2998a 1½mm long.

Issued: #2998a, 2000.

Republic of Palau

A2312

1995, Sept. 29 Litho. *Perf. 11.1*

2999 A2312 32c multicolored .60 .20

Comic Strips

A2313

Designs: a, The Yellow Kid. b, Katzenjammer Kids. c, Little Nemo in Slumberland. d, Bringing Up Father. e, Krazy Kat. f, Rube Goldberg's Inventions. g, Toonerville Folks. h, Gasoline Alley. i, Barney Google. j, Little Orphan Annie. k, Popeye. l, Blondie. m, Dick Tracy. n, Alley Oop. o, Nancy. p, Flash Gordon. q, Li'l Abner. r, Terry and the Pirates. s, Prince Valiant. t, Brenda Starr, Reporter.

1995, Oct. 1 Photo. *Perf. 10.1*

3000 A2313 Pane of 20 12.00 —
a.-t. 32c any single .60 .20
u. As No. 3000, a.-h. imperf., i.-l. part perf —
v. As No. 3000, m.-t. imperf., i.-l. part perf —
w. As No. 3000, a.-l. imperf., m.-t. imperf vert. —

Inscriptions on back of each stamp describe the comic strip.

U.S. Naval Academy, 150th Anniv.

A2314

1995, Oct. 10 Litho. *Perf. 10.9*

3001 A2314 32c multicolored .60 .20

Literary Arts Series

Tennessee Williams (1911-83) A2315

1995, Oct. 13 Litho. *Perf. 11.1*

3002 A2315 32c multicolored .60 .20

Christmas

Madonna and Child — A2316

Santa Claus Entering Chimney A2317

Child Holding Jumping Jack A2318

Child Holding Tree — A2319

Santa Claus Working on Sled — A2320

Midnight Angel A2321

Children Sledding A2322

1995 Litho. & Engr. *Perf. 11.2*

3003 A2316 32c multicolored .60 .20
c. Black (engr. denomination) omitted 250.00

Booklet Stamp
Perf. 9.8x10.9

3003A A2316 32c multicolored .65 .20
b. Booklet pane of 10 6.50 4.00

Lithographed

3004 A2317 32c multicolored .60 .20
3005 A2318 32c multicolored .60 .20
3006 A2319 32c multicolored .60 .20
3007 A2320 32c multicolored .60 .20
a. Block or strip of 4, #3004-3007 2.40 1.25
b. Bklt. pane, 3 ea #3004-3005, 2 ea #3006-3007 6.00 4.00
c. Bklt. pane, 2 ea #3004-3005, 3 ea #3006-3007 6.00 4.00
d. As "a," imperf. 600.00

Self-Adhesive Stamps
Photogravure
Serpentine Die Cut

3008 A2320 32c multicolored .75 .20
3009 A2318 32c multicolored .75 .20
3010 A2317 32c multicolored .75 .20
3011 A2319 32c multicolored .75 .20
a. Booklet pane of 20, 5 each #3008-3011 + label 15.00

Lithographed

3012 A2321 32c multicolored .60 .20
a. Bklt. pane of 20 + label 12.00
c. Bklt. pane of 15 + label 9.00
d. Booklet pane of 15 —

No. 3003, Madonna and Child, by Giotto di Bondone.

No. 3012a comes either with no die cutting in the label (1995 printing) or with die cutting (and deeper colors) from the 1996 printing.

No. 3012d is a pane of 16 with one stamp removed. The missing stamp can be from either row 1, 2, 3, 7 or 8 of the pane. The missing stamp is from the second row, either from the top or bottom, of the pane. No. 3012d cannot be made from No. 3012c, a pane of 15 + label. The label is die cut. If the label is removed, an impression of the die cutting appears on the backing paper.

Photogravure
Die Cut

3013 A2322 32c multicolored .60 .20
a. Booklet pane of 18 11.00

Self-Adhesive Coil Stamps
Serpentine Die Cut Vert.

3014 A2320 32c multicolored .60 .30
3015 A2318 32c multicolored .60 .30
3016 A2317 32c multicolored .60 .30
3017 A2319 32c multicolored .60 .30
a. Strip of 4, #3014-3017 2.40

Lithographed

3018 A2321 32c multicolored .60 .30

#3014-3018 were only available through the Philatelic Fullfillment Center in Kansas City.

Issued: #3003-3003A, 3012-3013, 3018, 10/19; #3004-3011, 3014-3017, 9/30.

Antique Automobiles

1893 Duryea A2323

1894 Haynes A2324

1898 Columbia A2325

1899 Winton A2326

1901 White A2327

1995, Nov. 3 Photo. *Perf. 10.1x11.1*

3019 A2323 32c multicolored .60 .20
3020 A2324 32c multicolored .60 .20
3021 A2325 32c multicolored .60 .20
3022 A2326 32c multicolored .60 .20
3023 A2327 32c multicolored .60 .20
a. Vert. or horiz. strip of 5, #3019-3023 3.00 2.00

Vert. or horiz. strips are all in different order.

Utah Statehood Centenary

Delicate Arch, Arches Natl. Park — A2328

1996, Jan. 4 Litho. *Perf. 11.1*

3024 A2328 32c multicolored .60 .20

Garden Flowers

A2329

A2330

A2331 A2332

A2333

Perf. 10.9 Vert.

1996, Jan. 19 Litho. & Engr.

Booklet Stamps

3025 A2329 32c Crocus .60 .20
3026 A2330 32c Winter Aconite .60 .20
3027 A2331 32c Pansy .60 .20
3028 A2332 32c Snowdrop .60 .20
3029 A2333 32c Anemone .60 .20
a. Booklet pane, #3025-3029 3.00 2.50
b. As "a," imperf —

Love

Cherub from Sistine Madonna — A2334

Serpentine Die Cut 11¼x11¾

1996, Jan. 20

Self-Adhesive
Booklet Stamp

3030 A2334 32c by Raphael .60 .20
a. Booklet pane of 20 + label 12.00
b. Booklet pane of 15 + label 9.00
c. Red (engr.) omitted 350.00
d. Red (engr.) missing (CM) —

No. 3030d must be collected se-tenant with a stamp bearing the red engraving.

Flora and Fauna Series

Kestrel Type of 1995 and

Red-headed Woodpecker A2335

Eastern Bluebird A2336

Red Fox A2339

Ring-necked Pheasant A2350

Coral Pink Rose — A2351

Serpentine Die Cut 10¾

1996-2000 Litho.

Self-Adhesive

3031 A1841 1c multicolored .20 .20

Serpentine Die Cut 11¼

3031A A1841 1c multicolored .20 .20

No. 3031A has blue inscription and year.

Perf. 11

3032 A2335 2c multicolored .20 .20
3033 A2336 3c multicolored .20 .20

Serpentine Die Cut 11½x11¼

Self-Adhesive

3036 A2339 $1 multicolored 2.00 .50
a. Serpentine die cut 11¾x11 2.00 .50

COIL STAMPS

Perf. 9¾ Vert.

3044 A1841 1c small date .20 .20
a. Large date .20 .20
3045 A2335 2c multicolored .20 .20

The tagging of No. 3036 has a bright yellow-green appearance under shortwave ultraviolet light while that of No. 3036a appears light blue green.

Date on #3044 is 1mm long, on #3044a 1.5mm.

Issued: #3032, 2/2/96; #3033, 4/3/96; #3044, 1/20/96; #3036, 8/14/98; #3045, 6/22/99; #3031, 11/19/99; #3031A, 10/00.

Blue Jay & Rose Types of 1993-95

Serpentine Die Cut 10½x10¾ on 3 Sides

1996-2000 Photo.

Self-Adhesive

Booklet Stamps

3048 A1847 20c multicolored .40 .20
a. Booklet pane of 10 4.00
b. Booklet pane of 4 1.60
c. Booklet pane of 6 2.40

Nos. 3048b-3048c are from the vending machine booklet No. BK237 that has a glue strip at the top edge of the top pane, the peelable strip removed and the rouletting line 2mm lower than on No. 3048a, when the panes are compared with the bottoms aligned.

Serpentine Die Cut 11¼x11¾

3049 A1853 32c yel, org, grn & blk .60 .20
a. Booklet pane of 20 + label 12.00
b. Booklet pane of 4 2.75
c. Booklet pane of 5 + label 3.00
d. Booklet pane of 6 3.60

Serpentine Die Cut 11¼ on 3 Sides

3050 A2350 20c multicolored .40 .20
a. Bklt. pane of 10, all stamps upright 4.00
b. Serpentine die cut 11 .40 .20
c. As "b," booklet pane of 10, all stamps upright 4.00

Serpentine Die Cut 10½x11 on 3 Sides

3051 A2350 20c multicolored .60 .20

Serpentine die cut 10.6x10.4 on 3 sides

3051A A2350 20c multicolored 3.75 .50
b. Booklet pane of 5, 4 #3051, 1 #3051A turned sideways at top 6.00
c. Booklet pane of 5, 4 #3051, 1 #3051A turned sideways at bottom 6.00

No. 3051 represents the eight upright stamps on the booklet panes Nos. 3051Ab and 3051Ac. The two stamps turned sideways on those panes are No. 3051A.

Serpentine Die Cut 11½x11¼ on 2, 3 or 4 Sides

3052 A2351 33c multicolored .80 .20
a. Booklet pane of 4 3.20
b. Booklet pane of 5 + label 4.00
c. Booklet pane of 6 4.80
d. Booklet pane of 20 + label 13.00
i. Imperf, pair —

Serpentine Die Cut 10¾x10½ on 2 or 3 sides

3052E A2351 33c multicolored .65 .20
f. Booklet pane of 20 13.00
g. As "f," all 12 stamps on one side with black ("33 USA," etc.) omitted —
h. Horiz. pair, imperf between —

COIL STAMPS

Serpentine Die Cut 11½ Vert.

3053 A1847 20c multicolored .40 .20

Serpentine Die Cut 9¾ Vert.

Litho.

Self-Adhesive

3054 A1853 32c yel, mag, blk & grn .60 .20
a. Imperf, pair 90.00
b. Blk, yel & grn omitted —
c. Blk, yel & grn omitted, imperf pair —
d. Black omitted —
e. Black omitted, imperf pair —

Nos. 3054b and 3054d also are miscut and with shifted die cuttings.

3055 A2350 20c multicolored .40 .20
a. Imperf, pair 200.00

Issued: #3048, 3053, 8/2/96; #3049, 10/24/96; #3054, 8/1/97; #3050, 3055, 7/31/98; #3051, 7/99; #3052, 8/13/99; #3052E, 4/7/00.

Black Heritage Series

Ernest E. Just (1883-1941), Marine Biologist — A2358

1996, Feb. 1 Litho. *Perf. 11.1*

3058 A2358 32c gray & black .60 .20

Smithsonian Institution, 150th Anniv.

A2359

1996, Feb. 7 *Perf. 11.1*

3059 A2359 32c multicolored .60 .20

Chinese New Year

Year of the Rat — A2360

1996, Feb. 8 Photo. *Perf. 11.1*

3060 A2360 32c multicolored .60 .20
a. Imperf, pair —

Pioneers of Communication

Eadweard Muybridge A2361

Ottmar Mergenthaler — A2362

Frederic E. Ives A2363

William Dickson A2364

1996, Feb. 22 Litho. *Perf. 11.1x11*

3061 A2361 32c multicolored .60 .20
3062 A2362 32c multicolored .60 .20
3063 A2363 32c multicolored .60 .20
3064 A2364 32c multicolored .60 .20
a. Block or strip, #3061-3064 2.40 2.00

Muybridge (1830-1904), Photographer; Mergenthaler (1854-99), Inventor of Linotype; Ives (1856-1937), Developer of Halftone Process; Dickson (1860-1935), Co-developer of Kinetoscope.

Fulbright Scholarships, 50th Anniv.

A2365

Litho. & Engr.

1996, Feb. 28 *Perf. 11.1*

3065 A2365 32c multicolored .60 .20

Jacqueline Cochran

A2366

Litho. & Engr.

1996, Mar. 9 *Perf. 11.1*

3066 A2366 50c multicolored 1.00 .20
a. Black (eng.) omitted 60.00

Cochran (1910-80), Pilot.

Marathon

A2367

1996, Apr. 11 Litho. *Perf. 11.1*

3067 A2367 32c multicolored .60 .20

1996 Summer Olympic Games

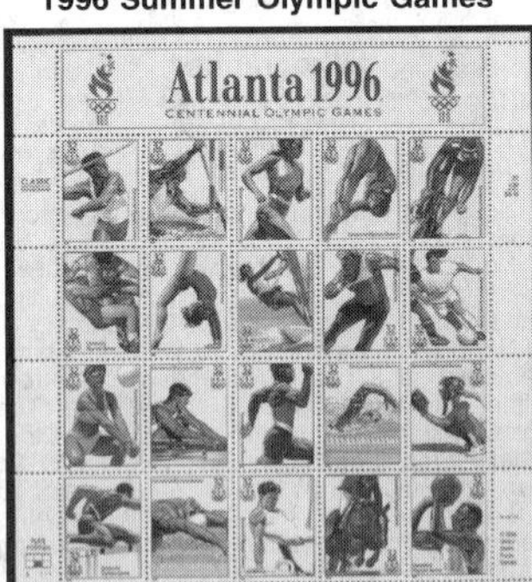

A2368

Designs: a, Decathlon (javelin). b, Canoeing. c, Women's running. d, Women's diving. e, Cycling. f, Freestyle wrestling. g, Women's gymnastics. h, Women's sailboarding. i, Shot put. j, Women's soccer. k, Beach volleyball. l, Rowing. m, Sprints. n, Women's swimming. o, Women's softball. p, Hurdles. q, Swimming. r, Gymnastics (pommel horse). s, Equestrian. t, Basketball.

1996, May 2 Photo. *Perf. 10.1*

3068 A2368 Pane of 20 12.00 —
a.-t. 32c any single .60 .20
u. As No. 3068, imperf 1,400.
v. As No. 3068, back inscriptions omitted on a, f, k, p, incorrect back inscriptions on others —

Inscription on back of each stamp describes the sport shown.

Georgia O'Keeffe (1887-1986)

A2369

Perf. 11.6x11.4

1996, May 23 Photo.

3069 A2369 32c multicolored .65 .20
a. Imperf, pair 175.00

Tennessee Statehood Bicentennial

A2370

1996, May 31 Photo. *Perf. 11.1*

3070 A2370 32c multicolored .60 .20

Booklet Stamp

Self-Adhesive

Serpentine Die Cut 9.9x10.8

3071 A2370 32c multicolored .60 .30
a. Booklet pane of 20 12.00
b. Horiz. pair, no die cutting btwn. —
c. Imperf., pair —
d. Horiz. pair, imperf vert. —

American Indian Dances

A2371

A2372

A2373

A2374

A2375

1996, June 7 Litho. *Perf. 11.1*

3072 A2371 32c Fancy .60 .20
3073 A2372 32c Butterfly .60 .20
3074 A2373 32c Traditional .60 .20
3075 A2374 32c Raven .60 .20
3076 A2375 32c Hoop .60 .20
a. Strip of 5, #3072-3076 3.00 2.00

Prehistoric Animals

A2376

A2377

A2378

A2379

1996, June 8 Litho. *Perf. 11.1x11*

3077 A2376 32c Eohippus .60 .20
3078 A2377 32c Woolly Mammoth .60 .20
3079 A2378 32c Mastodon .60 .20
3080 A2379 32c Saber-tooth Cat .60 .20
a. Block or strip, #3077-3080 2.40 1.50

A2380

A2381

Breast Cancer Awareness

1996, June 15 Litho. *Perf. 11.1*

3081 A2380 32c multicolored .60 .20

Legends of Hollywood

James Dean (1931-55)

1996, June 24 Photo. *Perf. 11.1*

3082 A2381 32c multicolored .60 .20
a. Imperf. pair *325.00*
b. As "a," red (USA 32c) missing (CM) and tan ("JAMES DEAN") omitted —
c. As "a," tan ("JAMES DEAN") omitted —
d. As "a," top stamp red missing (CM) and tan ("JAMES DEAN") omitted, bottom stamp tan omitted —

Nos. 3082c-3082d come from the same error pane. The top row is No. 3082b, rows 2-4 are No. 3082c. No. 3082d is a vertical pair with one stamp from No. 3082b at top and one stamp from 3082c at bottom.

Folk Heroes

A2382

A2383

A2384

A2385

1996, July 11 Litho. *Perf. 11.1x11*

3083 A2382 32c multicolored .60 .20
3084 A2383 32c multicolored .60 .20
3085 A2384 32c multicolored .60 .20
3086 A2385 32c multicolored .60 .20
a. Block or strip, #3083-3086 2.40 2.00

Myron's Discobolus A2386

Young Corn, by Grant Wood A2387

Centennial Olympic Games

1996, July 19 Engr. *Perf. 11.1*

3087 A2386 32c brown .65 .20

Sheet margin of the pane of 20 is lithographed.

Iowa Statehood, 150th Anniversary

1996, Aug. 1 Litho. *Perf. 11.1*

3088 A2387 32c multicolored .60 .20

Booklet Stamp
Self-Adhesive
Serpentine Die Cut 11.6x11.4

3089 A2387 32c multicolored .60 .30
a. Booklet pane of 20 12.00

Rural Free Delivery, Cent.

A2388

Litho. & Engr.

1996, Aug. 7 *Perf. 11.2x11*

3090 A2388 32c multicolored .60 .20

Riverboats

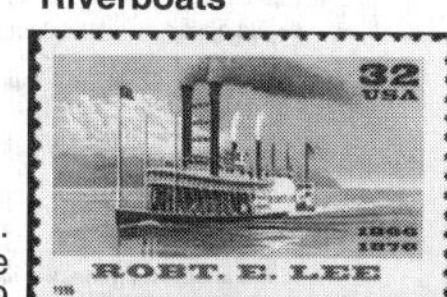

Robt. E. Lee A2389

Sylvan Dell A2390

Far West A2391

Rebecca Everingham — A2392

Bailey Gatzert A2393

Self-Adhesive
Serpentine Die Cut 11x11.1

1996, Aug. 22 Photo.

3091 A2389 32c multicolored .60 .20
3092 A2390 32c multicolored .60 .20
3093 A2391 32c multicolored .60 .20
3094 A2392 32c multicolored .60 .20
3095 A2393 32c multicolored .60 .20
a. Vert. strip of 5, #3091-3095 3.00
b. As "a," with special die cutting *75.00 50.00*

The serpentine die cutting runs through the peelable backing to which Nos. 3091-3095 are affixed. No. 3095a exists with stamps in different sequences.

On the long side of each stamp in No. 3095b, the die cutting is missing 3 "perforations" between the stamps, one near each end and one in the middle. This allows a complete strip to be removed from the backing paper for use on a first day cover.

American Music Series
Big Band Leaders

Count Basie A2394

Tommy & Jimmy Dorsey A2395

Glenn Miller A2396

Benny Goodman A2397

Songwriters

Harold Arlen A2398

Johnny Mercer A2399

Dorothy Fields A2400

Hoagy Carmichael A2401

1996, Sept. 11 Litho. *Perf. 11.1x11*

3096 A2394 32c multicolored .60 .20
3097 A2395 32c multicolored .60 .20
3098 A2396 32c multicolored .60 .20
3099 A2397 32c multicolored .60 .20
a. Block or strip, #3096-3099 2.40 1.75
3100 A2398 32c multicolored .70 .20
3101 A2399 32c multicolored .70 .20
3102 A2400 32c multicolored .70 .20
3103 A2401 32c multicolored .70 .20
a. Block or strip, #3100-3103 2.80 1.75

Literary Arts Series

F. Scott Fitzgerald (1896-1940) — A2402

1996, Sept. 27 Photo. *Perf. 11.1*

3104 A2402 23c multicolored .45 .20

Endangered Species

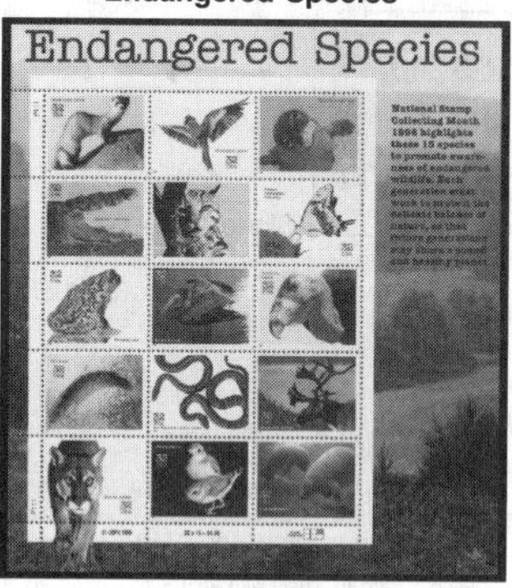

A2403

a, Black-footed ferret. b, Thick-billed parrot. c, Hawaiian monk seal. d, American crocodile. e, Ocelot. f, Schaus swallowtail butterfly. g, Wyoming toad. h, Brown pelican. i, California condor. j, Gila trout. k, San Francisco garter snake. l, Woodland caribou. m, Florida panther. n, Piping plover. o, Florida manatee.

1996, Oct. 2 Litho. *Perf. 11.1x11*

3105 A2403 Pane of 15 9.00 —
a.-o. 32c any single .60 .20

See Mexico No. 1995.

Computer Technology

A2404

Perf. 10.9x11.1

1996, Oct. 8 Litho. & Engr.

3106 A2404 32c multicolored .60 .20

Christmas

Madonna and Child from Adoration of the Shepherds, by Paolo de Matteis — A2405

Family at Fireplace A2406

Decorating Tree A2407

Dreaming of Santa Claus A2408

Holiday Shopping A2409

Skaters — A2410

1996 Litho. & Engr. *Perf. 11.1x11.2*

3107 A2405 32c multicolored .60 .20

Litho.

Perf. 11.3

3108 A2406 32c multicolored .60 .20
3109 A2407 32c multicolored .60 .20
3110 A2408 32c multicolored .60 .20
3111 A2409 32c multicolored .60 .20
a. Block or strip, #3108-3111 2.40 1.75
b. Strip of 4, #3110-3111, 3108-3109, with #3109 imperf, #3108 imperf at right —

Self-Adhesive Booklet Stamps

Litho. & Engr.

Serpentine Die Cut 10 on 2, 3 or 4 Sides

3112 A2405 32c multicolored .60 .20
a. Booklet pane of 20 + label 12.00
b. No die cutting, pair *75.00*
c. As "a," no die cutting —

Litho.

Serpentine Die Cut 11.8x11.5 on 2, 3 or 4 Sides

3113 A2406 32c multicolored .60 .20
3114 A2407 32c multicolored .60 .20
3115 A2408 32c multicolored .60 .20
3116 A2409 32c multicolored .60 .20
a. Bklt. pane, 5 ea #3113-3116 12.00
b. As "a," no die cutting *3,000.*

Photo.

Die Cut

3117 A2410 32c multicolored .60 .20
a. Booklet pane of 18 11.00

Issued: #3108-3111, 3113-3117, 10/8; #3107, 3112, 11/1.

Hanukkah

A2411

Serpentine Die Cut 11.1

1996, Oct. 22 Photo.

Self-Adhesive

3118 A2411 32c multicolored .60 .20

See Nos. 3352, 3547. See Israel No. 1289.

Cycling

Souvenir Sheet

A2412

1996, Nov. 1 Photo. *Perf. 11x11.1*

3119 A2412 Sheet of 2 2.00 2.00
a. 50c orange & multi 1.00 1.00
b. 50c blue green & multi 1.00 1.00

Chinese New Year

Year of the Ox A2413

1997, Jan. 5 Photo. *Perf. 11.2*

3120 A2413 32c multicolored .60 .20

Black Heritage Series

Brig. Gen. Benjamin O. Davis, Sr. (1880-1970) A2414

Self-Adhesive

Serpentine Die Cut 11.4

1997, Jan. 28 Litho.

3121 A2414 32c multicolored .60 .20

Statue of Liberty Type of 1994

Serpentine Die Cut 11 on 2, 3 or 4 Sides

1997, Feb. 1 Photo.

Self-Adhesive

3122 A1951 32c red, lt bl, dk bl & yel .60 .20
a. Booklet pane of 20 + label 12.00
b. Booklet pane of 4 2.50
c. Booklet pane of 5 + label 3.20
d. Booklet pane of 6 3.60
h. As "a," no die cutting —

Serpentine Die Cut 11.5x11.8 on 2, 3 or 4 Sides

1997 Photo.

Self-Adhesive

3122E A1951 32c red, lt bl, dk bl & yel 1.10 .20
f. Booklet pane of 20 + label 35.00
g. Booklet pane of 6 7.00

Love

A2415

Swans — A2416

Serpentine Die Cut 11.8x11.6 on 2, 3 or 4 Sides

1997, Feb. 4 Litho.

Self-Adhesive

3123 A2415 32c multicolored .60 .20
a. Booklet pane of 20 + label 12.00
b. No die cutting, pair *175.00*
c. As "a," no die cutting *1,750.*
d. As "a," black omitted —

Serpentine Die Cut 11.6x11.8 on 2, 3 or 4 Sides

3124 A2416 55c multicolored 1.00 .20
a. Booklet pane of 20 + label 21.00

Helping Children Learn

A2417

Serpentine Die Cut 11.6x11.7

1997, Feb. 18 Photo.

Self-Adhesive

3125 A2417 32c multicolored .60 .20

Merian Botanical Prints

Citron, Moth, Larvae, Pupa, Beetle A2418

Flowering Pineapple, Cockroaches A2419

No. 3128 (r), No. 3129 (l), No. 3128a below

Serpentine Die Cut 10.9x10.2 on 2, 3 or 4 Sides

1997, Mar. 3 Photo.

Self-Adhesive

3126 A2418 32c multicolored .60 .20
3127 A2419 32c multicolored .60 .20
a. Booklet pane of 20, 10 ea #3126-3127 + label 12.00
b. Pair, #3126-3127 1.20
c. Vert. pair, imperf between 500.00

Size: 18.5x24mm

Serpentine Die Cut 11.2x10.8 on 2 or 3 Sides

3128 A2418 32c multicolored .75 .20
a. See footnote 1.25 .25
b. Booklet pane of 5, 2 ea #3128-3129, 1 #3128a 4.50

3129 A2419 32c multicolored .75 .20
a. See footnote 1.25 .25
b. Booklet pane of 5, 2 ea #3128-3129, 1 #3129a 4.50
c. Pair, #3128-3129 1.50

Nos. 3128a-3129a are placed sideways on the pane and are serpentine die cut 11.2 on top and bottom, 10.8 on left side. The right side is 11.2 broken by a large perf where the stamp meets the vertical perforations of the two stamps above it. See illustration above.

Pacific 97

Sailing Ship — A2420

Stagecoach — A2421

1997, Mar. 13 Engr. *Perf. 11.2*

3130 A2420 32c blue .60 .20
3131 A2421 32c red .60 .20
a. Pair, #3130-3131 1.25 .60

Juke Box and Flag Over Porch Types of 1995

COIL STAMPS

1997, Mar. 14 Photo. *Imperf.*

Self-Adhesive

3132 A2225 (25c) brt org red, brt yel grn & multi .50 .50

Tagged

Serpentine Die Cut 9.9 Vert.

3133 A2212 32c dk bl, tan, brn, red & lt bl .60 .20

Nos. 3132-3133 were issued without backing paper. No. 3132 has simulated perforations ending in black bars at the top and bottom edges of the stamp.

Sky on No. 3133 shows color gradation at lower right that is not on Nos. 2915A or 2915D, and it has blue "1996" at left bottom.

Literary Arts

Thornton Wilder (1897-1975) — A2422

1997, Apr. 17 Litho. *Perf. 11.1*

3134 A2422 32c multicolored .60 .20

Raoul Wallenberg (1912-47)

Wallenberg and Jewish Refugees A2423

1997, Apr. 24 Litho. *Perf. 11.1*

3135 A2423 32c multicolored .60 .20

Dinosaurs

A2424

Designs: a, Ceratosaurus. b, Camptosaurus. c, Camarasaurus. d, Brachiosaurus. e, Goniopholis. f, Stegosaurus. g, Allosaurus. h, Opisthias. i, Edmontonia. j, Einiosaurus. k, Daspletosaurus. l, Palaeosaniwa. m, Corythosaurus. n, Ornithominus. o, Parasaurolophus.
Illustration reduced.

1997, May 1 Litho. *Perf. 11x11.1*

3136	A2424	Sheet of 15	9.00	—
a.-o.		32c any single	.60	.20
p.		As #3136, bottom seven stamps imperf	—	
q.		As #3136, top eight stamp imperf	—	
r.		As #3136, all colors and tagging missing (EP)	—	

Bugs Bunny

A2425

Serpentine Die Cut 11

1997, May 22 Photo.

3137	Pane of 10	6.00	
a.	A2425 32c single	.60	.20
b.	Booklet pane of 9	5.40	
c.	Booklet pane of 1	.60	

Die cutting on #3137b does not extend through the backing paper.

3138	Pane of 10	*125.00*	
a.	A2425 32c single	*2.00*	
b.	Booklet pane of 9	—	
c.	Booklet pane of 1, imperf	—	

Die cutting on #3138b extends through the backing paper. Used examples of #3138a are identical to those of #3137a.

An untagged promotional piece similar to No. 3137c exists on the same backing paper as the booklet pane, with the same design image, but without Bugs' signature and the single stamp. Replacing the stamp is an enlarged "32 / USA" in the same style as used on the stamp.

Pacific 97

Franklin A2426

Washington A2427

1997 Litho. & Engr. *Perf. 10.5x10.4*

3139	Pane of 12	12.00	—
a.	A2426 50c single	1.00	.50
3140	Pane of 12	14.50	—
a.	A2427 60c single	1.20	.60

Selvage on Nos. 3139-3140 is lithographed.
Issued: No. 3139, 5/29; No. 3140, 5/30.

Marshall Plan, 50th Anniv.

Gen. George C. Marshall, Map of Europe — A2428

1997, June 4 *Perf. 11.1*

3141	A2428	32c multicolored	.60	.20

Classic American Aircraft

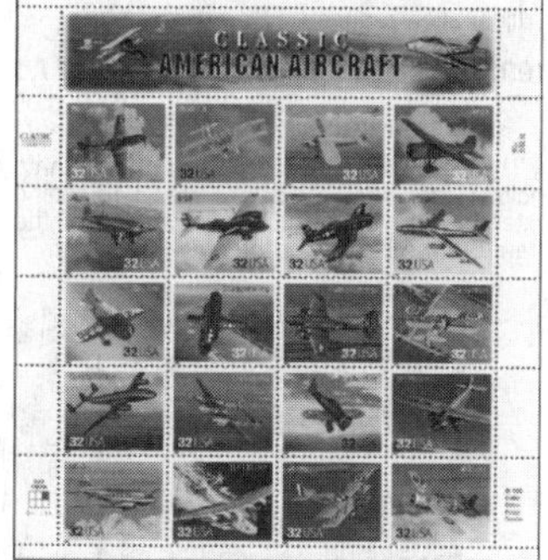

A2429

Designs: a, Mustang. b, Model B. c, Cub. d, Vega. e, Alpha. f, B-10. g, Corsair. h, Stratojet. i, GeeBee. j, Staggerwing. k, Flying Fortress. l, Stearman. m, Constellation. n, Lightning. o, Peashooter. p, Tri-Motor. q, DC-3. r, 314 Clipper. s, Jenny. t, Wildcat.
Illustration reduced.

1997, July 19 Photo. *Perf. 10.1*

3142	A2429	Pane of 20	12.00	—
a.-t.		32c any single	.60	.20

Inscriptions on back of each stamp describe the airplane.

Football Coaches

Bear Bryant A2430

Pop Warner A2431

Vince Lombardi A2432

George Halas A2433

1997 Litho. *Perf. 11.2*

3143	A2430	32c multicolored	.60	.20
3144	A2431	32c multicolored	.60	.20
3145	A2432	32c multicolored	.60	.20
3146	A2433	32c multicolored	.60	.20
a.		Block or strip, #3143-3146	2.40	1.75

With Red Bar Above Coach's Name

Perf. 11

3147	A2432	32c multicolored	.60	.30
3148	A2430	32c multicolored	.60	.30
3149	A2431	32c multicolored	.60	.30
3150	A2433	32c multicolored	.60	.30

Issued: #3143-3146, 7/25; #3147, 8/5; #3148, 8/7; #3149, 8/8; #3150, 8/16.

American Dolls

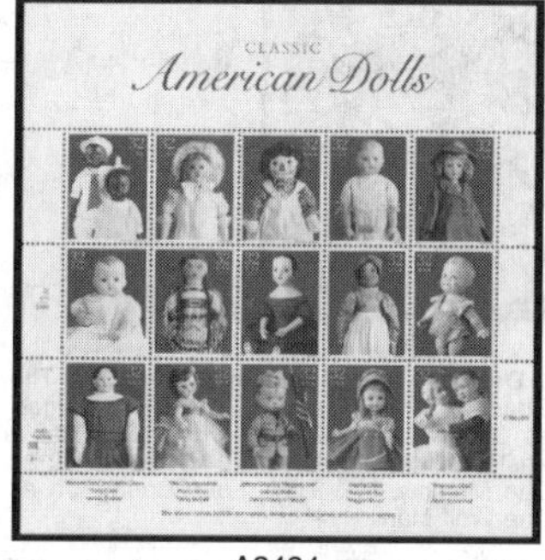

A2434

Designs: a, "Alabama Baby," and doll by Martha Chase. b, "Columbian Doll." c, Johnny Gruelle's "Raggedy Ann." d, Doll by Martha Chase. e, "American Child." f, "Baby Coos." g, Plains Indian. h, Doll by Izannah Walker. i, "Babyland Rag." j, "Scootles." k, Doll by Ludwig Greiner. l, "Betsy McCall." m, Percy Crosby's "Skippy." n, "Maggie Mix-up." o, Dolls by Albert Schoenhut.
Illustration reduced.

1997, July 28 *Perf. 10.9x11.1*

3151	A2434	Pane of 15	11.00	—
a.-o.		32c any single	.70	.20

A2435

A2436

Legends Of Hollywood

Humphrey Bogart (1899-1957)

1997, July 31 Photo. *Perf. 11.1*

3152	A2435	32c multicolored	.60	.20

Perforations in corner of each stamp are star-shaped.

"The Stars and Stripes Forever!"

1997, Aug. 21 *Perf. 11.1*

3153	A2436	32c multicolored	.60	.20

American Music Series
Opera Singers

Lily Pons A2437

Richard Tucker A2438

Lawrence Tibbett A2439

Rosa Ponselle A2440

Classical Composers & Conductors

Leopold Stokowski A2441

Arthur Fiedler A2442

George Szell A2443

Eugene Ormandy A2444

Samuel Barber A2445

Ferde Grofé A2446

Charles Ives A2447

Louis Moreau Gottschalk A2448

1997 Litho. *Perf. 11*

3154	A2437	32c multicolored	.65	.20
3155	A2438	32c multicolored	.65	.20
3156	A2439	32c multicolored	.65	.20
3157	A2440	32c multicolored	.65	.20
a.		Block or strip, #3154-3157	2.60	1.75
3158	A2441	32c multicolored	.65	.20
3159	A2442	32c multicolored	.65	.20
3160	A2443	32c multicolored	.65	.20
3161	A2444	32c multicolored	.65	.20

3162 A2445 32c multicolored .65 .20
3163 A2446 32c multicolored .65 .20
3164 A2447 32c multicolored .65 .20
3165 A2448 32c multicolored .65 .20
a. Block of 8, #3158-3165 5.25 4.00

Issued: #3154-3157, 9/10; #3158-3165, 9/12.

Padre Félix Varela (1788-1853)

A2449

1997, Sept. 15 Litho. ***Perf. 11.2***
3166 A2449 32c purple .60 .20

Department of the Air Force, 50th Anniv.

Thunderbirds Aerial Demonstration Squadron — A2450

Perf. 11.2x11.1
1997, Sept. 18 Litho.
3167 A2450 32c multicolored .60 .20

Beginning with #3167, a hidden 3-D design can be seen on some stamps when they are viewed with a special viewer sold by the post office.

Classic Movie Monsters

A2451

A2452

A2453

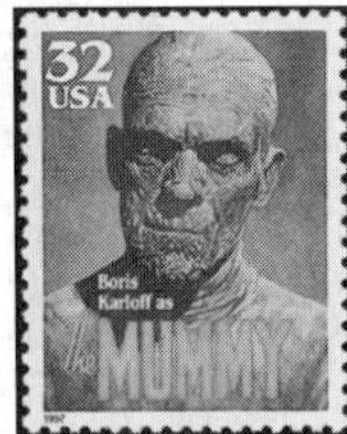

A2454

A2455

Designs: No. 3168, Lon Chaney as The Phantom of the Opera. No. 3169, Bela Lugosi as Dracula. No. 3170, Boris Karloff as Frankenstein's Monster. No. 3171, Boris Karloff as The Mummy. No. 3172, Lon Chaney, Jr. as The Wolf Man.

1997, Sept. 30 Photo. ***Perf. 10.2***
3168 A2451 32c multicolored .60 .20
3169 A2452 32c multicolored .60 .20
3170 A2453 32c multicolored .60 .20
3171 A2454 32c multicolored .60 .20
3172 A2455 32c multicolored .60 .20
a. Strip of 5, #3168-3172 3.00 2.25

First Supersonic Flight, 50th Anniv.

A2456

Serpentine Die Cut 11.4
1997, Oct. 14 Litho.
Self-Adhesive
3173 A2456 32c multicolored .60 .20

Women In Military Service

A2457

1997, Oct. 18 Litho. ***Perf. 11.1***
3174 A2457 32c multicolored .60 .20

Kwanzaa

A2458

Serpentine Die Cut 11
1997, Oct. 22 Photo.
Self-Adhesive
3175 A2458 32c multicolored .60 .20

See Nos. 3368, 3548.

Christmas

Madonna and Child A2459

Holly A2460

Serpentine Die Cut 9.9 on 2, 3 or 4 Sides
1997 Litho.
Booklet Stamps
Self-Adhesive
3176 A2459 32c multicolored .60 .20
a. Booklet pane of 20 + label 12.00

Serpentine Die Cut 11.2x11.8 on 2, 3 or 4 Sides
3177 A2460 32c multicolored .60 .20
a. Booklet pane of 20 + label 12.00
b. Booklet pane of 4 2.50
c. Booklet pane of 5 + label 3.00
d. Booklet pane of 6 3.75

Madonna and Child, by Sano di Pietro.

Issued: No. 3176, 10/27; No. 3177, 10/30.

Mars Pathfinder
Souvenir Sheet

Mars Rover Sojourner — A2461

Illustration reduced.

1997, Dec. 10 Photo. ***Perf. 11x11.1***
3178 A2461 multicolored 6.00 3.00
a. $3 single stamp 5.50 2.75

The perforations at the bottom of the stamp include the letters "USA." Vertical rouletting extends from the vertical perforations of the stamp to the bottom of the souvenir sheet.

Chinese New Year

Year of the Tiger — A2462

1998, Jan. 5 Photo. ***Perf. 11.2***
3179 A2462 32c multicolored .60 .20

A2463

A2464

Alpine Skiing
1998, Jan. 22 Litho. ***Perf. 11.2***
3180 A2463 32c multicolored .60 .20

Black Heritage Series
Serpentine Die Cut 11.6x11.3
1998, Jan. 28
Self-Adhesive
3181 A2464 32c sepia & black .60 .20

Madam C.J. Walker (1867-1919), entrepreneur.

Celebrate the Century

1900s — A2465

No. 3182: a, Model T Ford. b, Theodore Roosevelt. c, Motion picture "The Great Train Robbery," 1903. d, Crayola Crayons introduced, 1903. e, St. Louis World's Fair, 1904. f, Design used on Hunt's Remedy stamp (#RS56), Pure Food & Drug Act, 1906. g, Wright Brothers first flight, Kitty Hawk, 1903. h, Boxing match shown in painting "Stag at Sharkey's," by George Bellows of the Ash Can School. i, Immigrants arrive. j, John Muir, preservationist. k, "Teddy" Bear created. l, W.E.B. Du Bois, social activist. m, Gibson Girl. n, First baseball World Series, 1903. o, Robie House, Chicago, designed by Frank Lloyd Wright.

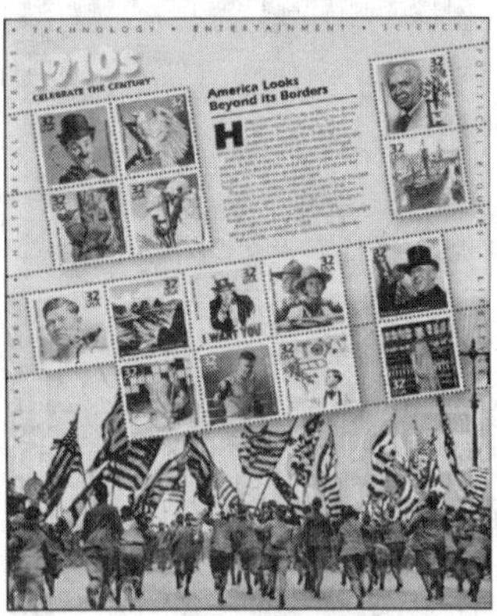

1910s — A2466

No. 3183: a, Charlie Chaplin as the Little Tramp. b, Federal Reserve System created, 1913. c, George Washington Carver. d, Avant-garde art introduced at Armory Show, 1913. e, First transcontinental telephone line, 1914. f, Panama Canal opens, 1914. g, Jim Thorpe wins decathlon at Stockholm Olympics, 1912. h, Grand Canyon National Park, 1919. i, U.S. enters World War I. j, Boy Scouts started in 1910, Girl Scouts formed in 1912. k, Woodrow Wilson. l, First crossword puzzle published, 1913. m, Jack Dempsey wins heavyweight title, 1919. n, Construction toys. o, Child labor reform.

1920s — A2467

No. 3184: a, Babe Ruth. b, The Gatsby style. c, Prohibition enforced. d, Electric toy trains. e, 19th Amendment (woman voting). f, Emily Post's Etiquette. g, Margaret Mead, anthropologist. h, Flappers do the Charleston. i, Radio entertains America. j, Art Deco style (Chrysler Building). k, Jazz flourishes. l, Four Horsemen of Notre Dame. m, Lindbergh flies the Atlantic. n, American realism (The Automat, by Edward Hopper). o, Stock Market crash, 1929.

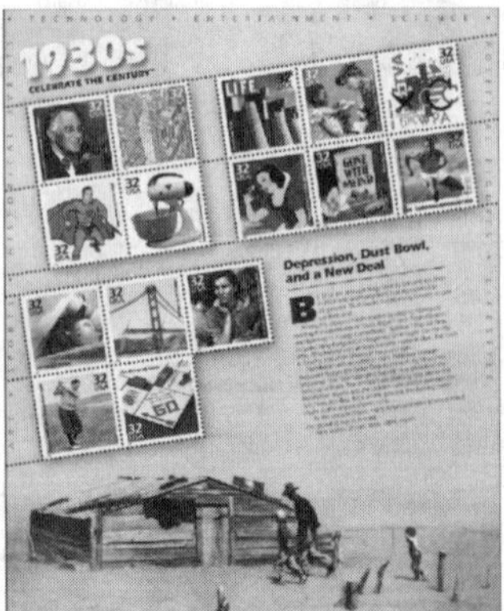

1930s — A2468

No. 3185: a, Franklin D. Roosevelt. b, The Empire State Building. c, 1st Issue of Life Magazine, 1936. d, Eleanor Roosevelt. e, FDR's New Deal. f, Superman arrives, 1938. g, Household conveniences. h, "Snow White and the Seven Dwarfs," 1937. i, "Gone with the Wind," 1936. j, Jesse Owens. k, Streamline design. l, Golden Gate Bridge. m, America survives the Depression. n, Bobby Jones wins Grand Slam, 1938. o, The Monopoly Game.

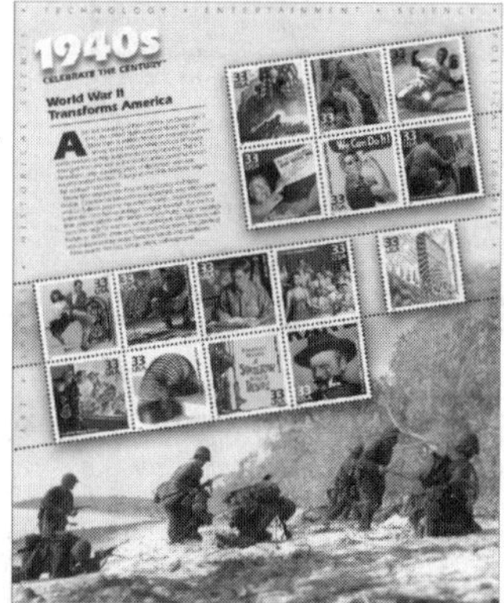

1940s — A2469

No. 3186: a, World War II. b, Antibiotics save lives. c, Jackie Robinson. d, Harry S Truman. e, Women support war effort. f, TV entertains America. g, Jitterbug sweeps nation. h, Jackson Pollock, Abstract Expressionism. i, GI Bill, 1944. j, Big Band Sound. k, Intl. style of architecture (UN Headquarters). l, Postwar baby boom. m, Slinky, 1945. n, "A Streecar Named Desire," 1947. o, Orson Welles' "Citizen Kane."

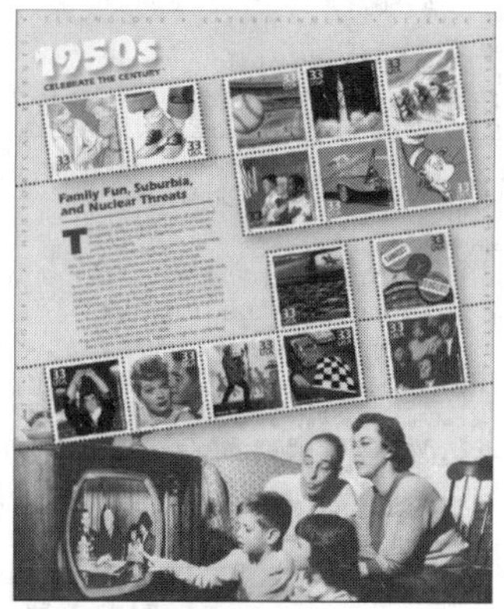

1950s — A2470

No. 3187: a, Polio vaccine developed. b, Teen fashions. c, The "Shot Heard 'Round the World." d, US launches satellites. e, Korean War. f, Desegregating public schools. g, Tail fins, chrome. h, Dr. Seuss' "The Cat in the Hat." i, Drive-in movies. j, World Series rivals. k, Rocky Marciano, undefeated. l, "I Love Lucy." m, Rock 'n Roll. n, Stock car racing. o, Movies go 3-D.

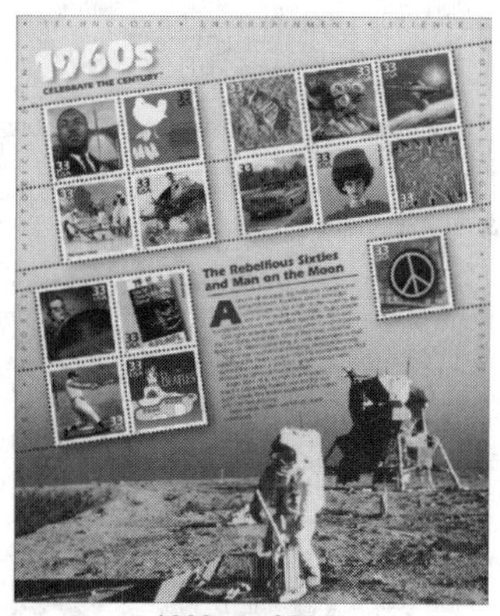

1960s — A2471

No. 3188: a, Martin Luther King, Jr., "I Have a Dream." b, Woodstock. c, Man walks on the moon. d, Green Bay Packers. e, Star Trek. f, The Peace Corps. g, Viet Nam War. h, Ford Mustang. i, Barbie Doll. j, Integrated circuit. k, Lasers. l, Super Bowl I. m, Peace symbol. n, Roger Maris, 61 in '61. o, The Beatles "Yellow Submarine."

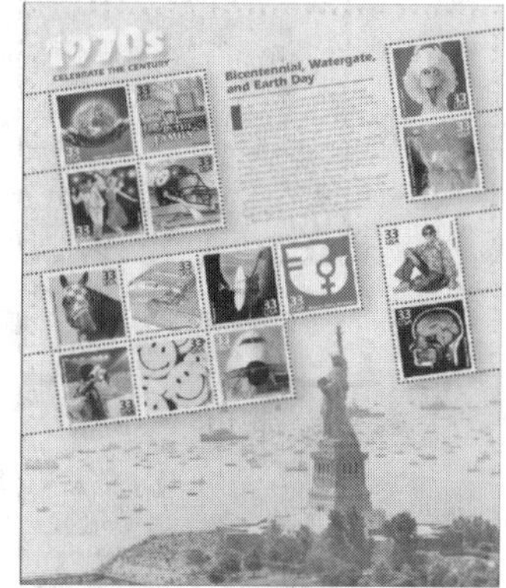

1970s — A2472

No. 3189: a, Earth Day celebrated. b, "All in the Family" television series. c, "Sesame Street" television series character, Big Bird. d, Disco music. e, Pittsburgh Steelers win four Super Bowls. f, US Celebrates 200th birthday. g, Secretariat wins Triple Crown. h, VCRs transform entertainment. i, Pioneer 10. j, Women's rights movement. k, 1970s fashions. l, "Monday Night Football." m, Smiley face buttons. n, Jumbo jets. o, Medical imaging.

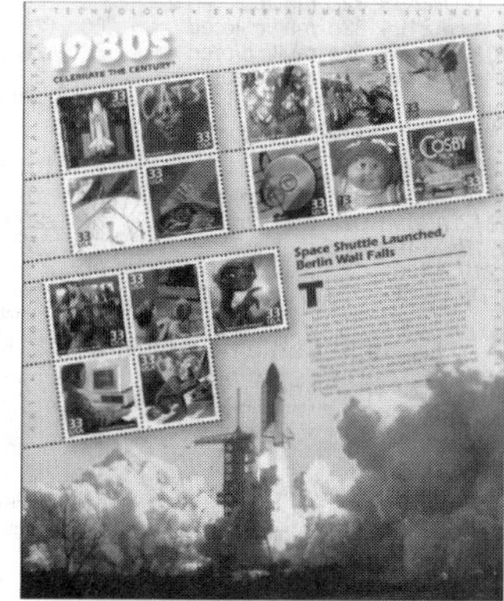

1980s — A2473

No. 3190: a, Space shuttle program. b, "Cats" Broadway show. c, San Francisco 49ers. d, Hostages in Iran come home. e, Figure skating. f, Cable TV. g, Vietnam Veterans Memorial. h, Compact discs. i, Cabbage Patch Kids. j, "The Cosby Show" television series. k, Fall of the Berlin Wall. l, Video games. m, "E. T. The Extra-Terrestrial" movie. n, Personal computers. o, Hip-hop culture.

1990s — A2474

No. 3191: a, New baseball records. b, Gulf War. c, "Seinfeld" television series. d, Extreme sports. e, Improving education. f, Computer art and graphics. g, Recovering species. h, Return to space. i, Special Olympics. j, Virtual reality. k, Movie "Jurassic Park." l, Movie "Titanic." m, Sport utility vehicles. n, World Wide Web. o, Cellular phones.

Litho.; Litho. & Engr. (#3182m, 3183f, 3184m, 3185b, 3186k, 3187a, 3188c, 3189h)

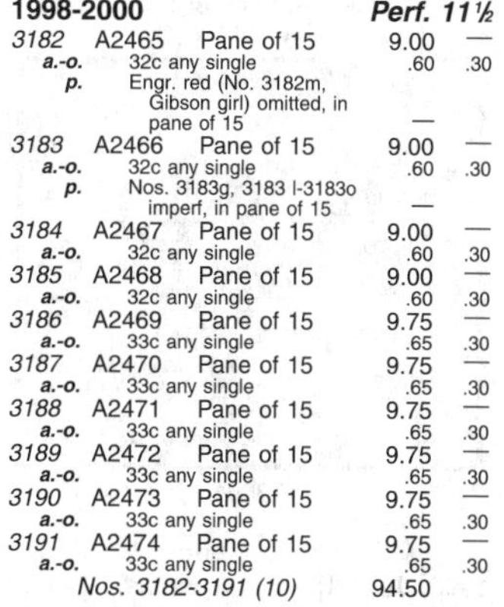

1998-2000			***Perf. 11½***	
3182	A2465	Pane of 15	9.00	—
a.-o.		32c any single	.60	.30
p.		Engr. red (No. 3182m, Gibson girl) omitted, in pane of 15	—	
3183	A2466	Pane of 15	9.00	—
a.-o.		32c any single	.60	.30
p.		Nos. 3183g, 3183 l-3183o imperf, in pane of 15	—	
3184	A2467	Pane of 15	9.00	—
a.-o.		32c any single	.60	.30
3185	A2468	Pane of 15	9.00	—
a.-o.		32c any single	.60	.30
3186	A2469	Pane of 15	9.75	—
a.-o.		33c any single	.65	.30
3187	A2470	Pane of 15	9.75	—
a.-o.		33c any single	.65	.30
3188	A2471	Pane of 15	9.75	—
a.-o.		33c any single	.65	.30
3189	A2472	Pane of 15	9.75	—
a.-o.		33c any single	.65	.30
3190	A2473	Pane of 15	9.75	—
a.-o.		33c any single	.65	.30
3191	A2474	Pane of 15	9.75	—
a.-o.		33c any single	.65	.30
		Nos. 3182-3191 (10)	94.50	

Issued: #3182-3183, 2/3; #3184, 5/28; #3185, 9/10; #3186, 2/18/99; #3187, 5/26/99; #3188, 9/17/99; #3189, 11/18/99; #3190, 1/12/00; #3191, 5/2/00.

"Remember The Maine"

A2475

Litho. & Engr.

1998, Feb. 15			***Perf. 11.2x11***	
3192	A2475	32c red & black	.60	.20

Flowering Trees

Southern Magnolia A2476

Blue Paloverde A2477

Yellow Poplar — A2478

Prairie Crab Apple — A2479

Pacific Dogwood A2480

Die Cut Perf 11.3

1998, Mar. 19 **Litho.**

Self-Adhesive

3193	A2476	32c multicolored	.60	.20
3194	A2477	32c multicolored	.60	.20
3195	A2478	32c multicolored	.60	.20
3196	A2479	32c multicolored	.60	.20
3197	A2480	32c multicolored	.60	.20
a.		Strip of 5, #3193-3197	3.00	

Alexander Calder, Sculptor

Black Cascade, 13 Verticals, 1959 — A2481

Untitled, 1965 — A2482

Rearing Stallion, 1928 — A2483

Portrait of a Young Man, c. 1945 — A2484

Un Effet du Japonais, 1945 — A2485

1998, Mar. 25		**Photo.**	***Perf. 10.2***	
3198	A2481	32c multicolored	.60	.20
3199	A2482	32c multicolored	.60	.20
3200	A2483	32c multicolored	.60	.20
3201	A2484	32c multicolored	.60	.20
3202	A2485	32c multicolored	.60	.20
a.		Strip of 5, #3198-3202	3.00	2.25

Cinco De Mayo

A2486

Serpentine Die Cut 11.7x10.9

1998, Apr. 16 Photo.

Self-Adhesive

3203 A2486 32c multicolored .60 .20

See No. 3309. See Mexico No. 2066.

A2487

A2488

Sylvester & Tweety

Serpentine Die Cut 11.1

1998, Apr. 27

Self-Adhesive

3204 Pane of 10 6.00
- ***a.*** A2487 32c single .60 .20
- ***b.*** Booklet pane of 9 #3204a 5.40
- ***c.*** Booklet pane of 1 #3204a .60

Die cutting on #3204b does not extend through the backing paper.

3205 Pane of 10 *10.00*
- ***a.*** A2487 32c single *.60*
- ***b.*** Booklet pane of 9 #3205a —
- ***c.*** Booklet pane of 1, imperf. —

Die cutting on #3205a extends through the backing paper. Used examples of No. 3205a are identical to those of No. 3204a.

Wisconsin Statehood

Serpentine Die Cut 10.8x10.9

1998, May 29 Photo.

Self-Adhesive

3206 A2488 32c multicolored .60 .30

See note after No. 3167.

Wetlands
A2489

Diner
A2490

COIL STAMPS

1998 Photo. ***Perf. 10 Vert.***

Self-Adhesive (#3207A, 3208A)

3207 A2489 (5c) multicolored .20 .20

Serpentine Die Cut 9.8 Vert.

3207A A2489 (5c) multicolored .20 .20

Perf. 10 Vert.

3208 A2490 (25c) multicolored .50 .50

Serpentine Die Cut 9.8 Vert.

3208A A2490 (25c) multicolored .50 .50

Issued: #3207-3208, 6/5; #3208A, 9/30; #3207A, 12/14.

1898 Trans-Mississippi Stamps, Centenary

A2491

Litho. & Engr.

1998, June 18 ***Perf. 12x12.4***

3209 A2491 Pane of 9 7.75 5.00
- ***a.*** A100 1c green & black .20 .20
- ***b.*** A108 2c red brown & black .20 .20
- ***c.*** A102 4c orange & black .20 .20
- ***d.*** A103 5c blue & black .20 .20
- ***e.*** A104 8c dark lilac & black .20 .20
- ***f.*** A105 10c purple & black .20 .20
- ***g.*** A106 50c green & black 1.00 .60
- ***h.*** A107 $1 red & black 2.00 1.25
- ***i.*** A101 $2 red brown & black 4.00 2.50

Vignettes on Nos. 3209b and 3209i are reversed in comparison to the original issue.

3210 A107 $1 Pane of 9 #3209h 18.00 —

Berlin Airlift, 50th Anniv.

A2492

1998, June 26 Photo. ***Perf. 11.2***

3211 A2492 32c multicolored .60 .20

American Music Series
Folk Singers

Huddie "Leadbelly" Ledbetter
A2493

Woody Guthrie
A2494

Sonny Terry
A2495

Josh White
A2496

Gospel Singers

Mahalia Jackson
A2497

Roberta Martin
A2498

Clara Ward
A2499

Sister Rosetta Tharpe
A2500

1998, June 26 ***Perf. 10.1x10.2***

3212 A2493 32c multicolored .60 .20
3213 A2494 32c multicolored .60 .20
3214 A2495 32c multicolored .60 .20
3215 A2496 32c multicolored .60 .20
- ***a.*** Block or strip, #3212-3215 2.50 2.00

Perf. 10.1x10.3

1998, July 15 Photo.

3216 A2497 32c multicolored .60 .20
3217 A2498 32c multicolored .60 .20
3218 A2499 32c multicolored .60 .20
3219 A2500 32c multicolored .60 .20
- ***a.*** Block or strip, #3216-3219 2.40 2.00

Spanish Settlement of the Southwest

La Mision de San Miguel de San Gabriel, Española, NM — A2501

1998, July 11 Litho. ***Perf. 11.2***

3220 A2501 32c multicolored .60 .20

Literary Arts Series

Stephen Vincent Benét — A2502

1998, July 22 Litho. ***Perf. 11.2***

3221 A2502 32c multicolored .60 .20

Tropical Birds

Antillean Euphonia — A2503

Green-throated Carib — A2504

Crested Honeycreeper — A2505

Cardinal Honeyeater
A2506

1998, July 29 Litho. ***Perf. 11.2***

3222 A2503 32c multicolored .60 .20
3223 A2504 32c multicolored .60 .20
3224 A2505 32c multicolored .60 .20
3225 A2506 32c multicolored .60 .20
- ***a.*** Block or strip of 4, #3222-3225 2.40 2.00

A2507

A2508

Legends of Hollywood

1998, Aug. 3 Photo. ***Perf. 11.1***

3226 A2507 32c multicolored .60 .20

Alfred Hitchcock (1899-1980). Perforations in corner of each stamp are star-shaped. Hitchcock's profile in the UL corner of each stamp is laser cut.

Organ & Tissue Donation

Serpentine Die Cut 11.7

1998, Aug. 5 Photo.

Self-Adhesive

3227 A2508 32c multicolored .60 .20

Modern Bicycle

A2509

COIL STAMPS

Serpentine Die Cut 9.8 Vert.

1998, Aug. 14 Photo. Untagged

Self-Adhesive

3228 A2509 (10c) multicolored, small "1998" year date .20 .20
- ***a.*** Large date .20 .20

Date on 3228a is approximately 1 ½mm; on 3228 approximately 1mm.

Perf. 9.9 Vert.

3229 A2509 (10c) multicolored .20 .20

Bright Eyes

Dog
A2510

Fish
A2511

Cat
A2512

Parakeet
A2513

Hamster
A2514

Serpentine Die Cut 9.9

1998, Aug. 20 Photo.

Self-Adhesive

3230	A2510	32c multicolored	.60	.20
3231	A2511	32c multicolored	.60	.20
3232	A2512	32c multicolored	.60	.20
3233	A2513	32c multicolored	.60	.20
3234	A2514	32c multicolored	.60	.20
a.		Strip of 5, #3230-3234	3.00	

See note after No. 3167.

Klondike Gold Rush, Centennial

A2515

1998, Aug. 21 Litho. *Perf. 11.1*

3235 A2515 32c multicolored .60 .20

American Art

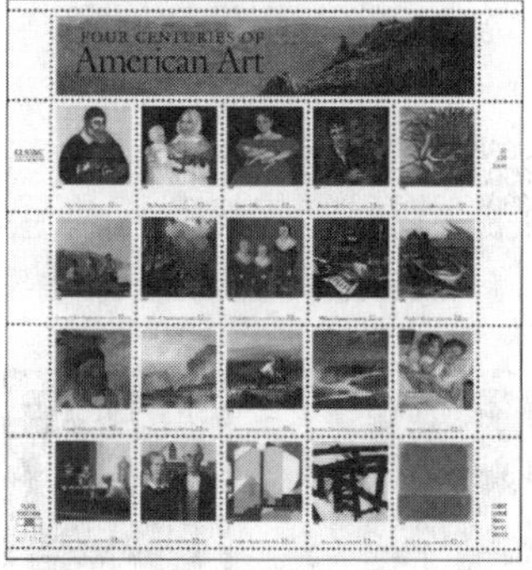

A2516

Paintings: a, "Portrait of Richard Mather," by John Foster. b, "Mrs. Elizabeth Freake and Baby Mary," by The Freake Limner. c, "Girl in Red Dress with Cat and Dog," by Ammi Phillips. d, "Rubens Peale with a Geranium," by Rembrandt Peale. e, "Long-billed Curlew, Numenius Longrostris," by John James Audubon. f, "Boatmen on the Missouri," by George Caleb Bingham. g, "Kindred Sprits," by Asher B. Durand. h, "The Westwood Children," by Joshua Johnson. i, "Music and Literature," by William Harnett. j, "The Fog Warning," by Winslow Homer. k, "The White Cloud, Head Chief of the Iowas," by George Catlin. l, "Cliffs of Green River," by Thomas Moran. m, "The Last of the Buffalo," by Albert Bierstadt. n, "Niagara," by Frederic Edwin Church. o, "Breakfast in Bed," by Mary Cassatt. p, "Nighthawks," by Edward Hopper. q, "American Gothic," by Grant Wood. r, "Two Against the White," by Charles Sheeler. s, "Mahoning," by Franz Kline. t, "No. 12," by Mark Rothko.

1998, Aug. 27 Photo. *Perf. 10.2*

3236	A2516	Pane of 20	12.00	—
a.-t.		32c any single	.60	.20

Inscriptions on the back of each stamp describe the painting and the artist.

American Ballet

A2517

Perf. 10.9x11.1

1998, Sept. 16 Litho.

3237 A2517 32c multicolored .60 .20

Space Discovery

A2518

A2519

A2520

A2521

A2522

1998, Oct. 1 Photo. *Perf. 11.1*

3238	A2518	32c multicolored	.60	.20
3239	A2519	32c multicolored	.60	.20
3240	A2520	32c multicolored	.60	.20
3241	A2521	32c multicolored	.60	.20
3242	A2522	32c multicolored	.60	.20
a.		Strip of 5, #3238-3242	3.00	2.25

See note after No. 3167.

Giving and Sharing

A2523

Serpentine Die Cut 11.1

1998, Oct. 7 Photo.

Self-Adhesive

3243 A2523 32c multicolored .60 .20

Christmas

Madonna and Child — A2524

Wreaths

Evergreen
A2525

Victorian
A2526

Chili Pepper
A2527

Tropical
A2528

1998, Oct. 15 Litho.

Booklet Stamps

Serpentine Die Cut 10.1x9.9 on 2, 3 or 4 Sides

3244	A2524	32c multicolored	.60	.20
a.		Booklet pane of 20 + label	12.00	
b.		Imperf, pair	—	

Serpentine Die Cut 11.3x11.6 on 2 or 3 Sides

3245	A2525	32c multicolored	1.50	.20
3246	A2526	32c multicolored	1.50	.20
3247	A2527	32c multicolored	1.50	.20
3248	A2528	32c multicolored	1.50	.20
a.		Bklt. pane of 4, #3245-3248	12.50	
b.		Bklt. pane of 5, #3245-3246, 3248, 2 #3247 + label	15.00	
c.		Booklet pane of 6, #3247-3248, 2 each #3245-3246	17.50	

Size: 23x30mm

Serpentine Die Cut 11.4x11.6 on 2, 3 or 4 Sides

3249	A2525	32c multicolored	.60	.20
3250	A2526	32c multicolored	.60	.20
3251	A2527	32c multicolored	.60	.20
3252	A2528	32c multicolored	.60	.20
a.		Block or strip, #3249-3252	2.40	
b.		Bklt. pane, 5 #3252a + label	12.00	
c.		As "a," red ("Greetings 32 USA" and "1998") omitted on #3249, 3252)		—

Madonna and Child, Florence, 15th Cent.

Weather
Vane — A2529

Uncle
Sam — A2530

Uncle Sam's Hat — A2531

Space Shuttle Landing — A2532

Piggyback Space Shuttle — A2533

1998 Litho. *Perf. 11.2*

Self-Adhesive (#3259, 3261-3263, 3265-3269)

3257	A2529	(1c) multi	.20	.20
a.		Black omitted	—	
3258	A2529	(1c) multi	.20	.20

No. 3257 is 18mm high, has thin letters, white USA, and black 1998. No. 3258 is 17mm high, has thick letters, pale blue USA and blue 1998.

Photo.

Serpentine Die Cut 10.8

3259	A2530	22c multi	.45	.20
a.		Die cut 10.8x10.5	1.00	.25

See No. 3353.

Perf. 11.2

3260 A2531 (33c) multi .65 .20

Litho.

Serpentine Die Cut 11.5

3261	A2532	$3.20 multi	6.00	3.00
3262	A2533	$11.75 multi	22.50	11.50

COIL STAMPS

Photo.

Serpentine Die Cut 9.9 Vert.

3263	A2530	22c multi	.45	.20
a.		Imperf., pair	—	

See No. 3353.

Perf. 9.8 Vert.

3264 A2531 (33c) multi .65 .20

Serpentine Die Cut 9.9 Vert.

3265	A2531	(33c) multi	.65	.20
a.		Imperf., pair	—	—
b.		Red omitted	—	
c.		Black omitted	—	
d.		Black omitted, imperf., pair	—	

Unused examples of No. 3265 are on backing paper the same size as the stamps.

On No. 3265b, the blue and gray colors are shifted down and to the right.

Serpentine Die Cut 9.9 Vert.

3266 A2531 (33c) multi .65 .20

Unused examples of No. 3266 are on backing paper larger than the stamps. Corners of stamps are rounded, and the stamps are spaced approximately 2mm apart.

BOOKLET STAMPS

Serpentine Die Cut 9.9 on 2 or 3 Sides

3267	A2531	(33c) multi	.65	.20
a.		Booklet pane of 10	6.50	

Serpentine Die Cut on 2, 3 or 4 Sides

11¼ (#3268, 3268a), 11 (#3268b, 3268c)

3268	A2531	(33c) multi	.65	.20
a.		Booklet pane of 10	6.50	
b.		Serpentine die cut 11	.65	.20
c.		As "b," bklt. pane of 20 + label	13.00	

Die Cut 8 on 2, 3 or 4 Sides

3269	A2531	(33c) multi	.65	.20
a.		Booklet pane of 18	12.00	

Issued: No. 3262, 11/19; others, 11/9.

A2534

COIL STAMPS

1998, Dec. 14 Photo. *Perf. 9.8 Vert.*

3270	A2534	(10c) Small date	.20	.20
a.		Large date	.20	.20

Serpentine Die Cut 9.9 Vert.

Self-Adhesive

3271	A2534	(10c) Small date	.20	.20
a.		Large date	.20	.20

Dates on Nos. 3270a and 3271a are approximately 1¾mm; on Nos. 3270-3271 approximately 1¼mm.

Compare to Nos. 2602-2604, 2907.

Chinese New Year

Year of the Rabbit — A2535

1999, Jan. 5 Photo. *Perf. 11.2*
3272 A2535 33c multicolored .65 .20

Black Heritage Series

Malcolm X — A2536

Serpentine Die Cut 11.4
1999, Jan. 20 Litho.
Self-Adhesive
3273 A2536 33c multicolored .65 .20

Malcolm X (1925-65), Civil Rights Activist.

Love

A2537

A2538

1999, Jan. 28 Photo. *Die Cut*
Booklet Stamp
Self-Adhesive
3274 A2537 33c multicolored .65 .20
a. Booklet pane of 20 13.00
b. Imperf., pair —
3275 A2538 55c multicolored 1.10 .20

Hospice Care

A2539

Serpentine Die Cut 11.4
1999, Feb. 9 Litho.
3276 A2539 33c multicolored .65 .20

Flag & City — A2540

1999 Photo. *Perf. 11.2*
Self-Adhesive (#3278-3279, 3281-3282)
3277 A2540 33c multicolored .65 .20

No. 3277 has red date.

Serpentine Die Cut 11 on 2, 3 or 4 Sides
3278 A2540 33c multicolored .65 .20
a. Booklet pane of 4 2.60
b. Booklet pane of 5 + label 3.25
c. Booklet pane of 6 3.90
d. Booklet pane of 10 6.50
e. Booklet pane of 20 + label 13.00
h. As "e," imperf —
i. Serpentine die cut 11¼ .65 .20
j. As "i," booklet pane of 10 6.50

No. 3278 has black date.

BOOKLET STAMPS
Serpentine Die Cut 11½x11¾ on 2, 3 or 4 Sides
3278F A2540 33c multicolored .65 .20
g. Booklet pane of 20 + label 13.00

No. 3278f has black date.

Serpentine Die Cut 9.8 on 2 or 3 Sides
3279 A2540 33c multicolored .65 .20
a. Booklet pane of 10 6.50

No. 3279 has red date.

COIL STAMPS
Perf. 9.9 Vert.
3280 A2540 33c multicolored, small "1999" year date .65 .20
a. Large date .65 .20
b. As No. 3280, imperf pair —

Date on 3280a is approximately 1¾mm; on No. 3280 approximately 1¼mm.

Serpentine Die Cut 9.8 Vert.
3281 A2540 33c large "1999" year date .65 .20
a. Imperf., pair 27.50
b. Light blue & yellow omitted *600.00*
c. Small date .65 .20

Corners are square on #3281. Unused examples are on backing paper the same size as the stamps.

Date on No. 3281 is approximately 1¾mm; on No. 3281c approximately 1¼mm.

3282 A2540 33c multicolored .65 .20

Corners are rounded on #3282. Unused examples are on backing paper larger than the stamps, and stamps are spaced approximately 2mm apart.

Flag & Chalkboard — A2541

Booklet Stamp
Serpentine Die Cut 7.9 on 2, 3 or 4 Sides
1999, Mar. 13 Photo.
Self-Adhesive
3283 A2541 33c multicolored .65 .20
a. Booklet pane of 18 12.00

Irish Immigration

A2542

1999, Feb. 26 Litho. *Perf. 11.2*
3286 A2542 33c multicolored .65 .20

See Ireland No. 1168.

Performing Arts Series

A2543

1999, Mar. 2 Litho. *Perf. 11.2*
3287 A2543 33c multicolored .65 .20

Alfred Lunt (1892-1977), Lynn Fontanne (1887-1983), Actors.

Arctic Animals

A2544

A2545

A2546

A2547

A2548

1999, Mar. 12 Litho. *Perf. 11*
3288 A2544 33c Arctic Hare .65 .20
3289 A2545 33c Arctic Fox .65 .20
3290 A2546 33c Snowy Owl .65 .20
3291 A2547 33c Polar Bear .65 .20
3292 A2548 33c Gray Wolf .65 .20
a. Strip of 5, #3288-3292 3.25 —

Sonoran Desert

A2549

Designs: a, Cactus wren, brittlebush, teddy bear cholla. b, Desert tortoise. c, White-winged dove, prickly pear. d, Gambel quail. e, Saguaro cactus. f, Desert mule deer. g, Desert cottontail, hedgehog cactus. h, Gila monster. i, Western diamondback rattlesnake, cactus mouse. i, Gila woodpecker.

Serpentine Die Cut Perf 11.2
1999, Apr. 6 Litho.
Self-Adhesive
3293 A2549 Pane of 10 6.50
a.-j. 33c any single .65 .20

Berries

Blueberries A2550

Raspberries A2551

Strawberries A2552

Blackberries A2553

Serpentine Die Cut 11½x11¾ on 2, 3 or 4 Sides
1999, Apr. 10 Photo.
Booklet Stamps
Self-Adhesive
3294 A2550 33c multicolored .65 .20
a. Dated "2000" .65 .20
3295 A2551 33c multicolored .65 .20
a. Dated "2000" .65 .20
3296 A2552 33c multicolored .65 .20
a. Dated "2000" .65 .20
3297 A2553 33c multicolored .65 .20
a. Dated "2000" .65 .20
b. Booklet pane, 5 each #3294-3297 + label 13.00
c. Block of 4, #3294-3297 2.60
d. Booklet pane, 5 #3297e + label 13.00
e. Block of 4, #3294a-3297a 2.60

No. 3297d is a double-sided booklet pane with 12 stamps on one side and 8 stamps plus label on the other side.

Serpentine Die Cut 9½x10 on 2 or 3 Sides
3298 A2550 33c multicolored .65 .20
3299 A2552 33c multicolored .65 .20
3300 A2551 33c multicolored .65 .20
3301 A2553 33c multicolored .65 .20
a. Bklt. pane of 4, #3298-3301 2.60
b. Bklt. pane of 5, #3298-3299, 3301, 2 #3300 + label 3.25
c. Booklet pane of 6, #3300-3301, 2 #3298-3299 4.00
d. Block of 4, #3298-3301 2.60

COIL STAMPS
Serpentine Die Cut 8.5 Vert.
3302 A2550 33c multicolored .65 .20
3303 A2551 33c multicolored .65 .20
3304 A2553 33c multicolored .65 .20
3305 A2552 33c multicolored .65 .20
a. Strip of 4, #3302-3305 2.60

Issued: #3294a-3297a, 3/15/00.

A2554

A2555

Daffy Duck

Serpentine Die Cut 11.1
1999, Apr. 16 Photo.
Self-Adhesive
3306 Pane of 10 6.50
a. A2554 33c single .65 .20
b. Booklet pane, 9 #3306a 5.85
c. Booklet pane, 1 #3306a .65

Die cutting on #3306b does not extend through the backing paper.

3307 Pane of 10 *6.50*
a. A2554 33c single *.65*
b. Booklet pane, 9 #3307a —
c. Booklet pane, 1 #3307a imperf. —

Die cutting on #3307a extends through the backing paper. Used examples of No. 3307a are identical to those of No. 3306a.

Nos. 3306b-3306c and 3307b-3307c are separated by a vertical line of microperforations.

Literary Arts Series

Ayn Rand (1905-82)

1999, Apr. 22 Litho. *Perf. 11.2*
3308 A2555 33c multicolored .65 .20

Cinco De Mayo Type of 1998

Serpentine Die Cut 11.6x11.3

1999, Apr. 27 **Litho.**

Self-Adhesive

3309 A2486 33c multicolored .65 .20

Tropical Flowers

Bird of Paradise A2556

Royal Poinciana A2557

Gloriosa Lily A2558

Chinese Hibiscus A2559

BOOKLET STAMPS

Serpentine Die Cut 10.9 on 2 or 3 Sides

1999, May 1 **Photo.**

Self-Adhesive

3310 A2556 33c multicolored .65 .20
3311 A2557 33c multicolored .65 .20
3312 A2558 33c multicolored .65 .20
3313 A2559 33c multicolored .65 .20
a. Block of 4, #3310-3313 2.60
b. Booklet pane, 5 #3313a 13.00

No. 3313b is a double-sided booklet pane.

A2560

A2561

John (1699-1777) & William (1739-1823) Bartram, Botanists

Franklinia Alatamaha, by William Bartram.

Serpentine Die Cut 11½

1999, May 18 **Litho.**

Self-Adhesive

3314 A2560 33c multicolored .65 .20

Prostate Cancer Awareness

Serpentine Die Cut 11

1999, May 28 **Photo.**

Self-Adhesive

3315 A2561 33c multicolored .65 .20

California Gold Rush, 150th Anniv.

A2562

1999, June 18 **Litho.** ***Perf. 11¼***

3316 A2562 33c multicolored .65 .20

Aquarium Fish

Reef Fish

A2563

A2564

A2565

A2566

#3317, Yellow fish, red fish, cleaner shrimp. #3318, Fish, thermometer. #3319, Red fish, blue & yellow fish. #3320, Fish, heater/airator.

Serpentine Die Cut 11½

1999, June 24 **Litho.**

Self-Adhesive

3317 A2563 33c multicolored .65 .20
3318 A2564 33c multicolored .65 .20
3319 A2565 33c multicolored .65 .20
3320 A2566 33c multicolored .65 .20
b. Strip of 4, #3317-3320 2.60

Extreme Sports

A2567

A2568

A2569

A2570

Serpentine Die Cut 11

1999, June 25 **Photo.**

Self-Adhesive

3321 A2567 33c Skateboarding .65 .20
3322 A2568 33c BMX Biking .65 .20
3323 A2569 33c Snowboarding .65 .20
3324 A2570 33c Inline Skating .65 .20
a. Block or strip of 4, #3321-3324 2.60

American Glass

Free-Blown Glass — A2571

Mold-Blown Glass — A2572

Pressed Glass — A2573

Art Glass — A2574

1999, June 29 **Litho.** ***Perf. 11***

3325 A2571 33c multicolored .65 .20
3326 A2572 33c multicolored .65 .20
3327 A2573 33c multicolored .65 .20
3328 A2574 33c multicolored .65 .20
a. Strip or block of 4, #3325-3328 2.60 —

A2575

A2576

Legends of Hollywood

James Cagney (1899-1986)

Perf. 11

1999, July 22 **Photo.** **Tagged**

3329 A2575 33c multicolored .65 .20

Perforations in corner of each stamp are star-shaped.

Gen. William "Billy" L. Mitchell (1879-1936), Aviation Pioneer

Serpentine Die Cut 9¾x10

1999, July 30 **Photo.**

Self-Adhesive

3330 A2576 55c multicolored 1.10 .20

Honoring Those Who Served

A2577

Serpentine Die Cut 11

1999, Aug. 16 **Photo.**

Self-Adhesive

3331 A2577 33c black, blue & red .65 .20

Universal Postal Union

A2578

1999, Aug. 25 **Litho.** ***Perf. 11***

3332 A2578 45c multicolored .90 .20

Famous Trains

Daylight A2579

Congressional — A2580

20th Century Limited A2581

Hiawatha A2582

Super Chief A2583

1999, Aug. 26 **Litho.** ***Perf. 11***

3333 A2579 33c multicolored .65 .20
3334 A2580 33c multicolored .65 .20
3335 A2581 33c multicolored .65 .20
3336 A2582 33c multicolored .65 .20
3337 A2583 33c multicolored .65 .20
a. Strip of 5, #3333-3337 3.25 —

Stamps in No. 3337a are arranged in four different orders.

Frederick Law Olmsted (1822-1903), Landscape Architect

A2584

1999, Sept. 12 **Litho.** ***Perf. 11***

3338 A2584 33c multicolored .65 .20

American Music Series Hollywood Composers

Max Steiner (1888-1971) — A2585

Dimitri Tiomkin (1894-1975) — A2586

Bernard Herrmann (1911-75) A2587

Franz Waxman (1906-67) A2588

Alfred Newman (1907-70) A2589

Erich Wolfgang Korngold (1897-1957) — A2590

1999, Sept. 16	Litho.	*Perf. 11*	
3339 A2585 33c multicolored		.65	.20
3340 A2586 33c multicolored		.65	.20
3341 A2587 33c multicolored		.65	.20
3342 A2588 33c multicolored		.65	.20
3343 A2589 33c multicolored		.65	.20
3344 A2590 33c multicolored		.65	.20
a. Block of 6, #3339-3344		3.90	—

Broadway Songwriters

Ira (1896-1983) & George (1898-1937) Gershwin — A2591

Alan Jay Lerner (1918-86) & Frederick Loewe (1901-88) A2592

Lorenz Hart (1895-1943) — A2593

Richard Rodgers (1902-79) & Oscar Hammerstein II (1895-1960) — A2594

Meredith Willson (1902-84) A2595

Frank Loesser (1910-69) A2596

1999, Sept. 21	Litho.	*Perf. 11*	
3345 A2591 33c multicolored		.65	.20
3346 A2592 33c multicolored		.65	.20
3347 A2593 33c multicolored		.65	.20
3348 A2594 33c multicolored		.65	.20
3349 A2595 33c multicolored		.65	.20
3350 A2596 33c multicolored		.65	.20
a. Block of 6, #3345-3350		3.90	—

Insects & Spiders

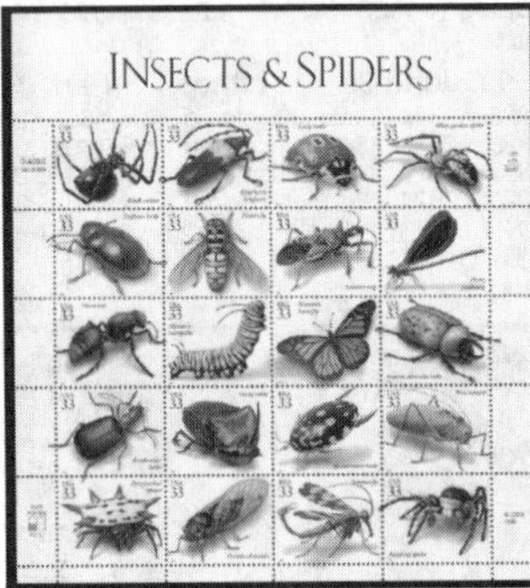

A2597

a, Black widow. b, Elderberry longhorn. c, Lady beetle. d, Yellow garden spider. e, Dogbane beetle. f, Flower fly. g, Assassin bug. h, Ebony jewelwing. i, Velvet ant. j, Monarch caterpillar. k, Monarch butterfly. l, Eastern Hercules beetle. m, Bombardier beetle. n, Dung beetle. o, Spotted water beetle. p, True katydid. q, Spinybacked spider. r, Periodical cicada. s, Scorpionfly. t, Jumping spider.

1999, Oct. 1	Litho.	*Perf. 11*	
3351 A2597 Pane of 20		13.00	—
a.-t. 33c any single		.65	.20

Hanukkah Type of 1996

Serpentine Die Cut 11

1999, Oct. 8 **Photo.**

Self-adhesive

3352 A2411 33c multicolored	.65	.20

Uncle Sam Type of 1998

COIL STAMP

1999, Oct. 8 Photo. ***Perf. 9¾ Vert.***

3353 A2530 22c multicolored	.45	.20

NATO, 50th Anniv.

A2598

1999, Oct. 13	Litho.	*Perf. 11¼*	
3354 A2598 33c multicolored		.65	.20

Christmas

Madonna and Child, by Bartolomeo Vivarini A2599

Deer A2600

Serpentine Die Cut 11¼ on 2 or 3 sides

1999, Oct. 20 **Litho.**

Booklet Stamp

Self-Adhesive

3355 A2599 33c multicolored	.65	.20
a. Booklet pane of 20	13.00	

Serpentine Die Cut 11¼

3356 A2600 33c gold & red	.65	.20
3357 A2600 33c gold & blue	.65	.20
3358 A2600 33c gold & purple	.65	.20
3359 A2600 33c gold & green	.65	.20
a. Block or strip, #3356-3359	2.60	

Booklet Stamps

Serpentine Die Cut 11¼ on 2, 3 or 4 sides

3360 A2600 33c gold & red	.65	.20
3361 A2600 33c gold & blue	.65	.20
3362 A2600 33c gold & purple	.65	.20
3363 A2600 33c gold & green	.65	.20
a. Booklet pane of 20, 5 each #3360-3363	13.00	

Size: 21x19mm

Serpentine Die Cut 11½x11¼ on 2 or 3 sides

3364 A2600 33c gold & red	.85	.20
3365 A2600 33c gold & blue	.85	.20
3366 A2600 33c gold & purple	.85	.20
3367 A2600 33c gold & green	.85	.20
a. Bklt. pane of 4, #3364-3367	3.50	
b. Bklt. pane, #3364, 3366, 3367, 2 #3365 + label	4.25	
c. Booklet pane of 6, #3365, 3367, 2 ea #3364, 3366	5.25	

The frame on Nos. 3356-3359 is narrow and the space between it and the hoof is a hairline. The frame on Nos. 3360-3363 is much thicker, and the space between it and the hoof is wider.

Kwanzaa Type of 1997

Serpentine Die Cut 11

1999, Oct. 29 **Photo.**

Self-Adhesive

3368 A2458 33c multicolored	.65	.20

Year 2000

Baby New Year — A2601

Serpentine Die Cut 11¼

1999, Dec. 27 **Litho.**

Self-Adhesive

3369 A2601 33c multicolored	.65	.20

Chinese New Year

Year of the Dragon — A2602

2000, Jan. 6	Litho.	*Perf. 11¼*	
3370 A2602 33c multicolored		.65	.20

Black Heritage

Patricia Roberts Harris — A2603

Serpentine Die Cut 11½x11¼

2000, Jan. 27 **Litho.**

Self-Adhesive

3371 A2603 33c indigo	.65	.20

Patricia Roberts Harris (1924-85), First Black Woman Cabinet Secretary.

Submarines

S Class A2604

Los Angeles Class A2605

Ohio Class A2606

USS Holland A2607

Gato Class — A2608

Illustration A2608 is reduced.

2000, Mar. 27	Litho.	*Perf. 11*	
3372 A2605 33c multi		.75	.20

Booklet Stamps

3373 A2604 22c multi	.55	.20
3374 A2605 33c multi, no microprint	.75	.30
3375 A2606 55c multi	1.25	.50
3376 A2607 60c multi	1.50	.55
3377 A2608 $3.20 multi	7.50	3.00
a. Booklet pane, #3373-3377	12.50	—

No. 3372 with microprinted "USPS" at base of sail. No. 3374 has no microprinting.

No. 3377a was issued with two types of text in the selvage.

Pacific Coast Rain Forest

A2609

Designs: a, Harlequin duck. b, Dwarf oregongrape, snail-eating ground beetle. c, American dipper, horiz. d, Cutthroat trout, horiz. e, Roosevelt elk. f, Winter wren. g,

Pacific giant salamander, Rough-skinned newt. h, Western tiger swallowtail, horiz. i, Douglas squirrel, foliose lichen. j, Foliose lichen, banana slug.

Serpentine Die Cut 11¼x11½, 11½ (horiz. stamps)

2000, Mar. 29 Litho.

Self-Adhesive

3378 A2609 Pane of 10 6.50
a.-j. 33c any single .65 .20

Louise Nevelson (1899-1988), Sculptor

Silent Music I — A2610

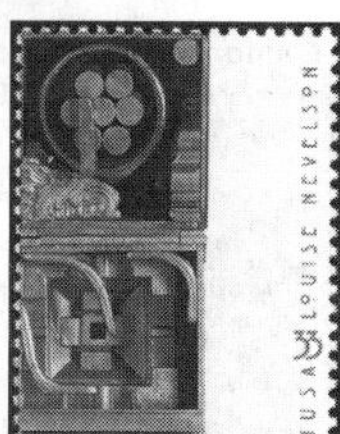

Royal Tide I — A2611

Black Chord — A2612

Nightsphere-Light — A2613

Dawn's Wedding Chapel I — A2614

2000, Apr. 6 Litho. *Perf. 11x11¼*

3379	A2610 33c multicolored	.65	.20
3380	A2611 33c multicolored	.65	.20
3381	A2612 33c multicolored	.65	.20
3382	A2613 33c multicolored	.65	.20
3383	A2614 33c multicolored	.65	.20
a.	Strip of 5, #3379-3383	3.25	—

Hubble Space Telescope Images

Eagle Nebula — A2615

Ring Nebula — A2616

Lagoon Nebula — A2617

Egg Nebula — A2618

Galaxy NGC 1316 — A2619

2000, Apr. 10 Photo. *Perf. 11*

3384	A2615 33c multicolored	.65	.20
3385	A2616 33c multicolored	.65	.20
3386	A2617 33c multicolored	.65	.20
3387	A2618 33c multicolored	.65	.20
3388	A2619 33c multicolored	.65	.20
a.	Strip of 5, #3384-3388	3.25	—
b.	As "a," imperf	*1,200.*	

American Samoa

Samoan Double Canoe A2620

2000, Apr. 17 Litho. *Perf. 11*

3389 A2620 33c multicolored .65 .20

Library of Congress

A2621

2000, Apr. 24 Litho. *Perf. 11*

3390 A2621 33c multicolored .65 .20

Design features interior dome & arched windows in Main Reading Room, Thomas Jefferson Building.

Road Runner & Wile E. Coyote

A2622

Serpentine Die Cut 11

2000, Apr. 26 Litho.

Self-Adhesive

3391	Pane of 10	6.50	
a.	A2622 33c single	.65	.20
b.	Booklet pane of 9 #3391a	5.85	
c.	Booklet pane of 1 #3391a	.65	
d.	All die cutting omitted, pane of 10	*8,500.*	

Die cutting on #3391 does not extend through the backing paper.

3392	Pane of 10	*6.50*
a.	A2622 33c single	*.65*
b.	Booklet pane of 9 #3392a	—
c.	Booklet pane of 1, imperf.	—

Die cutting on #3392b extends through the backing paper. Used examples of No. 3392a are identical to those of No. 3391a.

Distinguished Soldiers

A2623

A2624

A2625

A2626

Designs: No. 3393, Maj. Gen. John L. Hines. No. 3394, Gen. Omar N. Bradley. No. 3395, Sgt. Alvin C. York. No. 3396, Second Lt. Audie L. Murphy.

2000, May 3 Litho. *Perf. 11*

3393	A2623 33c multicolored	.65	.20
3394	A2624 33c multicolored	.65	.20
3395	A2625 33c multicolored	.65	.20
3396	A2626 33c multicolored	.65	.20
a.	Block or strip, #3393-3396	2.60	—

Summer Sports

Runners A2627

2000, May 5 Litho. *Perf. 11*

3397 A2627 33c multicolored .65 .20

Adoption

Stick Figures A2628

Serpentine Die Cut 11½

2000, May 10 Litho.

Self-Adhesive

3398 A2628 33c multicolored .65 .20

Youth Team Sports

A2629

A2630

A2631

A2632

2000, May 27 Litho. *Perf. 11*

3399	A2629 33c Basketball	.65	.20
3400	A2630 33c Football	.65	.20
3401	A2631 33c Soccer	.65	.20
3402	A2632 33c Baseball	.65	.20
a.	Block or strip, #3399-3402	2.60	—

The Stars and Stripes

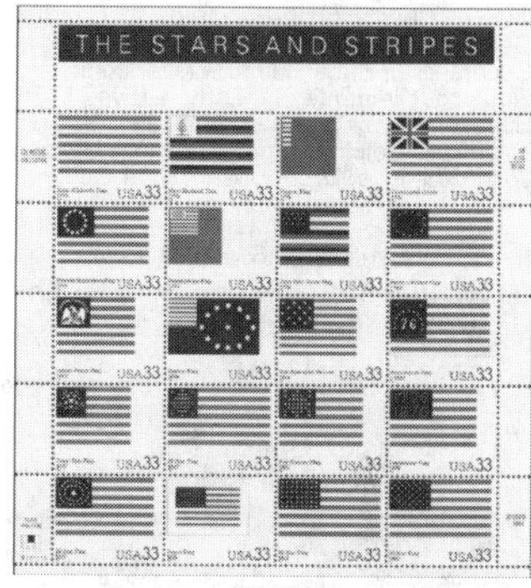

A2633

Designs: a, Sons of Liberty Flag, 1775. b, New England Flag, 1775. c, Forster Flag, 1775. d, Continental Colors, 1776. e, Francis Hopkinson Flag, 1777. f, Brandywine Flag, 1777. g, John Paul Jones Flag, 1779. h, Pierre L'Enfant Flag, 1783. i, Indian Peace Flag, 1803. j, Easton Flag, 1814. k, Star-Spangled Banner, 1814. l, Bennington Flag, c. 1820. m, Great Star Flag, 1837. n, 29-Star Flag, 1847. o, Fort Sumter Flag, 1861. p, Centennial Flag, 1876. q, 38-Star Flag, 1877. r, Peace Flag, 1891. s, 48-Star Flag, 1912. t, 50-Star Flag, 1960.

2000, June 14 Litho. *Perf. 10½x11*

3403 A2633 Pane of 20 13.00 —
a.-t. 33c any single .65 .30

Inscriptions on the back of each stamp describe the flag.

Berries

Blueberries A2634

Strawberries A2635

Blackberries
A2636

Raspberries
A2637

Serpentine Die Cut 8½ Horiz.

2000, June 16 **Photo.**

Self-Adhesive

Coil Stamps

3404	A2634 33c multicolored		.65	.20
3405	A2635 33c multicolored		.65	.20
3406	A2636 33c multicolored		.65	.20
3407	A2637 33c multicolored		.65	.20
	a.	Strip of 4, #3404-3407	2.60	

The adhesive on Nos. 3404-3407 is strong and can remove the ink from stamps in the roll.

Legends of Baseball

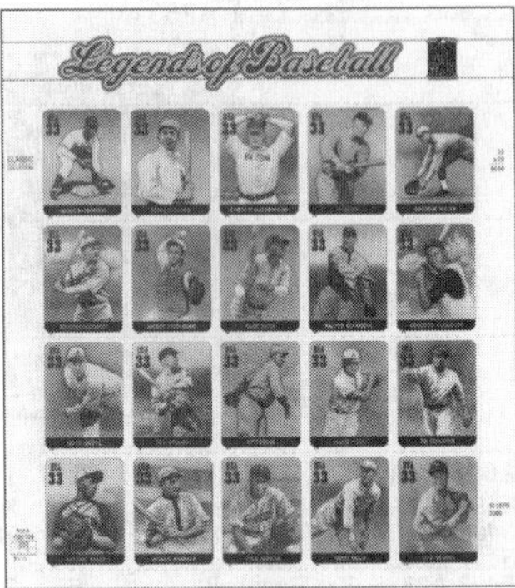

A2638

Designs: a, Jackie Robinson. b, Eddie Collins. c, Christy Mathewson. d, Ty Cobb. e, George Sisler. f, Rogers Hornsby. g, Mickey Cochrane. h, Babe Ruth. i, Walter Johnson. j, Roberto Clemente. k, Lefty Grove. l, Tris Speaker. m, Cy Young. n, Jimmie Foxx. o, Pie Traynor. p, Satchel Paige. q, Honus Wagner. r, Josh Gibson. s, Dizzy Dean. t, Lou Gehrig.

Serpentine Die Cut 11¼

2000, July 6 **Litho.**

Self-Adhesive

3408	A2638	Pane of 20	13.00	
a.-t.		33c any single	.65	.20

Space

Souvenir Sheets

A2639

A2640

A2641

A2642

A2643

No. 3409, Probing the Vastness of Space: a, Hubble Space Telescope. b, Radio interferometer very large array, New Mexico. c, Optical and infrared telescopes, Keck Observatory, Hawaii. d, Optical telescopes, Cerro Tololo Observatory, Chile. e, Optical telescope, Mount Wilson Observatory, California. f, Radio telescope, Arecibo Observatory, Puerto Rico.

No. 3410, Exploring the Solar System: a, Sun and corona. b, Cross-section of sun. c, Sun and earth. d, Sun and solar flare. e, Sun and clouds.

No. 3411, Escaping the Gravity of Earth: a, Space Shuttle and Space Station. b, Astronauts working in space.

No. 3412, Space Achievement & Exploration.

No. 3413, Landing on the Moon

Illustrations reduced.

2000 **Photo.** ***Perf. 10½x11***

3409	A2639	Sheet of 6	7.50	—
a.-f.		60c any single	1.25	.60

Perf. 10¾

3410	A2640	Sheet of 5 + label	10.00	—
a.-e.		$1 any single	2.00	1.00
f.		As #3410, imperf	—	
g.		As #3410, with hologram from #3411b applied	—	

Photogravure with Hologram Affixed

Perf. 10½, 10¾ (#3412)

3411	A2641	Sheet of 2	12.50	—
a.-b.		$3.20 any single	6.25	3.00
c.		Hologram omitted on right stamp	—	
3412	A2642	multi	22.50	11.50
a.		$11.75 Single stamp	20.00	10.00
b.		Hologram omitted	—	
c.		Hologram omitted on No. 3412 in uncut sheet of 5 panes	—	
3413	A2643	multi	22.50	11.50
a.		$11.75 Single stamp	20.00	10.00
b.		Double hologram	—	
c.		Double hologram on No. 3413 in uncut sheet of 5 panes	—	
d.		Hologram omitted on No. 3413 in uncut sheet of 5 panes	—	
		Nos. 3409-3413 (5)	75.00	

Issued: No. 3409, 7/10; No. 3410, 7/11; No. 3411, 7/9; No. 3412, 7/7; No. 3413, 7/8.

Warning: Soaking in water may affect holographic images.

Stampin' the Future Children's Stamp Design Contest Winners

by Zachary Canter
A2644

by Sarah Lipsey
A2645

by Morgan Hill
A2646

by Ashley Young
A2647

Serpentine Die Cut 11¼

2000, July 13 **Litho.**

Self-Adhesive

3414	A2644 33c multicolored		.65	.20
3415	A2645 33c multicolored		.65	.20
3416	A2646 33c multicolored		.65	.20
3417	A2647 33c multicolored		.65	.20
	a.	Horiz. strip of 4, #3414-3417	2.60	

Distinguished Americans

Gen. Joseph W. Stilwell
A2650

Sen. Claude Pepper
A2656

Sen. Hattie Caraway (1878-1950)
A2661

Edna Ferber (1887-1968), Writer
A2662

Perf. 11, Serpentine Die Cut 11 (#3431), 11½x11 (#3432) or 11x11½ (#3433)

2000-02 **Litho. & Engr.**

3420	A2650 10c red & black		.20	.20
	a.	Imperf, pair	*450.00*	
3426	A2656 33c red & black		.65	.20
3431	A2661 76c red & black		1.50	.20
3432	A2661 76c red & black		*3.00*	*3.00*
3433	A2662 83c red & black		1.60	.30

This is an ongoing set. Numbers may change. Issued: 10c, 8/24; 33c, 9/7, 75c, 2/21/01; 83c, 7/29/02.

California Statehood, 150th Anniv.

Big Sur and Iceplant — A2668

Serpentine Die Cut 11

2000, Sept. 8 **Photo.**

Self-Adhesive

3438	A2668 33c multicolored	.65	.20

Deep Sea Creatures

Fanfin Anglerfish
A2669

Sea Cucumber
A2670

Fangtooth
A2671

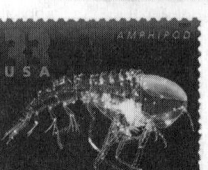

Amphipod
A2672

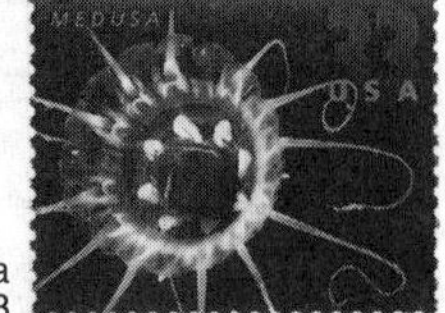

Medusa
A2673

2000, Oct. 2 **Photo.** ***Perf. 10x10¼***

3439	A2669 33c multicolored	.65	.20
3440	A2670 33c multicolored	.65	.20
3441	A2671 33c multicolored	.65	.20

3442 A2672 33c multicolored .65 .20
3443 A2673 33c multicolored .65 .20
a. Vert. strip of 5, #3439-3443 3.25 —

Literary Arts

Thomas Wolfe (1900-38), Novelist — A2674

2000, Oct. 3 Litho. *Perf. 11*
3444 A2674 33c multicolored .65 .20

White House, 200th Anniv.

A2675

Serpentine Die Cut 11¼
2000, Oct. 18 Litho.
Self-Adhesive
3445 A2675 33c multicolored .65 .20

Legends of Hollywood

A2676

2000, Oct. 24 Photo. *Perf. 11*
3446 A2676 33c multicolored .65 .20

Edward G. Robinson (1893-1973). Perforations in corner of each stamp are star-shaped.

New York Public Library Lion — A2677

Serpentine Die Cut 11½ Vert.
2000, Nov. 9 Photo.
Self-Adhesive
Coil Stamp
3447 A2677 (10c) multicolored .20 .20

Flag Over Farm — A2678

2000, Dec. 15 Litho. *Perf. 11¼*
3448 A2678 (34c) multicolored .65 .20

Self-Adhesive
Serpentine Die Cut 11¼
3449 A2678 (34c) multicolored .65 .20

Booklet Stamp
Self-Adhesive
Photo.
Serpentine Die Cut 8 on 2, 3 or 4 sides
3450 A2678 (34c) multicolored .65 .20
a. Booklet pane of 18 12.00

A2679

Statue of Liberty — A2680

PHOTOGRAVURE
Serpentine Die Cut 11 on 2, 3 or 4 sides
2000, Dec. 15 Photo.
Self-Adhesive (#3451, 3453)
Booklet Stamp
3451 A2679 (34c) multicolored .65 .20
a. Booklet pane of 20 13.00
b. Booklet pane of 4 2.60
c. Booklet pane of 6 3.90
d. As "a," imperf —

Coil Stamps
Perf. 9¾ Vert.
3452 A2680 (34c) multicolored .65 .20

Serpentine Die Cut 10 Vert.
3453 A2680 (34c) multicolored .65 .20
a. Imperf, pair —

A2681 A2682

A2683 A2684
Flowers

Serpentine Die Cut 10½x10¾ on 2 or 3 sides
2000, Dec. 15 Photo.
Booklet Stamps
Self-Adhesive
3454 A2681 (34c) pur & multi .65 .20
3455 A2682 (34c) tan & multi .65 .20
3456 A2683 (34c) green & multi .65 .20
3457 A2684 (34c) red & multi .65 .20
a. Block of 4, #3454-3457 2.60
b. Booklet pane of 4, #3454-3457 2.60
c. Booklet pane of 6, #3456, 3457, 2 each #3454-3455 3.90
d. Booklet pane of 6, #3454, 3455, 2 each #3456-3457 3.90
e. Booklet pane of 20, 5 each #3454-3457 + label 13.00

Serpentine Die Cut 11½x11¾ on 2 or 3 sides
2000, Dec. 15 Photo
3458 A2681 (34c) pur & multi .65 .20
3459 A2682 (34c) tan & multi .65 .20
3460 A2683 (34c) grn & multi .65 .20
3461 A2684 (34c) red & multi .65 .20
a. Block of 4, #3458-3461 2.60
b. Booklet pane of 20, 2 each #3461a, 3 each #3457a *25.00*
c. Booklet pane of 20, 2 each #3457a, 3 each #3461a *30.00*

Coil Stamps
Serpentine Die Cut 8½ Vert.
3462 A2683 (34c) green & multi .65 .20
3463 A2684 (34c) red & multi .65 .20
3464 A2682 (34c) tan & multi .65 .20
3465 A2681 (34c) pur & multi .65 .20
a. Strip of 4, #3462-3465 2.60

Lettering on No. 3462 has black outline not found on No. 3456. Zeroes of "2000" are rounder on Nos. 3454-3457 than on Nos. 3462-3465.

Statue of Liberty A2685

George Washington A2686

American Buffalo A2687

Flag Over Farm A2688

Statue of Liberty — A2689

A2690

A2691

A2692

Flowers A2693

Apple A2694

Orange A2695

Eagle A2696

Capitol Dome — A2697

Washington Monument A2698

Serpentine Die Cut 9¾ Vert.
2001 Photo.
Coil Stamp
Self-Adhesive
3466 A2685 34c multicolored .65 .20

Litho. *Perf. 11¼x11*
3467 A2687 21c multicolored .40 .20

Serpentine Die Cut 11
Self-Adhesive (#3468-3468A, 3470-3473)
3468 A2687 21c multicolored .40 .20

Serpentine Die Cut 11¼x11¾
3468A A2686 23c green .45 .20

Litho.
Perf. 11¼
3469 A2688 34c multicolored .65 .20

Serpentine Die Cut 11¼
3470 A2688 34c multicolored .65 .20

Photo.
Serpentine Die Cut 10¾
3471 A2696 55c multicolored 1.10 .20
3471A A2696 57c multicolored 1.10 .20

Serpentine Die Cut 11¼x11½
Self-Adhesive
3472 A2697 $3.50 multicolored 7.00 3.50
a. Imperf, pair —
3473 A2698 $12.25 multicolored 22.50 10.00

COIL STAMPS
Self-Adhesive (#3475-3475A, 3477-3481)
Photo.
Serpentine Die Cut 8½ Vert.
3475 A2687 21c multicolored .40 .20
3475A A2686 23c green .45 .20

Perf. 9¾ Vert.
3476 A2685 34c multicolored .65 .20

Serpentine Die Cut 9¾ Vert.
3477 A2685 34c multicolored .65 .20

No. 3477 has right angle corners and backing paper as high as the stamp. No. 3466 has rounded corners and is on backing paper larger than the stamp.

Serpentine Die Cut 8½ Vert.
3478 A2690 34c green & multi .65 .20
3479 A2691 34c red & multi .65 .20
3480 A2692 34c tan & multi .65 .20
3481 A2693 34c purple & multi .65 .20
a. Strip of 4, #3478-3481 2.60

BOOKLET STAMPS
Litho.
Self-Adhesive
Serpentine Die Cut 11¼ on 3 Sides
3482 A2686 20c dark carmine .40 .20
a. Booklet pane of 10 4.00
b. Booklet pane of 4 1.60
c. Booklet pane of 6 2.40

Serpentine Die Cut 10½x11¼ on 3 Sides
3483 A2686 20c dark carmine .40 .20
a. Booklet pane of 4, 2 #3482 at L, 2 #3483 at R *5.00*
b. Booklet pane of 6, 3 #3482 at L, 3 #3483 at R *8.00*
c. Booklet pane of 10, 5 #3482 at L, 5 #3483 at R *10.00*
d. Booklet pane of 4, 2 #3483 at L, 2 #3482 at R *5.00*
e. Booklet pane of 6, 3 #3483 at L, 3 #3482 at R *8.00*
f. Booklet pane of 10, 5 #3483 at L, 5 #3482 at R *10.00*
g. Pair, #3482 at L, #3483 at R *2.00*
h. Pair, #3483 at L, #3482 at R *2.00*

Nos. 3483a and 3483b have No. 3482 at L and No. 3483 at R.

Serpentine Die Cut 11¼ on 3 Sides
3484 A2687 21c multicolored .40 .20
b. Booklet pane of 4 1.60
c. Booklet pane of 6 2.40
d. Booklet pane of 10 4.00

Serpentine Die Cut 10½x11¼
3484A A2687 21c multicolored *1.00* .30
e. Booklet pane of 4, 2 #3484 at L, 2 #3484A at R *5.00*
f. Booklet pane of 6, 3 #3484 at L, 3 #3484A at R *8.00*
g. Booklet pane of 10, 5 #3484 at L, 5 #3484A at R *10.00*
h. Booklet pane of 4, 2 #3484A at L, 2 #3484 at R *5.00*

i. Booklet pane of 6, 3 #3484A at L, 3 #3484 at R 8.00
j. Booklet pane of 10, 5 #3484A at L, 5 #3484 at R 10.00
k. Pair, #3484 at L, #3484A at R 2.00
l. Pair, #3484A at L, #3484 at R 2.00

Photo.

Serpentine Die Cut 11 on 2, 3 or 4 Sides

3485 A2689 34c multicolored .65 .20
a. Booklet pane of 10 6.50
b. Booklet pane of 20 13.00
c. Booklet pane of 4 2.60
d. Booklet pane of 6 3.90
e. Imperf, pair (from No. 3485b) —

Photo.

Serpentine Die Cut 10½x10¾ on 2 or 3 Sides

3487 A2693 34c purple & multi .65 .20
3488 A2692 34c tan & multi .65 .20
3489 A2690 34c green & multi .65 .20
3490 A2691 34c red & multi .65 .20
a. Block of 4, #3487-3490 2.60
b. Booklet pane of 4, #3487-3490 2.60
c. Booklet pane of 6, #3489-3490, 2 each #3487-3488 3.90
d. Booklet pane of 6, #3487-3488, 2 each #3489-3490 3.90
e. Booklet pane of 20, 5 each #3490a + label 13.00

Litho.

Serpentine Die Cut 11¼ on 2, 3 or 4 Sides

3491 A2694 34c multicolored .65 .20
3492 A2695 34c multicolored .65 .20
a. Pair, #3491-3492 1.30
b. Booklet pane, 10 each #3491-3492 13.00
c. As "a," black ("34 USA") omitted —
d. As "a," imperf —

Serpentine Die Cut 11½x10¾ on 2 or 3 Sides

3493 A2694 34c multicolored .65 .20
3494 A2695 34c multicolored .65 .20
a. Pair, #3493-3494 1.30
b. Booklet pane, 2 each #3493-3494 2.60
c. Booklet pane, 3 each #3493-3494, #3493 at UL 3.90
d. Booklet pane, 3 each #3493-3494, #3494 at UL 3.90

Photo.

Serpentine Die Cut 8 on 2, 3 or 4 sides

3495 A2688 34c multicolored .65 .20
a. Booklet pane of 18 12.00

Issued: No. 3466, 1/7/01; Nos. 3472-3473, 1/29/01; Nos. 3468, 3471, 3475, 3482, 3483, 2/22; Nos. 3469, 3476-3481, 3485, 3487-3490, 2/7; Nos. 3470, 3491-3492, 3/6; 3493-3494, May; Nos. 3467, 3468A, 3471A, 3475A, 3484, 3484A, 9/20; 3495, 12/17.

Issued: $3.50, $12.25, 1/29.

Love

Rose, Apr. 20, 1763 Love Letter by John Adams A2699

Rose, Apr. 20, 1763 Love Letter by John Adams A2700

Rose, Aug. 11, 1763 Love Letter by Abigail Adams — A2701

Serpentine Die Cut 11¼ on 2, 3 or 4 Sides

2001 Litho.

Self-Adhesive

Booklet Stamp

3496 A2699 (34c) multicolored .65 .20
a. Booklet pane of 20 13.00
b. Vert. pair, imperf horiz. —

Serpentine Die Cut 11¼ on 2, 3 or 4 sides

3497 A2700 34c multicolored .65 .20
a. Booklet pane of 20 13.00

Size: 18x21mm

Serpentine Die Cut 11½x10¾ on 2 or 3 Sides

3498 A2700 34c multicolored .65 .20
a. Booklet pane of 4 2.60
b. Booklet pane of 6 3.90

Issued: Nos. 3497-3498, 2/14.

3499 A2701 55c multicolored 1.10 .20

Issued: No. 3496, 1/19; 55c, 2/14.

See No. 3551.

Chinese New Year

Year of the Snake A2702

2001, Jan. 20 Litho. *Perf. 11¼*

3500 A2702 34c multicolored .65 .20

Black Heritage

Roy Wilkins (1901-81), Civil Rights Leader — A2703

Serpentine Die Cut 11½x11¼

2001, Jan. 24 Litho.

Self-Adhesive

3501 A2703 34c blue .65 .20

American Illustrators

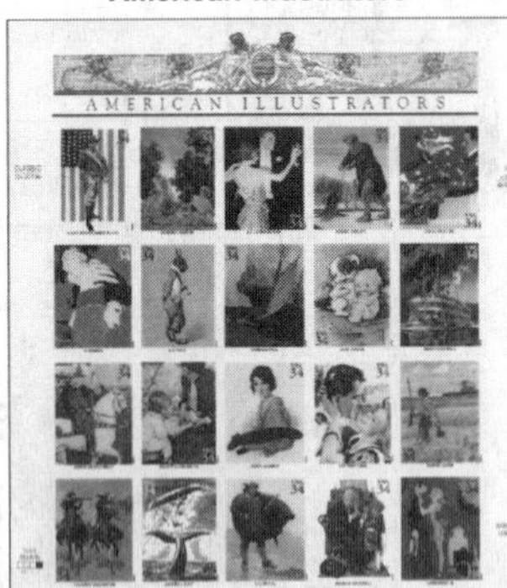

A2704

Designs: a, Marine Corps poster "First in the Fight, Always Faithful," by James Montgomery Flagg. b, "Interlude (The Lute Players)," by Maxfield Parrish. c, Advertisement for Arrow Collars and Shirts, by J. C. Leyendecker. d, Advertisement for Carrier Corp. Refrigeration, by Robert Fawcett. e, Advertisement for Luxite Hosiery, by Coles Phillips. f, Illustration for correspondence school lesson, by Al Parker. g, "Br'er Rabbit," by A. B. Frost. h, "An Attack on a Galleon," by Howard Pyle. i, Kewpie and Kewpie Doodle Dog, by Rose O'Neill. j, Illustration for cover of True Magazine, by Dean Cornwell. k, "Galahad's Departure," by Edwin Austin Abbey. l, "The First Lesson," by Jessie Willcox Smith. m, Illustration for cover of McCall's Magazine, by Neysa McMein. n, "Back Home For Keeps," by Jon Whitcomb. o, "Something for Supper," by Harvey Dunn. p, "A Dash for the Timber," by Frederic Remington. q, Illustration for "Moby Dick," by Rockwell Kent. r, "Captain Bill Bones," by N. C. Wyeth. s, Illustration for cover of The Saturday Evening Post, by Norman Rockwell. t, "The Girl He Left Behind," by John Held, Jr.

Serpentine Die Cut 11¼

2001, Feb. 1 Photo.

Self-Adhesive

3502 A2704 Pane of 20 13.00
a.-t. 34c any single .65 .30

Diabetes Awareness

A2705

Serpentine Die Cut 11¼x11½

2001, Mar. 16 Litho.

Self-Adhesive

3503 A2705 34c multicolored .65 .20

Nobel Prize Centenary

Alfred Nobel and Obverse of Medals A2706

Litho. & Engr.

2001, Mar. 22 *Perf. 11*

3504 A2706 34c multicolored .65 .20

See Sweden No. 2415.

Pan-American Exposition Invert Stamps, Cent.

A2707

Reproductions (dated 2001) of: a, #294a. b, #295a. c, #296a. d, Commemorative "cinderella" stamp depicting a buffalo.

Perf. 12 (#3505d), 12½x12 (others)

Litho. (#3505d), Engr. (others)

2001, Mar. 29

3505 A2707 Pane of 7, #3505a-3505c, 4 #3505d 6.75 —
a. A109 1c green & black .20 .20
b. A110 2c carmine & black .20 .20
c. A111 4c deep red brown & black .20 .20
d. 80c red & blue 1.60 .35

Great Plains Prairie

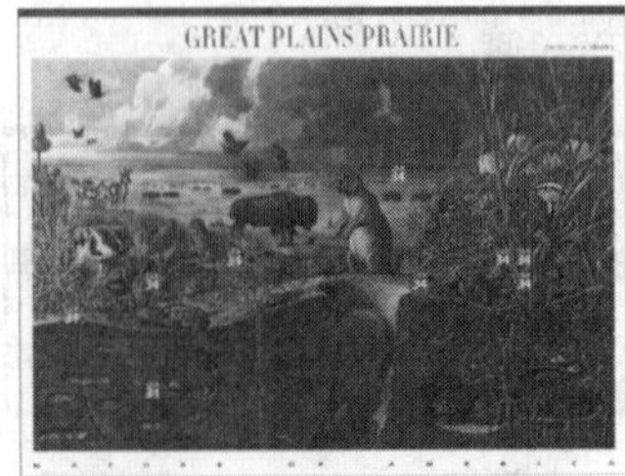

A2708

Wildlife and flowers: a, Pronghorns, Canada geese. b, Burrowing owls, American buffalos. c, American buffalo, Black-tailed prairie dogs, wild alfalfa, horiz. d, Black-tailed prairie dog, American buffalos,. e, Painted lady butterfly, American buffalo, prairie coneflowers, prairie wild roses, horiz. f, Western meadowlark, camel cricket, prairie coneflowers, prairie wild roses. g, Badger, harvester ants. h, Eastern short-horned lizard, plains pocket gopher. i, Plains spadefoot, dung beetle, prairie wild roses, horiz. j, Two-striped grasshopper, Ord's kangaroo rat.

Serpentine Die Cut 10

2001, Apr. 19 Litho.

Self-Adhesive

3506 A2708 Pane of 10 7.00
a.-j. 34c Any single .65 .20

Peanuts Comic Strip

Snoopy A2709

Serpentine Die Cut 11¼x11½

2001, May 17 Litho.

Self-Adhesive

3507 A2709 34c multicolored .65 .20

Honoring Veterans

A2710

Serpentine Die Cut 11¼x11½

2001, May 23 Litho.

Self-Adhesive

3508 A2710 34c multicolored .65 .20

Frida Kahlo (1907-54), Painter

Self-portrait A2711

2001, June 21 Litho. *Perf. 11¼*

3509 A2711 34c multicolored .65 .20

Legendary Playing Fields

Ebbets Field A2712

Tiger Stadium A2713

Crosley Field A2714

Yankee Stadium A2715

Polo Grounds A2716

Forbes Field A2717

Fenway Park A2718

Comiskey Park A2719

Shibe Park A2720

Wrigley Field A2721

Serpentine Die Cut 11¼x11½

2001, June 27 — Photo.

Self-Adhesive

3510	A2712 34c multicolored	.65	.20
3511	A2713 34c multicolored	.65	.20
3512	A2714 34c multicolored	.65	.20
3513	A2715 34c multicolored	.65	.20
3514	A2716 34c multicolored	.65	.20
3515	A2717 34c multicolored	.65	.20
3516	A2718 34c multicolored	.65	.20
3517	A2719 34c multicolored	.65	.20
3518	A2720 34c multicolored	.65	.20
3519	A2721 34c multicolored	.65	.20
a.	Block of 10, #3510-3519	6.50	

Atlas Statue, New York City

A2722

Serpentine Die Cut 8½ Vert.

2001, June 29 — Photo.

Self-Adhesive

Coil Stamp

3520 A2722 (10c) multicolored .20 .20

Leonard Bernstein (1918-90), Conductor

A2723

2001, July 10 — Litho. — *Perf. 11¼*

3521 A2723 34c multicolored .65 .20

Woody Wagon

A2724

Serpentine Die Cut 11½ Vert.

2001, Aug. 3 — Photo.

Self-Adhesive

Coil Stamp

3522 A2724 (15c) multicolored .30 .20

Legends of Hollywood

Lucille Ball (1911-89) — A2725

Serpentine Die Cut 11

2001, Aug. 6 — Litho.

Self-Adhesive

3523 A2725 34c multicolored .65 .20
a. As No. 3523, die cutting omitted —

American Treasures Series

Amish Quilts

Diamond in the Square, c. 1920 — A2726

Lone Star, c. 1920 — A2727

Sunshine and Shadow, c. 1910 — A2728

Double Ninepatch Variation A2729

Serpentine Die Cut 11¼x11½

2001, Aug. 9 — Litho.

Self-Adhesive

3524	A2726 34c multicolored	.65	.20
3525	A2727 34c multicolored	.65	.20
3526	A2728 34c multicolored	.65	.20
3527	A2729 34c multicolored	.65	.20
a.	Block or strip of 4, #3524-3527	2.60	

Carnivorous Plants

Venus Flytrap A2730

Yellow Trumpet A2731

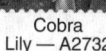

Cobra Lily — A2732

English Sundew — A2733

Serpentine Die Cut 11½

2001, Aug. 23 — Photo.

Self-Adhesive

3528	A2730 34c multicolored	.65	.20
3529	A2731 34c multicolored	.65	.20
3530	A2732 34c multicolored	.65	.20
3531	A2733 34c multicolored	.65	.20
a.	Block or strip of 4, #3528-3531	2.60	

Eid

"Eid Mubarak" — A2734

Serpentine Die Cut 11¼

2001, Sept. 1 — Photo.

Self-Adhesive

3532 A2734 34c multicolored .65 .20

Enrico Fermi (1901-54), Physicist

A2735

2001, Sept. 29 — Litho. — *Perf. 11*

3533 A2735 34c multicolored .65 .20

That's All Folks!

Porky Pig at Mailbox — A2736

Serpentine Die Cut 11

2001, Oct. 1 — Photo.

Self-Adhesive

3534	Pane of 10	6.50	
a.	A2736 34c single	.65	.20
b.	Booklet pane of 9 #3534a	5.85	
c.	Booklet pane of 1 #3534a	.65	

Die cutting on No. 3534b does not extend through the backing paper.

3535	Pane of 10	6.50	
a.	A2736 34c single	.65	
b.	Booklet pane of 9 #3535a	—	
c.	Booklet pane of 1, imperf.	—	

Die cutting on No. 3535a extends through backing paper. Used examples of No. 3535a are identical to those of No. 3534a.

Nos. 3534b-3534c and 3535b-3535c are separated by a vertical line of microperforations.

Christmas

Virgin and Child, by Lorenzo Costa — A2737

A2738 A2739 A2740 A2741

19th Century Chromolithographs of Santa Claus

Serpentine Die Cut 11½ on 2, 3 or 4 Sides

2001, Oct. 10 — Photo.

Self- Adhesive

Booklet Stamps (#3536, 3537a-3540a, 3541-3544)

3536 A2737 34c multicolored .65 .20
a. Booklet pane of 20 13.00

Serpentine Die Cut 10¾x11

Black Inscriptions

3537	A2738 34c multi, large date	.65	.20
a.	Small date (from booklet pane)	.65	.20
b.	Large date (from booklet pane)	.65	.20
3538	A2739 34c multi, large date	.65	.20
a.	Small date (from booklet pane)	.65	.20
b.	Large date (from booklet pane)	.65	.20
3539	A2740 34c multi, large date	.65	.20
a.	Small date (from booklet pane)	.65	.20
b.	Large date (from booklet pane)	.65	.20
3540	A2741 34c multi, large date	.65	.20
a.	Small date (from booklet pane)	.65	.20
b.	Block of 4, #3537-3540	2.60	
c.	Block of 4, small date, #3537a-3540a	2.60	
d.	Booklet pane, 5 #3540c + label	13.00	

e. Large date (from booklet pane) .65 .20
f. Block of 4, large date, #3537b-3539b, 3540e 2.60
g. Booklet pane, 5 #3540f + label 13.00

Numerals "3" and "4" are distinctly separate on Nos. 3537-3540, and touching or separated by a slight hairline on the booklet pane stamps.

Designs of Nos. 3537a-3540a are slightly taller than Nos. 3537-3540.

Serpentine Die Cut 11 on 2 or 3 Sides

Size: 21x18½mm

Green and Red Inscriptions

3541 A2738 34c multicolored .65 .20
3542 A2739 34c multicolored .65 .20
3543 A2740 34c multicolored .65 .20
3544 A2741 34c multicolored .65 .20
a. Block of 4, #3541-3544 2.60
b. Booklet pane of 4, #3541-3544 2.60
c. Booklet pane of 6, #3543-3544, 2 #3541-3542 3.90
d. Booklet pane of 6, #3541-3542, 2 #3543-3544 3.90
Nos. 3536-3544 (9) 5.85 1.80

James Madison (1751-1836)

Madison and His Home, Montpelier A2742

Litho. & Engr.

2001, Oct. 18 ***Perf. 11x11¼***

3545 A2742 34c green & black .65 .20

Thanksgiving

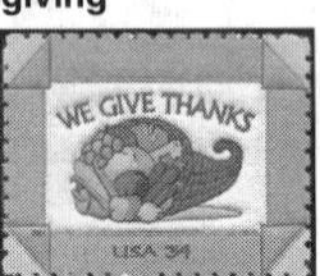

Cornucopia A2743

Serpentine Die Cut 11¼

2001, Oct. 19 **Litho.**

Self-Adhesive

3546 A2743 34c multicolored .65 .20

Hanukkah Type of 1996

Serpentine Die Cut 11

2001, Oct. 21 **Photo.**

Self-Adhesive

3547 A2411 34c multicolored .65 .20

Kwanzaa Type of 1997

Serpentine Die Cut 11

2001, Oct. 21 **Photo.**

Self-Adhesive

3548 A2458 34c multicolored .65 .20

United We Stand

A2744

Serpentine Die Cut 11¼ on 2, 3, or 4 Sides

2001, Oct. 24 **Litho.**

Self-Adhesive

Booklet Stamp

3549 A2744 34c multicolored .65 .20
a. Booklet pane of 20 13.00

United We Stand Type of 2001

Serpentine Die Cut 10½x10¾ on 2 or 3 Sides

2002, Jan. **Photo.**

Booklet Stamps

Self-Adhesive

3549B A2744 34c multicolored .65 .20
c. Booklet pane of 4 2.60
d. Booklet pane of 6 3.90
e. Booklet pane of 20 13.00

Issued No. 3549B, Jan. 2002 (first day covers are dated Oct. 24, 2001).

United We Stand Type of 2001

Serpentine Die Cut 9 ¾ Vert.

2001, Oct. 24 **Photo.**

Self-Adhesive

Coil Stamp

3550 A2744 34c multicolored .65 .20
3550A A2744 34c multicolored .65 .20

No. 3550 has right angle corners and backing paper as high as the stamp. No. 3550A has rounded corners, the backing paper larger than the stamp, and the stamps are spaced approximately 2mm apart.

Love Letters Type of 2001

Serpentine Die Cut 11¼

2001, Nov. 19 **Litho.**

Self-Adhesive

3551 A2701 57c multicolored 1.10 .20

Winter Olympics

Ski Jumping A2745

Snowboarding — A2746

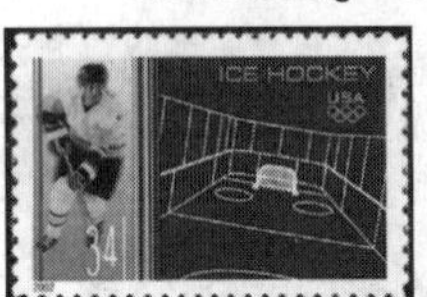

Ice Hockey A2747

Figure Skating A2748

Serpentine Die Cut 11½x10¾

2002, Jan. 8 **Photo.**

Self-Adhesive

3552 A2745 34c multicolored .65 .20
3553 A2746 34c multicolored .65 .20
3554 A2747 34c multicolored .65 .20
3555 A2748 34c multicolored .65 .20
a. Block or strip of 4, #3552-3555 2.60

Mentoring a Child

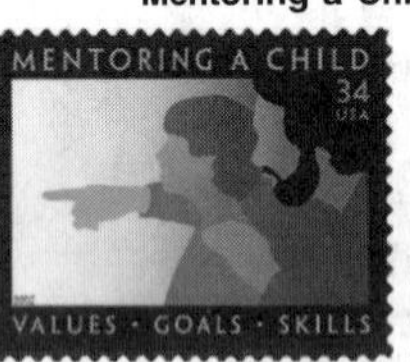

Child and Adult A2749

Serpentine Die Cut 11x10¾

2002, Jan. 10 **Photo.**

Self-Adhesive

3556 A2749 34c multicolored .65 .20

Black Heritage Series

Langston Hughes (1902-67), Writer — A2750

Serpentine Die Cut 10¼x10½

2002, Feb. 1 **Litho.**

Self-Adhesive

3557 A2750 34c multicolored .65 .20
a. Imperf, pair —

Beware of pairs/panes with extremely faint die cutting offered as imperf errors.

Happy Birthday

A2751

Serpentine Die Cut 11

2002, Feb. 8 **Photo.**

Self-Adhesive

3558 A2751 34c multicolored .65 .20

Chinese New Year

Year of the Horse A2752

Serpentine Die Cut 10½x10¼

2002, Feb. 11 **Litho.**

Self-Adhesive

3559 A2752 34c multicolored .65 .20

U.S. Military Academy, Bicent.

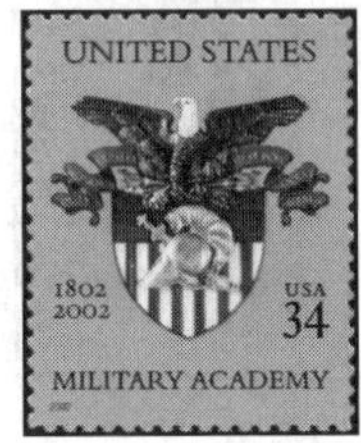

Military Academy Coat of Arms — A2753

Serpentine Die Cut 10½x11

2002, Mar. 16 **Photo.**

Self-Adhesive

3560 A2753 34c multicolored .65 .20

Greetings from America

A2754-A2803

Serpentine Die Cut 10¾

2002, Apr. 4 **Photo.**

Self-Adhesive

3561 A2754 34c Alabama .65 .20
3562 A2755 34c Alaska .65 .20
3563 A2756 34c Arizona .65 .20
3564 A2757 34c Arkansas .65 .20
3565 A2758 34c California .65 .20
3566 A2759 34c Colorado .65 .20
3567 A2760 34c Connecticut .65 .20
3568 A2761 34c Delaware .65 .20
3569 A2762 34c Florida .65 .20
3570 A2763 34c Georgia .65 .20
3571 A2764 34c Hawaii .65 .20
3572 A2765 34c Idaho .65 .20
3573 A2766 34c Illinois .65 .20
3574 A2767 34c Indiana .65 .20
3575 A2768 34c Iowa .65 .20
3576 A2769 34c Kansas .65 .20
3577 A2770 34c Kentucky .65 .20
3578 A2771 34c Louisiana .65 .20
3579 A2772 34c Maine .65 .20
3580 A2773 34c Maryland .65 .20
3581 A2774 34c Massachusetts .65 .20
3582 A2775 34c Michigan .65 .20
3583 A2776 34c Minnesota .65 .20
3584 A2777 34c Mississippi .65 .20
3585 A2778 34c Missouri .65 .20
3586 A2779 34c Montana .65 .20
3587 A2780 34c Nebraska .65 .20
3588 A2781 34c Nevada .65 .20
3589 A2782 34c New Hampshire .65 .20
3590 A2783 34c New Jersey .65 .20
3591 A2784 34c New Mexico .65 .20
3592 A2785 34c New York .65 .20
3593 A2786 34c North Carolina .65 .20
3594 A2787 34c North Dakota .65 .20
3595 A2788 34c Ohio .65 .20
3596 A2789 34c Oklahoma .65 .20
3597 A2790 34c Oregon .65 .20
3598 A2791 34c Pennsylvania .65 .20
3599 A2792 34c Rhode Island .65 .20
3600 A2793 34c South Carolina .65 .20
3601 A2794 34c South Dakota .65 .20
3602 A2795 34c Tennessee .65 .20
3603 A2796 34c Texas .65 .20
3604 A2797 34c Utah .65 .20
3605 A2798 34c Vermont .65 .20
3606 A2799 34c Virginia .65 .20
3607 A2800 34c Washington .65 .20
3608 A2801 34c West Virginia .65 .20
3609 A2802 34c Wisconsin .65 .20
3610 A2803 34c Wyoming .65 .20
a. Pane of 50, #3561-3610 32.50

Longleaf Pine Forest

A2804

Wildlife and flowers: a, Bachman's sparrow. b, Northern bobwhite, yellow pitcher plants. c, Fox squirrel, red-bellied woodpecker. d, Brown-headed nuthatch. e, Broadhead skink, yellow pitcher plants, pipeworts. f, Eastern towhee, yellow pitcher plants, Savannah meadow beauties, toothache grass. g, Gray fox, gopher tortoise, horiz. h, Blind click beetle, sweetbay, pine woods treefrog. i, Rosebud orchid, pipeworts, southern toad, yellow pitcher plants. j, Grass-pink orchid, yellow-sided skimmer, pipeworts, yellow pitcher plants, horiz.

Serpentine Die Cut 10½x10¾, 10¾x10½

2002, Apr. 26 **Photo.**

Self-Adhesive

3611 A2804 Pane of 10 7.00
a.-j. 34c Any single .65 .20
k. As #3611, imperf —

American Design Series

Toleware Coffeepot — A2805

2002, May 31 **Photo.** ***Perf. 10 Vert.***

Coil Stamp

3612 A2805 5c multicolored .20 .20

Star — A2806

, 10 (#3615)Serpentine Die Cut 11

2002, June 7 **Litho.**

Self-Adhesive (#3613-3614)

Year at Lower Left

3613 A2806 3c red, blue & black .20 .20
a. Imperf, pair —

Photo.
Serpentine Die Cut 10
Year at Lower Right

3614 A2806 3c red, blue & black .20 .20

Coil Stamp
Year at Lower Left

3615 A2806 3c red, blue & black .20 .20

Washington Type of 2001
Litho., Photo. (#3617)
2002, June 7 ***Perf. 11¼***

3616 A2686 23c green .45 .20

Self-Adhesive
Coil Stamp
Serpentine Die Cut 8½ Vert.

3617 A2686 23c gray green .45 .20

Compare No. 3617 with No. 3475A.

Booklet Stamps
Serpentine Die Cut 11¼ on 3 Sides

3618 A2686 23c green .45 .20
- *a.* Booklet pane of 4 1.80
- *b.* Booklet pane of 6 2.70
- *c.* Booklet pane of 10 4.50

Serpentine Die Cut 10½x11¼ on 3 Sides

3619 A2686 23c green .45 .20
- *a.* Booklet pane of 4, 2 #3619 at L, 2 #3618 at R 5.00
- *b.* Booklet pane of 6, 3 #3619 at L, 3 #3618 at R 8.00
- *c.* Booklet pane of 4, 2 #3618 at L, 2 #3619 at R 5.00
- *d.* Booklet pane of 6, 3 #3618 at L, 3 #3619 at R 8.00
- *e.* Booklet pane of 10, 5 #3619 at L, 5#3618 at R 10.00
- *f.* Booklet pane of 10, 5 #3618 at L, 5 #3619 at R 10.00
- *g.* Pair, #3619 at L, #3618 at R —
- *h.* Pair, #3618 at L, #3619 at R —

Flag — A2807

Litho., Photo. (#3622, 3624, 3625)
2002, June 7 ***Perf. 11¼x11***

3620 A2807 (37c) multicolored .70 .20

Self-Adhesive
Serpentine Die Cut 11¼x11

3621 A2807 (37c) multicolored .70 .20

Coil Stamp
Serpentine Die Cut 10 Vert.

3622 A2807 (37c) multicolored .70 .20
- *a.* Imperf, pair —

Booklet Stamps
Serpentine Die Cut 11¼ on 2, 3 or 4 Sides

3623 A2807 (37c) multicolored .70 .20
- *a.* Booklet pane of 20 14.00

Serpentine Die Cut 10½x10¾ on 2 or 3 Sides

3624 A2807 (37c) multicolored .70 .20
- *a.* Booklet pane of 4 2.80
- *b.* Booklet pane of 6 4.20
- *c.* Booklet pane of 20 14.00

Serpentine Die Cut 8 on 2, 3 or 4 Sides

3625 A2807 (37c) multicolored .70 .20
- *a.* Booklet pane of 18 13.00

Toy Mail Wagon A2808

Toy Locomotive A2809

Toy Taxicab A2810

Toy Fire Pumper A2811

Serpentine Die Cut 11 on 2, 3 or 4 Sides
2002, June 7 **Photo.**
Booklet Stamps
Self-Adhesive

3626 A2808 (37c) multicolored .70 .20
3627 A2809 (37c) multicolored .70 .20
3628 A2810 (37c) multicolored .70 .20
3629 A2811 (37c) multicolored .70 .20
- *a.* Block of 4, #3626-3629 2.80
- *b.* Booklet pane of 4, #3626-3629 2.80
- *c.* Booklet pane of 6, #3627, 3629, 2 each #3626, 3628 4.20
- *d.* Booklet pane of 6, #3626, 3628, 2 each #3627, 3629 4.20
- *e.* Booklet pane of 20, 5 each #3626-3629 14.00

Flag — A2812

Litho., Photo. (#3631-3633, 3636)
Serpentine Die Cut 11¼x11
2002, June 7
Self-Adhesive

3630 A2812 37c multicolored .70 .20

Coil Stamps
Water-Activated Gum
Perf. 10 Vert.

3631 A2812 37c multicolored .70 .20

Self-Adhesive
Serpentine Die Cut 10 Vert.

3632 A2812 37c multicolored .70 .20

Serpentine Die Cut 8½ Vert.

3633 A2812 37c multicolored .70 .20

Backing paper of No. 3633 is larger than the stamp.

Booklet Stamps
Serpentine Die Cut 11 on 3 Sides

3634 A2812 37c multicolored .70 .20
- *a.* Booklet pane of 10 7.00

Serpentine Die Cut 11¼ on 2, 3 or 4 Sides

3635 A2812 37c multicolored .70 .20
- *a.* Booklet pane of 20 14.00

Serpentine Die Cut 10½x10¾ on 2 or 3 Sides

3636 A2812 37c multicolored .70 .20
- *a.* Booklet pane of 4 2.80
- *b.* Booklet pane of 6 4.20
- *c.* Booklet pane of 20 14.00

Toy Locomotive A2813

Toy Mail Wagon A2814

Toy Fire Pumper A2815

Toy Taxicab A2816

Serpentine Die Cut 8½ Horiz.
2002, July 26 **Photo.**
Self-Adhesive
Coil Stamps

3638 A2813 37c multicolored .70 .20
3639 A2814 37c multicolored .70 .20
3640 A2815 37c multicolored .70 .20
3641 A2816 37c multicolored .70 .20
- *a.* Strip of 4, #3638-3641 2.80

Serpentine Die Cut 11 on 2, 3 or 4 Sides
Booklet Stamps

3642 A2814 37c multicolored .70 .20
3643 A2813 37c multicolored .70 .20
3644 A2816 37c multicolored .70 .20
3645 A2815 37c multicolored .70 .20
- *a.* Block of 4, #3642-3645 2.80
- *b.* Booklet pane of 4, #3642-3645 2.80
- *c.* Booklet pane of 6, #3643, 3645, 2 each #3642, 3644 4.20
- *d.* Booklet pane of 6, #3642, 3644, 2 each #3643, 3645 4.20
- *e.* Booklet pane of 20, 5 each #3642-3645 14.00

Coverlet Eagle — A2817

Serpentine Die Cut 11x11¼
2002, July 12 **Litho.**
Self-Adhesive

3646 A2817 60c multicolored 1.25 .25

Jefferson Memorial A2818

Capitol Dome — A2819

Serpentine Die Cut 11¼
2002, July 30 **Litho.**
Self-Adhesive

3647 A2818 $3.85 multicolored 7.50 3.75
3648 A2819 $13.65 multicolored 27.50 12.50

Masters of American Photography

A2820

Designs: a, Portrait of Daniel Webster, by Albert Sands Southworth and Josiah Johnson Hawes. b, Gen. Ulysses S. Grant and Officers, by Timothy H. O'Sullivan. c, "Cape Horn, Columbia River," by Carleton E. Watkins. d, "Blessed Art Thou Among Women," by Gertrude Käsebier. e, "Looking for Lost Luggage, Ellis Island," by Lewis W. Hine. f, "The Octopus," by Alvin Langdon Coburn. g, "Lotus, Mount Kisco, New York," by Edward Steichen. h, "Hands and Thimble," by Alfred Stieglitz. i, "Rayograph," by Man Ray. j, "Two Shells," by Edward Weston. k, "My Corsage," by James VanDerZee. l, "Ditched, Stalled, and Stranded, San Joaquin Valley, California," by Dorothea Lange. m, "Washroom and Dining Area of Floyd Burroughs' Home, Hale County, Alabama," by Walker Evans. n, "Frontline Soldier with Canteen, Saipan," by W. Eugene Smith. o, "Steeple," by Paul Strand. p, "Sand Dunes, Sunrise," by Ansel Adams. q, "Age and Its Symbols," by Imogen Cunningham. r, New York cityscape, by André Kertész. s, Photograph of pedestrians, by Garry Winogrand. t, "Bristol, Vermont," by Minor White.

Illustration reduced.

Serpentine Die Cut 10½x10¾
2002, June 13 **Photo.**
Self-Adhesive

3649 A2820 Pane of 20 14.00
- *a.-t.* 37c Any single .70 .30

American Treasures Series

Scarlet and Louisiana Tanagers, by John James Audubon — A2821

Serpentine Die Cut 10¾
2002, June 27 **Photo.**
Self-Adhesive

3650 A2821 37c multicolored .70 .20

Harry Houdini (1874-1926), Magician

A2822

Serpentine Die Cut 11¼
2002, July 3 **Litho.**
Self-Adhesive

3651 A2822 37c multicolored .70 .20

Andy Warhol (1928-87), Artist

Self-Portrait A2823

Serpentine Die Cut 10½x10¾
2002, Aug. 9 **Photo.**
Self-Adhesive

3652 A2823 37c multicolored .70 .20

Teddy Bears, Centennial

Bruin Bear, c. 1907 — A2824

"Stick" Bear, 1920s — A2825

Gund Bear, c. 1948 — A2826

Ideal Bear, c. 1905 — A2827

Serpentine Die Cut 10½

2002, Aug. 15 Photo.

Self-Adhesive

3653 A2824 37c multicolored .70 .20
3654 A2825 37c multicolored .70 .20
3655 A2826 37c multicolored .70 .20
3656 A2827 37c multicolored .70 .20
a. Block or vert. strip of 4, #3653-3656 2.80

Love

A2828

A2829

Serpentine Die Cut 11 on 2, 3 or 4 Sides

Litho. (#3657), Photo.

2002, Aug. 16

Booklet Stamp (#3657)

Self-Adhesive

3657 A2828 37c multicolored .70 .20
a. Booklet pane of 20 14.00

Serpentine Die Cut 11

3658 A2829 60c multicolored 1.25 .25

Ogden Nash (1902-7187), Poet

Nash and Poems A2830

Serpentine Die Cut 11

2002, Aug. 19 Photo.

Self-Adhesive

3659 A2830 37c multicolored .70 .20

Duke Kahanamoku (1890-1968), "Father of Surfing" and Olympic Swimmer

Kahanamoku and Surfers at Waikiki Beach — A2831

Serpentine Die Cut 11½x11¾

2002, Aug. 24 Photo.

Self-Adhesive

3660 A2831 37c multicolored .70 .20

American Bats

Red Bat A2832

Leaf-nosed Bat A2833

Pallid Bat A2834

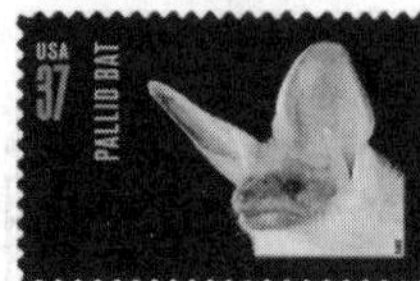

Spotted Bat A2835

Serpentine Die Cut 10¾

2002, Sept. 13 Photo.

Self-Adhesive

3661 A2832 37c multicolored .70 .20
3662 A2833 37c multicolored .70 .20
3663 A2834 37c multicolored .70 .20
3664 A2835 37c multicolored .70 .20
a. Block or horiz. strip of 4, #3661-3664 2.80

Women in Journalism

Nellie Bly (1864-1922) — A2836

Ida M. Tarbell (1857-1944) — A2837

Ethel L. Payne (1911-91) A2838

Marguerite Higgins (1920-66) A2839

Serpentine Die Cut 11x10½

2002, Sept. 14 Photo.

Self-Adhesive

3665 A2836 37c multicolored .70 .20
3666 A2837 37c multicolored .70 .20
3667 A2838 37c multicolored .70 .20
3668 A2839 37c multicolored .70 .20
a. Block or horiz. strip of 4, #3665-3668 2.80

Irving Berlin (1888-1989), Composer

Berlin and Score of "God Bless America" — A2840

Serpentine Die Cut 11

2002, Sept. 15 Photo.

Self-Adhesive

3669 A2840 37c multicolored .70 .20

Neuter and Spay

Kitten A2841

Puppy A2842

Serpentine Die Cut 10¾x10½

2002, Sept. 20 Photo.

Self-Adhesive

3670 A2841 37c multicolored .70 .20
3671 A2842 37c multicolored .70 .20
a. Horiz. or vert. pair, #3670-3671 1.40

Hanukkah Type of 1996

Serpentine Die Cut 11

2002, Oct. 10 Photo.

Self-Adhesive

3672 A2411 37c multicolored .70 .20

Kwanzaa Type of 1997

Serpentine Die Cut 11

2002, Oct. 10 Photo.

Self-Adhesive

3673 A2458 37c multicolored .70 .20

Eid Type of 2001

Serpentine Die Cut 11

2002, Oct. 10 Photo.

Self-Adhesive

3674 A2734 37c multicolored .70 .20

Christmas

Madonna and Child, by Jan Gossaert — A2843

Serpentine Die Cut 11x11¼ on 2, 3 or 4 Sides

2002, Oct. 10 Litho.

Self-Adhesive

Booklet Stamp

3675 A2843 37c multicolored .70 .20
a. Booklet pane of 20 14.00

Christmas

Snowman with Red and Green Plaid Scarf — A2844

Snowman with Blue Plaid Scarf — A2845

Snowman with Pipe — A2846

Snowman with Top Hat — A2847

Snowman with Blue Plaid Scarf — A2848

Snowman with Pipe — A2849

Snowman with Top Hat — A2850

Snowman with Red and Green Plaid Scarf — A2851

Serpentine Die Cut 11

2002, Oct. 28 Photo.

Self-Adhesive

3676 A2844 37c multicolored .70 .20
3677 A2845 37c multicolored .70 .20
3678 A2846 37c multicolored .70 .20
3679 A2847 37c multicolored .70 .20
a. Block or vert. strip of 4, #3676-3679 2.80

Coil Stamps

Serpentine Die Cut 8½ Vert.

3680 A2848 37c multicolored .70 .20
3681 A2849 37c multicolored .70 .20
3682 A2850 37c multicolored .70 .20
3683 A2851 37c multicolored .70 .20
a. Strip of 4, #3680-3683 2.80

Booklet Stamps

Serpentine Die Cut 10¾x11 on 2 or 3 Sides

3684 A2844 37c multicolored .70 .20
3685 A2845 37c multicolored .70 .20
3686 A2846 37c multicolored .70 .20
3687 A2847 37c multicolored .70 .20
a. Block of 4, #3684-3687 2.80
b. Booklet pane, 5 #3687a + label 14.00

Serpentine Die Cut 11 on 2 or 3 Sides

3688 A2851 37c multicolored .70 .20
3689 A2848 37c multicolored .70 .20
3690 A2849 37c multicolored .70 .20
3691 A2850 37c multicolored .70 .20
a. Block of 4, #3688-3691 2.80
b. Booklet pane of 4, #3688-3691 2.80
c. Booklet pane of 6, #3690-3691, 2 each #3688-3689 4.20
d. Booklet pane of 6, #3688-3689, 2 each #3690-3691 4.20
Nos. 3676-3691 (16) 11.20 3.20

Colors of Nos. 3684-3687 are deeper and designs are slightly smaller than those found on Nos. 3676-3679.

Legends of Hollywood

Cary Grant (1904-86), Actor — A2852

Serpentine Die Cut 10¾

2002, Oct. 15 Photo.

Self-Adhesive

3692 A2852 37c multicolored .70 .20

Sea Coast — A2853

Serpentine Die Cut 8½ Vert.

2002, Oct. 21 Photo.

Self-Adhesive

Coil Stamp

3693 A2853 (5c) multicolored .20 .20

Hawaiian Missionary Stamps

A2854

Designs: a, 2c stamp of 1851 (Hawaii Scott 1). b, 5c stamp of 1851 (Hawaii Scott 2) c, 13c stamp of 1851 (Hawaii Scott 3). d, 13c stamp of 1852 (Hawaii Scott 4).

2002, Oct. 24 Litho. *Perf. 11*

3694	A2854	Pane of 4	2.80	.80
a.-d.		37c Any single	.70	.20

Happy Birthday Type of 2002

Serpentine Die Cut 11

2002, Oct. 25 Photo.

Self-Adhesive

3695	A2751	37c multicolored	.70	.20

Greetings From America Type of 2002

Serpentine Die Cut 10¾

2002, Oct. 25 Photo.

Self-Adhesive

3696	A2754	37c Alabama	.70	.20
3697	A2755	37c Alaska	.70	.20
3698	A2756	37c Arizona	.70	.20
3699	A2757	37c Arkansas	.70	.20
3700	A2758	37c California	.70	.20
3701	A2759	37c Colorado	.70	.20
3702	A2760	37c Connecticut	.70	.20
3703	A2761	37c Delaware	.70	.20
3704	A2762	37c Florida	.70	.20
3705	A2763	37c Georgia	.70	.20
3706	A2764	37c Hawaii	.70	.20
3707	A2765	37c Idaho	.70	.20
3708	A2766	37c Illinois	.70	.20
3709	A2767	37c Indiana	.70	.20
3710	A2768	37c Iowa	.70	.20
3711	A2769	37c Kansas	.70	.20
3712	A2770	37c Kentucky	.70	.20
3713	A2771	37c Louisiana	.70	.20
3714	A2772	37c Maine	.70	.20
3715	A2773	37c Maryland	.70	.20
3716	A2774	37c Massachusetts	.70	.20
3717	A2775	37c Michigan	.70	.20
3718	A2776	37c Minnesota	.70	.20
3719	A2777	37c Mississippi	.70	.20
3720	A2778	37c Missouri	.70	.20
3721	A2779	37c Montana	.70	.20
3722	A2780	37c Nebraska	.70	.20
3723	A2781	37c Nevada	.70	.20
3724	A2782	37c New Hampshire	.70	.20
3725	A2783	37c New Jersey	.70	.20
3726	A2784	37c New Mexico	.70	.20
3727	A2785	37c New York	.70	.20
3728	A2786	37c North Carolina	.70	.20
3729	A2787	37c North Dakota	.70	.20
3730	A2788	37c Ohio	.70	.20
3731	A2789	37c Oklahoma	.70	.20
3732	A2790	37c Oregon	.70	.20
3733	A2791	37c Pennsylvania	.70	.20
3734	A2792	37c Rhode Island	.70	.20
3735	A2793	37c South Carolina	.70	.20
3736	A2794	37c South Dakota	.70	.20
3737	A2795	37c Tennessee	.70	.20
3738	A2796	37c Texas	.70	.20
3739	A2797	37c Utah	.70	.20
3740	A2798	37c Vermont	.70	.20
3741	A2799	37c Virginia	.70	.20
3742	A2800	37c Washington	.70	.20
3743	A2801	37c West Virginia	.70	.20
3744	A2802	37c Wisconsin	.70	.20
3745	A2803	37c Wyoming	.70	.20
a.		Pane of 50, #3696-3745	35.00	

Black Heritage Series

Thurgood Marshall (1908-93), Supreme Court Justice — A2855

Serpentine Die Cut 11½

2003, Jan. 7 Litho.

Self-Adhesive

3746	A2855	37c black & gray	.70	.20

SUBJECT INDEX OF REGULAR, COMMEMORATIVE & AIR POST ISSUES

UNITED STATES

SEMI-POSTAL STAMPS

Breast Cancer Awareness

SP1

Serpentine Die Cut 11

1998, July 29 **Photo.**

Self-Adhesive

B1 SP1 (32c+8c) multicolored	.80	.25

The 8c surtax was for cancer research. Copies of #B1 sold after the Jan. 10, 1999 1st class postage rate change were 33c stamps with 7c surtax; after Jan. 7, 2001, 34c stamps with 6c surtax.

Effective Mar. 23, 2002, the stamp was sold for 45c, but the face value remained at 34c until June 30, 2002, at which time the face value rose to 37c.

Heroes of 2001

Firemen Atop World Trade Center Rubble — SP2

Serpentine Die Cut 11¼

2002, June 7 **Litho.**

Self-Adhesive

B2 SP2 (34c+11c) multicolored	.90	.65

The 11c surtax was for assistance to families of emergency relief personnel killed or permanently disabled in the line of duty in connection with the terrorist attacks of Sept. 11, 2001. No. B2 became a 37c stamp with an 8c surtax June 30, 2002.

AIR POST STAMPS

For prepayment of postage on all mailable matter sent by airmail.

Curtiss Jenny — AP1

Engraved (Flat Plate Printing)

1918 **Unwmk.** ***Perf. 11***

C1 AP1 6c orange	65.00	30.00
Never hinged	110.00	
C2 AP1 16c green	80.00	35.00
Never hinged	140.00	
C3 AP1 24c car rose & bl	80.00	35.00
Never hinged	140.00	
a. Center inverted	*170,000.*	
Never hinged	*200,000.*	
Nos. C1-C3 (3)	225.00	100.00
Nos. C1-C3, never hinged	400.00	

Wooden Propeller and Radiator AP2

Emblem of Air Service AP3

De Havilland Biplane — AP4

1923

C4 AP2 8c dark green	22.50	14.00
Never hinged	40.00	
C5 AP3 16c dark blue	80.00	30.00
Never hinged	140.00	
C6 AP4 24c carmine	90.00	30.00
Never hinged	150.00	
Nos. C4-C6 (3)	192.50	74.00
Nos. C4-C6, never hinged	345.00	

Map of US and Two Mail Planes — AP5

1926-27

C7 AP5 10c dark blue	2.60	.35
Never hinged	4.50	
C8 AP5 15c olive brown	3.00	2.50
Never hinged	5.25	
C9 AP5 20c yellow green ('27)	7.50	2.00
Never hinged	13.50	
Nos. C7-C9 (3)	13.10	4.85
Nos. C7-C9, never hinged	23.25	

Lindbergh's Airplane "Spirit of St. Louis" — AP6

1927, June 18

C10 AP6 10c dark blue	7.25	2.50
Never hinged	12.50	
a. Booklet pane of 3	80.00	*65.00*
Never hinged	120.00	

Singles from No. C10a are imperf. at sides or imperf. at sides and bottom.

Nos. C1-C10 were available for ordinary postage.

Beacon on Rocky Mountains AP7

1928, July 25 ***Perf. 11***

C11 AP7 5c carmine & blue	5.00	.75
Never hinged	8.50	
a. Vertical pair, imperf. btwn.	*5,500.*	

Winged Globe — AP8

1930, Feb. 10 ***Perf. 11***

Size: 46½x19mm

C12 AP8 5c violet	10.00	.50
Never hinged	17.50	
a. Horiz. pair, imperf. btwn.	*4,500.*	

See Nos. C16-C17, C19.

Graf Zeppelin Issue

Zeppelin over Atlantic Ocean — AP9

Zeppelin between Continents — AP10

Zeppelin Passing Globe — AP11

1930, Apr. 19 ***Perf. 11***

C13 AP9 65c green	240.00	160.00
Never hinged	350.00	
C14 AP10 $1.30 brown	450.00	375.00
Never hinged	700.00	
C15 AP11 $2.60 blue	700.00	575.00
Never hinged	1,050.	
Nos. C13-C15 (3)	1,390.	1,110.
Nos. C13-C15, never hinged	2,160.	

Issued for use on mail carried on first Europe-Pan-America round-trip flight of Graf Zeppelin, May, 1930.

Type of 1930 Issue

Rotary Press Printing

1931-32 ***Perf. 10½x11***

Size: 47½x19mm

C16 AP8 5c violet	5.25	.60
Never hinged	8.75	
C17 AP8 8c olive bister ('32)	2.25	.40
Never hinged	3.75	

Century of Progress Issue

Airship "Graf Zeppelin" — AP12

Flat Plate Printing

1933, Oct. 2 ***Perf. 11***

C18 AP12 50c green	65.00	65.00
Never hinged	100.00	

Flight of the "Graf Zeppelin" in Oct. 1933, to Miami, Akron and Chicago, and from the last city to Europe.

Catalogue values for unused stamps in this section, from this point to the end of the section, are for Never Hinged items.

Type of 1930 Issue

Rotary Press Printing

1934, June 30 ***Perf. 10½x11***

C19 AP8 6c dull orange	3.50	.25

Transpacific Issues

The "China Clipper" over the Pacific AP13

Flat Plate Printing

1935, Nov. 22 ***Perf. 11***

C20 AP13 25c blue	1.40	1.00

Issued to pay postage on mail carried on the Transpacific air post service inaugurated Nov. 22, 1935.

The "China Clipper" over the Pacific AP14

1937, Feb. 15 ***Perf. 11***

C21 AP14 20c green	11.00	1.75
C22 AP14 50c carmine	10.00	5.00

Eagle Holding Shield, Olive Branch and Arrows AP15

1938, May 14 ***Perf. 11***

C23 AP15 6c dk blue & carmine	.50	.20
a. Vert. pair, imperf. horiz.	350.00	
b. Horiz. pair, imperf. vert.	*12,500.*	

Transatlantic Issue

Winged Globe — AP16

1939, May 16 ***Perf. 11***

C24 AP16 30c dull blue	10.50	1.50

Twin-Motored Transport Plane — AP17

Rotary Press Printing

1941-44 ***Perf. 11x10½***

C25 AP17 6c carmine	.20	.20
a. Booklet pane of 3 ('43)	5.00	*1.50*
b. Horiz. pair, imperf. between	*2,250.*	
C26 AP17 8c olive grn ('44)	.20	.20
C27 AP17 10c violet	1.25	.20
C28 AP17 15c brown carmine	2.25	.35
C29 AP17 20c bright green	2.25	.30
C30 AP17 30c blue	2.25	.35
C31 AP17 50c orange	11.00	3.25
Nos. C25-C31 (7)	19.40	4.85

Singles from No. C25a are imperf. at sides or imperf. at sides and bottom.

DC-4 Skymaster AP18

1946, Sept. 25 ***Perf. 11x10½***
C32 AP18 5c carmine .20 .20

DC-4 Skymaster — AP19

1947, Mar. 26 ***Perf. 10½x11***
C33 AP19 5c carmine .20 .20

See Nos. C37, C39, C41.

Pan American Union Building, Washington, DC — AP20

Statue of Liberty & New York Skyline AP21

Plane over San Francisco-Oakland Bay Bridge — AP22

1947 ***Perf. 11x10½***
C34 AP20 10c black .25 .20
C35 AP21 15c brt blue green .35 .20
a. Horiz. pair, imperf. between *2,250.*
C36 AP22 25c blue .90 .20
Nos. C34-C36 (3) 1.50 .60

No. C35a is valued in the grade of fine.

Coil Stamp

1948, Jan. 15 ***Perf. 10 Horiz.***
C37 AP19 5c carmine 1.00 .80

New York City Issue

Map of Five Boroughs, Circular Band & Planes — AP23

1948, July 31 ***Perf. 11x10½***
C38 AP23 5c bright carmine .20 .20

50th anniv. of the consolidation of the 5 boroughs of NYC.

Type of 1947

1949, Jan. 18 ***Perf. 10½x11***
C39 AP19 6c carmine .20 .20
a. Booklet pane of 6 10.00 *5.00*

Alexandria Bicentennial Issue

Home of John Carlyle, Alexandria Seal & Gadsby's Tavern AP24

Rotary Press Printing

1949, May 11 ***Perf. 11x10½***
C40 AP24 6c carmine .20 .20

Founding of Alexandria, Va, 200th anniv.

Type of 1947
Coil Stamp

1949, Aug. 25 ***Perf. 10 Horiz.***
C41 AP19 6c carmine 3.00 .20

Universal Postal Union Issue

Post Office Department Building AP25

Globe & Doves Carrying Messages AP26

Boeing Stratocruiser & Globe — AP27

1949 **Unwmk.** ***Perf. 11x10½***
C42 AP25 10c violet .20 .20
C43 AP26 15c ultramarine .30 .25
C44 AP27 25c rose carmine .60 .40
Nos. C42-C44 (3) 1.10 .85

75th anniv. of the UPU.

Wright Brothers Issue

Wilbur & Orville Wright and their Plane AP28

1949, Dec. 17 ***Perf. 11x10½***
C45 AP28 6c magenta .20 .20

46th anniv. of the Wright Brothers' 1st flight, Dec. 17, 1903.

Diamond Head, Honolulu, Hawaii AP29

1952, Mar. 26 ***Perf. 11x10½***
C46 AP29 80c brt red violet 5.00 1.25

First Plane and Modern Plane AP30

Powered Flight Issue

1953, May 29 ***Perf. 11x10½***
C47 AP30 6c carmine .20 .20

50th anniversary of powered flight.

Eagle in Flight — AP31

For Domestic Post Cards

1954, Sept. 3 ***Perf. 11x10½***
C48 AP31 4c bright blue .20 .20

See No. C50.

Air Force Issue

B-52 Stratofortress and F-104 Starfighters — AP32

Rotary Press Printing

1957, Aug. 1 ***Perf. 11x10½***
C49 AP32 6c blue .20 .20

50th anniv. of US Air Force.

Flying Eagle Type of 1954
For Domestic Post Cards

1958, July 31 ***Perf. 11x10½***
C50 AP31 5c rose red .20 .20

Silhouette of Jet Airliner — AP33

1958, July 31 ***Perf. 10½x11***
C51 AP33 7c blue .20 .20
a. Booklet pane of 6 13.00 *7.00*
b. Vert. pair, imperf btwn. (from bklt. pane) —

Coil Stamp

Perf. 10 Horizontally

C52 AP33 7c blue 2.00 .20

No. C51b resulted from a paper foldover after perforating and before cutting into panes. Two pairs are known.
See Nos. C60-C61.

Alaska Statehood Issue

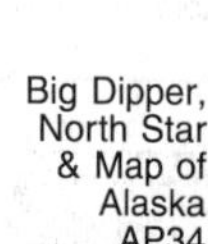

Big Dipper, North Star & Map of Alaska AP34

Rotary Press Printing

1959, Jan. 3 ***Perf. 11x10½***
C53 AP34 7c dark blue .20 .20

Alaska's admission to statehood.

Balloon Jupiter Issue

Balloon & Crowd — AP35

Giori Press Printing

1959, Aug. 17 ***Perf. 11***
C54 AP35 7c dark blue & red .20 .20

Cent. of the carrying of mail by the balloon Jupiter from Lafayette to Crawfordsville, Ind.

Hawaii Statehood Issue

Alii Warrior, Map of Hawaii & Star of Statehood AP36

Rotary Press Printing

1959, Aug. 21 ***Perf. 11x10½***
C55 AP36 7c rose red .20 .20

Hawaii's admission to statehood.

Pan American Games Issue

Runner Holding Torch — AP37

Giori Press Printing

1959, Aug. 27 ***Perf. 11***
C56 AP37 10c vio bl & brt red .25 .25

3rd Pan American Games, Chicago, Aug. 27-Sept. 7.

Liberty Bell AP38

Statue of Liberty AP39

Abraham Lincoln AP40

Giori Press Printing

1959-66 ***Perf. 11***
C57 AP38 10c blk & grn ('60) 1.10 .70
C58 AP39 15c black & orange .35 .20
C59 AP40 25c blk & mar ('60) .50 .20
a. Tagged ('66) .60 .30
Nos. C57-C59 (3) 1.95 1.10

Luminescence

See note following No. 1053. "Tagged" varieties of untagged airmail stamps start with No. C59a and end with No. C67a.

Airmail stamps starting with No. C69 are tagged unless otherwise noted.

Type of 1958

Rotary Press Printing

1960, Aug. 12 ***Perf. 10½x11***
C60 AP33 7c carmine .20 .20
a. Booklet pane of 6 16.00 *8.00*
b. Vert. pair, imperf btwn. (from bklt. pane) *5,500.*

No. C60b resulted from a paper foldover after perforating and before cutting into panes. Two pairs are known.

Type of 1958
Coil Stamp

1960, Oct. 22 ***Perf. 10 Horiz.***
C61 AP33 7c carmine 4.00 .25

Type of 1959-60 and

Statue of Liberty AP41

Giori Press Printing

1961-67 ***Perf. 11***
C62 AP38 13c black & red .40 .20
a. Tagged ('67) .75 .50

C63 AP41 15c black & orange .30 .20
a. Tagged ('67) .35 .20
b. As "a," horiz. pair, imperf. vert. *15,000.*

No. C63 has a gutter between the two parts of the design; No. C58 has none.

Jet Airliner Over Capitol — AP42

Rotary Press Printing

1962, Dec. 5 ***Perf. 10½x11***

C64 AP42 8c carmine .20 .20
a. Tagged ('63) .20 .20
b. Booklet pane 5 + label 7.00 *3.00*
c. As "b," tagged ('64) 2.00 *.75*

Three different messages are found on the label in No. C64b, and one on No. C64c.

Coil Stamp

Perf. 10 Horizontally

C65 AP42 8c carmine .40 .20
a. Tagged ('65) .35 .20

The 1st luminescent tagged US issue was No. C64a issued Aug. 1, 1963, at Dayton, OH. Initial experiments there used tagged stamps and an automated facer-canceler to extract airmail as an aid to dispatch.

Montgomery Blair Issue

Montgomery Blair — AP43

Giori Press Printing

1963, May 3 Unwmk. ***Perf. 11***

C66 AP43 15c car, dp cl & bl .60 .55

Blair (1813-1883), Postmaster Gen. (1861-64), who called the 1st Intl. Postal Conf., Paris, 1863, forerunner of the UPU.

Bald Eagle — AP44

For Domestic Post Cards

Rotary Press Printing

1963, July 12 ***Perf. 11x10½***

C67 AP44 6c red .20 .20
a. Tagged ('67) 4.00 3.00

Amelia Earhart Issue

Amelia Earhart & Lockheed Electra — AP45

Giori Press Printing

1963, July 24 ***Perf. 11***

C68 AP45 8c carmine & maroon .20 .20

Earhart (1898-1937), 1st woman to fly across the Atlantic.

Dr. Robert H. Goddard Issue

Robert H. Goddard, Atlas Rocket & Launching Tower, Cape Kennedy AP46

1964, Oct. 5 Unwmk. Tagged

C69 AP46 8c blue, red & bister .40 .20

Goddard (1882-1945), physicist and pioneer rocket researcher.

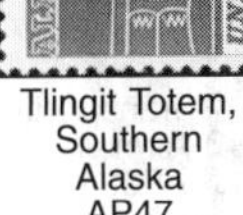

Tlingit Totem, Southern Alaska AP47

"Columbia Jays," by Audubon AP48

Alaska Purchase Issue

Giori Press Printing

1967, Mar. 30 ***Perf. 11***

C70 AP47 8c brown .25 .20

Cent. of the Alaska Purchase.

The Tlingit totem is from the Alaska State Museum, Juneau.

1967, Apr. 26 ***Perf. 11***

C71 AP48 20c multicolored .80 .20

See note after No. 1241.

50-Star Runway — AP49

Rotary Press Printing

1968, Jan. 5 Unwmk. ***Perf. 11x10½***

C72 AP49 10c carmine .20 .20
b. Booklet pane of 8 2.00 .75
c. Booklet pane of 5 + label 3.75 .75
d. Vert. pair, imperf btwn. (from bklt. pane) *8,000.*

Coil Stamp

Perf. 10 Vertically

C73 AP49 10c carmine .30 .20
a. Imperf., pair *600.00*

No. C72d resulted from a paper foldover after perforating and before cutting into panes. Only one pair is known.

The $1 Air Lift stamp is listed as No. 1341.

Air Mail Service Issue

Curtiss Jenny AP50

Lithographed, Engraved (Giori)

1968, May 15 ***Perf. 11***

C74 AP50 10c blue, black & red .25 .20

50th anniv. of regularly scheduled US air mail service.

USA and Jet — AP51

1968, Nov. 22 ***Perf. 11***

C75 AP51 20c red, blue & black .35 .20

See No. C81.

Moon Landing Issue

First Man on the Moon — AP52

Litho. & Engr. (Giori)

1969, Sept. 9 ***Perf. 11***

C76 AP52 10c multicolored .25 .20
a. Rose red (litho.) omitted *500.00* —

Man's 1st landing on the moon, July 20, 1969.

U.S. astronauts Neil A. Armstrong and Col. Edwin E. Aldrin, Jr., with Lieut. Col. Michael Collins piloting Apollo 11.

On No. C76a, the litho. rose red is missing from the entire vignette—the dots on top of the yellow areas as well as the flag shoulder patch.

Type of 1968 and:

Silhouette of Delta Wing Plane — AP53

Silhouette of Jet Airliner AP54

Winged Airmail Envelope AP55

Statue of Liberty AP56

Design: 21c, "USA" and jet (as #C75).

Rotary Press Printing

1971-73 ***Perf. 10½x11***

C77 AP53 9c red .20 .20

Perf. 11x10½

C78 AP54 11c carmine .20 .20
a. Booklet pane of 4 + 2 labels 1.25 *.75*
b. Untagged (Bureau precanceled) *.30*
C79 AP55 13c carmine ('73) .25 .20
a. Booklet pane of 5 + label ('73) 1.50 *.75*
b. Untagged (Bureau precanceled) *.30*

Giori Press Printing

Perf. 11

C80 AP56 17c bluish black, red & dark green .35 .20

Litho. & Engr. (Giori)

Perf. 11

C81 AP51 21c red, blue & black .40 .20
b. Black (engr.) missing (FO) —
Nos. C77-C81 (5) 1.40 1.00

Issued: 9c, 5/15; 11c, 5/7; 17c, 7/13; 21c, 5/21/71; 13c, 11/16/73.

The 9c was for use on domestic post cards.

No. C78b is precanceled "WASHINGTON D.C." (or "DC") and No. C79b "WASHINGTON DC" for the use of Congressmen and the public.

Coil Stamps

Rotary Press Printing

1971-73 ***Perf. 10 Vertically***

C82 AP54 11c carmine .25 .20
a. Imperf., pair *300.00*
C83 AP55 13c carmine ('73) .30 .20
a. Imperf., pair 75.00

Issue dates: 11c, May 7; 13c, Dec. 27.

National Parks Centennial Issue

Kii Statue & Temple, City of Refuge, Hawaii — AP57

Litho. & Engr. (Giori)

1972, May 3 ***Perf. 11***

C84 AP57 11c orange & multi .20 .20
a. Blue & green (litho) omitted *800.00*

Cent. of the Natl. Parks system. No. C84 shows view of the City of Refuge Natl. Historical Park at Honaunau.

Olympic Games Issue

Skiing & Olympic Rings AP58

Photogravure (Andreotti)

1972, Aug. 17 ***Perf. 11x10½***

C85 AP58 11c multicolored .20 .20

11th Winter Olympic Games, Sapporo, Japan, Feb. 3-13, and 20th Summer Olympic Games, Munich, Germany, Aug. 26-Sept. 11.

Electronics Progress Issue

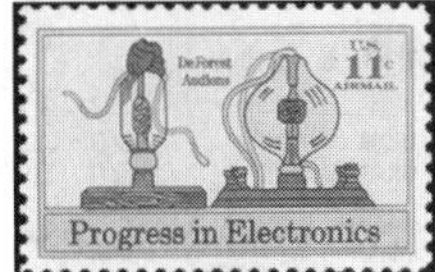

De Forest Audions AP59

Litho. & Engr. (Giori)

1973, July 10 ***Perf. 11***

C86 AP59 11c multicolored .20 .20
a. Vermilion & olive (litho.) omitted *1,400.*
c. Olive omitted —

Statue of Liberty AP60

Mt. Rushmore National Memorial AP61

1974 Giori Press Printing ***Perf. 11***

C87 AP60 18c car, black & ultra .35 .25
C88 AP61 26c ultra, black & car .50 .20

Issue dates: 18c, Jan. 11; 26c, Jan. 2.

Plane & Globes AP62

Plane, Globes & Flag AP63

Giori Press Printing

1976, Jan. 2 ***Perf. 11***

C89 AP62 25c ultra, red & black	.50	.20
C90 AP63 31c ultra, red & black	.60	.20

Wright Brothers Issue

Orville and Wilbur Wright, Flyer A AP64

Wright Brothers, Flyer A and Shed AP65

Litho. & Engr.

1978, Sept. 23 ***Perf. 11***

C91 AP64 31c ultra & multi	.65	.30
C92 AP65 31c ultra & multi	.65	.30
a. Vert. pair, #C91-C92	1.30	1.20
b. As "a," ultra & blk (engr.) omitted	*750.00*	
c. As "a," black (engr.) omitted	—	
d. As "a," blk, yel, mag, bl & brn (litho.) omitted	*2,250.*	

75th anniv. of 1st powered flight, Kill Devil Hill, NC, Dec. 17, 1903.

Octave Chanute Issue

Chanute & Biplane Hangglider AP66

Biplane Hanggliders & Chanute AP67

Litho. & Engr.

1979, Mar. 29 ***Perf. 11***

C93 AP66 21c ultra & multi	.70	.35
C94 AP67 21c ultra & multi	.70	.35
a. Vert. pair, #C93-C94	1.40	1.20
b. As "a," ultramarine & black (engr.) omitted	*4,500.*	

Octave Chanute (1832-1910), civil engineer and aviation pioneer.

Wiley Post Issue

Wiley Post & "Winnie Mae" AP68

NR-105 W, Post in Pressurized Suit, Portrait AP69

Litho. & Engr.

1979, Nov. 20 ***Perf. 11***

C95 AP68 25c ultra & multi	1.10	.45
C96 AP69 25c ultra & multi	1.10	.45
a. Vert. pair, #C95-C96	2.25	1.50

Post (1899-1935), 1st man to fly around the world alone and high-altitude flying pioneer.

Olympic Games Issue

High Jump AP70

1979, Nov. 1 **Photo.** ***Perf. 11***

C97 AP70 31c multicolored	.70	.30

22nd Olympic Games, Moscow, July 19-Aug. 3, 1980.

Philip Mazzei (1730-1816), Italian-born Political Writer — AP71

1980, Oct. 13 **Photo.** ***Perf. 11***

C98 AP71 40c multicolored	.80	.20
b. Imperf., pair	*2,750.*	

Perf. 10½x11¼

C98A AP71 40c multicolored	7.50	1.50
c. Horiz. pair, imperf. vert.	—	

Issued: #C98, 10/13; #C98A, 1982.

Blanche Stuart Scott (1886-1970) — AP72

Glenn Curtiss (1878-1930) — AP73

1980, Dec. 30

C99 AP72 28c multicolored	.60	.20
a. Imperf., pair	*3,250.*	
C100 AP73 35c multicolored	.65	.20

Scott, 1st woman pilot, and Curtiss, aviation pioneer and aircraft designer.

1984 Olympic Games

AP81

1983, June 17 ***Perf. 11***

C101 AP81 28c Gymnast	1.00	.30
C102 AP81 28c Hurdler	1.00	.30
C103 AP81 28c Basketball	1.00	.30
C104 AP81 28c Soccer	1.00	.30
a. Block of 4, #C101-C104	4.50	2.50
b. As "a," imperf. vert.	—	

Nos. C101-C104 are vertical.

1983, Apr. 8

C105 AP81 40c Shot put	.90	.40
C106 AP81 40c Gymnast	.90	.40
C107 AP81 40c Swimmer	.90	.40
C108 AP81 40c Weightlifting	.90	.40
b. Block of 4, #C105-C108	4.25	3.00
d. As "b," imperf.	*1,250.*	

1983, Nov. 4

C109 AP81 35c Women's fencing	.90	.55
C110 AP81 35c Cycling	.90	.55
C111 AP81 35c Women's volleyball	.90	.55
C112 AP81 35c Pole vaulting	.90	.55
a. Block of 4, #C109-C112	4.00	3.25

Alfred V. Verville AP86

Lawrence & Elmer Sperry AP87

1985, Feb. 13 **Photo.**

C113 AP86 33c multicolored	.65	.20
a. Imperf., pair	*850.00*	
C114 AP87 39c multicolored	.80	.25
a. Imperf., pair	*1,500.*	

Alfred V. Verville (1890-1970), aircraft designer, Lawrence Sperry (1892-1931), designer and pilot, and Elmer Sperry (1860-1930), inventor.

Transpacific Airmail AP88

1985, Feb. 15 **Photo.**

C115 AP88 44c multicolored	.85	.25
a. Imperf., pair	*850.00*	

Fr. Junipero Serra (1713-84)
California Missionary

Outline Map of Southern California, Portrait, San Gabriel Mission AP89

1985, Aug. 22 **Photo.** ***Perf. 11***

C116 AP89 44c multicolored	1.00	.35
a. Imperf., pair	*1,500.*	

Settling of New Sweden, 350th Anniv. AP90

17th Cent. European settler negotiating with 2 American Indians, map of New Sweden, the Swedish ships *Kalmar Nyckel* and *Fogel Grip*, based on an 18th cent. illustration from a Swedish book about the Colonies.

1988, Mar. 29 **Litho. & Engr.**

C117 AP90 44c multicolored	1.00	.25

See Finland No. 768 and Sweden No. 1672.

Samuel Pierpont Langley (1834-1906)
Astronomer, Aviation Pioneer and Inventor

Langley and Unmanned Aerodrome No. 5 AP91

Litho. & Engr.

1988, May 14 ***Perf. 11***

C118 AP91 45c multicolored	.90	.20

Igor Sikorsky (1889-1972)
Aeronautic Engineer

Sikorsky and VS300 Helicopter, 1939 AP92

1988, June 23 **Photo.** ***Perf. 11***

C119 AP92 36c multicolored	.70	.25

French Revolution, Bicent.

Liberty, Equality and Fraternity — AP93

Litho. & Engr.

1989, July 14 ***Perf. 11½x11***

C120 AP93 45c multicolored	.95	.20

See France Nos. 2143-2145a.

Pre-Columbian America Issue

UPAE Emblem & *Key Marco Cat* — AP94

Design features Southeastern Figure, *Key Marco Cat*, Calusa Culture, Pre-Columbian Mississippian Period, A.D. 700-1450

1989, Oct. 12 **Photo.** ***Perf. 11***

C121 AP94 45c multicolored	.90	.20

Discovery of America, 500th anniv. (in 1992).

Futuristic Mail Delivery

Spacecraft AP95

Air-suspended Hover Car — AP96

Moon Rover — AP97

Space Shuttle — AP98

1989, Nov. 27 *Perf. 11*
C122 AP95 45c multicolored 1.00 .50
C123 AP96 45c multicolored 1.00 .50
C124 AP97 45c multicolored 1.00 .50
C125 AP98 45c multicolored 1.00 .50
a. Block of 4, Nos. C122-C125 4.25 3.25
b. As "a," lt bl (engr.) omitted *800.00*

Litho. & Engr.

1989, Nov. 24 ***Imperf.***
C126 Sheet of 4 4.75 3.75
a. AP95 45c multicolored 1.00 .50
b. AP96 45c multicolored 1.00 .50
c. AP97 45c multicolored 1.00 .50
d. AP98 45c multicolored 1.00 .50

World Stamp Expo '89, 20th UPU Congress. See Russia No. 5837.

Pre-Columbian America Issue

Tropical Coast AP99

1990, Oct. 12 **Photo.** *Perf. 11*
C127 AP99 45c multicolored .90 .20

Harriet Quimby, Bleriot Aircraft AP100

1991, Apr. 27 **Photo.** *Perf. 11*
C128 AP100 50c multicolored 1.00 .25
a. Vert. pair, imperf. horiz. 1,900.
b. Perf. 11.2 ('93) 1.10 .25

William T. Piper, Piper Cub AP101

1991, May 17
C129 AP101 40c multicolored .80 .20

See No. C132.

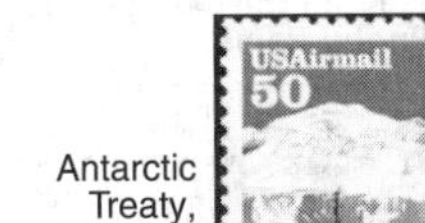

Antarctic Treaty, 30th Anniv. AP102

1991, June 21 **Photo.** *Perf. 11*
C130 AP102 50c multicolored 1.00 .35

Pre-Columbian America Issue

First Americans Crossed Over From Asia AP103

1991, Oct. 12 **Photo.** *Perf. 11*
C131 AP103 50c multicolored 1.00 .35

Piper Type of 1991

1993 **Photo.** *Perf. 11¼*
C132 AP101 40c multicolored 1.40 .35

Piper's hair touches top edge of design. Bullseye perf.

"All LC (Letters and Cards) mail receives First-Class Mail service in the United States, is dispatched by the fastest transportation available, and travels by airmail or priority service in the destination country. All LC mail should be marked 'AIRMAIL' or 'PAR AVION.'" (U.S. Postal Service, Pub. 51).

No. C133 listed below was issued to meet the LC rate to Canada and Mexico and is inscribed with the silhouette of a jet plane next to the denomination indicating the need for airmail service. This is unlike No. 2998, which met the LC rate to other countries, but contained no indication that it was intended for that use.

Future issues that meet a specific international airmail rate and contain the airplane silhouette will be treated by Scott as Air Post stamps. Stamps similar to No. 2998 will be listed in the Postage section.

Niagara Falls

AP104

1999, May 12 **Photo.** *Perf. 11*
Self-Adhesive
C133 AP104 48c multicolored .95 .20

Rio Grande

AP105

Serpentine Die Cut 11
1999, July 30 **Photo.**
Self-Adhesive
C134 AP105 40c multicolored .80 .60

Grand Canyon

AP106

Serpentine Die Cut 11¼x11½
2000, Jan. 20 **Litho.**
Self-Adhesive
C135 AP106 60c multicolored 1.25 .25
a. Imperf, pair —

Nine-Mile Prairie, Nebraska

AP107

Serpentine Die Cut 11¼x11½
2001, Mar. 6 **Litho.**
Self-Adhesive
C136 AP107 70c multicolored 1.40 .30

Mt. Mc Kinley

AP108

Serpentine Die Cut 11
2001, Apr. 17 **Photo.**
Self-Adhesive
C137 AP108 80c multicolored 1.60 .35

Acadia National Park

AP109

Serpentine Die Cut 11¼x11½
2001, May 30 **Litho.**
Self-Adhesive
C138 AP109 60c multicolored 1.25 .25

AIR POST SPECIAL DELIVERY STAMPS

To provide for the payment of both the postage and the special delivery fee in one stamp.

Great Seal of United States APSD1

Flat Plate Printing

1934 **Unwmk.** *Perf. 11*
CE1 APSD1 16c dark blue .60 .70
Never hinged .80

For imperforate variety see No. 771.

1936
CE2 APSD1 16c red & blue .40 .25
Never hinged .50
a. Horiz. pair, imperf. vert. *4,000.*

SPECIAL DELIVERY STAMPS

When affixed to any letter or article of mailable matter, secure immediate delivery, between 7 A. M. and midnight, at any post office.

Messenger Running SD1

Flat Plate Printing

1885 **Unwmk.** *Perf. 12*
E1 SD1 10c blue 375.00 50.00
Never hinged 800.00

Messenger Running SD2

1888
E2 SD2 10c blue 375.00 20.00
Never hinged 800.00

1893
E3 SD2 10c orange 225.00 25.00
Never hinged 475.00

Messenger Running SD3

Line under "Ten Cents"

1894
E4 SD3 10c blue 800.00 35.00
Never hinged 1,750.

1895 **Wmk. 191**
E5 SD3 10c blue 175.00 4.00
Never hinged 350.00
b. Printed on both sides —

Messenger on Bicycle SD4

1902
E6 SD4 10c ultramarine 150.00 4.50
Never hinged 350.00
a. 10c blue 150.00 4.50
Never hinged 350.00

Helmet of Mercury and Olive Branch — SD5

1908
E7 SD5 10c green 60.00 40.00
Never hinged 120.00

1911 **Wmk. 190** *Perf. 12*
E8 SD4 10c ultramarine 100.00 5.25
Never hinged 200.00
b. 10c violet blue 100.00 5.25
Never hinged 200.00

1914 *Perf. 10*
E9 SD4 10c ultramarine 180.00 7.50
Never hinged 375.00
a. 10c blue 210.00 8.50
Never hinged 425.00

1916 **Unwmk.** *Perf. 10*
E10 SD4 10c pale ultra 290.00 30.00
Never hinged 575.00
a. 10c blue 325.00 30.00
Never hinged 650.00

1917 *Perf. 11*
E11 SD4 10c ultramarine 22.50 .50
Never hinged 40.00
b. 10c gray violet 22.50 .50
Never hinged 40.00
c. 10c blue 60.00 2.50
Never hinged 110.00

Postman and Motorcycle SD6

Post Office Truck SD7

1922-25
E12 SD6 10c gray violet 35.00 .50
Never hinged 70.00
a. 10c deep ultramarine 42.50 .60
Never hinged 85.00
E13 SD6 15c deep orange ('25) 24.00 1.00
Never hinged 45.00
E14 SD7 20c black ('25) 1.75 1.00
Never hinged 3.00
Nos. E12-E14 (3) 60.75 2.50

No. E12 measures 36x21½mm
No. E15 measures 36½x21¾mm
No. E13 measures 36½x21½mm
No. E16 measures 36¾x22¼mm
No. E14 measures 35½x21½mm
No. E19 measures 36¼x22mm

Rotary Press Printing

1927-31 *Perf. 11x10½*
E15 SD6 10c gray violet .60 .20
Never hinged 1.00
a. 10c red lilac .60 .20
Never hinged 1.00
b. 10c gray lilac .60 .20

Never hinged 1.00
c. Horiz. pair, imperf. btwn. 300.00
E16 SD6 15c orange ('31) .70 .20
Never hinged 1.05

Catalogue values for unused stamps in this section, from this point to the end of the section, are for Never Hinged items.

1944-51
E17 SD6 13c blue .60 .20
E18 SD6 17c orange yellow 2.75 1.75
E19 SD7 20c black ('51) 1.25 .20
Nos. E17-E19 (3) 4.60 2.15

Special Delivery Letter, Hand to Hand SD8

1954-57 ***Perf. 11x10½***
E20 SD8 20c deep blue .40 .20
E21 SD8 30c lake ('57) .50 .20

Arrows SD9

Giori Press Printing

1969-71 ***Perf. 11***
E22 SD9 45c car & vio blue 1.25 .25
E23 SD9 60c vio blue & car ('71) 1.25 .20

Issue dates: 45c, Nov. 21; 60c, May 10.

REGISTRATION STAMP

Issued for the prepayment of registry fees; not usable for postage.

Eagle — RS1

Wmk. 190

1911, Dec. 1 Engr. ***Perf. 12***
F1 RS1 10c ultramarine 75.00 7.50
Never hinged 140.00

CERTIFIED MAIL STAMP

For use on first-class mail for which no indemnity value is claimed, but for which proof of mailing and proof of delivery are available at less cost than registered mail.

Catalogue values for unused stamps in this section are for Never Hinged items.

Letter Carrier — CM1

Rotary Press Printing

1955, June 6 Unwmk. ***Perf. 10½x11***
FA1 CM1 15c red .45 .30

POSTAGE DUE STAMPS

For affixing, by a postal clerk to any piece of mailable matter, to denote the amount to be collected from the addressee because of insufficient pre-payment of postage.

Unused values for all postage dues are for stamps with full original gum.

D1

D2

Printed by the American Bank Note Company

1879 Unwmk. Engraved ***Perf. 12***
J1 D1 1c brown 65.00 10.00
J2 D1 2c brown 400.00 10.00
J3 D1 3c brown 62.50 5.00
J4 D1 5c brown 700.00 50.00
J5 D1 10c brown 800.00 55.00
a. Imperf., pair *2,000.*
J6 D1 30c brown 350.00 55.00
J7 D1 50c brown 575.00 75.00
Nos. J1-J7 (7) 2,952. 260.00

Special Printing

1879
J8 D1 1c deep brown *17,500.*
J9 D1 2c deep brown *9,500.*
J10 D1 3c deep brown *14,000.*
J11 D1 5c deep brown *9,250.*
J12 D1 10c deep brown *4,500.*
J13 D1 30c deep brown *4,500.*
J14 D1 50c deep brown *4,500.*

1884
J15 D1 1c red brown 65.00 6.00
J16 D1 2c red brown 75.00 5.00
J17 D1 3c red brown 1,100. 225.00
J18 D1 5c red brown 575.00 35.00
J19 D1 10c red brown 575.00 30.00
J20 D1 30c red brown 175.00 55.00
J21 D1 50c red brown 1,750. 200.00
Nos. J15-J21 (7) 4,315. 556.00

1891
J22 D1 1c bright claret 30.00 1.00
J23 D1 2c bright claret 35.00 1.00
J24 D1 3c bright claret 70.00 12.50
J25 D1 5c bright claret 85.00 12.50
J26 D1 10c bright claret 140.00 25.00
J27 D1 30c bright claret 575.00 175.00
J28 D1 50c bright claret 575.00 175.00
Nos. J22-J28 (7) 1,510. 402.00

See Die and Plate Proofs in the Scott U.S. Specialized for imperfs. on stamp paper.

Printed by the Bureau of Engraving and Printing

1894
J29 D2 1c vermilion 2,000. 500.
Never hinged 4,250.
J30 D2 2c vermilion 800. 225.
Never hinged 1,600.

1894
J31 D2 1c deep claret 60.00 8.00
Never hinged 125.00
b. Vert. pair, imperf. horiz. —
J32 D2 2c deep claret 50.00 6.00
Never hinged 100.00
J33 D2 3c deep claret 200.00 35.00
Never hinged 425.00
J34 D2 5c deep claret 325.00 40.00
Never hinged 675.00
J35 D2 10c deep claret 325.00 30.00
Never hinged 675.00
J36 D2 30c deep claret 525.00 160.00
Never hinged 1,100.
a. 30c carmine 550.00 180.00
Never hinged 1,200.
b. 30c pale rose 425.00 110.00
Never hinged 900.00
J37 D2 50c deep claret 1,700. 600.00
Never hinged 3,500.
a. 50c pale rose 1,550. 500.00
Never hinged 3,250.
Nos. J31-J37 (7) 3,185. 879.00

Shades are numerous in the 1894 and later issues.

See Die and Plate Proofs in the Scott U.S. Specialized for 1c imperf. on stamp paper.

1895 **Wmk. 191**
J38 D2 1c deep claret 10.00 .75
Never hinged 20.00
J39 D2 2c deep claret 10.00 .70
Never hinged 20.00
J40 D2 3c deep claret 70.00 1.75
Never hinged 145.00
J41 D2 5c deep claret 75.00 1.75
Never hinged 160.00
J42 D2 10c deep claret 75.00 3.50
Never hinged 160.00
J43 D2 30c deep claret 600.00 50.00
Never hinged 1,300.
J44 D2 50c deep claret 425.00 37.50
Never hinged 900.00
Nos. J38-J44 (7) 1,265. 95.95

1910-12 **Wmk. 190**
J45 D2 1c deep claret 35.00 3.00
Never hinged 70.00
a. 1c rose carmine 32.50 3.00
Never hinged 65.00
J46 D2 2c deep claret 40.00 1.00
Never hinged 80.00
a. 2c rose carmine 35.00 1.00
Never hinged 70.00
J47 D2 3c deep claret 600.00 37.50
Never hinged 1,300.
J48 D2 5c deep claret 115.00 8.00
Never hinged 230.00
a. 5c rose carmine 110.00 8.50
Never hinged 220.00
J49 D2 10c deep claret 130.00 15.00
Never hinged 275.00
a. 10c rose carmine 125.00 15.00
Never hinged 260.00
J50 D2 50c deep claret ('12) 1,100. 140.00
Never hinged 2,350.
Nos. J45-J50 (6) 2,020. 204.50

1914 ***Perf. 10***
J52 D2 1c carmine lake 65.00 12.50
Never hinged 140.00
a. 1c dull rose 75.00 12.50
Never hinged 160.00
J53 D2 2c carmine lake 47.50 .40
Never hinged 105.00
a. 2c dull rose 52.50 .50
Never hinged 115.00
b. 2c vermilion 52.50 .50
Never hinged 115.00
J54 D2 3c carmine lake 950.00 55.00
Never hinged 2,250.
a. 3c dull rose 950.00 50.00
Never hinged 2,250.
J55 D2 5c carmine lake 37.50 3.50
Never hinged 80.00
a. 5c dull rose 37.50 2.50
Never hinged 80.00
J56 D2 10c carmine lake 57.50 2.00
Never hinged 115.00
a. 10c dull rose 70.00 3.00
Never hinged 140.00
J57 D2 30c carmine lake 240.00 17.50
Never hinged 480.00
J58 D2 50c carmine lake *12,500.* 1,100.
Never hinged *22,500.*
Nos. J52-J58 (7) 13,897. 1,190.

1916 Unwmk. ***Perf. 10***
J59 D2 1c rose 4,000. 500.00
Never hinged 8,000.
J60 D2 2c rose 200.00 45.00
Never hinged 450.00

1917 ***Perf. 11***
J61 D2 1c carmine rose 2.75 .25
Never hinged 5.00
a. 1c rose red 2.75 .25
Never hinged 5.00
b. 1c deep claret 2.75 .25
Never hinged 5.00
J62 D2 2c carmine rose 2.50 .25
Never hinged 5.00
a. 2c rose red 2.50 .25
Never hinged 5.00
b. 2c deep claret 2.50 .25
Never hinged 5.50
J63 D2 3c carmine rose 11.00 .25
Never hinged 22.00
a. 3c rose red 11.00 .25
Never hinged 22.00
b. 3c deep claret 11.00 .35
Never hinged 22.00
J64 D2 5c carmine 11.00 .25
Never hinged 22.00
a. 5c rose red 11.00 .25
Never hinged 22.00
b. 5c deep claret 11.00 .25
Never hinged 22.00
J65 D2 10c carmine rose 17.00 .30
Never hinged 35.00
a. 10c rose red 17.00 .25
Never hinged 35.00
b. 10c deep claret 17.00 .25
Never hinged 35.00
J66 D2 30c carmine rose 87.50 .75
Never hinged 175.00
a. 30c deep claret 87.50 .75
Never hinged 175.00
J67 D2 50c carmine rose 125.00 .30
Never hinged 250.00
a. 50c rose red 125.00 .30
Never hinged 250.00
b. 50c deep claret 125.00 .30
Never hinged 250.00
Nos. J61-J67 (7) 256.75 2.35

1925
J68 D2 ½c dull red 1.00 .25
Never hinged 1.90

D3

D4

1930 ***Perf. 11***
J69 D3 ½c carmine 4.50 1.40
Never hinged 8.00
J70 D3 1c carmine 3.00 .25
Never hinged 5.00
J71 D3 2c carmine 4.00 .25
Never hinged 7.00
J72 D3 3c carmine 21.00 1.75
Never hinged 37.50
J73 D3 5c carmine 19.00 2.50
Never hinged 35.00
J74 D3 10c carmine 40.00 1.00
Never hinged 70.00
J75 D3 30c carmine 140.00 2.00
Never hinged 225.00
J76 D3 50c carmine 190.00 1.00
Never hinged 325.00
J77 D4 $1 carmine 30.00 .25
Never hinged 50.00
a. $1 scarlet 25.00 .25
Never hinged 42.50
J78 D4 $5 carmine 37.50 .25
Never hinged 60.00
a. $5 scarlet 32.50 .25
Never hinged 52.50
Nos. J69-J78 (10) 489.00 10.65

Rotary Press Printing

1931-56 ***Perf. 11x10½***
J79 D3 ½c dull carmine .90 .20
Never hinged 1.30
J80 D3 1c dull carmine .20 .20
Never hinged .30
J81 D3 2c dull carmine .20 .20
Never hinged .30
J82 D3 3c dull carmine .25 .20
Never hinged .40
J83 D3 5c dull carmine .40 .20
Never hinged .60
J84 D3 10c dull carmine 1.10 .20
Never hinged 1.60
J85 D3 30c dull carmine 6.50 .25
Never hinged 10.00
J86 D3 50c dull carmine 9.00 .25
Never hinged 15.00

Perf. 10½x11
J87 D4 $1 scarlet ('56) 32.50 .25
Never hinged 47.50
Nos. J79-J87 (9) 51.05 1.95

J79a D3 ½c scarlet .90 .20
Never hinged 1.30
J80a D3 1c scarlet .20 .20
Never hinged .30
J81a D3 2c scarlet .20 .20
Never hinged .30
J82a D3 3c scarlet .25 .20
Never hinged .40
J83a D3 5c scarlet .40 .20
Never hinged .60
J84a D3 10c scarlet 1.10 .20
Never hinged 1.60
J85a D3 30c scarlet 32.50 .25
Never hinged 10.00
J86a D3 50c scarlet 9.00 .25
Never hinged 15.00
Nos. J79a-J86a (8) 44.55 1.70

Catalogue values for unused stamps in this section, from this point to the end of the section, are for Never Hinged items.

D5

Denominations added by rubber plates in an operation similar to precanceling.

Rotary Press Printing
Perf. 11x10½

1959, June 19 Unwmk.

Denomination in Black
J88 D5 ½c carmine rose 1.50 1.10
J89 D5 1c carmine rose .20 .20
a. "1 CENT" omitted 300.00
b. Pair, one without "1 CENT" *500.00*
J90 D5 2c carmine rose .20 .20
J91 D5 3c carmine rose .20 .20
a. Pair, one without "3 CENTS" *725.00*
J92 D5 4c carmine rose .20 .20
J93 D5 5c carmine rose .20 .20
a. Pair, one without "5 CENTS" 1,250.
J94 D5 6c carmine rose .20 .20
a. Pair, one without "6 CENTS" *850.00*
J95 D5 7c carmine rose .20 .20
J96 D5 8c carmine rose .20 .20
a. Pair, one without "8 CENTS" *850.00*
J97 D5 10c carmine rose .20 .20
J98 D5 30c carmine rose .75 .20
J99 D5 50c carmine rose 1.10 .20

Straight Numeral Outlined in Black
J100 D5 $1 carmine rose 2.00 .20
J101 D5 $5 carmine rose 9.00 .20
Nos. J88-J101 (14) 16.15 3.70

All single copies with value omitted are catalogued as No. J89a.

1978-85

Denomination in Black

J102 D5 11c carmine rose .25 .20
J103 D5 13c carmine rose .25 .20
J104 D5 17c carmine rose ('85) .40 .35
Nos. J102-J104 (3) .90 .75
Nos. J88-J104 (17) 17.05 4.45

Issue dates: Jan. 2, 1978, June 10, 1985.

UNITED STATES OFFICES IN CHINA

Issued for sale by the postal agency at Shanghai, at their surcharged value in local currency. Valid to the amount of their original values for the prepayment of postage on mail dispatched from the US postal agency at Shanghai to addresses in the US.

Nos. 498-499, 502-504, 506-510, 512, 514-518 Surcharged

1919 Unwmk. *Perf. 11*

K1 A140 2c on 1c green 25.00 *32.50*
Never hinged 50.00
K2 A140 4c on 2c rose, I 25.00 *32.50*
Never hinged 50.00
K3 A140 6c on 3c vio, II 52.50 *75.00*
Never hinged 115.00
K4 A140 8c on 4c brown 57.50 *75.00*
Never hinged 120.00
K5 A140 10c on 5c blue 65.00 *75.00*
Never hinged 140.00
K6 A140 12c on 6c red org 85.00 *110.00*
Never hinged 180.00
K7 A140 14c on 7c black 87.50 *125.00*
Never hinged 190.00
K8 A148 16c on 8c ol bis 65.00 *80.00*
Never hinged 140.00
a. 16c on 8c olive green 60.00 *60.00*
Never hinged 130.00
K9 A148 18c on 9c sal red 65.00 *85.00*
Never hinged 140.00
K10 A148 20c on 10c org yel 60.00 *70.00*
Never hinged 130.00
K11 A148 24c on 12c brn car 80.00 *80.00*
Never hinged 175.00
a. 24c on 12c claret brown 105.00 *125.00*
Never hinged 230.00
K12 A148 30c on 15c gray 87.50 *140.00*
Never hinged 190.00
K13 A148 40c on 20c dp ultra 130.00 *225.00*
Never hinged 275.00
K14 A148 60c on 30c org red 120.00 *175.00*
Never hinged 260.00
K15 A148 $1 on 50c lt vio 575.00 *650.00*
Never hinged 1,200.
K16 A148 $2 on $1 vio brown 450.00 *550.00*
Never hinged 950.00
a. Double surcharge *5,000.* *6,000.*
Never hinged *8,500.*
Nos. K1-K16 (16) 2,030. 2,580.

Nos. 498 and 528B Surcharged

1922, July 3

K17 A140 2c on 1c green 110.00 125.00
Never hinged 230.00
K18 A140 4c on 2c car, VII 100.00 110.00
Never hinged 210.00

OFFICIAL STAMPS

The franking privilege having been abolished, as of July 1, 1873, these stamps were provided for each of the departments of Government for the prepayment of postage on official matter.

These stamps were supplanted on May 1, 1879, by penalty envelopes and on July 5, 1884, were declared obsolete.

Designs, except Post Office, resemble those illustrated but are not identical. Each bears the name of Department. Portraits are as follows: 1c, Franklin; 2c, Jackson; 3c, Washington; 6c, Lincoln; 7c, Stanton; 10c, Jefferson; 12c, Clay; 15c, Webster; 24c, Scott; 30c, Hamilton; 90c, Perry.

Grade, condition and original gum are very important in valuing #O1-O120 unused.

Printed by the Continental Bank Note Co.
Thin Hard Paper

O1

1873 Unwmk. Engr. *Perf. 12*

AGRICULTURE

O1 O1 1c yellow 170.00 160.00
O2 O1 2c yellow 135.00 65.00
O3 O1 3c yellow 120.00 13.00
O4 O1 6c yellow 135.00 52.50
O5 O1 10c yellow 270.00 180.00
O6 O1 12c yellow 360.00 240.00
O7 O1 15c yellow 300.00 210.00
O8 O1 24c yellow 300.00 190.00
O9 O1 30c yellow 390.00 250.00
Nos. O1-O9 (9) 2,180. 1,360.

Special printings overprinted "SPECIMEN" follow No. O120.

EXECUTIVE

O10 O1 1c carmine 650.00 425.00
O11 O1 2c carmine 425.00 210.00
O12 O1 3c carmine 475.00 170.00
a. 3c violet rose 475.00 170.00
O13 O1 6c carmine 725.00 500.00
O14 O1 10c carmine 700.00 575.00
Nos. O10-O14 (5) 2,975. 1,880.

Special printings overprinted "SPECIMEN" follow No. O120.

INTERIOR

O15 O1 1c vermilion 37.50 8.50
O16 O1 2c vermilion 35.00 9.50
O17 O1 3c vermilion 50.00 5.25
O18 O1 6c vermilion 37.50 5.25
O19 O1 10c vermilion 37.50 16.00
O20 O1 12c vermilion 52.50 8.00
O21 O1 15c vermilion 100.00 18.00
O22 O1 24c vermilion 75.00 15.00
a. Double impression —
O23 O1 30c vermilion 100.00 15.00
O24 O1 90c vermilion 200.00 40.00
Nos. O15-O24 (10) 725.00 140.50

Special printings overprinted "SPECIMEN" follow No. O120.

JUSTICE

O25 O1 1c purple 120.00 90.00
O26 O1 2c purple 210.00 90.00
O27 O1 3c purple 210.00 22.50
O28 O1 6c purple 190.00 32.50
O29 O1 10c purple 225.00 75.00
O30 O1 12c purple 170.00 50.00
O31 O1 15c purple 325.00 160.00
O32 O1 24c purple 875.00 350.00
O33 O1 30c purple 850.00 275.00
O34 O1 90c purple 1,250. 525.00
Nos. O25-O34 (10) 4,425. 1,670.

Special printings overprinted "SPECIMEN" follow No. O120.

NAVY

O35 O1 1c ultramarine 80.00 42.50
a. 1c dull blue 85.00 45.00
O36 O1 2c ultramarine 65.00 18.00
a. 2c dull blue 70.00 16.00
O37 O1 3c ultramarine 125.00 10.00
a. 3c dull blue 120.00 11.00
O38 O1 6c ultramarine 62.50 15.00
a. 6c dull blue 67.50 15.00
O39 O1 7c ultramarine 450.00 190.00
a. 7c dull blue 450.00 190.00
O40 O1 10c ultramarine 85.00 32.50
a. 10c dull blue 85.00 32.50
O41 O1 12c ultramarine 110.00 32.50
O42 O1 15c ultramarine 180.00 60.00
O43 O1 24c ultramarine 220.00 70.00
a. 24c dull blue 200.00 —
O44 O1 30c ultramarine 160.00 37.50
O45 O1 90c ultramarine 725.00 240.00
a. Double impression *3,750.*
Nos. O35-O45 (11) 2,262. 748.00

Special printings overprinted "SPECIMEN" follow No. O120.

O6

POST OFFICE

O47 O6 1c black 14.00 8.00
O48 O6 2c black 17.50 7.50
a. Double impression 325.00 300.00
O49 O6 3c black 5.50 1.10
a. Printed on both sides *3,000.*
O50 O6 6c black 17.50 6.50
a. Diagonal half used as 3c on cover *3,000.*
O51 O6 10c black 75.00 42.50
O52 O6 12c black 37.50 8.75
O53 O6 15c black 50.00 15.00
O54 O6 24c black 65.00 18.00
O55 O6 30c black 75.00 18.00
O56 O6 90c black 95.00 15.00
Nos. O47-O56 (10) 452.00 140.35

Stamps of the POD are often on paper with a gray surface. This is due to insufficient wiping of the plates during printing.

Special printings overprinted "SPECIMEN" follow No. O120.

Seward — O8

STATE

O57 O1 1c dark green 140.00 57.50
O58 O1 2c dark green 225.00 80.00
O59 O1 3c bright green 110.00 18.00
O60 O1 6c bright green 100.00 24.00
O61 O1 7c dark green 170.00 55.00
O62 O1 10c dark green 130.00 42.50
O63 O1 12c dark green 210.00 100.00
O64 O1 15c dark green 220.00 70.00
O65 O1 24c dark green 450.00 190.00
O66 O1 30c dark green 425.00 150.00
O67 O1 90c dark green 800.00 300.00
O68 O8 $2 green & black 1,000. 1,000.
O69 O8 $5 green & black 6,000. 3,750.
O70 O8 $10 green & black 4,500. 2,600.
O71 O8 $20 green & black 3,500. 2,100.

Nos. O68-O71 with pen cancels sell for approximately 25-40% of the values shown.

Special printings overprinted "SPECIMEN" follow No. O120.

TREASURY

O72 O1 1c brown 40.00 5.50
O73 O1 2c brown 50.00 5.50
O74 O1 3c brown 50.00 1.40
a. Double impression —
O75 O1 6c brown 50.00 2.60
O76 O1 7c brown 95.00 26.00
O77 O1 10c brown 100.00 8.25
O78 O1 12c brown 95.00 6.50
O79 O1 15c brown 90.00 8.25
O80 O1 24c brown 500.00 75.00
O81 O1 30c brown 200.00 9.50
O82 O1 90c brown 200.00 10.50
Nos. O72-O82 (11) 1,470. 159.00

Special printings overprinted "SPECIMEN" follow No. O120.

WAR

O83 O1 1c rose 145.00 9.00
O84 O1 2c rose 130.00 10.00
O85 O1 3c rose 135.00 3.00
O86 O1 6c rose 450.00 6.50
O87 O1 7c rose 130.00 77.50
O88 O1 10c rose 45.00 16.00
O89 O1 12c rose 170.00 10.50
O90 O1 15c rose 40.00 12.00
O91 O1 24c rose 40.00 7.25
O92 O1 30c rose 42.50 7.25
O93 O1 90c rose 95.00 42.50
Nos. O83-O93 (11) 1,422. 201.50

Special printings overprinted "SPECIMEN" follow No. O120.

Printed by the American Bank Note Co.

1879 Soft Porous Paper

AGRICULTURE

O94 O1 1c yel, no gum 3,750.
O95 O1 3c yellow 375.00 70.00

INTERIOR

O96 O1 1c vermilion 250.00 230.00
O97 O1 2c vermilion 6.00 1.40
O98 O1 3c vermilion 5.50 1.10
O99 O1 6c vermilion 8.00 6.00
O100 O1 10c vermilion 85.00 65.00
O101 O1 12c vermilion 160.00 100.00
O102 O1 15c vermilion 325.00 240.00
O103 O1 24c vermilion *3,500.* —

JUSTICE

O106 O1 3c bluish purple 100.00 70.00
O107 O1 6c bluish purple 250.00 190.00

POST OFFICE

O108 O6 3c black 20.00 5.50

TREASURY

O109 O1 3c brown 60.00 7.25
O110 O1 6c brown 100.00 37.50
O111 O1 10c brown 175.00 55.00
O112 O1 30c brown 1,600. 300.00
O113 O1 90c brown 2,400. 300.00
Nos. O109-O113 (5) 4,335. 699.75

WAR

O114 O1 1c rose red 3.75 3.00
O115 O1 2c rose red 7.00 3.50
O116 O1 3c rose red 7.00 1.30
a. Imperf., pair *900.00*
b. Double impression *750.00*
O117 O1 6c rose red 7.00 1.10
O118 O1 10c rose red 40.00 37.50
O119 O1 12c rose red 35.00 11.00
O120 O1 30c rose red 110.00 75.00
Nos. O114-O120 (7) 209.75 132.40

SPECIAL PRINTINGS

Special printings of Official stamps were made in 1875 at the time the other Reprints, Re-issues and Special Printings were printed. They are ungummed.

Although perforated, these stamps were sometimes (but not always) cut apart with scissors. As a result the perforations may be mutilated and the design damaged.

All values exist imperforate.

Printed by the Continental Bank Note Co.

Overprinted in Block Letters

1875 *Perf. 12*

Thin, hard white paper
Type D

AGRICULTURE

Carmine Overprint

O1S D 1c yellow 15.00
a. "Sepcimen" error 1,000.
b. Small dotted "i" in "Specimen" 425.00
c. Horiz. ribbed paper 20.00
O2S D 2c yellow 27.50
a. "Sepcimen" error 1,000.
O3S D 3c yellow 75.00
a. "Sepcimen" error *4,000.*
O4S D 6c yellow 130.00
a. "Sepcimen" error *5,500.*
O5S D 10c yellow 130.00
a. "Sepcimen" error *4,000.*
O6S D 12c yellow 125.00
a. "Sepcimen" error *4,000.*
O7S D 15c yellow 125.00
a. "Sepcimen" error *4,000.*
O8S D 24c yellow 125.00
a. "Sepcimen" error *4,000.*
O9S D 30c yellow 125.00
a. "Sepcimen" error *4,000.*
Nos. O1S-O9S (9) 877.50

EXECUTIVE

Blue Overprint

O10S D 1c carmine 15.00
a. Small dotted "i" in "Specimen" 325.00
b. Ribbed paper 20.00
O11S D 2c carmine 30.00
O12S D 3c carmine 30.00
O13S D 6c carmine 30.00
O14S D 10c carmine 30.00
Nos. O10S-O14S (5) 135.00

INTERIOR

Blue Overprint

O15S D 1c vermilion 30.00
O16S D 2c vermilion 37.50
a. "Sepcimen" error *3,750.*
O17S D 3c vermilion 550.00
O18S D 6c vermilion 550.00
O19S D 10c vermilion 550.00
O20S D 12c vermilion 550.00
O21S D 15c vermilion 550.00
O22S D 24c vermilion 550.00
O23S D 30c vermilion 550.00
O24S D 90c vermilion 550.00
Nos. O15S-O24S (10) 4,467.

JUSTICE

Blue Overprint

O25S D 1c purple 15.00
a. "Sepcimen" error 675.00
b. Small dotted "i" in "Specimen" 275.00
c. Horiz. ribbed paper 20.00
O26S D 2c purple 30.00
a. "Sepcimen" error 1,200.

O27S D 3c purple 325.00
a. "Sepcimen" error 3,750.
O28S D 6c purple 325.00
O29S D 10c purple 325.00
O30S D 12c purple 325.00
a. "Sepcimen" error 4,000.
O31S D 15c purple 325.00
a. "Sepcimen" error 4,000.
O32S D 24c purple 350.00
a. "Sepcimen" error 4,000.
O33S D 30c purple 350.00
a. "Sepcimen" error 4,000.
O34S D 90c purple 350.00
Nos. O25S-O34S (10) 2,720.

NAVY

Carmine Overprint

O35S D 1c ultramarine 20.00
a. "Sepcimen" error 750.00
O36S D 2c ultramarine 35.00
a. "Sepcimen" error 1,000.
O37S D 3c ultramarine 375.00
O38S D 6c ultramarine 375.00
O39S D 7c ultramarine 150.00
a. "Sepcimen" error 3,000.
O40S D 10c ultramarine 375.00
a. "Sepcimen" error 4,250.
O41S D 12c ultramarine 400.00
a. "Sepcimen" error 4,000.
O42S D 15c ultramarine 400.00
a. "Sepcimen" error 7,500.
O43S D 24c ultramarine 400.00
a. "Sepcimen" error 4,000.
O44S D 30c ultramarine 400.00
a. "Sepcimen" error 4,500.
O45S D 90c ultramarine 400.00
Nos. O35S-O45S (11) 3,330.

POST OFFICE

Carmine Overprint

O47S D 1c black 25.00
a. "Sepcimen" error 900.00
b. Inverted overprint 1,000.
O48S D 2c black 65.00
a. "Sepcimen" error 1,750.
O49S D 3c black 500.00
a. "Sepcimen" error —
O50S D 6c black 500.00
O51S D 10c black 325.00
a. "Sepcimen" error 4,250.
O52S D 12c black 475.00
O53S D 15c black 500.00
a. "Sepcimen" error 4,250.
O54S D 24c black 500.00
a. "Sepcimen" error 4,250.
O55S D 30c black 500.00
O56S D 90c black 500.00
a. "Sepcimen" error 8,000.
Nos. O47S-O56S (10) 3,890.

STATE

Carmine Overprint

O57S D 1c bluish green 15.00
a. "Sepcimen" error 400.00
b. Small dotted "i" in "Specimen" 400.00
c. Horiz. ribbed paper 20.00
d. Double overprint —
O58S D 2c bluish green 30.00
a. "Sepcimen" error 750.00
O59S D 3c bluish green 45.00
a. "Sepcimen" error 2,500.
O60S D 6c bluish green 95.00
a. "Sepcimen" error 3,250.
O61S D 7c bluish green 47.50
a. "Sepcimen" error 2,500.
O62S D 10c bluish green 200.00
a. "Sepcimen" error 7,500.
O63S D 12c bluish green 210.00
a. "Sepcimen" error 3,500.
O64S D 15c bluish green 210.00
O65S D 24c bluish green 210.00
a. "Sepcimen" error 3,500.
O66S D 30c bluish green 210.00
a. "Sepcimen" error 3,750.
O67S D 90c bluish green 210.00
a. "Sepcimen" error 3,750.
O68S D $2 green & black 7,500.
O69S D $5 green & black 15,000.
O70S D $10 green & black 20,000.
O71S D $20 green & black 25,000.
Nos. O57S-O67S (11) 1,482.

TREASURY

Blue Overprint

O72S D 1c dark brown 27.50
O73S D 2c dark brown 130.00
O74S D 3c dark brown 500.00
O75S D 6c dark brown 500.00
O76S D 7c dark brown 325.00
O77S D 10c dark brown 500.00
O78S D 12c dark brown 550.00
O79S D 15c dark brown 550.00
O80S D 24c dark brown 450.00
O81S D 30c dark brown 550.00
O82S D 90c dark brown 550.00
Nos. O72S-O82S (11) 4,632.

WAR

Blue Overprint

O83S D 1c deep rose 17.50
a. "Sepcimen" error 750.00
O84S D 2c deep rose 35.00
a. "Sepcimen" error 1,250.
O85S D 3c deep rose 375.00
a. "Sepcimen" error 4,000.
O86S D 6c deep rose 375.00
a. "Sepcimen" error 4,250.
O87S D 7c deep rose 72.50
a. "Sepcimen" error 2,250.
O88S D 10c deep rose 375.00
a. "Sepcimen" error 4,250.
O89S D 12c deep rose 400.00
a. "Sepcimen" error 4,250.
O90S D 15c deep rose 400.00
a. "Sepcimen" error 4,250.
O91S D 24c deep rose 400.00
a. "Sepcimen" error 4,250.
O92S D 30c deep rose 400.00
a. "Sepcimen" error 4,250.
O93S D 90c deep rose 400.00
a. "Sepcimen" error 4,750.
Nos. O83S-O93S (11) 3,250.

SOFT POROUS PAPER

1881

EXECUTIVE

Blue Overprint

O10xS D 1c violet rose 47.50

NAVY

Carmine Overprint

O35xS D 1c gray blue 60.00
a. Double overprint 850.00

STATE

O57xS D 1c yellow green 225.00

OFFICIAL POSTAL SAVINGS MAIL

These stamps were used to prepay postage on official correspondence of the Postal Savings Division of the POD. Discontinued Sept. 23, 1914.

O11

1911 **Wmk. 191**

O121 O11 2c black 15.00 1.50
Never hinged 30.00
O122 O11 50c dark green 145.00 40.00
Never hinged 275.00
O123 O11 $1 ultra 135.00 11.00
Never hinged 250.00

Wmk. 190

O124 O11 1c dark violet 8.00 1.50
Never hinged 15.00
O125 O11 2c black 47.50 5.50
Never hinged 90.00
O126 O11 10c carmine 18.00 6.50
Never hinged 32.50
Nos. O121-O126 (6) 368.50 66.00

Catalogue values for unused stamps in this section, from this point to the end of the section, are for Never Hinged items.

Catalogue values for used stamps are for regularly used copies, not copies removed from first day covers.

From No. O127 onward, all official stamps are tagged unless noted.

OFFICIAL MAIL

O12

O13

Type O13 has frame line completely around blue design.

1983-85 **Unwmk.** ***Perf. 11***

O127 O12 1c red, bl & blk .20 .20
O128 O12 4c red, bl & blk .20 .25
O129 O12 13c red, bl & blk .45 .75
O129A O12 14c red, bl & blk ('85) .45 .50
O130 O12 17c red, bl & blk .60 .40
O132 O12 $1 red, bl & blk 2.00 1.00
O133 O12 $5 red, bl & blk 9.00 9.00
Nos. O127-O133 (7) 12.90 12.10

Coil Stamps

Perf. 10 Vert.

O135 O12 20c red, bl & blk 1.75 2.00
a. Imperf., pair 2,000.
O136 O12 22c red, bl & blk ('85) .80 2.00

#O129A does not have a "c" after the "14."

Inscribed: Postal Card Rate D

1985, Feb. 4 ***Perf. 11***

O138 O12 (14c) red, bl & blk 5.25 5.00

Coil Stamps

Inscribed: No. O139, Domestic Letter Rate D. No. O140, Domestic Mail E.

1985-88 ***Perf. 10 Vert.***

O138A O13 15c red, bl & blk .45 .50
O138B O13 20c red, bl & blk .45 .30
O139 O12 (22c) red, bl & blk 5.25 3.00
O140 O13 (25c) red, bl & blk .75 2.00
O141 O13 25c red, bl & blk .65 .50
a. Imperf., pair 1,750. —
Nos. O138A-O141 (5) 7.55 6.30

No. O139 is inscribed "D." No. O140 is inscribed "E."

Issue dates: 1985; E, Mar. 22, 1988; 15c, June 11; 20c, May 19; 25c, June 11.

See Nos. O143, O145-O151, O153-O156.

1989, July 5 **Litho.** ***Perf. 11***

O143 O13 1c red, blue & black .20 .20

O14

1991, Jan. 22 Litho. ***Perf. 10 Vert.***

Coil Stamp

O144 O14 (29c) red, blue & blk .75 .50

See No. O152.

Official Type of 1985

1991, May 24 Litho. ***Perf. 10 Vert.***

Coil Stamp

O145 O13 29c red, blue & blk .65 .30

1991-93 ***Perf. 11***

O146 O13 4c red, bl & blk .20 .30
O146A O13 10c red, bl & blk .25 .30
O147 O13 19c red, bl & blk .40 .50
O148 O13 23c red, bl & blk .45 .30
a. Imperf., pair 100.00
O151 O13 $1 red, bl & blk 2.00 .75

Nos. O146A, O151 have a line of microscopic printing below eagle.

Nos. O147 and O148 have blue background made up of crosshatched lines, thicker lettering and thinner numerals.

Issued: No. O146, 4/6; Nos. O147-O148, 5/24; 10c, 10/19/93; No. O151, 9/1993.

1994, Dec. 13 Litho. ***Perf. 9.8 Vert.***

COIL STAMP

Inscribed: For U.S. addresses only G.

O152 O14 (32c) red, blue & blk .65 —

Type of 1985

1995, May 9 Litho. ***Perf. 9¾ Vert.***

COIL STAMP

O153 O13 32c red, blue & black .65 .30

1995, May 9 ***Perf. 11.2***

O154 O13 1c red, blue & blk, untagged .20 .20
O155 O13 20c red, blue & black .45 .30
O156 O13 23c red, blue & black .50 .30

1999, Oct. 8 Litho. ***Perf. 9¾ Vert.***

COIL STAMP

O157 O13 33c red, blue & black .65 —

Nos. O153-O157 have a line of microscopic text below eagle.

Type of 1985

COIL STAMP

2001, Feb. 27 Litho. ***Perf. 9¾ Vert.***

O158 O13 34c red, blue & black .65 .30

Type of 1985

COIL STAMP

2002, Aug. 2 Photo. ***Perf. 10 Vert.***

O159 O13 37c red, blue & black .70 .35

NEWSPAPER STAMPS

For the prepayment of postage on bulk shipments of newspapers and periodicals. From 1875 on, the stamps were affixed to pages of receipt books, sometimes canceled and retained by the post office. Discontinued on July 1, 1898.

Virtually all used stamps of Nos. PR1-PR4 are canceled by blue brush strokes. All are rare. Most used stamps of Nos. PR9-PR32, PR57-PR79 and PR81-PR89 are pen canceled (or uncanceled).

Handstamp cancellations on any of these issues are rare and sell for much more than catalogue values which are for pen-canceled examples.

Used values for Nos. PR102-PR125 are for stamps with handstamp cancellations.

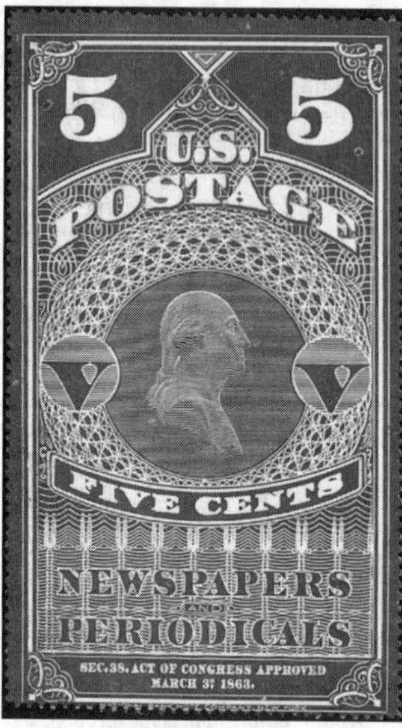

Washington — N1

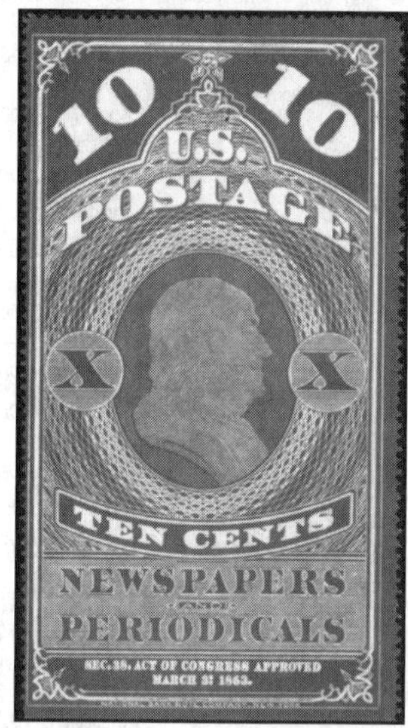

Franklin — N2

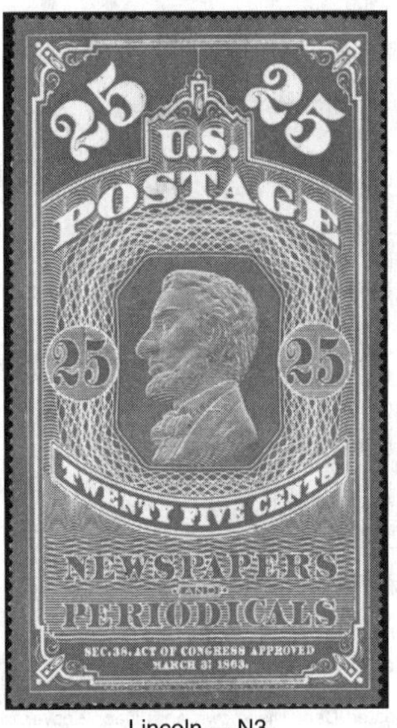

Lincoln — N3

Printed by the National Bank Note Co.

Thin Hard Paper, No Gum

1865 Unwmk. Typo. *Perf. 12*

Size: 51x95mm

Colored Border

PR1	N1	5c dark blue	500.00	—
a.		5c light blue	525.00	—
PR2	N2	10c blue green	200.00	—
a.		10c green	210.00	—
b.		Pelure paper	175.00	—
PR3	N3	25c orange red	260.00	—
a.		25c carmine red	290.00	—
b.		Pelure paper	200.00	

White Border

Yellowish Paper

PR4	N1	5c light blue	130.00	—
a.		5c dark blue	140.00	—
b.		Pelure paper	90.00	—
		Nos. PR1-PR4 (4)	1,090.	

Reprints of 1865 Issue Printed by the National Bank Note Co.

Hard White Paper, Without Gum

1875

PR5	N1	5c dull blue	135.00	
a.		Printed on both sides	—	
PR6	N2	10c dk bluish grn	145.00	
a.		Printed on both sides	*2,750.*	
PR7	N3	25c dark carmine	175.00	
		Nos. PR5-PR7 (3)	455.00	

The 5c has white border, 10c and 25c have colored borders.

Printed by the American Bank Note Co.

1880 Soft Porous Paper

White Border

PR8	N1	5c dark blue	375.00

Statue of Freedom — N4

"Justice" — N5

Ceres — N6

"Victory" — N7

Clio — N8

Minerva — N9

Vesta — N10

"Peace" — N11

"Commerce" N12

Hebe N13

Indian Maiden — N14

Printed by the Continental Bank Note Co.

Engraved Thin Hard Paper

1875 Size: 24x35mm

PR9	N4	2c black	75.00	22.50
PR10	N4	3c black	80.00	25.00
PR11	N4	4c black	80.00	22.50
PR12	N4	6c black	100.00	25.00
PR13	N4	8c black	115.00	35.00
PR14	N4	9c black	240.00	80.00
PR15	N4	10c black	140.00	30.00
PR16	N5	12c rose	325.00	75.00
PR17	N5	24c rose	375.00	90.00
PR18	N5	36c rose	450.00	100.00
PR19	N5	48c rose	750.00	160.00
PR20	N5	60c rose	550.00	90.00
PR21	N5	72c rose	850.00	210.00
PR22	N5	84c rose	1,200.	300.00
PR23	N5	96c rose	850.00	200.00
PR24	N6	$1.92 dark brn	950.00	275.00
PR25	N7	$3 vermilion	1,350.	290.00
PR26	N8	$6 ultra	2,100.	425.00
PR27	N9	$9 yellow	2,750.	475.00
PR28	N10	$12 blue grn	3,500.	600.00
PR29	N11	$24 dk gray vio	3,500.	600.00
PR30	N12	$36 brn rose	3,750.	750.00
PR31	N13	$48 red brn	4,500.	900.00
PR32	N14	$60 violet	5,250.	900.00

Special Printing of the 1875 Issue Printed by the Continental Bank Note Co.

Hard White Paper, Without Gum

PR33	N4	2c gray black	475.
a.		Horizontally ribbed paper	450.
PR34	N4	3c gray black	475.
a.		Horizontally ribbed paper	525.
PR35	N4	4c gray black	575.
a.		Horizontally ribbed paper	625.
PR36	N4	6c gray black	625.
PR37	N4	8c gray black	700.
PR38	N4	9c gray black	850.
PR39	N4	10c gray black	1,050.
a.		Horizontally ribbed paper	—
PR40	N5	12c pale rose	1,250.
PR41	N5	24c pale rose	1,800.
PR42	N5	36c pale rose	2,400.
PR43	N5	48c pale rose	2,800.
PR44	N5	60c pale rose	3,250.
PR45	N5	72c pale rose	3,750.
PR46	N5	84c pale rose	*4,000.*
PR47	N5	96c pale rose	*6,250.*
PR48	N6	$1.92 dk brown	*17,500.*
PR49	N7	$3 vermilion	*42,500.*
PR50	N8	$6 ultra	*47,500.*
PR51	N9	$9 yellow	—
PR52	N10	$12 blue green	*75,000.*
PR53	N11	$24 dk gray vio	—
PR54	N12	$36 brown rose	—
PR55	N13	$48 red brown	—
PR56	N14	$60 violet	—

Nos. PR33 to PR56 exist imperf. but were not regularly issued. (See the Scott U.S. Specialized Catalogue.)

The existence of No. PR39a has been questioned by specialists. The editors would like to see evidence of its existence.

Printed by the American Bank Note Co.

1879 Soft Porous Paper

PR57	N4	2c black	35.00	5.50
PR58	N4	3c black	40.00	7.00
PR59	N4	4c black	40.00	7.00
PR60	N4	6c black	75.00	15.00
PR61	N4	8c black	75.00	15.00
PR62	N4	10c black	75.00	15.00
PR63	N5	12c red	375.00	60.00
PR64	N5	24c red	375.00	60.00
PR65	N5	36c red	750.00	175.00
PR66	N5	48c red	700.00	130.00
PR67	N5	60c red	575.00	110.00
a.		Imperf., pair	*3,250.*	
PR68	N5	72c red	1,000.	210.00
PR69	N5	84c red	1,000.	160.00
PR70	N5	96c red	650.00	110.00
PR71	N6	$1.92 pale brn	450.00	105.00
PR72	N7	$3 red ver	500.00	105.00
PR73	N8	$6 blue	900.00	160.00
PR74	N9	$9 orange	600.00	110.00
PR75	N10	$12 yellow grn	750.00	150.00
PR76	N11	$24 dk violet	650.00	180.00
PR77	N12	$36 Indian red	800.00	200.00
PR78	N13	$48 yel brn	850.00	275.00
PR79	N14	$60 purple	850.00	275.00
		Nos. PR57-PR70 (14)	5,765.	1,079.

See the Scott U.S. Specialized Catalogue Die and Plate Proof section for other imperforates.

Special Printing of the 1879 Issue Printed by the American Bank Note Co.

1881

PR80	N4	2c intense black	1,000.

1885

PR81	N4	1c black	45.00	7.50
PR82	N5	12c carmine	120.00	17.50
PR83	N5	24c carmine	120.00	20.00
PR84	N5	36c carmine	160.00	30.00
PR85	N5	48c carmine	225.00	45.00
PR86	N5	60c carmine	300.00	65.00
PR87	N5	72c carmine	300.00	70.00
PR88	N5	84c carmine	600.00	160.00
PR89	N5	96c carmine	500.00	120.00
		Nos. PR81-PR89 (9)	2,370.	535.00

See the Scott U.S. Specialized Catalogue Die and Plate Proof section for imperforates.

Printed by the Bureau of Engraving and Printing

1894 Soft Wove Paper

PR90	N4	1c intense black	275.	—
PR91	N4	2c intense black	275.	
PR92	N4	4c intense black	325.	
PR93	N4	6c intense black	4,250.	
PR94	N4	10c intense black	750.	
PR95	N5	12c pink	2,000.	—
PR96	N5	24c pink	2,500.	
PR97	N5	36c pink	*50,000.*	
PR98	N5	60c pink	*60,000.*	—
PR99	N5	96c pink	*50,000.*	
PR100	N7	$3 scarlet	*60,000.*	
PR101	N8	$6 pale blue	*60,000.*	—

Nos. PR97-PR100 are valued in the grade of fine-very fine.

Statue of Freedom N15

"Justice" N16

"Victory" N17

Clio N18

Vesta — N19

"Peace" — N20

"Commerce" N21

Indian Maiden N22

1895 Unwmk.

Sizes: 1c-50c, 21x34mm, $2-$100, 24x35mm

PR102	N15	1c black	130.00	17.50
		Never hinged	250.00	
PR103	N15	2c black	130.00	17.50
		Never hinged	250.00	
PR104	N15	5c black	200.00	30.00
		Never hinged	375.00	
PR105	N15	10c black	400.00	75.00
		Never hinged	725.00	
PR106	N16	25c carmine	550.00	75.00
		Never hinged	1,100.	
PR107	N16	50c carmine	1,250.	150.00
		Never hinged	2,000.	
PR108	N17	$2 scarlet	1,350.	160.00
		Never hinged	2,150.	
PR109	N18	$5 ultra	1,750.	275.00
		Never hinged	3,000.	
PR110	N19	$10 green	1,900.	325.00
		Never hinged	3,250.	
PR111	N20	$20 slate	2,500.	550.00
		Never hinged	4,250.	
PR112	N21	$50 dull rose	2,500.	550.00
		Never hinged	4,250.	
PR113	N22	$100 purple	3,000.	650.00
		Never hinged	5,000.	
		Nos. PR102-PR113 (12)	15,660.	2,875.

1895-97 Wmk. 191

PR114	N15	1c black ('96)	6.00	6.00
		Never hinged	12.00	
PR115	N15	2c black	6.50	5.00
		Never hinged	12.00	
PR116	N15	5c black ('96)	10.00	7.50
		Never hinged	17.50	
PR117	N15	10c black	6.50	5.00
		Never hinged	12.00	
PR118	N16	25c carmine	12.50	15.00
		Never hinged	25.00	
PR119	N16	50c carmine	15.00	18.50
		Never hinged	30.00	
PR120	N17	$2 scar ('97)	20.00	30.00
		Never hinged	40.00	
PR121	N18	$5 dk bl ('96)	35.00	40.00
		Never hinged	70.00	
a.		$5 light blue	175.00	100.00
		Never hinged	350.00	
PR122	N19	$10 grn ('96)	35.00	40.00
		Never hinged	70.00	
PR123	N20	$20 slate ('96)	37.50	42.50
		Never hinged	75.00	
PR124	N21	$50 dl rose ('97)	50.00	42.50
		Never hinged	95.00	
PR125	N22	$100 pur ('96)	55.00	50.00
		Never hinged	100.00	
		Nos. PR114-PR125 (12)	289.00	302.00
		Nos. PR114-PR125, never hinged	506.50	

In 1899 the Government sold 26,989 sets of these stamps, but, as the stock of the high values was not sufficient to make up the required number, the $5, $10, $20, $50 and $100 were reprinted. These are virtually indistinguishable from earlier printings.

For overprints see Nos. R159-R160.

PARCEL POST STAMPS

Issued for the prepayment of postage on parcel post packages only.

Post Office Clerk — PP1

City Carrier PP2

Railway Postal Clerk — PP3

Rural Carrier PP4

Mail Train — PP5

Steamship and Mail Tender PP6

Automobile Service PP7

Airplane Carrying Mail — PP8

Manufacturing — PP9

Dairying PP10

Harvesting PP11

Fruit Growing PP12

1913 Engr. Wmk. 190 *Perf. 12*

Q1	PP1	1c carmine rose	5.75	1.50
		Never hinged	12.50	
Q2	PP2	2c carmine rose	6.75	1.25
		Never hinged	15.00	
Q3	PP3	3c carmine	13.50	5.75
		Never hinged	30.00	
Q4	PP4	4c carmine rose	37.50	3.00
		Never hinged	90.00	
Q5	PP5	5c carmine rose	32.50	2.25
		Never hinged	80.00	
Q6	PP6	10c carmine rose	52.50	3.00
		Never hinged	110.00	
Q7	PP7	15c carmine rose	67.50	12.00
		Never hinged	150.00	
Q8	PP8	20c carmine rose	140.00	25.00
		Never hinged	290.00	
Q9	PP9	25c carmine rose	67.50	6.75
		Never hinged	150.00	
Q10	PP10	50c carmine rose	280.00	40.00
		Never hinged	600.00	
Q11	PP11	75c carmine rose	95.00	35.00
		Never hinged	200.00	
Q12	PP12	$1 carmine rose	350.00	35.00
		Never hinged	750.00	
		Nos. Q1-Q12 (12)	1,148.	170.50
		Nos. Q1-Q12, never hinged	2,135.	

PARCEL POST POSTAGE DUE STAMPS

For affixing by a postal clerk, to any parcel post package, to denote the amount to be collected from the addressee because of insufficient prepayment of postage.

PPD1

1913 Engr. Wmk. 190 *Perf. 12*

JQ1	PPD1	1c dark green	11.00	4.50
		Never hinged	25.00	
JQ2	PPD1	2c dark green	85.00	17.50
		Never hinged	200.00	
JQ3	PPD1	5c dark green	15.00	5.50
		Never hinged	32.50	
JQ4	PPD1	10c dark green	175.00	45.00
		Never hinged	375.00	
JQ5	PPD1	25c dark green	105.00	5.00
		Never hinged	225.00	
		Nos. JQ1-JQ5 (5)	391.00	77.50
		Nos. JQ1-JQ5, never hinged	717.50	

SPECIAL HANDLING STAMPS

For use on fourth-class mail to secure the same expeditious handling accorded to first-class mail matter.

PP13

1925-29 Unwmk. Engr. *Perf. 11*

QE1	PP13	10c yel grn ('28)	1.60	1.00
		Never hinged	2.50	
QE2	PP13	15c yel grn ('28)	1.75	.90
		Never hinged	2.75	
QE3	PP13	20c yel grn ('28)	2.75	1.50
		Never hinged	4.40	
QE4	PP13	25c yel grn ('29)	20.00	7.50
		Never hinged	36.00	
	a.	25c deep green ('25)	32.50	5.50
		Never hinged	52.50	
		Nos. QE1-QE4 (4)	26.10	10.90
		Nos. QE1-QE4, never hinged	45.65	

COMPUTER VENDED POSTAGE

CVP1

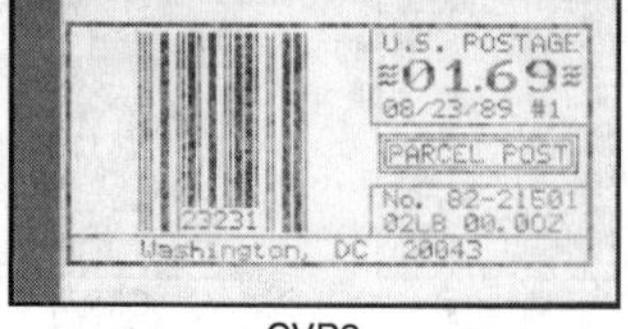

CVP2

1989, Aug. 23 Tagged *Guillotined* Self-Adhesive

Washington, DC, Machine 82

Date Other Than 1st Day

CVP1	CVP1	25c 1st Class	6.00	—
	a.	1st day dated, serial #12501-15500	4.50	—
	b.	1st day dated, serial #00001-12500	4.50	—
	c.	1st day dated, serial over #27500	—	—
CVP2	CVP1	$1 3rd Class	—	—
	a.	1st day dated, serial #24501-27500	—	—
	b.	1st day dated, serial over #27500	—	—
CVP3	CVP2	$1.69 Parcel Post	—	—
	a.	1st day dated, serial #21501-24500	—	—
	b.	1st day dated, serial over #27500	—	—
CVP4	CVP1	$2.40 Priority Mail	—	—
	a.	1st day dated, serial #18501-21500	—	—
	b.	Priority Mail ($2.74), with bar code (CVP2)	*100.00*	
	c.	1st day dated, serial over #27500	—	—
CVP5	CVP1	$8.75 Express Mail	—	—
	a.	1st day dated, serial #15501-18500	—	—
	b.	1st day dated, serial over #27500	—	—
		Nos. CVP1a-CVP5a (5)	82.50	—

Washington, DC, Machine 83

Date Other Than 1st Day

CVP6	CVP1	25c 1st Class	6.00	—
	a.	1st day dated, serial #12501-15500	4.50	—
	b.	1st day dated, serial #00001-12500	4.50	—
	c.	1st day dated, serial over #27500	—	—
CVP7	CVP1	$1 3rd Class	—	—
	a.	1st day dated, serial #24501-27500	—	—
	b.	1st day dated, serial over #27500	—	—
CVP8	CVP2	$1.69 Parcel Post	—	—
	a.	1st day dated, serial #21501-24500	—	—
	b.	1st day dated, serial over #27500	—	—
CVP9	CVP1	$2.40 Priority Mail	—	—
	a.	1st day dated, serial #18501-21500	—	—
	b.	1st day dated, serial over #27500	—	—
	c.	Priority Mail ($2.74), with bar code (CVP2)	*100.00*	
CVP10	CVP1	$8.75 Express Mail	—	—
	a.	1st day dated, serial #15501-18500	—	—
	b.	1st day dated, serial over #27500	—	—
		Nos. CVP6a-CVP10a (5)	57.50	—

1989, Sept. 1

Kensington, MD, Machine 82

Date Other Than 1st Day

CVP11	CVP1	25c 1st Class	6.00	—
	a.	1st day dated, serial #12501-15500	4.50	—
	b.	1st day dated, serial #00001-12500	4.50	—
	c.	1st day dated, serial over #27500	—	—
CVP12	CVP1	$1 3rd Class	—	—
	a.	1st day dated, serial #24501-27500	—	—
	b.	1st day dated, serial over #27500	—	—
CVP13	CVP2	$1.69 Parcel Post	—	—
	a.	1st day dated, serial #21501-24500	—	—
	b.	1st day dated, serial over #27500	—	—
CVP14	CVP1	$2.40 Priority Mail	—	—
	a.	1st day dated, serial #18501-21500	—	—
	b.	1st day dated, serial over #27500	—	—
	c.	Priority Mail ($2.74), with bar code (CVP2)	*100.00*	
CVP15	CVP1	$8.75 Express Mail	—	—
	a.	1st day dated, serial #15501-18500	—	—
	b.	1st day dated, serial over #27500	—	—
		Nos. CVP11a-CVP15a (5)	57.50	—
		Nos. CVP1b, CVP11b (2)	9.00	—

Kensington, MD, Machine 83

Date Other Than 1st Day

CVP16	CVP1	25c 1st Class	6.00	—
	a.	1st day dated, serial #12501-15500	4.50	—
	b.	1st day dated, serial #00001-12500	4.50	—
	c.	1st day dated, serial over #27500	—	—
CVP17	CVP1	$1 3rd Class	—	—
	a.	1st day dated, serial #24501-27500	—	—
	b.	1st day dated, serial over #27500	—	—
CVP18	CVP2	$1.69 Parcel Post	—	—
	a.	1st day dated, serial #21501-24500	—	—
	b.	1st day dated, serial over #27500	—	—
CVP19	CVP1	$2.40 Priority Mail	—	—
	a.	1st day dated, serial #18501-21500	—	—
	b.	1st day dated, serial over #27500	—	—
	c.	Priority Mail ($2.74), with bar code (CVP2)	100.00	
CVP20	CVP1	$8.75 Express Mail	—	—
	a.	1st day dated, serial #15501-18500	—	—
	b.	1st day dated, serial over #27500	—	—
		Nos. CVP16a-CVP20a (5)	57.50	—
		Nos. CVP6b, CVP16b (2)	9.00	—

1989, Nov.

Washington, DC, Machine 11

CVP21	CVP1	25c 1st Class	*150.00*	
	a.	1st Class, with bar code (CVP2)	—	

Stamps in CVP1 design, probably certified 1st class, with $1.10 denominations exist.

CVP22	CVP1	$1 3rd Class	*500.00*	
CVP23	CVP2	$1.69 Parcel Post	*500.00*	
CVP24	CVP1	$2.40 Priority Mail	*500.00*	
	a.	Priority Mail ($2.74), with bar code (CVP2)	—	
CVP25	CVP1	$8.75 Express Mail	*500.00*	

Washington, DC, Machine 12

CVP26	CVP1	25c 1st Class	*150.00*	

A $1.10 certified 1st Class stamp, dated Nov. 20, exists on cover.

CVP27	CVP1	$1 3rd Class	—	

A $1.40 Third Class stamp of type CVP2, dated Dec. 1 is known on a Dec. 2 cover.

CVP28	CVP2	$1.69 Parcel Post	—	
CVP29	CVP1	$2.40 Priority Mail	—	
	a.	Priority Mail ($2.74), with bar code (CVP2)	—	
CVP30	CVP1	$8.75 Express Mail	—	

An $8.50 Express Mail stamp, dated Dec. 2, exists on cover.

CVP3 — Type I

CVP3 — Type II

1992, Aug. 20 Engr. *Perf. 10 Horiz.*

Coil Stamp

CVP31	CVP3	29c red & blue, type I	.60	.25
	c.	32c, type II ('94)	.90	.40

No. CVP31 was available in all denominations from 1c to $99.99.

The listing is for the first class rate. Other denominations, se-tenant combinations, or "errors" will not be listed.

Type II denomination has large sans-serif numerals preceded by an asterisk measuring 2mm across. No. CVP31 has small numerals with serifs preceded by an asterisk 1½mm across.

CVP4

1994, Feb. 19 Photo. *Perf. 9.9 Vert.*

Coil Stamp

CVP32	CVP4	29c dk red & dk bl	.60	.25

No. CVP32 was available in all denominations from 19c to $99.99.

The listing is for the first class rate at time of issue. Other denominations, se-tenant combinations, or "errors" will not be listed.

1996, Jan. 26 Photo. *Perf. 9.9 Vert.*

CVP33	CVP4	32c brt red & bl	.60	.25

Letters in "USA" on No. CVP33 are thicker than on No. CVP32. Numerous other design differences exist in the moire pattern and in the bunting.

For No. CVP33, the 32c value has been listed because it was the first class rate at time of issue.

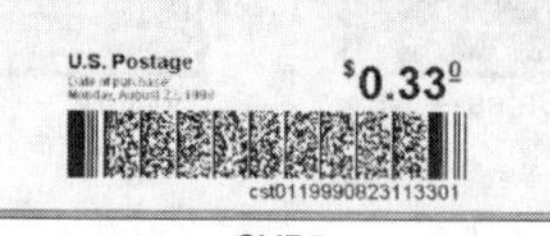

CVP5

Illustration reduced.

1999 Tagged Die Cut
Self-Adhesive

CVP34 CVP5 33c black — —

No. CVP34 was available from 15 NCR Automated Postal Center machines located in central Florida. Machines could produce values as low as 1c as well as values higher than 33c. The backing paper is taller and wider than the stamp.

CVP6

Illustration reduced.

1999 Tagged Die Cut
Self-Adhesive

CVP35 CVP6 33c black & red orange — —
a. With Priority Mail inscription instead of identification number at LL — —

No. CVP35 was available from 18 IBM machines located in central Florida. The backing paper is taller than the stamp. Machines could produce values as low as 1c as well as values higher than 33c.

CARRIERS' STAMPS

OFFICIAL ISSUES

Issued by the US Government to facilitate payment of fees for delivering and collecting letters.

Franklin
OC1

Eagle
OC2

1851 Unwmk. Engr. Imperf.

LO1 OC1 (1c) dull blue, *rose* 5,000. *5,000.*
LO2 OC2 1c blue 25.00 *50.00*

1875

REPRINTS OF 1851 ISSUE
Without Gum

LO3 OC1 (1c) blue, *rose*, imperf. 50.00
LO4 OC1 (1c) blue, perf. 12 *16,000.*
LO5 OC2 1c blue, imperf. 25.00
LO6 OC2 1c blue, perf. 12 160.00

Reprints of the Franklin Carrier are printed in dark blue, instead of the dull blue or deep blue of the originals.

The reprints of the Eagle carrier are on hard white paper, ungummed and sometimes perforated, and also on a coarse wove paper. Originals are on yellowish paper with brown gum.

SEMI-OFFICIAL ISSUES

Issued by officials or employees of the US Government for the purpose of securing or indicating payment of carriers' fees.

BALTIMORE, MD.

C1

1850-55 Typo. Imperf.

1LB1 C1 1c red, *bluish* 180. 160.
1LB2 C1 1c blue, *bluish* 200. 150.
a. Bluish laid paper — —
1LB3 C1 1c blue 160. 100.
a. Laid paper 200. 150.
b. Block of 14 containing three tete-beche gutter pairs (unique) *5,500.*
1LB4 C1 1c green — 850.
1LB5 C1 1c red 2,250. 1,750.

Ten varieties.

C2

C3

1856 Typo.

1LB6 C2 1c blue 130. 90.
1LB7 C2 1c red 130. 90.

Shades exist of Nos. 1LB6-1LB7.

1857

1LB8 C3 1c black 65. 50.
a. "SENT" 100. 75.
b. Short rays 100. 75.
1LB9 C3 1c red 100. 90.
a. "SENT" 140. 110.
b. Short rays 140. 110.
c. As "b," double impression —

Ten varieties of C3.

BOSTON, MASS.

C6

C7

1849-50 Typeset

3LB1 C6 1c blue 375. 180.
a. Wrong ornament at left *400.*
3LB2 C7 1c bl (shades), *slate* 190. 100.

CHARLESTON, S. C.

C8

C10

1849 Typo.

4LB1 C8 2c black, *brn rose* *10,000.*
Cut to shape 4,000. *4,000.*
4LB2 C8 2c black, *yellow*, cut to shape —

No. 4LB1 unused is a unique uncanceled stamp on piece. The used cut-to-shape stamp is also unique. In addition two covers exist bearing No. 4LB1.

No. 4LB2 unused (uncanceled) off cover is unique; four known on cover.

See the Scott U.S. Specialized Catalogue.

1854 Typeset

4LB3 C10 2c black *1,500.*

C11

1849-50 Typeset

4LB5 C11 2c black, *bluish*, pelure 750. 500.
a. "Ceuts" *5,750.*
4LB7 C11 2c black, *yellow* 750. *1,000.*
a. "Ccnts," ms. tied on cover *14,500.*

Several varieties of C11.

C13

C14

C15

1851-58 Typeset

4LB8 C13 2c blk, *bluish* 350. 175.
a. Period after "Paid" 500. 250.
b. "Cens" 700. *900.*
c. "Conours" and "Bents" —
4LB9 C13 2c blk, *bluish*, pelure *850.* *950.*
4LB11 C14 (2c) blk, *bluish* — *375.*
4LB12 C14 (2c) blk, *bluish*, pelure — —
4LB13 C15 (2c) blk, *bluish* ('58) 750. 400.
a. Comma after "PAID" *1,100.*
b. No period after "Post" *1,400.*

Several varieties of C13.

C16

C17

1851-58 Typeset

4LB14 C16 2c black, *bluish* *1,400.* *900.*
4LB15 C17 2c black, *bluish* *800.* *800.*

Several varieties of each.

C18

1858 Typeset

4LB16 C18 2c black, *bluish* *8,000.*

Several varieties.

Same as C19, but Inscribed "Beckmann's City Post"

1860

4LB17 C19 2c black —

One copy exists, on cover.

C19

C20

1859 Typeset

4LB18 C19 2c black, *bluish* *21,000.*
4LB19 C20 2c black, *bluish* *4,500.* —
4LB20 C20 2c black, *pink* 200. —
4LB21 C20 2c black, *yellow* 200.

CINCINNATI, OHIO

C20a

1854 Litho. Wove Paper

9LB1 C20a 2c brown — *3,000.*

CLEVELAND, OHIO

C20b

C20c

1854 Wove Paper Litho.

10LB1 C20b blue *5,000.* *2,000.*

Vertically Laid Paper

10LB2 C20c 2c black, *bluish* *7,000.* *3,750.*

LOUISVILLE, KY.

C21

C22

1857-58 Litho.

5LB1 C21 (2c) bluish green 125.
5LB2 C22 (2c) blue ('58) 250. *750.*
5LB3 C22 (2c) black ('58) *4,500.* *15,000.*

NEW YORK, N.Y.

C23

1842 Engr.

6LB1 C23 3c black, *grayish* *1,750.*

Used copies are Carriers' stamps only when canceled with the regular government cancellation "U.S." in octagonal frame (see illustration), "U.S.CITY DESPATCH POST," or New York circular postmark.

When canceled "FREE" in frame they were used as local stamps. See No. 40L1 in the Scott Specialized Catalogue of United States Stamps.

C24

1842-45 Engr.
Unsurfaced Paper, Colored Through

6LB2 C24 3c blk, *rosy buff* *2,500.*
6LB3 C24 3c blk, *light blue* *550.* 500.
6LB4 C24 3c black, *green* *11,500.*

Some authorities consider No. 6LB2 to be an essay, and No. 6LB4 to be a color changeling.

Glazed Paper, Surface Colored

6LB5 C24 3c blk, *bl grn* (*shades*) 200. 175.
a. Double impression *1,500.*
b. 3c, black, *blue* 650. *250.*
c. As "b," dbl. impression *850.*
d. 3c, black, *green* 1,000. *900.*
e. As "d," dbl. impression —
6LB6 C24 3c blk, *pink*, on cover front *14,500.*

No. 6LB6 is unique.

No. 6LB5 Surcharged in Red — C25

1846

6LB7 C25 2c on 3c, on cover *55,000.*

The City Despatch 2c red is listed in the Scott U.S. Specialized Catalogue as a Local stamp.

C27

1849-50 **Typo.**

6LB9	C27	1c black, *rose*	90.	90.
6LB10	C27	1c black, *yellow*	90.	90.
6LB11	C27	1c black, *buff*	90.	90.
a.		Pair, one stamp sideways	*2,250.*	

PHILADELPHIA, PA.

C28

C29

1849-50 **Typeset**

7LB1	C28	1c blk, *rose* (with letters L.P.)	450.	
7LB2	C28	1c black, *rose* (with letter S)	*3,000.*	
7LB3	C28	1c blk, *rose* (with letter H)	275.	
7LB4	C28	1c blk, *rose* (with letters L.S.)	400.	*500.*
7LB5	C28	1c black, *rose* (with letters J.J.)		*7,500.*
7LB6	C29	1c black, *rose*	300.	250.
7LB7	C29	1c blk, *blue*, glazed	*1,000.*	
7LB8	C29	1c blk, *ver*, glazed	*700.*	
7LB9	C29	1c blk, *yel*, glazed	*2,750.*	*2,250.*

Several varieties of each.

Nos. 7LB1-7LB9 normally received no cancellation.

Two examples reported of No. 7LB5, one uncanceled on a cover front, the other uncanceled on full cover with U.S. 5c (No. 1).

Value here is for stamp on cover front; for full cover see the Scott U.S. Specialized Catalogue.

The 1c black on buff (unglazed), type C29, is believed to be a color changeling.

C30

C31

C32

1850-52 **Litho.**

7LB11	C30	1c gold, *black*, glazed	175.	110.
7LB12	C30	1c blue	400.	275.
7LB13	C30	1c black	*750.*	*550.*

25 varieties of C30.

Handstamped

7LB14	C31	1c blue, *buff*	*3,000.*	
7LB16	C31	1c black		*5,000.*

1856(?)

7LB18	C32	1c black	*1,250.*	*2,000.*

P. O. PAID
1 Cent.

P. O. PAID,
One Cent.

Labels in these designs are not believed to be Carrier stamps.

ST. LOUIS, MO.

C36

C37

Illustrations enlarged to show details of the two types (note upper corners especially).

1849 **White Wove Paper** **Litho.**
Two Types

8LB1	C36	2c black	*7,000.*	—
8LB2	C37	2c black	*5,500.*	—

C38

1857 **Litho.**

8LB3	C38	2c blue		*22,500.*

Carrier stamps Nos. 9LB1, 10LB1-10LB2 are listed following No. 4LB21.

STAMPED ENVELOPES & WRAPPERS

VALUES

Values are for cut squares in a grade of very fine.

Very fine cut squares will have the design well centered within moderately large margins. Precanceled cut squares must include the entire precancellation.

Values for unused entires are for those without printed or manuscript address. Values for letter sheets are for folded entires. Unfolded copies sell for more. A "full corner" includes back and side flaps and commands a premium.

Entire envelopes and wrappers are listed in the Scott U.S. Specialized Catalogue.

Wrappers are listed with envelopes of corresponding designs, and indicated by prefix letter "W" instead of "U."

Envelopes with the stamp printed by error in colorless embossing from an uninked die, are "albinos." They are worth more than normal, inked impressions. Albinos of earlier issues, canceled while current, are scarce.

The papers of these issues vary greatly in texture, and in color from yellowish to bluish white and from amber to dark buff.

"+" Some authorities claim that Nos. U37, U48, U49, U110, U124, U125, U130, U133A, U137A, U137B, U137C, W138, U145, U162, U178A, U185, U220, U285, U286, U298, U299, UO3, UO32, UO38, UO45 and UO45A (each with "+" before number) were not regularly issued and are not known to have been used.

Washington
U1 U2

U1 — "THREE" in short label with curved ends; 13mm wide at top.

U2 — "THREE" in short label with straight ends; 15½mm wide at top.

U3

U4

U3 — "THREE" in short label with octagon ends.

U4 — "THREE" in wide label with straight ends; 20mm wide at top.

U5

U6

U5 — "THREE" in medium wide label with curved ends; 14½mm wide at top.

U7 U8

U7 — "TEN" in short label; 15⅓mm wide at top.

U8 — "TEN" in wide label 20mm wide at top.

On Diagonally Laid Paper

1853-55

U1	U1	3c red	325.00	30.00
U2	U1	3c red, *buff*	95.00	15.00
U3	U2	3c red	1,200.	40.00
U4	U2	3c red, *buff*	310.00	25.00
U5	U3	3c red ('54)	6,250.	500.00
U6	U3	3c red, *buff* ('54)	525.00	50.00
U7	U4	3c red	1,500.	90.00
U8	U4	3c red, *buff*	*8,000.*	125.00
U9	U5	3c red ('54)	37.50	3.50
U10	U5	3c red, *buff* ('54)	22.50	3.50
U11	U6	6c red	275.00	75.00
U12	U6	6c red, *buff*	160.00	65.00
U13	U6	6c green	325.00	120.00
U14	U6	6c green, *buff*	210.00	85.00
U15	U7	10c green ('55)	500.00	90.00
U16	U7	10c green, *buff* ('55)	125.00	55.00
a.		10c pale green, *buff*	110.00	50.00
U17	U8	10c green ('55)	350.00	125.00
a.		10c pale green	350.00	100.00
U18	U8	10c green, *buff* ('55)	400.00	75.00
a.		10c pale green, *buff*	375.00	75.00

Nos. U9, U10, U11, U12, U13, U14, U17 and U18 have been reprinted on white and buff papers, wove or vertically laid, and are not known entire. The originals are on diagonally laid paper. Value of 8 reprints on laid, $225. Reprints on wove sell for more.

Franklin, Period after "POSTAGE."
U9 U10

U10 — Bust touches inner frame-line at front and back.

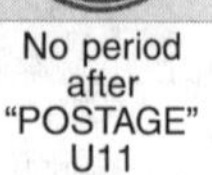

No period after "POSTAGE"
U11

Washington
U12

Envelopes are on diagonally laid paper. Wrappers on vert. or horiz. laid paper.

1860-61

W18B	U9	1c blue	*4,500.*	
U19	U9	1c blue, *buff*	40.00	15.00
W20	U9	1c blue, *buff* ('61)	70.00	50.00
W21	U9	1c bl, *man* ('61)	50.00	45.00
U21A	U9	1c blue, *org*, entire	*2,250.*	
W22	U9	1c blue, *org* ('61)	*3,750.*	
U23	U10	1c blue, *org*	750.00	350.00
U24	U11	1c blue, *amber*	375.00	125.00
W25	U11	1c bl, *man* ('61)	*7,500.*	*2,000.*
U26	U12	3c red	35.00	20.00
U27	U12	3c red, *buff*	26.00	13.00
U28	U12+9	3c + 1c red & blue	375.00	240.00
U29	U12+9	3c + 1c red & blue, *buff*	375.00	240.00
U30	U12	6c red	3,000.	1,250.
U31	U12	6c red, *buff*	3,750.	1,500.
U32	U12	10c green	1,600.	450.00
U33	U12	10c grn, *buff*	1,600.	275.00

Nos. U26, U27, U30 to U33 have been reprinted on the same vertically laid paper as the reprints of the 1853-55 issue, and are not known entire. Value, Nos. U26-U27, $160; Nos. U30-U33, $100.

U13

U14

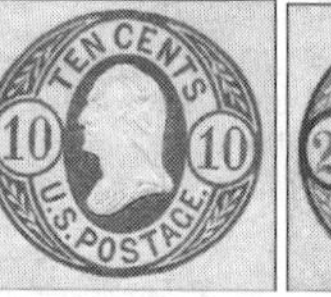

Washington
U15 U16

Envelopes are on diagonally laid paper. Nos. U36 and U45 come on vertically or horizontally laid paper.

1861

U34	U13	3c pink	27.00	5.75
U35	U13	3c pink, *buff*	25.00	5.25
U36	U13	3c pink, *bl* (letter sheet)	80.00	50.00
+U37	U13	3c pink, *org*	*5,000.*	
U38	U14	6c pink	120.00	80.00
U39	U14	6c pink, *buff*	70.00	62.50
U40	U15	10c yellow green	37.50	30.00
a.		10c blue green	37.50	27.50
U41	U15	10c yel green, *buff*	40.00	27.50
a.		10c blue green, *buff*	40.00	30.00
U42	U16	12c red & brown, *buff*	210.00	160.00
a.		12c lake & brown, *buff*	*1,400.*	
U43	U16	20c red & bl, *buff*	300.00	200.00
U44	U16	24c red & green, *buff*	240.00	200.00
a.		24c lake & green, *sal*	325.00	225.00
U45	U16	40c black & red, *buff*	375.00	350.00

Nos. U38 and U39 have been reprinted on the same papers as the reprints of the 1853-55 issue and are not known entire. Value of two reprints, $60.

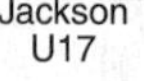

Jackson
U17

Jackson
U18

"U.S. POSTAGE" above

U17 — The downstroke and tail of the "2" unite near the point.

U18 — The downstroke and tail of the "2" touch but do not merge.

Jackson — U19

Jackson — U20

"U.S. POST" above

U19 — Stamp measures 24-25mm in width.

U20 — Stamp measures 25½-26¼mm in width.

Envelopes are on diagonally laid paper. Wrappers on vert. or horiz. laid paper.

1863-64

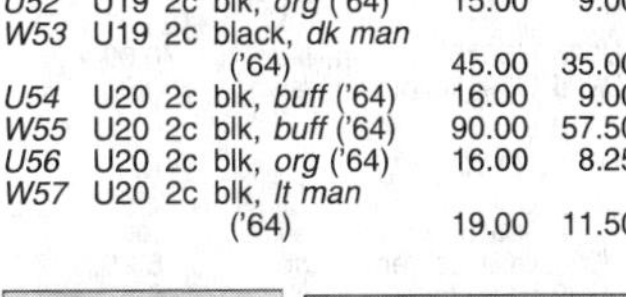

U46	U17	2c black, *buff*	45.00	20.00
W47	U17	2c black, *dk man*	65.00	45.00
+U48	U18	2c black, *buff*	3,250.	
+U49	U18	2c black, *orange*	1,500.	
U50	U19	2c blk, *buff* ('64)	17.00	9.00
W51	U19	2c blk, *buff* ('64)	350.00	160.00
U52	U19	2c blk, *org* ('64)	15.00	9.00
W53	U19	2c black, *dk man* ('64)	45.00	35.00
U54	U20	2c blk, *buff* ('64)	16.00	9.00
W55	U20	2c blk, *buff* ('64)	90.00	57.50
U56	U20	2c blk, *org* ('64)	16.00	8.25
W57	U20	2c blk, *lt man* ('64)	19.00	11.50

Washington U21

Washington U22

1864-65

U58	U21	3c pink	8.50	1.60
U59	U21	3c pink, *buff*	7.50	1.25
U60	U21	3c brown ('65)	60.00	30.00
U61	U21	3c brn, *buff* ('65)	47.50	26.00
U62	U21	6c pink	85.00	29.00
U63	U21	6c pink, *buff*	40.00	27.50
U64	U21	6c purple ('65)	55.00	26.00
U65	U21	6c pur, *buff* ('65)	50.00	20.00
U66	U22	9c lem, *buff* ('65)	450.00	250.00
U67	U22	9c org, *buff* ('65)	150.00	90.00
a.		9c orange yellow, *buff*	150.00	90.00
U68	U22	12c brn, *buff* ('65)	325.00	250.00
U69	U22	12c red brn, *buff* ('65)	125.00	55.00
U70	U22	18c red, *buff* ('65)	95.00	95.00
U71	U22	24c bl, *buff* ('65)	100.00	95.00
U72	U22	30c grn, *buff* ('65)	125.00	75.00
a.		30c yellow green, *buff*	125.00	*80.00*
U73	U22	40c rose, *buff* ('65)	125.00	*250.00*

Reay Issue

The engravings in this issue are finely executed.

Franklin — U23

Jackson — U24

U23 — Bust points to the end of the "N" of "ONE."

U24 — Bust narrow at back. Small, thick figures of value.

Washington U25

Lincoln U26

U25 — Queue projects below bust.

U26 — Neck very long at the back.

Stanton — U27

Jefferson — U28

U27 — Bust pointed at the back, figures "7" are normal.

U28 — Queue forms straight line with the bust.

Clay — U29

Webster — U30

U29 — Ear partly concealed by hair, mouth large, chin prominent.

U30 — Has side whiskers.

Scott — U31

Hamilton — U32

U31 — Straggling locks of hair at top of head; ornaments around the inner oval end in squares.

U32 — Back of bust very narrow, chin almost straight; labels containing figures of value are exactly parallel.

Perry — U33

U33 — Front of bust very narrow and pointed; inner lines of shields project very slightly beyond the oval.

1870-71

U74	U23	1c blue	45.00	30.00
a.		1c ultramarine	70.00	35.00
U75	U23	1c blue, *amber*	32.50	27.50
a.		1c ultramarine, *amb*	60.00	30.00
U76	U23	1c blue, *org*	20.00	15.00
W77	U23	1c blue, *man*	42.50	35.00
U78	U24	2c brown	40.00	16.00
U79	U24	2c brown, *amb*	20.00	9.00
U80	U24	2c brown, *org*	12.00	6.50
W81	U24	2c brown, *man*	27.50	21.00
U82	U25	3c green	8.00	1.00
a.		3c brown (error), entire	*13,000.*	
U83	U25	3c green, *amb*	6.75	2.00
U84	U25	3c green, *cream*	10.00	4.25
U85	U26	6c dark red	25.00	16.00
a.		6c vermilion	25.00	16.00
U86	U26	6c dk red, *amb*	25.00	15.00
a.		6c vermilion, *amber*	25.00	15.00
U87	U26	6c dk red, *cr*	32.50	16.00
a.		6c vermilion, *cream*	32.50	16.00
U88	U27	7c ver, *amb* ('71)	50.00	*190.00*
U89	U28	10c olive black	900.00	750.00
U90	U28	10c ol blk, *amb*	900.00	900.00
U91	U28	10c brown	77.50	70.00
U92	U28	10c brn, *amb*	87.50	50.00
a.		10c dark brown, *amb*	87.50	50.00
U93	U29	12c plum	100.00	82.50
U94	U29	12c plum, *amb*	125.00	110.00
U95	U29	12c plum, *cr*	275.00	250.00
U96	U30	15c red orange	75.00	
a.		15c orange	75.00	
U97	U30	15c red org, *amb*	210.00	*300.00*
a.		15c orange, *amber*	210.00	
U98	U30	15c red org, *cr*	325.00	350.00
a.		15c orange, *cream*	325.00	
U99	U31	24c purple	140.00	140.00
U100	U31	24c pur, *amb*	200.00	*325.00*
U101	U31	24c pur, *cream*	260.00	*500.00*
U102	U32	30c black	80.00	*110.00*
U103	U32	30c blk, *amb*	250.00	*500.00*
U104	U32	30c blk, *cream*	225.00	*500.00*
U105	U33	90c carmine	150.00	*350.00*
U106	U33	90c car, *amb*	300.00	*450.00*
U107	U33	90c car, *cream*	250.00	*2,500.*

Plimpton Issue

The profiles in this issue are inferior to the fine engraving of the Reay issue.

U34

U35

U34 — Bust forms an angle at the back near the frame. Lettering poorly executed. Distinct circle in "O" of "POSTAGE."

U35 — Lower part of bust points to the end of the "E" in "ONE." Head inclined downward.

U36

U37

U36 — Bust narrow at back. Thin figures of value. The head of the "P" in "POSTAGE" is very narrow. The bust at front is broad and ends in sharp corners.

U37 — Bust broad. Figures of value in long ovals.

U38

U39

U38 — Similar to U37 but the figure "2" at the left touches the oval.

U39 — Similar to U37 but the "O" of "TWO" has the center netted instead of plain. The "G" of "POSTAGE" and the "C" of "CENTS" have diagonal crossline.

U40

U41

U40 — Bust broad; numerals in ovals short and thick.

U41 — Similar to U40 but the ovals containing the numerals are much heavier. A diagonal line runs from the upper part of the "U" to the white frame-line.

U42

U43

U42 — Similar to U40 but the middle stroke of "N" in "CENTS" is as thin as the vertical strokes.

U43 — Bottom of bust cut almost semi-circularly.

U44

U45

U44 — Thin lettering, long thin figures of value.

U45 — Thick lettering, well-formed figures of value, queue does not project below bust.

U46

U46 — Top of head egg-shaped; knot of queue well marked and projects triangularly.

Taylor — U47

Die 1

Die 2

Die 1: Figures of value with thick curved tops.

Die 2: Figures of value with long, thin tops.

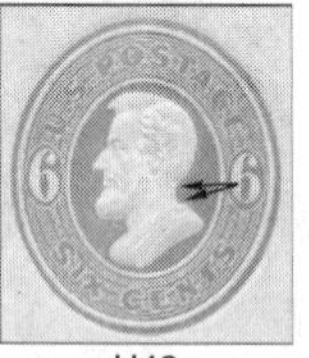

U48

U49

U48 — Neck very short at the back.

U49 — Figures of value turned up at the ends.

U50

U51

U50 — Very large head.

U51 — Knot of queue stands out prominently.

U52

U53

U52 — Ear prominent, chin receding.

U53 — No side whiskers, forelock projects above head.

U54

U55

U54 — Hair does not project; ornaments around the inner oval end in points.

U55 — Back of bust rather broad, chin slopes considerably; labels containing figures of value are not exactly parallel.

U56

U56 — Front of bust sloping; inner lines of shields project considerably into the inner oval.

1874-86

No.	Type	Description	Unused	Used
U108	U34	1c dk blue	200.00	70.00
a.		1c light blue	200.00	70.00
U109	U34	1c dk blue, *amb*	180.00	75.00
+U110	U34	1c dk blue, *cr*	1,600.	
U111	U34	1c dk blue, *org*	25.00	17.50
a.		1c light blue, *org*	25.00	17.50
W112	U34	1c dk blue, *man*	60.00	40.00
U113	U35	1c light blue	1.75	1.00
a.		1c dark blue	8.50	7.50
U114	U35	1c lt bl, *amb*	4.25	4.00
a.		1c dark blue, *amb*	19.00	10.00
U115	U35	1c blue, *cr*	5.00	4.50
a.		1c dark blue, *cr*	19.00	8.50
U116	U35	1c lt bl, *org*	.80	.40
a.		1c dark blue, *org*	4.00	2.50
U117	U35	1c lt bl, *bl* ('80)	8.00	5.25
U118	U35	1c lt bl, *fawn* ('79)	8.00	5.25
U119	U35	1c lt bl, *man* ('86)	8.50	3.25
W120	U35	1c lt bl, *man*	1.60	1.10
a.		1c dark blue, *man*	8.50	8.00
U121	U35	1c lt blue, *amb man* ('86)	14.50	10.00
U122	U36	2c brown	110.00	40.00
U123	U36	2c brn, *amb*	62.50	40.00
+U124	U36	2c brn, *cr*	1,250.	
+U125	U36	2c brn, *org*	25,000.	
W126	U36	2c brn, *man*	140.00	80.00
W127	U36	2c ver, *man*	1,900.	250.00
U128	U37	2c brown	47.50	32.50
U129	U37	2c brn, *amb*	72.50	37.50
+U130	U37	2c brn, *cr*	50,000.	
W131	U37	2c brn, *man*	18.00	16.00
U132	U38	2c brown	72.50	27.50
U133	U38	2c brn, *amb*	350.00	65.00
+U133A	U38	2c brn, *cr*	75,000.	
U134	U39	2c brown	1,400.	150.00
U135	U39	2c brn, *amb*	525.00	125.00
U136	U39	2c brn, *org*	50.00	29.00
W137	U39	2c brn, *man*	67.50	35.00
+U137A	U39	2c vermilion	35,000.	
+U137B	U39	2c ver, *amb*	35,000.	
+U137C	U39	2c ver, *org*	35,000.	
+W138	U39	2c ver, *man*	32,500.	
U139	U40	2c brown ('75)	52.50	35.00
U140	U40	2c brn, *amb* ('75)	87.50	60.00
+U140A	U40	2c reddish brown, *org* ('75)	25,000.	
W141	U40	2c brn, *man* ('75)	35.00	26.00
U142	U40	2c ver ('75)	7.00	3.00
a.		2c pink	7.50	5.00
U143	U40	2c ver, *amb* ('75)	7.00	3.00
U144	U40	2c ver, *cr* ('75)	14.50	6.25
+U145	U40	2c ver, *org* ('75)	40,000.	
U146	U40	2c ver, *bl* ('80)	140.00	40.00
U147	U40	2c ver, *fawn* ('75)	7.00	4.50
W148	U40	2c ver, *man* ('75)	3.75	3.75
U149	U41	2c ver ('78)	55.00	30.00
a.		2c pink	55.00	30.00
U150	U41	2c ver, *amb* ('78)	32.50	17.50
U151	U41	2c ver, *bl* ('80)	13.00	9.25
a.		2c pink, *blue*	10.00	9.00
U152	U41	2c ver, *fawn* ('78)	11.00	4.75
U153	U42	2c ver ('76)	70.00	26.00
U154	U42	2c ver, *amb* ('76)	400.00	90.00
W155	U42	2c ver, *man* ('76)	22.50	9.50
U156	U43	2c ver ('81)	1,400.	150.00
U157	U43	2c ver, *amb* ('81)	57,500.	35,000.
W158	U43	2c ver, *man* ('81)	100.00	60.00
U159	U44	3c green	27.50	6.75
U160	U44	3c grn, *amb*	30.00	10.50
U161	U44	3c green, *cr*	37.50	15.00
+U162	U44	3c grn, *blue*	—	
U163	U45	3c green	1.40	.30
U164	U45	3c grn, *amb*	1.50	.70
U165	U45	3c green, *cr*	9.00	6.50
U166	U45	3c grn, *blue*	8.25	6.25
U167	U45	3c grn, *fawn* ('75)	5.00	3.50
U168	U46	3c grn ('81)	1,500.	75.00
U169	U46	3c grn, *amb* ('81)	275.00	110.00
U170	U46	3c grn, *bl* ('81)	12,500.	3,750.
U171	U46	3c grn, *fawn* ('81)	45,000.	3,250.
U172	U47	5c bl, die 1 ('75)	12.00	8.00
U173	U47	5c bl, die 1, *amb* ('75)	12.00	9.00
U174	U47	5c bl, die 1, *cr* ('75)	110.00	40.00
U175	U47	5c bl, die 1, *bl* ('75)	32.50	15.00
U176	U47	5c bl, die 1, *fawn* ('75)	140.00	57.50
U177	U47	5c bl, die 2 ('75)	10.00	6.75
U178	U47	5c bl, die 2, *amb* ('75)	10.00	7.50
+U178A	U47	5c bl, die 2, *cr* ('76)	14,000.	
U179	U47	5c bl, die 2, *blue* ('75)	24.00	9.00
U180	U47	5c bl, die 2, *fawn* ('75)	120.00	45.00
U181	U48	6c red	7.00	6.25
a.		6c vermilion	7.00	6.25
U182	U48	6c red, *amb*	11.50	6.25
a.		6c vermilion, *amber*	11.00	6.25
U183	U48	6c red, *cr*	42.50	13.00
a.		6c vermilion, *cream*	42.50	13.00
U184	U48	6c red, *fawn* ('75)	20.00	13.00
+U185	U49	7c vermilion	1,800.	
U186	U49	7c ver, *amb*	125.00	62.50
U187	U50	10c brown	37.50	20.00
U188	U50	10c brn, *amb*	70.00	32.50
U189	U51	10c choc ('75)	7.50	4.00
a.		10c bister brown	8.50	5.00
b.		10c yellow ocher	4,500.	
U190	U51	10c choc, *amb* ('75)	8.00	7.00
a.		10c bister brn, *amb*	8.50	7.50
b.		10c yel ocher, *amb*	3,000.	
U191	U51	10c brn, *oriental buff* ('86)	12.00	8.25
U192	U51	10c brn, *bl* ('86)	15.00	8.25
a.		10c gray black, *blue*	15.00	8.25
b.		10c red brown, *blue*	15.00	8.25
U193	U51	10c brn, *man* ('86)	16.00	10.00
a.		10c red brown, *man*	16.00	10.00
U194	U51	10c brn, *amb man* ('86)	19.00	8.50
a.		10c red brown, *amber manila*	21.00	9.00
U195	U52	12c plum	450.00	100.00
U196	U52	12c plum, *amb*	275.00	175.00
U197	U52	12c plum, *cr*	225.00	150.00
U198	U53	15c orange	47.50	37.50
U199	U53	15c org, *amb*	160.00	100.00
U200	U53	15c org, *cr*	600.00	350.00
U201	U54	24c purple	175.00	150.00
U202	U54	24c pur, *amb*	190.00	125.00
U203	U54	24c pur, *cr*	175.00	125.00
U204	U55	30c black	62.50	27.50
U205	U55	30c blk, *amb*	72.50	60.00
U206	U55	30c blk, *cr*	375.00	375.00
U207	U55	30c blk, *oriental buff* ('86)	100.00	82.50
U208	U55	30c blk, *bl* ('86)	110.00	82.50
U209	U55	30c blk, *man* ('86)	95.00	80.00
U210	U55	30c blk, *amb man* ('86)	175.00	85.00
U211	U56	90c car ('75)	110.00	85.00
U212	U56	90c car, *amb* ('75)	225.00	300.00
U213	U56	90c car, *cr* ('75)	1,250.	
U214	U56	90c car, *oriental buff* ('86)	200.00	275.00
U215	U56	90c car, *bl* ('86)	190.00	250.00
U216	U56	90c car, *man* ('86)	175.00	250.00
U217	U56	90c car, *amb man* ('86)	125.00	200.00

See Nos. U336-U347.

United States Centennial Issue

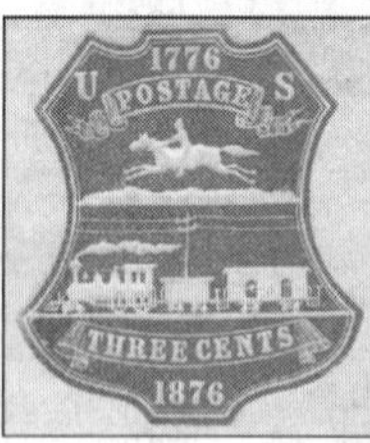

Single line under "POSTAGE" U57

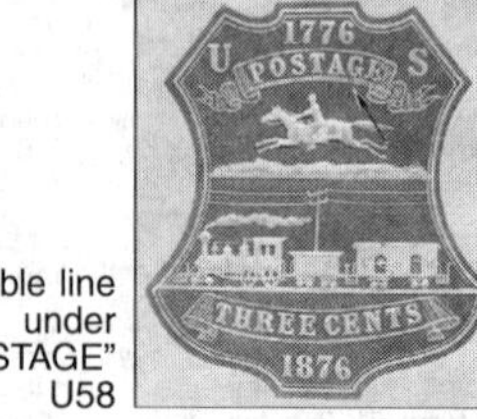

Double line under "POSTAGE" U58

1876

No.	Type	Description	Unused	Used
U218	U57	3c red	50.00	25.00
U219	U57	3c green	45.00	17.50
+U220	U58	3c red	42,500.	
U221	U58	3c green	52.50	21.00

Cent. of the US, and the World's Fair at Philadelphia.

See No. U582.

Garfield U59

Washington U60

1882-86

No.	Type	Description	Unused	Used
U222	U59	5c brown	4.75	2.75
U223	U59	5c brown, *amb*	5.00	3.25
U224	U59	5c brn, *oriental buff* ('86)	125.00	72.50
U225	U59	5c brown, *blue*	70.00	35.00
U226	U59	5c brown, *fawn*	350.00	

1883, Oct.

No.	Type	Description	Unused	Used
U227	U60	2c red	4.25	2.25
a.		2c brown (error), entire	10,000.	
U228	U60	2c red, *amber*	5.25	2.75
U229	U60	2c red, *blue*	8.00	5.00
U230	U60	2c red, *fawn*	9.00	5.25

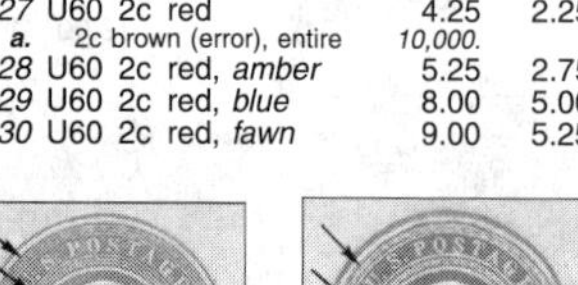

Wavy lines fine and clear — U61

Wavy lines thick and blurred — U62

Four Wavy Lines in Oval

1883, Nov.

No.	Type	Description	Unused	Used
U231	U61	2c red	4.25	2.25
U232	U61	2c red, *amber*	5.25	3.75
U233	U61	2c red, *blue*	9.00	7.25
U234	U61	2c red, *fawn*	6.50	4.75
W235	U61	2c red, *manila*	19.00	6.25

1884, June

No.	Type	Description	Unused	Used
U236	U62	2c red	10.50	4.00
U237	U62	2c red, *amber*	13.00	10.00
U238	U62	2c red, *blue*	22.50	10.00
U239	U62	2c red, *fawn*	16.00	10.00

See Nos. U260-W269.

3½ links over left "2" — U63

2 links below right "2" — U64

Round "O" in "TWO" — U65

No.	Type	Description	Unused	Used
U240	U63	2c red	95.00	42.50
U241	U63	2c red, *amber*	950.00	325.00
U242	U63	2c red, *fawn*		35,000.
U243	U64	2c red	100.00	57.50
U244	U64	2c red, *amber*	300.00	75.00
U245	U64	2c red, *blue*	450.00	200.00
U246	U64	2c red, *fawn*	400.00	140.00
U247	U65	2c red	2,750.	450.00
U248	U65	2c red, *amber*	4,250.	1,000.
U249	U65	2c red, *fawn*	1,100.	400.00

See Nos. U270-U276.

Jackson — U66

Die 1

Die 2

Die 1: Numeral at left is 2¾mm wide. Die 2: Numeral at left is 3¼mm wide.

1883-86

U250	U66	4c grn, die 1	3.75	3.50
U251	U66	4c grn, die 1, *amb*	4.75	3.50
U252	U66	4c grn, die 1, *oriental buff* ('86)	10.00	9.00
U253	U66	4c grn, die 1, *bl* ('86)	10.00	6.50
U254	U66	4c grn, die 1, *man* ('86)	12.50	7.50
U255	U66	4c grn, die 1, *amb man* ('86)	21.00	10.00
U256	U66	4c grn, die 2	8.50	5.00
U257	U66	4c grn, die 2, *amb*	14.50	7.00
U258	U66	4c grn, die 2, *man* ('86)	14.50	7.50
U259	U66	4c grn, die 2, *amb man* ('86)	14.50	7.50

1884, May

U260	U61	2c brown	14.50	5.75
U261	U61	2c brn, *amber*	14.50	6.50
U262	U61	2c brn, *blue*	17.00	10.00
U263	U61	2c brn, *fawn*	14.50	9.25
W264	U61	2c brn, *manila*	16.00	10.50

1884, June **Retouched Die**

U265	U62	2c brown	16.00	6.25
U266	U62	2c brn, *amber*	67.50	40.00
U267	U62	2c brn, *blue*	19.00	6.25
U268	U62	2c brn, *fawn*	16.00	11.00
W269	U62	2c brn, *manila*	24.00	15.00

2 Links Below Right "2"

U270	U64	2c brown	110.00	40.00
U271	U64	2c brn, *amber*	450.00	95.00
U272	U64	2c brn, *fawn*	*9,000.*	*2,500.*

Round "O" in "Two"

U273	U65	2c brown	275.00	100.00
U274	U65	2c brn, *amber*	275.00	85.00
U275	U65	2c brn, *blue*		*20,000.*
U276	U65	2c brn, *fawn*	1,000.	700.00

Washington
U67 U68

U67 — Extremity of bust below the queue forms a point.

U68 — Extremity of bust is rounded.

Similar to U61
Two wavy lines in oval

1884-86

U277	U67	2c brown	.50	.20
a.		2c brown lake	22.50	21.00
U278	U67	2c brn, *amber*	.65	.50
a.		2c brown lake, *amber*	35.00	25.00
U279	U67	2c brn, *oriental buff* ('86)	4.25	2.10
U280	U67	2c brn, *blue*	2.50	2.10
U281	U67	2c brn, *fawn*	3.00	2.40
U282	U67	2c brn, *man* ('86)	11.50	4.00
W283	U67	2c brn, *man*	7.25	5.00
U284	U67	2c brn, *amb man* ('86)	7.25	5.75
+U285	U67	2c red	750.00	
+U286	U67	2c red, *blue*	325.00	
W287	U67	2c red, *man*	125.00	
U288	U68	2c brown	350.00	42.50
U289	U68	2c brn, *amb*	16.00	12.50

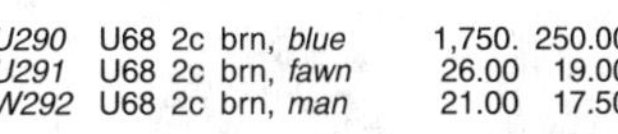

U290	U68	2c brn, *blue*	1,750.	250.00
U291	U68	2c brn, *fawn*	26.00	19.00
W292	U68	2c brn, *man*	21.00	17.50

Grant — US1

1886 **Letter Sheet**

U293	US1	2c green, entire	27.50	17.00

See the Scott U.S. Specialized Catalogue for perforation and inscription varieties..

Franklin
U69

Washington
U70

U70 — Bust points between 3rd and 4th notches of inner oval; "G" of "POSTAGE" has no bar.

U71

U72

U71 — Bust points between second and third notches of inner oval; "G" of "POSTAGE" has a bar; ear is indicated by one heavy line; one vertical line at corner of mouth.

U72 — Frame same as U71; upper part of head more rounded; ear indicated by two curved lines with two locks of hair in front; two vertical lines at corner of mouth.

Jackson — U73

Grant — U74

U75

U74 — There is a space between the beard and the collar of the coat. A button is on the collar.

U75 — The collar touches the beard and there is no button.

1887-94

U294	U69	1c blue	.55	.20
U295	U69	1c dk bl ('94)	7.50	2.50
U296	U69	1c bl, *amb* ('94)	3.50	1.25
U297	U69	1c dk blue, *amb* ('94)	47.50	22.50
+U298	U69	1c bl, *oriental buff* ('94)	*14,000.*	
+U299	U69	1c bl, *bl* ('94)	*20,000.*	
U300	U69	1c bl, *man* ('94)	.65	.35
W301	U69	1c bl, *man* ('94)	.45	.30
U302	U69	1c dk blue, *man* ('94)	27.50	11.00
W303	U69	1c dk blue, *man* ('94)	15.00	9.50
U304	U69	1c bl, *amb man*	7.50	4.25
U305	U70	2c green	16.00	9.00
U306	U70	2c grn, *amb*	32.50	14.00
U307	U70	2c grn, *oriental buff*	80.00	30.00
U308	U70	2c grn, *blue*	*9,000.*	1,250.
U309	U70	2c grn, *man*	*17,500.*	750.00
U310	U70	2c grn, *amb man*	2,500.	1,250.
U311	U71	2c green	.35	.20
a.		2c dark green ('94)	.50	.30
U312	U71	2c grn, *amb*	.45	.20
a.		Double impression	—	
b.		2c dk grn, *amber* ('94)	.60	.35
U313	U71	2c grn, *oriental buff*	.60	.25
a.		2c dk grn, *oriental buff* ('94)	2.00	1.00
U314	U71	2c grn, *blue*	.65	.30
a.		2c dk grn, *blue* ('94)	.85	.40
U315	U71	2c grn, *man*	1.75	.50
a.		2c dk grn, *man* ('94)	2.75	.75
W316	U71	2c grn, *man*	4.00	2.50
U317	U71	2c grn, *amb man*	2.75	1.90
a.		2c dk grn, *amb man* ('94)	4.00	3.00
U318	U72	2c green	150.00	12.50
U319	U72	2c grn, *amb*	190.00	25.00
U320	U72	2c grn, *oriental buff*	175.00	40.00
U321	U72	2c grn, *blue*	190.00	65.00
U322	U72	2c grn, *man*	275.00	65.00
U323	U72	2c grn, *amb man*	575.00	80.00
U324	U73	4c carmine	2.75	1.75
a.		4c lake	3.00	2.00
b.		4c scarlet ('94)	3.00	2.00
U325	U73	4c car, *amb*	3.25	2.25
a.		4c lake, *amber*	3.50	2.50
b.		4c scarlet, *amber* ('94)	3.50	3.25
U326	U73	4c car, *oriental buff*	6.50	3.00
a.		4c lake, *oriental buff*	7.50	3.50
U327	U73	4c car, *blue*	6.00	4.00
a.		4c lake, *blue*	6.00	4.00
U328	U73	4c car, *man*	7.50	5.50
a.		4c lake, *manila*	8.50	6.00
b.		4c pink, *manila*	14.00	4.50
U329	U73	4c car, *amb man*	6.00	2.75
a.		4c lake, *amb manila*	7.00	3.25
b.		4c pink, *amb manila*	15.00	3.75
U330	U74	5c blue	3.75	4.00
U331	U74	5c bl, *amber*	5.25	2.25
U332	U74	5c bl, *oriental buff*	5.75	3.75
U333	U74	5c bl, *blue*	10.00	5.50
U334	U75	5c blue ('94)	25.00	7.50
U335	U75	5c bl, *amb* ('94)	14.00	7.50
U336	U55	30c red brown	55.00	40.00
a.		30c yellow brown	60.00	45.00
b.		30c chocolate	67.50	47.50
U337	U55	30c red brn, *amb*	57.50	55.00
a.		30c yel brown, *amber*	55.00	55.00
b.		30c choc, *amber*	67.50	55.00
U338	U55	30c red brn, *oriental buff*	52.50	47.50
a.		30c yel brn, *oriental buff*	52.50	47.50
U339	U55	30c red brn, *bl*	52.50	47.50
a.		30c yellow brown, *blue*	52.50	47.50
U340	U55	30c red brn, *manila*	55.00	45.00
a.		30c brown, *manila*	52.50	40.00
U341	U55	30c red brown, *amb man*	60.00	30.00
a.		30c yel brn, *amb man*	60.00	30.00
U342	U56	90c purple	77.50	75.00
U343	U56	90c pur, *amb*	92.50	80.00
U344	U56	90c pur, *oriental buff*	92.50	85.00
U345	U56	90c pur, *blue*	92.50	90.00
U346	U56	90c pur, *man*	100.00	92.50
U347	U56	90c pur, *amb manila*	100.00	92.50

Columbian Exposition Issue

Columbus and Liberty — U76

1893

U348	U76	1c deep blue	2.25	1.25
U349	U76	2c violet	1.75	.50
a.		2c dark slate (error)	*2,500.*	
U350	U76	5c chocolate	8.50	7.50
a.		5c slate brown (error)	800.00	950.00
U351	U76	10c slate brown	35.00	30.00
		Nos. U348-U351 (4)	47.50	39.25

Franklin
U77

Washington
U78

U78 — Bust points to first notch of inner oval and is only slightly concave below.

U79

U80

U79 — Bust points to middle of second notch of inner oval and is quite hollow below. Queue has ribbon around it.

U80 — Same as U79 but hair flowing and no ribbon around queue.

Lincoln — U81

Pointed but not draped.

U82

U83

U82 — Bust broad and draped.

U83 — Head larger, inner oval has no notches.

Grant — U84

Similar to designs of 1887-95 but smaller

1899

U352	U77	1c green	.85	.20
U353	U77	1c grn, *amb*	5.50	1.50
U354	U77	1c grn, *oriental buff*	14.00	2.75
U355	U77	1c grn, *bl*	14.00	7.50
U356	U77	1c grn, *man*	2.25	.95
W357	U77	1c grn, *man*	2.50	1.10
U358	U78	2c carmine	3.00	1.75
U359	U78	2c car, *amb*	22.50	14.00
U360	U78	2c car, *oriental buff*	22.50	8.00
U361	U78	2c car, *blue*	62.50	27.50
U362	U79	2c carmine	.35	.20
a.		2c dark lake	30.00	30.00
U363	U79	2c car, *amb*	1.40	.20
U364	U79	2c car, *oriental buff*	1.20	.20
U365	U79	2c car, *blue*	1.50	.55
W366	U79	2c car, *man*	8.00	3.25
U367	U80	2c carmine	6.00	2.75
U368	U80	2c car, *amber*	9.00	6.75
U369	U80	2c car, *oriental buff*	25.00	12.50
U370	U80	2c car, *blue*	12.50	10.00
U371	U81	4c brown	19.00	11.00
U372	U81	4c brn, *amb*	19.00	12.50
U373	U82	4c brown	*12,500.*	1,100.
U374	U83	4c brown	14.00	8.00
U375	U83	4c brn, *amb*	52.50	17.50
W376	U83	4c brn, *man*	17.50	8.25
U377	U84	5c blue	12.50	9.50
U378	U84	5c blue, *amb*	16.00	10.00

Franklin U85 — Washington U86

U86 — "D" of "UNITED" contains vertical line at right that parallels the left vertical line. One short and two long vertical lines at right of "CENTS."

Grant — U87

Lincoln — U88

1903

U379	U85 1c green	.70	.20
U380	U85 1c green, *amb*	13.50	2.00
U381	U85 1c grn, *oriental buff*	16.00	2.50
U382	U85 1c green, *blue*	21.00	2.50
U383	U85 1c grn, *manila*	4.00	.90
W384	U85 1c grn, *manila*	2.50	.40
U385	U86 2c carmine	.40	.20
U386	U86 2c carmine, *amb*	1.90	.20
U387	U86 2c car, *oriental buff*	1.75	.30
U388	U86 2c carmine, *blue*	1.30	.50
W389	U86 2c car, *manila*	17.50	9.50
U390	U87 4c chocolate	22.50	11.00
U391	U87 4c choc, *amber*	20.00	12.50
W392	U87 4c choc, *manila*	20.00	12.50
U393	U88 5c blue	20.00	12.50
U394	U88 5c blue, *amber*	20.00	12.50

U89

"D" of "UNITED" is well rounded at right. The three lines at the right of "CENTS" and at the left of "TWO" are usually all short; the lettering is heavier and the ends of the ribbons slightly changed.

1904 **Re-cut Die**

U395	U89 2c carmine	.55	.20
U396	U89 2c car, *amber*	8.00	1.00
U397	U89 2c car, *oriental buff*	5.50	1.10
U398	U89 2c carmine, *blue*	3.50	.90
W399	U89 2c car, *manila*	12.00	9.50

Franklin — U90

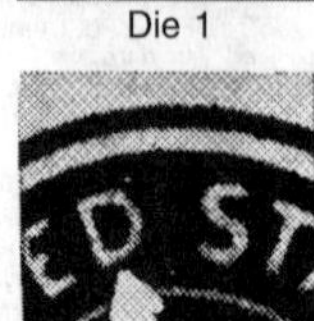

Die 1

Die 2

Die 3

Die 4

Die 1. Wide "D" in "UNITED."
Die 2. Narrow "D" in "UNITED."
Die 3. Wide "S-S" in "STATES" (1910).
Die 4. Sharp angle at back of bust, "N" and "E" of "ONE" are parallel (1912).

1907-16 **Die 1**

U400	U90 1c green	.30	.20
a.	Die 2	.80	.25
b.	Die 3	.80	.35
c.	Die 4	.75	.30
U401	U90 1c green, *amber*	1.75	.40
a.	Die 2	1.90	.70
b.	Die 3	2.40	.75
c.	Die 4	1.90	.65
U402	U90 1c grn, *oriental buff*	8.50	1.00
a.	Die 2	10.50	1.50
b.	Die 3	12.00	1.50
c.	Die 4	9.25	1.50
U403	U90 1c green, *blue*	9.25	1.50
a.	Die 2	9.25	1.50
b.	Die 3	9.25	3.00
c.	Die 4	8.00	1.25
U404	U90 1c grn, *manila*	3.00	1.90
a.	Die 3	3.75	3.00
W405	U90 1c grn, *manila*	.80	.25
a.	Die 2	40.00	25.00
b.	Die 3	7.50	4.00
c.	Die 4	40.00	—

Die 1, Washington—U91

Die 2

Die 3

Die 4

Die 5

Die 6

Die 7

Die 8

Die 1. Oval "O" in "TWO" and "C" in "CENTS," front of bust broad.

Die 2. Similar to 1 but hair in two distinct locks at top of head.

Die 3. Round "O" in "TWO" and "C" in "CENTS," coarse lettering.

Die 4. Similar to 3 but lettering fine and clear, hair lines clearly embossed. Inner oval thin and clear.

Die 5. All "S's" wide (1910).

Die 6. Similar to 1 but front of bust narrow (1913).

Die 7. Similar to 6 but upper corner of front of bust cut away (1916).

Die 8. Similar to 7 but lower stroke of "S" in "CENTS" is a straight line. Hair as in Die 2 (1916).

Die I

U406	U91 2c brown red	.80	.20
a.	Die 2	40.00	6.25
b.	Die 3	.60	.20
U407	U91 2c brn red, *amb*	5.75	2.00
a.	Die 2	250.00	45.00
b.	Die 3	3.75	1.00
U408	U91 2c brown red, *oriental buff*	7.25	1.50
a.	Die 2	150.00	55.00
b.	Die 3	6.75	2.50
U409	U91 2c brn red, *blue*	4.75	1.75
a.	Die 2	300.00	100.00
b.	Die 3	4.50	1.50
W410	U91 2c brn red, *man*	40.00	32.50
U411	U91 2c carmine	.25	.20
a.	Die 2	.45	.20
b.	Die 3	.75	.35
c.	Die 4	.40	.20
d.	Die 5	.55	.30
e.	Die 6	.40	.20
f.	Die 7	35.00	25.00
g.	Die 8	37.50	25.00
h.	Die 1, with added impression of 1c grn (#U400), entire	350.00	
i.	Die 1, with added impression of 4c blk (#U416a), entire	325.00	
U412	U91 2c carmine, *amb*	.25	.20
a.	Die 2	.90	.25
b.	Die 3	1.75	.45
c.	Die 4	.40	.25
d.	Die 5	.70	.35
e.	Die 6	.55	.35
f.	Die 7	30.00	20.00
U413	U91 2c car, *oriental buff*	.45	.20
a.	Die 2	1.25	.45
b.	Die 3	7.00	3.00
c.	Die 4	.40	.20
d.	Die 5	3.25	1.25
e.	Die 6	.55	.35
f.	Die 7	95.00	42.50
g.	Die 8	30.00	21.00
U414	U91 2c carmine, *blue*	.50	.20
a.	Die 2	1.10	.35
b.	Die 3	1.75	.60
c.	Die 4	.50	.25
d.	Die 5	1.75	.30
e.	Die 6	.55	.30
f.	Die 7	32.50	19.00
g.	Die 8	32.50	19.00
W415	U91 2c car, *manila*	4.50	2.00
a.	Die 2	4.50	1.10
b.	Die 5	4.50	2.25
c.	Die 7	110.00	87.50

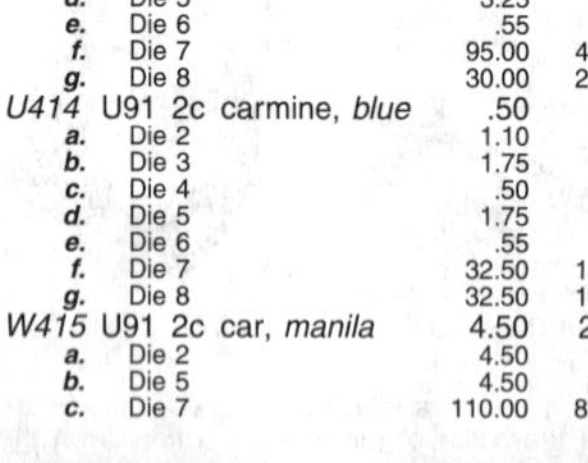

U90 4c Die 1

U90 4c Die 2

U416	U90 4c black, die 2	4.75	2.25
a.	Die 1	4.75	3.00
U417	U90 4c black, *amb*, die 2	6.50	2.50
a.	Die 1	6.50	2.50

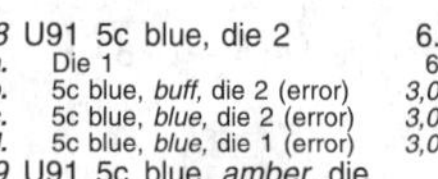

Die 1-Tall "F" in "FIVE" — Die 2-Short "F" in "FIVE"

U418	U91 5c blue, die 2	6.50	2.25
a.	Die 1	6.50	2.25
b.	5c blue, *buff*, die 2 (error)	*3,000.*	
c.	5c blue, *blue*, die 2 (error)	*3,000.*	
d.	5c blue, *blue*, die 1 (error)	*3,000.*	
U419	U91 5c blue, *amber*, die 2	15.00	11.00
a.	Die 1	13.50	11.00

Franklin — U92

Die 1

Die 2

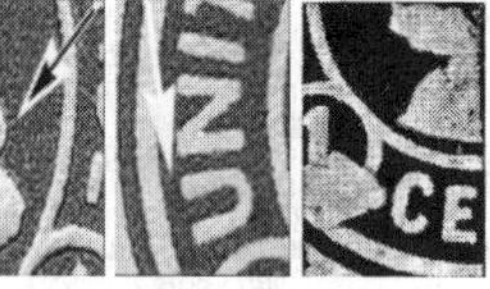

Die 3 — Die 4 — Die 5

(The 1c and 4c dies are the same except for figures of value.)

Die 1. UNITED nearer inner circle than outer circle.

Die 2. Large U; large NT closely spaced.

Die 3. Knob of hair at back of neck. Large NT widely spaced.

Die 4. UNITED nearer outer circle than inner circle.

Die 5. Narrow oval C, (also O and G).

1915-32 **Die 1**

U420	U92 1c green ('16)	.20	.20
a.	Die 2	140.00	55.00
b.	Die 3	.30	.20
c.	Die 4	.40	.40
d.	Die 5	.40	.35
U421	U92 1c grn, *amber* ('16)	.50	.30
a.	Die 2	450.00	175.00
b.	Die 3	1.10	.65
c.	Die 4	1.50	.85
d.	Die 5	1.00	.55
U422	U92 1c grn, *oriental buff* ('16)	2.00	.90
a.	Die 4	4.25	1.25
U423	U92 1c grn, *bl* ('16)	.45	.35
a.	Die 3	.75	.45
b.	Die 4	1.25	.65
c.	Die 5	.80	.35
U424	U92 1c grn, (unglazed), *manila* ('16)	6.50	4.00
W425	U92 1c grn, (unglazed), *manila* ('16)	.20	.20
a.	Die 3	160.00	125.00
U426	U92 1c grn, (glazed) *brown* ('20)	30.00	15.00
W427	U92 1c grn, (glazed) *brown* ('20)	65.00	
U428	U92 1c grn, (unglazed) *brown* ('20)	8.00	7.50
W428A	U92 1c grn, (unglazed) *brown*, die 1 ('20), entire		*3,000.*

Washington — U93

Die 1

Die 2

Die 3

Die 4

Die 5

Die 6

Die 7

Die 8

Die 9

(The 1½c, 2c, 3c, 5c, and 6c are the same except for figures of value.)

Die 1. Letters broad. Numerals vertical. Large head (9¼mm) from tip of nose to back of neck. E closer to inner circle than N of cents.

Die 2. Similar to 1; but U far from left circle.

Die 3. Similar to 2; but all inner circles very thin (Rejected Die).

Die 4. Similar to 1; but C very close to left circle.

Die 5. Small head (8¾mm) from tip of nose to back of neck. T and S of CENTS close at bottom.

Die 6. Similar to 5; but T and S of CENTS far apart at bottom. Left numeral slopes to right.

Die 7. Large head. Both numerals slope to right. Clean cut lettering. All letters T have short top strokes.

Die 8. Similar to 7; but all letters T have long top strokes.

Die 9. Narrow oval C (also O and G).

Die 1

U429 U93 2c car, *Dec. 20, 1915* .20 .20
- *a.* Die 2 14.00 6.00
- *b.* Die 3 45.00 25.00
- *c.* Die 4 30.00 15.00
- *d.* Die 5 .50 .35
- *e.* Die 6 .60 .30
- *f.* Die 7 .65 .25
- *g.* Die 8 .45 .20
- *h.* Die 9 .40 .20
- *i.* 2c grn, error, die 1, entire *14,000.*
- *j.* 2c car, die 1 with added impression of 1c grn (#U420), die 1 650.00
- *k.* Die 1, with added impression of 4c blk (#U416a), entire 1,000.
- *l.* Die 1, with added impression of 1c grn (#U400), die 1, entire 1,000.
- *m.* As No. U429, double impression, entire 1,750.

U430 U93 2c car, *amber* ('16) .25 .20
- *a.* Die 2 15.00 7.50
- *b.* Die 4 50.00 20.00
- *c.* Die 5 1.10 .35
- *d.* Die 6 .95 .40
- *e.* Die 7 .70 .35
- *f.* Die 8 .65 .30
- *g.* Die 9 .60 .20

U431 U93 2c car, *oriental buff* ('16) 2.25 .65
- *a.* Die 2 160.00 40.00
- *b.* Die 4 75.00 60.00
- *c.* Die 5 2.75 1.75
- *d.* Die 6 3.00 2.00
- *e.* Die 7 2.75 1.75

U432 U93 2c carmine, *blue* ('16) .25 .20
- *b.* Die 2 32.50 20.00
- *c.* Die 3 150.00 90.00
- *d.* Die 4 65.00 50.00
- *e.* Die 5 .80 .30
- *f.* Die 6 .85 .40
- *g.* Die 7 .75 .35
- *h.* Die 8 .60 .25
- *i.* Die 9 .90 .30

U432A U93 2c car, *manila*, die 7, entire *35,000.*

W433 U93 2c car, *manila* ('16) .25 .20

W434 U93 2c car, (glazed) *brn* ('20) 90.00 50.00

W435 U93 2c car, (unglazed) *brn* ('20) 95.00 50.00

U436 U93 3c purple ('32) .30 .20
- *a.* 3c dk vio, die 1 ('17) .55 .20
- *b.* 3c dark violet, die 5 1.65 .75
- *c.* 3c dark violet, die 6 2.00 1.40
- *d.* 3c dark violet, die 7 1.40 .95
- *e.* 3c purple, die 7 ('32) .65 .30
- *f.* 3c purple, die 9 ('32) .40 .20
- *g.* 3c car (error), die 1 32.50 27.50
- *h.* 3c car (error), die 5 35.00 30.00
- *i.* 3c dk vio, die 1, with added impression of 1c grn (#U420), die 1, entire 800.00
- *j.* 3c dk vio, die 1, with added impression of 2c car (#U429), die 1, entire 900.00 950.00

U437 U93 3c purple, *amb* .35 .20
- *a.* 3c dk vio, die 1 ('32) 3.25 1.25
- *b.* 3c dark vio, die 5 6.00 2.50
- *c.* 3c dark vio, die 6 6.00 2.50
- *d.* 3c dark vio, die 7 5.50 2.25
- *e.* 3c purple, die 7 ('32) .75 .20
- *f.* 3c purple, die 9 ('32) .50 .20
- *g.* 3c car (error), die 5 475.00 275.00
- *h.* 3c black (error), die 1 175.00 —

U438 U93 3c dk vio, *oriental buff* 22.50 1.50
- *a.* Die 5 22.50 1.00
- *b.* Die 6 32.50 1.65
- *c.* Die 7 32.50 3.50

U439 U93 3c purple, *bl* ('32) .30 .20
- *a.* 3c dk violet, die 1 ('17) 6.50 2.00
- *b.* 3c dark violet, die 5 7.50 4.00
- *c.* 3c dark violet, die 6 7.00 4.25
- *d.* 3c dark violet, die 7 10.00 5.50
- *e.* 3c purple, die 7 ('32) .75 .25
- *f.* 3c purple, die 9 ('32) .50 .20
- *g.* 3c car (error), die 5 350.00 300.00

U440 U92 4c black ('16) 1.50 .60
- *a.* 4c black with added impression of 2c car (#U429), die 1, entire 400.00

U441 U92 4c black, *amb* ('16) 3.00 .85

U442 U92 4c blk, *bl* ('21) 3.25 .85

U443 U93 5c blue ('16) 3.25 2.75

U444 U93 5c blue, *amber* ('16) 3.75 1.60

U445 U93 5c bl, *blue* ('21) 4.00 3.25

See Nos. U481-U485, U529-U531.

Listings of double or triple surcharges of 1920-25 are for specimens with the surcharges directly or partly upon the stamp.

Surcharged

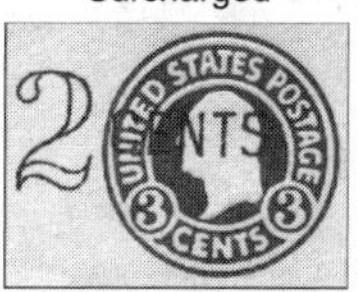

Type 1

1920-21

U446 U93 2c on 3c dk vio (U436, die 1) 15.00 10.00
- *a.* Die 5 (U436b) 14.00 10.00

Surcharged

Type 2

Rose Surcharge

U447 U93 2c on 3c dk vio (U436, die 1) 7.75 6.50
- *b.* Die 6 (U436c) 10.00 8.50

Black Surcharge

U447A U93 2c on 2c car (U429, die 1) —

U447C U93 2c on 2c car, *amb* (U430, die 1) —

U448 U93 2c on 3c dk vio (U436, die 1) 2.50 2.00
- *a.* Die 5 (U436b) 2.50 2.00
- *b.* Die 6 (U436c) 3.25 2.00
- *c.* Die 7 (U436d) 2.50 2.00

U449 U93 2c on 3c dk vio, *amb* (U437, die 1) 6.50 6.00
- *a.* Die 5 (U437b) 10.00 7.50
- *b.* Die 6 (U437c) 7.50 6.00
- *c.* Die 7 (U437d) 7.00 6.50

U450 U93 2c on 3c dk vio, *oriental buff* (U438, die 1) 17.50 14.00
- *a.* Die 5 (U438a) 17.50 14.00
- *b.* Die 6 (U438b) 17.50 14.00
- *c.* Die 7 (U438c) 100.00 90.00

U451 U93 2c on 3c dk vio, *blue* (U439, die 1) 12.50 10.00
- *b.* Die 5 (U439b) 12.50 10.00
- *c.* Die 6 (U439c) 12.50 10.00
- *d.* Die 7 (U439d) 25.00 20.00

Surcharged

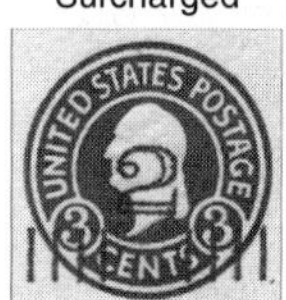

Type 3

Bars 2mm apart

U451A U90 2c on 1c grn (U400, die 1) *30,000.*

U452 U92 2c on 1c grn (U420, die 1) 3,500.
- *a.* Die 3 (U420b) 3,500.
- *b.* As No. U452, dbl. surch. 4,000.

U453 U91 2c on 2c car (U411b, die 3) 4,250.
- *a.* Die 1 (U411) 4,250.

U453B U91 2c on 2c car, *bl* (U414e, die 6) 2,750.

U453C U91 2c on 2c car, *oriental buff* (U413e, die 6) 2,100. 750.00
- *d.* Die 1 (U413) 2,100.

U454 U93 2c on 2c car (U429e, die 6) 100.00
- *a.* Die 1 (U429) 350.00
- *b.* Die 5 (U429d) 500.00
- *c.* Die 7 (U429f) 100.00

U455 U93 2c on 2c car, *amb* (U430, die 1) 2,000.
- *a.* Die 6 (U430d) 2,250.
- *b.* Die 7 (U430e) 2,250.

U456 U93 2c on 2c car, *oriental buff* (U431a, die 2) 300.00
- *a.* Die 5 (U431c) 325.00
- *b.* Die 7 (U431e) 800.00
- *c.* As #U456, dbl. surch. 500.00

U457 U93 2c on 2c car, *bl* (U432f, die 6) 350.00
- *a.* Die 5 (U432e) 350.00
- *b.* Die 7 (U432g) 750.00

U458 U93 2c on 3c dk vio (U436, die 1) .50 .35
- *a.* Die 5 (U436b) .50 .40
- *b.* Die 6 (U436c) .50 .35
- *c.* Die 7 (U436d) .50 .35
- *d.* As #U458, dbl. surch. 25.00 7.50
- *e.* As #U458, trip. surch. 110.00
- *f.* As #U458, dbl. surch., one in magenta 100.00
- *g.* As #U458, dbl. surch., types 2 & 3 125.00
- *h.* As "a," dbl. surch. 25.00 15.00
- *i.* As "a," triple surcharge 100.00
- *j.* As "a," dbl. surch., both magenta 100.00
- *k.* As "b," dbl. surch. 25.00 8.00
- *l.* As "c," dbl. surch. 25.00 8.00
- *m.* As "c," triple surcharge 100.00

U459 U93 2c on 3c dk vio, *amb* (U437c, die 6) 3.00 1.00
- *a.* Die 1 (U437) 4.00 1.00
- *b.* Die 5 (U437b) 4.00 1.00
- *c.* Die 7 (U437d) 3.00 1.00
- *d.* As #U459, dbl. surch. 35.00
- *e.* As "a," dbl. surch. 35.00
- *f.* As "b," dbl. surch. 35.00
- *g.* As "b," dbl. surch., types 2 & 3 125.00
- *h.* As "c," dbl. surch. 35.00

U460 U93 2c on 3c dk vio, *oriental buff* (U438a, die 5) 2.75 1.00
- *a.* Die 1 (U438) 3.00 1.50
- *b.* Die 6 (U438b) 3.00 2.00
- *c.* As #U460, dbl. surch. 20.00
- *d.* As "a," dbl. surch. 20.00
- *e.* As "b," dbl. surch. 20.00
- *f.* As "b," triple surcharge 150.00

U461 U93 2c on 3c dk vio, *bl* (U439, die 1) 4.25 1.00
- *a.* Die 5 (U439b) 4.25 1.00
- *b.* Die 6 (U439c) 4.25 1.00
- *c.* Die 7 (U439d) 10.00 2.00
- *d.* As #U461, dbl. surch. 20.00
- *e.* As "a," dbl. surch. 20.00
- *f.* As "b," dbl. surch. 20.00
- *g.* As "c," dbl. surch. 20.00

U462 U87 2c on 4c choc (U390) 625.00 250.00

U463 U87 2c on 4c choc, *amb* (U391) 575.00 250.00

U463A U90 2c on 4c blk (U416, die 2) 1,300. 400.00

U464 U93 2c on 5c bl (U443) 1,250.

Surcharged

Type 4

Similar to Type 3, but bars 1½mm apart.

U465 U92 2c on 1c grn (U420, die 1) 1,500.
- *a.* Die 3 (U420b) 1,600.

U466 U91 2c on 2c car (U411e, die 6) *14,000.*

U466A U93 2c on 2c car (U429, die 1) 750.00
- *c.* Die 5 (U429d) 1,250.
- *d.* Die 6 (U429e) 1,250.
- *e.* Die 7 (U429f) 1,250.

U466B U93 2c on 2c car, *amb* (U430) *12,500.*

U466C U93 2c on 2c car, *oriental buff* (U431), entire —

U467 U45 2c on 3c grn (U163) 350.00

U468 U93 2c on 3c dk vio (U436, die 1) .70 .45
- *a.* Die 5 (U436b) .70 .50
- *b.* Die 6 (U436c) .70 .50
- *c.* Die 7 (U436d) .70 .50
- *d.* As #U468, dbl. surch. 20.00
- *e.* As #U468, trip. surch. 100.00
- *f.* As #U468, dbl. surch., types 2 & 4 125.00
- *g.* As "a," double surcharge 20.00
- *h.* As "b," double surcharge 20.00
- *i.* As "c," double surcharge 20.00
- *j.* As "c," triple surcharge 100.00
- *k.* As "c," inverted surch. 75.00
- *l.* 2c on 3c car (error) (U436h) 650.00

U469 U93 2c on 3c dk vio, *amber* (U437, die 1) 3.50 2.25
- *a.* Die 5 (U437b) 3.50 2.25
- *b.* Die 6 (U437c) 3.50 2.25

c. Die 7 (U437d) 3.50 2.25
d. As No. U469, dbl. surch. 30.00
e. As "a," double surcharge 30.00
f. As "a," double surcharge, types 2 & 4 100.00
g. As "b," double surcharge 30.00
h. As "c," double surcharge 30.00

U470 U93 2c on 3c dk vio, *oriental buff* (U438, die 1) 4.50 2.50
a. Die 5 (U438a) 4.50 2.50
b. Die 6 (U438b) 4.50 2.50
c. Die 7 (U438c) 35.00 32.50
d. As No. U470, dbl. surch. 25.00
e. As No. U470, double surcharge, types 2 & 4 100.00
f. As "a," double surcharge 25.00
g. As "b," double surcharge 25.00

U471 U93 2c on 3c dk vio, *bl* (U439, die 1) 4.50 1.75
a. Die 5 (U439b) 4.50 1.75
b. Die 6 (U439c) 4.50 1.75
c. Die 7 (U439d) 10.00 6.00
d. As No. U471, dbl. surch. 30.00
e. As No. U471, double surcharge, types 2 & 4 175.00
f. As "a," double surcharge 30.00
g. As "b," double surcharge 30.00

U472 U87 2c on 4c choc (U390) 12.00 8.00
a. Double surcharge 150.00

U473 U87 2c on 4c choc, *amb* (U391) 16.00 10.00

Dbl. Surch., "1" and Type 4

U474 U93 2c on 1c on 3c dk vio (U436, die 1) 275.00
a. Die 5 (U436b) 325.00
b. Die 7 (U436d) 750.00

U475 U93 2c on 1c on 3c dk vio, *amb* (U437, die 1) 275.00

Surcharged

Type 5

U476 U93 2c on 3c dk vio, *amb* (U437, die 1) 275.00
a. Die 6 (U437c) 750.00
b. As #U476, double surch. —

Surcharged

Type 6

U477 U93 2c on 3c dk vio (U436, die 1) 125.00
a. Die 5 (U436b) 200.00
b. Die 6 (U436c) 200.00
c. Die 7 (U437d) 200.00

U478 U93 2c on 3c dk vio, *amb* (U437, die 1) 300.00

Handstamped Surcharge in Black or Violet—Type 7

U479 U93 2c on 3c dk vio (Bk) (U436, die 1) 450.00
a. Die 5 (U436b) 900.00
b. Die 7 (U436d) 450.00

U480 U93 2c on 3c dk vio (V) (U436d, die 7) 5,500.
a. Double overprint —

Expertization by competent authorities is recommended for Nos. U479-U480.

Type of 1916-32 Issue

1925-34

Die 1

U481 U93 1½c brown .20 .20
a. Die 8 .60 .25
b. 1½c purple (error) ('34) 90.00

U482 U93 1½c brown, *amber* .90 .40
a. Die 8 1.40 .75

U483 U93 1½c brn, *bl* 1.50 .95
a. Die 8 1.75 1.25

U484 U93 1½c brown, *manila* 6.00 3.00

W485 U93 1½c brown, *manila* .80 .20
a. With added impression of No. W433 120.00 —

Surcharged Type 8

1925

U486 U71 1½c on 2c grn (U311) 725.00

U487 U71 1½c on 2c grn, *amb* (U312) 1,250.

U488 U77 1½c on 1c grn (U352) 625.00

U489 U77 1½c on 1c grn, *amb* (U353) 110.00 60.00

U490 U90 1½c on 1c grn (U400, die 1) 5.00 3.50
a. Die 2 (U400a) 14.00 9.00
b. Die 3 (U400b) 30.00 17.50
c. Die 4 (U400c) 7.50 2.50

U491 U90 1½c on 1c grn, *amb* (U401c, die 4) 5.25 2.25
a. Die 1 (U401) 9.00 2.50
b. Die 2 (U401a) 90.00 65.00
c. Die 3 (U401b) 42.50 30.00

U492 U90 1½c on 1c grn, *oriental buff* (U402a, die 2) 500.00 100.00
a. Die 4 (U402c) 1,000. 100.00

U493 U90 1½c on 1c grn, *bl* (U403c, die 4) 100.00 55.00
a. Die 2 (U403a) 100.00 55.00

U494 U90 1½c on 1c grn, *man* (U404, die 1) 350.00 80.00
a. Die 3 (U404a) 1,000.

U495 U92 1½c on 1c grn (U420, die 1) .75 .25
a. Die 2 (U420a) 70.00 52.50
b. Die 3 (U420b) 1.60 .60
c. Die 4 (U420c) 1.75 .75
d. As No. U495, dbl. surch. 10.00 1.90
e. As "b," double surcharge 10.00 3.00
f. As "c," double surcharge 10.00 3.00

U496 U92 1½c on 1c grn, *amb* (U421, die 1) 17.50 12.50
a. Die 3 (U421b) 600.00
b. Die 4 (U421c) 17.50 12.50

U497 U92 1½c on 1c grn, *oriental buff* (U422, die 1) 3.25 1.90
a. Die 4 (U422b) 52.50

U498 U92 1½c on 1c grn, *bl* (U423c, die 4) 1.25 .75
a. Die 1 (U423) 2.25 1.50
b. Die 3 (U423b) 1.75 1.50

U499 U92 1½c on 1c grn, *man* (U424) 12.50 6.00

U500 U92 1½c on 1c grn, *brn* (unglazed) (U428) 75.00 30.00

U501 U93 1½c on 1c grn, *brn* (glazed) (U426) 75.00 25.00

U502 U93 1½c on 2c car (U429, die 1) 275.00 —
a. Die 5 (U429d) 375.00
b. Die 7 (U429f) 375.00
c. Die 6 (U429e) —
d. Die 8 (U429g) —

U503 U93 1½c on 2c car, *oriental buff* (U431c, die 5) 375.00 —
a. Double surcharge —
b. Dbl. surch., one inverted *700.00*

U504 U93 1½c on 2c car, *bl* (U432, die 1) 400.00 —
a. Die 7 (U432g) 350.00

On Envelopes of 1925

U505 U93 1½c on 1½c brn (U481, die 1) 450.00
a. Die 8 (U481a) 450.00

U506 U93 1½c on 1½c brn, *bl* (U483a, die 8) 450.00

The paper of No. U500 is not glazed and appears to be the same as that used for wrappers of 1920.

Surcharged Type 9

Black Surcharge

U507 U69 1½c on 1c bl (U294) 3,000.

U508 U77 1½c on 1c grn, *amb* (U353) 67.50

U508A U85 1½c on 1c grn (U379) 4,750.

U509 U85 1½c on 1c grn, *amb* (U380) 15.00 10.00
a. Double surcharge 75.00

U509B U85 1½c on 1c grn, *oriental buff* (U381) 60.00 40.00

U510 U90 1½c on 1c grn (U400, die 1) 2.40 1.25
b. Die 2 (U400a) 6.50 4.00
c. Die 3 (U400b) 25.00 8.00
d. Die 4 (U400c) 3.25 1.25
e. As No. U510, double surcharge 15.00

U511 U90 1½c on 1c grn, *amb* (U401, die 1) 225.00 72.50

U512 U90 1½c on 1c grn, *oriental buff* (U402, die 1) 7.00 4.00
a. Die 4 (U402c) 17.50 14.00

U513 U90 1½c on 1c grn, *bl* (U403, die 1) 5.25 2.50
a. Die 4 (U403c) 5.25 4.00

U514 U90 1½c on 1c grn, *man* (U404, die 1) 27.50 9.00
a. Die 3 (U404a) 60.00 37.50

U515 U92 1½c on 1c grn (U420, die 1) .35 .20
a. Die 2 (U420a) 20.00 15.00
b. Die 3 (U420b) .35 .20
c. Die 4 (U420c) .35 .20
d. As No. U515, dbl. surch. 10.00
e. As No. U515, inverted surch. 20.00
f. As No. U515, trip. surch. 20.00
g. As No. U515, dbl. surch., one invtd., entire —
h. As "b," double surcharge 10.00
i. As "b," inverted surcharge 20.00
j. As "b," triple surcharge 20.00
k. As "c," double surcharge 10.00
l. As "c," inverted surcharge 20.00

U516 U92 1½c on 1c grn, *amb* (U421c, die 4) 42.50 25.00
a. Die 1 (U421) 47.50 30.00

U517 U92 1½c on 1c grn, *oriental buff* (U422, die 1) 4.25 1.25
a. Die 4 (U422a) 5.50 1.50

U518 U92 1½c on 1c grn, *bl* (U423b, die 4) 4.50 1.25
a. Die 1 (U423) 6.50 2.50
b. Die 3 (U423a) 20.00 7.50
c. As "a," double surcharge 20.00

U519 U92 1½c on 1c grn, *man* (U424) 25.00 10.00
a. Double surcharge 100.00

U520 U93 1½c on 2c car (U429, die 1) 350.00 —
a. Die 5 (U429d) 350.00
b. Die 6 (U429e) 350.00
c. Die 7 (U429f) 400.00

U520D U93 1½c on 2c car, *amber* (U430c, die 5), entire —

Magenta Surcharge

U521 U92 1½c on 1c grn (U420b, die 3) 4.50 3.50
a. Double surcharge 75.00

Sesquicentennial Exposition Issue

Liberty Bell — U94

Die 1. The center bar of "E" of "POSTAGE" is shorter than top bar.

Die 2. The center bar of "E" of "POSTAGE" is of same length as top bar.

1926

U522 U94 2c carmine, die 1 1.10 .50
a. Die 2 7.00 3.75

See note below No. 627.

Washington Bicentennial Issue

Mount Vernon — U95

2 cent:
Die 1. "S" of "POSTAGE" normal.
Die 2. "S" of "POSTAGE" raised.

1932

U523 U95 1c olive green 1.00 .80
U524 U95 1½c chocolate 2.00 1.50
U525 U95 2c car, die 1 .40 .20
a. Die 2 70.00 16.00
b. Die 1, *blue*, entire (error) *27,500.*
U526 U95 3c violet 2.00 .35
U527 U95 4c black 18.00 16.00
U528 U95 5c dark blue 4.00 3.50
Nos. U523-U528 (6) 27.40 22.35

Bicen. of the birth of Washington.

1932 **Die 7**

U529 U93 6c orange 5.50 4.00
U530 U93 6c orange, *amber* 11.00 8.00
U531 U93 6c orange, *blue* 11.00 10.00

Franklin — U96

Die 1

Die 2

Die 3

Die 1. Short (3½mm) and thick "1" in thick circle.

Die 2. Tall (4½mm) and thin "1" in thin circle; upper and lower bars of E in ONE long and 1mm from circle.

Die 3. As in Die 2, but E normal and 1½mm from circle.

1950

U532 U96 1c green, die 1 5.50 1.75
a. Die 2 7.00 3.00
b. Die 3 7.00 3.00
Die 3, precanceled 1.25

Washington — U97

Die 1

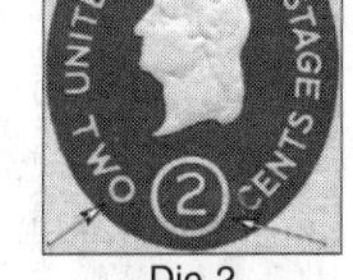
Die 2

Die 3

Die 4

Die 1. Thick "2" in circle; toe of "2" is an acute angle.
Die 2. Thin "2" in thin circle; toe of "2" is almost right angle; line through stand of "E" in POSTAGE goes considerably below tip of chin; "N" of UNITED is tall; "O" of TWO is high.
Die 3. Thin "2" in thin circle; toe of "2" is almost right angle; short UN in UNITED: thin crossbar in A of STATES.
Die 4. Tall UN in UNITED; thick crossbar in A of STATES; otherwise like Die 3.

U533	U97	2c carmine, die 3	.75	.25
a.		Die 1	.85	.30
b.		Die 2	1.50	.85
c.		Die 4	1.40	.60

Die 1

Die 2

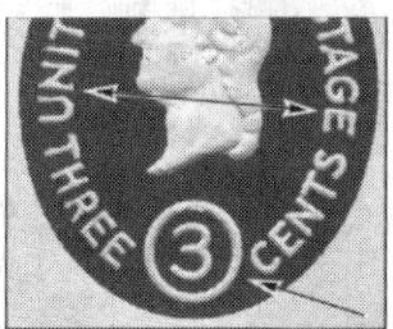
Die 3

Die 4

Die 5

Die 1. Thick and tall (4½mm) "3" in thick circle; long top bars and short stems in T's of STATES.
Die 2. Thin and tall (4½mm) "3" in medium circle; short top bars and long stems in T's of STATES.
Die 3. Thin and short (4mm) "3" in thin circle; lettering wider than Dies 1 and 2; line from left stand of N to stand of E is distinctly below tip of chin.
Die 4. Figure and letters as in Die 3. Line hits tip of chin; short N in UNITED and thin crossbar in A of STATES.
Die 5. Figure, letter and chin line as in Die 4; but tall N in UNITED and thick crossbar in A of STATES.

U534	U97	3c dk violet, die 4	.40	.20
a.		Die 1	2.00	.70
b.		Die 2	.80	.50
c.		Die 3	.60	.25
d.		Die 5	.80	.45

Washington — U98

1952

U535	U98	1½c brown	5.50	3.50
		Precanceled		1.25

Die 1

Die 2

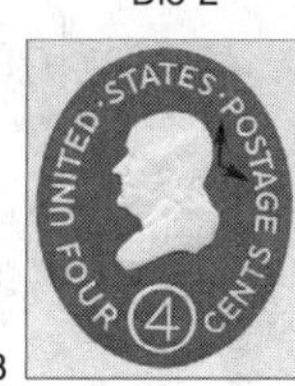
Die 3

Die 1. Head high in oval (2mm below T of STATES). Circle near (1mm) bottom of colored oval.
Die 2. Head low in oval (3mm). Circle 1½mm from edge of oval. Right leg of A of POSTAGE shorter than left. Short leg on P.
Die 3. Head centered in oval (2½mm). Circle as in Die 2. Legs of A of POSTAGE about equal. Long leg on P.

1958

U536	U96	4c red violet, die 1	.80	.20
a.		Die 2	1.05	.20
b.		Die 3	1.05	.20

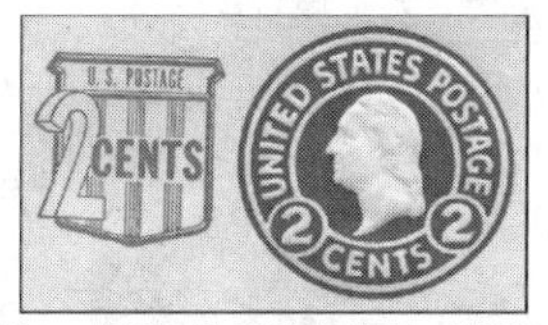
Nos. U429, U429f, U429h, U533, U533a-U533c Surcharged in Red - b

1958

U537	U93	2c + 2c car, die 1	3.50	1.50
a.		2c + 2c carmine, die 7	11.00	7.00
b.		2c + 2c carmine, die 9	5.50	5.00
U538	U97	2c + 2c car, die 1	.75	.20
a.		2c + 2c carmine, die 2	1.00	—
b.		2c + 2c carmine, die 3	.80	.25
c.		2c + 2c carmine, die 4	.80	—

Nos. U436a, U436e-U436f, U534a-U534d Surcharged in Green - a

U539	U93	3c + 1c pur, die 1	15.00	11.00
a.		3c + 1c purple, die 7	12.00	9.00
b.		3c + 1c purple, die 9	30.00	15.00
U540	U97	3c + 1c dk violet, die 3	.50	.20
a.		3c + 1c dk vio, die 2, entire	*2,500.*	—
b.		3c + 1c dark violet, die 4	.75	.20
c.		3c + 1c dark violet, die 5	.75	.20

See No. U545.

Benjamin Franklin U99

George Washington U100

Die 1 Die 2

Dies of 1¼c

Die 1. The "4" is 3mm high. Upper leaf in left cluster 2mm from "U."
Die 2. The "4" is 3½mm high. Leaf clusters are larger. Upper leaf at left is 1mm from "U."

1960

U541	U99	1¼c turquoise, die 1	.75	.50
		Die 1, precanceled		.20
a.		Die 2, precanceled		1.50
U542	U100	2½c dull blue	.85	.50
		Precanceled		.25

Precanceled Cut Squares

Precanceled envelopes do not normally receive another cancellation. Since the lack of a cancellation makes it impossible to distinguish between cut squares from used and unused envelopes, they are valued here as used only.

Pony Express Centennial Issue

Pony Express Rider — U101

Envelope White Outside, Blue Inside

1960, July 19

U543	U101	4c brown	.60	.30

Abraham Lincoln — U102

Die 1

Die 2

Die 3

Die 1. Center bar of E of POSTAGE is above the middle. Center bar of E of STATES slants slightly upward. Nose sharper, more pointed. No offset ink specks inside envelope on back of die impression.
Die 2. Center bar of E in POSTAGE in middle. P of POSTAGE has short stem. Ink specks on back of die impression.
Die 3. FI of FIVE closer than Die 1 or 2. Second T of STATES seems taller than ES. Ink specks on back of die impression.

1962, Nov. 19

U544	U102	5c dark blue, die 2	.85	.20
a.		Die 1	.85	.25
b.		Die 3	.90	.35
c.		Die 2 with albino impression of 4c (#U536)	65.00	—
d.		Die 3 with albino impression of 4c (#U536)	85.00	—
e.		Die 3 on complete impression of 4c (#U536)		—

No. U536 Surcharged Type "a" in Green at Left of Stamp

Two types of surcharge "a":
Type I. "U.S. POSTAGE" 18½mm high. Serifs on cross of T both diagonal. Two lines of shading in C of CENT.
Type II. "U.S. POSTAGE" 17½mm high. Right serif on cross of T is vertical. Three shading lines in C.

1962, Nov.

U545	U96	4c + 1c red vio, type I	1.40	.50
a.		Type II	1.10	.50

New York World's Fair (1964-65)

Globe with Satellite Orbit — U103

1964, Apr. 22

U546	U103	5c carmine rose	.60	.40

Liberty Bell — U104

Old Ironsides — U105

Eagle — U106

Head of Statue of Liberty — U107

1965-69 **Tagged (6c)**

U547	U104	1¼c brown		.20
U548	U104	1 4/10c brown ('68)		.20
U548A	U104	1 6/10c orange ('69)		.20
b.		1 6/10c brown (error), entire		—
U549	U105	4c bright blue	.75	.20
U550	U106	5c bright purple	.75	.20
a.		Tagged ('67)	2.00	.50
U551	U107	6c lt green ('68)	.70	.20

Issue dates: 5c, Jan. 5; 1¼c, Jan. 6; 6c, Jan. 4; 1 4/10c, Mar. 26; 1 6/10c, June 16.
No. U550a has a luminescent panel 9x29mm at left of stamp. It glows yellow green under ultraviolet light.

Nos. U549-U550 Surcharged Types "b" and "a" in Red or Green at Left of Stamp

1968, Feb. 5

U552	U105	4c + 2c brt blue (R)	3.75	2.00
U553	U106	5c + 1c brt pur (G)	3.50	2.50
a.		Tagged	3.50	2.75

Tagging

Envelopes from No. U554 onward are tagged, with the tagging element in the ink unless otherwise noted.

Herman Melville Issue

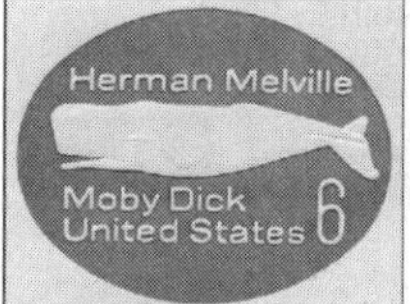

Moby Dick — U108

1970, Mar. 7

U554	U108	6c light blue	.50	.20

Herman Melville (1819-91), writer, and the whaling industry.

Youth Conference Issue

Youth Conference Emblem U109

1971, Feb. 24

U555	U109	6c light blue	.75	.20

White House Conference on Youth, Estes Park, Colo., Apr. 18-22.

Bell Type of 1965-69 and

Eagle — U110

1971 **Untagged (1 7/10c)**

U556	U104	1 7/10c deep lilac		.20
U557	U110	8c bright ultra	.40	.20

Issue dates: 1 7/10c, May 10; 8c, May 6.

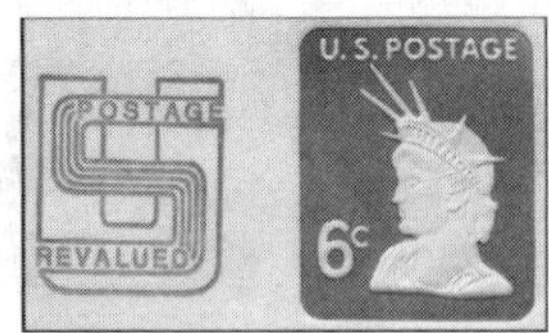

Nos. U551 and U555 Surcharged in Green

1971, May 16

U561 U107 6c + (2c) light green 1.00 .30
U562 U109 6c + (2c) light blue 2.00 1.60

Bowling Issue

Bowling Ball and Pin — U111

1971, Aug. 21

U563 U111 8c rose red .70 .20

Salute to bowling and 7th World Tournament of the Intl. Bowling Fed., Milwaukee, WI.

Aging Conference Issue

Conference Symbol — U112

1971, Nov. 5

U564 U112 8c light blue .50 .20

White House Conference on Aging, Washington, DC, Nov. 28-Dec. 2, 1971.

International Transportation Exhibition Issue

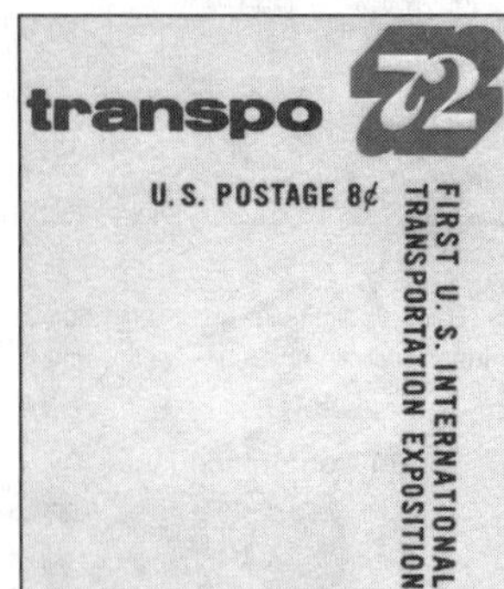

Transportation Exhibition Emblem — U113

Illustration ⅗ actual size.

1972, May 2

U565 U113 8c ultra & rose red .50 .20

US Intl. Transportation Exhib., Dulles Intl. Airport, Washington, May 27-June 4.

No. U557 Surcharged Type "b" in Ultramarine at Left of Stamp

1973, Dec. 1

U566 U110 8c + 2c bright ultra .40 .20

Liberty Bell — U114

1973, Dec. 5

U567 U114 10c emerald .40 .20

"Volunteer Yourself" U115

1974, Aug. 23 **Untagged**

U568 U115 1 8/10c blue green .20

US Tennis Centenary Issue

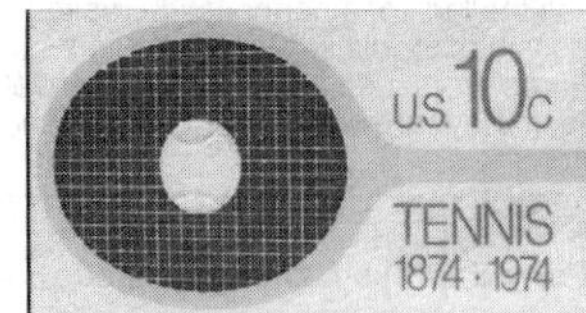

Tennis Racquet — U116

1974, Aug. 31

U569 U116 10c yel, brt bl & lt grn .65 .20

Bicentennial Era Issue

The Seafaring Tradition--Compass Rose — U118

The American Homemaker--Quilt Pattern — U119

The American Farmer--Sheaf of Wheat — U120

The American Doctor — U121

The American Craftsman--Tools, c. 1750 — U122

Designs (in brown on left side of envelope): 10c, Norwegian sloop Restaurationen. No. U572, Spinning wheel. No. U573, Plow. No. U574, Colonial era medical instruments and bottle. No. U575, Shaker rocking chair.

Light Brown Diagonally Laid Paper

1975-76

U571 U118 10c brown & blue .30 .20
 a. Brown ("10c/USA," etc.) omitted, entire *150.00*
U572 U119 13c brn & bl grn .35 .20
 a. Brown ("13c/USA," etc.) omitted, entire *150.00*
U573 U120 13c brn & brt grn .35 .20
 a. Brown ("13c/USA," etc.) omitted, entire *150.00*
U574 U121 13c brown & orange .35 .20
 a. Brown ("13c/USA," etc.) omitted, entire —
U575 U122 13c brown & car .35 .20
 a. Brown ("13c/USA," etc.) omitted, entire *150.00*

Issued: 10c, 10/13; #U572, 2/2/76; #U573, 3/15/76; #574, 6/30/76; #U575, 8/6/76.

Liberty Tree, Boston, 1646 U123

1975, Nov. 8

U576 U123 13c orange brown .30 .20

Precanceled Cut Squares
See note following No. U542.

Star and Pinweel U124

U125

U126

Eagle — U127

"Uncle Sam" — U128

1976-78 **Untagged (2c, 2.1c, 2.7c)**

U577 U124 2c red ('76) .20
U578 U125 2.1c yel grn ('77) .20
U579 U126 2.7c grn ('78) .20
U580 U127 (15c) orange ('78) .40 .20
U581 U128 15c red ('78) .40 .20

Issued: 2c, 9/10; 2.1c 6/3; 2.7c, 7/5; A, 5/22; 15c, 6/3.

Bicentennial Issue

Centennial Envelope, 1876 — U129

1976, Oct. 15

U582 U129 13c emerald .35 .20

See Nos. U218-U221.

Golf Issue

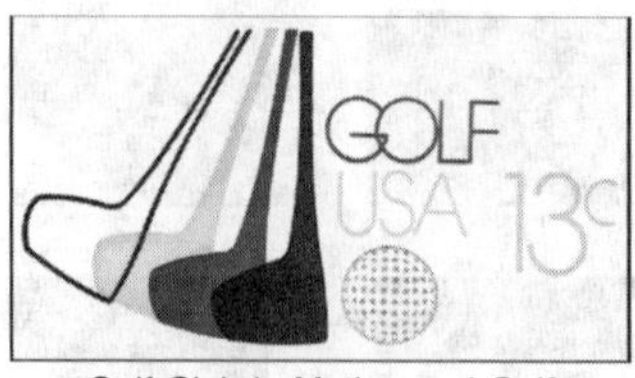

Golf Club in Motion and Golf Ball — U130

1977, Apr. 7

U583 U130 13c blk, bl & yel green .65 .20
 a. Black omitted, entire *650.00*
 b. Black & blue omitted, entire *550.00*

Energy Issue

Energy Conservation U131

Energy Development U132

1977, Oct. 20

U584 U131 13c blk, red & yel .40 .20
 a. Red & yel omitted, entire *250.00*
 b. Yellow omitted, entire *175.00*
 c. Black omitted, entire *175.00*
 d. Black & red omitted, entire *425.00*
U585 U132 13c blk, red & yel .40 .20

Nos. U584-U585 have a luminescent panel at left of stamp.

Olive Branch and Star — U133

1978, July 28

U586 U133 15c on 16c blue .35 .20
 a. Surcharge omitted, entire *375.00* —
 b. Surcharge on #U581, entire 100.00 —
 c. As "a," with surcharge printed on envelope flap 175.00 —

Auto Racing Issue

Indianapolis 500 Racing Car — U134

1978, Sept. 2

U587 U134 15c red, blue & black .35 .20
 a. Black omitted, entire *120.00*
 b. Black & blue omitted, entire —
 c. Red omitted, entire *120.00*
 d. Red & blue omitted, entire —

No. U576 Surcharged at left of Stamp Like No. U586

1978, Nov. 28 **Embossed**

U588 U123 15c on 13c org brn .35 .20

Precanceled Cut Squares
See note following No. U542.

U135

Weaver Violins — U136

U137

Eagle — U138

Star — U139

Eagle — U140

1979-82

Untagged (3.1c, 3.5c, 5.9c)

U589	U135	3.1c ultramarine		.20
U590	U136	3.5c purple		.20
U591	U137	5.9c brown		.20
U592	U138	(18c) violet	.45	.20
U593	U139	18c dark blue	.45	.20
U594	U140	(20c) brown	.45	.20

Issued: 3.1c, 5/18; 3.5c, 6/23; 5.9c, 2/17/82; #U592, 3/15/81; #U593, 4/2/81; #U594, 10/11/81.

Veterinary Medicine Issue

Seal of Veterinarians U141

Design on left side of envelope shows 5 animals and a bird in brown and "Veterinary Medicine" in gray.

1979, July 24

U595	U141	15c brown & gray	.50	.20
a.		Gray omitted, untagged, entire	750.00	
b.		Brown omitted, entire	1,050.	
c.		Gray & brown omitted, entire	—	

Olympic Games Issue

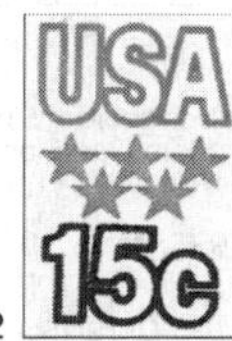

U142

Design (multicolored on left side of envelope) shows two soccer players with ball.

1979, Dec. 10

U596	U142	15c red, grn & blk	.60	.20
a.		Red & green omitted, untagged, entire	225.00	
b.		Blk omitted, untagged, entire	225.00	
c.		Blk & grn omitted, entire	225.00	
d.		Red omitted, untagged, entire	400.00	

22nd Olympic Games, Moscow, 7/19-8/3/80.

Bicycling Issue

Highwheeler Bicycle — U143

Design (on left side of envelope) shows racing bicycle.

1980, May 16

U597	U143	15c bl & rose claret	.40	.20
a.		Blue ("15c USA") omitted	100.00	

America's Cup Yacht Races Issue

Racing Yacht — U144

1980, Sept. 15

U598	U144	15c light blue	.40	.20

Italian Honeybee and Orange Blossoms U145

Bee & Petals Colorless Embossed

1980, Oct. 10

U599	U145	15c multicolored	.35	.20
a.		Brown ("USA 15c") omitted, entire	125.00	

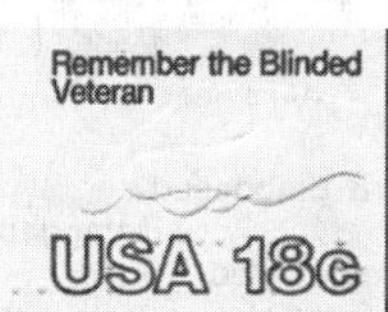

U146

Hand & Braille Colorless Embossed

1981, Oct. 11

U600	U146	18c blue & red	.45	.20
a.		Blue omitted, untagged, entire	—	
b.		Red omitted, entire	—	

Capitol Dome U147

1981, Nov. 13

U601	U147	20c deep magenta	.45	.20

U148

Illustration reduced.

1982, June 15

U602	U148	20c dk bl, blk & mag	.45	.20
a.		Dark blue omitted, entire	150.00	
b.		Dk bl & mag omitted, entire	—	

U149

1982, Aug. 6

U603	U149	20c purple & black	.65	.20
a.		Black omitted, entire	—	
b.		Purple omitted, entire	—	

U150

1983, Mar. 21 **Untagged**

U604	U150	5.2c orange		.20

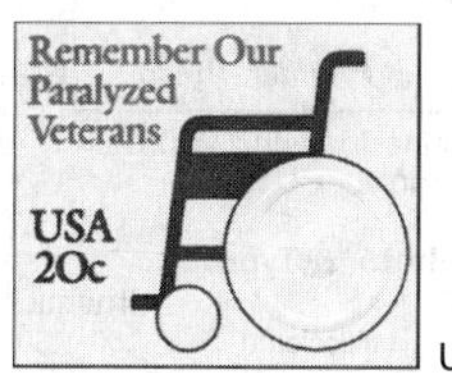

U151

1983, Aug. 3

U605	U151	20c red, bl & blk	.45	.20
a.		Red omitted, entire	—	
b.		Blue omitted, entire	—	
c.		Red & black omitted, entire	140.00	
d.		Blue & black omitted, entire	140.00	
e.		Black omitted, entire	225.00	

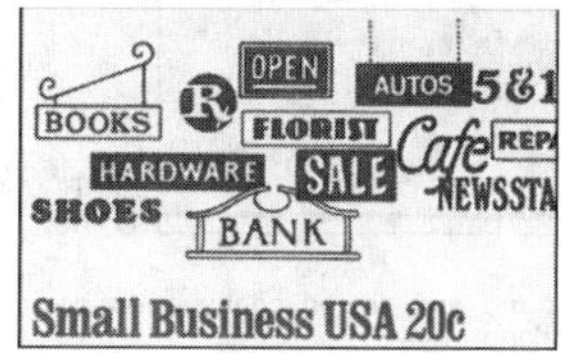

U152

Design shows storefronts at lower left.

Stamp and design continue on back of envelope.

1984, May 7 **Photo.**

U606	U152	20c multicolored	.50	.20

U153

1985, Feb. 1 **Embossed**

U607	U153	(22c) deep green	.55	.20

American Buffalo U154

1985, Feb. 25 **Embossed**

U608	U154	22c violet brown	.55	.20
a.		Untagged, precanceled with 3 blue lines		.20

Frigate U.S.S. Constitution, "Old Ironsides" — U155

Embossed

1985, May 3 **Untagged**

U609	U155	6c green blue		.20

Mayflower — U156

Embossed

1986, Dec. 4 **Untagged**

Precanceled

U610	U156	8.5c black & gray		.20

Stars U157

1988, Mar. 26 **Embossed & Typo.**

U611	U157	25c dk bl & dk red	.60	.20
a.		Dk red ("25") omitted, entire	75.00	—

Sea Gulls, Frigate USS Constellation — U158

Embossed & Typo.

1988, Apr. 12 **Untagged**

Precanceled

U612	U158	8.4c blk & brt bl		.20
a.		Black omitted, entire	600.00	

Snowflake — U159

"Holiday Greetings!" inscribed at lower left.

1988, Sept. 8 **Typo.**

U613	U159	25c dark red & green	.60	.25

Stars and "*Philatelic Mail*" Continuous in Dark Red Below Vignette — U160

1989, Mar. 10 **Typo.**

U614	U160	25c dk red & dp bl	.50	.25

"USA" and Stars — U161

1989, July 10 **Typo.** **Unwmk.**

U615	U161	25c dk red & dp bl	.50	.25
a.		Dark red omitted, entire	—	

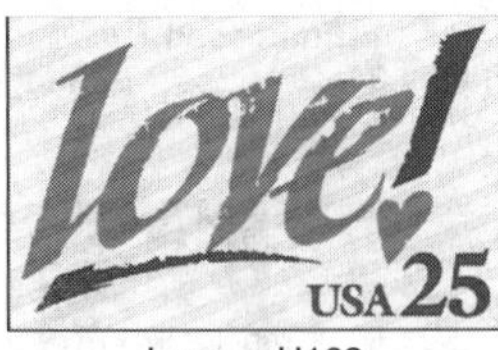

Love — U162

Litho. & Typo.

1989, Sept. 25 Unwmk.

U616 U162 25c dk red & br blue .50 .25
a. Dark red & bright blue omitted, entire 175.00

No. U616 has light blue lines printed diagonally over the entire surface of the envelope.

Shuttle Docking at Space Station — U163

1989, Dec. 3 Typo. Unwmk.

U617 U163 25c ultramarine .90 .60
a. Ultramarine omitted, entire 600.00

A hologram, visible through the die cut window to the right of "USA 25," is affixed to the inside of the envelope. Available only in No. 9 size. No. 9 envelopes are 225mm by 100mm.
See Nos. U625, U639.

Vince Lombardi Trophy, Football Players — U164

1990, Sept. 9 Litho. Unwmk.

U618 U164 25c vermilion .90 .60

A hologram, visible through the die cut window to the right of "USA 25," is affixed to the inside of the envelope.

Star — U165

Has embossed bars above and below the design.

1991, Jan. 24 Embossed & Typo.

U619 U165 29c ultra & rose .60 .30
a. Ultramarine omitted, entire 600.00
b. Rose omitted, entire 400.00

Precanceled Cut Squares
See note following No. U542.

Birds — U166

Stamp and design continue on back of envelope.

1991, May 3 Typo. Wmk.
Untagged
Precanceled

U620 U166 11.1c blue & red .20

Love — U167

1991, May 9 Litho.

U621 U167 29c lt bl, mar & brt rose .60 .30
a. Bright rose omitted, entire 500.00

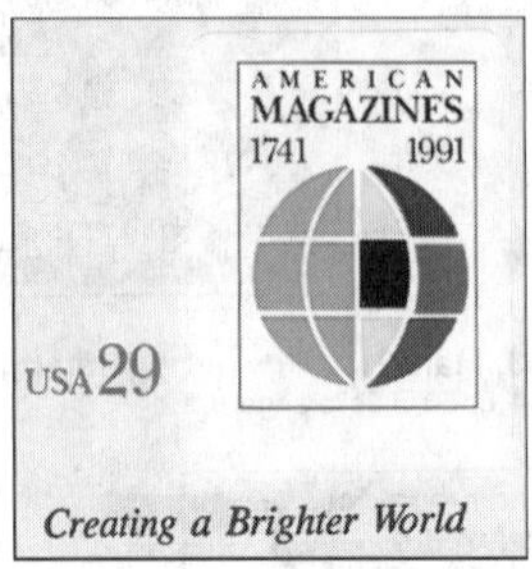

Magazine Industry, 250th Anniv. — U168

Photo. & Typo.

1991, Oct. 7 Unwmk.

U622 U168 29c multicolored .60 .30

The photogravure vignette, visible through the die cut window to the right of "USA 29," is affixed to the inside of the envelope. Available only in No. 10 size.

Star U169

Stamp and design continue on back of envelope.

1991, July 20 Typo.

U623 U169 29c ultra & rose .60 .30
a. Ultra omitted, entire —
b. Rose omitted, entire —

Lined with a blue design to provide security for enclosures. Available only in No. 9 size.

Country Geese U170

1991, Nov. 8 Litho. & Typo. Wmk.

U624 U170 29c blue gray & yel .60 .60

Space Shuttle Type of 1989

1992, Jan. 21 Typo. Unwmk.

U625 U163 29c yellow green .90 .50

A hologram, visible through the die cut window to the right of "USA 29," is affixed to the inside of the envelope. Available only in No. 10 size.
See No. U617a for envelopes with hologram only.

U171

Typo. & Litho.

1992, Apr. 10 Unwmk. *Die Cut*

U626 U171 29c multicolored .60 .30

The lithographed vignette, visible through the die cut window to the right of "USA 29," is affixed to the inside of the envelope.

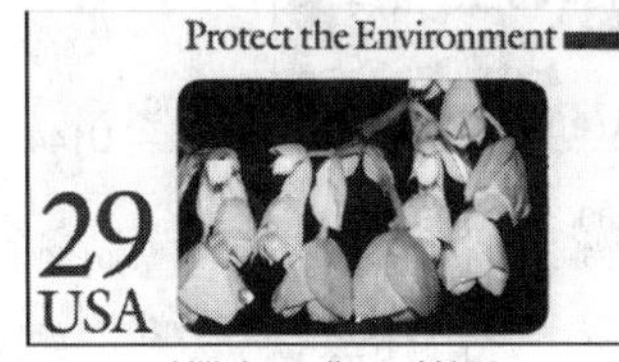

Hillebrandia — U172

Illustration reduced.

1992, Apr. 22

U627 U172 29c multicolored .60 .30

The lithographed vignette, visible through the die cut window to the right of "29 USA," is affixed to the inside of the envelope.

U173

Typo. & Embossed

1992, May 19 Untagged
Precanceled

U628 U173 19.8c red & blue .40

Disabled Americans

U174

1992, July 22 Typo. Unwmk.

U629 U174 29c red & blue .60 .30

U175

Illustration reduced.

Typo. & Litho.

1993, Oct. 2 Unwmk. *Die Cut*

U630 U175 29c multicolored .90 .50

The lithographed vignette, visible through the die cut window to the right of "USA 29," is affixed to the inside of the envelope.

U176

Typo. & Embossed

1994, Sept. 17 Unwmk.

U631 U176 29c brown & black .60 .30
a. Blk ("29/USA") omitted, entire 400.00

See No. U638.

Liberty Bell — U177

Typo. & Embossed

1995, Jan. 3 Unwmk.

U632 U177 32c greenish bl & bl .65 .30
a. Greenish bl omitted, entire 500.00
b. Blue ("USA 32") omitted, entire 150.00

U178

Design size: 49x38mm (#U633), 53x44mm (#U634).
Stamp and design continue on back of envelope.

1995 Typo. Unwmk.

U633 U178 (32c) blue & red .65 .30
U634 U178 (32c) blue & red .65 .30
a. Red and tagging omitted, entire 500.00
b. Blue omitted, entire 500.00

Originally, Nos. U633-U634 were only available through the Philatelic Fulfillment Center after their announcement 1/12/95.

U179

Design size: 58x25mm.
Stamp and design continue on back of envelope.

1995, Mar. 10 Typo. Unwmk.
Precanceled

U635 U179 (5c) grn & red brn .20

Graphic Eagle — U180

1995, Mar. 10 Typo. Unwmk.
Precanceled

U636 U180 (10c) dark car & bl .20

Spiral Heart — U181

1995, May 12 Typo. Unwmk.

U637 U181 32c red, *light blue* .65 .30

Liberty Bell Type of 1995

1995, May 16 Typo. Unwmk.

U638 U177 32c greenish bl & bl .65 .30
 a. Greenish blue omitted, entire —

Space Shuttle Type of 1989
Unwmk.

1995, Sept. 22 Typo. *Die Cut*

U639 U163 32c carmine rose .65 .35

A hologram, visible through the die cut window to the right of "USA 32," is affixed to the inside of the envelope.

U182

Typo. & Litho.

1996, Apr. 20 Unwmk. *Die Cut*

U640 U182 32c multicolored .60 .30

The lithographed vignette, visible through the die cut window to the right of "USA 32c," is affixed to the inside of the envelope.

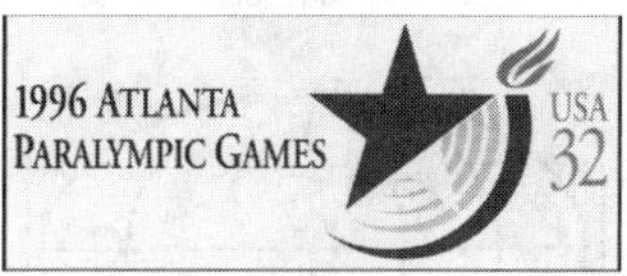

U183

1996, May 2

U641 U183 32c multicolored .60 .30
 a. Blue & red omitted, entire —
 b. Blue & gold omitted, entire *500.00*
 c. Red omitted, entire —
 d. Black & red omitted, entire *500.00*

U184

Typo. & Embossed

1999, Jan. 11 Unwmk.

U642 U184 33c yel, bl & red .65 .30
 a. Tagging bar to right of design .65 .30
 b. Blue omitted, entire —
 c. Yellow omitted, entire —

Typo.

U643 U184 33c blue & red .65 .30

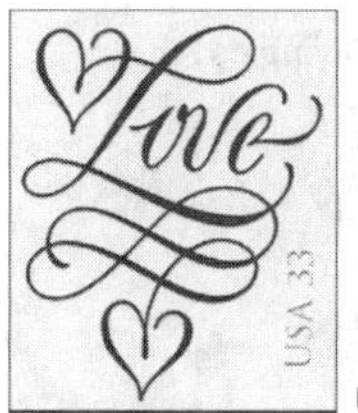

U185

1999, Jan. 28 Litho.

U644 U185 33c violet .65 .30

Lincoln — U186

Typo. & Litho.

1999, June 5 Unwmk.

U645 U186 33c blue & black .65 .30

Eagle U187

Unwmk.

2001, Jan. 7 Typo. Tagged

U646 U187 34c blue gray & gray .65 .30
 a. Blue gray omitted, entire —

Many color shades known.

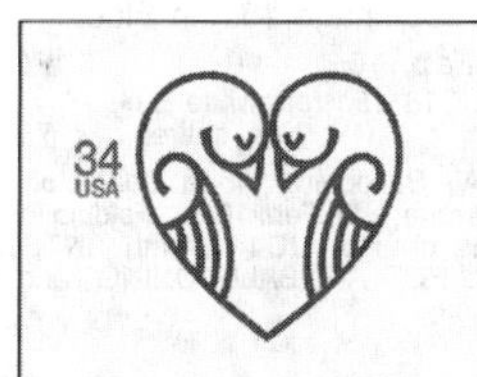

Lovebirds — U188

2001, Feb. 14 Litho. Unwmk.

U647 U188 34c rose & dull violet .65 .30

Community Colleges, Cent. — U189

2001, Feb. 20 Typo. Unwmk.

U648 U189 34c dk bl & org brn .65 .30

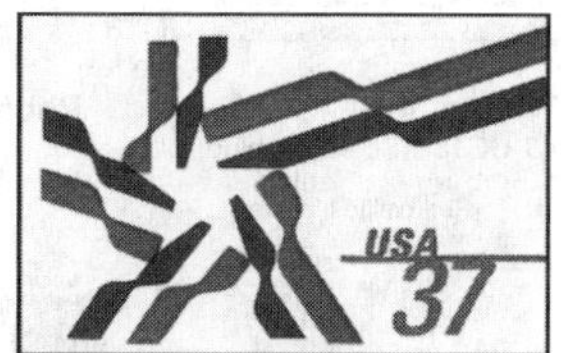

Ribbon Star — U190

2002, June 7 Typo. Unwmk.

U649 U190 37c red, blue & gray .75 .35

Type of 1995 Inscribed "USA / Presorted / Standard"

2002, Aug. 8 Typo. Unwmk.
Precanceled

U650 U180 (10c) dark carmine & blue .20

AIR POST STAMPED ENVELOPES & AIR LETTER SHEETS

UC1

UC2

UC1 — Vertical rudder is not semi-circular but slopes down to the left. The tail of the plane projects into the G of POSTAGE.

UC2 — Vertical rudder is semi-circular. The tail of the plane touches but does not project into the G of POSTAGE.

6c — Same as UC2 except 3 types of numeral:
Die 2a—Numeral "6" 6½mm wide.
Die 2b—Numeral "6" 6mm wide.
Die 2c—Numeral "6" 5½mm wide.
Die 3—Vertical rudder leans forward. "S" closer to "O" than to "T" of POSTAGE. "E" of POSTAGE has short center bar.

1929-44 Embossed

UC1 UC1 5c blue 3.50 2.00
 a. Orange & blue border, type b 350.00
UC2 UC2 5c blue 11.00 5.00
UC3 UC2 6c org, die 2a ('34) 1.50 .40
 a. See footnote *4,000.*
UC4 UC2 6c org, die 2b ('42) 2.75 2.00
UC5 UC2 6c org, die 2c ('44) .75 .30
UC6 UC2 6c org, die 3 ('42) 1.00 .35
 a. 6c org, *blue* (error), entire *3,500.* *2,400.*
UC7 UC2 8c ol grn ('32) 13.00 3.50

No. UC3a is similiar in design to UC3, with added impression of 3c pur (#U436a).
The entire is without border.

Surcharged in black on envelopes indicated by numbers in parentheses

1945

UC8 U93 6c on 2c (U429) 1.25 .65
 a. On U429f, die 7 2.25 1.50
 b. On U429g die 8 2.25 1.75
 c. On U429h, die 9 10.00 7.50
 d. 6c on 1c grn, error, (U420) *1,750.*
 e. 6c on 3c pur, error, (U436a) *2,000.*
 f. 6c on 3c purple, error, *amb* (U437a) *3,000.*
 g. 6c on 3c vio, error, (U526) *3,000.*
UC9 U95 6c on 2c (U525) 70.00 35.00

Surcharged in Black

Surcharged on 6c Orange Air Post Envelopes without borders

1946

UC10 UC2 5c on 6c, die 2a 2.75 1.50
 a. Double surcharge 60.00
UC11 UC2 5c on 6c, die 2b 9.00 5.50
UC12 UC2 5c on 6c, die 2c .75 .50
 a. Double surcharge 60.00 60.00
UC13 UC2 5c on 6c, die 3 .80 .60
 a. Double surcharge 60.00

The 6c borderless envelopes and the revalued envelopes were issued primarily for use to and from members of the armed forces.
The 5c rate came into effect Oct. 1, 1946.

DC-4 Skymaster UC3

Die 1. The end of the wing at the right is a smooth curve. The juncture of the front end of the plane and the engine forms an acute angle. The first T of STATES and the E's of UNITED STATES lean to the left.

Die 2. The end of the wing at the right is a straight line. The juncture of the front end of the plane and the engine is wide open. The first T of STATES and the E's of UNITED STATES lean to the right.

1946 Embossed

UC14 UC3 5c carmine, die 1 .75 .20
UC15 UC3 5c carmine, die 2 .85 .25

See Nos. UC18, UC26.

DC-4 Skymaster — UC4

Letter Sheet for Foreign Postage

"Air Letter" on face, 2-line inscription on back.

1947, Apr. 29 Typo.

UC16 UC4 10c brt red, *pale bl*, entire 8.50 6.00
 a. "Air Letter" on face, 4-line inscription on back ('51), entire 17.50 14.00
 b. As "a," 10c chocolate, *pale bl*, entire 450.00
 c. "Air Letter" and "Aerogramme" on face, 4-line inscription on back ('53), entire 45.00 12.50
 d. As "c," 3-line inscription on back ('55), entire 9.00 8.00

Washington & Franklin, Early and Modern Mail-carrying Vehicles — UC5

Embossed, Rotary Press Printing

1947, May 21

UC17 UC5 5c car, (22¼mm high) .40 .25
 a. Flat plate (21¾mm high) .50 .30

Cent. of the 1st postage stamps issued by the U.S. Government.

Type of 1946

Type I- 6's lean to right.
Type II- 6's upright.

1950, Sept. 22

UC18 UC3 6c carmine, type I .35 .20
 a. Type II .75 .25

Several other types differ slightly from the two listed.

Nos. UC14, UC15, UC18 Surcharged in Red

1951

UC19 UC3 6c on 5c car, die 1 .85 .50
UC20 UC3 6c on 5c car, die 2 .80 .50
 a. 6c on 6c car, error, entire *1,500.*
 b. 6c on 5c, double surcharge *500.00* —

Nos. UC14, UC15 and UC17 Surcharged in Red at Left of Stamp

1952

UC21 UC3 6c on 5c, die 1 27.50 17.50
UC22 UC3 6c on 5c, die 2 4.00 2.50
 a. Double surcharge 200.00
UC23 UC5 6c on 5c *1,250.*

The 6c on 4c black (No. U440) is believed to be a favor printing.

Eagle in Flight — UC6

1956, May 2 **Embossed**
UC25 UC6 6c red .75 .50

FIPEX, NYC, Apr. 28-May 6. Two types exist, differing mainly in the clouds at top.

Skymaster Type of 1946

1958, July 31
UC26 UC3 7c blue .65 .50

Nos. UC3-UC5, UC18 and UC25 Surcharged in Green

1958
UC27 UC2 6c + 1c, die 2a 325.00 225.00
UC28 UC2 6c + 1c, die 2b 75.00 75.00
UC29 UC2 6c + 1c, die 2c 45.00 50.00
UC30 UC3 6c + 1c, type I 1.00 .50
a. Type II 1.00 .50
UC31 UC6 6c + 1c 1.00 .50

Jet Airliner UC7

Letter Sheet for Foreign Postage.

Two types:
Type I - Back inscription in 3 lines.
Type II - Back inscription in 2 lines.

1958-59 **Typo.**
UC32 UC7 10c bl & red, *bl*, II ('59), entire 6.00 5.00
a. Type I ('58), entire 10.00 5.00
b. Red omitted, II, entire —
c. Blue omitted, II, entire 1,000.
d. Red omitted, I, entire 1,000.

Silhouette of Jet Airliner—UC8

1958, Nov. 21 **Embossed**
UC33 UC8 7c blue .60 .25

1960, Aug. 18
UC34 UC8 7c carmine .60 .25

Jet Plane and Globe UC9

Letter Sheet for Foreign Postage

1961, Nov. 16 **Typo.**
UC35 UC9 11c red & bl, *bl*, entire 2.75 1.50
a. Red omitted, entire 1,000.
b. Blue omitted, entire 1,000.

UC10

UC11

1962, Nov. 17 **Embossed**
UC36 UC10 8c red .55 .20

1965, Jan. 7
UC37 UC11 8c red .35 .20
a. Tagged ('67) 3.50 .30

No. UC37a has a luminescent panel ⅜x1 inches at left of stamp. It glows orange red under ultraviolet light.

Pres. John F. Kennedy and Jet Plane UC12

Letter Sheets for Foreign Postage

1965-67 **Typo.**
UC38 UC12 11c red & dk bl, *blue*, entire 3.25 1.50
UC39 UC12 13c red & dk bl, *blue*, entire 3.00 1.50
a. Red omitted 900.00
b. Dark blue omitted 500.00

Issued: 11c, 5/29/65; 13c, 5/29/67.

UC13

1968, Jan. 8 **Tagged** **Embossed**
UC40 UC13 10c red .50 .20

No. UC37 Surcharged in Red

1968, Feb. 5
UC41 UC11 8c + 2c red .65 .20

Tagging

Envelopes and Letter Sheets from No. UC42 onward are tagged unless otherwise noted.

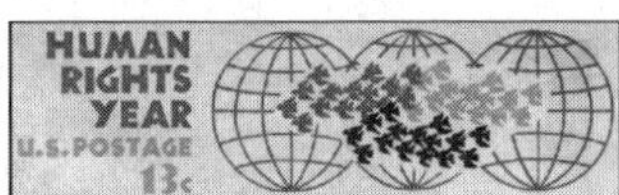

Globes and Flock of Birds — UC14

Letter Sheet for Foreign Postage

1968, Dec. 3 **Photo.**
UC42 UC14 13c gray, brn, org & blk, *blue*, entire 8.00 4.00
a. Orange omitted, entire —
b. Brown omitted, entire 500.00
c. Black omitted, entire —

Intl. Human Rights Year, and 20th anniv. of the UN Declaration of Human Rights.

UC15

1971, May 6 **Embossed**
UC43 UC15 11c red & blue .50 .20

Birds in Flight and "usa" — UC16

Letter Sheet for Foreign Postage
"postage 15c" in Gray

1971, May 28 **Photo.**
UC44 UC16 15c gray, red, white & blue, *blue*, entire 1.50 1.10
a. "AEROGRAMME" added, entire 1.50 1.10

Folding instructions (2 steps) in capitals on No. UC44; (4 steps) in upper and lower case on No. UC44a. No. UC44a issued Dec. 13.
See No. UC46.

No. UC40 Surcharged in Green

1971, June 28 **Embossed**
UC45 UC13 10c + (1c) red 1.50 .20

Letter Sheet for Foreign Postage
"usa" Type of 1971

Design: Three balloons and cloud at left in address section; no birds beside stamp.

"postage 15c" in Blue

1973, Feb. 10 **Photo.**
UC46 UC16 15c red, white & bl, *blue*, entire .75 .40

Hot Air Ballooning World Championships, Albuquerque, NM, Feb. 10-17. Folding instructions as on No. UC44a, with "INTERNATIONAL HOT AIR BALLOONING" added to inscription.

Bird in Flight — UC17

1973, Dec. 1 **Embossed**
UC47 UC17 13c rose red .30 .20

Beginning with No. UC48 all letter sheets are for Foreign Postage unless noted otherwise.

UC18

1974, Jan. 4 **Photo.**
UC48 UC18 18c red & blue, *blue*, entire .90 .30
a. Red omitted, entire —

UC19

Design: "NATO" and NATO emblem in multicolor at left in address section.

1974, Apr. 4 **Photo.**
UC49 UC19 18c red & blue, *blue*, entire .90 .40

25th anniv. of NATO.

UC20

1976, Jan. 16 **Photo.**
UC50 UC20 22c red & blue, *blue*, entire .90 .40

UC21

1978, Nov. 3 **Photo.**
UC51 UC21 22c bl, *bl*, entire .70 .25

UC22

Design (multicolored in bottom left corner) shows discus thrower.

1979, Dec. 5 **Photo.**
UC52 UC22 22c red, blk & grn, *bluish*, entire 1.50 .25

22nd Olympic Games, Moscow, July 19-Aug. 3, 1980.

UC23

Design shows Statue of Liberty at lower left. Inscribed "Tour the United States," folding area shows tourist attractions.

1980-81 **Photo.**
UC53 UC23 30c bl, red & brn, *bl*, entire .65 1.00
a. Red ("30c") omitted, entire 70.00
UC54 UC23 30c yel, magenta, bl & blk, *bl*, entire ('81) .65 1.00

Issued: Dec. 29, 1980; Sept. 21, 1981.

UC24

"Made in USA . . . world's best buys."

1982, Sept. 16 **Photo.**
UC55 UC24 30c multi, *bl*, entire .65 1.00

World Communications Year Issue

World Map Showing Locations of Satellite Tracking Stations — UC25

1983, Jan. 7 **Photo.**
UC56 UC25 30c multi, *bl*, entire .65 1.00

1984 Olympics

UC26

1983, Oct. 14 **Photo.**
UC57 UC26 30c multi, *bl*, entire .65 1.00

UC27

Design: Satellite over Earth at lower left, with Landsat photographs on folding area. Inscribed: Landsat views the Earth.

1985, Feb. 14 **Photo.**

UC58 UC27 36c multi, *bl*, entire .70 *1.00*

National Tourism Week

Urban Skyline UC28

1985, May 21 **Photo.**

UC59 UC28 36c multi, *bl*, entire .70 *1.00*
a. Black omitted, entire —

Mark Twain (1835-1910) and Halley's Comet

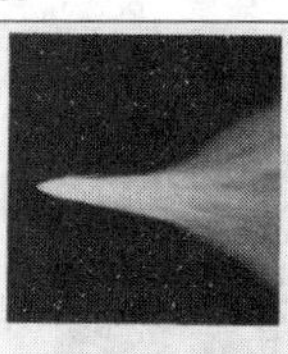

Comet Tail Viewed from Space — UC29

1985, Dec. 4 **Photo.**

UC60 UC29 36c multi, entire .90 *1.50*

UC30

1988, May 9 **Litho.**

UC61 UC30 39c multi, entire .80 *1.00*
a. Tagging bar to left of design ('89) .80 *1.00*

On No. UC61, the tagging bar is between "USA" and "39."

Montgomery Blair and Pres. Lincoln — UC31

Design: Mail bags and text at lower left. Globe, locomotive, bust of Blair, UPU emblem and text contained on reverse folding area.

1989, Nov. 20 **Litho.**

UC62 UC31 39c multi, entire .80 *1.00*

UC32

1991, May 17 **Litho.**

UC63 UC32 45c gray, red & bl, *blue*, entire .90 *1.00*
a. White paper, entire .90 *1.00*

Thaddeus Lowe (1832-1913), Balloonist — UC33

1995, Sept. 23 **Litho.**

UC64 UC33 50c multi, *blue*, entire 1.00 1.00

Voyageurs Natl. Park, Minnesota UC34

1999, May 15 **Litho.** **Tagged**

UC65 UC34 60c multi, *blue*, entire 1.25 1.00

POSTAL CARDS
"R.F." CONTROL OVERPRINT
STAMPED ENVELOPES
are listed in the Scott Specialized Catalogue of United States Stamps.
NEWSPAPER WRAPPERS
included in listings of Stamped Envelopes with prefix "W" instead of "U"
LETTER SHEETS included with Stamped Envelopes

OFFICIAL STAMPED ENVELOPES

Post Office Department

"2" 9mm high — UO1

"3" 9mm high — UO2

"6" 9½mm high — UO3

1873

UO1	UO1	2c black, *lemon*	20.00	9.00
UO2	UO2	3c black, *lemon*	12.00	6.00
+UO3	UO2	3c black	*22,500.*	
UO4	UO3	6c black, *lemon*	22.50	15.00

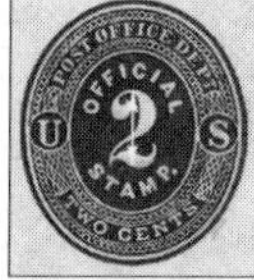
"2" 9¼mm high — UO4

"3" 9¼mm high — UO5

"6" 10½mm high — UO6

1874-79

UO5	UO4	2c black, *lemon*	8.50	4.00
UO6	UO4	2c black	110.00	32.50
UO7	UO5	3c black, *lemon*	3.25	.85
UO8	UO5	3c black	3,000.	2,250.
UO9	UO5	3c black, *amber*	85.00	35.00
UO10	UO5	3c black, *blue*	*45,000.*	
UO11	UO5	3c blue, *blue*	*45,000.*	
UO12	UO6	6c black, *lemon*	10.00	5.50
UO13	UO6	6c black	3,000.	1,500.

Postal Service

UO7

1877

UO14	UO7	black	6.50	3.75
UO15	UO7	black, *amber*	200.00	27.50
UO16	UO7	blue, *amber*	175.00	30.00
UO17	UO7	blue, *blue*	8.50	6.00
		Nos. UO14-UO17 (4)	390.00	67.25

War Department

Franklin UO8

Jackson UO9

UO8 — Bust points to the end of "N" of "ONE."

UO9 — Bust narrow at the back.

Washington UO10

Lincoln UO11

UO10 — Queue projects below the bust.

UO11 — Neck very long at the back.

Jefferson UO12

Clay UO13

UO12 — Queue forms straight line with bust.

UO13 — Ear partly concealed by hair, mouth large, chin prominent.

Webster UO14

Scott UO15

UO14 — Has side whiskers.

Hamilton — UO16

Back of bust very narrow, chin almost straight; the labels containing the letters "U S" are exactly parallel.

1873

Reay Issue

UO18	UO8	1c dark red	600.00	300.00
UO19	UO9	2c dark red	1,900.	400.00
UO20	UO10	3c dark red	62.50	40.00
UO21	UO10	3c dark red, *amb*	*40,000.*	
UO22	UO10	3c dark red, *cr*	800.00	250.00
UO23	UO11	6c dark red	275.00	90.00
UO24	UO11	6c dark red, *cr*	8,250.	425.00
UO25	UO12	10c dark red	*17,500.*	1,500.
UO26	UO13	12c dark red	150.00	50.00
UO27	UO14	15c dark red	140.00	55.00
UO28	UO15	24c dark red	150.00	50.00
UO29	UO16	30c dark red	500.00	150.00

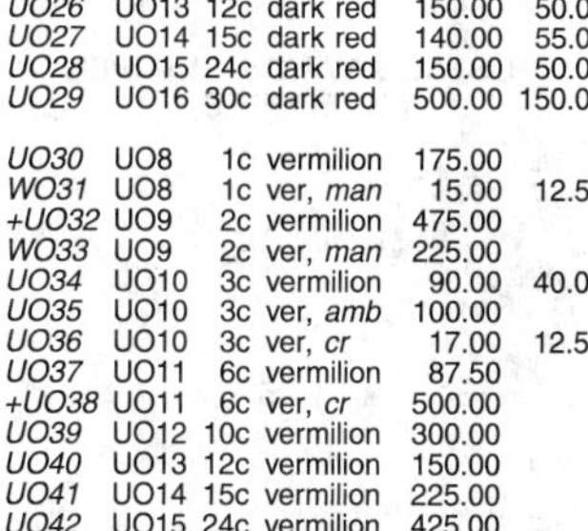

UO30	UO8	1c vermilion	175.00	
WO31	UO8	1c ver, *man*	15.00	12.50
+UO32	UO9	2c vermilion	475.00	
WO33	UO9	2c ver, *man*	225.00	
UO34	UO10	3c vermilion	90.00	40.00
UO35	UO10	3c ver, *amb*	100.00	
UO36	UO10	3c ver, *cr*	17.00	12.50
UO37	UO11	6c vermilion	87.50	
+UO38	UO11	6c ver, *cr*	500.00	
UO39	UO12	10c vermilion	300.00	
UO40	UO13	12c vermilion	150.00	
UO41	UO14	15c vermilion	225.00	
UO42	UO15	24c vermilion	425.00	
UO43	UO16	30c vermilion	500.00	

UO17

UO18

UO17--Bottom serif on "S" is thick and short, bust at bottom below hair forms sharp point.

UO18--Bottom serif on "S" is thick and short front part of bust is rounded.

UO19

UO20

UO19--Bottom serif on "S" is short, queue does not project below bust.

UO20--Neck very short at the back.

UO21

UO22

UO21--Knot of queue stands out prominently.

UO22--Ear prominent, chin receding.

UO23

UO24

UO23--Has no side whiskers, forelock projects above head.

UO24--Back of bust rather broad; chin slopes considerably; the labels containing letters "U S" are not exactly parallel.

1875

Plimpton Issue

UO44 UO17 1c red 150.00 80.00
+UO45 UO17 1c red, *amb* 925.00
+UO45A UO17 1c red, *org* *37,500.*
WO46 UO17 1c red, *man* 4.25 2.75
UO47 UO18 2c red 110.00 —
UO48 UO18 2c red, *amb* 30.00 14.00
UO49 UO18 2c red, *org* 50.00 13.50
WO50 UO18 2c red, *man* 87.50 40.00
UO51 UO19 3c red 14.00 9.00
UO52 UO19 3c red, *amb* 17.00 9.00
UO53 UO19 3c red, *cr* 7.00 3.75
UO54 UO19 3c red, *bl* 3.75 2.75
UO55 UO19 3c red, *fawn* 4.75 2.75
UO56 UO20 6c red 50.00 30.00
UO57 UO20 6c red, *amb* 80.00 40.00
UO58 UO20 6c red, *cr* 210.00 85.00
UO59 UO21 10c red 225.00 80.00
UO60 UO21 10c red, *amb* 1,100.
UO61 UO22 12c red 52.50 40.00
UO62 UO22 12c red, *amb* 700.00
UO63 UO22 12c red, *cr* 650.00
UO64 UO23 15c red 225.00 140.00
UO65 UO23 15c red, *amb* 950.00
UO66 UO23 15c red, *cr* 750.00
UO67 UO24 30c red 190.00 140.00
UO68 UO24 30c red, *amb* 950.00
UO69 UO24 30c red, *cr* 1,000.

POSTAL SAVINGS STAMPED ENVELOPES

UO25

1911

UO70 UO25 1c green 70.00 20.00
UO71 UO25 1c grn, *oriental buff* 200.00 67.50
UO72 UO25 2c carmine 11.50 3.75
a. 2c car, *manila* (error) *1,750.* *1,000.*

Used Values

Catalogue values for regularly used entires. Those with first day cancels generally sell for much less.

OFFICIAL MAIL

UO26

1983, Jan. 12

UO73 UO26 20c blue, entire 1.25 *30.00*

UO27

1985, Feb. 26

UO74 UO27 22c blue, entire .90 *10.00*

UO28

1987, Mar. 2 **Typo.**

UO75 UO28 22c blue, entire 1.00 *20.00*

Used exclusively to mail US Savings Bonds.

UO29

1988, Mar. 22 **Typo.**

UO76 UO29 (25c) blk & bl, entire 1.10 *20.00*

Used exclusively to mail US Saving Bonds.

UO30

1988, Apr. 11 **Embossed & Typo.**

UO77 UO30 25c blk & bl, entire .80 *15.00*
a. Denomination & lettering as No. UO78 .80 *15.00*

UO31

1988, Apr. 11 **Typo.**

UO78 UO31 25c blk & bl, entire .90 *25.00*
a. Denomination & lettering as No. UO77 .90 *25.00*

Used exclusively to mail US Saving Bonds.

Used Values

The appearance in the marketplace of postally used examples of the entires used to mail passports (Nos. UO79-UO82, UO86-UO87) is so infrequent that it currently is not possible to establish accurate values.

1990, Mar. 17 **Typo.**

UO79 UO31 45c blk & bl, entire 1.25 *85.00*
UO80 UO31 65c blk & bl, entire 1.75 *150.00*

Used exclusively to mail US passports.

UO32

Type UO32: sharp impression, stars and "E Pluribus Unum" are clear and distinct. Official is 14½mm long, USA is 17mm long.

1990, Aug. 10 **Typo.**

UO81 UO32 45c blk & bl, entire 1.25 *75.00*
UO82 UO32 65c blk & bl, entire 1.60 *125.00*

Used exclusively to mail US passports.

UO33

1991, Jan. 22 **Typo.** **Wmk.**

UO83 UO33 (29c) blk & bl, entire 1.10 *20.00*

Used exclusively to mail US Saving Bonds.

UO34

1991, Apr. 6 **Typo. & Embossed**

UO84 UO34 29c blk & bl, entire .75 *2.00*

UO35

1991, Apr. 17 **Typo.** **Wmk.**

UO85 UO35 29c blk & bl, entire .70 *20.00*

Used exclusively to mail US Saving Bonds.

Consular Service, Bicent. UO36

1992, July 10 **Litho.** **Unwmk.**

UO86 UO36 52c bl & red, entire 1.60 —
a. 52c bl & red, *blue-white, entire* 1.50 —
UO87 UO36 75c bl & red, entire 3.00 —
a. 75c bl & red, *blue-white, entire* 2.50 —

Used exclusively to mail US passports.

Original issues have "USPS copyright" on left under flap. Reissues (Nos. UO86a and UO87a) have it at right.

UO37

Typo. & Embossed

1995-99 **Unwmk.**

UO88 UO37 32c bl & red, entire .80 *10.00*
UO89 UO37 33c bl & red, entire .70 *10.00*
UO90 UO37 34c bl & red, entire .85 —

Issued: 32c, 5/9; 33c, 2/22/99; 34c, 2/27/01.

Type of 1995

2002 **Typo. & Embossed** **Unwmk.**

UO91 UO37 37c blue & red, entire .90 —

Issued: 37c, 8/2/02.

OFFICIAL WRAPPERS

Included in listings of Official Stamped Envelopes with prefix letters "WO" instead of "UO"

REVENUE STAMPS

Nos. R1-R102 were used to pay taxes on documents and proprietary articles including playing cards. Until Dec. 25, 1862, the law stated that a revenue stamp could be used only for payment of the tax upon the particular instrument or article specified on its face. After that date stamps, except the Proprietary, could be used indiscriminately.

Values quoted are for pen-canceled copies. Stamps with handstamped cancellations sell at higher prices. Stamps canceled with cuts, punches or holes sell for less. See the Scott U.S. Specialized Catalogue.

General Issue

First Issue. Head of Washington in Oval. Various Frames as Illustrated.

Nos. R1b to R42b, part perforate, occur perforated sometimes at sides only and sometimes at top and bottom only. The higher values, part perforate, are perforated at sides only. Imperforate and part perforate revenues often bring much more in pairs or blocks than as single copies.

The experimental silk paper is a variety of the old paper and has only a very few minute fragments of fiber.

Some of the stamps were in use eight years and were printed several times. Many color variations occurred, particularly when unstable pigments were used and the color was intended to be purple or violet, such as the 4c Proprietary, 30c and $2.50 stamps. Before 1868 dull colors predominate on these and the early red stamps. In later printings of the 4c Proprietary, 30c and $2.50 stamps, red predominates in the mixture, and on the dollar values the red is brighter. The early $1.90 stamp is dull purple, imperf. or perforated. In a later printing, perforated only, the purple is darker.

R1

R2

R3

R4 R5

1862-71 **Engr.** ***Perf. 12***

Old Paper

R1c R1 1c Express, red 1.25
a. Imperf. 60.00
b. Part perf. 40.00
d. Silk paper 100.00
e. Vertical pair, imperf. between, old paper *200.00*
R2c R1 1c Playing Cards, red 160.00
a. Imperf. 1,200.
b. Part perf. 1,250.
R3c R1 1c Proprietary, red .50
a. Imperf. 775.00
b. Part perf. 175.00
d. Silk paper 27.50
R4c R1 1c Telegraph, red 12.00
a. Imperf. 450.00
R5c R2 2c Bank Check, blue .25
a. Imperf. 1.00
b. Part perf. 1.75
e. Vert. pair, imperf btwn., old paper *400.00*
R6c R2 2c Bank Check, orange .25
b. Part perf. 55.00
d. Silk paper 250.00
e. Old paper, *green* 475.00
R7c R2 2c Certificate, blue 30.00
a. Imperf. 12.50
R8c R2 2c Certificate, orange 27.50
R9c R2 2c Express, blue .40
a. Imperf. 12.50
b. Part perf. 20.00
R10c R2 2c Express, orange 8.50
b. Part perf. *750.00*
d. Silk paper 90.00
R11c R2 2c Playing Cards, blue 4.00
b. Part perf. 200.00
R12c R2 2c Playing Cards, org 42.50
R13c R2 2c Proprietary, blue .40
a. Imperf. *500.00*
b. Part perf. 150.00
d. Silk paper 70.00
e. Ultramarine 200.00
R14c R2 2c Proprietary, orange 40.00
R15c R2 2c U.S. Int. Rev., orange ('64) .20
a. Imperf —
d. Silk paper .25
e. Old paper, *green* 650.00
R16c R3 3c For. Exch., green 4.50
b. Part perf. 300.00
d. Silk paper 70.00
R17c R3 3c Playing Cards, green ('63) 140.00
a. Imperf. *12,500.*
R18c R3 3c Proprietary, green 4.25
b. Part perf. 350.00
d. Silk paper 45.00
e. Printed on both sides, old paper *3,500.*
R19c R3 3c Telegraph, green 2.75
a. Imperf. 75.00
b. Part perf. 27.50

R20c R3 4c Inland Exch., brown ('63) 1.75
d. Silk paper 70.00
R21c R3 4c Playing Cards, slate ('63) 500.00
R22c R3 4c Proprietary, purple 6.50
a. Imperf. —
b. Part perf. 250.00
d. Silk paper 90.00

Many shade and color variations of Nos. R21-R22. See foreword, "Revenue Stamps."

R23c R3 5c Agreement, red .30
d. Silk paper 1.50
R24c R3 5c Certificate, red .30
a. Imperf. 2.50
b. Part perf. 13.00
d. Silk paper .35
R25c R3 5c Express, red .30
a. Imperf. 5.00
b. Part perf. 7.00
R26c R3 5c Foreign Exch., red .30
b. Part perf. —
d. Silk paper 300.00
R27c R3 5c Inland Exch., red .25
a. Imperf. 7.50
b. Part perf. 5.00
d. Silk paper 17.50
R28c R3 5c Playing Cards, red ('63) 25.00
R29c R3 5c Proprietary, red ('64) 25.00
d. Silk paper 140.00
R30c R3 6c Inland Exch., org ('63) 1.75
d. Silk paper 85.00
R31c R3 6c Proprietary, org ('71) *1,700.*

Nearly all copies of No. R31 are faulty or repaired and poorly centered.

The Catalogue value is for a fine centered copy with minor faults which do not detract from its appearance.

R32c R3 10c Bill of Lading, blue 1.00
a. Imperf. 47.50
b. Part perf. 325.00
R33c R3 10c Certificate, blue .25
a. Imperf. 150.00
b. Part perf. 350.00
d. Silk paper 5.00
R34c R3 10c Contract, blue .50
b. Part perf. 225.00
d. Silk paper 2.25
e. Ultramarine, part perf. 425.00
f. Ultramarine, old paper 1.00
R35c R3 10c For. Exch., blue 10.00
d. Silk paper —
e. ultra, old paper 12.50
R36c R3 10c Inland Exch., blue .20
a. Imperf. 250.00
b. Part perf. 4.00
d. Silk paper 40.00
R37c R3 10c Power of Attorney, blue .75
a. Imperf. 500.00
b. Part perf. 25.00
R38c R3 10c Proprietary, blue ('64) 17.50
R39c R3 15c For. Exch., brown ('63) 15.00
R40c R3 15c Inland Exch., brown 1.25
a. Imperf. 37.50
b. Part perf. 12.50
R41c R3 20c For. Exch., red 40.00
a. Imperf. 50.00
R42c R3 20c Inland Exch., red .35
a. Imperf. 15.00
b. Part perf. 17.50
d. Silk paper —
R43c R4 25c Bond, red 2.50
a. Imperf. 175.00
b. Part perf. 6.00
R44c R4 25c Certificate, red .25
a. Imperf. 10.00
b. Part perf. 6.00
d. Silk paper 2.75
e. Printed on both sides, old paper *4,500.*
f. Impression of No. R48 on back, old paper —
R45c R4 25c Entry of Goods, red .75
a. Imperf. 17.50
b. Part perf. 80.00
d. Silk paper 35.00
R46c R4 25c Insurance, red .25
a. Imperf. 10.00
b. Part perf. 10.00
d. Silk paper 4.50
R47c R4 25c Life Insurance, red 6.50
a. Imperf. 35.00
b. Part perf. 325.00
R48c R4 25c Power of Attorney, red .30
a. Imperf. 7.50
b. Part perf. 27.50
R49c R4 25c Protest, red 6.75
a. Imperf. 30.00
b. Part perf. 400.00
R50c R4 25c Warehouse Receipt, red 30.00
a. Imperf. 47.50
b. Part perf. 350.00
R51c R4 30c For. Exch., lilac 52.50
a. Imperf. 75.00
b. Part perf. 1,150.
d. Silk paper —
R52c R4 30c Inland Exch., lilac 3.50
a. Imperf. 60.00
b. Part perf. 70.00
d. Silk paper —

Many shade and color variations of Nos. R51-R52. See foreword, "Revenue Stamps."

R53c R4 40c Inland Exch., brown 3.50
a. Imperf. 650.00
b. Part perf. 7.00
f. Double impression —
R54c R5 50c Conveyance, blue .20
a. Imperf. 17.00
b. Part perf. 1.60
d. Silk paper 3.00
e. Ultramarine, old paper .25
f. Ultramarine, silk paper —
R55c R5 50c Entry of Goods, blue .40
b. Part perf. 12.00
d. Silk paper 50.00
R56c R5 50c For. Exch., blue 6.50
a. Imperf. 55.00
b. Part perf. 65.00
R57c R5 50c Lease, blue 8.50
a. Imperf. 25.00
b. Part perf. 85.00
R58c R5 50c Life Insurance, blue 1.00
a. Imperf. 40.00
b. Part perf. 50.00
R59c R5 50c Mortgage, blue .50
a. Imperf. 17.00
b. Part perf. 2.50
d. Silk paper —
R60c R5 50c Original Process, blue .60
a. Imperf. 3.75
b. Part perf. *600.00*
d. Silk paper 1.60
R61c R5 50c Passage Ticket, blue 1.25
a. Imperf. 75.00
b. Part perf. 200.00
R62c R5 50c Probate of Will, blue 19.00
a. Imperf. 40.00
b. Part perf. 80.00
R63c R5 50c Surety Bond, blue .30
a. Imperf. 210.00
b. Part perf. 2.50
e. Ultramarine, old paper .75
R64c R5 60c Inland Exch., org 6.00
a. Imperf. 90.00
b. Part perf. 50.00
d. Silk paper 40.00
R65c R5 70c For. Exch., green 11.00
a. Imperf. 400.00
b. Part perf. 110.00
d. Silk paper 65.00

R6

R7

R8

R9

R10

(Illustration sideways)
R11

Old Paper

R66c R6 $1 Conveyance, red 24.00
a. Imperf. 17.50
b. Part perf. 500.00
d. Silk paper 100.00
R67c R6 $1 Entry of Goods, red 1.90
a. Imperf. 37.50
d. Silk paper 70.00
R68c R6 $1 For. Exch., red .60
a. Imperf. 80.00
d. Silk paper 65.00
R69c R6 $1 Inland Exch., red .45
a. Imperf. 15.00
b. Part perf. 375.00
d. Silk paper 3.00
R70c R6 $1 Lease, red 3.00
a. Imperf. 35.00
R71c R6 $1 Life Insurance, red 6.50
a. Imperf. 150.00
R72c R6 $1 Manifest, red 35.00
a. Imperf. 42.50
R73c R6 $1 Mortgage, red 175.00
a. Imperf. 25.00
R74c R6 $1 Passage Ticket, red 250.00
a. Imperf. 275.00
R75c R6 $1 Power of Attorney, red 2.10
a. Imperf. 75.00
R76c R6 $1 Probate of Will, red 45.00
a. Imperf. 75.00
R77c R7 $1.30 For. Exch., orange ('63) 60.00
a. Imperf. *4,000.*
R78c R7 $1.50 Inland Exch., blue 4.50
a. Imperf. 27.50
R79c R7 $1.60 For. Exch., green ('63) 120.00
a. Imperf. 1,000.
R80c R7 $1.90 For. Exch., pur ('63) 100.00
a. Imperf. *7,000.*
d. Silk paper —

Many shade and color variations of No. R80. See foreword, "Revenue Stamps."

R81c R8 $2 Conveyance, red 2.75
a. Imperf. 150.00
b. Part perf. 1,500.
d. Silk paper 27.50
R82c R8 $2 Mortgage, red 4.50
a. Imperf. 120.00
d. Silk paper 55.00
R83c R8 $2 Probate of Will, red ('63) 60.00
a. Imperf. *4,500.*
R84c R8 $2.50 Inland Exch., pur ('63) 11.00
a. Imperf. 5,500.
d. Silk paper 25.00
R85c R8 $3 Charter Party, green 6.50
a. Imperf. 140.00
d. Silk paper 110.00
e. Printed on both sides *2,000.*
g. Impression of #RS208 on back *4,000.*
R86c R8 $3 Manifest, green 40.00
a. Imperf. 140.00
R87c R8 $3.50 Inland Exch., blue ('63) 60.00
a. Imperf. *5,500.*
e. Printed on both sides *4,000.*

Many shade and color variations of the $2.50. See foreword, "Revenue Stamps." The $3.50 has stars in upper corners.

R88c R9 $5 Charter Party, red 6.00
a. Imperf. 250.00
d. Silk paper 75.00
R89c R9 $5 Conveyance, red 8.50
a. Imperf. 37.50
d. Silk paper 80.00
R90c R9 $5 Manifest, red 90.00
a. Imperf. 150.00
R91c R9 $5 Mortgage, red 20.00
a. Imperf. 125.00
R92c R9 $5 Probate of Will, red 20.00
a. Imperf. 500.00
R93c R9 $10 Charter Party, green 32.50
a. Imperf. 650.00
R94c R9 $10 Conveyance, green 70.00
a. Imperf. 110.00
R95c R9 $10 Mortgage, green 30.00
a. Imperf. 450.00
R96c R9 $10 Probate of Will, green 30.00
a. Imperf. 1,250.
R97c R10 $15 Mortgage, blue 150.00
a. Imperf. 1,500.
e. Ultramarine, old paper 200.00
R98c R10 $20 Conveyance, org 90.00
a. Imperf. 140.00
d. Silk paper 140.00
R99c R10 $20 Probate of Will, orange 1,500.
a. Imperf. 1,500.
R100c R10 $25 Mortgage, red ('63) 150.00
a. Imperf. 1,000.
d. Silk paper 200.00
e. Horiz. pair, imperf. btwn., old paper *1,100.*
R101c R10 $50 U.S. Int. Rev., green ('63) 100.00
a. Imperf. 200.00
R102c R11 $200 U.S. Int. Rev., green & red ('64) 725.00
a. Imperf. 1,750.

DOCUMENTARY STAMPS

Second Issue

After release of the First Issue revenue stamps, the Bureau of Internal Revenue received many reports of fraudulent cleaning and re-use. The Bureau ordered a Second Issue with new designs and colors, using a patented "chameleon" paper which is usually slightly violet or pinkish, with silk fibers.

R12

R12a

R13

R13a

R13b

Head of Washington in Black within Octagon. Various Frames and Numeral Arrangements.

1871 ***Perf. 12***

R103 R12 1c blue & black 50.00
Cut cancel 20.00
a. Inverted center *1,500.*
R104 R12 2c blue & black 2.00
Cut cancel .20
a. Inverted center *6,000.*
R105 R12a 3c blue & black 20.00
Cut cancel 10.00
R106 R12a 4c blue & black 65.00
Cut cancel 30.00
R107 R12a 5c blue & black 1.50
Cut cancel .50
a. Inverted center *2,750.*
R108 R12a 6c blue & black 110.00
Cut cancel 55.00
R109 R12a 10c blue & black 1.00
Cut cancel .20
a. Inverted center *2,000.*
R110 R12a 15c blue & black 30.00
Cut cancel 17.50
R111 R12a 20c blue & black 6.00
Cut cancel 2.75
a. Inverted center *8,000.*

Nos. R109a, R111a are valued in the grade of fine.

Head of Washington in Black within Circle

Various Frames

R112 R13 25c blue & black .60
Cut cancel .20
a. Inverted center *10,000.*
b. Sewing machine perf. 110.00
c. Perf. 8 275.00
R113 R13 30c blue & black 80.00
Cut cancel 42.50
R114 R13 40c blue & black 65.00
Cut cancel 22.50
R115 R13a 50c blue & black .60
Cut cancel .20
a. Sewing machine perf. 75.00
b. Inverted center 850.00
Punch cancellation 275.00
R116 R13a 60c blue & black 100.00
Cut cancel 50.00
R117 R13a 70c blue & black 45.00
Cut cancel 17.50
a. Inverted center *3,500.*
Cut cancel *2,000.*
R118 R13b $1 blue & black 4.00
Cut cancel 1.60
a. Inverted center *5,000.*
Punch cancel *900.00*
R119 R13b $1.30 blue & black 350.00
Cut cancel 150.00
R120 R13b $1.50 blue & black 16.00
Cut cancel 8.00
a. Sewing machine perf. 450.00
R121 R13b $1.60 blue & black 450.00
Cut cancel 300.00
R122 R13b $1.90 blue & black 250.00
Cut cancel 110.00
R123 R13b $2 blue & black 15.00
Cut cancel 7.50
R124 R13b $2.50 blue & black 30.00
Cut cancel 16.00
R125 R13b $3 blue & black 35.00
Cut cancel 17.50
R126 R13b $3.50 blue & black 200.00
Cut cancel 100.00
R127 R13b $5 blue & black 22.50
Cut cancel 9.00
a. Inverted center *3,250.*
Punch cancel *950.00*
R128 R13b $10 blue & black 150.00
Cut cancel 70.00
R129 R13b $20 blue & black 400.00
Cut cancel 260.00
R130 R13b $25 blue & black 450.00
Cut cancel 260.00
R131 R13b $50 blue & black 500.00
Cut cancel 275.00
R132 R13b $200 red, bl & blk *5,000.*
Cut cancel *2,800.*
R133 R13b $500 red org, grn & blk *13,000.*

Fraudulently produced inverted centers exist, some excellently made.

Value for No. R133 is for a very fine appearing example with a light circular cut cancel or with minor flaws.

Third Issue

Violet "Chameleon" Paper with Silk Fibers. Various Frames and Numeral Arrangements.

1871-72 ***Perf. 12***

R134 R12 1c claret & blk ('72) 35.00
Cut cancel 19.00
R135 R12 2c orange & blk .20
Cut cancel .20
a. 2c vermilion & black (error) *650.00*
b. Inverted center 375.00
c. Imperf., pair —
R136 R12a 4c brown & blk ('72) 45.00
Cut cancel 21.00
R137 R12a 5c orange & black .25
Cut cancel .20
a. Inverted center *3,500.*

No. R137a is valued in the grade of fine.

R138 R12a 6c orange & blk ('72) 50.00
Cut cancel 25.00
R139 R12a 15c brown & blk ('72) 10.00
Cut cancel 5.00
a. Inverted center *15,000.*
R140 R13 30c orange & blk ('72) 15.00
Cut cancel 7.50
a. Inverted center *2,750.*
Cut cancel *1,750.*
R141 R13 40c brown & blk ('72) 40.00
Cut cancel 20.00
R142 R13a 60c orange & blk ('72) 75.00
Cut cancel 32.50
R143 R13a 70c green & blk ('72) 55.00
Cut cancel 22.50
R144 R13b $1 green & blk ('72) 1.35
Cut cancel .55
a. Inverted center *5,500.*
R145 R13b $2 ver & black ('72) 22.50
Cut cancel 14.00
R146 R13b $2.50 claret & blk ('72) 40.00
Cut cancel 22.00
a. Inverted center *20,000.*
R147 R13b $3 green & blk ('72) 40.00
Cut cancel 21.00
R148 R13b $5 ver & black ('72) 27.50
Cut cancel 12.50
R149 R13b $10 green & blk ('72) 100.00
Cut cancel 45.00
R150 R13b $20 org & blk ('72) 525.00
Cut cancel 260.00
a. $20 vermilion & black (error) 625.00

1874 ***Perf. 12***

R151 R12 2c org & blk, *grn* .20
Cut cancel .20
a. Inverted center 400.00

Liberty — R14

1875-78 ***Perf. 12***

R152a R14 2c bl, *blue,* silk paper .20
b. Wmk. 191R ('78) .20
c. Wmk. 191R, rouletted 32.50
d. Vert. pair, imperf. horiz. 500.00
e. As "b," imperf., pair *250.00*

The rouletted stamps probably were introduced in 1881.

Nos. 279, 267a, 267, 279Bg, 279B, 272-274 Overprinted in Red or Blue

I. R. (a) I.R. (b)

1898 **Wmk. 191** ***Perf. 12***

R153 A87(a) 1c grn (R) 3.75 2.50
R154 A87(b) 1c grn (R) .20 .20
a. Overprint inverted 20.00 *17.50*
b. Ovpt. on back instead of face, invtd. —
c. Pair, one without ovpt. —
R155 A88(b) 2c pink, III (Bl) .20 .20
b. 2c carmine, III .25 *.20*
c. As #R155, ovpt. invtd. 4.50 *2.75*
d. Vert. pair, one without ovpt. *750.00*
e. Horiz. pair, one without ovpt. —
f. As #R155, ovpt. on back instead of face, invtd. —
R155A A88(b) 2c pink, IV (Bl) .20 .20
g. 2c carmine, IV .20 *.20*
h. As #R155A, ovpt. invtd. 2.50 *1.75*

Handstamped Type "b"

R156 A93 8c vio brn *4,500.*
R157 A94 10c dark grn *3,750.*
R158 A95 15c dark blue *5,000.*

Nos. R156-R158 were emergency provisionals, privately prepared, not officially issued.

Privately Prepared Provisionals

No. 285 Overprinted in Red **I. R.** L. H. C.

1898 **Wmk. 191** ***Perf. 12***

R158A A100 1c dk yel grn *12,500. 10,000.*

Same Overprinted "I.R./P.I.D. & Son" in Red

R158B A100 1c dk yel grn *25,000. 22,500.*

No. R158B is valued with small faults as each of the four recorded examples have faults.

Nos. R158A-R158B were overprinted with federal government permission by the Purvis Printing Co. upon order of Capt. L.H. Chapman of the Chapman Steamboat Line. Both the Chapman line and P.I. Daprix & Son operated freight-carrying steamboats on the Erie Canal. The Chapman Line touched at Syracuse, Utica, Little Falls and Fort Plain; the Daprix boat ran between Utica and Rome. 250 of each stamp were overprinted.

Dr. Kilmer & Co. provisional overprints are listed in the Scott Specialized Catalogue of United States Stamps under Private Die uMedicine Stamps, Nos. RS307-RS315.

Newspaper Stamp No. PR121 Surcharged Vertically in Red

1898 **Wmk. 191** ***Perf. 12***

Reading Down

R159 N18 $5 on $5 dk blue 425.00 175.00

Reading Up

R160 N18 $5 on $5 dk blue 110.00 95.00

Battleship—R15

Inscribed: "Series of 1898" and "Documentary."

There are 2 styles of rouletting for the 1898 proprietary and documentary stamps, an ordinary roulette 5½ and one where small rectangles of the paper are cut out, called hyphen hole perf. 7.

1898 **Wmk. 191R** ***Rouletted 5½***

R161 R15 ½c orange 2.50 *10.00*
R162 R15 ½c dark gray .25 .20
a. Vert. pair, imperf. horiz. 75.00
R163 R15 1c pale blue .20 .20
a. Vert. pair, imperf. horiz. 7.50
b. Imperf., pair *400.00*
R164 R15 2c car rose .25 .25
a. Vert. pair, imperf. horiz. 75.00
b. Imperf., pair 200.00
c. Horiz. pair, imperf. vert. —
R165 R15 3c dark blue 2.00 .20
R166 R15 4c pale rose 1.25 .20
a. Vert. pair, imperf. horiz. 125.00
R167 R15 5c lilac .50 .20
a. Pair, imperf. horiz. or vert. 200.00 150.00
b. Horiz. pair, imperf. btwn. *450.00*
R168 R15 10c dark brown 1.50 .20
a. Vert. pair, imperf. horiz. 35.00 30.00
b. Horiz. pair, imperf. vert. —
R169 R15 25c pur brown 2.50 .20
R170 R15 40c blue lilac 125.00 1.00
Cut cancellation .30
R171 R15 50c slate violet 17.50 .20
a. Imperf., pair *300.00*
R172 R15 80c bister 100.00 .25
Cut cancellation .20

No. R167b may not be genuine.

Hyphen Hole Perf. 7

R163p 1c .25 .20
R164p 2c .30 .20
R165p 3c 20.00 1.00
R166p 4c 7.50 1.50
R167p 5c 7.50 .20
R168p 10c 5.00 .20
R169p 25c 8.00 .25
R170p 40c 175.00 35.00
R171p 50c 35.00 .75
b. Horiz. pair, imperf. btwn. — *250.00*
R172p 80c 200.00 50.00

Commerce — R16

1898 ***Rouletted 5½***

R173 R16 $1 dark green 10.00 .20
a. Vert. pair, imperf. horiz. —
b. Horiz. pair, imperf. vert. — 300.00
p. Hyphen hole perf. 7 20.00 .65
R174 R16 $3 dark brown 25.00 1.00
Cut cancellation .20
a. Horiz. pair, imperf. vert. 450.00
p. Hyphen hole perf. 7 40.00 2.25
Cut cancellation .20 .25
R175 R16 $5 orange red 35.00 1.75
Cut cancellation .20
R176 R16 $10 black 90.00 3.00
Cut cancellation .50
a. Horiz. pair, imperf. vert. —
R177 R16 $30 red 300.00 120.00
Cut cancellation 45.00
R178 R16 $50 gray brown 140.00 5.50
Cut cancellation 2.00

See Nos. R182-R183.

John Marshall R17

Alexander Hamilton R18

James Madison R19

Inscribed "Series of 1898"

1899 **Without Gum** ***Imperf.***

R179 R17 $100 yel brn & black 175.00 30.00
Cut cancellation 20.00
R180 R18 $500 car lake & black 1,200. 800.00
Cut cancellation 275.00
R181 R19 $1000 grn & blk 900.00 300.00
Cut cancellation 125.00

See #R224-R227, R246-R252, R282-R286.

Type of 1898

1900 ***Hyphen-Hole Perf. 7***

R182 R16 $1 carmine 20.00 .50
Cut cancellation .25
R183 R16 $3 lake 150.00 45.00
Cut cancellation 7.00

Warning: The ink on No. R183 will run in water.

Surcharged in Black

a

b

Surcharged type "a"

1900

R184 R16 $1 gray 15.00 .25
Cut cancellation .20
a. Horiz. pair, imperf. vert. —
b. Surcharge omitted 125.00
As "b", cut cancellation 80.00
R185 R16 $2 gray 15.00 .20
Cut cancellation .20
R186 R16 $3 gray 75.00 11.00
Cut cancellation 4.00
R187 R16 $5 gray 50.00 7.50
Cut cancellation 1.25
R188 R16 $10 gray 90.00 20.00
Cut cancellation 3.00
R189 R16 $50 gray 900.00 450.00
Cut cancellation 90.00

Surcharged type "b"

1902

R190 R16 $1 green 22.50 2.50
Cut cancellation .20
a. Inverted surcharge 175.00
R191 R16 $2 green 20.00 1.30
Cut cancellation .25
a. Surcharged as #R185 100.00 75.00
b. Surch. as #R185, in vio 1,300. —
c. As "a," double surcharge 125.00
d. As "a," triple surcharge —
R192 R16 $5 green 160.00 25.00
Cut cancellation 4.00
a. Surcharge omitted 190.00
b. Pair, one without surch. 375.00
R193 R16 $10 green 350.00 125.00
Cut cancellation 45.00
R194 R16 $50 green 950.00 800.00
Cut cancellation 250.00

Warning: If Nos. R190-R194 are soaked, the center part of the surcharged numeral may wash off. Before surcharging, a square of soluble varnish was applied to the middle of some stamps.

R20

Liberty — R21

Inscribed "Series of 1914"

Offset Printing

1914 **Wmk. 190** ***Perf. 10***

R195 R20 ½c rose 9.00 3.50
R196 R20 1c rose 1.75 .25
R197 R20 2c rose 2.25 .25
R198 R20 3c rose 55.00 30.00
R199 R20 4c rose 16.00 2.00
R200 R20 5c rose 5.00 .25
R201 R20 10c rose 4.00 .25
R202 R20 25c rose 35.00 .55
R203 R20 40c rose 20.00 1.25
R204 R20 50c rose 7.00 .25
R205 R20 80c rose 110.00 10.00
Nos. R195-R205 (11) 265.00 48.55

Wmk. 191R

R206 R20 ½c rose 1.50 .50
R207 R20 1c rose .25 .20
R208 R20 2c rose .25 .20
R209 R20 3c rose 1.50 .25
R210 R20 4c rose 3.50 .45
R211 R20 5c rose 1.75 .25
R212 R20 10c rose .75 .20
R213 R20 25c rose 5.00 1.25
R214 R20 40c rose 90.00 12.50
Cut cancellation .45
R215 R20 50c rose 17.50 .25
R216 R20 80c rose 125.00 20.00
Cut cancellation 1.00
Nos. R206-R216 (11) 247.00 36.05

Engr.

R217 R21 $1 green 35.00 .40
Cut cancellation .20
a. $1 yellow green 35.00 .20
R218 R21 $2 carmine 55.00 .75
Cut cancellation .20
R219 R21 $3 purple 70.00 3.50
Cut cancellation .45
R220 R21 $5 blue 60.00 2.75
Cut cancellation .50
R221 R21 $10 orange 140.00 5.00
Cut cancellation .75
R222 R21 $30 vermilion 300.00 11.00
Cut cancellation 2.00
R223 R21 $50 violet 1,300. 800.00
Cut cancellation 350.00

See #R240-R245, R257-R259, R276-R281.

Portrait Types of 1899 Inscribed "Series of 1915" (#R224), or "Series of 1914"

1914-15 **Without Gum** ***Perf. 12***

R224 R19 $60 brn *(Lincoln)* 175.00 125.00
Cut cancellation 65.00
R225 R17 $100 grn *(Washington)* 60.00 40.00
Cut cancellation 15.00
R226 R18 $500 blue — 600.00
Cut cancellation 250.00
R227 R19 $1000 orange — 500.00
Cut cancellation 275.00

The stamps of types R17, R18 and R19 in this and subsequent issues are issued in vert. strips of 4 which are imperf. at the top, bottom and right side; therefore, single copies are always imperf. on 1 or 2 sides.

R22

Offset Printing

1917 **Wmk. 191R** ***Perf. 11***

R228 R22 1c carmine rose .20 .20
R229 R22 2c carmine rose .20 .20
R230 R22 3c carmine rose 1.25 .35
R231 R22 4c carmine rose .65 .20
R232 R22 5c carmine rose .25 .20
R233 R22 8c carmine rose 2.00 .30
R234 R22 10c carmine rose .35 .20
R235 R22 20c carmine rose .60 .20
R236 R22 25c carmine rose 1.10 .20
R237 R22 40c carmine rose 2.00 .40
R238 R22 50c carmine rose 2.00 .20
R239 R22 80c carmine rose 5.00 .20
Nos. R228-R239 (12) 15.60 2.85

Type of 1914 without "Series 1914"

1917-33 **Engr.**

R240 R21 $1 yellow green 6.50 .20
a. $1 green 6.50 .20
R241 R21 $2 rose 11.00 .20
R242 R21 $3 violet 35.00 1.00
Cut cancellation .25
R243 R21 $4 yel brn ('33) 25.00 1.75
Cut cancellation .20
R244 R21 $5 dark blue 17.50 .30
Cut cancellation .20
R245 R21 $10 orange 30.00 1.25
Cut cancellation .20

Portrait Types of 1899-1915 without "Series of" and Date

Portraits: $30, Grant. $100, Washington.

1917 **Without Gum** ***Perf. 12***

R246 R17 $30 dp org, grn numerals 45.00 12.50
Cut cancellation 2.00
a. Imperf., pair 750.00
b. Numerals in blue 70.00 1.90
As "b," cut cancellation 1.25
R247 R19 $60 brown 55.00 7.00
Cut cancellation .80
R248 R17 $100 green 32.50 1.00
Cut cancellation .35
R249 R18 $500 blue, red numerals 300.00 35.00
Cut cancellation 12.00
a. Numerals in orange 350.00 50.00
R250 R19 $1000 orange 140.00 12.50
Cut cancellation 4.00
a. Imperf., pair 1,250.

See note after No. R227.

1928-29 **Offset Printing** ***Perf. 10***

R251 R22 1c carmine rose 2.00 1.50
R252 R22 2c carmine rose .60 .30
R253 R22 4c carmine rose 7.00 3.75
R254 R22 5c carmine rose 1.50 .50
R255 R22 10c carmine rose 2.25 1.25
R256 R22 20c carmine rose 5.50 4.50
Nos. R251-R256 (6) 18.85 11.80

Engr.

R257 R21 $1 green 110.00 30.00
Cut cancellation 5.00
R258 R21 $2 rose 45.00 2.50
R259 R21 $10 orange 150.00 40.00
Cut cancellation 25.00

1929 **Offset Printing** ***Perf. 11x10***

R260 R22 2c carmine rose 2.75 2.50
R261 R22 5c carmine rose 2.00 1.75
R262 R22 10c carmine rose 9.00 6.50
R263 R22 20c carmine rose 15.00 8.00

Used values for Nos. R264-R734 are for copies which are neither cut nor perforated with initials. Copies with cut cancellations or perforated initials are valued in the Scott U. S. Specialized Catalogue.

Types of 1917-33 Overprinted in Black **SERIES 1940**

1940 **Offset Printing** ***Perf. 11***

R264 R22 1c rose pink 3.25 2.25
R265 R22 2c rose pink 2.75 1.75
R266 R22 3c rose pink 8.25 4.00
R267 R22 4c rose pink 3.50 .55
R268 R22 5c rose pink 3.75 .90
R269 R22 8c rose pink 16.00 12.50
R270 R22 10c rose pink 1.75 .60
R271 R22 20c rose pink 2.25 .60
R272 R22 25c rose pink 5.50 1.00
R273 R22 40c rose pink 5.50 .65
R274 R22 50c rose pink 6.00 .50
R275 R22 80c rose pink 11.00 .90
Nos. R264-R275 (12) 69.50 26.20

Engr.

R276 R21 $1 green 45.00 .80
R277 R21 $2 rose 45.00 1.00
R278 R21 $3 violet 60.00 25.00
R279 R21 $4 yellow brown 110.00 30.00
R280 R21 $5 dark blue 65.00 11.00
R281 R21 $10 orange 150.00 32.50

Types of 1917 Handstamped in Green (Nos. R282-R284, R286) or Violet (No. R285) Like No. R264-R281

Perf. 12

Without Gum

R282 R17 $30 vermilion 700.
a. With black 2-line handstamp in larger type 9,000.
R283 R19 $60 brown 1,000.
a. As #R282a, cut cancel —
R284 R17 $100 green 2,250.
R285 R18 $500 blue 1,750.
a. As #R282a 3,250. 3,250.
b. Blue handstamp, double transfer —
c. Violet handstamp, double transfer 1,500.
R286 R19 $1000 orange 650.
a. Double overprint (cut cancel) —

Alexander Hamilton — R23

Levi Woodbury — R24

Thomas Corwin — R25

Portraits: 2c, Oliver Wolcott, Jr. 3c, Samuel Dexter. 4c, Albert Gallatin. 5c, George Washington Campbell. 8c, Alexander Dallas. 10c, William H. Crawford. 20c, Richard Rush. 25c, Samuel D. Ingham. 40c, Louis McLane. 50c, William J. Duane. 80c, Roger B. Taney. $2, Thomas Ewing. $3, Walter Forward. $4, John Canfield Spencer. $5, George M. Bibb. $10, Robert J. Walker. $20, William M. Meredith. $50, James Guthrie. $60, Howell Cobb. $100, P. F. Thomas. $500, John Adams Dix. $1,000, Salmon P. Chase.

Overprinted in Black Like Nos. R264-R281

1940 ***Perf. 11***

Various Portraits

R288 R23 1c carmine 4.50 3.25
R289 R23 2c carmine 5.00 3.00
R290 R23 3c carmine 19.00 10.00
R291 R23 4c carmine 50.00 22.50
R292 R23 5c carmine 3.25 .65
R293 R23 8c carmine 72.50 50.00
R294 R23 10c carmine 2.75 .50
R295 R23 20c carmine 4.25 2.75
R296 R23 25c carmine 3.00 .55
R297 R23 40c carmine 50.00 22.50
R298 R23 50c carmine 5.00 .45
R299 R23 80c carmine 110.00 .65
R300 R24 $1 carmine 35.00 .55
R301 R24 $2 carmine 47.50 .75
R302 R24 $3 carmine 135.00 85.00
R303 R24 $4 carmine 80.00 30.00
R304 R24 $5 carmine 47.50 2.00
R305 R24 $10 carmine 85.00 6.00
R305A R24 $20 carmine 2,000. 900.00
b. Imperf., pair 600.00

Various Frame Designs

Perf. 12

Without Gum

R306 R25 $30 carmine 130.00 45.00
R306A R25 $50 carmine — 3,250.
R307 R25 $60 carmine 260.00 60.00
a. Vert. pair, imperf btwn. 2,500. 1,450.
R308 R25 $100 carmine 190.00 65.00
R309 R25 $500 carmine — 3,250.
R310 R25 $1000 carmine — 425.00

The $30 to $1,000 denominations in this and following similar issues, and the $2,500, $5,000 and $10,000 stamps of 1952-58 have straight edges on one or two sides. They were issued without gum through No. R723.

Overprinted in Black "SERIES 1941"

1941 **Size: 19x22mm** ***Perf. 11***

R311 R23 1c carmine 3.00 2.25
R312 R23 2c carmine 3.00 .90
R313 R23 3c carmine 7.50 3.50
R314 R23 4c carmine 5.00 1.25
R315 R23 5c carmine 1.00 .25
R316 R23 8c carmine 14.00 7.50
R317 R23 10c carmine 1.25 .20
R318 R23 20c carmine 3.00 .45
R319 R23 25c carmine 1.75 .50
R320 R23 40c carmine 11.00 2.50
R321 R23 50c carmine 2.50 .25
R322 R23 80c carmine 55.00 10.00
Nos. R311-R322 (12) 108.00 29.55

Size: 21½x36¼mm

R323 R24 $1 carmine 10.00 .25
R324 R24 $2 carmine 12.50 .45
R325 R24 $3 carmine 20.00 2.75
R326 R24 $4 carmine 35.00 17.50
R327 R24 $5 carmine 40.00 .90
R328 R24 $10 carmine 60.00 3.50
R329 R24 $20 carmine 800.00 275.00

Size: 28½x42mm

Perf. 12

Without Gum

R330 R25 $30 carmine 125.00 40.00
R331 R25 $50 carmine 375.00 325.00
R332 R25 $60 carmine 175.00 60.00
R333 R25 $100 carmine 75.00 27.50
R334 R25 $500 carmine — 240.00
R335 R25 $1000 carmine — 125.00

Overprinted in Black "SERIES 1942"

1942 **Size: 19x22mm** ***Perf. 11***

R336 R23 1c carmine .50 .45
R337 R23 2c carmine .45 .45
R338 R23 3c carmine .70 .60
R339 R23 4c carmine 1.20 .90
R340 R23 5c carmine .45 .25
R341 R23 8c carmine 5.50 4.25
R342 R23 10c carmine 1.20 .25
R343 R23 20c carmine 1.20 .45
R344 R23 25c carmine 2.10 .45
R345 R23 40c carmine 4.75 1.20
R346 R23 50c carmine 3.00 .25
R347 R23 80c carmine 17.50 10.00
Nos. R336-R347 (12) 38.55 19.50

Size: 21½x36¼mm

R348 R24 $1 carmine 9.00 .25
R349 R24 $2 carmine 10.00 .25
R350 R24 $3 carmine 17.50 2.50
R351 R24 $4 carmine 25.00 5.00
R352 R24 $5 carmine 27.50 1.10
R353 R24 $10 carmine 65.00 2.50
R354 R24 $20 carmine 120.00 35.00

Size: 28½x42mm

Perf. 12

Without Gum

R355	R25	$30 carmine	70.00	30.00
R356	R25	$50 carmine	1,250.	650.00
R357	R25	$60 carmine	1,500.	850.00
R358	R25	$100 carmine	160.00	120.00
R359	R25	$500 carmine	*1,500.*	225.00
R360	R25	$1000 carmine	—	100.00

Overprinted in Black "SERIES 1943"

1943 Size: 19x22mm *Perf. 11*

R361	R23	1c carmine	.60	.50
R362	R23	2c carmine	.45	.40
R363	R23	3c carmine	3.00	2.75
R364	R23	4c carmine	1.25	1.25
R365	R23	5c carmine	.50	.30
R366	R23	8c carmine	4.25	3.00
R367	R23	10c carmine	.70	.25
R368	R23	20c carmine	1.90	.65
R369	R23	25c carmine	2.00	.35
R370	R23	40c carmine	5.00	2.50
R371	R23	50c carmine	1.50	.25
R372	R23	80c carmine	17.50	5.50
		Nos. R361-R372 (12)	38.65	17.70

Size: 21½x36¼mm

R373	R24	$1 carmine	6.00	.35
R374	R24	$2 carmine	11.00	.25
R375	R24	$3 carmine	20.00	2.25
R376	R24	$4 carmine	27.50	5.00
R377	R24	$5 carmine	35.00	.60
R378	R24	$10 carmine	55.00	4.00
R379	R24	$20 carmine	110.00	27.50

Size: 28½x42mm

Perf. 12

Without Gum

R380	R25	$30 carmine	55.00	18.00
R381	R25	$50 carmine	110.00	30.00
R382	R25	$60 carmine	260.00	85.00
R383	R25	$100 carmine	25.00	12.50
R384	R25	$500 carmine	—	200.00
R385	R25	$1000 carmine	—	160.00

Overprinted in Black "Series 1944"

1944 Size: 19x22mm *Perf. 11*

R386	R23	1c carmine	.40	.35
R387	R23	2c carmine	.45	.45
R388	R23	3c carmine	.50	.35
R389	R23	4c carmine	.55	.55
R390	R23	5c carmine	.30	.25
R391	R23	8c carmine	1.75	1.50
R392	R23	10c carmine	.40	.25
R393	R23	20c carmine	.75	.25
R394	R23	25c carmine	1.40	.25
R395	R23	40c carmine	2.75	.60
R396	R23	50c carmine	3.00	.25
R397	R23	80c carmine	15.00	4.00
		Nos. R386-R397 (12)	27.25	9.05

Size: 21½x36¼mm

R398	R24	$1 carmine	7.50	.25
R399	R24	$2 carmine	10.00	.35
R400	R24	$3 carmine	16.00	2.00
R401	R24	$4 carmine	22.50	10.00
R402	R24	$5 carmine	25.00	.35
R403	R24	$10 carmine	50.00	1.40
R404	R24	$20 carmine	100.00	15.00

Size: 28½x42mm

Perf. 12

Without Gum

R405	R25	$30 carmine	75.00	27.50
R406	R25	$50 carmine	35.00	17.50
R407	R25	$60 carmine	200.00	60.00
R408	R25	$100 carmine	40.00	10.00
R409	R25	$500 carmine	—	2,500.
R410	R25	$1000 carmine	—	275.00

Overprinted in Black "Series 1945"

1945 Size: 19x22mm *Perf. 11*

R411	R23	1c carmine	.25	.25
R412	R23	2c carmine	.25	.25
R413	R23	3c carmine	.50	.45
R414	R23	4c carmine	.30	.30
R415	R23	5c carmine	.35	.25
R416	R23	8c carmine	4.25	2.00
R417	R23	10c carmine	.80	.25
R418	R23	20c carmine	5.25	1.00
R419	R23	25c carmine	1.25	.30
R420	R23	40c carmine	5.50	1.00
R421	R23	50c carmine	2.75	.25
R422	R23	80c carmine	20.00	8.00
		Nos. R411-R422 (12)	41.45	14.30

Size: 21½x36¼mm

R423	R24	$1 carmine	8.50	.25
R424	R24	$2 carmine	9.00	.35
R425	R24	$3 carmine	17.50	2.25
R426	R24	$4 carmine	25.00	3.00
R427	R24	$5 carmine	25.00	.45
R428	R24	$10 carmine	50.00	1.40
R429	R24	$20 carmine	100.00	12.50

Size: 28½x42mm

Without Gum

Perf. 12

R430	R25	$30 carmine	125.00	32.50
R431	R25	$50 carmine	150.00	35.00
R432	R25	$60 carmine	250.00	55.00
R433	R25	$100 carmine	50.00	15.00
R434	R25	$500 carmine	300.00	175.00
R435	R25	$1000 carmine	200.00	90.00

Overprinted in Black "Series 1946"

1946 Wmk. 191R *Perf. 11*

Size: 19x22mm

R436	R23	1c carmine	.20	.25
R437	R23	2c carmine	.35	.30
R438	R23	3c carmine	.35	.30
R439	R23	4c carmine	.60	.50
R440	R23	5c carmine	.35	.35
R441	R23	8c carmine	1.25	1.10
R442	R23	10c carmine	.85	.25
R443	R23	20c carmine	1.25	.40
R444	R23	25c carmine	4.00	.25
R445	R23	40c carmine	2.50	.75
R446	R23	50c carmine	3.75	.25
R447	R23	80c carmine	12.50	4.25
		Nos. R436-R447 (12)	27.95	8.95

Size: 21½x36¼mm

R448	R24	$1 carmine	11.00	.25
R449	R24	$2 carmine	12.50	.25
R450	R24	$3 carmine	19.00	5.00
R451	R24	$4 carmine	25.00	10.00
R452	R24	$5 carmine	25.00	.45
R453	R24	$10 carmine	50.00	1.50
R454	R24	$20 carmine	100.00	12.50

Size: 28½x42mm

Without Gum

Perf. 12

R455	R25	$30 carmine	45.00	13.50
R456	R25	$50 carmine	35.00	10.00
R457	R25	$60 carmine	70.00	17.50
R458	R25	$100 carmine	50.00	10.00
R459	R25	$500 carmine	—	105.00
R460	R25	$1000 carmine	—	110.00

Overprinted in Black "Series 1947"

1947 Wmk. 191R *Perf. 11*

Size: 19x22mm

R461	R23	1c carmine	.65	.50
R462	R23	2c carmine	.55	.50
R463	R23	3c carmine	.65	.50
R464	R23	4c carmine	.70	.60
R465	R23	5c carmine	.35	.30
R466	R23	8c carmine	1.20	.70
R467	R23	10c carmine	1.10	.25
R468	R23	20c carmine	1.80	.50
R469	R23	25c carmine	2.40	.60
R470	R23	40c carmine	3.75	.90
R471	R23	50c carmine	3.00	.30
R472	R23	80c carmine	8.25	6.00
		Nos. R461-R472 (12)	24.40	11.65

Size: 21½x36¼mm

R473	R24	$1 carmine	6.00	.25
R474	R24	$2 carmine	9.50	.60
R475	R24	$3 carmine	12.00	5.00
R476	R24	$4 carmine	14.00	4.50
R477	R24	$5 carmine	21.00	.50
R478	R24	$10 carmine	50.50	2.00
R479	R24	$20 carmine	75.00	10.00

Size: 28½x42mm

Perf. 12

Without Gum

R480	R25	$30 carmine	100.00	20.00
R481	R25	$50 carmine	50.00	14.00
R482	R25	$60 carmine	120.00	40.00
R483	R25	$100 carmine	50.00	11.00
R484	R25	$500 carmine	—	150.00
R485	R25	$1000 carmine	—	80.00

Overprinted in Black "Series 1948"

1948 Wmk. 191R *Perf. 11*

Size: 19x22mm

R486	R23	1c carmine	.25	.25
R487	R23	2c carmine	.35	.35
R488	R23	3c carmine	.45	.35
R489	R23	4c carmine	.40	.30
R490	R23	5c carmine	.35	.25
R491	R23	8c carmine	.75	.35
R492	R23	10c carmine	.75	.25
R493	R23	20c carmine	1.75	.30
R494	R23	25c carmine	1.50	.25
R495	R23	40c carmine	4.50	1.75
R496	R23	50c carmine	2.25	.25
R497	R23	80c carmine	7.50	4.50
		Nos. R486-R497 (12)	20.80	9.15

Size: 21½x36¼mm

R498	R24	$1 carmine	7.50	.25
R499	R24	$2 carmine	12.50	.25
R500	R24	$3 carmine	17.50	2.50
R501	R24	$4 carmine	25.00	2.75
R502	R24	$5 carmine	21.00	.50
R503	R24	$10 carmine	50.00	1.00
a.		Pair, one dated "1946"		—
R504	R24	$20 carmine	95.00	12.50

Size: 28½x42mm

Perf. 12

Without Gum

R505	R25	$30 carmine	65.00	22.50
R506	R25	$50 carmine	65.00	20.00
a.		Vert. pair, imperf. btwn.	—	
R507	R25	$60 carmine	125.00	35.00
a.		Vert. pair, imperf. btwn.	*1,100*	
R508	R25	$100 carmine	55.00	10.00
a.		Vert. pair, imperf. btwn.	*850.00*	
R509	R25	$500 carmine	250.00	125.00
R510	R25	$1000 carmine	175.00	75.00

Overprinted in Black "Series 1949"

1949 Wmk. 191R *Perf. 11*

Size: 19x22mm

R511	R23	1c carmine	.25	.25
R512	R23	2c carmine	.55	.35
R513	R23	3c carmine	.40	.35
R514	R23	4c carmine	.60	.50
R515	R23	5c carmine	.35	.20
R516	R23	8c carmine	.70	.60
R517	R23	10c carmine	.40	.25
R518	R23	20c carmine	1.30	.60
R519	R23	25c carmine	1.80	.70
R520	R23	40c carmine	4.25	2.10
R521	R23	50c carmine	3.50	.30
R522	R23	80c carmine	10.00	4.75
		Nos. R511-R522 (12)	24.10	10.95

Size: 21½x36¼mm

R523	R24	$1 carmine	8.50	.55
R524	R24	$2 carmine	11.00	2.00
R525	R24	$3 carmine	17.50	6.00
R526	R24	$4 carmine	21.00	6.00
R527	R24	$5 carmine	21.00	2.75
R528	R24	$10 carmine	50.00	3.50
R529	R24	$20 carmine	95.00	11.00

Size: 28½x42mm

Perf. 12

Without Gum

R530	R25	$30 carmine	85.00	25.00
R531	R25	$50 carmine	100.00	40.00
R532	R25	$60 carmine	175.00	45.00
R533	R25	$100 carmine	50.00	15.00
R534	R25	$500 carmine	—	200.00
R535	R25	$1000 carmine	—	125.00

Overprinted in Black "Series 1950"

1950 Wmk. 191R *Perf. 11*

Size: 19x22mm

R536	R23	1c carmine	.25	.25
R537	R23	2c carmine	.30	.25
R538	R23	3c carmine	.35	.30
R539	R23	4c carmine	.50	.40
R540	R23	5c carmine	.30	.20
R541	R23	8c carmine	1.25	.65
R542	R23	10c carmine	.60	.25
R543	R23	20c carmine	1.00	.35
R544	R23	25c carmine	1.50	.35
R545	R23	40c carmine	3.25	1.75
R546	R23	50c carmine	4.00	.25
R547	R23	80c carmine	9.00	4.75
		Nos. R536-R547 (12)	22.30	9.75

Size: 21½x36¼mm

R548	R24	$1 carmine	9.00	.35
R549	R24	$2 carmine	11.00	2.00
R550	R24	$3 carmine	12.50	4.75
R551	R24	$4 carmine	17.50	6.00
R552	R24	$5 carmine	21.00	.85
R553	R24	$10 carmine	47.50	9.00
R554	R24	$20 carmine	95.00	10.00

Size: 28½x42mm

Perf. 12

Without Gum

R555	R25	$30 carmine	70.00	47.50
R556	R25	$50 carmine	65.00	17.50
a.		Vert. pair, imperf. horiz.		—
R557	R25	$60 carmine	150.00	55.00
R558	R25	$100 carmine	55.00	17.50
R559	R25	$500 carmine	—	100.00
R560	R25	$1000 carmine	—	75.00

Overprinted in Black "Series 1951"

1951 Wmk. 191R *Perf. 11*

Size: 19x22mm

R561	R23	1c carmine	.25	.25
R562	R23	2c carmine	.30	.25
R563	R23	3c carmine	.25	.25
R564	R23	4c carmine	.30	.25
R565	R23	5c carmine	.30	.25
R566	R23	8c carmine	1.00	.35
R567	R23	10c carmine	.55	.25
R568	R23	20c carmine	1.25	.45
R569	R23	25c carmine	1.50	.40
R570	R23	40c carmine	3.75	1.25
R571	R23	50c carmine	2.75	.35
R572	R23	80c carmine	5.50	2.50
		Nos. R561-R572 (12)	17.70	6.80

Size: 21½x36¼mm

R573	R24	$1 carmine	10.00	.20
R574	R24	$2 carmine	14.00	.50
R575	R24	$3 carmine	20.00	3.50
R576	R24	$4 carmine	25.00	5.00
R577	R24	$5 carmine	17.50	.65
R578	R24	$10 carmine	42.50	2.25
R579	R24	$20 carmine	90.00	10.00

Size: 28½x42mm

Perf. 12

Without Gum

R580	R25	$30 carmine	70.00	12.50
a.		Imperf., pair	*1,750.*	*750.00*
R581	R25	$50 carmine	85.00	22.50
R582	R25	$60 carmine	140.00	45.00
R583	R25	$100 carmine	45.00	12.50
R584	R25	$500 carmine	250.00	100.00
R585	R25	$1000 carmine	—	100.00

Overprinted in Black "Series 1952"

Designs: 55c, $1.10, $1.65, $2.20, $2.75, $3.30, L. J. Gage; $2500, William Windom; $5000, C. J. Folger; $10,000, W. Q. Gresham.

1952 Wmk. 191R *Perf. 11*

Size: 19x22mm

R586	R23	1c carmine	.25	.25
R587	R23	2c carmine	.35	.25
R588	R23	3c carmine	.30	.25
R589	R23	4c carmine	.35	.25
R590	R23	5c carmine	.25	.25
R591	R23	8c carmine	.75	.45
R592	R23	10c carmine	.40	.25
R593	R23	20c carmine	1.00	.35
R594	R23	25c carmine	1.50	.40
R595	R23	40c carmine	3.00	1.25
R596	R23	50c carmine	2.75	.25
R597	R23	55c carmine	20.00	10.00
R598	R23	80c carmine	12.50	3.00
		Nos. R586-R598 (13)	43.40	17.20

Size: 21½x36¼mm

R599	R24	$1 carmine	5.00	1.50
R600	R24	$1.10 carmine	42.50	25.00
R601	R24	$1.65 carmine	140.00	45.00
R602	R24	$2 carmine	11.00	.65
R603	R24	$2.20 carmine	125.00	60.00
R604	R24	$2.75 carmine	140.00	60.00
R605	R24	$3 carmine	25.00	4.00
a.		Horiz. pair, imperf. btwn.	*1,200.*	
R606	R24	$3.30 carmine	125.00	60.00
R607	R24	$4 carmine	22.50	4.00
R608	R24	$5 carmine	22.50	1.25
R609	R24	$10 carmine	45.00	1.25
R610	R24	$20 carmine	70.00	10.00

Size: 28½x42mm

Perf. 12

Without Gum

R611	R25	$30 carmine	47.50	18.00
R612	R25	$50 carmine	42.50	15.00
R613	R25	$60 carmine	300.00	50.00
R614	R25	$100 carmine	37.50	8.00
R615	R25	$500 carmine	—	100.00
R616	R25	$1000 carmine	—	30.00
R617	R25	$2500 carmine	—	165.00
R618	R25	$5000 carmine	—	3,000.
R619	R25	$10,000 carmine	—	*1,250.*

Overprinted in Black "Series 1953"

1953 Wmk. 191R *Perf. 11*

Size: 19x22mm

R620	R23	1c carmine	.25	.25
R621	R23	2c carmine	.25	.25
R622	R23	3c carmine	.30	.25
R623	R23	4c carmine	.50	.35
R624	R23	5c carmine	.35	.25
a.		Vert. pair, imperf. horiz.		*650.00*
R625	R23	8c carmine	.85	.35
R626	R23	10c carmine	.50	.20
R627	R23	20c carmine	1.00	.40
R628	R23	25c carmine	1.10	.50
R629	R23	40c carmine	2.00	.75
R630	R23	50c carmine	2.50	.25
R631	R23	55c carmine	4.25	2.00
a.		Horiz. pair, imperf. vert.	*350.00*	
R632	R23	80c carmine	6.75	2.00
		Nos. R620-R632 (13)	20.60	7.80

Size: 21½x36¼mm

R633	R24	$1 carmine	4.00	.25
R634	R24	$1.10 carmine	8.00	2.50
a.		Horiz. pair, imperf. vert.	600.00	
b.		Imperf., pair	*600.00*	
R635	R24	$1.65 carmine	8.00	4.00
R636	R24	$2 carmine	6.00	.65
R637	R24	$2.20 carmine	14.00	6.00
R638	R24	$2.75 carmine	20.00	7.00
R639	R24	$3 carmine	12.00	3.00
R640	R24	$3.30 carmine	26.00	8.00
R641	R24	$4 carmine	25.00	8.50
R642	R24	$5 carmine	20.00	1.00
R643	R24	$10 carmine	45.00	1.75
R644	R24	$20 carmine	85.00	18.00

Size: 28½x42mm

Perf. 12

Without Gum

R645	R25	$30 carmine	65.00	15.00
R646	R25	$50 carmine	120.00	30.00
R647	R25	$60 carmine	450.00	200.00
R648	R25	$100 carmine	37.50	12.50
R649	R25	$500 carmine	500.00	140.00
R650	R25	$1000 carmine	250.00	65.00
R651	R25	$2500 carmine	1,750.	1,100.
R652	R25	$5000 carmine	—	*3,750.*
R653	R25	$10,000 carmine	—	*3,250.*

Types of 1940 without Overprint

1954 Wmk. 191R *Perf. 11*

Size: 19x22mm

R654	R23	1c carmine	.25	.25
a.		Horiz. pair, imperf. vert.		—
R655	R23	2c carmine	.25	.25
R656	R23	3c carmine	.25	.25
R657	R23	4c carmine	.30	.25
R658	R23	5c carmine	.25	.25
R659	R23	8c carmine	.25	.25
R660	R23	10c carmine	.25	.25

R661 R23 20c carmine .50 .35
R662 R23 25c carmine .60 .40
R663 R23 40c carmine 1.25 .60
R664 R23 50c carmine 1.75 .25
a. Horiz. pair, imperf. vert 240.00
R665 R23 55c carmine 1.50 1.25
R666 R23 80c carmine 2.25 1.75
Nos. R654-R666 (13) 9.65 6.35

Size: 21½x36¼mm

R667 R24 $1 carmine 1.50 .30
R668 R24 $1.10 carmine 3.25 2.50
R669 R24 $1.65 carmine 100.00 70.00
R670 R24 $2 carmine 1.75 .45
R671 R24 $2.20 carmine 4.50 3.75
R672 R24 $2.75 carmine 100.00 65.00
R673 R24 $3 carmine 3.00 2.00
R674 R24 $3.30 carmine 6.50 5.00
R675 R24 $4 carmine 4.00 3.50
R676 R24 $5 carmine 5.50 .50
R677 R24 $10 carmine 10.00 1.50
R678 R24 $20 carmine 32.50 6.00

Overprinted in Black "Series 1954"

Perf. 12

Size: 28½x42mm

Without Gum

R679 R25 $30 carmine 50.00 14.00
R680 R25 $50 carmine 65.00 20.00
R681 R25 $60 carmine 100.00 22.50
R682 R25 $100 carmine 50.00 7.00
R683 R25 $500 carmine — 75.00
R684 R25 $1000 carmine 300.00 60.00
R685 R25 $2500 carmine — 210.00
R686 R25 $5000 carmine — 850.00
R687 R25 $10,000 carmine — 1,000.

Overprinted in Black "Series 1955"
Without Gum

1955 Wmk. 191R *Perf. 12*

Size: 28½x42mm

R688 R25 $30 carmine 65.00 12.50
R689 R25 $50 carmine 65.00 16.00
R690 R25 $60 carmine 110.00 30.00
R691 R25 $100 carmine 55.00 7.50
R692 R25 $500 carmine 700.00 125.00
R693 R25 $1000 carmine — 35.00
R694 R25 $2500 carmine — 140.00
R695 R25 $5000 carmine *1,750.* 1,250.
R696 R25 $10,000 carmine — 1,100.

Overprinted in Black
"Series 1956"
Without Gum

1956 Size: 28½x42mm

R697 R25 $30 carmine 85.00 15.00
R698 R25 $50 carmine 90.00 22.50
R699 R25 $60 carmine 110.00 40.00
R700 R25 $100 carmine 85.00 14.00
R701 R25 $500 carmine — 85.00
R702 R25 $1000 carmine 550.00 65.00
R703 R25 $2500 carmine — 475.00
R704 R25 $5000 carmine — 1,700.
R705 R25 $10,000 carmine — 700.00

Overprinted in Black "Series 1957"
Without Gum

1957 Size: 28½x42mm

R706 R25 $30 carmine 105.00 30.00
R707 R25 $50 carmine 85.00 32.50
R708 R25 $60 carmine — 175.00
R709 R25 $100 carmine 75.00 15.00
R710 R25 $500 carmine 350.00 100.00
R711 R25 $1000 carmine — 80.00
R712 R25 $2500 carmine — 750.00
R713 R25 $5000 carmine *2,250.* 1,100.
R714 R25 $10,000 carmine — 450.00

Overprinted in Black "Series 1958"
Without Gum

1958 Size: 28½x42mm

R715 R25 $30 carmine 80.00 20.00
R716 R25 $50 carmine 65.00 20.00
R717 R25 $60 carmine 110.00 30.00
R718 R25 $100 carmine 55.00 10.00
R719 R25 $500 carmine 250.00 75.00
R720 R25 $1000 carmine — 67.50
R721 R25 $2500 carmine — 900.00
R722 R25 $5000 carmine — 3,000.
R723 R25 $10,000 carmine — 1,500.

Documentary Stamps and Type of 1940 Without Overprint
With Gum

1958 Size: 28½x42mm

R724 R25 $30 carmine 37.50 7.00
a. Vert. pair, imperf. horiz. *2,250.*
R725 R25 $50 carmine 42.50 7.00
a. Vert. pair, imperf. horiz. —
R726 R25 $60 carmine 80.00 20.00
R727 R25 $100 carmine 19.00 4.75
R728 R25 $500 carmine 85.00 25.00
R729 R25 $1000 carmine 55.00 20.00
a. Vert. pair, imperf. horiz. *1,500.*
R730 R25 $2500 carmine — 160.00
R731 R25 $5000 carmine — 150.00
R732 R25 $10,000 carmine — 125.00

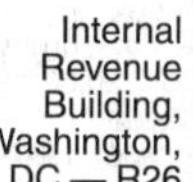

Internal Revenue Building, Washington, DC — R26

Giori Press Printing

1962, July 1 Unwmk. *Perf. 11*

R733 R26 10c vio bl & brt grn .80 .35
Never hinged 1.10

Centenary of Internal Revenue Service.

"Established 1862" Removed

1963

R734 R26 10c vio bl & brt grn 2.50 .60
Never hinged 4.50

Documentary revenue stamps were no longer required after Dec. 31, 1967.

PROPRIETARY STAMPS

Stamps for use on proprietary articles were included in the first general issue of 1862-71. They are Nos. R3, R13-R14, R18, R22, R29, R31, R38.

Washington — RB1

Various Frames and Sizes
Violet or Green Paper with Silk Threads

1871-74 Engr. *Perf. 12*

a. left column = Violet Paper (1871)

b. right column = Green Paper (1874)

RB1 RB1 1c grn & blk 5.00 10.00
c. Imperf. 80.00
d. Inverted center *3,000.*
RB2 RB1 2c grn & blk 6.00 22.50
c. Invtd. center *40,000.* *8,500.*

RB2c is valued with small faults.

RB3 RB1 3c grn & blk 22.50 50.00
c. Sewing machine perf. 275.00
d. Inverted center *16,000.*

No. RB3d is valued with small faults as 6 of the 7 recorded examples have faults.

RB4 RB1 4c grn & blk 12.50 17.50
c. Inverted center *19,000.*

No. RB4c is valued with small faults as all recorded examples have faults.

RB5 RB1 5c grn & blk 150.00 160.00
c. Inverted center *130,000.*

No. RB5c is unique. Value represents price realized in 2000 auction sale.

RB6 RB1 6c grn & blk 45.00 110.00
RB7 RB1 10c green & blk ('73) 175.00 55.00
RB8 RB1 50c green & blk ('73) 600.00 1,000.
RB9 RB1 $1 green & blk ('73) *1,100.* *8,000.*
RB10 RB1 $5 green & blk ('73) *7,000.* *25,000.*

No. RB10b is valued with small faults.

Washington — RB2

Various Frames and Sizes
Green Paper

Wmk. 191R, Unwmkd. (Silk Paper) 1875-81

b. left column = Perf.

c. right column = Rouletted 6

RB11 RB2 1c green .40 90.00
a. Silk paper 1.90
d. Vert. pair, imperf btwn. *250.00*
RB12 RB2 2c brown 1.40 110.00
a. Silk paper 2.50
RB13 RB2 3c orange 3.00 110.00
a. Silk paper 12.50
d. Horiz. pair, imperf. btwn. —
RB14 RB2 4c red brown 5.50
a. Silk paper 6.75
RB15 RB2 4c red 4.50 175.00
RB16 RB2 5c black 100.00 *1,500.*
a. Silk paper 125.00
RB17 RB2 6c violet blue 20.00 300.00
a. Silk paper 25.00
RB18 RB2 6c violet 30.00 —
RB19 RB2 10c blue ('81) 300.00

Many fraudulent roulettes exist.

The existence of No. RB18c has been questioned by specialists. The editors would like to see authenticated evidence proving its existence.

Battleship — RB3

Rouletted 5½

1898 Wmk. 191R Engr.

RB20 RB3 ⅛c yel grn .20 .20
a. Vert. pair, imperf. horiz. —
RB21 RB3 ¼c brown .20 .20
a. ¼c red brown .20 .20
b. ¼c yellow brown .20 .20
c. ¼c orange brown .20 .20
d. ¼c bister .20 .20
e. Vert. pair, imperf. horiz. — —
f. Printed on both sides —
RB22 RB3 ⅜c dp org .20 .20
a. Horiz. pair, imperf. vert. 10.00
b. Vert. pair, imperf. horiz. —
RB23 RB3 ⅝c deep ultra .20 .20
a. Vert. pair, imperf. horiz. 75.00 —
b. Horiz. pair, imperf. btwn. *300.00*
RB24 RB3 1c dark green 2.00 .20
a. Vert. pair, imperf. horiz. *300.00*
RB25 RB3 1¼c violet .20 .20
a. 1¼c brown violet .20 .20
b. Vert. pair, imperf. btwn. —
RB26 RB3 1⅞c dull blue 11.50 1.50
RB27 RB3 2c vio brown 1.00 .20
a. Horiz. pair, imperf. vert. 50.00
RB28 RB3 2½c lake 4.00 .20
a. Vert. pair, imperf. horiz. 175.00
RB29 RB3 3¾c olive gray 40.00 10.00
RB30 RB3 4c purple 12.50 1.00
RB31 RB3 5c brown org 12.50 1.00
a. Vert. pair, imperf. horiz. — *300.00*
b. Horiz. pair, imperf. vert. — *400.00*
Nos. RB20-RB31 (12) 84.50 15.10

Hyphen Hole Perf. 7

RB20p ⅛c .20 .20
RB21p ¼c .20 .20
g. ¼c yellow brown .20 .20
h. ¼c orange brown .20 .20
RB22p ⅜c .25 .20
RB23p ⅝c .25 .20
RB24p 1c 25.00 12.50
RB25p 1¼c .25 .20
c. 1¼c brown violet .25 .20
RB26p 1⅞c 30.00 7.50
RB27p 2c 6.00 .75
RB28p 2½c 5.00 .25
RB29p 3¾c 70.00 20.00
RB30p 4c 60.00 17.50
RB31p 5c 65.00 20.00

See note before No. R161.

RB4

RB5

Offset Printing

1914 Wmk. 190 *Perf. 10*

RB32 RB4 ⅛c black .20 .20
RB33 RB4 ¼c black 2.00 1.00
RB34 RB4 ⅜c black .20 .20
RB35 RB4 ⅝c black 4.50 1.75
RB36 RB4 1¼c black 3.00 1.00
RB37 RB4 1⅞c black 40.00 15.00
RB38 RB4 2½c black 9.00 2.50
RB39 RB4 3⅛c black 90.00 50.00
RB40 RB4 3¾c black 40.00 20.00
RB41 RB4 4c black 60.00 27.50
RB42 RB4 4⅜c black *1,500.* —
RB43 RB4 5c black 120.00 70.00
Nos. RB32-RB41,RB43 (11) 368.90 189.15

Wmk. 191R

RB44 RB4 ⅛c black .20 .20
RB45 RB4 ¼c black .20 .20
RB46 RB4 ⅜c black .60 .30
RB47 RB4 ½c black 3.25 2.75
RB48 RB4 ⅝c black .20 .20
RB49 RB4 1c black 4.25 4.00
RB50 RB4 1¼c black .35 .25
RB51 RB4 1½c black 3.00 2.25
RB52 RB4 1⅞c black 1.00 .60
RB53 RB4 2c black 5.00 4.00
RB54 RB4 2½c black 1.25 1.00
RB55 RB4 3c black 4.00 2.75
RB56 RB4 3⅛c black 5.00 3.00
RB57 RB4 3¾c black 11.00 7.50
RB58 RB4 4c black .30 .20
RB59 RB4 4⅜c black 15.00 8.00
RB60 RB4 5c black 3.00 2.50
RB61 RB4 6c black 55.00 40.00
RB62 RB4 8c black 17.50 11.00
RB63 RB4 10c black 11.00 7.00
RB64 RB4 20c black 22.50 17.50
Nos. RB44-RB64 (21) 163.60 115.20

1919 *Perf. 11*

RB65 RB5 1c dark blue .20 .20
RB66 RB5 2c dark blue .20 .20
RB67 RB5 3c dark blue 1.00 .60
RB68 RB5 4c dark blue 1.50 .50
RB69 RB5 5c dark blue 1.25 .60
RB70 RB5 8c dark blue 14.00 9.00
RB71 RB5 10c dark blue 5.00 2.00
RB72 RB5 20c dark blue 7.50 3.00
RB73 RB5 40c dark blue 45.00 10.00
Nos. RB65-RB73 (9) 75.65 26.10

FUTURE DELIVERY STAMPS

Issued to facilitate the collection of a tax upon each sale, agreement of sale or agreement to sell any products or merchandise at any exchange or board of trade, or other similar place for future delivery.

Documentary Stamps Nos. R228-R250 Overprinted in Black or Red

Offset Printing

1918-34 Wmk. 191R *Perf. 11*

Overprint Horizontal (Lines 8mm apart)

RC1 R22 2c car rose 5.50 .20
RC2 R22 3c car rose ('34) 30.00 22.50
Cut cancellation 12.50
RC3 R22 4c car rose 9.00 .20
RC3A R22 5c car rose ('33) 75.00 6.00
RC4 R22 10c car rose 15.00 .20
a. Double overprint — 5.00
b. "FUTURE" omitted — *200.00*
c. "DELIVERY FUTURE" 35.00
RC5 R22 20c car rose 20.00 .20
a. Double overprint 20.00
RC6 R22 25c car rose 45.00 .40
Cut cancellation .20
RC7 R22 40c car rose 50.00 .75
Cut cancellation .20
RC8 R22 50c car rose 11.50 .20
a. "DELIVERY" omitted — *100.00*
RC9 R22 80c car rose 95.00 10.00
Cut cancellation 1.00
a. Double overprint 35.00
Cut cancellation 6.00
Nos. RC1-RC9 (10) 356.00 40.65

Overprint Vertical, Reading Up (Lines 2mm apart)

Engr.

RC10 R21 $1 green (R) 40.00 .25
Cut cancellation .20
a. Overprint reading down *275.00*
b. Black overprint —
Cut cancellation 125.00
RC11 R21 $2 rose 45.00 .25
Cut cancellation .20
RC12 R21 $3 violet (R) 100.00 2.50
Cut cancellation .20
a. Overprint reading down — 50.00
RC13 R21 $5 dk bl (R) 80.00 .35
Cut cancellation .20
RC14 R21 $10 orange 100.00 .75
Cut cancellation .20
a. "DELIVERY FUTURE" *100.00*
RC15 R21 $20 olive bis 190.00 6.00
Cut cancellation .50
Nos. RC10-RC15 (6) 555.00 10.10

Perf. 12

Overprint Horizontal (Lines 11½mm apart)

Without Gum

RC16 R17 $30 ver, green numerals 80.00 3.50
Cut cancellation 1.25
a. Numerals in blue 70.00 3.50
Cut cancellation 1.50
b. As "a," imperf. *100.00*
RC17 R19 $50 olive grn 52.50 1.25
Cut cancellation .60
a. $50 olive bister 52.50 2.00
Cut cancellation .40
RC18 R19 $60 brown 80.00 2.25
Cut cancellation .75
a. Vert. pair, imperf. horiz. *400.00*
RC19 R17 $100 yel green ('34) 125.00 30.00
Cut cancellation 7.00
RC20 R18 $500 blue, red numerals (R) 90.00 11.00
Cut cancellation 4.50
a. Numerals in orange — 50.00
Cut cancellation 11.00
RC21 R19 $1000 orange 110.00 5.50
Cut cancellation 1.50
a. Vert. pair, imperf. horiz. *1,000.*
Nos. RC16-RC21 (6) 537.50 53.50

See note after No. R227.

1923-24 Offset Printing *Perf. 11*
Overprint Horiz.
(Lines 2mm apart)

RC22 R22 1c carmine rose 1.00 .20
RC23 R22 80c carmine rose 82.50 1.75
Cut cancellation .35

Documentary Stamps of 1917 Overprinted in Red or Black

1925-34 Engr.

RC25 R21 $1 green (R) 40.00 .75
Cut cancellation .20
RC26 R21 $10 orange (Bk) ('34) 110.00 15.00
Cut cancellation 10.00

Overprinted like Nos. RC1-RC9

1928-29 Offset Printing *Perf. 10*

RC27 R22 10c carmine rose *2,500.*
RC28 R22 20c carmine rose *2,500.*

STOCK TRANSFER STAMPS

Issued to facilitate the collection of a tax on all sales or agreements to sell, or memoranda of sales or delivery of, or transfers of legal title to shares or certificates of stock.

Documentary Stamps Nos. R228-R259 Overprinted in Black or Red

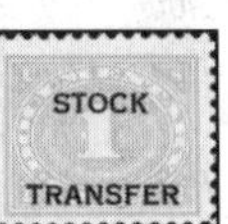

Offset Printing
1918-29 Wmk. 191R *Perf. 11*
Overprint Horiz. (Lines 8mm apart)

RD1 R22 1c car rose .85 .20
a. Double overprint — —
RD2 R22 2c car rose .20 .20
a. Double overprint — 5.00
Cut cancellation 2.50
RD3 R22 4c car rose .20 .20
a. Double overprint — 4.00
Cut cancellation 2.00
b. "STOCK" omitted 10.00
d. Overprint lines 10mm apart —
RD4 R22 5c car rose .25 .20
RD5 R22 10c car rose .25 .20
a. Double overprint — 5.00
Cut cancellation 2.50
b. "STOCK" omitted —
RD6 R22 20c car rose .50 .20
a. Double overprint 6.00
b. "STOCK" double —
RD7 R22 25c car rose 1.50 .20
Cut cancellation .20
RD8 R22 40c car rose ('22) 1.25 .20
RD9 R22 50c car rose .65 .20
a. Double overprint —
RD10 R22 80c car rose 3.00 .30
Cut cancellation .20
Nos. RD1-RD10 (10) 8.65 2.10

Overprint Vertical, Reading Up
(Lines 2mm apart)
Engr.

RD11 R21 $1 green (R) 85.00 20.00
Cut cancellation 3.00
a. Ovpt. reading down 125.00 20.00
Cut cancellation 7.50
RD12 R21 $1 green (Bk) 2.50 .25
a. Pair, one without ovpt. — *150.00*
b. Ovptd. on back instead of face, inverted — *100.00*
c. Ovpt. reading down — 6.00
d. $1 yellow green 2.75 .20
RD13 R21 $2 rose 2.50 .20
a. Ovpt. reading down 10.00
Cut cancellation 1.50
b. Vert. pair, imperf. horiz. *500.00*
RD14 R21 $3 violet (R) 17.50 4.25
Cut cancellation .20
RD15 R21 $4 yellow brn 9.00 .20
Cut cancellation .20
RD16 R21 $5 dk blue (R) 6.00 .20
Cut cancellation .20
a. Ovpt. reading down 20.00 1.00
Cut cancellation .20
RD17 R21 $10 orange 16.00 .30
Cut cancellation .20
RD18 R21 $20 ol bis ('21) 85.00 17.50
Cut cancellation 3.00
Nos. RD11-RD18 (8) 223.50 42.90

1918 Without Gum *Perf. 12*
Overprint Horizontal (Lines 11½mm apart)

RD19 R17 $30 ver, green numerals 17.50 4.50
Cut cancellation 1.00
a. Numerals in blue 55.00
RD20 R19 $50 olive green, *(Cleveland)* 110.00 55.00
Cut cancellation 20.00
RD21 R19 $60 brown 110.00 20.00
Cut cancellation 9.00
RD22 R17 $100 green 22.50 5.50
Cut cancellation 2.25
RD23 R18 $500 blue (R) 300.00 125.00
Cut cancellation 65.00
a. Numerals in orange 140.00
RD24 R19 $1000 orange 165.00 72.50
Cut cancellation 25.00

See note after No. R227.

1928-32 Offset Printing *Perf. 10*
Overprint Horiz. (Lines 8mm apart)

RD25 R22 2c carmine rose 2.50 .25
RD26 R22 4c carmine rose 2.50 .25
RD27 R22 10c carmine rose 2.00 .25
a. Inverted overprint *1,000.*
RD28 R22 20c carmine rose 3.00 .25
RD29 R22 50c carmine rose 3.50 .25

Overprint Vertical, Reading Up
(Lines 2mm apart)
Engr.

RD30 R21 $1 green 30.00 .20
a. $1 yellow green 30.00 .40
RD31 R21 $2 car rose 30.00 .20
a. Pair, one without ovpt. *200.00 175.00*
RD32 R21 $10 orange 32.50 .35
Cut cancellation .20
Nos. RD25-RD32 (8) 106.00 2.00

Overprinted Horiz. in Black

STOCK
TRANSFER

1920-28 Offset Printing *Perf. 11*

RD33 R22 2c carmine rose 7.50 .70
RD34 R22 10c carmine rose 2.50 .30
b. Inverted overprint *1,500.*
RD35 R22 20c carmine rose 5.00 .20
a. Horiz. pair, one without overprint *175.00*
d. Invtd. ovpt. (perf. initials) —
RD36 R22 50c carmine rose 3.00 .20

Engr.

RD37 R21 $1 green 50.00 9.50
Cut cancellation .25
RD38 R21 $2 rose 45.00 8.00
Cut cancellation .25
Nos. RD33-RD38 (6) 113.00 18.90

Shifted overprints on the 10c, 20c and 50c result in "TRANSFER STOCK," "TRANSFER" omitted, "STOCK" omitted, pairs, one without overprint and other varieties.

Perf. 10
Offset Printing

RD39 R22 2c carmine rose 6.50 .90
RD40 R22 10c carmine rose 1.50 .50
RD41 R22 20c carmine rose 2.50 .25
Nos. RD39-RD41 (3) 10.50 1.65

Used values for Nos. RD42-RD372 are for copies which are neither cut nor perforated with initials. Copies with cut cancellations or perforated initials are valued in the Scott U.S. Specialized Catalogue.

Documentary Stamps of 1917-33 Overprinted in Black

1940 *Perf. 11*

RD42 R22 1c rose pink 3.00 .45
a. "Series 1940" inverted — 250.00

No. RD42a always comes with a natural straight edge at left.

RD43 R22 2c rose pink 3.00 .50
RD45 R22 4c rose pink 3.00 .30
RD46 R22 5c rose pink 3.50 .20
RD48 R22 10c rose pink 4.50 .20
RD49 R22 20c rose pink 7.50 .20
RD50 R22 25c rose pink 7.50 .60
RD51 R22 40c rose pink 5.00 .75
RD52 R22 50c rose pink 6.00 .25
RD53 R22 80c rose pink 95.00 60.00
Nos. RD42-RD53 (10) 138.00 63.45

Engr.

RD54 R21 $1 green 30.00 .35
RD55 R21 $2 rose 30.00 .60
RD56 R21 $3 violet 160.00 12.50
RD57 R21 $4 yel brown 65.00 1.10
RD58 R21 $5 dark blue 55.00 1.25
RD59 R21 $10 orange 120.00 8.00
RD60 R21 $20 olive bister 260.00 75.00
Nos. RD54-RD60 (7) 720.00 98.80

Stock Transfer Stamps of 1918 Handstamped in Blue "Series 1940"

1940 Without Gum *Perf. 12*

RD61 R17 $30 vermilion *900.* 700.00
RD62 R19 $50 olive grn *900.* 2,000.
a. Dbl. ovpt. (perf. initials canc.) *500.*
RD63 R19 $60 brown *2,250.* 2,100.
RD64 R17 $100 green 1,000. 600.
RD65 R18 $500 blue *2,250.*
RD66 R19 $1000 orange *2,750.*

Alexander Hamilton ST1

Levi Woodbury ST2

Thomas Corwin — ST3

Portraits (see R23-R25): 2c, Wolcott. 4c, Gallatin. 5c, Campbell. 10c, Crawford. 20c, Rush. 25c, Ingham. 40c, McLane. 50c, Duane. 80c, Taney. $2, Ewing. $3, Forward. $4, Spencer. $5, Bibb. $10, Walker. $20, Meredith. $50, Guthrie. $60, Cobb. $100, Thomas. $500, Dix. $1,000, Chase.

Overprinted in Black **SERIES 1940**

1940 Wmk. 191R *Perf. 11*
Various Portraits
Size: 19x22mm

RD67 ST1 1c brt green 11.00 3.00
RD68 ST1 2c brt green 7.00 1.60
RD70 ST1 4c brt green 12.50 4.25
RD71 ST1 5c brt green 7.50 1.60
a. Without overprint (cut canc.) *250.00*
RD73 ST1 10c brt green 11.00 2.00
RD74 ST1 20c brt green 12.50 2.25
RD75 ST1 25c brt green 35.00 9.00
RD76 ST1 40c brt green 65.00 32.50
RD77 ST1 50c brt green 11.00 2.00
RD78 ST1 80c brt green 85.00 55.00
Nos. RD67-RD78 (10) 257.50 113.20

Size: 21½x36¼mm

RD79 ST2 $1 brt green 37.50 4.00
a. Without overprint (perf. initials canc.) *225.00*
RD80 ST2 $2 brt green 42.50 10.00
RD81 ST2 $3 brt green 65.00 12.50
RD82 ST2 $4 brt green 280.00 210.00
RD83 ST2 $5 brt green 60.00 14.00
RD84 ST2 $10 brt green 145.00 40.00
RD85 ST2 $20 brt green 900.00 80.00

Perf. 12
Without Gum
Size: 28½x42mm
Various Frame Designs

RD86 ST3 $30 brt green 650.00 150.00
RD87 ST3 $50 brt green 650.00 450.00
RD88 ST3 $60 brt green 3,000. 1,050.
RD89 ST3 $100 brt green — 300.00
RD90 ST3 $500 brt green — 2,000.
RD91 ST3 $1000 brt green — 2,000.

Overprinted in Black "Series 1941" **SERIES 1941**

1941 Size: 19x22mm *Perf. 11*

RD92 ST1 1c brt green .65 .50
RD93 ST1 2c brt green .45 .25
RD95 ST1 4c brt green .50 .25
RD96 ST1 5c brt green .45 .25
RD98 ST1 10c brt green .75 .25
RD99 ST1 20c brt green 1.75 .25
RD100 ST1 25c brt green 1.75 .40
RD101 ST1 40c brt green 2.50 .75
RD102 ST1 50c brt green 3.75 .35
RD103 ST1 80c brt green 22.50 7.50
Nos. RD92-RD103 (10) 35.05 10.75

Size: 21½x36¼mm

RD104 ST2 $1 brt green 15.00 .20
RD105 ST2 $2 brt green 16.00 .25
RD106 ST2 $3 brt green 24.00 1.50
RD107 ST2 $4 brt green 42.50 6.50
RD108 ST2 $5 brt green 42.50 .60
RD109 ST2 $10 brt green 90.00 4.00
RD110 ST2 $20 brt green 250.00 65.00
Nos. RD104-RD110 (7) 480.00 78.05

Perf. 12
Without Gum
Size: 28½x42mm

RD111 ST3 $30 brt green 225.00 225.00
RD112 ST3 $50 brt green 800.00 400.00
RD113 ST3 $60 brt green 1,200. 325.00
RD114 ST3 $100 brt green — 150.00
RD115 ST3 $500 brt green 1,750. *1,500.*
RD116 ST3 $1000 brt green — *1,400.*

Overprinted in Black "Series 1942"

1942 Size: 19x22mm *Perf. 11*

RD117 ST1 1c brt green .50 .30
RD118 ST1 2c brt green .40 .35
RD119 ST1 4c brt green 3.00 1.00
RD120 ST1 5c brt green .40 .20
a. Ovpt. invtd. (cut cancel) *225.00*
RD121 ST1 10c brt green 1.75 .20
RD122 ST1 20c brt green 2.00 .20
RD123 ST1 25c brt green 2.00 .20
RD124 ST1 40c brt green 4.25 .35
RD125 ST1 50c brt green 5.25 .20
RD126 ST1 80c brt green 22.50 5.75
Nos. RD117-RD126 (10) 42.05 8.75

Size: 21½x36¼mm

RD127 ST2 $1 brt green 15.00 .35
RD128 ST2 $2 brt green 25.00 .35
RD129 ST2 $3 brt green 30.00 1.00
RD130 ST2 $4 brt green 42.50 20.00
RD131 ST2 $5 brt green 37.50 .35
a. Dbl. ovpt. (perf. initials cancel) —
RD132 ST2 $10 brt green 70.00 8.00
RD133 ST2 $20 brt green 160.00 35.00
Nos. RD127-RD133 (7) 380.00 65.05

Perf. 12
Without Gum
Size: 28½x42mm

RD134 ST3 $30 brt green 200.00 60.00
RD135 ST3 $50 brt green 350.00 125.00
RD136 ST3 $60 brt green 400.00 190.00
RD137 ST3 $100 brt green *500.00* 80.00
RD138 ST3 $500 brt green — *12,500.*
RD139 ST3 $1000 brt green — 550.00

Overprinted in Black "Series 1943"

1943 Size: 19x22mm *Perf. 11*

RD140 ST1 1c brt green .40 .30
RD141 ST1 2c brt green .50 .40
RD142 ST1 4c brt green 1.75 .20
RD143 ST1 5c brt green .50 .20
RD144 ST1 10c brt green 1.00 .20
RD145 ST1 20c brt green 1.75 .20
RD146 ST1 25c brt green 4.50 .35
RD147 ST1 40c brt green 3.75 .25
RD148 ST1 50c brt green 3.75 .20
RD149 ST1 80c brt green 15.00 4.50
Nos. RD140-RD149 (10) 32.90 6.80

Size: 21½x36¼mm

RD150 ST2 $1 brt green 15.00 .20
RD151 ST2 $2 brt green 17.50 .35
RD152 ST2 $3 brt green 21.00 1.25
RD153 ST2 $4 brt green 42.50 15.00
RD154 ST2 $5 brt green 65.00 .35
RD155 ST2 $10 brt green 85.00 4.50
RD156 ST2 $20 brt green 150.00 37.50
Nos. RD150-RD156 (7) 396.00 59.15

Perf. 12
Without Gum
Size: 28½x42mm

RD157 ST3 $30 brt green 325.00 140.00
RD158 ST3 $50 brt green 650.00 140.00
RD159 ST3 $60 brt green — 1,000.

RD160 ST3 $100 brt green 110.00 60.00
RD161 ST3 $500 brt green — 1,100.
RD162 ST3 $1000 brt green — 250.00

Overprinted in Black "Series 1944"

Portraits: $2,500, William Windom. $5,000, C. J. Folger. $10,000, Walter Q. Gresham.

1944 Wmk. 191R *Perf. 11*

Size: 19x22mm

RD163 ST1 1c brt green .65 .60
RD164 ST1 2c brt green .45 .20
RD165 ST1 4c brt green .60 .25
RD166 ST1 5c brt green .50 .20
RD167 ST1 10c brt green .75 .20
RD168 ST1 20c brt green 1.25 .20
RD169 ST1 25c brt green 2.00 .30
RD170 ST1 40c brt green 8.00 5.00
RD171 ST1 50c brt green 4.50 .20
RD172 ST1 80c brt green 9.00 4.50
Nos. RD163-RD172 (10) 27.70 11.65

Size: 21½x36¼mm

RD173 ST2 $1 brt green 10.00 .40
RD174 ST2 $2 brt green 37.50 .60
RD175 ST2 $3 brt green 35.00 1.25
RD176 ST2 $4 brt green 40.00 5.00
RD177 ST2 $5 brt green 37.50 1.00
RD178 ST2 $10 brt green 75.00 4.50
RD179 ST2 $20 brt green 125.00 9.00
Nos. RD173-RD179 (7) 360.00 21.75

Perf. 12

Without Gum

Size: 28½x42mm

Bright Green

RD180 ST3 $30 200.00 75.00
RD181 ST3 $50 140.00 60.00
RD182 ST3 $60 240.00 140.00
RD183 ST3 $100 200.00 60.00
RD184 ST3 $500 — 500.00
RD185 ST3 $1000 — 800.00
RD185A ST3 $2500 —
RD185B ST3 $5000 —
RD185C ST3 $10,000 Cut cancel —

Overprinted in Black "Series 1945"

1945 Wmk. 191R *Perf. 11*

Size: 19x22mm

RD186 ST1 1c brt green .25 .20
RD187 ST1 2c brt green .25 .25
RD188 ST1 4c brt green .25 .20
RD189 ST1 5c brt green .25 .20
RD190 ST1 10c brt green .75 .35
RD191 ST1 20c brt green 1.25 .30
RD192 ST1 25c brt green 2.00 .35
RD193 ST1 40c brt green 3.00 .25
RD194 ST1 50c brt green 3.50 .30
RD195 ST1 80c brt green 7.50 3.00
Nos. RD186-RD195 (10) 19.00 5.40

Size: 21½x36¼mm

RD196 ST2 $1 brt green 14.00 .25
RD197 ST2 $2 brt green 22.50 .45
RD198 ST2 $3 brt green 37.50 .90
RD199 ST2 $4 brt green 37.50 2.50
RD200 ST2 $5 brt green 24.00 .50
RD201 ST2 $10 brt green 55.00 6.50
RD202 ST2 $20 brt green 125.00 12.50

Perf. 12

Without Gum

Size: 28½x42mm

Bright green

RD203 ST3 $30 140.00 70.00
RD204 ST3 $50 65.00 25.00
RD205 ST3 $60 240.00 150.00
RD206 ST3 $100 85.00 40.00
RD207 ST3 $500 — 900.00
RD208 ST3 $1000 *1,500.* 1,000.
RD208A ST3 $2500 Cut cancel *20,000.*
RD208B ST3 $5000 20,000.
RD208C ST3 $10,000 Cut cancel *20,000.*

Overprinted in Black "Series 1946"

1946 Wmk. 191R *Perf. 11*

Size: 19x22mm

RD209 ST1 1c brt green .20 .20
a. Pair, one dated "1945" *475.00*
RD210 ST1 2c brt green .35 .20
RD211 ST1 4c brt green .30 .20
RD212 ST1 5c brt green .35 .20
RD213 ST1 10c brt green .75 .20
RD214 ST1 20c brt green 1.50 .20
RD215 ST1 25c brt green 1.75 .25
RD216 ST1 40c brt green 3.50 .60
RD217 ST1 50c brt green 4.50 .25
RD218 ST1 80c brt green 11.00 6.00
Nos. RD209-RD218 (10) 24.20 8.30

Size: 21½x36¼mm

RD219 ST2 $1 brt green 10.00 .50
RD220 ST2 $2 brt green 11.00 .50
RD221 ST2 $3 brt green 21.00 1.25
RD222 ST2 $4 brt green 21.00 6.25
RD223 ST2 $5 brt green 32.50 1.25
RD224 ST2 $10 brt green 60.00 2.60
RD225 ST2 $20 brt green 150.00 45.00
Nos. RD219-RD225 (7) 305.50 57.35

Perf. 12

Without Gum

Size: 28½x42mm

RD226 ST3 $30 brt grn 125.00 42.50
RD227 ST3 $50 brt grn 90.00 47.50
RD228 ST3 $60 brt grn 210.00 100.00
RD229 ST3 $100 brt grn 125.00 55.00
RD230 ST3 $500 brt grn — 175.00
RD231 ST3 $1000 brt grn — 200.00
RD232 ST3 $2500 brt grn *20,000.*
(cut cancel) *13,500.*
RD233 ST3 $5000 brt grn, cut cancel *12,500.*
RD234 ST3 $10,000 brt grn, cut cancel 10,000.

Overprinted in Black "Series 1947"

1947 Wmk. 191R *Perf. 11*

Size: 19x22mm

RD235 ST1 1c brt green 1.25 .55
RD236 ST1 2c brt green 1.25 .50
RD237 ST1 4c brt green 1.00 .40
RD238 ST1 5c brt green 1.00 .35
RD239 ST1 10c brt green 1.25 .50
RD240 ST1 20c brt green 2.00 .50
RD241 ST1 25c brt green 3.00 .60
RD242 ST1 40c brt green 3.50 .75
RD243 ST1 50c brt green 4.00 .30
RD244 ST1 80c brt green 21.00 10.00
Nos. RD235-RD244 (10) 39.25 14.45

Size: 21½x36¼mm

RD245 ST2 $1 brt green 11.00 .50
RD246 ST2 $2 brt green 17.50 .75
RD247 ST2 $3 brt green 32.50 1.50
RD248 ST2 $4 brt green 40.00 6.00
RD249 ST2 $5 brt green 35.00 1.50
RD250 ST2 $10 brt green 55.00 5.00
RD251 ST2 $20 brt green 100.00 30.00
Nos. RD245-RD251 (7) 291.00 45.25

Perf. 12

Without Gum

Size: 28½x42mm

RD252 ST3 $30 brt grn 100.00 50.00
RD253 ST3 $50 brt grn 200.00 110.00
RD254 ST3 $60 brt grn 300.00 150.00
RD255 ST3 $100 brt grn 110.00 45.00
RD256 ST3 $500 brt grn — 400.00
RD257 ST3 $1000 brt grn — 100.00
RD258 ST3 $2500 brt grn —
(cut cancel) *450.00*
RD259 ST3 $5000 brt grn —
(cut cancel) *325.00*
RD260 ST3 $10,000 brt grn —
(cut cancel) 55.00
a. Horiz. pair, imperf. vert. (cut canc.) —

Overprinted in Black "Series 1948"

1948 Wmk. 191R *Perf. 11*

Size: 19x22mm

RD261 ST1 1c brt green .25 .25
RD262 ST1 2c brt green .25 .25
RD263 ST1 4c brt green .45 .30
RD264 ST1 5c brt green .30 .25
RD265 ST1 10c brt green .30 .25
RD266 ST1 20c brt green 1.40 .35
RD267 ST1 25c brt green 1.40 .40
RD268 ST1 40c brt green 2.25 .75
RD269 ST1 50c brt green 4.25 .30
RD270 ST1 80c brt green 17.50 6.00
Nos. RD261-RD270 (10) 28.35 9.10

Size: 21½x36¼mm

RD271 ST2 $1 brt green 12.00 .40
RD272 ST2 $2 brt green 20.00 .60
RD273 ST2 $3 brt green 25.00 3.75
RD274 ST2 $4 brt green 27.50 11.00
RD275 ST2 $5 brt green 32.50 2.50
RD276 ST2 $10 brt green 55.00 4.50
RD277 ST2 $20 brt green 95.00 18.00
Nos. RD271-RD277 (7) 267.00 40.75

Perf. 12

Without Gum

Size: 28½x42mm

RD278 ST3 $30 brt grn 150.00 60.00
RD279 ST3 $50 brt grn 100.00 60.00
RD280 ST3 $60 brt grn 250.00 140.00
RD281 ST3 $100 brt grn 85.00 22.50
RD282 ST3 $500 brt grn — 240.00
RD283 ST3 $1000 brt grn — 125.00
RD284 ST3 $2500 brt grn 650.00 350.00
RD285 ST3 $5000 brt grn — 275.00
RD286 ST3 $10,000 brt grn —
(cut cancel) 50.00

Overprinted in Black "Series 1949"

1949 Wmk. 191R *Perf. 11*

Size: 19x22mm

RD287 ST1 1c brt green 1.50 .45
RD288 ST1 2c brt green 1.50 .45
RD289 ST1 4c brt green 1.75 .50
RD290 ST1 5c brt green 1.75 .50
RD291 ST1 10c brt green 3.00 .75
RD292 ST1 20c brt green 5.00 .60
RD293 ST1 25c brt green 6.00 .85
RD294 ST1 40c brt green 12.50 1.50
RD295 ST1 50c brt green 15.00 .25
RD296 ST1 80c brt green 20.00 6.50
Nos. RD287-RD296 (10) 68.00 12.35

Size: 21½x36¼mm

RD297 ST2 $1 brt green 17.50 .75
RD298 ST2 $2 brt green 25.00 .90
RD299 ST2 $3 brt green 40.00 4.50
RD300 ST2 $4 brt green 37.50 7.50
RD301 ST2 $5 brt green 47.50 2.00
RD302 ST2 $10 brt green 65.00 4.00
RD303 ST2 $20 brt green 140.00 15.00
Nos. RD297-RD303 (7) 372.50 34.65

Perf. 12

Without Gum

Size: 28½x42mm

RD304 ST3 $30 brt grn 160.00 85.00
RD305 ST3 $50 brt grn 225.00 125.00
RD306 ST3 $60 brt grn 375.00 250.00
RD307 ST3 $100 brt grn 150.00 70.00
RD308 ST3 $500 brt grn — 250.00
RD309 ST3 $1000 brt grn — 100.00
RD310 ST3 $2500 brt grn —
(cut cancel) *450.00*
RD311 ST3 $5000 brt grn —
(cut cancel) *450.00*
RD312 ST3 $10,000 brt grn — 400.00
a. Pair, one without ovpt. (cut cancel) *8,000.*

No. RD312a is unique.

Overprinted in Black "Series 1950"

1950 Wmk. 191R *Perf. 11*

Size: 19x22mm

RD313 ST1 1c brt green .60 .35
RD314 ST1 2c brt green .50 .30
RD315 ST1 4c brt green .40 .35
RD316 ST1 5c brt green .50 .20
RD317 ST1 10c brt green 2.50 .30
RD318 ST1 20c brt green 3.75 .50
RD319 ST1 25c brt green 5.00 .70
RD320 ST1 40c brt green 7.50 1.00
RD321 ST1 50c brt green 8.25 .35
RD322 ST1 80c brt green 15.00 5.00
Nos. RD313-RD322 (10) 44.00 9.05

Size: 21½x36¼mm

RD323 ST2 $1 brt green 15.00 .50
RD324 ST2 $2 brt green 27.50 .75
RD325 ST2 $3 brt green 35.00 4.00
RD326 ST2 $4 brt green 42.50 9.00
RD327 ST2 $5 brt green 42.50 1.75
RD328 ST2 $10 brt green 140.00 5.00
RD329 ST2 $20 brt green 140.00 25.00
Nos. RD323-RD329 (7) 442.50 46.00

Perf. 12

Without Gum

Size: 28½x42mm

RD330 ST3 $30 brt grn 140.00 70.00
RD331 ST3 $50 brt grn 175.00 90.00
RD332 ST3 $60 brt grn 250.00 140.00
RD333 ST3 $100 brt grn 100.00 50.00
a. Vert. pair, imperf btwn. *2,250.* *1,750.*
RD334 ST3 $500 brt grn — 250.00
RD335 ST3 $1000 brt grn — 75.00
RD336 ST3 $2500 brt grn — *1,200.*
RD337 ST3 $5000 brt grn — 725.00
RD338 ST3 $10,000 brt grn — 800.00

Overprinted in Black "Series 1951"

1951 Wmk. 191R *Perf. 11*

Size: 19x22mm

RD339 ST1 1c brt green 2.00 .35
RD340 ST1 2c brt green 1.75 .30
RD341 ST1 4c brt green 2.00 .50
RD342 ST1 5c brt green 1.50 .35
RD343 ST1 10c brt green 2.00 .35
RD344 ST1 20c brt green 5.00 .90
RD345 ST1 25c brt green 7.50 .90
RD346 ST1 40c brt green 30.00 9.00
RD347 ST1 50c brt green 12.50 .90
RD348 ST1 80c brt green 25.00 10.00
Nos. RD339-RD348 (10) 89.25 23.55

Size: 21½x36¼mm

RD349 ST2 $1 brt green 26.00 .80
RD350 ST2 $2 brt green 32.50 1.25
RD351 ST2 $3 brt green 42.50 10.00
RD352 ST2 $4 brt green 50.00 12.00
RD353 ST2 $5 brt green 60.00 2.50
RD354 ST2 $10 brt green 95.00 8.50
RD355 ST2 $20 brt green 160.00 17.50
Nos. RD349-RD355 (7) 466.00 52.55

Perf. 12

Without Gum

Size: 28½x42mm

RD356 ST3 $30 brt grn 160.00 75.00
RD357 ST3 $50 brt grn 150.00 65.00
RD358 ST3 $60 brt grn — *1,400.*
RD359 ST3 $100 brt grn 150.00 65.00
RD360 ST3 $500 brt grn — 350.00
RD361 ST3 $1000 brt grn — 100.00
RD362 ST3 $2500 brt grn — *3,000.*
RD363 ST3 $5000 brt grn — *1,400.*
RD364 ST3 $10,000 brt grn *1,500.* 150.00

Overprinted in Black "Series 1952"

1952 Wmk. 191R *Perf. 11*

Size: 19x22mm

RD365 ST1 1c brt green 35.00 17.50
RD366 ST1 10c brt green 35.00 17.50
RD367 ST1 20c brt green 400.00 —
RD368 ST1 25c brt green 500.00 —
RD369 ST1 40c brt green 100.00 40.00

Size: 21½x36¼mm

RD370 ST2 $4 brt green 1,500. 550.
RD371 ST2 $10 brt green *3,000.* —
RD372 ST2 $20 brt green *5,750.* —

Stock Transfer stamps were discontinued in 1952.

See the *Scott United States Specialized Catalogue* for other categories of Revenue stamps.

HUNTING PERMIT STAMPS

The receipts of the sales of these "Migratory Bird Hunting" stamps help to maintain waterfowl life in the United States.

Unused values are for stamps with never-hinged original gum.

Minor natural gum skips and bends are normal on Nos. RW1-RW20.

No gum stamps are without signature or other cancel.

Used Values

Used value for No. RW1 is for stamp with handstamp or manuscript cancel, though technically it was against regulations to deface the stamp or to apply a postal cancellation..

Beginning with No. RW2, the used value is for stamps with manuscript signature.

Catalogue values for unused stamps in this section are for Never Hinged items.

Department of Agriculture

Various Designs Inscribed "U. S. Department of Agriculture"

HP1

Engraved; Flat Plate Printing

1934 Unwmk. *Perf. 11*

"Void after June 30, 1935"

RW1 HP1 $1 blue 775.00 125.00
Hinged 350.00
No gum 160.00
a. Imperf., pair —
b. Vert. pair, imperf. horiz. —

1935 "Void after June 30, 1936"

RW2 $1 Canvasback Ducks Taking to Flight 700.00 140.00
Hinged 350.00
No gum 190.00

1936 "Void after June 30, 1937"

RW3 $1 Canada Geese in Flight 350.00 75.00
Hinged 175.00
No gum 110.00

1937 "Void after June 30, 1938"

RW4 $1 Scaup Ducks Taking to Flight 300.00 57.50
Hinged 150.00
No gum 75.00

1938 "Void after June 30, 1939"

RW5 $1 Pintail Drake and Duck Alighting 425.00 57.50
Hinged 200.00
No gum 75.00

Department of the Interior
Various Designs Inscribed
"U. S. Department of the Interior"

Green-Winged Teal — HP2

1939 "Void after June 30, 1940"
RW6 HP2 $1 chocolate 250.00 45.00
Hinged 110.00
No gum 50.00

1940 "Void after June 30, 1941"
RW7 $1 Black Mallards 225.00 45.00
Hinged 110.00
No gum 50.00

1941 "Void after June 30, 1942"
RW8 $1 Family of Ruddy Ducks 225.00 45.00
Hinged 110.00
No gum 50.00

1942 "Void after June 30, 1943"
RW9 $1 Baldpates 225.00 45.00
Hinged 110.00
No gum 50.00

1943 "Void after June 30, 1944"
RW10 $1 Wood Ducks 90.00 32.50
Hinged 50.00
No gum 35.00

1944 "Void after June 30, 1945"
RW11 $1 White-fronted Geese 90.00 25.00
Hinged 50.00
No gum 32.50

1945 "Void after June 30, 1946"
RW12 $1 Shoveller Ducks in Flight 60.00 25.00
Hinged 35.00
No gum 27.50

1946 "Void after June 30, 1947"
RW13 $1 Redhead Ducks 45.00 16.00
No gum 18.00
a. $1 bright rose pink —

1947 "Void after June 30, 1948"
RW14 $1 Snow Geese 45.00 16.00
No gum 18.00

1948 "Void after June 30, 1949"
RW15 $1 Bufflehead Ducks in Flight 50.00 15.00
No gum 21.00

Goldeneye Ducks — HP3

1949 "Void after June 30, 1950"
RW16 HP3 $2 bright green 65.00 14.00
No gum 22.50

1950 "Void after June 30, 1951"
RW17 $2 Trumpeter Swans in Flight 75.00 11.00
No gum 22.50

1951 "Void after June 30, 1952"
RW18 $2 Gadwall Ducks 75.00 11.00
No gum 22.50

1952 "Void after June 30, 1953"
RW19 $2 Harlequin Ducks 75.00 11.00
No gum 22.50

1953 "Void after June 30, 1954"
RW20 $2 Blue-winged Teal 75.00 11.00
No gum 22.50

1954 "Void after June 30, 1955"
RW21 $2 Ring-necked Ducks 75.00 10.50
No gum 22.50

1955 "Void after June 30, 1956"
RW22 $2 Blue Geese 75.00 10.50
No gum 22.50
a. Back inscription inverted —

1956 "Void after June 30, 1957"
RW23 $2 American Merganser 75.00 10.50
No gum 22.50

1957 "Void after June 30, 1958"
RW24 $2 American Eiders 75.00 10.50
No gum 22.50
a. Back inscription inverted —

1958 "Void after June 30, 1959"
RW25 $2 Canada Geese 75.00 10.50
No gum 22.50

Labrador Retriever Carrying Mallard Drake — HP4

1959 Giori Press Printing
"Void after June 30, 1960"
RW26 HP4 $3 blue, ocher & blk 100.00 10.50
No gum 35.00
a. Back inscription inverted —

Redhead Ducks — HP5

1960 "Void after June 30, 1961"
RW27 HP5 $3 red brn, dk bl & bister 85.00 10.50
No gum 35.00

1961 "Void after June 30, 1962"
RW28 $3 Mallard Hen & Ducklings 85.00 10.50
No gum 38.00

Pintail Drakes — HP6

1962 "Void after June 30, 1963"
RW29 HP6 $3 Coming in for Landing 100.00 10.50
No gum 55.00
a. Back inscription omitted —

1963 "Void after June 30, 1964"
RW30 $3 Pair of Brant landing 100.00 10.50
No gum 55.00

1964 "Void after June 30, 1965"
RW31 $3 Hawaiian Nene Geese 100.00 10.50
No gum 55.00

1965 "Void after June 30, 1966"
RW32 $3 3 Canvasback Drakes 100.00 10.50
No gum 55.00

Whistling Swans — HP7

1966 "Void after June 30, 1967"
RW33 HP7 $3 ultra, sl grn & blk 100.00 10.50
No gum 55.00

1967 "Void after June 30, 1968"
RW34 $3 Old Squaw Ducks 125.00 10.00
No gum 55.00

1968 "Void after June 30, 1969"
RW35 $3 Hooded Mergansers 65.00 10.00
No gum 25.00

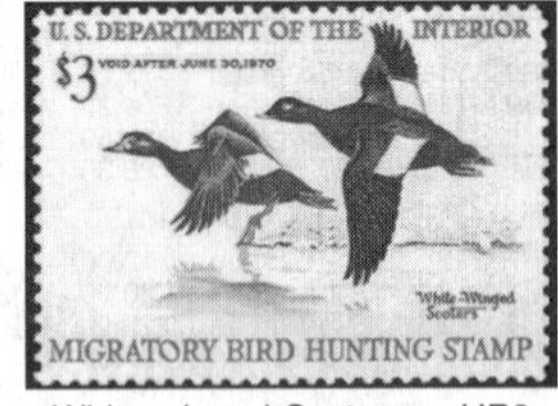

White-winged Scoters — HP8

1969 "Void after June 30, 1970"
RW36 HP8 $3 gray, brn, indigo & brn red 65.00 7.00
No gum 25.00

1970 Litho. & Engr.
"Void after June 30, 1971"
RW37 $3 Ross' Geese 65.00 7.00
No gum 24.00

1971 "Void after June 30, 1972"
RW38 $3 3 Cinnamon Teal 42.50 7.75
No gum 21.00

1972 "Void after June 30, 1973"
RW39 $5 Emperor Geese 25.00 7.00
No gum 12.50

1973 "Void after June 30, 1974"
RW40 $5 Steller's Eiders 18.00 7.00
No gum 11.50

1974 "Void after June 30, 1975"
RW41 $5 Wood Ducks 18.00 6.00
No gum 9.50

1975 "Void after June 30, 1976"
RW42 $5 Weathered canvas-back duck decoy & flying ducks 15.00 6.00
No gum 7.50

1976 Engr.
"Void after June 30, 1977"
RW43 $5 Family of Canada Geese 15.00 6.00
No gum 7.50

1977 Engr. & Litho.
"Void after June 30, 1978"
RW44 $5 Ross' Geese, pair 15.00 6.00
No gum 7.50

Hooded Merganser — HP9

1978 "Void after June 30, 1979"
RW45 HP9 $5 multicolored 12.50 6.00
No gum 7.00

1979 "Void after June 30, 1980"
RW46 $7.50 Green-winged teal 14.00 7.00
No gum 9.00

1980 "Void after June 30, 1981"
RW47 $7.50 Mallards 14.00 7.00
No gum 8.50

1981 "Void after June 30, 1982"
RW48 $7.50 Ruddy Ducks 14.00 7.00
No gum 8.50

1982 "Void after June 30, 1983"
RW49 $7.50 Canvasbacks 15.00 7.00
No gum 8.50
a. Orange & violet omitted —

1983 "Void after June 30, 1984"
RW50 $7.50 Pintails 15.00 7.00
No gum 8.50

1984 "Void after June 30, 1985"
RW51 $7.50 Widgeons 15.00 7.00
No gum 8.50

1985 "Void after June 30, 1986"
RW52 $7.50 Cinnamon Teal 15.00 7.00
No gum 8.50

1986 "Void after June 30, 1987"
RW53 $7.50 Fulvous Whistling Duck 15.00 7.00
No gum 8.50
a. Black omitted *3,750.*

1987 *Perf. 11½x11*
"Void after June 30, 1988"
RW54 $10 Redheads 17.50 9.50
No gum 10.00

1988 "Void after June 30, 1989"
RW55 $10 Snow Goose 17.00 10.00
No gum 11.00

1989 "Void after June 30, 1990"
RW56 $12.50 Lesser Scaups 19.00 10.00
No gum 12.00

1990 "Void after June 30, 1991"
RW57 $12.50 Black Bellied Whistling Duck 19.00 10.00
No gum 12.00
a. Back inscription omitted *425.00*

The back inscription is on top of the gum so beware of copies with gum removed. Used examples of No. RW57a cannot exist.

King Eiders — HP10

1991 "Void after June 30, 1992"

RW58	HP10 $15 multicolored	24.00	11.00
	No gum	15.00	
a.	Black (engr.) omitted	8,500.	

1992 "Void after June 30, 1993"

RW59	$15 Spectacled Eider	24.00	12.50
	No gum	15.00	

1993 "Void after June 30, 1994"

RW60	$15 Canvasbacks	24.00	11.00
	No gum	15.00	
a.	Black (engr.) omitted	3,250.	

1994 "Void after June 30, 1995"

RW61	$15 Red-breasted mergansers	24.00	11.00
	No gum	15.00	

1995 "Void after June 30, 1996"

RW62	$15 Mallards	24.00	11.00
	No gum	15.00	

1996 "Void after June 30, 1997"

RW63	$15 Surf Scoters	24.00	11.00
	No gum	15.00	

1997 "Void after June 30, 1998"

RW64	$15 Canada Goose	22.50	11.00
	No gum	15.00	

Nos. RW65 and later issues were sold in panes of 30 (RW65 and RW66) or 20 (RW67 and later issues). The self-adhesives starting with No. RW65A were sold in panes of 1. The self-adhesives are valued unused as complete panes and used as single stamps.

1998 "Void after June 30, 1999"

RW65	$15 Barrow's Goldeneye	24.00	11.00
	No gum	15.00	

Self-Adhesive

Serpentine Die Cut

RW65A	$15 Barrow's Goldeneye	22.50	12.50

1999 "Void after June 30, 2000"

RW66	$15 Greater Scaup	22.50	11.00
	No gum	15.00	

Self-Adhesive

Die Cut 10

RW66A	$15 Greater Scaup	22.50	12.50

2000 ***Perf. 11¼***

"Void after June 30, 2001"

RW67	$15 Mottled Duck	22.50	11.00
	No gum	15.00	

Self-Adhesive

Die Cut 10

RW67A	$15 Mottled Duck	22.50	12.50

2001 ***Perf. 11¼***

"Void after June 30, 2002"

RW68	$15 Northern pintail	22.50	11.00
	No gum	15.00	

Self-Adhesive

Die Cut 10

RW68A	$15 Northern pintail	22.50	12.50

Hunting Permit Type of 1991

2002 ***Perf. 11¼***

Inscribed "Void after June 30, 2003"

RW69	$15 *Black Scoters*	22.50	11.00
	No gum	15.00	

Self-Adhesive

Serpentine Die Cut 11x10¾

RW69A	$15 *Black Scoters*	22.50	11.00

No. RW69 was sold in panes of 20. No. RW69A was sold in panes of 1. No. RW69A is valued unused as a complete pane and used as a single stamp.

CONFEDERATE STATES

3c 1861 POSTMASTERS' PROVISIONALS

With the secession of South Carolina from the Union on Dec. 20, 1860, a new era began in U.S. history as well as its postal history. Other Southern states quickly followed South Carolina's lead, which in turn led to the formation of the provisional government of the Confederate States of America on Feb. 4, 1861.

President Jefferson Davis' cabinet was completed Mar. 6, 1861, with the acceptance of the position of Postmaster General by John H. Reagan of Texas. The provisional government had already passed regulations that required payment for postage in cash and that effectively carried over the U.S. 3c rate until the new Confederate Post Office Department took over control of the system.

Soon after entering on his duties, Reagan directed the postmasters in the Confederate States and in the newly seceded states to "continue the performance of their duties as such, and render all accounts and pay all moneys (sic) to the order of the Government of the U.S. as they have heretofore done, until the Government of the Confederate States shall be prepared to assume control of its postal affairs."

As coinage was becoming scarce, postal patrons began having problems buying individual stamps or paying for letters individually, especially as stamp stocks started to run short in certain areas. Even though the U.S. Post Office Department was technically in control of the postal system and southern postmasters were operating under Federal authority, the U.S.P.O. was hesitant in re-supplying seceded states with additional stamps and stamped envelopes.

The U.S. government had made the issuance of postmasters' provisionals illegal many years before, but the southern postmasters had to do what they felt was necessary to allow patrons to pay for postage and make the system work. Therefore, a few postmasters took it upon themselves to issue provisional stamps in the 3c rate then in effect.

Interestingly, these were stamps and envelopes that the U.S. government did not recognize as legal, but they did do postal duty unchallenged in the Confederate States. Yet the proceeds were to be remitted to the U.S. government in Washington! Six authenticated postmasters' provisionals in the 3c rate have been recorded.

On May 13, 1861, Postmaster General Reagan issued his proclamation "assuming control and direction of postal service within the limits of the Confederate States of America on and after the first day of June," with new postage rates and regulations.

The Federal government suspended operations in the Confederate States (except for western Virginia and the seceding state of Tennessee) by a proclamation issued by Postmaster General Montgomery Blair on May 27, 1861, effective from May 31, 1861, and June 10 for western and middle Tennessee.

As Tennessee did not join the Confederacy until July 2, 1861, the unissued 3c Nashville provisional was produced in a state that was in the process of seceding, while the other provisionals were used in the Confederacy before the June 1 assumption of control of postal service by the Confederate States of America.

Illustrations are reduced in size.

XU numbers are envelope entires.

HILLSBORO, N.C.

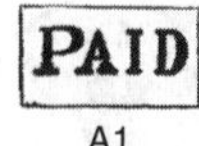

A1

Handstamped Adhesive

1AX1	A1 3c bluish blk, on cover		—

This is the same handstamp used for No. 39X1. 3c usage is determined from the May 27, 1861 circular date stamp.

No. 1AX1 is unique.

See Nos. 39X1, 39XU1.

JACKSON, MISS.

E1

Handstamped Envelope

2AXU1	E1	3c black	1,000.

See Nos. 43XU1-43XU4.

MADISON COURT HOUSE, FLA.

A1

"CNETS"

Typeset Adhesive

3AX1	A1	3c gold	—	10,000.
a.		"CNETS"		14,000.

No. 3AX1a is unique.

See No. 137XU1.

NASHVILLE, TENN.

A1

Typeset Adhesive (5 varieties)

4AX1	A1	3c carmine	150.

No. 4AX1 was prepared by Postmaster McNish with the U.S. rate, but the stamp was never issued.

See Nos. 61X2-61XU2.

SELMA, ALA.

E1

Handstamped Envelope

5AXU1	E1	3c black	1,750.

See Nos. 77XU1-77XU3.

TUSCUMBIA, ALA.

E1

Handstamped Envelope

Impression at upper right

6AXU1 E1 3c dull red, *buff* *16,500.*

See Nos. 84XU1-84XU3.

POSTMASTERS' PROVISIONAL ISSUES

These stamps and envelopes were issued by individual postmasters generally between June 1, 1861, when the use of U.S. stamps stopped in the Confederacy, and Oct. 16, 1861, when the 1st Confederate Government stamps were issued.

They were occasionally issued at later periods, especially in Texas, when regular issues of Government stamps were unavailable.

Canceling stamps of the post offices were often used to produce envelopes, some of which were supplied in advance by private citizens.

These envelopes and other stationery therefore may be found in a wide variety of papers, colors, sizes & shapes, including patriotic and semi-official types.

It is often difficult to determine whether the impression made by the canceling stamp indicates provisional usage or merely postage paid at the time the letter was deposited in the post office. Occasionally the same mark was used for both purposes.

The *press-printed* provisional envelopes are in a different category. They were produced in quantity, using envelopes procured in advance by the postmaster, such as those of Charleston, Lynchburg, Memphis, etc.

The press-printed envelopes are listed and valued on all known papers.

The handstamped provisional envelopes are listed and valued according to type and variety of handstamp, but not according to paper. Many exist on such a variety of papers that they defy accurate, complete listing.

The value of a handstamped provisional envelope is determined *primarily* by the clarity of the markings and its overall condition and attractiveness, rather than type of paper.

All handstamped provisional envelopes, when used, should also show the postmark of the town of issue.

Most handstamps are impressed at top right, although they exist from some towns in other positions.

Illustrations in this section are reduced in size.

XU numbers are envelope entires.

ABERDEEN, MISS.

E1

Handstamped Envelopes

1XU1 E1 5c black *6,000.*
1XU2 E1 10c (ms.) on 5c blk 12,500.

No. 1XU2 is unique.

ABINGDON, VA.

E1

Handstamped Envelopes

2XU1 E1 2c black *11,000.*
2XU2 E1 5c black 1,000.
2XU3 E1 10c black *2,200.* *3,500.*

No. 2XU3 unused and used are each unique.

ALBANY, GA.

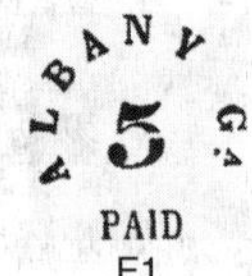

E1

E2

Handstamped Envelopes

3XU1 E1 5c grnsh blue 700.
3XU2 E1 10c grnsh blue *2,000.*
3XU3 E1 10c on 5c grnsh blue *3,500.*
3XU5 E2 5c grnsh blue —
3XU6 E2 10c grnsh blue *2,500.*

Only one example each recorded of Nos. 3XU2, 3XU3 and 3XU6.

ANDERSON COURT HOUSE, S.C.

E1

Handstamped Envelopes

4XU1 E1 5c black 500. 2,250.
4XU2 E1 10c (ms.) black *3,000.*

ATHENS, GA.

A1 - Type I

A1 - Type II

Typographed Adhesives

Two types of Type A1 exist.

5X1 A1 5c purple (shades) 900. 1,100.
a. Vertical tete beche pair *7,500.*
5X2 A1 5c red — 4,250.

ATLANTA, GA.

E1

E2

E3

Handstamped Adhesives

6XU1 E1 5c red 3,500.
6XU2 E1 5c black 175. 600.
6XU3 E1 10c on 5c black 1,500.
6XU4 E2 2c black *3,000.*
6XU5 E2 5c black 1,500.
6XU6 E2 10c black 850.
6XU7 E2 10c on 5c black 2,500.
6XU8 E3 5c black 3,500.
6XU9 E3 10c blk ("10" upright) 2,750.

Only one example each recorded of Nos. 6XU1 and 6XU8.

AUGUSTA, GA.

E1

Handstamped Envelope

7XU1 E1 5c black

Provisional status questioned. Indistinguishable from a handstamp paid cover when used.

The only known example purported to be a postmaster Provisional has a general CSA issue used over the marking.

The editors intend to delist this item unless evidence of a certified unused envelope with the marking is furnished.

AUSTIN, MISS.

E1

Press-printed Envelope (typeset)

8XU1 E1 5c red, *amber* *75,000.*

No. 8XU1 is unique.

AUSTIN, TEX.

E1a

Handstamped Adhesive

9X1 E1a 10c black —

Handstamped Envelope

9XU1 E1a 10c black 1,500.

AUTAUGAVILLE, ALA.

E1

E2

Handstamped Envelopes

10XU1 E1 5c black *10,000.*
10XU2 E2 5c black *12,500.*

No. 10XU2 is unique.

BALCONY FALLS, VA.

E1

Handstamped Envelope

122XU1 E1 5c black *1,500.*

BARNWELL COURT HOUSE, S.C.

E1

Handstamped Envelope

123XU1 E1 5c black *1,500.*

These are two separate handstamps.

BATON ROUGE, LA.

A1

A2

A3

A4

Ten varieties each of A1, A2 & A3

Typeset Adhesives

11X1 A1 2c green *5,250.* *5,000.*
a. "McCcrmick" *14,000.* *8,500.*
11X2 A2 5c green & car 1,500. 1,250.
a. "McCcrmick" — *2,000.*
11X3 A3 5c green & car *4,500.* *2,500.*
a. "McCcrmick" *3,250.*
11X4 A4 10c blue *6,000.*

Only one example each is recorded of No. 11X1a unused, used and on cover.

BEAUMONT, TEX.

A1

A2

Several varieties of A1

Typeset Adhesives

12X1 A1 10c black, *yellow,* *12,500.*
12X2 A1 10c black, *pink* *12,500.*
12X3 A2 10c blk, *yel,* on cover *90,000.*

Only one example is recorded of No. 12X3.

E1

A1

BLUFFTON, S.C.

Handstamped Envelope

124XU1 E1 5c black *3,500.*

Only one example recorded of No. 124XU1.

BRIDGEVILLE, ALA.

Handstamped Adhesive

13X1 A1 5c black & red *20,000.*

CAMDEN, S.C.

E1

E2

Handstamped Envelopes

125XU1 E1 5c black *3,500.*
125XU2 E2 10c black *450.*

No. 125XU2 unused was privately carried and is addressed but has no postal markings.
No. 125XU2 is indistinguishable from a handstamp paid cover when used.

CANTON, MISS.

E1

Handstamped Envelopes

14XU1 E1 5c black 2,750.
14XU2 E1 10c (ms.) on 5c black 5,000.

CAROLINA CITY, N.C.

E1

Handstamped Envelope

118XU1 E1 5c black *3,500.*

CARTERSVILLE, GA.

E1

Handstamped Envelope

126XU1 E1 (5c) red *1,250.*

CHAPEL HILL, N.C.

E1

Handstamped Envelope

15XU1 E1 5c black 3,000.

CHARLESTON, S.C.

A1

E1

E2

Lithographed Adhesive

16X1 A1 5c blue 900. 750.

Press-printed Envelopes (typographed from woodcut)

16XU1 E1 5c blue 1,100. *3,500.*
16XU2 E1 5c blue, *amber* 1,100. *3,500.*
16XU3 E1 5c blue, *org* 1,100. *3,500.*
16XU4 E1 5c blue, *buff* 1,100. *3,500.*
16XU5 E1 5c blue, *blue* 1,100. *3,500.*
16XU6 E2 10c blue, *org* *77,500.*

Handstamped Cut Square

16XU7 E2 10c black *3,000.*

The No. 16XU6 entire is unique.
There is also only one copy known of No. 16XU7. It is a cut-out, not an entire. It may not have been mailed from Charleston and may not have paid postage.

CHARLOTTESVILLE, VA.

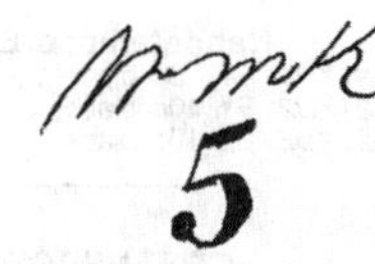

E1

Handstamped Envelopes Manuscript Initials

127XU1 E1 5c blue —
127XU2 E1 10c blue —

CHATTANOOGA, TENN.

E1

Handstamped Envelopes

17XU2 E1 5c black 1,600.
17XU3 E1 5c on 2c black *3,250.*

CHRISTIANSBURG, VA.

E1

Handstamped Envelopes

Impressed at top right

99XU1 E1 5c black, *blue* *2,000.*
99XU2 E1 5c blue *1,400.*
99XU3 E1 5c black, *orange* *2,000.*
99XU4 E1 5c green, on US envelope #U27 *4,500.*
99XU5 E1 10c blue *3,500.*

COLAPARCHEE, GA.

E1

Control

Handstamped Envelope

119XU1 E1 5c black *3,500.*

COLUMBIA, S.C.

E1

E2

Handstamped Envelopes

18XU1 E1 5c blue 500. *900.*
18XU2 E1 5c black 600. *900.*
18XU3 E1 10c on 5c blue *3,500.*
18XU4 E2 5c blue (seal on front) *2,500.*
a. Seal on back *1,000.*
18XU5 E2 10c blue (seal on back) *2,750.*

Three types of "PAID" for Nos. 18XU4-18XU5, one in circle.

Circular Seal similar to E2, 27mm diameter

18XU6 E2 5c blue (seal on back) *4,000.*

E1

E1a

COLUMBIA, TENN.

Handstamped Envelope

113XU1 E1 5c red *3,500.*

COLUMBUS, GA.

Handstamped Envelopes

19XU1 E1a 5c blue 700.
19XU2 E1a 10c red *2,250.*

E1

E1a

COURTLAND, ALA.

Handstamped Envelopes from Woodcut

103XU1 E1 5c black —
103XU2 E1 5c red *10,000.*

Provisional status of #103XU1 questioned.

DALTON, GA.

Handstamped Envelopes

20XU1 E1a 5c black 500.
a. Denomination omitted (5c rate) *650.*
20XU2 E1a 10c black 700.
20XU3 E1a 10c (ms.) on 5c black 1,500.

DANVILLE, VA.

A1

Design measures 60x37mm — E1

E2

E3

PAID 10

E4

Typeset Adhesives

21X1 A1 5c red, wove paper *5,500.*

One of the four recorded cut-to-shape examples is reported to be on laid paper.

Press-printed Envelopes (typographed)

Design E1 measures 60x37mm.
Two types: "SOUTHERN" in straight or curved line.

21XU1 E1 5c black *5,500.*
21XU2 E1 5c black, *amber* *5,500.*
21XU3 E1 5c blk, *dark buff* *5,250.*

Unissued 10c envelopes (type E1, in red) are known. All recorded examples are envelopes on which added stamps paid the postage.

Handstamped Envelopes

21XU3A E4 5c blk (ms "WBP") *1,000.*
21XU4 E2 10c black *2,000.*
21XU5 E2 10c blue
21XU6 E3 10c black *2,750.*
21XU7 E4 10c blk (ms "WBP") —

The existence of #21XU5 has been questioned.

DEMOPOLIS, ALA.

PAID
5

E1

Handstamped Envelopes Ms Signature

22XU1 E1 5c black ("Jno. Y. Hall") *3,500.*
22XU2 E1 5c black ("J. Y. Hall") *3,500.*
22XU3 E1 5c (ms.) blk ("J. Y. Hall") *4,000.*

EATONTON, GA.

E1

Handstamped Envelopes

23XU1 E1 5c black *3,000.*
23XU2 E1 5c + 5c black *4,500.*

Only one example is recorded of No. 23XU2.

EMORY, VA.

A1

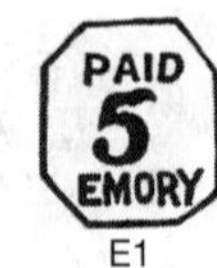

E1

E2

Handstamped Adhesive
On sheet selvage of US 1857
1c stamps
Perf. 15 on Three Sides

24X1 A1 5c blue 15,000.

No. 24X1 exists with "5" above or below "PAID."

Handstamped Envelopes

24XU1 E1 5c blue 2,000.
24XU2 E2 10c blue 10,000.

Only one example recorded of No. 24XU2.

E1

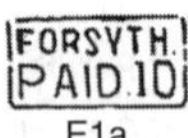

E1a

FINCASTLE, VA.

Press-printed Envelope (typeset)

104XU1 E1 10c black 20,000.

No. 104XU1 is unique.

FORSYTH, GA.

Handstamped Envelope

120XU1 E1a 10c black 1,350.

Only one example is recorded of No. 120XU1.

E1

E1a

FRANKLIN, N.C.

Press-printed Envelope (typeset)

25XU1 E1 5c blue, *buff* 30,000.

No. 25XU1 is unique.

FRAZIERSVILLE, S.C.

Handstamped Envelope
Manuscript "5"

128XU1 E1a 5c black 2,250.

Only one example is recorded of No. 128XU1.

FREDERICKSBURG, VA.

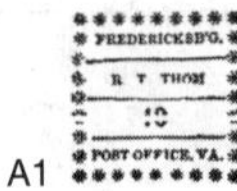
A1

Typeset Adhesives
Ten varieties
Thin Bluish Paper

26X1 A1 5c blue, *bluish* 250. 750.
26X2 A1 10c red (shades), *bluish* 900.

GAINESVILLE, ALA.

E1

E2

Handstamped Envelopes

27XU1 E1 5c black 5,000.
27XU2 E2 10c black 6,000.

GALVESTON, TEX.

E1

E2

Handstamped Envelopes

98XU1 E1 5c black 500. 1,500.
98XU2 E1 10c black 2,000.
98XU3 E2 10c black 550. 2,400.
98XU4 E2 20c black 3,500.

GASTON, N.C.

E1

Handstamped Envelope

129XU1 E1 5c black 4,500.

Only one example is recorded of No. 129XU1.

GEORGETOWN, S.C.

E1

Control

Handstamped Envelope

28XU1 E1 5c black 800.

GOLIAD, TEX.

A1

A2

Typeset Adhesives
Several varieties of A1 and A2

29X1 A1 5c black 7,000.
29X2 A1 5c black, *gray* 6,500.
29X3 A1 5c black, *rose* 7,000.
29X4 A1 10c black — 7,000.
29X5 A1 10c black, *rose* 7,000.

Type A1 stamps bear ms. control: "Clarke P.M."

29X6 A2 5c black, *gray* 10,000.
a. "Goilad" 12,000.
29X7 A2 10c black, *gray* 7,500.
a. "Goilad" 8,000.
29X8 A2 5c blk, *dk bl,* on cover 7,000.
29X9 A2 10c black, *dark blue* —

GONZALES, TEX.

A1

Lithographed Adhesives
on colored glazed paper

30X1 A1 (5c) gold, *dark blue* 15,000.
30X2 A1 (10c) gold, *garnet,* on cover, *1864* 12,500.
30X3 A1 (10c) gold, *black,* on cover, *1865* —

No. 30X1 must bear double-circle town cancel as validating control.
The control was applied to the labels in the sheet before their sale as stamps.
When used, the stamps bear an additional Gonzales double-circle postmark.

GREENSBORO, ALA.

E1

E2

Handstamped Envelopes

31XU1 E1 5c black 3,000.
31XU2 E1 10c black 2,750.
31XU3 E2 10c black 4,250.

GREENSBORO, N.C.

E1

Handstamped Envelope

32XU1 E1 10c red 1,250.

GREENVILLE, ALA.

A1

A2

Typeset Adhesives
on pinkish surface-colored
glazed paper

33X1 A1 5c blue & red 22,500.
33X2 A2 10c red & blue —

Nos. 33X1-33X2 exist used on cover.

GREENVILLE COURT HOUSE, S.C.

E1 Control

Handstamped Envelopes
Several types

34XU1 E1 5c black 2,000.
34XU2 E1 10c black 2,250.
34XU3 E1 20c (ms.) on 10c blk 3,000.

Envelopes must bear the black circle control on the back.

GREENWOOD DEPOT, VA.

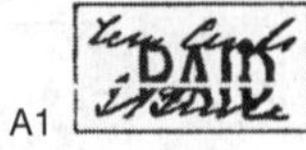

A1

Handstamped "PAID" Adhesive
Ms Value & Signature
Laid Paper
Uncanceled

35X1 A1 10c black, *gray blue,* on cover 20,000.

Six examples are known of No. 35X1, all on covers.
On only one cover is the stamp tied.

GRIFFIN, GA.

E1

Handstamped Envelope

102XU1 E1 5c black 2,000.

A1

A1a

GROVE HILL, ALA.

Handstamped Adhesive
(from woodcut)

36X1 A1 5c black —

Two examples are recorded:
One is on cover tied by the postmark.
The other is canceled by magenta pen on a cover front.

HALLETTSVILLE, TEX.

Handstamped Adhesive
Ruled Letter Paper

37X1 A1a 10c black, *gray blue,* on cover 15,000.

HAMBURGH, S.C.

E1

Handstamped Envelope

112XU1 E1 5c black 2,000.

HARRISBURGH (Harrisburg), TEX.

E1

Handstamped Envelope

130XU1 E1 5c black —

No. 130XU1 is indistinguishable from a handstamp paid cover when used.

A1

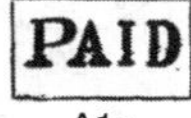

A1a

HELENA, TEX.

Typeset Adhesives

Several varieties

38X1 A1 5c black, *buff* 7,500. 6,000.
38X2 A1 10c black, *gray* 5,000.

On 10c "Helena" is in upper and lower case italics.

Used examples are valued with small faults or repairs, as all recorded have faults.

HILLSBORO, N.C.

Handstamped Adhesive

39X1 A1a 5c black, on cover 15,000.

Manuscript Envelope

39XU1 10c "paid 10" —

No. 39XU1 has undated town cancel as control on face.

See 3c 1861 Postmaster Provisional No. 1AX1.

E1

E1a

HOLLANDALE, TEX.

Handstamped Envelope

132XU1 E1 5c black —

HOUSTON, TEX.

Handstamped Envelopes

40XU1 E1a 5c red — 700.
40XU2 E1a 10c red — *1,500.*
40XU3 E1a 10c black *2,250.*
40XU4 E1a 5c + 10c red 2,500.
40XU5 E1a 10c + 10c red *2,500.*
40XU6 E1a 10c (ms.) on 5c red *3,000.*

HUNTSVILLE, TEX.

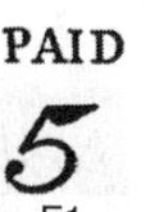

E1

Control

Handstamped Envelope

92XU1 E1 5c black *5,000.*

No. 92XU1 exists with "5" outside or within control circle.

A1

E1

INDEPENDENCE, TEX.

Handstamped Adhesives

41X1 A1 10c blk, *buff,* on cover 20,000.
41X2 A1 10c blk, *dull rose,* on cover
41X3 A1 10c blk, *buff* 32,500.

No. 41X1 is unique.

All known examples of Nos. 41X1-41X3 are uncanceled on covers with black "INDEPENDANCE TEX." (sic) postmark.

The existence of No. 41X2 has been questioned by specialists.

The editors would like to see authenticated evidence of the existence of this item.

No. 41X3 small "10," Manuscript "Pd," on cover, cut to shape.

ISABELLA, GA.

Handstamped Envelope Manuscript "5"

133XU1 E1 5c black *2,000.*

Only one example is recorded of No. 133XU1.

I-U-KA PAID 5CTS
E1

PAID 5 CENTS
E1a

IUKA, MISS.

Handstamped Envelope

42XU1 E1 5c black 1,600.

JACKSON, MISS.

Handstamped Envelopes

43XU1 E1a 5c black 500.
43XU2 E1a 10c black 2,000.
43XU3 E1a 10c on 5c black *2,750.*
43XU4 E1a 10c on 5c blue *2,750.*

The 5c also exists on a lettersheet.

See 3c 1861 Postmaster Provisional No. 2AXU1.

E1

E1a

JACKSONVILLE, ALA.

Handstamped Envelope

110XU1 E1 5c black — 3,000.

JACKSONVILLE, FLA.

Handstamped Envelope

134XU1 E1a 5c black —

Undated double circle postmark control on reverse.

A1

E1

JETERSVILLE, VA.

Handstamped "5"; Ms "AHA." Adhesive

Laid Paper

44X1 A1 5c black, vert. pair on cover, uncanceled *16,000.*

JONESBORO, TENN.

Handstamped Envelopes

45XU1 E1 5c black *3,750.*
45XU2 E1 5c dark blue *7,000.*

KINGSTON, GA.

PAID 5 CENTS
E1

PAID c 5 s CENTS
E2

E4

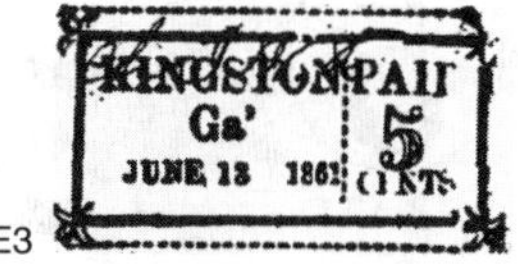

E3

Envelopes Typeset (probably impressed by hand, possibly press printed)

46XU1 E1 5c black 2,000.
46XU2 E2 5c black — 3,250.
a. No "C" or "S" at sides of numeral —
46XU3 E2 5c black, *amber* *2,750.*
46XU4 E3 5c black —

Handstamped

46XU5 E4 5c black 2,000.

Only one example of No. 46XU3 is recorded.

KNOXVILLE, TENN.

A1

Typographed Adhesives (stereotype from woodcut) Grayish White Laid Paper

47X1 A1 5c brick red *1,250.* 900.
47X2 A1 5c carmine *1,750.* 1,500.
47X3 A1 10c grn, on cover *57,750.*

The 5c has been reprinted in red, brown and chocolate on white and bluish wove and laid paper.

E1

E2

Press-printed Envelopes (typographed)

47XU1 E1 5c blue 750. *1,750.*
47XU2 E1 5c blue, *orange* 750. *2,000.*
47XU3 E1 10c red *3,000.*
47XU4 E1 10c red, *orange* *3,000.*

Handstamped Envelopes

47XU5 E2 5c black 750. *1,500.*
47XU6 E2 10c on 5c black *3,500.*

Type E2 exists with "5" above or below "PAID."

Nos. 47XU3 and 47XU4 are cut to shape. Each is unique.

LA GRANGE, TEX.

E1

Handstamped Envelopes

48XU1 E1 5c black — 2,000.
48XU2 E1 10c black 2,500.

LAKE CITY, FLA.

PAID 10
E1

Control

Handstamped Envelope

96XU1 E1 10c black *2,000.*

Envelopes have black circle control mark, or printed name of E.R. Ives, postmaster, on face or back.

LAURENS COURT HOUSE, S.C.

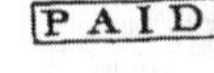

E1

Handstamped Envelope

116XU1 E1 5c black *1,500.*

LENOIR, N.C.

LENOIR N 5 C PAID
A1

LENOIR PAID 5 N. C.
E1

Handstamped Adhesive from Woodcut

Paper has ruled lines in orange

49X1 A1 5c blue *3,250.* *2,750.*

Handstamped Envelopes

49XU1 A1 5c black *3,500.*
49XU2 A1 10c (5c + 5c) blue *25,000.*
49XU3 E1 5c blue *4,500.*
49XU4 E1 5c black

The existence of No. 49XU4 has been questioned.

No. 49XU2 is unique.

LEXINGTON, MISS.

E1

Handstamped Envelopes

50XU1 E1 5c black *5,000.*
50XU2 E1 10c black *5,000.*

LEXINGTON, VA.

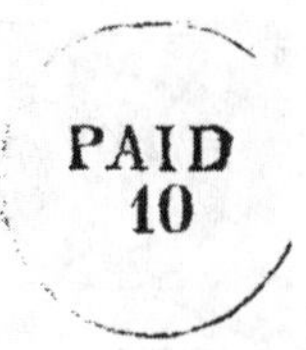

E1

Handstamped Envelopes

135XU1	E1	5c blue	*500.*
135XU2	E1	10c blue	*750.*

Nos. 135XU1-135XU2 by themselves are indistinguishable from a handstamp paid cover when used.

LIBERTY, VA.
(and SALEM, VA.)

PAID 5cts. A1

5 A1a

Typeset Adhesive
Laid Paper

74X1	A1 5c blk, on cover, uncanceled	*35,000.*

Three known on covers:
Two on covers with Liberty, Va. postmark;
One on cover with Salem, Va. postmark.

LIMESTONE SPRINGS, S.C.

Handstamped Adhesive

121X1	A1a 5c black, on cover	10,000.

Stamps are cut round, square or rectangular. Covers are not postmarked.

LIVINGSTON, ALA.

A1

Lithographed Adhesive

51X1	A1 5c blue	*8,000.*

LYNCHBURG, VA.

A1

E1

Typographed Adhesives
(stereotype from woodcut)

52X1	A1 5c blue (shades)	*1,500.*	*1,000.*

Press-printed Envelopes
(typographed)

52XU1	E1 5c black		*2,500.*
52XU2	E1 5c black, *amber*	650.	*2,500.*
52XU3	E1 5c black, *buff*		*2,500.*
52XU4	E1 5c black, *brown*	900.	*2,500.*

MACON, GA.

A1

A2

A3 A4

E1

Several varieties of each. Ten of A2.

Typeset Adhesives
Wove Paper

53X1	A1 5c blk, *lt blue green* (shades)	850.	600.
53X3	A2 5c black, *yellow*	2,500.	800.
53X4	A3 5c black, *yel* (shades)	2,750.	1,250.
a.	Vertical tete beche pair		—
53X5	A4 2c black, *gray grn*		—

No. 53X4a is unique.

Laid Paper

53X6	A2 5c black, *yellow*	*3,000.*	*3,500.*
53X7	A3 5c black, *yellow*	*6,000.*	
53X8	A1 5c blk, *lt blue green*	1,750.	*2,000.*

Handstamped Envelope

Two types of "PAID" and "5"

53XU1	E1 5c black	250.	*500.*

E1

E1a

MADISON, GA.

Handstamped Envelope

136XU1	E1 5c red	*500.*

No. 136XU1 is indistinguishable from a handstamp paid cover when used.

MADISON COURT HOUSE, FLA.

Typeset Envelope

137XU1	E1a 5c black, *yellow*	*23,000.*

No. 137XU1 is unique.

See 3c 1861 Postmaster Provisional No. 3AX1.

MARIETTA, GA.

E1

E2

Handstamped Envelopes

Two types of "PAID" and numerals

54XU1	E1 5c black	300.
54XU2	E1 10c on 5c black	*1,750.*
54XU3	E1 10c black	
54XU4	E2 5c black	*2,000.*

The existence of No. 54XU3 is questioned.

MARION, VA.

A1

Adhesives with Typeset frame
Handstamped Numeral in center
Wove Paper

55X1	A1 5c black	*6,500.*
55X2	A1 10c black	*16,500.* *10,000.*

Bluish Laid Paper

55X3	A1 5c black	—	—

The 2c, 3c, 15c and 20c are believed to be bogus items printed later using the original typeset frame.

MEMPHIS, TENN.

A1

A2

Typographed Adhesives
(stereotyped from woodcut)

56X1	A1 2c blue (shades)	90.	*1,250.*
56X2	A2 5c red (shades)	140.	*175.*
a.	Tete beche pair		1,500.
b.	Pair, one sideways	750.	
c.	Pelure paper	—	—

Press-printed Envelopes
(typographed)

56XU1	A2 5c red	2,500.
56XU2	A2 5c red, *amber*	4,000.
56XU3	A2 5c red, *orange*	2,500.

MICANOPY, FLA.

E1

Handstamped Envelope

105XU1	E1 5c black	*11,500.*

No. 105X1 is unique.

MILLEDGEVILLE, GA.

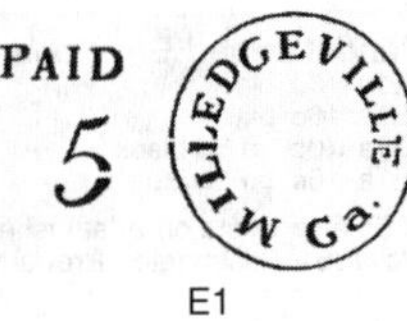

E1

E2

E3

Handstamped Envelopes

57XU1	E1 5c black		250.
a.	Wide spacing between "I" and "D" of "PAID"		400.
57XU2	E1 5c blue		800.
57XU3	E1 10c on 5c black		1,000.
57XU4	E2 10c black	225.	*1,000.*
a.	Wide spacing between "I" and "D" of "PAID"		1,000.
57XU5	E3 10c black		700.

The existence of 57XU2 as a provisional has been questioned by specialists. The editors would like to see authenticated evidence of provisional use of this marking.

N.B.PATTON
PAID 5

E1

A1

MILTON, N.C.

Handstamped Envelope
Manuscript "5"

138XU1	E1 5c black	*2,000.*

Two examples of No. 138XU1 are recorded.

MOBILE, ALA.

Lithographed Adhesives

58X1	A1 2c black	2,000.	1,000.
58X2	A1 5c blue	275.	275.

MONTGOMERY, ALA.

E1

E2

E3

Handstamped Envelopes

59XU1	E1 5c red		1,000.
59XU2	E1 5c blue	400.	*900.*
59XU3	E1 10c red		800.
59XU4	E1 10c blue		*1,500.*
59XU5	E1 10c black		800.
59XU6	E1 10c on 5c red		*2,750.*

The 10c design is larger than the 5c.

59XU7	E2 2c red	*2,500.*
59XU7A	E2 2c blue	*3,500.*
59XU8	E2 5c black	*2,250.*
59XU9	E3 10c black	*2,750.*
59XU10	E3 10c red	*1,500.*

MT. LEBANON, LA.

A1

Woodcut Adhesive
(mirror image of design)

60X1	A1 5c red brn, on cover	*385,000.*

No. 60X1 is unique. Value represents sale price at 1999 auction.

NASHVILLE, TENN.

A2

E1

Typographed Adhesives
(stereotyped from woodcut)
Gray Blue Ribbed Paper

61X2	A2 5c car (shades)	850.	500.
a.	Vertical tete beche pair		*3,000.*
61X3	A2 5c brick red	850.	450.
61X4	A2 5c gray (shades)	950.	625.
61X5	A2 5c violet brown	750.	475.
a.	Vertical tete beche pair	*3,500.*	*2,500.*
61X6	A2 10c green	*3,000.*	*3,000.*

Handstamped Envelopes

61XU1	E1 5c blue	850.
61XU2	E1 5c + 10c blue	*2,750.*

See 3c Postmaster Provisional No. 4AX1.

NEW ORLEANS, LA.

A1

A2

J.L.RIDDELL.P.M
PD 5 CTS
N O.P.O
E1

Stereotyped Adhesives from Woodcut

62X1 A1 2c blue 150. 500.
a. Printed on both sides —
62X2 A1 2c red (shades) 125. 1,000.
62X3 A2 5c brown, *white* 250. 175.
a. Printed on both sides 2,250.
b. 5c ocher 650. 600.
62X4 A2 5c red brn, *bluish* 280. 175.
a. Printed on both sides 2,750.
62X5 A2 5c yel brn, *off-white* 125. 225.
62X6 A2 5c red — 7,500.
62X7 A2 5c red, *bluish* 10,000.

Handstamped Envelopes

62XU1 E1 5c black 4,500.
62XU2 E1 10c black 12,500.

"J L. RIDDELL, P.M." omitted

62XU3 E1 2c black 9,500.

A1

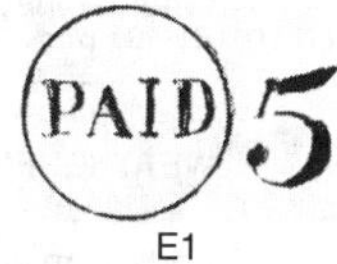

E1

NEW SMYRNA, FLA.

Handstamped Adhesive

63X1 A1 10c ("01") on 5c black 45,000.

No. 63X1 is unique.

NORFOLK, VA.

Handstamped Envelopes Ms Initials on Front or Back

139XU1 E1 5c blue — 1,250.
139XU2 E1 10c blue 1,750.

A1

E1

OAKWAY, S.C.

Handstamped Adhesive (from woodcut)

115X1 A1 5c black, on cover 66,000.

Two used examples of No. 115X1 are recorded, both on cover.

Value represents 1997 auction realization for the cover on which the stamp is tied by manuscript "Paid."

PENSACOLA, FLA.

Handstamped Envelopes

106XU1 E1 5c black 3,750.
106XU2 E1 10c (ms.) on 5c black 4,250.

A1

A1a

PETERSBURG, VA.

Typeset Adhesive (10 varieties)

65X1 A1 5c red (shades) 1,750. 500.

PITTSYLVANIA COURT HOUSE, VA.

Typeset Adhesives

66X1 A1a 5c red, wove paper 6,000. 5,000.
66X2 A1a 5c red, laid paper 6,500.

PLAINS OF DURA, GA.

E1

Handstamped Envelopes Ms. initials

140XU1 E1 5c black —
140XU2 E1 10c black —

A1

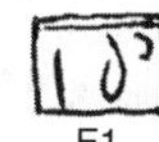

E1

PLEASANT SHADE, VA.

Typeset Adhesive (5 varieties)

67X1 A1 5c blue 2,750. 20,000.

PLUM CREEK, TEX.

Manuscript Adhesive

141X1 E1 10c black, *blue*, on cover —

The ruled lines and "10" are done by hand. Size and shape of the stamp varies.

PORT GIBSON, MISS.

PAID 5
E1

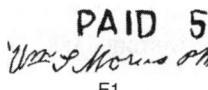

Handstamped Envelope Ms Signature

142XU1 E1 5c black —

A1

E1

PORT LAVACA, TEX.

Typeset Adhesive

107X1 A1 10c black, on cover 25,000.

No. 107X1 is unique.

RALEIGH, N.C.

Handstamped Envelopes

68XU1 E1 5c red 500.
68XU2 E1 5c blue 2,500.

A1

E1

RHEATOWN, TENN.

Typeset Adhesive Three varieties

69X1 A1 5c red 2,000. 2,750.

RICHMOND, TEX.

Handstamped Envelopes or Letter Sheets

70XU1 E1 5c red 1,500.
70XU2 E1 10c red 1,000.
70XU3 E1 10c on 5c red 5,000.
70XU4 E1 15c (ms.) on 10c red 5,000.

E1

E1a

RINGGOLD, GA.

Handstamped Envelope

71XU1 E1 5c blue black 3,000.

RUTHERFORDTON, N.C.

Handstamped Adhesive "Paid 5cts" in ms. Cut round

72X1 E1a 5c black, on cover (uncanceled) 25,000.

No. 72X1 is unique.

SALEM, N.C.

"Paid 5" in Ms.—E1

"Paid 5" Handstamped—E2

Handstamped Envelopes

73XU1 E1 5c black 1,150.
73XU2 E1 10c black 1,500.
73XU3 E2 5c black 1,500.
73XU4 E2 10c on 5c black 2,800.

Reprints exist on various papers. They either lack the "Paid" and value or have them counterfeited.

Salem, Va.
See No. 74X1 under Liberty, Va.

SALISBURY, N.C.

SALISBURY, N. C. POSTAGE FIVE CENTS P.M.
E1

Press-printed Envelope (Typeset)

Impressed at top left

75XU1 E1 5c black, *grnsh* 5,000.

One example known with part of envelope torn away, leaving part of design missing. Illustration E1 partly suppositional.

SAN ANTONIO, TEX.

E1 E2

Control

Handstamped Envelopes

76XU1 E1 10c black 275. 2,000.
76XU1A E2 5c black 1,500.
76XU2 E2 10c black 2,500.

Black circle control mark is on front or back.

SAVANNAH, GA.

E1

Control

PAID 10
E2

Handstamped Envelopes

101XU1 E1 5c black 300.
101XU2 E2 5c black 600.
101XU3 E1 10c black 750.
101XU4 E2 10c black 750.
101XU5 E1 10c on 5c black 1,500.
101XU6 E2 20c on 5c black 2,000.

Envelope must bear octagonal control mark. One example is known of No. 101XU6.

E1

E1a

SELMA, ALA.

Handstamped Envelopes Ms Signature

77XU1 E1 5c black 1,250.
77XU2 E1 10c black 2,500.
77XU3 E1 10c on 5c black 3,000.

See 3c Postmaster Provisional No. 5AXU1.

SPARTA, GA.

Handstamped Envelopes

93XU1 E1a 5c red — 1,750.
93XU2 E1a 10c red 2,500.

Only one example is recorded of No. 93XU2.

SPARTANBURG, S.C.

A1

A2

Handstamped Adhesives on Ruled or Plain Wove Paper

78X1 A1 5c black 3,500.
a. "5" omitted —
78X2 A2 5c black, *bluish* 4,000.
78X3 A2 5c black, *brown* 4,000.

Most examples of Nos. 78X1-78X3 are cut round.

Cut square examples in sound condition are worth much more.

STATESVILLE, N.C.

E1

Handstamped Envelopes

79XU1 E1 5c black 250. *600.*
79XU2 E1 10c on 5c black *2,250.*

Fakes exist of No. 79XU1 unused.

SUMTER, S.C.

E1

Handstamped Envelopes

80XU1 E1 5c black 400.
80XU2 E1 10c black 500.
80XU3 E1 10c on 5c black *800.*
80XU4 E1 2c (ms.) on 10c black *1,100.*

Used examples of Nos. 80XU1-80XU2 are indistinguishable from handstamped "Paid" covers.

TALBOTTON, GA.

E1

Handstamped Envelopes

94XU1 E1 5c black 1,000.
94XU2 E1 10c black 1,000.
94XU3 E1 10c on 5c black *2,000.*

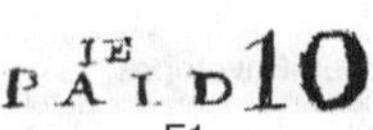

E1

A1

TALLADEGA, ALA.

Handstamped Envelopes

143XU1 E1 5c black — —
143XU2 E1 10c black — —

TELLICO PLAINS, TENN.

Typeset Adhesives

Laid Paper

81X1 A1 5c red 1,250. —
81X2 A1 10c red 2,500.

THOMASVILLE, GA.

PAID 
E1

Control

E2

Handstamped Envelopes

82XU1 E1 5c black 500.
82XU2 E2 5c black 900.

On No. 82XU1, the control is on the reverse of the cover.

TULLAHOMA, TENN.

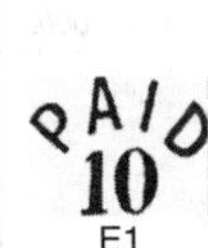

E1

Control

Handstamped Envelope

111XU1 E1 10c black *3,000.*

E1

E1a

TUSCALOOSA, ALA.

Handstamped Envelopes

83XU1 E1 5c black 250.
83XU2 E1 10c black 250.

Used examples of Nos. 83XU1-83XU2 are indistinguishable from handstamped "Paid" covers.

TUSCUMBIA, ALA.

Handstamped Envelopes

84XU1 E1a 5c black 2,250.
84XU2 E1a 5c red 3,000.
84XU3 E1a 10c black 3,500.

See 3c 1861 Postmasters Provisional No. 6AXU1.

Union City, Tenn.

E1

The use of E1 to produce provisional envelopes is doubtful.

A1

A1a

UNIONTOWN, ALA.

Typeset Adhesives in settings of 4 (2x2) Laid Paper (4 varieties of each value)

86X1 A1 2c dk bl, *gray bl* on cover —
86X2 A1 2c dk blue, sheet of 4 *57,500.*
86X3 A1 5c grn, *gray bl* 3,000. 2,000.
86X4 A1 5c green 3,000. 2,000.
86X5 A1 10c red, *gray blue* —

The only recorded examples of No. 86X2 are in a unique sheet of 4.

No. 86X5 used is an uncanceled stamp on a large piece with part of addressee's name in manuscript.

Another example also known on full cover.

UNIONVILLE, S.C.

Handstamped Adhesive Wove Paper with Blue Ruled Lines

87X1 A1a 5c black, *grayish* —

VALDOSTA, GA.

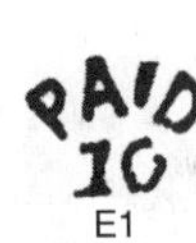

E1

Control

Handstamped Envelopes

100XU1 E1 10c black *2,000.*
100XU2 E1 5c + 5c black —

The black circle control must appear on front or back of envelope. There is one recorded cover each of Nos. 100XU1-100XU2.

VICTORIA, TEX.

A1

A2

Typeset Adhesives

88X1 A1 5c red brn, *grn* *9,000.*
88X2 A1 10c red brn, *grn* *10,000.* *5,500.*

Pelure Paper

88X3 A2 10c red brn, *grn* *10,000.* *10,000.*

No. 88X3, "10" is in bold face type.

WALTERBOROUGH, S.C.

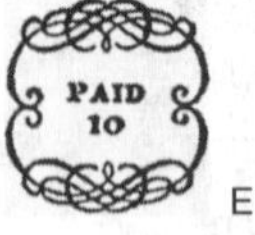

E1

Handstamped Envelopes

108XU1 E1 10c black, *buff* *4,250.*
108XU2 E1 10c carmine *4,250.*

WARRENTON, GA.

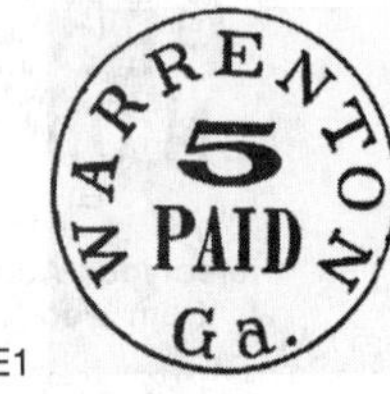

E1

Handstamped Envelopes

89XU1 E1 5c black 1,250.
89XU2 E1 10c (ms.) on 5c black 850.

Fakes of the Warrenton provisional marking based on the illustration shown are known on addressed but postally unused covers.

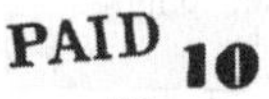

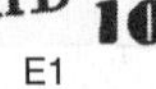

E1

E1a

WASHINGTON, GA.

Handstamped Envelope

117XU1 E1 10c black *2,000.*

WEATHERFORD, TEX.

Handstamped Envelopes Woodcut with "PAID" inserted in type

109XU1 E1a 5c black *2,000.*
109XU2 E1a 5c + 5c black *11,000.*

One example is known of No. 109XU2.

WINNSBOROUGH, S.C.

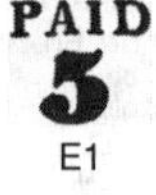

E1

Control

Handstamped Envelopes

97XU1 E1 5c black *1,500.*
97XU2 E1 10c black *3,500.*

Envelopes must bear black circle control on front or back.

WYTHEVILLE, VA.

E1

Control

Handstamped Envelope

114XU1 E1 5c black 900.

For later additions, listed out of numerical sequence, see:

#74X1, Liberty, Va. (& Salem, Va.)
#92XU1, Huntsville, Tex.
#93XU1, Sparta, Ga.
#94XU1, Talbotton, Ga.
#96XU1, Lake City, Fla.
#97XU1, Winnsborough, S.C.
#98XU1, Galveston, Tex.

#99XU1, Christiansburg, Va.
#100XU1, Valdosta, Ga.
#101XU1, Savannah, Ga.
#102XU1, Griffin, Ga.
#103XU1, Courtland, Ala.
#104XU1, Fincastle, Va.
#105XU1, Micanopy, Fla.
#106XU1, Pensacola, Fla.
#107X1, Port Lavaca, Tex.
#108XU1, Walterborough, S.C.
#109XU1, Weatherford, Tex.
#110XU1, Jacksonville, Ala.
#111XU1, Tullahoma, Tenn.
#112XU1, Hamburgh, S.C.
#113XU1, Columbia, Tenn.
#114XU1, Wytheville, Va.
#115X1, Oakway, S.C.
#116XU1, Laurens Court House, S.C.
#117XU1, Washington, Ga.
#118XU1, Carolina City, N.C.
#119XU1, Colaparchee, Ga.
#120XU1, Forsyth, Ga.
#121XU1, Limestone Springs, S.C.
#122XU1, Balcony Falls, Va.
#123XU1, Barnwell Court House, S.C.
#124XU1, Bluffton, S.C.
#125XU1, Camden, S.C.
#126XU1, Cartersville, Ga.
#127XU1, Charlottesville, Va.
#128XU1, Fraziersville, S.C.
#129XU1, Gaston, N.C.
#130XU1, Harrisburgh, Tex.
#132XU1, Hollandale, Tex.
#133XU1, Isabella, Ga.
#134XU1, Jacksonville, Fla.
#135XU1, Lexington, Va.
#136XU1, Madison, Ga.
#137XU1, Madison Court House, Fla.
#138XU1, Milton, N.C.
#139XU1, Norfolk, Va.
#140XU1, Plains of Dura, Ga.
#141X1, Plum Creek, Tex.
#142XU1, Port Gibson, Miss.
#143XU1, Talladega, Ala.

GENERAL ISSUES

Jefferson Davis
A1

Thomas Jefferson
A2

1861 Unwmk. Litho. ***Imperf.***

1	A1	5c green	250.00	150.00
		No gum	175.00	
a.		5c light green	250.00	150.00
		No gum	175.00	
b.		5c dark green	300.00	175.00
		No gum	210.00	
c.		5c olive green	350.00	175.00
		No gum	240.00	
2	A2	10c blue	280.00	190.00
		No gum	200.00	
a.		10c light blue	280.00	190.00
		No gum	200.00	
b.		10c dark blue	550.00	240.00
		No gum	400.00	
c.		10c indigo	*2,750.*	*2,250.*
		No gum	*2,000.*	
d.		Printed on both sides	—	—
e.		10c greenish blue	650.00	300.00
		No gum	450.00	

The earliest printings of No. 2 were made by Hoyer & Ludwig, the later ones by J. T. Paterson & Co.

Stamps of the later printings usually have a small colored dash below the lowest point of the upper left spandrel.

See Nos. 4-5.

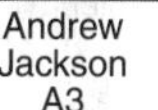

Andrew Jackson
A3

Jefferson Davis
A4

1862

3	A3	2c green	700.00	650.00
		No gum	500.00	
a.		2c bright yellow green	*1,750.*	—
		No gum	*1,300.*	
4	A1	5c blue	180.00	110.00
		No gum	125.00	
a.		5c dark blue	240.00	160.00
		No gum	170.00	
b.		5c light milky blue	270.00	200.00
		No gum	190.00	
5	A2	10c rose	1,400.	500.00
		No gum	1,000.	
a.		10c carmine	*2,800.*	*1,750.*
		No gum	*2,000.*	

Typo.

6	A4	5c lt blue (London print)	10.00	*27.50*
		No gum	6.50	
7	A4	5c blue (local print)	13.00	*20.00*
		No gum	8.50	
a.		5c deep blue	16.00	*35.00*
		No gum	12.50	
b.		Printed on both sides	*2,500.*	950.00

No. 6 has fine, clear impression. No. 7 has coarser impression and the color is duller and often blurred.

Both 2c and 10c stamps, types A4 and A10, were privately printed in various colors.

Andrew Jackson — A5

1863 Engr.

8	A5	2c brown red	70.00	*350.00*
		No gum	52.50	
a.		2c pale red	90.00	*450.00*
		No gum	65.00	

A6

Jefferson Davis — A6a

Thick or Thin Paper

9	A6	10c blue	850.	525.
		No gum	600.	
a.		10c milky blue	850.	525.
		No gum	600.	
b.		10c gray blue	900.	625.
		No gum	650.	
10	A6a	10c blue (with frame line)	5,000.	1,400.
		No gum	3,750.	
a.		10c milky blue	5,000.	1,400.
		No gum	3,750.	
b.		10c greenish blue	5,500.	1,500.
		No gum	4,000.	
c.		10c dark blue	5,500.	1,500.
		No gum	4,000.	

Values of Nos. 10, 10a, 10b and 10c are for copies showing parts of lines on at least three sides. Stamps showing 4 complete lines sell for 300%-400% of the values given.

A7

A8

There are many slight differences between A7 and A8, the most noticeable being the additional line outside the ornaments at the corners of A8.

11	A7	10c blue	9.00	*16.00*
		No gum	6.00	
a.		10c milky blue	22.50	*37.50*
		No gum	15.00	
b.		10c dark blue	18.50	*25.00*
		No gum	12.50	
c.		10c greenish blue	17.50	18.00
		No gum	12.00	
d.		10c green	80.00	*75.00*
		No gum	55.00	
e.		Officially perforated 12½	300.00	275.00
12	A8	10c blue	11.00	*18.00*
		No gum	7.50	
a.		10c milky blue	25.00	*35.00*
		No gum	17.00	
b.		10c light blue	11.00	*18.00*
		No gum	7.50	
c.		10c greenish blue	20.00	*45.00*
		No gum	13.50	
d.		10c dark blue	11.00	*20.00*
		No gum	7.50	
e.		10c green	175.00	*150.00*
		No gum	130.00	
f.		Officially perforated 12½	325.00	300.00

The paper of Nos. 11 and 12 varies from thin hard to thick soft. The so-called laid paper is probably due to thick streaky gum.

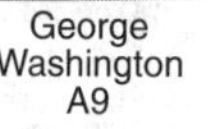

George Washington
A9

John C. Calhoun
A10

13	A9	20c green	37.50	*400.00*
		No gum	27.50	
a.		20c yellow green	70.00	*450.00*
		No gum	50.00	
b.		20c dark green	65.00	*500.00*
		No gum	45.00	
c.		Diag. half used as 10c on cover		*2,000.*
d.		Horiz. half used as 10c on cover		*3,500.*

1862 Typo.

14	A10	1c orange	100.00	
		No gum	70.00	
a.		1c deep orange	125.00	
		No gum	90.00	

The 1c was never put in use.

CANAL ZONE

kə-ˈnal ˈzōn

LOCATION — A strip of land 10 miles wide, extending through the Republic of Panama, between the Atlantic and Pacific Oceans.

GOVT. — From 1904-79 a US Government Reservation; from 1979-99 under joint control of the Republic of Panama and the US.

AREA — 552.8 sq. mi.

POP. — 41,800 (est. 1976)

The Canal Zone, site of the Panama Canal, was leased in perpetuity to the US for a cash payment of $10,000,000 and a yearly rental. Treaties between the two countries provided for joint jurisdiction by the US and Panama, 1979-1999, with Panama handling postal service. At the end of 1999, the canal, in its entirety, reverted to Panama.

100 Centavos = 1 Peso
100 Centesimos = 1 Balboa
100 Cents = 1 Dollar

Catalogue values for unused stamps in this country are for Never Hinged items, beginning with Scott 118 in the regular postage section and Scott C6 in the air post section.

Watermarks

Wmk. 190- "USPS" in Single-lined Capitals

Wmk. 191- Double-lined "USPS" in Capitals

Map of Panama — A1

Violet to Violet-blue Handstamp, "CANAL ZONE," on Panama Nos. 72-72c, 78 and 79

1904 Unwmk. Engr. ***Perf. 12***

1	A1	2c rose, both "PANAMA" up or down	550.00	425.00
a.		"CANAL ZONE" inverted	*950.00*	850.00
b.		"CANAL ZONE" double	*2,500.*	2,000.
c.		"CANAL ZONE" double, both inverted	*15,000.*	
d.		"PANAMA" reading down and up	700.00	650.00
e.		As "d," "CANAL ZONE" inverted	6,500.	6,500.
f.		Vert. pair, "PANAMA" reading up on top 2c, down on other	2,100.	2,100.
2	A1	5c blue	250.00	175.00
a.		"CANAL ZONE" inverted	725.00	600.00
b.		"CANAL ZONE" double	2,250.	1,500.
c.		Pair, one without "CANAL ZONE"	5,000.	5,000.
d.		"CANAL ZONE" diagonal, running down to right	750.00	700.00
3	A1	10c yellow	375.00	250.00
a.		"CANAL ZONE" inverted	725.00	600.00
b.		"CANAL ZONE" double		*15,000.*
c.		Pair, one without "CANAL ZONE"	*6,000.*	*5,000.*
		Nos. 1-3 (3)	1,175.	850.00

On the 2c stamp "PANAMA" is normally about 13mm; on the 5c and 10c about 15mm.

Varieties of "PANAMA" overprint exist on the 2c with inverted "V" for "A," accent on "A," inverted "N," etc.

Counterfeit "CANAL ZONE" overprints exist.

U.S. Nos. 300, 319, 304, 306 and 307 Overprinted in Black

CANAL ZONE
PANAMA

1904 Wmk. 191

4	A115	1c blue green	32.50	22.50
5	A129	2c carmine	30.00	25.00
a.		2c scarlet	35.00	30.00
6	A119	5c blue	110.00	65.00
7	A121	8c violet black	175.00	85.00
8	A122	10c pale red brown	150.00	90.00
		Nos. 4-8 (5)	497.50	287.50

Beware of fake overprints.

A2

A3

CANAL
ZONE
Regular Type

CANAL
ZONE
Antique Type

Black Overprint on Stamps of Panama

1904-06 Unwmk.

9	A2	1c green	2.75	2.25
a.		"CANAL" in antique type	100.00	100.00
b.		"ZONE" in antique type	70.00	70.00
c.		Inverted overprint	*5,000.*	*2,250.*
d.		Double overprint	*2,000.*	*1,500.*
10	A2	2c rose	4.50	3.00
a.		Inverted overprint	225.00	275.00
b.		"L" of "CANAL" sideways	2,500.	2,500.

Overprinted "CANAL ZONE" in Black, "PANAMA" and Bar in Red on Panama Nos. 77-79 "PANAMA" 15mm long

11	A3	2c rose	7.50	5.00
a.		"ZONE" in antique type	200.00	200.00
b.		"PANAMA" inverted, bar at bottom	350.00	350.00
12	A3	5c blue	8.00	3.75
a.		"CANAL" in antique type	75.00	65.00
b.		"ZONE" in antique type	75.00	65.00
c.		"CANAL ZONE" double	600.00	600.00
d.		"PANAMA" ovpt. dbl.	1,050.	1,000.
e.		"PANAMA" inverted, bar at bottom		1,250.
13	A3	10c yellow	22.50	12.50
a.		"CANAL" in antique type	200.00	200.00
b.		"ZONE" in antique type	175.00	160.00
c.		"PANAMA" ovpt. dbl.	650.00	650.00
d.		"PANAMA" overprint in red brown	27.50	27.50
		Nos. 11-13 (3)	38.00	21.25

With Added Surcharge in Red on Panama No. 81

8 cts

14 A3 8c on 50c bis brn 32.50 22.50
- **a.** "ZONE" in antique type 1,100. 1,100.
- **b.** "CANAL ZONE" invtd. 425.00 400.00
- **c.** Rose brown overprint 40.00 40.00
- **d.** As "c," "CANAL" in antique type 2,250.
- **e.** As "c," "ZONE" in antique type 2,250.
- **f.** As "c," "8 cts" double *850.00*
- **g.** As "c," "8" omitted *4,250.*

Panama No. 74 Overprinted "CANAL ZONE" in Regular Type in Black and Surch. Like No. 14 in Red. Both "PANAMA" Reading Up. "PANAMA" 13mm long.

1905

15 A3 8c on 50c bis brn 2,600. *4,500.*
- **a.** "PANAMA" reading down & up 6,500. —

On No. 15 with original gum the gum is almost always disturbed.

Panama Nos. 19 and 21 Surcharged in Black:

a — PANAMA CANAL ZONE 1 ct. PANAMA

b — PANAMA CANAL ZONE 1 ct. PANAMA

c — PANAMA CANAL ZONE 1 ct. PANAMA

d — PANAMA CANAL ZONE 2 cts. PANAMA

e — PANAMA CANAL ZONE 2 cts. PANAMA

f — PANAMA CANAL ZONE 2 cts. PANAMA

There were 3 printings of each denomination differing mainly in the relative position of the various parts of the surcharges. Varieties occur with invtd. "V" for the 3rd "A" in "PANAMA," "CA" spaced, "ZO" spaced, "2c" spaced, accents in various positions, and with bars shifted so that 2 bars appear on top or bottom of the stamp (either with or without the corresponding bar on top or bottom) and sometimes with only 1 bar at top or bottom.

1906

16 A4 1c on 20c vio, type a 2.00 1.60
- **a.** Surcharge type b 2.00 1.60
- **b.** Surcharge type c 2.00 1.60
- **c.** As #16, double surcharge *2,000.*

17 A4 2c on 1p lake, type d 2.75 2.75
- **a.** Surcharge type e 2.75 2.75
- **b.** Surcharge type f 20.00 20.00

Panama No. 74 Overprinted "CANAL ZONE" in Regular Type in Black and Surcharged in Red

8 cts. (b) — 8 cts (c)

Both "PANAMA" reading up

1905-06

18 A3 (b) 8c on 50c bis brn 55.00 50.00
- **a.** "ZONE" in antique type 200.00 180.00
- **b.** "PANAMA" down & up 175.00 160.00

19 A3 (c) 8c on 50c bis brn ('06) 55.00 45.00
- **a.** "CANAL" in antique type 210.00 180.00
- **b.** "ZONE" in antique type 210.00 180.00
- **c.** "8 cts." double *1,100.* *1,100.*
- **d.** "PANAMA" down & up 110.00 90.00

On Nos. 18-19 with original gum the gum is usually disturbed.

Panama No. 81 Overprinted "CANAL ZONE" in Regular Type in Black and Surcharged in Red Type "c" plus Period.

"PANAMA" reading up and down

20 A3 8c on 50c bis brn 45.00 40.00
- **a.** "CANAL" in antique type 200.00 180.00
- **b.** "ZONE" in antique type 200.00 180.00
- **c.** "8 cts" omitted 750.00 750.00
- **d.** "8 cts" double *1,500.*
- **e.** "cts 8" —

Numerous minor varieties of all these surcharges exist. Nos. 14, 18, 19 and 20 exist without CANAL ZONE overprint but were not regularly issued.

Vasco Nunez de Balboa A5

Francisco Hernandez de Cordoba A6

Justo Arosemena A7

Manuel J. Hurtado A8

Jose de Obaldia — A9

Stamps of Panama Ovptd. in Black

1906-07

Overprint Reading Up

21 A6 2c red & black 25.00 25.00
- **a.** "CANAL" only *4,000.*

Overprint Reading Down

22 A5 1c green & black 2.25 1.25
- **a.** Horiz. pair, imperf. btwn. 1,300. 1,300.
- **b.** Vert. pair, imperf. btwn. *1,750.* *1,750.*
- **c.** Vert. pair, imperf. horiz. *2,250.* *1,750.*
- **d.** Invtd. ovpt., reading up 550.00 550.00
- **e.** Double overprint 275.00 275.00
- **f.** Dbl. ovpt., one reading up 1,350. 1,350.
- **g.** Inverted center and ovpt. reading up *4,000.* *3,500.*
- **h.** Horiz. pair, imperf vert. —

23 A6 2c red & black 3.25 1.40
- **a.** Horiz. pair, imperf. btwn. 2,000. 1,750.
- **b.** Vertical pair, one without overprint 1,750. 1,750.
- **c.** Double overprint 500.00 500.00
- **d.** Dbl. ovpt., one diagonal 750.00 750.00
- **e.** Pair, Nos. 23, 23d 1,750.
- **f.** 2c carmine red & black 5.00 2.75
- **g.** As "f," inverted center and overprint reading up *5,000.*
- **h.** As "d," one "ZONE CANAL" *4,000.*
- **i.** "CANAL" double *3,250.*

24 A7 5c ultra & black 6.50 2.25
- **c.** Double overprint 450.00 350.00
- **d.** "CANAL" only *3,500.*
- **e.** "ZONE CANAL" *4,500.*

25 A8 8c purple & black 22.50 8.00
- **a.** Horizontal pair, imperf. between and at left margin 2,000. —

26 A9 10c violet & black 20.00 8.00
- **a.** Dbl. ovpt., one reading up *3,750.*
- **b.** Overprint reading up *4,000.*

Nos. 22-26 (5) 54.50 20.90

Nos. 22 to 25 occur with "CA" spaced.

Cordoba A11

Arosemena A12

Hurtado A13

Jose de Obaldia A14

Overprint Reading Down

1909

27 A11 2c ver & blk 12.50 6.50
- **a.** Horiz. pair, one without ovpt. *2,600.*
- **b.** Vert. pair, one without ovpt. *2,750.*

28 A12 5c dp bl & blk 45.00 12.50

29 A13 8c violet & black 37.50 14.00

30 A14 10c violet & black 40.00 15.00
- **a.** Horiz. pair, one without ovpt. *2,400.*
- **b.** Vert. pair, one without ovpt. *2,600.*

Nos. 27-30 (4) 135.00 48.00

Nos. 27-30 occur with "CA" spaced.

Do not confuse #27 with #39d or 53a.

For designs A11-A14 with overprints reading up, see Nos. 32-35, 39-41, 47-48, 53-54, 56-57.

Vasco Nunez de Balboa — A15

CANAL ZONE

Type I

Black Overprint, Reading Up

Type I Overprint: "C" with serifs both top and bottom. "L" "Z" and "E" with slanting serif.

Compare Type I overprint with Types II to V illustrated before Nos. 38, 46, 52 and 55. Illustrations of Types I to V are considerably enlarged and do not show actual spacing between lines of overprint.

1909-10

31 A15 1c dk green & blk 4.00 1.60
- **a.** Inverted center and overprint reading down *15,000.*
- **c.** Bklt. pane of 6 handmade, perf. margins 575.00

32 A11 2c vermilion & blk 4.50 1.60
- **a.** Vert. pair, imperf. horiz 1,000. 1,000.
- **c.** Bklt. pane of 6, handmade, perf. margins 750.00
- **d.** Double overprint —

33 A12 5c dp blue & blk 15.00 4.00
- **a.** Double overprint 375.00 375.00

34 A13 8c vio & blk ('10) 11.00 5.25
- **a.** Vert. pair, one without ovpt. *1,500.*

35 A14 10c violet & black 50.00 20.00

Nos. 31-35 (5) 84.50 32.45

See Nos. 38, 46, 52, 55.

A16

A17

Black Surcharge

1911

36 A16 10c on 13c gray 6.00 2.25
- **a.** "10 cts." inverted 325.00 275.00
- **b.** "10 cts." omitted 275.00

1914

37 A17 10c gray 55.00 12.50

Type II: "C" with serif at top only. "L" and "E" with vertical serifs. "O" tilts to left

Black Overprint, Reading Up

1912-16

38 A15 1c grn & blk ('13) 11.00 3.00
- **a.** Vert. pair, one without ovpt. 1,750. 1,750.
- **b.** Booklet pane of 6 625.00
- **c.** As "b," handmade, perf. margins 1,000.

39 A11 2c vermilion & blk 8.50 1.40
- **a.** Horiz. pair, right stamp without ovpt. 1,250.
- **b.** Horiz. pair, left stamp without ovpt. 1,750.
- **c.** Booklet pane of 6 500.00
- **d.** Overprint reading down 175.00
- **e.** As "d," inverted center 600.00 *750.00*
- **f.** As "e," booklet pane of 6 handmade, perf. margins *8,000.*
- **g.** As "c," handmade, perf. margins 1,000.
- **h.** As #39, "CANAL" only 1,100.

40 A12 5c dp blue & blk 22.50 3.25
- **a.** With portrait of 2c *8,750.*

41 A14 10c vio & blk ('16) 47.50 8.50

Nos. 38-41 (4) 89.50 16.15

Map of Panama Canal — A18

Balboa Takes Possession of the Pacific Ocean — A19

Gatun Locks — A20

Culebra Cut — A21

Blue Overprint, Type II

1915

42 A18 1c dark green & black 8.50 6.50

43 A19 2c carmine & black 10.00 4.25

44 A20 5c blue & black 11.00 5.75

45 A21 10c orange & black 22.50 11.00

Nos. 42-45 (4) 52.00 27.50

Type III: Similar to Type I but letters appear thinner, particularly the lower bar of "L," "Z" and "E." Impressions are often light, rough and irregular

Black Overprint, Reading Up

1915-20

46 A15 1c green & black 160.00 95.00
- **a.** Overprint reading down 375.00
- **b.** Double overprint 275.00
- **c.** "ZONE" double *4,250.*
- **d.** Dbl. ovpt., one "ZONE CANAL" 1,750.

47 A11 2c orange ver & blk 3,250. 100.00

48 A12 5c dp blue & black 500.00 175.00

Nos. 46-48 (3) 3,910. 370.00

S.S. "Panama" in Culebra Cut — A22

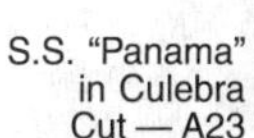

S.S. "Panama" in Culebra Cut — A23

S.S. "Cristobal" in Gatun Locks — A24

Blue Overprint, Type II

1917

49 A22	12c purple & black	17.50	5.50
50 A23	15c brt blue & black	55.00	25.00
51 A24	24c yel brown & black	45.00	15.00
	Nos. 49-51 (3)	117.50	45.50

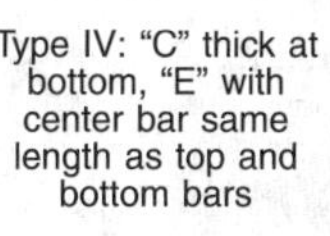

Type IV: "C" thick at bottom, "E" with center bar same length as top and bottom bars

Black Overprint, Reading Up

1918-20

52 A15	1c green & black	32.50	11.00
a.	Overprint reading down	175.00	—
b.	Booklet pane of 6	650.00	
c.	Bklt. pane of 6, left vert. row of 3 without ovpt.	7,500.	
d.	Bklt. pane of 6, right vert. row of 3 with dbl. ovpt.	7,500.	
e.	Horiz. bklt. pair, left stamp without overprint	3,000.	
f.	Horiz. bklt. pair, right stamp with dbl. overprint	3,000.	
53 A11	2c vermilion & blk	115.00	7.00
a.	Overprint reading down	150.00	150.00
b.	Horizontal pair, right stamp without overprint	2,000.	
c.	Booklet pane of 6	1,000.	
d.	Bklt. pane of 6, left vert. row of 3 without ovpt.	8,000.	
e.	Horiz. bklt. pair, left stamp without overprint	3,000.	4,500.
54 A12	5c dp blue & black ('20)	175.00	35.00
	Nos. 52-54 (3)	322.50	53.00

Normal spacing between words of overprint on Nos. 52 and 53 is 9¼mm. On No. 54 and the booklet printings of Nos. 52 and 53, the normal spacing is 9mm. Minor spacing varieties are known.

No. 53e used is unique and is on cover.

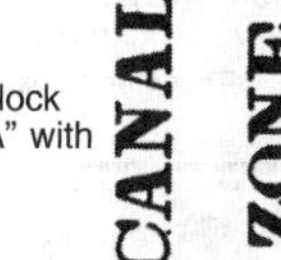

Type V: Smaller block type 1¾mm high. "A" with flat top

Black Overprint, Reading Up

1920-21

55 A15	1c lt green & black	22.50	3.50
a.	Overprint reading down	300.00	225.00
b.	Horiz. pair, right stamp without ovpt.	1,750.	
c.	Horiz. pair, left stamp without ovpt.	1,000.	
d.	"ZONE" only	2,750.	
e.	Booklet pane of 6	1,750.	
f.	"CANAL" double	1,400.	
56 A11	2c orange ver & blk	8.50	2.25
a.	Double overprint	600.00	
b.	Double overprint, one reading down	650.00	
c.	Horiz. pair, right stamp without ovpt.	1,500.	
d.	Horiz. pair, left stamp without ovpt.	1,250.	
e.	Vert. pair, one without overprint	1,500.	
f.	"ZONE" double	1,250.	
g.	Booklet pane of 6	850.00	
h.	"CANAL" double	1,000.	
57 A12	5c dp blue & black	300.00	55.00
a.	Horiz. pair, right stamp without ovpt.	2,500.	
b.	Horiz. pair, left stamp without ovpt.	2,500.	
	Nos. 55-57 (3)	331.00	60.75

Drydock at Balboa — A25

Ship in Pedro Miguel Locks — A26

Black Overprint, Type V

1920

58 A25	50c orange & black	275.00	160.00
59 A26	1b dk violet & black	160.00	65.00

Jose Vallarino A27

The "Land Gate" A28

Bolivar's Tribute — A29

Municipal Building in 1821 and 1921 — A30

Statue of Balboa A31

Tomas Herrera A32

Jose de Fabrega — A33

Black or Red Overprint, Type V

1921

60 A27	1c green	3.75	1.40
a.	"CANAL" double	2,500.	
b.	Booklet pane of 6	900.00	
61 A28	2c carmine	3.00	1.50
a.	Overprint reading down	200.00	225.00
b.	Double overprint	900.00	
c.	Vert. pair, one without overprint	3,500.	
d.	"CANAL" double	1,900.	
f.	Booklet pane of 6	2,100.	
62 A29	5c blue (R)	11.00	4.50
a.	Overprint reading down (R)	60.00	
63 A30	10c violet	18.00	7.50
a.	Overprint reading down	90.00	
64 A31	15c light blue	47.50	17.50
65 A32	24c black brown	70.00	22.50
66 A33	50c black	150.00	100.00
	Nos. 60-66 (7)	303.25	154.90

Experts question the status of the 5c blue with a small type V overprint in red or black.

Black Overprint, Type III

1924

67 A27	1c green	500.	200.
a.	"ZONE CANAL" reading down	850.	
b.	"ZONE" reading down	1,900.	

Coat of Arms — A34

Black Overprint

1924

68 A34	1c dark green	11.00	4.50
69 A34	2c carmine	8.25	2.75

The 5c to lb values were prepared but never issued. See listing in the Scott U.S. Specialized Catalogue.

US Nos. 551-554, 557, 562, 564-566, and 569-571 Overprinted in Red or Black

Type A

Letters "A" with Flat Tops

Flat Plate Printing

1924-25 ***Perf. 11***

70 A154	½c olive brown (R)	1.25	.75
71 A155	1c deep green	1.40	.90
a.	Inverted overprint	500.00	500.00
b.	"ZONE" inverted	350.00	325.00
c.	"CANAL" only	1,750.	
d.	"ZONE CANAL"	500.00	
e.	Booklet pane of 6	80.00	
72 A156	1½c yellow brown	1.90	1.70
73 A157	2c carmine	7.50	1.70
a.	Booklet pane of 6	175.00	
74 A160	5c dark blue	19.00	8.50
75 A165	10c orange	45.00	25.00
76 A167	12c brown violet	35.00	32.50
a.	"ZONE" inverted	3,750.	3,000.
77 A168	14c dark blue	30.00	22.50
78 A169	15c gray	50.00	37.50
79 A172	30c olive brown	35.00	22.50
80 A173	50c lilac	77.50	45.00
81 A174	$1 violet brown	225.00	95.00
	Nos. 70-81 (12)	528.55	293.55

The space between the two lines of the overprint, on both type A and B, varies on some settings.

US Nos. 554, 555, 557, 562, 564-567, 569-571 and 623 Overprinted in Black or Red

Type B

Letters "A" with Sharp Pointed Tops

1925-26

84 A157	2c carmine	30.00	8.00
a.	"CANAL" ONLY	1,600.	
b.	"ZONE CANAL"	325.00	
c.	Horiz. pair, one without overprint	3,500.	
d.	Booklet pane of 6	175.00	
85 A158	3c violet	4.00	3.25
a.	"ZONE ZONE"	600.00	550.00
86 A160	5c dark blue	4.00	2.25
a.	"ZONE ZONE"	1,250.	
b.	"CANAL" inverted	950.00	
c.	Inverted overprint	500.00	
d.	Pair, one without overprint	3,250.	
e.	"ZONE CANAL"	325.00	
f.	"ZONE" only	2,000.	
g.	Pair, one without ovpt., other ovpt. invtd.	2,250.	
h.	"CANAL" only	2,250.	
87 A165	10c orange	35.00	12.00
a.	"ZONE ZONE"	3,000.	
88 A167	12c brown violet	22.50	14.00
a.	"ZONE ZONE"	5,250.	
89 A168	14c dark blue	20.00	16.00
90 A169	15c gray	7.00	4.50
a.	"ZONE ZONE"	5,500.	
91 A187	17c black (R)	4.00	3.00
a.	"ZONE" only	900.00	
b.	"CANAL" only	1,700.	
c.	"ZONE CANAL"	175.00	
92 A170	20c carmine rose	7.25	3.25
a.	"CANAL" inverted	3,600.	
b.	"ZONE" inverted	3,850.	
c.	"ZONE CANAL"	3,600.	
93 A172	30c olive brown	5.00	4.00
94 A173	50c lilac	225.00	165.00
95 A174	$1 violet brown	125.00	60.00
	Nos. 84-95 (12)	488.75	295.25

Overprint Type B on US Sesquicentennial Stamp No. 627

1926

96 A188	2c carmine rose	4.50	3.75

On this stamp there is a space of 5mm between the two words of the overprint.

Overprint Type B on US Nos. 583, 584 and 591

1927 ***Perf. 10***

97 A157	2c carmine	62.50	11.00
a.	Pair, one without overprint	3,250.	
b.	Booklet pane of 6	525.00	
c.	"CANAL" only	2,000.	
d.	"ZONE" only	2,750.	
98 A158	3c violet	8.00	4.25
99 A165	10c orange	17.50	7.50
	Nos. 97-99 (3)	88.00	22.75

Overprint Type B on US Nos. 632, 634, 635, 637 and 642

1927-31 ***Perf. 11x10½***

100 A155	1c green	2.25	1.40
a.	Pair, one without overprint	4,000.	
101 A157	2c carmine	2.50	1.00
a.	Booklet pane of 6	175.00	
102 A158	3c violet	4.25	2.75
a.	Booklet pane of 6, hand-made, perf. margins	6,500.	
103 A160	5c dark blue	30.00	10.00
104 A165	10c orange	17.50	10.00
	Nos. 100-104 (5)	56.50	25.15

Wet and Dry Printings

Canal Zone stamps printed by both the "wet" and "dry" process are Nos. 105, 108-109, 111-114, 117, 138-140, C21-C24, C26, J25, J27. Starting with Nos. 147 and C27, the Bureau of Engraving and Printing used the "dry" method exclusively. See note following US Scott 1029.

Maj. Gen. William Crawford Gorgas A35

Maj. Gen. George Washington Goethals A36

Gaillard Cut — A37

Maj. Gen. Harry Foote Hodges A38

Lt. Col. David D. Gaillard A39

Maj. Gen. William L. Sibert — A40

Jackson Smith — A41

Rear Adm. Harry H. Rousseau A42

Col. Sydney B. Williamson A43

J.C.S. Blackburn — A44

1928-40 ***Perf. 11***

105 A35	1c green	.20	.20
106 A36	2c carmine	.20	.20
a.	Booklet pane of 6	15.00	20.00
107 A37	5c blue ('29)	1.00	.40
108 A38	10c orange ('32)	.20	.20
109 A39	12c violet brown ('29)	.75	.60
110 A40	14c blue ('37)	.85	.85
111 A41	15c gray ('32)	.40	.35
112 A42	20c olive brown ('32)	.60	.20

113 A43 30c brown black ('40) .80 .70
114 A44 50c lilac ('29) 1.50 .65
Nos. 105-114 (10) 6.50 4.35

For surcharges & overprints see #J21-J24, O1-O8.

United States Nos. 720 and 695 Overprinted type B

1933 ***Perf. 11x10½***

115 A226 3c deep violet 2.75 .25
b. "CANAL" only *2,600.*
c. Bklt. pane of 6, handmade, perf. margins 210.00
116 A168 14c dark blue 4.50 3.50
a. "ZONE CANAL" *1,500.*

Gen. George Washington Goethals — A45

1934, Aug. 15 ***Perf. 11***

117 A45 3c deep violet .20 .20
a. Booklet pane of 6 45.00 *32.50*
b. As "a," handmade, perf. margins 175.00 —

20th anniv. of the Panama Canal opening. See No. 153.

Catalogue values for unused stamps in this section, from this point to the end of the section, are for Never Hinged items.

US Nos. 803 and 805 Overprinted in Black

1939 ***Perf. 11x10½***

118 A275 ½c deep orange .20 .20
119 A277 1½c bister brown .20 .20

Panama Canal Anniversary Issue

Balboa-Before — A46

Balboa-After — A47

Gaillard Cut-Before A48

Gaillard Cut-After A49

Bas Obispo-Before — A50

Bas Obispo-After A51

Gatun Locks-Before — A52

Gatun Locks-After A53

Canal Channel-Before A54

Canal Channel-After — A55

Gamboa-Before A56

Gamboa-After — A57

Pedro Miguel Locks-Before — A58

Pedro Miguel Locks-After A59

Gatun Spillway-Before A60

Gatun Spillway-After — A61

1939, Aug. 15 ***Perf. 11***

120 A46 1c yellow green .65 .30
121 A47 2c rose carmine .65 .35
122 A48 3c purple .65 .20
123 A49 5c dark blue 1.60 1.25
124 A50 6c red orange 3.00 3.00
125 A51 7c black 3.25 3.00
126 A52 8c green 4.75 3.50
127 A53 10c ultramarine 3.50 3.00
128 A54 11c blue green 8.00 8.00
129 A55 12c brown carmine 7.50 7.50
130 A56 14c dark violet 7.50 7.50
131 A57 15c olive green 10.00 6.00
132 A58 18c rose pink 10.00 8.50
133 A59 20c brown 12.50 7.50
134 A60 25c orange 17.50 17.50
135 A61 50c violet brown 22.50 6.00
Nos. 120-135 (16) 113.55 83.10

25th anniv. of the Panama Canal.

Maj. Gen. George W. Davis A62

Gov. Charles E. Magoon A63

Theodore Roosevelt A64

John F. Stevens A65

John F. Wallace — A66

1946-49 Size: 19x22mm ***Perf. 11***

136 A62 ½c bright red ('48) .40 .25
137 A63 1½c chocolate ('48) .40 .25
138 A64 2c rose carmine ('49) .20 .20
139 A65 5c deep blue .35 .20
140 A66 25c yellow green ('48) .85 .55
Nos. 136-140 (5) 2.20 1.45

See #155, 162, 164. For overprint see #O9.

Map of Biological Area and Coati-Mundi A67

1948, Apr. 17 ***Perf. 11***

141 A67 10c black 1.25 .80

Establishment of the Canal Zone Biological Area on Barro Colorado Is., 25th anniv.

"Forty-niners" Arriving at Chagres A68

Journey by "Bungo" to Las Cruces A69

Las Cruces Trail to Panama A70

Departure for San Francisco A71

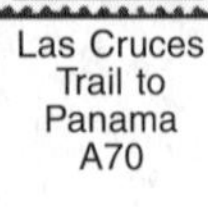

1949, June 1 ***Perf. 11***

142 A68 3c blue .50 .25
143 A69 6c violet .65 .30
144 A70 12c bright green 1.10 .90
145 A71 18c deep red lilac 2.00 1.50
Nos. 142-145 (4) 4.25 2.95

Centenary of the California Gold Rush.

Workers in Culebra Cut — A72

Early Railroad Scene — A73

1951, Aug. 15

146 A72 10c carmine 2.25 1.50

Contribution of West Indian laborers in the construction of the Canal.

1955, Jan. 28 ***Perf. 11***

147 A73 3c violet .60 .50

Cent. of the completion of the Panama Railroad and the 1st transcontinental railroad trip in Americas.

Gorgas Hospital and Ancon Hill — A74

1957, Nov. 17

148 A74 3c black, *blue green* .45 .35

75th anniv. of Gorgas Hospital. Printed on two shades of blue green paper.

S.S. Ancon A75

1958, Aug. 30 **Unwmk.**

149 A75 4c greenish blue .40 .30

Roosevelt Medal and Map — A76

1958, Nov. 15 ***Perf. 11***

150 A76 4c brown .40 .30

Theodore Roosevelt (1858-1919).

Boy Scout Badge — A77

Administration Building — A78

1960, Feb. 8 ***Perf. 11***

151 A77 4c dk blue, red & bister .50 .40

Boy Scouts of America, 50th anniv.

1960, Nov. 1 ***Perf. 11***

152 A78 4c rose lilac .20 .20

Types of 1934, 1960 and 1946 Coil Stamps

1960-62 ***Perf. 10 Vert.***

153 A45 3c deep violet .20 .20

Perf. 10 Horizontally

154 A78 4c deep rose lilac .20 .20

Perf. 10 Vertically

155 A65 5c deep blue .25 .20
Nos. 153-155 (3) .65 .00

Issued: 3c, 4c, 1960; 5c, Feb. 10, 1962.

Girl Scout Badge and Camp at Gatun Lake A79

1962, Mar. 12 ***Perf. 11***

No.	Type	Description	Unused	Used
156	A79	4c bl, dk grn & bister	.40	.30

50th anniv. of Girl Scouts.

Thatcher Ferry Bridge and Map of Western Hemisphere A80

1962, Oct. 12

No.	Type	Description	Unused	Used
157	A80	4c black & silver	.35	.25
a.		Silver (bridge) omitted	*7,500.*	

Opening of the Thatcher Ferry Bridge, spanning the Panama Canal.

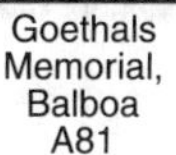

Goethals Memorial, Balboa A81

Fort San Lorenzo A82

1968-71 ***Perf. 11***

No.	Type	Description	Unused	Used
158	A81	6c green & ultra	.30	.30
159	A82	8c multicolored	.35	.20

Issued: 6c, Mar. 15, 1968; 8c, July 14, 1971.

Portrait Type of 1928-48

Coil Stamps

1975, Feb. 14 ***Perf. 10 Vert.***

No.	Type	Description	Unused	Used
160	A35	1c green	.20	.20
161	A38	10c orange	.70	.40
162	A66	25c yellow green	2.75	2.75
		Nos. 160-162 (3)	3.65	3.35

Dredge Cascadas A83

1976, Feb. 23 ***Perf. 11***

No.	Type	Description	Unused	Used
163	A83	13c multicolored	.35	.20
a.		Booklet pane of 4	3.00	—

Stevens Type of 1946

1977 ***Perf. 11x10½***

Size: 19x22½mm

No.	Type	Description	Unused	Used
164	A65	5c deep blue	.60	.85
a.		Tagged	12.00	15.00

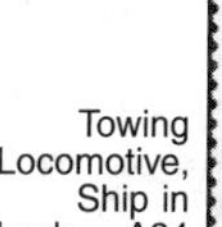

Towing Locomotive, Ship in Lock — A84

1978, Oct. 25 ***Perf. 11***

No.	Type	Description	Unused	Used
165	A84	15c dp grn & bl grn	.35	.20

AIR POST STAMPS

Nos. 105-106 Surcharged in Dark Blue

Type I- Flag of "5" pointing up **15**

Type II- Flag of "5" curved **15**

1929 Engr. Unwmk. ***Perf. 11***

No.	Type	Description	Unused	Used
C1	A35	15c on 1c green, I	8.00	5.50
C2	A35	15c on 1c green, II	75.00	60.00
C3	A36	25c on 2c carmine	3.50	2.00
		Nos. C1-C3 (3)	86.50	67.50

Nos. 114 and 106 Surcharged

1929, Dec. 31

No.	Type	Description	Unused	Used
C4	A44	10c on 50c lilac	7.50	6.50
C5	A36	20c on 2c carmine	5.00	1.75
a.		Dropped "2" in surcharge	80.00	60.00

Catalogue values for unused stamps in this section, from this point to the end of the section, are for Never Hinged items.

Gaillard Cut — AP1

1931-49 **Engr.**

No.	Type	Description	Unused	Used
C6	AP1	4c red violet ('49)	.75	.70
C7	AP1	5c yellow green	.60	.45
C8	AP1	6c yellow brown ('46)	.75	.35
C9	AP1	10c orange	1.00	.35
C10	AP1	15c blue	1.25	.30
C11	AP1	20c red violet	2.00	.30
C12	AP1	30c rose lake ('41)	3.50	1.00
C13	AP1	40c yellow	3.50	1.10
C14	AP1	$1 black	8.50	1.90
		Nos. C6-C14 (9)	21.85	6.45

For overprints see Nos. CO1-CO14.

Panama Canal Anniversary Issue

Douglas Plane over Sosa Hill — AP2

Planes and Map of Central America AP3

Pan American Clipper and Scene near Fort Amador AP4

Pan American Clipper at Cristobal Harbor AP5

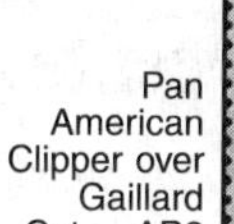

Pan American Clipper over Gaillard Cut — AP6

Pan American Clipper Landing AP7

1939, July 15

No.	Type	Description	Unused	Used
C15	AP2	5c greenish black	3.75	2.25
C16	AP3	10c dull violet	3.00	2.25
C17	AP4	15c light brown	4.25	1.25
C18	AP5	25c blue	13.00	8.00
C19	AP6	30c rose carmine	12.00	6.75
C20	AP7	$1 green	35.00	22.50
		Nos. C15-C20 (6)	71.00	43.00

10th anniv. of Air Mail service and the 25th anniv. of the opening of the Panama Canal.

Globe and Wing — AP8

1951, July 16 Unwmk. ***Perf. 11***

No.	Type	Description	Unused	Used
C21	AP8	4c red violet	.75	.35
C22	AP8	6c brown	.50	.25
C23	AP8	10c red orange	.90	.35
C24	AP8	21c blue	7.50	4.00
C25	AP8	31c cerise	7.50	3.75
a.		Horiz. pair, imperf. vert.	1,000.	—
C26	AP8	80c gray black	4.50	1.50
		Nos. C21-C26 (6)	21.65	10.20

1958, Aug. 16

No.	Type	Description	Unused	Used
C27	AP8	5c yellow green	1.00	.60
C28	AP8	7c olive	1.00	.45
C29	AP8	15c brown violet	3.75	2.75
C30	AP8	25c orange yellow	10.00	2.75
C31	AP8	35c dark blue	6.25	2.75
		Nos. C27-C31 (5)	22.00	9.30
		Nos. C21-C31 (11)	43.65	19.50

See No. C34.

Emblem of US Army Caribbean School AP9

1961, Nov. 21 ***Perf. 11***

No.	Type	Description	Unused	Used
C32	AP9	15c red & dk blue	1.25	.75

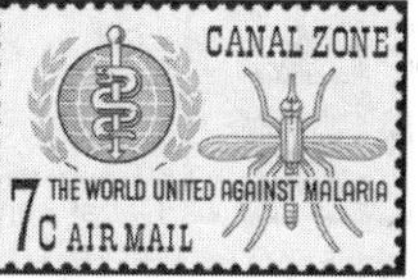

Malaria Eradication Emblem and Mosquito AP10

1962, Sept. 24 Unwmk. ***Perf. 11***

No.	Type	Description	Unused	Used
C33	AP10	7c yellow & black	.45	.40

WHO drive to eradicate malaria.

Type of 1951

1963, Jan. 7 ***Perf. 10½x11***

No.	Type	Description	Unused	Used
C34	AP8	8c carmine	.40	.30

Alliance Emblem AP11

1963, Aug. 17 Unwmk. ***Perf. 11***

No.	Type	Description	Unused	Used
C35	AP11	15c gray, green & dk ultra	1.10	.85

2nd anniv. of the Alliance for Progress, which aims to stimulate economic growth and raise living standards in Latin America.

Jet over Cristobal AP12

Designs: 8c, Gatun Locks. 15c, Madden Dam. 20c, Gaillard Cut. 30c, Miraflores Locks. 80c, Balboa.

1964, Aug. 15 ***Perf. 11***

No.	Type	Description	Unused	Used
C36	AP12	6c green & black	.45	.35
C37	AP12	8c rose red & black	.45	.35
C38	AP12	15c blue & black	1.00	.75
C39	AP12	20c rose lilac & blk	1.50	1.00
C40	AP12	30c redsh brn & blk	2.25	2.25
C41	AP12	80c ol bister & black	3.75	3.00
		Nos. C36-C41 (6)	9.40	7.70

50th anniv. of the Panama Canal.

Seal and Jet Plane AP13

1965, July 15 Unwmk. ***Perf. 11***

No.	Type	Description	Unused	Used
C42	AP13	6c green & black	.35	.30
C43	AP13	8c rose red & black	.30	.20
C44	AP13	15c blue & black	.50	.20
C45	AP13	20c lilac & black	.55	.30
C46	AP13	30c redsh brn & blk	.80	.30
C47	AP13	80c bister & black	2.00	.75
		Nos. C42-C47 (6)	4.50	2.05

1968-76

No.	Type	Description	Unused	Used
C48	AP13	10c dull orange & blk	.25	.20
a.		Booklet pane of 4 ('70)	4.25	—
C49	AP13	11c gray olive & blk	.25	.20
a.		Booklet pane of 4	3.50	—
C50	AP13	13c emerald & black	.80	.25
a.		Booklet pane of 4	6.00	—
C51	AP13	22c violet & black	.75	*2.00*
C52	AP13	25c pale yel green & blk	.60	.70
C53	AP13	35c salmon & black	.90	*2.00*
		Nos. C48-C53 (6)	3.55	*5.35*

Issued: 10c, 25c, 3/15/68; 11c, 9/24/71; 13c, 2/11/74; 22c, 35c, 5/10/76.

AIR POST OFFICIAL STAMPS

Officials and Air Post Officials were sold to the public only with a Balboa Heights, Canal Zone wavy line parcel post cancel while current. After being withdrawn from use, unused copies (except for Nos. CO8-CO12, O3 and O8) were sold at face value for three months beginning Jan. 2, 1952.

Used values are for the CTO copies, postally used copies being worth more.

Nos. C7, C9-C14 Overprinted in Black

Two Types of Overprint

1941-42 Unwmk. Engr. ***Perf. 11***

"PANAMA CANAL" 19-20mm

No.	Type	Description	Unused	Used
CO1	AP1	5c yellow green	5.50	1.50
CO2	AP1	10c orange	8.50	2.00
CO3	AP1	15c blue	11.00	2.00
CO4	AP1	20c red violet	12.50	4.00
CO5	AP1	30c rose lake ('42)	17.50	5.00
CO6	AP1	40c yellow	17.50	7.50
CO7	AP1	$1 black	20.00	10.00
		Nos. CO1-CO7 (7)	92.50	32.00

Overprint varieties occur on Nos. CO1-CO7 and CO14: "O" over "N" of "PANAMA" (entire 3rd row). "O" broken at top (pos. 31). "O" over 2nd "A" of "PANAMA" (pos. 45). 1st "F" of "OFFICIAL" over 2nd "A" of "PANAMA" (pos. 50).

1941

"PANAMA CANAL" 17mm long

No.	Type	Description	Unused	Used
CO8	AP1	5c light green	—	160.00
CO9	AP1	10c orange	—	275.00
CO10	AP1	20c red violet	—	175.00
CO11	AP1	30c rose lake	—	65.00
CO12	AP1	40c yellow	—	180.00
		Nos. CO8-CO12 (5)		855.00

Same Overprint on No. C8

1947, Nov.

"PANAMA CANAL" 19-20mm long

No.	Type	Description	Unused	Used
CO14	AP1	6c yellow brown	12.50	5.00
a.		Inverted overprint		*2,500.*

POSTAGE DUE STAMPS

Postage Due Stamps of the US Nos. J45a, J46a and J49a Overprinted in Black

CANAL ZONE

Wmk. 190

1914, Mar. Engr. *Perf. 12*

J1 D2 1c rose carmine 85.00 15.00
J2 D2 2c rose carmine 250.00 45.00
J3 D2 10c rose carmine 850.00 40.00
Nos. J1-J3 (3) 1,185. 100.00

Castle Gate (See footnote) — D1

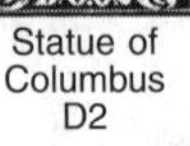

Statue of Columbus
D2

Pedro J. Sosa
D3

Blue Overprint, Type II, on Postage Due Stamps of Panama

1915 Unwmk.

J4 D1 1c olive brown 12.50 5.00
J5 D2 2c olive brown 225.00 17.50
J6 D3 10c olive brown 50.00 10.00
Nos. J4-J6 (3) 287.50 32.50

The 1c was intended to show a gate of San Lorenzo Castle, Chagres. By error the stamp actually shows the main gate of San Geronimo Castle, Portobelo.

Surcharged in Red

CANAL 2 ZONE

J7 D1 1c on 1c olive brn 110.00 15.00
J8 D2 2c on 2c olive brn 25.00 7.00
J9 D3 10c on 10c olive brn 22.50 5.00
Nos. J7-J9 (3) 157.50 27.00

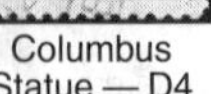

Columbus Statue — D4

Capitol, Panama City — D5

Carmine Surcharge

1919

J10 D4 2c on 2c olive brown 30.00 12.50
J11 D5 4c on 4c olive brown 35.00 15.00
a. "ZONE" omitted *7,500.*
b. "4" omitted *7,500.*

Blue Overprint, Type V, on Postage Due Stamp of Panama

1922

J11C D1 1c dark olive brown — 10.00
d. "CANAL ZONE" reading down 200.00

US Postage Due Stamps Nos. J61, J62b and J65b Overprinted in Black

Type A

CANAL
ZONE

Letters "A" with Flat Tops

1924 *Perf. 11*

J12 D2 1c carmine rose 100.00 27.50
J13 D2 2c deep claret 55.00 10.00
J14 D2 10c deep claret 225.00 50.00
Nos. J12-J14 (3) 380.00 87.50

US Postage Stamps Nos. 552, 554 and 562 Overprinted Type A and additional Overprint in Red or Blue

POSTAGE
DUE

1925

J15 A155 1c deep green 90.00 13.00
J16 A157 2c carmine (Bl) 22.50 7.00
J17 A165 10c orange 50.00 11.00
a. "POSTAGE DUE" double 500.00
b. "E" of "POSTAGE" missing 450.00
c. As "a" and "b" *3,250.*
Nos. J15-J17 (3) 162.50 31.00

"CANAL ZONE" Type B Overprinted on US Nos. J61, J62, J65, J65a
Letters "A" with Sharp Pointed Tops

1925

J18 D2 1c carmine rose 8.00 3.00
a. "ZONE ZONE" 1,250.
J19 D2 2c carmine rose 15.00 4.00
a. "ZONE ZONE" 1,500.
J20 D2 10c carmine rose 150.00 20.00
a. Pair, one without overprint *1,750.*
b. 10c rose red *250.00* 150.00
c. As "b," double overprint *450.00* —
Nos. J18-J20 (3) 173.00 27.00

No. 107 Surcharged in Black

1929-30

J21 A37 1c on 5c blue 4.50 1.75
a. "POSTAGE DUE" omitted *5,500.*
J22 A37 2c on 5c blue 7.50 2.50
J23 A37 5c on 5c blue 7.50 2.75
J24 A37 10c on 5c blue 7.50 2.75
Nos. J21-J24 (4) 27.00 9.75

On No. J23 the horizontal bars in the lower corners of the surcharge are omitted.

Canal Zone Seal — D6

1932-41

J25 D6 1c claret .20 .20
J26 D6 2c claret .20 .20
J27 D6 5c claret .35 .20
J28 D6 10c claret 1.40 1.50
J29 D6 15c claret ('41) 1.10 1.00
Nos. J25-J29 (5) 3.25 3.10

The 1c and 5c are found in both "wet" and "dry" printings. (See note after US No. 1029.) The dry printings are in red violet.

OFFICIAL STAMPS

See note at beginning of Air Post Official Stamps.

Regular Issues of 1928-34 Overprinted in Black

OFFICIAL
PANAMA
CANAL
Type 1

OFFICIAL
PANAMA CANAL
Type 2

Type 1 - "PANAMA" 10mm long.
Type 1A - "PANAMA" 9mm long.

1941 Unwmk. Engr. *Perf. 11*

O1 A35 1c ycl green (1) 2.25 .40
O2 A45 3c deep violet (1) 4.00 .75
O3 A37 5c blue (2) *1,000.* 32.50
O4 A38 10c orange (1) 7.00 1.90
O5 A41 15c gray (1) 12.50 2.25
O6 A42 20c olive brown (1) 15.00 2.75
O7 A44 50c lilac (1) 37.50 5.50
O8 A44 50c rose lilac (1A) 550.00

Same Overprint on No. 139

1947

O9 A65 5c deep blue (1) 9.00 3.50

CUBA

'kyü-bə

LOCATION — The largest island of the West Indies; south of Florida.
GOVT. — socialist; under US military governor 1899-1902 and US provisional governor 1906-1909.
AREA — 44,206 sq. mi.
POP. — 9,710,000 (1981)
CAPITAL — Havana

Formerly a Spanish possession, Cuba's attempts to gain freedom led to US intervention in 1898. Under Treaty of Paris of that year, Spain relinquished the island to US trust. In 1902, a republic was established and Cuban Congress took over government from US military authorities.

100 Cents = 1 Dollar

Watermark

Wmk. 191- Double-lined "USPS" in Capitals

Values for Nos. 176-220 are for stamps in the grade of fine and in sound condition where such exist. Values for Nos. 221-J4 are for very fine examples.

King Alfonso XIII
A19 N2

United States Administration
Puerto Principe Issue

Issues of Cuba of 1898 & 1896 Surcharged

HABILITADO 1 cent. — a
HABILITADO 1 cents. — b
HABILITADO 2 cents. — c
HABILITADO 2 cents. — d
HABILITADO 3 cents. — e
HABILITADO 3 cents. — f
HABILITADO 5 cents. — g
HABILITADO 5 cents. — h
HABILITADO 5 cents. — i
HABILITADO 5 cents. — j
HABILITADO 3 cents. — k
HABILITADO 3 cents. — l
HABILITADO 10 cents. — m

Types a, c, d, e, f, g and h are 17½mm high, the others are 19½mm high.

Black Surcharge on #156-158, 160

1898-99

#176-189 are Orange Brown

176 A19 (a) 1c on 1m 50. 30.
177 A19 (b) 1c on 1m 45. 35.
a. Broken figure "1" 75. 65.
b. Inverted surcharge 200.
d. As "a," inverted *250.*
178 A19 (c) 2c on 2m 22.50 18.
a. Inverted surcharge 250. 50.
179 A19 (d) 2c on 2m 40. 35.
a. Inverted surcharge 350. 100.
179B A19 (k) 3c on 1m 300. 175.
c. Double surcharge 1,500. 750.
179D A19 (l) 3c on 1m *1,500.* *750.*
e. Double surcharge — —
179F A19 (e) 3c on 2m *1,500.*

Value for No. 179F is for copies with minor faults.

179G A19 (f) 3c on 2m — *2,000.*

Value for No. 179G is for copies with minor faults.

180 A19 (e) 3c on 3m 27.50 30.
a. Inverted surcharge 110.
181 A19 (f) 3c on 3m 75. 75.
a. Inverted surcharge *200.*
182 A19 (g) 5c on 1m 700. 200.
a. Inverted surcharge *500.*
183 A19 (h) 5c on 1m *1,300.* *500.*
a. Inverted surcharge *700.*
184 A19 (g) 5c on 2m 750. 250.
185 A19 (h) 5c on 2m 1,500. 500.
186 A19 (g) 5c on 3m 650. 175.
a. Inverted surcharge 1,200. 700.
187 A19 (h) 5c on 3m 400.
a. Inverted surcharge 1,000.
188 A19 (g) 5c on 5m 80. 60.
a. Inverted surcharge 400. 200.
b. Double surcharge — —
189 A19 (h) 5c on 5m 350. 250.
a. Inverted surcharge 400.
b. Double surcharge — —

Values for Nos. 188, 189 are for the 1st printing.
The 2nd printing was surcharged using a shiny ink.

189C A19 (i) 5c on 5m org brn *7,500.*

Black Surcharge on No. P25

190 N2 (g) 5c on ½m bl grn 250. 75.
a. Inverted surcharge 500. 150.
b. Pair, one without surch. 500.

Value for No. 190b is for pair with unsurcharged copy at right. Exists with unsurcharged stamp at left.

191 N2 (h) 5c on ½m bl grn 300. 90.
a. Inverted surcharge 200.
192 N2 (i) 5c on ½m bl grn 550. 200.
a. Dbl. surch., one diagonal *11,500.*
193 N2 (j) 5c on ½m bl grn 800. 300.

Red Surcharge on No. 161

196 A19 (k) 3c on 1c blk vio 65. 35.
a. Inverted surcharge 300.
197 A19 (l) 3c on 1c blk vio 125. 55.
a. Inverted surcharge 300.

198	A19 (i)	5c on 1c blk vio	25.	30.
a.		Inverted surcharge		125.
b.		Vert. surch., reading up		*3,500.*
c.		Double surcharge	*400.*	*600.*
d.		Double invtd. surcharge		—

No. 198b exists reading down.

199	A19 (j)	5c on 1c blk vio	55.	55.
a.		Inverted surcharge		250.
b.		Vertical surcharge		*2,000.*
c.		Double surcharge	1,000.	600.
200	A19 (m)	10c on 1c blk vio	20.	*50.*
a.		Broken figure "1"	40.	*100.*

Black Surcharge on Nos. P26-P30

201	N2 (k)	3c on 1m bl grn	350.	350.
a.		Inverted surcharge		450.
b.		"EENTS"	550.	450.
c.		As "b," inverted		850.
202	N2 (l)	3c on 1m bl grn	550.	400.
a.		Inverted surcharge		850.
203	N2 (k)	3c on 2m bl grn	850.	350.
a.		"EENTS"	1,250.	500.
b.		Inverted surcharge		850.
c.		As "a," inverted		950.
204	N2 (l)	3c on 2m bl grn	1,250.	600.
a.		Inverted surcharge		750.
205	N2 (k)	3c on 3m bl grn	900.	350.
a.		Inverted surcharge		500.
b.		"EENTS"	1,250.	450.
c.		As "b," inverted		700.
206	N2 (l)	3c on 3m bl grn	1,200.	550.
a.		Inverted surcharge		700.
211	N2 (i)	5c on 1m bl grn		1,800.
a.		"EENTS"	—	2,500.
212	N2 (j)	5c on 1m bl grn		2,250.
213	N2 (i)	5c on 2m bl grn		1,800.
a.		"EENTS"	—	1,900.
214	N2 (j)	5c on 2m bl grn		1,750.
215	N2 (i)	5c on 3m bl grn		550.
a.		"EENTS"		1,000.
216	N2 (j)	5c on 3m bl grn	—	1,000.
217	N2 (i)	5c on 4m bl grn	*2,500.*	900.
a.		"EENTS"	*3,000.*	1,500.
b.		Inverted surcharge		*2,000.*
c.		As "a," inverted		2,000.
218	N2 (j)	5c on 4m bl grn		*1,250.*
a.		Inverted surcharge		*2,000.*
219	N2 (i)	5c on 8m bl grn	*2,500.*	1,250.
a.		Inverted surcharge		1,500.
b.		"EENTS"	—	1,800.
c.		As "b," inverted		2,500.
220	N2 (j)	5c on 8m bl grn		2,000.
a.		Inverted surcharge		2,500.

U.S. Nos. 279, 267, 267b, 279Bf, 279Bh, 268, 281, 282C and 283 Surcharged in Black

1899		**Wmk. 191**		***Perf. 12***
221	A87	1c on 1c yel grn	5.25	.35
222	A88	2c on 2c reddish car, III	10.00	.75
b.		2c on 2c vermilion, III	10.00	.75
222A	A88	2c on 2c reddish car, IV	5.75	.40
c.		2c on 2c vermilion, IV	5.75	.40
d.		As #222A, inverted surcharge	*3,500.*	*3,500.*
223	A88	2½c on 2c reddish car, III	5.00	.80
b.		2½c on 2c vermilion, III	5.00	.80
223A	A88	2½c on 2c reddish car, IV	3.50	.50
c.		2½c on 2c vermilion, IV	3.50	.50
224	A89	3c on 3c purple	12.50	1.75
a.		"CUB.A"	37.50	35.00
225	A91	5c on 5c blue	12.50	2.00
226	A94	10c on 10c brn, I	22.50	6.50
b.		"CUBA" omitted	*4,000.*	*4,000.*
226A	A94	10c on 10c brn, II	*6,000.*	
		Nos. 221-226 (8)	77.00	13.05

The 2½c was sold and used as a 2 centavo stamp.

Excellent counterfeits of this and the preceding issue exist, especially inverted and double surcharges.

Issues of the Republic under U.S. Military Rule

Statue of Columbus A20

Royal Palms A21

"Cuba" A22

Ocean Liner A23

Cane Field — A24

Wmk. U S-C (191C)

1899		**Engr.**		***Perf. 12***
227	A20	1c yellow green	3.50	.20
228	A21	2c carmine	3.50	.20
a.		2c scarlet	3.50	.20
b.		Booklet pane of 6	*2,000.*	
229	A22	3c purple	3.50	.20
230	A23	5c blue	4.50	.20
231	A24	10c brown	11.00	.50
		Nos. 227-231 (5)	26.00	1.30

Unwatermarked stamps of designs A20-A24 were re-engraved and issued by the Cuban Republic. See Volume 2 for details of the re-engraving.

SPECIAL DELIVERY STAMPS

United States Administration

U.S. No. E5 Surcharged in Red

1899		**Wmk. 191**		***Perf. 12***
E1	SD3	10c on 10c blue	130.00	100.00
a.		No period after "CUBA"	450.00	400.00

Issues of the Republic under U.S. Military Rule

Special Delivery Messenger SD2

Inscribed: "Immediata"

1899		**Wmk. 191C**		**Engr.**
E2	SD2	10c orange	50.00	15.00

POSTAGE DUE STAMPS

United States Administration

Postage Due Stamps of the US Nos. J38, J39, J41 & J42 Surcharged in Black Like Nos. 221-226A

1899		**Wmk. 191**		***Perf. 12***
J1	D2	1c on 1c dp claret	45.00	5.25
J2	D2	2c on 2c dp claret	45.00	5.25
a.		Inverted surcharge		*2,750.*
J3		5c on 5c dp claret	45.00	5.25
J4	D2	10c on 10c deep cl	27.50	2.50
		Nos. J1-J4 (4)	162.50	18.25

DANISH WEST INDIES

'dā-nish 'west 'in-dēs

LOCATION — Group of islands in the West Indies, lying east of Puerto Rico
GOVT. — Danish colony
AREA — 132 sq. mi.
POP. — 27,086 (1911)
CAPITAL — Charlotte Amalie

The US bought these islands in 1917 and they became the US Virgin Islands, using US stamps and currency.

100 Cents = 1 Dollar
100 Bit = 1 Franc (1905)

Watermarks

Wmk. 111- Small Crown

Wmk. 112- Crown

Wmk. 113- Crown

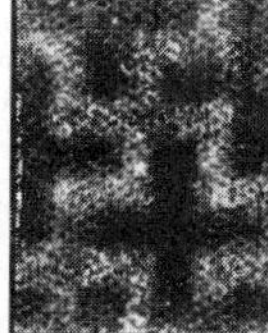

Wmk. 114- Multiple Crosses

Coat of Arms — A1

Yellowish Paper
Yellow Wavy-line Burelage, UL to LR

1856		**Wmk. 111**	**Typo.**	***Imperf.***
1	A1	3c dk car, brn gum	175.	190.
a.		3c dark car, yellow gum	200.	210.
b.		3c carmine, white gum	*4,000.*	—

Reprint: 1981, carmine, back-printed across two stamps ("Reprint by Dansk Post og Telegrafmuseum 1978"), value, pair, $10.

White Paper Yellow Wavy-line Burelage, UR to LL

1866				
2	A1	3c rose	40.00	*60.00*

No. 2 reprints unwatermarked: 1930 carmine, value $100. 1942 rose carmine, back-printed across each row ("Nytryk 1942 G. A. Hagemann Danmark og Dansk Vestindiens Friemaerker Bind 2"), value $50.

1872				***Perf. 12½***
3	A1	3c rose	75.00	*175.00*

1873

Without Burelage

4	A1	4c dull blue	175.00	*350.00*
a.		Imperf., pair	750.00	
b.		Horiz. pair, imperf. vert.	550.00	

#4 reprints, unwatermarked, imperf.: 1930, ultramarine, value $85. 1942, blue back-printed like 1942 reprint of #2, value $50.

A2

Normal Frame

Inverted Frame

The arabesques in the corners have a main stem and a branch. When the frame is in normal position, in the upper left corner the branch leaves the main stem half way between two little leaflets. In the lower right corner the branch starts at the foot of the second leaflet. When the frame is inverted the corner designs are, of course, transposed.

White Wove Paper Varying from Thin to Thick

1874-79		**Wmk. 112**		***Perf. 14x13½***
5	A2	1c green & brn red	15.00	*22.50*
a.		1c grn & rose lilac, thin paper	75.00	*125.00*
b.		1c grn & red vio, medium paper	40.00	65.00
c.		1c green & violet, thick paper	15.00	*22.50*
e.		Inverted frame	15.00	*22.50*
6	A2	3c blue & carmine	19.00	*14.00*
a.		3c lt bl & rose car, thin paper	65.00	50.00
b.		3c dp bl & dk car, medium paper	35.00	16.00
c.		3c greenish blue & lake, thick paper	19.00	14.00
d.		Imperf., pair	325.00	—
e.		Inverted frame	19.00	14.00
7	A2	4c brn & dull blue	13.00	13.00
b.		4c brown & ultramarine	150.00	200.00
c.		Diagonal half used as 2c on cover		110.00
d.		As "b," inverted frame	*750.00*	*1,250.*
8	A2	5c grn & gray ('76)	17.50	15.00
a.		5c yel grn & dk gray, thin paper	45.00	30.00
b.		Inverted frame	17.50	15.00
9	A2	7c lilac & orange	22.50	*77.50*
a.		7c lilac & yellow	77.50	77.50
b.		Inverted frame	52.50	*125.00*
10	A2	10c blue & brn ('76)	21.00	21.00
a.		10c dk bl & blk brn, thin paper	70.00	45.00
b.		"cent.s"	30.00	30.00
c.		Inverted frame	21.00	*25.00*
11	A2	12c red lilac & yel green ('77)	37.50	*125.00*
a.		12c lilac & deep green	125.00	*140.00*
12	A2	14c lilac & green	500.00	*850.00*
a.		Inverted frame	*2,000.*	*2,750.*
13	A2	50c violet, thin paper ('79)	160.00	*250.00*
a.		50c gray vio, thick porous paper	210.00	*325.00*
		Nos. 5-13 (9)	805.50	*1,388.*

The central element in the fan-shaped scrollwork at the outside of the lower left corner of Nos. 5a and 7b looks like an elongated diamond.

See Nos. 16-20. For surcharges see Nos. 14-15, 23-28, 40.

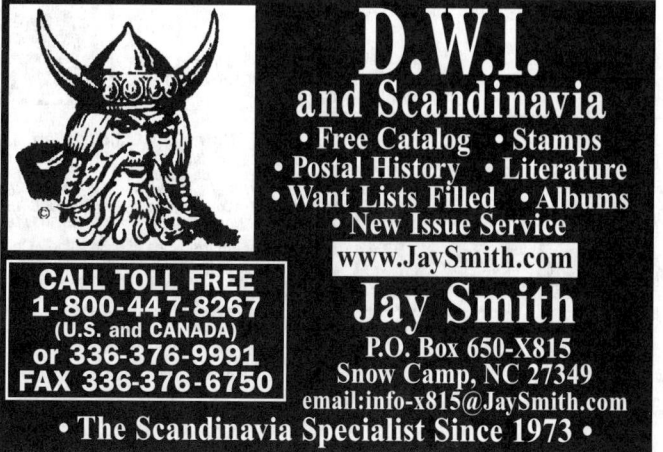

Nos. 9 & 13 Surcharged in Black

1887-95
14 A2 1c on 7c lilac & org 72.50 175.00
a. 1c on 7c lilac & yellow 72.50 175.00
b. Double surcharge 175.00 350.00
c. Inverted frame 90.00 300.00
15 A2 10c on 50c violet, thin paper ('95) 35.00 60.00

Type of 1874-79

1896-1901 *Perf. 13*
16 A2 1c grn & red vio ('98) 12.00 17.00
a. Normal frame 225.00 325.00
17 A2 3c blue & lake ('98) 10.00 13.00
a. Normal frame 200.00 325.00
18 A2 4c bis & dl bl ('01) 11.00 11.00
a. Diagonal half used as 2c on cover 90.00
b. Inverted frame 45.00 75.00
c. As "b," diagonal half used as 2c on cover 300.00
19 A2 5c green & gray 30.00 30.00
a. Normal frame 600.00 850.00
20 A2 10c blue & brn ('01) 65.00 110.00
a. Inverted frame 750.00 1,300.
b. "cent.s" 160.00 150.00
Nos. 16-20 (5) 128.00 181.00

Arms — A5

1900
21 A5 1c light green 2.50 2.50
22 A5 5c light blue 15.00 20.00

See #29-30. For surcharges see #41-42.

Nos. 6, 17, 20 Surcharged

c

d

Surcharge "c" in Black

1902 *Perf. 14x13½*
23 A2 2c on 3c blue & car 300.00 350.00
a. "2" in date with straight tail 325.00 375.00
b. Normal frame 3,500.

Perf. 13
24 A2 2c on 3c blue & lake 9.00 20.00
a. "2" in date with straight tail 11.50 22.50
b. Dated "1901" 375.00 400.00
c. Normal frame 150.00 225.00
d. Dark green surcharge 1,750.
e. As "d" & "a" — —
f. As "d" & "c" —
25 A2 8c on 10c blue & brn 20.00 32.50
a. "2" with straight tail 22.50 35.00
b. On No. 20b 20.00 37.50
c. Inverted frame 200.00 325.00

Only one copy of No. 24f can exist.

Surcharge "d" in Black
27 A2 2c on 3c blue & lake 11.00 30.00
a. Normal frame 225.00 375.00
28 A2 8c on 10c blue & brn 11.00 11.00
a. On No. 20b 17.50 20.00
b. Inverted frame 175.00 350.00
Nos. 23-28 (5) 351.00 443.50

1903 **Wmk. 113**
29 A5 2c carmine 6.00 17.50
30 A5 8c brown 22.50 42.50

King Christian IX — A8

St. Thomas Harbor — A9

1905 **Typo.** *Perf. 13*
31 A8 5b green 3.50 3.00
32 A8 10b red 3.50 3.00
33 A8 20b green & blue 8.00 7.00
34 A8 25b ultramarine 8.00 8.00
35 A8 40b red & gray 8.00 7.00
36 A8 50b yellow & gray 9.00 9.00

Frame Typo., Center Engr.
Wmk. Two Crowns (113)
Perf. 12
37 A9 1fr green & blue 17.50 37.50
38 A9 2fr org red & brown 30.00 50.00
39 A9 5fr yellow & brown 75.00 210.00
Nos. 31-39 (9) 162.50 334.50

Favor cancels exist on #37-39. Value 25% less.

Nos. 18, 22, 30 Surcharged in Black

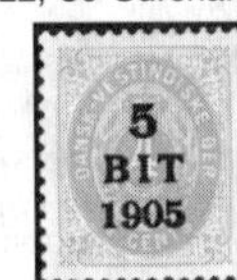

1905 **Wmk. 112** *Perf. 13*
40 A2 5b on 4c bis & dl bl 13.50 40.00
a. Inverted frame 40.00 75.00
41 A5 5b on 5c light blue 12.50 32.50

Wmk. 113
42 A5 5b on 8c brown 12.50 32.50
Nos. 40-42 (3) 38.50 105.00

Favor cancels exist on #40-42. Value 25% less.

Frederik VIII
A10

Christian X
A11

Frame Typo., Center Engr.

1907-08 **Wmk. 113** *Perf. 13*
43 A10 5b green 1.75 1.25
44 A10 10b red 1.75 1.25
45 A10 15b violet & brown 3.50 3.50
46 A10 20b green & blue 30.00 22.50
47 A10 25b blue & dk blue 1.50 1.75
48 A10 30b claret & slate 42.50 42.50
49 A10 40b ver & gray 4.50 5.25
50 A10 50b yellow & brown 4.50 9.00
Nos. 43-50 (8) 90.00 87.00

1915 **Wmk. 114** *Perf. 14x14½*
51 A11 5b yellow green 3.50 3.00
52 A11 10b red 3.50 35.00
53 A11 15b lilac & red brown 3.50 40.00
54 A11 20b green & blue 3.50 40.00
55 A11 25b blue & dark blue 3.50 10.00
56 A11 30b claret & black 3.50 50.00
57 A11 40b orange & black 3.50 50.00
58 A11 50b yellow & brown 3.50 50.00
Nos. 51-58 (8) 28.00 278.00

Forged and favor cancellations exist.

POSTAGE DUE STAMPS

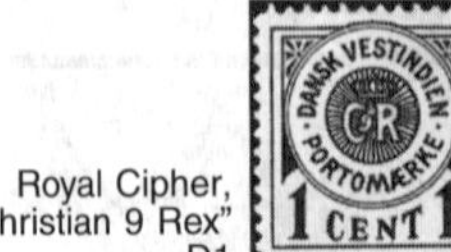
Royal Cipher, "Christian 9 Rex" D1

1902 **Unwmk.** **Litho.** *Perf. 11½*
J1 D1 1c dark blue 4.00 11.00
J2 D1 4c dark blue 9.00 17.50
J3 D1 6c dark blue 17.50 45.00
J4 D1 10c dark blue 15.00 45.00
Nos. J1-J4 (4) 45.50 118.50

There are five types of each value. On the 4c they may be distinguished by differences in the figures "4"; on the other values the differences are minute.

Used values of Nos. J1-J4 are for canceled copies. Uncanceled examples without gum have probably been used. Value 60% of unused.

Counterfeits of Nos. J1-J4 exist.

D2

1905-13 *Perf. 13*
J5 D2 5b red & gray 4.00 6.25
J6 D2 20b red & gray 7.00 12.50
J7 D2 30b red & gray 6.00 12.50
J8 D2 50b red & gray 5.50 32.50
a. Perf. 14x14½ ('13) 35.00 125.00
b. Perf. 11½ 300.00
Nos. J5-J8 (4) 22.50 63.75

All values of this issue are known imperforate, but were not regularly issued.

Used values of Nos. J5-J8 are for canceled copies. Uncanceled examples without gum have probably been used. Value 60% of unused.

Counterfeits of Nos. J5-J8 exist.

Danish West Indies stamps were replaced by those of the US in 1917, after the US bought the islands.

GUAM

ˈgwäm

LOCATION — One of the Mariana Islands in the Pacific Ocean, about 1450 miles east of the Philippines
GOVT. — United States Possession
AREA — 206 sq. mi.
POP. — 9,000 (est. 1899)
CAPITAL — Agaña

Formerly a Spanish possession, Guam was ceded to the United States in 1898 following the Spanish-American War. Stamps overprinted "Guam" were superseded by the regular postage stamps of the United States in 1901.

100 Cents = 1 Dollar

US Nos. 279, 279B, 279Bc, 268, 280a, 281, 282, 272, 282C, 283, 284, 275, 275a, 276 and 276A Overprinted in Black (1c-50c) or Red ($1)

1899 **Wmk. 191** *Perf. 12*
1 A87 1c deep green 20.00 25.00
2 A88 2c red, type IV 17.50 25.00
a. 2c rose carmine, type IV 22.50 30.00
3 A89 3c purple 125.00 175.00
4 A90 4c lilac brown 135.00 175.00
5 A91 5c blue 30.00 45.00
6 A92 6c lake 125.00 200.00
7 A93 8c violet brown 125.00 200.00
8 A94 10c brown, type I 45.00 55.00
9 A94 10c brown, type II 4,000. —
10 A95 15c olive green 150.00 175.00
11 A96 50c orange 350.00 425.00
a. 50c red orange 550.00 —
12 A97 $1 black, type I 350.00 400.00
13 A97 $1 black, type II 4,500.
Nos. 1-8,10-12 (11) 1,472. 1,900.

SPECIAL DELIVERY STAMP

United States No. E5 Overprinted in Red

1899 **Wmk. 191** *Perf. 12*
E1 SD3 10c blue 150.00 200.00

Guam Guard Mail stamps of 1930 are listed in the Scott Specialized United States Catalogue.

HAWAII

hə-ˈwä-yē

LOCATION — Group of 20 islands in the Pacific Ocean, about 2,000 miles southwest of San Francisco.
GOVT. — Former Kingdom and Republic
AREA — 6,435 sq. mi.
POP. — 150,000 (est. 1899)
CAPITAL — Honolulu

Until 1893 an independent kingdom, from 1893 to 1898 a republic, the Hawaiian Islands were annexed to the US in 1898. The Territory of Hawaii achieved statehood in 1959.

100 Cents = 1 Dollar

Values for Nos. 1-4 are for examples with minor damage that has been skillfully repaired.

A1

A2

A3

Pelure Paper

1851-52 **Unwmk.** **Typeset** *Imperf.*
1 A1 2c blue 660,000. 200,000.
2 A1 5c blue 45,000. 25,000.
3 A2 13c blue 22,500. 18,000.
4 A3 13c blue 40,000. 27,500.

Two varieties of each.
No. 1 unused is unique.

King Kamehameha III
A4 A5

Thick White Wove Paper

1853 **Engr.**
5 A4 5c blue 1,350. 1,050.
a. Line through "Honolulu" (Pos. 2) 2,750. 2,500.
6 A5 13c dark red 600. 1,100.

See Nos. 8-11.

A6

1857
7 A6 5c on 13c dark red 6,750. 9,000.

1857
Thin White Wove Paper
8 A4 5c blue 650. 625.
a. Line through "Honolulu" (Pos. 2) 1,250. 1,250.
b. Double impression 3,500. 3,500.

1861
Thin Bluish Wove Paper
9 A4 5c blue 350. 250.
a. Line through "Honolulu" (Pos. 2) 750. 900.

Re-issues

1868

Ordinary White Wove Paper

No.	Design	Description	Unused	Used
10	A4	5c blue	25.00	
a.		Line through "Honolulu" (Pos. 2)	55.00	
11	A5	13c dull rose	250.00	

Reprints:

5c — Originals have two small dots near the left side of the square in the upper right corner. These dots are missing in the reprints.

13c — The bottom of the 3 of 13 in the upper left corner is flattened in the originals and rounded in the reprints. The "t" of "Cts" on the left side is as tall as the "C" in the reprints, but shorter in the originals.

1889

No.	Design	Description	Unused	Used
10R	A4	5c blue	60.00	
11R	A5	13c orange red	250.00	

On August 19, 1892, the remaining supply of reprints was overprinted in black "REPRINT." The reprints (both with and without overprint) were sold at face value. See Scott's U.S. Specialized Catalogue.

Unused values for the Numeral stamps, Nos. 12-26, are for examples without gum.

A7

A8

A9

1859-62 **Typeset**

No.	Design	Description	Unused	Used
12	A7	1c lt blue, *bluish white*	9,000.	7,500.
a.		"1 Ce" omitted		16,500.
b.		"nt" omitted	—	—
13	A7	2c lt blue, *bluish white*	6,250.	3,750.
a.		2c dark blue, *grayish white*	6,750.	4,000.
b.		Comma after "Cents"	—	6,250.
c.		No period after "Leta"	—	—
14	A7	2c blk, *grnsh blue* ('62)	7,500.	4,500.
a.		"2-Cents."	—	—

1863

No.	Design	Description	Unused	Used
15	A7	1c black, *grayish*	475.	1,050.
a.		Tete beche pair	3,750.	
b.		"NTER"	—	
c.		Period omitted after "Postage"	725.	
16	A7	2c black, *grayish*	925.	700.
a.		"2" at top of rectangle	3,750.	3,750.
b.		Printed on both sides	—	21,000.
c.		"NTER"	3,250.	3,250.
d.		2c black, *grayish white*	975.	725.
e.		Period omitted after "Cents"	—	
f.		Overlapping impressions	—	—
g.		"TAGE."	—	—
17	A7	2c dk blue, *bluish*	7,750.	6,750.
a.		"ISL"	—	—
18	A7	2c black, *blue gray*	3,250.	4,750.

1864-65

No.	Design	Description	Unused	Used
19	A7	1c black	475.	1,000.
20	A7	2c black	725.	1,200.
21	A8	5c blue, *blue* ('65)	775.	575.
a.		Tete beche pair	10,500.	
b.		5c bluish black, *grayish white*	12,500.	
22	A9	5c blue, *blue* ('65)	550.	875.
a.		Tete beche pair	8,750.	
b.		5c blue, *grayish white*	—	
c.		Overlapping impressions	—	

1864 **Laid Paper**

No.	Design	Description	Unused	Used
23	A7	1c black	275.	2,100.
a.		HA instead of HAWAIIAN	3,750.	
b.		Tete beche pair	6,250.	
c.		Tete beche pair, #23, 23a	18,000.	
24	A7	2c black	300.	1,050.
a.		"NTER"	3,750.	
b.		"S" of "POSTAGE" omitted	1,500.	
c.		Tete beche pair	5,500.	

A10

1865 **Wove Paper**

No.	Design	Description	Unused	Used
25	A10	1c dark blue	300.	
a.		Double impression	—	
b.		With invtd. impression of #21	11,000.	
26	A10	2c dark blue	300.	

Nos. 12 to 26 were typeset and were printed in settings of ten, each stamp differing from the others.

King Kamehameha IV — A11

1861-63 **Litho.**

Horizontally Laid Paper

No.	Design	Description	Unused	Used
27	A11	2c pale rose	275.	250.
a.		2c carmine rose ('63)	2,000.	2,000.

Vertically Laid Paper

No.	Design	Description	Unused	Used
28	A11	2c pale rose	275.	150.
a.		2c carmine rose ('63)	300.	350.

1869 **Engr.** **Thin Wove Paper**

No.	Design	Description	Unused	Used
29	A11	2c red	45.00	—

No. 29 was a re-issue sold only at the Honolulu post office, at first without overprint and later with overprint "CANCELLED."

See #50-51 and note following #51.

Princess Victoria Kamamalu — A12

King Kamehameha IV — A13

King Kamehameha V
A14 A15

Mataio Kekuanaoa — A16

1864-86 **Engr.** ***Perf. 12***

Wove Paper

No.	Design	Description	Unused	Used
30	A12	1c purple ('86)	9.00	7.50
a.		1c mauve ('71)	40.00	20.00
b.		1c violet ('78)	17.50	10.00
31	A13	2c rose vermilion	15.00	9.00
a.		2c vermilion ('86)	35.00	12.50
b.		Half used as 1c on cover with #32		8,500.
32	A14	5c blue ('66)	175.00	30.00
33	A15	6c yel grn ('71)	25.00	9.00
a.		6c bluish green ('78)	25.00	9.00
34	A16	18c dull rose ('71)	85.00	35.00
		Nos. 30-34 (5)	309.00	90.50

No. 32 has traces of rectangular frame lines surrounding the design. Nos. 39 and 52C have no such frame lines.

For overprints see #53, 58-60, 65, 66C, 71.

King David Kalakaua A17

Prince William Pitt Leleiohoku A18

1875

No.	Design	Description	Unused	Used
35	A17	2c brown	7.50	3.00
36	A18	12c black	55.00	27.50

See Nos. 38, 43, 46. For overprints see Nos. 56, 62-63, 66, 69.

Princess Likelike A19

King David Kalakaua A20

Queen Kapiolani — A21

Statue of King Kamehameha I — A22

King William Lunalilo — A23

Queen Emma Kaleleonalani — A24

1882

No.	Design	Description	Unused	Used
37	A19	1c blue	6.00	10.00
38	A17	2c lilac rose	125.00	45.00
39	A14	5c ultramarine	15.00	3.25
a.		Vert. pair, imperf. horiz.	4,250.	4,250.
40	A20	10c black	35.00	20.00
41	A21	15c red brown	55.00	25.00
		Nos. 37-41 (5)	236.00	103.25

1883-86

No.	Design	Description	Unused	Used
42	A19	1c green	2.75	1.90
43	A17	2c rose ('86)	4.00	1.00
a.		2c dull red	62.50	21.00
44	A20	10c red brown ('84)	30.00	10.00
45	A20	10c vermilion	32.50	12.50
46	A18	12c red lilac	75.00	32.50
47	A22	25c dark violet	140.00	60.00
48	A23	50c red	160.00	85.00
49	A24	$1 rose red	240.00	140.00
		Maltese cross cancellation		100.00
		Nos. 42-49 (8)	684.25	342.90

Other fiscal cancellations exist on No. 49. For overprints see Nos. 54-55, 57, 61-61B, 64, 67-68, 70, 72-73.

Reproduction and Reprint

Yellowish Wove Paper

1886-89 ***Imperf.***

No.	Design	Description	Unused	Used
50	A11	2c orange vermilion	160.00	
51	A11	2c carmine ('89)	25.00	

In 1885 the Postmaster General wished to have on sale complete sets of Hawaii's stamps as far back as type A11, but was unable to find either the stone from which Nos. 27 and 28, or the plate from which No. 29 was printed. He therefore sent a copy of No. 29 to the American Bank Note Co., with an order to engrave a new plate and print 10,000 stamps, of which 5000 were overprinted "Specimen" in blue.

The original No. 29 was printed in sheet of 15 (5x3), but the plate of these "Official Imitations" was made up of 50 stamps (10x5). Later, in 1887, the original die for No. 29 was discovered, and after retouching, a new plate was made and 37,500 stamps were printed. These, like the originals, were printed in sheets of 15. They were delivered during 1889 and 1890. In 1892 all remaining unsold in the Post Office were overprinted "Reprint."

No. 29 is red in color, and printed on very thin white wove paper. No. 50 is orange vermilion in color, on medium, white to buff paper. In No. 50 the vertical line on the left side of the portrait touches the horizontal line over the label "Elua Keneta", while in the other two varieties, Nos. 29 and 51, it does not touch the horizontal line by half a millimeter. In No. 51 there are three parallel lines on the left side of the King's nose, while in No. 29 and No. 50 there are are no such lines. No. 51 is carmine in color and printed on thick, yellowish to buff wove paper.

It is claimed that both Nos. 50 and 51 were available for postage, although not made to fill a postal requirement.

Queen Liliuokalani — A25

1890-91 ***Perf. 12***

No.	Design	Description	Unused	Used
52	A25	2c dull violet ('91)	4.50	1.50
a.		Vert. pair, imperf. horiz.	4,000.	
52C	A14	5c deep indigo	110.00	140.00

Stamps of 1864-91 Overprinted in Red

Three categories of double overprints:

I. Both overprints heavy.

II. One overprint heavy, one of moderate strength.

III. One overprint heavy, one of light or weak strength.

1893

No.	Design	Description	Unused	Used
53	A12	1c purple	7.50	12.50
a.		"189" instead of "1893"	475.00	—
b.		No period after "GOVT"	210.00	210.00
f.		Double overprint (III)	550.00	
54	A19	1c blue	6.00	12.50
b.		No period after "GOVT"	140.00	140.00
e.		Double overprint (II)	1,500.	
f.		Double overprint (III)	400.00	
55	A19	1c green	1.50	3.00
d.		Double overprint (I)	625.00	450.00
f.		Double overprint (III)	200.00	
g.		Pair, one without ovpt.	10,000.	
56	A17	2c brown	10.00	20.00
b.		No period after "GOVT"	300.00	—
57	A25	2c dull violet	1.50	1.25
a.		"18 3" instead of "1893"	650.00	500.00
d.		Double overprint (I)	1,250.	650.00
f.		Double overprint (III)	160.00	
g.		Inverted overprint	4,000.	3,500.
58	A14	5c deep indigo	10.00	25.00
b.		No period after "GOVT"	225.00	250.00
f.		Double overprint (III)	1,250.	
59	A14	5c ultramarine	6.00	2.50
d.		Double overprint (I)	6,500.	
e.		Double overprint (II)	4,000.	4,000.
f.		Double overprint (III)		600.00
g.		Inverted overprint	1,500.	1,500.
60	A15	6c green	15.00	25.00
e.		Double overprint (II)	1,000.	
61	A20	10c black	9.00	15.00
e.		Double overprint (II)	750.00	
f.		Double overprint (III)	200.00	
61B	A20	10c red brown	14,000.	29,000.
62	A18	12c black	9.00	17.50
d.		Double overprint (I)	2,000.	
e.		Double overprint (II)	1,750.	
63	A18	12c red lilac	150.00	250.00
64	A22	25c dark violet	26.00	40.00
b.		No period after "GOVT"	325.00	325.00
f.		Double overprint (III)	1,000.	
		Nos. 53-61,62-64 (12)	251.50	424.25

Overprinted in Black

No.	Design	Description	Unused	Used
65	A13	2c vermilion	67.50	75.00
b.		No period after "GOVT"	250.00	250.00
66	A17	2c rose	1.25	2.25
b.		No period after "GOVT"	50.00	60.00
d.		Double overprint (I)	4,000.	
e.		Double overprint (II)	2,750.	
f.		Double overprint (III)	300.00	
66C	A15	6c green	14,000.	29,000.
67	A20	10c vermilion	15.00	30.00
f.		Double overprint (III)	1,250.	
68	A20	10c red brown	7.50	12.50
f.		Double overprint (III)	1,750.	
69	A18	12c red lilac	275.00	500.00
70	A21	15c red brown	20.00	30.00
e.		Double overprint (II)	2,000.	
71	A16	18c dull rose	25.00	35.00
a.		"18 3" instead of "1893"	475.00	475.00
b.		No period after "GOVT"	300.00	300.00
d.		Double overprint (I)	475.00	
f.		Double overprint (III)	225.00	
g.		Pair, one without ovpt.	2,500.	

72 A23 50c red 60.00 *90.00*
b. No period after "GOVT" *400.00 400.00*
f. Double overprint (III) *1,000.*
73 A24 $1 rose red 110.00 *175.00*
b. No period after "GOVT" *450.00* 425.00
Nos. 65-66,67-73 (9) 581.25 *949.75*

Coat of Arms — A26

View of Honolulu — A27

Statue of Kamehameha I — A28

Stars and Palms — A29

S.S. Arawa — A30

Pres. Sanford Ballard Dole — A31

"CENTS" Added — A32

1894
74 A26 1c yellow 2.00 1.25
75 A27 2c brown 2.25 .60
76 A28 5c rose lake 4.00 1.50
77 A29 10c yellow green 6.00 4.50
78 A30 12c blue 12.50 *17.50*
79 A31 25c deep blue 12.50 *17.50*
Nos. 74-79 (6) 39.25 *42.85*

1899
80 A26 1c dark green 1.50 1.25
81 A27 2c rose 1.40 1.00
a. 2c salmon 1.50 1.25
b. Vert. pair, imperf. horiz. *4,500.*
82 A32 5c blue 5.50 3.00
Nos. 80-82 (3) 8.40 5.25

OFFICIAL STAMPS

Lorrin Andrews Thurston — O1

1896 Unwmk. Engr. *Perf. 12*
O1 O1 2c green 40.00 17.50
O2 O1 5c black brown 40.00 17.50
O3 O1 6c deep ultra 40.00 17.50
O4 O1 10c bright rose 40.00 17.50
O5 O1 12c orange 40.00 17.50
O6 O1 25c gray violet 40.00 17.50
Nos. O1-O6 (6) 240.00 105.00

Used values for #O1-O6 are for copies cto "FOREIGN OFFICE/HONOLULU H.I." in double circle without date.

The stamps of Hawaii were replaced by those of the United States.

PHILIPPINES

ˌfi-lə-ˈpēnz

LOCATION — Group of 7,100 islands and islets in the Malay Archipelago, north of Borneo, in the North Pacific Ocean
GOVT. — US Admin., 1898-1946
AREA — 115,748 sq. mi.
POP. — 16,971,100 (est. 1941)
CAPITAL — Quezon City

The islands were ceded to the US by Spain in 1898. On Nov. 15, 1935, they were given their independence, subject to a transition period which ended July 4, 1946. On that date the Commonwealth became the "Republic of the Philippines."

100 Cents = 1 Dollar (1899)
100 Centavos = 1 Peso (1906)

Watermarks

Wmk. 191PI- Double-lined PIPS

Wmk. 190PI- Single-lined PIPS

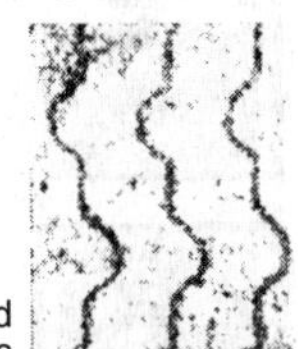
Wmk. 257- Curved Wavy Lines

Issued under US Administration

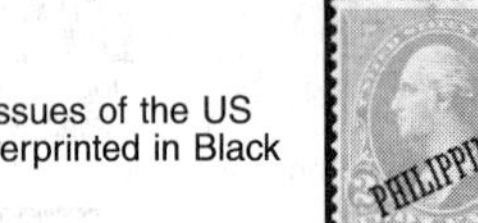

Issues of the US Overprinted in Black

On No. 260

1899-1901 Unwmk. *Perf. 12*
212 A96 50c orange 400.00 250.00

On Nos. 279, 279B, 279Bd, 279Be, 279Bf, 279Bc, 268, 281, 282C, 283, 284, 275 and 275a

Wmk. 191
213 A87 1c yellow green 3.00 .60
a. Inverted overprint *13,500.*
214 A88 2c red, IV 1.25 .60
a. 2c orange red, IV ('01) 1.25 .60
b. Bklt. pane of 6, red, IV ('00) 250.00 200.00
c. 2c reddish car, IV 1.90 .90
d. 2c rose car, IV 2.25 1.10
215 A89 3c purple 5.75 1.25
216 A91 5c blue 5.50 .90
a. Inverted overprint *3,750.*
217 A94 10c brown, I 17.50 4.00
217A A94 10c org brn, II 160.00 27.50
218 A95 15c olive green 32.50 8.00
219 A96 50c orange 125.00 37.50
a. 50c red orange 250.00
Nos. 213-219 (8) 350.50 80.35

No. 216a is valued in the grade of fine.

On Nos. 280b, 282 and 272

1901
220 A90 4c orange brown 22.50 5.00
221 A92 6c lake 29.00 7.00
222 A93 8c violet brown 29.00 7.50
Nos. 220-222 (3) 80.50 19.50

On Nos. 276, 276A, 277a and 278

Red Overprint
223 A97 $1 black, I 475. 275.
223A A97 $1 black, II 2,400. 750.
224 A98 $2 dark blue 475. 350.
225 A99 $5 dark green 825. *900.*

On Nos. 300-313 and shades

1903-04

Black Overprint
226 A115 1c blue green 4.00 .30
227 A116 2c carmine 7.50 1.10
228 A117 3c bright violet 67.50 12.50
229 A118 4c brown ('04) 75.00 22.50
a. 4c orange brown 75.00 20.00
230 A119 5c blue 11.00 1.00
231 A120 6c brnsh lake ('04) 80.00 22.50
232 A121 8c vio blk ('04) 45.00 15.00
233 A122 10c pale red brn ('04) 20.00 2.25
a. 10c red brown 25.00 3.00
b. Pair, one without ovpt. *1,500.*
234 A123 13c purple black 32.50 17.50
a. 13c brown violet 32.50 17.50
235 A124 15c olive green 60.00 15.00
236 A125 50c orange 125.00 35.00
Nos. 226-236 (11) 527.50 144.65

Red Overprint
237 A126 $1 black 475. 275.
238 A127 $2 dk blue ('04) 800. 850.
239 A128 $5 dk green ('04) 975. *3,000.*

On Nos. 319, 319c in Black

1904
240 A129 2c carmine 5.50 2.25
a. Booklet pane of 6 *1,100.*
b. 2c scarlet 6.25 2.75
c. As "b," booklet pane of 6 —

Jose Rizal — A40

Arms of Manila — A41

Designs: 4c, McKinley. 6c, Magellan. 8c, Miguel Lopez de Legaspi. 10c, Gen. Henry W. Lawton. 12c, Lincoln. 16c, Adm. William T. Sampson. 20c, Washington. 26c, Francisco Carriedo. 30c, Franklin.

Each Inscribed "Philippine Islands/United States of America"

1906, Sept. 8 Engr. Wmk. 191PI
241 A40 2c deep green .25 .20
a. 2c yellow green ('10) .40 .20
b. Booklet pane of 6 475.00
242 A40 4c carmine .30 .20
a. 4c carmine lake ('10) .60 .20
b. Booklet pane of 6 *650.00*
243 A40 6c violet 1.25 .20
244 A40 8c brown 2.50 .70
245 A40 10c blue 1.75 .20
a. 10c dark blue 1.75 .20
246 A40 12c brown lake 5.00 2.00
247 A40 16c violet black 3.75 .20
248 A40 20c orange brown 4.00 .30
249 A40 26c violet brown 6.00 2.25
250 A40 30c olive green 4.75 1.50
251 A41 1p orange 27.50 7.00
252 A41 2p black 35.00 1.25
253 A41 4p dark blue 100.00 15.00
254 A41 10p dark green 225.00 70.00
Nos. 241-254 (14) 417.05 101.00

Change of Colors

1909-13 *Perf. 12*
255 A40 12c red orange 8.50 2.50
256 A40 16c olive green 3.50 .75
257 A40 20c yellow 7.50 1.25
258 A40 26c blue green 1.75 .75
259 A40 30c ultramarine 10.00 3.25
260 A41 1p pale violet 30.00 5.00
260A A41 2p vio brown ('13) 85.00 2.75
Nos. 255-260A (7) 146.25 16.25

1911 Wmk. 190PI *Perf. 12*
261 A40 2c green .65 .20
a. Booklet pane of 6 *550.00*
262 A40 4c carmine lake 2.50 .20
a. 4c carmine — —
b. Booklet pane of 6 *600.00*
263 A40 6c deep violet 2.00 .20
264 A40 8c brown 8.50 .45
265 A40 10c blue 3.25 .20
266 A40 12c orange 2.50 .45
267 A40 16c olive green 2.50 .20
a. 16c pale olive green 2.50 .20
268 A40 20c yellow 2.00 .20
a. 20c orange 2.00 .20
269 A40 26c blue green 3.00 .20
270 A40 30c ultramarine 3.50 .40
271 A41 1p pale violet 22.50 .55
272 A41 2p violet brown 27.50 .75
273 A41 4p deep blue 625.00 80.00
274 A41 10p deep green 225.00 25.00
Nos. 261-274 (14) 930.40 109.00

1914
275 A40 30c gray 10.00 .40

1914-23 *Perf. 10*
276 A40 2c green 1.75 .20
a. Booklet pane of 6 *450.00*
277 A40 4c carmine 1.75 .20
a. Booklet pane of 6 *450.00*
278 A40 6c light violet 37.50 9.00
a. 6c deep violet 42.50 6.00
279 A40 8c brown 40.00 10.00
280 A40 10c dark blue 25.00 .20
281 A40 16c olive green 75.00 4.50
282 A40 20c orange 22.50 .85
283 A40 30c gray 55.00 2.75
284 A41 1p pale violet 110.00 3.00
Nos. 276-284 (9) 368.50 30.70

1918-26 *Perf. 11*
285 A40 2c green 20.00 4.25
a. Booklet pane of 6 *750.00*
286 A40 4c carmine 25.00 2.50
a. Booklet pane of 6 *1,350.*
287 A40 6c deep violet 35.00 1.75
287A A40 8c light brown 200.00 25.00
288 A40 10c dark blue 52.50 1.50
289 A40 16c olive green 90.00 6.75
289A A40 20c orange 60.00 7.50
289C A40 30c gray 55.00 12.50
289D A41 1p pale violet 70.00 14.00
Nos. 285-289D (9) 607.50 75.75

1917-25 Unwmk. *Perf. 11*
290 A40 2c yellow green .20 .20
a. 2c dark green .20 .20
b. Vert. pair, imperf. horiz. *1,500.*
c. Horiz. pair, imperf. btwn. *1,500.* —
d. Vert. pair, imperf. btwn. *1,750.*
e. Booklet pane of 6 27.50
291 A40 4c carmine .20 .20
a. 4c light rose .20 .20
b. Booklet pane of 6 17.50 —
292 A40 6c deep violet .30 .20
a. 6c lilac .35 .20
b. 6c red violet .35 .20
c. Booklet pane of 6 *550.00* —
293 A40 8c yellow brown .20 .20
a. 8c orange brown .20 .20
294 A40 10c deep blue .20 .20
295 A40 12c red orange .30 .20
296 A40 16c light olive green 55.00 .25
a. 16c olive bister 55.00 .40
297 A40 20c orange yellow .30 .20
298 A40 26c green .45 .45
a. 26c blue green .55 .25
299 A40 30c gray .55 .20
300 A41 1p pale violet 27.50 1.00
a. 1p red lilac 27.50 1.00
b. 1p pale rose lilac 27.50 1.10
301 A41 2p violet brown 25.00 .75
302 A41 4p blue 22.50 .45
a. 4p dark blue 22.50 .45
Nos. 290-302 (13) 132.70 4.50

1923-26

Design: 16c, Adm. George Dewey.

303 A40 16c olive bister .90 .20
a. 16c olive green 1.25 .20
304 A41 10p deep green ('26) 45.00 5.00

See Nos. 326-353. For surcharges see Nos. 368-369, 450. For overprints see Nos. C1-C28, C36-C46, C54-C57, O5-O14.

Legislative Palace A42

1926, Dec. 20 Unwmk. *Perf. 12*
319 A42 2c green & black .40 .25
a. Horiz. pair, imperf. btwn. *300.00*
b. Vert. pair, imperf. between *550.00*
320 A42 4c car & black .40 .35
a. Horiz. pair, imperf. btwn. *300.00*
b. Vert. pair, imperf. between *575.00*
321 A42 16c ol grn & black .75 .65
a. Horiz. pair, imperf. btwn. *350.00*
b. Vert. pair, imperf. between *625.00*
c. Double impression of center *675.00*
322 A42 18c lt brn & black .85 .50
a. Double impression of center *850.00*
b. Vert. pair, imperf. between *675.00*
323 A42 20c orange & black 1.25 .80
a. 20c orange & brown *600.00* —
b. Imperf., pair *575.00 575.00*
c. As "a," imperf., pair *950.00*
d. Vert. pair, imperf. between *675.00*
324 A42 24c gray & black .85 .55
a. Vert. pair, imperf. between *675.00*
325 A42 1p rose lilac & blk 45.00 30.00
a. Vert. pair, imperf. between *675.00*
Nos. 319-325 (7) 49.50 33.10

Opening of the Legislative Palace. For overprints see Nos. O1-O4.

Coil Stamp
Rizal Type of 1906

1928 *Perf. 11 Vertically*
326 A40 2c green 7.50 15.00

Types of 1906-23

1925-31 Unwmk. *Imperf.*
340 A40 2c yel grn ('31) .20 .20
a. green ('25) .25 .20
341 A40 4c car rose ('31) .20 .20
a. carmine ('25) .40 .20
342 A40 6c violet ('31) 1.00 1.00
a. deep violet ('25) 8.00 4.00
343 A40 8c brown ('31) .90 .90
a. yellow brown ('25) 6.00 3.00
344 A40 10c blue ('31) 1.75 1.40
a. deep blue ('25) 25.00 7.00
345 A40 12c dp org ('31) 2.50 2.10
a. red orange ('25) 25.00 7.00

346	A40 16c olive green (*Dewey*) ('31)	2.00	1.50
a.	bister green ('25)	20.00	5.50
347	A40 20c dp yel org ('31)	2.00	1.50
a.	yellow orange ('25)	20.00	5.50
348	A40 26c green ('31)	2.00	1.50
a.	blue green ('25)	25.00	7.00
349	A40 30c light gray ('31)	2.25	1.75
a.	gray ('25)	25.00	7.00
350	A41 1p lt violet ('31)	4.00	4.00
a.	violet ('25)	90.00	35.00
351	A41 2p brn vio ('31)	10.00	10.00
a.	violet brown ('25)	200.00	75.00
352	A41 4p blue ('31)	35.00	30.00
a.	deep blue ('25)	1,000.	375.00
353	A41 10p green ('31)	100.00	100.00
a.	deep green ('25)	2,000.	750.00
	Nos. 340-353 (14)	163.80	156.05
	Nos. 340a-353a (14)	3,444.	1,281.

Mount Mayon, Luzon A43

Post Office, Manila A44

Pier No. 7, Manila Bay — A45

(See footnote) — A46

Rice Planting A47

Rice Terraces A48

Baguio Zigzag A49

1932, May 3 *Perf. 11*

354	A43 2c yellow green	.40	.20
355	A44 4c rose carmine	.35	.25
356	A45 12c orange	.50	.50
357	A46 18c red orange	25.00	9.00
358	A47 20c yellow	.65	.55
359	A48 24c deep violet	1.00	.65
360	A49 32c olive brown	1.00	.70
	Nos. 354-360 (7)	28.90	11.85

The 18c vignette was intended to show Pagsanjan Falls in Laguna, central Luzon, and is so labeled. Through error, the stamp pictures Vernal Falls in Yosemite Natl. Park, CA.

For overprints see #C29-C35, C47-C51, C63.

Nos. 302, 302a Surcharged in Orange or Red

1932

368	A41 1p on 4p blue (O)	2.00	.45
a.	1p on 4p dark blue (O)	2.75	1.25
369	A41 2p on 4p dark blue (R)	3.50	.75
a.	2p on 4p blue (R)	3.50	.75

Baseball A50

Tennis — A51

Basketball — A52

1934, Apr. 14 **Typo.** *Perf. 11½*

380	A50 2c yellow brown	1.50	.80
381	A51 6c ultramarine	.25	.20
a.	Vert. pair, imperf. between	*1,250.*	
382	A52 16c violet brown	.50	.50
a.	Vert. pair, imperf. horiz.	*1,250.*	
	Nos. 380-382 (3)	2.25	1.50

Tenth Far Eastern Championship Games.

Jose Rizal — A53

Woman and Carabao A54

La Filipina — A55

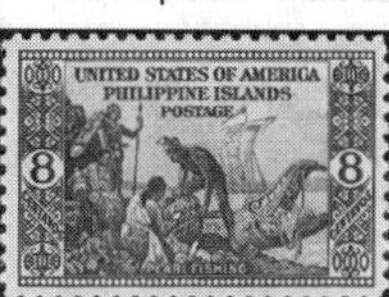
Pearl Fishing A56

Fort Santiago A57

Salt Spring — A58

Magellan's Landing, 1521 — A59

"Juan de la Cruz" — A60

Rice Terraces A61

"Blood Compact," 1565 — A62

Barasoain Church, Malolos A63

Battle of Manila Bay, 1898 A64

Montalban Gorge A65

George Washington A66

1935, Feb. 15 **Engr.** *Perf. 11*

383	A53 2c rose	.20	.20
384	A54 4c yellow green	.20	.20
385	A55 6c dark brown	.20	.20
386	A56 8c violet	.20	.20
387	A57 10c rose carmine	.20	.20
388	A58 12c black	.25	.20
389	A59 16c dark blue	.25	.20
390	A60 20c light olive green	.25	.20
391	A61 26c indigo	.30	.25
392	A62 30c orange red	.30	.25
393	A63 1p red orange & black	1.75	1.25
394	A64 2p bister brn & black	4.50	1.25
395	A65 4p blue & black	5.00	3.00
396	A66 5p green & black	10.00	3.00
	Nos. 383-396 (14)	23.60	10.60

For overprints & surcharges see #411-424, 433-446, 449, 463-466, 468, 472-474, 478-484, 485-494, C52-C53, O15-O36, O38, O40-O43, N2-N9, N28, NO2-NO6.

Commonwealth Issues

The Temples of Human Progress — A67

1935, Nov. 15

397	A67 2c carmine rose	.20	.20
398	A67 6c deep violet	.20	.20
399	A67 16c blue	.20	.20
400	A67 36c yellow green	.35	.30
401	A67 50c brown	.55	.55
	Nos. 397-401 (5)	1.50	1.45

Inauguration of the Philippine Commonwealth, Nov. 15th, 1935.

Jose Rizal — A68

President Manuel L. Quezon — A69

1936, June 19 *Perf. 12*

402	A68 2c yellow brown	.20	.20
403	A68 6c slate blue	.20	.20
a.	Horiz. pair, imperf. vert.	*1,350.*	
404	A68 36c red brown	.50	.45
	Nos. 402-404 (3)	.90	.85

75th anniv. of the birth of Jose Rizal.

1936, Nov. 15 *Perf. 11*

408	A69 2c orange brown	.20	.20
409	A69 6c yellow green	.20	.20
410	A69 12c ultramarine	.20	.20
	Nos. 408-410 (3)	.60	.60

1st anniv. of the Commonwealth.
For overprints see Nos. 467, 475.

Nos. 383-396 Overprinted in Black

a

b

COMMONWEALTH

1936-37 *Perf. 11*

411	A53 (a) 2c rose	.20	.20
a.	Booklet pane of 6	2.50	2.00
412	A54 (b) 4c yel grn ('37)	.50	*4.00*
413	A55 (a) 6c dark brown	.20	.20
414	A56 (b) 8c violet ('37)	.25	.20
415	A57 (b) 10c rose carmine	.20	.20
a.	"COMMONWEALT"		—
416	A58 (b) 12c black ('37)	.20	.20
417	A59 (b) 16c dark blue	.20	.20
418	A60 (a) 20c lt ol grn ('37)	.65	.40
419	A61 (b) 26c indigo ('37)	.45	.35
420	A62 (b) 30c orange red	.35	.20
421	A63 (b) 1p red org & black	.65	.20
422	A64 (b) 2p bister brn & black ('37)	5.00	2.75
423	A65 (b) 4p blue & blk ('37)	22.50	5.00
424	A66 (b) 5p grn & blk ('37)	3.00	1.50
	Nos. 411-424 (14)	34.35	15.60

Map of Philippines A70

Arms of Manila A71

1937, Feb. 3

425	A70 2c yellow green	.20	.20
426	A70 6c light brown	.20	.20
427	A70 12c sapphire	.20	.20
428	A70 20c deep orange	.25	.20

429 A70 36c deep violet .50 .40
430 A70 50c carmine .65 .35
Nos. 425-430 (6) 2.00 1.55

33rd Eucharistic Congress.

1937, Aug. 27 ***Perf. 11***
431 A71 10p gray 4.25 2.00
432 A71 20p henna brown 2.25 1.40

For overprints see Nos. 495-496. For surcharges see Nos. 451, C58.

Nos. 383-396 Overprinted in Black

COMMON-
WEALTH
a

COMMONWEALTH
b

1938-40 ***Perf. 11***
433 A53 (a) 2c rose ('39) .20 .20
a. Booklet pane of 6 3.50 2.50
b. As "a," lower left hand satamp overprinted "WEALTH COMMON-" *4,000.*
c. Hyphen omitted — —
434 A54 (b) 4c yel grn ('40) 1.25 *30.00*
435 A55 (a) 6c dk brn ('39) .20 .20
a. 6c golden brown .20 .20
436 A56 (b) 8c violet ('39) .20 .20
a. "COMMONWEALT" (LR 31) 90.00
437 A57 (b) 10c rose car ('39) .20 .20
a. "COMMONWEALT" (LR 31) —
438 A58 (b) 12c black ('40) .20 .20
439 A59 (b) 16c dark blue .20 .20
440 A60 (a) 20c lt ol grn ('39) .20 .20
441 A61 (b) 26c indigo ('40) .20 .20
442 A62 (b) 30c org red ('39) 1.40 .70
443 A63 (b) 1p red org & blk .40 .20
444 A64 (b) 2p bis brn & blk 2.75 .75
445 A65 (b) 4p bl & blk ('40) 150.00 150.00
446 A66 (b) 5p grn & blk ('40) 6.00 3.25
Nos. 433-446 (14) 163.40
Nos. 433,435-446 (13) 156.50

Overprint "b" measures 18½x1¾mm. No. 433b occurs in booklet pane, No. 433a, position 5; all copies are straight-edged, left and bottom.

Stamps of 1917-37 Surcharged in Red, Violet or Black

1939, July 5
449 A54 2c on 4c yel green (R) .20 .20
450 A40 6c on 26c blue grn (V) .20 .20
a. 6c on 26c green .65 .30
451 A71 50c on 20p henna brn (Bk) 1.00 1.00
Nos. 449-451 (3) 1.40 1.40

Foreign Trade Week.

Triumphal Arch — A72

Malacanan Palace A73

1939, Nov. 15 ***Perf. 11***
452 A72 2c yellow green .20 .20
453 A72 6c carmine .20 .20
454 A72 12c bright blue .20 .20
Nos. 452-454 (3) .60 .60

For overprints see Nos. 469, 476.

1939, Nov. 15
455 A73 2c green .20 .20
456 A73 6c orange .20 .20
457 A73 12c carmine .20 .20
Nos. 455-457 (3) .60 .60

#452-457 for 4th anniv. of the Commonwealth.
For overprint see No. 470.

Quezon Taking Oath of Office — A74

Jose Rizal — A75

1940, Feb. 8
458 A74 2c dark orange .20 .20
459 A74 6c dark green .20 .20
460 A74 12c purple .25 .20
Nos. 458-460 (3) .65 .60

4th anniversary of Commonwealth.
For overprints see Nos. 471, 477.

Rotary Press Printing

1941, Apr. 14 ***Perf. 11x10½***

Size: 19x22½mm

461 A75 2c apple green .20 *.50*

Flat Plate Printing

1941-43 ***Perf. 11***

Size: 18¾x22mm

462 A75 2c apple green ('43) .20 *.50*
a. 2c pale apple green .20 *.50*
b. Bklt. pane of 6 #462 ('43) 1.25 *5.00*
c. Bklt. pane of 6 #462a 2.50 *2.75*

No. 462 was issued only in booklet panes and all copies have straight edges.

Further printings were made in 1942 and 1943 in different shades from the first supply of stamps sent to the islands.

For type A75 overprinted see Nos. 464, O37, O39, N1, NO1.

Philippine Stamps of 1935-41, Handstamped in Violet

1944 ***Perf. 11, 11x10½***
463 A53 2c (#411) *325.00* *160.00*
a. Booklet pane of 6 *3,250.00*
463B A53 2c (#433) *1,400.* *1,350.*
464 A75 2c (#461) 3.75 3.00
465 A54 4c (#384) *42.50* *42.50*
466 A55 6c (#385) *2,000.* *2,000.*
467 A69 6c (#409) *150.00* *110.00*
468 A55 6c (#413) *875.00* *825.00*
469 A72 6c (#453) *225.00* *125.00*
470 A73 6c (#456) *850.00* *725.00*
471 A74 6c (#459) *225.00* *200.00*
472 A56 8c (#436) 17.50 *24.00*
473 A57 10c (#415) *140.00* *90.00*
474 A57 10c (#437) *175.00* *140.00*
475 A69 12c (#410) *1,000.* *400.00*
476 A72 12c (#454) *4,000.* *2,250.*
477 A74 12c (#460) *275.00* *190.00*
478 A59 16c (#389) *800.00*
479 A59 16c (#417) *650.00* *550.00*
480 A59 16c (#439) *300.00* *200.00*
481 A60 20c (#440) 35.00 35.00
482 A62 30c (#420) *350.00* *325.00*
483 A62 30c (#442) *500.00* *375.00*
484 A63 1p (#443) *6,250.* *4,500.*

Nos. 463-484 are valued in the grade of fine to very fine.

Types of 1935-37 Overprinted

a

b

1945 ***Perf. 11***
485 A53 (a) 2c rose .20 .20
486 A54 (b) 4c yellow green .20 .20
487 A55 (a) 6c golden brown .20 .20
488 A56 (b) 8c violet .20 .20
489 A57 (b) 10c rose carmine .20 .20
490 A58 (b) 12c black .20 .20
491 A59 (b) 16c dark blue .25 .20
492 A60 (a) 20c lt olive green .30 .20
493 A62 (b) 30c orange red .40 .35
494 A63 (b) 1p red org & black 1.10 .25

Nos. 431-432 Overprinted in Black

495 A71 10p gray 40.00 13.50
496 A71 20p henna brown 35.00 15.00
Nos. 485-496 (12) 78.25 30.70

Jose Rizal — A76

1946, May 28 ***Perf. 11x10½***
497 A76 2c sepia .20 .20

For overprints see No. 503 (Philippines, Vol. 5) and No. O44.

Succeeding issues, released by the Philippine Republic on and after July 4, 1946, are listed in Vol. 5.

AIR POST STAMPS

Madrid-Manila Flight Issue

Regular Issue of 1917-26 Overprinted in Red or Violet

1926, May 13 **Unwmk.** ***Perf. 11***
C1 A40 2c green (R) 8.75 8.75
C2 A40 4c carmine 11.50 11.50
a. Inverted overprint *2,500.* —
C3 A40 6c lilac (R) 55.00 55.00
C4 A40 8c org brown 57.50 57.50
C5 A40 10c deep blue (R) 57.50 57.50
C6 A40 12c red orange 57.50 57.50
C7 A40 16c lt olive green *(Sampson)* *2,100.* *1,600.*
C8 A40 16c ol bister *(Sampson)* (R) *3,750.* *3,000.*
C9 A40 16c olive green *(Dewey)* 70.00 30.00
C10 A40 20c orange yellow 70.00 70.00
C11 A40 26c blue green 70.00 70.00
C12 A40 30c gray 70.00 70.00
C13 A41 2p vio brown (R) 550.00 300.00
C14 A41 4p dark blue (R) 750.00 500.00
C15 A41 10p deep green 1,350. 700.00

Same Overprint on No. 269

Wmk. 190PI

Perf. 12

C16 A40 26c blue green *3,000.*

Same Overprint on No. 284

Perf. 10

C17 A41 1p pale violet 200.00 175.00

Flight of Spanish aviators Gallarza and Loriga from Madrid to Manila.

London-Orient Flight Issue

Regular Issue of 1917-25 Overprinted in Red

1928, Nov. 9 **Unwmk.** ***Perf. 11***
C18 A40 2c green .50 .30
C19 A40 4c carmine .60 .50
C20 A40 6c violet 2.10 1.75
C21 A40 8c orange brown 2.25 1.90
C22 A40 10c deep blue 2.25 1.90
C23 A40 12c red orange 3.25 2.75
C24 A40 16c ol green *(Dewey)* 2.40 1.90
C25 A40 20c orange yellow 3.25 2.75
C26 A40 26c blue green 9.50 6.50
C27 A40 30c gray 9.50 6.50

Same Overprint on No. 271

Wmk. 190PI

Perf. 12

C28 A41 1p pale violet 50.00 25.00
Nos. C18-C28 (11) 85.60 51.75

Flight from London to Manila.

Nos. 354-360 Overprinted

1932, Sept. 27 **Unwmk.** ***Perf. 11***
C29 A43 2c yellow green .40 .30
C30 A44 4c rose carmine .40 .30
C31 A45 12c orange .60 .50
C32 A46 18c red orange 3.50 3.25
C33 A47 20c yellow 1.75 1.50
C34 A48 24c deep violet 1.75 1.50
C35 A49 32c olive brown 1.75 1.50
Nos. C29-C35 (7) 10.15 8.85

Visit of Capt. Wolfgang von Gronau on his round-the-world flight.

Regular Issue of 1917-25 Overprinted

1933, Apr. 11
C36 A40 2c green .40 .35
C37 A40 4c carmine .45 .35
C38 A40 6c deep violet .80 .75
C39 A40 8c orange brown 2.50 1.50
C40 A40 10c dark blue 2.25 1.00
C41 A40 12c orange 2.00 1.00
C42 A40 16c ol green *(Dewey)* 2.00 1.00
C43 A40 20c yellow 2.00 1.00
C44 A40 26c green 2.25 1.50
a. 26c blue green 3.00 1.75
C45 A40 30c gray 3.00 1.75
Nos. C36-C45 (10) 17.65 10.20

Flight from Madrid to Manila of aviator Fernando Rein y Loring.

Stamp of 1917 Overprinted

1933, May 26 **Unwmk.** ***Perf. 11***
C46 A40 2c green .50 .40

Regular Issue of 1932 Overprinted

C47 A44 4c rose carmine .20 .20
C48 A45 12c orange .30 .20
C49 A47 20c yellow .30 .20
C50 A48 24c deep violet .40 .25
C51 A49 32c olive brown .50 .35
Nos. C46-C51 (6) 2.20 1.60

Nos. 387 & 392 Overprinted in Gold

1935, Dec. 2
C52 A57 10c rose carmine .30 .20
C53 A62 30c orange red .50 .35

China Clipper flight from Manila to San Francisco, Dec. 2-5, 1935.

Regular Issue of 1917-25 Surcharged in Various Colors

1936, Sept. 6 ***Perf. 11***
C54 A40 2c on 4c carmine (Bl) .20 .20
C55 A40 6c on 12c red org (V) .20 .20
C56 A40 16c on 26c bl grn (Bk) .25 .20
a. 16c on 26c green (Bk) 1.25 .70
Nos. C54-C56 (3) .65 .60

Manila-Madrid flight by aviators Antonio Arnaiz and Juan Calvo.

Regular Issue of 1917-37 Surcharged in Black or Red

1939, Feb. 17
C57 A40 8c on 26c blue green .75 .40
a. 8c on 26c green 1.60 .55
C58 A71 1p on 10p gray (R) 3.00 2.25

1st Air Mail Exhib., Feb. 17-19, 1939.

Moro Vinta and Clipper AP1

1941, June 30
C59 AP1 8c carmine 1.00 .60
C60 AP1 20c ultramarine 1.25 .45
C61 AP1 60c blue green 1.75 1.00
C62 AP1 1p sepia .70 .50
Nos. C59-C62 (4) 4.70 2.55

For overprint see No. NO7. For surcharges see Nos. N10-N11, N35-N36.

No. C47 Handstamped in Violet **VICTORY**

1944, Dec. 3 Unwmk. *Perf. 11*
C63 A44 4c rose carmine *2,750. 2,750.*

SPECIAL DELIVERY STAMPS

U.S. No. E5 Overprinted in Red

1901, Oct. 15 Wmk. 191 *Perf. 12*
E1 SD3 10c dark blue 125.00 100.00

Special Delivery Messenger — SD2

1906 Engr. Wmk. 191Pl
E2 SD2 20c ultramarine 30.00 7.50
b. 20c pale ultramarine 30.00 7.50

See Nos. E3-E6. For overprints see Nos. E7-E10, EO1.

Special Printing

Ovptd. in Red as #E1 on US #E6

1907
E2A SD4 10c ultramarine *2,750.*

1911 Wmk. 190Pl
E3 SD2 20c deep ultramarine 20.00 1.75

1916 *Perf. 10*
E4 SD2 20c deep ultra 175.00 75.00

1919 Unwmk. *Perf. 11*
E5 SD2 20c ultramarine .60 .20
a. 20c pale blue .75 .20
b. 20c dull violet .60 .20

Type of 1906 Issue

1925-31 *Imperf.*
E6 SD2 20c dull violet ('31) 20.00 *50.00*
a. 20c violet blue ('25) 40.00 27.50

Type of 1919 Overprinted in Black

1939 *Perf. 11*
E7 SD2 20c blue violet .25 .20

Nos. E5b and E7, Handstamped in Violet

1944 *Perf. 11*
E8 SD2 20c (On #E5b) *800.00 550.00*
E9 SD2 20c (On #E7) *300.00 225.00*

Type SD2 Overprinted "VICTORY" As No. 486

1945
E10 SD2 20c blue violet .70 .55
a. "IC" close together 3.25 2.75

SPECIAL DELIVERY OFFICIAL STAMP

Type of 1906 Issue Overprinted

1931 Unwmk. *Perf. 11*
EO1 SD2 20c dull violet .65 *75.00*
a. No period after "B" 20.00 15.00
b. Double overprint —

It is recommended that expert opinion be acquired for No. EO1 used.

POSTAGE DUE STAMPS

Postage Due Stamps of the U.S. Nos. J38-J44 Overprinted in Black

1899, Aug. 16 Wmk. 191 *Perf. 12*
J1 D2 1c deep claret 6.50 1.50
J2 D2 2c deep claret 6.50 1.25
J3 D2 5c deep claret 15.00 2.50
J4 D2 10c deep claret 19.00 5.50
J5 D2 50c deep claret 200.00 100.00

No. J1 was used to pay regular postage Sept. 5-19, 1902.

1901, Aug. 31
J6 D2 3c deep claret 17.50 7.00
J7 D2 30c deep claret 225.00 110.00
Nos. J1-J7 (7) 489.50 227.75

Post Office Clerk — D3

Unwmk.

1928, Aug. 21 Engr. *Perf. 11*
J8 D3 4c brown red .20 .20
J9 D3 6c brown red .20 .20
J10 D3 8c brown red .20 .20
J11 D3 10c brown red .20 .20
J12 D3 12c brown red .20 .20
J13 D3 16c brown red .20 .20
J14 D3 20c brown red .20 .20
Nos. J8-J14 (7) 1.40 1.40

For overprints see Nos. O16-O22, NJ1. For surcharge see No. J15.

No. J8 Surcharged in Blue

1937
J15 D3 3c on 4c brown red .20 .20

Nos. J8-J14 Handstamped in Violet **VICTORY**

1944
J16 D3 4c brown red *140.00* —
J17 D3 6c brown red *90.00* —
J18 D3 8c brown red *95.00* —
J19 D3 10c brown red *90.00* —
J20 D3 12c brown red *90.00* —
J21 D3 16c brown red *95.00* —
J22 D3 20c brown red *95.00* —
Nos. J16-J22 (7) *695.00*

OFFICIAL STAMPS

Official Handstamped Overprints

"Officers purchasing stamps for government business may, if they so desire, overprint them with the letters "O.B." either in writing with black ink or by rubber stamps but in such a manner as not to obliterate the stamp that postmasters will be unable to determine whether the stamps have been previously used." C. M. Cotterman, Director of Posts, Dec. 26, 1905.

Beginning Jan. 1, 1906, all branches of the Insular Government used postage stamps to prepay postage instead of franking them as before. Some officials used manuscript, some utilized typewriting machines, some made press-printed overprints, but by far the larger number provided themselves with rubber stamps.

The majority of these read "O.B." but other forms were: "OFFICIAL BUSINESS" or "OFFICIAL MAIL" in 2 lines, with variations on many of these.

These "O.B." overprints are known on US 1899-1901 stamps; on 1903-06 stamps in red and blue; on 1906 stamps in red, blue, black, yellow and green.

"O.B." overprints were also made on the centavo and peso stamps of the Philippines, per order of May 25, 1907.

Beginning in 1926, the Bureau of Posts issued press-printed official stamps, but many government offices continued to handstamp ordinary postage stamps "O.B."

Regular Issue of 1926 Overprinted in Red

1926, Dec. 20 Unwmk. *Perf. 12*
O1 A42 2c green & black 2.25 1.00
O2 A42 4c carmine & black 2.25 1.25
a. Vertical pair, imperf. between 750.00
O3 A42 18c lt brown & black 7.00 4.00
O4 A42 20c orange & black 6.75 1.75
Nos. O1-O4 (4) 18.25 8.00

Opening of the Legislative Palace.

Regular Issue of 1917-26 Overprinted

1931 *Perf. 11*
O5 A40 2c green .20 .20
a. No period after "B" 15.00 5.00
b. No period after "O" —
O6 A40 4c carmine .20 .20
a. No period after "B" 15.00 5.00
O7 A40 6c deep violet .20 .20
O8 A40 8c yellow brn .20 .20
O9 A40 10c deep blue .30 .20
O10 A40 12c red orange .25 .20
a. No period after "B" 32.50
O11 A40 16c lt ol green (Dewey) .25 .20
a. 16c olive bister 1.25 .20
O12 A40 20c orange yellow .25 .20
a. No period after "B" 22.50 15.00
O13 A40 26c green .40 .30
a. 26c blue green 1.00 .65
O14 A40 30c gray .30 .25
Nos. O5-O14 (10) 2.55 2.15

Same Overprint on Nos. 383-392

1935
O15 A53 2c rose .20 .20
a. No period after "B" 15.00 5.00
O16 A54 4c yellow green .20 .20
a. No period after "B" 15.00 8.50
O17 A55 6c dark brown .20 .20
a. No period after "B" 20.00 17.50
O18 A56 8c violet .20 .20
O19 A57 10c rose carmine .20 .20
O20 A58 12c black .20 .20
O21 A59 16c dark blue .20 .20
O22 A60 20c lt olive green .20 .20
O23 A61 26c indigo .25 .25
O24 A62 30c orange red .30 .20
Nos. O15-O24 (10) 2.15 2.05

Same Overprint on Nos. 411 and 418

1937-38 *Perf. 11*
O25 A53 2c rose .20 .20
a. No period after "B" 4.25 2.25
b. Period after "B" raised (UL 4) 175.00
O26 A60 20c lt olive green ('38) .65 .50

Nos. 383-392 Overprinted in Black:

a

b

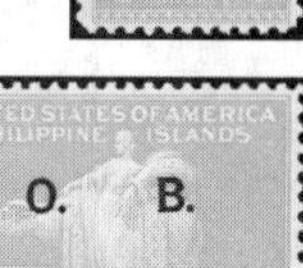

1938-40

O27 A53(a) 2c rose	.20	.20
a. Hyphen omitted	20.00	20.00
b. No period after "B"	25.00	25.00
O28 A54(b) 4c yellow green	.20	.20
O29 A55(a) 6c dark brown	.20	.20
O30 A56(b) 8c violet	.20	.20
O31 A57(b) 10c rose carmine	.20	.20
a. No period after "O"	30.00	30.00
O32 A58(b) 12c black	.20	.20
O33 A59(b) 16c dark blue	.20	.20
O34 A60(a) 20c lt ol grn ('40)	.25	.25
O35 A61(b) 26c indigo	.30	.30
O36 A62(b) 30c orange red	.25	.25
Nos. O27-O36 (10)	2.20	2.20

No. 461 Overprinted in Black

Perf. 11x10½

1941, Apr. 14 **Unwmk.**

O37 A75 2c apple green .20 .20

Official Stamps Handstamped in Violet

1944 ***Perf. 11, 11x10½***

O38 A53 2c #O27	*250.00*	*150.00*
O39 A75 2c #O37	6.50	3.00
O40 A54 4c #O16	*42.50*	*30.00*
O40A A55 6c #O29	*5,000.*	—
O41 A57 10c #O31	*150.00*	
a. No period after "O"	—	
O42 A60 20c #O22	*6,000.*	
O43 A60 20c #O26	*1,550.*	

No. 497 Overprinted Like No. O37 in Black

Perf. 11x10½

1946, June 19 **Unwmk.**

O44 A76 2c sepia .20 .20

OCCUPATION STAMPS

Issued under Japanese Occupation

Nos. 461, 438 and 439 Overprinted with Bars in Black

1942-43 Unwmk. ***Perf. 11x10½, 11***

N1 A75 2c apple green	.20	.20
a. Pair, one without overprint	—	
N2 A58 12c black ('43)	.20	.20
N3 A59 16c dark blue	5.00	3.75
Nos. N1-N3 (3)	5.40	4.15

Nos. 435, 442, 443 and 423 Surcharged in Black

a

b

c

d

Perf. 11

N4 A55 5c on 6c golden brn	.20	.20
a. Top bar shorter, thinner	.20	.20
b. 5c on 6c dark brown	.20	.20
c. As "b" and"a"	.20	.20
N5 A62 16c on 30c orange red ('43)	.25	.25
N6 A63 50c on 1p red org & black ('43)	.60	.60
a. Double surcharge		*300.00*
N7 A65 1p on 4p blue & black ('43)	125.00	*200.00*
Nos. N4-N7 (4)	126.05	*201.05*

On Nos. N4 and N4b, the top bar measures 1½x22½mm. On Nos. N4a and N4c, the top bar measures 1x21mm and the "5" is smaller and thinner.

No. N7 used is valued with a postal cancellation. Used examples exist with first day cancellations and these are worth somewhat less.

No. 384 Surcharged in Black

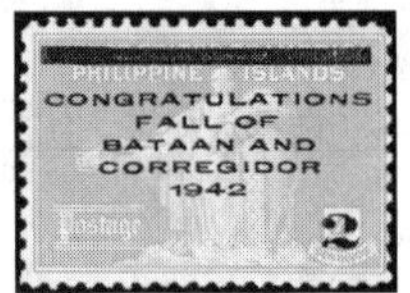

1942, May 18

N8 A54 2c on 4c yellow green 6.00 6.00

Japan's capture of Bataan and Corregidor. The American-Filipino forces finally surrendered May 7, 1942.

No. 384 Surcharged in Black

1942, Dec. 8

N9 A54 5c on 4c yellow green .50 .50

1st anniv. of the "Greater East Asia War."

Nos. C59 and C62 Surcharged in Black

1943, Jan. 23

N10 AP1 2(c) on 8c carmine	.25	.25
N11 AP1 5c on 1p sepia	.50	.50

Philippine Executive Commission, 1st anniv.

Nipa Hut OS1

Rice Planting OS2

Mt. Mayon and Mt. Fuji — OS3

Moro Vinta — OS4

Engr., Typo. (2, 6, 25c)

1943-44 **Wmk. 257** ***Perf. 13***

N12 OS1 1c deep orange	.20	.20
N13 OS2 2c bright green	.20	.20
N14 OS1 4c slate green	.20	.20
N15 OS3 5c orange brown	.20	.20
N16 OS2 6c red	.20	.20
N17 OS3 10c blue green	.20	.20
N18 OS4 12c steel blue	1.00	1.00
N19 OS4 16c dark brown	.20	.20
N20 OS1 20c rose violet	1.25	1.25
N21 OS3 21c violet	.20	.20
N22 OS2 25c pale brown	.20	.20
N23 OS3 1p deep carmine	.75	.75
N24 OS4 2p dull violet	5.50	5.50
N25 OS4 5p dark olive	14.00	9.00
Nos. N12-N25 (14)	24.30	19.30

For surcharges see Nos. NB5-NB7.

Map of Manila Bay Showing Bataan and Corregidor OS5

1943, May 7 **Photo.** **Unwmk.**

N26 OS5 2c carmine red	.20	.20
N27 OS5 5c bright green	.25	.25

Fall of Bataan and Corregidor, 1st anniv.

No. 440 Surcharged in Black

1943, June 20 **Engr.** ***Perf. 11***

N28 A60 12c on 20c lt olive green .20 .20
a. Double surcharge —

350th anniv. of the printing press in the Philippines. "Limbagan" is Tagalog for "printing press."

Rizal Monument, Filipina and Philippine Flag — OS6

1943, Oct. 14 **Photo.** ***Perf. 12***

N29 OS6 5c light blue	.20	.20
a. Imperf.	.20	.20
N30 OS6 12c orange	.20	.20
a. Imperf.	.20	.20
N31 OS6 17c rose pink	.20	.20
a. Imperf.	.20	.20
Nos. N29-N31 (3)	.60	.60

"Independence of the Philippines." Japan granted "independence" Oct. 14, 1943, when the puppet republic was founded.

The imperforate stamps were issued without gum.

Jose Rizal — OS7

Rev. Jose Burgos — OS8

Apolinario Mabini — OS9

1944, Feb. 17 **Litho.** ***Perf. 12***

N32 OS7 5c blue	.20	.20
a. Imperf.	.20	.20
N33 OS8 12c carmine	.20	.20
a. Imperf.	.20	.20
N34 OS9 17c deep orange	.20	.20
a. Imperf.	.20	.20
Nos. N32-N34 (3)	.60	.60

Nos. C60 and C61 Surcharged in Black

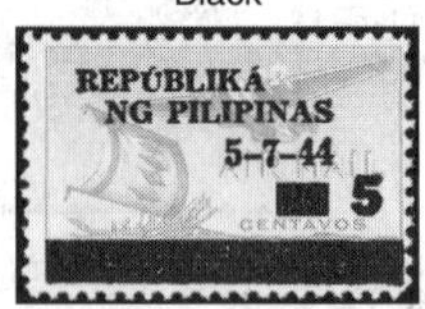

1944, May 7 ***Perf. 11***

N35 AP1 5c on 20c ultra	.50	.35
N36 AP1 12c on 60c blue green	1.25	.85

Fall of Bataan and Corregidor, 2nd anniv.

Jose P. Laurel — OS10

Without Gum

1945, Jan. 12 **Litho.** ***Imperf.***

N37 OS10 5c dull violet brown	.20	.20
N38 OS10 7c blue green	.20	.20
N39 OS10 20c chalky blue	.20	.20
Nos. N37-N39 (3)	.60	.60

1st anniv. of the puppet Philippine Republic (Oct. 14, 1944). "S" stands for "sentimos."

OCCUPATION SEMI-POSTAL STAMPS

Woman, Farming and Cannery — OSP1

Unwmk.

1942, Nov. 12 **Litho.** ***Perf. 12***

NB1 OSP1 2c + 1c pale vio	.20	.20
NB2 OSP1 5c + 1c brt green	.25	.20
NB3 OSP1 16c + 2c orange	32.50	32.50
Nos. NB1-NB3 (3)	32.95	32.90

Campaign to produce and conserve food. The surtax aided the Red Cross.

Souvenir Sheet

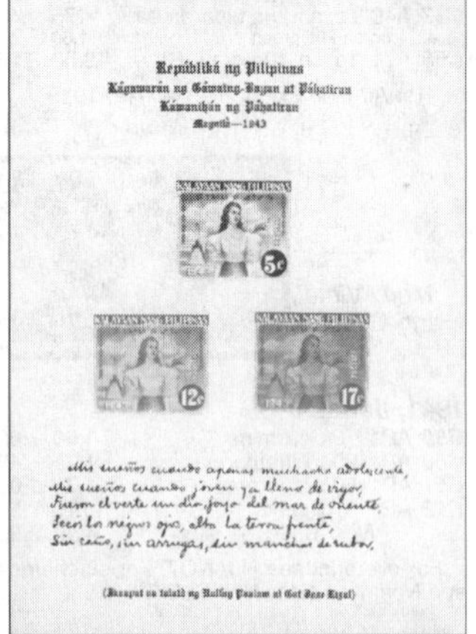
OSP2

Without Gum

1943, Oct. 14 ***Imperf.***

NB4 OSP2 Sheet of 3 50.00 *10.00*

"Independence of the Philippines."

No. NB4 contains Nos. N29a-N31a. Lower inscription from Rizal's "Last Farewell." Sold for 2.50p.

Nos. N18, N20 and N21 Surcharged in Black

1943, Dec. 8 Wmk. 257 *Perf. 13*

NB5	OS4 12c + 21c steel blue	.20	.20
NB6	OS1 20c + 36c rose violet	.20	.20
NB7	OS3 21c + 40c violet	.20	.20
	Nos. NB5-NB7 (3)	.60	.60

The surtax was for the benefit of victims of a Luzon flood.

"Baha" is Tagalog for "flood."

Souvenir Sheet

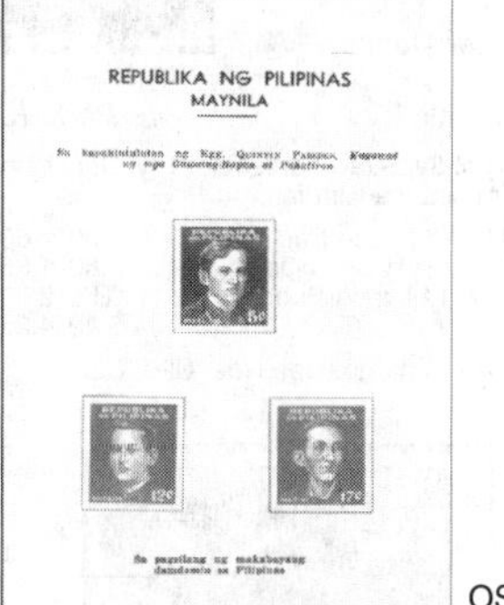

OSP3

Without Gum

Unwmk.

1944, Feb. 9 Litho. *Imperf.*

NB8	OSP3 Sheet of 3	5.00	*3.00*

No. NB8 contains Nos. N32a-N34a.

Sheet sold for 1p, surtax going to a fund for the care of heroes' monuments.

OCCUPATION POSTAGE DUE STAMP

No. J15 Ovptd. with Bar in Blue

1942, Oct. 14 Unwmk. *Perf. 11*

NJ1	D3 3c on 4c brown red	35.00	20.00

On copies of No. J15, two lines were drawn in India ink with a ruling pen across "United States of America" by employees of the Short Paid Section of the Manila Post Office.

This was to make a provisional 3c postage due stamp which was used from Sept. 1, 1942, (when the letter rate was raised from 2c to 5c) until Oct. 14 when No. NJ1 went on sale.

OCCUPATION OFFICIAL STAMPS

Nos. 461, 413, 435, 435a & 442 Overprinted or Surcharged in Black with Bars and

1943-44 Unwmk. *Perf. 11x10½, 11*

NO1	A75 2c apple green	.20	.20
a.	Double overprint	*500.00*	
NO2	A55 5c on 6c dk brown (#413, '44)	45.00	45.00
NO3	A55 5c on 6c gldn brn (No. 435a)	.20	.20
a.	Narrower spacing btwn. bars	.20	.20
b.	5c on 6c dark brown (#435)	.20	.20
c.	As "b," narrower spacing between bars	.20	.20
d.	Double surcharge	—	
NO4	A62 16c on 30c org red	.30	.30
a.	Wider spacing btwn bars	.30	.30
	Nos. NO1-NO4 (4)	45.70	45.70

On Nos. NO3 and NO3b, the bar deleting "United States of America" is 9¾-10mm above the bar deleting "Common-." On Nos. NO3a and NO3c, the spacing is 8-8½mm.

On No. NO4 the center bar is 19mm long, 3½mm below the top bar and 6mm above the Japanese characters.

On No. NO4a, the center bar is 20½mm long, 9mm below the top bar and 1mm above the Japanese characters.

"K. P." (Kagamitang Pampamahalaan) is Tagalog for "Official Business."

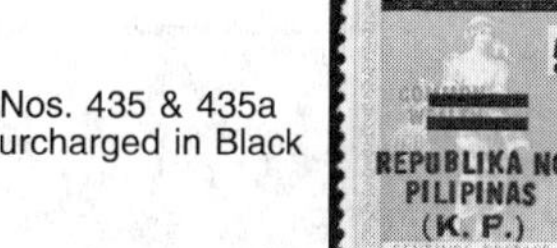

Nos. 435 & 435a Surcharged in Black

1944 *Perf. 11*

NO5	A55 5c on 6c golden brown	.20	.20
a.	5c on 6c dark brown	.20	.20

Nos. O34 & C62 Overprinted in Black

a

b

NO6	A60(a) 20c lt olive green	.25	.25
NO7	AP1(b) 1p sepia	.65	.65

PUERTO RICO

ˌpwer-tə-ˈrē-ˌ(ˌ)kō

(Porto Rico)

LOCATION — Large island in the West Indies, east of Hispaniola
GOVT. — Former Spanish possession
AREA — 3,435 sq. mi.
POP. — 953,243 (1899)
CAPITAL — San Juan

The island was ceded to the US by the Treaty of 1898.

Spanish issues of 1855-73 used in both Puerto Rico and Cuba are listed as Cuba Nos. 1-4, 9-14, 18-21, 32-34, 35A-37, 39-41, 43-45, 47-49, 51-53, 55-57.

Spanish issues of 1873-1898 for Puerto Rico only are listed in Vol. 4 of this Catalogue.

100 Cents = 1 Dollar (1898)

Issued under US Administration

Ponce Issue

A11

1898 Unwmk. *Imperf.*

200	A11 5c violet, *yellowish*	*7,000.*	

The only way No. 200 is known used is handstamped on envelopes.

Both unused stamps and used envelopes have a violet control mark.

Counterfeits exist of Nos. 200-201.

Coamo Issue

CORREOS
5 CTS.
COAMO

A12

1898 Unwmk. *Imperf.*

201	A12 5c black	650.	*1,050.*

There are ten varieties in the setting (see the Scott United States Specialized Catalogue).

The stamps bear the control mark "F. Santiago" in violet.

U.S. Nos. 279, 279Bf, 281, 272 & 282C Overprinted in Black at 36 degree angle

1899 Wmk. 191 *Perf. 12*

210	A87 1c yellow green	5.00	1.40
a.	Ovpt. at 25 degree angle	7.50	2.25
211	A88 2c redsh car, IV	4.25	1.25
a.	Ovpt. at 25 degree angle	5.50	2.25
212	A91 5c blue	9.00	2.50
213	A93 8c violet brown	27.50	17.50
a.	Ovpt. at 25 degree angle	32.50	19.00
c.	"PORTO RIC"	125.00	110.00
214	A94 10c brown, I	17.50	6.00
	Nos. 210-214 (5)	63.25	28.65

Misspellings of the overprint, actually broken letters (PORTO RICU, PORTU RICO, FORTO RICO), are found on 1c, 2c, 8c and 10c.

U.S. Nos. 279 and 279B Overprinted Diagonally in Black

1900

215	A87 1c yellow green	6.50	1.40
216	A88 2c red, IV	4.75	2.00
b.	Inverted overprint		*8,250.*

POSTAGE DUE STAMPS

U.S. Nos. J38, J39, J42 Overprinted like Nos. 210-214

1899 Wmk. 191 *Perf. 12*

J1	D2 1c deep claret	22.50	5.50
a.	Overprint at 25 degree angle	22.50	7.50
J2	D2 2c deep claret	20.00	6.00
a.	Overprint at 25 degree angle	20.00	7.00
J3	D2 10c deep claret	160.00	60.00
a.	Overprint at 25 degree angle	175.00	85.00
	Nos. J1-J3 (3)	202.50	71.50

Stamps of Puerto Rico were replaced by those of the US.

RYUKYU ISLANDS

rē-ˈyü-ˌ(ˌ)kyü ˈī-ləndz

LOCATION — Chain of 63 islands between Japan and Formosa, separating the East China Sea from the Pacific Ocean
GOVT. — Semi-autonomous under United States administration
AREA — 848 sq. mi.
POP. — 945,465 (1970)
CAPITAL — Naha, Okinawa

The Ryukyus were part of Japan until American forces occupied them in 1945. The islands reverted to Japan May 15, 1972.

Before the general issue of 1948, a number of provisional stamps were used. These included a mimeographed-handstamped adhesive for Kume Island, and various current stamps of Japan handstamped with chops by the postmasters of Okinawa, Amami, Miyako and Yaeyama. Although authorized by American authorities, these provisionals were local in nature, so are omitted in the listings that follow. They are listed in the *Scott United States Specialized Catalogue.*

100 Sen = 1 Yen

100 Cents = 1 Dollar (1958)

Catalogue values for all unused stamps in this country are for Never Hinged items.

Watermark

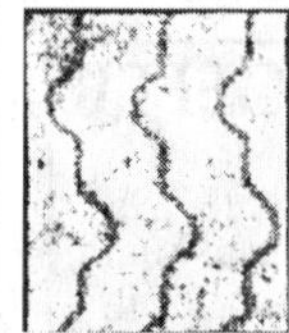

Wmk. 257

Cycad — A1

Lily — A2

Sailing Ship — A3

Farmer — A4

Wmk. 257

1949, July 18 Typo. *Perf. 13*

Second Printing

1	A1 5s magenta	1.50	1.50
2	A2 10s yellow green	6.00	5.50
3	A1 20s yellow green	3.50	3.50
4	A3 30s vermilion	1.50	1.50
5	A2 40s magenta	1.50	1.50
6	A3 50s ultramarine	3.00	3.25
7	A4 1y ultramarine	6.00	5.50
	Nos. 1-7 (7)	23.00	22.25

First Printing

1948, July 1

1a	A1 5s magenta	2.50	3.50
2a	A2 10s yellow green	1.40	2.00
3a	A1 20s yellow green	1.40	2.00
4a	A3 30s vermilion	2.50	3.25

5a	A2	40s magenta	50.00	50.00
6a	A3	50s ultramarine	2.50	3.50
7a	A4	1y ultramarine	450.00	325.00
		Nos. 1a-7a (7)	510.30	389.25

First printing: thick yellow gum, dull colors, rough perforations, grayish paper.

Second printing: white gum, sharp colors, cleancut perforations, white paper.

Tile Rooftop and Shishi — A5

1y, Ryukyu girl. 2y, Shuri Castle. 3y, Guardian dragon. 4y, Two women. 5y, Sea shells.

Perf. 13x13½

1950, Jan. 21 Unwmk. Photo.

8	A5	50s dark carmine rose	.20	.20
a.		White paper	.50	.50
b.		"White Sky" variety (pos. 76)	2.50	2.50
9	A5	1y deep blue	2.50	2.00
10	A5	2y rose violet	11.00	6.00
11	A5	3y carmine rose	25.00	11.00
12	A5	4y grnsh gray	15.00	11.00
13	A5	5y blue green	7.50	5.00
		Nos. 8-13 (6)	61.20	35.20

No. 8a is on whiter paper with colorless gum. Issued Sept. 6, 1958.

No. 8 is on toned paper with yellowish gum.

For surcharges see Nos. 16-17.

Ryukyu University A6

1951, Feb. 12 ***Perf. 13½x13***

14	A6	3y red brown	55.00	20.00

Opening of Ryukyu University, Feb. 12.

Pine Tree — A7

1951, Feb. 19 ***Perf. 13***

15	A7	3y dark green	55.00	25.00

Reforestation Week, Feb. 18-24.

Three types of 10y surcharge:
I - Narrow-spaced rules, "10" normal spacing.
II - Wide-spaced rules, "10" normal spacing.
III - Rules and "10" both wide-spaced.

1952 ***Perf. 13x13½***

16	A5	10y on 50s, type II	10.00	10.00
e.		Surcharge transposed	600.00	—
f.		Legend of surcharge only (no obliteration bars)	600.00	
16A	A5	10y on 50s, type I	40.00	40.00
b.		Bottom two bars inverted (pos. 17)	100.00	100.00
16B	A5	10y on 50s, type III	50.00	40.00
17	A5	100y on 2y rose vio	2,000.	1,600.
		Hinged	1,600.	

Surcharge forgeries are known of No. 17. Authentication by competent experts is recommended.

Dove, Bean Sprout and Map — A8

1952, Apr. 1 ***Perf. 13½x13***

18	A8	3y deep plum	120.00	40.00

Establishment of the Government of the Ryukyu Islands (GRI), Apr. 1, 1952.

Madanbashi Bridge — A9

1952-53

Designs: 2y, Main Hall, Shuri Castle. 3y, Shurei Gate. 6y, Stone Gate, Sogenji temple, Naha. 10y, Benzaiten-do temple. 30y, Sonohan Utaki (altar) at Shuri Castle. 50y, Tamaudum (royal mausoleum), Shuri. 100y, Stone Bridge, Hosho Pond.

19	A9	1y red	.20	.20
20	A9	2y green	.25	.25
21	A9	3y aqua	.30	.30
22	A9	6y blue	1.75	1.75
23	A9	10y crimson rose	2.50	.90
24	A9	30y olive green	12.00	6.50
a.		30y light olive green ('58)	40.00	
25	A9	50y rose violet	15.00	8.25
26	A9	100y claret	20.00	6.25
		Nos. 19-26 (8)	52.00	24.40

Issued: 1y, 2y, 3y, 11/20/52; others, 1/20/53.

Reception at Shuri Castle — A10

Perry and American Fleet A11

1953, May 26 ***Perf. 13½x13, 13x13½***

27	A10	3y deep magenta	12.50	6.50
28	A11	6y dull blue	1.25	1.25

Centenary of the arrival of Commodore Matthew Calbraith Perry at Naha, Okinawa.

Chofu Ota and Pencil-shaped Matrix — A12

1953, Oct. 1 ***Perf. 13½x13***

29	A12	4y yellow brown	10.00	5.00

3rd Newspaper Week.

Shigo Toma and Pen — A13

1954, Oct. 1

30	A13	4y blue	13.00	7.50

4th Newspaper Week.

Ryukyu Pottery — A14

Noguni Shrine and Sweet Potato Plant — A15

15y, Lacquerware. 20y, Textile design.

1954-55 Photo. ***Perf. 13***

31	A14	4y brown	1.00	.60
32	A14	15y vermilion	4.00	2.00
33	A14	20y yellow orange	2.50	2.00
		Nos. 31-33 (3)	7.50	4.60

Issue dates: June 25, 1954, June 20, 1955.

For surcharges see Nos. C19, C21, C23.

1955, Nov. 26

34	A15	4y blue	12.00	7.00

350th anniv. of the introduction of the sweet potato to the Ryukyu Islands.

Stylized Trees — A16

1956, Feb. 18 Unwmk.

35	A16	4y bluish green	10.00	5.00

Arbor Week, Feb. 18-24.

Willow Dance — A17

1956, May 1 ***Perf. 13***

Design: 8y, Straw hat dance. 14y, Dancer in warrior costume with fan.

36	A17	5y rose lilac	.90	.60
37	A17	8y violet blue	2.00	1.65
38	A17	14y reddish brown	3.50	2.00
		Nos. 36-38 (3)	6.40	4.25

For surcharges see Nos. C20, C22.

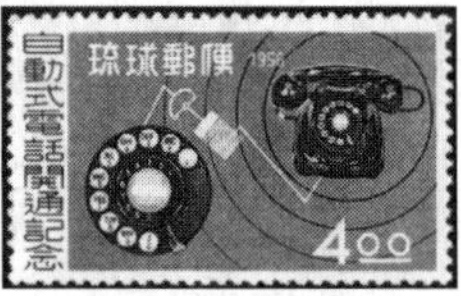

Telephone — A18

1956, June 8

39	A18	4y violet blue	15.00	8.00

Establishment of dial telephone system.

Garland of Pine, Bamboo and Plum — A19

1956, Dec. 1 ***Perf. 13½x13***

40	A19	2y multicolored	2.00	2.00

New Year, 1957.

Map of Okinawa and Pencil Rocket — A20

1957, Oct. 1 Photo. ***Perf. 13½x13***

41	A20	4y deep violet blue	.75	.75

7th annual Newspaper Week, Oct. 1-7.

Phoenix — A21

1957, Dec. 1 Unwmk. ***Perf. 13***

42	A21	2y multicolored	.25	.25

New Year, 1958.

Ryukyu Stamps — A22

1958, July 1 *Perf. 13½*

43	A22	4y multicolored	.80	.80

10th anniversary of first Ryukyu stamps.

Yen Symbol and Dollar Sign — A23

1958, Sept. 16 Typo. *Perf. 11*
Without Gum

44	A23	½c orange	.90	.90
a.		Imperf., pair	*1,000.*	
b.		Horiz. pair, imperf. btwn.	100.00	
c.		Vert. pair, imperf. btwn.	150.00	
d.		Vert. strip of 4, imperf. btwn.	500.00	
45	A23	1c yellow green	1.40	1.40
a.		Horiz. pair, imperf. btwn.	150.00	
b.		Vert. pair, imperf. btwn.	110.00	
c.		Vert. strip of 3, imperf. btwn.	450.00	
d.		Vert. strip of 4, imperf. btwn.	500.00	
e.		Block of 4, imperf. btwn. vert & horiz.	—	
46	A23	2c dark blue	2.25	2.25
a.		Horiz. pair, imperf. btwn.	150.00	
b.		Vert. pair, imperf. btwn.	*1,500.*	
c.		Horiz. strip of 3, imperf. btwn.	300.00	
d.		Horiz. strip of 4, imperf. btwn.	500.00	
47	A23	3c deep carmine	1.75	1.50
a.		Horiz. pair, imperf. btwn.	150.00	
b.		Vert. pair, imperf. btwn.	110.00	
c.		Vert. strip of 3, imperf. btwn.	300.00	
d.		Vert. strip of 4, imperf. btwn.	550.00	
e.		Block of 4, imperf. btwn. vert & horiz.	—	
48	A23	4c bright green	2.25	2.25
a.		Horiz. pair, imperf. btwn.	*500.00*	
b.		Vert. pair, imperf. btwn.	150.00	
49	A23	5c orange	4.25	3.75
a.		Horiz. pair, imperf. btwn.	150.00	
b.		Vert. pair, imperf. btwn.	*750.00*	
50	A23	10c aqua	5.75	4.75
a.		Horiz. pair, imperf. btwn.	200.00	
b.		Vert. pair, imperf. btwn.	150.00	
c.		Vert. strip of 3, imperf. btwn.	550.00	
51	A23	25c brt vio blue	8.00	6.00
a.		Gummed paper ('61)	9.50	8.50
b.		Horiz. pair, imperf. btwn.	*1,400.*	
c.		Vert. pair, imperf. btwn.	—	
d.		Vert. strip of 3, imperf. btwn.	600.00	
52	A23	50c gray	*17.50*	10.00
a.		Gummed paper ('61)	10.50	10.00
b.		Horiz. pair, imperf. btwn.	*1,200.*	
53	A23	$1 rose lilac	12.50	5.50
a.		Horiz. pair, imperf. btwn.	400.00	
b.		Vert. pair, imperf. btwn.	*1,750.*	
		Nos. 44-53 (10)	56.55	38.30

Printed locally. Perforation, paper and shade varieties exist. See chart in the *Scott United States Specialized Catalogue.*

Nos. 51a, 52a are on off-white paper and perf 10.3.

Gate of Courtesy — A24

1958, Oct. 15 Photo. *Perf. 13½*

54	A24	3c multicolored	1.25	1.25

Restoration of Shureimon, Gate of Courtesy, on road leading to Shuri City.
Counterfeits exist.

Lion Dance — A25

1958, Dec. 10 Unwmk. *Perf. 13½*

55	A25	1½c multicolored	.30	.30

New Year, 1959.

Trees and Mountains — A26

1959, Apr. 30 Litho. *Perf. 13½x13*

56	A26	3c bl, yel grn, grn & red	.70	.60

"Make the Ryukyus Green" movement.

Yonaguni Moth A27

1959, July 23 Photo. *Perf. 13*

57	A27	3c multicolored	1.10	1.00

Meeting of the Japanese Biological Education Society in Okinawa.

Hibiscus — A28

3c, Fish (Moorish idol). 8c, Sea shell (Phalium bandatum). 13c, Butterfly (Kallima Inachus Eucerca), denomination at left, butterfly going up. 17c, Jellyfish (Dactylometra pacifera Goette).

Inscribed 琉球郵便

1959, Aug. 10 *Perf. 13x13½*

58	A28	½c multicolored	.20	.20
59	A28	3c multicolored	.75	.40
60	A28	8c lt ultra, blk & ocher	11.00	5.50
61	A28	13c lt bl, gray & org	2.50	1.75
62	A28	17c vio bl, red & yel	22.50	9.00
		Nos. 58-62 (5)	36.95	16.85

Four-character inscription measures 10x2mm on ½c; 12x3mm on 3c, 8c; 8½x2mm on 13c, 17c. See Nos. 76-80.

Toy (Yakaji) — A29

1959, Dec. 1 Litho.

63	A29	1½c gold & multi	.55	.45

New Year, 1960.

University Badge A30

1960, May 22 Photo. *Perf. 13*

64	A30	3c multicolored	.95	.75

Opening of Ryukyu University, 10th anniv.

Dancer — A31

Designs: Various Ryukyu Dances.

1960, Nov. 1 Photo. *Perf. 13*
Dark Gray Background

65	A31	1c yellow, red & vio	1.50	.80
66	A31	2½c crimson, bl & yel	3.00	1.00
67	A31	5c dk blue, yel & red	.65	.50
68	A31	10c dk blue, yel & car	.80	.65
		Nos. 65-68 (4)	5.95	2.95

See Nos. 81-87, 220.

Torch and Nago Bay A32

Runners at Starting Line A33

1960, Nov. 8

72	A32	3c lt bl, grn & red	5.50	3.00
73	A33	8c orange & slate grn	.75	.75

8th Kyushu Inter-Prefectural Athletic Meet, Nago, Northern Okinawa, Nov. 6-7.

Little Egret and Rising Sun A34

1960, Dec. 1 Unwmk. *Perf. 13*

74	A34	3c reddish brown	5.50	3.50

National census.

Okinawa Bull Fight — A35

1960, Dec. 10 *Perf. 13½*

75	A35	1½c bis, dk bl & red brn	1.75	1.50

New Year, 1961.

Type of 1959 With Japanese Inscription Redrawn:

1960-61 Photo. *Perf. 13x13½*

76	A28	½c multicolored ('61)	.45	.45
77	A28	3c multicolored ('61)	.90	.35
78	A28	8c lt ultra, blk & ocher	.90	.80
79	A28	13c blue, brn & red	1.10	.90
80	A28	17c violet bl, red & yel	15.00	6.00
		Nos. 76-80 (5)	18.35	8.50

Size of Japanese inscription on Nos. 78-80 is 10½x11½mm. On No. 79 the denomination is at right, butterfly going down.

Issued: 8c-17c, July 1; 3c, Aug. 23; ½c, Oct.

Dancer Type of 1960 with "RYUKYUS" Added in English

1961-64 *Perf. 13*

81	A31	1c multicolored	.20	.20
82	A31	2½c multicolored ('62)	.20	.20
83	A31	5c multicolored ('62)	.25	.25
84	A31	10c multicolored ('62)	.45	.40
84A	A31	20c multicolored ('64)	3.25	1.40
85	A31	25c multicolored ('62)	1.00	.90
86	A31	50c multicolored	2.50	1.40
87	A31	$1 multicolored	6.00	.25
		Nos. 81-87 (8)	13.85	5.00

Issued: 50c, $1, Sept. 1; 1c, Dec. 5; 25c, Feb. 1; 2½c, 5c, 10c, June 20; 20c, Jan. 20.

Pine Tree — A36

1961, May 1 Photo. *Perf. 13*

88	A36	3c yellow green & red	1.60	1.25

"Make the Ryukyus Green" movement.

Naha, Steamer and Sailboat A37

1961, May 20

89	A37	3c aqua	2.10	1.50

40th anniversary of Naha.

White Silver Temple — A38

1961, Oct. 1 Typo. *Perf. 11*

90	A38	3c red brown	2.25	1.50
a.		Horiz. pair, imperf. between	*500.00*	
b.		Vert. pair, imperf. between	*600.00*	

Merger of townships Takamine, Kanegushiku and Miwa with Itoman.

A 3-cent stamp to commemorate the merger of two cities, Shimoji-cho and Hirara-shi of Miyako Island, was scheduled to be issued on Oct. 30, 1961. However, the merger was called off and the stamp never issued. It features a white chaplet on Kiyako linen on a blue background.

Books and Bird — A39

1961, Nov. 12 Litho. *Perf. 13*

91	A39	3c multicolored	1.10	.90

Issued for Book Week.

Rising Sun and Eagles — A40

1961, Dec. 10 Photo. *Perf. 13½*

92	A40	1½c gold, ver & blk	2.00	2.00

New Year, 1962.

Symbolic Steps, Trees and Government Building — A41

1962, Apr. 1 Unwmk. *Perf. 13½*

Design: 3c, Government Building.

93 A41 1½c multicolored .60 .60
94 A41 3c brt grn, red & gray .80 .80

10th anniv. of the Government of the Ryukyu Islands (GRI).

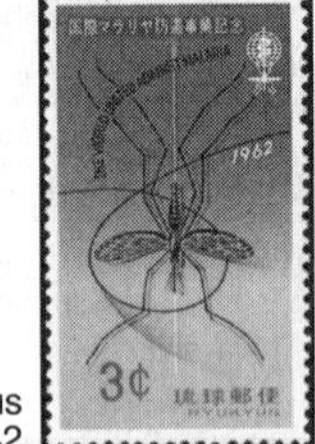
Anopheles Hyrcanus Sinensis — A42

8c, Malaria eradication emblem, Shurei gate.

1962, Apr. 7 *Perf. 13½x13*

95 A42 3c multicolored .60 .60
96 A42 8c multicolored .90 .75

WHO drive to eradicate malaria.

Dolls and Toys — A43

1962, May 5 Litho. *Perf. 13½*

97 A43 3c red, blk, bl & buff 1.10 1.00

Issued for Children's Day.

Linden or Sea Hibiscus — A44

1962, June 1 Photo.

Flowers: 3c, Indian coral tree. 8c, Iju (Schima liukiuensis Nakai). 13c, Touch-me-not (garden balsam). 17c, Shell flower (Alpinia speciosa).

98 A44 ½c multicolored .20 .20
99 A44 3c multicolored .35 .20
100 A44 8c multicolored .40 .40
101 A44 13c multicolored .60 .55
102 A44 17c multicolored 1.00 .80
Nos. 98-102 (5) 2.55 2.15

See #107, 114 for other flower stamps.
For surcharge see No. 190.

Earthenware A45

1962, July 5 *Perf. 13½x13*

103 A45 3c multicolored 3.50 2.50

Issued for Philatelic Week.

Japanese Fencing (Kendo) A46

1962, July 25 *Perf. 13*

104 A46 3c multicolored 4.00 3.00

All-Japan Kendo Meeting, Okinawa, July 25.

Rabbit Playing near Water, Bingata Cloth Design — A47

1962, Dec. 10 *Perf. 13x13½*

105 A47 1½c gold & multi 1.00 .80

New Year, 1963.

Young Man and Woman, Stone Relief — A48

1963, Jan. 15 Photo. *Perf. 13½*

106 A48 3c gold, black & blue .90 .80

Issued for Adult Day.

Gooseneck Cactus — A49

1963, Apr. 5 *Perf. 13x13½*

107 A49 1½c dk bl, grn, yel & pink .20 .20

Trees and Wooded Hills — A50

1963, Mar. 25 *Perf. 13½x13*

108 A50 3c ultra, grn & red brn 1.00 .80

"Make the Ryukyus Green" movement.

Map of Okinawa — A51

1963, Apr. 30 Unwmk. *Perf. 13½*

109 A51 3c multicolored 1.25 1.00

Opening of the Round Road on Okinawa.

Hawks over Islands — A52

1963, May 10 Photo.

110 A52 3c multicolored 1.10 .95

Issued for Bird Day, May 10.

Shioya Bridge — A53

1963, June 5

111 A53 3c multicolored 1.10 .95

Opening of Shioya Bridge over Shioya Bay.

Tsuikin-wan Lacquerware Bowl — A54

1963, July 1 Unwmk. *Perf. 13½*

112 A54 3c multicolored 3.00 2.50

Issued for Philatelic Week.

Map of Far East and JCI Emblem A55

1963, Sept. 16 Photo. *Perf. 13½*

113 A55 3c multicolored .70 .70

Meeting of the Intl. Junior Chamber of Commerce (JCI), Naha, Okinawa, Sept. 16-19.

Mamaomoto — A56

1963, Oct. 15 *Perf. 13x13½*

114 A56 15c multicolored 2.00 .80

Site of Nakagusuku Castle — A57

1963, Nov. 1 *Perf. 13½x13*

115 A57 3c multicolored .70 .60

Protection of national cultural treasures.

Flame — A58

1963, Dec. 10 *Perf. 13½*

116 A58 3c red, dk bl & yel .70 .60

15th anniversary of the Universal Declaration of Human Rights.

Dragon — A59

1963, Dec. 10 Photo.

117 A59 1½c Bingata Pattern .60 .50

New Year, 1964.

Carnation — A60

1964, May 10 *Perf. 13½*

118 A60 3c blue, yel, blk & car .40 .35

Issued for Mother's Day.

Pineapples and Sugar Cane — A61

1964, June 1

119 A61 3c multicolored .40 .35

Agricultural census.

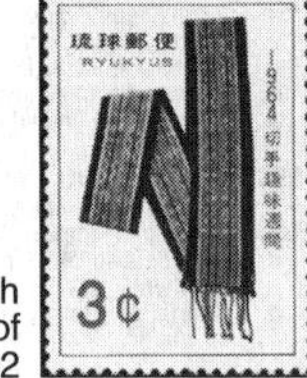
Minsah Obi (Sash Woven of Kapok) — A62

1964, July 1 Unwmk. *Perf. 13½*

120 A62 3c dp bl, rose pink & ocher .55 .50
a. 3c dp bl, dp car & ocher .70 .65

Issued for Philatelic Week.

Girl Scout and Emblem A63

1964, Aug. 31 Photo.

121 A63 3c multicolored .40 .35

10th anniversary of Ryukyuan Girl Scouts.

Shuri Relay Station — A64

Parabolic Antenna and Map — A65

1964, Sept. 1 Unwmk. *Perf. 13½*
Black Overprint

122 A64 3c deep green .65 .65
a. Figure "1" inverted 27.50 27.50
b. Overprint inverted *1,500.*
c. Overprint missing —
123 A65 8c ultra 1.25 1.25
a. Overprint missing —

Opening of the Ryukyu Islands-Japan microwave system carrying telephone & telegraph messages between the Ryukyus and Japan.

Many of the stamps with overprint errors listed above are damaged. Values are for stamps in very fine condition.

Gate of Courtesy, Olympic Torch and Emblem — A66

1964, Sept. 7 Photo. *Perf. 13½x13*

124 A66 3c ultra, yellow & red .20 .20

Relaying of the Olympic torch on Okinawa en route to Tokyo.

"Naihanchi," Karate Stance — A67

"Makiwara," Strengthening Hands and Feet — A68

"Kumite," Simulated Combat — A69

1964-65 Photo. *Perf. 13½*

125 A67 3c dull claret, yel & blk .50 .45
126 A68 3c yellow & multi ('65) .40 .40
127 A69 3c gray, red & blk ('65) .40 .40
Nos. 125-127 (3) 1.30 1.25

Karate, Ryukyuan self-defense sport. Issued: #125, 10/5; #126, 2/5; #127, 6/5.

Miyara Dunchí — A70

1964, Nov. 1 *Perf. 13½*

128 A70 3c multicolored .25 .25

Protection of national cultural treasures. Miyara Dunchi was built as a residence by Miyara-pechin Toen in 1819.

Snake and Iris (Bingata) — A71

1964, Dec. 10 Photo.

129 A71 1½c multicolored .30 .25

New Year, 1965.

Boy Scouts — A72

1965, Feb. 6 *Perf. 13½*

130 A72 3c lt blue & multi .45 .40

10th anniversary of Ryukyuan Boy Scouts.

Main Stadium, Onoyama A73

1965, July 1 *Perf. 13x13½*

131 A73 3c multicolored .25 .25

Inauguration of the main stadium of the Onoyama athletic facilities.

Samisen of King Shoko — A74

1965, July 1 Photo. *Perf. 13½*

132 A74 3c buff & multi .45 .40

Issued for Philatelic Week.

Kin Power Plant — A75

1965, July 1

133 A75 3c green & multi .25 .25

Completion of Kin power plant.

ICY Emblem, Ryukyu Map — A76

1965, Aug. 24 Photo. *Perf. 13½*

134 A76 3c multicolored .20 .20

UN, 20th anniv.; Intl. Cooperation Year, 1964-65.

Naha City Hall — A77

1965, Sept. 18 Unwmk. *Perf. 13½*

135 A77 3c blue & multi .20 .20

Completion of Naha City Hall.

Chinese Box Turtle — A78

Turtles: No. 137, Hawksbill turtle (denomination at top, country name at bottom). No. 138, Asian terrapin (denomination and country name on top).

1965-66 Photo. *Perf. 13½*

136 A78 3c gldn brn & multi .30 .30
137 A78 3c black, yel & brn .30 .30
138 A78 3c gray & multi .30 .30
Nos. 136-138 (3) .90 .90

Issue dates: No. 136, Oct. 20, 1965. No. 137, Jan. 20, 1966. No. 138, Apr. 20, 1966.

Horse (Bingata) — A79

1965, Dec. 10 Photo. *Perf. 13½*

139 A79 1½c multicolored .20 .20
a. Gold omitted 1,200. —

New Year, 1966.

There are 92 unused and 2 used examples of No. 139a known.

Noguchi's Okinawa Woodpecker A80

Sika Deer — A81

1966 Photo. *Perf. 13½*

140 A80 3c shown .20 .20
141 A81 3c shown .25 .25
142 A81 3c Dugong .25 .25
Nos. 140-142 (3) .70 .70

Nature conservation. Issued: #140, 2/15; #141, 3/15; #142, 4/20.

Ryukyu Bungalow Swallow — A82

1966, May 10 Photo. *Perf. 13½*

143 A82 3c sky blue, blk & brn .20 .20

4th Bird Week, May 10-16.

Lilies and Ruins A83

1966, June 23 *Perf. 13x13½*

144 A83 3c multicolored .20 .20

Memorial Day, commemorating the end of the Battle of Okinawa, June 23, 1945.

University of the Ryukyus A84

1966, July 1

145 A84 3c multicolored .20 .20

Transfer of the University of the Ryukyus from US authority to the Ryukyu Government.

Lacquerware, 18th Century — A85

1966, Aug. 1 *Perf. 13½*

146 A85 3c gray & multi .20 .20

Issued for Philatelic Week.

Tile-Roofed House and UNESCO Emblem — A86

1966, Sept. 20 Photo. *Perf. 13½*

147 A86 3c multicolored .20 .20

UNESCO, 20th anniv.

Government Museum and Dragon Statue — A87

1966, Oct. 6

148 A87 3c multicolored .20 .20

Completion of the GRI (Government of the Ryukyu Islands) Museum, Shuri.

Tomb of Nakasone-Tuimya Genga, Ruler of Miyako — A88

1966, Nov. 1 Photo. *Perf. 13½*

149 A88 3c multicolored .20 .20

Protection of national cultural treasures.

Ram in Iris Wreath (Bingata) — A89

1966, Dec. 10 Photo. *Perf. 13½*

150 A89 1½c dk blue & multi .20 .20

New Year, 1967.

Clown Fish — A90

1966-67

#152, Young boxfish (white numeral at lower left). #153, Forceps fish (pale buff numeral at lower right). #154, Spotted triggerfish (orange numeral). #155, Saddleback butterflyfish (carmine numeral, lower left).

151 A90 3c org red & multi .20 .20
152 A90 3c org yel & multi ('67) .20 .20
153 A90 3c multi ('67) .30 .25

154 A90 3c multi ('67)	.30	.25
155 A90 3c multi ('67)	.30	.25
Nos. 151-155 (5)	1.30	1.15

Issue dates: #151, Dec. 20. #152, Jan. 10. #153, Apr. 10. #154, May 25. #155, June 10.

A 3-cent stamp to commemorate Japanese-American-Ryukyuan Joint Arbor Day was scheduled for release on March 16, 1967. However, it was not released. The stamp in light blue and white features American and Japanese flags joined by a shield containing a tree.

Tsuboya Urn — A91

1967, Apr. 20

156 A91 3c yellow & multi	.20	.20

Issued for Philatelic Week.

Episcopal Miter — A92

1967-68 Photo. *Perf. 13½*

Seashells: No. 158, Venus comb murex. No. 159, Chiragra spider. No. 160, Green turban. No. 161, Euprotomus bulla.

157 A92 3c lt green & multi	.20	.20
158 A92 3c grnsh bl & multi	.20	.20
159 A92 3c emerald & multi	.25	.20
160 A92 3c lt blue & multi	.30	.25
161 A92 3c brt blue & multi	.60	.50
Nos. 157-161 (5)	1.55	1.35

Issued: #157, 7/20; #158, 8/30; #159, 1/18/68; #160, 2/20/68; #161, 6/5/68.

Red-tiled Roofs and ITY Emblem A93

1967, Sept. 11 Photo. *Perf. 13½*

162 A93 3c multicolored	.20	.20

International Tourist Year.

Mobile TB Clinic — A94

1967, Oct. 13 Photo. *Perf. 13½*

163 A94 3c lilac & multi	.20	.20

Anti-Tuberculosis Society, 15th anniv.

Hojo Bridge, Enkaku Temple, 1498 — A95

1967, Nov. 1

164 A95 3c blue grn & multi	.20	.20

Protection of national cultural treasures.

Monkey (Bingata) — A96

1967, Dec. 11 Photo. *Perf. 13½*

165 A96 1½c silver & multi	.25	.20

New Year 1968.

TV Tower and Map — A97

1967, Dec. 22

166 A97 3c multicolored	.25	.25

Opening of Miyako and Yaeyama television stations.

Dr. Kijin Nakachi and Helper — A98

1968, Mar. 15 Photo. *Perf. 13½*

167 A98 3c multicolored	.25	.25

120th anniv. of the first vaccination in the Ryukyu Islands, performed by Dr. Kijin Nakachi.

Pill Box (Inro) — A99

1968, Apr. 18

168 A99 3c gray & multi	.45	.45

Philatelic Week.

Young Man, Library, Book and Map of Ryukyu Islands A100

1968, May 13

169 A100 3c multicolored	.30	.25

10th International Library Week.

Mailmen's Uniforms and Stamp of 1948 A101

1968, July 1 Photo. *Perf. 13x13½*

170 A101 3c multicolored	.30	.25

1st Ryukyuan postage stamps, 20th anniv.

Main Gate, Enkaku Temple A102

Photo. & Engr.

1968, July 15 *Perf. 13½*

171 A102 3c multicolored	.30	.25

Restoration of the main gate of the Enkaku Temple, built 1492-1495, and destroyed during WWII.

Old Man's Dance — A103

1968, Sept. 15 Photo. *Perf. 13½*

172 A103 3c gold & multi	.30	.25

Issued for Old People's Day.

Mictyris Longicarpus A104

Crabs: #174, Uca dubia stimpson. #175, Baptozius vinosus. #176, Cardisoma carnifex. #177, Ocypode ceratophthalma pallas.

1968-69 Photo. *Perf. 13½*

173 A104 3c blue, ocher & blk	.30	.25
174 A104 3c lt bl grn & multi	.35	.30
175 A104 3c lt green & multi	.35	.30
176 A104 3c lt ultra & multi	.45	.40
177 A104 3c lt ultra & multi	.45	.40
Nos. 173-177 (5)	1.90	1.65

Issued: #173, 10/10; #174, 2/5/69; #175, 3/5/69; #176, 5/15/69; #177, 6/2/69.

Saraswati Pavilion A105

1968, Nov. 1 Photo. *Perf. 13½*

178 A105 3c multicolored	.30	.25

Restoration of the Saraswati Pavilion (in front of Enkaku Temple), destroyed during WWII.

Tennis Player — A106

1968, Nov. 3 Photo. *Perf. 13½*

179 A106 3c green & multi	.40	.35

35th All-Japan East-West Men's Soft-ball Tennis Tournament, Naha City, Nov. 23-24.

Cock and Iris (Bingata) — A107

1968, Dec. 10

180 A107 1½c orange & multi	.25	.20

New Year, 1969.

Boxer — A108

1969, Jan. 3

181 A108 3c gray & multi	.40	.30

20th All-Japan Amateur Boxing Championships, University of the Ryukyus, Jan. 3-5.

Ink Slab Screen — A109

1969, Apr. 17 Photo. *Perf. 13½*

182 A109 3c salmon, indigo & red	.40	.35

Philatelic Week.

Box Antennas and Map of Radio Link — A110

1969, July 1 Photo. *Perf. 13½*

183 A110 3c multicolored	.25	.20

Opening of the UHF (radio) circuit system between Okinawa and the outlying Miyako-Yaeyama Islands.

Gate of Courtesy and Emblems — A111

1969, Aug. 1 Photo. *Perf. 13½*

184 A111 3c Prus bl, gold & ver	.25	.20

22nd All-Japan Formative Education Study Conference, Naha, Aug. 1-3.

Tug of War Festival A112

Hari Boat Race A113

Izaiho Ceremony, Kudaka Island A114

Mortardrum Dance — A115

Sea God Dance A116

1969-70 Photo. *Perf. 13*
185 A112 3c multicolored .30 .25
186 A113 3c multicolored .35 .30
187 A114 3c multicolored .35 .30
188 A115 3c multicolored ('70) .50 .45
189 A116 3c multicolored ('70) .50 .45
Nos. 185-189 (5) 2.00 1.75

Folklore. Issued: #185, 8/1; #186, 9/5; #187, 10/3; #188, 1/20; #189, 2/27.

No. 99 Surcharged

1969, Oct. 15 Photo. *Perf. 13½*
190 A44 ½c on 3c multi .90 .90

Nakamura-ke Farm House, Built 1713-51 A117

1969, Nov. 1 Photo. *Perf. 13½*
191 A117 3c multicolored .20 .20

Protection of national cultural treasures.

Statue of Kyuzo Toyama, Maps of Hawaiian and Ryukyu Islands A118

1969, Dec. 5 Photo. *Perf. 13½*
192 A118 3c lt ultra & multi .40 .40
a. Without overprint 2,500.
b. Wide-spaced bars 725.00

Ryukyu-Hawaii emigration led by Kyuzo Toyama, 70th anniversary.
The overprint - "1969" at lower left and bars across "1970" at upper right - was applied before No. 192 was issued.

Dog and Flowers (Bingata) — A119

1969, Dec. 10
193 A119 1½c pink & multi .20 .20

New Year, 1970.

Sake Flask Made from Coconut A120

1970, Apr. 15 Photo. *Perf. 13½*
194 A120 3c multicolored .25 .25

Philatelic Week.

Classic Opera Issue

"The Bell" (Shushin Kaneiri) A121

Child and Kidnapper (Chu-nusudu) A122

Robe of Feathers (Mekarushi) A123

Vengeance of Two Young Sons (Nidotichiuchi) A124

The Virgin and the Dragon (Kokonomaki) A125

1970 Photo. *Perf. 13½*
195 A121 3c dull bl & multi .40 .40
196 A122 3c lt blue & multi .40 .40
197 A123 3c bluish grn & multi .40 .40
198 A124 3c dull bl grn & multi .40 .40
199 A125 3c multicolored .40 .40
Nos. 195-199 (5) 2.00 2.00
195a-199a, 5 sheets of 4 22.50 25.00

Issue dates: #195, Apr. 28; #196, May 29; #197, June 30; #198, July 30; #199, Aug. 25.

Underwater Observatory and Tropical Fish — A126

1970, May 22
200 A126 3c blue grn & multi .30 .25

Completion of the underwater observatory at Busena-Misaki, Nago.

Noboru Jahana (1865-1908), Politician — A127

Portraits: No. 202, Saion Gushichan Bunjaku (1682-1761), statesman. No. 203, Choho Giwan (1823-1876), regent and poet.

1970-71 Engr. *Perf. 13½*
201 A127 3c rose claret .50 .45
202 A127 3c dull blue green .75 .65
203 A127 3c black .50 .45
Nos. 201-203 (3) 1.75 1.55

Issued: #201, 9/25; #202, 12/22; #203, 1/22/71.

Map of Okinawa and People — A128

1970, Oct. 1 Photo.
204 A128 3c red & multi .25 .25

Oct. 1, 1970 census.

Great Cycad of Une — A129

1970, Nov. 2 Photo. *Perf. 13½*
205 A129 3c gold & multi .25 .25

Protection of national treasures.

Japanese Flag, Diet and Map of Ryukyus A130

1970, Nov. 15 Photo. *Perf. 13½*
206 A130 3c ultra & multi .80 .75

Citizens' participation in national administration according to Japanese law of 4/24/70.

Wild Boar and Cherry Blossoms (Bingata) — A131

1970, Dec. 10
207 A131 1½c multicolored .20 .20

New Year, 1971.

Low Hand Loom (Jibata) A132

Farmer Wearing Palm Bark Raincoat and Kuba Leaf Hat — A133

Fisherman's Wooden Box and Scoop A134

#209, Woman running a filature (reel). #211, Woman hulling rice with cylindrical "Shiri-ushi."

1971 Photo. *Perf. 13½*
208 A132 3c lt blue & multi .30 .25
209 A132 3c pale grn & multi .30 .25
210 A133 3c lt blue & multi .35 .30
211 A132 3c yellow & multi .40 .35
212 A134 3c gray & multi .35 .30
Nos. 208-212 (5) 1.70 1.45

Issue dates: #208, Feb. 16; #209, Mar. 16; #210, Apr. 30; #211, May 20; #212, June 15.

Water Carrier (Taku) — A135

1971, Apr. 15 Photo. *Perf. 13½*
213 A135 3c blue grn & multi .35 .30

Philatelic Week.

Old and New Naha, and City Emblem A136

1971, May 20 *Perf. 13*
214 A136 3c ultra & multi .25 .20

50th anniversary of Naha as a municipality.

Caesalpinia Pulcherrima — A137

Design: 2c, Madder (Sandanka).

1971 Photo. *Perf. 13*
215 A137 2c gray & multi .20 .20
216 A137 3c gray & multi .20 .20

Issue dates: 2c, Sept. 30; 3c, May 10.

View from Mabuni Hill — A138

Mt. Arashi from Haneji Sea — A139

Yabuchi Island from Yakena Port — A140

1971-72
217 A138 3c green & multi .20 .20
218 A139 3c blue & multi .20 .20
219 A140 4c multi ('72) .25 .20
Nos. 217-219 (3) .65 .60

Government parks. Issued: #217, July 30; #218, Aug. 30, 1971; #219, Jan. 20, 1972.

A 4-cent stamp picturing Iriomote Park was printed for release in 1971. Its use was changed, and it was used to validate Ryukyu Islands Emergency conversion confirmation certificates. See the Scott U.S. Specialized Catalogue.

Dancer — A141

1971, Nov. 1 Photo. *Perf. 13*
220 A141 4c Prus blue & multi .20 .20

Deva King, Torinji Temple — A142

1971, Dec. 1
221 A142 4c dp blue & multi .20 .20

Protection of national cultural treasures.

Rat and Chrysanthemums A143

1971, Dec. 10
222 A143 2c brown org & multi .20 .20

New Year 1972.

Student Nurse — A144

1971, Dec. 24
223 A144 4c lilac & multi .20 .20

Nurses' training, 25th anniversary.

Birds on Seashore A145

Sun over Islands A147

Coral Reef — A146

1972 Photo. *Perf. 13*
224 A145 5c brt blue & multi .40 .35
225 A146 5c gray & multi .40 .35
226 A147 5c ocher & multi .40 .35
Nos. 224-226 (3) 1.20 1.05

Issued: #224, 4/14; #225, 3/30; #226, 3/21.

Dove, US and Japanese Flags — A148

1972, Apr. 17 Photo. *Perf. 13*
227 A148 5c brt blue & multi .60 .60

Ratification of the Reversion Agreement with US under which the Ryukyu Islands were returned to Japan.

Antique Sake Pot (Yushibin) — A149

1972, Apr. 20
228 A149 5c ultra & multi .50 .50

Philatelic Week.

Ryukyu stamps were replaced by those of Japan after May 15, 1972.

AIR POST STAMPS

Dove and Map of Ryukyus — AP1

Perf. 13x13½
1950, Feb. 15 Unwmk. Photo.
C1 AP1 8y bright blue 150.00 60.00
C2 AP1 12y green 35.00 30.00
C3 AP1 16y rose carmine 15.00 15.00
Nos. C1-C3 (3) 200.00 105.00

Heavenly Maiden AP2

1951-54
C4 AP2 13y blue 2.50 1.50
C5 AP2 18y green 3.50 2.25
C6 AP2 30y cerise 6.00 1.75
C7 AP2 40y red violet 7.00 5.50
C8 AP2 50y yellow orange 9.00 6.50
Nos. C4-C8 (5) 28.00 17.50

Issue dates: Oct. 1, 1951, Aug. 16, 1954.

Heavenly Maiden Playing Flute — AP3

1957, Aug. 1 Engr. *Perf. 13½*
C9 AP3 15y blue green 9.00 3.50
C10 AP3 20y rose carmine 15.00 5.50
C11 AP3 35y yellow green 17.00 6.50
a. 35y light yellow green ('58) *150.00*
C12 AP3 45y reddish brown 18.00 8.00
C13 AP3 60y gray 21.00 10.00
Nos. C9-C13 (5) 80.00 33.50

Same Surcharged in Brown Red or Light Ultramarine

1959, Dec. 20
C14 AP3 9c on 15y (BrR) 2.50 1.50
a. Inverted surcharge *950.00*
b. Pair, one without surcharge —
C15 AP3 14c on 20y (LU) 3.00 3.00
C16 AP3 19c on 35y (BrR) 8.00 5.00
C17 AP3 27c on 45y (LU) 19.00 6.00
C18 AP3 35c on 60y (BrR) 16.00 9.00
Nos. C14-C18 (5) 48.50 24.50

Nos. 31-33, 36 and 38 Surcharged in Black, Brown, Red, Blue or Green

1960, Aug. 3 Photo. *Perf. 13*
C19 A14 9c on 4y 3.50 1.00
a. Surch. invtd. and trans-posed *15,000. 15,000.*
b. Invtd. surch. (legend only) *12,000.*
c. Surcharge transposed *1,500.*
d. Legend of surcharge only *4,000.*
e. Vert. pair, one without surch. —
C20 A17 14c on 5y (Br) 4.00 2.25
C21 A14 19c on 15y (R) 2.50 2.00
C22 A17 27c on 14y (Bl) 9.00 2.75
C23 A14 35c on 20y (G) 6.00 4.50
Nos. C19-C23 (5) 25.00 12.50

Nos. C19c and C19d are from a single sheet of 100 with surcharge shifted downward. Ten examples of No. C19c exist with "9c" also in bottom selvage. No. C19d is from the top row of the sheet.

No. C19e is unique, pos. 100, caused by paper foldover.

Wind God — AP4

9c, Heavenly Maiden (as on AP2). 14c, Heavenly Maiden (as on AP3). 27c, Wind God at right. 35c, Heavenly Maiden over treetops.

1961, Sept. 21 Photo. *Perf. 13½*
C24 AP4 9c multicolored .30 .20
C25 AP4 14c multicolored .70 .60
C26 AP4 19c multicolored .70 .70
C27 AP4 27c multicolored 3.50 .60
C28 AP4 35c multicolored 2.00 1.25
Nos. C24-C28 (5) 7.20 3.35

Jet over Gate of Courtesy AP5

Jet Plane AP6

1963, Aug. 28 *Perf. 13x13½*
C29 AP5 5½c multicolored .25 .25
C30 AP6 7c multicolored .25 .25

SPECIAL DELIVERY STAMP

Sea Horse and Map of Ryukyus — SD1

Perf. 13x13½
1950, Feb. 15 Unwmk. Photo.
E1 SD1 5y bright blue 30.00 16.00

UNITED NATIONS, OFFICES IN NEW YORK

yu-ˌnī-təd ˈnā-shənz

United Nations stamps are used on UN official mail sent from UN Headquarters in New York City, the UN European Office in Geneva, Switzerland, or from the Donaupark Vienna International Center or Atomic Energy Agency in Vienna, Austria to points throughout the world. They may be used on private correspondence sent through the UN post offices and are valid only at the individual UN post offices.

The UN stamps issued for use in Geneva and Vienna are listed in separate sections. Geneva issues were denominated in centimes and francs (now cents and euros) and Vienna issues in schillings and are valid only in Geneva or Vienna. The UN stamps issued for use in New York, denominated in cents and dollars, are valid only in New York.

Letters bearing Nos. 170-174 provide an exception as they were carried by the Canadian postal system.

See Switzerland Nos. 7O1-7O39 in Volume 6 of the Scott *Standard Postage Stamp Catalogue* for stamps issued by the Swiss Government for official use of the UN European Office in Geneva.

Catalogue values for all unused stamps in this section are for Never Hinged items.

Stamps are inscribed in English, French, or Spanish or are multilingual.

Watermark

Wmk. 309- Wavy Lines

Peoples of the World — A1

UN Headquarters Building — A2

"Peace, Justice, Security" — A3

UN Flag — A4

UN Children's Fund — A5

World Unity — A6

Perf. 13x12½, 12½x13, 12½x13½ (2c, 5c)

1951 Unwmk. Engr. & Photo.

1	A1	1c magenta	.20	.20
2	A2	1½c blue green	.20	.20
3	A3	2c purple	.20	.20
4	A4	3c magenta & blue	.20	.20
5	A5	5c blue	.20	.20
6	A1	10c chocolate	.25	.20
7	A4	15c violet & blue	.25	.20
8	A6	20c dark brown	.35	.20
9	A4	25c ol gray & blue	.40	.20
10	A2	50c indigo	2.25	1.50
11	A3	$1 red	1.50	.70
		Nos. 1-11 (11)	6.00	4.00

See Offices in Geneva Nos. 4, 14.

Veteran's War Memorial Building, San Francisco A7

1952, Oct. 24 Engr. *Perf. 12*

12	A7	5c blue	.20	.20

7th anniv. of the signing of the UN charter.

Globe and Encircled Flame A8

1952, Dec. 10 *Perf. 13½x14*

13	A8	3c deep green	.20	.20
14	A8	5c blue	.20	.20

Fourth anniv. of the adoption of the Universal Declaration of Human Rights.

Refugee Family — A9

1953, Apr. 24 *Perf. 12½x13*

15	A9	3c dk red brn & rose brn	.20	.20
16	A9	5c indigo & blue	.25	.25

"Protection for Refugees."

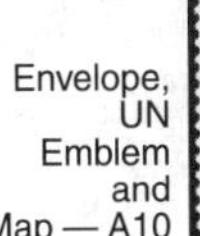

Envelope, UN Emblem and Map — A10

1953, June 12 Unwmk. *Perf. 13*

17	A10	3c black brown	.20	.20
18	A10	5c dark blue	.50	.45

Issued to honor the UPU.

Gearwheels and UN Emblem — A11

1953, Oct. 24 *Perf. 13x12½*

19	A11	3c dark gray	.20	.20
20	A11	5c dark green	.30	.30

UN activities in the field of technical assistance.

Hands Reaching Toward Flame — A12

Ear of Wheat — A13

1953, Dec. 10 *Perf. 12½x13*

21	A12	3c bright blue	.20	.20
22	A12	5c rose red	1.00	.50

Human Rights Day.

1954, Feb. 11

23	A13	3c dark green & yellow	.40	.20
24	A13	8c indigo & yellow	.85	.50

Issued to honor the FAO.

UN Emblem and Anvil — A14

1954, May 10 *Perf. 12½x13*

25	A14	3c brown	.20	.20
26	A14	8c magenta	1.25	.75

Honoring the ILO.

UN European Office, Geneva A15

1954, Oct. 25 *Perf. 14*

27	A15	3c dark blue violet	1.90	1.10
28	A15	8c red	.25	.25

UN Day.

Mother and Child — A16

1954, Dec. 10 *Perf. 14*

29	A16	3c red orange	6.75	2.00
30	A16	8c olive green	.25	.25

Human Rights Day.

Symbol of Flight A17

1955, Feb. 9 *Perf. 13½x14*

31	A17	3c blue	1.75	.65
32	A17	8c rose carmine	.75	.75

International Civil Aviation Organization.

UNESCO Emblem A18

1955, May 11 *Perf. 13½x14*

33	A18	3c lilac rose	.20	.20
34	A18	8c light blue	.20	.20

Honoring the UN Educational, Scientific and Cultural Organization.

UN Charter A19

1955, Oct. 24 *Perf. 13½x14*

35	A19	3c deep plum	.90	.50
36	A19	4c dull green	.35	.20
37	A19	8c bluish black	.20	.20
		Nos. 35-37 (3)	1.45	.90

Souvenir Sheet

Imperf

Wmk. 309

38	Sheet of 3	100.00	18.00
	Hinged	75.00	
a.	A19 3c deep plum	3.00	.50
b.	A19 4c dull green	3.00	.50
c.	A19 8c bluish black	3.00	.50

10th anniv. of the UN.

Two printings were made of No. 38. The first may be distinguished by the broken line of background shading on the 8c. It leaves a small white spot below the left leg of the "n" of "Unies." For the 2nd printing, the broken line was retouched, eliminating the white spot.

Hand Holding Torch — A20

1955, Dec. 9 Unwmk. *Perf. 14x13½*

39	A20	3c ultra	.20	.20
40	A20	8c green	.20	.20

Human Rights Day, Dec. 10.

Symbols of Telecommunication — A21

1956, Feb. 17 *Perf. 14*

41	A21	3c turquoise blue	.20	.20
42	A21	8c deep carmine	.30	.30

Honoring the ITU.

Globe & Caduceus — A22

1956, Apr. 6 *Perf. 14*

43	A22	3c bright greenish blue	.20	.20
44	A22	8c golden brown	.20	.20

Honoring the World Health Organization.

General Assembly A23

1956, Oct. 24 *Perf. 14*

45	A23	3c dark blue	.20	.20
46	A23	8c gray olive	.20	.20

UN Day, Oct. 24.

Flame and Globe A24

1956, Dec. 10 *Perf. 14*

47	A24	3c plum	.20	.20
48	A24	8c dark blue	.20	.20

Human Rights Day.

Weather Balloon — A25

1957, Jan. 28 *Perf. 14*

49	A25	3c violet blue	.20	.20
50	A25	8c dark carmine rose	.20	.20

Honoring the World Meteorological Organization.

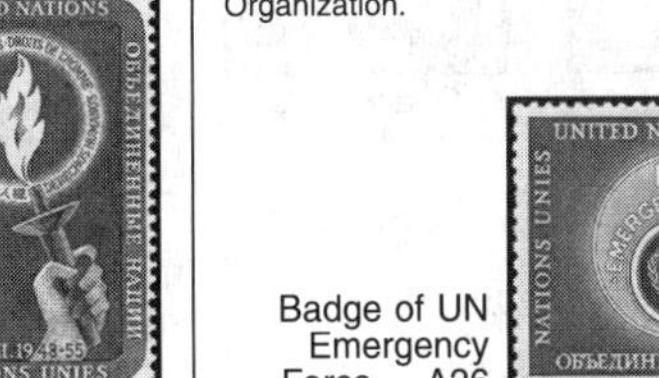

Badge of UN Emergency Force — A26

1957, Apr. 8 *Perf. 14x12½*

51	A26	3c light blue	.20	.20
52	A26	8c rose carmine	.20	.20

UN Emergency Force.

Re-engraved

1957, Apr.-May

53	A26	3c blue	.20	.20
54	A26	8c rose carmine	.35	.20

On Nos. 53-54 the background within and around the circles is shaded lightly, giving a halo effect. The letters are more distinct with a line around each letter.

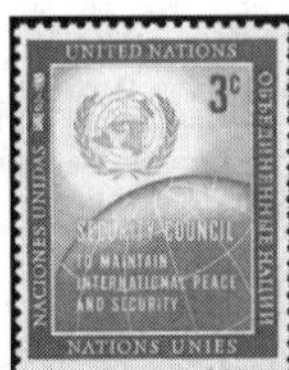

UN Emblem and Globe — A27

1957, Oct. 24 Engr. *Perf. 12½x13*

55	A27	3c orange brown	.20	.20
56	A27	8c dark blue green	.20	.20

Honoring the Security Council.

Flaming Torch — A28

1957, Dec. 10 ***Perf. 14***

57	A28	3c red brown	.20	.20
58	A28	8c black	.20	.20

Human Rights Day.

Atom & UN Emblem — A29

1958, Feb. 10 ***Perf. 12***

59	A29	3c olive	.20	.20
60	A29	8c blue	.20	.20

Honoring the International Atomic Energy Agency.

Central Hall, Westminster — A30

1958, Apr. 14 ***Perf. 12***

61	A30	3c violet blue	.20	.20
62	A30	8c rose claret	.20	.20

Central Hall, Westminster, London, was the site of the first session of the UN General Assembly 1946.

UN Seal A31

Gearwheels A32

1958 ***Perf. 13½x14***

63	A31	4c red orange	.20	.20

Perf. 13x14

64	A31	8c bright blue	.20	.20

Issue dates: 4c, Oct. 24; 8c, June 2.

1958, Oct. 24 **Engr.** ***Perf. 12***

65	A32	4c dark blue green	.20	.20
66	A32	8c vermilion	.20	.20

Honoring the Economic and Social Council.

Hands Upholding Globe — A33

1958, Dec. 10 **Unwmk.**

67	A33	4c yellow green	.20	.20
68	A33	8c red brown	.20	.20

Human Rights Day and the 10th anniv. of the signing of the Universal Declaration of Human Rights.

New York City Building, Flushing Meadows A34

1959, Mar. 30 ***Perf. 12***

69	A34	4c light lilac rose	.20	.20
70	A34	8c aqua	.20	.20

Site of many General Assembly meetings, 1946-50.

UN Emblems and Symbols of Agriculture, Industry and Trade — A35

Figure Adapted from Rodin's "Age of Bronze" — A36

1959, May 18 ***Perf. 12***

71	A35	4c blue	.20	.20
72	A35	8c red orange	.20	.20

Honoring the UN Economic Commission for Europe.

1959, Oct. 23 **Engr.** ***Perf. 12***

73	A36	4c bright red	.20	.20
74	A36	8c dark olive green	.20	.20

Honor the Trusteeship Council.

World Refugee Year Emblem — A37

1959, Dec. 10 **Unwmk.**

75	A37	4c olive & red	.20	.20
76	A37	8c ol & brt greenish bl	.20	.20

World Refugee Year,7/1/59-6/30/60.

Chaillot Palace, Paris — A38

1960, Feb. 29 ***Perf. 14***

77	A38	4c rose lilac & blue	.20	.20
78	A38	8c dull green & brown	.20	.20

Chaillot Palace in Paris was the site of General Assembly meetings in 1948 and 1951.

Map of Far East and Steel Beam A39

1960, Apr. 11 **Photo.** ***Perf. 13x13½***

79	A39	4c dp cl, bl grn & dl yel	.20	.20
80	A39	8c ol green, blue & rose	.20	.20

Honoring the Economic Commission for Asia and the Far East (ECAFE).

Tree, FAO and UN Emblems — A40

1960, Aug. 29 ***Perf. 13½***

81	A40	4c green, dk blue & org	.20	.20
a.		Imperf., pair	—	
82	A40	8c yel green, black & org	.20	.20

5th World Forestry Congress, Seattle, Wash., Aug. 29-Sept. 10.

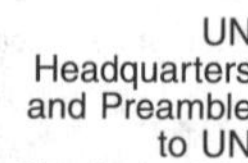

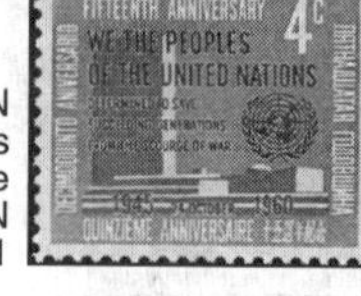

UN Headquarters and Preamble to UN Charter — A41

1960, Oct. 24 **Engr.** ***Perf. 11***

83	A41	4c blue	.20	.20
84	A41	8c gray	.20	.20

Souvenir Sheet

Imperf

85	Sheet of 2	.50	.50
a.	A41 4c blue	.25	.20
b.	A41 8c gray	.25	.20

15th anniv. of the UN.

Block and Tackle — A42

Scales of Justice — A43

1960, Dec. 9 **Photo.** ***Perf. 13½x13***

86	A42	4c multicolored	.20	.20
87	A42	8c multicolored	.20	.20
a.		Imperf., pair	—	

Honoring the International Bank for Reconstruction and Development.

No. 86 exists imperf.

1961, Feb. 13 **Unwmk.**

88	A43	4c yel, org brn & blk	.20	.20
89	A43	8c yellow, green & black	.20	.20

Honoring the International Court of Justice. The design was taken from Raphael's "Stanze."

Nos. 88-89 exist imperf.

Seal of International Monetary Fund — A44

1961, Apr. 17 ***Perf. 13x13½***

90	A44	4c bright bluish green	.20	.20
91	A44	7c fawn & yellow	.20	.20

Honoring the International Monetary Fund.

No. 90 exists imperf.

Abstract Group of Flags — A45

1961, June 5 ***Perf. 11½***

92	A45	30c multicolored	.40	.20

See Offices in Geneva No. 10.

Cogwheel and Map of Latin America — A46

1961, Sept. 18 ***Perf. 13½***

93	A46	4c blue, red & citron	.20	.20
94	A46	11c green, lilac & org ver	.25	.20

Honoring the Economic Commission for Latin America.

Africa House, Addis Ababa, and Map — A47

1961, Oct. 24 **Photo.** ***Perf. 11½***

95	A47	4c ultra, org, yel & brown	.20	.20
96	A47	11c emer, org, yel & brn	.25	.20

Honoring the Economic Commission for Africa.

Mother Bird Feeding Young and UNICEF Seal — A48

1961, Dec. 4 **Unwmk.** ***Perf. 11½***

97	A48	3c brown, gold, org & yel	.20	.20
98	A48	4c brn, gold, bl & emer	.20	.20
99	A48	13c dp grn, gold, pur & pink	.20	.20
		Nos. 97-99 (3)	.60	.60

15th anniv. of the UN Children's Fund.

Family and Symbolic Buildings A49

1962, Feb. 28 **Photo.** ***Perf. 14½x14***

Central design multicolored

100	A49	4c bright blue	.20	.20
a.		Black omitted	200.00	
b.		Yellow omitted	—	
c.		Brown omitted	—	
101	A49	7c orange brown	.20	.20
a.		Red omitted	—	
b.		Black omitted	—	

UN program for housing and urban development.

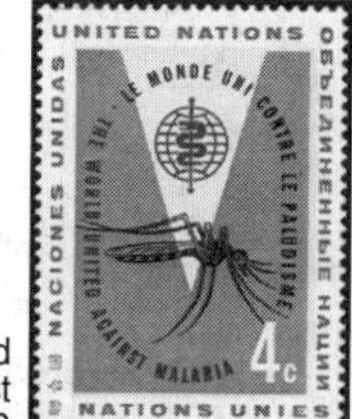

"The World Against Malaria" — A50

1962, Mar. 30 ***Perf. 14x14½***

Word frame in gray

102	A50	4c org, yel, green & black	.20	.20
103	A50	11c green, yel, brn & ind	.25	.20

Honoring the WHO and to call attention to the international campaign to eradicate malaria from the world.

"Peace" — A51

UN Flag — A52

Hands Combining "UN" and Globe — A53

UN Emblem over Globe A54

Photogravure; Engraved (5c)

1962, May 25 ***Perf. 14x14½***

104 A51 1c ver, blue, black & gray .20 .20
105 A52 3c lt green, Prus blue, yel & gray .20 .20

Perf. 12

Size: 36½x23½mm

106 A53 5c dark carmine rose .20 .20

Perf. 12½

107 A54 11c dk & lt blue & gold .25 .20
Nos. 104-107 (4) .85 .80

See #167 and UN Offices in Geneva #2, 6. Compare A51 with A76.

Flag at Half-mast and UN Headquarters A55

World Map Showing Congo A56

1962, Sept. 17 **Unwmk.** ***Perf. 11½***

108 A55 5c black, lt blue & blue .20 .20
109 A55 15c black, gray ol & blue .20 .20

1st anniv. of the death of Dag Hammarskjold, Secretary General of the UN 1953-61, in memory of those who died in the service of the UN.

1962, Oct. 24

110 A56 4c olive, org, black & yel .20 .20
111 A56 11c bl grn, org, blk & yel .20 .20

UN Operation in the Congo.

Globe in Universe and Palm Frond — A57

1962, Dec. 3 **Engr.** ***Perf. 14x13½***

112 A57 4c violet blue .20 .20
113 A57 11c rose claret .25 .20

Honoring the Committee on Peaceful Uses of Outer Space.

Development Decade Emblem — A58

Perf. 11½

1963, Feb. 4 **Unwmk.** **Photo.**

114 A58 5c pale grn, mar, dk blue & Prus blue .20 .20
115 A58 11c yel, mar, dk blue & Prus blue .20 .20

UN Development Decade and the UN Conference on the Application of Science and Technology for the Benefit of the Less Developed Areas, Geneva, Feb. 4-20.

Stalks of Wheat — A59

1963, Mar. 22 ***Perf. 11½***

116 A59 5c ver, green & yellow .20 .20
117 A59 11c ver, dp claret & yel .25 .20

"Freedom from Hunger" campaign of the FAO.

Bridge over Map of New Guinea — A60

1963, Oct. 1 **Unwmk.** ***Perf. 11½***

118 A60 25c blue, green & gray .45 .30

1st anniv. of the UN Temporary Executive Authority (UNTEA) in West New Guinea (West Irian).

General Assembly Building, New York — A61

1963, Nov. 4 **Photo.** ***Perf. 13***

119 A61 5c violet blue & multi .20 .20
120 A61 11c green & multi .20 .20

Since Oct. 1955 all sessions of the General Assembly have been held in the General Assembly Hall, UN Headquarters, N.Y.

Flame — A62

1963, Dec. 10 ***Perf. 13***

121 A62 5c green, gold, red & yel .20 .20
122 A62 11c car, gold, blue & yel .20 .20

15th anniv. of the signing of the Universal Declaration of Human Rights.

Ships at Sea and IMCO Emblem A63

1964, Jan. 13 ***Perf. 11½***

123 A63 5c blue, ol, ocher & yel .20 .20
124 A63 11c bl, dk grn, emer & yel .20 .20

Honoring the Intergovernmental Maritime Consultative Organization.

Map of the World — A64

UN Emblem — A65

Three Men United Before Globe — A66

Stylized Globe and Weather Vane — A67

1964 **Unwmk.** **Photo.** ***Perf. 14***

125 A64 2c lt bl, dk blue, org & yel green .20 .20
a. Perf. 13x13½ ('71) .20 .20

Perf. 11½

126 A65 7c dk bl, org brn & blk .20 .20
127 A66 10c bl grn, ol grn & blk .20 .20
128 A67 50c multicolored .75 .40
Nos. 125-128 (4) 1.35 1.00

Issued: 2c, 7c, 10c, May 29; 50c, Mar. 6.
See UN Offices in Geneva Nos. 3, 12.

Arrows Showing Global Flow of Trade A68

1964, June 15 ***Perf. 13***

129 A68 5c black, red & yellow .20 .20
130 A68 11c black, olive & yellow .20 .20

UN Conference on Trade and Development, Geneva, Mar. 23-June 15.

Poppy Capsule and Hands A69

1964, Sept. 21 **Engr.** ***Perf. 12***

131 A69 5c rose red & black .20 .20
132 A69 11c emerald & black .20 .20

International efforts and achievements in the control of narcotics.

Padlocked Atomic Blast — A70

Photogravure and Engraved

1964, Oct. 23 ***Perf. 11x11½***

133 A70 5c dark red & dk brown .20 .20

Signing of the nuclear test ban treaty pledging an end to nuclear explosions in the atmosphere, outer space and under water.

"Education for Progress" A71

1964, Dec. 7 **Photo.** ***Perf. 12½***

134 A71 4c multicolored .20 .20
135 A71 5c multicolored .20 .20
136 A71 11c multicolored .20 .20
Nos. 134-136 (3) .60 .60

UNESCO world campaign for universal literacy and for free compulsory primary education.

Progress Chart, Key & Globe — A72

Perf. 13½x13

1965, Jan. 25 **Unwmk.**

137 A72 5c multicolored .20 .20
138 A72 11c multicolored .20 .20
a. Black omitted (UN emblem on key) —

Special Fund Program, which aims to speed economic growth and social advancement in low-income countries.

Leaves & View of Cyprus — A73

1965, Mar. 4 **Photo.** ***Perf. 11½***

139 A73 5c org, olive & black .20 .20
140 A73 11c yel grn, blue grn & blk .20 .20

UN Peace-keeping Force on Cyprus.

"From Semaphore to Satellite" A74

1965, May 17 **Unwmk.** ***Perf. 11½***

141 A74 5c multicolored .20 .20
142 A74 11c multicolored .20 .20

Cent. of the ITU.

ICY Emblem — A75

1965, June 26 **Engr.** ***Perf. 14x13½***

143 A75 5c dark blue .20 .20
144 A75 15c lilac rose .20 .20

Souvenir Sheet

145 A75 Sheet of 2, #143-144 .35 .30

UN 25th anniv. and Intl. Cooperation Year.

"Peace" — A76

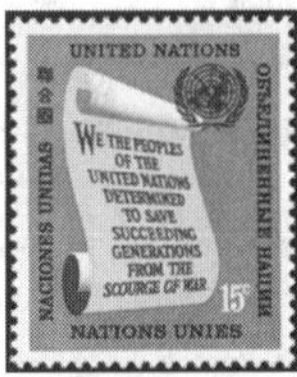

Opening Words, UN Charter — A77

UN Headquarters, Emblem — A78

UN Emblem — A79

UN Emblem A80

1965-66 **Photo.** ***Perf. 13½***

146 A76 1c ver, bl, blk & gray .20 .20

Perf. 14

147 A77 15c ol bis, dull yel, blk & dp claret .25 .20

Perf. 12

148 A78 20c dk bl, bl, red & yel .30 .20
a. Yellow omitted —

Lithographed and Embossed

Perf. 14

149 A79 25c lt bl & dk blue .35 .20

Photo.

Perf. 11½

150 A80 $1 aqua & sapphire 1.75 1.50
Nos. 146-150 (5) 2.85 2.30

Issued: 1c, 25c, 9/20; 15c, 20c, 10/25; $1, 3/25/66.

See UN Offices in Geneva Nos. 5, 9, 11.

Fields & People — A81

1965, Nov. 29 Photo. *Perf. 12*

151 A81 4c multicolored .20 .20
152 A81 5c multicolored .20 .20
153 A81 11c multicolored .20 .20
Nos. 151-153 (3) .60 .60

Emphasize the importance of the world's population growth and its problems and to call attention to population trends and developments.

Globe & Flags of UN Members — A82

1966, Jan. 31 Photo. *Perf. 11½*

154 A82 5c multicolored .20 .20
155 A82 15c multicolored .20 .20

World Federation of UN Associations.

WHO Headquarters, Geneva — A83

1966, May 26 Photo. *Perf. 12½x12*

Granite Paper

156 A83 5c multicolored .20 .20
157 A83 11c multicolored .20 .20

WHO Headquarters, Geneva.

Coffee — A84

1966, Sept. 19 *Perf. 13½x13*

158 A84 5c multicolored .20 .20
159 A84 11c multicolored .20 .20

International Coffee Agreement of 1962.

UN Observer — A85

1966, Oct. 24 Photo. *Perf. 11½*

Granite Paper

160 A85 15c multicolored .25 .20

Peace Keeping UN Observers.

Children of Various Races — A86

1966, Nov. 28 Litho. *Perf. 13x13½*

Designs: 5c, Children riding locomotive and tender. 11c, Children in open railroad car playing medical team.

161 A86 4c pink & multi .20 .20
162 A86 5c pale green & multi .20 .20
a. Yellow omitted — —
163 A86 11c ultra & multi .20 .20
a. Imperf., pair —
b. Dark blue omitted —
Nos. 161-163 (3) .60 .60

20th anniv. of UNICEF.

Hand Rolling up Sleeve & Chart Showing Progress A87

1967, Jan. 23 Photo. *Perf. 12½*

164 A87 5c multicolored .20 .20
165 A87 11c multicolored .20 .20

UN Development Program.

Type of 1962 and

UN Headquarters, New York & World Map — A88

1967 Photo. *Perf. 11½*

166 A88 1½c ultra, blk, org & ocher .20 .20

Size: 33x23mm

167 A53 5c red brn, brn & org yel .20 .20

Issue dates: 1½c, Mar. 17; 5c, Jan. 23.
See UN Offices in Geneva No. 1.

Fireworks — A89

1967, Mar. 17 *Perf. 14x14½*

168 A89 5c dark blue & multi .20 .20
169 A89 11c brown lake & multi .20 .20

Honoring all nations which gained independence since 1945.

"Peace" — A90

UN Pavilion, EXPO '67 — A91

Litho. & Engr.; Litho. (8c)

1967, Apr. 28 *Perf. 11*

170 A90 4c shown .20 .20
171 A90 5c Justice .20 .20
172 A91 8c shown .20 .20
173 A90 10c Fraternity .20 .20
174 A90 15c Truth .20 .20
Nos. 170-174 (5) 1.00 1.00

Montreal World's Fair, EXPO '67, Apr. 28-Oct. 27. Under special agreement with the Canadian Government Nos. 170-174 were valid for postage only on mail posted at the UN pavilion during the fair. The denominations are expressed in Canadian currency.

Luggage Tags and UN Emblem A92

Unwmk.

1967, June 19 Litho. *Perf. 14*

175 A92 5c multicolored .20 .20
176 A92 15c multicolored .25 .20

International Tourist Year, 1967.

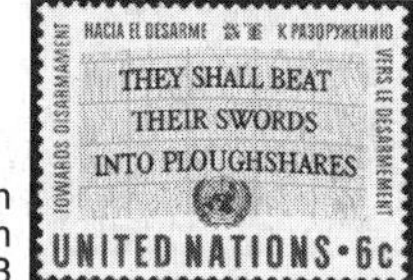

Quotation from Isaiah 2:4 — A93

1967, Oct. 24 Photo.

177 A93 6c multicolored .20 .20
178 A93 13c multicolored .20 .20

UN General Assembly's resolutions on general and complete disarmament and for suspension of nuclear and thermonuclear tests.

Art at UN Issue

Miniature Sheet

Memorial Window — A94

"The Kiss of Peace" — A95

Sizes: a, 41x46mm. b, 24x46mm. c, 41x33½mm. d, 36x33½mm. e, 29x33½mm. f, 41½x47mm.

1967, Nov. 17 Litho. *Rouletted 9*

179 A94 Sheet of 6, a.-f. .40 .30

Perf. 12½x13½

180 A95 6c multicolored .20 .20

No. 179 contains six 6c stamps, each rouletted on 3 sides, imperf. on fourth side. On Nos. 179a-179c, "United Nations. 6c" appears at top; on Nos. 179d-179f, at bottom. No. 179f includes name "Marc Chagall."

Globe and Major UN Organs A96

1968, Jan. 16 Photo. *Perf. 11½*

181 A96 6c multicolored .20 .20
182 A96 13c multicolored .20 .20

Honoring the UN Secretariat.

Statue by Henrik Starcke — A97

Art at UN Issue

1968, Mar. 1 Photo. *Perf. 11½*

183 A97 6c blue & multi .20 .20
184 A97 75c rose lake & multi 1.10 .85

The 6c is part of the "Art at UN" series. The 75c belongs to the definitive series. The 6c exists imperforate.

The Starcke statue represents mankind's search for freedom and happiness.

See UN Offices in Geneva No. 13.

Factories and Chart — A98

1968, Apr. 18 Litho. *Perf. 12*

185 A98 6c multicolored .20 .20
186 A98 13c multicolored .20 .20

UN Industrial Development Organization.

UN Headquarters A99

1968, May 31 Litho. *Perf. 13½*

187 A99 6c multicolored .20 .20

Radarscope and Globes A100

1968, Sept. 19 Photo. *Perf. 13x13½*

188 A100 6c green & multi .20 .20
189 A100 20c lilac & multi .30 .20

World Weather Watch, a new weather system directed by the World Meterological Organization.

Human Rights Flame — A101

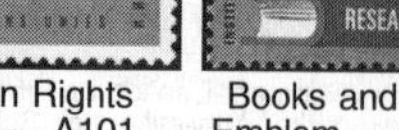

Books and UN Emblem — A102

Photogravure; Foil Embossed

1968, Nov. 22 *Perf. 12½*

190 A101 6c brt bl, dp ultra & gold .20 .20
191 A101 13c rose red, dk red & gold .20 .20

International Human Rights Year.

1969, Feb. 10 Litho. *Perf. 13½*
192 A102 6c yel green & multi .20 .20
193 A102 13c bluish lilac & multi .25 .20

UN Institute for Training and Research (UNITAR).

UN Building, Santiago, Chile A103

1969, Mar. 14 Litho. *Perf. 14*
194 A103 6c lt blue, vio bl & lt grn .20 .20
195 A103 15c pink, cr & red brown .25 .20

The UN Building in Santiago, Chile is the seat of the UN Economic Commission for Latin America and of the Latin American Institute for Economic and Social Planning.

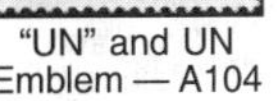

"UN" and UN Emblem — A104

UN Emblem and Scales of Justice — A105

1969, Mar. 14 Photo. *Perf. 13½*
196 A104 13c brt blue, black & gold .20 .20

See UN Offices in Geneva No. 7.

1969, Apr. 21 Photo. *Perf. 11½*
Granite Paper
197 A105 6c brt grn, ultra & gold .20 .20
198 A105 13c crim, lilac & gold .20 .20

20th anniv. session of the UN Intl. Law Commission.

Allegory of Labor, Emblems of UN and ILO A106

1969, June 5 Photo. *Perf. 13*
199 A106 6c bl, dp bl, yel & gold .20 .20
200 A106 20c org ver, mag, yel & gold .25 .20

"Labor and Development" and the 50th anniv. of the ILO.

Art at UN Issue

Ostrich, Tunisian Mosaic, 3rd Century — A107

Design: 13c, Pheasant.

1969, Nov. 21 Photo. *Perf. 14*
201 A107 6c blue & multi .20 .20
202 A107 13c red & multi .20 .20

Art at UN Issue

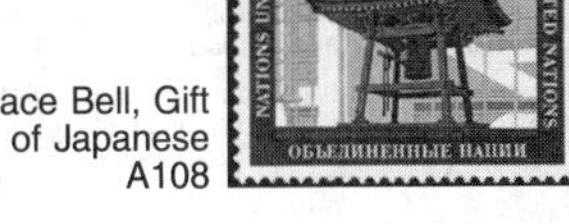

Peace Bell, Gift of Japanese A108

1970, Mar. 13 Photo. *Perf. 13½x13*
203 A108 6c vio blue & multi .20 .20
204 A108 25c claret & multi .35 .25

Mekong River, Power Lines and Map of Delta — A109

1970, Mar. 13 *Perf. 14*
205 A109 6c dk blue & multi .20 .20
206 A109 13c dp plum & multi .20 .20

Lower Mekong Basin, Viet Nam, Development project under UN auspices.

"Fight Cancer" A110

1970, May 22 Litho. *Perf. 14*
207 A110 6c blue & black .20 .20
208 A110 13c olive & black .20 .20

Fight against cancer in connection with the 10th Intl. Cancer Congress of the International Union Against Cancer, Houston, Texas, May 22-29.

UN Emblem and Olive Branch A111

UN Emblem — A112

1970, June 26 Photo. *Perf. 11½*
209 A111 6c red, gold, dk & lt bl .20 .20
210 A111 13c dk bl, gold, grn & red .20 .20

Perf. 12½
211 A112 25c dk bl, gold & lt bl .35 .25
Nos. 209-211 (3) .75 .65

Souvenir Sheet
Imperf
212 Sheet of 3 .60 .60
a. A111 6c multicolored .20 .20
b. A111 13c multicolored .20 .20
c. A112 25c multicolored .30 .20

25th anniv. of the UN.

Scales, Olive Branch, Progress Symbol A113

Sea Bed, Fish, Underwater Research A114

1970, Nov. 20 Photo. *Perf. 13½*
213 A113 6c gold & multi .20 .20
214 A113 13c silver & multi .20 .20

publicizing "Peace, Justice and Progress" in connection with the 25th anniv. of the UN.

Photogravure and Engraved
1971, Jan. 25 *Perf. 13*
215 A114 6c blue & multi .20 .20

Peaceful uses of the sea bed. See Offices in Geneva No. 15.

Refugees, Sculpture by Kaare K. Nygaard A115

1971, Mar. 12 Litho. *Perf. 13x12½*
216 A115 6c brown, ocher & black .20 .20
217 A115 13c ultra, grnsh bl & blk .20 .20

International support for refugees. See Offices in Geneva No. 16.

Wheat and Globe — A116

1971, Apr. 13 Photo. *Perf. 14*
218 A116 13c brn red, gold & grn .20 .20

Publicizing the UN World Food Program. See Offices in Geneva No. 17.

UPU Headquarters, Bern — A117

1971, May 28 Photo. *Perf. 11½*
219 A117 20c brown org & multi .35 .25

Opening of new UPU Headquarters, Bern. See Offices in Geneva No. 18.

"Eliminate Racial Discrimination" A118

A119

1971, Sept. 21 Photo. *Perf. 13½*
220 A118 8c yel green & multi .20 .20
221 A119 13c blue & multi .20 .20

International Year Against Racial Discrimination. See Offices in Geneva Nos. 19-20.

UN Headquarters, New York — A120

UN Emblem and Symbolic Flags A121

1971, Oct. 22 *Perf. 13½; 13 (60c)*
222 A120 8c vio blue & multi .20 .20
223 A121 60c ultra & multi .75 .75

Maia by Pablo Picasso — A122

1971, Nov. 19 Photo. *Perf. 11½*
224 A122 8c olive & multi .20 .20
225 A122 21c ultra & multi .30 .20

UN Intl. School. See Off. in Geneva No. 21.

Letter Changing Hands A123

1972, Jan. 5 Litho. *Perf. 14*
226 A123 95c blue & multi 1.25 1.00

"No More Nuclear Weapons" A124

1972, Feb. 14 Photo. *Perf. 13½x14*
227 A124 8c dull rose, blk, bl & gray .20 .20

To promote non-proliferation of nuclear weapons. See Offices in Geneva No. 23.

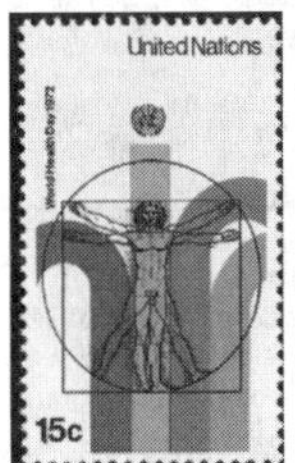

Proportions of Man (c. 1509), by Leonardo da Vinci A125

"Human Environment" A126

Lithographed and Engraved
1972, Apr. 7 *Perf. 13x13½*
228 A125 15c black & multi .25 .20

World Health Day, Apr. 7. See Offices in Geneva No. 24.

Lithographed and Embossed
1972, June 5 *Perf. 12½x14*
229 A126 8c multicolored .20 .20
230 A126 15c multicolored .25 .20

UN Conference on Human Environment, Stockholm, June 5-16, 1972.
See Offices in Geneva Nos. 25-26.

"Europe" and UN Emblem — A127

The Five Continents, by José Maria Sert — A128

1972, Sept. 11 Litho. *Perf. 13x13½*
231 A127 21c yel brown & multi .35 .25

Economic Commission for Europe, 25th anniv.
See Offices in Geneva No. 27.

Art at UN Issue

1972, Nov. 17 Photo. *Perf. 12x12½*

232 A128 8c gold, brn & gldn brn .20 .20
233 A128 15c gold, brn & blue grn .30 .20

See Offices in Geneva Nos. 28-29.

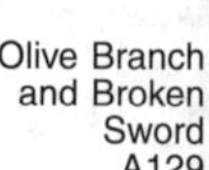

Olive Branch and Broken Sword A129

1973, Mar. 9 Litho. *Perf. 13½x13*

234 A129 8c blue & multi .20 .20
235 A129 15c lilac rose & multi .35 .20

Disarmament Decade, 1970-79.
Nos. 234-235 exist imperf. See Offices in Geneva Nos. 30-31.

Poppy Capsule and Skull — A130

1973, Apr. 13 Photo. *Perf. 13½*

236 A130 8c multicolored .20 .20
237 A130 15c multicolored .35 .25

Fight against drug abuse. See Offices in Geneva No. 32.

Honeycomb A131

1973, May 25 Photo. *Perf. 14*

238 A131 8c olive bister & multi .20 .20
239 A131 21c gray blue & multi .35 .25

5th anniv. of the UN Volunteer Program. See UN Offices in Geneva No. 33.

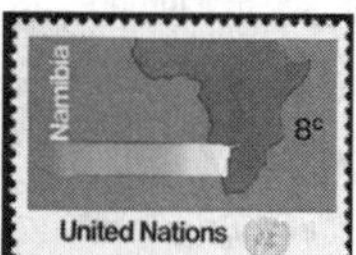

Map of Africa with Namibia A132

1973, Oct. 1 Photo. *Perf. 13½*

240 A132 8c emerald & multi .20 .20
241 A132 15c brt rose & multi .35 .25

To publicize Namibia (South-West Africa), for which the UN General Assembly ended the mandate of South Africa and established the UN Council for Namibia to administer the territory until independence. See Offices in Geneva No. 34.

UN Emblem, Human Rights Flame A133

1973, Nov. 16 Photo. *Perf. 13½*

242 A133 8c dp carmine & multi .20 .20
243 A133 21c blue green & multi .35 .25

25th anniv. of the adoption and proclamation of the Universal Declaration of Human Rights. See Offices in Geneva Nos. 35-36.

ILO Headquarters, Geneva A134

1974, Jan. 11 Photo. *Perf. 14*

244 A134 10c ultra & multi .20 .20
245 A134 21c blue green & multi .35 .25

New Headquarters of Intl. Labor Organization. See Offices in Geneva Nos. 37-38.

Post Horn Encircling Globe A135

1974, Mar. 22 Photo. *Perf. 14*

246 A135 10c multicolored .25 .20

UPU, cent. See Off. in Geneva #39-40.

Art at UN Issue

Peace Mural, by Candido Portinari A136

1974, May 6 Photo. *Perf. 14*

247 A136 10c gold & multi .20 .20
248 A136 18c ultra & multi .40 .30

See Offices in Geneva Nos. 41-42.

Dove & UN Emblem A137

UN Headquarters A138

Globe, UN Emblem, Flags A139

1974, June 10 Photo. *Perf. 14*

249 A137 2c dk bl & lt blue .20 .20
250 A138 10c multicolored .20 .20
251 A139 18c multicolored .30 .20
Nos. 249-251 (3) .70 .60

Children of the World — A140

Law of the Sea — A141

1974, Oct. 18 Photo. *Perf. 14*

252 A140 10c lt blue & multi .20 .20
253 A140 18c lilac & multi .40 .25

World Population Year. See Offices in Geneva Nos. 43-44.

1974, Nov. 22 Photo. *Perf. 14*

254 A141 10c green & multi .20 .20
255 A141 26c multicolored .40 .25

UN General Assembly declared the sea bed common heritage of mankind, exempt from arms race. See Offices in Geneva No. 45.

Satellite and Globe — A142

1975, Mar. 14 Litho. *Perf. 13*

256 A142 10c multicolored .20 .20
257 A142 26c multicolored .40 .30

Peaceful uses of outer space (meteorology, industry, fishing, communications). See Offices in Geneva Nos. 46-47.

Equality Between Men and Women — A143

1975, May 9 Litho. *Perf. 15*

258 A143 10c multicolored .20 .20
259 A143 18c multicolored .40 .25

International Women's Year 1975. See Offices in Geneva Nos. 48-49.

UN Flag and "XXX" — A144

1975, June 26 Litho. *Perf. 13*

260 A144 10c multicolored .20 .20
261 A144 26c purple & multi .50 .35

Souvenir Sheet

Imperf

262 Sheet of 2 .65 .50
  a. A144 10c olive bister & multi .20 .20
  b. A144 26c purple & multi .40 .25

30th anniv. of the UN. See Offices in Geneva Nos. 50-52.

Hand Reaching up over Map of Africa & Namibia — A145

1975, Sept. 22 Photo. *Perf. 13½*

263 A145 10c multicolored .20 .20
264 A145 18c multicolored .35 .20

"Namibia—United Nations direct responsibility." See note after No. 241. See Offices in Geneva Nos. 53-54.

Wild Rose Growing from Barbed Wire — A146

1975, Nov. 21 Engr. *Perf. 12½*

265 A146 13c ultramarine .25 .20
266 A146 26c rose carmine .50 .45

UN Peace-keeping Operations. See Offices in Geneva Nos. 55-56.

Symbolic Flags Forming Dove — A147

UN Emblem — A149

People of All Races A148

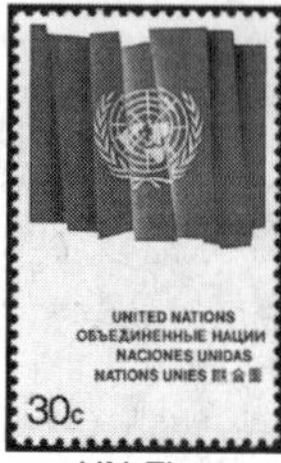

UN Flag A150

Dove and Rainbow A151

Perf. 13x13½, 13½x13, 14 (9c)

1976 Litho.; Photo. (9c)

267 A147 3c multicolored .20 .20
268 A148 4c multicolored .20 .20
269 A149 9c multicolored .20 .20
270 A150 30c blue, emer & black .40 .35
271 A151 50c multicolored .70 .65
Nos. 267-271 (5) 1.70 1.60

Issue dates: 9c, Nov. 19; others, Jan. 9.
See Offices in Vienna No. 8.

Interlocking Bands — A152

1976, Mar. 12 Photo. *Perf. 14*

272 A152 13c blue, green & black .20 .20
273 A152 26c green & multi .35 .30

World Federation of UN Association. See Offices in Geneva No. 57.

Cargo, Globe and Graph — A153

Houses Around Globe — A154

1976, Apr. 23 Photo. *Perf. 11½*

274 A153 13c multicolored .20 .20
275 A153 31c multicolored .40 .30

UN Conference on Trade and Development (UNCTAD), Nairobi, Kenya, May 1976. See Offices in Geneva No. 58.

1976, May 28 Photo. *Perf. 14*

276 A154 13c multicolored .20 .20
277 A154 25c green & multi .40 .30

Habitat, UN Conference on Human Settlements, Vancouver, Canada, May 31-June 11. See Offices in Geneva Nos. 59-60.

Magnifying Glass, Sheet of Stamps, UN Emblem
A155

1976, Oct. 8 Photo. *Perf. 11½*

278 A155 13c blue & multi .20 .20
279 A155 31c green & multi 1.25 1.25

UN Postal Administration, 25th anniv. Sheets of 20. See Offices in Geneva #61-62.

Grain — A156

1976, Nov. 19 Litho. *Perf. 14½*

280 A156 13c multicolored .25 .20

World Food Council. See Off. in Geneva #63.

WIPO Headquarters, Geneva — A157

1977, Mar. 11 Photo. *Perf. 14*

281 A157 13c citron & multi .20 .20
282 A157 31c brt green & multi .45 .30

World Intellectual Property Organization. See Geneva No. 64.

Drops of Water Falling into Funnel — A158

1977, Apr. 22 Photo. *Perf. 13½x13*

283 A158 13c yellow & multi .20 .20
284 A158 25c salmon & multi .45 .30

UN Water Conf., Mar del Plata, Argentina, Mar. 14-25. See Offices in Geneva #65-66.

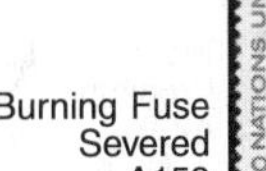

Burning Fuse Severed
A159

1977, May 27 Photo. *Perf. 14*

285 A159 13c purple & multi .20 .20
286 A159 31c dk blue & multi .45 .30

UN Security Council. See Geneva #67-68.

"Combat Racism"
A160

1977, Sept. 19 Litho. *Perf. 13½x13*

287 A160 13c black & yellow .20 .20
288 A160 25c black & vermilion .40 .30

Fight against racial discrimination. See Geneva Nos. 69-70.

Atom, Grain, Fruit and Factory — A161

1977, Nov. 18 Photo.

289 A161 13c yellow bister & multi .20 .20
290 A161 18c dull green & multi .35 .25

Peaceful uses of atomic energy. See Geneva Nos. 71-72.

Opening Words of UN Charter
A162

"Live Together in Peace"
A163

People of the World — A164

1978, Jan. 27 Litho. *Perf. 14½*

291 A162 1c gold, brown & red .20 .20
292 A163 25c multicolored .35 .30
293 A164 $1 multicolored 1.10 1.10
Nos. 291-293 (3) 1.65 1.60

See Offices in Geneva No. 73.

Smallpox Virus — A165

1978, Mar. 31 Photo. *Perf. 12x11½*

294 A165 13c rose & black .20 .20
295 A165 31c blue & black .45 .40

Global eradication of smallpox. See Offices in Geneva Nos. 74-75.

Open Handcuff
A166

Multicolored Bands and Clouds
A167

1978, May 5 Photo. *Perf. 12*

296 A166 13c multicolored .20 .20
297 A166 18c multicolored .30 .20

Liberation, justice and cooperation for Namibia. See Offices in Geneva No. 76.

1978, June 12 Photo. *Perf. 14*

298 A167 13c multicolored .20 .20
299 A167 25c multicolored .40 .30

Intl. Civil Aviation Organization for "Safety in the Air." See Offices in Geneva #77-78.

General Assembly
A168

1978, Sept. 15 Photo. *Perf. 13½*

300 A168 13c multicolored .20 .20
301 A168 18c multicolored .35 .25

See Offices in Geneva Nos. 79-80.

Hemispheres as Cogwheels
A169

1978, Nov. 17 Photo. *Perf. 14*

302 A169 13c multicolored .20 .20
303 A169 31c multicolored .50 .40

Technical Cooperation Among Developing Countries Conf., Buenos Aires, Argentina, Sept. 1978. See Offices in Geneva No. 81.

Hand Holding Olive Branch — A170

Tree of Various Races — A171

Globe, Dove with Olive Branch — A172

Birds and Globe — A173

1979, Jan. 19 Photo. *Perf. 14*

304 A170 5c multicolored .20 .20
305 A171 14c multicolored .20 .20
306 A172 15c multicolored .30 .25
307 A173 20c multicolored .30 .25
Nos. 304-307 (4) 1.00 .90

UNDRO Against Fire and Water — A174

1979, Mar. 9 Photo. *Perf. 14*

308 A174 15c multicolored .25 .20
309 A174 20c multicolored .35 .30

Office of the UN Disaster Relief Coordinator. See Offices in Geneva Nos. 82-83.

Child and ICY Emblem
A175

1979, May 4 Photo. *Perf. 14*

310 A175 15c multicolored .20 .20
311 A175 31c multicolored .35 .30

International Year of the Child. See Offices in Geneva Nos. 84-85.

Map of Namibia, Olive Branch — A176

Scales and Sword of Justice — A177

1979, Oct. 5 Litho. *Perf. 13½*

312 A176 15c multicolored .20 .20
313 A176 31c multicolored .40 .35

For a free and independent Namibia. See Offices in Geneva No. 86.

1979, Nov. 9 Litho. *Perf. 13x13½*

314 A177 15c multicolored .20 .20
315 A177 20c multicolored .40 .35

Intl. Court of Justice, The Hague, Netherlands. See Offices in Geneva Nos. 87-88.

Graph of Economic Trends — A178

Key — A179

1980, Jan. 11 *Perf. 15x14½*

316 A178 15c multicolored .20 .20
317 A179 31c multicolored .50 .35

New International Economic Order. See Offices in Geneva No. 89; Vienna No. 7.

Women's Year Emblems
A180

1980, Mar. 7 Litho. *Perf. 14½x15*

318 A180 15c multicolored .20 .20
319 A180 20c multicolored .30 .25

UN Decade for Women. See Offices in Geneva Nos. 90-91; Vienna Nos. 9-10.

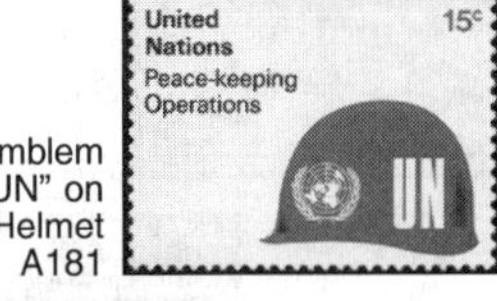

UN Emblem and "UN" on Helmet
A181

Arrows and UN Emblem
A182

1980, May 16 Litho. *Perf. 14x13*

320 A181 15c black & brt blue .25 .20
321 A182 31c multicolored .45 .40

UN Peace-keeping Operations. See Offices in Geneva No. 92; Vienna No. 11.

"35" and Flags — A183

Globe and Laurel — A184

1980, June 26 Litho. *Perf. 13*

322 A183 15c multicolored .20 .20
323 A184 31c multicolored .40 .30

Souvenir Sheet

Imperf

324 Sheet of 2 .70 .60
a. A183 15c multicolored .20
b. A184 31c multicolored .40

35th anniv. of the UN. See Offices in Geneva Nos. 93-95; Vienna Nos. 12-14.

Flag of Turkey A185

1980, Sept. 26 Litho. *Perf. 12*

Granite Paper

325 A185 15c shown .20 .20
326 A185 15c Luxembourg .20 .20
327 A185 15c Fiji .20 .20
328 A185 15c Viet Nam .20 .20
a. Se-tenant block of 4 .80 —
329 A185 15c Guinea .20 .20
330 A185 15c Surinam .20 .20
331 A185 15c Bangladesh .20 .20
332 A185 15c Mali .20 .20
a. Se-tenant block of 4 .80 —
333 A185 15c Yugoslavia .20 .20
334 A185 15c France .20 .20
335 A185 15c Venezuela .20 .20
336 A185 15c El Salvador .20 .20
a. Se-tenant block of 4 .80 —
337 A185 15c Madagascar .20 .20
338 A185 15c Cameroon .20 .20
339 A185 15c Rwanda .20 .20
340 A185 15c Hungary .20 .20
a. Se-tenant block of 4 .80 —
Nos. 325-340 (16) 3.20 3.20

Issued in 4 sheets of 16. Each sheet contains 4 blocks of 4 (Nos. 325-328, 329-332, 333-336, 337-340). A se-tenant block of 4 designs centers each sheet.

See #350-365, 374-389, 399-414, 425-440, 450-465, 477-492, 499-514, 528-543, 554-569, 690-697; 719-726, 744-751, 795-802.

Symbolic Flowers A186

Symbols of Progress A187

1980, Nov. 21 Litho. *Perf. 13½x13*

341 A186 15c multicolored .30 .25
342 A187 20c multicolored .40 .35

Economic and Social Council (ECOSOC). See Offices in Geneva Nos. 96-97; Vienna Nos. 15-16.

Inalienable Rights of the Palestinian People A188

1981, Jan. 30 Photo.

343 A188 15c multicolored .25 .20

See Offices in Geneva #98; Vienna #17.

Interlocking Puzzle Pieces — A189

Stylized Person — A190

1981, Mar. 6 Photo.

344 A189 20c multicolored .30 .20
345 A190 35c multicolored .55 .40

Intl. Year of the Disabled. See Offices in Geneva Nos. 99-100; Vienna Nos. 18-19.

Divislava and Sebastocrator Kaloyan, Bulgarian Mural, 1259, Boyana Church, Sofia — A191

1981, Apr. 15 Photo. *Perf. 11½*

Granite Paper

346 A191 20c multicolored .30 .25
347 A191 31c multicolored .45 .35

See Offices in Geneva #101; Vienna #20.

Solar Energy A192

Conference Emblem — A193

1981, May 29 Litho. *Perf. 13*

348 A192 20c multicolored .30 .25
349 A193 40c multicolored .55 .50

Conference on New and Renewable Sources of Energy, Nairobi, Aug. 10-21. See Offices in Geneva No. 102; Vienna No. 21.

Flag Type of 1980

1981, Sept. 25 Litho.

Granite Paper

350 A185 20c Djibouti .25 .20
351 A185 20c Sri Lanka .25 .20
352 A185 20c Bolivia .25 .20
353 A185 20c Equatorial Guinea .25 .20
a. Se-tenant block of 4 1.40 —
354 A185 20c Malta .25 .20
355 A185 20c Czechoslovakia .25 .20
356 A185 20c Thailand .25 .20
357 A185 20c Trinidad & Tobago .25 .20
a. Se-tenant block of 4 1.40 —
358 A185 20c Ukrainian SSR .25 .20
359 A185 20c Kuwait .25 .20
360 A185 20c Sudan .25 .20
361 A185 20c Egypt .25 .20
a. Se-tenant block of 4 1.40 —
362 A185 20c US .25 .20
363 A185 20c Singapore .25 .20
364 A185 20c Panama .25 .20
365 A185 20c Costa Rica .25 .20
a. Se-tenant block of 4 1.40 —
Nos. 350-365 (16) 4.00 3.20

See note after No. 340.

Seedling and Tree Cross Section A194

"10" and Symbols of Progress A195

1981, Nov. 13 Litho.

366 A194 18c multicolored .35 .25
367 A195 28c multicolored .65 .50

UN Volunteers Program, 10th anniv. See Offices in Geneva #103-104; Vienna #22-23.

Respect for Human Rights — A196

Independence of Colonial Countries and People — A197

Second Disarmament Decade — A198

1982, Jan. 22 *Perf. 11½x12*

368 A196 17c multicolored .30 .20
369 A197 28c multicolored .50 .35
370 A198 40c multicolored .80 .60
Nos. 368-370 (3) 1.60 1.15

10th Anniv. of UN Environment Program

A199 A200

1982, Mar. 19 Litho. *Perf. 13½x13*

371 A199 20c multicolored .25 .25
372 A200 40c multicolored .75 .65

See Offices in Geneva #107-108; Vienna #25-26.

UN Emblem and Olive Branch in Outer Space A201

Perf. 13 x 13½

1982, June 11 Litho.

373 A201 20c multicolored .45 .35

Exploration and Peaceful Uses of Outer Space. See Offices in Geneva Nos. 109-110; Vienna No. 27.

Flag Type of 1980

1982, Sept. 24 Litho. *Perf. 12*

Granite Paper

374 A185 20c Austria .25 .20
375 A185 20c Malaysia .25 .20
376 A185 20c Seychelles .25 .20
377 A185 20c Ireland .25 .20
a. Se-tenant block of 4 1.40 —
378 A185 20c Mozambique .25 .20
379 A185 20c Albania .25 .20
380 A185 20c Dominica .25 .20
381 A185 20c Solomon Islands .25 .20
a. Se-tenant block of 4 1.40 —
382 A185 20c Philippines .25 .20
383 A185 20c Swaziland .25 .20
384 A185 20c Nicaragua .25 .20
385 A185 20c Burma .25 .20
a. Se-tenant block of 4 1.40 —
386 A185 20c Cape Verde .25 .20
387 A185 20c Guyana .25 .20
388 A185 20c Belgium .25 .20
389 A185 20c Nigeria .25 .20
a. Se-tenant block of 4 1.40 —
Nos. 374-389 (16) 4.00 3.20

See note after No. 340.

Conservation and Protection of Nature — A202

1982, Nov. 19 Photo. *Perf. 14*

390 A202 20c Leaf .35 .30
391 A202 28c Butterfly .50 .45

See Off. in Geneva #111-112; Vienna #28-29.

A203

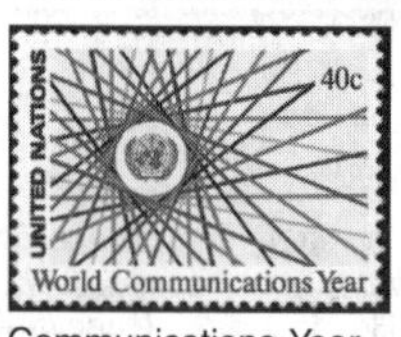

World Communications Year — A204

1983, Jan. 28 Litho. *Perf. 13*

392 A203 20c multicolored .25 .25
393 A204 40c multicolored .70 .65

See Offices in Geneva #113; Vienna #30.

Safety at Sea

A205 A206

1983, Mar. 18 Litho. *Perf. 14½*

394 A205 20c multicolored .30 .25
395 A206 37c multicolored .60 .50

See Off. in Geneva #114-115; Vienna #31-32.

World Food Program A207

1983, Apr. 22 Engr. *Perf. 13½*

396 A207 20c rose lake .35 .30

See Offices in Geneva #116; Vienna #33-34.

Trade and Development

A208 A209

1983, June 6 Litho. *Perf. 14*

397 A208 20c multicolored .40 .35
398 A209 28c multicolored .75 .65

See Off. in Geneva #117-118; Vienna #35-36.

Flag Type of 1980

1983, Sept. 23 Photo. *Perf. 12*

Granite Paper

399 A185 20c Great Britain .25 .20
400 A185 20c Barbados .25 .20
401 A185 20c Nepal .25 .20
402 A185 20c Israel .25 .20
a. Se-tenant block of 4 1.60 —
403 A185 20c Malawi .25 .20
404 A185 20c Byelorussian SSR .25 .20
405 A185 20c Jamaica .25 .20
406 A185 20c Kenya .25 .20
a. Se-tenant block of 4 1.60 —
407 A185 20c People's Republic of China .25 .20
408 A185 20c Peru .25 .20
409 A185 20c Bulgaria .25 .20
410 A185 20c Canada .25 .20
a. Se-tenant block of 4 1.60 —
411 A185 20c Somalia .25 .20
412 A185 20c Senegal .25 .20
413 A185 20c Brazil .25 .20
414 A185 20c Sweden .25 .20
a. Se-tenant block of 4 1.60 —
Nos. 399-414 (16) 4.00 3.20

See note after No. 340.

A210

35th Anniv. of the Universal Declaration of Human Rights — A211

Photogravure and Engraved

1983, Dec. 9 *Perf. 13½*

415 A210 20c Window Right .30 .25
416 A211 40c Peace Treaty with Nature .70 .65

See Off. in Geneva #119-120, Vienna #37-38.

Intl. Population Conference A212

1984, Feb. 3 Litho. *Perf. 14*

417 A212 20c multicolored .30 .25
418 A212 40c multicolored .60 .55

See Offices in Geneva #121; Vienna #39.

Tractor Plowing A213

Rice Paddy A214

1984, Mar. 15 Litho. *Perf. 14½*

419 A213 20c multicolored .40 .30
420 A214 40c multicolored .70 .65

World Food Day, Oct. 16. See Offices in Geneva Nos. 122-123; Vienna Nos. 40-41.

Grand Canyon A215

Ancient City of Polonnaruwa, Sri Lanka A216

1984, Apr. 18 Litho. *Perf. 14*

421 A215 20c multicolored .25 .20
422 A216 50c multicolored .70 .70

World Heritage (protection of world cultural and natural sites). See #601-602; Offices in Geneva #124-125, 211-212; Vienna #42-43, 125-126.

A217 A218

1984, May 29 Photo. *Perf. 11½*

423 A217 20c multicolored .40 .35
424 A218 50c multicolored 1.00 .85

Future for Refugees. See Offices in Geneva Nos. 126-127; Vienna Nos. 44-45.

Flag Type of 1980

1984, Sept. 21 Photo. *Perf. 12*

Granite Paper

425 A185 20c Burundi .55 .40
426 A185 20c Pakistan .55 .40
427 A185 20c Benin .55 .40
428 A185 20c Italy .55 .40
a. Se-tenant block of 4 2.75 —
429 A185 20c Tanzania .55 .40
430 A185 20c United Arab Emirates .55 .40
431 A185 20c Ecuador .55 .40
432 A185 20c Bahamas .55 .40
a. Se-tenant block of 4 2.75 —
433 A185 20c Poland .55 .40
434 A185 20c Papua New Guinea .55 .40
435 A185 20c Uruguay .55 .40
436 A185 20c Chile .55 .40
a. Se-tenant block of 4 2.75 —
437 A185 20c Paraguay .55 .40
438 A185 20c Bhutan .55 .40
439 A185 20c Central African Republic .55 .40
440 A185 20c Australia .55 .40
a. Se-tenant block of 4 2.75 —
Nos. 425-440 (16) 8.80 6.40

See note after No. 340.

Intl. Youth Year — A219

ILO Turin Center — A220

1984, Nov. 15 Litho. *Perf. 13½*

441 A219 20c multicolored .50 .35
442 A219 35c multicolored 1.50 1.10

See Offices in Geneva #128; Vienna #46-47.

1985, Feb. 1 Engr.

443 A220 23c Turin Center emblem .60 .45

See Off. in Geneva #129-130; Vienna #48.

UN University A221

1985, Mar. 15 Photo. *Perf. 13½*

444 A221 50c multicolored 1.25 1.00

See Off. in Geneva #131-132; Vienna #49.

Peoples of the World — A222

Painting UN Emblem A223

1985, May 10 Litho. *Perf. 14*

445 A222 22c multicolored .35 .30
446 A223 $3 multicolored 4.00 1.00

See Offices in Geneva #133-134; Vienna #50-51.

The Corner A224

Alvaro Raking Hay A225

Oil paintings (details) by American artist Andrew Wyeth.

1985, June 26 Photo. *Perf. 12x11½*

447 A224 22c multicolored .50 .35
448 A225 45c multicolored 1.25 .85

Souvenir Sheet

Imperf

449 Sheet of 2 1.60 1.25
a. A224 22c multicolored .50 —
b. A225 45c multicolored 1.00 —

40th anniv. of the UN. No. 449 has multicolored margin with inscription and UN emblem. Size: 75x83mm. See Offices in Geneva Nos. 135-137; Vienna Nos. 52-54.

Flag Type of 1980

1985, Sept. 20 Photo. *Perf. 12*

Granite Paper

450 A185 22c Grenada .55 .50
451 A185 22c Federal Republic of Germany .55 .50
452 A185 22c Saudi Arabia .55 .50
453 A185 22c Mexico .55 .50
a. Se-tenant block of 4 3.25 —
454 A185 22c Uganda .55 .50
455 A185 22c St. Thomas & Prince .55 .50
456 A185 22c USSR .55 .50
457 A185 22c India .55 .50
a. Se-tenant block of 4 3.25 —
458 A185 22c Liberia .55 .50
459 A185 22c Mauritius .55 .50
460 A185 22c Chad .55 .50
461 A185 22c Dominican Republic .55 .50
a. Se-tenant block of 4 3.25 —
462 A185 22c Sultanate of Oman .55 .50
463 A185 22c Ghana .55 .50
464 A185 22c Sierra Leone .55 .50
465 A185 22c Finland .55 .50
a. Se-tenant block of 4 3.25 —
Nos. 450-465 (16) 8.80 8.00

See note after No. 340.

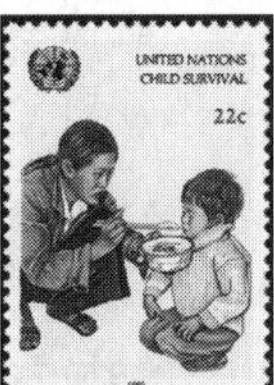

A226 A227

Photogravure and Engraved

1985, Nov. 22 *Perf. 13½*

466 A226 22c Asian child .35 .30
467 A226 33c Breastfeeding .65 .60

UNICEF Child Survival Campaign. See Offices in Geneva #138-139; Vienna #55-56.

1986, Jan. 31 Photo. *Perf. 11½*

468 A227 22c Abstract Painting by Wosene Kosrof .50 .45

Africa in Crisis, campaign against hunger. See Offices in Geneva #140; Vienna #57.

Water Resources A228

1986, Mar. 14 Photo. *Perf. 13½*

469 A228 22c Dam 1.25 1.10
470 A228 22c Irrigation 1.25 1.10
471 A228 22c Hygiene 1.25 1.10
472 A228 22c Well 1.25 1.10
a. Block of 4, #469-472 5.00 4.50

UN Development program. No. 472a has continuous design. See Offices in Geneva #141-144; Vienna #58-61.

Human Rights Stamp of 1954 — A229

Stamp collecting: 44c, Engraver.

1986, May 22 Engr. *Perf. 12½*

473 A229 22c dk violet & brt blue .30 .25
474 A229 44c brown & emer green .80 .70

See Offices in Geneva #146-147; Vienna #62-63.

Birds Nest in Tree — A230

Peace in Seven Languages A231

Photo. & Embossed

1986, June 20 *Perf. 13½*

475 A230 22c multicolored .50 .40
476 A231 33c multicolored 1.50 1.25

Intl. Peace Year. See Offices in Geneva Nos. 148-149; Vienna Nos. 64-65.

Flag Type of 1980

1986, Sept. 19 Photo. *Perf. 12*

Granite Paper

477 A185 22c New Zealand .60 .45
478 A185 22c Lao PDR .60 .45
479 A185 22c Burkina Faso .60 .45
480 A185 22c Gambia .60 .45
a. Se-tenant block of 4 3.25 —
481 A185 22c Maldives .60 .45
482 A185 22c Ethiopia .60 .45
483 A185 22c Jordan .60 .45
484 A185 22c Zambia .60 .45
a. Se-tenant block of 4 3.25 —

485 A185 22c Iceland .60 .45
486 A185 22c Antigua & Barbuda .60 .45
487 A185 22c Angola .60 .45
488 A185 22c Botswana .60 .45
a. Se-tenant block of 4 3.25 —
489 A185 22c Romania .60 .45
490 A185 22c Togo .60 .45
491 A185 22c Mauritania .60 .45
492 A185 22c Colombia .60 .45
a. Se-tenant block of 4 3.25 —
Nos. 477-492 (16) 9.60 7.20

See note after No. 340.

Souvenir Sheet

World Federation of UN Associations, 40th Anniv. — A232

22c, Mother Earth, by Edna Hibel, US. 33c, Watercolor by Salvador Dali (b. 1904), Spain. 39c, New Dawn, by Dong Kingman, US. 44c, Watercolor by Chaim Gross, US.

1986, Nov. 14 Litho. *Perf. 13x13½*

493 A232 Sheet of 4 4.75 2.50
a. 22c multicolored .60 —
b. 33c multicolored .75 —
c. 39c multicolored 1.10 —
d. 44c multicolored 1.25 —

See Offices in Geneva #150; Vienna #66.

Trygve Halvdan Lie (1896-1968), 1st Secretary-General A233

Photogravure and Engraved

1987, Jan. 30 *Perf. 13½*

494 A233 22c multicolored .90 .75

See Offices in Geneva #151; Vienna #67.

Intl. Year of Shelter for the Homeless A234

Perf. 13½x12½

1987, Mar. 13 Litho.

495 A234 22c Surveying, blueprint .50 .35
496 A234 44c Cutting lumber 1.50 1.25

See Offices in Geneva #154-155; Vienna #68-69.

Fight Drug Abuse A235

1987, June 12 Litho. *Perf. 14½x15*

497 A235 22c Construction .65 .50
498 A235 33c Education 1.25 1.00

See Offices in Geneva #156-157; Vienna #70-71.

Flag Type of 1980

1987, Sept. 18 Photo. *Perf. 12*

Granite Paper

499 A185 22c Comoros .60 .50
500 A185 22c Yemen PDR .60 .50
501 A185 22c Mongolia .60 .50
502 A185 22c Vanuatu .60 .50
a. Se-tenant block of 4 3.25 —
503 A185 22c Japan .60 .50
504 A185 22c Gabon .60 .50
505 A185 22c Zimbabwe .60 .50
506 A185 22c Iraq .60 .50
a. Se-tenant block of 4 3.25 —
507 A185 22c Argentina .60 .50
508 A185 22c Congo .60 .50
509 A185 22c Niger .60 .50
510 A185 22c St. Lucia .60 .50
a. Se-tenant block of 4 3.25 —
511 A185 22c Bahrain .60 .50
512 A185 22c Haiti .60 .50
513 A185 22c Afghanistan .60 .50
514 A185 22c Greece .60 .50
a. Se-tenant block of 4 3.25 —
Nos. 499-514 (16) 9.60 8.00

See note after No. 340.

UN Day — A236

Multinational people in various occupations.

1987, Oct. 23 Litho. *Perf. 14½x15*

515 A236 22c multicolored .40 .35
516 A236 39c multicolored .70 .65

See Offices in Geneva #158-159; Vienna #74-75.

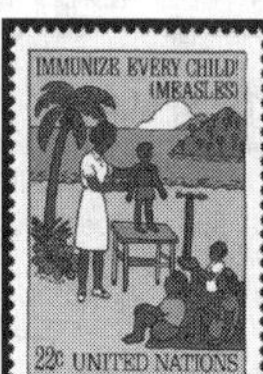

Immunize Every Child — A237

1987, Nov. 20 Litho. *Perf. 15x14½*

517 A237 22c Measles 1.25 .60
518 A237 44c Tetanus 2.50 1.75

See Offices in Geneva #160-161; Vienna #76-77.

Intl. Fund for Agricultural Development (IFAD) — A238

1988, Jan. 29 Litho. *Perf. 13½*

519 A238 22c Fishing .50 .40
520 A238 33c Farming 1.00 .85

See Offices in Geneva #162-163; Vienna #78-79.

A239

1988, Jan. 29 Photo. *Perf. 13½x14*

521 A239 3c multicolored ('88) .20 .20

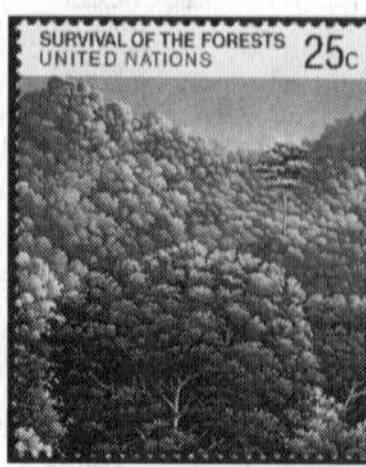

Survival of the Forests A240

1988, Mar. 18 Litho. *Perf. 14x15*

522 A240 25c multicolored 1.25 1.00
523 A240 44c multicolored 2.00 1.75
a. Pair, #522-523 3.75 3.25

#523a has continuous design. See Off. in Geneva #165-166; Vienna #80-81.

Intl. Volunteer Day — A241

1988, May 6 *Perf. 13x14, 14x13*

524 A241 25c Education, vert. .65 .50
525 A241 50c Vocational training 1.50 1.00

See Offices in Geneva #167-168; Vienna #82-83.

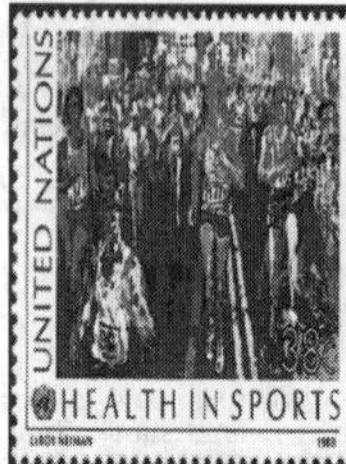

Health in Sports — A242

Perf. 13½x13, 13x13½

1988, June 17 Litho.

526 A242 25c Cycling, vert. .50 .45
527 A242 38c Marathon 1.25 1.10

See Offices in Geneva #169-170; Vienna #84-85.

Flag Type of 1980

1988, Sept. 16 Photo. *Perf. 12*

Granite Paper

528 A185 25c Spain .60 .45
529 A185 25c St. Vincent & Grenadines .60 .45
530 A185 25c Ivory Coast .60 .45
531 A185 25c Lebanon .60 .45
a. Se-tenant block of 4 3.25 —
532 A185 25c Yemen (Arab Republic) .60 .45
533 A185 25c Cuba .60 .45
534 A185 25c Denmark .60 .45
535 A185 25c Libya .60 .45
a. Se-tenant block of 4 3.25 —
536 A185 25c Qatar .60 .45
537 A185 25c Zaire .60 .45
538 A185 25c Norway .60 .45
539 A185 25c German Democratic Republic .60 .45
a. Se-tenant block of 4 3.25 —
540 A185 25c Iran .60 .45
541 A185 25c Tunisia .60 .45
542 A185 25c Samoa .60 .45
543 A185 25c Belize .60 .45
a. Se-tenant block of 4 3.25 —
Nos. 528-543 (16) 9.60 7.20

See note after No. 340.

A243

A244

1988, Dec. 9 Photo. & Engr.

544 A243 25c multicolored .55 .40

Souvenir Sheet

545 A243 $1 multicolored 1.25 1.25

Universal Declaration of Human Rights, 40th anniv.

See Offices in Geneva #171-172; Vienna #86-87.

1989, Jan. 27 Litho. *Perf. 13x14*

546 A244 25c Energy and nature .75 .45
547 A244 45c Agriculture 1.50 1.00

World Bank. See Offices in Geneva Nos. 173-174; Vienna Nos. 88-89.

UN Peace-Keeping Force, 1988 Nobel Peace Prize Winner — A245

1989, Mar. 17 Litho. *Perf. 14x13½*

548 A245 25c multicolored .50 .40

See Offices in Geneva #175, Vienna #90.

Aerial Photograph of New York Headquarters — A246

1989, Mar. 17 *Perf. 14½x14*

549 A246 45c multicolored .70 .60

World Weather Watch, 25th Anniv. (in 1988) — A247

Satellite photographs: 25c, Storm system off the East Coast, US. 36c, Typhoon Abby in the North-West Pacific.

1989, Apr. 21 Litho. *Perf. 13x14*

550 A247 25c multicolored .75 .50
551 A247 36c multicolored 1.50 1.25

See Offices in Geneva #176-177; Vienna #91-92.

A248 A249

Photo. & Engr., Photo.

1989, Aug. 23 *Perf. 14*

552 A248 25c multicolored 2.75 .50
553 A249 90c multicolored 2.25 1.75

Offices in Vienna, 10th anniv. See Offices in Geneva Nos. 178-179; Vienna Nos. 93-94.

Flag Type of 1980

1989, Sept. 22 Photo. *Perf. 12*

Granite Paper

554 A185 25c Indonesia .65 .55
555 A185 25c Lesotho .65 .55
556 A185 25c Guatemala .65 .55
557 A185 25c Netherlands .65 .55
a. Se-tenant block of 4 3.75 —
558 A185 25c South Africa .65 .55
559 A185 25c Portugal .65 .55
560 A185 25c Morocco .65 .55
561 A185 25c Syrian Arab Republic .65 .55
a. Se-tenant block of 4 3.75 —
562 A185 25c Honduras .65 .55
563 A185 25c Kampuchea .65 .55
564 A185 25c Guinea-Bissau .65 .55
565 A185 25c Cyprus .65 .55
a. Se-tenant block of 4 3.75 —
566 A185 25c Algeria .65 .55
567 A185 25c Brunei .65 .55
568 A185 25c St. Kitts and Nevis .65 .55
569 A185 25c United Nations .65 .55
a. Se-tenant block of 4 3.75 —
Nos. 554-569 (16) 10.40 8.80

See note after No. 340.

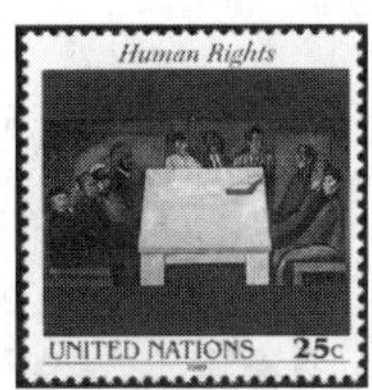

Declaration of Human Rights, 40th Anniv. (in 1988) — A250

Paintings: 25c, *The Table of Universal Brotherhood,* by Jose Clemente Orozco. 45c, *Study for Composition II,* by Vassily Kandinsky.

1989, Nov. 17 Litho. *Perf. 13½*

570 A250 25c multicolored .40 .30
571 A250 45c multicolored .90 .80

Printed in sheets of 12+12 se-tenant labels containing Articles 1 (25c) or 2 (45c) inscribed in English, French or German.

See Nos. 582-583, 599-600, 616-617, 627-628; Offices in Geneva Nos. 180-181, 193-194, 209-210, 224-225, 234-235; Vienna Nos. 95-96, 108-109, 123-124, 139-140, 150-151.

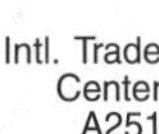
Intl. Trade Center A251

1990, Feb. 2 Litho. *Perf. 14½x15*

572 A251 25c multicolored 1.60 1.25

See Offices in Geneva #182; Vienna #97.

Fight AIDS Worldwide A252

Perf. 13½x12½

1990, Mar. 16 Litho.

573 A252 25c shown .50 .40
574 A252 40c Shadow over crowd 1.50 1.25

See Offices in Geneva #184-185; Vienna #99-100.

Medicinal Plants — A253

1990, May 4 Photo. *Perf. 11½*
Granite Paper

575 A253 25c *Catharanthus roseus* .75 .65
576 A253 90c *Panax quinquefolium* 2.00 1.50

See Off. in Geneva #186-187; Vienna #101-102.

United Nations, 45th Anniv. A254

1990, June 26 Litho. *Perf. 14½x13*

577 A254 25c shown .80 .70
578 A254 45c "45," emblem 2.75 2.50

Souvenir Sheet

579 Sheet of 2, #577-578 7.75 6.00

See Off. in Geneva #188-189; Vienna #103-104.

Crime Prevention — A255

1990, Sept. 13 Photo. *Perf. 14*

580 A255 25c Crimes of youth 1.10 .70
581 A255 36c Organized crime 2.50 1.25

See Off. in Geneva #191-192; Vienna #106-107.

Human Rights Type of 1989

Artwork: 25c, Fragment from the sarcophagus of Plotinus, c. 270 A.D. 45c, Combined Chambers of the High Court of Appeal by Charles Paul Renouard.

1990, Nov. 16 Litho. *Perf. 13½*

582 A250 25c black, gray & tan .45 .35
583 A250 45c black & brown .90 .75

See Off. in Geneva #193-194; Vienna #108-109.

Printed in sheets of 12+12 se-tenant labels containing Articles 7 (25c) or 8 (45c) inscribed in English, French or German.

Economic Commission for Europe A256

1991, Mar. 15 Litho. *Perf. 14*

584 A256 30c Two storks 1.10 .90
585 A256 30c Woodpecker, ibex 1.10 .90
586 A256 30c Capercaille, plover 1.10 .90
587 A256 30c Falcon, marmot 1.10 .90
a. Block of 4, #584-587 4.50 3.75

Namibian Independence A257

1991, May 10 Litho. *Perf. 14*

588 A257 30c Dunes, Namib Desert 1.00 .65
589 A257 50c Savanna 2.00 1.50

See Off. in Geneva #199-200; Vienna #114-115.

A258

The Golden Rule by Norman Rockwell — A259

1991, Sept. 11 Litho. *Perf. 13½*

590 A258 30c multicolored .90 .55

Photo.
Perf. 12x11½

591 A259 50c multicolored 1.50 1.00

UN Headquarters, New York — A260

1991, May 10 Engr. *Perf. 13½*

592 A260 $2 dark blue 3.00 2.50

Rights of the Child — A261

1991, June 14 Litho. *Perf. 14½*

593 A261 30c Children, globe 1.25 1.00
594 A261 70c Houses, rainbow 3.25 2.25

See Off. in Geneva #203-204; Vienna #117-118.

Banning of Chemical Weapons A262

90c, Hand holding back chemical drums.

1991, Sept. 11 Litho. *Perf. 13½*

595 A262 30c multicolored 1.75 1.40
596 A262 90c multicolored 5.50 4.00

See Off. in Geneva #205-206; Vienna #119-120.

UN Postal Administration, 40th Anniv. — A263

1991, Oct. 24 Litho. *Perf. 14x15*

597 A263 30c No. 1 1.10 .90
598 A263 40c No. 3 1.90 1.25

See Off. in Geneva #207-208; Vienna #121-122.

Human Rights Type of 1989

Artwork: 30c, The Last of England, by Ford Madox Brown. 50c, The Emigration to the East, by Tito Salas.

1991, Nov. 20 Litho. *Perf. 13½*

599 A250 30c multicolored .60 .45
600 A250 50c multicolored 1.25 1.00

Printed in sheets of 12+12 se-tenant labels containing Articles 13 (30c) or 14 (50c) inscribed in English, French or German.

See Off. in Geneva #209-210; Vienna #123-124.

World Heritage Type of 1984

Designs: 30c, Uluru Natl. Park, Australia. 50c, The Great Wall of China.

1992, Jan. 24 Litho. *Perf. 13*
Size: 35x28mm

601 A215 30c multicolored .70 .60
602 A215 50c multicolored 1.25 1.00

See Off. in Geneva #211-212; Vienna #125-126.

Clean Oceans — A264

1992, Mar. 13 Litho. *Perf. 14*

603 A264 29c Ocean surface .55 .55
604 A264 29c Ocean bottom .55 .55
a. Pair, #603-604 1.10 1.10

Printed in sheets of 12 containing 6 #604a.

See Off. in Geneva #214-215; Vienna #127-128.

Earth Summit — A265

#605, Globe at LR. #606, Globe at LL. #607, Globe at UR. #608, Globe at UL.

1992, May 22 Photo. *Perf. 11½*

605 A265 29c multicolored .50 .20
606 A265 29c multicolored .50 .20
607 A265 29c multicolored .50 .20
608 A265 29c multicolored .50 .20
a. Block of 4, #605-608 2.00 .80

See Off. in Geneva #216-219, Vienna #129-132.

Mission to Planet Earth — A266

#609, Satellites over city, sailboats, fishing boat. #610, Satellite over coast, passenger liner, dolphins, whale, volcano.

1992, Sept. 4 Photo. *Rouletted 8*
Granite Paper

609 A266 29c multicolored 3.25 3.00
610 A266 29c multicolored 3.25 3.00
a. Pair, #609-610 6.50 6.00

See Off. in Geneva #220-221, Vienna #133-134.

Science and Technology for Development — A267

Design: 50c, Animal, man drinking.

1992, Oct. 2 Litho. *Perf. 14*

611 A267 29c multicolored .50 .45
612 A267 50c multicolored .85 .70

See Off. in Geneva #222-223, Vienna #135-136.

UN University Building, Tokyo A268

UN Headquarters A269

40c, UN University Building, Tokyo, diff.

Perf. 14, 13½x13 (29c)

1992, Oct. 2 **Litho.**

613 A268 4c multicolored .20 .20
614 A269 29c multicolored .70 .55
615 A268 40c multicolored .90 .75
Nos. 613-615 (3) 1.80 1.50

Human Rights Type of 1989

Artwork: 29c, Lady Writing a Letter With her Maid, by Vermeer. 50c, The Meeting, by Ester Almqvist.

1992, Nov. 20 **Litho.** ***Perf. 13½***

616 A250 29c multicolored .90 .75
617 A250 50c multicolored 1.10 1.00

Printed in sheets of 12+12 se-tenant labels containing Articles 19 (29c) and 20 (50c) inscribed in English, French or German.

See Off. in Geneva #224-225; Vienna #139-140.

Aging With Dignity — A270

29c, Elderly couple, family. 52c, Old man, physician, woman holding fruit basket.

1993, Feb. 5 **Litho.** ***Perf. 13***

618 A270 29c multicolored 1.00 .75
619 A270 52c multicolored 1.75 1.40

See Off. in Geneva #226-227; Vienna #141-142.

Endangered Species A271

Designs: No. 620, Hairy-nosed wombat. No. 621, Whooping crane. No. 622, Giant clam. No. 623, Giant sable antelope.

1993, Mar. 3 **Litho.** ***Perf. 13x12½***

620 A271 29c multicolored .55 .50
621 A271 29c multicolored .55 .50
622 A271 29c multicolored .55 .50
623 A271 29c multicolored .55 .50
a. Block of 4, #620-623 2.25 2.25

See #639-642, 657-660, 674-677, 700-703, 730-733, 757-760, 773-776, 789-792; Offices in Geneva #228-231, 246-249, 264-267, 280-283, 298-301, 318-321, 336-339, 367-370; Vienna #143-146, 162-165, 180-183, 196-199, 214-217, 235-238, 253-256, 284-287.

Healthy Environment A272

Designs: 29c, Personal. 50c, Family.

1993, May 7 **Litho.** ***Perf. 15x14½***

624 A272 29c Man 1.00 .70
625 A272 50c Family 1.50 1.10

WHO, 45th anniv.

See Off. in Geneva #232-233; Vienna #147-148.

A273

1993, May 7 **Litho.** ***Perf. 15x14***

626 A273 5c multicolored .20 .20

Human Rights Type of 1989

Artwork: 29c, Shocking Corn, by Thomas Hart Benton. 35c, The Library, by Jacob Lawrence.

1993, June 11 **Litho.** ***Perf. 13½***

627 A250 29c multicolored .90 .65
628 A250 35c multicolored 1.25 1.00

Printed in sheets of 12 + 12 se-tenant labels containing Articles 25 (29c) and 26 (35c) inscribed in English, French or German.

See Off. in Geneva #234-235; Vienna #150-151.

Intl. Peace Day — A274

Denomination at: No. 629, UL. No. 630, UR. No. 631, LL. No. 632, LR.

Rouletted 12½

1993, Sept. 21 **Litho. & Engr.**

629 A274 29c blue & multi 2.00 1.50
630 A274 29c blue & multi 2.00 1.50
631 A274 29c blue & multi 2.00 1.50
632 A274 29c blue & multi 2.00 1.50
a. Block of 4, #629-632 9.00 7.00

See Off. in Geneva #236-239; Vienna #152-155.

Environment-Climate — A275

Designs: No. 633, Chameleon. No. 634, Palm trees, top of funnel cloud. No. 635, Bottom of funnel cloud, deer, antelope. No. 636, Bird of paradise.

1993, Oct. 29 **Litho.** ***Perf. 14½***

633 A275 29c multicolored 1.00 .90
634 A275 29c multicolored 1.00 .90
635 A275 29c multicolored 1.00 .90
636 A275 29c multicolored 1.00 .90
a. Strip of 4, #633-636 4.50 4.25

See Off. in Geneva #240-243; Vienna #156-159.

Intl. Year of the Family — A276

Designs: 29c, Mother holding child, two children, woman. 45c, People tending crops.

1994, Feb. 4 **Litho.** ***Perf. 13.1***

637 A276 29c green & multi 1.25 1.00
638 A276 45c blue & multi 2.00 1.50

See Off. in Geneva #244-245; Vienna #160-161.

Endangered Species Type of 1993

Designs: No. 639, Chimpanzee. No. 640, St. Lucia Amazon. No. 641, American crocodile. No. 642, Dama gazelle.

1994, Mar. 18 **Litho.** ***Perf. 12.7***

639 A271 29c multicolored .60 .50
640 A271 29c multicolored .60 .50
641 A271 29c multicolored .60 .50
642 A271 29c multicolored .60 .50
a. Block of 4, #639-642 2.50 2.25

See Off. in Geneva #246-249; Vienna #162-165.

Protection for Refugees — A277

1994, Apr. 29 **Litho.** ***Perf. 14.3x14.8***

643 A277 50c multicolored 1.25 1.00

See Offices in Geneva #250; Vienna #166.

Dove of Peace — A278

Sleeping Child, by Stanislaw Wyspianski A279

Mourning Owl, by Vanessa Isitt A280

1994, Apr. 29 **Litho.** ***Perf. 12.9***

644 A278 10c multicolored .20 .20
645 A279 19c multicolored .65 .30

Engr.

Perf. 13.1

646 A280 $1 red brown 2.50 .50

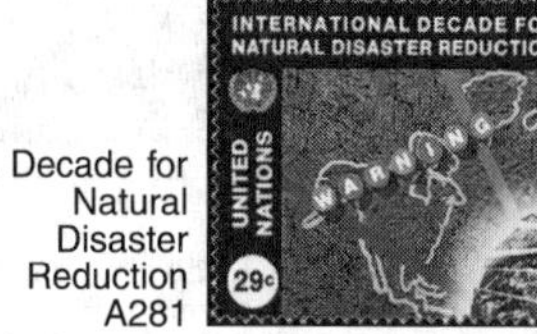

Intl. Decade for Natural Disaster Reduction A281

Earth viewed from space, outline map of: No. 647, North America. No. 648, Eurasia. No. 649, South America, No. 650, Australia and South Asia.

1994, May 27 **Litho.** ***Perf. 13.9x14.2***

647 A281 29c multicolored 1.00 .25
648 A281 29c multicolored 1.00 .25
649 A281 29c multicolored 1.00 .25
650 A281 29c multicolored 1.00 .25
a. Block of 4, #647-650 4.00 1.00

See Off. in Geneva #251-254; Vienna #170-173.

Population and Development — A282

Designs: 29c, Children playing. 52c, Family with house, car, other possessions.

1994, Sept. 1 **Litho.** ***Perf. 13.2x13.6***

651 A282 29c multicolored .75 .60
652 A282 52c multicolored 1.25 1.00

See Off. in Geneva #258-259; Vienna #174-175.

UNCTAD, 30th Anniv. A283

1994, Oct. 28

653 A283 29c multicolored .55 .50
654 A283 50c multi, diff. .95 .70

See Off. in Geneva #260-261; Vienna #176-177.

UN, 50th Anniv. — A284

Litho. & Engr.

1995, Jan. 1 ***Perf. 13.4***

655 A284 32c multicolored 1.25 .90

See Offices in Geneva #262; Vienna #178.

Social Summit, Copenhagen A285

Photo. & Engr.

1995, Feb. 3 ***Perf. 13.6x13.9***

656 A285 50c multicolored 1.10 1.00

See Offices in Geneva #263; Vienna #179.

Endangered Species Type of 1993

Designs: No. 657, Giant armadillo. No. 658, American bald eagle. No. 659, Fijian/Tongan banded iguana. No. 660, Giant panda.

1995, Mar. 24 **Litho.** ***Perf. 13x12½***

657 A271 32c multicolored .65 .55
658 A271 32c multicolored .65 .55
659 A271 32c multicolored .65 .55
660 A271 32c multicolored .65 .55
a. Block of 4, 657-660 2.75 2.25

See Off. in Geneva #264-267; Vienna #180-183.

Intl. Youth Year, 10th Anniv. — A286

32c, Seated child. 55c, Children cycling.

1995, May 26 **Litho.** ***Perf. 14.4x14.7***

661 A286 32c multicolored 1.00 .45
662 A286 55c multicolored 1.75 .85

See Off. in Geneva #268-269; Vienna #184-185.

UN, 50th Anniv. — A287

Designs: 32c, Hand with pen signing UN Charter, flags. 50c, Veterans' War Memorial, Opera House, San Francisco.

Perf. 13.3x13.6

1995, June 26 **Engr.**

663 A287 32c black 1.10 .85
664 A287 50c maroon 2.40 2.00

Souvenir Sheet

Litho. & Engr.

Imperf

665 Sheet of 2, #663-664 3.25 3.00
a. A287 32c black 1.25 .95
b. A287 50c maroon 1.60 1.40

See Off. in Geneva #270-271; Vienna #186-187.

4th World Conference on Women, Beijing A288

Designs: 32c, Mother and child. 40c, Seated woman, cranes flying above.

1995, Sept. 5 Photo. *Perf. 12*
666 A288 32c multicolored .80 .40

Size: 28x50mm
667 A288 40c multicolored 1.10 .50

See Off. in Geneva #273-274; Vienna #189-190.

UN Headquarters — A289

1995, Sept. 5 Litho. *Perf. 15*
668 A289 20c multicolored .35 .20

Miniature Sheet

United Nations, 50th Anniv. — A290

Designs: #669a-669 l, Various people in continuous design (2 blocks of six stamps with gutter between).

1995, Oct. 24 Litho. *Perf. 14*
669 Sheet of 12 17.00 6.00
a.-l. A290 32c any single 1.40 .20
670 Souvenir booklet 20.00
a. A290 32c Bklt. pane, vert. strip of 3 from UL of sheet 5.00 1.00
b. A290 32c Bklt. pane, vert. strip of 3 from UR of sheet 5.00 1.00
c. A290 32c Bklt. pane, vert. strip of 3 from LL of sheet 5.00 1.00
d. A290 32c Bklt. pane, vert. strip of 3 from LR of sheet 5.00 1.00

See Off. in Geneva #275-276; Vienna #191-192.

WFUNA, 50th Anniv. — A291

1996, Feb. 2 Litho. *Perf. 13x13½*
671 A291 32c multicolored .50 .35

See Offices in Geneva #277; Vienna #193.

Mural, by Fernand Leger — A292

1996, Feb. 2 Litho. *Perf. 14½x15*
672 A292 32c multicolored .50 .35
673 A292 60c multi, diff. 1.00 .75

Endangered Species Type of 1993

#674, Masdevallia veitchiana. #675, Saguaro cactus. #676, West Australian pitcher plant. #677, Encephalartos horridus.

1996, Mar. 14 Litho. *Perf. 12½*
674 A271 32c multicolored .75 .65
675 A271 32c multicolored .75 .65
676 A271 32c multicolored .75 .65
677 A271 32c multicolored .75 .65
a. Block of 4, #674-677 3.25 3.00

See Off. in Geneva #280-283; Vienna #196-199.

City Summit (Habitat II) — A293

Designs: No. 678, Deer. No. 679, Man, child, dog sitting on hill, overlooking town. No. 680, People walking in park, city skyline. No. 681, Tropical park, Polynesian woman, boy. No. 682, Polynesian village, orchids, bird.

1996, June 3 Litho. *Perf. 14x13½*
678 A293 32c multicolored 1.10 .80
679 A293 32c multicolored 1.10 .80
680 A293 32c multicolored 1.10 .80
681 A293 32c multicolored 1.10 .80
682 A293 32c multicolored 1.10 .80
a. Strip of 5, #678-682 5.50 4.00

See Off. in Geneva #284-288; Vienna #200-204.

Sport and the Environment A294

1996 Summer Olympic Games, Atlanta, GA: 32c, Men's basketball. 50c, Women's volleyball, horiz.

Perf. 14x14½, 14½x14
1996, July 19 Litho.
683 A294 32c multicolored 1.00 .75
684 A294 50c multicolored 2.00 1.50

Souvenir Sheet
685 A294 Sheet of 2, #683-684 3.00 1.25

See Off. in Geneva #289-291; Vienna #205-207.

Plea for Peace — A295

Designs: 32c, Doves. 60c, Stylized dove.

1996, Sept. 17 Litho. *Perf. 14½x15*
686 A295 32c multicolored .65 .45
687 A295 60c multicolored 1.25 .90

See Off. in Geneva #292-293; Vienna #208-209.

UNICEF, 50th Anniv. — A296

Fairy Tales: 32c, Yeh-Shen, China. 60c, The Ugly Duckling, by Hans Christian Andersen.

1996, Nov. 20 Litho. *Perf. 14½x15*
688 A296 32c multicolored .65 .50
689 A296 60c multicolored 1.50 1.25

Panes of 8 + label.

See Off. in Geneva #294-295; Vienna #210-211.

Flag Type of 1980

1997, Feb. 12 Photo. *Perf. 12*

Granite Paper
690 A185 32c Tadjikistan 1.00 .50
691 A185 32c Georgia 1.00 .50
692 A185 32c Armenia 1.00 .50
693 A185 32c Namibia 1.00 .50
a. Block of 4, #690-693 5.00 3.00
694 A185 32c Liechtenstein 1.00 .50
695 A185 32c Republic of Korea 1.00 .50
696 A185 32c Kazakhstan 1.00 .50
697 A185 32c Latvia 1.00 .50
a. Block of 4, #694-697 5.00 3.00

See note after No. 340.

Cherry Blossoms, UN Headquarters A297

Peace Rose — A298

1997, Feb. 12 Litho. *Perf. 14½*
698 A297 8c multicolored .40 .35
699 A298 55c multicolored 2.00 1.75

Endangered Species Type of 1993

Designs: No. 700, African elephant. No. 701, Major Mitchell's cockatoo. No. 702, Black-footed ferret. No. 703, Cougar.

1997, Mar. 13 Litho. *Perf. 12½*
700 A271 32c multicolored .65 .50
701 A271 32c multicolored .65 .50
702 A271 32c multicolored .65 .50
703 A271 32c multicolored .65 .50
a. Block of 4, #700-703 2.75 2.00

See Off. in Geneva #298-301; Vienna #214-217.

Earth Summit, 5th Anniv. A299

Designs: No. 704, Sailboat. No. 705, Three sailboats. No. 706, Two people watching sailboat, sun. No. 707, Person, sailboat.

$1, Combined design similar to #704-707.

1997, May 30 Photo. *Perf. 11.5*

Granite Paper
704 A299 32c multicolored 1.10 .20
705 A299 32c multicolored 1.10 .20
706 A299 32c multicolored 1.10 .20
707 A299 32c multicolored 1.10 .20
a. Block of 4, #704-707 4.50 1.00

Souvenir Sheet
708 A299 $1 multicolored 4.00 4.00
a. Ovptd. in sheet margin *20.00 20.00*

No. 708 contains one 60x43mm stamp. Overprint in sheet margin of No. 708a reads "PACIFIC 97 / World Philatelic Exhibition / San Francisco, California / 29 May - 8 June 1997."

See Off. in Geneva #302-306; Vienna #218-222.

Transportation A300

Ships: No. 709, Clipper ship. No. 710, Paddle steamer. No. 711, Ocean liner. No. 712, Hovercraft. No. 713, Hydrofoil.

1997, Aug. 29 Litho. *Perf. 14x14½*
709 A300 32c multicolored .75 .40
710 A300 32c multicolored .75 .40
711 A300 32c multicolored .75 .40
712 A300 32c multicolored .75 .40
713 A300 32c multicolored .75 .40
a. Strip of 5, #709-713 3.75 2.00

No. 713a has continuous design.

See Off. in Geneva #307-311; Vienna #223-227.

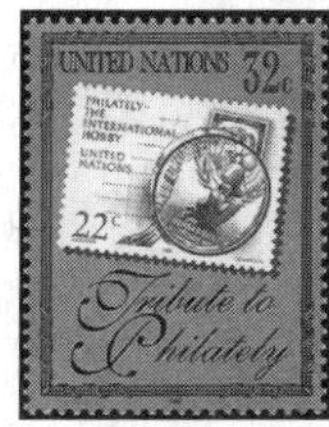

Philately — A301

1997, Oct. 14 Litho. *Perf. 13½x14*
714 A301 32c No. 473 2.50 2.25
715 A301 50c No. 474 4.00 3.50

See Off. in Geneva #312-313; Vienna #228-229.

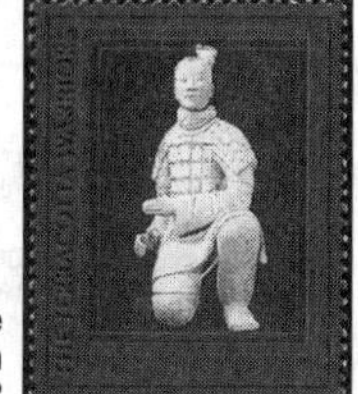

World Heritage Convention, 25th Anniv. — A302

Terracotta warriors of Xian: 32c, Single warrior. 60c, Massed warriors.

No. 718: a, like #716. b, like #717. c, like Geneva #314. d, like Geneva #315. e, like Vienna #230. f, like Vienna #231.

1997, Nov. 19 Litho. *Perf. 13½*
716 A302 32c multicolored 1.10 .75
717 A302 60c multicolored 2.10 1.75
718 Souvenir bklt. 8.50
a.-f. A302 8c any single .30 .30
g. Booklet pane of 4 #718a .75 .25
h. Booklet pane of 4 #718b .75 .25
i. Booklet pane of 4 #718c .75 .25
j. Booklet pane of 4 #718d .75 .25
k. Booklet pane of 4 #718e .75 .25
l. Booklet pane of 4 #718f .75 .25

See Off. in Geneva #314-316; Vienna #230-232.

Flag Type of 1980

1998, Feb. 13 Photo. *Perf. 12*

Granite Paper
719 A185 32c Micronesia .75 .50
720 A185 32c Slovakia .75 .50
721 A185 32c Democratic People's Republic of Korea .75 .50
722 A185 32c Azerbaijan .75 .50
a. Block of 4, #719-722 5.00 —
723 A185 32c Uzbekistan .75 .50
724 A185 32c Monaco .75 .50
725 A185 32c Czech Republic .75 .50
726 A185 32c Estonia .75 .50
a. Block of 4, #723-726 5.00 —

See note after No. 340.

A303

A304

A305

1998, Feb. 13 Litho. *Perf. 14½x15*

727	A303	1c multicolored	.20	.20
728	A304	2c multicolored	.20	.20

Perf. 15x14½

729	A305	21c multicolored	.45	.20

Endangered Species Type of 1993

#730, Lesser galago. #731, Hawaiian goose. #732, Golden birdwing. #733, Sun bear.

1998, Mar. 13 Litho. *Perf. 12½*

730	A271	32c multicolored	.65	.30
731	A271	32c multicolored	.65	.30
732	A271	32c multicolored	.65	.30
733	A271	32c multicolored	.65	.30
a.		Block of 4, #730-733	2.75	1.40

See Off. in Geneva #318-321; Vienna #235-238.

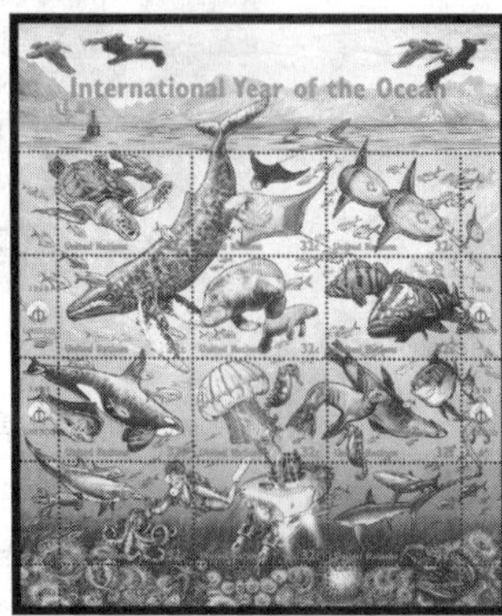

Intl. Year of the Ocean — A306

1998, May 20 Litho. *Perf. 13x13½*

734	A306	Sheet of 12	10.00	8.00
a.-l.		32c any single	.75	.60

See Offices in Geneva #322; Vienna #239.

Rain Forests A307

1998, June 19 Litho. *Perf. 13x13½*

735	A307	32c Jaguar	.75	.65

Souvenir Sheet

736	A307	$2 like #735	4.00	1.00

See Off. in Geneva #323-324; Vienna #240-241.

U.N. Peacekeeping Forces, 50th Anniv. — A308

Designs: 33c, Commander with binoculars. 40c, Two soldiers on vehicle.

1998, Sept. 15 Photo. *Perf. 12*

737	A308	33c multicolored	.85	.60
738	A308	40c multicolored	1.25	.90

See Off. in Geneva #325-326; Vienna #242-243.

Universal Declaration of Human Rights, 50th Anniv. — A309

Stylized people: 32c, Carrying flag. 55c, Carrying pens.

Litho. & Photo.

1998, Oct. 27 *Perf. 13*

739	A309	32c multicolored	.75	.65
740	A309	55c multicolored	1.25	1.25

See Off. in Geneva #327-328; Vienna #244-245.

Schönnbrun Palace, Vienna — A310

Designs: 33c, #743f, The Gloriette. 60c, #743b, Wall painting on fabric (detail), by Johann Wenzl Bergl, vert. No. 743a, Blue porcelain vase, vert. No. 743c, Porcelain stove, vert. No. 743d, Palace. No. 743e, Great Palm House (conservatory).

1998, Dec. 4 Litho. *Perf. 14*

741	A310	33c multicolored	.75	.50
742	A310	60c multicolored	1.50	.90
743		Souvenir bklt.	6.00	
a.-c.		A310 11c any single	.40	.40
d.-f.		A310 15c any single	.50	.50
g.		Booklet pane, 4 #743d	2.00	
h.		Booklet pane, 3 #743a	1.25	
i.		Booklet pane, 3 #743b	1.25	
j.		Booklet pane, 3 #743c	1.25	
k.		Booklet pane, 4 #743e	2.00	
l.		Booklet pane, 4 #743f	2.00	

See Off. in Geneva #329-331; Vienna #246-248.

Flag Type of 1980

1999, Feb. 5 Photo. *Perf. 12*

744	A185	33c Lithuania	.70	.50
745	A185	33c San Marino	.70	.50
746	A185	33c Turkmenistan	.70	.50
747	A185	33c Marshall Islands	.70	.50
a.		Block of 4, #744-747	5.00	—
748	A185	33c Moldova	.70	.50
749	A185	33c Kyrgyzstan	.70	.50
750	A185	33c Bosnia & Herzegovina	.70	.50
751	A185	33c Eritrea	.70	.50
a.		Block of 4, #748-751	5.00	—

See note after No. 340.

Flags and Globe — A311   Roses — A312

1999, Feb. 5 Litho. *Perf. 14x13½*

752	A311	33c multicolored	.65	.30

Photo.
Granite Paper
Perf. 11½x12

753	A312	$5 multicolored	8.50	1.00

World Heritage Sites, Australia A313

33c, #756f, Willandra Lakes region. 60c, #756b, Wet tropics of Queensland. No. 756a, Tasmanian wilderness. No. 756c, Great Barrier Reef. No. 756d, Uluru-Kata Tjuta Natl. Park. No. 756e, Kakadu Natl. Park.

1999, Mar. 19 Litho. *Perf. 13*

754	A313	33c multicolored	.85	.75
755	A313	60c multicolored	1.75	1.50
756		Souvenir booklet	5.00	
a.-c.		A313 5c any single	.20	.20
d.-f.		A313 15c any single	.30	.30
g.		Booklet pane of 4, #756a	.40	
h.		Booklet pane of 4, #756d	1.25	
i.		Booklet pane of 4, #756b	.40	
j.		Booklet pane of 4, #756e	1.25	
k.		Booklet pane of 4, #756c	.40	
l.		Booklet pane of 4, #756f	1.25	

See Off. in Geneva Nos. 333-335; Vienna Nos. 250-252.

Endangered Species Type of 1993

#757, Tiger. #758, Secretary bird. #759, Green tree python. #760, Long-tailed chinchilla.

1999, Apr. 22 Litho. *Perf. 12½*

757	A271	33c multicolored	.65	.20
758	A271	33c multicolored	.65	.20
759	A271	33c multicolored	.65	.20
760	A271	33c multicolored	.65	.20
a.		Block of 4, #757-760	2.60	

See Off. in Geneva Nos. 336-339; Vienna Nos. 253-256.

UNISPACE III, Vienna — A314

#761, Probe on planet's surface. #762, Planetary rover. #763, Composite of #761-762.

1999, July 7 Photo. *Rouletted 8*

761	A314	33c multicolored	.95	.60
762	A314	33c multicolored	.95	.60
a.		Pair, #761-762	2.00	1.50

Souvenir Sheet
Perf. 14½

763	A314	$2 multicolored	4.25	2.00
a.		Ovptd. in sheet margin	12.50	5.00

No. 763a was issued 7/7/00 and is overprinted in violet blue "WORLD STAMP EXPO 2000 / ANAHEIM, CALIFORNIA / U.S.A./ 7-16 JULY 2000."

See Off. in Geneva #340-342; Vienna #257-259.

UPU, 125th Anniv. — A315

Various people, 19th century methods of mail transportation, denomination at: No. 764, UL. No. 765, UR. No. 766, LL. No. 767, LR.

1999, Aug. 23 Photo. *Perf. 11¾*

764	A315	33c multicolored	.85	.50
765	A315	33c multicolored	.85	.50
766	A315	33c multicolored	.85	.50
767	A315	33c multicolored	.85	.50
a.		Block of 4, #764-767	3.50	—

See Off. in Geneva #343-346; Vienna #260-263.

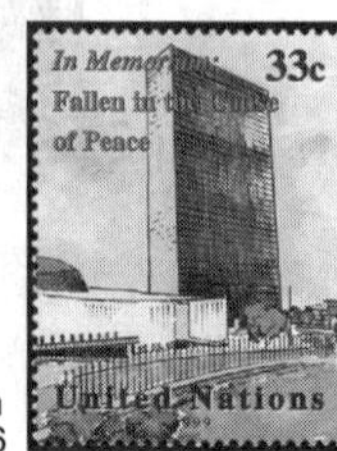

In Memoriam A316

UN Headquarters. Size of $1 stamp: 34x63mm.

1999, Sept. 21 Litho. *Perf. 14½x14*

768	A316	33c multicolored	2.00	1.75

Souvenir Sheet
Perf. 14

769	A316	$1 multicolored	2.00	1.00

See Off. in Geneva #347-348, Vienna #264-265.

Education, Keystone to the 21st Century — A317

Perf. 13½x13¾

1999, Nov. 18 Litho.

770	A317	33c Two readers	.65	.30
771	A317	60c Heart	1.25	.60

See Off. in Geneva #349-350, Vienna #266-267.

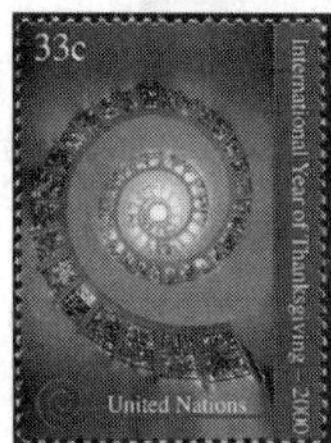

International Year of Thanksgiving A318

2000, Jan. 1 Litho. *Perf. 13¼x13½*

772	A318	33c multicolored	.90	.75

On No. 772 portions of the design were applied by a thermographic process producing a shiny, raised effect. See Off. in Geneva #351, Vienna #268.

Endangered Species Type of 1993

Designs: No. 773, Brown bear. No. 774, Black-bellied bustard. No. 775, Chinese crocodile lizard. No. 776, Pygmy chimpanzee.

2000, Apr. 6 Litho. *Perf. 12¾x12½*

773	A271	33c multicolored	.65	.30
774	A271	33c multicolored	.65	.30
775	A271	33c multicolored	.65	.30
776	A271	33c multicolored	.65	.30
a.		Block of 4, #773-776	2.60	2.00

See Off. in Geneva #352-355; Vienna #269-272.

Our World 2000 A319

Winning artwork in Millennium painting competition: 33c, Crawling Toward the Millennium, by Sam Yeates, US. 60c, Crossing, by Masakazu Takahata, Japan, vert.

Perf. 13x13½, 13½x13

2000, May 30 Litho.

777	A319	33c multicolored	.65	.30
778	A319	60c multicolored	1.25	.60

See Off. in Geneva #356-357, Vienna #273-274.

UN, 55th Anniv. — A320

Designs: 33c, Workmen removing decorative discs in General Assembly Hall, 1956. 55c, UN Building in 1951.

2000, July 7 Litho. *Perf. 13¼x13*

779 A320 33c multicolored .65 .30
780 A320 55c multicolored 1.10 .55

Souvenir Sheet

781 A320 Sheet of 2, #779-780 2.25 1.00

See Off. in Geneva #358-360, Vienna #275-277.

International Flag of Peace — A321

2000, Sept. 15 Litho. *Perf. 14½x14*

782 A321 33c multicolored .65 .30

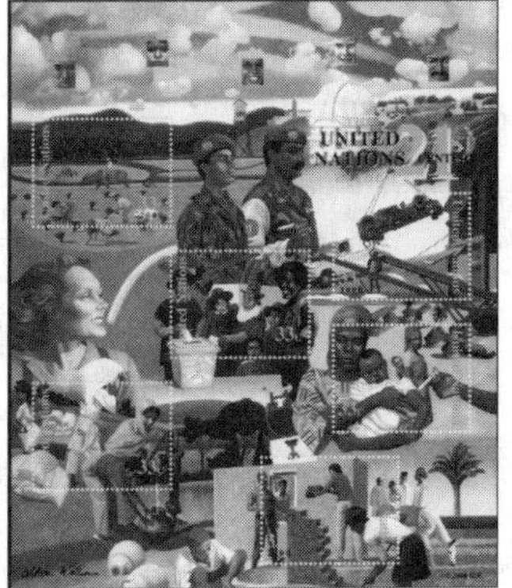

The UN in the 21st Century — A322

No. 783: a, Farmers, animals in rice paddy. b, Vehicle chassis being lifted. c, People voting. d, Baby receiving inoculation. e, Woman, man at pump. f, Mason, construction workers.

2000, Sept. 15 Litho. *Perf. 14*

783 A322 Sheet of 6 4.50 3.00
a.-f. 33c any single .75 .30

See Off. in Geneva #361; Vienna #278.

World Heritage Sites, Spain — A323

Designs: 33c, #786a, Alhambra, Generalife and Albayzin, Granada. 60c, #786d, Amphitheater of Mérida. #786b, Walled Town of Cuenca. #786c, Aqueduct of Segovia. #786e, Toledo. #786f, Güell Park, Barcelona.

2000, Oct. 6 Litho. *Perf. 14¾x14½*

784 A323 33c multicolored .65 .30
785 A323 60c multicolored 1.25 .60

Souvenir Booklet

786 Booklet 5.00
a.-c. A323 5c any single .20 .20
d.-f. A323 15c any single .30 .30
g. Booklet pane of 4, #786a .40 —
h. Booklet pane of 4, #786d 1.25 —
i. Booklet pane of 4, #786b .40 —
j. Booklet pane of 4, #786e 1.25 —
k. Booklet pane of 4, #786c .40 —
l. Booklet pane of 4, #786f 1.25 —

See Offices in Geneva Nos. 362-364, Vienna Nos. 279-281.

Respect for Refugees A324

2000, Nov. 9 Litho. *Perf. 13¼x12¾*

787 A324 33c multicolored .65 .30

Souvenir Sheet

788 A324 $1 multicolored 2.00 1.00

See Offices in Geneva Nos. 365-366, Vienna Nos. 282-283.

Endangered Species Type of 1993

Designs: No. 789, Common spotted cuscus. No. 790, Resplendent quetzal. No. 791, Gila monster. No. 792, Guereza.

2001, Feb. 1 Litho. *Perf. 12¾x12½*

789 A271 34c multicolored .65 .30
790 A271 34c multicolored .65 .30
791 A271 34c multicolored .65 .30
792 A271 34c multicolored .65 .30
a. Block of 4, #789-792 2.60 —

See Offices in Geneva Nos. 367-370; Vienna Nos. 284-287.

Intl. Volunteers Year — A325

Paintings by: 34c, Jose Zaragoza, Brazil. 80c, John Terry, Australia.

2001, Mar. 29 Litho. *Perf. 13¼*

793 A325 34c multicolored .65 .30
794 A325 80c multicolored 1.60 .80

See Offices in Geneva Nos. 371-372; Vienna Nos. 288-289.

Flag Type of 1980

2001, May 25 Photo. *Perf. 12*

Granite Paper

795 A185 34c Slovenia .65 .30
796 A185 34c Palau .65 .30
797 A185 34c Tonga .65 .30
798 A185 34c Croatia .65 .30
a. Block of 4, #795-798 2.60 —
799 A185 34c Former Yugoslav Republic of Macedonia .65 .30
800 A185 34c Kiribati .65 .30
801 A185 34c Andorra .65 .30
802 A185 34c Nauru .65 .30
a. Block of 4, #799-802 2.60 —
Nos. 795-802 (8) 5.20 2.40

Sunflower A326

Rose — A327

2001, May 25 Litho. *Perf. 13¼x13¾*

803 A326 7c multicolored .20 .20
804 A327 34c multicolored .65 .30

World Heritage Sites, Japan — A328

Designs: 34c, #807a, Kyoto. 70c, #807d, Shirakawa-Go and Gokayama. #807b, Nara. #807c, Himeji-Jo. #807e, Itsukushima Shinto Shrine. #807f, Nikko.

2001, Aug. 1 Litho. *Perf. 12¾x13¼*

805 A328 34c multicolored .65 .30
806 A328 70c multicolored 1.40 .70

Souvenir Booklet

807 Booklet 6.00
a.-c. A328 5c any single .20 .20
d.-f. A328 20c any single .40 .40
g. Booklet pane of 4, #807a .40 —
h. Booklet pane of 4, #807d 1.60 —
i. Booklet pane of 4, #807b .40 —
j. Booklet pane of 4, #807e 1.60 —
k. Booklet pane of 4, #807c .40 —
l. Booklet pane of 4, #807f 1.60 —

See Offices in Geneva Nos. 373-375, Vienna Nos. 290-292.

Dag Hammarskjöld (1905-61), UN Secretary General — A329

2001, Sept. 18 Engr. *Perf. 11x11¼*

808 A329 80c blue 1.60 .80

See Offices in Geneva No. 376, Vienna No. 293.

A330

UN Postal Administration, 50th Anniv. — A331

2001, Oct. 18 Litho. *Perf. 13½*

809 A330 34c Stamps, streamers .65 .30
810 A330 80c Stamps, gifts 1.60 .80

Souvenir Sheet

811 A331 Sheet of 2 #811a 4.00 2.00
a. $1 blue & light blue, 38mm diameter 2.00 1.00

See Offices in Geneva Nos. 377-379, Vienna Nos. 294-296.

Climate Change — A332

Designs: No. 812, Canada geese, greenhouses, butterfly, thistle. No. 813, Canada geese, iceberg, penguins, tomato plant. No. 814, Palm tree, solar collector. No. 815, Hand planting ginkgo cutting.

2001, Nov. 16 Litho. *Perf. 13¼*

812 A332 34c multicolored .65 .30
813 A332 34c multicolored .65 .30
814 A332 34c multicolored .65 .30
815 A332 34c multicolored .65 .30
a. Horiz. strip, #812-815 2.60 —

See Offices in Geneva Nos. 380-383, Vienna Nos. 297-300.

Awarding of Nobel Peace Prize to Secretary General Kofi Annan and UN — A333

2001, Dec. 10 Litho. *Perf. 13¼*

816 A333 34c multicolored .65 .30

See Offices in Geneva Nos. 384, Vienna Nos. 301.

Children and Stamps A334

2001, Mar. 1 Litho. *Perf. 13¾*

817 A334 80c multicolored 1.60 .80

Endangered Species Type of 1993

Designs: No. 818, Hoffmann's two-toed sloth. No. 819, Bighorn sheep. No. 820, Cheetah. No. 821, San Esteban Island chuckwalla.

2002, Apr. 4 Litho. *Perf. 12¾x12½*

818 A271 34c multicolored .65 .30
819 A271 34c multicolored .65 .30
820 A271 34c multicolored .65 .30
821 A271 34c multicolored .65 .30
a. Block of 4, #818-821 2.60 —

See Offices in Geneva Nos. 386-389; Vienna 308-311.

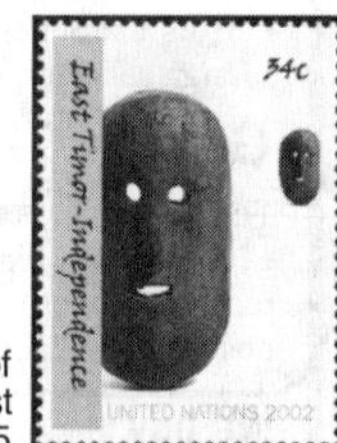

Independence of East Timor — A335

Designs: 34c, Wooden ritual mask. 57c, Decorative door panel.

2002, May 20 Litho. *Perf. 14x14½*

822 A335 34c multicolored .65 .30
823 A335 57c multicolored 1.10 .55

See Offices in Geneva Nos. 390-391; Vienna Nos. 312-313.

Intl. Year of Mountains A336

Designs: No. 824, Khan Tengri, Kyrgyzstan. No. 825, Mt. Kilimanjaro, Tanzania. No. 826, Mt. Foraker, US. No. 827, Paine Grande, Chile.

2002, May 24 Litho. *Perf. 13x13¼*

824	A336 34c multicolored	.65	.30
825	A336 34c multicolored	.65	.30
826	A336 80c multicolored	1.60	.80
827	A336 80c multicolored	1.60	.80
a.	Vert. strip or block of four, #824-827	4.50	2.25

See Offices in Geneva Nos. 392-395; Vienna Nos. 314-317.

World Summit on Sustainable Development, Johannesburg — A337

Designs: No. 828, Sun, Earth, planets, stars. No. 829, Three women. No. 830, Sailboat. No. 831, Three faceless people.

2002, June 27 Litho. *Perf. 14½x14*

828	A337 37c multicolored	.75	.35
829	A337 37c multicolored	.75	.35
830	A337 60c multicolored	1.25	.60
831	A337 60c multicolored	1.25	.60
a.	Vert. strip or block of four, #828-831	4.00	1.90

See Offices in Geneva Nos. 396-399; Vienna Nos. 318-321.

World Heritage Sites, Italy — A338

Designs: 37c, #834d, Florence. 70c, #834a, Amalfi Coast. #834b, Aeolian Islands. #834c, Rome. #834e, Pisa. #834f, Pompeii.

Perf. 13½x13¼

2002, Aug. 30 Litho.

832	A338 37c multicolored	.70	.30
833	A338 70c multicolored	1.40	.70

Souvenir Booklet

834	Booklet	5.00	
a.-c.	A338 5c any single	.20	.20
d.-f.	A338 15c any single	.30	.30
g.	Booklet pane of 4, #834d	1.25	—
h.	Booklet pane of 4, #834a	.40	—
i.	Booklet pane of 4, #834e	1.25	—
j.	Booklet pane of 4, #834b	.40	—
k.	Booklet pane of 4, #834f	1.25	—
l.	Booklet pane of 4, #834c	.40	—

See Offices in Geneva Nos. 400-402, Vienna Nos. 322-324.

AIDS Awareness A339

2002, Oct. 24 Litho. *Perf. 13½*

835	A339 70c multicolored	1.40	.70

See No. B1, Offices in Geneva Nos. 403, B1, Vienna Nos. 325, B1.

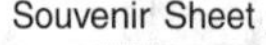

SEMI-POSTAL

Souvenir Sheet

AIDS Awareness — SP1

2002, Oct. 24 Litho. *Perf. 14½*

B1	SP1 37c + 6c multicolored	.90	.90

See Offices in Geneva No. B1, Vienna No. B1.

AIR POST

Plane and Gull — AP1

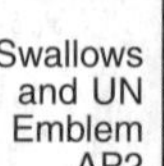

Swallows and UN Emblem AP2

Unwmk.

1951, Dec. 14 Engr. *Perf. 14*

C1	AP1 6c henna brown	.20	.20
C2	AP1 10c bright blue green	.20	.20
C3	AP2 15c deep ultra	.20	.25
a.	15c Prussian blue	100.00	
C4	AP2 25c gray black	.70	.35
	Nos. C1-C4 (4)	1.30	1.00

The 6c, 15c and 25c exist imperforate.

Airplane Wing and Globe — AP3

1957, May 27 *Perf. 12½x14*

C5	AP3 4c maroon	.20	.20

1959, Feb. 9 *Perf. 12½x13½*

C6	AP3 5c rose red	.20	.20

UN Flag and Plane AP4

1959, Feb. 9 *Perf. 13½x14*

C7	AP4 7c ultramarine	.20	.20

Outer Space — AP5

UN Emblem — AP6

"Flight Across Globe" — AP8

Bird of Laurel Leaves — AP7

Jet Plane and Envelope AP9

1963-64 Photo. *Perf. 11½*

C8	AP5 6c blk, blue & yel grn	.20	.20
C9	AP6 8c yel, ol green & red	.20	.20

Perf. 12½x12

C10	AP7 13c ultra, aqua, gray & car	.20	.20

Perf. 11½x12, 12x11½

C11	AP8 15c violet, buff, gray & pale grn ('64)	.25	.20
a.	Gray omitted	—	
C12	AP9 25c yel, org, gray, blue & red ('64)	.50	.30
	Nos. C8-C12 (5)	1.35	1.10

Dates of issue: 6c, 8c, 13c, June 17, 1963; 15c, 25c, May 1. See Offices in Geneva No. 8.

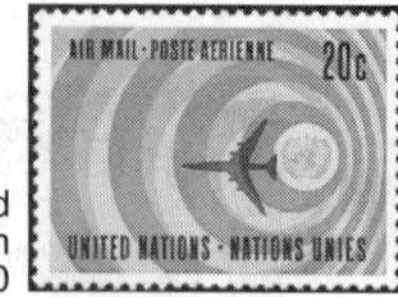

Jet Plane and UN Emblem AP10

1968, Apr. 18 Litho. *Perf. 13*

C13	AP10 20c multicolored	.30	.25

Wings, Envelopes and UN Emblem AP11

1969, Apr. 21 Litho.

C14	AP11 10c org ver, org, yel & black	.20	.20

UN Emblem and Stylized Wing — AP12

Birds in Flight — AP13

Clouds AP14

"UN" and Plane — AP15

Lithographed and Engraved

1972, May 1 *Perf. 13x13½*

C15	AP12 9c lt blue, dark red & vio blue	.20	.20

Photo. *Perf. 14x13½*

C16	AP13 11c blue & multi	.20	.20

Perf. 13½x14

C17	AP14 17c yel, red & org	.25	.20

Perf. 13

C18	AP15 21c silver & multi	.25	.25
	Nos. C15-C18 (4)	.90	.85

Globe and Jet — AP16

Pathways Radiating from UN Emblem AP17

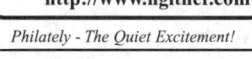

Bird in Flight, UN Headquarters AP18

Perf. 13, 12½x13 (18c)

1974, Sept. 16 Litho.

C19 AP16 13c multicolored .20 .20
C20 AP17 18c multicolored .25 .20
C21 AP18 26c blue & multi .35 .30
Nos. C19-C21 (3) .80 .70

Winged Airmail Letter — AP19

Symbolic Globe and Plane — AP20

1977, June 27 Photo. *Perf. 14*

C22 AP19 25c grnsh blue & multi .35 .25
C23 AP20 31c magenta .40 .30

U.N. OFFICES IN GENEVA, SWITZERLAND

For use only on mail posted at the Palais des Nations (UN European Office), Geneva. Inscribed in French unless otherwise stated.

100 Centimes = 1 Franc

Catalogue values for all unused stamps in this country are for Never Hinged items.

For use only on mail posted at the Palais des Nations (UN European Office), Geneva. Inscribed in French unless otherwise stated.

100 Centimes = 1 Franc

Types of UN Issues 1961-69 and

UN European Office, Geneva — G1

Designs: 5c, UN Headquarters, New York, and world map. 10c, UN flag. 20c, Three men united before globe. 50c, Opening words of UN Charter. 60c, UN emblem over globe. 70c, "UN" and UN emblem.

75c, "Flight Across Globe." 80c, UN Headquarters and emblem. 90c, Abstract group of flags. 1fr, UN Emblem. 2fr, Stylized globe and weather vane. 3fr, Statue by Henrik Starcke. 10fr, "Peace, Justice, Security."

Photogravure; Lithographed & Embossed (1fr); Engraved (10fr)

1969-70 Unwmk.

Perf. 13 (5c, 70c, 90c); Perf. 12½x12 (10c); Perf. 11½ (20c-60c, 3fr); Perf. 11½x12 (75c); Perf. 13½x14 (80c); Perf. 14 (1fr); Perf. 12x11½ (2fr); Perf. 12 (10fr)

1 A88 5c purple & multi .20 .20
a. Green omitted —
2 A52 10c salmon & multi .20 .20
3 A66 20c black & multi .20 .20
4 G1 30c dk blue & multi .20 .20
5 A77 50c ultra & multi .20 .20
6 A54 60c dk brown, sal & gold .20 .20
7 A104 70c red, black & gold .20 .20
8 AP8 75c car rose & multi .25 .25
9 A78 80c blue grn, red & yel .25 .25
10 A45 90c blue & multi .25 .25
11 A79 1fr lt & dk green .30 .30
12 A67 2fr blue & multi .60 .60
13 A97 3fr olive & multi .95 .95
14 A3 10fr deep blue 2.75 2.75
Nos. 1-14 (14) 6.75 6.75

The 20c, 80c and 90c are inscribed in French. The 75c and 10fr carry French inscription at top, English at bottom.

Issued: 60c, 10fr, 4/17/70; 70c, 80c, 90c, 2fr, 9/22/70; others, 10/4/69.

Sea Bed Type

Photogravure and Engraved

1971, Jan. 25 *Perf. 13*

15 A114 30c green & multi .20 .20

Refugee Type

1971, Mar. 12 Litho. *Perf. 13x12½*

16 A115 50c dp car, dp org & black .20 .20

Food Program Type

1971, Apr. 13 Photo. *Perf. 14*

17 A116 50c dk purple, gold & grn .20 .20

UPU Headquarters Type

1971, May 28 Photo. *Perf. 11½*

18 A117 75c green & multi .30 .30

Eliminate Discrimination Types

1971, Sept. 21 Photo. *Perf. 13½*

19 A118 30c blue & multi .20 .20
20 A119 50c multicolored .25 .25

Picasso Type

1971, Nov. 19 Photo. *Perf. 11½*

21 A122 1.10fr carmine & multi .75 .75

Palais des Nations, Geneva G2

1972, Jan. 5 Photo. *Perf. 11½*

22 G2 40c olive & multi .20 .20

Nuclear Weapons Type

1972, Feb. 14 Photo. *Perf. 13½x14*

23 A124 40c yel green, blk, rose & gray .25 .25

World Health Day Type

Lithographed and Engraved

1972, Apr. 7 *Perf. 13x13½*

24 A125 80c black & multi .40 .40

Environment Type

Lithographed and Embossed

1972, June 5 *Perf. 12½x14*

25 A126 40c multicolored .20 .20
26 A126 80c multicolored .40 .40

ECE Type

1972, Sept. 11 Litho. *Perf. 13x13½*

27 A127 1.10fr red & multi 1.00 1.00

Art at UN Type

1972, Nov. 17 Photo. *Perf. 12x12½*

28 A128 40c gold, brown & red .30 .30
29 A128 80c gold, brown & olive .60 .60

Disarmament Type

1973, Mar. 9 Litho. *Perf. 13½x13*

30 A129 60c violet & multi .40 .35
31 A129 1.10fr olive & multi .85 .85

Nos. 30-31 exist imperf.

Drug Abuse Type

1973, Apr. 13 Photo. *Perf. 13½*

32 A130 60c blue & multi .45 .40

Volunteers Type

1973, May 25 Photo. *Perf. 14*

33 A131 80c multicolored .35 .35

Namibia Type

1973, Oct. 1 Photo. *Perf. 13½*

34 A132 60c red & multi .35 .35

Human Rights Type

1973, Nov. 16 Photo. *Perf. 13½*

35 A133 40c ultra & multi .30 .30
36 A133 80c olive & multi .50 .50

ILO Headquarters Type

1974, Jan. 11 Photo. *Perf. 14*

37 A134 60c violet & multi .45 .45
38 A134 80c brown & multi .65 .60

UPU Type

1974, Mar. 22 Photo. *Perf. 14*

39 A135 30c multicolored .25 .20
40 A135 60c multicolored .60 .50

Art at UN Type

1974, May 6 Photo. *Perf. 14*

41 A136 60c dark red & multi .40 .40
42 A136 1fr green & multi .70 .70

WPY Type

1974, Oct. 18 Photo. *Perf. 14*

43 A140 60c brt green & multi .50 .45
44 A140 80c brown & multi .70 .70

Law of the Sea Type

1974, Nov. 22 Photo. *Perf. 14*

45 A141 1.30fr blue & multi 1.00 .95

Outer Space Type

1975, Mar. 14 Litho. *Perf. 13*

46 A142 60c multicolored .50 .50
47 A142 90c multicolored .75 .75

IWY Type

1975, May 9 Litho. *Perf. 15*

48 A143 60c multicolored .45 .40
49 A143 90c multicolored .65 .65

30th Anniv. Type

1975, June 26 Litho. *Perf. 13*

50 A144 60c green & multi .45 .40
51 A144 90c violet & multi .75 .70

Souvenir Sheet

Imperf

52 Sheet of 2 .75 .75
a. A144 60c green & multi .25 .25
b. A144 90c violet & multi .50 .50

Namibia Type

1975, Sept. 22 Photo. *Perf. 13½*

53 A145 50c multicolored .30 .30
54 A145 1.30fr multicolored .95 .95

Peace-keeping Operations Type

1975, Nov. 21 Engr. *Perf. 12½*

55 A146 60c greenish blue .35 .35
56 A146 70c bright violet .65 .60

WFUNA Type

1976, Mar. 12 Photo. *Perf. 14*

57 A152 90c multicolored .90 .85

UNCTAD Type

1976, Apr. 23 Photo. *Perf. 11½*

58 A153 1.10fr multicolored .90 .90

Habitat Type

1976, May 28 Photo. *Perf. 14*

59 A154 40c multicolored .20 .20
60 A154 1.50fr violet & multi .75 .75

UN Emblem, Post Horn and Rainbow — G3

1976, Oct. 8 Photo. *Perf. 11½*

61 G3 80c tan & multi .50 .50
62 G3 1.10fr lt green & multi 1.60 1.60

Sheets of 20.

Food Council Type

1976, Nov. 19 Litho. *Perf. 14½*

63 A156 70c multicolored .50 .45

WIPO Type

1977, Mar. 11 Photo. *Perf. 14*

64 A157 80c red & multi .65 .60

Drop of Water and Globe — G4

1977, Apr. 22 Photo. *Perf. 13½x13*

65 G4 80c ultra & multi .55 .50
66 G4 1.10fr dark car & multi .85 .75

UN Water Conference, Mar del Plata, Argentina, Mar. 14-25.

Hands Protecting UN Emblem — G5

1977, May 24 Photo. *Perf. 14*

67 G5 80c blue & multi .55 .50
68 G5 1.10fr emerald & multi .85 .75

UN Security Council.

Colors of Five Races Spun into One Firm Rope — G6

1977, Sept. 19 Litho. *Perf. 13*

69 G6 40c multicolored .25 .25
70 G6 1.10fr multicolored .65 .65

Fight against racial discrimination.

Atomic Energy Turning Partly into Olive Branch — G7

1977, Nov. 18 Photo.

71 G7 80c dark car & multi .60 .60
72 G7 1.10fr Prus blue & multi .80 .80

Peaceful uses of atomic energy.

"Tree" of Doves — G8

1978, Jan. 27 Litho. *Perf. 14½*

73 G8 35c multicolored .20 .20

Globes with Smallpox Distribution G9

1978, Mar. 31 Photo. *Perf. 12x11½*

74 G9 80c yellow & multi .60 .60
75 G9 1.10fr lt green & multi .90 .85

Global eradication of smallpox.

Namibia Type

1978, May 5 Photo. *Perf. 12*

76 A166 80c multicolored .85 .85

Jets and Flight Patterns — G10

1978, June 12 Photo. *Perf. 14*

77 G10 70c multicolored .40 .40
78 G10 80c multicolored .70 .70

International Civil Aviation Organization for "Safety in the Air."

General Assembly, Flags and Globe G11

1978, Sept. 15 Photo. *Perf. 13½*

79 G11 70c multicolored .50 .45
80 G11 1.10fr multicolored .90 .85

Technical Cooperation Type

1978, Nov. 17 Photo. *Perf. 14*

81 A169 80c multicolored .70 .70

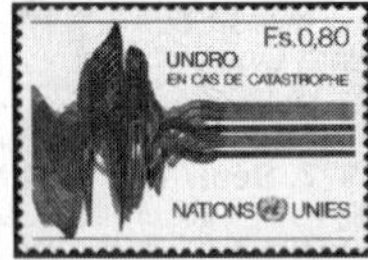

Seismograph Recording Earthquake G12

1979, Mar. 9 Photo. *Perf. 14*

82 G12 80c multicolored .50 .50
83 G12 1.50fr multicolored .80 .75

Office of the UN Disaster Relief Coordinator (UNDRO).

Children and Rainbow G13

1979, May 4 Photo. *Perf. 14*

84 G13 80c multicolored .35 .35
85 G13 1.10fr multicolored .65 .65

International Year of the Child.

Namibia Type

1979, Oct. 5 Litho. *Perf. 13½*

86 A176 1.10fr multicolored .50 .50

International Court of Justice, Scales — G14

1979, Nov. 9 Litho. *Perf. 13x13½*

87 G14 80c multicolored .40 .40
88 G14 1.10fr multicolored .60 .60

International Court of Justice, The Hague, Netherlands.

Economic Order Type

1980, Jan. 11 *Perf. 15x14½*

89 A179 80c multicolored .85 .85

Women's Year Emblem G15

1980, Mar. 7 Litho. *Perf. 14½x15*

90 G15 40c multicolored .30 .30
91 G15 70c multicolored .75 .75

UN Decade for Women.

Peace-keeping Operations Type

1980, May 16 Litho. *Perf. 14x13*

92 A181 1.10fr blue & green .85 .75

35th Anniv. Type and

Dove and "35" — G16

1980, June 26 Litho. *Perf. 13*

93 G16 40c multicolored .35 .30
94 A183 70c multicolored .65 .60

Souvenir Sheet

Imperf

95 Sheet of 2 .70 .70
 a. G16 40c multicolored .25 —
 b. A183 70c multicolored .45 —

35th anniv. of the UN.

ECOSOC Type and

Family Climbing Line Graph — G17

1980, Nov. 21 Litho. *Perf. 13½x13*

96 A186 40c multicolored .30 .25
97 G17 70c multicolored .60 .50

Palestinian Rights Type

1981, Jan. 30 Photo.

98 A188 80c multicolored .55 .50

Disabled Type of UN, Vienna

1981, Mar. 6 Photo.

99 A190 40c multicolored .25 .25
100 V4 1.50fr multicolored 1.00 1.00

Art Type

1981, Apr. 15 Photo. *Perf. 11½*

101 A191 80c multicolored .85 .85

Energy Type

1981, May 29 Litho. *Perf. 13*

102 A192 1.10fr multicolored .70 .70

Volunteers Program Type and Symbols of Science, Agriculture and Industry — G18

1981, Nov. 13 Litho. *Perf. 13½x13*

103 A194 40c multicolored .50 .50
104 G18 70c multicolored 1.00 1.00

Fight Against Apartheid G19

Flower of Flags G20

1982, Jan. 22 Photo. *Perf. 11½x12*

105 G19 30c multicolored .25 .20
106 G20 1fr multicolored .80 .70

Human Environment — G21

1982, Mar. 19 Litho. *Perf. 13½x13*

107 G21 40c multicolored .35 .25
108 A199 1.20fr multicolored 1.25 1.10

Outer Space Type and

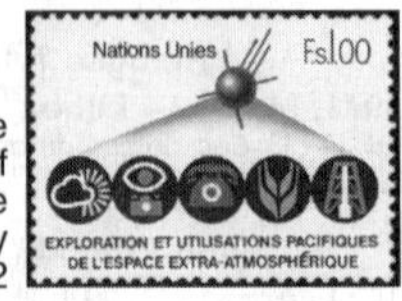

Satellite Applications of Space Technology G22

1982, June 11 Litho. *Perf. 13x13½*

109 A201 80c multicolored .70 .70
110 G22 1fr multicolored .90 .90

Conservation and Protection of Nature

1982, Nov. 19 Photo. *Perf. 14*

111 A202 40c Bird .50 .40
112 A202 1.50fr Reptile 1.25 1.10

World Communications Year Type

1983, Jan. 28 Litho. *Perf. 13*

113 A204 1.20fr multicolored 1.25 1.10

Safety at Sea Type and

Life Preserver and Radar — G23

1983, Mar. 18 Litho. *Perf. 14½*

114 A205 40c multicolored .40 .40
115 G23 80c multicolored .80 .80

World Food Program Type

1983, Apr. 22 Engr. *Perf. 13½*

116 A207 1.50fr blue 1.25 1.10

Type of UN and

G24

1983, June 6 Litho. *Perf. 14*

117 A208 80c multicolored .55 .55
118 G24 1.10fr multicolored .95 .90

35th Anniv. of the Universal Declaration of Human Rights

G25 G26

1983, Dec. 9 Photo. *Perf. 13½*

119 G25 40c Homo Humus Humanitas .45 .45
120 G26 1.20fr Right to Create .95 .90

Intl. Population Conference Type

1984, Feb. 3 Litho. *Perf. 14*

121 A212 1.20fr multicolored 1.00 1.00

Fishing G27

Women Farm Workers, Africa G28

1984, Mar. 15 Litho. *Perf. 14½*

122 G27 50c multicolored .35 .30
123 G28 80c multicolored .65 .55

World Food Day.

Valletta, Malta — G29

Los Glaciares Natl. Park, Argentina G30

1984, Apr. 18 Litho. *Perf. 14*

124 G29 50c multicolored .65 .60
125 G30 70c multicolored .90 .85

World Heritage. See Nos. 211-212.

G31

G32

1984, May 29 Photo. *Perf. 11½*

126 G31 35c multicolored .35 .30
127 G32 1.50fr multicolored 1.25 1.10

Refugees.

International Youth Year — G33

1984, Nov. 15 Litho. *Perf. 13½*

128 G33 1.20fr multicolored 1.40 1.40

ILO Type of UN and

Turin Center — G34

1985, Feb. 1 Engr.

129 A220 80c Turin Center emblem .70 .70
130 G34 1.20fr U Thant Pavilion 1.10 1.10

UN University Type

1985, Mar. 15 Photo. *Perf. 13½*

131 A221 50c Farmer, discussion group .65 .60
132 A221 80c As above 1.00 1.00

Postman G35

Doves — G36

1985, May 10 Litho. *Perf. 14*
133 G35 20c multicolored .25 .20
134 G36 1.20fr multicolored 1.60 1.50

40th Anniv. Type

1985, June 26 Photo. *Perf. 12x11½*
135 A224 50c multicolored .60 .60
136 A225 70c multicolored .90 .90

Souvenir Sheet

Imperf

137 Sheet of 2 2.50 2.25
a. A224 50c multicolored .85 —
b. A225 70c multicolored 1.10 —

UNICEF Child Survival Campaign

Photo. & Engr.

1985, Nov. 22 *Perf. 13½*
138 A226 50c Three girls *.40* .40
139 A226 1.20fr Infant drinking *1.00* 1.00

Africa in Crisis Type

Abstract painting by Alemayehou Gabremedhin.

1986, Jan. 31 Photo. *Perf. 11½*
140 A227 1.40fr Mother, hungry children 1.40 1.25

UN Development Program Type

1986, Mar. 14 Photo. *Perf. 13½*
141 A228 35c Erosion control 1.75 1.60
142 A228 35c Logging 1.75 1.60
143 A228 35c Lumber transport 1.75 1.60
144 A228 35c Nursery 1.75 1.60
a. Block of 4, #141-144 7.50 7.00

No. 144a has a continuous design.

Doves and Sun — G37

1986, Mar. 14 Litho. *Perf. 15x14½*
145 G37 5c multicolored .20 .20

UN Stamp Collecting Type

Designs: 50c, UN Human Rights stamp. 80c, UN stamps.

1986, May 22 Engr. *Perf. 12½*
146 A229 50c dk green & hn brn 1.25 .90
147 A229 80c dk green & yel org 1.75 1.40

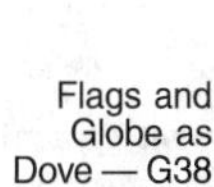

Flags and Globe as Dove — G38

Peace in French — G39

Photo. & Embossed

1986, June 20 *Perf. 13½*
148 G38 45c multicolored .75 .75
149 G39 1.40fr multicolored 1.60 1.60

Intl. Peace Year.

WFUNA Anniv. Type

Souvenir Sheet

Designs: 35c, Abstract by Benigno Gomez, Honduras. 45c, Abstract by Alexander Calder (1898-1976), US. 50c, Abstract by Joan Miro (b. 1893), Spain. 70c, Sextet with Dove, by Ole Hamann, Denmark.

1986, Nov. 14 Litho. *Perf. 13x13½*
150 Sheet of 4 4.00 3.75
a. A232 35c multicolored .55 —
b. A232 45c multicolored .75 —
c. A232 50c multicolored .95 —
d. A232 70c multicolored 1.25 —

Trygve Lie Type

Photo. & Engr.

1987, Jan. 30 *Perf. 13½*
151 A233 1.40fr multicolored 1.25 1.10

Sheaf of Colored Bands, by Georges Mathieu — G40

Armillary Sphere, Palais des Nations — G41

Photo., Photo. & Engr. (No. 153)

Perf. 11½x12, 13½ (No. 153)

1987, Jan. 30
152 G40 90c multicolored .75 .75
153 G41 1.40fr multicolored 1.40 1.40

Perf. 13½x12½

1987, Mar. 13 Litho.
154 A234 50c Construction .50 .45
155 A234 90c Finishing interior 1.00 .90

Fight Drug Abuse Type

1987, June 12 Litho. *Perf. 14½*
156 A235 80c Mother and child .75 .75
157 A235 1.20fr Workers in rice paddy 1.10 1.10

UN Day Type

Designs: Multinational people in various occupations.

1987, Oct. 23 Litho. *Perf. 14½x15*
158 A236 35c multicolored .60 .60
159 A236 50c multicolored .85 *.90*

Immunize Every Child Type

1987, Nov. 20 Litho. *Perf. 15x14½*
160 A237 90c Whooping cough 1.50 1.40
161 A237 1.70fr Tuberculosis 2.75 2.50

IFAD Type

1988, Jan. 29 Litho. *Perf. 13½*
162 A238 35c Flocks .40 .35
163 A238 1.40fr Fruit 1.40 1.25

G42

1988, Jan. 29 Photo. *Perf. 14*
164 G42 50c multicolored .90 .90

Survival of the Forests Type

1988, Mar. 18 Litho. *Perf. 14x15*
165 A240 50c Pine forest *1.50* 1.40
166 A240 1.10fr as 50c *4.00* 3.75
a. Pair, #165-166 *5.50* 5.25

No. 166a has a continuous design.

Intl. Volunteer Day Type

Perf. 13x14, 14x13

1988, May 6 Litho.
167 A241 80c Agriculture, vert. .80 .80
168 A241 90c Veterinary medicine 1.00 1.00

Health in Sports Type

Perf. 13½x13, 13x13½

1988, June 17 Litho.
169 A242 50c Soccer, vert. .40 .35
170 A242 1.40fr Swimming 1.40 1.25

Human Rights Declaration Anniv. Type

Photo. & Engr.

1988, Dec. 9 *Perf. 12*
171 A243 90c multicolored .75 .75

Souvenir Sheet

172 A243 2fr multicolored 3.00 3.00

World Bank Type

1989, Jan. 27 Litho. *Perf. 13x14*
173 A244 80c Telecommunications 1.00 1.00
174 A244 1.40fr Industry 2.25 2.25

Peace-Keeping Force Type

1989, Mar. 17 Litho. *Perf. 14x13½*
175 A245 90c multicolored 1.00 1.00

World Weather Watch Anniv. Type

Satellite photographs: 90c, Europe under the influence of Arctic air. 1.10fr, Surface temperatures of sea, ice and land surrounding the Kattegat between Denmark and Sweden.

1989, Apr. 21 Litho. *Perf. 13x14*
176 A247 90c multicolored 1.25 1.10
177 A247 1.10fr multicolored 2.00 1.90

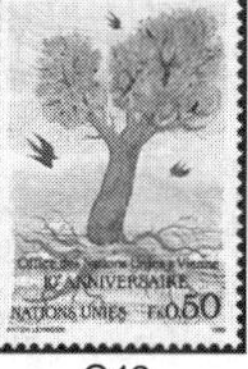

G43

G44

Photo. & Engr., Photo.

1989, Aug. 23 *Perf. 14*
178 G43 50c multicolored 1.10 1.10
179 G44 2fr multicolored 3.50 3.25

Offices in Vienna, 10th anniv.

Human Rights Type of 1989

Paintings and sculpture: 35c, *Young Mother Sewing,* by Mary Cassatt. 80c, *The Unknown Slave,* sculpture by Albert Mangones.

1989, Nov. 17 Litho. *Perf. 13½*
180 A250 35c multicolored .35 .30
181 A250 80c multicolored 1.00 .90

Printed in sheets of 12+12 se-tenant labels containing Articles 3 (35c) or 4 (80c) inscribed in French, German or English.

Intl. Trade Center Type

1990, Feb. 2 Litho. *Perf. 14½x15*
182 A251 1.50fr multicolored 2.50 2.40

G45

1990, Feb. 2 Photo. *Perf. 14x13½*
183 G45 5fr multicolored 5.00 4.75

G46

Fight AIDS Worldwide - G46a

Perf. 13½x12½

1990, Mar. 16 Litho.
184 G46 50c multicolored 1.10 1.10
185 G46a 80c multicolored 1.75 1.50

Medicinal Plants Type

1990, May 4 Photo. *Perf. 11½*

Granite Paper

186 A253 90c *Plumeria rubra* 1.10 1.10
187 A253 1.40fr *Cinchona officinalis* 2.25 2.00

UN 45th Anniv. Type

"45," emblem and: 90c, Symbols of clean environment, transportation and industry. 1.10fr, Dove in silhouette.

1990, June 26 Litho. *Perf. 14½x13*
188 A254 90c multicolored 1.25 1.25
189 A254 1.10fr multicolored 2.25 2.00

Souvenir Sheet

190 A254 Sheet of 2, #188-189 6.50 5.00

Crime Prevention Type

1990, Sept. 13 Photo. *Perf. 14*
191 A255 50c Official corruption 1.50 1.40
192 A255 2fr Environmental crime 3.50 3.25

Human Rights Type of 1989

Paintings: 35c, The Prison Courtyard by Vincent Van Gogh. 90c, Katho's Son Redeems the Evil Doer From Execution by Albrecht Durer.

1990, Nov. 16 Litho. *Perf. 13½*
193 A250 35c multicolored .50 .50
194 A250 90c black & brown 1.40 1.40

Printed in sheets of 12+12 se-tenant labels containing Articles 9 (35c) or 10 (90c) inscribed in French, German or English.

Economic Commission for Europe Type

1991, Mar. 15 Litho. *Perf. 14*
195 A256 90c Owl, gull 1.40 1.25
196 A256 90c Bittern, otter 1.40 1.25
197 A256 90c Swan, lizard 1.40 1.25
198 A256 90c Great crested grebe 1.40 1.25
a. Block of 4, #195-198 6.00 5.50

Namibian Independence Type

1991, May 10 Litho. *Perf. 14*
199 A257 70c Mountains 1.50 1.40
200 A257 90c Baobab tree 2.50 2.25

Ballots Filling Ballot Box — G47

UN Emblem — G48

1991, May 10 Litho. *Perf. 15x14½*
201 G47 80c multicolored 1.60 1.50
202 G48 1.50fr multicolored 3.00 2.75

G49

Rights of the Child G50

1991, June 14 Litho. *Perf. 14½*
203 G49 80c Hands holding infant 1.50 1.40
204 G50 1.10fr Children, flowers 2.25 2.00

G51

Banning of Chemical Weapons G52

1991, Sept. 11 Litho. *Perf. 13½*

205 G51 80c multicolored 2.00 1.60
206 G52 1.40fr multicolored 3.50 3.00

UN Postal Administration, 40th Anniv. Type

1991, Oct. 24 Litho. *Perf. 14x15*

207 A263 50c UN NY #7 1.25 1.10
208 A263 1.60fr UN NY #10 2.75 2.50

Human Rights Type of 1989

Artwork: 50c, Early Morning in Ro...1925, by Paul Klee. 90c, The Marriage of Giovanni Arnolfini and Fiovanna Cenami, by Jan Van Eyck.

1991, Nov. 20 Litho. *Perf. 13½*

209 A250 50c multicolored .90 .90
210 A250 90c multicolored 1.50 1.40

Printed in sheets of 12+12 se-tenant labels containing Articles 15 (50c) and 16 (90c) inscribed in French, German or English.

World Heritage Type of 1984

Designs: 50c, Sagarmatha Natl. Park, Nepal. 1.10fr, Stonehenge, United Kingdom.

1992, Jan. 24 Litho. *Perf. 13*
Size: 35x28mm

211 G29 50c multicolored 1.25 1.10
212 G29 1.10fr multicolored 2.50 2.25

G53

1992, Jan. 24 *Perf. 15x14½*

213 G53 3fr multicolored 3.75 3.50

Clean Oceans Type

1992, Mar. 13 Litho. *Perf. 14*

214 A264 80c Ocean surface, diff. .90 .90
215 A264 80c Ocean bottom, diff. .90 .90
a. Pair, #214-215 1.80 *2.00*

Printed in sheets of 12 containing 6 #215a.

Earth Summit Type

Designs: No. 216, Rainbow. No. 217, Faces shaped as clouds. No. 218, Two sailboats. No. 219, Woman with parasol, sailboat, flowers.

1992, May 22 Photo. *Perf. 11½*

216 A265 75c multicolored 1.10 1.00
217 A265 75c multicolored 1.10 1.00
218 A265 75c multicolored 1.10 1.00
219 A265 75c multicolored 1.10 1.00
a. Block of 4, #216-219 5.25 5.00

Mission to Planet Earth Type

Designs: No. 220, Space station. No. 221, Probes near Jupiter.

1992, Sept. 4 Photo. *Rouletted 8*
Granite Paper

220 A266 1.10fr multicolored 2.50 2.25
221 A266 1.10fr multicolored 2.50 2.25
a. Pair, #220-221 5.00 4.50

Science and Technology Type

Designs: 90c, Doctor, nurse. 1.60fr, Graduate seated before computer.

1992, Oct. 2 Litho. *Perf. 14*

222 A267 90c multicolored 1.50 1.40
223 A267 1.60fr multicolored 3.50 3.00

Human Rights Type of 1989

Artwork: 50c, The Oath of the Tennis Court, by Jacques Louis David. 90c, Rocking Chair I, by Henry Moore.

1992, Nov. 20 Litho. *Perf. 13½*

224 A250 50c multicolored 1.00 1.00
225 A250 90c multicolored 1.75 1.75

Printed in sheets of 12+12 se-tenant labels containing Articles 21 (50c) and 22 (90c) inscribed in French, German or English.

Aging With Dignity Type

Designs: 50c, Older man coaching soccer. 1.50fr, Older man working at computer terminal.

1993, Feb. 5 Litho. *Perf. 13*

226 A270 50c multicolored .75 .75
227 A270 1.50fr multicolored 2.40 2.40

Endangered Species Type

Designs: No. 228, Pongidae (gorilla). No. 229, Falco peregrinus (peregrine falcon). No. 230, Trichechus inunguis (Amazonian manatee). No. 231, Panthera uncia (snow leopard).

1993, Mar. 3 Litho. *Perf. 13x12½*

228 A271 80c multicolored 1.10 1.00
229 A271 80c multicolored 1.10 1.00
230 A271 80c multicolored 1.10 1.00
231 A271 80c multicolored 1.10 1.00
a. Block of 4, #228-231 4.50 4.25

Healthy Environment Type

1993, May 7 Litho. *Perf. 15x14½*

232 A272 60c Neighborhood 1.10 1.10
233 A272 1fr Urban skyscrapers 2.25 2.00

Human Rights Type of 1989

Artwork: 50c, Three Musicians, by Pablo Picasso. 90c, Voice of Space, by Rene Magritte.

1993, June 11 Litho. *Perf. 13½*

234 A250 50c multicolored .90 .90
235 A250 90c multicolored 2.00 1.90

Printed in sheets of 12 + 12 se-tenant labels containing Article 27 (50c) and 28 (90c) inscribed in French, German or English.

Intl. Peace Day Type

Denomination at: No. 236, UL. No. 237, UR. No. 238, LL. No. 239, LR.

Rouletted 12½
1993, Sept. 21 Litho. & Engr.

236 A274 60c purple & multi 2.25 2.00
237 A274 60c purple & multi 2.25 2.00
238 A274 60c purple & multi 2.25 2.00
239 A274 60c purple & multi 2.25 2.00
a. Block of 4, #236-239 9.00 8.00

Environment-Climate Type

Designs: No. 240, Polar bears. No. 241, Whale sounding. No. 242, Elephant seal. No. 243, Penguins.

1993, Oct. 29 Litho. *Perf. 14½*

240 A275 1.10fr multicolored 2.50 2.40
241 A275 1.10fr multicolored 2.50 2.40
242 A275 1.10fr multicolored 2.50 2.40
243 A275 1.10fr multicolored 2.50 2.40
a. Strip of 4, #240-243 10.00 9.75

Intl. Year of the Family Type of 1993

Designs: 80c, Parents teaching child to walk. 1fr, Two women and child picking plants.

1994, Feb. 4 Litho. *Perf. 13.1*

244 A276 80c rose violet & multi 1.25 1.25
245 A276 1fr brown & multi 1.75 1.75

Endangered Species Type of 1993

Designs: No. 246, Mexican prairie dog. No. 247, Jabiru. No. 248, Blue whale. No. 249, Golden lion tamarin.

1994, Mar. 18 Litho. *Perf. 12.7*

246 A271 80c multicolored 1.10 1.10
247 A271 80c multicolored 1.10 1.10
248 A271 80c multicolored 1.10 1.10
249 A271 80c multicolored 1.10 1.10
a. Block of 4, #246-249 4.50 4.50

Protection for Refugees Type of 1994

Design: 1.20fr, Hand lifting figure over chasm.

1994, Apr. 29 Litho. *Perf. 14.3x14.8*

250 A277 1.20fr multicolored 2.75 2.50

Intl. Decade for Natural Disaster Reduction Type of 1994

Earth seen from space, outline map of: No. 251, North America. No. 252, Eurasia. No. 253, South America. No. 254, Australia and South Pacific region.

1994, May 27 Litho. *Perf. 13.9x14.2*

251 A281 60c multicolored 2.00 1.75
252 A281 60c multicolored 2.00 1.75
253 A281 60c multicolored 2.00 1.75
254 A281 60c multicolored 2.00 1.75
a. Block of 4, #251-254 8.50 7.00

Palais des Nations, Geneva G54

Creation of the World, by Oili Maki — G55

1994, Sept. 1 Litho. *Perf. 14.3x14.6*

255 G54 60c multicolored .75 .75
256 G55 80c multicolored 1.00 1.00
257 G54 1.80fr multi, diff. 2.50 2.50

Population and Development Type of 1994

Designs: 60c, People shopping at open-air market. 80c, People on vacation crossing bridge.

1994, Sept. 1 Litho. *Perf. 13.2x13.6*

258 A282 60c multicolored 1.25 1.10
259 A282 80c multicolored 1.75 1.60

UNCTAD Type of 1994

1994, Oct. 28

260 A283 80c multi, diff. 1.25 1.25
261 A283 1fr multi, diff. 1.75 1.75
a. Grayish green omitted —

UN 50th Anniv. Type of 1995

Litho. & Engr.
1995, Jan. 1 *Perf. 13.4*

262 A284 80c multicolored 1.25 1.25

Social Summit Type of 1995

Photo. & Engr.
1995, Feb. 3 *Perf. 13.6x13.9*

263 A285 1fr multi, diff. 1.50 1.40

Endangered Species Type of 1993

Designs: No. 264, Crowned lemur, Lemur coronatus. No. 265, Giant Scops owl, Otus gurneyi. No. 266, Zetek's frog, Atelopus varius zeteki. No. 267, Wood bison, Bison bison athabascae.

1995, Mar. 24 Litho. *Perf. 13x12½*

264 A271 80c multicolored 1.40 1.25
265 A271 80c multicolored 1.40 1.25
266 A271 80c multicolored 1.40 1.25
267 A271 80c multicolored 1.40 1.25
a. Block of 4, 264-267 5.75 5.00

Intl. Youth Year Type of 1995

Designs: 80c, Farmer on tractor, fields at harvest time. 1fr, Couple standing by fields at night.

1995, May 26 Litho. *Perf. 14.4x14.7*

268 A286 80c multicolored 1.75 1.60
269 A286 1fr multicolored 2.75 2.00

UN, 50th Anniv. Type of 1995

Designs: 60c, Like No. 663. 1.80fr, Like No. 664.

Perf. 13.3x13.6
1995, June 26 Engr.

270 A287 60c maroon 1.00 .90
271 A287 1.80fr green 3.25 3.00

Souvenir Sheet
Litho. & Engr.
Imperf

272 Sheet of 2, #270-271 4.25 4.25
a. A287 60c maroon 1.00 1.00
b. A287 1.80fr green 3.25 3.25

Conference on Women Type of 1995

Designs: 60c, Black woman, cranes flying above. 1fr, Women, dove.

1995, Sept. 5 Photo. *Perf. 12*

273 A288 60c multicolored 1.50 1.25

Size: 28x50mm

274 A288 1fr multicolored 2.50 1.75

UN People, 50th Anniv. Type of 1995

1995, Oct. 24 Litho. *Perf. 14*

275 Sheet of 12 18.00 12.50
a.-l. A290 30c any single 1.40 1.25
276 Souvenir booklet 20.00
a. A290 30c Booklet pane of 3, vert. strip of 3 from UL of sheet 4.75 4.75
b. A290 30c Booklet pane of 3, vert. strip of 3 from UR of sheet 4.75 4.75
c. A290 30c Booklet pane of 3, vert. strip of 3 from LL of sheet 4.75 4.75
d. A290 30c Booklet pane of 3, vert. strip of 3 from LR of sheet 4.75 4.75

WFUNA, 50th Anniv. Type of 1996

1996, Feb. 2 Litho. *Perf. 13x13½*

277 A291 80c multicolored 1.50 1.25

The Galloping Horse Treading on a Flying Swallow, Chinese Bronzework, Eastern Han Dynasty (25-220 A.D.) — G56

Palais des Nations, Geneva G57

1996, Feb. 2 Litho. *Perf. 14½x15*

278 G56 40c multicolored .75 .60
279 G57 70c multicolored 1.25 1.10

Endangered Species Type of 1993

Designs: No. 280, Paphiopedilum delenatii. No. 281, Pachypodium baronii. No. 282, Sternbergia lutea. No. 283, Darlingtonia californica.

1996, Mar. 14 Litho. *Perf. 12½*

280 A271 80c multicolored 1.10 1.00
281 A271 80c multicolored 1.10 1.00
282 A271 80c multicolored 1.10 1.00
283 A271 80c multicolored 1.10 1.00
a. Block of 4, #280-283 4.50 4.25

City Summit Type of 1996

Designs: No. 284, Asian family. No. 285, Oriental garden. No. 286, Fruit, vegetable vendor, mosque. No. 287, Boys playing ball. No. 288, Couple reading newspaper.

1996, June 3 Litho. *Perf. 14x13½*

284 A293 70c multicolored 1.50 1.10
285 A293 70c multicolored 1.50 1.10
286 A293 70c multicolored 1.50 1.10
287 A293 70c multicolored 1.50 1.10
288 A293 70c multicolored 1.50 1.10
a. Strip of 5, #284-288 7.50 5.50

Sport and the Environment Type of 1996

Designs: 70c, Cycling, vert. 1.10fr, Sprinters.

Perf. 14x14½, 14½x14
1996, July 19 Litho.

289 A294 70c multicolored 1.40 1.40
290 A294 1.10fr multicolored 2.00 1.75

Souvenir Sheet

291 A294 Sheet of 2, #289-290 3.00 3.00

Plea for Peace Type of 1996

Designs: 90c, Tree filled with birds, vert. 1.10fr, Bouquet of flowers in rocket tail vase, vert.

1996, Sept. 17 Litho. *Perf. 15x14½*

292 A295 90c multicolored 1.75 1.50
293 A295 1.10fr multicolored 2.50 2.00

UNICEF Type of 1996

Fairy Tales: 70c, The Sun and the Moon, South America. 1.80fr, Ananse, Africa.

1996, Nov. 20 Litho. *Perf. 14½x15*
294 A296 70c multicolored 1.00 .90
295 A296 1.80fr multicolored 2.50 2.25

Panes of 8 + label.

UN Flag — G58

Palais des Nations Under Construction, by Massimo Campigli G59

1997, Feb. 12 Litho. *Perf. 14½*
296 G58 10c multicolored .20 .20
297 G59 1.10fr multicolored 1.50 1.50

Endangered Species Type of 1993

Designs: No. 298, Ursus maritimus (polar bear). No. 299, Goura cristata (blue-crowned pigeon). No. 300, Amblyrhynchus cristatus (marine iguana). No. 703, Lama guanicoe (guanaco).

1997, Mar. 13 Litho. *Perf. 12½*
298 A271 80c multicolored 1.10 1.00
299 A271 80c multicolored 1.10 1.00
300 A271 80c multicolored 1.10 1.00
301 A271 80c multicolored 1.10 1.00
a. Block of 4, #298-301 4.50 4.00

Earth Summit Anniv. Type of 1997

Designs: No. 302, Person flying over mountain. No. 303, Mountain, person's face. No. 304, Person standing on mountain, sailboats. No. 305, Person, mountain, trees.

1.10fr, Combined design similar to Nos. 302-305.

1997, May 30 Photo. *Perf. 11.5*
Granite Paper
302 A299 45c multicolored 1.50 1.25
303 A299 45c multicolored 1.50 1.25
304 A299 45c multicolored 1.50 1.25
305 A299 45c multicolored 1.50 1.25
a. Block of 4, #302-305 7.00 5.50

Souvenir Sheet
306 A299 1.10fr multicolored 3.50 3.50

Transportation Type of 1997

Air transportation: No. 307, Zeppelin, Fokker tri-motor. No. 308, Boeing 314 Clipper, Lockheed Constellation. No. 309, DeHavilland Comet. No. 310, Boeing 747, Illyushin jet. No. 311, Concorde.

1997, Aug. 29 Litho. *Perf. 14x14½*
307 A300 70c multicolored 1.10 1.00
308 A300 70c multicolored 1.10 1.00
309 A300 70c multicolored 1.10 1.00
310 A300 70c multicolored 1.10 1.00
311 A300 70c multicolored 1.10 1.00
a. Strip of 5, #307-311 5.50 5.00

No. 311a has continuous design.

Philately Type of 1997

Designs: 70c, No. 146. 1.10fr, No. 147.

1997, Oct. 14 Litho. *Perf. 13½x14*
312 A301 70c multicolored 2.00 1.75
313 A301 1.10fr multicolored 2.75 2.75

World Heritage Convention Type of 1997

Terracotta warriors of Xian: 45c, Single warrior. 70c, Massed warriors. No. 316a, like #716. No. 316b, like #717. No. 316c, like Geneva #314. No. 316d, like Geneva #315. No. 316e, like Vienna #230. No. 316f, like Vienna #231.

1997, Nov. 19 Litho. *Perf. 13½*
314 A302 45c multicolored 1.50 1.40
315 A302 70c multicolored 2.50 2.50
316 Souvenir booklet 8.50
a.-f. A302 10c any single .35 .35
g. Booklet pane of 4 #316a 1.40 1.40
h. Booklet pane of 4 #316b 1.40 1.40
i. Booklet pane of 4 #316c 1.40 1.40
j. Booklet pane of 4 #316d 1.40 1.40
k. Booklet pane of 4 #316e 1.40 1.40
l. Booklet pane of 4 #316f 1.40 1.40

Palais des Nations, Geneva G60

1998, Feb. 13 Litho. *Perf. 14½x15*
317 G60 2fr multicolored 2.75 2.25

Endangered Species Type of 1993

Designs: No. 318, Macaca thibetana (short-tailed Tibetan macaque). No. 319, Phoenicopterus ruber (Caribbean flamingo). No. 320, Ornithoptera alexandrae (Queen Alexandra's birdwing). No. 321, Dama mesopotamica (Persian fallow deer).

1998, Mar. 13 Litho. *Perf. 12½*
318 A271 80c multicolored 1.10 1.00
319 A271 80c multicolored 1.10 1.00
320 A271 80c multicolored 1.10 1.00
321 A271 80c multicolored 1.10 1.00
a. Block of 4, #318-321 4.50 4.00

Intl. Year of the Ocean — G61

1998, May 20 Litho. *Perf. 13x13½*
322 G61 Sheet of 12 12.00 11.00
a.-l. 45c any single .80 .80

Rain Forests Type

1998, June 19 *Perf. 13x13½*
323 A307 70c Orangutans 1.00 .75

Souvenir Sheet
324 A307 3fr like #323 6.00 5.50

Peacekeeping Type

Designs: 70c, Soldier with two children. 90c, Two soldiers, children.

1998, Sept. 15 Photo. *Perf. 12*
325 A308 70c multicolored 1.50 1.10
326 A308 90c multicolored 2.00 1.75

Declaration of Human Rights Type

Designs: 90c, Stylized birds. 1.80fr, Stylized birds flying from hand.

Litho. & Photo.

1998, Oct. 27 *Perf. 13*
327 A309 90c multicolored 1.40 1.40
328 A309 1.80fr multicolored 2.75 2.75

Schönnbrun Palace Type

Designs: 70c, #331b, Great Palm House. 1.10fr, #331d, Blue porcelain vase, vert. No. 331a, Palace. No. 331c, The Gloriette (archway). No. 331e, Wall painting on fabric (detail), by Johann Wenzl Bergl, vert. No. 331f, Porcelain stove, vert.

1998, Dec. 4 Litho. *Perf. 14*
329 A310 70c multicolored 1.00 1.00
330 A310 1.10fr multicolored 1.50 1.40
331 Souvenir booklet 7.00
a.-c. A310 10c any single .20 .20
d.-f. A310 30c any single .50 .40
g. Booklet pane, 4 #331a .75 .60
h. Booklet pane, 3 #331d 1.50 1.25
i. Booklet pane, 3 #331e 1.50 1.25
j. Booklet pane, 3 #331f 1.50 1.25
k. Booklet pane, 4 #331b .75 .60
l. Booklet pane, 4 #331c .75 .60

Palais Wilson, Geneva G62

1999, Feb. 5 Photo. *Perf. 11½*
Granite Paper
332 G62 1.70fr brown red 3.00 2.75

World Heritage, Australia Type

90c, #335e, Kakadu Natl. Park. 1.10fr, #335c, Great Barrier Reef. #335a, Tasmanian Wilderness. #335b, Wet tropics of Queensland. #335d, Uluru-Kata Tjuta Natl. Park. #335f, Willandra Lakes region.

1999, Mar. 19 Litho. *Perf. 13*
333 A313 90c multicolored 1.40 1.40
334 A313 1.10fr multicolored 1.50 1.40
335 Souvenir booklet 6.50
a.-c. A313 10c any single .20 .20
d.-f. A313 20c any single .40 .40
g. Booklet pane of 4, #335a .55 .40
h. Booklet pane of 4, #335d 1.60 1.40
i. Booklet pane of 4, #335b .55 .40
j. Booklet pane of 4, #335e 1.60 1.40
k. Booklet pane of 4, #335c .55 .40
l. Booklet pane of 4, #335f 1.60 1.40

Endangered Species Type of 1993

Designs: No. 336, Equus hemionus (Asiatic wild ass). No. 337, Anodorhynchus hyacinthinus (hyacinth macaw). No. 338, Epicrates subflavus (Jamaican boa). No. 339, Dendrolagus bennettianus (Bennetts' tree kangaroo).

1999, Apr. 22 Litho. *Perf. 12½*
336 A271 90c multicolored 1.40 1.25
337 A271 90c multicolored 1.40 1.25
338 A271 90c multicolored 1.40 1.25
339 A271 90c multicolored 1.40 1.25
a. Block of 4, #336-339 5.75 5.50

UNISPACE III Type

No. 340, Farm, satellite dish. No. 341, City, satellite in orbit. No. 342, Composite of #340-341.

1999, July 7 Photo. *Rouletted 8*
340 A314 45c multicolored .60 .60
341 A314 45c multicolored .60 .60
a. Pair, #340-341 2.00 2.00

Souvenir Sheet
Perf. 14½
342 A314 2fr multicolored 4.50 4.00
a. Ovptd. in sheet margin 9.50 8.00

No. 342a is overprinted in violet blue "PHILEXFRANCE 99 / LE MONDIAL DU TIMBRE / PARIS / 2 AU 11 JUILLET 1999."

UPU Type

Various people, early 20th century methods of mail transportation, denomination at: No. 343, UL. No. 344, UR. No. 345, LL. No. 346, LR.

1999, Aug. 23 Photo. *Perf. 11¾*
343 A315 70c multicolored 1.00 .75
344 A315 70c multicolored 1.00 .75
345 A315 70c multicolored 1.00 .75
346 A315 70c multicolored 1.00 .75
a. Block of 4, #343-346 4.00 3.50

In Memoriam Type

Armillary sphere, Palais de Nations. Size of 2fr stamp: 34x63mm.

1999, Sept. 21 Litho. *Perf. 14½x14*
347 A316 1.10fr multicolored 1.60 1.40

Souvenir Sheet
Perf. 14
348 A316 2fr multicolored 3.00 3.00

Education Type

Perf. 13½x13¾
1999, Nov. 18 Litho.
349 A317 90c Rainbow over globe 1.40 1.25
350 A317 1.80fr Fish, tree, globe, book 2.50 2.50

Intl. Year Of Thanksgiving Type

2000, Jan 1 Litho. *Perf. 13¼x13½*
351 A318 90c multicolored 1.40 1.25

On No. 351 portions of the design were applied by a thermographic process producing a shiny, raised effect.

Endangered Species Type of 1993

#352, Hippopotamus amphibius (hippopotamus). #353, Coscoroba coscoroba (Coscoroba swan). #354, Varanus prasinus (emerald monitor). #355, Enhydra lutris (sea otter).

2000, Apr. 6 Litho. *Perf. 12¾x12½*
352 A271 90c multicolored 1.25 1.00
353 A271 90c multicolored 1.25 1.00
354 A271 90c multicolored 1.25 1.00
355 A271 90c multicolored 1.25 1.00
a. Block of 4, #352-355 5.00 4.50

Our World 2000 Type

Winning artwork in Millennium painting competition: 90c, The Embrace, by Rita Adaimy, Lebanon. 1.10fr, Living Single, by Richard Kimanthi, Kenya, vert.

Perf. 13x13½, 13½x13
2000, May 30 Litho.
356 A319 90c multicolored 1.25 1.00
357 A319 1.10fr multicolored 1.50 1.25

55th Anniversary Type

Designs: 90c, Trygve Lie, Harry S Truman, workers at cornerstone dedication ceremony, 1949. 1.40fr, Window cleaner on Secretariat Building, General Assembly Hall under construction, 1951.

2000, July 7 Litho. *Perf. 13¼x13*
358 A320 90c multicolored 1.25 .60
359 A320 1.40fr multicolored 2.00 1.00

Souvenir Sheet
360 A320 Sheet of 2, #358-359 3.25 3.00

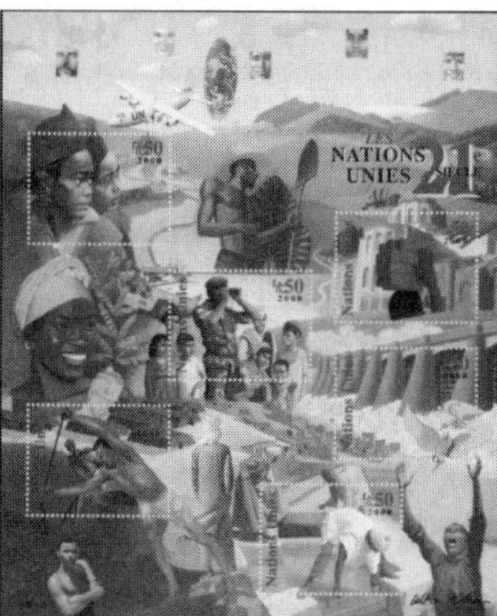

The UN in the 21st Century — G63

No. 361: a, Two people, terraced rice paddy. b, Man carrying bricks on head. c, UN Peacekeeper with binoculars. d, Dam, doves. e, Men with shovels. f, People working on irrigation system.

2000, Sept. 15 Litho. *Perf. 14*
361 G63 Sheet of 6 5.50 5.25
a.-f. 50c any single .65 .60

World Heritage, Spain Type

1fr, #364b, Walled Town of Cuenca. 1.20fr, #364e, Toledo. #364a, Alhambra, Generalife and Albayzin, Granada. #364c, Aqueduct of Segovia. #364d, Amphitheater of Mérida. #364f, Güell Park, Barcelona.

2000, Oct. 6 Litho. *Perf. 14¾x14½*
362 A323 1fr multicolored 1.40 .70
363 A323 1.20fr multicolored 1.60 .80

Souvenir Booklet
364 Booklet 5.50
a.-c. A323 10c any single .20 .20
d.-f. A323 20c any single .30 .30
g. Booklet pane of 4, #364a .55 .50
h. Booklet pane of 4, #364d 1.25 1.10
i. Booklet pane of 4, #364b .55 .50
j. Booklet pane of 4, #364e 1.25 1.10
k. Booklet pane of 4, #364c .55 .50
l. Booklet pane of 4, #364f 1.25 1.10

Respect for Refugees Type

Refugee with cane, four other refugees.

2000, Nov. 9 Litho. *Perf. 13¼x12¾*
365 A324 80c multicolored 1.10 .55

Souvenir Sheet
366 A324 1.80fr multicolored 2.40 1.25

Endangered Species Type of 1993

Designs: No. 367, Felis lynx canadensis (North American lynx). No. 368, Pavo muticus (green peafowl). No. 369, Geochelone elephantopus (Galapagos giant tortoise). No. 370, Lepilemur spp. (sportive lemur).

2001, Feb. 1 Litho. *Perf. 12¾x12½*
367 A271 90c multicolored 1.25 .60
368 A271 90c multicolored 1.25 .60
369 A271 90c multicolored 1.25 .60
370 A271 90c multicolored 1.25 .60
a. Block of 4, #367-370 5.00 —

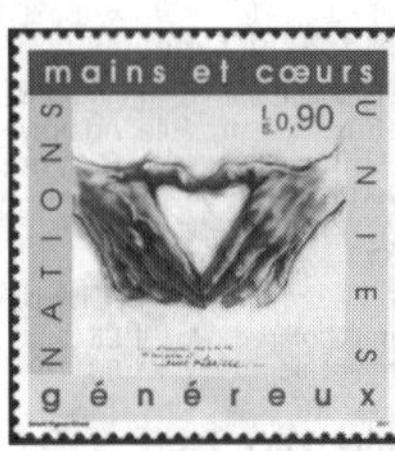

Intl. Volunteers Year — G64

Paintings by: 90c, Ernest Pignon-Ernest, France. 1.30fr, Paul Siché, France.

2001, Mar. 29 Litho. *Perf. 13¼*
371 G64 90c multicolored 1.10 .55
372 G64 1.10fr multicolored 1.60 .80

World Heritage, Japan Type

Designs: 1.10fr, #375b, Nara. 1.30fr, #375e, Itsukushima Shinto Shrine. #375a, Kyoto. #375c, Himeji-Jo. #375d, Shirakawa-Go and Gokayama. #375f, Nikko.

2001, Aug. 1 Litho. *Perf. 12¾x13¼*
373 A328 1.10fr multicolored 1.40 .70
374 A328 1.30fr multicolored 1.60 .80

Souvenir Booklet
375 Booklet 6.00
a.-c. A328 10c any single .20 .20
d.-f. A328 30c any single .35 .35
g. Booklet pane of 4, #375a .50 —
h. Booklet pane of 4, #375d 1.50 —
i. Booklet pane of 4, #375b .50 —
j. Booklet pane of 4, #375e 1.50 —
k. Booklet pane of 4, #375c .50 —
l. Booklet pane of 4, #375f 1.50 —

Dag Hammarskjöld Type

2001, Sept. 18 Engr. *Perf. 11x11¼*
376 A329 2fr carmine lake 2.50 1.25

UN Postal Administration, 50th Anniv. Types

2001, Oct. 18 Litho. *Perf. 13½*
377 A330 90c Stamps, globe 1.10 .55
378 A330 1.30fr Stamps, horns 1.60 .80

Souvenir Sheet
379 A331 Sheet of 2 4.00 2.00
a. 1.30fr red & light blue, 38mm diameter 1.75 .85
b. 1.80fr red & light blue, 38mm diameter 2.25 1.10

Climate Change Type

Designs: No. 380, Lizard, flowers, shoreline. No. 381, Windmills, construction workers. No. 382, Non-polluting factory. No. 383, Solar oven, city, village, picnickers.

2001, Nov. 16 Litho. *Perf. 13¼*
380 A332 90c multicolored 1.10 .55
381 A332 90c multicolored 1.10 .55
382 A332 90c multicolored 1.10 .55
383 A332 90c multicolored 1.10 .55
a. Horiz. strip, #380-383 4.50 —

Nobel Peace Prize Type

2001, Dec. 10 Litho. *Perf. 13¼*
384 A333 90c multicolored 1.10 .55

Palais des Nations — G65

2002, Mar. 1 Litho. *Perf. 13¾*
385 G65 1.30fr multicolored 1.75 .90

Endangered Species Type of 1993

Designs: No. 386, Cacajao calvus (white uakari). No. 387, Mellivora capensis (honey badger). No. 388, Otocolobus manul (manul). No. 389, Varanus exantematicus (Bosc's monitor).

2002, Apr. 4 Litho. *Perf. 12¾x12½*
386 A271 90c multicolored 1.25 .60
387 A271 90c multicolored 1.25 .60
388 A271 90c multicolored 1.25 .60
389 A271 90c multicolored 1.25 .60
a. Block of 4, #386-389 5.00 —

Independence of East Timor Type

Designs: 90c, Wooden statue of male figure. 1.30fr, Carved wooden container.

2002, May 20 Litho. *Perf. 14x14½*
390 A335 90c multicolored 1.25 .60
391 A335 1.30fr multicolored 1.75 .85

Intl. Year of Mountains Type

Designs: No. 392, Weisshorn, Switzerland. No. 393, Mt. Fuji, Japan. No. 394, Vinson Massif, Antarctica. No. 395, Mt. Kamet, India.

2002, May 24 Litho. *Perf. 13x13¼*
392 A336 70c multicolored .90 .45
393 A336 70c multicolored .90 .45
394 A336 1.20fr multicolored 1.60 .80
395 A336 1.20fr multicolored 1.60 .80
a. Vert. strip or block of four, #392-395 5.00 2.50

World Summit on Sustainable Development (Peter Max) Type

Designs: No. 396, Sun, birds, flowers, heart. No. 397, Three faceless people, diff. No. 398, Three women, diff. No. 399, Sailboat, mountain.

2002, June 27 Litho. *Perf. 14½x14*
396 A337 90c multicolored 1.25 .60
397 A337 90c multicolored 1.25 .60
398 A337 1.80fr multicolored 2.40 1.25
399 A337 1.80fr multicolored 2.40 1.25
a. Vert. strip or block of four, #396-399 7.50 3.75

World Heritage, Italy Type

Designs: 90c, #402e, Pisa. 1.30fr, #402b, Aeolian Islands. #402a, Amalfi Coast. #402c, Rome. #402d, Florence. #402f, Pompeii.

Perf. 13½x13¼
2002, Aug. 30 Litho.
400 A338 90c multicolored 1.25 .65
401 A338 1.30fr multicolored 1.90 .95

Souvenir Booklet
402 Booklet 5.00
a.-c. A338 10c any single .20 .20
d.-f. A338 20c any single .30 .30
g. Booklet pane of 4, #402d 1.25 —
h. Booklet pane of 4, #402a .40 —
i. Booklet pane of 4, #402e 1.25 —
j. Booklet pane of 4, #402b .40 —
k. Booklet pane of 4, #402f 1.25 —
l. Booklet pane of 4, #402c .40 —

AIDS Awareness Type

2002, Oct. 24 Litho. *Perf. 13½*
403 A339 1.30fr multicolored 1.90 .95

Entry of Switzerland into United Nations G66

2002, Oct. 24 Litho. *Perf. 14½x14¾*
404 G66 3fr multicolored 4.25 2.10

SEMI-POSTAL

AIDS Awareness Semi-postal Type

Souvenir Sheet

2002, Oct. 24 Litho. *Perf. 14½*
B1 SP1 90c + 30c multicolored 1.75 1.75

U.N. OFFICES IN VIENNA, AUSTRIA

For use only on mail posted at the Vienna International Center for the UN and the International Atomic Energy Agency.

100 Groschen = 1 Schilling
100 Cents = 1 Euro (2002)

Catalogue values for all unused stamps in this country are for Never Hinged items.

For use only on mail posted at the Vienna International Center for the UN and the International Atomic Energy Agency.

Type of Geneva 1978, UN Types of 1961-72 and

Donaupark, Vienna — V1

Aerial View — V2

Perf. 11½
1979, Aug. 24 Photo. Unwmk.
Granite Paper
1 G8 50g multicolored .20 .20
2 A52 1s multicolored .20 .20
3 V1 4s multicolored .20 .20
4 AP13 5s multicolored .25 .25
5 V2 6s multicolored .35 .35
6 A45 10s multicolored .50 .50
Nos. 1-6 (6) 1.70 1.70

No. 6 has no frame.

Economic Order Type

1980, Jan. 11 Litho. *Perf. 15x14½*
7 A178 4s multicolored .70 .70

Dove Type

1980, Jan. 11 Litho. *Perf. 13x13½*
8 A147 2.50s multicolored .25 .25

Women's Year Emblem on World Map — V3

1980, Mar. 7 Litho. *Perf. 14½x15*
9 V3 4s lt green & dk green .40 .40
10 V3 6s bister brown .75 .75

UN Decade for Women.

Peace-keeping Operations Type

1980, May 16 Litho. *Perf. 14x13*
11 A182 6s multicolored .40 .40

35th Anniv. Types of Geneva and UN

1980, June 26 Litho. *Perf. 13*
12 G16 4s multicolored .40 .40
13 A184 6s multicolored .65 .65

Souvenir Sheet
Imperf
14 Sheet of 2 .55 .55
a. G16 4s multicolored .20 —
b. A184 6s multicolored .35 —

35th anniv. of the UN.

ECOSOC Types of UN and Geneva

1980, Nov. 21 Litho. *Perf. 13½x13*
15 A187 4s multicolored .30 .30
16 G17 6s multicolored .60 .60

Palestinian Rights Type

1981, Jan. 30 Photo.
17 A188 4s multicolored .45 .45

Disabled Type of UN and

Interlocking Stitches — V4

1981, Mar. 6 Photo.
18 A189 4s multicolored .40 .40
19 V4 6s multicolored .60 .60

Art Type

1981, Apr. 15 Photo. *Perf. 11½*
20 A191 6s multicolored .75 .75

Energy Type

1981, May 29 Litho. *Perf. 13*
21 A193 7.50s multicolored .70 .70

Volunteers Program Types of UN and Geneva

1981, Nov. 13 Litho. *Perf. 13½x13*
22 A195 5s multicolored .50 .45
23 G18 7s multicolored 1.00 .90

"For a Better World" — V5

1982, Jan. 22 Photo. *Perf. 11½x12*
24 V5 3s multicolored .35 .35

Human Environment Types of UN and Geneva

1982, Mar. 19 Litho. *Perf. 13½x13*
25 A200 5s multicolored .40 .40
26 G21 7s multicolored .80 .80

Outer Space Type of Geneva

1982, June 11 Litho. *Perf. 13x13½*
27 G22 5s multicolored .60 .60

Conservation and Protection of Nature Type

1982, Nov. 19 Photo. *Perf. 14*
28 A202 5s Fish .50 .50
29 A202 7s Animal .70 .70

World Communications Year Type

1983, Jan. 28 Litho. *Perf. 13*
30 A203 4s multicolored .40 .40

Safety at Sea Types of Geneva and UN

1983, Mar. 18 Litho. *Perf. 14½*
31 G23 4s multicolored .40 .40
32 A206 6s multicolored .65 .65

World Food Program Type

1983, Apr. 22 Engr. *Perf. 13½*
33 A207 5s green .50 .50
34 A207 7s brown .70 .70

Trade and Development Types of Geneva and UN

1983, June 6 Litho. *Perf. 14*
35 G24 4s multicolored .30 .30
36 A209 8.50s multicolored .75 .75

35th Anniv. of the Universal Declaration of Human Rights
V6 V7

Photogravure and Engraved
1983, Dec. 9 *Perf. 13½*
37 V6 5s The Second Skin .50 .50
38 V7 7s Right to Think .75 .75

Intl. Population Conference Type

1984, Feb. 3 Litho. *Perf. 14*
39 A212 7s multicolored .65 .65

Field Irrigation V8

Pest Control V9

1984, Mar. 15 Litho. *Perf. 14½*
40 V8 4.50s multicolored .45 .45
41 V9 6s multicolored .70 .70

World Food Day.

Serengeti Park, Tanzania V10

Ancient City of Shiban, People's Democratic Rep. of Yemen — V11

1984, Apr. 18 Litho. *Perf. 14*
42 V10 3.50s multicolored .25 .25
43 V11 15s multicolored 1.40 1.40

World Heritage. See Nos. 125-126.

V12

V13

1984, May 29 Photo. *Perf. 11½*
44 V12 4.50s multicolored .55 .55
45 V13 8.50s multicolored 1.40 1.40

Refugees.

International Youth Year — V14

1984, Nov. 15 Litho. *Perf. 13½*
46 V14 3.50s multicolored .50 .50
47 V14 6.50s multicolored .75 .75

ILO Type of Geneva

1985, Feb. 1 Engr. *Perf. 13½*
48 G34 7.50s U Thant Pavilion .85 .85

UN University Type

1985, Mar. 15 Photo. *Perf. 13½*
49 A221 8.50s Rural scene, scientist .85 .85

Ship of Peace V15

Sharing Umbrella V16

1985, May 10 Litho. *Perf. 14*
50 V15 4.50s multicolored .35 .35
51 V16 15s multicolored 2.25 2.25

40th Anniv. Type

1985, June 26 Photo. *Perf. 12x11½*
52 A224 6.50s multicolored 1.00 1.00
53 A225 8.50s multicolored 1.50 1.50

Souvenir Sheet
Imperf

54 Sheet of 2 2.75 2.75
a. A224 6.50s multicolored .70 .70
b. A225 8.50s multicolored .90 .90

UNICEF Child Survival Campaign
Photogravure and Engraved

1985, Nov. 22 *Perf. 13½*
55 A226 4s Spoonfeeding children .75 .75
56 A226 6s Mother hugging infant 1.40 1.40

Africa in Crisis Type

Abstract painting by Tesfaye Tessema.

1986, Jan. 31 Photo. *Perf. 11½*
57 A227 8s multicolored .80 .80

UN Development Program Type

1986, Mar. 14 Photo. *Perf. 13½*
58 A228 4.50s Developing crop strains 1.50 1.25
59 A228 4.50s Animal husbandry 1.50 1.25
60 A228 4.50s Technical instruction 1.50 1.25
61 A228 4.50s Nutrition education 1.50 1.25
a. Block of 4, #58-61 6.25 5.50

No. 61a has a continuous design.

UN Stamp Collecting Type

Designs: 3.50s, UN stamps. 6.50s, Engraver.

1986, May 22 Engr. *Perf. 12½*
62 A229 3.50s dk ultra & dk brown .50 .45
63 A229 6.50s int blue & brt rose 1.10 1.10

Olive Branch, Rainbow, Earth — V17

Photogravure and Embossed

1986, June 20 *Perf. 13½*
64 V17 5s shown .90 .90
65 V17 6s Doves, UN emblem 1.10 1.10

Intl. Peace Year.

WFUNA Anniv. Type
Souvenir Sheet

Designs: 4c, White Stallion, by Elisabeth von Janota-Bzowski, Germany. 5s, Surrealistic landscape by Ernst Fuchs, Austria. 6s, Geometric abstract by Victor Vasarely (b. 1908), France. 7s, Mythological abstract by Wolfgang Hutter (b. 1928), Austria.

1986, Nov. 14 Litho. *Perf. 13x13½*
66 Sheet of 4 4.00 3.75
a. A232 4s multicolored .75 .60
b. A232 5s multicolored .85 .70
c. A232 6s multicolored 1.00 .80
d. A232 7s multicolored 1.25 1.00

Trygve Lie Type
Photogravure and Engraved

1987, Jan. 30 *Perf. 13½*
67 A233 8s multicolored 1.00 .95

Shelter for the Homeless Type
Perf. 13½x12½

1987, Mar. 13 Litho.
68 A234 4s Family, homes .65 .65
69 A234 9.50s Entering home 1.25 1.25

Fight Drug Abuse Type

1987, June 12 Litho. *Perf. 14½x15*
70 A235 5s Soccer players .60 .60
71 A235 8s Family 1.00 1.00

Donaupark, Vienna V18

Peace Embracing the Earth — V19

1987, June 12 *Perf. 14½x15*
72 V18 2s multicolored .35 .35
73 V19 17s multicolored 1.90 1.75

UN Day Type

1987, Oct. 23 Litho. *Perf. 14½x15*
74 A236 5s multicolored .85 .75
75 A236 6s multicolored 1.00 1.00

Immunize Every Child Type

1987, Nov. 20 *Perf. 15x14½*
76 A237 4s Polio .75 .75
77 A237 9.50s Diphtheria 2.00 1.75

IFAD Type

1988, Jan. 29 Litho. *Perf. 13½*
78 A238 4s Grains .50 .50
79 A238 6s Vegetables 1.00 1.00

Survival of the Forests Type

Deciduous forest in fall.

1988, Mar. 18 Litho. *Perf. 14x15*
80 A240 4s multicolored 2.25 2.25
81 A240 5s multicolored 3.25 3.25
a. Pair, #80-81 5.50 5.50

No. 81a has a continuous design.

Intl. Volunteer Day Type
Perf. 13x14, 14x13

1988, May 6 Litho.
82 A241 6s Medical care, vert. .85 .80
83 A241 7.50s Construction 1.25 1.25

Health in Sports Type
Perf. 13½x13, 13x13½

1988, June 17 Litho.
84 A242 6s Skiing, vert. .85 .85
85 A242 8s Tennis 1.25 1.25

Human Rights Declaration Anniv. Type
Photo. & Engr.

1988, Dec. 9 *Perf. 12*
86 A243 5s multicolored .50 .50

Souvenir Sheet

87 A243 11s multicolored 1.25 .50

World Bank Type

1989, Jan. 27 Litho. *Perf. 13x14*
88 A244 5.50s Transportation 1.25 1.25
89 A244 8s Health care, education 1.90 1.90

Peace-Keeping Force Type

1989, Mar. 17 Litho. *Perf. 14x13½*
90 A245 6s multicolored .90 .90

World Weather Watch Anniv. Type

Designs: 4s, Helical cloud formation over Italy, the eastern Alps and parts of Yugoslavia. 9.50s, Rainfall in Tokyo, Japan.

1989, Apr. 21 Litho. *Perf. 13x14*
91 A247 4s multicolored 1.00 1.00
92 A247 9.50s multicolored 2.25 2.25

V20

V21

Photo. & Engr., Photo.

1989, Aug. 23 *Perf. 14*
93 V20 5s multicolored 4.50 4.00
94 V21 7.50s multicolored 1.00 1.00

Offices in Vienna, 10th anniv.

Human Rights Type

Paintings: 4s, *The Prisoners*, by Kathe Kollwitz. 6s, *Justice*, by Raphael.

1989, Nov. 17 Litho. *Perf. 13½*
95 A250 4s multicolored .65 .65
96 A250 6s multicolored .90 .90

Printed in sheets of 12+12 se-tenant labels containing Articles 5 (4s) or 6 (6s) inscribed in German, English or French.

Intl. Trade Center Type

1990, Feb. 2 Litho. *Perf. 14½x15*
97 A251 12s multicolored 2.00 1.90

Painting by Kurt Regschek V22

1990, Feb. 2 Litho. *Perf. 13x13½*
98 V22 1.50s multicolored .30 .30

Fight AIDS Worldwide V23

Perf. 13½x12½

1990, Mar. 16 Litho.
99 V23 5s "AIDS" 1.50 1.40
100 V23 11s Stylized figures, ink blot 2.75 2.50

Medicinal Plants Type

1990, May 4 Photo. *Perf. 11½*
Granite Paper

101 A253 4.50s *Bixa orellana* 1.50 1.40
102 A253 9.50s *Momordica charantia* 2.75 2.50

UN 45th Anniv. Type

"45" and emblem.

1990, June 26 Litho. *Perf. 14½x13*
103 A254 7s multicolored 1.60 1.50
104 A254 9s multi, diff. 2.50 2.40

Souvenir Sheet

105 A254 Sheet of 2, #103-104 6.50 6.25

Crime Prevention Type

1990, Sept. 13 Photo. *Perf. 14*
106 A255 6s Domestic violence 1.25 1.25
107 A255 8s Crime against cultural heritage 2.50 2.25

Human Rights Type of 1989

Paintings: 4.50s, Before the Judge by Sandor Bihari. 7s, Young Man Greeted by a Woman Writing a Poem by Suzuki Harunobu.

1990, Nov. 16 Litho. *Perf. 13½*
108 A250 4.50s multicolored .40 .40
109 A250 7s multicolored 1.25 1.25

Printed in sheets of 12+12 se-tenant labels containing Articles 11 (4.50s) or 12 (7s) inscribed in German, English or French.

Economic Commission for Europe Type

1991, Mar. 15 Litho. *Perf. 14*
110 A256 5s Weasel, hoopoe 1.25 1.00
111 A256 5s Warbler, swans 1.25 1.00
112 A256 5s Badgers, squirrel 1.25 1.00
113 A256 5s Fish 1.25 1.00
a. Block of 4, #110-113 5.50 4.75

Namibian Independence Type

1991, May 10 Litho. *Perf. 14*
114 A257 6s Mountain, clouds 1.50 1.40
115 A257 9.50s Dune, Namib Desert 3.50 3.50

V24

1991, May 10 Litho. *Perf. 15x14½*
116 V24 20s multicolored 3.50 3.25

V25

Rights of the Child — V26

1991, June 14 Litho. *Perf. 14½*
117 V25 7s Stick drawings 1.50 1.50
118 V26 9s Child, clock, fruit 2.00 2.00

V27

Banning of Chemical Weapons V28

1991, Sept. 11 Litho. *Perf. 13½*
119 V27 5s multicolored 1.40 1.25
120 V28 10s multicolored 2.75 2.40

UN Postal Administration, 40th Anniv. Type

1991, Oct. 24 Litho. *Perf. 14x15*
121 A263 5s UN NY No. 8 .85 .85
122 A263 8s UN NY No. 5 2.00 2.00

Human Rights Type of 1989

Artwork: 4.50s, Pre-columbian Mexican pottery, c. 600 A.D. 7s, Windows, 1912, by Robert Delaunay.

1991, Nov. 20 Litho. *Perf. 13½*
123 A250 4.50s black & brown .75 .75
124 A250 7s multicolored 1.25 1.25

Printed in sheets of 12+12 se-tenant labels containing Articles 17 (4.50s) and 18 (7s) inscribed in German, English or French.

World Heritage Type of 1984

Designs: 5s, Iguacu Natl. Park, Brazil. 9s, Abu Simbel, Egypt.

1992, Jan. 24 Litho. *Perf. 13*
Size: 35x28mm
125 V10 5s multicolored 1.25 1.25
126 V10 9s multicolored 2.25 2.25

Clean Oceans Type

1992, Mar. 13 Litho. *Perf. 14*
127 A264 7s Ocean surface, diff. 1.10 1.10
128 A264 7s Ocean bottom, diff. 1.10 1.10
a. Pair, #127-128 2.25 2.25

Printed in sheets of 12 containing 6 #128a.

Earth Summit Type

1992, May 22 Photo. *Perf. 11½*
129 A265 5.50s Man in space 1.25 1.00
130 A265 5.50s Sun 1.25 1.00
131 A265 5.50s Man fishing 1.25 1.00
132 A265 5.50s Sailboat 1.25 1.00
a. Block of 4, #129-132 6.50 4.25

Mission to Planet Earth Type

Designs: No. 133, Satellite, person's mouth. No. 134, Satellite, person's ear.

1992, Sept. 4 Photo. *Rouletted 8*
Granite Paper
133 A266 10s multicolored 2.90 2.75
134 A266 10s multicolored 2.90 2.75
a. Pair, #133-134 6.00 5.50

Science and Technology Type

Designs: 5.50s, Woman emerging from computer screen. 7s, Green thumb growing flowers.

1992, Oct. 2 Litho. *Perf. 14*
135 A267 5.50s multicolored .80 .80
136 A267 7s multicolored 1.50 1.50

V29

Intl. Center, Vienna — V30

1992, Oct. 2 Litho. *Perf. 13x13½*
137 V29 5.50s multicolored 1.00 1.00
Perf. 13½x13
138 V30 7s multicolored 1.50 1.50

Human Rights Type of 1989

Artwork: 6s, Les Constructeurs, by Fernand Leger. 10s, Sunday Afternoon on the Island of La Grande Jatte, by Georges Seurat.

1992, Nov. 20 Litho. *Perf. 13½*
139 A250 6s multicolored 1.00 1.00
140 A250 10s multicolored 1.75 1.75

Printed in sheets of 12+12 se-tenant labels containing Articles 23 (6s) and 24 (10s) inscribed in German, English or French.

Aging With Dignity Type

Designs: 5.50s, Elderly couple, family working in garden. 7s, Older woman teaching.

1993, Feb. 5 Litho. *Perf. 13*
141 A270 5.50s multicolored 1.00 1.00
142 A270 7s multicolored 1.60 1.60

Endangered Species Type

Designs: No. 143, Equus grevyi (Grevy's zebra). No. 144, Spheniscus humboldti (Humboldt's penguins). No. 145, Varanus griseus (desert monitor). No. 146, Canis lupus (gray wolf).

1993, Mar. 3 Litho. *Perf. 13x12½*
143 A271 7s multicolored 1.25 1.10
144 A271 7s multicolored 1.25 1.10
145 A271 7s multicolored 1.25 1.10
146 A271 7s multicolored 1.25 1.10
a. Block of 4, #143-146 5.00 4.50

Healthy Environment Type

1993, May 7 Litho. *Perf. 15x14½*
147 A272 6s Wave in ocean 1.40 1.40
148 A272 10s Globe 2.25 2.00

V31

1993, May 7 Photo. *Perf. 11½*
Granite Paper
149 V31 13s multicolored 3.00 2.50

Human Rights Type of 1989

Artwork: 5s, Lower Austrian Peasants' Wedding, by Ferdinand G. Waldmuller. 6s, Outback, by Sally Morgan.

1993, June 11 Litho. *Perf. 13½*
150 A250 5s multicolored 1.25 1.25
151 A250 6s multicolored 1.50 1.50

Printed in sheets of 12 + 12 se-tenant labels containing Article 29 (5s) and 30 (6s) inscribed in German, English or French.

Intl. Peace Day Type

Denomination at: No. 152, UL. No. 153, UR. No. 154, LL. No. 155, LR.

Rouletted 12½
1993, Sept. 21 Litho. & Engr.
152 A274 5.50s green & multi 2.00 1.75
153 A274 5.50s green & multi 2.00 1.75
154 A274 5.50s green & multi 2.00 1.75
155 A274 5.50s green & multi 2.00 1.75
a. Block of 4, #152-155 8.50 7.00

Environment-Climate Type

Designs: No. 156, Monkeys. No. 157, Bluebird, industrial pollution, volcano. No. 158, Volcano, nuclear power plant, tree stumps. No. 159, Cactus, tree stumps, owl.

1993, Oct. 29 Litho. *Perf. 14½*
156 A275 7s multicolored 2.50 2.40
157 A275 7s multicolored 2.50 2.40
158 A275 7s multicolored 2.50 2.40
159 A275 7s multicolored 2.50 2.40
a. Strip of 4, #156-159 10.00 9.50

Intl. Year of the Family Type of 1993

Designs: 5.50s, Adults, children holding hands. 8s, Two adults, child planting crops.

1994, Feb. 4 Litho. *Perf. 13.1*
160 A276 5.50s blue green & multi 1.25 1.25
161 A276 8s red & multi 2.00 2.00

Endangered Species Type of 1993

Designs: No. 162, Ocelot. No. 163, White-breasted silver-eye. No. 164, Mediterranean monk seal. No. 165, Asian elephant.

1994, Mar. 18 Litho. *Perf. 12.7*
162 A271 7s multicolored 1.40 1.40
163 A271 7s multicolored 1.40 1.40
164 A271 7s multicolored 1.40 1.40
165 A271 7s multicolored 1.40 1.40
a. Block of 4, #162-165 5.75 5.75

Protection for Refugees Type of 1994

Design: 12s, Protective hands surround group of refugees.

1994, Apr. 29 Litho. *Perf. 14.3x14.8*
166 A277 12s multicolored 1.50 1.50

V32

V33

V34

1994, Apr. 29 Litho. *Perf. 12.9*
167 V32 50g multicolored .20 .20
168 V33 4s multicolored .70 .70
169 V34 30s multicolored 5.00 4.00
Nos. 167-169 (3) 5.90 4.90

Intl. Decade for Natural Disaster Reduction Type of 1994

Earth seen from space, outline map of: No. 170, North America. No. 171, Eurasia. No. 172, South America. No. 173, Australia and South Asia.

1994, May 27 Litho. *Perf. 13.9x14.2*
170 A281 6s multicolored 1.90 1.75
171 A281 6s multicolored 1.90 1.75
172 A281 6s multicolored 1.90 1.75
173 A281 6s multicolored 1.90 1.75
a. Block of 4, #170-173 8.00 7.00

Population and Development Type of 1994

Designs: 5.50s, Women teaching, running machine tool, coming home to family. 7s, Family on tropical island.

1994, Sept. 1 Litho. *Perf. 13.2x13.6*
174 A282 5.50s multicolored 1.75 1.60
175 A282 7s multicolored 2.25 2.10

UNCTAD Type of 1994

1994, Oct. 28
176 A283 6s multi, diff. 1.50 1.25
177 A283 7s multi, diff. 1.75 1.50

UN 50th Anniv. Type of 1995

Litho. & Engr.
1995, Jan. 1 *Perf. 13.4*
178 A284 7s multicolored 1.60 1.50

Social Summit Type of 1995

Photo. & Engr.
1995, Feb. 3 *Perf. 13.6x13.9*
179 A285 14s multi, diff. 2.50 2.50

Endangered Species Type of 1993

Designs: No. 180, Black rhinoceros, Diceros bicornis. No. 181, Golden conure, Aratinga guarouba. No. 182, Douc langur, Pygathrix nemaeus. No. 183, Arabian oryx, Oryx leucoryx.

1995, Mar. 24 Litho. *Perf. 13x12½*
180 A271 7s multicolored 1.25 1.25
181 A271 7s multicolored 1.25 1.25
182 A271 7s multicolored 1.25 1.25
183 A271 7s multicolored 1.25 1.25
a. Block of 4, 180-183 5.00 5.00

Intl. Youth Year Type of 1995

Designs: 6s, Village in winter. 7s, Teepees.

1995, May 26 Litho. *Perf. 14.4x14.7*
184 A286 6s multicolored 1.50 1.25
185 A286 7s multicolored 1.75 1.75

UN, 50th Anniv. Type of 1995

Designs: 7s, Like No. 663. 10s, Like No. 664.

Perf. 13.3x13.6
1995, June 26 Engr.
186 A287 7s green 1.40 1.40
187 A287 10s black 2.00 1.75

Souvenir Sheet
Litho. & Engr.
Imperf
188 Sheet of 2, #186-187 4.50 4.50
a. A287 7s green 1.75 1.75
b. A287 10s black 2.50 2.50

Conference on Women Type of 1995

Designs: 5.50s, Women amid tropical plants. 6s, Woman reading, swans on lake.

1995, Sept. 5 Photo. *Perf. 12*
189 A288 5.50s multicolored 1.25 1.25
Size: 28x50mm
190 A288 6s multicolored 2.25 2.00

UN People, 50th Anniv. Type of 1995

1995, Oct. 24 Litho. *Perf. 14*
191 Sheet of 12 19.00 19.00
a.-l. A290 3s any single 1.50 1.25
192 Souvenir booklet 21.00
a. A290 3s Booklet pane of 3, vert. strip of 3 from UL of sheet 5.00 5.00
b. A290 3s Booklet pane of 3, vert. strip of 3 from UR of sheet 5.00 5.00
c. A290 3s Booklet pane of 3, vert. strip of 3 from LL of sheet 5.00 5.00
d. A290 3s Booklet pane of 3, vert. strip of 3 from LR of sheet 5.00 5.00

WFUNA, 50th Anniv. Type of 1996

Design: 7s, Harlequin holding dove.

1996, Feb. 2 Litho. *Perf. 13x13½*
193 A291 7s multicolored 1.40 1.00

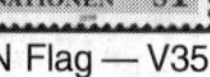
UN Flag — V35

Abstract, by Karl Korab — V36

1996, Feb. 2 Litho. *Perf. 15x14½*
194 V35 1s multicolored .20 .20
195 V36 10s multicolored 2.00 2.00

Endangered Species Type of 1993

Designs: No. 196, Cypripedium calceolus. No. 197, Aztekium ritteri. No. 198, Euphorbia cremersii. No. 199, Dracula bella.

1996, Mar. 14 Litho. *Perf. 12½*
196 A271 7s multicolored 1.25 1.00
197 A271 7s multicolored 1.25 1.00
198 A271 7s multicolored 1.25 1.00
199 A271 7s multicolored 1.25 1.00
a. Block of 4, #196-199 5.25 4.25

City Summit Type of 1996

Designs: No. 200, Arab family selling fruits, vegetables. No. 201, Woman beside stream, camels. No. 202, Woman carrying bundle on head, city skyline. No. 203, Woman threshing grain, yoke of oxen in field. No. 204, Native village, elephant.

1996, June 3 Litho. *Perf. 14x13½*
200 A293 6s multicolored 2.50 2.25
201 A293 6s multicolored 2.50 2.25
202 A293 6s multicolored 2.50 2.25
203 A293 6s multicolored 2.50 2.25
204 A293 6s multicolored 2.50 2.25
a. Strip of 5, #200-204 12.50 12.00

Sport and the Environment Type of 1996

Designs: 6s, Men's parallel bars (gymnastics), vert. 7s, Hurdles.

Perf. 14x14½, 14½x14
1996, July 19 Litho.
205 A294 6s multicolored 1.25 1.25
206 A294 7s multicolored 1.75 1.75

Souvenir Sheet

207 A294 Sheet of 2, #205-206 3.25 3.00

Plea for Peace Type of 1996

7s, Dove & butterflies. 10s, Stylized dove, diff.

1996, Sept. 17 Litho. *Perf. 14½x15*
208 A295 7s multicolored 1.25 1.25
209 A295 10s multicolored 1.90 1.75

UNICEF Type of 1996

Fairy Tales: 5.50s, Hansel and Gretel, by the Brothers Grimm. 8s, How Maui Stole Fire from the Gods, South Pacific.

1996, Nov. 20 Litho. *Perf. 14½x15*
210 A296 5.50s multicolored 1.00 .90
211 A296 8s multicolored 1.50 1.50

Panes of 8 + label.

V37

Phoenixes Flying Down (Detail), by Sagenji Yoshida — V38

1997, Feb. 12 Litho. *Perf. 14½*
212 V37 5s multicolored .85 .85
213 V38 6s multicolored 1.00 1.00

Endangered Species Type of 1993

No. 214, Macaca sylvanus (Barbary macaque). No. 215, Anthropoides paradisea (blue crane). No. 216, Equus przewalskii (Przewalski horse). No. 217, Myrmecophaga tridactyla (giant anteater).

1997, Mar. 13 Litho. *Perf. 12½*
214 A271 7s multicolored 1.50 1.25
215 A271 7s multicolored 1.50 1.25
216 A271 7s multicolored 1.50 1.25
217 A271 7s multicolored 1.50 1.25
a. Block of 4, #214-217 6.00 5.25

Earth Summit Anniv. Type of 1997

Designs: No. 218, Person running. No. 219, Hills, stream, trees. No. 220, Tree with orange leaves. No. 221, Tree with pink leaves.

11s, Combined design similar to Nos. 218-221.

1997, May 30 Photo. *Perf. 11.5*
Granite Paper
218 A299 3.50s multicolored 1.50 1.25
219 A299 3.50s multicolored 1.50 1.25
220 A299 3.50s multicolored 1.50 1.25
221 A299 3.50s multicolored 1.50 1.25
a. Block of 4, #218-221 6.00 5.25

Souvenir Sheet

222 A299 11s multicolored 2.75 2.75

Transportation Type of 1997

Ground transportation: No. 223, 1829 Rocket, 1901 Darraque. No. 224, Steam engine from Vladikawska Railway, trolley. No. 225, Double-decker bus. No. 226, 1950s diesel locomotive, semi-trailer. No. 227, High-speed train, electric car.

1997, Aug. 29 Litho. *Perf. 14x14½*
223 A300 7s multicolored 3.00 2.75
224 A300 7s multicolored 3.00 2.75
225 A300 7s multicolored 3.00 2.75
226 A300 7s multicolored 3.00 2.75
227 A300 7s multicolored 3.00 2.75
a. Strip of 5, #223-227 15.00 14.00

No. 227a has continuous design.

Philately Type of 1997

Designs: 6.50s, No. 62. 7s, No. 63.

1997, Oct. 14 Litho. *Perf. 13½x14*
228 A301 6.50s multicolored 1.25 1.25
229 A301 7s multicolored 1.75 1.75

World Heritage Convention Type of 1997

Terracotta warriors of Xian: 3s, Single warrior. 6s, Massed warriors. No. 232a, like #716. No. 232b, like #717. No. 232c, like Geneva #314. No. 232d, like Geneva #315. No. 232e, like Vienna #230. No. 232f, like Vienna #231.

1997, Nov. 19 Litho. *Perf. 13½*
230 A302 3s multicolored 1.25 1.25
231 A302 6s multicolored 2.50 2.25
232 Souvenir booklet 8.00
a.-f. A302 1s any single .30 .30
g. Booklet pane of 4 #232a 1.25 1.20
h. Booklet pane of 4 #232b 1.25 1.20
i. Booklet pane of 4 #232c 1.25 1.20
j. Booklet pane of 4 #232d 1.25 1.20
k. Booklet pane of 4 #232e 1.25 1.20
l. Booklet pane of 4 #232f 1.25 1.20

Japanese Peace Bell, Vienna — V39

Vienna Subway, Vienna Intl. Center — V40

1998, Feb. 13 Litho. *Perf. 15x14½*
233 V39 6.50s multicolored 1.00 1.00
234 V40 9s multicolored 1.50 1.50

Endangered Species Type of 1993

Designs: No. 235, Chelonia mydas (green turtle). No. 236, Speotyto cunicularia (burrowing owl). No. 237, Trogonoptera brookiana (Rajah Brooke's birdwing). No. 238, Ailurus fulgens (lesser panda).

1998, Mar. 13 Litho. *Perf. 12½*
235 A271 7s multicolored 1.50 1.25
236 A271 7s multicolored 1.50 1.25
237 A271 7s multicolored 1.50 1.25
238 A271 7s multicolored 1.50 1.25
a. Block of 4, #235-238 6.00 5.00

Intl. Year of the Ocean — V41

1998, May 20 Litho. *Perf. 13x13½*
239 V41 Sheet of 12 12.00 11.00
a.-l. 3.50s any single 1.00 1.00

Rain Forests Type

1998, June 19 *Perf. 13x13½*
240 A307 6.50s Ocelot 1.00 1.00

Souvenir Sheet

241 A307 22s like #240 3.50 3.25

Peacekeeping Type

Designs: 4s, Soldier passing out relief supplies. 7.50s, UN supervised voting.

1998, Sept. 15 Photo. *Perf. 12*
242 A308 4s multicolored .70 .70
243 A308 7.50s multicolored 1.25 1.25

Declaration of Human Rights Type

Designs: 4.50s, Stylized person. 7s, Gears.

Litho. & Photo.
1998, Oct. 27 *Perf. 13*
244 A309 4.50s multicolored .80 .80
245 A309 7s multicolored 1.25 1.25

Schönnbrun Palace Type

Designs: 3.50s, #248d, Palace. 7s, #248c, Porcelain stove, vert. No. 248a, Blue porcelain vase, vert. No. 248b, Wall painting on fabric (detail), by Johann Wenzl Bergl, vert. No. 248e, Great Palm House (conservatory). No. 248f, The Gloriette (archway).

1998, Dec. 4 Litho. *Perf. 14*
246 A310 3.50s multicolored .60 .60
247 A310 7s multicolored 1.10 1.10
248 Souvenir booklet 6.50
a.-c. A310 1s any single .25 .25
d.-f. A310 2s any single .35 .35
g. Booklet pane, 4 #248d 1.40 1.25
h. Booklet pane, 3 #248a .75 .65
i. Booklet pane, 3 #248b .75 .65
j. Booklet pane, 3 #248c .75 .65
k. Booklet pane, 4 #248e 1.40 1.25
l. Booklet pane, 4 #248f 1.40 1.25

Volcanic Landscape — V42

1999, Feb. 5 Litho. *Perf. 13x13½*
249 V42 8s multicolored 2.00 1.90

World Heritage, Australia Type

Designs: 4.50s, #252d, Uluru-Kata Tjuta Natl. Park. 6.50s, #252a, Tasmanian Wilderness. No. 252b, Wet tropics of Queensland. No. 252c, Great Barrier Reef. No. 252e, Kakadu Natl. Park. No. 252f, Willandra Lakes region.

1999, Mar. 19 Litho. *Perf. 13*
250 A313 4.50s multicolored .75 .75
251 A313 6.50s multicolored 1.10 1.10
252 Souvenir booklet 6.75
a.-c. A313 1s any single .20 .20
d.-f. A313 2s any single .35 .35
g. Booklet pane of 4, #252a .80
h. Booklet pane of 4, #252d 1.40
i. Booklet pane of 4, #252b .80
j. Booklet pane of 4, #252e 1.40
k. Booklet pane of 4, #252c .80
l. Booklet pane of 4, #252f 1.40

Endangered Specied Type of 1993

No. 253, Pongo pygmaeus (oran-utan). No. 254, Pelecanus crispus (Dalmatian pelican). No. 255, Eunectes notaeus (yellow anaconda). No. 256, Caracal.

1999, Apr. 22 Litho. *Perf. 12½*
253 A271 7s multicolored 1.10 1.10
254 A271 7s multicolored 1.10 1.10
255 A271 7s multicolored 1.10 1.10
256 A271 7s multicolored 1.10 1.10
a. Block of 4, #253-256 4.50 4.50

UNISPACE III Type

#257, Satellite over ships. #258, Satellite up close. #259, Composite of #257-258.

1999, July 7 Photo. *Rouletted 8*
257 A314 3.50s multicolored .75 .75
258 A314 3.50s multicolored .75 .75
a. Pair, #257-258 2.00 2.00

Souvenir Sheet
Perf. 14½

259 A314 13s multicolored 4.50 4.00

UPU Type

Various people, late 20th century methods of mail transportation, denomination at: No. 260, UL. No. 261, UR. No. 262, LL. No. 263, LR.

1999, Aug. 23 Photo. *Perf. 11¾*
260 A315 6.50s multicolored 1.10 1.10
261 A315 6.50s multicolored 1.10 1.10
262 A315 6.50s multicolored 1.10 1.10
263 A315 6.50s multicolored 1.10 1.10
a. Block of 4, #260-263 4.50 4.50

In Memoriam Type

Donaupark. Size of 14s stamp: 34x63mm.

1999, Sept. 21 Litho. *Perf. 14½x14*
264 A316 6.50s multicolored 1.10 1.10

Souvenir Sheet
Perf. 14

265 A316 14s multicolored 2.40 2.25

Education Type

Perf. 13½x13¾
1999, Nov. 18 Litho.
266 A317 7s Boy, girl, book 1.25 1.25
267 A317 13s Group reading 2.25 2.25

Intl. Year of Thanksgiving Type

2000, Jan. 1 Litho. *Perf. 13¼x13½*
268 A318 7s multicolored 1.25 1.25

On No. 268 portions of the design were applied by a thermographic process producing a shiny, raised effect.

Endangered Species Type of 1993

Designs: No. 269, Panthera pardus (leopard). No. 270, Platalea leucorodia (white spoonbill). No. 271, Hippocamelus bisulcus (huemal). No. 272, Orcinus orca (killer whale).

2000, Apr. 6 Litho. *Perf. 12¾x12½*
269 A271 7s multicolored 1.10 1.10
270 A271 7s multicolored 1.10 1.10
271 A271 7s multicolored 1.10 1.10
272 A271 7s multicolored 1.10 1.10
a. Block of 4, #269-272 4.50 4.50

Our World 2000 Type

Winning artwork in Millennium painting competition: 7s, Tomorrow's Dream, by Voltaire Perez, Philippines. 8s, Remembrance, by Dimitris Nalbandis, Greece, vert.

Perf. 13x13½, 13½x13
2000, May 30 Litho.
273 A319 7s multicolored 1.10 1.10
274 A319 8s multicolored 1.25 1.25

55th Anniversary Type

Designs: 7s, Secretariat Building, unfinished dome of General Assembly Hall, 1951. 9s, Trygve Lie and Headquraters Advisory Committee at topping-out ceremony, 1949.

2000, July 7 Litho. *Perf. 13¼x13*
275 A320 7s multicolored 1.10 1.10
276 A320 9s multicolored 1.50 1.50

Souvenir Sheet

277 A320 Sheet of 2, #275-276 2.60 2.25

The UN in the 21st Century — V43

No. 278: a, Farm machinery. b, UN Peacekeepers and children. c, Oriental farm workers. d, Peacekeepers searching for mines. e, Medical research. f, Handicapped people.

2000, Sept. 15 Litho. *Perf. 14*
278 V43 Sheet of 6 3.25 2.25
a.-f. 3.50s any single .50 .30

World Heritage, Spain Type

4.50s, #281c, Aqueduct of Segovia. 6.50s, #281f, Güell Park, Barcelona. #281a, Alhambra, Generalife and Albayzin, Granada. #281b, Walled Town of Cuenca. #281d, Amphitheater of Mérida. #281e, Toledo.

2000, Oct. 6 Litho. *Perf. 14¾x14½*

279 A323 4.50s multicolored .70 .35
280 A323 6.50s multicolored .95 .50

Souvenir Booklet

281 Booklet 5.50
a.-c. A323 1s any single .20 .20
d.-f. A323 2s any single .30 .30
g. Booklet pane of 4, #281a .55 .50
h. Booklet pane of 4, #281d 1.25 1.10
i. Booklet pane of 4, #281b .55 .50
j. Booklet pane of 4, #281e 1.25 1.10
k. Booklet pane of 4, #281c .55 .50
l. Booklet pane of 4, #281f 1.25 1.10

Respect for Refugees Type

Refugee with hat, three other refugees.

2000, Nov. 9 Litho. *Perf. 13¼x12¾*

282 A324 7s multicolored 1.10 .55

Souvenir Sheet

283 A324 25s multicolored 3.75 1.90

Endangered Species Type of 1993

Designs: No. 284, Tremarctos ornatus (spectacled bear). No. 285, Anas laysanensis (Laysan duck). No. 286, Proteles cristatus (aardwolf). No. 287, Trachypithecus cristatus (silvered leaf monkey).

2001, Feb. 1 Litho. *Perf. 12¾x12½*

284 A271 7s multicolored 1.00 .50
285 A271 7s multicolored 1.00 .50
286 A271 7s multicolored 1.00 .50
287 A271 7s multicolored 1.00 .50
a. Block of 4, #284-287 4.00 —

Intl. Volunteers Year — V44

Paintings by: 10s, Nguyen Thanh Chuong, Viet Nam. 12s, Ikko Tanaka, Japan.

2001, Mar. 29 Litho. *Perf. 13¼*

288 V44 10s multicolored 1.40 .70
289 V44 12s multicolored 1.75 .85

World Heritage, Japan Type

Designs: 7s, #290c, Himeji-Jo. 15s, #291f, Nikko. #292a, Kyoto. #292b, Nara. #292d, Shirakawa-Go and Gokayama. #292e, Itsukushima Shinto Shrine.

2001, Aug. 1 Litho. *Perf. 12¾x13¼*

290 A328 7s multicolored 1.00 .50
291 A328 15s multicolored 2.10 1.00

Souvenir Booklet

292 Booklet 5.00
a.-c. A328 1s any single .20 .20
d.-f. A328 2s any single .25 .25
g. Booklet pane of 4, #292a .55 —
h. Booklet pane of 4, #292d 1.10 —
i. Booklet pane of 4, #292b .55 —
j. Booklet pane of 4, #292e 1.10 —
k. Booklet pane of 4, #292c .55 —
l. Booklet pane of 4, #292f 1.10 —

Dag Hammarskjöld Type

2001, Sept. 18 Engr. *Perf. 11x11¼*

293 A329 7s green 1.00 .50

UN Postal Administration, 50th Anniv. Types

2001, Oct. 18 Litho. *Perf. 13½*

294 A330 7s Stamps, balloons 1.00 .50
295 A330 8s Stamps, cake 1.10 .55

Souvenir Sheet

296 A331 Sheet of 2 4.00 2.00
a. 7s green & light blue, 38mm diameter 1.00 .50
b. 21s green & light blue, 38mm diameter 3.00 1.50

Climate Change Type

Designs: No. 297, Solar panels, automobile at pump. No. 298, Blimp, bicyclists, horse and rider. No. 299, Balloon, sailboat, lighthouse, train. No. 300, Bird, train, traffic signs.

2001, Nov. 16 Litho. *Perf. 13¼*

297 A332 7s multicolored 1.00 .50
298 A332 7s multicolored 1.00 .50
299 A332 7s multicolored 1.00 .50
300 A332 7s multicolored 1.00 .50
a. Horiz. strip, #297-300 4.00 —

Nobel Peace Prize Type

2001, Dec. 10 Litho. *Perf. 13¼*

301 A333 7s multicolored 1.00 .50

100 Cents = 1 Euro (")

Austrian Tourist Attractions V45

Designs: 7c, Semmering Railway. 51c, Pferdschwemme, Salzburg. 58c, Aggstein an der Donau Ruins. 73c, Hallstatt. 87c, Melk Abbey. "2.03, Kapitelschwemme, Salzburg.

2002, Mar. 1 Litho. *Perf. 14½x14*

302 V45 7c multicolored .20 .20
303 V45 51c multicolored 1.00 .50
304 V45 58c multicolored 1.10 .55
305 V45 73c multicolored 1.50 .75
306 V45 87c multicolored 1.75 .85
307 V45 "2.03 multicolored 4.00 2.00
Nos. 302-307 (6) 9.55 4.85

Endangered Species Type of 1993

Designs: No. 308, Hylobates syndactylus (siamang). No. 309, Spheniscus demersus (jackass penguin). No. 310, Prionodon linsang (banded linsang). No. 311, Bufo retiformis (Sonoran green toad).

2002, Apr. 4 Litho. *Perf. 12¾x12½*

308 A271 51c multicolored 1.00 .50
309 A271 51c multicolored 1.00 .50
310 A271 51c multicolored 1.00 .50
311 A271 51c multicolored 1.00 .50
a. Block of 4, #308-311 4.00 —

Independence of East Timor Type

Designs: 51c, Deer horn container with carved wooden stopper. "1.09, Carved wooden tai weaving loom.

2002, May 20 Litho. *Perf. 14x14½*

312 A335 51c multicolored 1.00 .50
313 A335 "1.09 multicolored 2.10 1.00

Intl. Year of Mountains Type

Designs: No. 314, Mt. Cook, New Zealand. No. 315, Mt. Robson, Canada. No. 316, Mt. Rakaposhi, Pakistan. No. 317, Mt. Everest (Sagarmatha), Nepal.

2002, May 24 Litho. *Perf. 13x13¼*

314 A336 22c multicolored .45 .20
315 A336 22c multicolored .45 .20
316 A336 51c multicolored 1.00 .50
317 A336 51c multicolored 1.00 .50
a. Vert. strip or block of four, #392-395 3.00 1.50

World Summit on Sustainable Development (Peter Max) Type

Designs: No. 318, Rainbow. No. 319, Three women, diff. No. 320, Three faceless people. No. 321, Birds, wave.

2002, June 27 Litho. *Perf. 14½x14*

318 A337 51c multicolored 1.00 .50
319 A337 51c multicolored 1.00 .50
320 A337 58c multicolored 1.10 .55
321 A337 58c multicolored 1.10 .55
a. Vert. strip or block of four, #318-321 4.25 2.10

World Heritage, Italy Type

Designs: 51c, #324f, Pompeii. 58c, #324c, Rome. #324a, Amalfi Coast. #324b, Aeolian Islands. #324d, Florence. #324e, Pisa.

Perf. 13½x13¼

2002, Aug. 30 Litho.

322 A338 51c multicolored 1.10 .55
323 A338 58c multicolored 1.25 .60

Souvenir Booklet

324 Booklet 5.50
a.-c. A338 7c any single .20 .20
d.-f. A338 15c any single .30 .30
g. Booklet pane of 4, #324d 1.25 —
h. Booklet pane of 4, #324a .55 —
i. Booklet pane of 4, #324e 1.25 —
j. Booklet pane of 4, #324b .55 —
k. Booklet pane of 4, #324f 1.25 —
l. Booklet pane of 4, #324c .55 —

AIDS Awareness Type

2002, Oct. 24 Litho. *Perf. 13½*

325 A339 "1.53 multicolored 3.25 1.60

SEMI-POSTAL

AIDS Awareness Semi-postal Type

Souvenir Sheet

2002, Oct. 24 Litho. *Perf. 14½*

B1 SP1 51c + 25c multicolored 1.60 1.60

U.N., KOSOVO

These stamps were issued by the United Nations Interim Administration Mission in Kosovo and the Post & Telecommunications of Kosovo. Service was local for the first two months, with international use to start in mid-May.

100 pfennigs = 1 mark

Catalogue values for all unused stamps in this country are for Never Hinged items.

Peace in Kosovo — A1

Designs: 20pf, Mosaic depicting Orpheus, c. 5th-6th cent., Podujeve. 30pf, Dardinian idol, Museum of Kosovo. 50pf, Silver coin of Damastion from 4th cent. B.C. 1m, Statue of Mother Teresa, Prizren. 2m, Map of Kosovo.

Perf. 13½x13, 13½x13¼ (30pf)

2000, Mar. 14 Litho. Unwmk.

1 A1 20pf multicolored .20 .20
2 A1 30pf multicolored .30 .30
3 A1 50pf multicolored .50 .50
4 A1 1m multicolored 1.00 1.00
5 A1 2m multicolored 2.00 2.00
Nos. 1-5 (5) 4.00 4.00

Peace in Kosovo — A2

Designs: 20pf, Bird. 30pf, Street musician. 50pf, Butterfly and pear. 1m, Children and stars. 2m, Globe and handprints.

2001, Nov. 12 Litho. *Perf. 14*

6 A2 20pf multicolored .20 .20
7 A2 30pf multicolored .30 .30
8 A2 50pf multicolored .50 .50
9 A2 1m multicolored 1.10 1.10
10 A2 2m multicolored 2.10 2.10
Nos. 6-10 (5) 4.20 4.20

Nos. 6-10 were not available to collectors through the United Nations Postal Administration.

100 Cents = 1 Euro (")

Peace in Kosovo Type of 2001 With Denominations in Euros Only

2002, May 2 Litho. *Perf. 14*

11 A2 10c Like #6 .20 .20
12 A2 15c Like #7 .30 .30
13 A2 26c Like #8 .50 .50
14 A2 51c Like #9 .95 .95
15 A2 "1.02 Like #10 1.90 1.90
Nos. 11-15 (5) 3.85 3.85

Nos. 11-15 were not available to collectors through the United Nations Postal Administration.

U.N., WEST NEW GUINEA

Temporary Executive Authority

LOCATION — Western half of New Guinea, southwest Pacific Ocean
GOVT. — Province of Indonesia
AREA — In 1958, the size was 151,789 sq. mi.
POP. — estimated at 730,000 in 1958
CAPITAL — Hollandia

The former Netherlands New Guinea became a territory under the administration of the United Nations Temporary Executive Authority on Oct. 1, 1962.

The territory came under Indonesian administration on May 1, 1963. For stamps issued by Indonesia see West Irian in Vol. 6.

100 Cents = 1 Gulden

Catalogue values for all unused stamps in this country are for Never Hinged items.

Netherlands New Guinea Stamps of 1950-60 Overprinted

Type 2 Overprint

Perf. 12½x12, 12½x13½

1962-63 Photo. Unwmk.

1a	A4	1c	vermilion & yel	.25	.20
2a	A1	2c	deep orange	.35	.20
3a	A4	5c	choc & yel	.35	.20
4a	A5	7c	org red, bl & brn vio	.35	.20
5a	A4	10c	aqua & red brn	.35	.20
6a	A5	12c	grn, bl & brn vio	.35	.20
7a	A4	15c	dp yel & red brn	.60	.25
8a	A5	17c	brn vio & bl	.70	.35
9a	A4	20c	lt bl grn & red brn	.70	.35
10a	A6	25c	red	.60	.30
11a	A6	30c	deep blue	.95	.35
12a	A6	40c	deep orange	.95	.35
13a	A6	45c	dark olive	1.75	.75
14a	A6	55c	slate blue	1.25	.55
15a	A6	80c	dl gray vio	10.00	9.00
16a	A6	85c	dk vio brn	4.75	3.50
17a	A6	1g	plum	3.50	1.90

Engr.

18a	A3	2g	reddish brn	14.00	13.00
19a	A3	5g	green	6.00	3.50
			Nos. 1a-19a (19)	47.75	35.35

The overprint exists in four types:

1) Size 17½mm. Applied locally and sold in 1962 in West New Guinea. Top of "N" is slightly lower than the "U," and the base of the "T" is straight, or nearly so. This set sells for about $10 more than Nos. 1a-19a.

2) Size 17½mm. Applied in the Netherlands and sold in 1963 by the UN in New York. Top of the "N" is slightly higher than the "U," and the base of the "T" is concave. This is the set listed above.

3) Size 14mm. Exists on eight values.

4) Size 19mm. Exists on 1c and 10c.

Types 3 and 4 were applied in West New Guinea and it is doubtful whether they were regularly issued.

See the *U. S. Specialized Catalogue* for complete listings and values of the UNTEA overprints.

ABU DHABI

ˌä-bü-ˈthä-bē

LOCATION — Arabia, on Persian Gulf
GOVT. — Sheikdom under British protection
POP. — 25,000 (estimated)
CAPITAL — Abu Dhabi

Abu Dhabi is one of six Persian Gulf sheikdoms to join the United Arab Emirates, which proclaimed its independence Dec. 2, 1971. See United Arab Emirates.

100 Naye Paise = 1 Rupee
1000 Fils = 1 Dinar (1966)

Catalogue values for all unused stamps in this country are for Never Hinged items.

Sheik Shakbut bin Sultan — A1

Palace — A2

Designs: 40np, 50np, 75np, Gazelle. 5r, 10r, Oil rig and camels.

Perf. 14½

1964, Mar. 30 Photo. Unwmk.

1	A1	5np brt yellow green	1.10	.45
2	A1	15np brown	1.50	.45
3	A1	20np brt ultra	1.90	.65
4	A1	30np red orange	2.25	.65
5	A1	40np brt violet	4.00	.75
6	A1	50np brown olive	3.75	.65
7	A1	75np gray	4.00	1.25

Engr. ***Perf. 13x13½***

8	A2	1r light green	6.00	1.40
9	A2	2r black	9.00	4.75
10	A2	5r carmine rose	24.00	14.00
11	A2	10r dark blue	32.50	25.00
		Nos. 1-11 (11)	90.00	50.00

For surcharges see Nos. 15-25.

Falcon Perched on Wrist — A3

40np, Falcon facing left. 2r, Falcon facing right.

1965, Mar. 30 Photo. ***Perf. 14½***

12	A3	20np chlky blue & brn	10.00	1.75
13	A3	40np ultra & brown	12.50	2.75
14	A3	2r brt blue grn & gray brn	22.50	13.00
		Nos. 12-14 (3)	45.00	17.50

Nos. 1-11 Surcharged

a

b

c

1966, Oct. 1 Photo. ***Perf. 14½***

15	A1 (a)	5f on 5np	1.50	*2.50*
16	A1 (a)	15f on 15np	1.50	*2.10*
17	A1 (a)	20f on 20np	1.50	*2.50*
18	A1 (a)	30f on 30np	2.75	*6.00*
19	A1 (b)	40f on 40np	2.75	.90
20	A1 (b)	50f on 50np	12.00	*14.00*
21	A1 (b)	75f on 75np	12.00	*14.00*

Engr.

Perf. 13x13½

22	A2 (c)	100f on 1r	13.50	4.50
23	A2 (c)	200f on 2r	27.50	16.00
24	A2 (c)	500f on 5r	55.00	*52.50*
25	A2 (c)	1d on 10r	95.00	*110.00*
		Nos. 15-25 (11)	225.00	*225.00*

Overprint on No. 25 has "1 Dinar" on 1 line and 3 bars through old denomination.

Sheik Zaid bin Sultan al Nahayan
A4 A6

Dorcas Gazelle — A5

Designs: 5f, 15f, 20f, 35f, Crossed flags of Abu Dhabi. 200f, Falcon. 500f, 1d, Palace.

Engr.; Flags Litho.

1967, Apr. 1 ***Perf. 13x13½***

26	A4	5f dull grn & red	.20	.20
27	A4	15f dk brown & red	.30	.20
28	A4	20f dk blue & red	.30	.20
29	A4	35f purple & red	.60	.20

Engr.

30	A4	40f green	.75	.20
31	A4	50f brown	1.00	.30
32	A4	60f blue	1.25	.30
33	A4	100f car rose	2.25	.40

Litho.

34	A5	125f green & brn ol	2.75	1.25
35	A5	200f sky blue & brn	4.50	2.75
36	A5	500f org & brt pur	11.00	5.00
37	A5	1d green & vio bl	25.00	9.00
		Nos. 26-37 (12)	49.90	20.00

In 1969, the 15f was surcharged "25" in Arabic in black with a numbering machine.

1967, Aug. 6 Photo. ***Perf. 14½x14***

38	A6	40f Prussian green	1.00	.75
39	A6	50f brown	1.25	.60
40	A6	60f blue	2.25	.75
41	A6	100f carmine rose	5.50	1.40
		Nos. 38-41 (4)	10.00	3.50

Human Rights Flame and Sheik Zaid - A6a

Perf. 14½x14

1968, Apr. 1 Photo. Unwmk.

Emblem in Red and Green

42	A6a	35f peacock bl & gold	1.25	.50
43	A6a	60f dk blue & gold	2.00	.75
44	A6a	150f dk brown & gold	4.75	1.75
		Nos. 42-44 (3)	8.00	3.00

International Human Rights Year.

Sheik Zaid and Coat of Arms A7

Perf. 14x14½

1968, Aug. 6 Photo. Unwmk.

45	A7	5f multicolored	.45	.20
46	A7	10f multicolored	.70	.20
47	A7	100f multicolored	4.25	1.00
48	A7	125f multicolored	6.00	1.60
		Nos. 45-48 (4)	11.40	3.00

Accession of Sheik Zaid, 2nd anniversary.

Abu Dhabi Airport — A8

5f, Buildings under construction and earth-moving equipment. 35f, New bridge and falcon. Each stamp shows different portrait of Sheik Zaid.

Perf. 12, 12½x13 (10f)

1969, Mar. 28 Litho.

Size: 5f, 35f, 59x34mm

49	A8	5f multicolored	1.50	.25
50	A8	10f multicolored	3.00	.60
51	A8	35f multicolored	9.25	5.00
		Nos. 49-51 (3)	13.75	5.85

Issued to publicize progress made in Abu Dhabi during preceding 2 years.

Sheik Zaid and Abu Dhabi Petroleum Co. — A9

Designs: 60f, Abu Dhabi Marine Areas drilling platform and helicopter. 125f, Zakum Field separator at night. 200f, Tank farm.

1969, Aug. 6 Litho. ***Perf. 14x13½***

52	A9	35f olive grn & multi	1.00	.25
53	A9	60f yel brown & multi	1.75	.65
54	A9	125f multicolored	4.00	1.10
55	A9	200f red brown & multi	7.25	4.00
		Nos. 52-55 (4)	14.00	6.00

Accession of Sheik Zaid, 3rd anniversary.

Sheik Zaid — A10

Sheik Zaid and Stallion A11

5f, 25f, 60f, 90f, Oval frame around portrait. 150f, Gazelle and Sheik. 500f, Fort Jahili and Sheik. 1d, Grand Mosque and Sheik.

1970-71 Litho. ***Perf. 14***

56	A10	5f lt green & multi	.25	.20
57	A10	10f bister & multi	.35	.20
58	A10	25f lilac & multi	.65	.20
59	A10	35f violet & multi	.85	.30
60	A10	50f sepia & multi	1.25	.40
61	A10	60f violet & multi	1.40	.45
62	A10	70f rose red & multi	2.00	.65
63	A10	90f car rose & multi	3.00	.70
64	A11	125f multi ('71)	5.00	.90
65	A11	150f multi ('71)	6.00	2.00
66	A11	500f multi ('71)	17.50	5.00
67	A11	1d multi ('71)	30.00	9.00
		Nos. 56-67 (12)	68.25	20.00

For surcharge see No. 80.

Sheik Zaid and Mt. Fuji — A12

1970, Aug. Litho. ***Perf. 13½x13***

68	A12	25f multicolored	2.00	1.00
69	A12	35f multicolored	3.50	1.25
70	A12	60f multicolored	6.50	1.75
		Nos. 68-70 (3)	12.00	4.00

Issued to publicize EXPO '70 International Exhibition, Osaka, Japan, Mar. 15-Sept. 13.

Abu Dhabi Airport A13

Designs: 60f, Airport entrance. 150f, Aerial view of Abu Dhabi Town, vert.

Perf. 14x13½, 13½x14

1970, Sept. 22 Litho.

71	A13	25f multicolored	1.50	.50
72	A13	60f multicolored	4.00	1.25
73	A13	150f multicolored	9.00	3.00
		Nos. 71-73 (3)	14.50	4.75

Accession of Sheik Zaid, 4th anniversary.

Gamal Abdel Nasser — A14

1971, May 3 Litho. ***Perf. 14***

74	A14	25f deep rose & blk	3.50	2.00
75	A14	35f rose violet & blk	5.50	3.00

In memory of Gamal Abdel Nasser (1918-1970), President of UAR.

Scout Cars A15

Designs: 60f, Patrol boat. 125f, Armored car in desert. 150f, Meteor jet fighters.

1971, Aug. 6 Litho. ***Perf. 13***

76	A15	35f multicolored	2.50	.80
77	A15	60f multicolored	3.50	1.10
78	A15	125f multicolored	7.25	1.60
79	A15	150f multicolored	9.25	2.50
		Nos. 76-79 (4)	22.50	6.00

Accession of Sheik Zaid, 5th anniversary.

No. 60 Surcharged in Green

1971, Dec. 8 ***Perf. 14***

80	A10	5f on 50f multi	*75.00*	*50.00*

Dome of the Rock, Jerusalem — A16

Different views of Dome of the Rock.

1972, June 3 ***Perf. 13***

81	A16	35f lt violet & multi	12.50	2.50
82	A16	60f lt violet & multi	20.00	5.00
83	A16	125f lilac & multi	37.50	12.50
		Nos. 81-83 (3)	70.00	20.00

Nos. 80-83 were issued after Abu Dhabi joined the United Arab Emirates Dec. 2, 1971. Stamps of UAE replaced those of Abu Dhabi. UAE Nos. 1-12 were used only in Abu Dhabi except the 10f and 25f which were issued later in Dubai and Sharjah.

ADEN

'ä-dən

LOCATION — Southern Arabia
GOVT. — British colony and protectorate
AREA — 112,075 sq. mi.
POP. — 220,000 (est. 1964)
CAPITAL — Aden

Aden used India stamps before 1937.

In January, 1963, the colony of Aden (the port) and the sheikdoms and emirates of the Western Aden Protectorate formed the Federation of South Arabia. This did not include the Eastern Aden Protectorate with Kathiri and Qu'aiti States. Stamps of Aden, except those of Kathiri and Qu'aiti States, were replaced Apr. 1, 1965, by those of the Federation of South Arabia. See South Arabia and People's Democratic Republic of Yemen, Vol. 6.

12 Pies = 1 Anna
16 Annas = 1 Rupee
100 Cents = 1 Shilling (1951)

Catalogue values for unused stamps in this country are for Never Hinged items.

Dhow — A1

Perf. 13x11½

1937, Apr. 1 Engr. Wmk. 4

1	A1	½a lt green	3.25	1.25
2	A1	9p dark green	3.25	1.50
3	A1	1a black brown	3.25	.75
4	A1	2a red	3.25	1.75
5	A1	2½a blue	3.25	.75
6	A1	3a carmine rose	8.00	5.75
7	A1	3½a gray blue	6.75	1.75
8	A1	8a rose lilac	19.00	5.00
9	A1	1r brown	27.50	5.50
10	A1	2r orange yellow	42.50	13.50
11	A1	5r rose violet	80.00	62.50
12	A1	10r olive green	225.00	*250.00*
		Nos. 1-12 (12)	425.00	*350.00*
		Set, hinged	300.00	

Common Design Types pictured following the introduction.

Coronation Issue

Common Design Type

1937, May 12 ***Perf. 13½x14***

13	CD302	1a black brown	.65	*.75*
14	CD302	2½a blue	.85	*1.25*
15	CD302	3½a gray blue	1.25	*2.50*
		Nos. 13-15 (3)	2.75	*4.50*

Aidrus Mosque — A2

Designs: ¾a, 5r, Camel Corpsman. 1a, 2r, Aden Harbor. 1½a, 1r, Adenese dhow. 2½a, 8a, Mukalla. 3a, 14a, 10r, Capture of Aden, 1839.

1939-48 Engr. Wmk. 4 ***Perf. 12½***

16	A2	½a green	.45	*.45*
17	A2	¾a red brown ('46)	1.00	*1.00*
18	A2	1a brt lt blue	.20	.25
19	A2	1½a red	.50	*.55*
20	A2	2a dark brown ('46)	.20	.25
21	A2	2½a brt ultra	.35	.30
22	A2	3a rose car & dk brn	.55	.25
23	A2	8a orange	.50	.40
23A	A2	14a lt bl & brn blk ('45)	2.00	1.00
24	A2	1r bright green	2.00	*1.40*
25	A2	2r dp mag & bl blk ('44)	4.25	1.90
26	A2	5r dp ol & lake brn ('44)	10.50	7.25
27	A2	10r brt vio & brt sep	30.00	11.00
		Nos. 16-27 (13)	52.50	26.00

For shades, see the *Scott Classic Specialized Catalogue.*

Peace Issue

Common Design Type

Perf. 13½x14

1946, Oct. 15 Engr. Wmk. 4

28	CD303	1½a carmine	.20	*.90*
29	CD303	2½a deep blue	.20	*.40*

Return to peace at end of World War II.

Silver Wedding Issue

Common Design Types

1949, Jan. 17 Photo. ***Perf. 14x14½***

30	CD304	1½a scarlet	.40	*1.00*

Engraved; Name Typographed

Perf. 11½x11

31	CD305	10r purple	27.50	*30.00*

25th anniv. of the marriage of King George VI and Queen Elizabeth.

UPU Issue

Common Design Types
Surcharged with New Values in Annas and Rupees

Engr.; Name typo. on Nos. 33-34

1949, Oct. 10 ***Perf. 13½, 11x11½***

32	CD306	2½a on 20c dp ultra	.65	*1.25*
33	CD307	3a on 30c dp car	1.50	1.25
34	CD308	8a on 50c org	1.10	*1.25*
35	CD309	1r on 1sh blue	1.25	*2.25*
		Nos. 32-35 (4)	4.50	6.00

75th anniv. of the formation of the UPU.

Nos. 18 and 20-27 Surcharged with New Values in Black or Carmine

1951, Oct. 1 Wmk. 4 ***Perf. 12½***

36	A2	5c on 1a	.20	*.35*
37	A2	10c on 2a	.20	*.40*
38	A2	15c on 2½a	.20	*1.10*
a.		Double surcharge	*650.00*	
39	A2	20c on 3a	.25	*.35*
40	A2	30c on 8a (C)	.25	*.60*
41	A2	50c on 8a	.25	*.30*
42	A2	70c on 14a	1.50	1.40
43	A2	1sh on 1r	.40	*.25*
44	A2	2sh on 2r	6.75	2.50
45	A2	5sh on 5r	14.00	7.75
46	A2	10sh on 10r	21.00	10.00
		Nos. 36-46 (11)	45.00	25.00

Surcharge on No. 40 includes 2 bars.

Coronation Issue

Common Design Type

1953, June 2 Engr. ***Perf. 13½x13***

47	CD312	15c dark grn & black	.45	.35

Minaret — A10

Camel Transport — A11

15c, Crater. 25c, Mosque. 35c, Dhow. 50c, Map. 70c, Salt works. 1sh, Dhow building. 1sh, 25c, Colony Badge. 2sh, Aden Protectorate levy. 5sh, Crater Pass. 10sh, Tribesman. 20sh, Aden in 1572.

Perf. 12, 12x13½ ('56)

1953-59 Engr. Wmk. 4

Size: 29x23, 23x29mm

48	A10	5c grn, perf 12x13½ ('56)	.20	.20
a.		Perf. 12 ('55)	.20	.20
b.		5c bluish grn, perf 12x13½ ('56)	.50	*2.50*
49	A11	10c orange	.20	.20
a.		10c vermilion ('55)	.20	*.35*
50	A11	15c blue green	.90	.50
a.		15c grayish grn ('59)	4.25	*5.00*
51	A11	25c carmine	.60	.35
a.		25c deep rose red ('56)	2.25	1.00
52	A10	35c ultra, perf. 12	1.75	1.75
a.		35c dp bl, perf 12x13½ ('58)	3.00	2.00
b.		35c vio bl, perf 12x13½ ('59)	7.50	2.50
53	A10	50c blue, perf 12	.20	.20
a.		As "b," perf 12x13½ ('56)	.55	.20
b.		50c deep bl, perf 12 ('55)	1.00	*1.50*
54	A10	70c gray, perf 12	.20	.20
a.		As "b," perf 12x13½ ('56)	.60	.20
b.		70c grayish blk, perf 12 ('54)	1.00	.35
55	A11	1sh pur & sepia	.20	.20
55A	A11	1sh vio & black ('55)	1.10	.20
56	A10	1sh25c blk & lt blue ('56)	1.65	.50
57	A10	2sh car rose & sep	.90	.40
57A	A10	2sh car & black ('56)	4.25	.40
58	A10	5sh blue & sepia	.90	.40
58A	A10	5sh dk blue & blk ('56)	3.75	.50
59	A10	10sh olive & sepia	1.25	*6.75*
60	A10	10sh ol gray & blk ('54)	9.50	1.10

Size: 36½x27mm

Perf. 13½x13

61	A11	20sh rose vio & dk brn	4.75	*8.50*
61A	A11	20sh lt vio & blk ('57)	30.00	12.00
		Nos. 48-61A (18)	62.30	34.35

No. 60 has heavier shading on tribesman's lower garment than No. 59.

See #66-75. For overprints see #63-64.

Type of 1953

Inscribed: "Royal Visit 1954"

1954, Apr. 27 ***Perf. 12***

62	A11	1sh purple & sepia	.40	.40

Nos. 50 & 56 Overprinted in Red

No. 63

No. 64

1959, Jan. 26 ***Perf. 12, 12x13½***

63	A11	15c dark blue green	.30	.30
64	A10	1sh25c blk & light blue	.80	.80

Introduction of a revised constitution.

Freedom from Hunger Issue

Common Design Type

Perf. 14x14½

1963, June 4 Photo. Wmk. 314

65	CD314	1sh25c green	1.50	1.00

Types of 1953-57

Perf. 12x13½, 12 (#67-69, 73)

1964-65 Engr. Wmk. 314

66	A10	5c green ('65)	.50	*3.00*
67	A11	10c orange	.25	*.75*
68	A11	15c Prus green	.30	*2.75*
69	A11	25c carmine	.50	.35
70	A10	35c dk blue	2.50	2.50
71	A10	50c dull blue	1.00	.25
72	A10	70c gray	1.25	*1.50*
73	A11	1sh vio & black	8.00	2.00
74	A10	1sh25c blk & lt blue	8.00	1.90
75	A10	2sh car & blk ('65)	5.00	*20.00*
		Nos. 66-75 (10)	27.30	*35.00*

KATHIRI STATE OF SEIYUN

LOCATION — In Eastern Aden Protectorate
GOVT. — Sultanate
CAPITAL — Seiyun

The stamps of the Kathiri State of Seiyun were valid for use throughout Aden. Used copies generally bear Aden GPO or Aden Camp cancels. Examples with cancels from offices in the Eastern Protectorate command a premium.

Sultan Ja'far bin Mansur al Kathiri — A1

Seiyun — A2

Minaret at Tarim — A3

Designs: 2½a, Mosque at Seiyun. 3a, Palace at Tarim. 8a, Mosque at Seiyun, horiz. 1r, South Gate, Tarim. 2r, Kathiri House. 5r, Mosque at Tarim.

1942 Engr. Wmk. 4 ***Perf. 13¾x14***

1	A1	½a dark green	.20	*.45*
2	A1	¾a copper brown	.30	*.60*
3	A1	1a deep blue	.40	*.45*

Perf. 13x11½, 11½x13

4	A2	1½a carmine	.40	*.50*
5	A3	2a sepia brown	.30	*.75*
6	A3	2½a deep blue	.70	*1.00*
7	A2	3a dk car rose & dull brn	1.25	*1.75*
8	A2	8a orange red	.55	*.90*
9	A3	1r green	1.90	*1.50*
10	A2	2r rose vio & dk blue	6.50	*9.50*
11	A3	5r gray green & fawn	17.50	*12.50*
		Nos. 1-11 (11)	30.00	*29.90*

For surcharges see Nos. 20-27.

Nos. 4, 6 Ovptd. in Black or Red:

a

b

Perf. 13x11½, 11½x13

1946, Oct. 15 Wmk. 4

No.	Type	Description	Unused	Used
12	A2 (a)	1½a dark car rose	.20	*.50*
13	A3 (b)	2½a deep blue (R)	.20	*.25*
a.		Inverted overprint	*425.00*	
b.		Double overprint	—	

Victory of the Allied Nations in WWII.
All examples of No. 13b have the 2nd overprint almost directly over the 1st.

Silver Wedding Issue
Common Design Types

1949, Jan. 17 Photo. *Perf. 14x14½*

No.	Type	Description	Unused	Used
14	CD304	1½a scarlet	.50	*2.00*

Engraved; Name Typo.
Perf. 11½x11

No.	Type	Description	Unused	Used
15	CD305	5r green	14.00	10.00

25th anniv. of the marriage of King George VI and Queen Elizabeth.

UPU Issue
Common Design Types
Surcharged with New Values in Annas and Rupees
Engr.; Name Typo. on Nos. 17-18

1949, Oct. 10 *Perf. 13½, 11x11½*

No.	Type	Description	Unused	Used
16	CD306	2½a on 20c dp ultra	.25	*.50*
17	CD307	3a on 30c dp car	1.00	.65
18	CD308	8a on 50c orange	.55	*.75*
19	CD309	1r on 1sh blue	1.00	*1.10*
		Nos. 16-19 (4)	2.80	*3.00*

75th anniv. of the formation of the UPU.

Nos. 3 and 5-11 Surcharged with New Values in Carmine or Black
Perf. 14, 13x11½, 11½x13

1951, Oct. 1 Engr. Wmk. 4

No.	Type	Description	Unused	Used
20	A1	5c on 1a (C)	.20	.20
21	A3	10c on 2a	.30	.20
22	A3	15c on 2½a	.50	.50
23	A2	20c on 3a	.25	*.60*
24	A2	50c on 8a	.30	.25
25	A3	1sh on 1r	1.90	.75
26	A2	2sh on 2r	3.50	*15.00*
27	A3	5sh on 5r	14.50	*27.50*
		Nos. 20-27 (8)	21.45	*45.00*

Coronation Issue
Common Design Type

1953, June 2 *Perf. 13½x13*

No.	Type	Description	Unused	Used
28	CD312	15c dk green & blk	.30	*.50*

Sultan Hussein A10

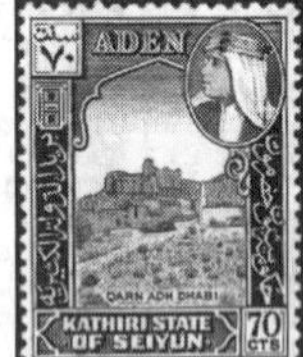

Qarn Adh Dhabi A11

15c, Seiyun scene, horiz. 25c, Minaret at Tarim. 35c, Mosque at Seiyun. 50c, Palace at Tarim, horiz. 1sh, Mosque at Seiyun, horiz. 2sh, South Gate, Tarim. 5sh, Kathiri house, horiz. 10sh, Mosque entrance, Tarim.

1954, Jan. 15 Engr. *Perf. 12½*

No.	Type	Description	Unused	Used
29	A10	5c dark brown	.20	.20
30	A10	10c deep blue	.20	.20

Perf. 13x11½, 11½x13

No.	Type	Description	Unused	Used
31	A11	15c dk blue green	.20	.20
32	A11	25c dk car rose	.20	.20
33	A11	35c deep blue	.20	.20
34	A11	50c dk car rose & dk brn	.20	.20
35	A11	1sh deep orange	.20	.20
36	A11	2sh gray green	3.25	*1.25*
37	A11	5sh vio & dk blue	5.25	*3.50*
38	A11	10sh vio & yel brn	5.25	*5.25*
		Nos. 29-38 (10)	15.15	*11.40*

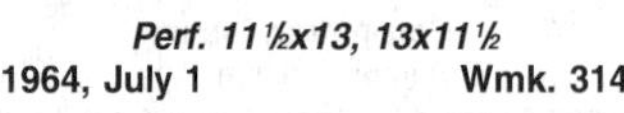
Perf. 11½x13, 13x11½

1964, July 1 Wmk. 314

Designs: 1sh25c, Seiyun, horiz. 1sh50c, View of Gheil Omer, horiz.

No.	Type	Description	Unused	Used
39	A11	70c black	1.50	1.00
40	A11	1sh25c bright green	1.50	*4.50*
41	A11	1sh50c purple	1.50	*4.50*
		Nos. 39-41 (3)	4.50	*10.00*

QUAITI STATE OF SHIHR AND MUKALLA

LOCATION — In Eastern Aden Protectorate
GOVT. — Sultanate
CAPITAL — Mukalla

The stamps of the Quaiti State of Shihr and Mukalla were valid for use throughout Aden. Used copies generally bear Aden GPO or Aden Camp cancels. Examples with cancels from offices in the Eastern Protectorate command a premium.

Sultan Sir Saleh bin Ghalib al Qu'aiti — A1

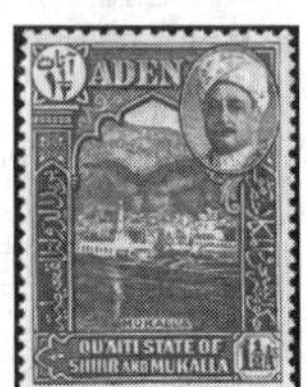

Mukalla Harbor — A2

Buildings at Shibam — A3

2a, Gateway of Shihr. 3a, Outpost of Mukalla. 8a, View of 'Einat. 1r, Governor's Castle, Du'an. 3r, Mosque in Hureidha. 5r, Meshhed.

1942 Engr. Wmk. 4 *Perf. 13¾x14*

No.	Type	Description	Unused	Used
1	A1	½a blue green	.60	.40
2	A1	¾a copper brown	1.00	.30
3	A1	1a deep blue	1.00	1.00

Perf. 13x11½, 11½x13

No.	Type	Description	Unused	Used
4	A2	1½a deep carmine	1.25	.60
5	A2	2a black brown	1.60	1.25
6	A3	2½a deep blue	.50	.30
7	A2	3a dk car rose & dl brn	.80	.75
8	A3	8a orange red	.50	.40
9	A2	1r green	3.25	2.50
10	A3	2r rose vio & dk blue	11.00	8.00
11	A3	5r gray green & fawn	13.50	10.50
		Nos. 1-11 (11)	35.00	26.00

For surcharges see Nos. 20-27.

Nos. 4, 6 Ovptd. in Black or Carmine like Kathiri Nos. 12-13

1946, Oct. 15 *Perf. 11½x13, 13x11½*

No.	Type	Description	Unused	Used
12	A2 (b)	1½a dk car rose	.20	*.50*
13	A3 (a)	2½a deep blue (C)	.20	.20

Victory of the Allied Nations in WWII.

Silver Wedding Issue
Common Design Types

1949, Jan. 17 Photo. *Perf. 14x14½*

No.	Type	Description	Unused	Used
14	CD304	1½a scarlet	.50	*2.25*

Engraved; Name Typo.
Perf. 11½x11

No.	Type	Description	Unused	Used
15	CD305	5r green	15.00	*10.50*

25th anniv. of the marriage of King George VI and Queen Elizabeth.

UPU Issue
Common Design Types
Surcharged with New Values in Annas and Rupees
Engr.; Name Typo. on Nos. 17 and 18

1949, Oct. 10 *Perf. 13½, 11x11½*

No.	Type	Description	Unused	Used
16	CD306	2½a on 20c dp ultra	.20	.20
17	CD307	3a on 30c dp car	1.00	.50
18	CD308	8a on 50c org	.80	.80
19	CD309	1r on 1sh blue	2.25	2.25
a.		Surcharge omitted	*1,250.*	
		Nos. 16-19 (4)	4.25	3.75

Nos. 3 and 5-11 Surcharged with New Values in Carmine or Black
Perf. 14, 13x11½, 11½x13

1951, Oct. 1 Engr. Wmk. 4

No.	Type	Description	Unused	Used
20	A1	5c on 1a (C)	.20	.20
21	A2	10c on 2a	.20	.20
22	A3	15c on 2½a	.20	.20
23	A2	20c on 3a	.30	.20
24	A3	50c on 8a	.20	*.40*
25	A2	1sh on 1r	.75	*.30*
26	A3	2sh on 2r	6.00	*8.75*
27	A3	5sh on 5r	9.00	*13.50*
		Nos. 20-27 (8)	16.85	*23.75*

Coronation Issue
Common Design Type

1953, June 2 Engr. *Perf. 13½x13*

No.	Type	Description	Unused	Used
28	CD312	15c dk blue & black	.60	.60

Qu'aiti State in Hadhramaut

Metal Work — A10

Fisheries A11

Designs: 10c, Mat making. 15c, Weaving. 25c, Pottery. 35c, Building. 50c, Date cultivation. 90c, Agriculture. 1sh25c, 10sh, Lime burning. 2sh, Dhow building. 5sh, Agriculture.

Perf. 11½x13, 13½x14

1955, Sept. 1 Engr. Wmk. 4

No.	Type	Description	Unused	Used
29	A10	5c greenish blue	.25	.20
30	A10	10c black	.40	.20
31	A10	15c dk green	.40	.20
32	A10	25c carmine	.35	.20
33	A10	35c ultra	.50	.20
34	A10	50c red orange	.35	.20
35	A10	90c brown	.40	.20
36	A11	1sh purple & blk	.40	.20
37	A11	1sh25c red org & blk	.45	.45
38	A11	2sh dk blue & blk	3.50	.80
39	A11	5sh green & blk	4.25	2.50
40	A11	10sh car & black	4.75	*5.50*
		Nos. 29-40 (12)	16.00	10.85

Types of 1955 with Portrait of Sultan Awadh Bin Saleh El-Qu'aiti

Design: 70c, Agriculture. Others as before.

1963, Oct. 20 Wmk. 314

No.	Type	Description	Unused	Used
41	A10	5c greenish blue	.20	*.50*
42	A10	10c black	.20	*.50*
43	A10	15c dark green	.20	*.50*
44	A10	25c carmine	.20	*.30*
45	A10	35c ultra	.30	*.65*
46	A10	50c red orange	.40	.35
47	A10	70c brown	.65	.35
48	A11	1sh purple & blk	.85	.20
49	A11	1sh25c red org & blk	1.00	*2.00*
50	A11	2sh dk blue & blk	2.50	.90
51	A11	5sh green & blk	10.00	*14.50*
52	A11	10sh car & black	12.50	*14.50*
		Nos. 41-52 (12)	29.00	*35.25*

AFARS AND ISSAS

French Territory of the

'ä-ˌfärz and ē-'säz

LOCATION — East Africa
GOVT. — French Overseas Territory
AREA — 8,880 sq. mi.
POP. — 150,000 (est. 1974)
CAPITAL — Djibouti (Jibuti)

The French overseas territory of Somali Coast was renamed the French Territory of the Afars and Issas in 1967. It became the Djibouti Republic (which see) on June 27, 1977.

100 Centimes = 1 Franc

Catalogue values for all unused stamps in this country are for Never Hinged items.

Imperforates

Most stamps of Afars and Issas exist imperforate in issued and trial colors, and also in small presentation sheets in issued colors.

Grayheaded Kingfisher — A48

1967 Engr. Unwmk. *Perf. 13*

No.	Type	Description	Unused	Used
310	A48	10fr Halcyon leucocephala	2.00	1.25
311	A48	15fr Haematopus ostralegus	2.50	1.75
312	A48	50fr Tringa nebularia	7.50	4.25
313	A48	55fr Coracias abyssinicus	10.00	5.50
314	A48	60fr Xerus rutilus, vert.	13.00	9.50
		Nos. 310-314 (5)	35.00	22.25
		Nos. 310-314,C50 (6)	51.00	29.75

Issued: 10fr, 55fr, Aug. 21; 15fr, 50fr, 60fr, Sept. 25. See No. C50.

Soccer A49

1967, Dec. 18 Engr. *Perf. 13*

No.	Type	Description	Unused	Used
315	A49	25fr shown	1.90	1.25
316	A49	30fr Basketball	2.40	1.75

Common Design Types
Pictured in section at front of book.

WHO Anniversary Issue
Common Design Type

1968, May 4 Engr. *Perf. 13*

No.	Type	Description	Unused	Used
317	CD126	15fr multicolored	1.25	1.10

20th anniv. of WHO.

Damerdjog Fortress A50

Administration Buildings: 25fr, Ali Adde. 30fr, Dorra. 40fr, Assamo.

1968, May 17 Engr. *Perf. 13*

No.	Type	Description	Unused	Used
318	A50	20fr slate, brn & emer	.90	.55
319	A50	25fr brt grn, bl & brn	1.00	.60
320	A50	30fr brn ol, brn org & sl	1.10	.80
321	A50	40fr brn ol, sl & brt grn	2.00	1.60
		Nos. 318-321 (4)	5.00	3.55

Human Rights Year Issue
Common Design Type

1968, Aug. 10 Engr. *Perf. 13*

No.	Type	Description	Unused	Used
322	CD127	10fr purple, ver & org	1.00	.65
323	CD127	70fr green, pur & org	1.75	1.10

International Human Rights Year.

Radio-television Station, Djibouti — A52

High Commission Palace, Djibouti — A53

Designs: 2fr, Justice Building. 5fr, Chamber of Deputies. 8fr, Great Mosque. 15fr, Monument of Free French Forces, vert. 40fr, Djibouti Post Office. 70fr, Residence of Gov. Léonce Lagarde at Obock. No. 332, Djibouti Harbormaster's Building. No. 333, Control tower, Djibouti Airport.

1968-70 Engr. *Perf. 13*

324	A52	1fr multicolored	.25	.20
325	A52	2fr multicolored	.25	.20
326	A52	5fr multicolored	.35	.20
327	A52	8fr multicolored	.40	.20
328	A52	15fr multicolored	3.00	2.00
329	A52	40fr multicolored	2.00	1.00
330	A53	60fr multicolored	2.25	1.50
331	A53	70fr multicolored	3.00	1.50
332	A53	85fr multicolored	4.00	2.00
333	A52	85fr multicolored	4.50	2.50
		Nos. 324-333 (10)	20.00	11.30

Issue years: 1968 - 60fr; 1969 - 1fr-15fr, 70fr, 85fr; 1970 - 40fr, 85fr.

Locust A54

Designs: 50fr, Pest control by helicopter. 55fr, Pest control by plane.

1969, Oct. 6 Engr. *Perf. 13*

334	A54	15fr brn, grn & slate	3.00	1.50
335	A54	50fr dk grn, bl & ol brn	1.60	1.10
336	A54	55fr red brn, bl & brn	2.40	1.50
		Nos. 334-336 (3)	7.00	4.10

Campaign against locusts.

ILO Issue

Common Design Type

1969, Nov. 24 Engr. *Perf. 13*

337 CD131 30fr org, gray & lil 1.40 .90

Afar Dagger in Ornamental Scabbard A56

1970, Apr. 3 Engr. *Perf. 13*

338	A56	10fr multicolored	.50	.35
339	A56	15fr multicolored	.60	.35
340	A56	20fr multicolored	.80	.55
341	A56	25fr multicolored	1.10	.55
		Nos. 338-341 (4)	3.00	1.80

See No. 364.

UPU Headquarters Issue

Common Design Type

1970, May 20 Engr. *Perf. 13*

342 CD133 25fr brn, brt grn & choc 1.10 .70

Trapshooting — A57

Motorboats A58

Designs: 50fr, Steeplechase. 55fr, Sailboat, vert. 60fr, Equestrians.

1970 Engr. *Perf. 13*

343	A57	30fr dp brn, yel grn & brt bl	1.40	.85
344	A58	48fr blue & multi	2.10	1.10
345	A58	50fr cop red, bl & pur	2.50	1.25
346	A58	55fr red brn, bl & ol	2.25	1.25
347	A58	60fr ol, blk & red brn	3.25	1.75
		Nos. 343-347 (5)	11.50	6.20

Issued: 30fr, 6/5; 48fr, 10/9; 50fr, 60fr, 11/6.

Automatic Ferry, Tadjourah A59

1970, Nov. 25

348 A59 48fr blue, brn & grn 2.25 1.40

Volcanic Geode A60

Diabase and Chrysolite A61

10fr, Doleritic basalt. 15fr, Olivine basalt.

1971 Photo. *Perf. 13*

349	A61	10fr black & multi	1.75	.75
350	A61	15fr black & multi	2.50	.75
351	A60	25fr black, crim & brn	5.00	2.25
352	A61	40fr black & multi	7.50	3.50
		Nos. 349-352 (4)	16.75	7.25

Issued: 10fr, 11/22; 15fr, 10/8; 25fr, 4/26; 40fr, 1/25.

A62 A63

1971, July 1 Photo. *Perf. 12x12½*

353	A62	4fr Manta birostris	1.25	.50
354	A62	5fr Coryphaena hippurus	1.25	.50
355	A62	9fr Pristis pectinatus	2.50	1.50
		Nos. 353-355 (3)	5.00	2.50

See No. C60.

De Gaulle Issue

Common Design Type

Designs: 60fr, Gen. Charles de Gaulle, 1940. 85fr, Pres. de Gaulle, 1970.

1971, Nov. 9 Engr. *Perf. 13*

356	CD134	60fr dk vio bl & blk	2.50	1.50
357	CD134	85fr dk vio bl & blk	3.00	1.50

1972, Mar. 8 Photo. *Perf. 12½x13*

Shells: 4fr, Strawberry Top. 9fr, Cypraea pantherina. 20fr, Bull-mouth helmet. 50fr, Ethiopian volute.

358	A63	4fr olive & multi	1.25	.40
359	A63	9fr dk blue & multi	1.50	.60
360	A63	20fr dp green & multi	3.75	1.00
361	A63	50fr dp claret & multi	7.50	1.50
		Nos. 358-361 (4)	14.00	3.50

Shepherd — A64

Design: 10fr, Dromedary breeding.

1973, Apr. 11 Photo. *Perf. 13*

362	A64	9fr blue & multi	1.00	.30
363	A64	10fr blue & multi	1.00	.30

Afar Dagger — A65

1974, Jan. 29 Engr. *Perf. 13*

364 A65 30fr slate grn & dk brn 1.10 .65

For surcharge see No. 379.

Flamingos, Lake Abbe — A66

Flamingos and different views of Lake Abbe.

1974, Feb. 22 Photo. *Perf. 13*

370	A66	5fr multicolored	1.25	.25
371	A66	15fr multicolored	.60	.50
372	A66	50fr multicolored	1.90	1.25
		Nos. 370-372 (3)	3.75	2.00

Soccer Ball — A67

1974, May 24 Engr. *Perf. 13*

373 A67 25fr black & emerald 1.25 .80

World Cup Soccer Championship, Munich, June 13-July 7.

Letters Around UPU Emblem — A68

Oleo Chrysophylla A69

1974, Oct. 9 Engr. *Perf. 13*

374	A68	20fr multicolored	1.00	.50
375	A68	100fr multicolored	2.50	2.00

Centenary of Universal Postal Union.

1974, Nov. 22 Photo.

376	A69	10fr shown	.75	.40
377	A69	15fr *Ficus species*	1.00	.60
378	A69	20fr *Solanum adoense*	2.25	1.00
		Nos. 376-378 (3)	4.00	2.00

Day Primary Forest.

No. 364 Surcharged with New Value and Two Bars in Red

1975, Jan. 1 Engr. *Perf. 13*

379 A65 40fr on 30fr multi 1.50 .90

Treasury — A70

Design: 25fr, Government buildings.

1975, Jan. 7 Engr. *Perf. 13*

380	A70	8fr blue, gray & red	.55	.35
381	A70	25fr red, blue & indigo	1.25	.75

Darioconus Textile — A71

Sea Shells: No. 383, Murex palmarosa. 10fr, Conus sumatrensis. 15fr, Cypraea pulchra. No. 386, 45fr, Murex scolopax. No. 387, Cypraea exhusta. 40fr, Ranella spinosa. 55fr, Cypraea erythraensis. 60fr, Conus taeniatus.

1975-76 Engr. *Perf. 13*

382	A71	5fr blue grn & brn	1.25	.60
383	A71	5fr blue & multi ('76)	1.50	.60
384	A71	10fr lilac, blk & brn	1.25	.60
385	A71	15fr blue, ind & brn	2.25	1.00
386	A71	20fr purple & lt brn	3.00	2.00
387	A71	20fr brt grn & multi ('76)	1.50	.60
388	A71	40fr green & brown	7.00	2.50
389	A71	45fr green, bl & bister	6.00	2.00
390	A71	55fr turq & multi ('76)	4.00	2.25
391	A71	60fr buff & sepia ('76)	7.00	3.00
		Nos. 382-391 (10)	34.75	15.15

Hypolimnas Misippus A72

Butterflies: 40fr, Papilio nireus. 50fr, Acraea anemosa. 65fr, Holocerina smilax menieri. 70fr, Papilio demodocus. No. 397, Papilio dardanus. No. 398, Balachowsky gonimbrasca. 150fr, Vanessa cardui.

1975-76 Photo. *Perf. 13*

392 A72 25fr emerald & multi 3.50 1.00
393 A72 40fr yellow & multi 3.50 1.00
394 A72 50fr ultra & multi ('76) 3.00 1.50
395 A72 65fr ol & multi ('76) 4.50 1.50
396 A72 70fr violet & multi 5.75 2.00
397 A72 100fr blue & multi 6.75 2.00
398 A72 100fr Prus bl & multi ('76) 6.75 2.00
399 A72 150fr grn & multi ('76) 6.25 2.00
Nos. 392-399 (8) 40.00 13.00

A73

Perf. 13x12½, 12½x13

1975-76 Photo.

400 A73 10fr Hyaena hyaena .55 .35
401 A73 15fr Cercopithecus aethiops 1.10 .50
402 A73 15fr Equus asinus somalicus 1.00 .50
403 A73 30fr Dorcatragus megalotis 1.60 .90
404 A73 50fr Ichneumia albicauda 2.25 1.00
405 A73 60fr Hystrix galasta 2.75 1.25
406 A73 70fr Ictonyx striatus 4.00 1.75
407 A73 200fr Orycteropus afar 6.75 3.75
Nos. 400-407 (8) 20.00 10.00

Nos. 401-402, 405 are vert.
Issued: 50fr, 60fr, 70fr, 2/21; No. 401, 200fr, 10/24; 10fr, No. 402, 30fr, 2/4/76.

A74

A75

1975-76 Photo. *Perf. 12½x13*

413 A74 20fr Vidua macroura 1.25 .80
414 A74 25fr Psittacula krameri 1.25 .40
415 A74 50fr Cinnyris venustus 2.50 1.50
416 A74 60fr Ardea goliath 4.00 1.75
417 A74 100fr Scopus umbretta 5.50 2.50
418 A74 100fr Oena capensis 4.00 1.75
419 A74 300fr Platalea alba 10.00 4.00
Nos. 413-419 (7) 28.50 12.70

Issued: 300fr, 6/15/76; 25fr, No. 418, 10/13/76; others 11/21 and 12/19/75.

1975, Dec. 19 Engr. *Perf. 13*

421 A75 20fr Palms 1.00 .40

Satellite and Alexander Graham Bell — A76

1976, Mar. 10 Engr. *Perf. 13*

422 A76 200fr dp bl, org & sl grn 4.50 2.25

Centenary of the first telephone call by Alexander Graham Bell, Mar. 10, 1876.

Basketball A77

1976, July 7 Litho. *Perf. 12½*

423 A77 10fr shown .45 .20
424 A77 15fr Bicycling .60 .30
425 A77 40fr Soccer 1.10 .50
426 A77 60fr Running 1.40 .80
Nos. 423-426 (4) 3.55 1.80

21st Olympic Games, Montreal, Canada, July 17-Aug. 1.

Pterois Radiata — A78

1976, Aug. 10 Photo. *Perf. 13x13½*

428 A78 45fr blue & multi 3.50 1.00

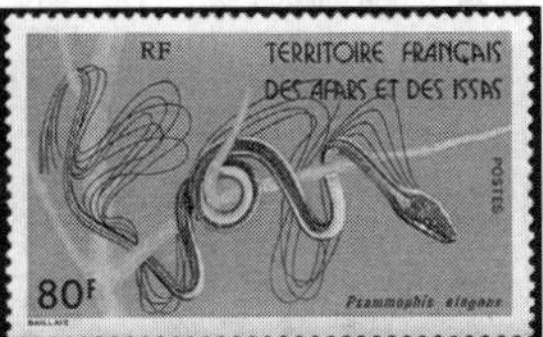

Psammophis Elegans — A79

Design: 70fr, Naja nigricollis, vert.

Perf. 13x13½, 13½x13

1976, Sept. 27 Photo.

430 A79 70fr ocher & multi 2.75 1.50
431 A79 80fr emerald & multi 3.25 1.75

Motorcyclist A80

1977, Jan. 27 Litho. *Perf. 12x12½*

432 A80 200fr multicolored 5.50 2.75

Moto-Cross motorcycle race.

Conus Betulinus — A81

Sea Shells: 5fr, Cyprea tigris. 70fr, Conus striatus. 85fr, Cyprea mauritiana.

1977 Engr. *Perf. 13*

433 A81 5fr multicolored 1.50 .50
434 A81 30fr multicolored 1.50 .60
435 A81 70fr multicolored 6.00 1.75
436 A81 85fr multicolored 6.00 2.00
Nos. 433-436 (4) 15.00 4.85

Gaterin Gaterinus A82

1977, Apr. 15 Photo. *Perf. 13x12½*

437 A82 15fr shown 1.10 .40
438 A82 65fr Barracudas 4.00 1.10

AIR POST STAMPS

AP16

AP17

Unwmk.

1967, Aug. 21 Engr. *Perf. 13*

C50 AP16 200fr Aquila rapax belisarius 16.00 7.50

1968 Engr. *Perf. 13*

C51 AP17 48fr Parachutists 2.75 1.50
C52 AP17 85fr Water skier & skin diver 3.75 2.50

Issue dates: 48fr, Jan. 5; 85fr, Mar. 15.

Aerial Map of the Territory — AP18

1968, Nov. 15 Engr. *Perf. 13*

C53 AP18 500fr bl, dk brn & ocher 22.50 7.00

Buildings Type of Regular Issue

100fr, Cathedral. 200fr, Sayed Hassan Mosque.

1969 Engr. *Perf. 13*

C54 A53 100fr multi, vert. 3.50 1.50
C55 A53 200fr multi, vert. 5.50 3.00

Issue dates: 100fr, Apr. 4; 200fr, May 8.

Concorde Issue

Common Design Type

1969, Apr. 17

C56 CD129 100fr org red & ol 18.00 10.00

Arta Ionospheric Station — AP19

Japanese Sword Guard, Fish Design — AP20

1970, May 8 Engr. *Perf. 13*

C57 AP19 70fr multicolored 3.00 2.00

Gold embossed

1970, Oct. 26 *Perf. 12½*

200fr, Japanese sword guard, horse design.

C58 AP20 100fr multicolored 7.50 5.00
C59 AP20 200fr multicolored 9.50 5.50

EXPO '70 International Exposition, Osaka, Japan, Mar. 15-Sept. 13.

Scarus vetula — AP21

1971, July 1 Photo. *Perf. 12½*

C60 AP21 30fr black & multi 4.00 2.50

Djibouti Harbor — AP22

1972, Feb. 3

C61 AP22 100fr blue & multi 4.00 2.25

New Djibouti harbor.

AP23

AP24

1972 Photo. *Perf. 12½x13*

C62 AP23	30fr Pterocles lichtensteini	2.50	1.40
C63 AP23	49fr Uppupa epops	4.50	2.50
C64 AP23	66fr Capella media	5.75	3.25
C65 AP23	500fr Francolinus ochropectus	24.00	9.00
	Nos. C62-C65 (4)	36.75	16.15

Issue dates: #C65, Nov. 3; others Apr. 21.

1972, June 8 Engr. *Perf. 13*

Olympic Rings and: 5fr, Running. 10fr, Basketball. 55fr, Swimming, horiz. 60fr, Olympic torch and Greek frieze, horiz.

C66 AP24	5fr multicolored	.45	.25
C67 AP24	10fr multicolored	.55	.40
C68 AP24	55fr multicolored	1.75	1.10
C69 AP24	60fr multicolored	2.25	1.25
	Nos. C66-C69 (4)	5.00	3.00

20th Olympic Games, Munich, 8/26-9/11.

Louis Pasteur — AP25

100fr, Albert Calmette and C. Guérin.

1972, Oct. 5 Engr. *Perf. 13*

C70 AP25	20fr multicolored	1.50	.50
C71 AP25	100fr multicolored	4.00	2.50

Pasteur, Calmette, Guerin, chemists and bacteriologists, benefactors of mankind.

Map and Views of Territory — AP26

200fr, Woman and Mosque of Djibouti, vert.

1973, Jan. 15 Photo. *Perf. 13*

C72 AP26	30fr brown & multi	4.50	3.50
C73 AP26	200fr multicolored	8.50	6.00

Visit of Pres. Georges Pompidou of France, Jan. 15-17.

AP27

1973, Feb. 26 Photo. *Perf. 13x12½*

C74 AP27	30fr Oryx beisa	2.00	1.00
C75 AP27	50fr Madogua saltiana	2.75	1.50
C76 AP27	66fr Felis caracal	3.75	2.00
	Nos. C74-C76 (3)	8.50	4.50

See Nos. C94-C96.

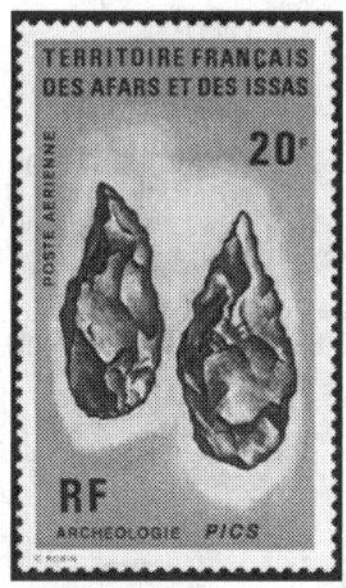

Celts — AP28

Various pre-historic flint tools. 40fr, 60fr, horiz.

1973 *Perf. 13*

C77 AP28	20fr yel grn, blk & brn	2.25	1.50
C78 AP28	40fr yellow & multi	2.75	2.00
C79 AP28	49fr lilac & multi	5.00	3.00
C80 AP28	60fr blue & multi	3.75	2.50
	Nos. C77-C80 (4)	13.75	9.00

Issued: 20fr, 49fr, 3/16; 40fr, 60fr, 9/7.

AP29

1973, Mar. 16

C81 AP29	40fr Octopus macropus	3.00	1.00
C82 AP29	60fr Halicore dugong	5.00	2.50

AP30

AP31

Copernicus: 8fr, Nicolaus Copernicus, Polish astronomer. 9fr, William C. Roentgen, physicist, X-ray discoverer. No. C85, Edward Jenner, physician, discoverer of vaccination. No. C86, Marie Curie, discoverer of radium and polonium. 49fr, Robert Koch, physician and bacteriologist. 50fr, Clement Ader (1841-1925), French aviation pioneer. 55fr, Guglielmo Marconi, Italian electrical engineer, inventor. 85fr, Moliere, French playwright. 100fr, Henri Farman (1874-1937), French aviation pioneer. 150fr, Andre-Marie Ampere (1775-1836), French physicist. 250fr, Michelangelo Buonarroti (1475-1564), Italian sculptor, painter and architect.

1973-75 Engr. *Perf. 13*

C83 AP30	8fr multicolored	1.00	.30
C84 AP30	9fr multicolored	1.00	.40
C85 AP30	10fr multicolored	1.25	.50
C86 AP30	10fr multicolored	.75	.40
C87 AP30	49fr multicolored	3.25	1.60
C88 AP30	50fr multicolored	2.50	1.25
C89 AP30	55fr multicolored	2.25	1.00
C90 AP30	85fr multicolored	4.00	1.75
C91 AP30	100fr multicolored	4.00	2.00
C92 AP30	150fr multicolored	4.00	2.00
C93 AP30	250fr multicolored	7.50	3.50
	Nos. C83-C93 (11)	31.50	14.70

Issued: 8fr, 85fr, 5/9/73; 9fr, #C85, 49fr, 10/12/73; 100fr, 1/29/74; 55fr, 3/22/74; #C86, 8/23/74; 150fr, 7/24/75; 250fr, 6/26/75; 50fr, 9/25/75.

Perf. 12½x13, 13x12½

1973, Dec. 12 Photo.

C94 AP31	20fr Papio anubis	1.50	.60
C95 AP31	50fr Genetta tigrina, horiz.	3.00	.90
C96 AP31	66fr Lapus habessinicus	4.25	1.50
	Nos. C94-C96 (3)	8.75	3.00

Spearfishing — AP32

1974, Apr. 14 Engr. *Perf. 13*

C97 AP32	200fr multicolored	7.50	4.50

No. C97 was prepared for release in Nov. 1972, for the 3rd Underwater Spearfishing Contest in the Red Sea. Dates were obliterated with a rectangle and the stamp was not issued without this obliteration.

Rock Carvings, Balho — AP33

1974, Apr. 26

C98 AP33	200fr carmine & slate	7.00	5.00

Lake Assal — AP34

Designs (Lake Assal): 50fr, Rock formations on shore. 85fr, Crystallized wood.

1974, Oct. 25 Photo. *Perf. 13*

C99 AP34	49fr multicolored	1.50	.75
C100 AP34	50fr multicolored	2.00	1.00
C101 AP34	85fr multicolored	4.00	2.25
	Nos. C99-C101 (3)	7.50	4.00

Columba Guinea — AP35

1975, May 23 Photo. *Perf. 13*

C102 AP35	500fr multicolored	18.00	6.50

Djibouti Airport — AP36

1977, Mar. 1 Litho. *Perf. 12*

C103 AP36	500fr multicolored	11.00	7.50

Opening of new Djibouti Airport.

Thomas A. Edison and Phonograph — AP37

Design: 75fr, Alexander Volta, electric train, lines and light bulb.

1977, May 5 Engr. *Perf. 13*

C104 AP37	55fr multicolored	3.25	1.50
C105 AP37	75fr multicolored	4.75	2.50

Famous inventors: Thomas Alva Edison and Alexander Volta (1745-1827).

POSTAGE DUE STAMPS

Nomad's Milk Jug — D3

Perf. 14x13

1969, Dec. 15 Engr. Unwmk.

J49 D3	1fr red brn, red lil & sl	.20	.20
J50 D3	2fr red brn, emer & sl	.20	.20
J51 D3	5fr red brn, bl & slate	.30	.30
J52 D3	10fr red brn, brn & slate	.80	.80
	Nos. J49-J52 (4)	1.50	1.50

AFGHANISTAN

af-ˈga-nə-ˌstan

LOCATION — Central Asia, bounded by Iran, Turkmenistan, Uzbekistan, Tajikistan, Pakistan, and China
GOVT. — Republic
AREA — 251,773 sq. mi.
POP. — 23,500,000 (1995 est.)
CAPITAL — Kabul

Afghanistan changed from a constitutional monarchy to a republic in July 1973.

12 Shahi = 6 Sanar = 3 Abasi =
2 Krans = 1 Rupee Kabuli
60 Paisas = 1 Rupee (1921)
100 Pouls = 1 Rupee Afghani (1927)

Catalogue values for unused stamps in this country are for Never Hinged items, beginning with Scott 364 in the regular postage section, Scott B1 in the semi-postal section, Scott C7 in the airpost section, Scott O8 in officials section, and Scott RA6 in the postal tax section.

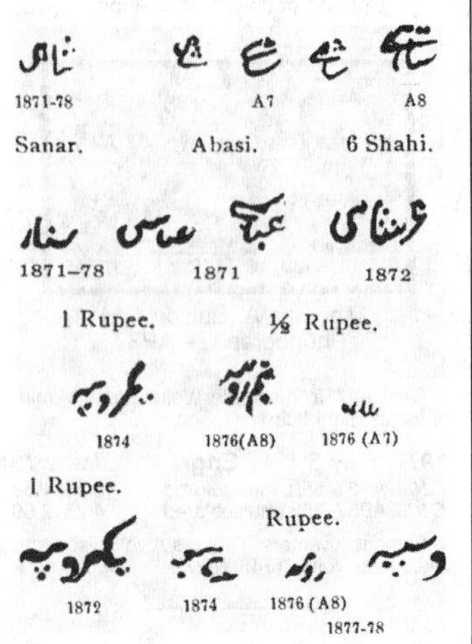

From 1871 to 1892 and 1898 the Moslem year date appears on the stamp. Numerals as follows:

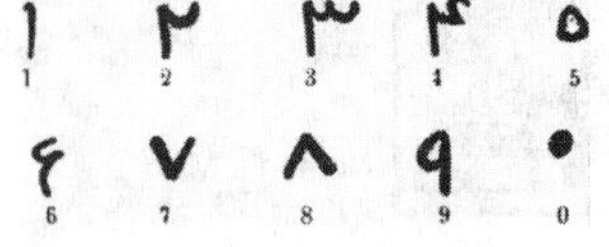

Until 1891 cancellation consisted of cutting or tearing a piece from the stamps. Such copies should not be considered as damaged.

Values are for cut square examples of good color. Cut to shape or faded copies sell for much less, particularly Nos. 2-10.

Nos. 2-108 are on laid paper of varying thickness except where wove is noted.

Until 1907 all stamps were issued ungummed.

The tiger's head on types A2 to A11 symbolizes the name of the contemporary amir, Sher (Tiger) Ali.

Kingdom of Kabul

Tiger's Head A2

(Both circles dotted)

1871 Unwmk. Litho. *Imperf.*

Dated "1288"

2	A2	1sh black	125.00	25.00
3	A2	1sa black	85.00	32.50
4	A2	1ab black	40.00	35.00
		Nos. 2-4 (3)	250.00	92.50

Thirty varieties of the shahi, 10 of the sanar and 5 of the abasi.

Similar designs without the tiger's head in the center are revenues.

A3

(Outer circle dotted)

Dated "1288"

5	A3	1sh black	175.00	35.00
6	A3	1sa black	75.00	27.50
7	A3	1ab black	37.50	22.50
		Nos. 5-7 (3)	287.50	85.00

Five varieties of each.

A4

1872

Toned Wove Paper

Dated "1289"

8	A4	6sh violet	*850.*	*750.*
9	A4	1rup violet	*1,300.*	*1,100.*

Two varieties of each. Date varies in location. Printed in sheets of 4 (2x2) containing two of each denomination.

Most used copies are smeared with a greasy ink cancel.

A4a

1873

White Laid Paper

Dated "1290"

10	A4a	1sh black	12.00	4.50
a.		Corner ornament missing	*450.00*	*375.00*
b.		Corner ornament retouched	*60.00*	*25.00*

15 varieties. Nos. 10a, 10b are the sixth stamp on the sheet.

A5

1873

11	A5	1sh black	2.25	2.00
11A	A5	1sh violet	*500.00*	

Sixty varieties of each.

1874

Dated "1291"

12	A5	1ab black	40.00	25.00
13	A5	½rup black	20.00	17.50
14	A5	1rup black	22.50	20.00
		Nos. 12-14 (3)	82.50	62.50

Five varieties of each.

Nos. 12-14 were printed on the same sheet. Se-tenant varieties exist.

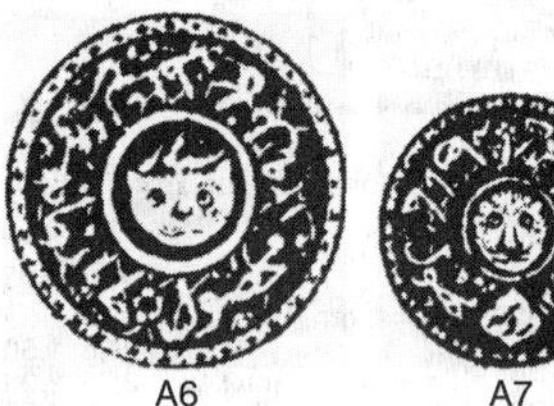

A6 A7

1875

Dated "1292"

15	A6	1sa black	*300.00*	*250.00*
a.		Wide outer circle	*600.00*	
16	A6	1ab black	350.00	300.00
17	A6	1sa brown violet	22.50	22.50
a.		Wide outer circle	110.00	
18	A6	1ab brown violet	40.00	25.00

Ten varieties of the sanar, five of the abasi.

Nos. 15-16 and 17-18 were printed in the same sheets. Se-tenant pairs exist.

1876

Dated "1293"

19	A7	1sh black	300.00	150.00
20	A7	1sa black	375.00	200.00
21	A7	1ab black	600.00	325.00
22	A7	½rup black	375.00	200.00
23	A7	1rup black	550.00	200.00
24	A7	1sh violet	375.00	200.00
25	A7	1sa violet	350.00	200.00
26	A7	1ab violet	425.00	200.00
27	A7	½rup violet	90.00	55.00
28	A7	1rup violet	90.00	75.00

12 varieties of the shahi and 3 each of the other values.

A8

1876

Dated "1293"

29	A8	1sh gray	5.00	4.00
30	A8	1sa gray	7.50	4.00
31	A8	1ab gray	15.00	7.50
32	A8	½rup gray	17.50	10.00
33	A8	1rup gray	22.50	10.00
34	A8	1sh olive blk	125.00	
35	A8	1sa olive blk	175.00	
36	A8	1ab olive blk	350.00	
37	A8	½rup olive blk	250.00	
38	A8	1rup olive blk	275.00	
39	A8	1sh green	22.50	3.75
40	A8	1sa green	35.00	15.00
41	A8	1ab green	50.00	37.50
42	A8	½rup green	100.00	40.00
43	A8	1rup green	100.00	80.00
44	A8	1sh ocher	22.50	7.50
45	A8	1sa ocher	35.00	15.00
46	A8	1ab ocher	60.00	27.50
47	A8	½rup ocher	75.00	60.00
48	A8	1rup ocher	125.00	110.00
49	A8	1sh violet	22.50	5.50
50	A8	1sa violet	22.50	7.50
51	A8	1ab violet	35.00	10.00
52	A8	½rup violet	60.00	22.50
53	A8	1rup violet	75.00	35.00

24 varieties of the shahi, 4 of which show denomination written:

12 varieties of the sanar, 6 of the abasi and 3 each of the ½ rupee and rupee.

A9

1877

Dated "1294"

54	A9	1sh gray	3.50	2.25
55	A9	1sa gray	6.00	3.00
56	A9	1ab gray	9.00	6.00
57	A9	½rup gray	12.00	12.00
58	A9	1rup gray	12.00	12.00
59	A9	1sh black	10.00	
60	A9	1sa black	17.50	
61	A9	1ab black	42.50	
62	A9	½rup black	45.00	
63	A9	1rup black	45.00	
64	A9	1sh green	4.50	3.50
a.		Wove paper	12.00	
65	A9	1sa green	7.50	3.50
a.		Wove paper	16.00	12.00
66	A9	1ab green	10.00	10.00
a.		Wove paper	27.50	
67	A9	½rup green	14.00	14.00
a.		Wove paper	30.00	30.00
68	A9	1rup green	14.00	14.00
a.		Wove paper	30.00	30.00
69	A9	1sh ocher	3.50	2.00
70	A9	1sa ocher	10.00	3.50
71	A9	1ab ocher	17.50	16.00
72	A9	½rup ocher	30.00	30.00
73	A9	1rup ocher	30.00	30.00
74	A9	1sh violet	3.75	2.00
75	A9	1sa violet	7.50	2.75
76	A9	1ab violet	11.00	7.50
77	A9	½rup violet	17.50	14.00
78	A9	1rup violet	17.50	14.00

25 varieties of the shahi, 8 of the sanar, 3 of the abasi and 2 each of the ½ rupee and rupee.

A10 A11

1878

Dated "1295"

79	A10	1sh gray	1.50	1.50
80	A10	1sa gray	1.75	1.75
81	A10	1ab gray	3.75	3.75
82	A10	½rup gray	10.00	7.50
83	A10	1rup gray	10.00	7.50
84	A10	1sh black	3.00	
85	A10	1sa black	3.00	
86	A10	1ab black	10.00	
87	A10	½rup black	20.00	
88	A10	1rup black	20.00	
89	A10	1sh green	21.00	20.00
90	A10	1sa green	3.00	3.00
91	A10	1ab green	11.00	10.00
92	A10	½rup green	21.00	17.50
93	A10	1rup green	21.00	17.50
94	A10	1sh ocher	10.00	3.00
95	A10	1sa ocher	3.00	2.25
96	A10	1ab ocher	11.00	10.00
97	A10	½rup ocher	21.00	21.00
98	A10	1rup ocher	16.00	16.00
99	A10	1sh violet	1.75	1.75
100	A10	1sa violet	1.75	1.75
101	A10	1ab violet	5.50	5.50
102	A10	½rup violet	21.00	17.50
103	A10	1rup violet	21.00	17.50
104	A11	1sh gray	2.00	1.75
105	A11	1sh black	*90.00*	
106	A11	1sh green	1.75	1.75
107	A11	1sh ocher	1.40	1.40
108	A11	1sh violet	2.00	1.75

40 varieties of the shahi, 30 of the sanar, 6 of the abasi and 2 each of the ½ rupee and 1 rupee.

The 1876, 1877 and 1878 issues were printed in separate colors for each main post office on the Peshawar-Kabul-Khulm (Tashkurghan) postal route. Some specialists consider the black printings to be proofs or trial colors.

There are many shades of these colors.

1ab, Type I (26mm) — A12

1ab, Type II (28mm) — A13

A14

A15

Dated "1298", numerals scattered through design

Handstamped, in watercolor

1881-90

Thin White Laid Batonne Paper

109	A12	1ab violet	1.75	1.10
109A	A13	1ab violet	3.50	2.50
110	A12	1ab black brn	3.50	1.75
111	A12	1ab rose	2.00	2.00
b.		Se-tenant with No. 111A	16.00	
111A	A13	1ab rose	2.50	2.00
112	A14	2ab violet	1.75	1.50
113	A14	2ab black brn	5.00	4.00
114	A14	2ab rose	3.00	3.00
115	A15	1rup violet	2.50	1.50
116	A15	1rup black brn	6.50	6.50
117	A15	1rup rose	3.00	3.00

Thin White Wove Batonne Paper

118	A12	1ab violet	6.50	4.00
119	A12	1ab vermilion	4.25	
120	A12	1ab rose		
121	A14	2ab violet		
122	A14	2ab vermilion	5.00	
122A	A14	2ab black brn		
123	A15	1rup violet	8.25	
124	A15	1rup vermilion	6.50	
125	A15	1rup black brn	8.25	

Thin White Laid Batonne Paper

126	A12	1ab brown org	2.50	2.50
126A	A13	1ab brn org (II)	3.50	3.50
127	A12	1ab carmine lake	2.50	2.50
a.		Laid paper		
128	A14	2ab brown org	2.50	2.50
129	A14	2ab carmine lake	3.00	3.00
130	A15	1rup brown org	10.00	10.00
131	A15	1rup car lake	4.25	4.25

Yellowish Laid Batonne Paper

132	A12	1ab purple		3.50
133	A12	1ab red	6.50	3.50

1884

Colored Wove Paper

133A	A13	1ab purple, *yel* (II)	17.50	17.50
134	A12	1ab purple, *grn*	20.00	
135	A12	1ab purple, *blue*	32.50	21.00
136	A12	1ab red, *grn*	37.50	
137	A12	1ab red, *yel*	1.75	
139	A12	1ab red, *rose*	6.00	
140	A14	2ab red, *yel*	6.00	
142	A14	2ab red, *rose*	5.50	
143	A15	1rup red, *yel*	6.50	6.50
145	A15	1rup red, *rose*	7.00	7.00

Thin Colored Ribbed Paper

146	A14	2ab red, *yellow*	3.00	
147	A15	1rup red, *yellow*	8.25	
148	A12	1ab lake, *lilac*	4.00	
149	A14	2ab lake, *lilac*	5.00	
150	A15	1rup lake, *lilac*	4.00	
151	A12	1ab lake, *green*	2.00	
152	A14	2ab lake, *green*	4.00	
153	A15	1rup lake, *green*	4.00	

1886-88

Colored Wove Paper

155	A12	1ab black, *magenta*	27.50	
156	A12	1ab claret brn, *org*	20.00	
156A	A12	1ab red, *org*	2.00	
156B	A14	2ab red, *org*	4.75	
156C	A15	1rup red, *org*	3.50	

Laid Batonné Paper

157	A12	1ab black, *lavender*	2.75	
158	A12	1ab cl brn, *grn*	6.50	
159	A12	1ab black, *pink*	17.50	
160	A14	2ab black, *pink*	35.00	
161	A15	1rup black, *pink*	20.00	

Laid Paper

162	A12	1ab black, *pink*	6.50	
163	A14	2ab black, *pink*	6.50	
164	A15	1rup black, *pink*	6.50	
165	A12	1ab brown, *yel*	6.50	
166	A14	2ab brown, *yel*	6.50	
167	A15	1rup brown, *yel*	6.50	
168	A12	1ab blue, *grn*	6.50	
169	A14	2ab blue, *grn*	6.50	
170	A15	1rup blue, *grn*	6.50	

1891

Colored Wove Paper

175	A12	1ab green, *rose*	22.50	
176	A15	1rup pur, *grn batonne*	22.50	

Nos. 109-176 fall into three categories:

1. Those regularly issued and in normal postal use from 1881 on, handstamped on thin white laid or wove paper in strip sheets containing 12 or more impressions of the same denomination arranged in two irregular rows, with the impressions often touching or overlappng.
2. The 1884 postal issues provisionally printed on smooth or ribbed colored wove paper as needed to supplement low stocks of the normal white paper stamps.
3. The "special" printings made in a range of colors on several types of laid or wove colored papers, most of which were never used for normal printings. These were produced periodically from 1886 to 1891 to meet philatelic demands. Although nominally valid for postage, most of the special printings were exported directly to fill dealers' orders, and few were ever postally used. Many of the sheets contained all three denominations with impressions separated by ruled lines. Sometimes different colors were used, so se-tenant multiples of denomination or color exist. Many combinations of stamp and paper colors exist besides those listed.

Various shades of each color exist.

Type A12 is known dated "1297."

Counterfeits, lithographed or typographed, are plentiful.

Kingdom of Afghanistan

A16

A17

A18

Dated "1309"

1891 Pelure Paper *Litho.*

177	A16	1ab slate blue	.85	.85
a.		Tete beche pair	14.00	
178	A17	2ab slate blue	6.00	5.00
179	A18	1rup slate blue	12.50	10.00
		Nos. 177-179 (3)	19.35	15.85

Revenue stamps of similar design exist in various colors.

Nos. 177-179 were printed in panes on the same sheet, so se-tenant gutter pairs exist. Examples in black or red are proofs.

A Mosque Gate and Crossed Cannons (National Seal) — A19

Dated "1310" in Upper Right Corner

1892

Flimsy Wove Paper

180	A19	1ab black, *green*	2.00	1.60
181	A19	1ab black, *orange*	2.50	2.50
182	A19	1ab black, *yellow*	2.00	1.60
183	A19	1ab black, *pink*	2.50	1.60
184	A19	1ab black, *lil rose*	2.50	2.50
185	A19	1ab black, *blue*	4.25	3.50
186	A19	1ab black, *salmon*	2.50	2.00
187	A19	1ab black, *magenta*	2.50	2.50
188	A19	1ab black, *violet*	2.50	2.50
188A	A19	1ab black, *scarlet*	2.50	1.75

Many shades exist.

A20

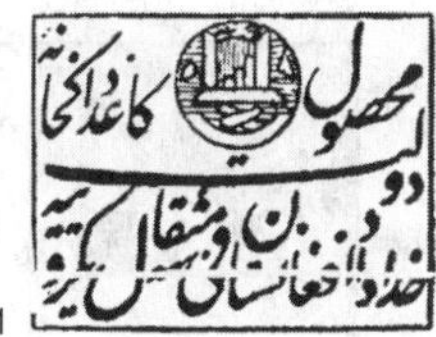
A21

Undated

1894

Flimsy Wove Paper

189	A20	2ab black, *green*	6.50	6.50
190	A21	1rup black, *green*	10.00	10.00

24 varieties of the 2 abasi and 12 varieties of the rupee.

Nos. 189-190 and F3 were printed se-tenant in the same sheet. Pairs exist.

A21a

Dated "1316"

1898

Flimsy Wove Paper

191	A21a	2ab black, *pink*	2.50	
192	A21a	2ab black, *magenta*	2.50	
193	A21a	2ab black, *yellow*	1.10	
193A	A21a	2ab black, *salmon*	3.00	
194	A21a	2ab black, *green*	1.40	
195	A21a	2ab black, *purple*	1.75	
195A	A21a	2ab black, *blue*	17.50	
		Nos. 191-195A (7)	29.75	

Nos. 191-195A were not regularly issued. Genuinely used copies are scarce. No. 195A was found in remainder stocks and probably was never released.

A22

A23

A24

1907 Engr. *Imperf.*

Medium Wove Paper

196	A22	1ab blue green	15.00	5.50
a.		1ab emerald	17.00	5.00
b.		Double impression	*125.00*	
197	A22	1ab brt blue	17.50	11.00
198	A23	2ab deep blue	7.50	7.50
199	A24	1rup green	35.00	*11.00*
a.		1rup blue green	35.00	*12.50*

Zigzag Roulette 10

200	A22	1ab green	125.00	35.00
201	A23	2ab blue	150.00	55.00
201A	A24	1rup blue green	*110.00*	*90.00*

1908 *Perf. 12*

202	A22	1ab green	15.00	*20.00*
203	A23	2ab deep blue	5.00	5.00
a.		Horiz. pair, imperf between	*175.00*	
204	A24	1rup blue green	35.00	17.50
		Nos. 202-204 (3)	55.00	42.50

Twelve varieties of the 1 abasi, 6 of the 2 abasi, 4 of the 1 rupee.

Nos. 196-204 were issued in small sheets containing 3 or 4 panes. Gutter pairs, normal and tête bêche, exist.

A25

A26

A27

1909-19 Typo. *Perf. 12*

205	A25	1ab ultra	3.00	1.00
a.		Imperf., pair	20.00	
206	A25	1ab red ('16)	.60	.60
a.		Imperf.	22.50	
207	A25	1ab rose ('18)	.80	.70
208	A26	2ab green	.50	.25
a.		Imperf., pair	20.00	
b.		Horiz. pair, imperf. btwn.		
208C	A26	2ab yellow ('16)	2.00	2.00
209	A26	2ab bis ('18-'19)	.90	*1.25*
210	A27	1rup lilac brn	4.00	4.00
a.		1rup red brown	4.00	4.00
211	A27	1rup ol bis ('16)	6.00	6.00
		Nos. 205-211 (8)	17.80	15.80

A28

1913

212	A28	2pa drab brown	10.00	2.00
a.		2pa red brown	10.00	2.00

No. 212 is inscribed "Tiket waraq dak" (Postal card stamps). It was usable only on postcards and not accepted for postage on letters.

Nos. 196-212 sometimes show letters of a papermaker's watermark, "Howard & Jones, London."

Royal Star — A29

1920, Aug. 24 *Perf. 12*

Size: 39x47mm

214	A29	10pa rose	40.00	20.00
215	A29	20pa red brown	60.00	40.00
216	A29	30pa green	125.00	100.00
		Nos. 214-216 (3)	225.00	160.00

Issued in sheets of two.

1921, Mar.

Size: 22½x28¼mm

217	A29	10pa rose	2.00	1.00
a.		Perf. 11 ('27)	18.00	10.00
218	A29	20pa red brown	3.50	2.00
219	A29	30pa yel green	5.00	2.50
a.		Tete beche pair	45.00	25.00
b.		30pa green	5.00	2.75
c.		As "b," Tete beche pair	45.00	25.00
		Nos. 217-219 (3)	10.50	5.50

Two types of the 10pa, three of the 20pa.

Crest of King Amanullah
A30 A32

1924, Feb. 26 *Perf. 12*

220 A30 10pa chocolate 27.50 27.50
a. Tete beche pair 90.00 70.00

6th Independence Day.

Printed in sheets of four consisting of two tete beche pairs, and in sheets of two. Two types exist.

Some authorities believe that Nos. Q15-Q16 were issued as regular postage stamps.

1925, Feb. 26 *Perf. 12*

Size: 29x37mm

222 A32 10pa light brown 45.00 35.00

7th Independence Day.
Printed in sheets of 8 (two panes of 4).

1926, Feb. 28

Wove Paper

Size: 26x33mm

224 A32 10pa dark blue 5.00 5.00
a. Imperf., pair 25.00
b. Horiz. pair, imperf. btwn. 40.00
c. Vert. pair, imperf. btwn.
d. Laid paper 25.00 10.00

7th anniv. of Independence. Printed in sheets of 4, and in sheets of 8 (two panes of 4). Tete beche gutter pairs exist.

Tughra and Crest of Amanullah — A33

1927, Feb.

225 A33 10pa magenta 9.00 9.00
a. Vertical pair, imperf. between 50.00 70

Dotted Background

226 A33 10pa magenta 15.00 10.00
a. Horiz. pair, imperf. between 65.00

The surface of No. 226 is covered by a net of fine dots.

8th anniv. of Independence. Printed in sheets of 8 (two panes of 4). Tete beche gutter pairs exist.

National Seal — A34

A35

A35a

A36

1927, Oct. *Imperf.*

227 A34 15p pink 1.00 1.00
228 A35 30p Prus green 2.00 .90
229 A36 60p light blue 3.00 2.50
a. Tete beche pair 7.50
Nos. 227-229 (3) 6.00 4.40

1927-30 *Perf. 11, 12*

230 A34 15p pink 1.00 1.00
231 A34 15p ultra ('29) 1.00 1.00
232 A35 30p Prus green 2.00 1.00
233 A35a 30p dp green ('30) 1.00 .90
234 A36 60p bright blue 2.00 1.00
a. Tete beche pair 9.00 9.00
235 A36 60p black ('29) 2.50 1.75
Nos. 230-235 (6) 9.50 6.65

Nos. 230, 232 and 234 are usually imperforate on one or two sides.

No. 233 has been redrawn. A narrow border of pearls has been added and "30," in European and Arabic numerals, inserted in the upper spandrels.

Tughra and Crest of Amanullah — A37

1928, Feb. 27

236 A37 15p pink 4.00 4.00
a. Tete beche pair 9.00 7.50
b. Horiz. pair, imperf. vert. 17.50 15.00
c. As "a," imperf. vert., block of 4 25.00

9th anniv. of Independence. This stamp is always imperforate on one or two sides.

A 15p blue of somewhat similar design was prepared for the 10th anniv., but was not issued due to Amanullah's dethronement. Value, $15.

A38

A39

A40

A41

A42

1928-30 *Perf. 11, 12*

237 A38 2p dull blue 2.50 1.60
a. Vertical pair, imperf. between 17.50
238 A38 2p lt rose ('30) .25 .25
239 A39 10p gray green 1.00 .20
a. Tete beche pair 12.00 5.00
b. Vert. pair, imperf. horiz. 10.00 10.00
c. Vertical pair, imperf. between
240 10p choc ('30) 1.25 1.00
a. 10p brown purple ('29) 8.00 4.00
241 A40 25p car rose 1.00 .25
242 A40 25p Prus green ('29) 1.50 1.00
243 A41 40p ultra 1.25 .35
a. Tete beche pair 13.00 *15.00*
244 A41 40p rose ('29) 1.50 1.25
a. Tete beche pair 12.50
b. Vert. pair, imperf. horiz. 10.00
245 A42 50p red .60 .50
246 A42 50p dk blue ('29) 1.75 1.25
Nos. 237-246 (10) 12.60 7.65

The sheets of these stamps are often imperforate at the outer margins.

Nos. 237-238 are newspaper stamps.

This handstamp was used for ten months by the Revolutionary Gov't in Kabul as a control mark on outgoing mail. It occasionally fell on the stamps but there is no evidence that it was officially used as an overprint. Unused copies were privately made.

Independence Monument
A46

Wmk. Large Seal in the Sheet

1931, Aug. **Litho.** *Perf. 12*

Laid Paper

Without Gum

262 A46 20p red 1.00 .60

13th Independence Day.

National Assembly Chamber
A47

A48

A50

National Assembly Building
A49

National Assembly Chamber
A51

National Assembly Building
A52

1932 **Unwmk.** **Typo.** *Perf. 12*

Wove Paper

263 A47 40p olive 1.00 .40
264 A48 60p violet .65 .50
265 A49 80p dark red 1.00 .80
266 A50 1af black 10.00 4.25
267 A51 2af ultra 3.50 2.75
268 A52 3af gray green 4.25 3.50
Nos. 263-268 (6) 20.40 12.20

Formation of the Natl. Council. Imperforate or perforated examples on ungummed chalky paper are proofs.

See Nos. 304-305.

Mosque at Balkh — A53

Kabul Fortress
A54

Parliament House, Darul Funun — A55

Parliament House, Darul Funun — A56

Arch of Qalai Bist — A57

Memorial Pillar of Knowledge and Ignorance
A58

Independence Monument — A59

Minaret at Herat — A60

Arch of Paghman
A61

Ruins at Balkh — A62

Minarets of Herat — A63

Great Buddha at Bamian — A64

1932 **Typo.** ***Perf. 12***

269	A53	10p brown	.50	.20
270	A54	15p dk brown	.60	.20
271	A55	20p red	.30	.20
272	A56	25p dk green	.75	.20
273	A57	30p red	.40	.30
274	A58	40p orange	.65	.35
275	A59	50p blue	.80	.35
a.		Tete beche pair	5.50	
276	A60	60p blue	1.50	.50
277	A61	80p violet	1.75	1.00
278	A62	1af dark blue	2.75	.60
279	A63	2af dk red violet	3.75	2.00
280	A64	3af claret	4.25	2.50
		Nos. 269-280 (12)	18.00	8.40

Counterfeits of types A53-A65 exist.

See Nos. 290-295, 298-299, 302-303.

Entwined 2's — A65

Two types:

Type I - Numerals shaded. Size about 21x29mm.

Type II - Numerals unshaded. Size about 21¾x30mm.

1931-38 ***Perf. 12, 11x12***

281	A65	2p red brn (I)	.25	.20
282	A65	2p olive blk (I) ('34)	.25	.20
283	A65	2p grnsh gray (I) ('34)	.35	.20
283A	A65	2p black (II) ('36)	.35	.20
284	A65	2p salmon (II) ('38)	.25	.20
284A	A65	2p rose (I) ('38)	.25	.20
b.		Imperf., pair	3.00	

Imperf

285	A65	2p black (II) ('37)	.75	.20
286	A65	2p salmon (II) ('38)	.25	.20
		Nos. 281-286 (8)	2.70	1.60

The newspaper rate was 2 pouls.

A66

A67

1932, Aug. ***Perf. 12***

287	A66	1af Independence Monument	2.75	1.50

14th Independence Day.

1932, Oct. **Typo.**

1929 Liberation Monument, Kabul.

288	A67	80p red brown	.85	.50

Arch of Paghman — A68

1933, Aug.

289	A68	50p light ultra	1.25	1.25

15th Independence Day.

Types of 1932 and

Royal Palace, Kabul A69

Darrah- Shikari Pass, Hindu Kush — A70

1934-38 **Typo.** ***Perf. 12***

290	A53	10p deep violet	.20	.20
291	A54	15p turq green	.20	.20
292	A55	20p magenta	.25	.20
293	A56	25p deep rose	.30	.20
294	A57	30p orange	.40	.20
295	A58	40p blue black	.75	.30
296	A69	45p dark blue	1.50	1.00
297	A69	45p red ('38)	.50	.20
298	A59	50p orange	.30	.20
299	A60	60p purple	.85	.20
300	A70	75p red	1.00	.35
301	A70	75p dk blue ('38)	.60	.40
302	A61	80p brown vio	1.00	.50
303	A62	1af red violet	1.60	1.00
304	A51	2af gray black	3.00	2.00
305	A52	3af ultra	5.00	3.00
		Nos. 290-305 (16)	17.45	10.15

Nos. 290, 292, 300, 304, 305 exist imperf.

Independence Monument — A71

1934, Aug. **Litho.**

Without Gum

306	A71	50p pale green	2.50	1.25
a.		Tete beche pair	10.00	3.50

16th year of Independence. Each sheet of 40 (4x10) included 4 tete beche pairs as lower half of sheet was inverted.

Independence Monument — A74

Fireworks Display A75

1935, Aug. 15

Laid Paper

309	A74	50p dark blue	1.25	1.25

17th year of Independence.

1936, Aug. 15 ***Perf. 12***

Wove Paper

310	A75	50p red violet	1.25	1.00

18th year of Independence.

Independence Monument and Nadir Shah — A76

1937

311	A76	50p vio & bis brn	1.00	.60
a.		Imperf., pair	2.25	

19th year of Independence.

Mohammed Nadir Shah
A77 A78

1938 ***Perf. 11x12***

Without Gum

315	A77	50p brt blue & sepia	5.00	2.50
a.		Imperf. pair	20.00	

20th year of Independence.

1939 ***Perf. 11, 12x11***

317	A78	50p deep salmon	1.75	1.00

21st year of Independence.

National Arms A79

Parliament House, Darul Funun — A80

Royal Palace, Kabul A81

Independence Monument — A82

Independence Monument and Nadir Shah — A83

Mohammed Zahir Shah — A84

Mohammed Zahir Shah A85

Perf. 11, 11x12, 12x11, 12

1939-61 **Typo.**

318	A79	2p intense blk	.20	.20
318A	A79	2p brt pink ('61)	1.50	.50
319	A80	10p brt purple	.20	.20
320	A80	15p brt green	.20	.20
321	A80	20p red lilac	.20	.20
322	A81	25p rose red	1.00	.25
322A	A81	25p green ('41)	.50	.20
323	A81	30p orange	.20	.20
324	A81	40p dk gray	.20	.20
325	A82	45p brt carmine	.20	.20
326	A82	50p dp orange	.30	.20
327	A82	60p violet	.60	.20
328	A83	75p ultra	3.00	.75
328A	A83	75p red vio ('41)	.75	.30
328C	A83	75p brt red ('44)	3.00	3.00
328D	A83	75p chnt brn ('49)	4.00	3.00
329	A83	80p chocolate	.50	.50
a.		80p dull red violet (error)		
330	A84	1af brt red violet	1.50	.75
330A	A85	1af brt red vio ('44)	3.00	1.50
331	A85	2af copper red	1.75	.50
a.		2af deep rose red	2.50	1.40
332	A84	3af deep blue	3.75	1.60
		Nos. 318-332 (21)	26.55	14.65

Many shades exist in this issue.

On No. 332 the King faces slightly left.

No. 318A issued with and without gum.

See #795A-795B. For similar design see #907A.

Mohammed Nadir Shah — A86

1940, Aug. 23 ***Perf. 11***

333	A86	50p gray green	.75	.60

22nd year of Independence.

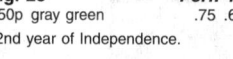

Independence Monument A87

Arch of Paghman A88

1941, Aug. 23 ***Perf. 12***

334	A87	15p gray green	5.00	2.75
335	A88	50p red brown	1.00	.85

23rd year of Independence.

Sugar Factory, Baghlan A89

1942, Apr. ***Perf. 12***

336 A89 1.25af blue (shades)		2.00	1.00
a. 1.25af ultra		2.00	1.50

In 1949, a 1.50af brown, type A89, was sold for 3af by the Philatelic Office, Kabul. It was not valid for postage. Value $3.50.

Independence Monument — A90

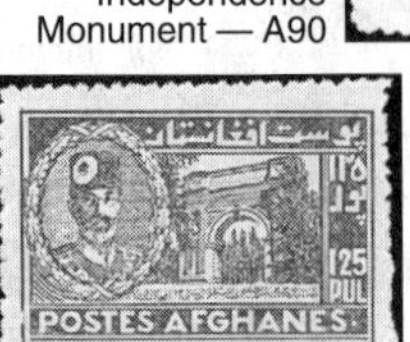
Mohammed Nadir Shah and Arch of Paghman A91

1942, Aug. 23 ***Perf. 12***

337 A90 35p bright green	2.75	2.00
338 A91 125p chalky blue	1.40	1.10

24th year of Independence.

Independence Monument and Nadir Shah — A92

Mohammed Nadir Shah — A93

Perf. 11x12, 12x11

1943, Aug. 25 Typo. Unwmk.

339 A92 35p carmine	9.75	8.00
340 A93 1.25af dark blue	2.25	1.90

25th year of Independence.

Tomb of Gohar Shad, Herat — A94

Ruins of Qalai Bist — A95

1944, May 1 ***Perf. 12, 11x12***

341 A94 35p orange	.50	.30
342 A95 70p violet	1.25	.50
a. 70p rose lilac	1.25	.50

A96

A97

1944, Aug. ***Perf. 12***

343 A96 35p crimson	.80	.60
344 A97 1.25af ultra	1.40	1.10

26th year of Independence.

A98

A99

1945, July

345 A98 35p deep red lilac	1.40	.65
346 A99 1.25af blue	2.40	1.50

27th year of Independence.

Mohammed Zahir Shah — A100

Independence Monument A101

Mohammed Nadir Shah A102

1946, July

347 A100 15p emerald	.80	.35
348 A101 20p dp red lilac	1.25	.55
349 A102 125p blue	2.10	1.75
Nos. 347-349 (3)	4.15	2.65

28th year of Independence.

Zahir Shah and Ruins of Qalai Bist — A103

A104

A105

1947, Aug.

350 A103 15p yellow green	.65	.20
351 A104 35p plum	.85	.20
352 A105 125p deep blue	2.25	1.40
Nos. 350-352 (3)	3.75	1.80

29th year of Independence.

Begging Child A106

A107

1948, May Unwmk. Typo. ***Perf. 12***

353 A106 35p yel green	3.50	3.00
354 A107 125p gray blue	3.50	3.00

Children's Day, May 29, 1948, and valid only on that day. Proceeds were used for Child Welfare.

A108 A109

A110

1948, Aug.

355 A108 15p green	.50	.20
356 A109 20p magenta	.70	.20
357 A110 125p dark blue	1.40	.70
Nos. 355-357 (3)	2.60	1.10

30th year of Independence.

United Nations Emblem — A111

1948, Oct. 24

358 A111 125p dk violet blue	7.00	7.00

UN, 3rd anniv. Valid one day only. Sheets of 9.

Maiwand Victory Column, Kandahar — A112

Zahir Shah and Ruins of Qalai Bist A113

Independence Monument and Nadir Shah — A114

1949, Aug. Typo. ***Perf. 12***

359 A112 25p green	.50	.20
360 A113 35p magenta	.65	.25
361 A114 1.25af blue	1.10	.75
Nos. 359-361 (3)	2.25	1.20

31st year of Independence.

Catalogue values for unused stamps in this section, from this point to the end of the section, are for Never Hinged items.

Nadir Shah — A117

1950, Aug.

364 A117 35p red brown	.50	.30
365 A117 125p blue	1.50	.65

32nd year of Independence.

Medical School and Nadir Shah A119

1950, Dec. 22 Typo. ***Perf. 12***

Size: 38x25mm

367 A119 35p emerald	.75	.60

Size: 46x30mm

368 A119 1.25af deep blue 2.75 1.90
a. 1.25af black (error) 6.00

19th anniv. of the founding of Afghanistan's Faculty of Medicine. On sale and valid for use on Dec. 22-28, 1950.

Minaret, Herat
A120

Zahir Shah
A121

Mosque of Khodja Abu Parsar, Balkh — A122

A123

A124

20p, Buddha at Bamian. 40p, Ruined arch. 45p, Maiwand Victory onument. 50p, View of Kandahar. 60p, Ancient tower. 70p, Afghanistan flag. 80p, 1af, Profile of Zahir Shah in uniform.

Photogravure, Engraved, Engraved and Lithographed

Perf. 12, 12½, 13x12½, 13½

1951, Mar. 21 Unwmk.

Imprint: "Waterlow & Sons Limited, London"

369 A120 10p yellow & brn .20 .20
370 A120 15p blue & brn .25 .20
371 A120 20p black 7.50 2.75
372 A121 25p green .30 .20
373 A122 30p cerise .35 .20
374 A121 35p violet .40 .20
375 A122 40p chestnut brn .40 .20
376 A120 45p deep blue .40 .20
377 A122 50p olive black 1.25 .20
378 A120 60p black 1.50 .50
379 A122 70p dk grn, blk, red & grn .50 .20
380 A123 75p cerise .75 .35
381 A123 80p carmine & blk 1.00 .35
382 A123 1af dp grn & vio .75 .35
383 A124 1.25af rose lil & blk *5.00* .35
384 A124 2af ultra 1.10 .35
385 A124 3af ultra & blk 2.50 .90
Nos. 369-385 (17) 24.15 7.70

Nos. 372, 374 and 381 to 385 are engraved, No. 379 is engraved and lithographed.

Imperfs. exist of the photogravure stamps.

See Nos. 445-451, 453, 552A-552D. For surcharges see Nos. B1-B2.

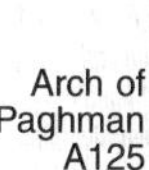

Arch of Paghman
A125

Nadir Shah and Independence Monument — A126

Overprint in Violet

Perf. 13½x13, 13

1951, Aug. 25 Engr.

386 A125 35p dk green & blk 1.00 .50
387 A126 1.25af deep blue 2.00 1.00

Overprint reads "Sol 33 Istiqlal" or "33rd Year of Independence." Overprint measures about 11mm wide.

See Nos. 398-399B, 441-442.

Proposed Flag of Pashtunistan — A127

Design: 125p, Flag and Pashtunistan warrior.

1951, Sept. 2 Litho. *Perf. 11½*

388 A127 35p dull chocolate 1.40 .65
389 A127 125p blue 2.40 1.75

Issued to publicize "Free Pashtunistan" Day.

Imperforates

From 1951 to 1958, quantities of nearly all locally-printed stamps were left imperforate and sold by the government at double face. From 1959 until March, 1964, many of the imperforates were sold for more than face value.

Avicenna — A128

1951, Nov. 4 Typo. *Perf. 11½*

390 A128 35p deep claret 2.00 .75
391 A128 125p blue .75 *2.25*

20th anniv. of the founding of the natl. Graduate School of Medicine.

A129

Dove and UN Symbols
A130

1951, Oct. 24

392 A129 35p magenta 1.40 1.00
393 A130 125p blue 3.50 2.75

7th anniv. of the UN.

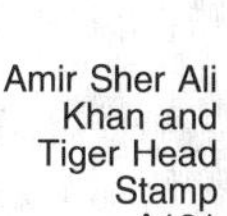

Amir Sher Ali Khan and Tiger Head Stamp
A131

Nos. 395, 397, Zahir Shah and stamp.

1951, Dec. 23 Litho.

394 A131 35p chocolate .50 .35
395 A131 35p rose lilac .50 .35
396 A131 125p ultra .85 .60
a. Cliche of 35p in plate of 125p 100.00 90.00
397 A131 125p aqua .85 .60
Nos. 394-397 (4) 2.70 1.90

76th anniv. of the UPU.

Stamps of 1951 Without Overprint

Perf. 13½x13, 13

1952, Aug. 24 Engr.

398 A125 35p dk green & blk 2.00 1.50
399 A126 1.25af deep blue 2.00 1.50

For overprints see #399A-399B, 441-442.

Same Overprinted in Violet

399A A125 35p dk grn & blk .60 .40
399B A126 1.25af deep blue 1.60 1.00

#398-399B issued for 34th Independence Day.

Globe — A132

Perf. 11½

1952, Oct. 25 Unwmk. Litho.

400 A132 35p rose .65 .45
401 A132 125p aqua 1.60 1.00

Issued to honor the United Nations.

Symbol of Medicine
A134

Tribal Warrior, Natl. Flag — A135

1952, Nov. *Perf. 11½*

403 A134 35p chocolate .55 .35
404 A134 125p violet blue 1.40 1.10

21st anniv. of the natl. Graduate School of Medicine.

No. 404 is inscribed in French with white letters on a colored background.

1952, Sept. 1 *Perf. 11*

405 A135 35p red .30 .30
406 A135 125p dark blue .60 .60

No. 406 is inscribed in French "Pashtunistan Day, 1952."

Flags of Afghanistan & Pashtunistan
A139

Badge of Pashtunistan
A140

Perf. 10½x11, 11

1953, Sept. 1 Unwmk.

411 A139 35p vermilion .35 .20
412 A140 125p blue .90 .45

Issued to publicize "Free Pashtunistan" Day.

Nadir Shah and Flag Bearer
A141

A142

1953, Aug. 24 *Perf. 11*

413 A141 35p green .20 .20
414 A142 125p violet .75 .60

35th anniv. of Independence.

United Nations Emblem — A143

1953, Oct. 24

415 A143 35p lilac .60 .50
416 A143 125p violet blue 1.50 1.00

United Nations Day, 1953.

A144

Nadir Shah — A145

1953, Nov. 29

417 A144 35p orange .90 .90
418 A145 125p chalky blue 2.10 2.10

22nd anniv. of the founding of the natl. Graduate School of Medicine.

Redrawn

35p. Original- Right character in second line of Persian inscription:

Redrawn- Persian character:

125p: Original- Inscribed "XXIII," "MADECINE" and "ANNIVERAIRE"
Redrawn- Inscribed "XXII," "MEDECINE" and "ANNIVERSAIRE"

1953

419	A144	35p deep orange	7.50	
420	A145	125p chalky blue	7.50	

Nadir Shah and Symbols of Independence — A146

1954, Aug. Typo. *Perf. 11*

421	A146	35p carmine rose	.50	.30
422	A146	125p violet blue	1.75	.80

36th year of Independence.

Raising Flag of Pashtunistan A147

1954, Sept. *Perf. 11½*

423	A147	35p chocolate	.50	.30
424	A147	125p blue	1.75	.80

Issued to publicize "Free Pashtunistan" Day.

UN Flag and Map — A148

1954, Oct. 24 *Perf. 11*

425	A148	35p carmine rose	.75	.75
426	A148	125p dk violet blue	2.25	2.25

9th anniv. of the United Nations.

UN Symbols A149

Design: 125p, UN emblem & flags.

1955, June 26 Litho. *Perf. 11*

Size: 26½x36mm

427	A149	35p dark green	.65	.40

Size: 28½x36mm

428	A149	125p aqua	1.60	.90

10th anniv. of the UN charter.

Nadir Shah (center) and Brothers A150

1929 Civil War Scene and Zahir Shah — A151

Tribal Elders' Council and Pashtun Flag — A152

1955, Aug. Unwmk. *Perf. 11*

429	A150	35p brt pink	.45	.30
430	A150	35p violet blue	.45	.30
431	A151	125p rose lilac	1.00	.75
432	A151	125p light violet	1.00	.75
		Nos. 429-432 (4)	2.90	2.10

37th anniv. of Independence.

1955, Sept. 5

433	A152	35p orange brown	.40	.20
434	A152	125p yellow green	1.00	.65

Issued for "Free Pashtunistan" Day.

UN Flag — A153

A154

1955, Oct. 24 Unwmk. *Perf. 11*

435	A153	35p orange brown	.75	.60
436	A153	125p brt ultra	1.40	1.10

10th anniv. of the United Nations.

1956, Aug. Litho.

437	A154	35p lt green	.50	.20
438	A154	140p lt violet blue	1.75	.75

38th year of Independence.

Jesh'n Exhibition Hall A155

1956, Aug. 25

439	A155	50p chocolate	.60	.30
440	A155	50p lt violet blue	.60	.30

International Exposition at Kabul.

Of the 50p face value, only 35p paid postage. The remaining 15p went to the Exposition.

Nos. 398-399 Handstamped in Violet

a

b

1957, Aug. Engr. *Perf. 13½x13, 13*

441	A125 (a)	35p dk green & blk	.75	.20
442	A126 (b)	1.25af deep blue	.85	.50

Arabic overprint measures 19mm.
39th year of independence.

Pashtunistan Flag — A156

1957, Sept. 1 Litho. *Perf. 11*

443	A156	50p pale lilac rose	.75	.40
444	A156	155p light violet	1.00	.75

Issued for "Free Pashtunistan" Day. French inscription on No. 444. 15p of each stamp went to the Pashtunistan Fund.

Types of 1951 and

Game of Buzkashi A157

Perf. 12, 12½, 12½x13, 13, 13x12, 13x12½, 13½x14

Photo., Engr., Engr.& Litho.

1957, Nov. 23 Unwmk.

Imprint: "Waterlow & Sons Limited, London"

445	A122	30p brown	.20	.20
446	A122	40p rose red	.20	.20
447	A122	50p yellow	.35	.20
448	A120	60p ultra	.40	.20
449	A123	75p brt violet	.50	.20
450	A123	80p violet & brn	.50	.20
451	A123	1af carmine & ultra	1.00	.20
452	A157	140p olive & dp claret	2.00	.50
453	A124	3af orange & blk	2.50	.50
		Nos. 445-453 (9)	7.65	2.40

No. 452 lacks imprint.

Nadir Shah and Flag-bearer A158

1958, Aug. 25 *Perf. 13½x14*

454	A158	35p dp yellow green	.40	.20
455	A158	140p brown	1.00	.60

40th year of Independence.

Exposition Buildings A159

1958, Aug. 23 Litho. *Perf. 11*

456	A159	35p brt blue green	.35	.20
457	A159	140p vermilion	.90	.40

International Exposition at Kabul.

Pres. Celal Bayar of Turkey — A160

Flags of UN and Afghanistan A161

1958, Sept. 13 Unwmk.

458	A160	50p lt blue	.35	.20
459	A160	100p brown	.60	.30

Visit of President Celal Bayar of Turkey.

1958, Oct. 24 Photo. *Perf. 14x13½*

Flags in Original Colors

460	A161	50p dark gray	.60	.60
461	A161	100p green	1.10	.90

United Nations Day, Oct. 24.

Atomic Energy Encircling the Hemispheres — A162

1958, Oct. 20 *Perf. 13½x14*

462	A162	50p blue	.45	.35
463	A162	100p dp red lilac	.80	.55

Issued to promote Atoms for Peace.

UNESCO Building, Paris A163

1958, Nov. 3

464	A163	50p dp yellow grn	.50	.40
465	A163	100p brown olive	.75	.60

UNESCO Headquarters in Paris opening, Nov. 3.

Globe and Torch A164

Perf. 13½x14

1958, Dec. 10 Unwmk.

466	A164	50p lilac rose	.35	.35
467	A164	100p maroon	.65	.65

10th anniv. of the signing of the Universal Declaration of Human Rights.

Nadir Shah and Flags A165

1959, Aug. Litho. *Perf. 11 Rough*

468	A165	35p light vermilion	.35	.20
469	A165	165p light violet	.90	.40

41st year of Independence.

Uprooted Oak Emblem — A166

1960, Apr. 7 *Perf. 11*

470	A166	50p deep orange	.20	.20
471	A166	165p blue	.35	.20

World Refugee Year, 7/1/59-6/30/60.

Two imperf. souvenir sheets exist. Both contain a 50p and a 165p, type A166, with marginal inscriptions and WRY emblem in maroon. On one sheet the stamps are in the colors of

Nos. 470-471 (size 108x81mm). On the other, the 50p is blue and the 165p is deep orange (size 107x80mm). Value $5 each.

For surcharges see Nos. B35-B36.

Buzkashi A167

1960, May 4 ***Perf. 11, Imperf.***

472 A167 25p rose red .35 .20
473 A167 50p bluish green .65 .35
a. Cliche of 25p in plate of 50p 20.00 20.00

See Nos. 549-550A.

Independence Monument A168

1960, Aug. ***Perf. 11, 12***

474 A168 50p light blue .35 .20
475 A168 175p bright pink .90 .30

42nd Independence Day.

Globe and Flags A169

1960, Oct. 24 Litho. ***Perf. 11, 12***

476 A169 50p rose lilac .25 .20
477 A169 175p ultra .75 .65

UN Day.

An imperf. souvenir sheet contains one each of Nos. 476-477 with marginal inscriptions ("La Journée des Nations Unies 1960" in French and Persian) and UN emblem in light blue. Size: 127x85½mm. Value $5.

This sheet was surcharged "+20ps" in 1962. Value $8.50.

Teacher Pointing to Globe A170

1960, Oct. 23 ***Perf. 11***

478 A170 50p brt pink .30 .20
479 A170 100p brt green .80 .45

Issued to publicize Teacher's Day.

Mohammed Zahir Shah — A171

1960, Oct. 15

480 A171 50p red brown .30 .20
481 A171 150p dk car rose .90 .30

Honoring the King on his 46th birthday.

Buzkashi A172

1960, Nov. 9 ***Perf. 11***

482 A172 175p lt red brown 1.75 .40

See Nos. 551-552.

No. 482 Overprinted "1960" and Olympic Rings in Bright Green.

1960, Dec. 24

483 A172 175p red brown 2.00 1.75
a. Souv. sheet of 1, imperf. 8.50

17th Olympic Games, Rome, 8/25-9/11.

Mir Wais — A173

1961, Jan. 5 Unwmk. ***Perf. 10½***

484 A173 50p brt rose lilac .50 .25
485 A173 175p ultra .90 .45
a. Souv. sheet, #484-485, imperf. 2.50 2.50

Mir Wais (1665-1708), national leader.

No Postal Need

existed for the 1p-15p denominations issued with sets of 1961-63 (between Nos. 486 and 649, B37 and B65).

The lowest denomination actually used for non-philatelic postage in that period was 25p (except for the 2p newspaper rate for which separate stamps were provided).

Horse, Sheep and Camel A174

#487, 175p, Rock partridge. 10p, 100p, Afghan hound. 15p, 150p, Grain & grasshopper, vert.

1961, Mar. 29 Photo. ***Perf. 13½x14***

486 A174 2p maroon & buff
487 A174 2p ultra & org
488 A174 5p brown & yel
489 A174 10p black & salmon
490 A174 15p blue grn & yel
491 A174 25p black & pink
492 A174 50p black & citron
493 A174 100p black & pink
494 A174 150p green & yel
495 A174 175p ultra & pink
Nos. 486-495 (10) 2.00

Two souvenir sheets, perf. and imperf., contain 2 stamps, 1 each of #492-493. Value $2 each.

Afghan Fencing A175

Designs: No. 497, 5p, 25p, 50p, Wrestlers. 10p, 100p, Man with Indian clubs. 15p, 150p, Afghan fencing. 175p, Children skating.

1961, July 6 ***Perf. 13½x14***

496 A175 2p green & rose lil
497 A175 2p brown & citron
498 A175 5p gray & rose
499 A175 10p blue & bister
500 A175 15p sl bl & dl lil
501 A175 25p black & dl bl
502 A175 50p sl grn & bis brn
503 A175 100p brown & bl grn
504 A175 150p brown & org yel
505 A175 175p black & blue
Nos. 496-505 (10) 3.00

Issued for Children's Day.

A souvenir sheet exists, perf. and imperf., containing one each of Nos. 502-503. Value $3.50 each.

For surcharges see Nos. B37-B41.

Bande Amir Lakes A176

1961, Aug. 7 Photo. ***Perf. 13½x14***

506 A176 3af brt blue .35 .20
507 A176 10af rose claret 1.10 .70

Nadir Shah — A177

Girl Scout — A178

1961, Aug. 23 ***Perf. 14x13½***

508 A177 50p rose red & blk .40 .25
509 A177 175p brt grn & org brn .85 .40

43rd Independence Day.

Two souvenir sheets, perf. and imperf., contain one each of Nos. 508-509. Value, each $2.50.

Perf. 14x13½

1961, July 23 Unwmk.

510 A178 50p dp car & dk gray .30 .20
511 A178 175p dp grn & rose brn .80 .40

Issued for Women's Day.

Two souvenir sheets exist, perf. and imperf., containing one each of Nos. 510-511. Value $3 each.

Exhibition Hall, Kabul A179

1961, Aug. 23 ***Perf. 13½x14***

512 A179 50p yel brn & yel grn .20 .20
513 A179 175p blue & brn .40 .30

International Exhibition at Kabul.

Pathan with Pashtunistan Flag — A180

1961, Aug. 31 Photo. ***Perf. 14x13½***

514 A180 50p blk, lil & red .25 .25
515 A180 175p brn, grnsh bl & red .45 .40

Issued for "Free Pashtunistan Day."

Souvenir sheets exist perf. and imperf. containing one each of Nos. 514-515. Value $2 each.

Assembly Building A181

1961, Sept. 10 ***Perf. 12***

516 A181 50p dk gray & brt grn .20 .20
517 A181 175p ultra & brn .45 .30

Anniv. of the founding of the Natl. Assembly.

Souvenir sheets exist, perf. and imperf., containing one each of Nos. 516-517. Value $1 each.

Exterminating Anopheles Mosquito — A182

1961, Oct. 5 ***Perf. 13½x14***

518 A182 50p blk & brn lil .50 .30
519 A182 175p maroon & brt grn 1.10 .50

Anti-Malaria campaign. Souvenir sheets exist, perf. and imperf., containing one each of Nos. 518-519. Value $3 each.

Zahir Shah — A183

1961, Oct. 15 ***Perf. 13½***

520 A183 50p lilac & blue .30 .20
521 A183 175p emerald & red brn .50 .35

Issued to honor King Mohammed Zahir Shah on his 47th birthday.

See Nos. 609-612.

Pomegranates — A184

Fruit: No. 523, 5p, 25p, 50p, Grapes. 10p, 150p, Apples. 15p, 175p, Pomegranates. 100p, Melons.

1961, Oct. 16 ***Perf. 13½x14***

Fruit in Natural Colors

522 A184 2p black
523 A184 2p green
524 A184 5p lilac rose
525 A184 10p lilac
526 A184 15p dk blue
527 A184 25p dull red
528 A184 50p purple
529 A184 100p brt blue
530 A184 150p brown
531 A184 175p olive gray
Nos. 522-531 (10) 2.10

For Afghan Red Crescent Society.

Souvenir sheets exist, perf. and imperf., containing one each of Nos. 528-529. Value $1.50 each.

For surcharges see Nos. B42-B46.

UN Headquarters, NY — A185

1961, Oct. 24 *Perf. 13½x14*

Vertical Borders in Emerald, Red and Black

532 A185 1p rose lilac
533 A185 2p slate
534 A185 3p brown
535 A185 4p ultra
536 A185 50p rose red
537 A185 75p gray
538 A185 175p brt green
Nos. 532-538 (7) 1.50

16th anniv. of the UN. Souvenir sheets exist, perf. and imperf., containing one each of Nos. 536-538. Value $2 each.

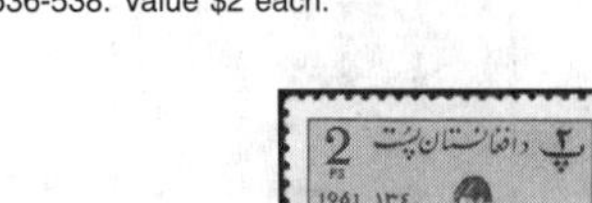

Children Giving Flowers to Teacher — A186

People Raising UNESCO Symbol — A187

#540, 5p, 25p, 50p, Tulips. 10p, 100p, Narcissus. 15p, 150p, Children giving flowers to teacher. 175p, Teacher with children in front of school.

1961, Oct. 26 **Photo.** *Perf. 12*

539 A186 2p multicolored
540 A186 2p multicolored
541 A186 5p multicolored
542 A186 10p multicolored
543 A186 15p multicolored
544 A186 25p multicolored
545 A186 50p multicolored
546 A186 100p multicolored
547 A186 150p multicolored
548 A186 175p multicolored
Nos. 539-548 (10) 2.50

Issued for Teacher's Day.

Souvenir sheets exist, perf. and imperf. containing one each of Nos. 545-546. Value, 2 sheets, $4.

For surcharges see Nos. B47-B51.

Buzkashi Types of 1960

1961-72 **Litho.** *Perf. 10½, 11*

549 A167 25p violet .20 .20
b. 25p brt vio, typo. ('72) .20 .20
549A A167 25p citron ('63) .20 .20
550 A167 50p blue .30 .20
550A A167 50p yel org ('69) .20 .20
551 A172 100p citron .45 .20
551A A172 150p orange ('64) .30 .20
552 A172 2af lt green 1.10 .45
Nos. 549-552 (7) 2.75 1.65

Zahir Shah Types of 1951

Photo., Engr., Engr. & Litho.

1962 *Perf. 13x12, 13*

Imprint: "Thomas De La Rue & Co. Ltd."

552A A123 75p brt purple 3.25 .25
552B A123 1af car & ultra 3.25 .35
552C A124 2af blue 4.25 .75
552D A124 3af orange & blk 6.25 1.10
Nos. 552A-552D (4) 17.00 2.45

1962, July 2 **Photo.** *Perf. 14x13½*

553 A187 2p rose lil & brn
554 A187 2p ol bis & brn
555 A187 5p dp org & dk grn
556 A187 10p gray & mag
557 A187 15p blue & brn
558 A187 25p org yel & pur
559 A187 50p lt grn & pur
560 A187 75p brt cit & brn
561 A187 100p dp org & brn
Nos. 553-561 (9) 1.60

15th anniv. of UNESCO. Souvenir sheets exist, perf. and imperf. One contains Nos. 558-559; the other contains Nos. 560-561. Value, $3 each.

For surcharges see Nos. B52-B60.

Ahmad Shah — A188

Afghan Hound — A189

1962, Feb. 24 **Photo.** *Perf. 13½*

562 A188 50p red brn & gray .20 .20
563 A188 75p green & salmon .25 .20
564 A188 100p claret & bister .40 .30
Nos. 562-564 (3) .85 .70

Ahmad Shah (1724-73), founded the Afghan kingdom in 1747 and ruled until 1773.

1962, Apr. 21 *Perf. 14x13½*

Designs: 5p, 75p, Afghan cock. 10p, 100p, Kondjid plant. 15p, 125p, Astrakhan skins.

565 A189 2p rose & brn
566 A189 2p lt green & brn
567 A189 5p dp rose & claret
568 A189 10p lt grn & sl grn
569 A189 15p blue grn & blk
570 A189 25p blue & brn
571 A189 50p gray & brn
572 A189 75p rose lil & lil
573 A189 100p gray & dl grn
574 A189 125p rose brn & blk
Nos. 565-574 (10) 2.00

Agriculture Day. Perf. and imperf. souvenir sheets exist. Set of 4 sheets, value $4.

Athletes with Flag and Nadir Shah — A190

Woman in National Costume — A191

1962, Aug. 23 *Perf. 12*

575 A190 25p multicolored .20 .20
576 A190 50p multicolored .20 .20
577 A190 150p multicolored .25 .20
Nos. 575-577 (3) .65 .60

44th Independence Day.

1962, Aug. 30 *Perf. 11½x12*

578 A191 25p lilac & brn .20 .20
579 A191 50p green & brn .25 .20
Nos. 578-579,C15-C16 (4) 1.90 1.85

Issued for Women's Day. A souvenir sheet exists containing one each of #578-579, C15-C16. Value $3.

Man and Woman with Flag — A192

Malaria Eradication Emblem and Swamp — A193

1962, Aug. 31 **Photo.**

580 A192 25p black, pale bl & red .20 .20
581 A192 50p black, grn & red .20 .20
582 A192 150p black, pink & red .45 .20
Nos. 580-582 (3) .85 .60

Issued for "Free Pashtunistan Day."

1962, Sept. 5 *Perf. 14x13½*

583 A193 2p dk grn & ol gray
584 A193 2p dk green & sal
585 A193 5p red brn & ol
586 A193 10p red brn & brt grn
587 A193 15p red brn & gray
588 A193 25p brt bl & bluish grn
589 A193 50p brt bl & rose lil
590 A193 75p black & blue
591 A193 100p black & brt pink
592 A193 150p black & bis brn
593 A193 175p black & orange
Nos. 583-593 (11) 2.50

WHO drive to eradicate malaria. Perf. and imperf. souvenir sheets exist. Set of 4 sheets, value $6.50.

For surcharges see Nos. B61-B71.

National Assembly Building — A194

Perf. 10½, 11 (100p)

1962, Sept. 10 **Unwmk.** **Litho.**

594 A194 25p lt green .35 .25
595 A194 50p blue .55 .35
596 A194 75p rose .75 .55
597 A194 100p violet 1.10 .90
598 A194 125p ultra 1.25 1.10
Nos. 594-598 (5) 4.00 3.15

Establishment of the National Assembly.

Horse Racing — A195

Designs: 2p, Pole vaulting. 3p, Wrestling. 4p, Weight lifting. 5p, Soccer.

1962, Sept. 22 **Photo.** *Perf. 12*

Black Inscriptions

599 A195 1p lt ol & red brn
600 A195 2p lt grn & red brn
601 A195 3p yellow & dk pur
602 A195 4p pale bl & grn
603 A195 5p bluish grn & dk brn
Nos. 599-603, C17-C22 (11) 2.50

4th Asian Games, Djakarta, Indonesia. Two souvenir sheets exist. A perforated one contains a 125p blue, dark blue and brown stamp in horse racing design. An imperf. one contains a 2af buff, purple and black stamp in soccer design. Value, $3.50 each.

Runners A196

1p, 2p, Diver, vert. 4p, Peaches. 5p, Iris, vert.

Perf. 11½x12, 12x11½

1962, Oct. 2 **Unwmk.**

604 A196 1p rose lil & brn
605 A196 2p blue & brn
606 A196 3p brt blue & lil
607 A196 4p ol gray & multi
608 A196 5p gray & multi
Nos. 604-608, C23-C25 (8) 2.00

Issued for Children's Day.

King Type of 1961, Dated "1962"

1962, Oct. 15 *Perf. 13½*

Various Frames

609 A183 25p lilac rose & brn .20 .20
610 A183 50p orange brn & grn .20 .20
611 A183 75p blue & lake .20 .20
612 A183 100p green & red brn .30 .20
Nos. 609-612 (4) .90 .80

Issued to honor King Mohammed Zahir Shah on his 48th birthday.

Grapes A197

1962, Oct. 16 *Perf. 12*

613 A197 1p shown
614 A197 2p Grapes
615 A197 3p Pears
616 A197 4p Wistaria
617 A197 5p Blossoms
Nos. 613-617, C26-C28 (8) 1.00

For the Afghan Red Crescent Society.

UN Headquarters, NY and Flags of UN and Afghanistan — A198

1962, Oct. 24 **Unwmk.**

618 A198 1p multicolored
619 A198 2p multicolored
620 A198 3p multicolored
621 A198 4p multicolored
622 A198 5p multicolored
Nos. 618-622, C29-C31 (8) 2.00

UN Day. Souvenir sheets exist. One contains a single 4af ultramarine stamp, perforated; the other, a 4af ocher stamp, imperf. Value, 2 sheets, $5.

Boy Scout — A199

Pole Vault — A200

1962, Oct. 18 **Photo.** *Perf. 12*

623 A199 1p yel, dk grn & sal
624 A199 2p dl yel, slate & sal
625 A199 3p rose, blk & sal
626 A199 4p multicolored
Nos. 623-626, C32-C35 (8) 2.25

Issued to honor the Boy Scouts.

1962, Oct. 25 Unwmk. *Perf. 12*

3p, High jump. 4p, 5p, Different blossoms.

627 A200 1p lilac & dk grn
628 A200 2p yellow grn & brn
629 A200 3p bister & vio
630 A200 4p sal pink, grn & ultra
631 A200 5p yellow, grn & bl
Nos. 627-631, C36-C37 (7) 1.25

Issued for Teacher's Day.

Rockets A201

1962, Nov. 29

632 A201 50p pale lil & dk bl .45
633 A201 100p lt blue & red brn .85

UN World Meteorological Day. A souvenir sheet contains one 5af pink and green stamp. Value $6.

Ansari Mausoleum, Herat — A202

Perf. 13½

1963, Jan. 3 Unwmk. Photo.

634 A202 50p purple & green .20 .20
635 A202 75p gray & magenta .20 .20
636 A202 100p orange brn & brn .30 .30
Nos. 634-636 (3) .70 .70

Khwaja Abdullah Ansari, Sufi, religious leader and poet, on the 900th anniv. of his death.

Sheep A203

Silkworm, Cocoons, Moth and Mulberry Branch A204

1963, Mar. 1 *Perf. 12*

637 A203 1p grnsh blue & blk
638 A203 2p yellow grn & blk
639 A203 3p lilac rose & blk
640 A204 4p gray, grn & brn
641 A204 5p red lil, grn & brn
Nos. 637-641, C42-C44 (8) 2.25

Issued for the Day of Agriculture.

Rice — A205

Designs: 3p, Corn. 300p, Wheat emblem.

1963, Mar. 27 Unwmk. *Perf. 14*

642 A205 2p gray, claret & grn .20 .20
643 A205 3p green, yel & ocher .20 .20
644 A205 300p dk blue & yel .30 .30
Nos. 642-644 (3) .70 .70

FAO "Freedom from Hunger" campaign.

Meteorological Measuring Instrument — A206

Designs: 3p, 10p, Weather station. 4p, 5p, Rockets in space.

1963, May 23 Photo. *Perf. 13½x14*

645 A206 1p dp magenta & brn
646 A206 2p brt blue & brn
647 A206 3p red & brown
648 A206 4p orange & lilac
649 A206 5p green & dl vio

Imperf

650 A206 10p red brn & grn
Nos. 645-650, C46-C50 (11) 7.50

3rd UN World Meteorological Day, Mar. 23.

Independence Monument A207

1963, Aug. 23 Litho. *Perf. 10½*

651 A207 25p lt green .20 .20
652 A207 50p orange .20 .20
653 A207 150p rose carmine .35 .20
Nos. 651-653 (3) .75 .60

45th Independence Day.

Pathans in Forest A208

1963, Aug. 31 Unwmk. *Perf. 10½*

654 A208 25p pale violet .20 .20
655 A208 50p sky blue .20 .20
655A A208 150p dull red brn .45 .35
Nos. 654-655A (3) .85 .75

Issued for "Free Pashtunistan Day."

4th Asian Games, Djakarta A208a

2p, 250p, 300p, Wrestling. 3p, 10p, Tennis. 4p, 500p, Javelin. 5p, 9af, Shot put.

1963, Sept. 3 Litho. *Perf. 12*

656 A208a 2p rose vio & brn
656A A208a 3p olive grn & brn
656B A208a 4p blue & brn
656C A208a 5p yel grn & brn
656D A208a 10p lt bl grn & brn
656E A208a 300p yellow & vio
656F A208a 500p lt yel bis & brn
656G A208a 9af pale grn & vio
Nos. 656-656G (8) 1.75

Souvenir Sheets

656H A208a 250p lilac & vio 1.50
656I A208a 300p blue & blk 1.50

Nos. 656-656F are airmail. Nos. 656-656I exist imperf.

National Assembly Building — A209

1963, Sept. 10 *Perf. 11*

657 A209 25p gray .20 .20
658 A209 50p dull red .20 .20
659 A209 75p brown .20 .20
660 A209 100p olive .30 .20
661 A209 125p lilac .40 .20
Nos. 657-661 (5) 1.30 1.00

Issued to honor the National Assembly.

Balkh Gate A210

1963, Oct. 8

662 A210 3af choc (screened margins) .40 .30
a. White margins 1.50 .50

In the original printing a halftone screen extended across the plate, covering the space between the stamps. A retouch removed the screen between the stamps (No. 662a).

Intl. Red Cross, Cent. A210a

4p, 5p, 200p, 3af, Nurse holding patient, vert. 10p, 4af, 6af, Crown Prince Ahmed Shah.

1963, Oct. 9 *Perf. 13½*

662B A210a 2p olive, blk & red
662C A210a 3p blue, blk & red
662D A210a 4p lt grn, blk & red
662E A210a 5p lt vio, blk & red
662F A210a 10p gray grn, red & blk
662G A210a 100p dull bl grn, red & blk
662H A210a 200p lt brn, blk & red
662I A210a 4af brt bl grn, red & blk
m. Souvenir sheet of 1 1.25
662J A210a 6af lt brn, red & blk
Nos. 662B-662J (9) 1.25

Souvenir Sheet

662K A210a 3af dl blue, blk & red 1.25

Nos. 662G-662K are airmail. Nos. 662B-662K exist imperf.

Zahir Shah — A211

Kemal Ataturk — A212

1963, Oct. 15 *Perf. 10½*

663 A211 25p green .20 .20
663A A211 50p gray .20 .20
663B A211 75p carmine rose .20 .20
663C A211 100p dull redsh brn .30 .20
Nos. 663-663C (4) .90 .80

King Mohammed Zahir Shah, 49th birthday.

1963, Oct. 10 *Perf. 10½*

664 A212 1af blue .20 .20
665 A212 3af rose lilac .40 .35

25th anniv. of the death of Kemal Ataturk, president of Turkey.

Protection of Nubian Monuments A213

Designs: 5af, 7.50af, 10af, Ruins, vert.

Perf. 12, Imperf. (150p, 250p, 10af)

1963, Nov. 16 Photo.

666 A213 100p lil rose & blk
666A A213 150p rose lil & blk
666B A213 200p brown & blk
666C A213 250p ultra & blk
666D A213 500p green & blk
666E A213 5af greenish blue & gray bl
666F A213 7.50af red brn & gray bl
666G A213 10af ver & gray bl
Nos. 666-666G (8) 2.50

#666E-666G are airmail. #666D exists imperf.

Women's Day — A213a

Boy and Girl Scouts — A213c

A213b

1964, Jan. 5 *Perf. 14x13½*

667 A213a 2p multicolored
667A A213a 3p multicolored
667B A213a 4p multicolored
667C A213a 5p multicolored
667D A213a 10p multicolored
Nos. 667-667D (5) 1.00

Exist imperf.

1964, Jan. 5 ***Perf. 13½x14, 14x13½***

#668F-668G, 668K-668M, Girl with flag.

668 A213b 2p multi
668A A213b 3p multi
668B A213b 4p multi
668C A213b 5p multi
668D A213b 10p multi
668E A213c 2af multi
668F A213c 2af multi
668G A213c 2.50af multi
668H A213c 3af multi
668I A213c 4af multi
668J A213c 5af multi
668K A213c 12af multi
Nos. 668-666K (12) 3.00

Souvenir Sheets

668L A213c 5af multi .75
668M A213c 6af multi .75
668N A213c 6af multi 1.25
668O A213c 10af multi 1.25

Nos. 668E-668O are airmail. Nos 668-668K, 668N-668O exist imperf.

Children — A213d

1964, Jan. 22 ***Perf. 12***

669 A213d 2p Playing ball
669A A213d 3p like #669
669B A213d 4p Swinging, jumping rope, vert.
669C A213d 5p Skiing, vert.
669D A213d 10p like #669
669E A213d 200p like #669C
669F A213d 300p like #669B
Nos. 669-666F (7) 2.00

Nos. 669E-669F are airmail. All exist imperf.

Red Crescent Society — A213e

Designs: 100p, 200p, Pierre and Marie Curie, physicists. 2.50af, 7.50af Nurse examining child. 3.50af, 5af, Nurse and patients.

Perf. 14, Imperf. (#670A, 670C-670D)

1964, Feb. 8

670 A213e 100p multi
670A A213e 100p multi
670B A213e 200p multi
670C A213e 2.50af multi
670D A213e 3.50af multi
670E A213e 5af multi
670F A213e 7.50af multi
Nos. 670-670F (7) 3.00

Nos. 670B-670D are airmail.

Teachers' Day — A213f

Flowers: 2p, 3p, 3af, 4af, Tulips. 4p, 5p, 3.50af, 6af, Flax. 10p, 1.50af, 2af, Iris.

Perf. 12, Imperf. (1.50af, 2af)

1964, Mar. 3

671 A213f 2p multicolored
671A A213f 3p multicolored
671B A213f 4p multicolored
671C A213f 5p multicolored
671D A213f 10p multicolored
671E A213f 1.50af multicolored
671F A213f 2af multicolored
671G A213f 3af multicolored
671H A213f 3.50af multicolored
Nos. 671-671H (9) 2.00

Souvenir Sheets

671I A213f 4af multi 1.50
671J A213f 6af multi, imperf 4.00

#671E-671J are airmail. #671-671D exist imperf.

A213g

UN Day: 5p, 10p, 2af, 3af, 4af, Doctor and nurse, vert.

1964, Mar. 9 ***Perf. 14***

672 A213g 2p multicolored
672A A213g 3p multicolored
672B A213g 4p multicolored
672C A213g 5p multicolored
672D A213g 10p multicolored
672E A213g 100p multicolored
672F A213g 2af multicolored
672G A213g 3af multicolored
Nos. 672-672G (8) 3.00 2.75

Souvenir Sheets

672H A213g 4af multi, imperf. 10.00
672I A213g 5af multi 3.00

Nos. 672E-672G are airmail. Nos. 672-672G exist imperf.
For surcharges see Nos. B71A-B71J.

UNICEF A213h

Design: 5af, 7.50af, 10af, Children eating.

Perf. 14x13½, Imperf. (150p, 250p, 10af)

1964, Mar. 15

673 A213h 100p multicolored
673A A213h 150p multicolored
673B A213h 200p multicolored
673C A213h 250p multicolored
673D A213h 5af multicolored
673E A213h 7.50af multicolored
673F A213h 10af multicolored
Nos. 673-673F (7) 10.00

Nos. 673D-673F are airmail.

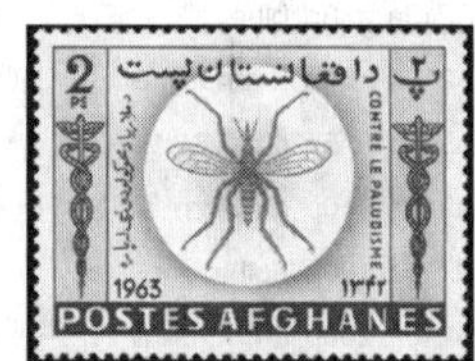

Eradication of Malaria — A213i

4p, 5p, 5af, 10af Spraying mosquitoes.

1964, Mar. 15 ***Perf. 13½***

674 A213i 2p lt red brn & yel grn
674A A213i 3p olive grn & buff
674B A213i 4p dk vio & bl grn
674C A213i 5p brn & grn
674D A213i 2af Prus bl & ver
h. Souvenir sheet of 1 .35
674E A213i 5af dk grn & lt red brn, imperf.
i. Souv. sheet of 1, imperf. 2.00
674F A213i 10af red brn & grnsh bl
Nos. 674-674F (7) 1.50

674G A213i 10p on 4p Prus bl & rose .60

No. 674G not issued without surcharge. Nos. 674-674C, 674G exist imperf. Nos. 674D-674F are airmail.
Exists imperf.

"Tiger's Head" of 1878 — A214

1964, Mar. 22 **Photo.** ***Perf. 12***

675 A214 1.25af gold, grn & blk .25 .20
676 A214 5af gold, rose car & blk .55 .35

Issued to honor philately.

Unisphere and Flags A215

1964, May 3 ***Perf. 13½x14***

677 A215 6af crimson, gray & grn .30 .20

New York World's Fair, 1964-65.

Hand Holding Torch — A216

1964, May 12 **Photo.** ***Perf. 14x13½***

678 A216 3.75af multicolored .20 .20

1st UN Seminar on Human Rights in Kabul, May 1964. The denomination in Persian at right erroneously reads "3.25" but the stamp was sold and used as 3.75af.

Kandahar Airport A217

1964, Apr. **Litho.** ***Perf. 10½, 11***

679 A217 7.75af dk red brown .40 .20
680 A217 9.25af lt green .50 .20
681 A217 10.50af lt green .50 .30
682 A217 13.75af carmine rose .70 .40
Nos. 679-682 (4) 2.10 1.10

Inauguration of Kandahar Airport.

Snow Leopard A218

50p, Ibex, vert. 75p, Head of argali. 5af, Yak.

1964, June 25 **Photo.** ***Perf. 12***

683 A218 25p yellow & blue .20 .20
684 A218 50p dl red & grn .20 .20
685 A218 75p Prus bl & lil .20 .20
686 A218 5af brt grn & dk brn .30 .30
Nos. 683-686 (4) .90 .90

View of Herat A219

Flag and Map of Afghanistan A220

Tourist publicity: 75p, Tomb of Queen Gowhar Shad, vert.

1964, July 12 ***Perf. 13½x14, 14x13½***

687 A219 25p sepia & bl .20 .20
688 A219 75p dp blue & buff .20 .20
689 A220 3af red, blk & grn .30 .20
Nos. 687-689 (3) .70 .60

Wrestling A221

25p, Hurdling, vert. 1af, Diving, vert. 5af, Soccer.

1964, July 26 ***Perf. 12***

690 A221 25p ol bis, blk & car .20 .20
691 A221 1af bl grn, blk & car .20 .20
692 A221 3.75af yel grn, blk & car .20 .20
693 A221 5af brn, blk & car .30 .30
a. Souv. sheet, #690-693, imperf. .90 .90
Nos. 690-693 (4) .90 .90

18th Olympic Games, Tokyo, Oct. 10-25, 1964. No. 693a sold for 15af. The additional 5af went to the Afghanistan Olympic Committee.

Flag and Outline of Nadir Shah's Tomb — A222

1964, Aug. 24 **Photo.**

695 A222 25p multicolored .20 .20
696 A222 75p multicolored .20 .20

Independence Day. The stamps were printed with an erroneous inscription in upper left corner: "33rd year of independence." This was locally obliterated with a typographed gold bar.

Pashtunistan Flag — A223

Zahir Shah — A225

1964, Sept. 1 **Unwmk.**

697 A223 100p gold, blk, red, bl & grn .20 .20

Issued for "Free Pashtunistan Day."

1964, Oct. 17 *Perf. 14x13½*

699 A225 1.25af gold & yel grn .20 .20
700 A225 3.75af gold & rose .20 .20
701 A225 50af gold & gray 2.00 1.75
Nos. 699-701 (3) 2.40 2.15

King Mohammed Zahir Shah, 50th birthday.

Coat of Arms of Afghanistan and UN Emblem A226

1964, Oct. 24 *Perf. 13½x14*

702 A226 5af gold, blk & dl bl .20 .20

Issued for United Nations Day.

Emblem of Afghanistan Women's Association A227

1964, Nov. 9 **Photo.** **Unwmk.**

703 A227 25p pink, dk bl & emer .50 .25
704 A227 75p aqua, dk bl & emer .75 .35
705 A227 1af sil, dk bl & emer 1.00 .50
Nos. 703-705 (3) 2.25 1.10

Issued for Women's Day.

Poet Mowlana Nooruddin Abdul Rahman Jami (1414-1492) A228

Perf. 11 Rough

1964, Nov. 23 **Litho.**

706 A228 1.50af blk, emer & yel .85 .85

Woodpecker A229

Birds: 3.75af, Black-throated jay, vert. 5af, Impeyan pheasant, vert.

Perf. 13½x14, 14x13½

1965, Apr. 20 **Photo.** **Unwmk.**

707 A229 1.25af multi 1.00 .50
708 A229 3.75af multi 1.75 .75
709 A229 5af multi 2.50 1.00
Nos. 707-709 (3) 5.25 2.25

ITU Emblem, Old and New Communication Equipment — A230

1965, May 17 *Perf. 13½x14*

710 A230 5af lt bl, blk & red .35 .35

Cent. of the ITU.

"Red City," Bamian — A231

Designs: 3.75af, Ruins of ancient Bamian city. 5af, Bande Amir, mountain lakes.

1965, May 30 *Perf. 13x13½*

711 A231 1.25af pink & multi .20 .20
712 A231 3.75af lt blue & multi .20 .20
713 A231 5af yellow & multi .30 .30
Nos. 711-713 (3) .70 .70

Issued for tourist publicity.

ICY Emblem A232

1965, June 25 *Perf. 13½x13*

714 A232 5af multicolored .25 .25

International Cooperation Year, 1965.

ARIANA Air Lines Emblem and DC-3 A233

5af, DC-6 at right. 10af, DC-3 on top.

Perf. 13½x14

1965, July 15 **Photo.** **Unwmk.**

715 A233 1.25af brt bl, gray & blk .20 .20
716 A233 5af red lil, blk & bl .30 .30
717 A233 10af bis, blk, bl gray & grn .75 .75
a. Souv. sheet, #715-717, imperf 1.00 1.00
Nos. 715-717 (3) 1.25 1.25

10th anniv. of Afghan Air Lines, ARIANA.

Nadir Shah — A234

1965, Aug. 23 *Perf. 14x13½*

718 A234 1af dl grn, blk & red brn .25 .20

For the 47th Independence Day.

Flag of Pashtunistan — A235

Perf. 13½x14

1965, Aug. 31 **Photo.** **Unwmk.**

719 A235 1af multicolored .25 .20

Issued for "Free Pashtunistan Day."

Zahir Shah Signing Constitution — A236

1965, Sept. 11 *Perf. 13x13½*

720 A236 1.50af brt grn & blk .25 .25

Promulgation of the new Constitution.

Zahir Shah and Oak Leaves — A237

1965, Oct. 14 *Perf. 14x13½*

721 A237 1.25af blk, ultra & salmon .20 .20
722 A237 6af blk, lt bl & rose lil .40 .35

King Mohammed Zahir Shah, 51st birthday.

Flags of UN and Afghanistan A238

1965, Oct. 24 *Perf. 13½x14*

723 A238 5af multicolored .20 .20

Issued for United Nations Day.

Dappled Ground Gecko A239

Designs: 4af, Caucasian agamid (lizard). 8af, Horsfield's tortoise.

Perf. 13½x14

1966, May 10 **Photo.** **Unwmk.**

724 A239 3af tan & multi .75 .35
725 A239 4af brt grn & multi .85 .40
726 A239 8af violet & multi 1.50 .75
Nos. 724-726 (3) 3.10 1.50

Soccer Player and Globe — A240

1966, July 31 **Litho.** *Perf. 14x13½*

727 A240 2af rose red & blk .65 .20
728 A240 6af violet bl & blk 1.10 .25
729 A240 12af bister brn & blk 2.25 .55
Nos. 727-729 (3) 4.00 1.00

World Cup Soccer Championship, Wembley, England, July 11-30.

Cotton Flower and Boll — A241

5af, Silkworm. 7af, Farmer plowing with oxen.

1966, July 31 *Perf. 13½x14*

730 A241 1af multicolored .50 .20
731 A241 5af multicolored 1.00 .30
732 A241 7af multicolored 1.40 .40
Nos. 730-732 (3) 2.90 .90

Issued for the Day of Agriculture.

Independence Monument — A242

1966, Aug. 23 **Photo.** *Perf. 13½x14*

733 A242 1af multicolored .25 .20
734 A242 3af multicolored .75 .25

Issued to commemorate Independence Day.

Flag of Pashtunistan — A243

Perf. 11 Rough

1966, Aug. 31 **Litho.**

735 A243 1af bright blue .50 .20

"Free Pashtunistan Day."

Bagh-i-Bala Park Casino A244

Tourist publicity: 2af, Map of Afghanistan. 8af, Tomb of Abd-er-Rahman. The casino on 4af is the former summer palace of Abd-er-Rahman near Kabul.

1966, Oct. 3 **Photo.** *Perf. 13½x14*

736 A244 2af red & multi .20 .20
737 A244 4af multicolored .40 .30
738 A244 8af multicolored .65 .60
a. Souvenir sheet of 3, #736-738, imperf. 3.50 3.50
Nos. 736-738 (3) 1.25 1.10

Zahir Shah — A245

UNESCO Emblem — A246

1966, Oct. 14 *Perf. 14x13½*
739 A245 1af dk slate grn .20 .20
740 A245 5af red brown .50 .25

King Mohammed Zahir Shah, 52nd birthday. See Nos. 760-761.

1967, Mar. 6 **Litho.** *Perf. 12*
741 A246 2af multicolored .60 .20
742 A246 6af multicolored .75 .20
743 A246 12af multicolored 1.50 .30
Nos. 741-743 (3) 2.85 .70

20th anniv. of UNESCO.

Zahir Shah and UN Emblem A247

1967 **Photo.**
744 A247 5af multicolored .40 .20
745 A247 10af multicolored .75 .30

UN Intl. Org. for Refugees, 20th anniv.

New Power Station A248

5af, Carpet, vert. 8af, Cement factory.

1967, Jan. 7 **Photo.** *Perf. 13½x14*
746 A248 2af red lil & ol grn .20 .20
747 A248 5af multicolored .20 .20
748 A248 8af blk, dk bl & tan .40 .25
Nos. 746-748 (3) .80 .65

Issued to publicize industrial development.

International Tourist Year Emblem A249

Designs: 6af, International Tourist Year emblem and map of Afghanistan.

1967, May 11 **Photo.** *Perf. 12*
749 A249 2af yel, blk & lt bl .20 .20
750 A249 6af bis brn, blk & lt bl .40 .20
a. Souv. sheet, #749-750, imperf 1.00 1.00

Intl. Tourist Year, 1967. No. 750a sold for 10af.

Power Dam, Dorunta A250

Macaque — A251

6af, Sirobi Dam, vert. 8af, Reservoir at Jalalabad.

1967, July 2 **Photo.** *Perf. 12*
751 A250 1af dk green & lil .20 .20
752 A250 6af red brn & grnsh bl .35 .35
753 A250 8af plum & dk bl .50 .50
Nos. 751-753 (3) 1.05 1.05

Progress in agriculture through electricity.

1967, July 28 **Photo.** *Perf. 12*

Designs: 6af, Striped hyena, horiz. 12af, Persian gazelles, horiz.

754 A251 2af dull yel & indigo .25 .20
755 A251 6af lt green & sepia .70 .35
756 A251 12af lt bl & red brn 1.50 .75
Nos. 754-756 (3) 2.45 1.30

Pashtun Dancers A252

1967, Sept. 1 **Photo.** *Perf. 12*
757 A252 2af magenta & violet .50 .20

Issued for "Free Pashtunistan Day."

Retreat of British at Maiwand A253

Fireworks and UN Emblem — A254

1967, Aug. 24
758 A253 1af dk brn & org ver .25 .20
759 A253 2af dk brn & brt pink .50 .20

Issued to commemorate Independence Day.

King Type of 1966

1967, Oct. 15 **Photo.** *Perf. 14x13½*
760 A245 2af brown red .20 .20
761 A245 8af dark blue .50 .25

Issued to honor King Mohammed Zahir Shah on his 53rd birthday.

1967, Oct. 24 **Litho.** *Perf. 12*
762 A254 10af violet bl & multi .65 .35

Issued for United Nations Day.

Greco-Roman Wrestlers A255

Said Jamalluddin Afghan — A256

Design: 6af, Free style wrestlers.

1967, Nov. 20 **Photo.**
763 A255 4af ol grn & rose lil .50 .20
764 A255 6af dp carmine & brn .80 .20
a. Souv. sheet, #763-764, imperf 5.00 5.00

1968 Olympic Games.

1967, Nov. 27
765 A256 1af magenta .20 .20
766 A256 5af brown .35 .20

Said Jamalluddin Afghan, politician (1839-97).

Bronze Vase, 11th-12th Centuries — A257

WHO Emblem A258

Design: 7af, Bronze vase, Ghasnavide era, 11th-12th centuries.

1967, Dec. 23 **Photo.** *Perf. 12*
767 A257 3af lt green & brn .20 .20
768 A257 7af yel & slate grn .40 .30
a. Souv. sheet, #767-768, imperf 2.50 2.50

1968, Apr. 7 **Photo.** *Perf. 12*
769 A258 2af citron & brt bl .20 .20
770 A258 7af rose & brt bl .30 .20

20th anniv. of the WHO.

Karakul A259

1968, May 20 **Photo.** *Perf. 12*
771 A259 1af yellow & blk .25 .20
772 A259 6af lt blue & blk .70 .20
773 A259 12af ultra & dk brn 1.25 .40
Nos. 771-773 (3) 2.20 .80

Issued for the Day of Agriculture.

Map of Afghanistan A260

Victory Tower, Ghazni — A261

Design: 16af, Mausoleum, Ghazni.

1968, June 3 *Perf. 13½x14, 12*
774 A260 2af red, blk, lt bl & grn .20 .20
775 A261 3af yel, dk brn & lt bl .20 .20
776 A261 16af pink & multi .95 .50
Nos. 774-776 (3) 1.35 .90

Issued for tourist publicity.

Cinereous Vulture — A262

6af, Eagle owl. 7af, Greater flamingoes.

1968, July 3 *Perf. 12*
777 A262 1af sky blue & multi .75 .20
778 A262 6af yellow & multi 1.50 .20
779 A262 7af multicolored 1.75 .30
Nos. 777-779 (3) 4.00 .70

Game of "Pegsticking" A263

2af, Olympic flame & rings, vert. 12af, Buzkashi.

1968, July 20 **Photo.** *Perf. 12*
780 A263 2af multicolored .20 .20
781 A263 8af orange & multi .65 .30
782 A263 12af multicolored 1.00 .45
Nos. 780-782 (3) 1.85 .95

19th Olympic Games, Mexico City, 10/12-27.

Flower-decked Armored Car — A264

1968, Aug. 23
783 A264 6af multicolored .40 .20

Issued to commemorate Independence Day.

Flag of Pashtunistan A265

1968 Aug. 31 **Photo.** *Perf. 12*
784 A265 3af multicolored .25 .20

Issued for "Free Pashtunistan Day."

Zahir Shah — A266

Human Rights Flame — A267

1968, Oct. 14 **Photo.** *Perf. 12*
785 A266 2af ultra .20 .20
786 A266 8af brown .45 .30

King Mohammed Zahir Shah, 54th birthday.

1968, Oct. 24
787 A267 1af multicolored .20 .20
788 A267 2af violet, bis & blk .20 .20
789 A267 6af vio blk, bis & vio .40 .20
Nos. 787-789 (3) .80 .60

Souvenir Sheet

Imperf

790 A267 10af plum, bis & red org 1.50 1.50

International Human Rights Year.

Maolana Djalalodine Balkhi — A268

Kushan Mural — A269

1968, Nov. 26 **Photo.** *Perf. 12*
791 A268 4af dk green & mag .25 .20

Balkhi (1207-73), historian.

1969, Jan. 2 ***Perf. 12***

Design: 3af, Jug shaped like female torso.

792 A269 1af dk grn, mar & yel .25 .20
793 A269 3af violet, gray & mar .75 .20
a. Souv. sheet, #792-793, imperf 1.50 1.50

Archaeological finds at Bagram, 1st cent. B.C. to 2nd cent. A.D.

ILO Emblem A270

1969, Mar. 23 **Photo.** ***Perf. 12***

794 A270 5af lt yel, lemon & blk .30 .20
795 A270 8af lt bl, grnsh bl & blk .50 .30

50th anniv. of the ILO.

Arms Type of 1939

1969, May (?) **Typo.**

795A A79 100p dark green .20 .20
795B A79 150p deep brown .25 .20

Nos. 795A-795B were normally used as newspaper stamps.

Badakhshan Scene A271

Tourist Publicity: 2af, Map of Afghanistan. 7af, Three men on mules ascending the Pamir Mountains.

1969, July 6 **Photo.** ***Perf. 13½x14***

796 A271 2af ocher & multi .20 .20
797 A271 4af multicolored .30 .20
798 A271 7af multicolored .75 .20
a. Souv. sheet, #796-798, imperf 1.75 1.75
Nos. 796-798 (3) 1.25 .60

No. 798a sold for 15af.

Bust, from Hadda Treasure, 3rd-5th Centuries — A272

Zahir Shah and Queen Humeira — A273

Designs: 5af, Vase and jug. 10af, Statue of crowned woman. 5af and 10af from Bagram treasure, 1st-2nd centuries.

1969, Aug. 3 **Photo.** ***Perf. 14x13½***

799 A272 1af olive grn & gold .20 .20
800 A272 5af purple & gold .20 .20
801 A272 10af dp blue & gold .40 .30
Nos. 799-801 (3) .80 .70

1969, Aug. 23 ***Perf. 12***

802 A273 5af gold, dk bl & red brn .35 .20
803 A273 10af gold, dp lil & bl grn .65 .35

Issued to commemorate Independence Day.

Map of Pashtunistan and Rising Sun — A274

1969, Aug. 31 **Typo.** ***Perf. 10½***

804 A274 2af lt blue & red .20 .20

Issued for "Free Pashtunistan Day."

Zahir Shah — A275

1969, Oct. 14 **Photo.** ***Perf. 12***
Portrait in Natural Colors

805 A275 2af dk brown & gold .20 .20
806 A275 6af brown & gold .45 .20

King Mohammed Zahir Shah, 55th birthday.

UN Emblem and Flag of Afghanistan — A276

1969, Oct. 24 **Litho.** ***Perf. 13½***

807 A276 5af blue & multi .25 .20

Issued for United Nations Day.

ITU Emblem — A277

Crested Porcupine A278

1969, Nov. 12

808 A277 6af ultra & multi .30 .20
809 A277 12af rose & multi .60 .35

Issued for World Telecommunications Day.

1969, Dec. 7 **Photo.** ***Perf. 12***

1af, Long-tailed porcupine. 8af, Red deer.

810 A278 1af yellow & multi .25 .20
811 A278 3af blue & multi .75 .50
812 A278 8af pink & multi 2.00 1.00
Nos. 810-812 (3) 3.00 1.70

Man's First Footprints on Moon, and Earth — A279

1969, Dec. 28 ***Perf. 13½x14***

813 A279 1af yel grn & multi .20 .20
814 A279 3af yellow & multi .25 .20
815 A279 6af blue & multi .40 .20
816 A279 10af rose & multi .65 .30
Nos. 813-816 (4) 1.50 .90

Moon landing. See note after Algeria #427.

Anti-cancer Symbol — A280

Mirza Abdul Quader Bedel — A281

1970, Apr. 7 **Photo.** ***Perf. 14***

817 A280 2af dk grn & rose car .20 .20
818 A280 6af dk bl & rose claret .40 .20

Issued to publicize the fight against cancer.

1970, May 6 ***Perf. 14x13½***

819 A281 5af multicolored .25 .20

Mirza Abdul Quader Bedel (1643-1720), poet.

Education Year Emblem A282

Mother and Child A283

1970, June 7 **Photo.** ***Perf. 12***

820 A282 1af black .20 .20
821 A282 6af deep rose .35 .20
822 A282 12af green .75 .35
Nos. 820-822 (3) 1.30 .75

International Education Year 1970.

1970, June 15 ***Perf. 13½***

823 A283 6af yellow & multi .25 .20

Issued for Mother's Day.

UN Emblem, Scales of Justice, Spacecraft A284

1970, June 26

824 A284 4af yel, dk bl & dp bl .20 .20
825 A284 6af pink, dk bl & brt bl .35 .20

25th anniversary of United Nations.

Mosque of the Amir of the two Swords, Kabul A285

2af, Map of Afghanistan. 7af, Arch of Paghman.

1970, July 6 ***Perf. 12***
Size: 30½x30½mm

826 A285 2af lt bl, blk & citron .20 .20

Size: 36x26mm

827 A285 3af pink & multi .20 .20
828 A285 7af yellow & multi .40 .20
Nos. 826-828 (3) .80 .60

Issued for tourist publicity.

Zahir Shah Reviewing Troops — A286

1970, Aug. 23 **Photo.** ***Perf. 13½***

829 A286 8af multicolored .60 .25

Issued to commemorate Independence Day.

Pathans — A287

1970, Aug. 31 **Typo.** ***Perf. 10½***

830 A287 2af ultra & red .20 .20

Issued for "Free Pashtunistan Day."

Quail — A288

4af, Golden eagle. 6af, Ringnecked pheasant.

1970, Sept. **Photo.** ***Perf. 12***

831 A288 2af multicolored .50 .25
832 A288 4af multicolored 1.00 .50
833 A288 6af multicolored 1.50 .75
Nos. 831-833 (3) 3.00 1.50

Zahir Shah — A289

Red Crescents
A290

1970, Oct. 14 Photo. ***Perf. 14x13½***
834 A289 3af green & vio .20 .20
835 A289 7af dk bl & vio brn .60 .25

King Mohammed Zahir Shah, 56th birthday.

1970, Oct. 16 Typo. ***Perf. 10½***
836 A290 2af black, gold & red .20 .20

Issued for the Red Crescent Society.

UN Emblem and Charter
A291

1970, Oct. 24 Photo. ***Perf. 14***
837 A291 1af gold & multi .20 .20
838 A291 5af gold & multi .20 .20

United Nations Day.

Tiger Heads of 1871 — A292

1970, Nov. 10 ***Perf. 12***
839 A292 1af sal, lt grnsh bl & blk .25 .20
840 A292 4af lt ultra, yel & blk .50 .20
841 A292 12af lilac, lt bl & blk .85 .35
Nos. 839-841 (3) 1.60 .75

Cent. of the 1st Afghan postage stamps. The postal service was established in 1870, but the 1st stamps were issued in May, 1871.

Globe and Waves
A293

1971, May 17 Photo. ***Perf. 13½***
842 A293 12af green, blk & bl .60 .35

3rd World Telecommunications Day.

Callimorpha Principalis
A294

Designs: 3af, Epizygaenella species. 5af, Parnassius autocrator.

1971, May 30 ***Perf. 13½x14***
843 A294 1af vermilion & multi 1.00 .50
844 A294 3af yellow & multi 2.25 1.00
845 A294 5af ultra & multi 3.00 1.50
Nos. 843-845 (3) 6.25 3.00

"UNESCO" and Half of Ancient Kushan Statue — A295

1971, June 26 Photo. ***Perf. 13½***
846 A295 6af ocher & vio .40 .20
847 A295 10af lt blue & mar .65 .30

UNESCO-sponsored Intl. Kushani Seminar.

Tughra and Independence Monument — A296

1971, Aug. 23
848 A296 7af rose red & multi .40 .20
849 A296 9af red orange & multi .65 .30

Independence Day.

Pashtunistan Square, Kabul — A297

1971, Aug. 31 Typo. ***Perf. 10½***
850 A297 5af deep rose lilac .25 .20

"Free Pashtunistan Day."

Zahir Shah — A298

A299

1971, Oct. 14 Photo. ***Perf. 12½x12***
851 A298 9af lt green & multi .40 .30
852 A298 17af yellow & multi .75 .55

King Mohammed Zahir Shah, 57th birthday.

1971, Oct. 16 ***Perf. 14x13½***

Design: Map of Afghanistan, red crescent, various activities.

853 A299 8af lt bl, red, grn & blk .45 .25

For Afghan Red Crescent Society.

Equality Year Emblem
A300

1971, Oct. 24 ***Perf. 12***
854 A300 24af brt blue 1.25 .70

International Year Against Racial Discrimination and United Nations Day.

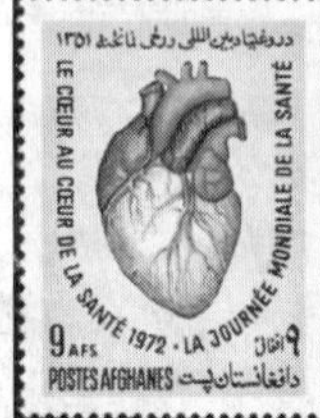

"Your Heart is your Health" — A301

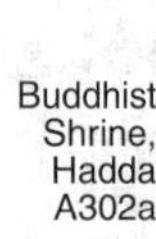

Tulip — A302

1972, Apr. 7 Photo. ***Perf. 14***
855 A301 9af pale yellow & multi .75 .30
856 A301 12af gray & multi 1.50 .35

World Health Day.

1972, June 5 Photo. ***Perf. 14***

Designs: 10af, Rock partridge, horiz. 12af, Lynx, horiz. 18af, Allium stipitatum (flower).

857 A302 7af green & multi .50 .25
858 A302 10af blue & multi .75 .35
859 A302 12af lt green & multi 1.00 .35
860 A302 18af blue grn & multi 1.25 .60
Nos. 857-860 (4) 3.50 1.55

Buddhist Shrine, Hadda
A302a

Designs: 7af, Greco-Bactrian animal seal, 250 B.C. 9af, Greco-Oriental temple, Ai-Khanoum, 3rd-2nd centuries B.C.

1972, July 16 Photo. ***Perf. 12***
861 A302a 3af brown & dl bl .50 .20
862 A302a 7af rose claret & dl grn .80 .20
863 A302a 9af green & lilac 1.10 .30
Nos. 861-863 (3) 2.40 .70

Tourist publicity.

King and Queen Reviewing Parade — A303

1972, Aug. 23 Photo. ***Perf. 13½***
864 A303 25af gold & multi 4.00 1.00

Independence Day.
Used as a provisional in 1978 with king and queen portion removed.

Wrestling
A304

10af, 19af, 21af, Wrestling, different hold.

1972, Aug. 26
865 A304 4af ol bis & multi .25 .20
866 A304 8af lt blue & multi .50 .25
867 A304 10af yel grn & multi .60 .30
868 A304 19af multicolored 1.25 .40
869 A304 21af lilac & multi 1.40 .45
a. Souv. sheet, #865-869, imperf 3.00 3.00
Nos. 865-869 (5) 4.00 1.60

20th Olympic Games, Munich, Aug. 26-Sept. 11. No. 869a sold for 60af.

Pathan and View of Tribal Territory — A305

Zahir Shah — A306

1972, Aug. 31 ***Perf. 12½x12***
870 A305 5af ultra & multi .25 .20

Pashtunistan day.

1972, Oct. 14 Photo. ***Perf. 14x13½***
871 A306 7af gold, blk & Prus bl 1.50 .30
872 A306 14af gold, blk & lt brn 2.50 .50

58th birthday of King Mohammed Zahir Shah.

City Destroyed by Earthquake, Refugees — A307

1972, Oct. 16 ***Perf. 13½***
873 A307 7af lt bl, red & blk .40 .20

For Afghan Red Crescent Society.

UN Emblem
A308

1972, Oct. 24
874 A308 12af lt ultra & blk .65 .35

UN Economic Commission for Asia and the Far East (ECAFE), 25th anniv.

Ceramics
A309

Designs: 9af, Leather coat, vert. 12af, Metal ware, vert. 16af, Inlaid artifacts.

1972, Dec. 10 Photo. *Perf. 12*

875 A309 7af gold & multi .40 .20
876 A309 9af gold & multi .55 .30
877 A309 12af gold & multi .70 .35
878 A309 16af gold & multi 1.00 .50
a. Souv. sheet, #875-878, imperf 2.25 2.25
Nos. 875-878 (4) 2.65 1.35

Handicraft industries. No. 878a sold for 45af.

WMO and National Emblems — A310

1973, Apr. 3 Photo. *Perf. 14*

879 A310 7af lt lil & dk grn .40 .20
880 A310 14af lt bl & dp claret .85 .45

Cent. of intl. meteorological cooperation.

Abu Rayhan al-Biruni — A311

Family — A312

1973, June 16 Photo. *Perf. 13½*

881 A311 10af multicolored .55 .30

Millennium of birth (973-1048), philosopher and mathematician.

1973, June 30 Photo. *Perf. 13½*

882 A312 9af orange & red lil .50 .30

Intl. Family Planning Fed., 21st anniv.

Republic

Impeyan Pheasant A313

Birds: 9af, Great crested grebe. 12af, Himalayan snow cock.

1973, July 29 Photo. *Perf. 12x12½*

883 A313 8af yellow & multi 1.25 .25
884 A313 9af blue & multi 1.75 .30
885 A313 12af multicolored 2.00 .35
Nos. 883-885 (3) 5.00 .90

Stylized Buzkashi Horseman A314

1973, Aug. *Perf. 13½*

886 A314 8af black .30 .25

Tourist publicity.

Fireworks A315

1973, Aug. 23 Photo. *Perf. 12*

887 A315 12af multicolored .45 .35

55th Independence Day.

Lake Abassine, Pashtunistan Flag — A316

1973, Aug. 31 *Perf. 14x13½*

888 A316 9af multicolored .50 .30

Pashtunistan Day.

Red Crescent A317

1973, Oct. 16 *Perf. 13½*

889 A317 10af red, blk & gold .60 .30

Red Crescent Society.

Kemal Ataturk A318

1973, Oct. 28 Litho. *Perf. 10½*

890 A318 1af blue .20 .20
891 A318 7af reddish brown .40 .20

50th anniversary of the Turkish Republic.

Human Rights Flame, Arms of Afghanistan A319

1973, Dec. 10 Photo. *Perf. 12*

892 A319 12af sil, blk & lt bl .45 .35

25th anniversary of the Universal Declaration of Human Rights.

Asiatic Black Bears A320

1974, Mar. 26 Litho. *Perf. 12*

893 A320 5af shown .35 .20
894 A320 7af Afghan hound .50 .20
895 A320 10af Persian goat .70 .30
896 A320 12af Leopard .90 .35
a. Souv. sheet, #893-896, imperf 5.00 5.00
Nos. 893-896 (4) 2.45 1.05

Worker and Farmer A321

1974, May 1 Photo. *Perf. 13½x12½*

897 A321 9af rose red & multi .40 .25

International Labor Day, May 1.

Independence Monument and Arch — A322

1974, May 27 Photo. *Perf. 12*

898 A322 4af blue & multi .20 .20
899 A322 11af gold & multi .35 .30

56th Independence Day.

Arms of Afghanistan and Symbol of Cooperation — A323

Pres. Mohammad Daoud Khan — A324

5af, Flag of Republic of Afghanistan. 15af, Soldiers, coat of arms of the Republic.

1974, July 25 *Perf. 13½x12½, 14*
Sizes: 4af, 15af, 36x22mm; 5af, 7af, 36x26, 26x36mm

900 A323 4af multicolored .20 .20
901 A323 5af multicolored .25 .20
902 A324 7af green, brn & blk .30 .20
a. Souv. sheet, #901-902, imperf .70 .70
903 A323 15af multicolored .65 .40
a. Souv. sheet, #900, 903, imperf 1.00 1.00
Nos. 900-903 (4) 1.40 1.00

1st anniv. of the Republic of Afghanistan.

Lesser Spotted Eagle A325

Birds: 6af, White-fronted goose, ruddy shelduck and gray-lag goose. 11af, European coots and European crane.

1974, Aug. 6 Photo. *Perf. 13½x13*

904 A325 1af car rose & multi .25 .20
905 A325 6af blue & multi .75 .20
906 A325 11af yellow & multi 1.50 .40
a. Strip of 3, #904-906 2.50 .80

Flags of Pashtunistan and Afghanistan — A326

1974, Aug. 31 Photo. *Perf. 14*

907 A326 5af multicolored .25 .20

Pashtunistan Day.

Natl. Arms A326a

1974, Aug. Typo. *Rough Perf. 11*

907A A326a 100p green

Coat of Arms A327

1974, Oct. 9

908 A327 7af gold, grn & blk .25 .20

Centenary of Universal Postal Union.

"un" and UN Emblem A328

1974, Oct. 24 Photo. *Perf. 14*

909 A328 5af lt ultra & dk bl .25 .20

United Nations Day.

Minaret of Jam — A329

Buddha, Hadda — A330

14af, Lady riding griffin, 2nd century, Bagram.

1975, May 5 Photo. *Perf. 13½*

910 A329	7af multicolored	.25	.20
911 A330	14af multicolored	.60	.30
912 A330	15af multicolored	.65	.30
a.	Souv. sheet, #910-912, imperf.	3.50	3.50
	Nos. 910-912 (3)	1.50	.80

South Asia Tourism Year 1975.

New Flag of Afghanistan A331

1975, May 27 Photo. *Perf. 12*

913 A331	16af multicolored	.75	.35

57th Independence Day.

Celebrating Crowd — A332

1975, July 17 Photo. *Perf. 13½*

914 A332	9af blue & multi	.45	.20
915 A332	12af carmine & multi	.55	.30

Second anniversary of the Republic.

Women's Year Emblems A333

1975, Aug. 24 Photo. *Perf. 12*

916 A333	9af car, lt bl & blk	.30	.20

International Women's Year 1975.

Pashtunistan Flag, Sun Rising Over Mountains A334

Mohammed Akbar Khan A335

1975, Aug. 31 *Perf. 13½*

917 A334	10af multicolored	.30	.25

Pashtunistan Day.

1976, Feb. 4 Photo. *Perf. 14*

918 A335	15af lt brown & multi	.45	.35

Mohammed Akbar Khan (1816-1846), warrior son of Amir Dost Mohammed Khan.

A336

Pres. Mohammad Daoud Khan — A337

1974-78 Photo. *Perf. 14*

919 A336	10af multi	.55	.20
920 A336	16af multi ('78)	2.00	*.75*
921 A336	19af multi	.75	.40
922 A336	21af multi	1.10	.45
923 A336	22af multi ('78)	3.00	*1.60*
924 A336	30af multi ('78)	4.00	*2.25*
925 A337	50af multi ('75)	2.25	1.10
926 A337	100af multi ('75)	4.50	2.00
	Nos. 919-926 (8)	18.15	8.75

Arms of Republic, Independence Monument — A338

1976, June 1 Photo. *Perf. 14*

927 A338	22af blue & multi	.65	.45

58th Independence Day.

Flag Raising — A339

1976, July 17 Photo. *Perf. 14*

928 A339	30af multicolored	.90	.75

Republic Day.

Mountain Peaks and Flag of Pashtunistan A340

1976, Aug. 31 Photo. *Perf. 14*

929 A340	16af multicolored	.50	.40

Pashtunistan Day.

Coat of Arms A340a

1976, Sept. Litho. *Perf. 11 Rough*

930 A340a	25p salmon	.25	.20
931 A340a	50p lt green	.25	.20
932 A340a	1af ultra	.25	.20
	Nos. 930-932 (3)	.75	.60

Flag and Views on Open Book A341

1977, May 27 Photo. *Perf. 14*

937 A341	20af green & multi	.60	.50

59th Independence Day.

Pres. Daoud and National Assembly — A342

President Taking Oath of Office A343

Designs: 10af, Inaugural address. 18af, Promulgation of Constitution.

1977, June 22

938 A342	7af multicolored	.65	.45
939 A343	8af multicolored	.70	.60
940 A343	10af multicolored	.90	.75
941 A342	18af multicolored	1.60	1.25
a.	Souvenir sheet of 4	3.00	3.00
	Nos. 938-941 (4)	3.85	3.05

Election of 1st Pres. and promulgation of Constitution. No. 941a contains 4 imperf. stamps similar to Nos. 938-941.

Jamalluddin Medal A344

1977, July 6 Photo. *Perf. 14*

942 A344	12af blue, blk & gold	.35	.30

Sajo Jamalluddin Afghani, reformer, 80th death anniversary.

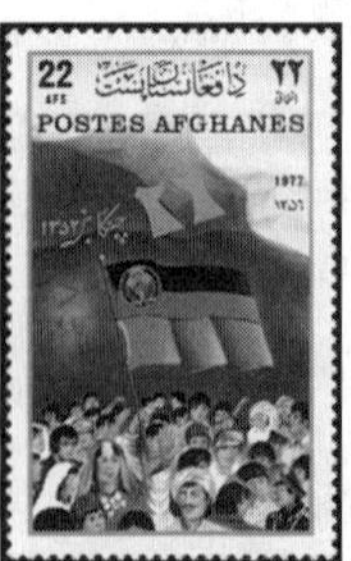

Afghanistan Flag over Crowd — A345

1977, July 17

943 A345	22af multicolored	.65	.55

Dancers, Fountain, Pashtunistan Flag — A346

1977, Aug. 31

944 A346	30af multicolored	.90	.75

Pashtunistan Day.

Arms and Carrier Pigeon A346a

1977, Oct. 30 Litho. *Perf. 11*

944A A346a	1af black & blue	.20	.20

Members of Parliament Congratulating Pres. Daoud — A347

1978, Feb. 5 Litho. *Perf. 14*

945 A347	20af multicolored	1.75	

Election of first president, first anniversary.

Map of Afghanistan, UPU Emblem — A348

1978, Apr. 1 Photo. *Perf. 14*

946 A348	10af green, blk & gold	.30	.25

Afghanistan's UPU membership, 50th anniv.

Wall Telephone and Satellite Station A349

1978, Apr. 12

947 A349	8af multicolored	.25	.20

Afghanistan's ITU membership, 50th anniv.

Democratic Republic

Arrows Pointing to Crescent, Cross and Lion — A350

1978, July 6 Litho. *Perf. 11 Rough*

948 A350	3af black	1.00	.50

50th anniv. of Afghani Red Crescent Soc.

Khalq Party Emblem — A350a

1978, Aug. Litho. *Perf. 11*

948A A350a 1af rose red & gold 1.25 .50
948B A350a 4af rose red & gold 1.75 .75

Qalai Bist Arch A351

1978, Aug. 19 *Perf. 14*

949 A351 16af Bamian Buddha 1.00 .40
949A A351 22af shown 1.25 .55
949B A351 30af Hazara Women 1.75 .90
Nos. 949-949B (3) 4.00 1.85

Men with Pashtunistan Flag — A352

Coat of Arms and Emblems A353

1978, Aug. 31 *Perf. 11 Rough*

950 A352 7af ultra & red .20 .20

Pashtunistan Day.

1978, Sept. 8 *Perf. 11*

951 A353 20af rose red .60 .50

World Literacy Day.

A354

Perf. 11½ Rough

1978, Oct. 25 Litho.

952 A354 18af light green .55 .45

Hero of Afghanistan.

Khalq Party Flag A355

1978, Oct. 19 Photo. *Perf. 11½*

953 A355 8af black, red & gold .25 .20
954 A355 9af black, red & gold .30 .20

"The mail serving the people."

Nour Mohammad Taraki — A356

1979, Jan. 1 Litho. *Perf. 12*

955 A356 12af multicolored .35 .20

Nour Mohammad Taraki, founder of People's Democratic Party of Afghanistan, installation as president.

Woman Breaking Chain — A357

1979, Mar. 8 Litho. *Perf. 11*

956 A357 14af red & ultra *1.50 .50*

Women's Day. Inscribed "POSSTES."

Map of Afghanistan, Census Emblem — A358

1979, Mar. 25 Litho. *Perf. 12*

957 A358 3af multicolored .75 .50

First comprehensive population census.

Farmers A359

1979, Mar. 21

958 A359 1af multicolored .50 .25

Agricultural advances.

Pres. Taraki Reading First Issue of Khalq — A360

1979, Apr. 11 *Perf. 12½x12*

959 A360 2af multicolored .25 .20

Khalq, newspaper of People's Democratic Republic of Afghanistan.

Pres. Noor Mohammad Taraki A361

Plaza with Tank Monument and Fountain — A362

House where Revolution Started — A363

Designs: 50p, Taraki, tank. 12af, House where 1st Khalq Party Congress was held.

Perf. 12, 12½x12 (A362)

1979, Apr. 27 Litho.

959A A363 50p multicolored .20 .20
960 A361 4af multicolored .20 .20
961 A362 5af multicolored .25 .20
962 A363 6af multicolored .30 .25
963 A363 12af multicolored .50 .45
Nos. 959A-963 (5) 1.45 1.30

1st anniversary of revolution.

Carpenter and Blacksmith A364

1979, May 1 *Perf. 12*

964 A364 10af multicolored .30 .25

Int'l Labor Day.

Children, Flag and Map of Afghanistan — A366

1979, June 1 Litho. *Perf. 12½x12*

966 A366 16af multicolored 1.50 .75

International Year of the Child.

Doves Circling Asia in Globe A366a

1979 Litho. *Perf. 11x10½*

966A A366a 2af red & blue 1.00 .20

Armed Afghans, Kabul Memorial and Arch — A367

Pashtunistan Citizens, Flag — A368

1979, Aug. 19 Litho. *Perf. 12*

967 A367 30af multicolored 1.25 .75

60th independence day.

1979, Aug. 31

968 A368 9af multicolored .30 .20

Pashtunistan Day.

UPU Day A369

1979, Oct. 9 Litho. *Perf. 12*

969 A369 15af multicolored .45 .40

Tombstone — A369a

1979, Oct. 25 Litho. *Perf. 12½x12*

969A A369a 22af multicolored 2.00 1.00

International Women's Day — A370

1980, Mar. 8 Litho. *Perf. 12*

970 A370 8af multicolored *1.25 .40*

Farmers' Day — A371

1980, Mar. 21 Litho. *Perf. 11½x12*

971 A371 2af multicolored 1.40 .45

Non-smoker and Smoker A372

1980, Apr. 7 ***Perf. 11½***
972 A372 5af multicolored 1.25 .40

Anti-smoking campaign; World Health Day.

Lenin, 110th Birth Anniversary A373

1980, Apr. 22 ***Perf. 12x12½***
973 A373 12af multicolored 1.75 .50

People and Fist on Map of Afghanistan — A374

1980, Apr. 27 Litho. ***Perf. 12½x12***
974 A374 1af multicolored .50 .20

Saur Revolution, 2nd anniversary.

International Workers' Solidarity Day — A375

1980, May 1
975 A375 9af multicolored .35 .20

Wrestling, Moscow '80 Emblem A376

1980, July 19 ***Perf. 12x12½, 12½x12***
976 A376 3af Soccer, vert. .55 .20
977 A376 6af shown .60 .20
978 A376 9af Buzkashi .65 .25
979 A376 10af Pegsticking .75 .25
Nos. 976-979 (4) 2.55 .90

22nd Summer Olympic Games, Moscow, July 19-Aug. 3.

61st Anniversary of Independence — A377

1980, Aug. 19 Litho. ***Perf. 12½x12***
980 A377 3af multicolored .45 .20

Pashtunistan Day — A378

1980, Aug. 30
981 A378 25af multicolored .75 .35

Intl. UPU Day A379

1980, Oct. 9 Litho. ***Perf. 12½x12***
982 A379 20af multicolored .60 .25

The resistance group headed by Amin Wardak released some stamps in 1980. Some of these are inscribed "WARDAK AFGHANISTAN," others "Solidarite Internationale Avec la Resistance Afghane." The status of these labels is questionable.

International Women's Day — A381

1981, Mar. 9 Litho. ***Perf. 12½x12***
984 A381 15af multicolored .90 .30

Farmers' Day — A382

1981, Mar. 20 Litho. ***Perf. 12½x12***
985 A382 1af multicolored .75 .25

Bighorn Mountain Sheep (Protected Species) A383

1981, Apr. 4 ***Perf. 12x12½***
986 A383 12af multicolored .90 .40

Saur Revolution, 3rd Anniversary A384

Intl. Workers' Solidarity Day — A385

1981, Apr. 27 ***Perf. 11***
987 A384 50p brown .45 .20

1981, May 1 ***Perf. 12½x12***
988 A385 10af multicolored .75 .25

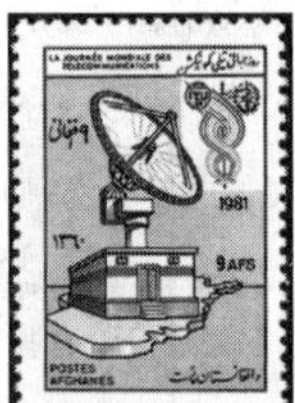
13th World Telecommunications Day — A387

1981, May 17 Litho. ***Perf. 12½x12***
990 A387 9af multicolored .40 .20

Intl. Children's Day — A388

1981, June 1 ***Perf. 12x12½***
991 A388 15af multicolored .75 .30

People's Independence Monument 62nd Anniv. of Independence — A389

1981, Aug. 19
992 A389 4af multicolored .75 .30

Pashtunistan Day — A390

1981, Aug. 31 Litho. ***Perf. 12***
992A A390 2af multicolored .45 .20

Intl. Tourism Day — A391

1981, Sept. 27 ***Perf. 12½x12***
993 A391 5af multicolored .45 .20

World Food Day — A392

1981, Oct. 16
995 A392 7af multicolored .50 .20

Asia-Africa Solidarity Meeting — A393

1981, Nov. 18 Litho. ***Perf. 11***
996 A393 8af blue .55 .20

Struggle Against Apartheid — A394

1300th Anniv. of Bulgaria A395

1981, Dec. 1 ***Perf. 12½x12***
997 A394 4af multicolored .35 .20

1981, Dec. 9 ***Perf. 12x12½***
998 A395 20af multicolored 1.00 .35

Buzkashi Game A395a

1980 Photo. ***Perf. 14***
998A A395a 50af multicolored 1.50 .75
998B A395a 100af multicolored 3.00 1.50

Intl. Women's Day A396

1982, Mar. 8 Litho. *Perf. 12*
999 A396 6af multicolored .40 .20

Farmers' Day — A397

1982, Mar. 21
1000 A397 4af multicolored .40 .20

Judas Trees — A398

Saur Revolution, 4th Anniv. — A399

Designs: Various local plants.

1982, Apr. 9 Litho. *Perf. 12*
1001 A398 3af shown .20 .20
1002 A398 4af Rose of Sharon .45 .20
1003 A398 16af Rhubarb plant .75 .25
Nos. 1001-1003 (3) 1.40 .65

1982, Apr. 27
1004 A399 1af multicolored .85 .30

George Dimitrov (1882-1947), First Prime Minister of Bulgaria — A400

Intl. Workers' Solidarity Day A401

1982, Apr. 30
1005 A400 30af multicolored 1.40 .50

1982, May 1
1006 A401 10af multicolored .60 .25

Storks — A402

1982, May 31
1007 A402 6af shown 1.00 .35
1008 A402 11af Nightingales 1.25 .45

Hedgehogs A403

1982, July 6 Litho. *Perf. 12*
1009 A403 3af shown .40 .20
1010 A403 14af Cobra 1.00 .35

See Nos. 1020-1022.

63rd Anniv. of Independence — A404

1982, Aug. 19
1011 A404 20af multicolored .85 .30

Pashtunistan Day — A405

1982, Aug. 31
1012 A405 32af multicolored 1.40 .50

World Tourism Day A406

1982, Sept. 27 Litho. *Perf. 12*
1013 A406 9af multicolored .65 .25

UPU Day A407

1982, Oct. 9
1014 A407 4af multicolored .50 .20

World Food Day A408

1982, Oct. 16
1015 A408 9af multicolored .75 .25

37th Anniv. of UN — A409

1982, Oct. 24
1016 A409 15af multicolored .60 .25

ITU Plenipotentiaries Conference, Nairobi, Sept. — A410

1982, Oct. 26
1017 A410 8af multicolored .40 .20

TB Bacillus Centenary A411

Human Rights Declaration, 34th Anniv. A412

1982, Nov. 24 Litho. *Perf. 12*
1018 A411 7af multicolored .35 .20

1982, Dec. 10
1019 A412 5af multicolored .35 .20

Animal Type of 1982

1982, Dec. 16
1020 A403 2af Lions .20 .20
1021 A403 7af Donkeys .45 .20
1022 A403 12af Marmots, vert. .75 .25
Nos. 1020-1022 (3) 1.40 .65

Intl. Women's Day — A413

Mir Alicher Nawai Research Decade — A414

1983, Mar. 8
1023 A413 3af multicolored .30 .20

1983, Mar. 19
1024 A414 22af multicolored .70 .25

Farmers' Day A415

1983, Mar. 21 Litho. *Perf. 12*
1025 A415 10af multicolored .40 .20

5th Anniv. of Saur Revolution A416

1983, Apr. 27 Litho. *Perf. 12*
1026 A416 15af multicolored .60 .25

Intl. Workers' Solidarity Day — A417

1983, May 1
1027 A417 2af multicolored .45 .20

World Communications Year — A418

1983, May 17
1028 A418 4af Modes of communication .25 .20
1029 A418 11af Building .50 .25

Intl. Children's Day — A419

1983, June 1 Litho. *Perf. 12*
1030 A419 25af multicolored .60 .25

2nd Anniv. of National Front — A420

1983, June 15
1031 A420 1af multicolored .20 .20

Local Butterflies A421

Various butterflies. 9af, 13af vert.

1983, July 6
1032 A421 9af multicolored .40 .30
1033 A421 13af multicolored 1.00 .55
1034 A421 21af multicolored 1.25 .65
Nos. 1032-1034 (3) 2.65 1.50

Struggle Against Apartheid — A422

1983, Aug. 1 Litho. *Perf. 12*
1035 A422 10af multicolored .30 .20

64th Anniv of Independence — A423

1983, Aug. 19

1036 A423 6af multicolored .25 .20

Parliament House A423a

1983, Sept. Litho. *Perf. 12*

1036A A423a 50af shown 2.00 .65
1036B A423a 100af Afghan Woman, Camel 4.00 1.25

A424

World Tourism Day — A425

1983, Sept. 27 Litho. *Perf. 12*

1037 A424 5af shown .25 .20
1038 A425 7af shown .35 .20
1039 A424 12af Golden statues .40 .20
1040 A425 16af Stone carving .50 .20
Nos. 1037-1040 (4) 1.50 .80

World Communications Year — A426

1983, Oct. 9 Litho. *Perf. 12*

1041 A426 14af Dish antenna, dove .50 .20
1042 A426 15af Building, flag .50 .20

World Food Day — A427

1983, Oct. 16 Litho. *Perf. 12*

1043 A427 14af multicolored .60 .25

Sports A428

1983, Nov. 1 Litho. *Perf. 12*

1044 A428 1af Soccer .20 .20
1045 A428 18af Boxing .70 .25
1046 A428 21af Wrestling .80 .25
Nos. 1044-1046 (3) 1.70 .70

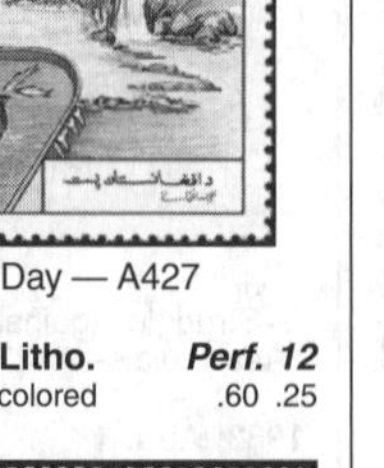

Pashtunistan Day — A428a

1983,Nov. Litho. *Perf. 12*

1046A A428a 3af Pathans Waving Flag .25 .20

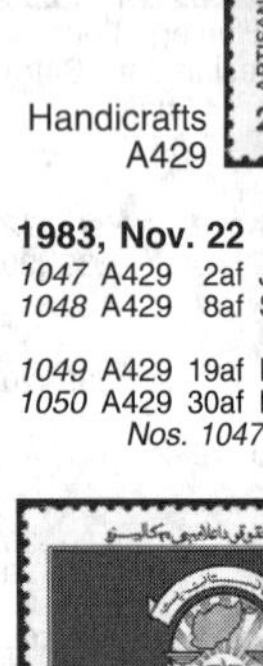

Handicrafts A429

1983, Nov. 22

1047 A429 2af Jewelry .20 .20
1048 A429 8af Stone ashtrays, dishes .30 .20
1049 A429 19af Furniture .55 .20
1050 A429 30af Leather goods 1.25 .40
Nos. 1047-1050 (4) 2.30 1.00

UN Declaration of Human Rights, 35th Anniv. A430

1983, Dec. 10 Litho. *Perf. 12*

1051 A430 20af multicolored .75 .25

Kabul Polytechnical Institute, 20th Anniv. — A431

1983, Dec. 28 *Perf. 12½x12*

1052 A431 30af multicolored 1.00 .35

1984 Winter Olympics A432

1984, Jan. *Perf. 12*

1053 A432 5af Figure skating .25 .20
1054 A432 9af Skiing .30 .20
1055 A432 11af Speed skating .40 .20
1056 A432 15af Hockey .50 .20
1057 A432 18af Biathlon .55 .20
1058 A432 20af Ski jumping .60 .25
1059 A432 22af Bobsledding .70 .25
Nos. 1053-1059 (7) 3.30 1.50

Intl. Women's Day — A433

1984, Mar. 8

1060 A433 4af multicolored .40 .25

Farmers' Day A434

Various agricultural scenes.

1984, Mar. 21 Litho. *Perf. 12*

1061 A434 2af multicolored .20 .20
1062 A434 4af multicolored 20 .20
1063 A434 7af multicolored 20 .20
1064 A434 9af multicolored 20 .20
1065 A434 15af multicolored .30 .20
1066 A434 18af multicolored .35 .20
1067 A434 20af multicolored .40 .20
Nos. 1061-1067 (7) 1.85 1.40

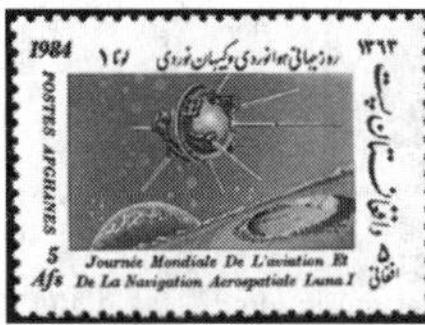

World Aviation Day A435

1984, Apr. 12

1068 A435 5af Luna 1 .25 .20
1069 A435 8af Luna 2 .35 .20
1070 A435 11af Luna 3 .45 .20
1071 A435 17af Apollo 11 .55 .20
1072 A435 22af Soyuz 6 .70 .25
1073 A435 28af Soyuz 7 .70 .25
1074 A435 34af Soyuz 6, 7, 8 1.00 .35
Nos. 1068-1074 (7) 4.00 1.65

Souvenir Sheet

Perf. 12x12½

1075 A435 25af S. Koroliov 1.00 .70

No. 1075 contains one 30x41mm stamp.

Saur Revolution, 6th Anniv. A436

1984, Apr. 27 *Perf. 12*

1076 A436 3af multicolored .25 .20

65th Anniv. of Independence — A437

1984, Aug. 19 Litho. *Perf. 12*

1077 A437 6af multicolored .30 .20

Pashto's and Balutchi's Day A438

1984, Aug. 31

1078 A438 3af Symbolic sun, tribal terr. .20 .20

Wildlife A439

Perf. 12½x12, 12x12½

1984, May 5 Litho.

1079 A439 1af Cape hunting dog, vert. .20 .20
1080 A439 2af Argali sheep, vert. .20 .20
1081 A439 6af Przewalski's horse .40 .20
1082 A439 8af Wild boar, vert. .55 .20
1083 A439 17af Snow leopard 1.00 .30
1084 A439 19af Tiger 1.25 .40
1085 A439 22af Indian elephant, vert. 1.40 .45
Nos. 1079-1085 (7) 5.00 1.95

19th UPU Congress, Hamburg A440

1984, June 18 *Perf. 12x12½*

1086 A440 25af German postman, 17th cent. .90 .30
1087 A440 35af Postrider, 16th cent. 1.40 .45
1088 A440 40af Carrier pigeon, letter 1.60 .55
Nos. 1086-1088 (3) 3.90 1.30

Souvenir Sheet

1089 A440 50af Hamburg No. 3 in black 2.50 1.50

No. 1089 contains one 30x40mm stamp.

Natl. Aviation, 40th Anniv. A441

Soviet civil aircraft.

1984, June 29

1090 A441 1af Antonov AN-2 .20 .20
1091 A441 4af Ilyushin IL-12 .25 .20
1092 A441 9af Tupolev TU-104 .55 .25
1093 A441 10af Ilyushin IL-18 .60 .25
1094 A441 13af Tupolev TU-134 .80 .25
1095 A441 17af Ilyushin IL-62 1.00 .30
1096 A441 21af Ilyushin IL-28 1.25 .40
Nos. 1090-1096 (7) 4.65 1.85

Ettore Bugatti (1881-1947), Type 43, Italy — A442

Classic automobiles and their designers: 5af, Henry Ford, 1903 Model A, US. 8af, Rene Panhard (1841-1908), 1899 Landau, France. 11af, Gottlieb Daimler (1834-1900), 1935 Daimler-Benz, Germany. 12af, Carl Benz (1844-1929), 1893 Victoris, Germany. 15af, Armand Peugeot (1848-1915), 1892 Vis-a-Vis, France. 22af, Louis Chevrolet (1879-1941), 1925 Sedan, US.

1984, June 30

1097 A442 2af multicolored .20 .20
1098 A442 5af multicolored .20 .20
1099 A442 8af multicolored .45 .20
1100 A442 11af multicolored .55 .20
1101 A442 12af multicolored .65 .25
1102 A442 15af multicolored .75 .25
1103 A442 22af multicolored 1.10 .35
Nos. 1097-1103 (7) 3.90 1.65

Qalai Bist Arch A443

World Tourism Day: 2af, Ornamental buckled harness. 5af, Victory Monument and Memorial Arch, Kabul. 9af, Standing sculpture of Afghani ruler and attendants. 15af, Buffalo riders in snow. 19af, Camel driver, tent, camel in caparison. 21af, Horsemen playing buzkashi.

1984, Sept. 27

1104	A443	1af	multicolored	.20	.20
1105	A443	2af	multicolored	.20	.20
1106	A443	5af	multicolored	.20	.20
1107	A443	9af	multicolored	20	.20
1108	A443	15af	multicolored	.40	.20
1109	A443	19af	multicolored	.65	.25
1110	A443	21af	multicolored	.65	.25
			Nos. 1104-1110 (7)	2.50	1.50

UN World Food Day — A444

Fruit-bearing trees.

1984, Oct. 16

1111	A444	2af	multicolored	.20	.20
1112	A444	4af	multicolored	.20	.20
1113	A444	6af	multicolored	.25	.20
1114	A444	9af	multicolored	.30	.20
1115	A444	13af	multicolored	.40	.20
1116	A444	15af	multicolored	.45	.20
1117	A444	26af	multicolored	.70	.25
			Nos. 1111-1117 (7)	2.50	1.45

People's Democratic Party, 20th Anniv. A445

1985, Jan. 1

1118	A445	25af	multicolored	1.00	.35

Farmer's Day A446

1985, Mar. 2

1119	A446	1af	Oxen	.20	.20
1120	A446	3af	Mare, foal	.20	.20
1121	A446	7af	Brown horse	.20	.20
1122	A446	8af	White horse, vert.	.35	.20
1123	A446	15af	Sheep, sheepskins	.40	.20
1124	A446	16af	Shepherd, cattle, sheep	.60	.25
1125	A446	25af	Family, camels	.85	.30
			Nos. 1119-1125 (7)	2.80	1.55

Geologist's Day — A447

1985, Apr. 5

1126	A447	4af	multicolored	.25	.20

Lenin Leading Red Army, 1917 — A448

Lenin and: 10af, Soviet Workers' Party deputies, Smolny. 15af, Revolutionaries, 1917, Leningrad. 50af, Portrait.

1985, Apr. 21 ***Perf. 12x12½***

1127	A448	10af	multicolored	.55	.20
1128	A448	15af	multicolored	.70	.25
1129	A448	25af	multicolored	1.25	.40
			Nos. 1127-1129 (3)	2.50	.85

Souvenir Sheet

1130	A448	50af	multicolored	1.50	1.25

Saur Revolution, 7th Anniv. — A449

1985, Apr. 27

1131	A449	21af	multicolored	.85	.30

Berlin-Treptow Soviet War Memorial, Red Army at Siege of Berlin, 1945 — A450

9af, Victorious Motherland monument, fireworks over Kremlin. 10af, Caecilienhof, site of Potsdam Treaty signing, Great Britain, USSR & US flags.

1985, May 9 ***Perf. 12½x12***

1132	A450	6af	multicolored	.40	.20
1133	A450	9af	multicolored	.55	.20
1134	A450	10af	multicolored	.65	.25
			Nos. 1132-1134 (3)	1.60	.65

End of World War II, defeat of Nazi Germany, 40th anniv.

INTELSAT, 20th Anniv. A451

Designs: 6af, INTELSAT satellite orbiting Earth. 9af, INTELSAT III. 10af, Rocket launch, Baikanur Space Center, vert.

Perf. 12x12½, 12½x12

1985, Apr. 6 **Litho.**

1135	A451	6af	multicolored	.40	.20
1136	A451	9af	multicolored	.45	.20
1137	A451	10af	multicolored	.60	.20
			Nos. 1135-1137 (3)	1.45	.60

12th World Youth Festival, Moscow — A452

1985, May 5

1138	A452	7af	Olympic stadium, Moscow	.20	.20
1139	A452	12af	Festival emblem	.45	.20
1140	A452	13af	Kremlin	.45	.20
1141	A452	18af	Folk doll, emblem	.65	.25
			Nos. 1138-1141 (4)	1.75	.85

Intl. Child Survival Campaign A453

1985, June 1

1142	A453	1af	Weighing child	.20	.20
1143	A453	2af	Immunization	.20	.20
1144	A453	4af	Breastfeeding	.25	.20
1145	A453	5af	Mother, child	.25	.20
			Nos. 1142-1145 (4)	.90	.80

Flowers A454

1985, July 5

1146	A454	2af	Oenothera affinis	.20	.20
1147	A454	4af	Erythrina crista-galli	.25	.20
1148	A454	8af	Tillandsia aeranthos	.40	.20
1149	A454	13af	Vinca major	.70	.25
1150	A454	18af	Mirabilis jalapa	1.00	.35
1151	A454	25af	Cypella herbertii	1.40	.45
1152	A454	30af	Clytostoma callistegioides	1.75	.60
			Nos. 1146-1152 (7)	5.70	2.25

Souvenir Sheet

Perf. 12½x11½

1153	A454	75af	Sesbania punicea, horiz.	4.00	3.00

ARGENTINA '85.

Independence, 66th Anniv. — A455

1985, Aug. 19 ***Perf. 12x12½***

1154	A455	33af	Mosque	1.40	.45

Pashto's and Baluchi's Day A456

1985, Aug. 30

1155	A456	25af	multicolored	1.00	.35

UN Decade for Women A457

1985, Sept. 22

1156	A457	10af	Emblems	.45	.20

World Tourism Day, 10th Anniv. A457a

1985, Sept. 27 **Litho.** ***Perf. 12***

1156A	A457a	1af	Guldara Stupa	.20	.20
1156B	A457a	2af	Mirwais Tomb, vert.	.20	.20
1156C	A457a	10af	Statue of Bamyan, vert.	.30	.20
1156D	A457a	13af	No Gumbad Mosque, vert.	.45	.20
1156E	A457a	14af	Pule Kheshti Mosque	.45	.20
1156F	A457a	15af	Bost Citadel	.50	.20
1156G	A457a	20af	Ghazni Minaret, vert.	.75	.25
			Nos. 1156A-1156G (7)	2.85	1.45

Sports A457b

Perf. 12x12½, 12½x12

1985, Oct. 3 **Litho.**

1156H	A457b	1af	Boxing	.20	.20
1156I	A457b	2af	Volleyball	.20	.20
1156J	A457b	3af	Soccer, vert.	.20	.20
1156K	A457b	12af	Buzkashi	.45	.20
1156L	A457b	14af	Weight lifting	.50	.20
1156M	A457b	18af	Wrestling	.60	.25
1156N	A457b	25af	Peg sticking	1.10	.35
			Nos. 1156H-1156N (7)	3.25	1.60

World Food Day A457c

1985, Oct. 16

1156O	A457c	25af	multicolored	.85	.30

UN 40th Anniv. — A458

Birds — A459

1985, Oct. 24 ***Perf. 12½x12***

1157	A458	22af	multicolored	.85	.30

1985, Oct. 25 ***Perf. 12½x12, 12x12½***

1158	A459	2af	Jay	.20	.20
1159	A459	4af	Plover, hummingbird	.60	.25
1160	A459	8af	Pheasant	.60	.25
1161	A459	13af	Hoopoe	.95	.30
1162	A459	18af	Falcon	1.25	.35
1163	A459	25af	Partridge	1.60	.50
1164	A459	30af	Pelicans, horiz.	2.10	.70
			Nos. 1158-1164 (7)	7.30	2.55

Souvenir Sheet

Perf. 12x12½

1165 A459 75af Parakeets 6.00 5.00

Mushrooms A460

1985, June 10 Litho. *Perf. 12½x12*

1165A A460 3af Tricholomopsis rutilans .20 .20
1166 A460 4af Boletus miniatoporus .25 .20
1167 A460 7af Amanita rubescens .45 .20
1168 A460 11af Boletus scaber .65 .25
1169 A460 12af Coprinus atramentarius .75 .25
1170 A460 18af Hypholoma 1.10 .35
1171 A460 20af Boletus aurantiacus 1.25 .40
Nos. 1165A-1171 (7) 4.65 1.85

World Wildlife Fund — A461

1985, Nov. 25

1172 A461 2af Leopard, cubs *.40 .20*
1173 A461 9af Adult's head *1.40 .45*
1174 A461 11af Adult *2.25 .75*
1175 A461 15af Cub *3.50 1.10*
Nos. 1172-1175 (4) 7.55 2.50

Motorcycle, Cent. — A462

Designs: Different makes and landmarks.

1985, Dec. 16

1176 A462 2af multicolored .20 .20
1177 A462 4af multicolored .20 .20
1178 A462 8af multicolored .25 .20
1179 A462 13af multicolored .65 .25
1180 A462 18af multicolored .80 .25
1181 A462 25af multicolored 1.10 .35
1182 A462 30af multicolored 1.25 .40
Nos. 1176-1182 (7) 4.45 1.85

Souvenir Sheet

Perf. 11½x12½

1183 A462 75af multicolored 3.50 2.50

People's Democratic Party, 21st Anniv. — A463

1986, Jan. 1 *Perf. 12½x12*

1184 A463 2af multicolored .30 .20

27th Soviet Communist Party Congress — A464

1986, Mar. 31

1185 A464 25af Lenin .75 .25

First Man in Space, 25th Anniv. — A465

Designs: 3af, Spacecraft. 7af, Soviet space achievement medal, vert. 9af, Rocket lift-off, vert. 11af, Yuri Gagarin, military decorations, vert. 13af, Gagarin, cosmonaut. 15af, Gagarin, politician. 17af, Gagarin wearing flight suit, vert.

Perf. 12½x12, 12x12½

1986, Apr. 12 Litho.

1186 A465 3af multicolored .20 .20
1187 A465 7af multicolored .25 .20
1188 A465 9af multicolored .40 .20
1189 A465 11af multicolored .45 .20
1190 A465 13af multicolored .50 .20
1191 A465 15af multicolored .55 .20
1192 A465 17af multicolored .65 .25
Nos. 1186-1192 (7) 4.50 4.50

Loya Jirgah (Grand Assembly) of the People's Democratic Republic, 1st Anniv. A465a

1986, Apr. 23 Litho. *Perf. 12x12½*

1192A A465a 3af multicolored .25 .20

Intl. Day of Labor Solidarity — A465b

1986, May 1 *Perf. 12½x12*

1192B A465b 5af multicolored .25 .20

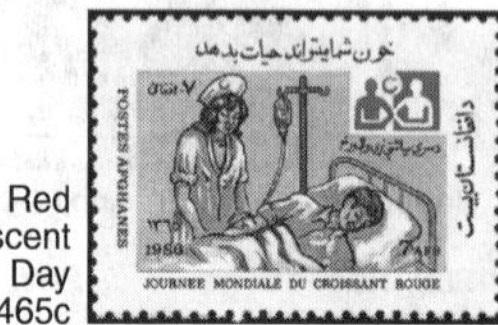

Intl. Red Crescent Day A465c

1986, May 8 *Perf. 12x12½*

1192C A465c 7af multicolored .40 .20

Intl. Children's Day A466

1986, June 1 *Perf. 12*

1193 A466 1af Mother, children, vert. .20 .20
1194 A466 3af Mother, child, vert. .20 .20
1195 A466 9af Children, map .30 .20
Nos. 1193-1195 (3) .70 .60

World Youth Day A466a

1986, July 31 *Perf. 12x12½*

1195A A466a 15af multicolored .60 .25

Pashtos' and Baluchis' Day A467

1986, Aug. 31 *Perf. 12x12½*

1196 A467 4af multicolored .25 .20

Intl. Peace Year — A468

1986, Sept. 30 Photo. *Perf. 12½x12*

1197 A468 12af black & Prus blue .50 .20

A469

1986 World Cup Soccer Championships, Mexico — A470

Various soccer plays.

1986, Apr. 15 Litho. *Perf. 12*

1198 A469 3af multi, vert. .20 .20
1199 A469 4af multicolored .20 .20
1200 A469 7af multicolored .25 .20
1201 A469 11af multi, vert. .40 .20
1202 A469 12af multicolored .45 .20
1203 A469 18af multi, vert. .70 .25
1204 A469 20af multi, vert. .80 .25
Nos. 1198-1204 (7) 4.50 4.50

Souvenir Sheet

Perf. 12½x12

1205 A470 75af multicolored 4.00 3.00

A471

A472

1986, Apr. 21 *Perf. 12½x12*

1206 A471 16af Lenin .60 .40

1986, Apr. 27 Litho. *Perf. 12½x12*

1207 A472 8af multicolored .30 .20

Saur revolution, 8th anniv.

Natl. Independence, 67th Anniv. — A473

1986, Aug. 19 Litho. *Perf. 12½x12*

1208 A473 10af multicolored .45 .20

Literacy Day A474

1986, Sept. 18 *Perf. 12x12½*

1209 A474 2af multicolored .25 .20

Dogs — A475

Lizards — A476

1986, May 19 Litho. *Perf. 12x12½*

1210 A475 5af St. Bernard .25 .20
1211 A475 7af Collie .30 .20
1212 A475 8af Pointer .35 .20
1213 A475 9af Golden retriever .40 .20
1214 A475 11af German shepherd .50 .20
1215 A475 15af Bulldog .65 .25
1216 A475 20af Afghan hound .85 .30
Nos. 1210-1216 (7) 4.50 4.50

1986, July 7 *Perf. 12x12½, 12½x12*

1217 A476 3af Cobra .20 .20
1218 A476 4af shown .25 .20
1219 A476 5af Praying mantis .25 .20
1220 A476 8af Beetle .30 .20
1221 A476 9af Tarantula .35 .20
1222 A476 10af Python .35 .20
1223 A476 11af Scorpions .40 .20
Nos. 1217-1223 (7) 3.00 3.00

Nos. 1217, 1219, 1221-1223 horiz.

STOCKHOLMIA '86 — A477

Ships.

1986, Aug. 28 *Perf. 12½x12*
1224 A477 4af multicolored .25 .20
1225 A477 5af multicolored .30 .20
1226 A477 6af multicolored .40 .20
1227 A477 7af multicolored .45 .20
1228 A477 8af multicolored .55 .20
1229 A477 9af multicolored .55 .20
1230 A477 11af multicolored .65 .25
Nos. 1224-1230 (7) 3.00 3.00

Souvenir Sheet

1231 A477 50af Galley 2.50 2.00

A479

A480

1986, Sept. 14 *Perf. 12*
1232 A479 3af lt blue, blk & olive gray .35 .20

Reunion of Afghan tribes under the Supreme Girgah.

1986, Oct. 25 *Perf. 12½x12*
1233 A480 3af black & brt ver .35 .20

Natl. youth solidarity.

Locomotives — A481

1986, June 21 *Perf. 12½x12*
1234 A481 4af multicolored .25 .20
1235 A481 5af multicolored .25 .20
1236 A481 6af multicolored .35 .20
1237 A481 7af multicolored .40 .20
1238 A481 8af multicolored .50 .20
1239 A481 9af multicolored .60 .20
1240 A481 11af multicolored .65 .25
Nos. 1234-1240 (7) 3.00 3.00

Fish A482

Various fish.

1986, May 25
1241 A482 5af multicolored .25 .20
1242 A482 7af multicolored .30 .20
1243 A482 8af multicolored .40 .20
1244 A482 9af multicolored .45 .20
1245 A482 11af multicolored .55 .20
1246 A482 15af multicolored .70 .25
1247 A482 20af multicolored .90 .30
Nos. 1241-1247 (7) 4.50 4.50

Saur Revolution, 9th Anniv. A483

1987, Apr. 27 *Perf. 12*
1248 A483 3af multicolored .25 .20

Natl. Reconciliation — A484

1987, May 27 *Perf. 12x12½*
1249 A484 3af multicolored .25 .20

A485

A486

UN Child Survival Campaign — A487

1987, June 1 *Perf. 12*
1250 A485 1af multicolored .20 .20
1251 A486 5af multicolored .20 .20
1252 A487 9af multicolored .25 .20
Nos. 1250-1252 (3) .65 .60

Conference of Clergymen and Ulema, 1st Anniv. A488

1987, June 30
1253 A488 5af multicolored .30 .20

Butterflies — A489 A490

1987, July 3
1254 A489 7af multicolored .30 .20
1255 A489 9af multi, diff. .40 .20
1256 A489 10af multi, diff. .45 .20
1257 A489 12af multi, diff. .50 .25
1258 A489 15af multi, diff. .55 .25
1259 A489 22af multi, diff. .80 .40
1260 A489 25af multi, diff. 1.00 .50
Nos. 1254-1260 (7) 6.00 6.00

10af, 15af and 22af horiz.

1987, Aug. 11
1261 A490 1af multicolored .20 .25

1st election of local representatives for State Power and Administration.

Natl. Independence, 68th Anniv. — A490a

1987, Aug. 19
1261A A490a 3af multicolored .20 .20

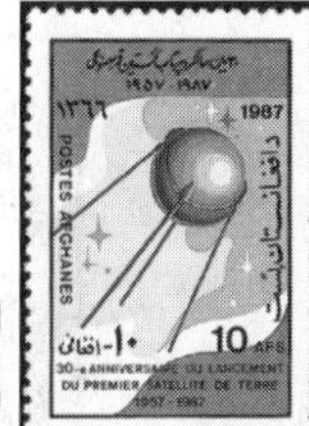

1st Artificial Satellite (Sputnik), 30th Anniv. — A491

1987, Oct. 4 **Litho.** *Perf. 12½x12*
1262 A491 10af Sputnik .35 .20
1263 A491 15af Rocket launch .50 .20
1264 A491 25af Soyuz .65 .25
Nos. 1262-1264 (3) 3.00 3.00

World Post Day A492

1987, Oct. 9 *Perf. 12x12½*
1265 A492 22af multicolored .75 .50

Intl. Communications and Transport Day — A493

1987, Oct. 24 *Perf. 12½x12*
1266 A493 42af multicolored 2.00 1.00

October Revolution in Russia, 70th Anniv. — A494

Mice — A495

1987, Nov. 7
1267 A494 25af Lenin .90 .50

1987, Dec. 6 *Perf. 12½x12, 12x12½*

Various mice. Nos. 1269-1272 horiz.

1268 A495 2af multicolored .20 .20
1269 A495 4af multi, diff. .25 .20
1270 A495 8af multi, diff. .30 .20
1271 A495 16af multi, diff. .55 .20
1272 A495 20af multi, diff. .70 .25
Nos. 1268-1272 (5) 3.00 3.00

Medicinal Plants — A496

Pashto's and Baluchis' Day — A497

1987, Nov. 11 **Litho.** *Perf. 12*
1273 A496 3af Castor bean .20 .20
1274 A496 6af Licorice .25 .20
1275 A496 9af Chamomile .40 .20
1276 A496 14af Datura .65 .25
1277 A496 18af Dandelion .75 .30
Nos. 1273-1277 (5) 2.25 1.15

1987, Aug. 30
1278 A497 4af multicolored .25 .20

Dinosaurs A498

Pashtos' and Baluchis' Day — A499

Perf. 12½x12, 12x12½

1988, June 6 **Litho.**
1279 A498 3af Mesosaurus .20 .20
1280 A498 5af Styracosaurus .25 .20
1281 A498 10af Uinatherium .45 .20
1282 A498 15af Protoceratops .70 .25
1283 A498 20af Stegosaurus .90 .30
1284 A498 25af Ceratosaurus 1.10 .35
1285 A498 30af Dinornis maximus 1.50 .60
Nos. 1279-1285 (7) 5.10 2.10

Nos. 1280-1283 horiz.

1988, Aug. 30 *Perf. 12½x12*
1286 A499 23af multicolored .75 .50

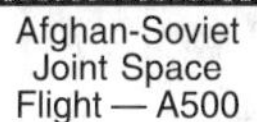

Afghan-Soviet Joint Space Flight — A500

Valentina Tereshkova, 1st Woman in Space, 25th Anniv. — A501

1988, Aug. 30
1287 A500 32af multicolored .75 .40

1988, Oct. 16 *Perf. 12x12½, 12½x12*
1288 A501 10af Portrait, rocket, horiz. .45 .25
1289 A501 15af Lift-off, dove .65 .30
1290 A501 25af Spacecraft, Earth, horiz. .90 .45
Nos. 1288-1290 (3) 2.00 1.00

Traditional Crafts — A502

Precious and Semiprecious Gems — A503

Perf. 12x12½, 12½x12

1988, Nov. 9 **Litho.**

1291	A502	2af	Pitcher, bowls	.20	.20
1292	A502	4af	Vases	.20	.20
1293	A502	5af	Dress	.20	.20
1294	A502	9af	Mats, napkins	.25	.20
1295	A502	15af	Pocketbooks	.40	.20
1296	A502	23af	Jewelry	.65	.25
1297	A502	50af	Furniture	1.25	.50
			Nos. 1291-1297 (7)	3.15	1.75

Nos. 1291-1292, 1294-1297 horiz.

1988, Dec. 5 ***Perf. 12½x12***

1298	A503	13af	Emeralds	.65	.25
1299	A503	37af	Lapiz lazuli	1.50	.60
1300	A503	40af	Rubies	1.75	.75
			Nos. 1298-1300 (3)	3.90	1.60

1988 Winter Olympics, Calgary — A504

1988, Dec. 25

1301	A504	2af	Women's figure skating	.20	.20
1301A	A504	5af	Skiing	.20	.20
1301B	A504	9af	Bobsledding	.30	.20
1301C	A504	22af	Biathlon	.80	.35
1301D	A504	37af	Speed skating	1.50	.65

Size: 80x60mm

1302	A504	75af	Ice hockey	2.50	2.50
			Nos. 1301-1302 (6)	5.50	4.10

A510

A511

A512

A513

A513a

Flowers — A514

Various flowering plants.

Perf. 12x12½, 12½x12

1988, Jan. 27 **Litho.**

1303	A510	3af	multicolored	.20	.20
1304	A511	5af	multicolored	.25	.20
1305	A511	7af	multi, vert.	.35	.20
1306	A512	9af	multicolored	.40	.20
1307	A513	12af	multicolored	.50	.20
1308	A513a	15af	multicolored	.60	.25
1309	A514	24af	multicolored	1.00	.50
			Nos. 1303-1309 (7)	3.30	1.75

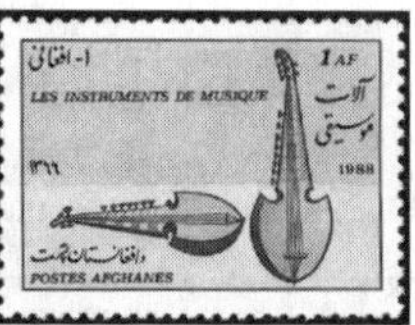

Traditional Musical Instruments A515

String and percussion instruments.

1988, Jan. 15 **Litho.** ***Perf. 12***

1310	A515	1af	shown	.20	.20
1311	A515	3af	drums	.20	.20
1312	A515	5af	multi, diff.	.20	.20
1313	A515	15af	multi, diff.	.50	.20
1314	A515	18af	multi, diff.	.55	.25
1315	A515	25af	multi, diff.	.85	.35
1316	A515	33af	multi, diff.	1.10	.45
			Nos. 1310-1316 (7)	3.60	1.85

Admission of Afghanistan to the ITU and UPU, 60th Anniv. — A516

1988, Apr. 13 **Litho.** ***Perf. 12***

1317	A516	20af	multicolored	.60	.30

Saur Revolution, 10th Anniv. A517

1988, Apr. 23

1318	A517	10af	multicolored	.45	.25

Fruit A518

1988, July 18 **Litho.** ***Perf. 12***

1319	A518	2af	Baskets, compote	.20	.20
1320	A518	4af	Four baskets	.20	.20
1321	A518	7af	Basket	.25	.20
1322	A518	8af	Grapes, vert.	.30	.20
1323	A518	16af	Market	.50	.20
1324	A518	22af	Market, diff.	.75	.30
1325	A518	25af	Vendor, vert.	.90	.40
			Nos. 1319-1325 (7)	3.10	1.70

Jawaharlal Nehru (1889-1964), 1st Prime Minister of Independent India — A519

1988, Nov. 14

1326	A519	40af	multicolored	1.50	.75

Natl. Independence, 69th Anniv. — A520

1988, Aug. 1

1327	A520	24af	multicolored	.80	.40

Intl. Red Cross and Red Crescent Organizations, 125th Annivs. — A521

1988, Sept. 26

1328	A521	10af	multicolored	.50	.25

Natl. Reconciliation Institute, 2nd Anniv. — A522

1989, Jan. 4

1329	A522	4af	multicolored	.20	.20

Chess A523

Boards, early matches and hand-made chessmen.

1989, Feb. 2 **Litho.** ***Perf. 12x12½***

1330	A523	2af	Bishop	.20	.20
1331	A523	3af	Queen	.25	.20
1332	A523	4af	King (bust)	.30	.20
1333	A523	7af	King, diff.	.35	.20
1334	A523	16af	Knight	.55	.20
1335	A523	24af	Pawn	.85	.30
1336	A523	45af	Bishop, diff.	1.50	.50
			Nos. 1330-1336 (7)	4.00	1.80

Paintings by Picasso — A524

Fauna — A525

Designs: 4af, *The Old Jew.* 6af, *The Two Mountebanks.* 8af, *Portrait of Ambrouse Vollar.* 22af, *Woman of Majorca.* 35af, *Acrobat on the Ball.* 75af, *Usine a Horta de Ebro.*

1989, Feb. 13 **Litho.** ***Perf. 12½x12***

1341	A524	4af	multicolored	.20	.20
1342	A524	6af	multicolored	.25	.20
1343	A524	8af	multicolored	.40	.20
1344	A524	22af	multicolored	.90	.30
1345	A524	35af	multicolored	1.25	.40

Size: 71x90mm

Imperf

1346	A524	75af	multicolored	3.00	2.50
			Nos. 1341-1346 (6)	6.00	3.80

1989, Feb. 20 **Litho.** ***Perf. 12½x12***

1347	A525	3af	*Allactaga euphratica*	.20	.20
1348	A525	4af	*Equus hemionus*	.25	.20
1349	A525	14af	*Felis lynx*	.70	.30
1350	A525	35af	*Gypaetus barbatus*	1.75	1.25
1351	A525	44af	*Capra falconeri*	1.75	1.00

Size: 71x91mm

Imperf

1352	A525	100af	*Naja oxiana*	4.50	3.00
			Nos. 1347-1352 (6)	9.15	5.95

Intl. Women's Day — A526

1989, Mar. 8 ***Perf. 12½x12***

1353	A526	8af	multicolored	.25	.20

Restoration and Development of San'a, Yemen — A527

1988, Dec. 27 **Litho.** ***Perf. 12***

1354	A527	32af	multicolored	1.00	.50

Agriculture Day
A528

1989, Mar. 21
1355 A528 1af Cattle .20 .20
1356 A528 2af Old and new plows .20 .20
1357 A528 3af Field workers .20 .20
Nos. 1355-1357 (3) .60 .60

World Meteorology Day — A529

1989, Mar. 23
1358 A529 27af shown .95 .50
1359 A529 32af Emblems 1.10 .60
1360 A529 40af Weather station, balloon, vert. 1.40 .75
Nos. 1358-1360 (3) 3.45 1.85

Saur Revolution, 11th Anniv.
A530

1989, Apr. 27
1361 A530 20af multicolored .75 .25

Classic Automobiles — A531

1989, Dec. 30 Litho. ***Perf. 12½x12***
1362 A531 5af 1910 Duchs, Germany .20 .20
1363 A531 10af 1911 Ford, US .35 .20
1364 A531 20af 1911 Renault, France .60 .30
1365 A531 25af 1911, Russo-Balte, Russia .85 .35
1366 A531 30af 1926 Fiat, Italy 1.00 .40

Asia-Pacific Telecommunity, 10th Anniv. — A532

1989, Aug. 3 ***Perf. 12***
1367 A532 3af shown .20 .20
1368 A532 27af Emblem, satellite dish .80 .50

Teacher's Day
A533

1989, May 30 Litho. ***Perf. 12***
1369 A533 42af multicolored 1.25 .60

French Revolution, Bicent. — A534

1989, July Litho. ***Perf. 12***
1370 A534 25af multicolored .90 .50

Natl. Independence, 70th Anniv. — A535

1989, Aug. 18 Litho. ***Perf. 12***
1371 A535 25af multicolored .90 .50

A536 Birds — A537

1989, Aug. 30
1372 A536 3af multicolored .20 .20

Pashtos' and Baluchis' Day.

1989, Dec. 5 Litho. ***Perf. 12***
1373 A537 3af Platalea leucorodia .20 .20
1374 A537 5af Porphyrio porhyrio .25 .20
1375 A537 10af Botaurus stellaris, horiz. .45 .20
1376 A537 15af Pelecanus onocrotalus .65 .35
1377 A537 20af Netta rufina .85 .40
1378 A537 25af Cygnus olor 1.10 .50
1379 A537 30af Phalacrocorax carbo, horiz. 1.25 .60
Nos. 1373-1379 (7) 4.75

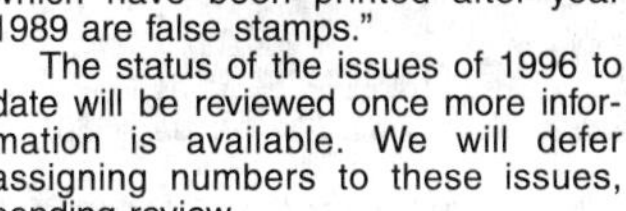
Tourism — A538

1989, Dec.
1380 A538 1af Mosque .20 .20
1381 A538 2af Minaret .20 .20
1382 A538 3af Buzkashi, horiz. .20 .20
1383 A538 4af Jet over Hendo Kush, horiz. .20 .20
Nos. 1380-1383 (4) .80

Mavlavi Allahdad Balkhi, President of Post of the Afghanistan Postal Administration, has declared that "the stamps which have been printed after year 1989 are false stamps."

The status of the issues of 1996 to date will be reviewed once more information is available. We will defer assigning numbers to these issues, pending review.

Mushrooms
A539

1996, July 20 Litho. ***Perf. 12½x13***

Designs: 100af, Suillus luteus. 300af, Russula virescens. 400af, Clitocybe inversa. 500af, Volvariella bombycina. 600af, Macrolepiota procera. 800af, Cystoderma cinnabarinum.
4000af, Lycoperdon umbrinum.

A539 Set of 6

Souvenir Sheet

A539 4000af multicolored

Souv. sheet contains one 32x40mm stamp.

Bears
A540

Designs: 500af, Ursus americanus, vert. 600af, Ursus maritimus. 800af, Helarctos malayanus. 900af, Ursus arctos horribilis. 1000af, Ursus arctos pyreneicus, vert.
4000af, Ursus arctos syriacus, vert.

Perf. 12½x13, 13x12½
1996, Aug. 15 Litho.
A540 Set of 5

Souvenir Sheet
Perf. 13

A540 4000af multicolored

Souv. sheet contains one 32x40mm stamp.

1998 World Cup Soccer Championships, France — A541

Various soccer players.

1996, Sept. 18 Litho. ***Perf. 13***
Background Color
A541 500af green
A541 600af purple
A541 700af brown

Size: 28x42mm
A541 800af yellow
A541 900af blue
A541 1000af vermilion

Souvenir Sheet
Perf. 12½

A541 4000d multicolored

Souv. sheet contains one 32x40mm stamp.

Silkworms
A542

Designs: 300af, Arctia caja. 400af, Sphinx ligustri. 500af, Zerynthia polyxema. 600af, Papilio machaon. 700af, Cerura vinula. 800af, Celerio euphorbiae.
3000af, Abraxes grossulariata.

1996, Oct. 7 ***Perf. 12½***
A542 Set of 6

Souvenir Sheet
Perf. 13

A542 3000af multicolored

Souv. sheet contains one 40x32mm stamp.

Domestic Cats — A543

Designs: 200af, American shorthair. 500af, Japanese bobtail. 600af, British shorthair. 800af, Devon rex. 1000af, Colorpoint shorthair. 1200af, Somali.
4000af, Sphinx.

1996 Litho. ***Perf. 12½***
A543 Set of 6

Souvenir Sheet

A543 4000af multicolored

Souv. sheet contains one 40x32mm stamp.

Horses
A544

200af, Eohippus. 300af, Miohippus. 400af, Merychippus. 500af, Pliohippus. 600af, Equus.

1996 Litho.1996, Nov. 5 ***Perf. 12½***
A544 Set of 5

Souvenir Sheet
Perf. 13

A544 3000af Trotter, sulky

Souvenir sheet contains one 40x32mm stamp. Inscription on 200af reads "Echippus."

Tulips — A545

Designs: 300af, Jewel of Spring. 400af, Mrs. John Scheepers. 500af, Absalon. 600af, Queen of Sheba. 800af, Marlette. 1000af, Mary Housley,
3000af, Fosteriana Purissima.

1997 Litho. ***Perf. 12½***
A545 Set of 6

Souvenir Sheet

A545 3000af multicolored

Souv. sheet contains one 32x40mm stamp.

Llamas and Camels
A546

Designs: 400af, Lama vicugna, vert. 600af, Lama guanicoe. 800af, Camelus dromedarius. 1000af, Lama guanicoe pacos, vert. 1200af,

Lama guanicoe glama. 1500af, Camelus ferus bactrianus.
4000af, Camelus dromedarius, vert.

1997
A546 Set of 6

Souvenir Sheet

A546 4000af multicolored

Souv. sheet contains one 32x40mm stamp.

Islamic Revolution, 4th Anniv. — A547

800af, shown. 1500af, Farmer plowing beside stream.

1996 **Litho.** ***Perf. 13***
A547 Set of 6

Independence, 77th Anniv. — A548

In Honor of Prophet Mohammed A549

A548, 700af. A549, 1500af.

1996
A548-A549 Set of 2

Domestic Cats A550

Designs: 30af, Norwegian forest. 50af, Ragdoll. 100af, Longhair Scottish fold. 200af, Oriental longhair. 300af, Manx. 500af, Sphinx. 1200af, Manx, diff.

1997 ***Perf. 12½***
A550 Set of 6

Souvenir Sheet

Perf. 13

A550 1200af multicolored

Souv. sheet contains one 40x32mm stamp.

Wildflowers A551

Designs: 50af, Nymphaea odorata. 100af, Nymphaea lotus. 200af, Aponogeton distachyus. 500af, Nymphaea capensis. 800af, Numphaea rubra. 1000af, Pontederia cordata.
3000af, Nymphaea daubenyana, horiz.

1997 **Litho.** ***Perf. 12½***
A551 Set of 6

Souvenir Sheet

A551 3000af multicolored

Souv. sheet contains one 40x32mm stamp.

Early Sailing Ships — A552

Designs: 400af, Hanseatic cog. 600af, Northern Europe dromond. 800af, Venetian cargo ship. 1000af, Northern Europe merchant ship. 1200af, Ladia Russian war ship. 1500af, Genoa merchant ship.
4000af, Egyptian merchant ship.

1997 **Litho.** ***Perf. 12½***
A552 Set of 3 pairs

Souvenir Sheet

A552 4000af multicolored

400af-600af, 800af-1000af, 1200af-1500af issued in setenant pairs.

1998 World Cup Soccer Championships, France — A553

French flag, various soccer plays.

1997 **Litho.** ***Perf. 12½***
A553 Set of 6

Souvenir Sheet

A553 4000af multicolored

Souv. sheet contains one 32x40mm stamp.

Mushrooms A554

Designs: 400af, Gomphidius glutinosus. 600af, Collybia fusipes. 800af, Stropharia aeruginosa. 1000af, Craterellus cornucopioides. 1200af, Guepinia helvelloides. 1500af, Ixocomus elegans.
4000af, Cantharellus cibarius.

1998 **Litho.** ***Perf. 12½***
A554 Set of 6

Souvenir Sheet

Perf. 13

A554 4000af multicolored

Souv. sheet contains one 40x32mm stamp.

Butterflies, Moths A556

Designs: 400af, Fabriciana adippe, vert. 600af, Nymphalis antiopa. 800af, Polygonia c-album. 1000af, Nymphalis polychloros. 1200af, Pararge aegeria. 1500af, Melitaea phoebe, vert.
4000af, Aglais urticae.

1998, July 3 **Litho.** ***Perf. 12½***
A556 Set of 6

Souvenir Sheet

Perf. 13

A556 4000af multicolored

Souv. sheet contains one 40x32mm stamp.

A sheet of 9 stamps memorializing Princess Diana also has been sold in the philatelic market.

Ovis Vignei A557

World Wildlife Fund: 800af, Male. 1000af, Female nursing young. 1200af, Two males walking. 10,000af, Two males butting heads.

1998 **Litho.** ***Perf. 12½***
A557 Strip of 4

Wildlife — A558

400af lilac, Panthera tigris, vert. 400af orange, Cepreolus capreolus, vert. 600af blue, Lutra lutra, vert. 600af brown, Cervus elaphus, vert. 800af blue green, Dama dama, vert. 800af red, Acinonyx jubatus, vert. 1000af violet, Panthera leo. 1000af green, Sus scrofa. 1200af brown, Martes foina. 1200af blue, Martes martes. 1500af black, Vulpes vulpes. 1500af green blue, Capra ibex.

1998 **Litho.** ***Perf. 12½***
A558 Set of 12

Dogs A559

400af, Bloodhound, vert.. 600af, St. Bernard, vert. 800af, Rottweiler, vert. 1000af, Borzoi, vert. 1200af, Basset hound. 1500af, Chow chow.

1998, Mar. 25 **Litho.** ***Perf. 12¾***
A559 Set of 6

Souvenir Sheet

Perf. 13

A559 4000af Vizsla, vert.

Souv. sheet contains one 32x40mm stamp.

Trains A560

400af, Large Bloomer, Great Britain. 600af, Mogul 2-6-0, US. 800af, Saddle Tank 0-4-0, US. 1000af, A4-4498, Great Britain. 1200af, 020201, Germany. 1500af, 3801, Australia.
4000af, Royal Hudson 2860, Canada.

1998, May **Litho.** ***Perf. 12¾***
A560 Set of 6 .05

Souvenir Sheet

Perf. 12½

A560 4000af multi

Souv. sheet contains one 36x28mm stamp.

Prehistoric Animals A561

400af, Mammuthu primigenius. 600af, Megaloceros. 800af, Ursus spelaeus. 1000af, Synthetoceras. 1200af, Coelodonta. 1500af, Hipparion.
4000af, Smilodon.

1998, May **Litho.** ***Perf. 12¾***
A561 Set of 6

Souvenir Sheet

Perf. 12½

A561 4000af multi

Souv. sheet contains one 32x40mm stamp.

SEMI-POSTAL STAMPS

Catalogue values for unused stamps in this section are for Never Hinged items.

No. 373 Surcharged in Violet

1952, July 12 **Unwmk.** ***Perf. 12½***

B1	A122	40p + 30p cerise	10.00	1.50
B2	A122	125p + 30p cerise	12.50	2.00

1000th anniv. of the birth of Avicenna.

Children at Play — SP1

1955, July 3 **Typo.** ***Perf. 11***

B3	SP1	35p + 15p dk green	.50	.35
B4	SP1	125p + 25p purple	1.00	.85

The surtax was for child welfare.

Amir Sher Ali Khan, Tiger Head Stamp and Zahir Shah — SP2

Children at Play — SP3

1955, July 2 **Litho.**
B5 SP2 35p + 15p carmine .40 .30
B6 SP2 125p + 25p pale vio bl .85 .55

85th anniv. of the Afghan post.

1956, June 20 **Typo.**
B7 SP3 35p + 15p brt vio bl .75 .25
B8 SP3 140p + 15p dk org brn 1.25 .75

Issued for Children's Day. The surtax was for child welfare. No. B8 inscribed in French.

Pashtunistan Monument, Kabul — SP4

1956, Sept. 1 **Litho.**
B9 SP4 35p + 15p dp violet .20 .20
B10 SP4 140p + 15p dk brown .60 .60

"Free Pashtunistan" Day. The surtax aided the "Free Pashtunistan" movement.

No. B9 measures 30½x19½mm; No. B10, 29x19mm. On sale and valid for use only on Sept. 1-2.

Globe and Sun — SP5

Children on Seesaw SP6

1956, Oct. 24 ***Perf. 11***
B11 SP5 35p + 15p ultra .65 .60
B12 SP5 140p + 15p red brown 1.25 1.00

Afghanistan's UN admission, 10th anniv.

1957, June 20 **Unwmk.**
B13 SP6 35p + 15p brt rose .75 .25
B14 SP6 140p + 15p ultra 1.50 .90

Children's Day. Surtax for child welfare.

UN Headquarters and Emblems SP7

1957, Oct. 24 ***Perf. 11 Rough***
B15 SP7 35p + 15p red brown .35 .20
B16 SP7 140p + 15p lt ultra .65 .55

United Nations Day.

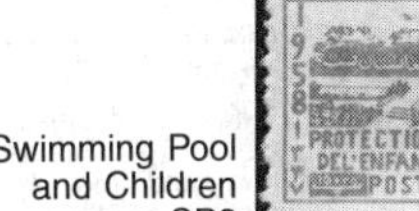

Swimming Pool and Children SP8

1958, June 22 ***Perf. 11***
B17 SP8 35p + 15p rose .25 .20
B18 SP8 140p + 15p dl red brn .75 .60

Children's Day. Surtax for child welfare.

Pashtunistan Flag — SP9

1958, Aug. 31
B19 SP9 35p + 15p lt blue .20 .20
B20 SP9 140p + 15p red brown .60 .60

Issued for "Free Pashtunistan Day."

Children Playing Tug of War — SP10

1959, June 23 **Litho.** ***Perf. 11***
B21 SP10 35p + 15p brown vio .50 .20
B22 SP10 165p + 15p brt pink 1.00 .60

Children's Day. Surtax for child welfare.

Pathans in Tribal Dance SP11

Perf. 11 Rough

1959, Sept. **Unwmk.**
B23 SP11 35p + 15p green .50 .20
B24 SP11 165p + 15p orange 1.00 .60

Issued for "Free Pashtunistan Day."

Afghan Cavalryman with UN Flag — SP12

1959, Oct. 24 ***Perf. 11 Rough***
B25 SP12 35p + 15p orange .20 .20
B26 SP12 165p + 15p lt bl grn .45 .40

Issued for United Nations Day.

Children SP13

1960, Oct. 23 **Litho.**
B27 SP13 75p + 25p lt ultra .75 .20
B28 SP13 175p + 25p lt green 1.50 .35

Children's Day. Surtax for child welfare.

Man with Spray Gun SP14

1960, Sept. 6 ***Perf. 11 Rough***
B29 SP14 50p + 50p orange .80 1.00
B30 SP14 175p + 50p red brown 2.25 2.25

11th anniversary of the WHO malaria control program in Afghanistan.

SP15

1960, Sept. 1 **Unwmk.**
B31 SP15 50p + 50p rose .25 .20
B32 SP15 175p + 50p dk blue .55 .45

Issued for "Free Pashtunistan Day."

Ambulance — SP16

1960, Oct. 16 ***Perf. 11***

Crescent in Red
B33 SP16 50p + 50p violet .40 .30
B34 SP16 175p + 50p blue .90 .75

Issued for the Red Crescent Society.

Nos. 470-471 Surcharged in Blue or Orange

1960, Dec. 31 **Litho.** ***Perf. 11***
B35 A166 50p + 25p dp org (Bl) 1.50 1.50
B36 A166 165p + 25p blue (O) 1.50 1.50

The souvenir sheets described after No. 471 were surcharged in carmine "+25 Ps" on each stamp. Value $5 each.

See general note after No. 485.

Nos. 496-500 Surcharged

1961 **Unwmk.** **Photo.** ***Perf. 13½x14***
B37 A175 2p + 25p green & rose lil
B38 A175 2p + 25p brown & cit
B39 A175 5p + 25p gray & rose
B40 A175 10p + 25p blue & bis
B41 A175 15p + 25p sl bl & dl lil
Nos. B37-B41 (5) 1.50

UNICEF. The same surcharge was applied to an imperf. souvenir sheet like that noted after No. 505. Value $4.50.

Nos. 522-526 Surcharged "+25PS" and Crescent in Red

1961, Oct. 16 ***Perf. 13½x14***
B42 A184 2p + 25p black
B43 A184 2p + 25p green
B44 A184 5p + 25p lilac rose
B45 A184 10p + 25p lilac
B46 A184 15p + 25p dk blue
Nos. B42-B46 (5) 2.00

Issued for the Red Crescent Society.

Nos. 539-543 Surcharged in Red: "UNESCO + 25PS"

1962 ***Perf. 12***
B47 A186 2p + 25p multi
B48 A186 2p + 25p multi
B49 A186 5p + 25p multi
B50 A186 10p + 25p multi
B51 A186 15p + 25p multi
Nos. B47-B51 (5) 1.50

UNESCO. The same surcharge was applied to the souvenir sheets mentioned after No. 548. Value, 2 sheets, $3.50.

Nos. 553-561 Surcharged: "Dag Hammarskjöld +20PS"

1962, Sept. 17 ***Perf. 14x13½***
B52 A187 2p + 20p
B53 A187 2p + 20p
B54 A187 5p + 20p
B55 A187 10p + 20p
B56 A187 15p + 20p
B57 A187 25p + 20p
B58 A187 50p + 20p
B59 A187 75p + 20p
B60 A187 100p + 20p
Nos. B52-B60 (5) 2.00

In memory of Dag Hammarskjold, Sec. Gen. of the UN, 1953-61. Perf. and imperf. souvenir sheets exist. Value, 2 sheets, $3.

Nos. 583-593 Surcharged "+15PS"

1963, Mar. 15 ***Perf. 14x13½***
B61 A193 2p + 15p
B62 A193 2p + 15p
B63 A193 5p + 15p
B64 A193 10p + 15p
B65 A193 15p + 15p
B66 A193 25p + 15p
B67 A193 50p + 15p
B68 A193 75p + 15p
B69 A193 100p + 15p
B70 A193 150p + 15p
B71 A193 175p + 15p
Nos. B61-B71 (11) 7.50

WHO drive to eradicate malaria.

Postally used copies of Nos. B37-B71 are uncommon and command a considerable premium over the values for unused copies.

Nos. 672-672G, 672I Surcharged in Various Positions

1964, Mar. 9
B71A A213g 2p + 50p
B71B A213g 3p + 50p
B71C A213g 4p + 50p
B71D A213g 5p + 50p
B71E A213g 10p + 50p
B71F A213g 100p + 50p
B71G A213g 2af + 50p
B71H A213g 3af + 50p

Souvenir Sheet
B71J A213g 5af + 50p

Nos. B71E-B71G are airmail semi-postals.

Blood Transfusion Kit — SP17

1964, Oct. 18 **Litho.** ***Perf. 10½***
B72 SP17 1af + 50p black & rose .50 .20

Issued for the Red Crescent Society and Red Crescent Week, Oct. 18-24.

First Aid Station SP18

1965, Oct. **Photo.** ***Perf. 13½x14***
B73 SP18 1.50af + 50p multi 1.00 .50

Issued for the Red Crescent Society.

Children Playing SP19

1966, Nov. 28 Photo. *Perf. 13½x14*

B74 SP19 1af + 1af yel grn & cl .35 .20
B75 SP19 3af + 2af yel & brn .75 .20
B76 SP19 7af + 3af rose lil & grn 1.25 .40
Nos. B74-B76 (3) 2.35 .80

Children's Day.

Nadir Shah Presenting Society Charter SP20

1967 Photo. *Perf. 13x14*

B77 SP20 2af + 1af red & dk grn .25 .20
B78 SP20 5af + 1af lil rose & brn .50 .25

Issued for the Red Crescent Society.

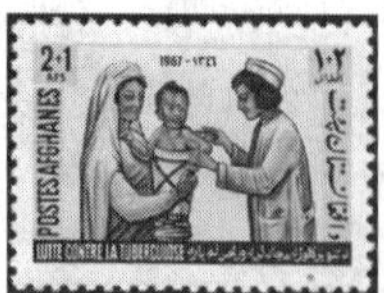

Vaccination SP21

Red Crescent — SP22

1967, June 6 Photo. *Perf. 12*

B79 SP21 2af + 1af yellow & blk .75 .20
B80 SP21 5af + 2af pink & brn 1.00 .25

The surtax was for anti-tuberculosis work.

1967, Oct. 18 Photo. *Perf. 12*
Crescent in Red

B81 SP22 3af + 1af gray ol & blk .50 .20
B82 SP22 5af + 1af dl bl & blk .75 .20

Issued for the Red Crescent Society.

Queen Humeira SP23

Red Crescent SP24

1968, June 14 Photo. *Perf. 12*

B83 SP23 2af + 2af red brown .25 .20
B84 SP23 7af + 2af dull green .75 .50

Issued for Mother's Day.

1968, Oct. 16 Photo. *Perf. 12*

B85 SP24 4af + 1af yel, blk & red .45 .25

Issued for the Red Crescent Society.

Red Cross, Crescent, Lion and Sun Emblems — SP25

Mother and Child — SP26

1969, May 5 Litho. *Perf. 14x13½*

B86 SP25 3af + 1af multicolored .75 .20
B87 SP25 5af + 1af multicolored 1.25 .30

League of Red Cross Societies, 50th anniv.

1969, June 14 Photo. *Perf. 12*

B88 SP26 1af + 1af yel org & brn .25 .20
B89 SP26 4af + 1af rose lil & pur .40 .25
a. Souvenir sheet of 2 1.00 1.00

Mother's Day. No. B89a contains 2 imperf. stamps similar to Nos. B88-B89. Sold for 10af.

Red Crescent — SP27

1969, Oct. 16 Photo. *Perf. 12*

B90 SP27 6af + 1af multi .75 .30

Issued for the Red Crescent Society.

UN and FAO Emblems, Farmer — SP28

1973, May 24 Photo. *Perf. 13½*

B91 SP28 14af + 7af grnsh bl & lil 1.10 .75

World Food Program, 10th anniversary.

Dome of the Rock, Jerusalem SP29

1977, Sept. 11 Photo. *Perf. 14*

B92 SP29 12af + 3af multi 1.50 .35

Surtax for Palestinian families and soldiers.

15 Cent. (lunar) of Islamic Pilgrimage (Hegira) — SP30

1981, Jan. 17 Litho. *Perf. 12½x12*

B93 SP30 13af + 2af multi 1.50 1.00

Red Crescent Aid Programs SP31

1981, May 8 *Perf. 12x12½*

B94 SP31 1af + 4af multi .50 .60

Intl. Year of the Disabled SP32

1981, Oct. 12 *Perf. 12x12½*

B95 SP32 6af + 1af multi .35 .25

AIR POST STAMPS

Plane over Kabul AP1

Perf. 12, 12x11, 11

1939, Oct. 1 Typo. Unwmk.

C1 AP1 5af orange 5.00 2.25
a. Imperf., pair ('47) 22.50 22.50
b. Horiz. pair, imperf. vert. 20.00
C2 AP1 10af blue 5.00 1.75
a. 10af lt bl 7.50 5.00
b. Imperf., pair ('47) 22.50
c. Horiz. pair, imperf. vert. 20.00
C3 AP1 20af emerald 10.00 5.00
a. Imperf., pair ('47) 22.50
b. Horiz. pair, imperf. vert. 20.00
c. Vert. pair, imperf. horiz. 22.50
Nos. C1-C3 (3) 20.00 9.00

These stamps come with clean-cut or rough perforations. Counterfeits exist.

1948, June 14 *Perf. 12x11½*

C4 AP1 5af emerald 15.00 15.00
C5 AP1 10af red orange 15.00 15.00
C6 AP1 20af blue 15.00 15.00
Nos. C4-C6 (3) 45.00 45.00

Imperforates exist.

Catalogue values for unused stamps in this section, from this point to the end of the section, are for Never Hinged items.

Plane over Palace Grounds, Kabul AP2

1951-54 Engr. *Perf. 13½*
Imprint: "Waterlow & Sons, Limited, London"

C7 AP2 5af henna brn 2.50 .55
C8 AP2 5af dp grn ('54) 3.50 .50
C9 AP2 10af gray 4.00 1.40
C10 AP2 20af dark blue 6.50 2.25

1957

C11 AP2 5af ultra .90 .35
C12 AP2 10af dark vio 1.75 .75
Nos. C7-C12 (6) 19.15 5.80

See No. C38.

Ariana Plane over Hindu Kush AP3

Perf. 11, Imperf.

1960-63 Litho. Unwmk.

C13 AP3 75p light vio .30 .30
C14 AP3 125p blue .40 .40

Perf. 10½, 11

C14A AP3 5af citron ('63) 1.10 1.10
Nos. C13-C14A (3) 1.80 1.80

Girl Scout — AP4

1962, Aug. 30 Photo. *Perf. 11½x12*

C15 AP4 100p ocher & brn .60 .60
C16 AP4 175p brt yel grn & brn .85 .85

Women's Day. See #578-579 and note on souvenir sheet.

Sports Type of Regular Issue, 1962

25p, 50p, Horse racing. 75p, 100p, Wrestling. 150p, Weight lifting. 175p, Soccer.

1962, Sept. 25 Unwmk. *Perf. 12*
Black Inscriptions

C17 A195 25p rose & red brn
C18 A195 50p gray & red brn
C19 A195 75p pale vio & dk grn
C20 A195 100p gray ol & dk pur
C21 A195 150p rose lil & grn
C22 A195 175p sal & brn
Nos. C17-C22 (6) 2.25

Children's Day Type of Regular Issue

Perf. 11½x12, 12x11½

1962, Oct. 14 Unwmk.

C23 A196 75p Runners
C24 A196 150p Peaches
C25 A196 200p Iris, vert.

A souvenir sheet contains one each of Nos. C23-C25. Value $2.50.

Red Crescent Type of Regular Issue

1962, Oct. 16 *Perf. 12*
Fruit and Flowers in Natural Colors; Carmine Crescent

C26 A197 25p Grapes
C27 A197 50p Pears
C28 A197 100p Wistaria

Two souvenir sheets exist. One contains a 150p gray brown stamp in blossom design, the other a 200p gray stamp in wistaria design, imperf. Value, each $5.

UN Type of Regular Issue

1962, Oct. 24 Photo.
Flags in Original Colors, Black Inscriptions

C29 A198 75p blue
C30 A198 100p lt brn
C31 A198 125p brt grn

Boy Scout Type of Regular Issue

1962, Oct. 25 Unwmk. *Perf. 12*

C32 A199 25p gray, blk, dl grn & sal
C33 A199 50p gri, brn & sal
C34 A199 75p bl grn, red brn & sal
C35 A199 100p bl, slate & sal

Teacher's Day Type of Regular Issue

1962, Oct. 25

C36 A200 100p Pole vault
C37 A200 150p High jump

A souvenir sheet contains one 250p pink and slate green stamp in design of 150p. Value $2.50.

Type of 1951-54

1962 Engr. *Perf. 13½*
Imprint: "Thomas De La Rue & Co. Ltd."

C38 AP2 5af ultra 6.00 1.00

Agriculture Types of Regular Issue
Unwmk.

1963, Mar. 1 Photo. *Perf. 12*

C42 A204 100p dk car, grn & brn
C43 A203 150p ocher & blk
C44 A204 200p ultra, grn & brn

Hands Holding Wheat Emblem AP5

1963, Mar. 27 Photo. *Perf. 14*

C45 AP5 500p lil, lt brn & brn 1.75 .60

FAO "Freedom from Hunger" campaign.

Two souvenir sheets exist. One contains a 1000p blue green, light brown and brown, type AP5, imperf. The other contains a 200p brown and green and 300p ultramarine, yellow and ocher in rice and corn designs, type A205. Values $6 and $2.50.

Meteorological Day Type of Regular Issue

Designs: 100p, 500p, Meteorological measuring instrument. 200p, 400p, Weather station. 300p, Rockets in space.

1963, May 23 ***Imperf.***

C46 A206 100p brn & bl

Perf. 13½x14

C47 A206 200p brt grn & lil
C48 A206 300p dk bl & rose
C49 A206 400p bl & dl red brn
C50 A206 500p car rose & gray grn

Nos. C47 and C50 printed se-tenant.
Two souvenir sheets exist. One contains a 125p red and brown stamp in rocket design. The other contains a 100p blue and dull red brown in "rockets in space" design. Values $5 and $7.50.

Kabul International Airport — AP8

Perf. 12x11½

1964, Apr. Unwmk. Photo.

C57 AP8 10af red lil & grn	.55	.20
C58 AP8 20af dk grn & red lil	.80	.40
a. Perf. 12 ('68)	5.00	3.00
C59 AP8 50af dk bl & grnsh bl	2.25	1.00
a. Perf. 12 ('68)	8.00	5.00
Nos. C57-C59 (3)	3.60	1.60

Inauguration of Kabul Airport Terminal.
Nos. C58a-C59a are 36mm wide. Nos. C58-C59 are 35½mm wide.

Zahir Shah and Kabul Airport — AP9

100af, Zahir Shah and Ariana Plane.

1971 Photo. ***Perf. 12½x13½***

C60 AP9 50af multi	10.00	8.00
C61 AP9 100af blk, red & grn	5.00	3.00

Remainders of No C60 were used, starting in 1978, with king's portrait removed.

REGISTRATION STAMPS

R1

Dated "1309"

1891 Unwmk. Litho. ***Imperf.***

Pelure Paper

F1 R1 1r slate blue	2.00
a. Tete beche pair	12.50

Genuinely used copies of No. F1 are rare. Counterfeit cancellations exist.

R2

Dated "1311"

1893 Thin Wove Paper

F2 R2 1r black, *green*	1.60

Genuinely used copies of No. F2 are rare. Counterfeit cancellations exist.

R3

Undated

1894

F3 R3 2ab black, *green*	7.50	*8.00*

12 varieties. See note below Nos. 189-190.

R4

Undated

1898-1900

F4 R4 2ab black, *deep rose*	3.50	3.50
F5 R4 2ab black, *lilac rose*	4.00	4.00
F6 R4 2ab black, *magenta*	5.00	4.00
F7 R4 2ab black, *salmon*	3.00	*3.50*
F8 R4 2ab black, *orange*	3.50	3.50
F9 R4 2ab black, *yellow*	3.50	*3.50*
F10 R4 2ab black, *green*	3.50	3.50
Nos. F4-F10 (7)	26.00	25.50

Many shades of paper.
Nos. F4-F10 come in two sizes, measured between outer frame lines: 52x36mm, 1st printing; 46x33mm, 2nd printing. The outer frame line (not pictured) is 3-6mm from inner frame line.
Used on P.O. receipts.

OFFICIAL STAMPS

(Used only on interior mail.)

Coat of Arms O1

1909 Unwmk. Typo. ***Perf. 12***

Wove Paper

O1 O1 red	1.00	1.00
a. Carmine ('19?)	2.25	*6.00*

Later printings of No. O1 in scarlet, vermilion, claret, etc., on various types of paper, were issued until 1927.

Coat of Arms — O2

1939-68? Typo. ***Perf. 11, 12***

O3 O2 15p emerald	.50	.50
O4 O2 30p ocher ('40)	.65	.65
O5 O2 45p dark carmine	.55	.55
O6 O2 50p brt car ('68)	.30	.30
a. 50p carmine rose ('55)	.50	.50
O7 O2 1af brt red violet	1.00	1.00
Nos. O3-O7 (5)	3.00	3.00

Size of 50p, 24x31mm, others 22½x28mm.

Catalogue values for unused stamps in this section, from this point to the end of the section, are for Never Hinged items.

1964-65 Litho. ***Perf. 11***

O8 O2 50p rose	.75	.75
a. 50p salmon ('65)	1.50	1.50

Stamps of this type are revenues.

PARCEL POST STAMPS

Coat of Arms — PP1

PP2

PP3

PP4

1909 Unwmk. Typo. ***Perf. 12***

Q1 PP1 3sh bister	1.00	*2.00*
a. Imperf., pair	*1.00*	
Q2 PP2 1kr olive gray	1.60	*3.00*
a. Imperf., pair		
Q3 PP3 1r orange	3.00	3.00
Q4 PP3 1r olive green	18.00	4.00
Q5 PP4 2r red	3.50	3.50
Nos. Q1-Q5 (5)	27.10	15.50

1916-18

Q6 PP1 3sh green	1.60	*3.00*
Q7 PP2 1kr pale red	2.50	1.25
a. 1kr rose red ('18)	3.25	3.25
Q8 PP3 1r brown org	1.25	1.25
a. 1r deep brown ('18)	10.00	2.50
Q9 PP4 2r blue	4.50	*5.00*
Nos. Q6-Q9 (4)	9.85	*10.50*

Nos. Q1-Q9 sometimes show letters of the papermaker's watermark "HOWARD & JONES LONDON."
Ungummed copies are remainders. They sell for one-third the price of mint examples.

Old Habibia College, Near Kabul — PP5

1921

Wove Paper

Q10 PP5 10pa chocolate	3.00	3.00
a. Tete beche pair	15.00	15.00
Q11 PP5 15pa light brn	6.00	5.00
a. Tete beche pair	20.00	
Q12 PP5 30pa red violet	9.00	7.00
a. Tete beche pair	30.00	
b. Laid paper	*15.00*	*10.00*
Q13 PP5 1r brt blue	10.00	9.00
a. Tete beche pair	50.00	
Nos. Q10-Q13 (4)	28.00	24.00

Stamps of this issue are usually perforated on one or two sides only.
The laid paper of No. Q12b has a papermaker's watermark in the sheet.

PP6

1924-26

Wove Paper

Q15 PP6 5kr ultra ('26)	35.00	35.00
Q16 PP6 5r lilac	15.00	15.00

A 15r rose exists, but is not known to have been placed in use.

PP7

PP8

1928-29 ***Perf. 11, 11xImperf.***

Q17 PP7 2r yellow orange	10.00	3.00
Q18 PP7 2r green ('29)	3.00	3.00
Q19 PP8 3r deep green	7.50	4.00
Q20 PP8 3r brown ('29)	5.00	5.00
Nos. Q17-Q20 (4)	25.50	15.00

POSTAL TAX STAMPS

Aliabad Hospital near Kabul PT1

Pierre and Marie Curie PT2

Perf. 12x11½, 12

1938, Dec. 22 Typo. Unwmk.

RA1 PT1 10p peacock grn 2.50 *4.00*
RA2 PT2 15p dull blue 2.50 *4.00*

Obligatory on all mail Dec. 22-28, 1938. The money was used for the Aliabad Hospital. See note with CD80.

PT3

Begging Child — PT4

1949, May 28 Typo. *Perf. 12*

RA3 PT3 35p red orange 2.50 1.60
RA4 PT4 125p ultra 2.75 1.60

United Nations Children's Day, May 28. Obligatory on all foreign mail on that date. Proceeds were used for child welfare.

Paghman Arch and UN Emblem PT5

1949, Oct. 24

RA5 PT5 125p dk blue green 10.00 6.00

4th anniv. of the UN. Valid one day only. Issued in sheets of 9 (3x3).

Catalogue values for unused stamps in this section, from this point to the end of the section, are for Never Hinged items.

Zahir Shah and Map of Afghanistan — PT6

1950, Mar. 30 Typo.

RA6 PT6 125p blue green 2.00 1.25

Return of Zahir Shah from a trip to Europe for his health. Valid for two weeks. The tax was used for public health purposes.

Hazara Youth — PT7

1950, May 28 Typo. *Perf. 11½*

RA7 PT7 125p dk blue green 2.00 1.50

Tax for Child Welfare. Obligatory and valid only on May 28, 1950, on foreign mail.

Ruins of Qalai Bist and Globe — PT8

1950, Oct. 24

RA8 PT8 1.25af ultramarine 7.50 4.00

5th anniv. of the UN. Proceeds went to Afghanistan's UN Projects Committee.

Zahir Shah and Medical Center PT9

1950, Dec. 22 Typo. *Perf. 11½*
Size: 38x25mm

RA9 PT9 35p carmine 1.00 1.00
RA10 PT9 1.25af black 4.50 2.25

The tax was for the national Graduate School of Medicine.

Koochi Girl with Lamb PT10

Kohistani Boy and Sheep — PT11

1951, May 28

RA11 PT10 35p emerald .75 .65
RA12 PT11 1.25af ultramarine .75 .65

The tax was for Child Welfare.

Distributing Gifts to Children — PT12

Qandahari Boys Dancing the "Attan" PT13

1952, May 28 Litho.

RA13 PT12 35p chocolate .25 .25
RA14 PT13 125p violet .75 .75

The tax was for Child Welfare.

Soldier Receiving First Aid — PT14

1952, Oct.

RA15 PT14 10p light green .50 .35

Stretcher-bearers and Wounded — PT15

Soldier Assisting Wounded — PT16

1953, Oct.

RA16 PT15 10p yel grn & org red .50 .40
RA17 PT16 10p vio brn & org red .50 .40

Prince Mohammed Nadir — PT17

Map and Young Musicians PT18

1953, May 28

RA18 PT17 35p orange yellow .20 .20
RA19 PT17 125p chalky blue .55 .55

No. RA19 is inscribed in French "Children's Day." The tax was for child welfare.

1954, May 28 Unwmk. *Perf. 11*

RA20 PT18 35p purple .30 .20
RA21 PT18 125p ultra 1.10 1.10

No. RA21 is inscribed in French. The tax was for child welfare.

PT19

Red Crescent PT20

1954, Oct. 17 *Perf. 11½*

RA22 PT19 20p blue & red .25 .20

1955, Oct. 18 *Perf. 11*

RA23 PT20 20p dull grn & car .50 .25

Zahir Shah and Red Crescent PT21

1956, Oct. 18

RA24 PT21 20p lt grn & rose car .25 .20

Red Crescent Headquarters, Kabul — PT22

1957, Oct. 17

RA25 PT22 20p lt ultra & car .75 .50

Map and Crescent PT23

1958, Oct. Unwmk. *Perf. 11*

RA26 PT23 25p yel grn & red .30 .30

PT24

1959, Oct. 17 Litho. *Perf. 11*

RA27 PT24 25p lt violet & red .20 .20

The tax on Nos. RA15-RA17, RA22-RA27 was for the Red Crescent Society. Use of these stamps was required for one week.

AGUERA, LA

LOCATION — An administrative district in southern Rio de Oro on the northwest coast of Africa.

GOVT. — Spanish possession

AREA — Because of indefinite political boundaries, figures for area and population are not available.

100 Centimos = 1 Peseta

Type of 1920 Issue of Rio de Oro Overprinted

1920, June Typo. Unwmk. *Perf. 13*

1	A8	1c blue green	1.90	1.90
2	A8	2c olive brown	1.90	1.90
3	A8	5c deep green	1.90	1.90
4	A8	10c light red	1.90	1.90
5	A8	15c yellow	1.90	1.90
6	A8	20c lilac	1.90	1.90
7	A8	25c deep blue	1.90	1.90
8	A8	30c dark brown	1.90	1.90
9	A8	40c pink	1.90	1.90
10	A8	50c bright blue	6.00	6.00
11	A8	1p red brown	11.00	11.00
12	A8	4p dark violet	32.50	32.50
13	A8	10p orange	65.00	65.00
		Nos. 1-13 (13)	131.60	131.60
		Set, never hinged	200.00	

Very fine examples of Nos. 1-13 will be somewhat off center. Well centered examples are uncommon and will sell for more.

King Alfonso XIII — A2

1922, June

14	A2	1c turquoise blue	.85	.85
15	A2	2c dark green	.85	.85
16	A2	5c blue green	.85	.85
17	A2	10c red	.85	.85
18	A2	15c red brown	.85	.85
19	A2	20c yellow	.85	.85
20	A2	25c deep blue	.85	.85
21	A2	30c dark brown	.85	.85
22	A2	40c rose red	1.10	1.10
23	A2	50c red violet	3.75	3.75
24	A2	1p rose	7.50	7.50
25	A2	4p violet	18.00	18.00
26	A2	10p orange	27.50	27.50
		Nos. 14-26 (13)	64.65	64.65
		Set, never hinged	100.00	

For later issues see Spanish Sahara.

AITUTAKI

ˌit-ə-ˈtäk-ē

LOCATION — One of the larger Cook Islands, in the South Pacific Ocean northeast of New Zealand

GOVT. — A dependency of New Zealand

AREA — 7 sq. mi.

POP. — 2,335 (1981)

The Cook Islands were attached to New Zealand in 1901. Stamps of Cook Islands were used in 1892-1903 and 1932-72.

Aitutaki acquired its own postal service in August 1972, though remaining part of Cook Islands.

12 Pence = 1 Shilling
100 Cents = 1 Dollar (1972)

Catalogue values for unused stamps in this country are for Never Hinged items, beginning with Scott 37.

Watermark

Wmk. 61- Single-lined NZ and Star Close Together

Stamps of New Zealand Surcharged in Red or Blue:

a

b

1903 Engr. Wmk. 61 *Perf. 14*

1	A18(a)	½p green (R)	4.25	*6.00*
2	A35(b)	1p rose car (Bl)	4.50	*6.25*

c

d

e

AITUTAKI.

Tai Tiringi.

f

Perf. 11

3	A22(c)	2½p blue (R)	9.75	*15.00*
4	A23(d)	3p yel brn (Bl)	16.00	14.00
5	A26(e)	6p red (Bl)	30.00	27.50
6	A29(f)	1sh scarlet (Bl)	55.00	*80.00*
a.		1sh orange red (Bl)	60.00	*87.50*

1911 Typo. *Perf. 14x15*

7	A41(a)	½p yellow grn (R)	1.00	*3.00*

Engr.

Perf. 14

9	A22(c)	2½p deep blue (R)	7.50	*16.00*

AITUTAKI. AITUTAKI.

Ono Pene. Tai Tiringi.

g h

1913-16 Typo.

10	A42(b)	1p rose (Bl)	2.75	*9.00*

Engr.

12	A41(g)	6p car rose (Bl) ('16)	42.50	*87.50*
13	A41(h)	1sh ver (Bl) ('14)	50.00	*125.00*

1916-17 *Perf. 14x13½, 14x14½*

17	A45(g)	6p car rose (Bl)	10.00	*24.00*
18	A45(h)	1sh ver (Bl) ('17)	32.50	*80.00*
		Nos. 1-18 (13)	265.75	*493.25*

New Zealand Stamps of 1909-19 Overprinted in Red or Dark Blue

1917-20 Typo. *Perf. 14x15*

19	A43	½p yellow grn ('20)	.95	*5.50*
20	A42	1p car (Bl) ('20)	3.00	*19.50*
21	A47	1½p gray black	3.50	*27.50*
22	A47	1½p brown org ('19)	.80	*6.50*
23	A43	3p choc (Bl) ('19)	3.25	*14.00*

Perf. 14x13½, 14x14½

Engr.

24	A44	2½p dull blue ('18)	1.60	*14.00*
25	A45	3p vio brn (Bl) ('18)	1.75	*17.50*
26	A45	6p car rose (Bl)	4.50	*19.00*
27	A45	1sh vermilion (Bl)	11.50	*26.00*
		Nos. 19-27 (9)	30.85	*149.50*

Landing of Capt. Cook A15

Avarua Waterfront A16

Capt. James Cook — A17

Palm — A18

Houses at Arorangi — A19

Avarua Harbor — A20

1920 Engr. Unwmk. *Perf. 14*

28	A15	½p green & black	3.25	*22.50*
29	A16	1p car & black	3.25	*16.00*
30	A17	1½p brown & blk	5.50	*11.00*
31	A18	3p dp blue & blk	2.25	*14.00*
32	A19	6p sl & red brn	6.25	*15.00*
33	A20	1sh claret & blk	9.00	*24.00*
		Nos. 28-33 (6)	29.50	*102.50*

Inverted centers, double frames, etc. are from printers waste.

Rarotongan Chief (Te Po) — A21

1924-27 Wmk. 61 *Perf. 14*

34	A15	½p green & blk ('27)	2.00	*9.00*
35	A16	1p carmine & blk	5.75	*6.00*
36	A21	2½p blue & blk ('27)	7.50	*47.50*
		Nos. 34-36 (3)	15.25	*62.50*

Catalogue values for unused stamps in this section, from this point to the end of the section, are for Never Hinged items.

Cook Islands Nos. 199-200, 202, 205-206, 210, 212-213, 215-217 Overprinted

1972 Photo. Unwmk. *Perf. 14x13½*

37	A34	½c gold & multi	.50	*.70*
38	A34	1c gold & multi	1.25	*1.25*
39	A34	2½c gold & multi	3.75	*6.25*
40	A34	4c gold & multi	1.25	*.75*
41	A34	5c gold & multi	4.25	*6.50*
42	A34	10c gold & multi	4.25	5.00
43	A34	20c gold & multi	2.10	*.90*
44	A34	25c gold & multi	1.25	*.90*
45	A34	50c gold & multi	4.75	*2.50*
46	A35	$1 gold & multi	7.00	*5.00*
47	A35	$2 gold & multi	.85	*.65*
		Nos. 37-47 (11)	31.20	*30.40*

Overprint horizontal on Nos. 46-47. On $2, overprint is in capitals of different font; size: 21x3mm.

Issued: Nos. 37-46, Aug. 9; No. 47, Nov. 24.

Same Overprint Horizontal in Silver On Cook Islands Nos. 330-332

1972, Oct. 27 *Perf. 13½*

48	A53	1c gold & multi	.20	.20
49	A53	5c gold & multi	.25	.25
50	A53	10c gold & multi	.40	.40
		Nos. 48-50 (3)	.85	.85

Fluorescence

Starting in 1972, stamps carry a "fluorescent security underprinting" in a multiple pattern of New Zealand's coat of arms with "Aitutaki" above, "Cook Islands" below and two stars at each side.

Silver Wedding Type of Cook Islands

1972, Nov. 20 Photo. *Perf. 13½*

Size: 29x40mm

51	A54	5c silver & multi	3.25	2.50

Size: 66x40mm

52	A54	15c silver & multi	1.50	1.10

25th anniversary of the marriage of Queen Elizabeth II and Prince Philip. Nos. 51-52 printed in sheets of 5 stamps and one label.

Flower Issue of Cook Islands Overprinted

1972, Dec. 11 Photo. *Perf. 14x13½*

53	A34	½c on #199	.20	.20
54	A34	1c on #200	.20	.20
55	A34	2½c on #202	.20	.20

56 A34 4c on #205 .25 .20
57 A34 5c on #206 .25 .20
58 A34 10c on #210 .40 .25
59 A34 20c on #212 1.00 .50
60 A34 25c on #213 .50 *.60*
61 A34 50c on #215 .75 *.90*
62 A35 $1 on #216 1.25 *2.00*
Nos. 53-62 (10) 5.00 *5.25*

See Nos. 73-76.

The Passion of Christ, by Mathias Grunewald — A22

Paintings: No. 63b, St. Veronica, by Rogier van der Weyden. No. 63c, Crucifixion, by Raphael. No. 63d, Resurrection, by della Francesca. No. 64a, Last Supper, by Master of Amiens. No. 64b, Condemnation of Christ, by Hans Holbein, the Elder. No. 64c, Crucifixion, by Rubens. No. 64d, Resurrection, by El Greco. No. 65a, Passion of Christ, by El Greco. No. 65b, St. Veronica, by Jakob Cornelisz. No. 65c, Crucifixion, by Rubens. No. 65d, Resurrection, by Dierik Bouts.

Perf. 13½

1973, Apr. 6 Photo. Unwmk.

63 Block of 4 .30 .30
a.-d. A22 1c any single .20 .20
64 Block of 4 .80 .80
a.-d. A22 5c any single .20 .20
65 Block of 4 1.90 1.90
a.-d. A22 10c any single .45 .45
Nos. 63-65 (3) 3.00 3.00

Easter. Printed in blocks of 4 in sheets of 40. Design descriptions in top and bottom margins.

Coin Type of Cook Islands

Queen Elizabeth II Coins: 1c, Taro leaf. 2c, Pineapples. 5c, Hibiscus. 10c, Oranges. 20c, Fairy terns. 50c, Bonito. $1, Tangaroa, Polynesian god of creation, vert.

1973, May 14 *Perf. 13x13½*

Size: 37x24mm

66 A55 1c dp car & multi .20 .20
67 A55 2c blue & multi .20 .20
68 A55 5c green & multi .20 .20

Size: 46x30mm

69 A55 10c vio blue & multi .20 .20
70 A55 20c green & multi .30 .25
71 A55 50c dp car & multi .60 .50

Size: 32x54½mm

72 A55 $1 blue, blk & sil 1.00 .75
Nos. 66-72 (7) 2.70 2.30

Cook Islands coinage commemorating silver wedding anniv. of Queen Elizabeth II.

Printed in sheets of 20 stamps and label showing Westminster Abbey.

Cook Islands Nos. 208, 210, 212 and 215 Overprinted Like Nos. 53-62 and: "TENTH ANNIVERSARY/ CESSATION/ OF/ NUCLEAR TESTING/ TREATY"

1973, July Photo. *Perf. 14x13½*

73 A34 8c gold & multi .20 .20
74 A34 10c gold & multi .20 .20
75 A34 20c gold & multi .50 .50
76 A34 50c gold & multi 1.10 1.10
Nos. 73-76 (4) 2.00 2.00

Nuclear Test Ban Treaty, 10th anniv., protest against French nuclear testing on Mururoa Atoll.

Princess Anne, Hibiscus A23

Design: 30c, Mark Phillips and hibiscus.

1973, Nov. 14 Photo. *Perf. 13½x14*

77 A23 25c gold & multi .30 .30
78 A23 30c gold & multi .40 .40
a. Souvenir sheet of 2, #77-78 .80 .80

Wedding of Princess Anne and Capt. Mark Phillips.

Virgin and Child, by Il Perugino — A24

Paintings of the Virgin and Child by various masters - #79: a, Van Dyck. b, Bartolommeo Montagna. c, Carlo Crivelli. d, Il Perugino. #80: a, Cima da Conegliano. b, Memling. c, Verones. d, Verones. #81: a, Raphael. b, Lorenzo Lotto. c, Del Colle. d, Memling.

1973, Dec. Photo. *Perf. 13*

79 A24 1c Block of 4, #a.-d. .25 .25
80 A24 5c Block of 4, #a.-d. .75 .75
81 A24 10c Block of 4, #a.-d. 2.00 2.00
Nos. 79-81 (3) 3.00 3.00

Christmas. Printed in blocks of 4 in sheets of 48. Design descriptions in margins.

Murex Ramosus A25

Terebra Maculata — A26

Pacific Shells: 1c, Nautilus macromphalus. 2c, Harpa major. 3c, Phalium strigatum. 4c, Cypraea talpa. 5c, Mitra stictica. 8c, Charonia tritonis. 10c, Murex triremis. 20c, Oliva sericea. 25c, Tritonalia rubeta. 60c, Strombus latissimus. $1, Biplex perca. $5, Cypraea hesitata.

1974-75 Photo. *Perf. 13*

82 A25 ½c silver & multi .50 .40
83 A25 1c silver & multi .50 .40
84 A25 2c silver & multi .50 .40
85 A25 3c silver & multi .50 .40
86 A25 4c silver & multi .50 .40
87 A25 5c silver & multi .50 .40
88 A25 8c silver & multi 1.10 .50
89 A25 10c silver & multi 1.10 .60
90 A25 20c silver & multi 1.50 1.00
91 A25 25c silver & multi 1.75 1.00
92 A25 60c silver & multi 6.00 1.75
93 A25 $1 silver & multi 4.75 3.00

Perf. 14

94 A26 $2 silver & multi 7.50 4.25
95 A26 $5 silver & multi 27.50 15.50
Nos. 82-95 (14) 54.20 30.00

Issued: #82-93, 1/31/74; $2, 1/20/75; $5, 2/28/75.

For overprints see Nos. O1-O16.

William Bligh and "Bounty" A27

1974, Apr. 11 Photo. *Perf. 13*

Size: 38x22mm

96 A27 1c shown .20 .20
97 A27 1c "Bounty" at sea .20 .20
a. Pair, #96-97 .20 .20
98 A27 5c Bligh and "Bounty" off Aitutaki .45 .45
99 A27 5c Chart of Aitutaki, 1856 .45 .45
a. Pair, #98-99 .90 .90
100 A27 8c James Cook and "Resolution" .95 .95
101 A27 8c Maps of Aitutaki and Pacific Ocean .95 .95
a. Pair, #100-101 1.90 1.90
Nos. 96-101,C1-C6 (12) 8.70 8.70

Capt. William Bligh (1754-1817), European discoverer of Aitutaki, Apr. 11, 1789.

Aitutaki Nos. 1 & 2 Map and UPU Emblem A28

Design: 50c, Aitutaki Nos. 4 and 28, map of Aitutaki and UPU emblem.

1974, July 15 Photo. *Perf. 13½*

102 A28 25c blue & multi .55 .55
103 A28 50c blue & multi 1.10 1.10
a. Souvenir sheet of 2, #102-103 2.00 2.00

UPU, cent. Printed in sheets of 5 plus label showing UPU emblem.

A29

Designs: Paintings of the Virgin and Child.

1974, Oct. 11 Photo. *Perf. 13½*

104 A29 1c Van der Goes .20 .20
105 A29 5c Giovanni Bellini .20 .20
106 A29 8c Gerard David .20 .20
107 A29 10c Antonello da Messina .20 .20
108 A29 25c Joos van Cleve .50 .50
109 A29 30c Maitre de St. Catherine .55 .55
a. Souvenir sheet of 6, #104-109 2.00 2.00
Nos. 104-109 (6) 1.85 1.85

Christmas. #104-109 printed in sheets of 15 stamps and corner label. See #B1-B6.

A30

1974, Nov. 29 Photo. *Perf. 14*

Designs: Churchill portraits.

110 A30 10c Dublin, Age 5 .20 .20
111 A30 25c As young man .25 .20
112 A30 30c Inspecting troops, WWII .35 .20
113 A30 50c Painting .70 .40
114 A30 $1 Giving V sign 1.40 .80
a. Souvenir sheet of 5, #110-114 + label, perf. 13½ 4.25 3.75
Nos. 110-114 (5) 2.90 1.80

Sir Winston Churchill (1874-1965). Nos. 110-114 printed in sheets of 5 stamps and corner label.

Emblem US & USSR Flags A31

50c, Icarus and Apollo Soyuz spacecraft.

1975, July 24 Photo. *Perf. 13x14½*

115 A31 25c multicolored .35 .35
116 A31 50c multicolored .90 .90
a. Souvenir sheet of 2 1.75 1.75

Apollo Soyuz space test project (Russo-American cooperation), launching July 15; link-up July 17. Nos. 115 and 116 each printed in sheets of 5 stamps and one label showing area of Apollo splash-downs. No. 116a contains one each of Nos. 115-116 with gold and black border and inscription.

Madonna and Child, by Pietro Lorenzetti — A32

Paintings: 7c, Adoration of the Kings, by Rogier van der Weyden. 15c, Madonna and Child, by Bartolommeo Montagna. 20c, Adoration of the Shepherds.

1975, Nov. 24 Photo. *Perf. 14x13½*

117 A32 Strip of 3 .30 .30
a. 6c St. Francis .20 .20
b. 6c Madonna and Child .20 .20
c. 6c St. John the Evangelist .20 .20
118 A32 Strip of 3 .30 .30
a. 7c One King .20 .20
b. 7c Madonna and Child .20 .20
c. 7c Two Kings .20 .20
119 A32 Strip of 3 .75 .75
a. 15c St. Joseph .25 .25
b. 15c Madonna and Child .25 .25
c. 15c St. John the Baptist .25 .25
120 A32 Strip of 3 1.25 1.25
a. 20c One Shepherd .40 .40
b. 20c Madonna and Child .40 .40
c. 20c Two Shepherds .40 .40
d. Souv. sheet of 12, #117-120, perf. 13½ 3.50 3.50
Nos. 117-120 (4) 2.60 2.60

Christmas. Nos. 117-120 printed in sheets of 30 (10 strips of 3).

For surcharges see Nos. B7-B10.

Descent from the Cross, detail — A33

Designs (Painting, Flemish School, 16th Century): 30c, Virgin Mary, disciple and body of Jesus. 35c, Mary Magdalene and disciple.

1976, Apr. 5 Photo. *Perf. 13½*

121 A33 15c gold & multi .20 .20
122 A33 30c gold & multi .30 .30
123 A33 35c gold & multi .70 .70
a. Souvenir sheet of 3 1.60 1.60
Nos. 121-123 (3) 1.20 1.20

Easter. No. 123a contains 3 stamps similar to Nos. 121-123, perf. 13, in continuous design without gold frames and white margins.

Declaration of Independence — A34

Paintings by John Trumbull: 35c, Surrender of Cornwallis at Yorktown. 50c, Washington's Farewell Address. a, "1976 BICENTENARY." b, "UNITED STATES." c, "INDEPENDENCE 1776."

1976, June 1 Photo. *Perf. 13½*

124 A34 Strip of 3 1.50 1.50
a.-c. 30c any single .50 .50
125 A34 Strip of 3 2.00 2.00
a.-c. 35c any single .65 .65
126 A34 Strip of 3 2.75 2.75
a.-c. 50c any single .90 .90
d. Souvenir sheet of 9 (3x3) 6.25 6.25
Nos. 124-126 (3) 6.25 6.25

American Bicentennial. Nos. 124-126 printed in sheets of 5 strips of 3 and 3-part corner label showing portrait of John Trumbull, commemorative inscription and portraits of Washington (30c), John Adams (35c) and Jefferson (50c). No. 126d contains 3 strips similar to Nos. 124-126.

Bicycling A35

Montreal Olympic Games Emblem and: 35c, Sailing. 60c, Field hockey. 70c, Running.

1976, July 15 Photo. *Perf. 13x14*

127 A35 15c multicolored .25 .20
128 A35 35c multicolored .55 .45
129 A35 60c multicolored .90 .75
130 A35 70c multicolored 1.10 .85
a. Souvenir sheet of 4 3.00 2.25
Nos. 127-130 (4) 2.80 2.25

21st Olympic Games, Montreal, Canada, July 17-Aug. 1. Nos. 127-130 printed in sheets of 5 stamps and label showing coat of Arms and Montreal Olympic Games emblem. No. 130a contains 4 stamps similar to Nos. 127-130 with gold margin around each stamp.

Nos. 127-130a Overprinted Diagonally: "ROYAL VISIT JULY 1976"

1976, July 30

131 A35 15c multicolored .20 .20
132 A35 35c multicolored .55 .55
133 A35 60c multicolored .75 .75
134 A35 70c multicolored 1.00 1.00
a. Souvenir sheet of 4 3.00 3.00
Nos. 131-134 (4) 2.50 2.50

Visit of Queen Elizabeth II to Montreal and official opening of the Games. Each stamp of No. 134a has diagonal overprint. Sheet margin has additional overprint: "ROYAL VISIT OF H.M. QUEEN ELIZABETH II/OFFICIALLY OPENED 17 JULY 1976."

Annunciation — A36

Designs: Nos. 137-138, Angel appearing to the shepherds. Nos. 139-140, Nativity. Nos. 141-142, Three Kings.

1976, Oct. 18 *Perf. 13½x13*

135 6c dk green & gold .20 .20
136 6c dk green & gold .20 .20
a. A36 Pair, #135-136 .20 .20
137 7c dk brown & gold .20 .20
138 7c dk brown & gold .20 .20
a. A36 Pair, #137-138 .25 .25
139 15c dk blue & gold .20 .20
140 15c dk blue & gold .20 .20
a. A36 Pair, #139-140 .30 .30
141 20c purple & gold .25 .25
142 20c purple & gold .25 .25
a. A36 Pair, #141-142 .50 .50
b. Souvenir sheet of 8 1.90 1.90
Nos. 135-142 (8) 1.70 1.70

Christmas. No. 142a contains 8 stamps similar to Nos. 135-142 with white margin around each pair of stamps.

A. G. Bell and 1876 Telephone — A38

Design: 70c, Satellite and radar.

1977, Mar. 3 Photo. *Perf. 13½x13*

143 A38 25c rose & multi .25 .25
144 A38 70c violet & multi .85 .85
a. Souvenir sheet of 2 1.65 1.65

Centenary of first telephone call by Alexander Graham Bell, Mar. 10, 1876. No. 144a contains a 25c in colors of 70c and 70c in colors of 25c.

Calvary (detail), by Rubens A39

Paintings by Rubens: 20c, Lamentation. 35c, Descent from the Cross.

1977, Mar. 31 Photo. *Perf. 13½x14*

145 A39 15c gold & multi .55 .55
146 A39 20c gold & multi .70 .70
147 A39 35c gold & multi 1.00 1.00
a. Souv. sheet, #145-147, perf. 13 2.75 2.75
Nos. 145-147 (3) 2.25 2.25

Easter, and 400th birth anniv. of Peter Paul Rubens (1577-1640), Flemish painter.

Capt. Bligh, "Bounty" and George III — A40

Designs: 35c, Rev. John Williams, George IV, First Christian Church. 50c, British flag, map of Aitutaki, Queen Victoria. $1, Elizabeth II and family on balcony after coronation.

1977, Apr. 21 *Perf. 13½*

148 A40 25c gold & multi .20 .20
149 A40 35c gold & multi .30 .30
150 A40 50c gold & multi .50 .50
151 A40 $1 gold & multi 3.00 3.00
a. Souvenir sheet of 4, #148-151 2.75 2.75
Nos. 148-151 (4) 4.00 4.00

Reign of Queen Elizabeth II, 25th anniv. For overprint & surcharge see #O11, O15.

Annunciation — A41

Designs: No. 154, Virgin, Child and ox. No. 155, Joseph and donkey (Nativity). No. 156, Three Kings. No. 157, Virgin and Child. No. 158, Joseph. No. 159, Virgin, Child and donkey (Flight into Egypt).

1977, Oct. 14 Photo. *Perf. 13½x14*

152 6c multicolored .20 .20
153 6c multicolored .20 .20
a. A41 Pair, #152-153 .25 .25
154 7c multicolored .20 .20
155 7c multicolored .20 .20
a. A41 Pair, #154-155 .25 .25
156 15c multicolored .20 .20
157 15c multicolored .20 .20
a. A41 Pair, #156-157 .40 .40
158 20c multicolored .25 .25
159 20c multicolored .25 .25
a. A41 Pair, #158-159 .50 .50
b. Souvenir sheet of 8, #152-159 1.60 1.60
Nos. 152-159 (8) 1.70 1.70

Christmas.

For surcharges see Nos. B19-B26a.

Hawaiian Wood Figurine — A43

Designs: 50c, Talbot hunting dog, figurehead of "Resolution", horiz. $1, Temple figure.

1978, Jan. 19 Litho. *Perf. 13½*

160 A43 35c multicolored .55 .55
161 A43 50c multicolored .75 .75
162 A43 $1 multicolored 1.40 1.40
a. Souvenir sheet of 3, #160-162 3.00 3.00
Nos. 160-162 (3) 2.70 2.70

Bicentenary of Capt. Cook's arrival in Hawaii. Nos. 160-162 issued in sheets of 6.

Jesus Carrying Cross, by Simone di Martini A44

Paintings: 20c, Avignon Pietà, 15th Century. 35c, Christ at Emmaus, by Rembrandt.

1978, Mar. 17 Photo. *Perf. 13½x14*

163 A44 15c gold & multi .20 .20
164 A44 20c gold & multi .30 .30
165 A44 35c gold & multi .50 .50
a. Souvenir sheet of 3 1.25 1.25
Nos. 163-165 (3) 1.00 1.00

Easter. No. 165a contains one each of Nos. 163-165, perf. 13½, and label showing Louvre, Paris. See Nos. B27-B29.

Elizabeth II — A45

Virgin and Child, by Dürer — A46

Souvenir Sheets

1978, June 15 Photo. *Perf. 13½x13*

166 Sheet of 6 2.75 2.75
a. A45 $1 Yale of Beaufort .25 .25
b. A45 $1 shown .25 .25
c. A45 $1 Ancestral statue .25 .25
d. Souvenir sheet of 6 1.50 1.50

25th anniv. of coronation of Queen Elizabeth II. No. 166 contains 2 each of Nos. 166a-166c, silver marginal inscription and coats of arms. No. 166d contains 2 strips of Nos. 166a-166c separated by horizontal slate green gutter showing Royal family on balcony, silver marginal inscription.

1978, Dec. 4 Photo. *Perf. 14½x13*

Designs: Various paintings of the Virgin and Child by Albrecht Dürer.

167 A46 15c multicolored .30 .25
168 A46 17c multicolored .35 .30
169 A46 30c multicolored .70 .50
170 A46 35c multicolored .90 .75
Nos. 167-170 (4) 2.25 1.80

Christmas; 450th death anniv. of Albrecht Dürer (1471-1528), German painter. Nos. 167-170 issued in sheets of 5 stamps and corner label. See No. B30.

Capt. Cook, by Nathaniel Dance — A47

Boy Holding Hibiscus, IYC Emblem — A48

Design: 75c, "Resolution" and "Adventure," by William Hodges.

1979, July 20 Photo. *Perf. 14x13½*

171 A47 50c multicolored 1.25 1.25
172 A47 75c multicolored 1.75 1.75
a. Souvenir sheet of 2, #171-172 2.50 2.50

Capt. James Cook (1728-1779), explorer, death bicentenary.

1979, Oct. 1 Photo. *Perf. 14x13½*

IYC Emblem and: 35c, Boy playing guitar. 65c, Boys in outrigger canoe.

173 A48 30c multicolored .20 .20
174 A48 35c multicolored .30 .30
175 A48 65c multicolored .55 .55
Nos. 173-175 (3) 1.05 1.05

See No. B31.

Aitutaki No. 102, Hill, Penny Black A49

Designs: Nos. 176, 178-179, 181, paintings of letter writers, Flemish School, 17th century.

1979, Nov. 14 Photo. *Perf. 13*

176 A49 50c Gabriel Metsu .45 .45
177 A49 50c shown .45 .45
178 A49 50c Jan Vermeer .45 .45
a. Strip of 3, #176-178 1.35 1.35
179 A49 65c Gerard Terborch .55 .55
180 A49 65c No. 103 (like No. 177) .55 .55
181 A49 65c Jan Vermeer .55 .55
a. Strip of 3, #179-181 1.65 1.65
Nos. 176-181 (6) 3.00 3.00

Souvenir Sheet

182 Sheet of 6 2.50 2.50
a. A49 30c like No. 176 .40 .40
b. A49 30c like No. 177 .40 .40
c. A49 30c like No. 178 .40 .40
d. A49 30c like No. 179 .40 .40
e. A49 30c like No. 180 .40 .40
f. A49 30c like No. 181 .40 .40

Sir Rowland Hill (1795-1879), originator of penny postage. Nos. 176-178 and 179-181 printed in sheets of 9.

Descent from the Cross, Detail — A50

Albert Einstein — A51

Easter: 30c, 35c, Descent from the Cross, by Quentin Metsys (details).

1980, Apr. 3 Photo. *Perf. 13x13½*
183 A50 20c multicolored .40 .40
184 A50 30c multicolored .50 .50
185 A50 35c multicolored .60 .60
Nos. 183-185 (3) 1.50 1.50

See No. B32.

1980, July 21 Photo. *Perf. 14*
186 A51 12c shown .55 .55
187 A51 12c Formula, atom structure .55 .55
a. Pair, #186-187 1.10 1.10
188 A51 15c Portrait, diff. .65 .65
189 A51 15c Atomic blast .65 .65
a. Pair, #188-189 1.30 1.30
190 A51 20c Portrait, diff. .90 .90
191 A51 20c Atomic blast, trees .90 .90
a. Pair, #190-191 1.80 1.80
b. Souv. sheet of 6, #186-191, perf. 13 4.25 4.25
Nos. 186-191 (6) 4.20 4.20

Albert Einstein (1879-1955), theoretical physicist.

A52

A53

1980, Sept. 26 Photo. *Perf. 14*
192 A52 6c Ancestral Figure, Aitutaki .20 .20
193 A52 6c God image staff, Rarotonga .20 .20
194 A52 6c Trade adze, Mangaia .20 .20
195 A52 6c Tangaroa carving, Rarotonga .20 .20
a. Block of 4, #192-195 .35 .35
196 A52 12c Wooden image, Aitutaki .20 .20
197 A52 12c Hand club, Rarotonga .20 .20
198 A52 12c Carved mace, Mangaia .20 .20
199 A52 12c Fisherman's god, Rarotonga .20 .20
a. Block of 4, #196-199 .70 .70
200 A52 15c Ti'i image, Aitutaki .20 .20
201 A52 15c Fisherman's god, diff. .20 .20
202 A52 15c Carved mace, Cook Islands .20 .20
203 A52 15c Tangaroa, diff. .20 .20
a. Block of 4, #200-203 .90 .90
204 A52 20c Chief's headdress, Aitutaki .30 .30
205 A52 20c Carved mace, diff. .30 .30
206 A52 20c God image staff, diff. .30 .30
207 A52 20c like #195 .30 .30
a. Block of 4, #2-4-207 1.20 1.20
b. Souvenir sheet of 16, #192-207 3.50

Third South Pacific Arts Festival, Port Moresby, Papua New Guinea.

1980, Nov. 21 Photo. *Perf. 13x13½*

Virgin and Child, Sculptures.

208 A53 15c 13th cent. .20 .20
209 A53 20c 14th cent. .20 .20
210 A53 25c 15th cent. .25 .25
211 A53 35c 15th cent., diff. .35 .35
Nos. 208-211 (4) 1.00 1.00

Christmas. See No. B33.

Mourning Virgin, by Pedro Roldan — A54

Sturnus Vulgaris — A55

Easter (Roldan Sculptures): 40c, Christ. 50c, Mourning St. John.

1981, Mar. 31 Photo. *Perf. 14*
212 A54 30c green & gold .35 .35
213 A54 40c brt purple & gold .45 .45
214 A54 50c dk blue & gold .60 .60
Nos. 212-214 (3) 1.40 1.40

See No. B34.

1981-82 *Perf. 14x13½, 13½x14*
215 A55 1c shown .45 .20
216 A55 1c Poephila gouldiae .45 .20
a. Pair, #215-216 .90 .20
217 A55 2c Petroica multicolor .50 .20
218 A55 2c Pachycephala pectoralis .50 .20
a. Pair, #217-218 1.00 .20
219 A55 3c Falco peregrinus .55 .20
220 A55 3c Rhipidura rufifrous .55 .20
a. Pair, #219-220 1.10 .20
221 A55 4c Tyto alba .65 .20
222 A55 4c Padda oryzivora .65 .20
a. Pair, #221-222 1.25 .30
223 A55 5c Artamus leucorhynchus .65 .20
224 A55 5c Vini peruviana .65 .20
a. Pair, #223-224 1.25 .35
225 A55 6c Columba livia .65 .20
226 A55 6c Porphyrio porphyria .65 .20
a. Pair, #225-226 1.25 .40
227 A55 10c Geopelia striata .85 .35
228 A55 10c Lonchura castaneothorax .85 .35
a. Pair, #227-228 1.75 .70
229 A55 12c Acridotheres tristis .95 .40
230 A55 12c Egretta sacra .95 .40
a. Pair, #229-230 1.90 .80
231 A55 15c Diomeda melanophris 1.25 .45
232 A55 15c Numenius phaeopus 1.25 .45
a. Pair, #231-232 2.50 .90
233 A55 20c Gygis alba 1.40 .65
234 A55 20c Pluvialis dominica 1.40 .65
a. Pair, #233-234 2.75 1.30
235 A55 25c Sula leucogaster 1.60 .80
236 A55 25c Anas superciliosa 1.60 .80
a. Pair, #235-236 3.25 1.60
237 A55 30c Anas acuta 1.90 .90
238 A55 30c Fregata minor 1.90 .90
a. Pair, #237-238 3.80 1.80
239 A55 35c Stercorarius pomarinus 2.10 1.10
240 A55 35c Conopoderas caffra 2.10 1.10
a. Pair, #239-240 4.25 2.20
241 A55 40c Lalage maculosa 2.50 1.10
242 A55 40c Gallirallus philippensis 2.50 1.10
a. Pair, #241-242 5.00 2.20
243 A55 50c Vini stepheni 2.75 1.50
244 A55 50c Diomedea epomophora 2.75 1.50
a. Pair, #243-244 5.50 3.00
245 A55 70c Ptilinopus victor 5.00 2.00
246 A55 70c Erythrura cyaneovirens 5.00 2.00
e. Pair, #245-246 10.50 4.00

Photo. *Perf. 13½*
Size: 35x47mm
246A A55 $1 Myiagra azureocapilla 4.75 3.50
246B A55 $2 Myiagra vanikorensis 5.75 *7.00*
246C A55 $4 Amandava amandava 10.00 *12.00*
246D A55 $5 Halcyon recurvirostris 11.00 *15.00*
Nos. 215-246D (36) 79.00 58.40

Issued: #215-230, 4/6; #231-238, 5/8; #239-246, 1/14/82; #246A-246B, 2/15/82.
Nos. 231-246 horiz.
For surcharges and overprint see Nos. 293-306, 452-454, O40-O41.

Prince Charles and Lady Diana — A56

Perf. 13x13½, 13½x13
1981, June 10 Photo.
247 A56 60c Charles, vert. .55 .55
248 A56 80c Lady Diana, vert. .70 .70
249 A56 $1.40 Shown 1.00 1.00
Nos. 247-249 (3) 2.25 2.25

Royal Wedding. Issued in sheets of 4.
For overprints and surcharges see Nos. 265-267, 307, 309, 355, 405-407, B35-B37.

1982 World Cup Soccer — A57

Designs: Various soccer players.

1981, Nov. 30 Photo. *Perf. 14*
250 A57 12c Pair, #250a-250b .85 .85
251 A57 15c Pair, #251a-251b 1.00 1.00
252 A57 20c Pair, #252a-252b 1.40 1.40
253 A57 25c Pair, #253a-253b 1.75 1.75
Nos. 250-253 (4) 5.00 5.00

See No. B38.

Christmas A58

Rembrandt Etchings: 15c, Holy Family, 1632, vert. 30c, Virgin with Child, 1634, vert. 40c, Adoration of the Shepherds, 1654. 50c, Holy Family with Cat, 1644.

1981, Dec. 10 *Perf. 14*
254 A58 15c gold & dk brown .40 .40
255 A58 30c gold & dk brown .65 .65
256 A58 40c gold & dk brown .85 .85
257 A58 50c gold & dk brown 1.10 1.10
Nos. 254-257 (4) 3.00 3.00

Souvenir Sheets
258 A58 80c + 5c like #254 .90 .90
259 A58 80c + 5c like #255 .90 .90
260 A58 80c + 5c like #256 .90 .90
261 A58 80c + 5c like #257 .90 .90

Nos. 258-261 have multicolored margins showing entire etching. Surtax on Nos. 258-261 was for local charities.

21st Birthday of Princess Diana — A59

1982, June 24 Photo. *Perf. 14*
262 A59 70c shown .75 1.60
263 A59 $1 Wedding portrait 1.90 1.00
264 A59 $2 Diana, diff. 3.50 2.25
a. Souvenir sheet of 3, #262-264 6.00 5.00
Nos. 262-264 (3) 6.15 4.85

See #268-270a. For surcharges see #308, 310.

Nos. 247-249 Overprinted: "21 June 1982 PRINCE WILLIAM OF WALES" or "COMMEMORATING THE ROYAL BIRTH"

1982, July 13 *Perf. 13x13½,13½x13*
265 A56 60c multicolored 1.00 1.00
266 A56 80c multicolored 1.50 1.50
267 A56 $1.40 multicolored 2.50 2.50
Nos. 265-267 (3) 5.00 5.00

Nos. 262-264a Inscribed: "ROYAL BIRTH 21 JUNE 1982 PRINCE WILLIAM OF WALES"

1982, Aug. 5 *Perf. 14*
268 A59 70c multicolored 1.10 1.10
269 A59 $1 multicolored 1.50 1.50
270 A59 $2 multicolored 3.00 3.00
a. Souvenir sheet of 3 6.00 6.00
Nos. 268-270 (3) 5.60 5.60

Christmas — A60

Madonna and Child Sculptures, 12th-15th Cent.

1982, Dec. 10 Photo. *Perf. 13*
271 A60 18c multicolored .55 .55
272 A60 36c multicolored .70 .70
273 A60 48c multicolored .90 .90
274 A60 60c multicolored 1.10 1.10
Nos. 271-274 (4) 3.25 3.25

Souvenir Sheet
275 Sheet of 4 4.00 4.00
a. A60 18c + 2c like 18c .45 .45
b. A60 36c + 2c like 36c .80 .80
c. A60 48c + 2c like 48c 1.10 1.10
d. A60 60c + 2c like 60c 1.25 1.25

Surtax was for children's charities.

Commonwealth Day — A61

1983, Mar. 14 Photo. *Perf. 13x13½*
276 A61 48c Bananas 1.25 1.25
277 A61 48c Ti'i statuette 1.25 1.25
278 A61 48c Boys canoeing 1.25 1.25
279 A61 48c Capt. Bligh, Bounty 1.25 1.25
a. Block of 4, #276-279 5.00 5.00

Scouting Year A62

1983, Apr. 18 Photo. *Perf. 14*
280 A62 36c Campfire .50 .50
281 A62 48c Salute .60 .60
282 A62 60c Hiking .65 .65
Nos. 280-282 (3) 1.75 1.75

Souvenir Sheet
Perf. 13½
283 Sheet of 3 3.00 3.00
a. A62 36c + 3c like #280 .75 .75
b. A62 48c + 3c like #281 .90 .90
c. A62 60c + 3c like #282 1.25 1.25

Surtax was for benefit of Scouting.

Nos. 280-283 Overprinted: "15th WORLD SCOUT JAMBOREE"

1983, July 11 Photo. *Perf. 14*
284 A62 36c multicolored .90 .90
285 A62 48c multicolored 1.10 1.10
286 A62 60c multicolored 1.25 1.25
Nos. 284-286 (3) 3.25 3.25

Souvenir Sheet
287 Sheet of 3 3.00 3.00
a. A62 36c + 3c like #284 .75 .75
b. A62 48c + 3c like #285 .90 .90
c. A62 60c + 3c like #286 1.25 1.25

A63

A64

Manned Flight Bicentenary: Modern sport balloons.

1983, July 22 Photo. Perf. 14x13

288 A63 18c multicolored .60 .60
289 A63 36c multicolored .80 .80
290 A63 48c multicolored 1.00 1.00
291 A63 60c multicolored 1.10 1.10
Nos. 288-291 (4) 3.50 3.50

Souvenir Sheet

292 A63 $2.50 multicolored 3.00 3.00

Nos. 233-246, 246D, 248-249, 263-264 Surcharged

1983, Sept. 22

293 A55 18c on 20c, #233 2.25 .35
294 A55 18c on 20c, #234 2.25 .35
a. Pair, #293-294 4.50 .70
295 A55 36c on 25c, #235 3.00 .70
296 A55 36c on 25c, #236 3.00 .70
a. Pair, #295-296 6.00 1.40
297 A55 36c on 30c, #237 3.00 .70
298 A55 36c on 30c, #238 3.00 .70
a. Pair, #297-298 6.00 1.40
299 A55 36c on 35c, #239 3.00 .70
300 A55 36c on 35c, #240 3.00 .70
a. Pair, #299-300 6.00 1.40
301 A55 48c on 40c, #241 3.50 .95
302 A55 48c on 40c, #242 3.50 .95
a. Pair, #301-302 7.00 1.90
303 A55 48c on 50c, #243 3.50 .95
304 A55 48c on 50c, #244 3.50 .95
a. Pair, #303-304 7.00 1.90
305 A55 72c on 70c, #245 6.25 1.50
306 A55 72c on 70c, #246 6.25 1.50
a. Pair, #305-306 12.50 3.00
307 A56 96c on 80c, #248 2.75 1.90
308 A59 96c on $1, #263 2.50 1.90
309 A56 $1.20 on $1.40, #249 2.50 2.50
310 A59 $1.20 on $2, #264 2.75 2.50

Size: 35x47mm

311 A55 $5.60 on $5, #246D 18.00 11.00
Nos. 293-311 (19) 77.50 31.50

Nos. 307-308, 310-311 vert.

1983, Sept. 29 Photo. Perf. 14

312 A64 48c shown .65 .65
313 A64 60c Global coverage .85 .85
314 A64 96c Communications satellite 1.50 1.50
a. Souvenir sheet of 3, #312-314 3.00 3.00
Nos. 312-314 (3) 3.00 3.00

World Communications Year.

Christmas A65

Raphael Paintings.

1983, Nov. 21 Photo. Perf. 13½x14

315 A65 36c Madonna of the Chair .75 .75
316 A65 48c Alba Madonna .95 .95
317 A65 60c Connestabile Madonna 1.25 1.25
Nos. 315-317 (3) 2.95 2.95

Souvenir Sheet

318 Sheet of 3 2.75 2.75
a. A65 36c + 3c like #315 .70 .70
b. A65 48c + 3c like #316 .85 .85
c. A65 60c + 3c like #317 1.00 1.00

1983, Dec. 15 Imperf.

Size: 46x46mm

319 A65 85c + 5c like #315 1.25 1.25
320 A65 85c + 5c like #316 1.25 1.25
321 A65 85c + 5c like #317 1.25 1.25
Nos. 319-321 (3) 3.75 3.75

Surtax was for children's charities.

Local Birds — A66

1984 Photo. Perf. 14

322 A66 2c as No. 216 .25 .25
323 A66 3c as No. 215 .25 .25
324 A66 5c as No. 217 .25 .25
325 A66 10c as No. 218 .25 .25
326 A66 12c as No. 220 .35 .35
327 A66 18c as No. 219 .45 .45
328 A66 24c as No. 221 .65 .65
329 A66 30c as No. 222 .75 .75
330 A66 36c as No. 223 .90 .90
331 A66 48c as No. 224 1.25 1.25
332 A66 50c as No. 225 .90 .90
333 A66 60c as No. 226 1.25 1.25
334 A66 72c as No. 227 1.50 1.50
335 A66 96c as No. 228 2.00 2.00
336 A66 $1.20 as No. 229 2.25 2.25
337 A66 $2.10 as No. 230 4.00 4.00
338 A66 $3 as No. 246A 5.75 5.75
339 A66 $4.20 as No. 246B 7.00 7.00
340 A66 $5.60 as No. 246C 7.50 7.50
341 A66 $9.60 as No. 246D 12.50 12.50
Nos. 322-341 (20) 50.00 50.00

For overprints and surcharges see Nos. O17-O39.

1984 Summer Olympics — A67

1984, July 24 Photo. Perf. 13x13½

342 A67 36c Javelin .35 .35
343 A67 48c Shot put .45 .45
344 A67 60c Hurdles .55 .55
345 A67 $2 Handball 1.75 1.75
Nos. 342-345 (4) 3.10 3.10

Souvenir Sheet

346 Sheet of 4 3.50 3.50
a. A67 36c + 5c like #342 .40 .40
b. A67 48c + 5c like #343 .50 .50
c. A67 60c + 5c like #344 .60 .60
d. A67 $2 + 5c like #345 1.75 1.75

Surtax was for benefit of local sports.

Nos. 342-345 Overprinted in Gold on Black with Winners' Names, Event, Nationality

1984, Aug. 21 Photo. Perf. 13x13½

347 A67 36c multicolored .40 .40
348 A67 48c multicolored .55 .55
349 A67 60c multicolored .65 .65
350 A67 $2 multicolored 1.90 1.90
Nos. 347-350 (4) 3.50 3.50

Ausipex '84 — A68

1984, Sept. 14 Photo. Perf. 14

351 A68 60c William Bligh, map 3.25 3.25
352 A68 96c Bounty, map 3.25 3.25
353 A68 $1.40 Stamps, map 3.25 3.25
Nos. 351-353 (3) 9.75 9.75

Souvenir Sheet

354 Sheet of 3 6.25 6.25
a. A68 60c + 5c like #351 1.40 1.40
b. A68 96c + 5c like #352 1.90 1.90
c. A68 $1.40 + 5c like #353 2.50 2.50

For overprint see No. 399.

No. 247 Surcharged with Black Bar and New Value in Gold and: "15.9.84 Birth/Prince Henry"

1984, Oct. 10 Photo. Perf. 13x13½

355 A56 $3 multicolored 4.00 4.00

Issued in sheets of 4.

A69

A70

1984, Nov. 16 Photo. Perf. 13

356 A69 36c Annunciation .40 .40
357 A69 48c Nativity .50 .50
358 A69 60c Epiphany .60 .60
359 A69 96c Flight into Egypt 1.00 1.00
Nos. 356-359 (4) 2.50 2.50

Souvenir Sheets

Size: 45x53mm

Imperf

360 A69 90c + 7c like #356 .90 .90
361 A69 90c + 7c like #357 .90 .90
362 A69 90c + 7c like #358 .90 .90
363 A69 90c + 7c like #359 .90 .90

Christmas.

1984, Dec. 10 Photo. Perf. 13½x14

364 A70 48c Diana, Henry 2.00 2.00
365 A70 60c William, Henry 2.00 2.00
366 A70 $2.10 Family 3.50 3.50
Nos. 364-366 (3) 7.50 7.50

Souvenir Sheet

367 Sheet of 3 7.00 7.00
a. A70 96c + 7c like #364 2.25 2.25
b. A70 96c + 7c like #365 2.25 2.25
c. A70 96c + 7c like #366 2.25 2.25

Christmas, Birth of Prince Henry, Sept. 15. Surtax was for benefit of local children's charities.

Audubon Birth Bicentenary A71

Illustrations of bird species by John J. Audubon.

1985, Mar. 22 Litho. Perf. 13

368 A71 55c Gray kingbird 1.25 1.25
369 A71 65c Bohemian waxwing 1.40 1.40
370 A71 75c Summer tanager 1.60 1.60
371 A71 95c Cardinal 1.75 1.75
372 A71 $1.15 White-winged crossbill 2.00 2.00
Nos. 368-372 (5) 8.00 8.00

Queen Mother, 85th Birthday A72

Photographs: 55c, Lady Elizabeth Bowes-Lyon, age 7. 65c, Engaged to the Duke of York, 75c, Duchess of York with daughter, Elizabeth. $1.30, Holding the infant Prince Charles. $3, Portrait taken on 63rd birthday.

1985-86 Perf. 13½x13

373 A72 55c multicolored .50 .50
374 A72 65c multicolored .60 .60
375 A72 75c multicolored .65 .65
376 A72 $1.30 multicolored 1.25 1.25
a. Souvenir sheet of 4, #373-376 3.25 3.25
Nos. 373-376 (4) 3.00 3.00

Souvenir Sheet

377 A72 $3 multicolored 2.25 2.25

Nos. 373-376 printed in sheets of 4.
Issued: #376a, 8/4/86; others, 6/14/85.

Intl. Youth Year A73

Designs: 75c, The Calmady Children, by Thomas Lawrence (1769-1830). 90c, Madame Charpentier's Children, by Renoir (1841-1919). $1.40, Young Girls at Piano, by Renoir.

1985, Sept. 16 Photo. Perf. 13

378 A73 75c multicolored 2.25 2.25
379 A73 90c multicolored 2.25 2.25
380 A73 $1.40 multicolored 3.00 3.00
Nos. 378-380 (3) 7.50 7.50

Souvenir Sheet

381 Sheet of 3 5.75 5.75
a. A73 75c + 10c like #378 1.25 1.25
b. A73 90c + 10c like #379 1.75 1.75
c. A73 $1.40 + 10c like #380 2.75 2.75

Surcharged for children's activities.

Adoration of the Magi, by Giotto di Bondone (1276-1337) — A74

1985, Nov. 15 Photo. Perf. 13½x13

382 A74 95c multicolored 1.75 1.75
383 A74 95c multicolored 1.75 1.75
a. Pair, #382-383 3.50 3.50
384 A74 $1.15 multicolored 1.75 1.75
385 A74 $1.15 multicolored 1.75 1.75
a. Pair, #384-385 3.50 3.50
Nos. 382-385 (4) 7.00 7.00

Souvenir Sheet

Imperf

386 A74 $6.40 multicolored 12.00 12.00

Christmas, return of Halley's Comet, 1985-86.

Halley's Comet A75

Designs: 90c, Halley's Comet, A.D. 684, wood engraving, Nuremberg Chronicles. $1.25, Sighting of 1066, Bayeux Tapestry, detail, c. 1092, France. $1.75, The Comet Inflicting Untold Disasters, 1456, Lucerne Chronicles, by Diebolt Schilling. $4.20, Melancolia I, engraving by Durer.

1986, Feb. 25 Photo. Perf. 13½x13

387 A75 90c multicolored 1.00 1.00
388 A75 $1.25 multicolored 1.50 1.50
389 A75 $1.75 multicolored 2.25 2.25
Nos. 387-389 (3) 4.75 4.75

Souvenir Sheets

390 Sheet of 3 + label 4.25 4.25
a. A75 95c, like #387 1.40 1.40
b. A75 95c, like #388 1.40 1.40
c. A75 95c, like #389 1.40 1.40

Imperf

391 A75 $4.20 multicolored 5.50 5.50

Elizabeth II, 60th Birthday — A76

1986, Apr. 21 Perf. 14

392 A76 95c Coronation portrait 1.10 1.10

Souvenir Sheet

Perf. 13½

393 A76 $4.20 Portrait, diff. 5.75 5.75

No. 392 printed in sheets of 5 with label picturing U.K. flag and Queen's flag for New Zealand.

Statue of Liberty, Cent. A77

1986, June 27 Photo. Perf. 14

394 A77 $1 Liberty head 1.10 1.10
395 A77 $2.75 Statue 3.00 3.00

Souvenir Sheet

Perf. 13½

396 Sheet of 2 3.00 3.00
a. A77 $1.25 like $1 1.50 1.50
b. A77 $1.25 like $2.75 1.50 1.50

For surcharges see Nos B44, B49.

Wedding of Prince Andrew and Sarah Ferguson — A78

1986, July 23 Perf. 14

397 A78 $2 multicolored 2.75 2.75

Souvenir Sheet

Perf. 13½

398 A78 $5 multicolored 6.25 6.25

No. 397 printed in sheets of 5 plus label picturing Westminster Abbey.
For surcharge see No. B48.

No. 354 Ovptd. with Gold Circle over AUSIPEX Emblem, Black and Gold STAMPEX '86 Emblem

1986, Aug. 4 Photo. Perf. 14

399 Sheet of 3 9.50 9.50
a. A68 60c + 5c like #351 2.00 2.00
b. A68 96c + 5c like #352 3.00 3.00
c. A68 $1.40 + 5c like #353 4.50 4.50

STAMPEX '86, Adelaide, Aug. 4-10.

Christmas A79

Paintings by Albrecht Durer: 75c, No. 404a, St. Anne with Virgin and Child. $1.35, No. 404b, Virgin and Child. $1.95, No. 404c, Adoration of the Magi. $2.75, No. 404d, Rosary Festivity.

1986, Nov. 21 Litho. Perf. 13½

400 A79 75c multicolored 1.60 1.60
401 A79 $1.35 multicolored 2.40 2.40
402 A79 $1.95 multicolored 3.00 3.00
403 A79 $2.75 multicolored 4.00 4.00
Nos. 400-403 (4) 11.00 11.00

Souvenir Sheet

404 Sheet of 4 13.00 13.00
a.-d. A79 $1.65 any single 3.25 3.25

For surcharges see Nos. B39-B44, B46-B47, B50-B54.

Nos. 247-249 Surcharged in Gold and Black

1987, Nov. 20 Photo. Perf. 13x12½

405 A56 $2.50 on 60c No. 247 2.75 2.75
406 A56 $2.50 on 80c No. 248 2.75 2.75
407 A56 $2.50 on $1.40 No. 249 2.75 2.75
Nos. 405-407 (3) 8.25 8.25

Issued in sheets of 4 with margin inscriptions overprinted with gold bar and "40th Anniversary of the Royal Wedding / 1947-1987" in black; "OVERPRINTED BY NEW ZEALAND GOVERNMENT PRINTER, / WELLINGTON, NOVEMBER 1987" at left.

A80

The Virgin with Garland, by Rubens — A81

Painting details.

1987, Dec. 10 Photo. Perf. 13x13½

408 A80 70c UL 1.90 1.90
409 A80 85c UR 2.00 2.00
410 A80 $1.50 LL 2.75 2.75
411 A80 $1.85 LR 3.25 3.25
Nos. 408-411 (4) 9.90 9.90

Souvenir Sheets

412 Sheet of 4 11.00 11.00
a. A80 95c like No. 408 2.75 2.75
b. A80 95c like No. 409 2.75 2.75
c. A80 95c like No. 410 2.75 2.75
d. A80 95c like No. 411 2.75 2.75

Perf. 13

413 A81 $6 multicolored 11.00 11.00

Christmas.

1988 Summer Olympics, Seoul — A82

Flags of Korea, Aitutaki, ancient and modern events, and Seoul Games emblem or $50 silver coin issued to commemorate the participation of Aitutaki athletes in the Olympics for the 1st time: 70c, No. 418a, Obverse of silver coin, chariot race, running. 85c, Emblem, running, soccer. 95c, Emblem, boxing, handball. $1.40, No. 418b, Reverse of coin, spearmen, women's tennis.

1988, Aug. 22 Photo. Perf. 14½x15

414 A82 70c multicolored 1.75 1.75
415 A82 85c multicolored 2.00 2.00
416 A82 95c multicolored 2.00 2.00
417 A82 $1.40 multicolored 2.75 2.75
Nos. 414-417 (4) 8.50 8.50

Souvenir Sheet

418 Sheet of 2 8.00 8.00
a.-b. A82 $2 any single 4.00 4.00

Nos. 414-417 Ovptd. with Names of 1988 Olympic Gold Medalists

a. "FLORENCE GRIFFTH JOYNER / UNITED STATES / 100 M AND 200 M"
b. "GELINDO BORDIN / ITALY / MARATHON"
c. "HITOSHI SAITO / JAPAN / JUDO"
d. "STEFFI GRAF / WEST GERMANY / WOMEN'S TENNIS"

1988, Oct. 10 Litho. Perf. 14½x15

419 A82 (a) 70c on No. 414 1.50 1.50
420 A82 (b) 85c on No. 415 1.75 1.75
421 A82 (c) 95c on No. 416 2.00 2.00
422 A82 (d) $1.40 on No. 417 3.00 3.00
Nos. 419-422 (4) 8.25 8.25

Griffith is spelled incorrectly on No. 419.

Christmas A83

Paintings by Rembrandt: 55c, Adoration of the Shepherds (detail), National Gallery, London. 70c, Holy Family, Alte Pinakothek, Munich. 85c, Presentation in the Temple, Kunsthalle, Hamburg. 95c, The Holy Family, Louvre, Paris. $1.15, Presentation in the Temple, diff., Mauritshuis, The Hague. $4.50, Adoration of the Shepherds (entire painting).

1988, Nov. 2 Photo. Perf. 13½

423 A83 55c multicolored 1.50 1.50
424 A83 70c multicolored 1.60 1.60
425 A83 85c multicolored 1.75 1.75
426 A83 95c multicolored 1.90 1.90
427 A83 $1.15 multicolored 3.25 3.25
Nos. 423-427 (5) 10.00 10.00

Souvenir Sheet

Perf. 14

428 A83 $4.50 multicolored 8.75 8.75

No. 428 contains one 52x34mm stamp.

A84

Mutiny on the *Bounty,* 200th Anniv. — A85

1989, July 3 Photo. Perf. 13½

429 A84 55c Ship, Capt. Bligh 2.10 2.10
430 A84 65c Breadfruit 2.40 2.40
431 A84 75c Bligh, chart 2.75 2.75
432 A84 95c *Bounty* off Aitutaki 3.00 3.00
433 A84 $1.65 Christian, Bligh 3.75 3.75
Nos. 429-433 (5) 14.00 14.00

Souvenir Sheet

434 A85 $4.20 Castaways 9.75 9.75

Discovery of Aitutaki by William Bligh, bicent.

1st Moon Landing, 20th Anniv. — A86

Apollo 11 mission emblem, American flag, eagle, "The Eagle has landed" and: 75c, Astronaut standing on the lunar surface. $1.15, Conducting an experiment in front of the lunar module. $1.80, Carrying equipment. $6.40, Raising the flag.

1989, July 28 Photo. Perf. 13½x13

435 A86 75c multicolored 2.00 2.00
436 A86 $1.15 multicolored 2.50 2.50
437 A86 $1.80 multicolored 3.25 3.25
Nos. 435-437 (3) 7.75 7.75

Souvenir Sheet

Perf. 13½

438 A86 $6.40 multicolored 9.50 9.50

No. 438 contains one 42x31mm stamp.

Christmas — A87

Details from *Virgin in Glory,* by Titian: 70c, Virgin. 85c, Christ child. 95c, Angel. $1.25, Cherubs. $6, Entire painting.

1989, Nov. 20 Photo. Perf. 13½x13

439 A87 70c multicolored 1.75 1.75
440 A87 85c multicolored 2.25 2.25
441 A87 95c multicolored 2.50 2.50
442 A87 $1.25 multicolored 3.00 3.00
Nos. 439-442 (4) 9.50 9.50

Souvenir Sheet

Perf. 13½

443 A87 $6 multicolored 10.50 10.500

No. 443 contains one 45x60mm stamp.

World Environmental Protection — A88

Designs: a, Human comet, World Philatelic Programs emblem. b, Comet tail and "Protect The Endangered Earth!" $3, Human comet, emblem and inscription.
Illustration reduced.

1990, Feb. 16 Photo. Perf. 13½x13

444 A88 Pair 4.50 4.50
a.-b. $1.75 any single 2.25 2.25

Souvenir Sheet

445 A88 $3 multicolored 4.00 4.00

No. 376a Ovptd. "Ninetieth / Birthday" in Black on Gold

Designs: 55c, Lady Elizabeth Bowes-Lyon, 1907. 65c, Lady Elizabeth engaged to Duke of York. 75c, As Duchess of York with daughter Elizabeth. $1.30, As Queen Mother with grandson.

1990, July 16 Litho. Perf. 13½x13

446 Sheet of 4 4.00 4.00
a. A72 55c multicolored .65 .65
b. A72 65c multicolored .75 .75
c. A72 75c multicolored .90 .90
d. A72 $1.30 multicolored 1.50 1.50

Christmas — A89

Paintings: 70c, Madonna of the Basket by Correggio. 85c, Virgin and Child by Morando. 95c, Adoration of the Child by Tiepolo. $1.75, Mystic Marriage of St. Catherine by Memling. $6, Donne Triptych by Memling.

1990, Nov. 28 Litho. *Perf. 14*

447 A89 70c multicolored .85 .85
448 A89 85c multicolored 1.00 1.00
449 A89 95c multicolored 1.10 1.10
450 A89 $1.75 multicolored 2.25 2.25
Nos. 447-450 (4) 5.20 5.20

Souvenir Sheet

451 A89 $6 multicolored 7.50 7.50

Nos. 246A-246B Overprinted

1990, Dec. 5 Photo. *Perf. 13½*

452 A55 $1 multicolored 1.90 1.90
453 A55 $2 multicolored 3.75 3.75

Birdpex '90, 20 Intl. Ornithological Congress, New Zealand.

No. 246D Overprinted "COMMEMORATING 65TH BIRTHDAY OF H.M. QUEEN ELIZABETH II"

1991, Apr. 22 Photo. *Perf. 13*

454 A55 $5 multicolored 6.25 6.25

Christmas — A90

Paintings: 80c, The Holy Family, by Mengs. 90c, Virgin and Child, by Fra Filippo Lippi. $1.05, Virgin and Child, by Durer. $1.75, Adoration of the Shepherds, by De La Tour. $6, The Holy Family, by Michelangelo.

1991, Nov. 13 Litho. *Perf. 14*

455 A90 80c multicolored .90 .90
456 A90 90c multicolored 1.10 1.10
457 A90 $1.05 multicolored 1.25 1.25
458 A90 $1.75 multicolored 2.00 2.00
Nos. 455-458 (4) 5.25 5.25

Souvenir Sheet

459 A90 $6 multicolored 7.00 7.00

1992 Summer Olympics, Barcelona — A91

1992, July 29 Litho. *Perf. 14*

460 A91 95c Hurdles 1.00 1.00
461 A91 $1.25 Weight lifting 1.40 1.40
462 A91 $1.50 Judo 1.75 1.75
463 A91 $1.95 Soccer 2.25 2.25
Nos. 460-463 (4) 6.40 6.40

6th Festival of Pacific Arts, Rarotonga — A92

Canoes: 30c, Vaka Motu. 50c, Hamatafua. 95c, Alia Kalia Ndrua. $1.75, Hokule'a Hawaiian. $1.95, Tuamotu Pahi.

1992, Oct. 16 Litho. *Perf. 14x15*

464 A92 30c multicolored .35 .35
465 A92 50c multicolored .55 .55
466 A92 95c multicolored 1.10 1.10
467 A92 $1.75 multicolored 2.00 2.00
468 A92 $1.95 multicolored 2.25 2.25
Nos. 464-468 (5) 6.25 6.25

For overprints see #524-528.

Overprinted "ROYAL VISIT"

1992, Oct. 16

469 A92 30c on #464 .35 .35
470 A92 50c on #465 .55 .55
471 A92 95c on #466 1.10 1.10
472 A92 $1.75 on #467 2.00 2.00
473 A92 $1.95 on #468 2.25 2.25
Nos. 469-473 (5) 6.25 6.25

Christmas A93

Designs: Different details from Virgin's Nativity, by Guido Reni.

1992, Nov. 19 Litho. *Perf. 13½*

474 A93 80c multicolored .90 .90
475 A93 90c multicolored 1.10 1.10
476 A93 $1.05 multicolored 1.25 1.25
477 A93 $1.75 multicolored 1.90 1.90
Nos. 474-477 (4) 5.15 5.15

Souvenir Sheet

478 A93 $6 like #476 6.50 6.50

No. 478 contains one 39x50mm stamp.

Discovery of America, 500th Anniv. — A94

Designs: $1.25, Columbus being blessed as he departs from Spain. $1.75, Map of Columbus' four voyages. $1.95, Columbus landing in New World.

1992, Dec. 11 *Perf. 14x15*

479 A94 $1.25 multicolored 1.40 1.40
480 A94 $1.75 multicolored 1.90 1.90
481 A94 $1.95 multicolored 2.25 2.25
Nos. 479-481 (3) 5.55 5.55

Coronation of Queen Elizabeth II, 40th Anniv. — A95

Designs: a, Victoria, Edward VII. b, George V, George VI. c, Elizabeth II.

1993, June 4 Litho. *Perf. 14*

482 A95 $1.75 Strip of 3, #a.-c. 6.00 6.00

Christmas — A96

Religious sculpture: 80c, Madonna and Child, by Nino Pisano. 90c, Virgin on Rosebush, by Luca Della Robbia. $1.15, Virgin with Child and St. John, by Juan Francisco Rustici. $1.95, Virgin with Child, by Michelangelo. $3, Madonna and Child, by Jacopo Della Quercia.

1993, Oct. 29 Litho. *Perf. 14*

483 A96 80c multicolored .90 .90
484 A96 90c multicolored 1.00 1.00
485 A96 $1.15 multicolored 1.25 1.25
486 A96 $1.95 multicolored 2.25 2.25

Size: 32x47mm

Perf. 13½

487 A96 $3 multicolored 3.50 3.50
Nos. 483-487 (5) 8.90 8.90

1994 Winter Olympics, Lillehammer — A97

Designs: a, Ice hockey. b, Ski jumping. c, Cross-country skiing.

1994, Feb. 11 Litho. *Perf. 14*

488 A97 $1.15 Strip of 3, #a.-c. 4.00 4.00

Flowers — A98

Hibiscus A98a

1994-97 Litho. *Perf. 13½*

489 A98 5c Prostrate morning glory .20 .20
490 A98 10c White frangipani .20 .20
491 A98 15c Red hibiscus .20 .20
492 A98 20c Yellow allamanda .20 .20
493 A98 25c Royal poinciana .25 .25
494 A98 30c White gardenia .35 .35
495 A98 50c Pink frangipani .55 .55
496 A98 80c Morning glory .90 .90
497 A98 85c Yellow mallow .95 .95
498 A98 90c Red coral tree 1.00 1.00
499 A98 $1 Cup of gold 1.10 1.10
500 A98 $2 Red cordia 2.25 2.25
501 A98a $3 multicolored 3.75 3.75
502 A98a $5 multicolored 6.25 6.25
503 A98a $8 multicolored 10.00 10.00
Nos. 489-503 (15) 28.15 28.15

Issued: 5c-90c, 2/17; $1, $2, 4/29; $3, $5, 11/18; $8, 11/21/97. This is an expanding set. Numbers may change.

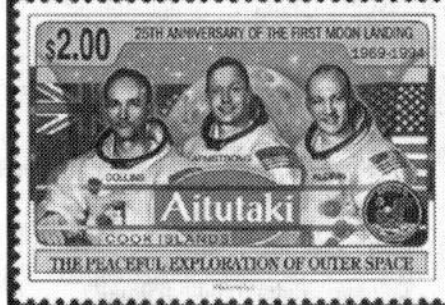

First Manned Moon Landing, 25th Anniv. A99

#506, Astronauts Collins, Armstrong, Aldrin. #507, Splash down in South Pacific.

1994, July 20 Litho. *Perf. 14*

506 A99 $2 multicolored 2.25 2.25
507 A99 $2 multicolored 2.25 2.25

Christmas — A100

Paintings: No. 508a, The Madonna of the Basket, by Corregio. b, Virgin & Child with Saints, by Hans Memling. c, The Virgin & Child with Flowers, by Dolci. d, Virgin & Child with Angels, by Bergognone.

No. 509a, The Adoration of the Kings, by Dosso. b, The Virgin & Child, by Bellini. c, The Virgin & Child, by Schiavone. d, Adoration of the Kings, by Dolci.

1994, Nov. 30 Litho. *Perf. 14*

508 A100 85c Block of 4, #a.-d. 3.75 3.75
509 A100 90c Block of 4, #a.-d. 4.00 4.00

End of World War II, 50th Anniv. — A101

Designs: a, Battle of Britain, 1940. b, Battle of Midway, June 1942.

1995, Sept. 4 Litho. *Perf. 13½x13*

510 A101 $4 Pair, #a.-b. 10.50 10.50

No. 510 issued in sheets of 4 stamps.

Queen Mother, 95th Birthday
A102

1995, Sept. 14 Litho. ***Perf. 13x13½***
511 A102 $4 multicolored 5.25 5.25

UN, 50th Anniv. — A103

1995, Oct. 18 Litho. ***Perf. 13½***
512 A103 $4.25 multicolored 5.50 5.50

Year of the Sea Turtle
A104

1995, Dec. 1 Litho. ***Perf. 14x13½***
513 A104 95c Green 1.25 1.25
514 A104 $1.15 Leatherback 1.50 1.50
515 A104 $1.50 Olive Ridley 2.00 2.00
516 A104 $1.75 Loggerhead 2.25 2.25
Nos. 513-516 (4) 7.00 7.00

Queen Elizabeth II, 70th Birthday
A105

1996, June 24 Litho. ***Perf. 14***
517 A105 $4.50 multicolored 6.00 6.00

No. 517 was issued in sheets of 4.

Modern Olympic Games, Cent.
A106

Designs: No. 518, Pierre de Coubertin, Olympic torch, parading athletes, 1896. No. 519, Modern sprinters, US flag, Atlanta, 1996.

1996, July 11 Litho. ***Perf. 14***
518 A106 $2 multicolored 2.75 2.75
519 A106 $2 multicolored 2.75 2.75
a. Pair, #518-519 5.50 5.50

Queen Elizabeth II and Prince Philip, 50th Wedding Anniv.
A107

$2.50, Queen Elizabeth II, Prince Philip, Queen Mother, and King George VI. $6, like #520, close-up.

1997, Nov. 20 Litho. ***Perf. 14***
520 A107 $2.50 multicolored 3.25 3.25

Souvenir Sheet

521 A107 $6 multicolored 7.75 7.75

No. 520 was issued in sheets of 4.

Diana, Princess of Wales (1961-97) — A108

1998, Apr. 15 Litho. ***Perf. 14***
522 A108 $1 multicolored 1.25 1.25

Souvenir Sheet

523 A108 $4 like #522 4.75 4.75

No. 522 was issued in sheets of 5 + label. No. 523 is a continuous design.
For surcharge see No. B55.

Nos. 464-468 Overprinted "KIA ORANA / THIRD MILLENNIUM"

1999, Dec. 31 Litho. ***Perf. 14x15***
524 A92 30c on #464 .30 .30
525 A92 50c on #465 .50 .50
526 A92 95c on #466 .95 .95
527 A92 $1.75 on #467 1.75 1.75
528 A92 $1.95 on #468 1.90 1.90
Nos. 524-528 (5) 5.40 5.40

Queen Mother, 100th Birthday — A109

No. 529: a, Wearing crown, blue-toned photograph. b, Wearing crown, color photograph. c, Wearing hat. d, With King George VI.
Illustration reduced.

2000, Oct. 20 Litho. ***Perf. 14***
529 A109 $3 Sheet of 4, #a-d 9.50 9.50

Souvenir Sheet

530 A109 $7.50 With flowers 6.00 6.00

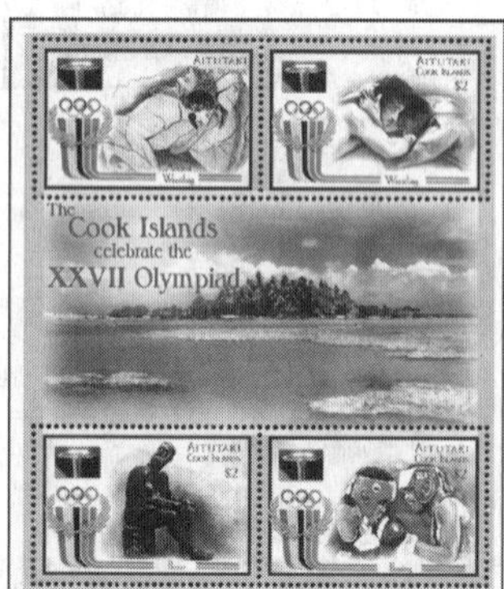

2000 Summer Olympics, Sydney — A110

No. 531: a, Ancient wrestling. b, Wrestling. c, Ancient boxer. d, Boxing.
Illustration reduced.

2000, Dec. 14 Litho. ***Perf. 14***
531 A110 $2 Sheet of 4, #a-d 7.25 7.25

Souvenir Sheet

532 A110 $2.75 Torch relay 2.50 2.50

Worldwide Fund for Nature (WWF)
A111

Various views of two blue lorikeets: 80c, 90c, $1.15, $1.95.

2002, Sept. 3 Litho. ***Perf. 14***
533-536 A111 Set of 4 4.75 4.75

SEMI-POSTAL STAMPS

Christmas Type of 1974

Designs: 1c+1c, like #104. 5c+1c, like #105. 8c+1c, like #106. 10c+1c, like #107. 25c+1c, like #108. 30c+1c, like #109.

1974, Dec. 2 Photo. ***Perf. 13½***
B1 A29 1c + 1c multicolored .20 .20
B2 A29 5c + 1c multicolored .20 .20
B3 A29 8c + 1c multicolored .20 .20
B4 A29 10c + 1c multicolored .20 .20
B5 A29 25c + 1c multicolored .30 .30
B6 A29 30c + 1c multicolored .30 .30
Nos. B1-B6 (6) 1.40 1.40

Surtax was for child welfare.

Nos. 117-120 Surcharged in Silver

1975, Dec. 19 Photo. ***Perf. 14x13½***
B7 A32 Strip of 3 .30 .30
a.-c. 6c+1c any single .20 .20
B8 A32 Strip of 3 .35 .35
a.-c. 7c+1c any single .20 .20
B9 A32 Strip of 3 .90 .90
a.-c. 15c+1c any single .30 .30
B10 A32 Strip of 3 1.25 1.25
a.-c. 20c+1c any single .40 .40
Nos. B7-B10 (4) 2.80 2.80

Christmas. The surtax was for children's activities during holiday season.

Nos. 135-142a Surcharged in Silver

1976, Nov. 19 Photo. ***Perf. 13½x13***
B11 A36 6c + 1c multicolored .20 .20
B12 A37 6c + 1c multicolored .20 .20
a. Pair, #B11-B12 .20 .20
B13 A36 7c + 1c multicolored .20 .20
B14 A37 7c + 1c multicolored .20 .20
a. Pair, #B13-B14 .25 .25
B15 A36 15c + 1c multicolored .20 .20
B16 A37 15c + 1c multicolored .20 .20
a. Pair, #B15-B16 .45 .45
B17 A36 20c + 1c multicolored .30 .30
B18 A37 20c + 1c multicolored .30 .30
a. Pair, #B17-B18 .60 .60
b. Souvenir sheet of 8 1.60 1.60

Surtax was for child welfare. Stamps of No. B18a each surcharged 2c.

Nos. 152-159a Surcharged in Black

1977, Nov. 15 ***Perf. 13½x14***
B19 A41 6c + 1c multicolored .20 .20
B20 A42 6c + 1c multicolored .20 .20
a. Pair, #B19-B20 .20 .20
B21 A41 7c + 1c multicolored .20 .20
B22 A42 7c + 1c multicolored .20 .20
a. Pair, #B21-B22 .25 .25
B23 A41 15c + 1c multicolored .20 .20
B24 A42 15c + 1c multicolored .20 .20
a. Pair, #B23-B24 .45 .45
B25 A41 20c + 1c multicolored .30 .30
B26 A42 20c + 1c multicolored .30 .30
a. Pair, #B25-B26 .60 .60
b. Souvenir sheet of 8 1.60 1.60
Nos. B19-B26 (8) 1.80 1.80

Surtax was for child welfare. Stamps of No. B26a each surcharged 2c.

Easter Type of 1978
Souvenir Sheets

Paintings: No. B27, like No. 163. No. B28, like No. 164. No. B29, like No. 165.

1978, Mar. 17 Photo. ***Perf. 14***
B27 A44 50c + 5c multicolored .70 .70
B28 A44 50c + 5c multicolored .70 .70
B29 A44 50c + 5c multicolored .70 .70

Nos. B27-B29 contain one stamp 33x25mm.

Christmas Type of 1978
Souvenir Sheet

1978, Dec. 4 Photo. ***Perf. 14½x13***
B30 Sheet of 4 2.25 2.25
a. A46 15c + 2c like #167 .30 .30
b. A46 17c + 2c like #168 .35 .35
c. A46 30c + 2c like #169 .55 .55
d. A46 35c + 2c like #170 .60 .60

Year of the Child Type
Souvenir Sheet

1979, Oct. 1 Photo. ***Perf. 14x13½***
B31 Sheet of 3 1.40 1.40
a. A48 30c + 3c like #173 .30 .30
b. A48 35c + 3c like #174 .35 .35
c. A48 65c + 3c like #175 .60 .60

Easter Type of 1980
Souvenir Sheet

#B32 shows entire painting in continuous design. #B32a-B32c similar to #183-185. Size of #B32a-B32c: 25x50mm.

1980, Apr. 3 Photo. ***Perf. 13x13½***
B32 Sheet of 3 1.40 1.40
a. A50 20c + 2c multicolored .35 .35
b. A50 30c + 2c multicolored .45 .45
c. A50 35c + 2c multicolored .55 .55

Christmas Type of 1980
Souvenir Sheet

1980, Nov. 21 Photo. ***Perf. 13x13½***
B33 Sheet of 4 1.40 1.40
a. A53 15c + 2c like #208 .20 .20
b. A53 20c + 2c like #209 .30 .30
c. A53 25c + 2c like #210 .35 .35
d. A53 35c + 2c like #211 .45 .45

Easter Type of 1981
Souvenir Sheet

1981, Mar. 31 Photo. ***Perf. 13½***
B34 Sheet of 3 1.65 1.65
a. A54 30c + 2c like #212 .35 .35
b. A54 40c + 2c like #213 .50 .50
c. A54 50c + 2c like #214 .65 .65

Nos. 247-249 Surcharged

1981, Nov. 23 Photo. ***Perf. 13x13½***
B35 A56 60 + 5c multi .70 .70
B36 A56 80 + 5c multi .80 .80
B37 A56 $1.40 + 5c multi 1.00 1.00
Nos. B35-B37 (3) 2.50 2.50

Intl. Year of the Disabled. Surtax was for the handicapped.

Soccer Type of 1981
Souvenir Sheet

1981, Nov. 30 ***Perf. 14***
B38 A57 Sheet of 8, multi 4.50 4.50

No. B38 contains stamps with 2c surtax similar to Nos. 250-253. Surtax was for local sports.

Nos. 400-404 Surcharged "NOVEMBER/21-24 1986/FIRST VISIT TO SOUTH/PACIFIC" and 10c in Silver

1986, Nov. 25 Litho. ***Perf. 13½***
B39 A79 75c + 10c multi 2.75 2.75
B40 A79 $1.35 + 10c multi 3.25 3.25
B41 A79 $1.95 + 10c multi 4.00 4.00
B42 A79 $2.75 + 10c multi 5.00 5.00
Nos. B39-B42 (4) 15.00 15.00

Souvenir Sheet

B43 Sheet of 4 15.00 15.00
a.-d. A79 $1.65 +10c on #404a-404d 3.75 3.75

State visit of Pope John Paul II.
For surcharges see Nos. B51-B54.

Nos. 394-395, 397 and 400-403 Surcharged "HURRICANE RELIEF/ + 50c" in Silver or Black

1987, Apr. 29 Litho. ***Perf. 13½, 14***
B44 A79 75c + 50c #400 2.00 2.00
B45 A77 $1 + 50c #394 (B) 2.50 2.50
B46 A79 $1.35 + 50c #401 3.00 3.00
B47 A79 $1.95 + 50c #402 3.25 3.25
B48 A78 $2 + 50c #397 3.25 3.25
B49 A77 $2.75 + 50c #395 (B) 4.25 4.25
B50 A79 $2.75 + 50c #403 4.25 4.25
Nos. B44-B50 (7) 22.50 22.50

Nos. B39-B42 Surcharged "HURRICANE RELIEF / +50c" in Silver

1987, Apr. 29 Litho. ***Perf. 13½***
B51 A79 75c + 50c No. B39 2.00 2.00
B52 A79 $1.35 + 50c No. B40 2.50 2.50
B53 A79 $1.95 + 50c No. B41 3.00 3.00
B54 A79 $2.75 + 50c No. B42 3.50 3.50
Nos. B51-B54 (4) 11.00 11.00

Souvenir Sheet
No. 523 Surcharged
"CHILDREN'S/CHARITIES" in Silver

1998, Nov. 19 Litho. *Perf. 14*

B55 A108 $4 + $1 multicolored 5.00 5.00

AIR POST STAMPS

Capt. Bligh Type of 1974

1974, Sept. 9 Litho. *Perf. 13*

Size: 46x26mm

C1 A27 10c Bligh and "Bounty" .75 .75
C2 A27 10c "Bounty" at sea .75 .75
a. Pair, #C1-C2 1.50 1.50
C3 A27 25c Bligh and "Bounty" .90 .90
C4 A27 25c Chart, 1856 .90 .90
a. Pair, #C3-C4 1.80 1.80
C5 A27 30c Cook and "Resolution" 1.10 1.10
C6 A27 30c Maps 1.10 1.10
a. Pair, #C5-C6 2.20 2.20
Nos. C1-C6 (6) 5.50 5.50

See note after No. 101.

OFFICIAL STAMPS

Nos. 83-90, 92-95, 150-151
Overprinted or Surcharged in Black, Silver or Gold

1978-79 Photo. *Perf. 13x13½*

O1 A25 1c multi .45 .25
O2 A25 2c multi .50 .25
O3 A25 3c multi .50 .25
O4 A25 4c multi (G) .50 .25
O5 A25 5c multi .50 .25
O6 A25 8c multi .65 .25
O7 A25 10c multi .85 .40
O8 A25 15c on 60c multi 1.25 .50
O9 A25 18c on 60c multi 1.25 .50
O10 A25 20c multi (G) 1.25 .50
O11 A40 50c multi .80 .80
O12 A25 60c multi 5.00 1.75
O13 A25 $1 multi 5.00 1.75
O14 A26 $2 multi 4.75 1.90
O15 A40 $4 on $1 multi (S) 2.00 1.90
O16 A26 $5 multi 5.75 3.00
Nos. O1-O16 (16) 31.00 14.50

Overprint on 4c, 20c, $1 diagonal.
Issued: #O14-O16, 2/20/79; others, 11/3/78.

Stamps of 1983-84 Ovptd. or Surcharged in Green

or Gold (#O29-O32)

1985, Aug. 9 *Perf. 14, 13x13½*

O17 A66 2c No. 322 .20 .20
O18 A66 5c No. 324 .20 .20
O19 A66 10c No. 325 .20 .20
O20 A66 12c No. 326 .20 .20
O21 A66 18c No. 327 .20 .20
O22 A66 20c on 24c No. 328 .20 .20
O23 A66 30c No. 329 .35 .35
O24 A66 40c on 36c No. 330 .45 .45
O25 A66 50c No. 332 .55 .55
O26 A66 55c on 48c No. 331 .65 .65
O27 A66 60c No. 333 .70 .70
O28 A66 65c on 72c No. 334 .75 .75
O29 A61 75c on 48c No. 276 .85 .85
O30 A61 75c on 48c No. 277 .85 .85
O31 A61 75c on 48c No. 278 .85 .85
O32 A61 75c on 48c No. 279 .85 .85
a. Block of 4, Nos. O29-O32 3.50 3.50
O33 A66 80c on 96c No. 335 .90 .90
Nos. O17-O33 (17) 8.95 8.95

Nos. 336-341, 246C-246D Overprinted or Surcharged Like Nos. O17-O28, O33 in Metallic Green or Blue

1986, Oct. 1 *Perf. 14*

O34 A66 $3 multi 3.00 3.00
O35 A66 $4.20 multi 4.25 4.25
O36 A66 $5.60 multi 5.75 5.75
O37 A66 $9.60 multi 10.00 10.00

1988-91 *Perf. 14*

O38 A66 $1.20 multi 1.50 1.50
O39 A66 $2.10 multi 2.50 2.50

Perf. 13½

O40 A55 $14 on $4 (B) 17.50 17.50
O41 A55 $18 on $5 (B) 22.50 22.50
Nos. O34-O41 (8) 67.00 67.00

Issue dates: July 2, 1991; others, June 15.

AJMAN

äj-'man

LOCATION — Oman Peninsula, Arabia, on Persian Gulf
GOVT. — Sheikdom under British Protection
AREA — 100 sq. mi.
POP. — 4,400
CAPITAL — Ajman

Ajman is one of six Persian Gulf sheikdoms to join the United Arab Emirates, which proclaimed its independence Dec. 2, 1971. See United Arab Emirates.

100 Naye Paise = 1 Rupee

Catalogue values for all unused stamps in this country are for Never Hinged items.

Sheik Rashid bin Humaid al Naimi & Arab Stallion
A1

Designs: 2np, 50np, Regal angelfish. 3np, 70np, Camel. 4np, 1r, Angelfish. 5np, 1.50r, Green turtle. 10np, 2r, Jewelfish. 15np, 3r, White storks. 20np, 5r, White-eyed gulls. 30np, 10r, Lanner falcon. 40np as 1np.

Photo. & Litho.

1964 Unwmk. *Perf. 14*

Size: 35x22mm

1 A1 1np gold & multi .20 .20
2 A1 2np gold & multi .20 .20
3 A1 3np gold & multi .20 .20
4 A1 4np gold & multi .20 .20
5 A1 5np gold & multi .20 .20
6 A1 10np gold & multi .20 .20
7 A1 15np gold & multi .20 .20
8 A1 20np gold & multi .20 .20
9 A1 30np gold & multi .20 .20

Size: 42x27mm

10 A1 40np gold & multi .20 .20
11 A1 50np gold & multi .25 .20
12 A1 70np gold & multi .25 .20
13 A1 1r gold & multi .40 .25
14 A1 1.50r gold & multi .50 .35
15 A1 2r gold & multi .85 .50

Size: 53x33½mm

16 A1 3r gold & multi 1.00 .75
17 A1 5r gold & multi 1.50 1.00
18 A1 10r gold & multi 3.25 2.50
Nos. 1-18 (18) 10.00 7.75

Issued: #1-9, 6/20; #10-15, 9/7; #16-18, 11/4.

Pres. and Mrs. John F. Kennedy with Caroline — A2

Pres. Kennedy: 10np, As a boy in football uniform. 15np, Diving. 50np, As navy lieutenant, receiving Navy and Marine Corps Medal from Capt. Frederic L. Conklin. 1r, Sailing with Jacqueline Kennedy. 2r, With Eleanor Roosevelt. 5r, With Lyndon B. Johnson and Hubert H. Humphrey. 10r, Portrait.

1964, Dec. 15 Photo. *Perf. 13½x14*

19 A2 10np grn & red lil .20 .20
20 A2 15np Prus bl & vio .20 .20
21 A2 50np org brn & dk bl .20 .20
22 A2 1r brn & Prus grn .30 .20
23 A2 2r red lil & dp ol .60 .20
24 A2 3r grn & red brn 1.00 .50
25 A2 5r vio & brn 1.50 1.50
26 A2 10r dk bl & red brn 4.00 2.25
Nos. 19-26 (8) 8.00 5.25

John F. Kennedy (1917-63). A souvenir sheet contains one each of Nos. 23-26.

Runners at Start — A3

10np, 1.50r, Boxing. 25np, 2r, Judo. 50np, 5r, Gymnast on vaulting horse. 1r, 3r, Sailing yacht.

1965, Jan. 12 Photo. *Perf. 13½x14*

27 A3 5np red brn, brt pink & Prus grn .20 .20
28 A3 10np dk ol grn, bl gray & red brn .20 .20
29 A3 15np dk vio, grn & sep .20 .20
30 A3 25np bl sal pink & blk .20 .20
31 A3 50np mar, bl & ind .20 .20
32 A3 1r dk grn, lil & ultra .40 .25
33 A3 1.50r lil, grn & brn .60 .40
34 A3 2r red org, bis & dk bl 1.00 .70
35 A3 3r dk brn, grnsh bl & lil 1.50 .95
36 A3 5r grn, yel & red brn 2.00 1.60
Nos. 27-36 (10) 6.50 4.90

18th Olympic Games, Tokyo, Oct. 10-25, 1964. A souvenir sheet contains four stamps similar to Nos. 33-36 in changed colors.

Stanley Gibbons Catalogue, 1865, U.S. No. 1X2 — A4

Designs: 10np, Austria, Scarlet Mercury 1856. 15np, British Guiana 1c, 1856. 25np, Canada 12p, 1851. 50np, Hawaii 2c, 1851. 1r, Mauritius 2p, 1847. 3r, Switzerland, Geneva 10c, 1843. 5r, Tuscany 31, 1860. 5np, 15np, 50np and 3r show first edition of Stanley Gibbons Catalogue; 10np, 25np, 1r and 5r show 1965 Elizabethan Catalogue.

1965, May 6 Unwmk. *Perf. 13*

37 A4 5np multi .20 .20
38 A4 10np multi .20 .20
39 A4 15np multi .20 .20
40 A4 25np multi .20 .20
41 A4 50np multi .20 .20
42 A4 1r multi .45 .20
43 A4 3r multi .75 .20
a. Souv. sheet of 4, #38-39, 42-43 2.50
44 A4 5r multi 1.25 .30
a. Souv. sheet of 4, #37, 40-41, 44 2.50
Nos. 37-44 (8) 3.45 1.70

Gibbons Catalogue Cent. Exhib., London, Feb. 17-20.Nos. 43a and 44a for 125th anniv. of 1st postage stamp. Sheets exist imperf.

Stamps of Ajman were replaced in 1972 by those of United Arab Emirates.

AIR POST STAMPS

Type of Regular Issue, 1964

Designs: 15np, Arab stallion. 25np, Regal angelfish. 35np, Camel. 50np, Angelfish. 75np, Green turtle. 1r, Jewelfish. 2r, White storks. 3r, White-eyed gulls. 5r, Lanner falcon.

Photo. & Litho.

1965 Unwmk. *Perf. 14*

Size: 42x25½mm

C1 A1 15np silver & multi .20 .20
C2 A1 25np silver & multi .20 .20
C3 A1 35np silver & multi .25 .20
C4 Al 50np silver & multi .30 .20
C5 A1 75np silver & multi .55 .20
C6 A1 1r silver & multi .40 .20

Size: 53x33½mm

C7 A1 2r silver & multi .75 .20
C8 A1 3r silver & multi 2.00 .20
C9 A1 5r silver & multi 3.25 .30
Nos. C1-C9 (9) 7.90 1.90

Issued: #C1-C6, Nov. 15; C7-C9, Dec 18.

AIR POST OFFICIAL STAMPS

Type of Regular Issue, 1964

Designs: 75np, Jewelfish. 2r, White storks. 3r, White-eyed gulls. 5r, Lanner falcon.

Photo. & Litho.

1965, Dec. 18 Unwmk. *Perf. 14*

Size: 42x25½mm

CO1 A1 75np gold & multi .35 .20

Size: 53x33½mm

CO2 A1 2r gold & multi 1.00 .20
CO3 A1 3r gold & multi 1.50 .20
CO4 A1 5r gold & multi 3.00 .35
Nos. CO1-CO4 (4) 5.85 .95

OFFICIAL STAMPS

Type of Regular Issue, 1964

25np, Arab stallion. 40np, Regal angelfish. 50np, Camel. 75np, Angelfish. 1r, Green turtle.

Photo. & Litho.

1965, Dec. 1 Unwmk. *Perf. 14*

Size: 42x25½mm

O1 A1 25np gold & multi .20 .20
O2 A1 40np gold & multi .20 .20
O3 A1 50np gold & multi .25 .20
O4 A1 75np gold & multi .30 .20
O5 A1 1r gold & multi .55 .20
Nos. O1-O5 (5) 1.50 1.00

ALAOUITES

'al-au-ˌwītz

LOCATION — A division of Syria, in Western Asia
GOVT. — Under French Mandate
AREA — 2,500 sq. mi.
POP. — 278,000 (approx. 1930)
CAPITAL — Latakia

This territory became an independent state in 1924, although still administered under the French Mandate. In 1930 it was renamed Latakia and Syrian stamps overprinted "Lattaquie" superseded the stamps of Alaouites. For these and subsequent issues see Latakia and Syria.

100 Centimes = 1 Piaster

Issued under French Mandate

Stamps of France Surcharged:

Nos. 1-6, 16-18

Nos. 7-15, 19-21

1925 Unwmk. *Perf. 14x13½*

No.	Type	Description	Unused	Used
1	A16	10c on 2c vio brn	1.00	1.00
2	A22	25c on 5c orange	.90	.90
3	A20	75c on 15c gray grn	2.25	2.25
4	A22	1p on 20c red brn	1.00	1.00
5	A22	1.25p on 25c blue	1.50	1.50
6	A22	1.50p on 30c red	5.00	5.00
7	A22	2p on 35c violet	1.60	1.60
8	A18	2p on 40c red & pale bl	2.25	2.25
9	A18	2p on 45c grn & bl	5.00	5.00
10	A18	3p on 60c vio & ultra	3.00	3.00
11	A20	3p on 60c lt vio	5.00	5.00
b.		Double surcharge	67.50	67.50
12	A20	4p on 85c vermilion	1.00	1.00
13	A18	5p on 1fr cl & ol grn	3.00	3.00
14	A18	10p on 2fr org & pale bl	4.50	4.50
15	A18	25p on 5fr bl & buff	5.50	5.50
		Nos. 1-15 (15)	42.50	42.50

For overprints see Nos. C1-C4.

Same Surcharges on Pasteur Stamps of France

No.	Type	Description	Unused	Used
16	A23	50c on 10c green	.95	.95
17	A23	75c on 15c green	.95	.95
18	A23	1.50p on 30c red	1.10	1.10
19	A23	2p on 45c red	1.50	1.50
20	A23	2.50p on 50c blue	1.75	1.75
21	A23	4p on 75c blue	2.25	2.25
		Nos. 16-21 (6)	8.50	8.50

Inverted Surcharges

No.	Type	Description	Unused
1a	A16	10c on 2c vio brn	10.00
2a	A22	25c on 5c orange	10.00
3a	A20	75c on 15c gray grn	10.00
4a	A22	1p on 20c red brn	10.00
5a	A22	1.25p on 25c blue	10.00
6a	A22	1.50p on 30c red	15.00
7a	A22	2p on 35c violet	15.00
8a	A18	2p on 40c red & pale bl	15.00
9a	A18	2p on 45c grn & bl	15.00
10a	A18	3p on 60c vio & ultra	10.00
11a	A20	3p on 60c lt vio	10.00
12a	A20	4p on 85c vermilion	10.00
13a	A18	5p on 1fr cl & ol grn	10.00
14a	A18	10p on 2fr org & pale bl	10.00
15a	A18	25p on 5fr bl & buff	10.00
16a	A23	50c on 10c green	9.50
17a	A23	75c on 15c green	9.50
18a	A23	1.50p on 30c red	9.50
19a	A23	2p on 45c red	9.50
20a	A23	2.50p on 50c blue	9.50
21a	A23	4p on 75c blue	9.50

Stamps of Syria, 1925, Overprinted in Red, Black or Blue:

On A3, A5

On A4

1925, Mar. 1 *Perf. 12½, 13½*

No.	Type	Description	Unused	Used
25	A3	10c dk violet (R)	.35	.35
a.		Double overprint	14.00	14.00
b.		Inverted overprint	11.00	
c.		Black overprint	12.00	12.00
26	A4	25c olive black (R)	.50	.50
a.		Inverted overprint	11.00	
b.		Blue overprint	15.00	15.00
27	A4	50c yellow green	.45	.45
a.		Inverted overprint	11.00	
b.		Blue overprint	15.00	15.00
c.		Red overprint	15.00	15.00
28	A4	75c brown orange	.45	.45
a.		Inverted overprint	11.00	
b.		Double overprint		*20.00*
29	A5	1p magenta	.65	.65
a.		Inverted overprint	11.00	
30	A4	1.25p deep green	.50	.50
a.		Red overprint	15.00	15.00
31	A4	1.50p rose red (Bl)	.50	.50
a.		Inverted overprint	11.00	
b.		Black overprint	17.50	17.50
32	A4	2p dk brown (R)	.45	.45
a.		Blue overprint	22.50	22.50
b.		Inverted overprint	11.00	
33	A4	2.50p pck blue (R)	.80	.80
a.		Black overprint	22.50	22.50
34	A4	3p orange brown	.45	.45
a.		Inverted overprint	11.00	
b.		Blue overprint	22.50	22.50
35	A4	5p violet	.60	.60
a.		Red overprint	22.50	22.50
36	A4	10p violet brown	1.00	1.00
37	A4	25p ultra (R)	2.00	2.00
		Nos. 25-37 (13)	8.70	8.70

For overprints see Nos. C5-C19.

Stamps of Syria, 1925, Surcharged in Black or Red:

Nos. 38-42

Nos. 43-45

1926

No.	Type	Description	Unused	Used
38	A4	3.50p on 75c brn org	.75	.60
a.		Surcharged on face and back	5.00	4.50
39	A4	4p on 25c ol blk (R)	1.00	.60
40	A4	6p on 2.50p pck bl (R)	.80	.60
41	A4	12p on 1.25p dp grn	.70	.60
a.		Inverted surcharge	10.00	10.00
42	A4	20p on 1.25p dp grn	1.25	1.10
43	A4	4.50p on 75c brn org	2.50	1.25
a.		Inverted surcharge	25.00	
44	A4	7.50p on 2.50p pck bl	2.00	1.25
45	A4	15p on 25p ultra	3.50	2.00
		Nos. 38-45 (8)	12.50	8.00

For overprint see No. C21.

Syria #199 Ovptd. like #25 in Red

1928

No.	Type	Description	Unused	Used
46	A3	5c on 10c dk violet	.30	.30
a.		Double surcharge	13.00	

Syria Nos. 178 and 174 Surcharged like Nos. 43-45 in Red

No.	Type	Description	Unused	Used
47	A4	2p on 1.25p dp green	6.00	3.50
48	A4	4p on 25c olive black	3.25	2.50

For overprint see No. C20.

No.	Type	Description	Unused	Used
49	A4	4p on 25c olive black	35.00	30.00
a.		Double impression		
		Nos. 46-49 (4)	44.55	36.30

AIR POST STAMPS

Nos. 8, 10, 13 & 14 with Additional Overprint in Black

1925, Jan. 1 Unwmk. *Perf. 14x13½*

No.	Type	Description	Unused	Used
C1	A18	2p on 40c	3.50	3.50
a.		Overprint reversed	60.00	
C2	A18	3p on 60c	5.25	5.25
a.		Overprint reversed	60.00	60.00
C3	A18	5p on 1fr	3.50	3.50
C4	A18	10p on 2fr	3.50	3.50
		Nos. C1-C4 (4)	15.75	15.75

Nos. 32, 34, 35 & 36 With Additional Overprint in Green

1925, Mar. 1 *Perf. 13½*

No.	Type	Description	Unused	Used
C5	A4	2p dark brown	1.00	1.00
C6	A4	3p orange brown	1.00	1.00
C7	A4	5p violet	1.00	1.00
C8	A4	10p violet brown	1.00	1.00
		Nos. C5-C8 (4)	4.00	4.00

Nos. 32, 34, 35 & 36 With Additional Overprint in Red

1926, May 1

No.	Type	Description	Unused	Used
C9	A4	2p dark brown	1.75	1.90
C10	A4	3p orange brown	1.75	1.90
C11	A4	5p violet	1.75	1.90
C12	A4	10p violet brown	1.75	1.90
		Nos. C9-C12 (4)	7.00	7.60

No. C9 has the original overprint in black.

Double or inverted overprints, original or plane, are known on most of Nos. C9-C12. Value, $8-$10.

The red plane overprint was also applied to Nos. C5-C8. These are believed to have been essays, and were not regularly issued.

Nos. 27, 37 and Syria No. 177 with Type A4 overprint, With Additional Overprint of Airplane in Red or Black

1929, June-July

No.	Type	Description	Unused	Used
C17	A4	50c yel grn (R)	.75	.75
a.		Plane overprint double	15.00	
b.		Plane ovpt. on face and back	11.00	
c.		Pair with plane overprint tete beche	35.00	
C18	A5	1p magenta (Bk)	2.75	2.75
C19	A4	25p ultra (R)	15.00	10.00
a.		Plane overprint inverted	60.00	60.00
		Nos. C17-C19 (3)	18.50	13.50

Nos. 47 and 45 With Additional Overprint of Airplane in Red

1929-30

No.	Type	Description	Unused	Used
C20	A4	2p on 1.25p ('30)	1.25	1.40
a.		Surcharge inverted	4.00	
b.		Double surcharge	3.50	
C21	A4	15p on 25p (Bk + R)	19.00	14.00
a.		Plane overprint inverted	35.00	35.00

POSTAGE DUE STAMPS

Postage Due Stamps of France, 1893-1920, Surcharged Like No. 1 (Nos. J1-J2) or No. 7 (Nos. J3-J5)

1925 Unwmk. *Perf. 14x13½*

No.	Type	Description	Unused	Used
J1	D2	50c on 10c choc	1.90	1.90
J2	D2	1p on 20c ol grn	1.90	1.90
J3	D2	2p on 30c red	1.90	1.90
J4	D2	3p on 50c vio brn	1.90	1.90
J5	D2	5p on 1fr red brn, *straw*	1.90	1.90
		Nos. J1-J5 (5)	9.50	9.50

Postage Due Stamps of Syria, 1925, Overprinted Like No. 26 (Type D5) or No. 25 (Type D6) in Black, Blue or Red

1925 *Perf. 13½*

No.	Type	Description	Unused	Used
J6	D5	50c brown, *yel*	.60	.60
J7	D6	1p vio, *rose* (Bl)	.60	.60
a.		Black overprint	9.00	9.00
b.		Double overprint (Bk + Bl)	14.00	14.00
J8	D5	2p blk, *blue* (R)	1.00	1.00
J9	D5	3p blk, *red org*	1.40	1.40
J10	D5	5p blk, *bl grn* (R)	2.40	2.40
		Nos. J6-J10 (5)	6.00	6.00

The stamps of Alaouites were superseded in 1930 by those of Latakia.

ALBANIA

al-'bā-nē-ə

LOCATION — Southeastern Europe
GOVT. — Republic
AREA — 11,101 sq. mi.
POP. — 3,364,571 (1999 est.)
CAPITAL — Tirana

After the outbreak of World War I, the country fell into a state of anarchy when the Prince and all members of the International Commission left Albania. Subsequently General Ferrero in command of Italian troops declared Albania an independent country. A constitution was adopted and a republican form of government was instituted which continued until 1928 when, by constitutional amendment, Albania was declared to be a monarchy. The President of the republic, Ahmed Zogu, became king of the new state. Many unlisted varieties or surcharges and lithographed labels are said to have done postal duty in Albania and Epirus during this unsettled period.

In March 1939, Italy invaded Albania. King Zog fled but did not abdicate. The King of Italy acquired the crown.

Germany occupied Albania from September, 1943, until late 1944 when it became an independent state. The People's Republic began in January, 1946.

40 Paras = 1 Piaster = 1 Grossion
100 Centimes = 1 Franc (1917)
100 Qintar = 1 Franc
100 Qintar (Qindarka) = 1 Lek (1947)

Catalogue values for unused stamps in this country are for Never Hinged items, beginning with Scott 458 in the regular postage section, Scott B34 in the semi-postal section, and Scott C67 in the airpost section.

Watermarks

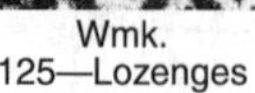
Wmk. 125—Lozenges

Wmk. 220—Double Headed Eagle

Stamps of Turkey Handstamped

Handstamped on Issue of 1908

Perf. 12, 13½ and Compound

1913, June Unwmk.

No.	Type	Description	Unused	Used
1	A19	2½pi violet brown	450.00	300.00

With Additional Overprint in Carmine

2 A19 10pa blue green 425.00 350.00

The eagle handstamp was applied to other Turkish stamps of 1908: 25pi green and 50 pi red brown. The 5pa ocher, Albania No. 4, was surcharged "2 paras." These three stamps were retained by officials. Values, $2,500, $5,750, $450.

Handstamped on Issue of 1909

4 A21 5pa ocher 250.00 240.00
5 A21 10pa blue green 200.00 110.00
6 A21 20pa car rose 175.00 110.00
7 A21 1pi ultra 150.00 110.00
8 A21 2pi blue black 190.00 175.00
10 A21 5pi dark violet 675.00 500.00
11 A21 10pi dull red 2,250. 2,000.

For surcharge see No. 19.

With Additional Overprint in Blue or Carmine

14 A21 20pa car rose (Bl) 450.00 *450.00*
15 A21 1pi brt blue (C) 900.00 800.00

Handstamped on Newspaper Stamp of 1911

17 A21 2pa olive green 250.00 240.00

Handstamped on Postage Due Stamp of 1908

18 A19 1pi black, *dp rose* 1,600. 1,250.

No. 18 was used for regular postage.

No. 6 Surcharged With New Value

19 A21 10pa on 20pa car rose 650.00 550.00

The overprint on #1-19 was handstamped and is found inverted, double, etc.
Nos. 6, 7 and 8 exist with the handstamp in red, blue or violet, but these varieties are not known to have been regularly issued.
Excellent counterfeits exist of Nos. 1 to 19.

A1

1913, July *Imperf.*

Handstamped on White Laid Paper Without Eagle and Value

20 A1 (1pi) black 210.00 *210.00*
Cut to shape 110.00 *110.00*
a. Sewing machine perf. 275.00 *275.00*

Counterfeits exist.

1913, Aug.

Value Typewritten in Violet With Eagle

21 A1 10pa violet 6.25 5.00
22 A1 20pa red & black 8.00 6.75
23 A1 1gr black 8.00 8.00
24 A1 2gr blue & violet 12.50 10.00
25 A1 5gr violet & blue 15.00 14.00
26 A1 10gr blue 21.00 20.00
Nos. 21-26 (6) 70.75 63.75

Nos. 21-26 exist with the eagle inverted or omitted and with numerous errors in the figures of value and the spelling of the word "grosh."

A2

Skanderbeg (George Castriota) — A3

1913, Nov. *Perf. 11½*

Handstamped on White Laid Paper Eagle and Value in Black

27 A2 10pa green 2.50 2.00
b. Eagle and value in green 650.00 650.00
c. 10pa red (error) 20.00 20.00
d. 10pa violet (error) 20.00 20.00
29 A2 20pa red 4.00 3.50
b. 20pa green (error) 20.00 20.00
30 A2 30pa violet 4.00 3.50
a. 30pa ultramarine (error) 20.00 20.00
b. 30pa red (error) 20.00 20.00
31 A2 1gr ultramarine 4.75 5.00
a. 1gr green (error) 20.00 20.00
b. 1gr black (error) 20.00 20.00
c. 1gr violet (error) 20.00 20.00
33 A2 2gr black 7.50 7.00
a. 2gr violet (error) 25.00 25.00
b. 2gr blue (error) 25.00 25.00
Nos. 27-33 (5) 22.75 21.00

The stamps of this issue are known with eagle or value inverted or omitted.
1st anniv. of Albanian independence.
Counterfeits exist.

1913, Dec. **Typo.** *Perf. 14*

35 A3 2q orange brn & buff 1.60 .80
36 A3 5q green & blue grn 1.60 .80
37 A3 10q rose red 1.60 .80
38 A3 25q dark blue 1.60 .80
39 A3 50q violet & red 4.25 2.00
40 A3 1fr deep brown 9.00 *4.50*
Nos. 35-40 (6) 19.65 *9.70*

For overprints and surcharges see Nos. 41-52, 105, J1-J9.

Nos. 35-40 Handstamped in Black or Violet

1914, Mar. 7

41 A3 2q orange brn & buff 22.50 *17.50*
42 A3 5q grn & bl grn (V) 22.50 *17.50*
43 A3 10q rose red 22.50 *17.50*
44 A3 25q dark blue (V) 22.50 *17.50*
45 A3 50q violet & red 22.50 *17.50*
46 A3 1fr deep brown 22.50 *17.50*
Nos. 41-46 (6) 135.00 *105.00*

Issued to celebrate the arrival of Prince Wilhelm zu Wied on Mar. 7, 1914.

Nos. 35-40 Surcharged in Black:

a

b

1914, Apr. 2

47 A3 (a) 5pa on 2q 1.10 1.10
48 A3 (a) 10pa on 5q 1.10 1.10
49 A3 (a) 20pa on 10q 1.75 1.50
50 A3 (b) 1gr on 25q 1.75 1.50
51 A3 (b) 2gr on 50q 1.75 1.50
52 A3 (b) 5gr on 1fr 10.00 8.50
Nos. 47-52 (6) 17.45 15.20

For overprints see Nos. 105, J6-J9.

Inverted Surcharge

47a A3 (a) 5pa on 2q 7.50 7.50
48a A3 (a) 10pa on 5q 7.00 7.00
49a A3 (a) 20pa on 10q 8.00 8.00
50a A3 (b) 1gr on 25q 8.00 8.00
51a A3 (b) 2gr on 50q 9.00 9.00
52b A3 (b) 5gr on 1fr 32.50 32.50
Nos. 47a-52b (6) 72.00 72.00

Korce (Korytsa) Issues

A4

1914 **Handstamped** *Imperf.*

52A A4 10pa violet & red 90.00 90.00
c. 10pa black & red 90.00 90.00
53 A4 25pa violet & red 90.00 90.00
a. 25pa black & red 150.00 150.00

Nos. 52A-53a originally were handstamped directly on the cover, so the paper varies. Later they were also produced in sheets; these are rarely found. Nos. 52A-53a were issued by Albanian military authorities.
Counterfeits exist of Nos. 52A and 53.

A5

A6

1917 **Typo. & Litho.** *Perf. 11½*

54 A5 1c dk brown & grn 12.00 10.00
55 A5 2c red & green 12.00 10.00
56 A5 3c gray grn & grn 12.00 10.00
57 A5 5c green & black 7.00 4.25
58 A5 10c rose red & black 7.00 4.25
59 A5 25c blue & black 7.00 4.25
60 A5 50c violet & black 12.00 9.00
61 A5 1fr brown & black 14.00 9.00
Nos. 54-61 (8) 83.00 60.75

1917-18

62 A6 1c dk brown & grn 2.75 2.50
63 A6 2c red brown & grn 2.75 2.50
a. "CTM" for "CTS" 30.00 25.00
64 A6 3c black & green 2.75 2.50
a. "CTM" for "CTS" 35.00 30.00
65 A6 5c green & black 4.25 4.25
66 A6 10c dull red & black 4.25 4.25
67 A6 50c violet & black 11.50 9.00
68 A6 1fr red brn & black 15.00 12.00
Nos. 62-68 (7) 43.25 37.00

Counterfeits abound of Nos. 54-68, 80-81.

No. 65 Surcharged in Red

QARKU
I
KORÇËS
25 CTS

1918

80 A6 25c on 5c green & blk 55.00 45.00

A7

1918

81 A7 25c blue & black 35.00 30.00

General Issue

A8

A9

Handstamped in Rose or Blue

XV I MCMXIX

1919 *Perf. 12½*

84 A8 (2)q on 2h brown 15.00 15.00
85 A8 5q on 16h green 15.00 15.00
86 A8 10q on 8h rose (Bl) 15.00 15.00
87 A8 25q on 64h blue 15.00 15.00
88 A9 25q on 64h blue 275.00 *275.00*
89 A8 50q on 32h violet 15.00 15.00
90 A8 1fr on 1.28k org, *bl* 15.00 15.00
Nos. 84-90 (7) *365.00 365.00*

See Nos. J10-J13. Compare with types A10-A14. For overprints see Nos 91-104.

Handstamped in Rose or Blue

1919, Jan. 16

91 A8 (2)q on 2h brown 8.50 8.50
92 A8 5q on 16h green 8.50 8.50
93 A8 10q on 8h rose (Bl) 8.50 8.50
94 A8 25q on 64h blue 35.00 35.00
95 A9 25q on 64h blue 35.00 35.00
96 A8 50q on 32h violet 8.50 8.50
97 A8 1fr on 1.28k org, *bl* 8.50 8.50
Nos. 91-97 (7) 112.50 112.50

Handstamped in Violet

1919

98 A8 (2)q on 2h brown 7.50 7.50
99 A8 5q on 16h green 7.50 7.50
100 A8 10q on 8h rose 7.50 7.50
101 A8 25q on 64h blue 10.00 10.00
102 A9 25q on 64h blue 75.00 65.00
103 A8 50q on 32h violet 7.50 7.50
104 A8 1fr on 1.28k org, *bl* 7.50 7.50
Nos. 98-104 (7) 122.50 112.50

No. 50 Overprinted in Violet

1919 *Perf. 14*

105 A3 1gr on 25q blue 5.00 *7.50*

A10

A11

1919, June 5 *Perf. 11½, 12½*

106 A10 10q on 2h brown 4.00 4.00
107 A11 15q on 8h rose 4.00 4.00
108 A11 20q on 16h green 4.00 4.00
109 A10 25q on 64h blue 4.00 4.00
110 A11 50q on 32h violet 8.50 8.50
111 A11 1fr on 96h orange 8.50 8.50
112 A10 2fr on 1.60k vio, *buff* 8.50 8.50
Nos. 106-112 (7) 41.50 41.50

Nos. 106-108, 110 exist with inverted surcharge.

A12

A13

Black or Violet Surcharge

1919

113 A12 10q on 8h car 4.00 4.00
114 A12 15q on 8h car (V) 4.00 4.00
115 A13 20q on 16h green 4.00 4.00
116 A13 25q on 35h violet 4.00 4.00
117 A13 50q on 64h blue 8.50 8.50
118 A13 1fr on 96h orange 8.50 8.50
119 A12 2fr on 1.60k vio, *buff* 8.50 8.50
Nos. 113-119 (7) 41.50 41.50

A14

A15

Overprinted in Blue or Black Without New Value

1920 *Perf. 12½*

120 A14 1q gray (Bl) 22.50 22.50
121 A14 10q rose (Bk) 1.75 2.75
a. Double overprint 24.00 *27.50*

122 A14 20q brown (Bl) 11.00 11.00
123 A14 25q blue (Bk) 110.00 *110.00*
124 A14 50q brown vio (Bk) 14.00 16.00
Nos. 120-124 (5) 159.25 *162.25*

Counterfeit overprints exist of Nos. 120-128.

Surcharged with New Value

125 A14 2q on 10q rose (R) 4.25 4.25
126 A14 5q on 10q rose (G) 4.25 4.25
127 A14 25q on 10q rose (Bl) 4.25 4.25
128 A14 50q on 10q rose (Br) 4.25 4.25
Nos. 125-128 (4) 17.00 17.00

Stamps of type A14 (Portrait of the Prince zu Wied) were not placed in use without overprint or surcharge.

Post Horn Overprinted in Black

1920 ***Perf. 14x13***

129 A15 2q orange 3.75 3.25
130 A15 5q deep green 6.25 6.00
131 A15 10q red 11.00 11.00
132 A15 25q light blue 20.00 11.00
133 A15 50q gray green 4.25 4.00
134 A15 1fr claret 4.25 4.00
Nos. 129-134 (6) 49.50 39.25

Type A15 was never placed in use without post horn or "Besa" overprint.

Stamps of Type A15 (No Post Horn) Overprinted

1921

135 A15 2q orange 3.00 3.00
136 A15 5q deep green 3.00 3.00
137 A15 10q red 6.00 6.00
138 A15 25q light blue 11.00 11.00
139 A15 50q gray green 6.00 6.00
140 A15 1fr claret 6.00 6.00
Nos. 135-140 (6) 35.00 35.00

For surcharge & overprints see #154, 156-157.

Stamps of these types, and with "TAKSE" overprint, were unauthorized and never placed in use. They are common.

Gjirokaster
A18

Korcha
A19

Designs: 5q, Kanina. 10q, Berati. 25q, Bridge at Vezirit. 50q, Rozafat. 2fr, Dursit.

1923 **Typo.** ***Perf. 12½, 11½***

147 A18 2q orange .60 .60
148 A18 5q yellow green .50 .50
149 A18 10q carmine .50 .50
150 A18 25q dark blue .50 .50
151 A18 50q dark green .65 .50
152 A19 1fr dark violet .65 .65
153 A19 2fr olive green 1.75 1.75
Nos. 147-153 (7) 5.00 5.00

For overprints & surcharges see #158-185, B1-B8.

No. 135 Surcharged

1922 ***Perf. 14x13***

154 A15 1q on 2q orange 3.00 3.00

Stamps of Type A15 (No Post Horn) Overprinted

1922

156 A15 5q deep green 3.00 2.50
157 A15 10q red 3.00 2.50

Nos. 147-151 Overprinted (top line in Black; diamond in Violet)

1924, Jan. ***Perf. 12½***

158 A18 2q red orange 4.00 3.75
159 A18 5q yellow green 4.00 3.75
160 A18 10q carmine 4.00 3.75
161 A18 25q dark blue 4.00 3.75
162 A18 50q dark green 4.00 3.75
Nos. 158-162 (5) 20.00 18.75

The words "Mbledhje Kushtetuese" are in taller letters on the 25q than on the other values. Opening of the Constituent Assembly. Counterfeits of Nos. 158 and 161 abound.

No. 147 Surcharged

1924

163 A18 1q on 2q red orange 2.25 2.25

Nos. 163, 147-152 Overprinted

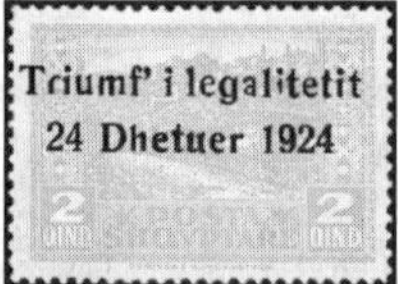

1924

164 A18 1g on 2q orange 1.75 *2.50*
165 A18 2g orange 1.75 *2.50*
166 A18 5g yellow green 1.75 *2.50*
167 A18 10g carmine 1.75 *2.50*
168 A18 25g dark blue 1.75 *2.50*
169 A18 50g dark green 1.75 *2.50*
170 A19 1fr dark violet 1.75 *2.50*
Nos. 164-170 (7) 12.25 *17.50*

Issued to celebrate the return of the Government to the Capital after a revolution.

Nos. 163, 147-152 Overprinted

1925

171 A18 1g on 2q orange 1.75 *2.50*
172 A18 2g orange 1.75 *2.50*
173 A18 5g yellow green 1.75 *2.50*
174 A18 10g carmine 1.75 *2.50*
175 A18 25g dark blue 1.75 *2.50*
176 A18 50g dark green 1.75 *2.50*
177 A19 1fr dark violet 1.75 *2.50*
Nos. 171-177 (7) 12.25 *17.50*

Proclamation of the Republic, Jan. 21, 1925. The date "1921" instead of "1925" occurs once in each sheet of 50.
Counterfeits exist.

Nos. 163, 147-153 Overprinted

1925

178 A18 1g on 2q orange .55 *.75*
a. Inverted overprint 7.00 7.00
179 A18 2g orange .55 *.75*
180 A18 5g yellow green .55 *.75*
a. Inverted overprint 7.00 7.00
181 A18 10g carmine .55 *.75*
182 A18 25g dark blue .55 *.75*
183 A18 50g dark green .55 *.75*
184 A19 1fr dark violet .65 *.90*
185 A19 2fr olive green .65 *.90*
Nos. 178-185 (8) 4.60 *6.30*

Counterfeits exist.

President Ahmed Zogu
A25 A26

1925 ***Perf. 13½, 13½x13***

186 A25 1q orange .20 .20
187 A25 2q red brown .20 .20
188 A25 5q green .20 .20
189 A25 10q rose red .20 .20
190 A25 15q gray brown 1.50 1.50
191 A25 25q dark blue .20 .20
192 A25 50q blue green .55 .55
193 A26 1fr red & ultra .95 .95
194 A26 2fr green & orange 1.25 1.25
195 A26 3fr brown & violet 2.00 2.00
196 A26 5fr violet & black 5.00 5.00
Nos. 186-196 (11) 12.25 12.25

No. 193 in ultramarine and brown, and No. 194 in green and brown were not regularly issued. Value, both $15.
For overprints & surcharges see #197-209, 238-248.

Nos. 186-196 Overprinted in Various Colors

1927

197 A25 1q orange (V) .60 .40
198 A25 2q red brn (G) .25 .20
199 A25 5q green (R) 1.25 .20
200 A25 10q rose red (Bl) .25 .20
201 A25 15q gray brn (G) 5.00 5.00
202 A25 25q dk blue (R) .60 .20
203 A25 50q blue grn (Bl) .60 .20
204 A26 1fr red & ultra (Bk) .90 *1.00*
205 A26 2fr green & org (Bk) .90 *1.50*
206 A26 3fr brown & vio (Bk) 1.40 *2.50*
207 A26 5fr violet & blk (Bk) 2.10 *3.00*
Nos. 197-207 (11) 13.85 14.40

No. 200 exists perf. 11.
For surcharges see Nos. 208-209, 238-240.

Nos. 200, 202 Surcharged in Black or Red

1928

208 A25 1q on 10q rose red .40 .30
a. Inverted surcharge 3.75 3.75
209 A25 5q on 25q dk blue (R) .40 .30
a. Inverted surcharge 3.75 3.75

A27

King Zog I — A28

1928 ***Perf. 14x13½***

Black Overprint

210 A27 1q orange brown 2.25 2.25
211 A27 2q slate 2.25 2.25
212 A27 5q blue green 2.25 2.25
213 A27 10q rose red 2.25 2.25
214 A27 15q bister 12.00 12.00
215 A27 25q deep blue 1.75 1.75
216 A27 50q lilac rose 2.25 2.25

Red Overprint

Perf. 13½x14

217 A28 1fr blue & slate 2.50 2.50
Nos. 210-217 (8) 27.50 27.50

Compare with types A29-A32.

A29

A30

1928 ***Perf. 14x13½***

Black or Red Overprint

218 A29 1q orange brown 8.25 8.25
219 A29 2q slate (R) 8.25 8.25
220 A29 5q blue green 7.00 7.00
221 A29 10q rose red 4.50 4.50
222 A29 15q bister 4.75 4.75
223 A29 25q deep blue (R) 4.75 4.75
224 A29 50q lilac rose 5.25 5.25

Perf. 13½x14

225 A30 1fr blue & slate (R) 7.75 7.75
226 A30 2fr green & slate (R) 9.50 9.50
Nos. 218-226 (9) 60.00 60.00

Proclamation of Ahmed Zogu as King of Albania.

A31

A32

1928 ***Perf. 14x13½***

Black Overprint

227 A31 1q orange brown .35 .35
228 A31 2q slate .35 .25
229 A31 5q blue green 3.00 .35
230 A31 10q rose red .35 .25
231 A31 15q bister 6.75 8.00
232 A31 25q deep blue .35 .25
233 A31 50q lilac rose .60 .25

Perf. 13½x14

Black Overprint

234 A32 1fr blue & slate 1.25 1.10
235 A32 2fr green & slate 1.25 1.25
236 A32 3fr dk red & ol bis 2.10 1.75
237 A32 5fr dull vio & gray 2.75 4.50
Nos. 227-237 (11) 19.10 18.30

The overprint reads "Kingdom of Albania."

Mbr. Shqiptare

■ 5 ■

Nos. 203, 202, 200 Surcharged in Black

1929				*Perf. 13½x13, 11½*	
238	A25	1q	on 50q blue green	.35	.35
239	A25	5q	on 25q dark blue	.35	.35
240	A25	15q	on 10q rose red	.55	.50
			Nos. 238-240 (3)	1.25	1.20

RROFT-MBRETI

Nos. 186-189, 191-194 Overprinted in Black or Red

8 X 1929.

1929				*Perf. 11½, 13½*	
241	A25	1q	orange	4.00	4.00
242	A25	2q	red brown	4.00	4.00
243	A25	5q	green	4.00	4.00
244	A25	10q	rose red	4.00	4.00
245	A25	25q	dark blue	4.00	4.00
246	A25	50q	blue green (R)	4.75	4.75
247	A26	1fr	red & white	7.00	7.00
248	A26	2fr	green & orange	8.75	8.75
			Nos. 241-248 (8)	40.50	40.50

34th birthday of King Zog. The overprint reads "Long live the King."

Lake Butrinto — A33

King Zog I — A34

Zog Bridge — A35

Ruin at Zog Manor — A36

Perf. 14, 14½

1930, Sept. 1			**Photo.**	**Wmk. 220**	
250	A33	1q	slate	.20	.20
251	A33	2q	orange red	.20	.20
252	A34	5q	yellow green	.20	.20
253	A34	10q	carmine	.20	.20
254	A34	15q	dark brown	.20	.20
255	A34	25q	dark ultra	.20	.20
256	A33	50q	slate green	.30	.30
257	A35	1fr	violet	.75	.75
258	A35	2fr	indigo	.85	.85
259	A36	3fr	gray green	1.90	1.90
260	A36	5fr	orange brown	3.25	3.25
			Nos. 250-260 (11)	8.25	8.25

2nd anniversary of accession of King Zog I.

For overprints see Nos. 261-270, 299-309, J39. For surcharges see Nos. 354-360.

Nos. 250-259 Overprinted in Black

1934, Dec. 24					
261	A33	1q	slate	8.50	8.50
262	A33	2q	orange red	8.50	8.50
263	A34	5q	yellow green	8.50	8.50
264	A34	10q	carmine	8.50	8.50
265	A34	15q	dark brown	8.50	8.50
266	A34	25q	dark ultra	8.50	8.50
267	A33	50q	slate green	8.50	8.50
268	A35	1fr	violet	8.50	8.50
269	A35	2fr	indigo	9.00	9.00
270	A36	3fr	gray green	12.50	12.50
			Nos. 261-270 (10)	89.50	89.50

Tenth anniversary of the Constitution.

Allegory of Death of Skanderbeg A37

Albanian Eagle in Turkish Shackles A38

5q, 25q, 40q, 2fr, Eagle with wings spread.

1937			**Unwmk.**	*Perf. 14*	
271	A37	1q	brown violet	.20	.20
272	A38	2q	brown	.30	.30
273	A38	5q	lt green	.35	.35
274	A37	10q	olive brown	.40	.40
275	A38	15q	rose red	.55	.55
276	A38	25q	blue	1.00	1.00
277	A37	50q	deep green	1.40	1.40
278	A38	1fr	violet	2.25	2.25
279	A38	2fr	orange brown	5.75	5.75
			Nos. 271-279 (9)	12.20	12.20

Souvenir Sheet

280			Sheet of 3	15.00	13.00
a.	A37	20q	red violet	3.00	3.00
b.	A38	30q	olive brown	3.00	3.00
c.	A38	40q	red	3.00	3.00

25th anniv. of independence from Turkey, proclaimed Nov. 26, 1912.

Queen Geraldine and King Zog — A40

1938				*Perf. 14*	
281	A40	1q	slate violet	.20	.20
282	A40	2q	red brown	.20	.20
283	A40	5q	green	.20	.20
284	A40	10q	olive brown	.35	.35
285	A40	15q	rose red	.60	.60
286	A40	25q	blue	.85	.85
287	A40	50q	Prus green	2.50	2.50
288	A40	1fr	purple	5.25	5.25
			Nos. 281-288 (8)	10.15	10.15

Souvenir Sheet

289			Sheet of 4	18.00	18.00
a.	A40	20q	dark red violet	1.75	1.75
b.	A40	30q	brown olive	1.75	1.75

Wedding of King Zog and Countess Geraldine Apponyi, Apr. 27, 1938.

No. 289 contains 2 each of Nos. 289a, 289b.

Queen Geraldine — A42

National Emblems — A43

Designs: 10q, 25q, 30q, 1fr, King Zog.

1938					
290	A42	1q	dp red violet	.20	.20
291	A43	2q	red orange	.20	.20
292	A42	5q	deep green	.20	.20
293	A42	10q	red brown	.20	.20
294	A42	15q	deep rose	.55	.55
295	A42	25q	deep blue	.70	.70
296	A43	50q	gray black	1.75	1.75
297	A42	1fr	slate green	6.00	6.00
			Nos. 290-297 (8)	9.80	9.80

Souvenir Sheet

298			Sheet of 3	18.00	18.00
b.	A43	20q	Prussian green	2.00	2.00
c.	A42	30q	deep violet	2.00	2.00

10th anniv. of royal rule. They were on sale for 3 days (Aug. 30-31, Sept. 1) only, during which their use was required on all mail.

No. 298 contains Nos. 294, 298b, 298c.

Issued under Italian Dominion

Nos. 250-260 Overprinted in Black

1939			**Wmk. 220**	*Perf. 14*	
299	A33	1q	slate	.20	.20
300	A33	2q	orange red	.20	.20
301	A34	5q	yellow green	.20	.20
302	A34	10q	carmine	.40	.40
303	A34	15q	dark brown	.40	.40
304	A34	25q	dark ultra	.60	.60
305	A33	50q	slate green	.90	.90
306	A35	1fr	violet	1.60	1.60
307	A35	2fr	indigo	2.50	2.50
308	A36	3fr	gray green	5.00	5.00
309	A36	5fr	orange brown	7.00	7.00
			Nos. 299-309 (11)	19.00	19.00

Resolution adopted by the Natl. Assembly, Apr. 12, 1939, offering the Albanian Crown to Italy.

A46

A47

Native Costumes — A48

King Victor Emmanuel III
A49 A50

Native Costume — A51

Monastery A52

Designs: 2fr, Bridge at Vezirit. 3fr, Ancient Columns. 5fr, Amphitheater.

1939			**Unwmk. Photo.**	*Perf. 14*	
310	A46	1q	blue gray	.20	.20
311	A47	2q	olive green	.20	.20
312	A48	3q	golden brown	.20	.20
313	A49	5q	green	.20	.20
314	A50	10q	brown	.20	.20
315	A50	15q	crimson	.25	.20
316	A50	25q	sapphire	.40	.25
317	A50	30q	brt violet	.55	.35
318	A51	50q	dull purple	.70	.35
319	A49	65q	red brown	1.00	1.00
320	A52	1fr	myrtle green	1.25	1.10
321	A52	2fr	brown lake	3.00	3.00
322	A52	3fr	brown black	5.75	5.75
323	A52	5fr	gray violet	12.00	12.00
			Nos. 310-323 (14)	25.90	25.00

For overprints and surcharges see Nos. 331-353.

King Victor Emmanuel III — A56

1942				**Photo.**	
324	A56	5q	green	.20	.20
325	A56	10q	brown	.25	.25
326	A56	15q	rose red	.35	.35
327	A56	25q	blue	.85	.85
328	A56	65q	red brown	1.25	1.25
329	A56	1fr	myrtle green	2.40	2.40
330	A56	2fr	gray violet	5.25	5.25
			Nos. 324-330 (7)	10.55	10.55

Conquest of Albania by Italy, 3rd anniv.

No. 311 Surcharged in Black

331	A47	1q	on 2q olive green	1.00	1.00

Issued under German Administration

Stamps of 1939 Overprinted in Carmine or Brown

1943					
332	A47	2q	olive green	1.10	2.25
333	A48	3q	golden brown	1.10	2.25
334	A49	5q	green	1.10	2.25
335	A50	10q	brown	1.10	2.25
336	A50	15q	crimson (Br)	1.10	2.25
337	A50	25q	sapphire	1.10	2.25
338	A50	30q	brt violet	1.10	2.25
339	A49	65q	red brown	1.25	4.50
340	A52	1fr	myrtle green	7.75	13.50
341	A52	2fr	brown lake	10.50	*45.00*
342	A52	3fr	brown black	45.00	*125.00*

Surcharged with New Values

343	A48	1q	on 3q gldn brn	1.10	2.25
344	A49	50q	on 65q red brn	1.25	4.50
			Nos. 332-344 (13)	74.55	*210.50*

Proclamation of Albanian independence.

The overprint "14 Shtator 1943" on Nos. 324 to 328 is private and fraudulent.

Independent State

Nos. 312 to 317 and 319 to 321 Surcharged with New Value and Bars in Black or Carmine, and:

1945					
345	A48	30q	on 3q gldn brn	3.00	3.00
346	A49	40q	on 5q green	3.00	3.00
347	A50	50q	on 10q brown	3.00	3.00
348	A50	60q	on 15q crimson	3.00	3.00
349	A50	80q	on 25q saph (C)	3.00	3.00
350	A50	1fr	on 30q brt violet	3.00	3.00
351	A49	2fr	on 65q red brn	3.00	3.00
352	A52	3fr	on 1fr myr green	3.00	3.00
353	A52	5fr	on 2fr brown lake	3.00	3.00
			Nos. 345-353 (9)	27.00	27.00

"DEMOKRATIKE" is not abbreviated on Nos. 352 and 353.

Nos. 250, 251, 256 and 258 Surcharged in Black or Carmine, and

1945				**Wmk. 220**	
354	A33	30q	on 1q slate	1.10	1.10
355	A33	60q	on 1q slate	1.25	1.25
356	A33	80q	on 1q slate	1.50	1.50
357	A33	1fr	on 1q slate	2.10	2.10
358	A33	2fr	on 2q org red	3.00	3.00
359	A33	3fr	on 50q sl grn	7.25	7.25
360	A35	5fr	on 2fr indigo	9.25	9.25
			Nos. 354-360 (7)	25.45	25.45

Albanian Natl. Army of Liberation, 2nd anniv.

The surcharge on No. 360 is condensed to fit the size of the stamp.

Country House, Labinot — A57

40q, 60q, Bridge at Berat. 1fr, 3fr, Permet.

Perf. 11½

1945, Nov. 28 Unwmk. Typo.

361	A57	20q bluish green	.20	.20
362	A57	30q deep orange	.40	.40
363	A57	40q brown	.40	.40
364	A57	60q red violet	.60	.60
365	A57	1fr rose red	1.40	1.40
366	A57	3fr dark blue	6.00	6.00
		Nos. 361-366 (6)	9.00	9.00

Counterfeits: lithographed; genuine: typographed.

For overprints and surcharges see Nos. 367-378, 418-423, B28-B33.

Nos. 361 to 366 Overprinted in Black

1946

367	A57	20q bluish green	.60	.60
368	A57	30q deep orange	.60	.60
369	A57	40q brown	.95	.95
370	A57	60q red violet	1.60	1.60
371	A57	1fr rose red	4.75	4.75
372	A57	3fr dark blue	7.50	7.50
		Nos. 367-372 (6)	16.00	16.00

Convocation of the Constitutional Assembly, Jan. 10, 1946.

People's Republic

#361-366 Overprinted in Black

1946 *Perf. 11*

373	A57	20q bluish green	.30	*.40*
374	A57	30q deep orange	.45	*.55*
375	A57	40q brown	.75	*1.10*
376	A57	60q red violet	1.50	*2.00*
377	A57	1fr rose red	4.50	*5.50*
378	A57	3fr dark blue	7.50	*8.00*
		Nos. 373-378 (6)	15.00	17.55

Proclamation of the Albanian People's Republic.

Some values exist perf 11½.

For surcharges see Nos. 418-423.

Globe, Dove and Olive Branch — A60

Perf. 11½, Imperf.

1946, Mar. 8 Typo.

Denomination in Black

379	A60	20q lilac & dull red	.20	.30
380	A60	40q dp lilac & dull red	.35	.50
381	A60	50q violet & dull red	.50	.75
382	A60	1fr lt blue & red	.80	1.00
383	A60	2fr dk blue & red	1.60	2.00
		Nos. 379-383 (5)	3.45	4.55

International Women's Congress.

Counterfeits exist.

Athletes with Shot and Indian Club A61

Perf. 11½

1946, Oct. 6 Litho. Unwmk.

384	A61	1q grnsh black	5.25	5.25
385	A61	2q green	5.25	5.25
386	A61	5q brown	5.25	5.25
387	A61	10q crimson	5.25	5.25
388	A61	20q ultra	5.25	5.25
389	A61	40q rose violet	5.25	5.25
390	A61	1fr deep orange	8.50	8.50
		Nos. 384-390 (7)	40.00	40.00

Balkan Games, Tirana, Oct. 6-13.

Qemal Stafa — A62

1947, May 5 *Perf. 12½x11½*

391	A62	20q brn & yel brn	4.00	*4.50*
392	A62	28q dk blue & blue	4.00	*4.50*
393	A62	40q brn blk & gray brn	4.00	*4.50*
a.		Souvenir sheet, #391-393	8.00	8.00
		Nos. 391-393 (3)	12.00	*13.50*

5th anniv. of the death of Qemal Stafa.

Young Railway Laborers A64

1947, May 16 *Perf. 11½*

395	A64	1q brn blk & gray brn	1.75	.60
396	A64	4q dk green & green	1.75	.60
397	A64	10q blk brn & bis brn	1.75	.60
398	A64	15q dk red & red	2.00	.60
399	A64	20q indigo & bl gray	2.75	.90
400	A64	28q dk blue & blue	4.25	.90
401	A64	40q brn vio & rose vio	11.00	4.25

Perf. 13x12½

402	A64	68q dk brn & org brn	17.50	7.75
		Nos. 395-402 (8)	42.75	16.20

Issued to publicize the construction of the Durres Elbasan Railway by Albanian youths.

The 4q, 20q, 28q and 40q exist perf 13x12½.

Citizens Led by Hasim Zeneli — A65

Enver Hoxha and Vasil Shanto — A66

Vojo Kushi — A68

Inauguration of Vithkuq Brigade A67

1947, July 10 Litho.

403	A65	16q brn org & red brn	3.25	3.25
404	A66	20q org brn & dk brn	3.25	3.25
405	A67	28q blue & dk blue	3.50	3.50
406	A68	40q lilac & dk brn	5.00	5.00
		Nos. 403-406 (4)	15.00	15.00

4th anniv. of the formation of Albania's army, July 10, 1943.

Conference Building Ruins, Peza — A69

Disabled Soldiers — A70

1947, Sept. 16

407	A69	2 l red violet	2.25	2.00
408	A69	2.50 l deep blue	2.25	2.00

Peza Conf., Sept. 16, 1942, 5th anniv.

1947, Nov. 17 *Perf. 12½x11½*

408A	A70	1 l red	6.00	6.00

Disabled War Veterans Cong., 11/14-20/47.

A71

A73

2 l, Banquet. 2.50 l, Peasants rejoicing.

Perf. 11½x12½, 12½x11½

1947, Nov. 17 Unwmk.

409	A71	1.50 l dull violet	2.50	2.50
410	A71	2 l brown	2.50	2.50
411	A71	2.50 l blue	2.50	2.50
412	A73	3 l rose red	2.50	2.50
		Nos. 409-412 (4)	10.00	10.00

Agrarian reform law of 11/17/46, 1st anniv.

Burning Farm Buildings A74

Designs: 2.50 l, Trench scene. 5 l, Firing line. 8 l, Winter advance. 12 l, Infantry column.

1947, Nov. 29 *Perf. 11½x12½*

413	A74	1.50 l red	1.75	1.50
414	A74	2.50 l rose brown	2.50	2.00
415	A74	5 l blue	3.00	2.50
416	A74	8 l purple	5.00	4.00
417	A74	12 l brown	7.50	6.00
		Nos. 413-417 (5)	19.75	16.00

3rd anniv. of Albania's liberation.

Nos. 373 to 378 Surcharged with New Value and Bars in Black

1948, Feb. 22 *Perf. 11*

418	A57	50q on 30q dp org	.35	.25
419	A57	1 l on 20q bluish grn	.70	.50
420	A57	2.50 l on 60q red vio	1.40	1.00
421	A57	3 l on 1fr rose red	1.75	1.25
422	A57	5 l on 3fr dk bl	3.25	2.25
423	A57	12 l on 40q brown	6.50	4.75
		Nos. 418-423 (6)	13.95	10.00

The two bars consist of four type squares each set close together.

Some values exist perf 11½.

Map, Train and Construction Workers A75

1948, June 1 Litho. *Perf. 11½*

424	A75	50q dk car rose	1.10	.55
425	A75	1 l lt green & blk	1.25	.55
426	A75	1.50 l deep rose	1.25	.55
427	A75	2.50 l org brn & dk brn	1.25	.55
428	A75	5 l dull blue	1.50	1.10
429	A75	8 l sal & dk brn	3.50	2.00
430	A75	12 l red vio & dk vio	4.75	2.25
431	A75	20 l olive gray	9.00	5.00
		Nos. 424-431 (8)	23.60	12.55

Issued to publicize the construction of the Durres-Tirana Railway.

Marching Soldiers A76

Design: 8 l, Battle scene.

1948, July 10

432	A76	2.50 l yellow brown	1.25	1.25
433	A76	5 l dark blue	1.75	1.75
434	A76	8 l violet gray	3.25	3.25
		Nos. 432-434 (3)	6.25	6.25

5th anniv. of the formation of Albania's army.

Bricklayer, Flag, Globe and "Industry" — A77

Map and Soldier — A78

1949, May 1 Photo. *Perf. 12½x12*

435	A77	2.50 l olive brown	.30	.30
436	A77	5 l blue	.70	.70
437	A77	8 l violet brown	1.10	1.10
		Nos. 435-437 (3)	2.10	2.10

Issued to publicize Labor Day, May 1, 1949.

1949, July 10 Unwmk.

438	A78	2.50 l brown	.50	.50
439	A78	5 l light ultra	.75	.75
440	A78	8 l brown orange	1.50	1.50
		Nos. 438-440 (3)	2.75	2.75

6th anniv. of the formation of Albania's army.

Enver Hoxha A79

Albanian Citizen and Spasski Tower, Kremlin A80

1949, Oct. 16 Engr. *Perf. 12½*

441	A79	50q purple	.20	.20
442	A79	1 l dull green	.20	.20
443	A79	1.50 l car lake	.20	.20
444	A79	2.50 l brown	.30	.20
445	A79	5 l violet blue	.65	.20
446	A79	8 l sepia	1.10	.90
447	A79	12 l rose lilac	2.50	1.50
448	A79	20 l gray blue	5.00	2.50
		Nos. 441-448 (8)	10.15	5.90

1949, Sept. 10 Photo. ***Perf. 12½x12***

449	A80	2.50 l	orange brown	.50	.50
450	A80	5 l	deep ultra	1.00	1.00

Albanian-Soviet friendship.

Albanian Soldier and Flag — A81

Battle Scene — A82

1949, Nov. 29 Unwmk. ***Perf. 12***

451	A81	2.50 l	brown	.25	.25
452	A82	3 l	dark red	.50	.50
453	A81	5 l	violet	.60	.60
454	A82	8 l	black	1.75	1.75
			Nos. 451-454 (4)	3.10	3.10

Fifth anniversary of Albania's liberation.

Joseph V. Stalin — A83

Symbols of UPU and Postal Transport A84

1949, Dec. 21

455	A83	2.50 l	dark brown	.45	.50
456	A83	5 l	violet blue	1.25	1.25
457	A83	8 l	rose brown	2.00	2.25
			Nos. 455-457 (3)	3.70	4.00

70th anniv. of the birth of Joseph V. Stalin.

Canceled to Order

Beginning in 1950, Albania sold some issues in sheets canceled to order. Values in second column when much less than unused are for "CTO" copies. Postally used stamps are valued at slightly less than, or the same as, unused.

Catalogue values for unused stamps in this section, from this point to the end of the section, are for Never Hinged items.

1950, July 1 Photo. ***Perf. 12x12½***

458	A84	8 l	blue	1.60	1.25
459	A84	8 l	rose brown	2.25	1.75
460	A84	12 l	sepia	2.75	2.25
			Nos. 458-460 (3)	6.60	5.25

75th anniv. (in 1949) of the UPU.

Sami Frasheri — A85

Arms and Albanian Flags — A86

Authors: 2.50 l, Andon Zako. 3 l, Naim Frasheri. 5 l, Kostandin Kristoforidhi.

1950, Nov. 5 ***Perf. 14***

461	A85	2 l	dark green	.70	.35
462	A85	2.50 l	red brown	.90	.40
463	A85	3 l	brown carmine	1.40	.60
464	A85	5 l	deep blue	2.00	.75
			Nos. 461-464 (4)	5.00	2.10

"Jubilee of the Writers of the Renaissance."

1951, Jan. 11 Engr. ***Perf. 14x13½***

465	A86	2.50 l	brown carmine	1.10	.25
466	A86	5 l	deep blue	2.00	.50
467	A86	8 l	sepia	3.00	1.00
			Nos. 465-467 (3)	6.10	1.75

5th anniv. of the formation of the Albanian People's Republic.

Skanderbeg — A87

Enver Hoxha and Congress of Permet — A88

1951, Mar. 1

468	A87	2.50 l	brown	.75	.25
469	A87	5 l	violet	1.50	.50
470	A87	8 l	olive bister	2.50	1.00
			Nos. 468-470 (3)	4.75	1.75

483rd anniv. of the death of George Castriota (Skanderbeg).

1951, May 24 Photo. ***Perf. 12***

471	A88	2.50 l	dark brown	.45	.20
472	A88	3 l	rose brown	.70	.30
473	A88	5 l	violet blue	1.10	.50
474	A88	8 l	rose lilac	1.90	.80
			Nos. 471-474 (4)	4.15	1.80

Congress of Permet, 7th anniversary.

Child and Globe — A89

Weighing Baby — A90

1951, July 16

475	A89	2 l	green	1.00	.75
476	A90	2.50 l	brown	1.50	.90
477	A90	3 l	red	2.00	1.10
478	A89	5 l	blue	3.00	1.25
			Nos. 475-478 (4)	7.50	4.00

Intl. Children's Day, June 1, 1951.

Enver Hoxha and Birthplace of Albanian Communist Party — A91

1951, Nov. 8 Photo. ***Perf. 14***

479	A91	2.50 l	olive brown	.30	.20
480	A91	3 l	rose brown	.45	.35
481	A91	5 l	dark slate blue	.70	.60
482	A91	8 l	black	1.00	.85
			Nos. 479-482 (4)	2.45	2.00

Albanian Communist Party, 10th anniv.

Battle Scene A92

Designs: 5 l, Schoolgirl, "Agriculture and Industry." 8 l, Four portraits.

1951, Nov. 28 ***Perf. 12x12½***

483	A92	2.50 l	brown	.40	.20
484	A92	5 l	blue	.65	.40
485	A92	8 l	brown carmine	1.40	.75
			Nos. 483-485 (3)	2.45	1.35

Albanian Communist Youth Org., 10th anniv.

Albanian Heroes (Haxhija, Lezhe, Giyebegej, Mezi and Dedej) — A93

#486-489 each show 5 "Heroes of the People"; #490 shows 2 (Stafa and Shanto).

1950, Dec. 25 Unwmk. ***Perf. 14***

486	A93	2 l	dark green	.60	.20
487	A93	2.50 l	purple	.80	.20
488	A93	3 l	scarlet	1.25	.25
489	A93	5 l	brt blue	1.75	.35
490	A93	8 l	olive brown	4.50	1.00
			Nos. 486-490 (5)	8.90	2.00

6th anniv. of Albania's liberation.

Tobacco Factory, Shkoder A94

Composite, Lenin Hydroelectric Plant — A95

Designs: 1 l, Canal. 2.50 l, Textile factory. 3 l, "8 November" Cannery. 5 l, Motion Picture Studio, Tirana. 8 l, Stalin Textile Mill, Tirana. 20 l, Central Hydroelectric Dam.

1953, Aug. 1 ***Perf. 12x12½, 12½x12***

491	A94	50q	red brown	.20	.20
492	A94	1 l	dull green	.30	.20
493	A94	2.50 l	brown	.50	.20
494	A94	3 l	rose brown	.65	.20
495	A94	5 l	blue	1.25	.20
496	A94	8 l	brown olive	1.75	.20
497	A95	12 l	deep plum	2.10	.30
498	A94	20 l	slate blue	3.25	.50
			Nos. 491-498 (8)	10.00	2.00

Liberation Scene — A96

1954, Nov. 29 ***Perf. 12x12½***

499	A96	50q	brown violet	.20	.20
500	A96	1 l	olive green	.25	.20
501	A96	2.50 l	yellow brown	.65	.20
502	A96	3 l	carmine rose	.80	.20
503	A96	5 l	gray blue	1.10	.20
504	A96	8 l	rose brown	2.00	.55
			Nos. 499-504 (6)	5.00	1.55

10th anniversary of Albania's liberation.

School — A97

Pandeli Sotiri, Petro Nini Luarasi, Nuci Naci — A98

1956, Feb. 23 ***Unwmk.***

505	A97	2 l	rose violet	.35	.20
506	A98	2.50 l	lt green	.50	.20
507	A98	5 l	ultra	1.10	.35
508	A97	10 l	brt grnsh blue	2.25	.65
			Nos. 505-508 (4)	4.20	1.40

Opening of the 1st Albanian school, 70th anniv.

Flags — A99

Designs: 5 l, Labor Party headquarters, Tirana. 8 l, Marx and Lenin.

1957, June 1 Engr. ***Perf. 11½x11***

509	A99	2.50 l	brown	.45	.20
510	A99	5 l	lt violet blue	.90	.20
511	A99	8 l	rose lilac	2.00	1.00
			Nos. 509-511 (3)	3.35	1.40

Albania's Labor Party, 15th anniv.

Congress Emblem A100

1957, Oct. 4 Unwmk. ***Perf. 11½***

512	A100	2.50 l	gray brown	.50	.20
513	A100	3 l	rose red	.70	.20
514	A100	5 l	dark blue	.90	.20
515	A100	8 l	green	1.60	.65
			Nos. 512-515 (4)	3.70	1.25

4th Intl. Trade Union Cong., Leipzig, 10/4-15.

Lenin and Cruiser "Aurora" A101

1957, Nov. 7 Litho. ***Perf. 10½***

516	A101	2.50 l	violet brown	.45	.20
517	A101	5 l	violet blue	.95	.20
518	A101	8 l	gray	1.25	.30
			Nos. 516-518 (3)	2.65	.70

40th anniv. of the Russian Revolution.

Albanian Fighter Holding Flag A102

Naum Veqilharxhj A103

1957, Nov. 28 *Perf. 10½*

519	A102	1.50 l	magenta	.40	.20
520	A102	2.50 l	brown	.60	.20
521	A102	5 l	blue	1.00	.35
522	A102	8 l	green	2.00	.65
			Nos. 519-522 (4)	4.00	1.40

Proclamation of independence, 45th anniv.

1958, Feb. 1 **Unwmk.**

523	A103	2.50 l	dark brown	.50	.20
524	A103	5 l	violet blue	1.00	.20
525	A103	8 l	rose lilac	2.00	.60
			Nos. 523-525 (3)	3.50	1.00

160th anniv. of the birth of Naum Veqilharxhj, patriot and writer.

Luigi Gurakuqi
A104

Soldiers
A105

1958, Apr. 15 **Photo.** *Perf. 10½*

526	A104	1.50 l	dark green	.30	.20
527	A104	2.50 l	brown	.45	.25
528	A104	5 l	blue	.75	.25
529	A104	8 l	sepia	1.50	.50
			Nos. 526-529 (4)	3.00	1.20

Transfer of the ashes of Luigi Gurakuqi.

1958, July 10 **Litho.**

2.50 l, 11 l, Airman, sailor, soldier and tank.

530	A105	1.50 l	blue green	.20	.20
531	A105	2.50 l	dark red brown	.30	.20
532	A105	8 l	rose red	1.00	.30
533	A105	11 l	bright blue	1.50	.50
			Nos. 530-533 (4)	3.00	1.20

15th anniversary of Albanian army.

Cerciz Topulli and Mihal Grameno
A106

Buildings and Tree
A107

1958, July 1

534	A106	2.50 l	dk olive bister	.35	.20
535	A107	3 l	green	.45	.20
536	A106	5 l	blue	.75	.20
537	A107	8 l	red brown	1.25	.40
			Nos. 534-537 (4)	2.80	1.00

50th anniversary, Battle of Mashkullore.

Ancient Amphitheater and Goddess of Butrinto
A108

1959, Jan. 25 **Litho.** *Perf. 10½*

538	A108	2.50 l	redsh brown	.65	.20
539	A108	6.50 l	lt blue green	1.60	.30
540	A108	11 l	dark blue	2.50	.75
			Nos. 538-540 (3)	4.75	1.25

Cultural Monuments Week.

Frederic Joliot-Curie and World Peace Congress Emblem
A109

Basketball
A110

1959, July 1 **Unwmk.**

541	A109	1.50 l	carmine rose	1.00	.20
542	A109	2.50 l	rose violet	1.75	.30
543	A109	11 l	blue	5.00	1.50
			Nos. 541-543 (3)	7.75	2.00

10th anniv. of the World Peace Movement.

1959, Nov. 20 *Perf. 10½*

Sports: 2.50 l, Soccer, 5 l, Runner. 11 l, Man and woman runners with torch and flags.

544	A110	1.50 l	bright violet	.40	.20
545	A110	2.50 l	emerald	.55	.20
546	A110	5 l	carmine rose	1.50	.25
547	A110	11 l	ultra	4.00	1.75
			Nos. 544-547 (4)	6.45	2.40

1st Albanian Spartacist Games.

Fighter and Flags — A111

Designs: 2.50 l, Miner with drill standing guard. 3 l, Farm woman with sheaf of grain. 6.50 l, Man and woman in laboratory.

1959, Nov. 29

548	A111	1.50 l	brt carmine	.50	.20
549	A111	2.50 l	red brown	.70	.20
550	A111	3 l	brt blue green	.90	.30
551	A111	6.50 l	bright red	2.00	.50
a.			Souvenir sheet	6.00	6.00
			Nos. 548-551 (4)	4.10	1.20

15th anniversary of Albania's liberation.

No. 551a contains one each of Nos. 548-551, imperf. and all in bright carmine. Inscribed ribbon frame of sheet and frame lines for each stamp are blue green.

Mother and Child, UN Emblem
A112

1959, Dec. 5 **Unwmk.**

552	A112	5 l	lt grnsh blue	3.00	1.00
a.			Miniature sheet	4.00	4.00

10th anniv. (in 1958) of the signing of the Universal Declaration of Human Rights.

No. 552a contains one imperf. stamp similar to No. 552; ornamental border.

Woman with Olive Branch
A113

Alexander Moissi
A114

1960, Mar. 8 **Litho.** *Perf. 10½*

553	A113	2.50 l	chocolate	.45	.20
554	A113	11 l	rose carmine	2.00	.50

50th anniv. of Intl. Women's Day, Mar. 8.

1960, Apr. 20

555	A114	3 l	deep brown	.35	.20
556	A114	11 l	Prus green	1.40	.35

80th anniversary of the birth of Alexander Moissi (Moisiu) (1880-1935), German actor.

Lenin — A115

School Building — A116

1960, Apr. 22

557	A115	4 l	Prus blue	1.10	.20
558	A115	11 l	lake	2.50	.40

90th anniversary of birth of Lenin.

1960, May 30 **Litho.** *Perf. 10½*

559	A116	5 l	green	1.25	.35
560	A116	6.50 l	plum	1.25	.35

1st Albanian secondary school, 50th anniv.

Soldier on Guard Duty
A117

Liberation Monument, Tirana, Family and Policeman
A118

1960, May 12 **Unwmk.** *Perf. 10½*

561	A117	1.50 l	carmine rose	.30	.20
562	A117	11 l	Prus blue	1.60	.40

15th anniversary of the Frontier Guards.

1960, May 14

563	A118	1.50 l	green	.30	.20
564	A118	8.50 l	brown	1.60	.40

15th anniversary of the People's Police.

Congress Site — A119

Pashko Vasa — A120

1960, Mar. 25

565	A119	2.50 l	sepia	.25	.20
566	A119	7.50 l	dull blue	1.00	.25

40th anniversary, Congress of Louchnia.

1960, May 5

Designs: 1.50 l, Jani Vreto. 6.50 l, Sami Frasheri. 11 l, Page of statutes of association.

567	A120	1 l	gray olive	.40	.20
568	A120	1.50 l	brown	.50	.20
569	A120	6.50 l	blue	1.10	.25
570	A120	11 l	rose red	2.00	.35
			Nos. 567-570 (4)	4.00	1.00

80th anniv. (in 1959) of the Association of Albanian Authors.

Albanian Fighter and Cannon
A121

TU-104 Plane, Clock Tower, Tirana, and Kremlin, Moscow
A122

1960, Aug. 2 **Litho.** *Perf. 10½*

571	A121	1.50 l	olive brown	.40	.20
572	A121	2.50 l	maroon	.50	.30
573	A121	5 l	dark blue	1.25	.40
			Nos. 571-573 (3)	2.15	.90

Battle of Viona (against Italian troops), 40th anniv.

1960, Aug. 18

574	A122	1 l	redsh brown	.40	.20
575	A122	7.50 l	brt grnsh blue	1.50	.35
576	A122	11.50 l	gray	2.75	.60
			Nos. 574-576 (3)	4.65	1.15

TU-104 flights, Moscow-Tirana, 2nd anniv.

Rising Sun and Federation Emblem
A123

Ali Kelmendi
A124

1960, Nov. 10 **Unwmk.** *Perf. 10½*

577	A123	1.50 l	ultra	.30	.20
578	A123	8.50 l	red	1.10	.30

Intl. Youth Federation, 15th anniv.

1960, Dec. 5 **Litho.** *Perf. 10½*

579	A124	1.50 l	pale gray grn	.30	.20
580	A124	11 l	dull rose lake	.70	.30

Ali Kelmendi, communist leader, 60th birthday.

Flags of Russia and Albania and Clasped Hands — A125

Marx and Lenin — A126

1961, Jan. 10 **Unwmk.** *Perf. 10½*

581	A125	2 l	violet	.30	.20
582	A125	8 l	dull red brown	.70	.30

15th anniv. of the Albanian-Soviet Friendship Society.

1961, Feb. 13 **Litho.**

583	A126	2 l	rose red	.30	.20
584	A126	8 l	violet blue	1.10	.20

Fourth Communist Party Congress.

Man from Shkoder — A127

Otter — A128

Costumes: 1.50 l, Woman from Shkoder. 6.50 l, Man from Lume. 11 l, Woman from Mirdite.

1961, Apr. 28 *Perf. 10½*

585	A127	1 l	slate	.35	.20
586	A127	1.50 l	dull claret	.60	.25
587	A127	6.50 l	ultra	1.90	.45
588	A127	11 l	red	3.25	1.25
			Nos. 585-588 (4)	6.10	2.15

1961, June 25 **Unwmk.** *Perf. 10½*

Designs: 6.50 l, Badger. 11 l, Brown bear.

589	A128	2.50 l	grayish blue	1.50	.25
590	A128	6.50 l	blue green	2.75	.50
591	A128	11 l	dark red brown	5.75	.85
			Nos. 589-591 (3)	10.00	1.60

Dalmatian Pelicans A129

Cyclamen A130

1961, Sept. 30 ***Perf. 14***

592 A129 1.50 l shown 2.00 .25
593 A129 7.50 l Gray herons 3.00 .60
594 A129 11 l Little egret 5.00 .75
Nos. 592-594 (3) 10.00 1.60

1961, Oct. 27 **Litho.**

595 A130 1.50 l shown 1.00 .20
596 A130 8 l Forsythia 2.75 .50
597 A130 11 l Lily 3.75 .60
Nos. 595-597 (3) 7.50 1.30

Milosh G. Nikolla — A131

Flag with Marx and Lenin — A132

1961, Oct. 30 ***Perf. 14***

598 A131 50q violet brown .30 .20
599 A131 8.50 l Prus green 1.25 .30

50th anniv. of the birth of Milosh Gjergi Nikolla, poet.

1961, Nov. 8

600 A132 2.50 l vermilion .50 .20
601 A132 7.50 l dull red brown 1.00 .30

20th anniv. of the founding of Albania's Communist Party.

Worker, Farm Woman and Emblem — A133

Yuri Gagarin and Vostok 1 — A134

1961, Nov. 23 **Unwmk.** ***Perf. 14***

602 A133 2.50 l violet blue .50 .20
603 A133 7.50 l rose claret 1.00 .30

20th anniv. of the Albanian Workers' Party.

1962, Feb. 15 **Unwmk.** ***Perf. 14***

604 A134 50q blue .40 .20
605 A134 4 l red lilac 1.60 .20
606 A134 11 l dk slate grn 2.00 .60
Nos. 604-606 (3) 4.00 1.00

1st manned space flight, made by Yuri A. Gagarin, Soviet astronaut, Apr. 12, 1961.

Nos. 604-606 were overprinted with an overall yellow tint and with "POSTA AJRORE" (Air Mail) in maroon in 1962. Value, set $50.

Petro Nini Luarasi — A135

Malaria Eradication Emblem — A136

1962, Feb. 28 **Litho.**

607 A135 50q Prus blue .25 .20
608 A135 8.50 l olive gray 1.50 .25

50th anniv. (in 1961) of the death of Petro Nini Luarasi, Albanian patriot.

1962, Apr. 30 **Unwmk.** ***Perf. 14***

609 A136 1.50 l brt green .20 .20
610 A136 2.50 l brown red .20 .20
611 A136 10 l red lilac .55 .25
612 A136 11 l blue .90 .35
Nos. 609-612 (4) 1.85 1.00

WHO drive to eradicate malaria.

Souvenir sheets, perf. and imperf., contain one each of Nos. 609-612. Value $20 each. Nos. 609-612 imperf., value, set $14.

Camomile A137

Woman Diver A138

Medicinal plants.

1962, May 10

613 A137 50q shown .20 .20
614 A137 8 l Linden .75 .25
615 A137 11.50 l Garden sage 1.75 .45
Nos. 613-615 (3) 2.70 .90

Value, imperf. set $12.

1962, May 31 ***Perf. 14***

2.50 l, Pole vault. 3 l, Mt. Fuji & torch, horiz. 9 l, Woman javelin thrower. 10 l, Shot putting.

616 A138 50q brt grnsh bl & blk .20 .20
617 A138 2.50 l gldn brn & sepia .20 .20
618 A138 3 l blue & gray .40 .20
619 A138 9 l rose car & dk brn 1.10 .25
620 A138 10 l olive & blk 1.25 .30
Nos. 616-620 (5) 3.15 1.15

1964 Olympic Games, Tokyo. Value, imperf. set $25. A 15 l (like 3 l) exists in souv. sheet, perf. and imperf.

Globe and Orbits — A139

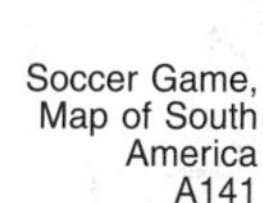

Dog Laika and Sputnik 2 — A140

Designs: 1.50 l, Rocket to the sun. 20 l, Lunik 3 photographing far side of the moon.

1962, June **Unwmk.** ***Perf. 14***

621 A139 50q violet & org .20 .20
622 A140 1 l blue grn & brn .35 .20
623 A140 1.50 l yellow & ver .50 .20
624 A139 20 l magenta & bl 3.50 .80
Nos. 621-624 (4) 4.55 1.40

Russian space explorations.

#621-624 exist imperf in changed colors.

Two miniature sheets exist, containing one 14-lek picturing Sputnik 1. The perforated 14-lek is yellow and brown; the imperf. red and brown.

Soccer Game, Map of South America A141

2.50 l, 15 l, Soccer game and globe as ball.

1962, July **Litho.**

625 A141 1 l org & dk pur .20 .20
626 A141 2.50 l emer & bluish grn .25 .20
627 A141 6.50 l lt brn & pink .90 .20
628 A141 15 l bluish grn & mar 1.50 .40
Nos. 625-628 (4) 2.85 1.00

World Soccer Championships, Chile, 5/30-6/17.

Exist imperforate in changed colors.

Two miniature sheets exist, each containing a single 20-lek in design similar to A141. The perf. sheet is brown and green; the imperf., brown and orange.

Map of Europe and Albania — A142

Woman of Dardhe — A143

Designs: 1 l, 2.50 l, Map of Adriatic Sea and Albania and Roman statue.

1962, Aug.

630 A142 50q multicolored .40 .35
631 A142 1 l ultra & red 1.00 .80
632 A142 2.50 l blue & red 3.00 2.50
633 A142 11 l multicolored 6.00 5.00
Nos. 630-633 (4) 10.40 8.65

Tourist propaganda. Imperforates in changed colors exist.

Miniature sheets containing a 7 l and 8 l stamp, perf. and imperf., exist.

1962, Sept.

Regional Costumes: 1 l, Man from Devoll. 2.50 l, Woman from Lunxheri. 14 l, Man from Gjirokaster.

635 A143 50q car, bl & pur .20 .20
636 A143 1 l red brn & ocher .20 .20
637 A143 2.50 l vio, yel grn & blk .65 .30
638 A143 14 l red brn & pale grn 2.25 .75
Nos. 635-638 (4) 3.30 1.45

Value, imperf. set $18.

Chamois A144

Ismail Qemali A145

Animals: 1 l, Lynx, horiz. 1.50 l, Wild boar, horiz. 15 l, 20 l, Roe deer.

1962, Oct. 24 **Unwmk.** ***Perf. 14***

639 A144 50q sl grn & dk pur .65 .20
640 A144 1 l orange & blk 1.10 .20
641 A144 1.50 l red brn & blk 1.50 .20
642 A144 15 l yel ol & red brn 7.75 1.00
Nos. 639-642 (4) 11.00 1.60

Miniature Sheet

643 A144 20 l yel ol & red brn 45.00 50.00

Imperfs. in changed colors, value #639-642 $25, #643 $25.

1962, Dec. 28 **Litho.**

Designs: 1 l, Albania eagle. 16 l, Eagle over fortress formed by "RPSH."

644 A145 1 l red & red brn .30 .20
645 A145 3 l org brn & blk .55 .20
646 A145 16 l dk car rose & blk 3.50 .50
Nos. 644-646 (3) 4.35 .90

50th anniv. of independence. Imperfs. in changed colors, value, set $12.50.

Monument of October Revolution — A146

Henri Dunant, Cross, Globe and Nurse — A147

1963, Jan. 5 **Unwmk.** ***Perf. 14***

647 A146 5 l shown .50 .20
648 A146 10 l Lenin statue 1.25 .35

October Revolution (Russia, 1917), 45th anniv.

1963, Jan 25 **Unwmk.** ***Perf. 14***

649 A147 1.50 l rose lake, red & blk .25 .20
650 A147 2.50 l lt bl, red & blk .30 .20
651 A147 6 l emerald, red & blk .75 .25
652 A147 10 l dull yel, red & blk 1.40 .50
Nos. 649-652 (4) 2.70 1.15

Cent. of the Geneva Conf., which led to the establishment of the Intl. Red Cross in 1864. Imperfs. in changed colors, value, set $20.

Stalin and Battle of Stalingrad A148

Andrian G. Nikolayev — A149

1963, Feb. 2

653 A148 8 l dk green & slate 2.75 .75

Battle of Stalingrad, 20th anniv. See #C67.

1963, Feb. 28 **Litho.**

Designs: 7.50 l, Vostoks 3 and 4 and globe, horiz. 20 l, Pavel R. Popovich. 25 l, Nikolayev, Popovich and globe with trajectories.

654 A149 2.50 l vio bl & sepia .40 .20
655 A149 7.50 l lt blue & blk .75 .20
656 A149 20 l violet & sepia 2.25 .70
Nos. 654-656 (3) 3.40 1.10

Miniature Sheet

657 A149 25 l vio bl & sepia 12.00 12.00

1st group space flight of Vostoks 3 and 4, Aug. 11-15, 1962. Imperfs. in changed colors, value #654-656 $12, #657 $12.

"Albania" Decorating Police Officer — A150

Polyphylla Fullo — A151

1963, Mar. 20 **Unwmk.** ***Perf. 14***

658 A150 2.50 l crim, mag & blk .40 .20
659 A150 7.50 l org ver, dk red & blk 1.40 .25

20th anniversary of the security police.

1963, Mar. 20

Beetles: 1.50 l, Lucanus cervus. 8 l, Procerus gigas. 10 l, Cicindela albanica.

660 A151 50q ol grn & brn .25 .20
661 A151 1.50 l blue & brn .55 .20
662 A151 8 l dl rose & blk vio 2.75 1.10
663 A151 10 l brt citron & blk 3.00 1.25
Nos. 660-663 (4) 6.55 2.75

1913 Stamp and Postmark A152

10 l, Stamps of 1913, 1937 and 1962.

1963, May 5

664 A152 5 l yel, buff, bl & blk .70 .25
665 A152 10 l car rose, grn & blk 1.40 .45

50th anniversary of Albanian stamps.

Boxer — A153 Crested Grebe — A154

Designs: 3 l, Basketball baskets. 5 l, Volleyball. 6 l, Bicyclists. 9 l, Gymnast. 15 l, Hands holding torch, and map of Japan.

1963, May 25 ***Perf. 13½***

666 A153 2 l yel, blk & red brn .25 .20
667 A153 3 l ocher, brn & bl .35 .20
668 A153 5 l gray bl, red brn & brn .60 .20
669 A153 6 l gray, dk gray & grn .80 .25
670 A153 9 l rose, red brn & bl 1.50 .30
Nos. 666-670 (5) 3.50 1.15

Miniature Sheet

671 A153 15 l lt bl, car, blk & brn 9.00 9.00

1964 Olympic Games in Tokyo. Value, imperfs. #666-670 $7.50, #671 $8.

1963, Apr. 20 Litho. *Perf. 14*

Birds: 3 l, Golden eagle. 6.50 l, Gray partridges. 11 l, Capercaillie.

672 A154 50q multicolored .20 .20
673 A154 3 l multicolored 1.10 .25
674 A154 6.50 l multicolored 2.50 .55
675 A154 11 l multicolored 4.00 .85
Nos. 672-675 (4) 7.80 1.85

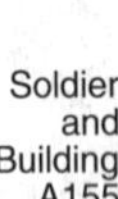

Soldier and Building A155

2.50 l, Soldier with pack, ship, plane. 5 l, Soldier in battle. 6 l, Soldier, bulldozer.

1963, July 10 Unwmk. *Perf. 12*

676 A155 1.50 l brick red, yel & blk .30 .20
677 A155 2.50 l bl, ocher & brn .40 .20
678 A155 5 l bluish grn, gray & blk .90 .20
679 A155 6 l red brn, buff & bl 1.25 .25
Nos. 676-679 (4) 2.85 .85

Albanian army, 20th anniversary.

Maj. Yuri A. Gagarin A156

Designs: 5 l, Maj. Gherman Titov. 7 l, Maj. Andrian G. Nikolayev. 11 l, Lt. Col. Pavel R. Popovich. 14 l, Lt. Col. Valeri Bykovski. 20 l, Lt. Valentina Tereshkova.

1963, July 30

Portraits in Yellow and Black

680 A156 3 l brt purple .30 .20
681 A156 5 l dull blue .45 .20
682 A156 7 l gray .60 .20
683 A156 11 l deep claret 1.10 .35
684 A156 14 l blue green 1.60 .55
685 A156 20 l ultra 2.25 1.00
Nos. 680-685 (6) 6.30 2.50

Man's conquest of space. Value, imperf. set $18.

Volleyball A157

1963, Aug. 31 ***Perf. 12x12½***

686 A157 2 l shown .20 .20
687 A157 3 l Weight lifting .35 .20
688 A157 5 l Soccer .65 .20
689 A157 7 l Boxing .80 .25
690 A157 8 l Rowing 1.50 .30
Nos. 686-690 (5) 3.50 1.15

European championships. Imperfs. in changed colors, value set $16.

Papilio Podalirius A158

1963, Sept. 29 Litho.

Various Butterflies and Moths in Natural Colors

691 A158 1 l red .20 *.20*
692 A158 2 l blue .75 *.20*
693 A158 4 l dull lilac 1.25 *.25*
694 A158 5 l pale green 2.25 *.40*
695 A158 8 l bister 2.75 *.55*
696 A158 10 l light blue 4.50 *.70*
Nos. 691-696 (6) 11.70 *2.30*

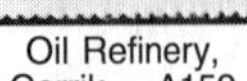

Oil Refinery, Cerrik — A159 Flag and Shield — A160

2.50 l, Food processing plant, Tirana, horiz. 30 l, Fruit canning plant. 50 l, Tannery, horiz.

1963, Nov. 15 Unwmk. *Perf. 14*

697 A159 2.50 l rose red, *pnksh* .20 .20
698 A159 20 l slate grn, *grnsh* .90 .20
699 A159 30 l dull pur, *grysh* 1.90 .50
700 A159 50 l ocher, *yel* 1.90 .75
Nos. 697-700 (4) 4.90 1.65

Industrial development in Albania.
For surcharges see #841-846.

1963, Nov. 24 ***Perf. 12½x12***

701 A160 2 l grnsh bl, blk, ocher & red .35 .20
702 A160 8 l blue, blk, ocher & red 1.00 .50

1st Congress of Army Aid Assn.

Chinese, Caucasian and Negro Men — A161

1963, Dec. 10 ***Perf. 12x11½***

703 A161 3 l bister & blk .50 .20
704 A161 5 l bister & ultra 1.00 .20
705 A161 7 l bister & vio 1.50 .30
Nos. 703-705 (3) 3.00 .70

15th anniv. of the Universal Declaration of Human Rights.

Slalom Ascent — A162 Lenin — A163

Designs: 50q, Bobsled, horiz. 6.50 l, Ice hockey, horiz. 12.50 l, Women's figure skating. No. 709A, Ski jumper.

1963, Dec. 25 ***Perf. 14***

706 A162 50q grnsh bl & blk .20 .20
707 A162 2.50 l red, gray & blk .30 .20
708 A162 6.50 l yel, blk & gray .75 .20
709 A162 12.50 l red, blk & yel grn 1.75 .50
Nos. 706-709 (4) 3.00 1.10

Miniature Sheet

709A A162 12.50 l multi 10.00 7.50

9th Winter Olympic Games, Innsbruck, Jan. 29-Feb. 9, 1964. Imperfs. in changed colors, value #706-709 $25, #709A $30.

1964, Jan. 21 ***Perf. 12½x12***

710 A163 5 l gray & bister .40 .20
711 A163 10 l gray & ocher .75 .30

40th anniversary, death of Lenin.

Hurdling — A164

Fish — A165

Designs: 3 l, Track, horiz. 6.50 l, Rifle shooting, horiz. 8 l, Basketball.

Perf. 12½x12, 12x12½

1964, Jan. 30 Litho.

712 A164 2.50 l pale vio & ultra .20 .20
713 A164 3 l lt grn & red brn .35 .20
714 A164 6.50 l blue & claret .60 .25
715 A164 8 l lt blue & ocher 1.00 .35
Nos. 712-715 (4) 2.15 1.00

1st Games of the New Emerging Forces, GANEFO, Jakarta, Indonesia, Nov. 10-22, 1963.

1964, Feb. 26 Unwmk. *Perf. 14*

716 A165 50q Sturgeon .20 .20
717 A165 1 l Gilthead .20 .20
718 A165 1.50 l Striped mullet .40 .20
719 A165 2.50 l Carp .60 .20
720 A165 6.50 l Mackerel 1.60 .40
721 A165 10 l Lake Ohrid trout 3.00 .50
Nos. 716-721 (6) 6.00 1.70

Wild Animals A166

1964, Mar. 28 ***Perf. 12½x12***

722 A166 1 l Red Squirrel .30 .20
723 A166 1.50 l Beech marten .60 .20
724 A166 2 l Red fox .60 .20
725 A166 2.50 l Hedgehog .90 .20
726 A166 3 l Hare 1.25 .20
727 A166 5 l Jackal 1.50 .25
728 A166 7 l Wildcat 2.40 .35
729 A166 8 l Wolf 3.00 .50
Nos. 722-729 (8) 10.55 2.10

Lighting Olympic Torch — A167

5 l, Torch, globes. 7 l, 15 l, Olympic flag, Mt. Fuji. 10 l, National Stadium, Tokyo.

1964, May 18 ***Perf. 12x12½***

730 A167 3 l lt yel grn, yel & buff .25 .20
731 A167 5 l red & vio blue .35 .20
732 A167 7 l lt bl, ultra & yel .55 .20
733 A167 10 l orange, bl & vio .75 .25
Nos. 730-733 (4) 1.90 .85

Miniature Sheet

734 A167 15 l lt bl, ultra & org 11.00 11.00

18th Olympic Games, Tokyo, Oct. 10-25, 1964. No. 734 contains one 49x62mm stamp. Imperfs. in changed colors, value #730-733 $11, #734 $14.
See No. 745.

Partisans — A168

5 l, Arms of Albania. 8 l, Enver Hoxha.

Perf. 12½x12

1964, May 24 Litho. Unwmk.

735 A168 2 l orange, red & blk .65 .20
736 A168 5 l multicolored 1.50 .30
737 A168 8 l red brn, blk & red 3.25 .85
Nos. 735-737 (3) 5.40 1.35

20th anniv. of the Natl. Anti-Fascist Cong. of Liberation, Permet, May 24, 1944. The label attached to each stamp, without perforations between, carries a quotation from the 1944 Congress.

Albanian Flag and Revolutionists A169

Full Moon — A170

Perf. 12½x12

1964, June 10 Litho. Unwmk.

738 A169 2.50 l red & gray .25 .20
739 A169 7.50 l lilac rose & gray .75 .25

Albanian revolution of 1924, 40th anniv.

1964, June 27 ***Perf. 12x12½***

Designs: 5 l, New moon. 8 l, Half moon. 11 l, Waning moon. 15 l, Far side of moon.

740 A170 1 l purple & yel .25 .20
741 A170 5 l violet & yel .60 .20
742 A170 8 l blue & yel 1.10 .30
743 A170 11 l green & yel 1.75 .45
Nos. 740-743 (4) 3.70 1.15

Miniature Sheet

Perf. 12 on 2 sides

744 A170 15 l ultra & yel 12.50 12.50

No. 744 contains one stamp, size: 35x36mm, perforated at top and bottom. Imperfs. in changed colors, value #740-743 $12.50, #744 $12.50.

No. 733 with Added Inscription: "Rimini 25-VI-64"

1964 ***Perf. 12x12½***

745 A167 10 l orange, bl & vio 3.50 3.00

"Toward Tokyo 1964" Phil. Exhib. at Rimini, Italy, June 25-July 6.

Wren — A171

Birds: 1 l, Penduline titmouse. 2.50 l, Green woodpecker. 3 l, Tree creeper.4 l, Nuthatch. 5 l, Great titmouse. 6 l, Goldfinch. 18 l, Oriole.

1964, July 31 ***Perf. 12x12½***

746 A171 50q multi .20 .20
747 A171 1 l orange & multi .40 .20
748 A171 2.50 l multi .60 .20
749 A171 3 l blue & multi .80 .20
750 A171 4 l yellow & multi 1.00 .25
751 A171 5 l blue & multi 1.25 .25
752 A171 6 l lt vio & multi 1.40 .50
753 A171 18 l pink & multi 3.00 1.25
Nos. 746-753 (8) 8.65 3.05

Running and Gymnastics A172

Sport: 2 l, Weight lifting, judo. 3 l, Equestrian, bicycling. 4 l, Soccer, water polo. 5 l, Wrestling, boxing. 6 l, Pentathlon, hockey. 7 l, Swimming, sailing. 8 l, Basketball, volleyball. 9 l, Rowing, canoeing. 10 l, Fencing, pistol shooting. 20 l, Three winners.

Perf. 12x12½

1964, Sept. 25 **Litho.** **Unwmk.**

754 A172 1 l lt bl, rose & emer .20 .20
755 A172 2 l bis brn, bluish grn & vio .20 .20
756 A172 3 l vio, red org & ol bis .20 .20
757 A172 4 l grnsh bl, ol & ultra .20 .20
758 A172 5 l grnsh bl, car & pale lil .30 .20
759 A172 6 l dk bl, org & lt bl .35 .20
760 A172 7 l dk bl, lt ol & org .35 .20
761 A172 8 l emer, gray & yel .50 .20
762 A172 9 l bl, yel & lil rose .65 .30
763 A172 10 l brt grn, org brn & yel grn 1.60 .50
Nos. 754-763 (10) 4.55 2.40

Miniature Sheet

Perf. 12

764 A172 20 l violet & lemon 16.00 16.00

18th Olympic Games, Tokyo, Oct. 10-25. No. 764 contains one stamp, size: 41x68mm. Imperfs. in changed colors, value #754-763 $12.50, #764 $12.50.

Arms of People's Republic of China — A173

Mao Tse-tung and Flag A174

1964, Oct. 1 ***Perf. 11½x12, 12x11½***

765 A173 7 l black, red & yellow 2.00 .40
766 A174 8 l black, red & yellow 3.00 .60

People's Republic of China, 15th anniv.

Karl Marx A175

Jeronim de Rada — A176

Designs: 5 l, St. Martin's Hall, London. 8 l, Friedrich Engels.

1964, Nov. 5 ***Perf. 12x11½***

767 A175 2 l red, lt vio & blk .55 .20
768 A175 5 l gray blue 1.10 .25
769 A175 8 l ocher, blk & red 2.25 .55
Nos. 767-769 (3) 3.90 1.00

Centenary of First Socialist International.

1964, Nov. 15 ***Perf. 12½x11½***

770 A176 7 l slate green 1.10 .35
771 A176 8 l dull violet 1.60 .55

Birth of Jeronim de Rada, poet, 150th anniv.

Arms of Albania — A177

Factories A178

Designs: 3 l, Combine harvester. 4 l, Woman chemist. 10 l, Hands holding Constitution, hammer and sickle.

Perf. 11½x12, 12x11½

1964, Nov. 29

772 A177 1 l multicolored .35 .20
773 A178 2 l red, yel & vio bl .45 .20
774 A178 3 l red, yel & brn .85 .20
775 A178 4 l red, yel & gray grn 1.00 .20
776 A177 10 l red, bl & blk 1.60 .45
Nos. 772-776 (5) 4.25 1.25

20th anniversary of liberation.

Planet Mercury — A179

Planets: 2 l, Venus and rocket. 3 l, Earth, moon and rocket. 4 l, Mars and rocket. 5 l, Jupiter. 6 l, Saturn. 7 l, Uranus. 8 l, Neptune. 9 l, Pluto. 15 l, Solar system and rocket.

1964, Dec. 15 ***Perf. 12x12½***

777 A179 1 l yellow & pur .20 .20
778 A179 2 l multicolored .20 .20
779 A179 3 l multicolored .20 .20
780 A179 4 l multicolored .25 .20
781 A179 5 l yel, dk pur & brn .45 .20
782 A179 6 l lt grn, vio brn & yel .60 .20
783 A179 7 l yellow & grn .70 .20
784 A179 8 l yellow & vio .85 .25
785 A179 9 l lt grn, yel & blk 1.25 .35
Nos. 777-785 (9) 4.70 2.00

Miniature Sheet

Perf. 12 on 2 sides

786 A179 15 l car, bl, yel & grn 15.00 15.00

No. 786 contains one stamp, size: 62x51mm, perforated at top and bottom. Imperfs. in changed colors. Value #777-785, $15; #786, $17.50.

European Chestnut A180

Symbols of Industry A181

1965, Jan. 25 ***Perf. 11½x12***

787 A180 1 l shown .20 .20
788 A180 2 l Medlars .25 .20
789 A180 3 l Persimmon .50 .20
790 A180 4 l Pomegranate .55 .20
791 A180 5 l Quince .80 .20
792 A180 10 l Orange 1.60 .35
Nos. 787-792 (6) 3.90 1.35

1965, Feb. 20

Designs: 5 l, Books, triangle and compass. 8 l, Beach, trees and hotel.

793 A181 2 l blk, car rose & pink 1.75 .50
794 A181 5 l yel, gray & blk 3.50 1.00
795 A181 8 l blk, vio bl & lt bl 5.75 1.60
Nos. 793-795 (3) 11.00 3.10

Professional trade associations, 20th anniv.

Water Buffalo A182

Various designs: Water buffalo.

1965, Mar. ***Perf. 12x11½***

796 A182 1 l lt yel grn, yel & brn blk .30 .20
797 A182 2 l lt bl, dk gray & blk .85 .20
798 A182 3 l yellow, brn & grn 1.10 .20
799 A182 7 l brt grn, yel & brn blk 2.75 .35
800 A182 12 l pale lil, dk brn & ind 4.00 .65
Nos. 796-800 (5) 9.00 1.60

Mountain View, Valbona — A183

1.50 l, Seashore. 3 l, Glacier and peak. 4 l, Gorge. 5 l, Mountain peaks. 9 l, Lake and hills.

1965, Mar. **Litho.** ***Perf. 12***

801 A183 1.50 l multi .60 .20
802 A183 2.50 l multi 1.40 .20
803 A183 3 l multi, vert. 1.40 .25
804 A183 4 l multi, vert. 1.75 .40
805 A183 5 l multi 2.10 .50
806 A183 9 l multi 6.00 .75
Nos. 801-806 (6) 13.25 2.30

Frontier Guard — A184

Small-bore Rifle Shooting, Prone — A185

1965, Apr. 25 **Unwmk.**

807 A184 2.50 l lt blue & multi .85 .20
808 A184 12.50 l lt ultra & multi 3.50 .90

20th anniversary of the Frontier Guards.

1965, May 10

Designs: 2 l, Rifle shooting, standing. 3 l, Target over map of Europe, showing Bucharest. 4 l, Pistol shooting. 15 l, Rifle shooting, kneeling.

809 A185 1 l lil, car rose, blk & brn .20 .20
810 A185 2 l bl, blk, brn & vio bl .35 .20
811 A185 3 l pink & car rose .45 .20
812 A185 4 l bis, blk & vio brn .60 .20
813 A185 15 l brt grn, brn & vio brn 2.25 .50
Nos. 809-813 (5) 3.85 1.30

European Shooting Championships, Bucharest.

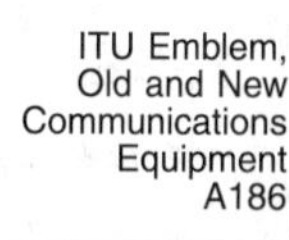
ITU Emblem, Old and New Communications Equipment A186

Col. Pavel Belyayev — A187

1965, May 17 ***Perf. 12½x12***

814 A186 2.50 l brt grn, blk & lil rose .50 .20
815 A186 12.50 l vio, blk & brt bl 3.25 .30

Centenary of the ITU.

1965, June 15 ***Perf. 12***

Designs: 2 l, Voskhod II. 6.50 l, Lt. Col. Alexei Leonov. 20 l, Leonov floating in space.

816 A187 1.50 l lt blue & brn .20 .20
817 A187 2 l dk bl, lt vio & lt ultra .20 .20
818 A187 6.50 l lilac & brn .70 .20

819 A187 20 l chlky bl, yel & blk 1.90 .40
Nos. 816-819 (4) 3.00 1.00

Miniature Sheet

Perf. 12 on 2 sides

820 A187 20 l brt bl, org & blk 6.00 6.00

Space flight of Voskhod II and 1st man walking in space, Lt. Col. Alexei Leonov. No. 820 contains one stamp, size: 51x59½mm, perforated at top and bottom. Imperf., brt grn background, value $6.

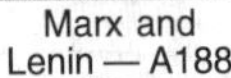

Marx and Lenin — A188

Mother and Child — A189

1965, June 21 ***Perf. 12***
821 A188 2.50 l dk brn, red & yel .85 .20
822 A188 7.50 l sl grn, org ver & buff 2.25 .25

6th Conf. of Postal Ministers of Communist Countries, Peking, June 21-July 15.

Perf. 12½x12, 12x12½
1965, June 29 Litho. Unwmk.

2 l, Pioneers. 3 l, Boy and girl at play, horiz. 4 l, Child on beach. 15 l, Girl with book.

823 A189 1 l brt bl, rose lil & blk .20 .20
824 A189 2 l salmon, vio & blk .35 .20
825 A189 3 l green, org & vio .50 .20
826 A189 4 l multicolored .70 .25
827 A189 15 l lil rose, brn & ocher 2.25 .50
Nos. 823-827 (5) 4.00 1.35

Issued for International Children's Day.

Statue of Magistrate A190

Flowers A191

Designs: 1 l, Amphora. 2 l, Illyrian armor. 3 l, Mosaic, horiz. 15 l, Torso, Apollo statue.

1965, July 20 ***Perf. 12***
828 A190 1 l lt ol, org & brn .20 .20
829 A190 2 l gray grn, grn & brn .25 .20
830 A190 3 l tan, brn, car & lil .50 .20
831 A190 4 l green, bis & brn .70 .25
832 A190 15 l gray & pale claret 1.75 .65
Nos. 828-832 (5) 3.40 1.50

1965, Aug. 11 ***Perf. 12½x12***
833 A191 1 l Fuchsia .20 .20
834 A191 2 l Cyclamen .30 .20
835 A191 3 l Tiger lily .50 .20
836 A191 3.50 l Iris .60 .25
837 A191 4 l Dahlia .70 .25
838 A191 4.50 l Hydrangea .80 .25
839 A191 5 l Rose 1.00 .30
840 A191 7 l Tulips 1.90 .35
Nos. 833-840 (8) 6.00 2.00

Nos. 698-700 Surcharged New Value and Two Bars

1965, Aug. 16 ***Perf. 14***
841 A159 5q on 30 l .20 .20
842 A159 15q on 30 l .30 .20
843 A159 25q on 50 l .45 .20
844 A159 80q on 50 l .80 .20
845 A159 1.10 l on 20 l 1.50 .30
846 A159 2 l on 20 l 2.75 .60
Nos. 841-846 (6) 6.00 1.70

White Stork — A192

"Homecoming," by Bukurosh Sejdini — A193

Migratory Birds: 20q, Cuckoo. 30q, Hoopoe. 40q, European bee-eater. 50q, European nightjar. 1.50 l, Quail.

1965, Aug. 31 ***Perf. 12***
847 A192 10q yel, blk & gray .20 .20
848 A192 20q brt pink, blk & dk bl .35 .20
849 A192 30q violet, blk & bis .65 .25
850 A192 40q emer, blk yel & org 1.40 .30
851 A192 50q ultra, brn & red brn 1.60 .35
852 A192 1.50 l bis, red brn & dp org 4.50 1.00
Nos. 847-852 (6) 8.70 2.30

1965, Sept. 26 Litho. ***Perf. 12x12½***
853 A193 25q olive black 1.25 .20
854 A193 65q blue black 3.75 .55
855 A193 1.10 l black 5.00 1.25
Nos. 853-855 (3) 10.00 2.00

Second war veterans' meeting.

Hunting — A194

Oleander — A195

1965, Oct. 6 Litho. Unwmk.
856 A194 10q Capercaillie .25 .20
857 A194 20q Deer .40 .20
858 A194 30q Pheasant .70 .20
859 A194 40q Mallards 1.10 .20
860 A194 50q Boar 1.25 .25
861 A194 1 l Rabbit 3.75 .55
Nos. 856-861 (6) 7.45 1.60

1965, Oct. 26 ***Perf. 12½x12***

Flowers: 20q, Forget-me-nots. 30q, Pink. 40q, White water lily. 50q, Bird's foot. 1 l, Corn poppy.

862 A195 10q brt bl, grn & car rose .20 .20
863 A195 20q org red, bl, brn & grn .40 .20
864 A195 30q vio, car rose & grn .60 .20
865 A195 40q emerald, yel & blk .80 .20
866 A195 50q org brn, yel & grn 1.00 .20
867 A195 1 l yel grn, blk & rose red 2.00 .70
Nos. 862-867 (6) 5.00 1.70

Hotel Turizmi, Fier — A196

Freighter "Teuta" — A197

Buildings: 10q, Hotel, Peshkopi. 15q, Sanatorium, Tirana. 25q, Rest home, Pogradec. 65q, Partisan Sports Arena, Tirana. 80q, Rest home, Mali Dajt. 1.10 l, Culture House, Tirana. 1.60 l, Hotel Adriatik, Durres. 2 l, Migjeni Theater, Shkoder. 3 l, Alexander Moissi House of Culture, Durres.

1965, Oct. ***Perf. 12x12½***
868 A196 5q blue & blk .20 .20
869 A196 10q ocher & blk .20 .20
870 A196 15q dull grn & blk .20 .20
871 A196 25q violet & blk .20 .20
872 A196 65q lt brn & blk .65 .20
873 A196 80q yel grn & blk .90 .20
874 A196 1.10 l lilac & blk 1.25 .20
875 A196 1.60 l lt vio bl & blk 1.90 .40
876 A196 2 l dull rose & blk 2.50 .50
877 A196 3 l gray & blk 4.00 .70
Nos. 868-877 (10) 12.00 3.00

1965, Nov. 16

Ships: 20q, Raft. 30q, Sailing ship, 19th cent. 40q, Sailing ship, 18th cent. 50q, Freighter "Vlora." 1 l, Illyric galleys.

878 A197 10q brt grn & dk grn .20 .20
879 A197 20q ol bis & dk grn .20 .20
880 A197 30q lt & dp ultra .35 .20
881 A197 40q vio & dp vio .60 .20
882 A197 50q pink & dk red .75 .20
883 A197 1 l bister & brn 1.50 .45
Nos. 878-883 (6) 3.60 1.45

Brown Bear — A198

Basketball and Players — A199

Various Albanian bears. 50q, 55q, 60q, horiz.

1965, Dec. 7 ***Perf. 11½x12***
884 A198 10q bister & dk brn .30 .20
885 A198 20q pale brn & dk brn .40 .20
886 A198 30q bis, dk brn & car .65 .20
887 A198 35q pale brn & dk brn .80 .20
888 A198 40q bister & dk brn 1.25 .20
889 A198 50q bister & dk brn 1.50 .20
890 A198 55q bister & dk brn 1.50 .30
891 A198 60q pale brn, dk brn & car 1.75 .50
Nos. 884-891 (8) 8.15 2.00

1965, Dec. 15 Litho. ***Perf. 12½x12***

10q, Games' emblem (map of Albania and basket). 30q, 50q, Players with ball (diff. designs). 1.40 l, Basketball medal on ribbon.

892 A199 10q blue, yel & car .20 .20
893 A199 20q rose lil, lt brn & blk .35 .20
894 A199 30q bis, lt brn, red & blk .45 .20
895 A199 50q lt grn, lt brn & blk .95 .20
896 A199 1.40 l rose, blk, brn & yel 1.75 .50
Nos. 892-896 (5) 3.70 1.30

7th Balkan Basketball Championships, Tirana, Dec. 15-19.

Arms of Republic and Smokestacks A200

Arms and: 10q, Book. 30q, Wheat. 60q, Book, hammer & sickle. 80q, Factories.

1966, Jan. 11 Litho. ***Perf. 11½x12***
Coat of Arms in Gold
897 A200 10q crimson & brn .20 .20
898 A200 20q blue & vio bl .20 .20
899 A200 30q org yel & brn .35 .20
900 A200 60q yel grn & brt grn .50 .20
901 A200 80q crimson & brn 1.10 .20
Nos. 897-901 (5) 2.35 1.00

Albanian People's Republic, 20th anniv.

Cow A201

1966, Feb. 25 ***Perf. 12½x12, 12x12½***
902 A201 10q shown .20 .20
903 A201 20q Pig .35 .20
904 A201 30q Ewe & lamb .45 .20
905 A201 35q Ram .65 .20
906 A201 40q Dog .95 .20
907 A201 50q Cat, vert. 1.00 .20
908 A201 55q Horse, vert. 1.25 .25
909 A201 60q Ass, vert. 1.50 .30
Nos. 902-909 (8) 6.35 1.75

Soccer Player and Map of Uruguay — A202

Andon Zako Cajupi — A203

5q, Globe in form of soccer ball. 15q, Player, map of Italy. 20q, Goalkeeper, map of France. 25q, Player, map of Brazil. 30q, Player, map of Switzerland. 35q, Player, map of Sweden. 40q, Player, map of Chile. 50q, Player, map of Great Britain. 70q, World Championship cup & ball.

1966, Mar. 20 Litho. ***Perf. 12***
910 A202 5q gray & dp org .20 .20
911 A202 10q lt brn, bl & vio .20 .20
912 A202 15q cit, dk bl & brt bl .20 .20
913 A202 20q org, vio bl & brt bl .25 .20
914 A202 25q salmon & sepia .30 .20
915 A202 30q lt yel grn & brn .30 .20
916 A202 35q lt ultra & emer .35 .20
917 A202 40q pink & brown .55 .20
918 A202 50q pale grn, mag & rose red .55 .20
919 A202 70q gray, brn, yel & blk .70 .30
Nos. 910-919 (10) 3.60 2.10

World Cup Soccer Championship, Wembley, England, July 11-30.

1966, Mar. 27 **Unwmk.**
920 A203 40q bluish blk .50 .20
921 A203 1.10 l dark green 1.50 .40

Andon Zako Cajupi, poet, birth centenary .

Painted Lady — A204

WHO Headquarters, Geneva, and Emblem — A205

Designs: 20q, Blue dragonfly. 30q, Cloudless sulphur butterfly. 35q, 40q, Splendid dragonfly. 50q, Machaon swallow-tail. 55q, Sulphur butterfly. 60q, Whitemarbled butterfly.

1966, Apr. 21 Litho. ***Perf. 11½x12***
922 A204 10q multicolored .25 .20
923 A204 20q yellow & multi .40 .20
924 A204 30q yellow & multi .65 .20
925 A204 35q sky blue & multi .80 .20
926 A204 40q multicolored .85 .20
927 A204 50q rose & multi 1.10 .20

928 A204 55q multicolored 1.25 .25
929 A204 60q multicolored 2.00 .35
Nos. 922-929 (8) 7.30 1.80

Perf. 12x12½, 12½x12

1966, May 3 Litho.

Designs (WHO Emblem and): 35q, Ambulance and stretcher bearers, vert. 60q, Albanian mother and nurse weighing infant, vert. 80q, X-ray machine and hospital.

930 A205 25q lt blue & blk .30 .20
931 A205 35q salmon & ultra .55 .20
932 A205 60q lt grn, bl & red .90 .20
933 A205 80q yel, bl, grn & lt brn 1.25 .25
Nos. 930-933 (4) 3.00 .85

Inauguration of the WHO Headquarters, Geneva.

Bird's Foot Starfish A206

Designs: 25q, Starfish. 35q, Brittle star. 45q, But-thorn starfish. 50q, Starfish. 60q, Sea cucumber. 70q, Sea urchin.

1966, May 10 ***Perf. 12x12½***

934 A206 15q multicolored .25 .20
935 A206 25q multicolored .45 .20
936 A206 35q multicolored .65 .20
937 A206 45q multicolored .90 .20
938 A206 50q multicolored 1.10 .20
939 A206 60q multicolored 1.25 .20
940 A206 70q multicolored 1.90 .35
Nos. 934-940 (7) 6.50 1.55

Luna 10 — A207

30q, 80q, Trajectory of Luna 10, earth & moon.

1966, June 10 ***Perf. 12x12½***

941 A207 20q blue, yel & blk .35 .20
942 A207 30q yel grn, blk & bl .50 .20
943 A207 70q vio, yel & blk .90 .25
944 A207 80q yel, vio, grn & blk 1.25 .50
Nos. 941-944 (4) 3.00 1.15

Launching of the 1st artificial moon satellite, Luna 10, Apr. 3, 1966.

Jules Rimet Cup and Soccer A208

Designs: Various scenes of soccer play.

1966, July 12 Litho. ***Perf. 12x12½***

Black Inscriptions

945 A208 10q ocher & lilac .20 .20
946 A208 20q lt blue & cit .20 .20
947 A208 30q brick red & Prus bl .25 .20
948 A208 35q lt ultra & rose .30 .20
949 A208 40q yel grn & lt red brn .35 .20
950 A208 50q lt red brn & yel grn .60 .20
951 A208 55q rose lil & yel grn .65 .20
952 A208 60q dp rose & ocher 1.25 .25
Nos. 945-952 (8) 3.80 1.65

World Cup Soccer Championship, Wembley, England, July 11-30.

Water Level Map of Albania — A209

30q, Water measure & fields. 70q, Turbine & pylon. 80q, Hydrological decade emblem.

1966, July ***Perf. 12½x12***

953 A209 20q brick red, blk & org .30 .20
954 A209 30q emer, blk & lt brn .50 .20
955 A209 70q brt violet & blk 1.10 .25
956 A209 80q brt bl, org, yel & blk 1.25 .45
Nos. 953-956 (4) 3.15 1.10

Hydrological Decade (UNESCO), 1965-74.

Greek Turtle — A210

Designs: 15q, Grass snake. 25q, European pond turtle. 30q, Wall lizard. 35q, Wall gecko. 45q, Emerald lizard. 50q, Slowworm. 90q, Horned viper (or sand viper).

1966, Aug. 10 Litho. ***Perf. 12½x12***

957 A210 10q gray & multi .20 .20
958 A210 15q yellow & multi .20 .20
959 A210 25q ultra & multi .30 .20
960 A210 30q multicolored .45 .20
961 A210 35q multicolored .60 .20
962 A210 45q multicolored .70 .25
963 A210 50q orange & multi .80 .30
964 A210 90q lilac & multi 1.75 .55
Nos. 957-964 (8) 5.00 2.10

Persian Cat A211

Cats: 10q, Siamese, vert. 15q, European tabby, vert. 25q, Black kitten. 60q, 65q, 80q, Various Persians.

Perf. 12x12½, 12½x12

1966, Sept. 20 Litho.

965 A211 10q multicolored .20 .20
966 A211 15q blk, sepia & car .25 .20
967 A211 25q blk, dk & lt brn .35 .20
968 A211 45q blk, org & yel .80 .20
969 A211 60q blk, brn & yel 1.40 .30
970 A211 65q multicolored 1.40 .40
971 A211 80q blk, gray & yel 1.60 .50
Nos. 965-971 (7) 6.00 2.00

Pjeter Budi, Writer — A212

1966, Oct. 5 ***Perf. 12x12½***

972 A212 25q buff & slate grn .25 .20
973 A212 1.75 l gray & dull claret 1.75 .45

UNESCO Emblem A213

Designs (UNESCO Emblem and): 15q, Open book, rose and school. 25q, Male folk dancers. 1.55 l, Jug, column and old building.

1966, Oct. 20 Litho. ***Perf. 12***

974 A213 5q lt gray & multi .20 .20
975 A213 15q dp blue & multi .30 .20
976 A213 25q gray & multi .50 .20
977 A213 1.55 l multi 2.00 .50
Nos. 974-977 (4) 3.00 1.10

20th anniv. of UNESCO.

A214

A215

Designs: 15q, Hand holding book with pictures of Marx, Engels, Lenin and Stalin. 25q, Map of Albania, hammer and sickle, symbols of agriculture and industry. 65q, Symbolic grain and factories. 95q, Fists holding rifle, spade, axe, sickle and book.

1966, Nov. 1 Litho. ***Perf. 11½x12***

978 A214 15q vermilion & gold .30 .20
979 A214 25q multicolored .55 .20
980 A214 65q brn, brn org & gold 1.25 .20
981 A214 95q yellow & multi 1.90 .40
Nos. 978-981 (4) 4.00 1.00

Albanian Communist Party, 5th Cong.

1966, Nov. 8

Designs: 15q, Hammer and sickle, Party emblem in sunburst. 25q, Partisan and sunburst. 65q, Steel worker and blast furnace. 95q, Combine harvester, factories, and pylon.

982 A215 15q orange & multi .30 .20
983 A215 25q red & multi .40 .20
984 A215 65q multicolored 1.10 .20
985 A215 95q blue & multi 1.50 .40
Nos. 982-985 (4) 3.30 1.00

25th anniv. of the founding of the Albanian Workers Party.

Russian Wolfhound — A216

Dogs: 15q, Sheep dog. 25q, English setter. 45q, English springer spaniel. 60q, Bulldog. 65q, Saint Bernard. 80q, Dachshund.

1966 Litho. ***Perf. 12½x12***

986 A216 10q green & multi .20 .20
987 A216 15q multicolored .30 .20
988 A216 25q lilac & multi .40 .20
989 A216 45q rose & multi .75 .35
990 A216 60q brown & multi 1.00 .40
991 A216 65q ultra & multi 1.10 .45
992 A216 80q blue grn & multi 1.50 .50
Nos. 986-992 (7) 5.25 2.30

Ndre Mjeda A217

Proclamation A218

1966 ***Perf. 12½x12***

993 A217 25q brt bl & dk brn .50 .20
994 A217 1.75 l brt grn & dk brn 2.00 .65

Birth Centenary of the priest Ndre Mjeda.

1966 ***Perf. 11½x12, 12x11½***

Designs: 10q, Banner, man and woman holding gun and axe, horiz. 1.85 l, man with axe and banner and partisan with gun.

995 A218 5q lt brn, red & blk .20 .20
996 A218 10q red, blk, gray & bl .20 .20
997 A218 1.85 l red, blk & salmon 1.50 .30
Nos. 995-997 (3) 1.90 .70

Albanian Communist Party, 25th anniv.

Golden Eagle — A219

Birds of Prey: 15q, European sea eagle. 25q, Griffon vulture. 40q, Common sparrowhawk. 50q, Osprey. 70q, Egyptian vulture. 90q, Kestrel.

1966, Dec. 20 Litho. ***Perf. 11½x12***

998 A219 10q gray & multi .20 .20
999 A219 15q multicolored .25 .20
1000 A219 25q citron & multi .45 .20
1001 A219 40q multicolored .80 .20
1002 A219 50q multicolored 1.00 .25
1003 A219 70q yellow & multi 1.40 .35
1004 A219 90q multicolored 1.90 .45
Nos. 998-1004 (7) 6.00 1.85

Hake A220

Fish: 15q, Red mullet. 25q, Opah. 40q, Atlantic wolf fish. 65q, Lumpfish. 80q, Swordfish. 1.15 l, Shorthorn sculpin.

1967, Jan. Photo. ***Perf. 12x11½***

Fish in Natural Colors

1005 A220 10q blue .20 .20
1006 A220 15q lt yellow grn .25 .20
1007 A220 25q Prus blue .35 .20
1008 A220 40q emerald .85 .20
1009 A220 65q brt blue grn .95 .25
1010 A220 80q blue 1.40 .35
1011 A220 1.15 l brt green 1.75 .60
Nos. 1005-1011 (7) 5.75 2.00

White Pelican A221

Designs: Various groups of pelicans.

1967, Feb. 22 Litho. ***Perf. 12***

1012 A221 10q pink & multi .20 .20
1013 A221 15q pink & multi .25 .20
1014 A221 25q pink & multi .55 .20

1015 A221 50q pink & multi 1.00 .20
1016 A221 2 l pink & multi 3.75 .75
Nos. 1012-1016 (5) 5.75 1.55

Camellia A222

Flowers: 10q, Chrysanthemum. 15q, Hollyhock. 25q, Flowering Maple. 35q, Peony. 65q, Gladiolus. 80q, Freesia. 1.15 l, Carnation.

Unwmk.

1967, Apr. 12 Litho. *Perf. 12*

Flowers in Natural Colors

1017 A222 5q pale brown .20 .20
1018 A222 10q lt lilac .20 .20
1019 A222 15q gray .25 .20
1020 A222 25q ultra .40 .20
1021 A222 35q lt blue .70 .20
1022 A222 65q lt blue grn 1.00 .20
1023 A222 80q lt bluish gray 1.50 .25
1024 A222 1.15 l dull yellow 2.00 .40
Nos. 1017-1024 (8) 6.25 1.85

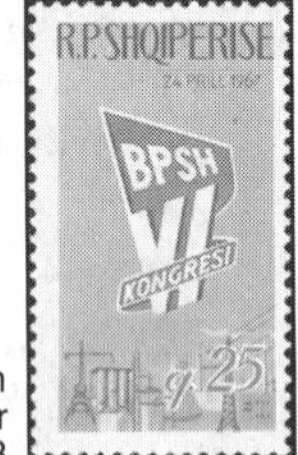

Congress Emblem and Power Station — A223

1967, Apr. 24 Litho. *Perf. 12*

1025 A223 25q multi .25 .20
1026 A223 1.75 l multi 2.25 .55

Cong. of the Union of Professional Workers, Tirana, Apr. 24.

Rose — A224

1967, May 15 *Perf. 12x12½*

Various Roses in Natural Colors.

1027 A224 5q blue gray .20 .20
1028 A224 10q brt blue .20 .20
1029 A224 15q rose violet .20 .20
1030 A224 25q lemon .35 .20
1031 A224 35q brt grnsh blue .45 .20
1032 A224 65q gray .85 .20
1033 A224 80q brown 1.10 .25
1034 A224 1.65 l gray green 2.50 .45
Nos. 1027-1034 (8) 5.85 1.90

Seashore, Bregdet Borsh — A225

Views: 15q, Buthrotum, vert. 25q, Shore, Fshati Piqeras. 45q, Shore, Bregdet. 50q, Shore, Bregdet Himare. 65q, Ship, Sarande (Santi Quaranta). 80q, Shore, Dhermi. 1 l, Sunset, Bregdet, vert.

Perf. 12x12½, 12½x12

1967, June 10

1035 A225 15q multicolored .20 .20
1036 A225 20q multicolored .25 .20
1037 A225 25q multicolored .30 .20
1038 A225 45q multicolored .80 .20
1039 A225 50q multicolored .90 .20
1040 A225 65q multicolored 1.25 .20
1041 A225 80q multicolored 1.40 .25
1042 A225 1 l multicolored 1.90 .35
Nos. 1035-1042 (8) 7.00 1.80

Fawn A226

Roe Deer: 20q, Stag, vert. 25q, Doe, vert. 30q, Young stag and doe. 35q, Doe and fawn. 40q, Young stag, vert. 65q, Stag and doe, vert. 70q, Running stag and does.

Perf. 12½x12, 12x12½

1967, July 20 Litho.

1043 A226 15q multicolored .35 .20
1044 A226 20q multicolored .35 .20
1045 A226 25q multicolored .55 .20
1046 A226 30q multicolored .65 .20
1047 A226 35q multicolored .80 .20
1048 A226 40q multicolored 1.10 .20
1049 A226 65q multicolored 1.60 .30
1050 A226 70q multicolored 1.60 .50
Nos. 1043-1050 (8) 7.00 2.00

Man and Woman from Madhe A227

Regional Costumes: 20q, Woman from Zadrimes. 25q, Dancer and drummer, Kukesit. 45q, Woman spinner, Dardhes. 50q, Farm couple, Myseqese. 65q, Dancer with tambourine, Tirana. 80q, Man and woman, Dropullit. 1 l, Piper, Laberise.

1967, Aug. 25 *Perf. 12*

1051 A227 15q tan & multi .20 .20
1052 A227 20q lt yellow grn .20 .20
1053 A227 25q multicolored .20 .20
1054 A227 45q sky blue & multi .35 .20
1055 A227 50q lemon & multi .55 .25
1056 A227 65q pink & multi .60 .35
1057 A227 80q multicolored .80 .40
1058 A227 1 l gray & multi 1.10 .55
Nos. 1051-1058 (8) 4.00 2.35

Fighters and Newspaper — A228

75q, Printing plant, newspapers, microphone. 2 l, People holding newspaper.

1967, Aug. 25 *Perf. 12½x12*

1059 A228 25q multicolored .40 .20
1060 A228 75q pink & multi .85 .25
1061 A228 2 l multicolored 2.25 .55
Nos. 1059-1061 (3) 3.50 1.00

Issued for the Day of the Press.

Street Scene, by Kolé Idromeno — A229

Hakmarrja Battalion, by Sali Shijaku — A230

Designs: 20q, David, fresco by Onufri, 16th century, vert. 45q, Woman's head, ancient mosaic, vert. 50q, Men on horseback from 16th century icon, vert. 65q, Farm Women, by Zef Shoshi. 80q, Street Scene, by Vangjush Mio. 1 l, Bride, by Kolé Idromeno, vert.

Perf. 12, 12x12½, (A230)

1967, Oct. 25 Litho.

1062 A229 15q multicolored .20 .20
1063 A229 20q multicolored .25 .20
1064 A230 25q multicolored .35 .20
1065 A229 45q multicolored .75 .20
1066 A229 50q multicolored .95 .20
1067 A230 65q multicolored 1.10 .20
1068 A230 80q multicolored 1.50 .25
1069 A230 1 l multicolored 2.40 .30
Nos. 1062-1069 (8) 7.50 1.75

Lenin at Storming of Winter Palace — A231

Rabbit — A232

Designs: 15q, Lenin and Stalin, horiz. 50q, Lenin and Stalin addressing meeting. 1.10 l, Storming of the Winter Palace, horiz.

1967, Nov. 7 *Perf. 12*

1070 A231 15q red & multi .25 .20
1071 A231 25q slate grn & blk .55 .20
1072 A231 50q brn, blk & brn vio .85 .20
1073 A231 1.10 l lilac, gray & blk 2.75 .25
Nos. 1070-1073 (4) 4.40 .85

50th anniv. of the Russian October Revolution.

1967, Nov. 25

Designs: Various hares and rabbits. The 15q, 25q, 35q, 40q and 1 l are horizontal.

1074 A232 15q orange & multi .20 .20
1075 A232 20q brt yel & multi .20 .20
1076 A232 25q lt brn & multi .25 .20
1077 A232 35q multicolored .35 .20
1078 A232 40q yellow & multi .65 .20
1079 A232 50q pink & multi .75 .20
1080 A232 65q multicolored 1.25 .30
1081 A232 1 l lilac & multi 2.00 .50
Nos. 1074-1081 (8) 5.65 2.00

University, Torch and Book — A233

1967 Litho. *Perf. 12*

1082 A233 25q multi .25 .20
1083 A233 1.75 l multi 1.50 .35

10th anniv. of the founding of the State University, Tirana.

Coat of Arms and Soldiers A234

65q, Arms, Factory, grain, flag, gun, radio tower. 1.20 l, Arms, hand holding torch.

1967 *Perf. 12x11½*

1084 A234 15q multi .20 .20
1085 A234 65q multi .55 .20
1086 A234 1.20 l multi 1.00 .20
Nos. 1084-1086 (3) 1.75 .60

25th anniversary of the Democratic Front.

Turkey A235

Designs: 20q, Duck. 25q, Hen. 45q, Rooster. 50q, Guinea fowl. 65q, Goose, horiz. 80q, Mallard, horiz. 1 l, Chicks, horiz.

Perf. 12x12½, 12½x12

1967, Nov. 25 Photo.

1087 A235 15q gold & multi .25 .20
1088 A235 20q gold & multi .25 .20
1089 A235 25q gold & multi .30 .20
1090 A235 45q gold & multi .50 .20
1091 A235 50q gold & multi .75 .20
1092 A235 65q gold & multi .95 .20
1093 A235 80q gold & multi 1.75 .30
1094 A235 1 l gold & multi 2.25 .40
Nos. 1087-1094 (8) 7.00 1.90

Skanderbeg A236

Designs: 10q, Arms of Skanderbeg. 25q, Helmet and sword. 30q, Kruje Castle. 35q, Petreles Castle. 65q, Berati Castle. 80q, Skanderbeg addressing national chiefs. 90q, Battle of Albulenes.

1967, Dec. 10 Litho. *Perf. 12x12½*

Medallion in Bister and Dark Brown

1095 A236 10q gold & violet .20 .20
1096 A236 15q gold & rose car .20 .20
1097 A236 25q gold & vio bl .20 .20
1098 A236 30q gold & dk blue .25 .20
1099 A236 35q gold & maroon .35 .20
1100 A236 65q gold & green .60 .20
1101 A236 80q gold & gray brn .95 .25
1102 A236 90q gold & ultra 1.75 .30
Nos. 1095-1102 (8) 4.50 1.75

500th anniv. of the death of Skanderbeg (George Castriota), national hero.

10th Winter Olympic Games, Grenoble, France, Feb. 6-18 — A237

Designs: 15q, 2 l, Winter Olympics emblem. 25q, Ice hockey. 30q, Women's figure skating. 50q, Slalom. 80q, Downhill skiing. 1 l, Ski jump.

1967-68

1103 A237 15q multicolored .20 .20
1104 A237 25q multicolored .20 .20
1105 A237 30q multicolored .20 .20
1106 A237 50q multicolored .30 .20
1107 A237 80q multicolored .60 .20
1108 A237 1 l multicolored 1.25 .25
Nos. 1103-1108 (6) 2.75 1.25

Miniature Sheet

Imperf

1109	A237	2 l red, gray & brt bl ('68)	6.00	6.00

Nos. 1103-1108 issued Dec. 29, 1967.

Skanderbeg Monument, Kruje — A238

Designs: 10q, Skanderbeg monument, Tirana. 15q, Skanderbeg portrait, Uffizi Galleries, Florence. 25q, engraved portrait of Gen. Tanush Topia. 35q, Portrait of Gen. Gjergj Arianti, horiz. 65q, Portrait bust of Skanderbeg by O. Paskali. 80q, Title page of "The Life of Skanderbeg." 90q, Skanderbeg battling the Turks, painting by S. Rrota, horiz.

Perf. 12x12½, 12½x12

1968, Jan. 17 **Litho.**

1110	A238	10q multicolored	.20	.20
1111	A238	15q multicolored	.25	.20
1112	A238	25q blk, yel & lt bl	.35	.20
1113	A238	30q multicolored	.40	.20
1114	A238	35q lt vio, pink & blk	.65	.20
1115	A238	65q multicolored	1.00	.25
1116	A238	80q pink, blk & yel	1.25	.45
1117	A238	90q beige & multi	1.75	.60
		Nos. 1110-1117 (8)	5.85	2.30

500th anniv. of the death of Skanderbeg (George Castriota), national hero.

Carnation A239

1968, Feb. 15 ***Perf. 12***

Various Carnations in Natural Colors

1118	A239	15q green	.20	.20
1119	A239	20q dk brown	.20	.20
1120	A239	25q brt blue	.20	.20
1121	A239	50q gray olice	.75	.20
1122	A239	80q bluish gray	1.10	.20
1123	A239	1.10 l violet gray	1.50	.40
		Nos. 1118-1123 (6)	3.95	1.40

"Electrification" A240

65q, Farm tractor, horiz. 1.10 l, Cow & herd.

1968, Mar. 5 **Litho.** ***Perf. 12***

1124	A240	25q multi	.25	.20
1125	A240	65q multi	.75	.25
1126	A240	1.10 l multi	1.00	.35
		Nos. 1124-1126 (3)	2.00	.80

Fifth Farm Cooperatives Congress.

Goat A241

Various goats. 15q, 20q, 25q are vertical.

1968, Mar. 25 ***Perf. 12x12½, 12½x12***

1127	A241	15q multi	.20	.20
1128	A241	20q multi	.20	.20
1129	A241	25q multi	.20	.20
1130	A241	30q multi	.30	.20
1131	A241	40q multi	.40	.20
1132	A241	50q multi	.45	.20
1133	A241	80q multi	.80	.20
1134	A241	1.40 l multi	2.00	.35
		Nos. 1127-1134 (8)	4.55	1.75

Zef N. Jubani — A242

Physician and Hospital — A243

1968, Mar. 30 ***Perf. 12***

1135	A242	25q yellow & choc	.25	.20
1136	A242	1.75 l lt violet & blk	1.25	.50

Sesquicentennial of the birth of Zef N. Jubani, writer and scholar.

Perf. 12½x12, 12x12½

1968, Apr. 7 **Litho.**

Designs (World Health Organization Emblem and): 65q, Hospital and microscope, horiz. 1.10 l, Mother feeding child.

1137	A243	25q green & claret	.20	.20
1138	A243	65q black, yel & bl	.55	.25
1139	A243	1.10 l black & dp org	1.00	.35
		Nos. 1137-1139 (3)	1.75	.80

20th anniv. of WHO.

Scientist A244

Women: 15q, Militia member. 60q, Farm worker. 1 l, Factory worker.

1968, Apr. 14 ***Perf. 12***

1140	A244	15q ver & dk red	.35	.20
1141	A244	25q blue grn & grn	.50	.20
1142	A244	60q dull yel & brn	.80	.20
1143	A244	1 l lt vio & vio	2.00	.40
		Nos. 1140-1143 (4)	3.65	1.00

Albanian Women's Organization, 25th anniv.

Karl Marx A245

Designs: 25q, Marx lecturing to students. 65q, "Das Kapital," "Communist Manifesto" and marching crowd. 95q, Full-face portrait.

1968, May 5 **Litho.** ***Perf. 12***

1144	A245	15q gray, dk bl & bis	.25	.20
1145	A245	25q brn vio, dk brn & dl yel	.50	.20
1146	A245	65q gray, blk, brn & car	1.25	.20
1147	A245	95q gray, ocher & blk	2.25	.50
		Nos. 1144-1147 (4)	4.25	1.10

Karl Marx, 150th birth anniversary.

Heliopsis A246

Flowers: 20q, Red flax. 25q, Orchid. 30q, Gloxinia. 40q, Turk's-cap lily. 80q, Amaryllis. 1.40 l, Red magnolia.

1968, May 10 ***Perf. 12x12½***

1148	A246	15q gold & multi	.20	.20
1149	A246	20q gold & multi	.20	.20
1150	A246	25q gold & multi	.30	.20
1151	A246	30q gold & multi	.35	.20
1152	A246	40q gold & multi	.35	.20
1153	A246	80q gold & multi	1.00	.40
1154	A246	1.40 l gold & multi	1.60	.60
		Nos. 1148-1154 (7)	4.00	2.00

Proclamation of Prizren — A247

25q, Abdyl Frasheri. 40q, House in Prizren.

1968, June 10 **Litho.** ***Perf. 12***

1155	A247	25q emerald & blk	.20	.20
1156	A247	40q multicolored	.45	.20
1157	A247	85q yellow & multi	.85	.25
		Nos. 1155-1157 (3)	1.50	.65

League of Prizren against the Turks, 90th anniv.

Shepherd, by A. Kushi — A248

Paintings from Tirana Art Gallery: 20q, View of Tirana, by V. Mio, horiz. 25q, Mountaineer, by G. Madhi. 40q, Refugees, by A. Buza. 80q, Guerrillas of Shahin Matrakut, by S. Xega. 1.50 l, Portrait of an Old Man, by S. Papadhimitri. 1.70 l, View of Scutari, by S. Rrota. 2.50 l, Woman in Scutari Costume, by Z. Colombi.

1968, June 20 ***Perf. 12x12½***

1158	A248	15q gold & multi	.20	.20
1159	A248	20q gold & multi	.20	.20
1160	A248	25q gold & multi	.25	.20
1161	A248	40q gold & multi	.45	.20
1162	A248	80q gold & multi	.75	.20
1163	A248	1.50 l gold & multi	1.25	.25
1164	A248	1.70 l gold & multi	1.50	.50
		Nos. 1158-1164 (7)	4.60	1.75

Miniature Sheet

Perf. 12½xImperf.

1165	A248	2.50 l multi	2.00	2.00

No. 1165 contains one stamp, size: 50x71mm.

Soldier and Guns — A249

25q, Sailor, warships. 65q, Aviator, planes, vert. 95q, Militiamen, woman.

1968, July 10 **Litho.** ***Perf. 12***

1166	A249	15q multicolored	.30	.20
1167	A249	25q multicolored	.45	.20
1168	A249	65q multicolored	1.25	.20
1169	A249	95q multicolored	2.50	.20
		Nos. 1166-1169 (4)	4.50	.80

25th anniversary of the People's Army.

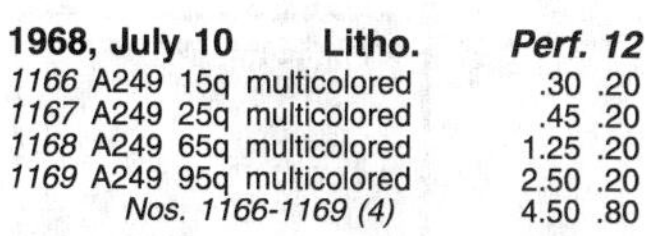

Squid A250

Designs: 20q, Crayfish. 25q, Whelk. 50q, Crab. 70q, Spiny lobster. 80q, Shore crab. 90q, Norway lobster.

1968, Aug. 20

1170	A250	15q multicolored	.20	.20
1171	A250	20q multicolored	.20	.20
1172	A250	25q multicolored	.25	.20
1173	A250	50q multicolored	.45	.20
1174	A250	70q multicolored	.75	.25
1175	A250	80q multicolored	.90	.30
1176	A250	90q multicolored	1.25	.35
		Nos. 1170-1176 (7)	4.00	1.70

Women's Relay Race — A251

Sport: 20q, Running. 25q, Women's discus. 30q, Equestrian. 40q, High jump. 50q, Women's hurdling. 80q, Soccer. 1.40 l, Woman diver. 2 l, Olympic stadium.

1968, Sept. 23 **Photo.** ***Perf. 12***

1177	A251	15q multicolored	.20	.20
1178	A251	20q multicolored	.20	.20
1179	A251	25q multicolored	.20	.20
1180	A251	30q multicolored	.20	.20
1181	A251	40q multicolored	.25	.20
1182	A251	50q multicolored	.35	.20
1183	A251	80q multicolored	.60	.20
1184	A251	1.40 l multicolored	1.00	.35
		Nos. 1177-1184 (8)	3.00	1.75

Souvenir Sheet

Perf. 12½ Horizontally

1185	A251	2 l multicolored	2.25	2.00

19th Olympic Games, Mexico City, Oct. 12-27. No. 1185 contains one rectangular stamp, size: 64x54mm. Value of imperfs., #1177-1184 $7, #1185 $5.

Enver Hoxha — A252

1968, Oct. 16 **Litho.** ***Perf. 12***

1186	A252	25q blue gray	.35	.20
1187	A252	35q rose brown	.50	.20
1188	A252	80q violet	.90	.35
1189	A252	1.10 l brown	1.10	.50
		Nos. 1186-1189 (4)	2.85	1.25

Souvenir Sheet

Imperf

1190	A252	1.50 l rose red, bl vio & gold	*55.00*	*40.00*

60th birthday of Enver Hoxha, First Secretary of the Central Committee of the Communist Party of Albania.

Book and Pupils A253

1968, Nov. 14 **Photo.**
1191 A253 15q mar & slate grn .45 .20
1192 A253 85q gray olive & sepia 2.75 .20

60th anniv. of the Congress of Monastir, Nov. 14-22, 1908, which adopted a unified Albanian alphabet.

Waxwing — A254

Birds: 20q, Rose-colored starling. 25q, Kingfishers. 50q, Long-tailed tits. 80q, Wallcreeper. 1.10 l, Bearded tit.

1968, Nov. 15 **Litho.**
Birds in Natural Colors
1193 A254 15q lt blue & blk .20 .20
1194 A254 20q bister & blk .30 .20
1195 A254 25q pink & blk .30 .20
1196 A254 50q lt yel grn & blk .60 .20
1197 A254 80q bis brn & blk 1.25 .30
1198 A254 1.10 l pale grn & blk 1.75 .50
Nos. 1193-1198 (6) 4.40 1.60

Mao Tse-tung — A255

1968, Dec. 26 **Litho.** ***Perf. 12½x12***
1199 A255 25q gold, red & blk .40 .20
1200 A255 1.75 l gold, red & blk 2.00 .30

75th birthday of Mao Tse-tung.

Adem Reka and Crane — A256

Portraits: 10q, Pjeter Lleshi and power lines. 15q, Mohammed Shehu and Myrteza Kepi. 25q, Shkurte Vata and women railroad workers. 65q, Agron Elezi, frontier guard. 80q, Ismet Bruçaj and mountain road. 1.30 l, Fuat Cela, blind revolutionary.

1969, Feb. 10 **Litho.** ***Perf. 12x12½***
1201 A256 5q multicolored .20 .20
1202 A256 10q multicolored .20 .20
1203 A256 15q multicolored .20 .20
1204 A256 25q multicolored .20 .20
1205 A256 65q multicolored .40 .20
1206 A256 80q multicolored .75 .20
1207 A256 1.30 l multicolored 1.25 .20
Nos. 1201-1207 (7) 3.20 1.40

Contemporary heroine and heroes.

Meteorological Instruments — A257

Designs: 25q, Water gauge. 1.60 l, Radar, balloon and isobars.

1969, Feb. 25 ***Perf. 12***
1208 A257 15q multicolored .25 .20
1209 A257 25q ultra, org & blk .45 .20
1210 A257 1.60 l rose vio, yel & blk 2.50 .60
Nos. 1208-1210 (3) 3.20 1.00

20th anniv. of Albanian hydrometeorology.

Partisans, 1944, by F. Haxmiu — A258

Paintings: 5q, Student Revolutionists, by P. Mele, vert. 65q, Steel Mill, by C. Ceka. 80q, Reconstruction, by V. Kilica. 1.10 l, Harvest, by N. Jonuzi. 1.15 l, Terraced Landscape, by S. Kaceli. 2 l, Partisans' Meeting.

Perf. 12x12½, 12½x12
1969, Apr. 25 **Litho.**
Size: 31½x41½mm
1211 A258 5q buff & multi .20 .20
Size: 51½x30½mm
1212 A258 25q buff & multi .20 .20
Size: 40½x32mm
1213 A258 65q buff & multi .30 .20
Size: 51½x30½mm
1214 A258 80q buff & multi .65 .20
1215 A258 1.10 l buff & multi .70 .20
1216 A258 1.15 l buff & multi .95 .20
Nos. 1211-1216 (6) 3.00 1.20

Miniature Sheet
Imperf
Size: 111x90mm
1217 A258 2 l ocher & multi 2.25 1.75

Leonardo da Vinci, Self-portrait A259

Designs (after Leonardo da Vinci): 35q, Lilies. 40q, Design for a flying machine, horiz. 1 l, Portrait of Beatrice. No. 1222, Portrait of a Noblewoman. No. 1223, Mona Lisa.

Perf. 12x12½, 12½x12
1969, May 2 **Litho.**
1218 A259 25q gold & sepia .20 .20
1219 A259 35q gold & sepia .40 .20
1220 A259 40q gold & sepia .45 .20
1221 A259 1 l gold & multi 1.25 .20
1222 A259 2 l gold & sepia 2.25 .55
Nos. 1218-1222 (5) 4.55 1.35

Miniature Sheet
Imperf
1223 A259 2 l gold & multi 3.25 2.25

Leonardo da Vinci (1452-1519), painter, sculptor, architect and engineer.

First Congress Meeting Place A260

Designs: 1 l, Albanian coat of arms. 2.25 l, Two partisans with guns and flag.

1969, May 24 ***Perf. 12***
1224 A260 25q lt grn, blk & red .35 .20
1225 A260 2.25 l multi 2.50 .85

Souvenir Sheet
1226 A260 1 l gold, bl, blk & red *25.00 20.00*

25th anniversary of the First Anti-Fascist Congress of Permet, May 24, 1944.

Albanian Violet — A261

Designs: Violets and Pansies.

1969, June 30 **Litho.** ***Perf. 12x12½***
1227 A261 5q gold & multi .20 .20
1228 A261 10q gold & multi .20 .20
1229 A261 15q gold & multi .30 .20
1230 A261 20q gold & multi .35 .20
1231 A261 25q gold & multi .35 .20
1232 A261 80q gold & multi 1.00 .35
1233 A261 1.95 l gold & multi 1.60 .65
Nos. 1227-1233 (7) 4.00 2.00

Plum, Fruit and Blossoms A262

Designs: Blossoms and Fruits.

1969, Aug. 10 **Litho.** ***Perf. 12***
1234 A262 10q shown .20 .20
1235 A262 15q Lemon .20 .20
1236 A262 25q Pomegranate .30 .20
1237 A262 50q Cherry .60 .20
1238 A262 80q Peach .95 .20
1239 A262 1.20 l Apple 1.75 .35
Nos. 1234-1239 (6) 4.00 1.35

Basketball A263

Designs: 10q, 80q, 2.20 l, Various views of basketball game. 25q, Hand aiming ball at basket and map of Europe, horiz.

1969, Sept. 15 **Litho.** ***Perf. 12***
1240 A263 10q multi .20 .20
1241 A263 15q buff & multi .20 .20
1242 A263 25q blue & multi .25 .20
1243 A263 80q multi .65 .20
1244 A263 2.20 l multi 1.60 .50
Nos. 1240-1244 (5) 2.90 1.30

16th European Basketball Championships, Naples, Italy, Sept. 27-Oct. 5.

Runner A264

Designs: 5q, Games' emblem. 10q, Woman gymnast. 20q, Pistol shooting. 25q, Swimmer at start. 80q, Bicyclist. 95q, Soccer.

1969, Sept. 30
1245 A264 5q multicolored .20 .20
1246 A264 10q multicolored .20 .20
1247 A264 15q multicolored .20 .20
1248 A264 20q multicolored .30 .20
1249 A264 25q multicolored .40 .20
1250 A264 80q multicolored .80 .20
1251 A264 95q multicolored 1.25 .20
Nos. 1245-1251 (7) 3.35 1.40

Second National Spartakiad.

Electronic Technicians, Steel Ladle — A265

25q, Mao Tse-tung with microphones. 1.40 l, Children holding Mao's red book.

1969, Oct. 1 **Litho.** ***Perf. 12***
1252 A265 25q multi, vert. .35 .20
1253 A265 85q multi 1.40 .40
1254 A265 1.40 l multi, vert. 2.25 .60
Nos. 1252-1254 (3) 4.00 1.20

People's Republic of China, 20th anniv.

Enver Hoxha A266

Designs: 80q, Pages from Berat resolution. 1.45 l, Partisans with flag.

1969, Oct. 20 **Litho.** ***Perf. 12***
1255 A266 25q multicolored .30 .20
1256 A266 80q gray & multi .60 .20
1257 A266 1.45 l ocher & multi 1.90 .40
Nos. 1255-1257 (3) 2.80 .80

25th anniv. of the 2nd reunion of the Natl. Antifascist Liberation Council, Berat.

Soldiers — A267

Designs: 30q, Oil refinery. 35q, Combine harvester. 45q, Hydroelectric station and dam. 55q, Militia woman, man and soldier. 1.10 l, Dancers and musicians.

1969, Nov. 29

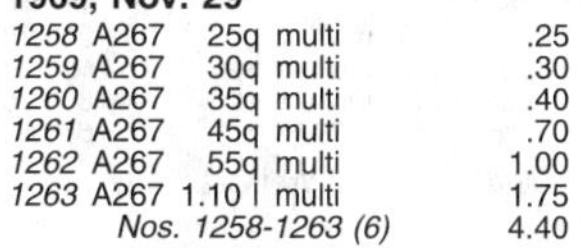

1258	A267	25q multi	.25	.20
1259	A267	30q multi	.30	.20
1260	A267	35q multi	.40	.20
1261	A267	45q multi	.70	.20
1262	A267	55q multi	1.00	.25
1263	A267	1.10 l multi	1.75	.40
		Nos. 1258-1263 (6)	4.40	1.45

25th anniv. of the socialist republic.

Joseph V. Stalin, (1879-1953), Russian Political Leader — A268

1969, Dec. 21 Litho. *Perf. 12*

1264	A268	15q lilac	.20	.20
1265	A268	25q slate blue	.20	.20
1266	A268	1 l brown	.75	.20
1267	A268	1.10 l violet blue	1.25	.20
		Nos. 1264-1267 (4)	2.40	.80

Head of Woman A269

Greco-Roman Mosaics: 25q, Geometrical floor design, horiz. 80q, Bird and tree, horiz. 1.10 l, Floor with birds and grapes, horiz. 1.20 l, Fragment with corn within oval design.

1969, Dec. 25 *Perf. 12½x12*

1268	A269	15q gold & multi	.20	.20
1269	A269	25q gold & multi	.20	.20
1270	A269	80q gold & multi	.45	.20
1271	A269	1.10 l gold & multi	.70	.20
1272	A269	1.20 l gold & multi	.95	.30
		Nos. 1268-1272 (5)	2.50	1.10

Cancellation of 1920 — A270

25q, Proclamation and congress site.

1970, Jan. 21 Litho. *Perf. 12*

1273	A270	25q red, gray & blk	.20	.20
1274	A270	1.25 l dk grn, yel & blk	1.25	.20

Congress of Louchnia, 50th anniversary.

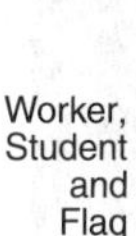

Worker, Student and Flag A271

1970, Feb. 11 *Perf. 12½x12*

1275	A271	25q red & multi	.25	.25
1276	A271	1.75 l red & multi	1.75	.50

Vocational organizations in Albania, 25th anniv.

Turk's-cap Lily — A272

Lilies: 5q, Cernum, vert. 15q, Madonna, vert. 25q, Royal, vert. 1.10 l, Tiger. 1.15 l, Albanian.

Perf. 11½x12, 12x11½

1970, Mar. 10 Litho.

1277	A272	5q multi	.20	.20
1278	A272	15q multi	.20	.20
1279	A272	25q multi	.35	.20
1280	A272	80q multi	.75	.20
1281	A272	1.10 l multi	1.10	.20
1282	A272	1.15 l multi	1.40	.25
		Nos. 1277-1282 (6)	4.00	1.25

Lenin A273

Designs (Lenin): 5q, Portrait, vert. 25q, As volunteer construction worker. 95q, Addressing crowd. 1.10 l, Saluting, vert.

1970, Apr. 22 Litho. *Perf. 12*

1283	A273	5q multi	.20	.20
1284	A273	15q multi	.20	.20
1285	A273	25q multi	.20	.20
1286	A273	95q multi	.60	.20
1287	A273	1.10 l multi	1.10	.20
		Nos. 1283-1287 (5)	2.30	1.00

Centenary of birth of Lenin (1870-1924).

Frontier Guard A274

1970, Apr. 25

1288	A274	25q multi	.25	.20
1289	A274	1.25 l multi	2.50	.50

25th anniversary of Frontier Guards.

Soccer Players — A275

Designs: 5q, Jules Rimet Cup and globes. 10q, Aztec Stadium, Mexico City. 25q, Defending goal. 65q, 80q, No. 1296, Two soccer players in various plays. No. 1297, Mexican horseman and volcano Popocatepetl.

1970, May 15 Litho. *Perf. 12½x12*

1290	A275	5q multicolored	.20	.20
1291	A275	10q multicolored	.20	.20
1292	A275	15q multicolored	.20	.20
1293	A275	25q lt green & multi	.20	.20
1294	A275	65q pink & multi	.30	.20
1295	A275	80q lt blue & multi	.55	.20
1296	A275	2 l yellow & multi	1.50	.25
		Nos. 1290-1296 (7)	3.15	1.45

Souvenir Sheet

Perf 12 x Imperf

1297	A275	2 l multicolored	2.25	1.75

World Soccer Championships for the Jules Rimet Cup, Mexico City, May 31-June 21, 1970. No. 1297 contains one large horizontal stamp. Nos. 1290-1297 exist imperf.

UPU Headquarters and Monument, Bern — A276

1970, May 30 Litho. *Perf. 12½x12*

1298	A276	25q ultra, gray & blk	.20	.20
1299	A276	1.10 l org, buff & blk	.65	.20
1300	A276	1.15 l grn, gray & blk	.90	.25
		Nos. 1298-1300 (3)	1.75	.65

Inauguration of the new UPU Headquarters in Bern.

Bird and Grapes Mosaic A277

Mosaics, 5th-6th centuries, excavated near Pogradec: 10q, Waterfowl and grapes. 20q, Bird and tree stump. 25q, Bird and leaves. 65q, Fish. 2.25 l, Peacock, vert.

1970, July 10 *Perf. 12½x12, 12x12½*

1301	A277	5q multi	.20	.20
1302	A277	10q multi	.20	.20
1303	A277	20q multi	.20	.20
1304	A277	25q multi	.30	.20
1305	A277	65q multi	.55	.20
1306	A277	2.25 l multi	1.75	.35
		Nos. 1301-1306 (6)	3.20	1.35

Fruit Harvest and Dancers A278

Designs: 25q, Contour-plowed fields and conference table. 80q, Cattle and newspapers. 1.30 l, Wheat harvest.

1970, Aug. 28 Litho. *Perf. 12x11½*

1307	A278	15q brt violet & blk	.20	.20
1308	A278	25q dp blue & blk	.20	.20
1309	A278	80q dp brown & blk	.60	.20
1310	A278	1.30 l org brn & blk	.90	.20
		Nos. 1307-1310 (4)	1.90	.80

25th anniv. of the agrarian reform law.

Attacking Partisans — A279

Designs: 25q, Partisans with horses and flag. 1.60 l, Partisans.

1970, Sept. 3 *Perf. 12*

1311	A279	15q org brn & blk	.20	.20
1312	A279	25q brn, yel & blk	.20	.20
1313	A279	1.60 l dp grn & blk	1.25	.30
		Nos. 1311-1313 (3)	1.65	.70

50th anniversary of liberation of Vlona.

Miners, by Nexhmedin Zajmi — A280

Paintings from the National Gallery, Tirana: 5q, Bringing in the Harvest, by Isuf Sulovari, vert. 15q, The Activists, by Dhimitraq Trebicka, vert. 65q, Instruction of Partisans, by Hasan Nallbani. 95q, Architectural Planning, by Vilson Kilica. No. 1319, Woman Machinist, by Zef Shoshi, vert. No. 1320, Partisan Destroying Tank, by Sali Shijaku, vert.

Perf. 12½x12, 12x12½

1970, Sept. 25 Litho.

1314	A280	5q multicolored	.20	.20
1315	A280	15q multicolored	.20	.20
1316	A280	25q multicolored	.20	.20
1317	A280	65q multicolored	.25	.20
1318	A280	95q multicolored	.40	.20
1319	A280	2 l multicolored	1.75	.30
		Nos. 1314-1319 (6)	3.00	1.30

Miniature Sheet

Imperf

1320	A280	2 l multicolored	2.00	1.25

Electrification Map of Albania — A281

Designs: 25q, Light bulb, hammer and sickle emblem, map of Albania and power graph. 80q, Linemen at work. 1.10 l, Use of electricity on the farm, in home and business.

1970, Oct. 25 Litho. *Perf. 12*

1321	A281	15q multi	.20	.20
1322	A281	25q multi	.20	.20
1323	A281	80q multi	.70	.20
1324	A281	1.10 l multi	1.00	.20
		Nos. 1321-1324 (4)	2.10	.80

Albanian village electrification completion.

Friedrich Engels A282

Designs: 1.10 l, Engels as young man. 1.15 l, Engels addressing crowd.

1970, Nov. 28 Litho. *Perf. 12x12½*

1325	A282	25q bister & dk bl	.20	.20
1326	A282	1.10 l bis & dp claret	.60	.20
1327	A282	1.15 l bis & dk ol grn	.70	.25
		Nos. 1325-1327 (3)	1.50	.65

150th anniv. of the birth of Friedrich Engels (1820-95), German socialist, collaborator with Karl Marx.

Factories—A282A

Designs: 10q, Tractor factory, Tirana. 15q, Fertilizer factory, Fier. 20q, Superphosphate factory, Lac. 25q, Cement factory, Elbasan. 80q, Coking plant, Qyteti Stalin.

1970-71 Litho. *Perf. 12*

1327A	A282A	10q multi	—	50.00
1327B	A282A	15q multi	—	50.00
1327C	A282A	20q multi	—	50.00
1327D	A282A	25q multi	—	50.00
1327E	A282A	80q multi	—	50.00
		Nos. 1327A-1327E (5)		250.00

Issue dates: 15q, 12/4/70. 10q, 20q, 25q, 80q, 1/20/71.

Ludwig van Beethoven A283

Designs: 5q, Birthplace, Bonn. 25q, 65q, 1.10 l, various portraits. 1.80 l, Scene from Fidelio, horiz.

1970, Dec. 16 Litho. *Perf. 12*

1328 A283 5q dp plum & gold .20 .20
1329 A283 15q brt rose lil & sil .20 .20
1330 A283 25q green & gold .20 .20
1331 A283 65q magenta & sil .30 .20
1332 A283 1.10 l dk blue & gold .60 .25
1333 A283 1.80 l black & sil 1.40 .45
Nos. 1328-1333 (6) 2.90 1.50

Ludwig van Beethoven (1770-1827), composer.

Coat of Arms A284

Designs: 25q, Proclamation. 80q, Enver Hoxha reading proclamation. 1.30 l, Young people and proclamation.

1971, Jan. 11 Litho. *Perf. 12*

1334 A284 15q lt bl, gold, blk & red .20 .20
1335 A284 25q rose lil, blk, gold & gray .20 .20
1336 A284 80q emerald, blk & gold .55 .20
1337 A284 1.30 l yel org, blk & gold .85 .25
Nos. 1334-1337 (4) 1.80 .85

Declaration of the Republic, 25th anniv.

"Liberty" A285 Black Men A286

Designs: 50q, Women's brigade. 65q, Street battle, horiz. 1.10 l, Execution, horiz.

Perf. 12x11½, 11½x12

1971, Mar. 18 Litho.

1338 A285 25q dk bl & bl .20 .20
1339 A285 50q slate green .35 .20
1340 A285 65q dk brn & chest .50 .20
1341 A285 1.10 l purple .75 .20
Nos. 1338-1341 (4) 1.80 .80

Centenary of the Paris Commune.

1971, Mar. 21 *Perf. 12x12½*

1.10 l, Men of 3 races. 1.15 l, Black protest.

1342 A286 25q blk & bis brn .20 .20
1343 A286 1.10 l blk & rose car .60 .20
1344 A286 1.15 l blk & ver .70 .20
Nos. 1342-1344 (3) 1.50 .60

Intl. year against racial discrimination.

Tulip — A287

Horseman, by Dürer — A288

Designs: Various tulips.

1971, Mar. 25

1345 A287 5q multi .20 .20
1346 A287 10q yellow & multi .20 .20
1347 A287 15q pink & multi .20 .20
1348 A287 20q lt blue & multi .20 .20
1349 A287 25q multi .25 .20
1350 A287 80q multi .50 .20
1351 A287 1 l multi .75 .20
1352 A287 1.45 l citron & multi 1.10 .25
Nos. 1345-1352 (8) 3.40 1.65

Perf. 11½x12, 12x11½

1971, May 15 Litho.

Art Works by Dürer: 15q, Three peasants. 25q, Dancing peasant couple. 45q, The bagpiper. 65q, View of Kalkrebut, horiz. 2.40 l, View of Trent, horiz. 2.50 l, Self-portrait.

1353 A288 10q blk & pale grn .20 .20
1354 A288 15q black & pale lil .20 .20
1355 A288 25q black & pale bl .25 .20
1356 A288 45q blk & pale rose .40 .20
1357 A288 65q black & multi .60 .20
1358 A288 2.40 l black & multi 2.25 .35
Nos. 1353-1358 (6) 3.90 1.35

Miniature Sheet

Imperf

1359 A288 2.50 l multi 3.00 1.75

Albrecht Dürer (1471-1528), German painter and engraver.

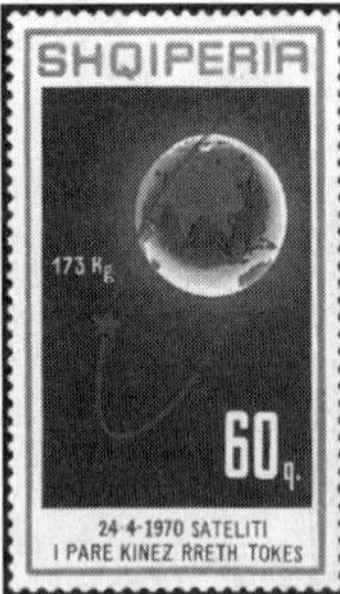

Satellite Orbiting Globe — A289

Designs: 1.20 l, Government Building, Tirana, and Red Star emblem. 2.20 l, like 60q, 2.50 l, Flag of People's Republic of China forming trajectory around globe.

1971, June 10 Litho. *Perf. 12x12½*

1360 A289 60q purple & multi .40 .20
1361 A289 1.20 l ver & multi 1.00 .25
1362 A289 2.20 l green & multi 1.60 .45

Imperf

1363 A289 2.50 l vio blk & multi 2.50 .90
Nos. 1360-1363 (4) 5.50 1.80

Space developments of People's Republic of China.

Mao Tse-tung A290

Designs: 1.05 l, House where Communist Party was founded, horiz. 1.20 l, Peking crowd with placards, horiz.

1971, July 1 *Perf. 12x12½, 12½x12*

1364 A290 25q silver & multi .30 .20
1365 A290 1.05 l silver & multi .95 .20
1366 A290 1.20 l silver & multi 1.25 .25
Nos. 1364-1366 (3) 2.50 .65

50th anniv. of Chinese Communist Party.

Crested Titmouse — A291

1971, Aug. 15 Litho. *Perf. 12½x12*

1367 A291 5q shown .20 .20
1368 A291 10q European serin .20 .20
1369 A291 15q Linnet .20 .20
1370 A291 25q Firecrest .45 .20
1371 A291 45q Rock thrush .70 .20
1372 A291 60q Blue tit 1.00 .50
1373 A291 2.40 l Chaffinch 4.25 2.50
a. Block of 7, #1367-1373 + label 10.00 5.00
Nos. 1367-1373 (7) 7.00 4.00

Continuous design with bird's nest label at upper left.

Olympic Rings and Running — A292

Designs (Olympic Rings and): 10q, Hurdles. 15q, Canoeing. 25q, Gymnastics. 80q, Fencing. 1.05 l, Soccer. 2 l, Runner at finish line. 3.60 l, Diving, women's.

1971, Sept. 15

1374 A292 5q green & multi .20 .20
1375 A292 10q multicolored .20 .20
1376 A292 15q blue & multi .20 .20
1377 A292 25q violet & multi .20 .20
1378 A292 80q lilac & multi .35 .20
1379 A292 1.05 l multicolored .45 .20
1380 A292 3.60 l multicolored 2.50 .50
Nos. 1374-1380 (7) 4.10 1.70

Souvenir Sheet

Imperf

1381 A292 2 l brt blue & multi 2.50 2.00

20th Olympic Games, Munich, Aug. 26-Sept. 10, 1972.

Workers with Flags A293

Designs: 1.05 l, Party Headquarters, Tirana, and Red Star. 1.20 l, Rifle, star, flag and "VI."

1971, Nov. 1 *Perf. 12*

1382 A293 25q multi .20 .20
1383 A293 1.05 l multi .65 .20
1384 A293 1.20 l multi, vert. .80 .25
Nos. 1382-1384 (3) 1.65 .65

6th Congress of Workers' Party.

Factories and Workers A294

Designs: 80q, "XXX" and flag, vert. 1.55 l, Enver Hoxha and flags.

1971, Nov. 8

1385 A294 15q gold, sil, lil & yel .20 .20
1386 A294 80q gold, sil & red .70 .20
1387 A294 1.55 l gold, sil, red & brn 1.40 .25
Nos. 1385-1387 (3) 2.30 .65

30th anniversary of Workers' Party.

Construction Work, by M. Fushekati — A295

Contemporary Albanian Paintings: 5q, Young Man, by R. Kuci, vert. 25q, Partisan, by D. Jukniu, vert. 80q, Fliers, by S. Kristo. 1.20 l, Girl in Forest, by A. Sadikaj. 1.55 l, Warriors with Spears and Shields, by S. Kamberi. 2 l, Freedom Fighter, by I. Lulani.

Perf. 12x12½, 12½x12

1971, Nov. 20

1388 A295 5q gold & multi .20 .20
1389 A295 15q gold & multi .20 .20
1390 A295 25q gold & multi .20 .20
1391 A295 80q gold & multi .40 .20
1392 A295 1.20 l gold & multi .90 .20
1393 A295 1.55 l gold & multi 1.10 .25
Nos. 1388-1393 (6) 3.00 1.25

Miniature Sheet

Imperf

1394 A295 2 l gold & multi 2.25 1.75

Young Workers' Emblem — A296

1971, Nov. 23 *Perf. 12x12½*

1395 A296 15q lt blue & multi .20 .20
1396 A296 1.35 l grnsh gray & multi 1.10 .25

Albanian Young Workers' Union, 30th anniv.

"Halili and Hajria" Ballet — A297

Scenes from "Halili and Hajria" Ballet: 10q, Brother and sister. 15q, Hajria before Sultan Suleiman. 50q, Hajria and husband. 80q, Execution of Halili. 1.40 l, Hajria killing her husband.

1971, Dec. 27 *Perf. 12½x12*

1397 A297 5q silver & multi .20 .20
1398 A297 10q silver & multi .20 .20
1399 A297 15q silver & multi .20 .20
1400 A297 50q silver & multi .45 .20

1401	A297	80q silver & multi	.70	.20
1402	A297	1.40 l silver & multi	1.10	.35
		Nos. 1397-1402 (6)	2.85	1.35

Albanian ballet Halili and Hajria after drama by Kol Jakova.

Biathlon and Olympic Rings — A298

Designs (Olympic Rings and): 10q, Sledding. 15q, Ice hockey. 20q, Bobsledding. 50q, Speed skating. 1 l, Slalom. 2 l, Ski jump. 2.50 l, Figure skating, pairs.

1972, Feb. 10

1403	A298	5q lt olive & multi	.20	.20
1404	A298	10q lt violet & multi	.20	.20
1405	A298	15q multicolored	.20	.20
1406	A298	20q pink & multi	.20	.20
1407	A298	50q lt blue & multi	.30	.20
1408	A298	1 l ocher & multi	.75	.20
1409	A298	2 l lilac & multi	1.50	.35
		Nos. 1403-1409 (7)	3.35	1.55

Souvenir Sheet

Imperf

1410	A298	2.50 l blue & multi	2.25	1.75

11th Winter Olympic Games, Sapporo, Japan, Feb. 3-13.

Wild Strawberries A299

Wild Fruits and Nuts: 10q, Blackberries. 15q, Hazelnuts. 20q, Walnuts. 25q, Strawberry-tree fruit. 30q, Dogwood berries. 2.40 l, Rowan berries.

1972, Mar. 20 Litho. *Perf. 12*

1411	A299	5q lt grn & multi	.20	.20
1412	A299	10q yellow & multi	.20	.20
1413	A299	15q lt vio & multi	.20	.20
1414	A299	20q pink & multi	.25	.20
1415	A299	25q multi	.25	.20
1416	A299	30q multi	.40	.20
1417	A299	2.40 l multi	2.50	.45
		Nos. 1411-1417 (7)	4.00	1.65

"Your Heart is your Health" A300

Worker and Student — A301

World Health Day: 1.20 l, Cardiac patient and electrocardiogram.

1972, Apr. 7 *Perf. 12x12½*

1418	A300	1.10 l multicolored	.75	.40
1419	A300	1.20 l rose & multi	3.00	1.25

1972, Apr. 24 Litho. *Perf. 11½x12½*

7th Trade Union Cong., May 8: 2.05 l, Assembly Hall, dancers and emblem.

1420	A301	25q multi	.25	.20
1421	A301	2.05 l blue & multi	1.50	.40

Qemal Stafa A302

Designs: 15q, Memorial flame. 25q, Monument "Spirit of Defiance," vert.

1972, May 5 *Perf. 12½x12, 12x12½*

1422	A302	15q gray & multi	.20	.20
1423	A302	25q sal rose, blk & gray	.20	.20
1424	A302	1.90 l dull yel & blk	1.10	.30
		Nos. 1422-1424 (3)	1.50	.70

30th anniversary of the murder of Qemal Stafa and of Martyrs' Day.

Camellia A303

Designs: Various camellias.

1972, May 10 *Perf. 12x12½*

Flowers in Natural Colors

1425	A303	5q lt blue & blk	.20	.20
1426	A303	10q citron & blk	.20	.20
1427	A303	15q grnsh gray & blk	.20	.20
1428	A303	25q pale sal & blk	.25	.20
1429	A303	45q gray & blk	.35	.20
1430	A303	50q sal pink & blk	.80	.20
1431	A303	2.50 l bluish gray & blk	3.00	.80
		Nos. 1425-1431 (7)	5.00	2.00

High Jump — A304

Designs (Olympic and Motion Emblems and): 10q, Running. 15q, Shot put. 20q, Bicycling. 25q, Pole vault. 50q, Hurdles, women's. 75q, Hockey. 2 l, Swimming. 2.50 l, Diving, women's.

1972, June 30 Litho. *Perf. 12½x12*

1432	A304	5q multicolored	.20	.20
1433	A304	10q lt brn & multi	.20	.20
1434	A304	15q lt lil & multi	.20	.20
1435	A304	20q multicolored	.20	.20
1436	A304	25q lt vio & multi	.20	.20
1437	A304	50q lt grn & multi	.40	.20
1438	A304	75q multicolored	.80	.20
1439	A304	2 l multicolored	1.50	.30
		Nos. 1432-1439 (8)	3.70	1.70

Miniature Sheet

Imperf

1440	A304	2.50 l multi	2.25	1.50

20th Olympic Games, Munich, Aug. 26-Sept. 11. Nos. 1432-1439 each issued in sheets of 8 stamps and one label (3x3) showing Olympic rings in gold.

Autobus A305

25q, Electric train. 80q, Ocean liner Tirana. 1.05 l, Automobile. 1.20 l, Trailer truck.

1972, July 25 Litho. *Perf. 12*

1441	A305	15q org brn & multi	.20	.20
1442	A305	25q gray & multi	.20	.20
1443	A305	80q dp grn & multi	.40	.20
1444	A305	1.05 l multi	.55	.20
1445	A305	1.20 l multi	.65	.20
		Nos. 1441-1445 (5)	2.00	1.00

Arm Wrestling A306

Folk Games: 10q, Piggyback ball game. 15q, Women's jumping. 25q, Rope game (srum). 90q, Leapfrog. 2 l, Women throwing pitchers.

1972, Aug. 18

1446	A306	5q multi	.20	.20
1447	A306	10q lt bl & multi	.20	.20
1448	A306	15q rose & multi	.20	.20
1449	A306	25q lt bl & multi	.20	.20
1450	A306	90q ocher & multi	.65	.20
1451	A306	2 l lt grn & multi	1.25	.25
		Nos. 1446-1451 (6)	2.70	1.25

1st National Festival of People's Games.

Mastheads — A307

30th Press Day: 25q, Printing press. 1.90 l, Workers reading paper.

1972, Aug. 25

1452	A307	15q lt bl & blk	.20	.20
1453	A307	25q red, grn & blk	.20	.20
1454	A307	1.90 l lt vio & blk	1.25	.35
		Nos. 1452-1454 (3)	1.65	.75

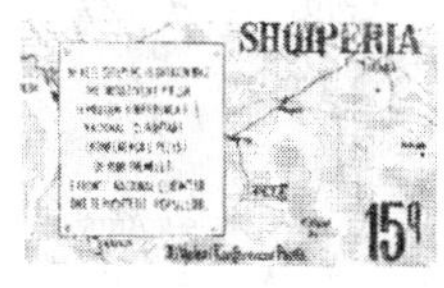

Map of Peza Area, Memorial Tablet A308

1972, Sept. 16

1455	A308	15q shown	.20	.20
1456	A308	25q Guerrillas with flag	.30	.20
1457	A308	1.90 l Peza Conference memorial	1.75	.35
		Nos. 1455-1457 (3)	2.25	.75

30th anniversary, Conference of Peza.

Partisans, by Sotir Capo — A309

Paintings: 10q, Woman, by Ismail Lulani, vert. 15q, "Communists," by Lec Shkreli, vert. 20q, View of Nendorit, 1941, by Sali Shijaku, vert. 50q, Woman with Sheaf, by Zef Shoshi, vert. 1 l, Landscape with Children, by Dhimitraq Trebicka. 2 l, Women on Bicycles, by Vilson Kilica. 2.30 l, Folk Dance, by Abdurrahim Buza.

Perf. 12½x12, 12x12½

1972, Sept. 25 Litho.

1458	A309	5q gold & multi	.20	.20
1459	A309	10q gold & multi	.20	.20
1460	A309	15q gold & multi	.20	.20
1461	A309	20q gold & multi	.20	.20
1462	A309	50q gold & multi	.35	.20
1463	A309	1 l gold & multi	.70	.20
1464	A309	2 l gold & multi	1.50	.35
		Nos. 1458-1464 (7)	3.35	1.55

Miniature Sheet

Imperf

1465	A309	2.30 l gold & multi	2.00	1.50

No. 1465 contains one 41x68mm stamp.

Congress Emblem — A310

Design: 2.05 l, Young worker with banner.

1972, Oct. 23 Litho. *Perf. 12*

1466	A310	25q silver, red & gold	.20	.20
1467	A310	2.05 l silver & multi	1.60	.45

Union of Working Youth, 6th Congress.

Hammer and Sickle A311

Ismail Qemali A312

Design: 1.20 l, Lenin as orator.

1972, Nov. 7 Litho. *Perf. 11½x12*

1468	A311	1.10 l multi	.55	.20
1469	A311	1.20 l multi	.60	.25

Russian October Revolution, 55th anniv.

Perf. 12x11½, 11½x12

1972, Nov. 29

Designs: 15q, Albanian fighters, horiz. 65q, Rally, horiz. 1.25 l, Coat of arms.

1470	A312	15q red, brt bl & blk	.20	.20
1471	A312	25q yel, blk & red	.20	.20
1472	A312	65q red, sal & blk	.50	.20
1473	A312	1.25 l dl red & blk	.95	.25
		Nos. 1470-1473 (4)	1.85	.85

60th anniv. of independence.

Cock, Mosaic A313

Mosaics, 2nd-5th centuries, excavated near Buthrotium and Apollonia: 10q, Bird, vert. 15q, Partridges, vert. 25q, Warrior's legs. 45q, Nymph riding dolphin, vert. 50q, Fish, vert. 2.50 l, Warrior with helmet.

1972, Dec. 10 *Perf. 12½x12, 12x12½*

1474	A313	5q silver & multi	.20	.20
1475	A313	10q silver & multi	.20	.20
1476	A313	15q silver & multi	.20	.20
1477	A313	25q silver & multi	.40	.20
1478	A313	45q silver & multi	.40	.20
1479	A313	50q silver & multi	.60	.20
1480	A313	2.50 l silver & multi	3.00	.70
		Nos. 1474-1480 (7)	5.00	1.90

Nicolaus Copernicus A314

Designs: 10q, 25q, 80q, 1.20 l, Various portraits of Copernicus. 1.60 l, Heliocentric solar system.

1973, Feb. 19 Litho. *Perf. 12x12½*

1481 A314 5q lil rose & multi .20 .20
1482 A314 10q dull ol & multi .20 .20
1483 A314 25q multicolored .20 .20
1484 A314 80q lt violet & multi .60 .20
1485 A314 1.20 l blue & multi .85 .25
1486 A314 1.60 l gray & multi 1.25 .35
Nos. 1481-1486 (6) 3.30 1.40

500th anniversary of the birth of Nicolaus Copernicus (1473-1543), Polish astronomer.

Flowering Cactus — A315

Designs: Various flowering cacti.

1973, Mar. 25 Litho. *Perf. 12*

1487 A315 10q multicolored .20 .20
1488 A315 15q multicolored .20 .20
1489 A315 20q beige & multi .20 .20
1490 A315 25q gray & multi .25 .20
1491 A315 30q beige & multi 3.75 1.25
1492 A315 65q gray & multi .55 .20
1493 A315 80q multicolored .60 .20
1494 A315 2 l multicolored 1.25 .50
a. Block of 8, #1487-1494 7.50 5.00
Nos. 1487-1494 (8) 7.00 2.95

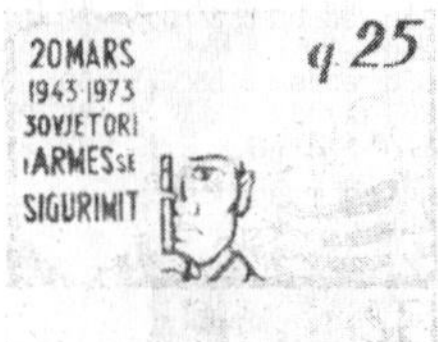

Guard and Factories A316

1.80 l, Guard and guards with prisoner.

1973, Mar. 20 Litho. *Perf. 12½x12*

1495 A316 25q ultra & blk .30 .20
1496 A316 1.80 l dk red & multi 1.40 .40

30th anniv. of the State Security Branch.

Common Tern — A317

Sea Birds: 15q, White-winged black terns, vert. 25q, Black-headed gull, vert. 45q, Great black-headed gull. 80q, Slender-billed gull, vert. 2.40 l, Sandwich terns.

1973, Apr. 30 *Perf. 12½x12, 12x12½*

1497 A317 5q gold & multi .20 .20
1498 A317 15q gold & multi .20 .20
1499 A317 25q gold & multi .30 .20
1500 A317 45q gold & multi .35 .20
1501 A317 80q gold & multi .80 .20
1502 A317 2.40 l gold & multi 2.50 .50
Nos. 1497-1502 (6) 4.35 1.50

Letters, 1913 Cancellation and Post Horn — A318

Design: 1.80 l, Mailman, 1913 cancel.

1973, May, 5 Litho. *Perf. 12x11½*

1503 A318 25q red & multi .40 .20
1504 A318 1.80 l red & multi 2.50 .50

60th anniversary of Albanian stamps.

Farmer, Worker, Soldier A319

Design: 25q, Woman and factory, vert.

1973, June 4 *Perf. 12*

1505 A319 25q carmine rose .25 .20
1506 A319 1.80 l yel, dp org & blk 1.50 .45

7th Congress of Albanian Women's Union.

Creation of General Staff, by G. Madhi — A320

Designs: 40q, "August 1949," sculpture by Sh. Haderi, vert. 60q, "Generation after Generation," sculpture by H. Dule, vert. 80q, "Defend Revolutionary Victories," by M. Fushekati.

1973, July 10 Litho. *Perf. 12½x12*

1507 A320 25q gold & multi *5.50* 5.50
1508 A320 40q gold & multi *5.50* 5.50
1509 A320 60q gold & multi *5.50* 5.50
1510 A320 80q gold & multi *5.50* 5.50
Nos. 1507-1510 (4) *22.00* 22.00

30th anniversary of the People's Army.

"Electrification," by S. Hysa — A321

Albanian Paintings: 10q, Woman Textile Worker, by N. Nallbani. 15q, Gymnasts, by M. Fushekati. 50q, Aviator, by F. Stamo. 80q, Fascist Prisoner, by A. Lakuriqi. 1.20 l, Workers with Banner, by P. Mele. 1.30 l, Farm Woman, by Zef Shoshi. 2.05 l, Battle of Tenda, by F. Haxhiu. 10q, 50q, 80q, 1.20 l, 1.30 l, vertical.

Perf. 12½x12, 12x12½

1973, Aug. 10

1511 A321 5q gold & multi .20 .20
1512 A321 10q gold & multi .20 .20
1513 A321 15q gold & multi .20 .20
1514 A321 50q gold & multi .25 .20
1515 A321 80q gold & multi .55 .20
1516 A321 1.20 l gold & multi .90 .20
1517 A321 1.30 l gold & multi .95 .20
Nos. 1511-1517 (7) 3.25 1.40

Souvenir Sheet

Imperf

1518 A321 2.05 l multi 2.25 1.25

Mary Magdalene, by Caravaggio A322

Paintings by Michelangelo da Caravaggio: 10q, The Lute Player, horiz. 15q, Self-portrait. 50q, Boy Carrying Fruit and Flowers. 80q, Still Life, horiz. 1.20 l, Narcissus. 1.30 l, Boy Peeling Apple. 2.05 l, Man with Feathered Hat.

Perf. 12x12½, 12½x12

1973, Sept. 28

1519 A322 5q gold & multi .20 .20
1520 A322 10q gold & multi .20 .20
1521 A322 15q gold, blk & gray .20 .20
1522 A322 50q gold & multi .25 .20
1523 A322 80q gold & multi .60 .20
1524 A322 1.20 l gold & multi .80 .25
1525 A322 1.30 l gold & multi .90 .25
Nos. 1519-1525 (7) 3.15 1.50

Souvenir Sheet

Imperf

1526 A322 2.05 l multi 3.75 2.00

Michelangelo da Caravaggio (Merisi; 1573?-1609), Italian painter. No. 1526 contains one stamp, size: 63x73mm.

Soccer — A323

Designs: 5q-1.25 l, Various soccer scenes. 2.05 l, Ball in goal and list of cities where championships were held.

1973, Oct. 30 Litho. *Perf. 12½x12*

1527 A323 5q multi .20 .20
1528 A323 10q multi .20 .20
1529 A323 15q multi .20 .20
1530 A323 20q multi .20 .20
1531 A323 25q multi .20 .20
1532 A323 90q multi .65 .20
1533 A323 1.20 l multi .95 .20
1534 A323 1.25 l multi 1.10 .20
Nos. 1527-1534 (8) 3.70 1.60

Minature Sheet

Imperf

1535 A323 2.05 l multi 2.00 1.50

World Soccer Cup, Munich 1974.

Weight Lifter — A324

Designs: Various stages of weight lifting. 1.20 l, 1.60 l, horiz.

1973, Oct. 30 Litho. *Perf. 12*

1536 A324 5q multi .20 .20
1537 A324 10q multi .20 .20
1538 A324 25q multi .20 .20
1539 A324 90q multi .55 .20
1540 A324 1.20 l multi .45 .20
1541 A324 1.60 l multi .95 .20
Nos. 1536-1541 (6) 2.55 1.20

Weight Lifting Championships, Havana, Cuba.

Ballet — A325

Harvester Combine A326

Designs: 5q, Cement factory, Kavaje. 10q, Ali Kelmendi truck factory and tank cars, horiz. 25q, "Communication." 35q, Skiers and hotel, horiz. 60q, Resort, horiz. 80q, Mountain lake. 1 l, Mao Tse-tung textile mill. 1.20 l, Steel workers. 2.40 l, Welder and pipe. 3 l, Skanderbeg Monument, Tirana. 5 l, Roman arches, Durres.

Perf. 12½x12, 12x12½

1973-74 Litho.

1543 A325 5q gold & multi .20 .20
1544 A325 10q gold & multi .20 .20
1545 A325 15q gold & multi .20 .20
1545A A326 20q gold & multi .20 .20
1546 A326 25q gold & multi .20 .20
1547 A326 35q gold & multi .20 .20
1548 A326 60q gold & multi .35 .20
1549 A326 80q gold & multi .50 .20
1549A A326 1 l gold & multi .45 .20
1549B A326 1.20 l gold & multi .75 .20
1549C A326 2.40 l gold & multi 1.50 .35
1550 A326 3 l gold & multi 1.75 .35
1551 A326 5 l gold & multi 2.75 .60
Nos. 1543-1551 (13) 9.25 3.30

Issue dates: Nos. 1545-1546, 1549-1550, Dec. 5, 1973; others, 1974.

Mao Tse-tung — A327

80th birthday of Mao Tse-tung: 1.20 l, Mao Tse-tung addressing crowd.

1973, Dec. 26 *Perf. 12*

1552 A327 85q multicolored .80 .20
1553 A327 1.20 l multicolored 1.25 .20

Old Man and Dog, by Gericault A328

Paintings by Jean Louis André Theodore Gericault: 10q, Horse's Head. 15q, Male Model. 25q, Head of Black Man. 1.20 l, Self-portrait. 2.05 l, Raft of the Medusa, horiz. 2.20 l, Battle of the Giants.

Perf. 12x12½, 12½x12

1974, Jan. 18 Litho.

1554 A328 10q gold & multi .20 .20
1555 A328 15q gold & multi .20 .20
1556 A328 20q gold & multi .20 .20
1557 A328 25q gold & blk .25 .20
1558 A328 1.20 l gold & multi .90 .20
1559 A328 2.20 l gold & multi 1.75 .35
Nos. 1554-1559 (6) 3.50 1.35

Souvenir Sheet

Imperf

1560 A328 2.05 l gold & multi 2.00 1.50

No. 1560 contains one 87x78mm stamp.

Lenin, by Pandi Mele — A329

Designs: 25q, Lenin with Sailors on Cruiser Aurora, by Dhimitraq Trebicka, horiz. 1.20 l, Lenin, by Vilson Kilica.

1974, Jan. 21 *Perf. 12½x12, 12x12½*

1561 A329 25q gold & multi .20 .25
1562 A329 60q gold & multi .60 .20
1563 A329 1.20 l gold & multi 1.75 .55
Nos. 1561-1563 (3) 2.55 1.00

50th anniv. of the death of Lenin.

Swimming Duck, Mosaic — A330

Designs: Mosaics from the 5th-6th Centuries A.D., excavated near Buthrotium, Pogradec and Apollonia.

1974, Feb. 20 Litho. *Perf. 12½x12*

1564 A330 5q shown .20 .20
1565 A330 10q Bird, flower .20 .20
1566 A330 15q Vase, grapes .20 .20
1567 A330 25q Duck .20 .20
1568 A330 40q Donkey, bird .30 .20
1569 A330 2.50 l Sea horse 1.50 .35
Nos. 1564-1569 (6) 2.60 1.35

Soccer — A331

Various scenes from soccer. 2.05 l, World Soccer Cup & names of participating countries.

1974, Apr. 25 Litho. *Perf. 12½x12*

1570 A331 10q gold & multi .20 .20
1571 A331 15q gold & multi .20 .20
1572 A331 20q gold & multi .20 .20
1573 A331 25q gold & multi .20 .20
1574 A331 40q gold & multi .30 .20
1575 A331 80q gold & multi .55 .20
1576 A331 1 l gold & multi .85 .25
1577 A331 1.20 l gold & multi 1.10 .35
Nos. 1570-1577 (8) 3.60 1.80

Souvenir Sheet

Imperf

1578 A331 2.05 l gold & multi 2.50 .90

World Cup Soccer Championship, Munich, June 13-July 7. No. 1578 contains one stamp (60x60mm) with simulated perforations. Nos. 1570-1577 exist imperf, No. 1578 with simulated perfs omitted.

Arms of Albania, Soldier — A332

Design: 1.80 l, Soldier and front page of 1944 Congress Book.

1974, May 24 Litho. *Perf. 12*

1579 A332 25q multicolored .20 .20
1580 A332 1.80 l multicolored 1.25 .25

30th anniversary of the First Anti-Fascist Liberation Congress of Permet.

Medicinal Plants A333

40q, 80q, 2.20 l, horiz.

1974, May 5 *Perf. 12x12½*

1581 A333 10q Bittersweet .20 .20
1582 A333 15q Arbutus .20 .20
1583 A333 20q Lilies of the valley .20 .20
1584 A333 25q Autumn crocus .20 .20
1585 A333 40q Borage .25 .20
1586 A333 80q Soapwort .85 .20
1587 A333 2.20 l Gentian 1.90 .40
Nos. 1581-1587 (7) 3.80 1.60

Revolutionaries with Albanian Flag — A334

1.80 l, Portraits of 5 revolutionaries, vert.

Perf. 12½x12, 12x12½

1974, June 10

1588 A334 25q red, blk & lil .30 .20
1589 A334 1.80 l yel, red & blk 1.25 .40

50th anniversary Albanian Bourgeois Democratic Revolution.

European Redwing — A335

Designs: Songbirds; Nos. 1597-1600 vert.

Perf. 12½x12, 12x12½

1974, July 15 Litho.

1594 A335 10q shown .20 .20
1595 A335 15q European robin .20 .20
1596 A335 20q Greenfinch .20 .20
1597 A335 25q Bullfinch .20 .20
1598 A335 40q Hawfinch .35 .20
1599 A335 80q Blackcap .85 .20
1600 A335 2.20 l Nightingale 1.90 .45
Nos. 1594-1600 (7) 3.90 1.65

Globe — A336

Cent. of UPU: 1.20 l, UPU emblem. 2.05 l, Jet over globe.

1974, Aug. 25 Litho. *Perf. 12x12½*

1601 A336 85q grn & multi .80 .20
1602 A336 1.20 l vio & ol grn 1.25 .20

Miniature Sheet

Imperf

1603 A336 2.05 l blue & multi 12.00 12.00

Widows, by Sali Shijaku — A337

Albanian Paintings: 15q, Drillers, by Danish Jukniu, vert. 20q, Workers with Blueprints, by Clirim Ceka. 25q, Call to Action, by Spiro Kristo, vert. 40q, Winter Battle, by Sabaudin Xhaferi. 80q, Comrades, by Clirim Ceka, vert. 1 l, Aiding the Partisans, by Guri Madhi. 1.20 l, Teacher with Pupils, by Kleo Nini Brezat. 2.05 l, Comrades in Arms, by Guri Madhi.

Perf. 12½x12, 12x12½

1974, Sept. 25

1604 A337 10q silver & multi .20 .20
1605 A337 15q silver & multi .20 .20
1606 A337 20q silver & multi .20 .20
1607 A337 25q silver & multi .20 .20
1608 A337 40q silver & multi .40 .20
1609 A337 80q silver & multi .75 .20
1610 A337 1 l silver & multi .95 .20
1611 A337 1.20 l silver & multi 1.00 .20
Nos. 1604-1611 (8) 3.90 1.60

Miniature Sheet

Imperf

1612 A337 2.05 l silver & multi 2.00 1.50

Crowd on Tien An Men Square A338

Design: 1.20 l, Mao Tse-tung, vert.

1974, Oct. 1 *Perf. 12*

1613 A338 85q gold & multi .80 .20
1614 A338 1.20 l gold & multi 1.25 .20

25th anniversary of the proclamation of the People's Republic of China.

Women's Volleyball A339

Spartakiad Medal and: 15q, Women hurdlers. 20q, Women gymnasts. 25q, Mass exercises in Stadium. 40q, Weight lifter. 80q, Wrestlers. 1 l, Military rifle drill. 1.20 l, Soccer.

1974, Oct. 9 *Perf. 12x12½*

1615 A339 10q multi .20 .20
1616 A339 15q multi .20 .20
1617 A339 20q multi .20 .20
1618 A339 25q gray & multi .20 .20
1619 A339 40q multi .25 .20
1620 A339 80q multi .50 .20
1621 A339 1 l multi .65 .20
1622 A339 1.20 l tan & multi 1.00 .20
Nos. 1615-1622 (8) 3.20 1.60

National Spartakiad, Oct. 9-17.

View of Berat — A340

Designs: 80q, Enver Hoxha addressing Congress, bas-relief, horiz. 1 l, Hoxha and leaders leaving Congress Hall.

Perf. 12x12½, 12½x12

1974, Oct. 20 Litho.

1623 A340 25q rose car & blk .30 .20
1624 A340 80q yel, brn & blk .70 .20
1625 A340 1 l dp lilac & blk 1.10 .30
Nos. 1623-1625 (3) 2.10 .70

30th anniversary of 2nd Congress of Berat.

Anniversary Emblem, Factory Guards — A341

35q, Chemical industry. 50q, Agriculture. 80q, Arts. 1 l, Atomic diagram & computer. 1.20 l, Youth education. 2.05 l, Crowd & History Book.

1974, Nov. 29 Litho. *Perf. 12½x12*

1626 A341 25q green & multi .20 .20
1627 A341 35q ultra & multi .20 .20
1628 A341 50q brown & multi .20 .20
1629 A341 80q multicolored .40 .20
1630 A341 1 l violet & multi .50 .20
1631 A341 1.20 l multicolored 1.00 .25
Nos. 1626-1631 (6) 2.50 1.25

Miniature Sheet

Imperf

1632 A341 2.05 l gold & multi 2.50 2.00

30th anniv. of liberation from Fascism.

Artemis, from Apolloni A342

1974, Dec. 25 Photo. *Perf. 12x12½*

1633 A342 10q shown .20 .20
1634 A342 15q Zeus statue .20 .20
1635 A342 20q Poseidon statue .20 .20
1636 A342 25q Illyrian helmet .25 .20
1637 A342 40q Amphora .30 .20
1638 A342 80q Agrippa .60 .25
1639 A342 1 l Demosthenes .80 .30
1640 A342 1.20 l Head of Bilia 1.50 .40
Nos. 1633-1640 (8) 4.05 1.95

Miniature Sheet

Imperf

1641 A342 2.05 l Artemis & amphora 2.50 1.50

Archaeological discoveries in Albania.

Workers and Factories A343

25q, Handshake, tools and book, vert.

1975, Feb. 11 Litho. *Perf. 12*

1642 A343 25q brown & multi .30 .20
1643 A343 1.80 l yellow & multi 1.50 .35

Albanian Trade Unions, 30th anniversary.

Chicory A344

1975, Feb. 15

1644 A344 5q shown .20 .20
1645 A344 10q Houseleek .20 .20
1646 A344 15q Columbine .20 .20
1647 A344 20q Anemone .20 .20
1648 A344 25q Hibiscus .20 .20
1649 A344 30q Gentian .20 .20
1650 A344 35q Hollyhock .50 .20
1651 A344 2.70 l Iris 2.50 .40
Nos. 1644-1651 (8) 4.20 1.80

Protected flowers.

Jesus, from Doni Madonna A345

Works by Michelangelo: 10q, Slave, sculpture. 15q, Head of Dawn, sculpture. 20q, Awakening Giant, sculpture. 25q, Cumaenian Sybil, Sistine Chapel. 30q, Lorenzo di Medici, sculpture. 1.20 l, David, sculpture. 2.05 l, Self-portrait. 3.90 l, Delphic Sybil, Sistine Chapel.

1975, Mar. 20 Litho. *Perf. 12x12½*

1652 A345 5q gold & multi .20 .20
1653 A345 10q gold & multi .20 .20
1654 A345 15q gold & multi .20 .20
1655 A345 20q gold & multi .20 .20
1656 A345 25q gold & multi .20 .20
1657 A345 30q gold & multi .30 .20
1658 A345 1.20 l gold & multi .50 .20
1659 A345 3.90 l gold & multi 2.00 .50
Nos. 1652-1659 (8) 3.80 1.90

Miniature Sheet

Imperf

1660 A345 2.05 l gold & multi 2.50 1.75

Michelangelo Buonarroti (1475-1564), Italian sculptor, painter and architect.

Two-wheeled Cart — A346

Albanian Transportation of the Past: 5q, Horseback rider. 15q, Lake ferry. 20q, Coastal three-master. 25q, Phaeton. 3.35 l, Early automobile on bridge.

1975, Apr. 15 Litho. *Perf. 12½x12*

1661 A346 5q bl grn & multi .20 .20
1662 A346 10q ol & multi .20 .20
1663 A346 15q lil & multi .20 .20
1664 A346 20q multi .20 .20
1665 A346 25q multi .20 .20
1666 A346 3.35 l ocher & multi 2.00 .50
Nos. 1661-1666 (6) 3.00 1.50

Guard at Frontier Stone — A347

Guardsman and Militia — A348

1975, Apr. 25 *Perf. 12*

1667 A347 25q multi .30 .20
1668 A348 1.80 l multi 1.50 .35

30th anniversary of Frontier Guards.

Posting Illegal Poster — A349

Designs: 60q, Partisans in battle. 1.20 l, Partisan killing German soldier, and Albanian coat of arms.

1975, May 9 *Perf. 12½x12*

1669 A349 25q multi .20 .20
1670 A349 60q multi .50 .20
1671 A349 1.20 l red & multi 1.00 .25
Nos. 1669-1671 (3) 1.70 .65

30th anniversary of victory over Fascism.

European Widgeons — A350

Waterfowl: 10q, Red-crested pochards. 15q, White-fronted goose. 20q, Northern pintails. 25q, Red-breasted merganser. 30q, Eider ducks. 35q, Whooper swan. 2.70 l, Shovelers.

1975, June 15 Litho. *Perf. 12*

1672 A350 5q brt blue & multi .20 .20
1673 A350 10q yel grn & multi .20 .20
1674 A350 15q brt rose lil & multi .20 .20
1675 A350 20q bl grn & multi .20 .20
1676 A350 25q multicolored .20 .20
1677 A350 30q multicolored .25 .20
1678 A350 35q orange & multi .40 .20
1679 A350 2.70 l multi 3.00 .75
Nos. 1672-1679 (8) 4.65 2.15

Shyqyri Kanapari, by Musa Qarri — A351

Albanian Paintings: 10q, Woman Saving Children in Sea, by Agim Faja. 15q, "November 28, 1912" (revolution), by Petrit Ceno, horiz. 20q, "Workers Unite," by Sali Shijaku. 25q, The Partisan Shota Galica, by Ismail Lulani. 30q, Victorious Resistance Fighters, 1943, by Nestor Jonuzi. 80q, Partisan Couple in Front of Red Flag, by Vilson Halimi. 2.05 l, Dancing Procession, by Abdurahim Buza. 2.25 l, Republic Day Celebration, by Fatmir Haxhiu, horiz.

Perf. 12x12½, 12½x12

1975, July 15 Litho.

1680 A351 5q gold & multi .20 .20
1681 A351 10q gold & multi .20 .20
1682 A351 15q gold & multi .20 .20
1683 A351 20q gold & multi .20 .20
1684 A351 25q gold & multi .20 .20
1685 A351 30q gold & multi .20 .20
1686 A351 80q gold & multi .40 .20
1687 A351 2.25 l gold & multi 1.40 .40
Nos. 1680-1687 (8) 3.00 1.80

Miniature Sheet

Imperf

1688 A351 2.05 l gold & multi 2.10 1.50

Nos. 1680-1687 issued in sheets of 8 stamps and gold center label showing palette and easel.

Farmer Holding Reform Law — A352

Design: 2 l, Produce and farm machinery.

1975, Aug. 28 *Perf. 12*

1689 A352 15q multicolored .25 .20
1690 A352 2 l multicolored 1.25 .50

Agrarian reform, 30th anniversary.

Alcynonium Palmatum A353

Corals: 10q, Paramuricea chamaeleon. 20q, Coralium rubrum. 25q, Eunicella covalini. 3.70 l, Cladocora cespitosa.

1975, Sept. 25 Litho. *Perf. 12*

1691 A353 5q blue, ol & blk .20 .20
1692 A353 10q blue & multi .20 .20
1693 A353 20q blue & multi .20 .20
1694 A353 25q blue & blk .20 .20
1695 A353 3.70 l blue & blk 2.50 .60
Nos. 1691-1695 (5) 3.30 1.40

Bicycling A354

Designs (Montreal Olympic Games Emblem and): 10q, Canoeing. 15q, Fieldball. 20q, Basketball. 25q, Water polo. 30q, Hockey. 1.20 l, Pole vault. 2.05 l, Fencing. 2.15 l, Montreal Olympic Games emblem and various sports.

1975, Oct. 20 Litho. *Perf. 12½*

1696 A354 5q multi .20 .20
1697 A354 10q multi .20 .20
1698 A354 15q multi .20 .20
1699 A354 20q multi .25 .20
1700 A354 25q multi .25 .20
1701 A354 30q multi .25 .20
1702 A354 1.20 l multi .75 .25
1703 A354 2.05 l multi 1.50 .40
Nos. 1696-1703 (8) 3.60 1.85

Miniature Sheet

Imperf

1704 A354 2.15 l org & multi 3.00 2.00

21st Olympic Games, Montreal, July 18-Aug. 8, 1976. Nos. 1696-1703 exist imperf.

Power Lines Leading to Village A355

Designs: 25q, Transformers and insulators. 80q, Dam and power station. 85q, Television set, power lines, grain and cogwheel.

1975, Oct. 25 *Perf. 12x12½*

1705 A355 15q ultra & yel .20 .20
1706 A355 25q brt vio & pink .20 .20
1707 A355 80q lt grn & gray .40 .20
1708 A355 85q ocher & brn 1.00 .40
Nos. 1705-1708 (4) 1.80 1.00

General electrification, 5th anniversary.

Child, Rabbit and Teddy Bear Planting Tree — A356

Fairy Tales: 10q, Mother fox. 15q, Ducks in school. 20q, Little pigs building house. 25q, Animals watching television. 30q, Rabbit and bear at work. 35q, Working and playing ants. 2.70 l, Wolf in sheep's clothes.

1975, Dec. 25 Litho. *Perf. 12½x12*

1709 A356 5q black & multi .20 .20
1710 A356 10q black & multi .20 .20
1711 A356 15q black & multi .20 .20
1712 A356 20q black & multi .20 .20
1713 A356 25q black & multi .20 .20
1714 A356 30q black & multi .25 .20
1715 A356 35q black & multi .25 .20
1716 A356 2.70 l black & multi 3.00 .60
Nos. 1709-1716 (8) 4.50 2.00

Arms, People, Factories A357

Design: 1.90 l, Arms, government building, celebrating crowd.

1976, Jan. 11 Litho. *Perf. 12*

1717 A357 25q gold & multi .25 .20
1718 A357 1.90 l gold & multi 1.25 .35

30th anniversary of proclamation of Albanian People's Republic.

Ice Hockey, Olympic Games' Emblem A358

Designs: 10q, Speed skating. 15q, Biathlon. 50q, Ski jump. 1.20 l, Slalom. 2.15 l, Figure skating, pairs. 2.30 l, One-man bobsled.

1976, Feb. 4

1719 A358 5q silver & multi .20 .20
1720 A358 10q silver & multi .20 .20
1721 A358 15q silver & multi .20 .20
1722 A358 50q silver & multi .25 .20
1723 A358 1.20 l silver & multi .65 .20
1724 A358 2.30 l silver & multi 1.50 .35
Nos. 1719-1724 (6) 3.00 1.35

Miniature Sheet

Perf. 12 on 2 sides x Imperf.

1725 A358 2.15 l silver & multi 2.10 1.75

12th Winter Olympic Games, Innsbruck, Austria, Feb. 4-15.

Meadow Saffron A359

Medicinal Plants: 10q, Deadly night-shade. 15q, Yellow gentian. 20q, Horse chestnut. 70q, Shield fern. 80q, Marshmallow. 2.30 l, Thorn apple.

1976, Apr. 10 Litho. *Perf. 12x12½*

1726 A359 5q black & multi .20 .20
1727 A359 10q black & multi .20 .20
1728 A359 15q black & multi .20 .20
1729 A359 20q black & multi .20 .20
1730 A359 70q black & multi .30 .20
1731 A359 80q black & multi .60 .20
1732 A359 2.30 l black & multi 1.60 .35
Nos. 1726-1732 (7) 3.30 1.55

Bowl and Spoon — A360

15q, Flask, vert. 20q, Carved handles, vert. 25q, Pistol and dagger. 80q, Wall hanging, vert. 1.20 l, Earrings and belt buckle. 1.40 l, Jugs, vert.

1976 Litho. *Perf. 12½x12, 12x12½*

1733 A360 10q lilac & multi .20 .20
1734 A360 15q gray & multi .20 .20
1735 A360 20q multi .20 .20
1736 A360 25q car & multi .20 .20
1737 A360 80q yellow & multi .50 .20
1738 A360 1.20 l multi .75 .25
1739 A360 1.40 l tan & multi 1.10 .35
Nos. 1733-1739 (7) 3.15 1.60

Natl. Ethnographic Conf., Tirana, June 28. For surcharge see No. 1873.

Founding of Cooperatives, by Zef Shoshi — A361

Paintings: 10q, Going to Work, by Agim Zajmi, vert. 25q, Crowd Listening to Loudspeaker, by Vilson Kilica. 40q, Woman Welder, by Sabaudin Xhaferi, vert. 50q, Factory, by Isuf Sulovari, vert. 1.20 l, 1942 Revolt, by Lec Shkreli, vert. 1.60 l, Coming Home from Work, by Agron Dine. 2.05 l, Honoring a Young Pioneer, by Andon Lakuriqi.

Perf. 12½x12, 12x12½

1976, Aug. 8 Litho.

1740 A361 5q gold & multi .20 .20
1741 A361 10q gold & multi .20 .20
1742 A361 25q gold & multi .20 .20
1743 A361 40q gold & multi .25 .20
1744 A361 50q gold & multi .25 .20
1745 A361 1.20 l gold & multi 1.00 .50
1746 A361 1.60 l gold & multi 1.50 .75
Nos. 1740-1746 (7) 3.60 2.25

Miniature Sheet **Perf.** *12 on 2 sides x Imperf.*

1747 A361 2.05 l gold & multi 2.50 2.00

Red Flag, Agricultural Symbols Enver Hoxha, Partisans and Albanian Flag

A362

A363

Design: 1.20 l, Red flag and raised pickax.

1976, Nov. 1

1748 A362 25q multi .25 .20
1749 A362 1.20 l multi 1.00 .50

7th Workers Party Congress.

1976, Oct. 28 *Perf. 12x12½*

1.90 l, Demonstrators with Albanian flag.

1750 A363 25q multi .25 .20
1751 A363 1.90 l multi 1.25 .65

Anti-Fascist demonstrations, 35th anniv.

Attacking Partisans, Meeting House A364

Designs (Red Flag and): 25q, Partisans, pickax and gun. 80q, Workers, soldiers, pickax and gun. 1.20 l, Agriculture and industry. 1.70 l, Dancers, symbols of science and art.

1976, Nov. 8 Litho. *Perf. 12x12½*

1752 A364 15q gold & multi .20 .20
1753 A364 25q gold & multi .20 .20
1754 A364 80q gold & multi .30 .20
1755 A364 1.20 l gold & multi .50 .20
1756 A364 1.70 l gold & multi 1.00 .20
Nos. 1752-1756 (5) 2.20 1.00

35th anniv. of 1st Workers Party Cong.

Young Workers and Track A365

1.25 l, Young soldiers and Albanian flag.

1976, Nov. 23 *Perf. 12*

1757 A365 80q yellow & multi .70 .35
1758 A365 1.25 l carmine & multi 1.00 .50

Union of Young Communists, 35th anniv.

"Cuca e Maleve" Ballet A366

Scenes from ballet "Mountain Girl."

1976, Dec. 14 *Perf. 12*

1759 A366 10q gold & multi .20 .20
1760 A366 15q gold & multi .20 .20
1761 A366 20q gold & multi .20 .20
1762 A366 25q gold & multi .20 .20
1763 A366 80q gold & multi .55 .20
1764 A366 1.20 l gold & multi .75 .20
1765 A366 1.40 l gold & multi .90 .25
Nos. 1759-1765 (7) 3.00 1.45

Miniature Sheet

Perf. 12 on 2 sides x Imperf.

1766 A366 2.05 l gold & multi 2.25 2.25

Bashtoves Castle A367

Albanian Castles: 15q, Gjirokastres. 20q, Ali Pash Tepelenes. 25q, Petreles. 80q, Beratit. 1.20 l, Durresit. 1.40 l, Krujes.

1976, Dec. 30 Litho. *Perf. 12*

1767 A367 10q black & dull bl .20 .20
1768 A367 15q black & grn .20 .20
1769 A367 20q black & gray .20 .20
1770 A367 25q black & brn .20 .20
1771 A367 80q black & rose .55 .30
1772 A367 1.20 l black & vio .90 .45
1773 A367 1.40 l black & brn red 1.00 .50
Nos. 1767-1773 (7) 3.25 2.05

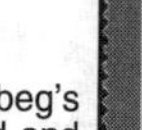

Skanderbeg's Shield and Spear — A368

Skanderbeg's Weapons: 80q, Helmet, sword and scabbard. 1 l, Halberd, quiver with arrows, crossbow and spear.

1977, Jan. 28 Litho. *Perf. 12*

1774 A368 15q silver & multi .75 .30
1775 A368 80q silver & multi 2.75 1.40
1776 A368 1 l silver & multi 4.25 2.25
Nos. 1774-1776 (3) 7.75 3.95

Skanderbeg (1403-1468), national hero.

Ilia Oiqi, Messenger in Storm — A369

Modern Heroes: 10q, Ilia Dashi, sailor in battle. 25q, Fran Ndue Ivanaj, fisherman in storm. 80q, Zeliha Allmetaj, woman rescuing child. 1 l, Ylli Zaimi, rescuing goats from flood. 1.90 l, Isuf Plloci, fighting forest fire.

1977, Feb. 28 Litho. *Perf. 12x12½*

1777 A369 5q brown & multi .20 .20
1778 A369 10q ultra & multi .20 .20
1779 A369 25q blue & multi .25 .20
1780 A369 80q ocher & multi .60 .30
1781 A369 1 l brown & multi .85 .40
1782 A369 1.90 l brown & multi 1.75 1.00
Nos. 1777-1782 (6) 3.85 2.30

Polyvinylchloride Plant, Vlore — A370

6th Five-year plan: 25q, Naphtha fractioning plant, Ballsh. 65q, Hydroelectric station and dam, Fjerzes. 1 l, Metallurgical plant and blast furance, Elbasan.

1977, Mar. 29 Litho. *Perf. 12½x12*

1783 A370 15q silver & multi .20 .20
1784 A370 25q silver & multi .30 .20
1785 A370 65q silver & multi .65 .30
1786 A370 1 l silver & multi 1.10 .60
Nos. 1783-1786 (4) 2.25 1.30

Qerime Halil Galica — A371

Victory Monument, Tirana — A372

Design: 1.25 l, Qerime Halil Galica "Shota" and father Azem Galica.

1977, Apr. 20 Litho. *Perf. 12*

1787 A371 80q dark red .65 .30
1788 A371 1.25 l gray blue 1.10 .60

"Shota" Galica, communist fighter.

1977, May 5 Litho. *Perf. 12*

Red Star and: 80q, Clenched fist, Albanian flag. 1.20 l, Bust of Qemal Stafa, poppies.

1789 A372 25q multi .30 .20
1790 A372 80q multi .90 .45
1791 A372 1.20 l multi 1.50 .75
Nos. 1789-1791 (3) 2.70 1.40

35th anniversary of Martyrs' Day.

Physician Visiting Farm, Mobile Clinic — A373

10q, Cowherd, cattle ranch. 20q, Militia woman helping with harvest, rifle, combine. 80q, Modern village, highway, power lines. 2.95 l, Tractor, greenhouses.

1977, June 18

1792 A373 5q multi .20 .20
1793 A373 10q multi .20 .20
1794 A373 20q multi .20 .20
1795 A373 80q multi .40 .20
1796 A373 2.95 l multi 3.00 1.50
Nos. 1792-1796 (5) 4.00 2.30

"Socialist transformation of the villages."

Armed Workers, Flag and Factory — A374

1.80 l, Workers with proclamation and flags.

1977, June 20

1797 A374 25q multi .20 .20
1798 A374 1.80 l multi 1.25 .65

9th Labor Unions Congress.

Kerchief Dance — A375

Designs: Various folk dances.

1977, Aug. 20 Litho. *Perf. 12*

1799 A375 5q multi .20 .20
1800 A375 10q multi .20 .20
1801 A375 15q multi .20 .20
1802 A375 25q multi .20 .20
1803 A375 80q multi .30 .20
1804 A375 1.20 l multi .60 .30
1805 A375 1.55 l multi .75 .40
Nos. 1799-1805 (7) 2.45 1.70

Miniature Sheet

Perf. 12 on 2 sides x Imperf.

1806 A375 2.05 l multi 1.75 1.75

See Nos. 1836-1840, 1884-1888.

Attack A376

Designs: 25q, Enver Hoxha addressing Army. 80q, Volunteers and riflemen. 1 l, Volunteers, hydrofoil patrolboat and MiG planes. 1.90 l, Volunteers and Albanian flag.

1977, July 10 Litho. *Perf. 12*

1807 A376 15q gold & multi .25 .20
1808 A376 25q gold & multi .25 .20
1809 A376 80q gold & multi .60 .30
1810 A376 1 l gold & multi .90 .45
1811 A376 1.90 l gold & multi 1.60 .75
Nos. 1807-1811 (5) 3.60 1.90

"One People-One Army."

Armed Workers, Article 3 of Constitution A377

Design: 1.20 l, Symbols of farming and fertilizer industry, Article 25 of Constitution.

1977, Oct.

1812 A377 25q red, gold & blk .25 .20
1813 A377 1.20 l red, gold & blk .95 .50

New Constitution.

Picnic — A378

Film Frames: 15q, Telephone lineman in winter. 25q, Two men and a woman. 80q, Workers. 1.20 l, Boys playing in street. 1.60 l, Harvest.

1977, Oct. 25 Litho. *Perf. 12½x12*

1814 A378 10q blue green .20 .20
1815 A378 15q multi .20 .20
1816 A378 25q black .25 .20
1817 A378 80q multi .75 .40
1818 A378 1.20 l deep claret 1.10 .60
1819 A378 1.60 l multi 1.50 .75
Nos. 1814-1819 (6) 4.00 2.35

Albanian films.

Farm Workers in Field, by V. Mio A379

Paintings by V. Mio: 10q, Landscape in Snow. 15q, Grazing Sheep under Walnut Tree in Spring. 25q, Street in Korce. 80q, Horseback Riders on Mountain Pass. 1 l, Boats on Shore. 1.75 l, Tractors Plowing Fields. 2.05 l, Self-portrait.

1977, Dec. 25 Litho. *Perf. 12½x12*

1820 A379 5q gold & multi .20 .20
1821 A379 10q gold & multi .20 .20
1822 A379 15q gold & multi .20 .20
1823 A379 25q gold & multi .20 .20
1824 A379 80q gold & multi .40 .20
1825 A379 1 l gold & multi .45 .20
1826 A379 1.75 l gold & multi .80 .20
Nos. 1820-1826 (7) 2.45 1.40

Miniature Sheet

Imperf.; Perf. 12 Horiz. between Vignette and Value Panel

1827 A379 2.05 l gold & multi 2.25 2.25

Pan Flute — A380

Albanian Flag, Monument and People — A381

Folk Musical Instruments: 25q, Single-string goat's-head fiddle. 80q, Woodwind. 1.20 l, Drum. 1.70 l, Bagpipe. Background shows various woven folk patterns.

1978, Jan. 20 *Perf. 12x12½*

1828 A380 15q multi .20 .20
1829 A380 25q multi .40 .20
1830 A380 80q multi 1.00 .50
1831 A380 1.20 l multi 2.00 1.00
1832 A380 1.70 l multi 3.75 2.00
Nos. 1828-1832 (5) 7.35 3.90

1978 *Perf. 12½x12, 12x12½*

25q, Ismail Qemali, fighters, horiz. 1.65 l, People dancing around Albanian flag, horiz.

1833 A381 15q multi .25 .20
1834 A381 25q multi .50 .25
1835 A381 1.65 l multi 2.00 1.00
Nos. 1833-1835 (3) 2.75 1.45

65th anniversary of independence.

Folk Dancing Type of 1977

Designs: Various dances.

1978, Feb. 15 Litho. *Perf. 12*

1836 A375 5q multi .20 .20
1837 A375 25q multi .20 .20
1838 A375 80q multi .50 .25
1839 A375 1 l multi .60 .30
1840 A375 2.30 l multi 1.25 .65
Nos. 1836-1840 (5) 2.75 1.60

Nos. 1836-1840 have white background around dancers, Nos. 1799-1805 have pinkish shadows.

Tractor Drivers, by Dhimitraq Trebicka A382

Working Class Paintings: 80q, Steeplejack, by Spiro Kristo. 85q, "A Point in the Discussion," by Skender Milori. 90q, Oil rig crew, by Anesti Cini, vert. 1.60 l, Metal workers, by Ramadan Karanxha. 2.20 l, Political discussion, by Sotiraq Sholla.

1978, Mar. 25 Litho. *Perf. 12*

1841 A382 25q multi .20 .20
1842 A382 80q multi .30 .20
1843 A382 85q multi .50 .25
1844 A382 90q multi .50 .25
1845 A382 1.60 l multi 1.25 .65
Nos. 1841-1845 (5) 2.75 1.55

Miniature Sheet

Perf. 12 on 2 sides x Imperf.

1846 A382 2.20 l multi 2.50 2.50

Woman with Rifle and Pickax A383

1.95 l, Farm & Militia women, industrial plant.

1978, June 1 Litho. *Perf. 12*

1847 A383 25q gold & red .25 .20
1848 A383 1.95 l gold & red 2.00 1.00

8th Congress of Women's Union.

Children and Flowers — A384

Designs: 10q, Children with rifle, ax, book and flags. 25q, Dancing children in folk costume. 1.80 l, Children in school.

1978, June 1 Litho.

1849 A384 5q multi .20 .20
1850 A384 10q multi .20 .20
1851 A384 25q multi .35 .20
1852 A384 1.80 l multi 1.75 .90
Nos. 1849-1852 (4) 2.50 1.50

International Children's Day.

Spirit of Skanderbeg as Conqueror A385

10q, Battle at Mostar Bridge. 80q, Marchers, Albanian flag. 1.20 l, Riflemen in winter battle. 1.65 l, Abdyl Frasheri (1839-92). 2.20 l, Rifles, scroll, pen, League building. 2.60 l, League headquarters, Prizren.

1978, June 10 Litho. *Perf. 12*

1853 A385 10q multi .20 .20
1854 A385 25q multi .20 .20
1855 A385 80q multi .50 .25
1856 A385 1.20 l multi .60 .30
1857 A385 1.65 l multi 1.00 .50
1858 A385 2.60 l multi 1.50 .75
Nos. 1853-1858 (6) 4.00 2.20

Miniature Sheet

Perf. 12 on 2 sides x Imperf.

1859 A385 2.20 l multi 2.50 2.50

Centenary of League of Prizren.

Guerrillas and Flag, 1943 — A386

Designs: 25q, Soldier, sailor, airman, militiaman, horiz. 1.90 l, Members of armed forces, civil guards, and Young Pioneers.

1978, July 10 *Perf. 11½x12½*

1860 A386 5q multi .50 .25
1861 A386 25q multi .75 .50
1862 A386 1.90 l multi 4.75 2.50
Nos. 1860-1862 (3) 6.00 3.25

35th anniversary of People's Army.

Woman with Machine Carbine — A387

Kerchief Dance — A388

25q, Man with target rifle, horiz. 95q, Man shooting with telescopic sights, horiz. 2.40 l, Woman target shooting with pistol.

Perf. 12½x12, 12x12½

1978, Sept. 20 Litho.

1863 A387 25q black & yel .25 .20
1864 A387 80q orange & blk .50 .25
1865 A387 95q red & blk .60 .30
1866 A387 2.40 l carmine & blk 1.40 .75
Nos. 1863-1866 (4) 2.75 1.50

32nd National Rifle-shooting Championships, Sept. 20.

1978, Oct. 6 *Perf. 12*

15q, Musicians. 25q, Fiddler with single-stringed instrument. 80q, Dancers, men. 1.20 l, Saber dance. 1.90 l, Singers, women.

1867 A388 10q multi .20 .20
1868 A388 15q multi .20 .20
1869 A388 25q multi .20 .20
1870 A388 80q multi .30 .20
1871 A388 1.20 l multi .60 .20
1872 A388 1.90 l multi .95 .25
Nos. 1867-1872 (6) 2.45 1.25

National Folklore Festival.
See Nos. 2082-2085, 2289-2290.

No. 1736 Surcharged with New Value, 2 Bars and "RICCIONE 78"

1978 Litho. *Perf. 12½x12*

1873 A360 3.30 l on 25q multi 6.50 4.00

Riccione 78 Philatelic Exhibition.

Enver Hoxha A389

1978, Oct. 16 Litho. *Perf. 12x12½*

1874 A389	80q	red & multi	.35	.20
1875 A389	1.20 l	red & multi	.55	.30
1876 A389	2.40 l	red & multi	1.10	.55
		Nos. 1874-1876 (3)	2.00	1.05

Miniature Sheet

Perf. 12½ on 2 sides x Imperf.

1877 A389 2.20 l red & multi 2.00 2.00

70th birthday of Enver Hoxha, First Secretary of Central Committee of the Communist Party of Albania.

Woman and Wheat — A390

25q, Woman with egg crates. 80q, Shepherd, sheep. 2.60 l, Milkmaid, cows.

1978, Dec. 15 *Perf. 12x12½*

1878 A390	15q	multicolored	.20	.20
1879 A390	25q	multicolored	.30	.20
1880 A390	80q	multicolored	1.25	.60
1881 A390	2.60 l	multicolored	4.25	2.25
		Nos. 1878-1881 (4)	6.00	3.25

Dora d'Istria — A391 Tower House — A392

Design: 1.10 l, Full portrait of Dora d'Istria, author; birth sesquicentennial.

1979, Jan. 22 Litho. *Perf. 12*

1882 A391	80q	lt grn & blk	.90	.45
1883 A391	1.10 l	vio brn & blk	1.10	.55

Costume Type of 1977

Designs: Various folk dances.

1979, Feb. 25

1884 A375	15q	multi	.20	.20
1885 A375	25q	multi	.30	.20
1886 A375	80q	multi	.50	.25
1887 A375	1.20 l	multi	.75	.40
1888 A375	1.40 l	multi	1.00	.50
		Nos. 1884-1888 (5)	2.75	1.55

#1884-1888 have white background. Denomination in UL on #1885, in UR on #1802; LL on #1886, UL on #1803.

1979, Mar. 20

Traditional Houses: 15q, Stone gallery house, horiz. 80q, House with wooden galleries, horiz. 1.20 l, Galleried tower house. 1.40 l, 1.90 l, Tower houses, diff.

1889 A392	15q	multi	.20	.20
1890 A392	25q	multi	.30	.20
1891 A392	80q	multi	.50	.25
1892 A392	1.20 l	multi	.75	.40
1893 A392	1.40 l	multi	1.00	.50
		Nos. 1889-1893 (5)	2.75	1.55

Miniature Sheet

Perf. 12 on 2 sides x Imperf.

1894 A392 1.90 l multi 3.25 3.25

See Nos. 2015-2018.

Soldier, Factories, Wheat A393

1.65 l, Soldiers, workers and coat of arms.

1979, May 14 Litho. *Perf. 12*

1895 A393	25q	multi	.75	.50
1896 A393	1.65 l	multi	2.50	1.25

Congress of Permet, 35th anniversary.

Albanian Flag A394

1979, June 4

1897 A394	25q	multi	1.00	.50
1898 A394	1.65 l	multi	3.00	1.50

5th Congress of Albanian Democratic Front.

Alexander Moissi, (1880-1935), Actor — A395

1979, Apr 2

1899 A396	80q	multi	1.00	.50
1900 A396	1.10 l	multi, diff.	1.25	.75

Vasil Shanto, (1913-44) A396

Design: 25q, 90q, Qemal Stafa (1921-42).

1979, May 5

1901 A395	15q	multi	.20	.20
1902 A395	25q	multi	.25	.20
1903 A395	60q	multi	.80	.40
1904 A395	90q	multi	1.50	.75
		Nos. 1901-1904 (4)	2.75	1.55

Shanto and Stafa, anti-Fascist fighters. For similar design see A410.

Winter Campaign, by Arben Basha — A397

Paintings of Military Scenes by: 25q, Ismail Lulani. 80q, Myrteza Fushekati. 1.20 l, Muhamet Deliu. 1.40 l, Jorgji Gjikopulli. 1.90 l, Fatmir Haxhiu.

1979, July 15 Litho. *Perf. 12½x12*

1905 A397	15q	multi	.20	.20
1906 A397	25q	multi	.20	.20
1907 A397	80q	multi	.50	.25
1908 A397	1.20 l	multi	.85	.50
1909 A397	1.40 l	multi	1.00	.50
		Nos. 1905-1909 (5)	2.75	1.65

Miniature Sheet

Perf. 12 on 2 sides x Imperf.

1910 A397 1.90 l multi 2.25 2.25

Athletes Surrounding Flag — A398

Literary Society Headquarters A399

1979, Oct. 1 Litho. *Perf. 12*

1911 A398	15q	shown	.20	.20
1912 A398	25q	Shooting	.20	.20
1913 A398	80q	Dancing	.55	.30
1914 A398	1.20 l	Soccer	.75	.40
1915 A398	1.40 l	High jump	.80	.50
		Nos. 1911-1915 (5)	2.50	1.60

Liberation Spartakiad, 35th anniversary.

1979, Oct. 12

Albanian Literary Society Centenary: 25q, Seal and charter. 80q, Founder. 1.55 l, 1879 Headquarters. 1.90 l, Founders.

1916 A399	25q	multi	.20	.20
1917 A399	80q	multi	.60	.30
1918 A399	1.20 l	multi	.90	.50
1919 A399	1.55 l	multi	1.00	.60
		Nos. 1916-1919 (4)	2.70	1.60

Miniature Sheet

Perf. 12½ on 2 sides x Imperf.

1920 A399 1.90 l multi 2.75 2.75

Congress Statute, Coat of Arms — A400

1979, Oct. 20 Photo. *Perf. 12x12½*

1921 A400	25q	multi	1.00	.50
1922 A400	1.65 l	multi	3.75	2.00

2nd Congress of Berat, 35th anniversary.

Children Entering School, Books — A401

1979 Litho. *Perf. 12½x12*

1923 A401	5q	shown	.20	.20
1924 A401	10q	Communications	.20	.20
1925 A401	15q	Steel workers	.20	.20
1926 A401	20q	Dancers, instruments	.20	.20
1927 A401	25q	Newspapers, radio, television	.20	.20
1928 A401	60q	Textile worker	.40	.20
1929 A401	80q	Armed forces	.55	.20
1930 A401	1.20 l	Industry	.80	.20
1931 A401	1.60 l	Transportation	1.00	.30
1932 A401	2.40 l	Agriculture	1.50	.35
1932A A401	3 l	Medicine	1.90	.50
		Nos. 1923-1932A (11)	7.15	2.75

Workers and Factory A402

Worker, Red Flag and: 80q, Hand holding sickle and rifle. 1.20 l, Red star and open book. 1.55 l, Open book and cogwheel.

1979, Nov. 29

1933 A402	25q	multi	.20	.20
1934 A402	80q	multi	.55	.30
1935 A402	1.20 l	multi	.90	.45
1936 A402	1.55 l	multi	1.10	.55
		Nos. 1933-1936 (4)	2.75	1.50

35th anniversary of independence.

Joseph Stalin — A403

Design: 1.10 l, Stalin on dais, horiz.

1979, Dec. 21 Litho. *Perf. 12*

1937 A403	80q	red & dk bl	.75	.20
1938 A403	1.10 l	red & dk bl	1.00	.20

Joseph Stalin (1879-1953), birth centenary.

Fireplace and Pottery, Korcar A404

Home Furnishings: 80q, Cupboard bed, dagger, pistol, ammunition pouch, Shkodar. 1.20 l, Stool, pot, chair, Mirdit. 1.35 l, Chimney, dagger, jacket, Gjirokaster.

1980, Feb. 27 Litho. *Perf. 12*

1939 A404	25q	multi	.20	.20
1940 A404	80q	multi	.35	.20
1941 A404	1.20 l	multi	.85	.45
1942 A404	1.35 l	multi	1.10	.60
		Nos. 1939-1942 (4)	2.50	1.45

See Nos. 1985-1988.

Pipe, Painted Flask A405

1980, Mar. 4

1943 A405	25q	shown	.20	.20
1944 A405	80q	Leather handbags	.40	.20
1945 A405	1.20 l	Carved eagle, embroidered rug	.90	.45
1946 A405	1.35 l	Lace	1.10	.55
		Nos. 1943-1946 (4)	2.60	1.40

Prof. Aleksander Xhuvanit Birth Centenary A406

1980, Mar. 14

1947 A406 80q multi 1.00 .50
1948 A406 1 l multi 1.25 .75

Revolutionaries on Horseback — A407

Insurrection at Kosove, 70th Anniversary: 1 l, Battle scene.

1980, Apr. 4

1949 A407 80q red & black 1.00 .50
1950 A407 1 l red & black 1.50 .75

Soldiers and Workers Laboring to Aid the Stricken Populations, by D. Jukinui and I. Lulani — A408

1980, Apr. 15 Litho. *Perf. 12½*

1951 A408 80q lt blue & multi 1.00 .50
1952 A408 1 l lt blue grn & multi 1.50 .75

Lenin, 110th Birth Anniversary A409

1980, Apr. 22

1953 A409 80q multi 1.00 .50
1954 A409 1 l multi 1.75 1.00

Misto Mame and Ali Demi, War Martyrs A410

War Martyrs: 80q, Sadik Staveleci, Vojo Kusji, Hoxhi Martini. 1.20 l, Bule Naipi, Persefoni Kokedhima. 1.35 l, Ndoc Deda, Hydajet Lezha, Naim Gyylbegu, Ndoc Mazi, Ahmed Haxha.

1980, May 5

1955 A410 25q multi .20 .20
1956 A410 80q multi .55 .30
1957 A410 1.20 l multi 1.00 .50
1958 A410 1.35 l multi 1.25 .75
Nos. 1955-1958 (4) 3.00 1.75

See Nos. 2012A-2012D, 2025-2028, 2064-2067, 2122-2125, 2171-2174, 2207-2209.

Scene from "Mirela" A411

1980, June 7

1959 A411 15q shown .20 .20
1960 A411 25q The Scribbler .20 .20
1961 A411 80q Circus Bears .50 .30
1962 A411 2.40 l Waterdrops 1.75 1.00
Nos. 1959-1962 (4) 2.65 1.70

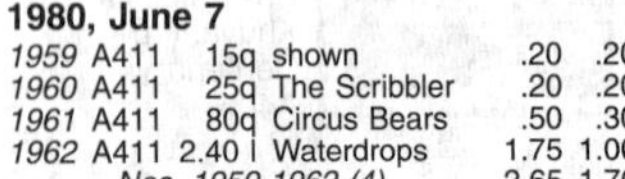

Carrying Iron Castings in the Enver Hoxha Tractor Combine, by S. Shijaku and M. Fushekati — A412

Paintings (Gallery of Figurative Paintings, Tirana): 80q, The Welder, by Harilla Dhima. 1.20 l, Steel Erectors, by Petro Kokushta. 1.35 l, Pandeli Lena, 1.80 l Communists, by Vilson Kilica.

1980, July 22

1963 A412 25q multi .20 .20
1964 A412 80q multi .55 .30
1965 A412 1.20 l multi .90 .50
1966 A412 1.35 l multi 1.10 .60
Nos. 1963-1966 (4) 2.75 1.60

Souvenir Sheet

1967 A412 1.80 l multi 2.25 2.25

Gate, Parchment Miniature, 11th Cent. — A413

Bas reliefs of the Middle Ages: 80q, Eagle, 13th cent. 1.20 l, Heraldic lion, 14th cent. 1.35 l, Pheasant, 14th cent.

1980, Sept. 27 Litho. *Perf. 12*

1968 A413 25q gold & blk .20 .20
1969 A413 80q gold & blk .35 .20
1970 A413 1.20 l gold & blk .65 .35
1971 A413 1.35 l gold & blk .80 .40
Nos. 1968-1971 (4) 2.00 1.15

Divjaka National Park A414

1980, Nov. 6 Photo.

1972 A414 80q shown .60 .30
1973 A414 1.20 l Lura .90 .50
1974 A414 1.60 l Thethi 1.50 .75
Nos. 1972-1974 (3) 3.00 1.55

Souvenir Sheet

Perf. 12½

1975 A414 1.80 l Llogara Park 2.75 2.75

Citizens, Flag and Arms of Albania A415

1981, Jan. 11 Litho. *Perf. 12*

1976 A415 80q shown .75 .35
1977 A415 1 l People's Party Headquarters, Tirana 1.00 .60

35th anniversary of the Republic.

Child's Bed A416

1981, Mar. 20 Litho. *Perf. 12*

1978 A416 25q shown .20 .20
1979 A416 80q Wooden bucket, brass bottle .50 .25
1980 A416 1.20 l Shoes .70 .35
1981 A416 1.35 l Jugs .85 .50
Nos. 1978-1981 (4) 2.25 1.30

A417

A419

1981, Apr. 20

1982 A417 80q Soldiers .60 .30
1983 A417 1 l Sword combat .90 .45

Souvenir Sheet

Perf. 12½ Vert.

1984 A417 1.80 l Soldier with pistol 1.75 1.75

Battle of Shtimje centenary.

Home Furnishings Type of 1980

1981, Feb. 25 Litho. *Perf. 12*

1985 A404 25q House interior, Labara .20 .20
1986 A404 80q Labara, diff. .30 .20
1987 A404 1.20 l Mat .65 .35
1988 A404 1.35 l Dibres .85 .45
Nos. 1985-1988 (4) 2.00 1.20

1981, June *Perf. 12*

Designs: Children's circus.

1989 A419 15q multi .20 .20
1990 A419 25q multi .20 .20
1991 A419 80q multi .35 .20
1992 A419 2.40 l multi 1.00 .60
Nos. 1989-1992 (4) 1.75 1.20

Soccer Players A420

1982 World Cup Soccer Elimination Games: Various soccer players.

1981, Mar. 31 Litho. *Perf. 12*

1993 A420 25q multi .25 .20
1994 A420 80q multi 1.90 .40
1995 A420 1.20 l multi 2.75 .60
1996 A420 1.35 l multi 3.50 .80
Nos. 1993-1996 (4) 8.40 2.00

Allies, by S. Hysa A421

Paintings: 80q, Warriors, by A. Buza. 1.20 l, Rallying to the Flag, Dec. 1911, by A. Zajmi, vert. 1.35 l, My Flag is My Heart, by L. Cefa, vert. 1.80 l, Circling the Flag in a Common Cause, by N. Vasia.

1981, July 10 *Perf. 12½x12*

1997 A421 25q multi .30 .20
1998 A421 80q multi .45 .30
1999 A421 1.20 l multi .65 .35
2000 A421 1.35 l multi .85 .45
Nos. 1997-2000 (4) 2.25 1.30

Souvenir Sheet

2001 A421 1.80 l multi 2.00 2.00

#2001 contains one 55x55mm stamp.

Rifleman A422

1981, Aug. 30 *Perf. 12*

2002 A422 25q shown .20 .20
2003 A422 80q Weight lifting .50 .40
2004 A422 1.20 l Volleyball .70 .40
2005 A422 1.35 l Soccer .85 .50
Nos. 2002-2005 (4) 2.25 1.50

Albanian Workers' Party, 8th Congress A423

1981, Nov. 1

2006 A423 80q Flag, star .60 .50
2007 A423 1 l Flag, hammer & sickle .90 .75

Albanian Workers' Party, 40th Anniv. — A424

Communist Youth Org., 40th Anniv. — A425

1981, Nov. 8

2008 A424 80q Symbols of industrialization .50 .50
2009 A424 2.80 l Fist, emblem 1.50 1.25

Souvenir Sheet

2010 A424 1.80 l Enver Hoxha, Memoirs 2.50 2.50

1981, Nov. 23

2011 A425 80q Star, ax, map .75 .75
2012 A425 1 l Flags, star 1.25 1.00

War Martyrs Type of 1980

25q, Perlat Rexhepi (1919-42) and Branko Kadia (1921-42). 80q, Xheladin Beqiri (1908-44) and Hajdar Dushi (1916-44). 1.20 l, Koci Bako (1905-41), Vasil Laci (1923-41) and Mujo Ulqinaku (1898-1939). 1.35 l, Mine Peza (1875-1942) and Zoja Cure (1920-44).

1981, May 5 Litho. *Perf. 12*

2012A A410 25q silver & multi .20 .20
2012B A410 80q gold & multi .75 .40
2012C A410 1.20 l silver & multi 1.25 .55
2012D A410 1.35 l gold & multi 1.40 .60
Nos. 2012A-2012D (4) 3.60 1.75

Fan S. Noli, Writer, Birth Centenary A426

1982, Jan. 6 Litho. *Perf. 12*

2013 A426 80q lt ol grn & gold .65 .40
2014 A426 1.10 l lt red brn & gold 1.10 .60

Traditional Houses Type of 1979

1982, Feb. *Perf. 12½x12*

2015 A392 25q Bulqize .20 .20
2016 A392 80q Lebush .75 .50
2017 A392 1.20 l Bicaj 1.00 .60
2018 A392 1.55 l Klos 1.40 .75
Nos. 2015-2018 (4) 3.35 2.05

TB Bacillus Centenary A428

1982, Mar. 24 *Perf. 12*

2019 A428 80q Globe 1.75 1.00
2020 A428 1.10 l Koch 2.75 1.75

Albanian League House, Prizren, by K. Buza — A429

Kosova Landscapes: 25q, Castle at Prizrenit, by G. Madhi. 1.20 l, Mountain Gorge at Rogove, by K. Buza. 1.55 l, Street of the Hadhji at Zekes, by G. Madhi. 25q, 1.20 l, 1.55 l vert.

Perf. 12x12½, 12½x12

1982, Apr. 15 Litho.

2021 A429 25q multi .30 .20
2022 A429 80q multi .80 .40
2023 A429 1.20 l multi 1.40 .75
2024 A429 1.55 l multi 2.00 1.00
Nos. 2021-2024 (4) 4.50 2.35

War Martyr Type of 1980

Designs: 25q, Hibe Palikuqi, Liri Gero. 80q, Mihal Duri, Kajo Karafili. 1.20 l, Fato Dudumi, Margarita Tutulani, Shejnaze Juka. 1.55 l, Memo Meto, Gjok Doci.

1982, May *Perf. 12*

2025 A410 25q multi .20 .20
2026 A410 80q multi .50 .30
2027 A410 1.20 l multi .80 .40
2028 A410 1.55 l multi 1.10 .75
Nos. 2025-2028 (4) 2.60 1.65

Loading Freighter — A430

Children's Paintings.

1982, June 15 *Perf. 12½x12*

2029 A430 15q shown .25 .20
2030 A430 80q Forest .55 .30
2031 A430 1.20 l City .80 .40
2032 A430 1.65 l Park 1.75 1.00
Nos. 2029-2032 (4) 3.35 1.90

9th Congress of Trade Unions A431

1982, June 6 Litho. *Perf. 12*

2033 A431 80q Workers, factories 1.50 1.00
2034 A431 1.10 l Emblem, flag 2.00 1.25

Alpine Village Festival, by Danish Jukniu A432

Industrial Development Paintings: 80q, Hydroelectric Station Builders, by Ali Miruku. 1.20 l, Steel Workers, by Clirim Ceka. 1.55 l, Oil drillers, by Pandeli Lena. 1.90 l, Trapping the Furnace, by Jorgji Gjikopulli.

1982, July *Perf. 12½*

2035 A432 25q multi .20 .20
2036 A432 80q multi .65 .50
2037 A432 1.20 l multi .90 .80
2038 A432 1.55 l multi 1.25 1.00
Nos. 2035-2038 (4) 3.00 2.50

Souvenir Sheet

Perf. 12

2039 A432 1.90 l multi 2.50 2.50

No. 2039 contains one 54x48mm stamp.

Communist Party Newspaper "Voice of the People," 40th Anniv. — A432a

1982, Aug. 25 Litho. *Perf. 12*

2039A A432a 80q Newspapers *25.00 15.00*
2039B A432a 1.10 l Paper, press *25.00 15.00*

40th Anniv. of Democratic Front A433

1982, Sept. 16 *Perf. 12*

2040 A433 80q Glory to the Heroes of Peza Monument 3.75 2.25
2041 A433 1.10 l Marchers 6.25 4.00

8th Youth Congress — A434

Handmade Shoulder Bags — A435

1982, Oct. 4

2042 A434 80q multi 3.50 2.75
2043 A434 1.10 l multi 5.50 4.00

1982, Nov.

2044 A435 25q Rug, horiz. .30 .20
2045 A435 80q shown .65 .40
2046 A435 1.20 l Wooden pots, bowls, horiz. .90 .50
2047 A435 1.55 l Jug 1.40 1.00
Nos. 2044-2047 (4) 3.25 2.10

70th Anniv. of Independence — A436

1982, Nov. 28

2048 A436 20q Ishamil Qemali .25 .20
2049 A436 1.20 l Partisans 1.00 .60
2050 A436 2.40 l Partisans, diff. 2.00 1.00
Nos. 2048-2050 (3) 3.25 1.80

Souvenir Sheet

2051 A436 1.90 l Independence Monument, Tirana 2.50 2.50

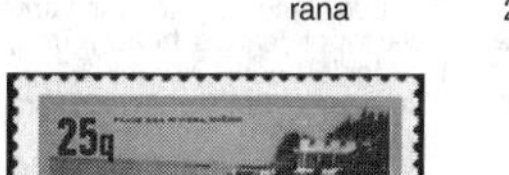

Dhermi Beach A437

1982, Dec. 20

2052 A437 25q shown .20 .20
2053 A437 80q Sarande .60 .30
2054 A437 1.20 l Ksamil .90 .45
2055 A437 1.55 l Lukove 1.40 .75
Nos. 2052-2055 (4) 3.10 1.70

Handkerchief Dancers — A438

Folkdancers.

1983, Feb. 20 Litho. *Perf. 12*

2056 A438 25q shown .20 .20
2057 A438 80q With kerchief, drum .40 .30
2058 A438 1.20 l With guitar, flute, tambourine .75 .50
2059 A438 1.55 l Women .90 .75
Nos. 2056-2059 (4) 2.25 1.75

A439

A440

1983, Mar. 14 Litho. *Perf. 12*

2060 A439 80q multi 1.10 .20
2061 A439 1.10 l multi 1.50 .25

Karl Marx (1818-83).

1983, Apr. 20

2062 A440 80q Electricity generation .75 .50
2063 A440 1.10 l Gas & oil production 1.25 .75

Energy development.

War Martyr Type of 1980

Designs: 25q, Asim Zeneli (1916-43), Nazmi Rushiti (1919-42). 80q, Shyqyri Ishmi (1922-42), Shyqyri Alimerko (1923-43), Myzafer Asqeriu (1918-42). 1.20 l, Qybra Sokoli (1924-44), Qeriba Derri (1905-44), Ylbere Bilibashi (1928-44). 1.55 l, Themo Vasi (1915-43), Abaz Shehu (1905-42).

1983, May 5 Litho. *Perf. 12*

2064 A410 25q multi .20 .20
2065 A410 80q multi .50 .30
2066 A410 1.20 l multi 1.00 .75
2067 A410 1.55 l multi 1.40 .90
Nos. 2064-2067 (4) 3.10 2.15

Women's Union, 9th Congress A441

1983, June 1 Litho. *Perf. 12x12½*

2068 A441 80q red & gold 1.10 .60
2069 A441 1.10 l blue & gold 1.50 .90

Bicycling A442

1983, June 20 *Perf. 12*

2070 A442 25q shown .20 .20
2071 A442 80q Chess .55 .35
2072 A442 1.20 l Gymnastics .90 .50
2073 A442 1.55 l Wrestling 1.10 .70
Nos. 2070-2073 (4) 2.75 1.75

40th Anniv. of People's Army — A443

1983, July 10

2074 A443 20q Armed services .25 .20
2075 A443 1.20 l Soldier, gun barrels 1.00 .50
2076 A443 2.40 l Factory guard, crowd 1.75 1.00
Nos. 2074-2076 (3) 3.00 1.70

Sunny Day, by Myrteza Fushekati — A444

Paintings: 80q, Messenger of the Grasp, by Niko Progi. 1.20 l, 29 November 1944, by Harilla Dhimo. 1.55 l, Fireworks, by Pandi Mele. 1.90 l, Partisan Assault, by Sali Shijaku and M. Fushekati.

1983, Aug. 28 Litho. *Perf. 12½x12*

2077 A444 25q multi .20 .20
2078 A444 80q multi .70 .40
2079 A444 1.20 l multi .85 .50
2080 A444 1.55 l multi 1.25 .75
Nos. 2077-2080 (4) 3.00 1.85

Souvenir Sheet

Perf. 12

2081 A444 1.90 l multi 4.00 4.00

Folklore Festival Type of 1978

Gjirokaster Folklore Festival: folkdances.

1983, Oct. 6 Litho. *Perf. 12*

2082 A388 25q Sword dance .20 .20
2083 A388 80q Kerchief dance .85 .45
2084 A388 1.20 l Shepherd flautists 1.10 .75
2085 A388 1.55 l Garland dance 1.60 1.00
Nos. 2082-2085 (4) 3.75 2.40

World Communications Year — A446

1983, Nov. 10

2086 A446 60q multi .50 .25
2087 A446 1.20 l multi 1.00 .50

75th Birthday of Enver Hoxha A447

1983, Oct. 16 Litho. *Perf. 12½*

2088 A447 80q multi .45 .25
2089 A447 1.20 l multi .80 .60
2090 A447 1.80 l multi 1.00 .75
Nos. 2088-2090 (3) 2.25 1.60

Souvenir Sheet

Perf. 12

2091 A447 1.90 l multi 2.00 2.00

The Right to a Joint Triumph, by J. Keraj A448

Era of Skanderbeg in Figurative Art: 80q, The Heroic Center of the Battle of Krujes, by N. Bakalli. 1.20 l, The Rights of the Enemy after our Triumph, by N. Progri. 1.55 l, The Discussion at Lezhes, by B. Ahmeti. 1.90 l, Victory over the Turks, by G. Madhi.

1983, Dec. 10 *Perf. 12½x12*

2092 A448 25q multi .25 .20
2093 A448 80q multi .80 .45
2094 A448 1.20 l multi 1.10 .65
2095 A448 1.55 l multi 1.60 1.00
Nos. 2092-2095 (4) 3.75 2.30

Souvenir Sheet

Perf. 12

2096 A448 1.90 l multi 4.00 3.50

Greco-Roman Ruins of Illyria — A449

1983, Dec. 28 *Perf. 12*

2097 A449 80q Amphitheater, Buthroxtum 1.00 .75
2098 A449 1.20 l Colonnade, Apollonium 1.50 1.00
2099 A449 1.80 l Vaulted gallery, amphitheater at Epidamnus 1.50 1.25
Nos. 2097-2099 (3) 4.00 3.00

Archeological Discoveries A450

Designs: Apollo, 3rd cent. 25q, Tombstone, Korce, 3rd cent. 80q, Apollo, diff. 1st cent. 1.10 l, Earthenware pot (child's head), Tren, 1st cent. 1.20 l, Man's head, Dyrrah, 2.20 l, Eros with Dolphin, statue Bronze Dyrrah, 3rd cent.

1984, Feb. 25 *Perf. 12x12½*

2100 A450 15q multi .20 .20
2101 A450 25q multi .20 .20
2102 A450 80q multi .55 .30
2103 A450 1.10 l multi .75 .50
2104 A450 1.20 l multi .90 .60
2105 A450 2.20 l multi 1.40 .75
Nos. 2100-2105 (6) 4.00 2.55

Clock Towers — A451

1984, Mar. 30 Litho. *Perf. 12*

2106 A451 15q Gjirokaster .20 .20
2107 A451 25q Kavaje .20 .20
2108 A451 80q Elbasan .50 .40
2109 A451 1.10 l Tirana .60 .45
2110 A451 1.20 l Peqin .90 .60
2111 A451 2.20 l Kruje 1.60 .90
Nos. 2106-2111 (6) 4.00 2.75

40th Anniv. of Liberation A452

1984, Apr. 20 Litho. *Perf. 12*

2112 A452 15q Student & microscope .20 .20
2113 A452 25q Guerrilla with flag .20 .20
2114 A452 80q Children with flag .60 .35
2115 A452 1.10 l Soldier .75 .50
2116 A452 1.20 l Workers with flag .90 .60
2117 A452 2.20 l Militia at dam 1.60 1.00
Nos. 2112-2117 (6) 4.25 2.85

Children — A453

1984, May Litho. *Perf. 12*

2118 A453 15q Children reading .30 .20
2119 A453 25q Young pioneers .60 .35
2120 A453 60q Gardening 1.10 .55
2121 A453 2.80 l Kite flying 2.50 1.50
Nos. 2118-2121 (4) 4.50 2.60

War Martyr Type of 1980

Designs: 15q, Manush Almani, Mustafa Matohiti, Kastriot Muco. 25q, Zaho Koka, Reshit Collaku, Maliq Muco. 1.20 l, Lefter Talo, Tom Kola, Fuat Babani. 2.20 l, Myslysm Shyri, Dervish Hexali, Skender Caci.

1984, May 5 Litho. *Perf. 12*

2122 A410 15q multi .30 .20
2123 A410 25q multi .60 .35
2124 A410 1.20 l multi 1.10 .70
2125 A410 2.20 l multi 2.00 1.25
Nos. 2122-2125 (4) 4.00 2.50

A454

A455

1984, May 24 Litho. *Perf. 12*

2126 A454 80q Enver Hoxha 1.50 .75
2127 A454 1.10 l Resistance fighter 2.00 1.50

40th anniv. of Permet Congress.

1984, June 12 Litho. *Perf. 12*

2128 A455 15q Goalkeeper .40 .30
2129 A455 25q Referee .60 .40
2130 A455 1.20 l Map of Europe 1.25 .60
2131 A455 2.20 l Field diagram 1.75 .90
Nos. 2128-2131 (4) 4.00 2.20

European soccer championships.

Freedom Came, by Myrteza Fushekati — A456

Paintings, Tirana Gallery of Figurative Art: 25q, Morning, by Zamir Mati, vert. 80q, My Darling, by Agim Zajmi, vert. 2.60 l, For the Partisans, by Arben Basha. 1.90 l, Eagle, by Zamir Mati, vert.

1984, June 12 *Perf. 12½*

2132 A456 15q multi .30 .20
2133 A456 25q multi .55 .45
2134 A456 80q multi 1.50 1.10
2135 A456 2.60 l multi 2.40 1.50
Nos. 2132-2135 (4) 4.75 3.25

Souvenir Sheet

Perf. 12 Horiz.

2136 A456 1.90 l multi 5.00 4.50

Flora — A457

1984, Aug. 20 Litho. *Perf. 12*

2137 A457 15q Moraceae L. .65 .35
2138 A457 25q Plantaginaceae L. 1.00 .50
2139 A457 1.20 l Hypericaceae L. 3.75 1.90
2140 A457 2.20 l Leontopodium alpinum 7.00 3.50
Nos. 2137-2140 (4) 12.40 6.25

AUSIPEX '84, Melbourne, Sept. 21-30 — A458

Perf. 12 Horiz.

1984, Sept. 21 Litho.

2141 A458 1.90 l Sword dancers, emblem 2.00 1.75

A459

A460

Forestry, logging, UNFAO emblem.

1984, Sept. 25 *Perf. 12*

2142 A459 15q Beech trees, transport .35 .20
2143 A459 25q Pine forest, logging cable .50 .35
2144 A459 1.20 l Firs, sawmill 1.75 1.00
2145 A459 2.20 l Forester clearing woods 2.40 1.50
Nos. 2142-2145 (4) 5.00 3.05

1984, Oct. 13 *Perf. 12½*

2146 A460 1.20 l View of Gjirokaster 2.00 .45

EURPHILA '84, Rome.

5th National Spartakiad A461

1984, Oct. 19 *Perf. 12*

2147 A461 15q Soccer .20 .20
2148 A461 25q Women's track & field .20 .20
2149 A461 80q Weight lifting .60 .30
2150 A461 2.20 l Pistol shooting 1.75 .90
Nos. 2147-2150 (4) 2.75 1.60

Souvenir Sheet

Perf. 12 Horiz.

2151 A461 1.90 l Opening ceremony, red flags 2.50 2.00

November 29 Revolution, 40th Anniv. A462

1984, Nov. 29 *Perf. 12*

2152 A462 80q Industrial reconstruction 1.25 .30
2153 A462 1.10 l Natl. flag, partisans 1.60 .40

Souvenir Sheet

Perf. 12 Horiz.

2154 A462 1.90 l Gen. Enver Hoxha reading 1944 declaration 2.50 2.00

Archaeological Discoveries from Illyria — A463

Designs: 15q, Iron Age water container. 80q, Terra-cotta woman's head, 6th-7th cent. B.C. 1.20 l, Aphrodite, bust, 3rd cent. B.C. 1.70 l, Nike, A.D. 1st-2nd cent. bronze statue.

1985, Feb. 25 *Perf. 12x12½*

2155 A463 15q multi .20 .20
2156 A463 80q multi .80 .40
2157 A463 1.20 l multi 1.10 .55
2158 A463 1.70 l multi 1.75 .85
Nos. 2155-2158 (4) 3.85 2.00

Hysni Kapo (1915-1980), Natl. Labor Party Leader — A464

1985, Mar. 4 *Perf. 12*

2159 A464 90q red & blk 1.25 .75
2160 A464 1.10 l chlky bl & blk 1.50 1.25

OLYMPHILEX '85, Lausanne — A465

1985, Mar. 18

2161 A465 25q Women's track & field .25 .20
2162 A465 60q Weight lifting .60 .30
2163 A465 1.20 l Soccer 1.10 .55
2164 A465 1.50 l Women's pistol shooting 1.25 .65
Nos. 2161-2164 (4) 3.20 1.70

Johann Sebastian Bach — A466

1985, Mar. 31

2165 A466 80q Portrait, manuscript 5.25 3.25
2166 A466 1.20 l Eisenach, birthplace 6.75 4.00

Gen. Enver Hoxha (1908-1985) A467

1985, Apr. 11 *Perf. 12½*

2167 A467 80q multicolored .80 .40

Souvenir Sheet

Imperf

2168 A467 1.90 l multicolored 2.00 1.00

Natl. Frontier Guards, 40th Anniv. A468

1985, Apr. 25 *Perf. 12*

2169 A468 25q Guardsman, family .75 .50
2170 A468 80q At frontier post 2.00 1.25

War Martyrs Type of 1980

25q, Mitro Xhani (1916-44), Nimete Progonati (1929-44), Kozma Nushi (1909-44). 40q, Ajet Xhindoli (1922-43), Mustafa Kacaci (1903-44), Estref Caka Osaja (1919-44). 60q, Celo Sinani (1929-44), Lt. Ambro Andoni (1920-44), Meleq Gosnishti (1913-44). 1.20 l, Thodhori Mastora (1920-44), Fejzi Micoli (1919-45), Hysen Cino (1920-44).

1985, May 5

2171 A410 25q multi .35 .20
2172 A410 40q multi .55 .40
2173 A410 60q multi 1.00 .60
2174 A410 1.20 l multi 1.60 1.00
Nos. 2171-2174 (4) 3.50 2.20

Victory over Fascism A469

25q, Rifle, red flag, inscribed May 9. 80q, Hand holding rifle, globe, broken swastika.

1985, May 9

2175 A469 25q multi *3.00 6.00*
2176 A469 80q multi *7.00 17.50*

End of World War II, 40th anniv.

Primary School, by Thoma Malo A470

Paintings, Tirana Gallery of Figurative Art: 80q, The Heroes, by Hysen Devolli, vert. 90q, In Our Days, by Angjelin Dodmasej, vert. 1.20 l, Going Off to Sow, by Ksenofon Dilo. 1.90 l, Foundry Workers, by Mikel Gurashi.

1985, June 25 *Perf. 12½*

2177 A470 25q multi .25 .20
2178 A470 80q multi .80 .40
2179 A470 90q multi .85 .45
2180 A470 1.20 l multi 1.10 .55
Nos. 2177-2180 (4) 3.00 1.60

Souvenir Sheet

Perf. 12 Horiz.

2181 A470 1.90 l multi 2.50 2.00

Basketball Championships, Spain — A471

Fruits — A472

Various plays.

1985, July 20 **Litho.** *Perf. 12*

2182 A471 25q dull bl & blk .25 .20
2183 A471 80q dull grn & blk .80 .40
2184 A471 1.20 l dl vio & blk 1.10 .60
2185 A471 1.60 l dl rose & blk 1.50 .80
Nos. 2182-2185 (4) 3.65 2.00

1985, Aug. 20

2186 A472 25q Oranges .20 .20
2187 A472 80q Plums .90 .60
2188 A472 1.20 l Apples 1.40 .75
2189 A472 1.60 l Cherries 2.00 1.25
Nos. 2186-2189 (4) 4.50 2.80

Architecture A473

1985, Sept. 20

2190 A473 25q Kruja .25 .20
2191 A473 80q Gjirokastra 1.10 .65
2192 A473 1.20 l Berati 1.40 1.00
2193 A473 1.60 l Shkodera 1.75 1.25
Nos. 2190-2193 (4) 4.50 3.10

Natl. Folk Theater Festival — A474

Various scenes from folk plays.

1985, Oct. 6

2194 A474 25q multi .25 .20
2195 A474 80q multi .80 .40
2196 A474 1.20 l multi 1.10 .60
2197 A474 1.60 l multi 1.50 .75

Size: 56x82mm

Imperf

2198 A474 1.90 l multi 3.50 1.90
Nos. 2194-2198 (5) 7.15 3.85

Socialist People's Republic, 40th Anniv. — A475

1986, Jan. 11 **Litho.** *Perf. 12½*

2199 A475 25q Natl. crest, vert. 1.25 .75
2200 A475 80q Proclamation, 1946 2.25 1.50

A476

A477

Designs: 25q, Dam, River Drin, Melgun. 80q, Bust of Enver Hoxha, dam power house.

1986, Feb. 20 *Perf. 12*

2201 A476 25q multi 2.50 1.00
2202 A476 80q multi 5.00 3.50

Enver Hoxha hydro-electric power station, Koman.

1986, Mar. 20 **Litho.** *Perf. 12*

Flowers: 25q, Gymnospermium shqipetarum. 1.20 l, Leucojum valentinum.

2203 A477 25q multi 1.00 .50
2204 A477 1.20 l multi 4.00 2.50
a. Pair, #2203-2204 12.00 8.00

No. 2204a sold only in booklets of 2; exists imperf.

A478

Famous Men — A479

Designs: 25q, Maxim Gorky, Russian author. 80q, Andre Marie Ampere, French physicist. 1.20 l, James Watt, English inventor of modern steam engine. 2.40 l, Franz Liszt, Hungarian composer.

1986, Apr. 20

2205		Strip of 4	5.00	2.20
a.	A478 25q dull red brown		.35	.20
b.	A478 80q dull violet		.85	.40
c.	A478 1.20 l blue green		1.40	.60
d.	A478 2.40 l dull lilac rose		2.40	.90

Size: 88x72mm

Imperf

2206	A479	1.90 l multi	2.50	2.25

No. 2206 has central area picturing Gorky, Ampere, Watt and Liszt, perf. 12½.

War Martyrs Type of 1980

25q, Ramiz Aranitasi (1923-43), Inajete Dumi (1924-44) and Laze Nuro Ferraj (1897-1944). 80q, Dine Kalenja (1919-44), Kozma Naska (1921-44), Met Hasa (1929-44) and Fahri Ramadani (1920-44). 1.20 l, Hiqmet Buzi (1927-44), Bajram Tusha (1922-42), Mumin Selami (1923-42) and Hajrfdin Bylyshi (1923-42).

1986, May 5 ***Perf. 12***

2207	A410	25q multi	.75	.35
2208	A410	80q multi	2.25	1.25
2209	A410	1.20 l multi	3.00	1.50
		Nos. 2207-2209 (3)	6.00	3.10

A480

1986 World Cup Soccer Championships, Mexico — A481

1986, May 31 **Litho.** ***Perf. 12***

2210	A480	25q Globe, world cup	.25	.20
2211	A480	1.20 l Player, soccer ball	1.25	.60

Size: 97x64mm

Imperf

2212	A481	1.90 l multi	1.75	.90
		Nos. 2210-2212 (3)	3.25	1.70

No. 2212 has central label, perf. 12½.

Transportation Workers' Day, 40th Anniv. — A482

1986, Aug. 10 **Litho.** ***Perf. 12***

2213	A482	1.20 l multi	3.75	2.75

Prominent Albanians A483

Designs: 30q, Naim Frasheri (1846-1900), poet. 60q, Ndre Mjeda (1866-1937), poet. 90q, Petro Nini Luarasi (1865-1911), poet, journalist. 1 l, Andon Zako Cajupi (1866-1930), poet. 1.20 l, Millosh Gjergj Nikolla Migjeni (1911-1938), novelist. 2.60 l, Urani Rumbo (1884-1936), educator.

1986, Sept. 20 **Litho.** ***Perf. 12***

2214	A483	30q multi	.30	.20
2215	A483	60q multi	.50	.30
2216	A483	90q multi	.85	.45
2217	A483	1 l multi	1.10	.70
2218	A483	1.20 l multi	1.25	.75
2219	A483	2.60 l multi	3.50	2.00
		Nos. 2214-2219 (6)	7.50	4.40

Albanian Workers' Party, 9th Congress, Tirana A484

1986, Nov. 3 **Litho.** ***Perf. 12***

2220	A484	30q multi	2.75	2.00

A485

A486

Albanian Workers' Party, 45th Anniv.: 30q, Handstamp, signature of Hoxha. 1.20 l, Marx, Engels, Lenin and Stalin, party building.

1986, Nov. 8

2221	A485	30q multi	1.00	.50
2222	A485	1.20 l multi	3.00	1.50

1986, Nov. 29 ***Perf. 12x12½***

Statue of Mother Albania.

2223	A486	10q peacock blue	.20	.20
2224	A486	20q henna brn	.20	.20
2225	A486	30q vermilion	.30	.20
2226	A486	50q dk olive bis	.50	.25
2227	A486	60q lt olive grn	.60	.30
2228	A486	80q rose	.80	.40
2229	A486	90q ultra	.90	.45
2230	A486	1.20 l green	1.10	.60
2231	A486	1.60 l red vio	1.50	.75
2232	A486	2.20 l myrtle grn	2.00	1.10
2233	A486	3 l brn org	2.75	1.40
2234	A486	6 l yel bister	5.50	2.25
		Nos. 2223-2234 (12)	16.35	8.10

For surcharges see Nos. 2435-2439.

Artifacts A487

Designs: 30q, Head of Aesoulapius, 5th cent. B.C. Byllis, marble. 80q, Aphrodite, 3rd cent. B.C., Fier, terracotta. 1 l, Pan, 3rd-2nd cent. B.C., Byllis, bronze. 1.20 l, Jupiter, A.D. 2nd cent., Tirana, limestone.

1987, Feb. 20

2235	A487	30q multi	.50	.25
2236	A487	80q multi	.90	.45
2237	A487	1 l multi	1.10	.75
2238	A487	1.20 l multi	1.50	1.00
		Nos. 2235-2238 (4)	4.00	2.45

A488

A489

Gun, quill pen, book of the alphabet and: 30q, Monument, vert. 80q, School, Korca. 1.20 l, Students.

1987, Mar. 7 ***Perf. 12***

2239	A488	30q multi	.35	.20
2240	A488	80q multi	.85	.40
2241	A488	1.20 l multi	1.25	.60
		Nos. 2239-2241 (3)	2.45	1.20

First Albanian school, cent.

1987, Apr. 20

Famous Men: 30q, Victor Hugo, French author. 80q, Galileo Galilei, Italian mathematician, philosopher. 90q, Charles Darwin, British biologist. 1.30 l, Miguel Cervantes, Spanish novelist.

2242	A489	30q multi	.30	.20
2243	A489	80q multi	.75	.40
2244	A489	90q multi	.90	.45
2245	A489	1.30 l multi	1.25	.80
		Nos. 2242-2245 (4)	3.20	1.85

World Food Day — A490

10th Trade Unions Cong. — A491

1987, May 20

2246	A490	30q Forsythia europaea	.30	.20
2247	A490	90q Moltkia doerfleri	.85	.45
2248	A490	2.10 l Wulfenia baldacii	2.00	1.00
		Nos. 2246-2248 (3)	3.15	1.65

1987, June 25

2249	A491	1.20 l multi	2.75	2.50

Sowing, by Bujar Asllani — A492

Paintings in the Eponymous Museum, Tirana: 30q, The Sustenance of Industry, by Myrteza Fushekati, vert. 80q, The Gifted Partisan, by Skender Kokobobo, vert. 1.20 l, At the Forging Block, by Clirim Ceka.

Perf. 12x12½, 12½x12

1987, July 20 **Litho.**

2250	A492	30q multi	.30	.20
2251	A492	80q multi	.80	.40
2252	A492	1 l shown	1.00	.50
2253	A492	1.20 l multi	1.25	.60
		Nos. 2250-2253 (4)	3.35	1.70

A493

OLYMPHILEX '87, Rome, Aug. 29-Sept. 6 — A494

Illustration A494 reduced.

1987, Aug. 29 **Litho.** ***Perf. 12½***

2254	A493	30q Hammer throw	.30	.20
2255	A493	90q Running	.90	.45
2256	A493	1.10 l Shot put	1.25	.60

Size: 85x60mm

2257	A494	1.90 l Runner, globe	2.00	1.00
		Nos. 2254-2257 (4)	4.45	2.25

Famous Men A495

Designs: 30q, Themistokli Germenji (1871-1917), author, politician. 80q, Bajram Curri (1862-1925), founder of the Albanian League. 90q, Aleks Stavre Drenova (1872-1947), poet. 1.30 l, Gjerasim D. Qiriazi (1861-1894), teacher, journalist.

1987, Sept. 30 ***Perf. 12***

2258	A495	30q multi	.20	.20
2259	A495	80q multi	.80	.40
2260	A495	90q multi	1.00	.60
2261	A495	1.30 l multi	1.75	1.00
		Nos. 2258-2261 (4)	3.75	2.20

Albanian Labor Party Congress, Tirana A496

1987, Oct. 22 **Litho.** ***Perf. 12***

2262	A496	1.20 l multi	3.00	2.50

Natl. Independence, 75th Anniv. — A497

Postal Administration, 75th Anniv. — A498

1987, Nov. 27

2263 A497 1.20 l State flag 3.25 2.50

1987, Dec. 5

2264 A498 90q P.O. emblem 2.50 1.50
2265 A498 1.20 l State seal 3.50 3.50

Art & Literature — A499

WHO, 40th Anniv. — A500

Portraits: 30q, Lord Byron (1788-1824), English Poet. 1.20 l, Eugene Delacroix (1798-1863), French painter.

1988, Mar. 10

2266 A499 30q org brn & blk 2.00 1.50
2267 A499 1.20 l pale vio & blk 5.50 4.00

1988, Apr. 7

2268 A500 90q multi 5.25 4.50
2269 A500 1.20 l multi 7.25 6.50

Flowers — A501

1988, May 20

Booklet Stamps

2270 A501 30q *Sideritis raeseri* 2.00 1.25
2271 A501 90q *Lunaria telekiana* 3.50 2.50
2272 A501 2.10 l *Sanguisorba albanica* 4.50 4.00
a. Bklt. pane of 3, plus label 10.00
Nos. 2270-2272 (3) 10.00 7.75

10th Women's Federation Congress A502

1988, June 6

2273 A502 90q blk, red & dark org 8.25 8.25

European Soccer Championships — A503

Various athletes.
1.90 l, Goalie designs of Nos. 2274-2276.

1988, June 10

2274 A503 30q multicolored .75 .75
2275 A503 80q multicolored 1.00 1.00
2276 A503 1.20 l multicolored 1.75 1.75

Size: 79x68mm

Imperf

2277 A503 1.90 l multicolored 4.50 4.50
Nos. 2274-2277 (4) 8.00 8.00

League of Prizren, 110th Anniv. — A504

People's Army, 45th Anniv. — A505

1988, June 10 Litho. *Perf. 12*

2278 A504 30q Hands — —
2279 A504 1.20q House — —

1988, July 10

2280 A505 60q shown — —
2281 A505 90q Soldier statue — —

Famous Albanians A506

Designs: 30q, Mihal Grameno (1871-1931), author. 90q, Bajo Topulli (1868-1930), freedom fighter. 1 l, Murat Toptani (1868-1917), poet. 1.20 l, Jul Variboba, poet.

1988, Aug. 15

2282 A506 30q multi — —
2283 A506 90q multi — —
2284 A506 1 l multi — —
2284A A506 1.20 l multi — —

Migjeni (1911-1938), Poet — A507

1988, Aug. 26 Litho. *Perf. 12*

2285 A507 90q silver & brown 3.50 3.50

Ballads A508

1988, Sept. 5

2286 A508 30q Dede Skurra 2.75 2.75
2287 A508 90q Omeri Iri 7.25 7.25
2288 A508 1.20 l Gjergj Elez Alia 10.00 10.00
Nos. 2286-2288 (3) 20.00 20.00

Folklore Festival Type of 1978

1988, Oct. 6

2289 A388 30q Kerchief Dance 9.50 9.50
2290 A388 1.20 l Dancers with raised arm 21.00 21.00

Enver Hoxha Museum A510

Perf. 12x12½, 12½x12

1988, Oct. 16 Litho.

2291 A510 90q Portrait, vert. 1.75 1.75
2292 A510 1.20 l shown 2.75 2.75

Hoxha (1908-85), Communist leader.

Monastir Congress, 80th Anniv. A511

1988, Nov. 14 Litho. *Perf. 12*

2293 A511 60q Scroll — —
2294 A511 90q Book, building — —

Locomotives, Map Showing Rail Network — A512

1989, Feb. 28 Litho. *Perf. 12½x12*

2295 A512 30q 1947 .20 .20
2296 A512 90q 1949 .65 .35
2297 A512 1.20 l 1978 .85 .40
2298 A512 1.80 l 1985 1.25 .65
2299 A512 2.40 l 1988 1.60 .85
Nos. 2295-2299 (5) 4.55 2.45

Archaeological Treasures — A513

30q, Illyrian grave. 90q, Warrior on horseback.

1989, Mar. 10 Litho. *Perf. 12*

2300 A513 30q blk & tan .20 .20
2301 A513 90q blk & dl grn .65 .35
2302 A513 2.10 l shown 1.50 .75
Nos. 2300-2302 (3) 2.35 1.30

Folklore A514

1989, Apr. 5 Litho. *Perf. 12x12½*

2303 A514 30q multicolored .20 .20
2304 A514 80q multi, diff. .55 .30
2305 A514 1 l multi, diff. .70 .35
2306 A514 1.20 l multi, diff. .85 .45
Nos. 2303-2306 (4) 2.30 1.30

Flowers — A515

Famous People — A516

Designs: 30q, *Aster albanicus.* 90q, *Orchis x paparisti.* 2.10 l, *Orchis albanica.*

1989, May 10 *Perf. 12*

2307 A515 30q multicolored .20 .20
2308 A515 90q multicolored .65 .35
2309 A515 2.10 l multicolored 1.50 .75
Nos. 2307-2309 (3) 2.35 1.30

1989, June 3

Designs: 30q, Johann Strauss the Younger (1825-1899), composer. 80q, Marie Curie (1867-1834), chemist. 1 l, Federico Garcia Lorca (1898-1936), poet. 1.20 l, Albert Einstein (1879-1955), physicist.

2310 A516 30q gold & blk brn .20 .20
2311 A516 80q gold & blk brn .60 .30
2312 A516 1 l gold & blk brn .75 .35
2313 A516 1.20 l gold & blk brn .85 .45
Nos. 2310-2313 (4) 2.40 1.30

6th Congress of Albanian Democratic Front A517

1989, June 26
2314 A517 1.20 l multicolored 1.50 .65

French Revolution, Bicent. — A518

90q, Storming of the Bastille. 1.20 l, Statue.

1989, July 7 Litho. *Perf. 12½*
2315 A518 90q multicolored .75 .40
2316 A518 1.20 l shown 1.00 .50

Illyrian Ship A519

1989, July 25 *Perf. 12*
2317 A519 30q shown .25 .20
2318 A519 80q Caravel .60 .30
2319 A519 90q 3-masted schooner .65 .35
2320 A519 1.30 l Modern cargo ship 1.00 .50
Nos. 2317-2320 (4) 2.50 1.35

A520

A521

Famous Men: 30q, Pjeter Bogdani (1625-1689), writer. 80q, Gavril Dara (1826-1889), poet. 90q, Thimi Mitko (1820-1890), writer. 1.30 l, Kole Idromeno (1860-1939), painter.

1989, Aug. 30 Litho. *Perf. 12*
2321 A520 30q multicolored .30 .20
2322 A520 80q multicolored .80 .40
2323 A520 90q multicolored .90 .45
2324 A520 1.30 l multicolored 1.25 .65
Nos. 2321-2324 (4) 3.25 1.70

1989, Sept. 29
2325 A521 90q shown .70 .35
2326 A521 1.20 l Workers .95 .50

First Communist International, 125th anniv.

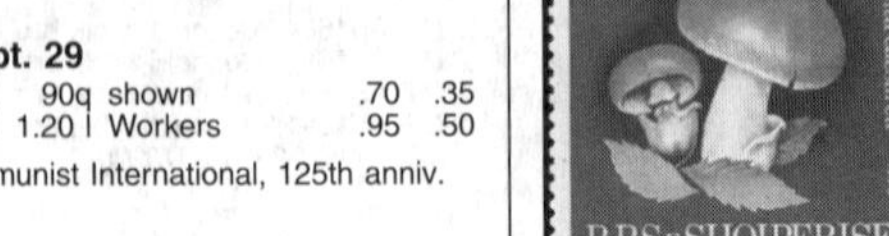

Spartakiad Games A522

1989, Oct. 27 *Perf. 12x12½*
2327 A522 30q Gymasnastics .20 .20
2328 A522 80q Soccer .55 .30
2329 A522 1 l Cycling .70 .35
2330 A522 1.20 l Running .85 .45
Nos. 2327-2330 (4) 2.30 1.30

Miniature Sheet

45th Anniv. of Liberation — A523

1989, Nov. 29 *Perf. 12x12½*
2331 A523 Sheet of 4 2.50 1.25
a. 30q Revolutionary .20 .20
b. 80q "45" .55 .30
c. 1 l Coat of arms .70 .35
d. 1.20 l Workers .85 .45

Rupicapra Rupicapra A524

1990, Mar. 15 *Perf. 12*
2332 A524 10q Two adults .25 .20
2333 A524 30q Adult, kid .50 .20
2334 A524 80q Adult 1.25 .60
2335 A524 90q Adult head 1.50 .75
a. Block of 4, #2332-2335 3.50 1.75

World Wildlife Fund.

Tribal Masks A525

1990, Apr. 4 *Perf. 12x12½*
2336 A525 30q shown .30 .20
2337 A525 90q multi, diff. .95 .50
2338 A525 1.20 l multi, diff. 1.25 .65
2339 A525 1.80 l multi, diff. 1.90 .95
Nos. 2336-2339 (4) 4.40 2.30

Mushrooms A526

1990, Apr. 28 Litho. *Perf. 12*
2340 A526 30q Amanita caesarea .25 .20
2341 A526 90q Lepiota procera .75 .40
2342 A526 1.20 l Boletus edulis 1.00 .50
2343 A526 1.80 l Clathrus cancelatus 1.50 .75
Nos. 2340-2343 (4) 3.50 1.85

First Postage Stamp, 150th Anniv. A527

1990, May 6 *Perf. 12*
2344 A527 90q shown 1.00 .50
2345 A527 1.20 l Post rider 1.25 .60
2346 A527 1.80 l Carriage 1.75 .90
a. Bklt. pane of 3, #2344-2346 + label 4.25
Nos. 2344-2346 (3) 4.00 2.00

World Cup Soccer, Italy A528

1990, June Litho. *Perf. 12*
2347 A528 30q multicolored .50 .25
2348 A528 90q multi, diff. 1.40 .75
2349 A528 1.20 l multi, diff. 2.00 1.00

Size: 80x63mm

Imperf

2350 A528 3.30 l multi, diff. 5.25 2.75
Nos. 2347-2350 (4) 9.15 4.75

Vincent Van Gogh, Death Cent. A529

Self portraits and: 30q, Details from various paintings. 90q, Woman in field. 2.10 l, Asylum. 2.40 l, Self-portrait.

1990, July 27
2351 A529 30q multicolored .50 .25
2352 A529 90q multicolored 1.40 .75
2353 A529 2.10 l multicolored 3.50 1.75

Size: 87x73mm

Imperf

2354 A529 2.40 l multicolored 1.90 .95
Nos. 2351-2354 (4) 7.30 3.70

Albanian Folklore — A530

Scenes from medieval folktale of "Gjergj Elez Alia": 30q, Alia lying wounded. 90q, Alia being helped onto horse. 1.20 l, Alia fighting Bajloz. 1.80 l, Alia on horseback over severed head of Bajloz.

1990, Aug. 30 *Perf. 12½x12*
2355 A530 30q multicolored .50 .25
2356 A530 90q multicolored 1.40 .70
2357 A530 1.20 l multicolored 2.00 .95
2358 A530 1.80 l multicolored 3.00 1.50
Nos. 2355-2358 (4) 6.90 3.40

Founding of Berat, 2400th Anniv. A531

Designs: 30q, Xhamia E Plumbit. 90q, Kisha E Shen Triadhes. 1.20 l, Ura E Beratit. 1.80 l, Onufri-Piktor Mesjetar. 2.40 l, Nikolla-Piktor Mesjetar.

1990, Sept. 20 *Perf. 12½*
2359 Block of 5 + 4 labels 4.25 2.10
a. A531 30q multi .20 .20
b. A531 90q multi .65 .30
c. A531 1.20 l multi .70 .35
d. A531 1.80 l multi 1.25 .65
e. A531 2.40 l multi 1.40 .70

No. 2359 was sold in souvenir folders for 9.90 l.

Illyrian Heroes — A532

1990, Oct. 20 *Perf. 12*
2360 A532 30q Pirroja .50 .25
2361 A532 90q Teuta 1.40 .70
2362 A532 1.20 l Bato 2.00 .95
2363 A532 1.80 l Bardhyli 3.00 1.50
Nos. 2360-2363 (4) 6.90 3.40

Intl. Literacy Year A533

1990, Oct. 30
2364 A533 90q lt bl & multi 1.40 .70
2365 A533 1.20 l pink & multi 2.00 .95

Albanian Horseman by Eugene Delacroix A534

Designs: 1.20 l, Albanian Woman by Camille Corot. 1.80 l, Skanderbeg by unknown artist.

1990, Nov. 30 *Perf. 12x12½*
2366 A534 30q multicolored .50 .25
2367 A534 1.20 l multicolored 1.90 .95
2368 A534 1.80 l multicolored 3.00 1.50
Nos. 2366-2368 (3) 5.40 2.70

A535 A536

1991, Jan. 23 Litho. *Perf. 12x12½*
2369 A535 90q shown .65 .30
2370 A535 1.20 l Boletini standing .90 .45

Isa Boletini (1864-1916), freedom fighter.

1991, Jan. 30 Litho. *Perf. 12*

Background Color

2371 A536 90q pale yellow — —
2372 A536 1.20 l pale gray — —

Arberi State, 800th anniv.

Pierre Auguste Renoir (1841-1919), Painter — A537

Paintings: 30q, Girl Reading, 1876, vert. 90q, The Swing, 1876, vert. 1.20 l, Boating Party, 1868-1869. 1.80 l, Flowers and grapes, 1878. 3 l, Self-portrait.

1991, Feb. 25 *Perf. 12½x12*

2373	A537	30q	multicolored	.20	.20
2374	A537	90q	multicolored	.65	.30
2375	A537	1.20 l	multicolored	.90	.45
2376	A537	1.80 l	multicolored	1.25	.65

Size: 95x75mm

Imperf

2377	A537	3 l	multicolored	4.75	2.50
			Nos. 2373-2377 (5)	7.75	4.10

Flowers — A538

1991, Mar. 30 *Perf. 12*

2378	A538	30q	Cistus albanicus	.50	.25
2379	A538	90q	Trifolium pilczii	1.40	.75
2380	A538	1.80 l	Lilium albanicum	3.00	1.50
			Nos. 2378-2380 (3)	4.90	2.50

Legend of Rozafa A539

Various scenes from legend.

1991, Sept. 30 Litho. *Perf. 12x12½*

2381	A539	30q	multicolored	.50	.25
2382	A539	90q	multicolored	1.40	.70
2383	A539	1.20 l	multicolored	2.00	.95
2384	A539	1.80 l	multicolored	3.00	1.50
			Nos. 2381-2384 (4)	6.90	3.40

For surcharges see #2586, 2604.

Wolfgang Amadeus Mozart, Death Bicent. — A540

1991, Oct. 5 Litho. *Perf. 12*

2385	A540	90q	Conducting	.70	.35
2386	A540	1.20 l	Portrait	.90	.45
2387	A540	1.80 l	Playing piano	1.40	.70

Size: 89x70mm

Imperf

2388	A540	3 l	Medal, score	4.00	4.00
			Nos. 2385-2388 (4)	7.00	5.50

Airplanes — A541

Designs: 30q, Glider, Otto Lilienthal, 1896. 80q, Avion III, Clement Ader, 1897. 90q, Flyer, Wright Brothers, 1903. 1.20 l, Concorde. 1.80 l, Tupolev 114. 2.40 l, Dornier 31 E.

1992, Jan. 27 Litho. *Perf. 12½x12*

2389	A541	30q	multicolored	.50	.25
2390	A541	80q	multicolored	1.25	.65
2391	A541	90q	multicolored	1.40	.70
2392	A541	1.20 l	multicolored	2.00	.90
2393	A541	1.80 l	multicolored	3.00	1.50
2394	A541	2.40 l	multicolored	4.00	2.00
			Nos. 2389-2394 (6)	12.15	6.00

No. 2393 misidentifies a Tupolev 144.

Explorers — A542

1992, Jan. 10

2395	A542	30q	Bering	.50	.25
2396	A542	90q	Columbus	1.40	.70
2397	A542	1.80 l	Magellan	3.00	1.50
			Nos. 2395-2397 (3)	4.90	2.45

1992 Winter Olympics, Albertville A543

1992, Feb. 15 Litho. *Perf. 12½*

2398	A543	30q	Ski jumping	.25	.20
2399	A543	90q	Cross country skiing	.70	.35
2400	A543	1.20 l	Pairs figure skating	.95	.50
2401	A543	1.80 l	Luge	1.40	.70
			Nos. 2398-2401 (4)	3.30	1.75

For surcharge see No. 2598.

Participation of Albania in Conference on Security and Cooperation in Europe, Berlin (1991) — A544

1992, Mar. 31 Litho. *Perf. 12½x12*

2402	A544	90q	shown	.95	.95
2403	A544	1.20 l	Flags, map	1.25	1.25
a.			Pair, #2402-2403	2.25	2.25

Dated 1991. Issued in sheets containing 2 #2403a, 3 each #2402-2403 + 2 labels.

Albanian Admission to CEPT — A545

1992, Apr. 25 Litho. *Perf. 12½*

2404	A545	90q	Envelopes, CEPT emblem	.80	.80
2405	A545	1.20 l	blk, pur & red lil	1.10	1.10
a.			Pair, #2404-2405	2.00	2.00

Issued in sheets containing 2 #2405a, 3 each #2404-2405 and 2 labels.

Martyrs' Day — A546

1992, May 5 *Perf. 12x12½*

2406	A546	90q	Freedom flame, vert.	*1.00*	*1.00*

Perf. 12½x12

2407	A546	4.10 l	Flowers	*4.50*	*4.50*

European Soccer Championships, Sweden'92 — A547

Various stylized designs of soccer plays.

1992, June 10 Litho. *Perf. 12*

2408	A547	30q	green & lt grn	.20	.20
2409	A547	90q	blue & pink	.25	.25
2410	A547	10.80 l	henna & tan	3.00	3.00

Size: 90x70mm

Imperf

2411	A547	5 l	tan, lt green & pink	1.40	1.40
			Nos. 2408-2411 (4)	4.85	4.85

1992 Summer Olympics, Barcelona A548

1992, June 14 Litho. *Perf. 12*

2412	A548	30q	Tennis	*.35*	*.35*
2413	A548	90q	Baseball	*1.00*	*1.00*
2414	A548	1.80 l	Table tennis	*2.00*	*2.00*

Size: 90x70mm

Imperf

2415	A548	5 l	Torch bearer	*1.50*	*1.50*
			Nos. 2412-2415 (4)	*4.85*	*4.85*

United Europe A549

1992, July 10 Litho. *Perf. 12*

2416	A549	1.20 l	multicolored	.75	.40

Horses A550

1992, Aug. 10 Litho. *Perf. 12*

2417	A550	30q	Native	*.20*	*.20*
2418	A550	90q	Nonius	*.25*	*.25*
2419	A550	1.20 l	Arabian, vert.	*.35*	*.35*
2420	A550	10.60 l	Haflinger, vert.	*2.75*	*2.75*
			Nos. 2417-2420 (4)	*3.55*	*3.55*

Discovery of America, 500th Anniv. A551

Map of North and South America and: 60q, Columbus, sailing ships. 3.20 l, Columbus meeting natives.

1992, Aug. 20

2421	A551	60q	blk, bl & gray	*.75*	*.75*
2422	A551	3.20 l	blk, brn & gray	*1.75*	*1.75*

Size: 90x70mm

Imperf

2423	A551	5 l	Map, Columbus	*50.00*	

Mother Theresa, Infant — A552

A553

1992, Oct. 4 Litho. *Perf. 12x12½*

2424	A552	40q	fawn	*.20*	*.20*
2425	A552	60q	brown	*.20*	*.20*
2426	A552	1 l	violet	*.20*	*.20*
2427	A552	1.80 l	gray	*.25*	*.25*
2428	A552	2 l	red	*.30*	*.30*
2429	A552	2.40 l	green	*.35*	*.35*
2430	A552	3.20 l	blue	*.50*	*.50*
2431	A552	5.60 l	rose violet	*1.00*	*1.00*
2432	A552	7.20 l	olive	*1.10*	*1.10*
2433	A552	10 l	org brn	*1.50*	*1.50*
			Nos. 2424-2433 (10)	*5.60*	*5.60*

See Nos. 2472-2476.

1993, Apr. 25 Litho. *Perf. 12*

2434	A553	16 l	multicolored	*2.50*	*2.50*

Visit of Pope John Paul II.

Nos. 2223-2226, 2229 Surcharged

1993, May 2 Litho. *Perf. 12x12½*

2435	A486	3 l	on 10q	*.60*	*.60*
2436	A486	6.50 l	on 20q	*1.25*	*1.25*
2437	A486	13 l	on 30q	*2.50*	*2.50*
2438	A486	20 l	on 90q	*4.00*	*4.00*
2439	A486	30 l	on 50q	*5.75*	*5.75*
			Nos. 2435-2439 (5)	*14.10*	*14.10*

Lef Nosi (1873-1945), Minister of Posts A554

1993, May 5 Litho. *Perf. 12*

2440 A554 6.50 l olive brn & bister *.90 .90*

First Albanian postage stamps, 80th anniv.

Europa A555

Contemporary paintings by: 3 l, A. Zajmi, vert. 7 l, E. Hila. 20 l, B. Ahmeti-Peizazh.

1993, May 28 Litho. *Perf. 12*

2441 A555 3 l multicolored *.75 .75*
2442 A555 7 l multicolored *1.75 1.75*

Size: 116x122mm

2443 A555 20 l multicolored *4.25 4.25*
Nos. 2441-2443 (3) *6.75 6.75*

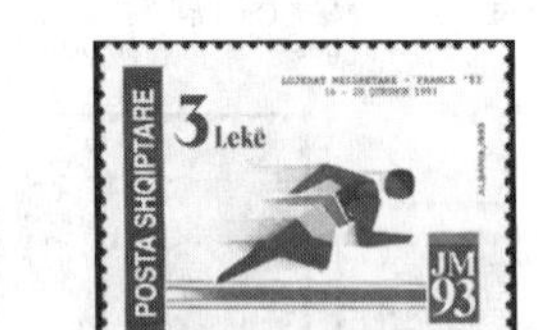

1993 Mediterranean Games, France — A556

1993, June 20 Litho. *Perf. 12*

2444 A556 3 l Running .55 .55
2445 A556 16 l Kayaking 3.00 3.00
2446 A556 21 l Cycling 3.75 3.75

Size: 111x78mm

Imperf

2447 A556 20 l Mediterranean map 3.50 3.50
Nos. 2444-2447 (4) 10.80 10.80

Frang Bardhi, Author, 350th Death Anniv. A557

1993, Aug. 20 Litho. *Perf. 12x12½*

2448 A557 6.50 l shown 1.10 1.10

Size: 89x101mm

Imperf

2449 A557 20 l Writing at desk 3.50 3.50

A558

A559

1994, July 17 Litho. *Perf. 12*

2450 A558 42 l shown 1.50 1.50
2451 A558 68 l Mascot, ball, US map 2.50 2.50

1994 World Cup Soccer Championships, US.

1994, Dec. 31 Litho. *Perf. 14*

European Inventors, Discoveries: 50 l, Gjovalin Gjadri, engineer. 100 l, Karl von Ghega, Austrian engineer. 150 l, Sketch of road project.

2452 A559 50 l multicolored 1.25 1.25
2453 A559 100 l multicolored 2.75 2.75

Size: 50x70mm

Imperf

2454 A559 150 l multicolored 4.00 4.00
Nos. 2452-2454 (3) 8.00 8.00

Europa (#2454).

Ali Pasa of Tepelene (Lion of Janina) (1744-1822) — A560

1995, Jan. 28 *Perf. 14*

2455 A560 60 l shown 2.50 2.50

Size: 70x50mm

Imperf

2456 A560 100 l Tepelene Palace 4.00 4.00

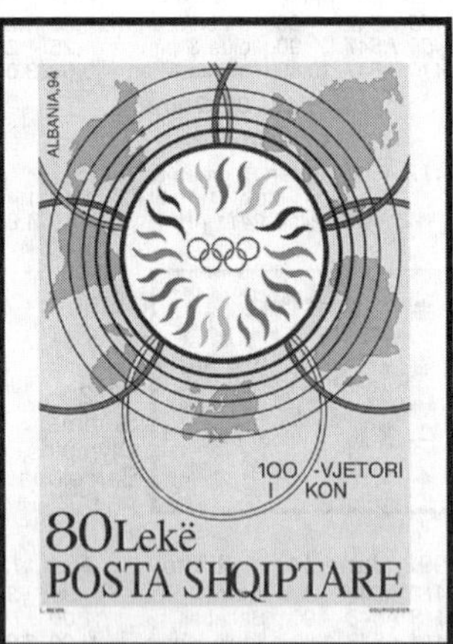

Intl. Olympic Committee, Cent. — A561

1995, Feb. 2 *Imperf.*

2457 A561 80 l multicolored 3.25 3.25

Karl Benz (1844-1929), Automobile Pioneer — A562

Designs: 5 l, Automobile company emblem, Benz. 10 l, Modern Mercedes Benz automobile. 60 l, First four-wheel Benz 1886 motor car. 125 l, Pre-war Mercedes touring car.

1995, Jan. 21 Litho. *Perf. 14*

2458 A562 5 l multicolored .20 .20
2459 A562 10 l multicolored .30 .30
2460 A562 60 l multicolored 1.60 1.60
2461 A562 125 l multicolored 3.50 3.50
Nos. 2458-2461 (4) 5.60 5.60

Liberation, 50th Anniv. (in 1994) A563

1995, Jan. 28 Litho. *Perf. 14*

2462 A563 50 l black, gray & red 2.00 2.00

Dated 1994.

Miniature Sheet

Albania '93 — A564

Composers: a, 3 l, Wagner. b, 6.50 l, Grieg. c, 11 l, Gounod. d, 20 l, Tchaikovsky.

1995, Jan. 26 *Perf. 12*

2463 A564 Sheet of 4, #a.-d. 2.00 2.00

Veskopoja Academy, 250th Anniv. — A565

Buildings of Veskopoja.

1995, Feb. 2

2464 A565 42 l multicolored 1.50 1.50
2465 A565 68 l multicolored 2.50 2.50
a. Pair, #2464-2465 4.00 4.00

Bleta Apricula — A566

Peace & Freedom — A567

1995, Aug. 20 Litho. *Perf. 12*

2466 A566 5 l On flower .20 .20
2467 A566 10 l Honeycomb, bee .40 .40
2468 A566 25 l Emerging from cell of honeycomb 1.00 1.00
Nos. 2466-2468 (3) 1.60 1.60

1995, Aug. 10 *Perf. 13½x14*

Stylized hands reaching for: 50 l, Olive branch. 100 l, Peace dove. 150 l, Stylized person.

2469 A567 50 l multicolored 1.25 1.25
2470 A567 100 l multicolored 2.50 2.50

Size: 80x60mm

Imperf

2471 A567 150 l multicolored 3.75 3.75
Nos. 2469-2471 (3) 7.50 7.50

Europa.

For surcharges, see Nos. B39-B40.

Mother Teresa Type of 1992

1994-95 Litho. *Perf. 12x12½*

2472 A552 5 l violet .25 .25
2473 A552 18 l orange .85 .85
2474 A552 20 l rose lilac .95 .95
2475 A552 25 l green 1.10 1.10
2476 A552 60 l olive 2.75 2.75
Nos. 2472-2476 (5) 5.90 5.90

Issued: 20 l, 1994; 60 l, 1995; others, 7/94.

Arctic Explorers — A568

Designs: a, Fridtjof Nansen (1861-1930), Norway. b, James Cook (1728-79), England. c, Roald Amundsen (1872-1928), Norway. d, Robert F. Scott (1872-1928), Great Britain.

1995, Sept. 14 Litho. *Perf. 13½x14*

2477 A568 25 l Block of 4, #a.-d. 4.25 4.25

UN, 50th Anniv. A569

1995, Sept. 14 Litho. *Perf. 14x13½*

2478 A569 2 l shown .20 .20
2479 A569 100 l like #2478, flags streaming to right 4.25 4.25

Poets — A570

1995 *Perf. 13½x14*

2480 A570 25 l Pol Elyar 1.10 1.10
2481 A570 50 l Sergej Esnin 2.25 2.25
a. Pair, #2480-2481 3.50 3.50

Entry into Council of Europe A571

Designs: 25 l, Doves flying from headquarters, Strasbourg. 85 l, Albanian eagle over map of Europe.

1995 *Perf. 14x13½*

2482 A571 25 l multicolored 1.10 1.10
2483 A571 85 l multicolored 3.75 3.75

For surcharge see No. 2583

Jan Kukuzeli, Composer A572

Stylized figure: 18 l, Writing. 20 l, Holding hand to head. 100 l, Holding up scroll of paper.

1995, Oct. 17 *Perf. 13½x14*

2484 A572 18 l multicolored .85 .85
2485 A572 20 l multicolored .95 .95

Size: 74x74mm

2486 A572 100 l multicolored 4.50 4.50
Nos. 2484-2486 (3) 6.30 6.30

World Tourism Organization, 20th Anniv. — A573

Stylized designs: 18 l, Church, saint holding scroll. 20 l, City, older buildings. 42 l, City, modern buildings.

1995, Oct. 17

2487 A573 18 l multicolored 1.00 1.00
2488 A573 20 l multicolored 1.10 1.10
2489 A573 42 l multicolored 2.50 2.50
Nos. 2487-2489 (3) 4.60 4.60

Fables of Jean de la Fontaine (1621-95) A574

Designs: 2 l, Raptor, turtle, wolf, goose, mouse, lion, rats. 3 l, Crow, goose, dog, foxes. 25 l, Insect, doves, frogs. 60 l, Drawings of Da la Fontaine, animals, birds.

1995, Aug. 20 Litho. *Perf. 14x13½*

2490 A574 2 l multicolored .20 .20
2491 A574 3 l multicolored .20 .20
2492 A574 25 l multicolored .85 .85

Imperf

Size: 73x56mm

2493 A574 60 l multicolored 2.75 2.75
Nos. 2490-2493 (4) 4.00 4.00

Folklore Festival, Berat — A575

Motion Pictures, Cent. — A576

Stylized designs: 5 l, Men's choir. 50 l, Costumed woman seated in chair.

1995, Oct. 17 Litho. *Perf. 13½x14*

2494 A575 5 l multicolored .20 .20
2495 A575 50 l multicolored 2.25 2.25

1995, Nov. 17

2496 A576 10 l Louis Lumiere .45 .45
2497 A576 85 l Auguste Lumiere 3.75 3.75
a. Pair, #2496-2497 4.20 4.20

Elvis Presley (1935-77) A577

1995, Nov. 20 Litho. *Perf. 14x13½*

2498 A577 3 l orange & multi .20 .20
2499 A577 60 l green & multi 2.50 2.50

A578

A579

1995, Nov. 25 *Perf. 13½x14*

2500 A578 10 l 1925 Bank notes .45 .45
2501 A578 25 l 1995 Bank notes 1.10 1.10

National Bank, 70th anniv.

1995, Nov. 27 Litho. *Perf. 13½x14*

2502 A579 5 l shown .20 .20
2503 A579 50 l Maiden planting tree 2.25 2.25

Democracy, 5th anniv.

A580

Designs: 25 l, Soccer ball, British flag, map of Europe, stadium. 100 l, Soccer ball, player.

1996, June 4 *Perf. 14*

2504 A580 25 l multicolored 1.10 1.10
2505 A580 100 l multicolored 4.50 4.50

Euro '96, European Soccer Championships, Great Britain.

Mother Teresa — A581

1996, May 5 *Perf. 13½x14*

2506 A581 25 l blue & multi .75 .75
2507 A581 100 l red & multi 2.75 2.75

Size: 52x74mm

Imperf

2508 A581 150 l Mother Teresa, diff. 5.00 5.00
Nos. 2506-2508 (3) 8.50 8.50

Europa. For overprints see Nos. 2551, 2582.

GSM Cellular Telephone Transmission A582

Designs: 10 l, Satellite transmitting signals. 60 l, Uses for cellular telephone, vert.

Perf. 13x13½, 13½x13

1996, Aug. 1 Litho.

2509 A582 10 l multicolored .45 .45
2510 A582 60 l multicolored 2.50 2.50

1996 Summer Olympic Games, Atlanta — A583

Stylized designs.

1996, Aug. 3 Litho. *Perf. 13x14*

2511 A583 5 l Runners .20 .20
2512 A583 25 l Throwers 1.00 1.00
2513 A583 60 l Jumpers 2.40 2.40

Size: 52x37mm

Imperf

2514 A583 100 l Emblem, US flag 4.00 4.00
Nos. 2511-2514 (4) 7.60 7.60

Gottfried Wilhelm Leibniz (1646-1716), Mathematician — A584

85 l, René Descartes (1596-1650), mathematician.

1996, Sept. 20 Litho. *Perf. 14*

2515 A584 10 l multicolored .40 .40
2516 A584 85 l multicolored 3.50 3.50

Paintings by Francisco Goya (1746-1828) A585

Designs: 10 l, The Naked Maja. 60 l, Dona Isabel Cobos de Porcel. 100 l, Self portrait.

1996, Sept. 25 *Perf. 14x13½*

2517 A585 10 l multicolored .40 .40
2518 A585 60 l multicolored 2.50 2.50

Souvenir Sheet

2519 A585 100 l multicolored 4.00 4.00

Religious Engravings — A586

Designs: a, 5 l, Book cover showing crucifixion, angels. b, 25 l, Medallion of crucifixion. c, 85 l, Book cover depicting life of Christ.

1996, Nov. 5 *Perf. 13x13½*

2520 A586 Block of 3, #a.-c. + label 4.75 4.75

UNICEF, 50th Anniv. — A587

1996, Nov. 11 *Perf. 13½*

Children's paintings: 5 l, Fairy princess. 10 l, Doll, sun. 25 l, Sea life. 50 l, House, people.

2521 A587 5 l multicolored .20 .20
2522 A587 10 l multicolored .45 .45
2523 A587 25 l multicolored 1.10 1.10
2524 A587 50 l multicolored 2.25 2.25
Nos. 2521-2524 (4) 4.00 4.00

Gjergj Fishta (1871-1940), Writer, Priest — A588

1996, Dec. 20 *Perf. 13½x14*

2525 A588 10 l shown .40 .40
2526 A588 60 l Battle scene, portrait 2.50 2.50

Omar Khayyam — A589

1997, Mar. 6 *Perf. 14*

2527 A589 20 l shown .70 .70
2528 A589 50 l Portrait, diff. 1.75 1.75

A590 A591

1997, Mar. 20 *Perf. 14x14½*

2529 A590 20 l Portrait .70 .70
2530 A590 60 l Printing press 2.15 2.15
a. Pair, #2529-2530 2.85 2.85

Johannes Gutenberg (1397?-1468).

1997, May 5 Litho. *Perf. 13x14*

The Azure Eye (Stories and Legends): 30 l, Dragon on rock looking at warrior, donkey. 100 l, Dragon drinking water from pond, warrior.

2531 A591 30 l multicolored .75 .75
2532 A591 100 l multicolored 3.00 3.00

Europa.

A592 A593

1997, Apr. 10 *Perf. 14*

2533 A592 10 l Pelicanus crispus .40 .40
2534 A592 80 l Pelicans, diff. 3.00 3.00
a. Pair, #2533-2534 3.40 3.40

No. 2534a is a continuous design.

1997, June 25 Litho. *Perf. 14*

2535 A593 10 l blk & dark brn .40 .40
2536 A593 25 l blk & blue blk 1.00 1.00

Souvenir Sheet

2537 A593 80 l gray brown 2.90 2.90

Faik Konica (1875-1942), writer and politician.

No. 2537 contains one 22x26mm stamp.

A594

1997 Mediterranean Games, Bari: 20 l, Man running. 30 l, Woman running, 3-man canoe. 100 l, Man breaking finish line, silhouettes of man and woman.

1997, June 13

2538 A594 20 l Man running .75 .75
2539 A594 30 l Woman running, canoe 1.10 1.10

Size: 52x74mm

Imperf

2540 A594 100 l multicolored 3.60 3.60

Skanderbeg — A595

1997, Aug. 25 Litho. *Perf. 13*

2541 A595 5 l red brn & red .20 .20
2542 A595 10 l dp ol & ol .40 .40
2543 A595 20 l dp grn & grn .80 .80
2544 A595 25 l dp mag & red lil 1.00 1.00
2545 A595 30 l dk vio & vio 1.25 1.25
2546 A595 50 l black 2.00 2.00
2547 A595 60 l brn & lt brn 2.40 2.40
2548 A595 80 l dk brown & brn 3.25 3.25
2549 A595 100 l dk red brown & red brn 4.00 4.00
2550 A595 110 l dark blue 4.25 4.25
Nos. 2541-2550 (10) 19.55 19.55

No. 2507 Ovptd. in Silver "HOMAZH / 1910-1997"

1997 *Perf. 13½x14*

2551 A581 100 l red & multi 6.50 6.50

Religious Manuscripts — A596

Albanian Codex: a, 10 l, 11th cent. b, 25 l, 6th cent. c, 60 l, 6th cent., diff.

1997, Nov. 15 Litho. *Perf. 13x14*

2552 A596 Block of 3, #a.-c. + label 3.50 3.50

See No. 2575.

Post and Telecommunications Administration, 85th Anniv. — A597

1997, Dec. 4 *Perf. 13½*

2553 A597 10 l multi .40 .40
2554 A597 30 l multi, diff. 1.10 1.10

A598

1998, Mar. 25 Litho. *Perf. 14*

2555 A598 30 l red brn & multi .75 .75
2556 A598 100 l tan & multi 2.75 2.75
a. Pair, #2555-2556 3.50 3.50

Nikete Dardani, musician.

A599

1998, Apr. 15

Legends of Pogradecit: a, 30 l, Old man seated at table. b, 50 l, Three Graces. c, 60 l, Two women, fountain. d, 80 l, Iceman.

2557 A599 Block of 4, #a.-d. 5.50 5.50

A600

1998, May 5 Litho. *Perf. 13x14*

2558 A600 60 l shown 1.00 1.00
2559 A600 100 l multi, diff. 2.00 2.00

Size: 50x72mm

Imperf

2560 A600 150 l multi, diff. 2.75 2.75

Europa (folk festivals).

A601

1998, June 10 Litho. *Perf. 13½x13*

Albanian League of Prizren, 120th anniv.: a, 30 l, Abdyl Frasheri. b, 50 l, Sulejman Vokshi. c, 60 l, Iljaz Pashe Dibra. d, 80 l, Ymer Prizreni.

2561 A601 Block of 4, #a.-d. 5.50 5.50

1998 World Cup Soccer Championships, France — A602

Perf. 13½

1998, June 10

Stylized soccer players.

2562 A602 60 l multicolored 1.50 1.50
2563 A602 100 l multicolored 2.50 2.50

Size: 50x73mm

Imperf

2564 A602 120 l Mascot 3.00 3.00

European Youth Greco-Roman Wrestling Championships, Albania — A603

1998, July 5 *Perf. 13½*

2565 A603 30 l shown .75 .75
2566 A603 60 l Wrestlers, diff. 1.50 1.50
a. Pair, #2565-2566 2.25 2.25

Eqerem Cabej (1908-1980), Albanian Etymologist — A604

1998, Aug. 7 *Perf. 14*

2567 A604 60 l yel brn & multi 1.50 1.50
2568 A604 80 l brn red & multi 2.00 2.00
a. Pair, #2567-2568 3.50 3.50

Paul Gauguin (1848-1903) A605

Paintings (details): 60 l, The Vision after the Sermon. 80 l, Ea Haere la Oe.

120 l, Stylized design to resemble self-portrait.

1998, Sept. 10 *Perf. 13½*

2569 A605 60 l multicolored 1.50 1.50
2570 A605 80 l multicolored 2.00 2.00
a. Pair, #2569-2570 3.50 3.50

Size: 50x73mm

Imperf

2571 A605 120 l multicolored 3.00 3.00

Epitaph of Gllavenica, 14th Cent. Depiction of Christ — A606

Designs: 30 l, Entire cloth showing artwork. 80 l, Closer view.

100 l, Upper portion of cloth, vert.

1998, Oct. 5 *Perf. 14½x14*

2572 A606 30 l multicolored .75 .75
2573 A606 80 l multicolored 2.00 2.00

Souvenir Sheet

Perf. 13

2574 A606 100 l multicolored 2.50 2.50

No. 2574 contains one 25x29mm stamp.

Religious Manuscripts Type of 1997

Illustrations from Purple Codex, Gold Codex: a, 30 l, Manuscript, columns on sides, arched top. b, 50 l, Manuscript cover with embossed pictures of icons. c, 80 l, Manuscript picturing cathedral, birds.

1998, Oct. 15 *Perf. 13x14*

2575 A596 Block of 3, #a.-c. + label 4.00 4.00

Mikel Koliqi (1902-97), First Albanian Cardinal — A607

1998, Nov. 28 ***Perf. 14***

2576 A607	30 l shown	.75	.75
2577 A607	100 l Portrait, facing	2.50	2.50
a.	Pair, #2576-2577	3.25	3.25

Mother Teresa (1910-97) — A608

Diana, Princess of Wales (1961-97) — A609

Perf. 14x13½, 13½x14

1998, Sept. 5 **Photo.**

2578 A608	60 l With child, horiz.	1.50	1.50
2579 A608	100 l shown	2.50	2.50

See Italy Nos. 2254-2255.

1998, Aug. 31 **Litho.** ***Perf. 13½***

2580 A609	60 l shown	1.50	1.50
2581 A609	100 l With Mother Teresa	2.50	2.50

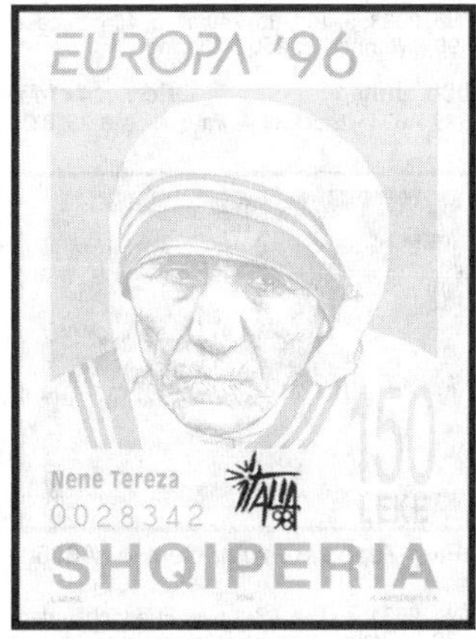

No. 2508 Ovptd. in Blue

1998, Oct. 23 **Litho.** ***Imperf.***

2582 A581	150 l multicolored	6.25	6.25

No. 2482 Surcharged

1999, Apr. 20 **Litho.** ***Perf. 14x13½***

2583 A571	150 l on 25 l multi	2.25	2.25

Famous Americans — A610

a, Washington. b, Lincoln. c. Martin Luther King, Jr.

1999, Mar. 15 ***Perf. 14***

2584 A610	150 l Block of 3, #a.-c. + label	6.25	6.25

Monacus Albiventris — A611

Seals: a, 110 l, One looking left, one looking right. b, 150 l, Both looking right. c, 110 l, Mirror image of #2585b. d, 150 l, Mirror image of #2585a.

1999, Apr. 10

2585 A611	Sheet of 4, #a.-d.	7.50	7.50

No. 2382 Surcharged

1999, Apr. 24 **Litho.** ***Perf. 12x12¼***

2586 A539	150 l on 90 l multi	4.00	4.00

IBRA '99, Nuremburg.

A612

1999, Apr. 25 **Litho.** ***Perf. 13½x13¾***

2587 A612	10 l blue & multi	.25	.25
2588 A612	100 l green & multi	2.50	2.50

Souvenir Sheet

Perf. 13

2589 A612	250 l green & multi	6.75	6.75

NATO, 50th anniv. No. 2589 contains one 30x50mm stamp.

A613

1999, Apr. 30 **Litho.** ***Perf. 13x13¾***

Cartoon mouse: a, 80 l, Writing. b, 110 l, Holding chin. c, 150 l, Wearing bow tie. d, 60 l, Pointing.

2590 A613	Strip of 4, #a.-d.	10.50	10.50

Animated films.

Europa A614

1999, May 1 **Litho.** ***Perf. 13¾x13***

2591 A614	90 l Thethi Park	1.75	1.75
2592 A614	310 l Lura Park	6.25	6.25

Imperf

Size: 80x60mm

2592A A614	350 l Kombetare Park	7.00	7.00
	Nos. 2591-2592A (3)	15.00	15.00

Illyrian Coins A615

Designs: a, 200 l, Kings of Illyria - Monumiou c. 300-280 BC cow suckling calf, square containing double stellate pattern, and Epidamos-Dyrrachium c. 623 BC, square with double stellate. b, 20 l, Damastion c. 395-380 BC siver drachm portable ingot, Byllis c. 238-168 BC AE13 serpent entwined around cornucopia, Skodra after 168 BC, AE17 war galley, and other war galley coin. c, 10l, Epirote Republic before 238 BC silver tetraobol with jugate busts of Zeus and Dione on obverse and thunderbolt within oak wreath reverse.

310 l, Kings of Illyria - Genthos c. 197-168 BC head wearing kausia.

1999, June 1 **Litho.** ***Perf. 13¾x13¼***

2593 A615	Strip of 3, #a.-c.	6.25	6.25

Souvenir Sheet

Perf. 13

2594 A615	310 l multicolored	8.50	8.50

Charlie Chaplin — A616

Designs: 30 l, Holding cigarette. 50 l, Tipping hat. 250 l, Dancing.

1999, June 20 **Litho.** ***Perf. 14x14¼***

2595 A616	30 l multicolored	.75	.75
2596 A616	50 l multicolored	1.25	1.25
2597 A616	250 l multicolored	6.75	6.75
a.	Booklet pane, 2 each #2595-2597, perf. 14¼ vert.	17.50	
	Complete booklet	17.50	
	Nos. 2595-2597 (3)	8.75	8.75

In No. 2597a, the 30 l stamps are at the ends of the pane and the 250 l stamps are in the middle.

No. 2398 Surcharged

1999, July 2 **Litho.** ***Perf. 12½***

2598 A543	150 l on 30q multi	4.25	4.25

PhilexFrance 99.

Holocaust — A617

1999, July 6 **Litho.** ***Perf. 14x14¼***

2599 A617	30 l brown & multi	.80	.80
2600 A617	150 l gray & multi	4.00	4.00

First Manned Moon Landing, 30th Anniv. — A618

No. 2601: a, 30 l, Astronaut, earth. b, 150 l, Lunar Module. c, 300 l, Astronaut, flag.

280 l, Lift-off.

1999, July 25 **Litho.** ***Perf. 13¼x14***

2601 A618	Strip of 3, #a.-c	13.00	13.00

Souvenir Sheet

Perf. 13

2602 A618	280 l multicolored	7.25	7.25

No. 2602 contains one 25x29mm stamp.

UPU, 125th Anniv. — A619

1999, Aug. 1 **Litho.** ***Perf. 14x14¼***

Background colors: a, 20 l, aquamarine and brown. b, 60 l, bister and dark blue.

2603 A619	Pair, #a.-b.	2.10	2.10

No. 2383 Surcharged in Brown, Symbol in Red and Green

1999 Method & Perf. as Before
2604 A539 150 l on 1.20 l multi 3.25 3.25

China 1999 World Philatelic Exhibition.

A620

A621

Background colors: a, 10 l, Yellow. b, 20 l, Orange. c, 200 l, Green.

1999, Sept. 2 Litho. *Perf. 14x14¼*
2605 A620 Strip of 3, #a.-c. 4.75 4.75

First Natl. Track & Field Championships, 70th anniv.

1999, Oct. 30 *Perf. 14*
2606 A621 30 l Madonna and Child .60 .60
2607 A621 300 l shown 6.00 6.00
a. Souv. sheet, 2 ea #2606-2607 14.00 14.00

Art by Onufri of Elbasan.

Famous Albanians — A622

Designs: a, 10 l, Bilal Golemi (1899-1955), veterinarian. b, 20 l, Azem Galica (1889-1924), freedom fighter. c, 50 l, Viktor Eftimiu (1889-1972), writer. d, 300 l, Lasgush Poradeci (1900-87), poet.

1999, Nov. 28 Litho. *Perf. 14¼x14*
2608 A622 Block of 4, #a.-d. 7.75 7.75

Carnival Masks — A623

1999, Dec. 1 *Perf. 13¾*
2609 A623 30 l shown .60 .60
2610 A623 300 l Turkey head 6.00 6.00

Millennium A624

2000, Mar. 27 Litho. *Perf. 13½x14*
2611 A624 40 l red & multi .90 .90
2612 A624 90 l blue & multi 2.00 2.00

Native Costumes — A625

a, 5 l, Librazhdi. b, 10 l, Malesia e Madhe woman. c, 15 l, Malesia e Madhe man. d, 20 l, Tropoje. e, 30 l, Dumrea. f, 35 l, Tirana man. g, 40 l, Tirana woman. h, 45 l, Arbereshe. i, 50 l, Gjirokaster. j, 55 l, Lunxheri. k, 70 l, Cameria. l, 90 l, Laberia.
Illustration reduced.

2000, Mar. 28 *Perf. 13x13¾*
2613 Booklet pane of 12 13.00 13.00
a.-l. A625 any single 1.10 1.10
Booklet, #2613 13.00

Gustave Mayer (1850-1900), Student of Albanian Culture — A626

Colors: a, 50 l, olive green. b, 130 l, carmine lake.
Illustration reduced.

2000, Mar. 30 *Perf. 13½x14*
2614 A626 Pair, #a-b 3.75 3.75

Cartoon Duck — A627

Duck with: a, 250 l, Top hat. b, 10 l, Ten-gallon hat. c, 30 l, Cap. d, 90 l, Bow.

2000, Apr. 6 Litho. *Perf. 13x13¾*
2615 A627 Strip of 4, #a-d 8.25 8.25

Grand Prix Race Cars — A628

Various cars.

2000, Apr. 10 Litho. *Perf. 14¼x14*
2616 Bklt. pane of 10 + 2 labels 9.25 9.25
a.-j. A628 30 l any single .90 .90
Booklet, #2616 9.25

Holy Year 2000 A629

Designs: 15 l, Church with bell tower. 40 l, Church with conical roof. 90 l, Ruins. 250 l, Aerial view of ruins.

2000, Apr. 22 Litho. *Perf. 13¾x14*
2617-2619 A629 Set of 3 3.25 3.25

Souvenir Sheet

Perf. 13¾

2620 A629 250 l multi 5.50 5.50

No. 2620 contains one 38x38mm stamp.

Europa, 2000
Common Design Type

2000, May 9 *Perf. 13x13¾*
2621 CD17 130 l multi 2.00 2.00

Souvenir Sheet

Perf. 13

2622 CD17 300 l Detail of #2621 4.50 4.50

No. 2622 contains one 25x29mm stamp.

Miniature Sheet

Wild Animals — A630

No. 2623: a, 10 l, Canis lupus. b, 40 l, Ursus arctos. c, 90 l, Sus scrofa. d, 220 l, Vulpes vulpes.
Illustration reduced.

2000, May 17 *Perf. 14¼x13¾*
2623 A630 Sheet of 4, #a-d 7.75 7.75

Gustav Mahler (1860-1911), Composer A631

2000, May 30 *Perf. 13½x14*
2624 A631 130 l multi 2.75 2.75

WIPA 2000 Stamp Exhibition, Vienna.

European Soccer Championships — A632

10 l, Goalie. 120 l, Player heading ball. 260 l, Player kicking ball.

2000, June 1 *Perf. 13¾x13¼*
2625-2626 A632 Set of 2 2.75 2.75

Imperf

Size: 81x60mm

2627 A632 260 l multi 5.50 5.50

Paintings by Pablo Picasso — A633

Various unnamed paintings or self-portraits: 30 l, Brown panel. 40 l, Green panel. 130 l, Self-portrait, with Espana 2000 philatelic exhibition emblem, vert. 250 l, Blue panel.

2000 Litho. *Perf. 13¾*
2628-2631 A633 Set of 4 9.50 9.50

Souvenir Sheet

Perf. 13

2632 A633 400 l Self-portrait 8.50 8.50

No. 2632 contains one 25x29mm stamp.
Issued: 130 l, 10/6; others 6/7.

2000 Summer Olympics, Sydney — A634

No. 2633: a, 10 l, Basketball. b, 40 l, Soccer. c, 90 l, Runner. d, 250 l, Cycling.

2000, July 1 *Perf. 14x14¼*
2633 A634 Block of 4, #a-d 8.25 8.25

First Zeppelin Flight, Cent. — A635

No. 2634: a, 15 l, LZ-1 over Friedrichshafen. b, 30 l, Airship over Paris. c, 300 l, R34 over New York.
Illustration reduced.

2000, July 2 *Perf. 13¾x13*
2634 A635 Sheet of 3, #a-c 7.50 7.50

Souvenir Sheet

Perf. 13

2635 A635 300 l Ferdinand von Zeppelin 6.50 6.50

No. 2634 contains three 40x28mm stamps.

Flowers — A636

No. 2636: a, 50 l, Gentiana lutea. b, 70 l, Gentiana cruciata.
Illustration reduced.

2000, Oct. 10 ***Perf. 13¼x14***
2636 A636 Pair, #a-b 2.60 2.60

Famous Albanians — A637

a, 30 l, Naim Frasheri, writer (1845-1900). b, 50 l, Bajram Curri, politician (1862-1925).
Illustration reduced.

2000, Nov. 28 ***Perf. 14¼x13¾***
2637 A637 Pair, #a-b 1.75 1.75

UN High Commissioner on Refugees, 50th Anniv. — A638

50 l, Mother & child. 90 l, Mother & child, diff.

2000, Dec. 14 ***Perf. 13¾x14¼***
2638-2639 A638 Set of 2 3.00 3.00

Famous Albanians — A639

No. 2640: a, Ahmed Myftar Dede. b, Sali Njazi Dede.
Illustration reduced.

2001, Feb. 22 Litho. ***Perf. 14¼x14***
2640 A639 90 l Horiz. pair, #a-b 3.00 3.00

Native Costumes — A640

No. 2641: a, Man from Tropoje. b, Woman from Lume. c, Woman from Mirdite. d, Man from Lume. e, Woman from Zadrime. f, Woman from Shpati. g, Man from Kruje. h, Woman from Macukulli. i, Woman from Dardhe. j, Man from Lushnje. k, Woman from Dropulli. l, Woman from Shmili.

2001, Mar. 15 ***Perf. 13x13¾***
2641 A640 20 l Sheet of 12, #a-l 4.00 4.00
Booklet, #2641 4.00

Flowers — A641

No. 2642: a, 10 l, Magnolia grandiflora. b, 20 l, Rosa virginiana. c, 90 l, Dianthus barbatus. d, 140 l, Syringa vulgaris.

2001, Mar. 30 ***Perf. 14x14¼***
2642 A641 Block of 4, #a-d 5.50 5.50

Cartoon Dog — A642

Denominations: a, 50 l. b, 90 l. c, 140 l, d, 20 l. Illustration reduced.

2001, Apr. 6 ***Perf. 13x13¾***
2643 A642 Strip of 4, #a-d 5.00 5.00

Opera Composers — A643

Designs: No. 2644, 90 l, Vincenzo Bellini (1801-35). No. 2645, 90 l, Giuseppe Verdi (1813-1901).
300 l, Bellini and Verdi.

2001, Apr. 20 ***Perf. 13¾x13***
2644-2645 A643 Set of 2 3.00 3.00

Souvenir Sheet

Perf. 13¾

2646 A643 300 l multi 5.00 5.00

Europa A644

Designs: 40 l, Waterfall, cliffs. 110 l, Waterfall, boulders. 200 l, Water, shoreline.
350 l, Ripples in water, vert.

2001, Apr. 29 ***Perf. 13¾x14***
2647-2649 A644 Set of 3 4.25 4.25

Souvenir Sheet

Perf. 12¾x13

2650 A644 350 l multi 4.25 4.25

No. 2650 contains one 25x29mm stamp.

Domestic Animals — A645

No. 2651: a, 10 l, Horse. b, 15 l, Donkey. c, 80 l, Cat. d, 90 l, Dog.
300 l, Cat.

2001, May 17 ***Perf. 14¼x14***
2651 A645 Sheet of 4, #a-d 3.25 3.25

Souvenir Sheet

Perf. 12¾x13

2652 A645 300 l shown 5.00 5.00

No. 2651 contains four 42x26mm stamps.

2001 Mediterranean Games, Tunis, Tunisia — A646

No. 2653: a, 10 l, Swimmer. b, 90 l, Runners. c, 140 l, Cyclists.
260 l, Discus thrower.

2001, June 1 ***Perf. 14¼x14***
2653 A646 Vert. strip of 3, #a-c 4.00 4.00

Souvenir Sheet

Perf. 13x12¾

2654 A646 260 l multi 4.50 4.50

No. 2654 contains one 29x25mm stamp.

History of Aviation — A647

No. 2655: a, Clement Ader's flight of Eole, Oct. 9, 1890. b, Louis Blériot's flight of Blériot IX over English Channel, July 25, 1909. c, Charles Lindbergh's solo transatlantic flight of Spirit of St. Louis, May, 1927. d, Flight over Tirana, May 30, 1925. e, Antonov AN-10, 1956. f, First Concorde flight, Feb. 9, 1969. g, First Boeing 747 flight, Jan. 22, 1970. h, First flight of Space Shuttle Columbia, Apr. 12, 1981.

2001, June 20 ***Perf. 13¾x13***
2655 A647 40 l Sheet of 8, #a-h 5.50 5.50

Bridges — A648

No. 2656: a, 10 l, Tabakeve. b, 20 l, Kamares. c, 40 l, Golikut. d, 90 l, Mesit.
250 l, Tabakeve.

2001, July 20 ***Perf. 13¾x13¼***
2656 A648 Sheet of 4, #a-d 2.75 2.75

Souvenir Sheet

Perf. 12¾x13

2657 A648 250 l shown 4.00 4.00

No. 2656 contains four 38x30mm stamps.

Coats of Arms — A649

Arms of: 20 l, Dimitri of Arber. 45 l, Balsha. 50 l, Muzaka. 90 l, George Castrioti (Skanderbeg).

2001, Sept. 12 ***Perf. 12¾x13***
2658 A649 20 l multi .35 .35
a. Booklet pane of 4 1.40
2659 A649 45 l multi .80 .80
a. Booklet pane of 4 3.25
2660 A649 50 l multi .85 .85
a. Booklet pane of 4 3.50
2661 A649 90 l multi 1.60 1.60
a. Booklet pane of 4 6.50
Booklet, #2658a-2661a 15.00
Nos. 2658-2661 (4) 3.60 3.60

Year of Dialogue Among Civilizations A650

Colors of denomination: 45 l, Green. 50 l, Black. 120 l, White.

2001, Oct. 6 ***Perf. 13½x14***

2662-2664 A650 Set of 3 3.50 3.50

Nobel Prizes, Cent. A651

Laureates: 10 l, Doctors Without Borders, Peace, 1999. 20 l , Wilhelm C. Roentgen, Physics, 1901. 90 l, Ferid Murad, Physiology or Medicine, 1988. 200 l, Mother Teresa, Peace, 1979.

2001, Dec. 1 ***Perf. 13¾x13¼***

2665-2668 A651 Set of 4 5.25 5.25

Europa — A654

Designs: 40 l, High wire act. 90 l, Acrobats. 220 l, Contortionist.
350 l, Trained horse act.

2002, May 1 Litho. ***Perf. 13x13¾***

2672-2674 A654 Set of 3 6.25 6.25

Souvenir Sheet

Perf. 13¾

2675 A654 350 l multi 6.25 6.25

No. 2675 contains one 37x37mm stamp.

SEMI-POSTAL STAMPS

Nos. 148-151 Surcharged in Red and Black

1924, Nov. 1

B1 A18 5g + 5q yel grn 5.00 *6.50*
B2 A18 10g + 5q carmine 5.00 *6.50*
B3 A18 25g + 5q dark blue 5.00 *6.50*
B4 A18 50g + 5q dark grn 5.00 *6.50*
Nos. B1-B4 (4) 20.00 *26.00*

Nos. B1 to B4 with Additional Surcharge in Red and Black

1924

B5 A18 5g + 5q + 5q yel grn 5.00 *6.50*
B6 A18 10g + 5q + 5q car 5.00 *6.50*
B7 A18 25g + 5q + 5q dk bl 5.00 *6.50*
B8 A18 50g + 5q + 5q dk grn 5.00 *6.50*
Nos. B5-B8 (4) 20.00 *26.00*

Issued under Italian Dominion

Nurse and Child — SP1

Unwmk.

1943, Apr. 1 Photo. ***Perf. 14***

B9 SP1 5q + 5q dark grn .25 .25
B10 SP1 10q + 10q olive brn .25 .25
B11 SP1 15q + 10q rose red .35 .35
B12 SP1 25q + 15q saphire .50 .50
B13 SP1 30q + 20q violet .60 .60
B14 SP1 50q + 25q dk org .75 .75
B15 SP1 65q + 30q grnsh blk 1.10 1.10
B16 SP1 1fr + 40q chestnut 2.50 2.50
Nos. B9-B16 (8) 6.30 6.30

The surtax was for the control of tuberculosis.

For surcharges see Nos. B24-B27.

Issued under German Administration

War Victims SP2

1944, Sept. 22

B17 SP2 5g + 5(q) dp grn 2.10 *2.75*
B18 SP2 10g + 5(q) dp brn 2.10 *2.75*
B19 SP2 15g + 5(q) car lake 2.10 *2.75*
B20 SP2 25g + 10(q) dp blue 2.10 *2.75*
B21 SP2 1fr + 50q dk olive 2.10 *2.75*
B22 SP2 2fr + 1(fr) purple 2.10 *2.75*
B23 SP2 3fr + 1.50(fr) dk org 2.10 *2.75*
Nos. B17-B23 (7) 14.70 *19.25*

Surtax for victims of World War II.

Independent State

Nos. B9 to B12 Surcharged in Carmine

1945, May 4 Unwmk. ***Perf. 14***

B24 SP1 30q +15q on 5q+5q 1.75 1.75
B25 SP1 50q +25q on 10q+10q 1.75 1.75
B26 SP1 1fr +50q on 15q+10q 5.00 5.00
B27 SP1 2fr +1fr on 25q+15q 8.75 8.75
Nos. B24-B27 (4) 17.25 17.25

The surtax was for the Albanian Red Cross.

People's Republic

Nos. 361 to 366 Overprinted in Red (cross) and Surcharged in Black

1946, July 16 ***Perf. 11***

B28 A57 20q + 10q bluish grn 6.50 6.50
B29 A57 30q + 15q dp org 6.50 6.50
B30 A57 40q + 20q brown 6.50 6.50
B31 A57 60q + 30q red vio 6.50 6.50
B32 A57 1fr + 50q rose red 6.50 6.50
B33 A57 3fr + 1.50fr dk bl 6.50 6.50
Nos. B28-B33 (6) 39.00 39.00

To honor and benefit the Congress of the Albanian Red Cross.

Counterfeits: lithographed; genuine: typographed.

Catalogue values for unused stamps in this section, from this point to the end of the section, are for Never Hinged items.

SP3

SP4

First Aid and Red Cross: 25q+5q, Nurse carrying child on stretcher. 65q+25q, Symbolic blood transfusion. 80q+40q, Mother and child.

1967, Dec. 1 Litho. ***Perf. 11½x12***

B34 SP3 15q + 5q blk, red & brn .90 .45
B35 SP3 25q + 5q multi 1.00 .60
B36 SP3 65q + 25q multi 3.00 .65
B37 SP3 80q + 40q multi 5.00 1.50
Nos. B34-B37 (4) 9.90 3.20

6th congress of the Albanian Red Cross.

1996, Aug. 5 Litho. ***Perf. 13½x13***

B38 SP4 50 l +10 l multi 2.50 2.50

Albanian Red Cross, 75th anniv.

Nos. 2469-2470 Surcharged

Methods and Perfs as Before

2001, Mar. 12

B39 A567 80 l +10 l on 50 l multi 3.00 3.00
B40 A567 130 l +20 l on 100 l multi 4.50 4.50

AIR POST STAMPS

Airplane Crossing Mountains AP1

Wmk. 125

1925, May 30 Typo. ***Perf. 14***

C1 AP1 5q green .50 .50
C2 AP1 10q rose red .50 .50
C3 AP1 25q deep blue .50 .50
C4 AP1 50q dark green 1.00 1.00
C5 AP1 1fr dk vio & blk 1.90 1.90
C6 AP1 2fr ol grn & vio 3.00 3.00
C7 AP1 3fr brn org & dk grn 5.25 5.25
Nos. C1-C7 (7) 12.65 12.65

Nos. C1-C7 exist imperf.

For overprint see Nos. C8-C28.

Nos. C1-C7 Overprinted

1927, Jan. 18

C8 AP1 5q green 3.00 3.00
a. Dbl. overprint, one invtd. 35.00
C9 AP1 10q rose red 3.00 3.00
a. Inverted overprint 30.00
b. Dbl. overprint, one invtd. 35.00
C10 AP1 25q deep blue 1.60 1.60
C11 AP1 50q dark grn 1.60 1.60
a. Inverted overprint 30.00
C12 AP1 1fr dk vio & blk 1.60 1.60
a. Inverted overprint 30.00
b. Double overprint 30.00
C13 AP1 2fr ol grn & vio 1.60 1.60
C14 AP1 3fr brn org & dk grn 2.75 2.75
Nos. C8-C14 (7) 15.15 15.15

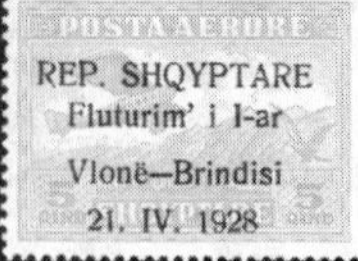

Nos. C1-C7 Overprinted

1928, Apr. 21

C15 AP1 5q green 1.40 1.50
a. Inverted overprint 22.50
C16 AP1 10q rose red 1.40 1.50
C17 AP1 25q deep blue 1.40 1.50
C18 AP1 50q dark green 3.00 2.50
C19 AP1 1fr dk vio & blk 15.00 19.00
C20 AP1 2fr ol grn & vio 15.00 19.00
C21 AP1 3fr brn org & dk grn 15.00 19.00
Nos. C15-C21 (7) 52.20 64.00

First flight across the Adriatic, Valona to Brindisi, Apr. 21, 1928.

The variety "SHQYRTARE" occurs once in the sheet for each value. Value 3 times normal.

Nos. C1-C7 Overprinted in Red Brown

1929, Dec. 1

C22 AP1 5q green 2.75 2.75
C23 AP1 10q rose red 2.75 2.75
C24 AP1 25q deep blue 5.75 5.75
C25 AP1 50q dk grn 17.00 17.00
C26 AP1 1fr dk vio & blk 80.00 80.00
C27 AP1 2fr ol grn 97.50 97.50
C28 AP1 3fr brn org & dk grn 190.00 190.00
Nos. C22-C28 (7) 395.75 395.75

Excellent counterfeits exist.

King Zog and Airplane over Tirana AP2

AP3

1930, Oct. 8 Photo. Unwmk.

C29 AP2 5q yellow green .35 .30
C30 AP2 15q rose red .45 .40
C31 AP2 20q slate blue .60 .55
C32 AP2 50q olive green .85 .75
C33 AP3 1fr dark blue 1.75 1.60
C34 AP3 2fr olive brown 5.50 5.25
C35 AP3 3fr purple 7.50 7.00
Nos. C29-C35 (7) 17.00 15.85

For overprints and surcharges see Nos. C36-C45.

Nos. C29-C35 Overprinted

1931, July 6

C36 AP2 5q yellow grn 2.10 2.10
a. Double overprint *65.00*
C37 AP2 15q rose red 2.10 2.10
C38 AP2 20q slate blue 2.10 2.10
C39 AP2 50q olive grn 2.10 2.10
C40 AP3 1fr dark blue 12.50 12.50
C41 AP3 2fr olive brn 12.50 12.50

C42 AP3 3fr purple 12.50 12.50
a. Inverted overprint *175.00*
Nos. C36-C42 (7) 45.90 45.90

1st air post flight from Tirana to Rome.

Only a very small part of this issue was sold to the public. Most of the stamps were given to the Aviation Company to help provide funds for conducting the service.

Issued under Italian Dominion

Nos. C29-C30 Overprinted in Black

1939, Apr. 19 Unwmk. *Perf. 14*
C43 AP2 5q yel green 1.25 1.10
C44 AP2 15q rose red 1.25 1.10

No. C32 With Additional Surcharge
C45 AP2 20q on 50q ol grn 2.00 2.00
a. Inverted overprint
Nos. C43-C45 (3) 4.50 4.20

See note after No. 309.

King Victor Emmanuel III and Plane over Mountains AP4

1939, Aug. 4 Photo.
C46 AP4 20q brown 13.00 4.00

Shepherds AP5

Map of Albania Showing Air Routes — AP6

Designs: 20q, Victor Emmanuel III and harbor view. 50q, Woman and river valley. 1fr, Bridge at Vezirit. 2fr, Ruins. 3fr, Women waving to plane.

1940, Mar. 20 Unwmk.
C47 AP5 5q green .25 .25
C48 AP6 15q rose red .25 .25
C49 AP5 20q deep blue .25 .25
C50 AP6 50q brown .75 .75
C51 AP5 1fr myrtle green 1.25 1.25
C52 AP6 2fr brown black 4.25 4.25
C53 AP6 3fr rose violet 10.00 10.00
Nos. C47-C53 (7) 17.00 17.00

People's Republic

Vuno-Himare AP12

Albanian Towns: 1 l, 10 l, Rozafat-Shkoder. 2 l, 20 l, Keshtjelle-Butrinto.

1950, Dec. 15 Engr. *Perf. 12½x12*
C54 AP12 50q gray black .25 .25
C55 AP12 1 l red brown .25 .25
C56 AP12 2 l ultra .50 .50
C57 AP12 5 l deep green 1.00 1.00
C58 AP12 10 l deep blue 2.25 2.25
C59 AP12 20 l purple 5.75 5.75
Nos. C54-C59 (6) 10.00 10.00

Nos. C56-C58 Surcharged with New Value and Bars in Red or Black

1952-53
C60 AP12 50q on 2 l (R) 40.00 40.00
C61 AP12 50q on 5 l 10.00 5.00
C62 AP12 2.50 l on 5 l (R) 60.00 60.00
C63 AP12 2.50 l on 10 l 10.00 5.00
Nos. C60-C63 (4) 120.00 110.00

Issued: #C60, C62, 12/26/52; #C61, C63, 3/14/53.

Catalogue values for unused stamps in this section, from this point to the end of the section, are for Never Hinged items.

Banner with Lenin, Map of Stalingrad and Tanks — AP13

1963, Feb. 2 Litho. *Perf. 14*
C67 AP13 7 l grn & dp car 3.00 .60

20th anniversary, Battle of Stalingrad.

Sputnik and Sun AP14

Designs: 3 l, Lunik 4. 5 l, Lunik 3 photographing far side of the Moon. 8 l, Venus space probe. 12 l, Mars 1.

1963, Oct. 31 Unwmk. *Perf. 12*
C68 AP14 2 l org, yel & blk .25 .30
C69 AP14 3 l multi .50 .30
C70 AP14 5 l rose lil, yel & blk .90 .45
C71 AP14 8 l multi 1.25 .85
C72 AP14 12 l blue & org 2.25 2.50
Nos. C68-72 (5) 5.15 4.40

Russian interplanetary explorations.

Nos. C68 and C71 Overprinted: "Riccione 23-8-1964"

1964, Aug. 23
C73 AP14 2 l org, yel & blk 5.50 5.50
C74 AP14 8 l multicolored 9.50 9.50

Intl. Space Exhib. in Riccione, Italy.

Plane over Berat AP15

1975, Nov. 25 Litho. *Perf. 12*
C75 AP15 20q multi .20 .20
C76 AP15 40q Gjirokaster .20 .20
C77 AP15 60q Sarande .20 .20
C78 AP15 90q Durres .50 .20
C79 AP15 1.20 l Kruje .80 .20
C80 AP15 2.40 l Boga 1.60 .35
C81 AP15 4.05 l Tirana 2.50 .65
Nos. C75-C81 (7) 6.00 2.00

SPECIAL DELIVERY STAMPS

Issued under Italian Dominion

King Victor Emmanuel III — SD1

1940 Unwmk. Photo. *Perf. 14*
E1 SD1 25q bright violet 1.40 .60
E2 SD1 50q red orange 2.40 2.00

Issued under German Administration

No. E1 Overprinted in Carmine

1943
E3 SD1 25q bright violet 15.00 17.50

Proclamation of Albanian independence.

POSTAGE DUE STAMPS

Nos. 35-39 Handstamped in Various Colors

1914, Feb. 23 Unwmk. *Perf. 14*
J1 A3 2q org brn & buff (Bl) 6.00 1.60
J2 A3 5q green (R) 6.00 2.50
J3 A3 10q rose red (Bl) 8.00 1.60
J4 A3 25q dark blue (R) 10.00 1.60
J5 A3 50q vio & red (Bk) 14.00 5.00
Nos. J1-J5 (5) 44.00 12.30

The two parts of the overprint are handstamped separately. Stamps exist with one or both handstamps inverted, double, omitted or in wrong color.

Nos. 48-51 Overprinted in Black

1914, Apr. 16
J6 A3 (a) 10pa on 5q green 2.75 2.25
J7 A3 (a) 20pa on 10q rose red 2.75 2.25
J8 A3 (b) 1gr on 25q blue 2.75 2.25
J9 A3 (b) 2gr on 50q vio & red 2.75 2.25
Nos. J6-J9 (4) 11.00 9.00

Same Design as Regular Issue of 1919, Overprinted

1919, Feb. 10 *Perf. 11½, 12½*
J10 A8 (4)q on 4h rose 5.00 4.50
J11 A8 (10)q on 10k red, *grn* 5.00 4.50
J12 A8 20q on 2k org, *gray* 5.00 4.50
J13 A8 50q on 5k brn, *yel* 5.00 4.50
Nos. J10-J13 (4) 20.00 18.00

Fortress at Scutari — D3

D5

Post Horn Overprinted in Black

1920, Apr. 1 *Perf. 14x13*
J14 D3 4q olive green .40 .40
J15 D3 10q rose red .85 .85
J16 D3 20q bister brn .85 .85
J17 D3 50q black 2.00 2.00
Nos. J14-J17 (4) 4.10 4.10

1922 *Perf. 12½, 11½*
Background of Red Wavy Lines
J23 D5 4q black, *red* 1.00 1.00
J24 D5 10q black, *red* 1.00 1.00
J25 D5 20q black, *red* 1.00 1.00
J26 D5 50q black, *red* 1.00 1.00
Nos. J23-J26 (4) 4.00 4.00

Same Overprinted in White

1925
J27 D5 4q black, *red* 1.00 1.00
J28 D5 10q black, *red* 1.00 1.00
J29 D5 20q black, *red* 1.00 1.00
J30 D5 50q black, *red* 1.00 1.00
Nos. J27-J30 (4) 4.00 4.00

The 10q with overprint in gold was a trial printing. It was not put in use.

D7

Coat of Arms — D8

Overprinted "QINDAR" in Red

1926, Dec. 24 *Perf. 13½x13*
J31 D7 10q dark blue .25 .20
J32 D7 20q green .50 .40
J33 D7 30q red brown .80 .60
J34 D7 50q dark brown 1.25 1.00
Nos. J31-J34 (4) 2.80 2.20

Wmk. Double Headed Eagle (220)
1930, Sept. 1 Photo. *Perf. 14, 14½*
J35 D8 10q dark blue 7.50 7.50
J36 D8 20q rose red 2.50 2.50
J37 D8 30q violet 2.50 2.50
J38 D8 50q dark green 2.50 2.50
Nos. J35-J38 (4) 15.00 15.00

Nos. J36-J38 exist with overprint "14 Shtator 1943" (see Nos. 332-344) which is private and fraudulent on these stamps.

No. 253 Overprinted **Taksë**

1936 *Perf. 14*
J39 A34 10q carmine 3.50 4.75
a. Hyphens on each side of "Takse" ('39) 20.00 20.00

Issued under Italian Dominion

Coat of Arms — D9

1940 Unwmk. Photo. *Perf. 14*
J40 D9 4q red orange *16.00 16.00*
J41 D9 10q bright violet *16.00 16.00*
J42 D9 20q brown *16.00 16.00*
J43 D9 30q dark blue *16.00 16.00*
J44 D9 50q carmine rose *16.00 16.00*
Nos. J40-J44 (5) *80.00 80.00*

ALEXANDRETTA

ˌa-lig-ˌₐzan-ˈdre-tə

LOCATION — A political territory in northern Syria, bordering on Turkey
GOVT. — French mandate
AREA — 10,000 sq. mi. (approx.)
POP. — 270,000 (approx.)

Included in the Syrian territory mandated to France under the Versailles Treaty, the name was changed to Hatay in 1938. The following year France returned the territory to Turkey in exchange for certain concessions. See Hatay.

100 Centimes = 1 Piaster

Stamps of Syria, 1930-36, Overprinted or Surcharged in Black or Red:

a

b

c

d

e

1938 Unwmk. *Perf. 12x12½*

1	A6(a)	10c vio brn	.60	.60
2	A6(a)	20c brn org	.60	.60

Perf. 13½

3	A9(b)	50c vio (R)	.75	.75
4	A10(b)	1p bis brn	.85	.85
5	A9(b)	2p dk vio (R)	1.25	1.25
6	A13(b)	3p yel grn (R)	2.00	2.00
7	A10(b)	4p yel org	2.50	2.50
8	A16(b)	6p grnsh blk (R)	2.25	2.25
9	A18(b)	25p vio brn	7.25	7.25
10	A15(c)	75c org red	1.10	1.10
11	A10(d)	2.50p on 4p yel org	1.50	1.50
12	AP2(e)	12.50p on 15p org red	3.25	3.25
		Nos. 1-12 (12)	23.90	23.90
		Set, never hinged	48.00	

Issue dates: #1-9, Apr. 14, #10-12, Sept. 2.

Nos. 4, 7, 10-12 Overprinted in Black

1938, Nov. 10

13	A15	75c	30.00	*32.50*
14	A10	1p	17.50	*19.00*
15	A10	2.50p on 4p	11.00	*12.50*
16	A10	4p	15.00	15.00
17	AP2	12.50p on 15p	30.00	*32.50*
		Nos. 13-17 (5)	103.50	111.50
		Set, never hinged	200.00	

Death of Kemal Ataturk, pres. of Turkey.

AIR POST STAMPS

Air Post Stamps of Syria, 1937, Overprinted Type "b" in Red or Black

1938, Apr. 14 Unwmk. *Perf. 13*

C1	AP14	½p dark vio (R)	.75	*.85*
C2	AP15	1p black (R)	.75	.50
C3	AP14	2p blue grn (R)	1.60	*1.75*
C4	AP15	3p deep ultra	1.75	*2.00*
C5	AP14	5p rose lake	4.00	*4.75*
C6	AP15	10p red brown	4.50	*5.25*
C7	AP14	15p lake brown	5.25	*6.00*
C8	AP15	25p dk blue (R)	7.25	*8.00*
		Nos. C1-C8 (8)	25.85	29.10
		Set, never hinged	47.50	

POSTAGE DUE STAMPS

Postage Due Stamps of Syria, 1925-31, Ovptd. Type "b" in Black or Red

1938, Apr. 14 Unwmk. *Perf. 13½*

J1	D5	50c brown, *yel*	*1.40*	2.00
J2	D6	1p violet, *rose*	*2.10*	2.25
J3	D5	2p blk, *blue* (R)	2.75	2.75
J4	D5	3p blk, *red org*	*4.50*	5.00
J5	D5	5p blk, *bl grn* (R)	*6.75*	7.00
J6	D7	8p blk, *gray bl* (R)	*7.50*	8.50
		Nos. J1-J6 (6)	25.00	27.50
		Set, never hinged	45.00	

On No. J2, the overprint is vertical, reading up, other denominations, horizontal.

Stamps of Alexandretta were discontinued in 1938 and replaced by those of Hatay.

ALGERIA

al-ˈjir-ē-ə

LOCATION — North Africa
GOVT. — Republic
AREA — 919,595 sq. mi.
POP. — 29,300,000 (1998 est.)
CAPITAL — Algiers

The former French colony of Algeria became an integral part of France on Sept. 1, 1958, when French stamps replaced Algerian stamps. Algeria became an independent country July 3, 1962.

100 Centimes = 1 Franc
100 Centimes = 1 Dinar (1964)

Catalogue values for unused stamps in this country are for Never Hinged items, beginning with Scott 109 in the regular postage section, Scott B27 in the semi-postal section, Scott C1 in the airpost section, Scott CB1 in the airpost semi-postal section, and Scott J25 in the postage due section.

Stamps of France Overprinted in Red, Blue or Black:

a

b

c

d

1924-26 Unwmk. *Perf. 14x13½*

1	A16(a)	1c dk gray (R)	.20	.20
2	A16(a)	2c violet brn	.20	.20
3	A16(a)	3c orange	.20	.20
4	A16(a)	4c yel brn (Bl)	.20	.20
5	A22(a)	5c orange (Bl)	.20	.20
6	A16(a)	5c green ('25)	.40	.30
7	A23(a)	10c green	.30	.20
b.		Booklet pane of 10	6.00	
8	A22(a)	10c green ('25)	.50	.20
9	A20(a)	15c slate grn	.20	.20
10	A23(a)	15c green ('25)	.60	.20
11	A22(a)	15c red brn (Bl) ('26)	.20	.20
12	A22(a)	20c red brn (Bl)	.25	.20
13	A22(a)	25c blue (R)	.20	.20
a.		Booklet pane of 10	45.00	
14	A23(a)	30c red (Bl)	.90	.20
15	A22(a)	30c cerise ('25)	.70	.50
a.		"ALGERIE" double	140.00	
16	A22(a)	30c lt bl (R) ('25)	.30	.20
a.		Booklet pane of 10	35.00	
17	A22(a)	35c violet	.30	.20
18	A18(b)	40c red & pale bl	.30	.20
19	A22(a)	40c ol brn (R) ('25)	.75	.50
20	A18(b)	45c grn & bl (R)	.40	.30
a.		Double overprint	175.00	
21	A23(a)	45c red (Bl) ('25)	.60	.20
22	A23(a)	50c blue (R)	.40	.20
23	A20(a)	60c lt violet	.65	.35
a.		Inverted overprint		*1,750.*
24	A20(a)	65c rose (Bl)	.35	.20
25	A23(a)	75c blue (R)	.60	.30
a.		Double overprint	150.00	
26	A20(a)	80c ver ('26)	.90	.40
27	A20(a)	85c ver (Bl)	.60	.20
28	A18(b)	1fr cl & ol grn	1.00	.30
29	A22(a)	1.05fr ver ('26)	1.00	.40
30	A18(c)	2fr org & pale bl	1.00	.55
31	A18(b)	3fr vio & bl ('26)	3.00	.80
32	A18(d)	5fr bl & buff (R)	8.00	4.75
		Nos. 1-32 (32)	25.40	13.45

No. 15 was issued precanceled only. Values for precanceled stamps in first column are for those which have not been through the post and have original gum. Values in second column are for postally used, gumless stamps.

For surcharges see Nos. 75, P1.

Street in Kasbah, Algiers
A1

Mosque of Sidi Abd-er-Rahman
A2

La Pêcherie Mosque — A3

Marabout of Sidi Yacoub
A4

1926-39 Typo. *Perf. 14x13½*

33	A1	1c olive	.20	.20
34	A1	2c red brown	.20	.20
35	A1	3c orange	.20	.20
36	A1	5c blue green	.20	.20
37	A1	10c brt violet	.20	.20
a.		Booklet pane of 10	25.00	
38	A2	15c orange brn	.20	.20
39	A2	20c green	.20	.20
40	A2	20c deep rose	.20	.20
41	A2	25c blue grn	.20	.20
42	A2	25c blue ('27)	.35	.20
43	A2	25c vio bl ('39)	.20	.20
44	A2	30c blue	.25	.20
45	A2	30c bl grn ('27)	.65	.40
46	A2	35c dp violet	1.00	.65
47	A2	40c olive green	.25	.20
a.		Booklet pane of 10	30.00	
48	A3	45c violet brn	.35	.20
49	A3	50c blue	.25	.20
a.		Booklet pane of 10	35.00	
50	A3	50c dk red ('30)	.20	.20
a.		Booklet pane of 10	40.00	
51	A3	60c yellow grn	.25	.20
52	A3	65c blk brn ('27)	1.60	1.10
53	A1	65c ultra ('38)	.25	.20
a.		Booklet pane of 10	25.00	
54	A3	75c carmine	.50	.35
55	A3	75c blue ('29)	2.00	.25
56	A3	80c orange red	.50	.25
57	A3	90c red ('27)	4.50	2.00
58	A4	1fr gray grn & red brn	.50	.25
59	A3	1.05fr lt brown	.50	.35
60	A3	1.10fr mag ('27)	4.50	1.25
61	A4	1.25fr dk bl & ultra	.80	.60
62	A4	1.50fr dk bl & ultra ('27)	2.40	.25
63	A4	2fr Prus bl & blk brn	1.90	.25
64	A4	3fr violet & org	3.50	.80
65	A4	5fr red & violet	6.00	2.25
66	A4	10fr ol brn & rose ('27)	37.50	22.50
67	A4	20fr vio & grn ('27)	4.50	3.50
		Nos. 33-67 (35)	77.00	40.60

Type A4, 50c blue and rose red, inscribed "CENTENAIRE-ALGERIE" is France No. 255.

See design A24. For stamps and types surcharged see Nos. 68-74, 131, 136, 187, B1-B13, J27, P2.

Stamps of 1926 Surcharged with New Values

1927

68	A2	10c on 35c dp violet	.20	.20
69	A2	25c on 30c blue	.20	.20
70	A2	30c on 25c blue grn	.20	.20
71	A3	65c on 60c yel grn	.75	.50
72	A3	90c on 80c org red	.50	.20
73	A3	1.10fr on 1.05fr lt brn	.30	.20
74	A4	1.50fr on 1.25fr dk bl & ultra	1.25	.75
		Nos. 68-74 (7)	3.40	2.25

Bars cancel the old value on #68, 69, 73, 74.

No. 4 Surcharged

1927

75	A16	5c on 4c yellow brown	*.50*	*.25*

Bay of Algiers
A5

1930, May 4 Engr. *Perf. 11, 12½*

78	A5	10fr red brown	9.50	7.50
a.		Imperf., pair	27.50	

Cent. of Algeria and for Intl. Phil. Exhib. of North Africa, May, 1930.

One copy of No. 78 was sold with each 10fr admission.

Travel across the Sahara A6

Arch of Triumph, Lambese A7

Admiralty Building, Algiers A8

Kings' Tombs near Touggourt A9

El-Kebir Mosque, Algiers A10

Oued River at Colomb-Bechar A11

Sidi Bon Medine Cemetery at Tlemcen A13

View of Ghardaia A12

1936-41 — Engr. — Perf. 13

No.	Type	Description	Unused	Used
79	A6	1c ultra	.20	.20
80	A11	2c dk violet	.20	.20
81	A7	3c dk blue grn	.20	.20
82	A12	5c red violet	.20	.20
83	A8	10c emerald	.20	.20
84	A9	15c red	.20	.20
85	A13	20c dk blue grn	.20	.20
86	A10	25c rose vio	.30	.20
87	A12	30c yellow grn	.30	.20
88	A9	40c brown vio	.20	.20
89	A13	45c deep ultra	.65	.40
90	A8	50c red	.40	.20
91	A6	65c red brn	3.25	2.10
92	A6	65c rose car ('37)	.35	.20
93	A6	70c red brn ('39)	.20	.20
94	A11	75c slate bl	.20	.20
95	A7	90c henna brn	1.00	.55
96	A10	1fr brown	.20	.20
97	A8	1.25fr lt violet	.35	.20
98	A8	1.25fr car rose ('39)	.30	.20
99	A11	1.50fr turq blue	1.25	.20
99A	A11	1.50fr rose ('40)	.35	.20
100	A12	1.75fr henna brn	.20	.20
101	A7	2fr dk brown	.20	.20
102	A6	2.25fr yellow grn	9.50	6.50
103	A12	2.50fr dk ultra ('41)	.30	.25
104	A13	3fr magenta	.25	.20
105	A10	3.50fr pck blue	2.10	1.75
106	A8	5fr slate blue	.30	.20
107	A11	10fr henna brn	.30	.20
108	A9	20fr turq blue	.70	.40
		Nos. 79-108 (31)	24.55	16.75

See Nos. 124-125, 162.

Nos. 82 and 100 with surcharge "E. F. M. 30frs" (Emergency Field Message) were used in 1943 to pay cable tolls for US and Canadian servicemen.

For other surcharges see Nos. 122, B27.

Catalogue values for unused stamps in this section, from this point to the end of the section, are for Never Hinged items.

Algerian Pavilion — A14

1937 — Perf. 13

No.	Type	Description	Unused	Used
109	A14	40c brt green	.30	.35
110	A14	50c rose carmine	.20	.20
111	A14	1.50fr blue	.50	.25
112	A14	1.75fr brown black	.60	.50
		Nos. 109-112 (4)	1.60	1.30

Paris International Exposition.

Constantine in 1837 — A15

1937

No.	Type	Description	Unused	Used
113	A15	65c deep rose	.30	.20
114	A15	1fr brown	2.50	.50
115	A15	1.75fr blue green	.40	.20
116	A15	2.15fr red violet	.20	.20
		Nos. 113-116 (4)	3.40	1.10

Taking of Constantine by the French, cent.

Ruins of a Roman Villa — A16

1938

No.	Type	Description	Unused	Used
117	A16	30c green	.50	.30
118	A16	65c ultra	.20	.20
119	A16	75c rose violet	.55	.40
120	A16	3fr carmine rose	1.40	1.40
121	A16	5fr yellow brown	2.25	2.25
		Nos. 117-121 (5)	4.90	4.55

Centenary of Philippeville.

No. 90 Surcharged in Black

1938

No.	Type	Description	Unused	Used
122	A8	25c on 50c red	.20	.20
a.		Double surcharge	35.00	30.00
b.		Inverted surcharge	20.00	18.00

Types of 1936

1939

Numerals of Value on Colorless Background

No.	Type	Description	Unused	Used
124	A7	90c henna brown	.20	.20
125	A10	2.25fr blue green	.20	.20

For surcharge see No. B38.

American Export Liner Unloading Cargo A17

1939

No.	Type	Description	Unused	Used
126	A17	20c green	.90	.65
127	A17	40c red violet	1.10	.50
128	A17	90c brown black	.60	.20
129	A17	1.25fr rose	3.50	.80
130	A17	2.25fr ultra	.90	.60
		Nos. 126-130 (5)	7.00	2.75

New York World's Fair.

Type of 1926, Surcharged in Black

Two types of surcharge:
I — Bars 6mm
II — Bars 7mm

1939-40 — Perf. 14x13½

No.	Type	Description	Unused	Used
131	A1	1fr on 90c crimson (I)	.20	.20
a.		Booklet pane of 10		
b.		Double surcharge (I)	50.00	
c.		Inverted surcharge (I)	27.50	
d.		Pair, one without surch. (I)	875.00	
e.		Type II ('40)	2.00	.50
f.		Inverted surcharge (II)	32.50	
g.		Pair, one without surch. (II)	875.00	

View of Algiers — A18

1941 — Typo.

No.	Type	Description	Unused	Used
132	A18	30c ultra	.20	.20
133	A18	70c sepia	.20	.20
134	A18	1fr carmine rose	.20	.20
		Nos. 132-134 (3)	.60	.60

See No. 163.

Marshal Pétain
A19 A20

1941 — Engr. — Perf. 13

No.	Type	Description	Unused	Used
135	A19	1fr dark blue	.30	.20

For stamp and type surcharged see #B36-B37.

No. 53 Surcharged in Black with New Value and Bars

1941 — Perf. 14x13½

No.	Type	Description	Unused	Used
136	A1	50c on 65c ultra	.30	.20
a.		Booklet pane of 10		
b.		Inverted surcharge	40.00	
c.		Pair, one without surch.	90.00	

1942 — Perf. 14x13

No.	Type	Description	Unused	Used
137	A20	1.50fr orange red	.20	.20

Four other denominations of type A20 exist (4, 5, 10, 20fr), but were not placed in use.

Constantine A21 Oran A22

Arms of Algiers — A23

Engraver's Name at Lower Left

1942-43 — Photo. — Perf. 12

No.	Type	Description	Unused	Used
138	A21	40c dark vio ('43)	.20	.20
139	A22	60c rose ('43)	.20	.20
140	A21	1.20fr yel grn ('43)	.20	.20
141	A23	1.50fr car rose	.20	.20
142	A22	2fr sapphire	.20	.20
143	A21	2.40fr rose ('43)	.20	.20
144	A23	3fr sapphire	.20	.20
145	A21	4fr blue ('43)	.20	.20
146	A22	5fr yel grn ('43)	.20	.20
		Nos. 138-146 (9)	1.80	1.80

For type surcharged see No. 166.

Imperforates

Nearly all of Algeria Nos. 138-285, B39-B96, C1-C12 and CB1-CB3 exist imperforate. See note after France No. 395.

Without Engraver's Name

1942-45 — Typo. — Perf. 14x13½

No.	Type	Description	Unused	Used
147	A23	10c dull brn vio ('45)	.20	.20
148	A22	30c dp bl grn ('45)	.20	.20
149	A21	40c dull brn vio ('45)	.20	.20
150	A22	60c rose ('45)	.20	.20
151	A21	70c deep bl ('45)	.20	.20
152	A23	80c dk bl grn ('43)	.25	.25
153	A21	1.20fr dp bl grn ('45)	.20	.20
154	A23	1.50fr brt rose ('43)	.20	.20
155	A22	2fr dp blue ('45)	.20	.20
156	A21	2.40fr rose ('45)	.30	.25
157	A23	3fr dp blue ('45)	.20	.20
158	A22	4.50fr brown vio	.20	.20
		Nos. 147-158 (12)	2.55	2.50

For surcharge see No. 190.

La Pêcherie Mosque — A24

1942 — Typo.

No.	Type	Description	Unused	Used
159	A24	50c dull red	.20	.20
a.		Booklet pane of 10	2.75	

1942 — Photo. — Perf. 12

No.	Type	Description	Unused	Used
160	A24	40c gray green	.20	.20
161	A24	50c red	.20	.20

Types of 1936-41, Without "RF"

1942 — Engr. — Perf. 13

No.	Type	Description	Unused	Used
162	A11	1.50fr rose	.30	.20

Typo. — Perf. 14x13½

No.	Type	Description	Unused	Used
163	A18	30c ultra	.20	.20

"One Aim Alone - Victory"
A25 A26

1943 — Litho. — Perf. 12

No.	Type	Description	Unused	Used
164	A25	1.50fr deep rose	.20	.20
165	A26	1.50fr dark blue	.20	.20

Type of 1942-3 Surcharged with New Value in Black

1943 — Photo.

No.	Type	Description	Unused	Used
166	A22	2fr on 5fr red orange	.20	.20
a.		Surcharge omitted	175.00	

Summer Palace, Algiers A27

1944, Dec. 1 — Litho.

No.	Type	Description	Unused	Used
167	A27	15fr slate	1.50	1.25
168	A27	20fr lt blue grn	1.00	.65
169	A27	50fr dk carmine	1.00	.65
170	A27	100fr deep blue	2.50	2.00
171	A27	200fr dull bis brn	4.00	2.00
		Nos. 167-171 (5)	10.00	6.55

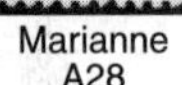
Marianne
A28

Gallic Cock
A29

1944-45

172 A28 10c gray .20 .20
173 A28 30c red violet .20 .20
174 A29 40c rose car ('45) .20 .20
175 A28 50c red .20 .20
176 A28 80c emerald .20 .20
177 A29 1fr green ('45) .20 .20
178 A28 1.20fr rose lilac .20 .20
179 A28 1.50fr dark blue .20 .20
a. Double impression 22.50
180 A29 2fr red .20 .20
a. Double impression 27.50
181 A29 2fr dk brown ('45) .20 .20
182 A28 2.40fr rose red .20 .20
183 A28 3fr purple .20 .20
184 A29 4fr ultra ('45) .20 .20
185 A28 4.50fr olive blk .30 .25
186 A29 10fr grnsh blk ('45) .50 .35
Nos. 172-186 (15) 3.40 3.20

No. 38 Surcharged in Black

1944 ***Perf. 14x13½***

187 A2 30c on 15c orange brn .20 .20
a. Inverted surcharge 10.00 4.00

This stamp exists precanceled only. See note below No. 32.

No. 154 Surcharged "RF" and New Value

1945

190 A23 50c on 1.50fr brt rose .20 .20
a. Inverted surcharge 15.00

Stamps of France, 1944, Overprinted Type "a" of 1924 in Black

1945-46

191 A99 80c yellow grn .20 .20
192 A99 1fr grnsh blue .20 .20
193 A99 1.20fr violet .25 .20
194 A99 2fr violet brown .35 .20
195 A99 2.40fr carmine rose .50 .20
196 A99 3fr orange .50 .20
Nos. 191-196 (6) 2.00 1.20

Same Overprint on Stamps of France, 1945-47, in Black, Red or Carmine

1945-47

197 A145 40c lilac rose .20 .20
198 A145 50c violet bl (R) .20 .20
199 A146 60c brt ultra (R) .25 .20
200 A146 1fr rose red ('47) .20 .20
201 A146 1.50fr rose lilac ('47) .20 .20
202 A147 2fr myr grn (R) ('46) .20 .20
203 A147 3fr deep rose .20 .20
204 A147 4.50fr ultra (C) ('47) .55 .20
205 A147 5fr lt green ('46) .20 .20
206 A147 10fr ultra .50 .35
Nos. 197-206 (10) 2.70 2.15

Same Overprint on France No. 383 and New Value Surcharged in Black

1946

207 A99 2fr on 1.50fr henna brn .20 .20
a. Without "2F" 150.00

Same Overprint on France Nos. 562 and 564, in Carmine or Blue

1947

208 A153 10c dp ultra & blk (C) .20 .20
209 A155 50c brown, yel & red (Bl) .40 .25

Constantine
A30

Algiers
A31

Arms of Oran — A32

Perf. 14x13½

1947-49 Unwmk. Typo.

210 A30 10c dk grn & brt red .20 .20
211 A31 50c black & orange .20 .20
212 A32 1fr ultra & yellow .20 .20
213 A30 1.30fr blk & grnsh bl .75 .45
214 A31 1.50fr pur & org yel .20 .20
215 A32 2fr blk & brt grn .20 .20
216 A30 2.50fr blk & brt red .60 .30
217 A31 3fr vio brn & grn .20 .20
218 A32 3.50fr lt grn & rose lil .20 .20
219 A30 4fr dk brn & brt grn .20 .20
220 A31 4.50fr ultra & scar .20 .20
221 A31 5fr blk & grnsh bl .20 .20
222 A32 6fr brown & scarlet .50 .20
223 A32 8fr choc & ultra ('48) .30 .20
224 A30 10fr car & choc ('48) .50 .20
225 A31 15fr black & red ('49) .60 .25
Nos. 210-225 (16) 5.25 3.60

See Nos. 274-280, 285.

Peoples of the World
A33

1949, Oct. 24 Engr. ***Perf. 13***

226 A33 5fr green 1.10 .80
227 A33 15fr scarlet 1.40 .80
228 A33 25fr ultra 3.00 2.50
Nos. 226-228 (3) 5.50 4.10

75th anniv. of the UPU.

Grapes
A34

Apollo of Cherchell
A35

25fr, Dates. 40fr, Oranges and lemons.

1950, Feb. 25

229 A34 20fr multicolored 1.25 .35
230 A34 25fr multicolored 1.40 .40
231 A34 40fr multicolored 2.75 .80
Nos. 229-231 (3) 5.40 1.55

1952 Unwmk. ***Perf. 13***

Designs: 12fr, 18fr, Isis statue, Cherchell. 15fr, 20fr, Child with eagle.

240 A35 10fr gray black .35 .20
241 A35 12fr orange brn .60 .25
242 A35 15fr deep blue .60 .20
243 A35 18fr rose red .60 .25
244 A35 20fr deep green .85 .20
245 A35 30fr deep blue 1.00 .40
Nos. 240-245 (6) 4.00 1.50

War Memorial, Algiers — A38

Fossilized Nautilus — A39

Phonolite Dike
A40

1952, Apr. 11

246 A38 12fr dark green .60 .40

Issued to honor the French Africa Army.

1952, Aug. 11

247 A39 15fr brt crimson 2.50 1.60
248 A40 30fr deep ultra 1.50 .90

19th Intl. Geological Cong., Algiers, 9/8-15.

French and Algerian Soldiers and Camel — A41

1952, Nov. 30

249 A41 12fr chestnut brown 1.50 1.00

50th anniv. of the establishment of the Sahara Companies.

Eugène Millon
A42

François C. Maillot — A43

Oranges — A44

Portrait: 50fr, Alphonse Laveran.

Unwmk.

1954, Jan. 4 Engr. ***Perf. 13***

250 A42 25fr dk grn & choc 1.50 .20
251 A43 40fr org brn & brn car 2.00 .60
252 A42 50fr ultra & indigo 2.00 .20
Nos. 250-252 (3) 5.50 1.00

Military Health Service.

1954, May 8

253 A44 15fr indigo & blue .75 .50

3rd Intl. Cong. on Agronomy, Algiers, 1954.

Type of France, 1954 Overprinted type "a" in Black

Unwmk.

1954, June 6 Engr. ***Perf. 13***

254 A240 15fr rose carmine .80 .60

Liberation of France, 10th anniversary.

Darguinah Hydroelectric Works
A45

Patio of Bardo Museum
A46

1954, June 19

255 A45 15fr lilac rose .75 .45

Opening of Darguinah hydroelectric works.

1954 Typo. ***Perf. 14x13½***

257 A46 12fr red brn & brn org .60 .25
258 A46 15fr dk blue & blue .60 .25

See Nos. 267-271.

Type of France, 1954, Overprinted type "a" in Carmine

1954 Engr. ***Perf. 13***

260 A247 12fr dark green .75 .50

150th anniv. of the 1st Legion of Honor awards at Camp de Boulogne.

St. Augustine — A47

1954, Nov. 11

261 A47 15fr chocolate .65 .65

1600th anniv. of the birth of St. Augustine.

Aesculapius Statue and El Kattar Hospital, Algiers
A48

1955, Apr. 3 Unwmk. ***Perf. 13***

262 A48 15fr red .50 .40

Issued to publicize the 30th French Congress of Medicine, Algiers, April 3-6, 1955.

Chenua Mountain and View of Tipasa
A49

1955, May 31

263 A49 50fr brown carmine .65 .20

2000th anniv. of the founding of Tipasa.

Type of France, 1955 Overprinted type "a" in Red

1955, June 13

264 A251 30fr deep ultra .90 .50

Rotary Intl., 50th anniv.

Marianne — A50

Great Kabylia Mountains A51

Perf. 14x13½

1955, Oct. 3 Typo. Unwmk.

265 A50 15fr carmine .30 .20

See No. 284.

1955, Dec. 17 Engr. *Perf. 13*

266 A51 100fr indigo & ultra 2.50 .35

Bardo Type of 1954, "Postes" and "Algerie" in White

Perf. 14x13½

1955-57 Unwmk. Typo.

267 A46 10fr dk brn & lt brn .25 .20
268 A46 12fr red brn & brn org ('56) .20 .20
269 A46 18fr crimson & ver ('57) .45 .20
270 A46 20fr grn & yel grn ('57) .35 .25
271 A46 25fr purple & brt purple .50 .20
Nos. 267-271 (5) 1.75 1.05

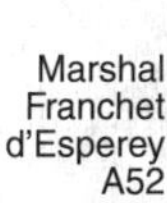

Marshal Franchet d'Esperey A52

1956, May 25 Engr. *Perf. 13*

272 A52 15fr sapphire & indigo 1.00 .70

Birth cent. of Marshal Franchet d'Esperey.

Marshal Jacques Leclerc A53

1956, Nov. 29

273 A53 15fr red brown & sepia .50 .50

Death of Marshal Leclerc.
For design surcharged see No. B90.

Type of 1947-49 and

Arms of Bône — A54

Arms: 2fr, Tizi-Quzou. 3fr, Mostaganem. 5fr, Tlemcen. 10fr, Setif. 12fr, Orleansville.

1956-58 Typo. *Perf. 14x13½*

274 A54 1fr green & ver .25 .20
275 A54 2fr ver & ultra ('58) .45 .25
276 A54 3fr ultra & emer ('58) .45 .25
277 A54 5fr ultra & yellow .25 .20
278 A31 6fr red & grn ('57) .45 .30
279 A54 10fr dp cl & emer ('58) .50 .30
280 A54 12fr ultra & red ('58) .50 .30
Nos. 274-280 (7) 2.85 1.80

Nos. 275 and 279 are inscribed "Republique Francaise." See No. 285.

View of Oran — A55

1956-58 Engr. *Perf. 13*

281 A55 30fr dull purple .60 .20
282 A55 35fr car rose ('58) .90 .45

Electric Train Crossing Bridge A56

1957, Mar. 25

283 A56 40fr dk blue grn & emer 1.00 .25

Marianne Type of 1955 Inscribed "Algerie" Vertically

Perf. 14x13½

1957, Dec. 2 Typo. Unwmk.

284 A50 20fr ultra .40 .20

Arms Type of 1947-49 Inscribed "Republique Francaise"

1958, July

285 A31 6fr red & green 17.50 15.00

Independent State

France Nos. 939, 968, 945-946 and 1013 Overprinted "EA" and Bars, Handstamped or Typographed, in Black or Red

1962, July 2

286 A336 10c brt green .25 .20
a. Typographed overprint .50 .20
287 A349 25c lake & gray .20 .20
a. Handstamped overprint .50 .20
288 A339 45c brt vio & ol gray 3.50 3.00
a. Handstamped overprint *18.00 11.00*
289 A339 50c sl grn & lt claret 5.00 3.00
a. Handstamped overprint *18.00 12.00*
290 A372 1fr dk bl, sl & bis 2.75 1.00
a. Handstamped overprint *3.50 1.50*
Nos. 286-290 (5) 11.70 7.40

Post offices were authorized to overprint their stock of these 5 French stamps. The size of the letters was specified as 3x6mm each, but various sizes were used. The post offices had permission to make their own rubber stamps. Typography, pen or pencil were also used. Many types exist. Colors of handstamped overprints include black, red, blue, violet. "EA" stands for Etat Algérien.

Mosque, Tlemcen — A57

Roman Gates of Lodi, Médéa A58

5c, Kerrata Gorge. 10c, Dam at Foum el Gherza. 95c, Oil field, Hassi Messaoud.

1962, Nov. 1 Engr. *Perf. 13*

291 A57 5c Prus grn, grn & choc .20 .20
292 A58 10c ol blk & dk bl .20 .20
293 A57 25c sl grn, brn & ver .40 .20
294 A57 95c dk bl, blk & bis 1.50 .55
295 A58 1fr green & blk 1.50 1.10
Nos. 291-295 (5) 3.80 2.25

The designs of Nos. 291-295 are similar to French issues of 1959-61 with "Republique Algerienne" replacing "Republique Francaise."

Flag, Rifle, Olive Branch — A59

Design: Nos. 300-303, Broken chain and rifle added to design A59.

1963, Jan. 6 Litho. *Perf. 12½*

Flag in Green and Red

296 A59 5c bister brown .20 .20
297 A59 10c blue .20 .20
298 A59 25c vermilion 1.50 .20
299 A59 95c violet 1.10 .45
300 A59 1fr green 1.00 .20
301 A59 2fr brown 2.50 .50
302 A59 5fr lilac 4.50 1.25
303 A59 10fr gray 17.00 7.00
Nos. 296-303 (8) 28.00 10.00

Nos. 296-299 for the successful revolution and Nos. 300-303 the return of peace.

Men of Various Races, Wheat Emblem and Globe A60

1963, Mar. 21 Engr. *Perf. 13*

304 A60 25c maroon, dl grn & yel .30 .25

FAO "Freedom from Hunger" campaign.

Map of Algeria and Emblems — A61

Physicians from 13th Century Manuscript — A62

1963, July 5 Unwmk. *Perf. 13*

305 A61 25c bl, dk brn, grn & red .40 .25

1st anniv. of Algeria's independence.

1963, July 29 Engr.

306 A62 25c brn red, grn & bis 1.00 .35

2nd Congress of the Union of Arab physicians.

Orange and Blossom — A63

Scales and Scroll A64

1963 *Perf. 14x13*

307 A63 8c gray grn & org .65 .65
308 A63 20c slate & org red .75 .75
309 A63 40c grnsh bl & org 1.00 1.00
310 A63 55c ol grn & org red 2.00 2.00
Nos. 307-310 (4) 4.40 4.40

Nos. 307-310 issued precanceled only. See note below No. 32.

1963, Oct. 13 Unwmk. *Perf. 13*

311 A64 25c blk, grn & rose red .40 .25

Issued to honor the new constitution.

Guerrillas — A65

Centenary Emblem — A66

1963, Nov. 1

312 A65 25c dk brn, yel grn & car .55 .25

9th anniversary of Algerian revolution.

1963, Dec. 8 Photo. *Perf. 12*

313 A66 25c lt vio bl, yel & dk red .55 .30

Centenary of International Red Cross.

UNESCO Emblem, Scales and Globe — A67

Workers — A68

1963, Dec. 16 Unwmk. *Perf. 12*

314 A67 25c lt blue & blk .55 .25

15th anniv. of the Universal Declaration of Human Rights.

1964, May 1 Engr. *Perf. 13*

315 A68 50c dull red, red org & bl .90 .50

Issued for the Labor Festival.

Map of Africa and Flags A69

1964, May 25 Unwmk. *Perf. 13*

316 A69 45c blue, orange & car .55 .30

Africa Day on the 1st anniv. of the Addis Ababa charter on African unity.

Ramses II Battling the Hittites (from Abu Simbel) — A70

Design: 30c, Two statues of Ramses II.

1964, June 28 Engr. *Perf. 13*

317 A70 20c choc, red & vio bl .55 .30
318 A70 30c brn, red & grnsh bl .65 .40

UNESCO world campaign to save historic monuments in Nubia.

A71

A72

5c, 25c, 85c, Tractors. 10c, 30c, 65c, Men working with lathe. 12c, 15c, 45c, Electronics center & atom symbol. 20c, 50c, 95c, Draftsman & bricklayer.

1964-65 Typo. *Perf. 14x13½*

319 A71	5c red lilac	.20	.20
320 A71	10c brown	.20	.20
321 A71	12c emerald ('65)	.40	.20
322 A71	15c dk blue ('65)	.25	.20
323 A71	20c yellow	.40	.20
324 A71	25c red	.50	.20
325 A71	30c purple ('65)	.40	.20
326 A71	45c rose car	.50	.20
327 A71	50c ultra	.60	.20
328 A71	65c orange	.80	.20
329 A71	85c green	1.40	.25
330 A71	95c car rose	1.75	.30
	Nos. 319-330 (12)	7.40	2.55

For surcharges see Nos. 389, 424.

1964, Aug. 30 Engr. *Perf. 13*

331 A72 85c Communications tower 1.50 .75

Inauguration of the Hertzian cable telephone line Algiers-Annaba.

Industrial & Agricultural Symbols — A73

1964, Sept. 26 Typo. *Perf. 13½x14*

332 A73 25c lt ultra, yel & red .60 .45

1st Intl. Fair at Algiers, Sept. 26-Oct. 11.

Gas Flames and Pipes — A74

1964, Sept. 27

333 A74 30c violet, blue & yel .45 .35

Arzew natural gas liquification plant opening.

Planting Trees — A75

Children and UNICEF Emblem — A76

1964, Nov. 29 Unwmk.

334 A75 25c slate grn, yel & car .30 .20

National reforestation campaign.

1964, Dec. 13 *Perf. 13½x14*

335 A76 15c pink, vio bl & lt grn .25 .20

Issued for Children's Day.

Decorated Camel Saddle — A77

1965, May 29 Typo. *Perf. 13½x14*

336 A77 20c blk, red, emer & brn .25 .20

Handicrafts of Sahara.

ICY Emblem A78

1965, Aug. 29 Engr. *Perf. 13*

337 A78 30c blk, mar & bl grn .45 .30
338 A78 60c blk, brt bl & bl grn .85 .40

International Cooperation Year, 1965.

ITU Emblem A79

1965, Sept. 19

339 A79 60c purple, emer & buff .45 .30
340 A79 95c dk brn, mar & buff .65 .35

Cent. of the ITU.

Musicians A80

Miniatures by Mohammed Racim: 60c, Two female musicians. 5d, Algerian princess and antelope.

1965, Dec. 27 Photo. *Perf. 11½*

341 A80	30c multicolored	1.10	.45
342 A80	60c multicolored	1.50	.85
343 A80	5d multicolored	9.00	5.25
	Nos. 341-343 (3)	11.60	6.55

Bulls, Painted in 6000 B.C. — A81

Wall Paintings from Tassili-N-Ajjer, c. 6000 B.C.: No. 345, Shepherd, vert. 2d, Fleeing ostriches. 3d, Two girls, vert.

1966, Jan. 29 Photo. *Perf. 11½*

344 A81	1d brn, bis & red brn	3.00	1.75
345 A81	1d gray, blk, ocher & dk brn	3.00	1.75
346 A81	2d brn, ocher & red brn	6.50	3.00
347 A81	3d buff, blk, ocher & brn red	7.50	4.00
	Nos. 344-347 (4)	20.00	10.50

See Nos. 365-368.

Pottery — A82

Handicrafts from Great Kabylia: 50c, Weaving, woman at loom, horiz. 70c, Jewelry.

1966, Feb. 26 Engr. *Perf. 13*

348 A82	40c Prus bl, brn red & blk	.30	.25
349 A82	50c dk red, ol & ocher	.40	.30
350 A82	70c vio bl, blk & red	.65	.40
	Nos. 348-350 (3)	1.35	.95

Weather Balloon, Compass Rose and Anemometer — A83

1966, Mar. 23 Engr. Unwmk.

351 A83 1d claret, brt bl & grn .85 .40

World Meteorological Day.

Book, Grain, Cogwheel and UNESCO Emblem — A84

Design: 60c, Grain, cogwheel, book and UNESCO emblem.

1966, May 2 Typo. *Perf. 13x14*

352 A84 30c yellow bis & blk .25 .20
353 A84 60c dk red, gray & blk .40 .25

Literacy as basis for development.

WHO Headquarters, Geneva — A85

1966, May 30 Engr. *Perf. 13*

354 A85 30c multicolored .35 .30
355 A85 60c multicolored .70 .40

Inauguration of the WHO Headquarters, Geneva.

Algerian Scout Emblem — A86

Arab Jamboree Emblem — A87

1966, July 23 Photo. *Perf. 12x12½*

356 A86 30c multicolored .65 .50
357 A87 1d multicolored 1.75 1.25

No. 356 commemorates the 30th anniv. of the Algerian Mohammedan Boy Scouts. No. 357, the 7th Arab Boy Scout Jamboree, held at Good Daim, Libya, Aug. 12.

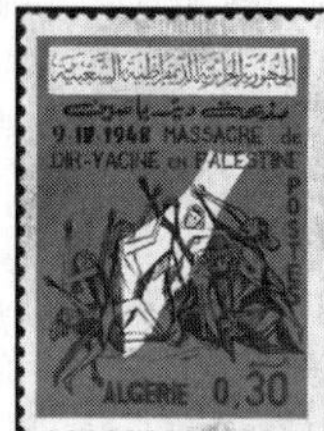

Map of Palestine and Victims A88

Abd-el-Kader A89

1966, Sept. 26 Typo. *Perf. 10½*

358 A88 30c red & black .80 .40

Deir Yassin Massacre, Apr. 9, 1948.

1966, Nov. 2 Photo. *Perf. 11½*

359 A89 30c multicolored .40 .20
360 A89 95c multicolored 1.10 .35

Transfer from Damascus to Algiers of the ashes of Abd-el-Kader (1807?-1883), Emir of Mascara. See Nos. 382-387.

UNESCO Emblem — A90

1966, Nov. 19 Typo. *Perf. 10½*

361 A90 1d multicolored 1.00 .35

20th anniv. of UNESCO.

Horseman A91

Miniatures by Mohammed Racim: 1.50d, Woman at her toilette. 2d, The pirate Barbarossa in front of the Admiralty.

1966, Dec. 17 Photo. *Perf. 11½*
Granite Paper

362 A91	1d multicolored	3.25	1.00
363 A91	1.50d multicolored	4.25	1.50
364 A91	2d multicolored	7.00	2.50
	Nos. 362-364 (3)	14.50	5.00

Wall Paintings Type of 1966

Wall Paintings from Tassili-N-Ajjer, c. 6000 B.C.: 1d, Cow. No. 366, Antelope. No. 367, Archers. 3d, Warrior, vert.

1967, Jan. 28 Photo. *Perf. 11½*

365 A81	1d brn, bis & dl vio	2.75	1.50
366 A81	2d brn, ocher & red brn	4.00	2.25
367 A81	2d brn, yel & red brn	4.50	2.75
368 A81	3d blk, gray, yel & red brn	6.25	3.50
	Nos. 365-368 (4)	17.50	10.00

Bardo Museum A92

La Kalaa Minaret — A93

Design: 1.30d, Ruins at Sedrata.

1967, Feb. 27 Photo. *Perf. 13*
369 A92 35c multicolored .20 .20
370 A93 95c multicolored .45 .30
371 A92 1.30d multicolored .75 .40
Nos. 369-371 (3) 1.40 .90

Moretti and International Tourist Year Emblem A94

Design: 70c, Tuareg riding camel, Tassili, and Tourist Year Emblem, vert.

1967, Apr. 29 Litho. *Perf. 14*
372 A94 40c multi .50 .25
373 A94 70c multi 1.00 .35

International Tourist Year, 1967.

Spiny-tailed Agamid A95

Designs: 20c, Ostrich, vert. 40c, Slender-horned gazelle, vert. 70c, Fennec.

1967, June 24 Photo. *Perf. 11½*
374 A95 5c bister & blk .60 .50
375 A95 20c ocher, blk & pink 1.25 .80
376 A95 40c ol bis, blk & red brn 2.00 1.00
377 A95 70c gray, blk & dp org 3.50 2.00
Nos. 374-377 (4) 7.35 4.30

Dancers — A96

Typographed and Engraved
1967, July 4 *Perf. 10½*
378 A96 50c gray vio, yel & blk .45 .35

National Youth Festival.

Map of the Mediterranean and Sport Scenes — A97

1967, Sept. 2 Typo. *Perf. 10½*
379 A97 30c black, red & blue .25 .20

Issued to publicize the 5th Mediterranean Games, Tunis, Sept. 8-17.

Skiers — A98

Olympic Emblem and Sports A99

1967, Oct. 21 Engr. *Perf. 13*
380 A98 30c brt blue & ultra .35 .20
381 A99 95c brn org, pur & brt grn .80 .55

Issued to publicize the 10th Winter Olympic Games, Grenoble, Feb. 6-18, 1968.

Abd-el-Kader Type of 1966
Lithographed, Photogravure
1967-71 *Perf. 13½, 11½*
382 A89 5c dull pur ('68) .20 .20
383 A89 10c green .85 .35
383A A89 10c sl grn (litho., '69) .20 .20
383B A89 25c orange ('71) .20 .20
384 A89 30c black ('68) .50 .20
385 A89 30c lt violet ('68) .75 .30
386 A89 50c rose claret .65 .20
387 A89 70c violet blue .85 .25
Nos. 382-387 (8) 4.20 1.90

No. 383, 50c and 70c, issued Nov. 13, 1967, are on granite paper, photo. The 5c, No.383A, 25c and 30c are litho., perf. 13½; others, perf. 11½.

The three 1967 stamps (No. 383, 50c, 70c) have numerals thin, narrow and close together; the Arabic inscription at lower right is 2mm high. The 5 litho. stamps are redrawn, with numerals thicker and spaced more widely; Arabic at lower right 3mm high.

Boy Scouts Holding Jamboree Emblem A100

1967, Dec. 23 Engr. *Perf. 13*
388 A100 1d multicolored 1.00 .80

12th Boy Scout World Jamboree, Farragut State Park, Idaho, Aug. 1-9.

No. 324 Surcharged
1967 Typo. *Perf. 14x13½*
389 A71 30c on 25c red .50 .20

Mandolin — A101

1968, Feb. 17 Photo. *Perf. 12½x13*
390 A101 30c shown .35 .25
391 A101 40c Lute .40 .25
392 A101 1.30d Rebec 1.40 .65
Nos. 390-392 (3) 2.15 1.15

Nememcha Rug — A102

Algerian Rugs: 70c, Guergour. 95c, Djebel-Amour. 1.30d, Kalaa.

1968, Apr. 13 Photo. *Perf. 11½*
393 A102 30c multi .75 .75
394 A102 70c multi 1.50 1.50
395 A102 95c multi 2.00 2.00
396 A102 1.30d multi 2.50 2.50
Nos. 393-396 (4) 6.75 6.75

Human Rights Flame A103

1968, May 18 Typo. *Perf. 10½*
397 A103 40c blue, red & yel .40 .30

International Human Rights Year, 1968.

WHO Emblem A104

1968, May 18
398 A104 70c blk, lt bl & yel .55 .30

20th anniv. of the WHO.

Welder — A105

Athletes, Olympic Flame and Rings — A106

1968, June 15 Engr. *Perf. 13*
399 A105 30c gray, brn & ultra .25 .20

Algerian emigration to Europe.

Perf. 12½x13, 13x12½
1968, July 4 Photo.

50c, Soccer player. 1d, Mexican pyramid, emblem, Olympic flame, rings & athletes, horiz.

400 A106 30c green, red & yel .35 .30
401 A106 50c rose car & multi .60 .30
402 A106 1d dk grn, org, brn & red 1.10 .65
Nos. 400-402 (3) 2.05 1.25

19th Olympic Games, Mexico City, 10/12-27.

Scouts and Emblem — A107

Barbary Sheep — A108

1968, July 4 *Perf. 13*
403 A107 30c multicolored .50 .20

8th Arab Boy Scout Jamboree, Algiers, 1968.

1968, Oct. 19 Photo. *Perf. 11½*
404 A108 40c shown .50 .25
405 A108 1d Red deer 1.25 .60

Hunting Scenes, Djemila A109

"Industry" A110

Design: 95c, Neptune's chariot, Timgad, horiz. Both designs are from Roman mosaics.

Perf. 12½x13, 13x12½
1968, Nov. 23 Photo.
406 A109 40c gray & multi .35 .25
407 A109 95c gray & multi .85 .50

1968, Dec. 14 *Perf. 11½*

Designs: No. 409, Miner with drill. 95c, "Energy" (circle and rays).

408 A110 30c dp orange & sil .25 .20
409 A110 30c brown & multi .25 .20
410 A110 95c silver, red & blk .75 .35
Nos. 408-410 (3) 1.25 .75

Issued to publicize industrial development.

Opuntia Ficus Indica — A111

Flowers: 40c, Carnations. 70c, Roses. 95c, Bird-of-paradise flower.

1969, Jan. Photo. *Perf. 11½*
Flowers in Natural Colors
411 A111 25c pink & blk .55 .25
412 A111 40c yellow & blk .65 .35
413 A111 70c gray & blk 1.25 .45
414 A111 95c brt blue & blk 2.00 .80
Nos. 411-414 (4) 4.45 1.85

See Nos. 496-499.

Irrigation Dam at Djorf Torba-Oued Guir — A112

Design: 1.50d, Truck on Highway No. 51 and camel caravan.

1969, Feb. 22 Photo. *Perf. 11½*
415 A112 30c multi .25 .20
416 A112 1.50d multi 1.25 .65

Public works in the Sahara.

Mail Coach A113

1969, Mar. 22 Photo. *Perf. 11½*
417 A113 1d multicolored 1.10 .60

Issued for Stamp Day, 1969.

Capitol, Timgad — A114

1d, Septimius Temple, Djemila, horiz.

1969, Apr. 5 Photo. *Perf. 13x12½*
418 A114 30c gray & multi .35 .20
419 A114 1d gray & multi .85 .35

Second Timgad Festival, Apr. 4-8.

ILO Emblem A115

Arabian Saddle — A116

1969, May 24 Photo. *Perf. 11½*
420 A115 95c dp car, yel & blk 1.00 .40

50th anniv. of the ILO.

1969, June 28 Photo. *Perf. 12x12½*

Algerian Handicrafts: 30c, Bookcase. 60c, Decorated copper plate.

Granite Paper

421 A116 30c multicolored .30 .20
422 A116 60c multicolored .55 .25
423 A116 1d multicolored 1.00 .45
Nos. 421-423 (3) 1.85 .90

No. 321 Surcharged

1969 Typo. *Perf. 14x13½*
424 A71 20c on 12c emerald .25 .20

Pan-African Culture Festival Emblem — A117

African Development Bank Emblem — A118

1969, July 19 Photo. *Perf. 12½*
425 A117 30c multicolored .35 .20

1st Pan-African Culture Festival, Algiers, 7/21-8/1.

1969, Aug. 23 Typo. *Perf. 10½*
426 A118 30c dull blue, yel & blk .35 .20

5th anniv. of the African Development Bank.

Astronauts and Landing Module on Moon — A119

Perf. 12½x11½
1969, Aug. 23 Photo.
427 A119 50c gold & multi .60 .35

Man's 1st landing on the moon, July 20, 1969. US astronauts Neil A. Armstrong and Col. Edwin E. Aldrin, Jr., with Lieut. Col. Michael Collins piloting Apollo 11.

Algerian Women, by Dinet — A120

1.50d, The Watchmen, by Etienne Dinet.

1969, Nov. 29 Photo. *Perf. 14½*
428 A120 1d multi 1.75 .90
429 A120 1.50d multi 2.75 1.40

Mother and Child — A121

1969, Dec. 27 Photo. *Perf. 11½*
430 A121 30c multicolored .35 .25

Issued to promote mother and child protection.

Agricultural Growth Chart, Tractor and Dam A122

30c, Transportation and development. 50c, Abstract symbols of industrialization.

1970, Jan. 31 Photo. *Perf. 12½*
Size: 37x23mm
431 A122 25c dk brn, yel & org .20 .20

Litho. *Perf. 14*
Size: 49x23mm
432 A122 30c blue & multi .25 .20

Photo. *Perf. 12½*
Size: 37x23mm
433 A122 50c rose lilac & blk .30 .20
Nos. 431-433 (3) .75 .60

Four-Year Development Plan.

Old and New Mail Delivery — A123

Spiny Lobster — A124

1970, Feb. 28 Photo. *Perf. 11½*
Granite Paper
434 A123 30c multicolored .30 .20

Issued for Stamp Day.

1970, Mar. 28

Designs: 40c, Mollusks. 75c, Retepora cellulosa. 1d, Red coral.

435 A124 30c ocher & multi .35 .20
436 A124 40c multicolored .50 .25
437 A124 75c ultra & multi .90 .35
438 A124 1d lt blue & multi 1.25 .50
Nos. 435-438 (4) 3.00 1.30

Oranges, EXPO '70 Emblem A125

Designs (EXPO '70 Emblem and): 60c, Algerian pavilion. 70c, Grapes.

1970, Apr. 25 Photo. *Perf. 12½x12*
439 A125 30c lt blue, grn & org .50 .20
440 A125 60c multicolored .65 .20
441 A125 70c multicolored 1.00 .35
Nos. 439-441 (3) 2.15 .75

EXPO '70 International Exhibition, Osaka, Japan, Mar. 15-Sept. 13, 1970.

Olives, Oil Bottle — A126

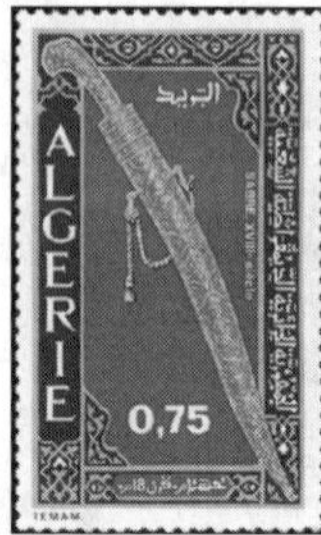

Saber — A127

1970, May 16 Photo. *Perf. 12½x12*
442 A126 1d yellow & multi 1.00 .65

Olive Year, 1969-1970.

Common Design Types pictured following the introduction.

UPU Headquarters Issue
Common Design Type

1970, May 30 *Perf. 13*
Size: 36x26mm
443 CD133 75c multicolored .50 .40

1970, June 27 Photo. *Perf. 12½*

Designs: 40c, Guns, 18th century, horiz. 1d, Pistol, 18th century, horiz.

444 A127 40c yellow & multi .65 .25
445 A127 75c red & multi .80 .40
446 A127 1d multicolored 1.25 .50
Nos. 444-446 (3) 2.70 1.15

Map of Arab Countries and Arab League Flag A128

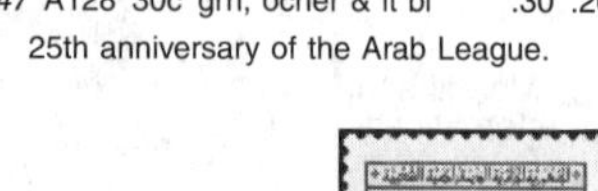

Typographed and Engraved
1970, July 25 *Perf. 10½*
447 A128 30c grn, ocher & lt bl .30 .20

25th anniversary of the Arab League.

Lenin — A129

1970, Aug. 29 Litho. *Perf. 11½x12*
448 A129 30c brown & buff .25 .20

Lenin (1870-1924), Russian communist leader.

Exhibition Hall and Algiers Fair Emblem — A130

1970, Sept. 11 Engr. *Perf. 14x13½*
449 A130 60c lt olive green .40 .30

New Exhibition Hall for Algiers Intl. Fair.

Education Year Emblem, Blackboard, Atom Symbol — A131

Koran Page — A132

1970, Oct. 24 Photo. *Perf. 14*
450 A131 30c pink, blk, gold & lt bl .25 .20
451 A132 3d multicolored 2.50 1.50

Issued for International Education Year.

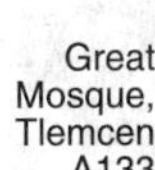

Great Mosque, Tlemcen A133

Design: 40c, Ketchaoua Mosque, Algiers, vert. 1d, Mosque, Sidi-Okba, vert.

1970-71 Litho. *Perf. 14*

456 A133 30c multicolored	.20	.20
457 A133 40c sepia & lemon ('71)	.25	.20
458 A133 1d multicolored	.65	.30
Nos. 456-458 (3)	1.10	.70

Symbols of the Arts A134

1970, Dec. 26 Photo. *Perf. 13x12½*

459 A134 1d grn, lt grn & org .80 .45

Main Post Office, Algiers A135

1971, Jan. 23 *Perf. 11½*

460 A135 30c multicolored .30 .20

Stamp Day, 1971.

Hurdling A136

40c, Vaulting, vert. 75c, Basketball, vert.

1971, Mar. 7 Photo. *Perf. 11½*

461 A136 20c lt blue & slate	.25	.20
462 A136 40c lt ol grn & slate	.35	.35
463 A136 75c salmon pink & slate	.65	.50
Nos. 461-463 (3)	1.25	1.05

Mediterranean Games, Izmir, Turkey, Oct. 1971.

Symbolic Head — A137

1971, Mar. 27 *Perf. 12½*

464 A137 60c car rose, blk & sil .30 .20

Intl. year against racial discrimination.

Emblem and Technicians A138

1971, Apr. 24 Photo. *Perf. 12½x12*

465 A138 70c cl, org & bluish blk .40 .30

Founding of the Institute of Technology.

Woman from Aurès — A139

Regional Costumes: 70c, Man from Oran. 80c, Man from Algiers. 90c, Woman from Amour Mountains.

1971, Oct. 16 *Perf. 11½*

466 A139 50c gold & multi	1.50	.65
467 A139 70c gold & multi	1.75	1.00
468 A139 80c gold & multi	2.25	1.10
469 A139 90c gold & multi	2.50	1.25
Nos. 466-469 (4)	8.00	4.00

See Nos. 485-488, 534-537.

UNICEF Emblem, Birds and Plants — A140

1971, Dec. 6 *Perf. 11½*

470 A140 60c multicolored .55 .30

25th anniv. of UNICEF.

Lion of St. Mark A141

1.15d, Bridge of Sighs, Venice, vert.

1972, Jan. 24 Litho. *Perf. 12*

471 A141 80c multi	.60	.35
472 A141 1.15d multi	.90	.50

UNESCO campaign to save Venice.

Javelin — A142

Book and Book Year Emblem — A143

Designs: 25c, Bicycling, horiz. 60c, Wrestling. 1d, Gymnast on rings.

1972, Mar. 25 Photo. *Perf. 11½*

473 A142 25c maroon & multi	.30	.20
474 A142 40c ocher & multi	.35	.25
475 A142 60c ultra & multi	.40	.40
476 A142 1d rose & multi	1.00	.50
Nos. 473-476 (4)	2.05	1.35

20th Olympic Games, Munich, 8/26-9/11.

1972, Apr. 15

477 A143 1.15d bister, brn & red .65 .50

International Book Year 1972.

Mailmen A144

Flowers A145

1972, Apr. 22

478 A144 40c gray & multi .25 .20

Stamp Day 1972.

1972, May 27

479 A145 50c Jasmine	.65	.30
480 A145 60c Violets	.75	.35
481 A145 1.15d Tuberose	1.50	.55
Nos. 479-481 (3)	2.90	1.20

Olympic Stadium, Chéraga A146

1972, June 10

482 A146 50c gray, choc & grn .60 .30

New Day, Algerian Flag — A147

1972, July 5

483 A147 1d green & multi .65 .40

10th anniversary of independence.

Festival Emblem — A148

Mailing a Letter — A149

1972, July 5 Litho. *Perf. 10½*

484 A148 40c grn, dk brn & org .25 .20

1st Arab Youth Festival, Algiers, July 5-11.

Costume Type of 1971

Regional Costumes: 50c, Woman from Hoggar. 60c, Kabyle woman. 70c, Man from Mzab. 90c, Woman from Tlemcen.

1972, Nov. 18 Photo. *Perf. 11½*

485 A139 50c gold & multi	.80	.70
486 A139 60c gold & multi	1.10	.90
487 A139 70c gold & multi	1.25	1.10
488 A139 90c gold & multi	1.75	1.25
Nos. 485-488 (4)	4.90	3.95

1973, Jan. 20 Photo. *Perf. 11*

489 A149 40c orange & multi .40 .20

Stamp Day.

Ho Chi Minh, Map of Viet Nam — A150

1973, Feb. 17 Photo. *Perf. 11½*

490 A150 40c multicolored .75 .50

To honor the people of Viet Nam.

Embroidery from Annaba A151

Designs: 60c, Tree of Life pattern from Algiers. 80c, Constantine embroidery.

1973, Feb. 24

491 A151 40c gray & multi	.75	.40
492 A151 60c blue and multi	1.00	.60
493 A151 80c dk red, gold & blk	1.50	.80
Nos. 491-493 (3)	3.25	1.80

Stylized Globe and Wheat — A152

1973, Mar. 26 Photo. *Perf. 11½*

494 A152 1.15d brt rose lil, org & grn .75 .40

World Food Program, 10th anniversary.

Soldier and Flag A153

1973, Apr. 23 Photo. *Perf. 14x13½*

495 A153 40c multicolored .25 .20

Honoring the National Service.

Flower Type of 1969

30c, Opuntia ficus indica. 40c, Roses. 1d, Carnations. 1.15d, Bird-of-paradise flower.

1973, May 21 Photo. *Perf. 11½*

Flowers in Natural Colors

496 A111 30c pink & blk	.40	.20
497 A111 40c gray & blk	.50	.20
498 A111 1d yellow & multi	.90	.40
499 A111 1.15d multi	1.25	.50
Nos. 496-499 (4)	3.05	1.30

For overprints and surcharges see #518-519, 531.

OAU Emblem — A154

1973, May 28 Photo. ***Perf. 12½x13***
500 A154 40c multicolored .40 .20

Org. for African Unity, 10th anniv.

Desert and Fruitful Land, Farmer and Family A155

1973, June 18 ***Perf. 11½***
501 A155 40c gold & multi .50 .40

Agricultural revolution.

Map of Africa, Scout Emblem — A156

1973, July 16 Litho. ***Perf. 10½***
502 A156 80c purple 1.00 .50

24th Boy Scout World Conference (1st in Africa), Nairobi, Kenya, July 16-21.

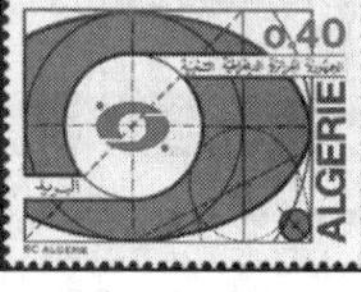
Algerian PTT Emblem A157

1973, Aug. 6 ***Perf. 14***
503 A157 40c blue & orange .25 .20

Adoption of new emblem for Post, Telegraph and Telephone System.

Conference Emblem — A158

Perf. 13½x12½

1973, Sept. 5 Photo.
504 A158 40c dp rose & multi .20 .20
505 A158 80c blue grn & multi .50 .25

4th Summit Conference of Non-aligned Nations, Algiers, Sept. 5-9.

Port of Skikda A159

1973, Sept. 29 Photo. ***Perf. 11½***
506 A159 80c ocher, blk & ultra .50 .25

New port of Skikda.

Young Workers — A160

1973, Oct. 22 Photo. ***Perf. 13***
507 A160 40c multicolored .25 .20

Voluntary work service.

Arms of Algiers A161

1973, Dec. 22 Photo. ***Perf. 13***
508 A161 2d gold & multi 1.60 1.10

Millennium of Algiers.

Infant — A162

1974, Jan. 7 Litho. ***Perf. 10½x11***
509 A162 80c orange & multi .60 .35

Fight against tuberculosis.

Man and Woman, Industry and Transportation — A163

1974, Feb. 18 Photo. ***Perf. 11½***
510 A163 80c multicolored .50 .20

Four-year plan.

A164

1974, Feb. 25 Photo. ***Perf. 11½***
511 A164 1.50d multi 1.10 .65

Millennium of the birth of abu-al-Rayhan al-Biruni (973-1048), philosopher and mathematician.

Map and Colors of Algeria, Tunisia, Morocco A165

1974, Mar. 4 Photo. ***Perf. 13***
512 A165 40c gold & multi .30 .20

Maghreb Committee for Coordination of Posts and Telecommunications.

Hand Holding Rifle — A166

Mother and Children — A167

1974, Mar. 25 ***Perf. 11½***
513 A166 80c red & black .30 .20

Solidarity with the struggle of the people of South Africa.

1974, Apr. 8 ***Perf. 13½***
514 A167 85c multicolored .35 .25

Honoring Algerian mothers.

Village A168

Designs: 80c, Harvest. 90c, Tractor and sun. Designs after children's drawings.

1974, June 15

Size: 45x26mm

515 A168 70c multicolored .40 .20

Size: 48x33mm

516 A168 80c multicolored .50 .30
517 A168 90c multicolored .60 .40
Nos. 515-517 (3) 1.50 .90

Nos. 498-499 Overprinted "FLORALIES/1974"

1974, June 22 Photo. ***Perf. 11½***
518 A111 1d multi .65 .35
519 A111 1.15d multi .70 .40

1974 Flower Show.

Stamp Vending Machine — A169

1974, Oct. 7 Photo. ***Perf. 13***
520 A169 80c multicolored .40 .20

Stamp Day 1974.

UPU Emblem and Globe A170

1974, Oct. 14 ***Perf. 14***
521 A170 80c multicolored .50 .30

Centenary of Universal Postal Union.

"Revolution" — A171

Soldiers and Mountains A172

Raising New Flag — A173

Design: 1d, Algerian struggle for independence (people, sun and fields).

1974, Nov. 4 Photo. ***Perf. 14***
522 A171 40c multicolored .30 .20
523 A172 70c multicolored .40 .20
524 A173 95c multicolored .50 .25
525 A171 1d multicolored .60 .30
Nos. 522-525 (4) 1.80 .95

20th anniv. of the start of the revolution.

"Horizon 1980" — A174

Ewer and Basin — A175

1974, Nov. 23 Photo. ***Perf. 13***
526 A174 95c ocher, dk red & blk .55 .25

10-year development plan, 1971-1980.

1974, Dec. 21 *Perf. 11½*

527 A175 50c shown .25 .20
528 A175 60c Coffee pot .30 .20
529 A175 95c Sugar bowl .45 .30
530 A175 1d Bath tub .50 .35
Nos. 527-530 (4) 1.50 1.05

17th century Algerian copperware.

No. 497 Surcharged with New Value and Heavy Bar

1975, Jan. 4

531 A111 50c on 40c multi .50 .40

Mediterranean Games' Emblem — A176

1975, Jan. 27 *Perf. 13½*

532 A176 50c purple, yel & grn .30 .20
533 A176 1d orange, bl & mar .60 .25

Mediterranean Games, Algiers, 1975.

Costume Type of 1971

Regional Costumes: No. 534, Woman from Hoggar. No. 535, Woman from Algiers. No. 536, Woman from Oran. No. 537, Man from Tlemcen.

1975, Feb. 22 **Photo.** *Perf. 11½*

534 A139 1d gold & multi .90 .80
535 A139 1d gold & multi .90 .80
536 A139 1d gold & multi .90 .80
537 A139 1d gold & multi .90 .80
Nos. 534-537 (4) 3.60 3.20

Map of Arab Countries, ALO Emblem A177

1975, Mar. 10 **Litho.** *Perf. 10½x11*

538 A177 50c red brown .25 .20

Arab Labor Organization, 10th anniversary.

Blood Transfusion A178

1975, Mar. 15 *Perf. 14*

539 A178 50c car rose & multi .30 .20

Blood donation and transfusions.

Post Office, Al-Kantara A179

Policeman and Map of Algeria A180

1975, May 10 **Photo.** *Perf. 11½*
Granite Paper

540 A179 50c multicolored .25 .20

Stamp Day 1975.

1975, June 1 **Photo.** *Perf. 13*

541 A180 50c multicolored .75 .40

Natl. Security and 10th Natl. Police Day.

Ground Receiving Station A181

Designs: 1d, Map of Algeria with locations of radar sites, transmission mast and satellite. 1.20d, Main and subsidiary stations.

1975, June 28 **Photo.** *Perf. 13*

542 A181 50c blue & multi .30 .20
543 A181 1d blue & multi .55 .20
544 A181 1.20d blue & multi .60 .25
Nos. 542-544 (3) 1.45 .65

National satellite telecommunications network.

Revolutionary with Flag — A182

1975, Aug. 20 **Photo.** *Perf. 11½*

545 A182 1d multicolored .50 .25

August 20th Revolutionary Movement (Skikda), 20th anniversary.

Swimming and Games' Emblem A183

Perf. 13x13½, 13½x13

1975, Aug. 23 **Photo.**

546 A183 25c shown .20 .20
547 A183 50c Judo, map .25 .20
548 A183 70c Soccer, vert. .50 .20
549 A183 1d Running, vert. .55 .25
550 A183 1.20d Handball, vert. .70 .40
a. Souv. sheet, #546-550, perf 13 4.50 4.50
Nos. 546-550 (5) 2.20 1.25

7th Mediterranean Games, Algiers, 8/23-9/46.

No. 550a sold for 4.50d. Exists imperf., same value.

Setif, Guelma, Kherrata — A184

1975 **Litho.** *Perf. 13½x14*

551 A184 5c orange & blk .20 .20
552 A184 10c emerald & brn .20 .20
553 A184 25c dl blue & blk .20 .20
554 A184 30c lemon & blk .20 .20
555 A184 50c brt grn & blk .25 .20
556 A184 70c fawn & blk .35 .20
557 A184 1d vermilion & blk .50 .25
Nos. 551-557 (7) 1.90 1.45

30th anniv. of victory in World War II. Issued: 50c, 1d, Nov. 3; others, Dec. 17.

For surcharge see No. 611.

Map of Maghreb and APU Emblem A185

1975, Nov. 20 **Photo.** *Perf. 11½*

558 A185 1d multicolored .55 .30

10th Cong. of Arab Postal Union, Algiers.

Mosaic, Bey Constantine's Palace A186

Dey-Alger Palace — A187

Famous buildings: 2d, Prayer niche, Medersa Sidi-Boumediene, Tlemcen.

1975, Dec. 22

559 A186 1d lt blue & multi .60 .25
560 A186 2d buff & multi 1.10 .60
561 A187 2.50d buff & blk 1.60 .90
Nos. 559-561 (3) 3.30 1.75

Al-Azhar University A188

Perf. 11½x12½

1975, Dec. 29 **Litho.**

562 A188 2d multicolored 1.10 .60

Millennium of Al-Azhar University.

Red-billed Firefinch — A189

Birds: 1.40d, Black-headed bush shrike, horiz. 2d, Blue tit. 2.50d, Blackbellied sand-grouse, horiz.

1976, Jan. 24 **Photo.** *Perf. 11½*

563 A189 50c multi .35 .20
564 A189 1.40d multi .85 .55
565 A189 2d multi 1.10 .65
566 A189 2.50d multi 1.50 .90
Nos. 563-566 (4) 3.80 2.30

See Nos. 595-598.

Telephones 1876 and 1976 — A190

Map of Africa with Angola and its Flag — A191

1976, Feb. 23 **Photo.** *Perf. 13½x13*

567 A190 1.40d rose, dk & lt bl .65 .40

Centenary of first telephone call by Alexander Graham Bell, Mar. 10, 1876.

1976, Feb. 23 *Perf. 11½*

568 A191 50c brown & multi .25 .20

Algeria's solidarity with the People's Republic of Angola.

A192

A193

Sahraoui flag and child, map of former Spanish Sahara.

1976, Mar. 15 **Photo.** *Perf. 11½*

569 A192 50c multicolored .25 .20

Algeria's solidarity with Sahraoui Arab Democratic Republic, former Spanish Sahara.

1976, Mar. 22

570 A193 1.40d Mailman .60 .30

Stamp Day 1976.

Microscope, Slide with TB Bacilli, Patients A194

1976, Apr. 26 *Perf. 13x13½*

571 A194 50c multicolored .40 .20

Fight against tuberculosis.

"Setif, Guelma, Kherrata" — A195

1976, May 24 **Photo.** *Perf. 13½x13*

572 A195 50c blue & yellow .35 .20
a. Booklet pane of 6 4.75
b. Booklet pane of 10 4.00

No. 572 was issued in booklets only.

Ram's Head over Landscape
A196

People Holding Torch, Map of Algeria
A197

1976, June 17 Photo. *Perf. 11½*
573 A196 50c multicolored .40 .20

Livestock breeding.

1976, June 29 Photo. *Perf. 14x13½*
574 A197 50c multicolored .25 .20

National Charter.

Palestine Map and Flag — A198

Map of Africa — A199

1976, July 12 *Perf. 11½*
Granite Paper
575 A198 50c multicolored 2.00 1.00

Solidarity with the Palestinians.

1976, Oct. 3 Litho. *Perf. 10½x11*
576 A199 2d dk blue & multi 1.00 .50

2nd Pan-African Commercial Fair, Algiers.

Blind Brushmaker
A200

The Blind, by Dinet
A201

1976, Oct. 23 Photo. *Perf. 14½*
577 A200 1.20d blue & multi .65 .35
578 A201 1.40d gold & multi 1.50 .75

Rehabilitation of the blind.

"Constitution 1976" — A202

1976, Nov. 19 Photo. *Perf. 11½*
579 A202 2d multicolored 1.00 .55

New Constitution.

Soldiers Planting Seedlings
A203

1976, Nov. 25 Litho. *Perf. 12*
580 A203 1.40d multicolored .75 .35

Green barrier against the Sahara.

Ornamental Border and Inscription — A204

1976, Dec. 18 Photo. *Perf. 11½*
Granite Paper
581 A204 2d multicolored 1.25 .75

Re-election of Pres. Houari Boumediene. See No. 627.

Map with Charge Zones and Dials
A205

People and Buildings
A206

1977, Jan. 22 *Perf. 13*
582 A205 40c silver & multi .30 .20

Inauguration of automatic national and international telephone service.

1977, Jan. 29 Photo. *Perf. 11½*
583 A206 60c on 50c multi .35 .20

2nd General Population and Buildings Census. No. 583 was not issued without the typographed red brown surcharge, date, and bars.

Sahara Museum, Uargla
A207

1977, Feb. 12 Litho. *Perf. 14*
584 A207 60c multicolored .35 .20

El-Kantara Gorge — A208

Perf. 12½x13½
1977, Feb. 19 Photo.
585 A208 20c green & yellow .20 .20
a. Bklt. pane, 3 #585, 4 #586 + label 8.00
b. Bklt. pane, 5 #585, 2 #587 + label 6.50
586 A208 60c brt lilac & yel .20 .20
587 A208 1d brown & yellow .40 .20
Nos. 585-587 (3) .80 .60

National Assembly — A209

1977, Feb. 27 *Perf. 11½*
588 A209 2d multicolored 1.00 .60

People and Flag — A210

Soldier and Flag — A211

Perf. 13½, 11½ (3d)
1977, Mar. 12 Photo.
589 A210 2d multicolored 1.25 .40
590 A211 3d multicolored 1.75 .65

Solidarity with the peoples of Zimbabwe (Rhodesia), 2d; Namibia, 3d.

Winter, Roman Mosaic
A212

The Seasons from Roman Villa, 2nd century A.D.: 1.40d, Fall. 2d, Summer. 3d, Spring.

1977, Apr. 21 Photo. *Perf. 11½*
Granite Paper
591 A212 1.20d multi .95 .50
592 A212 1.40d multi 1.25 .55
593 A212 2d multi 1.65 .95
594 A212 3d multi 2.50 1.60
a. Souv. sheet, #591-594 10.00 10.00
Nos. 591-594 (4) 6.35 3.60

No. 594a sold for 8d and exists imperf.

Bird Type of 1976

Birds: 60c, Tristram's warbler. 1.40d, Moussier's redstart, horiz. 2d, Temminck's horned lark, horiz. 3d, Eurasian hoopoe.

1977, May 21 Photo. *Perf. 11½*
595 A189 60c multi .75 .25
596 A189 1.40d multi 1.25 .40
597 A189 2d multi 1.75 .65
598 A189 3d multi 2.50 1.10
Nos. 595-598 (4) 6.25 2.40

Horseman — A213

Design: 5d, Attacking horsemen, horiz.

1977, June 25 Photo. *Perf. 11½*
599 A213 2d multicolored 1.75 .75
600 A213 5d multicolored 3.50 2.00

Flag Colors, Games Emblem — A214

Wall Painting, Games Emblem
A215

1977, Sept. 24 Photo. *Perf. 11½*
601 A214 60c multi .35 .25
602 A215 1.40d multi .80 .45

3rd African Games, Algiers 1978.

Village and Tractor
A216

1977, Nov. 12 *Perf. 14x13*
603 A216 1.40d multi .90 .65

Socialist agricultural village.

Almohades Dirham, 12th Century — A217

Ancient Coins: 1.40d, Almohades coin, 12th century. 2d, Almoravides dinar, 11th century.

1977, Dec. 17 Photo. *Perf. 11½*
604 A217 60c ultra, sil & blk .50 .35
605 A217 1.40d grn, gold & brn 1.10 .50
606 A217 2d red brn, gold & brn 1.50 .90
Nos. 604-606 (3) 3.10 1.75

Flowering Trees — A218

1978, Feb. 11 Photo. *Perf. 11½*

607 A218	60c Cherry	.35	.25
608 A218	1.20d Peach	.85	.50
609 A218	1.30d Almond	.85	.50
610 A218	1.40d Apple	.90	.55
	Nos. 607-610 (4)	2.95	1.80

No. 555 Surcharged with New Value and Bar

1978, Feb. 11 Litho. *Perf. 13½x14*

611 A184 60c on 50c .50 .20

Children with Traffic Signs and Car — A219

1978, Apr. 29 Photo. *Perf. 11½*

612 A219 60c multicolored .30 .20

Road safety and protection of children.

Sports and Games Emblems A220

Designs (Games Emblem and): 60c, Rower, vert. 1.20d, Flag colors. 1.30d, Fireworks, vert. 1.40d, Map of Africa and dancers, vert.

1978, July 13 Photo. *Perf. 11½*

613 A220	40c mul	.20	.20
614 A220	60c multi	.30	.20
615 A220	1.20d multi	.60	.30
616 A220	1.30d multi	.60	.35
617 A220	1.40d multi	.65	.35
	Nos. 613-617 (5)	2.35	1.40

3rd African Games, Algiers, July 13-28.

TB Patient Returning to Family — A221

1978, Oct. 5 Photo. *Perf. 13½x14*

618 A221 60c multicolored .35 .20

Anti-tuberculosis campaign.

Holy Kaaba — A222

1978, Oct. 28 Photo. *Perf. 11½*

619 A222 60c multicolored .30 .20

Pilgrimage to Mecca.

National Servicemen Building Road — A223

1978, Nov. 4

620 A223 60c multicolored .30 .20

African Unity Road from El Goleah to In Salah, inauguration.

Fibula A224

Pres. Boumediene A225

Jewelry: 1.35d, Pendant. 1.40d, Ankle ring.

1978, Dec. 21 Photo. *Perf. 12x11½*

621 A224	1.20d multi	.65	.30
622 A224	1.35d multi	.70	.30
623 A224	1.40d multi	1.10	1.10
	Nos. 621-623 (3)	2.45	1.70

1979, Jan. 7 Photo. *Perf. 12x11½*

624 A225 60c green, red & brown .30 .20

Houari Boumediene, pres. of Algeria 1965-1978.

Torch and Books A226

1979, Jan. 27 Photo. *Perf. 11½*

625 A226 60c multicolored .30 .20

Natl. Front of Liberation Party Cong.

Pres. Boumediene — A227

1979, Feb. 4 Photo. *Perf. 11½*

626 A227 1.40d multi .65 .30

40 days after death of Pres. Houari Boumediène.

Ornamental Type of 1976

Proclamation of new President.

1979, Feb. 10

627 A204 2d multicolored 1.00 .35

Election of Pres. Chadli Bendjedid.

A229

A230

1979, Apr. 18 Photo. *Perf. 11½*

628 A229 60c multicolored .30 .20

Sheik Abdul-Hamid Ben Badis (1889-1940).

1979, May 19 Photo. *Perf. 13½x14*

Designs: 1.20d, Telephone dial, map of Africa. 1.40d, Symbolic Morse key and waves.

629 A230	1.20d multi	.55	.20
630 A230	1.40d multi	.60	.25

Telecom '79 Exhib., Geneva, Sept. 20-26.

Harvest, IYC Emblem A231

1.40d, Dancers and IYC emblem, vert.

Perf. 11½x11, 11x11½

1979, June 21

631 A231	60c multi	.40	.20
632 A231	1.40d multi	.60	.45

International Year of the Child.

A232

A233

1979, Oct. 20 Photo. *Perf. 11½*

633 A232 1.40d Nuthatch .90 .40

1979, Nov. 1 Photo. *Perf. 12½*

Designs: 1.40d, Flag, soldiers and workers. 3d, Revolutionaries and emblem.

634 A233 1.40d multi .90 .25

Size: 37x48mm

Perf. 11½

635 A233 3d multi 2.25 .65

November 1 revolution, 25th anniversary.

Hegira, 1500 Anniv. A234

1979, Dec. 2 Photo. *Perf. 11½*

636 A234 3d multicolored 1.25 .65

Camels, Lion, Men and Slave — A235

Dionysian Procession (Setif Mosaic): 1.35d, Elephants, tigers and women. Men in tiger-drawn cart. No. 639a has continuous design.

1980, Feb. 16 Photo. *Perf. 11½*

Granite Paper

637 A235	1.20d multi	.55	.20
638 A235	1.35d multi	.60	.35
639 A235	1.40d multi	.65	.55
a.	Strip of 3, #637-639	1.80	1.25

Science Day — A236

1980, Apr. 19 Photo. *Perf. 12*

640 A236 60c multicolored .30 .20

Dam and Workers A237

1980, June 17 Photo. *Perf. 11½*

641 A237 60c multicolored .30 .20

Extraordinary Congress of the National Liberation Front Party.

Olympic Sports, Moscow '80 Emblem A238

1980, June 28

642 A238	50c Flame, rings, vert.	.25	.20
643 A238	1.40d shown	.65	.35

22nd Summer Olympic Games, Moscow, July 19-Aug. 3.

20th Anniversary of OPEC — A239

Perf. 11x10½, 10½x11

1980, Sept. 15 **Engr.**

644	A239	60c Men holding OPEC emblem, vert.	.30	.20
645	A239	1.40d shown	.65	.35

Aures Valley A240

1980, Sept. 25 **Litho.** ***Perf. 13½x14***

646	A240	50c shown	.25	.20
647	A240	1d El Oued Oasis	.40	.20
648	A240	1.40d Tassili Rocks	.60	.25
649	A240	2d View of Algiers	.90	.40
		Nos. 646-649 (4)	2.15	1.05

World Tourism Conf., Manila, Sept. 27.

Avicenna (980-1037), Philosopher and Physician A241

1980, Oct. 25 **Photo.** ***Perf. 12***

650	A241	2d multicolored	1.50	.75

Ruins of El Asnam A242

1980, Nov. 13 **Photo.** ***Perf. 12***

651	A242	3d multicolored	1.25	.45

Earthquake relief.

Crown A243

1980, Dec. 20 **Photo.** ***Perf. 12***

Granite Paper

652	A243	60c Necklace, vert.	.30	.20
653	A243	1.40d Earrings, bracelet, vert.	.60	.30
654	A243	2d shown	.80	.45
		Nos. 652-654 (3)	1.70	.95

See Nos. 705-707.

1980-1984 Five-Year Plan — A244

1981, Jan. 29 **Litho.** ***Perf. 14***

655	A244	60c multicolored	.25	.20

Basket Weaving — A245

1981, Feb. 19 **Photo.** ***Perf. 12½***

Granite Paper

656	A245	40c shown	.20	.20
657	A245	60c Rug weaving	.30	.20
658	A245	1d Coppersmith	.40	.20
659	A245	1.40d Jeweler	.60	.30
		Nos. 656-659 (4)	1.50	.90

Cedar Tree A246

Arbor Day: 1.40d, Cypress tree, vert.

1981, Mar. 19 **Photo.** ***Perf. 12***

Granite Paper

660	A246	60c multi	.30	.20
661	A246	1.40d multi	.60	.30

Mohamed Bachir el Ibrahimi (1869-1965) A247

Children Going to School A248

1981, Apr. 16

Granite Paper

662	A247	60c multicolored	.25	.20
663	A248	60c multicolored	.25	.20

Science Day.

12th International Hydatidological Congress, Algiers — A249

1981, Apr. 23 ***Perf. 14x13½***

664	A249	2d multicolored	.80	.30

13th World Telecommunications Day — A250

1981, May 14 **Photo.** ***Perf. 14x13½***

665	A250	1.40d multi	.60	.20

Disabled People and Hand Offering Flower — A251

Perf. 12½x13, 13x12½

1981, June 20 **Litho.**

666	A251	1.20d Symbolic globe, vert.	.55	.20
667	A251	1.40d shown	.60	.20

Intl. Year of the Disabled.

Papilio Machaon A252

1981, Aug. 20 **Photo.** ***Perf. 11½***

Granite Paper

668	A252	60c shown	.25	.20
669	A252	1.20d Rhodocera rhamni	.55	.20
670	A252	1.40d Charaxes jasius	.60	.25
671	A252	2d Papilio podalirius	.80	.40
		Nos. 668-671 (4)	2.20	1.05

Monk Seal — A253

1981, Sept. 17 ***Perf. 14x13½***

672	A253	60c shown	.25	.20
673	A253	1.40d Macaque	.60	.35

World Food Day — A254

Cave Drawings of Tassili — A255

1981, Oct. 16 **Photo.** ***Perf. 14x14½***

674	A254	2d multicolored	.65	.35

1981, Nov. 21 ***Perf. 11½***

Various cave drawings. 1.60d, 2d horiz.

675	A255	60c multi	.30	.20
676	A255	1d multi	.50	.20
677	A255	1.60d multi	.75	.35
678	A255	2d multi	.90	.40
		Nos. 675-678 (4)	2.45	1.15

Galley, 17-18th Cent. A256

1981, Dec. 17 **Photo.** ***Perf. 11½***

679	A256	60c shown	.40	.20
680	A256	1.60d Ship, diff.	.90	.35

1982 World Cup Soccer A257

Designs: Various soccer players.

Perf. 13x12½x 12½x13

1982, Feb. 25 **Litho.**

681	A257	80c multi, vert.	.35	.20
682	A257	2.80d multi	1.10	.50

TB Bacillus Centenary A258

1982, Mar. 20 **Photo.** ***Perf. 14½x14***

683	A258	80c multi	.35	.20

Painted Stand A259

1982, Apr. 24 **Photo.** ***Perf. 11½***

Granite Paper

684	A259	80c Mirror, vert.	.30	.20
685	A259	2d shown	.75	.40

Size: 48x33mm

686	A259	2.40d Chest	.90	.55
		Nos. 684-686 (3)	1.95	1.15

Djamaael Djadid Mosque, Algiers A260

1982, May 15 **Litho.** ***Perf. 14***

687	A260	80c shown	.30	.20
688	A260	2.40d Sidi Boumediene Mosque, Tlemcen	.80	.50
689	A260	3d Garden of Dey, Algiers	1.00	.55
		Nos. 687-689 (3)	2.10	1.25

See Nos. 731-734, 745-747, 774, 778-783.

A261

A262

Designs: Medicinal plants.

1982, May 27 Photo. *Perf. 11½*
Granite Paper

690 A261 50c Callitris articulata .25 .20
691 A261 80c Artemisia herba-alba .30 .20
692 A261 1d Ricinus communis .60 .20
693 A261 2.40d Thymus fontanesii 1.10 .45
Nos. 690-693 (4) 2.25 1.05

1982, July 5
Granite Paper

694 A262 50c Riflemen .20 .20
695 A262 80c Soldiers, horiz. .35 .20
696 A262 2d Symbols, citizens, horiz. .80 .45
Nos. 694-696 (3) 1.35 .85

Souvenir Sheet

697 A262 5d Emblem 2.25 2.25

Independence, 20th anniv.
No. 697 contains one 32x39mm stamp.

Soummam Congress A263

1982, Aug. 20 Litho.
698 A263 80c Congress building .35 .20

Scouting Year — A264

1982, Oct. 21 Photo.
Granite Paper

699 A264 2.80d multi 1.00 .45

Palestinian Child — A265

Chlamydotis Undulata — A266

1982, Nov. 25 Litho. *Perf. 10½*
700 A265 1.60d multi 3.00 .75

Perf. 15x14, 14x15
1982, Dec. 23 Photo.

Protected birds. 50c, 2d horiz.

701 A266 50c Geronticus eremita .40 .20
702 A266 80c shown .65 .20
703 A266 2d Aguila rapax 1.25 .40
704 A266 2.40d Gypaetus barbatus 1.75 .45
Nos. 701-704 (4) 4.05 1.25

Jewelry Type of 1980

1983, Feb. 10 *Perf. 11½*
Granite Paper

705 A243 50c Picture frame .20 .20
706 A243 1d Flaska .35 .25
707 A243 2d Brooch, horiz. .65 .45
Nos. 705-707 (3) 1.20 .90

A267

A268

1983, Mar. 17 Photo.
Granite Paper

708 A267 80c Abies numidica, vert. .25 .20
709 A267 2.80d Acacia raddiana .75 .60

Intl. Arbor Day.

Perf. 12x12½, 12½x12
1983, Apr. 21 Photo.

Various minerals. 1.20d, 2.40d horiz.

Granite Paper

710 A268 70c multi .30 .20
711 A268 80c multi .35 .20
712 A268 1.20d multi .50 .30
713 A268 2.40d multi 1.00 .60
Nos. 710-713 (4) 2.15 1.30

30th Anniv. of Intl. Customs Cooperation Council A269

1983, May 14 Photo. *Perf. 11½*
Granite Paper

714 A269 80c multi .35 .20

Emir Abdelkader Death Centenary — A270

1983, May 22 Photo. *Perf. 12*
Granite Paper

715 A270 4d multi 1.60 .75

A271

A272

Local mushrooms.

1983, July 21 *Perf. 14x15*
716 A271 50c Amanita muscaria .25 .20
717 A271 80c Amanita phalloides .50 .25
718 A271 1.40d Pleurotus eryngii 1.00 .50
719 A271 2.80d Tefezia leonis 2.25 1.00
Nos. 716-719 (4) 4.00 1.95

1983, Sept. 1 Photo. *Perf. 11½*
720 A272 80c multi .35 .20

ibn-Khaldun, historian, philosopher.

World Communications Year — A273

Perf. 11½x12½
1983, Sept. 22 Litho.
721 A273 80c Post Office, Algiers .35 .20
722 A273 2.40d Telephone, circuit box 1.00 .40

Goat and Tassili Mountains A274

1983, Oct. 20 Litho. *Perf. 12½x13*
723 A274 50c shown .20 .20
724 A274 80c Tuaregs in native costume .30 .20
725 A274 2.40d Animals, rock painting 1.00 .40
726 A274 2.80d Rock formation 1.00 .60
Nos. 723-726 (4) 2.50 1.40

Sloughi Dog — A275

Perf. 14x14½, 14½x14
1983, Nov. 24 Photo.
727 A275 80c shown .60 .40
728 A275 2.40d Sloughi, horiz. 1.50 .75

Natl. Liberation Party, 5th Congress — A276

1983, Dec. 19 Photo. *Perf. 11½*
729 A276 80c Symbols of development .35 .25

Souvenir Sheet

730 A276 5d Emblem 3.00 2.50

No. 730 contains one 32x38mm stamp.

View Type of 1982

1984, Jan. 26 Litho. *Perf. 14*
731 A260 10c View of Oran, 1830 .20 .20
732 A260 1d Sidi Abderahman and Taalibi Mosques .40 .20
733 A260 2d Bejaia, 1830 .80 .35
734 A260 4d Constantine, 1830 2.00 .60
Nos. 731-734 (4) 3.40 1.35

See Nos. 745-747, 781, 783.

Pottery A278

Perf. 11½x12, 12x11½
1984, Feb. 23 Photo.
Granite Paper

735 A278 80c Jug, vert. .35 .20
736 A278 1d Platter .50 .25
737 A278 2d Oil lamp, vert. 1.00 .45
738 A278 2.40d Pitcher 1.50 .60
Nos. 735-738 (4) 3.35 1.50

Fountains of Old Algiers — A279

1984 Summer Olympics — A280

Various fountains.

1984, Mar. 22 Photo. *Perf. 11½*
Granite Paper

739 A279 50c multi .20 .20
740 A279 80c multi .35 .20
741 A279 2.40d multi 1.00 .60
Nos. 739-741 (3) 1.55 1.00

1984, May 19 Photo. *Perf. 11½*
Granite Paper

742 A280 1d multi .45 .30

Brown Stallion A281

1984, June 14 Photo. *Perf. 11½*
Granite Paper

743 A281 80c shown .35 .20
744 A281 2.40d White mare 1.00 .60

View Type of 1982

1984 Litho. *Perf. 14*
745 A260 5c Mustapha Pacha .20 .20
746 A260 20c Bab Azzoun .20 .20
746A A260 30c Algiers .20 .20
746B A260 40c Kolea .20 .20
746C A260 50c Algiers .20 .20
747 A260 70c Mostaganem .35 .20
Nos. 745-747 (6) 1.35 1.20

Issued: #745, 746, 747, 7/19; #746A-746C, 10/20.

Lute A282

Native musical instruments.

1984, Sept. 22 Litho. *Perf. 15x14*
748 A282 80c shown .20 .20
749 A282 1d Drum .25 .20
750 A282 2.40d Fiddle .60 .35
751 A282 2.80d Bagpipe .70 .40
Nos. 748-751 (4) 1.75 1.15

30th Anniv. of Algerian Revolution — A284

1984, Nov. 3 Photo. *Perf. 11½x12*

757 A284 80c Partisans .20 .20

Souvenir Sheet

758 A284 5d Algerian flags, vert. 2.00 1.00

M'Zab Valley A285

1984, Dec. 15 *Perf. 15x14, 14x15*

759 A285 80c Map of valley .20 .20
760 A285 2.40d Town of M'Zab, vert. .50 .30

18th and 19th Century Metalware — A286

1985, Jan. 26 Photo. *Perf. 11½*

761 A286 80c Coffee pot .20 .20
762 A286 2d Bowl, horiz. .50 .25
763 A286 2.40d Covered bowl .65 .30
Nos. 761-763 (3) 1.35 .75

Fish A287

1985, Feb. 23 Photo. *Perf. 15x14*

764 A287 50c Thunnus thynnus .20 .20
765 A287 80c Sparus aurata .20 .20
766 A287 2.40d Epinephelus guaza .60 .30
767 A287 2.80d Mustelus mustelus .65 .35
Nos. 764-767 (4) 1.65 1.05

National Games A288

1985, Mar. 28 *Perf. 11½x12*

Granite Paper

768 A288 80c Doves, emblem .20 .20

Environmental Conservation — A289

1985, Apr. 25 *Perf. 13½*

769 A289 80c Stylized trees .20 .20
770 A289 1.40d Stylized waves .35 .20

View Type of 1982 and

The Casbah A290

View of Constantine A290a

Street Scene in Algiers — A290b

Designs: 2.50d, Djamaael Djadid Mosque, Algiers. 2.90d, like #746. 5d, like #746A. 1.50d, like #746B. 4.20d, like #764.

Perf. 13½x12½, 13 (#774, 4.20d), Perf. 13½x14 (#775) Perf. 14½x14 (2d)

Photo., Litho. (2d, 6,20d, 7.50d, #775)

1985-94

771 A290 20c dk blue & buff .20 .20
772 A290 80c sage grn & buff .20 .20
773 A290a 1d dk olive grn .50 .25
a. Bklt. pane of 5 + label 2.50
774 A260 1.50d dull red .55 .30
775 A290b 1.50d red brn & brn .25 .20
a. Booklet pane of 6 1.50
776 A290b 2d dk bl & lt bl .20 .20
a. Booklet pane of 5 + label .95
777 A290 2.40d chestnut & buff .60 .30
a. Bklt. pane of 5 (20c, 3 80c, 2.40d) + label 1.40
778 A260 2.50d bluish green 1.00 .50
779 A260 2.90d slate 1.15 .60
780 A260 4.20d gray green 1.60 .85
781 A260 5d dp bis & blk 2.00 1.00

Perf. 14

782 A260 6.20d like #731 1.00 .50
783 A260 7.50d like #745 1.25 .65
Nos. 771-783 (13) 10.50 5.75

Nos. 771-772, 777 issued only in booklet panes.

Issued: 20c, 80c, 2.40d, 6/1/85; 1d, 1/26/89; 2.50d, 2.90d, 5d, 2/23/89; #774, 4.20d, 3/21/91; #775, 5/20/92; 6.20d, 7.50d, 4/22/92; 2d, 10/21/93; #776a, 10/21/94.

See No. 1010.

UN, 40th Anniv. — A291

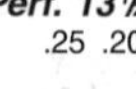

Natl. Youth Festival — A292

1985, June 26 Photo. *Perf. 14*

784 A291 1d Dove, emblem, 40 .25 .20

1985, July 5 Litho. *Perf. 13½*

785 A292 80c multicolored .25 .20

Intl. Youth Year A293

1985, July 5

786 A293 80c Silhouette, globe, emblem, vert. .25 .20
787 A293 1.40d Doves, globe .45 .20

World Map, OPEC — A294

1985, Sept. 14 Photo. *Perf. 12½x13*

788 A294 80c multicolored .25 .20

Organization of Petroleum Exporting Countries, 25th anniv.

Family Planning — A295

1985, Oct. 3 Litho. *Perf. 14*

789 A295 80c Mother and sons .20 .20
790 A295 1.40d Weighing infant .35 .20
791 A295 1.70d Breast-feeding .45 .20
Nos. 789-791 (3) 1.00 .60

El-Meniaa Township — A296

1985, Oct. 24 Engr. *Perf. 13*

792 A296 80c Chetaibi Bay, horiz. .20 .20
793 A296 2d shown .50 .25
794 A296 2.40d Bou Noura Town, horiz. .65 .30
Nos. 792-794 (3) 1.35 .75

The Palm Grove, by N. Dinet — A297

1985, Nov. 21 Photo. *Perf. 11½x12*

Granite Paper

795 A297 2d multi .50 .25
796 A297 3d multi, diff. .85 .40

Tapestries A298

Various designs.

1985, Dec. 19

Granite Paper

797 A298 80c multi .20 .20
798 A298 1.40d multi .40 .20
799 A298 2.40d multi .60 .30
800 A298 2.80d multi .75 .40
Nos. 797-800 (4) 1.95 1.10

Wildcats A299

1986, Jan. 23 *Perf. 12x11½, 11½x12*

Granite Paper

801 A299 80c Felis margarita .50 .20
802 A299 1d Felis caracal .70 .20
803 A299 2d Felis sylvestris 1.40 .80
804 A299 2.40d Felis serval, vert. 1.90 .95
Nos. 801-804 (4) 4.50 2.15

UN Child Survival Campaign — A300

Algerian General Worker's Union, 30th Anniv. — A301

1986, Feb. 13 Litho. *Perf. 13½*

805 A300 80c Oral vaccine .25 .20
806 A300 1.40d Mother, child, sun .60 .25
807 A300 1.70d Three children 1.00 .35
Nos. 805-807 (3) 1.85 .80

1986, Feb. 24 *Perf. 12½*

Granite Paper

808 A301 2d multi .50 .25

National Charter — A302

Natl. Day of the Disabled — A303

1986, Mar. 6 Photo. *Perf. 11½*

Granite Paper

809 A302 4d multi 1.00 .45

1986, Mar. 15 *Perf. 12½x13*

810 A303 80c multi .20 .20

A304

A305

1986, Apr. 17 Litho. *Perf. 14x15*

811 A304 80c multi .20 .20

Anti-Tuberculosis campaign.

1986, Apr. 24 *Perf. 14*

812 A305 2d Soccer ball, sombrero .50 .25
813 A305 2.40d Soccer players .65 .30

1986 World Cup Soccer Championships, Mexico.

Inner Courtyards — A306

Blood Donation Campaign A307

1986, May 15 Photo. *Perf. 11½*
Granite Paper

814 A306 80c multi .20 .20
815 A306 2.40d multi, diff. .65 .30
816 A306 3d multi, diff. .80 .40
Nos. 814-816 (3) 1.65 .90

1986, June 26 Litho. *Perf. 13½*

817 A307 80c multi .25 .20

Southern District Radio Communication Inauguration A308

1986, July *Perf. 13*

818 A308 60c multi .20 .20

Mosque Gateways A309

1986, Sept. 27 Photo. *Perf. 12x11½*
Granite Paper

819 A309 2d Door .50 .25
820 A309 2.40d Ornamental arch .65 .30

Intl. Peace Year A310

Perf. 13½x14½
1986, Oct. 16 Photo.

821 A310 2.40d multi .65 .30

Folk Dancing A311

1986, Nov. 22 Litho. *Perf. 14x13½*

822 A311 80c Woman, scarf .25 .20
823 A311 2.40d Woman, diff. .65 .30
824 A311 2.80d Man, sword .70 .40
Nos. 822-824 (3) 1.60 .90

Flowers — A312

1986, Dec. 18 Photo. *Perf. 14*

825 A312 80c Narcissus tazetta .25 .20
826 A312 1.40d Iris unguicularis .40 .20
827 A312 2.40d Capparis spinosa .65 .30
828 A312 2.80d Gladiolus segetum .70 .40
Nos. 825-828 (4) 2.00 1.10

See Nos. 936-938.

Abstract Paintings by Mohammed Issia Khem — A313

Perf. 11½x12, 12x11½
1987, Jan. 29 Litho.

829 A313 2d Man and woman, vert. .65 .35
830 A313 5d Man and books 1.60 .80

Jewelry from Aures A314

1987, Feb. 27 Photo. *Perf. 12*
Granite Paper

831 A314 1d Earrings .35 .20
832 A314 1.80d Bracelets .60 .30
833 A314 2.90d Nose rings 1.00 .50
834 A314 3.30d Necklace 1.10 .55
Nos. 831-834 (4) 3.05 1.55

Nos. 831-833 vert.

Petroglyphs, Atlas — A315

1987, Mar. 26 Litho. *Perf. 12x11½*
Granite Paper

835 A315 1d Man and woman .35 .20
836 A315 2.90d Goat 1.00 .50
837 A315 3.30d Horse, bull 1.10 .60
Nos. 835-837 (3) 2.45 1.30

Syringe as an Umbrella — A316

1987, Apr. 7 *Perf. 11½*
Granite Paper

838 A316 1d multi .35 .20

Child Immunization Campaign, World Health Day.

Volunteers A317

Third General Census — A318

1987, Apr. 23 *Perf. 10½*

839 A317 1d multi .35 .20

1987, May 21 *Perf. 13½*

840 A318 1d multi .35 .20

Algerian Postage, 25th Anniv. — A319

War Orphans' Fund label (1fr + 9fr) of 1962.

1987, July 5 Photo. *Perf. 11½x12*
Granite Paper

841 A319 1.80d multi .60 .30

A320

A321

1987, July 5
Granite Paper

842 A320 1d multi .35 .20

Souvenir Sheet

843 A321 5d multi 1.75 1.60

Natl. independence, 25th anniv.

Amateur Theater Festival, Mostaganem A322

1987, July 20 *Perf. 12x11½*
Granite Paper

844 A322 1d Actors on stage .35 .20
845 A322 1.80d Theater .60 .30
a. Pair, #844-845 1.00 .50

No. 845a has continuous design.

Mediterranean Games, Latakia — A323

1987, Aug. 6 *Perf. 13x12½, 12½x13*

846 A323 1d Discus .35 .20
847 A323 2.90d Tennis, vert. 1.00 .50
848 A323 3.30d Team handball 1.50 .55
Nos. 846-848 (3) 2.85 1.25

Birds — A324

1987 Litho. *Perf. 13½*

849 A324 1d Phoenicopterus ruber roseus .50 .25
850 A324 1.80d Porphyrio porphyrio .90 .50
851 A324 2.50d Elanus caeruleus 1.25 .65
852 A324 2.90d Milvus milvus 1.50 .75
Nos. 849-852 (4) 4.15 2.15

Agriculture A325

Perf. 10½x11, 11x10½

1987, Nov. 26 **Litho.**

853 A325 1d Planting .35 .20
854 A325 1d Reservoir .35 .20
855 A325 1d Harvesting crop, vert. .35 .20
856 A325 1d Produce, vert. .35 .20
Nos. 853-856 (4) 1.40 .80

African Telecommunications Day — A326

1987, Dec. 7 ***Perf. 10½***

857 A326 1d multi .35 .20

Transportation — A327

1987, Dec. 18 Litho. ***Perf. 10½x11***

858 A327 2.90d shown 1.00 .50
859 A327 3.30d Diesel train 1.10 .55

Algerian Universities A328

Various campuses.

1987, Dec. 26 ***Perf. 10½x11, 11x10½***

860 A328 1d shown .35 .20
861 A328 2.50d multi, diff. 1.00 .40
862 A328 2.90d multi, diff. 1.50 .50
863 A328 3.30d multi, diff., vert. 1.75 .55
Nos. 860-863 (4) 4.60 1.65

Intl. Rural Development Fund, 10th Anniv. — A329

1988, Jan. 27 ***Perf. 10½x11***

864 A329 1d multi .50 .25

Autonomy of State-owned Utilities — A330

1988, Feb. 27 Litho. ***Perf. 11x10½***

865 A330 1d multi .50 .25

Intl. Women's Day — A331

Arab Scouts, 75th Anniv. — A332

1988, Mar. 10 Litho. ***Perf. 11x10½***

866 A331 1d multi .50 .25

1988, Apr. 7 Litho. ***Perf. 10½***

867 A332 2d multi .95 .50

1988 Summer Olympics, Seoul — A333

Hot Springs — A334

1988, July 23 Litho. ***Perf. 10½***

868 A333 2.90d multi 1.40 .70

1988, July 16

869 A334 1d shown .50 .25
870 A334 2.90d Caverns, horiz. 1.40 .70
871 A334 3.30d Gazebo, fountain, horiz. 1.60 .80
Nos. 869-871 (3) 3.50 1.75

World Wildlife Fund A335

Barbary apes, *Macaca sylvanus.*

1988, Sept. 17 Litho. ***Perf. 10½***

872 A335 50c Adult .25 .20
873 A335 90c Family .45 .25
874 A335 1d Close-up, vert. .50 .25
875 A335 1.80d Seated on branch, vert. .90 .45
Nos. 872-875 (4) 2.10 1.15

Intl. Literacy Day — A336

WHO, 40th Anniv. — A337

1988, Sept. 10 Photo. ***Perf. 10½***

876 A336 2.90d multi 1.40 .70

1988, Oct. 15

877 A337 2.90d multi 1.40 .70

Fight Apartheid A338

1988, Nov. 19 Litho. ***Perf. 10½x11***

878 A338 2.50d multi 1.25 .60

Natl. Front Congress — A339

1988, Nov. 29 ***Perf. 11x10½***

879 A339 1d multi .50 .25

Agriculture A340

1988, Dec. 24 ***Perf. 10½***

880 A340 1d Irrigation .50 .25
881 A340 1d Orchard, fields, livestock .50 .25

Natl. Goals — A342

Airports — A343

1989, Mar. 9 Litho. ***Perf. 11½***

Granite Paper

886 A342 1d shown .50 .25
887 A342 1d Ancient fort .50 .25
888 A342 1d Telecommunications .50 .25
889 A342 1d Modern buildings .50 .25
Nos. 886-889 (4) 2.00 1.00

Nos. 887-889 horiz.

1989, Mar. 23 ***Perf. 10½x11, 11x10½***

890 A343 2.90d Oran Es Senia, horiz. 1.25 .70
891 A343 3.30d Tebessa, horiz. 1.50 .80
892 A343 5d shown 2.25 1.25
Nos. 890-892 (3) 5.00 2.75

Development of the South — A344

1989, Apr. 24 Litho. ***Perf. 13½***

893 A344 1d Irrigation .45 .25
894 A344 1.80d Building .90 .45
895 A344 2.50d Fossil fuel extraction, vert. 1.25 .60
Nos. 893-895 (3) 2.60 1.30

Eradicate Locusts A345

1989, May 25 ***Perf. 10½***

896 A345 1d multi .50 .25

National Service — A346

1989, May 11 Litho. ***Perf. 13½***

897 A346 2d multicolored .80 .40

1st Moon Landing, 20th Anniv. A347

4d, Astronaut, lunar module, Moon's surface.

1989, July 23 Litho. ***Perf. 13½***

898 A347 2.90d shown 1.00 .55
899 A347 4d multi, vert. 1.40 .75

Interparliamentary Union, Cent. — A348

1989, Sept. 4 ***Perf. 10½***

900 A348 2.90d gold, brt rose lil & blk 1.10 .55

Produce A349

1989, Sept. 23 Litho. *Perf. 11½*
Granite Paper

901 Strip of 3 4.00 2.00
a. A349 2d multi, diff. .75 .40
b. A349 3d multi, diff. 1.10 .55
c. A349 5d shown 2.00 1.00

Fish — A350

1989, Oct. 27 Litho. *Perf. 13½*

902 A350 1d *Sarda sarda* .30 .20
903 A350 1.80d *Zeus faber* .50 .35
904 A350 2.90d *Pagellus bogaraveo* .90 .55
905 A350 3.30d *Xiphias gladius* 1.00 .65
Nos. 902-905 (4) 2.70 1.75

Algerian Revolution, 35th Anniv. — A351

1989, Nov. 4 Litho. *Perf. 13½*

906 A351 1d multicolored .40 .20

African Development Bank, 25th Anniv. — A352

Mushrooms A353

1989, Nov. 18 *Perf. 10½*

907 A352 1d multicolored .40 .20

1989, Dec. 16 *Perf. 13½*

908 A353 1d *Boletus satanas* .30 .20
909 A353 1.80d *Psalliota xanthoderma* .60 .35
910 A353 2.90d *Lepiota procera* 1.00 .55
911 A353 3.30d *Lactarius deliciosus* 1.10 .65
Nos. 908-911 (4) 3.00 1.75

A354 A355

1990, Jan. 18 Litho. *Perf. 10½*

912 A354 1d multicolored .40 .20

Pan-African Postal Union, 10th anniv.

1990, Feb. 22 Litho. *Perf. 14*

913 A355 1d Energy conservation .25 .20

A356 A357

1990, Mar. 2 Photo. *Perf. 11½*

914 A356 3d multicolored .65 .30

African Soccer Championships.

1990, May 17 Litho. *Perf. 13½*

917 A357 2.90d shown .75 .40
918 A357 5d Trophy 1.25 .65

World Cup Soccer Championships, Italy.

Rural Electrification — A358

1990, June 21

919 A358 2d multicolored .50 .25

Youth A359

Youth Holding Rainbow — A360

1990, July 6 *Perf. 13½*

920 A359 2d multicolored .50 .25
921 A360 3d multicolored .75 .35

Maghreb Arab Union — A361

1990 *Perf. 14x13½*

922 A361 1d multicolored .40 .20

Vocations A362

1990, Apr. 26 Litho. *Perf. 12½*

923 A362 2d Craftsmen .75 .40
924 A362 2.90d Auto mechanics 1.10 .60
925 A362 3.30d Deep sea fishing 1.25 .65
Nos. 923-925 (3) 3.10 1.65

Organization of Petroleum Exporting Countries (OPEC), 30th Anniv. — A363

1990 *Perf. 13½*

926 A363 2d multicolored .75 .40

Savings Promotion A364

1990, Oct. 31 Litho. *Perf. 14*

927 A364 1d multicolored .20 .20

Namibian Independence — A365

1990, Nov. 8

928 A365 3d multicolored .60 .50

A366

A367

Farm animals.

1990, Nov. 29 *Perf. 13½*

929 A366 1d Duck .35 .20
930 A366 2d Rabbit, horiz. .65 .40
931 A366 2.90d Turkey .90 .55
932 A366 3.30d Rooster, horiz. 1.10 .65
Nos. 929-932 (4) 3.00 1.80

1990, Dec. 11

933 A367 1d multicolored .25 .20

Anti-French Riots, 30th anniv.

A368

A369

1990, Dec. 20 *Perf. 14*

934 A368 1d multicolored .25 .20

Fight against respiratory diseases.

1991, Feb. 24 Litho. *Perf. 13½*

935 A369 1d multicolored .25 .20

Constitution, 2nd anniv.

Flower Type of 1986

1991, May 23 Litho. *Perf. 13½*
Size: 26x36mm

936 A312 2d Jasminum fruticans .60 .30
937 A312 4d Dianthus crinitus 1.10 .65
938 A312 5d Cyclamen africanum 1.50 .85
Nos. 936-938 (3) 3.20 1.80

Children's Drawings A370

1991, June 3 Litho. *Perf. 13½*

939 A370 3d shown 1.00 .50
940 A370 4d Children playing 1.25 .65

Maghreb Arab Union Summit — A371

1991, June 10

941 A371 1d multicolored .30 .20

Geneva Convention on Refugees, 40th Anniv. — A372

1991, July 28 Litho. *Perf. 14½x13½*

942 A372 3d multicolored 1.00 .50

Postal Service A373

1991, Oct. 12 *Perf. 14*

943 A373 1.50d shown .55 .25
944 A373 4.20d Expo emblem, vert. 1.50 .75

Telecom '91, 6th World Forum and Exposition on Telecommunications, Geneva, Switzerland (No. 944).

Butterflies A374

1991, Nov. 21 Litho. *Perf. 11½*
Granite Paper

945 A374 2d Zerynthia rumina .30 .20
946 A374 4d Melitaea didyma .65 .30
947 A374 6d Vanessa atalanta 1.00 .50
948 A374 7d Nymphalis polychloros 1.10 .55
Nos. 945-948 (4) 3.05 1.55

A375

A376

1991, Dec. 21 *Perf. 12*
Granite Paper

949 A375 3d Necklace .40 .25
950 A375 4d Jewelry of Southern Tuaregs .60 .30
951 A375 5d Brooch .70 .40
952 A375 7d Rings, horiz. 1.00 .55
Nos. 949-952 (4) 2.70 1.50

1992, Mar. 8 Litho. *Perf. 14*

953 A376 1.50d Algerian Women .20 .20

Gazelles A377

Designs: 1.50d, Gazella dorcas. 6.20d, Gazella cuvieri. 8.60d, Gazella dama.

1992, May 13 *Perf. 14½x13*

954 A377 1.50d multicolored .25 .20
955 A377 6.20d multicolored .95 .50
956 A377 8.60d multicolored 1.25 .65
Nos. 954-956 (3) 2.45 1.35

1992 Summer Olympics, Barcelona A379

1992, June 24 Litho. *Perf. 14*

958 A379 6.20d Runners 1.00 .55

A381

A382

1992, July 7 Litho. *Perf. 14*

960 A381 5d multicolored .90 .45

Independence, 30th anniv.

1992, Sept. 23 Litho. *Perf. 14*

Designs: Medicinal plants.

961 A382 1.50d Ajuga iva .20 .20
962 A382 5.10d Rhamnus alaternus .60 .35
963 A382 6.20d Silybum marianum .70 .40
964 A382 8.60d Lavandula stoechas 1.00 .55
Nos. 961-964 (4) 2.50 1.50

Post Office Modernization A383

1992, Oct. 10 Litho. *Perf. 14*

965 A383 1.50d multicolored .20 .20

Marine Life — A384

Designs: 1.50d, Hippocampus hippocampus. 2.70d, Caretta caretta. 6.20d, Muraena helena. 7.50d, Palinurus elephas.

1992, Dec. 23

966 A384 1.50d multicolored .20 .20
967 A384 2.70d multicolored .35 .20
968 A384 6.20d multicolored .85 .40
969 A384 7.50d multicolored 1.00 .50
Nos. 966-969 (4) 2.40 1.30

Pres. Mohammad Boudiaf (1919-92) — A385

1992, Nov. 3 Litho. *Perf. 11½*
Granite Paper

970 A385 2d green & multi .30 .20
971 A385 8.60d blue & multi 1.10 .55

Coins A386

1992, Dec. 16 Litho. *Perf. 11½*
Granite Paper

972 A386 1.50d Numidia, 2nd cent. BC .20 .20
973 A386 2d Dinar, 14th cent. .30 .20
974 A386 5.10d Dinar, 11th cent. .65 .35
975 A386 6.20d Abdelkader, 19th cent. .85 .40
Nos. 972-975 (4) 2.00 1.15

Door Knockers — A387

Flowering Trees — A388

1993, Feb. 17 Litho. *Perf. 14*

976 A387 2d Algiers .30 .20
977 A387 5.60d Constantine .75 .40
978 A387 8.60d Tlemcen 1.10 .60
Nos. 976-978 (3) 2.15 1.20

1993, Mar. 17 *Perf. 12x11½, 11½x12*
Granite Paper

979 A388 4.50d Neflier (medlar), horiz. .50 .30
980 A388 8.60d Cognassier (quince) 1.00 .60
981 A388 11d Abricotier (apricot) 1.25 .75
Nos. 979-981 (3) 2.75 1.65

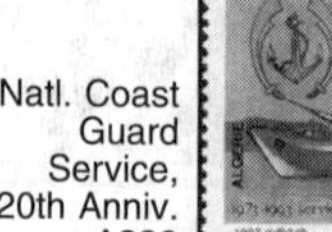

Natl. Coast Guard Service, 20th Anniv. A389

1993, Apr. 3 Litho. *Perf. 14*

982 A389 2d multicolored .30 .20

Traditional Grain Processing A390

1993, May 19 Litho. *Perf. 14*

983 A390 2d Container .25 .20
984 A390 5.60d Millstone .75 .40
985 A390 8.60d Press 1.00 .55
Nos. 983-985 (3) 2.00 1.15

Royal Mausoleums — A391

1993, June 16 Litho. *Perf. 14*

986 A391 8.60d Mauretania 1.10 .60
987 A391 12d El Khroub 1.60 .80

Ports A392

1993, Oct. 20 Litho. *Perf. 14x13½*

988 A392 2d Annaba .20 .20
989 A392 8.60d Arzew 1.00 .55

Varanus Griseus A393

Design: 2d, Chamaeleo vulgaris, vert.

Perf. 13½x14, 14x13½
1993, Nov. 20

990 A393 2d multicolored .25 .20
991 A393 8.60d multicolored 1.10 .55

Tourism A394

1993, Dec. 18 Litho. *Perf. 14x13½*

992 A394 2d Tipaza .20 .20
993 A394 8.60d Kerzaz .80 .40

A395

Chahid Day — A396

1994, Jan. 2 *Perf. 13½x14*

994 A395 2d multicolored .20 .20

SONATRACH (Natl. Society for Research, Transformation, and Commercialization of Hydrocarbons), 30th anniv.

1994, Feb. 18 Litho. *Perf. 13½x14*

995 A396 2d multicolored .20 .20

1994 World Cup Soccer Championships, US — A397

1994, Mar. 16 *Perf. 14x13½*

996 A397 8.60d multicolored .80 .40

A398

A399

Orchids: 5.60d, Orchis simia lam. 8.60d, Ophrys lutea cavan. 11d, Ophrys apifera huds.

1994, Apr. 20 Litho. *Perf. 11½*
Granite Paper

997	A398	5.60d multicolored	.55	.30
998	A398	8.60d multicolored	.85	.40
999	A398	11d multicolored	1.10	.55
		Nos. 997-999 (3)	2.50	1.25

1994, May 21 Litho. *Perf. 13x14*

Ancient petroglyphs.

1000	A399	3d Inscriptions	.35	.20
1001	A399	10d Man on horse	1.25	.60

A400

A401

1994, June 25

1002	A400	12d multicolored	1.25	.65

Intl. Olympic Committee, cent.

1994, July 13

1003	A401	3d multicolored	.35	.20

World Population Day.

Views of Algiers Type of 1992

Design: 3d, like #775.

1994, July 13 Litho. *Perf. 14*

1010	A290b	3d dk blue & lt blue	.35	.20

This is an expanding set. Number may change.

Jewelry from Saharan Atlas Region A402

Perf. 13½x14, 14x13½

1994, Oct. 18 Litho.

1019	A402	3d Fibules, vert.	.20	.20
1020	A402	5d Belt	.25	.20
1021	A402	12d Bracelets	.55	.30
		Nos. 1019-1021 (3)	1.00	.70

A403

A404

1994, Nov. 3 Litho. *Perf. 13½x14*

1022	A403	3d multicolored	.40	.20

Algerian Revolution, 40th anniv.

1994, Nov. 16 Litho. *Perf. 13½x14*

1023	A404	3d Ladybugs	.20	.20
1024	A404	12d Beetles	.55	.30

Fight Against AIDS A405

1994, Dec. 1 Litho. *Perf. 14x13½*

1025	A405	3d multicolored	.38	.20

Folk Dances — A406

Minerals — A407

1994, Dec. 17 Litho. *Perf. 13½x14*

1026	A406	3d Algeroise	.20	.20
1027	A406	10d Constantinoise	.50	.25
1028	A406	12d Alaoui	.55	.30
		Nos. 1026-1028 (3)	1.25	.75

See Nos. 1170-1172.

1994, Sept. 21

1029	A407	3d Gres lite-erode	.20	.20
1030	A407	5d Cipolin	.25	.20
1031	A407	10d Marne a turitella	.50	.25
		Nos. 1029-1031 (3)	.95	.65

World Tourism Organization, 20th Anniv. — A408

1995, Jan. 28 Litho. *Perf. 14x13½*

1032	A408	3d multicolored	.35	.20

Honey Bees — A409

Flowers — A410

1995, Feb. 22 *Perf. 13½x14, 14x13½*

1033	A409	3d shown	.35	.20
1034	A409	13d On flower, horiz.	1.50	.75

1995, Mar. 29 Photo. *Perf. 11½*
Granite Paper

1035	A410	3d Dahlias	.25	.20
1036	A410	10d Zinnias	1.00	.55
1037	A410	13d Lilacs	1.25	.75
		Nos. 1035-1037 (3)	2.50	1.50

Decorative Stonework — A411

Various patterns.

1995, Apr. 19 *Perf. 14*

1039	A411	3d brown	.35	.20
1040	A411	4d green	.45	.25
1041	A411	5d deep claret	.55	.30
		Nos. 1039-1041 (3)	1.35	.75

This is an expanding set. Numbers may change.

End of World War II, 50th Anniv. A413

1995, May 3 *Perf. 14x13½*

1048	A413	3d multicolored	.35	.20

Souvenir Sheet

VE Day, 50th Anniv. — A414

Illustration reduced.

1995, May 10 Litho. *Perf. 13½x14*

1049	A414	13d multicolored	1.50	.85

Volleyball, Cent. — A415

Environmental Protection — A416

1995, June 14

1050	A415	3d multicolored	.40	.20

1995, June 5

1051	A416	3d Air, water pollution	.35	.20
1052	A416	13d Air pollution	1.50	.85

General Electrification A417

1995, July 5 Litho. *Perf. 13½x14*

1053	A417	3d multicolored	.45	.20

UN, 50th Anniv. A418

1995, Oct. 24 *Perf. 14x13½*

1054	A418	13d multicolored	2.00	1.00

Pottery — A419

10d, Pot, Lakhdaria. 20d, Pitcher, Aokas. 21d, Jar, Larbaa Nath Iraten. 30d, Vase, Ouadhia.

1995, Nov. 14 Litho. *Perf. 14*

1055	A419	10d dark brown	1.50	.75
1056	A419	20d dull maroon	3.00	1.50
1057	A419	21d golden brown	3.25	1.60
1058	A419	30d dark rose brown	4.50	2.25
		Nos. 1055-1058 (4)	12.25	6.10

Aquatic Birds A420

1995, Dec. 20 Litho. *Perf. 14x13½*

1059	A420	3d Tadorna tadorna	.40	.20
1060	A420	5d Gallinago gallinago	.70	.35

1996 Summer Olympics, Atlanta A421

1996, Jan. 24 Litho. *Perf. 14x13½*

1061	A421	20d multicolored	2.50	1.25

Touareg Leather Crafts A422

Perf. 14x13½, 13½x14

1996, Feb. 14 **Litho.**

1062 A422 5d shown .60 .40
1063 A422 16d Saddle bag, vert. 2.25 1.00

Pasteur Institute of Algeria — A423

1996, Mar. 20 Litho. *Perf. 13½x14*

1064 A423 5d multicolored .75 .40

Youm El Ilm — A424

Designs: 16d, Dove, stylus, vert. 23d, Open book showing pencil, stylus, compass, satellite in earth orbit, vert.

Perf. 14x13½,13½x14

1996, Apr. 16 **Litho.**

1065 A424 5d multicolored .50 .40
1066 A424 16d multicolored 2.00 1.00
1067 A424 23d multicolored 3.00 1.50
Nos. 1065-1067 (3) 5.50 2.90

Minerals A425

Mineral, region: 10d, Iron, Djebel-Ouenza. 20d, Gold, Tirek-Amesmessa.

1996, May 6 Litho. *Perf. 14x13½*

1068 A425 10d multicolored .75 .25
1069 A425 20d multicolored 2.00 .60

Butterflies A426

Designs: 5d, Pandoriana pandora. 10d, Coenonympha pamphilus. 20d, Cynthia cardui. 23d, Melanargia galathea.

1996, June 12 Litho. *Perf. 11½*

Granite Paper

1070 A426 5d multicolored .30 .20
1071 A426 10d multicolored .75 .20
1072 A426 20d multicolored 1.50 .35
1073 A426 23d multicolored 2.00 .40
Nos. 1070-1073 (4) 4.55 1.15

Civil Protection A427

5d, Giving medical aid, ambulance. 23d, Prevention of natural disasters, vert.

Perf. 14x13½, 13½x14

1996, Oct. 9 **Litho.**

1074 A427 5d multicolored .40 .20
1075 A427 23d multicolored 1.25 .40

World Day Against Use of Illegal Drugs A428

1996, June 26 Litho. *Perf. 14x13½*

1076 A428 5d multicolored .40 .20

UNICEF, 50th Anniv. — A429

Stylized designs: 5d, Two children, wreath, pencils, flowers. 10d, Five children, pencil, key, flower, flag, hypodermic.

1996, Nov. 20 Litho. *Perf. 13½x14*

1077 A429 5d multicolored .30 .20
1078 A429 10d multicolored .50 .20

4th General Census A430

1997, Feb. 12 Litho. *Perf. 14x13½*

1079 A430 5d multicolored .20 .20

Protest at Ouargla, 35th Anniv. — A431

1997, Feb. 27 ***Perf. 13½x14***

1080 A431 5d multicolored .20 .20

Interior Courts of Algerian Dwellings A432

1996, Dec. 18 Litho. *Perf. 13½x14*

Designs: 5d, Palace of Hassan Pasha. 10d, Khedaouj El-Amia, Algiers. 20d, Palace of Light. 30d, Abdellatif Villa.

1081 A432 5d multicolored .20 .20
1082 A432 10d multicolored .35 .20
1083 A432 20d multicolored .70 .35
1084 A432 30d multicolored 1.10 .55
Nos. 1081-1084 (4) 2.35 1.30

Paintings by Ismail Samson (1934-88) A433

20d, Woman with Pigeons. 30d, Interrogation.

1996, Dec. 25 ***Perf. 14***

1085 A433 20d multicolored 1.00 .35
1086 A433 30d multicolored 1.50 .55

Victory Day, 35th Anniv. A434

1997, Mar. 19 ***Perf. 14x13½***

1087 A434 5d multicolored .20 .20

Flowers — A435

Designs: 5d, Ficaria verna. 16d, Lonicera arborea. 23d, Papaver rhoeas.

1997, Apr. 23 Litho. *Perf. 13½x14*

1088 A435 5d multicolored .20 .20
1089 A435 16d multicolored .55 .30
1090 A435 23d multicolored .80 .40
Nos. 1088-1090 (3) 1.55 .90

World Day to Stop Smoking — A436

1997, May 31 Litho. *Perf. 13½x14*

1091 A436 5d multicolored .20 .20

Legislative Elections — A437

1997, June 4

1092 A437 5d multicolored .20 .20

Scorpions A438

Designs: 5d, Buthus occitanus tunetanus. 10d, Androctonus australis hector.

1997, June 18 ***Perf. 14x13½***

1093 A438 5d multicolored .20 .20
1094 A438 10d multicolored .35 .20

Natl. Independence, 35th Anniv. — A439

Designs: 5d, Crowd celebrating, flags. 10d, Doves, broken chain, "35," flag.

1997, July 5 Litho. *Perf. 14x13½*

1095 A439 5d multicolored .20 .20

Souvenir Sheet

Perf. 14

1096 A439 10d multicolored .35 .20

No. 1096 contains one 30x40mm stamp.

Wood Carvings — A440

Designs: 5d, Inscription, Nedroma Mosque. 23d, Door, Ketchaoua Mosque.

1997, Jan. 15 Litho. *Perf. 13½x14*

1097 A440 5d multicolored .20 .20
1098 A440 23d multicolored .80 .40

Moufdi Zakaria (1908-77), poet. — A441

1997, Aug. 17 Litho. *Perf. 13½x14*

1099 A441 5d multicolored .20 .20

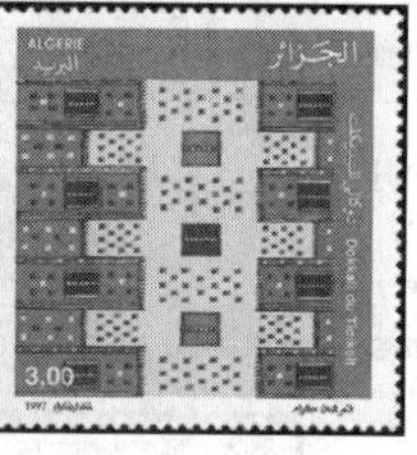
Textile Patterns A442

1997, Sept. 17 Litho. *Perf. 14*

1100 A442 3d Dokkali .20 .20
1101 A442 5d Tellis .20 .20
1102 A442 10d Bou-Taleb .35 .20
1103 A442 20d Ddil .70 .35
Nos. 1100-1103 (4) 1.45 .95

Natl. Police Force, 25th Anniv. A443

1997, Oct. 6 ***Perf. 14x13½***

1104 A443 5d multicolored .20 .20

Express Mail Service A444

1997, Oct. 9
1105 A444 5d multicolored .20 .20

Local Elections — A445

1997, Oct. 23 ***Perf. 13½x14***
1106 A445 5d multicolored .20 .20

Lighthouses A446

Perf. 14x13½, 13½x14
1997, Nov. 5 **Litho.**
1107 A446 5d Tenes .20 .20
1108 A446 10d Cape Caxine, vert. .35 .20

New Airpost Service, 1st Anniv. A447

1997, Nov. 17 ***Perf. 14x13½***
1109 A447 5d multicolored .20 .20

Shells A448

Designs: 5d, Chlamys varia. 10d, Bolinus brandaris. 20d, Hinia reticulata, vert.

Perf. 14x13½, 13½x14
1997, Dec. 17 **Litho.**
1110 A448 5d multicolored .20 .20
1111 A448 10d multicolored .35 .20
1112 A448 20d multicolored .70 .35
Nos. 1110-1112 (3) 1.25 .75

A449

A450

1997, Dec. 25 ***Perf. 13½x14***
1113 A449 5d multicolored .20 .20

Election of the Natl. Council.

1997, Dec. 30 **Litho.** ***Perf. 13½x14***

Completion of Government Reforms: a, Natl. flag, people, book, ballot box. b, People, open book, torch. c, Ballot box. d, Flag, rising sun, flower. e, Ballots, building, flag.

1114 A450 5d Strip of 5, #a.-e. .85 .45

Bombing of Sakiet Sidi Youcef, 40th Anniv. A451

1998, Feb. 8 **Litho.** ***Perf. 14x13½***
1115 A451 5d multicolored .20 .20

National Archives A452

1998, Feb. 16
1116 A452 5d multicolored .20 .20

Intl. Women's Day A453

1998, Mar. 8 **Litho.** ***Perf. 14x13½***
1117 A453 5d multicolored .20 .20

Expo '98, Lisbon A454

1998, Jan. 21 **Litho.** ***Perf. 14x13½***
1118 A454 5d shown .25 .20

Size: 80x75mm

Imperf

1119 A454 24d Mosaic 1.25 .60

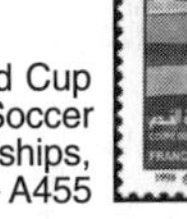
1998 World Cup Soccer Championships, Paris — A455

1998, Apr. 15 **Litho.** ***Perf. 13½x14***
1120 A455 24d multi 1.25 .60

Algiers Casbah A456

Designs: 5d, Aerial view, vert. 10d, Buildings, vert. 24d, Aerial view, diff.

1998, Apr. 22 ***Perf. 13½x14, 14x13½***
1121 A456 5d multi .25 .20
1122 A456 10d multi .50 .20
1123 A456 24d multi 1.25 .60
Nos. 1121-1123 (3) 2.00 1.00

Zaatcha Resistance — A457

1998, May 20 ***Perf. 13¼x13***
1124 A457 5d multi .25 .20

Tourism A458

5d, Mountains, farm, desert, vert. 10d, Youths, modes of transportation. 24d, Taghit.

Perf. 13½x14, 14x13½
1998, June 4 **Litho.**
1125 A458 5d multi .25 .20
1126 A458 10d multi .50 .25
1127 A458 24d multi 1.25 .60
Nos. 1125-1127 (3) 2.00 1.05

Arab Post Day A459

1998, Aug. 3 **Litho.** ***Perf. 14x13½***
1128 A459 5d multi .25 .20

Interpol, 75th Anniv. A460

1998, Sept. 7 **Litho.** ***Perf. 14x13½***
1129 A460 5d multi .25 .20

Creation of Provisional Government, 40th Anniv. — A461

1998, Sept. 19 ***Perf. 13¼x13***
1130 A461 5d multi .25 .20

Natl. Diplomacy Day A462

1998, Oct. 8 ***Perf. 14***
1131 A462 5d multi .25 .20

Algerian Olympic Committee, 35th Anniv. A463

1998, Oct. 18 ***Perf. 14x13½***
1132 A463 5d multi .25 .20

Birds A464

Designs: 5d, Pandion haliaetus. 10d, Larus audouinii. 24d, Phalacrocorax aristotelis, vert. 30d, Phalacrocorax carbo, vert.

Perf. 14x13½, 13½x14
1998, Nov. 11
1133 A464 5d multi .25 .20
1134 A464 10d multi .50 .25
1135 A464 24d multi 1.25 .60
1136 A464 30d multi 1.50 .75
Nos. 1133-1136 (4) 3.50 1.80

See Nos. 1204-1207.

Universal Declaration of Human Rights, 50th Anniv. A465

1998, Dec. 10 **Litho.** ***Perf. 14x13½***
1137 A465 5d Profiles, emblem .25 .20
1138 A465 24d shown 1.25 .60

Spinning and Weaving Tools A466

Designs: 5d, Comb, vert. 10d, Cards. 20d, Spindle, vert. 24d, Loom, vert.

1999, Jan. 20 ***Perf. 13½x14, 14x13½***
1139 A466 5d multi .25 .20
1140 A466 10d multi .50 .25
1141 A466 20d multi 1.00 .50
1142 A466 24d multi 1.25 .60
Nos. 1139-1142 (4) 3.00 1.55

Natl. Chahid Day — A467

1999, Feb. 18 ***Perf. 13x13¼***
1143 A467 5d multi .25 .20

Flowering Trees A468

1999, Mar. 17 ***Perf. 14x13½, 13½x14***
1144 A468 5d Pear .25 .20
1145 A468 10d Plum .50 .25
1146 A468 24d Orange, vert. 1.25 .60
Nos. 1144-1146 (3) 2.00 1.05

Presidential Elections A469

1999, Apr. 15 ***Perf. 13x13¼***
1147 A469 5d multi .25 .20

Handicrafts A470

Designs: 5d, Tlemcen mosaic, 14th cent., vert. 10d, Mosaic, Al Qal'a of Beni Hammad, 11th cent, vert. 20d, Cradle. 24d, Table.

1999, Apr. 18 ***Perf. 13¼x14, 14x13¼***
1148 A470 5d multi .25 .20
1149 A470 10d multi .50 .25
1150 A470 20d multi 1.00 .50
1151 A470 24d multi 1.25 .60
Nos. 1148-1151 (4) 3.00 1.55

7th African Games, Johannesburg — A471

Stylized athletes and: 5d, Map of Africa, vert. 10d, South African flag.

1999, May 12 ***Perf. 13¼x14, 14x13¼***
1152 A471 5d multi .25 .20
1153 A471 10d multi .50 .25

A472

A473

1999, June 6 ***Perf. 13¼x14***
Rocks.
1154 A472 5d Gneiss .25 .20
1155 A472 20d Granite 1.00 .50
1156 A472 24d Schist 1.25 .60
Nos. 1154-1156 (3) 2.50 1.30

1999, July 12 ***Perf. 13x13¼***
1157 A473 5d multi .25 .20
Organization of African Unity, 35th summit.

A474

A475

1999, July 12 ***Perf. 13¼x14***
1158 A474 5d multi .25 .20
Organization of African Unity Convention on Refugees.

1999, July 22 ***Perf. 13x13¼***
1159 A475 5d Police Day .25 .20

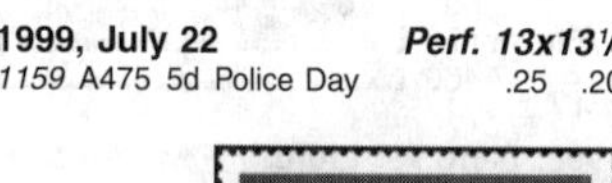

Intl. Year of Culture and Peace (in 2000) A476

1999, Sept. 14 **Litho.** ***Perf. 14***
1160 A476 5d multi .25 .20

Fish A477

Designs: 5d, Dentex dentex. 10d, Mullus surmuletus. 20d, Dentex gibbosus. 24d, Diplodus sargus.

1999, Sept. 15 ***Perf. 14x13¼***
1161 A477 5d multi .25 .20
1162 A477 10d multi .50 .25
1163 A477 20d multi 1.00 .50
1164 A477 24d multi 1.25 .60
Nos. 1161-1164 (4) 3.00 1.55

Civil Peace Referendum A478

1999, Sept. 16 ***Perf. 13¼x14***
1165 A478 5d multi .25 .20

UPU, 125th Anniv. A479

1999, Oct. 9 ***Perf. 14x13¼***
1166 A479 5d multi .25 .20

World Post Day A480

1999, Oct. 9 **Litho.** ***Perf. 14x13½***
1167 A480 5d multi .25 .20

Intl. Rural Women's Day A481

1999, Oct. 14 **Litho.** ***Perf. 14x13¼***
1168 A481 5d multi .25 .20

Algerian Revolution, 45th Anniv. — A482

Soldiers and : a, Helicopters, burning flag. b, Burning flag
Illustration reduced.

1999, Nov. 1 ***Perf. 13x13¼***
1169 A482 5d Pair, #a.-b. .50 .25

Folk Dances Type of 1994

1999, Dec. 15 ***Perf. 13¼x14***
1170 A406 5d Chaoui .25 .20
1171 A406 10d Targuie .50 .25
1172 A406 24d Mzab 1.25 .60
Nos. 1170-1172 (3) 2.00 1.05

Millennium — A483

No. 1173: a, Doves, UN emblem. b, Sun, plant, trees. c, Umbrella over wheat and corn plants. d, Microscope and flasks. e, Crane, ship, truck. f, Train, Concorde, satellite dish, satellite, Moon. g, Windmills. h, Globe, ballot box. i, Apollo 15 astronauts on Moon. j, Film, inkwell, musical instrument and notes.

No. 1174: a, Dove with olive branch. b, Hand, flora, fauna. c, Satellites, computer, map of Africa and Europe. d, Heart, staff of Aesculapius, Red Cross, Red Crescent. e, Stylized globe and arrows. f, Animals, film, violin, painting, book. g, Flame, sun, water. h, Hand holding plant. i, symbols of democracy. j, Satellite, planets, space shuttle, astronaut.

Sawtooth Die Cut 6¼ Vert.

2000, Jan. 19

Self-Adhesive

Booklet Stamps

1173 Bklt. pane of 10+2 labels 2.50
a.-j. A483 5d any single .25 .20
1174 Bklt. pane of 10+2 labels 2.50
a.-j. A483 5d any single .25 .20

Expo 2000, Hanover A485

2000, Feb. 16 **Litho.** ***Perf. 14x13¼***
1179 A485 5d multi .25 .20

2000 Summer Olympics, Sydney A486

2000, Mar. 22
1180 A486 24d multi 1.25 .60

Telethon 2000 — A487

2000, Apr. 8 ***Perf. 13¼x14***
1181 A487 5d multi .25 .20

Civil Concord A488

Designs: 5d, Dove, handshake, crowd, vert. 10d, Handshake, hands releasing dove. 20d, Handshake, doves, flowers. 24d, Doves, flowers, handshake, vert.

Perf. 11½x11¾, 11¾x11½

2000, Apr. 15
1182-1185 A488 Set of 4 3.00 1.50

National Library — A489

2000, Apr. 16 ***Perf. 13½x13***
1186 A489 5d multi .25 .20

Blood Donation — A490

2000, May 2 ***Perf. 13¼x14***
1187 A490 5d multi .25 .20

Tuareg Handicrafts A491

Background colors: 5d, Rose. 10d, Buff, vert.

2000, May 17 ***Perf. 14***
1188-1189 A491 Set of 2 .75 .40

Famous Men — A492

#1190, Mohammed Dib (b. 1920), writer. #1191, Mustapha Kateb (1920-89), actor. #1192, Ali Maachi (1927-58), musician. #1193, Mohamed Racim (1896-1975), artist.

2000, June 8 ***Perf. 13¼x13***
1190-1193 A492 10d Set of 4 2.00 1.00

Insects — A493

#1194, 5d, Hanneton. #1195, 5d, Anthrene. 10d, Vrillete du pain. 24d, Carabe.

2000, Sept. 20 ***Perf. 13¼x14***
1194-1197 A493 Set of 4 2.25 1.10

Roman Cinerary Urns Found at Tipasa — A494

2000, Oct. 18 **Litho.** ***Perf. 14***
1198-1200 A494 Set of 3, 5d, 10d, 24d 1.90 1.90

Orchids — A495

Designs: 5d, Limodorum abortivum. 10d, Orchis papilionacea. 24d, Orchis provincialis.

2000, Dec. 13 **Litho.** ***Perf. 14***
1201-1203 A495 Set of 3 1.00 1.00

Bird Type of 1998

Designs: No. 1204, 5d, Anser anser. No. 1205, 5d, Recurvirostra avosetta, vert. 10d, Botaurus stellaris, vert. 24d, Numenius arquata.

2001, Jan. 24
1204-1207 A464 Set of 4 1.10 1.10

Handicrafts — A496

Designs: 5d, Skampla, vert. 10d, Etagere. 24d, Mirror, vert.

2001, Feb. 21
1208-1210 A496 Set of 3 1.00 1.00

National Parks A497

Designs: 5d, Belezma, vert. 10d, Gouraya. 20d, Théniet el Had. 24d, El Kala, vert.

2001, Mar. 21 ***Perf. 13¼x14, 14x13¼***
1211-1214 A497 Set of 4 1.50 1.50

1st Intl. Colloquium on St. Augustine of Hippo — A498

Designs: 5d, Statue of St. Augustine (25x37mm). 24d, Mosaic.

Perf. 13¼x14, 13¼x13 (24d)

2001, Mar. 31
1215-1216 A498 Set of 2 .75 .75

Silver Coins — A499

Designs: 5d, 1830 Ryal boudjou. 10d, 1826 Double boudjou. 24d, 1771 Ryal drahem.

2001, Apr. 25 **Litho.** ***Perf. 13½x13***
1217-1219 A499 Set of 3 1.00 1.00

Natl. Scouting Day — A500

2001, May 27 **Litho.** ***Perf. 14***
1220 A500 5d multi .20 .20

Palestinian Intifada — A501

2001, June 2
1221 A501 5d multi .20 .20

Children's Games A502

Designs: No. 1222, 5d, Jacks. No. 1223, 5d, Hopscotch. No. 1224, 5d, Top spinning. No. 1225, 5d, Marbles.

2001, June 2
1222-1225 A502 Set of 4 .50 .50

Natl. Asthma Day — A503

2001, June 9
1226 A503 5d multi .20 .20

14th Mediterranean Games, Tunis, Tunisia — A504

Designs: No. 1227, 5d, Map, "50." No. 1228, 5d, Runners, emblem.

2001, July 25 **Litho.** ***Perf. 14***
1227-1228 A504 Set of 2 .30 .30

15th World Festival of Youth and Students — A505

2001, Aug. 8
1229 A505 5d multi .20 .20

Natl. Mujahedeen Day — A506

2001, Aug. 20 ***Perf. 13¼x14***
1230 A506 5d multi .20 .20

Intl. Teachers' Day — A507

2001, Oct. 6 **Litho.** ***Perf. 13¼x14***
1231 A507 5d multi .20 .20

Year of Dialogue Among Civilizations A508

2001, Oct. 9
1232 A508 5d multi .20 .20

Natl. Emigration Day — A509

2001, Oct. 17 ***Perf. 14x13¼***
1233 A509 5d multi .20 .20

19th Cent. Revolt Leaders — A510

Designs: No. 1234, 5d, Sheik El-Mokrani, 1871-73. No. 1235, 5d, Sheik Bouamama, 1881-1908.

2001, Nov. 1 ***Perf. 13¼x14***
1234-1235 A510 Set of 2 .30 .30

Jewelry From Aurès Region — A511

Designs: No. 1236, 5d, Fibula. No. 1237, 5d, Earring. 24d, Pendant.

2002, Jan. 23
1236-1238 A511 Set of 3 .90 .90

2002 World Cup Soccer Championships, Japan and Korea — A512

Designs: 5d, Goalie, ball, net, pagoda. 24d, Oriental man, ball, vert.

2002, Feb. 27 ***Perf. 14x13¼, 13¼x14***
1239-1240 A512 Set of 2 .75 .75

Ceasefire With French Forces, 40th Anniv. — A513

2002, Mar. 19 ***Perf. 13x13½***
1241 A513 5d multi .20 .20

Villages A514

Designs: No. 1242, 5d, Sidi-Ouali. No. 1243, 5d, Casbah of Ighzar.

2002, Apr. 17 **Litho.** ***Perf. 14x13¼***
1242-1243 A514 Set of 2 .25 .25

World Basketball Championships, Indianapolis A515

2002, May 15 ***Perf. 13¼x14***
1244 A515 5d multi .20 .20

Children's Day — A516

Children's art: No. 1245, 5d, Shown. No. 1246, 5d, Two girls, one waving.

2002, June 1 ***Perf. 14x13¼***
1245-1246 A516 Set of 2 .25 .25

Mohamed Temmam (1915-88), Artist — A517

Designs: No. 1247, 10d, Self-portrait. No. 1248, 10d, Tailor.

2002, June 8 ***Perf. 13x13¼***
1247-1248 A517 Set of 2 .50 .50

Independence, 40th Anniv. — A518

Designs: 5d, Emblem. 24d, People with flag.

2002, July 5 **Litho.** ***Perf. 14***
1249-1250 A518 Set of 2 .75 .75

Rocks and Minerals A519

Designs: No. 1251, 5d, Conglomerate rock. No. 1252, 5d, Galena. No. 1253, 5d, Calcite, vert. No. 1254, 5d, Feldspar, vert.

2002, July 24
1251-1254 A519 Set of 4 .50 .50

Lighthouses A520

Designs: 5d, Cherchell. 10d, Cap de Fer. 24d, Ile de Rachgoun.

2002, Sept. 11
1255-1257 A520 Set of 3 1.00 1.00

Reorganization of Postal Service — A521

2002, Oct. 9
1258 A521 5d multi .20 .20

Pottery — A522

Designs: No. 1259, 5d, Oil lamp. No. 1260, 5d, Jar with handles, Iraten. No. 1261, 5d, Jar, Miliana. No. 1262, 5d, Cooking pot and couscousier, Lakhdaria.

2002, Oct. 23
1259-1262 A522 Set of 4 .50 .50

SEMI-POSTAL STAMPS

Regular Issue of 1926 Surcharged in Black or Red

1927 **Unwmk.** ***Perf. 14x13½***
B1 A1 5c +5c bl grn .50 .50
B2 A1 10c +10c lilac .50 .50
B3 A2 15c +15c org brn .50 .50
B4 A2 20c +20c car rose .50 .50
B5 A2 25c +25c bl grn .50 .50
B6 A2 30c +30c lt bl .50 .50
B7 A2 35c +35c dp vio .55 .55
B8 A2 40c +40c ol grn .60 .60
B9 A3 50c +50c dp bl (R) .60 .60
a. Double surcharge 225.00 225.00
B10 A3 80c +80c red org .60 .60
B11 A4 1fr +1fr gray grn & red brn .65 .65
B12 A4 2fr +2fr Prus bl & blk brn 15.00 15.00
B13 A4 5fr +5fr red & vio 21.00 21.00
Nos. B1-B13 (13) 42.00 42.00

The surtax was for the benefit of wounded soldiers. Government officials speculated in this issue.

Railroad Terminal, Oran SP1

Ruins at Djemila SP2

Mosque of Sidi Abd-er-Rahman SP3

Designs: 10c+10c, Rummel Gorge, Constantine. 15c+15c, Admiralty Buildings, Algiers. 25c+25c, View of Algiers. 30c+30c, Trajan's Arch, Timgad. 40c+40c, Temple of the North, Djemila. 75c+75c Mansourah Minaret, Tlemcen. 1f+1f, View of Ghardaia. 1.50f+1.50f, View of Tolga. 2f+2f, Tuareg warriors. 3f+3f, Kasbah, Algiers.

1930 **Engr.** ***Perf. 12½***
B14 SP1 5c +5c orange 5.00 5.00
B15 SP1 10c +10c ol grn 5.00 5.00
B16 SP1 15c +15c dk brn 5.00 5.00
B17 SP1 25c +25c black 5.00 5.00
B18 SP1 30c +30c dk red 5.00 5.00
B19 SP1 40c +40c ap grn 5.00 5.00
B20 SP2 50c +50c ultra 5.00 5.00
B21 SP2 75c +75c red pur 5.00 5.00
B22 SP2 1fr +1fr org red 5.00 5.00
B23 SP2 1.50fr +1.50fr deep ultra 5.00 5.00
B24 SP2 2fr +2fr dk car 5.00 5.00
B25 SP2 3fr +3fr dk grn 5.00 5.00
B26 SP3 5fr +5fr grn & car 12.00 12.00
a. Center inverted 325.00
Nos. B14-B26 (13) 72.00 72.00

Centenary of the French occupation of Algeria. The surtax on the stamps was given to the funds for the celebration.

Nos. B14-B26 exist imperf. Value, set in pairs, $350.

Catalogue values for unused stamps in this section, from this point to the end of the section, are for Never Hinged items.

No. 102 Surcharged in Red

1938 ***Perf. 13***
B27 A6 65c +35c on 2.25fr yel grn .50 .50

20th anniversary of Armistice.

René Caillié, Charles Lavigerie and Henri Duveyrier SP14

1939 **Engr.**
B28 SP14 30c +20c dk bl grn 1.00 1.00
B29 SP14 90c +60c car rose 1.00 1.00
B30 SP14 2.25fr +75c ultra 10.00 10.00
B31 SP14 5fr +5fr brn blk 20.00 20.00
Nos. B28-B31 (4) 32.00 32.00

Pioneers of the Sahara.

French and Algerian Soldiers SP15

1940 **Photo.** ***Perf. 12***
B32 SP15 1fr +1fr bl & car .50 .40
B33 SP15 1fr +2fr brn rose & blk .50 .40
B34 SP15 1fr +4fr dp grn & red .70 .60
B35 SP15 1fr +9fr brn & car 1.00 1.00
Nos. B32-B35 (4) 2.70 2.40

The surtax was used to assist the families of mobilized men.

Type of Regular Issue, 1941 Surcharged in Carmine

1941 **Engr.** ***Perf. 13***
B36 A19 1fr +4fr black .20 .20

No. 135 Surcharged in Carmine

B37 A19 1fr +4fr dark blue .20 .20

The surtax was for National Relief.

No. 124 Surcharged in Black "+60c"

1942
B38 A7 90c +60c henna brn .20 .20
a. Double surcharge 55.00

The surtax was used for National Relief. The stamp could also be used as 1.50 francs for postage.

Mother and Child — SP16

1943, Dec. 1 Litho. *Perf. 12*

B39 SP16 50c +4.50fr brt pink .50 .25
B40 SP16 1.50fr +8.50fr lt grn .50 .25
B41 SP16 3fr +12fr dp bl .50 .25
B42 SP16 5fr +15fr vio brn .50 .25
Nos. B39-B42 (4) 2.00 1.00

The surtax was for the benefit of soldiers and prisoners of war.

Planes over Fields SP17

Unwmk.

1945, July 2 Engr. *Perf. 13*

B43 SP17 1.50fr +3.50fr lt ultra, red org & blk .25 .25

The surtax was for the benefit of Algerian airmen and their families.

France No. B192 Overprinted Type "a" of 1924 in Black

1945

B44 SP146 4fr +6fr dk vio brn .35 .20

The surtax was for war victims of the P.T.T.

Overprinted in Blue on Type of France, 1945

1945, Oct. 15

B45 SP150 2fr +3fr dk brn .40 .40

For Stamp Day.

Overprinted in Blue on Type of France, 1946

1946, June 29

B46 SP160 3fr +2fr red .45 .45

For Stamp Day.

Children Playing by Stream SP18

Girl — SP19

Athlete — SP20

Repatriated Prisoner and Bay of Algiers SP21

1946, Oct. 2 Engr. *Perf. 13*

B47 SP18 3fr +17fr dark grn .65 .65
B48 SP19 4fr +21fr red .65 .65
B49 SP20 8fr +27fr rose lilac 2.75 2.75
B50 SP21 10fr +35fr dark blue .70 .70
Nos. B47-B50 (4) 4.75 4.75

Type of France, 1947, Overprinted type "a" of 1924 in Carmine

1947, Mar. 15

B51 SP172 4.50fr +5.50fr dp ultra .40 .40

For Stamp Day.

Same on Type of France, 1947, Surcharged Like No. B36 in Carmine

1947, Nov. 13

B52 A173 5fr +10fr dk Prus grn .55 .40

Type of France, 1948, Overprinted in Dark Green—f

1948, Mar. 6

B53 SP176 6fr +4fr dk grn .55 .45

For Stamp Day.

Type of France, 1948, Overprinted type "a" of 1924 in Blue and New Value

1948, May

B54 A176 6fr +4fr red .55 .35

Battleship Richelieu and the Admiralty, Algiers SP22

Aircraft Carrier Arromanches — SP23

Unwmk.

1949, Jan. 15 Engr. *Perf. 13*

B55 SP22 10fr +15fr dp blue 4.50 4.50
B56 SP23 18fr +22fr red 4.50 4.50

The surtax was for naval charities.

Type of France, 1949, Overprinted in Blue—g

1949, Mar. 26

B57 SP180 15fr +5fr lilac rose 1.25 1.10

For Stamp Day, Mar. 26-27.

Type of France, 1950, Overprinted type "f" in Green

1950, Mar. 11

B58 SP183 12fr +3fr blk brn 1.25 1.10

For Stamp Day, Mar. 11-12.

Foreign Legionary — SP24

1950, Apr. 30

B59 SP24 15fr +5fr dk grn 1.10 1.10

Charles de Foucauld and Gen. J. F. H. Laperrine SP25

1950, Aug. 21 Unwmk. *Perf. 13*

B60 SP25 25fr +5fr brn ol & brn blk 3.00 3.00

50th anniversary of the presence of the French in the Sahara.

Emir Abd-el-Kader and Marshal T. R. Bugeaud — SP26

1950, Aug. 21

B61 SP26 40fr +10fr dk brn & blk brn 3.00 3.00

Unveiling of a monument to Emir Abd-el-Kader at Cacheron.

Col. Colonna d'Ornano and Fine Arts Museum, Algiers SP27

1951, Jan. 11

B62 SP27 15fr +5fr blk brn, vio brn & red brn .65 .65

Death of Col. Colonna d'Ornano, 10th anniv.

Type of France, 1951, Overprinted type "a" of 1924 in Black

1951, Mar. 10

B63 SP186 12fr +3fr brown .85 .85

For Stamp Day.

Type of France, 1952, Overprinted type "g" in Dark Blue

1952, Mar. 8 Unwmk. *Perf. 13*

B64 SP190 12fr +3fr dk bl 1.25 1.25

For Stamp Day.

French Military Medal — SP28

Unwmk.

1952, July 5 Engr. *Perf. 13*

B65 SP28 15fr +5fr grn, yel & brn 1.75 1.25

Centenary of the creation of the French Military Medal.

Type of France 1952, Surcharged type "g" and Surtax in Black

1952, Sept. 15

B66 A222 30fr +5fr dp ultra 1.40 1.25

10th anniv. of the defense of Bir-Hakeim.

View of El Oued SP29

Design: 12fr+3fr, View of Bou-Noura.

1952, Nov. 15 Engr.

B67 SP29 8fr +2fr ultra & red 1.25 1.10
B68 SP29 12fr +3fr red 2.25 1.90

The surtax was for the Red Cross.

Type of France, 1953, Overprinted type "a" of 1924 in Black

1953, Mar. 14 Engr.

B69 SP193 12fr +3fr purple 1.00 .90

For Stamp Day. Surtax for Red Cross.

Victory of Cythera — SP30

Unwmk.

1953, Dec. 18 Engr. *Perf. 13*

B70 SP30 15fr +5fr blk brn & brn .65 .60

The surtax was for army welfare work.

Type of France, 1954, Overprinted type "a" of 1924 in Black

1954, Mar. 20 Unwmk. *Perf. 13*

B71 SP196 12fr +3fr scarlet .75 .65

For Stamp Day.

Soldiers and Flags SP31

Foreign Legionary SP32

1954, Mar. 27

B72 SP31 15fr +5fr dk brn .65 .50

The surtax was for old soldiers.

1954, Apr. 30

B73 SP32 15fr +5fr dk grn 1.25 1.00

The surtax was for the welfare fund of the Foreign Legion.

Nurses and Verdun Hospital, Algiers SP33

15fr+5fr, J. H. Dunant & ruins at Djemila.

1954, Oct. 30

B74 SP33 12fr +3fr indigo & red 2.00 1.75
B75 SP33 15fr +5fr pur & red 2.50 2.00

The surtax was for the Red Cross.

Earthquake Victims and Ruins — SP34

First Aid — SP35

Design: #B80-B81, Removing wounded.

1954, Dec. 5

B76 SP34 12fr +4fr dk vio brn	1.00	1.00
B77 SP34 15fr +5fr dp bl	1.00	1.00
B78 SP35 18fr +6fr lil rose	1.75	1.75
B79 SP35 20fr +7fr violet	1.75	1.75
B80 SP35 25fr +8fr rose brn	2.00	2.00
B81 SP35 30fr +10fr brt bl grn	2.00	2.00
Nos. B76-B81 (6)	9.50	9.50

The surtax was for victims of the Orleansville earthquake disaster of September 1954.

Type of France, 1955, Overprinted type "a" of 1924 in Black

1955, Mar. 19

B82 SP199 12fr +3fr dp ultra 1.00 1.00

For Stamp Day, Mar. 19-20.

Women and Children SP36

Cancer Victim SP37

1955, Nov. 5

B83 SP36 15fr +5fr blue & indigo .60 .60

The tax was for war victims.

1956, Mar. 3 Unwmk. *Perf. 13*

B84 SP37 15fr +5fr dk brn .75 .50

The surtax was for the Algerian Cancer Society. The male figure in the design is Rodin's "Age of Bronze."

Type of France, 1956, Overprinted type "a" of 1924 in Black

1956, Mar.

B85 SP202 12fr +3fr red .90 .60

For Stamp Day, Mar. 17-18.

Foreign Legion Rest Home SP38

1956, Apr. 29

B86 SP38 15fr +5fr dk bl grn .90 .90

Honoring the French Foreign Legion.

Type of France, 1957, Overprinted type "f" in Black

1957, Mar. 16 Engr. *Perf. 13*

B87 SP204 12fr +3fr dull purple .70 .70

For Stamp Day and to honor the Maritime Postal Service.

Fennec SP39

Design: 15fr+5fr, Stork flying over roofs.

1957, Apr. 6

B88 SP39 12fr +3fr red brn & red	3.75	3.75
B89 SP39 15fr +5fr sepia & red	3.75	3.75

The surtax was for the Red Cross.

Type of Regular Issue, 1956 Surcharged in Dark Blue

1957, June 18

B90 A53 15fr +5fr scar & rose red .95 .95

17th anniv. of General de Gaulle's appeal for a Free France.

The Giaour, by Delacroix — SP40

On the Banks of the Oued, by Fromentin SP41

Design: 35fr+10fr, Dancer, by Chasseriau.

Unwmk.

1957, Nov. 30 Engr. *Perf. 13*

B91 SP40 15fr +5fr dk car	3.75	3.75
B92 SP41 20fr +5fr grn	3.75	3.75
B93 SP40 35fr +10fr dk bl	3.75	3.75
Nos. B91-B93 (3)	11.25	11.25

Surtax for army welfare organizations.

Type of France Overprinted type "f" in Blue

1958, Mar. 15 Unwmk. *Perf. 13*

B94 SP206 15fr +5fr org brn .75 .75

For Stamp Day.

Bird-of-Paradise Flower — SP42

Arms & Marshal's Baton — SP43

1958, June 14 Engr. *Perf. 13*

B95 SP42 20fr +5fr grn, org & vio 2.25 2.25

The surtax was for Child Welfare.

1958, July 20

B96 SP43 20fr +5fr ultra, car & grn 1.00 1.00

Marshal de Lattre Foundation.

Independent State

Clasped Hands, Wheat, Olive Branch — SP44

Burning Books — SP45

1963, May 27 Unwmk. *Perf. 13*

B97 SP44 50c +20c sl grn, brt grn & car .80 .60

Surtax for the Natl. Solidarity Fund.

1965, June 7 Engr. *Perf. 13*

B98 SP45 20c +5c ol grn, red & blk .50 .40

Burning of the Library of Algiers, 6/7/62.

Soldiers and Woman Comforting Wounded Soldier — SP46

1966, Aug. 20 Photo. *Perf. 11½*

B99 SP46 30c +10c multi	1.25	.70
B100 SP46 95c +10c multi	1.75	1.10

Day of the Moudjahid (Moslem volunteers).

Red Crescent, Boy and Girl — SP47

1967, May 27 Litho. *Perf. 14*

B101 SP47 30c +10c brt grn, brn & car .45 .35

Algerian Red Crescent Society.

Flood Victims — SP48

Design: 95c+25c, Rescuing flood victims.

1969, Nov. 15 Typo. *Perf. 10½*

B102 SP48 30c +10c multi .45 .35

Litho.

B103 SP48 95c +25c multi 1.00 .65

Red Crescent Flag SP49

1971, May 17 Engr. *Perf. 10½*

B104 SP49 30c +10c slate grn & car .35 .30

Algerian Red Crescent Society.

Intl. Children's Day — SP50

1989, June 1 Litho. *Perf. 10½x11*

B105 SP50 1d +30c multi .65 .50

Surtax for child welfare.

Solidarity with Palestinians SP51

1990, Dec. 9 Litho. *Perf. 10½x11*

B106 SP51 1d +30c multi .50 .30

Natl. Solidarity with Education SP52

1995, Sept. 20 Litho. *Perf. 13x14*

B107 SP52 3d +50c multi .50 .25

Red Crescent Society SP53

1998, May 2 Litho. *Perf. 13x13¼*

B108 SP53 5d +1d multi .30 .20

World Children's Day SP54

1998, June 1 *Perf. 14x13½, 13½x14*

B109 SP54 5d +1d shown	.30	.20
B110 SP54 5d +1d Flower, child, adult, vert.	.30	.20

Flood Victim Relief — SP55

2001, Dec. 24 Litho. *Perf. 13¼x14*

B111 SP55 5d +5d multi .25 .25

AIR POST STAMPS

Catalogue values for unused stamps in this section are for Never Hinged items.

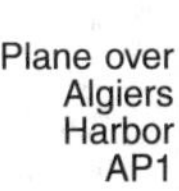

Plane over Algiers Harbor AP1

Two types of 20fr:

Type I - Monogram "F" without serifs. "POSTE" indented 3mm.

Type II - Monogram "F" with serifs. "POSTE" indented 4½mm.

Unwmk.

1946, June 20 Engr. *Perf. 13*

C1	AP1	5fr red	.25	.20
C2	AP1	10fr deep blue	.25	.20
C3	AP1	15fr deep green	.45	.20
C4	AP1	20fr brown (II)	.25	.20
C4A	AP1	20fr brown (I)	100.00	65.00
C5	AP1	25fr violet	.55	.20
C6	AP1	40fr gray black	.75	.20
		Nos. C1-C4,C5-CC6 (6)	2.50	1.20

For surcharges see Nos. C7, CB1-CB2.

No. C1 Surcharged in Black

1947, Jan. 18

C7 AP1 (4.50fr) on 5fr red .25 .20

Storks over Mosque — AP2

Plane over Village AP3

1949-53

C8	AP2	50fr green	2.00	.25
C9	AP3	100fr brown	1.75	.25
C10	AP2	200fr bright red	4.00	3.00
C11	AP3	500fr ultra ('53)	14.00	10.00
		Nos. C8-C11 (4)	21.75	13.50

Beni Bahdel Dam — AP4

1957, July 1 Unwmk. *Perf. 13*

C12 AP4 200fr dark red 3.25 .75

Caravelle over Ghardaia — AP5

Designs: 2d, Caravelle over El Oued. 5d, Caravelle over Tipasa.

1967-68 Engr. *Perf. 13*

C13	AP5	1d lil, org brn & emer	1.00	.50
C14	AP5	2d brt bl, org brn & emer	2.50	1.25
C15	AP5	5d brt bl, grn & org brn ('68)	6.00	2.75
		Nos. C13-C15 (3)	9.50	4.50

Plane over Casbah, Algiers — AP6

Designs: 3d, Plane over Oran. 4d, Plane over Rhumel Gorge.

1971-72 Photo. *Perf. 12½*

C16	AP6	2d grysh blk & multi	1.60	.80
C17	AP6	3d violet & blk	2.50	1.40
C18	AP6	4d blk & multi	3.25	1.75
		Nos. C16-C18 (3)	7.35	3.95

Issued: 2d, 6/12/71; 3d, 4d, 2/28/72.

Storks and Plane — AP7

1979, Mar. 24 Photo. *Perf. 11½*

C19 AP7 10d multi 4.00 1.60

Plane Approaching Coastal City — AP8

1991, Apr. 26 Litho. *Perf. 13½*

C20	AP8	10d shown	3.00	1.50
C21	AP8	20d Plane over city	6.00	3.00

Plane Over Djidjelli Corniche — AP9

1993, Sept. 25 Engr. *Perf. 13½x14*

C22 AP9 50d blue, grn & brn 6.25 3.25

AIR POST SEMI-POSTAL STAMPS

Catalogue values for unused stamps in this section are for Never Hinged items.

No. C2 Surcharged in Carmine

1947, June 18 *Perf. 13*

CB1 AP1 10fr +10fr deep blue .75 .60

7th anniv. of Gen. Charles de Gaulle's speech in London, June 18, 1940.

No. C1 Surcharged in Blue

1948, June 18

CB2 AP1 5fr +10fr red .70 .60

8th anniv. of Gen. Charles de Gaulle's speech in London, June 18, 1940.

Monument, Clock Tower and Plane — SPAP1

1949, Nov. 10 Engr. Unwmk.

CB3 SPAP1 15fr +20fr dk brn 3.50 3.50

25th anniv. of Algeria's 1st postage stamps.

POSTAGE DUE STAMPS

D1

D2

Perf. 14x13½

1926-27 Typo. Unwmk.

J1	D1	5c light blue	.20	.20
J2	D1	10c dk brn	.20	.20
J3	D1	20c olive grn	.20	.20
J4	D1	25c car rose	.35	.35
J5	D1	30c rose red	.20	.20
J6	D1	45c blue grn	.50	.50
J7	D1	50c brn vio	.20	.20
J8	D1	60c green ('27)	1.25	.30
J9	D1	1fr red brn, *straw*	.20	.20
J10	D1	2fr lil rose ('27)	.20	.20
J11	D1	3fr deep blue ('27)	.20	.20
		Nos. J1-J11 (11)	3.70	2.75

See Nos. J25-J26, J28-J32. For surcharges, see Nos. J18-J20.

1926-27

J12	D2	1c olive grn	.20	.20
J13	D2	10c violet	.40	.20
J14	D2	30c bister	.25	.20
J15	D2	60c dull red	.20	.20
J16	D2	1fr brt vio ('27)	11.00	1.75
J17	D2	2fr lt bl ('27)	7.50	.65
		Nos. J12-J17 (6)	19.55	3.20

See note below France No. J51.
For surcharges, see Nos. J21-J24.

Stamps of 1926 Surcharged

1927

J18	D1	60c on 20c olive grn	.90	.25
J19	D1	2fr on 45c blue grn	1.10	.65
J20	D1	3fr on 25c car rose	.75	.25
		Nos. J18-J20 (3)	2.75	1.15

Recouvrement Stamps of 1926 Surcharged

1927-32

J21	D2	10c on 30c bis ('32)	2.25	1.50
J22	D2	1fr on 1c olive grn	.65	.60
J23	D2	1fr on 60c dl red ('32)	11.00	.25
J24	D2	2fr on 10c violet	6.25	6.25
		Nos. J21-J24 (4)	20.15	8.60

Catalogue values for unused stamps in this section, from this point to the end of the section, are for Never Hinged items.

Type of 1926, Without "R F"

1942 Typo. *Perf. 14x13½*

J25	D1	30c dark red	.20	.20
J26	D1	2fr magenta	.20	.20

Type of 1926 Surcharged in Red

1944 *Perf. 14x13½*

J27 A2 50c on 20c yel grn .20 .20

- *a.* Inverted surcharge 3.50
- *b.* Double surcharge 9.50

No. J27 was issued precanceled only. See note after No. 32.

Type of 1926

1944 Litho. *Perf. 12*

J28	D1	1.50fr brt rose lilac	.30	.20
J29	D1	2fr greenish blue	.30	.20
J30	D1	5fr rose carmine	.30	.20
		Nos. J28-J30 (3)	.90	.60

Type of 1926

1947 Typo. *Perf. 14x13½*

J32 D1 5fr green .60 .45

France Nos. J80-J81 Overprinted Type "a" of 1925 in Carmine or Black

1947

J33	D5	10c sepia (C)	.20	.20
J34	D5	30c bright red violet	.20	.20

D3

Perf. 14x13

1947-55 Unwmk. Engr.

J35	D3	20c red	.20	.20
J36	D3	60c ultra	.25	.20
J37	D3	1fr dk org brn	.20	.20
J38	D3	1.50fr dull green	.40	.40
J39	D3	2fr red	.20	.20
J40	D3	3fr violet	.20	.20
J41	D3	5fr ultra ('49)	.25	.20
J42	D3	6fr black	.25	.20

J43	D3	10fr	lil rose	.35	.20
J44	D3	15fr	ol grn ('55)	.45	.45
J45	D3	20fr	brt grn	.25	.20
J46	D3	30fr	red org ('55)	.65	.40
J47	D3	50fr	indigo ('51)	1.25	.95
J48	D3	100fr	brt bl ('53)	5.50	3.50
			Nos. J35-J48 (14)	10.40	7.50

Independent State

France Nos. J93-J97 Overprinted "EA" in Black like Nos. 286-290

Perf. 14x13½

1962, July 2 Typo. Unwmk.

Handstamped Overprint

J49	D6	5c	bright pink	2.25	1.60
J50	D6	10c	red orange	2.25	1.40
J51	D6	20c	olive bister	2.25	1.40
J52	D6	50c	dark green	3.00	2.75
J53	D6	1fr	deep green	4.25	4.00
			Nos. J49-J53 (5)	14.00	11.15

Typographed Overprint

J49a	D6	5c	bright pink	6.00	6.00
J50a	D6	10c	red orange	6.00	6.00
J51a	D6	20c	olive bister	5.50	5.50
J52a	D6	50c	dark green	14.00	14.00
J53a	D6	1fr	deep green	25.00	25.00
			Nos. J49a-J53a (5)	56.50	56.50

See note after No. 290.

Scales — D4

Grain — D5

1963, June 25 ***Perf. 14x13½***

J54	D4	5c	car rose & blk	.20	.20
J55	D4	10c	olive & car	.20	.20
J56	D4	20c	ultra & blk	.20	.20
J57	D4	50c	bister brn & grn	.50	.30
J58	D4	1fr	lilac & org	.90	.50
			Nos. J54-J58 (5)	2.00	1.40

#J58 Surcharged with New Value & 3 Bars

1968, Mar. 28 Typo. ***Perf. 14x13½***

J59	D4	60c	on 1fr lilac & org	.40	.30

1972-93 Litho. ***Perf. 13½x14***

J60	D5	10c	bister	.20	.20
J61	D5	20c	deep brown	.20	.20
J62	D5	40c	orange	.20	.20
J63	D5	50c	dk vio blue	.20	.20
J64	D5	80c	dk olive gray	.40	.20
J65	D5	1d	green	.45	.25
J66	D5	2d	blue	.95	.40
J67	D5	3d	violet	.45	.20
J68	D5	4d	lilac rose	.60	.30
			Nos. J60-J68 (9)	3.65	2.15

Issued: 3d, 4d, 1/21/93; others, 10/21/72.

NEWSPAPER STAMPS

Nos. 1 and 33 Surcharged in Red

1924-26 Unwmk. ***Perf. 14x13½***

P1	A16	½c	on 1c dk gray	.20	.20
a.			Triple surcharge	87.50	
P2	A1	½c	on 1c olive ('26)	.20	.20

ALLENSTEIN

'a-lən-ˌshtin

LOCATION — In East Prussia
AREA — 4,457 sq. mi.
POP. — 540,000 (estimated 1920)
CAPITAL — Allenstein

Allenstein, a district of East Prussia, held a plebiscite in 1920 under the Versailles Treaty, voting to join Germany rather than Poland. Later that year, Allenstein became part of the German Republic.

100 Pfennig = 1 Mark

Stamps of Germany, 1906-20, Overprinted

Perf. 14, 14½, 14x14½, 14½x14

1920 Wmk. 125

1	A16	5pf	green	.20	*.30*
2	A16	10pf	carmine	.20	*.30*
3	A22	15pf	dk vio	.20	*.30*
4	A22	15pf	vio brn	4.50	*5.50*
5	A16	20pf	bl vio	.20	*.50*
6	A16	30pf	org & blk, *buff*	.25	*.30*
7	A16	40pf	lake & blk	.20	*.30*
8	A16	50pf	pur & blk, *buff*	.20	*.30*
9	A16	75pf	grn & blk	.20	*.30*
10	A17	1m	car rose	.55	.55
a.			Double overprint	—	—
11	A17	1.25m	green	.50	*1.10*
a.			Double overprint	—	—
12	A17	1.50m	yel brn	.50	*1.10*
13	A21	2.50m	lilac rose	1.00	*5.25*
14	A19	3m	blk vio	1.25	1.25
a.			Double overprint	250.00	*925.00*
			Never hinged	500.00	
b.			Inverted overprint	—	—
			Nos. 1-14 (14)	9.95	*17.35*
			Set, never hinged	18.00	

The 5pf brown (Germany #118), 10pf orange (#119), 20pf green (#121), 30pf blue (#123) and 40pf (#124) exist with this overprint but were not regularly issued. Value, each: $60 hinged, $120 never hinged.

Overprinted

15	A16	5pf	green	.20	*.30*
16	A16	10pf	carmine	.20	*.30*
17	A22	15pf	dark vio	.20	*.35*
18	A22	15pf	vio brn	17.50	*24.00*
19	A16	20pf	blue vio	.20	*.35*
20	A16	30pf	org & blk, *buff*	.30	.30
21	A16	40pf	lake & blk	.30	.30
22	A16	50pf	pur & blk, *buff*	.20	*.30*
23	A16	75pf	grn & blk	.20	*.45*
24	A17	1m	car rose	.55	.55
a.			Inverted overprint	500.00	*650.00*
			Never hinged	650.00	
25	A17	1.25m	green	.65	*1.10*
26	A17	1.50m	yel brn	.65	*1.10*
27	A21	2.50m	lilac rose	1.10	*2.75*
28	A19	3m	blk vio	.85	1.00
a.			Inverted overprint	325.00	*775.00*
			Never hinged	575.00	
b.			Double overprint	160.00	*475.00*
			Never hinged	475.00	
			Nos. 15-28 (14)	23.10	*33.15*
			Set, never hinged	47.50	

The 40pf carmine rose (Germany No. 124) exists with this oval overprint, but it is doubtful whether it was regularly issued. Value $85 hinged, $175 never hinged.

ANDORRA, SPANISH ADMIN.

an-'dor-ə

LOCATION — On the southern slope of the Pyrenees Mountains between France and Spain.
GOVT. — Co-principality
AREA — 179 sq. mi.
POP. — 72,766 (July 1, 1996)
CAPITAL — Andorra la Vella

Andorra is subject to the joint control of France and the Spanish Bishop of Urgel and pays annual tribute to both. The country has no monetary unit of its own, the peseta and franc both being in general use.

100 Centimos = 1 Peseta
100 Centimes = 1 Franc
100 Cents = 1 Euro (2002)

Catalogue values for unused stamps in the Spanish Administration for this country are for Never Hinged items, beginning with Scott 50 in the regular postage section and Scott C2 in the airpost section; for the French Administration of this country, Never Hinged items begin at Scott 78 for regular postage, Scott B1 for the semi-postal section, Scott C1 for the airpost section, and Scott J21 for the postage due section.

A majority of the Spanish Andorra stamps issued to about 1950 are poorly centered. The very fine examples that are valued will be somewhat off center. Very poorly centered examples (perfs cutting design) sell for less. Well centered stamps are scarce and sell for approximately twice the values shown (#1-24, E1-E3), or 50% more (#25-49, E4-E5).

Stamps of Spain, 1922-26, Overprinted in Red or Black

Perf. 13½x12½, 12½x11½, 14

1928 Unwmk.

1	A49	2c	olive green	.35	.30

Control Numbers on Back

2	A49	5c	car rose (Bk)	.45	.35
3	A49	10c	green	.45	.35
4	A49	15c	slate blue	2.00	2.00
5	A49	20c	violet	2.25	2.00
6	A49	25c	rose red (Bk)	2.00	2.00
7	A49	30c	black brown	10.00	8.25
8	A49	40c	deep blue	10.00	5.75
9	A49	50c	orange (Bk)	10.00	7.50
10	A49a	1p	blue blk	12.00	*12.50*
11	A49a	4p	lake (Bk)	80.00	*90.00*
12	A49a	10p	brown (Bk)	140.00	140.00
			Nos. 1-12 (12)	269.50	271.00
			Set, never hinged	425.00	

Counterfeit overprints exist.

#1-12 perf 14 are worth much more. See the *Scott Classic Specialized Catalogue.*

La Vall — A1

St. Juan de Caselles — A2

St. Julia de Loria — A3

St. Coloma — A4

General Council — A5

1929, Nov. 25 Engr. ***Perf. 14***

13	A1	2c	olive green	1.00	.50

Control Numbers on Back

14	A2	5c	carmine lake	2.25	1.25
15	A3	10c	yellow green	2.25	2.50
16	A4	15c	slate green	2.25	2.50
17	A3	20c	violet	2.25	2.50
18	A4	25c	carmine rose	5.50	5.50
19	A1	30c	olive brown	100.00	100.00
20	A2	40c	dark blue	4.50	2.75
21	A3	50c	deep orange	4.50	3.50
22	A5	1p	slate	11.00	11.00
23	A5	4p	deep rose	65.00	65.00
24	A5	10p	bister brown	75.00	*85.00*
			Nos. 13-24 (12)	275.50	282.00
			Set, never hinged	375.00	

Nos. 13-24 exist imperforate. Value, $700.

1931-38

Perf. 11½

13a	A1	2c		4.00	1.25

Control Numbers on Back

14a	A2	5c		7.00	5.25
15a	A3	10c		7.00	3.00
16a	A4	15c		20.00	16.00
17a	A3	20c		9.00	7.00
18a	A4	25c		6.50	4.00
19a	A1	30c	('33)	100.00	55.00
20a	A2	40c	('35)	10.00	8.00
22a	A5	1p	('38)	25.00	16.00
			Nos. 13a-22a (9)	188.50	115.50
			Set, never hinged	250.00	

Without Control Numbers

1936-43 ***Perf. 11½x11***

25	A1	2c	red brown ('37)	2.00	1.00
26	A2	5c	dark brown	2.00	1.00
27	A3	10c	blue green	9.00	4.00
a.			10c yellow green	72.50	60.00
			Never hinged	92.50	
28	A4	15c	blue green ('37)	4.00	3.50
a.			15c yellow green	5.75	3.75
29	A3	20c	violet	6.00	3.50
30	A4	25c	deep rose ('37)	2.00	*3.00*
31	A1	30c	carmine	3.00	2.75
31A	A2	40c	dark blue	*600.00*	—
			Never hinged	850.00	
32	A1	45c	rose red ('37)	3.00	1.75
33	A3	50c	deep orange	7.00	4.00
34	A1	60c	deep blue ('37)	5.00	3.50
34A	A5	1p	slate	1,500.	—
			Never hinged	2,250.	
35	A5	4p	deep rose ('43)	35.00	35.00
36	A5	10p	bister brn ('43)	35.00	*45.00*
			Nos. 25-31,32-34,35-36 (12)	113.00	108.00
			Set, never hinged	160.00	

Exist imperforate. Value hinged, $175.

Edelweiss — A6

Provost — A7

Coat of Arms — A8

Plaza of Ordino — A9

Chapel of Meritxell — A10

Map — A11

1948-53 Unwmk. Photo. ***Perf. 12½***

37	A6	2c	dark ol grn ('51)	.40	.70
38	A6	5c	deep org ('53)	.40	.70
39	A6	10c	deep blue ('53)	.45	.70

Engr. ***Perf. 9½x10***

40	A7	20c	brown vio	6.25	2.75
41	A7	25c	org, perf. 12½ ('53)	4.50	2.10
42	A8	30c	dk slate grn	8.00	3.25
43	A9	50c	deep green	9.50	4.75
44	A10	75c	dark blue	14.00	4.75
45	A9	90c	dp car rose	6.25	3.75
46	A10	1p	brt orange ver	9.50	4.75
47	A8	1.35p	dk blue vio	6.25	5.75

Perf. 10

48	A11	4p ultra ('53)	9.50	9.50
49	A11	10p dk vio brn ('51)	20.00	9.50
		Nos. 37-49 (13)	95.00	52.95
		Set, never hinged	125.00	

Catalogue values for unused stamps in this section, from this point to the end of the section, are for Never Hinged items.

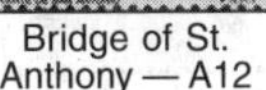
Bridge of St. Anthony — A12

Madonna of Meritxell, 8th Century — A13

Designs: 70c, Aynos pasture. 1p, View of Canillo. 2p, St. Coloma. 2.50p, Arms of Andorra. 3p, Old Andorra, horiz. 5p, View of Ordino, horiz.

1963-64 Unwmk. Engr. *Perf. 13*

50	A12	25c dk gray & sepia	.20	.20
51	A12	70c dk sl grn & brn blk	.20	.20
52	A12	1p slate & dull pur	.25	.20
53	A12	2p violet & dull pur	.25	.20
54	A12	2.50p rose claret	.55	.50
55	A12	3p blk & grnsh gray	1.00	.50
56	A12	5p dk brn & choc	1.60	1.00
57	A13	6p sepia & car	2.50	1.00
		Nos. 50-57 (8)	6.55	3.80

Issued: 25c-2p, 7/20/63; 2.50p-6p, 2/29/64.

Narcissus — A14

Encamp Valley — A15

1966, June 10 Engr. *Perf. 13*

58	A14	50c shown	.20	.20
59	A14	1p Pinks	.20	.20
60	A14	5p Jonquils	.80	.50
61	A14	10p Hellebore	1.90	.60
		Nos. 58-61 (4)	3.10	1.50

Common Design Types pictured following the introduction.

Europa Issue 1972

Common Design Type

1972, May 2 Photo. *Perf. 13*

Size: 25½x38mm

62	CD15	8p multicolored	110.00	62.50

1972, July 4 Photo. *Perf. 13*

Tourist publicity: 1.50p, Massana (village). 2p, Skiing on De La Casa Pass. 5p, Pessons Lake, horiz.

63	A15	1p multicolored	.20	.20
64	A15	1.50p multicolored	.55	.40
65	A15	2p multicolored	1.40	.40
66	A15	5p multicolored	1.75	.75
		Nos. 63-66 (4)	3.90	1.75

Butterfly Stroke A16

Design: 2p, Volleyball, vert.

1972, Oct. Photo. *Perf. 13*

67	A16	2p lt blue & multi	.20	.20
68	A16	5p multicolored	.25	.20

20th Olympic Games, Munich, 8/26-9/11.

St. Anthony Singers A17

1972, Dec. 5 Photo. *Perf. 13*

69	A17	1p shown	.20	.20
70	A17	1.50p Les Caramelles (boys' choir)	.20	.20
71	A17	2p Nativity scene	.20	.20
72	A17	5p Man holding giant cigar, vert	.40	.20
73	A17	8p Hermit of Meritxell, vert	.55	.30
74	A17	15p Marratxa dancers	1.25	.45
		Nos. 69-74 (6)	2.80	1.55

Andorran customs. No. 71 is for Christmas.

Europa Issue 1973

Common Design Type and

Symbol of Unity A18

1973, Apr. 30 Photo. *Perf. 13*

75	A18	2p ultra, red & blk	.20	.20

Size: 37x25mm

76	CD16	8p tan, red & blk	.65	.40

Nativity — A19

Virgin of Ordino — A20

Christmas: 5p, Adoration of the Kings. Designs are from altar panels of Meritxell Parish Church.

1973, Dec. 14 Photo. *Perf. 13*

77	A19	2p multicolored	.20	.20
78	A19	5p multicolored	.50	.35

1974, Apr. 29 Photo. *Perf. 13*

Europa: 8p, Les Banyes Cross.

79	A20	2p multicolored	.90	.30
80	A20	8p slate & brt blue	2.75	.85

Cupboard — A21

Crowns of Virgin and Child of Roser — A22

1974, July 30 Photo. *Perf. 13*

81	A21	10p multicolored	1.25	.40
82	A22	25p dark red & multi	3.25	1.25

UPU Monument, Bern A23

1974, Oct. 9 Photo. *Perf. 13*

83	A23	15p multicolored	1.10	.50

Centenary of Universal Postal Union.

Nativity A24

Christmas: 5p, Adoration of the Kings.

1974, Dec. 4 Photo. *Perf. 13*

84	A24	2p multicolored	.40	.20
85	A24	5p multicolored	1.40	.40

Mail Delivery, Andorra, 19th Century — A25

12th Century Painting, Ordino Church — A26

1975, Apr. 4 Photo. *Perf. 13*

86	A25	3p multicolored	.20	.20

Espana 75 Intl. Philatelic Exhibition, Madrid, 4/4-13.

1975, Apr. 28 Photo. *Perf. 13*

Design: 12p, Christ in Glory, 12th century Romanesque painting, Ordino church.

87	A26	3p multicolored	1.00	.30
88	A26	12p multicolored	2.25	.70

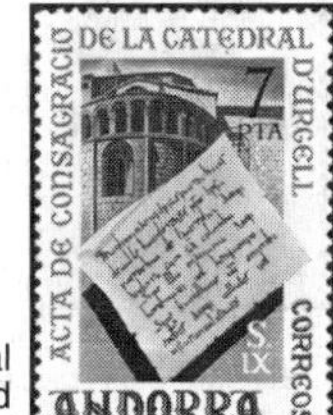
Urgel Cathedral and Document — A27

1975, Oct. 4 Photo. *Perf. 13*

89	A27	7p multicolored	.75	.60

Millennium of consecration of Urgel Cathedral, and Literary Festival 1975.

Nativity, Ordino A28

Christmas: 7p, Adoration of the Kings, Ordino.

1975, Dec. 3 Photo. *Perf. 13*

90	A28	3p multicolored	.20	.20
91	A28	7p multicolored	.30	.25

Caldron and CEPT Emblem — A29

Slalom and Montreal Olympic Emblem — A30

Europa: 12p, Chest and CEPT emblem.

1976, May 3 Photo. *Perf. 13*

92	A29	3p bister & multi	.20	.20
93	A29	12p yel & multi, horioz.	.40	.20

1976, July 9 Photo. *Perf. 13*

Design: 15p, One-man canoe and Montreal Olympic emblem, horiz.

94	A30	7p multicolored	.20	.20
95	A30	15p multicolored	.30	.25

21st Olympic Games, Montreal, Canada, July 17-Aug. 1.

Nativity A31

Christmas: 25p, Adoration of the Kings. Wall paintings in La Massana Church.

1976, Dec. 7 Photo. *Perf. 13*

96	A31	3p multicolored	.20	.20
97	A31	25p multicolored	.30	.25

View of Ansalonge — A32

Europa: 12p, Xuclar, valley, mountains.

1977, May 2 Litho. *Perf. 13*

98	A32	3p multicolored	.20	.20
99	A32	12p multicolored	.35	.25

Cross of Terme — A33

Map of Post Offices — A34

Christmas: 12p, Church of St. Miguel d'Engolasters.

1977, Dec. 2 Photo. *Perf. 13x12½*

100	A33	5p multicolored	.25	.25
101	A33	12p multicolored	.55	.40

Souvenir Sheet

Designs: 10p, Mail delivery. 20p, Post Office, 1928. 25p, Andorran coat of arms.

1978, Mar. 31 Photo. *Perf. 13x13½*

102	Sheet of 4	.75	.75
a.	A34 5p multicolored	.20	.20
b.	A34 10p multicolored	.20	.20
c.	A34 20p multicolored	.20	.20
d.	A34 25p multicolored	.25	.25

Spanish postal service in Andorra, 50th anniv.

La Vall — A35

Europa: 12p, St. Juan de Caselles.

1978, May 2 *Perf. 13*

103 A35 5p multicolored .20 .20
104 A35 12p multicolored .20 .20

Crown, Bishop's Mitre and Staff A36

1978, Sept. 24 Photo. *Perf. 13*

105 A36 5p brown, car & yel .25 .20

700th anniversary of the signing of treaty establishing Co-Principality of Andorra.

Holy Family — A37

Christmas: 25p, Adoration of the Kings. Both designs after frescoes in the Church of St. Mary d'Encamp.

1978, Dec. 5 Photo. *Perf. 13*

106 A37 5p multicolored .20 .20
107 A37 25p multicolored .30 .20

Young Woman — A38

1979, Feb. 14 Photo. *Perf. 13*

Designs: 5p, Young man. 12p, Bridegroom and bride riding mule.

108 A38 3p multicolored .20 .20
109 A38 5p multicolored .20 .20
110 A38 12p multicolored .20 .20
Nos. 108-110 (3) .60 .60

Old Mail Truck A39

Europa: 12p, Stampless covers of 1846 & 1854.

1979, Apr. 30 Engr. *Perf. 13*

111 A39 5p yel grn & dk blue .20 .20
112 A39 12p dk red & violet .20 .20

Children Holding Hands A40

1979, Oct. 18 Photo. *Perf. 13*

113 A40 19p multicolored .25 .20

International Year of the Child.

St. Coloma's Church — A41

Christmas: 25p, Agnus Dei roundel, St. Coloma's Church.

1979, Nov. 28 Photo. *Perf. 13½*

114 A41 8p multicolored .20 .20
115 A41 25p multicolored .30 .25

Bishop Pere d'Arg A42

Bishops of Urgel: 5p, Josep Caixal. 13p, Joan Benlloch.

1979, Dec. 27 Engr.

116 A42 1p dk blue & brown .20 .20
117 A42 5p rose lake & purple .20 .20
118 A42 13p brown & dk green .20 .20
Nos. 116-118 (3) .60 .60

See Nos. 132-133, 159, 175, C4.

Antoni Fiter, Magistrate — A43

Europa: 19p, Francesc Cairat, magistrate.

1980, Apr. 28 Photo. *Perf. 13x13½*

119 A43 8p bister, blk & brn .20 .20
120 A43 19p lt green & blk .25 .20

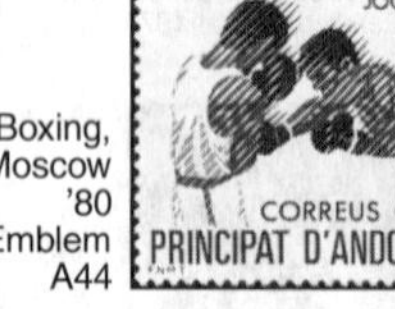
Boxing, Moscow '80 Emblem A44

1980, July 23 Photo. *Perf. 13½x13*

121 A44 5p Downhill skiing .20 .20
122 A44 8p shown .20 .20
123 A44 50p Target shooting .50 .40
Nos. 121-123 (3) .90 .80

12th Winter Olympic Games, Lake Placid, NY, Feb. 12-24 (5p); 22nd Summer Olympic Games, Moscow, July 19-Aug. 3.

Nativity A45

1980, Dec. 12 Litho. *Perf. 13*

124 A45 10p Nativity, vert. .20 .20
125 A45 22p shown .25 .20

Christmas 1980.

Children Dancing at Santa Anna Feast A46

Europa: 30p, Going to church on Aplec de la Verge de Canolich Day.

1981, May 7 Photo. *Perf. 13*

126 A46 12p multicolored .20 .20
127 A46 30p multicolored .30 .25

50th Anniv. of Police Force A47

1981, July 2 Photo. *Perf. 13½x13*

128 A47 30p multicolored .35 .20

Intl. Year of the Disabled A48

1981, Oct. 8 Photo. *Perf. 13½*

129 A48 50p multicolored .55 .25

Christmas 1981 A49

Designs: Encamp Church retable.

1981, Dec. 3 Photo. *Perf. 13½*

130 A49 12p Nativity .20 .20
131 A49 30p Adoration .35 .20

Bishops of Urgel Type of 1979

1981, Dec. 12 Engr. *Perf. 13½*

132 A42 7p Salvador Casanas .20 .20
133 A42 20p Josep de Boltas .25 .20

Natl. Arms — A51

1982, Feb. 17 Photo. *Perf. 13x13½*

134 A51 1p bright pink .20 .20
135 A51 3p bister brown .20 .20
136 A51 7p red orange .20 .20
137 A51 12p lake .20 .20
138 A51 15p ultra .20 .20
139 A51 20p blue green .25 .20
140 A51 30p crimson rose .30 .20

Perf. 13½x12½

1982, Sept. 30 Engr.

Size: 25½x30½mm

141 A51 50p dark green .70 .20
142 A51 100p dark blue 1.40 .45
Nos. 134-142 (9) 3.65 2.05

For type A51 without "PTA" see #192-198.

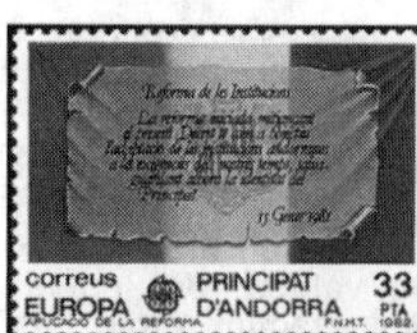
Europa 1982 A52

1982, May 12 Photo. *Perf. 13*

143 A52 14p New Reforms, 1866, vert. .20 .20
144 A52 33p Reform of Institutions, 1981 .40 .25

1982 World Cup — A53

Designs: Various soccer players.

1982, June 13 Photo. *Perf. 13x13½*

145 A53 14p multicolored .40 .40
146 A53 33p multicolored .85 .85
a. Pair, #145-146 + label 1.25 1.25

A54

A55

Anniversaries: 9p, Permanent Spanish and French delegations, cent. 14p, 50th anniv. of Andorran stamps. 23p, St. Francis of Assisi (1182-1226). 33p, Anyos Pro-Vicarial District membership centenary (Relacio sobre la Vall de Andorra titlepage).

1982, Sept. 7 Engr. *Perf. 13*

147 A54 9p dk blue & brown .20 .20
148 A54 14p black & green .40 .20
149 A54 23p dk blue & brown .25 .20
150 A54 33p black & olive grn .45 .35
Nos. 147-150 (4) 1.30 .95

Perf. 13x13½, 13½x13

1982, Dec. 9 Photo.

Christmas: 14p, Madonna and Child, Andorra la Vieille Church, vert. 33p, El Tio de Nadal (children in traditional costumes striking hollow tree).

151 A55 14p multicolored .20 .20
152 A55 33p multicolored .35 .25

Europa 1983 A56

1983, June 7 Photo. *Perf. 13*

153 A56 16p La Cortinada Church, architect, 12th cent. .20 .20
154 A56 38p Water mill, 16th cent. .45 .35

Local Mushrooms — A57

1983, July 20 Photo. *Perf. 13x12½*

155 A57 16p Lactarius sanguifluus .75 .25

See Nos. 165, 169, 172.

Universal Suffrage, 50th Anniv. A58

Photogravure and Engraved

1983, Sept. 6 *Perf. 13*
156 A58 10p multicolored .20 .20

Visit of Monsignor Jacinto Verdaguer Bishop and Co-Prince A59

1983, Sept. 6
157 A59 50p multicolored .70 .40

Christmas 1983 — A60

Saint Cerni de Nagol, Romanesque fresco, Church of San Cerni de Nagol.

1983, Nov. 24 Photo. *Perf. 13½*
158 A60 16p multicolored .25 .20

Bishops of Urgel Type of 1979

1983, Dec. 7 Engr. *Perf. 13*
159 A42 26p Joan J. Laguarda Fenollera .30 .20

1984 Winter Olympics A62

1984, Feb. 17 Litho. *Perf. 13½x14*
160 A62 16p Ski jumping .30 .20

ESPANA '84 — A63

1984, Apr. 27 Photo. *Perf. 13*
161 A63 26p Emblems .30 .20

Europa (1959-84) A64

1984, May 5 Engr.
162 A64 16p brown .20 .20
163 A64 38p blue .50 .30

1984 Summer Olympics A65

1984, Aug. 9 Litho. *Perf. 13½x14*
164 A65 40p Running .50 .30

Mushroom Type of 1983

1984, Sept. 27 Photo. *Perf. 13x12½*
165 A57 11p Morchella esculenta *2.00* 2.00

Christmas 1984 A66

1984, Dec. 6 Photo. *Perf. 13½*
166 A66 17p Nativity carving .25 .20

Europa 1985 A67

18p, Mossen Enric Arfany, composer, natl. hymn score. 45p, Musician Playing Viol, Romanesque fresco detail, La Cortinada Church, vert.

1985, May 3 Engr. *Perf. 13½*
167 A67 18p dk vio, grn & chocolate .20 .20
168 A67 45p green & chocolate .65 .20

Mushroom Type of 1983

Perf. 13½x12½

1985, Sept. 19 Photo.
169 A57 30p Gyromitra esculenta .45 .20

Pal Village — A68

1985, Nov. 7 Engr. *Perf. 13½*
170 A68 17p brt ultra & dk blue .25 .20

Christmas 1985 A69

Fresco: Angels Playing Trumpet and Psaltery, St. Bartholomew Chapel.

1985, Dec. 11 Photo. *Perf. 13½x13*
171 A69 17p multicolored .25 .20

Mushroom Type of 1983

Perf. 13½x12½

1986, Apr. 10 Photo.
172 A57 30p Marasmius oreades .45 .20

Europa 1986 — A70

1986, May 5 Engr. *Perf. 13*
173 A70 17p Water .20 .20
174 A70 45p Soil and air .60 .20

Bishops of Urgel Type of 1979

1986, Sept. 11 Engr. *Perf. 13½*
175 A42 35p Justi Guitart .45 .20

A72

A73

Santa Roma de Les Bons Church bell.

1986, Dec. 11 Litho. *Perf. 14*
176 A72 19p multicolored .25 .20

Christmas.

1987, Mar. 27 Photo. *Perf. 14*

Contemporary Natl. Coat of Arms.

177 A73 48p multicolored .60 .35

Visit of the co-princes: the Bishop of Urgel and president of France, September 26, 1986.

Europa 1987 A74

Modern architecture: 19p, Meritxell Sanctuary interior. 48p, Sanctuary exterior, vert.

1987, May 15 Engr. *Perf. 14x13½*
178 A74 19p dark blue & brown .20 .20
179 A74 48p dark blue & brown .60 .20

Souvenir Sheet

1992 Summer Olympics, Barcelona A75

20p, House of the Valleys. 50p, Bell tower, Chapel of the Archangel Michael, and torchbearer.

1987, July 20 Photo. *Perf. 14*
180 Sheet of 2 3.50 3.50
a. A75 20p multicolored 1.00 1.00
b. A75 50p multicolored 2.40 2.40

Local Mushrooms — A76

1987, Sept. 11 *Perf. 13½x12½*
181 A76 100p Boletus edulis 1.25 .50

Christmas A77

Design: Detail from a Catalan manuscript, De Nativitat, by R. Llull.

1987, Nov. 18 Litho. *Perf. 14*
182 A77 20p multicolored .25 .20

Lance and Arrowhead (Bronze Age) A78

1988, Mar. 25 Photo. *Perf. 14*
183 A78 50p multicolored .65 .25

Europa 1988 — A79

Pyrenean Mastiff — A80

Transport and communications: 20p, Les Bons, a medieval road. 45p, Trader and pack mules, early 20th cent.

1988, May 5 Engr. *Perf. 14x13½*
184 A79 20p dark bl & dark red .20 .20
185 A79 45p dark bl & dark red .50 .20

1988, July 26 Litho. *Perf. 14x13½*
186 A80 20p multicolored .25 .20

Bishop of Urgel and Seigneur of Caboet Confirming Co-Principality, 700th Anniv. — A81

1988, Oct. 24 Litho. *Perf. 14x13½*
187 A81 20p gold, blk & int blue .25 .20

Christmas 1988 A82

1988, Nov. 30 Litho. *Perf. 14x13½*
188 A82 20p multicolored .25 .20

Arms Type of 1982 Without "PTA"

1988, Dec. 2 Photo. *Perf. 13x13½*
192 A51 20p brt blue green .25 .20

Size: 25x30½mm

Perf. 13½x12½

Engr.

194 A51 50p grnsh black .65 .25
196 A51 100p dark blue 1.25 .45
198 A51 500p dark brown 6.50 2.10
Nos. 192-198 (4) 8.65 3.00

This is an expanding set. Numbers will change if necessary.

Europa 1989 A83

Perf. 14x13½, 13½x14

1989, May 8 Litho. & Engr.

200 A83 20p Leapfrog, vert. .25 .20
201 A83 45p Tug of war .50 .20

Santa Roma Church, Les Bons A84

Litho. & Engr.

1989, June 20 Perf. 13½x14

202 A84 50p blk, dp bl & grn bl .55 .20

Anniv. Emblem — A85

Christmas — A86

1989, Oct. 26 Litho. Perf. 14x13½

203 A85 20p multicolored .25 .20

Intl. Red Cross and Red Crescent societies, 125th annivs.; Year for the Protection of Human Life.

1989, Dec. 1

204 A86 20p *The Immaculate Conception* .25 .20

Europa 1990 A87

Post offices.

Perf. 13½x14, 14x13½

1990, May 17 Photo.

205 A87 20p shown .25 .20
206 A87 50p Post office, vert. .60 .25

Gomphidius Rutilus — A88

1990, June 21 Litho. Perf. 13x13½

207 A88 45p multicolored .60 .30

Plandolit House — A89

Christmas — A90

Litho. & Engr.

1990, Oct. 17 Perf. 13x12½

208 A89 20p brown & org yel .30 .20

1990, Nov. 26 Litho. Perf. 14x13½

209 A90 25p lake, brn & bister .35 .20

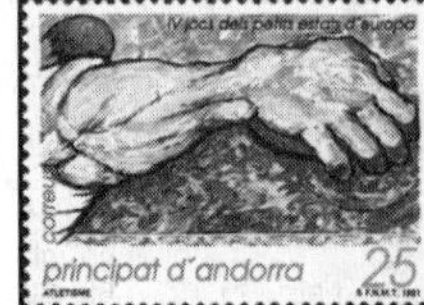

4th Games of the Small European States A91

1991, Apr. 29 Photo. Perf. 13½x14

210 A91 25p Discus .35 .20
211 A91 45p High jump, runner .65 .30

Europa — A92

Perf. 14x13½, 13½x14

1991, May 10 Litho.

212 A92 25p Olympus-1 satellite .40 .20
213 A92 55p Olympus-1, horiz. .80 .40

A93

Christmas — A94

1991, Sept. 20 Litho. Perf. 13x12½

214 A93 45p Macrolepiota procera .60 .30

1991, Nov. 29 Photo. Perf. 14x13½

215 A94 25p multicolored .35 .20

Woman Carrying Water Pails A95

1992, Feb. 14 Photo. Perf. 13½x14

216 A95 25p multicolored .35 .20

Discovery of America, 500th Anniv. A96

Perf. 14x13½, 13½x14

1992, May 8 Photo.

217 A96 27p Santa Maria, vert. .45 .20
218 A96 45p King Ferdinand .70 .30

Europa.

1992 Summer Olympics, Barcelona A97

1992, July 22 Photo. Perf. 13½x14

219 A97 27p Kayak .55 .25

Nativity Scene, by Fra Angelico — A98

1992, Nov. 18 Photo. Perf. 14

220 A98 27p multicolored .45 .20

Natl. Automobile Museum A99

Litho. & Engr.

1992, Sept. 10 Perf. 13½x14

221 A99 27p 1894 Benz .45 .25

Cantharellus Cibarius — A100

1993, Mar. 25 Photo. Perf. 13½x14

222 A100 28p multicolored .55 .25

Contemporary Paintings — A101

Europa: 28p, Upstream, by John Alan Morrison. 45p, Rhythm, by Angel Calvente, vert.

Perf. 13½x14, 14x13½

1993, May 20 Litho.

223 A101 28p multicolored .55 .25
224 A101 45p multicolored 1.00 .45

Art and Literature Society, 25th Anniv. — A102

1993, Sept. 23 Litho. Perf. 14

225 A102 28p multicolored .60 .25

Christmas — A103

Litho. & Engr.

1993, Nov. 25 Perf. 14x13½

226 A103 28p multi .60 .25

Souvenir Sheet

Constitution, 1st Anniv. — A104

1994, Mar. 14 Photo. Perf. 14

227 A104 29p multicolored .65 .65

Sir Alexander Fleming (1881-1955), Co-discoverer of Penicillin — A105

1994, May 6 Photo. Perf. 13½x14

228 A105 29p Portrait .60 .40
229 A105 55p AIDS virus 1.10 1.00

Europa.

Hygrophorus Gliocyclus — A106

1994, Sept. 27 Photo. Perf. 14

230 A106 29p multicolored .65 .65

Christmas — A107

1994, Nov. 29 Photo. Perf. 14x13½

231 A107 29p multicolored .65 .65

Nature Conservation in Europe — A108

1995, Mar. 23 Photo. Perf. 14

232 A108 30p Farm in valley .60 .50
233 A108 60p Stone fence, valley 1.25 1.10

Europa A109

1995, May 8 Photo. *Perf. 14*
234 A109 60p multicolored 1.25 1.10

Christmas — A110

1995, Nov. 8 Photo. *Perf. 14*
235 A110 30p Flight to Egypt .60 .50

Entrance Into Council of Europe A111

1995, Nov. 10
236 A111 30p multicolored .60 .50

Mushrooms — A112

1996, Apr. 30 Photo. *Perf. 14*
237 A112 30p Ramaria aurea .60 .50
238 A112 60p Tuber melanosporum 1.25 1.10

Isabelle Sandy (1884-1975), Writer — A113

1996, May 7
239 A113 60p brown & violet 1.25 1.10

Europa.

Intl. Museum Day A114

Design: Antique coal-heated iron.

1996, Sept. 12 Photo. *Perf. 14*
240 A114 60p multicolored .70 .60

Christmas A115

The Annunciation, by Andrew Martin, 1753, St. Eulalia d'Encamp Church.

1996, Nov. 26 Photo. *Perf. 14*
241 A115 30p multicolored .40 .40

Museums of Andorra A116

Early bicycles designed by: 32p, Karl Drais, 1818. 65p, Pierre Michaux, 1861.

1997, Apr. 28 Photo. *Perf. 14*
242 A116 32p multicolored .40 .40
243 A116 65p multicolored .75 .75

See Nos. 248-249.

A117

UNESCO — A118

Europa (Stories and Legends): Hikers watching family of bears crossing over river on fallen tree.

1997, May 6 Photo. *Perf. 14*
244 A117 65p multicolored .75 .75

1997, Sept. 30 Photo. *Perf. 14*
245 A118 32p multicolored .40 .40

Christmas — A119

1997, Nov. 25 Photo. *Perf. 14*
246 A119 32p multicolored .40 .40

1998 Winter Olympic Games, Nagano A120

1998, Feb. 23 Photo. *Perf. 14*
247 A120 35p Slalom skier .40 .40

Museums of Andorra Type of 1997

Early bicycles: 35p, Kangaroo, 1878. 70p, Hirondelle, 1889.

1998, Apr. 24 Photo. *Perf. 13½x14*
248 A116 35p multicolored .40 .40
249 A116 70p multicolored .75 .75

Harlequins, Canillas Carnival A121

1998, May 22 Photo. *Perf. 14*
250 A121 70p multicolored .80 .80

Europa.

Manual Digest, 250th Anniv. — A122

1998, Sept. 30 Photo. *Perf. 14*
251 A122 35p multicolored .45 .45

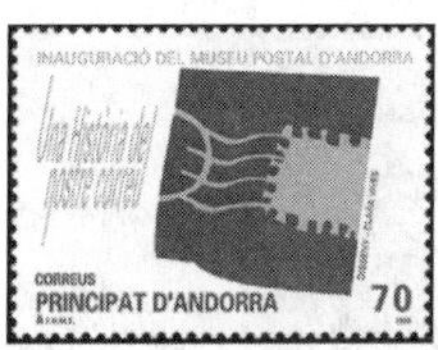
Inauguration of the Postal Museum of Andorra — A123

1998, Nov. 19 Photo. *Perf. 14*
252 A123 70p multicolored .85 .85

Christmas A124

1998, Nov. 26
253 A124 35p multicolored .45 .45

Museums of Andorra A125

Early bicycles designed by: 35p, Salvo, 1878, vert. 70p, Rudge, 1883.

1999, Jan. 29 Photo. *Perf. 14*
254 A125 35p multicolored .45 .45
255 A125 70p multicolored .85 .85

Council of Europe, 50th Anniv. A126

1999, Apr. 29 Photo. *Perf. 14*
256 A126 35p multicolored .40 .40

Incles Valley A127

1999, May 6
257 A127 70p multicolored .75 .75

Europa.

Transporting Mail on Horseback — A128

1999, Feb. 18 Photo. *Perf. 14*
258 A128 35p black & sepia .45 .45

Restoration of Casa Rull, Sispony, La Massana A129

1999, Sept. 22 Photo. *Perf. 13½x14*
259 A129 35p multicolored .40 .40

Christmas — A130

St. Coloma's Church — A131

1999, Nov. 10 Engr. *Perf. 14x13½*
260 A130 35p orange brn & brn .40 .40

1999, Nov. 12 Photo.
261 A131 35p multicolored .40 .40

European heritage.

Europa, 2000
Common Design Type

2000, May 11 Photo. *Perf. 13¾*
262 CD17 70p multi .75 .75

Angonella Lakes A132

2000, June 29 Photo. *Perf. 13¾x14*
263 A132 35p multi .40 .40

Casa Lacruz A133

2000, July 20 Photo. *Perf. 13¾x14*
264 A133 35p multi .40 .40

China, Areny-Plandolit Museum — A134

2000, July 27 *Perf. 14x13¾*
265 A134 70p multi .80 .80

2000 Summer Olympics, Sydney — A135

2000, Sept. 29 Photo. *Perf. 14x13½*
266 A135 70p multi .75 .75

European Convention on Human Rights, 50th Anniv. A136

2000, Nov. 3 *Perf. 13½x14*
267 A136 70p multi .75 .75

Natl. Archives, 25th Anniv. — A137

2000, Nov. 14 *Perf. 14x13½*
268 A137 35p multi .35 .35

Christmas — A138

2000, Nov. 22
269 A138 35p multi .35 .35

Rec de Solà — A139

2001, Mar. 30 Photo. *Perf. 14x13¾*
270 A139 40p multi .40 .40

Europa A140

2001, May 16 *Perf. 13¾x14*
271 A140 75p multi .80 .80

Casa Palau, Sant Julià de Lòria — A141

2001, June 20 Photo. *Perf. 14x13¾*
272 A141 75p multi .80 .80

Chapel of the Virgin of Meritxell, 25th Anniv. of Rebuilding — A142

2001, Sept. 7 Photo. *Perf. 14x13¾*
273 A142 40p multi .45 .45

Natl. Auditorium, 10th Anniv. A143

2001, Sept. 20 *Perf. 13¾x14*
274 A143 75p multi .85 .85

Christmas A144

2001, Nov. 20 Photo. *Perf. 13¾x14*
275 A144 40p multi .45 .45

100 Cents = 1 Euro (")

Coat of Arms — A145

2002, Jan. 2 Photo. *Perf. 12¾x13¼*
276 A145 25c brown orange .45 .45
277 A145 50c claret .90 .90

Birds A146

Designs: 25c, Prunella collaris. 50c, Montifringilla nivalis.

2002, Mar. 27 *Perf. 13¾x14*
278-279 A146 Set of 2 1.40 1.40

Intl. Year of Mountains A147

2002, Apr. 5
280 A147 50c multi .90 .90

Europa A148

2002, May 9
281 A148 50c multi .90 .90

AIR POST STAMPS

Catalogue values for unused stamps in this section, from this point to the end of the section, are for Never Hinged items.

AP1

Unwmk.
1951, June 27 Engr. *Perf. 11*
C1 AP1 1p dark violet brown 20.00 4.00

AP2 AP3

Litho. & Engr.
1983, Oct. 20 *Perf. 13*
C2 AP2 20p brown & bis brn .25 .20

Jaime Sansa Nequi, Episcopal Church official.

1984, Oct. 25 Photo. *Perf. 13*
C3 AP3 20p multicolored .30 .20

Pyrenees Art Center.

Bishops of Urgel Type of 1979

1985, June 13 Engr. *Perf. 13½*
C4 A42 20p Ramon Iglesias .30 .20

SPECIAL DELIVERY STAMPS

Special Delivery Stamp of Spain, 1905 Overprinted

1928 Unwmk. *Perf. 14*
Without Control Number on Back
E1 SD1 20c red 62.50 *65.00*
Never hinged 100.00

With Control Number on Back
E2 SD1 20c pale red 40.00 *45.00*
Never hinged 65.00

Eagle over Mountain Pass — SD2

1929 *Perf. 14*
With Control Number on Back
E3 SD2 20c scarlet 18.00 18.00
Never hinged 26.00

Perf 11½ examples are numbered A000.000 and are specimens. Value, $300.

1937 *Perf. 11½x11*
Without Control Number on Back
E4 SD2 20c red 6.75 6.50
Never hinged 7.50

Arms and Squirrel — SD3

1949 Unwmk. Engr. *Perf. 10x9½*
E5 SD3 25c red 4.00 4.00

ANDORRA, FRENCH ADMIN.

Stamps and Types of France, 1900-1929, Overprinted

Perf. 14x13½
1931, June 16 Unwmk.

1	A16	1c gray	.45	.60
a.		Double overprint	*1,000.*	*1,000.*
2	A16	2c red brown	.45	*.70*
3	A16	3c orange	.45	*.70*
4	A16	5c green	1.25	*1.25*
5	A16	10c lilac	2.25	*1.75*
6	A22	15c red brown	3.00	3.00
7	A22	20c red violet	4.25	4.00
8	A22	25c yellow brn	5.75	4.00
9	A22	30c green	4.75	4.00
10	A22	40c ultra	5.75	6.75
11	A20	45c lt violet	9.50	7.25
12	A20	50c vermilion	7.00	6.00
13	A20	65c gray green	14.00	*12.75*
14	A20	75c rose lilac	16.00	*14.75*
15	A22	90c red	20.00	17.50
16	A20	1fr dull blue	21.00	20.00
17	A22	1.50fr light blue	24.00	25.00

Overprinted

18	A18	2fr org & pale bl	15.00	*17.50*
19	A18	3fr brt vio & rose	57.50	*62.50*
20	A18	5fr dk bl & buff	72.50	100.00
21	A18	10fr grn & red	175.00	*210.00*
22	A18	20fr mag & grn	225.00	*275.00*
		Nos. 1-22 (22)	684.85	*795.00*

See No. P1 for ½c on 1c gray.
Nos. 9, 15 and 17 were not issued in France without overprint.

Chapel of Meritxell A50

Bridge of St. Anthony A51

St. Miguel d'Engolasters
A52

Gorge of St. Julia
A53

Old Andorra
A54

1932-43 Engr. *Perf. 13*

23 A50 1c gray blk .25 .25
24 A50 2c violet .40 .40
25 A50 3c brown .30 .30
26 A50 5c blue green .40 .40
27 A51 10c dull lilac .65 .60
28 A50 15c deep red 1.00 1.00
29 A51 20c lt rose 6.25 4.50
30 A52 25c brown 2.25 2.25
31 A51 25c brn car ('37) 4.50 6.50
32 A51 30c emerald 1.75 1.50
33 A51 40c ultra 5.00 4.25
34 A51 40c brn blk ('39) .65 .60
35 A51 45c lt red 6.00 5.00
36 A51 45c bl grn ('39) 3.00 2.50
37 A52 50c lilac rose 6.50 5.00
38 A51 50c lt vio ('39) 3.00 2.50
38A A51 50c grn ('40) 1.40 1.40
39 A51 55c lt vio ('38) 9.50 6.00
40 A51 60c yel brn ('38) .60 .50
41 A52 65c yel grn 35.00 35.00
42 A51 65c blue ('38) 6.50 5.50
43 A51 70c red ('39) 1.25 1.00
44 A52 75c violet 3.25 2.50
45 A51 75c ultra ('39) 2.50 2.25
46 A51 80c green ('38) 13.00 9.50
46A A53 80c bl grn ('40) .25 .30
47 A53 90c deep rose 3.25 2.25
48 A53 90c dk grn ('39) 2.25 2.25
49 A53 1fr blue grn 9.50 6.00
50 A53 1fr scarlet ('38) 15.00 15.00
51 A53 1fr dp ultra ('39) .25 .25
51A A53 1.20fr brt vio ('42) .25 .25
52 A50 1.25fr rose car ('33) 35.00 25.00
52A A50 1.25fr rose ('38) 3.00 1.40
52B A53 1.30fr sepia ('40) .25 .25
53 A54 1.50fr ultra 8.25 7.50
53A A53 1.50fr crim ('40) .25 .25
54 A53 1.75fr violet ('33) 80.00 80.00
55 A53 1.75fr dk bl ('38) 30.00 22.50
56 A53 2fr red violet 3.75 3.50
56A A50 2fr rose red ('40) 1.00 .65
56B A50 2fr dk bl grn ('42) .25 .20
57 A50 2.15fr dk vio ('38) 40.00 27.50
58 A50 2.25fr ultra ('39) 4.00 3.00
58A A50 2.40fr red ('42) .25 .20
59 A50 2.50fr gray blk ('39) 4.00 3.00
59A A50 2.50fr dp ultra ('40) 1.40 1.25
60 A53 3fr orange brn 3.75 3.50
60A A50 3fr red brn ('40) .30 .25
60B A50 4fr sl bl ('42) .30 .25
60C A50 4.50fr dp vio ('42) .75 .75
61 A54 5fr brown .40 .35
62 A54 10fr violet .45 .40
62B A54 15fr dp ultra ('42) .50 .40
63 A54 20fr rose lake .50 .40
63A A51 50fr turq bl ('43) 1.00 .50
Nos. 23-63A (56) 365.00 310.50

A 20c ultra exists. Value $12,500.

No. 37 Surcharged with Bars and New Value in Black

1935, Sept. 25

64 A52 20c on 50c lil rose 11.00 10.00
a. Double surcharge *1,900.*

Coat of Arms
A55 A56

1936-42 *Perf. 14x13*

65 A55 1c black ('37) .20 .20
66 A55 2c blue .20 .20
67 A55 3c brown .20 .20
68 A55 5c rose lilac .20 .20
69 A55 10c ultra ('37) .20 .20
70 A55 15c red violet .50 .50
71 A55 20c emerald ('37) .20 .20
72 A55 30c cop red ('38) .30 .30
72A A55 30c blk brn ('42) .20 .20
73 A55 35c Prus grn ('38) 30.00 30.00
74 A55 40c cop red ('42) .20 .20
75 A55 50c Prus grn ('42) .20 .20
76 A55 60c turq bl ('42) .20 .20
77 A55 70c vio ('42) .20 .20
Nos. 65-77 (14) 33.00 33.00

Catalogue values for unused stamps in this section, from this point to the end of the section, are for Never Hinged items.

1944

78 A56 10c violet .20 .20
79 A56 30c deep magenta .20 .20
80 A56 40c dull blue .20 .20
81 A56 50c orange red .20 .20
82 A56 60c black .20 .20
83 A56 70c brt red violet .20 .20
84 A56 80c blue green .20 .20
Nos. 78-84 (7) 1.40 1.40

See No. 114.

St. Jean de Caselles
A57

La Maison des Vallees
A58

Old Andorra
A59

Provost
A60

1944-47 *Perf. 13*

85 A57 1fr brown violet .35 .20
86 A57 1.20fr blue .20 .20
87 A57 1.50fr red .35 .20
88 A57 2fr dk blue grn .20 .20
89 A58 2.40fr rose red .30 .20
90 A58 2.50fr rose red ('46) 4.50 1.40
91 A58 3fr sepia .20 .20
92 A58 4fr ultra .35 .20
93 A59 4.50fr brown blk .40 .20
94 A58 4.50fr dk bl grn ('47) 7.00 3.50
95 A59 5fr ultra .30 .20
96 A59 5fr Prus grn ('46) .55 .30
97 A59 6fr rose car ('45) .40 .20
98 A59 10fr Prus green .20 .20
99 A59 10fr ultra ('46) .30 .20
100 A60 15fr rose lilac .65 .25
101 A60 20fr deep blue .75 .45
102 A60 25fr lt rose red ('46) 4.50 2.25
103 A60 40fr dk green ('46) 4.50 3.00
104 A60 50fr sepia 2.00 1.10
Nos. 85-104 (20) 28.00 14.65

1948-49

105 A58 4fr lt blue grn 1.00 .80
106 A59 6fr violet brn .50 .40
107 A59 8fr indigo 1.50 1.25
108 A59 12fr bright red 1.00 .90
109 A59 12fr blue grn ('49) 1.10 .90
110 A59 15fr crimson ('49) .60 .50
111 A60 18fr deep blue 3.75 2.00
112 A60 20fr dark violet 3.00 2.25
113 A60 25fr ultra ('49) 2.00 1.50
Nos. 105-113 (9) 14.45 10.50

1949-51 *Perf. 14x13, 13*

114 A56 1fr deep blue 1.25 .75
115 A57 3fr red ('51) 6.00 5.00
116 A57 4fr sepia 3.00 2.50
117 A58 5fr emerald 3.50 3.00
118 A58 5fr purple ('51) 6.00 5.00
119 A58 6fr blue grn ('51) 5.00 4.50
120 A58 8fr brown 1.50 1.00
121 A59 15fr blk brn ('51) 6.50 5.00
122 A59 18fr rose red ('51) 17.50 12.00
123 A60 30fr ultra ('51) 30.00 12.00
Nos. 114-123 (10) 80.25 50.75

Les Escaldres Spa — A61

St. Coloma Belfry
A62

Designs: 15fr-25fr, Gothic cross. 30fr-75fr, Village of Les Bons.

1955-58 Unwmk. Engr. *Perf. 13*

124 A61 1fr dk gray bl .20 .20
125 A61 2fr dp green .20 .20
126 A61 3fr red .25 .20
127 A61 5fr chocolate .25 .20
128 A62 6fr dk bl grn .50 .40
129 A62 8fr rose brown .50 .45
130 A62 10fr brt violet .80 .55
131 A62 12fr indigo .90 .60
132 A61 15fr red 1.25 .85
133 A61 18fr blue grn 1.25 .85
134 A61 20fr dp purple 1.90 1.50
135 A61 25fr sepia 2.25 1.50
136 A62 30fr deep blue 26.00 16.00
137 A62 35fr Prus bl ('57) 10.00 6.75
138 A62 40fr dk green 27.50 18.00
139 A62 50fr cerise 3.50 2.25
140 A62 65fr purple ('58) 9.50 5.75
141 A62 70fr chestnut ('57) 6.50 5.75
142 A62 75fr violet blue 45.00 32.50
Nos. 124-142 (19) 138.25 94.50

Issued: 35fr, 70fr, 8/19; 65fr, 2/10; others, 2/15.

Coat of Arms — A63

Gothic Cross, Meritxell
A64

65c, 85c, 1fr, Engolasters Lake.

1961, June 19 Typo. *Perf. 14x13*

143 A63 5c brt green & blk .20 .20
144 A63 10c red, pink & blk .20 .20
145 A63 15c blue & black .20 .20
146 A63 20c yellow & brown .20 .20

Engr. *Perf. 13*

147 A64 25c violet, bl & grn .25 .25
148 A64 30c mar, ol grn & brn .30 .30
149 A64 45c indigo, bl & grn 13.00 6.50
150 A64 50c pur, lt brn & ol grn 1.00 1.00
151 A64 65c bl, ol & brn 17.50 14.00
152 A64 85c rose lil, vio bl & brn 17.50 14.00
153 A64 1fr grnsh bl, ind & brn 1.00 1.00
Nos. 143-153 (11) 51.35 37.85

See Nos. 161-166A.

Imperforates

Most stamps of Andorra, French Administration, from 1961 onward exist imperforate in issued and trial colors, and also in small presentation sheets in issued colors.

Telstar and Globe Showing Andover and Pleumeur-Bodou — A65

1962, Sept. 29 Engr.

154 A65 50c ultra & purple .90 .90

1st television connection of the US and Europe through the Telstar satellite, 7/11-12.

"La Sardane"
A66

Charlemagne Crossing Andorra — A67

1fr, Louis le Debonnaire giving founding charter.

1963, June 22 Unwmk. *Perf. 13*

155 A66 20c lil rose, cl & ol grn 2.75 2.75
156 A67 50c sl grn & dk car rose 4.50 4.50
157 A67 1fr red brn, ultra & dk grn 7.00 7.00
Nos. 155-157 (3) 14.25 14.25

Old Andorra Church and Champs-Elysées Palace — A68

1964, Jan. 20 Engr.

158 A68 25c blk, grn & vio brn .90 .75

"PHILATEC," Intl. Philatelic and Postal Techniques Exhib., Paris, June 5-21, 1964.

Bishop of Urgel and Seigneur of Caboet Confirming Co-Principality, 1288 — A69

Design: 60c, Napoleon re-establishing Co-principality, 1806.

1964, Apr. 25 Engr. *Perf. 13*

159 A69 60c dk brn, red brn & sl grn 9.00 9.00
160 A69 1fr brt bl, org brn & blk 9.00 9.00

Arms Type of 1961

1964, May 16 Typo. *Perf. 14x13*

161 A63 1c dk blue & gray .25 .20
162 A63 2c black & orange .25 .20
163 A63 12c purple, emer & yel .50 .40
164 A63 18c black, lil & pink .50 .40
Nos. 161-164 (4) 1.50 1.20

Scenic Type of 1961

Designs: 40c, 45c, Gothic Cross, Meritxell. 60c, 90c, Pond of Engolasters.

1965-71 Engr. *Perf. 13*

165 A64 40c dk brn, org brn & sl grn .50 .50
165A A64 45c vio bl, ol bis & slate .90 .75
166 A64 60c org brn & dk brn .60 .60
166A A64 90c ultra, bl grn & bister .50 .50
Nos. 165-166A (4) 2.50 2.35

Issued: 40c, 60c, Apr. 24, 1965. 45c, June 13, 1970. 90c, Aug. 28, 1971.

Syncom Satellite over Pleumeur-Bodou Station — A70

1965, May 17 Unwmk.

167 A70 60c dp car, lil & bl 3.25 3.00

Cent. of the ITU.

Andorra House, Paris — A71

1965, June 5

168 A71 25c dk bl, org brn & ol gray .80 .65

Ski Lift — A72

Design: 25c, Chair lift, vert.

1966, Apr. 2 Engr. *Perf. 13*

169 A72 25c brt bl, grn & dk brn .80 .70
170 A72 40c mag, brt ultra & sep 1.10 1.00

Winter sports in Andorra.

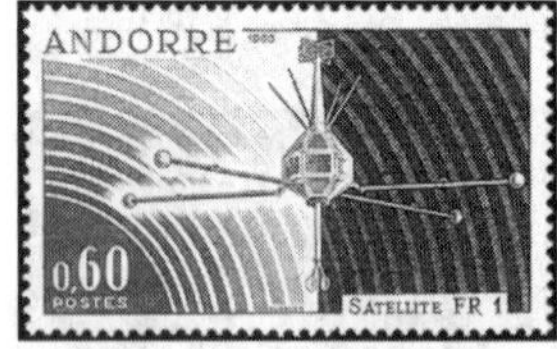

FR-1 Satellite — A73

1966, May 7 *Perf. 13*

171 A73 60c brt bl, grn & dk grn 1.25 1.10

Issued to commemorate the launching of the scientific satellite FR-1, Dec. 6, 1965.

Common Design Types pictured following the introduction.

Europa Issue, 1966

Common Design Type

1966, Sept. 24 Engr. *Perf. 13*

Size: 21½x35½mm

172 CD9 60c brown 3.25 2.00

Folk Dancers, Sculpture by Josep Viladomat — A74

Telephone Encircling the Globe — A75

1967, Apr. 29 Engr. *Perf. 13*

173 A74 30c ol grn, dp grn & slate .55 .30

Cent. (in 1966) of the New Reform, which reaffirmed and strengthened political freedom in Andorra.

Europa Issue, 1967

Common Design Type

1967, Apr. 29

Size: 22x36mm

174 CD10 30c bluish blk & lt bl *4.50* 2.50
175 CD10 60c dk red & brt pink *6.50* 3.50

1967, Apr. 29

176 A75 60c dk car, vio & blk .90 .60

Automatic telephone service.

Injured Father at Home A76

1967, Sept. 23 Engr. *Perf. 13*

177 A76 2.30fr ocher, dk red brn & brn red 6.00 4.50

Introduction of Social Security System.

Jesus in Garden of Gethsemane — A77

Designs (from 16th century frescoes in La Maison des Vallees): 30c, The Kiss of Judas. 60c, The Descent from the Cross (Pieta).

1967, Sept. 23

178 A77 25c black & red brn .40 .35
179 A77 30c purple & red lilac .40 .35
180 A77 60c indigo & Prus blue 1.00 .70
Nos. 178-180 (3) 1.80 1.40

See Nos. 185-187.

Downhill Skier — A78

1968, Jan. 27 Engr. *Perf. 13*

181 A78 40c org, ver & red lil .65 .55

10th Winter Olympic Games, Grenoble, France, Feb. 6-18.

Europa Issue, 1968

Common Design Type

1968, Apr. 27 Engr. *Perf. 13*

Size: 36x22mm

182 CD11 30c gray & brt bl *7.75* 3.50
183 CD11 60c brown & lilac *10.50* 4.75

High Jump A79

1968, Oct. 12 Engr. *Perf. 13*

184 A79 40c brt blue & brn .90 .70

19th Olympic Games, Mexico City, Oct. 12-27.

Fresco Type of 1967

Designs (from 16th century frescoes in La Maison des Vallees): 25c, The Scourging of Christ. 30c, Christ Carrying the Cross. 60c, The Crucifixion. (All horiz.)

1968, Oct. 12

185 A77 25c dk grn & gray grn .35 .35
186 A77 30c dk brown & lilac .40 .40
187 A77 60c dk car & vio brn 1.25 1.25
Nos. 185-187 (3) 2.00 2.00

Europa Issue, 1969

Common Design Type

1969, Apr. 26 Engr. *Perf. 13*

188 CD12 40c rose car, gray & dl bl *9.00* 4.00
189 CD12 70c indigo, dl red & ol *13.00* 6.00

10th anniv. of the Conf. of European Postal and Telecommunications Administrations.

Kayak on Isere River A80

Drops of Water & Diamond A80a

1969, Aug. 2 Engr. *Perf. 13*

190 A80 70c dk sl grn, ultra & ind 1.75 1.75

Intl. Canoe & Kayak Championships, Bourg-Saint-Maurice, Savoy, July 31-Aug. 6.

1969, Sept. 27 Engr. *Perf. 13*

191 A80a 70c blk, dp ultra & grnsh bl 3.50 2.00

European Water Charter.

St. John, the Woman and the Dragon A81

The Revelation (From the Altar of St. John, Caselles): 40c, St. John Hearing Voice from Heaven on Patmos. 70c, St. John and the Seven Candlesticks.

1969, Oct. 18

192 A81 30c brn, dp pur & brn red .40 .40
193 A81 40c gray, dk brn & brn ol .80 .80
194 A81 70c dk red, maroon & brt rose lilac 1.25 1.25
Nos. 192-194 (3) 2.45 2.45

See Nos. 199-201, 207-209, 214-216.

Field Ball — A82

Shot Put — A83

1970, Feb. 21 Engr. *Perf. 13*

195 A82 80c multi 1.60 1.10

Issued to publicize the 7th International Field Ball Games, France, Feb. 26-Mar. 8.

Europa Issue, 1970

Common Design Type

1970, May 2 Engr. *Perf. 13*

Size: 36x22mm

196 CD13 40c orange *7.50* 3.25
197 CD13 80c violet blue *15.00* 6.00

1970, Sept. 11 Engr. *Perf. 13*

198 A83 80c bl & dk brn 1.75 1.25

1st European Junior Athletic Championships, Colombes, France, Sept. 11-13.

Altar Type of 1969

The Revelation (from the Altar of St. John, Caselles): 30c, St. John recording angel's message. 40c, Angel erecting column symbolizing faithful in heaven. 80c, St. John's trial in kettle of boiling oil.

1970, Oct. 24

199 A81 30c dp car, dk brn & brt pur .60 .55
200 A81 40c violet & slate grn 1.00 .85
201 A81 80c ol, dk bl & car rose 1.75 1.50
Nos. 199-201 (3) 3.35 2.90

Ice Skating A84

1971, Feb. 20 Engr. *Perf. 13*

202 A84 80c dk red, red lil & pur 1.75 1.50

World Figure Skating Championships, Lyons, France, Feb. 23-28.

Capercaillie — A85

Nature protection: No. 204, Brown bear.

1971, Apr. 24 Photo. *Perf. 13*

203 A85 80c multicolored 2.00 1.50

Engr.

204 A85 80c blue, grn & brn 3.00 2.00

Europa Issue, 1971

Common Design Type

1971, May 8 Engr. *Perf. 13*

Size: 35½x22mm

205 CD14 50c rose red *9.00* 3.50
206 CD14 80c lt blue green *15.00* 6.00

Altar Type of 1969

The Revelation (from the Altar of St. John, Caselles): 30c, St. John preaching, Rev. 1:3. 50c, "The Sign of the Beast . . ." Rev. 16:1-2. 90c, The Woman, Rev. 17:1.

1971, Sept. 18

207 A81 30c dl grn, ol & brt grn .65 .55
208 A81 50c rose car, org & ol brn .75 .55
209 A81 90c blk, dk pur & bl 1.50 1.25
Nos. 207-209 (3) 2.90 2.35

Europa Issue 1972
Common Design Type

1972, Apr. 29 Photo. *Perf. 13*
Size: 21½x37mm

210 CD15 50c brt mag & multi *10.00* 3.50
211 CD15 90c multicolored *20.00* 6.50

Golden Eagle A86

1972, May 27 Engr.

212 A86 60c dk grn, olive & plum 3.25 2.00

Nature protection.

Shooting A87

1972, July 8

213 A87 1fr dk purple 2.00 1.50

20th Olympic Games, Munich, 8/26-9/11.

Altar Type of 1969

The Revelation (from the Altar of St. John, Caselles): 30c, St. John, bishop and servant. 50c, Resurrection of Lazarus. 90c, Angel with lance and nails.

1972, Sept. 16 Engr. *Perf. 13*

214 A81 30c dk ol, gray & red lil .65 .55
215 A81 50c vio blue & slate .75 .75
216 A81 90c dk Prus bl & sl grn 1.50 1.40
Nos. 214-216 (3) 2.90 2.70

De Gaulle as Coprince of Andorra — A88

90c, De Gaulle in front of Maison des Vallées.

1972, Oct. 23 Engr. *Perf. 13*

217 A88 50c violet blue 1.00 .90
218 A88 90c dk carmine 1.50 1.40
a. Pair, #217-218 + label 2.75 2.75

Visit of Charles de Gaulle to Andorra, 5th anniv.
See Nos. 399-400.

Europa Issue 1973
Common Design Type

1973, Apr. 28 Photo. *Perf. 13*
Size: 36x22mm

219 CD16 50c violet & multi 7.75 3.25
220 CD16 90c dk red & multi 13.00 6.00

Virgin of Canolich A89

1973, June 16 Engr. *Perf. 13*

221 A89 1fr ol, Prus bl & vio 1.40 1.10

Lily — A90

Blue Titmouse — A91

45c, Iris. 50c, Columbine. 65c, Tobacco. No. 226, Pinks. No. 227, Narcissuses.

1973-74 Photo. *Perf. 13*

222 A90 30c car rose & multi .30 .30
223 A90 45c yel grn & multi .20 .20
224 A90 50c buff & multi 1.00 1.00
225 A90 65c gray & multi .30 .30
226 A90 90c ultra & multi .75 .75
227 A90 90c grnsh bl & multi .65 .65
Nos. 222-227 (6) 3.20 3.20

See Nos. 238-240.

1973-74 Photo. *Perf. 13*

Nature protection: 60c, Citril finch and mistletoe. 80c, Eurasian bullfinch. 1fr, Lesser spotted woodpecker.

228 A91 60c buff & multi 3.00 1.50
229 A91 80c gray & multi 2.25 1.25
230 A91 90c gray & multi 1.75 1.00
231 A91 1fr yel grn & multi 1.75 1.25
Nos. 228-231 (4) 8.75 5.00

Europa Issue 1974

Virgin of Pal — A92

90c, Virgin of Santa Coloma. Statues are polychrome 12th cent. carvings by rural artists.

1974, Apr. 27 Engr. *Perf. 13*

232 A92 50c multicolored *10.50* 4.00
233 A92 90c multicolored *14.50* 6.00

Arms of Andorra and Cahors Bridge — A93

1974, Aug. 24 Engr. *Perf. 13*

234 A93 1fr blue, vio & org .90 .60

First anniv. of meeting of the co-princes of Andorra: Pres. Georges Pompidou of France and Msgr. Juan Marti Alanis, Bishop of Urgel.

Mail Box, Chutes and Globe — A94

1974, Oct. 5 Engr. *Perf. 13*

235 A94 1.20fr multi 1.00 .90

Centenary of Universal Postal Union.

Coronation of St. Marti, 16th Century — A95

Europa: 80c, Crucifixion, 16th cent., vert.

Perf. 11½x13, 13x11½

1975, Apr. 26 Photo.

236 A95 80c gold & multi *6.50* 4.00
237 A95 1.20fr gold & multi *8.50* 6.00

Flower Type of 1973

Designs: 60c, Gentian. 80c, Anemone. 1.20fr, Autumn crocus.

1975, May 10 Photo. *Perf. 13*

238 A90 60c olive & multi .25 .25
239 A90 80c brt rose & multi .80 .50
240 A90 1.20fr green & multi .50 .45
Nos. 238-240 (3) 1.55 1.20

Abstract Design — A96

1975, June 7 Engr. *Perf. 13*

241 A96 2fr bl, magenta & emer 1.40 1.25

ARPHILA 75 International Philatelic Exhibition, Paris, June 6-16.

A97

A98

1975, Aug. 23 Engr. *Perf. 13*

242 A97 80c violet bl & blk .65 .60

Georges Pompidou (1911-74), pres. of France and co-prince of Andorra (1969-74).

1975, Nov. 8 Engr. *Perf. 13*

243 A98 1.20fr Costume, IWY Emblem .90 .65

International Women's Year.

Skier and Snowflake A99

1976, Jan. 31 Engr. *Perf. 13*

244 A99 1.20fr multicolored .90 .65

12th Winter Olympic Games, Innsbruck, Austria, Feb. 4-15.

Telephone and Satellite — A100

1976, Mar. 20 Engr. *Perf. 13*

245 A100 1fr multicolored .70 .60

Centenary of first telephone call by Alexander Graham Bell, Mar. 10, 1976.

Catalan Forge A101

Europa: 1.20fr, Woolen worker.

1976, May 8 Engr. *Perf. 13*

246 A101 80c multi *2.00* 1.00
247 A101 1.20fr multi *3.00* 1.50

Thomas Jefferson A102

Trapshooting A103

1976, July 3 Engr. *Perf. 13*

248 A102 1.20fr multi .90 .70

American Bicentennial.

1976, July 17 Engr. *Perf. 13*

249 A103 2fr multi 1.40 .90

21st Olympic Games, Montreal, Canada, July 17-Aug. 1.

Meritxell Sanctuary and Old Chapel — A104

1976, Sept. 4 Engr. *Perf. 13*

250 A104 1fr multi .70 .60

Dedication of rebuilt Meritxell Church, Sept. 8, 1976.

Apollo — A105

Ermine — A106

Design: 1.40fr, Morio butterfly.

1976, Oct. 16 Photo. *Perf. 13*

251 A105 80c black & multi 1.60 1.00
252 A105 1.40fr salmon & multi 2.00 1.75

Nature protection.

1977, Apr. 2 Photo. *Perf. 13*

253 A106 1fr vio bl, gray & blk 1.40 1.25

Nature protection.

St. Jean de Caselles
A107

Manual Digest, 1748, Arms of Andorra
A108

Europa: 1.40fr, Sant Vicens Castle.

1977, Apr. 30 Engr. *Perf. 13*

254 A107 1fr multi *3.00* 1.25
255 A107 1.40fr multi *4.00* 1.75

1977, June 11 Engr. *Perf. 13*

256 A108 80c grn, bl & brn .65 .55

Establishment of Institute of Andorran Studies.

St. Romanus of Caesarea
A109

1977, July 23 Engr. *Perf. 12½x13*

257 A109 2fr multi 1.10 .90

Design from altarpiece in Church of St. Roma de les Bons.

General Council Chamber
A110

Guillem d'Arény Plandolit — A111

1977, Sept. 24 Engr. *Perf. 13*

258 A110 1.10fr multi 1.50 .90
259 A111 2fr car & dk brn 1.25 .80

Andorran heritage. Guillem d'Arény Plandolit started Andorran reform movement in 1866.

Squirrel — A112

1978, Mar. 18 Engr. *Perf. 13*

260 A112 1fr multi .80 .50

Flag and Valira River Bridge — A113

1978, Apr. 8

261 A113 80c multi .40 .30

Signing of the treaty establishing the Co-Principality of Andorra, 700th anniv.

Pal Church
A114

Europa: 1.40fr, Charlemagne's Castle, Charlemagne on horseback, vert.

1978, Apr. 29 Engr. *Perf. 13*

262 A114 1fr multi *3.00* 1.00
263 A114 1.40fr multi *4.50* 1.75

Virgin of Sispony
A115

1978, May 20 Engr. *Perf. 12x13*

264 A115 2fr multi 1.10 .90

Visura Tribunal
A116

1978, June 24 Engr. *Perf. 13*

265 A116 1.20fr multi .65 .40

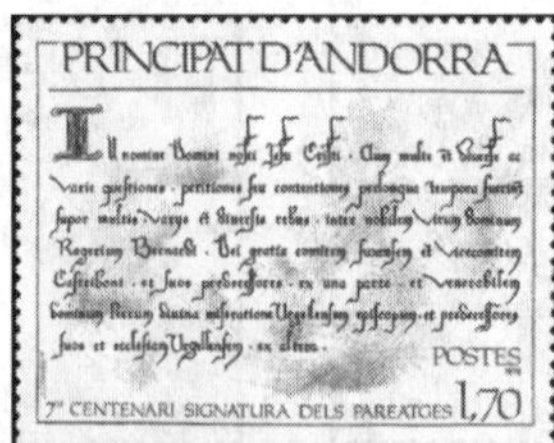

Preamble of 1278 Treaty — A117

1978, Sept. 2 Engr. *Perf. 13x12½*

266 A117 1.70fr multi .65 .40

700th anniversary of the signing of treaty establishing Co-Principality of Andorra.

Pyrenean Chamois
A118

White Partridges
A119

1979, Mar. 26 Engr. *Perf. 13*

267 A118 1fr multi .40 .35

1979, Apr. 9 Photo. *Perf. 13*

268 A119 1.20fr multi .75 .60

Nature protection. See Nos. 288-289.

French Mailman, 1900 — A120

Europa: 1.70fr, 1st French p.o. in Andorra.

1979, Apr. 28 Engr. *Perf. 13*

269 A120 1.20fr multi 1.25 .50
270 A120 1.70fr multi 2.75 .75

Falcon, Pre-Roman Painting
A121

1979, June 2 Engr. *Perf. 12½x13*

271 A121 2fr multi .90 .65

Child with Lambs, Church, IYC Emblem. — A122

1979, July 7 Photo. *Perf. 13*

272 A122 1.70fr multi .70 .50

International Year of the Child.

Bas-relief, Trobada Monument.
A123

1979, Sept. 29 Engr. *Perf. 13*

273 A123 2fr multi .90 .65

Co-Principality of Andorra, 700th anniv

Judo Hold
A124

Farm House, Cortinada
A125

1979, Nov. 24 Engr. *Perf. 13*

274 A124 1.30fr multi .65 .45

World Judo Championships, Paris, Dec. 1979.

1980, Jan. 26 Engr. *Perf. 13*

275 A125 1.10fr multi .35 .25

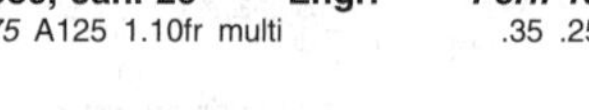

Cross-Country Skiing — A126

1980, Feb. 9

276 A126 1.80fr ultra & lil rose 1.10 .70

13th Winter Olympic Games, Lake Placid, NY, Feb. 12-24.

A128

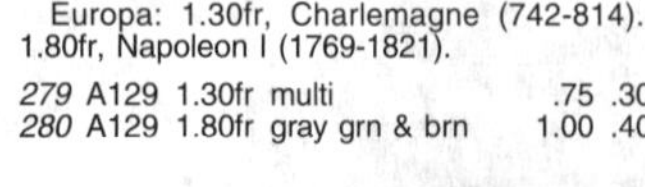

A129

1980, Aug. 30 Engr. *Perf. 13*

278 A128 1.20fr multi .40 .25

World Bicycling championships.

1980, Apr. 26 Engr. *Perf. 13*

Europa: 1.30fr, Charlemagne (742-814). 1.80fr, Napoleon I (1769-1821).

279 A129 1.30fr multi .75 .30
280 A129 1.80fr gray grn & brn 1.00 .40

Pyrenees Lily — A130

1980 Photo.

281 A130 1.10fr Dog-toothed violet .40 .25
282 A130 1.30fr shown .45 .30

Nature protection. Issue dates: 1.10fr, June 21; 1.30fr, May 17.

De La Vall House, 400th Anniversary of Restoration A131

1980, Sept. 6 Engr.

283 A131 1.40fr multi .40 .30

Angel, Church of St. Cerni de Nagol, Pre-Romanesque Fresco — A132

1980, Oct. 27 ***Perf. 13x12½***

284 A132 2fr multi .75 .60

Bordes de Mereig Mountain Village A133

1981, Mar. 21 Engr. ***Perf. 13***

285 A133 1.40fr bl gray & dk brn .45 .35

Europa Issue 1981

Ball de l'Ossa, Winter Game A134

1981, May 16 Engr.

286 A134 1.40fr shown .75 .40
287 A134 2fr El Contrapas dance .75 .55

Bird Type of 1979

1981, June 20 Photo.

288 A119 1.20fr Phylloscopus bonelli .50 .35
289 A119 1.40fr Tichodroma muraria .55 .40

World Fencing Championship, Clermont-Ferrand, July 2-13 — A135

1981, July 4 Engr.

290 A135 2fr bl & blk .60 .45

St. Martin, 12th Cent. Tapestry A136

1981, Sept. 5 Engr. ***Perf. 12x13***

291 A136 3fr multi 1.00 .75

Intl. Drinking Water Decade A137

Intl. Year of the Disabled A138

1981, Oct. 17 ***Perf. 13***

292 A137 1.60fr multi .45 .30

1981, Nov. 7

293 A138 2.30fr multi .70 .55

Europa 1982 A139

1982, May 8 Engr. ***Perf. 13***

294 A139 1.60fr Creation of Andorran govt., 1982 .75 .35
295 A139 2.30fr Land Council, 1419 1.25 .50

1982 World Cup — A140

Various soccer players.

1982, June 12 Engr. ***Perf. 13***

296 1.60fr red & dk brn .45 .35
297 2.60fr red & dk brn .60 .50
a. A140 Pair, #296-297 + label 1.25 .85

Souvenir Sheet

No. 52 — A141

1982, Aug. 21 Engr.

298 A141 5fr blk & rose car 1.25 1.25

1st Andorran Stamp Exhib., 8/21-9/19.

Horse, Roman Wall Painting — A142

1982, Sept. 4 Photo. ***Perf. 13x12½***

299 A142 3fr multi 1.00 .80

Wild Cat — A143

1982, Oct. 9 Engr. ***Perf. 13***

300 A143 1.80fr shown 1.10 .75
301 A143 2.60fr Pine trees .75 .55

TB Bacillus Centenary A144

St. Thomas Aquinas (1225-74) A145

1982, Nov. 13

302 A144 2.10fr Koch, lungs .55 .45

1982, Dec. 4

303 A145 2fr multi .55 .45

Manned Flight Bicentenary A146

1983, Feb. 26 Engr.

304 A146 2fr multi .55 .45

Nature Protection A147

1983, Apr. 16 Engr. ***Perf. 13***

305 A147 1fr Birch trees .35 .25
306 A147 1.50fr Trout .50 .35

See Nos. 325-326.

Europa 1983 A148

Catalane Gold Works.

1983, May 7 Engr. ***Perf. 13***

307 A148 1.80fr Exterior 1.00 .50
308 A148 2.60fr Interior 1.25 .60

30th Anniv. of Customs Cooperation Council — A149

1983, May 14

309 A149 3fr Letter of King Louis XIII 1.10 .75

First Arms of Valleys of Andorra A150

1983, Sept. 3 Engr. ***Perf. 13***

310 A150 5c olive grn & red .20 .20
311 A150 10c grn & olive grn .20 .20
312 A150 20c brt pur & red .20 .20
313 A150 30c brn vio & red .25 .20
314 A150 40c dk bl & vio .25 .20
315 A150 50c gray & red .20 .20
316 A150 1fr deep magenta .20 .20
317 A150 2fr org red & red brn .60 .40
318 A150 5fr dk brn & red 1.75 1.40
Nos. 310-318 (9) 3.85 3.20

See Nos. 329-335, 380-385, 464-465.

Painting, Cortinada Church A151

1983, Sept. 24 ***Perf. 12x13***

319 A151 4fr multi 1.25 .75

Plandolit House — A152

1983, Oct. 15 Photo. ***Perf. 13***

320 A152 1.60fr dp ultra & brn .45 .30

1984 Winter Olympics A153

1984, Feb. 18 Engr.

321 A153 2.80fr multicolored .75 .50

Pyrenees Region Work Community (Labor Org.) A154

1984, Apr. 28 **Engr.** ***Perf. 13***
322 A154 3fr brt blue & sepia .85 .60

Europa (1959-84) A155

1984, May 5 **Engr.**
323 A155 2fr brt grn .90 .40
324 A155 2.80fr rose car 1.10 .60

Nature Protection Type of 1983

1984, July 7 **Engr.** ***Perf. 13***
325 A147 1.70fr Chestnut tree .50 .30
326 A147 2.10fr Walnut tree .70 .50

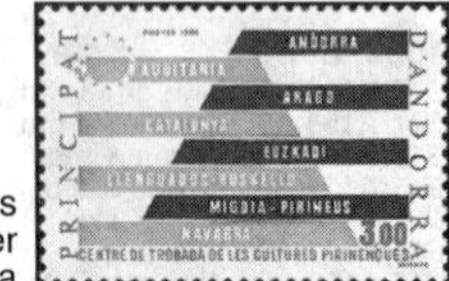

Pyrenees Art Center A155a

1984, Sept. 7 **Engr.**
327 A155a 3fr multi .90 .65

Romanesque Fresco, Church of St. Cerni de Nagol — A156

1984, Nov. 17 ***Perf. 12x13***
328 A156 5fr multi 1.60 1.25

First Arms Type of 1983

1984-87 **Engr.** ***Perf. 13***
329 A150 1.90fr emerald .90 .60
330 A150 2.20fr red orange .50 .35
a. Bklt. pane, 2 #329, 6 #330 5.50
331 A150 3fr bl grn & red brn 1.00 .65
332 A150 4fr brt org & brn 1.50 .90
333 A150 10fr brn org & blk 2.25 1.50
334 A150 15fr grn & dk grn 3.75 2.25
335 A150 20fr brt bl & red brn 4.75 3.00
Nos. 329-335 (7) 14.65 9.25

Nos. 329-330 issued in booklets only.
Issued: 3fr, 20fr, 12/1/84; 10fr, 2/9/85; 4fr, 15fr, 4/19/86; 1.90fr, 2.20fr, 3/28/87.

Saint Julia Valley A157

1985, Apr. 13 **Engr.**
336 A157 2fr multi .80 .45

Europa 1985 — A158

Intl. Youth Year — A159

1985, May 4 **Engr.**
337 A158 2.10fr Le Val D'Andorre 1.50 .85
338 A158 3fr Instruments 2.50 1.10

1985, June 8 **Engr.**
339 A159 3fr multi .90 .60

Wildlife Conservation — A160

1985, Aug. 3 **Photo.**
340 A160 1.80fr Anas platyrhynchos .65 .40
341 A160 2.20fr Carduelis carduelis .85 .60

Two Saints, Medieval Fresco in St. Cerni de Nagol Church A161

1985, Sept. 14 **Engr.** ***Perf. 12½x13***
342 A161 5fr multi 1.50 1.25

Postal Museum Inauguration A162

1986, Mar. 22 **Engr.** ***Perf. 13***
343 A162 2.20fr like No. 269 .80 .40

Europa 1986 A163

1986, May 3 **Engr.** ***Perf. 13***
344 A163 2.20fr Ansalonga 1.25 .75
345 A163 3.20fr Isard 2.00 1.25

1986 World Cup Soccer Championships, Mexico — A164

1986, June 14
346 A164 3fr multi 1.00 .50

Angonella Lake A165

1986, June 28
347 A165 2.20fr multi .65 .40

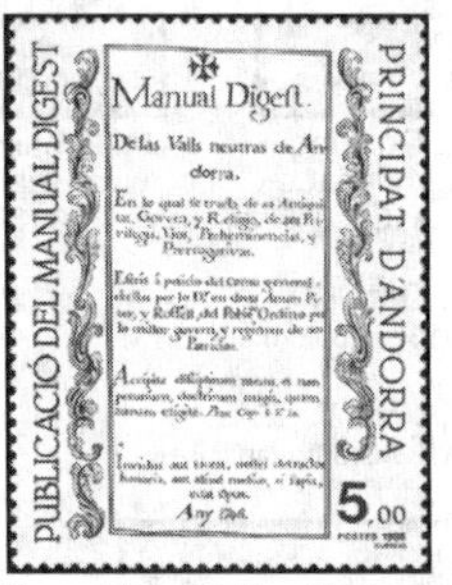

Manual Digest Frontispiece, 1748 — A166

1986, Sept. 6 **Engr.**
348 A166 5fr chnt brn, gray ol & blk 1.60 .90

Intl. Peace Year A167

1986, Sept. 29
349 A167 1.90fr bl gray & grnsh bl .65 .40

A168

1986, Oct. 18 **Engr.** ***Perf. 13½x13***
350 A168 1.90fr St. Vicenc D'Enclar .75 .40

Contemporary Natl. Coat of Arms — A169

1987, Mar. 27 **Litho.** ***Perf. 12½x13***
351 A169 2.20fr multi 1.50 .90

Visit of the French co-prince.

Europa 1987 A170

1987, May 2 **Engr.** ***Perf. 13***
352 A170 2.20fr Meritxell Sanctuary 1.25 .65
353 A170 3.40fr Pleta D'Ordino 1.75 .90

Ransol Village — A171

1987, June 13 **Photo.**
354 A171 1.90fr multicolored 1.00 .50

Nature A172

1987, July 4
355 A172 1.90fr Cavall rogenc 1.10 .60
356 A172 2.20fr Graellsia isabellae 1.40 .70

Aryalsu, Romanesque Painting, La Cortinada Church — A173

Litho. & Engr.

1987, Sept. 5 ***Perf. 12½x13***
357 A173 5fr multi 1.75 1.00

Hiker Looking at Map A174

1987, Sept. 19 **Engr.** ***Perf. 13***
358 A174 2fr olive, grn & dark brn vio .70 .45

Medieval Iron Key, La Cortinada A175

1987, Oct. 17 **Litho.**
359 A175 3fr multi 1.10 .60

Andorran Coat of Arms — A176

Booklet Stamp

1988, Feb. 6 Engr. *Perf. 13*

360 A176 2.20fr red .70 .40
a. Bklt. pane of 5 4.00
Complete bklt., 2 #360a 8.00

See Nos. 388-389B.

Shoemaker's Last from Roc de l'Oral — A177

1988, Feb. 13 Photo.

361 A177 3fr multi 1.00 .60

Rugby A178

1988, Mar. 19 Engr. *Perf. 13½x13*

362 A178 2.20fr emer grn, Prus grn & brn .95 .50

Europa 1988 A179

Hot Springs, Escaldes A180

Transport and communication: 2.20fr, Broadcast tower. 3.60fr, Computer graphics.

1988, May 2 Engr. *Perf. 13*

363 A179 2.20fr multicolored 2.00 .75
364 A179 3.60fr multicolored 3.00 1.25

1988, May 14 Engr.

365 A180 2.20fr Prus blue, org brn & emer .70 .50

Tor D'Ansalonga Farmhouse, Ansalonga Pass — A181

1988, June 13 Engr.

366 A181 2fr multi .65 .40

Sheepdog — A182

1988, July 2 Photo.

367 A182 2fr shown 1.25 .50
368 A182 2.20fr Hare 1.25 .50

Roman Fresco, 8th Cent., St. Steven's Church, Andorre-La-Vieille — A183

1988, Sept. 3 Engr. *Perf. 13x12½*

369 A183 5fr multicolored 1.75 .90

French Revolution, Bicent. — A184

1989, Jan. 1 Litho. *Perf. 13*

370 A184 2.20fr red & vio bl .85 .50

Poble de Pal Village A185

1989, Mar. 4 Engr. *Perf. 13*

371 A185 2.20fr indigo & lilac .70 .45

Europa 1989 A186

Children's games.

1989, June 9 Engr. *Perf. 13*

372 A186 2.20fr Human tower 1.25 .50
373 A186 3.60fr The handkerchief 1.50 .75

Red Cross A187

1989, May 6

374 A187 3.60fr multi 1.25 .65

Visigothic-Merovingian Age Cincture from a Column, St. Vicenc D'Anclar — A188

1989, June 3 Photo.

375 A188 3fr multi .90 .50

Wildlife A189

1989, Sept. 18 Engr. *Perf. 13*

376 A189 2.20fr Wild boar .90 .50
377 A189 3.60fr Newt 1.40 .75

Scene of Salome from the Retable of St. Michael of Mosquera, Encamp — A190

1989, Oct. 16 *Perf. 13x13½*

378 A190 5fr multi 1.50 .80

La Margineda Bridge A191

1990, Feb. 26 Engr. *Perf. 13*

379 A191 2.30fr multi .80 .45

Tourism.

Arms Types of 1983 and 1988

1990-93 Engr. *Perf. 13*

380 A150 2.10fr green .80 .30
381 A150 2.20fr green 1.50 .60
382 A150 2.30fr vermilion .85 .30
383 A150 2.40fr green .90 .40
384 A150 2.50fr vermilion 1.75 .70
385 A150 2.80fr vermilion 1.00 .40
Nos. 380-385 (6) 6.80 2.70

Booklet Stamps

Perf. 13

386 A176 2.30fr red .85 .30
a. Booklet pane of 5 4.25
387 A176 2.50fr vermilion 1.75 .65
a. Booklet pane of 5 8.50
388 A176 2.80fr red 1.00 .40
c. Booklet pane of 5 5.00
Nos. 386-388 (3) 3.60 1.35

Issued: 2.20fr, #384, 10/28/91; #387, 10/21/91; 2.40fr, 2.80fr, 8/9/93; 2.10fr, 2.30fr, 1990.

Llorts Mines A193

1990, Apr. 21 Engr. *Perf. 12½x13*

390 A193 3.20fr multicolored 1.25 .60

Europa A194

Designs: 2.30fr, Early post office. 3.20fr, Modern post office.

1990, May 5 *Perf. 13*

391 A194 2.30fr blk & scar 1.25 .50
392 A194 3.20fr scar & vio 2.25 .80

Otter A195

1990, May 25 *Perf. 12x13*

393 A195 2.30fr Roses, vert. .95 .50
394 A195 3.20fr shown 1.40 .75

Censer of St. Roma of Les Bons A196

1990, June 25 *Perf. 12½x13*

395 A196 3fr multicolored 1.10 .60

Tobacco Drying Sheds, Les Bons A197

1990, Sept. 15 Engr. *Perf. 12½x13*

396 A197 2.30fr multi .85 .50

St. Coloma (Detail) A198

1990, Oct. 8 *Perf. 12½x13*

397 A198 5fr multi 2.00 1.00

Coin from Church of St. Eulalia d'Encamp A199

1990, Oct. 27 Litho. *Perf. 13*

398 A199 3.20fr multi 1.10 .60

De Gaulle Type of 1972 Dated 1990

1990, Oct. 23 Engr. *Perf. 13*

399 A88 2.30fr vio bl 1.00 .55
400 A88 3.20fr dk car 1.40 .75
a. Pair, #399-400 + label 2.40 2.00

Birth centenary of De Gaulle.

4th Games of the Small European States — A200

1991, Apr. 8 Photo. *Perf. 13*

401 A200 2.50fr multicolored .90 .50

Chapel of St. Roma Dels Vilars A201

1991, Mar. 9 Engr. *Perf. 13*

402 A201 2.50fr multicolored .90 .50

Europa — A202

1991, Apr. 27 ***Perf. 13x12½, 12½x13***

403 A202 2.50fr TV satellite 1.25 .60
404 A202 3.50fr Telescope, horiz. 1.50 .75

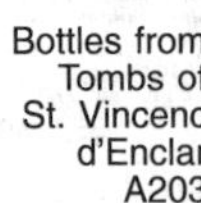

Bottles from Tombs of St. Vincenc d'Enclar A203

1991, May 11 **Photo.** ***Perf. 13***

405 A203 3.20fr multicolored 1.25 .60

Farm Animals A204

1991, June 22 **Engr.** ***Perf. 13***

406 A204 2.50fr Sheep .90 .50
407 A204 3.50fr Cow 1.25 .65

Petanque World Championships — A205

1991, Sept. 14 **Engr.** ***Perf. 13***

408 A205 2.50fr multicolored .90 .40

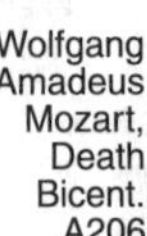

Wolfgang Amadeus Mozart, Death Bicent. A206

1991, Oct. 5

409 A206 3.40fr multicolored 1.40 .75

Virgin and Child of St. Julia and St. Germa A207

1991, Nov. 16 **Engr.** ***Perf. 12½x13***

410 A207 5fr multicolored 2.00 1.00

1992 Winter Olympics, Albertville — A208

1992, Feb. 10 **Litho.** ***Perf. 13***

411 A208 2.50fr Slalom skiing .95 .50
412 A208 3.40fr Figure skating 1.25 .75
a. Pair, #411-412 + label 2.25 1.10

Church of St. Andrew of Arinsal A209

1992, Mar. 21 **Engr.** ***Perf. 12x13***

413 A209 2.50fr black & tan 1.10 .60

Discovery of America, 500th Anniv. A210

1992, Apr. 25 ***Perf. 13***

414 A210 2.50fr Columbus' fleet 1.75 .60
415 A210 3.40fr Landing in New World 2.25 1.00

Europa.

1992 Summer Olympics, Barcelona A211

European Globeflower A212

1992, June 8 **Litho.** ***Perf. 13***

416 A211 2.50fr Kayaking 1.00 .60
417 A211 3.40fr Shooting 1.40 .90
a. Pair, #416-417 + label 2.40 2.00

1992, July 6

Design: 3.40fr, Vulture, horiz.

418 A212 2.50fr multicolored 1.00 .60
419 A212 3.40fr multicolored 1.40 .90

Martyrdom of St. Eulalia A213

1992, Sept. 14 **Photo.** ***Perf. 13***

420 A213 4fr multicolored 1.50 .80

Sculpture by Mauro Staccioli A214

1992, Oct. 5 **Engr.** ***Perf. 12½x13***

421 A214 5fr multicolored 2.00 1.00

Ordino Arcalis '91.

Tempest in a Tea Cup, by Dennis Oppenheim — A215

1992, Nov. 14 **Engr.** ***Perf. 13x12½***

422 A215 5fr multicolored 2.00 1.00

Skiing in Andorra — A216

Ski resorts: No. 423: a, 2.50fr, Soldeu El Tarter. b, 3.40fr, Arinsal.
No. 424: a, 2.50fr, Pas de la Casa-Grau Roig. b, 2.50fr, Ordino Arcalis. c, 3.40fr, Pal.

1993, Mar. 13 **Litho.** ***Perf. 13***

423 A216 Pair, #a.-b. + label 2.25 1.10
424 A216 Strip of 3, #a.-c. 3.25 1.75

Sculptures — A217

Europa: 2.50fr, "Estructures Autogeneradores," by Jorge du Bon, vert. 3.40fr, Sculpture, "Fisicromia per Andorra," by Carlos Cruz-Diez.

1993, May 15 **Engr.** ***Perf. 12½x13***

425 A217 2.50fr multicolored .75 .50

Litho.

Perf. 14x13½

426 A217 3.40fr multicolored 1.25 .75

Butterflies A218

1993, June 28 **Litho.** ***Perf. 13***

427 A218 2.50fr Polymmatus icarus .95 .50
428 A218 4.20fr Nymphalidae 1.50 .80

Tour de France Bicycle Race — A219

1993, July 20 **Litho.** ***Perf. 13***

429 A219 2.50fr multicolored .90 .50

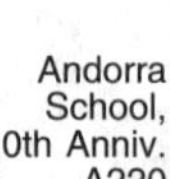

Andorra School, 10th Anniv. A220

1993, Sept. 20 **Litho.** ***Perf. 13***

430 A220 2.80fr multicolored 1.00 .60

Un Lloc Paga, by Michael Warren A221

1993, Oct. 18 **Engr.** ***Perf. 12½x13***

431 A221 5fr blue & black 1.75 1.00

Sculpture, by Erik Dietman A222

1993, Nov. 8 **Engr.** ***Perf. 12½x13***

432 A222 5fr multicolored 1.75 1.00

1994 Winter Olympics, Lillehammer A223

1994, Feb. 21 **Litho.** ***Perf. 13***

433 A223 3.70fr multicolored 1.25 .75

1st Anniversary of the Constitution — A224

Designs: 2.80fr, Monument, by Emili Armengol. 3.70fr, Stone tablet with inscription.

1994, Mar. 15 **Litho.** ***Perf. 13***

434 A224 2.80fr multicolored 1.00 .60
435 A224 3.70fr multicolored 1.40 .90
a. Pair, #434-435 + label 2.40 2.00

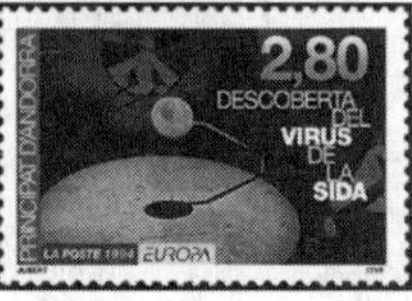

European Discoveries A225

Europa: 2.80fr, Discovery of AIDS virus. 3.70fr, Radio diffusion.

1994, May 9 **Litho.** ***Perf. 13***

436 A225 2.80fr multicolored 1.00 .60
437 A225 3.70fr multicolored 1.25 .75

1994 World Cup Soccer Championships, US — A226

1994, June 20
438 A226 3.70fr multicolored 1.50 .90

Tourist Sports — A227

#439, Mountain climbing. #440, Fishing. #441, Horseback riding. #442, Mountain biking.

1994, July 11
439 A227 2.80fr multicolored 1.10 .60
440 A227 2.80fr multicolored 1.10 .60
a. Pair, #439-440 + label 2.25 2.00
441 A227 2.80fr multicolored 1.10 .60
442 A227 2.80fr multicolored 1.10 .60
a. Pair, #441-442 + label 2.25 2.00
Nos. 439-442 (4) 4.40 2.40

Butterflies A228

1994, Sept. 5 Litho. *Perf. 13*
443 A228 2.80fr Iphiclides podalirus 1.10 .60
444 A228 4.40fr Aglais urticae 1.75 1.00

A229 A230

1994, Oct. 22 Litho. *Perf. 13*
445 A229 2.80fr multicolored 1.25 .75

Meeting of the Co-Princes, 1st anniv.

1995, Feb. 27 Litho. *Perf. 13*
446 A230 2.80fr multicolored 1.25 .75

European Nature Conservation Year

1995 World Cup Rugby Championships — A231

1995, Apr. 24 Litho. *Perf. 13*
447 A231 2.80fr multicolored 1.25 .75

Peace & Freedom A232

Europa: 2.80fr, Dove with olive branch. 3.70fr, Flock of doves.

1995, May 2
448 A232 2.80fr multicolored 1.00 .60
449 A232 3.70fr multicolored 1.25 .80

Caritas in Andorra, 15th Anniv. A233

1995, May 15 Litho. *Perf. 13*
450 A233 2.80fr multicolored 1.25 1.00

Caldea Health Spa — A234

1995, June 26 Litho. *Perf. 13*
451 A234 2.80fr multicolored 1.25 1.00

Ordino Natl. Auditorium A235

1995, July 10 Litho. & Engr.
452 A235 3.70fr black & buff 1.60 1.25

Virgin of Meritxell — A236

1995, Sept. 11 Litho. *Perf. 14*
453 A236 4.40fr multicolored 1.90 1.50

Protection of Nature A237

Butterflies: 2.80fr, Papallona llimonera, vert. 3.70fr, Papallona melanargia galathea.

1995, Sept. 25 *Perf. 13*
454 A237 2.80fr multicolored 1.25 1.00
455 A237 3.70fr multicolored 1.60 1.25

UN, 50th Anniv. — A238

1995, Oct. 21 Litho. *Perf. 13*
456 A238 2.80fr Flag, emblem 1.25 1.00
457 A238 3.70fr Emblem, "50," flag 1.60 1.25
a. Pair, #456-457 + label 3.00 3.00

Andorra's Entrance into Council of Europe A239

1995, Nov. 4
458 A239 2.80fr multicolored 1.25 1.00

World Skiing Championships, Ordino Arcalis — A240

1996, Jan. 29 Litho. *Perf. 13*
459 A240 2.80fr multicolored 1.25 1.25

Basketball in Andorra — A241

1996, Jan. 29 Litho. *Perf. 13*
460 A241 3.70fr multicolored 1.60 1.60

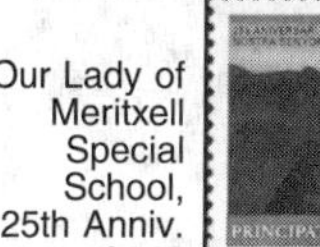
Our Lady of Meritxell Special School, 25th Anniv. A242

1996, Feb. 17 Litho. *Perf. 13*
461 A242 2.80fr multicolored 1.25 1.25

Songbirds A243

1996, Mar. 25
462 A243 3fr Pit riog 1.25 1.25
463 A243 3.80fr Mallarenga carbonera 1.60 1.60

First Arms Type of 1983

1996, Apr. 17 Engr. *Perf. 13*
464 A150 2.70fr green 1.25 1.25
465 A150 3fr red 1.40 1.40

Cross of St. James d'Engordany A244

1996, Apr. 20 Litho.
466 A244 3fr multicolored 1.40 1.40

Censer of St. Eulalia d'Encamp A245

1996, Apr. 20
467 A245 3.80fr multicolored 1.75 1.75

Europa — A246

Chess — A247

1996, May 6
468 A246 3fr Ermessenda de Castellbo 1.25 .50

1996, June 8 Litho. *Perf. 13*
469 A247 4.50fr multicolored 2.00 2.00

1996 Summer Olympic Games, Atlanta A248

1996, June 29 Litho. *Perf. 13*
470 A248 3fr multicolored 1.25 1.25

Arms of the Community of Canillo — A249

Serpentine Die Cut 7 Vert.
1996, June 10 Litho.
Self-Adhesive
471 A249 (3fr) multicolored 1.75 1.75
a. Booklet of 10 17.50

Natl. Children's Choir, 5th Anniv. A250

1996, Sept. 14 *Perf. 13*
472 A250 3fr multicolored 1.40 1.40

Livestock Fair A251

1996, Oct. 26 Engr. *Perf. 12x13*
473 A251 3fr multicolored 1.25 1.25

Churches A252

#474, St. Romá de Les Bons. #475, St. Coloma.

1996, Nov. 16 Litho. *Perf. 13*
474 A252 6.70fr multicolored 2.75 2.75
475 A252 6.70fr multicolored 2.75 2.75

A253

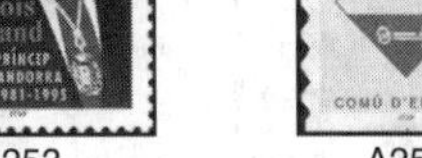
A254

1997, Jan. 7 Litho. *Perf. 13*

476 A253 3fr multicolored 1.25 1.25

Pres. Francois Mitterrand (1916-96).

Sawtooth Die Cut 7 Vert. x Straight Die Cut

1997, Feb. 24 Litho.

Self-Adhesive

477 A254 (3fr) Arms of Encamp 1.25 1.25
a. Booklet pane of 10 12.50

By its nature, No. 477a is a complete booklet. The peelable paper backing serves as a booklet cover.

A255

A256

1997, Mar. 22 *Perf. 13*

478 A255 3fr Volleyball 1.25 1.25

1997, May 12 Litho. *Perf. 13*

479 A256 3fr "The White Lady" 1.00 .50

Europa (Stories and Legends).

Oreneta Cuablanca A257

1997, May 31 Litho. *Perf. 13*

480 A257 3.80fr multicolored 1.60 1.60

Paintings of Mills A258

1997, Sept. 15 Litho. *Perf. 13*

481 A258 3fr Cal Pal, vert. 1.10 1.10
482 A258 4.50fr Mas d'en Sole 1.75 1.75

Religious Artifacts A259

Designs: 3fr, Monstrance of St. Iscle and St. Victoria. 15.50fr, Altar piece of St. Pierre d'Alxirivall.

1997, Oct. 27

483 A259 3fr multicolored 1.10 1.10
484 A259 15.50fr multicolored 5.75 5.75
a. Pair, #483-484 + label 7.00 7.00

Legends — A260

Designs: No. 485, Legend of Meritxell. No. 486, The cross of seven arms. 3.80fr, The fountain of Esmelicat.

1997, Nov. 22 Litho. *Perf. 13*

485 A260 3fr multicolored 1.10 1.10
486 A260 3fr multicolored 1.10 1.10
487 A260 3.80fr multicolored 1.40 1.40
a. Strip of 3, #485-487 3.75 3.75

Monaco Intl. Philatelic Exhibition — A261

1997, Nov. 28 Litho. *Perf. 13*

488 A261 3fr Chapel of St. Miguel d'Engolasters 1.10 1.10

Happy Anniversary A262

1998 Winter Olympic Games, Nagano A263

1998, Jan. 3 Litho. *Perf. 13*

489 A262 3fr Juggling candles 1.10 1.10

1998, Feb. 14

490 A263 4.40fr multicolored 1.75 1.75

Arms of Ordino — A264

Serpentine Die Cut Vert.

1998, Mar. 7 Litho.

Booklet Stamp

Self-Adhesive

491 A264 (3fr) multicolored 1.10 1.10
a. Booklet pane of 10 11.00
Complete booklet, #491a 11.00

See Nos. 504, 518, 531.

Mesa de Vila Church — A265

1998, Mar. 28 *Perf. 13*

492 A265 4.50fr multicolored 1.75 1.75

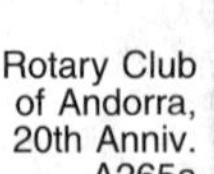

Rotary Club of Andorra, 20th Anniv. A265a

1998, Apr. 11

493 A265a 3fr multicolored 1.10 1.10

Finch A266

1998 Litho. *Perf. 13*

494 A266 3.80fr multicolored 1.40 1.40

1998 World Cup Soccer Championships, France — A267

1998, June 6 Litho. *Perf. 13*

495 A267 3fr multicolored 1.10 1.10

For overprint see No. 499.

Music Festival A268

1998, June 20 Litho. *Perf. 13*

496 A268 3fr multicolored 1.00 .60

Europa.

Expo '98, Lisbon A269

1998, July 6

497 A269 5fr multicolored 1.75 1.75

Chalice, House of the Valleys — A270

1998, Sept. 19 Litho. *Perf. 13*

498 A270 4.50fr multicolored 1.60 1.60

No. 495 Ovptd. "FINAL / FRANCA/BRASIL / 3-0"

1998, Nov. 16

499 A267 3fr multicolored 1.10 1.10

Early Maps of Andorra A271

1998, Nov. 16

500 A271 3fr 1717, vert. 1.10 1.10
501 A271 15.50fr 1777 5.75 5.75

Inauguration of the Postal Museum — A272

1998, Nov. 19 Litho. *Perf. 13*

502 A272 3fr multicolored 1.10 1.10

Manual Digest, 250th Anniv. A273

1998, Dec. 7

503 A273 3.80fr multicolored 1.40 1.40

Arms Type of 1998

Serpentine Die Cut Vert.

1999, Jan. 18

Booklet Stamp

Self-Adhesive

504 A264 (3fr) La Massana 1.10 1.10
a. Booklet pane of 10 11.00

No. 504a is a complete booklet.

Recycling A274

1999, Mar. 13 Litho. *Perf. 13*

505 A274 5fr multicolored 1.75 1.75

Sorteny Valley — A275

Illustration reduced.

1999, Apr. 10

506 A275 3fr multicolored 1.00 .60

Europa.

Council of Europe, 50th Anniv. A276

1999, May 5 Litho. *Perf. 13*

507 A276 3.80fr multicolored 1.40 1.40

First Stage Coach — A277

1999, May 15

508 A277 2.70fr multi 1.00 1.00

1999 European National Soccer Championships — A278

1999, June 10 Photo. *Perf. 13*

509 A278 4.50fr multicolored 1.75 1.75

PhilexFrance 99 — A279

1999, July 2 Litho. *Perf. 13x13¼*

510 A279 3fr multicolored 1.10 1.10

Historic View of Pal — A280

Perf. 13x13¼, 13¼x13

1999, July 10 Litho.

511 A280 3fr shown 1.10 1.10

512 A280 3fr Different view, vert. 1.10 1.10

International Federation of Photographic Art, 50th Anniv. — A281

1999, July 24 Litho. *Perf. 13*

513 A281 4.40fr multicolored 1.60 1.60

Casa Rull, Sispony A282

1999, Sept. 6 Litho. *Perf. 13x13¼*

514 A282 15.50fr multi 5.50 5.50

Chest With Six Locks — A283

1999, Oct. 9 Litho. *Perf. 13x13¼*

515 A283 6.70fr multicolored 2.40 2.40

Christmas A284

1999, Nov. 27 Litho. *Perf. 13*

516 A284 3fr multi 1.00 1.00

Year 2000 A285

2000, Jan. 5 Litho. *Perf. 13x13¼*

517 A285 3fr multi .95 .95

Arms Type of 1998

Serpentine Die Cut 6½ Vert.

2000, Feb. 26

Booklet Stamp

Self-Adhesive

518 A264 (3fr) Andorra-la-Vielle .95 .95
a. Booklet pane of 10 9.50

No. 518a is a complete booklet.

Snowboarding A286

2000, Mar. 17 Litho. *Perf. 13*

519 A286 4.50fr multi 1.40 1.40

Montserrat Caballé Chant Competition A287

2000, Apr. 3 *Perf. 13x13¼*

520 A287 3.80fr multi 1.10 1.10

Campanula Cochlearifolia A288

2000, Apr. 17 Litho. *Perf. 13*

521 A288 2.70fr multi .75 .75

Europa, 2000

Common Design Type

2000, May 9 *Perf. 13½x13*

522 CD17 3fr multi .70 .70

Festivals A289

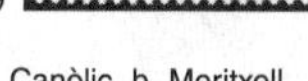

No. 523: a, Canòlic. b, Meritxell.

2000, May 27 Litho. *Perf. 13*

523 Pair + central label 1.75 1.75
a.-b. A289 3fr Any single .85 .85

Pardal Comú — A290

2000, July 7 Litho. *Perf. 13*

524 A290 4.40fr multi 1.25 1.25

A291 A292

2000, Sept. 11 Litho. *Perf. 13*

525 A291 5fr multi 1.40 1.40

2000 Summer Olympics, Sydney.

2000, Sept. 28

526 A292 3fr multi .85 .85

World Tourism Day.

Expo 2000, Hanover A293

2000, Oct. 6 Litho. *Perf. 13*

527 A293 3fr multi .80 .80

Arms Type of 1998

Serpentine Die Cut 6½ Vert.

2001, Feb. 19 Litho.

Booklet Stamp

Self-Adhesive

531 A264 (3fr) Sant Julià de Lòria .75 .75
a. Booklet, 10 #531 7.50

Canillo Aliga Mountain Station — A297

2001, Feb. 10 Litho. *Perf. 13*

532 A297 4.50fr multi 1.25 1.25

Casa Cristo Museum A298

2001, Feb. 17 *Perf. 13¼x13*

533 A298 6.70fr multi 1.90 1.90

Andorran Heritage — A299

No. 534: a, Legend of Engolasters Lake. b, Foundation of Andorra.

2001, Mar. 23 *Perf. 13*

534 A299 3fr Pair, #a-b, with central label 1.60 1.60

Intl. Book Day — A300 Europa — A301

2001, Apr. 23 Litho. *Perf. 13*

535 A300 3.80fr multi 1.00 1.00

2001, Apr. 28

536 A301 3fr multi .70 .70

A302

2001, May 12

537 A302 3fr Raspberries, vert. .80 .80

538 A302 4.40fr shown 1.10 1.10

European Language Year A303

2001, June 16 Litho. *Perf. 13*

539 A303 3.80fr multi 1.00 1.00

Escaldes-Engordany Jazz Festival — A304

2001, July 7

540 A304 3fr multi .85 .85

General Council's Kitchen
A305

2001, Aug. 10
541 A305 5fr multi 1.40 1.40

Chapel of the Virgin of Meritxell, 25th Anniv. of Rebuilding — A306

2001, Sept. 7 Litho. *Perf. 13*
542 A306 3fr multi .85 .85

Hotel Pla — A307

2001, Oct. 12
543 A307 15.50fr multi 4.25 4.25

Cross of Terme — A308

2001, Nov. 17 Litho. *Perf. 13½x13*
544 A308 2.70fr multi .80 .80

100 Cents = 1 Euro (")

National Arms — A309

Legends
A310 A311

Designs: 10c, Legend of Meritxell. 20c, Fountain of Esmelicat. 50c, The Cross with Seven Arms. "1, The Founding of Andorra. "2, Legend of Engolasters Lake. "5, The White Lady.

Perf. 13¼ (A309), 13¼x13
2002, Jan. 2 Photo. (A309), Litho.
545 A309 1c yel & multi .20 .20
546 A309 2c tan & multi .20 .20
547 A309 5c bl & multi .20 .20
548 A310 10c multi .20 .20
549 A310 20c multi .35 .35
550 A309 (46c) red & multi .80 .80
551 A310 50c multi .85 .85
552 A311 "1 multi 1.75 1.75
553 A311 "2 multi 3.50 3.50
554 A311 "5 multi 8.75 8.75
Nos. 545-554 (10) 16.8016.80

Traffic Safety Education in Schools — A312

2002, Jan. 25 Litho. *Perf. 13½x13*
555 A312 69c multi 1.25 1.25

2002 Winter Olympics, Salt Lake City — A313

2002, Feb. 2 Litho. *Perf. 13*
556 A313 58c multi 1.00 1.00

Hotel Rosaleda
A314

2002, Mar. 16 Litho. *Perf. 13*
557 A314 46c multi .80 .80

World Day for Water — A315

2002, Mar. 22 Litho. *Perf. 13*
558 A315 67c multi 1.25 1.25

Europa — A316

2002, May 10 Litho. *Perf. 13*
559 A316 46c multi .85 .85

Bilberries — A317

2002, July 6 Litho. *Perf. 13*
560 A317 46c multi .95 .95

Seated Nude, Sculpture by Josep Viladomat — A318

2002, Aug. 24 Litho. *Perf. 13¼x13*
561 A318 "2.36 multi 4.75 4.75

Envalira Tunnel
A319

2002, Sept. 2 *Perf. 13*
562 A319 46c multi .90 .90

Piper of Ordino — A320

2002, Sept. 27
563 A320 41c multi .80 .80

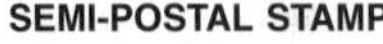

SEMI-POSTAL STAMP

Catalogue values for unused stamps in this section are for Never Hinged items.

Virgin of St. Coloma — SP1

Unwmk.
1964, July 25 Engr. *Perf. 13*
B1 SP1 25c + 10c multi 20.00 20.00

The surtax was for the Red Cross.

AIR POST STAMPS

Catalogue values for unused stamps in this section are for Never Hinged items.

Chamois
AP1

Unwmk.
1950, Feb. 20 Engr. *Perf. 13*
C1 AP1 100fr indigo 65.00 45.00

East Branch of Valira River — AP2

1955-57
C2 AP2 100fr dark green 8.50 6.50
C3 AP2 200fr cerise 17.50 14.00
C4 AP2 500fr dp bl ('57) 90.00 65.00
Nos. C2-C4 (3) 116.00 85.50

D'Inclès Valley
AP3

1961-64 Unwmk. *Perf. 13*
C5 AP3 2fr red, ol gray & cl 1.00 .65
C6 AP3 3fr bl, mar & slate grn 1.25 1.25
C7 AP3 5fr rose lil & red org 2.00 1.75
C8 AP3 10fr bl grn & slate grn 3.75 3.50
Nos. C5-C8 (4) 8.00 7.15

Issued: 10fr, 4/25/64; others, 6/19/61.

POSTAGE DUE STAMPS

Postage Due Stamps of France, 1893-1931, Overprinted

ANDORRE

On Stamps of 1893-1926

1931-33 Unwmk. *Perf. 14x13½*
J1 D2 5c blue 1.00 1.00
J2 D2 10c brown 1.00 1.00
J3 D2 30c rose red .40 .40
J4 D2 50c violet brn 1.00 1.00
J5 D2 60c green 10.00 10.00
J6 D2 1fr red brn, *straw* .50 .50
J7 D2 2fr brt violet 6.00 6.00
J8 D2 3fr magenta 1.10 1.10
Nos. J1-J8 (8) 21.00 21.00

On Stamps of 1927-31
J9 D4 1c olive grn 1.25 1.25
J10 D4 10c rose 2.75 2.75
J11 D4 60c red 16.00 16.00
J12 D4 1fr Prus grn ('32) 65.00 65.00
J13 D4 1.20fr on 2fr bl 50.00 50.00
J14 D4 2fr ol brn ('33) 140.00 140.00
J15 D4 5fr on 1fr vio 65.00 65.00
Nos. J9-J15 (7) 340.00 340.00

D5

D6

1935-41 Typo.
J16 D5 1c gray green 2.25 1.25
J17 D6 5c light blue ('37) 3.75 *4.50*
J18 D6 10c brown ('41) 3.00 *4.50*
J19 D6 2fr violet ('41) 6.00 3.25
J20 D6 5fr red orange ('41) 11.00 3.25
Nos. J16-J20 (5) 26.00 16.75

Catalogue values for unused stamps in this section, from this point to the end of the section, are for Never Hinged items.

Wheat Sheaves — D7

1943-46 *Perf. 14x13½*

J21 D7 10c sepia 1.00 1.00
J22 D7 30c brt red vio 1.50 1.50
J23 D7 50c blue grn 1.75 1.75
J24 D7 1fr brt ultra .80 .80
J25 D7 1.50fr rose red 5.75 5.75
J26 D7 2fr turq blue 1.50 1.50
J27 D7 3fr brown org 2.75 2.75
J28 D7 4fr dp vio ('45) 4.50 4.50
J29 D7 5fr brt pink 4.50 4.50
J30 D7 10fr red org ('45) 5.75 5.75
J31 D7 20fr olive brn ('46) 6.00 6.00
Nos. J21-J31 (11) 35.80 35.80

Inscribed: "Timbre Taxe"

1946-53

J32 D7 10c sepia ('46) 1.10 1.10
J33 D7 1fr ultra .75 .75
J34 D7 2fr turq blue 1.00 1.00
J35 D7 3fr orange brn 2.00 2.00
J36 D7 4fr violet 2.75 2.75
J37 D7 5fr brt pink 1.75 1.75
J38 D7 10fr red orange 2.75 2.75
J39 D7 20fr olive brn 6.25 6.25
J40 D7 50fr dk green ('50) 16.50 16.50
J41 D7 100fr dp green ('53) 87.50 87.50
Nos. J32-J41 (10) 122.35 122.35

Inscribed: "Timbre Taxe"

1961, June 19 *Perf. 14x13½*

J42 D7 5c rose pink 3.00 3.00
J43 D7 10c red orange 6.00 6.00
J44 D7 20c olive 9.00 9.00
J45 D7 50c dark slate green 15.00 15.00
Nos. J42-J45 (4) 33.00 33.00

D8

D9

1964-71 **Typo.** *Perf. 14x13½*

J46 D8 5c Centaury ('65) .20 .20
J47 D8 10c Gentian ('65) .20 .20
J48 D8 15c Corn poppy .20 .20
J49 D8 20c Violets ('71) .20 .20
J50 D8 30c Forget-me-not .20 .20
J51 D8 40c Columbine ('71) .20 .20
J52 D8 50c Clover ('65) .30 .30
Nos. J46-J52 (7) 1.50 1.50

1985, Oct. 21 **Engr.** *Perf. 13*

J53 D9 10c Holly .20 .20
J54 D9 20c Blueberries .20 .20
J55 D9 30c Raspberries .20 .20
J56 D9 40c Bilberries .20 .20
J57 D9 50c Blackberries .20 .20
J58 D9 1fr Broom .35 .30
J59 D9 2fr Rosehips .65 .35
J60 D9 3fr Nightshade 1.00 .60
J61 D9 4fr Nabiu 1.40 .75
J62 D9 5fr Strawberries 1.75 1.00
Nos. J53-J62 (10) 6.15 4.00

NEWSPAPER STAMP

France No. P7 Overprinted

1931 **Unwmk.** *Perf. 14x13½*

P1 A16 ½c on lc gray .75 .75

ANGOLA

aŋ-'gō-lə

LOCATION — S.W. Africa between Zaire and Namibia.
GOVT. — Republic
AREA — 481,351 sq. mi.
POP. — 11,177,537 (1999 est.)
CAPITAL — Luanda

Angola was a Portuguese overseas territory until it became independent November 11, 1975, as the People's Republic of Angola.

1000 Reis = 1 Milreis
100 Centavos = 1 Escudo (1913, 1954)
100 Centavos = 1 Angolar (1932)
10 Lweys = 1 Kwanza (1977)

Catalogue values for unused stamps in this country are for Never Hinged items, beginning with Scott 328 in the regular postage section, Scott C26 in the airpost section, Scott J31 in the postage due section, and Scott RA7 in the postal tax section.

Watermark

Wmk. 232—Maltese Cross

Portuguese Crown — A1

Perf. 12½, 13½

1870-77 **Typo.** **Unwmk.**

1 A1 5r black 2.00 1.00
a. Perf. 13½ 8.00 3.00
2 A1 10r yellow 20.00 9.00
3 A1 20r bister 2.00 1.10
a. Perf. 13½ 275.00 200.00
4 A1 25r red 8.00 4.25
c. 25r rose, perf. 14 225.00 125.00
d. Perf. 13½ 18.00 11.00
5 A1 40r blue ('77) 150.00 100.00
6 A1 50r green 40.00 10.00
a. Perf. 13½ 200.00 85.00
7 A1 100r lilac 3.00 1.75
a. Perf. 12½ 7.00 3.00
8 A1 200r orange ('77) 2.75 1.75
a. Perf. 12½ 4.00 2.10
9 A1 300r choc ('77) 3.00 2.00
a. Perf. 12½ 13.00 6.50

1881-85

10 A1 10r green ('83) 4.00 1.50
a. Perf. 12½ 21.00 10.00
11 A1 20r carmine rose ('85) 10.00 7.00
12 A1 25r violet ('85) 4.50 2.25
a. Perf. 13½ 6.75 3.25
13 A1 40r buff ('82) 6.25 2.25
a. Perf. 13½ 17.50 2.25
15 A1 50r blue 17.50 3.50
a. Perf. 13½ 27.50 3.00
Nos. 10-15 (5) 42.25 16.50

Two types of numerals are found on #2, 11, 13, 15.

The cliche of 40r in plate of 20r error, was discovered before the stamps were issued. All copies were defaced by a blue pencil mark. Value, $750.00.

In perf. 12½, Nos. 1-4, 4a and 6, as well as 7a, were printed in 1870 on thicker paper and 1875 on normal paper. Stamps of the earlier printing sell for 2 to 5 times more than those of the 1875 printing.

Some reprints of the 1870-85 issues are on a smooth white chalky paper, ungummed and perf. 13½.

Other reprints of these issues are on thin ivory paper with shiny white gum and clear-cut perf. 13½.

King Luiz — A2

King Carlos — A3

1886 **Embossed** *Perf. 12½*

16 A2 5r black 3.50 2.50
a. Perf. 13½ 11.50 8.50
17 A2 10r green 3.50 2.50
a. Perf. 13½ 13.00 7.25
18 A2 20r rose 10.00 6.25
a. Perf. 13½ 12.50 6.50
19 A2 25r red violet 7.50 1.50
20 A2 40r chocolate 8.00 5.00
21 A2 50r blue 10.50 2.00
22 A2 100r yellow brn 14.00 5.00
23 A2 200r gray violet 18.00 8.00
24 A2 300r orange 20.00 9.00
Nos. 16-24 (9) 95.00 41.75

For surcharges see #61-69, 172-174, 208-210.

Reprints of 5r, 20r & 100r have cleancut perf. 13½.

1893-94 **Typo.** *Perf. 11½, 12½, 13½*

25 A3 5r yellow 1.00 .85
26 A3 10r redsh violet 2.00 .90
27 A3 15r chocolate 2.75 1.25
28 A3 20r lavender 2.75 1.25
29 A3 25r green 1.25 1.00
a. Perf. 12½ 4.00 2.00
30 A3 50r light blue 3.25 1.25
a. Perf. 13½ 5.00 2.75
31 A3 75r carmine 6.00 3.50
a. Perf. 11½ 8.00 6.25
32 A3 80r lt green 7.50 3.50
33 A3 100r brown, *buff* 6.75 3.50
a. Perf. 11½ 50.00 32.50
34 A3 150r car, *rose* 12.00 10.00
35 A3 200r dk blue, *lt bl* 14.00 11.00
36 A3 300r dk blue, *sal* 15.00 11.00
Nos. 25-36 (12) 74.25 49.00

For surcharges see Nos. 70-81, 175-179, 213-216, 234.

No. P1 Surcharged in Blue

1894, Aug.

37 N1 25r on 2½r brown 80.00 22.50

King Carlos — A5

1898-1903 *Perf. 11½*

Name and Value in Black except 500r

38 A5 2½r gray .20 .20
39 A5 5r orange .20 .20
40 A5 10r yellow grn .20 .20
41 A5 15r violet brn 1.50 .70
42 A5 15r gray grn ('03) .65 .50
43 A5 20r gray violet .25 .20
44 A5 25r sea green 1.00 .40
45 A5 25r car ('03) .50 .20
46 A5 50r blue 1.60 .35
47 A5 50r brown ('03) 3.00 2.00
48 A5 65r dull blue ('03) 12.00 7.00
49 A5 75r rose 4.50 1.60
50 A5 75r red violet ('03) 1.25 .90
51 A5 80r violet 4.50 2.00
52 A5 100r dk blue, *blue* .90 .65
53 A5 115r org brn, *pink* ('03) 9.00 6.50
54 A5 130r brn, *straw* ('03) 9.00 6.50
55 A5 150r brn, *straw* 8.00 5.00
56 A5 200r red vio, *pink* 2.25 1.00
57 A5 300r dk blue, *rose* 3.25 3.25
58 A5 400r dull bl, *straw* ('03) 5.00 3.50
59 A5 500r blk & red, *bl* ('01) 3.50 3.00
60 A5 700r vio, *yelsh* ('01) 14.00 10.00
Nos. 38-60 (23) 86.25 55.85

For surcharges & overprints see #83-102, 113-117, 159-171, 181-183, 217-218, 221-225.

Stamps of 1886-94 Surcharged in Black or Red

Two types of surcharge:
I - 3mm between numeral and REIS.
II - 4½mm spacing.

1902 *Perf. 12½*

61 A2 65r on 40r choc 4.50 3.50
62 A2 65r on 300r org, I 4.50 3.50
a. Type II 32.50 25.00
63 A2 115r on 10r green 4.00 3.25
a. Inverted surcharge 30.00 20.00
b. Perf. 13½ 18.00 17.00
64 A2 115r on 200r gray vio 4.00 2.75
65 A2 130r on 50r blue 6.50 4.75
66 A2 130r on 100r brown 5.00 3.00
67 A2 400r on 20r rose 60.00 30.00
a. Perf. 13½ 60.00 45.00
68 A2 400r on 25r violet 9.00 6.00
69 A2 400r on 5r black (R) 8.00 6.25
a. Double surcharge 30.00 20.00
Nos. 61-69 (9) 105.50 63.00

For surcharges see Nos. 172-174, 208-210.

Perf. 11½, 12½, 13½

70 A3 65r on 5r yel, I 4.00 2.75
a. Type II 10.00 10.00
71 A3 65r on 10r red vio, I 3.25 2.25
a. Type II 13.00 5.25
b. Perf. 11½, type I 8.75 5.25
c. Perf. 11½, type II 3.50 2.50
72 A3 65r on 20r lav 5.00 3.00
a. Type II 6.50 6.00
73 65r on 25r green 4.00 2.50
a. Perf. 11½ 9.25 7.25
74 A3 115r on 80r lt grn 6.00 4.00
75 A3 115r on 100r brn, *buff* 6.00 3.50
a. Perf. 13½ 9.25 6.50
76 A3 115r on 150r car, *rose* 8.50 5.25
a. Perf. 13½ 10.00 6.00
77 A3 130r on 15r choc 3.50 2.00
78 A3 130r on 75r carmine 3.50 2.25
a. Perf. 13½ 14.00 11.50
79 A3 130r on 300r dk bl, *sal* 9.00 6.50
80 A3 400r on 50r lt bl 3.00 2.75
81 A3 400r on 200r bl, *bl* 3.00 3.25
a. Perf. 13½ 21.00 8.75
82 N1 400r on 2½r brn 1.75 1.10
a. Type II 2.50 2.25
Nos. 70-82 (13) 60.50 41.10

For surcharges see #175-180, 211-216, 234-235.

Reprints of Nos. 65, 67, 68 and 69 have clean-cut perforation 13½.

Stamps of 1898 Overprinted—a

1902 *Perf. 11½*

83 A5 15r brown 1.25 .60
84 A5 25r sea green 1.00 .35
85 A5 50r blue 1.75 .85
86 A5 75r rose 3.00 2.00
Nos. 83-86 (4) 7.00 3.80

For surcharge see No. 116.

No. 48 Surcharged in Black

1905

87 A5 50r on 65r dull blue 3.00 1.25

For surcharge see No. 183.

Stamps of 1898-1903 Overprinted in Carmine or Green—b

1911

88 A5 2½r gray .20 .20
89 A5 5r orange yel .20 .20
90 A5 10r light green .25 .20
91 A5 15r gray green .25 .20

92 A5 20r gray violet .25 .20
93 A5 25r carmine (G) .25 .20
94 A5 50r brown 1.50 .90
95 A5 75r lilac 2.50 2.50
96 A5 100r dk blue, *bl* 2.50 2.50
97 A5 115r org brn, *pink* 1.00 .60
98 A5 130r brown, *straw* 1.00 .60
99 A5 200r red lil, *pnksh* 1.00 .60
100 A5 400r dull bl, *straw* 1.50 .65
101 A5 500r blk & red, *bl* 1.25 .65
102 A5 700r violet, *yelsh* 1.75 .70
Nos. 88-102 (15) 15.40 10.90

Inverted and double overprints of Nos. 88-102 were made intentionally.

For surcharges see #217-218, 221-222, 224.

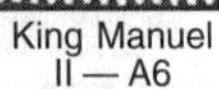

King Manuel II — A6

Ceres — A7

Overprinted in Carmine or Green

1912 ***Perf. 11½x12***
103 A6 2½r violet .25 *.50*
104 A6 5r black .25 *.50*
105 A6 10r gray green .35 .30
106 A6 20r carmine (G) .35 .30
107 A6 25r violet brown .35 .30
108 A6 50r dk blue .60 .50
109 A6 75r bister brown .65 *1.00*
110 A6 100r brown, *lt green* 1.60 .70
111 A6 200r dk green, *salmon* 1.10 .70
112 A6 300r black, *azure* 1.10 .70
Nos. 103-112 (10) 6.60 5.50

For surcharges see Nos. 219-220, 226-227.

No. 91 Surcharged with New Values as

1912, June ***Perf. 11½***
113 A5 2½r on 15r gray green 2.25 2.25
114 A5 5r on 15r gray green 1.75 1.50
115 A5 10r on 15r gray green 1.75 1.50
Nos. 113-115 (3) 5.75 5.25

Inverted and double surcharges of Nos. 113-115 were made intentionally.

Nos. 86 and 50 Surcharged "25" in Black and Overprinted in Violet—c

1912
116 A5 25r on 75r rose 70.00 50.00
117 A5 25r on 75r red violet 2.75 1.50
a. "REUPBLICA" 22.50 20.00
b. "25" omitted 27.50 25.00
c. "REPUBLICA" omitted 32.50 27.50

1914-26 Typo. *Perf. 12x11½, 15x14*
Name and Value in Black
118 A7 ¼c olive brown .20 *.20*
a. Inscriptions inverted 8.00
119 A7 ½c black .20 *.20*
120 A7 1c blue green .20 *.20*
121 A7 1c yel grn ('22) .20 .20
122 A7 1½c lilac brown .20 .20
123 A7 2c carmine .20 .20
124 A7 2c gray ('25) .30 *1.00*
125 A7 2½c lt violet .20 .20
126 A7 3c orange ('21) .20 *.60*
127 A7 4c dull rose ('21) .20 .20
128 A7 4½c gray ('21) .20 *.80*
130 A7 5c blue .20 .20
131 A7 6c lilac ('21) .20 .20
132 A7 7c ultra ('21) .20 .20
133 A7 7½c yellow brn .20 .20
134 A7 8c slate .20 .20
135 A7 10c orange brn .20 .20
136 A7 12c olive brn ('21) .35 .25
137 A7 12c dp green ('25) .20 .20
138 A7 15c plum .75 .20
139 A7 15c brn rose ('21) .20 .20
140 A7 20c yel green .25 .20
141 A7 24c ultra ('25) 1.25 .75
142 A7 25c choc ('25) 1.25 .75
143 A7 30c brown, *green* 2.00 *2.00*
144 A7 30c gray grn ('21) .75 .20
145 A7 40c brown, *pink* 3.50 2.00
146 A7 40c turq blue ('21) .75 .20
147 A7 50c orange, *sal* 6.00 4.25
148 A7 50c lt violet ('25) 1.50 .20
149 A7 60c dk blue ('22) 1.25 .20
150 A7 60c dp rose ('26) 25.00 *50.00*
151 A7 80c pink ('22) 1.25 .20
152 A7 1e green, *blue* 3.50 2.25
153 A7 1e rose ('22) 2.25 .20
154 A7 1e dp blue ('25) 4.00 3.00
155 A7 2e dk violet ('22) 1.25 .50
156 A7 5e buff ('25) 15.00 2.25
157 A7 10e pink ('25) 30.00 10.00
158 A7 20e pale turq ('25) 55.00 35.00
Nos. 118-158 (40) 160.75 120.20

Two kinds of paper, chalky-surfaced paper and ordinary, were used for Nos. 118-120, 122-123, 125, 130, 133-135, 138 and 140. Those on coated paper sell unused for 10 to 40 times the values listed; used for about 5 to 20 times.

All but #143, 145, 147 come perf 12x11½. All but #124, 137, 141-142, 146, 148, 151, 153-154, 156-158 come perf 15x14.

For surcharges see Nos. 228-229, 236-239.

Stamps of 1898-1903 Overprinted type "c" in Red or Green

On Stamps of 1898-1903

1914 ***Perf. 11½, 12***
159 A5 10r yel green (R) 3.25 2.75
160 A5 15r gray green (R) 3.25 2.75
161 A5 20r gray violet (G) .80 1.00
163 A5 75r red violet (G) .80 1.00
164 A5 100r blue, *blue* (R) 1.25 1.25
165 A5 115r org brn, *pink* (R) *80.00*
167 A5 200r red vio, *pnksh* (G) .90 .50
169 A5 400r dl bl, *straw* (R) 40.00 30.00
170 A5 500r blk & red, *bl* (R) 5.00 3.00
171 A5 700r vio, *yelsh* (G) 15.00 12.00

Inverted and double overprints were made intentionally. No. 165 was not regularly issued. Red overprints on the 20r, 75r, 200r were not regularly issued. The 130r was not regularly issued without surcharge (No. 225).

On Nos. 63-65, 74-76, 78-79, 82
Perf. 11½, 12½, 13½
172 A2 115r on 10r (R) 20.00 10.00
a. Perf. 13½ 30.00 20.00
173 A2 115r on 200r (R) 20.00 10.00
174 A2 130r on 50r (R) 35.00 20.00
175 A3 115r on 80r (R) 100.00 75.00
176 A3 115r on 100r (R) 250.00 150.00
177 A3 115r on 150r (G) 165.00 125.00
178 A3 130r on 75r (G) 1.75 1.60
179 A3 130r on 300r (R) 4.00 3.25
a. Perf. 12½ 7.00 4.50
180 N1 400r on 2½r (R) .40 .40
a. Perf. 11½ 1.60 1.25
Nos. 172-180 (9) 596.15 395.25

Overprinted

On Stamps of 1902
Perf. 11½, 12
181 A5 50r blue (R) .90 .60
182 A5 75r rose (G) 2.75 2.00

On No. 87
183 A5 50r on 65r dull blue (R) 2.50 2.50
Nos. 181-183 (3) 6.15 5.10

Inverted and double surcharges of Nos. 181-183 were made intentionally.

Common Design Types pictured following the introduction.

Vasco da Gama Issue of Various Portuguese Colonies

Common Design Types Surcharged

On Stamps of Macao

1913 ***Perf. 12½ to 16***
184 CD20 ¼c on ½a 4.00 4.00
185 CD21 ½c on Ia 3.00 3.00
186 CD22 1c on 2a 3.00 3.00
187 CD23 2½c on 4a 2.00 2.00
188 CD24 5c on 8a 2.00 2.00
189 CD25 7½c on 12a 5.50 5.50
190 CD26 10c on 16a 4.00 4.00
191 CD27 15c on 24a 4.00 4.00
Nos. 184-191 (8) 27.50 27.50

On Stamps of Portuguese Africa
Perf. 14 to 15
192 CD20 ¼c on 2½r .75 .75
193 CD21 ½c on 5r .75 .75
194 CD22 1c on 10r .75 .75
195 CD23 2½c on 25r .75 .75
196 CD24 5c on 50r .75 .75
197 CD25 7½c on 75r 2.50 2.50
198 CD26 10c on 100r 1.25 1.25
199 CD27 15c on 150r 1.75 1.75
Nos. 192-199 (8) 9.25 9.25

On Stamps of Timor
200 CD20 ¼c on ½a 2.00 2.00
201 CD21 ½c on 1a 2.00 2.00
202 CD22 1c on 2a 2.00 2.00
203 CD23 2½c on 4a 2.00 2.00
204 CD24 5c on 8a 2.00 2.00
205 CD25 7½c on 12a 3.00 3.00
206 CD26 10c on 16a 2.00 2.00
207 CD27 15c on 24a 2.00 2.00
Nos. 200-207 (8) 17.00 17.00
Nos. 184-207 (24) 53.75 53.75

Provisional Issue of 1902 Overprinted in Carmine

1915 ***Perf. 11½, 12½, 13½***
208 A2 115r on 10r green 1.00 *2.00*
209 A2 115r on 200r gray vio .90 *2.00*
210 A2 130r on 100r brown .70 *2.00*
211 A3 115r on 80r lt green 1.10 *2.00*
212 A3 115r on 100r brn, *buff* .90 *2.00*
a. Perf. 11½ 17.00 *17.00*
213 A3 115r on 150r car, *rose* 1.75 *2.00*
214 A3 130r on 15r choc .65 *2.00*
a. Perf. 12½ 7.00 7.00
215 A3 130r on 75r carmine 1.50 *1.75*
216 A3 130r on 300r dk bl, *sal* 1.10 *1.75*
Nos. 208-216 (9) 9.60 *17.50*

Stamps of 1911-14 Surcharged in Black:

d

e

On Stamps of 1911

1919 ***Perf. 11½***
217 A5 (d) ½c on 75r red lilac 1.50 *2.00*
218 A5 (d) 2½c on 100r blue, *grysh* 1.75 *2.00*

On Stamps of 1912
Perf. 11½x12
219 A6 (e) ½c on 75r bis brn .65 .60
220 A6 (e) 2½c on 100r brn, *lt grn* .75 .40

On Stamps of 1914
221 A5 (d) ½c on 75r red lil .65 .40
222 A5 (d) 2½c on 100r bl, *grysh* .70 .60
Nos. 217-222 (6) 6.00 *6.00*

Inverted and double surcharges were made for sale to collectors.

Nos. 163, 98 and Type of 1914 Surcharged with New Values and Bars in Black

1921
223 A5 (c) 00.5c on 75r *350.00 350.00*
224 A5 (b) 4c on 130r (#98) .70 *.70*
225 A5 (c) 4c on 130r brn, *straw* 2.75 2.50

Nos. 109 and 108 Surcharged with New Values and Bars in Black
226 A6 00.5c on 75c .85 .85
227 A6 1c on 50r .75 .65

Nos. 133 and 138 Surcharged with New Values and Bars in Black
228 A7 00.5c on 7½c .70 .60
229 A7 04c on 15c 1.10 1.10
Nos. 224-229 (6) 6.85 6.40
Nos. 223-229 (7) *356.85 356.40*

The 04c surcharge exists on the 15c brown rose, perf 12x11½, No. 139. Vale, 30 cents.

Nos. 81-82 Surcharged

1925 ***Perf. 12½***
234 A3 40c on 400r on 200r bl, *bl* .80 .65
a. Perf. 13½ 3.25 2.25
235 N1 40c on 400c on 2½r brn .60 .60
a. Perf. 13½ .60 .60

Nos. 150-151, 154-155 Surcharged

70 C.

1931 ***Perf. 11½***
236 A7 50c on 60c deep rose 1.50 .80
237 A7 70c on 80c pink 3.00 1.00
238 A7 70c on 1e deep blue 4.00 1.10
239 A7 1.40e on 2e dark violet 5.00 1.10
Nos. 236-239 (4) 13.50 4.00

Ceres — A14

Perf. 12x11½
1932-46 Typo. Wmk. 232
243 A14 1c bister brn .20 .20
244 A14 5c dk brown .20 .20
245 A14 10c dp violet .20 .20
246 A14 15c black .20 .20
247 A14 20c gray .25 .20
248 A14 30c myrtle grn .25 .20
249 A14 35c yel grn ('46) 4.50 2.00
250 A14 40c dp orange .25 .20
251 A14 45c lt blue .85 .65
252 A14 50c lt brown .20 .20
253 A14 60c olive grn .30 .20
254 A14 70c orange brn .65 .20
255 A14 80c emerald .25 .20
256 A14 85c rose 2.00 2.00
257 A14 1a claret .65 .20
258 A14 1.40a dk blue 4.50 1.10
258A A14 1.75a dk blue ('46) 6.00 1.10
259 A14 2a dull vio 2.25 .35
260 A14 5a pale yel grn 3.00 .50
261 A14 10a olive bis 10.00 .90
262 A14 20a orange 17.50 2.00
Nos. 243-262 (21) 54.20 13.00
Set, never hinged 75.00

For surcharges see Nos. 263-267, 271-273, 294A-300, J31-J36.

Surcharged with New Value and Bars

5½mm between bars and new value.

1934
263 A14 10c on 45c lt bl 1.25 .70
264 A14 20c on 85c rose 1.10 .70
265 A14 30c on 1.40a dk bl 1.10 .70
266 A14 70c on 2a dl vio 2.00 1.10
267 A14 80c on 5a pale yel grn 3.50 1.00
Nos. 263-267 (5) 8.95 4.20
Set, never hinged 14.00

See Nos. 294A-300.

Nos. J26, J30 Surcharged in Black

CORREIOS
5
CENTAVOS

1935 Unwmk. *Perf. 11½*
268 D2 5c on 6c lt brown .90 .60
269 D2 30c on 50c gray .90 .60
270 D2 40c on 50c gray .90 .60
Nos. 268-270 (3) 2.70 1.80
Set, never hinged 4.25

No. 255 Surcharged in Black

0,15 Cent.

1938 Wmk. 232 Perf. 12x11½

271 A14	5c on 80c emerald	.40	*1.00*
272 A14	10c on 80c emerald	.50	*1.75*
273 A14	15c on 80c emerald	.65	*2.50*
	Nos. 271-273 (3)	1.55	*5.25*
	Set, never hinged	2.60	

Vasco da Gama Issue

Common Design Types

Engr.; Name & Value Typo. in Black
Perf. 13½x13

1938, July 26 Unwmk.

274 CD34	1c gray green	.20	.20
275 CD34	5c orange brn	.20	.20
276 CD34	10c dk carmine	.20	.20
277 CD34	15c dk violet brn	.20	.20
278 CD34	20c slate	.20	.20
279 CD35	30c rose violet	.25	.20
280 CD35	35c brt green	.35	.20
281 CD35	40c brown	.25	.20
282 CD35	50c brt red vio	.25	.20
283 CD36	60c gray black	.35	.20
284 CD36	70c brown vio	.30	.20
285 CD36	80c orange	.30	.20
286 CD36	1a red	.30	.20
287 CD37	1.75a blue	.85	.30
288 CD37	2a brown car	1.50	.30
289 CD37	5a olive grn	3.00	.30
290 CD38	10a blue vio	6.50	.60
291 CD38	20a red brown	15.00	1.10
	Nos. 274-291 (18)	30.20	5.20
	Set, never hinged	50.00	

For surcharges see Nos. 301-304.

Marble Column and Portuguese Arms with Cross — A20

1938, July 29 Perf. 12½

292 A20	80c blue green	1.00	1.00
293 A20	1.75a deep blue	5.00	1.00
294 A20	20a dk red brown	11.00	6.00
	Nos. 292-294 (3)	17.00	8.00
	Set, never hinged	25.00	

Visit of the President of Portugal to this colony in 1938.

Stamps of 1932 Surcharged with New Value and Bars

8mm between bars and new value.

1941-45 Wmk. 232 Perf. 12x11½

294A A14	5c on 80c emer ('45)	.25	.20
295 A14	10c on 45c lt blue	.65	.55
296 A14	15c on 45c lt blue	1.00	.70
297 A14	20c on 85c rose	.65	.55
298 A14	35c on 85c rose	.65	.55
299 A14	50c on 1.40a dk blue	.65	.55
300 A14	60c on 1a claret	8.00	4.00
	Nos. 294A-300 (7)	11.85	7.10
	Set, never hinged	19.00	

Nos. 285 to 287 Surcharged with New Values and Bars in Black or Red

1945 Unwmk. Perf. 13½x13

301 CD36	5c on 80c org	.30	.20
302 CD36	50c on 1a red	.60	.20
303 CD37	50c on 1.75a bl (R)	.40	.20
304 CD37	50c on 1.75a bl	.60	.20
	Nos. 301-304 (4)	1.90	.80
	Set, never hinged	3.00	

Sao Miguel Fort, Luanda — A21

John IV — A22

Designs: 10c, Our Lady of Nazareth Church, Luanda. 50c, Salvador Correia de Sa e Bene vides. 1a, Surrender of Luanda. 1.75a, Diogo Cao. 2a, Manuel Cerveira Pereira. 5a, Stone Cliffs, Yelala. 10a, Paulo Dias de Novais. 20a, Massangano Fort.

Perf. 14½

1948, May Unwmk. Litho.

305 A21	5c dk violet	.20	.20
306 A21	10c dk brown	.25	.20
307 A22	30c blue grn	.20	.20
308 A22	50c vio brown	.20	.20
309 A21	1a carmine	.35	.20
310 A22	1.75a slate blue	.65	.20
311 A22	2a green	.65	.20
312 A21	5a gray black	1.25	.35
313 A22	10a rose lilac	2.50	.35
314 A21	20a gray blue	6.00	1.10
a.	Sheet of 10, #305-314	40.00	40.00
	Never hinged	65.00	
	Nos. 305-314 (10)	12.25	3.20
	Set, never hinged	20.00	

300th anniv. of the restoration of Angola to Portugal. No. 314a sold for 42.50a.

Lady of Fatima Issue

Common Design Type

1948, Dec.

315 CD40	50c carmine	.65	.50
316 CD40	3a ultra	2.00	1.00
317 CD40	6a red orange	5.00	2.00
318 CD40	9a dp claret	12.00	2.50
	Nos. 315-318 (4)	19.65	6.00
	Set, never hinged	30.00	

Our Lady of the Rosary at Fatima, Portugal.

Chiumbe River — A24

Black Rocks — A25

Designs: 50c, View of Luanda. 2.50a, Sa da Bandeira. 3.50a, Mocamedes. 15a, Cubal River. 50a, Duke of Bragança Falls.

1949 Unwmk. Perf. 13½

319 A24	20c dk slate blue	.20	.20
320 A25	40c black brown	.20	.20
321 A24	50c rose brown	.20	.20
322 A24	2.50a blue violet	1.10	.25
323 A24	3.50a slate gray	1.10	.25
323A A24	15a dk green	8.25	1.50
324 A24	50a dp green	22.50	3.75
	Nos. 319-324 (7)	33.55	6.35
	Set, never hinged	55.00	

Sailing Vessel — A26

UPU Symbols — A27

1949, Aug. Perf. 14

325 A26	1a chocolate	2.00	.35
326 A26	4a dk Prus green	5.00	.85
	Set, never hinged	11.00	

Centenary of founding of Mocamedes.

1949, Oct.

327 A27	4a dk grn & lt grn	2.50	1.50
	Never hinged	4.50	

75th anniv. of the UPU.

Catalogue values for unused stamps in this section, from this point to the end of the section, are for Never Hinged items.

Stamp of 1870 — A28

1950, Apr. 2 Perf. 11½x12

328 A28	50c yellow green	.80	.25
329 A28	1a fawn	.80	.25
330 A28	4a black	3.25	.70
a.	Sheet of 3, #328-330	7.50	7.50
	Nos. 328-330 (3)	4.85	1.20

Angola's first philatelic exhibition, marking the 80th anniversary of Angola's first stamps.

No. 330a contains Nos. 328, 329 (inverted), 330, perf. 11½ and sold for 6.50a. All copies carry an oval exhibition cancellation in the margin but the stamps were valid for postage.

Holy Year Issue

Common Design Types

1950, May Perf. 13x13½

331 CD41	1a dull rose vio	.35	.20
332 CD42	4a black	3.00	.35

Dark Chanting Goshawk — A31

European Bee Eater — A32

10c, Racquet-tailed roller. 15c, Bataleur eagle. 50c, Giant kingfisher. 1a, Yellow-fronted barbet. 1.50a, Openbill (stork). 2a, Southern ground hornbill. 2.50a, African skimmer. 3a, Shikra. 3.50a, Denham's bustard. 4a, African golden oriole. 4.50a, Long-tailed shrike. 5a, Red-shouldered glossy starling. 6a, Sharp-tailed glossy starling. 7a, Red-shouldered widow bird. 10a, Half-colored kingfisher. 12.50a, White-crowned shrike. 15a, White-winged babbling starling. 20a, Yellow-billed hornbill. 25a, Amethyst starling. 30a, Orange-breasted shrike. 40a, Secretary bird. 50a, Rosy-faced lovebird.

Photogravure and Lithographed

1951 Unwmk. Perf. 11½

Birds in Natural Colors

333 A31	5c lt blue	.20	*.50*
334 A32	10c aqua	.20	.20
335 A32	15c salmon pink	.25	*1.00*
336 A32	20c pale yellow	.50	.25
337 A31	50c gray blue	.30	.20
338 A31	1a lilac	.30	.20
339 A31	1.50a gray buff	.40	.20
340 A31	2a cream	.40	.20
341 A32	2.50a gray	.40	.20
342 A32	3a lemon yel	.40	.20
343 A31	3.50a lt gray	.40	.20
344 A31	4a rose buff	1.25	.20
345 A32	4.50a rose lilac	1.25	*3.00*
346 A31	5a green	5.00	.20
347 A31	6a blue	5.00	.55
348 A31	7a orange	5.00	.75
349 A31	10a lilac rose	15.00	1.10
350 A32	12.50a slate gray	6.00	1.75
351 A31	15a pale olive	6.00	1.75
352 A31	20a pale bis brn	20.00	4.50
353 A31	25a lilac rose	15.00	2.50
354 A32	30a pale salmon	15.00	3.00
355 A31	40a yellow	30.00	3.75
356 A31	50a turquoise	50.00	8.00
	Nos. 333-356 (24)	178.25	34.40
	Set, never hinged	125.00	

Holy Year Extension Issue

Common Design Type

1951, Oct. Litho. Perf. 14

357 CD43	4a orange + label	1.25	.50

Sheets contain alternate vertical rows of stamps and labels bearing quotations from Pope Pius XII or the Patriarch Cardinal of Lisbon. Stamp without label attached sells for less.

Medical Congress Issue

Common Design Type

Design: Medical examination

1952, June Perf. 13½

358 CD44	1a vio blue & brn blk	.40	.20

Head of Christ — A35

1952, Oct. Unwmk. Perf. 13

359 A35	10c dk blue & buff	.20	.20
360 A35	50c dk ol grn & ol gray	.20	.20
361 A35	2a rose vio & cream	1.25	.20
	Nos. 359-361 (3)	1.65	.60

Exhibition of Sacred Missionary Art, Lisbon, 1951.

Leopard — A36

Sable Antelope — A37

Animals: 20c, Elephant. 30c, Eland. 40c, African crocodile. 50c, Impala. 1a, Mountain zebra. 1.50a, Sitatunga. 2a, Black rhinoceros. 2.30a, Gemsbok. 2.50a, Lion. 3a, Buffalo. 3.50a, Springbok. 4a, Brindled gnu. 5a, Hartebeest. 7a, Wart hog. 10a, Defassa waterbuck. 12.50a, Hippopotamus. 15a, Greater kudu. 20a, Giraffe.

1953, Aug. 15 Perf. 12½

362 A36	5c multicolored	.20	.20
363 A37	10c multicolored	.20	.20
364 A37	20c multicolored	.20	.20
365 A37	30c multicolored	.20	.20
366 A36	40c multicolored	.20	.20
367 A37	50c multicolored	.20	.20
368 A37	1a multicolored	.20	.20
369 A37	1.50a multicolored	.20	.20
370 A36	2a multicolored	.20	.20
371 A37	2.30a multicolored	.25	.20
372 A37	2.50a multicolored	.30	.20
373 A36	3a multicolored	.30	.20
374 A37	3.50a multicolored	.20	.20
375 A37	4a multicolored	3.00	.25
376 A37	5a multicolored	.35	.20
377 A37	7a multicolored	.75	.25
378 A37	10a multicolored	1.25	.20
379 A37	12.50a multicolored	4.00	2.50
380 A37	15a multicolored	4.00	2.00
381 A37	20a multicolored	5.00	.35
	Nos. 362-381 (20)	21.20	8.35

Stamp of Portugal and Arms of Colonies — A38

1953, Nov. Photo. Perf. 13

Stamp and Arms Multicolored

382 A38	50c gray & dark gray	.55	.35

Cent. of Portugal's 1st postage stamps.

Map and Plane — A39

Typographed and Lithographed

1954, May 27 Perf. 13½

383 A39	35c multicolored	.20	.20
384 A39	4.50e multicolored	.70	.30

Visit of Pres. Francisco H C. Lopes.

Sao Paulo Issue

Common Design Type

1954 Litho.

385 CD46	1e bister & gray	.32	.20

Map of Angola — A41

Artur de Paiva — A42

1955, Aug. Unwmk. *Perf. 13½*

386 A41 5c multicolored .20 .20
387 A41 20c multicolored .20 .20
388 A41 50c multicolored .20 .20
389 A41 1e multicolored .20 .20
390 A41 2.30e multicolored .30 .20
391 A41 4e multicolored .50 .20
392 A41 10e multicolored .50 .20
393 A41 20e multicolored 1.00 .20
Nos. 386-393 (8) 3.10 1.60

For overprints see Nos. 593, 598, 604.

1956, Oct. 9 *Perf. 13½x12½*

394 A42 1e blk, dk bl & ocher .20 .20

Cent. of the birth of Col. Artur de Paiva.

Man of Malange — A43

Jose M. Antunes — A44

Various Costumes in Multicolor; Inscriptions in Black Brown

1957, Jan. 1 Photo. *Perf. 11½*

Granite Paper

395 A43 5c gray .20 .20
396 A43 10c orange yel .20 .20
397 A43 15c lt blue grn .20 .20
398 A43 20c pale rose vio .20 .20
399 A43 30c brt rose .20 .20
400 A43 40c blue gray .20 .20
401 A43 50c pale olive .20 .20
402 A43 80c lt violet .20 .20
403 A43 1.50e buff 1.00 .20
404 A43 2.50e lt yel grn 1.00 .20
405 A43 4e salmon .50 .20
406 A43 10e salmon pink 1.00 .25
Nos. 395-406 (12) 5.10 2.45

1957, Apr. *Perf. 13½*

407 A44 1e aqua & brown .65 .20

Birth cent. of Father Jose Maria Antunes.

Fair Emblem, Globe and Arms — A45

1958, July Litho. *Perf. 12x11½*

408 A45 1.50e multicolored .25 .20

World's Fair, Brussels, Apr. 17-Oct. 19.

Tropical Medicine Congress Issue

Common Design Type

Design: Securidaca longipedunculata.

1958, Dec. 15 *Perf. 13½*

409 CD47 2.50e multicolored 1.10 .70

Medicine Man — A47

Welwitschia Mirabilis A48

Designs: 1.50e, Early government doctor. 2.50e, Modern medical team.

1958, Dec. 18 *Perf. 11½x12*

410 A47 1e blue blk & brown .20 .20
411 A47 1.50e gray, blk & brown .50 .20
412 A47 2.50e multicolored .75 .40
Nos. 410-412 (3) 1.45 .80

75th anniversary of the Maria Pia Hospital, Luanda.

1959, Oct. 1 Litho. *Perf. 14½*

Various Views of Plant and Various Frames

413 A48 1.50e lt brn, grn & blk .55 .45
414 A48 2.50e multicolored .85 .50
415 A48 5e multicolored 1.10 .75
416 A48 10e multicolored 2.75 1.00
Nos. 413-416 (4) 5.25 2.70

Centenary of discovery of Welwitschia mirabilis, desert plant.

Map of West Africa, c. 1540, by Jorge Reinel — A49

1960, June 25 *Perf. 13½*

417 A49 2.50e multicolored .20 .20

500th anniv. of the death of Prince Henry the Navigator.

Distributing Medicines A50

Girl of Angola — A51

1960, Oct. Litho. *Perf. 14½*

418 A50 2.50e multicolored .30 .20

10th anniv. of the Commission for Technical Co-operation in Africa South of the Sahara (C.C.T.A.).

1961, Nov. 30 Unwmk. *Perf. 13*

Various portraits.

419 A51 10c multicolored .20 .20
420 A51 15c multicolored .20 .20
421 A51 30c multicolored .20 .20
422 A51 40c multicolored .20 .20
423 A51 60c multicolored .20 .20
424 A51 1.50e multicolored .20 .20
425 A51 2e multicolored .60 .20
426 A51 2.50e multicolored .85 .20
427 A51 3e multicolored 2.00 .20
428 A51 4e multicolored 1.25 .20
429 A51 5e multicolored 1.00 .20
430 A51 7.50e multicolored 1.25 .50
431 A51 10e multicolored 1.00 .25
432 A51 15e multicolored 1.00 .40
432A A51 25e multicolored 2.00 .65
432B A51 50e multicolored 4.00 1.00
Nos. 419-432B (16) 16.15 5.00

Sports Issue

Common Design Type

Sports: 50c, Flying. 1e, Rowing. 1.50e, Water polo. 2.50e, Hammer throwing. 4.50e, High jump. 15e, Weight lifting.

1962, Jan. 18 *Perf. 13½*

Multicolored Design

433 CD48 50c lt blue .40 .20
434 CD48 1e olive bister 1.00 .20
435 CD48 1.50e salmon .50 .20
436 CD48 2.50e lt green .50 .20
437 CD48 4.50e pale blue .50 .25
438 CD48 15e yellow 1.75 .65
Nos. 433-438 (6) 4.65 1.70

For overprint see No. 608.

Anti-Malaria Issue

Common Design Type

Design: Anopheles funestus.

1962, April Litho. *Perf. 13½*

439 CD49 2.50e multicolored .85 .50

Gen. Norton de Matos — A54

Locusts — A56

1962, Aug. 8 Unwmk. *Perf. 14½*

440 A54 2.50e multicolored .40 .20

50th anniv. of the founding of Nova Lisboa.

1963, June 2 Litho. *Perf. 14*

447 A56 2.50e multicolored .55 .25

15th anniv. of the Intl. Anti-Locust Organ.

Arms of Luanda A57

Vila de Santo Antonio do Zaire — A58

Coats of Arms (Provinces and Cities): 10c, Massangano. 15c, Sanza-Pombo. 25c, Ambriz. 30c, Muxima. 40c, Ambrizete. 50c, Carmona. 60c, Catete. 70c, Quibaxe. No. 458, Maquelo do Zombo. 1e, Salazar. 1.20e, Bembe. No. 461, Malanje. No. 462, Caxito. 1.80e, Dondo. 2e, Henrique de Carvalho. No. 465, Moçamedes. No. 466, Damba. 3e, Novo Redondo. 3.50e, S. Salvador do Congo. 4e, Cuimba. 5e, Luso. 6.50e, Negage. 7e, Quitexe. 7.50e, S. Filipe de Benguela. 8e, Mucaba. 9e, 31 de Janeiro. 10e, Lobito. 11e, Nova Caipemba. 12.50e, Gabela. 14e, Songo. 15e Sá da Bandeira. 17e, Quimbele. 17.50e, Silva Porto. 20e, Nova Lisboa. 22.50e, Cabinda. 25e, Noqui. 30e, Serpa Pinto. 35e, Santa Cruz. 50e, General Freire.

1963 *Perf. 13½*

Arms in Original Colors; Red and Violet Blue Inscriptions

448 A57 5c tan .20 .20
449 A57 10c lt blue .20 .20
450 A58 15c salmon .20 .20
451 A58 20c olive .20 .20
452 A58 25c lt blue .20 .20
453 A57 30c buff .20 .20
454 A58 40c gray .20 .20
455 A57 50c lt green .20 .20
456 A58 60c brt yellow .20 .20
457 A58 70c dull rose .20 .20
458 A57 1e pale lilac .30 .20
459 A58 1e dull yellow .20 .20
460 A58 1.20e rose .20 .20
461 A57 1.50e pale salmon .60 .20
462 A58 1.50e lt green .40 .20
463 A58 1.80e yel olive .25 .20
464 A57 2e lt yel green .30 .20
465 A57 2.50e lt gray 1.50 .20
466 A58 2.50e dull blue 1.25 .20
467 A57 3e yel olive .45 .20
468 A57 3.50e gray .50 .20
469 A58 4e citron .35 .20
470 A57 5e citron .40 .25
471 A58 6.50e tan .40 .25
472 A58 7e rose lilac .45 .25
473 A57 7.50e pale lilac 1.25 *2.00*
474 A58 8e lt aqua .45 .30
475 A58 9e yellow 1.25 *1.50*
476 A57 10e dp salmon .70 .35
477 A58 11e dull yel grn 2.00 1.50
478 A57 12.50e pale blue .90 .45
479 A58 14e lt gray 2.00 1.00
480 A57 15e lt blue 1.00 .45
481 A58 17e pale blue 3.00 2.00
482 A57 17.50e dull yellow 1.50 1.00
483 A57 20e lt aqua 1.50 .70
484 A57 22.50e gray 1.50 1.00
485 A58 25e citron 1.50 .70
486 A57 30e yellow 2.00 1.25
487 A58 35e grysh blue 2.00 1.50
488 A58 50e dp yellow 3.00 1.25
Nos. 448-488 (41) 35.10 22.10

Pres. Américo Rodrigues Thomaz — A59

1963, Sept. 16 Litho.

489 A59 2.50e multicolored .40 .20

Visit of the President of Portugal.

Airline Anniversary Issue

Common Design Type

1963, Oct. 5 Unwmk. *Perf. 14½*

490 CD50 1e lt blue & multi .50 .20

Cathedral of Sá da Bandeira — A61

Malange Cathedral A62

Churches: 20c, Landana. 30c, Luanda Cathedral. 40c, Gabela. 50c, St. Martin's Chapel, Baia dos Tigres. 1.50e, St. Peter, Chibia. 2e, Church of Our Lady, Benguela. 2.50e, Church of Jesus, Luanda. 3e, Camabatela. 3.50e, Mission, Cabinda. 4e, Vila Folgares. 4.50e, Church of Our Lady, Lobito. 5e, Church of Cabinda. 7.50e, Cacuso Church, Malange. 10e, Lubango Mission. 12.50e, Huila Mission. 15e, Church of Our Lady, Luanda Island.

1963, Nov. 1 Litho.

Multicolored Design and Inscription

491 A61 10c gray blue .20 .20
492 A61 20c pink .20 .20
493 A61 30c lt blue .20 .20
494 A61 40c tan .20 .20
495 A61 50c lt green .20 .20
496 A62 1e buff .20 .20
497 A61 1.50e lt vio blue .20 .20
498 A62 2e pale rose .20 .20
499 A61 2.50e gray .20 .20
500 A62 3e buff .20 .20
501 A61 3.50e olive .25 .20
502 A62 4e buff .25 .20
503 A62 4.50e pale blue .40 .25
504 A61 5e tan .50 .25
505 A62 7.50e gray .70 .30
506 A61 10e dull yellow .80 .35
507 A62 12.50e bister 1.00 .70
508 A62 15e pale gray vio 2.00 .60
Nos. 491-508 (18) 7.90 4.85

National Overseas Bank Issue

Common Design Type

Design: Antonio Teixeira de Sousa.

1964, May 16 *Perf. 13½*

509 CD51 2.50e multicolored .40 .25

Commerce Building and Arms of Chamber of Commerce A64

1964, Nov. Litho. *Perf. 12*
510 A64 1e multicolored .20 .20

Luanda Chamber of Commerce centenary.

ITU Issue
Common Design Type

1965, May 17 Unwmk. *Perf. 14½*
511 CD52 2.50e gray & multi .70 .25

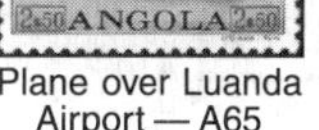

Plane over Luanda Airport — A65

Harquebusier, 1539 — A66

1965, Dec. 3 Litho. *Perf. 13*
512 A65 2.50e multicolored .25 .20

25th anniv. of DTA, Direccao dos Transportes Aereos.

1966, Feb. 25 Litho. *Perf. 14½*

50c, Harquebusier, 1539. 1e, Harquebusier, 1640. 1.50e, Infantry officer, 1777. 2e, Standard bearer, infantry, 1777. 2.50e, Infantry soldier, 1777. 3e, Cavalry officer, 1783. 4e, Cavalry soldier, 1783. 4.50e, Infantry officer, 1807. 5e, Infantry soldier, 1807. 6e, Cavalry officer, 1807. 8e, Cavalry soldier, 1807. 9e, Infantry soldier, 1873.

513 A66 50c multicolored .20 .20
514 A66 1e multicolored .20 .20
515 A66 1.50e multicolored .20 .20
516 A66 2e multicolored .20 .20
517 A66 2.50e multicolored .20 .20
518 A66 3e multicolored .20 .20
519 A66 4e multicolored .35 .25
520 A66 4.50e multicolored .35 .25
521 A66 5e multicolored .50 .20
522 A66 6e multicolored .65 .45
523 A66 8e multicolored 1.00 .75
524 A66 9e multicolored 1.25 .90
Nos. 513-524 (12) 5.30 4.00

National Revolution Issue
Common Design Type

Design: St. Paul's Hospital and Commercial and Industrial School.

1966, May 28 Litho. *Perf. 12*
525 CD53 1e multicolored .20 .20

Emblem of Holy Ghost Society — A68

1966 Litho. *Perf. 13*
526 A68 1e blue & multi .20 .20

Centenary of the Holy Ghost Society.

Navy Club Issue
Common Design Type

Designs: 1e, Mendes Barata and cruiser Dom Carlos I. 2.50e, Capt. Augusto de Castilho and corvette Mindelo.

1967, Jan. 31 Litho. *Perf. 13*
527 CD54 1e multicolored .40 .20
528 CD54 2.50e multicolored .65 .20

Fatima Basilica — A70

Angola Map, Manuel Cerveira Pereira — A71

1967, May 13 Litho. *Perf. 12½x13*
529 A70 50c multicolored .20 .20

50th anniv. of the apparition of the Virgin Mary to 3 shepherd children at Fatima.

1967, Aug. 15 Litho. *Perf. 12½x13*
530 A71 50c multicolored .20 .20

350th anniv. of the founding of Benguela.

Administration Building, Carmona — A72

1967 Litho. *Perf. 12*
531 A72 1e multicolored .20 .20

50th anniv. of the founding of Carmona.

Military Order of Valor — A73

Our Lady of Hope — A74

50c, Ribbon of the Three Orders. 1.50e, Military Order of Avis. 2e, Military Order of Christ. 2.50e, Military Order of St. John of Espada. 3e, Order of the Empire. 4e, Order of Prince Henry. 5e, Order of Benemerencia. 10e, Order of Public Instruction. 20e, Order for Industrial & Agricultural Merit.

1967, Oct. 31 *Perf. 14*
532 A73 50c lt gray & multi .20 .20
533 A73 1e lt green & multi .20 .20
534 A73 1.50e yellow & multi .20 .20
535 A73 2e multicolored .20 .20
536 A73 2.50e multicolored .20 .20
537 A73 3e lt olive & multi .20 .20
538 A73 4e gray & multi .20 .20
539 A73 5e multicolored .40 .20
540 A73 10e lilac & multi .55 .20
541 A73 20e lt blue & multi 1.25 .45
Nos. 532-541 (10) 3.60 2.25

1968, Apr. 22 Litho. *Perf. 14*

1e, Belmonte Castle, horiz. 1.50e, St. Jerome's Convent. 2.50e, Cabral's Armada.

542 A74 50c yellow & multi .20 .20
543 A74 1e gray & multi .25 .20
544 A74 1.50e lt blue & multi .40 .20
545 A74 2.50e buff & multi .60 .20
Nos. 542-545 (4) 1.45 .80

500th anniv. of the birth of Pedro Alvares Cabral, navigator who took possession of Brazil for Portugal.

Francisco Inocencio de Souza Coutinho — A75

1969, Jan. 7 Litho. *Perf. 14*
546 A75 2e multicolored .25 .20

Founding of Novo Redondo, 200th anniv.

Admiral Coutinho Issue
Common Design Type

Design: Adm. Gago Coutinho and his first ship.

1969, Feb. 17 Litho. *Perf. 14*
547 CD55 2.50e multicolored .30 .20

Compass Rose A77

Portal of St. Jeronimo's Monastery A79

1969, Aug. 29 Litho. *Perf. 14*
548 A77 1e multicolored .20 .20

500th anniv. of the birth of Vasco da Gama (1469-1524), navigator.

Administration Reform Issue
Common Design Type

1969, Sept. 25 Litho. *Perf. 14*
549 CD56 1.50e multicolored .20 .20

1969, Dec. 1 Litho. *Perf. 14*
550 A79 3e multicolored .20 .20

500th anniv. of the birth of King Manuel I.

Angolasaurus Bocagei — A80

Fossils and Minerals: 1e, Ferrometeorite. 1.50e, Dioptase crystals. 2e, Gondwanidium. 2.50e, Diamonds. 3e, Estromatolite. 3.50e, Procarcharodon megalodon. 4e, Microceratodus angolensis. 4.50e, Moscovite. 5e, Barite. 6e, Nostoceras. 10e, Rotula orbiculus angolensis.

1970, Oct. 31 Litho. *Perf. 13*
551 A80 50c tan & multi .20 .20
552 A80 1e multicolored .25 .20
553 A80 1.50e multicolored .30 .20
554 A80 2e multicolored .50 .20
555 A80 2.50e lt gray & multi .60 .20
556 A80 3e multicolored .75 .20
557 A80 3.50e blue & multi 1.00 .20
558 A80 4e lt gray & multi .70 .20
559 A80 4.50e gray & multi 1.00 .20
560 A80 5e gray & multi 1.00 .25
561 A80 6e pink & multi 1.50 .30
562 A80 10e lt blue & multi 2.00 .50
Nos. 551-562 (12) 9.80 2.85

Marshal Carmona Issue
Common Design Type

1970, Nov. 15 *Perf. 14*
563 CD57 2.50e multicolored .25 .20

Arms of Malanje, Cotton Boll and Field — A82

1970, Nov. 20 *Perf. 13*
564 A82 2.50e multicolored .25 .20

Centenary of the municipality of Malanje.

Mail Ships and Angola No. 1 A83

4.50e, Steam locomotive and Angola No. 4.

1970, Dec. 1 *Perf. 13½*
565 A83 1.50e multicolored .40 .25
566 A83 4.50e multicolored .75 .40

Cent. of stamps of Angola. See No. C36. For overprint see No. 616B.

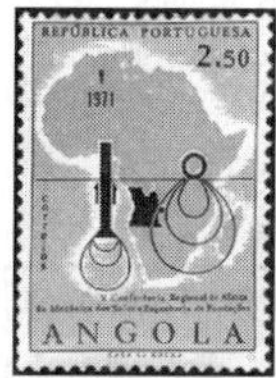

Map of Africa, Diagram of Seismic Tests — A84

Galleon on Congo River — A85

1971, Aug. 22 Litho. *Perf. 13*
567 A84 2.50e multicolored .20 .20

5th Regional Conference of Soil and Foundation Engineers, Luanda, Aug. 22-Sept. 5.

1972, May 25 Litho. *Perf. 13*
568 A85 1e emerald & multi .20 .20

4th centenary of the publication of The Lusiads by Luiz Camoens.

Olympic Games Issue
Common Design Type

1972, June 20 *Perf. 14x13½*
569 CD59 50c multicolored .20 .20

Lisbon-Rio de Janeiro Flight Issue
Common Design Type

1972, Sept. 20 Litho. *Perf. 13½*
570 CD60 1e multicolored .20 .20

WMO Centenary Issue
Common Design Type

1973, Dec. 15 Litho. *Perf. 13*
571 CD61 1e dk gray & multi .20 .20

Radar Station A89

1974, June 25 Litho. *Perf. 13*
572 A89 2e multicolored .25 .20

Establishment of satellite communications network via Intelsat among Portugal, Angola and Mozambique.
For overprint see No. 616A

Harpa Doris — A90

Designs: Sea shells.

1974, Oct. 25 Litho. *Perf. 12x12½*
573 A90 25c shown .20 .20
574 A90 30c Murex melanamathos .20 .20
575 A90 50c Venus foliaceo lamellosa .20 .20
576 A90 70c Lathyrus filosus .20 .20
577 A90 1e Cymbium cisium .20 .20
578 A90 1.50e Cassis tesselata .20 .20
579 A90 2e Cypraea stercoraria .20 .20
580 A90 2.50e Conus prometheus .20 .20
581 A90 3e Strombus latus .20 .20
582 A90 3.50e Tympanotonus fuscatus .20 .20
583 A90 4e Cardium costatum .25 .20
584 A90 5e Natica fulminea .25 .20
585 A90 6e Lyropecten nodosus .35 .20
586 A90 7e Tonna galea .75 .25
587 A90 10e Donax rugosus .90 .30
588 A90 25e Cymatium trigonum 1.50 .40

589 A90 30e Olivancilaria acuminata 2.50 .75
590 A90 35e Semifusus morio 2.50 .75
591 A90 40e Clavatula lineata 3.00 1.00
592 A90 50e Solarium granulatum 4.00 1.50
Nos. 573-592 (20) 18.00 7.55

For overprints see Nos. 605-607, 617-630.

No. 386 Overprinted in Blue: "1974 / FILATELIA / JUVENIL"

1974, Dec. 21 Litho. *Perf. 13½*
593 A41 5c multicolored .20 .20

Youth philately.

Republic

Star and Hand Holding Rifle — A91

1975, Nov. 11 Litho. *Perf. 13x13½*
594 A91 1.50e red & multi .20 .20

Independence in 1975.

Diquiche Mask — A92

Design: 3e, Bui ou Congolo mask.

1976, Feb. 6 *Perf. 13½*
595 A92 50c lt blue & multi .20 .20
596 A92 3e multicolored .20 .20

Workers — A93

President Agostinho Neto — A94

1976, May 1 Litho. *Perf. 12*
597 A93 1e red & multi .20 .20

International Workers' Day.

No. 392 Overprinted Bar and: "DIA DO SELO / 15 Junho 1976 / REP. POPULAR / DE"

1976, June 15 Litho. *Perf. 13½*
598 A41 10e multicolored .40 .25

Stamp Day.

1976, Nov. 11 Litho. *Perf. 13*
599 A94 50c yel & dk brown .20 .20
600 A94 2e lt gray & plum .20 .20
601 A94 3e gray & indigo .20 .20
602 A94 5e buff & brown .20 .20
603 A94 10e tan & sepia .40 .20
a. Souv. sheet of 1, imperf. 2.00 1.25
Nos. 599-603 (5) 1.20 1.00

First anniversary of independence.

Nos. 393, 588-589, 592 Overprinted with Bar over Republica Portuguesa and: "REPUBLICA POPULAR DE"

1977, Feb. 9 *Perf. 13½, 12x12½*
604 A41 20e multicolored 1.75 .25
605 A90 25e multicolored 2.25 .35
606 A90 30e multicolored 2.75 .50
607 A90 50e multicolored 4.50 .75
Nos. 604-607 (4) 11.25 1.85

Overprint in 3 lines on No. 604, in 2 lines on others.

No. 438 Overprinted with Bar over Republica Portuguesa and: "S. Silvestre / 1976 / Rep. Popular / de"

1976, Dec. 31 *Perf. 13½*
608 CD48 15e multicolored 3.50 .25

Child and WHO Emblem — A95

Map of Africa, Flag of Angola — A96

1977 Litho. *Perf. 10½*
609 A95 2.50k blk & lt blue .20 .20

Campaign for vaccination against poliomyelitis.

1977 Photo.
610 A96 6k blk, red & blue .20 .20

First Congress of Popular Movement for the Liberation of Angola.

Anti-Apartheid Emblem — A97

1979, June 20 Litho. *Perf. 13½*
611 A97 1k multicolored .20 .20

Anti-Apartheid Year.

Human Rights Emblem — A98

Child Flowers, Globe, IYC Emblem — A99

1979, June 15 Litho. *Perf. 13½*
612 A98 2.50k multicolored .20 .20

Declaration of Human Rights, 30th anniv. (in 1975).

1980, May 1 Litho. *Perf. 14x14½*
613 A99 3.50k multicolored .20 .20

International Year of the Child (1979).

Running, Moscow '80 Emblem — A100

5th Anniv. of Independence A101

1980, Dec. 15 Litho. *Perf. 13½*
614 A100 9k shown .30 .20
615 A100 12k Swimming, horiz. .40 .20

22nd Summer Olympic Games, Moscow, July 19-Aug. 3.

1980, Nov. 11
616 A101 5.50k multicolored .20 .20

Nos. 572, 566 Overprinted with Bar and: "REPUBLICA POPULAR / DE"

1980-81 Litho. *Perf. 13½x13*
616A A89 2e multi (bar only) .50
616B A83 4.50e multicolored 1.00

Issued: 2e, 5/17/81; 4.50e, 6/15/80.
See No. C37.

Nos. 577-580, 582-591 Overprinted with Black Bar over "Republica Portuguesa"

1981, June 15 Litho. *Perf. 12x12½*
617 A90 1e multicolored
618 A90 1.50e multicolored
619 A90 2e multicolored
620 A90 2.50e multicolored
621 A90 3.50e multicolored
622 A90 4e multicolored
623 A90 5e multicolored
624 A90 6e multicolored
625 A90 7e multicolored
626 A90 10e multicolored
627 A90 25e multicolored
628 A90 30e multicolored
629 A90 35e multicolored
630 A90 40e multicolored
Nos. 617-630 (14) 15.00 8.00

Man Walking with Canes, Tchibinda Ilunga Statue — A102

1981, Sept. 5 Litho. *Perf. 13½*
631 A102 9k multicolored .30 .20

Turipex '81 tourism exhibition.

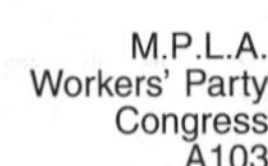

M.P.L.A. Workers' Party Congress A103

1980, Dec. 23 Litho. *Perf. 14*
632 A103 50 l Millet .20 .20
633 A103 5k Coffee .20 .20
634 A103 7.50k Sunflowers .30 .20
635 A103 13.50k Cotton .40 .20
636 A103 14k Oil .45 .25
637 A103 16k Diamonds .45 .25
Nos. 632-637 (6) 2.00 1.30

People's Power — A104

Natl. Heroes' Day — A105

1980, Nov. 11
638 A104 40k lt blue & blk 1.25 .40

1980, Sept. 17 *Perf. 14x13½*
639 A105 4.50k Former Pres. Neto .20 .20
640 A105 50k Neto, diff. 1.50 .65

Soweto Uprising, 5th Anniv. A106

1981
641 A106 4.50k multicolored .20 .20

2nd Central African Games — A107

1981, Sept. 3 Litho. *Perf. 13½*
642 A107 50 l Bicycling, tennis .20 .20
643 A107 5k Judo, boxing .20 .20
644 A107 6k Basketball, volleyball .25 .20
645 A107 10k Handball, soccer .35 .25
Nos. 642-645 (4) 1.00 .85

Souvenir Sheet

Imperf

646 A107 15k multicolored *2.00*

Charaxes Kahldeni A108

1982, Feb. 26 Litho. *Perf. 13½*
647 A108 50 l shown .20 .20
648 A108 1k Abantis zambesiaca .20 .20
649 A108 5k Catacroptera cloanthe .20 .20
650 A108 9k Myrina ficedula, vert. .40 .20
651 A108 10k Colotis danae .40 .20
652 A108 15k Acraea acrita .55 .25
653 A108 100k Precis hierta 2.75 1.25
a. Souvenir sheet 3.00 2.00
Nos. 647-653 (7) 4.70 2.50

No. 653a contains Nos. 647-653, imperf., and sold for 30k (stamps probably not valid individually).

5th Anniv. of UN Membership — A109

5.50k, The Silence of the Night, by Musseque Catambor. 7.50k, Cotton picking, Catete.

1982, Sept. 22 **Litho.**

654 A109 5.50k multicolored .20 .20
655 A109 7.50k multicolored .25 .20

20th Anniv. of Engineering Laboratory A110

1982, Dec. 21 **Litho.** ***Perf. 14***

656 A110 9k Lab .25 .20
657 A110 13k Worker, vert. .40 .20
658 A110 100k Equipment, vert. 3.25 1.25
Nos. 656-658 (3) 3.90 1.65

Local Flowers — A111

1983, Feb. 18 ***Perf. 13½***

659 A111 5k Dichrostachys glomerata .20 .20
660 A111 12k Amblygonocarpus obtusangulus .40 .20
661 A111 50k Albizzia versicolor 2.00 .60
Nos. 659-661 (3) 2.60 1.00

Women's Org., First Congress A112

1983 **Litho.** ***Perf. 13½***

662 A112 20k multicolored .80 .80

Africa Day — A113

1983, June 30 ***Perf. 13***

663 A113 6.5k multi .25 .25

World Communications Year — A114

1983, June 30 **Litho.** ***Perf. 13½***

664 A114 6.5k M'pungi .25 .25
665 A114 12k Mondu .40 .40

BRASILIANA '83 Stamp Exhibition, Rio de Janeiro, July 29-Aug. 7 — A115

Crop-eating insects.

1983, July 29 **Litho.** ***Perf. 13***

666 A115 4.5k Antestiopsis lineaticollis .20 .20
667 A115 6.5k Stephanoderes hampei ferr. .25 .25
668 A115 10k Zonocerus variegatus .40 .40
Nos. 666-668 (3) .85 .85

25th Anniv. of Economic Commission for Africa — A116

1983, Aug. 2

669 A116 10k Map, emblem .40 .40

185th Anniv. of Post Office A117

1983, Dec. 7 **Litho.** ***Perf. 13½***

670 A117 50 l Mail collection, vert. .20 .20
671 A117 3.5k Unloading mail plane .20 .20
672 A117 5k Sorting mail .20 .20
673 A117 15k Mailing letter, vert. .60 .60
674 A117 30k Post office box delivery 1.25 1.25
a. Min. sheet of 3, #671-672, 674 4.00 4.00
Nos. 670-674 (5) 2.45 2.45

No. 674a sold for 100k.

Local Butterflies A118

1984, Jan. 20 **Litho.** ***Perf. 13½***

675 A118 50 l Parasa karschi .20 .20
676 A118 1k Diaphone angolensis .20 .20
677 A118 3.5k Choeropasis jucunda .20 .20
678 A118 6.5k Hespagarista rendalli .40 .25
679 A118 15k Euchromia guineensis .75 .60
680 A118 17.5k Mazuca roseistriga 1.00 .70
681 A118 20k Utetheisa callima 1.50 .85
Nos. 675-681 (7) 4.25 3.00

A119

A120

1984, Apr. 11 **Litho.** ***Perf. 13½***

682 A119 30k multicolored 1.25 1.25

First Natl. Worker's Union Congress, Apr. 11-16 .

1984, Oct. 24 **Litho.** ***Perf. 13½***

Local birds.

683 A120 10.50k Bucorvos leadbeateri .45 .35
684 A120 14k Gypohicax angolensis .55 .50
685 A120 16k Ardea goliath .75 .50
686 A120 19.50k Pelicanus onocrotalus 1.00 .75
687 A120 22k Platelea alba 1.25 .90
688 A120 26k Balearica pavonnia 2.00 1.00
Nos. 683-688 (6) 6.00 4.00

Local Animals A121

1984, Nov. 12

689 A121 1k Tragelephus strepsicerus .20 .20
690 A121 4k Antidorcas marsupialis angolensis .20 .20
691 A121 5k Pan troglodytes .20 .20
692 A121 10k Sycerus caffer .40 .40
693 A121 15k Hippotragus niger variani .60 .60
694 A121 20k Orycteropus afer .80 .80
695 A121 25k Crocuta crocuta 1.00 1.00
Nos. 689-695 (7) 3.40 3.40

Angolese Monuments A122

1985, Feb. 21 **Litho.** ***Perf. 13½***

696 A122 5k San Pedro da Barra .25 .25
697 A122 12.5k Nova Oeiras .55 .55
698 A122 18k M'Banza Kongo .80 .80
699 A122 26k Massangano 1.10 1.10
700 A122 39k Escravatura Museum 1.60 1.60
Nos. 696-700 (5) 4.30 4.30

United Workers' Party, 25th Anniv. A123

1985, May **Litho.** ***Perf. 12***

701 A123 77k XXV, red flags 1.50 1.50

Printed in sheets of 5.

A124

A125

1985, May

702 A124 1k Flags .20 .20
703 A124 11k Oil drilling platform, Cabinda .25 .25
704 A124 57k Conference 1.10 1.10
a. Strip of 3, #702-704 1.40 1.40

Southern African Development Council, 5th anniv.

Lithographed and Typographed

1985, July 5 ***Perf. 11***

Medicinal plants.

705 A125 1k Lonchocarpus sericeus .20 .20
706 A125 4k Gossypium .20 .20
707 A125 11k Cassia occidentalis .25 .25
708 A125 25.50k Gloriosa superba .50 .50
709 A125 55k Cochlospermum angolensis 1.10 1.10
Nos. 705-709 (5) 2.25 2.25

ARGENTINA '85 exhibition.

5th Natl. Heroes Day A126

Natl. flag and: 10.50k, Portrait of Agostinho Neto, party leader. 36.50k, Neto working.

1985 **Litho.** ***Perf. 13½***

710 A126 10.50k multicolored .20 .20
711 A126 36.50k multicolored .70 .70

Ministerial Conference of Non-Aligned Countries, Luanda — A127

1985, Sept. 4 **Photo.** ***Perf. 11***

712 A127 35k multicolored 1.50 1.50

UN, 40th Anniv. A128

1985, Oct. 29 **Litho.** ***Perf. 11***

713 A128 12.50k multicolored .55 .55

Industry and Natural Resources — A129

1985, Nov. 11

714 A129 50 l Cement Factory .20 .20
715 A129 5k Logging .25 .25
716 A129 7k Quartz .30 .30
717 A129 10k Iron mine .45 .45
a. Souvenir sheet of 4, #714-717, imperf. 2.00 2.00
Nos. 714-717 (4) 1.20 1.20

Natl. independence, 10th anniv.

2nd Natl. Workers' Party Congress (MPLA) — A130

1985, Nov. 28 ***Perf. 13½***

718 A130 20k multicolored .85 .85

Demostenes de Almeida Clington Races, 30th Anniv. — A131

Various runners.

1985, Dec. 13

719 A131 50 l multicolored .20 .20
720 A131 5k multicolored .25 .25
721 A131 6.50k multicolored .30 .30
722 A131 10k multicolored .40 .40
Nos. 719-722 (4) 1.15 1.15

1986 World Cup Soccer Championships, Mexico — A132

Map, soccer field and various plays.

1986, May 6 Litho. ***Perf. 11½x11***

723 A132 50 l multi .20 .20
724 A132 3.50k multi .20 .20
725 A132 5k multi .25 .25
726 A132 7k multi .30 .30
727 A132 10k multi .45 .45
728 A132 18k multi .85 .85
Nos. 723-728 (6) 2.25 2.25

Struggle Against Portugal, 25th Anniv. A133

1986, May 6 ***Perf. 11x11½***

729 A133 15k multicolored .65 .65

First Man in Space, 25th Anniv. A134

1986, Aug. 21 Litho. ***Perf. 11x11½***

730 A134 50 l Skylab, US .20 .20
731 A134 1k Spacecraft .20 .20
732 A134 5k A. Leonov space-walking .25 .25
733 A134 10k Lunokhod on Moon .40 .40
734 A134 13k Apollo-Soyuz link-up .60 .60
Nos. 730-734 (5) 1.65 1.65

Admission of Angola to UN, 10th Anniv. A135

1986, Dec. 1 Litho. ***Perf. 11x11½***

735 A135 22k multi .90 .90

Liberation Movement, 30th Anniv. — A136

Angolese at work, fighting and: No. 736a, "1956." No. 736b, Congress emblem, "1980." No. 736c, Labor Party emblem, "1985."

1986, Dec. 3 ***Perf. 11½x11***

736 A136 Strip of 3 .65 .65
a.-c. 5k any single .20 .20

Agostinho Neto University, 10th Anniv. A137

1986, Dec. 30 Litho. ***Perf. 11x11½***

737 A137 50 l Mathematics .20 .20
738 A137 1k Law .20 .20
739 A137 10k Medicine .45 .45
Nos. 737-739 (3) .85 .85

Tribal Hairstyles — A138

1987, Apr. 15 Litho. ***Perf. 11½x11***

740 A138 1k Ouioca .20 .20
741 A138 1.50k Luanda .20 .20
742 A138 5k Humbe .20 .20
743 A138 7k Muila .20 .20
744 A138 20k Muila, diff. .45 .45
745 A138 30k Dilolo .75 .75
Nos. 740-745 (6) 2.00 2.00

Landscapes A139

Lenin — A140

Perf. 11½x12, 12x11½

1987, July 7 **Litho.**

746 A139 50 l Pambala Shore .20 .20
747 A139 1.50k Dala Waterfalls .20 .20
748 A139 3.50k Black Stones .20 .20
749 A139 5k Cuango River .20 .20
750 A139 10k Luanda coast .25 .25
751 A139 20k Hills of Leba .50 .50
Nos. 746-751 (6) 1.55 1.55

Nos. 746-747, 749 and 751 horiz.

1987, Nov. 25 ***Perf. 12x12½***

752 A140 15k multi .60 .60

October Revolution, Russia, 70th anniv.

2nd Congress of the Organization of Angolan Women (OMA) — A141

1988, May 30 Litho. ***Perf. 13x13½***

753 A141 2k shown .20 .20
754 A141 10k Soldier, nurse, technician, student .35 .35

Victory Carnival, 10th Anniv. A142

Various carnival scenes.

1988, June 15 Litho. ***Perf. 13½x13***

755 A142 5k shown .20 .20
756 A142 10k multi, diff. .35 .35

Augusto N'Gangula (1956-1968), Youth Pioneer Killed by Portuguese Colonial Army — A143

Agostinho Neto Pioneers' Organization (OPA), 25th Anniv. — A144

1989, Oct. 2 Litho. ***Perf. 12x11½***

757 A143 12k multicolored .40 .40
758 A144 15k multicolored .50 .50

Pioneer Day.

10th Natl. Soccer Championships, Benguela, May 1 — A145

1989, Oct. 16

759 A145 5k shown .20 .20
760 A145 5k Luanda, 3 years .20 .20
761 A145 5k Luanda, 5 years .20 .20
Nos. 759-761 (3) .60 .60

Intl. Fund for Agricultural Development, 10th Anniv. — A146

1990, Feb. 15 Litho. ***Perf. 11½x12***

762 A146 10k multicolored .70 .70

Ingombotas' Houses — A147

Architecture: 2k, Alta Train Station. 5k, National Museum of Anthropology. 15k, Ana Joaquina Palace. 23k, Iron Palace. 36k, Meteorological observatory, vert. 50k, People's Palace.

1990, Feb. 20 ***Perf. 12x11½, 11½x12***

763 A147 1k shown .20 .20
764 A147 2k multicolored .20 .20
765 A147 5k multicolored .35 .35
766 A147 15k multicolored 1.00 1.00
767 A147 23k multicolored 1.50 1.50
768 A147 36k multicolored 2.25 2.25
769 A147 50k multicolored 3.25 3.25
Nos. 763-769 (7) 8.75 8.75

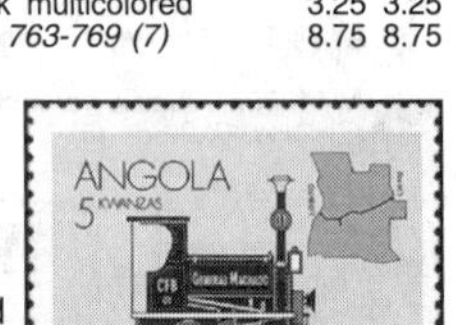

Luanda and Benguela Railways A148

Various maps and locomotives.

1990, Mar. 1 ***Perf. 12x11½***

770 A148 5k shown .35 .35
771 A148 12k Garrat T (left) .80 .80
772 A148 12k Garrat T (right) .80 .80
a. Pair, #771-772 1.60 1.60
773 A148 14k Mikado .95 .95
Nos. 770-773 (4) 2.90 2.90

Souvenir Sheet

774 A148 25k Diesel electric 2.35 2.35

No. 772a has a continuous design.

Southern Africa Development Coordinating Conf. (SADCC), 10th Anniv. — A149

1990, Apr. 1 Litho. ***Perf. 14***

775 A149 5k shown *7.00 4.00*
776 A149 9k Floating oil rig *10.00 6.00*

Pan-African Postal Union (PAPU), 10th Anniv. A150

1990, Apr. 6

777 A150 4k shown .75 .75
778 A150 10k Simulated stamp, map 1.50 1.50

Paintings by Raul Indipwo A151

1990, Apr. 24

779 A151 6k *Tres Gracas* .40 .40
780 A151 9k *Muxima*, vert. .65 .65

Stamp World London 90.

Hippotragus Niger Variani, Adult Male and Female — A152

1990, May 9 ***Perf. 14x13½***

781 A152 5k Adult male .35 .35
782 A152 5k shown .35 .35
783 A152 5k Adult female .35 .35
784 A152 5k Female, calf .35 .35
Nos. 781-784 (4) 1.40 1.40

World Wildlife Fund. Various combinations available in blocks or strips of four.

Rosa de Porcelana A153

1990, June 2 **Litho.** ***Perf. 14***

785 A153 5k shown .35 .35
786 A153 8k Cravo burro .55 .55
787 A153 10k Alamandra .70 .70
Nos. 785-787 (3) 1.60 1.60

Souvenir Sheet

788 A153 40k Hibiscus 2.70 2.70

Belgica '90.

Miniature Sheet

Intl. Literacy Year — A154

Various animals and forest scenes.

1990, July 26 **Litho.** ***Perf. 14***

789 A154 Sheet of 30 6.00 6.00
a.-ad. 1k any single .50 .50
790 A154 5k Zebra .35 .35
791 A154 5k Butterfly .35 .35
792 A154 5k Horse .35 .35
a. Block of 3, #790-792 + label 1.10 1.10

People's Assembly, 10th Anniv. A155

1990, Nov. 11 ***Perf. 14***

793 A155 10k multicolored .70 .70

3rd Natl. Labor Congress A156

1990 **Litho.** ***Perf. 13½***

794 A156 14k multicolored 1.40 1.40

War of Independence, 30th Anniv. — A157

Uniforms.

1991, Feb. 28 **Litho.** ***Perf. 14***

795 A157 6k Machete, 1961 .40 .40
a. Perf. 13½ vert. .40 .40
796 A157 6k Rifle, 1962-63 .40 .40
a. Perf. 13½ vert. .40 .40
797 A157 6k Rifle, 1968 .40 .40
a. Perf. 13½ vert. .40 .40
798 A157 6k Automatic rifle, 1972 .40 .40
a. Perf. 13½ vert. .40 .40
b. Bklt. pane of 4, #795a-798a 1.70
Nos. 795-798 (4) 1.60 1.60

Musical Instruments A158

Designs: a, Marimba. b, Mucupela. c, Ngoma la Txina. d, Kissange.

1991, Apr. 5 **Litho.** ***Perf. 14***

799 A158 6k Block or strip of 4, #799a-799d 1.75 1.75

Tourism A159

Designs: 3k, Iona National Park. 7k, Kalandula Waterfalls. 35k, Lobito Bay. 60k, Weltwitschia Mirabilis plant.

1991, June 25 **Litho.** ***Perf. 14***

800 A159 3k multi .20 .20
801 A159 7k multi .25 .25
802 A159 35k multi 1.10 1.10
803 A159 60k multi 2.00 2.00
Nos. 800-803 (4) 3.55 3.55

Dogs A160

1991, July 5 **Litho.** ***Perf. 14***

804 A160 5k Kabir of dembos .20 .20
805 A160 7k Ombua .25 .25
806 A160 11k Kabir massongo .40 .40
807 A160 12k Kawa tchowe .40 .40
Nos. 804-807 (4) 1.25 1.25

1992 Summer Olympics, Barcelona A161

1991, July 26 ***Perf. 13***

808 A161 4k Judo .20 .20
809 A161 6k Sailing .20 .20
810 A161 10k Running .35 .35
811 A161 100k Swimming 3.50 3.50
Nos. 808-811 (4) 4.25 4.25

Navigation Aids A162

1991, Nov. 8 **Litho.** ***Perf. 12***

812 A162 5k Quadrant .20 .20
813 A162 15k Astrolabe .50 .50
814 A162 20k Cross-staff .70 .70
815 A162 50k Portolano 1.75 1.75
Nos. 812-815 (4) 3.15 3.15

Iberex '91.

Rays A163

1992, Mar. 30 **Litho.** ***Perf. 14***

816 A163 40k Myliobatis aquila .20 .20
817 A163 50k Aetobatus narinari .20 .20
818 A163 66k Manta birostris .25 .25
819 A163 80k Raja miraletus .35 .35
Nos. 816-819 (4) 1.00 1.00

Souvenir Sheet

Perf. 13½

820 A163 25k Manta birostris, diff. .20 .20

A164

A165

Quioca masks.

1992, Apr. 30 **Litho.** ***Perf. 13½***

821 A164 60k Kalelwa .20 .20
822 A164 100k Mukixe Wa Kino .40 .40
823 A164 150k Cikunza .50 .50
824 A164 250k Mukixi Wa Mbwesu .90 .90
Nos. 821-824 (4) 2.00 2.00

See #854-857, 868-871, 883-886, 895-898.

1992, May 8 ***Perf. 14***

Medicinal Plants: 200k, Ptaeroxylon obliquum. 300k, Spondias mombin. 500k, Parinari curatellifolia. 600k, Cochlospermum angolense.

825 A165 200k brown & pale yel .75 .75
826 A165 300k brown & pale yel 1.10 1.10
827 A165 500k brown & pale yel 1.90 1.90
828 A165 600k brown & pale yel 2.25 2.25
a. Block or strip of 4, #825-828 6.00 6.00

Evangelization of Angola, 500th Anniv. — A166

1992, May 10 ***Perf. 13½***

829 A166 150k King, missionaries .55 .55
830 A166 420k Ruins of M'banza Congo 1.50 1.50
831 A166 470k Maxima Church 1.75 1.75
832 A166 500k Faces of people 1.90 1.90
Nos. 829-832 (4) 5.70 5.70

Traditional Houses — A167

Perf. 14, 13½ Vert. (#832A)

1992, May 22

832A A167 150k Dimbas 4.00 4.00
b. Bklt. pane of 4, #832A, 833a-835a 10.00
833 A167 330k Cokwe 1.25 1.25
a. Perf. 13½ vert. 1.25 1.25
834 A167 360k Mbali 1.40 1.40
a. Perf. 13½ vert. 1.40 1.40
835 A167 420k Ambwelas 1.60 1.60
a. Perf. 13½ vert. 1.60 1.60
836 A167 500k Upper Zambezi 1.90 1.90
Nos. 832A-836 (5) 10.15 10.15

Expo '92, Seville.

Agapornis Roseicollis A168

1992, June 2 ***Perf. 12x11½***

837 A168 150k Two birds on branch .55 .55
838 A168 200k Birds feeding .75 .75
839 A168 250k Hand holding bird .90 .90
840 A168 300k Bird on perch 1.10 1.10
a. Strip of 4, #837-840 3.35 3.35

Expo '92, Seville.

Souvenir Sheet

Visit of Pope John Paul II to Angola — A169

Abstract paintings: a, 340k, The Crucifixion. b, 370k, The Resurrection.

1992, June 4 Litho. *Perf. 13½*

841 A169 Sheet of 2, #a.-b. + 2 labels 1.75 1.75

1992 Summer Olympics, Barcelona A170

1992, July 30 *Perf. 14*

842 A170 120k Hurdles .30 .30
843 A170 180k Cycling .50 .50
844 A170 240k Roller hockey .65 .65
845 A170 360k Basketball 1.00 1.00
Nos. 842-845 (4) 2.45 2.45

Native Fishing — A171

1992, Aug. 5 *Perf. 11½x12*

846 A171 65k Building traps .20 .20
847 A171 90k Using nets .25 .25
848 A171 100k Laying traps .30 .30
849 A171 120k Fisherman in boats .35 .35
Nos. 846-849 (4) 1.10 1.10

Souvenir Sheet

Discovery of America, 500th Anniv. — A172

1992, Sept. 18 Litho. *Perf. 12*

850 A172 500k multicolored 1.75 1.75

Genoa '92.

First Free Elections in Angola — A173

Designs: 120k, People voting. 150k, Map, ballot box, peace doves. 200k, People, dove, hand dropping ballot into ballot box.

1992, Oct. 27 Litho. *Perf. 11½x12*

851 A173 120k multicolored .30 .30
852 A173 150k multicolored .40 .40
853 A173 200k multicolored .55 .55
Nos. 851-853 (3) 1.25 1.25

Quioca Mask Type of 1992

1992, Nov. 6 *Perf. 13½*

854 A164 72k Cihongo .30 .30
855 A164 80k Mbwasu .35 .35
856 A164 120k Cinhanga .45 .45
857 A164 210k Kalewa .80 .80
Nos. 854-857 (4) 1.90 1.90

Inauguration of Express Mail Service — A174

1992, Dec. 14 Litho. *Perf. 12x11½*

858 A174 450k Truck 1.10 1.10
859 A174 550k Airplane 1.25 1.25

Meteorological Instruments A175

1993, Mar. 23 Litho. *Perf. 11½x12*

860 A175 250k Weather balloon .65 .65
861 A175 470k Actinometer 1.10 1.10
862 A175 500k Rain gauge 1.25 1.25
Nos. 860-862 (3) 3.00 3.00

Seashells A176

1993, Apr. 6 *Perf. 12x11½*

863 A176 210k Trochita trochiformis .50 .50
864 A176 330k Strombus latus .75 .75
865 A176 400k Aporrhais pesgallinae .95 .95
866 A176 500k Fusos aff. albinus 1.25 1.25
Nos. 863-866 (4) 3.45 3.45

Souvenir Sheet

867 A176 1000k Pusionella nifat 2.25 2.25

Quioca Art Type of 1992

1993, June 7 Litho. *Perf. 12*

868 A164 72k Men with vehicles .20 .20
869 A164 210k Cavalier .45 .45
870 A164 420k Airplane .90 .90
871 A164 600k Men carrying stretcher 1.25 1.25
Nos. 868-871 (4) 2.80 2.80

Flowering Plants — A177

1993, June 28 *Perf. 11½x12*

872 A177 360k Sansevieria cylindrica .75 .75
873 A177 400k Euphorbia tirucalli .90 .90
874 A177 500k Opuntia ficus-indica 1.10 1.10
875 A177 600k Dracaena aubryana 1.25 1.25
Nos. 872-875 (4) 4.00 4.00

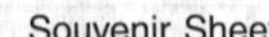

Souvenir Sheet

Africa Day — A178

1993, May 31 *Perf. 12*

876 A178 1500k Leopard 3.15 3.15

Tribal Pipes — A179

1993, Aug. 16 Litho. *Perf. 11½x12*

877 A179 72k Vimbundi .20 .20
878 A179 200k Vimbundi, diff. .45 .45
879 A179 420k Mutopa .90 .90
880 A179 600k Pexi 1.25 1.25
Nos. 877-880 (4) 2.80 2.80

Souvenir Sheet

Union of Portuguese Speaking Capitals — A180

1993, July 30 *Perf. 12x11½*

881 A180 1500k multicolored 3.25 3.25

Turtles — A181

Designs: a, 180k, Chelonia mydas (b). b, 450k, Eretmochelys imbricata. c, 550k, Dermochelys coriacea. d, 630k, Caretta caretta.

1993, July 9 Litho. *Perf. 12½x12*

882 A181 Block of 4, #a.-d. 3.50 3.50

Quioca Art Type of 1992

1993, Sept. 1 Litho. *Perf. 12*

883 A164 300k Leopard .65 .65
884 A164 600k Malhado 1.25 1.25
885 A164 800k Birds 1.60 1.60
886 A164 1000k Chickens 2.00 2.00
Nos. 883-886 (4) 5.50 5.50

Mushrooms A182

1993, Dec. 5 Litho. *Perf. 12*

887 A182 300k Tricholoma georgii .55 .55
a. Perf. 11½ vert. .55 .55
888 A182 500k Amanita phalloides .95 .95
a. Perf. 11½ vert. .95 .95
889 A182 600k Amanita vaginata 1.10 1.10
a. Perf. 11½ vert. 1.10 1.10
890 A182 1000k Macrolepiota procera 1.90 1.90
a. Perf. 11½ vert. 1.90 1.90
b. Booklet pane of 4, #887a-890a 4.50
Nos. 887-890 (4) 4.50 4.50

A183

1994, Jan. 10 Litho. *Perf. 12*

Natl. Culture Day: 500k, Cinganji, wood carving of dancer. 1000k, Ohunya yo soma, staff with woman's face. 1200k, Ongende, sculpture of man on donkey. 2200k, Upi, corn pestle.

891 A183 500k multicolored .45 .45
892 A183 1000k multicolored .90 .90
893 A183 1200k multicolored 1.10 1.10
894 A183 2200k multicolored 2.00 2.00
Nos. 891-894 (4) 4.45 4.45

Hong Kong '94.

Quioca Art Type of 1992

1994, Feb. 21 Litho. *Perf. 12*

895 A164 500k Bird on flower .30 .30
896 A164 2000k Plant with roots 1.25 1.25
897 A164 2500k Feto 1.60 1.60
898 A164 3000k Plant 2.00 2.00
Nos. 895-898 (4) 5.15 5.15

Social Responsibilities of AIDS — A184

500k, Mass of people. 1000k, Witchdoctor receiving AIDS through needle, people being educated. 3000k, Stylized man, woman.

1994, May 5 Litho. *Perf. 12*

899 A184 500k multicolored .35 .35
900 A184 1000k multicolored .65 .65
901 A184 3000k multicolored 2.00 2.00
Nos. 899-901 (3) 3.00 3.00

1994 World Cup Soccer Championships, US — A185

1994, June 17 *Perf. 14*

902 A185 500k Large arrows, small ball .30 .30
903 A185 700k Small arrows, large ball .45 .45
904 A185 2200k Ball in goal 1.50 1.50
905 A185 2500k Ball, foot 1.60 1.60
Nos. 902-905 (4) 3.85 3.85

Dinosaurs A186

1994, Aug. 16 Litho. *Perf. 12*

906 A186 1000k Brachiosaurus .20 .20
907 A186 3000k Spinosaurus .55 .55
908 A186 5000k Ouranosaurus .90 .90
909 A186 10,000k Lesothosaurus 1.90 1.90
Nos. 906-909 (4) 3.55 3.55

Souvenir Sheet

910 A186 19,000k Lesothosaurus, map of Africa 3.50 3.50

PHILAKOREA '94, SINGPEX '94. No. 910 contains one 44x34mm stamp.

Tourism A187

1994, Sept. 27 Litho. *Perf. 12x11½*

911 A187 2000k Birds .20 .20
912 A187 4000k Wild animals .35 .35
913 A187 8000k Native women .75 .75
914 A187 10,000k Native men .90 .90
Nos. 911-914 (4) 2.20 2.20

Post Boxes — A188

Designs: 5000k, Letters, bundled mail wall box. 7500k, Wall box for letters. 10,000k, Pillar box. 21,000k, Multi-function units.

1994, Oct. 7 *Perf. 14½*

915 A188 5000k multicolored .45 .45
916 A188 7500k multicolored .75 .75
917 A188 10,000k multicolored .90 .90
918 A188 21,000k multicolored 1.90 1.90
Nos. 915-918 (4) 4.00 4.00

Cotton Pests — A189

Insects: 5000k, Heliothis armigera. 6000k, Bemisia tabasi. 10,000k, Dysdercus. 27,000k, Spodoptera exigua.

1994, Nov. 11 Litho. *Perf. 14*

919 A189 5000k multicolored .45 .45
920 A189 6000k multicolored .55 .55
921 A189 10,000k multicolored .95 .95
922 A189 27,000k multicolored 2.50 2.50
Nos. 919-922 (4) 4.45 4.45

Intl. Olympic Committee, Cent. A190

1994, Dec. 15

923 A190 27,000k multicolored 2.75 2.75

Tribal Culture A191

Designs: 10,000k. Rubbing sticks to start fire. 15,000k, Extracting sap from tree. 20,000k, Smoking tribal pipe. 25,000k, Shooting bow & arrow. 28,000k, Mothers, children. 30,000k, Cave art.

1995, Jan. 6 Litho. *Perf. 14*

924 A191 10,000k multicolored .40 .40
925 A191 15,000k multicolored .65 .65
926 A191 20,000k multicolored .85 .85
927 A191 25,000k multicolored 1.00 1.00
928 A191 28,000k multicolored 1.10 1.10
929 A191 30,000k multicolored 1.25 1.25
Nos. 924-929 (6) 5.25 5.25

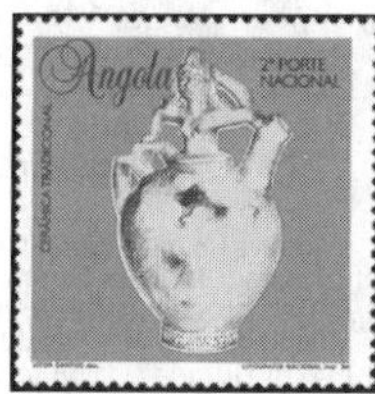

Traditional Ceramics A192

Designs: No. 930, Pitcher with bust of a woman as stopper. No. 931, Cone-shaped vase. No. 932, Bird-shaped vase. No. 933, Pitcher with bust of a man as stopper.

1995, Jan. 2 Litho. *Perf. 14½*

930 A192 (2) 2nd class natl.
931 A192 (1) 1st class natl.
932 A192 (2) 2nd class intl.
933 A192 (1) 1st class intl.
Nos. 930-933 (4) 3.25

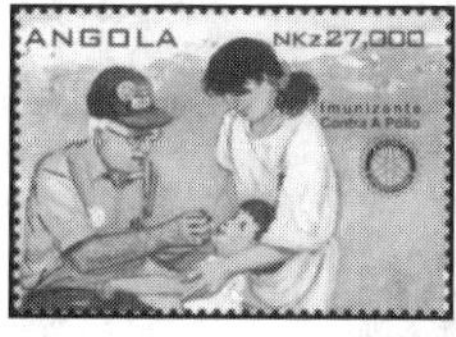

Rotary Intl., 90th Anniv. A193

a, Immunizing boy against polio. b, Medical examination. c, Immunizing girl against polio.

No. 936, Dove over map.

1995, Feb. 23 Litho. *Perf. 14*

934 Strip of 3 2.25 2.25
a.-c. A193 27,000k any single .75 .75
935 Strip of 3 2.25 2.25
a.-c. A193 27,000k any single .75 .75

Souvenir Sheet

936 A193 81,000k multicolored 4.00 4.00
a. English inscription 4.00 4.00

No. 934 has Portuguese inscriptions. No. 935 has English inscriptions. Both were issued in sheets of 9 stamps.

No. 936 contains Portuguese inscription in sheet margin.

Rotary Intl., 90th Anniv. — A194

Illustration reduced.

Litho. & Embossed

1995, Feb. 23 *Perf. 11½x12*

937 A194 81,000k gold

World Telecommunications Day — A195

Designs: No. 938, 1957 Sputnik 1. No. 939, Shuttle, Intelsat satellite.

1995 Litho. *Perf. 14*

938 A195 27,000k multicolored 1.50 1.50
939 A195 27,000k multicolored 1.50 1.50
a. Souvenir sheet, #938-939 3.00 3.00

Independence, 20th Anniv. — A196

1995, Nov. 11 Litho. *Perf. 14*

940 A196 2900k multicolored 1.50 1.50

4th World Conference on Women, Beijing — A197

Designs: 375k, Women working in fields. 1106k, Woman teaching, girls with book. 1265k, Woman in industry, career woman. 2900k, Woman in native headdress, vert.

1500k, Native mother, children, vert.

1996, Jan. 29 Litho. *Perf. 14*

941 A197 375k multicolored .20 .20
942 A197 1106k multicolored .35 .35
943 A197 1265k multicolored .45 .45
944 A197 2900k multicolored 1.00 1.00
Nos. 941-944 (4) 2.00 2.00

Souvenir Sheet

945 A197 1500k multicolored .50 .50

UN Assistance Programs — A198

Designs: 200k, Boy, highlift moving supplies. 1265k, Supply ship arriving. No. 948, Two high lifts. No. 949, Tractor-trailer traveling past vultures, native girl.

No. 950, Man, ship.

1996 Litho. *Perf. 14*

946 A198 200k multicolored .20 .20
947 A198 1265k multicolored .50 .50
948 A198 2583k multicolored 1.00 1.00
949 A198 2583k multicolored 1.00 1.00
Nos. 946-949 (4) 2.70 2.70

Souvenir Sheet

950 A198 1265k multicolored .50 .50

Flora and Fauna A199

1500k, Verdant hawkmoth. 4400k, Water lily. 5100k, Panther toad. 6000k, African wild dog.

1500k: a, Western honey buzzard. b, Bateleuer. c, Common kestrel.

4400k; d, Red-crested turaco. e, Giraffe. f, Elephant.

5100k: g, Hippopotamus. h, Cattle egret. i, Lion.

6000k: j, Helmeted turtle. k, African pygmy goose. l, Egyptian plover.

12,000k, Spotted hyena.

1996, Apr. 20 Litho. *Perf. 14*

951-954 A199 Set of 4 1.00 1.00
955 A199 Sheet of 12, #a.-l. 4.00 4.00

Souvenir Sheet

956 A199 12,000k multicolored .80 .80

Sheets of 12

Birds — A200

Fowl: No. 957a, California quail. b, Greater prairie chicken. c, Painted quail. d, Golden pheasant. e, Roulroul partridge. f, Ceylon sourfowl. g, Himalayan snowcock. h, Temminicks tragopan. i, Lady Amherst's pheasant. j, Great curassow. k, Red-legged partridge. l, Impeyan pheasant.

Hummingbirds: No. 958a, Anna's. b, Blue-throated. c, Broad-tailed. d, Costa's. e, White-eared. f, Calliope. g, Violet-crowned. h, Rufous. i, Crimson topaz. j, Broad-billed. k, Frilled coquette. l, Ruby-throated.

No. 959, Ring-necked pheasant. No. 960, Racquet-tail hummingbird.

1996, Apr. 20

957-958 A200 5500k #a.-l., ea 4.25 4.25

Souvenir Sheets

959-960 A200 12,000k each .80 .80

Lubrapex '96 A201

Wild animals: a, 180k, Lions attacking zebra. b, 450k, Zebras, lions, diff. c, 180k, Zebras grazing, lions stalking. d, 450k, Panthera leo. e, 550k, Cheetah. f, 630k, Cheetah running. g, 550k, Cheetah chasing antilope. h, 630k, Cheetah attacking antelope. i, 180k, Antilope (gnu) being attacked by wild dogs. j, 450k, Antelope, wild dogs. k, 180k, Pack of wild dogs. l, 450k, Licaon pictus. m, 550k, Panthera pardus. n, 630k, Oryx. o, 550k, Oryx, diff. p, 630k, Leopard attacking oryx.

1996, Apr. 27

961 A201 Sheet of 16, #a.-p. 6.00 6.00

Sheets of 6

Ships A202

Designs: No. 962a, Styrbjorn, Sweden, 1789. b, Constellation, US, 1797. c, Taureau, France, 1865. d, Bomb Ketch, France, 1682. e, Sardegna, Italy, 1881. f, HMS Glasgow, England, 1867.

No. 963a, Essex, US, 1812. b, HMS Inflexible, England, 1881. c, HMS Minotaur, England, 1863. d, Napoleon, France, 1854. e, Sophia Amalia, Denmark, 1650. f, Massena, France, 1887.

No. 964, HMS Tremendous, England, 1806, vert. No. 965, Royal Prince, England, 1666.

1996, May 4

962-963 A202 6000k #a.-f., ea 2.50 2.50

Souvenir Sheets

964-965 A202 12,000k each .80 .80

UN, 50th Anniv. (in 1995) A203

Designs: No. 966, Boys pumping water. No. 967, Man, woman with girl.

8000k, Unloading supplies from ship.

1996, Apr. 27 Litho. *Perf. 14*

966 A203 3500k multicolored 1.00 1.00

967 A203 3500k multicolored 1.00 1.00

Souvenir Sheet

968 A203 8000k multicolored 1.00 1.00

Sonangol, 20th Anniv. A204

Face in traditional mask, costume, native birds, and: No. 969, Oil derricks. No. 970, Oil storage tanks, ship. 2500k, Refinery equipment. 5000k, Cargo shipment, jet.

1996, May 12

969 A204 1000k multicolored .20 .20
970 A204 1000k multicolored .20 .20
971 A204 2500k multicolored .25 .25
972 A204 5000k multicolored .55 .55
Nos. 969-972 (4) 1.20 1.20

Brapex '96 — A205

#973, Slaves in hold. #974, Slaves fleeing ship as it's overturned. #975, Slave boats approaching ship. #976, Slaves talking with captain.
50,000k, like #975.

1996, Oct. 19 Litho. *Perf. 14*

973 A205 20,000k multicolored 1.25 1.25
974 A205 20,000k multicolored 1.25 1.25
975 A205 30,000k multicolored 1.90 1.90
976 A205 30,000k multicolored 1.90 1.90
Nos. 973-976 (4) 6.30 6.30

Souvenir Sheet

977 A205 50,000k multicolored 3.25 3.25

Churches — A206

5,000k, Mission, Huila. #979, Church of the Nazarene. #980, Church of Our Lady of Pó Pulo. 25,000k, St. Adriáo Church.

1996, Dec. 6 Litho. *Perf. 14*

978 A206 5,000k multicolored .30 .30
979 A206 10,000k multicolored .65 .65
980 A206 10,000k multicolored .65 .65
981 A206 25,000k multicolored 1.60 1.60
Nos. 978-981 (4) 3.20 3.20

1996 Summer Olympic Games, Atlanta A207

1996, Dec. 9

982 A207 5,000k Handball, vert. .30 .30
983 A207 10,000k Swimming .65 .65
984 A207 25,000k Track & field, vert. 1.60 1.60
985 A207 35,000k Shooting 2.25 2.25
Nos. 982-985 (4) 4.80 4.80

Souvenir Sheet

986 A207 65,000k Basketball 4.00 4.00

From this point the value of Angolan currency is in question.

MPLA (Liberation Movement), 40th Anniv. — A208

1996, Dec. 10 Litho. *Perf. 14*

987 A208 30,000k Dolphins, map *1.75 1.75*

Trains A209

Trains A209a

No. 988: a, AVE, Spain. b, Bullet Train, Japan. c, GM F7 Warbonnet, US. d, Deltic, Great Britain. e, Eurostar, France/Great Britain. f, ETR 450, Italy.
No. 989: a, Class E1300, Morocco. b, ICE, Germany. c, X2000, Sweden. d, TGV Duplex, France.
No. 989E: f, Steam engine. g, Garrat. h, General Electric.
No. 990, Canadian Pacific 4-4-0, Canada. No. 991, Via Rail Canadian, Canada.

1997, May 29 Litho. *Perf. 14*

Sheets of 6, 4 or 3

988 A209 100,000k #a.-f. *6.00 6.00*
989 A209 140,000k #a.-d. *6.00 6.00*
989E A209a 250,000k Sheet of 3, #f.-h. *5.75 5.75*

Souvenir Sheets

Perf. 13½

990-991 A209 110,000k each *4.00 4.00*

Nos. 990-991 contain one 38x50 or 50x38mm stamp, respectively.
PACIFIC 97.

Horses A210

No. 992: a, Thoroughbred. b, Palomino, appaloosa. c, Arabians. d, Arabian colt. e, Thoroughbred colt. f, Mustang. g, Mustang, diff. h, Furioso.
No. 993: a, Thoroughbred. b, Arabian, palomino. c, Arabian, chincoteague. d, Pintos. e, Przewalski's horse. f, Thoroughbred colt. g, Arabians. h, New forest pony.
No. 994: a, Selle Francais. b, Fjord. c, Percheron. d, Italian heavy draft. e, Shagya Arab. f, Avelignese. g, Czechoslovakian warmblood. h, New forest pony.
215,000k, Thoroughbreds. 220,000k, Thoroughbreds, diff.

1997, July 5 Litho. *Perf. 14*

Sheets of 8

992 A210 100,000k #a.-h. *4.00 4.00*
993 A210 120,000k #a.-h. *5.00 5.00*
994 A210 140,000k #a.-h. *5.50 5.50*

Souvenir Sheets

995 A210 215,000k multicolored *4.00 4.00*
996 A210 220,000k multicolored *4.00 4.00*

PACIFIC 97.

1998 World Cup Soccer Championships, France — A211

Winners holding World Cup trophy: No. 997: a, Uruguay, 1930. b, Germany, 1954. c, Brazil, 1970. d, Argentina, 1986. e, Brazil, 1994.
Winning team pictures: No. 998a, Germany, 1954. b, Uruguay, 1958. c, Italy, 1938. d, Brazil, 1962. e, Brazil, 1970. f, Uruguay, 1930.
220,000k, Angolan team members standing. 250,000k, 1997 Angolan team picture.

1997, July 5 Litho. *Perf. 14*

Sheets of 5 or 6

997 A211 100,000k #a.-e. + label *5.00 5.00*
998 A211 100,000k #a.-f. *6.00 6.00*

Souvenir Sheets

999 A211 220,000k multicolored *3.50 3.50*
1000 A211 250,000k multicolored *4.00 4.00*

ENSA (Security System), 20th Anniv. — A212

"Star" emblem, and stylized protection of "egg:" #1001, Industry. #1002, Recreation. #1003, Homes, shelters. #1004, Accident prevention.
350,000k, Emblem.

1998 Litho. *Perf. 13½*

1001-1004 A212 240,000k Set of 4 *7.50 7.50*

Souvenir Sheet

Perf. 13½x13

1005 A212 350,000k multicolored *2.75 2.75*

No. 1005 contains one 60x40mm stamp.

GURN (Natl. Unity & Reconciliation Government), 1st Anniv. — A213

Emblem, portion of country map and: 100,000k, a, Sea, swordfish, ships, oil derrick. b, Sea, swordfish. c, Sea, swordfish, ships, mining car on railroad track. d, Sea, power lines.
200,000k: e, Train on track, antelope. f, Mining cars on track, tractor pulling cart. g, Railroad track across rivers, tractor plowing. h, Power lines. i, UR corner of map, crystals. j, Train on track. k, Elephant, tree. l, Trunk of tree, bottom edge of map.

1998

1006 A213 Sheet of 12, #a.-l. 15.00 15.00

Souvenir Sheet

Education in Angola — A214

Illustration reduced.

1998

1007 A214 400,000k multicolored *3.25 3.25*

Diana, Princess of Wales (1961-97) — A215

Various portraits, color of sheet margin: No. 1008, pale green. No. 1009, pale yellow.
400,000k, Wearing protective clothing.

1998, May 21 Litho. *Perf. 14*

Sheets of 6

1008-1009 A215 100,000k #a.-f., each *4.75 4.75*

Souvenir Sheet

1010 A215 400,000k multicolored *3.25 3.25*

See No. 1028.

Expo '98, Lisbon A216

Marine life: No. 1011, 100,000k, Anemones. No. 1012, 100,000k, Sea urchin. No. 1013, 100,000k, Sea horses. No. 1014, 100,000k, Coral (Caravela). No. 1015, 240,000k, Sea slug. No. 1016, 240,000k, Worms (Tunicados).

1998, May 21 *Perf. 13½*

1011-1016 A216 Set of 6 7.00 7.00

Butterflies — A217

No. 1017: a, Metamorpha stelene. b, Papilio glaucus. c, Danaus plexippus. d, Catonephele numili. e, Plebejus argus. f, Hypolimnas bolina.
No. 1018: a, Terinos terpander. b, Bematistes aganice. c, Hebomoia glaucippe. d, Colias eurytheme. e, Pereute leucodrosime. f, Lycaena dispar.
No. 1019, horiz.: a, Dynastor napolean. b, Zeuxidia amethystus. c, Battus philenor. d, Phoebis philea. e, Danaus chrysippus. f, Glaucopsyche alexis.
No. 1020, Euphaedra neophron. No. 1021, Thecla betulae, horiz. No. 1022, Uraneis ucubis, armillaria staminea.

1998, May 21 *Perf. 14*

Sheets of 6

1017-1019 A217 120,000k #a.-f., each *6.00 6.00*

Souvenir Sheets

1020-1022 A217 250,000k each *4.00 4.00*

Cats and Dogs A218

Cats: No. 1023a, British tortoiseshell. b, Chinchilla. c, Russian blue. d, Black Persian (longhair). e, British red tabby. f, Birman.
Dogs: No. 1024a, West Highland terrier. b, Irish setter. c, Dachshund. d, St. John water dog. e, Shetland sheep dog. f, Dalmatian.
No. 1025, Turkish van (swimming cat). No. 1026, Labrador retriever.

1998, May 21 Litho. *Perf. 14x13½*

Sheets of 6

1023-1024 A218 140,000k #a.-f., each *6.75 6.75*

Souvenir Sheets

1025-1026 A218 500,000k each *4.00 4.00*

Wild Animals A219

100,000k: a, Panthera leo. b, Hippopotamus amphibius. c, Loxodonta africana. d, Giraffa camelopardalis.

220,000k: e, Syncerus caffer-caffer. f, Gorilla gorilla. g, Ceratotherim simum. h, Oryx gazella.

1998, July 24 Litho. *Perf. 14*

1027 A219 Sheet of 8, #a.-h. 10.00 10.00

Diana, Princes of Wales Type of 1998

Pictures showing Diana's campaign to ban land mines: a, With girl. b, With two boys. c, Wearing protective clothing.

1998, Aug. 31 Litho. *Perf. 14*

1028 A215 150,000k Strip of 3, #a.-c. *4.75 4.75*

No. 1028 was issued in sheets of 6 stamps.

Intl. Year of the Ocean — A220

Marine life: No. 1029a, Pagurites. b, Callinectes marginatus. c, Thais forbesi. d, Ostrea tulipa. e, Balanus amohitrite. f, Uca tangeri.

No. 1030: a, Littorina angulifera. b, Semifusus morio. c, Thais coronata. d, Cerithium atratum (red branch). e, Ostrea tulipa. f, Cerithium atratum (green branch).

No. 1031, Goniopsis, horiz. No. 1032, Unidentified shell.

1998, Sept. 4

Sheets of 6

1029 A220 100,000k #a.-f. *3.00 3.00*
1030 A220 170,000k #a.-f. *5.00 5.00*

Souvenir Sheets

1031-1032 A220 300,000k each *4.00 4.00*

Souvenir Sheet

Battle Against Polio in Angola — A221

Illustration reduced.

1998, Aug. 28 Litho. *Perf. 13½*

1033 A221 500,000k multicolored *2.50 2.50*

Traditional Boats A222

Designs: No. 1034, 250,000k, Boat, Bimba. No. 1035, 250,000k, Canoe with sail, Ndongo. 500,000k, Constructing boat, Ndongo.

1998, Sept. 4 *Perf. 14*

1034-1036 A222 Set of 3 5.00 5.00

Titanic A223

Views of Titanic: a, Under tow. b, Stern. c, Starboard side at night. d, At dock.

1998, Sept. 4

1037 A223 350,000k Sheet of 4, #a.-d. *7.00 7.00*

#1037c is 76x30mm, #1037d is 38x61mm.

Angolan Food A224

Various vegetables, fruits: #1038, 100,000k, 4 fruits. #1039, 100,000k, Squash sliced in half. #1040, 120,000k, Ears of corn. #1041, 120,000k, Green beans. #1042, 140,000k, Fruit with red seeds sliced in half. #1043, 140,000k, Sliced bananas.

1998

1038-1043 A224 Set of 6 5.50 5.50

Portugal '98.

Airplanes A225

No. 1044, IL-62 M. No. 1045, B737 100.

No. 1046: a, Ultralight. b, Gyroplane. c, Business jet. d, onvertible plane (e). e, Chuterplane (a, b, d). f, Twin rotors (e). g, Skycrane. h, Aerospatiale Concorde (i). i, Flying boat.

No. 1047: a, Pedal power (b). b, Sail plane (a, e). c, Aerobatic (f). d, Hang gliding (g). e, Balloon (h). f, Glidercraft (e, i). g, Model airplane. h, Air racing (i). i, Solar cells.

No. 1048, Boeing 777. No. 1049, Columbia Space Shuttle, vert. No. 1049A, Boeing 737-200. No. 1049B, Boeing 747-300.

1998-99 Litho. *Perf. 14*

1044 A225 200,000k multicolored *1.50 1.50*
1045 A225 200,000k multicolored *1.50 1.50*

Sheets of 9

1046 A225 150,000k #a.-i. *4.50 4.50*
1047 A225 250,000k #a.-i. *6.00 6.00*

Souvenir Sheets

1048-1049B A225 1,000,000k ea *5.00 5.00*

Nos. 1048-1049B each contain one 85x28mm stamp.

Issued: Nos. 1049A-1049B, 3/25/99; others 12/24/98.

Dinosaurs — A226

Designs, vert: No. 1050, Parasaurolophus. No. 1051, Maiasaura. No. 1052, Iguanodon. No. 1053, Elaphosaurus.

No. 1054, vert: a, Brontosaurus. b, Plateosaurus. c, Brachiosaurus. d, Anatosaurus. e, Tyrannosaurus. f, Carnotaurus. g, Corythosaurus. h, Stegosaurus. i, Iguanodon, diff.

No. 1055: a, Hadrosaurus. b, Ouranosaurus. c, Hypsilophodon. d, Brachiosaurus. e, Shunosaurus. f, Amargasaurus. g, Tuojiangosaurus. h, Monoclonius. i, Struthiosaurus.

No. 1056, Triceratops, vert. No. 1057, Tyrannosaurus, vert.

1998, Dec. 28

1050-1053 A226 120,000k Set of 4 *6.00 6.00*

Sheets of 9

1054-1055 A226 120,000k #a.-i., each *7.50 7.50*

Souvenir Sheets

1056-1057 A226 550,000k each *2.00 2.00*

World Wildlife Fund — A227

Lesser flamingo: a, Facing left. b, Body facing forward. c, Head and neck. d, With wings spread.

1999 Litho. *Perf. 14*

Strip of 4

1058 A227 300,000k #a.-d. *3.25 3.25*

No. 1058 was issued in sheets of 16 stamps.

Fauna A228

Designs: No. 1059, Equis caballus przewalski. No. 1060, Sphenisciformes, vert. No. 1061, Haliaeetus leucocephalus, vert. No. 1062, Anodorhynchus hyacinthinus.

No. 1063: a, Vulpes velox hebes. b, Odocoileus. c, Pongo pygmaeus. d, Leontopitecus rosalia. e, Panthera tigris. f, Tragelaphus eurycerus.

No. 1064: a, Tremarctos ornatus. b, Aphelocoma. c, Otus insularis. d, Balaeniceps rex. e, Lepidochelys kempii. f, Lutra canadensis.

No. 1065, Ailuropoda melanoleuca, vert. No. 1066, Ursus arctos horribilis.

1999

1059-1062 A228 300,000k Set of 4 *9.25 9.25*

Sheets of 6

1063-1064 A228 300,000k #a.-f., each *6.00 6.00*

Souvenir Sheets

1065-1066 A228 1,000,000k each *4.00 4.00*

These Flora and Fauna stamps, formerly Nos. 1067-1078, were not authorized by Angola postal authorities.

Other items inscribed "Angola" that were not authorized but which have appeared on the market include sheets with the themes of Disney and History of Animation, Millennium, Animals, Trains, Flora, Muhammad Ali & Lennox Lewis, Bruce Lee, Albert Einstein / Moon Landing, Elvis Presley and other entertainers, Great Personalities, John Kennedy and Marilyn Monroe, Martin Luther King, Jr., Payne Stewart, Colin Montgomerie, Babe Ruth, Cardinal John O'Connor, Pope John Paul II / Mother Teresa and Queen Elizabeth II / Winston Churchill.

World Telecommunications Day — A230

1999, May 17 Litho. *Perf. 14*

1079 A230 500,000k multi *.50 .50*

Souvenir Sheet

Waterfalls A231

a, Andulo. b, Chiumbo. c, Ruacaná. d, Coemba.

1999, June 5 Sheet of 4

1080 A231 500,000k #a.-d. *2.00 2.00*

A232

African Men's Basketball Championships - No. 1081: a, Poster. b, Basketball, hoop, tan background. c, Basketball, hoop, green background. d, Welwitschia plant holding basketball.

2,500,000k, Similar to No. 1081c.

1999, July 29 *Perf. 13½*

Sheet of 4

1081 A232 1,500,000k #a.-d. *3.00 3.00*

Souvenir Sheet

Perf. 13x13½

1082 A232 2,500,000k multi *2.00 2.00*

No. 1082 contains one 40x30mm stamp.

A233

1999, Aug. 17 *Perf. 14*

1083 A233 1,000,000k multi *.80 .80*

Southern African Development Community. Issued in sheets of 4.

A234

A235

Tribal kings - No. 782: a, Ekuikui II. b, Mvemba Nzinga. c, Mwata Yamvu Naweji II. d, Njinga Mbande.
1,000,000k, Mandume Ndemufayo.

1999, Sept. 17 **Sheet of 4**
1084 A234 500,000k #a.-d. *2.00 2.00*

Souvenir Sheet
1085 A234 1,000,000k multi *1.00 1.00*

1999, Sept. 17 Litho. *Perf. 14*

Queen Mother (b. 1900) - No. 1086: a, With King George VI. b, Wearing brooch. c, Wearing tiara. d, Wearing hat.
500,000k, Wearing academic gown.

Sheet of 4
1086 A235 200,000k #a.-d. *6.00 6.00*

Souvenir Sheet
Perf. 13¾
1087 A235 500,000k multi *3.75 3.75*

No. 1087 contains one 38x51mm stamp.

Ships A236

No. 1088: a, Egyptian bark, 1300 B.C. b, Flemish carrack, 1480. c, Beagle, 1830. d, North Star, 1852. e, Fram, 1892. f, Unyon Maru, 1909. g, Juan Sebastian de Elcano, 1927. h, Tovarishch, 1933.
No. 1089: a, Bucentauro, 1728. b, Clermont, 1807. c, Savannah, 1819. d, Dromedary, 1844. e, Iberia, 1881. f, S.S. Gluckauf, 1886. g, City of Paris, 1888. h, Mauretania, 1906.
No. 1090: a, Gloire, 1859. b, L'Ocean, 1868. c, Dandalo, 1876, stern of HMS Dreadnought, 1906. d, Bow of Dreadnought. e, Bismarck, 1939, stern of USS Cleveland, 1946. f, Bow of Cleveland. g, USS Boston, 1942, stern of USS Long Beach, 1959. h, Bow of Long Beach.
No. 1091, Chinese junk. No. 1092, Madre de Deus, 1609. No. 1093, Catamaran, 1861. No. 1094, Natchez, 1870.

1999, Sept. 23 Litho. *Perf. 14*

Sheets of 8
1088-1090 A236 950,000k #a.-h., each *6.00 6.00*

Souvenir Sheets
1091-1094 A236 5,000,000k each *3.00 3.00*

Mushrooms A237

#1095, Amanita caesarea. #1096, Psalliota xanthoderma. #1097, Hygrocybe conica. #1098, Boletus chrysenteron. #1099, Coprinus comatus. #1100, Boletus luteus.
#1101: a, Morchella crassipes. b, Boletus rufescens. c, Amanita phalloides. d, Collybia iocephala. e, Tricholoma aurantium. f, Cortinarius violaceus. g, Mycena polygramma. h, Psalliota augusta.
#1102: a, Amanita muscaria. b, Boletus aereus. c, Coprinus comatus. d, Amanita rubescens. e, Cortinarius collinitus. f, Boletus satanas. g, Lepiota procera. h, Clitocybe geotropa.
#1103: a, Russula nigricans. b, Boletus granulatus. c, Mycena strobilinoides. d, Amanita caesarea. e, Amanita muscaria. f, Boletus, crocipodius. g, Russula virescens. h, Lactarius deliciosus.
#1104, Psalliota haemorrhoidaria.
#1105, Mycena lilacifolia.

1999, Sept. 23 Litho. *Perf. 14*
1095 A237 1,250,000k multi .95 .95
1096 A237 1,250,000k multi .95 .95
1097 A237 1,250,000k multi .95 .95
1098 A237 1,250,000k multi .95 .95
1099 A237 1,250,000k multi .95 .95
1100 A237 1,250,000k multi .95 .95
Nos. 1095-1100 (6) 5.70 5.70

Sheets of 8
1101 A237 1,000,000k #a-h 6.50 6.50
1102 A237 1,000,000k #a-h 6.50 6.50
1103 A237 1,000,000k #a-h 6.50 6.50

Souvenir Sheets
1104 A237 5,000,000k multi 3.00 3.00
1105 A237 5,000,000k multi 3.00 3.00

A238

First Manned Moon Landing, 30th Anniv. A239

No. 1107: a, Astronaut spacewalking. b, Mariner 8. c, Viking 10. d, GINGA satellite. e, Soyuz 19. f, Voyager.
No. 1108, vert.: a, Space telescope. b, Space shuttle Atlantis. c, Uhuru satellite. d, Mir space station. e, Gemini 7. f, Venera 7.
No. 1109: a, Mercury, Venus. b, Jupiter. c, Neptune, Pluto. d, Earth, Mars. e, Saturn. f, Uranus.
No. 1110: a, Explorer 17. b, Intelsat 4A. c, GOES-D Satellite. d, Intelsat 2. e, Navstar. f, S.M.S.
No. 1111, Lunar rover, vert. No. 1112, Apollo 17 astronaut on moon, vert. No. 1113, Neil Armstrong, vert. No. 1114, Space shuttle Columbia. No. 1115, SBS-4, vert.

Perf. 13¾ (A238), 14 (A239)
1999, Nov. 15 Litho.

Sheets of 6, #a.-f.
1107-1108 A238 3,500,000k 7.25 7.25
1109-1110 A239 3,500,000k 7.25 7.25

Souvenir Sheets
1111-1112 A238 6,000,000k ea 1.60 1.60
1113-1115 A239 12,000,000k ea 3.25 3.25

Hokusai Paintings — A240

No. 1116: a, Night attack. b, Usigafuchi No Kudan. c, Drawing of man and bowl. d, Wildlife. e, Pheasant. f, People on bridge.
No. 1117: a, Tree and shoreline. b, Kabuki theater. c, Hen. d, Cooper. e, Trip to Enoshima. f, Sumida River landscape.
No. 1118, Yama-uba and Kintori, vert. No. 1119, Woman, vert.

1999, Dec. 13 Litho. *Perf. 13¾*

Sheets of 6, #a.-f.
1116-1117 A240 3,500,000k ea 4.50 4.50

Souvenir Sheets
1118-1119 A240 12,000,000k ea 4.00 4.00

On Dec. 13, the date of issue of these stamps, Angola devalued its currency, with approximately 1,000,000k being the equivalent of 1k after the devaluation.

Souvenir Sheets

PhilexFrance 99 — A241

No. 1120, 4-8-4 Linder Compound express. No. 1121, Hovertrain prototype.

Illustration reduced.

2000, Mar. 13 Litho. *Perf. 13¾*
1120-1121 A241 12k Set of 2 8.00 8.00

A242

Wildlife — A243

1.50k, Zebra. 2k, Fruit bat. 3k, California condor. 5.50k, Lion.
No. 1126, horiz.: a, Equus zebra. b, Ploceus xanthops. c, Lycaon protus. d, Acinonyx jubatus. e, Oryx gazella. f, Nursing Otocyon megalotis. g, Giraffa camelopardalis. h, Canis adustus. i, Perodicticus potto. j, Panthera leo. k, Coracius caudata. l, Pair of Otocyon megalotis.
No. 1127, horiz.: a, Struthio camelus. b, Felis lybica. c, Aepyceros melampus. d, Cercopithecus aethiops. e, Diceros bicornis. f, Papio sp. g, Felis caracal. h, Sagittarius serpentarius. i, Phacochoerus aethiopicus. j, Arctocephalus pusillus. k, Alcedo cristata. l, Hippopotamus amphibius.
No. 1128: a, Deer. b, Turkey. c, Beaver. d, Frog. e, Manatee. f, Trout.
No. 1129: a, Macaque. b, Toucan. c, Bothriopsis bilineata. d, Hyla leucopyliata. e, Tamarin. f, Eagle.
No. 1130, vert.: a, Mountain gorilla. b, Rhinoceros. c, Water buffalo. d, Chameleon. e, Cobra. f, Meerkats.
No. 1131, vert.: a, Kangaroo. b, Koala. c, Kingfishers. d, Frog on tree root. e, Three fish. f, Turtle.
No. 1132, Sloth. No. 1133, Lemur, vert. No. 1134, Cheetah, vert. No. 1135, Orangutan, vert. No. 1136, Cercopithecus aethiops, diff. No. 1137, Loxodonta africana.
Illustration A243 reduced.

2000, Apr. 7 *Perf. 14*
1122-1125 A242 Set of 4 2.50 2.50

Sheets of 12
1126 A243 1.50k #a-l 3.75 3.75
1127 A243 2k #a-l 5.00 5.00

Sheets of 6, #a-f
1128-1131 A242 3.50k Set of 4 17.00 17.00

Souvenir Sheets
1132-1135 A242 12k Set of 4 10.00 10.00
1136-1137 A243 12k Set of 4 10.00 10.00

Birds of Prey A244

1.50k, Harpy eagle. 2k, Unidentified bird. 3k, Vulture, vert. 5.50k, King vulture, vert.
No. 1142: a, Acolpiler gentilis. b, Surnis ulula. c, Falco peregrinus. d, Otus asio. e, Haliaetus vocifer. f, Herpetothers cachinnans.
No. 1143: a, Falco sperterius. b, Pulsetrix perspicillata. c, Elemus leucurus. d, Ninox novaseelandiae. e, Polemactus bellicosus. f, Polyborus plancus.
No. 1144: a, Verreaux's eagle. b, Aguia gigante. c, Aguia peixe.
No. 1145, vert.: a, Aguia despeida. b, Aguia dourada. c, Aguia devoradora de macacos.
No. 1146, King vulture, diff. No. 1147, Falcon, vert. No. 1148, Sagittarius serpentarius. No. 1149, Aquila chrysectos.

2000, Apr. 10
1138-1141 A244 Set of 4 2.75 2.75

Sheets of 6, #a-f
1142-1143 A244 3.50k Set of 2 8.50 8.50

Sheets of 3, #a-c
1144-1145 A244 6.50k Set of 2 8.00 8.00

Souvenir Sheets
1146-1147 A244 12k Set of 2 5.00 5.00
1148-1149 A244 15k Set of 2 6.50 6.50

Millennium — A245

Highlights of the 16th Century: a, Paintings by Lai-Ji. b, The Last Judgment, by Luca Signorelli. c, Garden of Earthly Delights by Hieronymus Bosch. d, The Prince, written by Niccolò Machiavelli. e, Utopia, written by Sir Thomas More. f, Martin Luther. g, Charles I of Spain becomes Holy Roman Emperor Charles V. h, The School of Athens, by Raphael. i, Juan Sebastián de Elcano circumnavigates globe. j, Henry VIII of England. k, Spanish conquest of Aztecs and Incas. l, Placentia Cathedral. m, Potatoes introduced to Europe. n, Heliocentric theory of Copernicus. o, Portuguese reach Japan. p, Death of Albrecht Dürer (60x40mm). q, Bartolomé de Las Casas promotes rights for Indians.
Illustration reduced.

2000, Oct. 2 Litho. *Perf. 12¾x12½*
1150 A245 2.50k Sheet of 17, #a-q, + label 6.00 6.00

War Damage in Angola A246

#1151, 3k, B.N.A. Building, Kuito. #1152, 3k, Kunje St., Kuito. #1153, 4k, Post office. #1154, 4k, Police headquarters. #1155, 5k, Apartment house. #1156, 5k, Independence Square. #1157, 6k, Child waving from upper floor of apartment house. #1158, 6k, Building, man carrying pack.

2000, Sept. 29 Litho. *Perf. 14*
1151-1158 A246 Set of 8 4.25 4.25

Popes — A247

#1159: a, Nicholas II, 1059-61. b, Paschal II, 1099-1118. c, Sergius IV, 1009-1012. d, Victor II, 1055-57. e, Victor III, 1086-87. f, Urban III, 1185-87.

#1160: a, Innocent II, 1130-43. b, John XIII, 965-72. c, Agapetus II, 946-55. d, John XV, 985-96. e, John XVIII, 1003-09. f, Lucius II, 1144-45.

#1161: a, Celestine II, 1143-44. b, Clement II, 1046-47. c, Clement III, 1187-91. d, Gelasius II, 1118-19. e, Benedict VII, 974-83. f, Gregory V, 996-99.

#1162, Leo IX, 1049-54. #1163, Gregory VII, 1073-85. #1164, Leo XIII, 1878-1903.

Illustration reduced.

2000, Oct. 2 ***Perf. 12x12¼***

Sheets of 6, #a-f

1159-1161 A247 Set of 3 6.25 6.25

Souvenir Sheets

1162-1164 A247 Set of 3 4.25 4.25

Monarchs — A248

#1165: a, Henry II, King of Germany and Holy Roman Emperor, 1002-24. b, Marina Mniszek, wife of false Russian czar Dmitri, 1605-06. c, Ivan IV of Russia, 1533-84. d, Ivan III of Russia, 1462-1505.

#1166: a, Charles II of Great Britain, 1660-85. b, Lady Jane Grey of England, 1533. c, Leopold III of Belgium, 1934-51. d, Louis XV of France, 1715-74.

#1167: a, James I of Great Britain, 1603-25. b, James II of Great Britain, 1685-88. c, James IV of Scotland, 1567-1625. d, Brian Boru of Ireland, 1002-14. e, Wilhelm I, King of Prussia and German Emperor, 1861-88. f, Edward VI of England, 1547-53.

#1168, Feodor I of Russia, 1584-98. #1169, False Russian czar Dmitri, 1605-06. #1170, William IV of Great Britain, 1830-37

Illustration reduced.

2000, Oct. 2

Sheets of 4, #a-d

1165-1166 A248 Set of 2 2.75 2.75

Sheet of 6

1167 A248 #a-f 2.10 2.10

Souvenir Sheets

1168-1170 A248 Set of 3 4.25 4.25

Children's Drawings A249

Various designs. Denominations: 3k, 4k, 5k.

2000, Nov. 7 ***Perf. 14***

1171-1173 A249 Set of 3 1.40 1.40

Post Office Buildings A250

Designs: No. 1174, 5k, Former Secretary of Communications Building, Luanda. No. 1175, 5k, Mbanza Congo Post Office. No. 1176, 5k, Namibe Post Office. No. 1177, 8k, Facade of Luanda Post Office. No. 1178, 8k, Luanda Post Office, diff. No. 1179, 8k, Lobito Post Office.

2000, Sept. 29 **Litho.** ***Perf. 14***

1174-1179 A250 Set of 6 6.00 6.00

National Radio and Television, 25th Anniv. — A251

No. 1180, 9.50k: a, Woman at computer in newsroom. b, Reporter with tape recorder reporting on tank battle. c, Rescuing victims from airplane crash.

No. 1181, 9.50k: a, People and equipment in newsroom. b, Cameraman filming tank battle. c, Refugees.

No. 1182, 20k, Reporter with tape recorder. No. 1183, 20k, Cameraman, vert.

Perf. 13¼x13½, 13½x13¼

2000, Dec. 7

Sheets of 3, #a-c

1180-1181 A251 Set of 2 8.50 8.50

Souvenir Sheets

1182-1183 A251 Set of 2 6.00 6.00

Souvenir Sheet

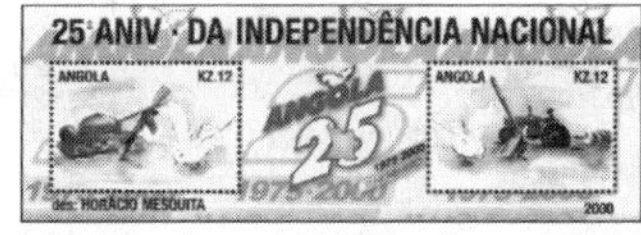

Independence, 25th Anniv. — A252

No. 1184: a, Tank, rifle, dove. b, Dove, hoe, tractor.

2001, Feb. 13 **Litho.** ***Perf. 14¼x14***

1184 A252 12k Sheet of 2, #a-b 2.60 2.60

Africa Day A253

Designs: No. 1185, 10k, Shown. No. 1186, 10k, Xylophone.

30k, Map, musical instruments, native with mask, elephant, satellite dishes and computer.

2001, May 25 ***Perf. 13x13¼***

1185-1186 A253 Set of 2 2.00 2.00

Souvenir Sheet

1187 A253 30k multi 3.00 3.00

Flowers A254

Butterfly and: 8k, Nicolaia speciosa. 9k, Allamanda cathartica. No. 1190, 10k, Welwitschia mirabilis. No. 1191, 10k, Tagetes patula.

30k, Welwitschia mirabilis.

2001, June 9

1188-1191 A254 Set of 4 3.75 3.75

Souvenir Sheet

1192 A254 30k multi 3.00 3.00

Belgica 2001 Intl. Stamp Exhibition, Brussels (#1192).

Souvenir Sheet

Total Solar Eclipse, June 21 — A255

2001, June 21

1193 A255 30k multi 3.25 3.25

SEMI-POSTAL STAMPS

Angolan Red Cross — SP1

1991, Sept. 19 **Litho.** ***Perf. 14***

B1 SP1 20k +5k Mother and child 1.00 1.00
B2 SP1 40k +5k Zebra and foal 2.50 2.50

AIR POST STAMPS

Common Design Type

Perf. 13½x13

1938, July 26 **Engr.** **Unwmk.**

Name and Value in Black

C1	CD39	10c red orange	.20	.20
C2	CD39	20c purple	.25	.20
C3	CD39	50c orange	.20	.20
C4	CD39	1a ultra	.40	.20
C5	CD39	2a lilac brn	.85	.20
C6	CD39	3a dk green	2.25	.25
C7	CD39	5a red brown	3.25	.35
C8	CD39	9a rose carmine	4.25	1.10
C9	CD39	10a magenta	5.50	1.10
		Nos. C1-C9 (9)	17.15	3.80

No. C7 exists with overprint "Exposicao Internacional de Nova York, 1939-1940" and Trylon and Perisphere.

AP2

Planes Circling Globe — AP3

1947, Aug. **Litho.** ***Perf. 10½***

C10	AP2	1a red brown	6.25	1.60
C11	AP2	2a yellow grn	6.25	1.60
C12	AP2	3a orange	8.00	1.60
C13	AP2	3.50a orange	10.00	4.00
C14	AP2	5a olive grn	90.00	15.00
C15	AP2	6a rose	90.00	17.50
C16	AP2	9a red	275.00	200.00
C17	AP2	10a green	175.00	60.00
C18	AP2	20a blue	175.00	60.00
C19	AP2	50a black	400.00	200.00
C20	AP2	100a yellow	750.00	600.00
		Nos. C10-C20 (11)	1,985.	1,161.

1949, May 1 **Photo.** ***Perf. 11½***

C21	AP3	1a henna brown	.20	.20
C22	AP3	2a red brown	.40	.20
C23	AP3	3a plum	.65	.20
C24	AP3	6a dull green	2.00	.40
C25	AP3	9a violet brown	3.00	1.00
		Nos. C21-C25 (5)	6.25	2.00

Catalogue values for unused stamps in this section, from this point to the end of the section, are for Never Hinged items.

Cambambe Dam AP4

Designs: 1.50e, Oil refinery, vert. 3e, Salazar Dam. 4e, Capt. Teófilo Duarte Dam. 4.50e, Craveiro Lopes Dam. 5e, Cuango Dam. 6e, Quanza River Bridge. 7e, Capt. Teófilo Duarte Bridge. 8.50e, Oliveira Salazar Bridge. 12.50e, Capt. Silva Carvalho Bridge.

Perf. 11½x12, 12x11½

1965, July 12 **Litho.** **Unwmk.**

C26	AP4	1.50e multicolored	1.00	.20
C27	AP4	2.50e multicolored	.60	.20
C28	AP4	3e multicolored	1.00	.20
C29	AP4	4e multicolored	.40	.20
C30	AP4	4.50e multicolored	.40	.20
C31	AP4	5e multicolored	.65	.20
C32	AP4	6e multicolored	.65	.20
C33	AP4	7e multicolored	1.00	.20
C34	AP4	8.50e multicolored	1.25	.55
C35	AP4	12.50e multicolored	1.50	.65
		Nos. C26-C35 (10)	8.45	2.80

Stamp Centenary Type

Design: 2.50e, Boeing 707 jet & Angola #2.

1970, Dec. 1 **Litho.** ***Perf. 13½***

C36 A83 2.50e multicolored .45 .20
a. Souv. sheet of 3, #565-566, C36 2.50 2.50

No. C36a sold for 15e.

No. C36 Overprinted with Bar and: "REPUBLICA POPULAR / DE"

1980, June 15 **Litho.** ***Perf. 13½***

C37 A83 2.50e multicolored .20

POSTAGE DUE STAMPS

D1 D2

1904 **Unwmk.** **Typo.** ***Perf. 11½x12***

J1	D1	5r yellow grn	.25	.20
J2	D1	10r slate	.25	.20
J3	D1	20r yellow brn	.35	.30
J4	D1	30r orange	.60	.60
J5	D1	50r gray brown	.60	.60
J6	D1	60r red brown	4.00	2.50
J7	D1	100r lilac	1.75	1.60
J8	D1	130r dull blue	1.75	1.60
J9	D1	200r carmine	4.00	3.00
J10	D1	500r gray violet	4.00	3.00
		Nos. J1-J10 (10)	17.55	13.60

Postage Due Stamps of 1904 Overprinted in Carmine or Green

1911

J11	D1	5r yellow grn	.20	.20
J12	D1	10r slate	.20	.20
J13	D1	20r yellow brn	.20	.20
J14	D1	30r orange	.30	.30
J15	D1	50r gray brown	.30	.30
J16	D1	60r red brown	.60	.60
J17	D1	100r lilac	.60	.60
J18	D1	130r dull blue	.60	.60
J19	D1	200r carmine (G)	.60	.60
J20	D1	500r gray violet	.70	.70
		Nos. J11-J20 (10)	4.30	4.30

1921 *Perf. 11½*

No.	Type	Description	Unused	Used
J21	D2	½c yellow green	.20	.20
J22	D2	1c slate	.20	.20
J23	D2	2c orange brown	.20	.20
J24	D2	3c orange	.20	.20
J25	D2	5c gray brown	.20	.20
J26	D2	6c lt brown	.20	.20
J27	D2	10c red violet	.20	.20
J28	D2	13c dull blue	.20	.20
J29	D2	20c carmine	.20	.20
J30	D2	50c gray	.20	.20
		Nos. J21-J30 (10)	2.00	2.00

For surcharges see Nos. 268-270.

Catalogue values for unused stamps in this section, from this point to the end of the section, are for Never Hinged items.

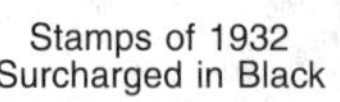
Stamps of 1932 Surcharged in Black

1948 **Wmk. 232** *Perf. 12x11½*

No.	Type	Description	Unused	Used
J31	A14	10c on 20c gray	.20	.20
J32	A14	20c on 30c myrtle grn	.40	.20
J33	A14	30c on 50c lt brown	.60	.45
J34	A14	40c on 1a claret	.75	.45
J35	A14	50c on 2a dull vio	1.25	.45
J36	A14	1a on 5a pale yel grn	3.00	1.00
		Nos. J31-J36 (6)	6.20	2.75

Common Design Type

Photogravure and Typographed

1952 **Unwmk.** *Perf. 14*

Numeral in Red, Frame Multicolored

No.	Type	Description	Unused	Used
J37	CD45	10c red brown	.20	.20
J38	CD45	30c olive green	.20	.20
J39	CD45	50c chocolate	.20	.20
J40	CD45	1a dk vio blue	.20	.20
J41	CD45	2a red brown	.20	.20
J42	CD45	5a black brown	.35	.35
		Nos. J37-J42 (6)	1.35	1.35

NEWSPAPER STAMP

N1

Perf. 11½, 12½, 13½

1893 **Typo.** **Unwmk.**

No.	Type	Description	Unused	Used
P1	N1	2½r brown	1.00	.70

No. P1 was also used for ordinary postage.
For surcharges see Nos. 37, 82, 180, 235.

POSTAL TAX STAMPS

Pombal Issue

Common Design Types

1925, May 8 **Unwmk.** *Perf. 12½*

No.	Type	Description	Unused	Used
RA1	CD28	15c lilac & black	.35	.25
RA2	CD29	15c lilac & black	.35	.25
RA3	CD30	15c lilac & black	.35	.25
		Nos. RA1-RA3 (3)	1.05	.75

"Charity" PT1

Coat of Arms PT2

1929 **Litho.** *Perf. 11*

Without Gum

No.	Type	Description	Unused	Used
RA4	PT1	50c dark blue	2.00	.70

1939 **Without Gum** *Perf. 10½*

No.	Type	Description	Unused	Used
RA5	PT2	50c turq green	1.00	.20
RA6	PT2	1a red	6.00	1.50

A 1.50a, type PT2, was issued for fiscal use.

Catalogue values for unused stamps in this section, from this point to the end of the section, are for Never Hinged items.

Old Man — PT3

Mother and Child — PT4

Designs: 1e, Boy. 1.50e, Girl.

Imprint: "Foto-Lito-E.G.A.-Luanda"

1955 **Unwmk.** *Perf. 13*

Heads in dark brown

No.	Type	Description	Unused	Used
RA7	PT3	50c dk ocher	.20	.20
RA8	PT3	1e orange ver	.75	.40
RA9	PT3	1.50e brt yel grn	.50	.25
		Nos. RA7-RA9 (3)	1.45	.85

A 2.50e, type PT3 showing an old woman, was issued for revenue use.
See Nos. RA16, RA19-RA21, RA25-RA27.

No. RA7 Surcharged with New Values and two Bars in Red or Black

1957-58

Head in dark brown

No.	Type	Description	Unused	Used
RA11	PT3	10c on 50c dk ocher (R)	.25	.25
RA12	PT3	10c on 50c dk ocher ('58)	.20	.20
RA13	PT3	30c on 50c dk ocher	.25	.25
		Nos. RA11-RA13 (3)	.70	.70

1959 **Litho.** *Perf. 13*

Design: 30c, Boy and girl.

No.	Type	Description	Unused	Used
RA14	PT4	10c orange & blk	.20	.20
RA15	PT4	30c slate & blk	.20	.20

Type of 1955 Redrawn

Design: 1e, Boy.

1961, Nov. *Perf. 13*

No.	Type	Description	Unused	Used
RA16	PT3	1e salmon pink & dk brn	.20	.20

Denomination in italics.

Yellow, White and Black Men — PT5

1962, July 1 **Typo.** *Perf. 10½*

Without Gum

No.	Type	Description	Unused	Used
RA17	PT5	50c multicolored	.65	.65
RA18	PT5	1e multicolored	.35	.35

Issued for the Provincial Settlement Committee (Junta Provincial do Povoamento). The tax was used to promote Portuguese settlement in Angola, and to raise educational and living standards of recent immigrants.

Denominations higher than 1e were used for revenue purposes.

Head Type of 1955
Without Imprint

Designs: 50c, Old man. 1e, Boy. 1.50e, Girl.

1964-65 **Litho.** *Perf. 11½*

Heads in dark brown

No.	Type	Description	Unused	Used
RA19	PT3	50c orange	.20	.20
RA20	PT3	1e dull red org ('65)	.20	.20
RA21	PT3	1.50e yel grn ('65)	.25	.25
		Nos. RA19-RA21 (3)	.65	.65

No. RA20 is second redrawing of 1e, with bolder lettering and denomination in gothic. Space between "Assistencia" and denomination on RA19-RA21 is ½mm; on 1955 issue space is 2mm.

Map of Angola, Industrial and Farm Workers — PT6

1965, Sept. 1 **Litho.** *Perf. 13*

No.	Type	Description	Unused	Used
RA22	PT6	50c multicolored	.35	.20
RA23	PT6	1e multicolored	.35	.25

The 2e was used for revenue purposes.

Head Type of 1955
Imprint: "I.N.A." or "INA" (1e)

Designs: 50c, Old man. 1e, Boy. 1.50e, Girl.

1966

Heads in dark brown

No.	Type	Description	Unused	Used
RA25	PT3	50c dull orange	.20	.20
RA26	PT3	1e dull brick red	.20	.20
RA27	PT3	1.50e lt yel grn	.35	.20
		Nos. RA25-RA27 (3)	.75	.60

Woman Planting Tree — PT7

1972 **Litho.** *Perf. 13*

No.	Type	Description	Unused	Used
RA28	PT7	50c shown	.20	.20
RA29	PT7	1e Workers	.20	.20
RA30	PT7	2e Produce	.20	.20
		Nos. RA28-RA30 (3)	.60	.60

POSTAL TAX DUE STAMPS

Pombal Issue

Common Design Types

1925, May 8 **Unwmk.** *Perf. 12½*

No.	Type	Description	Unused	Used
RAJ1	CD28	30c lilac & black	.50	*1.25*
RAJ2	CD29	30c lilac & black	.50	*1.25*
RAJ3	CD30	30c lilac & black	.50	*1.25*
		Nos. RAJ1-RAJ3 (3)	1.50	*3.75*

See note after Portugal No. RAJ4.

ANGRA

'aŋ-grə

LOCATION — An administrative district of the Azores, consisting of the islands of Terceira, Sao Jorge and Graciosa.
GOVT. — A district of Portugal
AREA — 275 sq. mi.
POP. — 70,000 (approx.)
CAPITAL — Angra do Heroismo

1000 Reis = 1 Milreis

King Carlos
A1 A2

1892-93 **Typo.** **Unwmk.** *Perf. 12½*

No.	Type	Description	Unused	Used
1	A1	5r yellow	2.25	1.25
a.		Perf. 11½	8.00	4.25
b.		Perf. 13½	2.50	1.25
2	A1	10r redsh violet	2.25	1.25
a.		Perf. 13½	3.25	1.90
3	A1	15r chocolate	2.75	2.00
a.		Perf. 13½	3.25	2.10
4	A1	20r lavender	4.50	2.00
a.		Perf. 13½	3.25	2.10
5	A1	25r green	3.50	.55
a.		Perf. 13½	7.00	2.50
b.		Perf. 11½	4.50	1.00
7	A1	50r blue	7.50	3.00
a.		Perf. 13½	10.00	4.75
8	A1	75r carmine	8.00	4.00
9	A1	80r yellow green	9.50	7.50
10	A1	100r brown, *yel,* perf. 13½ ('93)	32.50	11.00
a.		Perf. 12½	125.00	95.00
11	A1	150r car, *rose* ('93)	45.00	32.50
a.		Perf. 13½	50.00	37.50
12	A1	200r dk blue, *bl* ('93)	45.00	32.50
a.		Perf. 13½	50.00	37.50
13	A1	300r dk blue, *sal* ('93)	45.00	32.50
a.		Perf. 13½	50.00	37.50
		Nos. 1-13 (12)	207.75	130.05

Reprints of 50r, 150r, 200r and 300r, made in 1900, are perf. 11½ and ungummed. Value, each $7.50. Reprints of all values, made in 1905, have shiny white gum and clean-cut perf. 13½.

1897-1905 *Perf. 11½*

Name and Value in Black except Nos. 26 and 35

No.	Type	Description	Unused	Used
14	A2	2½r gray	.55	.35
15	A2	5r orange	.55	.35
a.		Diagonal half used as 2½r on cover		*22.50*
16	A2	10r yellow grn	.55	.35
17	A2	15r brown	7.00	4.50
18	A2	15r gray grn ('99)	1.25	.60
19	A2	20r gray violet	1.40	1.00
20	A2	25r sea green	2.25	2.25
21	A2	25r car rose ('99)	.75	.55
22	A2	50r dark blue	4.00	1.25
23	A2	50r ultra ('05)	10.00	8.00
24	A2	65r slate bl ('98)	.90	.55
25	A2	75r rose	2.50	1.25
26	A2	75r gray brn & car, *straw* ('05)	10.00	*8.00*
27	A2	80r violet	1.40	.90
28	A2	100r dk blue, *bl*	2.40	1.25
29	A2	115r org brn, *pink* ('98)	1.90	1.50
30	A2	130r gray brn, *straw* ('98)	1.90	1.50
31	A2	150r lt brn, *straw*	1.90	1.40
32	A2	180r sl, *pnksh* ('98)	2.40	2.25
33	A2	200r red vio, *pnksh*	4.50	3.75
34	A2	300r blue, *rose*	8.00	5.00
35	A2	500r blk & red, *bl*	12.50	10.00
a.		Perf. 12½	16.00	12.50
		Nos. 14-35 (22)	78.60	56.55

Azores stamps were used in Angra from 1906 to 1931, when they were superseded by those of Portugal.

ANGUILLA

aŋ,gwi-lə

LOCATION — In the West Indies southeast of Puerto Rico
GOVT. — British territory
AREA — 60 sq. mi.
POP. — 10,663 (est. 1997)
CAPITAL — The Valley

Anguilla separated unilaterally from the Associated State of St. Kitts-Nevis-Anguilla in 1967, formalized in 1980 following direct United Kingdom intervention some years before. A British Commissioner exercises executive authority.

100 Cents = 1 Eastern Caribbean Dollar

Catalogue values for all unused stamps in this country are for Never Hinged items.

St. Kitts-Nevis Nos. 145-160 Overprinted

Independent
Anguilla
On Type A14

Independent
Anguilla
On Type A15

Wmk. 314

1967, Sept. 4 Photo. Perf. 14

1	A14	½c blue & dk brn	25.00	22.50
2	A15	1c multicolored	25.00	7.00
3	A14	2c multicolored	25.00	2.00
4	A14	3c multicolored	25.00	5.00
5	A15	4c multicolored	25.00	6.00
6	A15	5c multicolored	100.00	20.00
7	A15	6c multicolored	50.00	10.00
8	A15	10c multicolored	25.00	7.50
9	A14	15c multicolored	55.00	12.00
10	A15	20c multicolored	85.00	20.00
11	A14	25c multicolored	70.00	22.50
12	A15	50c multicolored	*2,000.*	*500.00*
13	A14	60c multicolored	*2,500.*	*900.00*
14	A14	$1 multicolored	*1,600.*	*425.00*
15	A15	$2.50 multicolored	*1,600.*	*325.00*
16	A14	$5 multicolored	*1,300.*	*325.00*
		Nos. 1-16 (16)	*9,510.*	*2,609.*

Counterfeit overprints exist.

Mahogany Tree, The Quarter — A1

Designs: 2c, Sombrero Lighthouse. 3c, St. Mary's Church. 4c, Valley Police Station. 5c, Old Plantation House, Mt. Fortune. 6c, Valley Post Office. 10c, Methodist Church, West End. 15c, Wall-Blake Airport. 20c, Plane over Sandy Ground. 25c, Island Harbor. 40c, Map of Anguilla. 60c, Hermit crab and starfish. $1, Hibiscus. $2.50, Coconut harvest. $5, Spiny lobster.

Perf. 12½x13

1967-68 Litho. Unwmk.

17	A1	1c orange & multi	.20	.35
18	A1	2c gray green & blk	.20	.35
19	A1	3c emerald & blk	.20	.20
20	A1	4c brt blue & blk	.20	.20
21	A1	5c lt blue & multi	.20	.20
22	A1	6c ver & black	.20	.20
23	A1	10c multicolored	.20	.20
24	A1	15c multicolored	.50	.20
25	A1	20c multicolored	.70	.55
26	A1	25c multicolored	.50	.20
27	A1	40c blue & multi	.70	.25
28	A1	60c yellow & multi	2.50	2.25
29	A1	$1 lt green & multi	1.50	2.40
30	A1	$2.50 multicolored	1.75	2.75
31	A1	$5 multicolored	2.75	3.50
		Nos. 17-31 (15)	12.30	13.80

Issued: 1c, 5c, 10c, 20c, 25c, 40c, 11/27/67; 3c, 4c, 15c, 60c, $1, $5, 2/10/68; 2c, 6c, $2.50, 3/21/68.

For overprints see Nos. 53-67, 78-82.

Sailboats — A2

Designs: 15c, Boat building. 25c, Schooner Warspite. 40c, Yacht Atlantic Star.

1968, May 11 *Perf. 14*

32	A2	10c rose & multi	.40	.20
33	A2	15c olive & multi	.45	.20
34	A2	25c lilac rose & multi	.65	.30
35	A2	40c dull blue & multi	.75	.50
		Nos. 32-35 (4)	2.25	1.20

Purple-throated Carib — A3

Girl Guide Badge — A4

Anguillan Birds: 15c, Bananaquit. 25c, Black-necked stilt, horiz. 40c, Royal tern, horiz.

1968, July 8

36	A3	10c dull yel & multi	.90	.20
37	A3	15c yel green & multi	1.10	.30
38	A3	25c multicolored	1.40	.30
39	A3	40c multicolored	1.60	.40
		Nos. 36-39 (4)	5.00	1.20

1968, Oct. 14 *Perf. 13x13½, 13½x13*

10c, Girl Guide badge, horiz. 25c, Badge and Headquarters, horiz. 40c, Merit Badges.

40	A4	10c lt green & multi	.20	.20
41	A4	15c lt blue & multi	.20	.20
42	A4	25c multicolored	.30	.20
43	A4	40c multicolored	.40	.20
		Nos. 40-43 (4)	1.10	.80

Anguillan Girl Guides, 35th anniversary.

Three Kings — A5

Christmas: 10c, Three Kings seeing Star, vert. 15c, Holy Family, vert. 40c, Shepherds seeing Star. 50c, Holy Family and donkey.

1968, Nov. 18

44	A5	1c lilac rose & black	.20	.20
45	A5	10c blue & black	.20	.20
46	A5	15c brown & black	.20	.20
47	A5	40c brt ultra & black	.20	.20
48	A5	50c green & black	.20	.20
		Nos. 44-48 (5)	1.00	1.00

Bagging Salt — A6

Salt Industry: 15c, Packing salt. 40c, Salt pond. 50c, Loading salt.

1969, Jan. 4 *Perf. 13*

49	A6	10c red & multi	.30	.20
50	A6	15c lt blue & multi	.35	.20
51	A6	40c emerald & multi	.40	.20
52	A6	50c purple & multi	.45	.20
		Nos. 49-52 (4)	1.50	.80

Nos. 17-31 Overprinted: "INDEPENDENCE/JANUARY, 1969"

1969, Jan. 9 *Perf. 12½x13*

53	A1	1c orange & multi	.20	.20
54	A1	2c gray green & blk	.20	.20
55	A1	3c emerald & blk	.20	.20
56	A1	4c brt blue & blk	.20	.20
57	A1	5c lt blue & multi	.20	.20
58	A1	6c vermilion & blk	.20	.20
59	A1	10c multicolored	.20	.20
60	A1	15c multicolored	.20	.20
61	A1	20c multicolored	.25	.25
62	A1	25c multicolored	.35	.35
63	A1	40c blue & multi	.45	*.50*
64	A1	60c yellow & multi	.60	*.70*
65	A1	$1 lt green & multi	1.00	*1.25*
66	A1	$2.50 multicolored	2.50	*3.00*
67	A1	$5 multicolored	5.50	*6.25*
		Nos. 53-67 (15)	12.25	*13.90*

Crucifixion, School of Quentin Massys — A7

Easter: 40c, The Last Supper, ascribed to Roberti.

1969, Mar. 31 Litho. *Perf. 13½*

68	A7	25c multicolored	.30	.20
69	A7	40c multicolored	.50	.20

Amaryllis — A8

1969, June 10 *Perf. 14*

70	A8	10c shown	.25	.20
71	A8	15c Bougainvillea	.30	.30
72	A8	40c Hibiscus	.60	.50
73	A8	50c Cattleya orchid	1.60	1.00
		Nos. 70-73 (4)	2.75	2.00

Turban and Star Shells — A9

Sea Shells: 15c, Spiny oysters. 40c, Scotch, royal and smooth bonnets. 50c, Triton trumpet.

1969, Sept. 22

74	A9	10c multicolored	.30	.20
75	A9	15c multicolored	.45	.25
76	A9	40c multicolored	.85	.30
77	A9	50c multicolored	1.10	.35
		Nos. 74-77 (4)	2.70	1.10

Nos. 17, 25-28 Overprinted "CHRISTMAS 1969" and Various Christmas Designs

1969, Oct. 27 *Perf. 12½x13*

78	A1	1c orange & multi	.20	.20
79	A1	20c multicolored	.20	.20
80	A1	25c multicolored	.25	.20
81	A1	40c blue & multi	.50	.25
82	A1	60c yellow & multi	1.10	.30
		Nos. 78-82 (5)	2.25	1.15

Red Goatfish — A10

Designs: 15c, Blue-striped grunts. 40c, Mutton grouper. 50c, Banded butterfly-fish.

1969, Dec. 1 *Perf. 14*

83	A10	10c multicolored	.25	.20
84	A10	15c multicolored	.35	.20
85	A10	40c multicolored	1.00	.40
86	A10	50c multicolored	1.25	.60
		Nos. 83-86 (4)	2.85	1.40

Morning Glory — A11

1970, Feb. 23

87	A11	10c shown	.40	.20
88	A11	15c Blue petrea	.60	.20
89	A11	40c Hibiscus	.90	.25
90	A11	50c Flamboyant	1.10	.35
		Nos. 87-90 (4)	3.00	1.00

The Way to Calvary, by Tiepolo — A12

Easter: 20c, Crucifixion, by Masaccio, vert. 40c, Descent from the Cross, by Rosso Fiorentino, vert. 60c, Jesus Carrying the Cross, by Murillo.

1970, Mar. 26 *Perf. 13½*

91	A12	10c multicolored	.20	.20
92	A12	20c multicolored	.25	.20
93	A12	40c multicolored	.40	.25
94	A12	60c multicolored	.60	.35
		Nos. 91-94 (4)	1.45	1.00

ANGUILLA 10c

Anguilla Map, Scout Badge — A13

Designs: 15c, Cub Scouts practicing first aid. 40c, Monkey bridge. 50c, Scout Headquarters, The Valley, and Lord Baden-Powell.

1970, Aug. 10 *Perf. 13*

95	A13	10c multicolored	.25	.20
96	A13	15c multicolored	.35	.25
97	A13	40c multicolored	.45	.40
98	A13	50c multicolored	.70	.40
		Nos. 95-98 (4)	1.75	1.25

Anguilla Boy Scouts, 40th anniversary.

1c ANGUILLA

Boat Building — A14

Designs: 2c, Road construction. 3c, Blowing Point dock. 4c, Radio announcer. 5c, Cottage Hospital extension. 6c, Valley secondary school. 10c, Hotel extension. 15c, Sandy Ground. 20c, Supermarket and movie house. 25c, Bananas and mangoes. 40c, Wall-Blake airport. 60c, Sandy Ground jetty. $1, Administration building. $2.50, Cow and calf. $5, Sandy Hill Bay.

1970, Nov. 23 Litho. *Perf. 14*

99	A14	1c	multicolored	.35	.20
100	A14	2c	multicolored	.35	.20
101	A14	3c	multicolored	.35	.20
102	A14	4c	multicolored	.35	.20
103	A14	5c	multicolored	.50	.20
104	A14	6c	multicolored	.35	.20
105	A14	10c	multicolored	.35	.20
106	A14	15c	multicolored	.35	.25
107	A14	20c	multicolored	.70	.30
108	A14	25c	multicolored	.40	.35
109	A14	40c	multicolored	.60	.55
110	A14	60c	multicolored	3.00	.90
111	A14	$1	multicolored	.80	1.50
112	A14	$2.50	multicolored	1.50	3.50
113	A14	$5	multicolored	1.90	7.25
			Nos. 99-113 (15)	11.85	16.00

Adoration of the Shepherds, by Guido Reni — A15

Christmas: 20c, Virgin and Child, by Benozzo Gozzoli. 25c, Nativity, by Botticelli. 40c, Santa Margherita Madonna, by Mazzola. 50c, Adoration of the Kings, by Tiepolo.

1970, Dec. 11 *Perf. 13½*

114	A15	1c	multicolored	.20	.20
115	A15	20c	multicolored	.25	.20
116	A15	25c	multicolored	.30	.25
117	A15	40c	multicolored	.50	.35
118	A15	50c	multicolored	.55	.45
			Nos. 114-118 (5)	1.80	1.45

Angels Weeping over the Dead Christ, by Guercino — A16

Easter: 10c, Ecce Homo, by Correggio, vert. 15c, Christ Appearing to St. Peter, by Carracci, vert. 50c, The Supper at Emmaus, by Caravaggio.

1971, Mar. 29

119	A16	10c	pink & multi	.20	.20
120	A16	15c	lt blue & multi	.25	.20
121	A16	40c	yel green & multi	.45	.20
122	A16	50c	violet & multi	.55	.20
			Nos. 119-122 (4)	1.45	.80

Hypolimnas Misippus — A17

Butterflies: 15c, Junonia lavinia. 40c, Agraulis vanillae. 50c, Danaus plexippus.

1971, June 21 *Perf. 14x14½*

123	A17	10c	multicolored	1.75	.90
124	A17	15c	multicolored	1.75	1.00
125	A17	40c	multicolored	2.25	1.60
126	A17	50c	multicolored	2.25	1.90
			Nos. 123-126 (4)	8.00	5.40

Magnanime and Aimable in Battle — A18

Ships: 15c, HMS Duke and Agamemnon against Glorieux. 25c, HMS Formidable and Namur against Ville de Paris. 40c, HMS Canada. 50c, HMS St. Albans and wreck of Hector.

1971, Aug. 30 Litho. *Perf. 14*

127	A18	10c	multicolored	.35	.35
128	A18	15c	multicolored	.60	.65
129	A18	25c	multicolored	1.25	1.40
130	A18	40c	multicolored	2.00	2.25
131	A18	50c	multicolored	2.75	3.00
a.			Strip of 5, #127-131	7.25	7.25

West Indies sea battles.

Ansidei Madonna, by Raphael — A19

Christmas: 25c, Mystic Nativity, by Botticelli. 40c, Virgin and Child, School of Seville, inscribed Murillo. 50c, Madonna of the Iris, ascribed to Dürer.

1971, Nov. 29 *Perf. 14x13½*

132	A19	20c	green & multi	.25	.30
133	A19	25c	blue & multi	.25	.30
134	A19	40c	lilac rose & multi	.35	.40
135	A19	50c	violet & multi	.40	.50
			Nos. 132-135 (4)	1.25	1.50

Map of Anguilla and St. Maarten, by Jefferys, 1775 — A20

Jesus Buffeted, Stained-glass Window — A21

Maps of Anguilla by: 15c, Samuel Fahlberg, 1814. 40c, Thomas Jefferys, 1775, horiz. 50c, Capt. E. Barnett, 1847, horiz.

1972, Jan. 24 *Perf. 14x13½, 13½x14*

136	A20	10c	lt blue & multi	.20	.20
137	A20	15c	lt green & multi	.35	.25
138	A20	40c	lt green & multi	.75	.50
139	A20	50c	lt ultra & multi	1.00	.50
			Nos. 136-139 (4)	2.30	1.45

1972, Mar. 14 *Perf. 14x13½*

Easter (19th cent. Stained-glass Windows, Bray Church): 15c, Jesus Carrying the Cross. 25c, Crucifixion. 40c, Descent from the Cross. 50c, Burial.

140	A21	10c	multicolored	.30	.30
141	A21	15c	multicolored	.40	.40
142	A21	25c	multicolored	.40	.40
143	A21	40c	multicolored	.45	.45
144	A21	50c	multicolored	.55	.55
a.			Strip of 5, #140-144	2.50	2.50

Spear Fishing — A22

Sandy Ground — A23

1972-75 *Perf. 13½*

145	A22	1c	shown	.20	.20
146	A23	2c	Loblolly tree, vert.	.20	.20
147	A23	3c	shown	.20	.20
148	A23	4c	Ferry, Blowing Point, vert.	1.00	.20
149	A23	5c	Agriculture	.20	.50
150	A23	6c	St. Mary's Church, vert.	.20	.20
151	A23	10c	St. Gerard's Church	.20	.20
152	A22	15c	Cottage Hospital	.30	.30
153	A23	20c	Public Library	.35	.35
154	A23	25c	Sunset, Blowing Point	.50	*1.50*
155	A22	40c	Boat building	3.00	1.50
156	A22	60c	Hibiscus	3.75	3.00
157	A23	$1	Man-o-war bird	7.75	7.00
158	A23	$2.50	Frangipani	5.50	*8.00*
159	A23	$5	Brown pelican	13.50	12.00
160	A22	$10	Green-back turtle	13.50	*16.00*
			Nos. 145-160 (16)	50.35	*51.35*

Issued: $10, 5/20/75; others 10/30/72.
For overprints see Nos. 229-246.

Common Design Types pictured following the introduction.

Silver Wedding Issue, 1972
Common Design Type

Design: Queen Elizabeth II, Prince Philip, schooner and dolphin.

Perf. 14x14½

1972, Nov. 20 Photo. Wmk. 314

161	CD324	25c	olive & multi	*1.00*	*.75*
162	CD324	40c	maroon & multi	*1.00*	*.75*

Flight into Egypt — A24

Perf. 13½

1972, Dec. 4 Litho. Unwmk.

163	A24	1c	shown	.20	.20
164	A24	20c	Star of Bethlehem	.20	.20
165	A24	25c	Nativity	.20	.20
166	A24	40c	Three Kings	.20	*.25*
167	A24	50c	Adoration of the Kings	.25	*.30*
a.			Vert. strip of 4, #164-167	1.00	1.00
			Nos. 163-167 (5)	1.05	1.15

Christmas.

Betrayal of Jesus — A25

1973, Mar. 26

168	A25	1c	shown	.20	.20
169	A25	10c	Man of Sorrow	.20	.20
170	A25	20c	Jesus Carrying Cross	.20	.25
171	A25	25c	Crucifixion	.25	.25
172	A25	40c	Descent from Cross	.25	.25
173	A25	50c	Resurrection	.25	.35
a.			Souvenir sheet of 6	1.25	*1.50*
b.			Vert. strip of 5, #169-173	1.00	1.00
			Nos. 168-173 (6)	1.35	1.50

Easter. #173a contains 6 stamps similar to #168-173 with bottom panel in lilac rose.

Santa Maria A26

1973, Sept. 10

174	A26	1c	shown	.20	.20
175	A26	20c	Old West Indies map	1.25	1.25
176	A26	40c	Map of voyages	1.50	1.50
177	A26	70c	Sighting land	1.75	1.75
178	A26	$1.20	Columbus landing	2.40	2.40
a.			Souvenir sheet of 5, #174-178	7.00	*7.75*
b.			Horiz. strip of 4, #175-178	7.00	7.00
			Nos. 174-178 (5)	7.10	7.10

Discovery of West Indies by Columbus.

Princess Anne's Wedding Issue
Common Design Type

1973, Nov. 14 Wmk. 314 *Perf. 13½*

179	CD325	60c	blue grn & multi	.20	.20
180	CD325	$1.20	lilac & multi	.40	.30

Wedding of Princess Anne and Capt. Mark Phillips, Nov. 14, 1973.

Adoration of the Shepherds, by Guido Reni — A27

Paintings: 10c, Virgin and Child, by Filippino Lippi. 20c, Nativity, by Meester Van de Brunswijkse Diptiek. 25c, Madonna of the Meadow, by Bellini. 40c, Virgin and Child, by Cima. 50c, Adoration of the Kings, by Geertgen Tot Sint Jans.

1973, Dec. 2 Unwmk.

181	A27	1c	multicolored	.20	.20
182	A27	10c	multicolored	.20	.20
183	A27	20c	multicolored	.20	.20
184	A27	25c	multicolored	.20	.20
185	A27	40c	multicolored	.20	.20
186	A27	50c	multicolored	.20	.20
a.			Souvenir sheet of 6, #181-186	1.25	1.25
b.			Horiz. strip of 5, #182-186	1.00	1.00
			Nos. 181-186 (6)	1.20	1.20

Christmas.

Crucifixion, by Raphael — A28

Easter (Details from Crucifixion by Raphael): 15c, Virgin Mary and St. John. 20c, The Two Marys. 25c, Left Angel. 40c, Right Angel. $1, Christ on the Cross.

1974, Mar. 30

187 A28 1c lilac & multi .20 .20
188 A28 15c gray & multi .20 .20
189 A28 20c salmon & multi .20 .20
190 A28 25c yel green & multi .20 .20
191 A28 40c orange & multi .20 .20
192 A28 $1 lt blue & multi .25 .25
a. Souvenir sheet of 6, #187-192 1.50 *1.75*
b. Vert. strip of 5, #188-192 1.00 1.00
Nos. 187-192 (6) 1.25 1.25

Churchill Making Victory Sign — A29

20c, Roosevelt, Churchill, US, British flags. 25c, Churchill broadcasting during the war. 40c, Blenheim Palace. 60c, Churchill Statue & Parliament. $1.20, Chartwell.

1974, June 24

193 A29 1c multicolored .20 .20
194 A29 20c multicolored .25 .25
195 A29 25c multicolored .35 .35
196 A29 40c multicolored .40 .40
197 A29 60c multicolored .40 .40
198 A29 $1.20 multicolored .50 .50
a. Souvenir sheet of 6, #193-198 2.25 *2.50*
b. Horiz. strip of 5, #194-198 2.25 2.25
Nos. 193-198 (6) 2.10 2.10

Sir Winston Spencer Churchill (1874-1965).

UPU Emblem, Map of Anguilla — A30

1974, Aug. 27

199 A30 1c black & ultra .20 .20
200 A30 20c black & orange .20 .20
201 A30 25c black & yellow .20 .20
202 A30 40c black & brt lilac .25 .25
203 A30 60c black & lt green .35 .35
204 A30 $1.20 black & blue .55 .55
a. Souvenir sheet of 6 1.75 *2.00*
b. Horiz. strip of 5, #200-204 1.50 1.50
Nos. 199-204 (6) 1.75 1.75

UPU, centenary. No. 204a contains one each of Nos. 199-204 with second row (40c, 60c, $1.20) perf. 15 at bottom.

Fishermen Seeing Star — A31

Christmas: 20c, Nativity. 25c, King offering gift. 40c, Star over map of Anguilla. 60c, Family looking at star. $1.20, Two angels with star and "Peace."

1974, Dec. 16 Litho. *Perf. 14½*

205 A31 1c brt blue & multi .20 .20
206 A31 20c dull grn & multi .20 .20
207 A31 25c gray & multi .20 .20
208 A31 40c car & multi .20 .20
209 A31 60c dp blue & multi .20 .20
210 A31 $1.20 ultra & multi .25 .25
a. Souvenir sheet of 6, #205-210 1.50 *1.75*
b. Horiz. strip of 5, #206-210 1.25 1.25
Nos. 205-210 (6) 1.25 1.25

Virgin Mary, St. John, Mary Magdalene — A32

Paintings from Isenheim Altar, by Matthias Grunewald: 10c, Crucifixion. 15c, John the Baptist. 20c, St. Sebastian and Angels. $1, Burial of Christ, horiz. $1.50, St. Anthony, the Hermit.

1975, Mar. 25 *Perf. 13½*

211 A32 1c multicolored .20 .20
212 A32 10c multicolored .20 .20
213 A32 15c multicolored .20 .20
214 A32 20c multicolored .20 .20
215 A32 $1 multicolored .25 *.35*
216 A32 $1.50 multicolored .30 *.45*
a. Souvenir sheet of 6 1.75 *2.00*
b. Horiz. strip of 5, #212-216 1.25 1.25
Nos. 211-216 (6) 1.35 1.60

Easter. No. 216a contains 6 stamps similar to Nos. 211-216 with simulated perforations.

Statue of Liberty, N.Y. Skyline — A33

10c, Capitol, Washington, DC. 15c, Congress voting independence. 20c, Washington, map & his battles. $1, Boston Tea Party. $1.50, Bicentennial emblem, historic US flags.

1975, Nov. 10

217 A33 1c multicolored .20 .20
218 A33 10c multicolored .20 .20
219 A33 15c multicolored .30 .20
220 A33 20c multicolored .35 .20
221 A33 $1 multicolored .50 .45
222 A33 $1.50 multicolored .55 *.70*
a. Souvenir sheet of 6 1.75 *2.50*
b. Horiz. strip of 5, #218-222 2.00 *2.00*
Nos. 217-222 (6) 2.10 1.95

American Bicentennial. No. 222a contains one each of Nos. 217-222 with second row (20c, $1, $1.50) perf. 15 at bottom.

Virgin and Child with St. John, by Raphael — A34

Paintings, Virgin and Child by: 10c, Cima. 15c, Dolci. 20c, Durer. $1, Bellini. $1.50, Botticelli.

1975, Dec. 8 *Perf. 14x13½*

223 A34 1c ultra & multi .20 .20
224 A34 10c Prus blue & multi .20 .20
225 A34 15c plum & multi .20 .20
226 A34 20c car rose & multi .20 .20
227 A34 $1 brt grn & multi .35 .25
228 A34 $1.50 blue grn & multi .45 .40
a. Souvenir sheet of 6, #223-228 2.75 2.75
b. Horiz. strip of 5, #224-228 1.50 1.50
Nos. 223-228 (6) 1.60 1.45

Christmas.

Nos. 145-146, 148, 150-160 Overprinted "NEW CONSTITUTION 1976"

1976 Litho. *Perf. 13½*

229 A22 1c #145 .25 *.35*
230 A22 2c on 1c #145 .25 *.35*
231 A23 2c #146 4.25 1.60
232 A22 3c on 40c #155 .65 .60
233 A23 4c #148 .85 *.90*
234 A22 5c on 40c #155 .25 *.45*
235 A23 6c #150 .25 *.45*
236 A23 10c on 20c #153 .25 *.45*
237 A23 10c #151 4.25 3.75
238 A22 15c #152 .25 *.80*
239 A23 20c #153 .25 *.45*
240 A23 25c #154 .25 *.45*
241 A22 40c #155 .85 .65
242 A22 60c #156 .60 *.65*
243 A23 $1 #157 5.25 2.00
244 A23 $2.50 #158 2.00 2.00
245 A23 $5 #159 6.50 6.00
246 A22 $10 #160 2.50 *5.50*
Nos. 229-246 (18) 29.70 *27.40*

Flowering Trees — A35

1976, Feb. 16 *Perf. 13½x14*

247 A35 1c Almond .20 .20
248 A35 10c Clusia rosea .30 .30
249 A35 15c Calabash .30 .30
250 A35 20c Cordia .30 .30
251 A35 $1 Papaya .40 .40
252 A35 $1.50 Flamboyant .50 .50
a. Souvenir sheet of 6, #247-252 2.25 2.25
b. Horiz. strip of 5, #248-252 2.00 2.00
Nos. 247-252 (6) 2.00 2.00

The Three Marys — A36

Designs: 10c, Crucifixion. 15c, Two soldiers. 20c, Annunciation. $1, Altar tapestry, 1470, Monastery of Rheinau, Switzerland, horiz. $1.50, "Noli me Tangere" (Jesus and Mary Magdalene). Designs of vertical stamps show details from tapestry shown on $1 stamp.

1976, Apr. 5 *Perf. 14x13½, 13½x14*

253 A36 1c multicolored .20 .20
254 A36 10c multicolored .20 .20
255 A36 15c multicolored .20 .20
256 A36 20c multicolored .20 .20
257 A36 $1 multicolored .65 .65
258 A36 $1.50 multicolored .80 .80
a. Souvenir sheet of 6 2.50 *2.75*
b. Horiz. strip of 5, #254-258 2.25 2.25
Nos. 253-258 (6) 2.25 2.25

Easter. No. 258a contains 6 stamps similar to Nos. 253-258 with simulated perforations.

Le Desius and La Vaillante Approaching Anguilla — A37

Sailing Ships: 3c, Sailboat leaving Anguilla for Antigua to get help. 15c, HMS Lapwing in battle with frigate Le Desius and brig La Vaillante. 25c, La Vaillante aground off St. Maarten. $1, Lapwing. $1.50, Le Desius burning.

1976, Nov. 8 Litho. *Perf. 13½x14*

259 A37 1c multicolored .20 .20
260 A37 3c multicolored 1.10 .40
261 A37 15c multicolored 1.25 .55
262 A37 25c multicolored 1.25 .85
263 A37 $1 multicolored 1.75 1.25
264 A37 $1.50 multicolored 2.00 1.75
a. Souvenir sheet of 6, #259-264 7.50 7.50
b. Strip of 5, #260-264 7.50 7.50
Nos. 259-264 (6) 7.55 5.00

Bicentenary of Battle of Anguilla between French and British ships.

Christmas Carnival — A38

Children's Paintings: 3c, 3 children dreaming of Christmas gifts. 15c, Caroling. 25c, Candlelight procession. $1, Going to Church on Christmas Eve. $1.50, Airport, coming home for Christmas.

1976, Nov. 22

265 A38 1c multicolored .20 .20
266 A38 3c multicolored .20 .20
267 A38 15c multicolored .20 .20
268 A38 25c multicolored .25 .25
269 A38 $1 multicolored .35 .35
270 A38 $1.50 multicolored .50 .50
a. Souvenir sheet of 6, #265-270 1.75 *2.00*
b. Strip of 5, #266-270 1.00 1.00
Nos. 265-270 (6) 1.70 1.70

Christmas. For overprints and surcharges see Nos. 305-310a.

Prince Charles and HMS Minerva, 1973 — A39

Designs: 40c, Prince Philip landing at Road Bay, 1964. $1.20, Homage to Queen at Coronation. $2.50, Coronation regalia and map of Anguilla.

1977, Feb. 9

271 A39 25c multicolored .20 .20
272 A39 40c multicolored .20 .20
273 A39 $1.20 multicolored .25 .20
274 A39 $2.50 multicolored .35 .30
a. Souvenir sheet of 4, #271-274 1.00 *1.50*
Nos. 271-274 (4) 1.00 .90

25th anniv. of reign of Queen Elizabeth II. For overprints see Nos. 297-300.

Yellow-crowned Night Heron — A40

Designs: 2c, Great barracuda. 3c, Queen conch. 4c, Spanish bayonet (Yucca). 5c, Trunkfish. 6c, Cable and telegraph building. 10c, American sparrow hawk. 15c, Ground orchids. 20c, Parlorfish. 22c, Lobster fishing boat. 35c, Boat race. 50c Sea bean (flowers). $1, Sandy Island with palms. $2.50, Manchineel (fruit). $5, Ground lizard. $10, Red-billed tropic bird.

1977-78 Litho. *Perf. 13½x14*

275 A40 1c multicolored .30 *.75*
276 A40 2c multicolored .30 *1.25*
277 A40 3c multicolored 1.10 *1.90*
278 A40 4c multicolored .35 .30
279 A40 5c multicolored 1.40 .30
280 A40 6c multicolored .30 *.35*
281 A40 10c multicolored 3.75 2.25
282 A40 15c multicolored 2.50 1.90
283 A40 20c multicolored 1.90 .80
284 A40 22c multicolored .40 *.65*
285 A40 35c multicolored 1.25 .75
286 A40 50c multicolored .85 .50
287 A40 $1 multicolored .60 .50
288 A40 $2.50 multicolored 1.00 1.00
289 A40 $5 multicolored 1.75 1.75
290 A40 $10 multicolored 8.25 4.75
Nos. 275-290 (16) 26.00 19.70

Issued: #275-280, 290, 4/18/77; others 2/20/78.

For overprints and surcharges see Nos. 319-324, 337-342, 387-390, 402-404, 407-415, 417-423.

Crucifixion, by Quentin Massys — A41

Easter (Paintings): 3c, Betrayal of Christ, by Ugolino. 22c, Way to Calvary, by Ugolino. 30c, The Deposition, by Ugolino. $1, Resurrection, by Ugolino. $1.50, Crucifixion, by Andrea del Castagno.

1977, Apr. 25

291 A41 1c multicolored .20 .20
292 A41 3c multicolored .20 .20
293 A41 22c multicolored .20 .20
294 A41 30c multicolored .25 .25
295 A41 $1 multicolored .55 .55
296 A41 $1.50 multicolored .70 .70
a. Souvenir sheet of 6, #291-296 2.00 *2.25*
b. Strip of 5, #292-296 1.75 1.75
Nos. 291-296 (6) 2.10 2.10

Nos. 271-274, 274a Overprinted: "ROYAL VISIT/TO WEST INDIES"

1977, Oct. 26 Litho. *Perf. 13½x14*

297 A39 25c multicolored .20 .20
298 A39 40c multicolored .20 .20
299 A39 $1.20 multicolored .50 *.60*
300 A39 $2.50 multicolored 1.00 *1.25*
a. Souvenir sheet of 4 1.75 2.00
Nos. 297-300 (4) 1.90 *2.25*

Visit of Queen Elizabeth II to West Indies.

Suzanne Fourment in Velvet Hat, by Rubens — A42

Rubens Paintings: 40c, Helena Fourment with her Children. $1.20, Rubens with his wife. $2.50, Marchesa Brigida Spinola-Doria.

1977, Nov. 1 *Perf. 14x13½*

301 A42 25c black & multi .20 .20
302 A42 40c black & multi .25 .25
303 A42 $1.20 multicolored .80 .80
304 A42 $2.50 black & multi 1.00 1.00
a. Souvenir sheet of 4, #301-304 2.40 2.40
Nos. 301-304 (4) 2.25 2.25

Peter Paul Rubens, 400th birth anniv. Nos. 301-304 printed in sheets of 5 stamps and blue label with Rubens' portrait.

Nos. 265-270b Overprinted 1977 and Surcharged

1977, Nov. 7 *Perf. 13½x14*

305 A38 1c multicolored .20 .20
306 A38 5c on 3c multi .20 .20
307 A38 12c on 15c multi .20 .20
308 A38 18c on 25c multi .25 .25
309 A38 $1 multicolored .60 .60
310 A38 $2.50 on $1.50 multi 1.25 1.25
a. Souvenir sheet of 6, #305-310 3.00 3.00
b. Strip of 5, #306-310 2.50 2.50
Nos. 305-310 (6) 2.70 2.70

Christmas. Stamps and souvenir sheets have "1976" and old denomination obliterated with variously shaped rectangles.

Nos. 301-304a Ovptd. in Gold: "EASTER 1978"

1978, Mar. 6 *Perf. 14x13½*

311 A42 25c black & multi .20 .20
312 A42 40c black & multi .20 .20
313 A42 $1.20 black & multi .50 .50
314 A42 $2.50 black & multi .60 .60
a. Souvenir sheet of 4, #311-314 2.00 *2.25*
Nos. 311-314 (4) 1.50 1.50

Buckingham Palace — A43

Designs: 50c, Coronation procession. $1.50, Royal family on balcony. $2.50, Royal coat of arms.

1978, Apr. 6 *Perf. 14*

315 A43 22c multicolored .20 .20
316 A43 50c multicolored .20 .20
317 A43 $1.50 multicolored .45 .45
318 A43 $2.50 multicolored .70 .70
a. Souvenir sheet of 4, #315-318 2.00 2.00
Nos. 315-318 (4) 1.55 1.55

25th anniv. of coronation of Queen Elizabeth II.

#315-318 each exist in a booklet pane of 2.

Nos. 284-285 and 288 Ovptd. and Surcharged: "VALLEY / SECONDARY / SCHOOL / 1953-1978"

1978, Aug. 14 Litho. *Perf. 13½x14*

319 A40 22c multicolored .20 .20
320 A40 35c multicolored .25 .20
321 A40 $1.50 on $2.50 multi .55 .55
Nos. 319-321 (3) 1.00 .95

Valley Secondary School, 25th anniv. Surcharge on No. 321 includes heavy bar over old denomination.

Nos. 286-287, 289 Ovptd. and Surcharged: "ROAD / METHODIST / CHURCH / 1878-1978"

1978, Aug. 14

322 A40 50c multicolored .30 .30
323 A40 $1 multicolored .35 .35
324 A40 $1.20 on $5 multi .50 .50
Nos. 322-324 (3) 1.15 1.15

Road Methodist Church, centenary. Surcharge on No. 324 includes heavy bar over old denomination.

Mother and Child — A44

Christmas: 12c, Christmas masquerade. 18c, Christmas dinner. 22c, Serenade. $1, Star over manger. $2.50, Family going to church.

1978, Dec. 11 Litho. *Perf. 13½*

325 A44 5c multicolored .20 .20
326 A44 12c multicolored .20 .20
327 A44 18c multicolored .20 .20
328 A44 22c multicolored .20 .20
329 A44 $1 multicolored .30 .30
330 A44 $2.50 multicolored .65 .65
a. Souvenir sheet of 6, #325-330 2.00 *2.25*
Nos. 325-330 (6) 1.75 1.75

Type A44 in Changed Colors with IYC Emblem and Inscription.

1979, Jan. 15 Litho. *Perf. 13½*

331 A44 5c multicolored .20 .20
332 A44 12c multicolored .20 .20
333 A44 18c multicolored .20 .20
334 A44 22c multicolored .20 .20
335 A44 $1 multicolored .35 .35
336 A44 $2.50 multicolored .60 .60
a. Souvenir sheet of 4, #331-336 2.50 *2.75*
Nos. 331-336 (6) 1.75 1.75

Intl. Year of the Child. For overprint see #416

Nos. 275-278, 280-281 Surcharged

1979, Feb. 8 Litho. *Perf. 13½x14*

337 A40 12c on 2c multi *.45 .45*
338 A40 14c on 4c multi *.35 .55*
339 A40 18c on 3c multi *.70 .70*
340 A40 25c on 6c multi *.50 .50*
341 A40 38c on 10c multi *2.00 .90*
342 A40 40c on 1c multi *2.00 .90*
Nos. 337-342 (6) *6.00 4.00*

Valley Methodist Church A45

Church Interiors: 12c, St. Mary's Anglican Church, The Valley. 18c, St. Gerard's Roman Catholic Church, The Valley. 22c, Road Methodist Church. $1.50, St. Augustine's Anglican Church, East End. $2.50, West End Methodist Church.

1979, Mar. 30 Litho. *Perf. 14*

343 A45 5c multicolored .20 .20
344 A45 12c multicolored .20 .20
345 A45 18c multicolored .20 .20
346 A45 22c multicolored .20 .20
347 A45 $1.50 multicolored .70 .70
348 A45 $2.50 multicolored .90 .90
a. Souvenir sheet of 6 2.25 2.25
b. Strip of 6, #343-348 2.00 2.00

Easter. No. 348a contains Nos. 343-348 in 2 horizontal rows of 3.

US No. C3a A46

No. 350, Cape of Good Hope #1. No. 351, Penny Black. No. 352, Germany #C36. No. 353, US #245. No. 354, Great Britain #93.

1979, Apr. 23 Litho. *Perf. 14*

349 A46 1c multicolored .20 .20
350 A46 1c multicolored .20 .20
351 A46 22c multicolored .20 .20
352 A46 35c multicolored .25 .25
353 A46 $1.50 multicolored .50 .50
354 A46 $2.50 multicolored .75 .75
a. Souvenir sheet of 6, #349-353 2.00 *2.25*
Nos. 349-354 (6) 2.10 2.10

Sir Rowland Hill (1795-1879), originator of penny postage.

Wright's Flyer A — A47

History of Aviation: 12c, Louis Bleriot landing at Dover, 1909. 18c, Vickers Vimy, 1919. 22c, Spirit of St. Louis, 1927. $1.50, LZ127 Graf Zeppelin, 1928. $2.50, Concorde, 1979.

1979, May 21 Litho. *Perf. 14*

355 A47 5c multicolored .20 .20
356 A47 12c multicolored .20 .20
357 A47 18c multicolored .25 .20
358 A47 22c multicolored .25 .20
359 A47 $1.50 multicolored .90 .90
360 A47 $2.50 multicolored 1.90 1.90
a. Souvenir sheet of 6, #355-360 4.00 3.75
Nos. 355-360 (6) 3.70 3.60

Map of Anguilla, Map and View of Sombrero Island A48

Map of Anguilla, Map and View of: 12c, Anguillita Island. 18c, Sandy Island. 25c, Prickly Pear Cays. $1, Dog Island. $2.50, Scrub Island.

1979 Litho. *Perf. 14*

361 A48 5c multicolored .20 .20
362 A48 12c multicolored .20 .20
363 A48 18c multicolored .20 .20
364 A48 25c multicolored .20 .20
365 A48 $1 multicolored .40 .40
366 A48 $2.50 multicolored .65 .65
a. Souvenir sheet of 6, #361-366 2.75 2.75
Nos. 361-366 (6) 1.85 1.85

Anguilla's Outer Islands.

Red Poinsettia — A49

1979, Oct. 22 Litho. *Perf. 14½*

367 A49 22c shown .20 .20
368 A49 35c Kalanchoe .25 .25
369 A49 $1.50 Cream poinsettia .50 .50
370 A49 $2.50 White poinsettia .80 .80
a. Souvenir sheet of 4, #367-370 2.25 2.25
Nos. 367-370 (4) 1.75 1.75

Christmas.

Booths and Frames A50

50c, Earls Court Exhibition Hall. $1.50, Penny Black, Great Britain #2. $2.50, Exhibition emblem.

1979, Dec. 10 Litho. *Perf. 13*

371 A50 35c multicolored .25 .25
372 A50 50c multicolored .25 .25
373 A50 $1.50 multicolored .45 .45
374 A50 $2.50 multicolored .80 .80
b. Souvenir sheet of 4, #371-374 2.25 2.25
Nos. 371-374 (4) 1.75 1.75

Perf. 14½

371a A50 35c .25 .25
372a A50 50c .25 .25
373a A50 $1.50 .45 .45
374a A50 $2.50 .80 .80
c. Souvenir sheet of 4, #371-374 2.25 2.25
Nos. 371a-374a (4) 1.75 1.75

London 1980 Intl. Stamp Exhibition, May 6-14, 1980.

Lake Placid and Olympic Rings — A51

Olympic Rings and: 18c, Ice Hockey. 35c, Figure skating. 50c, Bobsledding. $1, Ski jump. $2.50, Luge.

1980, Jan. Litho. *Perf. 13½, 14½*

375 A51 5c multicolored .20 .20
376 A51 18c multicolored .20 .20
377 A51 35c multicolored .20 .20
378 A51 50c multicolored .20 .20
379 A51 $1 multicolored .35 .35
380 A51 $2.50 multicolored .60 .60
a. Souvenir sheet of 6, #375-380 2.25 2.25
Nos. 375-380 (6) 1.75 1.75

13th Winter Olympic Games, Lake Placid, NY, Feb. 12-24.

Salt Field A52

1980, Apr. 14 Litho. *Perf. 14*

381 A52 5c shown .20 .20
382 A52 12c Tallying salt .20 .20
383 A52 18c Unloading salt flats .20 .20
384 A52 22c Storage pile .20 .20
385 A52 $1 Bagging and grinding .35 .35
386 A52 $2.50 Loading onto boats .85 .85
a. Souvenir sheet of 6, #381-386 2.00 2.00
Nos. 381-386 (6) 2.00 2.00

Salt industry.

Nos. 281, 288 Overprinted: "50th Anniversary / Scouting 1980"

1980, Apr. 16 *Perf. 13½x14*

387 A40 10c multicolored 1.10 .25
388 A40 $2.50 multicolored 2.00 1.25

Nos. 283, 289 Overprinted: "75th Anniversary / Rotary 1980" and Rotary Emblem

1980, Apr. 16 *Perf. 13½x14*

389 A40 20c multicolored .75 .25
390 A40 $5 multicolored 2.50 2.00

Rotary International, 75th anniversary.

Big Ben, Great Britain #643, London 1980 Emblem — A53

Designs: $1.50, Canada #756. $2.50, Statue of Liberty, US #1632.

1980, May

391 A53 50c multicolored .50 .50
392 A53 $1.50 multicolored .75 .75
393 A53 $2.50 multicolored 1.00 1.00
a. Souvenir sheet of 3, #391-393 2.75 2.75
Nos. 391-393 (3) 2.25 2.25

London 1980 International Stamp Exhibition, May 6-14.

Queen Mother Elizabeth, 80th Birthday — A54

1980, Aug. 4 Litho. *Perf. 14*

394 A54 35c multicolored .55 .35
395 A54 50c multicolored .70 .40
396 A54 $1.50 multicolored 1.25 1.00
397 A54 $3 multicolored 1.75 1.75
a. Souvenir sheet of 4, #394-397 5.50 4.00
Nos. 394-397 (4) 4.25 3.50

Pelicans — A55

1980, Nov. 10 Litho. *Perf. 14*

398 A55 5c shown .35 .20
399 A55 22c Great gray herons .90 .20
400 A55 $1.50 Swallows 2.00 .60
401 A55 $3 Hummingbirds 2.75 1.50
a. Souvenir sheet of 4, #398-401 9.00 7.50
Nos. 398-401 (4) 6.00 2.50

Christmas. For overprints see #405-406.

Nos. 275, 278, 280-290, 334, 400-401 Overprinted: "SEPARATION 1980"

Perf. 13½x14, 14 (A55)

1980, Dec. 18 Litho.

402 A40 1c #275 .20 .20
403 A40 2c on 4c #278 .20 .20
404 A40 5c on 15c #282 .20 .20
405 A55 5c on $1.50 #400 .20 .20
406 A55 5c on $3 #401 .20 .20
407 A40 10c #281 .20 .20
408 A40 12c on $1 #287 .25 .20
409 A40 14c on $2.50 #288 .25 .20
410 A40 15c #282 .30 .20
411 A40 18c on $5 #289 .30 .20
412 A40 20c #283 .30 .20
413 A40 22c #284 .30 .20
414 A40 25c on 15c #282 .35 .20
415 A40 35c #285 .35 .25
416 A44 38c on 22c #334 .35 .30
417 A40 40c on 1c #275 .30 .35
418 A40 50c #286 .40 .40
419 A40 $1 #287 .55 .65
420 A40 $2.50 #288 1.10 2.00
421 A40 $5 #289 2.50 4.00
422 A40 $10 #290 5.75 8.00
423 A40 $10 on 6c #280 5.75 8.00
Nos. 402-423 (22) 20.30 26.55

Petition for Separation, 1825 — A56

1980, Dec. 18 *Perf. 14*

424 A56 18c shown .20 .20
425 A56 22c Referendum ballot, 1967 .20 .20
426 A56 35c Airport blockade, 1967 .25 .25
427 A56 50c Anguilla flag .30 .30
428 A56 $1 Separation celebration, 1980 .50 .50
a. Souvenir sheet of 5, #424-428 1.50 1.60
Nos. 424-428 (5) 1.45 1.45

Separation from St. Kitts-Nevis.

Nelson's Dockyard, by R. Granger Barrett A57

Ship Paintings: 35c, Agamemnon, Vanguard, Elephant, Captain and Victory, by Nicholas Pocock. 50c, Victory, by Monamy Swaine. $3, Battle of Trafalgar, by Clarkson Stanfield. $5, Lord Nelson, by L.F. Abbott and Nelson's arms.

1981, Mar. 2 Litho. *Perf. 14*

429 A57 22c multicolored 1.25 .75
430 A57 35c multicolored 1.50 1.00
431 A57 50c multicolored 2.00 1.25
432 A57 $3 multicolored 2.50 1.75
Nos. 429-432 (4) 7.25 4.75

Souvenir Sheet

433 A57 $5 multicolored 4.50 4.50

Lord Horatio Nelson (1758-1805), 175th death anniversary (1980).

Minnie Mouse A58

Easter: Various Disney characters in Easter outfits.

1981, Mar. 30 Litho. *Perf. 13½*

434 A58 1c multicolored .20 .20
435 A58 2c multicolored .20 .20
436 A58 3c multicolored .20 .20
437 A58 5c multicolored .20 .20
438 A58 7c multicolored .20 .20
439 A58 9c multicolored .20 .20
440 A58 10c multicolored .20 .20
441 A58 $2 multicolored 1.50 1.50
442 A58 $3 multicolored 2.00 2.00
Nos. 434-442 (9) 4.90 4.90

Souvenir Sheet

443 A58 $5 multicolored 5.50 5.50

Prince Charles, Lady Diana, St. Paul's Cathedral A59

1981, June 15 Litho. *Perf. 14*

444 A59 50c shown .20 .25
a. Souvenir sheet of 2 .30 .30
b. Wmk. 380 .30 .30
c. Booklet pane of 4 #444b 1.25 1.25
445 A59 $2.50 Althorp .45 .60
a. Souvenir sheet of 2 1.60 1.60
446 A59 $3 Windsor Castle .55 .75
a. Souvenir sheet of 2 2.00 2.00
b. Wmk. 380 2.00 2.00
c. Booklet pane of 4 #446b 8.00 8.00
Nos. 444-446 (3) 1.20 1.60

Souvenir Sheet

447 A59 $5 Buckingham Palace 2.00 2.00

Royal Wedding. Nos. 444a-446a contain stamps in different colors.

Boys Climbing Tree A60

1981 Litho. *Perf. 14*

448 A60 5c shown .20 .20
449 A60 10c Boys sailing boats .25 .25
450 A60 15c Children playing instruments .35 .35
451 A60 $3 Children with animals 2.50 2.50
Nos. 448-451 (4) 3.30 3.30

Souvenir Sheet

452 A60 $4 Boys playing soccer, vert. 5.00 5.00

UNICEF, 35th anniv.
Issued: 5c-15c, July 31; $3-$4, Sept. 30.

"The Children were Nestled all Snug in their Beds" — A61

Christmas: Scenes from Walt Disney's The Night Before Christmas.

1981, Nov. 2 Litho. *Perf. 13½*

453 A61 1c multicolored .20 .20
454 A61 2c multicolored .20 .20
455 A61 3c multicolored .20 .20
456 A61 5c multicolored .20 .20
457 A61 7c multicolored .20 .20
458 A61 10c multicolored .20 .20
459 A61 12c multicolored .20 .20
460 A61 $2 multicolored 3.00 1.75
461 A61 $3 multicolored 3.00 2.25
Nos. 453-461 (9) 7.40 5.40

Souvenir Sheet

462 A61 $5 multicolored 6.00 6.00

Red Grouper — A62

1982, Jan. 1 Litho. *Perf. 14*

463 A62 1c shown .20 *.60*
464 A62 5c Ferries, Blowing Point .30 *.60*
465 A62 10c Racing boats .20 *.60*
466 A62 15c Majorettes .20 *.60*
467 A62 20c Launching boat, Sandy Hill .40 *.60*
468 A62 25c Coral 1.25 .60
469 A62 30c Little Bay cliffs .30 *.75*
470 A62 35c Fountain Cave 1.25 .80
471 A62 40c Sandy Isld. .30 *.75*
472 A62 45c Landing, Sombrero .50 *.80*
473 A62 50c on 45c, #472 .50 .35
474 A62 60c Seine fishing 3.00 2.25
475 A62 75c Boat race, Sandy Ground .85 *1.75*
476 A62 $1 Bagging lobster, Island Harbor 2.25 1.75
477 A62 $5 Pelicans 14.00 10.00
478 A62 $7.50 Hibiscus 11.00 11.00
479 A62 $10 Queen triggerfish 14.00 12.00
Nos. 463-479 (17) 50.50 45.80

For overprints & surcharges see #507-510, 546A-546D, 578-582, 606-608, 640-647.

Easter — A63

Princess Diana, 21st Birthday — A64

Designs: Butterflies on flowers.

1982, Apr. 5

480 A63 10c Zebra, anthurium .50 .20
481 A63 35c Caribbean buckeye 1.25 .35
482 A63 75c Monarch, allamanda 1.50 .75
483 A63 $3 Red rim, orchid 2.25 2.25
Nos. 480-483 (4) 5.50 3.55

Souvenir Sheet

484 A63 $5 Flambeau, amaryllis 4.25 4.25

1982, May 17

Designs: Portraits, 1961-1981.

485 A64 10c 1961 .20 .20
486 A64 30c 1968 .20 .20
487 A64 40c 1970 .25 .25
488 A64 60c 1974 .40 .40
489 A64 $2 1981 1.40 1.40
490 A64 $3 1981 2.00 2.00
a. Souvenir sheet of 6, #485-490 4.50 4.50
Nos. 485-490 (6) 4.45 4.45

Souvenir Sheet

491 A64 $5 1981 5.00 5.00

For overprints see Nos. 639A-639G.

1982 World Cup — A65

Various Disney characters playing soccer.

1982, Aug. 3 Litho. *Perf. 11*

492 A65 1c multicolored .20 .20
493 A65 3c multicolored .20 .20
494 A65 4c multicolored .20 .20
495 A65 5c multicolored .20 .20
496 A65 7c multicolored .20 .20
497 A65 9c multicolored .20 .20
498 A65 10c multicolored .20 .20
499 A65 $2.50 multicolored 2.50 2.25
500 A65 $3 multicolored 2.50 2.25
Nos. 492-500 (9) 6.40 5.90

Souvenir Sheet

Perf. 14

501 A65 $5 multicolored 7.00 7.00

Scouting Year A66

1982, July 5
502 A66 10c Pitching tent .60 .50
503 A66 35c Marching band 1.00 .75
504 A66 75c Sailing 1.50 1.25
505 A66 $3 Flag bearers 4.00 3.00
Nos. 502-505 (4) 7.10 5.50

Souvenir Sheet

506 A66 $5 Camping 6.00 6.00

Nos. 465, 474-475, 477 Overprinted: "COMMONWEALTH / GAMES 1982"

1982, Oct. 18 Litho. *Perf. 14*
507 A62 10c multicolored .20 .20
508 A62 60c multicolored .55 .55
509 A62 75c multicolored .75 .75
510 A62 $5 multicolored 4.00 4.00
Nos. 507-510 (4) 5.50 5.50

12th Commonwealth Games, Brisbane, Australia, Sept. 30-Oct. 9.

Christmas — A67

Scenes from Walt Disney's Winnie the Pooh.

1982, Nov. 29
511 A67 1c multicolored .20 .20
512 A67 2c multicolored .20 .20
513 A67 3c multicolored .20 .20
514 A67 5c multicolored .25 .20
515 A67 7c multicolored .25 .20
516 A67 10c multicolored .25 .20
517 A67 12c multicolored .35 .25
518 A67 20c multicolored .60 .50
519 A67 $5 multicolored 6.00 5.00
Nos. 511-519 (9) 8.30 6.95

Souvenir Sheet

520 A67 $5 multicolored 7.50 7.50

Commonwealth Day (Mar. 14) — A68

1983, Feb. 28 Litho. *Perf. 14*
521 A68 10c Carnival procession .20 .20
522 A68 35c Flags .50 .50
523 A68 75c Economic cooperation 1.00 1.00
524 A68 $2.50 Salt pond 4.00 4.00
Nos. 521-524 (4) 5.70 5.70

Souvenir Sheet

525 A68 $5 Map showing Commonwealth 4.50 4.00

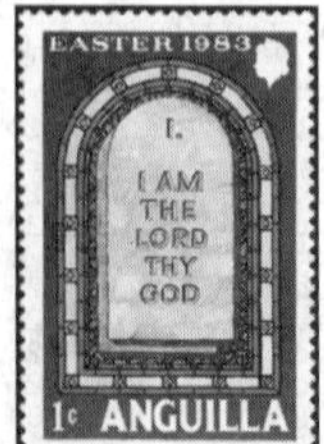

Easter — A69

Ten Commandments.

1983, Mar. 31 Litho. *Perf. 14*
526 A69 1c multicolored .20 .20
527 A69 2c multicolored .20 .20
528 A69 3c multicolored .20 .20
529 A69 10c multicolored .25 .20
530 A69 35c multicolored .55 .30
531 A69 60c multicolored 1.00 .50
532 A69 75c multicolored 1.10 .55
533 A69 $2 multicolored 2.75 2.00
534 A69 $2.50 multicolored 3.00 2.00
535 A69 $5 multicolored 4.75 3.00
Nos. 526-535 (10) 14.00 9.15

Souvenir Sheet

536 A69 $5 Moses Taking Tablets 4.00 4.00

Local Turtles and World Wildlife Fund Emblem — A70

1983, Aug. 10 Litho. *Perf. 13½*
537 A70 10c Leatherback *2.00 1.00*
538 A70 35c Hawksbill *4.00 2.00*
539 A70 75c Green *5.50 2.75*
540 A70 $1 Loggerhead *6.50 3.25*
Nos. 537-540 (4) *18.00 9.00*

Souvenir Sheet

541 A70 $5 Leatherback, diff. *11.00 5.50*

1983, Aug. 10 Litho. *Perf. 12*
537a A70 10c Leatherback *2.00 1.00*
538a A70 35c Hawksbill *7.00 3.50*
539a A70 75c Green *9.00 4.50*
540a A70 $1 Loggerhead *11.00 5.50*
Nos. 537a-540a (4) *29.00 14.50*

Manned Flight Bicentenary A71

1983, Aug. 22 *Perf. 14*
542 A71 10c Montgolfiere, 1783 .35 .25
543 A71 60c Blanchard & Jeffries, 1785 1.00 .60
544 A71 $1 Giffard's airship, 1852 1.50 1.00
545 A71 $2.50 Lilienthal's glider, 1890 2.25 1.75
Nos. 542-545 (4) 5.10 3.60

Souvenir Sheet

546 A71 $5 Wright Brothers' plane, 1909 4.00 4.00

Nos. 465, 471, 476-477 Overprinted: 150TH ANNIVERSARY / ABOLITION OF SLAVERY ACT

1983, Oct. 24 Litho. *Perf. 14*
546A A62 10c Racing boats .20 .20
546B A62 40c Sandy Isld .40 .35
546C A62 $1 Bagging lobster, Island Harbor 1.00 .90
546D A62 $5 Pelicans 4.75 4.50
Nos. 546A-546D (4) 6.35 5.95

Jiminy Cricket A72

Designs: Various Disney productions.

1983, Nov. 14 *Perf. 13½*
547 A72 1c shown .20 .20
548 A72 2c Jiminy Cricket, kettle .20 .20
549 A72 3c Jiminy Cricket, toys .20 .20
550 A72 4c Mickey and Morty .20 .20
551 A72 5c Scrooge McDuck .20 .20
552 A72 6c Minnie and Goofy .20 .20
553 A72 10c Goofy and Elf .20 .20
554 A72 $2 Scrooge McDuck, diff. 3.00 2.25
555 A72 $3 Disney characters 3.50 2.50
Nos. 547-555 (9) 7.90 6.15

Souvenir Sheet

556 A72 $5 Scrooge McDuck 7.50 7.50

Boys' Brigade Centenary — A73

1983, Sept. 12 Litho. *Perf. 14*
557 A73 10c Anguilla company, banner .25 .25
558 A73 $5 Marching with drummer 4.25 4.25
a. Souvenir sheet of 2, #557-558 4.00 4.00

1984 Olympics, Los Angeles — A74

Mickey Mouse Competing in Decathlon.

1984, Feb. 20 Litho. *Perf. 14*
559 A74 1c 100-meter run .20 .20
560 A74 2c Long jump .20 .20
561 A74 3c Shot put .20 .20
562 A74 4c High jump .20 .20
563 A74 5c 400-meter run .20 .20
564 A74 6c Hurdles .20 .20
565 A74 10c Discus .20 .20
566 A74 $1 Pole vault 2.50 2.50
567 A74 $4 Javelin 4.50 4.50
Nos. 559-567 (9) 8.40 8.40

Souvenir Sheet

568 A74 $5 1500-meter run 8.00 8.00

1984, Apr. 24 *Perf. 12½x12*
559a A74 1c .20 .20
560a A74 2c .20 .20
561a A74 3c .20 .20
562a A74 4c .20 .20
563a A74 5c .20 .20
564a A74 6c .20 .20
565a A74 10c .20 .20
566a A74 $1 3.00 3.00
567a A74 $4 5.50 5.50
Nos. 559a-567a (9) 9.90 9.90

Souvenir Sheet

568a A74 $5 With Olympic rings emblem 8.00 8.00

Nos. 559a-567a inscribed with Olympic rings emblem. Printed in sheets of 5 plus label.

Easter A75

Ceiling and Wall Frescoes, La Stanze della Segnatura, by Raphael (details).

1984, Apr. 19 Litho. *Perf. 13½x14*
569 A75 10c Justice .20 .20
570 A75 25c Poetry .30 .30
571 A75 35c Philosophy .40 .40
572 A75 40c Theology .40 .40
573 A75 $1 Abraham & Paul 1.10 1.10
574 A75 $2 Moses & Matthew 2.25 2.25
575 A75 $3 John & David 3.00 3.00
576 A75 $4 Peter & Adam 3.50 3.50
Nos. 569-576 (8) 11.15 11.15

Souvenir Sheet

577 A75 $5 Astronomy 4.50 4.50

Nos. 463, 469, 477-479 Surcharged

1984 Litho. *Perf. 14*
578 A62 25c on $7.50 #478 .45 .45
579 A62 35c on 30c #469 .50 .50
580 A62 60c on 1c #463 .55 .55
581 A62 $2.50 on $5 #477 2.25 2.25
582 A62 $2.50 on $10 #479 1.75 1.75
Nos. 578-582 (5) 5.50 5.50

Issue dates: 25c, May 17, others, Apr. 24.

Ausipex '84 — A76

Australian stamps.

1984, July 16 Litho. *Perf. 13½*
583 A76 10c No. 2 .40 .40
584 A76 75c No. 18 1.25 1.25
585 A76 $1 No. 130 1.75 1.75
586 A76 $2.50 No. 178 2.25 2.25
Nos. 583-586 (4) 5.65 5.65

Souvenir Sheet

587 A76 $5 Nos. 378, 379 5.50 5.50

Slavery Abolition Sesquicentennial — A77

Abolitionists and Vignettes: 10c, Thomas Fowell Buxton, planting sugar cane. 25c, Abraham Lincoln, cotton field. 35c, Henri Christophe, armed slave revolt. 60c, Thomas Clarkson, addressing Anti-Slavery Society. 75c, William Wilberforce, Slave auction. $1, Olaudah Equiano, slave raid on Benin coast. $2.50, General Gordon, slave convoy in Sudan. $5, Granville Sharp, restraining ship captain from boarding slave.

1984, Aug. 1 *Perf. 12*
588 A77 10c multicolored .20 .20
589 A77 25c multicolored .35 .35
590 A77 35c multicolored .50 .50
591 A77 60c multicolored .65 .65
592 A77 75c multicolored .90 .90
593 A77 $1 multicolored 1.00 1.00
594 A77 $2.50 multicolored 2.00 2.00
595 A77 $5 multicolored 4.00 4.00
a. Miniature sheet of 8, #588-595 9.50 9.50
Nos. 588-595 (8) 9.60 9.60

For overprints see Nos. 688-695a.

Christmas — A78

Various Disney characters and celebrations.

Perf. 14, 12½x12 ($2)

1984, Nov. 12 Litho.
596 A78 1c multicolored .20 .20
597 A78 2c multicolored .20 .20
598 A78 3c multicolored .20 .20
599 A78 4c multicolored .20 .20
600 A78 5c multicolored .20 .20
601 A78 10c multicolored .20 .20
602 A78 $1 multicolored 2.75 2.50
603 A78 $2 multicolored 3.50 3.25
604 A78 $4 multicolored 5.50 5.00
Nos. 596-604 (9) 12.95 11.95

Souvenir Sheet

605 A78 $5 multicolored 7.50 7.50

Nos. 464-465, 477 Overprinted or Surcharged: "U.P.U. CONGRESS / HAMBURG 1984"

1984, Aug. 13

606 A62 5c #464 .30 .20
607 A62 20c on 10c #465 .45 .30
608 A62 $5 #477 6.00 4.00
Nos. 606-608 (3) 6.75 4.50

Intl. Civil Aviation Org., 40th Anniv. A79

1984, Dec. 3 Litho. *Perf. 14*

609 A79 60c Icarus, by Hans Erni .75 .75
610 A79 75c Sun Princess, by Sadiou Diouf 1.00 1.00
611 A79 $2.50 Anniv. emblem, vert. 2.50 2.50
Nos. 609-611 (3) 4.25 4.25

Souvenir Sheet

612 A79 $5 Map of the Caribbean 4.50 4.50

Audubon Birth Bicent. — A80

Queen Mother 85th Birthday — A81

Illustrations by artist and naturalist J. J. Audubon (1785-1851).

1985, Apr. 30 Litho. *Perf. 14*

613 A80 10c Hirundo rustica .60 .50
614 A80 60c Mycteria americana 1.10 1.00
615 A80 75c Sterna dougallii 1.10 1.00
616 A80 $5 Pandion haliaetus 4.25 3.75
Nos. 613-616 (4) 7.05 6.25

Souvenir Sheets

617 A80 $4 Vireo solitarus, horiz. 3.75 3.75
618 A80 $4 Piranga ludoviciana, horiz. 3.75 3.75

1985, July 2

Photographs: 10c, Visiting the children's ward at King's College Hospital. $2, Inspecting Royal Marine Volunteer Cadets at Deal. $3, Outside Clarence House in London. $5, In an open carriage at Ascot.

619 A81 10c multicolored .20 .20
620 A81 $2 multicolored 1.25 1.25
621 A81 $3 multicolored 1.90 1.90
Nos. 619-621 (3) 3.35 3.35

Souvenir Sheet

622 A81 $5 multicolored 3.25 3.25

Nos. 619-621 printed in sheetlets of 5.

Birds A82

1985-86 Litho. *Perf. 13½x14*

623 A82 5c Brown pelican 1.60 1.00
624 A82 10c Turtle dove 1.60 1.00
625 A82 15c Man-o-war 1.60 1.00
626 A82 20c Antillean crested hummingbird 1.60 1.00
627 A82 25c White-tailed tropicbird 1.60 1.25
628 A82 30c Caribbean elaenia 1.60 1.25
629 A82 35c Black-whiskered vireo 6.25 5.00
629A A82 35c Lesser Antillean bullfinch ('86) 1.60 1.25
630 A82 40c Yellow-crowned night heron 1.60 1.25
631 A82 45c Pearly-eyed thrasher 1.60 1.25
632 A82 50c Laughing bird 1.60 1.25
633 A82 65c Brown booby 1.60 1.25
634 A82 80c Gray kingbird 2.10 *2.75*
635 A82 $1 Audubon's shearwater 2.10 *2.75*
636 A82 $1.35 Roseate tern 1.60 *2.75*
637 A82 $2.50 Bananaquit 4.75 *6.00*
638 A82 $5 Belted kingfisher 4.00 *7.00*
639 A82 $10 Green heron 6.75 *9.00*
Nos. 623-639 (18) 45.15 *48.00*

Issued: 25c, 65c, $1.35, $5, 7/22; 45c, 50c, 80c, $1, $10, 9/30; 5c-20c, 30c, #629, 40c, $2.50, 11/11; #629A, 3/10.

For overprints & surcharges see #678-682, 713-716, 723-739, 750-753, 764-767.

Nos. 485-491 Overprinted "PRINCE HENRY / BIRTH 15.9.84."

1985, Oct. 31 Litho. *Perf. 14*

639A A64 10c multicolored .20 .20
639B A64 30c multicolored .20 .20
639C A64 40c multicolored .30 .30
639D A64 60c multicolored .45 .45
639E A64 $2 multicolored 1.50 1.50
639F A64 $3 multicolored 4.25 4.25
h. Souv. sheet of 6, #639A-639F 4.80 4.80
Nos. 639A-639F (6) 6.90 6.90

Souvenir Sheet

639G A64 $5 multicolored 3.50 3.50

Nos. 464, 469 and 477 Ovptd. with Anniversary Emblem and "GIRL GUIDES 75th ANNIVERSARY / 1910-1985"

1985, Oct. 14 Litho. *Perf. 14*

640 A62 5c multicolored .20 .20
641 A62 30c multicolored .40 .30
642 A62 75c multicolored .55 .50
643 A62 $5 multicolored 6.00 5.00
Nos. 640-643 (4) 7.15 6.00

Nos. 465 and 469 Overprinted or Surcharged with Organization Emblem and "80th ANNIVERSARY ROTARY 1985."

1985, Nov. 18

644 A62 10c multicolored .20 .20
645 A62 35c on 30c multi .30 .30

Nos. 476, 469 Surcharged or Ovptd. with Emblem, Text and "INTERNATIONAL YOUTH YEAR"

1985, Nov. 18

646 A62 $1 multicolored 1.00 1.00
647 A62 $5 on 30c multi 4.50 4.50

Brothers Grimm — A83

Christmas: Disney characters in Hansel and Gretel.

1985, Nov. 11 Litho. *Perf. 14*

648 A83 5c multicolored .20 .20
649 A83 50c multicolored .75 .70
650 A83 90c multicolored 1.25 1.10
651 A83 $4 multicolored 3.50 3.25
Nos. 648-651 (4) 5.70 5.25

Souvenir Sheet

652 A83 $5 multicolored 6.25 6.25

Mark Twain (1835-1910), Author — A84

Disney characters in Huckleberry Finn.

1985, Nov. 11

653 A84 10c multicolored .30 .30
654 A84 60c multicolored 1.10 1.10
654A A84 $1 multicolored 1.75 1.75
655 A84 $3 multicolored 3.50 3.50
Nos. 653-655 (4) 6.65 6.65

Souvenir Sheet

656 A84 $5 multicolored 6.75 6.75

Christmas. No. 654A printed in sheets of 8.

Statue of Liberty Centennial A85

1985, Nov. 25

657 A85 10c Danmark, Denmark .55 *.65*
658 A85 20c Eagle, USA .75 *.90*
659 A85 60c Amerigo Vespucci, Italy 1.40 *1.50*
660 A85 75c Sir Winston Churchill, G.B. 1.40 *1.50*
661 A85 $2 Nippon Maru, Japan 2.00 *2.25*
662 A85 $2.50 Gorch, Germany 2.25 *2.50*
Nos. 657-662 (6) 8.35 *9.30*

Souvenir Sheet

663 A85 $5 Statue of Liberty, vert. 7.25 6.00

Easter — A86

Stained glass windows.

1986, Mar. 27 Litho. *Perf. 14*

664 A86 10c multicolored .25 .25
665 A86 25c multicolored .45 .45
666 A86 45c multicolored .80 .80
667 A86 $4 multicolored 4.00 4.00
Nos. 664-667 (4) 5.50 5.50

Souvenir Sheet

668 A86 $5 multi, horiz. 6.25 6.25

Halley's Comet A87

A88

Designs: 5c, Johannes Hevelius (1611-1687), Mayan temple observatory. 10c, US Viking probe landing on Mars, 1976. 60c, Theatri Cosmicum (detail), 1668. $4, Sighting, 1835. $5, Comet over Anguilla.

1986, Mar. 24

669 A87 5c multicolored .25 .25
670 A87 10c multicolored .30 .30
671 A87 60c multicolored 1.00 1.00
672 A87 $4 multicolored 4.00 4.00
Nos. 669-672 (4) 5.55 5.55

Souvenir Sheet

673 A88 $5 multicolored 5.25 5.25

Queen Elizabeth II, 60th Birthday

Common Design Type

1986, Apr. 21

674 CD339 20c Inspecting guards, 1946 .20 .20
675 CD339 $2 Garter Ceremony, 1985 1.75 1.75
676 CD339 $3 Trooping the color 2.50 2.50
Nos. 674-676 (3) 4.45 4.45

Souvenir Sheet

677 CD339 $5 Christening, 1926 4.50 4.50

Nos. 623, 631, 635, 637 and 639 Ovptd. "AMERIPEX 1986"

1986, May 22 *Perf. 13½x14*

678 A82 5c multicolored .45 .45
679 A82 45c multicolored .75 .75
680 A82 $1 multicolored 1.40 1.40
681 A82 $2.50 multicolored 2.50 2.50
682 A82 $10 multicolored 6.50 6.50
Nos. 678-682 (5) 11.60 11.60

Wedding of Prince Andrew and Sarah Ferguson — A89

1986, July 23 Litho. *Perf. 14, 12*

683 A89 10c Couple .20 *.25*
684 A89 35c Andrew .25 *.30*
685 A89 $2 Sarah 1.50 *1.75*
686 A89 $3 Couple, diff. 2.25 *2.75*
Nos. 683-686 (4) 4.20 *5.05*

Souvenir Sheet

687 A89 $6 Westminster Abbey 7.00 7.00

Nos. 588-595 Ovptd. "INTERNATIONAL / YEAR OF / PEACE"

1986, Sept. 29 Litho. *Perf. 12*

688 A77 10c multicolored .30 .30
689 A77 25c multicolored .50 .50
690 A77 35c multicolored .60 .60
691 A77 60c multicolored .90 .90
692 A77 75c multicolored 1.10 1.10
693 A77 $1 multicolored 1.25 1.25
694 A77 $2.50 multicolored 2.25 2.25
695 A77 $5 multicolored 3.50 3.50
a. Miniature sheet, #688-695 12.50 12.50
Nos. 688-695 (8) 10.40 10.40

Ships A90

1986, Nov. 29 Litho. *Perf. 14*

696 A90 10c Trading Sloop .75 .75
697 A90 45c Lady Rodney 1.25 1.25
698 A90 80c West Derby 1.75 1.75
699 A90 $3 Warspite 3.50 3.50
Nos. 696-699 (4) 7.25 7.25

Souvenir Sheet

700 A90 $6 Boat Race Day, vert. 10.00 10.00

Christmas.

Discovery of America, 500th Anniv. (in 1992) — A91

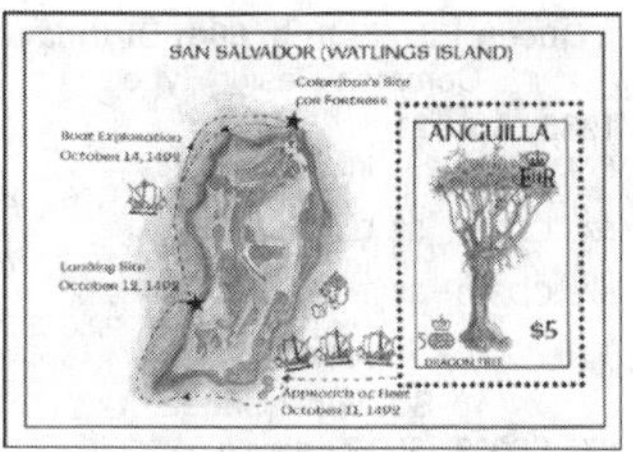

Dragon Tree — A92

5c, Christopher Columbus, astrolabe. 10c, Aboard ship. 35c, Santa Maria. 80c, Ferdinand, Isabella. $4, Indians. No. 707, Caribbean manatee.
Illustration A92 reduced.

1986, Dec. 22

701 A91 5c multi .30 *.35*
702 A91 10c multi .50 *.55*
703 A91 35c multi 1.25 *1.40*
704 A91 80c multi, horiz. 1.50 *1.75*
705 A91 $4 multi 3.25 *3.50*
Nos. 701-705 (5) 6.80 *7.55*

Souvenir Sheets

706 A92 $5 shown 6.50 6.50
707 A92 $5 multi, horiz. 6.50 6.50

Butterflies A93

1987, Apr. 14 Litho. *Perf. 14*

708 A93 10c Monarch .75 .75
709 A93 80c White peacock 2.25 2.25
710 A93 $1 Zebra 2.50 2.50
711 A93 $2 Caribbean buckeye 4.00 4.00
Nos. 708-711 (4) 9.50 9.50

Souvenir Sheet

712 A93 $6 Flambeau 9.00 9.00

Easter.

Nos. 629A, 631, 634 and 639 Ovptd. with CAPEX '87 Emblem in Red

1987, May 25 Litho. *Perf. 13½x14*

713 A82 35c on No. 629A .75 *.80*
714 A82 45c on No. 631 .85 *.90*
715 A82 80c on No. 634 1.25 *1.40*
716 A82 $10 on No. 639 7.00 *7.50*
Nos. 713-716 (4) 9.85 10.60

Separation from St. Kitts and Nevis, 20th Anniv. — A94

10c, Old goose iron, electric iron. 35c, Old East End School, Albena Lake-Hodge Comprehensive College. 45c, Old market place, People's Market. 80c, Old ferries & modern ferry at Blowing Point. $1, Old & new cable & wireless offices. $2, Public meeting at Burrowes Park, House of Assembly.

1987, May 25 *Perf. 14*

717 A94 10c multicolored .20 .20
718 A94 35c multicolored .30 .30
719 A94 45c multicolored .35 .35
720 A94 80c multicolored .65 .65
721 A94 $1 multicolored .80 .80
722 A94 $2 multicolored 1.75 1.75
a. Souvenir sheet of 6, #717-722 5.25 5.25
Nos. 717-722 (6) 4.05 4.05

Nos. 623, 625-628, 629A-639 Ovptd. "20 YEARS OF PROGRESS / 1967-1987" in Red or Surcharged in Red & Black

1987, Sept. 4 Litho. *Perf. 13½x14*

723 A82 5c No. 623 .75 *.80*
724 A82 10c on 15c No. 625 .75 *.80*
725 A82 15c No. 625 1.00 *1.10*
726 A82 20c No. 626 1.00 *1.10*
727 A82 25c No. 627 1.00 *1.10*
728 A82 30c No. 628 1.00 *1.10*
729 A82 35c No. 629A 1.00 *1.10*
730 A82 40c No. 630 1.00 *1.10*
731 A82 45c No. 631 1.00 *1.10*
732 A82 50c No. 632 1.00 *1.10*
733 A82 65c No. 633 1.40 *1.50*
734 A82 80c No. 634 1.50 *1.60*
735 A82 $1 No. 635 1.60 *1.75*
736 A82 $1.35 No. 636 2.00 *2.25*
737 A82 $2.50 No. 637 2.25 *2.50*
738 A82 $5 No. 638 3.50 *3.75*
739 A82 $10 No. 639 6.00 *6.50*
Nos. 723-739 (17) 27.75 *30.25*

Cricket World Cup — A95

Various action scenes.

1987, Oct. 5 *Perf. 14*

740 A95 10c multicolored .65 .60
741 A95 35c multicolored 1.10 1.00
742 A95 45c multicolored 1.25 1.10
743 A95 $2.50 multicolored 3.00 2.75
Nos. 740-743 (4) 6.00 5.45

Souvenir Sheet

744 A95 $6 multicolored 8.00 *8.50*

Sea Shells, Crabs A96

1987, Nov. 2

745 A96 10c West Indian top shell .50 .50
746 A96 35c Ghost crab .80 .80
747 A96 50c Spiny Caribbean vase 1.50 1.50
748 A96 $2 Great land crab 2.50 2.50
Nos. 745-748 (4) 5.30 5.30

Souvenir Sheet

749 A96 $6 Queen conch 7.00 *7.50*

Christmas.

Nos. 629A, 635-636 and 639 Ovptd. "40TH WEDDING ANNIVERSARY / H.M. QUEEN ELIZABETH II / H.R.H. THE DUKE OF EDINBURGH" in Scarlet

1987, Dec. 14 Litho. *Perf. 13½x14*

750 A82 35c multicolored .30 .30
751 A82 $1 multicolored .70 .75
752 A82 $1.35 multicolored 1.00 1.00
753 A82 $10 multicolored 7.00 7.50
Nos. 750-753 (4) 9.00 9.55

Easter (Lilies) — A97

1988, Mar. 28 Litho. *Perf. 14*

754 A97 30c Crinum erubescens .30 .30
755 A97 45c Hymenocallis caribaea .40 .40
756 A97 $1 Crinum macowanii .90 .90
757 A97 $2.50 Hemerocallis fulva 2.25 2.25
Nos. 754-757 (4) 3.85 3.85

Souvenir Sheet

758 A97 $6 Lilium longiflorum 5.00 *5.50*

1988 Summer Olympics, Seoul — A98

1988, July 25 Litho. *Perf. 14*

759 A98 35c 4x100-Meter relay .30 .25
760 A98 45c Windsurfing .45 .40
761 A98 50c Tennis 1.10 1.00
762 A98 80c Basketball 2.00 1.75
Nos. 759-762 (4) 3.85 3.40

Souvenir Sheet

763 A98 $6 Women's 200 meters 5.00 *6.00*

Nos. 629A, 634-635 and 637 Ovptd. "H.R.H. PRINCESS / ALEXANDRA'S / VISIT NOVEMBER 1988"

1988, Dec. 14 Litho. *Perf. 13½x14*

764 A82 35c multicolored .75 *.60*
765 A82 80c multicolored 1.25 *1.40*
766 A82 $1 multicolored 1.50 *1.60*
767 A82 $2.50 multicolored 2.50 *2.75*
Nos. 764-767 (4) 6.00 *6.35*

Marine Life — A99

1988, Dec. 5 Litho. *Perf. 14*

768 A99 35c Common sea fan .35 .35
769 A99 80c Coral crab .75 .75
770 A99 $1 Grooved brain coral 1.00 1.00
771 A99 $1.60 Old wife 1.75 1.75
Nos. 768-771 (4) 3.85 3.85

Souvenir Sheet

772 A99 $6 West Indies spiny lobster 5.00 5.00

Christmas.

Lizards — A100

1989, Feb. 20 Litho. *Perf. 13½x14*

773 A100 45c Wood slave .50 .35
774 A100 80c Slippery back .75 .70
775 A100 $2.50 Iguana 2.25 *2.75*
Nos. 773-775 (3) 3.50 *3.80*

Souvenir Sheet

776 A100 $6 Tree lizard 4.75 *5.00*

Easter — A101

Paintings: 35c, Christ Crowned with Thorns, by Hieronymous Bosch (c. 1450-1516. 80c, Christ Bearing the Cross, by David. $1, The Deposition, by David. $1.60, Pieta, by Rogier van der Weyden (1400-1464). $6, Crucified Christ with the Virgin Mary and Saints, by Raphael.

1989, Mar. 23 Litho. *Perf. 14x13½*

777 A101 35c multicolored .30 *.35*
778 A101 80c multicolored .60 *.70*
779 A101 $1 multicolored .75 .75
780 A101 $1.60 multicolored 1.25 *1.75*
Nos. 777-780 (4) 2.90 *3.55*

Souvenir Sheet

781 A101 $6 multicolored 4.75 *5.50*

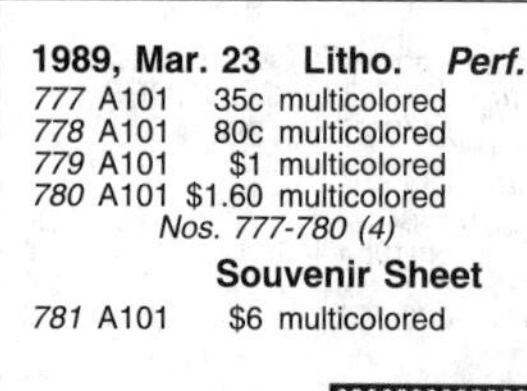

University of the West Indies, 40th Anniv. — A102

1989, Apr. 24 Litho. *Perf. 14x13½*

782 A102 $5 Coat of arms 4.00 *4.50*

Nos. 634-636 and 638 Ovptd. "20th / ANNIVERSARY / MOON / LANDING"

1989, July 3 Litho. *Perf. 13½X14*

783 A82 80c multicolored .60 .60
784 A82 $1 multicolored .75 .75
785 A82 $1.35 multicolored 1.00 1.00
786 A82 $5 multicolored 3.75 3.75
Nos. 783-786 (4) 6.10 6.10

Christmas — A103

Well-known and historic houses.

1989, Dec. 4 Litho. *Perf. 13½x14*

787 A103 5c Lone Star, 1930 .20 .20
788 A103 35c Whitehouse, 1906 .30 .30
789 A103 45c Hodges House .35 .35
790 A103 80c Warden's Place .60 .60
Nos. 787-790 (4) 1.45 1.45

Souvenir Sheet

791 A103 $6 Wallblake House, 1787 4.50 4.50

Fish A104

1990, Apr. 2 Litho. *Perf. 13½x14*

792 A104 5c Blear eye .20 .20
793 A104 10c Redman .20 .20
794 A104 15c Speckletail .20 .20
795 A104 25c Grunt .20 .20
796 A104 30c Amber jack .20 .20
797 A104 35c Red hind .25 .25
798 A104 40c Goatfish .30 .30
799 A104 45c Old wife .35 .35
800 A104 50c Butter fish .40 .40
801 A104 65c Shell fish .50 .50
802 A104 80c Yellowtail snapper .60 .60
803 A104 $1 Katy .75 .75
804 A104 $1.35 Mutton grouper 1.00 1.00
805 A104 $2.50 Doctor fish 1.90 1.90
806 A104 $5 Angelfish 3.75 3.75
807 A104 $10 Barracuda 7.50 7.50
Nos. 792-807 (16) 18.30 18.30

Nos. 792-793, 797 exist inscribed 1992.
For overprints and surcharge see #821-824, 849. For booklet see #890.

Easter — A105

1990, Apr. 2 *Perf. 14x13½*

811 A105 35c Last Supper .25 .25
812 A105 45c Trial .35 .35
813 A105 $1.35 Calvary 1.00 1.00
814 A105 $2.50 Empty tomb 1.90 1.90
Nos. 811-814 (4) 3.50 3.50

Souvenir Sheet

815 A105 $6 The Resurrection 4.50 4.50

See Nos. 834-838.

Cape of Good Hope #7 A106

Stamps of Great Britain and exhibition emblem: 25c, #1, vert. 50c, #2, vert. $2.50, #93. $6, #1-2.

1990, Apr. 30 *Perf. 14*

816 A106 25c multicolored .20 .20
817 A106 50c multicolored .35 .35
818 A106 $1.50 shown 1.10 1.10
819 A106 $2.50 multicolored 1.90 1.90
Nos. 816-819 (4) 3.55 3.55

Souvenir Sheet

820 A106 $6 multicolored 4.50 4.50

Stamp World London '90, Penny Black 150th anniv.

Nos. 803-806 Overprinted:

a. EXPO '90
b. 1990 INTERNATIONAL / LITERACY YEAR
c. WORLD CUP FOOTBALL / CHAMPIONSHIPS 1990
d. 90TH BIRTHDAY / H.M. THE QUEEN MOTHER

1990, Sept. 24 Litho. *Perf. 13½x14*

821 A104(a) $1 Katy .75 .75
822 A104(b) $1.35 Mutton grouper 1.00 1.00
823 A104(c) $2.50 Doctor fish 1.90 1.90
824 A104(d) $5 Angelfish 3.75 3.75
Nos. 821-824 (4) 7.40 7.40

Christmas — A107

Birds.

1990, Dec. 3 *Perf. 14*

825 A107 10c Laughing gull .20 .20
826 A107 35c Brown booby .35 .35
827 A107 $1.50 Bridled tern 1.40 1.40
828 A107 $3.50 Brown pelican 3.50 3.50
Nos. 825-828 (4) 5.45 5.45

Souvenir Sheet

829 A107 $6 Least tern 7.00 7.00

Flags A108

1991, Nov. 5 Litho. *Perf. 13½x14*

830 A108 50c Mermaid .40 .40
831 A108 80c New Anguilla official .60 .60
832 A108 $1 Three dolphins .75 .75
833 A108 $5 Governor's official 3.75 3.75
Nos. 830-833 (4) 5.50 5.50

Nos. 811-815 Inscribed or Overprinted "1991"

1991, Apr. 30 Litho. *Perf. 14x13½*

834 A105 35c like #811 .25 .25
835 A105 45c like #812 .35 .35
836 A105 $1.35 like #813 1.00 1.00
837 A105 $2.50 like #814 1.90 1.90
Nos. 834-837 (4) 3.50 3.50

Souvenir Sheet

838 A105 $6 like #815 7.75 7.75

Easter. "1990" obliterated by black bar in souvenir sheet margin.

Christmas — A109

Perf. 14x13½, 13½x14

1991, Dec. **Litho.**

839 A109 5c Angel, vert. .20 .20
840 A109 35c Santa, vert. .25 .25
841 A109 80c shown .60 .60
842 A109 $1 Palm trees, poinsettias .75 .75
Nos. 839-842 (4) 1.80 1.80

Souvenir Sheet

843 A109 $5 Homes, holly 3.75 3.75

Easter A110

Designs: 35c, Church, angels holding palms, vert. 45c Church, angels singing, vert. 80c, Village. $1, People going to church, vert. $5, People at beach, sailboats.

1992 Litho. *Perf. 14*

844 A110 35c multicolored .30 .30
845 A110 45c multicolored .40 .40
846 A110 80c multicolored .70 .70
847 A110 $1 multicolored .85 .85
848 A110 $5 multicolored 4.25 4.25
Nos. 844-848 (5) 6.50 6.50

No. 796 Surcharged

1992, June 10 Litho. *Perf. 13½x14*

849 A104 $1.60 on 30c #796 1.40 1.40

No. 849 inscribed "1992."

Independence, 25th Anniv. — A111

1992, Aug. 10 Litho. *Perf. 14*

850 A111 80c Official seal, flag .60 .60
851 A111 $1 Official seal .70 .70
852 A111 $1.60 Flags, airport 1.25 1.25
853 A111 $2 First seal 1.40 1.40
Nos. 850-853 (4) 3.95 3.95

Souvenir Sheet

854 A111 $10 #1, 8-11, 15-16 8.50 8.50

No. 854 contains one 85x85mm stamp. For booklet see No. 970.

Sailboat Racing — A112

Designs: 20c, On course. 35c, Stylized boat poster. 45c, Start of race. No. 858, Blue Bird, 1971, vert. No. 859, Construction plans for Blue Bird, vert. $1, Stylized boat poster, diff. $6, Like Nos. 855 & 857.

Perf. 13½x14, 14x13½

1992, Oct. 12 **Litho.**

855 A112 20c multicolored .20 .20
856 A112 35c multicolored .25 .25
857 A112 45c multicolored .35 .35
858 A112 80c multicolored .55 .55
859 A112 80c multicolored .55 .55
a. Pair, #858-859 1.10 1.10
860 A112 $1 multicolored .70 .70
Nos. 855-860 (6) 2.60 2.60

Souvenir Sheet

861 A112 $6 multicolored 4.55 4.55

No. 861 contains one 96x31mm stamp.

Discovery of America, 500th Anniv. A113

1992, Dec. 15 Litho. *Perf. 14*

862 A113 80c Landfall .70 .70
863 A113 $1 Columbus, vert. .85 .85
864 A113 $2 Fleet 1.75 1.75
865 A113 $3 Pinta 2.50 2.50
Nos. 862-865 (4) 5.80 5.80

Souvenir Sheet

866 A113 $6 Map of voyage, vert. 5.00 5.00

Christmas A114

Various Christmas trees and: 20c, Mucka Jumbie on stilts. 70c, Masquerading house to house. $1.05, Christmas baking, old oven style. $2.40, $5, Collecting presents.

1992, Dec. 7

867 A114 20c multicolored .20 .20
868 A114 70c multicolored .60 .60
869 A114 $1.05 multicolored .90 .90
870 A114 $2.40 multicolored 2.00 2.00
Nos. 867-870 (4) 3.70 3.70

Souvenir Sheet

871 A114 $5 Sheet of 1 + 3 labels 4.25 4.25

Labels on No. 871 are similar to Nos. 867-869, but without denomination.

Easter — A115

Children's drawings: 20c, Kite flying. 45c, Cliff top village service. 80c, Morning devotion on Sombrero. $1.50, Hilltop church service. $5, Good Friday kites.

1993, Mar. 29 Litho. *Perf. 14*

872 A115 20c multicolored .20 .20
873 A115 45c multicolored .40 .40
874 A115 80c multicolored .65 .65
875 A115 $1.50 multicolored 1.25 1.25
Nos. 872-875 (4) 2.50 2.50

Souvenir Sheet

876 A115 $5 multicolored 4.25 4.25

No. 876 contains one 42x56mm stamp.

Native Industries A116

1993, June 23 Litho. *Perf. 14*

877 A116 20c Salt .20 .20
878 A116 80c Tobacco .65 .65
879 A116 $1 Cotton .80 .80
880 A116 $2 Sugar cane 1.60 1.60
Nos. 877-880 (4) 3.25 3.25

Souvenir Sheet

881 A116 $6 Fishing 4.75 4.75

Coronation of Queen Elizabeth II, 40th Anniv. — A117

Designs: 80c, Lord Great Chamberlain presents the spurs of chivalry. $1, The benediction. $2, Queen Elizabeth II, coronation photograph. $3, St. Edward's Crown. $6, Queen, Prince Philip in Gold State Coach.

1993, Aug. 16 Litho. *Perf. 14*

882 A117 80c multicolored .65 .65
883 A117 $1 multicolored .80 .80
884 A117 $2 multicolored 1.75 1.75
885 A117 $3 multicolored 2.50 2.50
Nos. 882-885 (4) 5.70 5.70

Souvenir Sheet

886 A117 $6 multicolored 4.75 4.75

Anguilla Carnival — A118

1993, Aug. 23 Litho. *Perf. 14*

887 A118 20c Pan musician .20 .20
888 A118 45c Pirates .35 .35
889 A118 80c Stars .65 .65
890 A118 $1 Playing mas .80 .80
Booklet, 5 ea #796, 890 5.00
891 A118 $2 Masqueraders 1.75 1.75
892 A118 $3 Commandos 2.50 2.50
Nos. 887-892 (6) 6.25 6.25

Souvenir Sheet

893 A118 $5 Carnival fantasy 4.00 4.00

Christmas A119

Mail Delivery — A120

Traditional Christmas customs: 20c, Mucka Jumbies. 35c, Serenaders. 45c, Baking. $3, Five-fingers Christmas tree. $4, Mucka Jumbies and serenaders.

1993, Dec. 7 Litho. *Perf. 14x13½*

894 A119 20c multicolored .20 .20
895 A119 35c multicolored .30 .30
896 A119 45c multicolored .40 .40
897 A119 $3 multicolored 2.50 2.50
Nos. 894-897 (4) 3.40 3.40

Souvenir Sheet

Perf. 14

898 A119 $4 multicolored 3.50 3.50

No. 898 contains one 54x42mm stamp.

1993, Feb. 11 Litho. *Perf. 14*

Designs: 20c, Traveling Branch mail van, Sandy Ground, horiz. 45c, Mail boat, Betsy R, The Forest. 80c, Old post office, horiz. $1, Mail by jeep, Island Harbor. $4, New post office, 1993, horiz.

899 A120 20c multicolored .20 .20
900 A120 45c multicolored .40 .40
901 A120 80c multicolored .70 .70
902 A120 $1 multicolored .85 .85
903 A120 $4 multicolored 3.50 3.50
Nos. 899-903 (5) 5.65 5.65

Royal Visits — A121

1994, Feb. 18

904 A121 45c Princess Alexandra .35 .35
905 A121 50c Princess Alice .45 .45
906 A121 80c Prince Philip .70 .70
907 A121 $1 Prince Charles .85 .85
908 A121 $2 Queen Elizabeth II 1.75 1.75
a. Souvenir sheet of 4, #904-908 4.00 4.00
Nos. 904-908 (5) 4.10 4.10

Easter — A122

1994, Apr. 6 Litho. *Perf. 14x15*

Stained glass windows: 20c, Crucifixion. 45c, Empty tomb. 80c, Resurrection. $3, Risen Christ with disciples.

909 A122 20c multicolored .20 .20
910 A122 45c multicolored .40 .40
911 A122 80c multicolored .75 .75
912 A122 $3 multicolored 2.75 2.75
Nos. 909-912 (4) 4.10 4.10

Christmas — A123

Designs: 20c, Adoration of the shepherds. 30c, Magi, shepherds. 35c, The Annunciation. 45c, Nativity Scene. $2.40, Flight into Egypt.

1994, Nov. 22 Litho. *Perf. 14*

913 A123 20c multicolored .20 .20
914 A123 30c multicolored .30 .30
915 A123 35c multicolored .35 .35
916 A123 45c multicolored .45 .45
917 A123 $2.40 multicolored 2.50 2.50
Nos. 913-917 (5) 3.80 3.80

1994 World Cup Soccer Championships, US — A124

Soccer player and: 20c, Pontiac Silverdome, Detroit. 70c, Foxboro Stadium, Boston. $1.80, RFK Memorial Stadium, Washington. $2.40, Soldier Field, Chicago.
$6, Two players.

1994, Oct. 3 Litho. *Perf. 13½x14*

918 A124 20c multicolored .20 .20
919 A124 70c multicolored .65 .65
920 A124 $1.80 multicolored 1.60 1.60
921 A124 $2.40 multicolored 1.90 1.90
Nos. 918-921 (4) 4.35 4.35

Souvenir Sheet

922 A124 $6 multicolored 5.50 5.50

Easter A125

Turtle dove: 45c, One on tree branch. 50c, One on nest, one on branch. $5, Mother with young.

1995, Apr. 10 Litho. *Perf. 14*

923 A125 20c multicolored .20 .20
924 A125 45c multicolored .40 .40
925 A125 50c multicolored .45 .45
926 A125 $5 multicolored 4.75 4.75
Nos. 923-926 (4) 5.80 5.80

UN, 50th Anniv. A126

Secretaries general and: 20c, Trygve Lie (1946-53), general assembly. 80c, UN flag, UN headquarters with "50" (no portrait). $1, Dag Hammarskjold (1953-61), charter, U Thant (1961-71). $5, UN complex, New York, vert. (no portrait).

Perf. 13½x14, 14x13½

1995, June 26 Litho.

927 A126 20c multicolored .20 .20
928 A126 80c multicolored .75 .75
929 A126 $1 multicolored .95 .95
930 A126 $5 multicolored 4.75 4.75
Nos. 927-930 (4) 6.65 6.65

Caribbean Development Bank, 25th Anniv. — A127

Designs: 45c, Emblem, map of Anguilla. $5, Local headquarters along waterfront.

1995, Aug. 15 Litho. *Perf. 13½x14*

931 A127 45c multicolored .45 .45
932 A127 $5 multicolored 5.00 5.00
a. Pair, #931-932 5.45 5.45

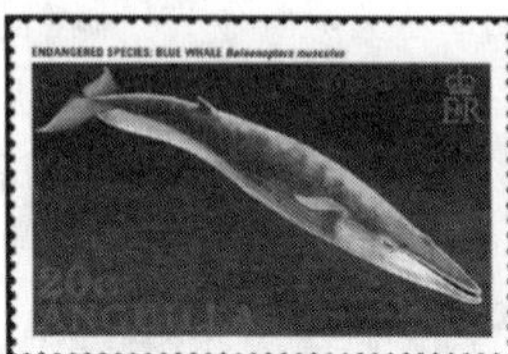
Whales — A128

Perf. 13½x14, 14x13½

1995, Nov. 24 Litho.

933 A128 20c Blue whale .20 .20
934 A128 45c Right whale, vert. .40 .40
935 A128 $1 Sperm whale .90 .90
936 A128 $5 Humpback whale 4.25 4.25
Nos. 933-936 (4) 5.75 5.75

Christmas A129

1995, Dec. 12 *Perf. 14½*

937 A129 10c Palm tree .20 .20
938 A129 25c Fish net floats .20 .20
939 A129 45c Sea shells .40 .40
940 A129 $5 Fish 4.25 4.25
Nos. 937-940 (4) 5.05 5.05

Corals A130

1996, June 21 Litho. *Perf. 14x14½*

941 A130 20c Deep water gorgonia .20 .20
942 A130 80c Common sea fan .70 .70
943 A130 $5 Venus sea fern 4.25 4.25
Nos. 941-943 (3) 5.15 5.15

A131 A132

1996 Summer Olympic Games, Atlanta: 20c, Running. 80c, Javelin, wheelchair basketball. $1, High jump. $3.50, Olympic torch, Greek, US flags.

1996, Dec. 12 Litho. *Perf. 14*

944 A131 20c multicolored .20 .20
945 A131 80c multicolored .65 .65
946 A131 $1 multicolored .80 .80
947 A131 $3.50 multicolored 2.75 2.75
Nos. 944-947 (4) 4.40 4.40

1996, Dec. 12

Battle for Anguilla, bicent.: 60c, Sandy Hill Fort, HMS Lapwing. 75c, French troops destroy church, horiz. $1.50, HMS Lapwing defeats Valiant, Decius, horiz. $4, French troops land, Rendezvous Bay.

948 A132 60c multicolored .50 .50
949 A132 75c multicolored .60 .60
950 A132 $1.50 multicolored 1.25 1.25
951 A132 $4 multicolored 3.25 3.25
Nos. 948-951 (4) 5.60 5.60

Fruits and Nuts A133

1997, Apr. 30 Litho. *Perf. 14*

952 A133 10c Gooseberry .20 .20
953 A133 20c West Indian cherry .20 .20
954 A133 40c Tamarind .25 *.30*
955 A133 50c Pomme-surette .30 *.40*
956 A133 60c Sea almond .40 *.50*
957 A133 75c Sea grape .55 *.65*
958 A133 80c Banana .55 *.65*
959 A133 $1 Genip .70 *.80*
960 A133 $1.10 Coco plum .80 *.85*
961 A133 $1.25 Pope .90 *.95*
962 A133 $1.50 Papaya 1.00 *1.10*
963 A133 $2 Sugar apple 1.40 1.40
964 A133 $3 Soursop 2.00 *2.25*
965 A133 $4 Pomegrante 2.75 *3.00*
966 A133 $5 Cashew 3.25 *3.50*
967 A133 $10 Mango 6.75 *7.00*
Nos. 952-967 (16) 22.00 *23.75*

Iguanas — A134

World Wildlife Fund: a, 20c, Baby iguanas emerging from eggs, juvenile iguana. b, 50c, Adult on rock. c, 75c, Two iguanas on tree limbs. d, $3, Adult up close, adult on tree branch.

1997, Oct. 13 Litho. *Perf. 13½x14*

968 A134 Strip of 4, #a.-d. 4.00 4.00

Diana, Princess of Wales (1961-67) A135

Designs: a, 15c, In red & white. b, $1, In yellow. c, $1.90, Wearing tiara. d, $2.25, Wearing blouse with Red Cross emblem.

1998, Apr. 14 Litho. *Perf. 14*

969 A135 Strip of 4, #a.-d. 4.00 4.00

No. 969 was issued in sheets of 16 stamps.

Fountain Cavern Carvings A136

30c, Rainbow Deity (Juluca). $1.25, Lizard. $2.25, Solar Chieftan. $2.75, Creator.

1997, Nov. 17 Litho. *Perf. 14x14½*

970 A136 30c multicolored .25 .25
Booklet, 5 ea #851, 970 4.75

971 A136 $1.25 multicolored	1.10	1.10
972 A136 $2.25 multicolored	1.90	1.90
973 A136 $2.75 multicolored	2.25	2.25
Nos. 970-973 (4)	5.50	5.50

1998 Intl. Arts Festival A137

Paintings: 15c, "Treasure Island." 30c, "Posing in the Light." $1, "Pescadores de Anguilla." $1.50, "Fresh Catch." $1.90, "The Bell Tower of St. Mary's."

1998, Aug. 24 Litho. *Perf. 14*

974 A137 15c multi	.20	.20
975 A137 30c multi, vert.	.25	.25
976 A137 $1 multi, vert.	.80	.80
Booklet, 5 ea #975-976	5.25	
977 A137 $1.50 multi	1.25	1.25
978 A137 $1.90 multi, vert.	1.50	1.50
Nos. 974-978 (5)	4.00	4.00

Christmas A138

Paintings of "Hidden beauty of Anguilla:" 15c, Woman cooking over open fire, girl seated on steps. $1, Person looking over fruits and vegetables. $1.50, Underwater scene. $3, Cacti growing along shore.

1998

979 A138 15c multicolored	.20	.20
980 A138 $1 multicolored	.80	.80
981 A138 $1.50 multicolored	1.25	1.25
982 A138 $3 multicolored	2.40	2.40
Nos. 979-982 (4)	4.65	4.65

Royal Air Force, 80th Anniv. A139

Designs: 30c, Sopwith Camel, Bristol F2B. $1, Supermarine Spitfire II, Hawker Hurricane Mk1. $1.50, Avro Lancaster. $1.90, Harrier GR7, Panavia Tornado F3.

1998 Litho. *Perf. 13½*
Granite Paper (No. 983)

983 A139 30c multicolored	.25	.25
984 A139 $1 multicolored	.80	.80
985 A139 $1.50 multicolored	1.25	1.25
986 A139 $1.90 multicolored	1.50	1.50
Nos. 983-986 (4)	3.80	3.80

University of the West Indies, 50th Anniv. — A140

Designs: $1.50, Anguilla campus. $1.90, Anguilla campus, torchbearer, University arms.

1998 Litho. *Perf. 13¼*
Granite Paper (#988)

987-988 A140 Set of 2	2.60	2.60

First Manned Moon Landing, 30th Anniv. — A141

Designs: 30c, Lift-off of Apollo 11, Command and Service Modules in lunar orbit. $1, Buzz Aldrin on Moon, footprint. $1.50, Lunar Module leaving Moon. $1.90, Splashdown.

1999, May 6 Litho. *Perf. 13¾*

989 A141 30c multi	.25	.25
990 A141 $1 multi	.75	.75
991 A141 $1.50 multi	1.10	1.10
992 A141 $1.90 multi	1.40	1.40
Nos. 989-992 (4)	3.50	3.50

Heroes of Anguilla's Revolution A142

Designs: 30c, Albena Lake Hodge (1920-85). $1, Collins O. Hodge (1926-78). $1.50, Edwin W. Rey (1906-80). $1.90, Walter G. Hodge (1920-89).

1999, July 5 *Perf. 14½x14¼*

993 A142 30c multi	.25	.25
994 A142 $1 multi	.75	.75
995 A142 $1.50 multi	1.10	1.10
996 A142 $1.90 multi	1.40	1.40
Nos. 993-996 (4)	3.50	3.50

Modern Architecture A143

Designs: No. 997, 30c, Library and resource center. No. 998, 65c, Parliamentary building and court house. No. 999, $1, Caribbean Commercial Bank. No. 999A, $1.50, Police headquarters. No. 1000, $1.90, Post office.

1999 Litho. *Perf. 14x14½*

997-1000 A143 Set of 5	4.00	4.00

Christmas and Millennium Celebrations — A144

Designs: 30c, Fireworks display and barbecue. $1, Globe, musicians. $1.50, Family dinner. $1.90, Decorated tree.

1999 Litho. *Perf. 13¼*

1001 A144 30c multi	.25	.25
1002 A144 $1 multi	.75	.75
1003 A144 $1.50 multi	1.10	1.10
1004 A144 $1.90 multi	1.40	1.40
Nos. 1001-1004 (4)	3.50	3.50

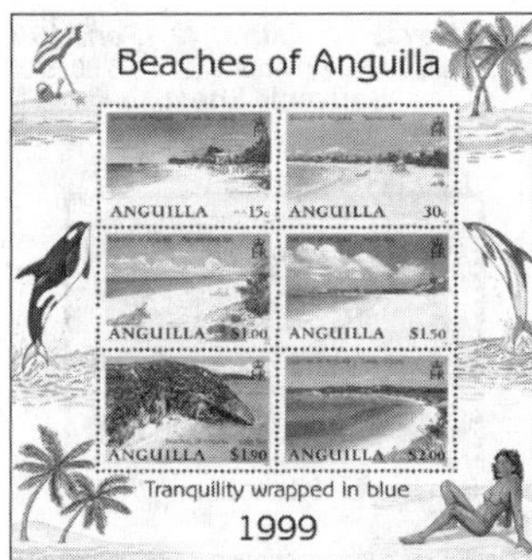

Beaches — A145

1005, 15c, Shoal Bay. 1006, 30c, Maundys Bay. 1007, $1, Rendezvous Bay. 1008, $1.50, Meads Bay. 1009, $1.90, Little Bay. 1010, $2, Sandy Ground.

1999 *Perf. 12*

1005-1010 A145 Set of 5	5.00	5.00
a. Sheet of 6, #1005-1010	5.00	5.00
b. As "a," with show emblem in margin	5.00	5.00

The Stamp Show 2000, London (No. 1010b). Issued: No. 1010b, 5/22/00.

Easter A146

Toys: 25c, Banjo. 30c, Top. $1.50, Slingshot. $1.90, Roller. $2.50, Killy ban.

No. 1016: a, 75c, Rag doll. b, $1, Kite. c, $1.25, Cricket ball. d, $4, Pond boat.

2000 *Perf. 13¼*

1011 A146 25c multi	.20	.20
1012 A146 30c multi	.25	.25
1013 A146 $1.50 multi	1.10	1.10
1014 A146 $1.90 multi	1.40	1.40
1015 A146 $2.50 multi	1.90	1.90
Nos. 1011-1015 (5)	4.85	4.85

Souvenir Sheet

1016 A146 Sheet of 4, #a-d	5.25	5.25

100th Test Match at Lord's Ground — A147

$2, Lanville Harrigan. $4, Cardigan Connor.

2000, May 5 Litho. *Perf. 13¾x13¼*

1017-1018 A147 Set of 2	4.50	4.50

Souvenir Sheet

Design: $6, Lord's Ground, horiz.

1018A A147 $6 multi	4.50	4.50

Prince William, 18th Birthday — A148

Prince William and: 30c, Queen Elizabeth II, Princes Philip and Charles. $1, Princess Diana, Princes Harry and Charles. $1.90, Princes Harry and Charles. $2.25, Princes Charles and Harry, in winter wear.

2000, July 20 *Perf. 13¼*

1019-1022 A148 Set of 4	4.00	4.00

Souvenir Sheet

1023 A148 $8 Prince William, vert.	6.00	6.00

Queen Mother, 100th Birthday — A149

Queen Mother and: 30c, Prince William. $1.50, Anguilla shoreline. $1.90, Clarence House. $5, Castle of Mey.

2000, Aug. 4

1024-1027 A149 Set of 4	6.50	6.50

Intl. Arts Festival A150

Artwork: 15c, Anguilla Montage, by Weme Caster. 30c, Serenity, by Damien Carty. 65c, Inter-island Cargo, by Paula Walden. $1.50, Rainbow City Where Spirits Find Form, by Fiona Percy. $1.90, Sailing Silver Seas, by Valerie Carpenter.

$7, Historic Anguilla, by Melsadis Fleming.

2000, Sept. 21 *Perf. 14¼x14½*

1028-1032 A150 Set of 5	3.50	3.50

Souvenir Sheet
Perf. 14¼

1033 A150 $7 multi	5.25	5.25

No. 1033 contains one 43x28mm stamp.

Christmas A151

Flower and Garden Show flower arrangements by: 15c, Rowena Carty. 25c, Yvonda Hodge. 30c, Carty, diff. $1, Simon Rogers. $1.50, Lady Josephine Gumbs. $1.90, Carty, diff.

2000, Nov. 22 *Perf. 13¼*

1034-1039 A151 Set of 6	3.75	3.75

Natl. Bank of Anguilla, 15th Anniv. — A152

Designs: 30c, Soccer team in annual primary school tournament. $1, Sponsored sailboat, De Chan, vert. $1.50, Bank's crest, vert. $1.90, New bank building.

2000, Nov. 27

1040-1043 A152 Set of 4	3.50	3.50

Ebenezer Methodist Church, 170th Anniv. — A153

Church in: 30c, Sepia tones. $1.90, Full color.

2000, Dec. 4
1044-1045 A153 Set of 2 1.60 1.60

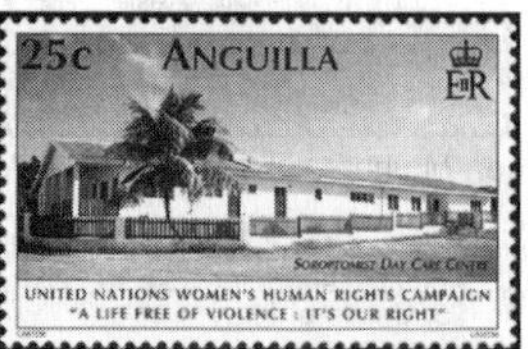

UN Women's Human Rights Campaign — A154

Designs: 25c, Soroptimist Day Care Center. 30c, Britannia Idalla Gumbs, vert. $2.25, Woman, vert.

2001 Litho. *Perf. 13¼*
1046-1048 A154 Set of 3 2.10 2.10

American Revolution, 225th Anniv. — A155

Designs: 30c, John Paul Jones, USS Ranger. $1, George Washington, Battle of Yorktown. $1.50, Thomas Jefferson, Submission of Declaration of Independence. $1.90, John Adams, Adams and Benjamin Franklin signing peace treaty.

2001, July 4 Litho. *Perf. 13¼*
1049-1052 A155 Set of 4 3.75 3.75

Birds A156

Designs: 30c, White-cheeked pintail. $1, Black-faced grassquits, vert. $1.50, Brown noddy. $2, Black-necked stilts, vert. $3, Snowy plovers.

No. 1058: a, 25c, Snowy egret. b, 65c, Red-billed tropicbird. $1.35, Greater yellowlegs. $2.25, Sooty tern.

2001, Aug. 7
1053-1057 A156 Set of 5 6.00 6.00

Souvenir Sheet

1058 A156 Sheet of 4, #a-d 3.50 3.50

Year of Dialogue Among Civilizations A157

2001, Oct. 9 *Perf. 13¼x13*
1059 A157 $1.90 multi 1.50 1.50

Christmas — A158

Musical instruments: 15c, Triangle. 25c, Maracas. 30c, Guiro, vert. $1.50, Marimba. $1.90, Tambu, vert. $2.50, Bath pan, vert.

No. 1066, vert.: a, 75c, Banjo. b, $1, Quatro. c, $1.25, Ukulele. d, $3, Cello.

2001, Nov. 5 Litho. *Perf. 13¼*
1060-1065 A158 Set of 6 5.00 5.00

Souvenir Sheet

1066 A158 Sheet of 4, #a-d 4.50 4.50

Sombrero Lighthouse — A159

Designs: 30c, Lighhouse in 1960s, vert. $1.50, Comparison of old and new lighthouses. $1.90, New lighthouse, 2001, vert.

2002, Apr. 2 Litho. *Perf. 13¼*
1067-1069 A159 Set of 3 2.75 2.75

Social Security Board, 20th Anniv. — A160

Social Security: 30c, Community service, vert. 75c, Benefits all ages, vert. $2.50, Benefits employees.

2002, May 28 Litho. *Perf. 13¼*
1070-1072 A160 Set of 3 2.75 2.75

Royal Navy Ships A161

Designs: 30c, HMS Antrim, 1967. 50c, HMS Formidable, 1939. $1.50, HMS Dreadnought, 1906. $2, HMS Warrior, 1860.

$7, HMS Ark Royal, 1981, vert.

2002, June 24 Litho. *Perf. 13¼*
1073-1076 A161 Set of 4 3.25 3.25

Souvenir Sheet

1077 A161 $7 multi 5.25 5.25

Reign of Queen Elizabeth II, 50th Anniv. — A162

Designs: 30c, Holding baby. $1.50, Wearing white dress. $1.90, Wearing tiara. $5, Wearing yellow hat.

$8, At desk.

2002, Oct. 14 Litho. *Perf. 13¼*
1078-1081 A162 Set of 4 6.50 6.50

Souvenir Sheet

1082 A162 $8 multi 6.00 6.00

Pan-American Health Organization, Cent. — A163

Designs: 30c, The Valley Health Center. $1.50, Emblem, "100."

2002, Nov. 11
1083-1084 A163 Set of 2 1.40 1.40

ANJOUAN

'an-jü-wän

LOCATION — One of the Comoro Islands in the Mozambique Channel between Madagascar and Mozambique.
GOVT. — French colony.
AREA — 89 sq. mi.
POP. — 20,000 (approx. 1912)
CAPITAL — Mossamondu

See Comoro Islands.

100 Centimes = 1 Franc

Navigation and Commerce — A1

Perf. 14x13½

1892-1907 Typo. Unwmk.

Name of Colony in Blue or Carmine

No.	Type	Value	Color	Unused	Used
1	A1	1c	black, *blue*	.85	.80
2	A1	2c	brown, *buff*	1.25	1.00
3	A1	4c	claret, *lav*	1.75	1.40
4	A1	5c	green, *grnsh*	3.25	2.75
5	A1	10c	blk, *lavender*	4.00	3.00
6	A1	10c	red ('00)	16.00	12.50
7	A1	15c	bl, quadrille paper	5.00	3.50
8	A1	15c	gray, *lt gray* ('00)	8.00	6.00
9	A1	20c	red, *green*	5.00	4.00
10	A1	25c	black, *rose*	6.00	4.00
11	A1	25c	blue ('00)	8.00	7.25
12	A1	30c	brn, *bister*	12.50	9.00
13	A1	35c	blk, *yel* ('06)	6.50	4.00
14	A1	40c	red, *straw*	22.50	13.50
15	A1	45c	blk, *gray grn* ('07)	75.00	70.00
16	A1	50c	car, *rose*	22.50	16.00
17	A1	50c	brn, *azure* ('00)	14.50	8.00
18	A1	75c	vio, *orange*	22.50	14.00
19	A1	1fr	brnz grn, *straw*	50.00	37.50
			Nos. 1-19 (19)	285.10	218.20

Perf. 13½x14 stamps are counterfeits.

Issues of 1892-1907 Surcharged in Black or Carmine

1912

No.	Type	Surcharge	Color	Unused	Used
20	A1	5c on 2c	brn, *buff*	.50	.50
21	A1	5c on 4c	claret, *lav* (C)	.65	.65
22	A1	5c on 15c	blue (C)	.65	.65
23	A1	5c on 20c	red, *green*	.65	.65
24	A1	5c on 25c	blk, *rose* (C)	.65	.65
25	A1	5c on 30c	brn, *bis* (C)	.65	.65
26	A1	10c on 40c	red, *straw*	.75	.75
27	A1	10c on 45c	blk, *gray grn* (C)	.85	.85
28	A1	10c on 50c	car, *rose*	2.00	2.00
29	A1	10c on 75c	vio, *org*	1.25	1.25
30	A1	10c on 1fr	brnz grn, *straw*	1.40	1.40
			Nos. 20-30 (11)	10.00	10.00

Nos. 21-23, 30 exist in pairs, one without surcharge. Value, $550 each.

Two spacings between the surcharged numerals are found on Nos. 20-30.

Nos. 20-30 were available for use in Madagascar and the Comoro archipelago.

The stamps of Anjouan were superseded by those of Madagascar, and in 1950 by those of Comoro Islands.

ANNAM AND TONKIN

a-'nam and 'tän-'kin

LOCATION — In French Indo-China bordering on the China Sea on the east and Siam on the west.
GOVT. — French Protectorate
AREA — 97,503 sq. mi.
POP. — 14,124,000 (approx. 1890)
CAPITAL — Annam: Hue; Tonkin: Hanoi

For administrative purposes, the Protectorates of Annam, Tonkin, Cambodia, Laos and the Colony of Cochin-China were grouped together and were known as French Indo-China.

100 Centimes = 1 Franc

Catalogue values for unused stamps are for examples without gum as most stamps were issued in that condition.

Stamps of French Colonies, 1881-86 Handstamped Surcharged in Black:

Perf. 14x13½

1888, Jan. 21 Unwmk.

No.	Type	Description	Unused	Used
1	A9	1c on 2c brn, *buff*	20.00	18.00
a.		Inverted surcharge	80.00	80.00
b.		Sideways surcharge	80.00	80.00
2	A9	1c on 4c claret, *lav*	16.00	15.00
a.		Inverted surcharge	80.00	80.00
b.		Double surcharge	100.00	100.00
c.		Sideways surcharge	80.00	80.00
3	A9	5c on 10c blk, *lav*	20.00	12.50
a.		Inverted surcharge	80.00	80.00
b.		Double surcharge	100.00	100.00

Hyphen between "A" and "T"

No.	Type	Description	Unused	Used
7	A9	1c on 2c brn, *buff*	175.00	160.00
a.		Inverted surcharge	350.00	
8	A9	1c on 4c claret, *lav*	325.00	*325.00*
9	A9	5c on 10c blk, *lav*	150.00	140.00

A 5c on 2c was prepared but not issued. Value $6,000.

In these surcharges there are different types of numerals and letters.

There are numerous other errors in the placing of the surcharges, including double one inverted, double both inverted, double one sideways, pair #1, 7, and pair one without surcharge. Such varieties command substantial premiums.

These stamps were superseded in 1892 by those of Indo-China.

ANTIGUA

an-'tēg-(w)ə

LOCATION — In the West Indies, southeast of Puerto Rico
GOVT. — Independent state
AREA — 171 sq. mi.
POP. — 64,246 (est. 1999)
CAPITAL — St. John's

Antigua was one of the presidencies of the former Leeward Islands colony until becoming a Crown Colony in 1956. It became an Associated State of the United Kingdom in 1967 and an independent nation on November 1, 1981, taking the name of Antigua and Barbuda.

Antigua stamps were discontinued in 1890 and resumed in 1903. In the interim, stamps of Leeward Islands were used. Between 1903-1956, stamps of Antigua and Leeward Islands were used concurrently.

12 Pence = 1 Shilling
20 Shillings = 1 Pound
100 Cents = 1 Dollar (1951)

Catalogue values for unused stamps in this country are for Never Hinged items, beginning with Scott 96.

Watermark

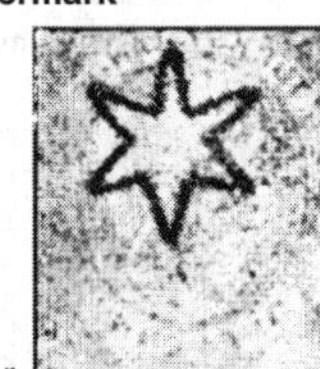

Wmk. 5- Star

Values for unused stamps are for examples with original gum as defined in the catalogue introduction. Any exceptions will be noted. Very fine examples of Nos. 1-8, 11, 18-20 will have perforations touching at least one frameline due to the narrow spacing of the stamps on the plates. Stamps with perfs clear of the framelines on all four sides are extremely scarce and will command higher prices.

Queen Victoria
A1 A2

Rough Perf. 14-16

1862 Engr. Unwmk.

1	A1	6p blue green	900.	575.
a.		Perf. 11-13	*5,000.*	
b.		Perf. 11-13x14-16	*2,750.*	
c.		Perf. 11-13 compound with 14-16	*3,000.*	

There is a question whether Nos. 1a-1c ever did postal duty.

Values for No. 1 are for stamps with perfs. cutting into the design. Values for No. 1b are for copies without gum.

1863-67 Wmk. 5

2	A1	1p lilac rose	110.00	32.50
a.		Vert. pair, imperf. btwn.	*15,000.*	
3	A1	1p vermilion ('67)	275.00	25.00
a.		Horiz. pair, imperf. btwn.	*16,000.*	
4	A1	6p green	400.00	27.50
a.		6p yellow green	*3,250.*	70.00
b.		Pair, imperf. between		—

1872 Wmk. 1 *Perf. 12½*

5	A1	1p lake	110.00	22.50
6	A1	1p vermilion	140.00	22.50
7	A1	6p blue green	525.00	9.00
		Nos. 5-7 (3)	775.00	54.00

1873-79 *Perf. 14*

8	A1	1p lake	110.00	11.00
a.		Half used as ½p on cover		*3,250.*

Typo.

9	A2	2½p red brown ('79)	600.00	160.00
10	A2	4p blue ('79)	275.00	16.00

Engr.

11	A1	6p blue green ('76)	325.00	13.00

1882-86 Typo. Wmk. 2

12	A2	½p green	2.50	11.00
13	A2	2½p red brown	140.00	55.00
14	A2	2½p ultra ('86)	7.00	*12.00*
15	A2	4p blue	275.00	16.00
16	A2	4p brown org ('86)	2.00	*3.00*
17	A2	1sh violet ('86)	160.00	125.00

Engr.

18	A1	1p carmine ('84)	1.75	*2.75*
19	A1	6p deep green	60.00	*125.00*

No. 18 was used for a time in St. Christopher and is identified by the "A12" cancellation.

1884 *Perf. 12*

20	A1	1p rose red	50.00	15.00

Seal of the Colony — A3

King Edward VII — A4

1903 Typo. Wmk. 1 *Perf. 14*

21	A3	½p blue grn & blk	3.50	*5.75*
a.		Bluish paper ('09)	100.00	100.00
22	A3	1p car & black	5.75	1.25
a.		Bluish paper ('09)	90.00	90.00
23	A3	2p org brn & vio	6.75	*22.50*
24	A3	2½p ultra & black	8.00	*14.00*
25	A3	3p ocher & gray green	10.50	*19.00*
26	A3	6p black & red vio	28.00	*45.00*
27	A3	1sh violet & ultra	40.00	*47.50*
28	A3	2sh pur & gray green	67.50	*85.00*
29	A3	2sh6p red vio & blk	20.00	*47.50*
30	A4	5sh pur & gray green	65.00	*90.00*
		Nos. 21-30 (10)	255.00	*377.50*

The 2½p, 1sh and 5sh exist on both ordinary and chalky paper.

1908-15 Wmk. 3

31	A3	½p green	2.50	*4.00*
32	A3	1p carmine	5.25	2.25
a.		1p scarlet ('15)	5.75	3.25
33	A3	2p org brn & dull vio ('12)	4.25	*26.00*
34	A3	2½p ultra	10.50	*14.00*
35	A3	3p ocher & grn ('12)	6.25	*18.00*
36	A3	6p blk & red vio ('11)	7.00	*37.50*
37	A3	1sh vio & ultra	14.00	*67.50*
38	A3	2sh vio & green ('12)	67.50	*80.00*
		Nos. 31-38 (8)	117.25	*249.25*

Nos. 33, 35-38 are on chalky paper.
For overprints see Nos. MR1-MR3.

George V — A6

St. John's Harbor — A7

1913

41	A6	5sh violet & green	70.00	*110.00*

1921-29 Wmk. 4

42	A7	½p green	1.90	.50
43	A7	1p rose red	1.75	.50
44	A7	1p dp violet ('23)	2.75	1.40
45	A7	1½p orange ('22)	2.75	*6.75*
46	A7	1½p rose red ('26)	4.00	1.75
47	A7	1½p fawn ('29)	2.75	.60
48	A7	2p gray	2.25	.75
49	A7	2½p ultra	3.75	*5.25*
50	A7	2½p orange ('23)	2.25	*16.00*

Chalky Paper

51	A7	3p violet, *yel* ('25)	4.00	*8.00*
52	A7	6p vio & red vio	3.00	*6.25*
53	A7	1sh black, *emer* ('29)	5.75	*7.50*
54	A7	2sh vio & ultra, *blue* ('27)	9.50	*52.50*
55	A7	2sh6p blk & red, *blue* ('27)	21.00	*25.00*
56	A7	3sh grn & vio ('22)	25.00	*80.00*
57	A7	4sh blk & red ('22)	45.00	*62.50*
		Nos. 42-57 (16)	137.40	*275.25*

Wmk. 3

Chalky Paper

58	A7	3p violet, *yel*	4.00	*10.50*
59	A7	4p black & red, *yel* ('22)	1.90	*5.25*
60	A7	1sh black, *emerald*	3.75	*7.50*
61	A7	2sh vio & ultra, *bl*	12.00	*18.00*
62	A7	2sh6p blk & red, *bl*	15.00	*47.50*
63	A7	5sh grn & red, *yel* ('22)	8.00	*45.00*
64	A7	£1 vio & black, *red* ('22)	190.00	*275.00*
		Nos. 58-64 (7)	234.65	*408.75*

Old Dockyard, English Harbour — A8

Govt. House, St. John's — A9

Nelson's "Victory," 1805 — A10

Sir Thomas Warner's Ship, 1632 — A11

Perf. 12½

1932, Jan. 27 Engr. Wmk. 4

67	A8	½p green	2.10	*6.25*
68	A8	1p scarlet	2.75	*5.25*
69	A8	1½p lt brown	3.00	*4.50*
70	A9	2p gray	3.75	*15.00*
71	A9	2½p ultra	3.75	*8.00*
72	A9	3p orange	4.00	*11.50*
73	A10	6p violet	14.00	*11.50*
74	A10	1sh olive green	18.00	*25.00*
75	A10	2sh6p claret	37.50	*47.50*
76	A11	5sh red brn & black	90.00	*110.00*
		Nos. 67-76 (10)	178.85	*244.50*

Tercentenary of the colony.

Common Design Types pictured following the introduction.

Silver Jubilee Issue
Common Design Type

1935, May 6 *Perf. 13½x14*

77	CD301	1p car & blue	1.90	2.40
78	CD301	1½p gray blk & ultra	2.75	.90
79	CD301	2½p blue & brn	6.25	*2.50*
80	CD301	1sh brt vio & ind	9.50	*12.50*
		Nos. 77-80 (4)	20.40	*18.30*
		Set, never hinged	27.50	

Coronation Issue
Common Design Type

1937, May 12 *Perf. 11x11½*

81	CD302	1p carmine	.50	*1.00*
82	CD302	1½p brown	.60	*1.00*
83	CD302	2½p deep ultra	1.25	*1.60*
		Nos. 81-83 (3)	2.35	*3.60*
		Set, never hinged	2.40	

English Harbour — A14

Nelson's Dockyard — A15

Fort James — A16

St. John's Harbor — A17

1938-48 Engr. *Perf. 12½*

84	A14	½p green	.30	*.90*
85	A15	1p red	2.50	*1.75*
86	A15	1½p brown violet	1.75	1.25
87	A14	2p dark gray	.30	*.50*
88	A15	2½p deep ultra	.50	*.75*
89	A16	3p pale orange	.45	*.80*
90	A17	6p purple	1.50	*1.00*
91	A17	1sh brown & blk	2.25	1.00
92	A16	2sh6p deep claret	15.00	7.50
93	A17	5sh grayish ol grn	10.00	6.50
94	A15	10sh red vio ('48)	11.00	*22.50*
95	A16	£1 Prus blue ('48)	17.00	*32.50*
		Nos. 84-95 (12)	62.55	*76.95*
		Set, never hinged	80.00	

See Nos. 107-113, 115-116, 118-121, 136-142, 144-145.
For overprint see Nos. 125-126.

Catalogue values for unused stamps in this section, from this point to the end of the section, are for Never Hinged items.

Peace Issue
Common Design Type

1946, Nov. 1 Wmk. 4 *Perf. 13½x14*

96	CD303	1½p brown	.25	.20
97	CD303	3p deep orange	.25	*.30*

Silver Wedding Issue
Common Design Types

1949, Jan. 3 Photo. *Perf. 14x14½*

98	CD304	2½p bright ultra	.40	*1.00*

Engraved; Name Typographed

Perf. 11½x11

99	CD305	5sh dk brown olive	8.00	7.25

UPU Issue
Common Design Types

Perf. 13½, 11x11½

1949, Oct. 10 Wmk. 4

Engr.; Name Typo. on 3p and 6p

100	CD306	2½p deep ultra	.40	*.50*
101	CD307	3p orange	1.40	*1.90*
102	CD308	6p purple	.90	*1.25*
103	CD309	1sh red brown	.90	*1.00*
		Nos. 100-103 (4)	3.60	4.65

University Issue
Common Design Types

Perf. 14x14½

1951, Feb. 16 Engr. Wmk. 4

104	CD310	3c chocolate & blk	.40	*.50*
105	CD311	12c purple & blk	.60	*.75*

Coronation Issue
Common Design Type

1953, June 2 *Perf. 13½x13*

106	CD312	2c dk green & blk	.50	*.75*

Types of 1938 with Portrait of Queen Elizabeth II

Martello Tower — A24

Perf. 13x13½, 13½x13

1953-56 Wmk. 4

No.	Type	Description	Unused	Used
107	A16	½c dk red brn ('56)	.25	*.25*
108	A14	1c gray	.25	*.50*
109	A15	2c deep green	.25	.20
110	A15	3c yellow & blk	.40	.20
111	A14	4c rose red (shades)	1.00	.20
112	A15	5c dull vio & blk	2.10	.35
113	A16	6c orange	1.60	.20
114	A24	8c deep blue	1.90	.20
115	A17	12c violet	1.90	.20
116	A17	24c chocolate & blk	2.10	.20
117	A24	48c dp bl & rose lil	5.75	2.25
118	A16	60c claret	6.25	.65
119	A17	$1.20 olive green	2.00	.60
120	A15	$2.40 magenta	9.25	*10.00*
121	A16	$4.80 greenish blue	12.50	*19.00*
		Nos. 107-121 (15)	47.50	*35.00*

See #143. For overprint see #125-126.

West Indies Federation

Common Design Type

Perf. 11½x11

1958, Apr. 22 Engr. Wmk. 314

No.	Type	Description	Unused	Used
122	CD313	3c green	.90	.25
123	CD313	6c blue	1.10	2.00
124	CD313	12c carmine rose	1.25	.50
		Nos. 122-124 (3)	3.25	2.75

Nos. 110 and 115 Overprinted in Red or Black: "Commemoration Antigua Constitution 1960"

Perf. 13x13½, 13½x13

1960, Jan. 1 Wmk. 4

No.	Type	Description	Unused	Used
125	A15	3c yellow & black	.20	.20
126	A17	12c violet (Blk)	.20	.20

Constitutional reforms effective Jan. 1, 1960.

Lord Nelson and Nelson's Dockyard A26

Perf. 11½x11

1961, Nov. 14 Wmk. 314

No.	Type	Description	Unused	Used
127	A26	20c brown & lilac	.90	.90
128	A26	30c dk blue & green	1.10	1.10

Completion of the restoration of Lord Nelson's headquarters, English Harbour.

Stamp of 1862 and Royal Mail Steam Packet in English Harbour A27

1962, Aug. 1 Engr. *Perf. 13*

No.	Type	Description	Unused	Used
129	A27	3c dull green & pur	.50	.20
130	A27	10c dull green & ultra	.60	.20
131	A27	12c dull green & blk	.65	.20
132	A27	50c dull grn & brn org	1.25	1.10
		Nos. 129-132 (4)	3.00	1.70

Centenary of first Antigua postage stamp.

Freedom from Hunger Issue

Common Design Type

Perf. 14x14½

1963, June 4 Photo. Wmk. 314

No.	Type	Description	Unused	Used
133	CD314	12c green	.30	.30

Red Cross Centenary Issue

Common Design Type

1963, Sept. 2 Litho. *Perf. 13*

No.	Type	Description	Unused	Used
134	CD315	3c black & red	.20	.25
135	CD315	12c ultra & red	.80	1.25

Types of 1938-53 with Portrait of Queen Elizabeth II

Perf. 13x13½, 13½x13

1963-65 Engr. Wmk. 314

No.	Type	Description	Unused	Used
136	A16	½c brown ('65)	1.40	.30
137	A14	1c gray ('65)	.90	.30
138	A15	2c deep green	.55	.20
139	A15	3c orange yel & blk	.40	.20
140	A14	4c brown red	.25	.35
141	A15	5c dull vio & black	.20	.35
142	A16	6c orange	.55	.40
143	A24	8c deep blue	.25	.45
144	A17	12c violet	.30	.50
145	A17	24c choc & black	3.50	.75
		Nos. 136-145 (10)	8.30	3.80

For surcharge see No. 152.

Shakespeare Issue

Common Design Type

Perf. 14x14½

1964, Apr. 23 Photo. Wmk. 314

No.	Type	Description	Unused	Used
151	CD316	12c red brown	.35	.20

No. 144 Surcharged with New Value and Bars

Perf. 13½x13

1965, Apr. 1 Engr. Wmk. 314

No.	Type	Description	Unused	Used
152	A17	15c on 12c violet	.25	.25

ITU Issue

Common Design Type

Perf. 11x11½

1965, May 17 Litho. Wmk. 314

No.	Type	Description	Unused	Used
153	CD317	2c blue & ver	.20	.20
154	CD317	50c orange & vio bl	1.40	1.10

Intl. Cooperation Year Issue

Common Design Type

1965, Oct. 25 *Perf. 14½*

No.	Type	Description	Unused	Used
155	CD318	4c blue grn & claret	.20	.20
156	CD318	15c lt vio & green	.40	.25

Churchill Memorial Issue

Common Design Type

1966, Jan. 24 Photo. *Perf. 14*

Design in Black, Gold and Carmine Rose

No.	Type	Description	Unused	Used
157	CD319	½c bright blue	.20	*1.25*
158	CD319	4c green	.25	.20
159	CD319	25c brown	.75	.30
160	CD319	35c violet	.85	.40
		Nos. 157-160 (4)	2.05	2.15

Royal Visit Issue

Common Design Type

1966, Feb. 4 Litho. *Perf. 11x12*

Portraits in Black

No.	Type	Description	Unused	Used
161	CD320	6c violet blue	1.25	.90
162	CD320	15c dark car rose	2.00	1.10

World Cup Soccer Issue

Common Design Type

1966, July 1 Wmk. 314 *Perf. 14*

No.	Type	Description	Unused	Used
163	CD321	6c multicolored	.20	.25
164	CD321	35c multicolored	.65	.25

WHO Headquarters Issue

Common Design Type

1966, Sept. 20 *Perf. 14*

No.	Type	Description	Unused	Used
165	CD322	2c multicolored	.20	.20
166	CD322	15c multicolored	.70	.35

Nelson's Dockyard A35

Designs: 1c, Old post office, St. John's. 2c, Health Center. 3c, Teachers' Training College. 4c, Martello Tower, Barbuda. 5c, Ruins of officers quarters, Shirley Heights. 6c, Government House, Barbuda. 10c, Princess Margaret School. 15c, Air terminal. 25c, General post office. 35c, Clarence House. 50c, Government House. 75c, Administration building. $1, Court House, St. John's. $2.50, Magistrates' Court. $5, St. John's Cathedral.

Perf. 11½x11

1966, Nov. 1 Engr. Wmk. 314

No.	Type	Description	Unused	Used
167	A35	½c green & blue	.20	.20
168	A35	1c purple & rose	.20	.25
169	A35	2c slate & org	.20	.25
170	A35	3c rose red & blk	.20	.25
171	A35	4c dull vio & brn	.20	.20
172	A35	5c vio bl & olive	.20	.20
a.		Booklet pane of 4 ('68)	.40	
173	A35	6c dp org & pur	.20	.20
174	A35	10c brt grn & rose red	.20	.20
a.		Booklet pane of 4 ('68)	1.00	
175	A35	15c brn & blue	1.00	.20
a.		Booklet pane of 4 ('68)	1.25	
176	A35	25c slate & brn	.50	.20
177	A35	35c dp rose & sep	1.00	.60
178	A35	50c green & black	.90	1.50
179	A35	75c Prus bl & vio blue	1.25	1.75
180	A35	$1 dp rose & olive	4.50	2.00
181	A35	$2.50 black & rose	3.75	5.50
182	A35	$5 ol grn & dl vio	5.50	6.50
		Nos. 167-182 (16)	20.00	20.00

For surcharge see No. 231.

1969 *Perf. 13½*

No.	Type	Description	Unused	Used
167a	A35	½c	.20	*.40*
168a	A35	1c	.20	*.50*
169a	A35	2c	.20	*.30*
170a	A35	3c	.20	.20
171a	A35	4c	.20	.20
172b	A35	5c	.20	.20
173a	A35	6c	.20	*.50*
174b	A35	10c	.20	.20
175b	A35	15c	.30	.30
176a	A35	25c	.50	.20
177a	A35	35c	.60	*.75*
178a	A35	50c	.95	*2.00*
180a	A35	$1	2.00	*3.00*
181a	A35	$2.50	5.50	*6.00*
182a	A35	$5	19.00	*24.00*
		Nos. 167a-182a (15)	30.45	*38.75*

The ½c, 3c, 6c are on ordinary paper. The 15c through $5 on glazed paper. The others exist on both papers.

UNESCO Anniversary Issue

Common Design Type

1966, Dec. 1 Litho. *Perf. 14*

No.	Type	Description	Unused	Used
183	CD323	4c "Education"	.20	.20
184	CD323	25c "Science"	.40	.20
185	CD323	$1 "Culture"	1.40	*2.00*
		Nos. 183-185 (3)	2.00	*2.40*

Independent State

Flag of Antigua, Spiny Lobster, Maps of Antigua and Barbuda A37

Designs: 15c, 35c, Flag of Antigua. 25c, Flag and Premier's Office Building.

1967, Feb. 27 Photo. *Perf. 14*

No.	Type	Description	Unused	Used
186	A37	4c multicolored	.20	.20
187	A37	15c multicolored	.20	.20
188	A37	25c multicolored	.20	*.20*
189	A37	35c multicolored	.20	*.20*
		Nos. 186-189 (4)	.80	*.80*

Antigua's independence, Feb. 27, 1967.

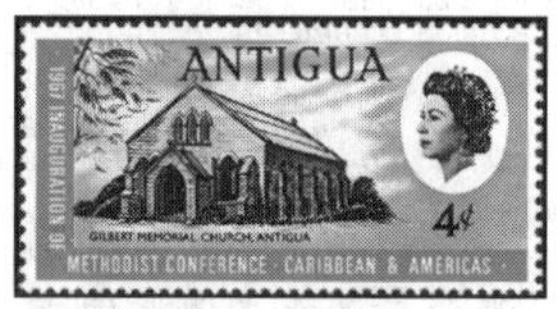
Gilbert Memorial Church, Antigua — A38

25c, Nathaniel Gilbert's House. 35c, Map of the Caribbean and Central America.

Perf. 14x13½

1967, May 18 Photo. Wmk. 314

No.	Type	Description	Unused	Used
190	A38	4c brt red & black	.20	.20
191	A38	25c emerald & black	.20	.20
192	A38	35c ultra & black	.20	.20
		Nos. 190-192 (3)	.60	.60

Attainment of autonomy by the Methodist Church in the Caribbean and the Americas, and the opening of headquarters near St. John's, Antigua, May 1967.

Antiguan and British Royal Arms — A39

1967, July 21 *Perf. 14½x14*

No.	Type	Description	Unused	Used
193	A39	15c dark green & multi	.20	.20
194	A39	35c deep blue & multi	.20	.20

Granting of a new coat of arms to the State of Antigua; 300th anniv. of the Treaty of Breda.

Sailing Ship, 17th Century A40

Design: 6c, 35c, Map of Barbuda from Jan Blaeu's Atlas, 1665.

Perf. 11½x11

1967, Dec. 14 Engr. Wmk. 314

No.	Type	Description	Unused	Used
195	A40	4c dark blue	.20	.20
196	A40	6c deep plum	.20	*.75*
197	A40	25c green	.30	.20
198	A40	35c black	.40	.30
		Nos. 195-198 (4)	1.10	*1.45*

Resettlement of Barbuda, 300th anniv.

Dow Hill Antenna — A41

Designs: 15c, Antenna and rocket blasting off. 25c, Nose cone orbiting moon. 50c, Reentry of space capsule.

Perf. 14½x14

1968, Mar. 29 Photo. Wmk. 314

No.	Type	Description	Unused	Used
199	A41	4c dk blue, org & black	.20	.20
200	A41	15c dk blue, org & black	.20	.20
201	A41	25c dk blue, org & black	.20	.20
202	A41	50c dk blue, org & black	.20	.20
		Nos. 199-202 (4)	.80	.80

Dedication of the Dow Hill tracking station in Antigua for the NASA Apollo project.

Beach and Sailfish A42

Designs: ½c, 50c, Limbo dancer, flames and dancing girls. 15c, Three girls on a beach and water skier. 35c, Woman scuba diver, corals and fish.

1968, July 1 Photo. *Perf. 14*

No.	Type	Description	Unused	Used
203	A42	½c red & multi	.20	.20
204	A42	15c sky blue & multi	.20	.20
205	A42	25c blue & multi	.30	.20
206	A42	35c brt blue & multi	.30	.20
207	A42	50c multicolored	.50	*.90*
		Nos. 203-207 (5)	1.50	*1.70*

Issued for tourist publicity.

St. John's Harbor, 1768 A43

St. John's Harbor: 15c, 1829. 25c, Map of deep-sea harbor, 1968. 35c, Dock, 1968. 2c, Like $1.

Engr. & Litho.; Engr. ($1)

1968, Oct. 31 Wmk. 314 *Perf. 13*

208 A43 2c dp car & lt blue .20 *.30*
209 A43 15c sepia & yel grn .35 .20
210 A43 25c dk blue & yel .40 .20
211 A43 35c dp green & sal .50 .20
212 A43 $1 black .90 *1.25*
Nos. 208-212 (5) 2.35 *2.15*

Opening of St. John's deep-sea harbor.

Mace and Parliament A44

Mace and: 15c, Mace bearer. 25c, House of Representatives, interior. 50c, Antigua coat of arms and great seal.

1969, Feb. 3 Photo. *Perf. 12½*

213 A44 4c crimson & multi .20 .20
214 A44 15c crimson & multi .20 .20
215 A44 25c crimson & multi .25 .20
216 A44 50c crimson & multi .35 *1.00*
Nos. 213-216 (4) 1.00 *1.60*

300th anniversary of Antigua Parliament.

CARIFTA Cargo — A45

4c, 15c, Ship, plane and trucks, horiz.

Perf. 13½x13, 13x13½

1969, Apr. 14 Litho. Wmk. 314

217 A45 4c blk & brt lilac rose .20 .20
218 A45 15c blk & brt grnsh blue .20 .20
219 A45 25c bister & black .20 .20
220 A45 35c tan & black .20 .25
Nos. 217-220 (4) .80 .85

1st anniv. of CARIFTA (Caribbean Free Trade Area).

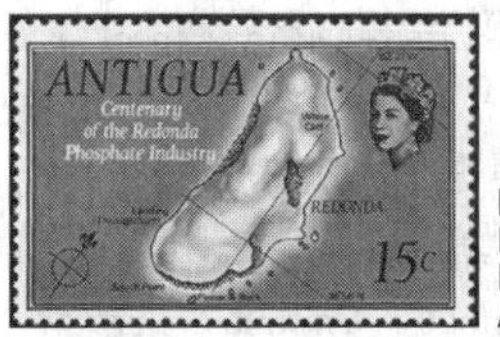

Map of Redonda Island A46

25c, View of Redonda from the sea & seagulls.

1969, Aug. 1 Photo. *Perf. 13x13½*

221 A46 15c ultra & multi .25 .20
222 A46 25c multicolored .25 .20
223 A46 50c salmon & multi .50 *.50*
Nos. 221-223 (3) 1.00 *.90*

Centenary of Redonda phosphate industry.

Adoration of the Kings, by Gugliemo Marcillat A47

Christmas: 10c, 50c, Holy Family, by anonymous German artist, 15th century.

1969, Oct. 15 Litho. *Perf. 13x14*

224 A47 6c bister brn & multi .20 .20
225 A47 10c fawn & multi .20 .20
226 A47 35c gray olive & multi .20 .20
227 A47 50c gray blue & multi .30 .20
Nos. 224-227 (4) .90 .80

Arms of Antigua — A48

Coil Stamps

Perf. 14½x14

1970, Jan. 30 Photo. Wmk. 314

228 A48 5c bright blue .20 .20
a. Wmk. 373 ('77) 7.00
229 A48 10c bright green .20 .20
a. Wmk. 373, invtd. ('77) .80
230 A48 25c deep magenta .45 .20
a. Wmk. 373 ('77) 12.50
Nos. 228-230 (3) .85 .60

No. 176 Surcharged

1970, Jan. 2 Engr. *Perf. 11½x11*

231 A35 20c on 25c slate & brown .25 .20

Sikorsky S-38 A49

Aircraft: 20c, Dornier DO-X. 35c, Hawker Siddeley 748. 50c, Douglas C-124C Globemaster II. 75c, Vickers VC 10.

1970, Feb. 16 Litho. *Perf. 14½*

232 A49 5c brt green & multi .40 .20
233 A49 20c ultra & multi 1.00 .20
234 A49 35c blue grn & multi 1.25 .20
235 A49 50c blue & multi 1.40 1.00
236 A49 75c vio blue & multi 1.50 1.75
Nos. 232-236 (5) 5.55 3.35

40th anniversary of air service.

Dickens and Scene from "Pickwick Papers" A50

Charles Dickens (1812-1870), English novelist and Scene from: 5c, "Nicholas Nickleby." 35c, "Oliver Twist." $1, "David Copperfield."

Wmk. 314

1970, May 19 Litho. *Perf. 14*

237 A50 5c olive & sepia .20 .20
238 A50 20c aqua & sepia .25 .20
239 A50 35c violet & sepia .30 .20
240 A50 $1 scarlet & sepia .75 .50
Nos. 237-240 (4) 1.50 1.10

Carib Indian and War Canoe A51

Ships: 1c, Columbus and "Nina." 2c, Sir Thomas Warner's arms and sailing ship. 3c, Viscount Hood and "Barfleur." 4c, Sir George Rodney and "Formidable." 5c, Capt. Horatio Nelson and "Boreas." 6c, King William IV and "Pegasus." 10c, Blackbeard (Edward Teach) and pirate ketch. 15c, Capt. Cuthbert Collingwood and "Pelican." 20c, Admiral Nelson and "Victoria." 25c, Paddle steamer "Solent" and Steam Packet Company emblem. 35c, King George V and corvette "Canada." 50c, Cruiser "Renown" and royal badge. 75c, S.S. "Federal Maple" and maple leaf. $1, Racing yacht "Sol-Quest" and Gallant 53 class emblem. $2.50, Missile destroyer "London" and her emblem. $5, Tug "Pathfinder" and arms of Antigua.

Wmk. 314 Sideways

1970, Aug. 19 Litho. *Perf. 14*

241 A51 ½c ocher & multi .20 *.55*
242 A51 1c Prus bl & multi .25 *.65*
243 A51 2c yel grn & multi .30 *1.25*
244 A51 3c ol bis & multi .30 *1.00*
245 A51 4c bl gray & multi .30 *1.25*
246 A51 5c fawn & multi .40 .35
247 A51 6c rose lil & multi .55 *1.40*
248 A51 10c brn org & multi .60 .20
249 A51 15c ultra & multi 3.00 .80
250 A51 20c ol grn & multi 1.00 .30
251 A51 25c olive & multi 1.00 .30
252 A51 35c dull red brn & multi 1.40 .65
253 A51 50c lt brn & multi 3.75 2.75
254 A51 75c beige & multi 5.50 *4.50*
255 A51 $1 Prus green & multi 5.50 1.60
256 A51 $2.50 gray & multi 5.50 *6.00*
257 A51 $5 yel & multi 5.50 *6.25*
Nos. 241-257 (17) 35.05 *29.80*

1972-74 Wmk. 314 Upright

241a A51 ½c .20 .25
242a A51 1c .20 .50
244a A51 3c .20 .40
245a A51 4c .20 1.00
246a A51 5c .20 .20
247a A51 6c .20 1.50
248a A51 10c .20 .20
249a A51 15c 1.60 .50
254a A51 75c 3.25 2.00
255a A51 $1 3.50 1.60
256a A51 $2.50 6.00 *7.50*
257a A51 $5 6.75 *10.50*
Nos. 241a-257a (12) 22.50 *26.15*

For surcharge see No. 368.

1975, Jan. 21 Wmk. 373

257b A51 $5 yellow & multi 5.00 *11.00*

Nativity, by Albrecht Dürer — A52

Private, 4th West India Regiment, 1804 — A53

Christmas: 10c, 50c, Adoration of the Magi, by Albrecht Dürer.

Engr. & Litho.

1970, Oct. 28 *Perf. 13½x14*

258 A52 3c brt grnsh blue & blk .20 .20
259 A52 10c pink & plum .20 .20
260 A52 35c brick red & black .25 .20
261 A52 50c lilac & violet .35 .25
Nos. 258-261 (4) 1.00 .85

Perf. 14x13½

1970, Dec. 1 Litho. Wmk. 314

Military Uniforms: ½c, Drummer Boy, 4th King's Own Regiment, 1759. 20c, Grenadier Company Officer, 60th Regiment, The Royal American, 1809. 35c, Light Company Officer, 93rd Regiment, The Sutherland Highlanders, 1826-1834. 75c, Private, 3rd West India Regiment, 1851.

262 A53 ½c lake & multi .20 .20
263 A53 10c brn org & multi .40 .20
264 A53 20c Prus grn & multi 1.00 .20
265 A53 35c dl pur & multi 1.25 .20
266 A53 75c dk ol grn & multi 3.00 2.00
a. Souv. sheet, #262-266 + label 8.00 *9.00*
Nos. 262-266 (5) 5.85 2.80

See #274-278, 283-287, 307-311, 329-333.

Market Woman Voting — A54

Voting by: 20c, Businessman. 35c, Mother (and child). 50c, Workman.

Perf. 14½x14

1971, Feb. 1 Photo. Wmk. 314

267 A54 5c brown .20 .20
268 A54 20c olive black .20 .20
269 A54 35c rose magenta .20 .20
270 A54 50c violet blue .20 .20
Nos. 267-270 (4) .80 .80

Adult suffrage, 20th anniversary.

Last Supper, from The Small Passion, by Dürer — A55

Woodcuts by Albrecht Dürer: 35c, Crucifixion from Eichstaff Missal. 75c, Resurrection from The Great Passion.

Perf. 14x13½

1971, Apr. 7 Litho. Wmk. 314

271 A55 5c gray, red & black .20 .20
272 A55 35c gray, violet & black .20 .20
273 A55 75c gray, gold & black .20 .20
Nos. 271-273 (3) .60 .60

Easter.

Military Uniform Type of 1970

Military Uniforms: ½c, Private, Suffolk Regiment, 1704. 10c, Grenadier, South Staffordshire, 1751. 20c, Fusilier, Royal Northumberland, 1778. 35c, Private, Northamptonshire. 1793, 75c, Private, East Yorkshire, 1805.

1971, July 12 Litho. Wmk. 314

274 A53 ½c gray grn & multi .20 .20
275 A53 10c bluish blk & multi .40 .25
276 A53 20c dk pur & multi .80 .30
277 A53 35c dk ol & multi 1.40 .35
278 A53 75c brown & multi 2.75 3.25
a. Souv. sheet, #274-278 + label 6.75 *7.50*
Nos. 274-278 (5) 5.55 4.35

Virgin and Child, by Veronese — A56

Christmas: 5c, 50c, Adoration of the Shepherds, by Bonifazio Veronese.

1971, Oct. 4 *Perf. 14x13½*

279 A56 3c multicolored .20 .20
280 A56 5c multicolored .20 .20
281 A56 35c multicolored .25 .20
282 A56 50c multicolored .45 .30
Nos. 279-282 (4) 1.10 .90

Uniform Type of 1970

Military Uniforms: ½c, Officer, King's Own Borderers Regiment, 1815. 10c, Sergeant, Buckinghamshire Regiment, 1837. 20c, Private, South Hampshire Regiment, 1853. 35c, Officer, Royal Artillery, 1854. 75c, Private, Worcestershire Regiment, 1870.

1972, July 1

283 A53 ½c ol brn & multi .20 .20
284 A53 10c dp grn & multi .35 .20
285 A53 20c brt vio & multi .70 .25
286 A53 35c mar & multi 1.25 .35
287 A53 75c dk vio bl & multi 2.50 *3.00*
a. Souvenir sheet of 5, #283-287 + label 7.50 *8.50*
Nos. 283-287 (5) 5.00 *4.00*

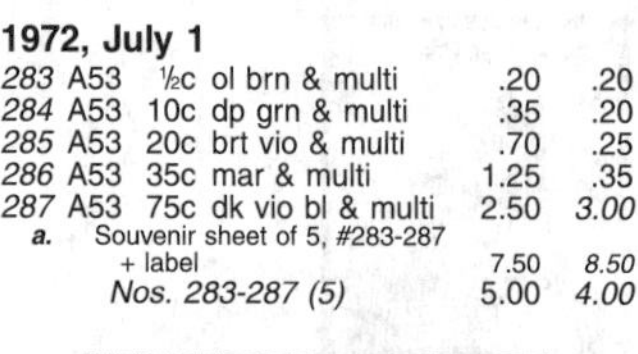

Reticulated Helmet Cowrie — A57

Sea Shells: 5c, Measled cowrie. 35c, West Indian fighting conch. 50c, Hawkwing conch.

1972, Aug. 1 ***Perf. 14½x14***

288 A57 3c multicolored .20 .20
289 A57 5c ver & multi .35 .20
290 A57 35c lt vio & multi 1.25 .25
291 A57 50c rose red & multi 2.00 *2.50*
Nos. 288-291 (4) 3.80 *3.15*

St. John's Cathedral, 1745-1843 — A58

Christmas: 50c, Interior of St. John's. 75c, St. John's rebuilt.

1972, Nov. 6 Litho. ***Perf. 14***

292 A58 35c org brn & multi .20 .20
293 A58 50c vio & multi .30 .30
294 A58 75c multicolored .50 *.50*
a. Souv. sheet, #292-294, perf 15 1.00 *1.25*
Nos. 292-294 (3) 1.00 *1.00*

Silver Wedding Issue, 1972

Common Design Type

1972, Nov. 20 Photo. ***Perf. 14x14½***

295 CD324 20c ultra & multi .20 .20
296 CD324 35c steel blue & multi .20 .20

Map of Antigua, Batsman Driving Ball — A60

Designs: 35c, Batsman and wicketkeeper. $1, Emblem of Rising Sun Cricket Club.

1972, Dec. 15 ***Perf. 13½x14***

297 A60 5c multicolored .25 .25
298 A60 35c multicolored 1.10 .50
299 A60 $1 multicolored 2.75 *3.25*
a. Souvenir sheet of 3, #297-299 5.50 *6.50*
Nos. 297-299 (3) 4.10 *4.00*

Rising Sun Cricket Club, St. John's, 50th anniv.

Map of Antigua and Yacht — A61

1972, Dec. 29 ***Perf. 14½***

300 A61 35c shown .20 .20
301 A61 50c Racing yachts .20 .20
302 A61 75c St. John's G.P.O. .30 .25
303 A61 $1 Statue of Liberty .30 .25
a. Souvenir sheet of 2, #301, 303 1.50 *1.50*
Nos. 300-303 (4) 1.00 .90

Opening of Antigua and Barbuda Information Office in New York City.

Window with Episcopal Coat of Arms — A62

Stained glass windows from Cathedral of St. John: 35c, Crucifixion. 75c, Arm of Rt. Rev. D.G. Davis, 1st bishop of Antigua.

1973, Apr. 16 Litho. ***Perf. 13½***

304 A62 5c yellow & multi .20 .20
305 A62 35c brt lilac & multi .20 .20
306 A62 75c blue & multi .30 .20
Nos. 304-306 (3) .70 .60

Easter.

Uniform Type of 1970

Military Uniforms: ½c, Private, Col. Zacharia Tiffin's Regiment, 1701. 10c, Private, 63rd Regiment, 1759. 20c, Officer, 35th Sussex Regiment, 1828. 35c, Private, 2nd West India Regiment, 1853. 75c, Sergeant, Princess of Wales Regiment, Hertfordshire, 1858.

Perf. 14x13½

1973, July 1 Wmk. 314

307 A53 ½c dp ultra & multi .20 .20
308 A53 10c rose lilac & multi .20 .20
309 A53 20c gray & multi .40 .25
310 A53 35c multicolored .60 .25
311 A53 75c multicolored 1.60 1.10
a. Souv. sheet, #307-311 + label 3.50 3.00
Nos. 307-311 (5) 3.00 2.00

Butterfly Costumes — A63

Designs: 20c, Carnival revelers. 35c, Costumed group. 75c, Carnival Queen.

Perf. 13½x14

1973, July 30 Unwmk.

312 A63 5c multicolored .20 .20
313 A63 20c multicolored .20 .20
314 A63 35c multicolored .20 .20
315 A63 75c multicolored .25 .20
a. Souvenir sheet of 4, #312-315 1.10 *1.25*
Nos. 312-315 (4) .85 .80

Carnival, July 29-Aug. 7.

Virgin of the Porridge, by David — A64

Christmas: 5c, Adoration of the Kings, by Stomer. 20c, Virgin of the Grand Duke, by Raphael. 35c, Nativity with God the Father and Holy Ghost, by Tiepolo. $1, Madonna and Child, by Murillo.

Perf. 14½

1973, Oct. 15 Photo. Unwmk.

316 A64 3c brt blue & multi .20 .20
317 A64 5c emerald & multi .20 .20
318 A64 20c gold & multi .20 .20
319 A64 35c violet & multi .25 .20
320 A64 $1 red & multi .40 .40
a. Souvenir sheet of 5, #316-320 1.75 *2.00*
Nos. 316-320 (5) 1.25 1.20

Princess Anne and Mark Phillips — A65

Design: $2, different border.

1973, Nov. 14 Litho. ***Perf. 13½***

321 A65 35c dull ultra & multi .20 .20
322 A65 $2 yel grn & multi .25 .25
a. Souvenir sheet of 2, #321-322 .75 .75

Wedding of Princess Anne and Capt. Mark Phillips.

Nos. 321-322 were issued in sheets of 5 plus label.

Nos. 321-322 and 322a Overprinted Vertically: "HONEYMOON / VISIT / DECEMBER 16th / 1973"

1973, Dec. 15 Litho. ***Perf. 13½***

323 A65 35c multicolored .20 .20
324 A65 $2 multicolored .50 .50
a. Souvenir sheet of 2, #323-324 .75 .75

Visit of Princess Anne and Mark Phillips to Antigua, Dec. 16. Same overprint in sheet margins of Nos. 323-324 and 324a.

Overprint lithographed. Also exists typographed.

Arms of Antigua and U.W.I. — A66

Designs: 20c, Dancers. 35c, Antigua campus. 75c, Chancellor Sir Hugh Wooding.

1974, Feb. 18 Wmk. 314

325 A66 5c multicolored .20 .20
326 A66 20c multicolored .20 .20
327 A66 35c multicolored .20 .20
328 A66 75c multicolored .20 .20
Nos. 325-328 (4) .80 .80

University of the West Indies, 24th anniv.

Uniform Type of 1970

Military Uniforms: ½c, Officer, 59th Foot, 1797. 10c, Gunner, Royal Artillery, 1800. 20c, Private, 1st West India Regiment, 1830. 35c, Officer, Gordon Highlanders, 1843. 75c, Private, Royal Welsh Fusiliers, 1846.

1974, May 1 ***Perf. 14x13½***

329 A53 ½c dull grn & multi .20 .20
330 A53 10c ocher & multi .40 .20
331 A53 20c multicolored .65 .20
332 A53 35c gray bl & multi .80 .20
333 A53 75c dk gray & multi 1.25 1.50
a. Souvenir sheet of 5, #329-333 3.00 2.50
Nos. 329-333 (5) 3.30 2.30

English Mailman and Coach, Helicopter — A67

UPU, Cent.: 1c, English bellman, 1846; Orinoco mailboat, 1851; telecommunications satellite. 2c, English mailtrain guard, 1852; Swiss post passenger bus, 1906; Italian hydrofoil. 5c, Swiss messenger, 16th century; Wells Fargo coach, 1800; Concorde. 20c, German position, 1820; Japanese mailmen, 19th century; carrier pigeon. 35c, Contemporary Antiguan mailman; radar station; aquaplane. $1, Medieval French courier; American train, 1884; British Airways jet.

1974, July 15 Litho. ***Perf. 14½***

334 A67 ½c multicolored .20 .20
335 A67 1c multicolored .20 .20
336 A67 2c multicolored .20 .20
337 A67 5c multicolored .20 .20
338 A67 20c multicolored .30 .20
339 A67 35c multicolored .65 .25
340 A67 $1 multicolored 1.75 1.50
a. Souvenir sheet of 7, #334-340 + label, perf. 13 4.50 3.50
Nos. 334-340 (7) 3.50 2.75

For surcharges see Nos. 365-367.

Traditional Steel Band — A68

Carnival 1974 (Steel Bands): 5c, Traditional players, vert. 35c, Modern steel band. 75c, Modern players, vert.

1974, Aug. 1, Wmk. 314 ***Perf. 14***

341 A68 5c rose red, dk red & blk .20 .20
342 A68 20c ocher, brn & blk .20 .20
343 A68 35c yel grn, grn & blk .20 .20
344 A68 75c dl bl, dk bl & blk .20 *.50*
a. Souvenir sheet of 4, #341-344 .75 .75
Nos. 341-344 (4) .80 *1.10*

Soccer — A69

Designs: Games' emblem and soccer.

1974, Sept. 23 Unwmk. ***Perf. 14½***

345 A69 5c multicolored .20 .20
346 A69 35c multicolored .20 .20
347 A69 75c multicolored .25 .25
348 A69 $1 multicolored .35 .35
a. Souvenir sheet of 4 1.25 1.25
Nos. 345-348 (4) 1.00 1.00

World Cup Soccer Championship, Munich, June 13-July 7. Nos. 345-348 issued in sheets of 5 plus label showing Soccer Cup. No. 348a contains one each of Nos. 345-348, perf. 13½, and 2 labels.

For overprints and surcharges see Nos. 361-364.

Winston Churchill (1874-1965) at Harrow — A70

Designs: 35c, St. Paul's during bombing and Churchill portrait. 75c, Churchill's coat of arms and catafalque. $1, Churchill during Boer war, warrant for arrest and map of his escape route.

1974, Oct. 20 Unwmk. ***Perf. 14½***

349 A70 5c multicolored .20 .20
350 A70 35c multicolored .20 .20
351 A70 75c multicolored .25 *.30*
352 A70 $1 multicolored .35 *.50*
a. Souvenir sheet of 4, #349-352 1.25 *1.75*
Nos. 349-352 (4) 1.00 *1.20*

Virgin and Child, by Giovanni Bellini — A71

Christmas: Paintings of the Virgin and Child.

1974, Nov. 18 Litho. ***Perf. 14½***

353 A71 ½c shown .20 .20
354 A71 1c Raphael .20 .20
355 A71 2c Van der Weyden .20 .20
356 A71 3c Giorgione .20 .20
357 A71 5c Andrea Mantegna .20 .20
358 A71 20c Alvise Vivarini .20 .20

359 A71 35c Bartolommeo Montagna .25 .20
360 A71 75c Lorenzo Costa .35 *.60*
a. Souv. sheet, #357-360, perf 13½ 1.25 *1.50*
Nos. 353-360 (8) 1.80 2.00

Nos. 346-348 Overprinted and No. 344 Surcharged and Overprinted: "EARTHQUAKE / RELIEF"

1974, Oct. 16 Litho. *Perf. 14½, 14*

361 A69 35c multicolored .30 .20
362 A69 75c multicolored .40 .25
363 A69 $1 multicolored .55 .35
364 A68 $5 on 75c multi 1.75 1.75
Nos. 361-364 (4) 3.00 2.55

Earthquake of Oct. 8, 1974.

Nos. 338-340 and 254a Surcharged with New Value and Two Bars

1974-75 Wmk. 314 *Perf. 14½*

365 A67 50c on 20c 1.25 *1.25*
366 A67 $2.50 on 35c 2.75 *3.75*
367 A67 $5 on $1 5.75 *5.25*

Perf. 14

368 A51 $10 on 75c 4.25 5.75
Nos. 365-368 (4) 14.00 *16.00*

Carib War Canoe, English Harbour A72

Designs (Nelson's Dockyard): 15c, Raising ship, 1770. 35c, Lord Nelson and "Boreas." 50c, Yachts arriving for Sailing Week, 1974. $1, "Anchorage" in Old Dockyard, 1970.

1975, Mar. 17 Unwmk. *Perf. 14½*

369 A72 5c multicolored .25 .20
370 A72 15c multicolored .75 .20
371 A72 35c multicolored 1.25 .25
372 A72 50c multicolored 1.25 1.00
373 A72 $1 multicolored 1.75 1.75
Nos. 369-373 (5) 5.25 3.40

Souvenir Sheet

Perf. 13½

373A A72 Sheet of 5, #369-373 4.00 3.00

Stamps in No. 373A are 43x28mm.

Lady of the Valley Church A73

Churches of Antigua: 20c, Gilbert Memorial. 35c, Grace Hill Moravian. 50c, St. Phillip's. $1, Ebenezer Methodist.

1975, May 19 Litho. *Perf. 14½*

374 A73 5c multicolored .20 .20
375 A73 20c multicolored .20 .20
376 A73 35c multicolored .20 .20
377 A73 50c multicolored .20 .20
378 A73 $1 multicolored .20 *.20*
a. Souvenir sheet of 3, #376-378, perf. 13½ 1.00 *1.50*
Nos. 374-378 (5) 1.00 1.00

Antigua, Senex's Atlas, 1721, and Hevelius Sextant, 1640 A74

Maps of Antigua: 20c, Jeffery's Atlas, 1775, and 18th century engraving of ship. 35c, Barbuda and Antigua, 1775 and 1975. $1, St. John's and English Harbour, 1973.

1975, July 21 Wmk. 314

379 A74 5c multicolored .30 .20
380 A74 20c multicolored .60 .20
381 A74 35c multicolored .75 .20
382 A74 $1 multicolored 1.50 *1.75*
a. Souvenir sheet of 4, #379-382 3.75 2.75
Nos. 379-382 (4) 3.15 *2.35*

Bugler and Sunset A75

Nordjamb 75 Emblem and: 20c, Black and white Scouts, tents and flags. 35c, Lord Baden-Powell and tents. $2, Dahomey dancers.

Unwmk.

1975, Aug. 26 Litho. *Perf. 14*

383 A75 15c multicolored .25 .20
384 A75 20c multicolored .35 .20
385 A75 35c multicolored .50 .25
386 A75 $2 multicolored 2.50 2.00
a. Souvenir sheet of 4, #383-386 4.00 4.25
Nos. 383-386 (4) 3.60 2.65

Nordjamb 75, 14th Boy Scout Jamboree, Lillehammer, Norway, July 29-Aug. 7.

Eurema Elathea A76

Butterflies: 1c, Danaus plexippus. 2c, Phoebis philea. 5c, Marpesia petreus thetys. 20c, Eurema proterpia. 35c, Papilio polydamas. $2, Vanessa cardui.

1975, Oct. 30 Litho. *Perf. 14*

387 A76 ½c multicolored .20 .20
388 A76 1c multicolored .20 .20
389 A76 2c multicolored .20 .20
390 A76 5c multicolored .25 .20
391 A76 20c multicolored 1.00 .50
392 A76 35c multicolored 1.60 1.25
393 A76 $2 multicolored 4.75 6.00
a. Miniature sheet of 4, #390-393 9.00 10.00
Nos. 387-393 (7) 8.20 8.55

Virgin and Child, by Correggio — A77

Christmas: Virgin and Child paintings.

1975, Nov. 17 Unwmk.

394 A77 ½c shown .20 .20
395 A77 1c El Greco .20 .20
396 A77 2c Durer .20 .20
397 A77 3c Antonello .20 .20
398 A77 5c Bellini .20 .20
399 A77 10c Durer .20 .20
400 A77 35c Bellini .40 .20
401 A77 $2 Durer .75 .60
a. Souvenir sheet of 4, #398-401 2.25 2.25
Nos. 394-401 (8) 2.35 2.00

West Indies Team A78

Designs: 5c, Batsman I.V.A. Richards and cup, vert. 35c, Bowler A.M.E. Roberts and cup, vert.

1975, Dec. 15 Litho. *Perf. 14*

402 A78 5c multicolored 1.10 .20
403 A78 35c multicolored 2.10 .50
404 A78 $2 multicolored 4.00 *7.00*
Nos. 402-404 (3) 7.20 *7.70*

World Cricket Cup, victory of West Indies team.

A number of unissued items, imperfs., part perfs., missing color varieties, etc., were made available when the Format International inventory was liquidated. Imperfs of some or all of the Antigua stamps in the following sets are included: #405-422, 503-507, 515-517, 703-707, 745-749, 755-759, 808-816, 819-826, 905-909, 934-937.

See footnote after #962.

Antillean Crested Hummingbird — A79

Irrigation System, Diamond Estate — A80

Designs: 1c, Imperial parrot. 2c, Zenaida dove. 3c, Loggerhead kingbird. 4c, Red-necked pigeon. 5c, Rufous-throated solitaire. 6c, Orchid tree. 10c, Bougainvillea. 15c, Geiger tree. 20c, Flamboyant. 25c, Hibiscus. 35c, Flame of the Woods. 50c, Cannon at Fort James. 75c, Premier's Office. $1, Potworks Dam. $5, Government House. $10, Coolidge International Airport.

1976, Jan. 19 Litho. *Perf. 15*

405 A79 ½c multicolored .20 .35
406 A79 1c multicolored .20 .35
407 A79 2c multicolored .20 .35
408 A79 3c multicolored .20 .40
409 A79 4c multicolored .20 .40
410 A79 5c multicolored .20 .20
411 A79 6c multicolored .20 .40
412 A79 10c multicolored .20 .20
413 A79 15c multicolored .20 .20
414 A79 20c multicolored .20 .20
415 A79 25c multicolored .20 .20
416 A79 35c multicolored .25 .25
417 A79 50c multicolored .35 .35
418 A79 75c multicolored .50 .60
419 A79 $1 multicolored .70 .80

Perf. 13½x14

420 A80 $2.50 rose & multi 1.50 *2.50*
421 A80 $5 lilac & multi 3.25 *4.50*
422 A80 $10 multicolored 6.75 *8.00*
Nos. 405-422 (18) 15.50 *20.25*

Nos. 405-422 exist inscribed "1978."

For overprints see Nos. 607-617.

Privates, Clark's Illinois Regiment — A81

1c, Riflemen, Pennsylvania Militia. 2c, Decorated American powder horn. 5c, Water bottle of Maryland troops. 35c, "Liberty Tree" and "Rattlesnake" flags. $1, American privateer Montgomery. $2.50, Congress Flag. $5, Continental Navy sloop Ranger.

1976, Mar. 17 Litho. *Perf. 14½*

423 A81 ½c multicolored .20 .20
424 A81 1c multicolored .20 .20
425 A81 2c multicolored .20 .20
426 A81 5c multicolored .20 .20
427 A81 35c multicolored .50 .20
428 A81 $1 multicolored 1.50 .25
429 A81 $5 multicolored 3.00 3.00
Nos. 423-429 (7) 5.80 4.25

Souvenir Sheet

Perf. 13

430 A81 $2.50 multicolored 2.50 3.50

American Bicentennial.

High Jump, Olympic Rings A82

Olympic Rings and: 1c, Boxing. 2c, Pole vault. 15c, Swimming. 30c, Running. $1, Bicycling. $2, Shot put.

1976, July 12 Litho. *Perf. 14½*

431 A82 ½c yellow & multi .20 .20
432 A82 1c purple & multi .20 .20
433 A82 2c emerald & multi .20 .20
434 A82 15c brt blue & multi .20 .20
435 A82 30c olive & multi .30 .20
436 A82 $1 orange & multi .50 .25
437 A82 $2 red & multi .75 .75
a. Souvenir sheet of 4 2.00 *2.50*
Nos. 431-437 (7) 2.35 2.00

21st Olympic Games, Montreal, Canada, July 17-Aug. 1. No. 437a contains one each of Nos. 434-437, perf. 13½.

Water Skiing A83

Water Sports: 1c, Sailfish sailing. 2c, Snorkeling. 20c, Deep-sea fishing. 50c, Scuba diving. $2, Swimming.

1976, Aug. 26 *Perf. 14*

438 A83 ½c yel grn & multi .20 .20
439 A83 1c sepia & multi .20 .20
440 A83 2c gray & multi .20 .20
441 A83 20c multicolored .20 .20
442 A83 50c brt vio & multi .35 .40
443 A83 $2 lt gray & multi 1.10 1.25
a. Souvenir sheet of 3, #441-443 2.00 2.50
Nos. 438-443 (6) 2.25 2.45

French Angelfish — A84

1976, Oct. 4 Litho. *Perf. 13½x14*

444 A84 15c shown .55 .20
445 A84 30c Yellowfish grouper .80 .25
446 A84 50c Yellowtail snappers 1.00 .45
447 A84 90c Shy hamlet 1.40 .75
Nos. 444-447 (4) 3.75 1.65

The Annunciation A85

Christmas: 10c, Flight into Egypt. 15c, Three Kings. 50c, Shepherds and star. $1, Kings presenting gifts to Christ Child.

1976, Nov. 15 Litho. *Perf. 14*

448 A85 8c multicolored .20 .20
449 A85 10c multicolored .20 .20
450 A85 15c multicolored .20 .20
451 A85 50c multicolored .20 .20
452 A85 $1 multi .20 .20
Nos. 448-452 (5) 1.00 1.00

Mercury and UPU Emblem A86

Designs: 1c, Alfred Nobel, symbols of prize categories. 10c, Viking spacecraft. 50c, Vivi Richards (batsman) and Andy Roberts (bowler). $1, Alexander G. Bell, telephones, 1876 and 1976. $2, Schooner Freelance.

1976, Dec. 28 Litho. *Perf. 14*

453 A86 ½c multicolored .20 .20
454 A86 1c multicolored .20 .20
455 A86 10c multicolored .25 .20
456 A86 50c multicolored 2.50 1.25
457 A86 $1 multicolored .75 1.25
458 A86 $2 multicolored 1.75 2.50
a. Souvenir sheet of 4, #455-458 6.00 *8.00*
Nos. 453-458 (6) 5.65 5.60

Special 1976 Events: UN Postal Admin., 25th anniv. (½c); Nobel Prize, 75th anniv. (1c); Viking Space Mission to Mars (10c); World Cricket Cup victory (50c); Telephone cent. ($1); Operation Sail, American Bicent. ($2).

Royal Family — A87

Designs: 30c, Elizabeth II and Prince Philip touring Antigua. 50c, Queen enthroned. 90c, Queen wearing crown. $2.50, Queen and Prince Charles. $5, Queen and Prince Philip.

1977, Feb. 7 *Perf. 13½x14*

459 A87 10c multicolored .20 .20
460 A87 30c multicolored .20 .20
461 A87 50c multicolored .20 .20
462 A87 90c multicolored .20 .20
463 A87 $2.50 multicolored .20 .40
Nos. 459-463 (5) 1.00 1.20

Souvenir Sheet

464 A87 $5 multicolored .80 1.00

Reign of Queen Elizabeth II, 25th anniv.

Nos. 459-463 were printed in sheets of 40. Sheets of 5 plus label, perf. 12, probably were not sold by the Antigua Post Office.

A booklet of self-adhesive stamps contains one pane of six rouletted and die cut 50c stamps in design of 90c, and one pane of one die cut $5. Stamps have changed colors. Panes have marginal inscriptions.

For overprints see Nos. 477-482.

Scouts Camping A88

Boy Scout Emblem and: 1c, Scouts on hike. 2c, Rock climbing. 10c, Cutting logs. 30c, Map and compass reading. 50c, First aid. $2, Scouts on raft.

1977, May 23 Litho. *Perf. 14*

465 A88 ½c multicolored .20 .20
466 A88 1c multicolored .20 .20
467 A88 2c multicolored .20 .20
468 A88 10c multicolored .20 .20
469 A88 30c multicolored .25 .20
470 A88 50c multicolored .45 .35
471 A88 $2 multicolored 1.50 1.75
a. Souvenir sheet of 3, #469-471 2.75 2.75
Nos. 465-471 (7) 3.00 3.10

Caribbean Boy Scout Jamboree, Jamaica.

Carnival Queen Holding Horseshoe — A89

30c, Carnival Queen in feather costume. 50c, Butterfly costume. 90c, Carnival Queen with ornaments. $1, Carnival King, Queen.

1977, July 18 Litho. *Perf. 14*

472 A89 10c multicolored .20 .20
473 A89 30c multicolored .20 .20
474 A89 50c multicolored .25 .25
475 A89 90c multicolored .50 .40
476 A89 $1 multicolored .60 .55
a. Souvenir sheet of 4, #473-476 1.75 *2.25*
Nos. 472-476 (5) 1.75 1.60

21st Summer Carnival.

Nos. 459-464 Overprinted: "ROYAL VISIT / 28th OCTOBER 1977"

Perf. 13½x14, 12

1977, Oct. 17 Litho.

477 A87 10c multicolored .20 .20
478 A87 30c multicolored .20 .20
479 A87 50c multicolored .20 .20
480 A87 90c multicolored .40 .40
481 A87 $2.50 multicolored 1.25 1.00
Nos. 477-481 (5) 2.25 2.00

Souvenir Sheet

482 A87 $5 multicolored 3.00 3.25

Visit of Queen Elizabeth II, Oct. 28.

Virgin and Child, by Cosimo Tura — A90

Virgin and Child by: 1c, $2, Carlo Crivelli (different). 2c, 25c, Lorenzo Lotto (different). 8c, Jacopo da Pontormo. 10c, Tura.

1977, Nov. 15 Litho. *Perf. 14*

483 A90 ½c multicolored .20 .20
484 A90 1c multicolored .20 .20
485 A90 2c multicolored .20 .20
486 A90 8c multicolored .20 .20
487 A90 10c multicolored .20 .20
488 A90 25c multicolored .20 .20
489 A90 $2 multicolored 1.00 .80
a. Souvenir sheet of 4, #486-489 1.50 *2.00*
Nos. 483-489 (7) 2.20 2.00

Christmas.

Pineapple A91

10th anniv. of Statehood: 15c, Flag of Antigua. 50c, Police band. 90c, Prime Minister V. C. Bird. $2, Coat of Arms.

1977, Dec. 28 Litho. *Perf. 13x13½*

490 A91 10c multicolored .20 .20
491 A91 15c multicolored .20 .20
492 A91 50c multicolored .75 .40
493 A91 90c multicolored .35 .40
494 A91 $2 multicolored .50 .60
a. Souv. sheet, #491-494, perf 14 2.00 1.75
Nos. 490-494 (5) 2.00 1.80

Wright Glider III, 1902 A92

1c, Flyer I in air, 1903. 2c, Weight and derrick launch system and Wright engine, 1903. 10c, Orville Wright, vert. 50c, Flyer III, 1905. 90c, Wilbur Wright, vert. $2, Wright Model B, 1910. $2.50, Flyer I, 1903, on ground.

1978, Mar. 28 *Perf. 14*

495 A92 ½c multicolored .20 .20
496 A92 1c multicolored .20 .20
497 A92 2c multicolored .20 .20
498 A92 10c multicolored .20 .20
499 A92 50c multicolored .25 .20
500 A92 90c multicolored .50 .30
501 A92 $2 multicolored 1.10 .90
Nos. 495-501 (7) 2.65 2.20

Souvenir Sheet

502 A92 $2.50 multicolored 2.00 *3.00*

1st powered flight by Wright brothers, 75th anniv.

Sunfish Regatta A93

Sailing Week 1978: 50c, Fishing and work boat race. 90c, Curtain Bluff race. $2, Powerboat rally. $2.50, Guadeloupe-Antigua race.

1978, Apr. 29 Litho. *Perf. 14½*

503 A93 10c multicolored .20 .20
504 A93 50c multicolored .30 .20
505 A93 90c multicolored .50 .35
506 A93 $2 multicolored 1.10 1.25
Nos. 503-506 (4) 2.10 2.00

Souvenir Sheet

507 A93 $2.50 multicolored 2.00 *2.25*

Elizabeth II and Prince Philip — A94

Designs: 30c, Coronation. 50c, State coach. 90c, Elizabth II and Archbishop. $2.50, Elizabeth II. $5, Elizabeth II, Prince Philip, Prince Charles and Princess Anne as children.

1978, June 2 Litho. *Perf. 14, 12*

508 A94 10c multicolored .20 .20
509 A94 30c multicolored .20 .20
510 A94 50c multicolored .20 .20
511 A94 90c multicolored .30 .30
512 A94 $2.50 multicolored .60 .60
Nos. 508-512 (5) 1.50 1.50

Souvenir Sheet

513 A94 $5 multicolored 2.00 2.00

25th anniv. of coronation of Queen Elizabeth II.

Nos. 508-512 were printed in sheets of 50 (2 panes of 25), perf. 14, and in sheets of 3 plus label, perf. 12, with frames in changed colors.

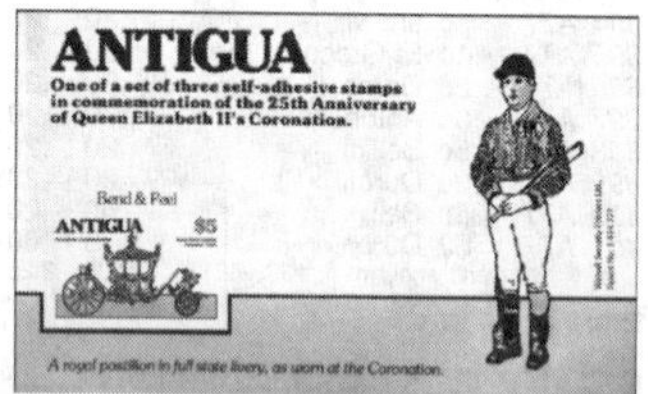

Glass Coach — A95

Royal Coaches: 50c, Irish state coach. $5, Coronation coach.

1978, June 2 Litho. *Imperf.*

Self-adhesive

514 Souvenir booklet 2.50
a. A95 Bklt. pane, 3 each 25c, 50c 1.00
b. A95 Bklt. pane, 1 $5 1.50

25th anniversary of coronation of Queen Elizabeth II. No. 514 contains 2 booklet panes printed on peelable paper backing showing royal processions.

Soccer — A96

Purple Wreath — A97

Designs: Various soccer scenes. Stamps in souvenir sheet horizontal.

1978, Aug. 18 Litho. *Perf. 15*

515 A96 10c multicolored .20 .20
516 A96 15c multicolored .20 .20
517 A96 $3 multicolored 2.00 1.75
Nos. 515-517 (3) 2.40 2.15

Souvenir Sheet

518 Sheet of 4 3.00 2.50
a. A96 25c multicolored .20 .20
b. A96 30c multicolored .30 .30
c. A96 50c multicolored .50 .50
d. A96 $2 multicolored 2.00 1.75

11th World Cup Soccer Championship, Argentina, June 1-25.

1978, Oct. Litho. *Perf. 14*

519 A97 25c shown .20 .20
520 A97 50c Sunflowers .30 .20
521 A97 90c Frangipani .60 .35
522 A97 $2 Passionflower 1.50 1.25
Nos. 519-522 (4) 2.60 2.00

Souvenir Sheet

523 A97 $2.50 Red hibiscus 2.00 *2.25*

St. Ildefonso Receiving Chasuble, by Rubens A98

Christmas: 25c, Flight of St. Barbara, by Rubens. $2, Holy Family, by Sebastiano del Piombo. $4, Annunciation, by Rubens.

1978, Oct. 30 Litho. *Perf. 14*

524 A98 8c multicolored .20 .20
525 A98 25c multicolored .25 .20
526 A98 $2 multicolored .80 .65
Nos. 524-526 (3) 1.25 1.05

Souvenir Sheet

527 A98 $4 multicolored 2.50 *3.00*

Antigua #2 — A99

Crucifixion, by Durer — A100

Designs: 50c, Great Britain Penny Black, 1840. $1, Woman posting letter in pillar box, and coach. $2, Mail train, ship, plane and Concorde. $2.50, Rowland Hill.

1979, Feb. 12 Litho. *Perf. 14*

528 A99 25c multicolored .20 .20
529 A99 50c multicolored .20 .20
530 A99 $1 multicolored .40 .25
531 A99 $2 multicolored .85 .50
Nos. 528-531 (4) 1.65 1.15

Souvenir Sheet

532 A99 $2.50 multicolored 1.25 *1.40*

Sir Rowland Hill (1795-1879), originator of penny postage.

Nos. 528-531 were printed in sheets of 50 (2 panes of 25), perf. 14, and in sheets of 5 plus label, perf. 12, with frames in changed colors.

For overprints, see Nos. 571A-571D.

1979, Mar. 15

Designs (after Dürer): 10c, Deposition. $2.50, Crucifixion. $4, Man of Sorrows.

533	A100	10c multicolored	.20	.20
534	A100	50c multicolored	.60	.25
535	A100	$4 multicolored	1.40	1.10
		Nos. 533-535 (3)	2.20	1.55

Souvenir Sheet

536	A100	$2.50 multicolored	1.25	1.25

Easter.

Child Playing with Sailboat — A101

IYC emblem, child's hand holding toy: 50c, Rocket. 90c, Automobile. $2, Train. $5, Plane.

1979, Apr. 9 Litho. *Perf. 14*

537	A101	25c multicolored	.20	.20
538	A101	50c multicolored	.25	.20
539	A101	90c multicolored	.50	.35
540	A101	$2 multicolored	1.25	1.10
		Nos. 537-540 (4)	2.20	1.85

Souvenir Sheet

541	A101	$5 multicolored	2.50	2.50

International Year of the Child.

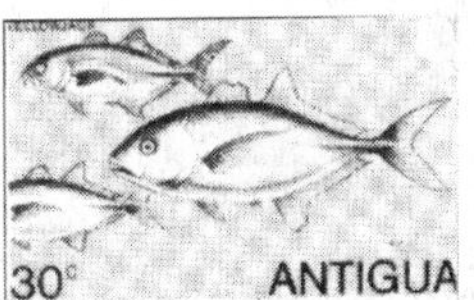

Yellowjacks — A102

Sport Fish: 50c, Bluefin tunas. 90c, Sailfish. $2.50, Barracuda. $3, Wahoos.

1979, May Litho. *Perf. 14½*

542	A102	30c multicolored	.40	.25
543	A102	50c multicolored	.50	.30
544	A102	90c multicolored	.75	.40
545	A102	$3 multicolored	2.25	1.50
		Nos. 542-545 (4)	3.90	2.45

Souvenir Sheet

546	A102	$2.50 multicolored	2.00	1.75

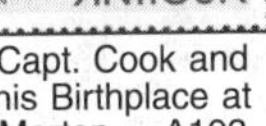

Capt. Cook and his Birthplace at Marton — A103

Holy Family — A104

Capt. James Cook (1728-1779) and: 50c, HMS Endeavour. 90c, Marine timekeeper. $2.50, HMS Resolution. $3, Landing at Botany Bay.

1979, July 2 Litho. *Perf. 14*

547	A103	25c multicolored	.40	.30
548	A103	50c multicolored	.50	.40
549	A103	90c multicolored	.50	.55
550	A103	$3 multicolored	1.75	2.50
		Nos. 547-550 (4)	3.15	3.75

Souvenir Sheet

551	A103	$2.50 multicolored	2.50	2.00

1979, Oct. 1 Litho. *Perf. 14*

Stained-glass Windows: 25c, Flight into Egypt. 50c, Shepherd and star. $3, Angel with trumpet. $4, Three Kings offering gifts.

552	A104	8c multicolored	.20	.20
553	A104	25c multicolored	.20	.20
554	A104	50c multicolored	.30	.30
555	A104	$4 multicolored	1.10	2.00
		Nos. 552-555 (4)	1.80	2.70

Souvenir Sheet

Perf. 12x12½

556	A104	$3 multicolored	1.50	2.00

Christmas.

Javelin, Olympic Rings — A105

1980, Feb. 7 Litho. *Perf. 14*

557	A105	10c shown	.20	.20
558	A105	25c Running	.25	.25
559	A105	$1 Pole vault	.55	.55
560	A105	$2 Hurdles	.75	.75
		Nos. 557-560 (4)	1.75	1.75

Souvenir Sheet

561	A105	$3 Boxing, horiz.	1.00	1.25

22nd Summer Olympic Games, Moscow, July 19-Aug. 3.

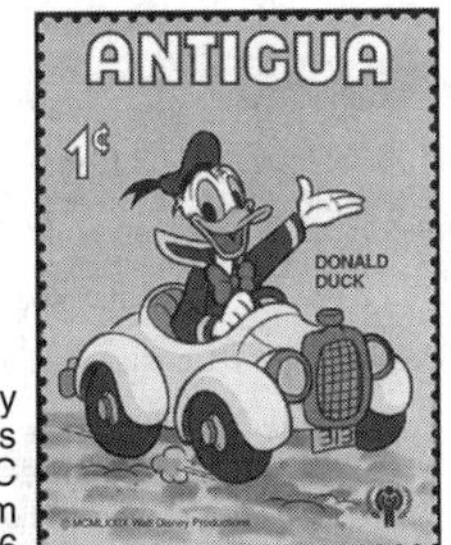

Disney Characters and IYC Emblem A106

Designs: Transportation scenes. ½c, 2c, 3c, 4c, 5c, $1, $2.50, horiz.

1980, Mar. 24 Litho. *Perf. 11*

562	A106	½c Mickey, plane	.20	.20
563	A106	1c Donald, car	.20	.20
564	A106	2c Goofy driving taxi	.20	.20
565	A106	3c Mickey, Minnie in sidecar	.20	.20
566	A106	4c Huey, Dewey and Louie	.20	.20
567	A106	5c Grandma Duck	.20	.20
568	A106	10c Mickey in jeep	.20	.20
569	A106	$1 Chip and Dale sailing	1.00	1.25
570	A106	$4 Donald on train	3.50	4.50
		Nos. 562-570 (9)	5.90	7.15

Souvenir Sheet

571	A106	$2.50 Goofy in glider	5.00	4.00

Nos. 528-531 in Changed Colors Overprinted "LONDON 1980"

1980, May 6 Litho. *Perf. 12*

571A	A99	25c multicolored	.20	.20
571B	A99	50c multicolored	.25	.25
571C	A99	$1 multicolored	.45	.45
571D	A99	$2 multicolored	2.10	2.10
		Nos. 571A-571D (4)	3.00	3.00

London '80 Intl. Stamp Exhib., May 6-14.

Birth of Venus, by Botticelli — A106a

10c, David, by Donatello. 50c, Reclining Couple, sarcophagus, Cerveteri. 90c, The Garden of Earthly Delights, by Hieronymus Bosch. $1, Portinari Altarpiece, by Hugo van der Goes. $4, Eleanora of Toledo and her Son Giovanni de Medici, by Bronzino. $5, The Holy Family, by Rembrandt.

Perf. 13½x14, 14x13½

1980, June 23 Litho.

572	A106a	10c multi, vert.	.20	.20
573	A106a	30c multi	.25	.20
574	A106a	50c multi	.35	.30
575	A106a	90c multi	.45	.45
576	A106a	$1 multi	.50	.50
577	A106a	$4 multi, vert.	2.75	3.00
		Nos. 572-577 (6)	4.50	4.65

Souvenir Sheet

Perf. 14

578	A106a	$5 multicolored	3.00	2.50

Anniversary Emblem, Intl. Headquarters, Evanston, IL — A107

1980, July 21 Litho. *Perf. 14*

579	A107	30c shown	.25	.25
580	A107	50c Antigua club banner	.30	.35
581	A107	90c Map of Antigua	.45	.60
582	A107	$3 Paul. P. Harris, emblem	2.00	2.75
		Nos. 579-582 (4)	3.00	3.95

Souvenir Sheet

583	A107	$5 Emblems, Antigua flags	2.25	2.75

Rotary International, 75th anniv.

A108

A109

1980, Sept. 15

584	A108	10c multicolored	.20	.20
585	A108	$2.50 multicolored	1.65	2.00

Souvenir Sheet

Perf. 12

586	A108	$3 multicolored	1.75	2.50

Queen Mother Elizabeth, 80th birthday.

1980, Nov. 3 Litho. *Perf. 14*

587	A109	10c Ringed Kingfisher	.50	.25
588	A109	30c Plain pigeon	.75	.40
589	A109	$1 Green-throated carib	1.00	1.00
590	A109	$2 Black-necked stilt	2.00	2.75
		Nos. 587-590 (4)	4.25	4.40

Souvenir Sheet

591	A109	$2.50 Roseate tern	5.75	5.25

Sleeping Beauty and the Prince — A110

Christmas: Various scenes from Walt Disney's Sleeping Beauty. $4 vert.

1980, Dec. 23 *Perf. 11, 13½x14 ($4)*

592	A110	½c multicolored	.20	.20
593	A110	1c multicolored	.20	.20
594	A110	2c multicolored	.20	.20
595	A110	4c multicolored	.20	.20
596	A110	8c multicolored	.20	.20
597	A110	10c multicolored	.20	.20
598	A110	25c multicolored	.25	.25
599	A110	$2 multicolored	1.75	1.75
600	A110	$2.50 multicolored	2.25	2.25
		Nos. 592-600 (9)	5.45	5.45

Souvenir Sheet

601	A110	$4 multicolored	5.25	4.50

Sugar-cane Railway Diesel Locomotive No. 15 — A111

1981, Jan. 12 *Perf. 14*

602	A111	25c shown	.20	.20
603	A111	50c Narrow-gauge steam locomotive	.35	.40
604	A111	90c Diesels #1, #10	.60	.65
605	A111	$3 Hauling sugar-cane	2.00	2.25
		Nos. 602-605 (4)	3.15	3.50

Souvenir Sheet

606	A111	$2.50 Sugar factory, train yard	2.50	2.50

Nos. 411-412, 414-422 Overprinted: "INDEPENDENCE 1981"

1981, Mar. 31 Litho.

607	A79	6c multicolored	.20	.20
608	A79	10c multicolored	.20	.20
609	A79	20c multicolored	.20	.20
610	A79	25c multicolored	.20	.20
611	A79	35c multicolored	.25	.25
612	A79	50c multicolored	.45	.45
613	A79	75c multicolored	.50	.50
614	A79	$1 multicolored	.75	.75
615	A80	$2.50 multicolored	1.25	1.50
616	A80	$5 multicolored	2.25	2.75
617	A80	$10 multicolored	4.50	5.75
		Nos. 607-617 (11)	10.75	12.75

Pipes of Pan, by Picasso — A112

Paintings by Pablo Picasso (1881-1973): 50c, Seated Harlequin. 90c, Paulo as Harlequin. $4, Mother and Child. $5, Three Musicians.

1981, May 5 Litho. *Perf. 14*

618	A112	10c multicolored	.20	.20
619	A112	50c multicolored	.35	.35
620	A112	90c multicolored	.60	.60
621	A112	$4 multicolored	2.50	2.50
		Nos. 618-621 (4)	3.65	3.65

Souvenir Sheet

Perf. 14x14½

622	A112	$5 multicolored	3.00	3.25

Royal Wedding Issue

Common Design Type

1981, June 16 Litho. *Perf. 14*

623	CD331	25c Couple	.20	.20
624	CD331	50c Glamis Castle	.20	.20
625	CD331	$4 Charles	1.40	1.40
		Nos. 623-625 (3)	1.80	1.80

Souvenir Sheet

626	CD331	$5 Glass coach	2.00	2.00
627	CD331	Booklet	9.00	
a.		Pane of 6 (2x25c, 2x$1, 2x$2), Charles	3.00	
b.		Pane of 1, $5, Couple	2.00	

No. 627 contains imperf., self-adhesive stamps.

Nos. 623-625 also printed in sheets of 5 plus label, perf. 12 in changed colors.

For surcharges see #792, 795, 802, 805.

Campfire Sing A113

1981, Oct. 28 Litho. *Perf. 15*

628 A113 10c Irene Joshua .20 .20
629 A113 50c shown .30 .25
630 A113 90c Sailing .65 .55
631 A113 $2.50 Milking cow 1.60 *1.75*
Nos. 628-631 (4) 2.75 2.75

Souvenir Sheet

632 A113 $5 Flag raising 5.00 4.00

Girl Guides, 50th anniv.

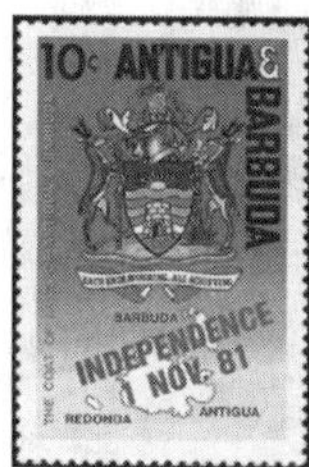

A114 A115

1981, Nov. 1 Litho. *Perf. 15*

633 A114 10c Arms .20 .20
634 A114 50c Flag .40 .20
635 A114 90c Prime Minister Bird .50 .45
636 A114 $2.50 St. John's Cathedral, horiz. 1.40 *2.25*
Nos. 633-636 (4) 2.50 *3.10*

Souvenir Sheet

637 A114 $5 Map 4.25 3.75

Independence .
No. 637 contains one 41x41mm stamp.

1981, Nov. 16

Christmas (Virgin and Child Paintings by): 8c, Holy Night, by Jacques Stella (1596-1657). 30c Julius Schnorr von Carolfeld (1794-1872). $1, Alonso Cano (1601-1667). $3, Lorenzo de Credi (1459-1537). $5, Holy Family, by Pieter von Avoni (1600-1652).

638 A115 8c multicolored .20 .20
639 A115 30c multicolored .55 .20
640 A115 $1 multicolored 1.10 *.85*
641 A115 $3 multicolored 1.90 *3.50*
Nos. 638-641 (4) 3.75 *4.75*

Souvenir Sheet

642 A115 $5 multicolored 3.75 *5.00*

Intl. Year of the Disabled A116

1981, Dec. 1 Litho. *Perf. 15*

643 A116 10c Swimming .20 .20
644 A116 50c Discus .25 *.30*
645 A116 90c Archery .45 *.50*
646 A116 $2 Baseball 1.10 *1.40*
Nos. 643-646 (4) 2.00 *2.40*

Souvenir Sheet

647 A116 $4 Basketball 4.50 2.50

1982 World Cup Soccer A117

Designs: Various soccer players.

1982, Apr. 15 Litho. *Perf. 14*

648 A117 10c multicolored .25 .20
649 A117 50c multicolored .50 .30
650 A117 90c multicolored .95 .65
651 A117 $4 multicolored 3.75 3.25
Nos. 648-651 (4) 5.45 4.40

Souvenir Sheet

652 A117 $5 multicolored 6.50 *7.50*

Also issued in sheetlets of 5 + label in changed colors, perf. 12.

A118 A119

1982, June 17 Litho. *Perf. 14½*

653 A118 10c A-300 Airbus .20 .20
654 A118 50c Hawker-Siddeley 748 .40 .40
655 A118 90c De Havilland Twin Otter DCH6 .65 .65
656 A118 $2.50 Britten-Norman Islander 1.75 1.75
Nos. 653-656 (4) 3.00 3.00

Souvenir Sheet

657 A118 $5 Jet, horiz. 3.50 *4.00*

Coolidge Intl. Airport opening.

1982, June 28 Litho. *Perf. 14½*

658 A119 10c Cordia, vert. .20 .20
659 A119 50c Golden spotted mongoose .35 .30
660 A119 90c Corallita, vert. .60 .60
661 A119 $3 Bulldog bats 2.00 *3.00*
Nos. 658-661 (4) 3.15 *4.10*

Souvenir Sheet

662 A119 $5 Caribbean monk seals 6.50 *7.00*

Charles Darwin's death centenary.

Princess Diana Issue
Common Design Type

1982, July 1 Litho. *Perf. 14½x14*

663 CD332 90c Greenwich Palace .90 .90
664 CD332 $1 Wedding 1.00 1.00
665 CD332 $4 Diana 4.00 4.00
Nos. 663-665 (3) 5.90 5.90

Souvenir Sheet

666 CD332 $5 Diana, diff. 5.00 4.75

For overprints and surcharges see Nos. 672-675, 797, 799, 803, 806.

Scouting Year A120

Designs: Independence Day celebration.

1982, July 15 *Perf. 14*

667 A120 10c Decorating buildings .20 .20
668 A120 50c Helping woman .45 .35
669 A120 90c Princess Margaret .75 .65
670 A120 $2.20 Cub Scout giving directions 1.60 *2.40*
Nos. 667-670 (4) 3.00 *3.60*

Souvenir Sheet

671 A120 $5 Baden-Powell 5.25 5.00

Nos. 663-666 Overprinted: "ROYAL BABY / 21.6.82"

1982, Aug. 30 Litho. *Perf. 14½x14*

672 CD332 90c multicolored .50 .50
673 CD332 $1 multicolored .60 .60
674 CD332 $4 multicolored 2.40 1.90
Nos. 672-674 (3) 3.50 3.00

Souvenir Sheet

675 CD332 $5 multicolored 3.25 3.25

For surcharges see Nos. 798, 800, 804, 807.

Roosevelt Driving by "The Little White House" A121

1982, Sept. 20 *Perf. 15*

676 A121 10c shown .20 .20
677 A121 25c Washington as blacksmith .35 .20
678 A121 45c Churchill, Roosevelt, Stalin .90 .35
679 A121 60c Washington crossing Delaware, vert. .90 .35
680 A121 $1 Roosevelt on train, vert. 1.25 .90
681 A121 $3 Roosevelt, vert. 1.40 *2.50*
Nos. 676-681 (6) 5.00 *4.50*

Souvenir Sheets

682 A121 $4 Washington, vert. 3.25 3.00
683 A121 $4 Eleanor and Franklin 3.25 3.00

George Washington's 250th birth anniv. and Franklin D. Roosevelt's birth centenary.

Christmas — A122

Raphael Paintings.

1982, Nov. Litho. *Perf. 14*

684 A122 10c Annunciation .20 .20
685 A122 30c Adoration of the Magi .20 .20
686 A122 $1 Presentation at the Temple .55 .55
687 A122 $4 Coronation of the Virgin 2.40 *2.40*
Nos. 684-687 (4) 3.35 *3.35*

Souvenir Sheet

688 A122 $5 Marriage of the Virgin 3.00 2.75

500th Birth Anniv. of Raphael — A123

1983, Jan. 28. Litho. *Perf. 14½*

689 A123 45c Galatea taking Reins of Dolphins, vert. .25 *.30*
690 A123 50c Sea Nymphs carried by Tritons, vert. .35 *.40*
691 A123 60c Winged Angel Steering Dolphins .40 *.45*
692 A123 $4 Cupids Shooting Arrows 2.25 *2.60*
Nos. 689-692 (4) 3.25 *3.75*

Souvenir Sheet

693 A123 $5 Galatea 3.00 3.25

A124

1983, Mar. 14 *Perf. 14*

694 A124 25c Pineapple crop .20 .20
695 A124 45c Carnival .35 .40
696 A124 60c Tourists, sailboat .45 .50
697 A124 $3 Control Tower 2.00 2.50
Nos. 694-697 (4) 3.00 3.60

Commonwealth Day.

World Communications Year — A125

1983, Apr. 5 Litho. *Perf. 14*

698 A125 15c TV screen, camera .35 .20
699 A125 50c Police radio, car 2.00 1.40
700 A125 60c Long distance phone call 2.00 1.40
701 A125 $3 Dish antenna, planets 4.00 *4.50*
Nos. 698-701 (4) 8.35 7.50

Souvenir Sheet

702 A125 $5 Comsat satellite 3.50 4.00

Imperforates
See note following No. 404.

Bottlenose Dolphin A126

1983, May 9 Litho. *Perf. 15*

703 A126 15c shown .75 .25
704 A126 50c Finback whale 1.60 1.25
705 A126 60c Bowhead whale 1.75 1.25
706 A126 $3 Spectacled porpoise 3.25 4.25
Nos. 703-706 (4) 7.35 7.00

Souvenir Sheet

707 A126 $5 Unicorn whale 7.50 6.00

Cashew Nut A127

1983, July 11 *Perf. 14*

708 A127 1c shown .20 *.45*
709 A127 2c Passion fruit .20 *.45*
710 A127 3c Mango .20 *.45*
711 A127 5c Grapefruit .20 .35
712 A127 10c Pawpaw .35 .20
713 A127 15c Breadfruit .40 .20
714 A127 20c Coconut .40 .20
715 A127 25c Oleander .45 .25
716 A127 30c Banana .50 .30
717 A127 40c Pineapple .60 .30
718 A127 45c Cordcia .65 .40
719 A127 50c Cassia .75 .45
720 A127 60c Poui 1.25 .75
721 A127 $1 Frangipani 1.90 1.25
722 A127 $2 Flamboyant 3.25 3.00
723 A127 $2.50 Lemon 3.75 4.00
724 A127 $5 Lignum vitae 6.00 8.00
725 A127 $10 Arms 9.25 11.50
Nos. 708-725 (18) 30.30 *32.50*

1985 *Perf. 12½x12*

708a A127 1c .20 *.45*
709a A127 2c .20 *.45*
710a A127 3c .20 *.45*
711a A127 5c .25 .35
712a A127 10c .30 .20
713a A127 15c .40 .20
714a A127 20c .50 .20
715a A127 25c .50 .20
716a A127 30c .60 .25
717a A127 40c .65 .25
718a A127 45c .70 .35
719a A127 50c 1.00 .35
720a A127 60c 1.25 .80
721a A127 $1 1.90 1.10
722a A127 $2 3.25 3.00
723a A127 $2.50 3.75 4.00
724a A127 $5 6.00 *8.00*
725a A127 $10 9.25 *11.50*
Nos. 708a-725a (18) 30.90 *32.10*

Issue dates: $2-$5, Dec; others Mar.

Manned Flight Bicentenary — A128

1983, Aug. 15 *Perf. 15*

726 A128 30c Dornier DoX .80 .30
727 A128 50c Supermarine S-6B .95 .60
728 A128 60c Curtiss F9C, USS Akron 1.00 .65
729 A128 $4 Pro Juventute balloon 3.25 *5.00*
Nos. 726-729 (4) 6.00 *6.55*

Souvenir Sheet

730 A128 $5 Graf Zeppelin 3.25 *3.50*

Christmas — A129

Raphael Paintings: 10c, 30c, $1, $4, Sybils and Angels details. $5, Vision of Ezekiel.

1983, Oct. 4 Litho. *Perf. 14*

731 A129 10c Angel flying with scroll .30 .20
732 A129 30c Angel, diff. .70 .30
733 A129 $1 Inscribing tablet 1.50 1.25
734 A129 $4 Angel showing tablet 3.25 *4.50*
Nos. 731-734 (4) 5.75 *6.25*

Souvenir Sheet

735 A129 $5 multicolored 2.00 2.50

Methodist Church, Anniv. — A130

1984 Olympics, Los Angeles — A131

Designs: 15c, John Wesley founder of Methodism. 50c, Nathaniel Gilbert, Antiguan founder. 60c, St. John's Methodist Church Steeple. $3, Ebenezer Methodist Church.

1983, Nov. Litho. *Perf. 14*

736 A130 15c multicolored .30 .20
737 A130 50c multicolored .85 .45
738 A130 60c multicolored .95 .60
739 A130 $3 multicolored 2.40 *3.75*
Nos. 736-739 (4) 4.50 *5.00*

1984, Jan. Litho. *Perf. 15*

740 A131 25c Discus .20 .20
741 A131 50c Gymnastics .30 .20
742 A131 90c Hurdling .60 *.65*
743 A131 $3 Bicycling 2.00 *2.25*
Nos. 740-743 (4) 3.10 *3.30*

Souvenir Sheet

744 A131 $5 Volleyball, horiz. 3.25 *4.00*

Booker Vanguard A132

1984, June 4 Litho. *Perf. 15*

745 A132 45c shown 1.00 .45
746 A132 50c Canberra 1.25 .70
747 A132 60c Yachts 1.60 .85
748 A132 $4 Fairwind 3.00 *6.00*
Nos. 745-748 (4) 6.85 *8.00*

Souvenir Sheet

749 A132 $5 Man-of-war, vert. 3.25 *4.00*

Local Flowers A133

US Presidents A134

1984, June 25 Litho. *Perf. 15*

755 A133 15c multicolored .30 .20
756 A133 50c multicolored .90 .60
757 A133 60c multicolored 1.00 .90
758 A133 $3 multicolored 2.75 *5.50*
Nos. 755-758 (4) 4.95 *7.20*

Souvenir Sheet

759 A133 $5 multicolored 3.25 3.25

1984, July 18 Litho. *Perf. 14*

760 A134 10c Lincoln .20 .20
761 A134 20c Truman .20 .20
762 A134 30c Eisenhower .25 .25
763 A134 40c Reagan .45 .45
764 A134 90c Lincoln, diff. .80 .80
765 A134 $1.10 Truman, diff. 1.10 1.10
766 A134 $1.50 Eisenhower, diff. 1.40 1.40
767 A134 $2 Reagan, diff. 1.50 1.50
Nos. 760-767 (8) 5.90 *5.90*

Slavery Abolition Sesquicentennial — A135

1984, Aug. 1

768 A135 40c Moravian Mission .70 .45
769 A135 50c Antigua Courthouse, 1823 .80 .60
770 A135 60c Sugar cane planting .85 .70
771 A135 $3 Boiling House, Delaps' Estate 3.50 *4.00*
Nos. 768-771 (4) 5.85 *5.75*

Souvenir Sheet

772 A135 $5 Willoughby Bay 6.00 6.00

Song Birds — A136

1984, Aug. 15 *Perf. 15*

773 A136 40c Rufous-sided towhee 1.10 .70
774 A136 50c Parula warbler 1.25 .90
775 A136 60c House wren 1.40 1.25
776 A136 $2 Ruby-crowned kinglet 1.75 *3.00*
777 A136 $3 Yellow-shafted flicker 2.50 *4.00*
Nos. 773-777 (5) 8.00 *9.85*

Souvenir Sheet

778 A136 $5 Yellow-breasted chat 3.75 *5.00*

AUSIPEX '84 — A137

The Blue Dancers, by Degas — A137a

1984, Sept. 21 *Perf. 15*

779 A137 $1 Grass skiing 1.50 1.50
780 A137 $5 Australian rules football 3.50 *5.00*

Souvenir Sheet

781 A137 $5 Boomerang 3.50 *4.00*

1984, Oct. Litho. *Perf. 15*

Paintings by Correggio: 25c, Virgin and Infant with Angels and Cherubs. 60c, The Four Saints. 90c, Saint Catherine. $3, The Campori Madonna. #790, St. John the Baptist.

Paintings by Degas: 50c, The Pink Dancers. 70c, Two Dancers. $4, Dancers at the Bar. #791, Folk Dancers.

782 A137a 15c multicolored .30 .20
783 A137a 25c multicolored .35 .20
784 A137a 50c multicolored .75 .50
785 A137a 60c multicolored .75 .40
786 A137a 70c multicolored 1.00 .70
787 A137a 90c multicolored 1.00 .75
788 A137a $3 multicolored 2.00 *3.50*
789 A137a $4 multicolored 2.25 *3.75*
Nos. 782-789 (8) 8.40 *10.00*

Souvenir Sheets

790 A137a $5 multicolored 3.00 3.00
791 A137a $5 multi, horiz. 3.00 3.00

Nos. 623-626, 663-666, 672-675, 694-697 Surcharged in Black or Gold

1984, June *Perf. 14, 14½x14*

792 CD331 $2 on 25c #623 2.75 2.75
793 CD334 $2 on 25c #694 2.10 1.10
794 CD334 $2 on 45c #695 2.10 1.10
795 CD331 $2 on 50c #624 2.75 2.75
796 CD334 $2 on 60c #696 2.10 1.10
797 CD332 $2 on 90c #663 (G) 2.25 2.00
798 CD332 $2 on 90c #672 (G) 2.25 2.00
799 CD332 $2 on $1 #664 (G) 2.25 2.00
800 CD332 $2 on $1 #673 (G) 2.25 2.00
801 CD334 $2 on $3 #697 2.10 1.10
802 CD331 $2 on $4 #625 2.75 2.75
803 CD332 $2 on $4 #665 (G) 2.25 2.00
804 CD332 $2 on $4 #674 (G) 2.25 2.00
Nos. 792-804 (13) 30.15 24.65

Souvenir Sheets

805 CD331 $2 on $5 #626 3.50 3.50
806 CD332 $2 on $5 #666 3.50 3.50
807 CD332 $2 on $5 #675 3.50 3.50

Nos. 797-800, 803-804 exist with silver surcharge.

Christmas 1984 and 50th Anniv. of Donald Duck A138

Scenes from various Donald Duck comics.

1984, Nov. Litho. *Perf. 11*

808 A138 1c multicolored .20 .20
809 A138 2c multicolored .20 .20
810 A138 3c multicolored .20 .20
811 A138 4c multicolored .20 .20
812 A138 5c multicolored .20 .20
813 A138 10c multicolored .20 .20
814 A138 $1 multicolored 1.50 1.00
815 A138 $2 multicolored 2.25 2.25
816 A138 $5 multicolored 3.25 *3.75*
Nos. 808-816 (9) 8.20 8.20

Souvenir Sheets

Perf. 14

817 A138 $5 multi, horiz. 4.50 *5.50*
818 A138 $5 Donald on beach 4.50 *5.50*

20th Century Leaders A139

1984, Nov. 19 Litho. *Perf. 15*

819 A139 60c John F. Kennedy (1917-1963), vert. 1.00 *1.25*
820 A139 60c Winston Churchill (1874-1965), vert. 1.00 *1.25*
821 A139 60c Mahatma Gandhi (1869-1948), vert. 1.00 *1.25*
822 A139 60c Mao Tse-Tung (1883-1976), vert. 1.00 *1.25*
823 A139 $1 Kennedy in Berlin 1.25 *1.50*
824 A139 $1 Churchill in Paris 1.25 *1.50*
825 A139 $1 Gandhi in Great Britain 1.25 *1.50*
826 A139 $1 Mao in Peking 1.25 *1.50*
Nos. 819-826 (8) 9.00 *11.00*

Souvenir Sheet

827 A139 $5 Flags of Great Britain, India, China, USA 7.00 4.50

Statue of Liberty Centennial A140

1985, Jan. 7

828 A140 25c Torch on display, 1885 .20 .20
829 A140 30c Restoration, 1984-1986, vert. .20 .20
830 A140 50c Bartholdi supervising construction, 1876 .30 .30
831 A140 90c Statue on Liberty Island .50 .50
832 A140 $1 Dedication Ceremony, 1886, vert. .80 .80
833 A140 $3 Operation Sail, 1976, vert. 1.50 *1.75*
Nos. 828-833 (6) 3.50 *3.75*

Souvenir Sheet

834 A140 $5 Port of New York 3.75 3.75

Traditional Scenes A141

1985, Jan. 21

835 A141 15c Ceramics, Arawak pot shard .20 .20
836 A141 50c Tatooing, body design .35 .40
837 A141 60c Harvesting Manioc, god Yocahu .45 .50
838 A141 $3 Caribs in battle, war club 2.00 *2.25*
Nos. 835-838 (4) 3.00 *3.35*

Souvenir Sheet

839 A141 $5 Tainos worshiping 3.25 *3.50*

Invention of the Motorcycle, Cent. — A142

1985, Mar. 7 *Perf. 14*

840 A142 10c Triumph 2HP Jap, 1903 .50 .50
841 A142 30c Indian Arrow, 1949 .85 .85
842 A142 60c BMW R100RS, 1976 1.40 1.40
843 A142 $4 Harley Davidson Model II, 1916 4.75 *4.75*
Nos. 840-843 (4) 7.50 *7.50*

Souvenir Sheet

844 A142 $5 Laverda Jota, 1975 *5.00* *6.00*

John J. Audubon, 200th Birth Anniv. A143

1985, Mar. 25 *Perf. 14*

845 A143 90c Horned grebe 1.25 .90
846 A143 $1 Least petrel 1.50 .90
847 A143 $1.50 Great blue heron 2.00 *2.40*
848 A143 $3 Double-crested cormorant 2.75 *4.25*
Nos. 845-848 (4) 7.50 *8.45*

Souvenir Sheet

849 A143 $5 White-tailed tropic bird, vert. 6.50 5.00

See Nos.910-914.

Butterflies
A144

1985, Apr. 16 *Perf. 14*
850 A144 25c Polygrapha cyanea .40 .20
851 A144 60c Leodonta dysoni 1.00 .50
852 A144 90c Junea doraete 1.25 .60
853 A144 $4 Prepona xenagoras 2.75 3.50
Nos. 850-853 (4) 5.40 4.80

Souvenir Sheet

854 A144 $5 Caerois gerdrudtus 5.50 *6.00*

Cessna 172 A145

1985, Apr. 30
855 A145 30c shown .40 .20
856 A145 90c Fokker DVII .90 .40
857 A145 $1.50 Spad VII 1.25 1.10
858 A145 $3 Boeing 747 1.75 *2.50*
Nos. 855-858 (4) 4.30 *4.20*

Souvenir Sheet

859 A145 $5 Twin Otter, Coolidge Intl. Airport 4.50 *5.50*

40th anniv. of the ICAO. Nos. 855, 858-859 show the ICAO and UN emblems.

Maimonides (1135-1204), Judaic Philosopher and Physician — A146

1985, June 17 **Litho.** *Perf. 14*
860 A146 $2 yellow green 1.75 1.25

Souvenir Sheet

861 A146 $5 deep brown 5.00 4.00

Intl. Youth Year A147

1985, July 1
862 A147 25c Agriculture .20 .20
863 A147 50c Hotel management .25 .30
864 A147 60c Environmental studies .30 .50
865 A147 $3 Windsurfing 2.50 *3.25*
Nos. 862-865 (4) 3.25 *4.25*

Souvenir Sheet

866 A147 $5 Youths, national flag 3.25 3.50

Queen Mother, 85th Birthday — A148

Designs: 90c, $1, Attending a church service. No. 867A, $1.50, Touring the London Gardens, children in a sandpit. $2.50, $3, Photograph (1979). $5, With Prince Edward at the wedding of Prince Charles and Lady Diana Spencer.

Perf. 14, 12x12½ (90c, $1, $3)

1985, July 15
866A A148 90c multi ('86) .65 .65
867 A148 $1 multi .75 .75
867A A148 $1 multi ('86) .75 .75
868 A148 $1.50 multi 1.10 1.10
869 A148 $2.50 multi 1.75 1.75
869A A148 $3 multi ('86) 2.00 2.00
Nos. 866A-869A (6) 7.00 7.00

Souvenir Sheet

870 A148 $5 multicolored 3.50 3.25

Nos. 866A, 867A, 869A issued in sheets of 5 plus label on Jan. 13, 1986.

Marine Life — A149

Johann Sebastian Bach — A150

1985, Aug. 1 *Perf. 14*
871 A149 15c Fregata magnificens .30 .20
872 A149 45c Diploria labyrinthiformis .50 .25
873 A149 60c Oreaster reticulatus .55 .45
874 A149 $3 Gymnothorax moringa 1.75 *2.25*
Nos. 871-874 (4) 3.10 *3.15*

Souvenir Sheet

875 A149 $5 Acropora palmata 3.75 3.25

1985, Aug. 26 **Litho.** *Perf. 14*
876 A150 25c Bass trombone .25 .20
877 A150 50c English horn .50 .30
878 A150 $1 Violino piccolo 1.00 .35
879 A150 $3 Bass rackett 2.25 *2.50*
Nos. 876-879 (4) 4.00 *3.35*

Souvenir Sheet

880 A150 $5 Portrait 4.50 4.75

Girl Guides, 75th Anniv. A151

Public service and growth-oriented activities.

1985, Sept. 10
881 A151 15c Public service .40 .20
882 A151 45c Guides meeting .50 .40
883 A151 60c Lord and Lady Baden-Powell .75 .50
884 A151 $3 Nature study 1.75 *2.25*
Nos. 881-884 (4) 3.40 *3.35*

Souvenir Sheet

885 A151 $5 Barn swallow 4.00 4.00

State Visit of Elizabeth II, Oct. 24 — A152

1985, Oct. 24 **Litho.** *Perf. 14½*
886 A152 60c National flags .45 .45
887 A152 $1 Elizabeth II, vert. .75 .75
888 A152 $4 HMY Britannia 3.00 *4.00*
Nos. 886-888 (3) 4.20 *5.20*

Souvenir Sheet

889 A152 $5 Map of Antigua 3.50 3.50

Mark Twain — A153

Disney characters in Roughing It.

1985, Nov. 4 *Perf. 14*
890 A153 25c Cowboys and Indians .30 .20
891 A153 50c Canoeing .50 .30
892 A153 $1.10 Pony Express .90 1.00
893 A153 $1.50 Buffalo hunt in Missouri 1.10 *1.50*
894 A153 $2 Nevada silver mine 1.75 *2.25*
Nos. 890-894 (5) 4.55 *5.25*

Souvenir Sheet

895 A153 $5 Stagecoach on Kansas plains 5.00 5.00

Jacob and Wilhelm Grimm, Fabulists and Philologists — A154

Disney characters in Spindle, Shuttle and Needle.

1985, Nov. 11
896 A154 30c multicolored .40 .30
897 A154 60c multicolored .50 .40
898 A154 70c multicolored .60 .45
899 A154 $1 multicolored 1.25 1.10
900 A154 $3 multicolored 2.50 *3.00*
Nos. 896-900 (5) 5.25 *5.25*

Souvenir Sheet

900A A154 $5 multicolored 5.00 5.00

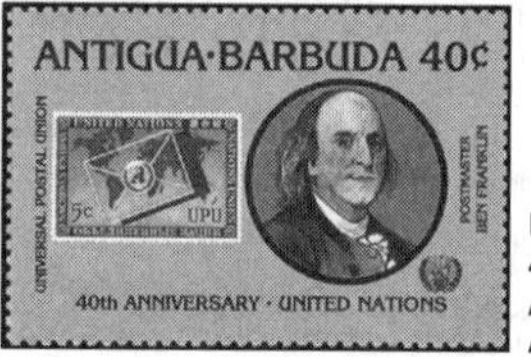

UN 40th Anniv. A155

Stamps of UN and portraits: 40c, No. 18 and Benjamin Franklin. $1, No. 391 and George Washington Carver, agricultural chemist. $3, No. 299 and Charles Lindbergh. $5, Marc Chagall, artist, vert.

1985, Nov. 18 *Perf. 13½x14*
901 A155 40c multicolored .30 .30
902 A155 $1 multicolored 1.00 1.00
903 A155 $3 multicolored 2.25 *2.50*
Nos. 901-903 (3) 3.55 *3.80*

Souvenir Sheet

Perf. 14x13½

904 A155 $5 multicolored 3.25 2.50

Christmas — A156

Religious paintings: 10c, Madonna and Child, by De Landi. 25c, Madonna and Child, by Bonaventura Berlingheiri (d. 1244). 60c, The Nativity, by Fra Angelico (1400-1455). $4, Presentation in the Temple, by Giovanni di Paolo Grazia (c.1403-1482). $5, The Nativity, by Antoniazzo Romano.

1985, Dec. 30 *Perf. 15*
905 A156 10c multicolored .20 .20
906 A156 25c multicolored .45 .20
907 A156 60c multicolored .60 .45
908 A156 $4 multicolored 2.00 *3.00*
Nos. 905-908 (4) 3.25 *3.85*

Souvenir Sheet

909 A156 $5 multicolored 3.25 *3.50*

Audubon Type of 1985

Illustrations of North American ducks.

1986, Jan. 6 *Perf. 12½x12*
910 A143 60c Mallard .45 .35
911 A143 90c Dusky duck .70 .65
912 A143 $1.50 Common pintail 1.10 *1.50*
913 A143 $3 Widgeon 2.25 *3.00*
Nos. 910-913 (4) 4.50 *5.50*

Souvenir Sheet

Perf. 14

914 A143 $5 Common eider 3.25 2.50

1986 World Cup Soccer Championships, Mexico — A157

1986, Mar. 17 **Litho.** *Perf. 14*
915 A157 30c shown .30 .20
916 A157 60c Heading the ball .45 .45
917 A157 $1 Referee .75 .60
918 A157 $4 Goal 3.00 *3.75*
Nos. 915-918 (4) 4.50 *5.00*

Souvenir Sheet

919 A157 $5 Action 3.50 3.00

Nos. 916-917 vert.
For overprints see Nos. 963-967.

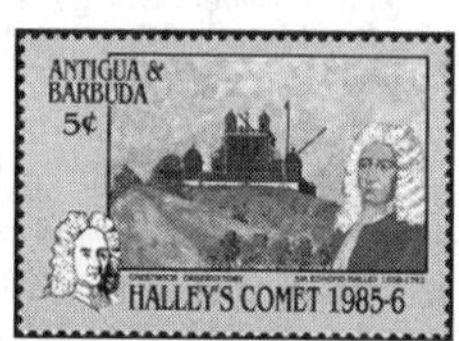

A158

Halley's Comet — A159

Designs: 5c, Edmond Halley, Greenwich Observatory. 10c, Me 163B Komet. German WWII fighter plane. 60c, Montezuma sighting comet, 1517. $4, Pocahontas saving Capt. John Smith's life, 1607 sighting as sign for Powhatan Indians to raid Jamestown. $5, Comet over Antigua.

1986, Mar. 24
920 A158 5c multicolored .20 .20
921 A158 10c multicolored .20 .20
922 A158 60c multicolored 1.00 .35
923 A158 $4 multicolored 2.50 *2.75*
Nos. 920-923 (4) 3.90 *3.50*

Souvenir Sheet

924 A159 $5 multicolored 3.50 3.50

For overprints see Nos. 973-977.

Queen Elizabeth II, 60th Birthday

Common Design Type

1986, Apr. 21
925 CD339 60c Wedding, 1947 .50 .50
926 CD339 $1 Trooping the color .75 .75
927 CD339 $4 Visiting Scotland 2.25 2.50
Nos. 925-927 (3) 3.50 *3.75*

Souvenir Sheet

928 CD339 $5 Held by Queen Mary, 1927 3.25 *4.00*

Boats — A160

1986, May 15

929 A160 30c Tugboat .25 .20
930 A160 60c Fishing boat .50 .35
931 A160 $1 Sailboat 2056 .75 .60
932 A160 $4 Lateen-rigged sailboat 2.75 3.00
Nos. 929-932 (4) 4.25 4.15

Souvenir Sheet

933 A160 $5 Boatbuilding 3.50 4.00

A number of unissued items, imperfs., part perfs., missing color varieties, etc., were made available when the Format International inventory was liquidated. Imperfs of some or all of the Antigua stamps in the following sets are included: #405-422, 503-507, 515-517, 703-707, 745-749, 755-759, 808-816, 819-826, 905-909, 934-937.

See footnote after #962.

AMERIPEX '86 — A161

American trains.

1986, May 22 *Perf. 15*

934 A161 25c Hiawatha .55 .20
935 A161 50c Grand Canyon .70 .40
936 A161 $1 Powhattan Arrow .75 .90
937 A161 $3 Empire State 2.00 3.00
Nos. 934-937 (4) 4.00 4.50

Souvenir Sheet

938 A161 $5 Daylight 3.50 5.50

Wedding of Prince Andrew and Sarah Ferguson

Common Design Type

1986, July 23 *Perf. 14*

939 CD340 45c Couple .30 .30
940 CD340 60c Prince Andrew .45 .45
941 CD340 $4 Princes Andrew, Philip 3.00 3.50
Nos. 939-941 (3) 3.75 4.25

Souvenir Sheet

942 CD340 $5 Couple, diff. 4.00 4.00

Conch Shells — A162

1986, Aug. 6 Litho. *Perf. 15*

943 A162 15c Say fly-specked cerith .35 .20
944 A162 45c Gmelin smooth scotch bonnet .80 .35
945 A162 60c Linne West Indian crown conch .85 .70
946 A162 $3 Murex ciboney 2.75 4.00
Nos. 943-946 (4) 4.75 5.25

Souvenir Sheet

947 A162 $5 Atlantic natica 4.75 5.00

Flowers A163

1986, Aug. 25 Litho. *Perf. 15*

948 A163 10c Water lily .20 .20
949 A163 15c Queen of the night .20 .20
950 A163 50c Cup of gold .50 .50
951 A163 60c Beach morning glory .75 .75
952 A163 70c Golden trumpet .85 .85
953 A163 $1 Air plant .90 1.10
954 A163 $3 Purple wreath 1.75 2.50
955 A163 $4 Zephyr lily 2.00 3.25
Nos. 948-955 (8) 7.15 9.35

Souvenir Sheets

956 A163 $4 Dozakie 2.50 3.00
957 A163 $5 Four o'clock 3.25 3.75

Fungi — A164

1986, Sept. 15

958 A164 10c Hygrocybe occidentalis scarletina .35 .25
959 A164 50c Trogia buccinalis .75 .60
960 A164 $1 Collybia subpruinosa 1.40 1.40
961 A164 $4 Leucocoprinus brebissonii 3.50 4.75
Nos. 958-961 (4) 6.00 7.00

Souvenir Sheet

962 A164 $5 Pyrrhoglossum pyrrhum 7.50 7.50

An unissued $3 stamp and #961 inscribed "4$" were made available when the Format International inventory was liquidated.

Nos. 915-919 Ovptd. "WINNERS Argentina 3 W. Germany 2" in Gold in 2 or 3 lines

1986, Sept. 15 *Perf. 14*

963 A157 30c multicolored .20 .20
964 A157 60c multicolored .30 .45
965 A157 $1 multicolored .75 .75
966 A157 $4 multicolored 3.75 4.00
Nos. 963-966 (4) 5.00 5.40

Souvenir Sheet

967 A157 $5 multicolored 4.00 4.00

Automobile, Cent. — A165

Carl Benz and classic automobiles.

1986, Oct. 20

968 A165 10c 1933 Auburn Speedster .20 .20
968A A165 15c 1986 Mercury Sable .20 .20
969 A165 50c 1959 Cadillac .40 .25
970 A165 60c 1950 Studebaker .50 .35
970A A165 70c 1939 Lagonda V-12 .60 .50
970B A165 $1 1930 Adler Standard .75 .60
970C A165 $3 1956 DKW 2.00 2.00
971 A165 $4 1936 Mercedes 500K 2.75 2.75
Nos. 968-971 (8) 7.40 6.85

Souvenir Sheets

972 A165 $5 1921 Mercedes Knight 3.50 3.25
972A A165 $5 1896 Daimler 3.50 3.25

Nos. 920-924 Ovptd. with Halley's Comet Emblem in Black or Silver

1986, Oct. 22 Litho. *Perf. 14*

973 A158 5c multicolored .20 .20
974 A158 10c multicolored .20 .20
975 A158 60c multicolored .45 .30
976 A158 $4 multicolored 3.00 2.75
Nos. 973-976 (4) 3.85 3.45

Souvenir Sheet

977 A159 $5 multicolored (S) 3.75 3.75

Christmas — A166

Disney characters as children.

1986, Nov. 4 *Perf. 11*

978 A166 25c Mickey .30 .25
979 A166 30c Mickey, Minnie .35 .30
980 A166 40c Aunt Matilda, Goofy .40 .35
981 A166 60c Goofy, Pluto .50 .55
982 A166 70c Pluto, Donald, Daisy .60 .65
983 A166 $1.50 Stringing popcorn 1.25 2.00
984 A166 $3 Grandma Duck, Minnie 2.25 2.75
985 A166 $4 Donald, Pete 2.75 3.25
Nos. 978-985 (8) 8.40 10.10

Souvenir Sheets

Perf. 14

986 A166 $5 Playing with presents 3.50 3.50
987 A166 $5 Reindeer 3.50 3.50

Nos. 985 printed in sheets of 8.

Coat of Arms A167

Natl. Flag A168

1986, Nov. 25 Litho. *Perf. 14x14½*

988 A167 10c bright blue .35 .35
989 A168 25c orange .40 .40

Marc Chagall (1887-1985), Artist A169

Designs: No. 990, The Profile, 1957. No. 991, Portrait of the Artist's Sister, 1910. No. 992, Bride with Fan, 1911. No. 993, David in Profile, 1914. No. 994, Fiancee with Bouquet, 1977. No. 995, Self-portrait with Brushes, 1909. No. 996, The Walk, 1973. No. 997, Candles, 1938. No. 998, Fall of Icarus, 1975. No. 999, Myth of Orpheus, 1977.

1987, Mar. 30 Litho. *Perf. 13½x14*

990 A169 10c multicolored .20 .20
991 A169 30c multicolored .20 .20
992 A169 40c multicolored .25 .25
993 A169 60c multicolored .35 .35
994 A169 90c multicolored .60 .60
995 A169 $1 multicolored .65 .65
996 A169 $3 multicolored 2.00 2.25
997 A169 $4 multicolored 2.75 3.00

Size: 110x95mm

Imperf

998 A169 $5 multicolored 3.25 3.25
999 A169 $5 multicolored 3.25 3.25
Nos. 990-999 (10) 13.50 14.00

A170

America's Cup — A171

1987, Feb. 5 *Perf. 15*

1000 A170 30c Canada I, 1981 .25 .20
1001 A170 60c Gretel II, 1970 .30 .30
1002 A170 $1 Sceptre, 1958 .70 .75
1003 A170 $3 Vigilant, 1893 2.00 2.50
Nos. 1000-1003 (4) 3.25 3.75

Souvenir Sheet

1004 A171 $5 Australia II, Liberty, 1983 3.75 4.50

Fish, World Wildlife Fund A172

Marine Birds A173

1987, Feb. 23 Litho. *Perf. 14*

1005 A172 15c Bridled burrfish 1.60 .35
1006 A173 30c Brown noddy 3.00 .40
1007 A172 40c Nassau grouper 1.90 .50
1008 A173 50c Laughing gull 3.50 1.00
1009 A172 60c French angelfish 2.25 1.00
1010 A172 $1 Porkfish 2.25 1.25
1011 A173 $2 Royal tern 4.50 4.00
1012 A173 $3 Sooty tern 4.50 5.50
Nos. 1005-1012 (8) 23.50 14.00

Souvenir Sheets

1013 A172 $5 Banded butterfly fish 6.00 6.00
1014 A173 $5 Brown booby 6.00 6.00

The 30c, 50c, $2, $3 and Nos. 1013-1014 do not picture the WWF emblem.

For overprints see Nos. 1137-1139A.

Statue of Liberty, Cent. A174

Photographs by Peter B. Kaplan.

1987, Apr. 20 *Perf. 14*

1015 A174 15c Lee Iacocca .20 .20
1016 A174 30c Statue at dusk .25 .25
1017 A174 45c Crown, head .45 .45
1018 A174 50c Iacocca, torch .50 .50
1019 A174 60c Crown observatory .50 .50
1020 A174 90c Interior restoration .70 .70
1021 A174 $1 Head .80 .80
1022 A174 $2 Statue at sunset 1.65 *1.75*
1023 A174 $3 Men on scaffold, flag 1.75 *2.50*
1024 A174 $5 Statue at night 3.00 *4.00*
Nos. 1015-1024 (10) 9.80 *11.65*

Nos. 1015-1018, 1021-1022, 1024 vert.

A175

Transportation Innovations — A175a

1987, Apr. 19 *Perf. 15*

1025 A175 10c Spirit of Australia, 1978 .20 .20
1026 A175a 15c Siemens' Electric locomotive, 1879 .20 .20
1027 A175 30c USS Triton, 1960 .25 .25
1028 A175a 50c Trevithick, 1801 .35 .35
1029 A175 60c USS New Jersey, 1942 .45 .45
1030 A175a 70c Draisine bicycle, 1818 .50 .50
1031 A175 90c SS United States, 1952 .70 .70
1032 A175a $1.50 Cierva C-4, 1923 1.25 *1.50*
1033 A175a $2 Curtiss NC-4, 1919 1.60 *2.50*
1034 A175 $3 Queen Elizabeth II, 1969 2.25 *2.50*
Nos. 1025-1034 (10) 7.75 *9.15*

Reptiles and Amphibians — A176

1987, June 15 *Perf. 14*

1035 A176 30c Eleutherodactylus martinicensis .50 .20
1036 A176 60c Thecadactylus bapicauda .70 .45
1037 A176 $1 Anolis bimaculatus leachi .90 .60
1038 A176 $3 Geochelone carbonaria 1.90 *2.50*
Nos. 1035-1038 (4) 4.00 *3.75*

Souvenir Sheet

1039 A176 $5 Ameiva griswoldi 3.25 3.25

Entertainers A177

1987, May 11

1040 A177 15c Grace Kelly .30 .20
1041 A177 30c Marilyn Monroe 1.00 .25
1042 A177 45c Orson Welles .35 .20
1043 A177 50c Judy Garland .35 .20
1044 A177 60c John Lennon 1.25 .35
1045 A177 $1 Rock Hudson .50 .35
1046 A177 $2 John Wayne 1.25 .70
1047 A177 $3 Elvis Presley 2.50 1.75
Nos. 1040-1047 (8) 7.50 4.00

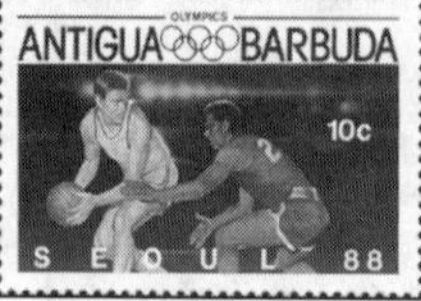
No. 1047 Overprinted

1987, Sept. 9 **Litho.** *Perf. 14*

1047A A177 $3 multicolored 4.00 3.00

1988 Summer Olympics, Seoul A178

1987, Mar. 23

1048 A178 10c Basketball .45 .20
1049 A178 60c Fencing .70 .30
1050 A178 $1 Women's gymnastics 1.00 .75
1051 A178 $3 Soccer 2.10 *3.25*
Nos. 1048-1051 (4) 4.25 *4.50*

Souvenir Sheet

1052 A178 $5 Boxing glove 3.50 *4.00*

16th World Scout Jamboree, Australia, 1987-88 A179

1987, Nov. 2 **Litho.** *Perf. 15*

1053 A179 10c Campfire, red kangaroo .65 .20
1054 A179 60c Kayaking, blue-winged kookaburra 1.25 .60
1055 A179 $1 Obstacle course, ring-tailed rock wallaby .95 .70
1056 A179 $3 Field kitchen, koalas 1.40 *3.25*
Nos. 1053-1056 (4) 4.25 *4.75*

Souvenir Sheet

1057 A179 $5 Flags 3.25 3.25

US Constitution Bicent. — A180

Designs: 15c, Virginia House of Burgesses exercising right of freedom of speech. 45c, Connecticut state seal. 60c, Delaware state seal. $4, Gouverneur Morris (1752-1816), principal writer of the Constitution, vert. $5, Roger Sherman (1721-1793), jurist and statesman, vert.

1987, Nov. 16 **Litho.** *Perf. 14*

1058 A180 15c multicolored .20 .20
1059 A180 45c multicolored .25 *.30*
1060 A180 60c multicolored .30 *.40*
1061 A180 $4 multicolored 2.25 *2.75*
Nos. 1058-1061 (4) 3.00 *3.65*

Souvenir Sheet

1062 A180 $5 multicolored 3.25 3.25

A181

A182

Christmas (Paintings): 45c, Madonna and Child, by Bernardo Daddi (1290-1355). 60c, Joseph, detail from The Nativity, by Sano Di Pietro (1406-1481). $1, Mary, detail from Di Pietro's The Nativity. $4, Music-making Angel, by Melozzo Da Forli (1438-1494). $5, The Flight into Egypt, by Di Pietro.

1987, Dec. 1

1063 A181 45c multicolored .30 .20
1064 A181 60c multicolored .45 .30
1065 A181 $1 multicolored .75 .70
1066 A181 $4 multicolored 2.25 *3.00*
Nos. 1063-1066 (4) 3.75 *4.20*

Souvenir Sheet

1067 A181 $5 multicolored 3.25 3.25

1988, Feb. 8 **Litho.** *Perf. 14*

1068 A182 25c Wedding portrait .20 .20
1069 A182 60c Elizabeth II, c. 1970 .45 *.50*
1070 A182 $2 Christening of Charles, 1948 1.25 *1.50*
1071 A182 $3 Elizabeth II, c. 1980 1.75 *2.00*
Nos. 1068-1071 (4) 3.65 *4.20*

Souvenir Sheet

1072 A182 $5 Royal family, c. 1951 3.25 3.25

40th wedding anniv. of Queen Elizabeth II and Prince Philip.

Tropical Birds A183

1988, Mar. 1

1073 A183 10c Great blue heron, vert. .25 .20
1074 A183 15c Ringed kingfisher .25 .20
1075 A183 50c Bananaquit .50 .40
1076 A183 60c Purple gallinule .50 .45
1077 A183 70c Blue-hooded euphonia .60 .55
1078 A183 $1 Caribbean parakeet, vert. .75 .65
1079 A183 $3 Troupial 3.00 2.50
1080 A183 $4 Hummingbird 3.00 *3.50*
Nos. 1073-1080 (8) 8.85 8.45

Souvenir Sheets

1081 A183 $5 Roseate flamingo, vert. 3.50 3.50
1082 A183 $5 Brown pelicans, vert. 3.50 3.50

Salvation Army — A184

1988, Mar. 7

1083 A184 25c Day-care, Antigua .60 .40
1084 A184 30c Penicillin inoculation, Indonesia .60 .45
1085 A184 40c Day-care Center, Bolivia .65 .55
1086 A184 45c Rehabilitation, India .65 .55
1087 A184 50c Training the blind, Kenya .75 *.90*
1088 A184 60c Infant care, Ghana .75 *.90*
1089 A184 $1 Job training, Zambia 1.00 *1.25*
1090 A184 $2 Food distribution, Sri Lanka 1.50 *2.50*
Nos. 1083-1090 (8) 6.50 *7.50*

Souvenir Sheet

1091 A184 $5 General Eva Burrows 3.25 3.25

A185

Discovery of America, 500th Anniv. (in 1992) — A186

Anniv. emblem and: 10c, Fleet. 30c, View of fleet in harbor from Paino Indian village. 45c, Caravel anchored in harbor, Paino village. 60c, Columbus, 3 Indians in canoe. 90c, Indian, parrot, Columbus. $1, Columbus in longboat. $3, Spanish guard, fleet in harbor. $4, Ships under full sail. No. 1100, Stone cross given to Columbus by Queen Isabella. No. 1101, Gold exelente.

1988, Mar. 14 **Litho.** *Perf. 14*

1092 A185 10c multicolored .50 .50
1093 A185 30c multicolored .50 .50
1094 A185 45c multicolored .55 .55
1095 A185 60c multicolored .55 .55
1096 A185 90c multicolored 1.00 1.00
1097 A185 $1 multicolored 1.00 1.00
1098 A185 $3 multicolored 1.75 1.75
1099 A185 $4 multicolored 2.00 2.00
Nos. 1092-1099 (8) 7.85 7.85

Souvenir Sheets

1100 A186 $5 multicolored 3.25 3.25
1101 A186 $5 multicolored 3.25 3.25

Paintings by Titian A187

Details: 30c, Bust of Christ. 40c, Scourging of Christ. 45c, Madonna in Glory with Saints. 50c, The Averoldi Polyptych. $1, Christ Crowned with Thorns. $2, Christ Mocked. $3, Christ and Simon of Cyrene. $4, Crucifixion with Virgin and Saints. No. 1110, Ecce Homo. No. 1111, Noli Me Tangere.

1988, Apr. 11 **Litho.** *Perf. 13½x14*

1102 A187 30c shown .35 .25
1103 A187 40c multicolored .40 .30
1104 A187 45c multicolored .40 .30
1105 A187 50c multicolored .45 .45
1106 A187 $1 multicolored .75 .75
1107 A187 $2 multicolored 1.25 *1.40*
1108 A187 $3 multicolored 2.00 *2.25*
1109 A187 $4 multicolored 2.25 *2.50*
Nos. 1102-1109 (8) 7.85 *8.20*

Souvenir Sheets

1110 A187 $5 multicolored 3.25 *3.75*
1111 A187 $5 multicolored 3.25 *3.75*

Sailing Week A188

1988, Apr. 18 *Perf. 15*

1112 A188 30c Canada I, 1980 .20 .20
1113 A188 60c Gretel II, Australia, 1970 .50 *.55*

1114 A188 $1 Sceptre, GB, 1958 .80 *.85*
1115 A188 $3 Vigilant, US, 1893 1.75 *3.00*
Nos. 1112-1115 (4) 3.25 *4.60*

Souvenir Sheet

1116 A188 $5 Australia II, 1983 3.25 *4.25*

Walt Disney Animated Characters and Epcot Center, Walt Disney World — A189

1988, May 3 ***Perf. 14x13½, 13½x14***

1116A A189 1c like 25c .20 .20
1116B A189 2c like 30c .20 .20
1116C A189 3c like 40c .20 .20
1116D A189 4c like 60c .20 .20
1116E A189 5c like 70c .20 .20
1116F A189 10c like $1.50 .20 .20
1117 A189 25c The Living Seas .20 .20
1118 A189 30c World of Motion .25 .25
1119 A189 40c Spaceship Earth .25 .25
1120 A189 60c Universe of Energy .30 .30
1121 A189 70c Journey to Imagination .40 .40
1122 A189 $1.50 The Land 1.25 1.25
1123 A189 $3 Communicore 2.25 2.25
1124 A189 $4 Horizons 2.50 2.50
Nos. 1116A-1124 (14) 8.60 8.60

Souvenir Sheets

1125 A189 $5 Epcot Center 3.50 *3.75*
1126 A189 $5 The Contemporary Resort Hotel 3.50 *3.75*

30c, 40c, $1.50, $3 and No. 1126 are vert.

Flowering Trees
A190 A186

1988, May 16 ***Perf. 14***

1127 A190 10c Jacaranda .30 .20
1128 A190 30c Cordia .35 .25
1129 A190 50c Orchid tree .50 .50
1130 A190 90c Flamboyant .60 .60
1131 A190 $1 African tulip tree .75 .75
1132 A190 $2 Potato tree 1.50 *1.75*
1133 A190 $3 Crepe myrtle 2.00 *2.25*
1134 A190 $4 Pitch apple 2.50 *3.00*
Nos. 1127-1134 (8) 8.50 *9.30*

Souvenir Sheets

1135 A190 $5 Cassia 3.25 *3.50*
1136 A190 $5 Chinaberry 3.25 *3.50*

Nos. 1135-1136 are continuous designs.

Nos. 1011-1012, 1014 and 1013 Ovptd. in Black for Philatelic Exhibitions

a

b

c

d

1988, May 9 **Litho.** ***Perf. 14***

1137 A173 (a) $2 multicolored 1.25 *1.50*
1138 A173 (b) $3 multicolored 2.00 *2.25*

Souvenir Sheets

1139 A173 (c) $5 multicolored 3.25 3.25
1139A A172 (d) $5 multicolored 3.25 3.25

1988 Summer Olympics, Seoul A192

1988, June 10

1140 A192 40c Gymnastic rings, vert. .30 .30
1141 A192 60c Weight lifting, vert. .45 .45
1142 A192 $1 Water polo .70 *.75*
1143 A192 $3 Boxing 1.75 *2.25*
Nos. 1140-1143 (4) 3.20 *3.75*

Souvenir Sheet

1144 A192 $5 Torch-bearer, vert. 3.25 *3.75*

Butterflies A193

1988-90 **Litho.** ***Perf. 14***

1145 A193 1c Monarch .20 *.35*
1146 A193 2c Jamaican clearwing .35 *.45*
1147 A193 3c Yellow-barred ringlet .35 *.45*
1148 A193 5c Cracker .45 .45
1149 A193 10c Jamaican mestra .55 .25
1150 A193 15c Mimic .65 .25
1151 A193 20c Silver spot .70 .25
1152 A193 25c Zebra .70 .25
1153 A193 30c Fiery sulphur .70 .25
1154 A193 40c Androgeus swallowtail .75 .25
1155 A193 45c Giant brimstone .75 .25
1156 A193 50c Orbed sulphur .80 .45
1157 A193 60c Blue-backed skipper .90 .50
1158 A193 $1 Common white skipper 1.40 .85
1159 A193 $2 Baracoa skipper 2.50 *2.75*
1160 A193 $2.50 Mangrove skipper 3.00 *3.50*
1161 A193 $5 Silver king 4.50 *5.00*
1161A A193 $10 Pygmy skipper 6.25 *7.50*
1162 A193 $20 Parides lycimenes 12.50 *13.50*
Nos. 1145-1162 (19) 38.00 *37.50*

Issued: $20, Feb. 19, 1990; others, Aug. 29.

John F. Kennedy A194

1988, Nov. 22 **Litho.** ***Perf. 14***

1162A A194 1c like 30c .20 .20
1162B A194 2c like $4 .20 .20
1162C A194 3c like $1 .20 .20
1162D A194 4c like 60c .20 .20
1163 A194 30c First family .25 .20
1164 A194 60c Motorcade, Mexico .45 .40
1165 A194 $1 Funeral procession .70 *.70*
1166 A194 $4 Aboard PT109 2.25 *2.50*
Nos. 1162A-1166 (8) 4.45 *4.60*

Souvenir Sheet

1167 A194 $5 Taking Oath of Office 3.25 *3.75*

Miniature Sheet

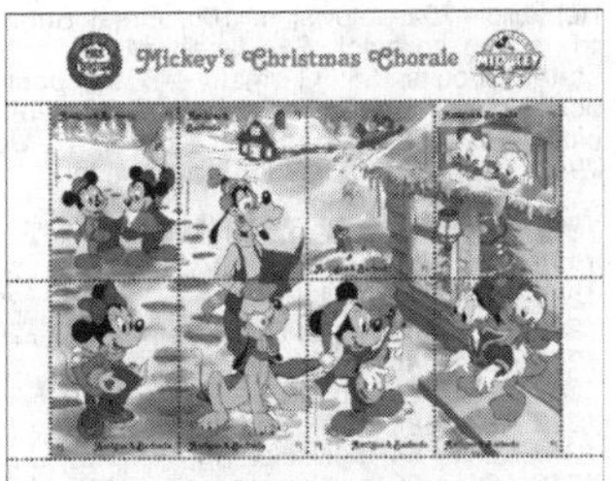

Christmas, Mickey Mouse 60th Anniv. — A195

Walt Disney characters - #1168: a, Morty and Ferdie. b, Goofy. c, Chip-n-Dale. d, Huey and Dewey. e, Minnie Mouse. f, Pluto. g, Mickey Mouse. h, Donald Duck and Louie.

No. 1169, Goofy driving Mickey and Minnie in a horse-drawn carriage. No. 1170, Characters on roller skates, caroling.

1988, Dec. 1 ***Perf. 13½x14, 14x13½***

1168 A195 Sheet of 8 6.00 6.00
a.-h. $1 any single .75 .75

Souvenir Sheets

1169 A195 $7 multicolored 5.00 5.00
1170 A195 $7 multi, horiz. 5.00 5.00

1988, Dec. 1 **Litho.** ***Perf. 14***

1171 A195 10c like No. 1168e .20 .20
1172 A195 25c like No. 1168f .20 .20
1173 A195 30c like No. 1168g .25 .25
1174 A195 70c like No. 1168h .50 .50
Nos. 1171-1174 (4) 1.15 1.15

Arawak Indian Whip Dance — A196

UPAE and discovery of America emblems and: a, Five adults. b, Eight adults. c, Seven adults. d, Three adults, three children.

1989, May 16 **Litho.** ***Perf. 14***

1175 Strip of 4 4.50 4.50
a.-d. A196 $1.50 any single 1.10 1.10

Souvenir Sheet

1176 A196 $6 Arawak chief 4.50 4.50

Discovery of America 500th anniv. (in 1992), pre-Columbian societies and customs.

Jet Flight, 50th Anniv. A197

Various jet aircraft.

1989, May 29 **Litho.** ***Perf. 14x13½***

1177 A197 10c DeHavilland Comet 4 .20 .20
1178 A197 30c Messerschmitt Me262 .25 .20
1179 A197 40c Boeing 707 .25 .30
1180 A197 60c Canadair F-86 Sabre .30 .25
1181 A197 $1 Lockheed F-104 Starfighter .40 .35
1182 A197 $2 McDonnell Douglas DC-10 .80 *1.00*
1183 A197 $3 Boeing 747 1.00 *1.10*
1184 A197 $4 McDonnell F-4 Phantom 1.00 *1.10*
Nos. 1177-1184 (8) 4.20 *4.50*

Souvenir Sheets

1185 A197 $7 Grumman F-14 Tomcat 4.75 *5.00*
1186 A197 $7 Concorde 4.75 *5.00*

Caribbean Cruise Ships A198

1989, June 20 **Litho.** ***Perf. 14***

1187 A198 25c TSS *Festivale* .20 .20
1188 A198 45c M.S. *Southward* .30 .20
1189 A198 50c M.S. *Sagafjord* .40 .20
1190 A198 60c MTS *Daphne* .45 .30
1191 A198 75c M.V. *Cunard Countess* .55 .45
1192 A198 90c M.S. *Song of America* .70 .65
1193 A198 $3 M.S. *Island Princess* 2.00 *2.25*
1194 A198 $4 S.S. *Galileo* 2.00 *2.25*
Nos. 1187-1194 (8) 6.60 *6.50*

Souvenir Sheets

1195 A198 $6 S.S. *Norway* 4.25 *4.75*
1196 A198 $6 S.S. *Oceanic* 4.25 *4.75*

Paintings by Hiroshige — A199

Designs: 25c, *Fish Swimming by Duck Half-submerged in Stream.* 45c, *Crane and Wave.* 50c, *Sparrows and Morning Glories.* 60c, *Crested Blackbird and Flowering Cherry.* $1, *Great Knot Sitting among Water Grass.* $2, *Goose on a Bank of Water.* $3, *Black Paradise Flycatcher and Blossoms.* $4, *Sleepy Owl Perched on a Pine Branch.* No. 1205, *Bullfinch Flying Near a Clematis Branch.* No. 1206, *Titmouse on a Cherry Branch.*

1989, July 3 ***Perf. 14x13½***

1197 A199 25c multicolored .45 .20
1198 A199 45c multicolored .55 .35
1199 A199 50c multicolored .60 .35
1200 A199 60c multicolored .70 .45
1201 A199 $1 multicolored .80 .60
1202 A199 $2 multicolored 1.75 1.75
1203 A199 $3 multicolored 2.00 2.00
1204 A199 $4 multicolored 2.00 2.00
Nos. 1197-1204 (8) 8.85 7.70

Souvenir Sheets

1205 A199 $5 multicolored 3.25 3.25
1206 A199 $5 multicolored 3.25 3.25

Hirohito (1901-1989) and enthronement of Akihito as emperor of Japan.

PHILEXFRANCE '89 — A200

Walt Disney characters, French landmarks: 1c, Helicopter over the Seine. 2c, Arc de Triomphe. 3c, Painting Notre Dame Cathedral. 4c, Entrance to the Metro. 5c, Fashion show. 10c, Follies. No. 1213, Shopping stalls on the Seine. $6, Sidewalk cafe, Left Bank. No. 1215, Hot air balloon *Ear Force One.* No. 1216, Dining.

1989, July 7 **Perf. 14x13½**

1207 A200 1c multicolored .20 .20
1208 A200 2c multicolored .20 .20
1209 A200 3c multicolored .20 .20
1210 A200 4c multicolored .20 .20
1211 A200 5c multicolored .20 .20
1212 A200 10c multicolored .20 .20
1213 A200 $5 multicolored 3.25 *3.75*
1214 A200 $6 multicolored 3.75 *4.00*
Nos. 1207-1214 (8) 8.20 *8.95*

Souvenir Sheets

1215 A200 $5 multicolored 3.25 3.25
1216 A200 $5 multicolored 3.25 3.25

1990 World Cup Soccer Championships, Italy — A201

Natl. flag, various actions of a defending goalie.

1989, Aug. 21 **Perf. 14**

1217 A201 15c multicolored .45 .20
1218 A201 25c multicolored .50 .20
1219 A201 $1 multicolored 1.00 .75
1220 A201 $4 multicolored 2.00 *3.50*
Nos. 1217-1220 (4) 3.95 *4.65*

Souvenir Sheets

1221 A201 $5 2 players, horiz. 3.25 *3.50*
1222 A201 $5 3 players, horiz. 3.25 *3.50*

For overprints see Nos. 1344-1349.

Mushrooms — A202

1989, Oct. 12 **Litho.** **Perf. 14**

1223 A202 10c Lilac fairy helmet .20 .20
1224 A202 25c Rough psathyrella, vert. .25 .20
1225 A202 50c Golden tops .60 .40
1226 A202 60c Blue cap, vert. .60 .45
1227 A202 75c Brown cap, vert. .75 .55
1228 A202 $1 Green gill, vert. 1.00 .75
1229 A202 $3 Red pinwheel 2.00 *2.50*
1230 A202 $4 Red chanterelle 2.00 *2.50*
Nos. 1223-1230 (8) 7.40 *7.55*

Souvenir Sheets

1231 A202 $6 Slender stalk 4.25 4.00
1232 A202 $6 Paddy straw mushroom 4.25 4.00

Nos. 1224, 1226-1228, 1231 vert.

Wildlife A203

1989, Oct. 19 **Litho.** **Perf. 14**

1233 A203 25c Hutia .30 .25
1234 A203 45c Caribbean monk seal .75 .40
1235 A203 60c Mustache bat, vert. .50 .45
1236 A203 $4 Manatee, vert. 1.50 *2.25*
Nos. 1233-1236 (4) 3.05 *3.35*

Souvenir Sheet

1237 A203 $5 West Indies giant rice rat 3.25 *3.75*

American Philatelic Soc. Emblem, Stamps on Stamps and Walt Disney Characters Promoting Philately A204

Designs: 1c, Israel #150, printing press. 2c, Italy #1238, first day cancel. 3c, US #143L4, Pony Express recruits. 4c, Denmark #566, early radio broadcast. 5c, German Democratic Republic #702, television. 10c, Great Britain #1, stamp collector. $4, Japan #1414, integrated circuits. $6, Germany #B667, boom box. No. 1246, US #1355, C3a, and Jenny biplane over Disneyland, horiz. No. 1247, US #940, 1421 and stamps for the wounded.

1989, Nov. 2 **Perf. 13½x14, 14x13½**

1238 A204 1c multicolored .20 .20
1239 A204 2c multicolored .20 .20
1240 A204 3c multicolored .20 .20
1241 A204 4c multicolored .20 .20
1242 A204 5c multicolored .20 .20
1243 A204 10c multicolored .20 .20
1244 A204 $4 multicolored 3.00 *3.25*
1245 A204 $6 multicolored 4.00 *4.25*
Nos. 1238-1245 (8) 8.20 *8.70*

Souvenir Sheets

1246 A204 $5 multicolored 3.50 *3.75*
1247 A204 $5 multicolored 3.50 *3.75*

Locomotives and Walt Disney Characters — A205

Perf. 14x13½, 13½x14

1989, Nov. 17

1248 A205 25c John Bull, 1831 .50 .50
1249 A205 45c Atlantic, 1832 .60 .50
1250 A205 50c William Crook's, 1861 .60 .50
1251 A205 60c Minnetonka, 1869 .70 .65
1252 A205 $1 Thatcher Perkins, 1863 .75 .75
1253 A205 $2 Pioneer, 1848 1.50 *2.00*
1254 A205 $3 Peppersass, 1869 1.75 *2.50*
1255 A205 $4 Gimbels Flyer 2.00 *2.50*
Nos. 1248-1255 (8) 8.40 *9.90*

Souvenir Sheets

1256 A205 $6 #6100 Class S-1 & 1835 Thomas Jefferson 4.25 *4.50*
1257 A205 $6 Jupiter & #119 4.25 *4.50*

New York World's Fair, 50th anniv., and World Stamp Expo '89, Washington, DC.

1st Moon Landing, 20th Anniv. A206

1989, Nov. 24 **Litho.** **Perf. 14**

1258 A206 10c Apollo 11 liftoff .20 .20
1259 A206 45c Aldrin walking on Moon .35 .20
1260 A206 $1 *Eagle* ascending from Moon .70 .60
1261 A206 $4 Recovery after splashdown 2.75 *3.25*
Nos. 1258-1261 (4) 4.00 *4.25*

Souvenir Sheet

1262 A206 $5 Armstrong 3.50 *3.75*

Nos. 1258-1259 and 1262, vert.

Souvenir Sheet

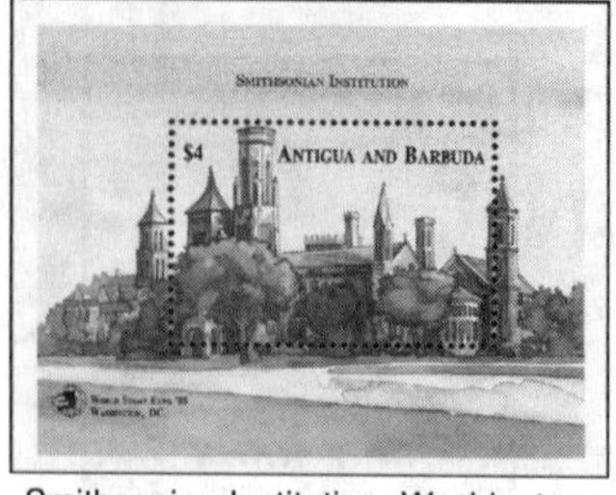

Smithsonian Institution, Washington, DC — A207

1989, Nov. 17 **Litho.** **Perf. 14**

1263 A207 $4 multicolored 3.00 3.00

World Stamp Expo '89.

Christmas — A208

Religious paintings: 10c, *The Small Cowper Madonna.* 25c, *Madonna of the Goldfinch.* 30c, *The Alba Madonna.* 50c, *Bologna Altarpiece* (attendant). 60c, *Bologna Altarpiece* (heralding angel). 70c, *Bologna Altarpiece* (archangel). $4, *Bologna Altarpiece* (saint holding ledger). No. 1271, *Madonna of Foligno.* No. 1272, *The Marriage of the Virgin.* No. 1273, *Bologna Altarpiece* (Madonna and Child).

Bologna Altarpiece by Giotto. Other paintings by Raphael.

1989, Dec. 11 **Litho.** **Perf. 14**

1264 A208 10c multicolored .20 .20
1265 A208 25c multicolored .20 .20
1266 A208 30c multicolored .20 .20
1267 A208 50c multicolored .45 .35
1268 A208 60c multicolored .50 .40
1269 A208 70c multicolored .55 .45
1270 A208 $4 multicolored 2.75 *3.00*
1271 A208 $5 multicolored 3.50 *4.00*
Nos. 1264-1271 (8) 8.35 *8.80*

Souvenir Sheets

1272 A208 $5 multicolored 3.50 *4.00*
1273 A208 $5 multicolored 3.50 *4.00*

America Issue — A210

Orchids — A211

UPAE, discovery of America 500th anniv. emblems and marine life: 10c, Star-eyed hermit crab. 20c, Spiny lobster. 25c, Magnificent banded fanworm. 45c, Cannonball jellyfish. 60c, Red-spiny sea star. $2, Peppermint shrimp. $3, Coral crab. $4, Branching fire coral. No. 1283, Common sea fan. No. 1284, Portuguese man-of-war.

1990, Mar. 26 **Litho.** **Perf. 14**

1275 A210 10c multicolored .20 .20
1276 A210 20c multicolored .20 .20
1277 A210 25c multicolored .25 .25
1278 A210 45c multicolored .45 .45
1279 A210 60c multicolored .70 .70
1280 A210 $2 multicolored 1.75 *2.00*
1281 A210 $3 multicolored 2.00 *2.25*
1282 A210 $4 multicolored 2.50 *2.75*
Nos. 1275-1282 (8) 8.05 *8.80*

Souvenir Sheets

1283 A210 $5 multicolored 3.50 *4.00*
1284 A210 $5 multicolored 3.50 *4.00*

1990, Apr. 17 **Perf. 14**

1285 A211 15c *Vanilla mexicana* .35 .25
1286 A211 45c *Epidendrum ibaguense* .50 .25
1287 A211 50c *Epidendrum secundum* .55 .30
1288 A211 60c *Maxillaria conferta* .60 .35
1289 A211 $1 *Oncidium altissimum* .90 .70
1290 A211 $2 *Spiranthes lanceolata* 1.25 *1.50*
1291 A211 $3 *Tonopsis utricularioides* 1.75 *2.25*
1292 A211 $5 *Epidendrum nocturnum* 3.50 *3.75*
Nos. 1285-1292 (8) 9.40 *9.35*

Souvenir Sheets

1293 A211 $6 *Octomeria graminifolia* 4.00 *4.50*
1294 A211 $6 *Rodriguezia lanceolata* 4.00 *4.50*

EXPO '90, Osaka.

Fish A212

1990, May 21 **Perf. 14**

1295 A212 10c Flamefish .35 .35
1296 A212 15c Coney .40 .35
1297 A212 50c Squirrelfish .60 .45
1298 A212 60c Sergeant major .60 .45
1299 A212 $1 Yellowtail snapper .85 .65
1300 A212 $2 Rock beauty 1.50 *1.75*
1301 A212 $3 Spanish hogfish 2.00 *2.25*
1302 A212 $4 Striped parrotfish 2.00 *2.25*
Nos. 1295-1302 (8) 8.30 *8.50*

Souvenir sheets

1303 A212 $5 Blackbar soldierfish 3.50 *4.00*
1304 A212 $5 Foureye butterflyfish 3.50 *4.00*

Victoria and Elizabeth II — A213

1990, May 3 **Litho.** **Perf. 15x14**

1305 A213 45c green .60 .30
1306 A213 60c bright rose .70 .50
1307 A213 $5 bright ultra 3.25 *4.00*
Nos. 1305-1307 (3) 4.55 *4.80*

Souvenir Sheet

1308 A213 $6 black 4.25 *4.75*

Penny Black, 150th anniv.

Royal Mail Transport A214

Designs: 50c, Steam packet *Britannia,* 1840. 75c, Railway mail car, 1892. $4, *Centaurus* seaplane, 1938. $6, Subway, 1927.

1990, May 3 **Perf. 13½**

1309 A214 50c red & deep green .55 .30
1310 A214 75c red & vio brn .75 .70
1311 A214 $4 red & brt ultra 3.00 *3.75*
Nos. 1309-1311 (3) 4.30 *4.75*

Souvenir Sheet

1312 A214 $6 red & black 4.25 *4.75*

Stamp World London '90.

Miniature Sheet

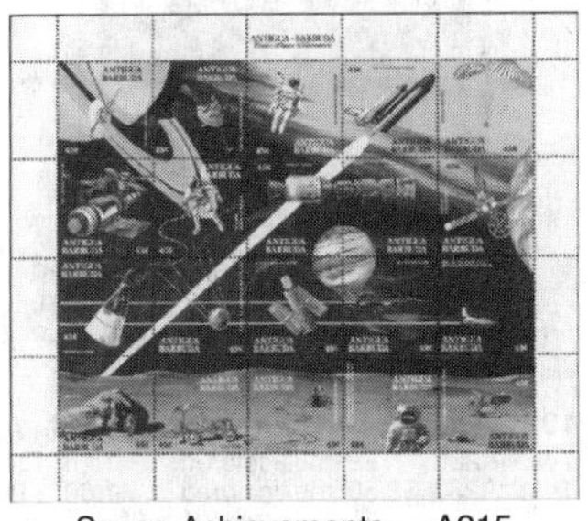

Space Achievements — A215

Designs: a, *Voyager 2* passing Saturn. b, *Pioneer 11* photographing Saturn. c, Manned maneuvering unit. d, *Columbia* space shuttle. e, Splashdown of Apollo 10 command module. f, *Skylab.* g, Ed White space walking, Gemini 4 mission. h, Apollo module, Apollo-Soyuz mission. i, Soyuz module, Apollo-Soyuz mission. j, *Mariner 1* passing Venus. k, Gemini 4 module. l, *Sputnik.* m, Hubble Space Telescope. n, X-15 rocket plane. o, Bell X-1 breaking sound barrier. p, Astronaut, Apollo 17 mission. r, American lunar rover. r, Lunar module, Apollo 14 mission. s, First men on the Moon, Apollo 11 mission. t, Lunokhod, Soviet lunar rover.

1990, June 11 Litho. *Perf. 14*

1313	A215	Sheet of 20	6.75	6.75
a.-t.		45c any single	.30	.30

Mickey Production Studios — A216

Walt Disney characters in Hollywood: 45c, Minnie Mouse reading script. 50c, Director Mickey Mouse, take 1 of Minnie. 60c, Make-up artist Daisy Duck. $1, Clarabelle as Cleopatra. $2, Mickey, Goofy, Donald Duck. $3, Goofy destroying set. $4, Mickey, Donald editing film. No. 1322, Mickey directs surfing film. No. 1323, Minnie, Daisy, Clarabelle in musical.

1990, Sept. 3 Litho. *Perf. 14x13½*

1314	A216	25c	shown	.25	.20
1315	A216	45c	multicolored	.45	.20
1316	A216	50c	multicolored	.55	.25
1317	A216	60c	multicolored	.60	.30
1318	A216	$1	multicolored	.80	.60
1319	A216	$2	multicolored	1.50	1.75
1320	A216	$3	multicolored	2.00	2.25
1321	A216	$4	multicolored	2.00	2.25
			Nos. 1314-1321 (8)	8.15	7.80

Souvenir Sheets

1322	A216	$5	multicolored	3.50	3.50
1323	A216	$5	multicolored	3.50	3.50

A217 A218

1990, Aug. 27 Litho. *Perf. 14*

1324	A217	15c	multicolored	.20	.20
1325	A217	35c	multi, diff.	.30	.20
1326	A217	75c	multi, diff.	.55	.55
1327	A217	$3	multi, diff.	2.00	2.50
			Nos. 1324-1327 (4)	3.05	3.45

Souvenir Sheet

1328	A217	$6	multi, diff.	4.00	4.50

Queen Mother, 90th birthday.

1990, Oct. 1 Litho. *Perf. 14*

1329	A218	50c	20-Kilometer Walk	.55	.30
1330	A218	75c	Triple jump	.70	.65
1331	A218	$1	10,000 meter run	.90	.85
1332	A218	$5	Javelin	3.00	4.25
			Nos. 1329-1332 (4)	5.15	6.05

Souvenir Sheet

1333	A218	$6	Opening ceremony, Los Angeles, 1984	4.25	*5.50*

1992 Summer Olympics, Barcelona.

Intl. Literacy Year — A219

Walt Disney characters in scenes from books by Charles Dickens: 15c, Huey and Dewey, Christmas Stories. 45c, Donald Duck, Bleak House. 50c, Dewey, Bad Pete, Oliver Twist. 60c, Daisy Duck, Old Curiosity Shop. $1, Little Nell. $2, Scrooge McDuck, Pickwick Papers. $3, Mickey and Minnie Mouse, Dombey and Son. $5, Minnie, Our Mutual Friend. No. 1342, Mickey and friends, David Copperfield. No. 1343, Pinocchio, Oliver Twist.

1990, Oct. 15 Litho. *Perf. 14*

1334	A219	15c	multicolored	.20	.20
1335	A219	45c	multicolored	.35	.35
1336	A219	50c	multicolored	.40	.40
1337	A219	60c	multicolored	.45	.45
1338	A219	$1	multicolored	.70	.70
1339	A219	$2	multicolored	1.25	1.75
1340	A219	$3	multicolored	1.75	2.25
1341	A219	$5	multicolored	2.50	3.00
			Nos. 1334-1341 (8)	7.60	9.10

Souvenir Sheets

1342	A219	$6	multicolored	4.25	4.50
1343	A219	$6	multicolored	4.25	4.50

Nos. 1217-1222 Overprinted

1990, Nov. 11

1344	A201	15c	multicolored	.40	.20
1345	A201	25c	multicolored	.40	.20
1346	A201	$1	multicolored	1.00	1.00
1347	A201	$4	multicolored	2.50	3.25
			Nos. 1344-1347 (4)	4.30	4.65

Souvenir Sheets

1348	A201	$5	on #1221	3.50	3.75
1349	A201	$5	on #1222	3.50	3.75

Overprint on Nos. 1348-1349 is 32x13mm.

Birds A220

1990, Nov. 19

1350	A220	10c	Pearly-eyed thrasher	.30	.30
1351	A220	25c	Purple-throated carib	.35	.35
1352	A220	50c	Common yellow-throat	.40	.40
1353	A220	60c	American kestrel	.70	.70
1354	A220	$1	Yellow-bellied sapsucker	.75	.75
1355	A220	$2	Purple gallinule	1.75	2.00
1356	A220	$3	Yellow-crowned night heron	2.25	2.50
1357	A220	$4	Blue-hooded euphonia	2.25	2.50
			Nos. 1350-1357 (8)	8.75	9.50

Souvenir Sheets

1358	A220	$6	Brown pelican	4.25	4.75
1359	A220	$6	Frigate bird	4.25	4.75

Christmas — A221

Paintings: 25c, Madonna and Child with Saints by del Piombo. 30c, Virgin and Child with Angels by Grunewald, vert. 40c, Holy Family and a Shepherd by Titian. 60c, Virgin and Child by Fra Filippo Lippi, vert. $1, Jesus, St. John and Two Angels by Rubens. $2, Adoration of the Shepherds by Catena. $4, Adoration of the Magi by Giorgione. $5, Virgin and Child Adored by a Warrior by Catena. No. 1368, Allegory of the Blessings of Jacob by Rubens, vert. No. 1369, Adoration of the Magi by Fra Angelico, vert.

Perf. 14x13½, 13½x14

1990, Dec. 10 Litho.

1360	A221	25c	multicolored	.25	.20
1361	A221	30c	multicolored	.30	.20
1362	A221	40c	multicolored	.40	.25
1363	A221	60c	multicolored	.55	.35
1364	A221	$1	multicolored	.75	.60
1365	A221	$2	multicolored	1.60	1.75
1366	A221	$4	multicolored	2.75	3.00
1367	A221	$5	multicolored	2.75	3.00
			Nos. 1360-1367 (8)	9.35	9.35

Souvenir Sheets

1368	A221	$6	multicolored	4.25	4.50
1369	A221	$6	multicolored	4.25	4.50

Peter Paul Rubens (1577-1640), Painter — A222

Entire paintings or different details from: 25c, Rape of the Daughters of Leucippus. 45c, $2, $4, Bacchanal. 50c, $1, $3, Rape of the Sabine Women. 60c, Battle of the Amazons. No. 1378, Rape of Hippodameia. No. 1379, Battle of the Amazons.

1991, Jan. 21 Litho. *Perf. 14*

1370	A222	25c	multicolored	.45	.30
1371	A222	45c	multicolored	.65	.45
1372	A222	50c	multicolored	.70	.50
1373	A222	60c	multicolored	.75	.65
1374	A222	$1	multicolored	.90	.90
1375	A222	$2	multicolored	1.25	1.50
1376	A222	$3	multicolored	2.00	2.25
1377	A222	$4	multicolored	2.75	3.00
			Nos. 1370-1377 (8)	9.45	9.55

Souvenir Sheets

1378	A222	$6	multicolored	4.25	4.50
1379	A222	$6	multicolored	4.25	4.50

World War II Milestones A223

Designs: 10c, US troops enter Germany, Sept. 11, 1944. 15c, All axis forces surrender in North Africa, May 12, 1943. 25c, US troops invade Kwajalein, Jan. 31, 1944. 45c, Roosevelt and Churchill meet in Casablanca, Jan. 14, 1943. 50c, Marshal Badoglio signs agreement with allies, Sept. 1, 1943. $1, Mountbatten appointed Supreme Allied Commander, Southeast Asia Command, Aug. 25, 1943. $2, Major Greek tactical victory, Koritza, Nov. 22, 1940. $4, Britain and USSR sign mutual assistance pact, July 12, 1941. $5, Operation Torch, Nov. 8, 1942. No. 1389, Japanese attack on Pearl Harbor, Dec. 7, 1941. No. 1390, American bombing attack on Schweinfurt, Oct. 14, 1943.

1991, Mar. 11 Litho. *Perf. 14*

1380	A223	10c	multicolored	.25	.25
1381	A223	15c	multicolored	.30	.20
1382	A223	25c	multicolored	.35	.35
1383	A223	45c	multicolored	.70	.50
1384	A223	50c	multicolored	.60	.45
1385	A223	$1	multicolored	.75	.65
1386	A223	$2	multicolored	1.50	1.75
1387	A223	$4	multicolored	2.25	2.50
1388	A223	$5	multicolored	2.25	2.50
			Nos. 1380-1388 (9)	8.95	9.15

Souvenir Sheets

1389	A223	$6	multicolored	4.25	4.50
1390	A223	$6	multicolored	4.25	4.50

Cog Railways of the World A224

Designs: 25c, Prince Regent, Middleton Colliery, 1812. 30c, Snowdon Mountain Railway, Wales. 40c, 1st Railcar at Hell Gate, Manitou and Pike's Peak Railway. 60c, PNKA Rack Railway, Amberawa, Java. $1, Green Mountain Railway, Mt. Desert Island, Maine, 1883. $2, Cog locomotive, Pike's Peak, 1891. $4, Vitznau-Rigi Cog Railway, Lake Lucerne. $5, Leopoldina Railway, Brazil. No. 1399, Electric Cog Donkey Engines, Panama Canal. No. 1400, Gornergratbahn, 1st electric cog railway in Switzerland, vert.

1991, Mar. 18 Litho. *Perf. 14*

1391	A224	25c	multicolored	.20	.20
1392	A224	30c	multicolored	.25	.25
1393	A224	40c	multicolored	.30	.30
1394	A224	60c	multicolored	.45	.45
1395	A224	$1	multicolored	1.00	.75
1396	A224	$2	multicolored	1.75	1.50
1397	A224	$4	multicolored	3.00	3.00
1398	A224	$5	multicolored	3.00	3.75
			Nos. 1391-1398 (8)	9.95	10.20

Souvenir Sheets

1399	A224	$6	multicolored	4.25	4.25
1400	A224	$6	multicolored	4.25	4.25

Butterflies A225

1991, Apr. 15 Litho. *Perf. 14*

1401	A225	10c	Zebra	.20	.20
1402	A225	35c	Southern daggertail	.25	.25
1403	A225	50c	Red anartia	.40	.40
1404	A225	75c	Malachite	.55	.55
1405	A225	$1	Polydamas swallowtail	.70	.75
1406	A225	$2	Orion	1.25	1.50
1407	A225	$4	Mimic	2.75	3.00
1408	A225	$5	Cracker	3.25	3.75
			Nos. 1401-1408 (8)	9.35	10.40

Souvenir Sheets

Caterpillars

1409	A225	$6	Monarch, vert.	4.25	4.25
1410	A225	$6	Painted lady, vert.	4.25	4.25

Voyages of Discovery A226

Designs: 10c, Hanno, Phoenicia, c. 450 B.C. 15c, Pytheas, Greece, 325 B.C. 45c, Eric the Red, Viking, A.D. 985. 60c, Leif Erikson, Viking, A.D. 1000. $1, Scylax, Greece, A.D. 518. $2, Marco Polo, A.D. 1259. $4, Queen Hatsheput, Egypt, 1493 B.C. $5, St. Brendan, Ireland, 500 A.D. No. 1419, Columbus, bare-headed. No. 1420, Columbus, wearing hat.

1991, Apr. 22

1411	A226	10c	multicolored	.20	.20
1412	A226	15c	multicolored	.20	.20
1413	A226	45c	multicolored	.35	.35
1414	A226	60c	multicolored	.45	.45
1415	A226	$1	multicolored	.70	.75
1416	A226	$2	multicolored	1.25	1.50
1417	A226	$4	multicolored	2.50	3.00
1418	A226	$5	multicolored	3.00	3.75
			Nos. 1411-1418 (8)	8.65	10.20

Souvenir Sheets

1419	A226	$6	multicolored	4.00	4.00
1420	A226	$6	multicolored	4.00	4.00

Discovery of America, 500th anniv. (in 1992).

Paintings by Vincent Van Gogh
A227

Designs: 5c, Portrait of Camille Roulin. 10c, Portrait of Armand Roulin. 15c, Young Peasant Woman with Straw Hat Sitting in the Wheat. 25c, Portrait of Adeline Ravoux. 30c, The Schoolboy (Camille Roulin). 40c, Portrait of Doctor Gachet. 50c, Portrait of a Man. 75c, Two Children. $2, Portrait of Postman Joseph Roulin. $3, The Seated Zouave. $4, L'arlesienne: Madame Ginoux with Books. No. 1432, Self Portrait, November/December 1888. No. 1433, Flowering Garden. No. 1434, Farmhouse in Provence. $6, The Bridge at Trinquetaille.

1991, May 13 ***Perf. 13½***

1421 A227 5c multicolored .20 .20
1422 A227 10c multicolored .20 .20
1423 A227 15c multicolored .20 .20
1424 A227 25c multicolored .20 .20
1425 A227 30c multicolored .25 .25
1426 A227 40c multicolored .30 .30
1427 A227 50c multicolored .35 .35
1428 A227 75c multicolored .55 .55
1429 A227 $2 multicolored 1.25 1.50
1430 A227 $3 multicolored 2.00 2.25
1431 A227 $4 multicolored 2.50 3.00
1432 A227 $5 multicolored 3.00 3.75
Nos. 1421-1432 (12) 11.00 12.75

Size: 102x76mm

Imperf

1433 A227 $5 multicolored 3.50 3.50
1434 A227 $5 multicolored 3.50 3.50
1435 A227 $6 multicolored 4.25 4.25

Phila Nippon '91 — A228

Walt Disney characters demonstrating Japanese martial arts: 10c, Mickey as champion sumo wrestler, vert. 15c, Goofy using tonfa. 45c, Ninja Donald in full field dress. 60c, Mickey using weapon in kung fu, vert. $1, Goofy tries kendo, vert. $2, Mickey, Donald demonstrating special technique of aikido. $4, Mickey flips Donald with judo throw. $5, Mickey demonstrates yabusame (target shooting from running horse), vert. No. 1444, Mickey using karate. No. 1445, Mickey demonstrating tamashiwara (powerbreaking), vert.

Perf. 13½x14, 14x13½

1991, June 29 **Litho.**

1436 A220 10c multicolored .20 .20
1437 A228 15c multicolored .20 .20
1438 A228 45c multicolored .35 .35
1439 A220 60c multicolored .45 .45
1440 A228 $1 multicolored .70 .75
1441 A220 $2 multicolored 1.25 1.50
1442 A220 $4 multicolored 2.50 3.00
1443 A228 $5 multicolored 3.00 3.75
Nos. 1436-1443 (8) 8.65 10.20

Souvenir Sheets

1444 A228 $6 multicolored 4.25 4.25
1445 A228 $6 multicolored 4.25 4.25

Royal Family Birthday, Anniversary
Common Design Type

1991, July 8 **Litho.** ***Perf. 14***

1446 CD347 10c multicolored .20 .20
1447 CD347 15c multicolored .20 .20
1448 CD347 20c multicolored .20 .20
1449 CD347 40c multicolored .30 .30
1450 CD347 $1 multicolored .70 .75
1451 CD347 $2 multicolored 1.25 1.50
1452 CD347 $4 multicolored 2.50 3.00
1453 CD347 $5 multicolored 3.00 3.75
Nos. 1446-1453 (8) 8.35 9.90

Souvenir Sheets

1454 CD347 $4 Elizabeth, Philip 2.75 2.75
1455 CD347 $4 Charles, Diana, sons 2.75 2.75

10c, 40c, $1, $5, No. 1455, Charles and Diana, 10th wedding anniversary. Others, Queen Elizabeth II, 65th birthday.

Walt Disney Characters Playing Golf — A229

Designs: 10c, Daisy Duck teeing off. 15c, Goofy using 3-Wood. 45c, Mickey using 3-Iron. 60c, Mickey missing ball using 6-Iron. $1, Donald trying 8-Iron to get out of pond. $2, Minnie using 9-Iron. $4, Donald digging hole with sand wedge. $5, Goofy trying new approach with putter. No. 1464, Grandma Duck using pitching wedge. No. 1465, Mickey cheering Minnie as she uses her 5-Wood, horiz.

Perf. 13½x14, 14x13½

1991, Aug. 7 **Litho.**

1456 A229 10c multicolored .20 .20
1457 A229 15c multicolored .20 .20
1458 A229 45c multicolored .35 .35
1459 A229 60c multicolored .45 .45
1460 A229 $1 multicolored .70 .75
1461 A229 $2 multicolored 1.25 1.50
1462 A229 $4 multicolored 2.50 3.00
1463 A229 $5 multicolored 3.00 3.75
Nos. 1456-1463 (8) 8.65 10.20

Souvenir Sheets

1464 A229 $6 multicolored 4.25 4.25
1465 A229 $6 multicolored 4.25 4.25

1992 Summer Olympics, Barcelona
A230

Archie Comics, 50th anniv.: 10c, Moose receiving gold medal. 25c, Archie, Veronica, Mr. Lodge, polo match, horiz. 40c, Archie & Betty, fencing. 60c, Archie, women's volleyball. $1, Archie, tennis. $2, Archie, marathon race. $4, Archie, judging women's gymnastics, horiz. $5, Archie, Betty, Veronica, basketball. No. 1474, Archie, soccer. No. 1475, Archie, Betty, baseball, horiz.

Perf. 13½x14, 14x13½

1991, Aug. 19

1466 A230 10c multicolored .20 .20
1467 A230 25c multicolored .20 .20
1468 A230 40c multicolored .30 .30
1469 A230 60c multicolored .45 .45
1470 A230 $1 multicolored .75 .75
1471 A230 $2 multicolored 1.50 1.50
1472 A230 $4 multicolored 3.00 3.00
1473 A230 $5 multicolored 3.75 3.75
Nos. 1466-1473 (8) 10.15 10.15

Souvenir Sheets

1474 A230 $6 multicolored 4.50 4.50
1475 A230 $6 multicolored 4.50 4.50

Charles de Gaulle, Birth Cent.
A231

Charles de Gaulle: 10c, and Pres. Kennedy, families, 1961. 15c, and Pres. Roosevelt, 1945, vert. 45c, and Chancellor Adenauer, 1962, vert. 60c, Liberation of Paris, 1944, vert. $1, Crossing the Rhine, 1945. $2, In Algiers, 1944. $4, and Pres. Eisenhower, 1960. $5, Returning from Germany, 1968, vert. No. 1484, and Churchill at Casablanca, 1943. No. 1485, and Citizens.

1991, Sept. 11 **Litho.** ***Perf. 14***

1476 A231 10c multicolored .20 .20
1477 A231 15c multicolored .20 .20
1478 A231 45c multicolored .35 .35
1479 A231 60c multicolored .45 .45
1480 A231 $1 multicolored .70 .75
1481 A231 $2 multicolored 1.25 1.50
1482 A231 $4 multicolored 2.50 3.00
1483 A231 $5 multicolored 3.00 3.75
Nos. 1476-1483 (8) 8.65 10.20

Souvenir Sheets

1484 A231 $6 multicolored 4.25 4.25
1485 A231 $6 multicolored 4.25 4.25

Independence, 10th Anniv. — A232

Designs: 10c, Island maps, government building. $6, Old P. O., St. Johns, #1 & #635.

1991, Oct. 28

1486 A232 10c multicolored .20 .20

Souvenir Sheet

1487 A232 $6 multicolored 4.25 4.25

No. 1487 contains one 50x38mm stamp.

Miniature Sheet

Attack on Pearl Harbor, 50th Anniv.
A233

Designs: No. 1488a, Bow of Nimitz class carrier, Ticonderoga class cruiser. b, Tourist boat to Arizona Memorial. c, USS Arizona Memorial. d, Aircraft salute to missing men. e, White tern. f, Japanese Kate torpedo bombers. g, Japanese Zero fighters. h, Battleship row in flames. i, USS Nevada breaking out. j, Zeros returning to carriers.

1991, Dec. 9 ***Perf. 14½x15***

1488 A233 $1 Sheet of 10, #a.-j. 7.50 7.50

Inscription for No. 1488f incorrectly describes torpedo bombers as Zekes.

3rd Antigua Methodist Cub Scout Pack, 60th Anniv.
A234

Designs: $2, Lord Robert Baden-Powell, scouts, vert. $3.50, Scouts around campfire. $5, Antigua & Barbuda flag, Jamboree emblem, vert.

1991, Dec. 9 ***Perf. 14***

1489 A234 75c multicolored .60 .60
1490 A234 $2 multicolored 1.25 1.50
1491 A234 $3.50 multicolored 2.25 2.75
Nos. 1489-1491 (3) 4.10 4.85

Souvenir Sheet

1492 A234 $5 multicolored 3.25 3.25

17th World Scout Jamboree, Korea.

Wolfgang Amadeus Mozart, Death Bicent.
A235

Portrait of Mozart and: $1.50, Scene from opera, Don Giovanni. $4, St. Peter's Cathedral, Salzburg.

1991, Dec. 9

1493 A235 $1.50 multicolored 1.10 1.10
1494 A235 $4 multicolored 2.50 3.00

Anniversaries and Events — A236

Designs: $2, Otto Lilienthal's glider No. 5. $2.50, Locomotive cab, vert.

1991, Dec. 9 **Litho.** ***Perf. 14***

1495 A236 $2 multicolored 1.25 1.50
1496 A236 $2.50 multicolored 1.60 1.90

First glider flight, cent. (No. 1495). Trans-Siberian Railway, cent. (No. 1496). Numbers have been reserved for additional values in this set.

Brandenburg Gate, Bicent. — A237

25c, Demonstrators in autos, German flag. $2, Statue. $3, Portions of decorative frieze.

1991, Dec. 9 **Litho.** ***Perf. 14***

1499 A237 25c multicolored .20 .20
1500 A237 $2 multicolored 1.25 1.50
1501 A237 $3 multicolored 2.00 2.25
Nos. 1499-1501 (3) 3.45 3.95

Souvenir Sheet

1502 A237 $4 multicolored 3.00 3.00

Christmas
A238

Paintings by Fra Angelico: 10c, The Annunciation. 30c, Nativity. 40c, Adoration of the Magi. 60c, Presentation in the Temple. $1, Circumcision. $3, Flight into Egypt. $4, Massacre of the Innocents. $5, Christ Teaching in the Temple. No. 1511, Adoration of the Magi, diff. No. 1512, Adoration of the Magi (Cook Tondo).

1991, Dec. 12 ***Perf. 12***

1503 A238 10c multicolored .20 .20
1504 A238 30c multicolored .25 .25
1505 A238 40c multicolored .30 .30
1506 A238 60c multicolored .45 .45
1507 A238 $1 multicolored .70 .75
1508 A238 $3 multicolored 2.00 2.25
1509 A238 $4 multicolored 2.50 3.00
1510 A238 $5 multicolored 3.00 3.75
Nos. 1503-1510 (8) 9.40 10.95

Souvenir Sheets

1511 A238 $6 multicolored 4.25 4.25
1512 A238 $6 multicolored 4.25 4.25

Queen Elizabeth II's Accession to the Throne, 40th Anniv.
Common Design Type

Queen Elizabeth II and various island scenes.

1992, Feb. 6 **Litho.** ***Perf. 14***

1513 CD348 10c multicolored .20 .20
1514 CD348 30c multicolored .20 .20
1515 CD348 $1 multicolored .70 .75
1516 CD348 $5 multicolored 3.00 3.75
Nos. 1513-1516 (4) 4.10 4.90

Souvenir Sheets

1517 CD348 $6 Beach 4.25 4.25
1518 CD348 $6 Flora 4.25 4.25

Mushrooms A239

1992 Litho. *Perf. 14*

1519	A239	10c Amanita caesarea	.20	.20
1520	A239	15c Collybia fusipes	.20	.20
1521	A239	30c Boletus aereus	.20	.20
1522	A239	40c Laccaria amethystina	.30	.30
1523	A239	$1 Russula virescens	.70	.75
1524	A239	$2 Tricholoma auratum	1.25	1.50
1525	A239	$4 Calocybe gambosa	2.50	3.00
1526	A239	$5 Panus tigrinus	3.00	3.75
		Nos. 1519-1526 (8)	8.35	9.90

Souvenir Sheet

1527	A239	$6 Auricularia auricula	4.25	4.25
1528	A239	$6 Clavariadelphus truncatus	4.25	4.25

Issued: 10c, 30c, $1, $5, #1528, May 18; others, Mar.

Disney Characters at Summer Olympics, Barcelona A240

Designs: 10c, Mickey presenting gold medal to mermaid for swimming. 15c, Dewey and Huey watching Louie in kayak. 30c, Uncle McScrooge, Donald yachting. 50c, Donald, horse trying water polo. $1, Big Pete weight lifting. $2, Donald, Goofy fencing. $4, Mickey, Donald playing volleyball. $5, Goofy vaulting over horse. No. 1537, Mickey playing basketball, horiz. No. 1538, Minnie Mouse on uneven parallel bars, horiz. No. 1539, Mickey, Goofy, and Donald judging Minnie's floor exercise, horiz. No. 1540, Mickey running after soccer ball.

1992, Mar. 16 *Perf. 13*

1529	A240	10c multicolored	.20	.20
1530	A240	15c multicolored	.20	.20
1531	A240	30c multicolored	.20	.20
1532	A240	50c multicolored	.40	.40
1533	A240	$1 multicolored	.70	.75
1534	A240	$2 multicolored	1.25	1.50
1535	A240	$4 multicolored	2.50	3.00
1536	A240	$5 multicolored	3.00	3.75
		Nos. 1529-1536 (8)	8.45	10.00

Souvenir Sheets

1537-1540	A240	$6 each	4.25	4.25

Dinosaurs A241

1992, Apr. 6 *Perf. 14*

1541	A241	10c Pteranodon	.20	.20
1542	A241	15c Brachiosaurus	.20	.20
1543	A241	30c Tyrannosaurus rex	.20	.20
1544	A241	50c Parasaurolophus	.40	.40
1545	A241	$1 Deinonychus	.70	.75
1546	A241	$2 Triceratops	1.25	1.50
1547	A241	$4 Protoceratops	2.50	3.00
1548	A241	$5 Stegosaurus	3.00	3.75
		Nos. 1541-1548 (8)	8.45	10.00

Souvenir Sheets

1549	A241	$6 Apatosaurus	4.25	4.25
1550	A241	$6 Allosaurus	4.25	4.25

Nos. 1541-1544 are vert.

Easter — A242

Paintings: 10c, Supper at Emmaus, by Caravaggio. 15c, The Vision of St. Peter, by Francisco de Zurbaran. 30c, $1, Christ Driving the Money Changers from the Temple, by Tiepolo (detail on $1). 40c, Martyrdom of St. Bartholomew (detail), by Jusepe de Ribera. $2, Crucifixion (detail), by Albrecht Altdorfer. $4, $5, The Deposition (diff. detail), by Fra Angelico. No. 1559, Crucifixion, by Albrecht Altdorfer, vert. No. 1560, The Last Supper, by Vicente Juan Masip.

1992 *Perf. 14x13½*

1551	A242	10c multicolored	.20	.20
1552	A242	15c multicolored	.20	.20
1553	A242	30c multicolored	.20	.20
1554	A242	40c multicolored	.30	.30
1555	A242	$1 multicolored	.70	.75
1556	A242	$2 multicolored	1.25	1.50
1557	A242	$4 multicolored	2.50	3.00
1558	A242	$5 multicolored	3.00	3.75
		Nos. 1551-1558 (8)	8.35	9.90

Souvenir Sheet

Perf. 13½x14

1559	A242	$6 multicolored	4.25	4.25
1560	A242	$6 multicolored	4.25	4.25

Spanish Art — A243

Designs: 10c, The Miracle at the Well, by Alonso Cano. 15c, The Poet Luis de Gongora y Argote, by Velazquez. 30c, The Painter Francisco Goya, by Vincente Lopez Portana. 40c, Maria de Las Nieves Michaela Fourdiniere, by Luis Paret y Alcazar. $1, Charles III Eating before His Court, by Paret y Alcazar, horiz. $2, A Rain Shower in Granada, by Antonio Munoz Degrain, horiz. $4, Sarah Bernhardt, by Santiago Rusinol y Prats. $5, The Hermitage Garden, by Joaquin Mir Trinxet. No. 1569, Olympus: Battle with the Giants, by Francisco Bayeu y Subias. No. 1570, The Ascent of Monsieur Boucle's Montgolfier Balloon in the Gardens of Aranjuez, by Antonio Carnicero.

1992, May 11

1561	A243	10c multicolored	.20	.20
1562	A243	15c multicolored	.20	.20
1563	A243	30c multicolored	.20	.20
1564	A243	40c multicolored	.30	.30
1565	A243	$1 multicolored	.70	.75
1566	A243	$2 multicolored	1.25	1.50
1567	A243	$4 multicolored	2.50	3.00
1568	A243	$5 multicolored	3.00	3.75

Size: 120x95mm

Imperf

1569	A243	$6 multicolored	3.75	4.50
1570	A243	$6 multicolored	3.75	4.50
		Nos. 1561-1570 (10)	15.85	18.90

Granada '92.

Discovery of America, 500th Anniv. A244

Designs: 15c, San Salvador Island. 30c, Martin Alonzo Pinzon, captain of Pinta. 40c, Columbus, signature, coat of arms. $1, Pinta. $2, Nina. $4, Santa Maria. No. 1577, Sea monster. No. 1578, Map, sailing ship.

1992, May 25 Litho. *Perf. 14*

1571	A244	15c multicolored	.20	.20
1572	A244	30c multicolored	.20	.20
1573	A244	40c multicolored	.30	.30
1574	A244	$1 multicolored	.70	.75
1575	A244	$2 multicolored	1.25	1.50
1576	A244	$4 multicolored	2.50	3.00
		Nos. 1571-1576 (6)	5.15	5.95

Souvenir Sheets

1577	A244	$6 multicolored	4.25	4.25
1578	A244	$6 multicolored	4.25	4.25

World Columbian Stamp Expo '92, Chicago.

Hummel Figurines — A245

Wanderers: 15c, No. 1587a, Boy sitting on rock pointing to flower in cap. 30c, No. 1587b, Girl sitting on fence. 40c, No. 1587c, Boy holding binoculars. 50c, No. 1587d, Boy carrying umbrella. $1, No. 1588a, Two boys looking up at direction marker. $2, No. 1588b, Boy carrying basket on back, walking with stick. $4, No. 1588c, Two girls, goat. $5, No. 1588d, Boy carrying walking stick.

1993, Jan. 6 Litho. *Perf. 14*

1579	A245	15c multicolored	.20	.20
1580	A245	30c multicolored	.20	.20
1581	A245	40c multicolored	.30	.30
1582	A245	50c multicolored	.40	.40
1583	A245	$1 multicolored	.70	.75
1584	A245	$2 multicolored	1.25	1.50
1585	A245	$4 multicolored	2.50	3.00
1586	A245	$5 multicolored	3.00	3.75
		Nos. 1579-1586 (8)	8.55	10.10

Souvenir Sheets of 4

1587	A245	$1.50 #a.-d.	4.25	4.25
1588	A245	$1.50 #a.-d.	4.25	4.25

Hummingbirds and Flowers — A246

Designs: 10c, Antillean crested, wild plantain. 25c, Green mango, parrot's plantain. 45c, Purple-throated carib, lobster claws. 60c, Antillean mango, coral plant. $1, Vervain, cardinal's guard. $2, Rufous breasted hermit, heliconia. $4, Blue-headed, red ginger. $5, Green-throated carib, ornamental banana. No. 1597, Bee, jungle flame. No. 1598, Western streamertails, bignonia.

1992, Aug. 10 Litho. *Perf. 14*

1589	A246	10c multicolored	.20	.20
1590	A246	25c multicolored	.20	.20
1591	A246	45c multicolored	.35	.35
1592	A246	60c multicolored	.45	.45
1593	A246	$1 multicolored	.70	.75
1594	A246	$2 multicolored	1.25	1.50
1595	A246	$4 multicolored	2.50	3.00
1596	A246	$5 multicolored	3.00	3.75
		Nos. 1589-1596 (8)	8.65	10.20

Souvenir Sheets

1597	A246	$6 multicolored	6.75	6.75
1598	A246	$6 multicolored	6.75	6.75

Genoa '92.

Discovery of America, 500th Anniv. — A247

1992 Litho. *Perf. 14½*

1599	A247	$1 Coming ashore	.75	.75
1600	A247	$2 Natives, ships	1.25	1.50

Organization of East Caribbean States.

Souvenir Sheet

Madison Square Garden, NYC — A248

1992 Litho. *Perf. 14*

1601	A248	$6 multicolored	5.00	5.00

Postage Stamp Mega-Event, Jacob Javits Center, New York City.

Elvis Presley (1935-1977) A249

Various pictures of Elvis Presley.

1992 *Perf. 13½x14*

1602	A249	$1 Sheet of 9, #a.-i.	7.00	7.00

Inventors and Pioneers A250

Designs: 10c, Ts'ai Lun, paper. 25c, Igor I. Sikorsky, 4-engine airplane. 30c, Alexander Graham Bell, telephone. 40c, Johannes Gutenberg, printing press. 60c, James Watt, steam engine. $1, Anton van Leeuwenhoek, microscope. $4, Louis Braille, Braille printing. $5, Galileo, telescope. No. 1607, Phonograph. No. 1608, Steamboat.

1992, Oct. 19 Litho. *Perf. 14*

1603	A250	10c multicolored	.20	.20
1604	A250	25c multicolored	.20	.20
1605	A250	30c multicolored	.25	.25
1605A	A250	40c multicolored	.40	.40
1605B	A250	60c multicolored	.45	.45
1605C	A250	$1 multicolored	.75	.75
1605D	A250	$4 multicolored	3.00	3.00
1606	A250	$5 multicolored	3.75	3.75
		Nos. 1603-1606 (8)	9.00	9.00

Souvenir Sheet

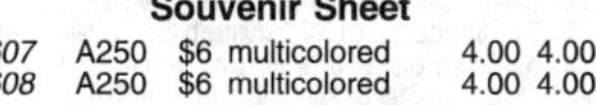

1607	A250	$6 multicolored	4.00	4.00
1608	A250	$6 multicolored	4.00	4.00

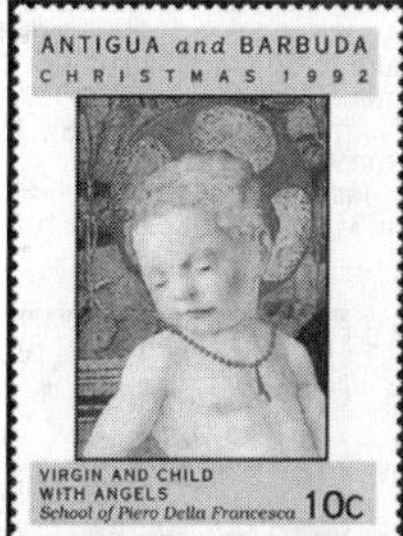

Christmas A251

Details from Paintings: 10c, Virgin and Child with Angels, by School of Piero Della Francesca. 25c, Madonna Degli Alberelli, by Giovanni Bellini. 30c, Madonna and Child with St. Anthony Abbot and St. Sigismund, by Neroccio di Landi. 40c, Madonna and the Grand Duke, by Raphael. 60c, The Nativity, by George de la Tour. $1, Holy Family, by Jacob Jordaens. $4, Madonna and Child Enthroned, by Margaritone. $5, Madonna and Child on a Curved Throne, by Byzantine artist. No. 1617, Madonna and Child, by Domenico Ghirlandaio (both names misspelled). No. 1618, The Holy Family, by Pontormo.

1992 ***Perf. 13½x14***

1609 A251 10c multicolored .20 .20
1610 A251 25c multicolored .20 .20
1611 A251 30c multicolored .25 .25
1612 A251 40c multicolored .30 .30
1613 A251 60c multicolored .45 .45
1614 A251 $1 multicolored .75 .75
1615 A251 $4 multicolored 3.00 3.00
1616 A251 $5 multicolored 3.75 3.75
Nos. 1609-1616 (8) 8.90 8.90

Souvenir Sheet

1617 A251 $6 multicolored 4.50 4.50
1618 A251 $6 multicolored 4.50 4.50

A252

A253

Anniversaries and Events: 10c, Cosomonauts. 40c, Graf Zeppelin, Goodyear blimp. 45c, Right Rev. Daniel C. Davis, St. John's Cathedral. 75c, Konrad Adenauer. $1, Bus Mosbacher, Weatherly. $1.50, Rain forest. No. 1625, Felis tigris. No. 1626, Flag, emblems, plant. No. 1627, Women acting on stage. $2.25, Women carrying baskets of food on their heads. $3, Lions Club emblem, club member. No. 1630, West German, NATO flags. No. 1631, China's Long March Booster Rocket. No. 1632, Dr. Hugo Eckener. No. 1633, The Hindenburg. No. 1634, Brandenburg Gate, German flag. No. 1635, Monarch butterfly. No. 1636, Hermes Shuttle, Columbus Space Station.

1992 **Litho.** ***Perf. 14***

1619 A252 10c multicolored .20 .20
1620 A252 40c multicolored .30 .30
1621 A253 45c multicolored .35 .35
1622 A252 75c multicolored .60 .60
1623 A252 $1 multicolored .75 .75
1624 A252 $1.50 multicolored 1.10 1.10
1625 A252 $2 multicolored 1.50 1.50
1626 A253 $2 multicolored 1.50 1.50
1627 A253 $2 multicolored 1.50 1.50
1628 A252 $2.25 multicolored 1.75 1.75
1629 A252 $3 multicolored 2.25 2.25
1630 A252 $4 multicolored 3.00 3.00
1631 A252 $4 multicolored 3.00 3.00
1632 A252 $6 multicolored 4.50 4.50
Nos. 1619-1632 (14) 22.30 22.30

Souvenir Sheets

1633-1636 A252 $6 each 4.50 4.50

Intl. Space Year (#1619, 1631, 1636). Count Zeppelin, 75th anniv. of death (#1620, 1632-1633). Diocese of Northeast Caribbean and Aruba District, 150th anniv. (#1621). Konrad Adenauer, 25th anniv. of death (#1622, 1630, 1634). 1962 winner of America's Cup (#1623). Earth Summit, Rio (#1624-1625, 1635). Inter-American Institute for Cooperation on Agriculture, 50th anniv. (#1626). Cultural Development, 40th anniv. (#1627). WHO Intl. Conf. on Nutrition, Rome (#1628). Lions Club, 75th anniv. (#1629).

Issued: #1619, 1621-1623, 1626-1631, 1634, 1636, Nov.; #1624-1625, 1635, Dec. 14.

Euro Disney, Paris — A254

Disney characters: 10c, Golf course. 25c, Davy Crockett Campground. 30c, Cheyenne Hotel. 40c, Santa Fe Hotel. $1, New York Hotel. $2, In car, map showing location. $4, Pirates of the Caribbean. $5, Adventureland. No. 1645, Mickey Mouse on map with star, vert. No. 1646, Roof turret at entrance, Mickey Mouse in uniform. No. 1646A, Mickey Mouse, colored spots on poster, vert. No. 1646B, Mickey on poster, vert., diff.

1992-93 **Litho.** ***Perf. 14x13½***

1637 A254 10c multicolored .20 .20
1638 A254 25c multicolored .20 .20
1639 A254 30c multicolored .25 .25
1640 A254 40c multicolored .30 .30
1641 A254 $1 multicolored .75 .75
1642 A254 $2 multicolored 1.50 1.50
1643 A254 $4 multicolored 3.00 3.00
1644 A254 $5 multicolored 3.75 3.75
Nos. 1637-1644 (8) 9.95 9.95

Souvenir Sheets

Perf. 13½x14

1645-1646B A254 $6 each 4.50 4.50

Issued: #1638-1639, 1642-1643, 1646-1646B, 2/22/93; others, 12/1992.

Miniature Sheets

Louvre Museum, Bicent. A255

Details or entire paintings, by Peter Paul Rubens: No. 1647a, Destiny of Marie de' Medici. b, Birth of Marie de'Medici. c, Marie's Education. d, Destiny of Marie de'Medici, diff. e, Henry IV Receives the Portrait. f, The Meeting at Lyons. g, The Marriage. h, The Birth of Louis XIII.

No. 1648a, The Capture of Juliers. b, The Exchange of Princesses. c, The Happiness of the Regency. d, The Majority of Louis XIII. e, The Flight from Blois. f, The Treaty of Angouleme. g, The Peace of Angers. h, The Queen's Reconciliation with Her Son.

$6, Helene Fourment Au Carosse.

1993, Mar. 22 **Litho.** ***Perf. 12***

Sheets of 8 + Label

1647 A255 $1 #a.-h. 6.00 6.00
1648 A255 $1 #a.-h. 6.00 6.00

Souvenir Sheet

Perf. 14½

1649 A255 $6 multicolored 4.50 4.50

No. 1649 contains one 55x88mm stamp.

Flowers — A256

1993, Mar. 15 **Litho.** ***Perf. 14***

1650 A256 15c Cardinal's guard .20 .20
1651 A256 25c Giant granadilla .20 .20
1652 A256 30c Spider flower .25 .25
1653 A256 40c Gold vine .30 .30
1654 A256 $1 Frangipani .75 .75
1655 A256 $2 Bougainvillea 1.50 1.50
1656 A256 $4 Yellow oleander 3.00 3.00
1657 A256 $5 Spicy jatropha 3.75 3.75
Nos. 1650-1657 (8) 9.95 9.95

Souvenir Sheets

1658 A256 $6 Bird lime tree 4.50 4.50
1659 A256 $6 Fairy lily 4.50 4.50

Endangered Species — A257

Designs: No. 1660a, St. Lucia parrot. b, Cahow. c, Swallow-tailed kite. d, Everglades kite. e, Imperial parrot. f, Humpback whale. g, Puerto Rican plain pigeon. h, St. Vincent parrot. i, Puerto Rican parrot. j, Leatherback turtle. k, American crocodile. l, Hawksbill turtle.

No. 1662, West Indian manatee.

1993, Apr. 5

1660 A257 $1 Sheet of 12, #a.-l. 9.00 9.00

Souvenir Sheets

1661 A257 $6 like #1660f 4.50 4.50
1662 A257 $6 multicolored 4.50 4.50

Philatelic Publishing Personalities — A258

Portrait, stamp: No. 1663, J. Walter Scott (1842-1919), US "#C3a," Antigua #1. No. 1664, Theodore Champion, France #8, Antigua #1. No. 1665, E. Stanley Gibbons (1856-1913), cover of his first price list and catalogue, Antigua #1. No. 1666, Hugo Michel (1866-1944), Bavaria #1, Antigua #1. No. 1667, Alberto (1877-1944) and Giulio (1902-1987) Bolaffi, Sardinia #1, Great Britain #3. No. 1668, Richard Borek (1874-1947), Brunswick #24, Bavaria #1.

Front pages, Mekeel's Weekly Stamp News: No. 1669a, Jan. 7, 1890. b, Feb. 12, 1993.

1993, June 14

1663 A258 $1.50 multicolored 1.10 1.10
1664 A258 $1.50 multicolored 1.10 1.10
1665 A258 $1.50 multicolored 1.10 1.10
1666 A258 $1.50 multicolored 1.10 1.10
1667 A258 $1.50 multicolored 1.10 1.10
1668 A258 $1.50 multicolored 1.10 1.10
Nos. 1663-1668 (6) 6.60 6.60

Souvenir Sheet of 2

1669 A258 $3 #a.-b. 4.50 4.50

Mekeel's Weekly Stamp News, cent. (in 1891; #1669).

Miniature Sheets

Coronation of Queen Elizabeth II, 40th Anniv. A259

Coronation: 1670a, 30c, Official photograph. b, 40c, Crown of Queen Elizabeth, the Queen Mother. c, $2, Dignataries attending ceremony. d, $4, Queen, Prince Edward.

$6, Portrait, by Denis Fildes.

First decade, 1953-1963: No. 1671a, Wedding photograph of Princess Margaret and Antony Armstrong-Jones. b, Queen opening Parliament, Prince Philip. c, Queen holding infant. d, Royal family. e, Queen Elizabeth II, formal portrait. f, Queen, Charles de Gaulle. g, Queen, Pope John XXIII. h, Queen inspecting troops.

Second decade, 1963-1973: No. 1672a, Investiture of Charles as Prince of Wales. b, Queen opening Parliament, Prince Philip, diff. c, Queen holding infant, diff. d, Queen, Prince Philip, children. e, Wearing blue robe, diadem. f, Prince Philip, Queen seated. g, Prince Charles, Queen at microphone. h, Queen conversing, model airplane.

Third decade, 1973-1983: No. 1673a, Wedding photograph of Prince Charles and Princess Diana. b, Queen opening Parliament, Prince Philip, diff. c, Princess Diana with infant. d, Princess Anne with infant. e, Portrait of Queen. f, Queen waving, Prince Philip. g, Queen, Pope John Paul II. h, Wedding portrait of Mark Phillips and Princess Anne.

Fourth decade, 1983-1993: No. 1674a, Wedding photograph of Sarah Ferguson and Prince Andrew. b, Queen opening Parliament, Prince Philip, diff. c, Princess Diana holding infant, diff. d, Sarah Ferguson, infant. e, Queen wearing blue dress. f, Queen waving from carriage, Prince Philip. g, Queen wearing military uniform. h, Queen Mother.

1993, June 2 **Litho.** ***Perf. 13½x14***

1670 A259 Sheet, 2 each #a.-d. 10.00 10.00

Sheets of 8

1671 A259 $1 #a.-h. + label 6.00 6.00
1672 A259 $1 #a.-h. + label 6.00 6.00
1673 A259 $1 #a.-h. + label 6.00 6.00
1674 A259 $1 #a.-h. + label 6.00 6.00

Souvenir Sheet

Perf. 14

1675 A259 $6 multicolored 4.50 4.50

No. 1675 contains one 28x42mm stamp.

Wedding of Japan's Crown Prince Naruhito and Masako Owada A260

Cameo photos of couple and: 40c, Crown Prince. $3, Princess.

$6, Princess wearing white coat, vert.

1993, Aug. 16 **Litho.** ***Perf. 14***

1676 A260 40c multicolored .30 .30
1677 A260 $3 multicolored 2.25 2.25

Souvenir Sheet

1678 A260 $6 multicolored 4.50 4.50

Picasso (1881-1973) — A261

Paintings: 30c, Cat and Bird, 1939. 40c, Fish on a Newspaper, 1957. $5, Dying Bull, 1934. $6, Woman with a Dog, 1953.

1993, Aug. 16 **Litho.** ***Perf. 14***

1679 A261 30c multicolored .25 .25
1680 A261 40c multicolored .30 .30
1681 A261 $5 multicolored 4.00 4.00
Nos. 1679-1681 (3) 4.55 4.55

Souvenir Sheet

1682 A261 $6 multicolored 4.50 4.50

Copernicus (1473-1543) A262

Designs: 40c, Astronomical devices. $4, Photograph of supernova. $5, Copernicus.

1993, Aug. 16

1683 A262 40c multicolored .30 .30
1684 A262 $4 multicolored 3.25 3.25

Souvenir Sheet

1685 A262 $5 multicolored 3.75 3.75

Willy Brandt (1913-1992), German Chancellor — A263

Designs: 30c, Helmut Schmidt, George Leber, Brandt. $4, Brandt, newspaper headlines. $6, Brandt at Warsaw Ghetto Memorial, 1970.

1993, Aug. 16

1686 A263 30c multicolored .25 .25
1687 A263 $4 multicolored 3.25 3.25

Souvenir Sheet

1688 A263 $6 multicolored 4.50 4.50

Polska '93 A264

Paintings: $1, Study of a Woman Combing Her Hair, by Wladyslaw Slewinski, 1897. $3, Artist's Wife with Cat, by Konrad Kryzanowski, 1912. $6, General Confusion, by S. I. Witkiewicz, 1930, vert.

1993, Aug. 16

1689 A264 $1 multicolored .80 .80
1690 A264 $3 multicolored 2.50 2.50

Souvenir Sheet

1691 A264 $6 multicolored 4.50 4.50

Inauguration of Pres. William J. Clinton — A265

Designs: $5, Pres. Clinton driving car. $6, Pres. Clinton, inauguration ceremony, vert.

1993, Aug. 16

1692 A265 $5 multicolored 4.00 4.00

Souvenir Sheet

1693 A265 $6 multicolored 4.50 4.50

No. 1693 contains one 43x57mm stamp.

1994 Winter Olympics, Lillehammer, Norway — A266

15c, Irina Rodnina, Alexei Ulanov, gold medalists, pairs figure skating, 1972. $5, Alberto Tomba, gold medal, giant slalom, 1988, 1992. $6, Yvonne van Gennip, Andrea Ehrig, gold, bronze medalists, speedskating, 1988.

1993, Aug. 16

1694 A266 15c multicolored .20 .20
1695 A266 $5 multicolored 4.00 4.00

Souvenir Sheet

1696 A266 $6 multicolored 4.50 4.50

1994 World Cup Soccer Championships, US — A267

English soccer players: No. 1697, Gordon Banks. No. 1698, 1709, Bobby Moore. No. 1699, Peter Shilton. No. 1700, Nobby Stiles. No. 1701, Bryan Robson. No. 1702, Geoff Hurst. No. 1703, Gary Lineker. No. 1704, Bobby Charlton. No. 1705, Martin Peters. No. 1706, John Barnes. No. 1707, David Platt. No. 1708, Paul Gascoigne. No. 1710, Player holding 1990 Fair Play Winners Trophy.

1993, July 30 Litho. *Perf. 14*

1697-1708 A267 $2 Set of 12 18.00 18.00

Souvenir Sheets

1709 A267 $6 multicolored 4.50 4.50
1710 A267 $6 multicolored 4.50 4.50

Nos. 1697-1708 issued in sheets of five plus label identifying player.

Aviation Anniversaries — A268

Designs: 30c, Dr. Hugo Eckener, Dr. Wm. Beckers, zeppelin over Lake George, NY. No. 1712, Chicago Century of Progress Exhibition seen from zeppelin. No. 1713, George Washington, Blanchard's balloon, vert. No. 1714, Gloster E.28/39, first British jet plane. $4, Pres. Wilson watching take-off of first scheduled air mail plane. No. 1716, Hindenburg over Ebbets Field, Brooklyn, NY, 1937. No. 1717, Gloster Meteor in combat. No. 1718, Eckener, vert. No. 1719, Alexander Hamilton, Pres. Washington, John Jay, gondola of Blanchard's balloon. No. 1720, PBY-5.

1993, Oct. 11

1711 A268 30c multicolored .20 .20
1712 A268 40c multicolored .30 .30
1713 A268 40c multicolored .30 .30
1714 A268 40c multicolored .30 .30
1715 A268 $4 multicolored 3.00 3.00
1716 A268 $5 multicolored 3.75 3.75
1717 A268 $5 multicolored 3.75 3.75
Nos. 1711-1717 (7) 11.60 11.60

Souvenir Sheets

1718 A268 $6 multicolored 4.50 4.50
1719 A268 $6 multicolored 4.50 4.50
1720 A268 $6 multicolored 4.50 4.50

Dr. Hugo Eckener, 125th anniv. of birth (#1711-1712, 1716, 1718). First US balloon flight, bicent. (#1713, 1715, 1719). Royal Air Force, 75th anniv. (#1714, 1717, 1720).

No. 1720 contains one 57x43mm stamp.

Mickey Mouse Movie Posters A269

Nos. 1721-1729: 10c, The Musical Farmer, 1932. 15c, Little Whirlwind, 1941. 30c, Pluto's Dream House, 1940. 40c, Gulliver Mickey, 1934. 50c, Alpine Climbers, 1936. $1, Mr. Mouse Takes a Trip, 1940. $2, The Nifty Nineties, 1941. $4, Mickey Down Under, 1948. $5, The Pointer, 1939.

#1730, The Simple Things, 1953. #1731, The Prince and the Pauper, 1990.

1993, Oct. 25 Litho. *Perf. 13½x14*

1721-1729 A269 Set of 9 12.00 12.00

Souvenir Sheets

1730-1731 A269 $6 each 4.50 4.50

St. John's Lodge #492, 150th Anniv. A270

Designs: 10c, W.K. Heath, Grand Inspector 1961-82, vert. 30c, Present Masonic Hall. 40c, 1st Masonic Hall. 60c, J.L.E. Jeffery, Grand Inspector 1953-61, vert.

1993, Aug. 16 Litho. *Perf. 14*

1732-1735 A270 Set of 4 1.10 1.10

First Ford Engine and Benz's First 4-Wheel Car, Cent. A271

30c, Lincoln Continental. 40c, 1914 Mercedes racing car. $4, 1966 Ford GT40. $5, 1954 Mercedes Benz gull wing coupe, street version. No. 1740, Mustang emblem. No. 1741, US #1286A, Germany #471.

1993, Oct. 11 Litho. *Perf. 14*

1736-1739 A271 Set of 4 7.00 7.00

Souvenir Sheets

1740-1741 A271 $6 each 4.50 4.50

Christmas — A272

Nos. 1742-1750, Disney characters in The Nutcracker: 10c, 15c, 20c, 30c, 40c, 50c, 60c, $3, $6. 1751, Minnie and Mickey. No. 1752, Mickey, vert.

1993, Nov. 8 *Perf. 14x13½, 13½x14*

1742-1750 A272 Set of 9 8.50 8.50

Souvenir Sheets

1751-1752 A272 $6 each 4.50 4.50

Fine Art — A273

Paintings by Rembrandt: No. 1753, 15c, Hannah and Samuel. 30c, Isaac & Rebecca (The Jewish Bride). 40c, Jacob Wrestling with the Angel. $5, Moses with the Tablets of the Law.

Paintings by Matisse: No. 1754, 15c, Guitarist. 60c, Interior with a Goldfish Bowl. $1, Portrait of Mlle. Yvonne Landsberg. $4, The Toboggan, Plate XX from Jazz. No. 1761, The Blinding of Samson by the Philistines, by Rembrandt. No. 1762, The Three Sisters, by Matisse.

1993, Nov. 22 *Perf. 13½x14*

1753-1760 A273 Set of 8 9.00 9.00

Souvenir Sheets

1761-1762 A273 $6 each 4.50 4.50

A274

Hong Kong '94 A275

Stamps, fishing boats at Shau Kei Wan: No. 1763, Hong Kong #370, bow of boat. No. 1764, Stern of boat, #1300.

Museum of Qin figures, Shaanxi Province, Tomb of Qin First Emperor: No. 1765a, Inside museum. b, Cavalryman, horse. c, Warriors in battle formation. d, Painted bronze horses, chariot. e, Pekingese dog (not antiquity). f, Chin warrior figures, horses.

1994, Feb. 18 Litho. *Perf. 14*

1763 A274 40c multicolored .30 .30
1764 A274 40c multicolored .30 .30
a. Pair, #1763-1764 .60 .60

Miniature Sheet

1765 A275 40c Sheet of 6, #a.-f. 1.75 1.75

Nos. 1763-1764 issued in sheets of 5 pairs. No. 1764a is a continuous design.

New Year 1994 (Year of the Dog) (#1765e).

Hong Kong '94 — A276

Disney characters: 10c, Mickey's "Pleasure Junk." 15c, Mandarin Minnie. 30c, Donald, Daisy journey by house boat. 50c, Mickey, Birdman of Mongkok. $1, Pluto encounters a good-luck dog. $2, Minnie, Daisy celebrate Bun Festival. $4, Goofy, the noodle maker. $5, Goofy pulls Mickey in a rickshaw.

No. 1774, Mickey celebrating New Year with Dragon Dance, horiz. No. 1775, View of Hong Kong Harbor, horiz.

1994, Feb. 18 Litho. *Perf. 13½x14*

1766-1773 A276 Set of 8 10.00 10.00

Souvenir Sheets

Perf. 14x13½

1774-1775 A276 $5 each 3.75 3.75

Miniature Sheets of 8

Sierra Club, Cent. — A277

No. 1776: a, Bactrian camel, emblem UR. b, Bactrian camel, emblem UL. c, African elephant, emblem UL. d, African elephant, emblem UR. e, Leopard, blue background. f, Leopard, emblem UR. g, Leopard, emblem UL. h, Club emblem.

No. 1777: a, Sumatran rhinoceros, lying on ground. b, Sumatran rhinoceros, looking straight ahead. c, Ring-tailed lemur standing. d, Ring-tailed lemur sitting on branch. e, Red-fronted brown lemur on branch. f, Red-fronted brown lemur. g, Red-fronted brown lemur, diff.

No. 1778, Sumatran rhinoceros, horiz. No. 1779, Ring-tailed lemur, horiz. No. 1780, Bactrian camel, horiz. No. 1781, African elephant, horiz.

1994, Mar. 1 Litho. *Perf. 14*

1776 A277 $1.50 #a.-h. 9.00 9.00
1777 A277 $1.50 #a.-g, #1776h 9.00 9.00

Souvenir Sheets

1778-1781 A277 $1.50 each 1.10 1.10

Miniature Sheets

New Year 1994 (Year of the Dog) — A278

Small breeds of dogs: No. 1782a, West highland white terrier. b, Beagle. c, Scottish terrier. d, Pekingese. e, Dachshund. f, Yorkshire terrier. g, Pomeranian. h, Poodle. i, Shetland sheepdog. j, Pug. k, Shih tzu. l, Chihuahua.

Large breeds of dogs: No. 1783a, Mastiff. b, Border collie. c, Samoyed. d, Airedale terrier. e, English setter. f, Rough collie. g, Newfoundland. h, Weimaraner. i, English springer spaniel. j, Dalmatian. k, Boxer. l, Old English sheepdog.

No. 1784, Welsh corgi. No. 1785, Labrador retriever.

1994, Apr. 5 *Perf. 14*

1782 A278 50c Sheet of 12, #a.-l. 4.50 4.50
1783 A278 75c Sheet of 12, #a.-l. 6.75 6.75

Souvenir Sheets

1784-1785 A278 $6 each 4.50 4.50

Orchids — A279 Butterflies — A280

Designs: 10c, Spiranthes lanceolata. 20c, Ionopsis utricularioides. 30c, Tetramicra canaliculata. 50c, Oncidium picturatum. $1, Epidendrum difforme. $2, Epidendrum ciliare. $4, Epidendrum ibaguense. $5, Epidendrum nocturnum.

No. 1794, Encyclia cochleata. No. 1795, Rodriguezia lanceolata.

1994, Apr. 11 *Perf. 14*

1786-1793 A279 Set of 8 10.00 10.00

Souvenir Sheets

1794-1795 A279 $6 each 4.50 4.50

1994, June 27 *Perf. 14*

Designs: 10c, Monarch. 15c, Florida white. 30c, Little sulphur. 40c, Troglodyte. $1, Common long-tail skipper. $2, Caribbean buckeye. $4, Polydamas swallowtail. $5, Zebra.

#1804, Cloudless sulphur. #1805, Hanno blue.

1796-1803 A280 Set of 8 10.00 10.00

Souvenir Sheets

1804-1805 A280 $6 each 4.50 4.50

Miniature Sheet of 9

Marine Life — A281

Designs: No. 1806a, Bottlenose dolphin. b, Killer whale (a). c, Spinner dolphin (b). d, Ocean sunfish (a). e, Caribbean reef shark, short fin pilot whale (d, f). f, Butterfly fish. g, Moray eel. h, Trigger fish. i, Red lobster (h).

#1807, Blue marlin, horiz. #1808, Sea horse.

1994, July 21 Litho. *Perf. 14*

1806 A281 50c a.-i. 3.50 3.50

Souvenir Sheets

1807-1808 A281 $6 each 4.50 4.50

Intl. Year of the Family A282

1994, Aug. 4

1809 A282 90c multicolored .70 .70

D-Day, 50th Anniv. A283

Designs: 40c, Short Sunderland attacks U-boat. $2, Lockheed P-38 Lightning attacks train. $3, B-26 Marauders of 9th Air Force. $6, Hawker Typhoon Fighter Bombers.

1994, Aug. 4

1810-1812 A283 Set of 3 4.25 4.25

Souvenir Sheet

1813 A283 $6 multicolored 4.50 4.50

A284

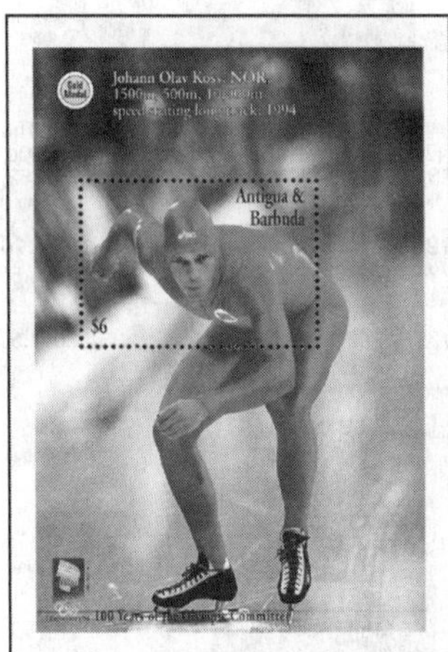

Intl. Olympic Committee, Cent. — A285

Designs: 50c, Edwin Moses, US, hurdles, 1984. $1.50, Steffi Graf, Germany, tennis, 1988. $6, Johann Olav Koss, Norway, speed skating, 1994.

1994, Aug. 4

1814 A284 50c multicolored .40 .40
1815 A284 $1.50 multicolored 1.10 1.10

Souvenir Sheet

1816 A285 $6 multicolored 4.50 4.50

English Touring Cricket, Cent. A286

35c, M.A. Atherton, England, Wisden Trophy. 75c, I.V.A. Richards, Leeward Islands, vert. $1.20, R.B. Richardson, Leeward Islands, Wisden Trophy.

$3, First English team, 1895.

1994, Aug. 4

1817-1819 A286 Set of 3 1.75 1.75

Souvenir Sheet

1820 A286 $3 multicolored 2.25 2.25

Miniature Sheets of 6

First Manned Moon Landing, 25th Anniv. A287

No. 1821: a, Edwin E. Aldrin, Jr. b, First footprint on Moon. c, Neil A. Armstrong. d, Aldrin descending to lunar surface. e, Aldrin deploys ALSET. f, Aldrin, US flag, Tranquility Base.

No. 1822: a, Scientific research, Tranquility Base. b, Plaque on Moon. c, Eagle ascending to docking. d, Command module in lunar orbit. e, US No. C76 made from die carried to Moon. f, Pres. Nixon, Apollo 11 crew.

$6, Armstrong, Aldrin, Postmaster General Blount.

1994, Aug. 4

1821-1822 A287 $1.50 #a.-f. 6.75 6.75

Souvenir Sheet

1823 A287 $6 multicolored 4.50 4.50

A288

PHILAKOREA '94 — A289

40c, Entrance bridge, Songgwangsa Temple. 90c, Song-op Folk Village, Cheju. $3, Panoramic view, Port Sogwip'o.

Ceramics, Koryo & Choson Dynasties: No. 1827a, Long-necked bottle. b, Jar. c, Jar, diff. d, Ewer in form of bamboo shoot. e, Jar, diff. f, Pear-shaped bottle. g, Porcelain jar with dragon design. h, Porcelain jar with bonsai design.

$4, Ox, ox herder, vert.

1994, Aug. 4 *Perf. 14, 13½ (#1827)*

1824-1826 A288 Set of 3 3.50 3.50

Miniature Sheet of 8

1827 A289 75c #a.-h. 6.00 6.00

Souvenir Sheet

1828 A288 $4 multicolored 3.00 3.00

Miniature Sheets of 8

Stars of Country & Western Music — A290

No. 1829: a, Patsy Cline. b, Tanya Tucker. c, Dolly Parton. d, Anne Murray. e, Tammy Wynette. f, Loretta Lynn. g, Reba McEntire. h, Skeeter Davis.

No. 1830a, Travis Tritt. b, Dwight Yoakam. c, Billy Ray Cyrus. d, Alan Jackson. e, Garth Brooks. f, Vince Gill. g, Clint Black. h, Eddie Rabbit.

No. 1831: a, Hank Snow. b, Gene Autry. c, Jimmie Rogers. d, Ernest Tubb. e, Eddy Arnold. f, Willie Nelson. g, Johnny Cash. h, George Jones.

No. 1832, Kitty Wells, horiz. No. 1833, Hank Williams, Sr. No. 1834, Hank Williams, Jr.

1994, Aug. 18 Litho. *Perf. 14*

1829-1831 A290 75c #a.-h, each 4.50 4.50

Souvenir Sheets

1832-1834 A290 $6 each 4.50 4.50

1994 World Cup Soccer Championships, US — A291

Designs: 15c, Hugo Sanchez, Mexico. 35c, Juergen Klinsman, Germany. 65c, Antigua player. $1.20, Cobi Jones, US. $4, Roberto Baggio, Italy. $5, Bwalya Kalusha, Zambia.

No. 1841, FIFA World Cup Trophy, vert. No. 1842, Maldive Islands player, vert.

1994, Sept. 19

1835-1840 A291 Set of 6 8.50 8.50

Souvenir Sheets

1841-1842 A291 $6 each 4.50 4.50

Order of the Caribbean Community — A292

First award recipients: 65c, Sir Shridath Ramphal, statesman, Guyana. 90c, William Demas, economist, Trinidad & Tobago. $1.20, Derek Walcott, writer, St. Lucia.

1994, Sept. 26

1843-1845 A292 Set of 3 2.00 2.00

Herman E. Sieger (1902-54) A293

Germany #C35, Graf Zeppelin, Sieger.

1994 Litho. *Perf. 14*

1846 A293 $1.50 multicolored 1.25 1.25

Birds A294

Designs: 10c, Magnificent frigate birds. 15c, Bridled quail dove. 30c, Magnificent frigate bird hatchling. 40c, Purple-throated carib, vert. No. 1851, $1, Antigua broad-wing hawk, vert. No. 1852, $1, Magnificent frigate bird, vert. $3, Magnificent frigate bird, white head. $4, Yellow warbler.

No. 1855, West Indian Whistling duck. No. 1856, Magnificent frigate bird, diff., vert.

1994, Dec. 12 Litho. *Perf. 14*

1847-1854 A294 Set of 8 7.50 7.50

Souvenir Sheets

1855-1856 A294 $6 each 4.50 4.50

World Wildlife Fund (#1847, 1849, 1852-1853).

Christmas A295

Paintings of Madonnas: 15c, The Virgin and Child by the Fireside, by Robert Campin. 35c, The Reading Madonna, by Giorgione. 40c, Madonna and Child, by Giovanni Bellini. 45c, The Litta Madonna, by da Vinci. 65c, The Virgin and Child Under the Apple Tree, by Lucas Cranach the Elder. 75c, Madonna and Child, by Master of the Female Half-Lengths. $1.20, An Allegory of the Church, by Alessandro Allori. $5, Madonna and Child Wreathed with Flowers, by Jacob Jordaens.

No. 1865, The Virgin Enthroned with Child, by Bohemian Master. No. 1866, Madonna and Child with (painting's) Commissioners, by Palma Vecchio.

1994, Dec. 12 *Perf. 13½x14*

1857-1864 A295 Set of 8 6.75 6.75

Souvenir Sheets

1865-1866 A295 $6 each 4.50 4.50

Birds — A296

Designs: 15c, Magnificent frigate bird. 25c, Blue-hooded euphonia. 35c, Meadowlark. 40c, Red-billed tropic bird. 45c, Greater flamingo. 60c, Yellow-faced grassquit. 65c, Yellow-billed cuckoo. 70c, Purple-throated carib. 75c, Bananaquit. 90c, Painted bunting. $1.20, Red-legged honeycreeper. $2, Jacana. $5, Greater antillean bullfinch. $10, Caribbean elaenia. $20, Trembler.

1995, Feb. 6 *Perf. 14½x14*

1867 A296 15c multicolored .20 .20
1868 A296 25c multicolored .20 .20
1869 A296 35c multicolored .20 .20
1870 A296 40c multicolored .20 .20
1871 A296 45c multicolored .30 .30
1872 A296 60c multicolored .35 .35
1873 A296 65c multicolored .45 .45
1874 A296 70c multicolored .45 .45
1875 A296 75c multicolored .50 .50
1876 A296 90c multicolored .60 .60
1877 A296 $1.20 multicolored .75 .75
1878 A296 $2 multicolored 1.25 1.25
1879 A296 $5 multicolored 3.00 3.00
1880 A296 $10 multicolored 6.25 6.25
1881 A296 $20 multicolored 13.00 13.00
Nos. 1867-1881 (15) 27.70 27.70

Prehistoric Animals A297

Designs, vert: 15c, Pachycephalosaurus. 20c, Afrovenator. 65c, Centrosaurus. 90c, Pentaceratops. $1.20, Tarbosaurus. $5, Styracosaur.

No. 1888a, Kronosaur. b, Ichthyosaur. c, Plesiosaur. d, Archelon. e, Two tyrannosaurs. f, One tyrannosaur. g, One parasaurolophus. h, Two parasaurolophuses. i, Oviraptor. j, Protoceratops with eggs. k, Pteranodon, protoceratops. l, Protoceratops.

#1889, Carnotaurus. #1890, Corythosaurus.

1995, May 15 **Litho.** *Perf. 14*

1882-1887 A297 Set of 6 6.25 6.25

Miniature Sheet of 12

1888 A297 75c #a.-l. 6.75 6.75

Souvenir Sheets

1889-1890 A297 $6 each 4.50 4.50

1996 Summer Olympics, Atlanta A298

Gold medalists: 15c, Al Oerter, US, discus. 20c, Greg Louganis, US, diving. 65c, Naim Suleymanoglu, Turkey, weight lifting. 90c, Louise Ritter, US, high jump. $1.20, Nadia Comaneci, Romania, gymnastics. $5, Olga Boldarenko, USSR, 10,000-meter run.

No. 1897, Lutz Hessilch, Germany, 1000-meter sprint cycling, vert. No. 1898, US team, eight-oared shell, 800-, 1500-meters.

1995, June 6 **Litho.** *Perf. 14*

1891-1896 A298 Set of 6 6.00 6.00

Souvenir Sheets

1897-1898 A298 $6 each 4.50 4.50

Miniature Sheets of 6 or 8

End of World War II, 50th Anniv. A299

No. 1899: a, Chiang Kai-Shek. b, Gen. MacArthur. c, Gen. Chennault. d, Brigadier Orde C. Wingate. e, Gen. Stillwell. f, Field Marshall William Slim.

No. 1900: a, Map of Germany showing battle plan. b, Tanks, infantry advance. c, Red Army at gates of Berlin. d, German defenses smashed. e, Airstrikes on Berlin. f. German soldiers give up. g, Berlin falls to Russians. h, Germany surrenders.

$3, Plane, ship, Adm. Chester Nimitz. $6, Gen. Konev at command post outside Berlin, vert.

1995, July 20

1899 A299 $1.20 #a.-f. + label 5.50 5.50
1900 A299 $1.20 #a.-h. + label 7.25 7.25

Souvenir Sheets

1901 A299 $3 multicolored 2.25 2.25
1902 A299 $6 multicolored 4.50 4.50

UN, 50th Anniv. — A300

FAO, 50th Anniv. — A301

No. 1903: a, 75c, Earl of Halifax, signatures. b, 90c, Virginia Gildersleeve. c, $1.20, Harold Stassen.

$6, Franklin D. Roosevelt.

1995, July 20 **Litho.** *Perf. 14*

1903 A300 Strip of 3, #a.-c. 2.25 2.25

Souvenir Sheet

1904 A300 $6 multicolored 4.50 4.50

No. 1903 is a continuous design.

1995, July 20

Street market scene: No. 1905a, 75c, Two women, bananas. b, 90c, Women, crates, produce. c, $1.20, Women talking, one with box of food on head.

$6, Tractor.

1905 A301 Strip of 3, #a.-c. 2.25 2.25

Souvenir Sheet

1906 A301 $6 multicolored 4.50 4.50

No. 1905 is a continuous design.

Rotary Intl., 90th Anniv. — A302

1995, July 20

1907 A302 $5 shown 3.75 3.75

Souvenir Sheet

1908 A302 $6 Natl. flag, Rotary emblem 4.50 4.50

Queen Mother, 95th Birthday A303

#1909: a, Drawing. b, White & dark pink hat. c, Formal portrait. d, Blue green hat, dress.

#1910, Light blue dress, pearls.

1995, July 20 *Perf. 13½x14*

1909 A303 $1.50 Strip or block of 4, #a.-d. 4.50 4.50

Souvenir Sheet

1910 A303 $6 multicolored 4.50 4.50

No. 1909 was issued in sheets of 2 each.

Sheets of 1909-1910 exist with black frame overprinted in margin, with text "In Memoriam/1900-2002."

Miniature Sheet of 12

Ducks — A304

No. 1911: a, Ring-necked duck. b, Ruddy duck. c, Green-winged teal (d). d, Wood duck. e, Hooded merganser (f). f, Lesser scaup (g). g, West Indian tree duck (h, k, l). h, Fulvous whistling duck (l). i, Bahama pintail. j, Shoveler (i). k, Masked duck (l). l, American widgeon.

$6, Blue-winged teal.

1995, Aug. 31 **Litho.** *Perf. 14*

1911 A304 75c #a.-l. 6.75 6.75

Souvenir Sheet

1912 A304 $6 multicolored 4.50 4.50

Bees A305

Designs: 90c, Mining bee. $1.20, Solitary bee. $1.65, Leaf-cutter. $1.75, Honey bee.

$6, Solitary mining bee.

1995, Sept. 7

1913-1916 A305 Set of 4 4.25 4.25

Souvenir Sheet

1917 A305 $6 multicolored 4.50 4.50

Miniature Sheet of 12

Domestic Cats A306

Designs: a, Somali. b, Persian. c, Devon rex. d, Turkish angora. e, Himalayan. f, Maine coon. g, Nonpedigree. h, American wirehair. i, British shorthair. j, American curl. k, Black nonpedigree. l, Birman.

$6, Siberian, vert.

1995, Sept. 7

1918 A306 45c #a.-l. 4.00 4.00

Souvenir Sheet

1919 A306 $6 multicolored 4.50 4.50

Miniature Sheet

Tourism A307

Stylized paintings depicting: a, Caring. b, Marketing. c, Working. d, Enjoying life.

1995, July 31 **Litho.** *Perf. 14*

1920 A307 $2 Sheet of 4, #a.-d. 6.00 6.00

Date of issue is in question. First day cover of Aug. 10, 1995, has been seen.

Greenbay Moravian Church, 150th Anniv. — A308

20c, 1st structure, wood & stone. 60c, 1st stone, concrete building, 3/67. 75c, $2, Present structure. 90c, John A. Buckley, 1st minister of African descent. $1.20, John Ephraim Knight, longest serving minister. $6, Front of present structure.

1995, Sept. 4

1921-1926 A308 Set of 6 4.25 4.25

Souvenir Sheet

1927 A308 $6 multicolored 4.50 4.50

Miniature Sheet of 12

Flowers — A309

No. 1928: a, Narcissus. b, Camellia. c, Iris. d, Tulip. e, Poppy. f, Peony. g, Magnolia. h, Oriental lily. i, Rose. j, Pansy. k, Hydrangea. l, Azaleas.

$6, Bird of paradise, calla lily.

1995, Sept. 7

1928 A309 75c #a.-l. 6.75 6.75

Souvenir Sheet

1929 A309 $6 multicolored 4.50 4.50

1995 Boy Scout Jamboree, Holland — A310

Tents - #1930: a, Explorer. b, Camper. c, Wall.
#1931: a, Trail tarp. b, Miner's. c, Voyager.
#1932, Scout with camping equipment, vert. #1933, Scout making camp fire.

1995, Oct. 5

Strip of 3

1930-1931 A310 $1.20 #a.-c, ea 2.75 2.75

Souvenir Sheets

1932-1933 A310 $6 each 4.50 4.50

For overprints see Nos. 1963-1966.

Trains A311

Designs: 35c, Gabon. 65c, Canadian. 75c, US. 90c, British high-speed. $1.20, French high-speed. No. 1939, American high-speed (Amtrak).
No. 1940: a, Australian diesel. b, Italian high-speed. c, Thai diesel. d, US steam. e, South African steam. f, Natal steam. g, US war train. h, British steam. i, British steam, diff.
No. 1941, Australian diesel, vert. No. 1942, Asian steam, vert.

1995, Oct. 23 Litho. *Perf. 14*

1934-1939 A311 Set of 6 7.50 7.50

Miniature Sheet of 9

1940 A311 $1.20 #a.-i. 8.25 8.25

Souvenir Sheets

1941-1942 A311 $6 each 4.50 4.50

Birds — A312

No. 1943: a, Purple-thoated carib. b, Antillean crested hummingbird. c, Bananaquit (d). d, Mangrove cuckoo. e, Troupial. f, Green-throated carib (e, g). g, Yellow warbler (h). h, Blue-hooded Euphonia. i, Scally-breasted thrasher. j, Burrowing owl (i). k, Caribbean crackle (k). l, Adelaide's warbler.
$6, Purple gallinule.

1995

Miniature Sheet of 12

1943 A312 75c #a.-l. 6.75 6.75

Souvenir Sheet

1944 A312 $6 multicolored 4.50 4.50

Miniature Sheets of 9

Nobel Prize Fund Established, Cent. — A313

Recipients: No. 1945a, S.Y. Agnon, literature, 1966. b, Kipling, literature, 1907. c, Aleksandr Solzhenitsyn, literature, 1970. d, Jack Steinberger, physics, 1988. e, Andrei Sakharov, peace, 1975. f, Otto Stern, physics, 1943. g, Steinbeck, literature, 1962. h, Nadine Gordimer, literature, 1991. i, Faulkner, literature, 1949.

No. 1946: a, Hammarskjold, peace, 1961. b, Georg Wittig, chemistry, 1979. c, Wilhelm Ostwald, chemistry, 1909. d, Koch, physiology or medicine, 1945. e, Karl Ziegler, chemistry, 1963. f, Fleming, physiology or medicine, 1945. g, Hermann Staudinger, chemistry, 1953. h, Manfred Eigen, chemistry, 1967. i, Arno Penzias, physics, 1978.
No. 1947, Elie Wiesel, peace, 1986, vert. No. 1948, Dalai Lama, peace, 1989, vert.

1995, Nov. 8

1945-1946 A313 $1 #a.-i. + label, each 6.75 6.75

Souvenir Sheets

1947-1948 A313 $6 each 4.50 4.50

Christmas A314

Details or entire paintings: 15c, Rest on the Flight into Egypt, by Veronese. 35c, Madonna with The Child, by Van Dyck. 65c, Sacred Conversation Piece, by Veronese. 75c, Vision of Saint Anthony, by Van Dyck. 90c, The Virgin and the Infant, by Van Eyck. No. 1954, The Immaculate Conception, by Tiepolo.
$5, Christ Appearing to His Mother, by Van Der Weyden. No. 1956, Infant Jesus and the Young St. John, by Murillo.

1995, Dec. 18 Litho. *Perf. 13½x14*

1949-1954 A314 Set of 6 6.75 6.75

Souvenir Sheets

1955 A314 $5 multicolored 3.75 3.75
1956 A314 $6 multicolored 4.50 4.50

Miniature Sheet

Elvis Presley (1935-77) A315

Nos. 1957-1958, Various portraits depicting Presley's life.

1995, Dec. 8 *Perf. 14*

1957 A315 $1 Sheet of 9, #a.-i. 6.75 6.75

Souvenir Sheet

1958 A315 $6 multicolored 4.50 4.50

John Lennon (1940-80), Entertainer — A316

45c, 50c, 65c, 75c, Various portraits of Lennon.

1995, Dec. 8

1959-1962 A316 Set of 4 1.75 1.75

Souvenir Sheet

1962A A316 $6 like 75c 4.50 4.50

Nos. 1959-1962 were each issued in miniature sheets of 16.
No. 1962A has a continuous design.

Nos. 1930-1933 Ovptd.

1995, Dec. 14

Strips of 3

1963-1964 A310 $1.20 #a.-c., ea 2.75 2.75

Souvenir Sheets

1965-1966 A310 $6 each 4.50 4.50

Size and location of overprint varies.

Mushrooms A317

#1967: a, Hygrophoropsis aurantiaca. b, Hygrophorus bakerensis. c, Hygrophorus conicus. d, Hygrophorus miniatus.
#1968: a, Suillus brevipes. b, Suillus luteus. c, Suillus granulatus. d, Suillus caerulescens.
No. 1969, Conocybe filaris. No. 1970, Hygrocybe flavescens.

1996, Apr. 22 Litho. *Perf. 14*

Strip of 4

1967-1968 A317 75c #a.-d., ea 2.25 2.25

Souvenir Sheets

1969-1970 A317 $6 each 4.50 4.50

#1967-1968 were each issued in sheets of 12 stamps.

Sailing Ships A318

Designs: 15c, Resolution. 25c, Mayflower. 45c, Santa Maria. No. 1970D, 75c, Aemilia, Holland, 1630. No. 1970E, 75c, Sovereign of the Seas, England, 1637. 90c, HMS Victory, England, 1765.
Battleships: No. 1971: a, Aemila, Holland, 1630. b, Sovereign of the Seas, England, 1637. c, Royal Louis, France, 1692. d, HMS Royal George, England, 1715. e, Le Protecteur, France, 1761. f, HMS Victory, England, 1765.
Ships of exploration: No. 1972: a, Santa Maria. b, Victoria. c, Golden Hinde. d, Mayflower. e, Griffin. f, Resolution.
No. 1973, Grande Hermine. No. 1974, USS Constitution, 1797.

1996, Apr. 25

1970A-1970F A318 Set of 6 2.50 2.50

Sheets of 6

1971 A318 $1.20 #a.-f. 5.50 5.50
1972 A318 $1.50 #a.-f. 6.75 6.75

Souvenir Sheets

1973-1974 A318 $6 each 4.50 4.50

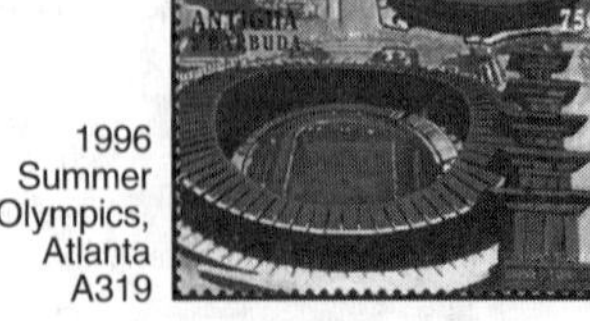

1996 Summer Olympics, Atlanta A319

Designs: 65c, Florence Griffith Joyner, women's track, vert. 75c, Olympic Stadium, Seoul, 1988. 90c, Allison Jolly, yachting. $1.20, 2000m Tandem cycling,
Medalists: No. 1979a, Wolfgang Nordwig, pole vault. b, Shirley Strong, women's 100m hurdles. c, Sergei Bubka, pole vault. d, Filbert Bayi, 3000m steeplechase. e, Victor Saneyev, triple jump. f, Silke Renk, women's javelin. g, Daley Thompson, decathlon. h, Bob Richards, pole vault. i, Parry O'Brien, shot put.
Diving medalists: No. 1980a, Ingrid Kramer, women's platform. b, Kelly McCormick, women's springboard. c, Gary Tobian, men's springboard. d, Greg Louganis, men's diving. e, Michelle Mitchell, women's platform. f, Zhou Jihong, women's platform. g, Wendy Wyland, women's platform. h, Xu Yanmei, women's platform. i, Fu Mingxia, women's platform.
$5, Bill Toomey, decathlon. $6, Mark Lenzi, men's springboard.

1996, May 6

1975-1978 A319 Set of 4 2.50 2.50

Sheets of 9

1979-1980 A319 90c #a.-i., each 6.25 6.25

Souvenir Sheets

1981 A319 $5 multicolored 3.75 3.75
1982 A319 $6 multicolored 4.50 4.50

Sea Birds A320

No. 1983: a, Black skimmer. b, Black-capped petrel. c, Sooty tern. d, Royal tern.
No. 1984 a, Pomarina jaegger. b, White-tailed tropicbird. c, Northern gannet. d, Laughing gull.
$5, Great frigatebird. $6, Brown pelican.

1996, May 13

Vertical Strip of 4

1983-1984 A320 75c #a.-d., ea 2.25 2.25

Souvenir Sheets

1985 A320 $5 multicolored 3.75 3.75
1986 A320 $6 multicolored 4.50 4.50

Nos. 1983-1984 were each issued in sheets of 12 stamps with each strip in sheet having a different order.

Disney Characters In Scenes from Jules Verne's Science Fiction Novels — A321

Designs: 1c, Around the World in Eighty Days. 2c, Journey to the Center of the Earth. 5c, Michel Strogoff. 10c, From the Earth to the Moon. 15c, Five Weeks in a Balloon. 20c, Around the World in Eighty Days, diff. $1, The Mysterious Island. $2, From the Earth to the Moon, diff. $3, Captain Grant's Children. $5, Twenty Thousand Leagues Under the Sea.
No. 1997, Twenty Thousand Leagues Under the Sea, diff. No. 1998, Journey to the Center of the Earth, diff.

1996, June 6 Litho. *Perf. 14x13½*

1987-1996 A321 Set of 10 8.75 8.75

Souvenir Sheets

1997-1998 A321 $6 each 4.50 4.50

Bruce Lee (1940-73), Martial Arts Expert — A322

Various portraits.

1996, June 13 *Perf. 14*

1999 A322 75c Sheet of 9, #a.-i. 5.25 5.25

Souvenir Sheet

2000 A322 $5 multicolored 3.75 3.75

China '96 (#1999).

Queen Elizabeth II, 70th Birthday — A323

Designs: a, In blue dress, pearls. b, Carrying bouquet of flowers. c, In uniform.
$6, Painting as younger woman.

1996, July 17 ***Perf. 13½x14***
2001 A323 $2 Strip of 3, #a.-c. 4.50 4.50

Souvenir Sheet

2002 A323 $6 multicolored 4.50 4.50

No. 2001 was issued in sheets of 9 stamps.

Traditional Cavalry A324

a, Ancient Egyptian. b, 13th cent. English. c, 16th cent. Spanish. d, 18th cent. Chinese.
$6, 19th cent. French.

1996, July 24 **Litho.** ***Perf. 14***
2003 A324 60c Block of 4, #a.-d. 1.75 1.75

Souvenir Sheet

2004 A324 $6 multicolored 4.50 4.50

No. 2003 was issued in sheets of 16 stamps.

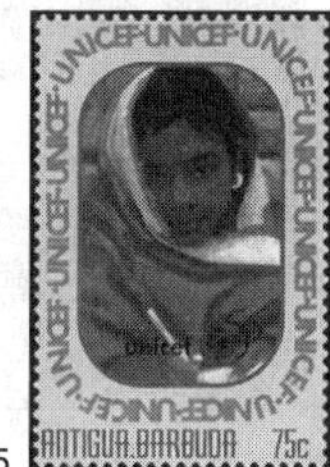

A325

A326

UNICEF, 50th Anniv.: 75c, Girl. 90c, Children. $1.20, Woman holding baby. $6, Girl, diff.

1996, July 30
2005-2007 A325 Set of 3 2.00 2.00

Souvenir Sheet

2008 A325 $6 multicolored 4.50 4.50

1996, July 30

Site, flower: 75c, Tomb of Zachariah, verbascum sinuatum. 90c, Pool of Siloam, hyacinthus orientalis. $1.20, Hurva Synagogue, ranunculus asiaticus.
$6, Model of Herod's Temple.

2009-2011 A326 Set of 3 2.25 2.25

Souvenir Sheet

2012 A326 $6 multicolored 4.50 4.50

Jerusalem, 3000th anniv.

Radio, Cent. A327

Entertainers: 65c, Kate Smith. 75c, Dinah Shore. 90c, Rudy Vallee. $1.20, Bing Crosby.
$6, Jo Stafford.

1996, July 30
2013-2016 A327 Set of 4 2.75 2.75

Souvenir Sheet

2017 A327 $6 multicolored 4.50 4.50

Christmas A328

Details or entire paintings, by Filippo Lippi: 60c, Madonna Enthroned. 90c, Adoration of the Child and Saints. $1, Annunciation. $1.20, Birth of the Virgin. $1.60, Adoration of the Child. $1.75, Madonna and Child.
No. 2024, Madonna and Child, diff. No. 2025, Circumcision.

1996, Nov. 25 ***Perf. 13½x14***
2018-2023 A328 Set of 6 5.25 5.25

Souvenir Sheets

2024-2025 A328 $6 each 4.50 4.50

Disney Pals — A329

1c, Goofy, Wilbur. 2c, Donald, Goofy. 5c, Donald, Panchito, Jose Carioca. 10c, Mickey, Goofy. 15c, Dale, Chip. 20c, Pluto, Mickey. $1, Daisy, Minnie at ice cream shop. $2, Daisy, Minnie. $3, Gus Goose, Donald.
No. 2035, Donald, vert. No. 2036, Goofy.

1997, Feb. 17 **Litho.** ***Perf. 14x13½***
2026-2034 A329 Set of 9 5.00 5.00

Souvenir Sheets

Perf. 13½x14, 14x13½

2035-2036 A329 $6 each 4.50 4.50

Salute to Broadway A330

Stars, show: No. 2037: a, Robert Preston, The Music Man. b, Michael Crawford, Phantom of the Opera. c, Zero Mostel, Fiddler on the Roof. d, Patti Lupone, Evita. e, Raul Julia, Threepenny Opera. f, Mary Martin, South Pacific. g, Carol Channing, Hello Dolly. h, Yul Brynner, The King and I. i, Julie Andrews, My Fair Lady.
$6, Mickey Rooney, Sugar Babies.

1997 ***Perf. 14***
2037 A330 $1 Sheet of 9, #a.-i. 6.80 6.80

Souvenir Sheet

2038 A330 $6 multicolored 4.50 4.50

Butterflies — A331

Designs: 90c, Charaxes porthos. $1.20, Aethiopana honorius. $1.60, Charaxes hadrianus. $1.75, Precis westermanni.
No. 2043: a, Charaxes protoclea. b, Byblia ilithyia. c, Black-headed tchagra (bird). d, Charaxes nobilis. e, Pseudacraea boisduvali. f, Charaxes smaragdalis. g, Charaxes lasti. h, Pseudacraea poggei. i, Graphium colonna.
No. 2044a, Carmine bee-eater (bird). b, Pseudacraea eurytus. c, Hypolimnas monteironis. d, Charaxes anticlea. e, Graphium leonidas. f, Graphium illyris. g, Nepheronia argia. h, Graphium policenes. i, Papilio dardanus.
No. 2045, Euxanthe tiberius, horiz. No. 2046, Charaxes lactitinctus, horiz. No. 2047, Euphaedra neophron.

1997, Mar. 10
2039-2042 A331 Set of 4 4.00 4.00

Sheets of 9

2043-2044 A331 $1.10 #a.-i., ea 7.50 7.50

Souvenir Sheets

2045-2047 A331 $6 each 4.50 4.50

UNESCO, 50th Anniv. — A332

World Heritage Sites: 60c, Convent of the Companions of Jesus, Morelia, Mexico. 90c, Fortress, San Lorenzo, Panama, vert. $1, Canaima Natl. Park, Venezuela, vert. $1.20, Huascarán Natl. Park, Peru, vert. $1.60, Church of San Francisco, Guatemala, vert. $1.75, Santo Domingo, Dominican Republic, vert.
No. 2054, vert: a-c, Guanajuato, Mexico. d, Jesuit missions of the Chiquitos, Bolivia. e, Huascarán Natl. Park, Peru. f, Jesuit missions, La Santisima, Paraguay. g, Cartagena, Colombia. h, Old Havana fortification, Cuba.
No. 2055: a, Tikal Natl. Park, Guatemala. b, Rio Platano Reserve, Honduras. c, Ruins of Copán, Honduras. d, Church of El Carmen, Antigua, Guatemala. e, Teotihuacán, Mexico.
No. 2056, Teotihuacán, Mexico, diff. No. 2057, Tikal Natl. Park, Guatemala, diff.

1997, Apr. 10 **Litho.** ***Perf. 14***
2048-2053 A332 Set of 6 5.25 5.25

Sheets of 8 or 5

2054 A332 $1.10 #a.-h. + label 6.75 6.75
2055 A332 $1.65 #a.-e. + label 6.25 6.25

Souvenir Sheets

2056-2057 A332 $6 each 4.50 4.50

Fauna — A333

No. 2058: a, Red bishop. b, Yellow baboon. c, Superb starling. d, Ratel. e, Hunting dog. f, Serval.
No. 2059: a, Okapi. b, Giant forest squirrel. c, Masked weaver. d, Common genet. e, Yellow-billed stork. f, Red-headed agama.
No. 2060, Malachite kingfisher. No. 2061, Gray crowned crane. No. 2062, Bat-eared fox.

1997, Apr. 24

Sheets of 6

2058 A333 $1.20 #a.-f. 5.50 5.50
2059 A333 $1.65 #a.-f. 7.50 7.50

Souvenir Sheets

2060-2062 A333 $6 each 4.50 4.50

Charlie Chaplin (1889-1977), Comedian, Actor A334

Various portraits.

1997, Feb. 24 **Litho.** ***Perf. 14***
2063 A334 $1 Sheet of 9, #a.-i. 6.75 6.75

Souvenir Sheet

2064 A334 $6 multicolored 4.50 4.50

Paul P. Harris (1868-1947), Founder of Rotary, Intl. — A335

Designs: $1.75, Service above self, James Grant, Ivory Coast, 1994, portrait of Harris.
$6, Group study exchange, New Zealand.

1997, June 12 **Litho.** ***Perf. 14***
2065 A335 $1.75 multicolored 1.25 1.25

Souvenir Sheet

2066 A335 $6 multicolored 4.50 4.50

Heinrich von Stephan (1831-97) A336

Portrait of Von Stephan and: No. 2067: a, Kaiser Wilhelm I. b, UPU emblem. c, Pigeon Post.
$6, Von Stephan, Basel messenger, 1400's.

1997, June 12
2067 A336 $1.75 Sheet of 3, #a.-c. 4.00 4.00

Souvenir Sheet

2068 A336 $6 multicolored 4.50 4.50

PACIFIC 97.

Queen Elizabeth II, Prince Philip, 50th Wedding Anniv. A337

No. 2069: a, Queen. b, Royal arms. c, Queen, Prince in royal attire. d, Queen, King riding in open carriage. e, Balmoral Castle. f. Prince Philip.
$6, Early portrait of Queen, King in royal attire.

1997, June 12
2069 A337 $1 Sheet of 6, #a.-f. 4.50 4.50

Souvenir Sheet

2070 A337 $6 multicolored 4.50 4.50

Grimm's Fairy Tales A338

Scenes from "Cinderella:" No. 2071: a, Mother, stepsisters. b, Cinderella, fairy godmother. c, Cinderella, Prince Charming.
$6, Prince trying shoe on Cinderella.

1997, June 13 ***Perf. 13½x14***

2071 A338 $1.75 Sheet of 3, #a.-c. 4.00 4.00

Souvenir Sheet

2072 A338 $6 multicolored 4.50 4.50

Chernobyl Disaster, 10th Anniv. A339

Designs: $1.65, UNESCO. $2, Chabad's Children of Chernobyl.

1997, June 12

2073 A339 $1.65 multicolored 1.25 1.25
2074 A339 $2 multicolored 1.50 1.50

Mushrooms — A340

Designs: 45c, Marasmius rotula. 65c, Cantharellus cibarius. 70c, Lepiota cristata. 90c, Auricularia mesenterica. $1, Pholiota alnicola. $1.65, Leccinum aurantiacum.

No. 2081: a, Entoloma serrulatum. b, Panaeolus sphinctrinus. c, Volvariella bombycina. d, Conocybe percincta. e, Pluteus cervinus. f, Russula foetens.

No. 2082, Panellus serotinus. No. 2083, Amanita cothurnata.

1997, Aug. 12 Litho. ***Perf. 14***

2075-2080 A340 Set of 6 4.00 4.00

Sheets of 6

2081 A340 $1.75 #a.-f. 8.00 8.00

Souvenir Sheets

2082-2083 A340 $6 each 4.50 4.50

Orchids — A341

Designs: 45c, Odontoglossum cervantesii. 65c, Medford star. 75c, Motes resplendent. 90c, Debutante. $1, Apple blossom. $2, Dendrobium.

No. 2090: a, Angel lace. b, Precious stones. c, Orange theope butterfly. d, Promenaea xanthina. e, Lycaste macrobulbon. f, Amesiella philippinensis. g, Machu Picchu. h, Zuma urchin.

No. 2091: a, Sophia Martin. b, Dogface butterfly. c, Mini purple. d, Showgirl. e, Mem. Dorothy Bertsch. f, Black II. g, Leeanum. h, Paphiopedilum macranthum.

No. 2092, Seine. No. 2093, Paphiopedilum gratrixianum.

1997, Aug. 19 Litho. ***Perf. 14***

2084-2089 A341 Set of 6 4.25 4.25

Sheets of 8

2090-2091 A341 $1.65 #a.-h., each 5.00 5.00

Souvenir Sheets

2092-2093 A341 $6 each 4.50 4.50

1998 World Cup Soccer Championships, France — A342

Designs: 60c, Maradona, Argentina, 1986. 75c, Fritzwalter, W. Germany, 1954. 90c, Zoff, Italy, 1982. $1.20, Moore, England, 1966. $1.65, Alberto, Brazil, 1970. $1.75, Matthäus, W. Germany.

No. 2100, vert: a, Ademir, Brazil, 1950. b, Eusebio, Portugal, 1966. c, Fontaine, France, 1958. d, Schillaci, Italy, 1990. e, Leonidas, Brazil, 1938. f, Stabile, Argentina, 1930. g, Nejedly, Czechoslovakia, 1934. h, Muller, W. Germany, 1970.

No. 2101, Players, W. Germany, 1990. No. 2102, Bebeto, Brazil, vert.

1997, Oct. 6 Litho. ***Perf. 14***

2094-2099 A342 Set of 6 6.00 6.00

Sheet of 8 + Label

2100 A342 $1 #a.-h. 6.00 6.00

Souvenir Sheets

2101-2102 A342 $6 each 4.50 4.50

Domestic Animals A343

Dogs: No. 2103: a, Dachshund. b, Staffordshire terrier. c, Sharpei. d, Beagle. e, Norfolk terrier. f, Golden retriever.

Cats: No. 2104: a, Scottish fold. b, Japanese bobtail. c, Tabby manx. d, Bicolor American shorthair. e, Sorrel abyssinian. f, Himalayan blue point.

No. 2105, Siberian husky, vert. No. 2106, Red tabby American shorthair kitten, vert.

1997, Oct. 27 Litho. ***Perf. 14***

Sheets of 6

2103-2104 A343 $1.65 #a.-f., ea 7.50 7.50

Souvenir Sheets

2105-2106 A343 $6 each 4.50 4.50

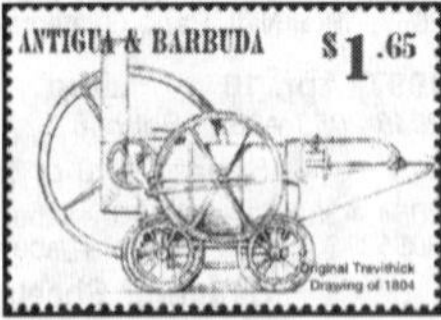

Early Trains A344

No. 2107: a, Original Trevithick drawing, 1804. b, "Puffing Billy," William Hedley, 1860. c, Crampton locomotive, Northern Railway, France, 1858. d, Twenty-five ton locomotive, Lawrence Machine Shop, 1860's. e, First locomotive, "Mississippi," built in England. f, "Coppernob," locomotive by Edward Bury, Furness Railway.

No. 2108: a, "Jenny Lind," by David Joy for E.B. Wilson. b, "Atlantic" type locomotive, by Schenectady Locomotive Works, 1899. c, British built tank engine, Japan, by Kisons of Leeds, 1881. d, Express freight locomotive, 4-8-2 type, Pennsylvania Railroad. e, Four-cylinder locomotive, by Karl Golsdorf, Austria. f, "E" series 0-10-0 locomotive, produced by Lugansk Works, Russia, 1930.

No. 2109, "Patente" George Stephenson, 1843. No. 2110, Brunel's Trestle, Lynher River.

1997, Nov. 10

Sheets of 6

2107-2108 A344 $1.65 #a.-f., ea 7.50 7.50

Souvenir Sheets

2109-2110 A344 $6 each 4.50 4.50

Christmas A345

Entire paintings or details: 15c, The Angel Leaving Tobias and His Family, by Rembrandt. 25c, The Resurrection, by Martin Knoller. 60c, Astronomy, by Raphael. 75c, Music-making Angel, by Melozzo da Forli. 90c, Amor, by Parmigianino. $1.20, Madonna and Child with Saints John the Baptist, Anthony, Stephen and Jerome, by Rosso Fiorentino.

No. 2117, The Portinari Altarpiece, by Hugo Van Der Goes. No. 2118, The Wedding of Tobiolo, by Gianantonio and Francesco Guardi.

1997, Dec. 2 Litho. ***Perf. 14***

2111-2116 A345 Set of 6 5.25 5.25

Souvenir Sheets

2117-2118 A345 $6 each 4.50 4.50

Diana, Princess of Wales (1961-97) — A346

Various portraits, color of sheet margin: No. 2119, Pale green. No. 2120, Pale pink.

No. 2121, With her sons (in margin). No. 2122, With Pope John Paul II (in margin).

1998, Jan. 19 Litho. ***Perf. 14***

Sheets of 6

2119-2120 A346 $1.65 #a.-f., ea 7.50 7.50

Souvenir Sheets

2121-2122 A346 $6 each 4.50 4.50

Fish A347

Designs: 75c, Yellow damselfish. 90c, Barred hamlet. $1, Jewelfish. $1.20, Bluehead wrasse. $1.50, Queen angelfish. $1.75, Queen triggerfish.

No. 2129: a, Jack-knife fish. b, Cuban hogfish. c, Sergeant major. d, Neon goby. e, Jawfish. f, Flamefish.

No. 2130: a, Rock beauty. b, Yellowtail snapper. c, Creole wrasse. d, Slender filefish. e, Squirrel fish. f, Fairy basslet.

No. 2131, Black-capped gramma. No. 2132, Porkfish.

1998, Feb. 19

2123-2128 A347 Set of 6 5.50 5.50

Sheets of 6

2129-2130 A347 $1.65 #a.-f., ea 7.50 7.50

Souvenir Sheets

2131-2132 A347 $6 each 4.50 4.50

Cedar Hall Moravian Church, 175th Anniv. A348

Designs: 20c, First church, manse, 1822-40. 45c, Cedar Hall School, 1840. 75c, Hugh A. King, former minister. 90c, Present structure. $1.20, Water tank, 1822. $2, Former manse demolished, 1978.

$6, Present structure, diff.

1998, Mar. 16 Litho. ***Perf. 14***

2133-2138 A348 Set of 6 4.25 4.25

Souvenir Sheet

2139 A348 $6 multicolored 4.50 4.50

No. 2139 contains one 50x37mm stamp.

Lighthouses — A349

Lighthouse, location: 45c, Trinity, Europa Point, Gibraltar, vert. 65c, Tierra Del Fuego, Argentina. 75c, Point Loma, California, US. 90c, Groenpoint, South Africa, vert. $1, Youghal, County Cork, Ireland, vert. $1.20, Launceston, Tasmania, Australia, vert. $1.65, Point Abino, Ontario, Canada. $1.75, Great Inagua, Bahamas.

$6, Capa Hatteras, North Carolina, US.

1998, Apr. 20

2140-2147 A349 Set of 8 6.50 6.50

Souvenir Sheet

2148 A349 $6 multi, vert. 4.50 4.50

Winnie the Pooh A350

No. 2149: a, Pooh, Tigger in January. b, Pooh, Piglet in February. c, Piglet in March. d, Tigger, Pooh, Piglet in April. e, Kanga, Roo in May. f, Pooh, Owl in June.

No. 2150: a, Pooh, Eeyore, Tigger, Piglet in July. b, Pooh, Piglet in August. c, Christopher Robin in September. d, Eeyore in October. e, Pooh, Rabbit in November. f, Pooh, Piglet in December.

No. 2151, Pooh, Rabbit holding blanket, Spring. No. 2152, Pooh holding hand to mouth, Summer. No. 2153, Pooh holding rake, Fall. No. 2154, Eeyore, Pooh, Winter.

1998, May 11 Litho. ***Perf. 13½x14***

Sheets of 6

2149-2150 A360 $1 #a.-f., each 4.50 4.50

Souvenir Sheet

2151-2154 A350 $6 each 4.50 4.50

Thomas Oliver Robinson Memorial High School, Cent. A351

Designs: 20c, $6, Nellie Robinson (1880-1972), founder, vert. 45c, School picture, 1985. 65c, Former building, 1930-49. 75c, Students with present headmistress, Natalie Hurst. 90c, Ina Loving (1908-96), educator, vert. $1.20, Present building, 1950.

1998, July 23 Litho. ***Perf. 14***

2155-2160 A351 Set of 6 3.25 3.25

Souvenir Sheet

2161 A351 $6 multicolored 4.50 4.50

No. 2161 is a continuous design.

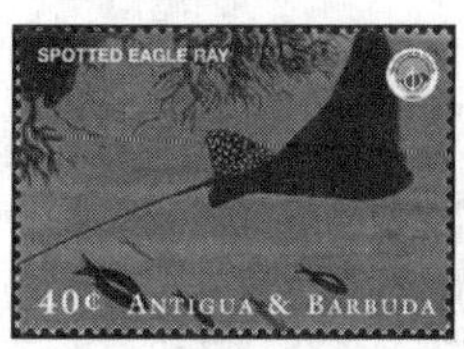
Intl. Year of the Ocean A352

Marine life, "20,000 Leagues Under the Sea:" No. 2162: a, Spotted eagle ray. b, Manta ray. c, Hawksbill turtle. d, Jellyfish. e, Queen angelfish. f, Octopus. g, Emperor angelfish. h, Regal angelfish. i, Porkfish. j, Raccoon butterfly fish. k, Atlantic barracuda. l, Sea horse. m, Nautilus. n, Trumpet fish. o, White tip shark. p, Spanish galleon. q, Black tip shark. r, Long-nosed butterfly fish. s, Green moray eel. t, Captain Nemo. u, Treasure chest. v, Hammer-head shark. w, Divers. x, Lion fish. y, Clown fish.

Wildlife and birds: No. 2163: a, Maroon tailed conure. b, Cocoi heron. c, Common tern. d, Rainbow lorikeet. e, Saddleback butterfly fish. f, Goatfish, cat shark. g, Blue shark, stingray. h, Majestic snapper. i, Nassau grouper. j, Black-cap gramma, blue tang. k, Stingrays. l, Stingrays, giant starfish.

#2164, Fiddler ray. #2165, Humpback whale.

1998, Aug. 17

2162 A352 40c Sheet of 25, #a.-y. 7.50 7.50
2163 A352 75c Sheet of 12, #a.-l. 6.75 6.75

Souvenir Sheets

2164-2165 A352 $6 each 4.50 4.50

Ships A353

No. 2166: a, Savannah. b, Viking ship. c, Greek warship.

No. 2167: a, Clipper. b, Dhow. c, Fishing cat.

No. 2168, Dory, vert. No. 2169, Baltimore clipper. No. 2170, English warship, 13th cent.

1998, Aug. 18 ***Perf. 14x14½***

Sheets of 3

2166-2167 A353 $1.75 #a.-c., ea 4.00 4.00

Souvenir Sheets

Perf. 14

2168-2170 A353 $6 each 4.50 4.50

CARICOM, 25th Anniv. — A354

1998, Aug. 20 Litho. ***Perf. 13½***

2171 A354 $1 multicolored .75 .75

Antique Automobiles — A355

No. 2172: a, 1911 Torpedo. b, 1913 Mercedes 22. c, 1920 Rover. d, 1956 Mercedes Benz. e, 1934 Packard V12. f, 1924 Opel.

Fords: No. 2173: a, 1896. b, 1903 Model A. c, 1928 Model T. d, 1922 Model T. e, 1929 Blackhawk. f, 1934 Sedan. #2174, 1908. #2175, 1929.

1998, Sept. 1 ***Perf. 14***

Sheets of 6

2172-2173 A355 $1.65 #a.-f., ea 7.50 7.50

Souvenir Sheets

2174-2175 A355 $6 each 4.50 4.50

Nos. 2174-2175 each contain one 60x40mm stamp.

Aircraft A356

No. 2176: a, NASA Space Shuttle. b, Saab Grippen. c, Eurofighter EF2000. d. Sukhoi SU 27. e, Northrop B-2. f, Lockheed F-117 Nighthawk.

No. 2177: a, Lockheed-Boeing General Dynamics Yf-22. b, Dassault-Breguet Rafale BO 1. c, MiG 29. d, Dassault-Breguet Mirage 2000D. e, Rockwell B-1B Lancer. f, McDonnell-Douglas C-17A.

No. 2178, Sukhoi SU 35. No. 2179, F18 Hornet.

1998, Sept. 21

Sheets of 6

2176-2177 A356 $1.65 #a.-f., ea 7.50 7.50

Souvenir Sheets

2178-2179 A356 $6 each 4.50 4.50

Famous People of the 20th Cent. — A357

Inventors and their inventions: No. 2180: a, Rudolf Diesel (1858-1913). b, Internal combustion, diesel engines. c, Zeppelin war balloon, Intrepid. d, Ferdinand von Zeppelin (1838-1917). e, Wilhelm Conrad Röntgen (1845-1923). f, X-ray machine. g, Saturn rocket. h, Wernher von Braun (1912-77).

No. 2181: a, Carl Benz (1844-1929). b, Internal combustion engine, automobile. c, Atomic bomb. d, Albert Einstein. e, Leopold Godowsky, Jr. (1901-83) and Leopold Damrosch Mannes (1899-1964). f, Kodachrome film. g, First turbo jet airplane. h, Hans Pabst von Ohain (1911-98).

No. 2182, Hans Geiger (1882-1945), inventor of the Geiger counter. No. 2183, William Shockley (1910-89), developer of transistors.

1998, Nov. 10 Litho. ***Perf. 14***

Sheets of 8

2180-2181 A357 $1 #a.-h., each 6.00 6.00

Souvenir Sheets

2182-2183 A357 $6 each 4.50 4.50

Nos. 2180b-2180c, 2180f-2180g, 2181b-2181c, 2181f-2181g are 53x38mm.

Diana, Princess of Wales (1961-97) A358

1998, Nov. 18

2184 A358 $1.20 multicolored .90 .90

No. 2184 was issued in sheets of 6.

Gandhi — A359

Portraits: 90c, Up close, later years. $1, Seated with hands clasped. $1.20, Up close, early years. $1.65, Primary school, Rajkot, age 7. $6, With stick, walking with boy (in margin).

1998, Nov. 18

2185-2188 A359 Set of 4 2.75 2.75

Souvenir Sheet

2189 A359 $6 multicolored 4.50 4.50

Picasso — A360

Paintings: $1.20, Figures on the Seashore, 1931, horiz. $1.65, Three Figures Under a Tree, 1907. $1.75, Two Women Running on the Beach, 1922, horiz.

$6, Bullfight, 1900, horiz.

1998, Nov. 18

2190-2192 A360 Set of 3 3.50 3.50

Souvenir Sheet

2193 A360 $6 multicolored 4.50 4.50

1998 World Scouting Jamboree, Chile A361

90c, Handshake. $1, Scouts hiking. $1.20, Sign.

$6, Lord Baden-Powell.

1998, Oct. 8 Litho. ***Perf. 14***

2194-2196 A361 Set of 3 2.50 2.50

Souvenir Sheet

2197 A361 $6 multicolored 4.50 4.50

Organization of American States, 50th Anniv. A362

1998, Nov. 18 ***Perf. 13½***

2198 A362 $1 multicolored .75 .75

Enzo Ferrari (1898-1988), Automobile Manufacturer — A363

No. 2199: a, Top view of Dino 246 GT-GTS. b, Front view of Dino 246 GT-GTS. c, 1977 365 GT4 BB.

$6, Dino 246 GT-GTS.

1998, Nov. 18 ***Perf. 14***

2199 A363 $1.75 Sheet of 3, #a.-c. 4.00 4.00

Souvenir Sheet

2200 A363 $6 multicolored 4.50 4.50

No. 2200 contains one 92x35mm stamp.

Royal Air Force, 80th Anniv. A364

No. 2201: a, McDonnell Douglas Phantom FGR1. b, Sepecat Jaguar GR1A. c, Panavia Tornado F3. d, McDonnell Douglas Phantom FGR2.

No. 2202, Eurofighter 2000, Hurricane. No. 2203, Hawk, biplane.

1998, Nov. 18

2201 A364 $1.75 Sheet of 4, #a.-d. 4.00 4.00

Souvenir Sheets

2202-2203 A364 $6 each 4.50 4.50

Sea Birds A365

Designs: 15c, Brown pelican. 25c, Dunlin. 45c, Atlantic puffin. 90c, Pied cormorant.

No. 2208: a, King eider. b, Inca tern. c, Dovekie. d, Ross's bull. e, Brown noddy. f, Marbled murrelet. g, Northern gannet. h, Razorbill. i, Long-tailed jaeger. j, Black guillemot. k, Whimbrel. l, Oystercatcher.

No. 2209, Rhynchops niger. No. 2210, Diomedea exulans.

1998, Nov. 24

2204-2207 A365 Set of 4 1.25 1.25
2208 A365 75c Sheet of 12, #a.-l. 6.75 6.75

Souvenir Sheets

2209-2210 A365 $6 each 4.50 4.50

Christmas A366

Dogs with Christmas decorations: 15c, Border collie. 25c, Dalmatian. 65c, Weimaraner. 75c, Scottish terrier. 90c, Long-haired dachshund. $1.20, Golden retriever. $2, Pekingese.

No. 2218, Dalmatian, diff. No. 2219, Jack Russell terrier.

1998, Dec. 10

2211-2217 A366 Set of 7 4.50 4.50

Souvenir Sheet

2218-2219 A366 $6 each 4.50 4.50

Disney Characters in Water Sports A367

Water skiing - No. 2220: a, Goofy, maroon skis. b, Mickey. c, Goofy, Mickey. d, Donald. e, Goofy, blue skis. f, Minnie.

Surfing - No. 2221: a, Goofy running with board. b, Mickey. c, Donald holding board. d, Donald, riding board. e, Minnie. f, Goofy in water.

Sailing & sailboarding - No. 2221G: h, Mickey wearing cap. i, Mickey, Goofy, counter-balancing boat. j, Goofy sailboarding. k, Mickey, seagull overhead. l, Goofy puffing at sail. m, Mickey sailboarding.

No. 2222, Mickey. No. 2223, Minnie. No. 2224, Goofy. No. 2225, Donald.

1999, Jan. 11 Litho. ***Perf. 13½x14***

Sheets of 6

2220-2221 A367 $1 #a.-f., each 4.50 4.50
2221G A367 $1 #h.-m. 4.50 4.50

Souvenir Sheets

2222-2225 A367 $6 each 4.50 4.50

Mickey Mouse, 70th anniv.

Hell's Gate Steel Orchestra, 50th Anniv. A368

Designs: 20c, Nelson's Dockyard, 1996. 60c, Holiday Inn, Rochester, New York, 1992. 75c, Early years, 1950. 90c, World's Fair, 1964, Eustace Henry (AKA Manning). $1.20, Alston Henry playing double tenor.
No. 2231, like #2229, vert. No. 2232, The early years, vert.

1999, Feb. 1 Litho. *Perf. 14*
2226-2230 A368 Set of 5 2.75 2.75

Souvenir Sheets
2231-2232 A368 $4 each 3.00 3.00

Flowers A369

Designs, vert: 60c, Tulip. 75c, Fuschia. $1.20, Calla lily. $1.65, Sweet pea.
No. 2237: a, Morning glory. b, Geranium. c, Blue hibiscus. d, Marigolds. e, Sunflower. f, Impatiens. g, Petunia. h, Pansy. i, Saucer magnolia.
No. 2238: a, Primrose. b, Bleeding heart. c, Pink dogwood. d, Peony. e, Rose. f, Hellebores. g, Lily. h, Violet. i, Cherry blossoms.
No. 2239, Lily, vert. no. 2240, Zinnias, vert.

1999, Apr. 19 Litho. *Perf. 14*
2233-2236 A369 Set of 4 3.25 3.25

Sheets of 9
2237 A369 90c #a.-i. 6.00 6.00
2238 A369 $1 #a.-i. 6.75 6.75

Souvenir Sheets
2239-2240 A369 $6 each 4.50 4.50

Elle Macpherson, Model — A370

Various portraits.

1999, Apr. 26 *Perf. 13½*
2241 A370 $1.20 Sheet of 8, #a.-h. 7.25 7.25

Australia '99 World Stamp Expo.

John Glenn's Space Flight — A371

John Glenn, 1962 - No. 2242: a, Climbing into Mercury Capsule. b, Formal portrait. c, Having helmet adjusted. d, Entering pressure chamber.
No. 2243: a, Luna 2. b, Mariner 2. c, Giotto space probe. d, Rosat. e, Intl. Ultraviolet Explorer. f, Ulysses Space Probe.
No. 2244: a, Mariner 10. b, Luna 9. c, Advanced X-ray Astrophysics Facility. d, Magellan Spacecraft. e, Pioneer-Venus 2. f, Infra-red Astronomy Satellite.
No. 2245, Salyut 1, horiz. No. 2246, MIR, horiz.

1999, May 6 Litho. *Perf. 14*
2242 A371 $1.75 Sheet of 4, #a.-d. 5.25 5.25

Space Exploration A372

Sheets of 6
2243-2244 A372 $1.65 #a.-f., ea 7.50 7.50

Souvenir Sheets
2245-2246 A372 $6 each 4.50 4.50

Nos. 2245-2246 are incorrectly inscribed.

Prehistoric Animals A373

Designs: 65c, Brachiosaurus. 75c, Oviraptor, vert. $1, Homotherium. $1.20, Macrauchenia, vert.
No. 2251: a, Leptictidium. b, Ictitherium. c, Plesictis. d, Hemicyon. e, Diacodexis. f, Stylinodon. g, Kanuites. h, Chriacus. i, Argyrolagus.
No. 2252: a, Struthiomimus. b, Corythosaurus. c, Dsungaripterus. d, Compognathus. e, Prosaurolophus. f, Montanoceratops. g, Stegosaurus. h, Deinonychus. i, Ouranosaurus.
No. 2253, Pteranodon. No. 2254, Eurhinodelphus.

1999, May 26
2247-2250 A373 Set of 4 3.50 3.50

Sheets of 9
2251-2252 A373 $1.65 #a.-i., each 11.50 11.50

Souvenir Sheets
2253-2254 A373 $6 each 4.50 4.50

Illustrations on Nos. 2247-2248 are switched.

IBRA'99, World Stamp Exhibition, Nuremberg — A374

Exhibition emblem, Leipzig-Dresden Railway and: No. 2255, $1, Caroline Islands #19. No. 2257, $1.65, Caroline Islands #4.
Emblem, Gölsdorf 4-4-0 and: No. 2256, $1.20, Caroline Islands #16. No. 2258, $1.90, Caroline Islands #8, #10.
$6, Registered label on cover.
Illustration reduced.

1999, June 24 Litho. *Perf. 14*
2255-2258 A374 Set of 4 4.50 4.50

Souvenir Sheet
2259 A374 $6 multicolored 5.00 5.00

Paintings by Hokusai (1760-1849) — A375

Details or entire paintings: No. 2260: a, Asakusa Honganji. b, Dawn at Isawa in Kai Province. c, Samurai with Bow and Arrow (bows level). d, Samurai with Bow and Arrow (bows at different angles). e, Kajikazawa in Kai Province. f, A Great Wave.
No. 2261: a, People on the Balcony of the Sazaido. b, Nakahara in Sagami Province. c, Defensive Positions (2 men). d, Defensive Positions (3 men). e, Mount Fuji in Clear Weather. f, Nihonbashi in Edo.
No. 2262, Cotenyama At Shinagawa on Tokaido Highway, vert. No. 2263, A Netsuke Workshop, vert.

1999, June 24

Sheets of 6
2260-2261 A375 $1.65 #a.-f., ea 7.50 7.50

Souvenir Sheets
2262-2263 A375 $6 each 4.50 4.50

Johann Wolfgang von Goethe (1749-1832), Poet — A376

No. 2264: a, Three archangels in "Faust." b, Portraits of Goethe and Friedrich von Schiller (1759-1805). c, Faust reclining in landscape with spirits.
$6, Profile portrait of Goethe.

1999, June 24 Litho. *Perf. 14*
2264 A376 $1.75 Sheet of 3, #a.-c. 4.00 4.00

Souvenir Sheet
2265 A376 $6 multicolored 4.50 4.50

Souvenir Sheets

Philexfrance '99, World Philatelic Exhibition — A377

Locomotives: #2266, Crampton 1855-69. #2267, 232-U1 4-Cylinder Compound 4-6-4, 1949.
Illustration reduced.

1999, June 24 *Perf. 13¾*
2266 A377 $6 multicolored 4.50 4.50
2267 A377 $6 multicolored 4.50 4.50

A378

Wedding of Prince Edward and Sophie Rhys-Jones - No. 2268: a, Sophie. b. Sophie, Edward. c, Edward.
$6, Horse and carriage, couple.

1999, June 24 *Perf. 13½*
2268 A378 $3 Sheet of 3, #a.-c. 6.75 6.75

Souvenir Sheet
2269 A378 $6 multicolored 4.50 4.50

A379

1999, May 25 Litho. *Perf. 14½x14*

Various white kittens: 35c, 45c, 60c, 75c, 90c, $1.
No. 2276: a, One holding paw on another. b, Black & white. c, White kitten, black kitten. d, One with yarn. e, Two in basket. f, One looking up.
No. 2277: a, One playing with red yarn. b, Two long-haired. c, Yellow tabby. d, One with mouse. e, Yellow tabby on pillow. f, Black & gray tabby.
No. 2278, Tabby cat carrying kitten. No. 2279, Yellow kitten in tree.

2270-2275 A379 Set of 6 3.00 3.00

Sheets of 6
2276-2277 A379 $1.65 #a.-f., ea 7.50 7.50

Souvenir Sheets
2278-2279 A379 $6 each 4.50 4.50

Australia '99, World Stamp Expo (#2276-2279).

A380

UN Rights of the Child Convention, 10th Anniv. - No. 2280: a, Three children. b, Adult hand taking child's hand, silhouette of mother holding infant. c, UN Building, member flags, dove.
$6, Dove.

1999, June 22 *Perf. 14*
2280 A380 $3 Sheet of 3, #a.-c. 6.75 6.75

Souvenir Sheet
2281 A380 $6 multicolored 4.50 4.50

A381

1999, June 24 Litho. *Perf. 13x11*

Boats and ships: 25c, Missa Ferdie. 45c, Sailboats. 60c, Jolly Roger Pirate Ship. 90c, $4, Freewinds. $1.20, Monarch of the Seas.

2282-2286 A381 Set of 5 2.60 2.60
2286a Souvenir sheet, #2282-2286 2.60 2.60

Souvenir Sheet
Perf. 13¾
2287 A381 $4 multicolored 3.00 3.00

No. 2287 contains one 51x38mm stamp.

A382

Butterflies: 65c, Fiery jewel. 75c, Hewitson's blue hairstreak. $1.20, Scarce bamboo page, horiz. $1.65, Paris peacock, horiz.
No. 2292, horiz.: a, California dog face. b, Small copper. c, Zebra swallowtail. d, White M hairstreak. e, Old world swallowtail. f, Buckeye. g, Apollo. h, Sonoran blue. i, Purple emperor.
No. 2293, Monarch. No. 2294, Cairns birdwing, horiz.

1999, Aug. 16 *Perf. 14*
2288-2291 A382 Set of 4 3.25 3.25
2292 A382 $1 Sheet of 9, #a.-i. 6.75 6.75

Souvenir Sheets
2293-2294 A382 $6 each 4.50 4.50

Christmas A383

15c, Madonna and child in a Wreath of Flowers by Peter Paul Rubens. 25c, Shroud of Christ Held by Two Angels, by Albrecht Dürer. 45c, Madonna and Child Enthroned Between Two Saints, by Raphael. 60c, Holy Family with the Lamb, by Raphael. $2, The Transfiguration, by Raphael. $4, Three Putti Holding a Coat of Arms, by Dürer.

$6, The Coronation of the Holy St. Catherine, by Rubens.

1999, Nov. 22 Litho. *Perf. 13¾*

2295-2300 A383 Set of 6 5.50 5.50

Souvenir Sheet

2301 A383 $6 multicolored 4.50 4.50

Famous Elderly People A384

Designs: a, Katharine Hepburn. b, Martha Graham. c, Eubie Blake. d, Agatha Christie. e, Eudora Welty. f, Helen Hayes. g, Vladimir Horowitz. h, Katharine Graham. i, Pablo Casals. j, Pete Seeger. k, Andres Segovia. l, Frank Lloyd Wright.

2000, Jan. 18 Litho. *Perf. 14*

2302 A384 90c Sheet of 12, #a-l 8.00 8.00

Charlie Chaplin A385

Designs: a, "Modern Times," street scene. b, "The Gold Rush," with other actor. c, Unidentified film. d, "Modern Times," on gears. e, "The Gold Rush," arms akimbo. f, "The Gold Rush," with cane.

2000, Jan. 18 *Perf. 13¾*

2303 A385 $1.65 Sheet of 6, #a-f 7.25 7.25

Sir Cliff Richard, Rock Musician A386

2000, Jan. 18 *Perf. 13¼*

2304 A386 $1.65 multi 1.25 1.25

Issued in sheets of 6.

Birds A387

Designs: 75c, Streamertail. 90c, Yellow-bellied sapsucker. $1.20, Rufous-tailed jacamar. $2, Spectacled owl.

No. 2309: a, Ground dove. b, Wood stork. c, Saffron finch. d, Green-backed heron. e, Lovely cotinga. f, St. Vincent parrot. g, Cuban grassquit. h, Red-winged blackbird.

No. 2310: a, Scarlet macaw. b, Yellow-fronted amazon. c, Queen-of-Bavaria. d, Nanday conure. e, Jamaican tody. f, Smooth-billed ani. g, Puerto Rican woodpecker. h, Ruby-throated hummingbird.

No. 2311, Vermilion flycatcher. No. 2312, Red-capped manakin, vert.

2000, Apr. 17 Litho. *Perf. 14*

2305-2308 A387 Set of 4 3.75 3.75

Sheets of 8, #a-h

Perf. 13¾x14

2309-2310 A387 $1.20 Set of 2 14.00 14.00

Souvenir Sheets

Perf. 13¾

2311-2312 A387 $6 Set of 2 9.00 9.00

The Stamp Show 2000, London (Nos. 2309-2312). Size of stamps: Nos. 2309-2310, 48x31mm; No. 2311, 50x38mm; No. 2312, 38x50mm.

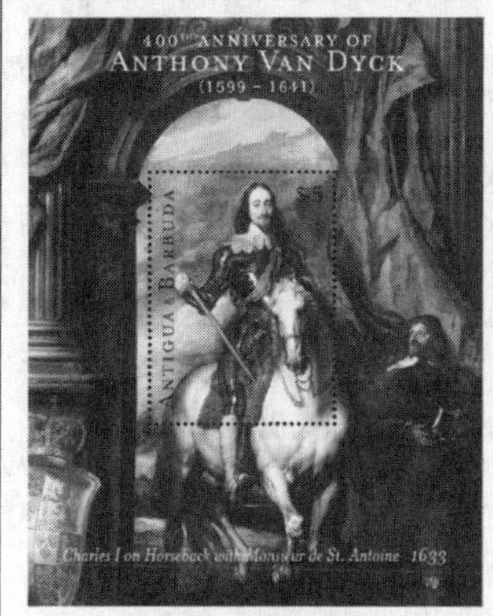
Paintings of Anthony Van Dyck — A388

No. 2313: a, Arthur Goodwin. b, Sir Thomas Wharton. c, Mary Villers (as Venus), Daughter of the Duke of Buckingham. d, Christina Bruce, Countess of Devonshire. e, James Hamilton, 3rd Marquis and 1st Duke of Hamilton. f, Henry Danvers, Earl of Danby.

No. 2314: a, Charles I in Robes of State. b, Henrietta Maria. c, Queen Henrietta Maria with Her Dwarf Sir Jeffrey Hudson. d, Charles I in Armor. e, Henrietta Maria in Profile, facing right. f. Queen Henrietta Maria.

No. 2315: a, Marie de Raet, Wife of Philippe le Roy. b, Jacomo de Cachiopin. c, Princess Henrietta of Lorraine Attended by a Page. d, Portrait of a Man. e, Portrait of a Woman. f, Philippe le Roy, Seigneur de Ravels.

No. 2316, Charles I on Horseback with Monsieur de St. Antoine. No. 2317, Le Roi a La Chasse (Charles I hunting). No. 2318, Charles I in Three Positions. No. 2319, Charles I and Queen Henrietta. No. 2320, Portrait of Two Young English Gentlemen, Sons of the Duke of Lenox. No. 2321, George, Lord Digby, and William, Lord Russell.

Illustration reduced.

2000, May 15 *Perf. 13¾*

Sheets of 6, #a-f

2313-2315 A388 $1.20 Set of 3 15.00 15.00

Souvenir Sheets

2316-2319 A388 $5 Set of 4 15.00 15.00

2320-2321 A388 $6 Set of 2 9.00 9.00

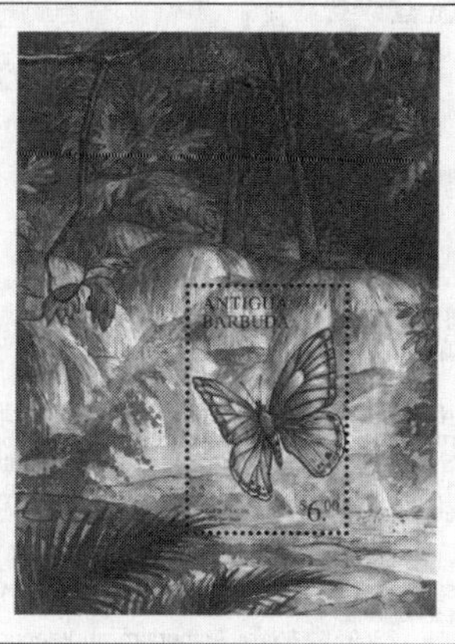
Butterflies — A389

No. 2322: a, Orange theope. b, Sloane's urania. c, Gold-drop helicopis. d, Papilio velovis. e, Graphium androcles. f, Cramer's mesene.

No. 2323, horiz.: a, Euploea miniszeki. b, Doris. c, Evenus coronata. d, Anchisiades swallowtail. e, White-spotted tadpole. f, Morpho patroclus.

No. 2324, horiz.: a, Mesosemia loruhama. b, Bia actorion. c, Ghost brimstone. d, Blue tharops. e, Catasticta manco. f, White-tailed page.

No. 2325, Reakirt's blue. No. 2326, Graphium encelades, horiz. No. 2327, Graphium milon, horiz.

Illustration reduced.

2000, May 29 *Perf. 14*

Sheets of 6, #a-f

2322-2324 A389 $1.65 Set of 3 22.50 22.50

Souvenir Sheets

2325-2327 A389 $6 Set of 3 13.00 13.00

Prince William, 18th Birthday — A390

Prince William - No. 2328: a, With checked shirt, waving. b, In jacket and white shirt. c, With arms clasped. d, In striped shirt, waving.

$6, With Prince Harry, Princess Diana and unidentified man.

Illustration reduced.

2000, June 21 *Perf. 14*

2328 A390 $1.65 Sheet of 4, #a-d 5.00 5.00

Souvenir Sheet

Perf. 13¾

2329 A390 $6 multi 4.50 4.50

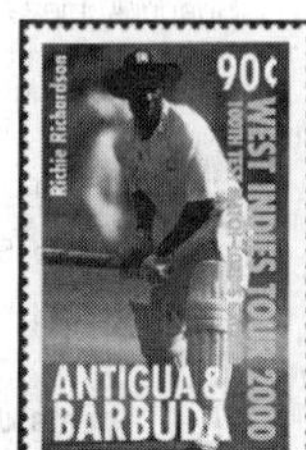
100th Test Cricket Match at Lord's Ground — A391

90c, Richie Richardson. $5, Viv Richard.

$6, Lord's Ground, horiz.

2000, June 26 *Perf. 14*

2330-2331 A391 Set of 2 4.50 4.50

Souvenir Sheet

2332 A391 $6 multi 4.50 4.50

Souvenir Sheet

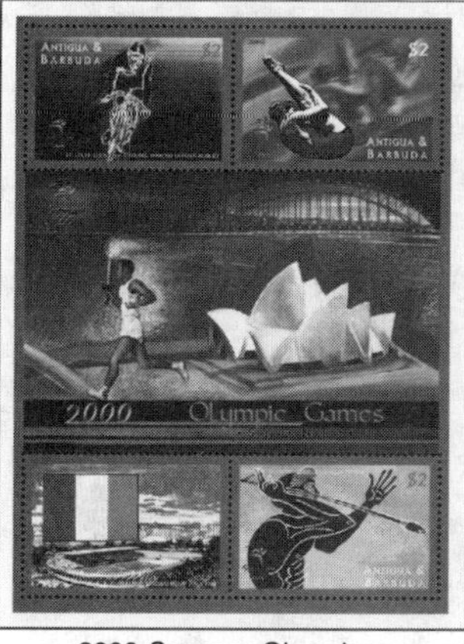
2000 Summer Olympics, Sydney — A392

Designs: a, Cyclist. b, Diver. c, Italian flag, Flaminio Stadium, Rome. d, Ancient Greek javelin thrower.

Illustration reduced.

2000, June 26

2333 A392 $2 Sheet of 4, #a-d 6.00 6.00

First Zeppelin Flight, Cent. — A393

No. 2334: a, LZ-1. b, LZ-2. c, LZ-3.

$6, LZ-7.

Illustration reduced.

2000, June 26 *Perf. 13½*

2334 A393 $3 Sheet of 3, #a-c 6.75 6.75

Souvenir Sheet

Perf. 14¼

2335 A393 $6 multi 4.50 4.50

No. 2334 contains three 45x27mm stamps.

Cats — A394

No. 2336: a, Long-haired blue & white. b, Snow shoe. c, Persian. d, Chocolate lynx point. e, Brown & white sphynx. f, White tortoiseshell.

$6, Lavender tortie.

Illustration reduced.

2000, May 29 Litho. *Perf. 14*

2336 A394 $1.65 Sheet of 6, #a-f 7.50 7.50

Souvenir Sheet

2337 A394 $6 multi 4.50 4.50

Souvenir Sheet

Public Railways, 175th Anniv. — A395

Designs: a, Locomotion No. 1, George Stephenson. b, John Bull.
Illustration reduced.

2000, June 26

2338 A395 $3 Sheet of 2, #a-b 4.50 4.50

The Stamp Show 2000, London.

Souvenir Sheet

Johann Sebastian Bach (1685-1750) — A396

Illustration reduced.

2000, June 26

2339 A396 $6 multi 4.50 4.50

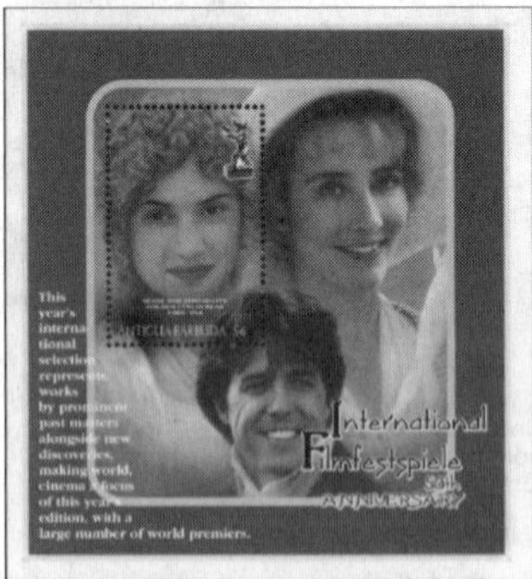

Berlin Film Festival, 50th Anniv. — A397

No. 2340: a, Une Femme Est Une Femme. b, Carmen Jones. c, Die Ratten. d, Die Vier im Jeep. e, Lilies of the Field. f, Invitation to the Dance.
$6, Sense and Sensibility.
Illustration reduced.

2000, June 26

2340 A397 $1.65 Sheet of 6, #a-f 7.50 7.50

Souvenir Sheet

2341 A397 $6 multi 4.50 4.50

Flowers — A398

Designs: 45c, Epidendrum pseudepidndrum. 65c, Odontoglossum cervantesii. 75c, Cattleya dowiana. 90c, Beloperone guttata. $1, Colliandra haematocephala. $1.20, Brassavola nodosa.
No. 2348, $1.65: a, Masdevallia coccinea. b, Paphinia cristata. c, Vanilla planifolia. d, Cattleya forbesii. e, Lycaste skinneri. f, Cattleya percivaliana.
No. 2349, $1.65: a, Anthurium andreanum. b, Doxantha unguiscati. c, Hibiscus rosasinensis. d, Canna indica. e, Heliconius umilis. f, Strelitzia reginae.
No. 2350, $1.65: a, Pseudocalymna alliaceum. b, Datura candida. c, Ipomoea tuberosa. d, Allamanda cathartica. e, Aspasia epidendroides. f, Maxillaria cucullata.
No. 2351, Strelitzia reginae. No. 2352, Cattleya leopoldii. No. 2353, Rossioglossum grande.

2000, May 29 Litho. *Perf. 14*

2342-2347 A398 Set of 6 3.75 3.75

Sheets of 6, *#a-f*

2348-2350 A398 Set of 3 22.50 22.50

Souvenir Sheets

2351-2353 A398 $6 Set of 3 13.50 13.50

Dogs — A399

Designs: 90c, Boxer. $1, Wire-haired pointer (inscribed Alaskan malamute). $2, Alaskan malamute (inscribed Wire-haired pointer). $4, Saluki.
No. 2358: a, Bearded collie. b, Cardigan Welsh corgi. c, Saluki. d, Basset hound. e, Standard poodle. f, Boston terrier.
No. 2359, Cavalier King Charles Spaniel.

2000, May 29

2354-2357 A399 Set of 4 6.00 6.00

2358 A399 $1.65 Sheet of 6, #a-f 7.25 7.25

Souvenir Sheet

2359 A399 $6 multi 4.50 4.50

Space Achievements — A400

No. 2360, $1.65: a, Sputnik 1. b, Explorer 1. c, Mars Express. d, Luna 1. e, Ranger 7. f, Mariner 4.
No. 2361, $1.65: a, Mariner 10. b, Soho. c, Mariner 2. d, Giotto. e, Exosat. f, Pioneer.
No. 2362, Hubble Space Telescope. No. 2363, Vostok 1.
Illustration reduced.

2000, June 26

Sheets of 6, *#a-f*

2360-2361 A400 Set of 2 15.00 15.00

Souvenir Sheets

2362-2363 A400 $6 Set of 2 9.00 9.00

World Stamp Expo 2000, Anaheim.

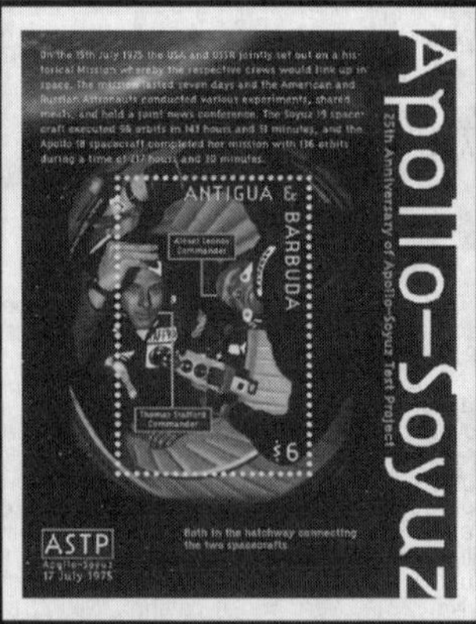

Apollo-Soyuz Mission, 25th Anniv. — A401

No. 2364: a, Alexei Leonov. b, Soyuz 19. c, Valeri Kubasov.
$6, Leonov and Thomas Stafford.
Illustration reduced.

2000, June 26

2364 A401 $3 Sheet of 3, #a-c 6.75 6.75

Souvenir Sheet

2365 A401 $6 multi 4.50 4.50

Souvenir Sheet

Albert Einstein (1879-1955) — A402

Illustration reduced.

2000, June 26 *Perf. 14¼*

2366 A402 $6 multi 4.50 4.50

Girls' Brigade A403

Designs: 20c, Outreach program to Sunshine Home for Girls. 60c, Ullida Rawlins Gill, Intl. vice-president, vert. 75c, Officers and girls. 90c, Raising the flag, vert. $1.20, Members with 8th Antigua Company flag.
$5, Emblem, vert.

2000, July 13 *Perf. 14*

2367-2371 A403 Set of 5 2.75 2.75

Souvenir Sheet

2372 A403 $5 multi 3.75 3.75

A404

Queen Mother, 100th Birthday — A405

No. 2373: a, As child. b, In 1940. c, With Princess Anne, 1951. d, In Canada, 1989.
$6, Inspecting the troops. $20, In gardens.
Illustration reduced.

Litho., Margin Embossed

2000, Aug. 4 *Perf. 14*

2373 A404 $2 Sheet of 4, #a-d, + label 6.00 6.00

Souvenir Sheet

Perf. 13¾

2374 A404 $6 multi 4.50 4.50

Without Gum

Litho. & Embossed

Die Cut 8¾x9

2375 A405 $20 gold & multi

No. 2374 contains one 38x51mm stamp.

Popes — A406

No. 2376: a, Alexander VI, 1492-1503, hands clasped. b, Benedict XIII, 1724-30. c, Boniface IX, 1389-1404. d, Alexander VI, no hands. e, Clement VIII, 1592-1605. f, Clement VI, 1342-52.
No. 2377: a, John Paul II, 1978-present. b, Benedict XV, 1914-22. c, John XXIII, 1958-63. d, Pius XI, 1922-39. e, Pius XII, 1939-58. f, Paul VI, 1963-78.
No. 2378, Pius II, 1458-1464. No. 2379, Pius VII, 1800-23.
Illustration reduced.

2000, Aug. 21 Litho. *Perf. 13¾*

Sheets of 6, *#a-f*

2376-2377 A406 $1.65 Set of 2 15.00 15.00

Souvenir Sheets

2378-2379 A406 $6 Set of 2 9.00 9.00

Monarchs — A407

No. 2380: a, Donaldbane of Scotland, 1093-97. b, Duncan I of Scotland, 1034-40. c, Duncan II of Scotland, 1094. d, Macbeth of Scotland, 1040-57. e, Malcolm III of Scotland, 1057-93. f, Edgar of Scotland, 1097-1107.

No. 2381: a, Charles I of Great Britain, 1625-49. b, Charles II of Great Britain, 1660-85. c, George III of Great Britain, 1760-1820. d, James II of Great Britain, 1685-89. e, James II of Scotland, 1437-60. f, James III of Scotland, 1460-88.

No. 2382, Robert I of Scotland, 1306-29. No. 2383, Anne of Great Britain, 1702-14.

Illustration reduced.

2000, Aug. 21

Sheets of 6, #a-f

2380-2381 A407 $1.65 Set of 2 15.00 15.00

Souvenir Sheets

2382-2383 A407 $6 Set of 2 9.00 9.00

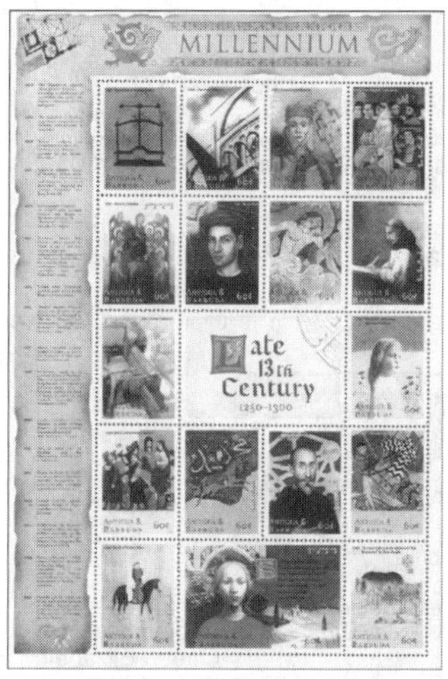

Millennium (#2385) — A408

No. 2384 - Chinese paintings: a, Admonitions of the Instructress to the Court Ladies, attributed to Ku K'ai-chih. b, Ink drawing on silk, 3rd cent. B.C. c, Ink and color drawing on silk, 2nd cent. B.C. d, Scholars of the Northern Qi Collating Texts (detail), attributed to Yang Zihua. e, Sprinting Outing (detail), attributed to Zhan Ziqian. f, Portrait of the Emperors (detail), attributed to Yen Liben. g, Sailing Boats and a Riverside Mansion, attributed to Li Sixun. h, Two Horses and a Groom (detail), by Han Kan. i, King's Portrait (detail), attributed to Wu Daozi. j, Court Ladies Wearing Flowered Headdresses (detail), attributed to Zhou Fang. k, Distant Mountain Forest (view of cliffs), by Juran. l, Mount Kuanglu, by Jiang Hao. m, Pheasant and Small Birds by a Jujube Shrub, by Huang Jucai. n, Deer Among Red Maples, by anonymous painter. o, Distant Mountain Forest (hills in foreground). p, Literary Gathering, by Han Huang (60x40mm). q, Sketches of Birds and Insects (detail), by Huang Quan.

Perf. 12¾x12½

2000, Aug. 21 **Litho.**

2384 A408 25c Sheet of 17, #a-q, + label 3.25 3.25

Highlights of 1250-1300: a, Expansion of the Inquisition. b, Chartres Cathedral. c, Sculptures in Naumburg Cathedral. d, 1st English Parliament. e, The Madonna in Majesty (Maestà), by Cimabue. f, Marco Polo. g Divine wind. h, Death of St. Thomas Aquinas. i, Arezzo Cathedral. j, Margaret, Queen of Scotland. k, Jewish exodus from England. l, Fall of Acre to Muslims. m, Moses de León writes much of The Zohar. n, German Civil War. o, Death of Kublai Khan. p, Dante writes La Vita Nuova (60x40mm). q, Chao Meng-fu paints Autumn Colors on the Quiao and Hua Mountains.

2000, Aug. 21

2385 A408 60c Sheet of 17, #a-q + label 7.50 7.50

Battle of Britain, 60th Anniv. — A409

No. 2386, $1.20: a, Bristol Blenheim. b, Winston Churchill. c, Bristol Blenheim and barrage balloon. d, Heinkel. e, Spitfire. f, German rescue vessel. g, Messerschmitt 109. h, RAF air and sea rescue launch.

No. 2387, $1.20: a, German lookout. b, Children being evacuated. c, Youngsters evacuated from hospitals. d, Hurricane. e, Rescue workers. f, British political cartoon. g, King George VI and Queen Elizabeth inspect wreckage. h, Barrage balloon over Tower Bridge.

No. 2388, $6, Spitfires. No. 2389, $6, Junkers 87B.

2000, Oct. 16 **Litho.** ***Perf. 14***

Sheets of 8, #a-h

2386-2387 A409 Set of 2 14.50 14.50

Souvenir Sheets

2388-2389 A409 Set of 2 9.00 9.00

Rainforest Fauna — A410

Designs: 75c, Agouti. 90c, Capybara. $1.20, Basilisk lizard. $2, Heliconid butterfly.

No. 2394, $1.65: a, Green violet-ear hummingbird. b, Harpy eagle. c, Three-toed sloth. d, White uakari monkey. e, Anteater. f, Coati.

No. 2395, $1.75: a, Red-eyed tree frog. b, Black spider monkey. c, Emerald toucanet. d, Kinkajou. e, Spectacled bear. f, Tapir.

No. 2396, $6, Keel-billed toucan, horiz. No. 2397, $6, Scarlet macaw, horiz.

2000, Sept. 25 **Litho.** ***Perf. 14***

2390-2393 A410 Set of 4 3.75 3.75

Sheets of 6, #a-f

2394-2395 A410 Set of 2 15.00 15.00

Souvenir Sheets

2396-2397 A410 Set of 2 9.00 9.00

Submarines — A411

Designs: 65c, Sea Cliff. 75c, Beaver Mark IV. 90c, Reef Ranger. $1, Cubmarine. $1.20, Alvin. $3, Argus.

No. 2404, $2: a, Revenge. b, Walrus. c, Los Angeles. d, Daphne. e, USS Ohio. f, USS Skipjack.

No. 2405, $6, Trieste. No. 2406, $6, German Type 209.

2000, Oct. 2

2398-2403 A411 Set of 6 5.50 5.50

2404 A411 $2 Sheet of 6, #a-f 9.00 9.00

Souvenir Sheets

2405-2406 A411 Set of 2 9.00 9.00

Paintings from the Prado — A412

No. 2407, $1.65: a, Three men. b, Man's head. c, Three women. d, Man on white horse. e, Man on brown horse. f, Man leading horse. a-c from Family Portrait, by Adriaen Thomasz Key. d-f from The Devotion of Rudolf I, by Peter Paul Rubens and Jan Wildens.

No. 2408, $1.65: a, Seated man. b, Man with sash. c, Group of men. d, Laureated figure. e, Men working at anvil. f, Two workers. a-c from The Defense of Cadiz Against the English by Francisco de Zurbaran. d-f from Vulcan's Forge, by Diego Velázquez

No. 2409, $1.65: a, Mandolin player. b, Woman with fan. c, Two men. d, Bald man. e, Two Magi. f, Jesus, Mary and Joseph. a-c from The Concert, by Vicente Palmaroli y Gonzalez. d-f from The Adoration of the Magi, by Juan Bautista Maino

No. 2410, $6, The Seller of Fans, by José del Castillo. No. 2411, $6, Portrati of a Family in a Garden, by Jan van Kessel, the Younger. No. 2412, $6, The Deliverance of St. Peter, by José de Ribera, horiz.

Illustration reduced.

2000, Oct. 6 ***Perf. 12x12¼, 12¼x12***

Sheets of 6, #a-f

2407-2409 A412 Set of 3 22.50 22.50

Souvenir Sheets

2410-2412 A412 Set of 3 13.50 13.50

España 2000 Intl. Philatelic Exhibition.

Christmas — A413

Designs (background): 25c, #2417a, Angels, full body (blue). 45c, #2417b, Angel's heads (orange). 90c, #2417c, Angel's heads (blue). $5, #2417d, Angels, full body (yellow).

2000, Dec. 4 ***Perf. 14***

2413-2416 A413 Set of 4 5.00 5.00

2417 A413 $1.75 Sheet of 4, #a-d 5.25 5.25

Souvenir Sheet

2418 A413 $6 Jesus 4.50 4.50

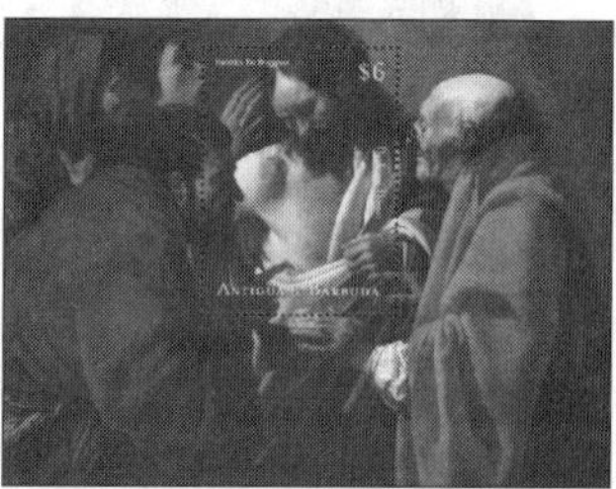

Rijksmuseum, Amsterdam, Bicent. (in 2000) — A414

No. 2419, $1: a, Dr. Ephraim Bueno, by Rembrandt. b, Woman Writing a Letter, by Frans van Mieris, the Elder. c, Mary Magdalene, by Jan van Scorel. d, Portrait of a Woman (inscribed Anna Coddle), by Maarten van Heemskerck. e, Cleopatra's Banquet, by Gerard Lairesse. f, Titus van Rijn in Friar's Habit, by Rembrandt.

No. 2420, $1.20: a, Saskia van Uylenburgh, by Rembrandt. b, In the Month of July, by Paul Joseph Constantin Gabriel. c, Maria Trip, by Rembrandt. d, Still Life with Flowers, by Jan van Huysum. e, Hesje van Cleyburgh, by Rembrandt. f, Girl in a White Kimono, by George Hendrik Breitner.

No. 2421, $1.65: a, Man and woman at spinning wheel, by Pieter Pietersz. b, Self-portrait, by Rembrandt. c, Jeremiah Lamenting the Destruction of Jerusalem, by Rembrandt. d, The Jewish Bride, by Rembrandt. e, Tobit and Anna with a Kid, by Rembrandt. f, The Prophetess Anna, by Rembrandt.

No. 2422, $6, Doubting Thomas, by Hendrick ter Brugghen. No. 2423, $6, Still Life with Cheeses, by Floris van Dijck. No. 2424, $6, Isaac Blessing Jacob, by Govert Flinck.

2001, Jan. 15 **Litho.** ***Perf. 13¾***

Sheets of 6, #a-f

2419-2421 A414 Set of 3 17.50 17.50

Souvenir Sheets

2422-2424 A414 Set of 3 13.50 13.50

Pokémon — A415

No. 2425: a, Starmie. b, Misty. c, Brock. d, Geodude. e, Krabby. f, Ash.

2001, Feb. 13

2425 A415 $1.75 Sheet of 6, #a-f 8.00 8.00

Souvenir Sheet

2426 A415 $6 Charizard 4.50 4.50

Mushrooms A416

Designs: 25c, Blue-toothed entoloma. 90c, Common morel. $1, Red cage fungus. $1.75, Fawn shield-cap.

No. 2431, $1.65: a, Lilac bonnet. b, Silky volvar. c, Poplar field cap. d, St. George's mushroom. e, Red-stemmed tough shank. f, Fly agaric.

No. 2432, $1.65: a, Copper trumpet. b, Meadow mushroom. c, Green-gilled parasol. d, Panther. e, Death cap. f, King bolete.

No. 2433, $6, Yellow parasol. No. 2434, Mutagen milk cap.

2001, Mar. 26 ***Perf. 13¾x13¼***

2427-2430 A416 Set of 4 3.00 3.00

Sheets of 6, #a-f

2431-2432 A416 Set of 2 15.00 15.00

Souvenir Sheets

2433-2434 A416 Set of 2 9.00 9.00

Hong Kong 2001 Stamp Exhibition (2431-2434).

Population and Housing Census — A417

Map of Antigua with various graphs. Denominations: 15c, 25c, 65c, 90c.

2001, Apr. 2 ***Perf. 13¾***
2435-2438 A417 Set of 4 1.50 1.50

Souvenir Sheet

2439 A417 $6 Map, emblem 4.50 4.50

Phila Nippon '01, Japan — A418

Designs: 45c Two women facing right, from Yuna (Bath-house Women). 60c, Woman facing left, from Yuna. 65c, Two women, from Yuna. 75c, Man with stringed instrument at top, from Hikone Screen. $1, Woman with stringed instrument at bottom, from Hikone Screen. $1.20, Two people, from Hikone Screen.

No. 2446 - Namban Screen, by Naizen Kano: a, Ship's stern. b, Ship's bow. c, Man with closed umbrella. d, Man with open umbrella.

No. 2447 - Merry Making Under the Cherry Blossoms, by Naganobu Kano: a, Steps. b, Tree. c, Four people near building. d, Four people, mountains. e, Three people. f, One person.

No. 2448, $6, Visiting a Shrine on a Rainy Night, by Harunobu Suzuki. No. 2449, $6, Harunobu Suzuki, by Kokan Shiba. No. 2450, $6, Daruma, by Tsujo Kano.

2001, May 28 Litho. ***Perf. 14¼x14***
2440-2445 A418 Set of 6 3.50 3.50
2446 A418 $1.65 Sheet of 4, #a-d 5.00 5.00
2447 A418 $1.65 Sheet of 6, #a-f 7.50 7.50

Souvenir Sheets

Perf. 13¾

2448-2450 A418 Set of 3 13.50 13.50

Nos. 2448-2450 each contain one 38x51mm stamp.

No. 2449 is incorrectly inscribed. It actually depicts "Courtesan on a Veranda Upstairs," by Kokan.

Orchids A419

Designs: 45c, Hintleya burtii. 75c, Neomoovea irrovata. 90c, Comparettia speciosa. $1, Cypripedium crapeanum.

No. 2455, $1.20, vert.: a, Trichoceuos muralis. b, Dracula rampira. c, Psychopsis papilio. d, Lycaste clenningiana. e, Telipogon nevuosus. f, Masclecallia ayahbacana.

No. 2456, $1.65, vert.: a, Rhyncholaelia glanca. b, Oncidium barbatum. c, Phaius tankervillege. d, Ghies brechtiana. e, Angraecum leonis. f, Cychnoches loddigesti.

No. 2457, $1.65, vert.: a, Cattleya dowiana. b, Dendrobium cruentum. c, Bulbophyllum lobbi. d, Chysis laevis. e, Ancistrochilus rothschildicanus. f, Angraecum sororium.

No. 2458, $6, Trichopilia fragrans, vert. No. 2459, $6, Symphalossum sanguinem, vert.

2001, June 11 ***Perf. 14***
2451-2454 A419 Set of 4 2.40 2.40

Sheets of 6, #a-f

2455-2457 A419 Set of 3 20.00 20.00

Souvenir Sheets

2458-2459 A419 Set of 2 9.00 9.00

Souvenir Sheets

I Love Lucy — A420

Designs: No. 2460, $6, Fred and Ricky. No. 2461, $6, Lucy and Ethel. No. 2462, $6, Lucy and fireplace. No. 2463, $6, Lucy and open door.

2001, Mar. 5 Litho. ***Perf. 13¾***
2460-2463 A420 Set of 4 18.00 18.00

See Nos. 2522-2525.

Marine Life and Birds A421

Designs: 25c, Yellowtail damselfish. 45c, Indigo hamlet. 65c, Great white shark. No. 2467, 90c, Bottlenose dolphin. No. 2468, 90c, Palette surgeonfish. $1, Octopus.

No. 2470, $1.20: a, Common dolphin. b, Franklin's gull. c, Rock beauty. d, Bicolor angelfish. e, Beaugregory. f, Banded butterflyfish.

No. 2471, $1.20: a, Common tern. b, Flying fish. c, Queen angelfish. d, Blue-striped grunt. e, Porkfish. f, Blue tang.

No. 2472, $1.65: a, Dugong. b, White-tailed tropicbird. c, Bull shark and Spanish grunt. d, Manta ray. e, Green turtle. f, Spanish grunt.

No. 2473, $1.65: a, Red-footed booby. b, Bottlenose dolphin. c, Hawksbill turtle. d, Monk seal. e, Bull shark and coral. f, Lemon shark.

No. 2474, $5, Sailfish. No. 2475, $5, Beaugregory and brown pelican, vert. No. 2476, $6, Hawksbill turtle. No. 2477, $6, Queen triggerfish.

2001, June 11 ***Perf. 14***
2464-2469 A421 Set of 6 3.25 3.25

Sheets of 6, #a-f

2470-2473 A421 Set of 4 26.00 26.00

Souvenir Sheets

2474-2477 A421 Set of 4 16.00 16.00

Ship Freewinds — A422

Designs: 30c, Maiden voyage anniversary in Antigua. 45c, In St. Barthelemy. 75c, In Caribbean at sunset. 90c, In Bonaire. $1.50, In Bequia.

No. 2483, $4, With lights on during eclipse. No. 2484, $4, In Curacao.

2001, June 15
2478-2482 A422 Set of 5 3.00 3.00

Souvenir Sheets

2483-2484 A422 Set of 2 6.00 6.00

Toulouse-Lautrec Paintings — A423

No. 2485: a, Monsieur Georges-Henri Manuel Standing. b, Monsieur Louis Pascal. c, Roman Coolus. d, Monsieur Fourcade.

$5, Dancing at the Moulin de la Galette.

2001, July 3 ***Perf. 13¾***
2485 A423 $2 Sheet of 4, #a-d 6.00 6.00

Souvenir Sheet

2486 A423 $5 multi 3.75 3.75

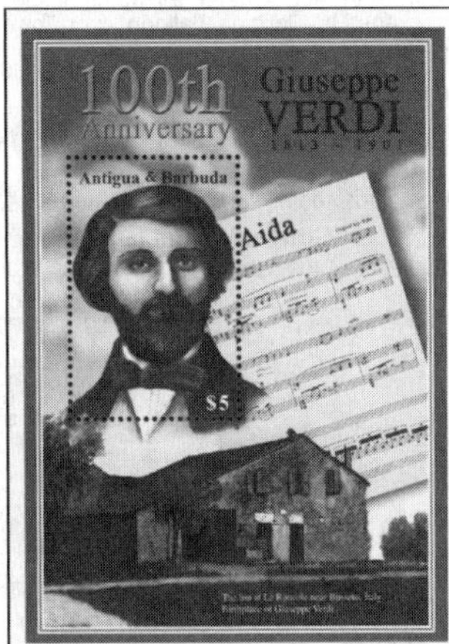

Giuseppe Verdi (1813-1901), Opera Composer — A424

No. 2487: a, Verdi in hat. b, Character and score from Don Carlos. c, Conductor and score for Aida. d, Musicians and score for Rigoletto.

2001, July 3 ***Perf. 14***
2487 A424 $2 Sheet of 4, #a-d 6.00 6.00

Souvenir Sheet

2488 A424 $5 Verdi, score 3.75 3.75

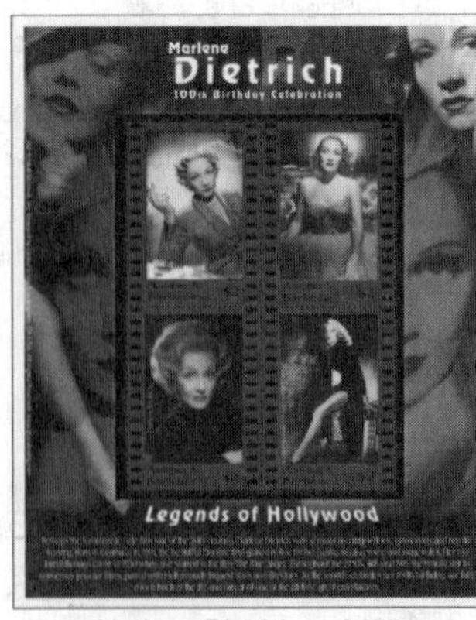

Marlene Dietrich — A425

No. 2489: a, With cigarette. b, On sofa. c, Color photograph. d, With piano.

2001, July 3 ***Perf. 13¾***
2489 A425 $2 Sheet of 4, #a-d 6.00 6.00

Queen Victoria (1819-1901) — A426

No. 2490: a, Blue dress. b, Red hat. c, Crown. d, Crown and blue sash.

2001, July 3 ***Perf. 14***
2490 A426 $2 Sheet of 4, #a-d 6.00 6.00

Souvenir Sheet

2491 A426 $5 As old woman 3.75 3.75

Queen Elizabeth II, 75th Birthday — A427

No. 2492: a, At birth, 1926. b, In 1938. c, In 1939. d, At coronation, 1953. e, In 1956. f, In 1985.

2001, July 3
2492 A427 $1 Sheet of 6, #a-f 4.50 4.50

Souvenir Sheet

2493 A427 $6 In 1940 4.50 4.50

Photomosaic of Queen Elizabeth II — A428

2001, July 3 Litho. ***Perf. 14***
2494 A428 $1 multi .75 .75

Queen Elizabeth II, 75th birthday. Issued in sheets of 8.

Monet Paintings — A429

No. 2495, horiz.: a, Water Lilies. b, Rose Portals, Giverny. c, The Water Lily Pond, Harmony in Green. d, The Artist's Garden, Irises.

$5, Jerusalem Artichokes.

2001, July 3 ***Perf. 13¾***
2495 A429 $2 Sheet of 4, #a-d 6.00 6.00

Souvenir Sheet

2496 A429 $5 multi 3.75 3.75

Endangered Animals — A430

Designs: 25c, Collared peccary. 30c, Baird's tapir. 45c, Agouti. 75c, Bananaquit. 90c, Six-banded armadillo. $1, Roseate spoonbill.

No. 2503: a, Mouse opossum. b, Magnificent black frigatebird. c, Northern jacana. d, Painted bunting. e, Haitian solenodon. f, St. Lucia iguana.

No. 2504: a, West Indian iguana. b, Scarlet macaw. c, Cotton-topped tamarin. d, Kinkajou.

No. 2505, $6, Ocelot, vert. No. 2506, $6, King vulture, vert.

2001, Sept. 10 ***Perf. 14***

2497-2502 A430 Set of 6 2.75 2.75
2503 A430 $1.80 Sheet of 6, #a-f 8.25 8.25
2504 A430 $2.50 Sheet of 4, #a-d 7.50 7.50

Souvenir Sheets

2505-2506 A430 Set of 2 9.00 9.00

Rudolph Valentino (1895-1926), Actor — A431

No. 2507, $1: a, Blood and Sand. b, Eyes of Youth. c, All Night. d, Last known photo of Valentino. e, Camille. f, Cobra.

No. 2508, $1: a, The Son of the Sheik. b, The Young Rajah. c, The Eagle. d, The Sheik. e, A Sainted Devil. f, Monsieur Beaucaire.

No. 2509, $6, The Four Horsemen of the Apocalypse. No. 2510, $6, Valentino with Natasha Rambova.

2001, Oct. 2 ***Perf. 13¾***

Sheets of 6, #a-f

2507-2508 A431 Set of 2 9.00 9.00

Souvenir Sheets

2509-2510 A431 Set of 2 9.00 9.00

Scenes From Shirley Temple Movies — A432

No. 2511, $1.65 - Scenes from Baby, Take a Bow, with Temple: a, In polka-dot dress. b, With man on steps. c, With man holding gun. d, With woman.

No. 2512, $1.80, horiz. - Scenes from The Little Princess, with Temple: a, With man. b, Washing floor. c, With woman and child. d, With old woman.

No. 2513, $1.50 - Scenes from The Little Princess, with Temple: a, With woman. b, In pink dress. c, Holding doll. d, On throne. e, With man. f, With birthday cake.

No. 2514, $1.65, horiz. - Scenes from Baby, Take a Bow, with Temple: a, With woman and five children. b, With arms around man. c, Being tucked in bed. d, With man. e, Standing with man and woman. f, Looking in cradle.

No. 2515, $6, In polka-dot dress, from Baby, Take a Bow. No. 2516, With soldiers, from The Little Princess.

2001, Oct. 2 **Sheets of 4, #a-d**

2511-2512 A432 Set of 2 10.50 10.50

Sheets of 6, #a-f

2513-2514 A432 Set of 2 14.00 14.00

Souvenir Sheets

2515-2516 A432 Set of 2 9.00 9.00

Nobel Prizes, Cent. — A433

No. 2517, $1.50 - Chemistry laureates: a, Melvin Calvin, 1961. b, Linus C. Pauling, 1954. c, Vincent du Vigneaud, 1955. d, Richard Synge, 1952. e, Archer Martin, 1952. f, Alfred Werner, 1913.

No. 2518, $1.50 - Chemistry laureates: a, Robert F. Curl, Jr., 1996. b, Alan J. Heeger, 2000. c, Michael Smith, 1993. d, Sidney Altman, 1989. e, Elias James Corey, 1990. f, William Francis Giauque, 1949.

No. 2519, $6, Ernest Rutherford, Chemistry, 1908. No. 2520, $6, International Red Cross, Peace, 1944. No. 2521, $6, Ernst Otto Fischer, Chemistry, 1973.

2001, Nov. 29 ***Perf. 14***

Sheets of 6, #a-f

2517-2518 A433 Set of 2 13.50 13.50

Souvenir Sheets

2519-2521 A433 Set of 3 13.50 13.50

I Love Lucy Type of 2001

Designs: No. 2522, $6, Fred at desk. No. 2523, $6, Lucy and Fred. No. 2524, $6, Lucy, closed door. No. 2525, $6, Fred and Ricky at desk, horiz.

2001 ***Perf. 13¾***

2522-2525 A420 Set of 4 18.00 18.00

Christmas — A434

Paintings: 25c, Madonna and Child with Angels, by Filippo Lippi. 45c, Madonna of Corneto Tarquinia, by Lippi. 50c, Madonna and Child, by Domenico Ghirlandaio. 75c, Madonna and Child, by Lippi. $4, Madonna Delceppo, by Lippi.

$6, Madonna Enthroned with Angels and Saints, by Lippi.

2001, Dec. 4 **Litho.** ***Perf. 14***

2526-2530 A434 Set of 5 4.50 4.50

Souvenir Sheet

2531 A434 $6 multi 4.50 4.50

2002 World Cup Soccer Championships, Japan and Korea — A435

No. 2532, $1.50: a, Scene from final game, 1950. b, Ferenc Puskas, 1954. c, Raymond Kopa, 1958. d, Mauro, 1962. e, Gordon Banks, 1966. f, Pelé, 1970.

No. 2533, $1.50: a, Daniel Passarella, 1978. b, Karl-Heinz Rummenigge, 1982. c, World Cup trophy, 1986. d, Diego Maradona, 1990. e, Roger Milla, 1994. f, Zinedine Zidane, 1998.

No. 2534, $6, Head from Jules Rimet Cup, 1930. No. 2535, $6, Head and globe from World Cup trophy, 2002.

2001, Dec. 17 ***Perf. 13¾x14¼***

Sheets of 6, #a-f

2532-2533 A435 Set of 2 13.50 13.50

Souvenir Sheets

Perf. 14¼

2534-2535 A435 Set of 2 9.00 9.00

Queen Mother Type of 2000 Redrawn

No. 2536: a, As child. b, In 1940. c, With Princess Anne, 1951. d, In Canada, 1989.

$6, Inspecting the troops.

2001, Dec. ***Perf. 14***

Yellow Orange Frames

2536 A404 $2 Sheet of 4, #a-d, + label 6.00 6.00

Souvenir Sheet

Perf. 13¾

2537 A404 $6 multi 4.50 4.50

Queen Mother's 101st birthday. No. 2537 contains one 38x51mm stamp with a darker appearance than that found on No. 2374. Sheet margins of Nos. 2536-2537 lack embossing and gold arms found on Nos. 2373-2374.

US Civil War — A436

No. 2538: a, Battle of Nashville. b, Battle of Atlanta. c, Battle of Spotsylvania. d, Battle of the Wilderness. e, Battle of Chickamauga Creek. f, Battle of Gettysburg. g, Battle of Chancellorsville. h, Battle of Fredericksburg. i, Battle of Antietam. j, Second Battle of Bull Run. k, Battle of Five Forks. l, Seven Days' Battle. m, Battle of Bull Run. n, Battle of Shiloh. o, Battle of Seven Pines. p, Battle of Fort Sumter. q, Battle of Chattanooga. r, Surrender at Appomattox.

No. 2539, vert.: a, Gen. Ulysses S. Grant. b, Pres. Abraham Lincoln. c, Confederate Pres. Jefferson Davis. d, Gen. Robert E. Lee. e, Gen. George A. Custer. f, Adm. Andrew Hull Foote. g, General Thomas "Stonewall" Jackson. h, Gen. J.E.B. Stuart. i, Gen. George G. Meade. j, Gen. Philip H. Sheridan. k, Gen. James Longstreet. l, Gen. John S. Mosby.

No. 2540, $6, Monitor. No. 2541, $6, Merrimack.

2002, Jan. 28 ***Perf. 14¾***

2538 A436 45c Sheet of 18, #a-r 6.00 6.00
2539 A436 50c Sheet of 12, #a-l 4.50 4.50

Souvenir Sheets

Perf. 14½x14¾ (#2540), 13¾

2540-2541 A436 Set of 2 9.00 9.00

No. 2541 contains one 50x38mm stamp.

Reign of Queen Elizabeth II, 50th Anniv. — A437

No. 2542: a, Striped dress. b, Green patterned dress. c, Orange patterned dress. d, White jacket.

$6, Queen with Princess Margaret.

2002, Feb. 6 ***Perf. 14¼***

2542 A437 $2 Sheet of 4, #a-d 6.00 6.00

Souvenir Sheet

2543 A437 $6 multi 4.50 4.50

United We Stand — A438

2002, Feb. 11 ***Perf. 13½x13¼***

2544 A438 $2 multi 1.50 1.50

Printed in sheets of 4.

Cricket Player Sir Vivian Richards, 50th Birthday — A439

Designs: 25c, Raising bat. 30c, Receiving gift. 50c, With arms raised. 75c, At bat. $1.50, Wearing sash, with woman. $1.80, Standing next to photograph of himself.

No. 2551, $6, Holding sword. No. 2552, $6, With Antigua color guard.

2002, Mar. 7 ***Perf. 13½x13¼***

2545-2550 A439 Set of 6 4.00 4.00

Souvenir Sheets

2551-2552 A439 Set of 2 9.00 9.00

Flora and Fauna A440

Designs: 50c, Thick-billed parrot. 75c, Lesser long-nosed bat. $1.50, Montserrat oriole. $1.80, Miss Perkin's blue butterfly.

No. 2557, 90c: a, Quetzals. b, Two-toed sloth. c, Lovely cotinga. d, Giant hairstrak butterfly. e, Magenta-throated woodstar. f, Bull's-eye silk moth. g, Golden toads. h, Collared peccaries. i, Tamandua anteater.

No. 2558, $1: a, St. Lucia parrot. b, Cuban kite. c, West Indian whistling duck. d, Poey's sulphur butterfly. e, Scarlet ibis. f, Black-capped petrel. g, St. Lucia whiptail. h, Cuban

Solenodon. i, False androgeus swallowtail butterfly.
No. 2559, $6, Margay. No. 2560, $6, Olive Ridley turtle.

2002, Apr. 8 ***Perf. 14***
2553-2556 A440 Set of 4 3.50 3.50

Sheets of 9, *#a-i*
2557-2558 A440 Set of 2 13.00 13.00

Souvenir Sheets
2559-2560 A440 Set of 2 9.00 9.00

Antigua Community Players, 50th Anniv. — A441

Various photos: 20c, 25c, 30c, 75c, 90c, $1.50, $1.80.
No. 2568, $4, Former Pres. Edie Hill-Thibou, vert. No. 2569, $4, Acting Pres. and Music Director Yvonne Maginley, vert.

Perf. 13½x13¾
2002, June 11 **Litho.**
2561-2567 A441 Set of 7 4.25 4.25

Souvenir Sheets
Perf. 14
2568-2569 A441 Set of 2 6.00 6.00

Endangered Animals — A442

No. 2570: a, Red-billed tropicbird. b, Brown pelican. c, Magnificent frigatebird. d, Ground lizard. e, West Indian whistling duck. f, Antiguan racer snake. g, Spiny lobster. h, Hawksbill turtle. i, Queen conch.

2002, July 12 ***Perf. 14***
2570 A442 $1.50 Sheet of 9, #a-i 10.00 10.00

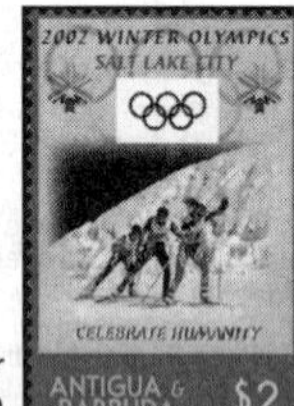

2002 Winter Olympics, Salt Lake City — A443

Designs: No. 2571, $2, Cross-country skiing. No. 2572, $2, Pairs figure skating.

2002, July 15 ***Perf. 13½x13¼***
2571-2572 A443 Set of 2 3.00 3.00
2572a Souvenir sheet, #2571-2572 3.00 3.00

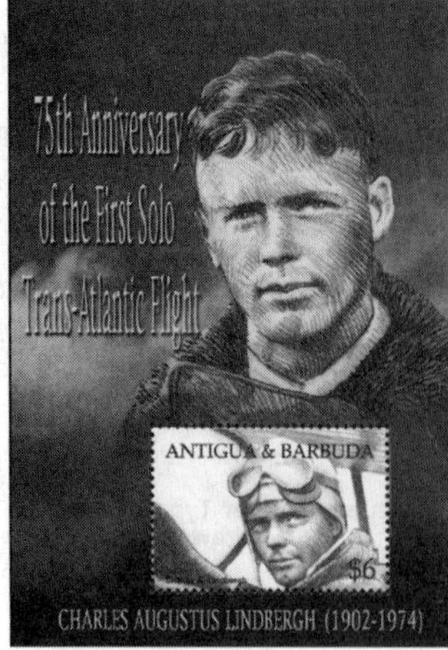

First Solo Transatlantic Flight, 75th Anniv. — A444

No. 2573: a, Charles Lindbergh and The Spirit of St. Louis. b, Arrival at Le Bourget Airport, Paris. c, Lindbergh receiving hero's welcome, New York.
$6, Lindbergh in airplane.

2002, July 15 ***Perf. 13¼x13½***
2573 A444 $2.50 Sheet of 3, #a-c 5.75 5.75

Souvenir Sheet
2574 A444 $6 multi 4.50 4.50

Intl. Year of Mountains — A445

No. 2575: a, Mt. Fuji. b, Machu Picchu. c, Matterhorn.

2002, July 15 ***Perf. 13½x13¼***
2575 A445 $2 Sheet of 3, #a-c 4.50 4.50

Amerigo Vespucci (1454-1512), Explorer — A446

No. 2576, horiz.: a, Vespucci with gray head covering. b, Vespucci with red head covering. c, Hands and map.
$6, Vespucci and compass.

Perf. 13¼x13½, 13½x13¼
2002, July 15
2576 A446 $2.50 Sheet of 3, #a-c 5.75 5.75

Souvenir Sheet
2577 A446 $6 multi 4.50 4.50

Princess Diana (1961-97) — A447

No. 2578: a, Wearing seven-strand pearl necklace. b, Wearing tiara and white dress. c, Wearing hat. d, Wearing earrings and black dress. e, Wearing tiara, no dress seen. f, Wearing earrings, no dress seen.
$6, Wearing white dress.

2002, July 29 ***Perf. 14***
2578 A447 $1.80 Sheet of 6, #a-f 8.25 8.25

Souvenir Sheet
2579 A447 $6 multi 4.50 4.50

Presidents John F. Kennedy and Ronald Reagan — A448

No. 2580, $1.50, horiz.: a, John, Robert and Edward Kennedy. b, Kennedy with Danny Kaye. c, Kennedy addressing nation. d, With wife, Jacqueline. e, Shaking hands with young Bill Clinton. f, Family members at funeral.
No. 2581, $1.50, horiz.: a, Reagan with wife, Nancy, and Pope John Paul II. b, As George Gipp in movie *Knute Rockne, All American.* c, With Gen. Matthew Ridgeway at Bitburg Cemetery. d, With Vice-president George H. W. Bush and Mikhail Gorbachev. e, With Presidents Ford, Carter, and Nixon. f, On horseback, with Queen Elizabeth II.
No. 2582, $6, Kennedy and flag. No. 2583, $6, Reagan.

2002, July 29 **Litho.**

Sheets of 6, *#a-f*
2580-2581 A448 Set of 2 13.50 13.50

Souvenir Sheets
2582-2583 A448 Set of 2 9.00 9.00

Elvis Presley (1935-77) A449

2002, Aug. 20 ***Perf. 13¾***
2584 A449 $1 multi .75 .75

Printed in sheets of 9.

Teddy Bears, Cent. — A450

No. 2585: a, Cheerleader bear. b, Figure skater bear. c, Ballet dancer bear. d, Aerobics instructor bear.

2002, Aug. 26
2585 A450 $2 Sheet of 4, #a-d 6.00 6.00

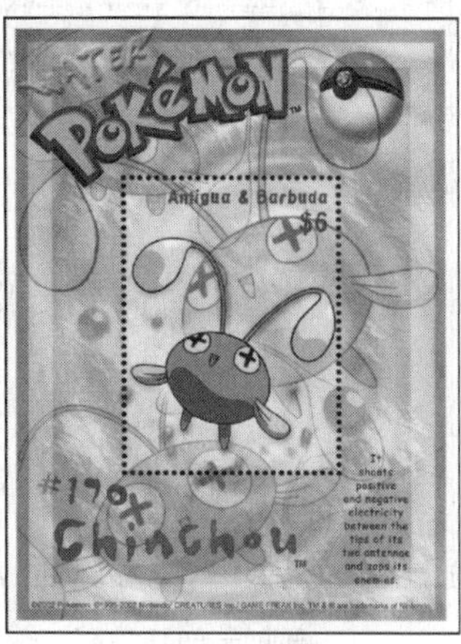

Pokémon — A451

No. 2586: a, Croconau. b, Mantine. c, Feraligatr. d, Quilfish. e, Remoraid. f, Quagsire.
$6, Chinchou.

2002, Aug. 26
2586 A451 $1.50 Sheet of 6, #a-f 6.75 6.75

Souvenir Sheet
2587 A451 $6 multi 4.50 4.50

Lee Strasberg (1901-82), Movie Actor and Director — A452

2002, Sept. 16 ***Perf. 14***
2588 A452 $1 multi .75 .75

Printed in sheets of 9.

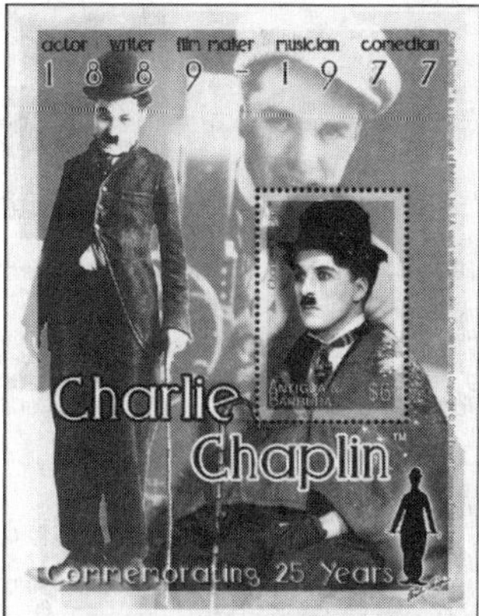

Charlie Chaplin (1889-1977), Actor — A453

No. 2589: a, Wearing bowler hat, facing forward. b, Wearing suit and vest. c, Wearing top hat. d, Wearing bowler hat, profile. e, Wearing bow tie and suit. f, With hand at chin.
$6, Wearing bowler hat, diff.

2002, Sept. 16
2589 A453 $1.80 Sheet of 6, #a-f 8.25 8.25

Souvenir Sheet

2590 A453 $6 multi 4.50 4.50

Marlene Dietrich (1901-92), Actress — A454

No. 2591: a, With hands at side of face. b, Wearing top hat. c, Faciing forward. d, With hand on chin. e, Wearing black hat. f, Wearing gloves.
$6, Facing forward, diff.

2002, Sept. 16
2591 A454 $1.50 Sheet of 6, #a-f 6.75 6.75

Souvenir Sheet

2592 A454 $6 multi 4.50 4.50

Bob Hope — A455

No. 2593: a, Wearing red cap. b, Wearing hat with strap. c, Wearing top hat. d, Wearing black cap. e, Wearing camouflage. f, Wearing white cap.

2002, Sept. 16
2593 A455 $1.50 Sheet of 6, #a-f 6.75 6.75

Ferrari Race Cars A456

Designs: 20c, 1957 801. 25c, 1959 256 F1. 30c, 1960 246P F1. 90c, 1966 246 F1. $1, 1971 312 B2. $1.50, 1969 312 F1. $2, 1997 F310B. $4, 2002 F2002.

2002, Oct. 14 **Litho.**
2594-2601 A456 Set of 8 7.75 7.75

Independence, 21st Anniv. — A457

Designs: 25c, Flag. 30c, Arms, vert. $1.50, Mt. St. John's Hospital nearing completion. $1.80, Parliament Building.
No. 2606, $6, Prime Minister Lester B. Bird, vert. No. 2607, $6, Sir Vere C. Bird, vert.

2002, Oct. 31 ***Perf. 14***
2602-2605 A457 Set of 4 3.00 3.00

Souvenir Sheets

2606-2607 A457 Set of 2 9.00 9.00

Nos. 2606-2607 each contain one 38x50mm stamp.

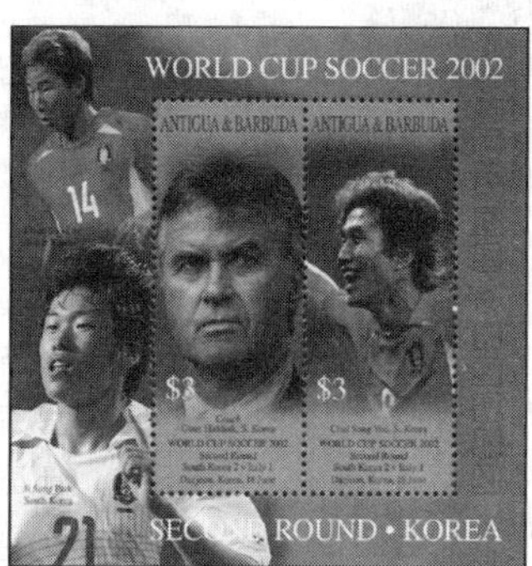

Second Round of World Cup Soccer Championships — A458

No. 2608, $1.65: a, Pyo Lee. b, Ji Sung Park. c, Jung Hwan Ahn. d, Filippo Inzaghi. e, Paolo Maldini. f, Damiano Tommasi.
No. 2609, $1.65: a, Juan Valeron. b, Iker Casillas. c, Fernando Hierro. d, Gary Kelly. e, Damien Duff. f, Matt Holland.
No. 2610, $3: a, South Korean coach Guus Hiddink. b, Chul Sang Yoo.
No. 2611, $3: a, Francesco Totti. b, Italy coach Giovanni Trapattoni.
No. 2612, $3: a, Spain coach Jose Antonio Camacho. b, Carlos Gamarra.
No. 2613, $3: a, Robbie Keane. b, Ireland coach Mick McCarthy.

2002, Nov. 4 ***Perf. 13½x13¼***

Sheets of 6, #a-f

2608-2609 A458 Set of 2 15.00 15.00

Souvenir Sheets, #a-b

2610-2613 A458 Set of 4 18.00 18.00

Christmas A459

Designs: 25c, Coronation of the Virgin, by Domenico Ghirlandaio. 45c, Adoration of the Magi (detail), by Ghirlandaio. 75c, Annunciation (detail), by Simone Martini, vert. 90c, Adoration of the Magi (detail, diff.) by Ghirlandaio. $5, Madonna and Child, by Giovanni Bellini.
$6, Madonna and Child, by Martini.

2002, Nov. 18 ***Perf. 14***
2614-2618 A459 Set of 5 5.50 5.50

Souvenir Sheet

2619 A459 $6 multi 4.50 4.50

Worldwide Fund for Nature (WWF) A460

Antiguan racer snake: a, Head. b, Snake with head near tail. c, Snake and dried leaves. d, Snake on rocks.

2002, Nov. 25
2620 Strip of 4 3.00 3.00
a.-d. A460 $1 Any single .75 .75

Printed in sheets of 4 strips.

Flora & Fauna — A461

No. 2621, $1.50: a, Magnificent frigatebird. b, Sooty tern. c, Bananaquit. d, Yellow-crowned night heron. e, Greater flamingo. f, Belted kingfisher.
No. 2622, $1.50: a, Killer whale. b, Sperm whale. c, Minke whale. d, Blainville's beaked whale. e, Blue whale. f, Cuvier's beaked whale.
No. 2623, $1.80: a, Hieroglyphic moth. b, Hypocrita dejanira. c, Snowy eupseudosoma moth. d, Composia credula. e, Giant silkworm moth. f, Diva moth.
No. 2624, $1.80: a, Epidendrum fragrans. b, Dombeya. c, Yellow poul. d, Milky wave plant. e, Cinderella plant. f, Coral orchid.
No. 2625, $5, Snowy egret. No. 2626, $5, Rothschildia orizaba. No. 2627, $6, Humpback whale. No. 2628, $6, Ionopsis utriculariodes.

2002, Nov. 25 **Litho.**

Sheets of 6, #a-f

2621-2624 A461 Set of 4 30.00 30.00

Souvenir Sheets

2625-2628 A461 Set of 4 16.00 16.00

Souvenir Sheet

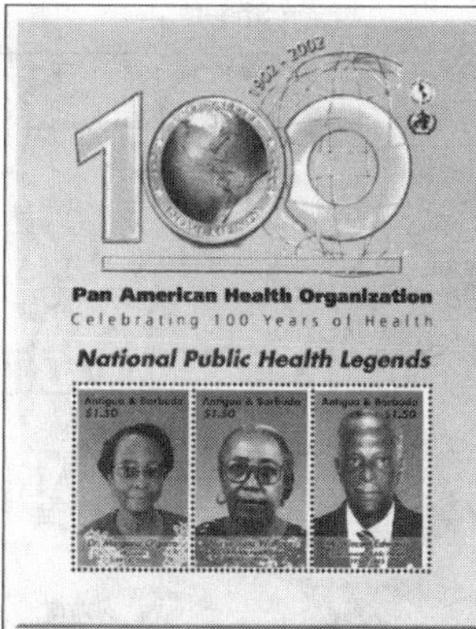

Pan-American Health Organization, Cent. — A462

No. 2629: a, Dr. Margaret O'Garro. b, Nurse Ineta Wallace. c, Public Health Worker Vincent Edwards.

2002, Dec. 2
2629 A462 $1.50 Sheet of 3, #a-c 3.50 3.50

Souvenir Sheets

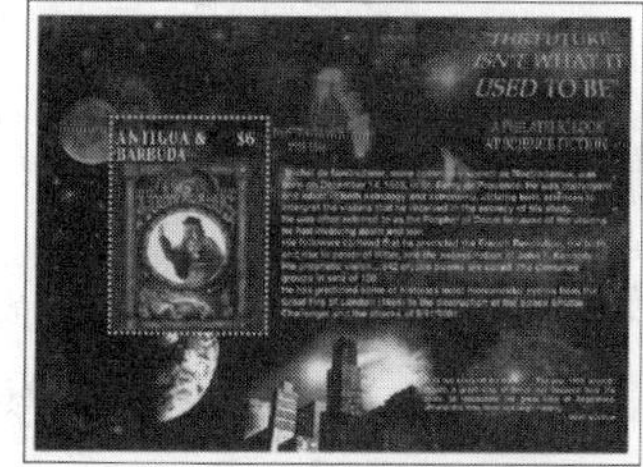

Science Fiction — A463

No. 2630, $6, Writings of Nostradamus. No. 2631, $6, *2001: A Space Odyssey*, by Arthur C. Clarke. No. 2632, $6, Are We Alone?

2002, Dec. 12 ***Perf. 13¾***
2630-2632 A463 Set of 3 13.50 13.50

WAR TAX STAMPS

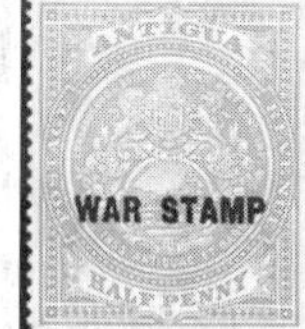

No. 31 and Type A3 Overprinted in Black or Red

1916-18 **Wmk. 3** ***Perf. 14***
MR1 A3 ½p green 1.00 *1.90*
MR2 A3 ½p green (R) ('17) 1.40 *1.90*
MR3 A3 1½p orange ('18) 1.00 *1.25*
Nos. MR1-MR3 (3) 3.40 *5.05*

ARGENTINA

ˌär-jən-ˈtē-nə

LOCATION — In South America
GOVT. — Republic
AREA — 1,084,120 sq. mi.
POP. — 36,737,664 (est. 1999)
CAPITAL — Buenos Aires

100 Centavos = 1 Peso (1858, 1992)
100 Centavos = 1 Austral (1985)

Catalogue values for unused stamps in this country are for Never Hinged items, beginning with Scott 587 in the regular postage section, Scott B12 in the semi-postal section, Scott C59 in the airpost section, Scott CB1 in the airpost semi-postal section and Scott O79 in the officials section.

Watermarks

Wmk. 84- Italic RA

Wmk. 85- Small Sun, 4½mm

Wmk. 86- Large Sun, 6mm

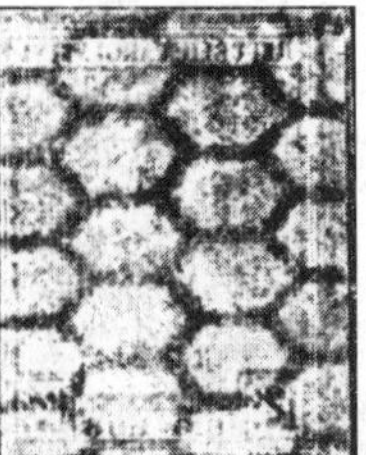

Wmk. 87- Honeycomb

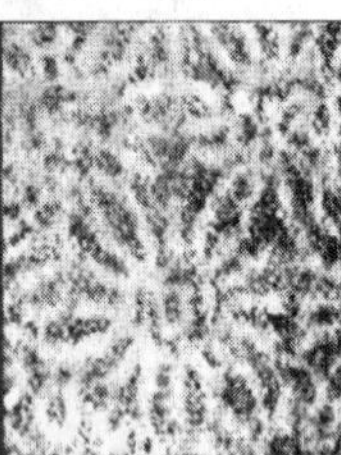

Wmk. 88- Multiple Suns

Wmk. 89- Large Sun

In this watermark the face of the sun is 7mm in diameter, the rays are heavier than in the large sun watermark of 1896-1911 and the watermarks are placed close together, so that parts of several frequently appear on one stamp. This paper was intended to be used for fiscal stamps and is usually referred to as "fiscal sun paper."

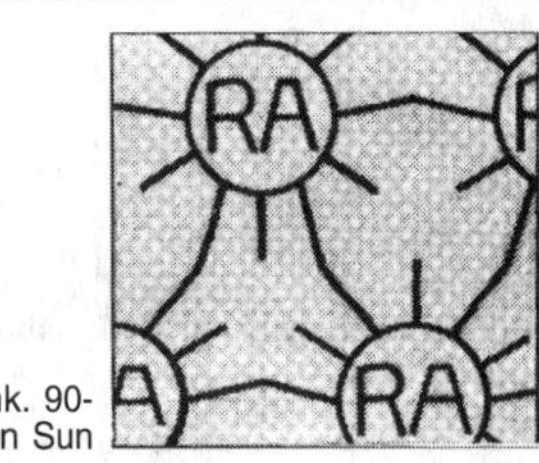

Wmk. 90- RA in Sun

In 1928 watermark 90 was slightly modified, making the diameter of the Sun 9mm instead of 10mm. Several types of this watermark exist.

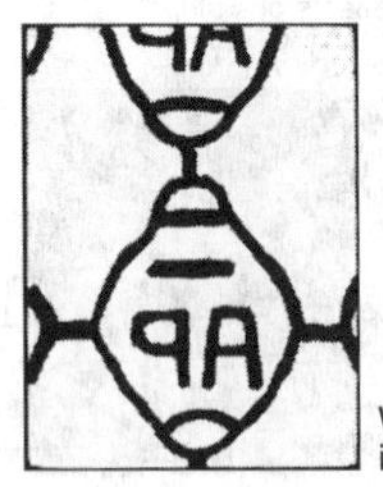

Wmk. 205- AP in Oval

The letters "AP" are the initials of "AHORRO POSTAL." This paper was formerly used exclusively for Postal Savings stamps.

Wmk. 287- Double Circle and Letters in Sheet

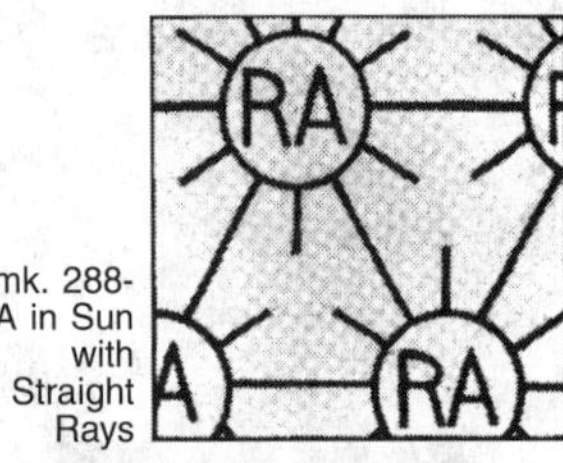

Wmk. 288- RA in Sun with Straight Rays

Wmk. 365- Argentine Arms, "Casa de Moneda de la Nacion" & "RA" Multiple

Values for Unused
Unused values for Nos. 5-17 are for examples without gum. Examples with original gum command higher prices. Unused values of Nos. 1-4B and stamps after No. 17 are for examples with original gum as defined in the catalogue introduction.

Argentine Confederation

Symbolical of the Argentine Confederation
A1 A2

Unwmk.

1858, May 1 Litho. *Imperf.*

1	A1	5c red	1.50	*24.00*
a.		Colon after "5"	1.75	*32.50*
b.		Colon after "V"	1.75	*32.50*
2	A1	10c green	2.50	*57.50*
f.		Diagonal half used as 5c on cover		*800.00*
3	A1	15c blue	16.00	*160.00*
c.		One-third used as 5c on cover		*6,500.*
		Nos. 1-3 (3)	20.00	*241.50*

There are nine varieties of Nos. 1, 2 and 3. Counterfeits and forged cancellations of Nos. 1-3 are plentiful.

1860, Jan.

4	A2	5c red	3.25	*72.50*
4A	A2	10c green	7.00	
4B	A2	15c blue	25.00	
		Nos. 4-4B (3)	35.25	

Nos. 4A and 4B were never placed in use. Some compostitions of Nos. 4-4B contain 8 different types across the sheet. Other settings exist with minor variations. Counterfeits and forged cancellations of Nos. 4-4B are plentiful.

Argentine Republic

Seal of the Republic — A3

Broad "C" in "CENTAVOS," Accent on "U" of "REPUBLICA"

1862, Jan. 11

5	A3	5c rose	40.00	37.50
a.		5c rose lilac	87.50	35.00
6	A3	10c green	140.00	65.00
b.		Diagonal half used as 5c on cover		*4,250.*
7	A3	15c blue	275.00	225.00
a.		Without accent on "U"	*7,000.*	*3,000.*
b.		Tete beche pair	*55,000.*	
i.		15c ultramarine	425.00	325.00
j.		Diagonal third used as 5c on cover		*5,000.*

Only one used example of No. 7b is known. It has faults. Two unused examples are known. One is sound with origional gum, the other is in a block, without gum, and has tiny faults.

Broad "C" in "CENTAVOS," No Accent on "U"

1863

7C	A3	5c rose	18.00	*21.00*
d.		5c rose lilac	100.00	110.00
m.		Worn plate (rose)	200.00	52.50
7F	A3	10c yellow green	350.00	140.00
g.		10c olive green	*500.00*	250.00
q.		10c green, ribbed paper	425.00	200.00
r.		Worn plate (green)	325.00	150.00
s.		Worn plate (olive green)	425.00	160.00

Narrow "C" in "CENTAVOS," No Accent on "U"

1864

7H	A3	5c rose red	160.00	32.50

The so-called reprints of 10c and 15c are counterfeits. They have narrow "C" and straight lines in shield. Nos. 7C and 7H have been extensively counterfeited.

Rivadavia Issue

Bernardino Rivadavia
A4 A5

Rivadavia — A6

1864-67 Engr. Wmk. 84 *Imperf.*

Clear Impressions

8	A4	5c brown rose	*1,300.*	*160.*
a.		5c orange red ('67)	*1,500.*	*160.*
9	A5	10c green	*2,000.*	*1,200.*
10	A6	15c blue	*7,500.*	*4,000.*

Perf. 11½

Dull to Worn Impressions

11	A4	5c brown rose ('65)	30.00	12.00
11B	A4	5c lake ('65)	77.50	17.50
12	A5	10c green	80.00	30.00
a.		Half used as 5c on cover		*900.00*
c.		Horiz. pair, imperf vert.		*1,750.*
13	A6	15c blue	275.00	110.00

1867-72 Unwmk. *Imperf.*

14	A4	5c carmine ('72)	250.	65.
15	A4	5c rose	200.	100.
15A	A5	10c green	*4,000.*	*4,000.*
16	A6	15c blue	*2,000.*	*1,750.*

Nos. 15A-16 issued without gum.

1867 *Perf. 11½*

17	A4	5c carmine	350.00	150.00

Nos. 14, 15 and 17 exist with part of papermaker's wmk. "LACROIX FRERES." Unused values, $600, $500 and $1,000, respectively.

Rivadavia
A7

Manuel Belgrano
A8

Jose de San Martin — A9

Groundwork of Horizontal Lines

1867-68 *Perf. 12*

18	A7	5c vermilion	200.00	10.00
18A	A8	10c green	30.00	4.50
b.		Diag. half used as 5c on cover		*750.00*
19	A9	15c blue	65.00	15.00

Groundwork of Crossed Lines

20	A7	5c vermilion	10.50	.80
21	A9	15c blue	92.50	12.00

See Nos. 27, 33-34, 39 and types A19, A33, A34, A37. For surcharges and overprints see Nos. 30-32, 41-42, 47-51, O6-O7, O26.

Gen. Antonio G. Balcarce
A10

Mariano Moreno
A11

Carlos Maria de Alvear
A12

Gervasio Antonio Posadas
A13

Cornelio Saavedra — A14

1873

22 A10 1c purple 5.00 2.00
a. 1c gray violet 6.25 2.00
23 A11 4c brown 5.00 .40
a. 4c red brown 17.50 2.00
24 A12 30c orange 100.00 16.00
a. Vert. pair, imperf horiz. 4,000.
25 A13 60c black 100.00 4.75
26 A14 90c blue 25.00 2.50
Nos. 22-26 (5) 235.00 25.65

For overprints see Nos. O5, O12-O14, O19-O21, O25, O29.

1873

Laid Paper

27 A8 10c green 200.00 20.00

Nos. 18, 18A Surcharged in Black

Nos. 30-31

No. 32

1877, Feb.

Wove Paper

30 A7 1c on 5c vermilion 47.50 15.00
a. Inverted surcharge 350.00 200.00
31 A7 2c on 5c vermilion 92.50 60.00
a. Inverted surcharge 700.00 500.00
32 A8 8c on 10c green 125.00 30.00
b. Inverted surcharge 500.00 425.00
Nos. 30-32 (3) 265.00 105.00

Varieties also exist with double and triple surcharges, surcharge on reverse, 8c on No. 27, all made clandestinely from the original cliches of the surcharges.

Forgeries of these surcharges include the inverted and double varieties.

1876-77 ***Rouletted***

33 A7 5c vermilion 150.00 60.00
34 A7 8c lake ('77) 25.00 .40

Belgrano A17

Dalmacio Vélez Sarsfield A18

San Martín — A19

1878 ***Rouletted***

35 A17 16c green 8.00 1.10
36 A18 20c blue 10.00 3.00
37 A19 24c blue 17.50 3.00
Nos. 35-37 (3) 35.50 7.10

See No. 56. For overprints see Nos. O9-O10, O15-O17, O22, O28.

Vicente Lopez — A20

Alvear — A21

1877-80 ***Perf. 12***

38 A20 2c yellow green 4.25 .90
39 A7 8c lake ('80) 4.25 .40
a. 8c brown lake 30.00 .40
40 A21 25c lake ('78) 22.50 6.00
Nos. 38-40 (3) 31.00 7.30

For overprints see Nos. O4, O11, O18, O24.

No. 18 Surcharged in Black

Large "P" Wide "V"

Small "P" Narrow "V"

1882

41 A7 ½c on 5c ver 1.60 1.60
a. Double surcharge 80.00 80.00
b. Inverted surcharge 20.00 20.00
c. "PROVISORIO" omitted 80.00 80.00
d. Fraction omitted 50.00
e. "PROVISOBIO" 32.50 32.50
f. Pair, one without surcharge 200.00
g. Small "P" in "PROVISORIO" 2.50 2.50
h. As "a," small "P" in "PROVISORIO" 32.50 32.50
i. As "b," small "P" in "PROVISORIO" 40.00 40.00
j. As "d," small "P" in "PROVISORIO" 15.00 15.00

Perforated across Middle of Stamp

42 A7 ½c on 5c ver 3.25 3.25
a. "PROVISORIO" 40.00 40.00
b. Large "P" in "PROVISORIO" 30.00 22.50

A23

1882 **Typo.** ***Perf. 12***

43 A23 ½c brown 1.40 .80
a. Imperf., pair 40.00 40.00
44 A23 1c red, perf. 14 3.50 1.00
a. Perf. 12 9.00 4.25
45 A23 12c ultra, perf 14 45.00 8.75
a. Perf. 12 55.00 8.75

Engr.

46 A23 12c grnsh blue, perf. 14 125.00 11.00
Nos. 43-46 (4) 174.90 21.55

See type A29. For overprints see Nos. O2, O8, O23, O27.

No. 21 Surcharged in Red:

a

b

c

1884 **Engr.** ***Perf. 12***

47 A9 (a) ½c on 15c blue 1.90 1.50
a. Groundwork of horiz. lines 100.00 80.00
b. Inverted surcharge 27.50 20.00
48 A9 (b) 1c on 15c blue 16.00 13.00
a. Groundwork of horiz. lines 10.00 6.50
b. Inverted surcharge 80.00 57.50
c. Double surcharge 40.00 32.50
d. Triple surcharge 350.00

Nos. 20-21 Surcharged in Black

49 A7 (a) ½c on 5c ver 4.00 3.25
a. Inverted surcharge 160.00 110.00
b. Date omitted 150.00 —
c. Pair, one without surcharge 375.00
d. Double surcharge 550.00
50 A9 (a) ½c on 15c blue 10.00 8.00
a. Groundwork of horiz. lines 32.50 26.00
b. Inverted surcharge 72.50 55.00
c. Pair, one without surcharge 325.00
51 A7 (c) 4c on 5c ver 10.00 6.50
a. Inverted surcharge 26.00 20.00
b. Double surcharge 325.00 200.00
c. Pair, one without surcharge but with "4" in manuscript 550.00 350.00

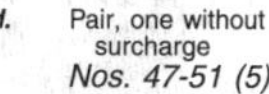

d. Pair, one without surcharge 250.00
Nos. 47-51 (5) 41.90 32.25

A29

1884-85 **Engr.** ***Perf. 12***

52 A29 ½c red brown 1.00 .45
a. Horiz. pair, imperf vert. 300.00 250.00
53 A29 1c rose red 5.25 .45
a. Horiz. pair, imperf vert. 300.00 250.00
54 A29 12c deep blue 25.00 1.25
a. 12c grnish blue ('85) 30.00 1.25
b. Horiz. pair, imperf vert. 300.00 250.00
Nos. 52-54 (3) 31.25 2.15

For overprints see Nos. O1, O3, O9.

San Martin Type of 1878

1887 **Engr.**

56 A19 24c blue 17.50 1.40

Justo Jose de Urquiza — A30

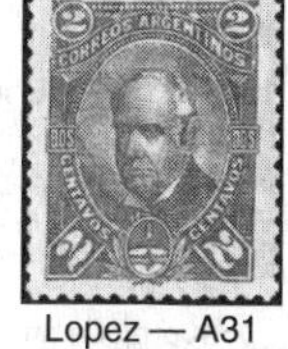

Lopez — A31

Miguel Juarez Celman A32

Rivadavia (Large head) A33

Rivadavia (Small head) A34

Domingo F. Sarmiento A35

Nicolas Avellaneda — A36

San Martin—A37

Julio A. Roca — A37a

Belgrano A37b

Manuel Dorrego A38

Moreno — A39

Bartolome Mitre — A40

CINCO CENTAVOS.

A33 - Shows collar on left side only.

A34 - Shows collar on both sides. Lozenges in background larger and clearer than in A33.

1888-90 **Litho.** ***Perf. 11½***

57 A30 ½c blue .80 .45
b. Vert. pair, imperf. horiz. 125.00 65.00
c. Horiz. pair, imperf. vert. 125.00 65.00
58 A31 2c yel green 10.00 6.00
b. Vert. pair, imperf. horiz. 80.00
c. Horiz. pair, imperf. vert. 200.00
59 A32 3c blue green 1.75 .65
b. Horiz. pair, imperf. vert. 80.00
c. Horiz. pair, imperf. btwn. 100.00
d. Vert. pair, imperf. btwn. 25.00 25.00
60 A33 5c carmine 8.00 .60
b. Vert. pair, imperf. horiz. 100.00
61 A34 5c carmine 12.50 1.25
b. Vert. pair, imperf. btwn.
c. Vert. pair, imperf. horiz. 400.00
62 A35 6c red 25.00 15.00
b. Vert. pair, imperf. btwn. 80.00
c. Perf. 12 52.50 42.50
63 A36 10c brown 15.00 1.10
64 A37 15c orange 15.00 1.60
d. Vert. pair, imperf. btwn. 600.00
64A A37a 20c green 12.00 1.25
64B A37b 25c purple 15.00 2.00
65 A38 30c brown 21.00 2.50
b. 30c reddish choc brn 400.00 80.00
c. Horiz. pair, imperf. btwn. 400.00 325.00
66 A39 40c sl, perf 12 25.00 3.00
a. Perf. 11½ 80.00 16.00
b. Horiz. pair, imperf. btwn. (#66) 600.00
67 A40 50c blue 100.00 8.25
Nos. 57-67 (13) 261.05 43.65

In this issue there are several varieties of each value, the difference between them being in the relative position of the head to the frame.

Imperf., Pairs

57a	A30	½c	75.00	60.00
58a	A31	2c	55.00	
59a	A32	3c	35.00	25.00
61a	A34	5c		100.00
62a	A35	6c	55.00	
63a	A36	10c	55.00	
64c	A37	15c		200.00
65a	A38	30c	275.00	200.00

Urquiza A41

Velez Sarsfield A42

Miguel Juarez Celman A43

Rivadavia (Large head) A44

Sarmiento A45

Juan Bautista Alberdi A46

1888-89 **Engr.** ***Perf. 11½, 11½x12***

68 A41 ½c ultra .40 .25
a. Vert. pair, imperf. horiz. —
b. Imperf., pair 30.00 —
69 A42 1c brown .90 .40
a. Vert. pair, imperf. horiz. 65.00
b. Vert. pair, imperf. btwn. —
c. Imperf., pair 30.00
d. Horiz. pair, imperf. btwn. 100.00
70 A43 3c blue green 2.50 .75
71 A44 5c rose 2.75 .40
a. Imperf., pair 40.00 —
72 A45 6c blue black 1.75 .55
b. Perf. 11½x12 12.50 3.00

73	A46	12c blue	5.50	1.75
a.		Imperf., pair	30.00	
b.		bluish paper	8.00	2.00
c.		Perf. 11½	8.25	3.00
		Nos. 68-73 (6)	13.80	4.10

#69-70 exist with papermakers' watermarks.

See #77, designs A50, A61. For surcharges see #83-84.

Jose Maria Paz — A48

Santiago Derqui — A49

Rivadavia (Small head) A50

Avellaneda A51

Moreno A53

Mitre A54

Posadas — A55

1890 Engr. *Perf. 11½*

75	A48	¼c green	.40	.30
76	A49	2c violet	.85	.20
a.		2c purple	.85	.20
b.		2c slate	1.25	.30
c.		Horiz. pair, imperf. btwn.	25.00	20.00
d.		Imperf., pair	35.00	
e.		Perf. 11½x12	5.00	.50
77	A50	5c carmine	2.00	.25
a.		Imperf., pair	50.00	25.00
b.		Perf. 11½x12	5.00	.30
c.		Vert. pair, imperf. btwn.	75.00	60.00
d.		Horiz. pair, imperf. btwn.	75.00	60.00
78	A51	10c brown	2.50	.40
b.		Imperf., pair	150.00	—
c.		Vert. pair, imperf. btwn.	225.00	
80	A53	40c olive green	5.00	.80
a.		Imperf., pair	40.00	
b.		Horiz. pair, imperf. btwn.		*250.00*
81	A54	50c orange	5.00	.80
a.		Imperf., pair	60.00	
b.		Perf. 11½x12	16.00	1.60
82	A55	60c black	15.00	2.75
a.		Imperf., pair	—	
b.		Vert. pair, imperf. btwn.	125.00	100.00
		Nos. 75-82 (7)	30.75	5.50

Type A50 differs from type A44 in having the head smaller, the letters of "Cinco Centavos" not as tall, and the curved ornaments at sides close to the first and last letters of "Republica Argentina."

Lithographed Surcharge on No. 73 in Black or Red

1890 *Perf. 11½x12*

83	A46	¼c on 12c blue	.40	.40
a.		Perf. 11½	37.50	25.00
b.		Double surcharge	75.00	35.00
c.		Inverted surcharge	80.00	
84	A46	¼c on 12c blue (R)	.40	.40
a.		Double surcharge	52.50	52.50
b.		Perf. 11½	7.00	5.00

Surcharge is different on #83 and 84.

Nos. 83-84 exist as pairs, one without surcharge. These were privately produced.

Rivadavia A57

Jose de San Martin A58

Gregorio Araoz de Lamadrid A59

Admiral Guillermo Brown A60

1891 Engr. *Perf. 11½*

85	A57	8c carmine rose	1.25	.25
a.		Imperf., pair	75.00	
86	A58	1p deep blue	40.00	7.50
87	A59	5p ultra	200.00	21.00
88	A60	20p green	300.00	60.00
		Nos. 85-88 (4)	541.25	88.75

A 10p brown and a 50p red were prepared but not issued. Values: 10p $1,500 for fine, 50p $1,000 with rough or somewhat damaged perfs.

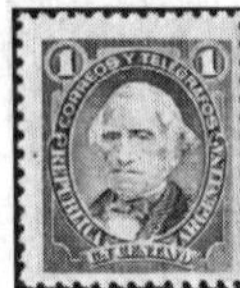

Velez Sarsfield A61

"Santa Maria," "Nina" and "Pinta" A62

1890 *Perf. 11½*

89	A61	1c brown	.80	.40
b.		Horiz. pair, imperf. btwn.		*550.00*

Type A61 is a re-engraving of A42. The figure "1" in each upper corner has a short horizontal serif instead of a long one pointing downward. In type A61 the first and last letters of "Correos y Telegrafos" are closer to the curved ornaments below than in type A42. Background is of horizontal lines (cross-hatching on No. 69).

1892, Oct. 12 Wmk. 85 *Perf. 11½*

90	A62	2c light blue	6.00	3.00
a.		Double impression	190.00	
91	A62	5c dark blue	8.50	5.00

Discovery of America, 400th anniv. Counterfeits of Nos. 90-91 are litho.

Rivadavia A63

Belgrano A64

San Martin — A65

Perf. 11½, 12 and Compound

1892-95 Wmk. 85

92	A63	½c dull blue	.35	.20
a.		½c bright ultra	50.00	25.00
93	A63	1c brown	.50	.20
94	A63	2c green	.60	.25
95	A63	3c orange ('95)	1.25	.20
96	A63	5c carmine	1.50	.25
b.		5c green (error)	650.00	650.00
98	A64	10c carmine rose	10.00	.40
99	A64	12c dp bl ('93)	7.50	.40
100	A64	16c gray	12.50	.55
101	A64	24c gray brown	12.50	.55
b.		Perf. 12	27.50	15.00
102	A64	50c blue green	18.00	.55
b.		Perf. 12	27.50	5.00
103	A65	1p lake ('93)	10.00	.75
a.		1p red brown	17.50	5.00
104	A65	2p dark green	21.00	2.25
a.		Perf. 12	110.00	37.50
105	A65	5p dark blue	37.50	2.75
		Nos. 92-105 (13)	133.20	9.30

The high values of this and succeeding issues are frequently punched with the word "INUTILIZADO," parts of the letters showing on each stamp. These punched stamps sell for only a small fraction of the catalogue values.

Reprints of No. 96b have white gum. The original stamp has yellowish gum. Value $125.

Imperf., Pairs

92b	A63	½c	55.00	—
93a	A63	1c	55.00	—
94a	A63	2c	27.50	—
96a	A63	5c	27.50	—
98a	A64	10c	55.00	—
99a	A64	12c	55.00	—
100a	A64	16c	55.00	—
101a	A64	24c	55.00	—
102a	A64	50c	55.00	—
103b	A65	1p	60.00	—
105a	A65	5p	140.00	—

Nos. 102a, 103b and 105a exist only without gum; the other imperfs are found with or without gum, and values are the same for either condition.

Vertical Pairs, Imperf. Between

92c	A63	½c	125.00	
93b	A63	1c	100.00	
94b	A63	2c	50.00	
95a	A63	3c	250.00	
96c	A63	5c	45.00	—
98b	A64	10c	100.00	
99b	A64	12c	100.00	

Horizontal Pairs, Imperf. Between

93c	A63	1c	110.00	
94c	A63	2c	55.00	
96d	A63	5c	55.00	45.00
98c	A64	10c	110.00	

1896-97 Wmk. 86

106	A63	½c slate	.50	.25
a.		½c gray blue	.50	.25
b.		½c indigo	.50	.25
107	A63	1c brown	.50	.25
108	A63	2c yellow green	.50	.25
109	A63	3c orange	.50	.25
110	A63	5c carmine	.50	.25
a.		Imperf., pair	100.00	
111	A64	10c carmine rose	8.00	.25
112	A64	12c deep blue	4.00	.25
113	A64	16c gray	10.00	.80
114	A64	24c gray brown	10.00	1.00
a.		Imperf., pair	100.00	—
115	A64	30c orange ('97)	10.00	.60
116	A64	50c blue green	10.00	.60
117	A64	80c dull violet	18.00	.80
118	A65	1p lake	25.00	.80
119	A65	1p20c black ('97)	10.00	3.50
120	A65	2p dark green	16.00	8.00
121	A65	5p dark blue	90.00	10.00
a.		Perf. 12	325.00	90.00
		Nos. 106-121 (16)	213.50	27.85

Vertical Pairs, Imperf. Between

106c	A63	½c	200.00	
107a	A63	1c	125.00	
108a	A63	2c	125.00	
109a	A63	3c	200.00	
110b	A63	5c	125.00	125.00
112b	A64	12c	125.00	100.00

Horizontal Pairs, Imperf. Between

107b	A63	1c	125.00	
108b	A63	2c	125.00	
110c	A63	5c	125.00	80.00
111a	A64	10c	125.00	
112c	A64	12c	125.00	

Allegory, Liberty Seated
A66 A67

Perf. 11½, 12 and Compound

1899-1903

122	A66	½c yellow brown	.35	.25
123	A66	1c green	.50	.25
124	A66	2c slate	.50	.25
125	A66	3c orange ('01)	.85	.40
126	A66	4c yellow ('03)	1.50	.50
127	A66	5c carmine rose	.50	.25
128	A66	6c black ('03)	1.00	.50
129	A66	10c dark green	1.50	.35
130	A66	12c dull blue	1.00	.50
131	A66	12c olive grn ('01)	1.00	.50
132	A66	15c sea green ('01)	2.75	.50
132B	A66	15c dull blue ('01)	3.00	.50
133	A66	16c orange	7.50	5.00
134	A66	20c claret	2.00	.25
135	A66	24c violet	3.50	.80
136	A66	30c rose	7.50	.50
137	A66	30c vermilion ('01)	3.75	.40
a.		30c scarlet	50.00	2.50
138	A66	50c brt blue	4.75	.40
139	A67	1p bl & blk, perf. 11½	14.00	.65
a.		Center inverted	*1,500.*	*525.00*
b.		Perf. 12	250.00	125.00
140	A67	5p orange & blk	57.50	7.00
		Punch cancellation		1.60
a.		Center inverted	*2,750.*	—
141	A67	10p green & blk	50.00	9.25
		Punch cancellation		1.75
a.		Center inverted	*3,600.*	
		Punch cancellation		675.00
142	A67	20p red & black	200.00	21.00
		Punch cancellation		1.75
a.		Center invtd.(punch cancel)		*2,000.*
		Nos. 122-142 (22)	364.95	50.00

Imperf., Pairs

122a	A66	½c	30.00	
123a	A66	1c	45.00	
124a	A66	2c	15.00	
125a	A66	3c	250.00	
127a	A66	5c	15.00	
128a	A66	6c	45.00	
129a	A66	10c	45.00	
132a	A66	15c	45.00	

Vertical Pairs, Imperf. Between

122b	A66	½c	10.00	10.00
123b	A66	1c	10.00	10.00
124b	A66	2c	5.00	5.00
125b	A66	3c	200.00	150.00
126a	A66	4c	250.00	200.00
127b	A66	5c	5.00	3.00
128b	A66	6c	12.00	10.00
129b	A66	10c	75.00	
132c	A66	15c	12.00	10.00

Horizontal Pairs, Imperf. Between

122c	A66	½c	30.00	20.00
123c	A66	1c	50.00	20.00
124c	A66	2c	10.00	5.00
125c	A66	3c	225.00	150.00
126b	A66	4c	275.00	
127c	A66	5c	10.00	5.00
128c	A66	6c	17.50	10.00
129c	A66	10c	17.50	10.00
132d	A66	15c	35.00	20.00
138a	A66	50c	160.00	

River Port of Rosario A68

1902, Oct. 26 *Perf. 11½, 11½x12*

143	A68	5c deep blue	4.50	2.50
a.		Imperf., pair	95.00	
b.		Vert. pair, imperf. btwn.	95.00	
c.		Horiz. pair, imperf. btwn.	75.00	

Completion of port facilities at Rosario.

San Martin
A69 A70

1908-09 Typo. *Perf. 13½, 13½x12½*

144	A69	½c violet	.20	.20
145	A69	1c brnsh buff	.20	.20
146	A69	2c chocolate	.55	.20
147	A69	3c green	.70	.30
148	A69	4c redsh violet	1.40	.30
149	A69	5c carmine	.30	.20
150	A69	6c olive bister	.80	.25
151	A69	10c gray green	1.50	.20
152	A69	12c yellow buff	.40	.40
153	A69	12c dk blue ('09)	1.25	.20
154	A69	15c apple green	1.75	.85
155	A69	20c ultra	1.25	.20
156	A69	24c red brown	3.25	.60
157	A69	30c dull rose	5.00	.60
158	A69	50c black	4.75	.40
159	A70	1p sl bl & pink	11.00	1.75
		Nos. 144-159 (16)	34.30	6.85

The 1c blue was not issued. Value $250.

Wmk. 86 appears on ½, 1, 6, 20, 24 and 50c. Other values have similar wmk. with wavy rays.

Stamps lacking wmk. are from outer rows printed on sheet margin.

Pyramid of May — A71

Nicolas Rodriguez Pena & Hipolito Vieytes — A72

Meeting at Pena's Home — A73

3c, Miguel de Azcuenaga (1754-1833) & Father Manuel M. Alberti (1763-1811). 4c, Viceroy's house & Fort Buenos Aires. 5c, Cornelio Saavedra (1759-1829). 10c, Antonio Luis Beruti (1772-1842) & French distributing badges. 12c, Congress building. 20c, Juan Jose Castelli (1764-1812) & Domingo Matheu (1765-1831). 24c, 1st council. 30c, Manuel Belgrano (1770-1820) & Juan Larrea (1782-1847). 50c, 1st meeting of republican government, May 25, 1810. 1p, Mariano Moreno (1778-1811) & Juan Jose Paso (1758-1833). 5p, Oath of the Junta. 10p, Centenary Monument. 20p, Jose Francisco de San Martin (1778-1850).

Inscribed "1810 1910"
Various Frames

1910, May 1 Engr. *Perf. 11½*

160 A71 ½c bl & gray bl .30 .20
161 A72 1c blue grn & blk .30 .20
b. Horiz. pair, imperf. btwn. *65.00*
162 A73 2c olive & gray .20 .20
163 A72 3c green .70 .20
164 A73 4c dk bl & grn .70 .25
165 A71 5c carmine .40 .20
166 A73 10c yel brn & blk 1.75 .20
167 A73 12c brt blue 1.40 .25
168 A72 20c gray brn & blk 3.25 .35
169 A73 24c org brn & bl 1.75 .90
170 A72 30c lilac & blk 1.75 .65
171 A71 50c car & blk 4.50 .90
172 A72 1p brt blue 10.00 3.50
173 A73 5p orange & vio 70.00 30.00
Punch cancel 2.50
174 A71 10p orange & blk 90.00 65.00
Punch cancel 3.00
175 A71 20p dp bl & ind 150.00 90.00
Punch cancel 4.50
Nos. 160-175 (16) 337.00 193.00

Centenary of the republic.

Center Inverted

160a A71 ½c *800.00*
161a A72 1c *800.00*
162a A73 2c *800.00*
164a A73 4c *550.00*
167a A73 12c *700.00*
171a A71 50c *700.00*
173a A73 5p *700.00*

Domingo F. Sarmiento A87

Agriculture A88

1911, May 15 Typo. *Perf. 13½*

176 A87 5c gray brn & blk .75 .50

Domingo Faustino Sarmiento (1811-88), pres. of Argentina, 1868-74.

Wmk. 86, without Face

1911 Engr. *Perf. 12*

Size: 19x25mm

177 A88 5c vermilion .40 .20
178 A88 12c deep blue 5.00 .20

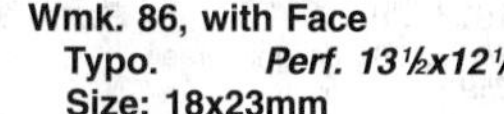

Wmk. 86, with Face

1911 Typo. *Perf. 13½x12½*

Size: 18x23mm

179 A88 ½c violet .20 .20
180 A88 1c brown ocher .20 .20
181 A88 2c chocolate .20 .20
a. Perf. 13½ 4.25 1.75
b. Imperf., pair *26.00*
182 A88 3c green .40 .20
183 A88 4c brown violet .35 .25
184 A88 10c gray green .50 .20
185 A88 20c ultra 4.25 1.00
186 A88 24c red brown 5.25 3.50
187 A88 30c claret 1.75 .50
188 A88 50c black 8.00 .85
Nos. 179-188 (10) 21.10 7.10

The 5c dull red is a proof. In this issue Wmk. 86 comes: straight rays (4c, 20c, 24c) and wavy rays (2c). All other values exist with both forms.

Wmk. 87 (Horiz. or Vert.)

1912-14 *Perf. 13½x12½*

189 A88 ½c violet .20 .20
190 A88 1c ocher .20 .20
191 A88 2c chocolate .30 .20
192 A88 3c green .60 .20
193 A88 4c brown violet .60 .20
194 A88 5c red .20 .20
195 A88 10c deep green 1.40 .20
196 A88 12c deep blue 1.40 .20
197 A88 20c ultra 8.00 .70
198 A88 24c red brown 3.25 1.60
199 A88 30c claret 8.00 .60
200 A88 50c black 5.00 .60
Nos. 189-200 (12) 29.15 5.10

See Nos. 208-212. For overprints see Nos. OD1-OD8, OD47-OD54, OD102-OD108, OD146-OD152, OD183-OD190, OD235-OD241, OD281-OD284, OD318-OD323.

Perf. 13½

189a A88 ½c .80 .25
190a A88 1c .80 .25
191a A88 2c .80 .20
192a A88 3c 35.00 16.00
193a A88 4c 1.60 .70
194a A88 5c .30 .20
196a A88 12c 3.25 .80
197a A88 20c 5.00 .70
Nos. 189a-197a (8) 47.55 19.10

A89

1912-13 *Perf. 13½*

201 A89 1p dull bl & rose 6.00 1.00
Punch cancel .30
202 A89 5p slate & ol grn 19.00 6.00
Punch cancel .60
203 A89 10p violet & blue 75.00 9.00
Punch cancel 1.40
204 A89 20p blue & claret 175.00 60.00
Punch cancel 2.00
Nos. 201-204 (4) 275.00 76.00

1915 Unwmk. *Perf. 13½x12½*

208 A88 1c ocher .50 .20
209 A88 2c chocolate .50 .20
212 A88 5c red .50 .20
Nos. 208-212 (3) 1.50 .60

Only these denominations were printed on paper without watermark.

Other stamps of the series are known unwatermarked but they are from the outer rows of sheets the other parts of which are watermarked.

Francisco Narciso de Laprida A90

Declaration of Independence A91

Jose de San Martin—A92a
A92

Perf. 13½, 13½x12½

1916, July 9 Litho. Wmk. 87

215 A90 ½c violet .20 .20
216 A90 1c buff .25 .20

Perf. 13½x12½

217 A90 2c chocolate .20 .20
218 A90 3c green .45 .20
219 A90 4c red violet .65 .20

Perf. 13½

220 A91 5c red .30 .20
a. Imperf., pair *40.00*
221 A91 10c gray green 1.50 .20
222 A92 12c blue .65 .20
223 A92 20c ultra 1.00 .25
224 A92 24c red brown 1.60 .75
225 A92 30c claret 1.60 .40
226 A92 50c gray black 3.25 .50
227 A92a 1p sl bl & red 9.25 4.00
Punch cancel .50
a. Imperf., pair *325.00*
228 A92a 5p black & gray grn 110.00 40.00
Punch cancel 3.25
229 A92a 10p violet & blue 110.00 75.00
Punch cancel 2.50
230 A92a 20p dull blue & cl 160.00 67.50
Punch cancel 1.00
a. Imperf., pair *650.00*
Nos. 215-230 (16) 400.90 190.00

Cent. of Argentina's declaration of independence of Spain, July 9, 1816.

The watermark is either vert. or horiz. on Nos. 215-220, 222; only vert. on No. 221, and only horiz. on Nos. 223-230.

For overprints see #OD9, OD55-OD56, OD109, OD153, OD191-OD192, OD285, OD324.

A93

A94

A94a

Juan Gregorio Pujol — A95

1917 *Perf. 13½, 13½x12½*

231 A93 ½c violet .20 .20
232 A93 1c buff .25 .20
233 A93 2c brown .25 .20
234 A93 3c lt green .75 .20
235 A93 4c red violet .80 .40
236 A93 5c red .25 .20
a. Imperf., pair *14.00*
237 A93 10c gray green 1.50 .20

Perf. 13½

238 A94 12c blue 1.00 .20
239 A94 20c ultra 1.50 .20
240 A94 24c red brown 4.50 2.00
241 A94 30c claret 4.50 .60
242 A94 50c gray black 4.00 .60
243 A94a 1p sl bl & red 4.00 .35
244 A94a 5p black & gray grn 20.00 3.00
Punch cancel 1.50
245 A94a 10p violet & blue 47.50 9.25
Punch cancel 1.00
246 A94a 20p dull bl & cl 77.50 15.00
Punch cancel .80
a. Center inverted 1,200. 875.00
Nos. 231-246 (16) 168.50 32.80

The watermark is either vert. or horiz. on Nos. 231-236, 238; only vert. on No. 237, and only horiz. on Nos. 239-246.

All known examples of No. 246a are off-center to the right.

1918, June 15 Litho. *Perf. 13½*

247 A95 5c bister & gray .70 .25

Cent. of the birth of Juan G. Pujol (1817-61), lawyer and legislator.

Perf. 13½, 13½x12½

1918-19 Unwmk.

248 A93 ½c violet .20 .20
249 A93 1c buff .20 .20
a. Imperf., pair *14.00*
250 A93 2c brown .20 .20
251 A93 3c lt green .25 .20
252 A93 4c red violet .25 .20
253 A93 5c red .20 .20
254 A93 10c gray green 1.10 .20

Perf. 13½

255 A94 12c blue 1.25 .20
256 A94 20c ultra 1.60 .20
257 A94 24c red brown 2.00 .50
258 A94 30c claret 2.50 .30
259 A94 50c gray black 5.50 .25
Nos. 248-259 (12) 15.25 2.85

The stamps of this issue sometimes show letters of papermakers' watermarks.

There were two printings, in 1918 and 1923, using different ink and paper.

1920 Wmk. 88 *Perf. 13½, 13½x12½*

264 A93 ½c violet .20 .20
265 A93 1c buff .25 .20
266 A93 2c brown .25 .20
267 A93 3c green 1.50 .30
268 A93 4c red violet 2.00 1.25
269 A93 5c red .40 .20
270 A93 10c gray green 3.25 .20

Perf. 13½

271 A94 12c blue 1.75 .20
272 A94 20c ultra 2.50 .20
274 A94 30c claret 8.25 .70
275 A94 50c gray black 5.00 .90
Nos. 264-275 (11) 25.35 4.55

See #292-300, 304-307A, 310-314, 318, 322.

For overprints see Nos. OD10-OD20, OD57-OD71, OD74, OD110-OD121, OD154-OD159, OD161-OD162, OD193-OD207, OD209-OD211, OD242-OD252, OD254-OD255, OD286-OD290, OD325-OD328, OD330.

Belgrano's Mausoleum A96

Creation of Argentine Flag A97

Gen. Manuel Belgrano — A98

1920, June 18 *Perf. 13½*

280 A96 2c red .35 .20
a. Perf. 13½x12½ .35 .20
281 A97 5c rose & blue .40 .20
282 A98 12c green & blue .75 .75
Nos. 280-282 (3) 1.50 1.15

Belgrano (1770-1820), Argentine general, patriot and diplomat.

Gen. Justo Jose de Urquiza — A99

Bartolome Mitre — A100

1920, Nov. 11

283 A99 5c gray blue .25 .20

Gen. Justo Jose de Urquiza (1801-70), pres. of Argentina, 1854-60. See No. 303.

1921, June 26 Unwmk.

284 A100 2c violet brown .25 .20
285 A100 5c light blue .25 .20

Bartolome Mitre (1821-1906), pres. of Argentina, 1862-65.

Allegory, Pan-America — A101

1921, Aug. 25 *Perf. 13½*

286 A101 3c violet .55 .30
287 A101 5c blue .80 .20
288 A101 10c vio brown 1.40 .35
289 A101 12c rose 2.00 .75
Nos. 286-289 (4) 4.75 1.60

Inscribed "Buenos Aires-Agosto de 1921" A102

Inscribed "Republica Argentina" A103

1921, Oct. *Perf. 13½x12½*

290 A102 5c rose .30 .20
a. Perf. 13½ 1.25 .20
291 A103 5c rose 1.50 .20
a. Perf. 13½ 2.50 .20

1st Pan-American Postal Cong., Buenos Aires, Aug., 1921.
See Nos. 308-309, 319. For overprints see Nos. OD72, OD160, OD208, OD253, OD329.

1920 Wmk. 89 *Perf. 13½, 13½x12½*

292 A93 ½c violet 2.00 .75
293 A93 1c buff 5.00 .75
294 A93 2c brown 3.00 .75
297 A93 5c red 4.00 .50
298 A93 10c gray green 4.00 .40

Perf. 13½

299 A94 12c blue *3,000.* 125.00
300 A94 20c ultra 12.00 .75
Nos. 292-298,300 (6) 30.00 3.90

1920

303 A99 5c gray blue 350.00 225.00

Perf. 13½, 13½x12½

1922-23 **Wmk. 90**

304 A93 ½c violet .20 .20
305 A93 1c buff .20 .20
306 A93 2c brown .20 .20
307 A93 3c green .40 .30
307A A93 4c red violet 3.75 1.00
308 A102 5c rose 2.25 .20
309 A103 5c red 1.50 .20
310 A93 10c gray green 4.75 .30

Perf. 13½

311 A94 12c blue .75 .20
312 A94 20c ultra 1.25 .20
313 A94 24c red brown 9.25 4.50
314 A94 30c claret 5.50 .50
Nos. 304-314 (12) 30.00 8.00

Paper with Gray Overprint RA in Sun
Perf. 13½, 13½x12½

1922-23 **Unwmk.**

318 A93 2c brown 3.00 1.00
319 A103 5c red 2.00 .30

Perf. 13½

322 A94 20c ultra 15.00 1.50
Nos. 318-322 (3) 20.00 2.80

San Martín
A104 A105
With Period after Value

1923, May **Litho.** **Wmk. 90**

323 A104 ½c red violet .20 .20
324 A104 1c buff .30 .20
325 A104 2c dark brown .30 .20
326 A104 3c lt green .30 .20
327 A104 4c red brown .30 .20
328 A104 5c red .30 .20
329 A104 10c dull green 2.50 .20
330 A104 12c deep blue .40 .20
331 A104 20c ultra 1.00 .20
332 A104 24c lt brown 2.50 1.50
333 A104 30c claret 7.75 .60
334 A104 50c black 4.00 .35

Without Period after Value

Wmk. 87 *Perf. 13½*

335 A105 1p blue & red 4.00 .20
336 A105 5p gray lilac & grn 16.00 1.75
Punch cancel .60
337 A105 10p claret & blue 55.00 10.50
Punch cancel 1.00
338 A105 20p sl & brn lake 90.00 30.00
Punch cancel .60
a. Center inverted
Nos. 323-338 (16) 184.85 46.70

Nos. 335-338 and 353-356 canceled with round or oval killers in purple (revenue cancellations) sell for one-fifth to one-half as much as postally used copies.
For overprints see Nos. 399-404.

Design of 1923
Without Period after Value
Perf. 13½, 13½x12½

1923-24 **Litho.** **Wmk. 90**

340 A104 ½c red violet .20 .20
341 A104 1c buff .20 .20
342 A104 2c dk brown .20 .20
343 A104 3c green .20 .20
a. Imperf., pair 8.00
344 A104 4c red brown .40 .20
345 A104 5c red .20 .20
346 A104 10c dull green .30 .20
347 A104 12c deep blue .50 .20
348 A104 20c ultra .65 .20
349 A104 24c lt brown 1.60 .70
350 A104 25c purple .80 .20
351 A104 30c claret 1.60 .20
352 A104 50c black 1.60 .20
353 A105 1p blue & red 2.00 .20
354 A105 5p dk vio & grn 15.00 .75
Punch cancel .20
355 A105 10p claret & blue 32.50 3.25
Punch cancel .20
356 A105 20p slate & lake 47.50 7.50
Punch cancel .20
Nos. 340-356 (17) 105.45 14.80

1931-33

Typographed

343b A104 3c 1.40 .25
345a A104 5c 2.50 .20
346a A104 10c 4.00 .20
347a A104 12c 8.50 1.50
348a A104 20c 32.50 1.60
350a A104 25c 20.00 .75
351a A104 30c 15.00 .40
Nos. 343b-351a (7) 83.90 4.90

The typographed stamps were issued only in coils and have a rough impression with heavy shading about the eyes and nose. Nos. 343 and 346 are known without watermark.
Nos. 341-345, 347-349, 351a may be found in pairs, one with period.
See note after No. 338. See Nos. 362-368. For overprints see Nos. OD21-OD33, OD75-OD87, OD122-OD133, OD163-OD175, OD212-OD226, OD256-OD268, OD291-OD304, OD331-OD345.

Rivadavia — A106

1926, Feb. 8 *Perf. 13½*

357 A106 5c rose .40 .20

Presidency of Bernardino Rivadavia, cent.

Rivadavia A108

San Martin A109

General Post Office, 1926 — A110

General Post Office, 1826 — A111

1926, July 1 *Perf. 13½x12½*

358 A108 3c gray green .20 .20
359 A109 5c red .20 .20

Perf. 13½

360 A110 12c deep blue .90 .20
361 A111 25c chocolate 1.60 .20
a. "1326" for "1826" 6.00 .75
Nos. 358-361 (4) 2.90 .80

Centenary of the Post Office.
For overprints see #OD34, OD88, OD134, OD227-OD228, OD269, OD305, OD346.

Type of 1923-31 Issue
Without Period after Value

1927 **Wmk. 205** *Perf. 13½x12½*

362 A104 ½c red violet .50 .40
a. Pelure paper 2.50 2.00
363 A104 1c buff .50 .40
364 A104 2c dark brown .30 .25
a. Pelure paper .70 .60
365 A104 5c red .50 .30
a. Period after value 9.00 6.00
b. Pelure paper .70 .60
366 A104 10c dull green 5.00 3.00
367 A104 20c ultra 47.50 5.00

Perf. 13½

368 A105 1p blue & red 35.00 6.00
Nos. 362-368 (7) 89.30 15.35

Arms of Argentina and Brazil A112

Wmk. RA in Sun (90)

1928, Aug. 27 *Perf. 12½x13*

369 A112 5c rose red 1.50 .50
370 A112 12c deep blue 2.50 .70

Cent. of peace between the Empire of Brazil and the United Provinces of the Rio de la Plata.

Allegory, Discovery of the New World — A113

"Spain" and "Argentina" — A114

"America" Offering Laurels to Columbus A115

1929, Oct. 12 **Litho.** *Perf. 13½*

371 A113 2c lilac brown 2.00 .40
372 A114 5c light red 2.00 .40
373 A115 12c dull blue 6.00 1.00
Nos. 371-373 (3) 10.00 1.80

Discovery of America by Columbus, 437th anniv.

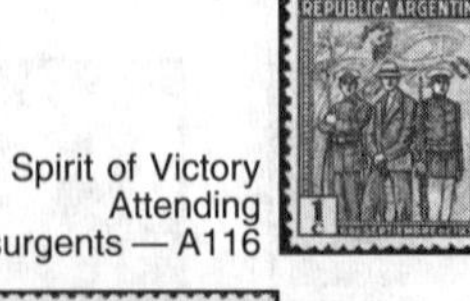
Spirit of Victory Attending Insurgents — A116

March of the Victorious Insurgents A117

Perf. 13½x12½ (A116), 12½x13 (A117)

1930

374 A116 ½c violet gray .20 .20
375 A116 1c myrtle green .20 .20
376 A117 2c dull violet .25 .20
377 A116 3c green .30 .25
378 A116 4c violet .25 .25
379 A116 5c rose red .20 .20
380 A116 10c gray black .70 .35
381 A117 12c dull blue .50 .25
382 A117 20c ocher .50 .25
383 A117 24c red brown 2.25 1.50
384 A117 25c green 2.50 1.50
385 A117 30c deep violet 4.50 2.00
386 A117 50c black 6.25 2.50
387 A117 1p sl bl & red 11.00 10.00
388 A117 2p black & org 22.50 10.00
389 A117 5p dull grn & blk 65.00 40.00
390 A117 10p dp red brn & dull blue 90.00 42.50
391 A117 20p yel grn & dl bl 225.00 100.00
392 A117 50p dk grn & vio 600.00 450.00
Nos. 374-390 (17) 207.10 112.15

Revolution of 1930.
Nos. 387-392 with oval (parcel post) cancellation sell for less.
For overprint see No. 405.

1931 *Perf. 12½x13*

393 A117 ½c red violet .20 .20
394 A117 1c gray black 1.25 .50
395 A117 3c green .60 .30
396 A117 4c red brown .35 .25
397 A117 5c red .20 .20
a. Plane omitted, top left corner 3.00 1.60
398 A117 10c dull green 1.25 .30
Nos. 393-398 (6) 3.85 1.75

Revolution of 1930.

Stamps of 1924-25 Overprinted in Red or Green

1931, Sept. 6 *Perf. 13½, 13½x12½*

399 A104 3c green .40 .40
400 A104 10c dull green .60 .60
401 A104 30c claret (G) 4.50 2.50
402 A104 50c black 4.50 3.00

Overprinted in Blue

403 A105 1p blue & red 5.00 3.50
404 A105 5p dk violet & grn 70.00 20.00

No. 388 Overprinted in Blue

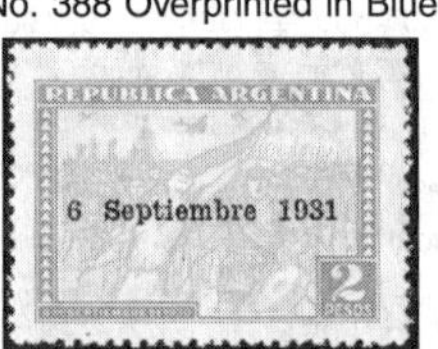

Perf. 12½x13

405 A117 2p black & orange 13.00 9.00
Nos. 399-405 (7) 98.00 39.00

1st anniv. of the Revolution of 1930.
See Nos. C30-C34.

Refrigeration Compressor — A118

Perf. 13½x12½

1932, Aug. 29 **Litho.**

406 A118 3c green 1.00 .50
407 A118 10c scarlet 2.00 .40
408 A118 12c gray blue 5.00 1.50
Nos. 406-408 (3) 8.00 2.40

6th Intl. Refrigeration Congress.

Port of La Plata A119

Pres. Julio A. Roca — A120

Municipal Palace A121

Cathedral of La Plata — A122

Dardo Rocha A123

Perf. 13½x13, 13x13½ (10c)

1933, Jan.

409	A119	3c	green & dk brn	.40	.30
410	A120	10c	orange & dk vio	.50	.20
411	A121	15c	dk bl & dp bl	3.50	1.75
412	A122	20c	violet & yel brn	1.60	1.00
413	A123	30c	dk grn & vio brn	14.00	5.50
			Nos. 409-413 (5)	20.00	8.75

50th anniv. of the founding of the city of La Plata, Nov. 19th, 1882.

Christ of the Andes — A124

Buenos Aires Cathedral A125

1934, Oct. 1 ***Perf. 13x13½, 13½x13***

414	A124	10c	rose & brown	.70	.20
415	A125	15c	dark blue	1.40	.45

32nd Intl. Eucharistic Cong., Oct. 10-14.

"Liberty" with Arms of Brazil and Argentina A126

Symbolical of "Peace" and "Friendship" A127

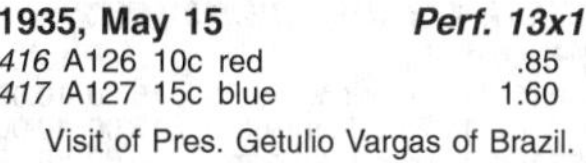

1935, May 15 ***Perf. 13x13½***

416	A126	10c	red	.85	.25
417	A127	15c	blue	1.60	.50

Visit of Pres. Getulio Vargas of Brazil.

Belgrano A128

Sarmiento A129

Urquiza — A130

Louis Braille — A131

San Martin — A132

Brown — A133

Moreno A134

Alberdi A135

Nicolas Avellaneda A136

Rivadavia A137

Mitre A138

Bull (Cattle Breeding) A139

Martin Güemes A140

Agriculture A141

Merino Sheep (Wool) A142

Sugar Cane A143

Oil Well (Petroleum) — A144

Map of South America A145 A146

Fruit — A147

Iguacu Falls (Scenic Wonders) A148

Grapes (Vineyards) A149

Cotton — A150

Two types of A140:
Type I - Inscribed Juan Martin Guemes.
Type II - Inscribed Martin Güemes.

Perf. 13, 13½x13, 13x13½

1935-51 **Litho.** **Wmk. 90**

418	A128	½c	red violet	.20	.20
419	A129	1c	buff	.20	.20
a.			Typo.	.20	.20
420	A130	2c	dark brown	.20	.20
421	A131	2½c	black ('39)	.20	.20
422	A132	3c	green	.20	.20
423	A132	3c	lt gray ('39)	.20	.20
424	A134	3c	lt gray ('46)	.20	.20
425	A133	4c	lt gray	.20	.20
426	A133	4c	sage green ('39)	.20	.20
427	A134	5c	yel brn, typo.	.20	.20
a.			Tete beche pair, typo.	4.50	2.25
b.			Booklet pane of 8, typo.		
c.			Booklet pane of 4, typo.		
d.			Litho.	1.40	.20
428	A135	6c	olive green	.20	.20
429	A136	8c	orange ('39)	.20	.20
430	A137	10c	car, typo.	.30	.20
431	A137	10c	brown ('42)	.20	.20
a.			Typo.	.40	.20
432	A138	12c	brown	.20	.20
433	A138	12c	red ('39)	.20	.20
434	A139	15c	slate bl ('36)	.85	.20
435	A139	15c	pale ultra ('39)	.50	.20
436	A140	15c	lt gray bl (II) ('42)	40.00	2.00
437	A140	20c	lt ultra (I)	.60	.20
438	A140	20c	lt ultra (II) ('36)	.35	.20
439	A140	20c	bl gray (II) ('39)	.35	.20
439A	A139	20c	dk bl & pale bl, ('42) 22x33mm	.85	.20
440	A139	20c	blue ('51)	.20	.20
a.			Typo.	.20	.20
441	A141	25c	car ('36)	.20	.20
442	A142	30c	org brn ('36)	.50	.20
443	A143	40c	dk vio ('36)	.40	.20
444	A144	50c	red & org ('36)	.35	.20
445	A145	1p	brn blk & lt bl ('36)	20.00	1.00
446	A146	1p	brn blk & lt bl ('37)	13.00	.50
a.			Chalky paper	100.00	2.00
447	A147	2p	brn lake & dk ultra ('36)	.85	.20
448	A148	5p	ind & ol grn ('36)	6.00	.25
449	A149	10p	brn lake & blk	35.00	2.00
450	A150	20p	bl grn & brn ('36)	47.50	7.50
			Nos. 418-450 (34)	170.80	18.85

See Nos. 485-500, 523-540, 659, 668. For overprints see Nos. O37-O41, O43-O51, O53-O56, O58-O78, O108, O112, OD35-OD46, OD89-OD101, OD135-OD145, OD176-OD182C, OD229-OD234F, OD270-OD280, OD306-OD317, OD347-OD357.

No. 439A exists with attached label showing medallion. Value $42.50 unused, $22.50 used.

Souvenir Sheet

A151

Without Period after Value

1935, Oct. 17 **Litho.** ***Imperf.***

452	A151	Sheet of 4	52.50	30.00
a.		10c dull green	7.00	4.00

Phil. Exhib. at Buenos Aires, Oct. 17-24, 1935. The stamps were on sale during the 8 days of the exhibition only. Sheets measure 83x101mm.

Plaque — A152

1936, Dec. 1 ***Perf. 13x13½***

453	A152	10c rose	.50	.25

Inter-American Conference for Peace.

Domingo Faustino Sarmiento A153

"Presidente Sarmiento" A154

1938, Sept. 5
454 A153 3c sage green .50 .50
455 A153 5c red .50 .50
456 A153 15c deep blue 1.00 .50
457 A153 50c orange 3.00 1.00
Nos. 454-457 (4) 5.00 2.50

50th anniv. of the death of Domingo Faustino Sarmiento, pres., educator and author.

1939, Mar. 16
458 A154 5c greenish blue .35 .20

Final voyage of the training ship "Presidente Sarmiento."

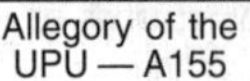

Allegory of the UPU — A155

Coat of Arms — A157

Post Office, Buenos Aires — A156

Iguacu Falls — A158

Bonete Hill, Nahuel Huapi Park — A159

Allegory of Modern Communications A160

Argentina, Land of Promise A161

Lake Frias, Nahuel Huapi Park — A162

Perf. 13x13½, 13½x13
1939, Apr. 1 **Photo.**
459 A155 5c rose carmine .20 .20
460 A156 15c grnsh black .40 .25
461 A157 20c brt blue .40 .20
462 A158 25c dp blue grn .85 .40
463 A159 50c brown 1.60 .65
464 A160 1p brown violet 1.90 .80
465 A161 2p magenta 8.75 5.25
466 A162 5p purple 35.00 16.00
Nos. 459-466 (8) 49.10 23.75

Universal Postal Union, 11th Congress.

Souvenir Sheets

A163

A164

1939, May 12 **Wmk. 90** ***Imperf.***
467 A163 Sheet of 4 6.00 4.25
a. 5c rose carmine (A155) 1.25 .75
b. 20c bright blue (A157) 1.25 .75
c. 25c deep blue green (A158) 1.25 .75
d. 50c brown (A159) 1.25 .75
468 A164 Sheet of 4 6.00 4.25

Issued in four forms:

a. Unsevered horizontal pair of sheets, type A163 at left, A164 at right 15.00 15.00
b. Unsevered vertical pair of sheets, type A163 at top, A164 at bottom 15.00 15.00
c. Unsevered block of 4 sheets, type A163 at left, A164 at right 52.50 52.50
d. Unsevered block of 4 sheets, type A163 at top, A164 at bottom 52.50 52.50

11th Cong. of the UPU and the Argentina Intl. Phil. Exposition (C.Y.T.R.A.).
No. 468 contains Nos. 467a-467d.

Family and New House A165

Perf. 13½x13
1939, Oct. 2 **Litho.** **Wmk. 90**
469 A165 5c bluish green .25 .20

1st Pan-American Housing Congress.

Bird Carrying Record A166

Head of Liberty and Arms of Argentina A167

Record and Winged Letter A168

Perf. 13x13½, 13½x13 (#472)
1939, Dec. 11 **Photo.**
470 A166 1.18p indigo 15.00 10.00
471 A167 1.32p bright blue 15.00 10.00
472 A168 1.50p dark brown 50.00 30.00
Nos. 470-472 (3) 80.00 50.00

These stamps were issued for the recording and mailing of flexible phonograph records.

Map of the Americas — A169

1940, Apr. 14 ***Perf. 13x13½***
473 A169 15c ultramarine .40 .20

50th anniv. of the Pan American Union.

Souvenir Sheet

1840-MAYO-1940
PRIMER CENTENARIO DEL SELLO POSTAL ADHESIVO
EXPOSICION FILATELICA DE CORDOBA

Reproductions of Early Argentine Stamps — A170

Wmk. RA in Sun (90)
1940, May 25 **Litho.** ***Imperf.***
474 A170 Sheet of 5 9.50 5.50
a. 5c dark blue (Corrientes A2) 1.10 .70
b. 5c red (Argentina A1) 1.10 .70
c. 5c dark blue (Cordoba #1) 1.10 .70
d. 5c red (Argentina A3) 1.10 .70
e. 10c dark blue (Buenos Aires A1) 1.10 .70

100th anniv. of the first postage stamp.

General Domingo French and Colonel Antonio Beruti A171

1941, Feb. 20 ***Perf. 13½x13***
475 A171 5c dk gray blue & lt blue .30 .20

Issued in honor of General French and Colonel Beruti, patriots.

Marco M. de Avellaneda A172

Statue of Gen. Julio Roca A173

1941, Oct. 3 ***Perf. 13x13½***
476 A172 5c dull slate blue .30 .20

Avellaneda, (1814-41), army leader and martyr.

1941, Oct. 19 **Photo.** **Wmk. 90**
477 A173 5c dark olive green .30 .20

Dedication of a monument to Lt. Gen. Julio Argentino Roca (1843-1914).

Carlos Pellegrini and Bank of the Nation A174

1941, Oct. 26 ***Perf. 13½x13***
478 A174 5c brown carmine .30 .20

Founding of the Bank of the Nation, 50th anniv.

Gen. Juan Lavalle — A175

1941, Dec. 5 ***Perf. 13x13½***
479 A175 5c bright blue .30 .20

Gen. Juan Galo de Lavalle (1797-1841).

National Postal Savings Bank A176

1942, Apr. 5 **Litho.** ***Perf. 13½x13***
480 A176 1c pale olive .20 .20

Jose Manuel Estrada — A177

1942, July 13 ***Perf. 13x13½***
481 A177 5c brown violet .30 .20

Jose Estrada (1842-1894), writer and diplomat.

No. 481 exists with label, showing medallion, attached. Value, pair $10.

Types of 1935-51
Perf. 13, 13x13½, 13½x13
1942-50 **Litho.** **Wmk. 288**

485	A128	½c	brown violet	4.75	1.00
486	A129	1c	buff ('50)	.20	.20
487	A130	2c	dk brown ('50)	.20	.20
488	A132	3c	lt gray	16.00	1.25
489	A134	3c	lt gray ('49)	.20	.20
490	A137	10c	red brn ('49)	.20	.20
491	A138	12c	red	.20	.20
492	A140	15c	lt gray blue (II)	.30	.20
493	A139	20c	dk sl bl & pale bl	1.25	.20
494	A141	25c	dull rose ('49)	.60	.20
495	A142	30c	org brn ('49)	1.25	.20
496	A143	40c	violet ('49)	8.00	.20
497	A144	50c	red & org ('49)	8.00	.20
498	A146	1p	brn blk & lt bl	6.50	.20
499	A147	2p	brn lake & bl ('49)	13.00	.85
500	A148	5p	ind & ol grn ('49)	50.00	4.50
			Nos. 485-500 (16)	110.65	10.00

No. 493 measures 22x33mm.

Post Office, Buenos Aires — A178

Proposed Columbus Lighthouse A179

Inscribed: "Correos y Telegrafos."

1942, Oct. 5 Litho. *Perf. 13*
503 A178 35c lt ultra 2.75 .20

See Nos. 541-543.

1942, Oct. 12 Wmk. 288
504 A179 15c dull blue 5.00 .50

Wmk. 90
505 A179 15c dull blue 65.00 10.00

450th anniv. of the discovery of America by Columbus.

Jose C. Paz — A180

Books and Argentine Flag — A181

1942, Dec. 15 Wmk. 288
506 A180 5c dark gray .35 .20

Cent. of the birth of Jose C. Paz, stateman and founder of the newspaper La Prensa.

1943, Apr. 1 Litho. *Perf. 13*
507 A181 5c dull blue .20 .20

1st Book Fair of Argentina.

Arms of Argentina Inscribed "Honesty, Justice, Duty" — A182

1943-50 Wmk. 288 *Perf. 13*
Size: 20x26mm
508 A182 5c red ('50) 6.00 .20

Wmk. 90
509 A182 5c red .25 .20
a. 5c dull red, unsurfaced paper 3.00 .20
510 A182 15c green .70 .20

Perf. 13x13½
Size: 22x33mm
511 A182 20c dark blue 1.10 .20
Nos. 508-511 (4) 8.05 .80

Change of political organization, 6/4/43.

Independence House, Tucuman A183

Liberty Head and Savings Bank A184

1943-51 Wmk. 90 *Perf. 13*
512 A183 5c blue green 1.00 .20

Wmk. 288
513 A183 5c blue green ('51) .50 .20

Restoration of Independence House.

1943, Oct. 25 Wmk. 90
514 A184 5c violet brown .50 .20

Wmk. 288
515 A184 5c violet brown 45.00 3.00

1st conference of National Postal Savings.

Port of Buenos Aires in 1800 — A185

1943, Dec. 11 Wmk. 90
516 A185 5c gray black .20 .20

Day of Exports.

Warship, Merchant Ship and Sailboat A186

Arms of Argentine Republic A187

1944, Jan. 31 *Perf. 13*
517 A186 5c blue .20 .20

Issued to commemorate Sea Week.

1944, June 4
518 A187 5c dull blue .20 .20

1st anniv. of the change of political organization in Argentina.

St. Gabriel A188

Cross at Palermo A189

1944, Oct. 11
519 A188 3c yellow green .20 .20
520 A189 5c deep rose .20 .20

Fourth national Eucharistic Congress.

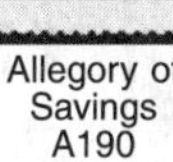
Allegory of Savings A190

Reservists A191

1944, Oct. 24
521 A190 5c gray .20 .20

20th anniv. of the National Savings Bank.

1944, Dec. 1
522 A191 5c blue .20 .20

Day of the Reservists.

Types of 1935-51

Perf. 13x13½, 13½x13

1945-47 Litho. Unwmk.
523 A128 ½c brown vio ('46) .20 .20
524 A129 1c yellow brown .20 .20
525 A130 2c sepia .20 .20
526 A132 3c lt gray (San Martin) .40 .20
527 A134 3c lt gray (Moreno) ('46) .20 .20
528 A135 6c olive grn ('47) .20 .20
529 A137 10c brown ('46) 1.25 .20
530 A140 15c lt gray bl (II) .75 .20
531 A139 20c dk sl bl & pale bl 1.25 .20
532 A141 25c dull rose 1.00 .20
533 A142 30c orange brown 1.00 .20
534 A143 40c violet 2.00 .20
535 A144 50c red & orange 3.00 .20
536 A146 1p brn blk & lt bl 3.00 .20
537 A147 2p brown lake & bl 30.00 1.00
538 A148 5p ind & ol grn ('46) 50.00 4.00
539 A149 10p dp cl & int blk 10.00 2.00
540 A150 20p bl grn & brn ('46) 10.00 2.00
Nos. 523-540 (18) 114.65 11.80

No. 531 measures 22x33mm.

Post Office Type Inscribed: "Correos y Telecommunicaciones"

1945 Unwmk. *Perf. 13x13½*
541 A178 35c lt ultra 2.50 .20

Wmk. 90
542 A178 35c lt ultra 1.25 .20

Wmk. 288
543 A178 35c lt ultra .35 .20
Nos. 541-543 (3) 4.10 .60

Bernardino Rivadavia
A192 A193

Mausoleum of Rivadavia A194

Perf. 13½x13
1945, Sept. 1 Litho. Unwmk.
544 A192 3c blue green .20 .20
545 A193 5c rose .20 .20
546 A194 20c blue .30 .20
Nos. 544-546 (3) .70 .60

Cent. of the death of Bernardino Rivadavia, Argentina's first president.

No. 546 exists with mute label attached. The pair sells for four times the price of the single stamp.

San Martin A195

Monument to Army of the Andes, Mendoza A196

1945-46 Wmk. 90 Typo. or Litho.
547 A195 5c carmine .20 .20
a. Litho. ('46) .20 .20

Wmk. 288
548 A195 5c carmine, litho. 125.00 20.00

Unwmk.
549 A195 5c carmine ('46) .50 .20
a. Litho. ('46) .20 .20

For overprints see Nos. O42, O57.

1946, Jan. 14 Litho. *Perf. 13½x13*
550 A196 5c violet brown .20 .20

Issued to honor the Unknown Soldier of the War for Independence.

A197 A198

1946, Apr. 12
551 A197 5c Franklin D. Roosevelt .20 .20

1946, June 4 *Perf. 13x13½*
Liberty Administering Presidential Oath.
552 A198 5c blue .20 .20

Inauguration of Pres. Juan D. Perón, 6/4/46.

Argentina Receiving Popular Acclaim A199

1946, Oct. 17 *Perf. 13½x13*
553 A199 5c rose violet .20 .20
554 A199 10c blue green .25 .20
555 A199 15c dark blue .45 .20
556 A199 50c red brown .70 .30
557 A199 1p carmine rose 1.40 .70
Nos. 553-557 (5) 3.00 1.60

First anniversary of the political organization change of Oct. 17, 1945.

Coin Bank and World Map — A200

1946, Oct. 31 Unwmk.
558 A200 30c dk rose car & pink .60 .20

Universal Day of Savings, October 31, 1946.

Argentine Industry — A201

International Bridge Connecting Argentina and Brazil A202

1946, Dec. 6 *Perf. 13x13½*
559 A201 5c violet brown .20 .20

Day of Argentine Industry, Dec. 6.

1947, May 21 Litho. *Perf. 13½x13*
560 A202 5c green .20 .20

Opening of the Argentina-Brazil International Bridge, May 21, 1947.

Map of Argentine Antarctic Claims — A203

Justice — A204

1947-49 Unwmk. *Perf. 13x13½*
561 A203 5c violet & lilac .30 .20
562 A203 20c dk car rose & rose .70 .20

Wmk. 90
563 A203 20c dk car rose & rose 2.00 .20

Wmk. 288

564 A203 20c dk car rose & rose ('49) 2.00 .20
Nos. 561-564 (4) 5.00 .80

1st Argentine Antarctic mail, 43rd anniv.

1947, June 4 **Unwmk.**

565 A204 5c brn vio & pale yel .20 .20

1st anniversary of the Peron government.

Icarus Falling A205

1947, Sept. 25 ***Perf. 13½x13***

566 A205 15c red violet .20 .20

Aviation Week.

Training Ship Presidente Sarmiento — A206

1947, Oct. 5 ***Perf. 13x13½***

567 A206 5c blue .20 .20

50th anniv. of the launching of the Argentine training frigate "Presidente Sarmiento."

Cervantes and Characters from Don Quixote A207

Perf. 13½x13

1947, Oct. 12 **Photo.** **Wmk. 90**

568 A207 5c olive green .20 .20

400th anniv. of the birth of Miguel de Cervantes Saavedra, playwright and poet.

Gen. Jose de San Martin A208

Perf. 13½x13

1947-49 **Unwmk.** **Litho.**

569 A208 5c dull green .20 .20

Wmk. 288

570 A208 5c dull green ('49) .20 .20

Transfer of the remains of Gen. Jose de San Martin's parents.

School Children — A209

Statue of Araucanian Indian — A210

1947-49 **Unwmk.** ***Perf. 13x13½***

571 A209 5c green .20 .20

Wmk. 90

574 A209 20c brown .35 .20

Wmk. 288

575 A209 5c green ('49) .35 .20
Nos. 571-575 (3) .90 .60

Argentine School Crusade for World Peace.

1948, May 21 **Wmk. 90**

576 A210 25c yellow brown .30 .20

American Indian Day, Apr. 19.

Cap of Liberty — A211

Manual Stop Signal — A212

1948, July 16

577 A211 5c ultra .20 .20

Revolution of June 4, 1943, 5th anniv.

1948, July 22

578 A212 5c chocolate & yellow .20 .20

Traffic Safety Day, June 10.

Post Horn and Oak Leaves — A213

Argentine Farmers — A214

1948, July 22 **Unwmk.**

579 A213 5c lilac rose .20 .20

200th anniversary of the establishment of regular postal service on the Plata River.

Perf. 13x13½

1948, Sept. 20 **Wmk. 288**

580 A214 10c red brown .20 .20

Agriculture Day, Sept. 8, 1948.

Liberty and Symbols of Progress — A215

Perf. 13x13½

1948, Nov. 23 **Photo.** **Wmk. 287**

581 A215 25c red brown .20 .20

3rd anniversary of President Juan D. Peron's return to power, October 17, 1945.

Souvenir Sheets

A216

15c, Mail coach. 45c, Buenos Aires in 18th cent. 55c, 1st train, 1857. 85c, Sailing ship, 1767.

1948, Dec. 21 **Unwmk.** ***Imperf.***

582 A216 Sheet of 4 3.00 3.00
a. 15c dark green .45 .45
b. 45c orange brown .45 .45
c. 55c lilac brown .45 .45
d. 85c ultramarine .45 .45

A217

Designs: 85c, Domingo de Basavilibaso (1709-75). 1.05p, Postrider. 1.20p, Sailing ship, 1798. 1.90p, Courier in the Andes, 1772.

583 A217 Sheet of 4 14.00 11.00
a. 85c brown 3.00 2.50
b. 1.05p dark green 3.00 2.50
c. 1.20p dark blue 3.00 2.50
d. 1.90p red brown 3.00 2.50

200th anniversary of the establishment of regular postal service on the Plata River.

Winged Wheel — A218

Perf. 13½x13

1949, Mar. 1 **Wmk. 288**

584 A218 10c blue .25 .20

Railroad nationalization, 1st anniv.

Liberty A219

1949, June 20 **Engr.** **Wmk. 90**

585 A219 1p red & red violet .40 .20

Ratification of the Constitution of 1949.

Allegory of the UPU A220

1949, Nov. 19

586 A220 25c dk grn & yel grn .25 .20

75th anniv. of the UPU.

Catalogue values for unused stamps in this section, from this point to the end of the section, are for Never Hinged items.

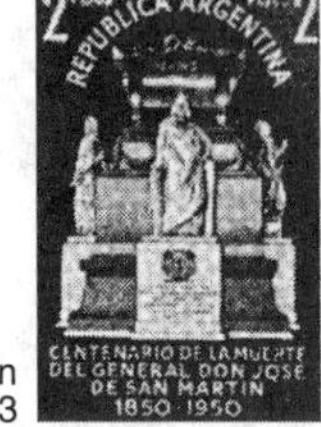

Gen. Jose de San Martin — A221

San Martin at Boulogne sur Mer — A222

Mausoleum of San Martin — A223

20c, 50c, 75c, Different portraits of San Martin. 1p, House where San Martin died.

Engr., Photo. (25c, 1p, 2p)

1950, Aug. 17 **Wmk. 90** ***Perf. 13½***

587 A221 10c indigo & dk pur .20 .20
588 A221 20c red brn & dk brn .20 .20
589 A222 25c brown .20 .20
590 A221 50c dk green & ind .40 .20
591 A221 75c choc & dk grn .40 .20
a. Souv. sheet of 4, #587, 588, 590, 591, imperf. 1.25 .80
592 A222 1p dark green .85 .25
593 A223 2p dp red lilac .75 .35
Nos. 587-593 (7) 3.00 1.60

Death cent. of General Jose de San Martin.

Map Showing Antarctic Claims — A224

1951, May 21 **Litho.** ***Perf. 13x13½***

594 A224 1p choc & lt blue .70 .20

For overprint see No. O52.

Pegasus and Train A225

Communications Symbols — A226

Design: 25c, Ship and dolphin.

1951, Oct. 17 Photo. *Perf. 13½*
595 A225 5c dark brown .20 .20
596 A225 25c Prus green .25 .20
597 A226 40c rose brown .30 .20
Nos. 595-597 (3) .75 .60

Close of Argentine Five Year Plan.

Woman Voter and "Argentina" A227

1951, Dec. 14 *Perf. 13½x13*
598 A227 10c brown violet .20 .20

Granting of women's suffrage.

Eva Peron
A228 A229

Litho. or Engraved (#605)
1952, Aug. 26 Wmk. 90 *Perf. 13*
599 A228 1c orange brown .20 .20
600 A228 5c gray .20 .20
601 A228 10c rose lilac .20 .20
602 A228 20c rose pink .20 .20
603 A228 25c dull green .20 .20
604 A228 40c dull violet .20 .20
605 A228 45c deep blue .20 .20
606 A228 50c dull brown .20 .20

Photo.
607 A229 1p dark brown .25 .20
608 A229 1.50p deep green 1.50 .20
609 A229 2p brt carmine .45 .20
610 A229 3p indigo .75 .20
Nos. 599-610 (12) 4.55 2.40

For overprints see Nos. O79-O85.

Inscribed: "Eva Peron"
1952-53 *Perf. 13x13½*
611 A229 1p dark brown .30 .20
612 A229 1.50p deep green 1.10 .20
613 A229 2p brt car ('53) 1.10 .20
614 A229 3p indigo 2.75 .20

Engr.
Perf. 13½x13
Size: 30x40mm
615 A229 5p red brown 2.75 .35
616 A228 10p red 7.00 1.40
617 A229 20p green 11.00 4.00
618 A228 50p ultra 20.00 10.00
Nos. 611-618 (8) 46.00 16.55

For overprints see Nos. O86-O93.

Indian Funeral Urn — A230

1953, Aug. 28 Photo. *Perf. 13x13½*
619 A230 50c blue green .20 .20

Founding of Santiago del Estero, 400th anniv.

Rescue Ship "Uruguay" — A231

1953, Oct. 8 *Perf. 13½*
620 A231 50c ultra .85 .20

50th anniv. of the rescue of the Antarctic expedition of Otto C. Nordenskjold.

Planting Argentine Flag in the Antarctic A232

1954, Jan. 20 Engr. *Perf. 13½x13*
621 A232 1.45p blue 1.25 .20

50th anniv. of Argentina's 1st antarctic p.o. and the establishing of the La Hoy radio p.o. in the South Orkneys.

Wired Communications A233

Television A234

Perf. 13x13½, 13½x13
1954, Apr. Photo. Wmk. 90
622 A233 1.50p shown .35 .25
623 A233 3p Radio 1.10 .30
624 A234 5p shown 1.40 .55
Nos. 622-624 (3) 2.85 1.10

Intl. Plenipotentiary Conf. of Telecommunications, Buenos Aires, 1952.

Pediment, Buenos Aires Stock Exchange A235

1954, July 13 *Perf. 13½x13*
625 A235 1p dark green .30 .20

Cent. of the establishment of the Buenos Aires Stock Exchange.

Eva Peron — A236

1954 Wmk. 90
626 A236 3p dp car rose 2.00 .50

Wmk. 288
627 A236 3p dp car rose 225.00 40.00

2nd anniv. of the death of Eva Peron.

Jose de San Martin — A237

Wheat — A238

Industry - A238a

Eva Peron Foundation Building A239

Cliffs of Humahuaca — A240

Gen. Jose de San Martin — A241

Designs: 50c, Buenos Aires harbor. 1p, Cattle ranch (Ganaderia). 3p, Nihuil Dam. 5p, Iguacu Falls, vert. 20p, Mt. Fitz Roy, vert.

Engraved (#632, 638-642), Photogravure (#634-637)
Perf. 13½, 13x13½ (80c), 13½x13 (#639, 641-642)
1954-59 Wmk. 90
628 A237 20c brt red, typo. .20 .20
629 A237 20c red, litho. ('55) 1.00 .20
630 A237 40c red, litho. ('56) .20 .20
631 A237 40c brt red, typo. ('55) .25 .20
632 A239 50c blue ('56) .30 .20
633 A239 50c bl, litho. ('59) 1.00 .20
634 A238 80c brown .30 .20
635 A239 1p brown ('58) .30 .20
636 A238a 1.50p ultra ('58) .30 .20
637 A239 2p dk rose lake .40 .20
638 A239 3p violet brn ('56) .40 .20
639 A240 5p gray grn ('55) 8.00 .20
a. Perf. 13½ 10.00 .20
640 A240 10p yel grn ('55) 6.00 .80
641 A240 20p dull vio ('55) 12.00 .20
a. Perf. 13½ 15.00 .20
642 A241 50p ultra & ind ('55) 10.00 .20
a. Perf. 13½ 12.00 .20
Nos. 628-642 (15) 40.65 3.60

See Nos. 699-700. For similar designs inscribed "Republica Argentina" see Nos. 823-827, 890, 935, 937, 940, 990, 995, 1039, 1044, 1048.

For overprints see Nos. O94-O106, O142, O153-O157.

Allegory A242

1954, Aug. 26 Typo. *Perf. 13½*
643 A242 1.50p slate black .65 .20

Cent. of the establishment of the Buenos Aires Grain Exchange.

Clasped Hands and Congress Medal — A243

1955, Mar. 21 Photo. *Perf. 13½x13*
644 A243 3p red brown .80 .20

Issued to publicize the National Productivity and Social Welfare Congress.

Allegory of Aviation — A244

Argentina Breaking Chains — A245

1955, June 18 Wmk. 90 *Perf. 13½*
645 A244 1.50p olive gray .65 .20

Commercial aviation in Argentina, 25th anniv.

1955, Oct. 16 Litho.
647 A245 1.50p olive green .30 .20

Liberation Revolution of Sept. 16, 1955.

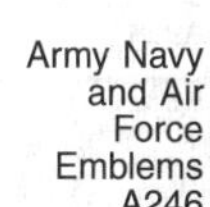

Army Navy and Air Force Emblems A246

Perf. 13½x13
1955, Dec. 31 Photo. Wmk. 90
648 A246 3p blue .40 .20

"Brotherhood of the Armed Forces."

A247

1956, Feb. 3 *Perf. 13½*
649 A247 1.50p Justo Jose de Urquiza .30 .20

Battle of Caseros, 104th anniversary.

A248

1956, July 28 Engr. *Perf. 13½x13*

650 A248 2p Coin and die .30 .20

75th anniversary of the Argentine Mint.

1856 Stamp of Corrientes A249

Juan G. Pujol — A250

Design: 2.40p, Stamp of 1860-78.

1956, Aug. 21

651 A249 40c dk grn & blue .20 .20
652 A249 2.40p brn & lil rose .30 .20

Photo.

653 A250 4.40p brt blue .65 .20
a. Souv. sheet, #651-653, imperf. 2.25 2.00
Nos. 651-653 (3) 1.15 .60

Centenary of Argentine postage stamps.
No. 653a for the Argentine stamp cent. and Philatelic Exhib. for the Cent. of Corrientes Stamps, Oct. 12-21. The 4.40p is photo., the other two stamps and border litho. Colors of 40c and 2.40p differ slightly from engraved stamps.

Felling Trees, La Pampa A251

Maté Herb and Gourd, Misiones — A252

1p, Cotton plant and harvest, Chaco.

1956, Sept. 1 *Perf. 13½*

654 A251 50c ultra .20 .20
655 A251 1p magenta .20 .20
656 A252 1.50p green .25 .20
Nos. 654-656 (3) .65 .60

Elevation of the territories of La Pampa, Chaco and Misiones to provinces.

"Liberty" A253

Florentino Ameghino A254

Perf. 13½

1956, Sept. 15 Wmk. 90 Photo.

657 A253 2.40p lilac rose .30 .20

1st anniv. of the Revolution of Liberation.

1956, Nov. 30

658 A254 2.40p brown .30 .20

Issued to honor Florentino Ameghino (1854-1911), anthropologist.
For overprint see No. O110.

Adm. Brown Type of 1935-51

1956 Litho. *Perf. 13*

Two types:
I. Bust touches upper frame line of name panel at bottom.
II. White line separates bust from frame line.

Size: 19½-20½x26-27mm

659 A133 20c dull purple (I) .20 .20
a. Type II .20 .20
b. Size 19½x25¼mm (I) .20 .20

For overprint see No. O108.

Benjamin Franklin A255

1956, Dec. 22 Photo. *Perf. 13½*

660 A255 40c intense blue .30 .20

250th anniv. of the birth of Benjamin Franklin.

Frigate "Hercules" A256

Guillermo Brown A257

1957, Mar. 2

661 A256 40c brt blue .20 .20
662 A257 2.40p gray black .35 .20
Nos. 661-662,C63-C65 (5) 1.20 1.00

Admiral Guillermo (William) Brown (1777-1857), founder of the Argentine navy.

Roque Saenz Pena (1851-1914) A258

Church of Santo Domingo, 1807 A259

1957, Apr. 1

663 A258 4.40p grnsh gray .45 .20

Roque Saenz Pena, pres. 1910-14.

For overprint see No. O111.

1957, July 6 Wmk. 90

664 A259 40c brt blue green .20 .20

150th anniv. of the defense of Buenos Aires.

"La Portena" A260

1957, Aug. 31 Wmk. 90 *Perf. 13½*

665 A260 40c pale brown .20 .20

Centenary of Argentine railroads.

Esteban Echeverria A261

"Liberty" A262

1957, Sept. 2 *Perf. 13x13½*

666 A261 2p claret .25 .20

Esteban Echeverria (1805-1851), poet.
For overprint see No. O109.

1957, Sept. 28 *Perf. 13½*

667 A262 40c carmine rose .20 .20

Constitutional reform convention.

Portrait Type of 1935-51

1957, Oct. 28 Litho. *Perf. 13½*

Size: 16½x22mm

668 A128 5c Jose Hernandez .20 .20

For overprint see No. O112.

Oil Derrick and Hands Holding Oil — A263

Perf. 13½

1957, Dec. 21 Wmk. 90 Photo.

669 A263 40c bright blue .20 .20

50th anniv. of the national oil industry.

Museum, La Plata — A264

1958, Jan. 11

670 A264 40c dark gray .20 .20

City of La Plata, 75th anniversary.

A265

A266

40c, Locomotive & arms of Argentina & Bolivia. 1p, Map of Argentine-Bolivian boundary & plane.

1958, Apr. 19 Wmk. 90 *Perf. 13½*

671 A265 40c slate & dp car .30 .20
672 A266 1p dark brown .30 .20

Argentine-Bolivian friendship. No. 671 for the opening of the Jacuiba-Santa Cruz railroad; No. 672, the exchange of presidential visits.

Symbols of the Republic A267

1958, Apr. 30 Photo. & Engr.

673 A267 40c multicolored .20 .20
674 A267 1p multicolored .20 .20
675 A267 2p multicolored .25 .20
Nos. 673-675 (3) .65 .60

Transmission of Presidential power.

Flag Monument — A268

1958, June 21 Litho. Wmk. 90

676 A268 40c blue & violet bl .20 .20

1st anniv. of the Flag Monument of Rosario.

Map of Antarctica — A269

1958, July 12 *Perf. 13½*

677 A269 40c car rose & blk .50 .20

International Geophysical Year, 1957-58.

Stamp of Cordoba and Mail Coach A270

1958, Oct. 18

678 A270 40c pale blue & slate .20 .20
Nos. 678,C72-C73 (3) .65 .60

Centenary of Cordoba postage stamps.

"Slave" by Michelangelo and UN Emblem — A271

Engraved and Lithographed

1959, Mar. 14 Wmk. 90 *Perf. 13½*

679 A271 40c violet brn & gray .20 .20

10th anniv. (in 1958) of the signing of the Universal Declaration of Human Rights.

Orchids and Globe — A272

1959, May 23 Photo. *Perf. 13½*

680	A272	1p dull claret	.25	.20

1st International Horticulture Exposition.

Pope Pius XII — A273

1959, June 20 Engr. *Perf. 13½*

681	A273	1p yellow & black	.20	.20

Pope Pius XII, 1876-1958.

William Harvey — A274

1959, Aug. 8 Litho. Wmk. 90

1p, Claude Bernard. 1.50p, Ivan P. Pavlov.

682	A274	50c green	.20	.20
683	A274	1p dark red	.20	.20
684	A274	1.50p brown	.25	.20
		Nos. 682-684 (3)	.65	.60

21st Intl. Cong. of Physiological Sciences, Buenos Aires.

Type of 1958 and

Domestic Horse — A275

Jose de San Martin — A276

Tierra del Fuego A277

Inca Bridge, Mendoza — A278

Ski Jumper A279

Mar del Plata A280

Designs: 10c, Cayman. 20c, Llama. 50c, Puma. No. 690, Sunflower. 3p, Zapata Slope, Catamarca. 12p, 23p, 25p, Red Quebracho tree. 20p, Nahuel Huapi Lake. 22p, "Industry" (cogwheel and factory).

Two overall paper sizes for 1p, 5p:
I - 27x37½mm or 37½x27mm.
II - 27x39mm or 39x27mm.

Perf. 13x13½

1959-70 Litho. Wmk. 90

685	A275	10c slate green	.20	.20
686	A275	20c dl red brn ('61)	.20	.20
687	A275	50c bister ('60)	.20	.20
688	A275	50c bis, typo. ('60)	.20	.20
689	A275	1p rose red	.20	.20

Perf. 13½

690	A278	1p brn, photo., I ('61)	.20	.20
a.		Paper II ('69)	1.00	.20
690B	A278	1p brown, I	.80	.20
691	A276	2p rose red ('61)	.25	.20
692	A276	2p red, typo. (19½ x 26mm) ('61)	.30	.20
a.		Redrawn (19½ x 25mm)	4.75	.20
693	A277	3p dk bl, photo. ('60)	.20	.20
694	A276	4p red, typo ('62)	.20	.20
694A	A276	4p red ('62)	.40	.20
695	A277	5p gray brn, photo., I	.40	.20
e.		5p dark brown, paper II ('70)	8.00	.20
695A	A276	8p ver ('65)	1.25	.20
695B	A276	8p red, typo. ('65)	.30	.20
695C	A276	10p ver ('66)	.65	.20
695D	A276	10p red, typo. ('66)	.50	.20

Photo.

696	A278	10p lt red brn ('60)	.50	.20
697	A278	12p dk brn vio ('62)	.80	.20
697A	A278	12p dk brn, litho. ('64)	8.00	.20
698	A278	20p Prus grn ('60)	2.75	.20
698A	A276	20p red, typo. ('67)	.25	.20
699	A238a	22p ultra ('62)	1.50	.20
700	A238a	22p ultra, litho. ('62)	24.00	.20
701	A278	23p green ('65)	4.75	.20
702	A278	25p dp vio ('66)	1.25	.20
703	A278	25p pur, litho. ('66)	6.25	.20
704	A279	100p blue ('61)	8.00	.20
705	A280	300p dp vio ('62)	6.00	.20
		Nos. 685-705 (29)	70.50	5.80

See Nos. 882-887, 889, 892, 923-925, 928-930, 938, 987-989, 991.

For overprints and surcharges see Nos. 1076, C82-C83, O113-O118, O122-O124, O126-O141, O143-O145, O163.

The 300p remained on sale as a 3p stamp after the 1970 currency exchange.

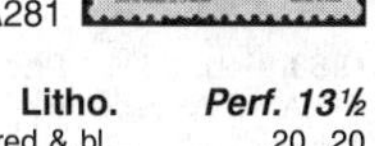

Symbolic Sailboat — A281

1959, Oct. 3 Litho. *Perf. 13½*

706	A281	1p blk, red & bl	.20	.20

Red Cross sanitary education campaign.

Child Playing with Doll — A282

1959, Oct. 17

707	A282	1p red & blk	.20	.20

Issued for Mother's Day, 1959.

Buenos Aires 1p Stamp of 1859 — A283

1959, Nov. 21 Wmk. 90 *Perf. 13½*

708	A283	1p gray & dk bl	.20	.20

Issued for the Day of Philately.

Bartolomé Mitre and Justo José de Urquiza — A284

1959, Dec. 12 Photo. *Perf. 13½*

709	A284	1p purple	.20	.20

Treaty of San Jose de Flores, centenary.

WRY Emblem — A285

Abraham Lincoln — A286

1960, Apr. 7 Litho. Wmk. 90

710	A285	1p bister & car	.20	.20
711	A285	4.20p apple grn & dp claret	.30	.20

World Refugee Year, July 1, 1959-June 30, 1960. See No. B25.

1960, Apr. 14 Photo. *Perf. 13½*

712	A286	5p ultra	.40	.20

Sesquicentennial (in 1959) of the birth of Abraham Lincoln.

Cornelio Saavedra and Cabildo, Buenos Aires — A287

"Cabildo" and: 2p, Juan José Paso. 4.20p, Manuel Alberti and Miguel Azcuénaga. 10.70p, Juan Larrea and Domingo Matheu.

Perf. 13½

1960, May 28 Wmk. 90 Photo.

713	A287	1p rose lilac	.20	.20
714	A287	2p bluish grn	.20	.20
715	A287	4.20p gray & grn	.25	.20
716	A287	10.70p gray & ultra	.45	.20
		Nos. 713-716,C75-C76 (6)	1.65	1.20

150th anniversary of the May Revolution. Souvenir sheets are Nos. C75a and C76a.

Luis Maria Drago — A288

Juan Bautista Alberdi — A289

1960, July 8

717	A288	4.20p brown	.25	.20

Ccentenary of the birth of Dr. Luis Maria Drago, statesman and jurist.

1960, Sept. 10 Wmk. 90 *Perf. 13½*

718	A289	1p green	.20	.20

150th anniversary of the birth of Juan Bautista Alberdi, statesman and philosopher.

Map of Argentina and Antarctic Sector — A290

Caravel and Emblem A291

1960, Sept. 24 Litho. *Perf. 13½*

719	A290	5p violet	.85	.25

National census of 1960.

1960, Oct. 1 Photo.

720	A291	1p dk olive grn	.20	.20
721	A291	5p brown	.45	.20
		Nos. 720-721,C78-C79 (4)	1.25	.80

8th Congress of the Postal Union of the Americas and Spain.

Virgin of Luján, Patroness of Argentina A292

Argentine Boy Scout Emblem A293

1960, Nov. 12 Wmk. 90 *Perf. 13½*

722	A292	1p dark blue	.20	.20

First Inter-American Marian Congress.

1961, Jan. 17 Litho.

723	A293	1p car rose & blk	.30	.20

International Patrol Encampment of the Boy Scouts, Buenos Aires.

"Shipment of Cereals," by Quinquela Martin — A294

1961, Feb. 11 Photo. *Perf. 13½*

724 A294 1p red brown .30 .20

Export drive: "To export is to advance."

Naval Battle of San Nicolás — A295

1961, Mar. 2 *Perf. 13½*

725 A295 2p gray .30 .20

Naval battle of San Nicolas, 150th anniv.

Mariano Moreno by Juan de Dios Rivera A296

1961, Mar. 25 *Perf. 13½*

726 A296 2p blue .20 .20

Mariano Moreno (1778-1811), writer, politician, member of the 1810 Junta.

Emperor Trajan Statue — A297

Rabindranath Tagore — A298

1961, Apr. 11

727 A297 2p slate green .20 .20

Visit of Pres. Giovanni Gronchi of Italy to Argentina, April 1961.

1961, May 13 Photo. *Perf. 13½*

728 A298 2p purple, *grysh* .20 .20

Centenary of the birth of Rabindranath Tagore, Indian poet.

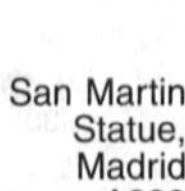

San Martin Statue, Madrid A299

1961, May 24 Wmk. 90

729 A299 1p olive gray .20 .20

Unveiling of a statue of General José de San Martin in Madrid.

Manuel Belgrano A300

1961, June 17 *Perf. 13½*

730 A300 2p violet blue .20 .20

Erection of a monument by Hector Rocha, to General Manuel Belgrano in Buenos Aires.

Explorers, Sledge and Dog Team A301

1961, Aug. 19 Photo. Wmk. 90

731 A301 2p black .70 .25

10th anniversary of the General San Martin Base, Argentine Antarctic.

Spanish Conquistador and Sword — A302

Sarmiento Statue by Rodin, Buenos Aires — A303

1961, Aug. 19 Litho.

732 A302 2p red & blk .20 .20

First city of Jujuy, 400th anniversary.

1961, Sept. 9 Photo.

733 A303 2p violet .20 .20

Domingo Faustino Sarmiento (1811-88), political leader and writer.

Symbol of World Town Planning A304

1961, Nov. 25 Litho. *Perf. 13½*

734 A304 2p ultra & yel .20 .20

World Town Planning Day, Nov. 8.

Manuel Belgrano Statue, Buenos Aires — A305

Grenadier, Flag and Regimental Emblem — A306

1962, Feb. 24 Photo.

735 A305 2p Prus blue .20 .20

150th anniversary of the Argentine flag.

1962, Mar. 31 Wmk. 90 *Perf. 13½*

736 A306 2p carmine rose .20 .20

150th anniversary of the San Martin Grenadier Guards regiment.

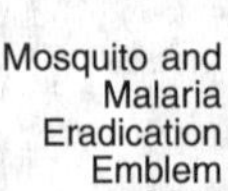

Mosquito and Malaria Eradication Emblem A307

1962, Apr. 7 Litho.

737 A307 2p vermilion & blk .20 .20

WHO drive to eradicate malaria.

Church of the Virgin of Lujàn — A308

Bust of Juan Jufrè — A309

1962, May 12 *Perf. 13½*

738 A308 2p org brn & blk .20 .20

75th anniversary of the pontifical coronation of the Virgin of Lujan.

1962, June 23 Photo.

739 A309 2p Prus blue .20 .20

Founding of San Juan, 4th cent.

"Soaring into Space" — A310

Juan Vucetich — A311

1962, Aug. 18 Litho. *Perf. 13½*

740 A310 2p maroon, blk & bl .20 .20

Argentine Air Force, 50th anniversary.

1962, Oct. 6 Photo. Wmk. 90

741 A311 2p green .20 .20

Juan Vucetich (1864-1925), inventor of the Argentine system of fingerprinting.

Domingo F. Sarmiento A312

February 20th Monument, Salta A313

Design: 4p, Jose Hernandez.

1962-66 Photo. *Perf. 13½*

742 A312 2p deep green .65 .20

Litho.

742A A312 2p lt green ('64) .55 .20

Photo.

742B A312 4p dull red ('65) .45 .20

Litho.

742C A312 4p rose red ('66) .60 .20

Nos. 742-742C (4) 2.25 .80

See No. 817-819. For overprints see Nos. O119-O121, O125, O149.

1963, Feb. 23 Photo. Wmk. 90

743 A313 2p dark green .20 .20

150th anniversary of the Battle of Salta, War of Independence.

Gear Wheels A314

1963, Mar. 16 Litho. *Perf. 13½*

744 A314 4p gray, blk & brt rose .20 .20

Argentine Industrial Union, 75th anniv.

National College, Buenos Aires — A315

Child Draining Cup — A316

1963, Mar. 16 Wmk. 90

745 A315 4p dull org & blk .20 .20

National College of Buenos Aires, cent.

1963, Apr. 6

746 A316 4p multicolored .20 .20

FAO "Freedom from Hunger" campaign.

Frigate "La Argentina," 1817, by Emilio Biggeri A317

1963, May 18 Photo.

747 A317 4p bluish green .30 .20

Issued for Navy Day, May 17.

Seat of 1813 Assembly and Official Seal — A318

1963, July 13 Litho. *Perf. 13½*

748 A318 4p lt blue & blk .20 .20

150th anniversary of the 1813 Assembly.

Battle of San Lorenzo, 1813 A319

1963, Aug. 24

749 A319 4p grn & blk, *grnsh* .20 .20

Sesquicentennial of the Battle of San Lorenzo.

Queen Nefertari Offering Papyrus Flowers, Abu Simbel A320

1963, Sept. 14 *Perf. 13½*

750 A320 4p ocher, blk & bl grn .30 .20

Campaign to save the historic monuments in Nubia.

Government House, Buenos Aires — A321

1963, Oct. 12 Wmk. 90 ***Perf. 13½***

751 A321 5p rose & brown .20 .20

Inauguration of President Arturo Illia.

"Science" A322

Francisco de las Carreras, Supreme Court Justice A323

1963, Oct. 16 Litho.

752 A322 4p org brn, bl & blk .20 .20

10th Latin-American Neurosurgery Congress.

1963, Nov. 23 Photo. ***Perf. 13½***

753 A323 5p bluish green .20 .20

Centenary of judicial power.

Blackboards A324

1963, Nov. 23 Litho.

754 A324 5p red, blk & bl .20 .20

Issued to publicize "Teachers for America" through the Alliance for Progress program.

Kemal Atatürk A325

"Payador" by Juan Carlos Castagnino A326

1963, Dec. 28 Photo. ***Perf. 13½***

755 A325 12p dark gray .30 .20

25th anniversary of the death of Kemal Atatürk, president of Turkey.

1964, Jan. 25 Litho.

756 A326 4p ultra, blk & lt bl .30 .20

Fourth National Folklore Festival.

Maps of South Georgia, South Orkney and South Sandwich Islands A327

4p, Map of Argentina & Antarctic claims, vert.

1964, Feb. 22 Wmk. 90 ***Perf. 13½***

Size: 33x22mm

757 A327 2p lt & dk bl & bister 1.25 .25

Size: 30x40mm

758 A327 4p lt & dk bl & ol grn 1.75 .30

Nos. 757-758,C92 (3) 4.75 1.25

Argentina's claim to Antarctic territories, 60th anniv.

Jorge Newbery in Cockpit A328

1964, Feb. 23 Photo.

759 A328 4p deep green .20 .20

Newbery, aviator, 50th death anniv.

John F. Kennedy A329

1964, Apr. 14 Engr. Wmk. 90

760 A329 4p claret & dk bl .35 .20

President John F. Kennedy (1917-63).

José Brochero by José Cuello — A330

1964, May 9 Photo. ***Perf. 13½***

761 A330 4p light sepia .20 .20

50th anniversary of the death of Father Jose Gabriel Brochero.

Soldier of Patricios Regiment A331

1964, May 29 Litho. Wmk. 90

762 A331 4p blk, ultra & red .40 .20

Issued for Army Day. Later Army Day stamps, inscribed "Republica Argentina," are of type A340a.

Pope John XXIII — A332

1964, June 27 Engr.

763 A332 4p orange & blk .25 .20

Issued in memory of Pope John XXIII.

University of Cordoba Arms — A333

Pigeons and UN Building, NYC — A334

1964, Aug. 22 Litho. Wmk. 90

764 A333 4p blk, ultra & yel .20 .20

350th anniv. of the University of Cordoba.

1964, Oct. 24 ***Perf. 13½***

765 A334 4p dk blue & lt blue .20 .20

Issued for United Nations Day.

Joaquin V. Gonzalez A335

Julio Argentino Roca A336

1964, Nov. 14 Photo.

766 A335 4p dk rose carmine .20 .20

Centenary (in 1963) of the birth of Joaquin V. Gonzalez, writer.

1964, Dec. 12 ***Perf. 13½***

767 A336 4p violet blue .20 .20

General Julio A. Roca, (1843-1914), president of Argentina, (1880-86, 1898-1904).

Market at Montserrat Square, by Carlos Morel — A337

1964, Dec. 19 Photo.

768 A337 4p sepia .30 .20

19th century Argentine painter Carlos Morel.

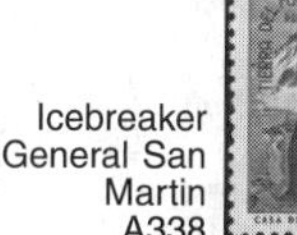

Icebreaker General San Martin A338

2p, General Belgrano Base, Antarctica.

1965 ***Perf. 13½***

769 A338 2p dull purple .40 .20

770 A338 4p ultra .50 .20

Issued to publicize the natl. territory of Tierra del Fuego, Antarctic and South Atlantic Isles.

Issue dates: 4p, Feb. 27; 2p, June 5.

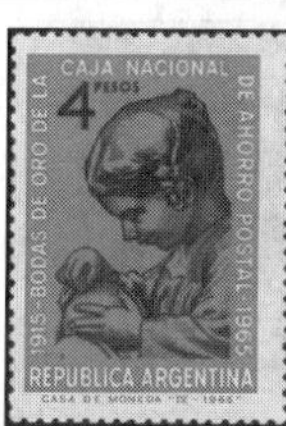

Girl with Piggy Bank — A339

1965, Apr. 3 Litho.

771 A339 4p red org & blk .20 .20

National Postal Savings Bank, 50th anniv.

Sun and Globe A340

1965, May 29

772 A340 4p blk, org & dl bl .25 .20

Nos. 772,C98-C99 (3) 1.65 .90

International Quiet Sun Year, 1964-65.

Hussar of Pueyrredon Regiment A340a

1965, June 5 Wmk. 90 ***Perf. 13½***

773 A340a 8p dp ultra, blk & red .50 .20

Issued for Army Day. See Nos. 796, 838, 857, 893, 944, 958, 974, 1145.

Ricardo Rojas (1882-1957) A341

1965, June 26 Photo.

Portraits: No. 775, Ricardo Guiraldes (1886-1927). No. 776, Enrique Larreta (1873-1961). No. 777, Leopoldo Lugones (1874-1938). No. 778, Roberto J. Payro (1867-1928).

774 A341 8p brown .35 .20

775 A341 8p brown .35 .20

776 A341 8p brown .35 .20

777 A341 8p brown .35 .20

778 A341 8p brown .35 .20

Nos. 774-778 (5) 1.75 1.00

Issued to honor Argentine writers. Printed se-tenant in sheets of 100 (10x10); 2 horizontal rows of each design with Guiraldes in top rows and Rojas in bottom rows.

Hipolito Yrigoyen A342

1965, July 3 Litho.

779 A342 8p pink & black .20 .20

Hipolito Yrigoyen (1852-1933), president of Argentina 1916-22, 1928-30.

Children Looking Through Window A343

1965, July 24 **Photo.**
780 A343 8p salmon & blk .25 .20

International Seminar on Mental Health.

Child's Funerary Urn and 16th Century Map A344

1965, Aug. 7 **Litho.**
781 A344 8p lt grn, dk red, brn & ocher .30 .20

City of San Miguel de Tucuman, 400th anniv.

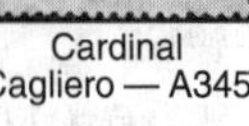

Cardinal Cagliero — A345

Dante Alighieri — A346

1965, Aug. 21 **Photo.**
782 A345 8p violet .20 .20

Juan Cardinal Cagliero (1839-1926), missionary to Argentina and Bishop of Magida.

1965, Sept. 16 **Wmk. 90** ***Perf. 13½***
783 A346 8p light ultra .30 .20

Dante Alighieri (1265-1321), Italian poet.

Clipper "Mimosa" and Map of Patagonia A347

1965, Sept. 25 **Litho.**
784 A347 8p red & black .30 .20

Centenary of Welsh colonization of Chubut, and the founding of the city of Rawson.

Map of Buenos Aires, Cock and Compass Emblem of Federal Police A348

1965, Oct. 30 **Photo.** ***Perf. 13½***
785 A348 8p carmine rose .30 .20

Issued for Federal Police Day.

Child's Drawing of Children A349

1965, Nov. 6 **Litho.** **Wmk. 90**
786 A349 8p lt yel grn & blk .30 .20

Public education law, 81st anniversary.

Church of St. Francis, Catamarca A350

Ruben Dario A351

1965, Dec. 8
787 A350 8p org yel & red brn .20 .20

Brother Mamerto de la Asuncion Esquiu, preacher, teacher and official of 1885 Provincial Constitutional Convention.

Litho. and Photo.

1965, Dec. 22 ***Perf. 13½***
788 A351 15p bl vio, *gray* .20 .20

Ruben Dario (pen name of Felix Ruben Garcia Sarmiento, 1867-1916), Nicaraguan poet, newspaper correspondent and diplomat.

"The Orange Seller" A352

Pueyrredon Paintings: No. 790, "Stop at the Grocery Store." No. 791, "Landscape at San Fernando" (sailboats). No. 792, "Bathing Horses at River Plata."

1966, Jan. 29 **Photo.** ***Perf. 13½***
789 A352 8p bluish green .70 .40
790 A352 8p bluish green .70 .40
791 A352 8p bluish green .70 .40
792 A352 8p bluish green .70 .40
a. Block of 4, #789-792 + 2 labels 2.80 1.60

Prilidiano Pueyrredon (1823-1870), painter.

Sun Yat-sen, Flags of Argentina and China — A353

1966, Mar. 12 **Wmk. 90** ***Perf. 13½***
793 A353 8p dk red brown .70 .25

Dr. Sun Yat-sen (1866-1925), founder of the Republic of China.

Souvenir Sheet

Rivadavia Issue of 1864 — A354

Wmk. 90

1966, Apr. 20 **Litho.** ***Imperf.***
794 A354 Sheet of 3 .95 .95
a. 4p gray & red brown .20 .20
b. 5p gray & green .20 .20
c. 8p gray & dark blue .20 .20

2nd Rio de la Plata Stamp Show, Buenos Aires, Mar. 16-24.

People of Various Races and WHO Emblem A355

1966, Apr. 23 ***Perf. 13½***
795 A355 8p brown & black .30 .20

Opening of the WHO Headquarters, Geneva.

Soldier Type of 1965

Army Day: 8p, Cavalryman, Guemes Infernal Regiment.

1966, May 28 **Litho.**
796 A340a 8p multicolored .55 .30

Coat of Arms — A356

Arms: a, National. b, Buenos Aires. c, La Rioja. d, Catamarca. e, Cordoba. f, Corrientes. g, Chaco. h, Chubut. i, Entre Rios. j, Formosa. k, Jujuy. l, La Pampa. m, Federal Capital. n, Mendoza. o, Misiones. p, Neuquen. q, Salta. r, San Juan. s, San Luis. t, Santa Cruz. u, Santa Fe. v, Santiago del Estero. w, Tucuman. x, map of Rio Negro. y, Map of Tierra del Fuego, Antarctica, South Atlantic Islands.

1966, July 30 **Wmk. 90** ***Perf. 13½***
797 Sheet of 25 40.00
a.-y. A356 10p black & multi 1.00 .65

150th anniv. of Argentina's Declaration of Independence.

Three Crosses, Caritas Emblem A357

1966, Sept. 10 **Litho.** ***Perf. 13½***
798 A357 10p ol grn, blk & lt bl .25 .20

Caritas, charity organization.

Hilario Ascasubi (1807-75) — A358

Portraits: #800, Estanislao del Campo (1834-80). #801, Miguel Cane (1851-1905). #802, Lucio V. Lopez (1848-94). #803, Rafael Obligado (1851-1920). #804, Luis Agote (1868-1954), M.D. #805, Juan B. Ambrosetti (1865-1917), naturalist and archaeologist. #806, Miguel Lillo (1862-1931), botanist and chemist. #807, Francisco P. Moreno (1852-1919), naturalist and paleontologist. #808, Francisco J. Muñiz (1795-1871), physician.

1966 **Photo.** **Wmk. 90**
799 A358 10p dk blue green .40 .35
800 A358 10p dk blue green .40 .35
801 A358 10p dk blue green .40 .35
802 A358 10p dk blue green .40 .35
803 A358 10p dk blue green .40 .35
804 A358 10p deep violet .40 .35
805 A358 10p deep violet .40 .35
806 A358 10p deep violet .40 .35
807 A358 10p deep violet .40 .35
808 A358 10p deep violet .40 .35
Nos. 799-808 (10) 4.00 3.50

Nos. 799-803 issued Sept. 17 to honor Argentine writers. Printed se-tenant in sheets of 100 (10x10); 2 horizontal rows of each portrait. Nos. 804-808 issued Oct. 22 to honor Argentine scientists; 2 horizontal rows of each portrait. Scientists set has value at upper left, frame line with rounded corners.

Anchor A359

1966, Oct. 8 **Litho.**
809 A359 4p multicolored .25 .20

Argentine merchant marine.

Flags and Map of the Americas A360

1966, Oct. 29 ***Perf. 13½***
810 A360 10p gray & multi .25 .20

7th Conference of American Armies.

Argentine National Bank — A361

1966, Nov. 5 **Photo.**
811 A361 10p brt blue green .20 .20

75th anniv. of the Argentine National Bank.

La Salle Monument and College, Buenos Aires — A362

1966, Nov. 26 **Litho.** ***Perf. 13½***
812 A362 10p brown org & blk .20 .20

75th anniv. of the Colegio de la Salle, Buenos Aires, and to honor Saint Jean Baptiste de la Salle (1651-1719), educator.

Map of Argentine Antarctica and Expedition Route — A363

1966, Dec. 10 **Wmk. 90**
813 A363 10p multicolored .70 .45

1965 Argentine Antarctic expedition, which planted the Argentine flag on the South Pole. See No. 851.

Juan Martin de Pueyrredon — A364

1966, Dec. 17 Photo. *Perf. 13½*

814 A364 10p dull red brn .20 .20

Issued to honor Juan Martin de Pueyrredon (1777-1850), Governor of Cordoba and of the United Provinces of the River Plata.

Gen. Juan de Las Heras — A365

1966, Dec. 17 Engr.

815 A365 10p black .20 .20

Issued to honor Gen. Juan Gregorio de Las Heras (1780-1866), Peruvian field marshal and aide-de-camp to San Martin.

Inscribed "Republica Argentina" Types of 1955-61 and

Jose Hernandez — A366

Designs: 50p, Gen. Jose de San Martin. 90p, Guillermo Brown. 500p, Red deer in forest.

Two overall paper sizes for 6p, 50p (No. 827) and 90p:
I - 27x37½mm
II - 27x39mm

Perf. 13½

1965-68 Wmk. 90 Photo.

817 A366 6p rose red, litho, I ('67) 1.25 .20
818 A366 6p rose red ('67), II 2.25 .20
819 A366 6p brn, 15x22mm ('68) .20 .20
823 A238a 43p dk car rose 6.25 .20
824 A238a 45p brn ('66) 4.25 .20
825 A238a 45p brn, litho ('67) 7.00 .20
826 A241 50p dk bl, 29x40mm 7.00 .20
827 A241 50p dk bl, 22x31½mm, I ('67) 4.75 .20
 a. Paper II 2.75 .20
828 A366 90p ol bis, I ('67) 3.00 .20
 a. Paper II 12.00 .20

Trout Leaping in National Park — A366a

Engr.

829 A495 500p yellow grn ('66) 1.50 .50
829A A366a 1,000p vio bl ('68) 6.00 2.00
 Nos. 817-829A (11) 43.45 4.30

The 500p and 1,000p remained on sale as 5p and 10p stamps after the 1970 currency exchange.

See Nos. 888, 891, 939, 941, 992, 1031, 1040, 1045-1047. For surcharge and overprints see Nos. 1077, O153-O158, O162.

Pre-Columbian Pottery — A367

1967, Feb. 18 Litho. *Perf. 13½*

830 A367 10p multicolored .30 .20

20th anniv. of UNESCO.

"The Meal" by Fernando Fader — A368

1967, Feb. 25 Photo. Wmk. 90

831 A368 10p red brown .30 .20

Issued in memory of the Argentine painter Fernando Fader (1882-1935).

Col. Juana Azurduy de Padilla (1781-1862), Soldier — A369

Famous Argentine Women: #833, Juana Manuela Gorriti, writer. #834, Cecilia Grierson (1858-1934), physician. #835, Juana Paula Manso (1819-75), writer and educator. #836, Alfonsina Storni (1892-1938), writer and educator.

1967, May 13 Photo. *Perf. 13½*

832 A369 6p dark brown .30 .20
833 A369 6p dark brown .30 .20
834 A369 6p dark brown .30 .20
835 A369 6p dark brown .30 .20
836 A369 6p dark brown .30 .20
 Nos. 832-836 (5) 1.50 1.00

Printed se-tenant in sheets of 100 (10x10); 2 horizontal rows of each portrait.

Schooner "Invencible," 1811 — A370

1967, May 20 Litho.

837 A370 20p multicolored .85 .35

Issued for Navy Day.

Soldier Type of 1965

Army Day: 20p, Highlander (Arribeños Corps).

1967, May 27

838 A340a 20p multicolored .70 .30

Souvenir Sheet

Manuel Belgrano and José Artigas — A371

1967, June 22 *Imperf.*

839 A371 Sheet of 2 .40 .40
 a. 6p gray & brown .20 .20
 b. 22p brown & gray .25 .25

Third Rio de la Plata Stamp Show, Montevideo, Uruguay, June 18-25.

Peace Dove and Valise — A372

PADELAI Emblem — A373

1967, Aug. 5 Litho. *Perf. 13½*

840 A372 20p multicolored .25 .20

Issued for International Tourist Year 1967.

1967, Aug. 12 Litho.

841 A373 20p multicolored .25 .20

75th anniv. of the Children's Welfare Association (Patronato de la Infancia-PADELAI).

Stagecoach and Modern City — A374

1967, Sept. 23 Wmk. 90 *Perf. 13½*

842 A374 20p rose, yel & blk .25 .20

Centenary of Villa Maria, Cordoba.

San Martin by Ibarra — A375

"Battle of Chacabuco" by P. Subercaseaux — A376

1967, Sept. 30 Litho.

843 A375 20p blk brn & pale yel .55 .20

Engr.

844 A376 40p blue black .85 .20

Battle of Chacabuco, 150th anniversary.

Exhibition Rooms — A377

1967, Oct. 11 Photo.

845 A377 20p blue gray .20 .20

Government House Museum, 10th anniv.

Pedro L. Zanni, Fokker and 1924 Flight Route A378

1967, Oct. 21 Litho. *Perf. 13½*

846 A378 20p multicolored .30 .20

Issued for Aviation Week and to commemorate the 1924 flight of the Fokker seaplane "Province of Buenos Aires" from Amsterdam, Netherlands, to Osaka, Japan.

Training Ship General Brown, by Emilio Biggeri A379

1967, Oct. 28 Wmk. 90

847 A379 20p multicolored .85 .35

Issued to honor the Military Naval School.

Ovidio Lagos and Front Page — A380

1967, Nov. 11 Photo.

848 A380 20p sepia .20 .20

Centenary of La Capital, Rosario newspaper.

St. Barbara A381

1967, Dec. 2 *Perf. 13½*

849 A381 20p rose red .30 .20

St. Barbara, patron saint of artillerymen.

Portrait of his Wife, by Eduardo Sivori — A382

1968, Jan. 27 Photo. *Perf. 13½*
850 A382 20p blue green .30 .20

Eduardo Sivori (1847-1918), painter.

Antarctic Type of 1966 and

Admiral Brown Scientific Station A383

Planes over Map of Antarctica — A384

6p, Map showing radio-postal stations 1966-67.

1968, Feb. 17 Litho. Wmk. 90
851 A363 6p multicolored .40 .20
852 A383 20p multicolored .60 .25
853 A384 40p multicolored 1.00 .30
Nos. 851-853 (3) 2.00 .75

Issued to publicize Argentine research projects in Argentine Antarctica.

The Annunciation, by Leonardo da Vinci — A385

Children and WHO Emblem — A387

Man in Wheelchair and Factory — A386

1968, Mar. 23 Photo. *Perf. 13½*
854 A385 20p lilac rose .20 .20

Issued for the Day of the Army Communications System and its patron saint, Gabriel.

1968, Mar. 23 Litho.
855 A386 20p green & black .20 .20

Day of Rehabilitation of the Handicapped.

1968, May 11 Wmk. 90 *Perf. 13½*
856 A387 20p dk vio bl & ver .20 .20

20th anniv. of WHO.

Soldier Type of 1965

Army Day: 20p, Uniform of First Artillery Regiment "General Iriarte."

1968, June 8 Litho.
857 A340a 20p multicolored .75 .25

Frigate "Libertad," Painting by Emilio Biggeri — A388

1968, June 15 Wmk. 90
858 A388 20p multicolored .75 .25

Issued for Navy Day.

Guillermo Rawson and Old Hospital A389

1968, July 20 Photo. *Perf. 13½*
859 A389 6p olive bister .20 .20

Cent. of Rawson Hospital, Buenos Aires.

Student Directing Traffic for Schoolmates A390

1968, Aug. 10 Litho. *Perf. 13½*
860 A390 20p lt bl, blk, buff & car .20 .20

Traffic safety and education.

O'Higgins Joining San Martin at Battle of Maipu, by P. Subercaseaux — A391

1968, Aug. 15 Engr.
861 A391 40p bluish black .65 .30

Sesquicentennial of the Battle of Maipu.

Osvaldo Magnasco (1864-1920), Lawyer, Professor of Law and Minister of Justice — A392

1968, Sept. 7 Photo. *Perf. 13½*
862 A392 20p brown .25 .20

Grandmother's Birthday, by Patricia Lynch — A393

The Sea, by Edgardo Gomez — A394

1968, Sept. 21 Litho.
863 A393 20p multicolored .25 .20
864 A394 20p multicolored .25 .20

The designs were chosen in a competition among kindergarten and elementary school children.

Mar del Plata at Night A395

1968, Oct. 19 Litho. *Perf. 13½*
865 A395 20p black, ocher & bl .25 .20
Nos. 865,C113-C114 (3) 1.30 .70

4th Plenary Assembly of the Intl. Telegraph and Telephone Consultative Committee, Mar del Plata, Sept. 23-Oct. 25.

Frontier Gendarme A396

Patrol Boat A397

1968, Oct. 26
866 A396 20p multicolored .30 .20
867 A397 20p blue, vio bl & blk .30 .20

No. 866 honors the Gendarmery; No. 867 the Coast Guard.

Aaron de Anchorena and Pampero Balloon A398

1968, Nov. 2 Photo.
868 A398 20p blue & multi .30 .20

22nd Aeronautics and Space Week.

St. Martin of Tours, by Alfredo Guido — A399

1968, Nov. 9 Litho.
869 A399 20p lilac & dk brn .20 .20

St. Martin of Tours, patron saint of Buenos Aires.

Municipal Bank Emblem A400

1968, Nov. 16
870 A400 20p multicolored .20 .20

Buenos Aires Municipal Bank, 90th anniv.

Anniversary Emblem A401

1968, Dec. 14 Wmk. 90 *Perf. 13½*
871 A401 20p car rose & dk grn .20 .20

ALPI (Fight Against Polio Assoc.), 25th anniv.

Shovel and State Coal Fields Emblem — A402

Pouring Ladle and Army Manufacturing Emblem — A403

1968, Dec. 21 Litho.
872 A402 20p orange, bl & blk .25 .20
873 A403 20p dl vio, dl yel & blk .25 .20

Issued to publicize the National Coal and Steel industry at the Rio Turbio coal fields and the Zapla blast furnaces.

Woman Potter, by Ramon Gomez Cornet — A404

1968, Dec. 21 Photo. *Perf. 13½*
874 A404 20p carmine rose .50 .40

Centenary of the Witcomb Gallery.

View of Buenos Aires and Rio de la Plata by Ulrico Schmidl A405

1969, Feb. 8 Litho. Wmk. 90
875 A405 20p yellow, blk & ver .50 .35

Ulrico Schmidl (c. 1462-1554) who wrote "Journey to the Rio de la Plata and Paraguay."

Types of 1955-67

Designs: 50c, Puma. 1p, Sunflower. 3p, Zapata Slope, Catamarca. 5p, Tierra del Fuego. 6p, José Hernandez. 10p, Inca Bridge, Mendoza. 50p, José de San Martin. 90p, Guillermo Brown. 100p, Ski jumper.

Photo.; Litho. (50c, 3p, 10p)
1969-70 Wmk. 365 *Perf. 13½*
882 A275 50c bister ('70) .70 .20
883 A277 5p brown 1.25 .20
884 A279 100p blue 26.00 1.40

Unwmk.

885 A278 1p brown ('70) .65 .20
886 A277 3p dk blue ('70) .65 .20
a. Wmk. 90 5.25 .35
887 A277 5p brown ('70) .75 .20
888 A366 6p red brn, 15x22mm ('70) 1.25 .20
889 A278 10p dull red ('70) .50 .20
a. Wmk. 90 475.00 47.50
890 A241 50p dk bl, 22x31½mm ('70) 1.75 .20
891 A366 90p ol brn, 22x32mm ('70) 3.50 .20
892 A279 100p blue ('70) 9.00 .30
Nos. 882-892 (11) 46.00 3.50

For surcharges see Nos. 1076-1077.

Soldier Type of 1965

Army Day: 20p, Sapper (gastador) of Buenos Aires Province, 1856.

Wmk. 365

1969, May 31 Litho. ***Perf. 13½***
893 A340a 20p multicolored .85 .35

Frigate Hercules, by Emilio Biggeri — A406

1969, May 31
894 A406 20p multicolored 1.00 .30

Issued for Navy Day.

"All Men are Equal" — A407

ILO Emblem — A408

1969, June 28 Wmk. 90
895 A407 20p black & ocher .20 .20

International Human Rights Year.

1969, June 28 Litho. Wmk. 365
896 A408 20p lt green & multi .20 .20

50th anniv. of the ILO.

Pedro N. Arata (1849-1922), Chemist — A409

Radar Antenna, Balcarce Station and Satellite — A410

Portraits: No. 898, Miguel Fernandez (1883-1950), zoologist. No. 899, Angel P. Gallardo (1867-1934), biologist. No. 900, Cristobal M. Hicken (1875-1933), botanist. No. 901, Eduardo Ladislao Holmberg, M.D. (1852-1937), natural scientist.

1969, Aug. 9 Wmk. 365 ***Perf. 13½***
897 A409 6p Arata .40 .20
898 A409 6p Fernandez .40 .20
899 A409 6p Gallardo .40 .20

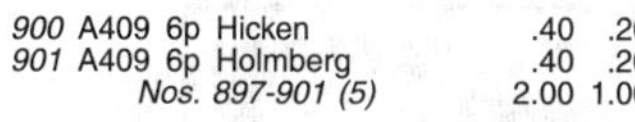

900 A409 6p Hicken .40 .20
901 A409 6p Holmberg .40 .20
Nos. 897-901 (5) 2.00 1.00

Argentine scientists. See No. 778 note.

1969, Aug. 23 Wmk. 99
902 A410 20p yellow & blk .30 .20

Communications by satellite through Intl. Telecommunications Satellite Consortium (INTELSAT). See No. C115.

Nieuport 28, Flight Route and Map of Buenos Aires Province A411

1969, Sept. 13 Litho. Wmk. 90
903 A411 20p multicolored .30 .20

50th anniv. of the first Argentine airmail service from El Palomar to Mar del Plata, flown Feb. 23-24, 1919, by Capt. Pedro L. Zanni.

Military College Gate and Emblem A412

1969, Oct. 4 Wmk. 365 ***Perf. 13½***
904 A412 20p multicolored .30 .20

Cent. of the National Military College, El Palomar (Greater Buenos Aires).

Gen. Angel Pacheco — A413

1969, Nov. 8 Photo. Wmk. 365
905 A413 20p deep green .25 .20

Gen. Angel Pacheco (1795-1869).

La Farola, Logotype of La Prensa — A414

1969, Nov. 8 Litho. ***Perf. 13½***

#907, Bartolomé Mitre & La Nacion logotype.

906 A414 20p orange, yel & blk .70 .25
907 A414 20p brt green & blk .70 .25

Cent. of newspapers La Prensa and La Nacion.

Julian Aguirre — A415

Musicians: No. 909, Felipe Boero. No. 910, Constantino Gaito. No. 911, Carlos Lopez Buchardo. No. 912, Alberto Williams.

Wmk. 365

1969, Dec. 6 Photo. ***Perf. 13½***
908 A415 6p Aguirre .55 .30
909 A415 6p Boero .55 .30
910 A415 6p Gaito .55 .30
911 A415 6p Buchardo .55 .30
912 A415 6p Williams .55 .30
Nos. 908-912 (5) 2.75 1.50

Argentine musicians. See No. 778 note.

Lt. Benjamin Matienzo and Nieuport Plane — A416

1969, Dec. 13 Litho.
913 A416 20p multicolored .55 .35

23rd Aeronautics and Space Week.

High Power Lines and Map A417

Design: 20p, Map of Santa Fe Province and schematic view of tunnel.

1969, Dec. 13
914 A417 6p multicolored .50 .20
915 A417 20p multicolored 1.00 .20

Completion of development projects: 6p for the hydroelectric dams on the Limay and Neuquen Rivers, the 20p the tunnel under Rio Grande from Sante Fe to Parana.

Lions Emblem A418

1969, Dec. 20 Wmk. 365 ***Perf. 13½***
916 A418 20p black, emer & org .60 .25

Argentine Lions Intl. Club, 50th anniv.

Madonna and Child, by Raul Soldi — A419

1969, Dec. 27 Litho.
917 A419 20p multicolored .70 .30

Christmas 1969.

Manuel Belgrano, by Jean Gericault A420

The Creation of the Flag, Bas-relief by Jose Fioravanti — A421

Perf. 13½

1970, July 4 Unwmk. Photo.
918 A420 20c deep brown .35 .20

Litho. ***Perf. 12½***
919 A421 50c bister, blk & bl .85 .50

Gen. Manuel Belgrano (1770-1820), Argentine patriot.

San Jose Palace A422

1970, Aug. 9 Litho. ***Perf. 13½***
920 A422 20c yellow grn & multi .25 .20

Gen. Justo Jose de Urquiza (1801-70), pres. of Argentina, 1854-60.

Schooner "Juliet" — A423

1970, Aug. 8 Unwmk.
921 A423 20c multicolored 1.00 .40

Issued for Navy Day.

Receiver of 1920 and Waves A424

1970, Aug. 29
922 A424 20c lt blue & multi .30 .20

50th anniv. of Argentine broadcasting.

Types of 1955-67 Inscribed "Republica Argentina" and Types A425, A426

Belgrano A425

Lujan Basilica A426

Designs: 1c, Sunflower. 3c, Zapata Slope, Catamarca. 5c, Tierra del Fuego. 8c, No. 931, Belgrano. 10c, Inca Bridge, Mendoza. 25c, 50c, 70c, Jose de San Martin. 65c, 90c, 1.20p, San Martin. 1p, Ski jumper. 1.15p, 1.80p, Adm. Brown.

1970-73 Photo. Unwmk. *Perf. 13½*

923 A278 1c dk green ('71) .20 .20
924 A277 3c car rose ('71) .20 .20
925 A277 5c blue ('71) .20 .20
926 A425 6c deep blue .20 .20
927 A425 8c green ('72) .20 .20
928 A278 10c dull red ('71) .40 .20
929 A278 10c brn, litho. ('71) .50 .20
930 A278 10c org brn ('72) .45 .20
931 A425 10c brown ('73) .20 .20
932 A426 18c yel & dk brn, litho ('73) .20 .20
933 A425 25c brown ('71) .30 .20
934 A425 50c scarlet ('72) 1.25 .20
935 A241 65c brn, 22x31½mm, paper II ('71) .65 .20
936 A425 70c dk blue ('73) .30 .20
937 A241 90c emer, 22x31½mm ('72) 3.25 .20
938 A279 1p brn, 22½x29½mm ('71) 1.90 .20
939 A366 1.15p dk bl, 22½x32mm ('71) 1.10 .20
940 A241 1.20p org, 22x31½mm ('73) 1.10 .20
941 A366 1.80p brown ('73) 1.10 .20
Nos. 923-941 (19) 13.70 3.80

The imprint "Casa de Moneda de la Nacion" (in capitals) appears on 3c, 5c, Nos. 928-929; 65c, 90c, 1p, 1.20p.

On type A425 only the 6c is inscribed "Ley 18.188" below denomination.

Fluorescent paper was used in printing the 25c, 50c, and 70c. The 3c, 5c, 8c, No. 931 and 65c were issued on both ordinary and fluorescent paper.

See Nos. 987-996, 1032-1038, 1042-1043, 1089-1107. For overprint and surcharge see Nos. 1010, 1078.

Soldier Type of 1965

Galloping messenger of Field Army, 1879.

1970, Oct. 17 Litho. *Perf. 13½*

944 A340a 20c multicolored .80 .25

Dome of Cathedral of Cordoba A430

1970, Nov. 7 Unwmk.

945 A430 50c gray & blk .80 .20

Bishopric of Tucuman, 400th anniv. See #C131.

People Around UN Emblem A431

1970, Nov. 7

946 A431 20c tan & multi .20 .20

25th anniversary of the United Nations.

State Mint and Medal A432

1970, Nov. 28 Unwmk. *Perf. 13½*

947 A432 20c gold, grn & blk .20 .20

Inauguration of the State Mint Building, 25th anniversary.

St. John Bosco and Dean Funes College A433

1970, Dec. 19 Litho.

948 A433 20c olive & blk .20 .20

Honoring the work of the Salesian Order in Patagonia.

Nativity, by Horacio Gramajo Gutierrez — A434

1970, Dec. 19

949 A434 20c multicolored .55 .35

Christmas 1970.

Argentine Flag, Map of Argentine Antarctica A435

1971, Feb. 20 Litho. *Perf. 13½*

950 A435 20c multicolored 1.25 .50

Argentine South Pole Expedition, 5th anniv.

Phosphorescent Sorting Code and Albert Einstein — A436

1971, Apr. 30 Unwmk. *Perf. 13½*

951 A436 25c multicolored .50 .30

Electronics in postal development.

Symbolic Road Crossing A437

1971, May 29 Litho.

952 A437 25c blue & blk .25 .20

Inter-American Regional Meeting of the Intl. Federation of Roads, Buenos Aires, 3/28-31.

Elias Alippi — A438

Actors: No. 954, Juan Aurelio Casacuberta. No. 955, Angelina Pagano. No. 956, Roberto Casaux. No. 957, Florencio Parravicini. See No. 778 note.

1971, May 29 Litho.

953 A438 15c Alippi .35 .20
954 A438 15c Casacuberta .35 .20
955 A438 15c Pagano .35 .20
956 A438 15c Casaux .35 .20
957 A438 15c Parravicini .35 .20
Nos. 953-957 (5) 1.75 1.00

Soldier Type of 1965

Army Day, May 29: Artilleryman, 1826.

1971, July 3 Unwmk. *Perf. 13½*

958 A340a 25c multicolored 1.25 .50

Bilander "Carmen," by Emilio Biggeri — A439

1971, July 3

959 A439 25c multicolored 1.25 .25

Navy Day

Peruvian Order of the Sun A440

1971, Aug. 28

960 A440 31c multicolored .30 .20

Sesquicentennial of Peru's independence.

Güemes in Battle, by Lorenzo Gigli A441

#962, Death of Güemes, by Antonio Alice.

1971, Aug. 28

Size: 39x29mm

961 A441 25c multicolored .50 .30

Size: 84x29mm

962 A441 25c multicolored .50 .30

Sesquicentennial of the death of Martin Miguel de Güemes, leader in Gaucho War, Governor and Captain General of Salta Province.

Stylized Tulip — A442

1971, Sept. 18

963 A442 25c tan & multi .25 .20

3rd Intl. and 8th Natl. Horticultural Exhib.

Father Antonio Saenz, by Juan Gut — A443

1971, Sept. 18

964 A433 25c gray & multi .25 .20

Sesquicentennial of University of Buenos Aires, and to honor Father Antonio Saenz, first Chancellor and Rector.

Fabricaciones Militares Emblem — A444

1971, Oct. 16 Unwmk. *Perf. 13½*

965 A444 25c brn, gold, bl & blk .25 .20

30th anniv. of military armament works.

Cars and Trucks A445

Design: 65c, Tree converted into paper.

1971, Oct. 16

966 A445 25c dull bl & multi .50 .20
967 A445 65c green & multi 1.25 .50
Nos. 966-967,C134 (3) 2.35 .95

Nationalized industries.

Luis C. Candelaria and his Plane, 1918 — A446

1971, Nov. 27

968 A446 25c multicolored .25 .20

25th Aeronautics and Space Week.

Observatory and Nebula of Magellan — A447

1971, Nov. 27

969 A447 25c multicolored .25 .20

Cordoba Astronomical Observatory, cent.

Christ in Majesty A448

1971, Dec. 18 **Litho.**

970 A448 25c blk & multi .25 .20

Christmas 1971. Design is from a tapestry by Horacio Butler in Basilica of St. Francis, Buenos Aires.

Mother and Child, by J. C. Castagnino A449

1972, May 6 **Unwmk.** ***Perf. 13½***

971 A449 25c fawn & black .25 .20

25th anniv. (in 1971) of UNICEF.

Mailman's Bag — A450

1972, Sept. 2 **Litho.** ***Perf. 13½***

972 A450 25c lemon & multi .20 .20

Bicentenary of appointment of first Argentine mailman.

Adm. Brown Station, Map of Antarctica — A451

1972, Sept. 2

973 A451 25c blue & multi .70 .35

10th anniv. (in 1971) of Antarctic Treaty.

Soldier Type of 1965

Army Day: 25c, Sergeant, Negro and Mulatto Corps, 1806-1807.

1972, Sept. 23

974 A340a 25c multicolored .75 .35

Brigantine "Santisima Trinidad" — A452

1972, Sept. 23

975 A452 25c multicolored .75 .35

Navy Day. See No. 1006.

A453

1972, Sept. 30 **Litho.** ***Perf. 13½***

976 A453 45c Oil pump .90 .20

50th anniv. of the organ. of the state oil fields (Yacimientos Petroliferos Fiscales).

A454

1972, Sept. 30

977 A454 25c Sounding balloon .25 .20

Cent. of Natl. Meteorological Service.

Trees and Globe — A455

1972, Oct. 14 ***Perf. 13x13½***

978 A455 25c bl, blk & lt bl .70 .20

7th World Forestry Congress, Buenos Aires, Oct. 4-18.

Arms of Naval School, Frigate "Presidente Sarmiento" — A456

1972, Oct. 14

979 A456 25c gold & multi .65 .35

Centenary of Military Naval School.

Early Balloon and Plane, Antonio de Marchi — A457

1972, Nov. 4 ***Perf. 13½***

980 A457 25c multicolored .50 .30

Aeronautics and Space Week, and in honor of Baron Antonio de Marchi (1875-1934), aviation pioneer.

Bartolomé Mitre — A458

1972, Nov. 4 **Engr.**

981 A458 25c dark blue .50 .30

Pres. Bartolome Mitre (1821-1906), writer, historian, soldier.

Flower and Heart — A459

1972, Dec. 2 **Litho.** ***Perf. 13½***

982 A459 90c lt bl, ultra & blk .60 .35

"Your heart is your health," World Health Day.

"Martin Fierro," by Juan C. Castignano A460

"Spirit of the Gaucho," by Vicente Forte — A461

1972, Dec. 2 **Litho.** ***Perf. 13½***

983 A460 50c multicolored .30 .20
984 A461 90c multicolored .65 .35

Intl. Book Year 1972, and cent. of publication of the poem, Martin Fierro, by Jose Hernandez (1834-86).

Iguacu Falls and Tourist Year Emblem — A462

1972, Dec. 16 ***Perf. 13x13½***

985 A462 45c multicolored .30 .20

Tourism Year of the Americas.

King, Wood Carving, 18th Century A463

1972, Dec. 16 ***Perf. 13½***

986 A463 50c multicolored .50 .25

Christmas 1972.

Types of 1955-73 Inscribed "Republica Argentina" and

Moon Valley, San Juan Province A463a

Designs: 1c, Sunflower. 5c, Tierra del Fuego. 10c, Inca Bridge, Mendoza. 50c, Lujan Basilica. 65c, 22.50p, San Martin. 1p, Ski jumper. 1.15p, 4.50p, Guillermo Brown. 1.80p, Manuel Belgrano.

Litho.; Photo. (1c, 65c, 1p)
Perf. 13½, 12½ (1.80p)

1972-75 **Wmk. 365**

987	A278	1c	dk green	.20	.20
988	A277	5c	dark blue	.20	.20
989	A278	10c	bister brn	.20	.20
989A	A426	50c	dull pur ('75)	.20	.20
990	A241	65c	gray brown	3.25	.20
991	A279	1p	brown	1.40	.20
992	A366	1.15p	dk gray bl	1.40	.20
993	A425	1.80p	blue ('75)	.20	.20
994	A366	4.50p	green ('75)	.65	.20
995	A241	22.50p	vio bl ('75)	1.40	.20
996	A463a	50p	multi ('75)	2.75	.30
			Nos. 987-996 (11)	11.85	2.30

Paper size of 1c is 27½x39mm; others of 1972, 37x27, 27x37mm.
Size of 22.50p, 50p: 26½x38½mm.
See Nos. 1050, 1108.

Cock (Symbolic of Police) — A464

1973, Feb. 3 Litho. Unwmk.
997 A464 50c lt green & multi .30 .20

Sesqui. of Federal Police of Argentina.

First Coin of Bank of Buenos Aires — A465

1973, Feb. 3 *Perf. 13½*
998 A465 50c purple, yel & brn .20 .20

Sesquicentennial of the Bank of Buenos Aires Province.

DC-3 Planes Over Antarctica — A466

1973, Apr. 28 Litho. *Perf. 13½*
999 A466 50c lt blue & multi 1.50 .60

10th anniversary of Argentina's first flight to the South Pole.

Rivadavia's Chair, Argentine Arms and Colors — A467

1973, May 19 Litho. *Perf. 13½*
1000 A467 50c multicolored .25 .20

Inauguration of Pres. Hector J. Campora, May 25, 1973.

San Martin, by Gil de Castro — A468

San Martin and Bolivar A469

1973, July 7 Litho. *Perf. 13½*
1001 A468 50c lt green & multi .35 .20
1002 A469 50c yellow & multi .35 .20

Gen. San Martin's farewell to the people of Peru and his meeting with Simon Bolivar at Guayaquil July 26-27, 1822.

Eva Peron A470

1973, July 26 Litho. *Perf. 13½*
1003 A470 70c black, org & bl .20 .20

Maria Eva Duarte de Peron (1919-1952), political leader.

House of Viceroy Sobremonte, by Hortensia de Virgilion — A471

1973, July 28 *Perf. 13x13½*
1004 A471 50c blue & multi .20 .20

400th anniversary of the city of Cordoba.

Woman, by Lino Spilimbergo A472

1973, Aug. 28 Litho. *Perf. 13½*
1005 A472 70c multicolored .70 .20

Philatelists' Day. See Nos. B60-B61.

Ship Type of 1972

Navy Day: 70c, Frigate "La Argentina."

1973, Oct. 27 Litho. *Perf. 13½*
1006 A452 70c multicolored .60 .35

New and Old Telephones — A473

1973, Oct. 27
1007 A473 70c brt blue & multi .40 .20

Natl. telecommunications system, 25th anniv.

Plume Made of Flags of Participants A474

1973, Nov. 3 *Perf. 13½*
1008 A474 70c yellow bis & multi .25 .20

12th Cong. of Latin Notaries, Buenos Aires.

No. 940 Overprinted

1973, Nov. 30 Photo.
1010 A241 1.20p orange .85 .20

Assumption of presidency by Juan Peron, Oct. 12.

Virgin and Child, Window, La Plata Cathedral A476

Christmas: 1.20p, Nativity, by Bruno Venier, b. 1914.

1973, Dec. 15 Litho. *Perf. 13½*
1011 A476 70c gray & multi .35 .20
1012 A476 1.20p black & multi .70 .35

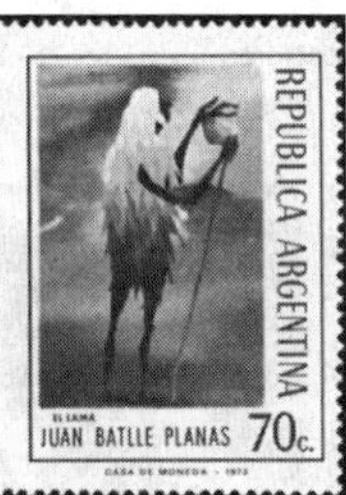
The Lama, by Juan Batlle Planas — A477

Paintings: 50c, Houses in Boca District, by Eugenio Daneri, horiz. 90c, The Blue Grotto, by Emilio Pettoruti, horiz.

1974, Feb. 9 Litho. *Perf. 13½*
1013 A477 50c multicolored .30 .20
1014 A477 70c multicolored .35 .20
1015 A477 90c multicolored .60 .30
Nos. 1013-1015,B64 (4) 1.55 .95

Argentine painters.

Mar del Plata A478

1974, Feb. 9
1016 A478 70c multicolored .30 .20

Centenary of Mar del Plata.

Weather Symbols — A479

1974, Mar. 23 Litho. *Perf. 13½*
1017 A479 1.20p multicolored .35 .20

Cent. of intl. meteorological cooperation.

Justo Santa Maria de Oro — A480

1974, Mar. 23
1018 A480 70c multicolored .20 .20

Bicentenary of the birth of Brother Justo Santa Maria de Oro (1772-1836), theologian, patriot, first Argentine bishop.

Belisario Roldan (1873-1922), Writer — A481

1974, June 29 Photo. Unwmk.
1019 A481 70c bl & brn .20 .20

Poster with Names of OAS Members — A482

1974, June 29 Litho.
1020 A482 1.38p multicolored .20 .20

Organization of American States, 25th anniv.

ENCOTEL Emblem — A483

1974, Aug. 10 Litho. *Perf. 13*
1021 A483 1.20p blue, gold & blk .40 .20

ENCOTEL, Natl. Post and Telegraph Press.

Flags of Argentina, Bolivia, Brazil, Paraguay, Uruguay A484

1974, Aug. 16 *Perf. 13½*
1022 A484 1.38p multicolored .25 .20

6th Meeting of Foreign Ministers of Rio de la Plata Basin Countries.

El Chocon Hydroelectric Complex, Limay River — A485

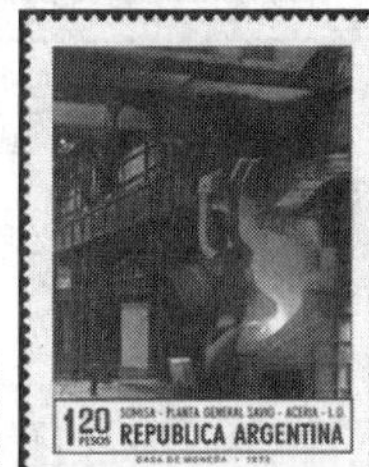

Somisa Steel Mill, San Nicolas A486

Gen. Belgrano Bridge, Chaco-Corrientes — A487

Perf. 13½, 13x13½ (4.50p)

1974, Sept. 14

1023	A485	70c	multicolored	.40	.20
1024	A486	1.20p	multicolored	.60	.30
1025	A487	4.50p	multicolored	2.00	.50
	Nos. 1023-1025 (3)			3.00	1.00

Development projects.

Brigantine Belgrano, by Emilio Biggeri — A488

1974, Oct. 26 Litho. *Perf. 13½*

1026 A488 1.20p multicolored .60 .30

Departure into exile in Chile of General San Martin, Sept. 22, 1822.

Alberto R. Mascias and Bleriot Plane — A489

1974, Oct. 26 Unwmk.

1027 A489 1.20p multicolored .50 .25
a. Wmk 365 — —

Air Force Day, Aug. 10, and to honor Alberto Roque Garcias (1878-1951), aviation pioneer.

Hussar, 1812, by Eleodoro Marenco A490

1974, Oct. 26

1028 A490 1.20p multicolored .50 .25

Army Day.

Post Horn and Flags A491

1974, Nov. 23 Unwmk. *Perf. 13½*

1029 A491 2.65p multicolored .85 .20
a. Wmk 365 — —

Centenary of Universal Postal Union.

Franciscan Monastery — A492

1974, Nov. 23 Litho.

1030 A492 1.20p multicolored .40 .20

400th anniversary, city of Santa Fe.

Trout Type of 1968

1974 Engr. Unwmk.

1031 A366a 1000p vio bl 3.25 .80

Due to a shortage of 10p stamps a quantity of this 1,000p was released for use as 10p.

Types of 1954-73 Inscribed "Republica Argentina" and

Red Deer in Forest — A495

Congress Building — A497

Designs: 30c, 60c, 1.80p, Manuel Belgrano. 50c, Lujan Basilica. 1.20p, 2p, 6p, San Martin (16x22½mm). 2.70p, 7.50p, 22.50p, San Martin (22x31½mm). 4.50p, 13.50p, Guillermo Brown. 10p, Leaping trout.

1974-76 Unwmk. Photo. *Perf. 13½*

1032	A425	30c	brown vio	.20	.20
1033	A426	50c	blk & brn red	.20	.20
1034	A426	50c	bister & bl	.20	.20
1035	A425	60c	ocher	.20	.20
1036	A425	1.20p	red	.30	.20
1037	A425	1.80p	deep blue	.20	.20
1038	A425	2p	dark purple	.20	.20
1039	A241	2.70p	dk bl, 22x31½mm	.25	.20
1040	A366	4.50p	green	.85	.20
1041	A495	5p	yel green	.40	.20
1042	A425	6p	red orange	.20	.20
1043	A425	6p	emerald	.20	.20
1044	A241	7.50p	grn, 22x31½mm	.85	.20
1045	A366a	10p	violet blue	1.00	.20
1046	A366	13.50p	scar, 16x22½mm	.85	.20
1047	A366	13.50p	scar, 22x31½mm	.85	.20
1048	A241	22.50p	dp bl, 22x31½mm	.75	.20
1049	A497	30p	yel & dk red brn	1.10	.20
1050	A463a	50p	multicolored	1.50	.20
	Nos. 1032-1050 (19)			10.30	3.80

Issued: 10p, 5/74; 30c, 1.20p, 2.70p, 5/15/74; 5p, 11/20/74; 30p, 12/10/74; 2p, 3/1/75; 60c, 7.50p, 4/30/75; 4.50p, 7/21/75; 1.80p, #1042, 1047, 22.50p, 8/14/75; #1046, 10/10/75; #1034, 10/30/75; #1043, 11/6/75; 50p, 2/76.

Fluorescent paper was used in printing No. 1036, 2p, Nos. 1044 and 1047. The 30p was issued on both ordinary and fluorescent paper.

See No. 829. For type of A495 overprinted see No. 1144.

Miniature Sheet

A498

1974, Dec. 7 Litho. *Perf. 13½*

1052	A498	Sheet of 6	3.50	2.75
a.	1p	Mariano Necochea	.25	.20
b.	1.20p	Jose de San Martin	.25	.20
c.	1.70p	Manuel Isidoro Suarez	.35	.25
d.	1.90p	Juan Pascual Pringles	.40	.30
e.	2.70p	Latin American flags	.65	.35
f.	4.50p	Jose Felix Bogado	1.10	.50

Sesqui. of Battles of Junin and Ayacucho.

Dove, by Vito Campanella — A499

St. Anne, by Raul Soldi — A500

1974, Dec. 21 Litho. *Perf. 13½*

1053 A499 1.20p multicolored .50 .20
1054 A500 2.65p multicolored .75 .30

Christmas 1974.

Boy Looking at Stamp — A501

1974, Dec. 21

1055 A501 1.70p black & yel .40 .20

World Youth Philately Year.

Space Monsters, by Raquel Forner — A502

Argentine modern art: 4.50p, Dream, by Emilio Centurion.

1975, Feb. 22 Litho. *Perf. 13½*

1056 A502 2.70p multi .90 .25
1057 A502 4.50p multi 1.75 .40

Indian Woman and Cathedral, Catamarca — A503

Tourist Publicity: #1059, Carved chancel and street scene. #1060, Grazing cattleand monastery yard. #1061, Painted pottery and power station. #1062, Farm cart and colonial mansion. #1063, Perito Moreno glacier and spinning mill. #1064, Lake Lapataia and scientific surveyor. #1065, Los Alerces National Park and oil derrick.

1975 Litho. Unwmk. *Perf. 13½*

1058	A503	1.20p	shown	.25	.20
1059	A503	1.20p	Jujuy	.25	.20
1060	A503	1.20p	Salta	.25	.20
1061	A503	1.20p	Santiago del Estero	.25	.20
1062	A503	1.20p	Tucuman	.25	.20
1063	A503	6p	Santa Cruz	.50	.20
1064	A503	6p	Tierra del Fuego	.50	.20
1065	A503	6p	Chubut	.50	.20
	Nos. 1058-1065 (8)			2.75	1.60

Issue dates: 1.20p, Mar. 8; 6p, Dec. 20.

"We Have Been Inoculated" A504

1975, Apr. 26 Unwmk. *Perf. 13½*

1066 A504 2p multi .45 .25

Children's inoculation campaign (child's painting).

Hugo A. Acuña and South Orkney Station — A505

Designs: No. 1068, Francisco P. Moreno and Lake Nahuel Huapi. No. 1069, Lt. Col. Luis Piedra Buena and cutter, Luisito. No. 1070, Ensign José M. Sobral and Snow Hill House. No. 1071, Capt. Carlos M. Moyano and Cerro del Toro (mountain).

1975, June 28 Litho. *Perf. 13*

1067 A505 2p grnsh bl & multi	.25	.20
1068 A505 2p yel grn & multi	.25	.20
1069 A505 2p lt vio & multi	.25	.20
1070 A505 2p gray bl & multi	.25	.20
1071 A505 2p pale grn & multi	.25	.20
Nos. 1067-1071 (5)	1.25	1.00

Pioneers of Antarctica.

Frigate "25 de Mayo" A506

1975, Sept. 27 Unwmk. *Perf. 13½*

1072 A506 6p multi .40 .25

Navy Day 1975.

Eduardo Bradley and Balloon A507

1975, Sept. 27 Wmk. 365

1073 A507 6p multi .40 .25

Air Force Day.

Declaration of Independence, by Juan M. Blanes — A508

1975, Oct. 25

1074 A508 6p multi .30 .20

Sesquicentennial of Uruguay's declaration of independence.

Flame A509

1975, Oct. 17 Unwmk.

1075 A509 6p gray & multi .30 .20

Loyalty Day, 30th anniversary of Pres. Peron's accession to power.

Nos. 886, 891 and 932 Surcharged

1975 Lithographed, Photogravure

1076 A277 6c on 3p	.20	.20
1077 A366 30c on 90p	.20	.20
1078 A426 5p on 18c	.35	.20
Nos. 1076-1078 (3)	.75	.60

Issued: 6c, 10/30; 30c, 11/20; 5p, 10/24. The 6c also exists on No. 886a.

International Bridge, Flags of Argentina & Uruguay — A510

1975, Oct. 25 Litho. Wmk. 365

1081 A510 6p multi .35 .20

Opening of bridge connecting Colon, Argentina, and Paysandu, Uruguay.

Post Horn, Surcharged A511

1975, Nov. 8

1082 A511 10p on 20c multi .45 .20

Introduction of postal code. Not issued without surcharge.

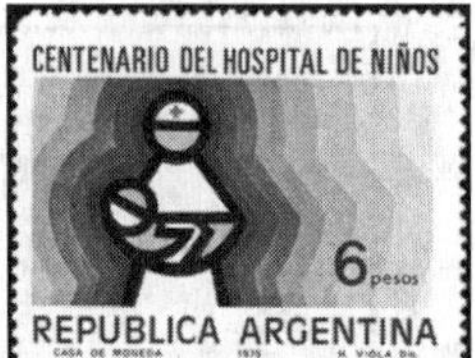

Nurse Holding Infant A512

1975, Dec. 13 Litho. *Perf. 13½*

1083 A512 6p multi .45 .20

Children's Hospital, centenary.

Nativity, Nueva Pompeya Church — A513

1975, Dec. 13 Litho. Unwmk.

1084 A513 6p multicolored .30 .20

Christmas 1975.

Types of 1970-75 and

Church of St. Francis, Salta — A515

Designs: 3p, No. 1099, 60p, 90p, Manuel Belgrano. 12p, 15p, 20p, 30p, No. 1100, 100p, 110p, 120p, 130p, San Martin. 15p, 70p, Guillermo Brown. 300p, Moon Valley (lower inscriptions italic). 500p, Adm. Brown Station, Antarctica.

1976-78 Photo. Unwmk. *Perf. 13½*

1089 A425 3p slate	.20	.20
1090 A425 12p rose red	.25	.20

Perf. 12½x13

Litho. Wmk. 365

1091 A425 12p rose red	.20	.20
1092 A425 12p emerald	.20	.20

Perf. 13½

Photo. Unwmk.

1093 A425 12p emer ('77)	.20	.20
1094 A425 15p rose red	.20	.20
1095 A425 15p vio bl ('77)	.20	.20
1097 A425 20p rose red ('77)	.35	.20
1098 A425 30p rose red ('77)	.35	.20
1099 A425 40p dp grn	.50	.20
1100 A425 40p rose red ('77)	.35	.20
1101 A425 60p dk bl ('77)	.70	.20
1102 A425 70p dk bl ('77)	1.00	.20
1103 A425 90p emer ('77)	1.00	.30
1104 A425 100p red	.75	.25
1105 A425 110p rose red ('78)	.50	.20
1106 A425 120p rose red ('78)	.60	.20
1107 A425 130p rose red ('78)	.70	.25

Litho.

1108 A463a 300p multi	3.50	1.50
a. Wmk 365	—	—
1109 A515 500p multi ('77)	8.25	1.40
a. Wmk 365	—	—
1110 A515 1000p multi ('77)	10.00	2.00
Nos. 1089-1110 (21)	30.00	8.70

Fluorescent paper was used in printing both 12p rose red, 15p rose red, 20p, 30p, 40p rose red, 100p, 110p, 120p, 130p.

No. 1099 and the 300p were issued on both ordinary and fluorescent paper.

See Nos. B73-B74.

A516

1976 Photo. Unwmk. *Perf. 13½*

1112 A516 12c gray & blk	.20	.20
1113 A516 50c gray & grn	.20	.20
1114 A516 1p red & blk	.20	.20
1115 A516 4p bl & blk	.20	.20
1116 A516 5p org & blk	.20	.20
1117 A516 6p dp brn & blk	.20	.20
1118 A516 10p gray & vio bl	.25	.20
1119 A516 27p lt grn & blk	.50	.20
1120 A516 30p lt bl & blk	.90	.20
1121 A516 45p yel & blk	.90	.20
1122 A516 50p dl grn & blk	1.25	.20
1123 A516 100p brt grn & red	1.60	.20

Perf. 13x12½

1976 Litho. Wmk. 365

1124 A516 5p org & blk	.20	.20
1125 A516 27p lt grn & blk	.50	.20
1126 A516 45p yel & blk	1.25	.20
Nos. 1112-1126 (15)	8.55	3.00

The 1p, 6p, 10p, 50p and No. 1116 were issued on both ordinary and fluorescent paper.

Jet and Airlines Emblem — A517

Perf. 13x13½

1976, Apr. 24 Litho. Unwmk.

1130 A517 30p bl, lt bl & dk bl 1.00 .20

Argentine Airlines, 25th anniversary.

Frigate Heroina & Map of Falkland Islands — A518

1976, Apr. 26

1131 A518 6p multi 1.00 .40

Argentina's claim to Falkland Islands.

Louis Braille — A519

Wmk. 365

1976, May 22 Engr. *Perf. 13½*

1132 A519 19.70 deep blue .30 .20

Sesquicentennial of the invention of the Braille system of writing for the blind by Louis Braille (1809-1852).

Private, 7th Infantry Regiment A520

1976, May 29 Litho. Unwmk.

1133 A520 12p multi .40 .20

Army Day.

Schooner Rio de la Plata, by Emilio Biggeri — A521

1976, June 19

1134 A521 12p multi .40 .20

Navy Day.

Dr. Bernardo Houssay — A522

Argentine Nobel Prize Winners:
10p, Bernardo Houssay, medicine and physiology, 1947. 15p, Luis F. Leloir, chemistry, 1970. 20p, Carlos Saavedra Lamas, peace, 1936.

1976, Aug. 14 Litho. *Perf. 13½*

1135 A522 10p org & blk .25 .20
1136 A522 15p yel & blk .30 .20
1137 A522 20p ocher & blk .45 .25
Nos. 1135-1137 (3) 1.00 .65

Rio de la Plata International Bridge — A523

1976, Sept. 18 Litho. *Perf. 13½*

1138 A523 12p multi .30 .20

Inauguration of International Bridge connecting Puerte Unzue, Argentina, and Fray Bentos, Uruguay.

Pipelines & Cooling Tower, Gen. Mosconi Plant A524

1976, Nov. 20 Litho. *Perf. 13½*

1139 A524 28p multi .40 .20

Pablo Teodoro Fels & Bleriot Monoplane, 1910 — A525

1976, Nov. 20

1140 A525 15p multi .30 .20

Air Force Day.

Nativity A526

1976, Dec. 18 Litho. *Perf. 13½*

1141 A526 20p multi .65 .30

Christmas. Painting by Edith Chiapetto.

Water Conference Emblem — A527

1977, Mar. 19 Litho. *Perf. 13½*

1142 A527 70p multi .70 .25

UN Water Conf., Mar del Plata, Mar. 14-25.

Dalmacio Velez Sarsfield — A528

1977, Mar. 19 Engr.

1143 A528 50p blk & red brn .70 .30

Dalmacio Velez Sarsfield (1800-1875), author of Argentine civil code.

Red Deer Type of 1974 Surcharged

1977, July 30 Photo. *Perf. 13½*

1144 A495 100p on 5p brn 1.40 .35

Sesquicentennial of Uruguayan postal service. Not issued without surcharge.

Soldier, 16th Lancers A529

1977, July 30

1145 A529 30p multi .40 .20

Army Day.

Schooner Sarandi, by Emilio Biggeri — A530

1977, July 30

1146 A530 30p multi .40 .25

Navy Day.

Soccer Games' Emblem A531

70p, Argentina '78 emblem, flags & soccer field.

1977, May 14

1147 A531 30p multi .40 .20
1148 A531 70p multi .85 .40

11th World Cup Soccer Championship, Argentina, June 1-25, 1978.

The Visit, by Horacio Butler A532

Consecration, by Miguel P. Caride — A533

1977, Mar. 26 Litho.

1149 A532 50p multi .50 .25
1150 A533 70p multi .65 .40

Argentine artists.

Sierra de la Ventana — A534

Views: #1152, Civic Center, Santa Rosa. #1153, Skiers, San Martin de los Andes. #1154, Boat on Lake Fonck, Rio Negro.

1977, Oct. 8 Litho. *Perf. 13x13½*

1151 A534 30p multi .30 .20
1152 A534 30p multi .30 .20
1153 A534 30p multi .30 .20
1154 A534 30p multi .30 .20
Nos. 1151-1154 (4) 1.20 .80

Guillermo Brown, by R. del Villar — A535

1977, Oct. 8 *Perf. 13½*

1155 A535 30p multi .40 .25

Adm. Guillermo Brown (1777-1857), leader in fight for independence, bicentenary of birth.

Jet A536

Double-decker, 1926 — A537

1977 Litho. *Perf. 13½*

1156 A536 30p multi .25 .20
1157 A537 40p multi .30 .20

50th anniversary of military plane production (30p); Air Force Day (40p).

Issue dates: 30p, Dec. 3; 40p, Nov. 26.

Adoration of the Kings — A538

1977, Dec. 17

1158 A538 100p multi 1.00 .30

Christmas 1977.

Historic City Hall, Buenos Aires — A539

Chapel of Rio Grande Museum, Tierra del Fuego A540

5p, 20p, La Plata Museum. 10p, Independence Hall, Tucuman. 40p, City Hall, Salta. #1165, City Hall, Buenos Aires. 100p, Columbus Theater, Buenos Aires. 200p, flag Monument, Rosario. 280p, 300p, Chapel of Rio Grande Museum, Tierra del Fuego. 480p, 520p, 800, Ruins of Jesuit Mission Church of San Ignacio, Misiones. 500p, Candonga Chapel, Cordoba. 1000p, G.P.O., Buenos Aires. 2000p, Civic Center, Bariloche, Rio Negro.

Three types of 10p: I. Nine vertical window bars; small imprint "E. MILIAVACA Dib." II. Nine bars; large imprint "E. MILIAVACA DIB." III. Redrawn; 5 bars; large imprint.

1977-81 Photo. Unwmk. *Perf. 13½*
Size: 32x21mm, 21x32mm

1159	A540	5p	gray & blk	.20	.20
1160	A540	10p	lt ultra & blk, I	.20	.20
a.	Type II			.20	.20
1161	A540	10p	lt bl & blk, III	.20	.20
1162	A540	20p	citron & blk, litho.	.20	.20
1163	A540	40p	gray bl & blk	.25	.20
1164	A539	50p	yel & blk	.30	.20
1165	A540	50p	citron & blk	.20	.20
1166	A540	100p	org & blk, litho.	.35	.20
a.	Wmk. 365			92.50	24.00
1167	A540	100p	red org & blk	.20	.20
1168	A540	100p	turq & blk	.20	.20
1169	A539	200p	lt bl & blk	.50	.25
1170	A540	280p	rose & blk	14.00	.20
1171	A540	300p	lemon & blk	.95	.20
1172	A540	480p	org & blk	1.75	.25
1173	A540	500p	yel grn & blk	1.75	.20
1174	A540	520p	org & blk	1.75	.30
1175	A540	800p	rose lil & blk	2.25	.30
1176	A540	1000p	lem bis & blk	2.50	.40
1177	A540	1000p	gold & blk, 40x29mm	3.75	.40
1178	A540	2000p	multi	2.25	.40
	Nos. 1159-1178 (20)			33.75	4.90

#1161, 1163, 1165, 1167, 1169, 1171, 1173, 1176, 1177 were issued on both ordinary and fluorescent paper. No. 1174 was issued only on fluorescent paper. All others were issued only on ordinary paper.

Issued: #1164, 5/30/77; 280p, 12/15/77; #1160, 3/14/78; 480p, 5/22/78; 5p, 7/25/78; 20p, 500p, 9/8/78; #1166, 9/20/78; #1177, 9/28/78; 520p, 9/30/78; 300p, 10/5/78; 40p, 12/1/78; #1161/79; #1165, 1/8/79; 800p, 3/20/79; #1167, 4/25/79; 200p, 6/23/79; #1176, 12/15/79; 2000p, 6/25/80; #1168, 5/26/81.

For overprints see Nos. 1253, 1315.

Soccer Games' Emblem A544

1978, Feb. 10 Photo. *Perf. 13½*

1179	A544 200p yel grn & bl	.85	.30
a.	Wmk 365	*100.00*	

11th World Cup Soccer Championship, Argentina, June 1-25.

View of El Rio, Rosario — A545

Designs (Argentina '78 Emblem and): 100p, Rio Tercero Dam, Cordoba. 150p, Cordillera Mountains, Mendoza. 200p, City Center, Mar del Plata. 300p, View of Buenos Aires.

1978, May 6 Litho. *Perf. 13*

1180	A545 50p multi	.20	.20
1181	A545 100p multi	.30	.20
1182	A545 150p multi	.50	.20
1183	A545 200p multi	.50	.25
1184	A545 300p multi	1.10	.30
	Nos. 1180-1184 (5)	2.60	1.15

Sites of 11th World Cup Soccer Championship, June 1-25.

Children — A546

1978, May 20

1185	A546 100p multi	.35	.20

50th anniversary of Children's Institute.

Labor Day, by B. Quinquela Martin — A547

Design: No. 1187, Woman's torso, sculpture by Orlando Pierri.

1978, May 20 *Perf. 13½*

1186	A547 100p multi	.35	.20
1187	A547 100p multi	.35	.20

Argentina, Hungary, France, Italy and Emblem — A548

Stadium — A549

Teams and Argentina '78 Emblem: 200p, Poland, Fed. Rep. of Germany, Tunisia, Mexico. 300p, Austria, Spain, Sweden, Brazil. 400p, Netherlands, Iran, Peru, Scotland.

1978 Litho. *Perf. 13*

1188	A548 100p multi	.30	.20
1189	A548 200p multi	.65	.20
1190	A548 300p multi	.95	.25
1191	A548 400p multi	1.25	.35
	Nos. 1188-1191 (4)	3.15	1.00

Souvenir Sheet
Lithographed and Engraved
Perf. 13½

1192	A549 700p buff & blk	2.50	1.40

11th World Cup Soccer Championship, Argentina, June 1-25. Issued: #1188-1191, 6/6; #1192, 6/3.

Stadium Type of 1978 Inscribed in Red: "ARGENTINA / CAMPEON"

Lithographed and Engraved

1978, Sept. 2 *Perf. 13½*

1193	A549 1000p bulf, blk & red	3.25	1.40

Argentina's victory in 1978 Soccer Championship. No. 1193 has margin similar to No. 1192 with Rimet Cup emblem added in red.

Young Tree Nourished by Old Trunk, UN Emblem — A550

1978 Sept. 2 Litho.

1194	A550 100p multi	.35	.25

Technical Cooperation among Developing Countries Conf., Buenos Aires, Sept. 1978.

Emblems of Buenos Aires & Bank — A551

1978, Sept. 16

1195	A551 100p multi	.35	.25

Bank of City of Buenos Aires, centenary.

General Savio & Steel Production — A552

1978, Sept. 16

1196	A552 100p multi	.35	.25

Gen. Manuel N. Savio (1892-1948), general manager of military heavy industry.

San Martin — A553

1978, Oct. Engr.

1197	A553 2000p grnsh blk	6.25	1.10

1979 Wmk. 365

1198	A553 2000p grnsh blk	4.75	.35

Gen Jose de San Martin (1778-1850), soldier and statesman. See No. 1292.

Globe & Argentine Flag — A554

1978, Oct. 7 Litho. *Perf. 13½*

1199	A554 200p multi	.70	.30

12th Intl. Cancer Cong., Buenos Aires, Oct. 5-11.

Chessboard, Queen & Pawn — A555

1978, Oct. 7

1200	A555 200p multi	2.00	.65

23rd National Chess Olympics, Buenos Aires, Oct. 25-Nov. 12.

Correct Positioning of Stamps A557

50p, Use correct postal code number.

1978 Photo. *Perf. 13½*

1201	A557 20p ultra	.20	.20
1203	A557 50p carmine	.25	.20

No. 1201 issued on both ordinary and fluorescent paper.

A558

A559

1978-82 Photo. *Perf. 13½*

1204	A558	150p bl & ultra	.35	.20
1205	A558	180p bl & ultra	.45	.20
1206	A558	200p bl & ultra	.30	.20
1207	A559	240p ol bis & bl ('79)	.40	.20
1208	A559	260p blk & lt bl ('79)	.40	.20
1209	A559	290p blk & lt bl ('79)	.45	.20
1210	A559	310p mag & bl ('79)	.50	.20
1211	A559	350p ver & bl ('79)	.65	.20
1212	A559	450p ultra & bl	.50	.20
1213	A559	600p grn & bl ('80)	.70	.25
1214	A559	700p blk & bl ('80)	.70	.25
1215	A559	800p red & bl ('81)	.65	.20
1216	A559	1100p gray & bl ('81)	.90	.20
1217	A559	1500p blk & bl ('81)	.35	.20
1218	A559	1700p grn & bl ('82)	.45	.20
		Nos. 1204-1218 (15)	7.75	3.10

No. 1204 issued on fluorescent and ordinary paper. No. 1206 issued only on fluorescent paper.

For overprint see No. 1338.

Balsa "24" A561

Ships: 200p, Tug Legador. 300p, River Parana tug No. 34. 400p, Passenger ship Ciudad de Parana.

1978, Nov. 4 Litho. *Perf. 13½*

1220	A561 100p multi	.25	.20
1221	A561 200p multi	.50	.20
1222	A561 300p multi	.70	.30
a.	Pair, #1221-1222	1.25	
1223	A561 400p multi	.95	.40
a.	Pair, #1220, 1223	1.25	
	Nos. 1220-1223 (4)	2.40	1.10

20th anniversary of national river fleet. Issued on fluorescent paper.

View and Arms of Bahia Blanca A562

1978, Nov. 25 Litho. *Perf. 13½*

1224	A562 20p multi	.50	.20

Sesquicentennial of Bahia Blanca.

"Spain," (Queen Isabella and Columbus) by Arturo Dresco — A563

1978, Nov. 25

1225	A563 300p multi	2.75	.30

Visit of King Juan Carlos and Queen Sofia of Spain to Argentina, Nov. 26.

Virgin and Child, San Isidro Cathedral A564

1978, Dec. 16

1226	A564 200p gold & multi	.55	.30

Christmas 1978.

Slope at Chacabuco, by Pedro Subercaseaux — A565

Painting: 1000p, The Embrace of Maipu (San Martin and O'Higgins), by Pedro Subercaseaux, vert.

1978, Dec. 16 Litho. *Perf. 13½*

1227 A565 500p multi 1.00 .25
1228 A565 1000p multi 2.00 .40

José de San Martin, 200th birth anniversary.

Adolfo Alsina A566

Design: No. 1230, Mariano Moreno.

1979, Jan. 20

1229 A566 200p lt bl & blk .30 .20
1230 A566 200p yel red & blk .30 .20

Adolfo Alsina (1828-1877), political leader, vice-president; Mariano Moreno (1778-1811), lawyer, educator, political leader.

Argentina No. 37 and UPU Emblem — A567

1979, Jan. 20

1231 A567 200p multi .25 .20

Centenary of Argentina's UPU membership.

Still-life, by Carcova A568

Painting: 300p, The Laundresses, by Faustino Brughetti.

1979, Mar. 3

1232 A568 200p multi .45 .20
1233 A568 300p multi .60 .20

Ernesto de la Carcova (1866-1927) and Faustino Brughetti (1877-1956), Argentine painters.

A569

1979, Mar. 3

1234 A569 200p Balcarce Earth station .55 .25

Third Inter-American Telecommunications Conference, Buenos Aires, March 5-9.

A570

1979

1235 A570 30p Stamp collecting .20 .20

Printed on ordinary and fluorescent paper.

European Olive — A571

1979, June 2 Litho. *Perf. 13½*

1236 A571 100p shown .25 .20
1237 A571 200p Tea .55 .25
1238 A571 300p Sorghum .85 .40
1239 A571 400p Common flax 1.10 .55
Nos. 1236-1239 (4) 2.75 1.40

Laurel and Regimental Emblem A572

1979, June 9

1240 A572 200p gold & multi .40 .25

Founding of Subteniente Berdina Village in memory of Sub-lieutenant Rodolfo Hernan Berdina, killed by terrorists in 1975.

"75" and Automobile Club Emblem — A573

1979, June 9

1241 A573 200p gold & multi .40 .20

Argentine Automobile Club, 75th anniv.

Exchange Building and Emblem — A574

1979, June 9

1242 A574 200p bl, blk & gold .40 .20

Grain Exchange, 125th anniversary.

Cavalry Officer, 1817 — A575

1979, July 7 Litho. *Perf. 13½*

1243 A575 200p multi 1.00 .30

Army Day.

Corvette Uruguay and Navy Emblem — A576

#1245, Hydrographic service ship & emblem.

1979 *Perf. 13*

1244 A576 250p multi .85 .35
1245 A576 250p multi .85 .35

Navy Day; Cent. of Naval Hydrographic Service. Issued: #1244, July 28; #1245, July 7.

Tree and Man — A577

1979, July 28 *Perf. 13½*

1246 A577 250p multi .60 .25

Protection of the Environment Day, June 5.

"Spad" Flying over Andes, and Vicente Almandos Almonacid — A578

1979, Aug. 4

1247 A578 250p multi .70 .25

Air Force Day.

Gen. Julio A. Roca Occupying Rio Negro, by Juan M. Blanes — A579

1979, Aug. 4

1248 A579 250p multi .70 .25

Conquest of Rio Negro Desert, centenary.

Rowland Hill — A580

1979, Sept. 29 Litho. *Perf. 13½*

1249 A580 300p gray red & blk .55 .25

Sir Rowland Hill (1795-1879), originator of penny postage.

Viedma Navarez Monument A581

1979, Sept. 29

1250 A581 300p multi .60 .25

Viedma and Carmen de Patagones towns, bicentenary.

Pope Paul VI — A582

Design: No. 1252, Pope John Paul I.

1979, Oct. 27 Engr. *Perf. 13½*

1251 A582 500p black 1.00 .30
1252 A582 500p sepia 1.00 .30

No. 1169 Overprinted in Red: "75 ANIV. / SOCIEDAD/ FILATELICA / DE ROSARIO"

1979, Nov. 10 Photo. *Perf. 13½*

1253 A539 200p lt blue & blk .60 .20

Rosario Philatelic Society, 75th anniversary.

A583

1979, Nov. 10 Litho.

1254 A583 300p multi .70 .30

Frontier resettlement.

A584

1979, Dec. 1 Litho. *Perf. 13½*
1255 A584 300p multi .70 .30

Military Geographic Institute centenary.

Christmas 1979 — A585

1979, Dec. 1
1256 A585 300p multi .55 .25

General Mosconi Birth Centenary — A586

1979, Dec. 15 Engr. *Perf. 13½*
1257 A586 1000p blk & bl 1.50 .25

Rotary Emblem and Globe A587

1979, Dec. 29 Litho.
1258 A587 300p multi 1.75 .35

Rotary International, 75th anniversary.

Child and IYC Emblem A588

Family, by Pablo Menicucci — A589

1979, Dec. 29
1259 A588 500p lt bl & sepia .75 .20
1260 A589 1000p multi 1.50 .25

International Year of the Child.

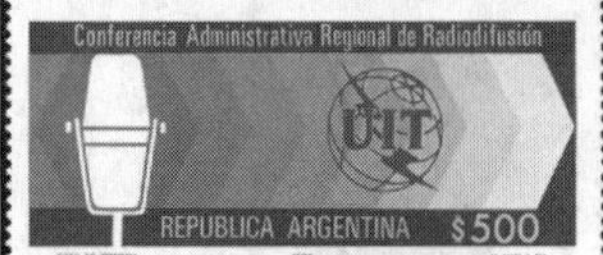

Microphone, Waves, ITU Emblem — A590

1980, Mar. 22 Litho. *Perf. 13x13½*
1261 A590 500p multi .95 .25

Regional Administrative Conference on Broadcasting by Hectometric Waves for Area 2, Buenos Aires, Mar. 10-29.

Guillermo Brown — A591

1980 Engr. *Perf. 13½*
1262 A591 5000p black 4.50 .20

See No. 1372.

Argentine Red Cross Centenary — A592

1980, Apr. 19 Litho. *Perf. 13½*
1263 A592 500p multi .50 .20

OAS Emblem A593

1980, Apr. 19
1264 A593 500p multi .55 .25

Day of the Americas, Apr. 14.

Dish Antennae, Balcarce — A594

1980, Apr. 26 Litho. & Engr.
1265 A594 300p shown .40 .20
1266 A594 300p Hydroelectric Station, Salto Grande .40 .20
1267 A594 300p Bridge, Zarate-Brazo Largo .40 .20
Nos. 1265-1267 (3) 1.20 .60

Capt. Hipolito Bouchard, Frigate "Argentina" — A595

1980, May 31 Litho. *Perf. 13x13½*
1268 A595 500p multicolored .70 .30

Navy Day.

"Villarino," San Martin, by Theodore Gericault — A596

1980, May 31
1269 A596 500p multicolored .70 .30

Return of the remains of Gen. Jose de San Martin to Argentina, centenary.

Buenos Aires Gazette, 1810, Signature — A597

1980, June 7 *Perf. 13½*
1270 A597 500p multicolored .55 .25

Journalism Day.

Miniature Sheet

Coaches in Victoria Square — A598

1980 June 14
1271 Sheet of 14 9.00 9.00
a.-n. A598 500p any single .60 .60

Buenos Aires, 400th anniv. No. 1271 shows ceramic mural of Victoria Square by Rodolfo Franco in continuous design. See No. 1285.

Gen. Pedro Aramburu A599

1980, July 12 Litho. *Perf. 13½*
1272 A599 500p yel & blk .55 .25

Gen. Pedro Eugenio Aramburu (1903-1970), provisional president, 1955.

Army Day A600

1980, July 12
1273 A600 500p multicolored .85 .30

Gen. Juan Gregorio de Las Heras (1780-1866), Hero of 1817 War of Independence — A601

Grandees of Argentina Bicentenary: No. 1275, Rivadavia. No. 1276, Brig. Gen Jose Matias Zapiola (1780-1874), naval commander and statesman.

1980, Aug. 2 Litho. *Perf. 13½*
1274 A601 500p tan & blk .55 .25
1275 A601 500p multicolored .55 .25
1276 A601 500p lt lilac & blk .55 .25
Nos. 1274-1276 (3) 1.65 .75

Avro "Gosport" Biplane, Maj. Francisco de Artega — A602

1980, Aug. 16 *Perf. 13*
1277 A602 500p multicolored .70 .25

Air Force Day. Artega (1882-1930) was first director of Military Aircraft Factory where Avro "Gosport" was built (1927).

University of La Plata, 75th Anniversary — A603

1980, Aug. 16 *Perf. 13½*
1278 A603 500p multi .55 .25

Souvenir Sheets

Emperor Penguin A604

South Orkneys Argentine Base — A605

No. 1279 (A604): a, shown. b, Bearded penguin. c, Adelie penguins. d, Papua penguins. e, Sea elephants. f, A605 shown. g, A606 shown. h, Fur seals. i, Giant petrels. j, Blue-eyed cororants. k, Stormy petrels. m, Anarctic doves.

1980, Sept. 27 Litho. *Perf. 13½*

1279	Sheet of 12	11.00	11.00
a.-m.	A604 500p, any single	.75	.60
1280	Sheet of 12	11.00	11.00
a.	A605 500p Puerto Soledad	.75	.60
b.	A605 500p Building close	.75	.60

75th anniv. of Argentina's presence in the South Orkneys and 150th anniv. of political and military command in the Falkland Islands. Nos. 1279-1280 each contain 12 stamps (4x3) with landscape designs in center of sheets. Silhouettes of Argentine exploration ships in margins. #1280 contains #1279a-1279e, 1279h-1279m, 1280a-1280b.

Anti-smoking Campaign A608

1980, Oct. 11

1282	A608 700p multi	.90	.25

National Census — A609

1980, Sept.

1283	A609 500p blk & bl	1.00	.20

Madonna and Child (Congress Emblem) — A610

1980, Oct. 1 Litho.

1284	A610 700p multi	.85	.20

National Marian Cong., Mendoza, Oct. 8-12

Mural Type of 1980
Miniature Sheet

1980, Oct. 25

1285	Sheet of 14	9.00	9.00
a.-n.	A598 500p, any single	.60	.50

Buenos Aires, 400th anniv./Buenos Aires '80 Stamp Exhib., Oct. 24-Nov. 2. No. 1285 shows ceramic mural Arte bajo la Ciudad by Alfredo Guido in continuous design.

Technical Military Academy, 50th Anniversary A611

1980, Nov. 1

1286	A611 700p multi	.75	.20

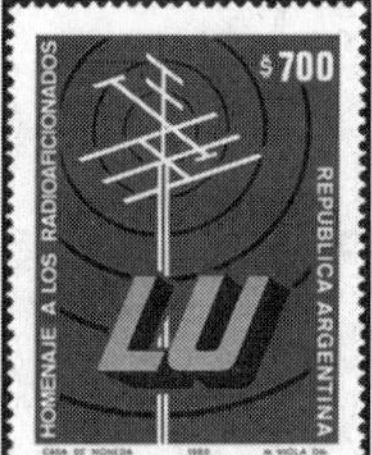

Amateur Radio Operation A612

1980, Nov. 1

1287	A612 700p multi	.75	.20

Medal — A613

Lujan Cathedral Floor Plan — A614

1980, Nov. 29 Litho. *Perf. 13½*

1288	A613 700p multi	.75	.25
1289	A614 700p olive & brn	.75	.25

Christmas 1980. 150th anniv. of apparition of Holy Virgin to St. Catherine Laboure, Paris (No. 1288), 350th anniv. of apparition at Lujan.

150th Death Anniversary of Simon Bolivar — A615

1980, Dec. 13

1290	A615 700p multi	.75	.25

Soccer Gold Cup Championship, Montevideo, 1980 — A616

1981, Jan. 3 Litho.

1291	A616 1000p multi	1.10	.25

San Martin Type of 1978

1981, Jan. 20 Engr. *Perf. 13½*

1292	A553 10,000p dark blue	7.25	.20

Landscape in Lujan, by Marcos Tiglio — A617

Paintings: No. 1304, Expansion of Light along a Straight Line, by Miguel Angel Vidal, vert.

1981, Apr. 11 Litho.

1303	A617 1000p multi	.85	.30
1304	A617 1000p multi	.85	.30

Intl. Sports Medicine Congress, June 7-12 — A618

1981, June 6 Litho. *Perf. 13½*

1305	A618 1000p bl & dk brn	.75	.20

Esperanza Base, Antarctica — A619

Cargo Plane, Map of Vice-Commodore Marambio Island — A620

Perf. 13½, 13x13½ (No. 1308)

1981, June 13

1306	A619 1000p shown	1.40	.40
1307	A619 2000p Almirante Irizar	2.50	.55
1308	A620 2000p shown	2.50	.85
	Nos. 1306-1308 (3)	6.40	1.80

Antarctic Treaty 20th anniv.

Antique Pistols (Military Club Centenary) — A621

1981, June 27 *Perf. 13½*

1309	A621 1000p Club building	.80	.20
1310	A621 2000p shown	.80	.20

Gen. Juan A. Alvarez de Arenales (1770-1831) A622

Famous Men: No. 1312, Felix G. Frias (1816-1881), writer. No. 1313, Jose E. Uriburu (1831-1914), statesman.

1981, Aug. 8 Litho. *Perf. 13½*

1311	A622 1000p multi	.70	.20
1312	A622 1000p multi	.70	.20
1313	A622 1000p multi	.70	.20
	Nos. 1311-1313 (3)	2.10	.60

Naval Observatory Centenary — A623

1981, Aug. 15 Litho. *Perf. 13x13½*

1314	A623 1000p multi	.75	.25

No. 1176 Overprinted in Red: "50 ANIV. DE LA ASOCIACION / FILATELICA Y NUMISMATICA / DE BAHIA BLANCA"

1981, Aug. 15 Photo. *Perf. 13½*

1315	A540 1000p lem & blk	2.00	1.00

50th anniv. of Bahia Blanca Philatelic and Numismatic Society.

St. Cayetano, Stained-glass Window, Buenos Aires — A624

1981, Sept. 5 Litho. *Perf. 13½*

1316	A624 1000p multi	.70	.20

St. Cayetano, founder of Teatino Order, 500th birth anniv.

Pablo Castaibert (1883-1909) and his Monoplane (Air Force Day) — A625

1981, Sept. 5 *Perf. 13x13½*

1317	A625 1000p multi	.65	.20

Intl. Year of the Disabled A626

1981, Sept. 10 *Perf. 13½*

1318	A626 1000p multi	.65	.20

22nd Latin-American Steelmakers' Congress, Buenos Aires, Sept. 21-23 — A627

1981, Sept. 19

1319	A627 1000p multi	.65	.20

Army Regiment No. 1 (Patricios), 175th Anniv. — A628

1981, Oct. 10 Litho. *Perf. 13½*

1320 1500p Natl. arms .45 .20
1321 1500p shown .45 .20
a. A628 Pair, #1320-1321 .90 .30

A629

San Martin as artillery Captain in Battle of Bailen, 1808.

1981, Oct. 5

1322 Sheet of 8 + 4 labels 4.75 1.75
a. A629 1000p multi .35 .20
b. A629 1500p multi .50 .20

Espamer '81 Intl. Stamp Exhib. (Americas, Spain, Portugal), Buenos Aires, Nov. 13-22.

No. 1322 contains 2 each se-tenant pairs with label between.

A630

1981, Oct. 5

1323 A630 1000p multi 2.25 .30

Anti-indiscriminate whaling.

Espamer '81 Emblem and Ship A631

1981

1324 A631 1300p multi 1.00 .40

No. 1324 Overprinted in Blue: "CURSO SUPERIOR DE ORGANIZACIONES DE FILATELICOS-UPAE-BUENOS AIRES-1981"

1981, Nov. 7 Photo. *Perf. 13½*

1325 A631 1300p multi 1.25 .20

Postal Administration philatelic training course.

Soccer Players A632

Designs: Soccer players.

1981, Nov. 13 Litho.

1326 Sheet of 4 + 2 labels 7.25 7.25
a. A632 2000p multi .50 .50
b. A632 3000p multi .65 .65
c. A632 5000p multi 1.10 1.10
d. A632 15,000p multi 3.25 3.25

Espamer '81.

"Peso" Coin Centenary — A633

1981, Nov. 21

1327 A633 2000p Patacon, 1881 .40 .20
1328 A633 3000p Argentine Oro, 1881 .60 .20

Christmas 1981 — A634

1981, Dec. 12

1329 A634 1500p multi .85 .25

Traffic Safety A635

1981, Dec. 19 Litho.

1330 A635 1000p Observe traffic lights, vert. .75 .40
1331 A635 2000p Drive carefully, vert. .75 .40
1332 A635 3000p Cross at white lines .75 .40
1333 A635 4000p Don't shine headlights 1.50 .40
Nos. 1330-1333 (4) 3.75 1.60

Francisco Luis Bernardez, Ciuda Laura — A636

Writers and title pages from their works: 2000p, Lucio V. Mansilla, Excursion a los indios ranqueles. 3000p, Conrado Nale Roxlo, El Grillo. 4000p, Victoria Ocampo, Sur.

1982, Mar. 20 Litho.

1334 A636 1000p shown .60 .20
1335 A636 2000p multi .85 .20
1336 A636 3000p multi 1.25 .30
1337 A636 4000p multi 1.75 .30
Nos. 1334-1337 (4) 4.45 1.00

No. 1218 Overprinted: "LAS / MALVINAS / SON/ ARGENTINAS"

1982, Apr. 17 Photo. *Perf. 13½*

1338 A559 1700p green & blue .50 .20

Argentina's claim on Falkland Islands.

Robert Koch — A637

1982, Apr. 17 Litho. Wmk. 365

1339 A637 2000p multi .50 .25

TB bacillus centenary and 25th Intl. Tuberculosis Conference.

American Airforces Commanders' 22nd Conf. — A638

1982, Apr. 17

1340 A638 2000p multi .70 .30

Stone Carving, City Founder's Signature (Don Hernando de Lerma) — A639

1982, Apr. 17

1341 A639 2000p multi .70 .30

Souvenir Sheet

1342 A639 5000p multi 2.00 2.00

City of Salta, 400th anniv. No. 1342 contains one 43x30mm stamp.

Naval Center Centenary — A640

1982, Apr. 24 *Perf. 13x13½*

1343 A640 2000p multi .70 .30

Chorisia Speciosa — A641

1982 Unwmk. Photo. *Perf. 13½*

1344 A641 200p Zinnia peruviana .20 .20
1345 A641 300p Ipomoea purpurea .20 .20
1346 A641 400p Tillandsia aeranthos .20 .20
1347 A641 500p shown .20 .20
1348 A641 800p Oncidium bifolium .20 .20
1349 A641 1000p Erythrina crista-galli .20 .20
1350 A641 2000p Jacaranda mimosi-folia .25 .20
1351 A641 3000p Bauhinia candicans .30 .20
1352 A641 5000p Tecoma stans .50 .20
1353 A641 10,000p Tabebuia ipe 1.00 .25
1354 A641 20,000p Passiflora coerulea 2.25 .35
1355 A641 30,000p Aristolochia littoralis 3.25 .50
1356 A641 50,000p Oxalis en-neaphylla 5.25 .70
Nos. 1344-1356 (13) 14.00 3.60

Nos. 1344-1346, 1348-1350 issued on fluorescent paper. Nos. 1353-1356 issued on ordinary paper. Others issued on both fluorescent and ordinary paper.

Issued: 500p, 2000p, 5000p, 10,000p, 5/22; 200p, 300p, 1000p, 20,000p, 9/25; 400p, 800p, 30,000p, 50,000p, 12/4; 3000p, 12/18.

See Nos. 1429-1443A, 1515-1527, 1683-1691. For overprint see No. 1382.

10th Death Anniv. of Gen. Juan C. Sanchez A641a

1982, May 29 Litho. Wmk. 365

1364 A641a 5000p grn & blk .90 .30

Luis Venet, First Commander — A641b

1982, June 12

1365 A641b 5000p org & blk 1.10 .45

Size: 83x28mm

1366 A641b 5000p Map .75 .30
a. Pair, Nos. 1365-1366 2.00 2.00

153rd Anniv. of Malvinas Political and Military Command District.

Compare with No. 1411.

Visit of Pope John Paul II A641c

1982, June 12

1367 A641c 5000p multi 1.75 .55

Organ Grinder, by Aldo Severi (b. 1928) — A641d

3000p, Still Life, by Santiago Cogorno (b. 1915).

1982, July 3 Wmk. 365

1368 A641d 2000p shown .25 .20
1369 A641d 3000p multi .40 .20

Guillermo Brown Type of 1980 and:

Jose de San Martin A641e

Litho. and Engr.

1982	Unwmk.	Perf. 13½		
1372 A591	30,000p blk & bl		3.25	.65
1376 A641e	50,000p sepia & car		6.50	.85

Issue dates: 30,000p, June; 50,000p, July.

Scouting Year A641f

Wmk. 365

1982, Aug. 7 Litho. *Perf. 13½*

1380 A641f 5000p multi 1.25 .20

Alconafta Fuel Campaign A641g

1982, Aug. 7 Wmk. 365

1381 A641g 2000p multi .30 .20

No. 1352 Overprinted: "50 ANIVERSARIO SOCIEDAD FILATELICA DE TUCUMAN"

1982, Aug. 7 Photo. Unwmk.

1382 A641 5000p multi 1.50 1.25

Rio III Central Nuclear Power Plant, Cordoba A642

Wmk. 365

1982, Sept. 4 Litho. *Perf. 13½*

1383 A642 2000p shown .30 .20
1384 A642 2000p Control room .30 .20

Namibia Day — A643

1982, Sept. 4

1385 A643 5000p Map .75 .20

Formosa Cathedral — A644

Churches and Cathedrals of the Northeast: 2000p, Our Lady of Itati, Corrientes, vert. 3000p, Resistencia Cathedral, Chaco, vert. 10,000p, St. Ignatius Church ruins, Misiones.

1982, Sept. 18 Litho. & Engr.

1386 A644	2000p	dk grn & blk	.50	.50
1387 A644	3000p	dk brn & brn	.50	.50
1388 A644	5000p	dk bl & brn	1.00	.50
1389 A644	10,000p	dp org & blk	1.50	.50
	Nos. 1386-1389 (4)		3.50	2.00

Tension Sideral, by Mario Alberto Agatiello A645

Sculpture (Espamer '81 and Juvenex '82 Exhibitions): 3000p, Sugerencia II, by Eduardo Mac Entyre. 5000p, Storm, by Carlos Silva.

1982, Oct. 2 Litho. *Perf. 13½*

1390 A645	2000p	multi	.25	.20
1391 A645	3000p	multi	.45	.20
1392 A645	5000p	multi	.60	.20
	Nos. 1390-1392 (3)		1.30	.60

Sante Fe Bridge A646

1982, Oct. 16 Litho. & Engr.

1393 A646 2000p bl & blk .40 .20

2nd Southern Cross Games, Santa Fe and Rosario, Nov. 26-Dec. 5.

10th World Men's Volleyball Championship — A647

1982, Oct. 16 Litho. Wmk. 365

1394 A647 2000p multi .40 .30
1395 A647 5000p multi .60 .30

Los Andes Newspaper Centenary — A648

Design: Army of the Andes Monument, Hill of Glory, Mendoza.

1982, Oct. 30

1396 A648 5000p multi .50 .20

A649

1982, Oct. 30 Wmk. 365

1397 A649 5000p Signs .55 .25

50th Anniv. of Natl. Roads, Administration.

A650

1982, Nov. 20 Litho.

La Plata City Cent.: No. 1400: a, Cathedral, diff. b, Head, top. c, Observatory. d, City Hall, diff. e, Head, bottom. f, University.

1398 A650	5000p	Cathedral	.75	.20
1399 A650	5000p	City Hall	.75	.20
1400		Sheet of 6	2.25	1.00
a.-f.	A650 2500p any single		.30	.20

Well, Natl. Hydrocarbon Congress Emblem — A651

1982, Nov. 20

1401 A651 5000p multi .50 .20

Oil Discovery, Comodoro Rivadavia, 75th anniv.

Jockey Club of Buenos Aires Centenary A652

#1403, Carlos Pellegrini, first president.

1982, Dec. 4 Litho.

1402 A652 5000p Emblem .50 .20
1403 A652 5000p multi .50 .20

Christmas A653

1982, Dec. 18 *Perf. 13½*

1404 A653 3000p St. Vincent de Paul 1.50 .20

Size: 29x38mm

1405 A653 5000p St. Francis of Assisi 1.25 .20

Pedro B. Palacios (1854-1917), Writer — A654

Writers: 2000p, Leopoldo Marechal (1900-1970). 3000p, Delfina Bunge de Galvez (1881-1952). 4000p, Manuel Galvez (1882-1962). 5000p, Evaristo Carriego (1883-1912).

1983, Mar. 26 Litho. *Perf. 13½*

1406 A654	1000p	multi	.20	.20
1407 A654	2000p	multi	.25	.20
1408 A654	3000p	multi	.30	.20
1409 A654	4000p	multi	.40	.20
1410 A654	5000p	multi	.55	.20
a.	Strip of 5, #1406-1410		1.75	1.00

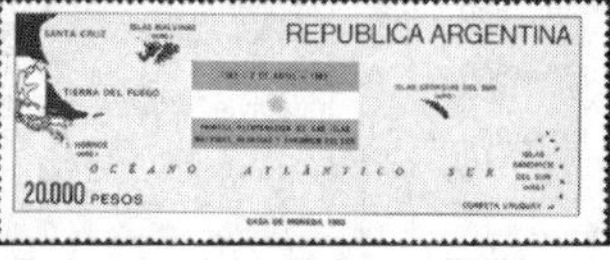

Recovery of the Malvinas (Falkland Islands) — A655

1983, Apr. 9 Litho. *Perf. 13½*

1411 A655 20,000p Map, flag 1.50 .50

Compare No. 1411 with No. 1366.

Telecommunications Systems — A656

1983, Apr. 16 Wmk. 365

1412 A656 5000p SITRAM 1.00 .50
1413 A656 5000p RED ARPAC 1.50 .50

Naval League Emblem A657

1983, May 14 Litho. *Perf. 13½*

1414 A657 5000p multi .35 .20

Navy Day and 50th anniv. of Naval League.

Allegory, by Victor Rebuffo A658

1983, May 14

1415 A658 5000p multi .35 .20

Natl. Arts Fund, 25th Anniv.

75th Anniv. of Colon Opera House, Buenos Aires — A659

1983, May 28 **Wmk. 365**

1416 A659 5000p Main hall .70 .20
1417 A659 10000p Stage 1.00 .20

Protected Species — A660

1983, July 2 **Litho.** ***Perf. 13½***

1418 A660 1p Chrysocyon brachtyurus .30 .20
1419 A660 1.50p Ozotocerus bezoarticus .50 .20
1420 A660 2p Myrmecophaga tridactyla .55 .20
1421 A660 2.50p Leo onca .65 .20
Nos. 1418-1421 (4) 2.00 .80

City of Catamarca, 300th Anniv. — A661

Foundation of the City of Catamarca, by Luis Varela Lezana (1900-1982).

1983, July 16 **Litho.** ***Perf. 13½***

1422 A661 1p multi .30 .20

Mamerto Esquiu (1826-1883) A662

1983, July 16

1423 A662 1p multi .30 .20

Bolivar, by Herrera Toro — A663

Bolivar, Engraving by Kepper — A664

Perf. 13 (A663), 13½ (A664)

1983 **Unwmk.**

1424 A663 1p multi .30 .20
1425 A664 2p black .60 .20
1426 A664 10p San Martin 3.00 1.50
Nos. 1424-1426 (3) 3.90 1.90

Issue dates: 1p, 2p, July 23. 10p, Aug. 20. See Nos. 1457-1462B.

Gen. Toribio de Luzuriaga (1782-1842) A665

1983, Aug. 20 **Litho.** ***Perf. 13½***

1427 A665 1p multi .30 .20

50th Anniv. of San Martin National Institute A666

1983, Aug. 20 **Engr.** **Unwmk.**

1428 A666 2p sepia .60 .20

Flower Type of 1982 in New Currency

1983-85 **Photo.** ***Perf. 13½***

1429 A641 5c like #1347 .20 .20
1430 A641 10c like #1349 .20 .20
1431 A641 20c like #1350 .20 .20
1432 A641 30c like #1351 .20 .20
1433 A641 40c Eichhornia crassipes .20 .20
1434 A641 50c like #1352 .20 .20
1435 A641 1p like #1353 .20 .20
1435A A641 1.80p Mutisia retusa .20 .20
1436 A641 2p like #1354 .25 .20
1437 A641 3p like #1355 .30 .20
1438 A641 5p like #1356 .55 .20
1439 A641 10p Alstroemeria aurantiaca 1.10 .80
1440 A641 20p like #1345 .55 .20
1441 A641 30p Embothrium coccineum 3.50 2.50
1442 A641 50p like #1346 1.10 .40
1443 A641 100p like #1348 1.60 .50
1443A A641 300p Cassia carnaval .80 .25
Nos. 1429-1443A (17) 11.35 6.85

Issued: 20p, 8/27/84; 50p, 10/19/84; 100p, 12/84; 300p, 6/15/85.

Nos. 1429, 1433, 1435A issued on fluorescent paper. Nos. 1443, 1443A issued on ordinary paper. Others issued on both ordinary and fluorescent paper.

For overprint and surcharge see #1489, 1530.

Intl. Rotary South American Regional Conference, Buenos Aires, Sept. 25-28 — A667

1983, Sept. 24 **Litho.**

1444 A667 1p multi .55 .25

9th Pan American Games, Caracas, Aug. 13-28 — A668

1983, Sept. 24

1445 A668 1p Track .30 .20
1446 A668 2p Emblem .65 .30

World Communications Year — A669

1983, Oct. 8 ***Perf. 13½***

1447 A669 2p multi .60 .25

Squash Peddler by Antonio Berni (1905-1981) A670

2p, Figure in Yellow by Luis Seoane (1910-79).

1983, Oct. 15 ***Perf. 13½***

1448 A670 1p multi .30 .20
1449 A670 2p multi .50 .25

World Communications Year — A671

Designs: 1p, Wagon, 18th cent. 2p, Post chaise, 19th cent. 4p, Steam locomotive, 1857. 5p, Tramway, 1910.

1983, Nov. 19 **Litho.** ***Perf. 13½***

1450 A671 1p multi .20 .20
1451 A671 2p multi .25 .20
1452 A671 4p multi .50 .20
1453 A671 5p multi .65 .25
Nos. 1450-1453 (4) 1.60 .85

World Communications Year — A672

1983, Nov. 26 **Litho.** ***Perf. 12½x12***

1454 A672 2p General Post Office .40 .20

Return to Elected Government A673

1983, Dec. 10 **Photo.** ***Perf. 13½***

1455 A673 2p Coin, 1813 .30 .20

Eudyptes Crestatus A674

Designs: b, Diomedea exulans. c, Diomedea melanophris. d, Eudyptes chrysolophus. e, Luis Piedra Buena. f, Carlos Maria Moyano. g, Luis Py. h, Augusto Lasserre. i, Phoebetria palpebrata. j, Hydrurga leptonyx. k, Lobodon carcinophagus. l, Leptonychotes weddelli.

1983, Dec. 10 **Litho.**

1456 Sheet of 12 4.50 2.25
a.-l. A674 2p any single .35 .20

Southern pioneers and fauna. Margin depicts various airplanes and emblems.

Bolivar Type of 1983

Famous men: 10p, Angel J. Carranza (1834-99), historian. No. 1458, 500p, Guillermo Brown. No. 1459, Estanislao del Campo (1834-80), poet. 30p, Jose Hernandez (1834-86), author. 40p, Vicente Lopez y Planes (1784-1856), poet and patriot. 50p, San Martin. 200p, Belgrano.

1983-85 **Litho. & Engr.** ***Perf. 13½***

1457 A664 10p pale bl & dk bl .50 .30
1458 A664 20p dk bl & blk 2.75 1.40
1459 A664 20p dl brn ol & ol blk .50 .30
1460 A664 30p pale bl & bluish blk .60 .30
1461 A664 40p lt bl grn & blk .90 .40
1462 A664 50p Prus & choc 1.10 .25
1462A A664 200p int bl & blk 3.00 .95
1462B A664 500p brn & int bl 2.00 .50
Nos. 1457-1462B (8) 11.35 4.40

Issued: #1458, 10/6; 10p, #1459, 30p, 40p, 3/23/85; 50p, 4/23/85; 200p, 11/2/85; 500p, 5/2/85.

Christmas 1983 — A675

Nativity Scenes: 2p, Tapestry, by Silke. 3p, Stained-glass window, San Carlos de Bariloche's Wayn Church, vert.

1983, Dec. 17 Litho. *Perf. 13½*

1463 A675 2p multi .30 .20
1464 A675 3p multi .55 .30

Centenary of El Dia Newspaper A676

1984, Mar. 24 Litho.

1465 A676 4p Masthead, printing roll .40 .20

Alejandro Carbo Teachers' College Centenary — A677

1984, June 2 Litho. *Perf. 13½*

1466 A677 10p Building .40 .25

1984 Olympics A678

#1468, Weightlifting, discus, shot put. #1469, Javelin, fencing. #1470, Bicycling, swimming.

1984, July 28 Litho. *Perf. 13½*

1467 A678 5p shown .25 .20
1468 A678 5p multicolored .25 .20
1469 A678 10p multicolored .45 .25
1470 A678 10p multicolored .45 .25
Nos. 1467-1470 (4) 1.40 .90

Rosario Stock Exchange Centenary A679

1984, Aug. 11

1471 A679 10p multicolored .45 .25

Wheat A680

1984, Aug. 11

1472 A680 10p shown .50 .25
1473 A680 10p Corn .50 .25
1474 A680 10p Sunflower .50 .25
Nos. 1472-1474 (3) 1.50 .75

18th FAO Regional Conference for Latin America and Caribbean (No. 1472); 3rd Natl. Corn Congress (No. 1473); World Food Day (No. 1474).

Wildlife Protection — A681

1984, Sept. 22 Litho. *Perf. 13½*

1475 A681 20p Hippocamelus bisulcus .40 .20
1476 A681 20p Vicugna vicugna .40 .20
1477 A681 20p Aburria jacutinga .40 .20
1478 A681 20p Mergus octosetaceus .40 .20
1479 A681 20p Podiceps gallardoi .40 .20
Nos. 1475-1479 (5) 2.00 1.00

First Latin American Theater Festival, Cordoba, Oct. — A682

1984, Oct. 13 Litho. *Perf. 13½*

1480 A682 20p Mask .25 .20

Intl. Eucharistic Congress, 50th Anniv. — A683

Apostles' Communion, by Fra Angelico.

1984, Oct. 13

1481 A683 20p multicolored .30 .20

Glaciares Natl. Park (UNESCO World Heritage List) — A684

1984, Nov. 17 Litho.

1482 A684 20p Sea .25 .20
1483 A684 30p Glacier .40 .20

City of Puerto Deseado Centenary — A685

1984, Nov. 17 *Perf. 13½*

1484 A685 20p shown .30 .20
1485 A685 20p Ushuaia centenary .30 .20

Childrens' Paintings, Christmas 1984 — A686

1984, Dec. 1 Litho. *Perf. 13½*

1486 A686 20p Diego Aguero .30 .20
1487 A686 30p Leandro Ruiz .60 .20
1488 A686 50p Maria Castillo, vert. .60 .20
Nos. 1486-1488 (3) 1.50 .60

No. 1439 Overprinted

1984, Dec. 1 Photo. *Perf. 13½*

1489 A641 10p multicolored .40 .40

Buenos Aires Philatelic Center, 50th anniv.

Vista Del Jardin Zoologico, by Fermin Eguia — A687

Paintings: No. 1491, El Congreso Iluminado, by Francisco Travieso. No. 1492, Galpones (La Boca), by Marcos Borio.

1984, Dec. 15 *Perf. 13½*

1490 A687 20p multi .30 .20
1491 A687 20p multi, vert. .30 .20
1492 A687 20p multi, vert. .30 .20
Nos. 1490-1492 (3) .90 .60

Gen. Martin Miguel de Guemes (1785-1821) — A688

1985, Mar. 23 Litho. *Perf. 13½*

1493 A688 30p multicolored .25 .20

ARGENTINA '85 Exhibition — A689

First airmail service from: 20p, Buenos Aires to Montevideo, 1917. 40p, Cordoba to Villa Dolores, 1925. 60p, Bahia Blanca to Comodoro Rivadavia, 1929. 80p, Argentina to Germany, 1934. 100p, naval service to the Antarctic, 1952.

1985, Apr. 27

1494 A689 20p Bleriot Gnome .20 .20
1495 A689 40p Junker F-13L .30 .20
1496 A689 60p Latte 25 .50 .20
1497 A689 80p L.Z. 127 Graf Zeppelin .65 .30
1498 A689 100p Consolidated PBY Catalina .85 .40
Nos. 1494-1498 (5) 2.50 1.30

Central Bank, 50th Anniv. A690

1985, June 1

1499 A690 80p Bank Bldg., Buenos Aires .55 .20

Jose A. Ferreyra (1889-1943), Director of Munequitas Portenas — A691

Famous directors and their films: No. 1501, Leopoldo Torre Nilsson (1924-1978), scene from Martin Fierro.

1985, June 1

1500 A691 100p shown .60 .20
1501 A691 100p multi .60 .20

Carlos Gardel (1890-1935), Entertainer A692

Paintings: No. 1502, Gardel playing the guitar on stage, by Carlos Alonso (b. 1929). No. 1503, Gardel in a wide-brimmed hat, by Hermegildo Sabat (b. 1933). No. 1504, Portrait of Gardel in an ornamental frame, by Aldo Severi (b. 1928) and Martiniano Arce (b. 1939).

1985, June 15

1502 A692 200p multi .95 .45
1503 A692 200p multi .95 .45
1504 A692 200p multi .95 .45
Nos. 1502-1504 (3) 2.85 1.35

The Arrival, by Pedro Figari A693

A Halt on the Plains, by Prilidiano Pueyrredon — A693a

Oil paintings (details): 30c, The Wagon Square, by C. B. de Quiros. Illustration A693a is reduced.

1985, July 6 Litho. *Perf. 13½*

1505 A693 20c multi 1.00 .25
1506 A693 30c multi 1.25 .25

Souvenir Sheet
Perf. 12

1507 A693a Sheet of 2 2.50 2.50
a. 20c Pilgrims, vert. .30 .30
b. 30c Wagon .40 .40

ARGENTINA '85. No. 1507 contains 2 30x40mm stamps. See No. 1542.

Buenos Aires to Montevideo, 1917 Teodoro Fels Flight — A694

Historic flight covers: #1509, Villa Dolores to Cordoba, 1925. #1510, Buenos Aires to France, 1929 St. Exupery flight. #1511, Buenos Aires to Bremerhaven, 1934 Graf Zeppelin flight. #1512, 1st Antarctic flight, 1952.

1985, July 13 ***Perf. 12x12½***

1508 A694 10c emer & multi .40 .20
1509 A694 10c ultra & multi .40 .20
1510 A694 10c lt choc & multi .40 .20
1511 A694 10c chnt & multi .40 .20
1512 A694 10c ap grn & multi .40 .20
Nos. 1508-1512 (5) 2.00 1.00

ARGENTINA '85.

Illuminated Fruit, by Fortunato Lacamera (1887-1951) — A695

Paintings: 20c, Woman with Bird, by Juan del Prete, vert.

1985, Sept. 7 ***Perf. 13½***

1513 A695 20c multi .85 .30
1514 A695 30c multi 1.00 .30

Flower Types of 1982-85

Designs: 1a, Begonia micranthera var. hieronymi. 5a, Gymnocalycium bruchii.

1985-88 **Photo.** ***Perf. 13½***

1515 A641 ½c like #1356 .20 .20
1516 A641 1c like #1439 .20 .20
1517 A641 2c like #1345 .20 .20
1518 A641 3c like #1441 .20 .20
1519 A641 5c like #1346 .25 .20
1520 A641 10c like #1348 .35 .20
1521 A641 20c like #1347 .80 .20
1522 A641 30c like #1443A 1.10 .25
1523 A641 50c like #1344 1.75 .30
1524 A641 1a multi 3.50 .65
1525 A641 2a like #1351 .40 .20
1526 A641 5a multi 6.75 3.00

Size: 15x23mm

1527 A641 8½c like #1349 .30 .20
Nos. 1515-1527 (13) 16.00 6.00

Issued: ½c, 1c, 12/16; 2c, 8½c, 30c, 9/18; 3c, 5c, 10c, 50c, 1a, 9/7; 20c, 10/17; 5a, 3/21/87; 2a, 12/5/88.

No. 1435 Surcharged

1986, Nov. 4 **Photo.** ***Perf. 13½***

1530 A641 10c on 1p No. 1435 .20 .20

Folk Musical Instruments A699

1985, Sept. 14 **Litho.** ***Perf. 13½***

1531 A699 20c Frame drum .55 .25
1532 A699 20c Long flute .55 .25
1533 A699 20c Jew's harp .55 .25
1534 A699 20c Pan flutes .55 .25
1535 A699 20c Musical bow .55 .25
Nos. 1531-1535 (5) 2.75 1.25

Juan Bautista Alberdi (1810-1884), Historian, Politician A700

Famous men: Nicolas Avellaneda (1836-1885), President in 1874. 30c, Fr. Luis Beltran (1784-1827), military and naval engineer. 40c, Ricardo Levene (1885-1959), historian, author.

1985, Oct. 5

1536 A700 10c multi .25 .20
1537 A700 20c multi .45 .25
1538 A700 30c multi .65 .30
1539 A700 40c multi 1.10 .45
Nos. 1536-1539 (4) 2.45 1.20

Type of 1985 and

Skaters A701

Deception, by J. H. Rivoira — A702

1985, Oct. 19 **Litho.** ***Perf. 13½***

1540 A701 20c multi .35 .30
1541 A702 30c multi .50 .50

Size: 147x75mm

Imperf

1542 A693a 1a multi 1.90 1.50

IYY. No. 1542 is inscribed in silver with the UN 40th anniversary and IYY emblems.

Provincial Views — A703

#1543, Rock Window, Buenos Aires. #1544, Forclaz Windmill, Entre Rios. #1545, Lake Potrero de los Funes, San Luis. #1546, Mission church, north-east province. #1547, Penguin colony, Punta Tombo, Chubut. #1548, Water Mirrors, Cordoba.

1985, Nov. 23 ***Perf. 13½***

1543 A703 10c multi .25 .25
1544 A703 10c multi .25 .25
1545 A703 10c multi .25 .25
1546 A703 10c multi .25 .25
1547 A703 10c multi .25 .25
1548 A703 10c multi .25 .25
Nos. 1543-1548 (6) 1.50 1.50

Christmas 1985 — A704

Designs: 10c, Birth of Our Lord, by Carlos Cortes. 20c, Christmas, by Hector Viola.

1985, Dec. 7

1549 A704 10c multi .25 .20
1550 A704 20c multi .50 .45

Natl. Campaign for the Prevention of Blindness — A705

1985, Dec. 7

1551 A705 10c multi .25 .20

Rio Gallegos City, Cent. — A716

1985, Dec. 21 **Litho.** ***Perf. 13½***

1552 A716 10c Church .80 .40

Natl. Grape Harvest Festival, 50th Anniv. A717

1986, Mar. 15

1553 A717 10c multi .25 .20

Exists with Wmk. 265, Value $10.

Historical Architecture in Buenos Aires — A718

Designs: No. 1554, Valentin Alsina House, Italian Period, 1860-70. No. 1555, House on Cerrito Street, French influence, 1880-1900. No. 1556, House on the Avenida de Mayo y Santiago del Estero, Art Nouveau, 1900-10. No. 1557, Customs Building, academic architecture, 1900-15. No. 1558, Isaac Fernandez Blanco Museum, house of architect Martin Noel, natl. restoration, 1910-30. Nos. 1554-1556 vert.

1986, Apr. 19

1554 A718 20c multi .40 .30
1555 A718 20c multi .40 .30
1556 A718 20c multi .40 .30
1557 A718 20c multi .40 .30
1558 A718 20c multi .40 .30
Nos. 1554-1558 (5) 2.00 1.50

Antarctic Bases, Pioneers and Fauna — A719

Designs: a, Base, Jubany. b, Arctocephalus gazella. c, Otaria byronia. d, Gen. Belgrano Base. e, Daption capensis. f, Diomedia melanophris. g, Apterodytes patagonica. h, Macronectes giganteus. i, Hugo Alberto Acuna (1885-1953). j, Spheniscus magellanicus. k, Gallinago gallinage. l, Capt. Agustin del Castillo (1855-89).

1986, May 31

1559 Sheet of 12 9.00 9.00
a.-l. A719 10c any single .75 .75

Famous People — A720

#1560, Dr. Alicia Moreau de Justo, human rights activist. #1561, Dr. Emilio Ravignani (1886-1954), historian. #1562, Indira Gandhi.

1986, July 5 **Litho.** ***Perf. 13½***

1560 A720 10c multi .45 .25
1561 A720 10c multi .45 .25
1562 A720 30c multi 1.10 .65
Nos. 1560-1562 (3) 2.00 1.15

Statuary, Buenos Aires — A721

1986, July 5

20c, Fountain of the Nereids, by Dolores Lola Mora (1866-1936). 30c, Lamenting at Work, by Rogelio Yrurtia (1879-1950), horiz.

1563 A721 20c multi .50 .45
1564 A721 30c multi .80 .65

Famous Men — A722

#1565, Francisco N. Laprida (1786-1829), politician. #1566, Estanislao Lopez (1786-1838), brigadier general. #1567, Francisco Ramirez (1786-1821), general.

1986, Aug. 9 **Litho.** ***Perf. 13***

1565 A722 20c dl yel, brn & blk .40 .40
1566 A722 20c dl yel, brn & blk .40 .40
1567 A722 20c dl yel, brn & blk .40 .40
Nos. 1565-1567 (3) 1.20 1.20

Fr. Ceferino Namuncura (1886-1905) A723

1986, Aug. 30 ***Perf. 13½***
1568 A723 20c multi .60 .40

Miniature Sheets

Natl. Team Victory, 1986 World Cup Soccer Championships, Mexico — A724

Designs: No. 1569a-1569d, Team. Nos. 1569e-1569h, Shot on goal. Nos. 1570a-1570d, Action close-up. Nos. 1570e-1570h, Diego Maradona holding soccer cup.

1986, Nov. 8 **Litho.** ***Perf. 13½***
1569 A724 Sheet of 8 10.00 *10.00*
a.-h. 75c any single 1.10 *1.10*
1570 A724 Sheet of 8 10.00 *10.00*
a.-h. 75c any single 1.10 *1.10*

San Francisco (Cordoba), Cent. — A725

1986, Nov. 8
1571 A725 20c Municipal Building .50 .45

Trelew City (Chubut), Cent. — A726

1986, Nov. 22 **Litho.** ***Perf. 13½***
1572 A726 20c Old railroad station, 1865 .50 .45

Mutualism Day — A727

1986, Nov. 22
1573 A727 20c multi .60 .45

Christmas — A728

Designs: 20c, Naif retable, by Aniko Szabo (b. 1945). 30c, Everyone's Tree, by Franca Delacqua (b. 1947).

1986, Dec. 13 **Litho.** ***Perf. 13½***
1574 A728 20c multicolored .50 .35
1575 A728 30c multicolored .60 .35

Santa Rosa de Lima, 400th Birth Anniv. — A729

1986, Dec. 13
1576 A729 50c multicolored 1.75 .75

Rio Cuarto Municipal Building A730

1986, Dec. 20
1577 A730 20c shown .40 .25
1578 A730 20c Court Building, Cordoba .40 .25

Rio Cuarto City, bicent. Court Building, Cordoba, 50th anniv.

Antarctic Treaty, 25th Anniv. — A731

1987, Mar. 7 **Litho.** ***Perf. 13½***
1579 A731 20c Marine biologist .35 .20
1580 A731 30c Ornithologist .60 .25

Souvenir Sheet

Perf. 12

1581 Sheet of 2 3.00 3.00
a. A731 20c like No. 1579 .40 .20
b. A731 30c like No. 1580 .55 .25

No. 1581 contains 2 stamps, size: 40x50mm.

Natl. Mortgage Bank, Cent. — A732

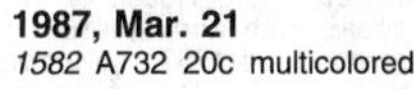

1987, Mar. 21 ***Perf. 13½***
1582 A732 20c multicolored .65 .45

Natl. Cooperative Associations Movement — A733

1987, Mar. 21
1583 A733 20c multicolored .65 .45

Second State Visit of Pope John Paul II — A734

Engr., Litho. (No. 1585)

1987, Apr. 4 ***Perf. 13½***
1584 A734 20c shown .35 .25
1585 A734 80c Papal blessing 1.40 .70

Souvenir Sheet

Perf. 12

1586 A734 1a like 20c 2.25 2.25

No. 1586 contains one 40x50mm stamp.

Intl. Peace Year A735

30c, Pigeon, abstract sculpture by Victor Kaniuka.

1987, Apr. 11 **Litho.**
1587 A735 20c multicolored .35 .20
1588 A735 30c multicolored .55 .35

Low Handicap World Polo Championships A736

Polo Players, painting by Alejandro Moy.

1987, Apr. 11
1589 A736 20c multicolored .75 .20

Miniature Sheet

ICOM '86 — A737

Designs: a, Emblem. b, Family crest, National History Museum, Buenos Aires. c, St. Bartholomew, Enrique Larreta Museum of Spanish Art, Buenos Aires. d, Zoomorphic club, Patagonian Museum, San Carlos de Bariloche. e, Supplication, anthropomorphic sculpture, Natural Sciences Museum, La Plata. f, Wrought iron lattice from the house of J. Urquiza, president of the Confederation of Argentina, Entre Rios History Museum, Parana. g, St. Joseph, 18th cent. wood figurine, Northern History Museum, Salta. h, Funerary urn, Provincial Archaeological Museum, Santiago del Estero.

1987, May 30
1590 Sheet of 8 3.50 3.50
a.-h. A737 25c any single .40 .30

Intl. Council of Museums, 14th general conf.

Natl. College of Monserrat, Cordoba, 300th Anniv. — A738

1987, July 4 ***Imperf.***
1591 A738 1a multicolored 1.40 1.40

Monserrat '87 Philatelic Exposition.

Fight Drug Abuse A739

The Proportions of Man, by da Vinci.

1987, Aug. 15 ***Perf. 13½***
1592 A739 30c multicolored .45 .20

Famous Men A740

Portraits and quotations: 20c, Jorge Luis Borges (1899-1986), writer. 30c, Armando Discepolo (1887-1971), playwright. 50c, Carlos A. Pueyrredon (1887-1962), professor, Legion of Honor laureate.

1987, Aug. 15

1593	A740	20c multicolored	.30	.20
1594	A740	30c multicolored	.50	.25
1595	A740	50c multicolored	.75	.35
		Nos. 1593-1595 (3)	1.55	.80

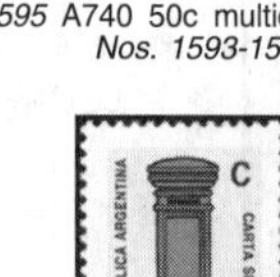

Pillar Boxes
A741 A742

1987 Photo. *Perf. 13½*

1596	A741	(30c) yel, blk & dark red	2.00	.30
		Booklet with 10 stamps	20.00	
1597	A742	(33c) lt blue grn, blk & yel	.85	.35

Issue dates: (30c), June 8; (33c), July 13.

The Sower, by Julio Vanzo A743

1987, Sept. 12

1598	A743	30c multicolored	.35	.20

Argentine Agrarian Federation, 75th anniv.

10th Pan American Games, Indianapolis, Aug. 7-25 — A744

1987, Sept. 26

1599	A744	20c Basketball	.25	.20
1600	A744	30c Rowing	.35	.20
1601	A744	50c Yachting	.55	.20
		Nos. 1599-1601 (3)	1.15	.60

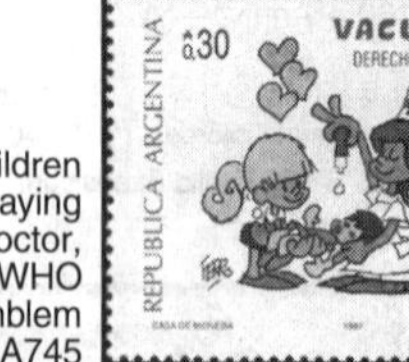

Children Playing Doctor, WHO Emblem A745

1987, Oct. 7

1602	A745	30c multi	.35	.20

Vaccinate every child campaign.

Heroes of the Revolution A746

Signing of the San Nicolas Accord, 1852, by Rafael del Villar A747

Independence anniversaries and historic events: No. 1603, Maj.-Col. Ignacio Alvarez Thomas (1787-1857). No. 1604, Col. Manuel Crispulo Bernabe Dorrego (1787-1829). No. 1606, 18th cent. Spanish map of the Falkland Isls., administered by Jacinto de Altolaguirre.

1987, Oct. 17

1603	A746	25c shown	.30	.20
1604	A746	25c multi	.30	.20
1605	A747	50c shown	.55	.30
1606	A747	50c multi	.55	.30
		Nos. 1603-1606 (4)	1.70	1.00

Museum established in the House of the San Nicholas Accord, 50th anniv. (#1605); Jacinto de Altolaguirre (1754-1787), governor the Malvinas Isls. for the King of Spain (#1606).

Celedonio Galvan Moreno, 1st Director — A748

1987, Nov. 21

1607	A748	50c multicolored	.55	.40

Postas Argentinas magazine, 50th anniv.

LRA National Radio, Buenos Aires, 50th Anniv. — A749

1987, Nov. 21

1608	A749	50c multicolored	.55	.40

Natl. Philatelic Society, Cent. A750

1987, Nov. 21

1609	A750	1a Jose Marco del Pont	1.10	.55

Christmas A751

Tapestries: 50c, *Navidad,* by Alisia Frega. 1a, *Vitral,* by Silvina Trigos.

1987, Dec. 5

1610	A751	50c multicolored	.55	.20
1611	A751	1a multicolored	1.10	.55

Natl. Parks — A752

1987, Dec. 19 *Perf. 13x13½*

1612	A752	50c Baritu	.55	.35
1613	A752	50c Nahuel Huapi	.55	.35
1614	A752	50c Rio Pilcomayo	.55	.35
1615	A752	50c Tierra del Fuego	.55	.35
1616	A752	50c Iguacu	.55	.35
		Nos. 1612-1616 (5)	2.75	1.75

See #1647-1651, 1715-1719, 1742-1746.

Landscapes in Buenos Aires Painted by Jose Cannella — A753

1988-89 Litho. *Perf. 13½*

1617	A753	5a Caminito	2.00	1.10
1618	A753	10a Viejo Almacen	4.00	2.25
1618A	A753	10a like No. 1618	1.10	.50
1618B	A753	50a like No. 1617	1.10	.50
c.		Wmk 365	*125.00*	20.00
		Nos. 1617-1618B (4)	8.20	4.35

No. 1618 inscribed "Viejo Almacen"; No. 1618A inscribed "El Viejo Almacen."
Issue dates: 5a, #1618, 3/15; #1618A, 10/20; 50a, 5/30/89.
For overprint see No. 1635.

Minstrel in a Tavern, by Carlos Morel A754

Paintings: No. 1620, Interior of Curuzu, by Candido Lopez.

1988, Mar. 19 Litho. *Perf. 13½*

1619	A754	1a shown	.60	.30
1620	A754	1a multicolored	.60	.30

See Nos. 1640-1641.

Argentine-Brazilian Economic Cooperation and Integration Program for Mutual Growth — A755

1988, Mar. 19

1621	A755	1a multicolored	.50	.25

Cities of Alta Gracia and Corrientes, 400th Annivs. — A756

1988, Apr. 9 Litho. *Perf. 13½*

1622	A756	1a Alta Gracia Church	.75	.40
1623	A756	1a Chapel of St. Anne, Corrientes	.75	.40

Labor Day — A757

Grain Carriers, a tile mosaic by Alfredo Guido, Line D of Nueve de Julio station, Buenos Aires subway: a, (UL). b, (UR). c, (LL). d, (LR).

1988, May 21

1624	A757	Block of 4	3.00	2.00
a.-d.		50c any single	.50	.50

1988 Summer Olympics, Seoul — A758

1988, July 16 Litho. *Perf. 13½*

1625	A758	1a Running	.30	.20
1626	A758	2a Soccer	.75	.30
1627	A758	3a Field hockey	1.10	.50
1628	A758	4a Tennis	1.40	.65
		Nos. 1625-1628 (4)	3.55	1.65

Mendoza Bank, Cent. — A759

Natl. Gendarmerie, Cent. — A760

1988, Aug. 13

1629	A759	2a multicolored	.65	.45
1630	A760	2a multicolored	.65	.45

Sarmiento and Cathedral School to the North, Buenos Aires — A761

1988, Sept. 10 Litho. *Perf. 13½*

1631	A761	3a multicolored	.65	.45

Domingo Faustino Sarmiento (1811-1888), educator, politician.

St. Cayetano, Patron of Workers A762

El Amor, by Antonio Berni, Pacific Gallery, Buenos Aires — A763

1988, Sept. 10 **Litho.**

1632 A762 2a multicolored .45 .45
1633 A762 3a Our Lady of Carmen, Cuyo .70 .70

Souvenir Sheet

Perf. 12

1634 A763 5a multicolored 1.00 1.00

Liniers Philatelic Circle and the Argentine Western Philatelic Institution (IFADO), 50th annivs.

No. 1634 contains one 40x30mm stamp.

No. 1617 Ovptd. with Congress Emblem and: "XXI CONGRESO DE LA SOCIEDAD INTERNACIONAL DE UROLOGIA"

1988, Oct. 29 **Litho.** ***Perf. 13½***

1635 A753 5a multicolored *3.50* .40

21st Congress of the Intl. Urology Soc.

Tourism A763a

1988, Nov. 1 **Litho.** ***Perf. 13½***

1635A A763a 3a Purmamarca, Jujuy .50 .25

Size: 28½x38mm

1635B A763a 20a Ushuaia 3.35 1.60

Buenos Aires Subway, 75th Anniv. A764

1988, Dec. 17 **Litho.** ***Perf. 13½***

1636 A764 5a Train, c. 1913 1.10 .55

Christmas A765

Frescoes in Ucrania Cathedral, Buenos Aires: No. 1637, *Virgin Patron.* No. 1638, *Virgin of Tenderness.*

1988, Dec. 17

1637 A765 5a multicolored 1.25 .50
1638 A765 5a multicolored 1.25 .50

St. John Bosco (1815-1888), Educator, and Church in Ushuaia — A766

1989, Apr. 8 **Litho.** ***Perf. 13½***

1639 A766 5a multicolored .30 .20

Dated 1988.

Art Type of 1988

Paintings: No. 1640, *Blancos,* by Fernando Fader (1882-1935). No. 1641, *Rincon de los Areneros,* by Justo Lynch (1870-1953).

1989, Apr. 8

1640 A754 5a multicolored .50 .20
1641 A754 5a multicolored .50 .20

Holy Week A767

Sculpture and churches: No. 1642, *The Crown of Thorns,* Calvary of Tandil, and Church of Our Lady Carmelite, Tandil. No. 1643, *Jesus the Nazarene* and Metropolitan Cathedral, Buenos Aires. No. 1644, *Jesus Encounters His Mother* (scene of the crucifixion), La Quebrada Village, San Luis. No. 1645, *Our Lady of Sorrow* and Church of Humahuaca, Jujuy.

1989, Apr. 22 **Litho.** ***Perf. 13½***

1642 A767 2a multicolored .20 .20
1643 A767 2a multicolored .20 .20
1644 A767 3a multicolored .30 .20
1645 A767 3a multicolored .30 .20
Nos. 1642-1645 (4) 1.00 .80

Printed in sheets of 16+4 labels containing blocks of 4 of each design. Labels picture Jesus's arrival in Jerusalem (Palm Sunday).

Prevent Alcoholism — A768

1989, Apr. 22

1646 A768 5a multicolored .30 .20

Natl. Park Type of 1987

1989, May 6 ***Perf. 13x13½***

1647 A752 5a Lihue Calel .70 .20
1648 A752 5a El Palmar .70 .20
1649 A752 5a Calilegua .70 .20
1650 A752 5a Chaco .70 .20
1651 A752 5a Los Glaciares .70 .20
Nos. 1647-1651 (5) 3.50 1.00

Admission of Argentina to the ITU, Cent. — A769

1989, May 6 ***Perf. 13½***

1652 A769 10a multicolored .45 .20

World Model Aircraft Championships — A770

1989, May 27 **Litho.** ***Perf. 13½***

1653 A770 5a F1A glider .20 .20
1654 A770 5a F1B rubber band motor .20 .20
1655 A770 10a F1C gas motor .35 .20
Nos. 1653-1655 (3) .75 .60

French Revolution, Bicent. — A771

Designs: 10a, "All men are born free and equal." 15a, French flag and *La Marianne,* by Gandon. 25a, *Liberty Guiding the People,* by Delacroix.

1989, July 1 **Litho.** ***Perf. 13½***

1656 A771 10a shown .50 .20
1657 A771 15a multicolored .50 .20

Souvenir Sheet

Perf. 12

1658 A771 25a multicolored .25 .20

No. 1658 contains one 40x30mm stamp.

The Republic, a Bronze Bust in the Congreso de la Nacion, Buenos Aires — A772

1989, Aug. 12 **Litho.** ***Perf. 13½***

1659 A772 300a on 50a multi .75 .50

Peaceful transition of power (presidential office). Not issued without surcharge.

Immigration to Argentina — A773

1989, Aug. 19 ***Perf. 13½***

1660 A773 150a S.S. *Weser,* 1889 .65 .35
1661 A773 200a Immigrant hotel, 1889 .75 .45

Souvenir Sheet

Perf. 12

1662 Sheet of 2 1.60 1.60
a. A773 150a like No. 1660 .65 .35
b. A773 200a like No. 1661 .75 .45

No. 1662 contains 40c30mm stamps.

Famous Men A774

Designs: No. 1663, Fr. Guillermo Furlong (1889-1974), historian, and title page of *The Jesuits.* No. 1664, Dr. Gregorio Alvarez (1889-1986), physician, and title page of *Canto a Chos Malal.* 200a, Brig.-Gen. Enrique Martinez (1789-1870) and lithograph *La Batalla de Maipu,* by Teodoro Gericault.

1989, Oct. 7 **Litho.** ***Perf. 13½***

1663 A774 150a multicolored .35 .20
1664 A774 150a multicolored .35 .20
1665 A774 200a multicolored .35 .20
Nos. 1663-1665 (3) 1.05 .60

America Issue — A775

Emblem of the Postal Union of the Americas and Spain (PUAS) and pre-Columbian art from Catamarca Province: 200a, Wooden mask from Atajo, Loma Morada. 300a, Urn of the Santa Maria Culture (Phase 3) from Punta de Balastro, Santa Maria Department.

1989, Oct. 14

1666 A775 200a multicolored .50 .35
1667 A775 300a multicolored .75 .50

Federal Police Week — A776

Children's drawings: No. 1668, Diego Molinari, age 13. No. 1669, Carlos Alberto Sarago, age 8. No. 1670, Roxana Andrea Osuna, age 7. No. 1671, Pablo Javier Quaglia, age 9.

1989, Oct. 28 **Litho.** ***Perf. 13½***

1668 A776 100a multi .25 .20
1669 A776 100a multi .25 .20
1670 A776 150a multi .40 .20
1671 A776 150a multi .40 .20
Nos. 1668-1671 (4) 1.30 .80

Battle of Vuelta de Obligado, 1845 — A777

Illustration reduced.

1989, Dec. 2 **Litho.** ***Perf. 13x13½***

1672 A777 300a multicolored .40 .20

Paintings — A778

Cristo de los Cerros, Sculpture by Chipo Cespedes A779

1989, Dec. 2 ***Perf. 13½***

1673 A778 200a Gato Frias .35 .20
1674 A778 200a Maria Carballido .35 .20
1675 A779 300a shown .35 .20
Nos. 1673-1675 (3) 1.05 .60

Christmas.

Buenos Aires Port, Cent. — A780

Illustration reduced.

1990, Mar. 3 **Litho.** ***Perf. 13½***

1676 A780 Strip of 4 7.50 6.00
a.-d. 200a any single 1.25 .65

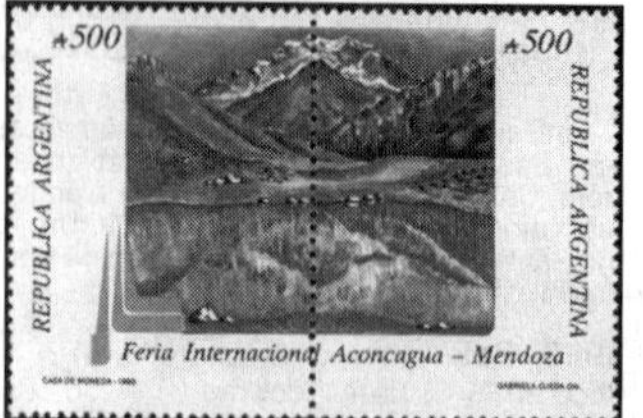

Aconcagua Intl. Fair, Mendoza — A781

Design: Aconcagua mountain, Los Horcones Lagoon and fair emblem.
Illustration reduced.

1990, Mar. 3

1677 A781 Pair, #a.-b. 2.00 1.50

Natl. Savings and Insurance Fund, 75th Anniv. — A782

1990, May 5 **Litho.** ***Perf. 13½***

1678 A782 1000a multicolored .35 .20

Miniature Sheet

1990 World Cup Soccer Championships, Italy — A783

Designs: a, Athlete's torso (striped jersey). b, Athlete's torso (solid jersey). c, Players' feet, soccer ball. d, Player (knee to waist).

1990, May 5

1679 A783 Sheet of 4 5.00 5.00
a.-d. 2500a multicolored 1.00 1.00

Carlos Pellegrini, Commercial High School Founder, Cent. — A784

1990, June 2 **Litho.** ***Perf. 13½***

1680 A784 2000a multicolored .30 .20

Youth Against Drugs A785

1990, June 2

1681 A785 2000a multicolored .30 .20

Intl. Literacy Year A786

1990, July 14 **Litho.** ***Perf. 13½***

1682 A786 2000a multicolored .30 .20

Flower Type of 1982 in New Currency

1989-90 **Photo.** ***Perf. 13½***

1683 A641	10a	like #1433	.20	.20
1684 A641	20a	like #1435A	.20	.20
1685 A641	50a	like #1354	.20	.20
1686 A641	100a	like #1439	.20	.20
1687 A641	300a	like #1345	.40	.20
1688 A641	500a	like #1441	.65	.35
1689 A641	1000a	like #1355	.20	.20
1690 A641	5000a	like #1349	1.00	.70
1691 A641	10,000a	like #1350	1.50	1.00
Nos. 1683-1691 (9)			4.55	3.25

Issued: 20a, 100a, 300a, 500a, 8/1/89; 10a, 8/24/89; 50a, 8/30/89; 1000, 3/8/90; 5000a, 4/6/90; 10,000a, 7/2/90.

World Basketball Championships A787

1990, Aug. 11 **Litho.** ***Perf. 13½***

1703 A787 2000a multicolored 2.00 1.50

Souvenir Sheet

Perf. 12

1704 A787 5000a Jump ball 3.75 2.75

Postal Union of the Americas and Spain, 14th Congress — A788

1990, Sept. 15 **Litho.** ***Perf. 13½***

1705 A788 3000a Arms, seal 1.50 .75
1706 A788 3000a Sailing ships 1.50 .75
1707 A788 3000a Modern freighter 1.50 .75
1708 A788 3000a Van, cargo plane 1.50 .75
Nos. 1705-1708 (4) 6.00 3.00

America Issue A789

1990, Oct. 13

1709 A789 3000a Iguacu Falls, hamelia erecta 1.50 .60
1710 A789 3000a Puerto Deseado, elephant seal 1.50 .60

Natl. Parks Type of 1987

1990, Oct. 27 ***Perf. 13x13½***

1715 A752 3000a Lanin 1.50 .65
1716 A752 3000a Laguna Blanca 1.50 .65
1717 A752 3000a Perito Moreno 1.50 .65
1718 A752 3000a Puelo 1.50 .65
1719 A752 3000a El Rey 1.50 .65
Nos. 1715-1719 (5) 7.50 3.25

Stamp Day A790

1990, Oct. 27 ***Perf. 13½***

1720 A790 3000a multicolored 1.50 .60

Salvation Army, Cent. — A793

Designs: No. 1722, Natl. University of the Littoral, Santa Fe, cent.

1990, Dec. 1 **Litho.** ***Perf. 13½***

1721 A793 3000a multicolored 1.75 1.00
1722 A793 3000a multicolored 1.75 1.00
a. Pair, #1721-1722 + label 3.75 2.25

Miniature Sheets

Christmas — A794

Stained glass windows: No. 1723, The Immaculate Conception. No. 1724, The Nativity. No. 1725, Presentation of Jesus at the Temple.

1990, Dec. 1 ***Perf. 13½x13***

Sheets of 4

1723 A794 3000a #a.-d. 6.00 6.00
1724 A794 3000a #a.-d. 6.00 6.00
1725 A794 3000a #a.-d. 6.00 6.00

Landscapes — A795

Paintings: No. 1726, Los Sauces, by Atilio Malinverno. No. 1727, Paisaje, by Pio Collivadino, vert.

1991, May 4 **Litho.** ***Perf. 13½***

1726 A795 4000a multicolored 1.00 .85
1727 A795 4000a multicolored 1.00 .85

Return of Remains of Juan Manuel de Rosas (1793-1877) A796

1991, June 1 **Litho.** ***Perf. 13½***

1728 A796 4000a multicolored 1.00 .85

Swiss Confederation, 700th Anniv. — A797

1991, Aug. 3 **Litho.** ***Perf. 13½***

1729 A797 4000a multicolored .95 .80

Miniature Sheet

Cartoons A798

Designs: a, Hernan, the Corsair by Jose Luis Salinas. b, Don Fulgencio by Lino Palacio. c, Medical Rules of Salerno by Oscar Esteban Conti. d, Buenos Aires Undershirt by Alejandro del Prado. e, Girls! by Jose A.G. Divito. f, Langostino by Eduardo Carlos Ferro. g, Mafalda by Joaquin Salvador Lavoro. h, Mort Cinder by Alberto Breccia.

1991, Aug. 3

1730 A798 4000a Sheet of 8, #a.-h. 7.75 7.50

City of La Rioja, 400th Anniv. — A799

1991, Sept. 14 Litho. *Perf. 13½*

1731 A799 4000a multicolored 1.00 .85

First Balloon Flight over the Andes, 75th Anniv. — A800

Illustration reduced.

1991, Sept. 14

1732 A800 4000a multicolored 1.00 .85

America Issue A801

#1733, Magellan's caravel, Our Lady of Victory. #1734, Ships of Juan Diaz de Solis.

1991, Nov. 9 Litho. *Perf. 13½*

1733 A801 4000a multicolored 1.00 .80
1734 A801 4000a multicolored 1.00 .80

Anniversaries — A802

Designs: a, J. Enrique Pestalozzi, founder of newspaper, Daily Argentinian. b, Leandro N. Alem, founder of Radical People's Party. c, Man with rifle, emblem of Argentine Federal Shooting Club. d, Dr. Nicasio Etchepareborda, emblem of College of Odontology. e, Dalmiro Huergo, emblem of Graduate School of Economics.

1991, Nov. 30

1735 A802 4000a Strip of 5, #a.-e. 5.00 4.00

Christmas — A803

Stained glass windows from Our Lady of Lourdes Basilica, Buenos Aires: Nos. 1736a-1736b, Top and bottom portions of Virgin of the Valley, Catamarca. Nos. 1736c-1736d, Top and bottom portions of Virgin of the Rosary of the Miracle, Cordoba.

1991, Nov. 30

1736 A803 4000a Block of 4, #a.-d. 5.00 3.50

Famous Men A804

Designs: a, Gen. Juan de Lavalle (1797-1841), Peruvian medal of honor. b, Brig. Gen. Jose Maria del Rosario Siriaco Paz (1791-1854), medal. c, Marco Manuel de Avellaneda (1813-1841), lawyer. d, Guillermo Enrique Hudson (1841-1922), author.

1991, Dec. 14 Litho. *Perf. 13½*

1737 A804 4000a Block of 4, #a.-d. 5.00 3.50

Birds — A805

1991, Dec. 28

1738 A805 4000a Pterocnemia pennata 1.25 .85
1739 A805 4000a Morphnu guianensis 1.25 .85
1740 A805 4000a Ara chloroptera 1.25 .85
Nos. 1738-1740 (3) 3.75 2.55

Miniature Sheet

Arbrafex '92, Argentina-Brazil Philatelic Exhibition — A806

Traditional costumes: a, Gaucho, woman. b, Gaucho, horse. c, Gaucho in store. d, Gaucho holding lariat.

1992 Litho. *Perf. 13½*

1741 A806 38c Sheet of 4, #a.-d. 5.00 4.00

Natl. Parks Type of 1987

1992, Apr. 4 Litho. *Perf. 13x13½*

1742 A752 38c Alerces .75 .55
1743 A752 38c Formosa Nature Reserve .75 .55
1744 A752 38c Petrified Forest .75 .55
1745 A752 38c Arrayanes .75 .55
1746 A752 38c Laguna de los Pozuelos .75 .55
Nos. 1742-1746 (5) 3.75 2.75

Mushrooms — A807

1992-94 Photo. *Perf. 13½*

1748 A807 10c Psilocybe cubensis .20 .20
1749 A807 25c Coprinus atramentarius .50 .35
a. Wmk. 365 30.00 30.00
1750 A807 38c like #1748 .75 .55
1751 A807 48c like #1749 .95 .65
1752 A807 50c Suillus granulatus 1.00 .70
1753 A807 51c Morchella esculenta 1.00 .70
1754 A807 61c Amanita muscaria 1.25 .85
1755 A807 68c Coprinus comatus 1.25 .85
1756 A807 1p like #1754 2.00 1.40
1757 A807 1.25p like #1752 2.50 1.75
1758 A807 1.77p Stropharia oeruginosa 3.50 2.50
1759 A807 2p like #1753 4.00 2.75
Nos. 1748-1759 (12) 18.90 13.25

No. 1758 not issued without overprint "Centro Filatelico de Neuquen y Rio Negro 50th Aniversario."

Issued: 38c, 4/4/92; 48c, 51c, 61c, 8/1/92; 1.77p, 11/7/92; 25c, 50c, 8/17/93; 1p, 2p, 8/26/93; 10c, 1/11/94; 68c, 1.25p, 10/10/92; #1749a, 1997.

See design A838.

Falkland Islands War, 10th Anniv. A808

1992, May 2 Litho. *Perf. 13½*

1767 A808 38c Pucara 1A-58 .75 .55
1768 A808 38c Cruiser Gen. Belgrano .75 .55
1769 A808 38c Soldier and truck .75 .55
Nos. 1767-1769 (3) 2.25 1.65

Miniature Sheet

Preserve the Environment — A809

a, Deer. b, Geese. c, Butterflies. d, Whale.

1992, June 6 Litho. *Perf. 12*

1770 A809 38c Sheet of 4, #a.-d. 5.00 4.00

Paintings by Florencio Molina Campos — A810

1992, June 6 *Perf. 13½*

1771 A810 38c A La Sombra .75 .55
1772 A810 38c Tileforo Areco, vert. .75 .55

Famous Men A811

Designs: No. 1773, Gen. Lucio N. Mansilla (1792-1871). No. 1774, Jose Manuel Estrada (1842-1894), writer. No. 1775, Brig. Gen. Jose I. Garmendia (1842-1915).

1992, July 4 Litho. *Perf. 13½*

1773 A811 38c multicolored .75 .55
1774 A811 38c multicolored .75 .55
1775 A811 38c multicolored .75 .55
Nos. 1773-1775 (3) 2.25 1.65

Fight Against Drugs — A812

1992, Aug. 1 *Perf. 13½x13*

1776 A812 38c multicolored .75 .55

Col. Jose M. Calaza, 140th Birth Anniv. A813

1992, Sept. 5 Litho. *Perf. 13½*

1777 A813 38c multicolored .75 .55

Discovery of America, 500th Anniv. — A814

Designs: a, Columbus, castle, ship. b, Native drawings, Columbus.

1992, Oct. 10 Litho. *Perf. 13½*

1778 A814 38c Pair, #a.-b. 1.50 1.50

Argentine Film Posters A815

1992, Nov. 7 Litho. *Perf. 13½*

1779 A815 38c Dios Se Lo Pague, 1948 .75 .55
1780 A815 38c Las Aguas Bajan Turbias, 1952 .75 .55
1781 A815 38c Un Guapo Del 900, 1960 .75 .55
1782 A815 38c La Tregua, 1974 .75 .55
1783 A815 38c La Historia Oficial, 1984 .75 .55
Nos. 1779-1783 (5) 3.75 2.75

Christmas
A816

1992, Nov. 28
1784 A816 38c multicolored .75 .55

Miniature Sheet

Iberoprenfil '92 — A817

Lighthouses: a, Punta Mogotes. b, Rio Negro. c, San Antonio. d, Cabo Blanco.

1992, Dec. 5
1785 A817 38c Sheet of 4, #a.-d. 5.00 3.00

Fight Against AIDS
A818 A819

1992, Dec. 12 Litho. *Perf. 13½*
1786 A818 10c multicolored 1.00 .30
1787 A819 26c multicolored 2.00 .50

Intl. Space Year
A820

1992, Dec. 19
1788 A820 38c multicolored .75 .55

Souvenir Sheet

Miraculous Lord Crucifix, 400th Anniv. of Arrival in America — A821

1992, Dec. 26 *Perf. 12*
1789 A821 76c multicolored 1.50 1.50

Jujuy City, 400th Anniv. — A822

1993, Apr. 24 Litho. *Perf. 13½*
1790 A822 38c multicolored .75 .55

Argentina Soccer Assoc., Cent. — A823

1993, Mar. 27
1791 A823 38c multicolored .75 .55

Souvenir Sheet

Intl. Philatelic Exhibitions
A824

Designs: a, 38c, City Hall, Poznan, Poland. b, 48c, Statue of Christ the Redeemer, Rio de Janeiro, Brazil. c, 76c, Royal Palace, Bangkok, Thailand.

1993, May 8 Litho. *Perf. 12*
1792 A824 Sheet of 3, #a.-c. 4.00 3.25

Polska '93 (#1792a), Brasiliana '93 (#1792b), Bangkok '92 (#1792c).

Luis C. Candelaria's Flight Over Andes Mountains, 75th Anniv. — A825

1993, June 26 Litho. *Perf. 13x13½*
1793 A825 38c multicolored .75 .55

Illustration reduced.

Order of San Martin, 50th Anniv. — A826

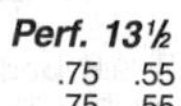
National History Academy, Cent. — A827

1993, May 29 *Perf. 13½*
1794 A826 38c multicolored .75 .55
1795 A827 38c multicolored .75 .55

Armed Forces Memorial Day — A828

1993, June 12
1796 A828 38c Natl. Gendarmerie .75 .55
1797 A828 38c Coast Guard .75 .55

Paintings — A829

#1798, Old House, by Norberto Russo. #1799, Pa'las Casas, by Adriana Zaefferer.

1993, Aug. 14 Litho. *Perf. 13½*
1798 A829 38c multicolored .75 .55
1799 A829 38c multicolored .75 .55

Pato — A830

1993, Aug. 28 Litho. *Perf. 12*
1800 A830 1p multicolored 2.00 1.40

Nut-Bearing Trees — A831

#1801, Enterolobium contortisiliquum. #1802, Prosopis alba. #1803, Magnolia grandiflora. #1804, Erythrina falcata. Illustration reduced.

1993, Sept. 25 Litho. *Perf. 13x13½*
1801 A831 75c multicolored 1.50 1.00
1802 A831 75c multicolored 1.50 1.00
1803 A831 1.50p multicolored 3.00 2.00
1804 A831 1.50p multicolored 3.00 2.00
Nos. 1801-1804 (4) 9.00 6.00

America Issue
A832

Whales: 50c, Eubalaena australis. 75c, Cephalorhynchus commersonii.

1993, Oct. 9 *Perf. 13½*
1805 A832 50c multicolored 1.00 .70
1806 A832 75c multicolored 1.50 1.10

Miniature Sheet

Christmas, New Year — A833

Denomination at: a, UL. b, UR. c, LL. d, LR.

1993, Dec. 4 Litho. *Perf. 13½*
1807 A833 75c Sheet of 4, #a.-d. 6.00 6.00

Cave of the Hands, Santa Cruz — A834

1993, Dec. 18
1808 A834 1p multicolored 2.00 1.40

New Emblem, Argentine Postal Service — A835

Illustration reduced.

1994, Jan. 8 ***Perf. 11½***

1809	A835	75c multicolored	6.00	.75

A836

1994 World Cup Soccer Championships, US — A837

Players from: 25c, Germany, 1990. 50c, Brazil, 1970. 75c, 1.50p, Argentina, 1986. 1p, Italy, 1982.

1994, June 11 **Litho.** ***Perf. 13½***

1810	A836	25c multicolored	.50	.20
1811	A836	50c multicolored	1.00	.70
1812	A836	75c multicolored	1.50	1.00
1813	A836	1p multicolored	2.00	1.40
		Nos. 1810-1813 (4)	5.00	3.30

Souvenir Sheet

Perf. 12

1814	A836	1.50p multicolored	3.00	3.00

No. 1814 contains one 40x50mm stamp with continuous design.

1994, July 23 ***Perf. 13½***

Drawings of championships by: No. 1815, Julian Lisenberg. No. 1816, Matias Taylor, vert. No. 1817, Torcuato S. Gonzalez Agote, vert. No. 1818, Maria Paula Palma.

1815	A837	75c multicolored	1.50	1.00
1816	A837	75c multicolored	1.50	1.00
1817	A837	75c multicolored	1.50	1.00
1818	A837	75c multicolored	1.50	1.00
		Nos. 1815-1818 (4)	6.00	4.00

Issued in sheet containing a block of 4 of each stamp + 4 labels.

A838

Molothrus Badius — A838a

1994-95 **Litho.** ***Perf. 13½***

1819	A838	10c like #1748	.20	.20
1820	A838	25c like #1749	.50	.35
1823	A838	50c like #1752	1.00	.70
1828	A838	1p like #1754	2.00	1.40
1832	A838	2p like #1753	4.00	2.75
1835	A838a	9.40p multicolored	19.00	13.00
		Nos. 1819-1835 (6)	26.70	18.40

See design A807.

Issued: 10c, 25c, 50c, 1p, 2p, 6/14/94; 9.40p, 4/12/95.

This is an expanding set. Numbers may change.

Wildlife of Falkland Islands A839

Designs: 25c, Melanodera melanodera. 50c, Pygoscelis papua. 75c, Tachyeres brachypterus. 1p, Mirounga leonina.

1994, Aug 6

1839	A839	25c multicolored	.50	.35
1840	A839	50c multicolored	1.00	.70
1841	A839	75c multicolored	1.50	1.00
1842	A839	1p multicolored	2.00	1.40
		Nos. 1839-1842 (4)	5.00	3.45

City of San Luis, 400th Anniv. — A840

1994, Aug. 20

1843	A840	75c multicolored	1.50	1.00

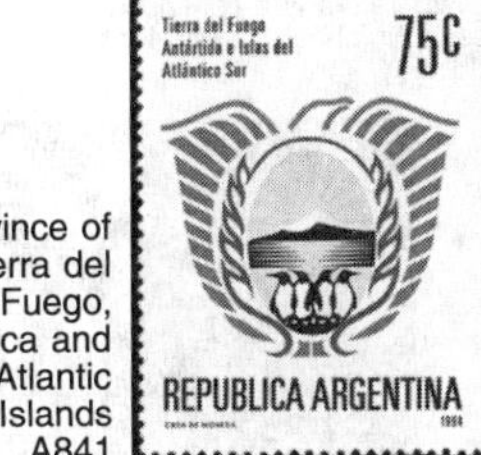

Province of Tierra del Fuego, Antarctica and South Atlantic Islands A841

1994, Aug. 20

1844	A841	75c multicolored	1.50	1.00

Argentine Inventors — A842

Designs: No. 1845, Ladislao Jose Biro (1899-1985), ball point pen. No. 1846, Raul Pateras de Pescara (1890-1966), helicopter. No. 1847, Quirino Cristiani (1896-1984), animated drawings. No. 1848, Enrique Finochietto (1881-1948), surgical instruments.

1994, Oct. 1

1845	A842	75c multicolored	1.50	1.00
1846	A842	75c multicolored	1.50	1.00
1847	A842	75c multicolored	1.50	1.00
1848	A842	75c multicolored	1.50	1.00
a.		Block of 4, #1845-1848	6.00	6.00

Issued in sheets containing 4 #1848a + 4 labels.

UNICEF Christmas A843

1994, Nov. 26 **Litho.** ***Perf. 11½***

1849	A843	50c shown	1.00	.70
1850	A843	75c Bell, bulb, star, diff.	1.50	1.00

Take Care of Our Planet A844

Children's paintings: No. 1851, Boy, girl holding earth, vert. No. 1852, Children outdoors, vert. No. 1853, World as house. No. 1854, People around "world" table.

1994, Dec. 3 ***Perf. 13½***

1851	A844	25c multicolored	.50	.35
1852	A844	25c multicolored	.50	.35
1853	A844	50c multicolored	1.00	.70
1854	A844	50c multicolored	1.00	.70
		Nos. 1851-1854 (4)	3.00	2.10

Christmas — A845

1994, Dec. 10

1855	A845	50c Annunciation	1.00	.70
1856	A845	75c Madonna & Child	1.50	1.00

Nos. 1855-1856 each issued in sheets of 20 + 5 labels.

12th Pan American Games, Mar del Plata — A846

1995 **Litho.** ***Perf. 13½***

1857	A846	75c Running	1.50	1.00
1858	A846	75c Cycling	1.50	1.00
1859	A846	75c Diving	1.50	1.00
1860	A846	1.25p Gymnastics, vert.	2.50	1.75
1861	A846	1.25p Soccer, vert.	2.50	1.75
		Nos. 1857-1861 (5)	9.50	6.50

Issued: No. 1857, 2/18; others, 3/11.

Natl. Constitution — A847

Design: 75c, Natl. Congress Dome, woman from statue The Republic Triumphant.

1995, Apr. 8

1862	A847	75c multicolored	1.50	1.00

21st Intl. Book Fair — A848

Illustration reduced.

1995, Apr. 8

1863	A848	75c multicolored	1.50	1.00

Birds A849

1995 **Litho.** ***Perf. 13½***

1876	A849	5p Carduelis magellanica	10.00	7.00
1880	A849	10p Zonotrichia capensis	20.00	14.00

Issued: 5p, 10p, 5/23/95. This is an expanding set. Numbers may change.

A850

1995, Mar. 25 **Litho.** ***Die Cut***

Self-Adhesive

1883A	A850	25c multicolored	8.00	.35
1884	A850	75c multicolored	2.00	1.00
a.		Booklet pane, 2 #1883A, 6 #1884	12.50	
		Complete booklet, #1884a	50.00	
b.		Booklet pane, 4 #1883A, 12 #1884	25.00	
		Complete booklet, #1884b	80.00	

Argentine Engineers' Center, Cent. — A851

1995, June 3 ***Perf. 13½***

1885	A851	75c multicolored	1.50	1.00

Jose Marti (1853-95) — A852

#1887, Antonio Jose de Sucre (1795-1830).

1995, Aug. 12 **Litho.** ***Perf. 13½***

1886	A852	1p multicolored	2.00	1.40
1887	A852	1p multicolored	2.00	1.40

Fauna — A853

1995, Sept. 1 **Litho.** ***Perf. 13½***

1888	A853	5c Ostrich	.20	.20
1889	A853	25c Penguin	.50	.35
1890	A853	50c Toucan	1.00	.70
1891	A853	75c Condor	1.50	1.00
1892	A853	1p Owl	2.00	1.40
1893	A853	2p Bigua	4.00	2.75
1894	A853	2.75p Tero	5.50	3.75

Booklet Stamps

Perf. 13½ on 2 or 3 Sides

1895 A853 25c Alligator .50 .35
1896 A853 50c Fox 1.00 .70
1897 A853 75c Anteater 1.50 1.00
1898 A853 75c Deer 1.50 1.00
1899 A853 75c Whale 1.50 1.00
a. Booklet pane, 1 each Nos. 1889-1891, 1895-1899 9.00
Complete booklet, #1899a 9.00
Nos. 1888-1899 (12) 20.70 14.20

See Nos. 1958, 2004-2004A.

Native Heritage — A854

a, Cave drawings, shifting sands. b, Stone mask. c, Anthropomorphous vessel. d, Woven textile.

1995, Sept. 9
1900 A854 75c Block of 4, #a.-d. 6.00 6.00

Sunflower, Postal Service Emblem — A855

1995, Oct. 7
1901 A855 75c multicolored 7.00 .75

Juan D. Peron (1895-1974) — A856

1995, Oct. 7
1902 A856 75c lt ol bis & dk bl 1.50 1.00

Miniature Sheet

Anniversaries — A857

Annivs: a, UN, 50th. b, ICAO, 50th (in 1994). c, FAO, 50th. d, ILO, 75th (in 1994).

1995, Oct. 14 ***Perf. 12***
1903 A857 75c Sheet of 4, #a.-d. 6.00 6.00

Christmas and New Year — A858

Designs: Nos. 1904, 1908, Christmas tree, presents. No. 1905, "1996." No. 1906, Champagne glasses. No. 1907, Present.

1995, Nov. 25 **Litho.** ***Perf. 13½***
1904 A858 75c multicolored 1.50 1.00

Booklet Stamps

Perf. 13½ on 1 or 2 Sides

1905 A858 75c multicolored 1.50 1.00
1906 A858 75c multicolored 1.50 1.00
1907 A858 75c multicolored 1.50 1.00
1908 A858 75c multicolored 1.50 1.00
a. Booklet pane, #1905-1908 + label 6.00
Complete booklet, #1908a 6.00
Nos. 1904-1908 (5) 7.50 5.00

No. 1908a is a continuous design. Ribbon extends from edge to edge on #1908 and stops at edge of package on #1905.

Miniature Sheet

Motion Pictures, Cent. A859

Black and white film clips, director: a, The Battleship Potemkin, Sergei Eisenstein (Soviet Union). b, Casablanca, Michael Curtiz (US). c, Bicycle Thief, Vittorio De Sica (Italy). d, Limelights, Charles Chaplin (England). e, The 400 Blows, Francois Truffaut (France). f, Chronicle of the Lonely Child, Leonardo Favio (Argentina).

1995, Dec. 2 ***Perf. 13½***
1909 A859 75c Sheet of 6, #a.-f. 9.00 9.00

The Sky — A860

1995, Dec. 16 ***Perf. 13½ on 3 Sides***

Booklet Stamps

1910 A860 25c Dirigible .50 .35
1911 A860 25c Kite .50 .35
1912 A860 25c Hot air balloon .50 .35
1913 A860 50c Balloons 1.00 .70
1914 A860 50c Paper airplane 1.00 .70
1915 A860 75c Airplane 1.50 1.00
1916 A860 75c Helicopter 1.50 1.00
1917 A860 75c Parachute 1.50 1.00
a. Booklet pane, #1910-1917 + label 8.00
Complete booklet, No. 1917a 8.00

Nos. 1910-1917 do not appear in Scott number order in No. 1917a, which has a continuous design.

America Issue A861

Postal vehicles from Postal &Telegraph Museum: #1918, Horse & carriage. #1919, Truck.

1995, Dec. 16 ***Perf. 13½***
1918 A861 75c multicolored 1.50 1.00
1919 A861 75c multicolored 1.50 1.00

Olympic Games, Cent. A862

1996, Mar. 30 **Litho.** ***Perf. 13½***
1920 A862 75c Running 1.50 1.00
1921 A862 1p Discus 2.00 1.40

Physicians A863

Designs: a, Francisco J. Muniz (1795-1871). b, Ricardo Gutierrez (1838-96). c, Ignacio Pirovano (1844-95). d, Esteban L. Maradona (1895-1995).

1996, Apr. 20 **Litho.** ***Perf. 12***
1922 A863 50c Sheet of 4 4.00 4.00
a.-d. Any single 1.00 1.00

Jerusalem, 3000th Anniv. — A864

7th cent. mosaic maps of city, denomination at: No. 1923, LL. No. 1924, LR.

1996, May 18 **Litho.** ***Perf. 13½***
1923 A864 75c multicolored 1.50 1.00
1924 A864 75c multicolored 1.50 1.00
a. Pair, #1923-1924 5.00 3.00

No. 1924a is a continuous design and was issued in sheets of 8 + 4 labels.

Endangered Fauna — A865

1996, June 15 **Litho.** ***Perf. 13½***
1925 A865 75c Capybara 1.50 1.00
1926 A865 75c Guanaco 1.50 1.00
a. Pair, #1925-1926 3.00 3.00

America Issue.

Summer Olympic Games A866

Designs: 75c, Torch bearer, Buenos Aires, candidate for 2004 Games. 1p, Men's eight with coxswain, Atlanta, 1996.

1996, July 6
1927 A866 75c multicolored 1.50 1.00
1928 A866 1p multicolored 2.00 1.40

National Parks — A867

Wildlife, national park: No. 1929, Mountain turkey, Diamante. No. 1930, Parrot, San Antonio Nature Reserve. No. 1931, Deer, Otamendi Natl. Reserve. No. 1932, Rabbit, El Leoncito Nature Reserve.

Illustration reduced.

1996, Aug. 24 **Litho.** ***Perf. 13x13½***
1929 A867 75c multicolored 1.50 1.00
1930 A867 75c multicolored 1.50 1.00
1931 A867 75c multicolored 1.50 1.00
1932 A867 75c multicolored 1.50 1.00
Nos. 1929-1932 (4) 6.00 4.00

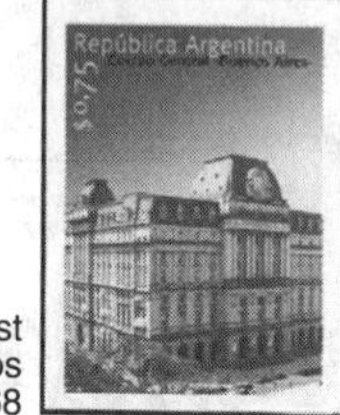

Central Post Office, Buenos Aires — A868

1996, Oct. 5 **Litho.** ***Die Cut***

Self-Adhesive

Size: 25x35mm

1933 A868 75c multicolored 1.50 1.50

Vignette of No. 1933 is broken by circular and rectangular die cut areas to guard against reuse.

See Nos. 1983-1984.

Carousel Figures — A869

#1934, Hand-carved decorative ornaments. #1935, Child on carousel horse. #1936, Carousel. #1937, Heads of horses. #1938, Child in airplane. #1939, Carousel pig. #1940, Boy in car.

1996, Oct. 5 ***Perf. 13½ Horiz.***

Booklet Stamps

1934 A869 25c multicolored .50 .50
1935 A869 25c multicolored .50 .50
1936 A869 25c multicolored .50 .50
1937 A869 50c multicolored 1.00 1.00
1938 A869 50c multicolored 1.00 1.00
1939 A869 50c multicolored 1.00 1.00
1940 A869 75c multicolored 1.50 1.50
a. Booklet pane, #1934-1940 6.00
Complete booklet, #1940a 6.00

Sequence of stamps in No. 1940a: No. 1940, 1934, 1937, 1935, 1938, 1936, 1939.

Port Belgrano Naval Base, Cent. — A870

Designs: 25c, LST "San Antonio." 50c, Corvette *Rosales.* 75c, Destroyer *Hercules.* 1p, Aircraft carrier, "25th of May."

1996-97 **Litho.** ***Perf. 13½***
1941 A870 25c multicolored .50 .50
1942 A870 50c multicolored 1.00 1.00
1943 A870 75c multicolored 1.50 1.50
1944 A870 1p multicolored 2.00 2.00
Nos. 1941-1944 (4) 5.00 5.00

Issued: 25c, 1p, 10/5/96; 50c, 75c, 2/1/97.

Christmas — A871

Tapestries: 75c, Nativity, by Gladys Angelica Rinaldi, vert. 1p, Candles, by Norma Bonet de Maekawa.

1996, Nov. 30 Litho. *Perf. 13½*
1945 A871 75c multicolored 1.50 1.50
1946 A871 1p multicolored 2.00 2.00

Exploration of Antarctica — A872

Designs: 75c, Melchior Base. 1.25p, Icebreaker ARA Alte. Irizar.

1996, Nov. 30
1947 A872 75c multicolored 1.50 1.50
1948 A872 1.25p multicolored 2.50 2.50

National Gallery, Cent. A873

Paintings of women by: 75c, Paul Gauguin, vert. No. 1950, Edouard Monet, vert. No. 1951, Amedeo Modigiliani, vert. 1.25p, Pablo Picasso.

1996, Dec. 14
1949 A873 75c multicolored 1.50 1.50
1950 A873 1p multicolored 2.00 2.00
1951 A873 1p multicolored 2.00 2.00
1952 A873 1.25p multicolored 2.50 2.50
Nos. 1949-1952 (4) 8.00 8.00

Mining Industry — A874

1997, Feb. 1 Litho. *Perf. 13½*
1953 A874 75c Granite 1.50 1.50
1954 A874 1.25p Borax 2.50 2.50

Traditional Costumes — A875

1997, Feb. 22 Litho. *Perf. 13½*
1955 A875 75c multicolored 1.50 1.50

America issue.

Repatriation of the Curved Sword of Gen. San Martin, Cent. — A876

1997, Mar. 15 Litho. *Perf. 13½*
1956 A876 75c multicolored 1.50 1.50

29th Youth Rugby World Championships — A877

1997, Mar. 22
1957 A877 75c multicolored 1.50 1.50

Fauna Type of 1995

1997, Feb. 22 Litho. *Perf. 13½*
1958 A853 10c Reddish sandpiper .20 .20

Buenos Aires-Rio de Janeiro Regatta, 50th Anniv. — A879

1997, Apr. 5 Litho. *Perf. 13½*
1960 A879 75c Fortuna II 1.50 1.50

Natl. History Museum, Cent. — A880

1997, May 17
1961 A880 75c multicolored 1.50 1.50

La Plata Natl. University, Cent. — A881

1997, May 17
1962 A881 75c multicolored 1.50 1.50

Lighthouses A882

a, Cabo Virgenes. b, Isla Pingüino. c, San Juan de Salvamento. d, Punta Delgada.

1997, May 31
1963 A882 75c Sheet of 4, #a.-d. 6.00 6.00

Ramón J. Cárcano (1860-1946), Developer of Postal and Telegraph System A883

1997, May 31
1964 A883 75c multicolored 1.50 1.50

Buenos Aires, Candidate for 2004 Summer Olympics — A884

1997, June 21
1965 A884 75c multicolored 1.50 1.50

First Electric Tram in Buenos Aires, Cent. A885

Designs: a, Lacroze Suburban Service Tram Co, 1912. b, Lacroze Urban Service Tram Co., 1907. c, Anglo Argentina Tram Co., 1930. d, Buenos Aires City Transportation Corp., 1942. e, Military Manufacture Tram, 1956. f, South Electric Tram, 1908.

1997, July 12
Sheet of 6
1966 A885 75c #a.-f. + 2 labels 9.00 9.00

Monument to Joaquín V. González (1863-1923), La Rioja — A886

1997, Aug. 9
1967 A886 75c multicolored 1.50 1.50

Musicians and Composers A887

Paintings: No. 1968, Alberto Ginastera (1916-83), by Carlos Nine. No. 1969, Astor Piazzolla (1921-92), by Carlos Alonso. No. 1970, Anibal Troilo (1914-75), by Hermenegildo Sabat. No. 1971, Atahualpa Yupanqui (b. 1908), by Luis Scafati.

1997, Aug. 9
1968 A887 75c multicolored 1.50 1.50
1969 A887 75c multicolored 1.50 1.50
1970 A887 75c multicolored 1.50 1.50
1971 A887 75c multicolored 1.50 1.50
Nos. 1968-1971 (4) 6.00 6.00

Argentine Authors — A888

#1972, Jorge Luis Borges (1899-1986), maze. #1973, Julio Cortázar (1914-84), hop scotch game.

1997, Aug. 30 Litho. *Perf. 13*
1972 A888 1p multicolored 2.00 2.00
1973 A888 1p multicolored 2.00 2.00

Women's Political Rights Law, 50th Anniv. A889

1997, Sept. 6 Litho. *Perf. 13½*
1974 A889 75c Eva Perón 3.00 1.50

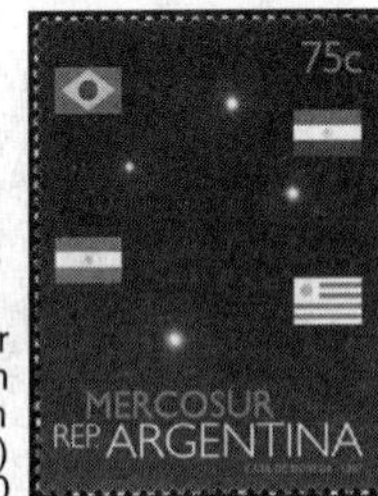
Mercosur (Common Market of Latin America) A890

1997, Sept. 27 Litho. *Perf. 13½*
1975 A890 75c multicolored 1.50 1.50

See Bolivia #1019, Brazil #2646, Paraguay #2564, Uruguay #1681.

Launching of Frigate President Sarmiento, Cent. — A891

#1976, Painting of ship by Hugo Leban.

#1977: a, Ship. b, Ship's figurehead, vert.

1997, Oct. 4

1976 A891 75c multicolored 1.50 1.50

Souvenir Sheet

Perf. 12

1977 A891 75c Sheet of 2, #a.-b. 5.00 3.00

No. 1977 contains two 40x30mm stamps.

Ernesto "Che" Guevara (1928-67) A892

1997, Oct. 18

1978 A892 75c multicolored 5.00 1.50

Ecology on Stamps — A893

Children's drawings: No. 1979, Animal, by J. Chiapparo, vert. No. 1980, Vicuna, by L.L. Portal, vert. No. 1981, Seal, by A. Lloren. No. 1982, Bird in flight, by J. Saccone.

1997, Nov. 8 Litho. *Perf. 13½*

1979 A893 50c multicolored 1.00 1.00
1980 A893 50c multicolored 1.00 1.00
1981 A893 75c multicolored 1.50 1.50
1982 A893 75c multicolored 1.50 1.50
Nos. 1979-1982 (4) 5.00 5.00

Central Post Office, Buenos Aires, Type of 1996

1997, July 24 Litho. *Die Cut*

Self-Adhesive

Size: 23x35mm

1983 A868 25c multicolored .50 .50
1984 A868 75c multicolored 1.50 1.50
a. Bklt. pane, 2 #1983, 6 #1984 10.00
Complete booklet, #1984a 10.00

Nos. 1983-1984 are broken at both the top and bottom of each stamp by three lines of wavy die cutting.

Christmas — A893a

Nativity scene tapestries by: #1984B, 1984G, Mary José. #1984C, Elena Aguilar. #1984D, Silvia Pettachi. #1984E, Ana Escobar. #1984F, Alejandra Martinez. #1984H, Nidia Martinez.

1997, Nov. 22 Litho. *Perf. 13½*

1984B A893a 75c multicolored 1.50 1.50

Booklet Stamps

Self-Adhesive

Size: 44x27mm

Die Cut

1984C A893a 25c multicolored .50 .50
1984D A893a 25c multicolored .50 .50
1984E A893a 50c multicolored 1.00 1.00
1984F A893a 50c multicolored 1.00 1.00
1984G A893a 75c multicolored 1.50 1.50
1984H A893a 75c multicolored 1.50 1.50
i. Booklet pane, #1984C-1984H 6.00

Nos. 1984C-1984H are broken at upper right by three die cut chevrons.

Mother Teresa (1910-97) A893b

1997, Dec. 27

1984J A893b 75c multicolored 1.60 1.50

Dr. Bernardo A. Houssay (1887-1971), 1947 Nobel Prize Winner in Medicine — A894

1998, Jan. 31 Litho. *Perf. 13½*

1985 A894 75c multicolored 1.50 1.50

First Ascension of Mount Aconcagua, Cent. — A895

Illustration reduced.

1998, Feb. 14 *Perf. 12*

1986 A895 1.25p multicolored 3.00 2.50

Founding of San Martin de los Andes, Cent. — A896

1998, Mar. 14 Litho. *Perf. 13½*

1987 A896 75c multicolored 1.60 1.50

Regimental Quarters of Gen. San Martin's Mounted Grenadiers A897

Designs: a, Statue. b, Large jar with painting of San Martin. c, Regimental seal. d, Regimental quarters.

1998, Mar. 21 Litho. *Perf. 13½*

1988 A897 75c Block of 4, #a.-d. 6.50 6.00

Protection of the Ozone A898

1998, Mar. 28 Litho. *Perf. 13½*

1989 A898 75c multicolored 1.50 1.50

America Issue — A899

Letter carriers: #1990, Wearing white uniform. #1991, Carrying letter bag with shoulder strap.

1998, Apr. 4

1990 A899 75c multicolored 1.50 1.50
1991 A899 75c multicolored 1.50 1.50

Characters from Stories by Maria Elena Walsh — A900

#1992, El Reino Del Reves. #1993, Zoo Loco. #1994, Dailan Kifki. #1995, Manuelita.

1998, Apr. 17 Litho. *Die Cut*

Booklet Stamps

Self-Adhesive

1992 A900 75c multicolored 1.50 1.50
1993 A900 75c multicolored 1.50 1.50
1994 A900 75c multicolored 1.50 1.50
1995 A900 75c multicolored 1.50 1.50
a. Complete booklet, #1992-1995 7.50

Historic Chapels A901

#1996, San Pedro de Fiambalá, Catamarca. #1997, Huacalera, Jujuy. #1998, Santo Domingo, La Rioja. #1999, Tumbaya, Jujuy.

1998, Apr. 25 Litho. *Perf. 13x13½*

1996 A901 75c multicolored 1.50 1.50
1997 A901 75c multicolored 1.50 1.50
1998 A901 75c multicolored 1.50 1.50
1999 A901 75c multicolored 1.50 1.50
Nos. 1996-1999 (4) 6.00 6.00

White Helmets, A Commitment to Humanity — A902

1998, May 23 Litho. *Perf. 13½*

2000 A902 1p multicolored 2.00 2.00

Beginning with No. 2001, many Argentine stamps are inscribed "Correo Official," but these are not Official stamps (i.e., for government use only).

1998 World Cup Soccer Championships, France — A903

Stylized players representing: a, Argentina. b, Croatia. c, Jamaica. d, Japan.

1998, May 30

2001 A903 75c Block of 4, #a.-d. 6.25 6.00

Journalist's Day — A904

1998, June 20

2002 A904 75c multicolored 1.50 1.50

Creation of Argentine Postal System, 250th Anniv. — A905

a, Corrientes design A2, peso coin. b, Building, post box.

1998, June 27

2003 A905 75c Pair, #a.-b. 3.25 3.00

Fauna Type of 1995

1998 Litho. *Die Cut*

Self-Adhesive (#2004)

2004 A853 60c Picaflor 1.25 1.25

Perf. 13½

2004A A853 3.25p Tero 6.50 6.50

#2004 is broken at bottom right by 3 or 5 lines of wavy die cutting.

Issued: 60c, 12/12; 3.25p, 7/22.

Ruins, Mission St. Ignacio A906

1998, July 25 Litho. *Perf. 13½*

2005 A906 75c multicolored 1.50 1.50

Mercosur.

Cattle A907

1998, Aug. 1

2006 A907 25c Brahman .50 .50
2007 A907 25c Aberdeen-Angus .50 .50
2008 A907 50c Hereford 1.00 1.00
2009 A907 50c Criolla 1.00 1.00
2010 A907 75c Holland-Argentina 1.60 1.50
2011 A907 75c Shorthorn 1.60 1.50
Nos. 2006-2011 (6) 6.20 6.00

Deception Island Base, Antarctica, 50th Anniv. — A908

1998, Aug. 15 Litho. *Perf. 14½*

2012 A908 75c multicolored 1.60 1.50

State of Israel, 50th Anniv. A909

1998, Sept. 5 Litho. *Perf. 13½*

2013 A909 75c multicolored 1.50 1.50

Argentine-Japan Friendship Treaty, Cent. — A910

1998, Oct. 3

2014 A910 75c multicolored 1.50 1.50

Post Office Building, Buenos Aires, 70th Anniv. A911

Designs: No. 2015, Building, clock, tile. No. 2016, Column ornamentation, tile, bench.

1998, Oct. 3

2015 A911 75c multicolored 1.50 1.50
2016 A911 75c multicolored 1.50 1.50
a. Pair, #2015-2016 3.25 3.00

Cartoons — A912

Designs: a, Patoruzu, by Quinterno. b, Matias, by Sendra. c, Clemente, by Caloi. d, El Eternauta, by Oesterheld and López. e, Loco Chavez, by Trillo and Altuna. f, Inodoro Pereyra, by Fontanarrosa. g, Tia Vicenta, by Landrú. h, Gaturro, by Nik.

1998, Oct. 17 Litho. *Perf. 13¾x13¼*

2017 A912 75c Sheet of 8, #a.-h. 13.00 12.00

Dr. Pedro de Elizalde's Children's Hospital, 220th Anniv. — A913

1998, Oct. 24 Litho. *Perf. 13½*

2025 A913 15c multicolored 2.25 1.00

Raoul Wallenberg (1912-47), Humanitarian — A914

1998, Nov. 21

2026 A914 75c multicolored 1.60 1.50

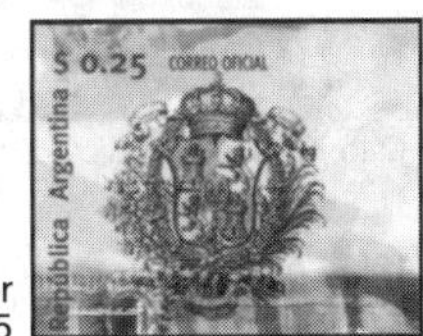

Espamer '98 — A915

25c, Spanish flags, arms. 75c, 18th cent. schooner. 75c+75c, Brigantine, gray sails. 1.25p+1.25p, Brigantine, white sails.

1998, Nov. 21 *Die Cut*

Booklet Stamps

Self-Adhesive

2027 A915 25c multicolored .50 .50
2028 A915 75c multicolored 1.50 1.50
2029 A915 75c +75c multi 3.00 3.00
2030 A915 1.25p +1.25p multi 5.00 5.00
a. Booklet pane, #2027-2030 12.00

Nos. 2027-2030 are broken at top right of each stamp by four lines of wavy die cutting. No. 2030a is a complete booklet.

Organization of American States, 50th Anniv. — A916

1998, Nov. 28 *Perf. 13½*

2031 A916 75c multicolored 1.50 1.50

Dinosaurs of Argentina — A917

Designs: a, Eoraptor. b, Gasparinisaura. c, Giganotosaurus. d, Patagosaurus.

1998, Nov. 28

2032 A917 75c Sheet of 4, #a.-d. 9.00 6.00

Christmas A918

1998, Dec. 5

2033 A918 75c multicolored 1.60 1.50

Newspaper El Liberal, Cent. A919

1998, Dec. 5

2034 A919 75c Juan A. Figueroa 1.60 1.50

La Nueva Provincia, Daily Newspaper, Cent. A920

1998, Dec. 12

2035 A920 75c Enrique Julio 1.60 1.50

Universal Declaration of Human Rights, 50th Anniv. — A921

1998, Dec. 12

2036 A921 75c multicolored 1.50 1.50

Holocaust Memorial, Cathedral of Buenos Aires — A922

1998, Dec. 12

2037 A922 75c multicolored 1.60 1.50

Southern Cross — A923

Inscriptions: 8.75p, Sur postal express. 17.50p, Sur postal 24.

1999-2000 Litho. *Die Cut*

Self-Adhesive

2038 A923 8.75p bl & silver 14.00 14.00
2039 A923 17.50p bl & gold 27.50 27.50

Issued: 8.75p, 7/1/99; 17.50p, 3/2/00. Nos. 2038-2039 are broken at right by five wavy lines of die cutting.

National Fund for the Arts, 40th Anniv. A925

1999, Mar. 6 Litho. *Perf. 13½*

2042 A925 75c multicolored 1.50 1.50

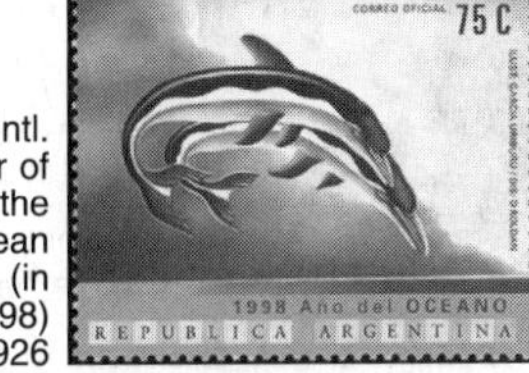

Intl. Year of the Ocean (in 1998) A926

1999, Mar. 6

2043 A926 50c Penguin, vert. 1.00 1.00
2044 A926 75c Dolphins 1.60 1.50

Postmen — A927

Designs: 25c, Early postman, city scene. 50c, Early postman, people on bicycles, factory. 75c, Modern postman, city buildings.

1998-99 Litho. *Die Cut*

Self-Adhesive

2045 A927 25c multicolored .50 .50
2046 A927 75c multicolored 1.50 1.50
a. Strip of 4, 1 #2045, 3 #2046 5.00

Booklet Stamps

Serpentine Die Cut

2047 A927 25c multicolored .50 .50
2048 A927 75c multicolored 1.50 1.50
a. Bklt. pane, 2 #2047, 6 #2048 10.00
Complete booklet, #2048a 10.00

Size: 21x27mm

Die Cut

2049 A927 25c multicolored .50 .50
2050 A927 50c multicolored 1.00 1.00
2051 A927 75c multicolored 1.50 1.50
a. Bklt. pane, 2 ea #2049-2051 6.00
Complete booklet, #2051a 6.00

Nos. 2045-2048 are broken at lower right by five lines of wavy die cutting. Nos. 2049-2051 are broken in center by five wavy lines of die cutting. Nos. 2045-2046 have darker vignettes than #2047-2048.

Issued: Nos. 2045-2048, 12/9/98. Nos. 2049-2051, 2/2/99.

25th Book Fair A928

Designs: a, Book. b, Obelisk, readers.

1999, Apr. 17 Litho. *Perf. 13¾x13½*

2052 A928 75c Pair, a.-b. 3.25 3.00

Argentine Rugby Union, Cent. — A929

75c, Player, balls. 1.50p, Old, modern players.

1999, Apr. 24 Litho. ***Perf. 13¾x13½***

2054 A929 75c multicolored 1.60 1.50

Souvenir Sheet

2055 A929 1.50p multi + 3 labels 3.00 3.00

Cafes of Buenos Aires — A930

Designs: a, Mug, Giralda Dairy. b, Two glasses, Homero Manzi Cafe. c, Hat hanging on rack, Ideal Sweet Shop. d, Cup and saucer, Tortoni Cafe.

Serpentine Die Cut

1999, Apr. 30 Litho.

Self-Adhesive

2056	Booklet pane of 4	6.50	
a.	A930 25c multicolored	.50	.50
b.-c.	A930 75c multi, each	1.50	1.50
d.	A930 1.25p multicolored	2.50	2.50
	Complete booklet, #2056	6.50	

Argentine Olympic Committee, 75th Anniv. — A931

1999, May 15 ***Perf. 14x13¼***

2057 A931 75c Pierre de Coubertin 1.50 1.50

Enrico Caruso (1873-1921), Opera Singer — A932

Designs: a, Portrait of Caruso. b, Singer, various musical instruments. c, Outside of Colon Theatre, Buenos Aires. d, Scene from opera, "El Matrero."

1999, May 15 ***Perf. 13½***

2058 A932 75c Sheet of 4, #a.-d. 6.00 6.00

Famous Women A933

Designs: a, Rosario Vera Penaloza (1873-1950), educator. b, Julieta Lanteri (1862-1932), physician.

1999, June 5 ***Perf. 14x13¼***

2059 A933 75c Pair, #a.-b. 3.00 3.00

Souvenir Sheets

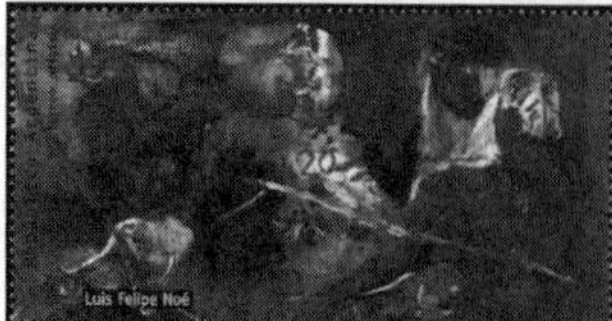

Paintings from Natl. Museum of Art, Buenos Aires — A934

No. 2060: a, Anarchy of Year 20, by Luis Felipe Noé. b, Retrato de L.E.S., by Carlos Alonso.

No. 2061: a, Typical Orchestra, by Antonio Berni. b, Untitled, (Woman seated), by Aída Carballo.

Illustration reduced.

1999, June 5 ***Perf. 14***

Sheets of 2

2060-2061 A934 75c #a.-b., each 3.00 3.00

No. 2060b is 40x40mm, No. 2061a, 70x50mm, No. 2061b, 40x50mm.

Carrier Pigeon A935

1999, June 12 ***Perf. 13¾x13½***

2062 A935 75c multicolored 1.50 1.50

Maps — A936

1999, June 12 ***Die Cut***

Self-Adhesive

2063	A936	35c Local highway	.70	.70
2064	A936	40c City street	.80	.80
2065	A936	50c Regional highway	1.00	1.00
		Nos. 2063-2065 (3)	2.50	2.50

Nos. 2063-2065 are broken at lower left by five wavy lines of die cutting.

Dogs A937

Designs: a, 25c, Boxer. b, 25c, English sheepdog. c, 50c, Collie. d, 50c, St. Bernard. e, 75c, German shepherd. f, 75c, Siberian husky.

1999, July 24 Litho. ***Perf. 13½***

2066 A937 Sheet of 6, #a.-f. 6.00 6.00

Natl. Telecommunications Day — A938

1999, July 24 ***Perf. 13½x13¾***

2067 A938 75c multicolored 1.50 1.50

Justo José de Urquiza School, Concepcion del Uruguay, 150th Anniv. — A939

1999, Aug. 7 ***Perf. 13¾x13½***

2068 A939 75c multicolored 1.50 1.50

Otto Krause Technical School, Buenos Aires, Cent. — A940

1999, Aug. 7 ***Perf. 13½x13¾***

2069 A940 75c multicolored 1.50 1.50

Bethlehem 2000 Project — A941

1999, Aug. 21 ***Perf. 13½***

2070 A941 75c multicolored 3.00 1.50

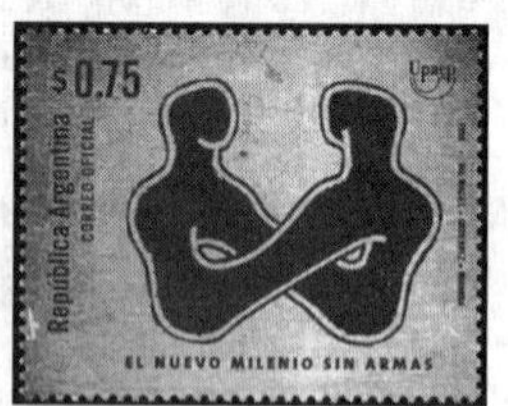

America Issue, A New Millennium Without Arms — A942

Perf. 13½x13¾, 13¾x13½

1999, Aug. 21

2071 A942 75c shown 1.50 1.50

2072 A942 75c Tree of hands, vert. 1.50 1.50

National Parks — A943

Parks and animals: No. 2073, Mburucuyá, coypu. No. 2074, Quebrada de Los Condoritos, condor. No. 2075, San Guillermo, vicuna. No. 2076, Sierra de las Quijadas, puma. No. 2077, Talampaya, gray fox.

Illustration reduced.

1999, Sept. 25 Litho. ***Perf. 14x13½***

2073	A943	50c multicolored	1.00	1.00
2074	A943	50c multicolored	1.00	1.00
2075	A943	50c multicolored	1.00	1.00
2076	A943	75c multicolored	1.50	1.50
2077	A943	75c multicolored	1.50	1.50
		Nos. 2073-2077 (5)	6.00	6.00

Inter-American Development Bank, 40th Anniv. — A944

1999, Oct. 9 Litho. ***Perf. 13½x13¾***

2078 A944 75c multi 1.50 1.50

UPU, 125th Anniv. A945

1999, Oct. 9 ***Perf. 13¾x13½***

2079 A945 1.50p multi 3.00 3.00

Trees — A946

a, Nothofagus pumilio. b, Prosopis caldenia. c, Schinopsis balansae. d, Cordia trichotoma.

1999, Oct. 16 ***Perf. 13½x13¾***

2080 A946 75c Strip of 4, #a-d 6.00 6.00

Sinking of A.R.A. Fournier, 50th Anniv. A947

1999, Oct. 16 ***Perf. 13¾x13½***

2081 A947 75c multi 1.50 1.50

Aviation Anniversaries — A948

Designs: No. 2082, Late 25 airplane. No. 2083, Parachutists.

1999, Oct. 30 ***Perf. 13¾x13½***

2082 A948 75c multi 1.50 1.50

2083 A948 75c multi 1.50 1.50

First Argentine airmail flight, 70th anniv. (#2082), Hundred consecutive jumps by Argentine Parachute Club, 50th anniv.

Souvenir Sheets

Millennium — A949

No. 2084: a, 75c, Head of soccer player. b, 50c, Machine as soccer player.
No. 2085: a, 50c, Cane, vert. b, 75c, Head of Jorge Luis Borges (1899-1986), writer.
No. 2086: a, 50c, Accordion player on bed, vert. b, 75c, Stylized tango dancers.

1999, Oct. 30 — ***Perf. 14***

2084 A949 Sheet of 2, #a.-b. 2.50 2.50
2085 A949 Sheet of 2, #a.-b. 2.50 2.50
2086 A949 Sheet of 2, #a.-b. 2.50 2.50

Size of 75c stamps: 40x40mm.

Argentine Soccer Teams — A950

Designs: No. 2087, Banner and flags of River Plate team. No. 2088, Banner of Boca Juniors team, balloons.
River Plate team (red and white team colors) - No. 2089: a, Stadium, emblem, soccer balls. b, Team on field. c, Fans. d, Emblem. e, Trophy. f, Banner in stadium. g, Player, ball.
Boca Juniors team (blue and yellow team colors) - No. 2090: a, Two players, ball. b, Emblem. c, Four players celebrating. d, Fans, balloons. e, Banner in stadium. f, Blurred shot of players in action. g, Blurred shot of players, diff.

1999 — ***Perf. 13½x13¼***

2087 A950 75c multi 1.50 1.50
2088 A950 75c multi 1.50 1.50

Self-Adhesive

Die Cut

2089 Pane of 7 10.00
a. A950 25c multi .50 .50
b.-c. A950 50c any single 1.00 1.00
d.-f. A950 75c any single 1.50 1.50
g. A950 1.50p multi 3.00 3.00
2090 Pane of 7 10.00
a. A950 25c multi .50 .50
b.-c. A950 50c any single 1.00 1.00
d.-f. A950 75c any single 1.50 1.50
g. A950 1.50p multi 3.00 3.00

Issued: Nos. 2087-2088, 11/13; Nos. 2089-2090, 11/15.
Sizes: #2089a-2089f, 2090a-2090f, 37x27mm; #2089g, 2090g, 37x37mm.

Canonization of Brother Héctor Valdivielso Sáez — A951

1999, Nov. 20 — ***Perf. 13¾x13½***

2091 A951 75c multi 1.50 1.50

Manuel Belgrano National Naval School, Bicent. — A952

1999, Nov. 27

2092 A952 75c multi 1.50 1.50

Souvenir Sheet

Launch of Corvette Uruguay, 125th Anniv. — A953

1999, Nov. 27 — **Litho.** — ***Perf. 14***

2093 A953 1.50p multi 3.00 3.00

A954

Christmas — A955

No. 2094, Figurines of Holy Family.
No. 2095: a, Magus. b, Bell. c, Two Magi, camels. d, Leaf. e, Angel with star. f, Nativity scene. g, Star. h, Ornaments.

1999, Dec. 4 — ***Perf. 13¾x13½***

2094 A954 75c multi 1.50 1.50

Perf. 14

2095 Sheet of 8 9.50 9.00
a.-b A955 25c any single .50 .50
c.-d. A955 50c any single 1.00 1.00
e.-h. A955 75c any single 1.50 1.50

Sizes: Nos. 2095a, 2095b, 2095g, 2095h, 30x30mm.

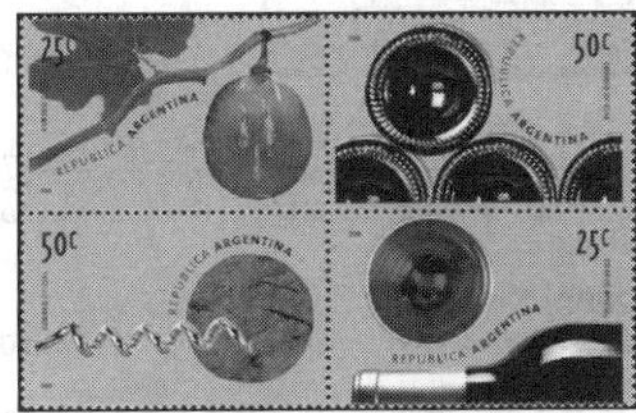

Viticulture — A956

Designs: a, 25c, Grape on vine. b, 50c, Bottoms of wine bottles. c, 50c, Cork and corkscrew. d, 25c, Glass of wine, wine bottle.
Illustration reduced.

2000, Feb. 26 — **Litho.** — ***Perf. 13¼***

2096 A956 Block of 4, #a-d 3.00 3.00

World Mathematics Year — A957

2000, Mar. 18 — ***Perf. 13¾x13½***

2097 A957 75c multi 1.50 1.50

Birds — A958

a, Leptotila verrauxi. b, Columba picazuro. c, Columbina picni. d, Zenaida auriculata.

2000, Mar. 18 — ***Die Cut***

Self-Adhesive

2098 Booklet of 4 6.00
a.-d. A958 75c any single 1.50 1.50

Souvenir Sheet

Bangkok 2000 Stamp Exhibition — A959

Designs: a, 25c, Vanda coerulea. b, 75c, Erythrina crista-galli.
Illustration reduced.

2000, Mar. 25 — ***Perf. 14***

2099 A959 Sheet of 2, #a-b 2.00 2.00

Miniature Sheet

Libraries — A960

Designs: a, 25c, National Public Library Protection Commission. b, 50c, Jujuy Public Library. c, 75c, Argentine Library for the Blind. d, Argentine National Library.
Illustration reduced.

Litho., Litho. & Embossed (#2100c)

2000, Apr. 15 — ***Perf. 13½***

2100 A960 Sheet of 4, #a-d 5.00 5.00

Gen. Luis Maria Campos Military School, Cent. — A961

2000, Apr. 29 — ***Perf. 13¾x13½***

2101 A961 75c multi 1.50 1.50

Discovery of Brazil, 500th Anniv. — A962

a, 75c, Pedro Cabral, 1558 map of Brazil coastline. b, 25c, Compass rose and ship.
Illustration reduced.

2000, Apr. 29

2102 A962 Pair, #a-b 2.00 2.00

Souvenir Sheet

The Stamp Show 2000, London — A963

Designs: a, 25c, Great Britain #1 and design A1, La Porteña, 1st locomotive in Argentina. b, 75c, Argentina No. 7, mail box.
Illustration reduced.

2000, May 20 — ***Perf. 14***

2103 A963 Sheet of 2, #a-b 2.00 2.00

91st Intl. Convention of Rotary International, Buenos Aires — A964

2000, June 3 — **Litho.** — ***Perf. 13½x13¾***

2104 A964 75c multi 1.50 1.50

Stampin' the Future — A965

Children's Stamp Design Contest Winners: 25c, Rocío Casado. 50c, Carolina Cáceres, vert. 75c, Valeria A. Pizarro. 1p, Cristina Ayala Castro, vert.

Perf. 13½x13¼, 13¼x13½

2000, June 24

2105-2108 A965 Set of 4 5.00 5.00

America Issue — A966

AIDS Prevention: No. 2109, Handshake. No. 2110, Heart and hands.

2000, July 8 — ***Perf. 13¾x13½***

2109-2110 A966 75c Set of 2 3.00 3.00

Antoine de Saint-Exupéry (1900-44), Pilot, Writer — A967

#2111, 2115, Potez 25. #2112, 2116, Late 28. #2113, Saint-Exupéry. #2114, Henri Guillaumet, Vicente A. Almonacid and Jean Mermoz. #2117, Map of southern Argentina, tail of Late 25 plane. 1p, Nose of Late 25 plane, cover from 1st airmail flight to Trelew.

2000, July 29 — ***Perf. 13½***

2111 A967 25c multi .50 .50

2112	A967 50c multi	1.00	1.00

Booklet Stamps

Perf. 14

Size: 30x30mm

2113	A967 25c multi	.50	.50
2114	A967 50c multi	1.00	1.00

Size: 60x20mm

2115	A967 25c multi	.50	.50
2116	A967 50c multi	1.00	1.00
a.	Booklet pane, #2113-2116	3.00	

Size: 40x30mm

2117	A967 50c multi	1.00	1.00
2118	A967 1p multi	2.00	2.00
a.	Booklet pane, #2117-2118	3.00	
	Booklet, #2116a, 2118a	6.00	
	Nos. 2111-2118 (8)	7.50	7.50

Argentine airmail service, 73rd anniv., Aerofila 2000 Philatelic Exhibition, Buenos Aires (No. 2118a).

President Arturo U. Illia (1900-82) A968

2000, Aug. 5 *Perf. 13½x13¼*

2119	A968 75c multi	1.50	1.50

José de San Martín (1778-1850) A969

2000, Aug. 26 *Perf. 13½*

2120	A969 75c multi	1.50	1.50

Dalmacio Vélez Sarsfield (1800-75), Writer of Civil Code — A970

Perf. 13½x13¼

2000, Sept. 23 **Litho.**

2121	A970 75c multi	1.50	1.50

2000 Summer Olympic, Sydney — A971

No. 2122: a, Windsurfing. b, Field hockey. c, Volleyball. d, Pole vault.

Illustration reduced.

2000, Sept. 23 *Perf. 13½*

2122	A971 75c Block of 4, #a-d	6.00	6.00

Horses A972

No. 2123: a, Argentine Petiso. b, Argentine Carriage Horse. c, Peruvian. d, Criolla. e, Argentine Saddle Horse. f, Argentine Polo.

No. 2124: a, Horse-drawn mail coach. b, Horse's head.

2000, Oct. 7 *Perf. 13¾x13½*

2123	Sheet of 6 + 2 labels	6.00	6.00
a.-b.	A972 25c Any single	.50	.50
c.-d.	A972 50c Any single	1.00	1.00
e.-f.	A972 75c Any single	1.50	1.50

Souvenir Sheet

Perf. 14

2124	Sheet of 2	2.00	2.00
a.	A972 25c multi	.50	.50
b.	A972 75c mutli	1.50	1.50

España 2000 Intl. Philatelic Exhibition.

Archaeological Artifacts — A973

Designs: 10c, Ceremonial hatchet, Santa Maria culture. 25c, Musical pipes. 50c, Loom, Mapuche culture. 60c, Poncho. 75c, Funerary mask, Tafi culture. 1p, Basket, Mbayá Indians. 2p, Drum, Mapuche culture. 3.25p, Ceremonial mask, Chané culture. 5p, Funerary urn, Belén culture. 9.40p, Rhea-feather costume.

Type A Syncopation (1st stamp #2125): On two longer sides, groups of 2 and 18 holes separated by a bracket-shaped hole equal in width to two holes.

Perf. 13½x13¾ Sync. Type A

2000 **Litho.**

2125	A973	10c multi	.20	.20
2126	A973	25c multi	.50	.50
2127	A973	50c multi	1.00	1.00
2128	A973	60c multi	1.25	1.25
2129	A973	75c multi	1.50	1.50
2130	A973	1p multi	2.00	2.00
2131	A973	2p multi	4.00	4.00
2132	A973	3.25p multi	7.50	7.50
2133	A973	5p multi	10.00	10.00
2134	A973	9.40p multi	19.00	19.00
	Nos. 2125-2134 (10)		46.95	46.95

Issued: 10c, 60c, 11/16; 25c, 50c, 75c, 9.40p, 10/26; 1p, 2p, 9/13; 3.25p, 5p, 8/30.

Natl. Atomic Energy Commission, 50th Anniv. A974

2000, Nov. 11 **Litho.** *Perf. 13½*

2135	A974 75c multi	1.50	1.50

Fileteado Art Style and the Tango — A975

No. 2136: a, Left side of Fileteado design. b, Right side of Fileteado design. c, Musicians. d, Tango dancers.

Illustration reduced.

2000, Nov. 11 *Perf. 13¾x13½*

2136	A975 75c Block of 4, #a-d	6.00	6.00

Organ Donation Campaign A976

2000, Nov. 25 *Perf. 13½*

2137	A976 75c multi	1.50	1.50

Christmas A977

2000, Nov. 25

2138	A977 75c multi	1.50	1.50

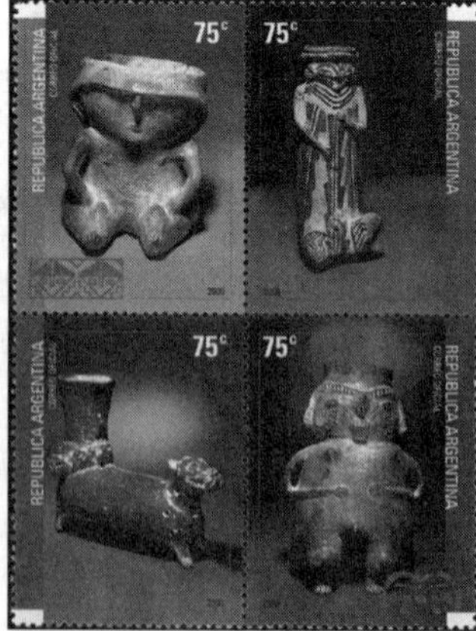

Medicinal Plants — A978

Designs: No. 2139, 75c, Mirabilis jalapa. No. 2140, 75c, Senna corymbosa. No. 2141, 75c, Eugenia uniflora. No. 2142, 75c, Commelina erecta.

2000, Nov. 25

2139-2142	A978 Set of 4	6.00	6.00

Pre-Columbian Art — A979

Various artifacts. Background colors: a, Bright orange. b, Red orange. c, Green. d, Red violet.

Illustration reduced.

2000, Dec. 9

2143	A979 75c Block of 4, #a-d	6.25	6.00

A979a

Serpentine Die Cut 11¼x11

2001, Feb. 6 **Litho.**

Self-Adhesive

Background Color

2143E	A979a	10c blue green	.20	.20
2143F	A979a	25c brt green	.50	.50
2143G	A979a	60c orange	1.25	1.25
2143H	A979a	75c red	1.50	1.50
2143I	A979a	1p blue	2.00	2.00
2143J	A979a	3p red brown	6.00	6.00
2143K	A979a	3.25p yel green	6.50	6.50
2143L	A979a	5.50p rose	11.00	11.00
	Nos. 2143E-2143L (8)		28.95	28.95

Nos. 2143E-2143L are broken at right by five die cut wavy lines. Sold at Unidad Postal outlets.

Miniature Sheet

Cenozoic Mammals — A980

No. 2144: a, Megaterio (Megatherium americanum). b, Gliptodonte (Doedicurus clavicaudatus). c, Macrauquenia (Macrauchenia patachonica). d, Toxodonte (Toxodon platensis).

2001, Mar. 10 *Perf. 13¾x13½*

2144	A980 75c Sheet of 4, #a-d	6.00	6.00

Antarctic Bases, 50th Anniv. — A981

Map and: No. 2145, 75c, Cormorant, Base Brown. No. 2146, 75c, Skua, Base San Martín.

Perf. 13¾x13½

2001, Mar. 24 **Litho.**

2145-2146	A981 Set of 2	3.00	3.00

Apiculture — A982

No. 2147: a, Bee on flower. b, Bees on honeycomb. c, Bees, apiarist, and hives. d, Honey, pollen.

2001, Apr. 7 *Perf. 13½x13¼*

2147	Block of 4	6.00	6.00
a.-d.	A982 75c Any single	1.50	1.50

Souvenir Sheet

Argentine Antarctic Institute, 50th Anniv. — A983

No. 2148: a, Scientist with fossils. b, Scientist with mapping equipment.

2001, Apr. 21 ***Perf. 14***
2148 A983 75c Sheet of 2, #a-b 3.00 3.00

Spain to Argentina Flight of Plus Ultra Seaplane, 75th Anniv. — A984

2001, Apr. 28 ***Perf. 13¾x13½***
2149 A984 75c multi 1.50 1.50

Art in Silver — A985

No. 2150: a, Bridle (Freno). b, Stirrups (Estribos). c, Spurs (Espuelas). d, Gaucho's ornament (Rastra).
Illustration reduced.

2001, May 19 Litho. ***Perf. 13¾x13½***
2150 A985 75c Block of 4, #a-d 6.00 6.00

World Youth Soccer Championships — A986

Designs: No. 2151, 75c, Player kicking ball. No. 2152, 75c, Goalie catching ball.

2001, June 16
2151-2152 A986 Set of 2 3.00 3.00

Souvenir Sheet

Belgica 2001 Intl. Stamp Exhibition, Brussels — A987

No. 2153: a, 25c, Washerwoman by the Banks of the Belgrano, by Prilidiano Pueyrredón. b, 75c, The Hay Harvest, by Pieter Breughel, the Elder.

2001, June 16 ***Perf. 14***
2153 A987 Sheet of 2, #a-b 2.00 2.00

2001 Census — A988

Perf. 13½x13¾ Syncopated
2001, July 14
2154 A988 75c multi 1.50 1.50

SAC-C Satellite, Birds and Flowers A989

2001, July 14 ***Perf. 13¾x13½***
2155 A989 75c multi 1.50 1.50

Environmental protection.

Bandoneón Recital - 1990, by Aldo Severi — A990

2001, July 28 ***Perf. 13½x13¾***
2156 A990 75c multi 1.50 1.50

The tango in art.

Souvenir Sheet

Phila Nippon '01, Japan — A991

No. 2157: a, Tango dancers, musical score. b, Kabuki dancer.

2001, July 28 ***Perf. 14***
2157 A991 75c Sheet of 2, #a-b 3.00 3.00

Miniature Sheet

Wild Cats — A992

No. 2158: a, 25c, Puma. b, 25c, Jaguar. c, 50c, Jaguarundi and young. d, 50c, Ocelot. e, 75c, Mountain cat. f, 75c, Huiña.

2001, July 28 ***Perf. 13¾x13½***
2158 A992 Sheet of 6, #a-f, +2 labels 6.00 6.00

Enrique Santos Discépolo (1901-51), Tango Lyricist — A993

2001, Aug. 4 ***Perf. 13½x13¾***
2159 A993 75c multi 1.50 1.50

America Issue - UNESCO World Heritage — A994

No. 2160 - Buildings and artifacts from Jesuit Block and Estancias of Cordoba: a, Denomination at UL. b, Denomination at UR.
Illustration reduced.

2001, Aug. 11 ***Perf. 13¾x13½***
2160 A994 75c Horiz. pair, #a-b 3.00 3.00

Prevention of Breast Cancer — A995

2001, Sept. 1 ***Perf. 13½x13¾***
2161 A995 75c multi 1.50 1.50

World Championship Race Cars of Juan Manuel Fangio — A996

No. 2162 - Cars and track layouts: a, Alfa Romeo 159 Alfetta, Barcleona, 1951. b, Mercedes-Benz W196, Reims, France, 1954. c, Lancia-Ferrari D50, Monte Carlo, Monaco, 1956. d, Maserati 250F, Nürburgring, Germany, 1957.
Illustration reduced.

2001, Oct. 6 ***Perf. 13¾x13½***
2162 A996 75c Block of 4, #a-d 6.00 6.00

Politicians A997

Designs: No. 2163, 75c, Roque Sáenz Peña (1851-1914). No. 2164, 75c, Justo José de Urquiza (1801-70).

2001, Oct. 20
2163-2164 A997 Set of 2 3.00 3.00

Bulnesia Sarmientoi A998

2001, Oct. 20 Litho. ***Perf. 13½x13¾***
2165 A998 75c multi 1.50 1.50

Souvenir Sheet

Hafnia 01 Philatelic Exhibition, Copenhagen — A999

No. 2166: a, 25c, Argentine post rider, 18th cent. b, 75c, European post rider, 17th cent.

2001, Oct. 27 Litho. ***Perf. 14***
2166 A999 Sheet of 2, #a-b 2.00 2.00

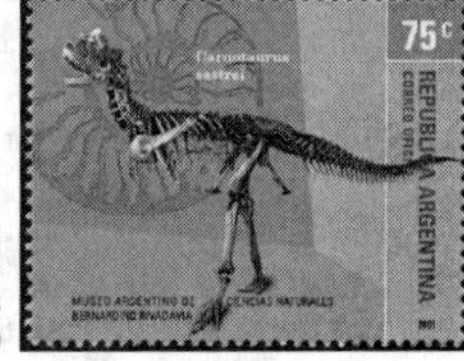

Items in Argentine Museums A1000

Designs: No. 2167, 75c, Ammonite, skeleton of Carnotaurus sastrei, from Argentine Naural Science Museum. No. 2168, 75c, Letter from Buenos Aires, stagecoach "La Pobladora," from Enrique Udaondo Graphic Museum Complex. No. 2169, 75c, Icons from

Averias culture, funerary urn from Las Mercedes culture, from Emilio and Duncan Wagner Museum of Anthropological and Natural Sciences, vert. No. 2170, 75c, Crucifix of Juan Martin de Pueyrredon, and detail, from Pueyrredon Museum, vert.

Perf. 13¾x13½, 13½x13¾

2001, Nov. 10 Litho.
2167-2170 A1000 Set of 4 6.00 6.00

Aviators and Their Airplanes A1001

Designs: No. 2171, 75c, Carola Lorenzini (1899-1941) and Focke Wulf 44-J. No. 2172, 75c, Jean Mermoz (1901-36) and "Arc-en-Ciel."

2001, Nov. 24 ***Perf. 13¾x13½***
2171-2172 A1001 Set of 2 3.00 3.00

Christmas A1002

2001, Nov. 24 ***Perf. 13½x13¾***
2173 A1002 75c multi 1.50 1.50

Dances A1003

No. 2174: a, Flamenco. b, Waltz. c, Zamba. d, Tango.

Perf. 13¾x13½

2001, Nov. 29 Litho.
2174 Booklet pane of 4 6.00 —
a.-d. A1003 75c Any single 1.50 1.50
Booklet, #2174 6.00

Dancers' Day A1004

2001, Dec. 1 Litho. ***Perf. 13¾x13½***
2175 A1004 75c multi 1.50 1.50

Argentine Television, 50th Anniv. — A1005

No. 2176: a, Television, camera, microphone, test pattern. b, Televisions and videotape reels. c, Television, astronaut and satellite dish. d, Televisions, cables and VCR remote control.

Illustration reduced.

2001, Dec. 1 ***Perf. 13¾x13½***
2176 A1005 75c Block of 4, #a-d 6.00 6.00

Argentina in the Antarctic A1006

Designs: No. 2177, 75c, Esperanza Base, 50th anniv. No. 2178, 75c, First air and sea courier service, 50th anniv.

2002, Mar. 9
2177-2178 A1006 Set of 2 1.25 1.25

America Issue - Education A1007

No. 2179: a, School and Argentine flag. b, Children playing hop scotch.

2002, Mar. 23
2179 A1007 75c Vert. pair, #a-b 1.00 1.00

Falkland Islands Birds A1008

Designs: No. 2180, 50c, Charadrius falklandicus. No. 2181, 50c, Larus scoresbii. No. 2182, 75c, Chloephaga rubidiceps, vert. No. 2183, 75c, Aptenodytes patagonicus, vert.

Perf. 13¾x13½, 13½x13¾

2002, Apr. 13 Litho.
2180-2183 A1008 Set of 4 1.60 1.60

Anniversaries — A1010

No. 2185, 25c: a, Rosario riverfront, Ship on Paraná River, arms. b, Rosario riverfront, National Flag Monument.

No. 2186, 50c: a, Mt. Fitzroy, Nahuel Huapi Natl. Park. b, Dr. Francisco P. Moreno.

No. 2187, 75c: a, Flower, aerial view of San Carlos de Bariloche. b, Church and town map.

Illustration reduced.

2002, May 11 Litho. ***Perf. 13½x13¾***
Horiz. Pairs, #a-b
2185-2187 A1010 Set of 3 1.90 1.90

Pan-American Health Organization, Cent. — A1011

2002, June 1
2188 A1011 75c multi .40 .40

Doctors — A1012

No. 2189: a, Cosme Mariano Argerich (1758-1820), founder of Military Health Service. b, José María Ramos Mejía (1849-1914), psychiatric educator. c, Salvador Mazza (1886-1946), Chagas' disease specialist. d, Carlos Arturo Gianantonio (1926-95), pediatrician.

Illustration reduced.

Perf. 13¾x13½

2002, June 15 Litho.
2189 A1012 50c Block of 4, #a-d 1.10 1.10

Landscapes — A1013

No. 2190: a, Seven-colored Mountain, Jujuy Province. b, Iguaçu Falls, Misiones Province. c, Talampaya Natl. Park, La Rioja Province. d, Mt. Aconcagua, Mendoza Province. e, Rose Garden, Buenos Aires. f, San Jorge Lighthouse, Chubut. g, Perito Moreno Glacier, Santa Cruz Province. h, Lapataia Bay, Tierra del Fuego Province.

Illustration reduced.

2002, July 29 ***Perf. 14x13½***
2190 Block of 8 3.25 3.25
a.-h. A1013 75c Any single .40 .40

Eva Perón (1919-52) A1014

No. 2191: a, Official portrait. b, Embossed profile. c, At microphone. d, Painting by Nicolas Garcia Uriburu.

Litho., Litho & Embossed (#2191b)

2002, July 27 ***Perf. 13½x13¾***
2191 Horiz. strip of 4 1.60 1.60
a.-d. A1014 75c Any single .40 .40

Worldwide Fund for Nature (WWF) — A1015

No. 2192: a, Ozotoceros bezoarticus. b, Vicugna vicugna. c, Pudu puda. d, Catagonus wagneri.

Illustration reduced.

2002, July 27 Litho. ***Perf. 13¾x13½***
2192 A1015 $1 Block of 4, #a-d 2.25 2.25

Souvenir Sheet

Philakorea 2002 World Stamp Exhibition, Seoul — A1016

No. 2193: a, Argentine soccer player (blue and white shirt). b, Korean soccer player (red shirt).

2002, Aug. 10 ***Perf. 14***
2193 A1016 1.50p Sheet of 2, #a-b 1.60 1.60

Valdés Peninsula Tourism — A1017

Whale breaching: a, Head. b, Tail.

Illustration reduced.

2002, Sept. 14 ***Perf. 13½x13¾***
2194 A1017 75c Horiz. pair, #a-b .85 .85

Insects A1018

Designs: 25c, Edessa meditabunda. 50c, Elaechlora viridis. 75c, Chrysodina aurata. 1p, Steirastoma breve.

2002, Sept. 21 ***Perf. 13¾x13½***
2195-2198 A1018 Set of 4 1.40 1.40

Men's Volleyball World Championships A1019

Various players with background colors of: No. 2199, 75c, Blue green (shown). No. 2200,

75c, Light blue. No. 2201, 75c, Yellow green. No. 2202, 75c, Orange.

Perf. 13½x13¾

2002, Sept. 28 **Litho.**

2199-2202	A1019	Set of 4	1.60	1.60

On Nos. 2199-2202 portions of the design were applied by a thermographic process producing a shiny, raised effect.

Argentine Highway Association, 50th Anniv. — A1020

2002, Oct. 5 ***Perf. 13¾x13½***

2203	A1020	75c multi	.40	.40

Argentine Personalities — A1021

Designs: No. 2204, 75c, Roberto Arlt (1900-42), novelist. No. 2205, 75c, Beatriz Guido (1924-88), writer. No. 2206, 75c, Niní Marshall (1903-96), actress. No. 2207, 75c, Luis Sandrini (1905-80), actor.

2002, Oct. 19

2204-2207	A1021	Set of 4	1.75	1.75

SEMI-POSTAL STAMPS

Samuel F. B. Morse — SP1

Globe — SP2

Landing of Columbus SP5

Map of Argentina SP6

Designs: 10c+5c, Alexander Graham Bell. 25c+15c, Rowland Hill.

Wmk. RA in Sun (90)

1944, Jan. 5 **Litho.** ***Perf. 13***

B1	SP1	3c +2c lt vio & sl bl	.35	.25
B2	SP2	5c +5c dl red & sl bl	.65	.20
B3	SP1	10c +5c org & slate bl	1.25	.70
B4	SP1	25c +15c red brn & sl bl	1.75	1.10
B5	SP5	1p +50c lt grn & sl bl	8.00	7.25
		Nos. B1-B5 (5)	12.00	9.50

The surtax was for the Postal Employees Benefit Association.

1944, Feb. 17 **Wmk. 90** ***Perf. 13***

B6	SP6	5c +10c ol yel & slate	.75	.50
B7	SP6	5c +50c vio brn & slate	3.25	2.00
B8	SP6	5c +1p dl org & slate	9.00	6.50
B9	SP6	5c +20p dp bl & slate	22.50	15.00
		Nos. B6-B9 (4)	35.50	24.00

The surtax was for the victims of the San Juan earthquake.

Souvenir Sheets

National Anthem and Flag — SP7

Illustration reduced.

1944, July 17 ***Imperf.***

B10	SP7	5c +1p vio brn & lt bl	1.90	1.90
B11	SP7	5c +50p bl blk & lt bl	350.00	250.00

Surtax for the needy in the provinces of La Rioja and Catamarca.

Catalogue values for unused stamps in this section, from this point to the end of the section, are for Never Hinged items.

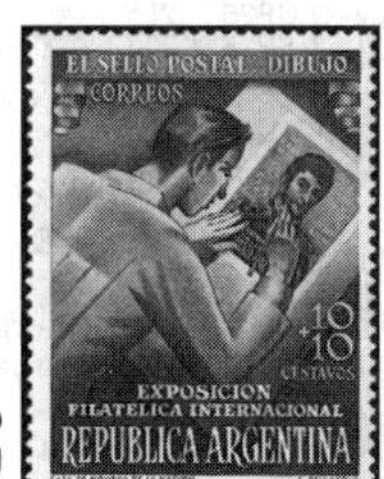

Stamp Designing SP8

1950, Aug. 26 **Photo.** ***Perf. 13½***

B12	SP8	10c +10c violet	.25	.25
		Nos. B12,CB1-CB5 (6)	20.45	15.65

Argentine Intl. Philatelic Exhibition, 1950.

Poliomyelitis Victim — SP9

1956, Apr. 14 ***Perf. 13½x13***

B13	SP9	20c +30c slate	.30	.20

The surtax was for the poliomyelitis fund. Head in design is from Correggio's "Antiope," Louvre.

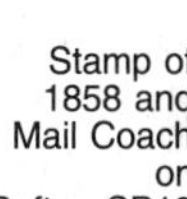

Stamp of 1858 and Mail Coach on Raft — SP10

Designs: 2.40p+1.20p, Album, magnifying glass and stamp of 1858. 4.40p+2.20p, Government seat of Confederation, Parana.

1958, Mar. 29 **Litho.** ***Perf. 13½***

B14	SP10	40c +20c brt grn & dl pur	.30	.25
B15	SP10	2.40p +1.20p ol gray & bl	.40	.25
B16	SP10	4.40p +2.20p lt bl & dp claret	.60	.40
		Nos. B14-B16,CB8-CB12 (8)	5.80	4.55

Surtax for Intl. Centennial Philatelic Exhibition, Paraná, Entre Rios, Apr. 19-27.

View of Flooded Land — SP11

1958, Oct. 4 **Photo.** ***Perf. 13½***

B17	SP11	40c +20c brown	.20	.20
		Nos. B17,CB13-CB14 (3)	1.25	1.15

The surtax was for flood victims in the Buenos Aires district.

Child Receiving Blood — SP12

1958, Dec. 20 **Litho.** **Wmk. 90**

B18	SP12	1p +50c blk & rose red	.20	.20

The surtax went to the Anti-Leukemia Foundation.

Runner SP13

1959, Sept. 5 ***Perf. 13½***

Designs: 50c+20c, Basketball players, vert. 1p+50c, Boxers, vert.

B19	SP13	20c +10c emer & blk	.20	.20
B20	SP13	50c +20c yel & blk	.20	.20
B21	SP13	1p +50c mar & blk	.20	.20
		Nos. B19-B21,CB15-CB16 (5)	1.60	1.35

3rd Pan American Games, Chicago, Aug. 27-Sept. 7, 1959.

Condor — SP14

Birds: 50c+20c, Fork-tailed flycatchers. 1p+50c, Magellanic woodpecker.

1960, Feb. 6

B22	SP14	20c +10c dk bl	.20	.20
B23	SP14	50c +20c dp vio bl	.20	.20
B24	SP14	1p +50c brn & buff	.20	.20
		Nos. B22-B24,CB17-CB18 (5)	1.35	1.15

The surtax was for child welfare work. See Nos. B30, CB29.

Souvenir Sheet

Uprooted Oak Emblem — SP15

1960, Apr. 7 **Wmk. 90** ***Imperf.***

B25	SP15	Sheet of 2	1.25	1.25
a.		1p + 50c bister & carmine	.55	.55
b.		4.20p + 2.10p apple grn & dp claret	.55	.55

WRY, July 1, 1959-June 30, 1960. The surtax was for aid to refugees.

Jacaranda — SP16

Flowers: 1p+1p, Passionflower. 3p+3p, Orchid. 5p+5p, Tabebuia.

1960, Dec. 3 **Photo.** ***Perf. 13½***

B26	SP16	50c +50c deep blue	.20	.20
B27	SP16	1p +1p bluish grn	.20	.20
B28	SP16	3p +3p henna brn	.30	.25
B29	SP16	5p +5p dark brn	.50	.35
		Nos. B26-B29 (4)	1.20	1.00

"TEMEX 61" (Intl. Thematic Exposition). For overprints see Nos. B31-B34.

Type of 1960

Bird: 4.20p+2.10p, Blue-eyed shag.

1961, Feb. 25 **Wmk. 90** ***Perf. 13½***

B30	SP14	4.20p +2.10p chestnut brn	.50	.30

Surtax for child welfare work. See #CB29.

Nos. B26-B29 Overprinted in Black, Brown, Blue or Red: "14 DE ABRIL DIA DE LAS AMERICAS"

1961, Apr. 15

B31	SP16	50c +50c deep blue	.20	.20
B32	SP16	1p +1p bluish grn (Brn)	.20	.20
B33	SP16	3p +3p henna brn (Bl)	.30	.25
B34	SP16	5p +5p dk brn (R)	.50	.35
		Nos. B31-B34 (4)	1.20	1.00

Day of the Americas, Apr. 14.

Cathedral, Cordoba SP17

Stamp of 1862 SP18

Flight into Egypt, by Ana Maria Moncalvo SP19

Design: 10p+10p, Cathedral, Buenos Aires.

Perf. 13½

1961, Oct. 21 Wmk. 90 Photo.

B35 SP17 2p +2p rose claret .25 .20
B36 SP18 3p +3p green .30 .20
B37 SP17 10p +10p brt blue .90 .50
a. Souvenir sheet of 3 1.75 1.10
Nos. B35-B37 (3) 1.45 .90

1962 International Stamp Exhibition.

No. B37a contains three imperf. stamps similar to Nos. B35-B37 in dark blue.

1961, Dec. 16 Litho.

B38 SP19 2p +1p lilac & blk brn .20 .20
B39 SP19 10p +5p light & deep claret .50 .20

The surtax was for child welfare.

Chalk-browed Mockingbird SP20

Design: 12p+6p, Rufous-collared sparrow.

1962, Dec. 29 ***Perf. 13½***

B40 SP20 4p +2p bis, brn & bl grn .90 .60
B41 SP20 12p +6p gray, yel, grn & brn 1.50 1.10

The surtax was for child welfare. See Nos. B44, B47, B48-B50, CB32, CB35-CB36.

Soccer — SP21

Perf. 13½

1963, May 18

B42 SP21 4p +2p multi .25 .20
B43 SP21 12p +6p Horseman-ship .45 .35
a. Dark carmine (jacket) omitted
Nos. B42-B43,CB31 (3) 1.25 1.05

4th Pan American Games, Sao Paulo.

Bird Type of 1962

Design: Vermilion flycatcher.

1963, Dec. 21 Litho.

B44 SP20 4p +2p blk, red, org & grn .60 .30

The surtax was for child welfare. See No. CB32.

Fencers — SP22

4p+2p, National Stadium, Tokyo, horiz.

1964, July 18 Wmk. 90 ***Perf. 13½***

B45 SP22 4p +2p red, ocher & brn .20 .20
B46 SP22 12p +6p bl grn & blk .40 .30
Nos. B45-B46,CB33 (3) 1.10 1.00

18th Olympic Games, Tokyo, Oct. 10-25, 1964. See No. CB33.

Bird Type of 1962

Design: Red-crested cardinal.

1964, Dec. 23 Litho.

B47 SP20 4p +2p dk bl, red & grn .60 .30

The surtax was for child welfare. See #CB35.

Bird Type of 1962
Inscribed "R. ARGENTINA"

Designs: 8p+4p, Lapwing. 10p+5p, Scarlet-headed marshbird, horiz. 20p+10p, Amazon kingfisher.

1966-67 ***Perf. 13½***

B48 SP20 8p +4p blk, ol, brt grn & red .80 .35
B49 SP20 10p +5p blk, bl, org & grn .80 .55
B50 SP20 20p +10p blk, yel, bl & pink .40 .35
Nos. B48-B50,CB36,CB38-CB39 (6) 4.30 3.25

The surtax was for child welfare.

Issue dates: 8p+4p, Mar. 26, 1966. 10p+5p, Jan. 14, 1967. 20p+10p, Dec. 23, 1967.

Grandmother's Birthday, by Patricia Lynch; Lions Emblem — SP23

Perf. 12½x13½

1968, Dec. 14 Litho. Wmk. 90

B51 SP23 40p + 20p multi .45 .40

1st Lions Intl. Benevolent Phil. Exhib. Surtax for the Children's Hospital Benevolent Fund.

White-faced Tree Duck — SP24

1969, Sept. 20 Wmk. 365 ***Perf. 13½***

B52 SP24 20p + 10p multi .50 .35

Surtax for child welfare. See No. CB40.

Slender-tailed Woodstar (Hummingbird) SP25

1970, May 9 Wmk. 365 ***Perf. 13½***

B53 SP25 20c + 10c multi .45 .40

The surtax was for child welfare. See Nos. CB41, B56-B59, B62-B63.

Dolphinfish — SP26

1971, Feb. 20 Unwmk. ***Perf. 12½***
Size: 75x15mm

B54 SP26 20c + 10c multi .50 .45

Surtax for child welfare. See No. CB42.

Children with Stamps, by Mariette Lydis — SP27

1971, Dec. 18 Litho. ***Perf. 13½***

B55 SP27 1p + 50p multi .50 .30

2nd Lions Intl. Solidarity Stamp Exhib.

Bird Type of 1970

Birds: 25c+10c, Saffron finch. 65c+30c, Rufous-bellied thrush, horiz.

1972, May 6 Unwmk. ***Perf. 13½***

B56 SP25 25c + 10c multi .30 .20
B57 SP25 65c + 30c multi .45 .30

Surtax was for child welfare.

Bird Type of 1970

Birds: 50c+25c, Southern screamer (chaja). 90c+45c, Saffron-cowled blackbird, horiz.

1973, Apr. 28

B58 SP25 50c + 25c multi .50 .30
B59 SP25 90c + 45c multi .70 .50

Surtax was for child welfare.

Painting Type of Regular Issue

Designs: 15c+15c, Still Life, by Alfredo Guttero, horiz. 90c+90c, Nude, by Miguel C. Victorica, horiz.

1973, Aug. 28 Litho. ***Perf. 13½***

B60 A472 15c + 15c multi .30 .20
B61 A472 90c + 90c multi 1.00 .70

Bird Type of 1970

Birds: 70c+30c, Blue seed-eater. 1.20p+60c, Hooded siskin.

1974, May 11 Litho. ***Perf. 13½***

B62 SP25 70c + 30c multi .50 .35
B63 SP25 1.20p + 60c multi .75 .40

Surtax was for child welfare.

Painting Type of 1974

Design: 70c+30c, The Lama, by Juan Batlle Planas.

1974, May 11 Litho. ***Perf. 13½***

B64 A477 70c + 30c multi .30 .25

PRENFIL-74 UPU, Intl. Exhib. of Phil. Periodicals, Buenos Aires, Oct. 1-12.

Plushcrested Jay — SP28

Designs: 13p+6.50p, Golden-collared macaw. 20p+10p, Begonia. 40p+20p, Teasel.

1976, June 12 Litho. ***Perf. 13½***

B65 SP28 7p + 3.50p multi .20 .20
B66 SP28 13p + 6.50p multi .30 .20
B67 SP28 20p + 10p multi .50 .30
B68 SP28 40p + 20p multi 1.00 .50
Nos. B65-B68 (4) 2.00 1.20

Argentine philately.

Telegraph, Communications Satellite — SP29

Designs: 20p+10p, Old and new mail trucks. 60p+30p, Old, new packet boats. 70p+35p, Biplane and jet.

1977, July 16 Litho. ***Perf. 13½***

B69 SP29 10p + 5p multi .25 .20
B70 SP29 20p + 10p multi .50 .60
B71 SP29 60p + 30p multi 1.00 .85
B72 SP29 70p + 35p multi 1.25 .85
Nos. B69-B72 (4) 3.00 2.50

Surtax was for Argentine philately.
No. B70 exists with wmk. 365.

Church of St. Francis Type, 1977,
Inscribed: "EXPOSICION ARGENTINA '77"

1977, Aug. 27

B73 A515 160p + 80p multi 2.50 2.00

Surtax was for Argentina '77 Philatelic Exhibition. Issued in sheets of 4.

No. B73 Overprinted with Soccer Cup Emblem

1978, Feb. 4 Litho. ***Perf. 13½***

B74 A515 160p + 80p multi 4.50 4.25
a. Souvenir sheet of 4 20.00 19.00

11th World Cup Soccer Championship, Argentina, June 1-25.

Spinus Magellanicus SP30

Birds: #B76, Variable seedeater. #B77, Yellow thrush. #B78, Pyrocephalus rubineus. #B79, Great kiskadee.

1978, Aug. 5 Litho. ***Perf. 13½***

B75 SP30 50p + 50p multi .90 .60
B76 SP30 100p + 100p multi 1.10 .90
B77 SP30 150p + 150p multi 1.40 1.25
B78 SP30 200p + 200p multi 1.75 1.75
B79 SP30 500p + 500p multi 8.50 7.25
Nos. B75-B79 (5) 13.65 11.75

ARGENTINA '78, Inter-American Philatelic Exhibition, Buenos Aires, Oct. 27-Nov. 5. Nos. B75-B79 issued in sheets of 4 with marginal inscriptions commemorating Exhibition and 1978 Soccer Championship.

Caravel "Magdalena," 16th Century — SP31

Sailing Ships: 500+500p, 3 master "Rio de la Plata," 17th cent. 600+600p, Corvette "Descubierta," 18th cent. 1500+1500p, Naval Academy yacht "A.R.A. Fortuna," 1979.

1979, Sept. 8 Litho. ***Perf. 13½***

B80 SP31 400p +400p multi 4.00 2.25
B81 SP31 500p +500p multi 4.75 2.50
B82 SP31 600p +600p multi 6.00 3.25
B83 SP31 1500p +1500p multi 15.00 8.00
Nos. B80-B83 (4) 29.75 16.00

Buenos Aires '80, Intl. Philatelic Exhibition, 10/24-11/2/80. Issued in sheets of 4.

Purmamarca Church SP32

Churches: 200p + 100p, Molinos. 300p + 150p, Animana. 400p + 200p, San Jose de Lules.

1979, Nov. 3 Litho. *Perf. 13½*

B84	SP32	100p + 50p multi	.25	.20
B85	SP32	200p + 100p multi	.45	.20
B86	SP32	300p + 150p multi	.60	.20
B87	SP32	400p + 200p multi	.90	.25
		Nos. B84-B87 (4)	2.20	.85

Buenos Aires No. 3, Exhibition and Society Emblems — SP33

Argentine Stamps: 750p+750p, type A580. 1000p+1000p, No. 91. 2000p+2000p, type A588.

1979, Dec. 15 Litho. *Perf. 13½*

B88	SP33	250p + 250p	.90	.75
B89	SP33	750p + 750p	2.25	1.75
B90	SP33	1000p + 1000p	3.00	2.50
B91	SP33	2000p + 2000p	6.00	5.00
		Nos. B88-B91 (4)	12.15	10.00

PRENFIL '80, Intl. Philatelic Literature and Publications Exhib., Buenos Aires, Nov. 7-16, 1980.

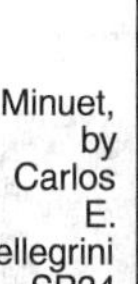

Minuet, by Carlos E. Pellegrini SP34

Paintings: 700p+350p, Media Cana, by Carlos Morel. 800p+400p, Cielito, by Pellegrini. 1000p+500p, El Gato, by Juan Leon Palliere.

1981, July 11 Litho. *Perf. 13½*

B92	SP34	500p + 250p multi	.70	.35
B93	SP34	700p + 350p multi	1.00	.70
B94	SP34	800p + 400p multi	1.10	.90
B95	SP34	1000p + 500p multi	1.40	1.25
		Nos. B92-B95 (4)	4.20	3.20

Espamer '81 Intl. Stamp Exhib. (Americas, Spain, Portugal), Buenos Aires, Nov. 13-22.

Canal, by Beatrix Bongliani (b. 1933) — SP35

Tapestries: 1000p+500p, Shadows, by Silvia Sieburger, vert. 2000p+1000p, Interpretation of a Rectangle, by Silke R. de Haupt, vert. 4000p+2000p, Tilcara, by Tana Sachs.

1982, July 31 Litho. *Perf. 13½*

B96	SP35	1000p + 500p multi	.20	.20
B97	SP35	2000p + 1000p multi	.40	.40
B98	SP35	3000p + 1500p multi	.60	.60
B99	SP35	4000p + 2000p multi	.80	.80
		Nos. B96-B99 (4)	2.00	2.00

Boy Playing Marbles SP36

1983, July 2 Litho. *Perf. 13½*

B100	SP36	20c + 10c shown	.20	.20
B101	SP36	30c + 15c Jumping rope	.45	.20
B102	SP36	50c + 25c Hopscotch	.85	.20
B103	SP36	1p + 50c Flying kites	1.10	.50
B104	SP36	2p + 1p Spinning top	1.60	.65
		Nos. B100-B104 (5)	4.20	1.75

Surtax was for natl. philatelic associations.
See Nos. B106-B110.

Compass, 15th Cent. — SP37

ARGENTINA '85 Intl. Stamp Show: b, Arms of Spain, Argentina. c, Columbus' arms. d-f, Columbus' arrival at San Salvador Island. Nos. B105d-B105f in continuous design; ships shown on singles range in size, left to right, from small to large. Surtax was for exhibition.

1984, Apr. 28 Litho. *Perf. 13½*

B105		Block of 6	3.75	3.75
a.-f.		SP37 5p + 2.50p, any single	.50	.25

Children's Game Type of 1983

1984, July 7 Litho. *Perf. 13½*

B106	SP36	2p + 1p Blind Man's Buff	.20	.20
B107	SP36	3p + 1.50p The Loop	.30	.25
B108	SP36	4p + 2p Leap Frog	.35	.30
B109	SP36	5p + 2.50p Rolling the loop	.45	.35
B110	SP36	6p + 3p Ball Mold	.55	.45
		Nos. B106-B110 (5)	1.85	1.55

Butterflies — SP38

1985, Nov. 9 Litho. *Perf. 13½*

B111	SP38	5c + 2c Rothschildia jacobaeae	.75	.20
B112	SP38	10c + 5c Heliconius erato phyllis	.75	.40
B113	SP38	20c + 10c Precis evarete hilaris	1.00	.75
B114	SP38	25c + 13c Cyanopepla pretiosa	1.50	1.00
B115	SP38	40c + 20c Papilio androgeus	2.00	1.50
		Nos. B111-B115 (5)	6.00	3.85

Children's Drawings — SP39

1986, Aug. 30 Litho.

B116	SP39	5c + 2c N. Pastor	.20	.20
B117	SP39	10c + 5c T. Valleistein	.35	.35
B118	SP39	20c + 10c J.M. Flores	.60	.60
B119	SP39	25c + 13c M.E. Pezzuto	.75	.75
B120	SP39	40c + 20c E. Diehl	1.10	1.10
		Nos. B116-B120 (5)	3.00	3.00

Surtax for natl. philatelic associations.

Miniature Sheets

Fresh-water Fish — SP40

No. B121: a, Metynnis maculatus. b, Cynolebias nigripinnis. c, Leporinus solarii. d, Aphyocharax rathbuni. e, Corydoras aeneus. f, Thoracocharax securis. g, Cynolebias melanotaenia. h, Cichlasoma facetum.

No. B122: a, Tetragonopterus argenteus. b, Hemigrammus caudovittatus. c, Astyanax bimaculatus. d, Gymnocorymbus ternetzi. e, Hoplias malabaricus. f, Aphyocharax rubripinnis. g, Apistogramma agassizi. h, Pyrrhulina rachoviana.

1987, June 27

B121		Sheet of 8	2.00	1.75
a.-h.		SP40 10c +5c, any single	.25	.20
B122		Sheet of 8	4.00	3.50
a.-h.		SP40 20c +10c, any single	.50	.40

PRENFIL '88, Intl. Philatelic Literature and Media Exhibition, Buenos Aires, Nov. 25-Dec. 2 — SP41

Locomotives and railroad car: No. B123, Yatay locomotive, 1888. No. B124, FCCA electric passenger car, 1914. No. B125, B-15 locomotive, 1942. No. B126, GT-22 No. 200 locomotive, 1988.

1988, June 4 Litho. *Perf. 13½*

B123	SP41	1a +50c multi	.65	.50
B124	SP41	1a +50c multi	.65	.50
B125	SP41	1a +50c multi	.65	.50
B126	SP41	1a +50c multi	.65	.50
		Nos. B123-B126 (4)	2.60	2.00

Nos. B123-B125 each issued in sheets of 4.

Horses SP42

Paintings: No. B127, *The Waiting,* by Gustavo Solari. No. B128, *Mare and Foal,* by E. Castro. No. B129, *Saint Isidor,* by Castro. No. B130, *At Lagoon's Edge,* by F. Romero Carranza. No. B131, *Under the Tail,* by Castro.

1988, Oct. 29 Litho. *Perf. 13½*

B127	SP42	2a +1a multi	.70	.50
B128	SP42	2a +1a multi	.70	.50
B129	SP42	2a +1a multi	.70	.50
B130	SP42	2a +1a multi	.70	.50
B131	SP42	2a +1a multi	.70	.50
		Nos. B127-B131 (5)	3.50	2.50

PRENFIL '88 — SP43

Covers of philatelic magazines.

1988, Nov. 26 Litho. *Perf. 13½*

B132	SP43	1a +1a *Cronaca Filatelica,* Italy	.40	.30
B133	SP43	1a +1a *CO-FI,* Brazil	.40	.30
B134	SP43	1a +1a *References de la Poste,* France	.40	.30
B135	SP43	2a +2a *Postas Argentinas*	.65	.50
		Nos. B132-B135 (4)	1.85	1.40

Souvenir Sheet

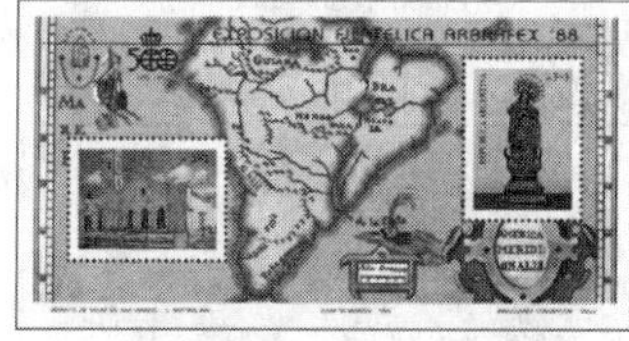

ARBRAPEX '88 — SP44

Designs: No. B136a, *Candel Delivery at San Ignacio,* by Leonie Matthis, Cornelio Saavedra Museum, Buenos Aires. No. B136b, *Immaculate Conception,* a statue in the Isaac Fernandez Blanco Museum, Buenos Aires.

1988, Nov. 26 *Perf. 12*

B136	SP44	Sheet of 2	1.60	1.25
a.		2a +2a multi	.65	.50
b.		3a +3a multi	.95	.70

Fish SP45

#B137, *Diplomystes viedmensis.* #B138, *Haplochiton taeniatus.* #B139, *Percichthys trucha.* #B140, *Galaxias platei.* #B141, *Salmo fario.*

1989, June 24 Litho. *Perf. 13½*

B137	SP45	10a +5a multi	.25	.20
B138	SP45	10a +5a multi	.25	.20
B139	SP45	10a +5a multi	.25	.20
B140	SP45	10a +5a multi	.25	.20
B141	SP45	10a +5a multi	.25	.20
		Nos. B137-B141 (5)	1.25	1.00

Printed in sheets of 4.

Discovery of America 500th Anniv. (in 1992) and ESPAMER '90 — SP46

Documents and chronicles: No. B142, Columbus's coat of arms, *Book of Privileges* title page. No. B143, Illustration from *New Chronicle and Good Government,* by Guaman Poma de Ayala. No. B144, Illustration from *Discovery and Conquest of Peru,* by Pedro de Cieza de Leon. No. B145, Illustration from *Travel to the River Plate,* by Ulrico Schmidl.

1989, Sept. 16 Litho. *Perf. 13½*
Yellow, Rose Violet & Black

B142	SP46	100a +50a	.90	.80
B143	SP46	150a +50a	.90	.80
B144	SP46	200a +100a	.90	.80
B145	SP46	250a +100a	.90	.80
		Nos. B142-B145 (4)	3.60	3.20

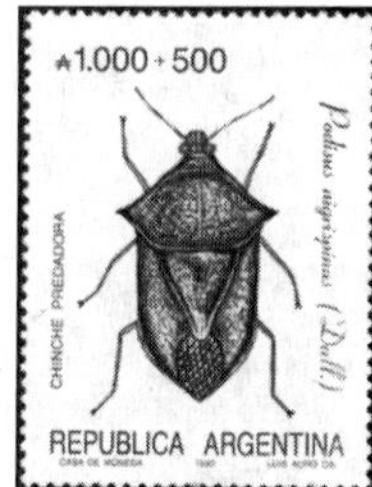

Insects SP47

Designs: No. B146, *Podisus nigrispinus.* No. B147, *Adalia bipunctata.* No. B148, *Nabis punctipennis.* No. B149, *Hippodamia convergens.* No. B150, *Calleida suturalis.*

1990, June 30 Litho. *Perf. 13½*

B146 SP47 1000a +500a multi	1.00	.85
B147 SP47 1000a +500a multi	1.00	.85
B148 SP47 1000a +500a multi	1.00	.85
B149 SP47 1000a +500a multi	1.00	.85
B150 SP47 1000a +500a multi	1.00	.85
Nos. B146-B150 (5)	5.00	4.25

Printed in sheets of 4.

Souvenir Sheet

First Natl. Exposition of Aerophilately — SP48

a, Lieut. Marcos A. Zar, Macchi seaplane. b, Capt. Antonio Parodi, Ansaldo SVA biplane. Illustration reduced.

1990, July 14 Litho. *Perf. 12*

B151 SP48 Sheet of 2	6.00	5.00
a. 2000a +2000a multi	3.00	2.50
b. 3000a +3000a multi	3.00	2.50

Souvenir Sheet

1992 Summer Olympics, Barcelona SP49

Designs: a, Shot put. b, High jump. c, Hurdles. d, Pole vault.

1990, Dec. 15 Litho. *Perf. 13½*

B152 Sheet of 4	9.00	9.00
a.-d. SP49 2000a +2000a multi	2.25	2.25

Espamer '91 Philatelic Exhibition. See No. B155.

Souvenir Sheet

Discovery of America, 500th Anniv. (in 1992) — SP50

Voyage of Alesandro Malaspina, 1789-1794: a, Sailing ship. b, Malaspina. c, Indian, hut. d, Indian, horse, artist drawing.

1990, Oct. 13 Litho. *Perf. 13½*

B153 Sheet of 4	6.00	6.00
a.-d. SP50 2000a +1000a, any single	1.50	1.50

Espamer '91, Buenos Aires.

Souvenir Sheet

Race Cars and Drivers — SP51

Designs: a, Juan Manuel Fangio. b, Juan Manuel Bordeu. c, Carlos Alberto Reutemann. d, Oscar and Juan Galvez.

1991 Litho. *Perf. 13½*

B154 SP51 Sheet of 4	4.75	4.75
a.-d. 2500a +2500a, any single	1.25	1.25

Espamer '91.

Souvenir Sheet

1992 Summer Olympics Type of 1990

Women's gymnastics routines: a, Floor exercise. b, Uneven parallel bars. c, Balance beam. d, Rhythmic gymnastics.

1991, June 29 Litho. *Perf. 13½*

B155 Sheet of 4	4.75	4.75
a.-d. SP49 2500a +2500a, any single	1.25	1.25

Espamer '91.

Iberoprenfil '92 — SP52

Designs: No. B156, Castor missile. No. B157, Satellite LUSAT 1.

1991, Dec. 28 Litho. *Perf. 13½*

B156 SP52 4000a +4000a multi	2.00	1.75
B157 SP52 4000a +4000a multi	2.00	1.75

Dinosaurs SP53

1992, May 2 Litho. *Perf. 13½*

B158 SP53 38c +38c Carnotaurus	2.00	2.00
B159 SP53 38c +38c Amargasaurus	2.00	2.00

Iberoprenfil '92, Buenos Aires — SP54

Paintings by Raul Soldi (b. 1905): No. B160, The Fiesta. No. B161, Church of St. Anne of Glew.

1992, Sept. 5 Litho. *Perf. 13½*

B160 SP54 76c +76c multi	3.50	3.50
B161 SP54 76c +76c multi	3.50	3.50

Parafil '92 — SP55

1992, Nov. 21 Litho. *Perf. 13½*

B162 SP55 76c +76c multi	3.00	3.00

2nd Argentine-Paraguayan Philatelic Exhibition, Buenos Aires.

Souvenir Sheet

Birds — SP56

a, Egretta thula. b, Amblyramphus holosericeus. c, Paroaria coronata. d, Chloroceryle amazona.

1993, July 17 Litho. *Perf. 13½*

B163 SP56 38c +38c Sheet of 4	8.00	8.00

Souvenir Sheet

Latin American Air Post Philatelic Exhibition — SP57

Designs: a, 25c+25c, Antoine de Saint-Exupery (1940-44), pilot, author. b, 75c+75c, "The Little Prince," vert. Illustration reduced.

1995, June 3 Litho. *Perf. 12*

B164 SP57 Sheet of 2, #a.-b.	7.00	7.00

For overprint see No. B180.

Souvenir Sheet

Exploration of Antarctica SP58

75c+25c, Transport ship ARA Bahia Aguirre. 1.25p+75c, Argentine Air Force Hercules C-130.

1995, July 8

B165 SP58 Sheet of 2, #a.-b.	9.00	9.00

Aerofila '96 SP59

Historic airplanes, pilots: No. B166, "Plus ultra," Ramón Franco Bahamonde (1896-1938). No. B167, 14 Bis, Alberto Santos-Dumont (1873-1932). No. B168, Spirit of St. Louis, Charles A. Lindbergh (1902-1974). No. B169, Buenos Aires, Eduardo A. Olivero (1896-1966).

1996, July 13 Litho. *Perf. 13½*

B166 SP59 25c +25c multi	1.50	1.50
B167 SP59 25c +25c multi	1.50	1.50
B168 SP59 50c +50c multi	3.00	3.00
B169 SP59 50c +50c multi	3.00	3.00
Nos. B166-B169 (4)	9.00	9.00

Ceramic Murals from Buenos Aires Subway SP60

1996, Sept. 21 Litho. *Perf. 13½*

B170 SP60 1p +50c Dragon	4.00	4.00
B171 SP60 1.50p +1p Bird	7.00	7.00

MEVIFIL '97, 1st Intl. Exhibition of Audio-Visual and Philatelic Information Media — SP61

Designs: No. B172, France Type A1. No. B173, Spain Type A3. No. B174, Argentina Type A4. No. B175, Buenos Aires Type A1.

1997, May 10 Litho. *Perf. 13½*

B172 SP61 50c +50c multi	2.00	2.00
B173 SP61 50c +50c multi	2.00	2.00
B174 SP61 50c +50c multi	2.00	2.00
B175 SP61 50c +50c multi	2.00	2.00
a. Block of 4, #B172-B175	8.00	8.00

Issued in sheets of 16 stamps + 4 labels.

Trains — SP62

Designs: No. B176, Las Nubes (Train to the Clouds), Salta. No. B177, Historical train, Buenos Aires. No. B178, Old Patagonian Express, Rio Negro-Chubut. No. B179, Southern Fueguino Railway, Tierra Del Fuego. Illustration reduced.

1997, Sept. 6 Litho. *Perf. 13*

B176 SP62 50c +50c multi	2.00	2.00
B177 SP62 50c +50c multi	2.00	2.00
B178 SP62 50c +50c multi	2.00	2.00
B179 SP62 50c +50c multi	2.00	2.00
Nos. B176-B179 (4)	8.00	8.00

No. B164 Ovptd. in Red Violet in Sheet Margin:

1997, Sept. 27 Litho. *Perf. 12*

B180 SP57 Sheet of 2	7.00	7.00

Cartography — SP63

Maps of the Buenos Aires area from: 25c+25c, 1546. No. B182, 17th century. No. B183, 1910. 75c+75c, 1999.

Perf. 13¾x13½

1999, Nov. 20 **Litho.**

B181 SP63 25c + 25c multi 1.00 1.00
B182 SP63 50c + 50c multi 2.00 2.00
B183 SP63 50c + 50c multi 2.00 2.00
B184 SP63 75c + 75c multi 3.00 3.00
a. Block of 4, #B181-B184 12.00 12.00

Methods of Transportation — SP64

No. B185: a, Bicycle. b, Graf Zeppelin. c, Train. d, Trolley.
Illustration reduced.

2000, Oct. 21 **Litho.** ***Perf. 14x13½***

B185 Block of 4 8.00 8.00
a. SP64 25c +25c multi 1.00 1.00
b.-c. SP64 50c +50c Any single 2.00 2.00
d. SP64 75c +75c multi 3.00 3.00

Cetaceans — SP65

No. B186: a, Burmeister's porpoise (Mariposa espinosa). b, River Plate dolphin. c, Minke whale. d, Humpback whale (Yubarta).
Illustration reduced.

2001, Sept. 15 **Litho.** ***Perf. 14x13½***

B186 Block of 4 8.00 8.00
a. SP65 25c +25c multi 1.00 1.00
b.-c. SP65 50c +50c Any single 2.00 2.00
d. SP65 75c +75c multi 3.00 3.00

Reptiles — SP66

No. B187: a, Boa constrictor occidentalis. b, Caiman yacare. c, Tupinambis merianae. d, Chelonoidis carbonaria.

2002, Aug. 24 **Litho.** ***Perf. 14x13½***

B187 Block of 4 2.25 2.25
a. SP66 25c +25c multi .30 .30
b.-c. SP66 50c +50c Either single .55 .55
d. SP66 75c +75c multi .85 .85

AIR POST STAMPS

Airplane Circles the Globe — AP1

Eagle — AP2

Wings Cross the Sea — AP3

Condor on Mountain Crag — AP4

Perforations of Nos. C1-C37 vary from clean-cut to rough and uneven, with many skipped perfs.

Perf. 13x13½, 13½x13

1928, Mar. 1 **Litho.** **Wmk. 90**

C1 AP1 5c lt red 1.25 .50
C2 AP1 10c Prus blue 2.25 1.00
C3 AP2 15c lt brown 2.25 .80
C4 AP1 18c lilac gray 3.00 2.75
a. 18c brown lilac 3.25 2.75
b. Double impression *375.00*
C5 AP2 20c ultra 2.25 .80
C6 AP2 24c deep blue 3.50 2.75
C7 AP3 25c brt violet 3.50 1.50
C8 AP3 30c rose red 5.25 1.00
C9 AP4 35c rose 3.50 1.00
C10 AP1 36c bister brn 2.50 1.50
C11 AP4 50c gray black 4.00 .50
C12 AP2 54c chocolate 3.50 2.00
C13 AP2 72c yellow grn 4.75 2.00
a. Double impression *300.00*
C14 AP3 90c dk brown 9.00 1.75
C15 AP3 1p slate bl & red 11.00 .65
C16 AP3 1.08p rose & dk bl 16.00 4.50
C17 AP4 1.26p dull vio & grn 20.00 8.00
C18 AP4 1.80p blue & lil rose 20.00 8.00
C19 AP4 3.60p gray & blue 42.50 19.00
Nos. C1-C19 (19) 160.00 60.00

The watermark on No. C4a is larger than on the other stamps of this set, measuring 10mm across Sun.

Zeppelin First Flight

Air Post Stamps of 1928 Overprinted in Blue

1930, May

C20 AP2 20c ultra 10.00 5.00
C21 AP4 50c gray black 20.00 10.00
a. Inverted overprint *475.00*
C22 AP3 1p slate bl & red 21.00 10.00
a. Inverted overprint *650.00*
C23 AP4 1.80p blue & lil rose 55.00 25.00
C24 AP4 3.60p gray & blue 150.00 70.00
Nos. C20-C24 (5) 256.00 120.00

Overprinted in Green

C25 AP2 20c ultra 10.00 6.00
C26 AP4 50c gray black 12.50 9.00
C27 AP3 90c dark brown 10.00 6.00
C28 AP3 1p slate bl & red 20.00 12.50
C29 AP4 1.80p blue & lil rose 600.00 400.00
a. Thick paper *850.00*
Nos. C25-C29 (5) 652.50 433.50

Air Post Stamps of 1928 Overprinted in Red or Blue

On AP1-AP2

On AP3-AP4

1931

C30 AP1 18c lilac gray 2.00 1.50
C31 AP2 72c yellow green 14.00 10.50
C32 AP3 90c dark brown 14.00 10.50
C33 AP4 1.80p bl & lil rose (Bl) 30.00 22.50
C34 AP4 3.60p gray & blue 57.50 40.00
Nos. C30-C34 (5) 117.50 85.00

1st anniv. of the Revolution of 1930.

Zeppelin Issue

Nos. C1, C4, C4a, C14 Overprinted in Blue or Red

On AP1

On AP3

1932, Aug. 4

C35 AP1 5c lt red (Bl) 3.00 2.00
C36 AP1 18c lilac gray (R) 12.50 9.00
a. 18c brown lilac (R) 100.00 60.00
C37 AP3 90c dark brown (R) 32.50 26.00
Nos. C35-C37 (3) 48.00 37.00

Plane and Letter — AP5

Mercury — AP6

Plane in Flight — AP7

Perf. 13½x13, 13x13½

1940, Oct. 23 **Photo.** **Wmk. 90**

C38 AP5 30c deep orange 5.00 .20
C39 AP6 50c dark brown 7.50 .20
C40 AP5 1p carmine 1.75 .20
C41 AP7 1.25p deep green .50 .20
C42 AP5 2.50p bright blue 1.25 .20
Nos. C38-C42 (5) 16.00 1.00

Plane and Letter — AP8

Mercury and Plane — AP9

Perf. 13½x13, 13x13½

1942, Oct. 6 **Litho.** **Wmk. 90**

C43 AP8 30c orange .20 .20
C44 AP9 50c dull brn & buff .40 .20

See Nos. C49-C52, C57, C61.

Plane over Iguaçu Falls — AP10

Plane over the Andes — AP11

Perf. 13½x13

1946, June 10 **Unwmk.**

C45 AP10 15c dull red brn .25 .20
C46 AP11 25c gray green .20 .20

See Nos. C53-C54.

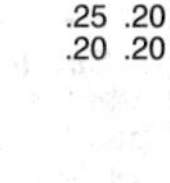

Allegory of Flight AP12

Astrolabe — AP13

Perf. 13½x13, 13x13½

1946, Sept. 25 **Litho.** **Unwmk.**

Surface-Tinted Paper

C47 AP12 15c sl grn, *pale grn* .55 .20
C48 AP13 60c vio brn, *ocher* .55 .35

Types of 1942

1946-48 **Unwmk.** ***Perf. 13½x13***

C49 AP8 30c orange 1.40 .20
C50 AP9 50c dull brn & buff 2.50 .20
C51 AP8 1p carmine ('47) 1.25 .20
C52 AP8 2.50p brt blue ('48) 5.50 .75
Nos. C49-C52 (4) 10.65 1.35

Types of 1946

1948 **Wmk. 90**

C53 AP10 15c dull red brn .20 .20
C54 AP11 25c gray green .25 .20

Atlas (National Museum, Naples) — AP14

Map of Argentine Republic, Globe and Caliper — AP15

Perf. 13½x13, 13x13½

1948-49 **Photo.** **Wmk. 288**

C55 AP14 45c dk brown ('49) .35 .20
C56 AP15 70c dark green .50 .25

4th Pan-American Reunion of Cartographers, Buenos Aires, Oct.-Nov., 1948.

Mercury Type of 1942

1949 **Litho.** ***Perf. 13x13½***

C57 AP9 50c dull brn & buff .40 .20

Marksmanship Trophy — AP16

1949, Nov. 4 **Photo.**
C58 AP16 75c brown .75 .20

World Rifle Championship, 1949.

Catalogue values for unused stamps in this section, from this point to the end of the section, are for Never Hinged items.

Douglas DC-3 and Condor AP17

Perf. 13x13½

1951, June 20 **Wmk. 90**
C59 AP17 20c dk olive grn .20 .20

10th anniversary of the State air lines.

Douglas DC-6 and Condor — AP18

1951, Oct. 17 ***Perf. 13½***
C60 AP18 20c blue .20 .20

End of Argentine 5-year Plan.

Plane-Letter Type of 1942

1951 **Litho.** ***Perf. 13½x13***
C61 AP8 1p carmine .40 .20

Jesus by Leonardo da Vinci (detail, "Virgin of the Rocks") AP19

Perf. 13½x13

1956, Sept. 29 **Photo.** **Wmk. 90**
C62 AP19 1p dull purple .35 .20

Issued to express the gratitude of the children of Argentina to the people of the world for their help against poliomyelitis.

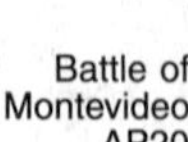

Battle of Montevideo AP20

Leonardo Rosales and Tomas Espora AP21

Guillermo Brown — AP22

Map of Americas & Arms of Buenos Aires — AP23

1957, Mar. 2 ***Perf. 13½***

C63 AP20	60c	blue gray	.20	.20
C64 AP21	1p	brt pink	.20	.20
C65 AP22	2p	brown	.25	.20
		Nos. C63-C65 (3)	.65	.60

Cent. of the death of Admiral Guillermo Brown, founder of the Argentine navy.

1957, Aug. 16
C66 AP23 2p rose violet .40 .20

Issued to publicize the Inter-American Economic Conference in Buenos Aires.

AP24

1957, Aug. 31 **Wmk. 90** ***Perf. 13½***
C67 AP24 60c Modern locomotive .20 .20

Centenary of Argentine railroads.

AP25

1957, Sept. 14

C68 AP25	1p	Globe, Flag, Compass Rose	.20	.20
C69 AP25	2p	Key	.30	.20

1957 International Congress for Tourism.

Birds Carrying Letters AP26

1957, Nov. 6
C70 AP26 1p bright blue .20 .20

Issued for Letter Writing Week, Oct. 6-12.

Early Plane AP27

1958, May 31 ***Perf. 13½***
C71 AP27 2p maroon .20 .20

50th anniv. of the Argentine Aviation Club.

Stamp Anniv. Type

Designs: 80c, Stamp of Buenos Aires and view of the Plaza de la Aduana. 1p, Stamp of 1858 and "The Post of Santa Fe."

1958 **Litho.** ***Perf. 13½***

C72 A270	80c	pale bis & sl bl	.20	.20
C73 A270	1p	red org & dk bl	.25	.20

Cent. of the 1st postage stamps of Buenos Aires & the Argentine Confederation.

Issue dates: 80c, Oct. 18; 1p, Aug. 23.

Comet Jet over World Map AP29

1959, May 16 ***Perf. 13½***
C74 AP29 5p black & olive .35 .20

Inauguration of jet flights by Argentine Airlines.

Type of Regular Issue, 1960.

"Cabildo" and: 1.80p, Mariano Moreno. 5p, Manuel Belgrano and Juan Jose Castelli.

Perf. 13½

1960, May 28 **Wmk. 90** **Photo.**

C75 A287	1.80p	red brown	.20	.20
a.		Souvenir sheet of 3	.65	.40
C76 A287	5p	buff & purple	.35	.20
a.		Souvenir sheet of 3	1.25	.80

Souvenir sheets are imperf. No. C75a contains one No. C75 and 1p and 2p resembling Nos. 713-714; stamps in reddish brown. No. C76a contains one No. C76 and 4.20p and 10.70p resembling Nos. 715-716; stamps are in green.

Symbolic of New Provinces — AP30

1960, July 8 **Litho.**
C77 AP30 1.80p dp car & blue .20 .20

Elevation of the territories of Chubut, Formosa, Neuquen, Rio Negro and Santa Cruz to provinces.

Type of Regular Issue, 1960

1960, Oct. 1 **Photo.** ***Perf. 13½***

C78 A291	1.80p	rose lilac	.20	.20
C79 A291	10.70p	brt grnsh blue	.40	.20

UNESCO Emblem AP31

1962, July 14 **Litho.**
C80 AP31 13p ocher & brown .40 .25

15th anniv. of UNESCO.

Mail Coach AP32

1962, Oct. 6 **Wmk. 90** ***Perf. 13½***
C81 AP32 5.60p gray brn & blk .20 .20

Mailman's Day, Sept. 14, 1962.

No. 695 and Type of 1959 Surcharged in Green

1962, Oct. 31 **Photo.**

C82 A277	5.60p	on 5p brown	.30	.20
C83 A277	18p	on 5p brn, *grnsh*	1.00	.20

UPAE Emblem — AP33

Skylark — AP34

1962, Nov. 24 **Photo.** ***Perf. 13½***
C84 AP33 5.60p dark blue .20 .20

50th anniv. of the founding of the Postal Union of the Americas and Spain, UPAE.

1963, Feb. 9 **Litho.**

Design: 11p, Super Albatros.

C85 AP34	5.60p	blue & black	.20	.20
C86 AP34	11p	blue, blk & red	.30	.20

9th World Gliding Championships.

Symbolic Plane AP35

1963-65 **Wmk. 90** ***Perf. 13½***

C87	AP35	5.60p	dk pur, car & brt grn	.40	.20
C88	AP35	7p	black & bis ('64)	.55	.20
C88A	AP35	7p	black & bis ('65)	4.00	.55
C89	AP35	11p	blk, dk pur & grn	.55	.25
C90	AP35	18p	dk pur, red & vio bl	1.10	.35
C91	AP35	21p	brown, red & gray	1.40	.55
			Nos. C87-C91 (6)	8.00	2.10

"Argentina" reads down on No. C88, up on No. C88A. See Nos. C101-C104, C108-C111, C123-C126, C135-C141. For overprint and surcharges see Nos. C96, C146-C150.

Type of Regular Issue, 1964

Map of Falkland Islands (Islas Malvinas).

1964, Feb. 22 ***Perf. 13½***

Size: 33x22mm

C92 A327 18p lt & dk bl & ol grn 1.75 .70

UPU Monument, Bern, and UN Emblem AP36

1964, May 23 **Engr.** ***Perf. 13½***
C93 AP36 18p red & dk brown .50 .25

15th UPU Cong., Vienna, Austria, 5-6/64.

Discovery of America, Florentine Woodcut
AP37

1964, Oct. 10 **Litho.**
C94 AP37 13p tan & black .35 .30

Day of the Race, Columbus Day.

Lt. Matienzo Base, Antarctica
AP38

1965, Feb. 27 **Photo.** ***Perf. 13½***
C95 AP38 11p salmon pink .50 .20

Issued to publicize the national territory of Tierra del Fuego, Antarctic and South Atlantic Isles.

No. C88A Overprinted in Silver: "PRIMERS / JORNADAS FILATELICAS / RIOPLATENSES"

1965, Mar. 17 **Litho.**
C96 AP35 7p black & bister .25 .20

1st Rio de la Plata Stamp Show, sponsored jointly by the Argentine and Uruguayan Philatelic Associations, Montevideo, Mar. 19-28.

ITU Emblem — AP39

Ascending Rocket — AP40

1965, May 11 **Wmk. 90** ***Perf. 13½***
C97 AP39 18p slate, blk & red .40 .25

Centenary of the ITU.

1965, May 29 **Photo.** ***Perf. 13½***

Design: 50p, Earth with trajectories and magnetic field, horiz.

C98 AP40 18p vermilion .40 .20
C99 AP40 50p dp violet blue 1.00 .50

6th Symposium on Space Research, held in Buenos Aires, and to honor the Natl. Commission of Space Research.

Type of 1963-65 Inscribed "Republica Argentina" Reading Down

1965, Oct. 13 **Litho.** **Wmk. 90**
C101 AP35 12p dk car rose & brn 1.40 .20
C102 AP35 15p vio blue & dk red .85 .25
C103 AP35 27.50p dk bl grn & gray 1.40 .40
C104 AP35 30.50p dk brown & dk bl 2.00 .60
Nos. C101-C104 (4) 5.65 1.45

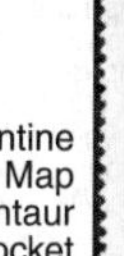

Argentine Antarctica Map and Centaur Rocket
AP41

1966, Feb. 19 ***Perf. 13½***
C105 AP41 27.50p bl, blk & dp org 1.00 .75

Launchings of sounding balloons and of a Gamma Centaur rocket in Antarctica during February, 1965.

Sea Gull and Southern Cross
AP42

1966, May 14 ***Perf. 13½***
C106 AP42 12p Prus blue, blk & red .30 .20

50th anniv. of the Naval Aviation School.

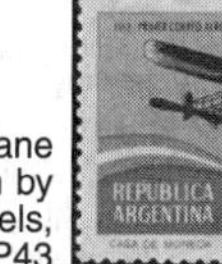

Blériot Plane Flown by Fels, 1917 — AP43

1967, Sept. 2 **Litho.** ***Perf. 13½***
C107 AP43 26p olive, bl & blk .25 .20

Flight by Theodore Fels from Buenos Aires to Montevideo, Sept. 2, 1917, allegedly the 1st intl. airmail flight.

Type of 1963-65 Inscribed "Republica Argentina" Reading Down

1967, Dec. 20 ***Perf. 13½***
C108 AP35 26p brown .60 .25
C109 AP35 40p violet 4.50 .30
C110 AP35 68p blue green 3.00 .45
C111 AP35 78p ultra 1.25 .60
Nos. C108-C111 (4) 9.35 1.60

Vito Dumas and Ketch "Legh II"
AP44

1968, July 27 **Litho.** **Wmk. 90**
C112 AP44 68p bl, blk, red & vio bl .65 .40

Issued to commemorate Vito Dumas's one-man voyage around the world in 1943.

Type of Regular Issue and

Assembly Emblem — AP45

40p, Globe and map of South America.

1968, Oct. 19 **Litho.** ***Perf. 13½***
C113 A395 40p brt pink, lt bl & blk .40 .20
C114 AP45 68p bl, lt bl, gold & blk .65 .30

4th Plenary Assembly of the Intl. Telegraph and Telephone Consultative Committee, Mar del Plata, Sept. 23-Oct. 25.

Radar Antenna, Balcarce Station
AP46

Perf. 13½

1969, Aug. 23 **Wmk. 90** **Photo.**
C115 AP46 40p blue gray .70 .25

Communications by satellite through Intl. Telecommunications Consortium (INTELSAT).

Atucha Nuclear Center
AP47

1969, Dec. 13 **Litho.** **Wmk. 365**
C116 AP47 26p blue & multi 1.40 .80

Completion of Atucha Nuclear Center.

Type of 1963-65 Inscribed "Republica Argentina" Reading Down

1969-71 ***Perf. 13½***
C123 AP35 40p violet 5.00 .30
C124 AP35 68p dk blue grn ('70) 2.00 .60

Unwmk.

C125 AP35 26p yellow brn ('71) .25 .20
C126 AP35 40p violet ('71) 2.75 .40
Nos. C123-C126 (4) 10.00 1.50

Old Fire Engine and Fire Brigade Emblem
AP48

1970, Aug. 8 **Litho.** **Unwmk.**
C128 AP48 40c green & multi .55 .30

Centenary of the Fire Brigade.

Education Year Emblem
AP49

1970, Aug. 29 ***Perf. 13½***
C129 AP49 68c blue & blk .40 .25

Issued for International Education Year.

Fleet Leaving Valparaiso, by Antonio Abel — AP50

1970, Oct. 17 **Litho.** ***Perf. 13½***
C130 AP50 26c multicolored 1.00 .35

150th anniv. of the departure for Peru of the liberation fleet from Valparaiso, Chile.

Sumampa Chapel — AP51

1970, Nov. 7 **Photo.**
C131 AP51 40c multicolored .95 .35

Bishopric of Tucuman, 400th anniversary.

Buenos Aires Planetarium — AP52

1970, Nov. 28 **Litho.** ***Perf. 13½***
C132 AP52 40c multicolored .60 .25

Jorge Newbery and Morane Saulnier Plane
AP53

1970, Dec. 19
C133 AP53 26c bl, blk, yel & grn .40 .25

24th Aeronautics and Space Week.

Industries Type of Regular Issue

Design: 31c, Refinery.

1971, Oct. 16 **Litho.** ***Perf. 13½***
C134 A445 31c red, blk & yel .60 .25

Type of 1963-65 Inscribed "Republica Argentina" Reading Down

1971-74 **Unwmk.**
C135 AP35 45c brown 3.25 .20
C136 AP35 68c red .50 .20
C137 AP35 70c vio blue ('73) .85 .20
C138 AP35 90c emerald ('73) 1.90 .20
C139 AP35 1.70p blue ('74) .50 .25
C140 AP35 1.95p emerald ('74) .50 .30
C141 AP35 2.65p dp claret ('74) .50 .40
Nos. C135-C141 (7) 8.00 1.75

Fluorescent paper was used for Nos. C135-C136, C138-C141. The 70c was issued on both papers.

Don Quixote, Drawing by Ignacio Zuloaga
AP54

1975, Apr. 26 **Photo.** ***Perf. 13½***
C145 AP54 2.75p yellow, blk & red .60 .35

Day of the Race and for Espana 75 Intl. Philatelic Exhibition, Madrid, Apr. 4-13.

No. C87 Surcharged

1975, Sept. 15 Litho. Wmk. 90

C146 AP35 9.20p on 5.60p .90 .20
C147 AP35 19.70p on 5.60p 1.25 .45
C148 AP35 100p on 5.60p 5.50 2.25
Nos. C146-C148 (3) 7.65 2.90

No. C87 Surcharged

1975, Oct. 15

C149 AP35 9.20p on 5.60p .70 .30
C150 AP35 19.70p on 5.60p 1.25 .60

Argentine State Airline, 50th Anniv. — AP55

1990, Sept. 15 Litho. *Perf. 13½*

C151 AP55 2500a Junkers JU52-3M 1.25 .90
C152 AP55 2500a Grumman SA-16 1.25 .90
C153 AP55 2500a Fokker F-27 1.25 .90
C154 AP55 2500a Fokker F-28 1.25 .90
Nos. C151-C154 (4) 5.00 3.60

AIR POST SEMI-POSTAL STAMPS

Catalogue values for unused stamps in this section are for Never Hinged items.

Philatelic Exhibition Type

#CB1, Stamp engraving. #CB2, Proofing stamp die. #CB3, Sheet of stamps. #CB4, The letter. #CB5, Gen. San Martin.

Perf. 13½

1950, Aug. 26 Wmk. 90 Photo.

CB1 SP8 45c + 45c vio bl .40 .25
CB2 SP8 70c + 70c dk brn .55 .40
a. Souv. sheet of 3, #B12, CB1, CB2, imperf. 3.00 3.00
CB3 SP8 1p + 1p cerise 1.50 1.50
CB4 SP8 2.50p + 2.50p ol gray 8.50 6.00
CB5 SP8 5p + 5p dull grn 9.25 7.25
Nos. CB1-CB5 (5) 20.20 15.40

Argentine Intl. Philatelic Exhib., 1950.

Pieta by Michelangelo SPAP2

1951, Dec. 22 *Perf. 13½x13*

CB6 SPAP2 2.45p +7.55p grnsh blk 21.00 14.00

Surtax as for the Eva Peron Foundation.

Flower and Child's Head SPAP3

1958, Mar. 15 *Perf. 13½*

CB7 SPAP3 1p +50c deep claret .30 .30

Surtax for National Council for Children.

Stamp of 1858 — SPAP4

1958, Mar. 29 Litho. Wmk. 90

CB8 SPAP4 1p + 50c gray ol & bl .40 .30
CB9 SPAP4 2p + 1p rose lilac & vio .50 .40
CB10 SPAP4 3p + 1.50p green & brown .60 .50
CB11 SPAP4 5p + 2.50p gray ol & car rose 1.00 .85
CB12 SPAP4 10p + 5p gray ol & brn 2.00 1.60
Nos. CB8-CB12 (5) 4.50 3.65

The surtax was for the Intl. Centennial Philatelic Exhibition, Buenos Aires, Apr. 19-27.

Type of Semi-Postal Issue, 1958

Designs: 1p+50c, Flooded area. 5p+2.50p, House and truck under water.

1958, Oct. 4 Photo. *Perf. 13½*

CB13 SP11 1p + 50c dull purple .25 .20
CB14 SP11 5p + 2.50p grnsh blue .80 .75

The surtax was for victims of a flood in the Buenos Aires district.

Type of Semi-Postal Issue

1959, Sept. 5 Litho. *Perf. 13½*

CB15 SP13 2p + 1p Rowing .40 .25
CB16 SP13 3p + 1.50p Woman diver .60 .50

Bird Type of Semi-Postal Issue

2p+1p, Rufous tinamou. 3p+1.50p, Rhea.

1960, Feb. 6 *Perf. 13½*

CB17 SP14 2p + 1p rose car & sal .30 .20
CB18 SP14 3p + 1.50p slate green .45 .35

The surtax was for child welfare work.
See No. CB29.

Buenos Aires Market Place, 1810 SPAP5

6p+3p, Oxcart water carrier. 10.70p+5.30p, Settlers landing. 20p+10p, The Fort.

1960, Aug. 20 Photo. Wmk. 90

CB19 SPAP5 2 + 1p rose brown .20 .20
CB20 SPAP5 6 + 3p gray .35 .25
CB21 SPAP5 10.70 + 5.30p blue .60 .35
CB22 SPAP5 20 + 10p bluish grn 1.00 .85
Nos. CB19-CB22 (4) 2.15 1.65

Inter-American Philatelic Exhibition EFIMAYO 1960, Buenos Aires, Oct. 12-24, held to for the sesquicentennial of the May Revolution of 1910.
For overprints see Nos. CB25-CB28.

Seibo, National Flower — SPAP6

1960, Sept. 10 *Perf. 13½*

#CB24, Copihue, Chile's national flower.

CB23 SPAP6 6 + 3p lilac rose .35 .30
CB24 SPAP6 10.70 + 5.30p ver .50 .40

The surtax was for earthquake victims in Chile.

Nos. CB19-CB22 Overprinted: "DIA DE LAS NACIONES UNIDAS 24 DE OCTUBRE"

1960, Oct. 8

CB25 SPAP5 2 + 1p rose brown .20 .20
CB26 SPAP5 6 + 3p gray .30 .30
CB27 SPAP5 10.70 + 5.30p blue .50 .40
CB28 SPAP5 20 + 10p bluish green .85 .75
Nos. CB25-CB28 (4) 1.85 1.65

United Nations Day, Oct. 24, 1960.

Type of Semi-Postal Issue, 1960

Design: Emperor penguins.

1961, Feb. 25 Photo. Wmk. 90

CB29 SP14 1.80p + 90c gray .30 .20

The surtax was for child welfare work.

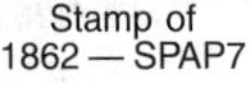

Stamp of 1862 — SPAP7

Crutch, Olympic Torch and Rings — SPAP8

1962, May 19 Litho.

CB30 SPAP7 6.50p + 6.50p Prus bl & grnsh bl .70 .65

Opening of the "Argentina 62" Philatelic Exhibition, Buenos Aires, May 19-29.

Type of Semi-Postal Issue, 1963

1963, May 18 Wmk. 90 *Perf. 13½*

CB31 SP21 11p + 5p Bicycling .55 .50

Type of Semi-Postal Issue, 1962

1963, Dec. 21 *Perf. 13½*

CB32 SP20 11p + 5p Great kiskadee .70 .60

The surtax was for child welfare.

Type of Semi-Postal Issue, 1964

1964, July 18 Litho.

CB33 SP22 11p + 5p Sailboat .50 .50

1964, Sept. 19 Litho. *Perf. 13½*

CB34 SPAP8 18p + 9p bluish grn, blk, red & yel .60 .60

13th "Olympic" games for the handicapped, Tokyo, 1964.

Bird Type of Semi-Postal Issue, 1962

1964, Dec. 23 Litho. Wmk. 90

CB35 SP20 18p + 9p Chilean swallow .90 .75

The surtax was for child welfare.

Bird Type of Semi-Postal Issue, 1962, Inscribed "R. ARGENTINA"

Design: Rufous ovenbird.

1966, Mar. 26 *Perf. 13½*

CB36 SP20 27.50p + 12.50p bl, ocher, yel & grn .80 .70

The surtax was for child welfare.

Coat of Arms — SPAP9

1966, June 25 Litho. *Perf. 13½*

CB37 SPAP9 10p + 10p multi 1.75 1.40

ARGENTINA '66 Philatelic Exhibition held in connection with the sesquicentennial celebration of the Declaration of Independence, Buenos Aires, July 16-23. The surtax was for the Exhibition. Issued in sheets of 4.

Bird Type of Semi-Postal Issue, 1962, Inscribed "R. ARGENTINA"

Designs: 15p+7p, Blue and yellow tanager. 26p+13p, Toco toucan.

1967 Litho. Wmk. 90

CB38 SP20 15p + 7p blk, bl, grn & yel 1.00 .90
CB39 SP20 26p + 13p blk, org, yel & bl .50 .40

The surtax was for child welfare.
Issued: 15p+7p, Jan. 14; 26p+13p, Dec. 23.

Bird Type of Semi-Postal Issue, 1969

Design: 26p+13p, Lineated woodpecker.

1969, Sept. 20 Wmk. 365 *Perf. 13½*

CB40 SP24 26p + 13p multi .50 .40

The surtax was for child welfare.

Bird Type of Semi-Postal Issue, 1970

Design: 40c+20c, Chilean flamingo.

1970, May 9 Litho. Wmk. 365

CB41 SP25 40c + 20c multi .45 .40

The surtax was for child welfare.

Fish Type of Semi-Postal Issue, 1971

Design: Pejerrey (atherinidae family).

1971, Feb. 20 Unwmk. *Perf. 12½*
Size: 75x15mm

CB42 SP26 40c + 20c multi .40 .40

The surtax was for child welfare.

OFFICIAL STAMPS

Regular Issues Overprinted in Black

1884-87 Unwmk. *Perf. 12, 14*

O1 A29 ½c brown 12.00 10.00
O2 A23 1c red 8.00 6.00
b. Perf. 12 40.00 32.50
O3 A29 1c red .50 .35
b. Double overprint 35.00 35.00
O4 A20 2c green .50 .35
b. Double overprint 75.00
O5 A11 4c brown .50 .35
O6 A7 8c lake .50 .35
O7 A8 10c green 40.00 25.00
O8 A23 12c ultra (#45) 6.50 4.00
a. Perf. 14 325.00 125.00
O9 A29 12c grnsh blue .80 .65
O10 A19 24c blue 1.25 1.00
O11 A21 25c lake 16.00 12.50
O12 A12 30c orange 32.50 20.00
O13 A13 60c black 20.00 12.50
O14 A14 90c blue 20.00 16.00
b. Double overprint 50.00 45.00
Nos. O1-O14 (14) 159.05 109.05

Inverted Overprint

O1a A29 ½c 16.00 12.50
O2a A23 1c Perf. 14 50.00 40.00
c. Perf. 12 32.50 30.00
O3a A29 1c 1.60 1.00
O4a A20 2c 65.00 40.00
O5a A11 4c 40.00 32.50
O6a A7 8c 60.00 60.00
O8b A23 12c Perf. 12 12.50
O9a A29 12c 125.00 65.00
O10a A19 24c 2.75 1.60
O13a A13 60c 90.00 50.00
O14a A14 90c 50.00 40.00

1884 ***Rouletted***

O15 A17 16c green 1.75 1.00
- *a.* Double overprint 16.00 —
- *b.* Inverted overprint 125.00

O16 A18 20c blue 8.00 7.00
- *a.* Inverted overprint 60.00 40.00

O17 A19 24c blue 1.25 1.00
- *a.* Inverted overprint 4.00 2.50
- *b.* Double ovpt., one inverted 250.00 —

Nos. O15-O17 (3) 11.00 9.00

Overprinted Diagonally in Red

1885 ***Perf. 12***

O18 A20 2c green 2.00 1.50
- *a.* Inverted overprint 40.00 32.50

O19 A11 4c brown 2.00 1.40
- *a.* Inverted overprint 40.00 32.50
- *b.* Double overprint 50.00

O20 A13 60c black 20.00 16.00
O21 A14 90c blue 200.00 150.00

1885 ***Rouletted***

O22 A19 24c blue 17.50 12.50

On all of these stamps, the overprint is found reading both upwards and downwards.

Counterfeits exist of No. O21 overprint and others.

Regular Issues Handstamped Horizontally in Black

1884 ***Perf. 12, 14***

O23 A23 1c red 50.00 17.00
- *a.* Perf. 12 150.00 100.00

O24 A20 2c green, diagonal overprint 25.00 15.00
- *a.* Horizontal overprint 150.00 125.00

O25 A11 4c brown 10.00 8.00
O26 A7 8c lake 10.00 10.00
O27 A23 12c ultra 27.50 20.00

Overprinted Diagonally

O28 A19 24c bl, rouletted 20.00 15.00
O29 A13 60c black 15.00 10.00

Counterfeit overprints exist.

Liberty Head — O1

Perf. 11½, 12 and Compound

1901, Dec. 1 **Engr.**

O31 O1 1c gray .25 .20
- *b.* Vert. pair, imperf. horiz. 50.00
- *c.* Horiz. pair, imperf. vert. 50.00

O32 O1 2c orange brown .30 .20
O33 O1 5c red .40 .20
- *b.* Vert. pair, imperf. horiz. 50.00

O34 O1 10c dark green .50 .20
O35 O1 30c dark blue 4.00 1.00
O36 O1 50c orange 2.00 1.00

Nos. O31-O36 (6) 7.45 2.80

Imperf, Pairs

O31a O1 1c 40.00
O32a O1 2c 40.00
O33a O1 5c 50.00
O34a O1 10c 40.00
O35a O1 30c 65.00
O36a O1 50c 50.00

Regular Stamps of 1935-51 Overprinted in Black

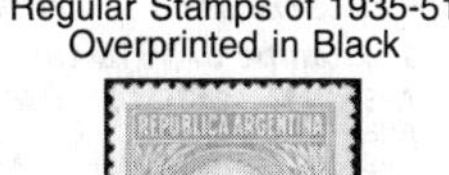

c

Perf. 13x13½, 13½x13, 13

1938-54 **Wmk. RA in Sun (90)**

O37 A129 1c buff ('40) .20 .20
O38 A130 2c dk brn ('40) .20 .20
O39 A132 3c grn ('39) .20 .20
O40 A132 3c lt gray ('39) .20 .20
O41 A134 5c yel brn .20 .20
O42 A195 5c car ('53) .20 .20
O43 A137 10c carmine .20 .20
O44 A137 10c brn ('39) .20 .20
O45 A140 15c lt gray bl, type II ('47) .20 .20
O46 A139 15c slate blue .50 .20
O47 A139 15c pale ultra ('39) .20 .20
O48 A139 20c blue ('53) .30 .20
O49 A141 25c carmine .20 .20
- *a.* Overprint 11mm .20 .20

O49B A143 40c dk violet .90 .20
O50 A144 50c red & org .20 .20
- *a.* Overprint 11mm .25 .20

O51 A146 1p brn blk & lt bl ('40) .20 .20
- *a.* Overprint 11mm .25 .25

O52 A224 1p choc & lt bl ('51) .20 .20
- *a.* Overprint 11mm .20 .20

O53 A147 2p brn lake & dk ultra (ovpt. 11mm) ('54) .70 .20

Nos. O37-O53 (18) 5.20 3.60

Overprinted in Black on Stamps and Types of 1945-47

Perf. 13x13½, 13½x13

1945-46 **Unwmk.**

O54 A130 2c sepia 2.75 .40
O55 A134 3c lt gray 2.25 .30
O56 A134 5c yel brn .65 .20
O57 A195 5c dp car .20 .20
O58 A137 10c brown .20 .20
- *a.* Double overprint

O59 A140 15c lt gray bl, type II .20 .20
O61 A141 25c dull rose .20 .20
O62 A144 50c red & org .55 .20
O63 A146 1p brn blk & lt bl .20 .20
O64 A147 2p brn lake & bl .40 .20
O65 A148 5p ind & ol grn .20 .20
O66 A149 10p dp cl & int blk .45 .20
O67 A150 20p bl grn & brn 1.00 .30

Nos. O54-O67 (13) 9.25 3.00

Overprinted in Black on Stamps and Types of 1942-50

Perf. 13, 13x13½

1944-51 **Wmk. 288**

O73 A134 3c lt gray 1.10 .50
O74 A134 5c yellow brown .20 .20
O75 A137 10c red brown .20 .20
O76 A140 15c lt gray bl, type II .25 .20
O77 A144 50c red & org (overprint 11 mm) 1.50 .50
O78 A146 1p brn blk & lt bl (overprint 11mm) 1.75 .40

Nos. O73-O78 (6) 5.00 2.00

Catalogue values for unused stamps in this section, from this point to the end of the section, are for Never Hinged items.

Nos. 600-606 Overprinted in Black

d

1953 **Wmk. 90** ***Perf. 13***

O79 A228 5c gray .20 .20
O80 A228 10c rose lilac .20 .20
O81 A228 20c rose pink .20 .20
O82 A228 25c dull green .20 .20
O83 A228 40c dull violet .20 .20
O84 A228 45c deep blue .20 .20
O85 A228 50c dull brown .20 .20

e

f

Nos. 611-617 Overprinted Type "e" in Blue

Perf. 13x13½, 13½x13

O86 A229 1p dk brown .20 .20
O87 A229 1.50p dp green .30 .20
O88 A229 2p brt carmine .20 .20
O89 A229 3p indigo .55 .25

Size: 30x40mm

O90 A229 5p red brown .60 .45
O91 A228 10p red 2.75 1.75
O92 A229 20p green 30.00 20.00

Nos. O79-O92 (14) 36.00 24.45

No. 612 Overprinted Type "f" in Blue

O93 A229 1.50p dp grn 1.00 .30

Regular Issues of 1954-59 Variously Overprinted in Black or Blue

g

h

Perf. 13½, 13x13½, 13½x13

1955-61 **Litho.** **Wmk. 90**

O94 A237(c) 20c red (#629) .20 .20
O95 A237(d) 20c red (#629) .20 .20
O96 A237(d) 40c red, ovpt. 15mm (#630) .20 .20

Engr.

O97 A239(g) 50c bl (#632) .20 .20

Photo.

O98 A239(h) 1p brn (#635) .20 .20
O99 A239(e) 1p brn (Bl, #635) .20 .20
O100 A239(e) 1p brn (Bk, #635) .20 .20

Engr.

O101 A239(h) 3p vio brn (#638) .20 .20
O102 A240(h) 5p gray grn (#639) .30 .20
O103 A240(e) 10p yel grn (#640) .50 .20
O104 A240(f) 20p dl vio (#641) .75 .30
O105 A240(h) 20p dl vio (#641) .75 .25
O106 A241(e) 50p ultra & ind (#642) 1.10 .20

Nos. O94-O106 (13) 5.00 2.75

The overprints on #O99-O100 & O103-O104 are horizontal; that on #O106 is vertical. On #O106 overprint measures 23mm.

Issued: #O102, 1957; #O97, O101, O103, O105, 1958; #O98-O99, O104, 1959; #O100, 1960; #O106, 1961.

No. 659 Overprinted Type "d"

1957 **Wmk. 90** **Litho.** ***Perf. 13***

O108 A133 20c dl pur (ovpt. 15mm) .20 .20

Nos. 666, 658 and 663 Variously Overprinted

1957 **Photo.** ***Perf. 13x13½, 13½***

O109 A261(g) 2p claret .20 .20
O110 A254(e) 2.40p brown .20 .20
O111 A258(c) 4.40p grnsh gray .25 .20

Nos. O109-O111 (3) .65 .60

Nos. 668, 685-687, 690-691, 693-705, 742, 742C and Types of 1959-65 Overprinted in Black, Blue or Red Types "e," "g," or

i

j

k

m

n

Lithographed; Photogravure

1960-68 ***Perf. 13x13½, 13½***

O112 A128(g) 5c buff (vert. ovpt.) .20 .20
O113 A275(j) 10c sl grn .20 .20
O114 A275(j) 20c dl red brn .20 .20
O115 A275(i) 50c bister .20 .20
O116 A278(k) 1p brn .20 .20
O117 A278(j) 1p brn, photo. (vert. ovpt.) .20 .20
O117A A278(j) 1p brn, litho., (down) .20 .20
O118 A276(j) 2p rose red .20 .20
O119 A312(m) 2p dp grn .25 .20
O120 A312(j) 2p brt grn (up) .20 .20
O121 A312(j) 2p grn litho. (down) .25 .20
O122 A277(e) 3p dk bl (horiz.) .20 .20
O123 A277(j) 3p dk blue .20 .20
O124 A276(j) 4p red, litho. .20 .20
O125 A312(j) 4p rose red, litho. (down) .20 .20
O126 A277(e) 5p brn (Bl) (horiz.) .25 .20
O127 A277(e) 5p brn (Bk) (horiz.) .25 .20
O128 A277(j) 5p sepia .20 .20
O129 A277(e) 5p sepia (horiz. ovpt.) .20 .20
O130 A276(j) 8p red .20 .20
O131 A278(i) 10p lt red brn .45 .20
O132 A276(j) 10p vermilion .20 .20
O133 A278(j) 10p brn car (up) .20 .20
O134 A278(m) 12p dk brn vio (horiz.) .40 .20
O135 A278(k) 20p Prus grn .50 .20
O136 A278(j) 20p Prus grn (up) .40 .20
O137 A276(j) 20p red, litho. .35 .20
O138 A276(m) 20p red, litho.(horiz.) .25 .20
O139 A278(j) 23p grn (vert. ovpt.) .50 .20
O140 A278(j) 25p dp vio, photo. (R) (up) .50 .20
O141 A278(j) 25p pur, litho. (R) (down) .50 .20
O142 A241(n) 50p dk blue 1.10 .20
O143 A279(m) 100p bl (horiz. ovpt.) 1.10 .35
O144 A279(m) 100p blue (up) 1.10 .35
O145 A280(m) 300p dp violet (horiz.) 2.25 .60

Nos. O112-O145 (35) 14.00 7.70

The "m" overprint measures 15½mm on 2p; 14½mm on 12p, 100p and 300p; 13mm on 20p.

Issued: #O122, O127, O135, 1961; #O112-O114, O116, O118, 1962; #O124, 1963; #O119, O134, O143, 1964; #O117, O125, O130, O139, O144, 1965; #O120, O128, O132-O133, O136, O140, O142, O145, 1966;

#O121, O129, O137-O138, O141, 1967; #O117A, 1968.

Nos. 699, 823-825, 827-829, and Type of 1962 Overprinted in Black or Red Types "j," "m," or "o"

o

Inscribed: "Republica Argentina"

Litho., Photo., Engr.

1964-67 Wmk. 90 *Perf. 13½*

O149 A312(j) 6p rose red (down) .25 .20
O153 A238a(m) 22p ultra .50 .20
O154 A238a(j) 43p dk car rose (down) .75 .20
O155 A238a(j) 45p brn, photo. (up) .75 .20
O156 A238a(j) 45p brn, litho. (up) 1.10 .20
O157 A241(j) 50p dk bl (up) (R) 2.25 .20
O158 A366(j) 90p ol bis (up) 2.75 .20
O162 A495(o) 500p yel grn 3.50 .80
Nos. O149-O162 (8) 11.85 2.20

Issued: No. O153, 1964; No. O155, 1966; Nos. O149, O156-O162, 1967.

Type of 1959-67 Ovptd. Type "j"

1969 Litho. Wmk. 365 *Perf. 13½*

O163 A276 20p vermilion .20 .20

Beginning with No. 2001, many Argentine stamps are inscribed "Correo Official," but are not official stamps.

OFFICIAL DEPARTMENT STAMPS

Regular Issues of 1911-37 Overprinted in Black

Type I

Type II

Ministry of Agriculture (M. A.)

Type I

1913-37

On Stamp of 1911

OD1 A88 2c #181 .20 .20

On Stamps of 1912-14

OD2 A88 1c #190 .20 .20
OD3 A88 2c #191 .20 .20
OD4 A88 5c #194 .30 .20
OD5 A88 12c #196 .20 .20
Nos. OD2-OD5 (4) .90 .80

On Stamps of 1915-16

OD6 A88 1c #208 .20 .20
OD7 A88 2c #209 .20 .20
OD8 A88 5c #212 .20 .20
OD9 A91 5c #220 .20 .20
Nos. OD6-OD9 (4) .80 .80

On Stamp of 1917

OD10 A94 12c #238 .30 .20

On Stamps of 1918-19

OD11 A93 1c #249 .20 .20
OD12 A93 2c #250 .20 .20
OD13 A93 5c #253 .20 .20
OD14 A94 12c #255 .20 .20
OD15 A94 20c #256 .20 .20
Nos. OD10-OD15 (6) 1.30 1.20

On Stamps of 1920

OD16 A93 1c #265 .30 .25
OD17 A93 2c #266 .50 .25
OD18 A93 5c #269 .20 .20
Nos. OD16-OD18 (3) 1.00 .70

On Stamps of 1922-23

OD19 A94 12c #311 1.00 .40
OD20 A94 20c #312 25.00

On Stamps of 1923

OD21 A104 1c #324 .20 .20
OD22 A104 2c #325 .25 .20
OD23 A104 5c #328 .20 .20
OD24 A104 12c #330 .20 .20
OD25 A104 20c #331 .20 .20
Nos. OD21-OD25 (5) 1.05 1.00

On Stamps of 1923-31

OD26 A104 1c #341 .20 .20
OD27 A104 2c #342, I .20 .20
a. Type II 1.50 .75
OD28 A104 3c #343 .20 .20
OD29 A104 5c #345, II .20 .20
a. Type I .20 .20
OD30 A104 10c #346, II .20 .20
a. Type I .20 .20
OD31 A104 12c #347 .20 .20
OD32 A104 20c #348, I .20 .20
a. Type II .20 .20
OD33 A104 30c #351 .20 .20
Nos. OD26-OD33 (8) 1.60 1.60

On Stamp of 1926

OD34 A110 12c #360 .20 .20

Type II

On Stamps of 1935-37

OD35 A129 1c #419 .20 .20
OD36 A130 2c #420 .20 .20
OD37 A132 3c #422 .20 .20
OD38 A134 5c #427 .20 .20
OD39 A137 10c #430 .20 .20
OD40 A139 15c #434 .50 .20
OD41 A140 20c #437 .30 .20
OD42 A140 20c #438 .20 .20
OD43 A141 25c #441 .25 .20
OD44 A142 30c #442 .20 .20
OD45 A145 1p #445 2.50 1.50
OD46 A146 1p #446 .50 .25
Nos. OD35-OD46 (12) 5.45 3.75

Ministry of War (M. G.)

Type I

On Stamp of 1911

OD47 A88 2c #181 .20 .20

On Stamps of 1912-14

OD48 A88 1c #190 .20 .20
OD49 A88 2c #191 .75 .20
OD50 A88 5c #194 .20 .20
OD51 A88 12c #196 .20 .20
Nos. OD48-OD51 (4) 1.35 .80

On Stamps of 1915-16

OD52 A88 1c #208 6.00 .75
OD53 A88 2c #209 .60 .20
OD54 A88 5c #212 .75 .20
OD55 A91 5c #220 1.00 .25
OD56 A92 12c #222 1.00 .35
Nos. OD52-OD56 (5) 9.35 1.75

On Stamps of 1917

OD57 A93 1c #232 .30 .20
OD58 A93 2c #233 .40 .20
OD59 A93 5c #236 .30 .20
OD60 A94 12c #238 .60 .20
Nos. OD57-OD60 (4) 1.60 .80

On Stamps of 1918-19

OD61 A93 1c #249 .20 .20
OD62 A93 2c #250 .20 .20
OD63 A93 5c #253 .20 .20
OD64 A94 12c #255 .40 .20
OD65 A94 20c #256 1.25 .20
Nos. OD61-OD65 (5) 2.25 1.00

On Stamps of 1920

OD66 A93 2c #266 .40 .20
OD67 A93 5c #269 .40 .20
OD68 A94 12c #271 .35 .20
Nos. OD66-OD68 (3) 1.15 .60

On Stamp of 1920

OD69 A94 12c #299 2.00 .25

On Stamps of 1922-23

OD70 A93 1c #305 .75 .20
OD71 A93 2c #306 1.50 .45
OD72 A103 5c #309 .75 .20
OD73 A94 20c #312 .30 .20
Nos. OD70-OD73 (4) 3.30 1.05

On Stamp of 1922-23

OD74 A93 2c #318 5.00 .50

On Stamps of 1923

OD75 A104 1c #324 .20 .20
OD76 A104 2c #325 .20 .20
OD77 A104 5c #328 .20 .20
OD78 A104 12c #330 .20 .20
OD79 A104 20c #331 1.00 .20
Nos. OD75-OD79 (5) 1.80 1.00

On Stamps of 1923-31

OD80 A104 1c #341 1.25 .45
OD81 A104 2c #342 .20 .20
OD82 A104 3c #343, I .20 .20
a. Type II .40 .20
OD83 A104 5c #345, I .20 .20
a. Type II .20 .20
OD84 A104 10c #346, II .20 .20
a. Type I .60 .20
OD85 A104 20c #348, I .20 .20
a. Type II .40 .20
OD86 A104 30c #351, II .20 .20
a. Type I 1.00 .20
OD87 A105 1p #353 2.00 .30
Nos. OD80-OD87 (8) 4.45 1.95

On Stamp of 1926

OD88 A109 5c #359 .60 .20

Type II

On Stamps of 1935-37

OD89 A129 1c #419 .20 .20
OD90 A130 2c #420 .20 .20
OD91 A132 3c #422 .20 .20
OD92 A134 5c #427 .20 .20
OD93 A137 10c #430 .20 .20
OD94 A139 15c #434 .25 .20
OD95 A140 20c #437 1.00 .20
OD96 A140 20c #438 .25 .20
OD97 A141 25c #441 .20 .20
OD98 A142 30c #442 .20 .20
OD99 A144 50c #444 .25 .20
OD100 A145 1p #445 1.25 .50
OD101 A146 1p #446 .50 .25
Nos. OD89-OD101 (13) 4.90 2.95

Ministry of Finance (M. H.)

Type I

On Stamp of 1911

OD102 A88 2c #181 .20 .20

On Stamps of 1912-14

OD103 A88 1c #190 .20 .20
OD104 A88 2c #191 .20 .20
OD105 A88 5c #194 .20 .20
OD106 A88 12c #196 .20 .20
Nos. OD103-OD106 (4) .80 .80

On Stamps of 1915-16

OD107 A88 2c #209 .20 .20
OD108 A88 5c #212 .20 .20
OD109 A91 5c #220 .20 .20
Nos. OD107-OD109 (3) .60 .60

On Stamps of 1917

OD110 A93 2c #233 .20 .20
OD111 A93 5c #236 1.25 .20
OD112 A94 12c #238 .20 .20
Nos. OD110-OD112 (3) 1.65 .60

On Stamps of 1918-19

OD113 A93 2c #250 25.00
OD114 A93 5c #253 .20 .20
OD115 A94 12c #255 .45 .20
OD116 A94 20c #256 .45 .20

On Stamps of 1920

OD117 A93 1c #265 .75 .45
OD118 A93 2c #266 1.25 .45
OD119 A93 5c #269 .30 .20
OD120 A94 12c #271 .60 .20
Nos. OD117-OD120 (4) 2.90 1.30

On Stamp of 1922-23

OD121 A94 20c #312 12.50 2.50

On Stamps of 1923

OD122 A104 1c #324 .75 .40
OD123 A104 2c #325 .20 .20
OD124 A104 5c #328 .20 .20
OD125 A104 12c #330 .20 .20
OD126 A104 20c #331 .20 .20
Nos. OD122-OD126 (5) 1.55 1.20

On Stamps of 1923-31

OD127 A104 3c #343 7.00 1.50
OD128 A104 5c #345 .20 .20
OD129 A104 10c #346 .20 .20
OD130 A104 12c #347 7.00 3.75
OD131 A104 20c #348, I .20 .20
a. Type II .35 .20
OD132 A104 30c #351 .25 .20
OD133 A105 1p #353 .40 .20
Nos. OD127-OD133 (7) 15.25 6.25

On Stamp of 1926

OD134 A110 12c #360 12.50 12.50

Type II

On Stamps of 1935-37

OD135 A129 1c #419 .20 .20
OD136 A130 2c #420 .20 .20
OD137 A132 3c #422 .20 .20
OD138 A134 5c #427 .20 .20
OD139 A137 10c #430 .20 .20
OD140 A139 15c #434 .45 .20
OD141 A140 20c #437 .20 .20
OD142 A140 20c #438 .20 .20
OD143 A142 30c #442 .20 .20
OD144 A145 1p #445 2.00 1.00
OD145 A146 1p #446 .50 .20
Nos. OD135-OD145 (11) 4.55 3.00

Ministry of the Interior (M. I.)

Type I

On Stamp of 1911

OD146 A88 2c #181 .25 .20

On Stamps of 1912-14

OD147 A88 1c #190 .20 .20
OD148 A88 2c #191 .20 .20
OD149 A88 5c #194 .20 .20
OD150 A88 12c #196 .20 .20
Nos. OD146-OD150 (5) 1.05 1.00

On Stamps of 1915-17

OD151 A88 2c #209 .80 .30
OD152 A88 5c #212 .75 .20
OD153 A91 5c #220 .60 .20
OD154 A93 5c #236 1.50 .20
Nos. OD151-OD154 (4) 3.65 .90

On Stamps of 1918-19

OD155 A93 2c #250 .20 .20
OD156 A93 5c #253 .20 .20

On Stamps of 1920

OD157 A93 1c #265 3.75 1.25
OD158 A93 5c #269 .75 .35

On Stamps of 1922-23

OD159 A93 2c #306 12.50 12.50
OD160 A103 5c #309 3.50 1.25
OD161 A94 12c #311 1.25 .40
OD162 A94 20c #312 1.25 .40
Nos. OD159-OD162 (4) 18.50 14.55

On Stamps of 1923

OD163 A104 1c #324 .20 .20
OD164 A104 2c #325 .20 .20
OD165 A104 5c #328 .20 .20
OD166 A104 12c #330 2.00 2.00
OD167 A104 20c #331 .75 .20
Nos. OD163-OD167 (5) 3.35 2.80

On Stamps of 1923-31

OD168 A104 1c #341 .20 .20
OD169 A104 2c #342 .20 .20
OD170 A104 3c #343, II .20 .20
a. Type I 1.25 .30
OD171 A104 5c #345, I .20 .20
a. Type II .20 .20
OD172 A104 10c #346, II .20 .20
OD173 A104 12c #347 .30 .20
OD174 A104 20c #348, II .20 .20
a. Type I .75 .20
OD175 A104 30c #351 .20 .20
Nos. OD168-OD175 (8) 1.70 1.60

Type II

On Stamps of 1935-37

OD176 A129 1c #419 .20 .20
OD177 A130 2c #420 .20 .20
OD178 A132 3c #422 .20 .20
OD178A A134 5c #427 .20 .20
OD179 A137 10c #430 .20 .20
OD180 A139 15c #434 .30 .20
OD181 A140 20c #437 .75 .20
OD182 A140 20c #438 .20 .20
OD182A A142 30c #442 .20 .20
OD182B A145 1p #445 2.00 1.00
OD182C A146 1p #446 .55 .20
Nos. OD176-OD182C (11) 5.00 3.00

Ministry of Justice and Instruction (M. J. I.)

Type I

On Stamp of 1911

OD183 A88 2c #181 1.25 .20

On Stamps of 1912-14

OD184 A88 1c #190 1.50 .20
OD185 A88 2c #191 1.00 .20
OD186 A88 5c #194 .45 .20
OD187 A88 12c #196 .45 .20
Nos. OD184-OD187 (4) 3.40 .80

On Stamps of 1915-17

OD188 A88 1c #208 .30 .20
OD189 A88 2c #209 .30 .20
OD190 A88 5c #212 1.00 .20
OD191 A91 5c #220 .25 .20
OD192 A92 12c #222 .75 .20
Nos. OD188-OD192 (5) 2.60 1.00

On Stamps of 1917

OD193 A93 1c #232 .25 .20
OD194 A93 2c #233 .75 .20
OD195 A93 5c #236 .25 .20
OD196 A94 12c #238 17.50 5.00
Nos. OD193-OD196 (4) 18.75 5.60

On Stamps of 1918-19

OD197 A93 1c #249 .20 .20
OD198 A93 2c #250 .20 .20
OD199 A93 5c #253 .20 .20
OD200 A94 12c #255 .20 .20
OD201 A94 20c #256 .50 .20
Nos. OD197-OD201 (5) 1.30 1.00

On Stamps of 1920

OD202 A93 1c #265 .25 .20
OD203 A93 2c #266 .20 .20
OD204 A93 5c #269 .20 .20
OD205 A94 12c #271 .40 .20
Nos. OD202-OD205 (4) 1.05 .80

On Stamps of 1922-23

OD206 A93 1c #305 .25 .20
OD207 A93 2c #306 1.50 .50
OD208 A103 5c #309 .25 .20
OD209 A94 12c #311 10.00 1.75
OD210 A94 20c #312 1.50 .35
Nos. OD206-OD210 (5) 13.50 3.00

On Stamp of 1922-23

OD211 A93 2c #318 2.50 2.50

On Stamps of 1923

OD212 A104 1c #324 .20 .20
OD213 A104 2c #325 .20 .20
OD214 A104 5c #328 .20 .20
OD215 A104 12c #330 .20 .20
OD216 A104 20c #331 .50 .20
Nos. OD212-OD216 (5) 1.30 1.00

On Stamps of 1923-31

OD217 A104 ½c #340 2.00 .75
OD218 A104 1c #341, I .20 .20
a. Type II .20 .20
OD219 A104 2c #342 .20 .20
OD220 A104 3c #343, I .20 .20
a. Type II .20 .20
OD221 A104 5c #345, I .20 .20
a. Type II .20 .20
OD222 A104 10c #346, II .20 .20
a. Type I .30 .20
OD223 A104 12c #347, I .20 .20
a. Type II .30 .20
OD224 A104 20c #348, I .20 .20
a. Type II .20 .20
OD225 A104 30c #351 .20 .20
OD226 A105 1p #353 .40 .50
Nos. OD217-OD226 (10) 4.00 2.85

On Stamps of 1926

OD227 A109 5c #359 .20 .20
OD228 A110 12c #360 .20 .20

Type II
On Stamps of 1935-37

OD229 A129 1c #419 .20 .20
OD230 A130 2c #420 .20 .20
OD231 A132 3c #422 .20 .20
OD232 A134 5c #427 .20 .20
OD233 A137 10c #430 .20 .20
OD234 A139 15c #434 .45 .20
OD234A A140 20c #437 .20 .20
OD234B A140 20c #438 .20 .20
OD234C A141 25c #441 .20 .20
OD234D A142 30c #442 .20 .20
OD234E A145 1p #445 1.00 .60
OD234F A146 1p #446 .30 .20
Nos. OD229-OD234F (12) 3.55 2.80

Ministry of Marine
(M. M.)
Type I
On Stamp of 1911

OD235 A88 2c #181 .20 .20

On Stamps of 1912-14

OD236 A88 1c #190 .20 .20
OD237 A88 2c #191 .20 .20
OD238 A88 5c #194 2.00 .20
OD239 A88 12c #196 .20 .20
Nos. OD236-OD239 (4) 2.60 .80

On Stamps of 1915-16

OD240 A88 2c #209 .60 .20
OD241 A88 5c #212 .40 .20

On Stamps of 1917

OD242 A93 1c #232 .20 .20
OD243 A93 2c #233 .20 .20
OD244 A93 5c #236 .20 .20
Nos. OD242-OD244 (3) .60 .60

On Stamps of 1918-19

OD245 A93 1c #249 .20 .20
OD246 A93 2c #250 .20 .20
OD247 A93 5c #253 .25 .20
OD248 A94 12c #255 .25 .20
OD249 A94 20c #256 3.00 .35
Nos. OD245-OD249 (5) 3.90 1.15

On Stamps of 1920

OD250 A93 1c #265 .20 .20
OD251 A93 2c #266 .20 .20
OD252 A93 5c #269 .25 .20
Nos. OD250-OD252 (3) .65 .60

On Stamps of 1922-23

OD253 A103 5c #309 1.00 .20
OD254 A94 12c #311 7.00 7.00
OD255 A94 20c #312 7.00 1.50
Nos. OD253-OD254 (2) 8.00 7.20

On Stamps of 1923

OD256 A104 1c #324 .20 .20
OD257 A104 2c #325 .20 .20
OD258 A104 5c #328 .30 .20
OD259 A104 12c #330 .65 .20
OD260 A104 20c #331 .65 .20
Nos. OD256-OD260 (5) 2.00 1.00

On Stamps of 1923-31

OD261 A104 1c #341 .75 .25
OD262 A104 2c #342 .20 .20
OD263 A104 3c #343 .65 .20
OD264 A104 5c #345, I .20 .20
a. Type II .60 .20
OD265 A104 10c #346 .60 .20
OD266 A104 20c #348, II .60 .20
a. Type I .75 .20
OD267 A104 30c #351 1.00 .20
OD268 A105 1p #353 11.00 3.00
Nos. OD261-OD268 (8) 15.00 4.45

On Stamp of 1926

OD269 A109 5c #359 .50 .20

Type II
On Stamps of 1935-37

OD270 A129 1c #419 .20 .20
OD271 A130 2c #420 .20 .20
OD272 A132 3c #422 .20 .20
OD273 A134 5c #427 .20 .20
OD274 A137 10c #430 .25 .20
OD275 A139 15c #434 .30 .20
OD276 A140 20c #437 .40 .20
OD277 A140 20c #438 .30 .20
OD278 A142 30c #442 .25 .20
OD279 A145 1p #445 3.25 1.00
OD280 A146 1p #446 .75 .20
Nos. OD270-OD280 (11) 6.30 3.00

Ministry of Public Works
(M. O. P.)
Type I
On Stamp of 1911

OD281 A88 2c #181 .30 .20

On Stamps of 1912-14

OD282 A88 1c #190 .30 .20
OD283 A88 5c #194 .20 .20
OD284 A88 12c #196 1.50 .35
Nos. OD282-OD284 (3) 2.00 .75

On Stamps of 1916-19

OD285 A91 5c #220 10.00 1.00
OD286 A94 12c #238 25.00
OD287 A94 20c #256 25.00

On Stamps of 1920

OD288 A93 2c #266 6.00 2.50
OD289 A93 5c #269 2.00 .20
OD290 A94 12c #271 20.00 6.00
Nos. OD288-OD290 (3) 28.00 8.70

On Stamps of 1923

OD291 A104 1c #324 .40 .20
OD292 A104 2c #325 .30 .20
OD293 A104 5c #328 .40 .20
OD294 A104 12c #330 .60 .20
OD295 A104 20c #331 1.00 .20
Nos. OD291-OD295 (5) 2.70 1.00

On Stamps of 1923-31

OD296 A104 1c #341 .20 .20
OD297 A104 2c #342 .20 .20
OD298 A104 3c #343 .20 .20
OD299 A104 5c #345, I .20 .20
a. Type II .20 .20
OD300 A104 10c #346 .20 .20
OD301 A104 12c #347 9.00 1.25
OD302 A104 20c #348, I .20 .20
a. Type II 2.50 .50
OD303 A104 30c #351 .40 .20
OD304 A105 1p #353 20.00 6.00
Nos. OD296-OD304 (9) 30.60 8.65

On Stamp of 1926

OD305 A109 5c #359 .60 .20

Type II
On Stamps of 1935-37

OD306 A129 1c #419 .20 .20
OD307 A130 2c #420 .20 .20
OD308 A132 3c #422 .20 .20
OD309 A134 5c #427 .20 .20
OD310 A137 10c #430 .30 .20
OD311 A139 15c #434 .60 .20
OD312 A140 20c #437 .75 .20
OD313 A140 20c #438 .20 .20
OD314 A142 30c #442 .20 .20
OD315 A144 50c #444 .20 .20
OD316 A145 1p #445 2.00 1.00
OD317 A146 1p #446 .50 .25
Nos. OD306-OD317 (12) 5.55 3.25

Ministry of Foreign Affairs and Religion
(M. R. C.)
Type I
On Stamp of 1911

OD318 A88 2c #181 5.00 1.25

On Stamps of 1912-14

OD319 A88 1c #190 .20 .20
OD320 A88 2c #191 .20 .20
OD321 A88 5c #194 .40 .20
OD322 A88 12c #196 1.50 .25
Nos. OD319-OD322 (4) 2.30 .85

On Stamps of 1915-19

OD323 A88 5c #212 .40 .20
OD324 A91 5c #220 .20 .20
OD325 A94 20c #256 2.00 .75
Nos. OD323-OD325 (3) 2.60 1.15

On Stamps of 1920

OD326 A93 1c #265 .40 .20
OD327 A93 5c #269 .20 .20

On Stamps of 1922-23

OD328 A93 2c #306 9.00 3.50
OD329 A103 5c #309 27.50
OD330 A93 10c #311 22.50
Nos. OD328-OD330 (3) 59.00

On Stamps of 1923

OD331 A104 1c #324 .20 .20
OD332 A104 2c #325 .20 .20
OD333 A104 5c #328 .20 .20
OD334 A104 12c #330 .20 .20
OD335 A104 20c #331 .20 .20
Nos. OD331-OD335 (5) 1.00 1.00

On Stamps of 1923-31

OD336 A104 ½c #340 1.00 .50
OD337 A104 1c #341 .20 .20
OD338 A104 2c #342 .20 .20
OD339 A104 3c #343 .20 .20
OD340 A104 5c #345 .20 .20
OD341 A104 10c #346, II .20 .20
a. Type I 1.50 .20
OD342 A104 12c #347 .20 .20
OD343 A104 20c #348, I .20 .20
a. Type II .20 .20
OD344 A104 30c #351, I .20 .20
a. Type II .20 .20
OD345 A105 1p #353 .40 .20
Nos. OD336-OD346 (11) 3.20 2.50

On Stamp of 1926

OD346 A110 12c #360 .20 .20

Type II
On Stamps of 1935-37

OD347 A129 1c #419 .20 .20
OD348 A130 2c #420 .20 .20
OD349 A132 3c #422 .20 .20
OD350 A134 5c #427 .20 .20
OD351 A137 10c #430 .20 .20
OD352 A139 15c #434 .20 .20
OD353 A140 20c #437 .20 .20
OD354 A140 20c #438 .20 .20
OD355 A142 30c #442 .20 .20
OD356 A145 1p #445 2.50 1.25
OD357 A146 1p #446 1.00 .50
Nos. OD347-OD357 (11) 5.30 3.55

BUENOS AIRES

The central point of the Argentine struggle for independence. At intervals Buenos Aires maintained an independent government but after 1862 became a province of the Argentine Republic.

8 Reales = 1 Peso

> Values of Buenos Aires Nos. 1-8 vary according to condition. Quotations are for fine copies. Very fine to superb specimens sell at much higher prices, and inferior or poor copies sell at reduced values, depending on the condition of the individual specimen.
> Nos. 1-8 were issued without gum.

Steamship — A1

1858 Unwmk. Typo. *Imperf.*

1 A1 1 (in) pesos lt brn 350. 250.
2 A1 2 (dos) pesos blue 175. 140.
b. Diagonal half used as 1p on cover 7,500.
3 A1 3 (tres) pesos grn 1,500. 750.
a. 3p dark green 1,800. 825.
4 A1 4 (cuatro) pesos ver 4,750. 1,750.
a. Half used as 2p on cover 15,000.
5 A1 5 (cinco) pesos org 4,250. 1,450.
a. 5p ocher 4,250. 1,450.
b. 5p olive yellow 4,250. 1,450.

Issued: #2-5, Apr. 29; #1, Oct. 26.

1858, Oct. 26

6 A1 4 (cuatro) reales brown 250. 200.
a. 4r gray brown 250. 200.
b. 4r yellow brown 250. 200.

1859, Jan. 1

7 A1 1 (in) pesos blue 160. 225.
a. 1p indigo 200. 250.
b. Impression on reverse of stamp in blue 3,000.
c. Double impression 250. 300.
d. Tete beche pair 65,000.
e. Half used as 4r on cover 7,500.
8 A1 1 (to) pesos blue 350. 225.

Nos. 1, 2, 3 and 7 have been reprinted on very thick, hand-made paper. The same four stamps and No. 8 have been reprinted on thin, hard, white wove paper.

Counterfeits of Nos. 1-8 are plentiful.

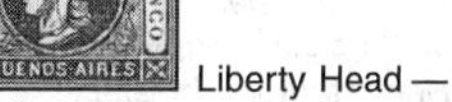

Liberty Head — A2

1859, Sept. 3

9 A2 4r green, *bluish* 250.00 160.00
10 A2 1p blue 35.00 17.50
11 A2 2p vermilion, fine impression 350.00 160.00
a. 2p red, blurred impression 300.00 125.00
b. Vert. half used as 1p on cover 2,000.

Both fine and blurred impressions of these stamps may be found. They have generally been called Paris and Local prints, respectively, but the opinion now obtains that the differences are due to the impression and that they do not represent separate issues. Values are for fine impressions, unless otherwise noted. Rough or blurred impressions sell for less.

Many shades exist of Nos. 1-11.

1862, Oct. 4

12 A2 1p rose 200.00 100.00
13 A2 2p blue 350.00 75.00

All three values have been reprinted in black, brownish black, blue and red brown on thin hard white paper. The 4r has also been reprinted in green on bluish paper.

Values are for fine impressions. Rough or blurred impressions sell for less.

CORDOBA

A province in the central part of the Argentine Republic.

100 Centavos = 1 Peso

Arms of Cordoba — A1

Unwmk.
1858, Oct. 28 Litho. *Imperf.*
Laid Paper

1 A1 5c blue 125.
2 A1 10c black 2,500.

Cordoba stamps were printed on laid paper, but stamps from edges of the sheets sometimes do not show any laid lines and appear to be on wove paper. Counterfeits are plentiful.

CORRIENTES

The northeast province of the Argentine Republic.

1 Real M(oneda) C(orriente) = 12½ Centavos M.C. = 50 Centavos
100 Centavos Fuertes = 1 Peso Fuerte

Nos. 1-2 were issued without gum. Nos. 3-8 were issued both with and without gum (values the same).

Ceres
A1 A2

Unwmk.
1856, Aug. 21 Typo. *Imperf.*

1 A1 1r black, *blue* 85.00 175.00

No. 1 used is valued with pen cancellation.

Pen Stroke Through "Un Real"

1860, Feb. 8

2 A1 (3c) black, *blue* 350.00 175.00

No. 2 used is valued with pen cancellation.

1860-78

3 A2 (3c) black, *blue* 9.50 30.00
4 A2 (2c) blk, *yel grn* ('64) 37.50 37.50
a. (2c) black, *blue green* 92.50 110.00
5 A2 (2c) blk, *yel* ('67) 7.50 19.00
6 A2 (3c) blk, *dk bl* ('71) 3.00 19.00
7 A2 (3c) blk, *rose red* ('76) 100.00 50.00
a. (3c) black, *lil rose* ('75) 140.00 80.00

8 A2 (3c) blk, *dk rose* ('79) 8.00 *32.50*
a. (3c) black, *red vio* ('77) 60.00 35.00
Nos. 3-8 (6) 165.50 188.00

Pen canceled examples of Nos. 3-8 that do not indicate the town of origin sell for much less.

Printed from settings of 8 varieties, 3 or 4 impressions constituting a sheet. Some impressions were printed inverted and tete beche pairs may be cut from adjacent impressions.

From Jan. 1 to Feb. 24, 1864, No. 4 was used as a 5 centavos stamp but copies so used can only be distinguished when they bear dated cancellations.

The reprints show numerous spots and small defects which are not found on the originals. They are printed on gray blue, dull blue, gray green, dull orange and light magenta papers.

ARMENIA

är-'mē-nē-ə

LOCATION — South of Russia bounded by Georgia, Azerbaijan, Iran and Turkey
GOVT. — Republic
AREA — 11,490 sq. mi.
POP. — 3,409,234 (est. 1999)
CAPITAL — Yerevan

With Azerbaijan and Georgia, Armenia made up the Transcaucasian Federation of Soviet Republics.

Stamps of Armenia were replaced in 1923 by those of Transcaucasian Federated Republics.

With the breakup of the Soviet Union on Dec. 26, 1991, Armenia and ten former Soviet republics established the Commonwealth of Independent States.

100 Kopecks = 1 Ruble
100 Luma = 1 Dram (1993)

Catalogue values for unused stamps in this country are for Never Hinged items, beginning with Scott 430 in the regular postage section.

Counterfeits abound of all overprinted and surcharged stamps.

Watermark

Wmk. 171- Diamonds

Perforations

Perforations are the same as the basic Russian stamps.

National Republic

Russian Stamps of 1902-19 Handstamped

At least thirteen types exist of both framed and unframed overprints ("a" and "c"). The device is the Armenian "H," initial of Hayasdan (Armenia). Inverted and double overprints are found.

Surcharged

Type I - Without periods (two types).
Type II - Periods after 1st "K" and "60."

Black Surcharge

1919 Unwmk. *Perf. 14x14½*

1 A14 60k on 1k orange (II) 2.50 .40
a. Imperf. (I) 1.00 .25
b. Imperf. (II) 1.00 .25

Violet Surcharge

2 A14 60k on 1k orange (II) .50 .50

Handstamped in Violet—a

Perf.

6 A15 4k carmine 2.00 2.00
7 A14 5k claret, imperf. 7.50 7.50
a. Perf. 5.00 5.00
9 A14 10k on 7k lt blue 5.00 1.25
10 A11 15k red brn & bl 3.00 .25
11 A8 20k blue & car 2.00 1.00
13 A11 35k red brn & grn 3.50 3.50
14 A8 50k violet & green 3.50 3.50
15 A14 60k on 1k orange (II) 2.00 2.00
a. Imperf. (I) 1.90 2.00
b. Imperf. (II) 8.50 9.00
18 A13 5r dk bl, grn & pale bl 3.50 4.25
a. Imperf. 1.00 1.00
19 A12 7r dk green & pink 1.75 2.00
20 A13 10r scar, yel & gray 1.75 2.00

Handstamped in Black

31 A14 2k green, imperf. 1.00 .20
a. Perf. 5.00 4.25
32 A14 3k red, imperf. 1.00 .20
a. Perf. 5.00 2.00
33 A15 4k carmine .20 .20
34 A14 5k claret 1.00 .20
a. Imperf. 5.00 5.00
36 A15 10k dark blue 2.00 .65
37 A14 10k on 7k lt blue .50 .20
38 A11 15k red brn & bl .50 .20
a. Imperf. 3.00 3.00
39 A8 20k blue & car 1.00 .20
40 A11 25k green & gray vio 1.00 .20
41 A11 35k red brn & grn 1.00 .20
42 A8 50k violet & green 1.00 .20
43 A14 60k on 1k orange (II) 2.50 2.50
43A A11 70k brown & org 1.00 .30
b. Imperf. .50 .30
44 A9 1r pale brn, dk brn & org 1.50 .30
a. Imperf. .50 .50
45 A12 3½r mar & lt grn, imperf. 5.00 .65
a. Perf. 5.00 .85
46 A13 5r dk bl, grn & pale bl .60 .65
a. Imperf. 6.00 1.00
47 A12 7r dk green & pink 6.00 1.10
48 A13 10r scar, yel & gray *50.00* 1.00

Handstamped in Violet—c

Unwmk. *Perf.*

Wove Paper

62 A14 2k green, imperf. .40 .40
a. Perf. 4.50 4.50
63 A14 3k red, imperf. .25 .25
a. Perf. 3.00 2.75
64 A15 4k carmine .50 .50
65 A14 5k claret 3.00 .40
a. Imperf. 3.00 .60
67 A15 10k dark blue 1.00 .85
68 A14 10k on 7k lt bl 1.00 .65
69 A11 15k red brn & bl 2.50 2.50
70 A8 20k blue & car .40 .40
71 A11 25k grn & gray vio 1.00 1.00
72 A11 35k red brn & grn 1.50 1.50
73 A8 50k violet & grn .50 .50
74 A14 60k on 1k org (II) 2.50 2.00
a. Imperf. (I) 1.65 1.65
b. Imperf. (II) 2.00 2.00
75 A9 1r pale brn, dk brn & org .60 .60
a. Imperf. 1.50 1.50
76 A12 3½r mar & lt grn, imperf. .75 .75
a. Perf. 1.00 1.00
77 A13 5r dk bl, grn & pale bl, imperf. 5.00 5.00
a. Perf. 4.00 4.00
78 A12 7r dk green & pink 7.50 7.50
79 A13 10r scar, yel & gray 2.25 1.90

Imperf

85 A11 70k brown & org 5.00 2.00

Handstamped in Black

Perf.

90 A14 1k orange 10.00 4.50
a. Imperf. 10.00 6.00
91 A14 2k green, imperf. 1.00 .20
a. Perf. 7.50 2.50
92 A14 3k red, imperf. 1.00 .20
a. Perf. 10.00 2.75
93 A15 4k carmine .50 .50
94 A14 5k claret 1.00 .20
a. Imperf. 3.00 .60
95 A14 7k light blue 15.00 15.00
96 A15 10k dark blue 12.00 12.00
97 A14 10k on 7k lt bl .20 .20
98 A11 15k red brn & bl .20 .20
99 A8 20k blue & car .20 .20
100 A11 25k grn & gray vio .50 .20
101 A11 35k red brn & grn .20 .20
102 A8 50k violet & grn .20 .20
102A A14 60k on 1k org, imperf. (I) .30 .30
b. Imperf. (II) .50 .50
c. Perf. (II) 2.50 1.25
103 A9 1r pale brn, dk brn & org 1.00 1.00
a. Imperf. .75 .75
104 A12 3½r maroon & lt grn 4.00 .50
a. Imperf. 5.00 .30
105 A13 5r dk bl, grn & pale bl 2.50 2.50
a. Imperf. 2.50 2.50
106 A12 7r dk green & pink 3.00 2.50
107 A13 10r scar, yel & gray 7.00 3.50

Imperf

113 A11 70k brown & org 1.00 .25

Handstamped in Violet or Black:

5r

f

10r

g

Violet Surcharge, Type f

1920 *Perf.*

120 A14 3r on 3k red, imperf. .85 .85
a. Perf. 2.50 2.50
121 A14 5r on 3k red 3.75 3.25
122 A15 5r on 4k car 10.00 8.00
123 A14 5r on 5k claret, imperf. 10.00 10.00
a. Perf. 10.00 8.00
124 A15 5r on 10k dk blue 10.00 8.00
125 A14 5r on 10k on 7k lt bl 10.00 8.00
126 A8 5r on 20k bl & car

Imperf

127 A14 5r on 2k green 7.00 7.00
128 A11 5r on 35k red brn & grn 7.00 7.00

Black Surcharge, Type f or Type g (#130)

Perf.

130 A14 1r on 1k orange .50 .50
a. Imperf. .75 .75
131 A14 3r on 3k red .20 .20
a. Imperf. .20 .20
132 A15 3r on 4k carmine 3.00 3.00
133 A14 5r on 2k grn, imperf. .20 .20
a. Perf. 2.00 2.00
134 A14 5r on 3k red 5.00 5.00
a. Imperf. 2.50 2.50
135 A15 5r on 4k carmine .40 .40
a. Imperf. 4.75 4.75
136 A14 5r on 5k claret .50 .50
a. Imperf. .50 .50
137 A14 5r on 7k lt blue 2.00 2.00
138 A15 5r on 10k dk blue .50 .50
139 A14 5r on 10k on 7k lt bl .50 .50
140 A11 5r on 14k bl & rose 2.00 2.00
141 A11 5r on 15k red brn & blue .50 .50
a. Imperf. 2.00 2.00
142 A8 5r on 20k bl & car .50 .50
a. Imperf. 10.00 10.00
143 A11 5r on 20k on 14k bl & rose 12.00 12.00
144 A11 5r on 25k grn & gray vio 12.00 12.00

Black Surcharge, Type g or Type f (#148A, 151)

145 A14 10r on 1k org, imperf. .90 .90
a. Perf. *225.00 225.00*
146 A14 10r on 3k red *175.00 175.00*
147 A14 10r on 5k claret 15.00 15.00
a. Imperf. 6.00
148 A8 10r on 20k bl & car 15.00 15.00
148A A11 10r on 25k grn & gray vio 8.00 8.00
149 A11 10r on 25k grn & gray vio 5.00 5.00
a. Imperf. 8.00 8.00
150 A11 10r on 35k red brn & grn .50 .50
151 A8 10r on 50k brn vio & grn 1.75 1.75
152 A8 10r on 50k brn vio & grn .45 .45
152A A11 10r on 70k brn & org, imperf. 3.00 3.00
b. Perf. *200.00 200.00*
152C A8 25r on 20k bl & car 4.00 4.00
153 A11 25r on 25k grn & gray vio 2.00 2.00
154 A11 25r on 35k red brn & grn 2.00 2.00
a. Imperf. 3.50 3.50
155 A8 25r on 50k vio & grn 4.00 4.00
a. Imperf. 5.00 5.00
156 A11 25r on 70k brn & org 8.00 8.00
a. Imperf. 5.00 5.00
157 A9 50r on 1r pale brn, dk brn & org, imperf. 1.00 1.00
a. Perf. 5.00 5.00
158 A13 50r on 5r dk bl, grn & lt bl 10.00 10.00
a. Imperf. 10.00 10.00
159 A12 100r on 3½r mar & lt grn 7.00 7.00
a. Imperf. 7.00 7.00
160 A13 100r on 5r dk bl, grn & pale bl 10.00 10.00
a. Imperf. 7.00 7.00
161 A12 100r on 7r dk grn & pink 10.00 10.00
a. Imperf. 35.00 35.00
162 A13 100r on 10r scar, yel & gray 10.00 10.00

Wmk. Wavy Lines (168)

Perf. 13½

Vertically Laid Paper

163 A12 100r on 3½r blk & gray *100.00 100.00*
164 A12 100r on 7r blk & yel *100.00 100.00*

1920 Unwmk. *Imperf.*

Wove Paper

166 A14 (g) 1r on 60k on 1k org (I) 12.00 12.00
168 A14 (f) 5r on 1k orange 9.00 9.00
173 A11 (f) 5r on 35k red brn & grn 2.50 2.50
177 A11 (g) 50r on 70k brn & org 5.00 5.00
179 A12 (g) 50r on 3½r mar & lt grn 2.00 2.00
181 A9 (g) 100r on 1r pale brn, dk brn & org 4.00 4.00

Romanov Issues Surcharged Type g or Type f (#185-187, 190)
On Stamps of 1913

1920 *Perf. 13½*

184 A16 1r on 1k brn org 10.00 10.00
185 A18 3r on 3k rose red 15.00 15.00
186 A19 5r on 4k dull red 10.00 10.00
187 A22 5r on 14k blue grn 60.00 60.00
187A A19 10r on 4k dull red 30.00
187B A26 10r on 35k gray vio & dk grn
187C A19 25r on 4k dull red 10.00 10.00
188 A26 25r on 35k gray vio & dk grn 2.75 2.75
189 A28 25r on 70k yel grn & brn 2.75 2.75
190 A31 50r on 3r dk vio 2.00 2.00
190A A16 100r on 1k brn org 100.00 100.00
190B A17 100r on 2k green 100.00 100.00
191 A30 100r on 2r brown 10.50 10.50
192 A31 100r on 3r dk vio 10.50 10.50

On Stamps of 1915, Type g

Thin Cardboard

Inscriptions on Back

Perf. 12

193 A21 100r on 10k blue 3.00
194 A23 100r on 15k brn 3.00
195 A24 100r on 20k ol grn 3.00

On Stamps of 1916, Type f

Perf. 13½

196 A20 5r on 10k on 7k brown 5.00 5.00
197 A22 5r on 20k on 14k bl grn 8.00 8.00

Surch. Type f or Type g (#204-205A, 207-207C, 210-211) over Type c in Violet

Perf.

200 A15 5r on 4k car 1.00 1.00
201 A15 5r on 10k dk bl 1.00 1.00
202 A11 5r on 15k red brn & bl 2.00 2.00
203 A8 5r on 20k blue & car 1.75 1.75
204 A11 10r on 25k grn & gray vio 1.50 1.50
205 A11 10r on 35k red brn & grn 3.00 3.00
205A A8 10r on 50k brn vio & grn 3.50 3.50

206 A8 25r on 50k brn vio & grn 150.00 150.00
207 A9 50r on 1r pale brn, dk brn & org, imperf. 3.50 3.50
a. Perf. 25.00 25.00
207B A12 100r on 3½r mar & lt grn 30.00
207C A12 100r on 7r dk grn & pink 9.00

Imperf

208 A14 5r on 2k green 25.00 25.00
209 A14 5r on 5k claret 25.00 25.00
210 A11 25r on 70k brn & org 5.50 5.50
211 A13 100r on 5r dk bl, grn & pale bl 1.00 1.00

Surcharged Type g or Type f (212-213, 215, 219-219A, 221-222) over Type c

Type c in Black

Perf.

212 A14 5r on 7k lt bl 150.00 150.00
213 A14 5r on 10k on 7k lt bl 5.00 5.00
214 A11 5r on 15k red brn & bl .50 .50
215 A8 5r on 20k blue & car 3.00 3.00
215A A11 10r on 5r on 25k grn & gray vio 5.00 5.00
216 A11 10r on 35k red brn & grn .50 .50
217 A8 10r on 50k brn vio & grn 1.00 1.00
217A A9 50r on 1r pale brn, dk brn & org 1.00 1.00
b. Imperf. 1.10 1.10
217C A12 100r on 3½r mar & lt grn 1.50 1.50
218 A13 100r on 5r dk bl, grn & pale bl 10.00 10.00
a. Imperf. 1.75 1.75
219 A12 100r on 7r dk grn & pink 15.00 15.00
219A A13 100r on 10r scar, yel & gray 10.00 10.00

Imperf

220 A14 1r on 60k on 1k org (I) 20.00 20.00
221 A14 5r on 2k green .80 .80
222 A14 5r on 5k claret 3.00 3.00
223 A11 10r on 70k brn & org 2.00 2.00
224 A11 25r on 70k brn & org 2.00 2.00

Surcharged Type g or Type f (#233) over Type a

Type a in Violet

Imperf

231 A9 50r on 1r pale brn, dk brn & org 140.00 140.00
232 A13 100r on 5r dk bl, grn & pale bl 10.50

Type a in Black

Perf.

233 A8 5r on 20k blue & car .80 .80
233A A11 10r on 25k grn & gray vio 55.00 55.00
234 A11 10r on 35k red brn & grn .90 .90
235 A12 100r on 3½r mar & lt grn 1.25 1.25
a. Imperf. 1.50 1.50

Imperf

237 A14 5r on 2k green 125.00 125.00
237A A11 10r on 70k brn & org

Surcharged Type a and New Value

Type a in Violet

Perf.

238 A11 10r on 15k red brn & blue .80 .80

Type a in Black

239 A8 5r on 20k blue & car 3.00 3.00
239A A8 10r on 20k blue & car 3.00 3.00
239B A8 10r on 50k brn red & grn 7.50

Imperf

240 A12 100r on 3½r mar & lt grn 1.90 1.90

Surcharged Type c and New Value

Type c in Black

1920 ***Perf.***

241 A15 5r on 4k red 1.75 1.75
242 A11 5r on 15k red brn & bl 1.00 1.00
243 A8 10r on 20k blue & car 1.75 1.75
243A A11 10r on 25k grn & gray vio 1.00 1.00
244 A11 10r on 35k red brn & grn 1.00 1.00
a. With additional surch. "5r" 1.50 1.50
245 A12 100r on 3½r mar & lt grn 1.50 1.50

Imperf

247 A14 3r on 3k red 4.75 4.75
248 A14 5r on 2k green .30 .30
249 A9 50r on 1r pale brn, dk brn & org .90 .90

Type c in Violet

249A A14 5r on 2k green 6.50

Postal Savings Stamps Surcharged

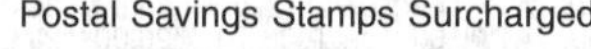

A1 A2 A3

Perf. 14½x15

Wmk. 171

250 A1 60k on 1k red & buff 50.00 50.00
251 A2 1r on 1k red & buff 5.00 5.00
252 A3 5r on 5k green & buff 7.25 7.25
253 A3 5r on 10k brn & buff 30.00 3.00

Russian Semi-Postal Stamps of 1914-18 Surcharged with Armenian Monogram and New Values like Regular Issues

On Stamps of 1914

Unwmk. ***Perf.***

255 SP5 25r on 1k red brn & dk grn, *straw* 60.00 60.00
256 SP5 25r on 3k mar & gray grn, *pink* 60.00 60.00
257 SP5 50r on 7 dk brn & dk grn, *buff* 20.00 20.00
258 SP5 100r on 1k red brn & dk grn, *straw* 25.00 25.00
259 SP5 100r on 3k mar & gray grn, *pink* 25.00 25.00
260 SP5 100r on 7k dk brn & dk grn, *buff* 25.00 25.00

On Stamps of 1915-19

261 SP5 25r on 1k org brn & gray 75.00 75.00
262 SP5 25r on 3k car & gray 30.00 30.00
263 SP5 50r on 10k dk bl & brn 25.00 25.00
264 SP5 100r on 1k org brn & gray 50.00 3.50
265 SP5 100r on 10k dk bl & brn 50.00 3.50

These surcharged semi-postal stamps were used for ordinary postage.

A set of 10 stamps in the above designs was prepared in 1920, but not issued for postal use, though some were used fiscally. Value of set, $4. Exist with "SPECIMEN" overprint and imperf. Reprints exist.

Soviet Socialist Republic

Hammer and Sickle — A7

Mythological Monster — A8

Symbols of Soviet Republics on Designs from old Armenian Manuscripts A9

Ruined City of Ani — A10

Mythological Monster — A11

Armenian Soldier — A12

Soviet Symbols, Armenian Designs — A14

Mythological Monster A13

Mt. Alagöz and Plain of Shirak A15

Fisherman on River Aras — A16

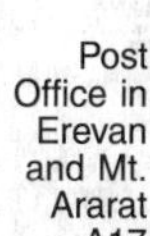

Post Office in Erevan and Mt. Ararat A17

Ruin in City of Ani — A18

Street in Erevan — A19

Lake Sevan and Sevan Monastery — A20

Mythological Subject from old Armenian Monument — A21

Mt. Ararat — A22

1921 Unwmk. ***Perf. 11½, Imperf.***

278 A7 1r gray green .30
279 A8 2r slate gray .30
280 A9 3r carmine .30
281 A10 5r dark brown .30
282 A11 25r gray .30 .20
283 A12 50r red .20
284 A13 100r orange .20
285 A14 250r dark blue .20
286 A15 500r brown vio .20
287 A16 1000r sea green .25
288 A17 2000r bister .75
289 A18 5000r dark brown .60
290 A19 10,000r dull red .60
291 A20 15,000r slate blue .60
292 A21 20,000r lake .60
293 A22 25,000r gray blue 1.25
294 A22 25,000r brown olive 6.50
Nos. 278-294 (17) 13.45

Except the 25r, Nos. 278-294 were not regularly issued and used. Counterfeits exist.

For surcharges see Nos. 347-390.

Russian Stamps of 1909-17 Surcharged

Wove Paper

Lozenges of Varnish on Face

1921, Aug. ***Perf. 13½***

295 A9 5000r on 1r 10.00
296 A12 5000r on 3½r 10.00
297 A13 5000r on 5r 10.00
298 A12 5000r on 7r 10.00
299 A13 5000r on 10r 10.00
Nos. 295-299 (5) 50.00

Nos. 295-299 were not officially issued. Counterfeits abound.

A23

Mt. Ararat & Soviet Star — A24

Soviet Symbols — A25

Crane — A26

Peasant — A27

Harpy — A28

Peasant Sowing — A29

Soviet Symbols — A30

Forging — A31

Plowing A32

1922 ***Perf. 11½***

No.	Type	Description	Value
300	A23	50r green & red	.50
301	A24	300r slate bl & buff	.60
302	A25	400r blue & pink	.60
303	A26	500r vio & pale lil	.60
304	A27	1000r dull bl & pale bl	.60
305	A28	2000r black & gray	.85
306	A29	3000r black & grn	.85
307	A30	4000r black & lt brn	.85
308	A31	5000r blk & dull red	.75
309	A32	10,000r black & pale rose	.75
a.		Tête bêche pair	35.00
		Nos. 300-309 (10)	6.95

Nos. 300-309 were not issued without surcharge.

Stamps of types A23 to A32, printed in other colors than Nos. 300 to 309, are essays.

Nos. 300-309 with Handstamped Surcharge of New Values in Rose, Violet or Black

1922

No.	Description	Unused	Used
310	10,000 on 50r (R)	45.00	60.00
311	10,000 on 50r (V)	8.50	11.00
312	10,000 on 50r	8.50	11.00
313	15,000 on 300r (R)	45.00	75.00
314	15,000 on 300r (V)	8.50	14.00
315	15,000 on 300r	8.50	14.00
316	25,000 on 400r (V)	8.50	14.00
317	25,000 on 400r	8.50	14.00
318	30,000 on 500r (R)	52.50	90.00
319	30,000 on 500r (V)	10.00	17.00
320	30,000 on 500r	10.00	17.00
321	50,000 on 1000r (R)	45.00	75.00
322	50,000 on 1000r (V)	8.50	14.00
323	50,000 on 1000r	8.50	14.00
324	75,000 on 3000r	11.00	20.00
325	100,000 on 2000r (R)	100.00	100.00
326	100,000 on 2000r (V)	20.00	20.00
327	100,000 on 2000r	20.00	20.00
328	200,000 on 4000r (V)	22.50	22.50
329	200,000 on 4000r	22.50	22.50
330	300,000 on 5000r (V)	30.00	45.00
331	300,000 on 5000r	30.00	45.00
332	500,000 on 10,000r (V)	30.00	30.00
333	500,000 on 10,000r	30.00	30.00
	Nos. 310-333 (24)	591.50	795.00

Forgeries exist.

Goose — A33

Armenian Woman at Well — A35

Armenian Village Scene A34

Mt. Ararat A36

Mt. Ararat A37

New Values in Gold Kopecks, Handstamped Surcharge in Black

1922 ***Imperf.***

No.	Type	Description	Unused	Used
334	A33	1(k) on 250r rose	12.50	12.50
335	A33	1(k) on 250r gray	20.00	20.00
336	A34	2(k) on 500r rose	8.00	8.00
337	A34	3(k) on 500r gray	8.00	8.00
338	A35	4(k) on 1000r rose	8.00	8.00
339	A35	4(k) on 1000r gray	15.00	15.00
340	A36	5(k) on 2000r gray	8.00	8.00
341	A36	10(k) on 2000r rose	8.00	8.00
342	A37	15(k) on 5000r rose	52.50	52.50
343	A37	20(k) on 5000r gray	8.00	8.00
		Nos. 334-343 (10)	148.00	148.00

Nos. 334-343 were issued for postal tax purposes.

Nos. 334-343 exist without surcharge but are not known to have been issued in that condition. Counterfeits exist of both sets.

Regular Issue of 1921 Handstamped with New Values in Black or Red Short, Thick Numerals

1922 ***Imperf.***

No.	Type	Description	Unused	Used
347	A8	2(k) on 2r (R)	50.00	50.00
350	A11	4(k) on 25r (R)	30.00	30.00
353	A13	10(k) on 100r (R)	20.00	20.00
354	A14	15(k) on 250r	10.00	10.00
355	A15	20(k) on 500r	15.00	15.00
a.		With "k" written in red	10.00	10.00
357	A22	50(k) on 25,000r bl (R)	12.00	12.00
358	A22	50(k) on 25,000r brn ol (R)	9.00	9.00
359	A22	50(k) on 25,000r brn ol		
		Nos. 347-358 (7)	146.00	146.00

Perf. 11½

No.	Type	Description	Unused	Used
360	A7	1(k) on 1r, imperf.	25.00	25.00
a.		Perf.	15.00	15.00
361	A7	1(k) on 1r (R)	35.00	35.00
a.		Imperf.	40.00	40.00
362	A8	2(k) on 2r, imperf.	40.00	40.00
a.		Perf.	40.00	40.00
363	A15	2(k) on 500r	35.00	35.00
a.		Imperf.	50.00	50.00
364	A15	2(k) on 500r (R)	9.00	9.00
365	A11	4(k) on 25r, imperf.	25.00	25.00
a.		Perf.	25.00	25.00
366	A12	5(k) on 50r, imperf.	1.75	1.75
a.		Perf.	2.50	2.50
367	A13	10(k) on 100r	20.00	20.00
a.		Imperf.	20.00	20.00
368	A21	35(k) on 20,000r, imperf.	50.00	50.00
a.		With "k" written in violet	50.00	50.00
b.		Perf.	65.00	65.00
c.		As "a," perf.	65.00	65.00
d.		With "kop" written in violet, imperf.		
		Nos. 360-368 (9)	240.75	240.75

Manuscript Surcharge in Red

Perf. 11½

No.	Type	Description	Unused	Used
371	A14	1k on 250r dk bl	40.00	40.00

Handstamped in Black or Red Tall, Thin Numerals

Imperf

No.	Type	Description	Unused	Used
377	A11	4(k) on 25r (R)	4.25	4.25
379	A13	10(k) on 100r	10.00	10.00
380	A15	20(k) on 500r	6.00	6.00
381	A22	50k on 25,000r bl	75.00	75.00
a.		Surcharged "50" only	50.00	50.00
382	A22	50k on 25,000r bl (R)	12.00	12.00
382A	A22	50k on 25,000r brn ol	24.00	24.00
		Nos. 377-382A (6)	131.25	131.25

On Nos. 381, 382 and 382A the letter "k" forms part of the surcharge.

Perf. 11½

No.	Type	Description	Unused	Used
383	A7	1(k) on 1r (R)	50.00	50.00
a.		Imperf.		
384	A14	1(k) on 250r	1.75	1.75
385	A15	2(k) on 500r	8.00	8.00
a.		Imperf.	20.00	20.00
386	A15	2(k) on 500r (R)	20.00	20.00
387	A9	3(k) on 3r	20.00	20.00
a.		Imperf.	20.00	20.00
388	A21	3(k) on 20,000r, imperf.	10.00	10.00
a.		Perf.	50.00	50.00
389	A11	4(k) on 25r	2.50	2.50
a.		Imperf.	4.25	4.25
390	A12	5(k) on 50r, imperf.	10.00	10.00
a.		Perf.	15.00	15.00
		Nos. 383-390 (8)	122.25	122.25

Catalogue values for unused stamps in this section, from this point to the end of the section, are for Never Hinged items.

Mt. Ararat — A45

a, 20k. b, 2r. c, 5r.

1992, May 28 **Litho.** ***Perf. 14***

No.	Type	Description	Unused	Used
430	A45	Strip of 3, #a.-c.	4.00	4.00

Souvenir Sheet

No.	Type	Description	Unused	Used
431	A45	7r Eagle & Mt. Ararat	55.00	55.00

AT & T Communications System in Armenia—A45a

1992, July 1 **Litho.** ***Perf. 13x13½***

No.	Type	Description	Unused	Used
431A	A45a	50k multicolored	4.50	3.50

A46

A47

1992 Summer Olympics, Barcelona: a, 40k, Ancient Greek wrestlers. b, 3.60r, Boxing. c, 5r, Weight lifting. d, 12r, Gymnastics.

1992, July 25 **Litho.** ***Perf. 14***

No.	Type	Description	Unused	Used
432	A46	Strip of 4, #a.-d.	3.50	3.50

1992-93 **Litho.** ***Perf. 14½, 15x14½***

20k, Natl. flag. 1r, Goddess Waroubini, Orgov radio telescope. 2r, Yerevan Airport. No. 436, Goddess Anahit. No. 437, Runic message, 7th cent B.C. 5r, UPU emblem. 20r, Silver cup.

No.	Type	Description	Unused	Used
433	A47	20k multicolored	.20	.20
434	A47	1r gray green	.20	.20
435	A47	2r blue	.30	.30
436	A47	3r brown	.50	.50
437	A47	3r bronze	.20	.20
438	A47	5r brown black	.75	.75
439	A47	20r gray	.20	.20
		Nos. 433-439 (7)	2.35	2.35

No. 435 is airmail. See Nos. 464-471, 521-524.

Issued: #436, 20k, 2r, 5r, 8/25/92; others, 5/12/93.

Religious Artifacts — A50

Yerevan '93 — A52

David of Sassoun, by Hakop Kojoian—A50a

Scenic Views — A51

1993, May 23 Litho. *Perf. 14*

448 A50 40k Marker	.20	.20
449 A50 80k Gospel page	.30	.25
450 A50 3.60r Bas-relief, 13th cent.	1.10	.90
451 A50 5r Icon of the Madonna	1.75	1.50
Nos. 448-451 (4)	3.35	2.85

Souvenir Sheet

Perf. 14x13½

451A A50a 12r multicolored	6.00	5.00

1993, May 24 *Perf. 14*

Designs (illustration reduced): 40k, Garni Canyon, vert. 80k, Shaki Waterfall, Zangezur, vert. 3.60r, Arpa River Canyon, vert. 5r, Lake Sevan. 12r, Mount Aragats.

452 A51 40k multicolored	.20	.20
453 A51 80k multicolored	.20	.20
454 A51 3.60r multicolored	.50	.50
455 A51 5r multicolored	.60	.60
456 A51 12r multicolored	1.50	1.50
Nos. 452-456 (5)	3.00	3.00

1993, May 25 *Perf. 14½*

457 A52 10r multicolored	.50	.50
a. Min. sheet of 6 + 2 labels	4.25	

For surcharges see Nos. 485-486.

Souvenir Sheet

Noah's Descent from Mt. Ararat, by Hovhannes Aivazovsky—A52a

1993, Aug. 4 Litho. *Perf. 14½*

458 A52a 7r multicolored	2.50	2.50

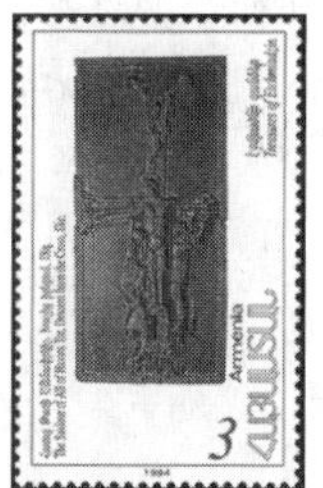

Religious Relics, Echmiadzin — A53

Designs: 3r, Wooden panel, descent from cross, 9th cent. 5r, Gilded silver reliquary for Holy Cross of Khotakerats. 12r, Cross depicting right hand of St. Karapet, 14th cent. 30r, Reliquary for arm of St. Thaddeus the Apostle, 17th cent. 50r, Gilded silver vessel for consecrated ointment, 1815.

1994, Aug. 4 Litho. *Perf. 14x14½*

459 A53 3d multicolored	.20	.20
460 A53 5d multicolored	.20	.20
461 A53 12d multicolored	.70	.70
462 A53 30d multicolored	1.40	1.40
463 A53 50d multicolored	2.00	2.00
Nos. 459-463 (5)	4.50	4.50

Artifacts and Landmarks Type of 1993

Gods of Van (Urartu): 10 l, Shivini, god of the sun. 50 l, Tayshaba, god of elements. 10d, Khaldi, supreme god.
25d, Natl. arms.

1994, Aug. 4 *Perf. 14½*

464 A47 10 l black & brown	.20	.20
465 A47 50 l black & red brown	.20	.20
469 A47 10d black & gray	.50	.50
471 A47 25d red & bister	1.25	1.25
Nos. 464-471 (4)	*2.15*	*2.15*

Issued: 10 l, 50 l, 10d, 25d, 8/4/94.
This is an expanding set. Numbers may change.

A54

1994, Dec. 31 Litho. *Perf. 14½x14*

479 A54 16d No. 1a	.45	.45

First Armenian postage stamp, 75th anniv.

A54a

A54b

1994, Dec. 30 Litho. *Perf. 14x14½*

480 A54a 30d Early printing press	.50	.50

First Armenian periodical, 200th anniv.

1994, Dec. 30 Litho. *Perf. 14x14½*

481 A54b 30d Natl. arms, stadium	.55	.55

Natl. Olympic Committee.

A54c

1994, Dec. 30 Litho. *Perf. 14x14½*

482 A54c 40d Olympic rings	.75	.75

Intl. Olympic Committee, Cent.

A54d

1994, Dec. 31 Litho. *Perf. 14x14½*

483 A54d 50d multi + label	.85	.85

Ervand Otian (1869-1926)

A54e

1994, Dec. 31 Litho. *Perf. 14½x14*

484 A54e 50d multi + label	.85	.85

Levon Shant (1869-1951).

No. 457 Surcharged in Blue or Red Brown

a

b

1994, Sept. 10 Litho. *Perf. 14*

485 A52(a) 40d on 10r (Bl)	3.50	3.50
486 A52(b) 40d on 10r (RB)	3.50	3.50

Yerevan '94.

A55

A56

Christianity in Armenia: 60d, Cross, 10th-11th cent. No. 488, Kings Abgar & Trdat, 1836. No. 489, St. Bartholomew, St. Thaddeus. 80d, St. Gregory, the Illuminator. 90d, Baptism of the Armenian people, 1892. 400d, Plan of Echmiadzin, c. 1660, engr. by Jakob Peeters.

1995, Apr. 3 Litho. *Perf. 14x15*

487 A55 60d multicolored	.85	.85
488 A55 70d multicolored	.90	.90
489 A55 70d multicolored	.90	.90
490 A55 80d multicolored	1.10	1.10
491 A55 90d multicolored	1.25	1.25
Nos. 487-491 (5)	5.00	5.00

Souvenir Sheet

492 A55 400d multicolored	4.00	4.00

Nos. 488-489 are 45x44mm.

1995, Apr. 3

493 A56 150d gray & black	1.25	1.25

Vazgen I (1908-94), Catholikos of All Armenians.

Armenia Fund A57

1995, Apr. 27 *Perf. 15x14*

494 A57 90d multicolored	.80	.80

UN, 50th Anniv. A58

1995, Apr. 28

495 A58 90d multicolored	.80	.80

Cultural Artifacts — A59

Designs: 30d, Black polished pottery, 14th-13th cent. B.C. 60d, Silver cup, 5th cent. B.C. 130d, Gohar carpet, 1700 A.D.

1995, Apr. 27 *Perf. 15x14*

496 A59 30d multicolored	.25	.25
497 A59 60d multicolored	.50	.50
498 A59 130d multicolored	1.25	1.25
Nos. 496-498 (3)	2.00	2.00

Birds — A60

1995, Apr. 27 *Perf. 14*

499 A60 40d Milvus milvus	.50	.50
500 A60 60d Aquila chrysaetos	.75	.75

End of World War II, 50th Anniv. A61

Designs: No. 501, P. Kitsook, 408th Armenian Rifle Division. No. 502, A. Sargissin, N. Safarian, 89th Taman Armenian Triple Order-Bearer Division. No. 503, B. Chernikov, N. Tavartkeladze, V. Penkovsky, 76th Armenian Alpine Rifle Red Banner (51st Guards) Division. No. 504, S. Zakian, H. Babayan, I. Lyudnikov, 390th Armenian Rifle Division. No. 505, A. Vasillian, M. Dobrovolsky, Y. Grechany, G. Sorokin, 409th Armenian Rifle Division.

No. 506, vert.: a, Marshal Hovhannes Baghramian. b, Adm. Hovhannes Issakov. c, Marshal Hamazasp Babajanian. d, Marshal Sergey Khoudyakov.

No. 507: Return of the Hero, by Mariam Aslamazian.

1995, Sept. 30 Litho. *Perf. 15x14*

501 A61 60d multicolored	.45	.45
502 A61 60d multicolored	.45	.45
503 A61 60d multicolored	.45	.45
504 A61 60d multicolored	.45	.45
505 A61 60d multicolored	.45	.45
Nos. 501-505 (5)	2.25	2.25

Miniature Sheet

Perf. 15x14½

506 A61 60d Sheet of 4, #a.-d.	3.00	3.00

Souvenir Sheet

Perf. 15x14

507 A61 300d multicolored	3.75	3.75

Authors A62

Designs: No. 508, Ghevond Alishan (1820-1901). No. 509, Gregor Artsruni (1845-92), vert. No. 510, Franz Werfel (1890-1945).

1995, Oct. 5 Litho. *Perf. 15x14*

508 A62 90d blue & black	.75	.75
509 A62 90d multicolored	.75	.75
510 A62 90d blue & maroon	.75	.75
Nos. 508-510 (3)	2.25	2.25

Nos. 508-510 issued with se-tenant label.

A64

Prehistoric artifacts: 40d, Four-wheeled carriages, 15th cent. BC. 60d, Bronze model of geocentric solar system, 11-10th cent. BC, vert. 90d, Tombstone, Red Tufa, 7-6th cent. BC, vert.

1995, Dec. 5 ***Perf. 14½x15, 15x14½***

512 A64 40d multicolored .25 .25
513 A64 60d multicolored .60 .60
514 A64 90d multicolored .90 .90
Nos. 512-514 (3) 1.75 1.75

A65

Christianity in Armenia — A66

Views of Yerevan: 60d, Brandy distillery, wine cellars. 80d, Abovian Street. 90d, Sports and concert complex. 100d, Baghramian Avenue. 120d, Republic Square.
400d, Panoramic photograph of Yerevan.

1995, Dec. 5 ***Perf. 15x14***

515 A65 60d salmon & black .35 .35
516 A65 80d pale org & blk .45 .45
517 A65 90d buff & black .50 .50

Size: 61x24mm

518 A65 100d pale yel bis & blk .85 .85
519 A65 120d dull org & blk 1.10 1.10
Nos. 515-519 (5) 3.25 3.25

Souvenir Sheet

520 A66 400d multicolored 3.50 3.50

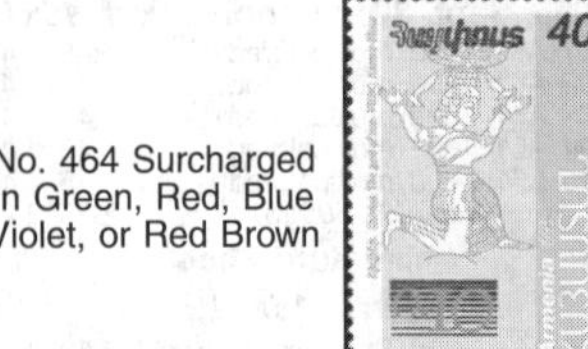
No. 464 Surcharged in Green, Red, Blue Violet, or Red Brown

1996, Mar. 30 Litho. ***Perf. 14½***

521 A47 40d on 10l (G) 1.00 1.00
522 A47 100d on 10l (R) 2.50 2.50
523 A47 150d on 10l (BV) 3.50 3.50
524 A47 200d on 10l (RB) 5.00 5.00
Nos. 521-524 (4) 12.00 12.00

Alexandre Griboyedov (1795-1829), Writer — A67

1996, Apr. 24 Litho. ***Perf. 14x14½***

525 A67 90d multi + label .70 .70

Khrimian Hayrik (1820-1907), Catholicos of All Armenians — A68

1996, Apr. 30 ***Perf. 14½x14***

526 A68 90d brown & blue .70 .70

No. 526 is printed se-tenant with label.

Admiral Lazar Serbryakov (1795-1862) — A69

1996, Apr. 30

527 A69 90d multi + label .70 .70

Armenian Red Cross, 75th Anniv. — A70

1996, May 4 ***Perf. 14x14½***

528 A70 60d multicolored .45 .45

Motion Pictures, Cent. A71

1996, May 4 ***Perf. 14½x14***

529 A71 60d multicolored .45 .45

Endangered Fauna — A72

1996, May 3 ***Perf. 14***

530 A72 40d Carpa aegagrus .30 .30
531 A72 60d Panthera pardus .45 .45

1996 Summer Olympics, Atlanta — A73

Modern Olympic Games, Cent. — A74

Designs: a, 40d, Cyclist. b, 60d, Athletic event. c, 90d, Wrestling.

1996, July 25

532 A73 Strip of 3, #a.-c. 1.25 1.25

1996, July 25 ***Perf. 14x14½***

533 A74 60d multicolored .45 .45

Fridtjof Nansen (1861-1930), Arctic Explorer — A75

1996, May 20 Litho. ***Perf. 14x14½***

534 A75 90d multicolored .60 .60

32nd Chess Olympiad, Yerevan — A76

#535, Petrosian-Botvinnik, World Championship match, Moscow, 1963. #536, Kasparov-Karpov, World Championship Match, Leningrad, 1986. #537, G. Kasparian, first prize winner, Contest of the Shakhmati v SSSR magazine, 1939. #538, 32nd Chess Olympiad, Yerevan.

1996, Sept. 15 Litho. ***Perf. 14***

535 A76 40d multicolored .35 .35
536 A76 40d multicolored .35 .35
537 A76 40d multicolored .35 .35
538 A76 40d multicolored .35 .35
a. Booklet pane, #535-538 *1.50*
Complete booklet, 2 #538a *3.00*
Nos. 535-538 (4) 1.40 1.40

No. 538a issued 9/24.
Nos. 535-538 also exist imperf.

Tigran Petrosian, World Chess Champion, Chess House, Yerevan — A77

1996, Sept. 20 ***Perf. 14x15***

539 A77 90d multicolored .75 .75

No. 539 also exists imperf.

Capra Aegagrus A78

World Wildlife Fund: 70d, Two running. 100d, One standing. 130d, One holding head down. 350d, Two facing forward.

1996, Oct. 20 Litho. ***Perf. 14½x14***

540 A78 70d multicolored .40 .40
541 A78 100d multicolored .50 .50
542 A78 130d multicolored .75 .75
543 A78 350d multicolored 2.00 2.00
a. Block of 4, #540-543 3.75 3.75
b. Booklet pane, 2 #543a 7.50
Complete booklet, #543b 7.50

Issued in sheets of 16 stamps.

Christianity in Armenia, 1700th Anniv. — A79

Armenian churches: No. 544, St. Catherine Church, St. Petersburg, 1780. No. 545, Church of the Holy Mother, Kishinev, 1803. No. 546, Church of the Holy Mother, Samarkand, 1903. No. 547, Armenian Church, Lvov, 1370. No. 548, St. Hripsime Church, Yalta, 1913.
500d, Church of St. Gevorg of Etchmiadzin, Tbilisi, 1805.

1996 Litho. ***Perf. 14x15***

544 A79 100d multicolored .50 .50
545 A79 100d multicolored .50 .50
546 A79 100d multicolored .50 .50
547 A79 100d multicolored .50 .50
548 A79 100d multicolored .50 .50
Nos. 544-548 (5) 2.50 2.50

Souvenir Sheet

549 A79 500d multicolored 2.50 2.50

First Armenian Printing Press, Etchmiadzin, 225th Anniv. — A80

1997, Mar. 26 Litho. ***Perf. 15x14***

550 A80 70d multicolored .35 .35

Armenian Entertainers — A81

#551, Folk singer, Jivani (1846-1909). #552, Arno Babajanian (1921-83), composer, vert.

1997, Mar. 26 ***Perf. 15x14, 14x15***

551 A81 90d multicolored .45 .45
552 A81 90d multicolored .45 .45

Paintings from Natl. Gallery of Armenia A82

#553, "One of my Dreams," by Eghishe Tadevossian. #554, "Countryside," by Gevorg Bashinjaghian. #555, "Portrait of Natalia Tehumian," by Hakob Hovnatanian. #556, "Salomé," by Vardges Surenians.

1997, May 28 Litho. ***Perf. 15x14***

553 A82 150d multi .70 .70
554 A82 150d multi .70 .70
555 A82 150d multi, vert. .70 .70
556 A82 150d multi, vert. .70 .70
Nos. 553-556 (4) 2.80 2.80

See Nos. 573-575.

Rouben Mamulian (1897-1987), Motion Picture Director — A83

1997, Oct. 8 Litho. ***Perf. 15x14***

557 A83 150d multicolored .70 .70

Moscow '97, World Philatelic Exhibition — A84

1997, Oct. 17 ***Perf. 14x15***

558 A84 170d St. Basil's Cathedral .80 .80

Eghishe Charents (1897-1937), Poet — A85

1997, Oct. 19 ***Perf. 15x14***
559 A85 150d multicolored .70 .70

A86 A87

Europa (Stories and Legends): 170d, Hayk, the Progenitor of the Armenians. 250d, Vahagn, the Dragon Slayer.

1997, Oct. 18 ***Perf. 14x15***
560 A86 170d multicolored .80 .80
561 A86 250d multicolored 1.10 1.10

1997, Dec. 19 Litho. ***Perf. 14***
562 A87 40d Iris lycotis .20 .20
563 A87 170d Iris elegantissima .85 .85

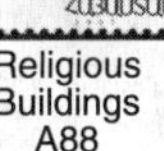

Religious Buildings A88

Christmas A89

#564, San Lazzaro, the Mekhitarian Congregation, Venice. #565, St. Gregory the Illuminator Cathedral, Anthelias. #566, St. Khach Armenian Church, Rostov upon Don. #567, St. James Monastery, Jerusalem. #568, Nercissian School, Tbilisi.
500d, Lazarian Seminary, Moscow.

1997, Dec. 22 ***Perf. 15x14, 14x15***
564 A88 100d multi, horiz. .50 .50
565 A88 100d multi .50 .50
566 A88 100d multi .50 .50
567 A88 100d multi, horiz. .50 .50

Size: 60x21mm

568 A88 100d multi, horiz. .50 .50
Nos. 564-568 (5) 2.50 2.50

Souvenir Sheet

569 A88 500d multicolored 2.50 2.50

Christianity in Armenia, 1700th anniv. (in 2001).

1997, Dec. 26 ***Perf. 14x15***
570 A89 40d multicolored .25 .25

Diana, Princess of Wales (1961-97) A90

1998, Apr. 8 Litho. ***Perf. 15x14***
571 A90 250d multicolored 1.00 1.00

No. 571 was issued in sheets of 5 + label.

Karabakh Movement, 10th Anniv. — A91

1998, Feb. 20 Litho. ***Perf. 13½x14***
572 A91 250d multicolored 1.00 1.00

Paintings from Natl. Gallery of Armenia Type of 1997

#573, "Tartar Women's Dance," by Alexander Bazhbeouk-Melikian. #574, "Family. Generations," by Yervand Kochar. #575, "Spring in Our Yard," by Haroutiun Kalents.

1998, Feb. 21 ***Perf. 15x14, 14x15***
573 A82 150d multi .65 .65
574 A82 150d multi, vert. .65 .65
575 A82 150d multi, vert. .65 .65
Nos. 573-575 (3) 1.95 1.95

1998 World Cup Soccer Championships, France — A92

1998, June 10 Litho. ***Perf. 14x15***
576 A92 250d multicolored 1.10 1.10

No. 576 was issued in sheetlets of 10 plus sheets of 8 + 2 labels.

National Holidays and Festivals A93

Europa: 170d, Couple jumping over fire, Trndez. 250d, Girls taking part in traditional ceremony, Ascension Day.

1998, June 24 Litho. ***Perf. 15x14***
577 A93 170d multicolored .75 .75
578 A93 250d multicolored 1.25 1.25

Butterflies A94

National Costumes A95

1998, June 26 ***Perf. 14***
579 A94 170d Papilio alexanor .75 .75
580 A94 250d Rethera komarovi 1.25 1.25

1998, July 16 Litho. ***Perf. 14x13½***
581 A95 170d Ayrarat .75 .75
582 A95 250d Vaspurakan 1.10 1.10

See Nos. 591-592.

Christianity in Armenia, 1700th Anniv. (in 2001) — A96

Churches: a, St. Forty Children's, 1958, Milan. b, St. Sargis, London, 1923. c, St. Vardan Cathedral, 1968, New York. d, St. Hovannes Cathedral, 1902, Paris. e, St. Gregory the Illuminator Cathedral, 1938, Buenos Aires.

1998, Sept. 25 Litho. ***Perf. 11½***
583 A96 100d Sheet of 5, #a.-e. 2.40 2.40

Memorial to Armenian Earthquake Victims A97

1998, Sept. 26 ***Perf. 15x14***
584 A97 250d multicolored 1.10 1.10

No. 584 was issued in sheets of 8 + 2 labels.

Minerals A98

1998, Oct. 23
585 A98 170d Pyrite .75 .75
586 A98 250d Agate 1.10 1.10

See Nos. 616-617.

Valery Bryusov (1873-1924), Writer — A99

1998, Dec. 1 ***Perf. 14x15***
587 A99 90d multicolored .45 .45

Souvenir Sheet

Sergei Parajanov, Film Director, 75th Birth Anniv. — A100

Illustration reduced.

1999, Apr. 19 Litho. ***Perf. 14x14¾***
588 A100 500d multicolored 2.25 2.25
a. IBRA 99 emblem in margin 2.25 2.25

State Reserves A101

1999, Apr. 22 ***Perf. 14¾x14¼***
589 A101 170d Khosrov .75 .75
590 A101 250d Kilijan 1.25 1.25

Europa.

National Costumes Type of 1998

1999, Apr. 20 Litho. ***Perf. 14x13½***
591 A95 170d Karin .75 .75
592 A95 250d Zangezour 1.25 1.25

Council of Europe, 50th Anniv. — A102

1999, June 12
593 A102 170d multicolored .80 .80

Cilician Ships A103

1999, Aug. 12 Litho. ***Perf. 14¾x14***

Sail Colors

594 A103 170d orange & blue .80 .80
595 A103 250d red & white 1.25 1.25

With PhilexFrance 99 Emblem at LR

596 A103 250d red & white 1.25 1.25
Nos. 594-596 (3) 3.30 3.30

Domesticated Animals — A104

1999, Aug. 19 ***Perf. 13¼x13¾***
597 A104 170d Armenian gampr dog .80 .80
598 A104 250d Van cat 1.25 1.25

With China 1999 World Philatelic Exhibition Emblem at LR

599 A104 250d Van cat 1.25 1.25
Nos. 597-599 (3) 3.30 3.30

Souvenir Sheet

First Pan-Armenian Games — A105

Illustration reduced.

1999, Aug. 28 ***Perf. 14¾x14***
600 A105 250d multicolored 3.00 3.00

Souvenir Sheet

Christianity in Armenia, 1700th Anniv. (in 2001) — A106

Churches: a, St. Gregory the Illuminator, Cairo. b, St. Gregory the Illuminator, Singapore. c, St. Khach, Suceava, Romania. d, St. Savior, Worcester, Mass. e, Church of the Holy Mother, Madras, India.

1999, Aug. Litho. ***Perf. 13¼x13¾***
601 A106 70d Sheet of 5, #a.-e. + label 1.60 1.60

UPU, 125th Anniv. A107

1999, Oct. ***Perf. 14¾x14¼***

602 A107 270d multicolored 1.40 1.40

Politicians Assassinated Oct. 27, 1999 — A108

Designs: No. 603, Parliament Speaker Karen Demirchyan, Parliament building. No. 604, Prime Minister Vazgen Sargsyan, troops. 540d, Demirchyan, Sargsyan, Yuri Bakhshyan, Ruben Miroyan, Henrik Abrahamyan, Armenak Armenakyan, Leonard Petrossyan and Mikael Kotanyan.

Perf. 14¾x14¼

2000, Feb. 21 **Litho.**

603 A108 250d multi 1.10 1.10
604 A108 250d multi 1.10 1.10
a. Sheet, 5 each #603-604 11.00 11.00

Imperf

Size: 60x44mm

605 A108 540d multi 2.50 2.50

Fish — A109

Designs: 50d, Salmo ischchan. 270d, Barbus goktschaicus.

2000, May 23 **Litho.** ***Perf. 13¼x13¾***

606 A109 50d multi .25 .25
607 A109 270d multi 1.25 1.25

Fairy Tales A110

2000, May 25 ***Perf. 14¾x14¼***

608 A110 70d The Liar Hunter .35 .35
609 A110 130d The King and the Peddler .60 .60

Europa, 2000

Common Design Type

2000, June 19 ***Perf. 14¼x14¾***

610 CD17 40d multi .20 .20
611 CD17 500d multi 2.25 2.25

Christianity as State Religion, 1700th Anniv. — A111

No. 612: a, St. Gayane Church, Vagharshapat. b, Etchmiadzin Cathedral, Vagharshapat. c, Church of the Holy Mother, Khor Virap. d, St. Shoghakat Church, Vagharshapat. e, St. Hripsime Church, Vagharshapat. Illustration reduced.

2000, July 10 **Litho.** ***Perf. 13¼x13¾***

612 A111 70d Sheet of 5, #a-e, + label 1.75 1.75

2000 Summer Olympics, Sydney — A112

Designs: 10d, Basketball. 30d, Tennis. 500d, Weight lifting.

2000, July 11 ***Perf. 13½x13¾***

613-615 A112 Set of 3 2.50 2.50

Mineral Type of 1998

Designs: 170d, Quartz. 250d, Molybdenite.

2000, Sept. 4 ***Perf. 14¾x14***

616-617 A98 Set of 2 1.90 1.90

A113

A114

2000, Sept. 11 ***Perf. 14x14¾***

618 A113 270d multi 1.25 1.25

Nerses Shnorhali (1100-73), poet and musician.

2000, Sept. 15

619 A114 170d multi .80 .80

Christmas.

Avetik Issahakian (1875-1957), Poet — A115

2000, Sept. 17 ***Perf. 14¾x14***

620 A115 130d multi .60 .60

Musical Instruments A116

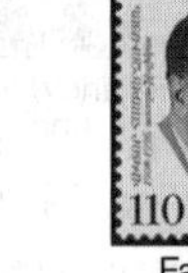
Famous Armenians A117

Designs: 170d, Dhol. 250d, Duduk.

2000, Dec. 22 **Litho.** ***Perf. 14x13¼***

621-622 A116 Set of 2 1.90 1.90

2000, Dec. 23 ***Perf. 14¾x14¼***

No. 623: a, Viktor Hambartsoumian (1908-96), cosmologist. b, Abraham Alikhanov (1904-70), physicist. c, Andranik Iossifian (1905-93), engineer. d, Sargis Saltikov (1905-83), metallurgist. e, Samuel Kochariants (1909-87), nuclear weapons scientist. f, Atrem Mikoyan (1905-70), aircraft designer. g, Norayr Sissakian (1907-66), biologist. h, Ivan Knunyants (1906-90), chemist. i, Nikoghayos Yenikolopian (1924-93), chemist.

No. 624: a, Nikoghayos Adonts (1871-1942), historian. b, Manouk Abeghian (1865-1944), grammarian. c, Hovhannes Toumanian (1869-1923), poet. d, Hrachya Ajarian (1876-1953), linguist. e, Gevorg Emin (1918-98), writer. f, Yervand Lalayan (1864-1931), anthropologist. g, Daniel Varoujan (1884-1915), poet. h, Paruyr Sevak (1924-71), writer. i, William Saroyan (1908-81), writer.

No. 625: a, Hamo Beknazarian (1892-1965), actor. b, Alexandre Tamanian (1878-1936), architect. c, Vahram Papazian (1888-1968), actor. d, Vassil Tahirov (1859-1938), viticulturist. e, Leonid Yengibarian (1935-72), mime. f, Haykanoush Danielian (1893-1958), singer. g, Sergo Hambartsoumian (1910-83) "Strongest man on Earth". h, Hrant Shahinian (1923-96), gymnast. i, Toros Toramanian (1864-1934), architectural historian.

No. 626: a, Komitas (1869-1935), composer. b, Aram Khachatourian (1903-78), composer. c, Martiros Sarian (1880-1972), artist. d, Avet Terterian (1929-94), composer. e, Alexandre Spendiarian (1871-1928), composer. f, Arshile Gorky (1904-48), artist. g, Minas Avetissian (1928-75), artist. h, Levon Orbeli (1882-1958), physiologist. i, Hripsimeh Simonian (1916-98), artist.

623 Booklet pane of 9 4.50
a.-i. A117 110d Any single .50 .50
624 Booklet pane of 9 4.50
a.-i. A117 110d Any single .50 .50
625 Booklet pane of 9 4.50
a.-i. A117 110d Any single .50 .50
626 Booklet pane of 9 4.50
a.-i. A117 110d Any single .50 .50
Booklet, #623-626 18.00

Souvenir Sheet

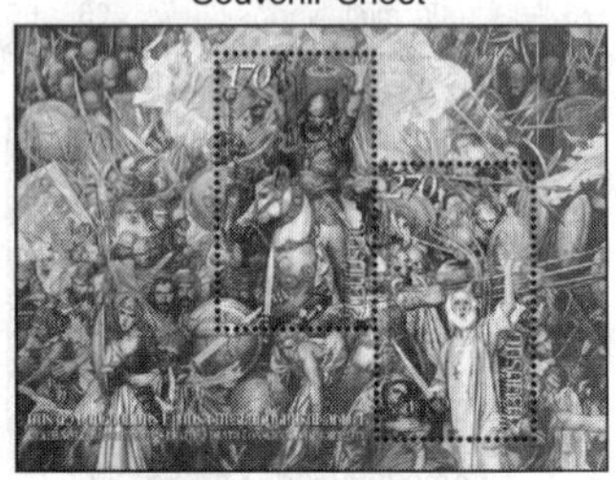
Battle of Avarayr, 1550th Anniv. — A118

No. 627: a, 170d, St. Vardan Mamikonian (388-451). b, 270d, Battle of Avarayr, 451.

2001, June 7 **Litho.** ***Perf. 14x14¾***

627 A118 Sheet of 2, #a-b 1.60 1.60

Record of Lamentations, by St. Grigor Narekatzi, 1000th Anniv. — A119

2001, June 8 **Litho.** ***Perf. 14¾x14***

628 A119 25d multi 1.00 1.00

Europa A120

Designs: 50d, Lake Sevan. 500d, Spandarian Reservoir.

2001, June 9

629-630 A120 Set of 2 2.60 2.60

Armenian Admission to Council of Europe A121

2001, June 11

631 A121 240d multi 1.10 1.10

Worldwide Fund for Nature (WWF) — A122

Sciurus persicus: a, 40d, On branch. b, 50d, Eating. c, 80d, Close-up. d, 120d, Digging. Illustration reduced.

Perf. 13¼x13¾

2001, Aug. 25 **Litho.**

632 A122 Block of 4, #a-d 2.10 2.10

Souvenir Sheet

Second Pan-Armenian Games — A123

2001, Aug. 18 **Litho.** ***Perf. 14¾x14***

633 A123 300d multi 1.10 1.10

Souvenir Sheet

Christianity in Armenia, 1700th Anniv. — A124

Views of St. Gregory the Illuminator Cathedral, Yerevan: a, 50d, Front. b, 205d, Side (45x30mm). c, 240d, Side, diff. (45x30mm).

Perf. 13¾x13¼, 13¼x13¾

2001, Aug. 27

634 A124 Sheet of 3, #a-c, + 6 labels 1.90 1.90
d. As No. 634, with brown inscriptions in margins 1.90 1.90

Marginal inscriptions on No. 634d read "INTERNATIONAL / PHILATELIC EXHIBITION / ARMENIA '01/ 10-16 September, 2001, Yerevan," in English, Armenian, Russian and French. Souvenir sheet can be formed into a box which shows cathedral from various angles.

Ivan Lazarev (1735-1801) and Institute of Eastern Languages, Moscow — A125

2001, Sept. 26 **Litho.** ***Perf. 14¾x14***

635 A125 300d multi 1.40 1.40

See Russia No. 6665.

Native Costumes — A126

Man and woman from: 50d, Javakhch. 250r, Artzakh.

2001, Sept. 27 ***Perf. 14x13½***
636-637 A126 Set of 2 1.40 1.40

6th World Wushu Championships A127

2001, Oct. 3 ***Perf. 13¼x13¾***
638 A127 180d black .85 .85

Year of Dialogue Among Civilizations — A128

2001, Oct. 9 ***Perf. 14x14¾***
639 A128 275d multi 1.40 1.40

Commonwealth of Independent States, 10th Anniv. — A129

2001, Nov. 29
640 A129 205d multi .95 .95

European Year of Languages A130

2001, Dec. 21 ***Perf. 14¾x14***
641 A130 350d multi 1.60 1.60

Independence, 10th Anniv. — A131

2001, Dec. 22
642 A131 300d multi 1.40 1.40

Transportation A132

Designs: 180d, Cart. 205d, Phaeton.

2001, Dec. 24 ***Perf. 13½x14***
643-644 A132 Set of 2 1.90 1.90

Medicinal Plants — A133

Designs: 85d, Hypericum perforatum. 205d, Thymus serpyllum.

2001, Dec. 25 ***Perf. 13¼x13¾***
645-646 A133 Set of 2 1.40 1.40

Eagle — A134

2002, Mar. 28 Litho. ***Perf. 14¾x14***
647 A134 10d brown .20 .20
648 A134 25d green .20 .20
649 A134 50d dk blue .20 .20
Nos. 647-649 (3) .60 .60

Industries A135

Designs: 120d, Calendar belt, 2nd cent. B.C., copper smelter. 350d, Containers, 7th cent. B.C., hops, barley, beer kettles.

2002, Apr. 26
650-651 A135 Set of 2 2.00 2.00

National Gallery Artworks — A136

Designs: No. 652, 200d, Lily, by Edgar Chahine. No. 653, 200d, Salomé, sculpture by Hakob Gurjian.

2002, Apr. 29 ***Perf. 14x14¾***
652-653 A136 Set of 2 1.60 1.60

2002 World Cup Soccer Championships, Japan and Korea — A137

2002, May 2 ***Perf. 14¾x14***
654 A137 350d multi 1.50 1.50

Souvenir Sheet

Hovsep Pushman (1877-1906), Artist — A138

2002, May 9
655 A138 650d multi 2.75 2.75

Hovhannes Tevossian (1902-58), Engineer — A139

2002, May 14
656 A139 350d multi 1.50 1.50

Europa — A140

Designs: 70d, Magician's hat. 500d, Clown.

2002, July 30 Litho. ***Perf. 14x14¾***
657-658 A140 Set of 2 2.75 2.75

Artemy Aivazian, Composer, Cent. of Birth A141

2002, July 31 ***Perf. 14¾x14***
659 A141 600d multi 2.75 2.75

Souvenir Sheet

Cathedral of Ani, 1000th Anniv. (in 2001) — A142

Perf. 13¼x13¾

2002, Sept. 24 **Litho.**
660 A142 550d multi 2.40 2.40

Intl. Year of Mountains A143

2002, Sept. 26 ***Perf. 14¾x14***
661 A143 350d multi 1.50 1.50

Reptiles — A144

Designs: 170d, Lacerta armeniaca. 220d, Vipera raddei.

2002, Sept. 27 ***Perf. 13¼x13¾***
662-663 A144 Set of 2 1.75 1.75

AIR POST STAMPS

AP1 AP2

Design: 90d, Artiom Katsian (1886-1943), world record holding pilot on range and altitude in 1909.

1995, Dec. 5 Litho. ***Perf. 14x15***
C1 AP1 90d multicolored .75 .75

1996, Apr. 30 Litho. ***Perf. 14x14½***
C2 AP2 90d multicolored .70 .70

Nelson Stepanian (1913-44), WWII fighter ace.

ARUBA

ə-'rü-bə

LOCATION — West Indies, north of Venezuela
AREA — 78 sq. mi.
POP. — 67,014
CAPITAL — Oranjestad

On Jan. 1, 1986 Aruba, formerly part of Netherlands Antilles, achieved a separate status within the Kingdom of the Netherlands.

100 Cents = 1 Gulden

Catalogue values for all unused stamps in this country are for Never Hinged items.

Used values are for CTO or stamps removed from first day covers. Postally used examples sell for more.

Traditional House — A1

Perf. 14x13

1986-87 Litho. Unwmk.

1	A1	5c	shown	.20	.20
2	A1	15c	King William III Tower	.20	.20
3	A1	20c	Loading crane	.20	.20
4	A1	25c	Lighthouse	.20	.20
5	A1	30c	Snake	.30	.25
6	A1	35c	Owl	.30	.25
7	A1	45c	Shell	.30	.25
8	A1	55c	Frog	.40	.35
9	A1	60c	Water skier	.50	.45
10	A1	65c	Net fishing	.60	.55
11	A1	75c	Music box	.60	.55
12	A1	85c	Pre-Columbian bisque pot	.65	.60
13	A1	90c	Bulb cactus	.70	.65
14	A1	100c	Grain	.75	.70
15	A1	150c	Watapana tree	1.25	1.10
16	A1	250c	Aloe plant	2.10	1.90
			Nos. 1-16 (16)	9.25	8.40

Issued: 5c, 30c, 60c, 150c, 1/1; 15c, 35c, 65c, 250c, 2/5; 20c, 45c, 75c, 100c, 4/7/87; 25c, 55c, 85c, 90c, 7/17/87.

Independence A2

1986, Jan. 1 ***Perf. 14x13, 13x14***

18 A2 25c Map .35 .30
19 A2 45c Coat of arms, vert. .60 .55
20 A2 55c Natl. anthem, vert. .70 .65
21 A2 100c Flag 1.00 .90
Nos. 18-21 (4) 2.65 2.40

Intl. Peace Year — A3

1986, Aug. 29 **Litho.** ***Perf. 14x13***

22 A3 60c shown .75 .55
23 A3 100c Barbed wire 1.00 .80

Princess Juliana and Prince Bernhard, 50th Wedding Anniv. — A4

1987, Jan. 7 **Photo.** ***Perf. 13x14***

24 A4 135c multicolored 1.25 1.10

State Visit of Queen Beatrix and Prince Claus of the Netherlands A5

1987, Feb. 16 **Litho.** ***Perf. 14x13***

25 A5 55c shown .55 .45
26 A5 60c Prince William-Alexander .60 .50

Tourism — A6

1987, June 5 **Litho.**

27 A6 60c Beach and sea .65 .60
28 A6 100c Rock and cacti 1.10 1.00

Aloe Vera Plant — A7

Coins — A8

1988, Jan. 27 **Litho.** ***Perf. 13x14***

29 A7 45c Field .40 .40
30 A7 60c Plant .60 .55
31 A7 100c Harvest 1.00 .90
Nos. 29-31 (3) 2.00 1.85

1988, Mar. 16 **Litho.** ***Perf. 13x14***

32 A8 25c 25-cent .25 .25
33 A8 55c 50-cent .50 .50
34 A8 65c 5 and 10-cent .75 .70
35 A8 150c 1-florin 1.50 1.40
Nos. 32-35 (4) 3.00 2.85

Love Issue — A9

A10

1988, May 4

36 A9 70c shown .50 .45
37 A9 135c Seashells, coastal scenery 1.10 1.00

1988, Aug. 24

38 A10 35c shown .40 .35
39 A10 100c Emblems 1.00 .90

Aruba, the 162nd member of the Intl. Olympic Committee (35c), 1988 Summer Olympics, Seoul (100c).

Carnival A11

1989, Jan. 5 ***Perf. 14x13***

40 A11 45c Two children .40 .40
41 A11 60c Girl .60 .55
42 A11 100c Entertainer 1.00 .90
Nos. 40-42 (3) 2.00 1.85

Maripampun, *Omphalophalmum Rubrum* — A12

1989, Mar. 16 **Litho.** ***Perf. 14x13***

43 A12 35c Leaves .35 .30
44 A12 55c Pods .55 .50
45 A12 200c Blossom 1.75 1.60
Nos. 43-45 (3) 2.65 2.40

New Year 1990 — A13

UPU — A14

Dande band members playing instruments or singing: 25c, Violin, tambor, cuatro, marimba. 70c, Lead singer, guitar. 150c, Accordion, urri, guitar.

1989, Nov. 16 **Litho.** ***Perf. 13x14***

46 A13 25c multicolored .25 .20
47 A13 70c multicolored .60 .55
48 A13 150c multicolored 1.25 1.10
Nos. 46-48 (3) 2.10 1.85

1989, June 8 **Litho.** ***Perf. 13x14***

49 A14 250c multicolored 2.25 2.00

Crotalus durissus unicolor A15

1989, Aug. 24 ***Perf. 14x13***

50 A15 45c shown .45 .40
51 A15 55c multi, diff. .50 .45
52 A15 60c multi, diff. .65 .60
Nos. 50-52 (3) 1.60 1.45

Snake species in danger of extinction.

Man Living in Harmony with Nature — A16

1990, Feb. 7 ***Perf. 13x14, 14x13***

53 A16 45c The land .45 .40
54 A16 55c shown .55 .50
55 A16 100c The sea 1.00 .90
Nos. 53-55 (3) 2.00 1.80

Environmental protection. #53, 55 horiz.

Marine Life — A17

Designs: 60c, Giant caribbean anemone, Pederson's cleaning shrimp. 70c, Queen angelfish, red and orange coral. 100c, Banded coral shrimp, fire sponge, yellow boring sponge.

1990, Apr. 4 **Litho.** ***Perf. 14x13***

56 A17 60c multicolored .65 .60
57 A17 70c multicolored .75 .70
58 A17 100c multicolored 1.10 1.00
Nos. 56-58 (3) 2.50 2.30

A18

A19

1990, May 30 **Litho.** ***Perf. 13x14***

59 A18 35c multicolored .30 .25
60 A18 200c Character trademark 1.75 1.60

World Cup Soccer Championships, Italy.

1990, Sept. 12

61 A19 45c Tools .40 .35
62 A19 60c Stone figure .60 .55
63 A19 100c Jar 1.00 .90
Nos. 61-63 (3) 2.00 1.80

Archeological discoveries.

Landscapes A20

1991, Jan. 31 **Litho.** ***Perf. 14x13***

64 A20 55c Seashore .50 .50
65 A20 65c Desert .65 .60
66 A20 100c Cactus, ocean view 1.00 .90
Nos. 64-66 (3) 2.15 2.00

Working Women — A21

Medicinal Plants — A22

Designs: 35c, Taking care of others. 70c, Housewife. 100c, Women in society.

1991, Mar. 28 **Litho.** ***Perf. 13x14***

67 A21 35c multicolored .30 .25
68 A21 70c multicolored .65 .60
69 A21 100c multicolored .90 .80
Nos. 67-69 (3) 1.85 1.65

Style of inscriptions varies.

1991, May 29

70 A22 65c Ocimum sanctum .55 .55
71 A22 75c Jatropha gossypifolia .65 .65
72 A22 95c Croton flavens .90 .80
Nos. 70-72 (3) 2.10 2.00

A23

A24

Aruban Handicrafts: 35c, Fish net, wood float, wooden needle. 250c, Straw hat, hat block.

1991, July 31 **Litho.** ***Perf. 13x14***

73 A23 35c lt bl, dk bl & blk .30 .25
74 A23 250c pink, lil rose & blk 2.25 2.00

1991, Nov. 29 **Litho.** ***Perf. 13x14***

75 A24 35c Toucan .35 .30
76 A24 70c People shaking hands .65 .60
77 A24 100c Windmill 1.00 .90
Nos. 75-77 (3) 2.00 1.80

Welcome to Aruba.

Aruba Postal Service, Cent. — A25

60c, Government decree, 1892, vert. 75c, First post office. 80c, Current post office.

Perf. 13x14, 14x13

1992, Jan. 31 **Litho.**

78 A25 60c multicolored .60 .55
79 A25 75c multicolored .75 .70
80 A25 80c multicolored .85 .75
Nos. 78-80 (3) 2.20 2.00

Equality Day — A26

1992, Mar. 25 **Litho.** ***Perf. 14x13***

81 A26 100c People of five races .95 .80
82 A26 100c Woman, man, scales .95 .80

Discovery of America, 500th Anniv. — A27

1992, July 30 **Litho.** ***Perf. 13x14***

83 A27 30c Columbus .30 .25
84 A27 40c Sailing ship .40 .35
85 A27 50c Natives, map .55 .50
Nos. 83-85 (3) 1.25 1.10

Natural Bridges in Aruba — A28

Designs: 70c, Seroe Colorado Bridge, south coast. 80c, Natural Bridge, north coast.

1992, Nov. 30 **Litho.** ***Perf. 14x13***

86 A28 70c multicolored .70 .65
87 A28 80c multicolored .80 .70

A29

A30

1993, Jan. 29 Litho. *Perf. 13x14*
88 A29 200c multicolored 1.90 1.90

Express mail service.

1993, Mar. 31 Litho. *Perf. 13x14*

Various rock formations found in Districts of Ayo and Casibari.

89 A30 50c multicolored .50 .50
90 A30 60c multicolored .60 .60
91 A30 100c multicolored .90 .90
Nos. 89-91 (3) 2.00 2.00

Folklore — A31

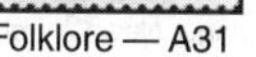
Sailing Sports — A32

40c, String instruments, drum. 70c, Traditional music & games. 80c, Dera Gai song lyrics.

1993, May 28 Litho. *Perf. 13x14*
92 A31 40c multicolored .40 .40
93 A31 70c multicolored .70 .70
94 A31 80c multicolored .80 .80
Nos. 92-94 (3) 1.90 1.90

1993, July 30 Litho. *Perf. 13x14*
95 A32 50c Sailboating .50 .50
96 A32 65c Land sailing .65 .65
97 A32 75c Wind surfing .75 .75
Nos. 95-97 (3) 1.90 1.90

Iguana Iguana — A33

Perf. 14x13, 13x14
1993, Sept. 1 Litho.
98 A33 35c Young .40 .40
99 A33 60c Almost grown .60 .60
100 A33 100c Mature, vert. 1.00 1.00
Nos. 98-100 (3) 2.00 2.00

Burrowing Owl — A34

Perf. 14x13, 13x14
1994, Jan. 28 Litho.
101 A34 5c Two adults .20 .20
102 A34 10c Two adults, young .35 .30
103 A34 35c Adult with prey, vert. .65 .55
104 A34 40c Adult, vert. .80 .70
Nos. 101-104 (4) 2.00 1.75

World Wildlife Fund.

A35

A36

Intl. Olympic Committee, Cent.: 90c, Baron Pierre de Coubertin (1863-1937), founder of modern Olympics.

1994, Mar. 29 Litho. *Perf. 13x14*
105 A35 50c multicolored .50 .45
106 A35 90c multicolored .75 .65

1994, July 7 Litho. *Perf. 13x14*
107 A36 65c shown .60 .55
108 A36 150c Mascot, soccer ball 1.40 1.25

1994 World Cup Soccer Championships, US.

Wild Fruit — A37

Designs: 40c, Malpighia punicifolia. 70c, Cordia sebestena. 85c, Pithecellobium unguis-cati. 150c, Coccoloba uvifera.

1994, Sept. 28 Litho. *Perf. 13x14*
109 A37 40c multicolored .40 .35
110 A37 70c multicolored .75 .65
111 A37 85c multicolored .90 .80
112 A37 150c multicolored 1.50 1.40
Nos. 109-112 (4) 3.55 3.20

Architectural Landmarks A38

Designs: 35c, Government building, 1888. 60c, Ecury residence, 1929, vert. 100c, Protestant Church, 1846, vert.

1995, Jan. 27 Litho. *Perf. 14x13*
113 A38 35c multicolored .35 .30
Perf. 13x14
114 A38 60c multicolored .65 .60
115 A38 100c multicolored 1.00 .90
Nos. 113-115 (3) 2.00 1.80

UN, 50th Anniv. — A39

Interpaso Horses — A40

Designs: 30c, Flags, sea, UN emblem, dove, text from UN charter. 200c, World with flags, doves, UN emblem.

1995, Mar. 29 Litho. *Perf. 13x14*
116 A39 30c multicolored .40 .35
117 A39 200c multicolored 2.00 1.90

1995, May 26 *Perf. 14x13, 13x14*

Designs: 25c, 10-time champion Casanova II, ribbons, horiz. 75c, Paso Fino, horiz. 80c, Horse doing figure 8. 90c, Girl on horse.

118 A40 25c multicolored .25 .25
119 A40 75c multicolored .70 .65
120 A40 80c multicolored .75 .70
121 A40 90c multicolored .85 .80
Nos. 118-121 (4) 2.55 2.40

Vegetables — A41

1995, July 28 Litho. *Perf. 13x14*
122 A41 25c Vigna sinensis .25 .25
123 A41 50c Cucumis anguria .50 .45
124 A41 70c Hibiscus esculentus .70 .65
125 A41 85c Cucurbita moschata .80 .75
Nos. 122-125 (4) 2.25 2.10

Turtles — A42

1995, Sept. 27 Litho. *Perf. 14x13*
126 A42 15c Hawksbill .30 .20
127 A42 50c Green .50 .35
128 A42 95c Loggerhead .90 .70
129 A42 100c Leatherback .95 .70
Nos. 126-129 (4) 2.65 1.95

Separate Status, 10th Anniv. — A43

Statesmen and politicians: No. 130, Jan Hendrik Albert Eman (1887-1957). No. 131, Juan Enrique Irausquin (1904-62). No. 132, Cornelis Albert Eman (1916-67). No. 133, Gilberto Francois Croes (1938-85).

1996, Jan. 1 Litho. *Perf. 13x14*
130 A43 100c multicolored .90 .85
131 A43 100c multicolored .90 .85
132 A43 100c multicolored .90 .85
133 A43 100c multicolored .90 .85
Nos. 130-133 (4) 3.60 3.40

The 1986 date on No. 133 is in error.

America Issue — A44

National dresswear: 65c, Woman wearing long, full dress, apron, vert. 70c, Man wearing hat, bow tie, white shirt, black pants, vert. 100c, Couple dancing.

Perf. 13x14, 14x13
1996, Mar. 25 Litho.
134 A44 65c multicolored .75 .75
135 A44 70c multicolored .80 .75
136 A44 100c multicolored 1.10 1.00
Nos. 134-136 (3) 2.65 2.50

1996 Summer Olympic Games, Atlanta — A45

1996, May 28 Litho. *Perf. 14x13*
137 A45 85c Runners .90 .85
138 A45 130c Cyclist 1.40 1.25

A46

A47

Famous Women: No. 139, Livia (Mimi) Ecury (1920-91), nurse. No. 140, Lolita Euson (1914-94), poet. No. 141, Laura Wernet-Paskel (1911-62), teacher.

1996, Sept. 27 Litho. *Perf. 13x14*
139 A46 60c multicolored .65 .65
140 A46 60c multicolored .65 .65
141 A46 60c multicolored .65 .65
Nos. 139-141 (3) 1.95 1.95

1997, Jan. 23 Litho. *Perf. 13x14*

Year of Papiamento 1997: 50c, Sign promoting use of Papiamento language, children playing on beach, people in water, boat. 140c, "Papiamento," sunrise.

142 A47 50c multicolored .50 .45
143 A47 140c multicolored 1.25 1.40

Mailman on Bicycle, 1936-57 A48

America issue: 70c, Mailman handing mail to woman, jeep, 1957-88. 80c, Mailman on motor scooter placing mail in mailbox, 1995.

1997, Mar. 27 Litho. *Perf. 14x13*
144 A48 60c multicolored .55 .55
145 A48 70c multicolored .65 .55
146 A48 80c multicolored .80 .65
Nos. 144-146 (3) 2.00 1.75

Aruban Architectrue A49

30c, Decorated cunucu house. 65c, Steps with "popchi's." 100c, Arends's Building, vert.

1997, May 22 Litho. *Perf. 14x13*
147 A49 30c multicolored .30 .30
148 A49 65c multicolored .70 .65
Perf. 13x14
149 A49 100c multicolored 1.00 .90
Nos. 147-149 (3) 2.00 1.85

Marine Life — A50

Designs: a, Marlin jumping out of water, lighthouse. b, Dolphin jumping out of water, trees, plants on beach. c, Iguana on rock, beach. d, Dolphin, fish. e, Two dolphins, fish. f, Fish, turtles, owl on beach. g, Various fish among coral. h, Diver, shipwreck, fish, coral. i, Various fish.

1997, May 29 Litho. *Perf. 12½x13*
150 A50 90c Sheet of 9, #a.-i. 9.00 9.00

PACIFIC 97.

Cruise Tourism A51

Designs: 35c, Ship at pier, tourists walking toward ship. 50c, Ship with gangway lowered, tourists. 150c, Ship out to sea, small boat.

1997, July 24 Litho. *Perf. 14x13*
151 A51 35c multicolored .40 .35
152 A51 50c multicolored .55 .50
153 A51 150c multicolored 1.60 1.40
Nos. 151-153 (3) 2.55 2.25

Aruban Wild Flowers A52

50c, Erythrina velutina. 60c, Cordia dentata. 70c, Tabebuia billbergii. 130c, Guaiacum officinale.

1997, Sept. 25

154 A52	50c multicolored	.55	.55
155 A52	60c multicolored	.70	.70
156 A52	70c multicolored	.80	.80
157 A52	130c multicolored	1.50	1.50
	Nos. 154-157 (4)	3.55	3.55

Fort Zoutman, Bicent. — A53

1998, Jan. 13 Litho. *Perf. 14x13*

158 A53	30c sepia & multi	.35	.35
159 A53	250c gray & multi	2.75	2.75

Total Solar Eclipse, 1998 — A54

1998, Feb. 26 Litho. *Perf. 13x14*

160 A54	85c shown	.90	.90
161 A54	100c Map, track of eclipse	1.10	1.10

Native Birds — A55

50c, Mimus gilvus. 60c, Falco sparverius. 70c, Icterus icterus. 150c, Coereba flaveola.

Perf. 14x13, 13x14

1998, July 10 Litho.

162 A55	50c multi	.55	.55
163 A55	60c multi, vert.	.70	.70
164 A55	70c multi, vert.	.80	.80
165 A55	150c multi	1.75	1.75
	Nos. 162-165 (4)	3.80	3.80

World Stamp 1998 — A56

1998, Sept. 8 Litho. *Perf. 14x13*

166 A56	225c multicolored	2.50	2.50

Endangered Animals A57

Equus asinus: 40c, Two standing on hill. 65c, Three standing, rocks, cacti, tree. 100c, Adult, foal standing among rocks, cacti.

1999, June 21 Litho. *Perf. 14x13*

167 A57	40c multicolored	.45	.45
168 A57	65c multicolored	.75	.75
169 A57	100c multicolored	1.10	1.10
	Nos. 167-169 (3)	2.30	2.30

Cacti — A58

Designs: 50c, Opuntia wentiana. 60c, Lemaireocereus griseus. 70c, Cephalocereus lanuginosus. 75c, Cephalocereus lanuginosus (in bloom).

1999, Mar. 31 Litho. *Perf. 14x13*

170 A58	50c multicolored	.60	.60
171 A58	60c multicolored	.70	.70
172 A58	70c multicolored	.80	.80
173 A58	75c multicolored	.90	.90
	Nos. 170-173 (4)	3.00	3.00

Dogs — A59

Various dogs, background: 40c, Trees. 60c, Cactus, aloe plant, rocks. 80c, Tree, sea. 165c, Sky, clouds.

1999, May 31 Litho. *Perf. 13x14*

174 A59	40c multicolored	.40	.40
175 A59	60c multicolored	.65	.65
176 A59	80c multicolored	.85	.85
177 A59	165c multicolored	1.60	1.60
	Nos. 174-177 (4)	3.50	3.50

Discovery of Aruba, 500th Anniv. — A60

1999, Aug. 9 Litho. *Perf. 14x13*

178 A60	150c shown	1.50	1.50
179 A60	175c Abstract paintings	2.00	2.00
a.	Souvenir sheet, #178-179	3.50	3.50

Natl. Library, 50th Anniv. — A61

1999, Aug. 20

180 A61	70c shown	.80	.80
181 A61	100c Original building	1.10	1.10

Christmas - A62

Die Cut Perf. 13x13½

1999, Dec. 1 Litho.

Self-Adhesive Coil Stamps

182 A62	40c Magi on shore	.50	.50
183 A62	70c Magi in desert	.85	.85
184 A62	100c Holy Family	1.40	1.40
	Nos. 182-184 (3)	2.75	2.75

Tourist Attractions A62a

Reptiles A63

Tourist Attractions: 25c, Guadirikiri Cave. 55c, Cactus landscape. 85c, Hooiberg. 500c, Conchi. Reptiles: 40c, Norops lineatus. 60c, Iguana iguana, vert. 75c, Leptodeira annulata, vert. 150c, Cnemidophorus murinus.

2000 Litho. *Perf. 14x13, 13x14*

185 A62a	25c multi	.30	.30
186 A63	40c multi	.45	.45
187 A62a	55c multi	.60	.60
188 A63	60c multi	.65	.65
189 A63	75c multi	.85	.85
190 A62a	85c multi	1.00	1.00
191 A63	150c multi	1.75	1.75
192 A62a	500c multi	5.75	5.75
	Nos. 185-192 (8)	11.35	11.35

Issued: 40c, 60c, 75c, 150c, 1/31; 25c, 55c, 85c, 500c, 6/5.

America Issue, Campaign Against AIDS — A64

Perf. 14x13, 13x14

2000, Mar. 2 Litho.

193 A64	75c Flags	.85	.85
194 A64	175c Ribbon on globe, vert.	2.00	2.00

Organization Anniversaries A65

Designs: 150c, Aruba Bank N.V., 75th anniv. 165c, Alto Vista Church, 250th anniv.

2000, Apr. 20 Litho. *Perf. 14x13*

195 A65	150c multi	1.60	1.60
196 A65	165c multi	1.90	1.90

Type of 2000

Animals: 5c, Cat. 15c, Shells. 30c, Tortoise. 35c, Mud house, vert. 50c, Rabbit. 100c, Balashi gold smelter, vert. 200c, Parakeet. 250c, Rock crystals.

Perf. 14x13, 13x14 (#200, 202)

2001 Litho.

197 A63	5c multi	.20	.20
198 A62a	15c multi	.20	.20
199 A63	30c multi	.35	.35
200 A62a	35c multi	.40	.40
201 A63	50c multi	.55	.55
202 A62a	100c multi	1.10	1.10
203 A63	200c multi	2.25	2.25
204 A62a	250c multi	2.75	2.75
	Nos. 197-204 (8)	7.80	7.80

Issued: 5c, 30c, 50c, 200c, 1/31. 15c, 35c, 100c, 250c, 8/6.

Mascaruba, 40th Anniv. — A66

Actors on stage and audience in: 60c: Background. 150c, Foreground.

2001, Mar. 26 Litho. *Perf. 14x13*

205-206 A66	Set of 2	2.40	2.40

Classic Motor Vehicles A67

Designs: 25c, 1930 Ford Crown Victoria Leatherback. 40c, 1933 Citroen Commerciale. 70c, 1948 Plymouth pickup truck. 75c, 1959 Ford Edsel.

2001, May 31

207-210 A67	Set of 4	2.40	2.40

Year of Dialogue Among Civilizations A68

2001, Oct. 9 Litho. *Perf. 14x13*

211 A68	175c multi	2.00	2.00

Airport Views — A69

Designs: 30c, Dakota Airport, 1950. 75c, Queen Beatrix Airport, 1972. 175c, Queen Beatrix Airport, 2000.

2002, Jan. 31 Litho. *Perf. 14x13*

212-214 A69	Set of 3	3.25	3.25

Royal Wedding A70

Prince Willem-Alexander, Maxima Zorreguieta and: 60c, Royal palace, golden coach. 300c, Bourse of Berlage, New Church.

2002, Feb. 2

215-216 A70	Set of 2	4.00	4.00

Water and Energy Company, 70th Anniv. — A71

Designs: 60c, Faucet and water drop, vert. 85c, Pipeline. 165c, Meter and meter-reading equipment, vert.

Perf. 13x14, 14x13

2002, June 3 Litho.

217-219 A71	Set of 3	3.50	3.50

America Issue - Youth, Education and Literacy — A72

Designs: 25c, Hand writing letters with quill pen. 100c, Child looking over wall of letters.

2002, July 15 Litho. *Perf. 14x12¾*

220-221 A72	Set of 2	1.40	1.40

Aruba in World War II — A73

Designs: 60c, Attack on Lago Oil Refinery by German U-boat U-156. 75c, Torpedoing of ships by U-156. 150c, Statue of "Boy" Ecury, Aruban resistance fighter, Arubian militiaman, vert.

Perf. 14x13, 13x14

2002, Sept. 9 Litho.

222-224 A73	Set of 3	3.25	3.25

SEMI-POSTAL STAMPS

Surtax for child welfare organizations unless otherwise stated.

Solidarity SP1

1986, May 7 Litho. *Perf. 14x13*

B1 SP1 30c + 10c shown .60 .30
B2 SP1 35c + 15c Three ropes .80 .55
B3 SP1 60c + 25c One rope 1.10 .75
Nos. B1-B3 (3) 2.50 1.60

Surtax for social and cultural projects.

Child Welfare SP2

1986, Oct. 29 Litho. *Perf. 14x13*

B4 SP2 45c + 20c Boy, caterpillar 1.00 .70
B5 SP2 70c + 25c Boy, cocoon 1.25 .90
B6 SP2 100c + 40c Girl, butterfly 1.75 1.40
Nos. B4-B6 (3) 4.00 3.00

Christmas (Child Welfare) SP3

1987, Oct. 27 Litho. *Perf. 14x13*

B7 SP3 25c +10c Boy on beach .45 .45
B8 SP3 45c +20c Drawing Christmas tree .65 .65
B9 SP3 70c +30c Child, creche figures 1.00 1.00
Nos. B7-B9 (3) 2.10 2.10

Solidarity SP4

YMCA emblem in various geometric designs.

1988, Aug. 3 Litho. *Perf. 14x13*

B10 SP4 45c +20c shown .60 .60
B11 SP4 60c +25c multi, diff. .80 .80
B12 SP4 100c +50c multi, diff. 1.40 1.40
Nos. B10-B12 (3) 2.80 2.80

11th YMCA world council.
Surtax for social and cultural projects.

Children's Toys (Child Welfare) — SP5

1988, Oct. 26 *Perf. 13x14*

B13 SP5 45c +20c Jacks .80 .80
B14 SP5 70c +30c Top 1.10 1.10
B15 SP5 100c +50c Kite 1.60 1.60
Nos. B13-B15 (3) 3.50 3.50

Child Welfare SP6

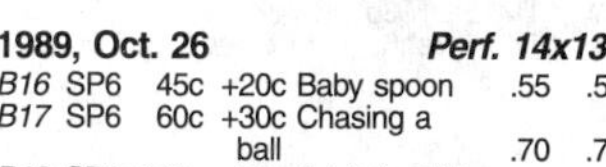

1989, Oct. 26 *Perf. 14x13*

B16 SP6 45c +20c Baby spoon .55 .55
B17 SP6 60c +30c Chasing a ball .70 .70
B18 SP6 100c +50c Adult & child holding hands 1.25 1.25
Nos. B16-B18 (3) 2.50 2.50

Solidarity SP7

1990, July 25

B19 SP7 55c +25c shown 1.00 1.00
B20 SP7 100c +50c Family, house 1.75 1.75

Surtax for social and cultural projects.

Child Welfare — SP8

Child Welfare — SP9

Christmas song.

1990, Oct. 24 Litho. *Perf. 13x14*

B21 SP8 45c +20c Wind surfboards .70 .70
B22 SP8 60c +30c shown .90 .90
B23 SP8 100c +50c Kites, lizard 1.50 1.50
Nos. B21-B23 (3) 3.10 3.10

1991, Oct. 25 Litho. *Perf. 13x14*

Literacy: 45c+25c, Discovery of reading. 60c+35c, Pointing to letter. 100c+50c, Child reading.

B24 SP9 45c +25c multi .75 .75
B25 SP9 60c +35c multi 1.00 1.00
B26 SP9 100c +50c multi 1.50 1.50
Nos. B24-B26 (3) 3.25 3.25

Solidarity SP10

55c+30c, Girl scouts, flag & emblem. 100c+50c, Hand holding cancer fund emblem, people.

1992, May 27 Litho. *Perf. 14x13*

B27 SP10 55c +30c multi .80 .80
B28 SP10 100c +50c multi 1.50 1.50

Surtax for social and cultural projects.

Postal Services of Aruba, Cent. (Child Welfare) SP11

Designs: 50c+30c, Heart. 70c+35c, Airplane, letters. 100c+55c, Pigeon with letter in beak, vert.

1992, Oct. 30 Litho. *Perf. 14x13*

B29 SP11 50c +30c multi .80 .80
B30 SP11 70c +35c multi 1.00 1.00

Perf. 13x14

B31 SP11 100c +50c multi 1.50 1.50
Nos. B29-B31 (3) 3.30 3.30

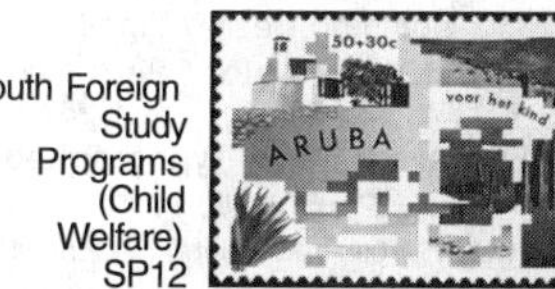

Youth Foreign Study Programs (Child Welfare) SP12

Abstract designs of: 50c+30c, Landscapes. 75c+40c, Young man, scenes of other countries, vert. 100c+50c, Integrating cultures.

1993, Oct. 27 *Perf. 14x13, 13x14*

B32 SP12 50c +30c multi .80 .80
B33 SP12 75c +40c multi 1.10 1.10
B34 SP12 100c +50c multi 1.50 1.50
Nos. B32-B34 (3) 3.40 3.40

Solidarity SP13

Intl. Year of the Family: 50c+35c, Family seated, reading, studying. 100c+50c, Family playing in front of house.

1994, May 30 Litho. *Perf. 14x13*

B35 SP13 50c +35c multi .90 .90
B36 SP13 100c +50c multi 1.50 1.50

Surtax for social and cultural projects.

Child Welfare SP14

Designs: 50c+30c, Children on anchor with umbrella. 80c+35c, Children inside Sun. 100c+50c, Child riding owl.

1994, Oct. 27 Litho. *Perf. 14x13*

B37 SP14 50c +30c multi .80 .80
B38 SP14 80c +35c multi 1.25 1.25
B39 SP14 100c +50c multi 1.50 1.50
Nos. B37-B39 (3) 3.55 3.55

Child Welfare SP15

Solidarity SP16

Children's drawings: 50c+25c, Children with balloons, house. 70c+35c, Three people with picnic basket on sunny day. 100c+50c, People gardening on sunny day.

1995, Oct. 26 Litho. *Perf. 13x14*

B40 SP15 50c +25c multi .70 .70
B41 SP15 70c +35c multi 1.00 1.00
B42 SP15 100c +50c multi 1.40 1.40
Nos. B40-B42 (3) 3.10 3.10

1996, July 26 Litho. *Perf. 13x14*

El Sol Naciente Lodge, 75th Anniv.: 60c+30c, Masonic emblems. 100c+ 50c, Columns, terrestrial and celestial globes.

B43 SP16 60c +30c multi .90 .90
B44 SP16 100c +50c multi 1.60 1.60

Surtax for social and cultural projects (Solidarity)

Child Welfare SP17

Cartoons: 50c+25c, Mother, baby rabbit waiting at school bus stop. 70c+35c, Mother, baby owl, outside school. 100c+50c, Children flying kite.

1996, Oct. 24 Litho. *Perf. 14x13*

B45 SP17 50c +25c multi .75 .75
B46 SP17 70c +35c multi 1.10 1.10
B47 SP17 100c +50c multi 1.40 1.40
Nos. B45-B47 (3) 3.25 3.25

Child Welfare SP18

Designs: 50c+25c, Girl sitting among aloe plants. 70c+35c, Boy, butterfly, cactus, vert. 100c+50c, Girl swimming under water, fish, coral.

Perf. 14x13, 13x14

1997, Oct. 23 Litho.

B48 SP18 50c +25c multi .85 .85
B49 SP18 70c +35c multi 1.25 1.25
B50 SP18 100c +50c multi 1.60 1.60
Nos. B48-B50 (3) 3.70 3.70

Solidarity SP19

Service Organizations: 60c+30c, Globe, emblem of Lions Intl., wheelchair balanced on map of Aruba. 100c+50c, Child reading book, emblem of Rotary Intl., woman in rocking chair.

1998, May 29 Litho. *Perf. 14x13*

B51 SP19 60c +30c multi 1.00 1.00
B52 SP19 100c +50c multi 1.75 1.75

Surtax for social and cultural projects.

Child Welfare — SP20

50c+25c, Girl performing traditional ribbon dance. 80c+40c, Boy playing a cuarta. 100c+50c, Two boys playing basketball.

1998, Oct. 22 Litho. *Perf. 13x14*

B53 SP20 50c +25c multi .85 .85
B54 SP20 80c +40c multi 1.25 1.25
B55 SP20 100c +50c multi 1.75 1.75
Nos. B53-B55 (3) 3.85 3.85

Child Welfare SP21

Designs: 60c+30c, Child on beach with man with fishing net. 80c+40c, Adult reading to children. 100c+50c, Mother, child, vert.

Perf. 14x13, 13x14

1999, Oct. 21 Litho.

B56 SP21 60c +30c multi .60 .60
B57 SP21 80c +40c multi .90 .90
B58 SP21 100c +50c multi 1.25 1.25
Nos. B56-B58 (3) 2.75 2.75

Solidarity SP22

75c+35c, Children on playground equipment. 100c+50c, Children playing in sand.

2000, Aug. 28 Litho. *Perf. 14x13*

B59-B60 SP22 Set of 2 2.75 2.75

Child Welfare SP23

Children's art: 60c+30c, House with solar collectors. 80c+40c, House, girl, garbage can. 100c+50c, Flying automobiles.

2000, Oct. 26

B61-B63 SP23 Set of 3 4.00 4.00

Child Welfare — SP24

Intl. Volunteers Year: 40c+20c, Children at crosswalk. 60c+30c, Boys walking dog. 100c+50c, Children depositing trash in can at beach.

2001, Oct. 31 Litho. *Perf. 13x14*

B64-B66	SP24	Set of 3	3.50	3.50

Child Welfare — SP25

Designs: 40c+20c, Boy, iguana and goat. 60c+30c, Girl, hawksbill turtle, red crab, horiz. 100c+50c, Boy, pelicans, parakeet, conch shell.

Perf. 13x14, 14x13

2002, Oct. 31 Litho.

B67-B69	SP25	Set of 3	3.50	3.50

ASCENSION

ə-ˈsen‸t‸-shən

LOCATION — An island in the South Atlantic Ocean, 900 miles from Liberia
GOVT. — A part of the British Crown Colony of St. Helena
AREA — 34 sq. mi.
POP. — 1,117 (1993)

In 1922 Ascension was placed under the administration of the Colonial Office and annexed to the British Crown Colony of St. Helena. The only post office is at Georgetown.

12 Pence = 1 Shilling
20 Shillings = 1 Pound
100 Pence = 1 Pound (1971)

Catalogue values for unused stamps in this country are for Never Hinged items, beginning with Scott 50.

Stamps and Types of St. Helena, 1912-22 Overprinted in Black or Red

1922 Wmk. 4 *Perf. 14*

1	A9	½p green & blk	3.75	*12.50*
2	A10	1p green	4.00	*11.50*
3	A10	1½p rose red	13.00	*42.50*
4	A9	2p gray & blk	13.00	11.50
5	A9	3p ultra	11.50	*14.00*
6	A10	8p dl vio & blk	22.50	*42.50*
7	A10	2sh ultra & blk, *blue*	70.00	*110.00*
8	A10	3sh vio & blk	110.00	*140.00*

Wmk. 3

9	A9	1sh blk, *gray grn* (R)	25.00	*42.50*
		Nos. 1-9 (9)	272.75	*427.00*

Seal of Colony — A3

1924-27 Typo. Wmk. 4 *Perf. 14*

Chalky Paper

10	A3	½p black & gray	3.25	*11.50*
11	A3	1p green & blk	5.00	*6.75*
12	A3	1½p rose red	6.75	*25.00*
13	A3	2p bluish gray & gray	10.50	5.50
14	A3	3p ultra	7.00	*11.50*
15	A3	4p blk & gray, *yel*	42.50	*70.00*
16	A3	5p ol & lil ('27)	9.50	*19.00*
17	A3	6p rose lil & gray	42.50	*75.00*
18	A3	8p violet & gray	13.50	*37.50*
19	A3	1sh brown & gray	17.50	*42.50*
20	A3	2sh ultra & gray, *blue*	50.00	*75.00*
21	A3	3sh blk & gray, *blue*	70.00	*77.50*
		Nos. 10-21 (12)	278.00	*456.75*

View of Georgetown — A4

Map of Ascension — A5

Sooty Tern Breeding Colony A9

1½p, Pier at Georgetown. 3p, Long Beach. 5p, Three Sisters. 5sh, Green Mountain.

1934, July 2 Engr.

23	A4	½p violet & blk	.85	.75
24	A5	1p lt grn & blk	1.60	1.10
25	A4	1½p red & black	1.60	*2.10*
26	A5	2p org & black	1.60	*2.40*
27	A4	3p ultra & blk	1.60	1.40
28	A4	5p blue & black	2.00	*3.00*
29	A5	8p dk brn & blk	3.75	*4.50*
30	A9	1sh carmine & blk	16.50	6.00
31	A5	2sh6p violet & blk	35.00	*40.00*
32	A4	5sh brown & blk	47.50	*65.00*
		Nos. 23-32 (10)	112.00	*126.25*

Common Design Types pictured following the introduction.

Silver Jubilee Issue

Common Design Type

1935, May 6 *Perf. 11x12*

33	CD301	1½p car & dk blue	3.25	*7.00*
34	CD301	2p blk & ultra	10.00	*20.00*
35	CD301	5p ind & grn	16.00	*22.50*
36	CD301	1sh brn vio & ind	22.50	*25.00*
		Nos. 33-36 (4)	51.75	*74.50*
		Set, never hinged	75.00	

25th anniv. of the reign of King George V.

Coronation Issue

Common Design Type

1937, May 19 *Perf. 13½x14*

37	CD302	1p deep green	.45	.70
38	CD302	2p deep orange	.90	.40
39	CD302	3p bright ultra	.90	.50
		Nos. 37-39 (3)	2.25	1.60
		Set, never hinged	3.50	

Georgetown — A11

Designs: No. 41, 41A, 2p, 4p, Green Mountain. No. 41D, 6p, 10sh, Three Sisters. 1½p, 2sh6p, Pier at Georgetown. 3p, 5sh, Long Beach.

Perf. 13, 13½(#41, 44, 45), 14 (#43C)

1938-53

Center in Black

40	A11	½p violet ('44)	.35	*1.60*
		Never hinged	.65	
a.		Perf. 13½	1.50	1.25
		Never hinged	3.25	
41	A11	1p green	19.00	7.50
		Never hinged	42.50	
41A	A11	1p org yel, ('42)	.35	*.60*
		Never hinged	.50	
b.		Perf. 14 ('49)	.50	*16.00*
		Never hinged	.80	
c.		Perf. 13½	7.50	*9.50*
		Never hinged	15.00	
41D	A11	1p green ('49)	.45	*.60*
		Never hinged	.60	
42	A11	1½p red, ('44)	.60	*.85*
		Never hinged	1.00	
a.		Perf. 14 ('49)	2.00	*15.00*
		Never hinged	3.00	
b.		Perf. 13½	1.75	1.40
		Never hinged	4.00	
42C	A11	1½p lilac rose ('53)	.35	*7.00*
		Never hinged	.50	
d.		Perf. 14 ('49)	.40	*.90*
		Never hinged	.55	
e.		1½p carmine, perf 14	6.00	5.50
		Never hinged	7.50	
43	A11	2p orange ('44)	.50	.40
		Never hinged	.90	
a.		Perf. 14 ('49)	2.25	*37.50*
		Never hinged	3.25	
b.		Perf. 13½	2.00	1.00
		Never hinged	4.50	
43C	A11	2p red ('49)	.75	.75
		Never hinged	1.00	
44	A11	3p ultra	60.00	25.00
		Never hinged	100.00	
44A	A11	3p black, ('44)	.55	*.85*
		Never hinged	.75	
c.		Perf. 13½ ('40)	7.50	.90
		Never hinged	18.00	
44B	A11	4p ultra, ('44)	3.50	3.00
		Never hinged	4.75	
d.		Perf. 13½	7.50	3.50
		Never hinged	15.00	
45	A11	6p gray blue	6.00	1.25
		Never hinged	10.00	
a.		Perf. 13 ('44)	6.00	5.00
		Never hinged	10.00	
46	A11	1sh dk brn ('44)	3.25	2.00
		Never hinged	5.50	
a.		Perf. 13½	7.00	1.75
		Never hinged	17.50	
47	A11	2sh6p car ('44)	24.00	*32.50*
		Never hinged	40.00	
a.		Perf. 13½	25.00	10.00
		Never hinged	42.50	
48	A11	5sh yel brn ('44)	35.00	30.00
		Never hinged	52.50	
a.		Perf. 13½	60.00	9.00
		Never hinged	100.00	
49	A11	10sh red vio ('44)	45.00	*57.50*
		Never hinged	70.00	
a.		Perf. 13½	80.00	50.00
		Never hinged	125.00	
b.		10sh brt analine red pur, perf 13	55.00	40.00
		Never hinged	110.00	
		Nos. 40-49 (16)	199.65	*171.40*
		Set, Never hinged	275.00	

Catalogue values for unused stamps in this section, from this point to the end of the section, are for Never Hinged items.

Peace Issue

Common Design Type

Perf. 13½x14

1946, Oct. 21 Engr. Wmk. 4

50	CD303	2p deep orange	.40	*.50*
51	CD303	4p deep blue	.40	.30

Silver Wedding Issue

Common Design Types

1948, Oct. 20 Photo. *Perf. 14x14½*

52	CD304	3p black	.50	.50

Engraved; Name Typographed

Perf. 11½x11

53	CD305	10sh red violet	42.50	40.00

The stamps formerly listed as Nos. 54-56 have been merged into the rest of the George VI definitive series as Nos. 41//43C.

UPU Issue

Common Design Types

Engr.; Name Typo. on Nos. 58, 59

1949, Oct. 10 *Perf. 13½, 11x11½*

57	CD306	3p rose carmine	1.00	*1.10*
58	CD307	4p indigo	3.25	1.25
59	CD308	6p olive	2.50	2.50
60	CD309	1sh slate	3.25	3.00
		Nos. 57-60 (4)	10.00	7.85

Coronation Issue

Common Design Type

1953, June 2 Engr. *Perf. 13½x13*

61	CD312	3p gray & black	1.50	1.50

Reservoir A16

Designs: 1p, Map of Ascension. 1½p, Georgetown. 2p, Map showing Ascension between South America and Africa and cable lines. 2½p, Mountain road. 3p, Yellow-billed tropic bird. 4p, Longfinned tuna. 6p, Waves. 7p, Young green turtles. 1sh, Land crab. 2sh6p, Sooty tern (wideawake). 5sh, Perfect Crater. 10sh, View from Northwest.

1956, Nov. 19 Wmk. 4 *Perf. 13*

Center in Black

62	A16	½p brown	.20	.25
63	A16	1p lilac rose	.35	.55
64	A16	1½p orange	.35	.55
65	A16	2p carmine	.55	.45
66	A16	2½p org brown	.65	.75
67	A16	3p blue	.90	.90
68	A16	4p turq blue	.85	1.25
69	A16	6p dark blue	1.10	.80
70	A16	7p olive	1.40	.90
71	A16	1sh scarlet	1.90	.80
72	A16	2sh6p brown violet	19.00	6.00
73	A16	5sh bright green	25.00	15.00
74	A16	10sh purple	50.00	32.50
		Nos. 62-74 (13)	102.25	60.70

Brown Booby — A17

Birds: 1½p, Black tern. 2p, Fairy tern. 3p, Red-billed tropic bird in flight. 4½p, Brown noddy. 6p, Sooty tern. 7p, Frigate bird. 10p, Blue-faced booby. 1sh, Yellow-billed tropic bird. 1sh6p, Red-billed tropic bird. 2sh6p, Madeiran storm petrel. 5sh, Red-footed booby (brown phase). 10sh, Frigate birds. £1, Red-footed booby (white phase).

Perf. 14x14½

1963, May 23 Photo. Wmk. 314

75	A17	1p multicolored	.75	.25
a.		Booklet pane of 4	1.00	
76	A17	1½p multicolored	1.00	.50
a.		Booklet pane of 4	1.25	
b.		Blue omitted	70.00	
77	A17	2p multicolored	1.00	.25
a.		Booklet pane of 4	1.50	
78	A17	3p multicolored	1.00	.25
a.		Booklet pane of 4	1.75	
79	A17	4½p multicolored	1.00	.25
80	A17	6p multicolored	1.00	.25
a.		Booklet pane of 4	4.50	
81	A17	7p multicolored	1.00	.25
82	A17	10p multicolored	1.00	.25
83	A17	1sh multicolored	1.00	.25
84	A17	1sh6p multicolored	3.75	1.50
a.		Booklet pane of 4	7.50	
85	A17	2sh6p multicolored	5.50	*6.75*
86	A17	5sh multicolored	6.00	6.00
87	A17	10sh multicolored	11.00	6.75
88	A17	£1 multicolored	17.00	8.50
		Nos. 75-88 (14)	52.00	32.00

Freedom from Hunger Issue

Common Design Type

1963, June 4 Wmk. 314

89	CD314	1sh6p car rose	2.00	1.00

Red Cross Centenary Issue

Common Design Type

1963, Sept. 2 Litho. *Perf. 13*

90	CD315	3p black & red	.90	.90
91	CD315	1sh6p ultra & red	6.00	6.00

ITU Issue
Common Design Type
Perf. 11x11½
1965, May 17 Litho. Wmk. 314
92 CD317 3p mag & violet .60 .40
93 CD317 6p grnsh bl & brn org 1.60 1.10

Intl. Cooperation Year Issue
Common Design Type
1965, Oct. 25 Wmk. 314 *Perf. 14½*
94 CD318 1p bl grn & claret .50 .50
95 CD318 6p lt vio & green 1.00 1.00

Churchill Memorial Issue
Common Design Type
1966, Jan. 24 Photo. *Perf. 14*
Design in Black, Gold and Carmine Rose
96 CD319 1p bright blue .35 .25
97 CD319 3p green 1.40 .85
98 CD319 6p brown 1.75 1.40
99 CD319 1sh6p violet 5.00 4.00
Nos. 96-99 (4) 8.50 6.50

World Cup Soccer Issue
Common Design Type
1966, July 1 Litho. *Perf. 14*
100 CD321 3p multicolored .70 .50
101 CD321 6p multicolored 1.40 1.25

WHO Headquarters Issue
Common Design Type
1966, Sept. 20 Litho. *Perf. 14*
102 CD322 3p multicolored 1.50 .75
103 CD322 1sh6p multicolored 3.50 2.00

Apollo Satellite Station, Ascension — A18

Wmk. 314
1966, Nov. 7 Photo. *Perf. 14*
104 A18 4p purple & black .20 .20
105 A18 8p blue grn & blk .20 .20
106 A18 1sh3p brn ol & blk .20 .20
107 A18 2sh6p brt grnsh blue & black .40 .40
Nos. 104-107 (4) 1.00 1.00

Opening of the Apollo communications satellite-earth station, part of the US Apollo program.

UNESCO Anniversary Issue
Common Design Type
1967, Jan. 3 Litho. *Perf. 14*
108 CD323 3p "Education" .65 .75
109 CD323 6p "Science" 1.50 1.75
110 CD323 1sh6p "Culture" 5.00 4.00
Nos. 108-110 (3) 7.15 6.50

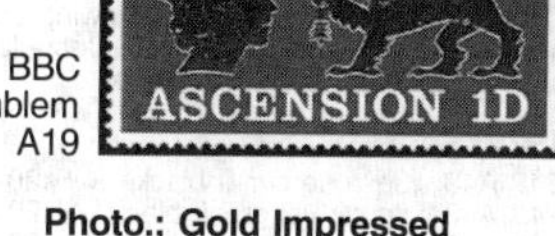

BBC Emblem A19

Photo.; Gold Impressed
1967, Dec. 1 Wmk. 314 *Perf. 14½*
111 A19 1p ultra & gold .20 .20
112 A19 3p dk green & gold .20 .20
113 A19 6p brt purple & gold .20 .20
114 A19 1sh6p brt red & gold .35 .35
Nos. 111-114 (4) .95 .95

Opening of the British Broadcasting Company's South Atlantic Relay Station on Ascension Island.

Human Rights Flame and Chain — A20

Perf. 14½x14
1968, July 8 Litho. Wmk. 314
115 A20 6p org, car & blk .20 .20
116 A20 1sh6p gray, mag & blk .30 .30
117 A20 2sh6p brt grn, plum & blk .40 .40
Nos. 115-117 (3) .90 .90

International Human Rights Year.

Blackfish A21

Fish: No. 119, Sailfish. 6p, Oldwife. 8p, Leather jacks. 1sh6p, Yellowtails. 1sh9p, Tuna. 2sh3p, Mako sharks. 2sh11p, Rock hind (jack).

Perf. 13x12½
1968-69 Wmk. 314 Litho.
118 A21 4p brt grnsh bl & blk .25 .20
119 A21 4p red & multi .30 .30
120 A21 6p yel olive & multi .35 .35
121 A21 8p brt rose lil & multi .50 .40
122 A21 1sh6p brown & multi 1.75 1.75
123 A21 1sh9p emer & multi 1.00 .90
124 A21 2sh3p ocher & multi 1.60 1.10
125 A21 2sh11p dp org & multi 3.25 3.00
Nos. 118-125 (8) 9.00 8.00

Issue dates: No. 119, 6p, 1sh6p, 2sh11p, Mar. 3, 1969; others, Oct. 23, 1968.
See Nos. 130-133.

Arms of R.N.S. Rattlesnake A22

Coats of Arms of Royal Naval Ships: 9p, Weston. 1sh9p, Undaunted. 2sh3p, Eagle.

Perf. 14x14½
1969, Oct. 1 Photo. Wmk. 314
126 A22 4p multicolored .50 .45
127 A22 9p multicolored .65 .55
128 A22 1sh9p multicolored 1.00 .70
129 A22 2sh3p multicolored 1.10 .80
a. Min. sheet of 4, #126-129 7.00 7.00
Nos. 126-129 (4) 3.25 2.50

See Nos. 134-137, 152-159, 166-169.

Fish Type of 1968

Deep-sea fish: 4p, Wahoo. 9p, Coalfish. 1sh9p, Dolphinfishes. 2sh3p, Soldierfish.

1970, Apr. 6 Litho. *Perf. 14*
130 A21 4p bluish grn & multi 2.50 2.00
131 A21 9p org & multi 3.25 2.00
132 A21 1sh9p ultra & multi 3.50 2.50
133 A21 2sh3p gray & multi 3.50 2.50
Nos. 130-133 (4) 12.75 9.00

Naval Arms Type of 1969

4p, Penelope. 9p, Carlisle. 1sh6p, Amphion. 2sh6p, Magpie.

Perf. 12½x12
1970, Sept. 7 Photo. Wmk. 314
134 A22 4p ultra, gold & blk 1.25 .25
135 A22 9p lt bl, blk, gold & red 1.75 .50
136 A22 1sh6p grnsh bl, gold & blk 2.00 1.25
137 A22 2sh6p lt grnsh bl, gold & blk 2.50 2.00
a. Miniature sheet of 4, #134-137 11.00 10.00
Nos. 134-137 (4) 7.50 4.00

Decimal Currency Issue

Tycho Brahe's Observatory, Quadrant and Supernova, 1572 — A23

Man into Space: ½p, Chinese rocket, 1232, vert. 1p, Medieval Arab astronomers, vert. 2p, Galileo, his telescope and drawing of moon, 1609. 2½p, Isaac Newton, telescope and apple. 3½p, Harrison's chronometer and ship, 1735. 4½p, First American manned orbital flight (Project Mercury, 1962, vert.). 5p, Reflector of Palomar telescope and ring nebula in Lyra, Messier 57. 7½p, Jodrell Bank telescope. 10p, Mariner 7, 1969, and telescopic view of Mars. 12½p, Sputnik 2 and dog Laika, 1957. 25p, Astronaut walking in space, 1965 (Gemini 4; vert.). 50p, US astronauts and moon landing module, 1969. £1, Future space research station.

1971, Feb. 15 Litho. *Perf. 14½*
138 A23 ½p multicolored .20 .20
a. Booklet pane of 4 .50
139 A23 1p multicolored .20 .20
a. Booklet pane of 4 .75
140 A23 1½p multicolored .25 .25
a. Booklet pane of 4 1.00
141 A23 2p multicolored .30 .25
a. Booklet pane of 4 1.90
142 A23 2½p multicolored .75 .60
a. Booklet pane of 4 2.50
143 A23 3½p multicolored 1.50 .60
a. Booklet pane of 4 3.50
144 A23 4½p multicolored 1.00 .60
145 A23 5p multicolored .75 .60
146 A23 7½p multicolored 3.00 1.40
147 A23 10p multicolored 2.75 1.50
148 A23 12½p multicolored 4.75 1.75
149 A23 25p multicolored 5.50 2.00
150 A23 50p multicolored 4.75 2.25
151 A23 £1 multicolored 4.75 4.00
Nos. 138-151 (14) 30.45 16.20

For overprints see Nos. 189-191.

Arms of H.M.S. Phoenix — A24

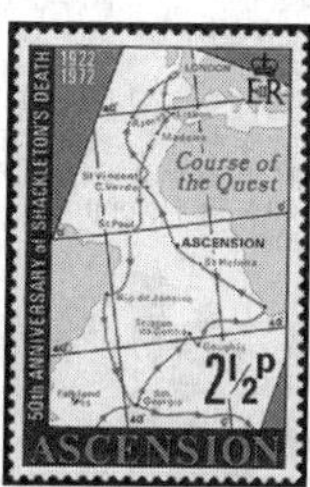
Course of Quest — A25

Coats of Arms of Royal Naval Ships: 4p, Milford. 9p, Pelican. 15p, Oberon.

1971, Nov. 15 Photo. *Perf. 13½x13*
152 A24 2p gold & multi 1.10 .20
153 A24 4p gold & multi 1.25 .45
154 A24 9p gold & multi 1.75 1.10
155 A24 15p gold & multi 1.90 1.75
a. Souvenir sheet of 4, #152-155 7.00 7.00
Nos. 152-155 (4) 6.00 3.50

Naval Arms Type of 1969

1½p, Lowestoft. 3p, Auckland. 6p, Nigeria. 17½p, Bermuda.

1972, May 22 Litho. *Perf. 14x14½*
156 A22 1½p bl, gold & blk .65 .65
157 A22 3p grnsh bl, gold & blk .70 .70
158 A22 6p grn, gold, blk & bl .80 .80
159 A22 17½p lil, gold, blk & red 1.60 1.60
a. Miniature sheet of 4, #156-159 4.00 4.00
Nos. 156-159 (4) 3.75 3.75

1972, Aug. 2 *Perf. 14*

Designs: 4p, Shackleton and "Quest", horiz. 7½p, Shackleton's cabin and Quest in pack ice, horiz. 11p, Shackleton statue, London, and memorial cairn, South Georgia.

160 A25 2½p multicolored .65 .50
161 A25 4p multicolored .70 .65
162 A25 7½p multicolored .75 .70
163 A25 11p multicolored .90 .90
a. Souvenir sheet of 4, #160-163 3.75 3.75
Nos. 160-163 (4) 3.00 2.75

Sir Ernest Henry Shackleton (1874-1922), explorer of Antarctica.

Silver Wedding Issue, 1972
Common Design Type

Design: Queen Elizabeth II, Prince Philip, land crab and shark.

1972, Nov. 20 Photo. *Perf. 14x14½*
164 CD324 2p violet & multi .20 .20
165 CD324 16p car rose & multi .55 .55

Naval Arms Type of 1969

2p, Birmingham. 4p, Cardiff. 9p, Penzance. 13p, Rochester.

1973, May 28 Litho. Wmk. 314
166 A22 2p blue & multi 2.25 1.40
167 A22 4p yel grn & multi 2.75 1.40
168 A22 9p lt blue & multi 3.50 1.60
169 A22 13p violet & multi 4.00 1.60
a. Min. sheet of 4, #166-169 22.50 15.00
Nos. 166-169 (4) 12.50 6.00

Turtles — A26

1973, Aug. 28 *Perf. 13½*
170 A26 4p Green 1.75 1.10
171 A26 9p Loggerhead 3.50 2.25
172 A26 12p Hawksbill 5.50 3.50
Nos. 170-172 (3) 10.75 6.85

Light Infanty Marine Sergeant, 1900 — A27

Uniforms (Royal Marines): 6p, Private, 1816. 12p, Officer, Light Infantry, 1880. 20p, Color Sergeant, Artillery, 1910.

1973, Oct. 31 *Perf. 14½*
173 A27 2p multicolored 2.00 1.50
174 A27 6p lt green & multi 2.75 1.75
175 A27 12p lt blue & multi 3.25 2.50
176 A27 20p lt lilac & multi 3.75 2.75
Nos. 173-176 (4) 11.75 8.50

Departure of the Royal Marines from Ascension, 50th anniv.

Princess Anne's Wedding Issue
Common Design Type
1973, Nov. 14 *Perf. 14*
177 CD325 2p ocher & multi .20 .20
178 CD325 18p multicolored .40 .40

Letter and UPU Emblem A29

UPU Cent.: 9p, Emblem and Mercury.

Wmk. 314
1974, Mar. 27 Litho. *Perf. 14½*
179 A29 2p multicolored .20 .20
180 A29 9p vio blue & multi .50 .50

Young Churchill and Blenheim Palace
A30

25p, Churchill and UN Headquarters, NYC.

1974, Nov. 30 Litho. Unwmk.

181	A30	5p slate grn & multi		.20	.20
182	A30	25p purple & multi		.80	.80
	a.	Souvenir sheet of 2, #181-182		2.00	2.25

Sir Winston Churchill (1874-1965).

Skylab over Photograph of Ascension Taken by Skylab 3 — A31

Skylab Space Station: 18p, Command module and photo of Ascension from Skylab 4.

1975, Mar. 20 Wmk. 314 *Perf. 14½*

183	A31	2p multicolored	.20	.20
184	A31	18p multicolored	.80	.80

US Air Force C-141A Starlifter — A32

Aircraft: 5p, Royal Air Force C-130 Hercules. 9p, Vickers VC-10. 24p, U.S. Air Force C-5A Galaxy.

Perf. 13½x14

1975, June 19 Litho. Wmk. 314

185	A32	2p multicolored	1.25	.55
186	A32	5p multicolored	1.50	.70
187	A32	9p multicolored	1.75	1.25
188	A32	24p multicolored	3.00	2.50
	a.	Souvenir sheet of 4, #185-188	13.00	13.00
		Nos. 185-188 (4)	7.50	5.00

Wideawake Airfield, Ascension Island.

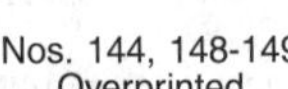

Nos. 144, 148-149 Overprinted

1975, Aug. Litho. *Perf. 14½*

189	A23	4½p multicolored	.25	.25
190	A23	12½p multicolored	.35	.35
191	A23	25p multicolored	.50	.50
		Nos. 189-191 (3)	1.10	1.10

Apollo Soyuz space test project (Russo-American cooperation), launching July 15; link-up, July 17.

HMS Peruvian and Zenobia Arriving Oct. 22, 1815
A33

Designs: 5p, Water Supply, Dampiers Drip. 9p, First Landing, Oct. 1815. 15p, The Garden on Green Mountain. All designs after paintings by Isobel McManus.

1975, Oct. 22 Wmk. 373 *Perf. 14½*

192	A33	2p lt blue & multi	.20	.20
193	A33	5p lt blue & multi	.30	.20
194	A33	9p red & multi	.45	.40
195	A33	15p red & multi	.90	.75
		Nos. 192-195 (4)	1.85	1.55

British occupation, 160th anniv.

Canaries
A34

2p, Fairy tern, vert. 3p, Waxbills. 4p, Black noddy. 5p, Brown noddy. 6p, Common mynah. 7p, Madeira storm petrels. 8p, Sooty terns. 9p, White booby. 10p, Red-footed booby. 15p, Red-throated francolin. 18p, Brown booby. 25p, Red-billed bo'sun bird. 50p, Yellow-billed bo'sun bird. £1, Ascension frigatebird. £2, Boatswain Island Bird Sanctuary and birds.

Perf. 14x14½, 14½x14

1976, Apr. 26 Litho. Wmk. 373

Size: 35x27mm, 27x35mm

196	A34	1p multi	.40	*1.25*
197	A34	2p multi	.45	*1.25*
198	A34	3p multi	.45	*1.25*
199	A34	4p multi, vert.	.50	*1.25*
200	A34	5p multi	.60	*1.25*
201	A34	6p multi	.60	*1.25*
202	A34	7p multi, vert.	.60	*1.25*
203	A34	8p multi	.60	*1.25*
204	A34	9p multi, vert.	.60	*1.25*
205	A34	10p multi	.60	*1.25*
206	A34	15p multi, vert.	1.10	*1.40*
207	A34	18p multi, vert.	1.10	*1.40*
208	A34	25p multi	1.25	*1.40*
209	A34	50p multi	2.00	*2.25*
210	A34	£1 multi, vert.	2.40	2.75

Perf. 13½

Size: 46x33mm

211	A34	£2 multicolored	4.75	*6.00*
		Nos. 196-211 (16)	18.00	27.70

Great Britain Type A1 with Ascension Cancel — A35

9p, Ascension No. 1, vert. 25p, Freighter Southampton Castle.

1976, May 4 *Perf. 13½x14, 14x13½*

212	A35	5p lt brn, car & blk	.20	.20
213	A35	9p gray grn, grn & blk	.30	.30
214	A35	25p blue & multi	.50	.50
		Nos. 212-214 (3)	1.00	1.00

Festival of Stamps 1976. See Tristan da Cunha #208a for souvenir sheet that contains one each of Ascension #214, St. Helena #297 and Tristan da Cunha #208.

US Base
A36

Designs: 9p, NASA Station, Devil's Ashpit. 25p, Viking satellite landing on Mars.

Wmk. 373

1976, July 4 Litho. *Perf. 13½*

215	A36	8p black & multi	.40	.40
216	A36	9p black & multi	.50	.50
217	A36	25p black & multi	1.10	1.10
		Nos. 215-217 (3)	2.00	2.00

American Bicentennial. No. 215 also for the 20th anniv. of Bahamas Long Range Proving Ground (extension) Agreement.

Queen in Coronation Coach — A37

Designs: 8p, Prince Philip on Ascension Island, 1957, vert. 12p, Queen leaving Buckingham Palace in coronation coach.

Perf. 14x13½, 13½x14

1977, Feb. 7 Litho. Wmk. 373

218	A37	8p multicolored	.20	.20
219	A37	12p multicolored	.25	.25
220	A37	25p multicolored	.45	.45
		Nos. 218-220 (3)	.90	.90

Reign of Queen Elizabeth II, 25th anniv.

Water Pipe in Tunnel — A38

5p, Breakneck Valley wells. 12p, Break tank in pipe line, horiz. 25p, Dam & reservoir, horiz.

1977, June 27 Litho. *Perf. 14½*

221	A38	3p multicolored	.20	.20
222	A38	5p multicolored	.20	.20
223	A38	12p multicolored	.50	.30
224	A38	25p multicolored	1.00	.60
		Nos. 221-224 (4)	1.90	1.30

Water supplies constructed by Royal Marines, 1832 and 1881.

Mars Bay Site, 1877
A39

Designs: 8p, Mars Bay and instrument sites. 12p, Prof. and Mrs. Gill before their tent. 25p, Map of Ascension.

Perf. 13½x14

1977, Oct. 3 Litho. Wmk. 373

225	A39	3p multicolored	.20	.20
226	A39	8p multicolored	.30	.25
227	A39	12p multicolored	.50	.45
228	A39	25p multicolored	1.00	.85
		Nos. 225-228 (4)	2.00	1.75

Centenary of visit of Prof. David Gill (1843-1914), astronomer, to Ascension.

Elizabeth II Coronation Anniversary Issue

Souvenir Sheet

Common Design Types

Unwmk.

1978, May 21 Litho. *Perf. 15*

229	Sheet of 6	2.50	2.50
a.	CD326 25p Lion of England	.40	.40
b.	CD327 25p Elizabeth II	.40	.40
c.	CD328 25p Green turtle	.40	.40

No. 229 contains 2 se-tenant strips of Nos. 229a-229c, separated by horizontal gutter with commemorative and descriptive inscriptions and showing central part of coronation procession with coach.

East Crater (Broken Tooth) — A40

Volcanoes: 5p, Hollands Crater (Hollow Tooth). 12p, Bears Back. 15p, Green Mountain. 25p, Two Boats village.

1978, Sept. 4 Litho. *Perf. 14½*

230	A40	3p multicolored	.20	.20
231	A40	5p multicolored	.20	.20
232	A40	12p multicolored	.40	.40
233	A40	15p multicolored	.50	.50
234	A40	25p multicolored	.80	.80
	a.	Souvenir sheet, 2 each #230-234	4.25	*5.00*
	b.	Strip of 5, #230-234	2.00	2.00

No. 234b shows panoramic view of volcanic terrain.

Resolution
A41

Capt. Cook's voyages: 8p, Cook's chronometer. 12p, Green turtle. 25p, Cook after Flaxman/Wedgwood medallion.

Litho.; Litho. & Engr. (25p)

1979, Jan. 8 *Perf. 11*

235	A41	3p multicolored	.20	.20
236	A41	8p multicolored	.30	.25
237	A41	12p multicolored	.55	.40
238	A41	25p multicolored	1.10	.85
		Nos. 235-238 (4)	2.15	1.70

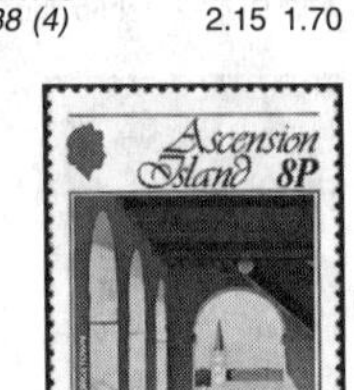

St. Mary's Church, Georgetown — A42

Designs: 12p, Old map of Ascension Island. 50p, Ascension, by Rembrandt.

Wmk. 373

1979, May 24 Litho. *Perf. 14½*

239	A42	8p multicolored	.20	.20
240	A42	12p multicolored	.20	.20
241	A42	50p multicolored	.60	.60
		Nos. 239-241 (3)	1.00	1.00

Ascension Day.

Landing Cable at Comfortless Cove — A43

Eastern Telegraph Co., 80th anniv.: 8p, Cable Ship Anglia. 12p, Map showing cables across the Atlantic, vert. 15p, Cable-laying ship. 25p, Cable and earth station.

1979, Sept. 15

242	A43	3p rose car & black	.20	.20
243	A43	8p dk yel grn & black	.20	.20
244	A43	12p yel bister & black	.30	.30
245	A43	15p violet & black	.35	.35
246	A43	25p deep org & black	.55	.55
		Nos. 242-246 (5)	1.60	1.60

Ascension No. 45 — A44

1979, Dec. 17 Wmk. 373 *Perf. 14*

247 A44 3p shown .20 .20
248 A44 8p No. 73 .20 .20
249 A44 12p No. 14 .20 .20
250 A44 50p Hill portrait, vert. .55 *.75*
Nos. 247-250 (4) 1.15 1.35

Sir Rowland Hill (1795-1879), originator of penny postage.

Anogramma Ascensionis A45

1980, Feb. 18 Litho. *Perf. 14½*

251 A45 3p shown .20 .20
252 A45 6p Xiphopteris ascensionense .20 .20
253 A45 8p Sporobolus caespitosus .20 .20
254 A45 12p Sporobolus durus, vert. .20 .20
255 A45 18p Dryopteris ascensionis, vert. .30 .30
256 A45 24p Marattia purpurascens, vert. .40 .40
Nos. 251-256 (6) 1.50 1.50

17th Century Bottle Post, London 1980 Emblem A46

1980, May 1 Wmk. 373 *Perf. 14*

257 A46 8p shown .20 .20
258 A46 12p 36-gun frigate, 19th century .25 .25
259 A46 15p "Garth Castle," 1863 .30 .30
260 A46 50p "St. Helena," Lockheed C141 .75 .75
a. Souvenir sheet of 4, #257-260 1.75 *2.50*
Nos. 257-260 (4) 1.50 1.50

London 1980 Intl. Stamp Exhib., May 6-14.

Queen Mother Elizabeth Birthday
Common Design Type

1980, Aug. 11 Litho. *Perf. 14*

261 CD330 15p multicolored .50 .50

Lubbock's Yellowtail A47

1980, Sept. 15 Litho. *Perf. 13½x14*

262 A47 3p shown .35 .35
263 A47 10p Resplendent angelfish .50 .50
264 A47 25p Hedgehog butterflyfish .80 .80
265 A47 40p Marmalade razorfish 1.10 1.10
Nos. 262-265 (4) 2.75 2.75

Tortoisen, by Thomas Maxon A48

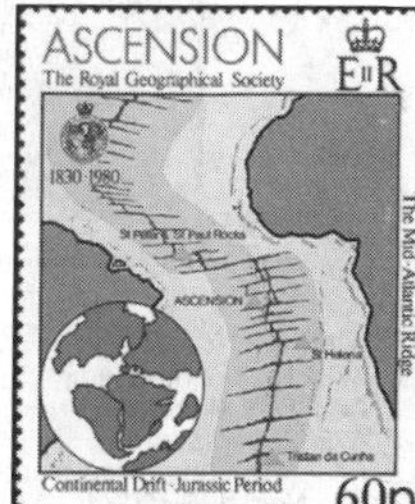

Map of South Atlantic Ridge and Contintental Drift — A49

15p, Wideawake Fair, by Linton Palmer, 1866.

1980, Nov. 17 *Perf. 13½, 14 (60p)*

266 A48 10p multicolored .20 .20
267 A48 15p multicolored .35 .35
268 A49 60p multicolored 1.25 1.25
Nos. 266-268 (3) 1.80 1.80

Royal Geographical Soc., 50th anniv.

Green Mountain Farm, 1881 — A50

Designs: 15p, Two Boats, 1881. 20p, Green Mountain and Two Boats farms, 1981. 30p, Green Mountain Farm, 1981.

1981, Feb. 15 Litho. *Perf. 14*

269 A50 12p multicolored .20 .20
270 A50 15p multicolored .30 .30
271 A50 20p multicolored .35 .35
272 A50 30p multicolored .65 .65
Nos. 269-272 (4) 1.50 1.50

Cable and Wireless Earth Station A51

1981, Apr. 27 Litho. *Perf. 14*

273 Sheet of 10 3.75 3.75
a. A51 15p multicolored .35 .35

Flight of Columbia space shuttle. Gutter contains story of Ascension and space shuttle; margin shows craft and dish antenna.

Poinsettia — A52

1981, May 11 Wmk. 373 *Perf. 13½*

274 A52 1p shown .55 .55
275 A52 2p Clustererd wax flower .65 .65
276 A52 3p Kolanchoe, vert. .65 .65
277 A52 4p Yellow pops .65 .65
278 A52 5p Camel's foot creeper .65 .65
279 A52 8p White oleander .65 .65
280 A52 10p Ascension lily, vert. 1.10 1.10
281 A52 12p Coral plant, vert. 1.25 1.25
282 A52 15p Yellow allamanda 1.00 1.00
283 A52 20p Ascention euphorbia 1.00 1.00
284 A52 30p Flame of the forest, vert. 1.00 1.00
285 A52 40p Bougainvillea 1.00 1.00

Size: 42x53mm

286 A52 50p Solanum 1.00 1.00
287 A52 £1 Ladies petticoat 1.60 1.60
288 A52 £2 Red hibiscus 3.00 3.00
Nos. 274-288 (15) 15.75 15.75

Nos. 275-276, 280, 282-283 and 287 also issued inscribed 1982.

For overprints see Nos. 321-322.

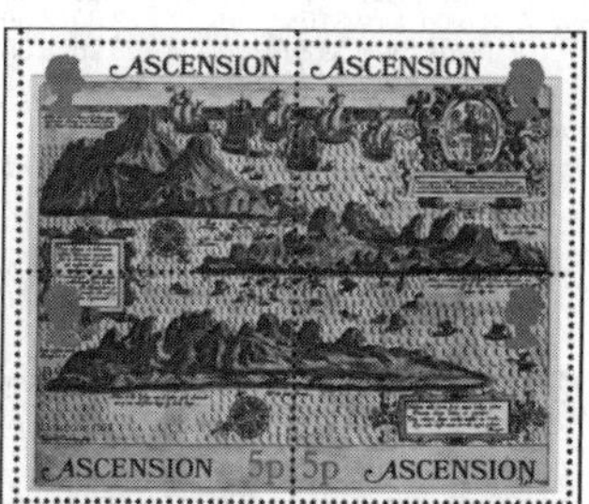

Linschoten's Map of Ascension, 1599 (Illustration reduced) — A53

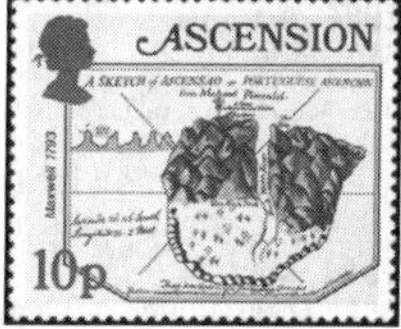

Maxwell's Map of Ascension, 1793 — A54

Designs: Old maps of Ascension.

1981, May 22 *Perf. 14½*

289 A53 Sheet of 4 .60 .60
a.-d. 5p any single .20 .20
290 A54 10p shown .25 .25
291 A54 12p Maxwell, 1793, diff. .35 .35
292 A54 15p Eckberg & Chapman, 1811 .40 .40
293 A54 40p Campbell, 1819 1.10 1.10
Nos. 289-293 (5) 2.70 2.70

Royal Wedding Issue
Common Design Type

1981, July 22 Wmk. 373 *Perf. 14*

294 CD331 10p Bouquet .20 .20
295 CD331 15p Charles .30 .30
296 CD331 50p Couple 1.00 1.00
Nos. 294-296 (3) 1.50 1.50

Nos. 294-296 each se-tenant with label.

Man Shining Cannon — A55

1981, Sept. 14 Litho. *Perf. 14*

297 A55 5p shown .20 .20
298 A55 10p Mountain climbing .20 .20
299 A55 15p First aid treatment .35 .35
300 A55 40p Duke of Edinburgh .80 .80
Nos. 297-300 (4) 1.55 1.55

Duke of Edinburgh's Awards, 25th anniv.

Scouting Year A56

1982, Feb. 22 Litho. *Perf. 14*

301 A56 10p Parallel rope walking .25 .25
302 A56 15p 1st Ascension scout flag .40 .40
303 A56 25p Radio operators .60 .60
304 A56 40p Baden-Powell .75 .75
a. Souvenir sheet of 4 2.25 2.25
Nos. 301-304 (4) 2.00 2.00

No. 304a contains stamps in designs of Nos. 301-304 (30x30mm, perf. 14½, diamond-shape).

Sesquicentennial of Charles Darwin's Visit — A57

1982, Apr. 19

305 A57 10p Portrait .30 .30
306 A57 12p Pistols .40 .40
307 A57 15p Rock crab .55 .55
308 A57 40p Beagle 1.25 1.25
Nos. 305-308 (4) 2.50 2.50

40th Anniv. of Wideawake Airfield — A58

1982, June 15 Litho. *Perf. 14*

309 A58 5p Fairey Swordfish .85 .85
310 A58 10p North American B25C Mitchell 1.00 1.00
311 A58 15p Boeing EC-135N Aria 1.25 1.25
312 A58 50p Lockheed Hercules 1.90 1.90
Nos. 309-312 (4) 5.00 5.00

Princess Diana Issue
Common Design Type
Perf. 14½x14

1982, July 1 Wmk. 373

313 CD333 12p Arms .45 .45
314 CD333 15p Diana .45 .45
315 CD333 25p Wedding .70 .70
316 CD333 50p Portrait 1.40 1.40
Nos. 313-316 (4) 3.00 3.00

Christmas and 50th Anniv. of BBC Overseas Broadcasting — A59

Anniv. Emblem and: 5p, Bush House (London headquarters). 10p, Atlantic relay station. 25p, Lord Reith, first director general. 40p, King George V delivering Christmas address, 1932.

1982, Dec. 20 Litho. *Perf. 14*

317 A59 5p multicolored .20 .20
318 A59 10p multicolored .30 .30
319 A59 25p multicolored .70 .70
320 A59 40p multicolored 1.10 1.10
Nos. 317-320 (4) 2.30 2.30

Nos. 282-283 Overprinted: "1st PARTICIPATION / COMMONWEALTH GAMES 1982"

1982 Litho. *Perf. 13½*

321 A52 15p multicolored .45 .45
322 A52 20p multicolored .55 .55

12th Commonwealth Games, Brisbane, Australia, Sept. 30-Oct. 9.

A60

1983, Mar. 1 *Perf. 14*

323 A60 7p Marasmius echinosphaerus .50 .25
324 A60 12p Chlorophyllum molybdites .75 .45
325 A60 15p Leucocoprinus cepaestipes .90 .55
326 A60 20p Lycoperdon marginatum 1.00 .75
327 A60 50p Marasmiellus distantifolius 1.60 1.50
Nos. 323-327 (5) 4.75 3.50

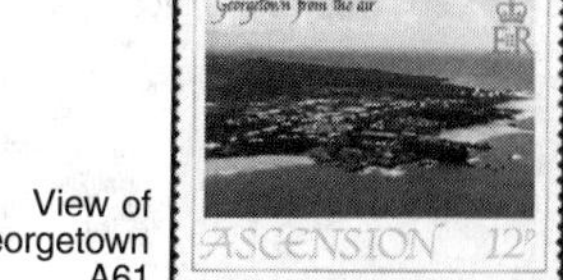

View of Georgetown A61

1983, May 12 Litho. *Perf. 14*

328 A61 12p shown .30 .30
329 A61 15p Farm, Green Mountain .30 .30
330 A61 20p Boatswain Bird Isld. .45 .45
331 A61 60p Telemetry Hill 1.25 1.25
Nos. 328-331 (4) 2.30 2.30

See Nos. 359-362.

Manned Flight Bicentenary — A62

Military Aircraft.

1983, Aug. 1 Wmk. 373 *Perf. 14*

332 A62 12p Wessex Five helicopter .75 .75
333 A62 15p Vulcan B2 .85 .85
334 A62 20p Nimrod MR2P 1.00 1.00
335 A62 60p Victor K2 1.75 1.75
Nos. 332-335 (4) 4.35 4.35

Introduced Species A63

1983, Sept. Litho. Wmk. 373

336 A63 12p Iguanid .40 .40
337 A63 15p Rabbit .50 .50
338 A63 20p Cat .60 .60
339 A63 60p Donkey 1.75 1.75
Nos. 336-339 (4) 3.25 3.25

Tellina Antonii Philippi A64

1983, Nov. 28 Litho. *Perf. 14½*

340 A64 7p shown .20 .20
341 A64 12p Nodipecten nodosus .35 .35
342 A64 15p Cypraea lurida oceanica .45 .45
343 A64 20p Nerita ascensionis gmelin .60 .60
344 A64 50p Micromelo undatus 1.50 1.50
Nos. 340-344 (5) 3.10 3.10

St. Helena Colony, 150th Anniv. — A65

Designs: First issue inscribed Ascension instead of overprinted.

1984, Jan. 10 Litho. *Perf. 14*

345 A65 12p No. 3 .30 .30
346 A65 15p No. 4 .40 .40
347 A65 20p No. 6 .55 .55
348 A65 60p No. 9 1.50 1.50
Nos. 345-348 (4) 2.75 2.75

Souvenir Sheet

Visit of Prince Andrew — A66

1984, Apr. 10 *Perf. 14½x14*

349 Sheet of 2 2.25 2.25
a. A66 12p Andrew .25 .25
b. A66 70p In naval uniform 1.75 1.75

Lloyd's List Issue
Common Design Type

1984, May 28

351 CD335 12p Naval semaphore .40 .25
352 CD335 15p "Southampton Castle" .45 .35
353 CD335 20p Pier Head .55 .45
354 CD335 70p Dane 1.60 1.50
Nos. 351-354 (4) 3.00 2.55

1984 Coins and Wildlife A67

1984, June *Perf. 14*

355 A67 12p One penny, yellowfin tuna .45 .45
356 A67 15p Two pence, donkeys .60 .60
357 A67 20p Fifty pence, green turtle .70 .70
358 A67 70p One pound, sooty terns 1.75 1.75
Nos. 355-358 (4) 3.50 3.50

View Type of 1983

1984, Oct. Litho. Wmk. 373

359 A61 12p Devil's Riding School .25 .25
360 A61 15p St. Mary's Church .35 .35
361 A61 20p Two Boats Village .50 .50
362 A61 70p Ascension Isld. 1.75 1.75
Nos. 359-362 (4) 2.85 2.85

Trees — A68

1985, Mar. 8 Litho. *Perf. 14½x14*

363 A68 7p Bermuda cypress .55 .50
364 A68 12p Norfolk Island pine .60 .55
365 A68 15p Screwpine .70 .65
366 A68 20p Eucalyptus .90 .80
367 A68 65p Spore tree 2.25 2.00
Nos. 363-367 (5) 5.00 4.50

Military Firearms A69

Large guns and insignia: 12p, Thirty-two pounder small bore muzzle loader, c. 1820; Royal Marines hat plate, c. 1816. 15p, Seven-inch rifled muzzle loader, c. 1866; royal cipher. 20p, Seven-pounder rifled muzzle loader, c. 1877; Royal Artillery badge. 70p, HMS Hood 5.5-inch gun; ship crest.

1985, July 21 Wmk. 373 *Perf. 14½*

368 A69 12p multicolored .70 .70
369 A69 15p multicolored .80 .80
370 A69 20p multicolored 1.00 1.00
371 A69 70p multicolored 2.50 2.50
Nos. 368-371 (4) 5.00 5.00

Queen Mother 85th Birthday
Common Design Type

12p, With Duke of York, Balmoral, 1924. 15p, With Princes Andrew and Edward. 20p, At Ascot. 70p, Christening of Prince Henry, Windsor Castle. 75p, Leaving the QEII, 1968.

Perf. 14½x14

1985, June 7 Wmk. 384

372 CD336 12p multicolored .45 .45
373 CD336 15p multicolored .45 .45
374 CD336 20p multicolored .60 .60
375 CD336 70p multicolored 1.50 1.50
Nos. 372-375 (4) 3.00 3.00

Souvenir Sheet

376 CD336 75p multicolored 2.00 2.00

Intl. Youth Year, Girl Guides 75th Anniv. — A70

1985, Oct. 4 Wmk. 373

377 A70 12p Guides' banner .85 .85
378 A70 15p First aid .90 .90
379 A70 20p Camping 1.00 1.00
380 A70 70p Lady Baden-Powell 2.75 2.75
Nos. 377-380 (4) 5.50 5.50

Wildflowers A71 Halley's Comet A72

Wmk. 384

1985, Dec. 6 Litho. *Perf. 14*

381 A71 12p Clerodendrum fragrans .40 .40
382 A71 15p Shell ginger .45 .45
383 A71 20p Cape daisy .60 .60
384 A71 70p Ginger lily 1.75 1.75
Nos. 381-384 (4) 3.20 3.20

1986, Mar. 7

Designs: 12p, Newton's reflector telescope. 15p, Edmond Halley, Old Greenwich Observatory. 20p, Short's Gregorian telescope, comet, 1759. 70p, ICE space probe, Ascension satellite tracking station.

385 A72 12p multicolored .55 .55
386 A72 15p multicolored .65 .65
387 A72 20p multicolored .70 .70
388 A72 70p multicolored 2.00 2.00
Nos. 385-388 (4) 3.90 3.90

Queen Elizabeth II 60th Birthday
Common Design Type

Designs: 7p, Infant photograph, 1926. 15p, 1st worldwide Christmas broadcast, 1952. 20p, Garter Ceremony, Windsor Castle, 1983. 35p, Royal Tour, New Zealand, 1981. £1, Visiting Crown Agents' offices, 1983.

1986, Apr. 21 *Perf. 14x14½*

389 CD337 7p scarlet, blk & sil .20 .20
390 CD337 15p ultra, blk & sil .25 .25
391 CD337 20p green & multi .35 .35
392 CD337 35p violet & multi .65 .65
393 CD337 £1 rose vio & multi 1.75 1.75
Nos. 389-393 (5) 3.20 3.20

For overprints see Nos. 431-435.

AMERIPEX '86 — A73

1986, May 22 *Perf. 14½*

394 A73 12p No. 183 .35 .35
395 A73 15p No. 260 .45 .45
396 A73 20p No. 215 .55 .55
397 A73 70p No. 310 2.00 2.00
Nos. 394-397 (4) 3.35 3.35

Souvenir Sheet

398 A73 75p Statue of Liberty, New York Harbor 2.25 2.25

Statue of Liberty, cent.

Royal Wedding Issue, 1986
Common Design Type

Designs: 15p, Couple kissing. 35p, Andrew in navy uniform, helicopter.

Wmk. 384

1986, July 23 Litho. *Perf. 14*

399 CD338 15p multicolored .45 .45
400 CD338 35p multicolored 1.00 1.00

Ships A74

1986, Oct. 14 Wmk. 384 *Perf. 14½*

401 A74 1p Ganymede, c. 1811 .20 .20
402 A74 2p Kangaroo, c. 1811 .20 .20
403 A74 4p Trinculo, c. 1811 .20 .20
404 A74 5p Daring, c. 1811 .20 .20
405 A74 9p Thais, c. 1811 .25 .25
406 A74 10p Pheasant, 1819 .35 .35
407 A74 15p Myrmidon, 1819 .45 .45
408 A74 18p Atholl, 1825 .55 .55
409 A74 20p Medina, 1830 .60 .60
410 A74 25p Saracen, 1840 .80 .80
411 A74 30p Hydra, c. 1845 .90 .90
412 A74 50p Sealark, 1840 1.40 1.40
413 A74 70p Rattlesnake, 1868 1.90 1.90
414 A74 £1 Penelope, 1889 3.00 3.00
415 A74 £2 Monarch, 1897 6.00 6.00
Nos. 401-415 (15) 17.00 17.00

For surcharges see Nos. 502-504.

Edible Bush Fruits A75

1987, Jan. 29 *Perf. 14*

416 A75 12p Cape gooseberry .35 .35
417 A75 15p Prickly pear .45 .45
418 A75 20p Guava .60 .60
419 A75 70p Loquat 2.00 2.00
Nos. 416-419 (4) 3.40 3.40

1st Manned Space Flight, 25th Anniv. — A76 Military Uniforms, 1815-20 — A77

1987, Mar. 30

420 A76 15p Ignition .45 .45
421 A76 18p Lift-off .55 .55
422 A76 25p Reentry .70 .70
423 A76 £1 Splashdown 3.00 3.00
Nos. 420-423 (4) 4.70 4.70

Souvenir Sheet

424 A76 70p Friendship 7 capsule 2.25 2.25

1987, June 29

Designs: a, Captains in full dress, 1st landing on Ascension. b, Surgeon and sailors at campsite. c, Seaman returning from Dampier's Drip with water supply. d, Midshipman at lookout post. e, Commander and surveyor.

425 Strip of 5 4.00 4.00
a.-e. A77 25p multicolored .80 .80

See Nos. 458, 474, 482, 507.

Butterflies A78

1987, Aug. 10 *Perf. 14½*

426 A78 15p Painted lady .60 .60
427 A78 18p Monarch .75 .75
428 A78 25p Diadem 1.00 1.00
429 A78 £1 Long-tailed blue 3.75 3.75
Nos. 426-429 (4) 6.10 6.10

See Nos. 436-439, 459-462.

Birds — A79

Designs: a, Ascension frigatebirds (males). b, Brown booby, frigatebird, white boobies. c, Frigatebird, white booby. d, Ascension frigatebirds (females). e, Adult frigatebird feeding young.

1987, Oct. 8 Wmk. 373 *Perf. 14*

430 Strip of 5 6.00 6.00
a.-e. A79 25p any single 1.25 1.25

No. 430 has continuous design.
See No. 453.

Nos. 389-393 Ovptd. "40TH WEDDING ANNIVERSARY" in Silver

Perf. 14x14½

1987, Dec. 9 Litho. Wmk. 384

431 CD337 7p scar, blk & sil .20 .20
432 CD337 15p ultra, blk & sil .40 .40
433 CD337 20p green & multi .65 .65
434 CD337 35p violet & multi 1.00 1.00
435 CD337 £1 rose vio & multi 2.75 2.75
Nos. 431-435 (5) 5.00 5.00

40th wedding anniv. of Queen Elizabeth II and Prince Philip.

Insects Type of 1987

1988, Jan. 18 *Perf. 14½*

436 A78 15p Field cricket .60 .60
437 A78 18p Bush cricket .75 .75
438 A78 25p Ladybug 1.00 1.00
439 A78 £1 Burnished brass moth 4.00 4.00
Nos. 436-439 (4) 6.35 6.35

Capt. William Bate (d. 1838), 1st Garrison Commander and Colonial Founder of Ascension
A80

Designs: 9p, Bate's Memorial, St. Mary's Church. 15p, Commodore's Cottage, Cross Hill. 18p, North East or Bate's Cottage, 1833. 25p, Landmarks on map. 70p, Bate and 3 soldiers.

1988, Apr. 14 Litho. *Perf. 14*

440 A80 9p multicolored .35 .35
441 A80 15p multicolored .55 .55
442 A80 18p multicolored .65 .65
443 A80 25p multicolored .90 .90
444 A80 70p multicolored 2.25 2.25
Nos. 440-444 (5) 4.70 4.70

Australia Bicentennial Emblem and Ships Named HMS Resolution — A81

1988, June 23 Litho. *Perf. 14*

445 A81 9p 3-Masted square-rigger, 1667 .35 .35
446 A81 18p 3-Masted square-rigger, 1772 .65 .65
447 A81 25p Navy cruiser, 1892 .90 .90
448 A81 65p Battleship, 1916 2.25 2.25
Nos. 445-448 (4) 4.15 4.15

Australia bicentennial.

Nos. 445-448 Overprinted

Wmk. 384

1988, July 30 Litho. *Perf. 14*

449 A81 9p multicolored .35 .35
450 A81 18p multicolored .65 .65
451 A81 25p multicolored .90 .90
452 A81 65p multicolored 2.25 2.25
Nos. 449-452 (4) 4.15 4.15

SYDPEX '88, July 30-Aug. 7.

Bird Type of 1987

Behaviors of the wideawake tern, Sterna fuscata: a, Two adults, flock overhead. b, Nesting (two birds). c, Nesting (three birds). d, Adult and young. e, Tern flapping its wings.

1988, Aug. 15 *Perf. 14*

453 Strip of 5 6.00 6.00
a.-e. A79 25p any single 1.25 1.25

No. 453 has continuous design.

Lloyds of London, 300th Anniv.

Common Design Type

8p, Lloyd's Coffee House, Tower Street, 1688. 18p, Cable ship Alert, horiz. 25p, Satellite recovery in space, horiz. 65p, Ship Good Hope Castle on fire off Ascension, 1973.

Wmk. 373

1988, Oct. 17 Litho. *Perf. 14*

454 CD341 8p multicolored .30 .30
455 CD341 18p multicolored .60 .60
456 CD341 25p multicolored .85 .85
457 CD341 65p multicolored 2.25 2.25
Nos. 454-457 (4) 4.00 4.00

Military Uniforms Type of 1987

Uniforms of the Royal Marines: a, Marines arrive in Ascension (marines), 1821. b, Semaphore station (officer, marine), 1829. c, Octagonal tank (sergeant), 1831. d, Water pipe tunnel (officers), 1833. e, Constructing barracks (officer), 1834.

1988, Nov. 21

458 Strip of 5 5.00 5.00
a.-e. A77 25p multicolored 1.00 1.00

Insect Type of 1987

Wmk. 384

1989, Jan. 16 Litho. *Perf. 14½*

459 A78 15p Plume moth .60 .60
460 A78 18p Green bottle .70 .70
461 A78 25p Weevil .95 .95
462 A78 £1 Paper wasp 3.75 3.75
Nos. 459-462 (4) 6.00 6.00

Land Crabs, Gecarcinus Lagostoma — A82

1989, Apr. 17

463 A82 15p multi .50 .50
464 A82 18p multi, diff. .65 .65
465 A82 25p multi, diff. .90 .90
466 A82 £1 multi, diff. 3.50 3.50
Nos. 463-466 (4) 5.55 5.55

Miniature Sheet

467 Sheet of 4 5.50 5.50
a. A82 15p like No. 463 .50 .50
b. A82 18p like No. 464 .65 .65
c. A82 25p like No. 465 .85 .85
d. A82 £1 like No. 466 3.50 3.50

Vignettes of Nos. 467a-467d do not have frame.

Moon Landing, 20th Anniv.

Common Design Type

Apollo 7: 15p, Tracking Station, Ascension Is. 18p, Launch, Cape Kennedy. 25p, Mission emblem. 70p, Expended Saturn IVB stage. £1, Lunar landing profile for the Apollo 11 mission.

1989, July 20 *Perf. 14x13½*

Size of Nos. 469-470: 29x29mm

468 CD342 15p multicolored .45 .45
469 CD342 18p multicolored .55 .55
470 CD342 25p multicolored .75 .75
471 CD342 70p multicolored 2.10 2.10
Nos. 468-471 (4) 3.85 3.85

Souvenir Sheet

472 CD342 £1 multicolored 3.00 3.00

Souvenir Sheet

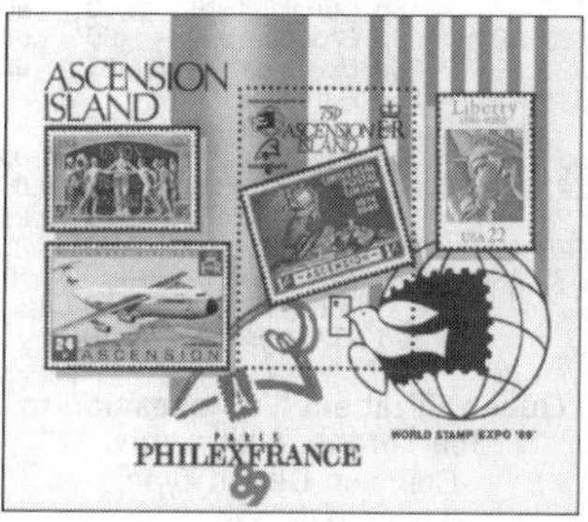

A83

1989, July 7 *Perf. 14x13½*

473 A83 75p Emblems, No. 60 2.50 2.50

Miniature Sheet

World Stamp Expo '89, Washington, DC, and PHILEXFRANCE '89, Paris — A84

The Statue of Liberty and scenes from the centenary celebrations, 1986: a, Operation Sail. b, Face. c, Upper body. d, Three crown points. e, Ships in harbor, view of lower Manhattan. f, Ship in port, New York City.

1989, Aug. 21 Wmk. 373

474 Sheet of 6 2.75 2.75
a.-f. A84 15p any single .45 .45

Devil's Ashpit Tracking Station
A85

1989, Sept. 30 Wmk. 384 *Perf. 14*

475 Sheet, 5 each #a.-b. 6.75 6.75
a. A85 18p shown .55 .55
b. A85 25p US space shuttle launch .80 .80

Termination of NASA tracking operations, begun in 1965, at the station.

Shells and Mollusks
A86

Wmk. 384

1989, Nov. 6 Litho. *Perf. 14*

476 A86 8p *Strombus latus* .30 .30
477 A86 18p *Tonna galea* .60 .60
478 A86 25p *Harpa doris* .85 .85
479 A86 £1 *Charonia variegata* 3.25 3.25
Nos. 476-479 (4) 5.00 5.00

Donkeys — A87

Perf. 14 on 3 Sides

1989, Nov. 17 Litho. Wmk. 384

Booklet Stamps

480 A87 18p shown .50 .50
a. Booklet pane of 6 3.00
481 A87 25p Green turtle .75 .75
a. Booklet pane of 4 3.00

No. 480a sold for £1.

Military Type of 1987

Royal Navy equipment, c. 1815-1820: a, Seaman's pistol, hat, cutlass. b, Midshipman's belt buckle, button, sword, hat. c, Surgeon's hat, sword, instrument chest. d, Captain's hat, telescope, sword. e, Admiral's epaulet, megaphone, hat, pocket.

1990, Feb. 12 Litho. *Perf. 14*

482 Strip of 5 4.75 4.75
a.-e. A77 25p any single .95 .95

World Wildlife Fund — A88

Frigate birds *(Fregata aquila)*: 9p, Family group. 10p, Chick. 11p, Male in flight. 15p, Female and immature in flight.

Perf. 14½x14

1990, Mar. 5 Litho. Wmk. 373

483 A88 9p multicolored *1.25* 1.00
484 A88 10p multicolored *1.50* 1.25
485 A88 11p multicolored *1.75* 1.50
486 A88 15p multicolored *2.50* 2.00
Nos. 483-486 (4) *7.00* 5.75

Great Britain Nos. 1-2
A89

Exhibition emblem and: 18p, Early Ascension cancellations. 25p, Unloading mail at Wideawake Airfield. £1, Main P.O., Royal Mail van.

1990, May 3 Litho. *Perf. 14*

487 A89 9p shown .30 .30
488 A89 18p multicolored .60 .60
489 A89 25p multicolored .85 .85
490 A89 £1 multicolored 3.25 3.25
Nos. 487-490 (4) 5.00 5.00

Penny Black 150th anniv., Stamp World London '90.

Queen Mother, 90th Birthday

Common Design Types

1990, Aug. 4 Wmk. 384 *Perf. 14x15*

491 CD343 25p Portrait, 1940 .85 .85

Perf. 14½

492 CD344 £1 King, Queen with soldiers 3.25 3.25

Garth Castle, 1910 — A90

Designs: 18p, RMS St. Helena, 1982. 25p, Launching new RMS St. Helena, 1989. 70p, Duke of York launching new RMS St. Helena. £1, New RMS St. Helena.

Wmk. 373

1990, Sept. 13 Litho. *Perf. 14½*
493 A90 9p multicolored .35 .35
494 A90 18p multicolored .65 .65
495 A90 25p multicolored .90 .90
496 A90 70p multicolored 2.50 2.50
Nos. 493-496 (4) 4.40 4.40

Souvenir Sheet

497 A90 £1 multicolored 3.50 3.50

See St. Helena Nos. 535-539, Tristan da Cunha Nos. 482-486.

Christmas — A91

Sculpture (8p) and paintings of Madonna and Child by: 8p, Felici. 18p, Unknown artist. 25p, Gebhard. 65p, Gritti.

1990, Oct. 24 *Perf. 14*
498 A91 8p multicolored .30 .30
499 A91 18p multicolored .65 .65
500 A91 25p multicolored .90 .90
501 A91 65p multicolored 3.25 3.25
Nos. 498-501 (4) 5.10 5.10

Nos. 410, 412 & 414 Ovptd. in Silver "BRITISH FOR 175 YEARS"

1991, Feb. 5 Wmk. 384 *Perf. 14½*
502 A74 25p on #410 1.00 1.00
503 A74 50p on #412 2.00 2.00
504 A74 £1 on #414 4.00 4.00
Nos. 502-504 (3) 7.00 7.00

Elizabeth & Philip, Birthdays
Common Design Types

1991, June 18
505 CD345 25p multicolored .80 .80
506 CD346 25p multicolored .80 .80
a. Pair, #505-506 + label 1.60 1.60

Military Uniforms Type of 1987

Royal Marines Equipment 1821-1844: a, Officer's shako, epaulettes, belt plate, button. b, Officer's cap, sword, epaulettes, belt plate. c, Drum Major's shako with cords, staff. d, Sergeant's shako, chevrons, belt plate, canteen. e, Drummer's drum, sticks, shako.

1991, Aug. 1 Wmk. 373 *Perf. 14*
507 A77 25p Strip of 5, #a.-e. 4.00 4.00

Atlantic Relay Station, 25th Anniv. A92

15p, BBC Atlantic relay station. 18p, English Bay transmitters. 25p, Satellite receiving station. 70p, Antenna support tower.

1991, Sept. 17 Wmk. 384 *Perf. 14½*
508 A92 15p multi .50 .50
509 A92 18p multi .60 .60
510 A92 25p multi, vert. .85 .85
511 A92 70p multi, vert. 2.50 2.50
Nos. 508-511 (4) 4.45 4.45

Christmas A93

Designs: 8p, St. Mary's Church, exterior. 18p, St. Mary's Church, interior. 25p, Grotto of Our Lady of Ascension, exterior. 65p, Grotto of Our Lady of Ascension, interior.

1991, Oct. 1 *Perf. 14*
512 A93 8p multicolored .30 .30
513 A93 18p multicolored .60 .60
514 A93 25p multicolored .85 .85
515 A93 65p multicolored 2.25 2.25
Nos. 512-515 (4) 4.00 4.00

Fish A94

Wmk. 373

1991, Dec. 10 Litho. *Perf. 14*
516 A94 1p Blackfish .20 .20
517 A94 2p Five finger .20 .20
518 A94 4p Resplendent angelfish .20 .20
519 A94 5p Silver fish .20 .20
520 A94 9p Gurnard .30 .30
521 A94 10p Blue dad .35 .35
522 A94 15p Cunning fish .50 .50
523 A94 18p Grouper .60 .60
524 A94 20p Moray eel .65 .65
525 A94 25p Hardback soldierfish .85 .85
526 A94 30p Blue marlin 1.00 1.00
527 A94 50p Wahoo 1.65 1.65
528 A94 70p Yellowfin tuna 2.25 2.25
529 A94 £1 Blue shark 3.25 3.25
530 A94 £2.50 Bottlenose dolphin 8.50 8.50
Nos. 516-530 (15) 20.70 20.70

Queen Elizabeth II's Accession to the Throne, 40th Anniv.
Common Design Type

Wmk. 373

1992, Feb. 6 Litho. *Perf. 14*
531 CD349 9p multicolored .30 .30
532 CD349 15p multicolored .50 .50
533 CD349 18p multicolored .60 .60
534 CD349 25p multicolored .85 .85
535 CD349 70p multicolored 2.25 2.25
Nos. 531-535 (5) 4.50 4.50

Discovery of America, 500th Anniv. — A95

Wmk. 373

1992, Feb. 18 Litho. *Perf. 14*
536 A95 9p STV Eye of the Wind .30 .30
537 A95 18p STV Soren Larsen .60 .60
538 A95 25p Pinta, Santa Maria, & Nina .85 .85
539 A95 70p Columbus, Santa Maria 2.25 2.25
Nos. 536-539 (4) 4.00 4.00

World Columbian Stamp Expo '92, Chicago and Genoa '92 Intl. Philatelic Exhibitions.

Wideawake Airfield, 50th Anniv. — A96

Wmk. 373

1992, May 5 Litho. *Perf. 14*
540 A96 15p Control tower .50 .50
541 A96 18p Nose hangar .60 .60
542 A96 25p Construction work .85 .85
543 A96 70p Laying fuel pipeline 2.25 2.25
Nos. 540-543 (4) 4.20 4.20

Ascension's Participation in Falkland Islands' Liberation, 10th Anniv. — A97

Wmk. 373

1992, June 12 Litho. *Perf. 14*
544 A97 15p Nimrod Mk.2 .50 .50
545 A97 18p VC10 .60 .60
546 A97 25p Wessex HU Mk.5 helicopter .85 .85
547 A97 65p Vulcan B2 2.25 2.25
Nos. 544-547 (4) 4.20 4.20

Souvenir Sheet

548 A97 Sheet of 4, #a.-d. 5.00 5.00

Surtax for Soldiers', Sailors' and Airmen's Families Association.

#548a, 15p + 3p like #544. b, 18p + 4p like #545. c, 25p + 5p like #546. d, 65p + 13p like #547.

Christmas A98

Children's drawings: 8p, Snowman, rocks, candle. 18p, Underwater Santa, Christmas tree. 25p, Hello, bells. 65p, Nativity Scene, angel.

Wmk. 384

1992, Oct. 13 Litho. *Perf. 14*
549 A98 8p multicolored .30 .30
550 A98 18p multicolored .70 .70
551 A98 25p multicolored .95 .95
552 A98 65p multicolored 2.50 2.50
Nos. 549-552 (4) 4.45 4.45

Yellow Canary — A99

Wmk. 373

1993, Jan. 12 Litho. *Perf. 14½*
553 A99 15p Singing male .40 .40
554 A99 18p Adult male, female .55 .55
555 A99 25p Young calling for food .80 .80
556 A99 70p Mixed flock 2.25 2.25
Nos. 553-556 (4) 4.00 4.00

Royal Air Force, 75th Anniv.
Common Design Type

Designs: 20p, Sopwith Snipe. No. 558, Supermarine Southampton. 30p, Avro Anson. 70p, Vickers Wellington 1C.

No. 561a, Westland Lysander. b, Gloster Meteor. c, DeHavilland Comet. d, British Aerospace Nimrod.

Wmk. 373

1993, Apr. 1 Litho. *Perf. 14*
557 CD350 20p multicolored .60 .60
558 CD350 25p multicolored .70 .70
559 CD350 30p multicolored .85 .85
560 CD350 70p multicolored 2.25 2.25
Nos. 557-560 (4) 4.40 4.40

Souvenir Sheet

561 CD350 25p Sheet of 4, #a.-d. 3.00 3.00

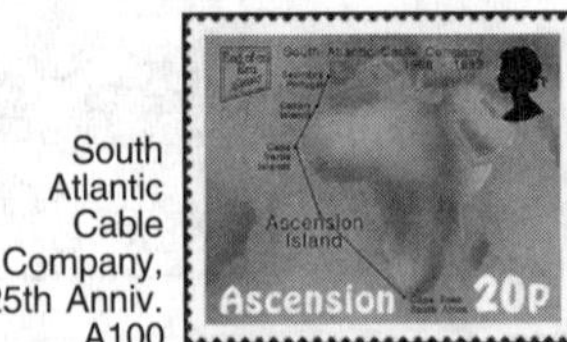

South Atlantic Cable Company, 25th Anniv. A100

Designs: 20p, Map showing cable route. 25p, Cable ship laying cable. 30p, Map of Ascension. 70p, Cable ship off Ascension.

Perf. 14x14½

1993, June 8 Litho. Wmk. 384
562 A100 20p multicolored .60 .60
563 A100 25p multicolored .75 .75
564 A100 30p multicolored .90 .90
565 A100 70p multicolored 2.00 2.00
Nos. 562-565 (4) 4.25 4.25

Flowers A101

Perf. 14x14½

1993, Aug. 3 Litho. Wmk. 384
566 A101 20p Lantana camara .60 .60
567 A101 25p Moonflower .75 .75
568 A101 30p Hibiscus .90 .90
569 A101 70p Frangipani 2.00 2.00
Nos. 566-569 (4) 4.25 4.25

Christmas A102

Designs: 12p, Child mailing Christmas card. 20p, Mail loaded onto Tristar. 25p, Plane in flight. 30p, Mail unloaded at Wideawake Airfield. 65p, Child reading card, Georgetown.

Perf. 14½x14

1993, Oct. 19 Litho. Wmk. 373
570 A102 12p multicolored .35 .35
571 A102 20p multicolored .60 .60
572 A102 25p multicolored .75 .75
573 A102 30p multicolored .90 .90
574 A102 65p multicolored 2.00 2.00
a. Souvenir sheet of 5, #570-574 4.50 4.50
Nos. 570-574 (5) 4.60 4.60

Stamps from No. 574a show a continuous design, while Nos. 570-574 have white borders on sides.

Prehistoric Aquatic Reptiles — A103

1994, Jan. 25 Wmk. 373 *Perf. 14*
575 A103 12p Ichthyosaurus .35 .35
576 A103 20p Metriorhynchus .60 .60
577 A103 25p Mosasaurus .75 .75
578 A103 30p Elasmosaurus .90 .90
579 A103 65p Plesiosaurus 1.90 1.90
Nos. 575-579 (5) 4.50 4.50

Ovptd. with Hong Kong '94 Emblem

1994, Feb. 18
580 A103 12p on #575 .35 .35
581 A103 20p on #576 .60 .60
582 A103 25p on #577 .75 .75
583 A103 30p on #578 .90 .90
584 A103 65p on #579 1.90 1.90
Nos. 580-584 (5) 4.50 4.50

Green Turtle A104

20p, Four on beach. 25p, Crawling in sand. #587, Crawling from sea. 65p, Swimming.

No. 589a, Side view, crawling from sea. b, Digging nest. c, Hatchlings heading to sea. d, Digging nest, diff.

1994, Mar. 22
585 A104 20p multicolored .60 .60
586 A104 25p multicolored .75 .75
587 A104 30p multicolored .90 .90
588 A104 65p multicolored 1.90 1.90
Nos. 585-588 (4) 4.15 4.15

Souvenir Sheet

589 A104 30p Sheet of 4, #a.-d. 3.50 3.50

Civilian Ships
A105

Ships serving during Falkland Islands War, 1982: 20p, Tug Yorkshireman. 25p, Minesweeper support ship RMS St. Helena. 30p, Oil tanker British ESK. 65p, Cruise liner Uganda, hospital ship.

1994, June 14

590 A105 20p multicolored .60 .60
591 A105 25p multicolored .75 .75
592 A105 30p multicolored .90 .90
593 A105 65p multicolored 1.90 1.90
Nos. 590-593 (4) 4.15 4.15

Sooty Tern
A106

1994, Aug. 16

594 A106 20p Chick .60 .60
595 A106 25p Juvenile .75 .75
596 A106 30p Brooding adult .90 .90
597 A106 65p Displaying male 1.90 1.90
Nos. 594-597 (4) 4.15 4.15

Souvenir Sheet

598 A106 £1 Dread 3.00 3.00

Christmas
A107

Donkeys: 12p, Mare with foal. 20p, Young adult. 25p, Foal. 30p, Adult, egrets. 65p, Adult.

1994, Oct. 11 ***Perf. 14x14½***

599 A107 12p multicolored .40 .40
600 A107 20p multicolored .60 .60
601 A107 25p multicolored .75 .75
602 A107 30p multicolored .95 .95
603 A107 65p multicolored 2.00 2.00
Nos. 599-603 (5) 4.70 4.70

Flowers
A108

20p, Leonurus japonicus. 25p, Periwinkle. 30p, Four o'clock. 65p, Blood flower.

1995, Jan. 10 ***Perf. 14***

604 A108 20p multi, vert. .60 .60
605 A108 25p multi .75 .75
606 A108 30p multi, vert. .95 .95
607 A108 65p multi 2.00 2.00
Nos. 604-607 (4) 4.30 4.30

Island Scenes, c. 1895
A109

Designs: 12p, Horse-drawn wagon, Two Boats, Green Mountain. 20p, Island stewards' store. 25p, Royal Navy headquarters, barracks. 30p, Police office. 65p, Pier head.

1995, Mar. 7 **Wmk. 384** ***Perf. 14½***

608 A109 12p sepia .35 .35
609 A109 20p sepia .60 .60
610 A109 25p sepia .75 .75
611 A109 30p sepia .90 .90
612 A109 65p sepia 2.00 2.00
Nos. 608-612 (5) 4.60 4.60

End of World War II, 50th Anniv.
Common Design Types

Designs: 20p, 5.5-inch guns taken from HMS Hood, 1941. 25p, Fairey Swordfish, first aircraft to land at Ascension. 30p, HMS Dorsetshire patrolling South Atlantic. 65p, HMS Devonshire patrolling South Atlantic.
£1, Reverse of War Medal, 1939-45.

1995, May 8 **Wmk. 373** ***Perf. 14***

613 CD351 20p multicolored .60 .60
614 CD351 25p multicolored .75 .75
615 CD351 30p multicolored .90 .90
616 CD351 65p multicolored 2.00 2.00
Nos. 613-616 (4) 4.25 4.25

Souvenir Sheet

617 CD352 £1 multicolored 3.00 3.00

Butterflies — A110

1995, Sept. 1 **Wmk. 384**

618 A110 20p Long-tailed blue .60 .60
619 A110 25p Painted lady .75 .75
620 A110 30p Diadem .90 .90
621 A110 65p African monarch 2.00 2.00
Nos. 618-621 (4) 4.25 4.25

Souvenir Sheet

622 A110 £1 Red admiral 3.00 3.00

Singapore '95 (#622).

Christmas
A111

Designs based on children's drawings:
12p, Santa on boat. 20p, Santa on wall. 25p, Santa in chimney. 30p, Santa on dolphin. 65p, South Atlantic run.

1995, Oct. 10 **Wmk. 373**

623 A111 12p multicolored .35 .35
624 A111 20p multicolored .60 .60
625 A111 25p multicolored .75 .75
626 A111 30p multicolored .90 .90
627 A111 65p multicolored 2.00 2.00
Nos. 623-627 (5) 4.60 4.60

Mollusks
A112

12p, Cypraea lurida. 25p, Cypraea spurca. 30p, Harpa doris. 65p, Umbraculum umbraculum.

Wmk. 384

1996, Jan. 10 **Litho.** ***Perf. 14***

628 A112 12p multicolored .35 .35
629 A112 25p multicolored .75 .75
630 A112 30p multicolored .90 .90
631 A112 65p multicolored 2.00 2.00
a. Strip of 4, #628-631 4.00 4.00

Queen Elizabeth II, 70th Birthday
Common Design Type

Various portraits of Queen, scenes of Ascension:
20p, St. Marys Church. 25p, The Residency. 30p, Roman Catholic Grotto. 65p, The Exiles Club.

Wmk. 384

1996, Apr. 22 **Litho.** ***Perf. 13½***

632 CD354 20p multicolored .65 .65
633 CD354 25p multicolored .80 .80
634 CD354 30p multicolored 1.00 1.00
635 CD354 65p multicolored 2.00 2.00
Nos. 632-635 (4) 4.45 4.45

CAPEX '96
A113

Island transport: 20p, US Army Jeep. 25p, 1924 Citreon 7.5HP two seater. 30p, 1930 Austin Ten-four Tourer. 65p, Series 1 Land Rover.

Wmk. 384

1996, June 8 **Litho.** ***Perf. 14***

636 A113 20p multicolored .65 .65
637 A113 25p multicolored .80 .80
638 A113 30p multicolored 1.00 1.00
639 A113 65p multicolored 2.00 2.00
Nos. 636-639 (4) 4.45 4.45

Birds and Their Young — A114

1p, Madeiran storm petrel. 2p, Red-billed tropicbird. 4p, Indian mynah. 5p, House sparrow. 7p, Common waxbill. 10p, White tern. 12p, Francolin. 15p, Brown noddy. 20p, Yellow canary. 25p, Black noddy. 30p, Red-footed booby. 40p, Yellow-billed tropicbird. 65p, Brown booby. £1, Masked booby. £2, Sooty tern. £3, Ascension frigate bird.

Wmk. 373

1996, Aug. 12 **Litho.** ***Perf. 13***

640 A114 1p multicolored .20 .20
641 A114 2p multicolored .20 .20
642 A114 4p multicolored .20 .20
643 A114 5p multicolored .20 .20
644 A114 7p multicolored .20 .20
645 A114 10p multicolored .30 .30
646 A114 12p multicolored .35 .35
647 A114 15p multicolored .45 .45
648 A114 20p multicolored .60 .60
649 A114 25p multicolored .70 .70
650 A114 30p multicolored .90 .90
651 A114 40p multicolored 1.10 1.10
652 A114 65p multicolored 1.90 1.90
a. Sheet of 1, perf. 14 2.10 2.10
653 A114 £1 multicolored 3.00 3.00
a. Souvenir sheet of 1 3.25 3.25
654 A114 £2 multicolored 6.00 6.00
655 A114 £3 multicolored 9.00 9.00
Nos. 640-655 (16) 25.30 25.30

No. 652a for Hong Kong '97. Issued 2/3/97.
No. 653a for return of Hong Kong to China. Issued 7/1/97.

BBC Atlantic Relay Station, 30th Anniv.
A115

Various views of relay station: 20p, 25p, Towers. 30p, Towers, buildings. 65p, Satellite dish, towers, beach.

1996, Sept. 9 **Wmk. 384** ***Perf. 14***

656 A115 20p multicolored .65 .65
657 A115 25p multicolored .80 .80
658 A115 30p multicolored 1.00 1.00
659 A115 65p multicolored 2.00 2.00
Nos. 656-659 (4) 4.45 4.45

Christmas
A116

Santa Claus: 12p, On satellite dish. 20p, Playing golf. 25p, By beach. 30p, On RAF Tristar. 65p, Aboard RMS St. Helena.

Perf. 14x14½

1996, Sept. 23 **Litho.** **Wmk. 373**

660 A116 12p multicolored .40 .40
661 A116 20p multicolored .65 .65
662 A116 25p multicolored .80 .80
663 A116 30p multicolored 1.00 1.00
664 A116 65p multicolored 2.00 2.00
Nos. 660-664 (5) 4.85 4.85

UNICEF, 50th anniv.

A117

Wmk. 373

1997, Jan. 7 **Litho.** ***Perf. 14½***

665 A117 20p Date palm .65 .65
666 A117 25p Mauritius hemp .80 .80
667 A117 30p Norfolk Island pine 1.00 1.00
668 A117 65p Dwarf palm 2.00 2.00
Nos. 665-668 (4) 4.45 4.45

Hong Kong '97.

A118

Wmk. 373

1997, Apr. 1 **Litho.** ***Perf. 14½***

Flag, ship or aircraft: 12p, Great Britain Red Ensign, tanker Maserk Ascension. 25p, RAF Ensign, Tristar. 30p, NASA emblem, Space Shuttle Atlantis. 65p, Royal Navy White Ensign, HMS Northumberland.

669 A118 12p multicolored .40 .40
670 A118 25p multicolored .80 .80
671 A118 30p multicolored .95 .95
672 A118 65p multicolored 2.00 2.00
Nos. 669-672 (4) 4.15 4.15

Herbs
A119

Designs: a, Solanum sodomaeum. b, Ageratum conyzoides. c, Leonurus sibricus. d, Cerastium vulgatum. e, Commelina diffusa.

Perf. 14x14½

1997, June 7 **Litho.** **Wmk. 373**

673 A119 30p Strip of 5, #a.-e. 5.00 5.00

A120

Birds — A121

Queen Elizabeth II and Prince Philip, 50th Wedding Anniv.: No. 674, Queen Elizabeth II. No. 675, Prince Philip playing polo. No. 676, Queen petting horse. No. 677, Prince Philip. No. 678, Prince Philip, Queen Elizabeth II. No.

679, Prince Harry, Prince William riding horses.

£1.50, Queen Elizabeth, Prince Philip riding in open carriage.

Wmk. 384

1997, July 10 Litho. *Perf. 13½*

674	A120	20p multicolored	.65	.65
675	A120	20p multicolored	.65	.65
a.		Pair, #674-675	1.40	1.40
676	A120	25p multicolored	.85	.85
677	A120	25p multicolored	.85	.85
a.		Pair, #676-677	1.75	1.75
678	A120	30p multicolored	1.00	1.00
679	A120	30p multicolored	1.00	1.00
a.		Pair, #678-679	2.00	2.00
		Nos. 674-679 (6)	5.00	5.00

Souvenir Sheet

680	A120	£1.50 multicolored	4.75	4.75

Perf. 14 on 3 Sides

1997, Sept. 1 Litho. Wmk. 373

Booklet Stamps

681	A121	15p like #644	.50	.50
682	A121	35p like #648	1.10	1.10
a.		Booklet pane, 2 ea #681-682	3.25	
		Complete booklet, #682a	3.25	

Game Fish — A122

Perf. 14x14½

1997, Sept. 3 Litho. Wmk. 373

683	A122	12p Black marlin	.35	.35
684	A122	20p Atlantic sailfish	.65	.65
685	A122	25p Swordfish	.80	.80
686	A122	30p Wahoo	.95	.95
687	A122	£1 Yellowfin tuna	3.25	3.25
		Nos. 683-687 (5)	6.00	6.00

A123

A124

St. Mary's Church (Christmas): 15p, Interior view. 35p, Stained glass window, Madonna and Child. 40p, Stained glass window, Falklands, 1982. 50p, Stained glass window.

Wmk. 384

1997, Oct. 1 Litho. *Perf. 14*

688	A123	15p multicolored	.50	.50
689	A123	35p multicolored	1.10	1.10
690	A123	40p multicolored	1.25	1.25
691	A123	50p multicolored	1.75	1.75
		Nos. 688-691 (4)	4.60	4.60

Wmk. 373

1998, Feb. 10 Litho. *Perf. 14*

Insects: 15p, Cactoblastis cactorum. 35p, Teleonemia scrupulosa. 40p, Neltumius arizonensis. 50p, Algarobius prosopis.

692	A124	15p multicolored	.50	.50
693	A124	35p multicolored	1.10	1.10
694	A124	40p multicolored	1.25	1.25
695	A124	50p multicolored	1.60	1.60
		Nos. 692-695 (4)	4.45	4.45

Diana, Princess of Wales (1961-97)

Common Design Type

a, In polka-dotted dress. b, In yellow blouse. c, With longer hair style. d, Holding flowers.

Perf. 14½x14

1998, Mar. 31 Litho. Wmk. 373

696	CD355	35p Sheet of 4, #a.-d.	5.25	5.25

No. 696 sold for £1.40 + 20p, with surtax from international sales being donated to the Princess Diana Memorial Fund and surtax from national sales being donated to designated local charity.

Royal Air Force, 80th Anniv.

Common Design Type of 1993 Re-inscribed

15p, Fairey Fawn. 35p, Vickers Vernon. 40p, Supermarine Spitfire F-22. 50p, Bristol Britannia C2.

No. 701: a, Blackburn Kangaroo. b, SE5a. c, Curtiss Kittyhawk III. d, Boeing Fortress II (B-17).

Wmk. 384

1998, Apr. 1 Litho. *Perf. 14*

697	CD350	15p multicolored	.70	.70
698	CD350	35p multicolored	1.60	1.60
699	CD350	40p multicolored	1.90	1.90
700	CD350	50p multicolored	2.25	2.25
		Nos. 697-700 (4)	6.45	6.45

Souvenir Sheet

701	CD350	50p Sheet of 4, #a.-d.	6.75	6.75

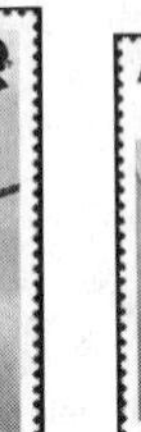

Birds — A125

Island Sports — A126

Wmk. 373

1998, June 15 Litho. *Perf. 14*

702	A125	15p Swallow	.50	.50
703	A125	25p House martin	.80	.80
704	A125	35p Cattle egret	1.10	1.10
705	A125	40p Swift	1.25	1.25
706	A125	50p Allen's gallinule	1.60	1.60
		Nos. 702-706 (5)	5.25	5.25

Wmk. 373

1998, Aug. 17 Litho. *Perf. 14*

707	A126	15p Cricket	.50	.50
708	A126	35p Golf	1.10	1.10
709	A126	40p Soccer	1.25	1.25
710	A126	50p Trapshooting	1.60	1.60
		Nos. 707-709 (3)	2.85	2.85

Christmas A127

Designs: 15p, Children's nativity play. 35p, Santa arriving on Ascension. 40p, Santa arriving at a party. 50p, Carol singers.

Wmk. 373

1998, Oct. 1 Litho. *Perf. 14*

711	A127	15p multicolored	.50	.50
712	A127	35p multicolored	1.10	1.10
713	A127	40p multicolored	1.25	1.25
714	A127	50p multicolored	1.60	1.60
		Nos. 711-714 (4)	4.45	4.45

World War II Aircraft A128

15p, Curtiss C-46 Commando. 35p, Douglas C-47 Dakota. 40p, Douglas C-54 Skymaster. 50p, Consolidated Liberator Mk.V. £1.50, Consolidated Liberator LB-30.

Wmk. 373

1999, Jan. 20 Litho. *Perf. 14*

715	A128	15p multicolored	.50	.50
716	A128	35p multicolored	1.10	1.10
717	A128	40p multicolored	1.25	1.25
718	A128	50p multicolored	1.60	1.60
		Nos. 715-718 (4)	4.45	4.45

Souvenir Sheet

719	A128	£1.50 multicolored	4.75	4.75

Winston Churchill, 125th birth anniv.

Australia '99, World Stamp Expo A129

Union Castle Mail Ships: 15p, SS Glengorm Castle. 35p, SS Gloucester Castle. 40p, SS Durham Castle. 50p, SS Garth Castle. £1, HMS Endeavour.

Perf. 14½x14

1999, Mar. 5 Litho. Wmk. 373

720	A129	15p multicolored	.50	.50
721	A129	35p multicolored	1.10	1.10
722	A129	40p multicolored	1.25	1.25
723	A129	50p multicolored	1.60	1.60
		Nos. 720-723 (4)	4.45	4.45

Souvenir Sheet

724	A129	£1 multicolored	3.25	3.25

World Wildlife Fund — A130

Fairy tern: No. 725, Two on branch. No. 726, One on branch. No. 727, Adult feeding chick. No. 728, Two in flight.

Wmk. 384

1999, Apr. 27 Litho. *Perf. 14½*

725	A130	10p multicolored	.35	.35
726	A130	10p multicolored	.35	.35
727	A130	10p multicolored	.35	.35
728	A130	10p multicolored	.35	.35
a.		Sheet of 16, 4 each #725-728	5.75	5.75
		Nos. 725-728 (4)	1.40	1.40

Wedding of Prince Edward and Sophie Rhys-Jones

Common Design Type

Perf. 13¾x14

1999, June 19 Litho. Wmk. 384

729	CD356	50p Separate portraits	1.60	1.60
730	CD356	£1 Couple	3.25	3.25

1st Manned Moon Landing, 30th Anniv.

Common Design Type

Designs: 15p, Command and service modules. 35p, Moon from Apollo 11. 40p, Devil's Ashpit Tracking Station. 50p, Lunar module lifts off moon.

£1.50, Looking at earth from moon.

Perf. 14x13¾

1999, July 20 Litho. Wmk. 384

731	CD357	15p multicolored	.50	.50
732	CD357	35p multicolored	1.10	1.10
733	CD357	40p multicolored	1.25	1.25
734	CD357	50p multicolored	1.60	1.60
		Nos. 731-734 (4)	4.45	4.45

Souvenir Sheet

Perf. 14

735	CD357	£1.50 multicolored	4.75	4.75

No. 735 contains one 40mm circular stamp.

Queen Mother's Century

Common Design Type

Queen Mother: 15p, With King George VI, Winston Churchill. 35p, With Prince Charles. 40p, At Clarence House, 88th birthday. 50p, With drummers at Clarence House.

£1.50, With Titanic.

Wmk. 384

1999, Aug. 20 Litho. *Perf. 13½*

736-739	CD358	Set of 4	4.50	4.50

Souvenir Sheet

740	CD358	£1.50 black	5.00	5.00

Christmas A131

Wmk. 384

1999, Oct. 6 Litho. *Perf. 13¾*

741	A131	15p 3 children	.50	.50
742	A131	35p 2 children, hats	1.10	1.10
743	A131	40p 2 children, bed	1.25	1.25
744	A131	50p 4 children	1.75	1.75
		Nos. 741-744 (4)	4.60	4.60

Cable and Wireless, Cent. A132

Perf. 13¼x13¾

1999, Dec. 13 Litho. Wmk. 373

745	A132	15p CS Anglia	.50	.50
746	A132	35p CS Cambria	1.10	1.10
747	A132	40p Map	1.25	1.25
748	A132	50p CS Colonia	1.60	1.60
		Nos. 745-748 (4)	4.45	4.45

Souvenir Sheet

749	A132	£1.50 CS Seine	5.00	5.00

Turtle Project — A133

15p, Young turtles. 35p, Turtle, trail at left. 40p, Turtle with tracking device on beach. 50p, Turtle with tracking device heading to sea.

No. 754: a, Turtle head, rock. b, Like 15p. c, Turtle on beach, sea. d, Turtle in surf.

2000, Mar. 8 Litho. *Perf. 13¾*

750	A133	15p multi	.50	.50
751	A133	35p multi	1.10	1.10
752	A133	40p multi	1.25	1.25
753	A133	50p multi	1.60	1.60
		Nos. 750-753 (4)	4.45	4.45

Souvenir Sheet

Perf. 14

754	A133	25p Sheet of 4, #a-d	3.25	3.25

No. 754 contains four 40x26mm stamps.

Prince William, 18th Birthday

Common Design Type

William: 15p, As toddler, vert. 35p, Wearing suit and wearing cap, vert. 40p, Holding flowers, and in parka. 50p, In suit and in checked shirt.

Perf. 13¾x14¼, 14¼x13¾

2000, June 21 Litho. Wmk. 373

Stamps With White Border

755	CD359	15p multi	.45	.45
756	CD359	35p multi	1.00	1.00
757	CD359	40p multi	1.25	1.25
758	CD359	50p multi	1.50	1.50
		Nos. 755-758 (4)	4.20	4.20

Souvenir Sheet

Stamps Without White Border

Perf. 14¼

759		Sheet of 5	4.50	4.50
a.	CD359	10p multi	.30	.30
b.	CD359	15p multi	.45	.45
c.	CD359	35p multi	1.00	1.00
d.	CD359	40p multi	1.25	1.25
e.	CD359	50p multi	1.50	1.50

Forts A134

Designs: 15p, 1815 fortifications. 35p, Fort Thornton, 1817. 40p, Fort Hayes, 1860. 50p, Fort Bedford, 1940.

Wmk. 373

2000, Aug. 14	**Litho.**	***Perf. 14***
760-763 A134 Set of 4		4.00 4.00

Christmas — A135

Carols: 15p, I Saw Three Ships. 25p, Silent Night. 40p, Away in a Manger. 90p, Hark, the Herald Angels Sing.

2000, Oct. 16	**Wmk. 384**
764-767 A135 Set of 4	5.00 5.00

Souvenir Sheet

New Year 2001 (Year of the Snake) — A136

Turtles: a, 25p, Green. b, 40p, Loggerhead. Illustration reduced.

Wmk. 373

2001, Feb. 1	**Litho.**	***Perf. 14½***
768 A136 Sheet of 2, #a-b		1.90 1.90

Hong Kong 2001 Stamp Exhibition.

Sinking of the Roebuck, Tercentenary A137

Designs: 15p, Capt. William Dampier. 35p, Drawing of the Roebuck, horiz. 40p, Cave dwelling at Dampier's Drip, horiz. 50p, Map.

2001, Feb. 25	**Litho.**	***Perf. 14***
769-772 A137 Set of 4		4.00 4.00

Discovery of Ascension Island, 500th Anniv. — A138

Designs: 15p, Alfonso de Albuquerque. 35p, Portuguese caravel. 40p, Cantino map. 50p, Rear admiral Sir George Cockburn.

Perf. 14¾x14¼

2001, Mar. 25	**Litho.**	**Wmk. 384**
773-776 A138 Set of 4		4.00 4.00

The Age of Victoria A139

Designs: 15p, Great Britain Type A1 with Ascension cancel, vert. 25p, Parade, 1901. 35p, HMS Phoebe. 40p, The Red Lion, 1863. 50p, Queen Victoria, vert. 65p, Sir Joseph Dalton Hooker, botanist, vert. £1.50, Queen Victoria's Funeral.

Wmk. 373

2001, May 24	**Litho.**	***Perf. 14***
777-782 A139 Set of 6		6.50 6.50

Souvenir Sheet

783 A139 £1.50 multi	4.25 4.25

Souvenir Sheet

Belgica 2001 Intl. Stamp Exhibition, Brussels — A140

Ascension tourist sites: a, 35p, Islander Hostel. b, 35p, The Residency. c, 40p, The Red Lion. d, 40p, Turtle Ponds.

Wmk. 373

2001, June 9	**Litho.**	***Perf. 14¼***
784 A140 Sheet of 4, #a-d		4.25 4.25

Birdlife International World Bird Festival A141

Ascension frigate bird: 15p, On rock with wings outstretched, vert. 35p, Chick, with mouth open, vert. 40p, Pair in flight. 50p, Close-up of bird.

Perf. 13¾x14¼, 14¼x13¾

2001, Oct. 1	**Litho.**	**Wmk. 373**
785-788 A141 Set of 4		4.00 4.00

Souvenir Sheet

789 Sheet, #785-788, 789a, perf. 14¼	4.25 4.25
a. A141 10p Two birds on rock	.25 .25

Reign Of Queen Elizabeth II, 50th Anniv. Issue

Common Design Type

Designs: Nos. 790, 794a, 15p, Princess Elizabeth with dog. Nos. 791, 794b, 35p, In 1978. Nos. 792, 794c, 40p, In 1946. Nos. 793, 794d, 50p, In 1998. No. 794e, 60p, 1955 portrait by Annigoni (38x50mm).

Perf. 14¼x14½, 13¾ (#794e)

2002, Feb. 6	**Litho.**	**Wmk. 373**

With Gold Frames

790-793 CD360 Set of 4	4.00 4.00

Souvenir Sheet

Without Gold Frames

794 CD360 Sheet of 5, #a-e	5.75 5.75

Falkland Islands War, 20th Anniv. A142

Designs: 15p, Troops landing at English Bay. 35p, Weapons testing at Ascension. 40p, HMS Hermes and helicopter. 50p, Vulcan bomber at Wideawake Airfield.

Wmk. 373

2002, June 14	**Litho.**	***Perf. 14***
795-798 A142 Set of 4		4.25 4.25

Queen Mother Elizabeth (1900-2002)

Common Design Type

Designs: 35p, Wearing flowered bonnet (sepia photograph). 40p, Wearing pink hat.

No. 801: a, 50p, Wearing hat (sepia photograph). b, £1, Wearing blue hat.

Wmk. 373

2002, Aug. 5	**Litho.**	***Perf. 14¼***

With Purple Frames

799-800 CD361 Set of 2	2.25 2.25

Souvenir Sheet

Without Purple Frames

Perf. 14½x14¼

801 CD361 Sheet of 2, #a-b	4.75 4.75

Flowers and Local Scenes A143

Designs: 10p, Vinca, Travellers palm. 15p, Mexican poppy, Broken Tooth. 20p, Ascension lily, St. Mary's Church. 25p, Goatweed, Boatswain Bird Island. 30p, Mauritius hemp, Cannon. 35p, Frangipani, Guest House. 40p, Ascension spurge, Wideawake tern. 50p, Lovechaste, Pier head. 65p, Yellowboy, Sisters Peak. 90p, Persian lilac, Two Boats School. £2, Wild currant, Green turtle. £5, Coral tree, Wideawake Airfield.

Wmk. 373

2002, Aug. 28		**Litho.**	***Perf. 14***	
802	A143 10p multi		.30	.30
803	A143 15p multi		.45	.45
804	A143 20p multi		.60	.60
805	A143 25p multi		.75	.75
806	A143 30p multi		.90	.90
807	A143 35p multi		1.10	1.10
808	A143 40p multi		1.25	1.25
809	A143 50p multi		1.50	1.50
810	A143 65p multi		2.00	2.00
811	A143 90p multi		2.75	2.75
812	A143 £2 multi		6.00	6.00
813	A143 £5 multi		15.00	15.00
	Nos. 802-813 (12)		32.60	32.60

Christmas — A144

Paintings: 15p, Ecce Ancilla Dominii, by Dante Gabriel Rossetti. 25p, The Holy Family and a Shepherd, by Titian, horiz. 35p, Christ Carrying the Cross, by Ambrogio Bergognone. 75p, Sketch for "The Ascension," by Benjamin West.

Perf. 14x14¼, 14¼x14

2002, Oct. 9	**Litho.**	**Wmk. 373**
814-817 A144 Set of 4		4.75 4.75

POSTAGE DUE STAMPS

Outline Map of Ascension — D1

1986		**Litho.**	***Perf. 15x14***	
J1	D1	1p beige & brown	.20	.20
J2	D1	2p orange & brown	.20	.20
J3	D1	5p org ver & brn	.20	.20
J4	D1	7p violet & black	.20	.30
J5	D1	10p ultra & black	.25	.35
J6	D1	25p pale green & blk	.60	.70
		Nos. J1-J6 (6)	1.65	1.95

AUSTRALIAN STATES

NEW SOUTH WALES

LOCATION — Southeast coast of Australia in the South Pacific Ocean
GOVT. — British Crown Colony
AREA — 309,432 sq. mi.
POP. — 1,500,000 (estimated, 1900)
CAPITAL — Sydney

In 1901 New South Wales united with five other British colonies to form the Commonwealth of Australia. Stamps of Australia are now used.

12 Pence = 1 Shilling
20 Shillings = 1 Pound

Watermarks

Wmk. 12- Crown and Single-lined A

Wmk. 13- Large Crown and Double-lined A

Wmk. 49- Double-lined Numerals Corresponding with the Value

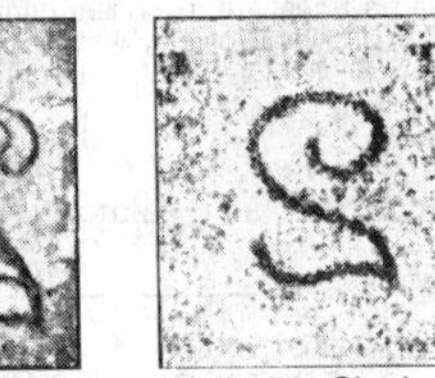

Wmk. 50- Single-lined Numeral

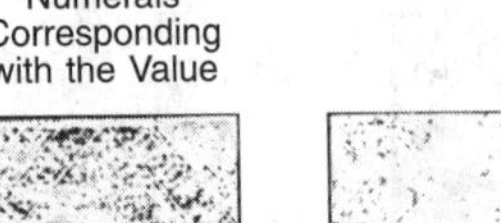

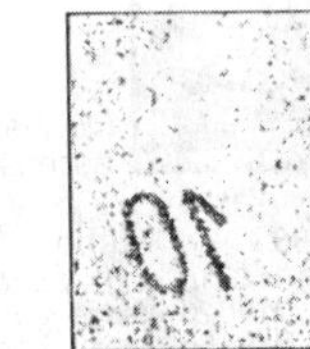

Wmk. 51- Single-lined Numeral

Wmk. 52- Single-lined Numeral

Wmk. 53- 5/-

Wmk. 54- Small Crown and NSW

Wmk. 55- Large Crown and NSW

Wmk. 56- NSW

Wmk. 57- 5/- NSW in Diamond

Wmk. 58- 20/- NSW in Circle

Wmk. 70- V and Crown

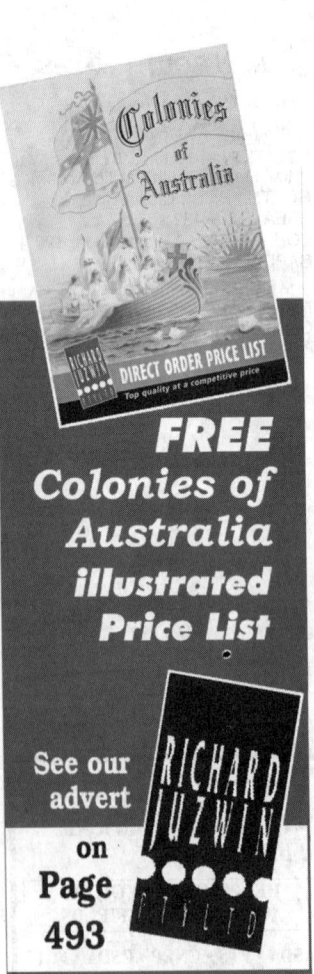

Wmk. 199- Crown and A in Circle

Values for unused stamps are for examples with original gum as defined in the catalogue introduction except for Nos. 1-20 which are rarely found with gum and are valued without gum. Very fine examples of Nos. 35-100, F3-F5, J1-J10 and O1-O40 will have perforations touching the framelines or design on one or more sides due to the narrow spacing of the stamps on the plates and imperfect perforation methods. Stamps with perfs clear of the design on all four sides are scarce and will command higher prices.

Seal of the Colony
A1 A2

A1 has no clouds. A2 has clouds added to the design, except in pos. 15.

1850 Unwmk. Engr. *Imperf.*

1	A1 1p red, *yelsh wove*	4,000.	400.
b.	1p red, *bluish wove*	4,000.	350.
2	A2 1p red, *yelsh wove*	2,500.	275.
b.	1p red, *yellowish laid*	4,000.	450.
c.	1p red, *bluish wove*	2,500.	275.
e.	1p red, *bluish laid*		
f.	Hill unshaded	4,250.	450.
g.	No clouds	4,250.	450.
h.	No trees	4,250.	450.

Twenty-five varieties.

Stamps from early impressions of the plate sell at considerably higher prices.

No. 1 was reproduced by the collotype process in a souvenir sheet distributed at the London International Stamp Exhibition 1950. The paper is white.

Plate I — A3

Plate II — A4

Plate I: Vertically lined background.

Plate I re-touched: Lines above and below "POSTAGE" and "TWO PENCE" deepened. Outlines of circular band around picture also deepened.

Plate II (First re-engraving of Plate I): Horizontally lined background; the bale on the left side is dated and there is a dot in the star in each corner.

Plate II retouched: Dots and dashes added in lower spandrels.

Plate I

Late (worn plate) Impressions

3	A3 2p blue, *yelsh wove*	1,675.	150.
a.	Early impressions	4,500.	375.

Twenty-four varieties.

Plate I, Retouched

4	A3 2p blue, *yelsh wove*	3,000.	275.

Twelve varieties.

Plate II

Late (worn plate) Impressions

5	A4 2p blue, *yelsh wove*	1,750.	160.
a.	2p blue, *bluish wove*	1,750.	160.
b.	2p blue, *grayish wove*	1,750.	160.
c.	"CREVIT" omitted	—	375.
d.	Pick and shovel omitted	—	300.
e.	No whip	*3,000.*	210.
h.	Early impressions	*3,000.*	225.

Plate II, Retouched

5F	A4 2p blue, *bluish wove*	2,350.	175.
g.	No whip	—	275.
i.	"CREVIT" omitted		375.

Eleven varieties.

Plate III
A5

Plate IV
A6

Plate III (Second re-engraving of Plate I): The bale is not dated and, with the exception of Nos. 7, 10 and 12, it is single-lined. There are no dots in the stars.

Plate IV (Third re-engraving of Plate I): The bale is double-lined and there is a circle in the center of each star.

1850-51

6	A5 2p bl, *grayish wove*	2,100.	175.
a.	Fan with 6 segments	—	350.
b.	Double-lined bale	—	225.
c.	No whip	—	250.
7	A6 2p blue, *bluish wove* ('51)	2,350.	150.
a.	2p ultra, *white laid*	3,000.	175.
b.	2p blue, *grayish wove*	2,350.	150.
c.	Fan with 6 segments	—	210.
d.	No clouds	—	210.

Twenty-four varieties.

Plate V — A7

A8

Plate V (Fourth re-engraving of Plate I): There is a pearl in the fan-shaped ornament below the central design.

1850-51

8	A7 2p blue, *grayish wove* ('51)	2,350.	150.
a.	2p ultra, *yellowish laid*	3,500.	275.
b.	Fan with 6 segments	—	250.
c.	Pick and shovel omitted	—	250.
9	A8 3p grn, *bluish wove*	2,350.	225.
a.	3p green, *yellowish wove*	3,500.	240.
b.	3p green, *yellowish laid*	4,650.	425.
c.	3p green, *bluish laid*	4,650.	425.
e.	No whip		350.

Twenty-four varieties of #8, twenty-five of #9.

Queen Victoria
A9 A10

TWO PENCE
Plate I - Background of wavy lines.
Plate II - Stars in corners.
Plate III (Plate I re-engraved) - Background of crossed lines.

SIX PENCE
Plate I - Background of fine lines.
Plate II (Plate I re-engraved) - Background of coarse lines.

1851 Yellowish Wove Paper

10	A9 1p carmine	1,675.	225.00
b.	No leaves to right of "SOUTH"	*3,250.*	360.00
c.	Two leaves to right of "SOUTH"	*3,250.*	450.00
d.	"WALE"	*3,250.*	450.00
11	A9 2p ultra, Plate I	800.00	90.00

1852 Bluish Laid Paper

12	A9 1p orange brown	3,000.	375.
a.	No leaves to right of "SOUTH"		550.
b.	Two leaves to right of "SOUTH"		650.
c.	"WALE"		650.

1852-55

Bluish or Grayish Wove Paper

13	A9 1p red	850.00	110.00
a.	1p carmine	1,000.	125.00
b.	No leaves to right of "SOUTH"		225.00
c.	Two leaves to right of "SOUTH"		290.00
d.	"WALE"		290.00
14	A9 2p blue, Plate I	650.00	30.00
a.	2p ultramarine	700.00	30.00
b.	2p slate	625.00	30.00
15	A10 2p blue, Plate II ('53)	1,050.	87.50
a.	"WAEES"	*2,250.*	425.00
16	A9 2p blue, Plate III ('55)	450.00	55.00
17	A9 3p green	1,250.	140.00
a.	3p emerald	1,550.	200.00
b.	"WACES"	—	350.00
18	A9 6p brown, Plate I	1,900.	250.00
a.	6p black brown	1,900.	275.00
b.	"WALLS"	*4,250.*	525.00
19	A9 6p brown, Plate II	1,900.	275.00
a.	6p bister brown	1,900.	275.00
20	A9 8p yellow ('53)	3,500.	600.00
a.	8p orange	3,600.	675.00
b.	No leaves to right of "SOUTH"		1,250.

The plates of the 1, 2, 3 and 8p each contained 50 varieties and those of the 6p 25 varieties.

The 2p, plate II, 6p, plate II, and 8p have been reprinted on grayish blue wove paper. The reprints of the 2p have the spandrels and background much worn. Most of the reprints of the 6p have no floreate ornaments to the right and left of "South." On all the values the wreath has been retouched.

Type of 1851 and:

A11

A12

A13

A14

1854-55 **Wmk. 49**

23 A9 1p orange 160.00 17.00
- **a.** No leaves to right of "SOUTH" 325.00 80.00
- **b.** Two leaves to right of "SOUTH" 450.00 110.00
- **c.** "WALE" 450.00 125.00

24 A9 2p blue 100.00 10.00
- **a.** 2p ultramarine 100.00 10.50

25 A9 3p green 190.00 27.50
- **a.** "WACES" 110.00
- **b.** Watermarked "2" 2,800. 1,500.

Value for No. 25b is for copy with the design cut into.

26 A11 5p green 950.00 575.00
27 A12 6p sage green 425.00 32.50
28 A12 6p brown 450.00 32.50
- **a.** Watermarked "8" 1,650. 100.00

29 A12 6p gray 425.00 52.50
- **a.** Watermarked "8" 1,650. 100.00

30 A13 8p orange ('55) 4,750. 1,000.
- **a.** 8p yellow 4,750. 1,000.

31 A14 1sh pale red brown 750.00 75.00
- **a.** 1sh red 700.00 75.00
- **b.** Watermarked "8" 2,000. 175.00

See Nos. 38-42, 56, 58, 65, 67.

Nos. 38-42 exist with wide margins. Copies with perforations trimmed are often offered as Nos. 26, 30, and 30a.

A15

A16

1856

32 A15 1p red 140.00 21.00
- **a.** 1p orange 140.00 21.00
- **b.** Printed on both sides *2,000.* *2,000.*

33 A15 2p blue 125.00 8.00
- **a.** Watermarked "1" *4,500.*
- **b.** Watermarked "5" 550.00 55.00
- **c.** Watermarked "8"

34 A15 3p green 800.00 80.00
- **a.** 3p yellow green 750.00 75.00
- **b.** Watermarked "2" *3,600.*

Nos. 32-34 (3) 1,065. 109.00

The two known copies of No. 33c are in museums. Both are used.

The 1p has been reprinted in orange on paper watermarked Small Crown and NSW, and the 2p in deep blue on paper watermarked single lined "2." These reprints are usually overprinted "SPECIMEN."

See Nos. 34C-37, 54, 63, 90.

1859 **Litho.**

34C A15 2p light blue 725.00

1860-63 Engr. Wmk. 49 ***Perf. 13***

35 A15 1p red 60.00 8.50
- **a.** 1p orange 100.00 8.50
- **b.** Perf. 12x13 *1,800.*
- **c.** Perf. 12 95.00 15.00

36 A15 2p blue, perf. 12 100.00 10.00
- **a.** Watermarked "1" *3,250.*
- **c.** Perf. 12x13 *2,400.* 225.00

37 A15 3p blue green 50.00 10.50
- **a.** 3p yellow green 52.50 9.00
- **b.** 3p deep green 52.50 10.00
- **c.** Watermarked "6" 95.00 12.50
- **d.** Perf. 12 600.00 45.00

38 A11 5p dark green 42.50 19.00
- **a.** 5p yellow green 80.00 32.50
- **b.** Perf. 12 160.00 45.00

39 A12 6p brown, perf. 12 275.00 52.50
- **a.** 6p gray, perf. 12 275.00 42.50

40 A12 6p violet 60.00 6.25
- **a.** 6p aniline lilac 950.00 140.00
- **b.** Watermarked "5" 360.00 30.00
- **c.** Watermarked "12" 1,200. 20.00
- **e.** Perf. 12 275.00 18.00

41 A13 8p yellow 150.00 40.00
- **a.** 8p orange 175.00 37.50
- **b.** Perf. 12 2,100. 625.00

42 A14 1sh rose 85.00 8.00
- **a.** 1sh carmine 80.00 7.50
- **c.** Perf. 12 425.00 50.00

Nos. 35-42 (8) 822.50 154.75

1864 **Wmk. 50** ***Perf. 13***

43 A15 1p red 45.00 15.00

1861-80 **Wmk. 53** ***Perf. 13***

44 A16 5sh dull violet 225.00 35.00
- **a.** 5sh purple 200.00 40.00
- **b.** 5sh dull violet, perf. 12 1,500. 360.00
- **c.** 5sh purple, perf. 12 — 45.00
- **d.** 5sh purple, perf. 10 225.00 45.00
- **e.** 5sh purple, perf. 12x10 400.00 60.00

See No. 101. For overprint see No. O11.

Reprints are perf. 10 and overprinted "REPRINT" in black.

A17

A18

1862-65 Typo. Unwmk. ***Perf. 13***

45 A17 1p red ('65) 95.00 30.00
- **a.** Perf. 14 72.50 50.00

46 A18 2p blue 57.50 3.00
- **a.** Perf. 14 75.00 37.50

1863-64 **Wmk. 50** ***Perf. 13***

47 A17 1p red 21.50 1.90
- **a.** Watermarked "2" 95.00 13.00

48 A18 2p blue 12.00 .65
- **a.** Watermarked "1" 140.00 4.50

1862 **Wmk. 49** ***Perf. 13***

49 A18 2p blue 52.50 7.50
- **a.** Watermarked "5" 125.00 16.00
- **b.** Perf. 12x13 *550.00*
- **c.** Perf. 12 140.00 30.00

See Nos. 52-53, 61-62, 70-76.

A19

A20

1867, Sept. Wmk. 51, 52 ***Perf. 13***

50 A19 4p red brown 45.00 3.25
- **a.** Imperf.

51 A20 10p lilac 12.00 3.50
- **b.** Horiz. pair, imperf. between *550.00*

No. 51 exists imperf, with Specimen overprint. Value $24.

See Nos. 55, 64, 91, 97, 117, 129.

A21

A22

A23

Typo.; Engr. (3p, 5p, 8p)

1871-84 **Wmk. 54** ***Perf. 13***

52 A17 1p red 6.50 .50
- **a.** Perf. 10 360.00 27.50
- **b.** Perf. 13x10 17.00 .50
- **c.** Horiz. pair imperf. between *625.00*

53 A18 2p blue 8.00 .50
- **a.** Imperf.
- **b.** Horiz. pair, imperf. vert. *725.00*
- **c.** Perf. 10 360.00 22.50
- **d.** Perf. 13x10 8.00 .50
- **e.** Perf. 12x13
- **f.** Perf. 11x12 240.00 37.50

54 A15 3p green ('74) 19.00 2.75
- **a.** Perf. 11 200.00 140.00
- **b.** Perf. 12 — 225.00
- **c.** Perf. 10x12 160.00 32.50
- **d.** Perf. 12x11 125.00 45.00
- **e.** Perf. 10 65.00 5.75
- **f.** Perf. 13x10 125.00 15.00

55 A19 4p red brown ('77) 57.50 6.50
- **a.** Perf. 10 275.00 47.50
- **b.** Perf. 13x10 75.00 4.00

56 A11 5p dk grn, perf. 10 ('84) 16.00 9.50
- **a.** Imperf.
- **b.** Perf. 12 300.00 125.00
- **c.** Perf. 10x12 110.00 40.00
- **d.** Perf. 13x10

57 A21 6p lilac ('72) 42.50 1.25
- **a.** Imperf.
- **b.** Perf. 13x10 52.50 1.60
- **c.** Perf. 10 300.00 13.50

58 A13 8p yellow ('77) 100.00 16.00
- **a.** Imperf.
- **b.** Perf. 10 300.00 25.00
- **c.** Perf. 13x10 200.00 22.50

59 A22 9p on 10p red brown, perf. 12 (Bk) 12.50 4.50
- **a.** Double surcharge, blk & bl 175.00
- **b.** Perf. 10x12 325.00 250.00
- **c.** Perf. 10 12.00 4.50
- **d.** Perf. 12x11 16.00 5.25
- **e.** Perf. 11x12 — —
- **f.** Perf. 13 22.50 5.75
- **g.** Perf. 11 35.00 7.25
- **h.** Perf. 10x11 45.00 10.50

60 A23 1sh black ('76) 75.00 3.00
- **a.** Imperf. — —
- **b.** Perf. 13x10 250.00 5.75
- **c.** Perf. 10 275.00 12.00
- **d.** Perf. 11 — —

Nos. 52-60 (9) 337.00 44.50

The surcharge on #59 measures 15mm. See #66, 68. For overprints see #O1-O10.

Typo.; Engr. (3p, 5p, 8p)

1882-91 **Wmk. 55** ***Perf. 11x12***

61 A17 1p red 5.25 .30
- **a.** Perf. 10 9.00 .30
- **b.** Perf. 10x13 125.00 6.25
- **c.** Perf. 10x12 300.00 75.00
- **d.** Perf. 12x11 140.00
- **e.** Perf. 10x11 *550.00* 140.00
- **f.** Perf. 11 175.00
- **g.** Perf. 13 750.00 375.00

62 A18 2p blue 11.50 .20
- **a.** Perf. 10 24.00 .30
- **b.** Perf. 13x10 80.00 2.25
- **c.** Perf. 13 550.00 125.00
- **d.** Perf. 12x10 375.00 95.00
- **e.** Perf. 11 125.00
- **f.** Perf. 12x11 375.00 125.00
- **g.** Perf. 11x10 550.00 140.00
- **h.** Perf. 12 250.00

63 A15 3p green 5.25 .95
- **a.** Imperf., pair 175.00
- **b.** Vert. pair, imperf. btwn. 200.00
- **c.** Horiz. pair, imperf. vert.
- **d.** Double impression —
- **e.** Perf. 10 6.50 .75
- **f.** Perf. 11 6.50 1.00
- **g.** Perf. 12 8.50 1.25
- **h.** Perf. 12x11 7.25 1.25
- **i.** Perf. 10x12 30.00 3.00
- **m.** Perf. 10x11 18.00 1.40
- **n.** Perf. 12x10 30.00 3.25

64 A19 4p red brown 27.50 1.25
- **a.** Perf. 10 45.00 3.00
- **b.** Perf. 10x12 190.00 75.00
- **c.** Perf. 12 240.00 95.00

65 A11 5p dk blue green 7.25 .70
- **a.** Imperf., pair 200.00
- **b.** Perf. 11 12.00 .65
- **c.** Perf. 10 12.00 .90
- **d.** Perf. 12 12.00 .90
- **e.** Perf. 10x12 30.00
- **f.** 5p green, perf. 12x11 7.50 .75
- **g.** 5p green, perf. 11x10 47.50 5.75
- **h.** 5p green, perf. 12x10 75.00 3.25
- **i.** 5p green, perf. 10x11 45.00 4.25
- **j.** 5p green, perf. 11 8.50 .65

66 A21 6p lilac, perf. 10 42.50 1.25
- **a.** Horiz. pair, imperf. between *750.00*
- **b.** Perf. 10x12 45.00 1.40
- **c.** Perf. 11x12 75.00 11.50
- **d.** Perf. 12 85.00 9.50
- **e.** Perf. 11x10 55.00 2.25
- **f.** Perf. 11 85.00 7.50
- **g.** Perf. 10x13 325.00

67 A13 8p yellow, perf. 10 95.00 15.00
- **a.** Perf. 11 95.00 18.00
- **b.** Perf. 12 160.00 26.00
- **c.** Perf. 10x12 125.00 32.50

68 A23 1sh black 60.00 2.75
- **a.** Perf. 10x13 — —
- **b.** Perf. 10 60.00 2.75
- **c.** Perf. 11 200.00 11.00
- **d.** Perf. 10x12 — 240.00

Nos. 61-68 (8) 254.25 22.40

Nos. 63 and 65 exist with two types of watermark 55 - spacings of 1mm or 2mm between crown and NSW.

See No. 90. For surcharges and overprints see Nos. 92-94, O12-O19.

The 1, 2, 4, 6, 8p and 1sh have been reprinted on paper watermarked Large Crown and NSW. The 1, 2, 4p and 1sh are perforated 11x12, the 6p is perforated 10 and the 8p 11. All are overprinted "REPRINT," the 1sh in red and the others in black.

Perf. 11x12

1886-87 **Typo.** **Wmk. 56**

Bluish Revenue Stamp Paper

70 A17 1p scarlet 5.50 1.60
- **a.** Perf. 10 16.00 4.25

71 A18 2p dark blue 14.00 2.25
- **a.** Perf. 10 57.50 5.75

For overprint, see No. O20.

A24

Perf. 12 (#73-75), 12x10 (#72, 75A) and Compound

1885-86

"POSTAGE" in Black

72 A24 5sh green & vio 400.00 75.00
- **a.** Perf. 10 — —

73 A24 10sh rose & vio 1,100. 225.00

74 A24 £1 rose & vio 2,500. —
- **a.** Perf. 13 — 2,100.

"POSTAGE" in Blue

Bluish Paper

75 A24 10sh rose & vio 175.00 62.50
- **b.** Perf. 10 675.00 175.00
- **c.** Perf. 12x11 — —

White Paper

75A A24 £1 rose & vio 3,400. *1,600.*

For overprints, see Nos. O21-O23.

The 5sh with black overprint and the £1 with blue overprint have been reprinted on paper watermarked NSW. They are perforated 12x10 and are overprinted "REPRINT" in black.

1894 **White Paper**

"POSTAGE" in Blue

76 A24 10sh rose & violet 160.00 40.00
- **a.** Double overprint

See No. 108B.

View of Sydney
A25

Emu
A26

Captain Cook — A27

Victoria and Coat of Arms — A28

Lyrebird
A29

Kangaroo
A30

1888-89 **Wmk. 55** ***Perf. 11x12***

77 A25 1p violet 3.75 .20
- **a.** Perf. 12 5.25 .20
- **b.** Perf. 12x11½ 16.00 .90

78 A26 2p blue 5.75 .20
- **a.** Imperf., pair 110.00
- **b.** Perf. 12 8.00 .20
- **c.** Perf. 12x11½ 11.50 .20

79 A27 4p brown 10.50 2.75
- **a.** Perf. 12x11½ 29.00 7.00
- **b.** Perf. 12 25.00 3.00
- **c.** Perf. 11 400.00 125.00
- **d.** Imperf.

80 A28 6p carmine rose 20.00 3.25
- **a.** Perf. 12 20.00 8.00
- **b.** Perf. 12x11½ 32.50 3.75

81 A29 8p red violet 16.00 2.75
- **a.** Perf. 12 16.00 2.75
- **b.** Perf. 12x11½ 37.50 10.50

82 A30 1sh vio brown ('89) 20.00 1.25
- **a.** Imperf., pair 650.00
- **b.** Perf. 12x11½ 21.00 1.25
- **c.** Perf. 12 24.00 1.25

Nos. 77-82 (6) 76.00 10.40

First British settlement in Australia, cent. For overprints see Nos. O24-O29.

1888 Wmk. 56 *Perf. 11x12*
83 A25 1p violet 13.00 1.25
84 A26 2p blue 60.00 6.00

See #104B-106C, 113-115, 118, 125-127, 130.

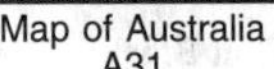
Map of Australia
A31

Governors Capt. Arthur Phillip (above) and Lord Carrington
A32

1888-89 Wmk. 53 *Perf. 10*
85 A31 5sh violet ('89) 200.00 50.00
86 A32 20sh ultra 250.00 125.00

See #88, 120. For overprints see #O30-O31.

1890 Wmk. 57 *Perf. 10*
87 A31 5sh violet 150.00 27.50
a. Perf. 11 190.00 35.00
b. Perf. 10x11 175.00 27.50
c. Perf. 12 300.00 40.00

Perf. 11x12
Wmk. 58
88 A32 20sh ultra 160.00 75.00
a. Perf. 11 185.00 80.00
b. Perf. 10, cobalt blue 290.00 125.00
c. Perf. 12 250.00 125.00

For overprints see Nos. O32-O33.

"Australia"
A33

Victoria
A37

1890, Dec. 22 Wmk. 55 *Perf. 11x12*
89 A33 2½p ultra 2.90 .50
a. Perf. 12 10.00 .50
b. Perf. 12x11½ 60.00 —

For overprint see No. O35.

Type of 1856

1891 Engr. Wmk. 52 *Perf. 10*
90 A15 3p green 6.00 *16.00*
a. Double impression

Type of 1867

1893 Typo. *Perf. 11*
91 A20 10p lilac 13.50 4.00
a. Perf. 10 14.50 5.00
b. Perf. 11x10 or 10x11 22.50 8.00
c. Perf. 12x11 125.00 16.00

Types of 1862-84 Surcharged in Black:

a

b

1891, Jan. 5 Wmk. 55 *Perf. 11x12*
92 A17(a) ½p on 1p gray 3.00 *3.25*
a. Imperf.
b. Surcharge omitted —
c. Double surcharge *250.00*
93 A21(b) 7½p on 6p brown 5.25 3.00
a. Perf. 10 5.25 3.00
b. Perf. 11 5.00 2.75
c. Perf. 12 6.25 3.00
d. Perf. 10x12 5.75 3.00

Perf. 12x11½
94 A23(b) 12½p on 1sh red 10.50 8.00
a. Perf. 11x12 11.50 8.00
b. Perf. 10 11.50 8.50
c. Perf. 11 12.00 8.50
d. Perf. 12 14.00 8.00
Nos. 92-94 (3) 18.75 14.25

For overprints see Nos. O34, O36-O37.

1892
95 A37 ½p slate 2.10 .20
a. Perf. 12x11½ 2.10 .20
b. Perf. 12 2.40 .20
c. Perf. 10 25.00 1.00
d. Perf. 10x12 75.00 8.00
e. Perf. 11 80.00 6.00

See #102, 109, 121. For overprint see #O38.

Types of 1867-71

1897 *Perf. 11x12*
96 A22 9p on 10p red brn (Bk) 8.00 5.25
a. 9p on 10p org brn (Bk) 8.00 5.25
b. Surcharge omitted —
c. Double surcharge 140.00 110.00
d. Perf. 11 11.00 8.00
e. Perf. 12 10.50 7.00
97 A20 10p violet 12.00 5.00
a. Perf. 12x11½ 12.00 5.00
b. Perf. 11 19.00 6.75
c. Perf. 12 14.00 5.50

The surcharge on No. 96 measures 13½mm. For overprints see Nos. O39-O40.

Seal
A38

Victoria
A39

A40

ONE PENNY:
Die I - The first pearl in the crown at the left is merged into the arch, the shading under the fleur-de-lis is indistinct, and the "s" of "WALES" is open.
Die II - The first pearl is circular, the vertical shading under the fleur-de-lis is clear, and the "s" of "WALES" not so open.

2½ PENCE:
Die I - There are 12 radiating lines in the star on the Queen's breast.
Die II - There are 16 radiating lines in the star. The eye is nearly full of color.

1897 *Perf. 12*
98 A38 1p rose red, II 2.25 .20
a. Die I, perf. 11x12 2.75 .20
b. Imperf., pair —
c. Imperf. horiz., pair 300.00
d. Die I, perf. 12x11½ 3.00 .20
e. Die I, perf. 12 5.00 .50
f. Die II, perf. 12x11½ 2.00 .20
g. Die II, perf. 11x12 2.50 .20
99 A39 2p deep blue 5.75 .20
a. Perf. 11x12 3.00 .20
b. Perf. 12x11½ 3.00 .20
100 A40 2½p dp purple, II 6.50 1.10
a. Die I, perf. 12x11 7.50 1.40
b. Die I, perf. 11 9.00 2.25
c. Die I, perf. 11½x12 9.50 1.10
d. Die II, perf. 11x12 6.50 1.10
e. Die II, perf. 11½x12 9.00 1.25
Nos. 98-100 (3) 14.50 1.50

Sixtieth year of Queen Victoria's reign.
See Nos. 103-104, 110-112, 122-124.

Type of 1861

1897 Engr. Wmk. 53 *Perf. 11*
101 A16 5sh red violet 37.50 13.50
a. Horiz. pair, imperf. btwn. *3,000.*
b. Perf. 11x12 or 12x11 40.00 18.00
c. Perf. 12 45.00 20.00

Perf. 12x11½, 11½x12

1899, Oct. Typo. Wmk. 55

HALF PENNY:
Die I - Narrow "H" in "HALF."

102 A37 ½p blue green, I 1.00 .20
a. Imperf., pair 62.50 *70.00*
103 A39 2p ultra 1.90 .20
a. Imperf., pair 62.50
104 A40 2½p dk blue, II 3.00 .65
a. Imperf., pair 90.00
104B A27 4p org brown 9.50 4.00
c. Imperf. pair 250.00
105 A28 6p emerald 70.00 21.00
a. Imperf., pair 200.00
106 A28 6p orange 12.00 1.75
a. 6p yellow 11.00 1.75
b. Imperf., pair 160.00
106C A29 8p magenta 19.00 3.00
Nos. 102-106C (7) 116.40 30.80

Lyrebird
A41

"Australia"
A42

1903 *Perf. 12x11½*
107 A41 2sh6p blue green 42.50 17.00

See Nos. 119, 131.

1903 Wmk. 70 *Perf. 12½*
108 A42 9p org brn & ultra 11.50 2.50
a. Perf. 11 500.00 300.00

See No. 128.

Type of 1885-86

1904 Wmk. 56 *Perf. 12x11*
"POSTAGE" in Blue
108B A24 10sh brt rose & vio 160.00 80.00
c. Perf. 11 160.00 45.00
e. Perf. 12, aniline crim & vio 175.00 45.00

The watermark (NSW) of No. 108B is 20x7mm, with rounded angles in "N" and "W." On No. 75, the watermark is 21x7mm, with sharp angles in the "N" and "W."

HALF PENNY:
Die II - Wide "H" in "HALF."

Perf. 11, 11x12½, 12x11½ and Compound

1905-06 Wmk. 12
109 A37 ½p blue grn, II 1.50 .40
a. ½p blue green, I 2.50 .40
b. Booklet pane of 12 —
110 A38 1p car rose, II 1.50 .20
a. Booklet pane of 6 —
b. Booklet pane of 12 —
111 A39 2p deep ultra 1.75 .20
112 A40 2½p dk blue, II 3.25 1.40
113 A27 4p org brown 8.50 3.25
114 A28 6p orange 11.50 1.60
a. 6p yellow 13.00 1.60
b. Perf. 11 225.00
115 A29 8p magenta 18.00 3.50
117 A20 10p violet 12.50 3.50
118 A30 1sh vio brown 16.00 1.60
119 A41 2sh6p blue green 27.50 16.00

Wmk. 199
120 A32 20sh ultra 160.00 67.50
Nos. 109-115,117-120 (11) 262.00 99.15

1906-07 Wmk. 13
121 A37 ½p green, I 4.00 .65
122 A38 1p rose, II 4.75 .75
123 A39 2p ultra 4.75 .75
124 A40 2½p blue, II 45.00
125 A27 4p org brown 12.00 6.25
126 A28 6p orange 27.50 9.00
127 A29 8p red violet 17.50 9.00
128 A42 9p org brn & ultra, perf. 12x12½ ('06) 8.00 1.75
a. Perf. 11 55.00 40.00
129 A20 10p violet 25.00 22.50
130 A30 1sh vio brown 27.50 5.00
131 A41 2sh6p blue green 50.00 30.00
Nos. 121-131 (11) 226.00
Nos. 121-123,125-128,130-131 (9) 63.15

Portions of some of the sheets on which the above are printed show the watermark "COMMONWEALTH OF AUSTRALIA." Stamps may also be found from portions of the sheet without watermark.

SEMI-POSTAL STAMPS

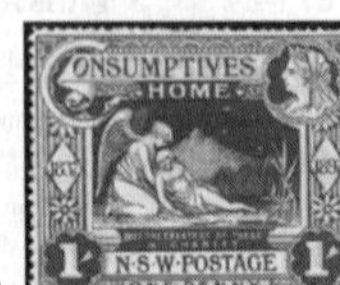
SP1

Allegory of Charity — SP2

Illustrations reduced.

1897, June Wmk. 55 *Perf. 11*
B1 SP1 1p (1sh) grn & brn 37.50 37.50
B2 SP2 2½p (2sh6p) rose, bl & gold 200.00 *200.00*

Diamond Jubilee of Queen Victoria.
The difference between the postal and face values of these stamps was donated to a fund for a home for consumptives.

REGISTRATION STAMPS

Queen Victoria — R1

Unwmk.

1856, Jan. 1 Engr. *Imperf.*
F1 R1 (6p) orange & blue 700.00 175.00
F2 R1 (6p) red & blue 700.00 150.00
a. Frame printed on back *2,750.* *2,000.*

1860 *Perf. 12, 13*
F3 R1 (6p) orange & blue 350.00 50.00
F4 R1 (6p) red & blue 260.00 40.00

Nos. F1 to F4 exist also on paper with papermaker's watermark in sheet.

1863 Wmk. 49
F5 R1 (6p) red & blue 75.00 15.00

Fifty varieties.
Nos. F1-F2 were reprinted on thin white wove unwatermarked paper and on thick yellowish wove unwatermarked paper; the former are usually overprinted "SPECIMEN."
No. F4 was reprinted on thin white wove unwatermarked paper; perf. 10 and overprinted "REPRINT" in black.

POSTAGE DUE STAMPS

D1

Perf. 10, 11, 11½, 12 and Compound

1891-92 Typo. Wmk. 55
J1 D1 ½p green, perf 10 3.25 2.75
J2 D1 1p green 5.75 1.00
a. Perf. 12 18.00 3.75
J3 D1 2p green 9.50 1.25
a. Perf. 10x12 17.00 4.00
J4 D1 3p green 16.00 3.50
J5 D1 4p green 12.00 1.40
J6 D1 6p green, perf 10 20.00 4.00
J7 D1 8p green, perf 10 70.00 12.00
J8 D1 5sh green, perf 10 150.00 37.50
a. Perf. 11 225.00 85.00

Perf. 12x10
J9 D1 10sh green 200.00 110.00
a. Perf. 10 325.00 52.50
J10 D1 20sh green 250.00 140.00
a. Perf. 10 350.00 90.00
b. Perf. 12 340.00
Nos. J1-J10 (10) 736.50 313.40

Nos. J1-J5 exist on both ordinary and chalky paper.
Used values for Nos. J8-J10 are for c-t-o copies.

OFFICIAL STAMPS

Regular Issues Overprinted in Black or Red

Perf. 10, 11, 12, 13 and Compound

1879-80 **Wmk. 54**

O1 A17 1p red 13.00 3.00
a. Perf. 10 300.00 35.00
b. Perf. 10x13 25.00 4.00
O2 A18 2p blue *17.00* 2.50
a. Perf. 11x12 225.00
b. Perf. 10 225.00 35.00
O3 A15 3p green (R) 425.00 275.00
O4 A15 3p green 200.00 32.50
a. Watermarked "6" — 450.00
b. Double overprint
O5 A19 4p red brown 200.00 10.00
a. Perf. 10x13 250.00 85.00
O6 A11 5p dark green 20.00 14.00
O7 A21 6p lilac 250.00 9.00
a. Perf. 10 325.00 45.00
b. Perf. 10x13 160.00 45.00
O8 A13 8p yellow (R) *1,000.* 225.00
O9 A13 8p yellow — 18.00
a. Perf. 10 325.00 80.00
O10 A23 1sh black (R) 275.00 10.00
a. Perf. 10 — 18.00
b. Perf. 10x13 — 25.00

1880 **Wmk. 53**

O11 A16 5sh lilac, perf. 11 200.00 75.00
a. Double overprint *1,600.*
b. Perf. 10 300.00 110.00
c. Perf. 12x10 400.00 110.00
d. Perf. 13 425.00 90.00
e. Perf. 10x12 —

1881 **Wmk. 55**

O12 A17 1p red 9.00 1.60
a. Perf. 10x13 150.00
O13 A18 2p blue 7.50 1.00
a. Perf. 10x13 300.00 80.00
O14 A15 3p green 7.00 3.25
a. Double overprint 450.00
b. Perf. 12 200.00 100.00
c. Perf. 11
O15 A19 4p red brown 12.00 3.50
a. Perf. 10x12 190.00 75.00
b. Perf. 12 200.00 175.00
O16 A11 5p dark green 12.50 *13.50*
a. Perf. 12 110.00
b. Perf. 10x12 — —
O17 A21 6p lilac 20.00 5.50
a. Perf. 12 55.00
b. Perf. 11x12 — —
O18 A13 8p yellow 25.00 11.00
a. Double overprint — —
b. Perf. 12 140.00 45.00
O19 A23 1sh black (R) 25.00 *6.50*
a. Double overprint 190.00
b. Perf. 10x13 65.00
c. Perf. 11 25.00 7.00
Nos. O12-O19 (8) 118.00 45.85

Beware of other red overprints on watermark 55 stamps.

1881 **Wmk. 56**

O20 A17 1p red 32.50 7.00

1887-90

O21 A24 10sh on #75 *1,500.*
O22 A24 £1 on #75A *5,500. 3,500.*

No. 75 Overprinted **O S**

1889

O23 A24 10sh rose & vio *1,450.* 600.00
a. Perf. 10 *2,750. 1,600.*

Overprinted

1888-89 **Wmk. 55**

O24 A25 1p violet 2.25 .30
a. Overprinted "O" only
O25 A26 2p blue 4.00 .30
O26 A27 4p red brown 10.50 3.00
O27 A28 6p carmine 8.00 4.50
O28 A29 8p red lilac 20.00 9.50
O29 A30 1sh vio brown 19.00 3.50
a. Double overprint
Nos. O24-O29 (6) 63.75 21.10

Wmk. 53

O30 A31 5sh violet (R) *625.00 500.00*
O31 A32 20sh ultra *1,600.* 825.00

1890 **Wmk. 57**

O32 A31 5sh violet *150.00* 65.00
a. Perf. 12 550.00 125.00

Wmk. 58

O33 A32 20sh ultra *1,850.* 600.00

Centenary of the founding of the Colony (Nos. O24-O33).

1891 **Wmk. 55**

O34 A17(a) ½p on 1p gray & black 55.00 47.50
a. Double overprint
O35 A33 2½p ultra 7.50 6.00
O36 A21(b) 7½p on 6p brn & black 35.00 35.00
O37 A23(b) 12½p on 1sh red & black 60.00 *62.50*
Nos. O34-O37 (4) 157.50 151.00

1892

O38 A37 ½p gray 5.75 *10.00*

1894 **Wmk. 54**

O39 A22 9p on 10p red brn 400.00 425.00

Wmk. 52

O40 A20 10p lilac, perf. 10 175.00 *125.00*
a. Perf. 11x10 250.00 *240.00*

The official stamps became obsolete on Dec. 31, 1894. In Aug., 1895, sets of 32 varieties of "O.S." stamps, together with some envelopes and postal cards, were placed on sale at the Sydney post office at £2 per set. These sets contained most of the varieties listed above and a few which are not known in the original issues. An obliteration consisting of the letters G.P.O. or N.S.W. in three concentric ovals was lightly applied to the center of each block of four stamps.

It is understood that the earlier stamps and many of the overprints were reprinted to make up these sets.

QUEENSLAND

ˈkwēnz-ˌland

LOCATION — Northeastern part of Australia
GOVT. — British Crown Colony
AREA — 670,500 sq. mi.
POP. — 498,129 (1901)
CAPITAL — Brisbane

Originally a part of New South Wales, Queensland was constituted a separate colony in 1859. It was one of the six British Colonies that united in 1901 to form the Commonwealth of Australia.

12 Pence = 1 Shilling
20 Shillings = 1 Pound

Values for unused stamps are for examples with original gum as defined in the catalogue introduction. Very fine examples of Nos. 4-73, 84-125, 128-140, and F1-F3b will have perforations touching the design on at least one or more sides due to the narrow spacing of the stamps on the plates. Stamps with perfs clear of the design on all four sides are scarce and will command higher prices.

Watermarks

Wmk. 5- Small Star

Wmk. 6- Large Star

Wmk. 12- Crown and Single-lined A

Wmk. 13- Crown and Double-lined A

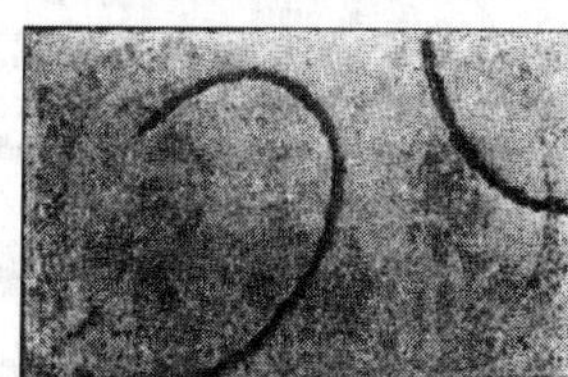

Wmk. 65- "Queensland Postage Stamps" in Sheet in Script Capitals

Wmks. 66 & 67- "Queensland" in Large Single-lined Roman Capitals in the Sheet and Short-pointed Star to Each Stamp (Stars Vary Slightly in Size and Shape)

Wmk. 68- Crown and Q

Wmk. 69- Large Crown and Q

There are two varieties of the watermark 68, differing slightly in the position and shape of the crown and the tongue of the "Q."

Wmk. 70- V and Crown

Queen Victoria — A1

Wmk. 6

1860, Nov. 1 **Engr.** ***Imperf.***

1 A1 1p deep rose 3,000. 750.
2 A1 2p deep blue 5,750. *2,000.*
3 A1 6p deep green 4,000. 750.

Clean-Cut Perf. 14 to 16

4 A1 1p deep rose 1,600. 240.
5 A1 2p deep blue 475. 100.00
a. Horiz. pair, imperf between — —
6 A1 6p deep green 525. 62.50

Clean-Cut Perf. 14 to 16

1860-61 **Wmk. 5**

6A A1 2p blue 475.00 100.00
b. Horiz. pair, imperf. vert 1,050.
6D A1 3p brown ('61) 275.00 62.50
6E A1 6p deep green 575.00 62.50
6F A1 1sh gray violet 525.00 80.00

Regular Perf. 14

6H A1 1p rose 125.00 40.00
6I A1 2p deep blue 300.00 52.50

Rough Perf. 14 to 16

7 A1 1p deep rose 70.00 32.50
8 A1 2p blue 100.00 32.50
a. Horiz. pair, imperf between 1,800.
9 A1 3p brown ('61) 50.00 30.00
a. Horiz. pair, imperf. vert. 1,800.
10 A1 6p deep green 140.00 25.00
a. 6p yellow green 210.00 25.00
11 A1 1sh dull violet 360.00 80.00

Thick Yellowish Paper

Square Perf. 12½ to 13

1862-67 **Unwmk.**

12 A1 1p Indian red 300.00 65.00
13 A1 1p orange ('63) 55.00 13.50
a. Perf. 13, round holes ('67) 55.00 13.50
b. Horiz. pair, imperf. between —
c. Imperf., pair — 525.00
14 A1 2p deep blue 35.00 13.50
a. 2p pale blue 80.00 27.50
b. Perf. 13, round holes ('67) 80.00 25.00
c. Imperf., pair — 550.00
e. Horiz. pair, imperf. between *950.00*
f. Vert. pair, imperf. between *1,150*
15 A1 3p brown ('63) 50.00 27.50
a. Imperf.
b. Perf. 13, round holes ('67) 55.00 32.50
16 A1 6p yellow grn ('63) 72.50 13.50
a. 6p green 125.00 25.00
b. Perf. 13, round holes ('67) 110.00 22.50
c. Imperf., pair — 550.00
d. Horiz. pair, imperf. between — 1,050.
17 A1 1sh gray ('63) 125.00 22.50
b. Imperf. horizontally
c. Horiz. pair, imperf. between — 1,100.
d. Perf. 13, round holes ('67)

White Wove Paper

1865 **Wmk. 5** ***Rough Perf. 13***

18 A1 1p orange 60.00 18.00
a. Horiz. pair, imperf. vert. 425.00
19 A1 2p light blue 50.00 14.50
a. Vert. pair, imperf. horiz. 875.00
b. Half used as 1p on cover *2,000.*
20 A1 6p yellow green 125.00 22.50
Nos. 18-20 (3) 235.00 55.00

Perf. 13, Round Holes

1866 **Wmk. 65**

21 A1 1p orange vermilion 140.00 25.00
22 A1 2p blue 50.00 16.00
b. Diagonal half used as 1p on cover —

1866 **Unwmk.** **Litho.** ***Perf. 13***

23 A1 4p lilac 100.00 16.00
a. 4p slate 150.00 20.00
24 A1 5sh pink 225.00 55.00
b. Vert. pair, imperf between *950.00*

Wmk. 66, 67

1868-74 **Engr.** ***Perf. 13***

25 A1 1p orange ('71) 40.00 4.50
26 A1 2p blue 40.00 2.50
27 A1 3p grnsh brn ('71) 90.00 5.00
a. 3p brown 80.00 5.00
b. 3p olive brown 80.00 5.50
28 A1 6p yel green ('71) 125.00 7.75
a. 6p deep green 160.00 14.50
30 A1 1sh grnsh gray ('72) 375.00 40.00
31 A1 1sh violet ('74) 225.00 20.00

Perf. 12

32 A1 1p orange 250.00 27.50
33 A1 2p blue 575.00 35.00
34 A1 3p brown 325.00 140.00
35 A1 6p deep green 850.00 45.00
36 A1 1sh violet 375.00 45.00

Perf. 13x12

36A A1 1p orange 225.00
37 A1 2p blue *1,250.* 50.00
37A A1 3p brown *1,100.*

The reprints are perforated 13 and the colors differ slightly from those of the originals.

1868-75 **Wmk. 68** ***Perf. 13***

38 A1 1p orange 45.00 4.50
a. Imperf pair 175.00
39 A1 1p rose ('74) 50.00 8.00
40 A1 2p blue 37.50 4.25
b. Imperf., pair 300.00
41 A1 3p brown ('75) 65.00 14.00
42 A1 6p yel green ('69) 100.00 7.50
a. 6p apple green 125.00 9.00
b. 6p deep green 125.00 9.00
43 A1 1sh violet ('75) *175.00* 30.00
Nos. 38-43 (6) *472.50* 68.25

No. 40 exists in vert. pair, imperf. btwn.

1876-78 ***Perf. 12***

44 A1 1p orange 35.00 4.50
a. Imperf. *350.00*

45 A1 1p rose 45.00 10.00
46 A1 2p blue 22.50 1.40
47 A1 3p brown 60.00 9.00
48 A1 6p yellow green 140.00 4.50
a. 6p apple green 140.00 6.50
b. 6p deep green 140.00 7.00
49 A1 1sh violet 42.50 9.00
m. Vert. pair, imperf between —
Nos. 44-49 (6) 345.00 38.40

#44, 49 exist in vertical pairs, imperf. between.

Perf. 13x12

49B A1 1p orange 150.00
49C A1 2p blue *1,600.* 250.00
49D A1 4p yellow 300.00
49E A1 6p deep green 300.00

Perf. 12½x13

49G A1 1p orange vermilion 325.00
49H A1 2p deep blue 350.00

The reprints are perforated 12 and are in paler colors than the originals.

1879 Unwmk. *Perf. 12*

50 A1 6p pale emerald 175.00 25.00
a. Horiz. pair, imperf. vert. 650.00

A2

A3

1875-81 Litho. Wmk. 68 *Perf. 13*

50B A1 4p yellow ('75) 800.00 42.50

Perf. 12

51 A1 4p buff ('76) 600.00 22.50
a. 4p yellow 600.00 24.00
52 A1 2sh pale blue ('81) 65.00 22.50
a. 2sh deep blue 75.00 22.50
b. Imperf.
53 A2 2sh6p lt red ('81) 110.00 40.00
54 A1 5sh orange brn ('81) 150.00 60.00
a. 5sh fawn 150.00 60.00
55 A1 10sh brown ('81) 325.00 110.00
a. Imperf., pair *800.00*
56 A1 20sh rose ('81) 650.00 125.00
Nos. 50B-56 (7) 2,700. 422.50

Nos. 53-56, 62-64, 74-83 with pen (revenue) cancellations removed are often offered as unused.

1879-81 Typo. Wmk. 68 *Perf. 12*

57 A3 1p rose red 13.50 1.75
a. 1p red orange 16.00 3.00
b. 1p brown orange 35.00 5.50
c. "QOEENSLAND" 100.00 30.00
d. Imperf.
e. Vert. pair, imperf. horiz. *325.00*
58 A3 2p gray blue 26.00 1.25
a. 2p deep ultra 29.00 1.25
b. Imperf.
c. "PENGE" 125.00 37.50
d. "TW" joined 25.00 1.75
e. Vert. pair, imperf. horiz. 450.00
59 A3 4p orange yellow 100.00 10.00
a. Imperf.
60 A3 6p yellow green 62.50 4.50
a. Imperf.
61 A3 1sh pale violet ('81) 50.00 5.50
a. 1sh deep violet 52.50 4.50
Nos. 57-61 (5) 252.00 23.00

The stamps of type A3 were electrotyped from plates made up of groups of four types, differing in minor details. Two dies were used for the 1p and 2p, giving eight varieties for each of those values.

Nos. 59-60 exist imperf. vertically.

For surcharge see No. 65.

Moire on Back

1878-79 Unwmk.

62 A3 1p brown org ('79) 375.00 55.00
a. "QOEENSLAND" 1,800.
63 A3 2p deep ultra ('79) 450.00 27.50
a. "PENGE" *4,250.* 700.00
64 A1 1sh red violet 100.00 47.50
Nos. 62-64 (3) 925.00 130.00

No. 57b Surcharged Vertically in Black **Half-penny**

1881 Wmk. 68

65 A3 ½p on 1p brn org 175.00 95.00
a. "QOEENSLAND" 950.00 750.00

A4

A5

1882-83 Typo. *Perf. 12*

66 A4 1p pale red 5.25 .35
a. 1p rose 5.25 .35
b. Imperf. pair —
67 A4 2p gray blue 8.00 .35
a. 2p deep ultra 8.00 .35
b. Imperf. —
68 A4 4p yellow ('83) 18.00 2.00
a. "PENGE" 125.00 45.00
b. Imperf., pair —
69 A4 6p yellow green 10.00 1.25
70 A4 1sh violet ('83) 19.00 2.25
Nos. 66-70 (5) 60.25 6.20

There are eight minor varieties of the 1p, twelve of the 2p and four each of the other values. On the 1p there is a period after "PENNY." On all values the lines of shading on the neck extend from side to side.

Compare design A4 with A6, A10, A11, A15, A16.

1883 *Perf. 9½x12*

71 A4 1p rose 140.00 25.00
72 A4 2p gray blue 310.00 50.00
73 A4 1sh pale violet 200.00 30.00
Nos. 71-73 (3) 650.00 105.00

Beware of faked perfs.

See Nos. 94, 95, 100.

Wmk. 68 Twice Sideways

1882-85 Engr. *Perf. 12*

Thin Paper

74 A5 2sh ultra 60.00 22.50
75 A5 2sh6p vermilion 50.00 22.50
76 A5 5sh car rose ('85) 50.00 25.00
77 A5 10sh brown 95.00 42.50
78 A5 £1 dk grn ('83) 225.00 125.00
Nos. 74-78 (5) 480.00 237.50

The 2sh, 5sh and £1 exist imperf.

There are two varieties of the watermark on Nos. 74-78, as in the 1879-81 issue.

Copies with revenue cancels sell for $3.25-6.50.

1886 Wmk. 69 *Perf. 12*

Thick Paper

79 A5 2sh ultra 90.00 32.50
80 A5 2sh6p vermilion 40.00 22.50
81 A5 5sh car rose 37.50 30.00
82 A5 10sh dark brown 100.00 42.50
83 A5 £1 dark green 175.00 60.00
Nos. 79-83 (5) 442.50 187.50

High value stamps with cancellations removed are offered as unused.

Copies with revenue cancels sell for $3.25-6.50.

See Nos. 126-127, 141-144.

A6

Redrawn

1887-89 Typo. Wmk. 68 *Perf. 12*

84 A6 1p orange 4.00 .35
85 A6 2p gray blue 8.00 .50
a. 2p deep ultra 11.50 1.00
86 A6 2sh red brown ('89) 65.00 37.50

Perf. 9½x12

88 A6 2p deep ultra *225.00* 90.00
Nos. 84-88 (4) *302.00* 128.35

The 1p has no period after the value.

In the redrawn stamps the shading lines on the neck are not completed at the left, leaving an irregular white line along that side.

Variety "LA" joined exists on Nos. 84-86, 88, 90, 91, 93, 97, 98, 102.

On No. 88 beware of faked perfs.

A7

A8

1890-92 *Perf. 12½, 13*

89 A7 ½p green 4.00 1.10
90 A6 1p orange red 2.75 .20
a. Imperf. 30.00 30.00
91 A6 2p gray blue 4.50 .20
92 A8 2½p rose carmine 10.00 1.10
93 A6 3p brown ('92) 9.00 2.00
94 A4 4p orange 16.00 1.75
a. 4p yellow 15.00 1.75
b. "PENGE" 75.00 25.00
95 A4 6p green 11.00 1.75
96 A6 2sh red brown 40.00 12.50
Nos. 89-96 (8) 97.25 20.60

The ½p and 3p exist imperf.

1895 Wmk. 69 *Perf. 12½, 13*

Thick Paper

98 A6 1p orange 3.25 .45
99 A6 2p gray blue 3.25 .45

Perf. 12

100 A4 1sh pale violet 16.00 3.75
Nos. 98-100 (3) 22.50 4.65

A9

A10

Moiré on Back

1895 Unwmk. *Perf. 12½, 13*

101 A9 ½p green 2.25 1.75
a. Without moire 55.00
102 A6 1p orange 2.25 1.00
a. "PE" missing 110.00 75.00

Wmk. 68

103 A9 ½p green 1.75 .75
a. ½p deep green 1.50 .75
b. Printed on both sides 80.00
104 A10 1p orange 3.25 .20
105 A10 2p gray blue 5.00 .35

Wmk. 69

Thick Paper

106 A9 ½p green 2.25 1.00

1895-96 Unwmk. Thin Paper

Crown and Q Faintly Impressed

107 A9 ½p green 2.50 1.10
108 A10 1p orange 3.50 1.00
108A A6 2p gray blue 11.00

A11

A12

A13

1895-96 Wmk. 68

109 A11 1p red 7.50 .20
110 A12 2½p rose 12.00 3.50
111 A13 5p violet brown 14.00 3.50
111A A11 6p yellow green

A14

A15

A16

A17

A18

A19

TWO PENCE:

Type I - Point of bust does not touch frame.

Type II - First redrawing. The top of the crown, the chignon and the point of the bust touch the frame. The forehead is completely shaded.

Type III - Second redrawing. The top of crown does not touch the frame, though the chignon and the point of the bust do. The forehead and the bridge of the nose are not shaded.

1897-1900 *Perf. 12½, 13*

112 A14 ½p deep green 3.50 3.50
a. Perf. 12 110.00
113 A15 1p red 2.00 .20
a. Perf. 12 2.75 .60
114 A16 2p gray blue (I) 2.00 .20
a. Perf. 12 2.00 .20
115 A17 2½p rose 16.00 12.50
116 A17 2½p violet, *blue* 9.00 1.10
117 A15 3p brown 8.00 1.40
118 A15 4p bright yellow 8.00 1.40
119 A18 5p violet brown 7.50 1.40
120 A15 6p yellow green 8.00 1.75
121 A19 1sh lilac 12.50 1.60
a. 1sh light violet 14.50 1.75
122 A19 2sh turq blue 30.00 14.00
Nos. 112-122 (11) 106.50 39.05

1898 *Serrated Roulette 13*

123 A15 1p scarlet 4.50 2.75
a. Serrated and perf. 13 6.00 3.75
b. Serrated in black 9.00 9.00
c. Serrated without color and in black 9.00 *11.00*
d. Same as "b," and perf. 13 80.00 80.00
e. Same as "c," and perf. 13 100.00 85.00

Victoria
A20

"Australia"
A21

1899 Typo. *Perf. 12, 12½, 13*

124 A20 ½p blue green 1.75 .65

Unwatermarked stamps are proofs.

1903 Wmk. 70 *Perf. 12½*

NINE PENCE:

Type I- "QUEENSLAND" 18x1½mm.

Type II- "QUEENSLAND" 17½x1¼mm.

125 A21 9p org brn & ultra, II 13.00 2.50
a. Type I 13.00 2.50

See No. 128.

Type of 1882

Perf. 12, 12½, 13

1906 Litho. Wmk. 68

126 A5 5sh rose 125.00 75.00
127 A5 £1 dark green 400.00 125.00

1907 Typo. Wmk. 13 *Perf. 12½*

128 A21 9p yel brn & ultra, I 13.50 3.00
a. Type II 25.00 3.75
b. Perf. 11, type II 225.00

1907 Wmk. 68 *Perf. 12½, 13*

129 A16 2p ultra, type II 8.00 2.50
129A A18 5p dark brown 9.00 2.25
b. 5p olive brown 10.00 2.50

1907-09 Wmk. 12

130 A20 ½p deep green 1.60 .90
131 A15 1p red 2.00 .20
a. Imperf., pair 200.00
132 A16 2p ultra, II 6.75 .20
133 A16 2p ultra, III 2.50 .20
134 A15 3p pale brown 10.00 1.25
135 A15 4p bright yellow 11.00 2.50
136 A15 4p gray black ('09) 12.00 2.00
137 A18 5p brown 7.75 2.50
a. 5p olive brown 12.50 3.25
138 A15 6p yellow green 11.00 2.25
139 A19 1sh violet 13.50 3.50
140 A19 2sh turquoise bl 32.50 11.00

Wmk. 12 Sideways
Litho.

141	A5	2sh6p	deep orange	45.00	35.00
142	A5	5sh	rose	50.00	35.00
143	A5	10sh	dark brown	90.00	45.00
144	A5	£1	blue green	200.00	125.00
	Nos. 130-144 (15)			495.60	266.50

POSTAL FISCAL STAMPS

Authorised for postal use from Jan. 1, 1880. Authorization withdrawn July 1, 1892.

Used values are for examples with postal cancellations used from Jan. 1, 1880 through June 30, 1892.

Beware of copies with a pen cancellation removed and a fake postmark added.

Queen Victoria
PF1 PF2

1866-74 Engr. Unwmk. *Perf. 13*

AR1	PF1	1p	blue	30.00	8.00
AR2	PF1	6p	violet	30.00	*35.00*
AR3	PF1	1sh	green	35.00	10.00
AR4	PF1	2sh	brown	100.00	50.00
AR5	PF1	2sh 6p	red	100.00	37.50
AR6	PF1	5sh	yellow	300.00	75.00
AR7	PF1	6sh	yellow		
AR8	PF1	10sh	yel grn	400.00	*175.00*
AR9	PF1	20sh	rose	500.00	*175.00*

Wmk. 68

AR10	PF1	1p	blue	20.00	20.00
AR11	PF1	6p	violet	27.50	*30.00*
AR12	PF1	6p	blue	27.50	17.50
AR13	PF1	1sh	green	35.00	17.50
AR14	PF1	2sh	brown	100.00	35.00
AR15	PF1	5sh	yellow	300.00	75.00
AR16	PF1	10sh	yel grn	400.00	*110.00*
AR17	PF1	20sh	rose	500.00	*175.00*

1872-73 Wmk. 69 *Perf. 13*

AR18	PF2	1p	lilac	12.00	8.00
AR19	PF2	6p	brown	25.00	12.50
AR20	PF2	1sh	green	35.00	15.00
AR21	PF2	2sh	blue	50.00	12.50
AR22	PF2	2sh 6p	ver	75.00	30.00
AR23	PF2	5sh	org brn	125.00	30.00
AR24	PF2	10sh	brown	300.00	*85.00*
AR25	PF2	20sh	rose	500.00	*150.00*

Perf. 12

AR26	PF2	1p	lilac	12.00	8.00
AR27	PF2	6p	brown	25.00	12.50
AR28	PF2	2sh	blue	50.00	12.50
AR29	PF2	2sh 6p	ver	75.00	30.00
AR30	PF2	5sh	org brn	125.00	30.00
AR31	PF2	10sh	brown	300.00	*85.00*
AR32	PF2	20sh	rose	500.00	*150.00*

Unwmk.
Perf. 13

AR33	PF2	1p	lilac	15.00	10.00
AR34	PF2	6p	lilac	75.00	37.50
AR35	PF2	6p	brown	25.00	12.50
AR36	PF2	1sh	green	35.00	15.00
AR37	PF2	2sh	blue	55.00	*60.00*
AR38	PF2	2sh 6p	ver	100.00	40.00
AR39	PF2	5sh	org brn	150.00	50.00
AR40	PF2	10sh	brown	300.00	100.00
AR41	PF2	20sh	rose	500.00	125.00

Perf. 12

AR42	PF2	1p	lilac	15.00	10.00
AR43	PF2	6p	lilac	90.00	50.00
AR44	PF2	6p	brown	50.00	40.00
AR45	PF2	1sh	green	35.00	15.00
AR46	PF2	2sh	blue	55.00	60.00
AR47	PF2	2sh 6p	ver	100.00	40.00
AR48	PF2	5sh	org brn	150.00	50.00
AR49	PF2	10sh	brown	300.00	100.00
AR50	PF2	20sh	rose	500.00	125.00

Queen Victoria — PF3

1878-79 Engr. Unwmk. *Perf. 12*

AR51	PF3	1p	violet	50.00	15.00

Wmk. 68

AR52	PF3	1p	violet	20.00	10.00

SEMI-POSTAL STAMPS

Queen Victoria, Colors and Bearers — SP1

SP2

Perf. 12, 12½
1900, June 19 Wmk. 68

B1	SP1	1p	red lilac	100.00	95.00
B2	SP2	2p	deep violet	250.00	225.00

These stamps were sold at 1sh and 2sh respectively. The difference was applied to a patriotic fund in connection with the Boer War.

REGISTRATION STAMPS

R1

Clean-Cut Perf. 14 to 16
1861 Wmk. 5 Engr.

F1	R1	(6p)	olive yellow	400.00	75.00
a.	Horiz. pair, imperf. vert.			*4,000.*	

Rough Perf. 14 to 16

F2	R1	(6p)	dull yellow	50.00	35.00

1864 *Perf. 12½ to 13*

F3	R1	(6p)	golden yellow	80.00	35.00
a.	Imperf.				
b.	Double impression			800.00	

The reprints are watermarked with a small truncated star and perforated 12.

SOUTH AUSTRALIA

'sauth o-'strāl-yə

LOCATION — Central part of southern Australia
GOVT. — British Colony
AREA — 380,070 sq. mi.
POP. — 358,346 (1901)
CAPITAL — Adelaide

South Australia was one of the six British colonies that united in 1901 to form the Commonwealth of Australia.

12 Pence = 1 Shilling
20 Shillings = 1 Pound

Values for unused stamps are for examples with original gum as defined in the catalogue introduction.

Very fine examples of Nos. 10-60 and O1-O60 will have perforations slightly cutting into the framelines or design on one or more sides due to the narrow spacing of the stamps on the plates.

Stamps with perfs clear on all sides are scarce to rare and will command higher to substantially higher prices.

Watermarks

Wmk. 6- Star with Long Narrow Points

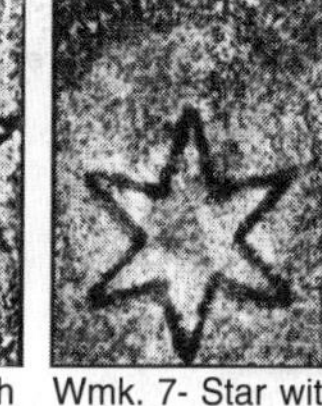

Wmk. 7- Star with Short Broad Points

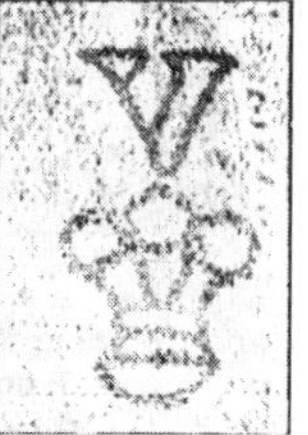

Wmk. 70- Crown and V

Wmk. 72- Crown and SA

Wmk. 73- Crown and SA, Letters Close

Wmk. 74- Crown and Single-lined A

Queen Victoria — A1

1855-56 Engr. Wmk. 6 *Imperf.*
London Print

1	A1	1p	dark green	2,800.	400.
2	A1	2p	dull carmine	600.	80.
3	A1	6p	deep blue	2,500.	150.
4	A1	1sh	violet ('56)	*4,500.*	

No. 4 was never put in use. Nos. 1 and 3 without watermark are proofs.

1856-59 Local Print

5	A1	1p	deep yel grn ('58)	*5,500.*	550.00
a.	1p yellow green ('58)			*4,000.*	525.00
6	A1	2p	blood red	1,350.	72.50
a.	Printed on both sides				*800.00*
b.	2p orange red ('56)			1,450.	80.00
7	A1	2p	pale red ('57)	650.00	55.00
a.	Printed on both sides				*625.00*
8	A1	6p	slate blue ('57)	2,250.	160.00
9	A1	1sh	orange ('57)	4,250.	350.00
a.	Printed on both sides			—	—
b.	1sh red orange			—	450.00

1858-59 *Rouletted*

10	A1	1p	yellow grn ('59)	475.00	47.50
a.	Horiz. pair, imperf. between			—	—
b.	1p pale yellow green			500.00	52.50
11	A1	2p	pale red ('59)	125.00	22.50
a.	Printed on both sides				*650.00*
12	A1	6p	slate blue	375.00	27.50
13	A1	1sh	orange ('59)	1,125.	37.50
c.	Printed on both sides				*1,250.*

See #14-16, 19-20, 25-26, 28-29, 32, 35-36, 41-43, 47, 51-52, 69-70, 73, 113, 118. For overprints see #O1-O2, O5, O7, O9, O11-O13, O17, O20, O27, O30, O32, O39-O40, O42, O52, O76, O85.

A2

A3

Surcharge on #22-24, 34, 49-50

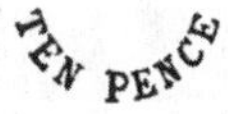

1860-69 *Rouletted*

14	A1	1p	dull blue green	45.00	24.00
a.	1p deep green			225.00	62.50
b.	1p bright green			45.00	25.00
15	A1	1p	sage green	67.50	27.50
16	A1	2p	vermilion ('62)	47.50	4.00
a.	Horiz. pair, imperf. btwn.			700.00	325.00
b.	Rouletted and perf. all around			—	*625.00*
c.	Printed on both sides			—	450.00
18	A2	4p	dull violet ('67)	67.50	17.00
19	A1	6p	grnsh bl ('63)	67.50	3.75
20	A1	6p	dull blue	95.00	6.00
a.	6p sky blue			110.00	6.50
b.	6p Prussian blue			675.00	47.50
c.	Horiz. pair, imperf btwn.				*775.00*
d.	6p ultramarine			62.50	3.75
e.	Horiz. pair, imperf. btwn. (#20f)			—	*375.00*
f.	6p indigo blue			—	55.00
g.	Rouletted and perf. all around (#20f)				*300.00*
21	A3	9p	gray lilac ('69)	52.50	9.00
a.	Double impression			—	—
c.	Rouletted and perf. all around			*1,750.*	*250.00*
22	A3	10p	on 9p red org (Bl) ('66)	190.00	27.50
23	A3	10p	on 9p yel (Bl) ('67)	225.00	24.00
24	A3	10p	on 9p yel (Blk) ('69)	1,300.	32.50
a.	Inverted surcharge			—	*2,750.*
c.	Printed on both sides			—	*1,000.*
d.	Rouletted x perf. 10				—
24E	A1	1sh	red brown	125.00	13.00
f.	Vert. pair, imperf. btwn.			—	1,250.
25	A1	1sh	lake brn ('65)	140.00	13.00
a.	Horiz. pair, imperf. btwn.			—	*425.00*
26	A1	1sh	brown ('63)	125.00	16.00
a.	1sh chestnut ('64)			140.00	11.00
27	A2	2sh	carmine ('67)	160.00	27.50
a.	Horiz. pair, imperf. btwn.				*900.00*

There are six varieties of the surcharge "TEN PENCE" in this and subsequent issues.

Nos. 16b, 20g, 21c, 28a, 32c, 33a are rouletted remainders that were later perforated.

See #31, 33, 46, 48, 53, 63, 68, 72, 74, 112, 113B, 119-120. For surcharges & overprints see #34, 44-45, 49-50, 59, 67, 71, O4, O6, O8, O10, O16-O19, O18, O21, O26, O28-O29, O31, O33, O36-O38, O41, O41B, O43, O53. Compare with design A6a.

1867-72 *Perf. 11½ to 12½xRoulette*

28	A1	1p	blue green	200.00	32.50
a.	Rouletted and perf. all around				575.00
29	A1	1p	yellow green	140.00	22.50
31	A2	4p	dull violet ('68)	1,400.	125.00
a.	4p purple ('69)			—	100.00
32	A1	6p	Prus blue	400.00	19.00
a.	6p sky blue			450.00	19.00
b.	Printed on both sides			—	—
c.	Rouletted and perf. all around			—	*275.00*
d.	6p indigo blue ('69)			475.00	24.00
33	A3	9p	gray lilac ('72)	—	*250.00*
34	A3	10p	on 9p yel (Bl) ('68)	725.00	32.50
a.	Printed on both sides			—	*575.00*
35	A1	1sh	chestnut ('68)	250.00	27.50
36	A1	1sh	lake brown ('69)	250.00	27.50

#44-45 **3-PENCE**

Perf. 10, 11½, 12½ and Compound
1867-74

41	A1	1p	yellow green	45.00	17.50
42	A1	1p	blue green	60.00	12.50
a.	Printed on both sides				

43 A1 2p vermilion 1,250.
44 A2 3p on 4p dp bl (Blk) ('70) 60.00 5.50
a. 3p on 4p ultra, black surcharge 125.00 5.50
b. Surcharge omitted *20,000.* *5,000.*
c. Double surcharge 4,500.
d. Surcharged on both sides 3,250.
45 A2 3p on 4p sl bl (Red) ('70) 425.00 62.50
46 A2 4p dull violet 60.00 9.00
47 A1 6p dark blue 90.00 8.00
a. 6p sky blue 350.00 9.25
b. Imperf. vert., pair
48 A3 9p red lilac ('72) 47.50 5.00
a. 9p violet 110.00 5.50
b. 9p red violet 110.00 5.50
c. Printed on both sides 350.00
49 A3 10p on 9p yel (Bl) ('68) 1,500. 26.00
50 A3 10p on 9p yel (Blk) ('69) 150.00 21.00
51 A1 1sh deep brown 150.00 12.00
52 A1 1sh red brown 100.00 12.00
a. 1sh chestnut 125.00 12.50
53 A2 2sh carmine 60.00 7.50
a. Printed on both sides 400.00
b. Horiz. pair, imperf. vert.

See Nos. 67, O14, O28, O36.

A6

A6a

1868 Typo. Wmk. 72 *Rouletted*
54 A6a 2p orange red 65.00 4.00
a. Imperf.
b. Printed on both sides 275.00
c. Horiz. pair, imperf. btwn. 275.00

1869 *Perf. 11½ to 12½xRoulette*
55 A6a 2p orange red 150.00

1870 *Perf. 10xRoulette*
56 A6a 2p orange red 350.00 30.00

Perf. 10, 11½, 12½ and Compound
1868-75
57 A6 1p bl grn ('75) 24.00 4.50
58 A6a 2p orange red 13.00 1.00
a. Printed on both sides 200.00
b. Horiz. pair, imperf. vert.

Engr.
59 A3 10p on 9p yel (Bl) *1,500.*

1869 Typo. Wmk. 6 *Rouletted*
60 A6a 2p orange red 65.00 11.50
a. Imperf.
b. Printed on both sides

Perf. 11½ to 12½xRoulette
61 A6a 2p orange red 125.00

Perf. 11½ to 12½
61B A6a 2p orange red

See #62, 64-66, 97-98, 105-106, 115-116, 133-134, 145-146. For surcharges & overprints see #75, O3, O22-O25, O34-O35, O44-O47, O49, O55-O56, O62-O63, O68-O69, O74, O78-O79.

1871 Wmk. 70 *Perf. 10*
62 A6a 2p orange red 75.00 16.00

Engr.
63 A2 4p dull violet 2,250. 350.00
a. Printed on both sides

Copies of the 4p from edge of sheet sometimes lack watermark.

Perf. 10, 11½, 12½ and Compound
1876-80 Typo. Wmk. 73
64 A6 1p green 6.00 .50
65 A6a 2p orange 4.25 .50
66 A6a 2p blood red ('80) 225.00 7.50
Nos. 64-66 (3) 235.25 8.50

See #97-98, 105-106, 115-116, 133-134, 145-146.

8 PENCE
No. 71

No. 75

1876-84 Engr. Wmk. 7
67 A2 3p on 4p ultra (Blk) 65.00 17.50
a. 3p on 4p deep blue 15.00
b. Double surcharge *1,500.*

68 A2 4p reddish violet 50.00 5.50
a. 4p dull violet 60.00 9.00
69 A1 6p deep blue 65.00 4.50
a. Horiz. pair, imperf. vert.
b. Imperf.
70 A1 6p pale ultra ('84) 40.00 2.25
71 A3 8p on 9p bister brn 65.00 5.50
a. 8p on 9p yellow brown 57.50 2.50
b. 8p on 9p gray brown ('80) 52.50 4.00
d. Double surcharge 375.00
72 A3 9p rose lilac 12.00 5.50
a. Printed on both sides 300.00
73 A1 1sh red brown 37.50 3.25
a. 1sh brown 40.00 2.50
b. Horiz. pair, imperf. btwn. 300.00
74 A2 2sh carmine 35.00 4.50
a. Horiz. pair, imperf. vert. *400.00*
b. Imperf., pair

For overprint see No. O41.

1882 Wmk. 73 *Perf. 10*
Black Surcharge
75 A6 ½p on 1p green 10.50 4.00

A9

A10

A11

A12

Perf. 10, 11½, 12½ and Compound
1883-90 Typo.
76 A9 ½p chocolate brown 2.25 .25
a. ½p red brown ('89) 2.25 .25
b. ½p bister brown 3.50 .25
78 A10 3p deep green ('86) 6.50 .75
a. 3p olive green ('90) 11.00 1.50
79 A11 4p violet ('90) 7.75 1.75
80 A12 6p blue ('87) 7.75 1.00
Nos. 76-80 (4) 24.25 3.75

See #96, 100-101, 104, 108-109, 111. For surcharges & overprints see #94-95, 99, O48, O50-O51, O54, O57-O61, O64, O66-O67, O71, O73, O75, O81-O82.

A13

1886-96 *Perf. 10, 11½ to 12½*
81 A13 2sh6p violet 27.50 6.50
82 A13 5sh rose 40.00 16.00
83 A13 10sh green 100.00 25.00
84 A13 15sh buff 200.00 140.00
85 A13 £1 blue 160.00 60.00
86 A13 £2 red brown 475.00 150.00
87 A13 50sh rose red 600.00 200.00
88 A13 £3 olive green 825.00
89 A13 £4 lemon 1,000.
90 A13 £5 gray *2,700.*
90A A13 £5 brown ('96) *2,600.*
91 A13 £10 bronze *3,000.* *700.00*
92 A13 £15 silver *6,500.*
93 A13 £20 lilac *8,250.*

For overprints see Nos. O83-O84.

#94, 99

#95

Perf. 10, 11½x12½ and Compound
1891
Brown Surcharge
94 A11 2½p on 4p green 8.00 1.40
a. "½" nearer the "2" 30.00 20.00
b. Pair, imperf. between 375.00

c. Fraction bar omitted 90.00 80.00

Carmine Surcharge
95 A12 5p on 6p red brn 17.00 6.00
a. No period after "D" 160.00

See #99. For overprints see #O48, O57, O59.

Many stamps of the issues of 1855-91 have been reprinted; they are all on paper watermarked Crown and SA, letters wide apart, and are overprinted "REPRINT."

1893 Typo. *Perf. 15*
96 A9 ½p brown 3.00 .20
a. Horiz. pair, imperf. btwn 125.00
b. Pair, perf. 12 btwn; perf. 15 around 200.00 50.00
97 A6 1p green 4.00 .20
98 A6a 2p orange 6.50 .20
a. Vert. pair, imperf. between 225.00
99 A11 2½p on 4p green 12.00 1.60
a. "½" nearer the "2" 40.00 35.00
b. Fraction bar omitted
100 A11 4p gray violet 13.00 2.00
101 A12 6p blue 32.50 4.25
Nos. 96-101 (6) 71.00 8.45

Kangaroo, Palm — A16

Coat of Arms — A17

1894, Mar. 1
102 A16 2½p blue violet 13.00 1.50
103 A17 5p dull violet 15.00 2.50

See Nos. 107, 110, 117, 135-136, 147, 151. For overprints see Nos. O65, O70, O72, O80.

1895-97 *Perf. 13*
104 A9 ½p pale brown 3.00 .25
105 A6 1p green 5.25 .50
a. Vert. pair, imperf. between
106 A6a 2p orange 4.25 .20
107 A16 2½p blue violet 7.50 .35
108 A10 3p olive green ('97) 5.00 .30
109 A11 4p bright violet 6.50 .35
110 A17 5p dull violet 7.00 .35
111 A12 6p blue 8.00 .40
Nos. 104-111 (8) 46.50 2.70

Some authorities regard the so-called redrawn 1p stamps with thicker lettering (said to have been issued in 1897) as impressions from a new or cleaned plate.

Perf. 11½, 12½, Clean-Cut, Compound
1896 Engr. Wmk. 7
112 A3 9p lilac rose 12.50 6.50
113 A1 1sh dark brown 26.00 5.50
a. Horiz. pair, imperf. vert.
c. Vert. pair, imperf. btwn. 180.00
113B A2 2sh carmine 32.50 8.00
Nos. 112-113B (3) 71.00 20.00

Adelaide Post Office — A18

1899 Typo. Wmk. 73 *Perf. 13*
114 A18 ½p yellow green 1.75 .25
115 A6 1p carmine 3.00 .20
a. 1p scarlet 2.75 .50
116 A6a 2p purple 2.25 .25
117 A16 2½p dark blue 7.00 .75
Nos. 114-117 (4) 14.00 1.45

See #132, 144. For overprint see #O77.

Perf. 11½, 12½
1901 Engr. Wmk. 72
118 A1 1sh dark brown 24.00 16.00
a. 1sh red brown 24.00 10.00
b. Horiz. pair, imperf. vert.
119 A2 2sh carmine 27.50 15.00

1902
120 A3 9p magenta 20.00 20.00

A19

A20

Perf. 11½, 12½ and Compound
1902-03 Typo. Wmk. 73
121 A19 3p olive green 4.75 .75
122 A19 4p red orange 7.50 1.50
123 A19 6p blue green 6.50 1.50
124 A19 8p ultra (value 19mm long) 8.50 2.25
124A A19 8p ultra (value 16½mm long) ('03) 13.00 3.00
b. "EIGNT" 900.00 *3,000.*
125 A19 9p claret 8.50 2.25
a. Pair, imperf. between 300.00
126 A19 10p org buff 11.00 3.50
127 A19 1sh brown ('03) 12.00 3.00
a. Horiz. or vert. pair, imperf. btwn. 700.00
128 A19 2sh6p purple 32.50 9.00
129 A19 5sh rose 75.00 52.50
130 A19 10sh green ('03) 110.00 65.00
131 A19 £1 blue 275.00 150.00
Nos. 121-131 (12) 564.25 294.25

1904 *Perf. 12x11½*
132 A18 ½p yellow green 3.00 .55
133 A6 1p rose 6.50 .60
134 A6a 2p purple 6.50 .60
135 A16 2½p dark blue 14.00 1.50
136 A17 5p dull violet 11.00 1.75
Nos. 132-136 (5) 41.00 5.00

1904-08 *Perf. 12 and 12x11½*
137 A20 6p blue green 8.25 1.75
138 A20 8p ultra ('06) 11.50 2.25
139 A20 9p claret 8.00 1.60
139A A20 10p org buff ('07) 20.00 5.25
b. Pair, imperf. between 325.00 225.00
140 A20 1sh brown 12.00 2.00
a. Pair, imperf. between 250.00
141 A20 2sh6p purple ('05) 55.00 8.25
142 A20 5sh scarlet 55.00 32.50
142B A20 10sh green ('08) 140.00 125.00
143 A20 £1 deep blue 200.00 140.00
Nos. 137-143 (9) 509.75 318.60

See Nos. 148-150, 152-157.

1906-12 Wmk. 74
144 A18 ½p green 1.50 .20
145 A6 1p carmine 1.50 .20
146 A6a 2p purple 2.50 .20
a. Horiz. pair, imperf. between
147 A16 2½p dk blue ('11) 10.50 1.50
148 A20 3p ol grn (value 19mm long) 6.50 1.25
a. Horiz. pair, imperf. between
149 A20 3p ol grn (value 17mm long) ('09) 8.50 1.50
150 A20 4p red orange 9.75 1.75
151 A17 5p dull vio ('08) 8.50 2.00
152 A20 6p blue grn ('07) 7.50 1.10
a. Vert. pair, imperf. between 240.00
153 A20 8p ultra ('09) 15.00 5.50
154 A20 9p claret 15.00 3.00
a. Vert. pair, imperf. between 195.00
b. Horiz. pair, imperf. between 225.00
155 A20 1sh brown 11.00 3.00
a. Pair, imperf. between 175.00
156 A20 2sh6p purple ('09) 32.50 10.50
157 A20 5sh lt red ('12) 82.50
Nos. 144-157 (14) 212.75 31.70

OFFICIAL STAMPS

For Departments
Regular Issues Overprinted in Red, Black or Blue:

A. (Architect), A. G. (Attorney General), A. O. (Audit Office), B. D. (Barracks Department), B. G. (Botanical Gardens), B. M. (Bench of Magistrates), C. (Customs), C. D. (Convict Department), C. L. (Crown Lands), C. O. (Commissariat Officer), C. S. (Chief Secretary), C. Sgn. (Colonial Surgeon), C. P. (Commissioner of Police), C. T. (Commissioner of Titles), D. B. (Destitute Board), D. R. (Deed Registry), E. (Engineer), E. B. (Education Board),

G. P. (Government Printer), G. S. (Government Storekeeper), G. T. (Goolwa Tramway), G. F. (Gold Fields), H. (Hospital), H. A. (House of Assembly), I. A. (Immigration Agent), I. E. (Intestate Estates), I. S. (Inspector of Sheep), L. A. (Lunatic Asylum), L. C. (Legislative

Council), L. L. (Legislative Library), L. T. (Land Titles), M. (Military), M. B. (Marine Board), M. R. (Manager of Railways), M. R. G. (Main Roads Gambierton), N. T. (Northern Territory), O. A. (Official Assignee), P. (Police), P. A. (Protector of Aborigines), P. O. (Post Office), P. S. (Private Secretary), P. W. (Public Works), R. B. (Road Board), R. G. (Registrar General of Births, &c.), S. (Sheriff), S. C. (Supreme Court), S.G. (Surveyor General), S. M. (Stipendiary Magistrate), S. T. (Superintendent of Telegraph), T. (Treasurer), T. R. (Titles Registry), V. (Volunteers), V. A. (Valuator), V. N. (Vaccination), W. (Waterworks).

1868-74 Wmk. 6 *Rouletted*

Item	Unused	Used
O1 A1 1p green		
O2 A1 2p pale red		
O3 A6a 2p vermilion		
O4 A2 4p dull violet		
O5 A1 6p slate blue		
O6 A3 9p gray lilac		
O7 A1 1sh brown		
O8 A2 2sh carmine		

Perf. 11½ to 12½ x Roulette

Item	Unused	Used
O9 A1 1p green		
O10 A2 4p dull violet		
O11 A1 6p blue		
O12 A1 1sh brown		

Perf. 10, 11½, 12½ and Compound

Item	Unused	Used
O13 A1 1p green		
O14 A2 3p on 4p slate blue (Red)		
O16 A2 4p dull violet		
O17 A1 6p deep blue		
O18 A3 9p violet		
O19 A3 10p on 9p yellow (Blk)		
O20 A1 1sh brown		
O21 A2 2sh carmine		

Rouletted
Wmk. 72

O22 A6a 2p orange

Perf. 10 x Roulette

O23 A6a 2p orange

Perf. 10, 11½, 12½ and Compound

O24 A6a 2p orange

Wmk. 70
Perf. 10

O25 A6a 2p orange
O26 A2 4p dull violet

For General Use

Overprinted in Black **O.S.**

Perf. 10, 11½, 12½ and Compound
1874 Wmk. 6

Item	Unused	Used
O27 A1 1p green	—	*450.00*
a. Printed on both sides		
O28 A2 3p on 4p ultra		150.00
a. No period after "S"		375.00
O29 A2 4p dull violet	27.50	9.50
a. Inverted overprint		
b. No period after "S"		25.00
c. Perf. 10	1,650.	400.00
O30 A1 6p deep blue	55.00	9.50
a. No period after "S"		22.50
O31 A3 9p violet	250.00	60.00
a. No period after "S"	300.00	
O32 A1 1sh red brown	55.00	16.00
a. Double overprint		27.50
b. No period after "S"	110.00	40.00
O33 A2 2sh carmine	67.50	14.00
a. Double overprint		
b. No period after "S"		32.50

1874-75 Wmk. 72

Item	Unused	Used
O34 A6 1p blue green	100.00	27.50
a. Inverted overprint		
O35 A6a 2p orange	14.00	1.40

1876-86 Wmk. 7

Item	Unused	Used
O36 A2 3p on 4p ultra		
O37 A2 4p dull violet	100.00	17.00
O38 A2 4p reddish vio	37.50	3.00
a. Double overprint		
b. Inverted overprint		
c. Dbl. ovpt., one inverted		
O39 A1 6p dark blue	62.50	5.00
a. Double overprint		37.50
b. Inverted overprint		
O40 A1 6p ultramarine	57.50	4.50
a. Double overprint		
b. Inverted overprint		
O41 A3 8p on 9p yel brn	425.00	125.00
a. Double overprint	750.00	
O41B A3 9p violet	*4,000.*	
O42 A1 1sh red brown	45.00	5.00
a. Inverted overprint	150.00	75.00
b. Double overprint		
O43 A2 2sh carmine	110.00	8.00
a. Double overprint		70.00
b. Inverted overprint		75.00

1880-91 Wmk. 73

Item	Unused	Used
O44 A6 1p blue green	11.00	.50
a. Inverted overprint		22.50
b. Double overprint	35.00	20.00
c. Dbl. ovpt., one inverted		
O45 A6 1p yellow green	12.00	.50
O46 A6a 2p orange	11.00	.25
a. Inverted overprint		10.00
b. Double overprint	70.00	25.00
c. Overprinted sideways		
d. Dbl. ovpt., one inverted		
e. Dbl. ovpt., both inverted		57.50
O47 A6a 2p blood red	52.50	5.00
O48 A11 2½p on 4p green	35.00	9.50
a. "½" nearer the "2"		75.00
b. Double overprint		
c. Pair, one without ovpt.		
Nos. O44-O48 (5)	121.50	15.75

1882-90 *Perf. 10*

Item	Unused	Used
O49 A6 ½p on 1p green	25.00	8.00
a. Inverted overprint		
O50 A11 4p violet	21.00	1.90
O51 A12 6p blue	12.00	1.25
a. Double overprint		
Nos. O49-O51 (3)	58.00	11.15

Overprinted in Black **O.S.**

Perf. 10, 11½, 12½ and Compound
1891 Wmk. 7

Item	Unused	Used
O52 A1 1sh red brown	42.50	3.50
O53 A2 2sh carmine	100.00	10.00
a. Double overprint		

1891-95 Wmk. 73

Item	Unused	Used
O54 A9 ½p brown	12.00	2.50
O55 A6 1p blue green	12.00	.30
a. Double overprint	80.00	
O56 A6a 2p orange	12.00	.30
O57 A11 2½p on 4p green	45.00	2.75
a. "½" nearer the "2"	52.50	18.00
b. Inverted overprint	100.00	
O58 A11 4p violet	17.50	1.25
a. Double overprint		
O59 A12 5p on 6p red brn	55.00	2.50
O60 A12 6p blue	9.75	.75
a. Double overprint		
Nos. O54-O60 (7)	163.25	10.35

1893 *Perf. 15*

Item	Unused	Used
O61 A9 ½p brown	15.00	1.75
O62 A6 1p green	11.00	.30
O63 A6a 2p orange	12.00	.20
a. Inverted overprint		18.00
b. Double overprint		32.50
O64 A11 4p gray violet	65.00	1.75
a. Double overprint		21.00
O65 A17 5p dull violet	80.00	4.50
O66 A12 6p blue	20.00	.70
Nos. O61-O66 (6)	203.00	9.20

1896 *Perf. 13*

Item	Unused	Used
O67 A9 ½p brown	12.50	1.75
a. Triple overprint		
O68 A6 1p green	16.00	.20
O69 A6a 2p orange	11.00	.20
O70 A16 2½p blue violet	60.00	1.40
O71 A11 4p brt violet	65.00	1.75
a. Double overprint	30.00	40.00
O72 A17 5p dull violet	60.00	4.25
O73 A12 6p blue	25.00	.90
Nos. O67-O73 (7)	249.50	10.45

On No. O67a, one overprint is upright, two sideways.

Same Overprint in Dark Blue

1891-95 *Perf. 10*

Item	Unused	Used
O74 A6 1p green	150.00	15.00
O75 A12 6p blue		

Black Overprint

Perf. 11½, 12½, Clean-Cut
1897 Wmk. 7

Item	Unused	Used
O76 A1 1sh brown	40.00	4.50
a. Double overprint		

Overprinted in Black **O. S.**

1900 Wmk. 73 *Perf. 13*

Item	Unused	Used
O77 A18 ½p yellow green	10.00	1.75
O78 A6 1p carmine rose	11.50	.20
a. Inverted overprint		
b. Double overprint		
O79 A6a 2p purple	11.50	.20
a. Inverted ovpt.	40.00	
O80 A16 2½p dark blue	82.50	1.40
a. Inverted overprint		30.00
O81 A11 4p violet	65.00	.70
a. Inverted overprint	125.00	
O82 A12 6p blue	20.00	.75
Nos. O77-O82 (6)	200.50	5.00

1901 *Perf. 10*

Item	Unused	Used
O83 A13 2sh6p violet	*3,000.*	*2,000.*
O84 A13 5sh rose	*2,250.*	*2,250.*

On Nos. O77-O82 the letters "O.S." are 11½mm apart; on Nos. O83-O84, 14½mm apart.

Overprinted in Black **O.S.**

1903 Wmk. 72 *Perf. 11½, 12½*

Item	Unused	Used
O85 A1 1sh red brown	40.00	25.00

Many of the official stamps are found with one or both the periods after "O.S." missing. This occurs more often in the later than in the earlier issues.

TASMANIA

taz-ˈmā-nē-ə

LOCATION — An island off the south-eastern coast of Australia
GOVT. — British Colony
AREA — 26,215 sq. mi.
POP. — 172,475 (1901)
CAPITAL — Hobart

Tasmania was one of the six British colonies that united in 1901 to form the Commonwealth of Australia. The island was originally named Van Diemen's Land by its discoverer, Abel Tasman, the present name having been adopted in 1853. Stamps of Australia are now used.

12 Pence = 1 Shilling
20 Shillings = 1 Pound

Watermarks

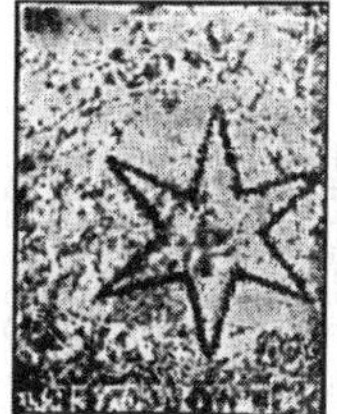
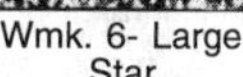

Wmk. 6- Large Star

Wmk. 49- Double-lined Numeral

Wmk. 75- Double-lined Numeral

Wmk. 50- Single-lined "2"

Wmk. 51- Single-lined "4"

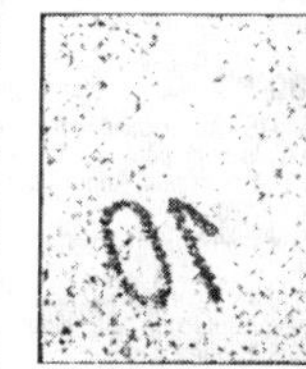

Wmk. 52- Single-lined "10"

Wmk. 70- V and Crown

Wmk. 13- Crown & Double-lined A

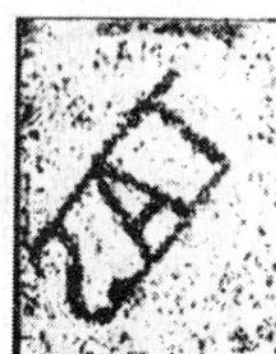

Wmk. 76- TAS

Wmk. 77- TAS

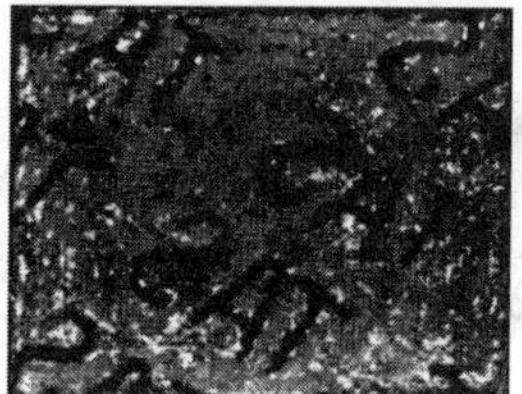

Wmk. 78- Multiple TAS

Values for unused stamps are for examples with original gum as defined in the catalogue introduction except for Nos. 1-2a and 10 which are valued without gum as few examples exist with any remaining original gum. Very fine examples of Nos. 17-75a will have perforations touching the design on one or more sides due to the narrow spacing of the stamps on the plates. Stamps with perfs clear of the design on all four sides are scarce and command higher prices.

Queen Victoria
A1 A2

Unwmk.

1853, Nov. 1 Engr. *Imperf.*

Item	Unused	Used
1 A1 1p blue	3,500.	850.00
2 A2 4p red orange	2,250.	400.00
a. 4p yellow orange	2,250.	325.00
Cut to shape		17.50

Twenty-four varieties of each.

The 4p on vertically laid paper is believed to be a proof. Value, unused, $5,000.

The reprints are made from defaced plates and show marks across the face of each stamp. They are on thin and thick, unwatermarked paper and thin cardboard; only the first are perforated. Nearly all the reprints of Tasmania may be found with and without the overprint "REPRINT."

Nos. 1-47A with pen or revenue cancellations sell for a small fraction of the price of postally used specimens. Copies are found with pen cancellation removed.

Queen Victoria — A3

1855 Wmk. 6 Wove Paper

Item	Unused	Used
4 A3 1p dark carmine	5,500.	825.00
5 A3 2p green	1,800.	500.00
a. 2p deep green	1,800.	600.00
6 A3 4p deep blue	1,250.	85.00

1856-57 Unwmk.

Item	Unused	Used
7 A3 1p pale red	5,500.	525.00
8 A3 2p emerald ('57)	6,500.	750.00
9 A3 4p blue ('57)	650.00	95.00

1856 Pelure Paper

Item	Unused	Used
10 A3 1p brown red	3,250.	625.00

1857 Wmk. 139, 49, 75

11 A3 1p carmine 85.00 17.00
a. 1p orange red 85.00 17.00
b. 1p brown red 400.00 22.50
c. Double impression 150.00
12 A3 2p sage green 150.00 57.50
a. 2p yellow green 260.00 70.00
b. 2p green — 37.50
13 A3 4p pale blue 110.00 14.00
b. Printed on both sides —
d. Double impression 150.00
Nos. 11-13 (3) 345.00

See #17-19, 23-25, 29-31, 35-37, 39-41, 45-47A.

A4

A4a

1858

14 A4 6p gray lilac 160.00 52.50
a. 6p red violet 625.00 150.00
b. Double impression 225.00
15 A4 6p blue gray 400.00 85.00
16 A4a 1sh vermilion 550.00 67.50
Nos. 14-16 (3) 1,110. 205.00

No. 15 watermarked large star was not regularly issued.

1864 ***Rouletted***

17 A3 1p carmine 375.00 125.00
a. 1p brick red — 175.00
18 A3 2p yellow grn — 400.00
19 A3 4p blue — 175.00
21 A4 6p gray lilac — 225.00
22 A4a 1sh vermilion — 625.00

1864-69 ***Perf. 10***

23 A3 1p brick red 50.00 19.00
a. 1p carmine 50.00 19.00
b. 1p orange red 50.00 19.00
c. As "b," double impression —
24 A3 2p yellow green 275.00 65.00
a. 2p sage green 375.00 150.00
25 A3 4p blue 125.00 9.00
a. Double impression 110.00
26 A4 6p lilac 140.00 12.50
a. 6p red lilac 375.00 55.00
27 A4 6p slate blue 190.00 47.50
28 A4a 1sh vermilion 100.00 19.00
a. Horiz. pair, imperf. vert.
Nos. 23-28 (6) 880.00 172.00

1864-69 ***Perf. 12, 12½***

29 A3 1p carmine 42.50 8.50
a. 1p orange red 52.50 —
b. 1p brick red 62.50 27.50
c. Double impression —
d. Wmkd. "2" 1,000.
As "d," pen cancel 125.00
30 A3 2p yellow green 125.00 42.50
a. 2p dark green 260.00 125.00
b. 2p sage green 275.00 125.00
31 A3 4p blue 80.00 15.00

Perf. 11½, 12½

32 A4 6p red lilac 75.00 35.00
a. 6p purple 75.00 35.00
b. 6p violet 140.00 22.50
d. Horiz. pair, imperf. vert. —
e. Double impression —
33 A4 6p slate blue, perf. 12½ 325.00 80.00
34 A4a 1sh vermilion 125.00 30.00
a. Double impression 160.00
b. Horiz. pair, imperf. vert. —
Nos. 29-34 (6) 772.50 211.00

The reprints are on unwatermarked paper, perforated 11½, and on thin cardboard, imperforate and perforated.

Pin-perf. 5½ to 9½, 13½ to 14½

1867

35 A3 1p carmine 350.00 77.50
36 A3 2p yellow green 300.00
37 A3 4p blue 160.00
38 A4 6p gray 150.00
38A A4 6p red lilac 450.00
38B A4a 1sh vermilion —

Oblique Roulette

39 A3 1p carmine 350.00
40 A3 2p yellow green 410.00
41 A3 4p blue 325.00
42 A4 6p gray 550.00
43 A4 6p red lilac —
44 A4a 1sh vermilion 750.00

1868 ***Serrate Perf. 19***

45 A3 1p carmine 275.00 125.00
46 A3 2p yellow green 250.00
47 A3 4p blue 650.00 110.00
47A A3 6p purple 500.00

Queen Victoria — A5

1870-71 Typo. Wmk. 50 ***Perf. 11½***

48 A5 2p blue green 52.50 4.00
a. Double impression —
b. Perf. 12 62.50 5.50
c. 2p green 95.00 6.50
d. As "d," perf. 12 57.50 5.50
e. As "d," imperf, pair —

See Nos. 49-75, 98, 108-109.

Wmk. 51

49 A5 1p rose ('71) 60.00 20.00
a. Imperf., pair 600.00 210.00
50 A5 4p blue 725.00 300.00

Wmk. 52

51 A5 1p rose 40.00 9.00
a. Imperf. pair 275.00 250.00
c. Perf. 11½ 1,000.
52 A5 10p black 20.00 17.00
a. Imperf. pair 125.00
b. Perf. 11½ 25.00 20.00

The reprints are on unwatermarked paper. The 4p has also been reprinted on thin cardboard, imperf and perf.

1871-76 Wmk. 76 ***Perf. 11½***

53 A5 1p rose 4.50 .60
a. Imperf.
c. Perf. 12 65.00 9.00
53B A5 1p vermilion ('73) 250.00 95.00
54 A5 2p dp grn ('72) 12.00 .60
a. 2p yellow green 125.00 1.25
b. 2p blue green 45.00 .60
c. Imperf. pair 125.00
d. 2p green, perf. 12 450.00 140.00
e. Double impression
55 A5 3p brown 37.50 4.50
a. 3p purple brown 37.50 4.50
b. As "a," imperf. pair 325.00
56 A5 3p red brown ('71) 37.50 4.50
a. 3p indian red 35.00 4.50
b. Imperf. pair 125.00
c. Vert. pair, imperf. horiz.
d. Perf. 12 85.00 21.00
57 A5 4p dull yellow ('76) 40.00 7.50
a. Perf. 12 225.00 15.00
58 A5 9p blue 20.00 7.50
a. Imperf. pair 125.00
b. Perf. 12 40.00 40.00
59 A5 5sh bright violet 125.00 37.50
a. Imperf.
b. Horiz. pair, imperf. vert.
c. Perf. 12 175.00 150.00
Pen cancel .30
Nos. 53-59 (8) 526.50 157.70

The reprints are on unwatermarked paper, the 5sh has also been reprinted on thin cardboard; all are perforated.

1878 Wmk. 77 ***Perf. 14***

60 A5 1p rose 4.50 .60
61 A5 2p deep green 4.50 .60
62 A5 8p violet brown 15.00 4.50
Nos. 60-62 (3) 24.00 5.70

The 8p has been reprinted on thin unwatermarked paper, perforated 11½.

1880-83 ***Perf. 12, 11½***

63 A5 3p indian red, perf. 12 9.00 2.00
a. Imperf. pair 85.00
b. Horiz. pair, imperf. between 600.00
c. Perf. 11½ 10.50 3.00
64 A5 4p lem, perf. 11½ ('83) 40.00 7.50
a. 4p olive yellow, perf. 11½ 95.00 21.00
b. Printed on both sides 210.00
c. Imperf.
d. 4p deep yellow, perf. 12 75.00 22.50

Type of 1871 Surcharged in Black

1889 ***Perf. 14***

65 A5 ½p on 1p carmine 9.00 1.75
a. "al" sideways in surcharge 825.00 *500.00*

No. 65 has been reprinted on thin cardboard, perforated 12, with the surcharge "Halfpenny" 19mm long.

1889-96 ***Perf. 11½***

66 A5 ½p red orange 2.25 .70
a. ½p yellow orange 2.25 .70
b. Perf. 12 2.00 .85
67 A5 1p dull red 8.25 2.00
a. 1p vermilion 5.00 2.00
68 A5 1p car, perf. 12 8.25 3.25
a. 1p pink, perf. 12 27.50 5.00
b. 1p salmon rose, perf. 12 8.25 3.25
c. Imperf. pair 92.50 92.50

Perf. 12

69 A5 4p bister ('96) 18.00 8.25
70 A5 9p chalky bl ('96) 10.00 3.25
Nos. 66-70 (5) 46.75 17.45

1891 Wmk. 76 ***Perf. 11½***

71 A5 ½p orange 16.00 8.25
a. ½p brown orange 16.00 8.25
b. Imperf. pair 75.00
c. Perf. 12 35.00 9.25
72 A5 1p salmon rose 21.00 11.50
a. 1p carmine, perf. 12 40.00 20.00
73 A5 4p ol bis, perf. 12 15.00 6.50
Nos. 71-73 (3) 52.00 26.25

See Nos. 98, 108-109.

Surcharged in Black

1891 Wmk. 77 ***Perf. 11½***

Surcharge 14mm High

74 A5 2½p on 9p lt blue 6.00 6.50
a. Dbl. surcharge, one invtd. 210.00 200.00
b. Imperf. pair 140.00

Perf. 12

Surcharge 15mm High

75 A5 2½p on 9p lt blue 5.50 5.00
a. Surcharged in blue

No. 74 has been reprinted on thin unwatermarked paper, imperforate. There is also a reprint on thin cardboard, in deep ultramarine, with surcharge 16½mm high, and perforated 12.

A8

A9

1892-99 Typo. ***Perf. 14***

76 A8 ½p orange & vio .85 .35
77 A9 2½p magenta 2.50 .65
78 A8 5p pale bl & brn 3.50 1.40
79 A8 6p blue vio & blk 3.50 1.50
80 A8 10p red brn & grn ('99) 6.75 5.50
81 A8 1sh rose & green 4.50 1.50
82 A8 2sh6p brown & blue 25.00 8.00
83 A8 5sh brn vio & red 37.50 17.00
84 A8 10sh brt vio & brn 75.00 45.00
85 A8 £1 green & yel 475.00 225.00
Nos. 76-85 (10) 634.10 305.90

No. 80 shows the numeral on white tablet. See #99, 110-111. For overprint see #AR35.

Lake Marion — A10

Mt. Wellington — A11

View of Hobart — A12

Tasman's Arch — A13

Spring River, Port Davey — A14

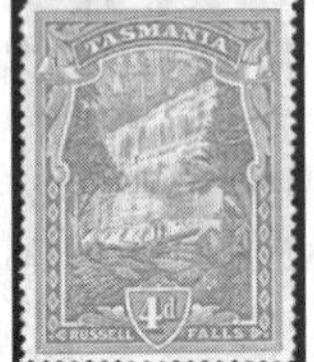

Russell Falls — A15

Mt. Gould and Lake St. Clair — A16

Dilston Falls — A17

1899-1900 Engr. Wmk. 78 ***Perf. 14***

86 A10 ½p dark green 5.00 1.75
87 A11 1p carmine 5.00 .60
88 A12 2p violet 5.50 .45
89 A13 2½p dark blue 11.00 5.00
90 A14 3p dark brown 8.50 1.75
91 A15 4p ocher 16.00 2.25
92 A16 5p ultramarine 16.00 7.50
93 A17 6p lake 20.00 6.50
Nos. 86-93 (8) 87.00 25.80

See Nos. 94-97, 102-107, 114-117.

Perf. 11, 12½, 11x12½

1902-03 Litho., Typo. Wmk. 70

94 A10 ½p green 2.25 .30
95 A11 1p carmine 5.50 .20
96 A11 1p dull red 5.00 .20
97 A12 2p violet 3.25 .20
98 A5 9p blue 9.00 3.00
a. 9p ultramarine 225.00
b. 9p indigo 90.00
c. Perf. 11 7.25 3.50
99 A8 1sh rose & green 12.00 3.75
a. Perf. 11 27.50 27.50
Nos. 94-99 (6) 37.00 7.65

Nos. 94, 97 are litho., Nos. 96, 98-99 typo. No. 95 was printed both ways.

No. 78 Surcharged in Black

1904 Wmk. 77 ***Perf. 14***

100 A8 1½p on 5p blue & brn 1.75 1.25

Perf. 11, 12, 12½ and Compound

1905-08 Typo. Wmk. 13

102 A10 ½p dull green 2.00 .20
a. Booklet pane of 12
103 A11 1p carmine 2.00 .20
a. Booklet pane of 18
104 A12 2p violet 3.50 .20
105 A14 3p dark brown 7.00 2.00
106 A15 4p ocher 13.00 2.25
107 A17 6p lake 40.00 5.00
108 A5 8p violet brown 19.00 5.00
109 A5 9p blue 8.00 3.00
110 A8 1sh rose & green 13.00 2.50

111 A8	10sh brt vio & brn	100.00	62.50
a.	Perf. 11	175.00	
	Nos. 102-111 (10)	207.50	82.85

Nos. 104-107 also printed litho.

1911 **Redrawn**

114 A12	2p bright violet	3.50	.30
115 A15	4p dull yellow	16.00	8.00
116 A17	6p lake	17.00	8.00
	Nos. 114-116 (3)	36.50	16.30

The redrawn 2p measures 33½x25mm instead of 32½x24½mm. There are many slight changes in the clouds and other parts of the design.

The 4p is much lighter, especially the waterfall and trees above it. This appears to be a new or cleaned plate rather than a redrawn one.

In the redrawn 6p there are more colored lines in the waterfall and the river and more white dots in the trees.

No. 114 Surcharged in Red

1912

117 A12	1p on 2p bright violet	.85	.50

POSTAL FISCAL STAMPS

Authorised for postal use by Act of November 1, 1882. Authorization withdrawn Nov. 30, 1900.

Used values are for examples with postal cancellations used from Nov. 1, 1882 through Nov. 30, 1900.

Beware of copies with a pen cancellation removed and a fake postmark added.

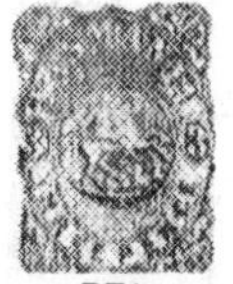

PF1

PF2

St. George and the Dragon
PF3 PF4

1863-64 Engr. Wmk. 139 *Imperf.*

AR1	PF1	3p green	75.00	50.00
AR2	PF2	2sh 6p car	80.00	50.00
AR3	PF3	5sh green	75.00	55.00
AR4	PF3	5sh brown	200.00	*150.00*
AR5	PF4	10sh orange	175.00	*150.00*

For overprint see No. AR32.

Perf. 10

AR6	PF1	3p green	40.00	22.50
AR7	PF2	2sh 6p car	50.00	
AR8	PF3	5sh brown	75.00	
AR9	PF4	10sh orange	42.50	

Perf. 12

AR10	PF1	3p green	45.00	27.50
AR11	PF2	2sh 6p car	45.00	35.00
AR12	PF3	5sh green	32.50	27.50
AR13	PF3	5sh brown	80.00	
AR14	PF4	10sh orange	35.00	27.50

Perf. 12½

AR15	PF1	3p green	80.00	
AR16	PF2	2sh 6p car	80.00	
AR17	PF3	5sh brown	100.00	
AR18	PF4	10sh orange	70.00	

Perf. 11½

AR19	PF1	3p green		
AR20	PF2	2sh 6p car	42.50	32.50
AR21	PF3	5sh green	32.50	22.50
AR22	PF4	10sh orange	55.00	40.00

Wmk. 77
Perf. 12

AR23	PF2	2sh 6p car	20.00	15.00

For overprint see No. AR33.

Duck-billed Platypus — PF5

1880 Engr. Wmk. 77 *Perf. 14*

AR24	PF5	1p slate	12.50	4.00
AR25	PF5	3p brown	12.50	3.00
AR26	PF5	6p lilac	65.00	2.50
AR27	PF5	1sh rose	75.00	6.00

For overprints see Nos. AR28-AR31.

Nos. AR24-AR27, AR2, AR23, 85 Overprinted "REVENUE"

1900, Nov. 15

AR28	PF5	1p slate	20.00	
AR29	PF5	3p brown	20.00	*20.00*
AR30	PF5	6p lilac	60.00	
AR31	PF5	1sh rose	100.00	
AR32	PF2	2sh 6p car (#AR2)		
AR33	PF2	2sh 6p car (#AR23)	200.00	
AR34	PF4	10sh orange		
AR35	A8	£1 grn & yel (#85)	200.00	*150.00*

Nos. AR28-AR35 were not supposed to be postally used. Because of imprecise terminology, postal use was tolerated until all postal use of revenues ceased on Nov. 30, 1900.

Other denominations and watermarks were overprinted after postal use was no longer allowed.

VICTORIA

vik-'tōr-ē-ə

LOCATION — In the extreme south-eastern part of Australia
GOVT. — British Colony
AREA — 87,884 sq. mi.
POP. — 1,201,341 (1901)
CAPITAL — Melbourne

Victoria was one of the six former British colonies which united on Jan. 1, 1901, to form the Commonwealth of Australia.

12 Pence = 1 Shilling
20 Shillings = 1 Pound

Unused values for Nos. 1-16 are for stamps without gum as these stamps are seldom found with original gum. Otherwise, unused values are for stamps with original gum as defined in the catalogue introduction.

Very fine examples of all rouletted, perforated and serrate perforated stamps from Nos. 9-109 and F2 will have roulettes, perforations or serrate perforations touching the design. Examples clear on four sides range from scarce to rare and will command higher prices.

Watermarks

Wmk. 6—Large Star

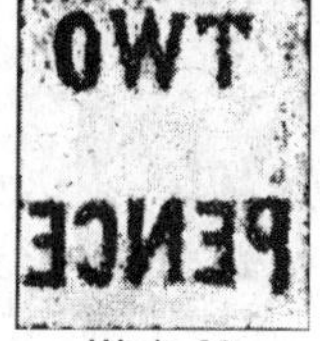

Wmk. 80

Wmk. 50

Wmk. 80a

Wmk. 81

Wmk. 139

Wmk. 49

Wmk. 75

Wmk. 70—V and Crown

Wmk. 13—Crown & Double-lined A

Queen Victoria
A1

Victoria on Throne
A2

1850 Litho. Unwmk. *Imperf.*

1	A1	1p dull red	1,150.	110.00
a.		1p vermilion	1,450.	400.00
2	A1	1p rose	700.00	125.00
a.		1p pink	550.00	100.00
3	A1	3p blue	*2,000.*	200.00
a.		3p light blue	550.00	45.00
4	A1	3p indigo	625.00	50.00
		Nos. 1-4 (4)	4,475.	485.00

Nos. 1-4 exist with and without frame line.

THREE TYPES OF 2p:

Type I - Border, two sets of nine wavy lines crisscrossing. Background, 22 groups of wavy triple lines below "VICTORIA."

Type II - Border, same. Background, 15 groups of wavy triple lines below "VICTORIA."

Type III - Border, two sets of five wavy lines crisscrossing. Background, same as type II.

5	A1	2p lilac, I	*3,000.*	300.00
a.		2p brn lilac, I	*3,250.*	325.00
6	A1	2p brn lilac, II	1,100.	100.00
a.		2p gray lilac, II	1,200.	110.00
7	A1	2p brn lilac, III	*800.00*	100.00
a.		2p gray lilac, III	*800.00*	275.00
b.		Value omitted, III		*2,500.*
8	A1	2p yel brn, III	550.00	100.00

Rouletted 7

9	A1	1p vermilion		*2,250.*
10	A1	3p blue		190.00
a.		3p deep blue	*1,600.*	200.00

Perf. 12

12	A1	3p blue	*1,500.*	125.00
a.		3p deep blue	*1,500.*	125.00

1852 Engr. *Imperf.*

14	A2	2p reddish brown	160.00	35.00

#14 was reprinted on paper with watermark 70, imperf. & perf. 12½, overprinted "REPRINT."

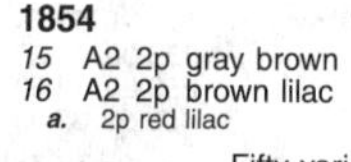

1854 Litho.

15	A2	2p gray brown	240.00	35.00
16	A2	2p brown lilac	200.00	30.00
a.		2p red lilac	250.00	35.00

Fifty varieties.

A3

A4

1854-58 Typo.

17	A3	6p orange	175.00	25.00
a.		6p red orange	240.00	30.00

See Nos. 19-20, 22-24A, 26-28

Lithographed

18	A4	1sh blue	725.00	22.50

See Nos. 21, 25.

Typographed

19	A3	2sh green	1,150.	150.00

1857-58 *Rouletted 7, 9½*

20	A3	6p orange	—	55.00

Lithographed

21	A4	1sh blue	—	90.00

Typographed

22	A3	2sh green ('58)	*4,000.*	350.00

Small Serrate Perf. 19

23	A3	6p orange	—	90.00

Large Serpentine Perf. 10½

24	A3	6p orange	—	75.00

Serrate x Serpentine Perf.

24A	A3	6p orange	—	125.00

1859 Litho. *Perf. 12*

25	A4	1sh blue	160.00	14.00

Typographed

26	A3	2sh green	260.00	37.50

1861 Wmk. "SIX PENCE" (80)

27	A3	6p black	250.00	52.50

Wmk. Single-lined "2" (50)

1864 *Perf. 12, 13*

28	A3	2sh blue, *green*	225.00	8.50

A5

Wmk. Large Star (6)

1856, Oct. Engr. *Imperf.*

29	A5	1p green	125.00	27.50

1858 *Rouletted 5½-6½*

30	A5	6p blue	125.00	12.50

Nos. 29 and 30 have been reprinted on paper watermarked V and Crown. They are imperforate and overprinted "REPRINT."

A6

A7

1857-61 Typo. *Imperf.*

31	A6	1p yellow green	100.00	13.50
a.		Printed on both sides		*825.00*
32	A6	4p vermilion	275.00	13.50
a.		Printed on both sides		*825.00*
33	A6	4p rose	225.00	11.00

Rouletted 7 to 9½

34	A6	1p yellow green	325.00	110.00
35	A6	4p rose	—	35.00

Perf. 12

36	A6	1p yellow green	—	300.00

Unwmk. *Imperf.*

37	A6 1p blue green	325.00	13.50
38	A6 2p lilac	250.00	13.50
39	A6 4p rose	*450.00*	35.00

Copies of No. 39 printed in dull carmine on thin paper are regarded as printer's waste and of little value. They are also found printed on both sides.

Rouletted 7 to 9½

40	A6 1p blue green	300.00	17.50
a.	1p yellow green		
b.	Horiz. pair, imperf. btwn.		
41	A6 2p lilac		
42	A6 4p rose	275.00	8.00
a.	Horiz. pair, imperf. btwn.		

Perf. 12

43	A6 1p blue green	150.00	10.00
a.	1p yellow green	175.00	13.50
b.	Horiz. pair, imperf. btwn.		—
44	A6 2p lilac		225.00
45	A6 4p rose	160.00	4.50
b.	Vert. pair, imperf. btwn.		

Serrate Perf. 19

45A	A6 2p lilac	600.00	350.00

Laid Paper

Imperf

46	A6 4p rose	550.00	22.50

Rouletted 5 to 7

47	A6 2p violet	150.00	5.50
a.	2p brown lilac	200.00	7.50
b.	2p dark lilac	200.00	17.50
48	A6 4p rose	150.00	4.75

Perf. 12

49	A6 1p green	225.00	12.50
50	A6 4p rose	140.00	10.00

Wove Paper

1860 Wmk. Value in Words (80)

51	A6 1p yellow green	65.00	7.00
a.	Wmk. "FOUR PENCE" (error)		—
52	A6 2p gray lilac	125.00	6.75
a.	2p brown lilac	—	24.00

Wmk. "THREE PENCE" (80)

53	A6 2p gray lilac	225.00	10.00

Single-lined "2" (50)

54	A6 2p lilac	160.00	12.50
a.	2p gray lilac	160.00	15.00
b.	2p brown lilac	160.00	14.00
c.	As "b," wmkd. single-lined "6"		*4,500.*

1860 Unwmk. Laid Paper

56	A7 3p deep blue	350.00	40.00

Wmk. Value in Words (80)

Perf. 11½ to 12

1860-62 Wove Paper

57	A7 3p blue	160.00	9.00
58	A7 3p claret	160.00	32.50
a.	Perf. 13	175.00	35.00
59	A7 4p rose	160.00	4.00
60	A7 6p orange	*3,000.*	300.00
61	A7 6p black	225.00	7.00

Wmk. "FIVE SHILLINGS" (80)

62	A7 4p rose	*1,500.*	20.00

Wmk. Single-lined "4" (80a)

1863 *Imperf.*

63	A7 4p rose		— 125.00

Rouletted

64	A7 4p rose	*2,400.*	225.00

Perf. 11½ to 12

65	A7 4p rose	100.00	7.25

1863 Unwmk. *Perf. 12*

66	A7 4p rose	400.00	10.50

A8

A9

1861-63 Wmk. 80 *Perf. 11½ to 12*

67	A8 1p green	80.00	8.00
68	A9 6p black	80.00	6.50

Wmk. Double-lined "1" (139)

69	A8 1p green	175.00	11.50

Wmk. Single-lined Figures (50)

70	A8 1p green	57.50	6.00
71	A9 6p black	160.00	6.00

The 1p and 6p of 1861-63 are known on paper without watermark but were probably impressions on the margins of watermarked sheets.

A10

A11

A12

A13

Wmk. Single-lined Figures (50, 80a, 81)

1863-67 *Perf. 11½ to 13*

74	A10 1p green	70.00	4.00
a.	Double impression		825.00
75	A10 2p gray lilac	67.50	4.00
a.	2p violet	60.00	5.75
76	A10 4p rose	100.00	3.00
a.	Double impression		825.00
77	A11 6p blue	80.00	3.00
78	A10 8p orange	300.00	52.50
79	A12 10p brn, *rose*	140.00	5.00
80	A13 1sh blue, *blue*	140.00	3.00
	Nos. 74-80 (7)	897.50	74.50

See Nos. 81-82, 84-96, 99-101, 108-112, 115-119, 124-126, 144, 188. Compare design A11 design A54.

A14

Wmk. Double-lined "1" (139)

81	A10 1p green	85.00	5.00
82	A10 2p gray lilac	225.00	7.50
83	A14 3p lilac	175.00	40.00
84	A11 6p blue	60.00	5.50
	Nos. 81-84 (4)	545.00	58.00

See Nos. 97, 113, 155, 186. Compare design A14 with design A51.

Wmk. Double-lined "2" (49)

85	A11 6p blue		

Wmk. Single-lined "4" (80a)

86	A10 1p green	140.00	11.00
87	A10 2p gray lilac	175.00	6.50
88	A11 6p blue		*1,600.*

Wmk. Double-lined "4" (75)

89	A10 1p green	1,300.	140.00
90	A10 2p gray lilac	180.00	5.50
91	A10 4p rose	200.00	6.50
92	A11 6p blue	300.00	16.00

Wmk. Single-lined "6" (50)

93	A10 1p green	225.00	20.00
94	A10 2p gray lilac	200.00	5.75

Wmk. Single-lined "8" (50)

95	A10 1p green	200.00	13.50
96	A10 2p gray lilac	225.00	7.00
97	A14 3p lilac	175.00	27.50
99	A12 10p slate	550.00	110.00

Wmk. "SIX PENCE" (80)

100	A10 1p green	675.00	21.00
101	A11 6p blue	325.00	15.00

All values of the 1864-67 series except the 3p and 8p are known on unwatermarked paper. They are probably varieties from watermarked sheets which have been so placed on the printing press that some of the stamps escaped the watermark.

One copy of the 2p gray lilac, design A10, is reported to exist with only "PENCE" of watermark 80 showing. Some believe this is part of the "SIX PENCE" watermark.

1870 Wmk. "THREE PENCE" (80)

108	A11 6p blue	225.00	6.25

Wmk. "FOUR PENCE" (80)

109	A11 6p blue	500.00	40.00

A15

1867-78 Wmk. (70) *Perf. 11½ to 13*

110	A10 1p green	60.00	2.00
111	A10 2p lilac	85.00	3.25
a.	2p gray lilac	62.50	2.00
112	A10 2p lilac, *lilac*	90.00	10.00
113	A14 3p red lilac	300.00	18.00
a.	3p lilac	350.00	20.00
114	A14 3p orange	22.50	2.00
a.	3p yellow	62.50	2.00
115	A10 4p rose	90.00	3.50
116	A11 6p blue	25.00	2.50
117	A11 6p ultra	27.50	2.50
a.	6p lilac blue	62.50	2.25
118	A10 8p brn, *rose*	125.00	5.00
119	A13 1sh bl, *blue*	250.00	10.00
120	A15 5sh bl, *yel*	1,700.	450.00
121	A15 5sh bl & rose	160.00	15.00
a.	Without blue line under crown	140.00	15.00
122	A15 5sh ultra & rose	175.00	20.00

See #126, 144, 188. For surcharge see #124.

See #191. Compare design A15 with design A58.

A16

A19

1870 *Perf. 13*

123	A16 2p lilac	40.00	2.00
a.	Perf. 12	40.00	1.25

No. 110 Surcharged in Red — ½ ½ HALF

1873, July 19 *Perf. 13, 12*

124	A10 ½p on 1p green	35.00	10.00

No. 79 Surcharged in Blue — 9 9 NINEPENCE

1871 Wmk. Single-lined "10" (81)

125	A12 9p on 10p brn, *rose*	375.00	11.00
a.	Double surcharge		*1,200.*

1873-78 Typo.

126	A10 8p brown, *rose* ('78)	125.00	6.50
127	A19 9p brown, *rose*	125.00	6.50

For additional stamps of design A19, see Nos. 128-129, 174-175. Compare design A19 with design A55.

1875 Wmk. V and Crown (70)

128	A19 9p brown, *rose*	140.00	11.00

No. 128 Surcharged in Black — 8d 8d EIGHTPENCE

1876

129	A19 8p on 9p brn, *rose*	175.00	14.00

A21

A22

A23

A24 A25

1873-81 *Perf. 13, 12*

130	A21 ½p rose ('74)	5.50	.35
131	A21 ½p rose, *rose* ('78)	20.00	8.00
132	A22 1p grn ('75)	15.00	1.00
133	A22 1p grn, *gray* ('78)	90.00	60.00
134	A22 1p grn, *yel* ('78)	60.00	15.00
135	A23 2p violet	15.00	.25
136	A23 2p vio, *grnsh* ('78)	125.00	15.00
137	A23 2p vio, *buff* ('78)	125.00	15.00
137A	A23 2p vio, *lil* ('78)		350.00
138	A24 1sh bl, *bl* ('76)	55.00	4.00
139	A25 2sh bl, *grn* ('81)	175.00	20.00

See Nos. 140, 156A-159, 184, 189-190. Compare design A21 with design A46, A24 with A56, A25 with A57.

1878

Double-lined Outer Oval

140	A23 2p violet	20.00	.25
a.	Imperf., pair		400.00
b.	Pair, imperf. btwn.		

A26

A27

A28

1881-83 *Perf. 12½*

141	A26 1p green ('83)	14.00	.90
142	A27 2p brown	27.50	.25
143	A27 2p lilac	12.00	.20
144	A10 4p car rose	200.00	2.75
145	A28 4p car rose	40.00	1.50
	Nos. 141-145 (5)	293.50	5.60

See Nos. 156, 185, 187. Compare design A26 with design A47, A27 with A49, A28 with A52.

A29

A30

A31 A32

A33

A34

1884-86

146	A29 ½p rose	6.00	.40
147	A30 1p green	6.00	.20
148	A31 2p violet	4.75	.20
a.	2p lilac rose	10.50	.20
149	A30 3p bister	8.00	.50
a.	3p ocher	6.50	.50
150	A32 4p magenta	32.50	2.25
a.	4p violet (error)	*4,000.*	400.00
151	A30 6p gray blue	42.50	1.40
a.	6p ultramarine	35.00	1.40
152	A33 8p rose, *rose*	22.50	4.50
153	A34 1sh blue, *yel*	47.50	3.25
154	A33 2sh olive, *grn*	22.50	2.00
	Nos. 146-154 (9)	192.25	14.70

See Nos. 177-178, 192A. Compare designs A31-A32 with designs A37-A38.

Nos. 114, 145, 138-139 Overprinted "STAMP / DUTY" Vertically in Blue or Black

1885

155	A14	3p orange (Bl)	60.00	21.00
156	A28	4p car rose (Bl)	50.00	12.50
156A	A24	1sh bl, *bl* (Bl)		1,250.
157	A24	1sh bl, *bl* (Bk)	95.00	22.50
158	A25	2sh bl, *grn* (Bk)	75.00	20.00
		Nos. 155-156,157-158 (4)	280.00	76.00

Reprints of 4p and 1sh have brighter colors than originals. They lack the overprint "REPRINT."

A35

A36

A37

A38

A39

A40

1886-87 ***Perf. 12½***

159	A35	½p lilac	16.00	3.00
160	A35	½p rose	4.50	.20
160A	A35	½p scarlet	5.00	.20
161	A36	1p green	5.00	.20
162	A37	2p violet	3.00	.20
a.		2p red lilac	2.00	.20
b.		Imperf.		
163	A38	4p red	6.00	.60
164	A39	6p blue	7.50	.40
165	A39	6p ultra	7.50	.20
166	A40	1sh lilac brown	22.50	1.50
		Nos. 159-166 (9)	77.00	6.50

See No. 180.

A41

A42

1889

167	A41	1sh6p blue	110.00	62.50
168	A41	1sh6p orange	15.00	4.00

Southern Cross A43

Queen Victoria A44

1890-95 ***Perf. 12½***

169	A42	1p org brn	2.25	.20
a.		1p chocolate brown	2.75	.20
170	A42	1p yel brn	2.00	.20
171	A42	1p brn org, *pink* ('91)	1.60	.50
172	A43	2½p brn red, *yel*	6.00	.50
173	A44	5p choc ('91)	7.00	.50
174	A19	9p green ('92)	20.00	5.00
175	A19	9p rose red	13.00	1.50
a.		9p rose ('95)	13.00	1.50
176	A40	1sh deep claret	15.00	.50
a.		1sh red brown	13.00	.40
b.		1sh maroon	20.00	1.00
177	A33	2sh yel grn	25.00	10.00
178	A33	2sh emerald	20.00	6.00
		Nos. 169-178 (10)	111.85	24.90

In 1891 many stamps of the early issues were reprinted. They are on paper watermarked V and Crown, perforated 12, 12½, and overprinted "REPRINT."

See Nos. 181, 183, 192. Compare design A43 with design A50, A44 with A53.

A45

1897

179	A45	1½p yellow green	4.00	1.75

See No. 182. Compare design A45 with design A48.

1899

180	A35	½p emerald	5.00	.20
181	A42	1p brt rose	4.00	.20
182	A45	1½p red, *yel*	2.75	1.50
183	A43	2½p dark blue	6.50	1.25
		Nos. 180-183 (4)	18.25	3.15

1901

184	A21	½p blue green	1.90	.50
a.		"VICTCRIA"	65.00	25.00
185	A27	2p violet	4.50	.20
186	A14	3p brown org	14.00	1.50
187	A28	4p bister	25.00	5.00
188	A11	6p emerald	9.00	2.75
189	A24	1sh orange yel	35.00	10.00
190	A25	2sh blue, *rose*	40.00	11.00
191	A15	5sh rose red & bl	60.00	20.00
		Nos. 184-191 (8)	189.40	50.95

1901

192	A42	1p olive green	6.50	5.00
192A	A30	3p sage green	21.00	12.00

Nos. 192-192A were available for postal use until June 30, 1901, and thereafter restricted to revenue use.

A46

A47

A48

A49

A50

A51

A52

A53

A54

A55

A56

A57

A58

1901 ***Perf. 11, 12½ and Compound***

193	A46	½p blue green	1.50	.20
194	A47	1p rose red	1.25	.20
a.		1p rose	1.25	.20
195	A48	1½p red, *yellow*	2.25	.50
a.		Perf. 11	50.00	32.50
196	A49	2p violet	2.75	.20
197	A50	2½p blue	3.25	.20
198	A51	3p brown org	6.00	.30
199	A52	4p bister	6.00	.35
200	A53	5p chocolate	5.25	.25
201	A54	6p emerald	8.00	.50
202	A55	9p rose	10.00	.75
203	A56	1sh org yel	11.50	.75
204	A57	2sh blue, *rose*	21.00	2.25
205	A58	5sh rose red & bl	65.00	12.50
a.		5sh car & blue	65.00	9.00
		Nos. 193-205 (13)	143.75	18.95

See Nos. 209-229, 232.

King Edward VII

A59 A60

1901-05

206	A59	£1 deep rose	325.00	125.00
a.		Perf. 11 ('05)	325.00	140.00
208	A60	£2 dk blue ('02)	750.00	275.00
a.		Perf. 11 ('05)	850.00	600.00

See Nos. 230-231.

1903 **Redrawn**

209	A56	1sh yellow	15.00	1.40
a.		1sh orange	13.00	1.40

No. 209 has the network lighter than No. 203. In the latter the "P" and "E" of "POSTAGE" are in a position more nearly horizontal than on No. 209.

Perf. 11, 12x12½, 12½, 12½x11

1905-10 **Wmk. 13**

218	A46	½p blue green	1.25	.60
219	A47	1p rose red	1.00	.20
a.		1p carmine rose	2.00	.20
220	A49	2p violet	3.25	.20
a.		2p purple	3.25	.20
221	A50	2½p blue	3.50	.25
222	A51	3p brown org	4.50	.30
a.		3p dull yellow	5.25	.25
223	A52	4p bister	6.50	.40
224	A53	5p chocolate	6.00	.30
225	A54	6p emerald	8.25	.50
226	A55	9p orange brown	10.00	1.10
a.		9p brown rose	13.00	1.10
227	A55	9p car rose	10.00	1.10
228	A56	1sh yellow ('08)	10.00	1.00
229	A58	5sh org red & ultra	62.50	12.50
a.		5sh rose red & ultra	70.00	12.50
230	A59	£1 pale red ('07)	325.00	110.00
a.		£1 rose ('10)	325.00	100.00
231	A60	£2 dull blue	750.00	300.00
		Nos. 218-229 (12)	126.75	18.45

No. 220 Surcharged in Red

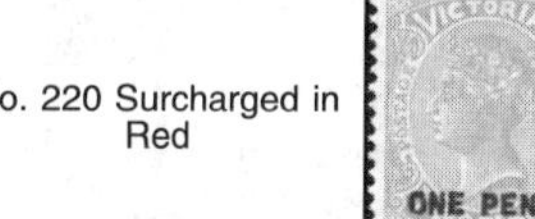

1912, July 1

232	A49	1p on 2p violet	.30	.20

POSTAL FISCAL STAMPS

On Jan. 1, 1884, all postage and fiscal stamps were made available for either purpose. Fiscal stamps became invalid after June 30, 1901.

Used values are for examples with postal cancellations used from Jan. 1, 1884 through June 30, 1901.

Beware of copies with a pen cancellation removed and a fake postmark added.

Stamps inscribed "Stamp Duty" that were issued primarily in postal rates in the normal postage stamp size are listed in the postage section (Nos. 146-178, 180-183, 192-192A). The stamps meeting primarily fiscal rates and in the larger fiscal stamp size, are listed here in the Postal-Fiscal section.

Stamps Inscribed "Stamp Statute"

Victoria — PF1

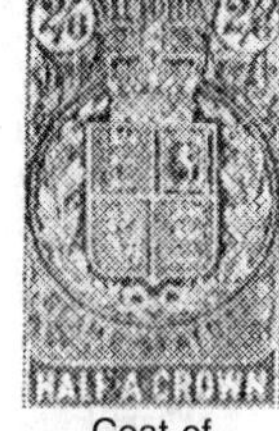

Coat of Arms — PF2

PF3

3p, denomination in center. Frames differ on design PF1.

Wmk. V and Crown (70)

1870-83 **Typo.** ***Perf. 13***

AR1	PF1	1p green	17.50	17.50
		Revenue cancel		2.00
a.		Perf. 12½	30.00	30.00
AR2	PF1	3p lilac	125.00	100.00
		Revenue cancel		45.00
AR3	PF1	4p red	125.00	75.00
		Revenue cancel		45.00
AR4	PF1	6p blue	50.00	15.00
		Revenue cancel		5.00
a.		Perf. 12	50.00	15.00
		Revenue cancel		5.00
AR5	PF1	1sh blue, *blue*	45.00	17.50
		Revenue cancel		6.00
a.		Perf. 12	50.00	22.50
		Revenue cancel		6.00
b.		Perf. 12½	45.00	17.50
		Revenue cancel		6.00
c.		Wmk. 50, perf. 13	40.00	17.50
		Revenue cancel		6.00
d.		Wmk. 50, perf. 12	65.00	22.50
		Revenue cancel		7.00
AR6	PF1	2sh blue, *grn*	65.00	42.50
		Revenue cancel		12.50
a.		Perf. 12	65.00	50.00
		Revenue cancel		12.50
b.		Wmk. 50, perf. 13	75.00	55.00
		Revenue cancel		12.50
c.		Wmk. 50, perf. 12	75.00	55.00
		Revenue cancel		12.50
AR7	PF2	2sh 6p orange, *yel*	125.00	55.00
		Revenue cancel		30.00
a.		Perf. 12	125.00	75.00
		Revenue cancel		30.00
b.		Perf. 12½	—	75.00
		Revenue cancel		30.00
AR8	PF1	5sh blue, *yel*	150.00	50.00
		Revenue cancel		30.00
a.		Perf. 12	175.00	
b.		Perf. 12½	150.00	50.00
		Revenue cancel		30.00
AR9	PF1	10sh brown, *rose*	600.00	125.00
		Revenue cancel		50.00
a.		Perf. 12		
b.		Wmk. 50, perf. 13	600.00	125.00
		Revenue cancel		50.00
c.		Wmk. 50, perf. 12		
AR10	PF1	£1 lilac, *yel*	350.00	100.00
		Revenue cancel		40.00
a.		Perf. 12	350.00	100.00
		Revenue cancel		40.00
b.		Perf. 12½	350.00	100.00
		Revenue cancel		40.00

AR11	PF3	£5 black, *grn*	3,000.	300.00
		Revenue cancel		70.00
a.		Perf. 12		
b.		Perf. 12½	3,000.	300.00
		Revenue cancel		70.00

Nos. AR1-AR12 distributed for postal use from Jan. 1, 1884 through Apr. 23, 1884.

No. AR1 Surcharged "½d/HALF"

1879-96

AR12	PF1	½p on 1p grn	75.00	50.00
		Revenue cancel		20.00

Stamps Inscribed "Stamp Duty"

PF4 PF5

PF6 PF7

PF8 PF9

PF10 PF11

PF12 PF13

PF14 PF15

PF16 PF17

PF18 PF23

PF19 PF24

PF20 PF25

PF21 PF26

PF22 PF27

PF28

Wmk. V and Crown (70)

1879-96 Litho. *Perf. 13*

AR13	PF4	1p green	50.00	10.00
		Revenue cancel		4.00
a.		Perf. 12	50.00	10.00
		Revenue cancel		4.00
b.		Perf. 12½		
AR14	PF8	1sh 6p pink	125.00	20.00
		Revenue cancel		8.00
a.		Perf. 12	—	27.50
		Revenue cancel		8.00
b.		Perf. 12½		
AR15	PF11	3sh violet, *blue*	350.00	27.50
		Revenue cancel		8.00
a.		Perf. 12	—	40.00
		Revenue cancel		8.00
b.		Perf. 12½		
AR16	PF12	4sh orange	80.00	17.50
		Revenue cancel		4.00
a.		Perf. 12	80.00	17.50
		Revenue cancel		4.00
b.		Perf. 12½		
AR17	PF4	6sh green	250.00	27.50
		Revenue cancel		8.00
a.		Perf. 12½		
AR18	PF15	10sh brn, *pink*	350.00	60.00
		Revenue cancel		30.00
a.		Perf. 12		
b.		Perf. 12½		
AR19	PF16	15sh lilac	1,000.	125.00
		Revenue cancel		40.00
AR20	PF17	£1 orange	400.00	65.00
		Revenue cancel		15.00
a.		Perf. 12½	400.00	
AR21	PF18	£1 5sh pink	850.00	150.00
		Revenue cancel		100.00
AR22	PF19	£1 10sh olive	900.00	100.00
		Revenue cancel		40.00
AR23	PF20	35sh lilac	3,500.	
		Revenue cancel		200.00
AR24	PF21	£2 blue	—	90.00
		Revenue cancel		15.00
AR25	PF22	45sh violet	1,500.	125.00
		Revenue cancel		35.00
AR26	PF23	£5 rose	1,250.	275.00
		Revenue cancel		70.00
AR27	PF24	£6 blue, *pink*	—	500.00
		Revenue cancel		100.00
AR28	PF25	£7 violet, *blue*	—	500.00
		Revenue cancel		100.00
AR29	PF26	£8 scarlet, *yel*	—	650.00
		Revenue cancel		110.00
AR30	PF27	£9 green, *grn*	—	650.00
		Revenue cancel		110.00

Typo.

AR31	PF4	1p green	30.00	10.00
		Revenue cancel		4.00
a.		Perf. 12	30.00	10.00
		Revenue cancel		4.00
b.		Perf. 12½		
AR32	PF5	1p brown	8.00	2.00
		Revenue cancel		.75
a.		Perf. 12	8.00	3.00
		Revenue cancel		.75
b.		Perf. 12½		
AR33	PF6	6p blue	40.00	6.00
		Revenue cancel		2.50
a.		Perf. 12	50.00	6.00
		Revenue cancel		2.50
b.		Perf. 12½		
AR34	PF7	1sh blue, *blue*	65.00	6.00
		Revenue cancel		2.50
a.		Perf. 12	65.00	6.00
		Revenue cancel		2.50
b.		Perf. 12½	65.00	6.00
		Revenue cancel		2.50
AR35	PF7	1sh blue, *yel,* perf 12½	90.00	20.00
		Revenue cancel		10.00
AR36	PF8	1sh 6p pink	150.00	25.00
		Revenue cancel		10.00
AR37	PF9	2sh blue, *grn*	100.00	15.00
		Revenue cancel		7.50
a.		Perf. 12	125.00	17.50
		Revenue cancel		7.50
b.		Perf. 12½	—	20.00
		Revenue cancel		7.50
AR38	PF10	2sh 6p orange, perf 12½	80.00	12.50
		Revenue cancel		2.00
AR39	PF11	3sh violet, *bl,* perf 12½	200.00	22.50
		Revenue cancel		7.50
AR40	PF11	3sh bister	60.00	17.50
		Revenue cancel		7.50
AR41	PF12	4sh org, perf 12½	90.00	10.00
		Revenue cancel		2.50
AR42	PF13	5sh claret, *yel*	55.00	6.00
		Revenue cancel		2.00
a.		Perf. 12	70.00	12.50
		Revenue cancel		2.00
b.		Perf. 12½	55.00	12.50
		Revenue cancel		2.00
AR43	PF13	5sh car rose	85.00	10.00
		Revenue cancel		4.00
AR44	PF14	6sh green	90.00	25.00
		Revenue cancel		8.00
AR45	PF15	10sh brn, *pink*	—	60.00
		Revenue cancel		30.00
a.		Perf. 12		
b.		Perf. 12½		
AR46	PF15	10sh green	110.00	17.50
		Revenue cancel		10.00
AR47	PF16	15sh brown	350.00	45.00
		Revenue cancel		8.00
AR48	PF17	£1 org, *yel,* perf 12½	375.00	65.00
		Revenue cancel		15.00
a.		Perf. 12	650.00	80.00
		Revenue cancel		15.00
AR49	PF18	£1 5sh pink	1,000.	90.00
		Revenue cancel		50.00
AR50	PF19	£1 10sh olive	700.00	80.00
		Revenue cancel		30.00
AR51	PF21	£2 blue	900.00	80.00
		Revenue cancel		15.00
a.		Perf. 12	—	100.00
		Revenue cancel		15.00
AR52	PF22	45sh gray lilac	2,500.	100.00
		Revenue cancel		30.00
AR53	PF23	£5 rose, perf. 12	—	250.00
		Revenue cancel		75.00
a.		perf. 12½	—	400.00
		Revenue cancel		100.00
AR54	PF28	£10 lilac	2,000.	100.00
		Revenue cancel		35.00
a.		Perf. 12	1,750.	110.00
		Revenue cancel		35.00

#AR49-AR52, AR54, used, are valued cto.

PF29

PF30

PF31

Wmk. V and Crown (70)

1879-1900 Engr. *Perf. 12½*

AR55	PF29	£25 green	—	500.00
		Revenue cancel		65.00
a.		Perf. 13		
b.		Perf. 12		
AR56	PF30	£50 violet	—	500.00
		Revenue cancel		75.00
a.		Perf. 13		
AR57	PF31	£100 red	—	475.00
		Revenue cancel		125.00
a.		Perf. 13		
b.		Perf. 12		
		Revenue cancel		125.00

Typo.

AR58	PF29	£25 green	—	110.00
a.		Lithographed		
		Revenue cancel		50.00
AR59	PF30	£50 violet	—	150.00
a.		Lithographed		
		Revenue cancel		70.00
AR60	PF31	£100 red	—	225.00
a.		Lithographed		
		Revenue cancel		100.00

Nos. AR55-AR60, used, are valued cto.

PF32

1887-90 Typo.

AR61	PF32	£5 cl & ultra	*1,250.*	100.00
		Revenue cancel		25.00
AR62	PF32	£6 blue & yel	*1,500.*	125.00
		Revenue cancel		30.00
AR63	PF32	£7 blk & red	*1,750.*	150.00
		Revenue cancel		40.00
AR64	PF32	£8 org & lilac	*1,900.*	175.00
		Revenue cancel		45.00
AR65	PF32	£9 red & green	*2,000.*	200.00
		Revenue cancel		50.00

Nos. AR61-AR65, used, are valued cto.

SEMI-POSTAL STAMPS

SP1

Queen Victoria and Figure of Charity SP2

Wmk. V and Crown (70)

1897, Oct. Typo. *Perf. 12½*

No.	Type	Description	Unused	Used
B1	SP1	1p deep blue	15.00	18.00
B2	SP2	2½p red brown	110.00	110.00

These stamps were sold at 1sh and 2sh6p respectively. The premium was given to a charitable institution.

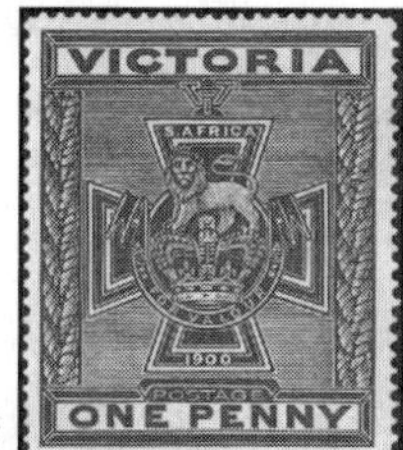
Victoria Cross — SP3

Scout Reporting SP4

1900

No.	Type	Description	Unused	Used
B3	SP3	1p brown olive	70.00	70.00
B4	SP4	2p emerald	140.00	140.00

These stamps were sold at 1sh and 2sh respectively. The premium was given to a patriotic fund in connection with the South African War.

REGISTRATION STAMPS

R1

Unwmk.

1854, Dec. 1 Typo. *Imperf.*

No.	Type	Description	Unused	Used
F1	R1	1sh rose & blue	1,000.	100.00

1857 *Rouletted 7*

No.	Type	Description	Unused	Used
F2	R1	1sh rose & blue	5,000.	150.00

LATE FEE STAMP

LF1

Unwmk.

1855, Jan. 1 Typo. *Imperf.*

No.	Type	Description	Unused	Used
I1	LF1	6p lilac & green	650.00	150.00

POSTAGE DUE STAMPS

D1

Wmk. V and Crown (70)

1890 Typo. *Perf. 12½*

No.	Type	Description	Unused	Used
J1	D1	½p claret & blue	2.00	1.60
J2	D1	1p claret & blue	3.25	1.25
J3	D1	2p claret & blue	5.00	1.50
J4	D1	4p claret & blue	6.00	1.75
J5	D1	5p claret & blue	5.50	1.60
J6	D1	6p claret & blue	6.25	1.50
J7	D1	10p claret & blue	60.00	32.50
J8	D1	1sh claret & blue	35.00	5.00
J9	D1	2sh claret & blue	92.50	42.50
J10	D1	5sh claret & blue	140.00	90.00
		Nos. J1-J10 (10)	355.50	179.20

1891

No.	Type	Description	Unused	Used
J11	D1	½p lake & blue	2.50	2.00
J12	D1	1p brown red & blue	4.25	1.25
J13	D1	2p brown red & blue	4.25	.90
J14	D1	4p lake & blue	6.50	4.50
		Nos. J11-J14 (4)	17.50	8.65

1894

No.	Type	Description	Unused	Used
J15	D1	½p bl grn & rose	1.60	1.40
J16	D1	1p bl grn & rose	.70	.35
J17	D1	2p bl grn & rose	1.50	.30
J18	D1	4p bl grn & rose	3.50	1.25
J19	D1	5p bl grn & rose	4.00	2.25
J20	D1	6p bl grn & rose	4.00	2.50
J21	D1	10p bl grn & rose	10.00	8.50
J22	D1	1sh bl grn & rose	5.00	2.75
J23	D1	2sh green & rose	60.00	20.00
J24	D1	5sh green & rose	100.00	35.00
		Nos. J15-J24 (10)	190.30	74.30

1906 Wmk. 13

No.	Type	Description	Unused	Used
J25	D1	½p yel grn & rose	1.60	1.60
J26	D1	1p yel grn & rose	3.00	.65
J27	D1	2p yel grn & rose	6.50	1.50
J28	D1	4p yel grn & rose	13.00	10.00
		Nos. J25-J28 (4)	24.10	13.75

A 5p with wmk. 13 exists but was not issued.

WESTERN AUSTRALIA

ˈwes-tərn o-ˈstrāl-yə

LOCATION — Western part of Australia, occupying about a third of that continent
GOVT. — British Colony
AREA — 975,920 sq. mi.
POP. — 184,124 (1901)
CAPITAL — Perth

Western Australia was one of the six British colonies that united on January 1, 1901, to form the Commonwealth of Australia.

12 Pence = 1 Shilling
20 Shillings = 1 Pound

Unused values for Nos. 1-10 are for stamps without gum as these stamps are seldom found with original gum. Otherwise, unused values are for stamps with original gum as defined in the catalogue introduction.

Very fine examples of all rouletted and perforated stamps from Nos. 6-34 have roulettes or perforations touching the design. Examples clear on all four sides range from scarce to rare and will command higher prices.

Watermarks

Wmk. 82- Swan

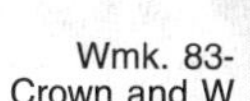
Wmk. 83- Crown and W A

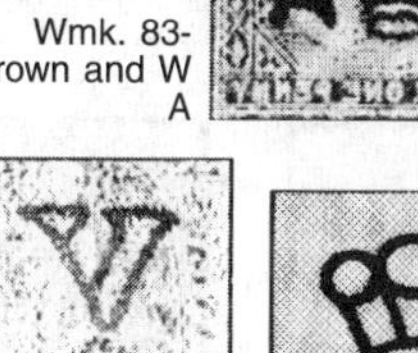
Wmk. 70- V and Crown

Wmk. 13- Crown & Double-lined A

Wmk. 74- Crown and Single-lined A

Swan
A1 A2

1854-57 Engr. Wmk. 82 *Imperf.*

No.	Type	Description	Unused	Used
1	A1	1p black	800.	190.

Litho.

No.	Type	Description	Unused	Used
2	A2	2p brown, *red* ('57)	2,000.	475.
a.		2p brown, *deep red* ('57)	2,250.	750.
b.		Printed on both sides	2,500.	850.

See Nos. 4, 6-7, 9, 14-39, 44-52, 54, 59-61. For surcharges see Nos. 41, 55-56.

A3

A4

No.	Type	Description	Unused	Used
3	A3	4p blue	240.	150.
a.		Frame inverted		*75,000.*
		As "a," cut to shape		*20,000.*
b.		4p slate blue	1,550.	750.
4	A2	6p bronze ('57)	*3,000.*	600.
5	A4	1sh pale brown	400.	275.
a.		1sh dark brown	500.	325.
b.		1sh dark red brown	1,000.	425.
c.		1sh pale red brown		1,750.

Engraved

Rouletted

No.	Type	Description	Unused	Used
6	A1	1p black	1,750.	450.00

Lithographed

No.	Type	Description	Unused	Used
7	A2	2p brown, *red* ('57)	*4,500.*	1,250.
a.		Printed on both sides		*1,450.*
8	A3	4p blue	—	425.00
9	A2	6p bronze ('57)	*4,000.*	825.00
10	A4	1sh brown	1,800.	725.00

The 1p, 2p, 4p and 6p are known with pin-perforation but this is believed to be unofficial. No. 7a is only recorded used and with pin perforations.

1860 Engr. *Imperf.*

No.	Type	Description	Unused	Used
14	A1	2p vermilion	90.00	80.00
a.		2p pale orange	90.00	65.00
15	A1	4p blue	275.00	*1,600.*
16	A1	6p dull green	1,100.	525.00

Rouletted

No.	Type	Description	Unused	Used
17	A1	2p vermilion	550.00	175.00
a.		2p pale orange	550.00	175.00
18	A1	4p deep blue	2,500.	—
19	A1	6p dull green	—	550.00

1861 *Clean-Cut Perf. 14 to 16*

No.	Type	Description	Unused	Used
20	A1	1p rose	325.00	95.00
a.		Imperf.		
21	A1	2p blue	70.00	25.00
a.		Imperf., pair		
b.		Horiz. pair, imperf. vert.		
22	A1	4p vermilion	575.00	*1,500.*
a.		Imperf.		
23	A1	6p purple brn	190.00	40.00
a.		Imperf.		
24	A1	1sh green	325.00	57.50
a.		Imperf.		

Rough Perf. 14 to 16

No.	Type	Description	Unused	Used
24B	A1	1p rose	200.00	37.50
24C	A1	6p pur brn, *bluish*	1,250.	275.00
24D	A1	1sh deep green	1,200.	250.00

Perf. 14

No.	Type	Description	Unused	Used
25	A1	1p rose	175.00	45.00
25A	A1	2p blue	75.00	30.00
25B	A1	4p vermilion	175.00	140.00

Unwmk. *Perf. 13*

No.	Type	Description	Unused	Used
26	A1	1p lake	55.00	5.00
28	A1	6p violet	110.00	40.00

1865-79 Wmk. 1 *Perf. 12½*

No.	Type	Description	Unused	Used
29	A1	1p bister	55.00	4.00
30	A1	1p yel ocher	65.00	6.75
31	A1	2p yellow	55.00	1.75
a.		2p lilac (error) ('79)	*7,500.*	*3,750.*
32	A1	4p carmine	62.50	5.00
a.		Double impression	*6,000.*	
33	A1	6p violet	70.00	6.00
a.		6p lilac	140.00	6.00
b.		6p red lilac	140.00	6.00
c.		Double impression		*7,000.*
34	A1	1sh bright green	95.00	11.50
a.		1sh sage green	275.00	24.00
		Nos. 29-34 (6)	402.50	35.00

1872-78 *Perf. 14*

No.	Type	Description	Unused	Used
35	A1	1p bister	75.00	3.25
36	A1	1p yellow ocher	55.00	1.25
37	A1	2p yellow	47.50	.75
38	A1	4p carmine	325.00	75.00
39	A1	6p lilac	95.00	3.25
		Nos. 35-39 (5)	597.50	83.50

A5

A8

1872 Typo.

No.	Type	Description	Unused	Used
40	A5	3p red brown	26.00	3.75
a.		3p brown	26.00	3.75

See #53, 92. For surcharges see #57, 69-72A.

No. 31 Surcharged in Green ONE PENNY

1875 Engr. *Perf. 12½*

No.	Type	Description	Unused	Used
41	A1	1p on 2p yellow	240.00	47.50
a.		Pair, one without surcharge		
b.		"O" of "ONE" omitted		
c.		Triple surcharge		*2,500.*

Forged surcharges exist.

1882 Wmk. 2 *Perf. 12*

No.	Type	Description	Unused	Used
44	A1	1p ocher yellow	77.50	3.00
46	A1	2p yellow	100.00	3.00
47	A1	4p carmine	150.00	27.50
48	A1	6p pale violet	250.00	27.50
		Nos. 44-48 (4)	577.50	61.00

1882 *Perf. 14*

No.	Type	Description	Unused	Used
49	A1	1p ocher yellow	17.50	1.00
50	A1	2p yellow	22.50	1.0
51	A1	4p carmine	85.00	10.00
52	A1	6p violet	72.50	3.00
a.		6p pale violet	72.50	4.00

Typographed

No.	Type	Description	Unused	Used
53	A5	3p red brown	8.50	1.50
a.		3p brown	13.50	1.50
		Nos. 49-53 (5)	211.00	16.50

1883 Engr. *Perf. 12x14*

No.	Type	Description	Unused	Used
54	A1	1p ocher yellow	1,500.	275.00

Nos. 44 and 49 Surcharged in Red

1884 *Perf. 12*

No.	Type	Description	Unused	Used
55	A1	½p on 1p ocher yel	9.00	*14.50*

Perf. 14

No.	Type	Description	Unused	Used
56	A1	½p on 1p ocher yel	13.00	*18.00*

No. 40 Surcharged in Green

1885 Typo. Wmk. 1

57	A5	1p on 3p red brown	40.00	9.50
a.		1p on 3p brown	47.50	11.00
b.		"1" with straight top	95.00	27.50

Wmk. Crown and C A (2)

1885 Typo. *Perf. 14*

58	A8	½p green	3.00	.50

See No. 89.

1888 Engr.

59	A1	1p rose	15.00	2.50
60	A1	2p slate	40.00	1.00
61	A1	4p red brown	82.50	18.00
		Nos. 59-61 (3)	137.50	21.50

A9

A10

A11

A12

1890-93 Typo.

62	A9	1p carmine rose	10.00	.20
63	A10	2p slate	14.00	.20
64	A11	2½p blue	6.00	.75
65	A12	4p orange brown	6.00	.80
66	A12	5p bister	8.25	1.00
67	A12	6p violet	14.00	.80
68	A12	1sh olive green	16.00	2.25
		Nos. 62-68 (7)	74.25	6.00

See Nos. 73-74, 76, 80, 90, 94.

Nos. 40 and 53a Surcharged in Green

1893 Wmk. Crown and C C (1)

69	A5	1p on 3p red brown	11.00	5.00
a.		1p on 3p brown	11.00	3.25
b.		Double surcharge	*725.00*	

Wmkd. Crown and C A (2)

70	A5	1p on 3p brown	40.00	9.00

Nos. 40a and 53a Surcharged in Green

1895 Wmk. Crown and C C (1)

71	A5	½p on 3p brown	7.00	3.00
a.		Double surcharge	*700.00*	

Green and Red Surcharge

72	A5	½p on 3p brown	125.00	

Wmk. Crown and C A (2)

72A	A5	½p on 3p brown	75.00	

After the supply of paper watermarked Crown and C C was exhausted, No. 72A was printed. Ostensibly this was to provide samples for Postal Union distribution, but a supply for philatelic demands was also made.

Types of 1890-93 and

A15

1899-1901 Typo. Wmk. 83

73	A9	1p carmine rose	3.50	.20
74	A10	2p yellow	9.00	.20
75	A15	2½p blue ('01)	6.00	.20
		Nos. 73-75 (3)	18.50	.60

A16

A17

A18

A19

A20

A21

A22

Southern Cross — A23

Queen Victoria
A24 A25

Perf. 12½, 12x12½

1902-05 Wmk. 70

76	A9	1p car rose	6.50	.20
a.		1p salmon		
b.		Perf. 11	100.00	5.00
c.		Perf. 12½x11		175.00
77	A16	2p yellow	3.25	.20
a.		Perf. 11	125.00	5.50
b.		Perf. 12½x11		225.00
79	A17	4p orange brn	6.00	.80
a.		Perf. 11	375.00	110.00
80	A12	5p ol bis, perf 12½ ('05)	72.50	40.00
a.		Perf. 11	45.00	21.00
81	A18	8p pale yel grn	20.00	2.75
82	A19	9p orange	27.50	4.00
b.		Perf. 11	60.00	40.00
83	A20	10p red	27.50	5.50
84	A21	2sh red, *yel*	42.50	8.25
a.		Perf. 11	125.00	55.00
85	A22	2sh6p dk bl, *rose*	40.00	7.75
86	A23	5sh blue green	70.00	19.00
87	A24	10sh violet	175.00	60.00
88	A25	£1 brown org	475.00	225.00
		Nos. 76-88 (12)	965.75	373.45

Perf. 12½, 12x12½

1905-12 Wmk. 13

89	A8	½p dp green ('10)	2.25	.35
90	A9	1p rose	3.00	.20
e.		Perf. 11	13.00	2.50
f.		Perf. 12½x11	200.00	82.50
91	A16	2p yellow	3.00	.20
a.		Perf. 11	11.00	4.50
b.		Perf. 12½x11	225.00	95.00
92	A5	3p brown	6.50	.40
a.		Perf. 11	12.00	2.75
b.		Perf. 12½x11	260.00	82.50
93	A17	4p orange brn	8.00	1.50
a.		4p bister brown	8.00	1.50
b.		Perf. 11	475.00	90.00
94	A12	5p olive bis	10.00	.70
a.		Perf. 11	25.00	8.50
95	A18	8p pale yel grn ('12)	16.00	17.00
96	A19	9p orange	21.00	3.00
b.		Perf. 11	65.00	55.00
97	A20	10p red orange	21.00	10.00
98	A23	5s blue green	140.00	40.00
		Nos. 89-98 (10)	230.75	73.35

For surcharge see No. 103.

A26

A27

1906-07 Wmk. 83 *Perf. 14*

99	A26	6p bright violet	18.00	.70
100	A27	1sh olive green	25.00	6.00

1912 Wmk. 74 *Perf. 11½x12*

101	A26	6p bright violet	11.00	3.00
102	A27	1sh gray green	22.50	4.00
a.		Perf. 12½		

No. 91 Surcharged

1912 Wmk. 13 *Perf. 12½*

103	A16	1p on 2p yellow	.75	.40

Stamps of Western Australia were replaced by those of Australia.

POSTAL FISCAL STAMPS

Postal use of the 1p telegraph stamp was authorized beginning Oct. 25, 1886.

Used values are for examples with postal cancellations.

Beware of copies with a pen cancellation removed and a fake postmark added.

PF1

PF2

1886 Wmk. 1 *Perf. 14*

AR1	PF1	1p bister	30.00	6.00

Perf. 12½

AR2	PF1	1p bister	27.50	4.00

The 6p is known postally used but was not authorized.

Authorized for postal use by the Post and Telegraph Act of Sept. 5, 1893 were the current revenue stamps through the 1sh value.

Beware of copies with a pen cancellation removed and a fake postmark added.

Because the Act specified current stamps, postally used examples from the provisional issue of of 1881 are not included here.

1882 Wmk. 2 *Perf. 14*

AR3	PF2	1p purple	10.00	1.50
AR4	PF2	2p purple	100.00	35.00
AR5	PF2	3p purple	35.00	2.25
AR6	PF2	6p purple	40.00	4.00
AR7	PF2	1sh purple	75.00	5.50

Wmk. 83

AR8	PF2	1p purple	6.50	1.50
AR9	PF2	3p purple	27.50	2.25
AR10	PF2	6p purple	27.50	2.50
AR11	PF2	1sh purple	75.00	10.00

Nos. AR7, AR11 have a rectangular outer frame and a circular frame around the swan.

Higher values are known with postal cancels, some postally used, but these were not authorized.

AUSTRALIA

o-'strāl-yə

LOCATION — Oceania, south of Indonesia, bounded on the west by the Indian Ocean
GOVT. — Self-governing dominion of the British Commonwealth
AREA — 2,967,909 sq. mi.
POP. — 17,892,423 (1996)
CAPITAL — Canberra

Australia includes the former British colonies of New South Wales, Victoria, Queensland, South Australia, Western Australia and Tasmania.

12 Pence = 1 Shilling
20 Shillings = 1 Pound
100 Cents = 1 Dollar (1966)

Catalogue values for unused stamps in this country are for Never Hinged items, beginning with Scott 197 in the regular postage section, Scott C6 in the air post section, Scott J71 in the postage due section, and all of the Australian Antarctic Territory.

Watermarks

Wmk. 8- Wide Crown and Wide A

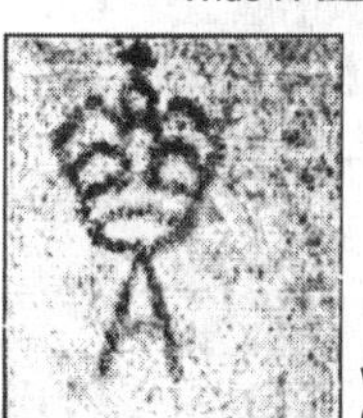
Wmk. 9- Wide Crown and Narrow A

Wmk. 10- Narrow Crown and Narrow A

Wmk. 11- Multiple Crown and A

Wmk. 12- Crown and Single-lined A

Wmk. 13- Large Crown and Double-lined A

Wmk. 55- Large Crown and NSW

Wmk. 203- Small Crown and A Multiple

Wmk. 228- Small Crown and C of A Multiple

Kangaroo and Map — A1

Die I - The inside frameline has a break at left, even with the top of the letters of the denomination.

Die II - The frameline does not show a break.

Die III - The left inside frameline shows a break parallel to the face of the kangaroo.

Die IV - As Die III, with a break in the top outside frameline above the "ST" of "AUSTRALIA." The upper right inside frameline has an incomplete corner.

Dies are only indicated when there are more than one for any denomination.

1913 Typo. Wmk. 8 ***Perf. 11½, 12***

No.	Type	Description	Unused	Used
1	A1	½p green	6.00	2.75
		Never hinged	10.00	
2	A1	1p car, die I	6.75	.75
		Never hinged	11.50	
h.		Die II	12.50	1.00
		Never hinged	22.50	
3	A1	2p gray	24.00	4.00
		Never hinged	45.00	
4	A1	2½p dark blue	27.50	12.50
		Never hinged	45.00	
5	A1	3p ol bis, die I	45.00	8.75
		Never hinged	95.00	
a.		Die II	150.00	47.50
		Never hinged	*300.00*	
6	A1	4p orange	47.50	21.00
		Never hinged	100.00	
7	A1	5p orange brown	40.00	30.00
		Never hinged	110.00	
8	A1	6p ultra (II)	45.00	18.00
		Never hinged	125.00	
b.		Die III	*1,000.*	*300.00*
9	A1	9p purple	42.50	22.50
		Never hinged	110.00	
10	A1	1sh blue green	45.00	15.00
		Never hinged	175.00	
11	A1	2sh brown	160.00	75.00
		Never hinged	500.00	
12	A1	5sh yellow & gray	250.00	140.00
		Never hinged	650.00	
13	A1	10sh pink & gray	600.00	425.00
		Never hinged	1,600.	
14	A1	£1 ultra & brown	1,300.	1,000.
		Never hinged	2,750.	
15	A1	£2 dp rose & blk	2,350.	1,550.
		Nos. 1-12 (12)	739.25	350.25

On No. 4 "2½d" is colorless in solid blue background.

See Nos. 38-59, 96-102, 121-129, 206.

King George V
A2

Kookaburra (Kingfisher)
A3

1913-14 Unwmk. Engr. ***Perf. 11***

No.	Type	Description	Unused	Used
17	A2	1p carmine	4.25	4.25
		Never hinged	5.75	
a.		Vert. pair, imperf. between	*2,000.*	
18	A3	6p lake brown ('14)	70.00	35.00
		Never hinged	150.00	

See No. 95.

A4

ONE PENNY

Die I - Normal die, having outside the oval band with "AUSTRALIA" a white line and a heavy colored line.

Die Ia - As die I with a small white spur below the right serif at foot of the "1" in left tablet.

Die II - A heavy colored line between two white lines back of the emu's neck. A white scratch crossing the vertical shading lines at the lowest point of the bust.

TWO PENCE

Die I - The numeral "2" is thin. The upper curve is 1mm. across and a very thin line connects it with the foot of the figure.

Die II - The "2" is thicker than in die I. The top curve is 1½mm across and a strong white line connects it with the foot of the figure. There are thin vertical lines across the ends of the groups of short horizontal lines at each side of "TWO PENCE."

THREE PENCE

Die I - The ends of the thin horizontal lines in the background run into the solid color of the various parts of the design. The numerals are thin and the letters of "THREE PENCE" are thin and irregular.

Die II - The oval about the portrait, the shields with the numerals, etc., are outlined by thin white lines which separate them from the horizontal background lines. The numerals are thick and the letters of "THREE PENCE" are heavy and regular.

FIVE PENCE

Die I - The top of the flag of the "5" is slightly curved.

Die II - The top of the flag of the "5" is flat. There are thin white vertical lines across the ends of the short horizontal lines at each side of "FIVE PENCE."

1914-24 Typo. Wmk. 9 ***Perf. 14***

No.	Type	Description	Unused	Used
19	A4	½p emerald ('15)	2.50	.40
		Never hinged	4.50	
a.		Thin "½" at right	*1,400.*	*700.00*
20	A4	½p orange ('23)	2.50	1.25
		Never hinged	3.50	
21	A4	1p red (I)	4.25	.20
		Never hinged	7.50	
a.		1p carmine rose (I)	8.25	.80
		Never hinged	20.00	
b.		1p red (Ia)	375.00	4.75
		Never hinged	500.00	
c.		1p carmine (II) ('18)	60.00	30.00
		Never hinged	95.00	
d.		1p scar (I), rough paper	18.00	2.00
e.		1p rose red (Ia), rough paper	250.00	20.00
f.		1p brt rose (Ia), rough paper	375.00	50.00
22	A4	1p vio (I) ('22)	4.50	.60
		Never hinged	8.00	
a.		1p red violet	6.50	1.50
		Never hinged	10.00	
23	A4	1p green (I) ('24)	3.50	.20
		Never hinged	4.50	
24	A4	1½p choc ('18)	5.00	.20
		Never hinged	8.00	
a.		1½p red brown	5.50	.20
		Never hinged	14.00	
b.		1½p black brown	4.50	.25
		Never hinged	7.50	
25	A4	1½p emerald ('23)	3.50	.20
		Never hinged	4.00	
26	A4	1½p scarlet ('24)	2.50	.20
		Never hinged	3.50	
27	A4	2p brn org (I) ('20)	10.00	.25
		Never hinged	17.00	
a.		2p orange (I) ('20)	12.00	.30
		Never hinged	19.00	
b.		Booklet pane of 6		
28	A4	2p red (I) ('22)	7.50	.20
		Never hinged	14.00	
29	A4	2p red brn (I) ('24)	15.00	3.75
		Never hinged	25.00	
30	A4	3p ultra (I) ('24)	25.00	2.25
		Never hinged	35.00	
31	A4	4p orange ('15)	40.00	2.25
		Never hinged	70.00	
a.		4p yellow	110.00	16.00

Never hinged 250.00
32 A4 4p violet ('21) 17.50 13.00
Never hinged 25.00
33 A4 4p lt ultra ('22) 45.00 4.50
Never hinged 60.00
34 A4 4p ol bis ('24) 27.50 4.00
Never hinged 37.50
35 A4 4½p violet ('24) 22.50 4.00
Never hinged 35.00
36 A4 5p org brn (I) ('15) 18.00 3.00
Never hinged 45.00
37 A4 1sh4p lt blue ('20) 65.00 19.00
Never hinged 125.00
Nos. 19-37 (19) 321.25 59.45

See Nos. 60-76, 113-120, 124.

1915 ***Perf. 11½, 12***

38 A1 2p gray 45.00 11.00
Never hinged 95.00
39 A1 2½p dark blue 45.00 15.00
Never hinged 110.00
40 A1 6p ultra (II) 125.00 19.00
Never hinged 275.00
a. Die III *900.00* 250.00
41 A1 9p violet 125.00 32.50
Never hinged 275.00
42 A1 1sh blue green 125.00 20.00
Never hinged 325.00
43 A1 2sh brown 400.00 90.00
Never hinged 900.00
44 A1 5sh yellow & gray 700.00 225.00
Never hinged 1,500.
Nos. 38-44 (7) 1,565. 412.50

1915-24 **Wmk. 10**

45 A1 2p gray (I) 25.00 6.00
Never hinged 40.00
a. Die II, shiny paper 35.00 8.00
46 A1 2½p dark blue 25.00 10.00
Never hinged 40.00
a. "1" of fraction omitted *10,000.* *3,500.*
47 A1 3p olive bister (I) 20.00 3.50
Never hinged 35.00
a. Die II 80.00 25.00
b. 3p lt olive (IV) 35.00 10.00
48 A1 6p ultra (II) 50.00 7.00
Never hinged 90.00
a. 6p chalky blue (III) 65.00 7.00
c. 6p ultra (IV) 50.00 6.00
49 A1 6p yel brn (IV, '23) 20.00 2.50
Never hinged 40.00
50 A1 9p lilac (III) 40.00 12.00
Never hinged 55.00
a. 9p violet (II) 35.00 6.00
Never hinged 55.00
51 A1 1sh blue grn (II, '16) 35.00 4.50
Never hinged 55.00
b. Die IV 35.00 3.00
52 A1 2sh brown ('16) 150.00 15.00
Never hinged 350.00
53 A1 2sh vio brn (II, '24) 50.00 25.00
Never hinged 100.00
54 A1 5sh yel & gray ('18) 190.00 80.00
Never hinged 350.00
55 A1 10sh brt pink & gray ('17) 400.00 150.00
Never hinged 750.00
56 A1 £1 ultra & brn ('16) 1,250. 700.00
Never hinged 2,500.
a. £1 ultra & brn org ('16) 1,300. 700.00
57 A1 £1 gray (IV, '24) 450.00 275.00
Never hinged 750.00
58 A1 £2 dp rose & blk ('19) 2,250. 1,250.
Never hinged 3,000.
59 A1 £2 rose & vio brn ('24) 1,750. 1,200.
Never hinged 2,750.
Nos. 45-54 (10) 605.00 165.50

Perf. 14, 14½, 14½x14

1918-23 **Wmk. 11**

60 A4 ½p emerald 3.00 1.00
Never hinged 4.25
a. Thin "½" at right 110.00 45.00
61 A4 1p rose (I) 25.00 9.00
Never hinged 32.50
62 A4 1p dl grn (I) ('24) 6.00 6.00
Never hinged 9.00
63 A4 1½p choc ('19) 5.00 1.00
Never hinged 11.00
a. 1½p red brown ('19) 8.00 1.00
Never hinged 15.00
Nos. 60-63 (4) 39.00 17.00

1924 **Unwmk.** ***Perf. 14***

64 A4 1p green (I) 4.25 3.75
Never hinged 5.50
65 A4 1½p carmine 4.25 3.00
Never hinged 6.75

Perf. 14, 13½x12½

1926-30 **Wmk. 203**

66 A4 ½p orange 1.40 1.00
Never hinged 3.00
a. Perf. 14 ('27) 6.50 5.25
Never hinged 8.50
67 A4 1p green (I) 1.50 .35
Never hinged 3.00
a. 1p green (Ia) 47.50 *60.00*
Never hinged 65.00
b. Perf. 14 2.75 .45
Never hinged 4.50
68 A4 1½p rose red ('27) 2.75 .20
Never hinged 3.50
c. Perf. 14 ('26) 6.00 .65
Never hinged 12.00
69 A4 1½p red brn ('30) 4.00 2.00
Never hinged 8.00
70 A4 2p red brn (II, '28) 7.00 4.00
Never hinged 10.50
a. Perf. 14 (I, '27) 27.50 20.00
Never hinged 40.00
71 A4 2p red (II) ('30) 4.00 .20
Never hinged 12.50
a. 2p red (I) ('30) 5.00 1.60
Never hinged 12.00
c. Unwmkd. (II) ('31) *1,500.* *1,000.*
72 A4 3p ultra (I) 30.00 10.00
Never hinged 55.00
a. 3p ultra (II) ('29) 17.50 2.00
Never hinged 30.00
b. Perf. 14 20.00 4.50
Never hinged 37.50
73 A4 4p ol bis ('29) 16.00 2.00
Never hinged 32.50
a. Perf. 14 ('28) 42.50 22.50
Never hinged 85.00
74 A4 4½p dk vio ('27) 17.00 3.75
Never hinged 25.00
a. Perf. 13½x12½ ('28) 47.50 13.00
Never hinged 67.50
75 A4 5p brn buff (II) ('30) 17.50 4.50
Never hinged 32.50
76 A4 1sh4p pale turq bl ('28) 85.00 20.00
Never hinged 175.00
a. Perf. 14 ('27) 125.00 70.00
Never hinged 300.00
Nos. 66-76 (11) 186.15 48.00

For surcharges & overprints see #106-107, O3-O4.

Parliament House, Canberra A5

Unwmk.

1927, May 9 **Engr.** ***Perf. 11***

94 A5 1½p brown red .60 .20
Never hinged 1.00
a. Vert. pair, imperf. btwn. *2,750.* *2,500.*

Opening of Parliament House at Canberra.

Melbourne Exhibition Issue
Kookaburra Type of 1914

1928, Oct. 29

95 A3 3p deep blue 3.75 3.00
Never hinged 5.25
a. Pane of 4 125.00 *150.00*
Never hinged 190.00

No. 95a was issued at the Melbourne Intl. Phil. Exhib. No marginal inscription. Printed in sheets of 60 stamps (15 panes). No. 95 was printed in sheets of 120 and issued Nov. 2 throughout Australia.

Kangaroo-Map Type of 1913
Perf. 11½, 12

1929-30 **Wmk. 203** **Typo.**

96 A1 6p brown 21.00 5.00
Never hinged 30.00
97 A1 9p violet 30.00 5.00
Never hinged 70.00
98 A1 1sh blue green 27.50 4.50
Never hinged 65.00
99 A1 2sh red brown 60.00 12.50
Never hinged 140.00
100 A1 5sh yel & gray 190.00 60.00
Never hinged 325.00
101 A1 10sh pink & gray 350.00 275.00
Never hinged 600.00
102 A1 £2 dl red & blk ('30) 1,800. 425.00
Never hinged 3,750.
Nos. 96-102 (7) 2,478.50 787.00

For overprint see No. O5.

Black Swan — A6

Unwmk.

1929, Sept. 28 **Engr.** ***Perf. 11***

103 A6 1½p dull red .75 .75
Never hinged 1.40

Centenary of Western Australia.

Capt. Charles Sturt — A7

1930, June 2

104 A7 1½p dark red .40 .20
Never hinged .45
105 A7 3p dark blue 3.50 3.00
Never hinged 6.00

Capt. Charles Sturt's exploration of the Murray River, cent.

Nos. 68 and 74a surcharged

1930 **Wmk. 203** ***Perf. 13½x12½***

106 A4 2p on 1½p rose red .75 .25
Never hinged 1.50
107 A4 5p on 4½p dark violet 5.00 5.00
Never hinged 10.00

"Southern Cross" over Hemispheres A8

Perf. 11, 11½

1931, Mar. 19 **Unwmk.**

111 A8 2p dull red .75 .20
Never hinged 1.10
112 A8 3p blue 4.75 2.00
Never hinged 8.00
Nos. 111-112,C2 (3) 12.50 9.20

Trans-oceanic flights (1928-1930) of Sir Charles Edward Kingsford-Smith (1897-1935).
See #C3 for similar design. For overprints see #CO1, O1-O2.

Types of 1913-23 Issues
Perf. 13½x12½

1931-36 **Typo.** **Wmk. 228**

113 A4 ½p orange ('32) 2.50 1.60
Never hinged 3.00
114 A4 1p green (I) 1.50 .20
Never hinged 2.25
115 A4 1½p red brn ('36) 6.00 4.50
Never hinged 8.00
116 A4 2p red (II) 1.75 .20
Never hinged 2.50
117 A4 3p ultra (II) ('32) 17.50 .30
Never hinged 25.00
118 A4 4p ol bis ('33) 17.50 .45
Never hinged 26.00
120 A4 5p brn buff (II) ('32) 12.00 .30
Never hinged 20.00

Perf. 11½, 12; 13½x12½ (1sh4p)

121 A1 6p yel brn ('36) 16.00 11.00
Never hinged 25.00
122 A1 9p violet ('32) 16.50 2.00
Never hinged 40.00
124 A4 1sh4p lt blue ('32) 60.00 6.00
Never hinged 140.00
125 A1 2sh red brn ('35) 4.00 .90
Never hinged 6.00
126 A1 5sh yel & gray ('32) 125.00 18.00
Never hinged 250.00
127 A1 10sh pink & gray ('32) 325.00 100.00
Never hinged 650.00
128 A1 £1 gray ('35) 450.00 165.00
Never hinged 650.00
129 A1 £2 dl rose & blk ('34) 2,000. 350.00
Never hinged 3,000.
Nos. 113-129 (15) 3,055.25 660.45

For redrawn 2sh see No. 206. For overprints see Nos. O6-O11.

Sydney Harbor Bridge — A9

Unwmk.

1932, Mar. 14 **Engr.** ***Perf. 11***

130 A9 2p red 1.90 .50
Never hinged 2.25
131 A9 3p blue 4.00 3.00
Never hinged 6.75
132 A9 5sh gray green 350.00 200.00
Never hinged 575.00

Wmk. 228
Perf. 10½
Typo.

133 A9 2p red 1.60 .80
Never hinged 2.75

Opening of the Sydney Harbor Bridge on Mar. 19, 1932.
Value for 5sh, used, is for CTO copies.
For overprints see Nos. O12-O13.

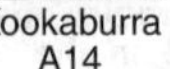
Kookaburra A14

Male Lyrebird A16

1932, June 1 ***Perf. 13½x12½***

139 A14 6p light brown 15.00 .50
Never hinged 25.00

1932, Feb. 15 **Unwmk.** ***Perf. 11***
Size: 21½x25mm

141 A16 1sh green 37.50 .75
Never hinged 75.00

See #175, 300. For overprint see #O14.

Yarra Yarra Tribesman, Yarra River and View of Melbourne A17

Wmk. 228

1934, July 2 **Engr.** ***Perf. 10½***

142 A17 2p vermilion 1.10 .30
Never hinged 1.75
a. Perf. 11½ 3.75 .75
Never hinged 6.50
143 A17 3p blue 2.75 2.50
Never hinged 5.25
a. Perf. 11½ 4.25 2.50
Never hinged 6.50
144 A17 1sh black 40.00 16.00
Never hinged 67.50
a. Perf. 11½ 40.00 20.00
Never hinged 72.50
Nos. 142-144 (3) 43.85 18.80

Centenary of Victoria.

Merino Sheep — A18

1934, Nov. 1 ***Perf. 11½***

147 A18 2p copper red, Die I 2.50 .20
Never hinged 3.50
a. Die II 20.00 1.50
148 A18 3p dark blue 10.00 6.00
Never hinged 15.00
149 A18 9p dark violet 35.00 25.00
Never hinged 67.50
Nos. 147-149 (3) 47.50 31.20

Capt. John Macarthur (1767-1834), "father of the New South Wales woolen industry."
Two dies of 2p: I, shading on hill in background uneven from light to dark. II, shading is uniformly dark.

Cenotaph in Whitehall, London — A19

George V on His Charger "Anzac" — A20

1935, Mar. 18 *Perf. 13½x12½*

150	A19	2p red	.65	.20
		Never hinged	.90	

Perf. 11

151	A19	1sh black	40.00	25.00
		Never hinged	70.00	
a.		Perf 13½x12½	*1,000.*	
		Never hinged	*1,400.*	

Anzacs' landing at Gallipoli, 20th anniv.

1935, May 2 *Perf. 11½*

152	A20	2p red	.75	.20
		Never hinged	2.00	
153	A20	3p blue	3.00	2.25
		Never hinged	7.50	
154	A20	2sh violet	37.50	30.00
		Never hinged	70.00	
		Nos. 152-154 (3)	41.25	32.45

25th anniv. of the reign of King George V.

Amphitrite Joining Cables between Australia and Tasmania A21

1936, Apr. 1

157	A21	2p red	.35	.20
		Never hinged	.60	
158	A21	3p dark blue	3.25	2.00
		Never hinged	5.25	

Australia/Tasmania telephone link.

Proclamation Tree and View of Adelaide, 1936 — A22

1936, Aug. 3

159	A22	2p red	.40	.20
		Never hinged	1.10	
160	A22	3p dark blue	3.25	3.25
		Never hinged	5.00	
161	A22	1sh green	12.00	6.00
		Never hinged	20.00	
		Nos. 159-161 (3)	15.65	9.45

Centenary of South Australia.

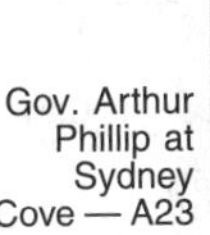

Gov. Arthur Phillip at Sydney Cove — A23

1937, Oct. 1 *Perf. 13x13½*

163	A23	2p red	.90	.20
		Never hinged	1.90	
164	A23	3p ultra	2.75	1.60
		Never hinged	4.50	
165	A23	9p violet	16.00	11.00
		Never hinged	25.00	
		Nos. 163-165 (3)	19.65	12.80

150th anniversary of New South Wales.

Kangaroo A24

Queen Elizabeth A25

King George VI A26 A27

Koala — A28

Merino Sheep — A29

Kookaburra (Kingfisher) A30

Platypus A31

Queen Elizabeth and King George VI in Coronation Robes A32 A33

King George VI and Queen Elizabeth A34

Two Types of A25 and A26:

Type I - Highlighted background. Lines around letters of Australia Postage and numerals of value.

Type II - Background of heavy diagonal lines without the highlighted effect. No lines around letters and numerals.

Perf. 13½x14, 14x13½

1937-46 **Engr.** **Wmk. 228**

166	A24	½p org, perf. 15x14 ('42)	.20	.20
		Never hinged	1.00	
a.		Perf. 13½x14 ('38)	.70	.25
		Never hinged	1.25	
167	A25	1p emerald (I)	.20	.20
		Never hinged	1.00	
168	A26	1½p dull red brn (II)	3.00	1.75
		Never hinged	4.50	
a.		Perf. 15x14 ('41)	4.25	3.50
		Never hinged	6.25	
169	A26	2p scarlet (I)	.30	.20
		Never hinged	1.00	
170	A27	3p ultramarine	12.00	.60
		Never hinged	30.00	
a.		3p dp ultra, thin paper ('38)	20.00	.80
		Never hinged	50.00	
171	A28	4p grn, perf. 15x14 ('42)	.85	.20
		Never hinged	1.25	
a.		Perf. 13½x14 ('38)	2.50	.90
		Never hinged	5.00	
172	A29	5p pale rose vio, perf. 14x15 ('46)	1.25	.50
		Never hinged	2.00	
a.		Perf. 14x13½ ('38)	2.50	.55
		Never hinged	4.00	
173	A30	6p vio brn, perf. 15x14 ('42)	.60	.20
		Never hinged	1.50	
a.		Perf. 13½x14	5.25	.85
		Never hinged	15.00	
b.		6p chocolate, perf. 15x14	1.00	.20
		Never hinged	1.50	
174	A31	9p sep, perf. 14x15 ('43)	1.75	.20
		Never hinged	2.50	
a.		Perf. 14x13½ ('38)	3.75	.90
		Never hinged	7.25	
175	A16	1sh gray grn, perf. 15x14 ('41)	1.10	.20
		Never hinged	1.50	
a.		Perf. 13½x14	22.50	2.00
		Never hinged	47.50	
176	A27	1sh4p magenta ('38)	1.50	.50
		Never hinged	2.00	

Perf. 13½

177	A32	5sh dl red brn ('38)	5.00	2.50
		Never hinged	10.00	
178	A33	10sh dl gray vio ('38)	30.00	13.00
		Never hinged	45.00	
179	A34	£1 bl gray ('38)	60.00	27.50
		Never hinged	90.00	
		Nos. 166-179 (14)	117.75	47.75

No. 175 measures 17½x21½mm.

See #223A, 293, 295, 298, 300. For surch. & overprints see #190, M1, M4-M5, M7.

1938-42 *Perf. 15x14*

180	A25	1p emerald (II)	.55	.25
181	A25	1p dl red brn (II) ('41)	.50	.20
181B	A26	1½p bl grn (II) ('41)	.60	.20
182	A26	2p scarlet (II)	.60	.20
182B	A26	2p red vio (II) ('41)	.20	.20
183	A27	3p dk ultra ('40)	15.00	.75
		Never hinged	30.00	
183A	A27	3p dk vio brn ('42)	.20	.20
		Nos. 180-183A (7)	17.65	2.00
		Set, never hinged	40.00	

No. 183 differs from Nos. 170-170a in the shading lines on the king's left eyebrow which go downward, left to right, instead of the reverse. Also, more of the left epaulette shows.

For surcharges & ovpt. see #188-189, M3.

Coil Perforation

A special perforation was applied to stamps intended for use in coils to make separation easier. It consists of small and large holes (2 small, 10 large, 2 small) on the stamps' narrow side. Some of the stamps so perforated were sold in sheets.

This coil perforation may be found on Nos. 166, 181, 182, 182B, 193, 215, 223A, 231, 257, 315-316, 319, 319a and others.

Nurse, Sailor, Soldier and Aviator — A35

Perf. 13½x13

1940, July 15 **Engr.** **Wmk. 228**

184	A35	1p green	1.00	.20
		Never hinged	2.00	
185	A35	2p red	1.00	.20
		Never hinged	2.00	
186	A35	3p ultra	4.00	3.00
		Never hinged	7.00	
187	A35	6p chocolate	12.50	10.00
		Never hinged	21.00	
		Nos. 184-187 (4)	18.50	13.40

Australia's participation in WWII.

No. 182 Surcharged in Blue

1941, Dec. 10 *Perf. 15x14*

188	A26	2½p on 2p red	.20	.20
		Never hinged	.25	

No. 183 Surcharged in Blue and Yellow

189 A27 3½p on 3p dk ultra .40 .35
Never hinged .50

No. 172a Surcharged in Purple

Perf. 14x13½

190 A29 5½p on 5p pale rose vio 4.00 4.00
Never hinged 4.75
Nos. 188-190 (3) 4.60 4.55

Queen Elizabeth
A36 A37

King George VI
A38 A39

George VI and Blue Wrens
A40

Emu
A41

1942-44 Engr. *Perf. 15x14*

191 A36 1p brown vio ('43) .20 .20
192 A37 1½p green .20 .20
193 A38 2p lt rose vio ('44) .20 .20
194 A39 2½p red .20 .20
195 A40 3½p ultramarine .20 .20
196 A41 5½p indigo .35 .20
Nos. 191-196 (6) 1.35 1.20
Set, never hinged 1.75

See #224-225. For overprint see #M2.

Catalogue values for unused stamps in this section, from this point to the end of the section, are for Never Hinged items.

Duke and Duchess of Gloucester
A42

1945, Feb. 19 Engr. *Perf. 14½*

197 A42 2½p brown red .20 .20
198 A42 3½p bright ultra .25 .25
199 A42 5½p indigo .25 .25
Nos. 197-199 (3) .70 .70

Inauguration of the Duke of Gloucester as Governor General.

Official Crest and Inscriptions
A43

Dove and Australian Flag
A44

Angel of Peace; "Motherhood" and "Industry"
A45

1946, Feb. 18 Wmk. 228 *Perf. 14½*

200 A43 2½p carmine .20 .20
201 A44 3½p deep ultra .20 .25
202 A45 5½p deep yellow green .40 .35
Nos. 200-202 (3) .80 .80

End of WWII. See #1456-1458.

Sir Thomas Mitchell and Map of Queensland
A46

1946, Oct. 14

203 A46 2½p dark carmine .20 .20
204 A46 3½p deep ultra .20 .25
205 A46 1sh olive green .80 .35
Nos. 203-205 (3) 1.20 .80

Sir Thomas Mitchell's exploration of central Queensland, cent.

Kangaroo-Map Type of 1913 Redrawn

1945, Dec. Typo. *Perf. 11½*

206 A1 2sh dk red brown 4.00 3.50

The R and A of AUSTRALIA are separated at the base and there is a single line between the value tablet and "Two Shillings." On No. 125 the tail of the R touches the A, while two lines appear between value tablet and "Two Shillings." There are many other minor differences in the design.

For overprint see No. M6.

John Shortland
A47

Pouring Steel
A48

Loading Coal — A49

1947, Sept. Engr. *Perf. 14½x14*

207 A47 2½p brown red .30 .20

Perf. 14½

208 A48 3½p deep blue .25 .30
209 A49 5½p deep green .35 .30
Nos. 207-209 (3) .90 .80

150th anniv. of the discovery of the Hunter River estuary, site of Newcastle by Lieut. John Shortland. By error the 2½p shows his father, Capt. John Shortland.

Princess Elizabeth — A50

Perf. 14x14½

1947, Nov. 20 Wmk. 228

210 A50 1p brown violet .20 .20

See No. 215.

Hereford Bull
A51

Crocodile
A52

1948, Feb. 16 *Perf. 14½*

211 A51 1sh3p violet brown 1.90 .70
212 A52 2sh chocolate 2.00 .50

See No. 302.

William J. Farrer — A53

Design: No. 214, Ferdinand von Mueller.

1948 *Perf. 14½x14*

213 A53 2½p red .20 .20
214 A53 2½p dark red .20 .20

William J. Farrer (1845-1906), wheat researcher, and Ferdinand von Mueller (1825-1896), German-born botanist.

Issue dates: #213, July 12. #214, Sept. 13.

Elizabeth Type of 1947

1948, Aug. Unwmk. *Perf. 14x14½*

215 A50 1p brown violet .20 .20

Scout in Uniform — A55

Arms of Australia — A56

1948, Nov. 15 Engr. Wmk. 228

216 A55 2½p brown red .20 .20

Pan-Pacific Scout Jamboree, Victoria, Dec. 29, 1948 to Jan. 9, 1949. See No. 249.

1949-50 Wmk. 228 *Perf. 14x13½*

218 A56 5sh dark red 3.50 .50
219 A56 10sh red violet 15.00 1.00
220 A56 £1 deep blue 35.00 4.00
221 A56 £2 green ('50) 100.00 15.00
Nos. 218-221 (4) 153.50 20.50

Henry Hertzberg Lawson (1867-1922), Author and Poet — A57

Perf. 14½x14

1949, June 17 Unwmk.

222 A57 2½p rose brown .20 .20

Outback Mail Carrier and Plane — A58

1949, Oct. 10

223 A58 3½p violet blue .25 .20

UPU, 75th anniv.

Types of 1938, 1942-44 & A59

Aborigine
A59

John Forrest
A60

1948-50 Unwmk. *Perf. 14½x14*

223A A24 ½p orange ('49) .20 .20
224 A37 1½p green ('49) .25 .20
225 A38 2p lt rose violet .30 .20

Wmk. 228

226 A59 8½p dark brown ('50) .50 .40
Nos. 223A-226 (4) 1.25 1.00

Issued: 2p, Dec.; ½p, Sept.; 1½p, 8/29; 8½p, 8/14.

See Nos. 248, 303.

1949, Nov. 28 Wmk. 228

227 A60 2½p brown red .20 .20

Forrest (1847-1918), explorer & statesman.

New South Wales
A61

Victoria
A62

First stamp designs.

Perf. 14½x14

1950, Sept. 27 Unwmk.

228 A61 2½p rose brown .25 .20
229 A62 2½p rose brown .25 .20
a. Pair, #228-229 .65 .40

Cent. of Australian adhesive postage stamps. Issued in sheets of 160 stamps containing alternate copies of Nos. 228 and 229.

Elizabeth
A63

George VI
A64

A65

A66

1950-51 Engr. Unwmk.

230 A63 1½p deep green .30 .20
231 A63 2p yellow grn ('51) .20 .20
232 A64 2½p violet brn ('51) .20 .20
233 A64 3p dull green ('51) .30 .20
Nos. 230-233 (4) 1.00 .80

Issued: 1½p, 6/19; 2p, 3/28; 2½p, 5/23; 3p, 11/14.

1950-52 Wmk. 228

234 A64 2½p red .20 .20
235 A64 3p red ('51) .20 .20
236 A65 3½p red brown ('51) .30 .20
237 A65 4½p scarlet ('52) .40 .35
238 A65 6½p choc ('52) .30 .30
238A A65 6½p blue green ('52) .40 .20
239 A66 7½p deep blue ('51) .45 .30
Nos. 234-239 (7) 2.25 1.75

Issued: 2½p, 4/12; 3p, 2/28; 7½p, 10/31; 3½p, 11/28; 4½p, #238, 2/20; #238A, 4/9.

A67

Founding of the Commonwealth of Australia, 50th Anniv. — A68

Designs: No. 240, Sir Edmund Barton. No. 241, Sir Henry Parkes. 5½p, Duke of York opening first Federal Parliament. 1sh6p, Parliament House, Canberra.

Perf. 14½x14

1951, May 1 Engr. Unwmk.

240 3p carmine	.40	.20
241 3p carmine	.40	.20
a. A67 Pair, #240, 241	.80	.65
242 A68 5½p deep blue	.40	*.70*
243 A68 1sh6p red brown	1.25	.90
Nos. 240-243 (4)	2.45	2.00

Edward Hammond Hargraves A69

King George VI A70

Design: No. 245, Charles Joseph Latrobe (1801-1875), first governor of Victoria.

1951, July 2

244 A69 3p rose brown	.25	.20
245 A69 3p rose brown	.25	.20
a. Pair, #244, 245	.65	.65

Discovery of gold in Australia, cent. (No. 244); Establishment of representative government in Victoria, cent. (No. 245). Sheets contain alternate rows of Nos. 244 and 245.

1952, Mar. 19 Wmk. 228 *Perf. 14½*

247 A70 1sh½p slate blue	1.60	.25

Aborigine Type of 1950 Redrawn

Size: 20½x25mm

248 A59 2sh6p dark brown	3.25	.40

Portrait as on A59; lettering altered and value repeated at lower left. See No. 303.

Scout Type of 1948

Dated "1952-53"

Perf. 14x14½

1952, Nov. 19 Wmk. 228

249 A55 3½p red brown	.20	.20

Pan-Pacific Scout Jamboree, Greystanes, Dec. 30, 1952, to Jan. 9, 1953.

Modern Dairy, Butter Production — A71

Perf. 14½

1953, Feb. 11 Unwmk. Typo.

250 A71 3p shown	.75	.20
251 A71 3p Wheat	.75	.20
252 A71 3p Beef	.75	.20
a. Strip of 3, #250-252	4.50	4.50
253 A71 3½p shown	.75	.20
254 A71 3½p Wheat	.75	.20
255 A71 3½p Beef	.75	.20
a. Strip of 3, #253-255	3.25	*3.25*
Nos. 250-255 (6)	4.50	1.20

Both the 3p and 3½p were printed in panes of 50 stamps: 17 Butter, 17 Wheat and 16 Beef. The stamps were issued to encourage food production.

Queen Elizabeth II — A72

Perf. 14½x14

1953-54 Unwmk. Engr.

256 A72 1p purple	.20	.20
256A A72 2½p deep blue ('54)	.25	.20
257 A72 3p dark green	.25	.20

Wmk. 228

258 A72 3½p dark red	.25	.20
258B A72 6½p orange ('54)	.90	.20
Nos. 256-258B (5)	1.85	1.00

Issued: 3½p, 4/21; 3p, 6/17; 1p, 8/19; 2½p, 6½p, 6/23.

See Nos. 292, 296.

Coronation Issue

Queen Elizabeth II A73

1953, May 25 Unwmk.

259 A73 3½p rose red	.25	.20
260 A73 7½p violet	.70	.45
261 A73 2sh dull green	2.25	1.10
Nos. 259-261 (3)	3.20	1.75

Boy and Girl with Calf — A74

1953, Sept. 3 *Perf. 14½*

262 A74 3½p dp green & red brn	.25	.20

Official establishment of Young Farmers' Clubs, 25th anniv.

Lieut. Gov. David Collins A75

Tasmania Stamp of 1853 A77

Sullivan Cove, Hobart A76

#264, Lieut. Gov. William Paterson (facing left).

1953, Sept. 23 *Perf. 14½x14*

263 A75 3½p red brown	.35	.20
264 A75 3½p red brown	.35	.20
a. Pair, #263-264	1.25	1.10
265 A76 2sh green	3.00	2.50
Nos. 263-265 (3)	3.70	2.90

Settlement in Tasmania, 150th anniv. Sheets contain alternate rows of Nos. 263 and 264.

1953, Nov. 11 *Perf. 14½*

266 A77 3p red	.20	.20

Tasmania's first postage stamps, cent.

Elizabeth II and Duke of Edinburgh — A78

Elizabeth II — A79

Telegraph Pole and Key — A80

1954, Feb. 2 *Perf. 14½x14, 14x14½*

267 A78 3½p rose red	.20	.20
268 A79 7½p purple	.30	*.80*
269 A78 2sh green	1.50	1.00
Nos. 267-269 (3)	2.00	2.00

Visit of Queen Elizabeth II and the Duke of Edinburgh, 1954.

1954, Apr. 7 Engr. *Perf. 14*

270 A80 3½p dark red	.25	.20

Inauguration of the telegraph in Australia, cent.

Red Cross and Globe — A81

Swan — A82

1954, June 9 *Perf. 14½x14*

271 A81 3½p deep blue & red	.20	.20

Australian Red Cross Society.

1954, Aug. 2 Unwmk. *Perf. 14½*

274 A82 3½p black	.20	.20

Western Australia's first postage stamp, cent.

Diesel and Early Steam Locomotives A83

1954, Sept. 13 *Perf. 14x14½*

275 A83 3½p red brown	.20	.20

Centenary of Australian railroads.

Antarctic Flora and Fauna and Map — A84

1954, Nov. 17 *Perf. 14*

276 A84 3½p black	.20	.20

Australia's interest in the Antarctic continent.

Olympic Circles and Arms of Melbourne — A85

1954, Dec. 1

277 A85 2sh dark blue	2.50	1.50

16th Olympic Games to be held in Melbourne Nov.-Dec. 1956. See No. 286.

Globe, Flags and Rotary Emblem — A86

1955, Feb. 23 *Perf. 14x14½*

278 A86 3½p carmine	.20	.20

Rotary International, 50th anniv.

Elizabeth II — A87

Top of US Monument, Canberra — A88

1955, Mar. 9 Wmk. 228 *Perf. 14½*

279 A87 1sh½p dk gray blue	3.50	.25

See No. 301.

1955, May 4 Unwmk. *Perf. 14x14½*

280 A88 3½p deep ultra	.20	.20

Friendship between Australia and the US.

Cobb and Company Mail Coach
A89

1955, July 6 ***Perf. 14½x14***

281 A89 3½p dark brown .20 .20
282 A89 2sh brown 2.50 1.90

Pioneers of Australia's coaching era.

World Map, YMCA Emblem
A90

Engr. and Typo.

1955, Aug. 10 ***Perf. 14***

283 A90 3½p Prus green & red .20 .20

Centenary of YMCA.

Florence Nightingale and Modern Nurse — A91

Queen Victoria — A92

1955, Sept. 21 Engr. ***Perf. 14x14½***

284 A91 3½p red violet .20 .20

Centenary of Florence Nightingale's work in the Crimea and of the founding of modern nursing.

1955, Oct. 17 ***Perf. 14½***

285 A92 3½p green .20 .20

South Australia's first postage stamps, cent.

Olympic Type of 1954

1955, Nov. 30 Unwmk. ***Perf. 14***

286 A85 2sh deep green 2.50 1.50

16th Olympic Games at Melbourne, Nov. 22-Dec. 8, 1956.

Queen Victoria, Queen Elizabeth II and Badges of Victoria, New South Wales and Tasmania
A93

1956, Sept. 26 ***Perf. 14½x14***

287 A93 3½p brown carmine .25 .20

Centenary of responsible government in Victoria, New South Wales and Tasmania.

Melbourne Coat of Arms — A94

Southern Cross, Olympic Torch — A95

Collins Street, Melbourne
A96

Design: 2sh, Melbourne across Yarra River.

1956, Oct. 31 Engr. ***Perf. 14½, 14***

288 A94 4p dark carmine .30 .20
289 A95 7½p ultramarine .55 .40

Photo.

Perf. 14x14½

290 A96 1sh multicolored .70 .45

Perf. 12x11½

Granite Paper

291 A96 2sh multicolored .95 .95
Nos. 288-291 (4) 2.50 2.00

16th Olympic Games, Melbourne, 11/22-12/8.

A lithographed souvenir sheet incorporating reproductions of Nos. 288-291 in reduced size was of private origin and not postally valid.

Types of 1938-55 and

Queen Elizabeth II — A97

Perf. 14½x14, 14x15, 15x14, 14½

1956-57 Engr. Unwmk.

292	A72	3½p	dark red	1.00	.20
293	A28	4p	green	1.60	.20
294	A97	4p	claret ('57)	.30	.20
a.			Booklet pane of 6 ('57)	7.50	
295	A30	6p	brown violet	2.75	.20
296	A72	6½p	orange	1.75	.20
297	A97	7½p	violet ('57)	3.00	.40
298	A31	9p	sepia	9.00	.55
299	A97	10p	gray blue ('57)	2.75	.20
300	A16	1sh	gray green	6.00	.30
301	A87	1sh7p	redsh brn ('57)	4.50	.30
302	A52	2sh	chocolate	12.00	.25
303	A59	2sh6p	brown ('57)	9.00	.25
			Nos. 292-303 (12)	53.65	3.25

No. 300 measures 17½x21½mm. No. 303 measures 20½x25mm and is the redrawn type of 1952.

Issued: 3½p, 7/2; 2sh, 7/21; #293, 6p, 8/18; 6½p, Sept. 9p, 1sh, 12/13; 2sh6p, 1/30; 10p, 3/6; #294, 1sh7p, 3/13; 7½p, 11/13.

South Australia Coat of Arms — A99

1957, Apr. 17 Unwmk. ***Perf. 14½***

304 A99 4p brown red .20 .20

Centenary of responsible government in South Australia.

There are two types of No. 304.

Caduceus and Map of Australia
A100

1957, Aug. 21 ***Perf. 14½x14***

305 A100 7p violet blue .60 .20

Royal Flying Doctor Service of Australia.

Star of Bethlehem and Praying Child
A101

1957, Nov. 6 **Engr.**

306 A101 3½p dull rose .25 .20
307 A101 4p pale purple .25 .20

Christmas.

Canberra War Memorial, Sailor and Airman
A102

#309, As #308 with soldier and service woman. Printed in alternate rows in sheet.

1958, Feb. 10 **Unwmk.**

308 A102 5½p brown carmine 1.25 .75
309 A102 5½p brown carmine 1.25 .75
a. Pair, #308-309 3.50 3.50

Sir Charles Kingsford-Smith and "Southern Cross" — A103

1958, Aug. 27 ***Perf. 14x14½***

310 A103 8p brt violet blue 1.00 .90

1st air crossing of the Tasman Sea, 30th anniv. See New Zealand No. 321.

Broken Hill Mine — A104

1958, Sept. 10 ***Perf. 14½x14***

311 A104 4p brown .25 .20

Broken Hill mining field, 75th anniv.

Nativity — A105

1958, Nov. 5 ***Perf. 14½x15***

312 A105 3½p dark red .20 .20
313 A105 4p dark purple .25 .20

Christmas.

A106

A107

A108

A109

A110

Platypus
A111

Tasmanian Tiger
A112

Flannel Flower — A113

Aboriginal Stockman Cutting Out a Steer
A114

Designs: 3p, Queen Elizabeth II facing right. 6p, Banded anteater. 8p, Tiger cat. 9p, Kangaroos. 11p, Rabbit bandicoot. 1sh6p, Christmas bells (flower). 2sh3p, Wattle (flower). 2sh5p, Banksia (flower). 3sh, Waratah (flower).

FIVE PENCE

Die I - Four short lines inside "5" at right of ball; six short lines left of ball; full length line above ball is seventh from bottom. Odd numbered horizontal rows in each sheet are in Die I.

Die II - Five short lines inside "5" at right of ball; seven at left; full length line above ball is eighth from bottom. Even numbered horizontal rows in each sheet are in Die II.

Perf. 14½x14, 14x14½, 14½

1959-64 Engr. Unwmk.

314	A106	1p	dull violet	.20	.20
315	A107	2p	red brown	.55	.20
316	A108	3p	bluish green	.20	.20
317	A108	3½p	dark green	.20	.20
318	A109	4p	carmine	1.90	.20
a.			Booklet pane of 6	25.00	
319	A110	5p	dark blue (I)	.90	.20
a.			5p dark blue (II)	.90	.20
b.			Booklet pane of 6 ('60)	11.00	
320	A111	6p	chocolate	2.10	.20
321	A111	8p	red brown	.80	.20
322	A111	9p	brown black	1.90	.20
323	A111	11p	dark blue	1.40	.20
324	A111	1sh	slate green	3.75	.20
325	A112	1sh2p	dk purple	1.40	.20
326	A113	1sh6p	red, *yellow*	2.75	.60
327	A113	2sh	dark blue	1.40	.20
328	A113	2sh3p	green, *yel*	1.40	.20
328A	A113	2sh3p	yellow grn	5.25	1.00
329	A113	2sh5p	brown, *yellow*	6.50	.40
330	A113	3sh	crimson	1.60	.35
			Wmk. 228		
331	A114	5sh	red brown	21.00	1.00
			Nos. 314-331 (19)	55.20	6.15

Issued: 1p, 4p, 2/2; 3½p, 3/18; 2sh, 4/8; 3p, 5/20; 3sh, 7/15; 1sh, #328, 9/9; 5p, 10/1; 9p, 10/21; 1sh6p, 2/3/60; 2sh5p, 3/16/60; 8p, 5/11/60; 6p, 9/30/60; 11p, 5/3/61; 5sh, 7/26/61; 2p, 1sh2p, 3/21/62; #328A, 10/28/64.

Luminescent Printings

Paper with an orange red phosphorescence (surface coating), was used for some printings of the Colombo Plan 1sh, No. 340, the Churchill 5p, No. 389, and several regular postage stamps. These include 2p, 3p, 6p, 8p, 9p, 11p, 1sh2p, 1sh6p and 2sh3p (Nos. 315, 316, 365, 367, 321, 368, 323, 325, 369, 328A).

Stamps printed only on phosphorescent paper include the Monash 5p, Hargrave 5p, ICY 2sh3p and Christmas 5p (Nos. 388, 390-393) and succeeding commemoratives; the 2sh, 2sh6p and 3sh regular birds (Nos. 370, 372, 373); and most of the regular series in decimal currency.

Ink with a phosphorescent content was used in printing most of the 5p red, No. 366, almost all of the 5p red booklets, No. 366a, most of the decimal 4c regular, No. 397, and its booklet pane, No. 397a, and all of No. 398.

Postmaster Isaac Nichols Boarding Vessel to Receive Mail — A115

1959, Apr. 22 ***Perf. 14½x14***

332 A115 4p dark gray blue .25 .20

First post office, Sydney, 150th anniv.

Parliament House, Brisbane, and Queensland Arms — A116

1959, June 5 ***Perf. 14x14½***

333 A116 4p dk green & violet .25 .20

Cent. of Queensland self-government.

Approach of the Magi — A117

1959, Nov. 4 ***Perf. 15x14½***

334 A117 5p purple .25 .20

Christmas.

Girl Guide and Lord Baden-Powell — A118

1960, Aug. 18 ***Perf. 14½x14***

335 A118 5p dark blue .30 .20

50th anniversary of the Girl Guides.

The Overlanders by Sir Daryl Lindsay — A119

1960, Sept. 21 ***Perf. 14½***

336 A119 5p lilac rose .30 .20

Exploration of Australia's Northern Territory, cent.

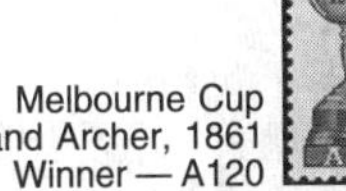

Melbourne Cup and Archer, 1861 Winner — A120

1960, Oct. 12 **Unwmk.**

337 A120 5p sepia .30 .20

Centenary of the Melbourne Cup.

Queen Victoria A121

Open Bible and Candle A122

1960 Nov. 2 **Engr.** ***Perf. 14½***

338 A121 5p dark green .20 .20

Centenary of the first Queensland stamps.

1960, Nov. 9 **Unwmk.**

339 A122 5p maroon .20 .20

Christmas; beginning of 350th anniv. year of the publication of the King James translation of the Bible.

Colombo Plan Emblem — A123

1961, June 30 ***Perf. 14x14½***

340 A123 1sh red brown .75 .20

Colombo Plan for the peaceful development of South East Asia countries, 10th anniv.

Dame Nellie Melba, by Sir Bertram Mackennal — A124

1961, Sept. 20 ***Perf. 14½***

341 A124 5p deep blue .30 .20

Dame Nellie Melba, singer, birth cent.

Page from Book of Hours, 15th Century A125

John McDouall Stuart — A126

1961, Nov. 8 ***Perf. 14½x14***

342 A125 5p reddish brown .30 .20

Christmas; end of the 350th anniv. year of the publication of the King James translation of the Bible.

1962, July 25 **Unwmk.** ***Perf. 14½***

345 A126 5p carmine .30 .20

First south-north crossing of Australia by John McDouall Stuart, cent.

Nurse and Rev. Flynn's Grave — A127

1962, Sept. 5 **Photo.** ***Perf. 13½***

346 A127 5p multicolored .30 .20

a. Red omitted 400.00

Australian Inland Mission founded by Rev. John Flynn, 50th anniv.

Woman and Globe — A128

Madonna and Child — A129

1962, Sept. 26 **Engr.** ***Perf. 14x14½***

347 A128 5p dark green .30 .20

World Conf. of the Associated Country Women of the World, Melbourne, Oct. 2-12.

1962, Oct. 17 ***Perf. 14½***

348 A129 5p deep violet .30 .20

Christmas.

View of Perth and Kangaroo Paw — A130

Arms of Perth A131

1962, Nov. 1 **Photo.** ***Perf. 14***

349 A130 5p multicolored .30 .20

a. Red omitted 750.00

Perf. 14½x14

350 A131 2sh3p emer, blk, red & ultra 4.00 4.00

British Empire and Commonwealth Games, Perth, Nov. 22-Dec. 1.

Elizabeth II — A132

Elizabeth II and Prince Philip — A133

1963, Feb. 18 **Engr.** ***Perf. 14½***

351 A132 5p dark green .30 .20

352 A133 2sh3 red brown 4.00 4.00

Visit of Elizabeth II and Prince Philip.

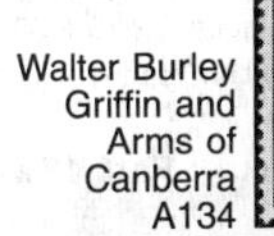

Walter Burley Griffin and Arms of Canberra A134

Red Cross Centenary Emblem — A135

1963, Mar. 8 **Unwmk.** ***Perf. 14½x14***

353 A134 5p dark green .35 .20

50th anniv. of Canberra; Walter Burley Griffin, American architect, who laid out plan for Canberra.

1963, May 8 **Photo.** ***Perf. 13½x13***

354 A135 5p dk blue, red & gray .35 .20

Centenary of the International Red Cross.

Explorers Blaxland, Lawson and Wentworth Looking West from Mt. York — A136

1963, May 28 **Engr.** ***Perf. 14½x14***

355 A136 5p dark blue .30 .20

1st crossing of the Blue Mts., 150th anniv.

Globe, Ship, Plane and Map of Australia A137

1963, Aug. 28 **Unwmk.**

356 A137 5p red .35 .20

Importance of exports to Australian economy.

Elizabeth II A138

Black-backed Magpie and Eucalyptus A139

Abel Tasman and Ship — A144

George Bass, Whaleboat — A145

Designs: 6p, Yellow-tailed thornbill, horiz. 1sh6p, Galah on tree stump. 2sh, Golden whistler. 2sh5p, Blue wren and bracken fern. 2sh6p, Scarlet robin, horiz. 3sh, Straw-necked ibis. 5sh, William Dampier and "Roebuck" sailing ship. 7sh6p, Capt. James Cook. 10sh, Matthew Flinders and three-master "Investigator." £2, Admiral Philip Parker King.

Perf. 15x14

1963-65 **Unwmk.** **Engr.**

365 A138 5p green .55 .20

a. Booklet pane of 6 ('64) 20.00

b. Pair, imperf. btwn. 1.50 1.50

366 A138 5p red .45 .20

a. Booklet pane of 6 25.00

Photo.

Perf. 13½

367 A139 6p multi .70 .20

a. Vert. pair, imperf. btwn.

368 A139 9p multi .90 *2.40*

369 A139 1sh6p multi .65 *1.25*

370 A139 2sh multi 1.50 .40

371 A139 2sh5p multi 2.25 *3.00*

372 A139 2sh6p multi 4.25 2.75

a. Red omitted *1,500.*

373 A139 3sh multi 4.25 1.50

Engr.

Perf. 14½x14, 14½x15

374 A144 4sh violet blue 2.50 .50

Wmk. 228

375 A145 5sh red brown 3.50 1.10

376 A144 7sh6p olive green 16.50 14.00

377 A144 10sh deep claret 26.00 4.00

378 A145 £1 purple 30.00 13.00

379 A145 £2 brn blk 55.00 *65.00*

Nos. 365-379 (15) 149.00 109.50

No. 365a was printed in sheets of 288 which were sold intact by the Philatelic Bureau. These sheets have been broken to obtain pairs and blocks which are imperf. between (see No. 365b).

Issued: #365, 4sh, 10/9/63; 10sh, £1, 2/26/64; 9p, 1sh6p, 2sh5p, 3/11/64; 6p, 8/19/64; 7sh6p, £2, 8/26/64; 5sh, 11/25/64; 2sh, 2sh6p, 3sh, 4/21/65; #366, 6/30/65.

See Nos. 400-401, 406-417, 1727-1728.

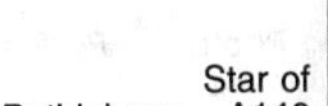

Star of Bethlehem — A146

1963, Oct. 25 **Unwmk.** ***Perf. 14½***

380 A146 5p blue .20 .20

Christmas.

Cable Around World and Under Sea — A147

1963, Dec. 3 Photo. *Perf. 13½*

381 A147 2sh3p gray, ver, blk & blue 4.50 3.50

Opening of the Commonwealth Pacific (telephone) cable service (COMPAC).
See New Zealand No. 364.

Bleriot 60 Plane, 1914 — A148

1964, July 1 Engr. *Perf. 14½x14*

382	A148	5p olive green	.20	.20
383	A148	2sh3p red	5.25	4.25

50th anniv. of the first air mail flight in Australia; Maurice Guillaux, aviator.

Child Looking at Nativity Scene — A149

1964, Oct. 21 Photo. *Perf. 13½*

384	A149	5p bl, blk, red & buff	.20	.20
a.		Red omitted	—	*475.00*
b.		Black omitted	*600.00*	

Christmas.

No. 384a used is valued on cover. The red ink can be removed from No. 384 by bleaching.

"Simpson and His Donkey" by Wallace Anderson — A150

1965, Apr. 14 Engr. *Perf. 14x14½*

385	A150	5p olive bister	.25	.20
386	A150	8p dark blue	1.25	.90
387	A150	2sh3p rose claret	4.75	4.25
		Nos. 385-387 (3)	6.25	5.35

50th anniv. of the landing of the Australian and New Zealand Army Corps (ANZAC) at Gallipoli, Turkey, Apr. 25, 1915. Private John Simpson Kirkpatrick saved the lives of many wounded soldiers. The statue erected in his honor stands in front of Melbourne's Shrine of Remembrance.

Radio Mast and Satellite Orbiting Earth A151

Winston Churchill A152

1965, May 10 Photo. *Perf. 13½*

388	A151	5p multicolored	.20	.20
a.		Black ("5d" and pylon) omitted	*850.00*	

ITU, cent.

1965, May 24

389 A152 5p lt blue, gray & blk .25 .20

Sir Winston Spencer Churchill (1874-1965), statesman and WWII leader.
See New Zealand No. 371.

John Monash and Transmission Tower — A153

Lawrence Hargrave and Sketch for 1902 Seaplane A154

1965, June 23 Photo. *Perf. 13½*

390 A153 5p red, yel, blk & lt brn .25 .20

Birth cent. of General Sir John Monash (1865-1931), soldier, Vice-Chancellor of University of Melbourne and chairman of the Victoria state electricity commission.

1965, Aug. 4 Unwmk. *Perf. 13½*

391	A154	5p multicolored	.25	.20
a.		Purple (5d) omitted	*225.00*	

50th anniv. of the death of Lawrence Hargrave (1850-1915), aviation pioneer.

ICY Emblem — A155

Nativity — A156

1965, Sept. 1 Photo. *Perf. 13½*

392 A155 2sh3p lt blue & green 2.75 2.50

International Cooperation Year.

1965, Oct. 20 Unwmk. *Perf. 13½*

393	A156	5p multicolored	.30	.20
a.		Gold omitted	*1,000.*	
b.		Ultramarine omitted	475.00	

Christmas.

Types of 1963-65 and

Elizabeth II — A157

Humbug Fish — A158

Designs: No. 400, Yellow-tailed thornbill, horiz. 6c, blue-faced honeyeater, horiz. 8c, Coral fish. 9c, Hermit crab. 10c Anemone fish. 13c, Red-necked avocet. 15c, Galah on tree stump. 20c, Golden whistler. 24c Azure kingfisher, horiz. 25c, Scarlet robin, horiz. 30c Straw-necked ibis. 40c Abel Tasman and ship. 50c, William Dampier and "Roebuck" sailing ship. 75c, Capt. James Cook. $1, Matthew Flinders and three-master "Investigator." $2, George Bass and whaleboat. $4, Admiral Philip Parker King.

Perf. 14½x14 (A157); 13½ (A158, A139)

Engr. (A157), Photo. (A158, A139)

1966-71

394	A157	1c red brown	.25	.20
395	A157	2c olive green	.65	.20
396	A157	3c Prus green	.65	.20
397	A157	4c red	.20	.20
a.		Booklet pane of 5 + label	30.00	
398	A157	5c on 4c red ('67)	.30	.20
a.		Booklet pane of 5 + label ('67)	5.50	
399	A157	5c dk blue ('67)	.65	.20
a.		Booklet pane of 5 + label	11.00	
400	A139	5c lt grn, blk, brn & yel	.25	.20
401	A139	6c gray, blk, lem & bl	.70	.30
401A	A157	6c orange ('70)	.50	.20
402	A158	7c brn, ver, blk & gray	.75	.20
402A	A157	7c dp rose lilac ('71)	.65	.20
403	A158	8c multicolored	.75	.30
404	A158	9c multicolored	.75	.20
405	A158	10c lt brn, blk, org & bl	.75	.20
406	A139	13c lt bl grn, blk, gray & red	1.60	.20
a.		Red omitted	1,000.	
b.		Gray omitted	750.00	
407	A139	15c lt grn, blk, gray & rose	1.40	.60
a.		Gray omitted	1,500.	
408	A139	20c pink, blk, yel & gray	2.75	.20
a.		Yellow omitted	900.00	
409	A139	24c tan, blk, vio bl & org	.80	*.85*
410	A139	25c gray, grn, blk & red	3.25	.20
a.		Red omitted	1,100.	
411	A139	30c lt grn, buff, blk & red	11.00	.55
a.		Red omitted	*900.00*	

Engr.

Perf. 14½x14, 14½x15

412	A144	40c violet blue	4.50	.20
413	A145	50c brown red	6.25	.20
414	A144	75c olive green	.90	.70
415	A144	$1 deep claret	1.60	.20
a.		Perf 15x14	75.00	15.00
416	A145	$2 purple	7.00	.50
417	A145	$4 sepia	6.00	5.50
		Nos. 394-417 (26)	54.85	12.90

No. 398 issued in booklets only.

Booklet panes of 10 of No. 399, and of 5 No. 400, are torn from sheets. They were issued for the use of "Australian Defence Forces," as the covers read, in Viet Nam.

Issued: #398, 399, 9/29/67; #401A, 9/28/70; #402A, 10/1/71; #415a, 1973; others, 2/14/66.

Coil Stamps

1966-67 Photo. *Perf. 15 Horiz.*

418	A157	3c emerald, blk & buff	.40	.35
419	A157	4c org red, blk & buff	.60	.20
420	A157	5c blue, black & buff	.75	.20
		Nos. 418-420 (3)	1.75	.75

Issued: 5c, 9/29/67; others, 2/14/66.

Rescue A159

1966, July 6 Photo. *Perf. 13½*

421 A159 4c blue, ultra & black .25 .20

Royal Life Saving Society, 75th anniv.

Adoration of the Shepherds A160

1966, Oct. 19 Photo. *Perf. 13½*

422 A160 4c olive & black .25 .20

Christmas.

Dutch Sailing Ship, 17th Century — A161

Hands Reaching for Bible — A162

1966, Oct. 24 Photo. *Perf. 13½*

423 A161 4c bl, blk, dp org & gold .25 .20

350th anniv. of Dirk Hartog's discovery of the Australian west coast, and his landing on the island named after him.

1967, Mar. 7 Photo. *Perf. 13½*

424 A162 4c multicolored .25 .20

British and Foreign Bible Soc., 150th anniv.

Combination Lock and Antique Keys — A163

1967, Apr. 5 Photo. *Perf. 13½*

425 A163 4c emerald, blk & lt blue .25 .20

150th anniv. of banking in Australia (Bank of New South Wales).

Lions Intl., 50th Anniv. — A164

1967, June 7 Photo. *Perf. 13½*

426 A164 4c ultra, black & gold .25 .20

YWCA Emblems and Flags A165

1967, Aug. 21 Photo. *Perf. 13½*

427 A165 4c dk blue, lt bl & lilac .25 .20

World Council Meeting of the YWCA, Monash University, Victoria, Aug. 14-Sept. 1.

Seated Women Symbolizing Obstetrics and Gynecology, Female Symbol A166

1967, Sept. 20 Photo. *Perf. 13½*

428 A166 4c lilac, dk blue & blk .25 .20

5th World Congress of Gynecology and Obstetrics, Sydney, Sept. 23-30.

Gothic Arches and Christmas Bell Flower A167

Cross, Stars of David and Yin Yang Forming Mandala — A168

1967 Photo. *Perf. 13½*

429	A167	5c multicolored	.25	.20
430	A168	25c multicolored	2.50	2.50

Christmas.

Issue dates: 5c, Oct. 18; 25c, Nov. 27.

Satellite Orbiting Earth — A169

Satellite and Antenna, Moree, N.S.W. — A170

Design: 20c, World weather map connecting Washington, Moscow and Melbourne, and computer and teleprinter tape spools.

1968, Mar. 20 Photo. *Perf. 13½*

431 A169 5c dull yel, red, bl & dk blue .25 .20
432 A169 20c blue, blk & red 3.00 3.00
433 A170 25c Prus blue, blk & lt green 3.50 3.50
Nos. 431-433 (3) 6.75 6.70

Use of satellites for weather observations and communications.

Kangaroo Paw, Western Australia A171

Sturt's Desert Rose, Northern Territory A171a

State Flowers: 13c, Pink heath, Victoria. 15c, Tasmanian blue gum, Tasmania. 20c, Sturt's desert pea, South Australia. 25c, Cooktown orchid, Queensland. 30c, Waratah, New South Wales.

1968, July 10 Photo. *Perf. 13½*
Flowers in Natural Colors

434 A171 6c bister & dk brn .75 .20
435 A171 13c lt grnsh blue .90 .20
436 A171 15c dk brn & yel 1.25 .25
437 A171 20c lemon & black 3.50 .20
438 A171 25c light ultra 2.75 .20
439 A171 30c chocolate .85 .20
Nos. 434-439 (6) 10.00 1.25

A 1971 reprinting of No. 439 shows more areas of white in the pink petals. This is scarcer than the first printing.

Coil Stamps

1970-75 *Perf. 14½ Horiz.*

Designs: 5c, Golden wattle, national flower. 7c, 10c, Sturt's desert pea.

439A A171a 2c dk grn & multi .20 .20
i. Lettering and value bolder .20 .20
439B A171a 4c gray & multi .50 .40
439C A171a 5c gray & multi .20 .20
439D A171a 6c gray & multi 1.10 .50
h. Green omitted 400.00
439E A171a 7c blk, red & grn .35 .20
f. Green omitted 150.00
439G A171a 10c blk, red & grn .30 .20
Nos. 439A-439G (6) 2.65 1.70

Issued: 4c, 5c, 4/27; 6c, 10/28; 2c, 7c, 10/1/71; 10c, 1/15/75; #439Ai, 11/73.

Soil Testing Through Chemistry & by Computer A172

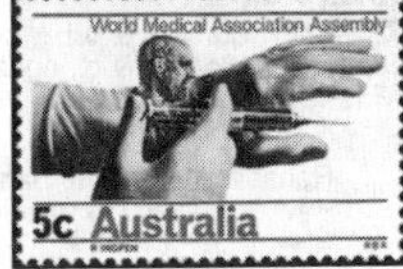

Hippocrates & Hands Holding Hypodermic A173

1968, Aug. 6 Photo. *Perf. 13½*

440 A172 5c multicolored .25 .20
441 A173 5c multicolored .25 .20

9th Intl. Congress of Soil Science, University of Adelaide, Aug. 6-16 (No. 440); General Assembly of World Medical Associations, Sydney, Aug. 6-9 (No. 441). Nos. 440-441 printed in sheets of 100 in two separate panes of 50 connected by a gutter. Each sheet contains 10 gutter pairs.

Runner and Aztec Calendar Stone — A174

Symbolic House and Money — A175

Design: 25c, Aztec calendar stone and Mexican flag, horiz.

1968, Oct. 2

442 A174 5c multicolored .20 .20
443 A174 25c multicolored 2.25 2.00

19th Olympic Games, Mexico City, Oct. 12-27. Nos. 442-443 printed in sheets of 100 in two separate panes of 50 connected by a gutter. Each sheet contains 10 gutter pairs.

1968, Oct. 16

444 A175 5c multicolored .25 .20

11th Triennial Congress of the Intl. Union of Building Societies and Savings Associations, Sydney, Oct. 20-27.

View of Bethlehem and Church Window — A176

1968, Oct. 23 Photo. *Perf. 13½*

445 A176 5c lt bl, red, grn & gold .20 .20
a. Red omitted 350.00

Christmas.

Edgeworth David (1858-1934), Geologist A177

Sir Edmund Barton (1849-1920) A178

Reginald C. and John R. Duigan, Aviators — A179

Famous Australians: #447, Caroline Chisholm (1808-77), social worker, reformer. #448, Albert Namatjira (1902-59), aborigine, artist. #449, Andrew Barton (Banjo) Paterson (1864-1941), poet, writer.

1968, Nov. 6 Engr. *Perf. 15x14*

446 A177 5c green, *greenish* .80 .20
a. Booklet pane of 5 + label 4.00
447 A177 5c purple, *pink* .80 .20
a. Booklet pane of 5 + label 4.00
448 A177 5c dark brown, *buff* .80 .20
a. Booklet pane of 5 + label 4.00
449 A177 5c indigo, *lt blue* .80 .20
a. Booklet pane of 5 + label 4.00
Nos. 446-449 (4) 3.20 .80

1969, Oct. 22 Engr. *Perf. 15x14*

Prime Ministers: #451, Alfred Deakin (1856-1919). #452, John C. Watson (1867-1941). #453, Sir George H. Reid (1845-1918).

450 A178 5c indigo, *greenish* .80 .20
a. Booklet pane of 5 + label 4.00
451 A178 5c indigo, *greenish* .80 .20
a. Booklet pane of 5 + label 4.00
452 A178 5c indigo, *greenish* .80 .20
a. Booklet pane of 5 + label 4.00
453 A178 5c indigo, *greenish* .80 .20
a. Booklet pane of 5 + label 4.00
Nos. 450-453 (4) 3.20 .80

1970, Nov. 16 Engr. *Perf. 15x14*

Famous Australians: #455, Lachlan Macquarie (1761-1824), Governor of New South Wales. #456, Adam Lindsay Gordon (1833-70), poet. #457, Edward John Eyre (1815-1901), explorer.

454 A179 6c dark blue .80 .20
a. Booklet pane of 5 + label 4.00
455 A179 6c dark brown, *salmon* .80 .20
a. Booklet pane of 5 + label 4.00
456 A179 6c magenta, *brt pink* .80 .20
a. Booklet pane of 5 + label 4.00
457 A179 6c brown red, *salmon* .80 .20
a. Booklet pane of 5 + label 4.00
Nos. 454-457 (4) 3.20 .80

Nos. 446-457 were issued in booklet panes only; all stamps have 1 or 2 straight edges.

Macquarie Lighthouse — A180

1968, Nov. 27 Engr. *Perf. 14½x13½*

458 A180 5c indigo, *buff* .35 .20

Macquarie Lighthouse, Outer South Head, Sydney, 150th anniv.

Surveyor George W. Goyder and Assistants, 1869; Building in Darwin, 1969 — A181

1969, Feb. 5 Photo. *Perf. 13½*

459 A181 5c black brn & dull yel .20 .20

First permanent settlement of the Northern Territory of Australia, cent.

Melbourne Harbor Scene A182

1969, Feb. 26 Photo. *Perf. 13½*

460 A182 5c dull blue & multi .20 .20

6th Biennial Conference of the Intl. Assoc. of Ports and Harbors, Melbourne, March 3-8.

Overlapping Circles A183

1969, June 5 Photo. *Perf. 13½*

461 A183 5c gray, vio bl, bl & gold .20 .20

ILO, 50th anniv.

Sugar Cane — A184

Primary industries: 15c, Eucalyptus (timber). 20c, Wheat. 25c, Ram, ewe, lamb (wool).

1969, Sept. 17 *Perf. 13½x13*

462 A184 7c blue & multi .75 .75
463 A184 15c emerald & multi 3.75 3.50
464 A184 20c org brn & multi 1.40 .60
465 A184 25c gray, black & yel 1.25 .70
Nos. 462-465 (4) 7.15 5.55

Nativity — A185

Tree of Life — A186

Perf. 13½x13, 13x13½
1969, Oct. 15 Photo.

466 A185 5c multicolored .20 .20
467 A186 25c multicolored 2.75 2.75

Christmas.

Vickers Vimy Flown by Ross Smith, England to Australia A187

#469, B.E. 2E plane, automobile, spectators. #470, Ford truck, surveyors Lieuts. Hudson Fysh & P.J. McGinness.

1969, Nov. 12 *Perf. 13x13½*

468 A187 5c bl, blk, cop red & ol .60 .35
469 A187 5c bl, blk, cop red & ol .60 .35
470 A187 5c cop red, black & ol .60 .35
a. Strip of 3, #468-470 3.50 3.00
Nos. 468-470 (3) 1.80 1.05

1st England to Australia flight by Capt. Ross Smith & Lieut. Keith Smith, 50th anniv.

No. 470a has various combinations possible.

Diesel Locomotive and New Track Linking Melbourne, Sydney and Brisbane with Perth A188

1970, Feb. 11 Photo. *Perf. 13x13½*

471 A188 5c multicolored .25 .20

Completion of the standard gauge railroad between Sydney and Perth.

EXPO '70 Australian Pavilion A189

Design: 20c, Southern Cross and Japanese inscription: "From the country of the south with warm feeling."

1970, Mar. 16 Photo. *Perf. 13x13½*

472 A189 5c bl, blk, red & brnz .25 .20
473 A189 20c red & black 1.00 .45

EXPO '70 Intl. Exhib., Osaka, Japan, Mar. 15-Sept. 13.

Queen Elizabeth II and Prince Philip
A190

Australian Flag — A191

1970, Mar. 31

474 A190 5c yel bister & black .25 .20
475 A191 30c vio blue & multi 2.25 2.00

Visit of Queen Elizabeth II, Prince Philip and Princess Anne to Australia.

Steer, Alfalfa and Native Spear Grass
A192

1970, Apr. 13 Photo. *Perf. 13x13½*

476 A192 5c emerald & multi .25 .20

11th Intl. Grasslands Congress, Surfers Paradise, Queensland, Apr. 13-23.

Capt. James Cook and "Endeavour" — A193

#478, Sextant, "Endeavour." #479, "Endeavour," landing party, kangaroo. #480, Daniel Charles Solander, Sir Joseph Banks, Cook, map, botanical drawing. #481, Cook taking possession with Union Jack; "Endeavour," coral. 30c, Cook, "Endeavour," sextant, kangaroo, aborigines.

1970, Apr. 20 *Perf. 13½x13*

Size: 24x35½mm

477 A193 5c org brn & multi .40 .20
478 A193 5c org brn & multi .40 .20
479 A193 5c org brn & multi .40 .20
480 A193 5c org brn & multi .40 .20
481 A193 5c org brn & multi .40 .20
a. Strip of 5, #477-481 2.00 2.00

Size: 62x29mm

482 A193 30c org brn & multi 2.50 2.50
a. Souv. sheet, #477-482, imperf 9.00 9.00
Nos. 477-482 (6) 4.50 3.50

Cook's discovery and exploration of the eastern coast of Australia, 200th anniv.

No. 481a has continuous design.

No. 482a with brown marginal overprint "Souvenir Sheet ANPEX 1970. . ." is of private origin.

Snowy Mountains Hydroelectric Project
A194

Designs: 8c, Ord River hydroelectric project (dam, cotton plant and boll). 9c, Bauxite and aluminum production (mine, conveyor belt and aluminum window frame). 10c, Oil and natural gas (off-shore drilling rig and pipelines).

1970, Aug. 31 Photo. *Perf. 13x13½*

483 A194 7c multicolored 1.60 .40
484 A194 8c multicolored .25 .20
485 A194 9c multicolored .25 .20
486 A194 10c multicolored 1.10 .20
Nos. 483-486 (4) 3.20 1.00

Australian economic development.

Flame Symbolizing Democracy and Freedom of Speech — A195

1970, Oct. 2 Photo. *Perf. 13½x13*

487 A195 6c green & multi .25 .20

16th Commonwealth Parliamentary Assoc. Conference, Canberra, Oct. 2-9.

Herd of Illawarra Shorthorns and Laboratory
A196

1970, Oct. 7 *Perf. 13x13½*

488 A196 6c multicolored .25 .20

18th Intl. Dairy Cong., Sydney, Oct. 12-16.

Madonna and Child, by William Beasley
A197

UN Emblem, Dove and Symbols
A198

1970, Oct. 14 *Perf. 13½x13*

489 A197 6c multicolored .25 .20

Christmas.

1970, Oct. 19

490 A198 6c blue & multi .25 .20

25th anniversary of the United Nations.

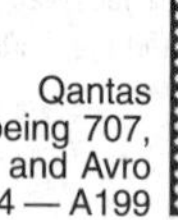

Qantas Boeing 707, and Avro 504 — A199

30c, Sunbeam Dyak powered Avro 504 on ground and Qantas Boeing 707 in the air.

1970, Nov. 2 *Perf. 13x13½*

491 A199 6c multicolored .20 .20
492 A199 30c multicolored 1.40 1.40

Qantas, Australian overseas airlines, 50th anniv.

Japanese Noh Actor, Australian Dancer and Chinese Opera Character — A200

15c, Chinese pipe, trumpet, Australian aboriginal didgeridoo, Thai fiddle, Indian double oboe, Tibetan drums. 20c, Red Sea dhow, Chinese junk, Australian lifeguard's surfboat, Malaysian & South Indian river boats.

1971, Jan. 6 Photo. *Perf. 13½x13*

493 A200 7c multicolored .50 *.55*
494 A200 15c multicolored .80 *.90*
495 A200 20c multicolored .70 *.80*
Nos. 493-495 (3) 2.00 2.25

Link between Australia and Asia; 28th Intl. Congress of Orientalists, Canberra, Jan. 6-12.

Southern Cross
A201

1971, Apr. 21 Photo. *Perf. 13x13½*

496 A201 6c multicolored .25 .20

Australian Natives Assoc., cent.

Symbolic Market Graphs — A202

Rotary Emblem
A203

1971, May 5 *Perf. 13½x13*

497 A202 6c silver & multi .25 .20

Centenary of Sydney Stock Exchange.

1971, May 17 *Perf. 13x13½*

498 A203 6c multicolored .25 .20

First Intl. Rotary Convention held in Australia, Sydney, May 16-20.

DH-9A, Australian Mirage Jet Fighters
A204

RSPCA Centenary
A205

1971, June 9 *Perf. 13½x13*

499 A204 6c multicolored .35 .20

Royal Australian Air Force, 50th anniv.

1971, July 5 Photo. *Perf. 13½x13*

Designs: 12c, Man and lamb (animal science). 18c, Kangaroo (fauna conservation). 24c, Seeing eye dog (animals' aid to man).

500 A205 6c blk, brown & org .25 .20
501 A205 12c blk, dk grn & yel .75 .20
502 A205 18c brown & multi .95 .30
503 A205 24c blue & multi 1.25 .50
Nos. 500-503 (4) 3.20 1.20

Royal Society for Prevention of Cruelty to Animals in Australia, cent.

Longnecked Tortoise, Painted on Bark — A206

Aboriginal Art: 25c, Mourners' body paintings, Warramunga tribe. 30c, Cave painting, Western Arnhem Land, vert. 35c, Graveposts, Bathurst and Melville Islands, vert.

Perf. 13x13½, 13½x13

1971, Sept. 29

504 A206 20c multicolored .65 .25
505 A206 25c multicolored .65 .45
506 A206 30c multicolored .90 .35
507 A206 35c multicolored .65 .40
Nos. 504-507 (4) 2.85 1.45

Three Kings and Star — A207

1971, Oct. 13 Photo. *Perf. 13½x13*

508 Block of 7 35.00
a. A207 7c brt grn, dk bl (Kings) & lil 6.25 .30
b. A207 7c lil, red brn, grn & dk bl 4.50 .20
c. A207 7c red brown & lilac 1.25 .20
d. A207 7c lilac, red brn & brt grn 2.00 .20
e. A207 7c red brown & dark blue 2.10 .20
f. A207 7c lilac, green & dk blue 14.00 1.40
g. A207 7c brt grn, dk bl & lilac (Kings) 2.50 .20

Christmas. Nos. 508a-508g printed se-tenant in sheets of 50. Each sheet contains 2 green crosses formed by 4 No. 508g and three No. 508a.

Andrew Fisher (1862-1928)
A208

Cameo Brooch
A209

Prime Ministers: No. 515, Joseph Cook (1860-1947). No. 516, William Morris Hughes (1864-1952). No. 517, Stanley Melbourne Bruce (1883-1967).

1972, Mar. 8 Engr. *Perf. 15x14*

514 A208 7c dark blue .50 .20
a. Booklet pane of 5 + label 2.50
515 A208 7c dark red .50 .20
a. Booklet pane of 5 + label 2.50
516 A208 7c dark blue .50 .20
a. Booklet pane of 5 + label 2.50
517 A208 7c dark red .50 .20
a. Booklet pane of 5 + label 2.50
Nos. 514-517 (4) 2.00 .80

Nos. 514-517 were issued in booklets only; all stamps have one or two straight edges.

1972, Apr. 18 Photo. *Perf. 13½*

518 A209 7c multicolored .25 .20

Country Women's Assoc., 50th anniv.

Apple and Banana
A210

1972, June 14

519 A210 20c shown 1.75 1.75
520 A210 25c Rice 1.75 1.75
521 A210 30c Fish 1.75 1.75
522 A210 35c Cattle 3.50 3.50
Nos. 519-522 (4) 8.75 8.75

Worker in Sheltered Workshop — A211

18c, Amputee assembling electrical circuit. 24c, Boy wearing Toronto splint, playing ball.

1972, Aug. 2 *Perf. 13½x13*

523 A211 12c grn & brn .25 .20
524 A211 18c org & ol, horiz. 1.25 .20
525 A211 24c brn & ultra .50 .20
Nos. 523-525 (3) 2.00 .60

Rehabilitation of the handicapped.

Overland Telegraph Line — A212

1972, Aug. 22 Photo. *Perf. 13x13½*

526 A212 7c dk red, blk & lemon .25 .20

Centenary of overland telegraph line.

Athlete, Olympic Rings — A213

1972, Aug. 28 *Perf. 13½x13*

527 A213	7c	shown	.20	.20
528 A213	7c	Swimming	.20	.20
529 A213	7c	Rowing	.20	.20
530 A213	35c	Equestrian	4.50	4.00
		Nos. 527-530 (4)	5.10	4.60

20th Olympic Games, Munich, 8/26-9/11.

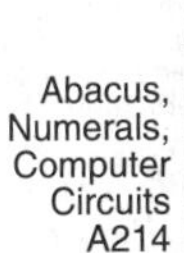

Abacus, Numerals, Computer Circuits A214

1972, Oct. 16 Photo. *Perf. 13x13½*

531 A214 7c multicolored .20 .20

10th Intl. Congress of Accountants.

19th Cent. Combine Harvester A215

Perf. 13½x13, 13x13½

1972, Nov. 15 Photo.

532 A215	5c	Pioneer family, vert.	.20	.20
533 A215	10c	Water pump, vert.	.45	.20
534 A215	15c	shown	.30	.20
535 A215	40c	Pioneer house	.65	.20
536 A215	50c	Cobb & Co. coach	1.10	.20
537 A215	60c	Early Morse key, vert.	1.00	.45
538 A215	80c	Paddle-wheel steamer	1.10	.45
		Nos. 532-538 (7)	4.80	1.90

Australian pioneer life.

Jesus and Children A216

Dove, Cross and "Darkness into Light" — A217

Metric Conversion, Mass — A218

Perf. 14½x14, 13½x13

1972, Nov. 29

539 A216	7c	tan & multi	.35	.20
540 A217	35c	blue & multi	7.50	7.50

Christmas.

1973, Mar. 7 Photo. *Perf. 14x14½*

Metric conversion: No. 542, Temperature, horiz. No. 543, Length. No. 544, Volume.

541 A218	7c	pale vio & multi	.80	.20
542 A218	7c	yellow & multi	.80	.20
543 A218	7c	yel green & multi	.80	.20
544 A218	7c	brt rose & multi	.80	.20
		Nos. 541-544 (4)	3.20	.80

Conversion to metric system.

Stylized Caduceus and Laurel A219

1973, Apr. 4 Photo. *Perf. 14½x14*

545 A219 7c dk bl, emer & lil rose .25 .20

WHO, 25th anniv.

Dame Mary Gilmore, Writer A220

Shipping Industry A221

Famous Australians: #547, William Charles Wentworth, explorer. #548, Sir Isaac Isaacs, lawyer, 1st Australian-born Governor-General. #549, Marcus Clarke, writer.

Engr. & Litho.

1973, May 16 *Perf. 15x14*

546 A220	7c	bister & black	1.00	.20
547 A220	7c	bister & black	1.00	.20
548 A220	7c	black & violet	1.00	.20
549 A220	7c	black & violet	1.00	.20
a.		Block of 4, #546-549	4.00	1.00

1973, June 6 Photo. *Perf. 13½x13*

Designs: 25c, Iron ore and steel. 30c, Truck convoy (beef road). 35c, Aerial mapping.

550 A221	20c	ultra & multi	2.00	1.50
551 A221	25c	red & multi	2.00	1.50
552 A221	30c	ol brn & multi	2.00	1.50
553 A221	35c	olive & multi	2.75	1.75
		Nos. 550-553 (4)	8.75	6.25

Australian economic development.

Banded Coral Shrimp A222

Chrysoprase—A223 558

Helichrysum Thomsonii A223a

Wombat A224

Radio Astronomy A225

Red Gums of the Far North, by Hans Heysen — A226

Coming South (Immigrants), by Tom Roberts — A226a

Paintings: $1, Sergeant of Light Horse, by George Lambert. No. 575, On the Wallaby Track. $4, Shearing the Rams, by Tom Roberts. No. 577, McMahon's Point, by Arthur Streeton. No. 578, Mentone.

Perf. 14x15, 15x14 (A222, A223, A223a); Perf. 14x14½ (A224); Perf. 13x13½ (A225, A226, $1)

1973-84 Photo.

554	A222	1c	shown	.20	.20
555	A222	2c	Fiddler crab	.20	.20
556	A222	3c	Coral crab	.20	.20
557	A222	4c	Mauve stinger	.20	.20
558	A223	6c	shown	.20	.20
559	A223	7c	Agate	.20	.20
560	A223	8c	Opal	.20	.20
561	A223	9c	Rhodonite	.20	.20
562	A223	10c	Star sapphire ('74)	.20	.20
563	A225	11c	Atomic absorption spectrophotometry ('75)	.55	.25
564	A223a	18c	shown ('75)	.50	.20
565	A224	20c	shown ('74)	.40	.20
566	A225	24c	shown ('75)	1.00	.40
567	A224	25c	Spiny anteater ('74)	1.25	.35
568	A224	30c	Brushtail possum ('74)	.70	.20
569	A225	33c	Immunology ('75)	1.00	1.00
570	A223a	45c	Callistemon teretifolius, horiz. ('75)	.65	.25
571	A225	48c	Oceanography ('75)	1.75	1.10
572	A224	75c	Feather-tailed glider ('74)	1.25	.75
573	A226a	$1	multi ('74)	1.50	.25
574	A226	$2	shown ('74)	2.75	.30
575	A226	$2	multi ('81)	2.50	.30
576	A226	$4	multi ('74)	5.00	2.25

Litho.

Perf. 14½

577	A226a	$5	multi ('79)	6.00	2.00
578	A226	$5	multi ('84)	6.00	1.25
579	A226a	$10	shown ('77)	12.00	3.25
			Nos. 554-579 (26)	46.60	16.10

Issued: 1c-9c, 7/11; 20c, 25c, 30c, 75c, 2/13; $1, #574, $4, 4/24; 10c, 10/16; 11c, 24c, 33c, 48c, 5/14; 18c, 45c, 8/27; $10, 10/19; #577, 3/14; #575, 6/17; #578, 4/4.

No. 560 Surcharged in Red

Perf. 15x14

580 A223 9c on 8c multi ('74) .20 .20

Hand Protecting Playing Children A227

1973, Sept. 5 Photo. *Perf. 13x13½*

581 A227 7c bis brn, grn & plum .25 .20

50th anniv. of Legacy, an ex-servicemen's organization concerned with the welfare of widows and children of servicemen.

Baptism of Christ A228

The Good Shepherd A229

1973, Oct. 3 *Perf. 14x14½*

582 A228 7c gold & multi .30 .20
a. Perf. 14x15 3.50 2.50

Perf. 13½

583 A229 30c gold & multi 2.50 2.50

Christmas.

Buchanan's Hotel, Townsville A230

St. James' Church, Sydney — A231

Designs: 7c, Opera House, Sydney. 40c, Como House, Melbourne.

1973, Oct. 17 Photo. *Perf. 14½x14*

584 A230 7c lt blue & ultra .40 .20
a. Perf. 15x14 4.00 .80
585 A230 10c bister & black .60 .35

Perf. 13x13½, 13½x13

586 A230	40c	dl pink, gray & blk	.75	.75
587 A231	50c	gray & multi	2.00	1.50
		Nos. 584-587 (4)	3.75	2.80

Australian architecture; opening of the Sydney Opera House, Oct. 14, 1973 (No. 584).

Radio and Gramophone Speaker A232

1973, Nov. 21 Photo. *Perf. 13½x13*

588 A232 7c dull blue, blk & brn .25 .20

Broadcasting in Australia, 50th anniv.

Supreme Court Judge on Bench
A233

Australian Football
A234

1974, May 15 Photo. *Perf. 14x14½*

589 A233 7c multicolored .25 .20

150th anniv. of the proclamation of the Charter of Justice in New South Wales and Van Diemen's Land (Australia's Third Charter).

1974, July 24 Photo. *Perf. 14x14½*

590 A234 7c shown .35 .20
591 A234 7c Cricket .35 .20
592 A234 7c Golf .35 .20
593 A234 7c Surfing .35 .20
594 A234 7c Tennis .35 .20
595 A234 7c Bowls, horiz. .35 .20
596 A234 7c Rugby, horiz. .35 .20
Nos. 590-596 (7) 2.45 1.40

Carrier Pigeon
A235

Designs: 30c, Carrier pigeons, vert.

1974, Oct. 9 Photo. *Perf. 14½x14*

597 A235 7c multicolored .25 .20
a. Perf. 15x14 .75 .20

Perf. 13½x13

598 A235 30c multicolored 1.00 1.00

UPU, cent. A booklet containing a strip of 5 each of Nos. 597-598 was produced and sold for $4 Australian by the National Stamp Week Promotion Council with government approval.

William Charles Wentworth
A236

Adoration of the Kings, by Dürer
A237

Typo. & Litho.

1974, Oct. 9 *Perf. 14x15*

599 A236 7c bister & black .35 .20
a. Perf. 14x14½ .90 .25

Sesquicentennial of 1st Australian independent newspaper. W. C. Wentworth and Dr. Robert Wardell were the editors and the "A" is type from masthead of "The Australian."

1974, Nov. 13 Engr. *Perf. 14x14½*

Christmas: 35c, Flight into Egypt, by Albrecht Dürer.

600 A237 10c buff & black .25 .20
601 A237 35c buff & black .90 .90

Pre-school Education
A238

Correspondence Schools — A239

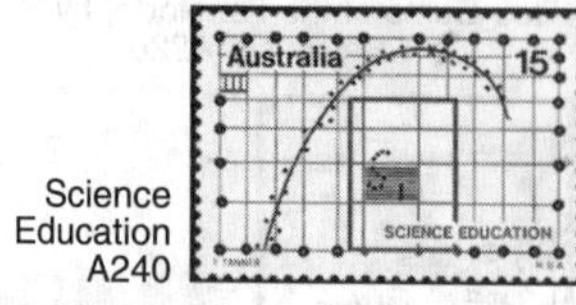

Science Education
A240

Advanced Education — A241

Perf. 13x13½, 13½x13

1974, Nov. 20 Photo.

602 A238 5c multicolored .25 .20
603 A239 11c multicolored .35 .25
604 A240 15c multicolored .40 .30
605 A241 60c multicolored 1.00 .95
Nos. 602-605 (4) 2.00 1.70

"Avoid Pollution"
A242

"Road Safety" — A243

Design: No. 607, "Avoid bush fires."

1975, Jan. 29 Photo. *Perf. 14½x14*

606 A242 10c multicolored .30 .20
a. Perf. 15x14 7.50 3.75
607 A242 10c multicolored .30 .20
a. Perf. 15x14 1.50 1.00

Perf. 14x14½

608 A243 10c multicolored .30 .20
Nos. 606-608 (3) .90 .60

Environmental dangers.

Symbols of Womanhood, Sun, Moon
A244

Joseph B. Chiefley (1885-1951)
A245

1975, Mar. 12 Photo. *Perf. 14x14½*

609 A244 10c dk vio blue & grn .25 .20

International Women's Year.

1975, Mar. 26

610 A245 10c shown .20 .20
611 A245 10c John Curtin, 1885-1945 .20 .20
612 A245 10c Arthur W. Fadden, 1895-1973 .20 .20
613 A245 10c Joseph A. Lyons, 1879-1939 .20 .20
614 A245 10c Earle Page, 1880-1963 .20 .20
615 A245 10c John H. Scullin, 1876-1953 .20 .20
Nos. 610-615 (6) 1.20 1.20

Australian Prime Ministers.

Australian Postal Commission
A246

Design: No. 617, Australian Telecommunications Commission.

1975, July 1 Photo. *Perf. 14½x14*

616 A246 10c red, black & gray .40 .20
a. Perf. 15x14 .50 .20
617 A246 10c yel, black & gray .40 .20
a. Pair, #616-617 .95 .75
b. Perf. 15x14 .50 .20
c. Pair, #616a, 617b 1.25 1.00

Formation of Australian Postal and Telecommunications Commissions. Printed checkerwise.

Edith Cowan, Judge and Legislator
A247

Truganini, Last Tasmanian Aborigine
A248

Portraits: No. 619, Louisa Lawson (1848-1920), journalist. No. 620, Ethel Florence (Henry Handel) Richardson (1870-1946), novelist. No. 621, Catherine Spence (1825-1910), teacher, journalist, voting reformer. No. 622, Emma Constance Stone (1856-1902), first Australian woman physician.

1975, Aug. 6 Photo. *Perf. 14x14½*

618 A247 10c olive grn & multi .30 .30
a. Perf. 14x15 .35 .35
619 A247 10c yel bister & multi .30 .30
a. Perf. 14x15 .35 .35
620 A248 10c olive & multi .30 .30
a. Perf. 14x15 .35 .35
621 A248 10c gray & multi .30 .30
a. Perf. 14x15 .35 .35
622 A247 10c violet & multi .30 .30
a. Perf. 14x15 .35 .35
623 A248 10c brown & multi .30 .30
a. Perf. 14x15 .35 .35
Nos. 618-623 (6) 1.80 1.80

Famous Australian women.

Spirit House (PNG) and Sydney Opera House — A249

Bird in Flight and Southern Cross
A250

1975, Sept. 16 Photo. *Perf. 13½*

624 A249 18c multicolored .40 .20
625 A250 25c multicolored .75 .55

Papua New Guinea independence, Sept. 16, 1975.

Adoration of the Kings — A251

"The Light Shineth in the Darkness"
A252

1975, Oct. 29 Photo. *Perf. 14½x14*

626 A251 15c multicolored .30 .20
627 A252 45c silver & multi 1.50 1.50

Christmas.

Australian Coat of Arms
A253

Type I - Kangaroo: eye is dot, right paw has 1 toe, left foot has 1 toe. Emu: feet have 1 toe.
Type II - Kangaroo: eye is line, right paw has 3 toes, left foot has 2 toes. Emu: feet have 2 toes.
Other differences exist.

1976, Jan. 5 Photo. *Perf. 14½x14*

628 A253 18c multicolored, type I .40 .20
a. Type II .75 .25

"Williams' Coffin" Telephone, 1878 — A254

1976, Mar. 10 Photo. *Perf. 13½*

629 A254 18c buff & multi .35 .20

Centenary of first telephone call by Alexander Graham Bell, Mar. 10, 1876.

John Oxley
A255

Designs: Australian explorers.

1976, June 9 Photo. *Perf. 13½*

630 A255 18c shown .25 .20
631 A255 18c Hamilton Hume and William Hovell .25 .20
632 A255 18c John Forrest .25 .20
633 A255 18c Ernest Giles .25 .20
634 A255 18c Peter Warburton .25 .20
635 A255 18c William Gosse .25 .20
Nos. 630-635 (6) 1.50 1.20

Survey Rule, Graph, Punched Tape — A256

1976, June 15 *Perf. 15x14*

636 A256 18c multicolored .30 .20

Commonwealth Scientific and Industrial Research Organization, 50th anniv.

Soccer Goalkeeper
A257

Olympic Rings and: No. 638, Woman gymnast, vert. 25c, Woman diver, vert. 40c, Bicycling.

Perf. 13x13½, 13½x13

1976, July 14	**Photo.**	
637 A257 18c multicolored	.30	.20
638 A257 18c multicolored	.30	.20
639 A257 25c multicolored	.45	.40
640 A257 40c multicolored	.65	.50
Nos. 637-640 (4)	1.70	1.30

21st Olympic Games, Montreal, Canada, July 17-Aug. 1.

Richmond Bridge, Tasmania A258

Mt. Buffalo, Victoria — A259

Designs: 25c, Broken Bay, New South Wales. 35c, Wittenoom Gorge, Western Australia. 70c, Barrier Reef, Queensland. 85c, Ayers Rock, Northern Territory.

Perf. 14½x14, 14x14½

1976, Aug. 25	**Photo.**	
641 A258 5c multicolored	.25	.20
642 A258 25c multicolored	.35	.20
643 A258 35c multicolored	.30	.30
644 A259 50c multicolored	.50	.25
645 A258 70c multicolored	.60	.35
646 A258 85c multicolored	1.00	.80
Nos. 641-646 (6)	3.00	2.10

Blamire Young and Australia No. 59 — A260

1976, Sept. 27	**Photo.**	***Perf. 13½***	
647 A260 18c apple grn & multi		.35	.20

Miniature Sheet

648	Sheet of 4	1.60	1.50
a.	A260 18c yellow & dark brown	.35	.35
b.	A260 18c rose, dk brown & yel	.35	.35
c.	A260 18c bl, dk brn, rose & yel	.35	.35

Natl. Stamp Week, Sept. 27-Oct. 3. Blamire Young (1862-1935), designer of Australia's 1st issue. No. 648 shows different stages of 4-color printing. The 4th stamp in sheet is identical with No. 647.

Virgin and Child, after Simone Cantarini A261

Holly, Toy Koala, Christmas Tree and Decoration, Partridge A262

1976, Nov. 1	**Photo.**	***Perf. 14½x14***	
649 A261 15c brt car & lt blue		.30	.20

Perf. 13½

650 A262 45c multicolored	.80	.75

Christmas.

John Gould (1804-1881) Ornithologist A263

Famous Australians: No. 652, Thomas Laby (1880-1946), nuclear scientist. No. 653, Sir Baldwin Spencer (1860-1929), anthropologist (aborigines). No. 654, Griffith Taylor (1880-1963), geographer and arctic explorer.

1976, Nov. 10	***Perf. 15x14***	
651 A263 18c shown	.30	.20
652 A263 18c Laby	.30	.20
653 A263 18c Spencer	.30	.20
654 A263 18c Taylor	.30	.20
Nos. 651-654 (4)	1.20	.80

Violinists — A264

1977, Jan. 19	**Photo.**	***Perf. 14x14½***	
655 A264 20c shown		.25	.20
656 A264 30c Dramatic scene		.30	.20
657 A264 40c Dancer		.55	.40
658 A264 60c Opera singer		.70	.20
Nos. 655-658 (4)		1.80	1.00

Performing arts in Australia.

Elizabeth II A265

Wicket Keeper, Slip Fieldsman A266

Design: 45c, Elizabeth II and Prince Philip.

1977, Feb. 2		
659 A265 18c multicolored	.30	.20
660 A265 45c multicolored	.75	.75

Reign of Queen Elizabeth II, 25th anniv.

1977, Mar. 9	**Photo.**	***Perf. 13½***

Cricket match, 19th century: No. 662, Umpire and batsman. No. 663, Two fieldsmen. No. 664, Batsman and umpire. No. 665, Bowler and fieldsman. 45c, Batsman facing bowler.

661 A266 18c gray & multi	.30	.25
662 A266 18c gray & multi	.30	.25
663 A266 18c gray & multi	.30	.25
664 A266 18c gray & multi	.30	.25
665 A266 18c gray & multi	.30	.25
a. Strip of 5, #661-665	1.50	1.50
666 A266 45c gray & multi	.80	.75
Nos. 661-666 (6)	2.30	2.00

Parliament House, Canberra A267

1977, Apr. 13	***Perf. 14½x14***	
667 A267 18c multicolored	.40	.20

Parliament House, Canberra, 50th anniv.

Trade Union Workers A268

1977, May 9	**Photo.**	***Perf. 13***	
668 A268 18c multicolored		.35	.20

Australian Council of Trade Unions (ACTU), 50th anniv.

Surfing Santa — A269

Virgin and Child — A270

1977, Oct. 31	**Photo.**	***Perf. 14x14½***	
669 A269 15c multicolored		.35	.20

Perf. 13½x13

670 A270 45c multicolored	.75	.75

Christmas.

Australian Flag — A271

1978, Jan. 26	**Photo.**	***Perf. 13x13½***	
671 A271 18c multicolored		.35	.20

Australia Day, 190th anniversary of first permament settlement in New South Wales.

Harry Hawker and Sopwith "Camel" A272

Australian Aviators and their Planes: No. 673, Bert Hinkler and Avro Avian. No. 674, Charles Kingsford-Smith and Fokker "Southern Cross." No. 675, Charles Ulm and "Southern Cross."

1978, Apr. 19	**Litho.**	***Perf. 15½***	
672 A272 18c ultra & multi		.30	.20
673 A272 18c blue & multi		.30	.20
674 A272 18c orange & multi		.30	.20
675 A272 18c yellow & multi		.30	.20
a. Souv. sheet, 2 each #674-675, imperf.		1.60	1.60
Nos. 672-675 (4)		1.20	.80

No. 675a for 50th anniv. of first Trans-Pacific flight from Oakland, Cal., to Brisbane.

Beechcraft Baron Landing A273

1978, May 15	**Photo.**	***Perf. 13½***	
676 A273 18c multicolored		.30	.20

Royal Flying Doctor Service, 50th anniv.

Illawarra Flame Tree A274

Sturt's Desert Rose, Map of Australia A275

Australian trees: 25c, Ghost gum. 40c, Grass tree. 45c, Cootamundra wattle.

1978, June 1		
677 A274 18c multicolored	.20	.20
678 A274 25c multicolored	.60	.60
679 A274 40c multicolored	.70	.70
680 A274 45c multicolored	.65	.65
Nos. 677-680 (4)	2.15	2.15

1978, June 19	**Litho.**	***Perf. 15½***	
681 A275 18c multicolored		.35	.20

Establishment of Government of the Northern Territory.

Hooded Dotterel — A276

Australian birds: 20c, Little grebe. 25c, Spur-wing Plover. 30c, Pied oystercatcher. 55c, Lotus bird.

1978	**Photo.**	***Perf. 13½***	
682 A276 5c multicolored		.20	.20
683 A276 20c multicolored		.25	.20
684 A276 25c multicolored		.35	.20
685 A276 30c multicolored		.40	.30
686 A276 55c multicolored		.70	.50
Nos. 682-686 (5)		1.90	1.40

Issued: Nos. 683, 686, July 3; others, July 17. See Nos. 713-718, 732-739, 768.

Australia No. 95 on Album Page — A277

1978, Sept. 25	**Litho.**	***Perf. 15½***	
687 A277 20c multicolored		.30	.20
a. Miniature sheet of 4		1.25	1.25

National Stamp Week; 50th anniv. of Melbourne Intl. Phil. Exhib., Oct. 1928.

Virgin and Child, by Simon Marmion — A278

1978	***Perf. 15***	

Paintings from National Gallery, Victoria: 15c, Virgin and Child, after Van Eyck. 55c, Holy Family, by Perino del Vaga.

688 A278 15c multicolored	.20	.20
689 A278 25c multicolored	.50	.50
690 A278 55c multicolored	.80	.80
Nos. 688-690 (3)	1.50	1.50

Christmas. Issued: 25c, 10/3; others, 11/1.

Tulloch
A279

Race horses: 35c, Bernborough, vert. 50c, Phar Lap, vert. 55c, Peter Pan.

Perf. 15x14, 14x15

1978, Oct. 18 Photo.

691 A279 20c multicolored .25 .20
692 A279 35c multicolored .45 .50
693 A279 50c multicolored .65 .65
694 A279 55c multicolored .65 .65
Nos. 691-694 (4) 2.00 2.00

Australian horse racing.

Flag Raising at Sydney Cove — A280

1979, Jan. 26 Litho. *Perf. 15½*

695 A280 20c multicolored .35 .20

Australia Day, Jan. 26.

Passenger Steamer Canberra
A281

Ferries and Murray River Steamers: 35c, M.V. Lady Denman. 50c, P.S. Murray River Queen. 55c, Hydrofoil Curl Curl.

1979, Feb. 14 Photo. *Perf. 13½*

696 A281 20c multicolored .30 .20
697 A281 35c multicolored .50 .40
698 A281 50c multicolored .75 .65
699 A281 55c multicolored .85 .85
Nos. 696-699 (4) 2.40 2.10

Port Campbell
A282

Designs: Australian National Parks.

1979, Apr. 9 Litho. *Perf. 15½*

700 A282 20c shown .30 .20
701 A282 20c Uluru .30 .20
702 A282 20c Royal .30 .20
703 A282 20c Flinders Ranges .30 .20
704 A282 20c Namburg .30 .20
  a. Strip of 5, #700-704 1.50
705 A282 20c Girraween, vert. .30 .20
706 A282 20c Mount Field, vert. .30 .20
  a. Pair, #705-706 .60
Nos. 700-706 (7) 2.10 1.40

Double Fairlie
A283

Australian steam locomotives: 35c, Puffing Billy. 50c, Pichi Richi. 55c, Zig Zag.

Perf. 13½, 15x14 (20c)

1979, May 16 Photo.

707 A283 20c multicolored .20 .20
708 A283 35c multicolored .40 .30
709 A283 50c multicolored .75 .60
710 A283 55c multicolored .80 .80
Nos. 707-710 (4) 2.15 1.90

"Black Swan"
A284

1979, June 6 Photo. *Perf. 13½*

711 A284 20c multicolored .35 .20

150th anniversary of Western Australia.

Children Playing, IYC Emblem
A285

1979, Aug. 13 Litho. *Perf. 13½x13*

712 A285 20c multicolored .30 .20

International Year of the Child.

Bird Type of 1978

Australian birds: 1c, Zebra finch. 2c, Crimson finch. 15c, Forest kingfisher, vert. 20c, Eastern yellow robin. 40c, Lovely wren, vert. 50c, Flame robin, vert.

1979, Sept. 17 Photo. *Perf. 13½*

713 A276 1c multicolored .20 .20
714 A276 2c multicolored .20 .20
715 A276 15c multicolored .30 .20
716 A276 20c multicolored .30 .20
717 A276 40c multicolored .50 .20
718 A276 50c multicolored .70 .20
Nos. 713-718 (6) 2.20 1.20

Christmas Letters, Flag-wrapped Parcels — A286

Trout Fishing — A287

Christmas: 15c, Nativity, icon. 55c, Madonna and Child, by Buglioni.

1979 Litho. *Perf. 13*

719 A286 15c multicolored .20 .20
720 A286 25c multicolored .30 .30
721 A286 55c multicolored .90 .90
Nos. 719-721 (3) 1.40 1.40

Issue dates: 25c, Sept. 24. Others, Nov. 1.

1979, Oct. 24 Photo. *Perf. 14x14½*

Sport fishing: 35c, Angler. 50c, Black marlin fishing. 55c, Surf fishing.

722 A287 20c multicolored .25 .20
723 A287 35c multicolored .45 .45
724 A287 50c multicolored .70 .45
725 A287 55c multicolored .75 .70
Nos. 722-725 (4) 2.15 1.80

Matthew Flinders, Map of Australia
A288
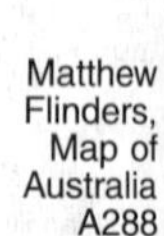

1980, Jan. 23 Litho. *Perf. 13½*

726 A288 20c multicolored .30 .20

Australia Day, Jan. 28.

Dingo
A289

1980, Feb. 20 Litho. *Perf. 13½x13*

727 A289 20c shown .30 .20
728 A289 25c Border collie .35 .35
729 A289 35c Australian terrier .60 .40
730 A289 50c Australian cattle dog .80 .70
731 A289 55c Australian kelpie .65 .65
Nos. 727-731 (5) 2.70 2.30

Bird Type of 1978

Perf. 13½, 14x15 (22c), 13x12½ (28c, 60c)

1980 Litho., Photo. (22c)

732 A276 10c Golden-shoulder parrot, vert. .20 .20
  a. Perf. 14½x14 1.50 .50
733 A276 22c White-tailed kingfisher, vert. .30 .20
734 A276 28c Rainbow bird, vert. .45 .20
735 A276 35c Regent bower bird, vert. .45 .20
736 A276 45c Masked woodswallow .95 .20
  a. Perf. 14x14½ 2.50 1.75
737 A276 60c King parrot, vert. .75 .25
738 A276 80c Rainbow pitta 1.00 .45
739 A276 $1 Western magpie, vert. 1.25 .30
Nos. 732-739 (8) 5.35 2.00

Issued: #733, 734, 737, 3/31; others, 7/1.

Queen Elizabeth II, 54th Birthday — A290

1980, Apr. 21 Litho. *Perf. 13x13½*

740 A290 22c multicolored .35 .20

Wanderer
A291

High Court Building, Canberra
A292

1980, May 7 Litho. *Perf. 13x13½*

741 Strip of 5 1.25 1.00
  a. A291 22c shown .25 .20
  b. A291 22c Stealing sheep .25 .20
  c. A291 22c Squatter on horseback .25 .20
  d. A291 22c Three troopers .25 .20
  e. A291 22c Wanderer's ghost .25 .20

"Waltzing Matilda", poem by Andrew Barton Patterson (1864-1941). No. 741 in continuous design.

1980, May 19

742 A292 22c multicolored .35 .20

Opening of High Court of Australia Building, Canberra, May 26.

Salvation Army Officers
A294

Perf. 13x13½, 13½x13

1980, Aug. 11

747 A294 22c shown .30 .20
748 A294 22c St. Vincent de Paul Society, vert. .30 .20
749 A294 22c Meals on Wheels, vert. .30 .20
750 A294 22c "Life. Be in it." (Joggers, bicyclists) .30 .20
Nos. 747-750 (4) 1.20 .80

Mailman c. 1900 — A295

Holy Family, by Prospero Fontana — A296

1980, Sept. 29 Litho. *Perf. 13x13½*

751 A295 22c Mailbox .30 .20
752 A295 22c shown .30 .20
753 A295 22c Mail truck .30 .20
754 A295 22c Mailman, mailbox .30 .20
755 A295 22c Mailman, diff. .30 .20
  a. Souvenir sheet of 3 1.00 1.00
  b. Strip of 5, #751-755 1.50 1.00

Natl. Stamp Week, Sept. 29-Oct. 5. #755a contains stamps similar to #751, 753, 755.

No. 755a overprinted "SYDPEX 80" was privately produced.

1980 *Perf. 13x13½*

Christmas: 15c, Virgin Enthroned, by Justin O'Brien. 60c, Virgin and Child, by Michael Zuern the Younger, 1680.

756 A296 15c multicolored .25 .20
757 A296 28c multicolored .45 .45
758 A296 60c multicolored .90 .65
Nos. 756-758 (3) 1.60 1.30

Issued: 15c, 60c, Nov. 3; 28c, Oct. 1.

CA-6 Wackett Trainer, 1941 — A297

Designs: Australian military training planes.

1980, Nov. 19 *Perf. 13½x14*

759 A297 22c shown .30 .30
760 A297 40c Winjeel, 1955 .60 .60
761 A297 45c Boomerang, 1944 .65 .50
762 A297 60c Nomad, 1975 1.00 .60
Nos. 759-762 (4) 2.55 2.00

Bird Type of 1978

1980, Nov. 17 Litho. *Perf. 13½*

768 A276 18c Spotted catbird, vert. .35 .20

Flag on Map of Australia
A298

1981, Jan. 21

771 A298 22c multicolored .35 .20

Australia Day, Jan. 21.

Jockey Darby Munro (1913-1966), by Tony Rafty — A299

Australian sportsmen (Caricatures by Tony Rafty): 35c, Victor Trumper (1877-1915), cricket batsman. 55c, Norman Brookes (1877-1968), tennis player. 60c, Walter Lindrum (1898-1960), billiards player.

1981, Feb. 18 *Perf. 14x13½*

772 A299 22c multicolored .25 .20
773 A299 35c multicolored .45 .40
774 A299 55c multicolored .65 .65
775 A299 60c multicolored .75 .75
Nos. 772-775 (4) 2.10 2.00

Australia No. C2 and Cover A300

Perf. 13x13½, 13½x13

1981, Mar. 25 Litho.

776 A300 22c Australia No. C2, vert. .30 .25
777 A300 60c shown .90 .80

Australia-United Kingdom official airmail service, 50th anniv.

Map of Australia, APEX Emblem A301

1981, Apr. 6 Photo. *Perf. 13x13½*

778 A301 22c multicolored .30 .20

50th anniv. of APEX (young men's service club).

Queen Elizabeth's Personal Flag of Australia A302

1981, Apr. 21 *Perf. 13*

779 A302 22c multicolored .35 .20

Queen Elizabeth II, 55th birthday.

License Inspected, Forrest Creek, by S.T. Gill — A303

Gold Rush Era (Sketches by S.T. Gill): No. 781, Puddling. No. 782, Quality of Washing Stuff. No. 783, Diggers on Route to Deposit Gold.

1981, May 20 Photo. *Perf. 13x13½*

780 A303 22c multicolored .30 .20
781 A303 22c multicolored .30 .20
782 A303 22c multicolored .30 .20
783 A303 22c multicolored .30 .20
Nos. 780-783 (4) 1.20 .80

Lace Monitor — A303a

Tasmanian Tiger — A304

Two Types of A304:
Type I - Indistinct line at right of ear, stripes even with base of tail.
Type II - Heavy line at right of ear, stripes longer.

1981-83 Litho.

784 A303a 1c shown .20 .20
785 A303a 3c Corroboree frog .20 .20
786 A304 5c Queensland hairy-nosed wombat, vert. .20 .20
787 A303a 15c Eastern snake-necked tortoise .20 .20
788 A304 24c Type I .35 .20
a. Shown, type II .35 .20
789 A304 25c Greater bilby, vert. .35 .20
790 A303a 27c Blue Mountains tree frog .35 .20
791 A304 30c Bridled nail-tailed wallaby, vert. .35 .20
792 A303a 40c Smooth knob-tailed gecko .45 .25
793 A304 50c Leadbeater's opossum .65 .40
794 A304 55c Stick-nest rat, vert. .75 .40
795 A303a 65c Yellow-faced whip snake .80 .45
796 A303a 70c Crucifix toad .90 .55
797 A303a 75c Eastern water dragon .90 .55
798 A303a 85c Centralian blue-tongued lizard 1.00 .65
799 A303a 90c Freshwater crocodile 1.10 .70
800 A303a 95c Thorny devil 1.25 .75
Nos. 784-800 (17) 10.00 6.30

Perfs: 1c, 70c, 85c, 95c, 13½; 3c, 15c, 27c, 40c, 50c, 65c, 75c, 90c, 12½x13; 5c, 25c, 30c, 55c, 13x12½; 24c, 13x13½.

Issued: 24c, 7/1/81; 5c, 25c, 30c, 50c, 55c, 7/15/81; 3c, 27c, 65c, 75c, 4/19/82; 15c, 40c, 90c, 6/16/82. 1c, 70c, 85c, 95c, 2/2/83.

1982-84 *Perf. 14x14½, 14½x14*

785a A303a 3c ('84) .30 .20
786a A304 5c ('84) 1.00 .20
787a A303a 15c ('84) .70 .25
789a A304 25c ('83) 1.10 .20
790a A303a 27c .75 .25
792a A303a 40c ('84) 2.00 .30
793a A304 50c ('83) 1.25 .40
795a A303a 65c ('84) 1.40 .60
797a A303a 75c ('84) 1.50 .80
Nos. 785a-797a (9) 10.00 3.20

Prince Charles and Lady Diana A305

1981, July 29 Litho. *Perf. 13*

804 A305 24c multicolored .30 .20
805 A305 60c multicolored .60 *1.00*

Royal Wedding.

Fungi — A306

Intl. Year of the Disabled — A307

1981, Aug. 19 Litho. *Perf. 13*

806 A306 24c Cortinarius cinnabarinus .25 .20
807 A306 35c Coprinus comatus .40 .30
808 A306 55c Armillaria luteobubalina .60 .45
809 A306 60c Cortinarius austrovenetus .75 .65
Nos. 806-809 (4) 2.00 1.60

1981, Sept. 16 *Perf. 14x13½*

810 A307 24c multicolored .25 .20

Christmas Bush for His Adorning A308

Globe A309

Christmas (Carols by William James and John Wheeler): 30c, The Silver Stars are in the Sky. 60c, Noeltime.

1981 Litho. *Perf. 13x13½*

811 A308 18c multicolored .25 .20
812 A308 30c multicolored .40 .30
813 A308 60c multicolored .60 .50
Nos. 811-813 (3) 1.25 1.00

Issue dates: 30c, Sept. 28; others, Nov. 2.

1981, Sept. 30

814 A309 24c multicolored .20 .20
815 A309 60c multicolored .65 *.90*

Commonwealth Heads of Government Meeting, Melbourne, Sept. 30-Oct. 7.

Yacht — A310

1981, Oct. 14 Litho. *Perf. 13x13½*

816 A310 24c Ocean racer .25 .20
817 A310 35c Lightweight sharpie .40 .30
818 A310 55c 12-Meter .60 .45
819 A310 60c Sabot .75 .60
Nos. 816-819 (4) 2.00 1.55

Australia Day, Jan. 26 A311

1982, Jan. 20 Litho. *Perf. 13x13½*

820 A311 24c multicolored .25 .20

Sperm Whale A312

1982, Feb. 17 *Perf. 13x13½, 13½x13*

821 A312 24c shown .35 .20
822 A312 35c Southern right whale, vert. .60 .60
823 A312 55c Blue whale, vert. .90 .75
824 A312 60c Humpback whale 1.00 1.00
Nos. 821-824 (4) 2.85 2.55

Elizabeth II, 56th Birthday — A313

Roses — A314

1982, Apr. 21 *Perf. 13½*

825 A313 27c multicolored .40 .20

1982, May 19 *Perf. 13x13½*

826 A314 27c Marjorie Atherton .30 .30
827 A314 40c Imp .55 .50
828 A314 65c Minnie Watson .80 .80
829 A314 75c Satellite .90 .85
Nos. 826-829 (4) 2.55 2.45

50th Anniv. of Australian Broadcasting Commission A315

1982, June 16 *Perf. 13½x13*

830 A315 27c Announcer, microphone .30 .25
831 A315 27c Emblem .30 .25
a. Pair, #830-831 .60 .50

#830-831 se-tenant in continuous design.

Alice Springs Post Office, 1872 — A316

1982, Aug. 4 *Perf. 13½x14, 14x13½*

832 A316 27c shown .30 .20
833 A316 27c Kingston, 1869 .30 .20
834 A316 27c York, 1893 .30 .20
835 A316 27c Flemington, 1890, vert. .30 .20
836 A316 27c Forbes, 1881, vert. .30 .20
837 A316 27c Launceston, 1889, vert. .30 .20
838 A316 27c Rockhampton, 1892, vert. .30 .20
Nos. 832-838 (7) 2.10 1.40

Christmas — A317

1st Australian Christmas cards, 1881. 21c, horiz.

1982 Litho. *Perf. 14½*

839 A317 21c multicolored .25 .20
840 A317 35c multicolored .35 .30
841 A317 75c multicolored .65 *.90*
Nos. 839-841 (3) 1.25 1.40

Issue dates: 35c, Sept. 15; others, Nov. 1.

12th Commonwealth Games, Brisbane, Sept. 30-Oct. 9 — A318

1982, Sept. 22 Litho. *Perf. 14x14½*

842 A318 27c Archery .30 .20
843 A318 27c Boxing .30 .20
844 A318 27c Weightlifting .30 .20
a. Souvenir sheet of 3, #842-844 1.00 1.00
845 A318 75c Pole vault .75 *1.00*
Nos. 842-845 (4) 1.65 1.60

Natl. Stamp Week A319

1982, Sept. 27 *Perf. 13x13½*

846 A319 27c No. 132 .30 .20

A320

A321

Design: Gurgurr (Moon Spirit), Bark Painting by Yirawala Gunwinggu Tribe.

1982, Oct. 12 *Perf. 14½*

847 A320 27c multicolored .30 .20

Opening of Natl. Gallery, Canberra.

Perf. 12½x13½

1982, Nov. 17 Photo.

Designs: Various eucalypts (gum trees).

848 A321 1c Pink-flowered marri .20 .20
849 A321 2c Gungurru .20 .20
850 A321 3c Red-flowering gum 1.00 *1.50*

851 A321 10c Tasmanian blue gum 1.00 *1.75*
852 A321 27c Forrest's marlock .50 .50
a. Bklt. pane, #850-851, 2 #848-849, 3 #852 + label 2.50
b. Bklt. pane, 2 ea #848-849, 852 1.00
Nos. 848-852 (5) 2.90 4.15

Nos. 848-852 issued in booklets only.

Mimi Spirits Singing and Dancing, by David Milaybuma A322

Aboriginal Bark Paintings: Music and dance of the Mimi Spirits, Gunwinggu Tribe.

1982, Nov. 17 Litho. *Perf. 13½x14*
853 A322 27c shown .25 .25
854 A322 40c Lofty Nabardayal .40 *.65*
855 A322 65c Jimmy Galareya .65 *.75*
856 A322 75c Dick Nguleingulei Murrumurru .70 *1.00*
Nos. 853-856 (4) 2.00 2.65

Historic Fire Engines A323

1983, Jan. 12 *Perf. 13½x14*
857 A323 27c Shand Mason Steam, 1891 .30 .25
858 A323 40c Hotchkiss, 1914 .45 *.65*
859 A323 65c Ahrens-Fox PS2, 1929 .75 *1.00*
860 A323 75c Merryweather Manual, 1851 .75 *1.00*
Nos. 857-860 (4) 2.25 2.90

Australia Day — A324

1983, Jan. 26 Litho. *Perf. 14½*
861 A324 27c Sirius .35 .20
862 A324 27c Supply .35 .20
a. Pair, #861-862 .90 .75

A325

A326

1983, Feb. 2 *Perf. 14x13½*
863 A325 27c multicolored .30 .20

Australia-New Zealand Closer Economic Relationship agreement (ANZCER).

1983, Mar. 9 Litho. *Perf. 14½*
864 A326 27c Equality, dignity .25 .20
865 A326 27c Social justice, co-operation .25 .20
866 A326 27c Liberty, freedom .25 .20
867 A326 75c Peace, harmony .75 *1.00*
Nos. 864-867 (4) 1.50 1.60

Commonwealth day.

Queen Elizabeth II, 57th Birthday A327

1983, Apr. 20 *Perf. 14½*
868 A327 27c Britannia .30 .20

World Communications Year — A328

1983, May 18 Litho. *Perf. 13½x14*
869 A328 27c multicolored .30 .20

50th Anniv. of Australian Jaycees Youth Organization A329

1983, June 8
870 A329 27c multicolored .30 .20

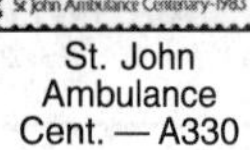

St. John Ambulance Cent. — A330

Regent Skipper — A331

1983, June 8 *Perf. 13½x14*
871 A330 27c multicolored .30 .20

1983 *Perf. 13½, 14½x14 (30c)*
872 A331 4c shown .20 .20
873 A331 10c Cairn's birdwing .20 .20
874 A331 20c Macleay's swallowtail .30 .20
875 A331 27c Ulysses .45 .20
875A A331 30c Chlorinda hair-streak .50 .20
876 A331 35c Blue tiger .55 .20
877 A331 45c Big greasy .60 .20
878 A331 60c Wood white .85 .30
879 A331 80c Amaryllis azure 1.00 .40
880 A331 $1 Sword grass brown 1.25 .20
Nos. 872-880 (10) 5.90 2.30

Issue dates: 30c, Oct. 24; others, June 15.

The Sentimental Bloke, by C.J. Dennis, 1909 — A332

Folktale scenes: a, The bloke. b, Doreen - the intro. c, The stror at coot. d, Hitched. e, The mooch of life.

1983, Aug. 3 *Perf. 14½*
881 Strip of 5 1.25 1.25
a.-e. A332 27c multi, any single .25 .25

Kookaburra Bird Wearing Santa Hat — A333

1983 Litho. *Perf. 13½x14*
882 A333 24c Nativity .30 .30
883 A333 35c multicolored .45 .35
884 A333 85c Holiday beach scene 1.00 .60
Nos. 882-884 (3) 1.75 1.25

Christmas. Issued: #883, 9/14; #882, 884, 11/2.

Inland Explorers — A334

Clay sculptures by Dianne Quinn: No. 885, Ludwig Leichhardt (1813-48). No. 886, William John Wills (1834-61), Robert O'Hara Burke (1821-61). No. 887, Paul Edmund de Strzelecki (1797-1873). No. 888, Alexander Forrest (1849-1901).

1983, Sept. 26 *Perf. 14½*
885 A334 30c multicolored .30 .20
886 A334 30c multicolored .30 .20
887 A334 30c multicolored .30 .20
888 A334 30c multicolored .30 .20
Nos. 885-888 (4) 1.20 .80

Australia Day — A335

1984, Jan. 26 Litho. *Perf. 13½x14*
889 A335 30c Cooks' Cottage .30 .20

50th Anniv. of Official Air Mail Service — A336

Pilot Charles Ulm (1898-1934); his plane, "Faith in Australia," and different flight covers.

1984, Feb. 22 Litho. *Perf. 13½*
890 A336 45c Australia-New Zealand .75 *1.25*
891 A336 45c Australia-Papua New Guinea .75 *1.25*
a. Pair, #890-891 1.50 *2.50*

Thomson, 1898 — A337

Australian-made vintage cars: b, Tarrant, 1906. c, Australian Six, 1919. d, Summit, 1923. e, Chic, 1924.

1984, Mar. 14 *Perf. 14½*
892 Strip of 5 1.75 1.00
a.-e. A337 30c any single .35 .20

Queen Elizabeth II, 58th Birthday A338

1984, Apr. 18 *Perf. 14½*
893 A338 30c multicolored .25 .20

Clipper Ships A339

1984, May 23 *Perf. 14x13½, 13½x14*
894 A339 30c Cutty Sark, 1869, vert. .35 .30
895 A339 45c Orient, 1853 .55 .55
896 A339 75c Sobraon, 1866 .90 .90
897 A339 85c Thermopylae, 1868, vert. 1.10 1.10
Nos. 894-897 (4) 2.90 2.85

Freestyle Skiing — A340

Coral Hopper — A341

1984, June 6 Litho. *Perf. 14½*
898 A340 30c shown .40 .20
899 A340 30c Slalom, horiz. .40 .20
900 A340 30c Cross-country, horiz. .40 .20
901 A340 30c Downhill .40 .20
Nos. 898-901 (4) 1.60 .80

Perf. 13½, 14x14½ (30c, 33c)

1984-86 Litho.
902 A341 2c shown .20 .20
903 A341 3c Jimble .20 .20
904 A341 5c Tasseled anglerfish .20 .20
905 A341 10c Stonefish .20 .20
906 A341 20c Red handfish .25 .20
907 A341 25c Orange-tipped cowrie .45 .25
908 A341 30c Choat's wrasse .55 .25
909 A341 33c Leafy sea dragon .45 .20
910 A341 40c Red velvet fish .55 .25
911 A341 45c Texile cone shell .65 .30
912 A341 50c Blue-lined surgeonfish .90 .50
913 A341 55c Bennett's nudibranch 1.00 .50
914 A341 60c Lionfish .85 .40
915 A341 65c Stingray .95 .40
916 A341 70c Blue-ringed octopus 1.00 .50
917 A341 80c Pineapple fish 1.10 .55
918 A341 85c Regal angelfish 1.50 .95
919 A341 90c Crab-eyed goby 1.25 .55
920 A341 $1 Crown of thorns starfish 1.50 .60
Nos. 902-920 (19) 13.75 7.20

Issued: 2c, 25c, 30c, 50c, 55c, 85c, 6/18; 33c, 1/20/85; 5c, 20c, 40c, 80c, 90c, 6/12/85; 3c, 10c, 45c, 60c, 65c, 70c, $1, 6/11/86.

1984 Summer Olympics A342

Event stages.

Perf. 13½x14, 14x13½

1984, July 25 Litho.
922 A342 30c Start (facing down) .35 .20
923 A342 30c Competing (facing right) .35 .20
924 A342 30c Finish, vert. .35 .20
Nos. 922-924 (3) 1.05 .60

Ausipex '84 A343

Christmas A344

#926: a, Victoria #3. b, New South Wales #1. c, Tasmania #1. d, South Australia #1. e, Western Australia #1. f, Queensland #3.

1984 Litho. *Perf. 14½*
925 A343 30c No. 2 .45 .20

Souvenir Sheet

926 Sheet of 7 3.50 3.00
a.-f. A343 30c any single .50 .20

#926 contains #925, 926a-926f. Issue dates: #925, Aug. 22; #926, Sept. 21.

1984 Litho. *Perf. 14x13½*

927 A344 24c Angel and Child .20 .20
928 A344 30c Veiled Virgin and Child .30 .20
929 A344 40c Angel .45 .40
930 A344 50c Three Kings .55 .45
931 A344 85c Madonna and Child .75 *1.00*
Nos. 927-931 (5) 2.25 2.25

Stained-glass windows. Issue dates: 40c, Sept. 17; others, Oct. 30.

European Settlement Bicentenary A345

Design: No. 932, Bicentennial Emblem.

Rock paintings: No. 933, Stick figures, Cobar Region, New South Wales. No. 934, Bunjil's Cave, Grampians, Western Victoria. No. 935, Quinkan Gallery, Cape York, Queensland. No. 936, Wandjina Spirit and Snake Babies, Gibb River, Western Australia. No. 937, Rock Python, Western Australia. No. 938, Silver Barramundi, Kakadu Natl. Park, Northern Territory. 85c, Rock Possum, Kakadu Natl. Park.

1984, Nov. 7 Litho. *Perf. 14½*

932 A345 30c multicolored .30 .20
933 A345 30c multicolored .40 .25
934 A345 30c multicolored .40 .25
935 A345 30c multicolored .40 .25
936 A345 30c multicolored .40 .25
937 A345 30c multicolored .40 .25
938 A345 30c multicolored .30 .20
939 A345 85c multicolored .90 *1.50*
Nos. 932-939 (8) 3.50 3.15

Settlement of Victoria Sesquicentenary A346

1984, Nov. 19

940 A346 30c Helmeted honeyeater .35 .20
941 A346 30c Leadbeater's possum .35 .20
a. Pair, #940-941 .70

Australia Day A347

1985, Jan. 25 Litho.

942 30c Musgrave Ranges, by Sidney Nolan .45 .20
a. Pair, #942 tete-beche 1.50
943 30c The Walls of China, by Russell Drysdale .45 .20
a. A347 Pair, #942-943 .90
b. Pair, #943 tete-beche 1.50

Intl. Youth Year — A348

1985, Feb. 13 Litho. *Perf. 14x13½*

944 A348 30c multicolored .40 .20

Royal Victorian Volunteer Artillery A349

District Nursing Service Centenary A350

Colonial military uniforms: b, Western Australian Pinjarrah Cavalry. c, New South Wales Lancers. d, New South Wales Contingent to the Sudan. e, Victorian Mounted Rifles.

1985, Feb. 25 *Perf. 14½*

945 Strip of 5 2.25 1.60
a.-e. A349 33c any single .45 .20

1985, Mar. 13

946 A350 33c multicolored .35 .20

Australian Cockatoo — A351

Perf. 14 Horiz. on 1 or 2 sides

1985, Mar. 13

947 A351 1c apple grn, yel & buff 1.25 1.25
948 A351 33c apple grn, yel, & lt grnsh blue .45 .20
a. Bklt. pane, 1 #947, 3 #948 2.75

Issued in booklets only.

A352

1985, Apr. 10 *Perf. 13*

949 A352 33c Abel Tasman, explorer .50 .25
950 A352 33c The Eendracht .50 .25
951 A352 33c William Dampier .50 .25
952 A352 90c Globe and hand 1.25 *1.50*
a. Souvenir sheet of 4, #949-952 3.00 3.00
Nos. 949-952 (4) 2.75 2.25

Queen Elizabeth II, 59th Birthday — A353

1985, Apr. 22 *Perf. 14x13½*

953 A353 33c Queen's Badge, Order of Australia .35 .20

A354

A356

1985, May 15 Litho. *Perf. 14x13*

954 A354 33c Soil .45 .25
955 A354 50c Air .65 *1.00*
956 A354 80c Water 1.00 *1.10*
957 A354 90c Energy 1.10 *1.40*
Nos. 954-957 (4) 3.20 3.75

Environmental conservation.

1985, July 17 Litho. *Perf. 14½*

Illustrations from classic children's books: a, Elves & Fairies, by Annie Rentoul. b, The Magic Pudding, text and illustrations by Norman Lindsay. c, Ginger Meggs, by James Charles Bancks. d, Blinky Bill, by Dorothy Wall. e, Snugglepot and Cuddlepie, by May Gibbs.

960 Strip of 5 1.75 1.25
a.-e. A356 33c any single .35 .20

Electronic Mail — A357

1985, Sept. 18 Litho.

961 A357 33c multicolored .40 .20

Christmas A358

Angel in a ship, detail from a drawing by Albrecht Durer (1471-1528).

1985, Sept. 18 Litho.

962 A358 45c multicolored .45 .35

See Nos. 967-970.

Coastal Shipwrecks A359

Salvaged antiquities: 33c, Astrolabe from Batavia, 1629. 50c, German beardman (Bellarmine) jug from Vergulde Draeck, 1656. 90c, Wooden bobbins from Batavia, and scissors from Zeewijk, 1727. $1, Silver buckle from Zeewijk.

1985, Oct. 2 Litho. *Perf. 13*

963 A359 33c multicolored .40 .20
964 A359 50c multicolored .60 *.75*
965 A359 90c multicolored 1.25 1.25
966 A359 $1 multicolored 1.75 1.25
Nos. 963-966 (4) 4.00 3.45

Christmas Type of 1985

Illustrations by Scott Hartshorne.

1985, Nov. 1 Litho. *Perf. 14*

967 A358 27c Angel with trumpet .30 .20
968 A358 33c Angel with bells .40 .25
969 A358 55c Angel with star .70 .65
970 A358 90c Angel with ornament 1.10 1.10
Nos. 967-970 (4) 2.50 2.20

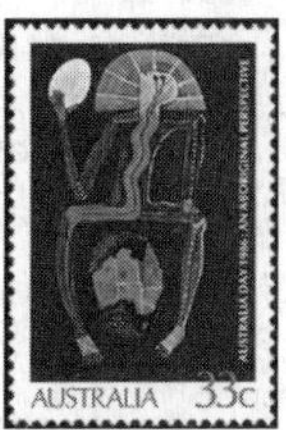

Australia Day — A360

AUSSAT — A361

1986, Jan. 24 Litho. *Perf. 14½*

971 A360 33c Aboriginal painting .35 .20

1986, Jan. 24

Various communications satellites.

972 A361 33c multicolored .35 .20
973 A361 80c multicolored 1.10 .75

South Australia, Sesquicent. A362

1986, Feb. 12 *Perf. 13½x14*

974 A362 33c Sailing ship Buffalo .40 .20
975 A362 33c City Sign, sculpture by O.H. Hajek .40 .20
a. Pair, #974-975 .80 .40

Cook's New Holland Expedition A363

1986, Mar. 12 *Perf. 13*

976 A363 33c Hibiscus merankensis .40 .25
977 A363 33c Banksia serrata .40 .25
978 A363 50c Dillenia alata .60 *1.00*
979 A363 80c Corria reflexa 1.10 1.00
980 A363 90c Parkinson 1.50 1.50
981 A363 90c Banks 1.50 1.50
Nos. 976-981 (6) 5.50 5.50

Australian bicentennial. Sydney Parkinson (d. 1775), artist. Sir Joseph Banks (1743-1820), naturalist.

Halley's Comet — A364

Elizabeth II, 60th Birthday — A365

1986, Apr. 9 *Perf. 14x13½*

982 A364 33c Radio telescope, trajectory diagram .35 .20

1986, Apr. 21 *Perf. 14½*

983 A365 33c multicolored .35 .20

Horses A366

1986, May 21

984 A366 33c Brumbies .45 .25
985 A366 80c Stock horse mustering 1.10 .65
986 A366 90c Show-jumping 1.25 .95
987 A366 $1 Australian pony 1.40 .95
Nos. 984-987 (4) 4.20 2.80

Click Go the Shears, Folk Song — A366a

Lines from the song: b, Old shearer stands. c, Ringer looks around. d, Boss of the board. e, Tar-boy is there. f, Shearing is all over.

1986, July 21 Litho. *Perf. 14½*

987A Strip of 5 2.50 1.25
b.-f. A366a 33c, any single .55 .20

Amalgamated Shearers' Union, predecessor of the Australian Workers' Union, cent.

Australia Bicentennial
A367

Settling of Botany Bay penal colony: No. 988, King George III, c. 1767, by A. Ramsay. No. 989, Lord Sydney, secretary of state, 1783-1789, by Gilbert Stuart. No. 990, Capt. Arthur Phillip, 1st penal colony governor, by F. Wheatley, 1786. $1, Capt. John Hunter, governor, 1795-1800, by W. B. Bennett, 1815.

1986, Aug. 6 Litho. *Perf. 13*

988 A367 33c multicolored .50 .30
989 A367 33c multicolored .50 .30
990 A367 33c multicolored .50 .30
991 A367 $1 multicolored 1.50 1.00
Nos. 988-991 (4) 3.00 1.90

Wildlife
A368

Alpine Wildflowers
A369

Designs: a, Red kangaroo. b, Emu. c, Koala. d, Kookaburra. e, Platypus.

1986, Aug. 13 *Perf. 14½x14*

992 Strip of 5 2.00 1.00
a.-e. A368 36c any single .40 .20

Rouletted 9½ Vert. on 1 or 2 sides

1986, Aug. 25

Booklet Stamps

993 A369 3c Royal bluebell .45 *.50*
994 A369 5c Alpine marsh marigold 1.00 *2.50*
995 A369 25c Mount Buffalo sunray 1.00 .75
996 A369 36c Silver snow daisy .90 .40
a. Bklt. pane, #993, #994, 2 #996 2.75
b. Bklt. pane, #993, #995, 2 #996 2.75
Nos. 993-996 (4) 3.35 4.15

Orchids — A370

America's Cup Triumph '83 — A371

1986, Sept. 18 *Perf. 14½*

997 A370 36c Elythranthera emarginata .50 .20
998 A370 55c Dendrobium nindii .80 .60
999 A370 90c Caleana major 1.40 1.00
1000 A370 $1 Thelymitra variegata 1.50 1.10
Nos. 997-1000 (4) 4.20 2.90

1986, Sept. 26 *Perf. 14x13½*

1001 A371 36c Australia II crossing finish line .60 .20
1002 A371 36c Trophy .60 .20
1003 A371 36c Boxing kangaroo .60 .20
Nos. 1001-1003 (3) 1.80 .60

Intl. Peace Year — A372

1986, Oct. 22 Litho. *Perf. 14x13½*

1004 A372 36c multicolored .50 .20

Christmas
A373

Kindergarten nativity play: No. 1005, Holy Family, vert. No. 1006, Three Kings, vert. No. 1007, Angels. No. 1008a, Angels, peasants. No. 1008b, Holy Family, angels, vert. No. 1008c, Shepherd, angels, vert. No. 1008d, Three Kings. No. 1008e, Shepherds.

1986, Nov. 3 Litho.

1005 A373 30c multicolored .35 .20
a. Perf 14x13½ 1.00 .50
1006 A373 36c multicolored .50 .20
1007 A373 60c multicolored .90 .50
Nos. 1005-1007 (3) 1.75 .90

Souvenir Sheet

1008 Sheet of 5 2.50 2.50
a.-e. A373 30c any single .50 .50

Perfs: Nos. 1005-1006, 1008c, 15x14½; Nos. 1007, 1008a 1008e, 14½x15.

No. 1008b, 15x14½x15x15; No. 1008d, 14½x15x14½x14½.

Australia Day — A374

1987, Jan. 23 Litho. *Perf. 13½x14*

1009 A374 36c Flag, circuit board .55 .20
1010 A374 36c Made in Australia campaign emblem .55 .20

America's Cup — A375

Fruits — A376

Views of yachts racing.

1987, Jan. 28 *Perf. 15x14½*

1011 A375 36c multicolored .40 .20
1012 A375 55c multicolored .60 *1.00*
1013 A375 90c multicolored 1.10 *1.25*
1014 A375 $1 multicolored 1.40 .75
Nos. 1011-1014 (4) 3.50 3.20

1987, Feb. 11 *Perf. 14x13½*

1015 A376 36c Melons, grapes .40 .20
1016 A376 65c Tropical fruit .60 .75
1017 A376 90c Pears, apples, oranges 1.10 1.10
1018 A376 $1 Berries, peaches 1.40 1.25
Nos. 1015-1018 (4) 3.50 3.30

Agricultural Shows — A377

1987, Apr. 10 Litho. *Perf. 14x13½*

1019 A377 36c Livestock .40 .20
1020 A377 65c Produce .60 .60
1021 A377 90c Carnival 1.10 1.00
1022 A377 $1 Farmers 1.40 1.10
Nos. 1019-1022 (4) 3.50 2.90

Queen Elizabeth II, 61st Birthday
A378

1987, Apr. 21 *Perf. 13½x14*

1023 A378 36c multicolored .45 .20

First Fleet Leaving England
A379

Continuous design: No. 1024a, Convicts awaiting transportation. b, Capt. Arthur Phillip, Mrs. Phillip, longboat on shore. c, Sailors relaxing and working. d, Longboats heading from and to fleet. 4e, Fleet in harbor.

No. 1025a, Longboat approaching Tenerife, The Canary Isls. b, Fishing in Tenerife Harbor. $1, Fleet, dolphins.

1987 *Perf. 13*

1024 Strip of 5 2.50 2.50
a.-e. A379 36c any single .50 .20
1025 Pair 1.00 1.00
a.-b. A379 36c any single .50 .20
1026 A379 $1 multicolored 1.50 1.50
Nos. 1024-1026 (3) 5.00 5.00

Australia bicent.; departure of the First Fleet, May 13, 1787; arrival at Tenerife, June 1787.

Issued: #1024, 5/13; #1025-1026, 6/3.

1987, Aug. 6

First Fleet arrives at Rio de Janeiro, Aug. 1787: a, Whale, storm in the Atlantic. b, Citrus grove. c, Market. d, Religious procession. e, Fireworks over harbor.

1027 Strip of 5 2.50 2.50
a.-e. A379 37c any single .50 .20

No. 1027 has a continuous design.

1987, Oct. 13

First Fleet arrives at Cape of Good Hope, Oct. 1787: No. 1028a, British officer surveys livestock and supplies, Table Mountain. No. 1028b, Ships anchored in Table Bay. No. 1029, Fishermen pull in nets as the Fleet approaches the Cape.

1028 Pair .90 .90
a.-b. A379 37c any single .45 .20
1029 A379 $1 multicolored 1.25 .50

No. 1028 has a continuous design.

1988, Jan. 26

Arrival of the First Fleet, Sydney Cove, Jan. 1788: a, Five aborigines on shore. b, Four aborigines on shore. c, Kangaroos. d, White cranes. e, Flag raising.

1030 Strip of 5 2.00 2.00
a.-e. A379 37c any single .40 .20

Printed se-tenant in a continuous design.

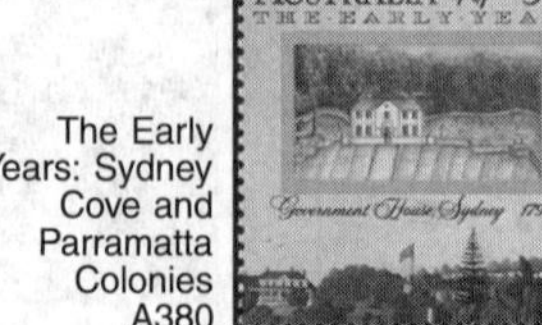

The Early Years: Sydney Cove and Parramatta Colonies
A380

Details from panorama "View of Sydney from the East Side of the Cove," 1808, painted by convict artist John Eyre to illustrate The Present Picture of New South Wales, published in London in 1811, and paintings in British and Australian museums: a, Government House, 1790, Sydney, by midshipman George Raper. b, Government Farm, Parramatta, 1791, attributed to the Port Jackson Painter. c, Parramatta Road, 1796, attributed to convict artist Thomas Watling. d, The Rocks and Sydney Cove, 1800, an aquatint engraving by Edward Dayes. e, Sydney Hospital, 1803, by George William Evans, an explorer and surveyor-general of New South Wales. Printed se-tenant in a continuous design.

1988, Apr. 13 Litho. *Perf. 13*

1031 Strip of 5 2.50 2.50
a.-e. A380 37c any single .50 .20

Australia Bicentennial.

The Man from Snowy River, 1890, Ballad by A.B. Paterson
A381

Fauna
A382

Excerpts: a, At the station. b, Mountain bred. c, Terrible descent. d, At their heels. e, Brought them back.

1987, June 24 *Perf. 14x13½*

1034 Strip of 5 2.25 2.25
a.-e. A381 36c any single .45 .30

Printed se-tenant in a continuous design.

1987, July 1 *Perf. 14½x14*

Designs: a, Possum. b, Cockatoo. c, Wombat. d, Rosella. e, Echidna.

1035 Strip of 5 1.75 1.75
a.-e. A382 37c any single .35 .20

Printed se-tenant in a continuous design.

Technology — A383

1987, Aug. 19 *Perf. 14½*

1036 A383 37c Bionic ear .40 .20
1037 A383 53c Microchips .55 .30
1038 A383 63c Robotics .70 .60
1039 A383 68c Zirconia ceramics .75 .70
Nos. 1036-1039 (4) 2.40 1.80

Children
A384

1987, Sept. 16

1040 A384 37c Crayfishing .35 .20
1041 A384 55c Cat's cradle .65 *.75*
1042 A384 90c Eating meat pies .90 .90
1043 A384 $1 Playing with a joey 1.10 .75
Nos. 1040-1043 (4) 3.00 2.60

Christmas
A385

Carolers: a, Woman, two girls. b, Man, two girls. c, Four children. d, Man, two women, boy. e, Six youths. 37c, three women, two men. Nos. 1044a-1044e are vert.

1987, Nov. 2 Litho. *Perf. 14½*

1044 Strip of 5 2.00 2.00
a.-e. A385 30c any single .40 .20

Perf. 13½x14

1045 A385 37c multicolored .45 .20
1046 A385 63c shown .80 .50
Nos. 1044-1046 (3) 3.25 2.70

Carols by Candlelight, Christmas Eve, Sidney Myer Bowl, Melbourne.

Aboriginal Crafts — A386

Designs: 3c, Spearthrower, Western Australia. 15c, Shield, New South Wales. No. 1049, Basket, Queensland. No. 1050, Bowl, Central Australia. No. 1051, Belt, Northern Territory.

Perf. 15½ Horiz.

1987, Oct. 13 Photo.

1047 A386 3c multicolored 1.10 *1.25*
1048 A386 15c multicolored 3.00 3.00
1049 A386 37c multicolored .55 .35
a. Bklt. pane, 2 ea #1047, 1049 4.00
1050 A386 37c multicolored .55 .35
1051 A386 37c multicolored .55 .35
a. Bklt. pane, #1048, 3 #1050, 2 #1051 8.00
Nos. 1047-1051 (5) 5.75 5.30

Issued only in booklets.

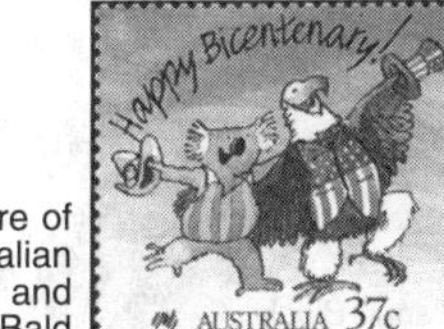

Caricature of Australian Koala and American Bald Eagle — A387

1988, Jan. 26 *Perf. 13*

1052 A387 37c multicolored .55 .20

Australia bicentennial. See No. 1086 and US No. 2370.

Living Together — A388

Cartoons.

1988 *Perf. 14*

1053 A388 1c Religion .20 .20
1054 A388 2c Industry .20 .20
1055 A388 3c Local government .20 .20
1056 A388 4c Trade unions .20 .20
1057 A388 5c Parliament .20 .20
1058 A388 10c Transportation .20 .20
1059 A388 15c Sports .20 .20
1060 A388 20c Commerce .30 .20
1061 A388 25c Housing .35 .20
1062 A388 30c Welfare .45 .20
1063 A388 37c Postal services .55 .20
a. Booklet pane of 10 5.50
1063B A388 39c Tourism .55 .20
c. Booklet pane of 10 5.50
1064 A388 40c Recreation .60 .30
1065 A388 45c Health .70 .35
1066 A388 50c Mining .75 .20
1067 A388 53c Primary industry .80 .30
1068 A388 55c Education .85 .30
1069 A388 60c Armed Forces .95 .20
1070 A388 63c Police 1.00 .75
1071 A388 65c Telecommunications 1.00 .40
1072 A388 68c The media 1.10 .40
1073 A388 70c Science and technology 1.10 .50
1074 A388 75c Visual arts 1.10 .25
1075 A388 80c Performing arts 1.25 .40
1076 A388 90c Banking 1.40 .50
1077 A388 95c Law 1.50 .60
1078 A388 $1 Rescue and emergency services 1.50 .55
Nos. 1053-1078 (27) 19.20 8.40

Issued: 1c, 2c, 3c, 5c, 30c, 40c, 55c, 60c, 63c, 65c, 68c, 75c, 95c, 3/16; 39c, 9/28; others, 2/17.

Queen Elizabeth II, 62nd Birthday A389

1988, Apr. 21 *Perf. 14½*

1079 A389 37c multicolored .60 .20

EXPO '88, Brisbane, Apr. 30-Oct. 30 — A390

1988, Apr. 29 *Perf. 13*

1080 A390 37c multicolored .60 .20

Opening of Parliament House, Canberra A391

1988, May 9 *Perf. 14½*

1081 A391 37c multicolored .60 .20

Australia Bicentennial A392

Designs: No. 1082, Colonist, clipper ship. No. 1083, British and Australian parliaments, Queen Elizabeth II. No. 1084, Cricketer W.G. Grace. No. 1085, John Lennon (1940-1980), William Shakespeare (1564-1616) and Sydney Opera House. #1083a, 1085a have continuous design picturing flag of Australia.

1988, June 21 Litho. *Perf. 13*

1082 A392 37c multicolored .75 .20
1083 A392 37c multicolored .75 .20
a. Pair, #1082-1083 1.50 .40
1084 A392 $1 multicolored 1.75 *2.75*
1085 A392 $1 multicolored 1.75 *2.75*
a. Pair, #1084-1085 3.50 5.50
Nos. 1082-1085 (4) 5.00 5.90

See Great Britain Nos. 1222-1225.

Caricature Type of 1988

Design: Caricature of an Australian koala and New Zealand kiwi.

1988, June 21 Litho. *Perf. 13½*

1086 A387 37c multicolored .60 .20

Australia bicentennial. See New Zealand No. 907.

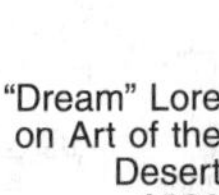

"Dream" Lore on Art of the Desert A393

Aboriginal paintings from Papunya Settlement in the Flinders University Art Museum: 37c, Bush Potato Country, by Turkey Tolsen Tjupurrula with by David Corby Tjapaltjarri. 55c, Courtship Rejected, by Limpi Puntungka Tjapangati. 90c, Medicine Story, anonymous. $1, Ancestor Dreaming, by Tim Leura Tjapaltjarri.

1988, Aug. 1 Litho. *Perf. 13*

1087 A393 37c multicolored .45 .20
1088 A393 55c multicolored .85 *1.00*
1089 A393 90c multicolored 1.10 *1.40*
1090 A393 $1 multicolored 1.40 1.25
Nos. 1087-1090 (4) 3.80 3.85

1988 Summer Olympics, Seoul — A394

1988, Sept. 14 *Perf. 14½*

1091 A394 37c Basketball .55 .55
1092 A394 65c Running .85 .85
1093 A394 $1 Rhythmic gymnastics 1.10 1.10
Nos. 1091-1093 (3) 2.50 2.50

34th Commonwealth Parliamentary Conference, Canberra — A395

1988, Sept. 19

1094 A395 37c Scepter and mace .50 .20

Works in the Contemporary Decorative Arts Collection at the Natl. Gallery — A396

Roulette 9 Horiz.

1988, Sept. 28 Litho.

1095 A396 2c "Australian Fetish," by Peter Tully 2.50 *5.00*
1096 A396 5c Vase by Colin Levy 2.50 *5.00*
1097 A396 39c Teapot by Frank Bauer .75 .35
a. Bklt. pane of 3 (2c, 2 39c) 4.00
b. Bklt. pane of 6 (5c, 5 39c) 5.00
Nos. 1095-1097 (3) 5.75 10.35

Nos. 1095-1097 issued in booklets only.

Views — A397

1988, Oct. 17 Photo. *Perf. 13*

1098 A397 39c The Desert .65 .20
1099 A397 55c The Top End .90 .30
1100 A397 65c The Coast 1.10 1.10
1101 A397 70c The Bush 1.10 1.10
Nos. 1098-1101 (4) 3.75 2.70

Christmas A398

Children's design contest winning drawings: 32c, Nativity scene, by Danielle Hush, age 7. 39c, Koala wearing a Santa hat, by Kylie Courtney, age 6. 63c, Cockatoo wearing a Santa hat, by Benjamin Stevenson, age 10.

1988, Oct. 31 *Perf. 13½x13*

1102 A398 32c multicolored .45 .20
1103 A398 39c multicolored .55 .20
1104 A398 63c multicolored 1.00 .70
Nos. 1102-1104 (3) 2.00 1.10

Sir Henry Parkes (1815-1896), Advocate of the Federation of the Six Colonies — A399

1989, Jan. 25 Litho. *Perf. 14x13½*

1105 A399 39c multicolored .60 .20

Australia Day.

Sports — A400

1989, Feb. 13 *Perf. 14x14½*

1106 A400 1c Bowls .20 .20
a. Perf. 13¼x13¾ ('90) .30 .30
1107 A400 2c Bowling .20 .20
a. Perf. 13¼x13¾ ('91) .20 .20
1108 A400 3c Football .20 .20
1109 A400 39c Fishing .40 .20
a. Booklet pane of 10 7.00
d. Perf. 13¼x13¾ on 3 or 4 sides ('90) .70 .20
e. Booklet pane of 10, #1109d 10.00
1109B A400 41c Cycling .35 .20
c. Booklet pane of 10 6.25
1110 A400 55c Kite-flying .35 .30
1111 A400 70c Cricket .95 .40
1112 A400 $1.10 Golf 1.10 .65

#1109d also exists perfed on 4 sides from sheets. These are scarcer

1990-94

1114 A400 5c Kayaking, canoeing .20 .20
a. Perf. 13¼x13¾ .20 .20
1115 A400 10c Windsurfing .20 .20
a. Perf. 13¼x13¾ .20 .20
1116 A400 20c Tennis .20 .20
a. Perf. 13¼x13¾ .30 .30
1117 A400 65c Rock climbing .65 .35
a. Perf. 13¼x13¾ 1.00 1.00
1118 A400 $1 Running .95 .55
a. Perf. 13¼x13¾ 3.75 2.00

Issued: #1114a, 1115a, 1116a, 1117a, 1118, 1/17/90; #1118a, 1/91; #1115, 1117, 2/92; #1116, 7/93; #1114, 3/94.

1990, Aug. 27

1119 A400 43c Skateboarding .45 .20
a. Booklet pane of 10 6.75

Perf. 13½

1120 A400 $1.20 Hang-gliding 2.10 .50

1991, Aug. 22 *Perf. 14x14½*

1121 A400 75c Netball .50 .40
1122 A400 80c Squash .55 .40
1123 A400 85c Diving 1.60 .40
1124 A400 90c Soccer 1.60 .45
Nos. 1106-1124 (19) 12.75 6.20

For self-adhesive stamps see #1185-1186.

Botanical Gardens — A401

Designs: $2, Nooroo, New South Wales. $5, Mawarra, Victoria. $10, Palm House, Adelaide Botanical Garden. $20, A View of the Artist's House and Garden in Mills Plains, Van Diemen's Land by John Glover.

1989-90 Litho. & Engr. *Perf. 14*

1132 A401 $2 multicolored 1.50 1.00
 a. Perf. 13¼x13¾ ('91) 3.50 1.00
1133 A401 $5 multicolored 4.50 2.00
 a. Perf. 13¼x13¾ 6.75 2.00
1134 A401 $10 multicolored 8.00 2.00

Perf. 14½x14

1135 A401 $20 multicolored 16.00 8.00
 Nos. 1132-1135 (4) 30.00 13.00

Issued: $10, 4/12; $2, $5, 9/13; $20, 8/15/90.

Sheep A402

1989, Feb. 27 *Perf. 13½x14*

1136 A402 39c Merino .55 .20
1137 A402 39c Poll Dorset .55 .20
1138 A402 85c Polwarth 1.25 *1.50*
1139 A402 $1 Corriedale 1.40 .75
 Nos. 1136-1139 (4) 3.75 2.65

World Sheep and Wool Congress, Tasmania, Feb. 27-Mar. 6.

Queen Elizabeth II, 63rd Birthday — A403

1989, Apr. 21 Litho. *Perf. 14½*

1140 A403 39c Statue by John Dowie .55 .20

Colonial Australia A404

Pastoral Era: a, Immigrant ship in port, c. 1835. b, Pioneer's hut, wool bales in dray. c, Squatter's homestead. d, Shepherds. e, Explorers.

1989, May 10

1141 Strip of 5 2.50 1.10
 a.-e. A404 39c any single .50 .20

Stars of Stage and Screen — A405

Performers and directors: 39c, Gladys Moncrieff and Roy Rene, the stage, 1920's. 85c, Charles Chauvel and Chips Rafferty, talking films. $1, Nellie Stewart and James Cassius Williamson, the stage, 1890's. $1.10, Lottie Lyell and Raymond Longford, silent films.

1989, July 12 Litho. *Perf. 14½*

1142 A405 39c multicolored .45 .20
 a. Perf. 14x13½ ('90) 5.00 5.00
1143 A405 85c multicolored 1.10 *1.50*
1144 A405 $1 multicolored 1.10 .75
1145 A405 $1.10 multicolored 1.10 .75
 Nos. 1142-1145 (4) 3.75 3.20

Impressionist Paintings A406

Paintings by Australian artists: No. 1146, *Impression for Golden Summer,* by Sir Arthur Streeton. No. 1147, *All on a Summer's Day,* by Charles Conder, vert. No. 1148, *Petit Dejeuner,* by Frederick McCubbin. No. 1149, *Impression,* by Tom Roberts.

Perf. 13½x14, 14x13½

1989, Aug. 23 Litho.

1146 A406 41c shown .45 .20
1147 A406 41c multicolored .45 .20
1148 A406 41c multicolored .45 .20
1149 A406 41c multicolored .45 .20
 Nos. 1146-1149 (4) 1.80 .80

The Urban Environment — A407

1989, Sept. 1 Litho. *Perf. 15½*

Booklet Stamps

1150 A407 41c Freeways .60 *.70*
1151 A407 41c Architecture .60 *.70*
1152 A407 41c Commuter train .60 *.70*
 a. Bklt. pane, 2 ea #1150, 1152, 3 #1151 5.00
 Nos. 1150-1152 (3) 1.80 2.10

No. 1152a sold for $3.

Australian Youth Hostels, 50th Anniv. A408

1989, Sept. 13 *Perf. 14½*

1153 A408 41c multicolored .65 .20

Street Cars — A409

Designs: No. 1154, Horse-drawn tram, Adelaide, 1878. No. 1155, Steam tram, Sydney, 1884. No. 1156, Cable car, Melbourne, 1886. No. 1157, Double-deck electric tram, Hobart, 1893. No. 1158, Combination electric tram, Brisbane, 1901.

1989, Oct. 11 Litho. *Perf. 13½x14*

1154 A409 41c multicolored .55 .20
1155 A409 41c multicolored .55 .20
1156 A409 41c multicolored .55 .20
 a. Perf. 14½ on 3 sides 1.25 1.25
 b. Booklet pane of 10, #1156a 11.50
1157 A409 41c multicolored .55 .20
1158 A409 41c multicolored .55 .20
 Nos. 1154-1158 (5) 2.75 1.00

Purchase of booklet containing No. 1156b included STAMPSHOW '89 admission ticket and a Melbourne one-day transit pass. Sold for $8.

Christmas A410

Radio Australia, 50th Anniv. A411

Illuminations: 36c, Annunciation, from the Nicholai Joseph Foucault Book of Hours, c. 1510-20. 41c, Annunciation to the Shepherds, from the Wharncliffe Hours, c. 1475. 80c, Adoration of the Magi, from Parisian Book of Hours, c. 1490-1500.

1989, Nov. 1 *Perf. 14x13½*

1159 A410 36c multicolored .45 .20
 a. Booklet pane of 10 4.00

Perf. 15x14½

1160 A410 41c multicolored .55 .20
1161 A410 80c multicolored 1.00 .60
 Nos. 1159-1161 (3) 2.00 1.00

1989, Nov. 1 *Perf. 14x13½*

1162 A411 41c multicolored .55 .20

Australia Day A412

Special Occasions A413

1990, Jan. 17 Litho. *Perf. 15x14½*

1163 A412 41c Golden wattle .65 .20

1990, Feb. 7 *Perf. 14x13½*

1164 A413 41c Thinking of You .65 .20
 a. Booklet pane of 10 6.50
 b. Perf. 14½ on 3 sides .65 .20
 c. Booklet pane of 10, #1164b 6.50

See No. 1193.

Women Practicing Medicine in Australia, Cent. A414

1990, Feb. 7 *Perf. 14½x15*

1165 A414 41c Constance Stone .65 .20

Dr. Constance Stone, Australia's first woman doctor.

A415

A416

Fauna of the High Country.

1990, Feb. 21 *Perf. 14x13½*

1166 A415 41c Greater glider .55 .20
1167 A415 65c Spotted-tailed quoll .80 .50
1168 A415 70c Mountain pygmy-possum 1.00 .60
1169 A415 80c Brush-tailed rock-wallaby 1.25 .70
 Nos. 1166-1169 (4) 3.60 2.00

1990, Mar. 14

1170 A416 41c Quit smoking .55 .20
1171 A416 41c Don't drink and drive .55 .20
1172 A416 41c Eat right .55 .20
1173 A416 41c Medical check-ups .55 .20
 Nos. 1170-1173 (4) 2.20 .80

Community health.

A417

A418

Scenes from WW II, 1940-41: #1174, Anzacs at the front. #1175, Women working in factories, aircraft at the ready. 65c, Veterans and memorial parade. $1, Helicopters picking up wounded, cemetery. $1.10, Anzacs reading mail from home, 5 women watching departure of 2 ships.

1990, Apr. 12 Litho. *Perf. 14½*

1174 A417 41c shown .55 .20
1175 A417 41c multicolored .55 .20
1176 A417 65c multicolored .80 .55
1177 A417 $1 multicolored 1.25 .65
1178 A417 $1.10 multicolored 1.40 .70
 Nos. 1174-1178 (5) 4.55 2.30

Australia and New Zealand Army Corps (ANZAC).

1990, Apr. 19 *Perf. 14½*

1179 A418 41c multicolored .60 .20

Queen Elizabeth's 64th birthday.

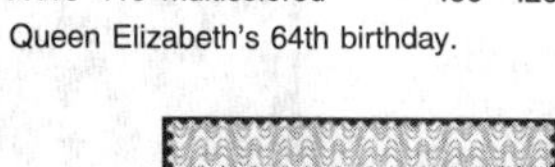

Penny Black, 150th Anniv. A419

Stamps on stamps: a, New South Wales #44. b, South Australia #4. c, Tasmania #2. d, Victoria #120. e, Queensland #111A. f, Western Australia #3a.

1990, May 1 *Perf. 13½x14*

1180 Block of 6 4.00 1.25
 a.-f. A419 41c any single .65 .20
 g. Souvenir sheet of 6 4.25 3.75

The Gold Rush — A420

a, Off to the diggings. b, The diggings. c, Panning for gold. d, Commissioner's tent. e, Gold escort.

1990, May 16 *Perf. 13*

1181 Strip of 5 2.50 2.50
 a.-e. A420 41c any single .50 .20

Cooperation in Antarctic Research A421

1990, June 13 Litho. *Perf. 14½x14*

1182 A421 41c Glaciology .60 .20
1183 A421 $1.10 Krill (marine biology) 1.60 .55
 a. Min. sheet of 2, #1182-1183 2.25 2.25
 b. #1183a overprinted 3.75 3.75

No. 1183 is overprinted in gold, in sheet margin only, for NZ 1990 International Stamp Exhibition, Auckland, Aug. 24-Sept. 2, 1990.

See Russia Nos. 5902-5903.

Colonial Australia A422

Boom Time: a, Land boom. b, Building boom. c, Investment boom. d, Retail boom. e, Factory boom.

1990, July 12 Litho. *Perf. 13*

1184 Strip of 5 2.50 2.50
a.-e. A422 41c any single .50 .25

Sports Type of 1989

1990-91 Typo. *Die Cut Perf. 11½*

Self-Adhesive

1185 A400 41c Cycling .75 .65
1186 A400 43c Skateboarding .70 .20
a. Litho. .70 .20

Blue background has large dots on No. 1186 and smaller dots on No. 1186a. No. 1186 is on waxed paper backing printed with 0 to 4 koalas. No. 1186a is on plain paper backing printed with one kangaroo.

Issued: 41c, 5/16; #1186, 8/27; #1186a, 1991.

This is an expanding set. Numbers will change if necessary.

Salmon Gums by Robert Juniper — A423

43c, The Blue Dress by Brian Dunlop.

Perf. 15½ Vert.

1990, Sept. 3 Litho.

Booklet Stamps

1191 A423 28c multicolored 2.25 1.75
a. Perf. 14½ vert. 2.25 1.75
1192 A423 43c multicolored .65 .50
a. Bklt. pane, #1191, 4 #1192 3.25
b. Perf. 14½ vert. .65 .50
c. Bklt. pane, #1191a, 4 #1192b 3.25

Thinking Of You Type

1990, Sept. 3 *Perf. 14½*

1193 A413 43c multicolored .50 .20
a. Booklet pane of 10 5.00

Christmas A424

1990, Oct. 31 Litho. *Perf. 14½*

1194 A424 38c Kookaburras .60 .20
a. Booklet pane of 10 6.25
1195 A424 43c Nativity, vert. .70 .20
1196 A424 80c Opossum 1.40 .60
Nos. 1194-1196 (3) 2.70 1.00

Local Government in Australia, 150th Anniv. — A425

1990, Oct. 31

1197 A425 43c Town Hall, Adelaide .70 .20

Flags A426

1991, Jan. 10 Litho. *Perf. 14½*

1199 A426 43c National flag .55 .20
1200 A426 90c White ensign 1.10 .55
1201 A426 $1 Air Force ensign 1.25 .65
1202 A426 $1.20 Red ensign 1.40 .75
Nos. 1199-1202 (4) 4.30 2.15

Australia Day.

Water Birds — A427

1991, Feb. 14

1203 A427 43c Black swan .55 .20
1204 A427 43c Black-necked stork, vert. .55 .20
1205 A427 85c Cape Barren goose, vert. 1.00 1.00
1206 A427 $1 Chestnut teal 1.10 .60
Nos. 1203-1206 (4) 3.20 2.00

Women's Wartime Services, 50th Anniv. A428

50th Anniv: #1208, Siege of Tobruk. $1.20, Australian War Memorial, Canberra.

1991, Mar. 14 Litho. *Perf. 14½*

1207 A428 43c shown .55 .20
1208 A428 43c multicolored .55 .20
1209 A428 $1.20 multicolored 1.40 .70
Nos. 1207-1209 (3) 2.50 1.10

Queen Elizabeth II's 65th Birthday — A429

1991, Apr. 11 Litho. *Perf. 14½*

1210 A429 43c multicolored .55 .20

Insects A430

1991, Apr. 11

1211 A430 43c Hawk moth .55 .20
1212 A430 43c Cotton harlequin bug .55 .20
1213 A430 80c Leichhardt's grasshopper 1.00 .60
1214 A430 $1 Jewel beetle 1.10 .70
Nos. 1211-1214 (4) 3.20 1.70

Australian Photography, 150th Anniv. — A431

Designs: No. 1215a, Bondi, by Max Dupain, 1939. No. 1215b, Gears for the Mining Industry, Vickers Ruwolt Melbourne, by Wolfgang Sievers, 1967. 70c, Wheel of Youth, by Harold Cazneaux, 1929. $1.20, Teacup Ballet, by Olive Cotton, 1935.

1991, May 13 Litho. *Perf. 14½*

1215 Pair 1.10 .40
a.-b. A431 43c any single .55 .20
1216 A431 70c blk, olive & cl .90 .50
1217 A431 $1.20 blk, gray & Prus bl 1.40 .75
Nos. 1215-1217 (3) 3.40 1.65

Golden Days of Radio — A432

Pets — A433

1991, June 13 Litho. *Perf. 14½*

1218 A432 43c Music & variety shows .70 .20
1219 A432 43c Soap operas .70 .20
1220 A432 85c Quiz shows 1.25 1.25
1221 A432 $1 Children's stories 1.50 .65
Nos. 1218-1221 (4) 4.15 2.30

1991, July 25 Litho. *Perf. 14½*

1222 A433 43c Puppy .65 .20
1223 A433 43c Kitten .65 .20
1224 A433 70c Pony 1.10 .40
1225 A433 $1 Cockatoo 1.50 .60
Nos. 1222-1225 (4) 3.90 1.40

George Vancouver (1757-1798) and Edward John Eyre (1815-1901), Explorers — A434

1991, Sept. 26 Litho. *Perf. 14½*

1226 A434 $1.05 multicolored 1.60 .55
a. Souvenir sheet of 1 1.60 1.60
b. As "a," overprinted in gold 2.75 2.75

Vancouver's visit to Western Australia, 200th anniv. and Eyre's journey to Albany, Western Australia, 150th anniv.

No. 1226b overprinted in sheet margin with show emblem and: "PHILANIPPON / WORLD STAMP / EXHIBITION / TOKYO / 16-24 NOV 1991" followed by Japanese inscription.

Issue date: #1226b, Nov. 16.

Australian Literature of the 1890's A435

Designs: 43c, Seven Little Australians by Ethel Turner. 75c, On Our Selection by Steele Rudd. $1, Clancy of the Overflow by A.B. "Banjo" Paterson, vert. $1.20, The Drover's Wife by Henry Lawson, vert.

1991, Oct. 10

1227 A435 43c multicolored .65 .20
1228 A435 75c multicolored 1.10 .50
1229 A435 $1 multicolored 1.60 .65
1230 A435 $1.20 multicolored 1.90 .80
Nos. 1227-1230 (4) 5.25 2.15

Christmas A436

1991, Nov. 1

1231 A436 38c Shepherd .50 .20
a. Booklet pane of 20 10.00
1232 A436 43c Baby Jesus .55 .20
1233 A436 90c Wise man, camel 1.10 .45
Nos. 1231-1233 (3) 2.15 .85

Thinking of You — A437

1992, Jan. 2 Litho. *Perf. 14½x15*

1234 A437 45c Wildflowers .50 .25
a. Booklet pane of 10 5.00

Threatened Species — A438

#1235: a, Parma wallaby. b, Ghost bat. c, Long-tailed dunnart. d, Little pygmy possum. e, Dusky hopping mouse. f, Squirrel glider.

1992, Jan. 2 Litho. *Perf. 14x14½*

1235 Block of 6 4.00 4.00
a.-f. A438 45c any single .65 .65

Die Cut

Perf. 11½

Self-Adhesive

Size: 31x22mm

1241 A438 45c like #1235a .65 .25
a. Typo. .65 .25
1242 A438 45c like #1235b .65 .25
a. Typo. .65 .25
1243 A438 45c like #1235c .65 .25
a. Typo. .65 .25
1244 A438 45c like #1235d .65 .25
a. Typo. .65 .25
1245 A438 45c like #1235e .65 .25
a. Typo. .65 .25
1246 A438 45c like #1235f .65 .25
a. Typo. .65 .25
b. Bklt. pane, 2 each #1241-1244, 1 each #1245-1246 6.25
c. Pane of 5, #1242-1246 3.25
d. Strip of 6, #1241-1246 4.00
e. Strip of 6, #1241a-1246a 4.00
f. #1246c overprinted 4.00
g. As "f," no die cutting 190.00

Litho. stamps are sharper in appearance than typo. stamps, most notably on the black lettering. Nos. 1246b and 1246c have tagging bars which make the right portion of the stamps appear toned.

No. 1246f - overprinted in Gold on sheet margin of No. 1246c with emblem of "WORLD COLUMBIAN / STAMP EXPO '92 / MAY 22-31, 1992 - CHICAGO." Issued in May.

See Nos. 1271-1293.

Wetlands A439

Perf. 14½ Horiz.

1992, Jan. 2 Photo.

Booklet Stamps

1247 A439 20c Noosa River, Queensland .55 .45
a. Perf. 14 horiz. .55 .55
1248 A439 45c Lake Eildon, Victoria .55 .45
a. Bklt. pane, #1247, 4 #1248 2.75
Complete booklet, #1248a 2.75
b. Perf. 14 horiz. .55 .55
c. Bklt. pane, #1247a, 4 #1248b 2.75
Complete booklet, #1248c 2.75

Sailing Ships A440

Perf. 14½x15, 15x14½

1992, Jan. 15 Litho.

1249 A440 45c Young Endeavour .70 .20
1250 A440 45c Britannia, vert. .70 .20
1251 A440 $1.05 Akarana, vert. 1.60 .60
1252 A440 $1.20 John Louis 1.75 .70
a. Sheet of 4, #1249-1252 4.75 4.75
b. As "a," overprinted 5.50 5.50
c. As "a," overprinted 7.50 7.50
Nos. 1249-1252 (4) 4.75 1.70

Australia Day. Discovery of America, 500th anniv. (No. 1252a).

Overprint in gold on sheet margin of No. 1252b contains emblem and "WORLD

COLUMBIAN / STAMP EXPO '92 / MAY 22-31, 1992-CHICAGO." No. 1252b issued in May.

Overprint in gold on sheet margin of No. 1252c contains emblem and "GENOVA '92 / 18-27 SEPTEMBER." No. 1252c issued in Sept.

Australian Battles, 1942 — A441

1992, Feb. 19 Litho. *Perf. 14½*

1253 A441 45c Bombing of Darwin .55 .20
1254 A441 75c Milne Bay .80 .60
1255 A441 75c Kokoda Trail .80 .60
1256 A441 $1.05 Coral Sea 1.25 .80
1257 A441 $1.20 El Alamein 1.40 .95
Nos. 1253-1257 (5) 4.80 3.15

Intl. Space Year — A442

1992, Mar. 19

1258 A442 45c Helix Nebula .65 .20
1259 A442 $1.05 The Pleiades 1.50 .65
1260 A442 $1.20 Spiral Galaxy NGC 2997 1.60 .70
a. Sheet of 3, #1258-1260 3.75 3.75
b. As "a," overprinted 5.00 5.00
Nos. 1258-1260 (3) 3.75 1.55

Overprint on sheet margin of No. 1260b contains emblem of "WORLD COLUMBIAN / STAMP EXPO '92 / MAY 22-31, 1992-CHICAGO." No. 1260b issued in May.

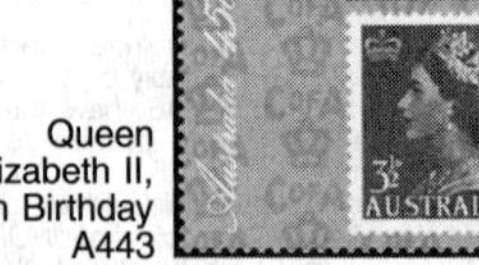

Queen Elizabeth II, 66th Birthday A443

1992, Apr. 9 *Perf. 14x14½*

1261 A443 45c Wmk. 228 & #258 .65 .20

Vineyard Regions A444

Designs: No. 1262, Hunter Valley New South Wales. No. 1263, North Eastern Victoria. No. 1264, Barossa Valley South Australia. No. 1265, Coonawarra South Australia. No. 1266, Margaret River Western Australia.

1992, Apr. 9

1262 A444 45c multicolored .65 .20
1263 A444 45c multicolored .65 .20
1264 A444 45c multicolored .65 .20
1265 A444 45c multicolored .65 .20
1266 A444 45c multicolored .65 .20
Nos. 1262-1266 (5) 3.25 1.00

Land Care — A445

a, Salt action. b, Farm planning. c, Erosion control. d, Tree planting. e, Dune care.

1992, June 11 Litho. *Perf. 14½x14*

1267 Strip of 5 2.75 2.25
a.-e. A445 45c Any single .55 .20

1992 Summer Olympics and Paralympics, Barcelona A446

1992, July 2 *Perf. 14½*

1268 A446 45c Cycling .50 .20
1269 A446 $1.20 Weight lifting 1.40 .60
1270 A446 $1.20 High jump 1.40 .60
Nos. 1268-1270 (3) 3.30 1.40

Threatened Species Type of 1992

1992-98 Litho. *Perf. 14x14½*

1271 A438 30c Saltwater crocodile .40 .20
1272 A438 35c Echidna .50 .20
1273 A438 40c Platypus .55 .20
1274 A438 45c Kangaroo .65 .20
1275 A438 45c Adult kangaroo with joey .65 .20
1276 A438 45c Two adult kangaroos .65 .20
a. Sheet of 3, #1274-1276 2.10 1.00
1277 A438 45c Four koalas .65 .20
1278 A438 45c Koala walking .65 .20
1279 A438 45c Koala in tree .65 .20
a. Block of 6, #1274-1279 4.00 1.40
b. Souv. sheet, #1274-1279 4.00 4.00
1280 A438 50c Koala .70 .25
1281 A438 60c Common brushtail possum .85 .30
1282 A438 70c Kookaburra .95 .35
a. "Australia 70c" in brn ('96) .95 .35
1283 A438 85c Pelican 1.25 .40
1284 A438 90c Eastern gray kangeroo 1.25 .40
1285 A438 95c Common wombat 1.40 .45
1286 A438 $1.20 Pink cockatoo 1.60 .55
a. "Australia $1.20" in brown ('98) 1.65 .55
1287 A438 $1.35 Emu 2.00 .65
Nos. 1271-1287 (17) 15.35 5.15

PHILAKOREA '94 (#1279b).

On No. 1279a Australia and denomination are orange, "KANGAROO" is 9mm long, and date is 1½mm long. Date is 1mm long and "KANGAROO" 8mm long on Nos. 1279d and 1279f.

"Australia" and denominations on Nos. 1282, 1286 are in orange.

No. 1276a inscribed in sheet margin with "CHINA '96 - 9th Asian International Exhibition" in Chinese and English and exhibition emblems.

No. 1282a comes from 3 Koala or 1 Kangaroo and 1 Koala printing. No. 1286a comes from 1 Kangaroo printing.

Issued: 35c, 50c, 60c, 95c, 8/13; 40c, 70c, 90c, $1.20, 8/12/93; 30c, 85c, $1.35, 3/10/94; 45c, 5/12/94; #1279b, 8/94; #1282a, 3/96; #1276a, 5/18/96; #1286a, 12/98.

1996 Litho. *Perf. 14x14½*

1274a A438 45c brown panel .60 .60
b. Bright orange panel .60 .60
1275a A438 45c brown panel .60 .60
b. Bright orange panel .60 .60
1276b A438 45c brown panel .60 .60
c. Bright orange panel .60 .60
1277a A438 45c brown panel .60 .60
b. Bright orange panel .60 .60
1278a A438 45c brown panel .60 .60
b. Bright orange panel .60 .60
1279c A438 45c brown panel .60 .60
d. Block, #1274a-1275a, 1276b, 1277a-1278a, 1279c 4.00 4.00
e. Bright orange panel .60 .60
f. Block, #1274b-1275b, 1276c, 1277b-1278b, 1279e 4.00 4.00

On No. 1279a Australia and denomination are orange, "KANGAROO" is 9mm lond, and date is 1½mm long. Date is 1mm long and "KANGAROO" 8mm long on Nos. 1279d and 1279f. No. 1279d comes from 2 Koala printing. No. 1279f comes from 3 Koala printing.

Die Cut Perf. 11

1994, May 12 Litho.

Self-Adhesive

1288 A438 45c like #1274 .65 .20
1289 A438 45c like #1275 .65 .20
1290 A438 45c like #1276 .65 .20
1291 A438 45c like #1277 .65 .20
1292 A438 45c like #1278 .65 .20
1293 A438 45c like #1279 .65 .20
a. Bklt. pane, #1290, 1293, 2 each #1288-1289, 1291-1292 6.50
b. Strip of 6, #1288-1293 4.00

Opening of Sydney Harbor Tunnel, August 29 — A447

Sydney Harbor Bridge and Tunnel: a, Left side. b, Right side.

1992, Aug. 28 Litho. *Perf. 14½*

1296 A447 45c Pair, #a.-b. 1.25 .45
c. Pair, #d.-e., perf 15½ 1.25 .45

Buildings in Western Australia Goldfield Towns A448

#1297, Warden's Courthouse, Coolgardie. #1298, Post Office, Kalgoorlie. $1.05, York Hotel, Kalgoorlie. $1.20, Town Hall, Kalgoorlie.

1992, Sept. 17 Litho. *Perf. 14x14½*

1297 A448 45c multicolored .50 .20
1298 A448 45c multicolored .50 .20
1299 A448 $1.05 multicolored 1.10 .50
1300 A448 $1.20 multicolored 1.25 .60
Nos. 1297-1300 (4) 3.35 1.50

Sheffield Shield Cricket Competition, Cent. — A449

Cricket match, 1890s: 45c, Bowler. $1.20, Batsman, wicket keeper.

1992, Oct. 15 Litho. *Perf. 14½*

1301 A449 45c multicolored .60 .20
1302 A449 $1.20 multicolored 1.60 .55

Christmas A450

Designs: 40c, Children dressed as Mary and Joseph with baby carriage. 45c, Boy jumping from bed Christmas morning. $1, Boy and girl singing Christmas carol.

1992, Oct. 30 Litho. *Perf. 14x14½*

1303 A450 40c multicolored .45 .45
a. Booklet pane of 20 9.00
1304 A450 45c multicolored .60 .20
1305 A450 $1 multicolored 1.25 .45
Nos. 1303-1305 (3) 2.30 1.10

Watercolor Paintings by Albert Namatjira A451

Designs: No. 1306a, Ghost Gum, Central Australia. b, Across the Plain to Mount Giles.

1993, Jan. 14 Litho. *Perf. 14x15*

1306 A451 45c Pair, #a.-b. 1.25 .40

Australia Day.

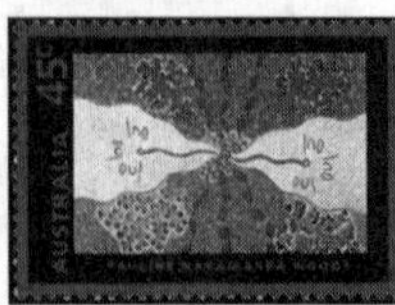

Dreamings A452

Aboriginal paintings: 45c, Wild Onion Dreaming, by Pauline Nakamarra Woods. 75c, Yam Plants, by Jack Wunuwun, vert. 85c, Goose Egg Hunt, by George Milpurrurru, vert. $1, Kalumpiwarra-Ngulalintji, by Rover Thomas.

Perf. 14x14½, 14½x14

1993, Feb. 4 Litho.

1307 A452 45c red & multi .55 .20
1308 A452 75c org yel & multi .80 .30
1309 A452 85c buff & multi .90 .35
1310 A452 $1 salmon & multi 1.00 .45
Nos. 1307-1310 (4) 3.25 1.30

World Heritage Sites in Australia — A453

1993, Mar. 4 Litho. *Perf. 14½x14*

1311 A453 45c Uluru (Ayers Rock) .55 .20
1312 A453 85c Fraser Island .90 .40
1313 A453 95c Shark Bay 1.00 .40
1314 A453 $2 Kakadu 2.00 .85
Nos. 1311-1314 (4) 4.45 1.85

See Nos. 1485-1488.

World War II Ships A454

45c, Cruiser HMAS Sydney II. 85c, Corvette HMAS Bathurst. $1.05, Destroyer HMAS Arunta. $1.20, Hospital Ship Centaur.

1993, Apr. 7 Litho. *Perf. 14x14½*

1315 A454 45c multicolored .60 .20
1316 A454 85c multicolored .90 .35
1317 A454 $1.05 multicolored 1.10 .60
1318 A454 $1.20 multicolored 1.40 .65
Nos. 1315-1318 (4) 4.00 1.80

A455 A456

1993, Apr. 7 *Perf. 14½x14*

1319 A455 45c multicolored .55 .20

Queen Elizabeth II, 67th birthday.

1993, May 7 Litho. *Perf. 14½x14*

Designs based on 19th cent. trade union banners: #1320, Baker, shoe maker. #1321, Stevedore, seamstresses. $1, Blacksmith, telephone operator, cook. $1.20, Carpenters.

1320 A456 45c multicolored .50 .20
1321 A456 45c multicolored .50 .20
1322 A456 $1 multicolored 1.00 .55
1323 A456 $1.20 multicolored 1.25 .65
Nos. 1320-1323 (4) 3.25 1.60

Working life in the 1890s.

Trains A457

#1324, Centenary Special, Tasmania. #1325, Spirit of Progress. #1326, Western Endeavour. #1327, Silver City Comet. #1328, Kuranda Tourist Train. #1329, The Ghan.

1993, June 1 ***Perf. 14x14½***

1324 A457 45c multicolored .60 .60
1325 A457 45c multicolored .60 .60
1326 A457 45c multicolored .60 .60
1327 A457 45c multicolored .60 .60
1328 A457 45c multicolored .60 .60
1329 A457 45c multicolored .60 .60
a. Block of 6, #1324-1329 3.75 3.75

Die Cut Perf. 12x11½

Self-Adhesive

1330 A457 45c like No. 1324 .60 .20
1331 A457 45c like No. 1325 .60 .20
1332 A457 45c like No. 1326 .60 .20
1333 A457 45c like No. 1327 .60 .20
1334 A457 45c like No. 1328 .60 .20
1335 A457 45c like No. 1329 .60 .20
a. Strip of 6, #1330-1335 3.75
b. Bklt. pane, #1332, 1335, 2 ea #1330-1331, 1333-1334 6.00

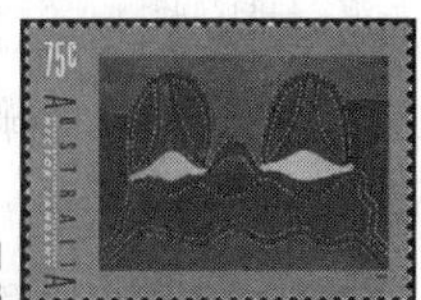

Aboriginal Art — A458

Aboriginal paintings: 45c, Black Cockatoo Feather, by Fiona Foley, vert. 75c, Ngarrgooroon Country, by Hector Jandany. $1, Ngak Ngak, by Ginger Riley. $1.05, Untitled work, by Robert Cole, vert.

Perf. 14½x14, 14x14½

1993, July 1 **Litho.**

1336 A458 45c henna brown & multi .60 .20
1337 A458 75c brown & multi 1.00 .30
1338 A458 $1 gray & multi 1.25 .55
1339 A458 $1.05 olive & multi 1.40 .60
Nos. 1336-1339 (4) 4.25 1.65

Dame Enid Lyons, MP, and Sen. Dorothy Tangney A459

No. 1340, Stylized globe, natl. arms, Inter-Parliamentary Conf. emblem.

1993, Sept. 2 **Litho.** ***Perf. 14½***

1340 A459 45c multicolored .60 .20
1341 A459 45c multicolored .60 .20
a. Pair, #1340-1341 1.25 .40

90th Inter-Parliamentary Union Conference (#1340). First women in Australian Federal Parliament, 50th anniv. (#1341). Nos. 1340-1341 printed in panes of 25 with 16 #1340 and 9 #1341. Panes with 16 #1341 and 9 #1340 were issued Nov. 19, but were available only through Philatelic Agency.

A460

A461

Dinosaurs: #1342, 1348, Ornithocheirus. #1343, 1349, Leaellynasaura. #1344, Allosaurus. #1345, Timimus. #1346, Muttaburrasaurus. #1347, Minmi.

1993, Oct. 1 ***Perf. 14x14½, 14½x14***

1342 A460 45c multi, horiz. .60 .60
1343 A460 45c multi .60 .60
1344 A461 45c multi .60 .60
1345 A461 45c multi .60 .60

Size: 29x50mm

1346 A461 75c multi .95 .35
1347 A461 $1.05 multi horiz. 1.40 .60
a. Souvenir sheet of 6, #1342-1347 4.75 4.75
b. As "a," overprinted 5.50 5.50
c. As "a," overprinted 5.50 5.50
Nos. 1342-1347 (6) 4.75 3.35

Self-Adhesive

Die Cut Perf. 11½

1348 A460 45c multi horiz. .60 .20
1349 A460 45c multi .60 .20
a. Bklt. pane, 5 each #1348-1349 6.00

Overprint in gold on sheet margin of No. 1347b contains "BANGKOK 1993" show emblem and "WORLD PHILATELIC / EXHIBITION / BANGKOK 1-10 OCTOBER 1993."

Overprint in gold on sheet margin of No. 1347c contains dinosaur and "Sydney / STAMP & COIN / SHOW / 15-17 October 1993."

Christmas — A462

1993, Nov. 1 **Litho.** ***Perf. 14½x14***

1354 A462 40c Goodwill .50 .20
a. Booklet pane of 20 10.50
1355 A462 45c Joy .60 .20
1356 A462 $1 Peace 1.25 .45
Nos. 1354-1356 (3) 2.35 .85

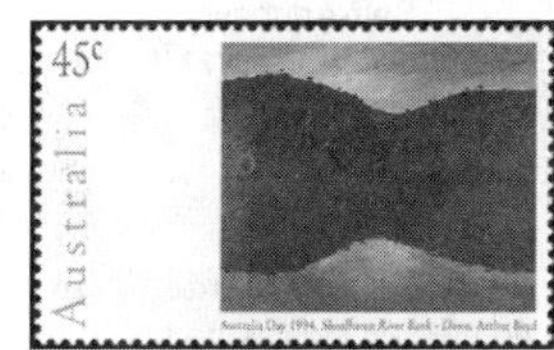

Australia Day — A463

Landscape paintings: 45c, Shoalhaven River Bank-Dawn, by Arthur Boyd. 85c, Wimmera (from Mt. Arapiles), by Sir Sidney Nolan. $1.05, Lagoon, Wimmera, by Nolan. $2, White Cockatoos in Paddock with Flame Trees, by Boyd, vert.

Perf. 14½x14, 14x14½

1994, Jan. 13 **Litho.**

1357 A463 45c multicolored .65 .20
1358 A463 85c multicolored 1.25 .40
1359 A463 $1.05 multicolored 1.50 .50
1360 A463 $2 multicolored 3.00 1.00
Nos. 1357-1360 (4) 6.40 2.10

See #1418-1421, 1476-1479, 1572-1574.

Royal Life Saving Society, Cent. A464

1994, Jan. 20 **Litho.** ***Perf. 14x14½***

1361 A464 45c Vigilance .55 .55
1362 A464 45c Education .55 .55
1363 A464 95c Drill 1.10 1.10
1364 A464 $1.20 Fitness 1.40 1.40
Nos. 1361-1364 (4) 3.60 3.60

Die Cut Perf. 11½

Self-Adhesive

1365 A464 45c like #1361 .65 .20
1366 A464 45c like #1362 .65 .20
a. Pair, #1365-1366 1.40
b. Booklet pane, 5 #1366a 7.00

Thinking of You — A465

1994, Feb. 3 **Litho.** ***Perf. 14½x14***

1367 A465 45c Rose .50 .20
1368 A465 45c Tulips .50 .20
1369 A465 45c Poppies .50 .20
a. Pair, #1368-1369 1.00 .40
b. Booklet pane, 5 #1369a 5.00
Nos. 1367-1369 (3) 1.50 .60

A466

A467

1994, Apr. 8 **Litho.** ***Perf. 14½***

1370 A466 45c multicolored .50 .20

Queen Elizabeth II, 68th birthday.

1994, Apr. 8 ***Perf. 14½x14***

1371 A467 95c multicolored 1.00 .45

Opening of Friendship Bridge, Thailand-Laos.

Intl. Year of the Family A468

Children's paintings of their families: 45c, Bobbie Lea Blackmore. 75c, Kathryn Teoh. $1, Maree McCarthy.

1994, Apr. 14 **Litho.** ***Perf. 14x14½***

1372 A468 45c multicolored .55 .20
1373 A468 75c multicolored .90 .30
1374 A468 $1 multicolored 1.25 .50
Nos. 1372-1374 (3) 2.70 1.00

Australian Women's Right to Vote, Cent. A469

1994, June 9 **Litho.** ***Perf. 14x14½***

1375 A469 45c multicolored .50 .20

Bunyips Folklore Creatures A470

Types of Bunyips: No. 1376, Aboriginal legend. No. 1377, Nature Spirit. 90c, Berkeley's Creek. $1.35, Natural history.

1994, July 14 **Litho.** ***Perf. 14x14½***

1376 A470 45c multicolored .55 .20
1377 A470 45c multicolored .55 .20
a. Pair, #1376-1377 1.00 .40
1378 A470 90c multicolored 1.00 .40
1379 A470 $1.35 multicolored 1.60 .65
Nos. 1376-1379 (4) 3.70 1.45

World War II Prime Ministers A471

Designs: a, Robert Menzies. b, Arthur Fadden. c, John Curtin. d, Francis (Frank) Forde. e, Joseph Benedict (Ben) Chifley.

1994, Aug. 11

1380 Strip of 5 2.75 1.10
a.-e. A471 45c any single .55 .20

Aviation Pioneers — A472

Designs: No. 1381, Lawrence Hargrave, box kites. No. 1382, Ross and Keith Smith, Vickers Vimy. $1.35, Ivor McIntyre, Stanley Globe, Fairey IIID A10-3 seaplane. $1.80, Freda Thompson, DeHavilland Moth Major.

1994, Aug. 29 **Engr.** ***Perf. 12***

1381 A472 45c multicolored .55 .20
1382 A472 45c multicolored .55 .20
1383 A472 $1.35 multicolored 1.60 .65
1384 A472 $1.80 multicolored 2.00 .85
Nos. 1381-1384 (4) 4.70 1.90

First England-Australia flight within 30-day time span (#1382). First aerial circumnavigation of Australia (#1383). First woman to fly solo from England-Australia (#1384).

A473

Australian Zoo Animals — A474

Perf. 14x14½, 14½x14

1994, Sept. 28 **Litho.**

1385 A473 45c Scarlet macaw .65 .65
1386 A473 45c Cheetah, vert. .65 .65
1387 A474 45c Fijian crested iguana .65 .65
1388 A474 45c Orangutan .65 .65

Size: 50x30mm

Perf. 14½x14

1389 A473 $1 Asian elephant 1.50 1.50
a. Souv. sheet of 5, #1385-1389, perf. 14½ 4.25 4.25
b. As "a," ovptd. 6.00 6.00
c. As "a," ovptd. 6.00 6.00
d. As "a," ovptd. 6.00 6.00
e. As "a," ovptd. 6.00 6.00
Nos. 1385-1389 (5) 4.10 4.10

Self-Adhesive

Die Cut Perf. 11½

1390 A473 45c like #1385 1.00 .25
1391 A473 45c like #1386 1.00 .25
a. Bklt. pane, 6 #1390, 4 #1391 10.00

Overprint in gold on sheet margin:

No. 1389b, show emblem and "Brisbane Stamp Show Zoos / October 21-23, 1994."

No. 1389c, show emblem and "SYDNEY / STAMP / AND / COIN / SHOW / 30/9/94 TO 2/10/94."

No. 1389d, show emblem and "Stampshow '94 Melbourne October 27-30 / National/State Centennial Exhibition 1894-1994."

No. 1389e, show emblem and "STAMP SHOW 94 / Fremantle Convention Centre / 5-6 November 1994."

Christmas A475

Details from Adoration of the Magi, by Giovanni Toscani: 40c, Madonna and Child, vert. 45c, One of Magi, horse and groom. $1, Joseph receiving frankincense from Magi. $1.80, Entire painting.

1994, Oct. 31 **Litho.** ***Perf. 14½x14***

1392 A475 40c multicolored .60 .20
a. Booklet pane of 20 12.00
Complete booklet, #1392a 12.00

Perf. 14x14½

1393 A475 45c multicolored .70 .25
1394 A475 $1 multicolored 1.60 .40

Size: 50x30mm

1395 A475 $1.80 multicolored 2.75 .80
Nos. 1392-1395 (4) 5.65 1.65

50th Sydney-Hobart Yacht Race — A476

Designs: a, Yachts bow-on, Sydney Opera House, Harbor Bridge. b, Two yachts abeam.

1994, Oct. 31 ***Perf. 14½***

1396 Pair 1.40 1.40
a.-b. A476 45c any single .70 .70

Self-Adhesive

Die Cut Perf. 11½

1397 A476 45c like #1396a 1.10 .25
1397A A476 45c like #1396b 1.10 .25

A477

Die Cut Perf. 17

1994, Nov. 2 **Litho.**

Self-Adhesive

Booklet Stamps

Background Color

1398 A477 45c bluish green .70 .20
1399 A477 45c blue .70 .20
1400 A477 45c purple .70 .20
1401 A477 45c yellow green .70 .20
1402 A477 45c pale yel green .70 .20
1403 A477 45c pale red brown .70 .20
1404 A477 45c rose .70 .20
1405 A477 45c orange yellow .70 .20
a. Booklet pane of 20 14.00
Nos. 1398-1405 (8) 5.60 1.60

No. 1405a contains 3 each #1399, 1401, 1403, 1405 and 2 each #1398, 1400, 1402, 1404. No. 1405a was sold in ATM machines, at the Natl. Philatelic Center, and Australian Philatelic Bureau.

Two printings differ slightly in shade and advertisement on back of pane.

Australia Day Type of 1994

Paintings: No. 1418, Back Verandah, by Russell Drysdale. No. 1419, Skull Springs Country, by Guy Grey-Smith. $1.05, Outcamp, by Robert Juniper. $1.20, Kite Flying, by Ian Fairweather.

1995, Jan. 12 **Litho.** ***Perf. 15x14½***

1418 A463 45c multicolored .70 .25
1419 A463 45c multicolored .70 .25
1420 A463 $1.05 multicolored 1.60 .40
1421 A463 $1.20 multicolored 1.75 .45
Nos. 1418-1421 (4) 4.75 1.35

St. Valentine's Day — A478

Various designs: a, Red heart. b, Red & gold heart. c, Gold heart.

1995, Feb. 6 **Litho.** ***Perf. 14½x14***

1422 Strip of 3 2.10 .75
a.-c. A478 45c any single .70 .25

See No. 1480.

Endeavour A479

#1423: a, Captain Cook's Endeavour. b, Replica.

1995, Feb. 9 **Litho.** ***Perf. 14x14½***

1423 Pair 1.40 .50
a.-b. A479 45c any single .70 .25

Booklet Stamps

Size: 44x26mm

Perf. 14 Horiz.

1424 A479 20c like #1423a 1.00 1.00
1425 A479 45c like #1423b .70 .25
a. Bklt. pane, #1424, 4 #1425 3.25
Complete booklet, #1425a 3.25

Natl. Trust, 50th Anniv. A480

Designs: No. 1426a, Coalport plate, Regency style bracket clock. No. 1426b, 15th-16th cent. x-frame Italian style chair, 19th cent. Steiner doll. $1, Advance Australia teapot, neo-classical parian-ware statuette. $2, China urn, silver bowl.

1995, Mar. 16 **Engr.** ***Perf. 14x14½***

1426 Pair 1.40 .50
a.-b. A480 45c any single .70 .25
1427 A480 $1 red brn & bl 1.50 .50
1428 A480 $2 blue & green 3.00 1.00
Nos. 1426-1428 (3) 5.90 2.00

Opals — A481

1995, Apr. 5 **Litho.** ***Perf. 14½x14***

1429 A481 $1.20 Light opal 1.75 .90
1430 A481 $2.50 Black opal 3.75 1.90

Nos. 1429-1430 each contain a holographic image. Soaking in water may affect the hologram.

See Nos. 1554-1555.

A482 A483

1995, Apr. 20 **Litho.** ***Perf. 14½***

1431 A482 45c multicolored .65 .20

Queen Elizabeth II, 69th birthday.

1995, Apr. 20 **Litho.** ***Perf. 14½x14***

Famous Australians from World War II.

1432 A483 45c Sir Edward Dunlop .65 .65
1433 A483 45c Mrs. Jessie Vasey .65 .65
1434 A483 45c Tom Derrick .65 .65
1435 A483 45c Rawdon Hume Middleton .65 .65
a. Block of 4, #1432-1435 2.60 2.60

Self-Adhesive

Die Cut Perf. 11½

1436 A483 45c like #1432 .65 .20
1437 A483 45c like #1433 .65 .20
1438 A483 45c like #1434 .65 .20
1439 A483 45c like #1435 .65 .20
a. Booklet pane, 4 #1436, 2 each #1437-1439 6.50
b. Strip of 4, #1436-1439 3.00
Nos. 1432-1439 (8) 5.20 3.40

See Nos. 1452-1455.

UN, 50th Anniv. A484

1995, May 11 **Litho.** ***Perf. 14x14½***

1440 A484 45c + label, multi .65 .20
a. Block of 4 + 4 labels 2.75 .90

No. 1440 was issued se-tenant with label in blocks of 4 + 4 labels in four designs. In alternating rows, labels appear on left or right side of stamp.

A485 A486

Poster, scene from: No. 1441, The Story of the Kelly Gang, 1906. No. 1442, On Our Selection, 1932. No. 1443, Jedda, 1955. No. 1444, Picnic at Hanging Rock, 1970s. No. 1445, Strictly Ballroom, 1992.

1995, June 8 **Litho.** ***Perf. 14½x14***

1441 A485 45c multicolored .65 .65
1442 A485 45c multicolored .65 .65
1443 A485 45c multicolored .65 .65
1444 A485 45c multicolored .65 .65
1445 A485 45c multicolored .65 .65
a. Strip of 5, #1441-1445 3.25 1.25

Self-Adhesive

Die Cut Perf. 11½

1446 A485 45c like #1441 .65 .20
1447 A485 45c like #1442 .65 .20
1448 A485 45c like #1443 .65 .20
1449 A485 45c like #1444 .65 .20
1450 A485 45c like #1445 .65 .20
a. Strip of 5, #1446-1450 3.50
b. Bklt. pane, 2 ea #1446-1450 6.50

Motion Pictures, cent.

By its nature No. 1450b constitutes a complete booklet. The peelable backing serves as a booklet cover.

1995, July 13 **Litho.** ***Perf. 14½x14***

People with Disabilities: No. 1451a, Person flying kite from wheelchair. b, Blind person playing violin, guide dog.

1451 Pair 1.25 .95
a.-b. A486 45c any single .60 .20

Famous Australians from World War II Type of 1995

1995, Aug. 10 **Litho.** ***Perf. 14½x14***

1452 A483 45c Leon Goldsworthy .65 .25
1453 A483 45c Len Waters .65 .25
1454 A483 45c Ellen Savage .65 .25
1455 A483 45c Percy Collins .65 .25
a. Block of 4, #1452-1455 2.60 2.25

Peace Types of 1946

Perf. 14x14½, 14½x14

1995, Aug. 10 **Engr.**

1456 A43 45c red brown .65 .20
1457 A45 45c dark green .65 .20
1458 A44 $1.50 dark blue 2.25 2.00
Nos. 1456-1458 (3) 3.55 2.40

End of World War II, 50th anniv.

Wildlife A487

Designs: a, Koalas. b, Pandas.

1995, Sept. 1 **Litho.** ***Perf. 14***

1459 Pair 1.25 .95
a.-b. A487 45c any single .60 .20
c. Souv. sheet #1459a, perf. 11x11½ .60 .60
d. Souv. sheet #1459b, perf. 11x11½ .60 .60
e. #1459c Ovptd. in sheet margin 1.00 1.00
f. #1459d Ovptd. in sheet margin 1.00 1.00

Overprints read: No. 1459e: "AUSTRALIAN STAMP EXHIBITION." No. 1459f: "INTERNATIONAL STAMP & COIN EXPO. / BEIJING '95."

Issued: No. 1459f, 9/14/95.

See People's Republic of China Nos. 2597-2598.

Australian Medical Discoveries A488

Designs: No. 1461a, Joseph Slattery, Thomas Lyle, Walter Filmer, x-ray pioneers. No. 1461b, Jean Macnamara, Macfarlane Burnet, viruses and immunology. No. 1461C, Fred Hollows, eye care, vert. $2.50, Howard Florey, co-discoverer of penicillin, vert.

1995, Sept. 7 ***Perf. 14x14½, 14½x14***

1461 Pair 1.25 .95
a.-b. A488 45c any single .60 .20
1461C A488 45c multicolored .60 .20
1461D A488 $2.50 multicolored 3.75 3.75
Nos. 1461-1461D (3) 5.60 4.90

No. 1461D exists in sheetlets of 10.

The World Down Under A489

Designs: Nos. 1462a, 1465a, Flatback turtle. Nos. 1462b, 1465b, Flame angelfish, nudibranch. Nos. 1463a, 1465c, Potato cod, giant maori wrasse. Nos. 1463b, 1465d, Giant trevally. Nos. 1464a, 1465e, Black marlin. Nos. 1464b, 1465f, Mako & tiger sharks.

1995, Oct. 3 **Litho.** ***Perf. 14x14½***

1462 Pair 1.25 1.25
a.-b. A489 45c any single .60 .60
1463 Pair 1.25 1.25
a.-b. A489 45c any single .60 .60
1464 Pair 1.25 1.25
a.-b. A489 45c any single .60 .60
Nos. 1462-1464 (3) 3.75 3.75

Miniature Sheet of 6

1465 A489 45c #a.-f. 4.00 3.75
g. Ovptd. in sheet margin 4.50
h. Ovptd. in sheet margin 4.50
i. Ovptd. in sheet margin 4.50
j. Ovptd. in sheet margin 4.50
k. Ovptd. in sheet margin 4.50

Nos. 1462-1464 have pale blue border on three sides. No. 1465 is a continuous design and does not have the pale border. Fish on No. 1465 are printed with additional phosphor ink producing a glow-in-the-dark effect under ultraviolet light.

Overprints in gold in sheet margin of No. 1465 include show emblems and text:

No. 1465g: "ADELAIDE / STAMP AND / COLLECTIBLES / FAIR / 14/10/95 - / 15/10/95."

No. 1465h: "SYDNEY / CENTREPOINT 95 / STAMPSHOW."

No. 1465i: "Brisbane Stamp Show / 20-22 October 1995."

No. 1465j: "Melbourne Stamp & Coin Fair / 27-29 October 1995."

No. 1465k: "Swanpex WA / 28-29 October 1995."

Booklet Stamps

Self-Adhesive

Die Cut Perf. 11½

1466 A489 45c like #1462a .65 .20
1467 A489 45c like #1462b .65 .20
1468 A489 45c like #1463a .65 .20
1469 A489 45c like #1463b .65 .20
1470 A489 45c like #1464a .65 .20
1471 A489 45c like #1464b .65 .20
a. Booklet pane, #1470-1471, 2 each #1466-1469 6.50
b. Strip of 6, #1466-1471 4.50

By its nature, No. 1471a constitutes a complete booklet. The peelable backing serves as a booklet cover.

Christmas — A490

Stained glass windows, Our Lady Help of Christians Church, Melbourne: 40c, Madonna and Child. 45c, Angel carrying banner. $1, Three rejoicing angels.

1995, Nov. 1 Litho. *Perf. 14½x14*

1472	A490 40c multicolored	.60	.60
1473	A490 45c multicolored	.65	.65
1474	A490 $1 multicolored	1.50	1.50
	Nos. 1472-1474 (3)	2.75	2.75

Booklet Stamp

Self-Adhesive

Die Cut Perf. 11½

1475 A490 40c multicolored	.60	.30
a. Booklet pane of 20	12.00	

Madonna and Child on No. 1475 are printed with additional phosphor ink giving parts of the stamp a rough texture.

By its nature, No. 1475a constitutes a complete booklet. The peelable backing serves as a booklet cover, which also contains 20 labels. The complete booklet is available with backing showing two different advertisements.

Australia Day Type of 1994

Paintings by Australian women: 45c, West Australian Banksia, by Margaret Preston, vert. 85c, The Babe is Wise, by Lina Bryans, vert. $1, The Bridge in Curve, by Grace Cossington Smith. $1.20, Beach Umbrellas, by Vida Lahey.

Perf. 14x14½, 14½x14

1996, Jan. 16 Litho.

1476 A463 45c multicolored	.65	.20
1477 A463 85c multicolored	1.25	.40
1478 A463 $1 multicolored	1.50	.50
1479 A463 $1.20 multicolored	1.75	.60
Nos. 1476-1479 (4)	5.15	1.70

Heart and Roses A491

1996, Jan. 30 *Perf. 14x14½*

1480 A491 45c gold & multi	.65	.20

See No. 1422.

Military Aviation A492

#1481, Firefly, Sea Fury. #1482, Beaufighter, Kittyhawk. #1483, Hornet. #1484, Kiowa.

1996, Feb. 26 Litho. *Perf. 14x14½*

1481 A492 45c multicolored	.70	.20
1482 A492 45c multicolored	.70	.20
1483 A492 45c multicolored	.70	.20
1484 A492 45c multicolored	.70	.20
a. Block of 4, #1481-1484	2.80	2.50

Australian World Heritage Sites Type of 1993

Designs: 45c, Tasmanian Wilderness. 75c, Willandra Lakes. 95c, Fossil Cave, Naracoorte. $1, Lord Howe Island.

1996, Mar. 14 Litho. *Perf. 14½x14*

1485 A453 45c multicolored	.70	.20
1486 A453 75c multicolored	1.25	.40
1487 A453 95c multicolored	1.40	.45
1488 A453 $1 multicolored	1.50	.50
Nos. 1485-1488 (4)	4.85	1.55

Indonesian Bear Cuscus — A493

No. 1489, Australian Spotted Cuscus.

1996, Mar. 22

1489 A493 45c multicolored	.70	.20
1490 A493 45c multicolored	.70	.20
a. Pair, Nos. 1489-1490	1.40	.95
b. Souvenir sheet, No. 1490a	1.40	1.40

No. 1490a has continuous design.

No. 1490b exists overprinted "WORLD PHILATELIC YOUTH EXHIBITION / PAMERAN FILATELI REMAJA DUNIA / INDONESIA '96." These were sold at the show, but apparently were never sold by the philatelic agency.

See Indonesia Nos. 1640-1642.

Queen Elizabeth II, 70th Birthday A494

Litho. & Engr.

1996, Apr. 11 *Perf. 14x14½*

1491 A494 45c multicolored	.70	.20

North Melbourne Kangaroos A495

Brisbane Bears A496

Sydney Swans — A497

Carlton Blues — A498

Adelaide Crows — A499

Fitzroy Lions — A500

Richmond Tigers — A501

St. Kilda Saints — A502

Melbourne Demons — A503

Collingwood Magpies — A504

Fremantle Dockers — A505

Footscray Bulldogs — A506

West Coast Eagles A507

Essendon Bombers A508

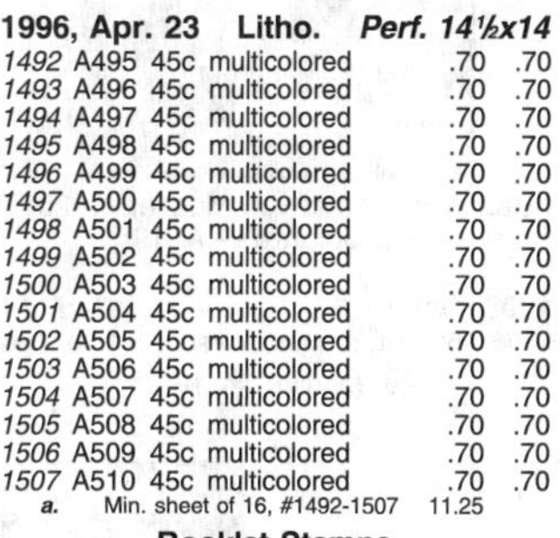

Geelong Cats — A509

Hawthorn Hawks — A510

1996, Apr. 23 Litho. *Perf. 14½x14*

1492 A495 45c multicolored	.70	.70
1493 A496 45c multicolored	.70	.70
1494 A497 45c multicolored	.70	.70
1495 A498 45c multicolored	.70	.70
1496 A499 45c multicolored	.70	.70
1497 A500 45c multicolored	.70	.70
1498 A501 45c multicolored	.70	.70
1499 A502 45c multicolored	.70	.70
1500 A503 45c multicolored	.70	.70
1501 A504 45c multicolored	.70	.70
1502 A505 45c multicolored	.70	.70
1503 A506 45c multicolored	.70	.70
1504 A507 45c multicolored	.70	.70
1505 A508 45c multicolored	.70	.70
1506 A509 45c multicolored	.70	.70
1507 A510 45c multicolored	.70	.70
a. Min. sheet of 16, #1492-1507	11.25	

Booklet Stamps

Self-Adhesive

Serpentine Die Cut 11½

1508 A495 45c multicolored	.70	.20
a. Booklet pane of 10	7.00	
1509 A496 45c multicolored	.70	.20
a. Booklet pane of 10	7.00	
1510 A497 45c multicolored	.70	.20
a. Booklet pane of 10	7.00	
1511 A498 45c multicolored	.70	.20
a. Booklet pane of 10	7.00	
1512 A499 45c multicolored	.70	.20
a. Booklet pane of 10	7.00	
1513 A500 45c multicolored	.70	.20
a. Booklet pane of 10	7.00	
1514 A501 45c multicolored	.70	.20
a. Booklet pane of 10	7.00	
1515 A502 45c multicolored	.70	.20
a. Booklet pane of 10	7.00	
1516 A503 45c multicolored	.70	.20
a. Booklet pane of 10	7.00	
1517 A504 45c multicolored	.70	.20
a. Booklet pane of 10	7.00	
1518 A505 45c multicolored	.70	.20
a. Booklet pane of 10	7.00	
1519 A506 45c multicolored	.70	.20
a. Booklet pane of 10	7.00	
1520 A507 45c multicolored	.70	.20
a. Booklet pane of 10	7.00	
1521 A508 45c multicolored	.70	.20
a. Booklet pane of 10	7.00	
1522 A509 45c multicolored	.70	.20
a. Booklet pane of 10	7.00	
1523 A510 45c multicolored	.70	.20
a. Booklet pane of 10	7.00	

By their nature, Nos. 1508a-1523a are complete booklets. The peelable paper backing serves as a booklet cover.

Australian Football League, cent.

Flora and Fauna — A511

Designs: 5c, Leadbeater's possum. 10c, Powerful owl. 20c, Saltwater crocodile, Kangkong flower. 25c, Northern dwarf tree frog, red lily. No. 1528, Little kingfisher. No. 1529, Jacana. No. 1530, Jabiru. No. 1531, Brolga. $1, Big greasy butterfly, water lily. $2, Blackwood wattle. $5, Mountain ash, fern. $10, Kakadu Wetlands during lightning storm, great egret, red lily.

Perf. 14x14½, 14½x14 (#1535)

1996-99 Litho.

1524 A511 5c multi	.20	.20
1525 A511 10c multi	.20	.20
1526 A511 20c multi	.30	.30
1527 A511 25c multi	.40	.40
1528 A511 45c multi	.70	.70
1529 A511 45c multi	.70	.70
1530 A511 45c multi	.70	.70
1531 A511 45c multi	.70	.70
a. Block of 4, #1528-1531	3.00	3.00
b. Souvenir sheet of 2, #1530-1531	1.20	
1532 A511 $1 multi	1.00	1.00
1533 A511 $2 multi	2.00	2.00

Size: 30x50mm

1534 A511 $5 multi, vert.	5.00	5.00

Size: 50x30mm

1535 A511 $10 multi	9.00	9.00
a. Souvenir sheet of 1	12.00	10.00
b. As "a," ovptd. in sheet margin	27.50	25.00
c. As "a," ovptd in sheet margin	11.00	11.00
Nos. 1524-1535 (12)	20.90	20.90

Self-Adhesive

Serpentine Die Cut 11½, 11¼ (#1539i)

1536 A511 45c like #1529	.70	.20
1537 A511 45c like #1528	.70	.20
1538 A511 45c like #1531	.70	.20
1539 A511 45c like #1530	.70	.20
a. Booklet pane, 3 ea #1536, #1538, 2 ea #1537, #1539	7.00	
b. Strip of 4, #1536-1539	2.80	
h. Sheet of 5, #1537-1539, 2 #1536	3.50	
i. Booklet pane, 5 each #1536-1539	14.00	

Serpentine Die Cut 12½x13

1539C A511 45c like #1529	.70	.20
1539D A511 45c like #1528	.70	.20
1539E A511 45c like #1531	.70	.20
1539F A511 45c like #1530	.70	.20
g. Strip of 4, #1539C-1539F	2.80	

Nos. 1536-1539 are booklet stamps.

No. 1531b is inscribed in sheet margin with Shanghai '97 emblem and "International Stamp & Coin Exposition Shanghai '97" in Chinese and English.

No. 1535b is overprinted in silver in sheet margin with PACIFIC 97 emblem and "Australia Post Exhibition Sheet No. 4."

No. 1535c is overprinted in copper in sheet margin with "PHILA NIPPON '01" and show emblem. Issued: No. 1535c, 8/1/01.

By its nature No. 1539a is a complete booklet. The peelable backing serves as a booklet cover.

Issued: 5c, 10c, $2, $5, 5/9/96; 20c, 25c, $1, $10, #1538a, 4/10/97; #1528-1531, 1536-1539, 6/2/97; #1531b, 11/17/97; #1539C-1539F, 11/13/99; No. 1539i, 9/1/98.

No. 1539i is a complete booklet.

See Nos. 1734-1746E, 1984-1995.

Modern Olympic Games, Cent. A512

#1540, Edwin Flack, 1st Australian gold medalist, runners. #1541, Fanny Durack, 1st Australian woman gold medalist, swimmers. $1.05, Paralympics, Atlanta.

Litho. & Engr.

1996, June 6 *Perf. 14x14½*

1540 A512 45c multicolored	.70	.20
1541 A512 45c multicolored	.70	.20
a. Pair, #1540-1541	1.40	1.25
1542 A512 $1.05 multicolored	1.60	1.60
Nos. 1540-1542 (3)	3.00	2.00

Transfer of Olympic Flag from Atlanta to Sydney A513

1996, July 22 Litho.

1543 A513 45c multicolored	.70	.20

Issued in sheets of 10.

Children's Book Council, 50th Anniv. A514

Covers from "Book of the Year" books: No. 1544, "Animalia." No. 1545, "Greetings from Sandy Beach." No. 1546, "Who Sank the Boat?" No. 1547, "John Brown, Rose and the Midnight Cat."

1996, July 4 Litho. *Perf. 14x14½*

1544 A514 45c multicolored .70 .70
1545 A514 45c multicolored .70 .70
1546 A514 45c multicolored .70 .70
1547 A514 45c multicolored .70 .70
a. Block of 4, #1544-1547 2.80 2.50

Serpentine Die Cut 11½

Self-Adhesive

1548 A514 45c like #1544 .70 .20
1549 A514 45c like #1546 .70 .20
1550 A514 45c like #1547 .70 .20
1551 A514 45c like #1545 .70 .20
a. Booklet pane, 4 #1548, 2 each #1549-1551 7.00
b. Strip of 4, #1548-1551 2.80

By its nature, No. 1551a is a complete booklet. The peelable paper backing serves as a booklet cover.

National Council of Women, Cent. — A515

Designs: 45c, Margaret Windeyer (1866-1939), honorary life president. $1, Rose Scott (1847-1925), founding executive member.

1996, Aug. 8 Litho. *Perf. 14½x14*

1552 A515 45c claret & yellow .70 .20
1553 A515 $1 blue & yellow 1.50 1.50

Gems Type of 1995

1996, Sept. 5 Litho. *Perf. 14½x14*

1554 A481 45c Pearl .70 .20
1555 A481 $1.20 Diamond 1.90 1.90

No. 1555 contains a round foil design. Soaking in water may affect the design.

Arts Councils in Regional Australia A516

Silhouettes of performing artists, outdoor scene: 20c, Ballet dancer, violinist, field, bales, trees. 45c, Violinist, hand holding flower, dancer, tree in field.

Perf. 14 Horiz.

1996, Sept. 12 Litho.

Booklet Stamps

1556 A516 20c multicolored 1.25 1.00
1557 A516 45c multicolored .70 .20
a. Bklt. pane, #1556, 4 #1557 3.25
Complete booklet, #1557a 3.25

A517

Pets — A518

1996-97 *Perf. 14x14½, 14½x14*

1558 A517 45c Cockatoo .70 .70
1559 A517 45c Ducks, vert. .70 .70
1560 A517 45c Dog, cat, vert. .70 .70
a. Pair, #1559-1560 1.40 1.40
1561 A518 45c Dog, puppy .70 .70
1562 A518 45c Kittens .70 .70
a. Pair, #1561-1562 1.40 1.40

Size: 29x49mm

1563 A518 45c Pony mare, foal .70 .20
a. Souvenir sheet, #1558-1563 4.25 4.25
b. As "a," ovptd. 4.25 4.25
c. As "a," ovptd. 4.25 4.25
d. As "a," ovptd. 4.25 4.25
e. As "a," ovptd. 4.25 4.25
f. As "a," ovptd. 4.25 4.25
g. As "a," ovptd. 4.25 4.25
h. As "a," ovptd. 4.25 4.25
Nos. 1558-1563 (6) 4.20 3.70

Self-Adhesive

Serpentine Die Cut 11½

1564 A518 45c like #1561 .70 .20
1565 A518 45c like #1562 .70 .20
a. Bklt. pane, 6 #1564, 4 #1565 7.00

No. 1563a is a continuous design.

Overprints in gold on sheet margin: No. 1563b, show emblem and "10TH ASIAN INTERNATIONAL PHILATELIC EXHIBITION 1996" in Chinese and English. No. 1563c, pets emblem and, "ASDA CENTREPOINT '96 STAMP AND COIN SHOW / 5-7 October 1996." No. 1563d, pets emblem and "ST PETERS STAMP & COLLECTIBLE FAIR / 12-13 OCTOBER 1996." No. 1563e, pets emblem and "MELBOURNE '96 NATIONAL PHILATELIC EXHIBITION / 17-20 OCTOBER 1996." No. 1563f, pets emblem and "QUEENSLAND SPRING STAMP AND COIN SHOW / 25-27 OCTOBER 1996." No. 1563g, pets emblem and "SWANPEX '96 / 26-27 OCTOBER 1996." No. 1563h: Hong Kong '97 emblem and "11TH ASIAN INTERNATIONAL STAMP EXHIBITION / 12-16 FEBRUARY 1997."

By its nature, No. 1565a is a complete booklet. The peelable paper backing serves as a booklet cover.

Issued: Nos. 1558-1563, 1563a, 1564-1465, 10/1/96; Nos. 1563b-1563g, 10/3/96; No. 1563h, 2/12/97.

Baron Ferdinand von Mueller (1825-96), Botanist — A519

1996, Oct. 9 *Perf. 14*

1566 A519 $1.20 multicolored 1.90 1.90

See Germany No. 1949.

Christmas — A520

1996, Nov. 1 *Perf. 14½x14*

1567 A520 40c Madonna and Child .65 .65
1568 A520 45c Wise man .70 .70
1569 A520 $1 Shepherd boy, lamb 1.50 1.50
Nos. 1567-1569 (3) 2.85 2.85

Self-Adhesive

Serpentine Die Cut 12

1570 A520 40c like #1567 .65 .20
a. Booklet pane of 20 13.00

By its nature, No. 1570a is a complete booklet. The peelable paper backing serves as a booklet cover.

Exploration of Australian Coast & Christmas Island by Willem de Vlamingh, 300th Anniv. — A521

Portrait of a Dutch Navigator, by Jan Verkolje.

1996, Nov. 1 *Perf. 14x14½*

1571 A521 45c multicolored .70 .20
a. Pair, #1571 & Christmas Is. #404 1.40 1.40

Australia Day Type of 1994

Paintings: 85c, Landscape '74, by Fred Williams. 90c, The Balcony 2, by Brett Whiteley. $1.20, Fire Haze at Gerringong, by Lloyd Rees.

1997, Jan. 16 Litho. *Perf. 14½x14*

1572 A463 85c multicolored 1.25 .40
1573 A463 90c multicolored 1.40 .45
1574 A463 $1.20 multicolored 1.90 .60
Nos. 1572-1574 (3) 4.55 1.45

Sir Donald Bradman, Cricketer A522

1997, Jan. 23 Litho. *Perf. 14½*

1575 A522 45c Portrait .70 .40
1576 A522 45c At bat .70 .40
a. Pair, No. 1575-1576 1.40 1.40

See #1634-1646, 1719-1722, 1800-1807, 1933-1936, 1941-1942.

Greetings — A523

1997, Jan. 29 *Perf. 14½x14*

1577 A523 45c Rose .70 .70

Serpentine Die Cut 11½

Booklet Stamp

Self-Adhesive

1578 A523 45c like #1577 .70 .20
a. Booklet pane of 10 7.00

By its nature, No. 1578a is a complete booklet. The peelable paper backing, which also contains 12 labels, serves as a booklet cover.

Classic Cars — A524

#1579, 1934 Ford Coupe Utility. #1580, 1948 GMH Holden 48-215 (FX). #1581, 1958 Austin Lancer. #1582, 1962 Chrysler Valiant R Series.

1997, Feb. 27 Litho. *Perf. 14x14½*

1579 A524 45c multicolored .70 .70
a. Booklet pane of 4 3.00
1580 A524 45c multicolored .70 .70
a. Booklet pane of 4 3.00
1581 A524 45c multicolored .70 .70
a. Booklet pane of 4 3.00
1582 A524 45c multicolored .70 .70
a. Booklet pane of 4 3.00
b. Block of 4, #1579-1582 3.00 3.00
Complete booklet, #1579a, 1580a, 1581a, 1582a 16.00

Complete booklet contains 2 postal cards and 16 self-adhesive labels.

Serpentine Die Cut 12

Booklet Stamps

Self-Adhesive

1583 A524 45c like #1579 .70 .20
1584 A524 45c like #1580 .70 .20
1585 A524 45c like #1581 .70 .20
1586 A524 45c like #1582 .70 .20
a. Bklt. pane, 2 ea #1583, 1585, 3 ea #1584, 1586 7.00
b. Strip of 4, #1583-1586 3.00

By its nature, No. 1586a is a complete booklet. The peelable backing serves as a booklet cover. The backing for No. 1586b is inscribed with a 3x8mm black vertical box and "SNP CAMBEC."

Circuses in Australia, 150th Anniv. — A525

#1591, Queen of the Arena, May Wirth (1894-1978). #1592, Wizard of the Wire, Con Colleano (1899-1973). #1593, Clowns. #1594, Tumblers.

1997, Mar. 13 Litho. *Perf. 14½x14*

1591 A525 45c multicolored .70 .20
1592 A525 45c multicolored .70 .20
1593 A525 45c multicolored .70 .20
1594 A525 45c multicolored .70 .20
a. Block of 4, #1591-1594 3.00 3.00

Queen Elizabeth II, 71st Birthday, 50th Wedding Anniv. A526

1997, Apr. 17 Engr. *Perf. 14x14½*

1595 A526 45c Design A50 .70 .20

A527

A528

1997, Apr. 17 *Perf. 14½x14*

1596 A527 45c multicolored .70 .20

Lions Clubs of Australia, 50th anniv.

1997, May 8 Litho. *Perf. 14½x14*

Dolls and Teddy Bears: No. 1597, Doll wearing red hat. No. 1598, Bear standing. No. 1599, Doll wearing white dress holding teddy bear. No. 1600, Doll in brown outfit. No. 1601, Teddy bear seated.

1597 A528 45c multicolored .70 .20
1598 A528 45c multicolored .70 .20
1599 A528 45c multicolored .70 .20
1600 A528 45c multicolored .70 .20
1601 A528 45c multicolored .70 .20
a. Strip of 5, #1597-1601 3.50 3.50

Nos. 1597-1601 were printed in sheets containing two strips of five. Some sheets exist overprinted in margin with picture of teddy bear and inscription "Brisbane Stamp & Coin Expo / 7-9 June 1997."

Emergency Services A529

#1602, Disaster victim evacuated. #1603, Police rescue hiker. $1.05, Rapid response saves home. $1.20, Ambulance dash saves life.

1997, July 10 Litho. *Perf. 14x14½*

1602 A529 45c multicolored .70 .20
1603 A529 45c multicolored .70 .20
a. Pair, #1602-1603 1.40 .40
1604 A529 $1.05 multicolored 1.60 1.60
1605 A529 $1.20 multicolored 1.75 1.75
Nos. 1602-1605 (4) 4.75 3.75

Arrival of Merino Sheep in Australia, Bicent. A530

Designs: No. 1606, George Peppin, Junior (1827-76), breeder, Merino sheep. No. 1607, "Pepe" chair, uses of wool.

1997, Aug. 7 Litho. *Perf. 14x14½*

1606 A530 45c multicolored .70 .20
1607 A530 45c multicolored .70 .20
a. Pair, #1606-1607 1.40 1.40

Scenes from "The Dreaming," Animated Stories for Children A531

Designs: 45c, Dumbi the Owl. $1, The Two Willy-Willies. $1.20, How Brolga Became a Bird. $1.80, Tuggan-Tuggan.

1997, Aug. 21 *Perf. 14½*

1608 A531 45c multicolored .70 .20
1609 A531 $1 multicolored 1.50 .40
1610 A531 $1.20 multicolored 1.75 .45
1611 A531 $1.80 multicolored 2.75 .70
Nos. 1608-1611 (4) 6.70 1.75

Prehistoric Animals — A532

#1612, Rhoetosaurus brownei. #1613, Mcnamaraspis kaprios. #1614, Ninjemys oweni. #1615, Paracyclotosaurus davidi. #1616, Woolungasaurus glendowerensis.

1997, Sept. 4 Litho. *Perf. 14½x14*

1612 A532 45c multicolored .65 .40
1613 A532 45c multicolored .65 .40
1614 A532 45c multicolored .65 .40
1615 A532 45c multicolored .65 .40
1616 A532 45c multicolored .65 .40
a. Strip of 5, #1612-1616 3.25 3.25

Printed in sheets of 10 stamps.

A533

Nocturnal Animals — A534

Perf. 14½x14, 14x14½

1997, Oct. 1 Litho.

1617 A533 45c Barking owl .65 .65
1618 A533 45c Spotted-tailed quoll .65 .65
a. Pair, #1617-1618 1.40 1.40
1619 A534 45c Platypus .65 .65
1620 A534 45c Brown antechinus .65 .65
1621 A534 45c Dingo .65 .65
a. Strip of 3, #1619-1621 2.00 2.00

Size: 49x29mm

1622 A534 45c Yellow-bellied glider .65 .65
a. Souvenir sheet, #1617-1622 4.00 4.00
Nos. 1617-1622 (6) 3.90 3.90

No. 1622a is printed with additional phosphor ink revealing a glow-in-the-dark spider and web under ultraviolet light.

Size: 21x32mm

Serpentine Die Cut Perf. 11½

Self-Adhesive

1623 A533 45c like #1617 .65 .20
1624 A533 45c like #1618 .65 .20
a. Booklet pane, 5 each #1623-1624 6.50
b. Pair, #1623-1624 1.40

By its nature No. 1624a is a complete booklet. The peelable paper backing serves as a booklet cover.

Breast Cancer Awareness A535

1997, Oct. 27 Litho. *Perf. 14x14½*

1625 A535 45c multicolored .65 .20

Christmas A536

Children in Christmas Nativity pageant: 40c, Angels. 45c, Mary holding Baby Jesus. $1, Three Wise Men.

1997, Nov. 3

1626 A536 40c multicolored .60 .60
1627 A536 45c multicolored .65 .65
1628 A536 $1 multicolored 1.40 1.40
Nos. 1626-1628 (3) 2.65 2.65

Booklet Stamps

Serpentine Die Cut Perf. 11½

Self-Adhesive

1629 A536 40c multicolored .60 .20
a. Booklet pane of 20 12.00

By its nature No. 1629a is a complete booklet. The peelable paper backing serves as a booklet cover, which also contains 20 labels.

Maritime Heritage — A537

1998, Jan. 15 Litho. *Perf. 14½x14*

1630 A537 45c Flying Cloud .60 .20
a. Sheet of 10 6.00 2.00
1631 A537 85c Marco Polo 1.10 .35
a. Sheet of 2, #1631 perf. 13½ & Canada #1779, perf. 13 1.75 1.75
1632 A537 $1 Chusan 1.25 .40
1633 A537 $1.20 Heather Belle 1.60 .50
Nos. 1630-1633 (4) 4.55 1.45

Australia '99 (#1630a). World Stamp Expo. (#1631a).
See Canada #1779a.
Issued: #1630a, 6/17/98; #1631a, 3/19/99.

Legends Type of 1997

Olympians: No. 1634: a, Betty Cuthbert. b, Cuthbert running. c, Herb Elliott. d, Elliott running. e, Dawn Fraser. f, Fraser swimming. g, Marjorie Jackson. h, Jackson running. i, Murray Rose. j, Rose swimming. k, Shirley Strickland. l, Strickland clearing hurdle.

1998, Jan. 21 *Perf. 14x14½*

Size: 34x27mm

1634 Sheet of 12 7.25 7.25
a.-l. A522 any single .60 .60

Booklet Stamps

Self-Adhesive

Serpentine Die Cut 11½

Size: 34x25mm

1635 A522 45c like #1634a .60 .20
1636 A522 45c like #1634b .60 .20
1637 A522 45c like #1634c .60 .20
1638 A522 45c like #1634d .60 .20
1639 A522 45c like #1634e .60 .20
1640 A522 45c like #1634f .60 .20
1641 A522 45c like #1634g .60 .20
1642 A522 45c like #1634h .60 .20
1643 A522 45c like #1634i .60 .20
1644 A522 45c like #1634j .60 .20
1645 A522 45c like #1634k .60 .20
1646 A522 45c like #1634l .60 .20
a. Bklt. pane of 12, #1635-1646 7.25

By its nature, No. 1646a is a complete booklet. The peelable backing serves as a booklet cover.

Greetings — A538

1998, Feb. 12 Litho. *Perf. 14½x14*

1647 A538 45c Champagne roses .60 .60

Booklet Stamp

Self-Adhesive

Serpentine Die Cut 11½

1648 A538 45c like #1647 .60 .20
a. Booklet pane of 10 6.00

By its nature No. 1648a is a complete booklet. The peelable paper backing, which contains 12 labels, serves as a booklet cover.

Queen Elizabeth II, 72nd Birthday A539

1998, Apr. 9 Litho. *Perf. 14x14½*

1649 A539 45c multicolored .60 .20

Royal Australian Navy Fleet Air Arm, 50th Anniv. A540

1998, Apr. 9

1650 A540 45c multicolored .60 .20

Farming in Australia A541

Designs: No. 1651, Sheep for producing wool. No. 1652, Sheaves of wheat. No. 1653, Herding cattle on horseback. No. 1654, Harvesting sugar cane. No. 1655, Dairy cattle, man on motorcycle.

1998, Apr. 21

1651 A541 45c multicolored .60 .60
1652 A541 45c multicolored .60 .60
1653 A541 45c multicolored .60 .60
1654 A541 45c multicolored .60 .60
1655 A541 45c multicolored .60 .60
a. Strip of 5, #1651-1655 3.00 3.00

Booklet Stamps

Self-Adhesive

Serpentine Die Cut 11½

Size: 37x25mm

1656 A541 45c like #1651 .60 .20
1657 A541 45c like #1652 .60 .20
1658 A541 45c like #1653 .60 .20
1659 A541 45c like #1654 .60 .20
1660 A541 45c like #1655 .60 .20
a. Bklt. pane, 2 ea #1656-1660 6.00

The peelable backing of No. 1660a serves as a booklet cover.

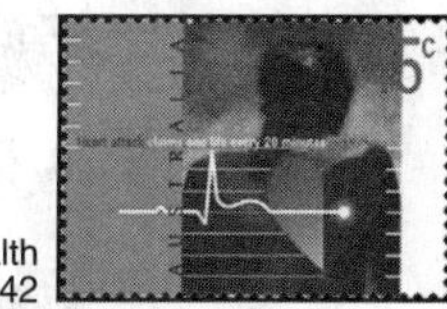

Heart Health A542

1998, May 4 Litho. *Perf. 14x14½*

1661 A542 45c multicolored .60 .20

Rock and Roll in Australia A543

a, "The Wild One," by Johnny O'Keefe, 1958. b, "Oh Yeah Uh Huh," by Col Joye and the Joye Boys, 1959. c, "He's My Blonde-headed Stompie Wompie Real Gone Surfer Boy," by Little Pattie, 1963. d, "Shakin' All Over," by Normie Rowe, 1965. e, "She's So Fine," by The Easybeats, 1965. f, "The Real Thing," by Russell Morris, 1969. g, "Turn Up Your Radio," by The Masters Apprentices, 1970. h, "Eagle Rock," by Daddy Cool, 1971. i, "Most People I Know Think That I'm Crazy," by Billy Thorpe & the Aztecs, 1972. j, "Horror Movie," by Skyhooks, 1974. k, "It's a Long Way to the Top," by AC/DC, 1975. l, "Howzat," by Sherbet, 1976.

1998, May 26

1662 A543 Sheet of 12 7.25 7.50
a.-l. 45c any single .60 .60

Coil Stamps

Self-Adhesive

Serpentine Die Cut 11½

Size: 37x25mm

1663 A543 45c like #1662a .60 .20
1664 A543 45c like #1662b .60 .20
1665 A543 45c like #1662c .60 .20
1666 A543 45c like #1662d .60 .20
1667 A543 45c like #1662e .60 .20
1668 A543 45c like #1662f .60 .20
1669 A543 45c like #1662g .60 .20
1670 A543 45c like #1662h .60 .20
1671 A543 45c like #1662i .60 .20
1672 A543 45c like #1662j .60 .20
1673 A543 45c like #1662k .60 .20
1674 A543 45c like #1662l .60 .20
a. Strip of 12 + label 7.25

Endangered Birds — A544

World Wildlife Fund: #1675, Helmeted honeyeater. #1676, Orange-bellied parrot. #1677, Red-tailed black cockatoo. #1678, Gouldian finch.

1998, June 25 *Perf. 14x14½*

1675 A544 5c multicolored .20 .20
1676 A544 5c multicolored .20 .20
a. Pair, #1675-1676 .20 .20
1677 A544 45c multicolored .60 .20
1678 A544 45c multicolored .60 .20
a. Pair, #1677-1678 1.25 1.25

Performing and Visual Arts — A545

Young people: No. 1679, Playing French horn. No. 1680, Dancing.

1998, July 16 Litho. *Perf. 14x14½*

1679 A545 45c multicolored .60 .20
1680 A545 45c multicolored .60 .20
a. Pair, #1679-1680 1.25 1.25

Orchids — A546

Designs: 45c, Phalaenopsis rosenstromii. 85c, Arundina graminifolia. $1, Grammatophyllum speciosum. $1.20, Dendrobium phalaenopsis.

1998, Aug. 6 Litho. *Perf. 14½x14*

1681 A546 45c multicolored .60 .20
1682 A546 85c multicolored 1.00 .35
1683 A546 $1 multicolored 1.25 .40
1684 A546 $1.20 multicolored 1.50 .50
a. Souvenir sheet, #1681-1684 4.50 4.50
Nos. 1681-1684 (4) 4.35 1.45

See Singapore Nos. 858-861b.

The Teapot of Truth, by Cartoonist Michael Leunig A547

#1685, Angel carrying teapot, bird with flower. #1686, Birds perched on heart-shaped vine. #1687, Characters using their heads to pour tea into cup. $1, Stylized family. $1.20, Stylized teapot with face & legs.

1998, Aug. 13 *Perf. 14x14½*

1685 A547 45c multicolored .60 .20
a. Booklet pane of 4 2.50
1686 A547 45c multicolored .60 .20
a. Booklet pane of 4 2.50
1687 A547 45c multicolored .60 .20
a. Booklet pane of 4 2.50

Size: 30x25mm

1688 A547 $1 multicolored 1.25 1.25
a. Booklet pane of 2 2.50
1689 A547 $1.20 multicolored 1.50 1.50
a. Booklet pane of 2 3.00
Complete booklet, #1685a, 1686a, 1687a, 1688a, 1689a, 1 postal card & 16 self-adhesive labels 14.00
Nos. 1685-1689 (5) 4.55 3.35

A548

A549

Butterflies.

1998, Sept. 3 Litho. *Perf. 14½x14*

1690 A548 45c Red lacewing .55 .55
1691 A548 45c Dull oakblue .55 .55
1692 A548 45c Meadow argus .55 .55
1693 A548 45c Ulysses .55 .55
1694 A548 45c Common red-eye .55 .55
a. Strip of 5, #1690-1694 2.75 2.75
b. Souv. sheet of 5, #1690-1694 3.00 3.00

No. 1694b for China 1999 World Philatelic Exhibition. Issued 8/21/99.

Self-Adhesive

Serpentine Die Cut 11½

1695 A548 45c like #1690 .55 .20
1696 A548 45c like #1691 .55 .20
1697 A548 45c like #1692 .55 .20
1698 A548 45c like #1693 .55 .20
1699 A548 45c like #1694 .55 .20
a. Strip of 5, #1695-1699 2.75

1998, Sept. 10

#1700, Sextant, map of Bass Strait. #1701, Telescope, map of Van Diemen's Land (Tasmania).

1700 A549 45c multicolored .55 .20
1701 A549 45c multicolored .55 .20
a. Pair, #1700-1701 1.10 1.10

Circumnavigation of Tasmania by George Bass (1771-c. 1803) and Matthew Flinders (1774-1814), bicent.

A550 Marine Life — A551

#1702, Fiery squid. #1703, Manta ray. #1704, Bottlenose dolphin. #1705, Weedy seadragon. #1706, Southern right whale. #1707, White pointer shark.

Perf. 14½x14, 14x14½

1998, Oct. 1 Litho.

1702 A550 45c multi .55 .55
1703 A550 45c multi, horiz. .55 .55
1704 A551 45c multi .55 .55
1705 A551 45c multi .55 .55
a. Pair, #1704-1705 1.10 1.10

Size: 50x30mm

1706 A551 45c multi, horiz. .55 .55
1707 A551 45c multi .55 .55
a. Souvenir sheet, #1702-1707 3.50 3.50
Nos. 1702-1707 (6) 3.30 3.30

Booklet Stamps

Self-Adhesive

Serpentine Die Cut Perf. 11½

1708 A551 45c like #1704 .55 .20
1709 A551 45c like #1705 .55 .20
a. Bklt. pane, 5 ea #1708-1709 5.50

No. 1709a is a complete booklet. The peelable paper backing serves as a booklet cover. Nos. 1708-1709 also exist in coils.

Universal Declaration of Human Rights, 50th Anniv. — A552

1998, Oct. 22 Litho. *Perf. 14½x14*

1712 A552 45c multicolored .60 .20

Christmas A553

40c, Magi. 45c, Nativity. $1, Journey to Bethlehem.

1998, Nov. 2 *Perf. 14x14½*

1713 A553 40c multicolored .50 .50
1714 A553 45c multicolored .60 .60
1715 A553 $1 multicolored 1.25 1.25
Nos. 1713-1715 (3) 2.35 2.35

Booklet Stamp

Self-Adhesive

Serpentine Die Cut Perf. 11½

1716 A553 40c multicolored .50 .20
a. Booklet pane of 20 10.00

No. 1716a is a complete booklet.

Nationality and Citizenship Act, 50th Anniv. A554

1999, Jan. 14 Litho. *Perf. 14x14½*

1717 A554 45c multicolored .55 .55

Die Cut Perf. 11¾

Self-Adhesive

1718 A554 45c multicolored .55 .20

Legends Type of 1997

Designs: Nos. 1719, 1721, Arthur Boyd, artist. Nos. 1720, 1722, "Nebuchadnezzar on Fire Falling over a Waterfall," by Boyd.

1999, Jan. 22 Litho. *Perf. 14x14½*

1719 A522 45c multicolored .60 .60
1720 A522 45c multicolored .60 .60
a. Pair, #1719-1720 1.25 1.25

Booklet Stamps

Self-Adhesive

Serpentine Die Cut Perf. 11½

1721 A522 45c multicolored .60 .20
1722 A522 45c multicolored .60 .20
a. Bklt. pane, 5 ea #1721-1722 6.00

No. 1722a is a complete booklet.

Love — A555

1999, Feb. 4 *Perf. 14x14½*

1723 A555 45c Red roses .60 .60

Booklet Stamp

Self-adhesive

Serpentine Die Cut Perf. 11½

1724 A555 45c like #1723 .60 .20
a. Booklet pane of 10 6.00

No. 1724a is a complete booklet.

Intl. Year of Older Persons A556

Designs: No. 1725, Woman walking with girl, man up close. No. 1726, Woman up close, man playing soccer with boy.

1999, Feb. 11 *Perf. 14x14½*

1725 A556 45c multicolored .60 .30
1726 A556 45c multicolored .60 .30
a. Pair, #1725-1726 1.25 1.25

Early Navigators Type of 1963

#1727: a, like #374. b, like #376. c, like #377.
#1728: a, like #375. b, like #379. c, like #378.

Perf. 14x14½, 14½x14

1999, Mar. 19 Litho.

1727 Sheet of 3 1.75 1.75
a.-c. A144 45c any single .55 .55
d. As #1727, imperf. 16.00 16.00
e. As #1727, perfin "A99" in sheet margin 42.50 42.50
1728 Sheet of 3 1.75 1.75
a.-c. A144 45c any single .55 .55
d. As #1728, imperf. 16.00 16.00
e. As #1728, perfin "A99" in sheet margin 42.50 42.50

Australia '99, World Stamp Expo.
Nos. 1727e-1728e were made from Nos. 1727d-1728d at Australia '99. Examples with the perforating and "A99" inverted were intentionally misperfed personally by patrons of the show.

Sailing Ships — A557

1999, Mar. 19 *Perf. 14½x14*

1729 A557 45c Polly Woodside .60 .20
a. Souvenir sheet of 2, #1729, Ireland #1173a 2.50 1.25
1730 A557 85c Alma Doepel 1.10 .35
1731 A557 $1 Enterprize 1.25 .40
1732 A557 $1.05 Lady Nelson 1.40 .45

Australia '99, World Stamp Expo (#1729a).
No. 1729 was issued in sheets of 20 with a se-tenant label showing Australia '99 logo. Panes of 10 #1729 with labels were sold only at the show, where patrons could have their photos printed on the label.

Olympic Torch — A558

1999, Mar. 22

1733 A558 $1.20 #289 1.60 .55

Flora & Fauna Type of 1996

Flowers: #1734, 1743, 1746B, Correa reflexa. #1735, 1744, 1746C, Hibbertia scandens. #1736, 1745, 1746D, Ipomoea pescaprae. #1737, 1746, 1746E, Wahlenbergia stricta.
70c, Humpback whales, zebra volute. #1739, Brahminy kite, checkerboard helmet shell. #1740, Fraser Island, chambered nautilus. $1.05, Loggerhead turtle, baler. $1.20, White-bellied sea eagle, Campbell's stromb.

1999 Litho. *Perf. 14x14½*

1734 A511 45c multicolored .60 .60
1735 A511 45c multicolored .60 .60
1736 A511 45c multicolored .60 .60
1737 A511 45c multicolored .60 .60
a. Block of 4, #1734-1737 2.40 2.40
1738 A511 70c multicolored .90 .30
1739 A511 90c multicolored 1.10 .40
1740 A511 90c multicolored 1.10 .40
a. Pair, #1739-1740 2.25 2.25
1741 A511 $1.05 multicolored 1.40 .45
1742 A511 $1.20 multicolored 1.50 .50
Nos. 1734-1742 (9) 8.40 4.45

Booklet Stamps

Serpentine Die Cut 11, 11¼ (#1742Df)

Self-Adhesive

1742A A511 45c like #1734 .60 .20
1742B A511 45c like #1735 .60 .20
1742C A511 45c like #1736 .60 .20
1742D A511 45c like #1737 .60 .20
e. Booklet pane, 3 each #1742A, 1742C, 2 each #1742B, 1742D 6.00
f. Booklet pane, 5 each #1742A-1742D 12.00

Die Cut perf. 12½x12¾

1743 A511 45c like #1734 .60 .20
1744 A511 45c like #1735 .60 .20
1745 A511 45c like #1736 .60 .20
1746 A511 45c like #1737 .60 .20
a. Booklet pane, 3 each #1743, 1745, 2 each #1744, #1746 6.00
g. Strip of 4, #1743-1746 2.40

Nos. 1742De, 1746a are complete booklets.

Coil Stamps

Serpentine Die Cut 11½

1746B A511 45c like #1734 .60 .20
1746C A511 45c like #1735 .60 .20
1746D A511 45c like #1736 .60 .20
1746E A511 45c like #1737 .60 .20
f. Strip of 4, #1746B-1746E 2.40
h. Pane, #1746B, 1746D-1746E, 2 #1746C 3.00

Issued: #1738-1742, 7/8; others, 4/8.
No. 1742Df is a complete booklet.

Queen Mother and Queen Elizabeth II — A559

1999, Apr. 15 *Perf. 14x14½*

1747 A559 45c multicolored .60 .20

Queen Elizabeth II, 73rd birthday.

Children's Television Programs — A560

Designs: #1748, 1753, "Here's Humphrey." #1749, 1754, "Bananas in Pajamas." #1750, 1755, "Mr. Squiggle." #1751, 1756, Teddy bears from "Play School." #1752, 1757, Clock, dog, boy from "Play School."

1999, May 6 Litho. *Perf. 14½x14*

1748	A560 45c multicolored	.60	.60
1749	A560 45c multicolored	.60	.60
1750	A560 45c multicolored	.60	.60
1751	A560 45c multicolored	.60	.60
1752	A560 45c multicolored	.60	.60
a.	Strip of 5, #1748-1752	3.00	3.00

Self-Adhesive

Serpentine Die Cut 11½x11¼

1753	A560 45c like #1748	.60	.20
1754	A560 45c like #1749	.60	.20
1755	A560 45c like #1750	.60	.20
1756	A560 45c like #1751	.60	.20
1757	A560 45c like #1752	.60	.20
a.	Bklt. pane, 2 ea #1753-1757	6.00	

No. 1757a is a complete booklet.

Perth Mint, Cent. A561

1999, May 13 Litho. *Perf. 14¼x14*

1758	A561 $2 gold & multi	2.50	1.25

Test Rugby in Australia, Cent. A562

#1759, 1763, Kicking ball, vert. #1760, 1764, Catching ball. $1, Diving with ball. $1.20, Being tackled.

1999, June 8 *Perf. 14½x14*

1759	A562 45c multi	.60	.60
1760	A562 45c multi, vert.	.60	.60
a.	Pair, #1759-1760	1.25	1.25

Perf. 14x14½

1761	A562 $1 multi	1.25	.40
1762	A562 $1.20 multi	1.50	.55

Serpentine Die Cut 11½

Self-Adhesive

Coil Stamps

1763	A562 45c like #1759	.60	.20
1764	A562 45c like #1760	.60	.20
a.	Pair, #1763-1764	1.25	

Snowy Mountains Hydroelectric Projects, 50th Anniv. A563

#1765, Rock bolters at Tumut 2 Power Station Hall, driller at Tooma-Tumut Tunnel. #1766, English class for migrant workers at Cooma. #1767, Eucumbene Dam, Tumut 2 Tailwater Tunnel. #1768, Island Bend Dam, German carpenters.

1999, Aug. 12 Litho. *Perf. 14x14½*

1765	A563 45c multicolored	.60	.60
1766	A563 45c multicolored	.60	.60
1767	A563 45c multicolored	.60	.60
1768	A563 45c multicolored	.60	.60
a.	Block of 4, #1765-1768	2.40	2.40

Self-Adhesive

Coil Stamps

Litho.

Serpentine Die Cut 11¾

1769	A563 45c Like #1765	.60	.30
1770	A563 45c Like #1766	.60	.30
1771	A563 45c Like #1767	.60	.30
1772	A563 45c Like #1768	.60	.30
a.	Strip of 4, #1769-1772	2.40	

Greetings A564

1999-2002 Litho. *Perf. 14½x14*

1773	A564 45c Teddy bear	.60	.20
1774	A564 45c Birthday cake	.60	.20
1775	A564 45c Roses, rings	.60	.20
a.	Booklet pane of 4 ('02)	2.40	—
	Booklet, 5 #1775a	12.00	
1776	A564 45c Pen, letter	.60	.20
1777	A564 45c Christmas ornament	.60	.20
1778	A564 $1 Koala	1.25	.40
	Nos. 1773-1778 (6)	4.25	1.40

Nos. 1773-1778 each were printed with a se-tenant label at right in sheets of 20. Size of label is 24mm wide on No. 1777, 19mm wide on No. 1775a, 17mm on others. Labels were inscribed with phrases appropriate to the stamp design, or blank, upon which Australia Post printed photographs, sent to them through special orders. No. 1775a comes with five different margins, each of which is found in the booklet, which sold for $9.95.

Issued: Nos. 1773-1778, 9/1/99; No. 1775a, 3/12/02.

See No. 1926.

2000 Olympic Games, Sydney — A565

1999, Sept. 14 Litho. *Perf. 14½x14*

1779	A565 45c multicolored	.60	.20

Sydney Design 99, Intl. Design Congress A566

Designs: 45c, Australia Post emblem. 90c, Embryo chair. $1.35, Possum skin textile design. $1.50, Storey Hall, Royal Melbourne Institute of Technology.

1999, Sept. 16 Litho. *Perf. 14x14½*

1780	A566 45c multicolored	.60	.20
1781	A566 90c multicolored	1.10	.40
1782	A566 $1.35 multicolored	1.75	.60
1783	A566 $1.50 multicolored	2.00	.65
	Nos. 1780-1783 (4)	5.45	1.85

Pond Fauna — A567

Designs: Nos. 1784, 1790c, Roth's tree frog. Nos. 1785, 1790d, Dragonfly. Nos. 1786, 1790b, Sacred kingfisher. Nos. 1787, 1790f, Magnificent tree frog. Nos. 1788, 1790e, 1791, Northern dwarf tree frog. Nos. 1789, 1790a, 1792, Javelin frog.

No. 1793, Sacred kingfisher. No. 1794, Magnificent tree frog.

1999, Oct. 1 Litho. *Perf. 14x14½*

1784	A567 45c multicolored	.60	.60
1785	A567 45c multicolored	.60	.60
a.	Pair, #1784-1785	1.25	1.25

Size: 26x38mm

Perf. 14½x14

1786	A567 45c multicolored	.60	.60
1787	A567 45c multicolored	.60	.60
a.	Pair, #1786-1787	1.25	1.25

Size: 24x30mm

1788	A567 50c multicolored	.70	.70
1789	A567 50c multicolored	.70	.70
a.	Pair, #1788-1789	1.40	1.40
	Nos. 1784-1789 (6)	3.80	3.80

Souvenir Sheet

Perf. 14½

1790	A567 Sheet of 6, #a-f	4.00	4.00
g.	Ovptd. in sheet margin	4.00	4.00

No. 1790d has foil impression on dragonfly's wings.

No. 1790 with overprints for Victorian and South Australian Philatelic Congresses in 1999 are unofficial.

No. 1790g issued 3/25/00 overprinted in sheet margin "BANGKOK 2000 / 25 March - 3 April 2000" and show emblem.

Self-Adhesive

Serpentine Die Cut 11¼

Size: 24x30mm

1791	A567 50c multicolored	.70	.25
1792	A567 50c multicolored	.70	.25
a.	Bklt. pane, 5 ea #1791-1792	7.00	

Nos. 1791-1792 are booklet stamps. No. 1792a is a complete booklet.

Die Cut Perf. 11¾

Size: 26x38mm

1793	A567 45c multi	.60	.20
1794	A567 45c multi	.60	.20
a.	Pair, #1793-1794	1.20	

Christmas A568

1999, Nov. 1 *Perf. 14½x14*

1795	A568 40c Madonna and child, vert.	.50	.50

Perf. 14x14½

1796	A568 $1 Tree	1.25	.40

Booklet Stamp

Self-Adhesive

Serpentine Die Cut 11¾

1797	A568 40c Like #1795	.50	.20
a.	Booklet pane of 20	10.00	

Celebrate 2000 — A569

1999, Nov. 1 Litho. *Perf. 14½x14*

1798	A569 45c multicolored	.60	.20

No. 1798 has a holographic image. Soaking in water may affect hologram. No. 1798 printed with a se-tenant label at right in sheets of 20. Labels were inscribed "Celebrate 2000" or blank, upon which Australia Post printed photographs, sent to them through special orders.

Sheets of 10 stamps plus 10 photo labels have been available at special events. These have the sheet selvage inscribed for each event. Most of these have been available only at the event and exist in very limited quantities.

Sheets of 10 also exist with 10 labels inscribed "Celebrate 2000."

Faces of Australia — A570

Ordinary people: a, Nicholle and Meghan Triandis, baby twins. b, David Willis, cattleman with hat. c, Natasha Bramley, with snorkel gear. d, Cyril Watson, Aboriginal boy. e, Mollie Dowdall, with red hat. f, Robin Dicks, in khaki uniform. g, Mary Simons, with gray hair. h, Peta and Samantha Nieuwerth, mother and daughter. i, Dr. John Matthews, with stethoscope. j, Edith Dizon-Fitzsimmons, with large earrings. k, Philippa Weir, with brown hat. l, John Thurgar, with suit, tie and hat. m, Miguel Alzona, with large, multicolored hat. n, Rachael Thomson, girl with wavy hair. o, Necip Akarsu, with mustache. p, Justin Allan, with HMAS Brisbane cap. q, Wadad Dennaoui, with checked blouse. r, Jack Laity, with hat and jacket. s, Kelsey Stubbin, with Australia cap. t, Gianna Rossi, with hand on chin. u, Paris Hansch, young girl. v, Donald George Whatham, in shirt and tie. w, Stacey Coull, Aboriginal girl in patterned blouse. x, Alex Payne, with bicycle helmet. y, John Lodge, with Salvation Army hat.

2000. Jan. 1 Litho. *Perf. 14¾x13¾*

1799	Sheet of 25	14.50	14.50
a.-y.	A570 45c Any single	.55	.40

Legends Type of 1997

Aging veterans of World War I: Nos. 1800, 1804, Walter Parker. Nos. 1801, 1805, Roy Longmore. Nos. 1802, 1806, Alec Campbell . Nos. 1803, 1807, 1914-15 Star.

2000, Jan. 21 Litho. *Perf. 14x14¾*

Size: 34x25mm

1800	A522 45c multi	.55	.55
1801	A522 45c multi	.55	.55
1802	A522 45c multi	.55	.55
1803	A522 45c multi	.55	.55
a.	Block of 4, #1800-1803	2.25	2.25

Self-Adhesive

Die Cut Perf. 11¾

1804	A522 45c multi	.55	.25
1805	A522 45c multi	.55	.25
1806	A522 45c multi	.55	.25
1807	A522 45c multi	.55	.25
a.	Complete booklet, 2 each #1804-1806, 4 #1807	5.50	

A571

A572

2000, Feb. 24 Litho. *Perf. 14¾x14*

Arts festivals.

1808	A571 45c Perth	.55	.25
1809	A571 45c Adelaide	.55	.25
1810	A571 45c Sydney	.55	.25
1811	A571 45c Melbourne	.55	.25
1812	A571 45c Brisbane	.55	.25
a.	Strip of 5, #1808-1812	2.75	1.25

2000, Mar. 23 Litho. *Perf. 14¾x14*

Gardens: #1813, 1818, 1823, Coast banksia, false sarsaparailla, swamp bloodwood (denomination at UR). #1814, 1819, 1824, Swamp bottlebrush, Eastern spinebill (denomination at UL). #1815, 1820, 1825, Canna X generalis varieties (denomination at LL). #1816, 1821, 1826, Pond, roses, purple swamphen (denomination at UR). #1817,

1822, 1927, Pond, hibiscus, nerium oleander (denomination at UL).

1813 A572 45c multi .55 .55
1814 A572 45c multi .55 .55
1815 A572 45c multi .55 .55
1816 A572 45c multi .55 .55
1817 A572 45c multi .55 .55
a. Horiz. strip, #1813-1817 2.75 2.75

Booklet Stamps
Self-Adhesive
Serpentine Die Cut 11½x11¼
Pale Green Frames

1818 A572 45c multi .55 .25
1819 A572 45c multi .55 .25
1820 A572 45c multi .55 .25
1821 A572 45c multi .55 .25
1822 A572 45c multi .55 .25
a. Booklet, 2 each #1818-1822 5.50
Nos. 1818-1822 (5) 2.75 1.25

Coil Stamps
Self-Adhesive
Serpentine Die Cut 11¾
Pale Green Frames

1823 A572 45c multi .55 .25
1824 A572 45c multi .55 .25
1825 A572 45c multi .55 .25
1826 A572 45c multi .55 .25
1827 A572 45c multi .55 .25
a. Strip of 5, #1823-1827 2.75

Queen Elizabeth II, 74th Birthday A573

2000, Apr. 13 Litho. *Perf. 14x14¾*
1828 A573 45c multi .55 .25

Korean War, 50th Anniv. A574

2000, Apr. 18
1829 A574 45c multi .55 .25

Daisy — A575

Australia on Globe, Southern Cross — A576

Kangaroo and Flag — A577

Sand, Sea and Sky — A578

Rainforest A579

2000, May 11 *Perf. 14½x14*
1830 A575 45c multi + label .55 .25
1831 A576 45c multi + label .55 .25
1832 A577 45c multi + label .55 .25
a. Sheet of 10 + 10 labels 10.50 10.50
1833 A578 45c multi + label .55 .25
1834 A579 45c multi + label .55 .25
Nos. 1830-1834 (5) 2.75 1.25

Nos. 1830-1834 each issued in sheets of 20 stamps and labels, with and without decorative selvage.

Sheets containing 10 No. 1831 with margins and ten labels that could be personalized were sold for $12, $2 of which was donated to volunteer organizations of the purchaser's choice. Volunteer organizations could purchase these sheets and offer them for resale in fundraising projects.

No. 1832a sold for $16. Sheet has decorative selvage and labels showing stock photo.

The Move Towards Federation — A580

Designs: No. 1835, Taking the vote. No. 1836, Waiting for the results. No. 1837, The fair new nation. No. 1838, Queen Victoria.

2000, May 22 *Perf. 14¾x14*
1835 A580 45c multi .55 .25
1836 A580 45c multi .55 .25
a. Pair, #1835-1836 1.10 .50

Size: 30x50mm
Perf. 14x14½

1837 A580 $1.50 multi 1.90 .95
1838 A580 $1.50 multi 1.90 .95
a. Pair, #1837-1838 3.80 1.90
b. Souvenir sheet, #1836a, 1838a 5.00 2.40
c. As "b," with marginal inscription for The Stamp Show 2000, London 5.00 2.40
Nos. 1835-1838 (4) 4.90 2.40

Tourist Attractions — A581

Designs: 50c, Sydney Opera House. $1, Nandroya Falls. $1.50, Sydney Harbour Bridge. $2, Cradle Mountain. $3, The Pinnacles. $4.50, Flinders Ranges. $5, Twelve Apostles. $10, Devils Marbles.

2000, June 20 Litho. *Perf. 14½x14*
1839 A581 50c multi .60 .30
1840 A581 $1 multi 1.25 .60
1841 A581 $1.50 multi 1.90 .95
1842 A581 $2 multi 2.50 1.25
1843 A581 $3 multi 3.75 1.90

Size: 56x25mm
Perf. 14x14½

1844 A581 $4.50 multi 5.50 2.75
1845 A581 $5 multi 6.00 3.00
1846 A581 $10 multi 12.00 6.00
Nos. 1839-1846 (8) 33.50 16.75

See No. 1925, 1979-1983.

2000 Paralympics, Sydney — A582

#1847, 1855, Wheelchair tennis. #1848, 1856, Amputee running. #1849, 1853, Wheelchair basketball. #1850, 1852, Cycling for the visually impaired. #1851, 1854, Amputee shot put.

2000, July 3 Litho. *Perf. 14¾x14*
1847 A582 45c multi .55 .55
1848 A582 45c multi .55 .55
a. Pair, #1847-1848 1.10 1.10
1849 A582 49c multi .60 .60
1850 A582 49c multi .60 .60
1851 A582 49c multi .60 .60
a. Strip of 3, #1849-1851 1.80 1.80

Booklet Stamps
Self-Adhesive
Die Cut Perf. 11½x11¾

1852 A582 49c multi .60 .30
1853 A582 49c multi .60 .30
1854 A582 49c multi .60 .30
a. Bklt., 4 ea #1852-1853, 2 #1854 6.00

Coil Stamps
Self-Adhesive
Serpentine Die Cut 11¾

1855 A582 45c multi .55 .25
1856 A582 45c multi .55 .25
a. Pair, #1855-1856 1.10

Australian Victoria Cross, Cent. — A583

#1857, Sir Neville Howse. #1858, Sir Arthur Roden Cutler. #1859, Victoria Cross. #1860, Edward Kenna. #1861, Keith Payne.

2000, July 24 Litho. *Perf. 14¾x14*
1857 A583 45c multi .55 .25
1858 A583 45c multi .55 .25
1859 A583 45c multi .55 .25
1860 A583 45c multi .55 .25
1861 A583 45c multi .55 .25
a. Horiz. strip of 5, #1857-1861 2.75 1.25

Olympic Sports — A584

#1862a, 1869, Water polo. #1862b, 1870, Women's field hockey. #1862c, 1863, Swimming. #1862d, 1865, Basketball. #1862e, 1866, Triathlon cycling. #1862f, 1871, Equestrian. #1862g, 1873, Tennis. #1862h, 1864, Rhythmic gymnastics. #1862i, 1867, Runner. #1862j, 1868, Rowing.

2000, Aug. 17 Litho. *Perf. 14¾x14*
1862 Sheet of 10 5.00 5.00
a.-j. A584 45c Any single .50 .50
k. As #1862, with inscription added in sheet margin 5.00 5.00

No. 1862k was issued 9/15/00 and has additional multicolored inscription in upper sheet margin reading "15-28 / September / 2000 / OLYMPHILEX 2000" and show emblem.

Booklet Stamps
Self-Adhesive
Serpentine Die Cut 11½x11¼

1863 A584 45c multi .50 .25
1864 A584 45c multi .50 .25
1865 A584 45c multi .50 .25
1866 A584 45c multi .50 .25
1867 A584 45c multi .50 .25
1868 A584 45c multi .50 .25
1869 A584 45c multi .50 .25
1870 A584 45c multi .50 .25
1871 A584 45c multi .50 .25
1872 A584 45c multi .50 .25
a. Booklet, #1863-1872 5.00

Sydney and Athens — A585

Olympic torch, flag and: 45c, Parthenon. $1.50, Sydney Opera House.

2000, Sept. 15 Litho. *Perf. 14½x14*
1873 A585 45c multi + label .50 .25
1874 A585 $1.50 multi + label 1.60 .80

See Greece Nos. 1968-1969.

Australian Gold Medalists at 2000 Olympics A586

Cathy Freeman Lighting Olympic Flame — A587

#1875, 1891, Ian Thorpe. #1876, 1892, Men's 4x100-meter freestyle relay swimming team. #1877, 1893, Michael Diamond. #1878, 1894, Three day event equestrian team. #1879, 1895, Susie O'Neill. #1880, 1896, Men's 4x200-meter freestyle relay swimming team. #1881, 1897, Simon Fairweather. #1882, 1898, Brett Aitken, Scott McGrory. #1883, 1899, Grant Hackett. #1884, 1900, Women's water polo team. #1885, 1901, Natalie Cook, Kerri Pottharst. #1886, 1902, Cathy Freeman. #1887, 1903, Lauren Burns. #1888, 1904, Women's field hockey team. #1889, 1905, Jenny Armstrong, Belinda Stowell. #1890, 1906, Tom King, Mark Turnbull.

2000 Digitally Printed *Perf. 14¼*
1875 A586 45c multi .50 .50
1876 A586 45c multi .50 .50
1877 A586 45c multi .50 .50
1878 A586 45c multi .50 .50
1879 A586 45c multi .50 .50
1880 A586 45c multi .50 .50
1881 A586 45c multi .50 .50
1882 A586 45c multi .50 .50
1883 A586 45c multi .50 .50
1884 A586 45c multi .50 .50
1885 A586 45c multi .50 .50
1886 A586 45c multi .50 .50
1887 A586 45c multi .50 .50
1888 A586 45c multi .50 .50
1889 A586 45c multi .50 .50
1890 A586 45c multi .50 .50

Litho.

1891 A586 45c multi .50 .40
1892 A586 45c multi .50 .40
1893 A586 45c multi .50 .40
1894 A586 45c multi .50 .40
1895 A586 45c multi .50 .40
1896 A586 45c multi .50 .40
1897 A586 45c multi .50 .40
1898 A586 45c multi .50 .40
1899 A586 45c multi .50 .40
1900 A586 45c multi .50 .40
1901 A586 45c multi .50 .40
1902 A586 45c multi .50 .40
1903 A586 45c multi .50 .40
1904 A586 45c multi .50 .40
1905 A586 45c multi .50 .40
1906 A586 45c multi .50 .40
1907 A587 45c multi .50 .40
Nos. 1875-1907 (33) 16.50 14.80

Issued: #1875, 1876, 1891, 1892, 9/17; #1877, 1893, 9/18; #1878-1880, 1894-1896, 9/20; #1881, 1897, 9/21; #1882, 1898, 9/22; #1883, 1884, 1899, 1900, 9/24; #1885, 1886, 1901, 1902, 9/26; #1887, 1903, 9/28; #1888, 1904, 9/30; #1889, 1890, 1905, 1906, 10/1; #1907, 10/10.

#1875-1890 have shinier appearance than #1891-1906. Olympic rings, flag stars and flag edge on #1875-1890 has a more ragged appearance than #1891-1906, which have crisp details.

#1875-1907 printed in sheets of 10. Sheets of #1875-1890 have rouletted right margin and one of six red animal imprints in lower right margin representing where the sheets were made (Platypus, Sydney; Kookaburra, Canberra; Koala, Brisbane; Swan, Perth; Kangaroo, Adelaide; Opossum, Melbourne). Sheets of #1875-1890 were placed on sale at 67 outlets within 24 hours of the awarding of the medals to the athletes. Sheets of #1891-1906, which have a straight-edged right margin and a red Australia map imprint in lower right margin, gradually became available nationwide as stocks were printed and shipped.

A sheet containing Nos. 1891-1907 and 8 labels was available only in the Australia Post annual collection. Value, $8.50.

Space — A588

#1908, 1914a, Flight crew. #1909, 1914b, Robots, vert. #1910, 1914c, 1915, 1917, Astronaut, vert. #1911, 1914d, 1916, 1918, Terrain, vert. #1912, 1914e, Spacecraft. #1913, 1914f, Launch site, vert.

Perf. 14x14½, 14½x14

2000, Oct. 3 Litho.

1908	A588 45c multi		.50	.50
1909	A588 45c multi		.50	.50

Size: 26x38mm

1910	A588 45c multi		.50	.50
1911	A588 45c multi		.50	.50
a.	Pair, #1910-1911		1.00	1.00

Size: 50x30mm

1912	A588 45c multi	.50	.50

Size: 30x50mm

1913	A588 45c multi	.50	.50
	Nos. 1908-1913 (6)	3.00	3.00

Souvenir Sheet

Litho. with Translucent Foil

Perf. 14½

1914	Sheet of 6	3.00	3.00
a.-f.	A588 45c any single	.50	.50
g.	As #1914, ovptd. in margin in gold	3.00	3.00

Booklet Stamps

Litho.

Self-Adhesive

Serpentine Die Cut 11½x11¼

1915	A588 45c multi	.50	.25
1916	A588 45c multi	.50	.25
a.	Booklet, 5 each #1915-1916	5.00	

Coil Stamps

Serpentine Die Cut 11½

1917	A588 45c multi	.50	.25
1918	A588 45c multi	.50	.25
a.	Pair, #1917-1918	1.00	.50

Nos. 1915-1918 have pink and gray frames.

No 1914g overprinted with emblem of Hong Kong 2001 Stamp Exhibition. Issued 2/1/01.

2000 Paralympics, Sydney — A589

Designs: No. 1919, Paralympics emblem. No. 1920, Runner with torch.

2000, Oct. 18 Litho. *Perf. 14½x14*

1919	A589 45c multi + label	.50	.25
1920	A589 45c multi + label	.50	.25

Siobhan Paton, Paralympian of the Year — A590

2000, Oct. 31 *Perf. 14¼*

1921	A590 45c multi	.50	.25

Christmas — A591

40c, Madonna and child. 45c, Manger.

2000, Nov. 1 Litho. *Perf. 14½x14*

1922	A591 40c multi	.45	.45
1923	A591 45c multi	.50	.25
a.	Souvenir sheet, #1922-1923	.95	.45

Booklet Stamp

Serpentine Die Cut 11¾

1924	A591 40c multi	.45	.20
a.	Booklet of 20 + 20 stickers	9.00	

Tourist Attractions Type of 2000

2000, Nov. 1 *Perf. 14½x14*

1925	A581 80c Byron Bay	.85	.45

No. 1778 Overprinted in Dark Blue

2001, Jan. Litho. *Perf. 14½x14*

1926	A564 $1 multi + label	1.10	.40

Federation of Australia, Cent. — A592

Designs: Nos. 1927, 1931, Federation Arch, Sydney. Nos. 1928, 1932, Sir Edmund Barton, first prime minister. No. 1929, National celebrations, horiz (50x30mm). No. 1930, State banquet (30x50mm).

Perf. 14¾x14, 14x14¾

2001, Jan. 1 Litho.

1927	A592 49c multi	.55	.55
1928	A592 49c multi	.55	.55
a.	Pair, #1927-1928	1.10	1.10
1929	A592 $2 multi	2.25	1.10
1930	A592 $2 multi	2.25	1.10
a.	Souvenir sheet, #1927-1930, perf. 14½	5.75	2.75

Self-Adhesive

Booklet Stamps

Serpentine Die Cut 11½x11

1931	A592 49c multi	.55	.25
1932	A592 49c multi	.55	.25
a.	Booklet, 5 each # 1931-1932	5.50	
	Nos. 1927-1932 (6)	6.70	3.80

Australian Legends Type of 1997

Slim Dusty, musician: Nos. 1933, 1935, With guitar. Nos. 1934, 1936, Wearing blue shirt.

2001, Jan. 25 *Perf. 14x14¾*

Size: 34x26mm

1933	A522 45c multi	.50	.50
1934	A522 45c multi	.50	.50
a.	Pair, #1933-1934	1.00	1.00

Self-Adhesive

Booklet Stamps

Serpentine Die Cut 11x11½

1935	A522 45c multi	.50	.25
1936	A522 45c multi	.50	.25
a.	Booklet, 5 each #1935-1936	5.00	
	Nos. 1933-1936 (4)	2.00	1.50

Australian Army, Cent. A593

Rising Sun badge and: No. 1937, Light Horse Brigade, 1940, soldiers in New Guinea, 1943. No. 1938, Soldier in UN peacekeeping mission carrying Rwandan child, 1995, soldiers on commando officer selection course, 1997.

2001, Feb. 15 *Perf. 14x14¾*

1937	A593 45c multi	.50	.25
1938	A593 45c multi	.50	.25
a.	Pair, #1937-1938	.50	.25

Opening of National Museum, Canberra A594

Designs: No. 1939, Museum floor plan. No. 1940, Pangk (wallaby sculpture), by George MacNaught and Joe Ngallametta.

2001, Mar. 8

1939	A594 49c multi	.50	.25
1940	A594 49c multi	.50	.25
a.	Pair, #1939-1940	1.00	.50

Australian Legends Type of 1997

Similar to Nos. 1575-1576, but with cropped designs and "1908-2001" inscription added.

2001, Mar. 13 *Perf. 14¼*

1941	A522 45c Like #1575	.45	.25
1942	A522 45c Like #1576	.45	.25
a.	Pair, #1941-1942	.90	.50

Rock Music A595

Designs: Nos. 1943a, 1953, Khe Sanh, by Cold Chisel, 1978. Nos. 1943b, 1952, Down Under, by Men at Work, 1981. Nos. 1943c, 1951, Power and the Passion, by Midnight Oil, 1983. Nos. 1943d, 1950, Original Sin, by INXS. Nos. 1943e, 1949, You're the Voice, by John Farnham, 1986. Nos. 1943f, 1948, Don't Dream It's Over, by Crowded House, 1986. Nos. 1943g, 1947, Treaty, by Yothu Yindi, 1991. Nos. 1943h, 1946, Tomorrow, by Silverchair, 1994. Nos. 1943i, 1945, Confide in Me, by Kylie Minogue, 1994. Nos. 1943j, 1944, Truly, Madly, Deeply, by Savage Garden, 1997.

2001, Mar. 20 Litho. *Perf. 14x14¾*

1943	Sheet of 10	4.50	4.50
a.-j.	A595 45c Any single	.45	.45

Self-Adhesive

Serpentine Die Cut 11¼x11½

1944	A595 45c multi	.45	.25
1945	A595 45c multi	.45	.25
1946	A595 45c multi	.45	.25
1947	A595 45c multi	.45	.25
1948	A595 45c multi	.45	.25
1949	A595 45c multi	.45	.25
1950	A595 45c multi	.45	.25
1951	A595 45c multi	.45	.25
1952	A595 45c multi	.45	.25
1953	A595 45c multi	.45	.25
a.	Horiz. strip of 10, #1944-1953	4.50	
b.	Booklet, #1944-1953	4.50	

Queen Elizabeth II, 75th Birthday — A596

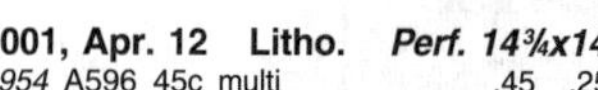

2001, Apr. 12 Litho. *Perf. 14¾x14*

1954	A596 45c multi	.45	.25

Flower — A597

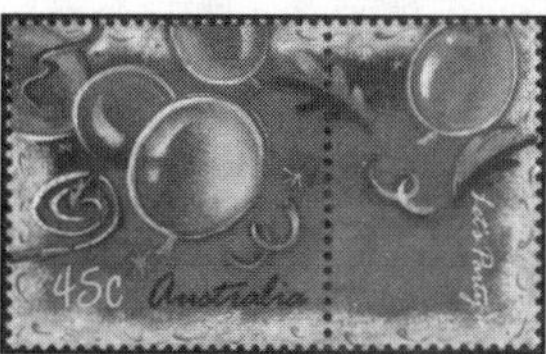

Balloons — A598

Streamers — A599

Kangaroos — A600

Bayulu Banner — A601

Litho., Litho with Hologram (#1957)

2001, Apr. 24 *Perf. 14½x14*

1955	A597 45c multi + label	.45	.25
1956	A598 45c multi + label	.45	.25
1957	A599 45c multi + label	.45	.25
1958	A600 $1 multi + label	1.00	.50
1959	A601 $1.50 multi + label	1.60	.80
	Nos. 1955-1959 (5)	3.95	2.05

Federal Parliament, Cent. — A602

Designs: No. 1960, The Opening of the First Federal Parliament, 9 May 1901, by Charles Nuttall. No. 1961, Opening of the First Parliament of the Commonwealth of Australia by H.R.H. The Duke of Cornwall and York (Later King George V), May 9, 1901, by Tom Roberts.

2001, May 3 Litho. *Perf. 14¼*

1960	A602 45c multi	.45	.25
a.	Souvenir sheet of 1	.45	.25
1961	A602 $2.45 multi	2.60	1.25
a.	Souvenir sheet of 1	2.60	1.25

Outback Services A603

Designs: Nos. 1962, 1967, 1972, Telecommunications. Nos. 1963, 1968, 1973, Transport. Nos. 1964, 1969, 1974, School of the Air. Nos. 1965, 1970, 1975, Postal service. Nos., 1966, 1971, 1976, Royal flying Doctor Service.

2001, June 5 *Perf. 14x14½*

1962	A603 45c multi	.45	.45
1963	A603 45c multi	.45	.45
1964	A603 45c multi	.45	.45
1965	A603 45c multi	.45	.45
1966	A603 45c multi	.45	.45
a.	Horiz. strip, #1962-1966	2.25	2.25

Self-Adhesive
Coil Stamps
Serpentine Die Cut 11¼

1967 A603 45c multi .45 .25
1968 A603 45c multi .45 .25
1969 A603 45c multi .45 .25
1970 A603 45c multi .45 .25
1971 A603 45c multi .45 .25
a. Horiz. strip, #1967-1971 2.25

Booklet Stamps
Serpentine Die Cut 11¾

1972 A603 45c multi .45 .25
1973 A603 45c multi .45 .25
1974 A603 45c multi .45 .25
1975 A603 45c multi .45 .25
1976 A603 45c multi .45 .25
a. Booklet, 2 each #1972-1976 4.50
Nos. 1962-1976 (15) 6.75 4.75

Dragon Boat Races A604

Dragon boats and: 45c, Hong Kong Convention and Exhibition Center. $1, Sydney Opera House.

2001, June 25 ***Perf. 14x14½***
1977 A604 45c multi .45 .25
1978 A604 $1 multi 1.00 .50
a. Souvenir sheet, #1977-1978 1.45 .75

See Hong Kong Nos. 938-939.

Tourist Attraction Type of 2000

Designs: 50c, Blue Mountains. $1, Murrumbidgee River. $1.50, Port Douglas. $20, Uluru.

Litho., Litho with Foil Application ($20)

2001, July 12 ***Perf. 14½x14***
1979 A581 50c multi .50 .50
1980 A581 $1 multi 1.00 1.00
1981 A581 $1.50 multi 1.50 1.50

Size: 56x25mm
Perf. 14x14½
1982 A581 $20 multi 20.00 10.00
Nos. 1979-1982 (4) 23.00 13.00

Booklet Stamp
Self-Adhesive
Serpentine Die Cut 11¼x10½
1983 A581 50c multi .50 .25
a. Booklet, 10 #1983 5.00

Flora & Fauna Type of 1996

Birds: Nos. 1984, 1988, 1992, Variegated fairy wren. Nos. 1985, 1989, 1993, Painted firetail. Nos. 1986, 1990, 1994, Crimson chat. Nos. 1987, 1991, 1995, Budgerigar.

2001-02 Litho. ***Perf. 14x14½***
1984 A511 45c multi .50 .50
1985 A511 45c multi .50 .50
1986 A511 45c multi .50 .50
1987 A511 45c multi .50 .50
a. Block of 4, #1984-1987 2.00 2.00

Self-Adhesive
Coil Stamps
Die Cut Perf. 12½x12¾
1988 A511 45c multi .50 .25
1989 A511 45c multi .50 .25
1990 A511 45c multi .50 .25
1991 A511 45c multi .50 .25
a. Horiz. strip of 4, #1988-1991 2.00

Booklet Stamps
Serpentine Die Cut 11¼
1992 A511 45c multi .50 .25
1993 A511 45c multi .50 .25
1994 A511 45c multi .50 .25
1995 A511 45c multi .50 .25
a. Booklet pane, #1993, 1995 1.00
b. Booklet pane, #1992-1995, rouletted at bottom 2.00
Booklet, #1995a, 2 #1995b 5.00
c. Booklet pane, #1992-1995, rouletted at side 2.00
Booklet, 5 #1995c 10.00
d. Pane, #1992-1994, 2 #1995 2.50
e. Coil strip, #1992-1995 2.00
f. As "d," with Philakorea 2002 ovpt. in margin ('02) 2.40
g. As "d," with China 2002 Stamp & Coin Expo ovpt. in margin ('02) 2.40
Nos. 1984-1995 (12) 6.00 4.00

Issued: No. 1995f, 8/2/02; No. 1995g, 9/28/02. Rest of set, 8/9/01.

Daniel Solander (1733-82), Botanist on Endeavour A605

Designs: 45c, Barringtonia calyptrata and Solander. $1.50, Cachlospermum gillivraei and Endeavour.

Perf. 12½x12¾
2001, Aug. 16 Litho. & Engr.
1996 A605 45c multi .50 .25
1997 A605 $1.50 multi 1.60 .80

See Sweden No. 2419.

Commonwealth Heads of Government Meeting, Brisbane — A606

2001, Sept. 4 Litho. ***Perf. 14½x14***
1998 A606 45c Southern Cross .45 .25
1999 A606 45c Australia on globe .45 .25
a. Pair, #1998-1999 .90 .50

Christmas — A607

2001, Sept. 4 ***Perf. 14½x14***
Stamp + Label
2000 A607 40c Christmas tree .40 .20
2001 A607 80c Star .80 .40

Birds of Prey — A608

Designs: No. 2002, Wedge-tailed eagle. No. 2003, Nankeen kestrel. No. 2004, Red goshawk, vert. No. 2005, Spotted harrier, vert.

Perf. 14x14½, 14½x14
2001, Sept. 11
2002 A608 49c multi .50 .25
2003 A608 49c multi .50 .25
a. Pair, #2002-2003 1.00 .50
2004 A608 98c multi .95 .50
2005 A608 98c multi .95 .50
a. Pair, #2004-2005 1.90 1.00
Nos. 2002-2005 (4) 2.90 1.50

Caricatures of Australian Wildlife by Roland Harvey — A609

Designs: Nos. 2006, 2012, Bilby and antechinus musicians, dancing cockatoo. Nos. 2007, 2013, Koala with birthday cake. Nos. 2008, 2014, Ring-tailed possums with drinks and food. Nos. 2009, 2015, Bilbies, crocodile, emu, koala and gifts. Nos. 2010, 2016, Wombat and ladder. Nos. 2011, 2017, Wallabies, echidnas, platypus and ladder.

2001, Oct. 2 ***Perf. 14½x14***
2006 A609 45c multi .45 .45
2007 A609 45c multi .45 .45
2008 A609 45c multi .45 .45
a. Horiz. strip of 3, #2006-2008 1.40 1.40
b. Souvenir sheet, #2006-2008 1.40 1.40
2009 A609 45c multi .45 .45
2010 A609 45c multi .45 .45
2011 A609 45c multi .45 .45
a. Horiz. strip, #2009-2011 1.35 .75
b. Souvenir sheet, #2009-2011 1.35 .75

Self-Adhesive
Serpentine Die Cut 11½x11
2012 A609 45c multi .45 .25
2013 A609 45c multi .45 .25
2014 A609 45c multi .45 .25
2015 A609 45c multi .45 .25
2016 A609 45c multi .45 .25
2017 A609 45c multi .45 .25
a. Coil strip, 2012-2017 2.70
b. Booklet, #2014-2015, 2 each #2012-2013, 2016-2017 4.50
Nos. 2006-2017 (12) 5.40 4.20

Christmas — A610

Illuminations from the Wharncliffe Hours, by Maitre Francois: 40c, Adoration of the Magi. 45c, Flight into Egypt.

2001, Nov. 1 ***Perf. 14½x14***
2018 A610 40c multi .40 .40
2019 A610 45c multi .45 .45

Self-Adhesive
Serpentine Die Cut 11½x11¼
2020 A610 40c multi .40 .20
a. Booklet of 20 + 20 labels 8.00

Australian Legends Type of 1997

Medical researchers: Nos. 2021, 2026, Sir Gustav Nossal. Nos. 2022, 2027, Nancy Mills. No. 2023, 2028, Peter Doherty. Nos. 2024, 2029, Fiona Stanley. Nos. 2025, 2030, Donald Metcalf.

2002, Jan. 23 Litho. ***Perf. 14x14¾***
Size: 34x26mm
2021 A522 45c multi .45 .45
2022 A522 45c multi .45 .45
2023 A522 45c multi .45 .45
2024 A522 45c multi .45 .45
2025 A522 45c multi .45 .45
a. Vert. strip, #2021-2025 2.25 2.25

Booklet Stamps
Self-Adhesive
Serpentine Die Cut 11x11½
2026 A522 45c multi .45 .25
2027 A522 45c multi .45 .25
2028 A522 45c multi .45 .25
2029 A522 45c multi .45 .25
2030 A522 45c multi .45 .25
a. Booklet, 2 each #2026-2030 4.50
Nos. 2021-2030 (10) 4.50 3.50

Reign of Queen Elizabeth II, 50th Anniv. — A611

Queen: 45c, As young woman. $2.45, In 2000.

2002, Feb. 6 ***Perf. 14¾x14***
2031 A611 45c multi .45 .35
2032 A611 $2.45 multi 2.50 1.90
a. Souvenir sheet, #2031-2032 3.00 3.00

Gold Medalists at 2002 Winter Olympics, Salt Lake City — A612

Designs: No. 2033, Steven Bradbury. No. 2034, Alisa Camplin.

2002 ***Perf. 14¼***
2033 A612 45c multi .45 .35
2034 A612 45c multi .45 .35

Issued: No. 2033, 2/20; No. 2034, 2/22.

Race Cars — A613

Designs: Nos. 2035, 2041, Victoria Austin 7 and Bugatti Type 40, Phillip Island, Victoria, 1928. Nos. 2036, 2042, Jaguar Mark II, Mallala, South Australia, 1963. Nos. 2037, 2043, Repco-Brabham, Sandown, Victoria, 1966. Nos. 2038, 2044, Holden Torana XU1 and Ford Falcon XY GTHO, Bathurst, New South Wales, 1972. Nos. 2039, 2045, Williams FW07 Ford, Calder, Victoria, 1980. Nos. 2040, 2046, Benetton-Renault, Albert Park, Victoria, 2001.

2002, Feb. 27 ***Perf. 14x14¾***
2035 A613 45c multi .50 .50
2036 A613 45c multi .50 .50
2037 A613 45c multi .50 .50
2038 A613 45c multi .50 .50
2039 A613 45c multi .50 .50
2040 A613 45c multi .50 .50
a. Block of 6, #2035-2040 3.00 3.00

Self-Adhesive
Serpentine Die Cut 11¼x11½
2041 A613 45c multi .50 .25
2042 A613 45c multi .50 .25
2043 A613 45c multi .50 .25
2044 A613 45c multi .50 .25
2045 A613 45c multi .50 .25
2046 A613 45c multi .50 .25
a. Coil strip, #2041-2046 3.00
b. Booklet, #2045-2046, 2 each #2041-2044 5.00
Nos. 2035-2046 (12) 6.00 4.50

Lighthouses and Maps — A614

Designs: 45c, Macquarie, New South Wales. Nos. 2048, 2051, Troubridge Island, South Australia. Nos. 2049, 2052, Cape Naturaliste, Western Australia. $1.50, Cape Bruny, Tasmania.

2002, Mar. 12 ***Perf. 14½x14***

2047 A614 45c multi .50 .35
a. Booklet pane of 4 2.00 —
2048 A614 49c multi .50 .50
a. Booklet pane of 2 1.00 —
2049 A614 49c multi .50 .50
a. Horiz. pair, #2048-2049 1.00 1.00
b. Booklet pane of 2 1.00 —
2050 A614 $1.50 multi 1.60 1.25
a. Booklet pane of 2 3.25 —
b. Booklet pane, #2047-2050 3.25 —
Booklet, #2047a, 2048a, 2049b, 2050a, 2050b 10.50

Booklet Stamps
Self-Adhesive
Serpentine Die Cut 11¾

2051 A614 49c multi .50 .25
2052 A614 49c multi .50 .25
a. Booklet, 5 each #2051-2052 5.00
Nos. 2047-2052 (6) 4.10 3.10

Booklet containing Nos. 2047a-2050b sold for $9.95.

Encounter of Matthew Flinders and Nicolas Baudin, Bicent. A615

Map, ship and: 45c, Baudin and kangaroo. $1.50, Flinders and Port Lincoln parrot.

2002, Apr. 4 ***Perf. 14x14¾***

2053 A615 45c multi .50 .35
2054 A615 $1.50 multi 1.60 1.25

See France Nos. 2882-2883.

Tourist Attractions Type of 2000

Designs: 50c, Walker Flat. $1, Mt. Roland. $1.50, Cape Leveque.

2002, May 1 ***Perf. 14½x14***

2055 A581 50c multi .55 .25
2056 A581 $1 multi 1.10 .25
2057 A581 $1.50 multi 1.60 .80

Booklet Stamps
Self-Adhesive
Serpentine Die Cut 11¼x10½

2058 A581 50c multi .55 .20
2059 A581 $1 multi 1.10 .20
a. Booklet, 6 #2058, 4 #2059 7.75
Nos. 2055-2059 (5) 4.90 1.70

Flora & Fauna Type of 1996

Designs: 50c, Desert star flower. $1, Bilby. $1.50, Thorny devil. $2, Great Sandy Desert.

2002, June 4 Litho. ***Perf. 14x14½***

2060 A511 50c multi .55 .25
2061 A511 $1 multi 1.10 .55
2062 A511 $1.50 multi 1.75 .85

Perf. 14½x14
Size: 50x30mm

2063 A511 $2 multi 2.25 1.10
Nos. 2060-2063 (4) 5.65 2.75

Paintings by Albert Namatjira (1902-59) A616

Designs: Nos. 2064, 2068, Ghost Gum Mt. Sonder, MacDonnel Ranges. Nos. 2065, 2069, Mt. Hermannsburg. Nos. 2066, 2070, Glen Helen Country. Nos. 2067, 2071, Simpsons Gap.

2002, July 2 Litho. ***Perf. 14x14¾***

2064 A616 45c multi .50 .50
a. Booklet pane of 4 2.00 —
2065 A616 45c multi .50 .50
a. Booklet pane of 4 2.00 —
2066 A616 45c multi .50 .50
a. Booklet pane of 4 2.00 —
2067 A616 45c multi .50 .50
a. Block of 4, #2064-2067 2.00 2.00
b. Souvenir sheet of 4, #2064-2067 2.00 2.00
c. Booklet pane of 4 2.00 —
d. Booklet pane, #2067b 2.00 —
Booklet, #2064a, 2065a, 2066a, 2067c, 2067d 10.00

Serpentine Die Cut 11x11½
Self-Adhesive

2068 A616 45c multi .50 .25
2069 A616 45c multi .50 .25
2070 A616 45c multi .50 .25
2071 A616 45c multi .50 .25
a. Booklet pane of 10, 3 each #2068-2069, 2 each #2070-2071 5.00
b. Coil strip of 4, #2068-2071 2.00
Nos. 2064-2071 (8) 4.00 3.00

Australia - Thailand Diplomatic Relations, 50th Anniv. A617

Designs: 45c, Nelumbo nucifera. $1, Nymphaea immutabilis.

2002, Aug. 6 Litho. ***Perf. 14x14½***

2072 A617 45c multi .50 .40
2073 A617 $1 multi 1.10 .80
a. Souvenir sheet, #2072-2073 1.60 1.60

See Thailand Nos. 2028-2029.

Christmas — A618

Koala A619

Puja, by Ngarralja Tommy May — A620

2002, Aug. 23 ***Perf. 14¼x14***

2074 A618 90c multi + label .95 .70
2075 A619 $1.10 multi + label 1.25 .95
2076 A620 $1.65 multi + label 1.75 1.25
Nos. 2074-2076 (3) 3.95 2.90

Nos. 2074-2076 were each printed in sheets of 20 stamps + 20 labels. Labels on some sheets could be personalized for an additional fee.

Tourist Attractions Type of 2000

Designs: $1.10, Coonawarra. $1.65, Gaiwerd-Grampians Natl. Park. $2.20, National Library. $3.30, Cape York.

2002, Aug. 23 Litho. ***Perf. 14½x14***

2077 A581 $1.10 multi 1.25 .25
2078 A581 $1.65 multi 1.75 .90
2079 A581 $2.20 multi 2.40 1.25
2080 A581 $3.30 multi 3.75 1.90
Nos. 2077-2080 (4) 9.15 4.30

Aboriginal Food Plants — A621

Designs: Nos. 2081, 2088, Murnong. Nos. 2082, 2087, Acacia seeds. Nos. 2083, 2086, Quandong. Nos. 2084, 2090, Honey grevillea. Nos. 2085, 2089, Lilly-pilly.

2002, Sept. 3 Litho. ***Perf. 14¾x14***

2081 A621 49c multi .55 .55
2082 A621 49c multi .55 .55
2083 A621 49c multi .55 .55
2084 A621 49c multi .55 .55
2085 A621 49c multi .55 .55
a. Horiz. strip of 5, #2081-2085 2.75 2.75

Booklet Stamps
Self-Adhesive
Serpentine Die Cut 11¾

2086 A621 49c multi .55 .25
2087 A621 49c multi .55 .25
2088 A621 49c multi .55 .25
2089 A621 49c multi .55 .25
2090 A621 49c multi .55 .25
a. Booklet pane, 2 each #2086-2090 5.50
Nos. 2081-2090 (10) 5.50 4.00

Bunyip — A622 Fairy — A623

Gnome — A624 Goblin — A625

Wizard — A626 Sprite — A627

2002, Sept. 25 ***Perf. 14¾x14***

2091 A622 45c multi .50 .50
2092 A623 45c multi .50 .50
2093 A624 45c multi .50 .50
a. Horiz. strip of 3, #2091-2093 1.50 1.50
2094 A625 45c multi .50 .50
2095 A626 45c multi .50 .50
2096 A627 45c multi .50 .50
a. Horiz. strip of 3, #2094-2096 1.50 1.50
b. Souvenir sheet, #2091-2096 3.00 3.00

Self-Adhesive
Serpentine Die Cut 11½x11

2097 A622 45c multi .50 .25
2098 A623 45c multi .50 .25
2099 A624 45c multi .50 .25
2100 A625 45c multi .50 .25
2101 A626 45c multi .50 .25
2102 A627 45c multi .50 .25
a. Vert. coil strip of 6, #2097-2102 3.00
b. Booklet pane, #2097, 2102, 2 each #2098-2101 5.00
Nos. 2091-2102 (12) 6.00 4.50

Characters from The Magic Rainforest, by John Marsden.

Race Horses A628

2002, Oct. 15 Litho. ***Perf. 14x14½***

2103 A628 45c Wakeful .50 .40
2104 A628 45c Rising Fast .50 .40
2105 A628 45c Manikato .50 .40
2106 A628 45c Might and Power .50 .40
2107 A628 45c Sunline .50 .40
a. Horiz. strip of 5, #2103-2107 2.50 2.00

Christmas — A629

2002, Nov. 1 ***Perf. 14½x14***

2108 A629 40c Nativity .45 .25
2109 A629 45c Magi .50 .25

Self-Adhesive
Booklet Stamp
Serpentine Die Cut 11¼

2110 A629 40c Nativity .45 .20
a. Booklet pane of 20 + 20 labels 9.00
Nos. 2108-2110 (3) 1.40 .70

AIR POST STAMPS

Airplane over Bush Lands — AP1

Unwmk.

1929, May 20 Engr. ***Perf. 11***

C1 AP1 3p deep green 6.50 3.75
Never hinged 12.50
a. Booklet pane of 4 ('30) 125.00

Kingsford-Smith Type of 1931

1931, Mar. 19

C2 A8 6p gray violet 7.00 7.00
Never hinged 10.00

AP3

1931, Nov. 4

C3 AP3 6p olive brown 15.00 12.00
Never hinged 22.50

For overprint see No. CO1.

Mercury and Hemispheres AP4

1934, Dec. 1 ***Perf. 11***

C4 AP4 1sh6p violet brown 20.00 3.00
Never hinged 55.00

Perf. 13x13½

1937, Oct. 22 **Wmk. 228**

C5 AP4 1sh6p violet brown 7.50 .25
Never hinged 12.50

Catalogue values for unused stamps in this section, from this point to the end of the section, are for Never Hinged items.

Mercury and Globe — AP5

1949, Sept. 1 ***Perf. 14½***

C6 AP5 1sh6p sepia 1.75 .20

1956, Dec. 6 **Unwmk.**

C7 AP5 1sh6p sepia 16.00 .85

Super-Constellation over Globe — AP6

1958, Jan. 6 *Perf. 14½x14*

C8 AP6 2sh dark violet blue 2.50 1.75

Inauguration of Australian "Round the World" air service.

AIR POST OFFICIAL STAMP

No. C3 Overprinted

Perf. 11, 11½

1931, Nov. 17 **Unwmk.**

CO1 AP3 6p olive brown 22.50 *22.50*
Never hinged 27.50

Issued primarily for official use, but to prevent speculation, a quantity was issued for public distribution.

POSTAGE DUE STAMPS

Very fine examples of Nos. J1-J38 will have perforations touching the design on one or more sides due to the narrow spacing of the stamps on the plates. Stamps with perfs clear of the design on all four sides are scarce and will command higher prices.

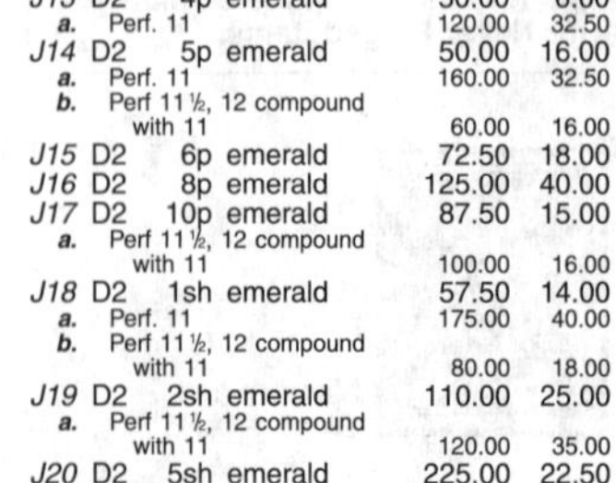

D1 D2

1902 Typo. Wmk. 55 *Perf. 11½, 12*

J1 D1 ½p emerald 3.00 *4.00*
J2 D1 1p emerald 12.00 6.00
a. Perf. 11 *750.00 300.00*
J3 D1 2p emerald 25.00 7.00
J4 D1 3p emerald 25.00 18.00
J5 D1 4p emerald 37.50 11.00
J6 D1 6p emerald 50.00 9.00
J7 D1 8p emerald 87.50 75.00
J8 D1 5sh emerald 160.00 70.00
Nos. J1-J8 (8) 400.00 200.00

The 1p, 2p and 4p, type D1, exist also in perforations compounding 11 with 11½ & 12.

Perf. 11½, 12, 11 and 11 Compound with 11½, 12

1902-04

J9 D2 ½p emerald 7.25 *8.50*
a. Perf. 11 140.00 100.00
J10 D2 1p emerald 4.50 2.75
a. Perf. 11 75.00 35.00
b. Perf 11½, 12 150.00 80.00
J11 D2 2p emerald 15.00 3.50
a. Perf. 11 110.00 25.00
b. Perf 11½, 12 85.00
J12 D2 3p emerald 55.00 8.75
b. Perf 11½, 12 175.00 65.00
J13 D2 4p emerald 50.00 6.00
a. Perf. 11 120.00 32.50
J14 D2 5p emerald 50.00 16.00
a. Perf. 11 160.00 32.50
b. Perf 11½, 12 compound with 11 60.00 16.00
J15 D2 6p emerald 72.50 18.00
J16 D2 8p emerald 125.00 40.00
J17 D2 10p emerald 87.50 15.00
a. Perf 11½, 12 compound with 11 100.00 16.00
J18 D2 1sh emerald 57.50 14.00
a. Perf. 11 175.00 40.00
b. Perf 11½, 12 compound with 11 80.00 18.00
J19 D2 2sh emerald 110.00 25.00
a. Perf 11½, 12 compound with 11 120.00 35.00
J20 D2 5sh emerald 225.00 22.50
a. Perf. 11 425.00 125.00

Perf. 11

J21 D2 10sh emerald *2,250. 1,500.*
J22 D2 20sh emerald *3,750. 2,750.*
Nos. J9-J20 (12) 859.25 180.00

Perf. 11½, 12 Compound with 11

1906 **Wmk. 12**

J23 D2 ½p emerald 14.00 7.00
J24 D2 1p emerald 30.00 2.50
a. Perf. 11 *850.00 350.00*
J25 D2 2p emerald 50.00 4.00
J26 D2 3p emerald 375.00 200.00
J27 D2 4p emerald 77.50 20.00
a. Perf. 11 *1,300. 600.00*
J28 D2 6p emerald 225.00 20.00
Nos. J23-J28 (6) 771.50 253.50

1907 Wmk. 13 ***Perf. 11½x11***

J29 D2 ½p emerald 24.00 *65.00*
J30 D2 1p emerald 70.00 37.50
J31 D2 2p emerald 125.00 92.50
J32 D2 4p emerald 200.00 95.00
J33 D2 6p emerald 240.00 110.00
Nos. J29-J33 (5) 659.00 400.00

D3 D4

Perf. 11 (2sh, 10sh, 20sh), 11½x11 (1sh, 5sh)

1908-09 **Wmk. 12**

J34 D3 1sh emer ('09) 110.00 16.00
J35 D3 2sh emerald *1,100. 1,100.*
J36 D3 5sh emerald 250.00 52.50
J37 D3 10sh emerald *1,900. 2,250.*
J38 D3 20sh emerald *5,500. 6,000.*

Perf. 11, 12x12½, 12½, 14

1909 **Wmk. 13**

J39 D4 ½p green & car 13.50 *26.00*
J40 D4 1p green & car 13.50 4.00
a. Perf 11 1,500. 600.00
J41 D4 2p green & car 22.50 3.50
a. Perf 11 6,000. 1,500.
J42 D4 3p green & car 22.50 12.50
J43 D4 4p green & car 21.00 4.50
J44 D4 6p green & car 26.00 7.25
a. Perf 11 6,000. 3,000.
J45 D4 1sh green & car 29.00 4.00
J46 D4 2sh green & car 67.50 13.50
J47 D4 5sh green & car 87.50 15.00
J48 D4 10sh green & car 240.00 150.00
J49 D4 £1 green & car 460.00 275.00
Nos. J39-J49 (11) 1,003. 515.25

1922-25 Wmk. 10 ***Perf. 14, 11 (4p)***

J50 D4 ½p grn & car ('23) 6.50 1.75
J51 D4 1p green & car 6.50 1.90
J52 D4 1½p yellow green & rose ('25) 3.75 3.25
J53 D4 2p green & car 8.00 3.75
J54 D4 3p green & car 15.00 2.75
J55 D4 4p green & car 19.00 2.25
J56 D4 6p green & car 22.50 13.00
Nos. J50-J56 (7) 81.25 28.65

No. J55 exists perf 14.

1931-37 Wmk. 228 ***Perf. 11, 14***

J57 D4 ½p yel green & rose ('34) 12.50 11.50
J58 D4 1p yel grn & rose 7.75 1.00
J59 D4 2p yel grn & rose 9.00 .50
J60 D4 3p yel green & rose ('37) 72.50 57.50
J61 D4 4p yel green & rose ('34) 6.75 1.90
J62 D4 6p yel green & rose ('36) 310.00 225.00
J63 D4 1sh yel green & rose ('34) 50.00 26.00
Nos. J57-J63 (7) 468.50 323.40

D5

Engraved; Value Typo.

1938 ***Perf. 14½x14***

J64 D5 ½p green & car .75 *1.25*
J65 D5 1p green & car 5.00 .50
J66 D5 2p green & car 4.50 .50
J67 D5 3p green & car 15.00 3.50
J68 D5 4p green & car 4.50 .25
J69 D5 6p green & car 45.00 17.50
J70 D5 1sh green & car 20.00 7.50
Nos. J64-J70 (7) 94.75 31.00

Catalogue values for unused stamps in this section, from this point to the end of the section, are for Never Hinged items.

Type of 1938
Value Tablet Redrawn

Original Redrawn

Pence denominations: "D" has melon-shaped center in redrawn tablet. The redrawn 3p differs slightly, having semi-melon-shaped "D" center, with vertical white stroke half filling it.

1sh. 1938: Numeral "1" narrow, with six background lines above.

1sh. 1947: Numeral broader, showing more white space around dotted central ornament. Three lines above.

1946-57 **Wmk. 228**

J71 D5 ½p grn & car ('56) 2.75 1.40
J72 D5 1p grn & car ('47) 1.40 .25
J73 D5 2p green & car .85 1.00
J74 D5 3p green & car 4.50 .35
J75 D5 4p grn & car ('52) 5.50 .50
J76 D5 5p grn & car ('48) 8.25 1.25
J77 D5 6p grn & car ('47) 8.25 .65
J78 D5 7p grn & car ('53) 5.50 3.00
J79 D5 8p grn & car ('57) 13.50 11.50
J80 D5 1sh grn & car ('47) 13.50 1.25
Nos. J71-J80 (10) 64.00 21.15

1953-54

White Tablet, Carmine Numeral

J81 D5 1sh grn & car ('54) 9.00 5.00
J82 D5 2sh green & car 12.50 10.00
J83 D5 5sh green & car 17.50 2.50
Nos. J81-J83 (3) 39.00 17.50

Issued: 2sh, 5sh, Aug. 26; 1sh, Feb. 17.

Redrawn Type of 1947-57

Two Types of Some Pence Values:
Type I - Background lines touch numeral, "D" and period.
Type II - Lines do not touch numeral, etc.
Second engraving of 1sh has sharper and thicker lines.
The ½p type II has 7 dots under the "2."
The 8p type II has distinct lines in centers of "8" and between "8" and "D."

Engr.; Value Typo.

1958-60 Unwmk. ***Perf. 14½x14***

J86 D5 ½p grn & car, II 2.25 1.10
a. Six dots under the "2" 3.75 .95
J87 D5 1p grn & car, II 2.25 .40
a. Type I 2.50 1.50
J88 D5 3p grn & car, II 1.50 .75
J89 D5 4p grn & car, I 4.00 4.00
a. Type II ('59) 3.00 *6.00*
J90 D5 5p grn & car, I 11.50 6.00
a. Type II ('59) 57.50 25.00
J91 D5 6p grn & car, II 2.40 1.75
J92 D5 8p grn & car, II 8.75 *15.00*
a. Indistinct lines 15.00 15.00
J93 D5 10p grn & car, II 4.00 3.25

White Tablet, Carmine Numeral

J94 D5 1sh green & car 4.75 2.50
a. 2nd redrawing ('60) 9.00 .60
J95 D5 2sh grn & car 19.00 5.50
Nos. J86-J95 (10) 60.40 40.25

Issued: 1sh, 9/8/58; 10p, 12/9/59; 2sh, 3/8/60; 3p, 6p, 5/25/60; others, 2/27/58.

MILITARY STAMPS

Nos. 166, 191, 183A, 173, 175, 206 and 177 Overprinted in Black:

a

b

c

Perf. 14½x14, 15x14, 11½, 13½x13

1946-47 **Wmk. 228**

M1 A24(a) ½p orange 2.10 2.00
Never hinged 3.25
M2 A36(b) 1p brown vio 1.75 1.50
Never hinged 2.75
a. Blue overprint 100.00 67.50
Never hinged 125.00
M3 A27(b) 3p dk vio brn 1.40 *1.50*
Never hinged 2.25
a. Double overprint 500.00
M4 A30(a) 6p brn violet 10.50 6.75
Never hinged 16.00
M5 A16(a) 1sh gray green 10.50 8.00
Never hinged 16.00
M6 A1 (c) 2sh dk red brn 30.00 *32.50*
Never hinged 40.00
M7 A32(c) 5sh dl red brn 77.50 *87.50*
Never hinged 110.00
Nos. M1-M7 (7) 133.75 139.75

"B.C.O.F." stands for "British Commonwealth Occupation Force."

Forged overprints of Nos. M6-M7 exist.

Issued: #M1-M3, 10/11/46; #M4-M7, 5/8/47.

OFFICIAL STAMPS

Perforated Initials

In 1913-31, postage stamps were perforated "OS" for federal official use. The Scott Standard Catalogues do not list officials with perforated initials, but listings for these Australian stamps will be found in the *Scott Classic Specialized Catalogue*.

Overprinted Official stamps are comparatively more difficult to find well centered than the basic issues on which they are printed. This is because poorly centered sheets that had been discarded were purposely chosen to be overprinted to save money.

Overprinted

On Regular Issue of 1931

1931, May 4 Unwmk. ***Perf. 11, 11½***

O1 A8 2p dull red 60.00 22.50
O2 A8 3p blue 175.00 35.00

These stamps were issued primarily for official use but to prevent speculation a quantity was issued for public distribution.

Used values are for cto copies.

Counterfeit overprints exist.

On Regular Issues of 1928-32

1932 Wmk. 203 ***Perf. 13½x12½***

O3 A4 2p red, II 10.00 .90
O4 A4 4p olive bister 30.00 6.00

Perf. 11½, 12

O5 A1 6p brown 67.50 35.00

1932-33 Wmk. 228 ***Perf. 13½x12½***

O6 A4 ½p orange 6.00 1.25
a. Inverted overprint *3,000. 1,500.*
O7 A4 1p green, I 2.00 .75
O8 A4 2p red, II 5.00 .60
a. Inverted overprint 2,250.
O9 A4 3p ultra, II ('33) 14.00 7.50
O10 A4 5p brown buff 42.50 21.00

Perf. 11½, 12

O11 A1 6p yellow brown 35.00 25.00
a. Inverted overprint —
Nos. O6-O11 (6) 104.50 56.10

1932 Unwmk. ***Perf. 11, 11½***

O12 A9 2p red 5.50 4.50
O13 A9 3p blue 18.00 18.00
O14 A16 1sh gray green 55.00 32.50
Nos. O12-O14 (3) 78.50 55.00

AUSTRALIAN ANTARCTIC TERRITORY

Catalogue values for all unused stamps in this section are for Never Hinged items.

All stamps are also valid for postage in Australia.

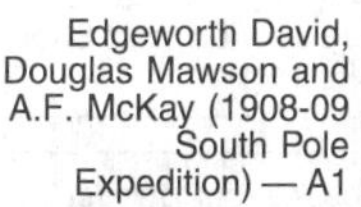

Edgeworth David, Douglas Mawson and A.F. McKay (1908-09 South Pole Expedition) — A1

Australian Explorers and Map of Antarctica — A2

Designs: 8p, Loading weasel (snow truck). 1sh, Dog team and iceberg, vert. 2sh3p, Emperor penguins and map, vert.

Perf. 14½, 14½x14, 14x14½

1957-59 Engr. Unwmk.

L1 A1 5p brown .60 .20
L2 A2 8p dark blue 3.00 2.00
L3 A2 1sh dark green 3.00 1.75
L4 A2 2sh ultra ('57) 1.40 .55
L5 A2 2sh3p green 7.00 4.50
Nos. L1-L5 (5) 15.00 9.00

Nos. L1 and L2 were printed as 4p and 7p stamps and surcharged typographically in black and dark blue before issuance.

Sizes of stamps: No. L2, 34x21mm; Nos. L3, L5, 21x34mm; No. L4, 43½x25½mm.

1961, July 5 ***Perf. 14½***

L6 A1 5p dark blue 1.10 .20

The denomination on No. L6 is not within a typographed circle, but is part of the engraved design.

Sir Douglas Mawson — A3

Lookout and Iceberg — A4

1961, Oct. 18

L7 A3 5p dark green .35 .20

50th anniv. of the 1911-14 Australian Antarctic Expedition.

Perf. 13½x13, 13x13½

1966-68 Photo. Unwmk.

Designs: 1c, Aurora australis and camera dome. 2c, Banding penguins. 5c, Branding of elephant seals. 7c, Measuring snow strata. 10c, Wind gauges. 15c, Weather balloon. 20c, Helicopter. 25c, Radio operator. 50c, Ice compression tests. $1, "Mock sun" (parahelion) and dogs. 20c, 25c, 50c and $1 horizontal.

L8 A4 1c multicolored .70 .35
L9 A4 2c multicolored 3.00 .80
L10 A4 4c multicolored .95 .90
L11 A4 5c multicolored 2.75 1.75
L12 A4 7c multicolored .80 .80
L13 A4 10c multicolored 1.00 .90
L14 A4 15c multicolored 5.00 2.00
L15 A4 20c multicolored 6.25 2.50
L16 A4 25c multicolored 3.00 3.00
L17 A4 50c multicolored 4.75 *5.50*
L18 A4 $1 multicolored 26.00 14.00
Nos. L8-L18 (11) 54.20 32.50

Issued: 5c, 9/25/68; others, 9/28/66.

Nos. L8-L18 are on phosphorescent helecon paper. Fluorescent orange is one of the colors used in printing the 10c, 15c, 20c and 50c.

Sastrugi Snow Formation A5

1971, June 23 Photo. ***Perf. 13x13½***

L19 A5 6c shown .75 .75
L20 A5 30c Pancake ice 4.25 *5.00*

10th anniv. of the Antarctic Treaty pledging peaceful uses of and scientific cooperation in Antarctica.

Capt. Cook, Sextant, Azimuth Compass A6

Design: 35c, Chart of Cook's circumnavigation of Antarctica, and "Resolution."

1972, Sept. 13 Photo. ***Perf. 13x13½***

L21 A6 7c bister & multi 1.50 1.50
L22 A6 35c buff & multi 4.00 *5.00*

Bicentenary of Capt. James Cook's circumnavigation of Antarctica.

Plankton and Krill Shrimp — A7

Mawson's D.H. Gipsy Moth, 1931 — A8

Food Chain (Essential for Survival): 7c, Adelie penguin feeding on krill shrimp. 9c, Leopard seal pursuing fish, horiz. 10c, Killer whale hunting seals, horiz. 20c, Wandering albatross, horiz. $1, Sperm whale attacking giant squid.

Explorers' Aircraft: 8c, Rymill's DH Fox Moth returning to Barry Island. 25c, Hubert Wilkins Lockheed Vega, horiz. 30c, Lincoln Ellsworth's Northrop Gamma. 35c, Lars Christensen's Avro Avian and Framnes Mountains, horiz. 50c, Richard Byrd's Ford Tri-Motor dropping US flag over South Pole.

Perf. 13½x13, 13x13½

1973, Aug. 15

L23 A7 1c multicolored .20 .20
L24 A8 5c multicolored .20 .20
L25 A7 7c multicolored 1.40 .60
L26 A8 8c multicolored .30 *.50*
L27 A7 9c multicolored .25 .25
L28 A7 10c multicolored 3.00 1.25
L29 A7 20c multicolored .35 .35
L30 A8 25c multicolored .35 .35
L31 A8 30c multicolored .35 *.50*
L32 A8 35c multicolored .30 .45
L33 A8 50c multicolored 1.25 1.25
L34 A7 $1 multicolored 2.25 1.25
Nos. L23-L34 (12) 10.20 7.15

Adm. Byrd, Plane, Mountains A9

Design: 20c, Adm. Byrd, Floyd Bennett trimotored plane, map of Antarctica.

1979, June 20 Litho. ***Perf. 15½***

L35 A9 20c multicolored .40 *.50*
L36 A9 55c multicolored .85 *1.00*

50th anniv. of first flight over South Pole by Richard Byrd (1888-1957).

"S.Y. Nimrod" A10

2c, 5c, 22c, 25c, 40c, 55c, $1 are vertical. No. L41 actually pictures the S.S. Morning.

Perf. 13½x13, 13x13½

1974-81 Litho.

L37 A10 1c S.Y. Aurora .20 .20
L38 A10 2c R.Y. Penola .20 .20
L39 A10 5c M.V. Thala Dan .20 .20
L40 A10 10c H.M.S. Challenger .20 .20
L41 A10 15c shown .95 .95
L42 A10 15c S.Y. Nimrod, stern view .25 .20
L43 A10 20c R.R.S. Discovery II .30 .30
L44 A10 22c R.Y.S. Terra Nova .30 .30
L45 A10 25c S.S. Endurance .40 .35
L46 A10 30c S.S. Fram .50 .50
L47 A10 35c M.S. Nella Dan .45 .40
L48 A10 40c M.S. Kista Dan .50 .50
L49 A10 45c L'Astrolabe .55 .55
L50 A10 50c S.S. Norvegia .70 .70
L51 A10 55c S.Y. Discovery .80 .80
L52 A10 $1 H.M.S. Resolution 1.25 .65
Nos. L37-L52 (16) 7.75 7.00

A11

A12

1982, May 5 Litho. ***Perf. 14x13½***

L53 A11 27c Mawson, landscape .35 .35
L54 A11 75c Mawson, map 1.25 1.25

Sir Douglas Mawson (1882-1958), explorer.

1983, Apr. 6 Litho. ***Perf. 14½***

Local Wildlife: a, Light-mantled sooty albatross. b, Macquarie Isld. shags. c, Elephant seals. d, Royal penguins. e, Antarctic prions.

L55 Strip of 5, multi 2.75 *2.75*
a.-e. A12 27c, any single .55 *.55*

12th Antarctic Treaty Consultative Meeting, Canberra, Sept. 13-27 — A13

1983, Sept. 7 Litho. ***Perf. 14½***

L56 A13 27c multicolored .45 .45

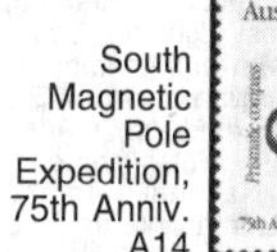
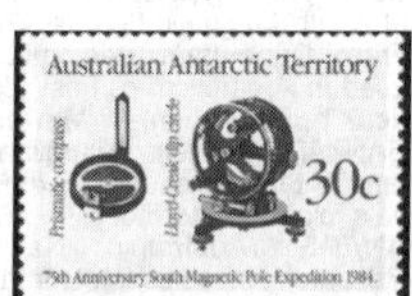

South Magnetic Pole Expedition, 75th Anniv. A14

1984, Jan. 16

L57 A14 30c Prismatic compass .50 .50
L58 A14 85c Aneroid barometer 1.25 *1.50*

Dog Team, Mawson Station A15

1984-87 Litho. ***Perf. 14½x15***

L60 A15 2c Summer afternoon .20 .20
L61 A15 5c shown .20 .20
L62 A15 10c Evening .20 .20
L63 A15 15c Prince Charles Mts. .20 .20
L64 A15 20c Morning .30 .30
L65 A15 25c Sea ice, iceberg .40 .40
L66 A15 30c Mt. Coates .50 .50

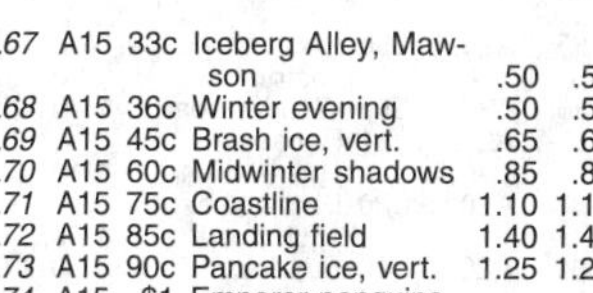

L67 A15 33c Iceberg Alley, Mawson .50 .50
L68 A15 36c Winter evening .50 .50
L69 A15 45c Brash ice, vert. .65 .65
L70 A15 60c Midwinter shadows .85 .85
L71 A15 75c Coastline 1.10 1.10
L72 A15 85c Landing field 1.40 1.40
L73 A15 90c Pancake ice, vert. 1.25 1.25
L74 A15 $1 Emperor penguins, Auster Rookery 1.50 1.50
Nos. L60-L74 (15) 9.75 9.75

Issued: 5, 25, 30, 75, 85c, 7/18/84; 15, 33, 45, 90c, $1, 8/7/85; 2, 10, 20, 36, 60c, 3/11/87.

Antarctic Treaty, 25th Anniv. — A16

1986, Sept. 17 Litho. ***Perf. 14x13½***

L75 A16 36c multicolored .85 .50

Environment, Conservation and Technology A17

No. L76: a, Hour-glass dolphins and the *Nella Dan.* b, Emperor penguins and Davis Station. c, Crabeater seal and helicopters. d, Adelie penguins and snow-ice transport vehicle. e, Gray-headed albatross and photographer.

1988, July 20 Litho. ***Perf. 13***

L76 Strip of 5 4.25 2.00
a.-e. A17 37c any single .75 .25

Paintings by Sir Sidney Nolan (b. 1917) — A18

1989, June 14 Litho. ***Perf. 14x13½***

L77 A18 39c *Antarctica* .65 .65
L78 A18 39c *Iceberg Alley* .65 .65
L79 A18 60c *Glacial Flow* 1.00 1.00
L80 A18 80c *Frozen Sea* 1.40 1.40
Nos. L77-L80 (4) 3.70 3.70

Aurora Australis A19

Design: $1.20, Research ship Aurora Australis.

1991, June 20 Litho. ***Perf. 14½***

L81 A19 43c multicolored .50 .50
L82 A19 $1.20 multicolored 1.75 1.75

Antarctic Treaty, 30th anniv. (No. L81).

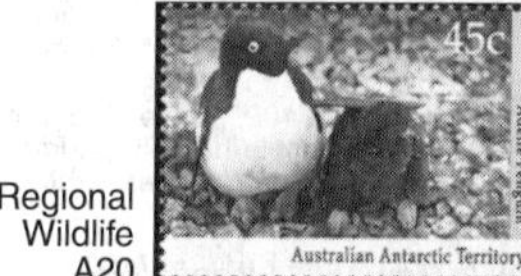

Regional Wildlife A20

Perf. 14x14½, 14½x14

1992-93 Litho.

L83 A20 45c Adelie penguin .55 .40
L84 A20 75c Elephant seal .85 .55

L85	A20	85c Northern giant petrel	.90	.60
L86	A20	95c Weddell seal	1.10	.70
L86A	A20	$1 Royal penguins	1.10	.75
L87	A20	$1.20 Emperor penguin, vert.	1.40	.90
L88	A20	$1.40 Fur seals	1.50	1.00
L89	A20	$1.50 King penguins, vert.	1.60	1.10
		Nos. L83-L89 (8)	9.00	6.00

Issued: $1, $1.40, $1.50, 1/14/93; others, 5/14/92.

The Last Huskies A21

1994, Jan. 13 Litho. *Perf. 14½*

L90 A21	45c Dog up close, vert.	.65	.35
L91 A21	75c Sled team	1.10	.90
L92 A21	85c Dog seated, vert.	1.25	1.00
L93 A21	$1.05 Three dogs	1.50	1.25
	Nos. L90-L93 (4)	4.50	3.50

Whales & Dolphins A22

1995, June 15 Litho. *Perf. 14½*

L94 A22	45c Humpback whale	.70	.45
L95 A22	45c Hourglass dolphin, vert.	.70	.45
L96 A22	45c Minke whale, vert.	.70	.45
a.	Pair, #L95-L96	1.40	1.10
L97 A22	$1 Killer whale	1.40	.50
a.	Souvenir sheet of 4, #L94-L97	3.50	3.50
b.	As "a," overprinted	8.00	8.00
c.	As "a," overprinted	8.00	8.00
	Nos. L94-L97 (4)	3.50	1.85

No. L97b is overprinted in gold in sheet margin with Singapore '95 emblem and: "Australia Post Exhibition Sheet No. 2," and, in both Chinese and English, with "Singapore 95 World Stamp Exhibition."

No. L97c is overprinted in gold in sheet margin with exhibition emblem, "Australian Post Exhibition Sheet No. 3" and "CAPEX '96 WORLD PHILATELIC EXHIBITION / EXPOSITION PHILATELIQUE MONDIALE"

Issued: #L97b, 9/1/95; #L97c, 6/15/96.

Landscapes, by Christian Clare Robertson — A23

#L98, Rafting sea ice. #L99, Shadow on the Plateau. $1, Ice cave. $1.20, Twelve Lake.

1996, May 16 Litho. *Perf. 14½x14*

L98 A23	45c multicolored	.70	.55
L99 A23	45c multicolored	.70	.55
a.	Pair, Nos. L98-L99	1.40	1.25
L100 A23	$1 multicolored	1.60	1.10
L101 A23	$1.20 multicolored	1.90	1.25
	Nos. L98-L101 (4)	4.90	3.45

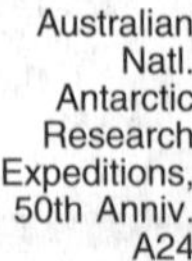

Australian Natl. Antarctic Research Expeditions, 50th Anniv. A24

Designs: No. L102, Apple field huts. No. L103, Inside an apple hut. 95c, Summer surveying. $1.05, Sea ice research. $1.20, Remote field camp.

1997, May 15 Litho. *Perf. 14x14½*

L102 A24	45c multicolored	.60	.45
L103 A24	45c multicolored	.60	.45
a.	Pair, #L102-L103	1.25	1.00
L104 A24	95c multicolored	.95	.90
L105 A24	$1.05 multicolored	1.10	1.00
L106 A24	$1.20 multicolored	1.25	1.10
	Nos. L102-L106 (5)	4.50	3.90

Modes of Transportion A25

Designs: No. L107, Snowmobile. No. L108, Ship, "Aurora Australis." $1, Helicopter airlifting a four-wheel drive ATV, vert. $2, Antarctic Hagglunds (rubber-tracked vehicles with fiberglass cabins), vert.

Perf. 14x14½, 14½x14

1998, Mar. 5 Litho.

L107 A25	45c multicolored	.55	.55
L108 A25	45c multicolored	.55	.55
a.	Pair, #L107-L108	1.25	1.00
L109 A25	$1 multicolored	1.40	1.25
L110 A25	$2 multicolored	2.50	1.50
	Nos. L107-L110 (4)	5.00	3.85

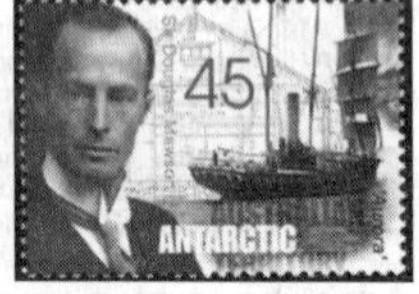

Preservation of Huts used During Mawson's Antarctic Expedition A26

#L111, Photograph of Mawson, sailing ship Aurora. #L112, Photograph, "Home of the Blizzard," by Frank Hurley. 90c, Photograph, "Huskie Team," by Xavier Mertz. $1.35, Huts restoration.

1999, May 13 Litho. *Perf. 14x14½*

L111 A26	45c multicolored	.50	.50
L112 A26	45c multicolored	.50	.50
a.	Pair, #L111-L112	1.25	1.00
L113 A26	90c multicolored	1.25	1.25
L114 A26	$1.35 multicolored	1.75	1.75
	Nos. L111-L114 (4)	4.00	4.00

Penguins A27

2000, July 24 Litho. *Perf. 13¾x14½*

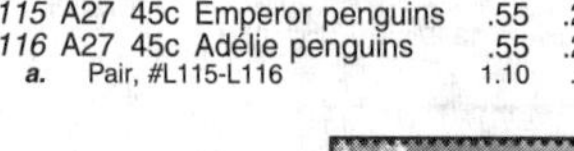

L115 A27	45c Emperor penguins	.55	.25
L116 A27	45c Adélie penguins	.55	.25
a.	Pair, #L115-L116	1.10	.50

Australians in the Antarctic, Cent. — A28

No. L117: a, Penguins and icicles. b, Louis Bernacchi, physicist. c, Nimrod. d, Scientists at South Magnetic Pole. e, Griffith Taylor and Frank Debenham, geologists. f, First radio used in Antarctica. g, First flight over Antarctica. h, Sir Douglas Mawson, explorer. i, BANZARE (British, Australian and New Zealand Antarctic Research Expedition). j, Australia's claim to territory. k, Establishment of ANARE (Australian National Antarctic Research Expeditions). l, Transport. m, Aurora Australis. n, Climate research. o, Cold-weather clothing. p, Nella Dan. q, First women on Antarctica. r, Communications. s, Tourism. t, Satellite view of Antarctica.

2001, May 17 Litho. *Perf. 14¾x14*

L117	Sheet of 20	4.50	4.50
a.-e.	A28 5c Any single	.20	.20
f.-j.	A28 10c Any single	.20	.20
k.-o.	A28 25c Any single	.25	.20
p.-t.	A28 45c Any single	.50	.25

Worldwide Frund for Nature (WWF) — A29

No. L118: a, Leopard seal and pup on ice. b, Leopard seal and penguin on ice. c, Penguins, two leopard seals in water. d, Penguins, leopard seal in water.

2001, Sept. 11 Litho. *Perf. 14x14½*

L118 A29	Block of 4	1.80	1.00
a.-d.	45c Any single	.45	.25

Antarctic Base Stations — A29

Maps showing station locations and : a, Light Detection and Ranging Instrument, aurora australis, Davis Station. b, Diatom, Casey Station. c, Wandering albatross, Macquarie Island Station. d, Adèlie penguin, Mawson Station.

2002, July 2 Litho. *Perf. 14x14¾*

L119 A29	Block of 4, #a-d	2.00	1.00
a.-d.	45c Any single	.50	.25

AUSTRIA

'os-trē-ə

LOCATION — Central Europe
GOVT. — Republic
AREA — 32,378 sq. mi.
POP. — 8,139,299 (1999 est.)
CAPITAL — Vienna

Before 1867 Austria was an absolute monarchy, which included Hungary and Lombardy-Venetia. In 1867 the Austro-Hungarian Monarchy was established, with Austria and Hungary as equal partners. After World War I, in 1918, the different nationalities established their own states and only the German-speaking parts remained, forming a republic under the name "Deutschosterreich" (German Austria), which name was shortly again changed to "Austria." In 1938 German forces occupied Austria, which became part of the German Reich. After the liberation by Allied troops in 1945, an independent republic was re-established.

60 Kreuzer = 1 Gulden
100 Neu-Kreuzer = 1 Gulden (1858)
100 Heller = 1 Krone (1899)
100 Groschen = 1 Schilling (1925)
100 Cents = 1 Euro (2002)

Catalogue values for unused stamps in this country are for Never Hinged items, beginning with Scott 432 in the regular postage section, Scott B165 in the semi-postal section, Scott C47 in the airpost section, Scott J175 in the postage due section, and Scott 4N1 in the AMG section.

Unused stamps without gum sell for about one-third or less of the values quoted.

Watermarks

Wmk. 91 - "BRIEF-MARKEN" In Double-lined Capitals Across the Middle of the Sheet

Wmk. 140 - Crown

Issues of the Austrian Monarchy (including Hungary)

Coat of Arms — A1

NINE KREUZER

Type I. One heavy line around coat of arms center. On the 9kr the top of "9" is about on a level with "Kreuzer" and not near the top of the label. Each cliche has the "9" in a different position.

Type IA. As type I, but with 1¼mm between "9" and "K."

Type II. One heavy line around coat of arms center. On the 9kr the top of "9" is much higher than the top of the word "Kreuzer" and nearly touches the top of the label.

Type III. As type II, but with two, thinner, lines around the center.

Wmk. K.K.H.M. in Sheet or Unwmk.
1850 Typo. *Imperf.*

The stamps of this issue were at first printed on a rough hand-made paper, varying in thickness and having a watermark in script letters K.K.H.M., the initials of Kaiserlich Königliches Handels-Ministerium (Imperial and Royal Ministry of Commerce), vertically in the gutter between the panes. Parts of these letters show on margin stamps in the sheet. From 1854 a thick, smooth machine-made paper without watermark was used.

Thin to Thick Paper

1	A1 1kr yellow	1,250.	85.00
a.	Printed on both sides	*1,750.*	125.00
b.	1kr orange	1,750.	110.00
c.	1kr brown orange	2,500.	475.00
2	A1 2kr black	1,050.	62.50
a.	Ribbed paper	—	*2,400.*
b.	2kr gray black	1,600.	90.00
d.	Half used as 1kr on cover		*27,500.*

3 A1 3kr red 625.00 3.25
a. Ribbed paper 2,750. 110.00
b. Laid paper — 11,250.
c. Printed on both sides 7,500.
4 A1 6kr brown 850.00 6.25
a. Ribbed paper 1,750.
c. Diagonal half used as 3kr on cover 13,000.
5 A1 9kr blue, type II 1,200. 9.00
a. 9kr blue, type I 1,600. 12.50
b. 9kr blue, type IA 13,500. 1,000.
c. Laid paper, type III 9,500.
d. Printed on both sides, type II 7,000.

1854

Machine-made Paper, Type III

1d A1 1kr yellow 1,000. 77.50
2c A1 2kr black 1,300. 60.00
3e A1 3kr red 375.00 2.25
f. 3kr red, type I 3,250. 40.00
4b A1 6kr brown 675.00 5.25
5e A1 9kr blue 750.00 2.25

In 1852-54, Nos. 1 to 5, rouletted 14, were used in Tokay and Homonna. A 12kr blue exists, but was not issued.

The reprints are type III in brighter colors, some on paper watermarked "Briefmarken" in the sheet.

For similar design see Lombardy-Venetia A1.

Emperor Franz Josef
A2 A3 A4

A5 A6

1858-59 Embossed *Perf. 14½*

Two Types of Each Value.

Type I. Loops of the bow at the back of the head broken, except the 2kr. In the 2kr, the "2" has a flat foot, thinning to the right. The frame line in the UR corner is thicker than the line below. In the 5kr the top frame line is unbroken.

Type II. Loops complete. Wreath projects further at top of head. In the 2kr, the "2" has a more curved foot of uniform thickness, with a shading line in the upper and lower curves. The frame line UR is thicker than the line below. In the 5kr the top frame line is broken.

6 A2 2kr yellow, type II 900.00 42.50
a. 2kr yellow, type I 1,900. 350.00
b. 2kr orange, type II 2,000. 225.00
c. Half used as 1kr on cover 30,000.
7 A3 3kr black, type II 2,100. 175.00
a. 3kr black, type I 1,300. 225.00
8 A3 3kr green, type II ('59) 1,100. 125.00
9 A4 5kr red, type II 325.00 1.00
a. 5kr red, type I 675.00 13.50
b. 5kr red, type II with type I frame 800.00 25.00
10 A5 10kr brown, type II 675.00 2.50
a. 10kr brown, type I 1,100. 32.50
b. Half used as 5kr on cover 12,500.
11 A6 15kr blue, type II 650.00 1.75
a. Type I 1,300. 13.50
b. Half used as 7kr on cover —

The reprints are of type II and are perforated 10½, 11, 12, 12½ and 13. There are also imperforate reprints of Nos. 6 to 8.

For similar designs see Lombardy-Venetia A2-A6.

Franz Josef — A7

Coat of Arms — A8

1860-61 Embossed *Perf. 14*

12 A7 2kr yellow 325.00 25.00
a. Half used as 1kr on cover 20,000.
13 A7 3kr green 300.00 20.00
14 A7 5kr red 200.00 .75
15 A7 10kr brown 275.00 1.75
a. Half used as 5kr on cover 7,500.
16 A7 15kr blue 350.00 1.00

The reprints are perforated 9, 9½, 10, 10½, 11, 11½, 12, 12½, 13 and 13½.

There are also imperforate reprints of the 2 and 3kr.

For similar design see Lombardy-Venetia A7. For overprints see Poland Nos. J11-J12.

1863

17 A8 2kr yellow 475.00 80.00
a. Half used as 1kr on cover —
18 A8 3kr green 400.00 75.00
19 A8 5kr rose 375.00 10.00
20 A8 10kr blue 1,000. 12.50
21 A8 15kr yellow brown 1,000. 13.00

For similar design see Lombardy-Venetia A1.

Wmk. 91, or, before July 1864, Unwmkd.

1863-64 *Perf. 9½*

22 A8 2kr yellow ('64) 150.00 10.00
a. Ribbed paper 375.00
b. Half used as 1kr on cover 17,000.
23 A8 3kr green ('64) 150.00 10.00
24 A8 5kr rose 42.50 .40
a. Ribbed paper 550.00
25 A8 10kr blue 175.00 2.50
a. Half used as 5kr on cover 15,000.
26 A8 15kr yellow brown 175.00 1.50
Nos. 22-26 (5) 692.50 24.40

The reprints are perforated 10½, 11½, 13 and 13½. There are also imperforate reprints of the 2 and 3kr.

Issues of Austro-Hungarian Monarchy

From 1867 to 1871 the independent postal administrations of Austria and Hungary used the same stamps.

A9

A10

5 kr:

Type I. In arabesques in lower left corner, the small ornament at left of the curve nearest the figure "5" is short and has three points at bottom.

Type II. The ornament is prolonged within the curve and has two points at bottom. The corresponding ornament at top of the lower left corner does not touch the curve (1872).

Type III. Similar to type II but the top ornament is joined to the curve (1881). Two different printing methods were used for the 1867-74 issues. The first produced stamps on which the hair and whiskers were coarse and thick, from the second they were fine and clear.

1867-72 Wmk. 91 Typo. *Perf. 9½*

Coarse Print

27 A9 2kr yellow 90.00 1.90
a. Half used as 1kr on cover —
28 A9 3kr green 100.00 2.00
29 A9 5kr rose, type II 67.50 .20
a. 5kr rose, type I 75.00 .20
b. Perf. 10½, type II 125.00
c. Cliché of 3kr in plate of 5kr 27,500.
30 A9 10kr blue 225.00 2.00
a. Half used as 5kr on cover —
31 A9 15kr brown 225.00 4.50
32 A9 25kr lilac 67.50 15.00
b. 25kr brown violet 250.00 40.00

Perf. 12

33 A10 50kr light brown 30.00 90.00
a. 50kr pale red brown 375.00 140.00
b. 50kr brownish rose 375.00 225.00
c. Pair, imperf. btwn., vert. or horizontal 650.00 1,500.

Issues for Austria only

1874-80 *Perf. 9½*

Fine Print

34 A9 2kr yellow ('76) 11.00 .75
35 A9 3kr green ('76) 45.00 .60
36 A9 5kr rose, type III 5.00 .20
37 A9 10kr blue ('75) 100.00 .40
38 A9 15kr brown ('77) 6.75 5.50
39 A9 25kr gray lil ('78) 1.00 125.00

Perf. 9

34a A9 2kr 175.00 42.50
35a A9 3kr 150.00 19.00
36a A9 5kr 62.50 2.25
37a A9 10kr 300.00 25.00
38a A9 15kr 450.00 75.00

Perf. 10½

34b A9 2kr 45.00 2.75
35b A9 3kr 80.00 1.75
36b A9 5kr 11.00 .75
37b A9 10kr 175.00 2.00
38b A9 15kr 190.00 16.00

Perf. 12

34c A9 2kr 200.00 100.00
35c A9 3kr 175.00 16.00
36c A9 5kr 45.00 3.75
37c A9 10kr 375.00 90.00
38c A9 15kr 625.00 140.00
40 A10 50kr brown ('80) 17.50 125.00

Perf. 13

34d A9 2kr 225.00 225.00
35d A9 3kr 160.00 22.50
36d A9 5kr 75.00 13.50
37d A9 10kr 200.00 65.00
38d A9 15kr 450.00 300.00
40a A10 50kr 27.50 150.00

Perf. 9x10½

34e A9 2kr 300.00 57.50
35e A9 3kr 250.00 50.00
36e A9 5kr 90.00 17.50
37e A9 10kr 275.00 65.00

Various compound perforations exist.

Values are for stamps that do not show the watermark. Stamps showing the watermark often sell for more.

For similar designs see Offices in the Turkish Empire A1-A2.

A11

Perf. 9, 9½, 10, 10½, 11½, 12, 12½

1883

Inscriptions in Black

41 A11 2kr brown 5.50 .40
42 A11 3kr green 5.00 .30
43 A11 5kr rose 25.00 .25
a. Vert. pair, imperf. btwn. 175.00 350.00
44 A11 10kr blue 4.00 .30
45 A11 20kr gray 47.50 3.50
46 A11 50kr red lilac 275.00 60.00

The last printings of Nos. 41-46 are watermarked "ZEITUNGS-MARKEN" instead of "BRIEF-MARKEN." Values are for stamps that do not show watermark. Stamps with watermarks that are identifiable as being from "BRIEF-MARKEN" sheets often sell for slightly more, while those with watermarks identifying stamps from "ZEITUNGS-MARKEN" sheets often sell for considerably more.

The 5kr has been reprinted in a dull red rose, perforated 10½.

For similar design see Offices in the Turkish Empire A3.

For surcharges see Offices in the Turkish Empire Nos. 15-19.

A12

A13

Perf. 9 to 13½, also Compound

1890-96 Unwmk.

Granite Paper

Numerals in black, Nos. 51-61

51 A12 1kr dark gray 1.25 .25
a. Pair, imperf. between 175.00 450.00
52 A12 2kr light brown .25 .25
53 A12 3kr gray green .40 .25
a. Pair, imperf. between 250.00 500.00
54 A12 5kr rose .40 .25
a. Pair, imperf. between 175.00 375.00
55 A12 10kr ultramarine .90 .25
a. Pair, imperf. between 275.00 550.00
56 A12 12kr claret 2.00 .35
a. Pair, imperf. between —
57 A12 15kr lilac 2.00 .35
a. Pair, imperf. between 350.00 750.00
58 A12 20kr olive green 30.00 2.00
59 A12 24kr gray blue 2.00 1.25
a. Pair, imperf. between 400.00 550.00
60 A12 30kr dark brown 2.50 .65
61 A12 50kr violet 5.00 7.50

Engr.

62 A13 1gld dark blue 2.50 2.25
63 A13 1gld pale lilac ('96) 37.50 3.50
64 A13 2gld carmine 3.00 16.00
65 A13 2gld gray green ('96) 13.50 32.50
Nos. 51-65 (15) 103.20 67.60

Nearly all values of the 1890-1907 issues are found with numerals missing in one or more corners, some with numerals printed on the back.

For surcharges see Offices in the Turkish Empire Nos. 20-25, 28-31.

A14

Perf. 9 to 13½, also Compound

1891 Typo.

Numerals in black

66 A14 20kr olive green 1.75 .25
67 A14 24kr gray blue 3.00 .75
68 A14 30kr brown 1.75 .25
a. Pair, imperf. between 250.00 625.00
b. Perf. 9 95.00 40.00
69 A14 50kr violet 1.75 .35
Nos. 66-69 (4) 8.25 1.60

For surcharges see Offices in the Turkish Empire Nos. 26-27.

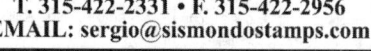

A15

A16

A17

A18

Perf. 10½ to 13½ and Compound

1899

Without Varnish Bars

Numerals in black, Nos. 70-82

70 A15 1h lilac .60 .20
 b. Imperf. 50.00 *110.00*
 c. Perf. 10½ 21.00 5.25
 d. Numerals inverted 1,500. *1,850.*
71 A15 2h dark gray 2.50 .50
72 A15 3h bister brown 5.50 .20
 b. "3" in lower right corner sideways *2,000.*
73 A15 5h blue green 6.50 .20
 c. Perf. 10½ 13.00 3.25
74 A15 6h orange .60 .20
75 A16 10h rose 14.00 .20
 b. Perf. 10½ 525.00 140.00
76 A16 20h brown 4.25 .20
77 A16 25h ultramarine 50.00 .30
78 A16 30h red violet 16.00 2.25
 b. Horiz. pair, imperf. btwn. 300.00 —
80 A17 40h green 26.00 2.75
81 A17 50h gray blue 15.00 3.50
 b. All four "50's" parallel *2,500.*
82 A17 60h brown 40.00 1.10
 b. Horiz. pair, imperf. btwn. 375.00 —
 c. Perf. 10½ 75.00 3.00

Engr.

83 A18 1k carmine rose 5.00 .20
 a. 1k carmine 5.00 .20
 b. Vert. pair, imperf. btwn. 225.00 *300.00*
84 A18 2k gray lilac 42.50 .40
 a. Vert. pair, imperf. btwn. 300.00 *550.00*
85 A18 4k gray green 8.75 *12.00*
 Nos. 70-85 (15) 237.20 24.20

For surcharges see Offices in Crete Nos. 1-7, Offices in the Turkish Empire Nos. 32-45.

1901 **With Varnish Bars**

70a A15 1h lilac 1.75 .40
71a A15 2h dark gray 1.75 .35
72a A15 3h bister brown .60 .20
73a A15 5h blue green .60 .20
74a A15 6h orange .60 .20
75a A16 10h rose .60 .20
76a A16 20h brown .65 .20
77a A16 25h ultra .85 .40
78a A16 30h red violet 1.75 .90
79 A17 35h green .85 .40
80a A17 40h green 1.60 *3.25*
81a A17 50h gray blue 4.00 *7.50*
82a A17 60h brown 2.00 .65
 Nos. 70a-78a,79,80a-82a (13) 17.60 14.85

The diagonal yellow bars of varnish were printed across the face to prevent cleaning.

A19

A20

A21

Perf. 12½ to 13½ and Compound

1905-07 **Typo.**

Colored Numerals

Without Varnish Bars

86 A19 1h lilac .20 *.35*
87 A19 2h dark gray .20 .20
88 A19 3h bister brown .20 .20
89b A19 5h dk blue green 3.50 .20
90 A19 5h yellow grn ('06) .40 .20
91 A19 6h deep orange .40 .20
92 A20 10h carmine ('06) .45 .20
93 A20 12h violet ('07) 1.00 .65
94 A20 20h brown ('06) 3.00 .20
95 A20 25h ultra ('06) 3.50 .40
96 A20 30h red violet ('06) 7.50 .25

Black Numerals

97b A20 10h carmine 4.50 .20
98b A20 20h brown 32.50 1.25
99b A20 25h ultra 30.00 1.25
100b A20 30h red violet 50.00 2.00

White Numerals

101 A21 35h green 2.50 .25
102 A21 40h deep violet 2.50 .75
103 A21 50h dull blue 2.50 2.75
104 A21 60h yellow brown 2.50 .75
105 A21 72h rose 2.50 1.75
 Nos. 86-105 (20) 149.85 14.00
 Set, never hinged 325.00

For surcharges see Offices in Crete #8-14.

1904

With Varnish Bars

86a A19 1h lilac .50 *1.00*
87a A19 2h dark gray 1.60 .80
88a A19 3h bister brown 1.75 .20
89a A19 5h dk blue green 3.50 .20
91a A19 6h deep orange 13.00 .30
97a A20 10h carmine 2.25 .20
98a A20 20h brown 32.50 1.00
99a A20 25h ultra 30.00 1.00
100a A20 30h red violet 40.00 2.00
101a A21 35h green 32.50 .75
102a A21 40h deep violet 30.00 3.50
103a A21 50h dull blue 30.00 8.00
104a A21 60h yellow brown 35.00 1.50
105a A21 72h rose 2.25 1.50
 Nos. 86a-105a (14) 254.85 21.95
 Set, never hinged 575.00

Stamps of the 1901, 1904 and 1905 issues perf. 9 or 10½, also compound with 12½, were not sold at any post office, but were supplied only to some high-ranking officials. This applies also to the contemporary issues of Austrian Offices Abroad.

Karl VI — A22

Franz Josef — A23

Schönbrunn Castle — A24

Franz Josef — A25

Designs: 2h, Maria Theresa. 3h, Joseph II. 5h, 10h, 25h, Franz Josef. 6h, Leopold II. 12h, Franz I. 20h, Ferdinand I. 30h, Franz Josef as youth. 35h, Franz Josef in middle age. 60h, Franz Josef on horseback. 1k, Franz Josef in royal robes. 5k, Hofburg, Vienna.

1908-13 **Typo.** ***Perf. 12½***

110a A22 1h gray black .30 .20
111a A22 2h violet .25 .20
112 A22 3h magenta ('13) .20 .20
113 A22 5h yel grn ('13) .20 .20
 a. Booklet pane of 6 *20.00*
114a A22 6h buff .75 .75
115 A22 10h rose ('13) .20 .20
 a. Booklet pane of 6 60.00
116a A22 12h scarlet 1.25 1.00
117 A22 20h choc ('13) 1.60 .20
118 A22 25h ultra ('13) 1.50 .25
119 A22 30h ol grn ('13) 4.50 .30
120 A22 35h slate 2.50 .20

Engr.

121 A23 50h dark green .65 .20
 a. Vert. pair, imperf. btwn. 225.00 *325.00*
 b. Horiz. pair, imperf. btwn. 225.00 *325.00*
122 A23 60h deep carmine .35 .20
 a. Vert. pair, imperf. btwn. 260.00 *375.00*
 b. Horiz. pair, imperf. btwn. 260.00 *375.00*
123 A23 72h dk brown ('13) 1.75 .30
124 A23 1k purple 12.00 .20
 a. Vert. pair, imperf. btwn. 225.00 *325.00*
 b. Horiz. pair, imperf. btwn. 225.00 *325.00*
125 A24 2k lake & ol grn 18.00 .35
126 A24 5k bis & dk vio 35.00 4.50
127 A25 10k blue, bis & dp brn 165.00 62.50
 Nos. 110a-127 (18) 246.00 71.95
 Set, never hinged 560.00

Definitive set issued for the 60th year of the reign of Emperor Franz Josef.

The 1h-35h exist on both ordinary (1913) and chalk-surfaced (1908) paper. The cheaper varieties are listed above. For detailed listings, see the Scott Classic Specialized Catalogue.

All values exist imperforate. They were not sold at any post office, but presented to a number of high government officials. This applies also to all imperforate stamps of later issues, including semi-postals, etc., and those of the Austrian Offices Abroad.

Litho. forgeries of No. 127 exist.

For overprint and surcharge see #J47-J48. For similar designs see Offices in Crete A5-A6, Offices in the Turkish Empire A16-A17.

Birthday Jubilee Issue

Similar to 1908 Issue, but designs enlarged by labels at top and bottom bearing dates "1830" and "1910"

1910 **Typo.**

128 A22 1h gray black 4.00 *7.50*
129 A22 2h violet 7.75 *10.00*
130 A22 3h magenta 4.50 *8.00*
131 A22 5h yellow green .20 .25
132 A22 6h buff 3.00 *8.00*
133 A22 10h rose .20 .25
134 A22 12h scarlet 3.00 *8.00*
135 A22 20h chocolate 8.00 *10.00*
136 A22 25h deep blue 2.00 2.00
137 A22 30h olive green 3.25 *6.75*
138 A22 35h slate 3.25 *6.75*

Engr.

139 A23 50h dark green 4.50 *9.25*
140 A23 60h deep carmine 4.50 *9.25*
141 A23 1k purple 5.00 *11.00*
142 A24 2k lake & ol grn 125.00 *190.00*
143 A24 5k bister & dk vio 92.50 *150.00*
144 A25 10k blue, bis & dp brn 425.00 *275.00*
 Nos. 128-144 (17) 695.65 *712.00*
 Set, never hinged 1,250.

80th birthday of Emperor Franz Josef.
All values exist imperforate.
Litho. forgeries of Nos. 142-144 exist.

Austrian Crown — A37

Franz Josef — A38

A39

Coat of Arms — A40

1916-18 **Typo.**

145 A37 3h brt violet .20 .20
146 A37 5h lt green .20 .20
 a. Booklet pane of 6 14.00
 b. Booklet pane of 4 + 2 labels 27.50
147 A37 6h deep orange .25 *.80*
148 A37 10h magenta .20 .20
 a. Booklet pane of 6 27.50
149 A37 12h light blue .25 *1.40*
150 A38 15h rose red .40 .20
 a. Booklet pane of 6 15.00
151 A38 20h chocolate 2.25 .20
152 A38 25h blue 3.75 .40
153 A38 30h slate 3.50 .65
154 A39 40h olive green .20 .20
155 A39 50h blue green .20 .20
156 A39 60h deep blue .20 .20
157 A39 80h orange brown .20 .20
158 A39 90h red violet .20 .20
159 A39 1k car, *yel* ('18) .25 .20

Engr.

160 A40 2k dark blue 1.25 .20
161 A40 3k claret 19.00 1.00
162 A40 4k deep green 3.50 1.50
163 A40 10k deep violet 21.00 *40.00*
 Nos. 145-163 (19) 57.00 *48.15*
 Set, never hinged 125.00

Stamps of type A38 have two varieties of the frame. Stamps of type A40 have various decorations about the shield.

Nos. 145-163 exist imperf. Value set, $500 hinged, $850 never hinged..

1917 **Ordinary Paper**

164 A40 2k light blue 1.25 .25
165 A40 3k carmine rose 32.50 .75
166 A40 4k yellow green 1.75 1.10
167 A40 10k violet 110.00 75.00
 Nos. 164-167 (4) 145.50 77.10
 Set, never hinged 275.00

Nos. 164-167 exist imperf. Value set, $325 hinged, $500 never hinged.

See Nos. 172-175 (granite paper). For overprints and surcharges see Nos. 181-199, C1-C3, J60-J63, N1-N5, N10-N19, N33-N37, N42-N51. Western Ukraine 2-7, 11-15, 19-28, 57-58, 85-89, 94-103, N3-N14, NJ13.

Emperor Karl I — A42

1917-18 **Typo.**

168 A42 15h dull red .20 .20
 a. Booklet pane of 6 14.00
169 A42 20h dk green ('18) .20 .20
 a. 20h green ('17) .50 .25
 Never hinged 3.50
170 A42 25h blue .50 .20
171 A42 30h dull violet .30 .20
 Nos. 168-171 (4) 1.20 .80
 Set, never hinged 6.50

Nos. 168-171 exist imperf. Value set, $125 hinged, $190 never hinged.

For overprints and surcharges see Nos. N6-N9, N20, N38-N41, N52, N64. Western Ukraine 1, 8, 16-18, 90-93, N15-N18.

1918-19 **Engr.**

Granite Paper

172 A40 2k light blue .20 *.35*
 a. Perf. 11½ 625.00 *750.00*
 Never hinged, #172a 925.00
173 A40 3k carmine rose .25 *.75*
174 A40 4k yellow green ('19) 3.00 *18.00*
175 A40 10k lt violet ('19) 6.25 *21.00*
 Nos. 172-175 (4) 9.70 *40.10*
 Set, never hinged 20.00

Issues of the Republic

Austrian Stamps of 1916-18 Overprinted

1918-19 **Unwmk.** ***Perf. 12½***

181 A37 3h bright violet .20 .20
182 A37 5h light green .20 .20
183 A37 6h deep orange .20 1.10
184 A37 10h magenta .20 .20
185 A37 12h light blue .25 *1.25*
186 A42 15h dull red .20 *1.00*
187 A42 20h deep green .20 .20
188 A42 25h blue .20 .20
189 A42 30h dull violet .20 .20
190 A39 40h olive green .20 .20
191 A39 50h deep green .45 *1.10*
192 A39 60h deep blue .45 *1.75*
193 A39 80h orange brown .20 .20
 a. Inverted overprint 200.00
 Never hinged, #193a 275.00
194 A39 90h red violet .20 *.45*
195 A39 1k carmine, *yel* .20 *.25*

Granite Paper

196 A40 2k light blue .20 .20
 a. Horiz. pair, imperf. between 240.00
 Never hinged, #196a 325.00
 b. Vert. pair, imperf. between 240.00
 Never hinged, #196b 325.00
 c. Perf. 11½ 65.00 62.50
 Never hinged, #196c 100.00
197 A40 3k carmine rose .30 *.75*
198 A40 4k yellow green .80 *1.90*
 a. Perf. 11½ 16.00 25.00
 Never hinged, #198a 27.50
199 A40 10k deep violet 7.25 *17.50*
 Nos. 181-199 (19) 12.10 *28.85*
 Set, never hinged 20.00

Nos. 181, 182, 184, 187-191, 194, 197 and 199 exist imperforate.

Post Horn — A43

Coat of Arms — A44

Allegory of New Republic — A45

1919-20 Typo. *Perf. 12½*

Ordinary Paper

200 A43 3h gray .20 .20
201 A44 5h yellow green .20 .20
202 A44 5h gray ('20) .20 .20
203 A43 6h orange .20 *.45*
204 A44 10h deep rose .20 .20
205 A44 10h red ('20) .20 .20
a. Thick grayish paper ('20) .20 .20
206 A43 12h grnsh blue .20 *.65*
207 A43 15h bister ('20) .20 *.55*
a. Thick grayish paper ('20) .20 .20
208 A45 20h dark green .20 .20
a. 20h yellow green .20 .20
b. As "a," thick grysh paper ('20) .50 2.00
209 A44 25h blue .20 .20
210 A43 25h violet ('20) .20 .20
211 A45 30h dark brown .20 .20
212 A45 40h violet .20 .20
213 A45 40h lake ('20) .20 .20
214 A44 45h olive green .20 *.60*
215 A45 50h dark blue .20 .20
a. Thick grayish paper ('20) .25 *.55*
216 A43 60h olive green ('20) .20 .20
217 A44 1k carmine, *yel* .20 .20
218 A44 1k light blue ('20) .20 .20
Nos. 200-218 (19) 3.80 5.25
Set, never hinged 4.25

All values exist imperf. (For regularly issued imperfs, see Nos. 227-235.)

For overprints and surcharge see Nos. B11-B19, B30-B38, J102, N21, N27, N53, N58, N65, N71.

Parliament Building A46

1919-20 Engr. *Perf. 12½, 11½*

Granite Paper

219 A46 2k ver & blk .25 *.55*
a. Center inverted *3,650.*
b. Perf. 11½ .75 *1.50*
220 A46 2½k olive bis ('20) .20 *.25*
221 A46 3k blue & blk brn .20 .20
a. Perf. 11½ 3.50 *6.75*
222 A46 4k carmine & blk .20 .20
a. Center inverted *2,250.* *1,450.*
b. Perf. 11½ 1.75 *3.50*
223 A46 5k black ('20) .20 .20
a. Perf. 11½x12½ 45.00 *67.50*
Never hinged 90.00
b. Perf. 11½ 2.75 *5.00*
224 A46 7½k plum .20 *.35*
a. Perf. 11½ 110.00 160.00
Never hinged 210.00
b. Perf. 11½x12½ 75.00 125.00
Never hinged 125.00
225 A46 10k olive grn & blk brn .20 *.35*
a. Perf. 11½x12½ 125.00 175.00
Never hinged 210.00
b. Perf. 11½ 14.50 25.00
Never hinged 25.00
226 A46 20k lil & red ('20) .20 *.45*
a. Center inverted *10,500.* *6,250.*
b. Perf. 11½ 62.50 110.00
Never hinged 110.00
Nos. 219-226 (8) 1.65 *2.55*
Set, never hinged 2.25

A number of values exist imperforate between. Values, $300 to $400 a pair.

See No. 248. For overprints and surcharge see Nos. B23-B29, B43-B49, N30, N60, N74.

1920 Typo. *Imperf.*

Ordinary Paper

227 A44 5h yellow green .20 *.45*
228 A44 5h gray .20 .20
229 A44 10h deep rose .20 .20
230 A44 10h red .20 .20
231 A43 15h bister .20 .20
232 A43 25h violet .20 .20
233 A45 30h dark brown .20 .20
234 A45 40h violet .20 .20
235 A43 60h olive green .20 .20
Nos. 227-235 (9) 2.05
Set, never hinged 1.40

Arms
A47 A48

1920-21 Typo. *Perf. 12½*

Ordinary Paper

238 A47 80h rose .20 .20
239 A47 1k black brown .20 .20
241 A47 1½k green ('21) .20 .20
242 A47 2k blue .20 .30
243 A48 3k yel grn & dk grn ('21) .20 *.30*
244 A48 4k red & claret ('21) .20 .20
245 A48 5k vio & claret ('21) .20 .20
246 A48 7½k yel & brn ('21) .20 *.25*
247 A48 10k ultra & blue ('21) .20 *.20*
Nos. 238-247 (9) 1.80 2.05
Set, never hinged 2.25

Nos. 238-245, 247 exist on white paper of good quality and on thick grayish paper of inferior quality; No. 246 only on white paper. Values are are for the cheaper varieties. See the Scott Classic Specialized Catalogue for detailed listings.

For overprints and surcharges see Nos. B20-B22, B39-B42, N22-N23, N31, N54-N55, N61-N62, N66-N67.

1921 Engr.

248 A46 50k dk violet, *yel* .35 *.80*
Never hinged .60
a. Perf. 11½ 15.00 *50.00*
Never hinged 25.00

Symbols of Agriculture A49

Symbols of Labor and Industry A50

1922-24 Typo. *Perf. 12½*

250 A49 ½k olive bister .20 *.60*
251 A50 1k brown .20 .20
252 A50 2k cobalt blue .20 .20
253 A49 2½k orange brown .20 .20
254 A50 4k dull violet .20 *1.00*
255 A49 5k gray green .20 .20
256 A49 7½k gray violet .20 .20
257 A50 10k claret .20 .20
258 A49 12½k gray green .20 .20
259 A49 15k bluish green .20 .20
260 A49 20k dark blue .20 .20
261 A49 25k claret .20 .20
262 A50 30k pale gray .20 .20
263 A50 45k pale red .20 .20
264 A50 50k orange brown .20 .20
265 A50 60k yellow green .20 .20
266 A50 75k ultramarine .20 .20
267 A50 80k yellow .20 .20
268 A49 100k gray .20 .20
269 A49 120k brown .20 .20
270 A49 150k orange .20 .20
271 A49 160k light green .20 .20
272 A49 180k red .20 .20
273 A49 200k pink .20 .20
274 A49 240k dark violet .20 .20
275 A49 300k light blue .20 .20
276 A49 400k deep green .85 .20
a. 400k gray green .85 .30
277 A49 500k yellow .20 .20
278 A49 600k slate .20 .20
279 A49 700k brown ('24) .70 .20
280 A49 800k violet ('24) .80 *1.50*
281 A50 1000k violet ('23) .55 .20
282 A50 1200k car rose ('23) .35 *.45*
283 A50 1500k orange ('24) 1.00 .20
284 A50 1600k slate ('23) 2.75 2.75
285 A50 2000k dp bl ('23) 3.50 1.50
286 A50 3000k lt blue ('23) 11.00 1.75
287 A50 4000k dk bl, *bl* ('24) 5.00 2.10
Nos. 250-287 (38) 32.10 17.65
Set, never hinged 92.50

Nos. 250-287 exist imperf. Value set, $500 hinged, $750 never hinged.

For overprints & surcharges see #N24-N26, N28-N29, N32, N56, N59, N63, N68-N70, N72-N73.

Symbols of Art and Science — A51

1922-24 Engr. *Perf. 12½*

288 A51 20k dark brn .20 .20
a. Perf. 11½ 1.10 *1.25*
Never hinged, #288a 1.60
289 A51 25k blue .20 .20
a. Perf. 11½ 1.00 *2.50*
Never hinged, #289a 1.90
290 A51 50k brown red .20 .20
a. Perf. 11½ 2.25 *3.50*
Never hinged, #290a 3.75
b. Vert. pair, imperf. btwn. 200.00 *250.00*
Never hinged 250.00
291 A51 100k deep grn .20 .20
a. Perf. 11½ 5.50 *7.00*
Never hinged, #291a 8.00
b. Vert. pair, imperf. btwn. — *375.00*
Never hinged —
292 A51 200k dark violet .20 .20
a. Perf. 11½ 8.00 *13.50*
Never hinged, #292a 12.00
b. Vert. pair, imperf. btwn. 300.00
Never hinged 375.00
293 A51 500k dp orange .20 *1.00*
294 A51 1000k blk vio, *yel* .20 .20
a. Perf. 11½ 160.00 *250.00*
Never hinged, #294a 400.00
b. Vert. pair, imperf. btwn. 240.00
Never hinged 300.00
c. Horiz. pair, imperf. btwn. 300.00
Never hinged 375.00
295 A51 2000k olive grn, *yel* .20 .20
a. Vert. pair, imperf. btwn. 275.00
Never hinged 325.00
296 A51 3000k claret brn ('23) 8.00 .65
297 A51 5000k gray black ('23) 1.50 1.50

Granite Paper

298 A51 10,000k red brown ('24) 3.25 *4.00*
Nos. 288-298 (11) 14.35 8.55
Set, never hinged 35.00

On Nos. 281-287, 291-298 "kronen" is abbreviated to "k" and transposed with the numerals.

Nos. 288-298 exist imperf. Value set, $375 hinged, $625 never hinged.

Numeral A52

Fields Crossed by Telegraph Wires A53

White-Shouldered Eagle — A54

Church of Minorite Friars — A55

1925-27 Typo. *Perf. 12*

303 A52 1g dark gray .20 .20
304 A52 2g claret .35 .20
305 A52 3g scarlet .70 .20
306 A52 4g grnsh blue ('27) 1.10 .20
307 A52 5g brown orange 1.50 .20
308 A52 6g ultramarine 1.25 .20
309 A52 7g chocolate 1.50 .20
310 A52 8g yellow green 5.75 .20
311 A53 10g orange .35 .20
313 A53 15g red lilac .35 .20
314 A53 16g dark blue .35 .20
315 A53 18g olive green 1.10 .55
316 A54 20g dark violet .35 .20
317 A54 24g carmine .70 .40
318 A54 30g dark brown .55 .20
319 A54 40g ultramarine 1.10 .20
320 A54 45g yellow brown 1.25 .20
321 A54 50g gray 1.50 .25
322 A54 80g turquoise blue 3.25 *4.50*

Perf. 12½

Engr.

323 A55 1s deep green 15.00 1.40
a. 1s light green 210.00 8.25
b As "a," pair, imperf between 425.00
Never hinged 550.00
Never hinged, #323a 625.00
324 A55 2s brown rose 6.25 *10.00*
Nos. 303-324 (21) 44.45 *20.10*
Set, never hinged 140.00

#303-324 exist imperf. Value, set $425.

For type A52 surcharged see Nos. B118.

Güssing — A56

National Library, Vienna — A57

15g, Hochosterwitz. 16g, 20g, Durnstein. 18g, Traunsee. 24g, Salzburg. 30g, Seewiesen. 40g, Innsbruck. 50g, Worthersee. 60g, Hohenems. 2s, St. Stephen's Cathedral, Vienna.

1929-30 Typo. *Perf. 12½*

Size: 25½x21½mm

326 A56 10g brown orange .90 .20
327 A56 10g bister ('30) .90 .20
328 A56 15g violet brown .70 *1.25*

329 A56 16g dark gray 1.75 .20
330 A56 18g blue green .40 .45
331 A56 20g dark gray ('30) .40 .20
332 A56 24g maroon 4.25 6.00
333 A56 24g lake ('30) 6.50 .45
334 A56 30g dark violet 4.25 .20
335 A56 40g dark blue 7.25 .20
336 A56 50g gray violet ('30) 27.50 .20
337 A56 60g olive green 22.50 .25

Engr.
Size: 21x26mm

338 A57 1s black brown 5.25 .25
a. Horiz. pair, imperf. btwn. 240.00
Never hinged 300.00
b. Vert. pair, imperf. btwn. 240.00
Never hinged 300.00
339 A57 2s dark green 9.25 8.75
a. Horiz. pair, imperf. btwn. 240.00
Never hinged 300.00
Nos. 326-339 (14) 91.80 18.80
Set, never hinged 290.00

#326, 328-330 and 332-339 exist imperf. Values, set of 12 unused hinged $1,300, never hinged $1,650.

Type of 1929-30 Issue

Designs: 12g, Traunsee. 64g, Hohenems.

1932 **Perf. 12**
Size: 21x16½mm

340 A56 10g olive brown .80 .20
341 A56 12g blue green 1.50 .20
342 A56 18g blue green 1.40 2.10
343 A56 20g dark gray 1.10 .20
344 A56 24g carmine rose 5.25 .20
345 A56 24g dull violet 3.50 .20
346 A56 30g dark violet 17.50 .20
347 A56 30g carmine rose 4.25 .20
a. Vert. pair, imperf. btwn. 40.00
Never hinged, #347a 50.00
348 A56 40g dark blue 19.00 .90
349 A56 40g dark violet 6.25 .30
350 A56 50g gray violet 24.00 .30
351 A56 50g dull blue 5.75 .30
352 A56 60g gray green 52.50 2.75
353 A56 64g gray green 12.00 .30
Nos. 340-353 (14) 154.80 8.35
Set, never hinged 500.00

For overprints and surcharges see Nos. B87-B92, B119-B121.

Nos. 340-353 exist imperf. Values, set unused hinged, $575, never hinged $725.

Burgenland A67

Tyrol A68

Costumes of various districts: 3g, Burgenland. 4g, 5g, Carinthia. 6g, 8g, Lower Austria. 12g, 20g, Upper Austria. 24g, 25g, Salzburg. 30g, 35g, Styria. 45g, Tyrol. 60g, Vorarlberg bridal couple. 64g, Vorarlberg. 1s, Viennese family. 2s, Military.

1934-35 **Typo.** **Perf. 12**

354 A67 1g dark violet .20 .20
355 A67 3g scarlet .20 .20
356 A67 4g olive green .20 .20
357 A67 5g red violet .20 .20
358 A67 6g ultramarine .20 .25
359 A67 8g green .20 .20
360 A67 12g dark brown .20 .20
361 A67 20g yellow brown .20 .20
362 A67 24g grnsh blue .20 .20
363 A67 25g violet .20 .25
364 A67 30g maroon .20 .20
365 A67 35g rose carmine .30 .45

Perf. 12½

366 A68 40g slate gray .40 .25
367 A68 45g brown red .35 .20
368 A68 60g ultramarine .60 .35
369 A68 64g brown .75 .20
370 A68 1s deep violet .90 .55
371 A68 2s dull green 35.00 65.00

Designs Redrawn
Perf. 12 (6g), 12½ (2s)

372 A67 6g ultra ('35) .20 .20
373 A68 2s emerald ('35) 3.25 5.25
Nos. 354-373 (20) 43.95 74.75
Set, never hinged 110.00

The design of No. 358 looks as though the man's ears were on backwards, while No. 372 appears correctly.

On No. 373 there are seven feathers on each side of the eagle instead of five.

Nos. 354-373 exist imperf. Values, set unused hinged $375, never hinged $450.

For surcharges see Nos. B128-B131.

Dollfuss Mourning Issue

Engelbert Dollfuss — A85

1934-35 **Engr.** **Perf. 12½**

374 A85 24g greenish black .40 .30
Never hinged 1.25
375 A85 24g indigo ('35) .75 .70
Never hinged 2.50

Nos. 374-375 exist imperf. Vale, each unused hinged $120, never hinged $150.

"Mother and Child," by Joseph Danhauser A86

"Madonna and Child," after Painting by Dürer — A87

1935, May 1

376 A86 24g dark blue .40 .20
Never hinged 1.00
a. Vert. pair, imperf. btwn. 200.00
Never hinged 250.00
b. Horiz. pair, imperf. btwn. 190.00
Never hinged 240.00

Mother's Day. No. 376 exists imperf. Value, unused hinged $150, never hinged $175.

1936, May 5 **Photo.**

377 A87 24g violet blue .20 .30
Never hinged .55

Mother's Day. No. 377 exists imperf. Value, unused hinged $150, never hinged $180.

Farm Workers — A88

Design: 5s, Factory workers.

1936, June **Engr.** **Perf. 12½**

378 A88 3s red orange 12.50 17.50
Never hinged 24.00
379 A88 5s brown black 30.00 42.50
Never hinged 45.00

Nos. 378-379 exist imperf. Values, set unused hinged $210, never hinged $250.

Engelbert Dollfuss A90

Mother and Child — A91

1936, July 25

380 A90 10s dark blue 675.00 800.00
Never hinged 900.00

Second anniv. of death of Engelbert Dollfuss, chancellor. Exists imperf. Value, $1,750, never hinged $2,000.

1937, May 5 **Photo.** **Perf. 12**

381 A91 24g henna brown .20 .25
Never hinged .55

Mother's Day. Exists imperf. Values, unused hinged $140, never hinged $165.

S.S. Maria Anna A92

Steamships: 24g, Uranus, 64g, Oesterreich.

1937, June 9

382 A92 12g red brown .60 .35
383 A92 24g deep blue .60 .35
384 A92 64g dark green .60 .80
Nos. 382-384 (3) 1.80 1.50
Set, never hinged 5.00

Centenary of steamship service on Danube River. Exist imperf. Values, set unused hinged $350, never hinged $450.

First Locomotive, "Austria" A95

Designs: 25g, Modern steam locomotive. 35g, Modern electric train.

1937, Nov. 22

385 A95 12g black brown .20 .20
386 A95 25g dark violet .65 1.00
387 A95 35g brown red 1.60 2.25
Nos. 385-387 (3) 2.45 3.45
Set, never hinged 7.00

Centenary of Austrian railways. Exist imperf. Values, set unused hinged $90, never hinged $110.

Rose and Zodiac Signs — A98

1937 **Engr.** **Perf. 13x12½**

388 A98 12g dark green .20 .20
389 A98 24g dark carmine .20 .20
Set, never hinged .40

Nos. 388-389 exist imperf. Values, set unused hinged $95, never hinged $120.

For Use in Vienna, Lower Austria and Burgenland

Germany Nos. 509-511 and 511B Overprinted in Black

a

b

1945 **Unwmk.** **Perf. 14**

390 A115(a) 5pf dp yellow green .20 .40
391 A115(b) 6pf purple .20 1.00
392 A115(a) 8pf red .20 .20
393 A115(b) 12pf carmine .20 .75
Nos. 390-393 (4) 2.35
Set, never hinged .40

Nos. 390-393 exist with overprint inverted or double.

Germany No. 507, the 3pf, with overprint "a" was prepared, not issued, but sold to collectors after the definitive Republic issue had been placed in use. Values, $30 hinged, $60 never hinged.

German Semi-Postal Stamps, #B207, B209, B210, B283 Surcharged in Black

c

d

1945 **Perf. 14, 14x13½, 13½x14**

394 SP181(c) 5pf on 12pf + 88pf .50 1.60
395 SP184(d) 6pf on 6pf + 14pf 3.00 11.00
396 SP242(d) 8pf on 42pf + 108pf .75 2.25
397 SP183(d) 12pf on 3pf + 7pf .50 1.25
Nos. 394-397 (4) 4.75 16.10
Set, never hinged 9.00

The surcharges are spaced to fit the stamps.

Stamps of Germany, Nos. 509 to 511, 511B, 519 and 529 Overprinted

e

f

1945 **Typo.** **Perf. 14**
Size: 18½x22½mm

398 A115(e) 5pf dp yel grn .25 1.75
399 A115(f) 5pf dp yel grn 4.75 17.50
400 A115(e) 6pf purple .20 1.25
401 A115(e) 8pf red .20 .75
402 A115(e) 12pf carmine .20 1.00

Engr.
Size: 21½x26mm

403 A115(e) 30pf olive green 6.25 10.00
a. Thin bar at bottom 15.00 17.50
a. Never hinged 25.00
404 A118(e) 42pf brt green 10.00 32.50
a. Thin bar at bottom 15.00 27.50
a. Never hinged 25.00
Nos. 398-404 (7) 21.85 64.75
Set, never hinged 55.00

On Nos. 403a and 404a, the bottom bar of the overprint is 2½mm wide, and, as the overprint was applied in two operations, "Osterreich" is usually not exactly centered in its diagonal slot. On Nos. 403 and 404, the bottom bar is 3mm wide, and "Osterreich" is always well centered.

Germany Nos. 524-527 (the 1m, 2m, 3m and 5m), overprinted with vertical bars and "Osterreich" similar to "e" and "f," were prepared, not issued, but sold to collectors after the definitive Republic issue had been placed in use. Value for set, $70 hinged, $150 ever hinged.

Counterfeits exist of Nos. 403-404, 403a-404a and 1m-5m overprints.

For Use in Styria

Stamps of Germany Nos. 506 to 511, 511A, 511B, 514 to 523 and 529 Overprinted in Black

1945 Unwmk. Typo. *Perf. 14*

Size: 18½x22½mm

405 A115 1pf gray black 1.50 *4.00*
406 A115 3pf lt brown 1.00 *4.00*
407 A115 4pf slate 5.00 *15.00*
408 A115 5pf dp yel grn 1.40 *4.00*
409 A115 6pf purple .20 *.40*
410 A115 8pf red .30 *1.00*
411 A115 10pf dark brown 1.25 *4.00*
412 A115 12pf carmine .20 *.50*

Engr.

413 A115 15pf brown lake .40 *2.25*
414 A115 16pf pck green 10.00 *37.50*
415 A115 20pf blue 1.00 *4.00*
416 A115 24pf org brn 10.00 *40.00*

Size: 22½x26mm

417 A115 25pf brt ultra 1.00 *4.00*
418 A115 30pf olive green 1.00 *4.00*
419 A115 40pf brt red violet 1.25 *4.00*
420 A118 42pf brt green 2.10 *6.50*
421 A115 50pf myrtle green 1.60 *5.00*
422 A115 60pf dk red brown 2.00 *5.75*
423 A115 80pf indigo 1.50 *5.25*
Nos. 405-423 (19) 42.70 *151.15*
Set, never hinged 65.00

Overprinted on Nos. 524-527

Perf. 12½, 14

424 A116 1m dk slate grn 7.50 *20.00*
a. Perf. 12½ 100.00
425 A116 2m violet 7.50 *25.00*
a. Perf. 14 12.00 *45.00*
426 A116 3m copper red 25.00 *55.00*
a. Perf. 14 125.00
427 A116 5m dark blue 225.00 *525.00*
a. Perf. 14 *575.00*
Nos. 424-427 (4) 265.00 *625.00*
Set, never hinged 450.00

On the preceding four stamps the innermost vertical lines are 10½mm apart; on the pfennig values 6½mm apart.

Counterfeits exist of Nos. 405-427 overprints.

Germany Nos. 524 to 527 Overprinted in Black

Perf. 14

428 A116 1m dk slate grn 10.50 *22.50*
429 A116 2m violet 12.00 *25.00*

Perf. 12½

430 A116 3m copper red 21.00 *55.00*
431 A116 5m dark blue 140.00 *425.00*
a. Perf. 14 *600.00*
Nos. 428-431 (4) 183.50 *527.50*
Set, never hinged 375.00

On the preceding four stamps, "Osterreich" is thinner, measuring 16mm. On the previous set of 23 values it measures 18mm.

Counterfeits exist of Nos. 428-431 overprints.

Catalogue values for unused stamps in this section, from this point to the end of the section, are for Never Hinged items.

For Use in Vienna, Lower Austria and Burgenland

Coat of Arms
A99 A100

Typographed or Lithographed

1945, July 3 Unwmk. *Perf. 14x13½*

Size: 21x25mm

432 A99 3pf brown .20 .20
433 A99 4pf slate .20 .20
434 A99 5pf dark green .20 .20
435 A99 6pf deep violet .20 .20
436 A99 8pf orange brown .20 .20
437 A99 10pf deep brown .20 .20
438 A99 12pf rose carmine .20 .20
439 A99 15pf orange red .20 .20
440 A99 16pf dull blue green .20 .35

Perf. 14

Size: 24x28½mm

441 A99 20pf light blue .20 .20
442 A99 24pf orange .20 .20
443 A99 25pf dark blue .20 .20
444 A99 30pf deep gray grn .20 .20
445 A99 38pf ultramarine .20 .20
446 A99 40pf brt red vio .20 .20
447 A99 42pf sage green .20 .20
448 A99 50pf blue green .20 *.60*
449 A99 60pf maroon .20 .20
450 A99 80pf dull lilac .20 .20

Engr. *Perf. 14x13½*

451 A100 1m dark green .20 *.35*
452 A100 2m dark purple .20 *.40*
453 A100 3m dark violet .20 *.60*
454 A100 5m brown red .25 *.75*
Nos. 432-454 (23) 4.65 *6.45*

Nos. 432, 433, 437, 439, 440, 443, 446, 448, 449 are typographed. Nos. 434, 435, 441, 442 are lithographed; the other values exist both ways.

For overprint see No. 604.

For General Use

Lermoos, Winter Scene — A101

The Prater Woods, Vienna — A105

Wolfgang See, near Salzburg A106

Lake Constance A110

Dürnstein, Lower Austria A124

Designs: 4g, Eisenerz surface mine. 5g, Leopoldsberg, near Vienna. 6g, Hohensalzburg, Salzburg Province. 10gr, Hochosterwitz, Carinthia. 15g, Forchtenstein Castle, Burgenland. 16g, Gesäuse Valley. 24g, Höldrichs Mill, Lower Austria. 25g, Oetz Valley Outlet, Tyrol. 30g, Neusiedler Lake, Burgenland. 35g, Belvedere Palace, Vienna. 38g, Langbath Lake. 40g, Mariazell, Styria. 42g, Traunkirchen. 45g, Hartenstein Castle. 50g, Silvretta Mountains, Vorarlberg. 60g, Railroad viaducts near Semmering. 70g, Waterfall of Bad-Gastein, Salzburg. 80g, Kaiser Mountains, Tyrol. 90g, Wayside Shrine, Tragöss, Styria. 2s, St. Christof am Arlberg, Tyrol. 3s, Heiligenblut, Carinthia. 5s, Schönbrunn, Vienna.

Perf. 14x13½

1945-46 Photo. Unwmk.

455 A101 3g sapphire .20 .20
456 A101 4g dp orange ('46) .20 .20
457 A101 5g dk carmine rose .20 .20
458 A101 6g dk slate green .20 .20
459 A105 8g golden brown .20 .20
460 A106 10g dark green .20 .20
461 A106 12g dark brown .20 .20
462 A106 15g dk slate bl ('46) .20 .20
463 A106 16g chnt brn ('46) .20 .20

Perf. 13½x14

464 A110 20g dp ultra ('46) .20 .20
465 A110 24g dp yellow grn ('46) .20 .20
466 A110 25g gray black ('46) .20 .20
467 A110 30g dark red .20 .20
468 A110 35g brown red ('46) .20 .20
469 A110 38g brn olive ('46) .20 .20
470 A110 40g gray .20 .20
471 A110 42g brn org ('46) .20 .20
472 A110 45g dark blue ('46) .25 *.35*
473 A110 50g dark blue .20 .20
474 A110 60g dark violet .20 .20
a. Imperf., pair 45.00 *60.00*
475 A110 70g Prus blue ('46) .20 *.25*
476 A110 80g brown .20 *.40*
477 A110 90g Prussian green .90 1.00
478 A124 1s dk red brn ('46) .50 .75
479 A124 2s blue gray ('46) 2.75 2.00
480 A124 3s dk slate grn ('46) .65 *.65*
481 A124 5s dark red ('46) 1.10 *1.25*
Nos. 455-481 (27) 10.35 10.45

See Nos. 486-488, 496-515. For overprints and surcharges see Nos. 492-493, B166, B280, B287.

No. 461 Overprinted in Carmine

1946, Sept. 26

482 A106 12g dark brown .20 .25

Meeting of the Soc. for Cultural and Economic Relations with the USSR, Vienna, Sept. 26-29.

City Hall Park, Vienna A128

Hochosterwitz, Carinthia A129

Perf. 14x13½

1946-47 Photo. Unwmk.

483 A128 8g deep plum .20 .20
484 A128 8g olive brown .20 .20
a. 8g dark olive green .20 .20
485 A129 10g dk brn vio ('47) .20 .20

Perf. 13½x14

486 A110 30g blue gray ('47) .35 .35
487 A110 50g brown violet ('47) .25 .30
488 A110 60g violet blue ('47) 1.60 1.40
Nos. 483-488 (6) 2.80 2.65

See No. 502.

Franz Grillparzer A130

1947 Engr. *Perf. 14x13½*

489 A130 18g chocolate .20 .20

Photo.

490 A130 18g dk violet brn .20 .20

Death of Grillparzer, dramatic poet, 75th anniv.

A second printing of No. 490 on thicker paper has a darker frame and clearer delineation of the portrait.

Issue dates: #489, Feb. 10; #490, Mar. 31.

Franz Schubert — A131

1947, Mar. 31 Engr.

491 A131 12g dark green .20 .20

150th birth anniv. of Franz Schubert, musician and composer.

Nos. 469 and 463 Surcharged in Brown

1947, Sept. 1 Photo. *Perf. 14*

492 A110 75g on 38g brown ol .20 *.50*
493 A106 1.40s on 16g chnt brn .20 .20

The surcharge on No. 493 varies from brown to black brown.

Symbols of Global Telegraphic Communication A132

1947, Nov. 5 Engr. *Perf. 14x13½*

495 A132 40g dark violet .20 .20

Centenary of the telegraph in Austria.

Scenic Type of 1946

1946, Aug. Photo. *Perf. 13½x14*

496 A124 1s dark brown .75 .50
497 A124 2s dark blue 5.00 3.25
498 A124 3s dark slate green 1.25 .75
499 A124 5s dark red 27.50 12.50
Nos. 496-499 (4) 34.50 17.00

On Nos. 478 to 481 the upper and lower panels show a screen effect. On Nos. 496 to 499 the panels appear to be solid color.

Scenic Types of 1945-46

1947-48 Photo. *Perf. 14x13½*

500 A101 3g bright red .20 .20
501 A101 5g bright red .20 .20
502 A129 10g bright red .20 .20
503 A106 15g brt red ('48) 1.25 1.25

Perf. 13½x14

504 A110 20g bright red .30 .20
505 A110 30g bright red .50 .20
506 A110 40g bright red .50 .20
507 A110 50g bright red .65 .20
508 A110 60g brt red ('48) 6.25 1.50
509 A110 70g brt red ('48) 2.25 .20
510 A110 80g brt red ('48) 2.50 .20
511 A110 90g brt red ('48) 3.00 .50
512 A124 1s dark violet .50 .20
513 A124 2s dark violet .65 .20
514 A124 3s dk violet ('48) 8.50 .90
515 A124 5s dk violet ('48) 8.50 1.25
Nos. 500-515 (16) 35.95 7.60

Carl Michael Ziehrer (1843-1922), Composer A133

#517, Adalbert Stifter (1805-68), novelist. #518, Anton Bruckner (1824-96), composer. 60g, Friedrich von Amerling (1803-87), painter.

1948-49 Engr.

516 A133 20g dull green .35 .25
517 A133 40g chocolate 5.00 2.50
518 A133 40g dark green 4.50 4.00
519 A133 60g rose brown .50 .25
Nos. 516-519 (4) 10.35 7.00

Issue dates: 20g, Jan. 21, No. 517, Sept. 6, No. 518, Sept. 3, 1949, 60g, Jan. 26.

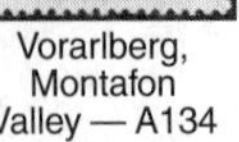

Vorarlberg, Montafon Valley — A134

Costume of Vienna, 1850 — A135

Austrian Costumes: 3g, Tyrol, Inn Valley. 5g, Salzburg, Pinzgau. 10g, Styria, Salzkammergut. 15g, Burgenland, Lutzmannsburg. 25g, Vienna, 1850. 30g, Salzburg, Pongau. 40g, Vienna, 1840. 45g, Carinthia, Lesach Valley. 50g, Vorarlberg, Bregenzer Forest. 60g, Carinthia, Lavant Valley. 70g, Lower Austria, Wachau. 75g, Styria, Salzkammergut. 80g, Styria, Enns Valley. 90g, Central Styria. 1s, Tyrol, Puster Valley. 1.20s, Lower Austria, Vienna Woods. 1.40s, Upper Austria, Inn District. 1.45s, Wilten. 1.50s, Vienna, 1853. 1.60s, Vienna, 1830. 1.70s, East Tyrol, Kals. 2s, Upper Austria. 2.20s, Ischl, 1820. 2.40s, Kitzbuhel. 2.50s, Upper Steiermark, 1850. 2.70s, Little Walser Valley. 3s, Burgenland. 3.50s, Lower Austria, 1850. 4.50s, Gail Valley. 5s, Ziller Valley. 7s, Steiermark, Sulm Valley.

Perf. 14x13½

1948-52 Unwmk. Photo.

520 A134 3g gray ('50) .40 .35
521 A134 5g dk grn ('49) .20 .20
522 A134 10g deep blue .20 .20
523 A134 15g brown .40 .20
524 A134 20g yellow green .20 .20
525 A134 25g brown ('49) .20 .20
526 A134 30g dk car rose 1.60 .20
527 A134 30g dk vio ('50) .30 .20
528 A134 40g violet 1.75 .20
529 A134 40g green ('49) .20 .20
530 A134 45g violet blue 1.75 .30
531 A134 50g org brn ('49) .30 .20
532 A134 60g scarlet .20 .20
533 A134 70g brt bl grn ('49) .20 .20
534 A134 75g blue 2.75 .40
535 A134 80g car rose ('49) .30 .20
536 A134 90g brn vio ('49) 21.00 .30
537 A134 1s ultramarine 4.00 .20
538 A134 1s rose red ('50) 55.00 .20
539 A134 1s dk grn ('51) .20 .20
540 A134 1.20s violet ('49) .30 .20
541 A134 1.40s brown 1.75 .20
542 A134 1.45s dk car ('51) .80 .20
543 A134 1.50s ultra ('51) .60 .20
544 A134 1.60s org red ('49) .20 .20
545 A134 1.70s vio bl ('50) 2.10 .55
546 A134 2s blue green .75 .20
547 A134 2.20s slate ('52) 4.75 .20
548 A134 2.40s blue ('51) .75 .20
549 A134 2.50s brown ('52) 2.00 .75
550 A134 2.70s dk brn ('51) .50 .45
551 A134 3s brn car ('49) 1.75 .20
552 A134 3.50s dull grn ('51) 12.50 .20
553 A134 4.50s brn vio ('51) .60 .60
554 A134 5s dark red vio .75 .20
555 A134 7s olive ('52) 3.00 .75

Engr.

556 A135 10s gray ('50) 22.50 3.50
Nos. 520-556 (37) 146.75 13.35
Set, hinged 65.00

In 1958-59, 21 denominations of this set were printed on white paper, differing from the previous grayish paper with yellowish gum.

Pres. Karl Renner — A136

1948, Nov. 12 *Perf. 14x13½*

557 A136 1s deep blue 1.75 1.00

Founding of the Austrian Republic, 30th anniv. See Nos. 573, 636.

Franz Gruber and Josef Mohr A137

1948, Dec. 18 *Perf. 13½x14*

558 A137 60g red brown 3.75 3.75

130th anniv. of the hymn "Silent Night, Holy Night".

Symbolical of Child Welfare — A138

1949, May 14 Photo. *Perf. 14x13½*

559 A138 1s bright blue 10.00 1.25

1st year of activity of UNICEF in Austria.

Johann Strauss, the Younger — A139

1949 Engr.

30g, Johann Strauss, the elder. #561, Johann Strauss, the younger. #562, Karl Millöcker.

560 A139 30g violet brown 1.75 1.25
561 A139 1s dark blue 2.50 2.00
562 A139 1s dark blue 10.00 6.00
Nos. 560-562 (3) 14.25 9.25

Johann Strauss, the elder (1804-49), Johann Strauss, the younger (1825-99), and Karl Millöcker (1842-1899), composers. See #574.

Esperanto Star, Olive Branches — A140

St. Gebhard — A141

1949, June 25 Photo.

563 A140 20g blue green .90 .50

Austrian Esperanto Congress at Graz.

1949, Aug. 6 Engr.

564 A141 30g dark violet 1.40 1.25

St. Gebhard (949-995), Bishop of Vorarlberg.

Letter, Roses and Post Horn A142

UPU, 75th Anniv.: 60g, Plaque. 1s, "Austria," wings and monogram.

1949, Oct. 8 *Perf. 13½x14*

565 A142 40g dark green 3.25 1.60
566 A142 60g dk carmine 3.25 1.60
567 A142 1s dk violet blue 6.00 4.75
Nos. 565-567 (3) 12.50 7.95

Moritz Michael Daffinger — A143

Andreas Hofer — A144

30g, Alexander Girardi. #569, Daffinger. #570, Hofer. #571, Josef Madersperger.

1950 Unwmk. *Perf. 14x13½*

568 A144 30g dark blue 1.40 .75
569 A143 60g red brown 6.00 3.25
570 A144 60g dark violet 10.00 6.50
571 A144 60g purple 4.50 2.25
Nos. 568-571 (4) 21.90 12.75

Alexander Girardi (1850-1918), actor; Moritz Michael Daffinger (1790-1849), painter; Andreas Hofer (1767-1810), patriot; Josef Madersperger (1768-1850), inventor.

Issue dates: 30g, Dec. 5; No. 569, Jan. 25; No. 570, Feb. 20; No. 571, Oct. 2.

Austrian Stamp of 1850 — A146

1950, May 20 *Perf. 14½*

572 A146 1s black, *straw* 1.50 .90

Centenary of Austrian postage stamps.

Renner Type of 1948
Frame and Inscriptions Altered

1951, Mar. 3

573 A136 1s black, *straw* 1.25 .20

In memory of Pres. Karl Renner, 1870-1950.

Strauss Type of 1949

Portrait: 60g, Joseph Lanner.

1951, Apr. 12

574 A139 60g dk blue green 3.50 1.10

Joseph Lanner (1801-43), composer.

Martin Johann Schmidt — A147

Boy Scout Emblem — A148

1951, June 28 Engr. *Perf. 14x13½*

575 A147 1sh brown red 4.50 2.00

150th death anniv. of Martin Johann Schmidt, painter.

1951, Aug. 3 Engr. and Litho.

576 A148 1sh dk grn, ocher & pink 3.25 2.50

7th World Scout Jamboree, Bad Ischl-St. Wolfgang, Aug. 3-13, 1951.

Wilhelm Kienzl — A149

Josef Schrammel A150

Design: 1s, Karl von Ghega.

1951-52 Engr. Unwmk.

577 A149 1s deep green ('52) 6.00 1.25
578 A149 1.50s indigo 2.50 .85
579 A150 1.50s violet blue ('52) 6.00 1.25
Nos. 577-579 (3) 14.50 3.35

Ghega (1802-60), civil engineer; Kienzl (1857-1941), composer; Schrammel (1852-95), composer. See #582.

Issued: 1s, 3/2; #578, 10/3; #579, 3/3.

Breakfast Pavilion, Schönbrunn A151

1952, May 24 ***Perf. 13½x14***

580 A151 1.50s dark green 4.75 1.00

Vienna Zoological Gardens, 200th anniv.

Globe as Dot Over "i" — A152

School Girl — A153

1952, July 1 ***Perf. 14x13½***

581 A152 1.50s dark blue 4.75 .65

Formation of the Intl. Union of Socialist Youth Camp, Vienna, July 1-10, 1952.

Type Similar to A150

Portrait: 1s, Nikolaus Lenau.

1952, Aug. 13

582 A150 1s deep green 5.00 1.10

Nikolaus Lenau, pseudonym of Nikolaus Franz Niembsch von Strehlenau (1802-50), poet.

1952, Sept. 6

583 A153 2.40s dp violet blue 8.50 1.75

Issued to stimulate letter-writing between Austrian and foreign school children.

Hugo Wolf — A154

Pres. Theodor Körner — A155

1953, Feb. 21 Engr. ***Perf. 14x13½***

587 A154 1.50s dark blue 5.25 .70

Hugo Wolf, composer, 50th death anniv.

1953, Apr. 24

588 A155 1.50s dk violet blue 5.25 .70

80th birthday of Pres. Theodor Körner. See Nos. 591, 614.

State Theater, Linz, and Masks A156

1953, Oct. 17 ***Perf. 13½x14***

589 A156 1.50s dark gray 13.50 1.50

State Theater at Linz, 150th anniv.

Child and Christmas Tree — A157

Karl von Rokitansky A158

1953, Nov. 30 ***Perf. 14x13½***

590 A157 1s dark green 1.00 .20

See No. 597.

Type Similar to A155

Portrait: 1.50s, Moritz von Schwind.

1954, Jan. 21 ***Perf. 14x13½***

591 A155 1.50s purple 10.00 1.10

Moritz von Schwind, painter, 150th birth anniv.

1954, Feb. 19

592 A158 1.50s purple 13.00 1.75

Karl von Rokitansky, physician, 150th birth anniv. See No. 595.

Esperanto Star and Wreath A159

Engr. and Photo.

1954, June 5 ***Perf. 13½x14***

593 A159 1s dk brown & emer 3.50 .25

Esperanto movement in Austria, 50th anniv.

A160

1954, Aug. 4 Engr. ***Perf. 14x13½***

594 A160 1s dark blue green 9.00 1.75

300th birth anniv. of Johann Michael Rottmayr von Rosenbrunn, painter.

Type Similar to A158

Portrait: 1.50s, Carl Auer von Welsbach.

1954, Aug. 4

595 A158 1.50s violet blue 27.50 1.50

25th death anniv. of Carl Auer von Welsbach (1858-1929), chemist.

2nd Intl. Congress for Catholic Church Music, Vienna, Oct. 4-10 — A161

1954, Oct. 2 Unwmk.

Organ, St. Florian Monastery and Cherub.

596 A161 1s brown 1.50 .25

Christmas Type of 1953

1954, Nov. 30

597 A157 1s dark blue 2.25 .30

Arms of Austria and Official Publication A162

1954, Dec. 18 Engr.

598 A162 1s salmon & black 1.90 .20

Austria's State Printing Plant, 150th anniv., and Wiener Zeitung, government newspaper, 250th year of publication.

Parliament Building A163

Designs: 1s, Western railroad station, Vienna. 1.45s, Letters forming flag. 1.50s, Public housing, Vienna. 2.40s, Limberg dam.

1955, Apr. 27 ***Perf. 13½x14***

599 A163 70g rose violet 1.25 .20
600 A163 1s deep ultra 4.75 .20
601 A163 1.45s scarlet 7.25 1.75
602 A163 1.50s brown 16.00 .25
603 A163 2.40s dk blue green 6.75 3.00
Nos. 599-603 (5) 36.00 5.40

10th anniv. of Austria's liberation.

Type of 1945 Overprinted in Blue

1955, May 15 *Perf. 14x13½*
604 A100 2s blue gray 1.75 .20

Signing of the state treaty with the US, France, Great Britain and Russia, 5/15/55.

Workers of Three Races Climbing Globe A164

1955, May 20 *Perf. 13½x14*
605 A164 1s indigo 1.75 1.50

4th congress of the Intl. Confederation of Free Trade Unions, Vienna, May.

Burgtheater, Vienna A165

Design: 2.40s, Opera House, Vienna.

1955, July 25
606 A165 1.50s light sepia 2.50 .20
607 A165 2.40s dark blue 3.00 1.25

Re-opening of the Burgtheater and Opera House in Vienna.

Symbolic of Austria's Desire to Join the UN — A166

1955, Oct. 24 **Unwmk.**
608 A166 2.40s green 11.00 1.40

Tenth anniversary of UN.

Wolfgang Amadeus Mozart, Birth Bicent. — A167

1956, Jan. 21 *Perf. 14x13½*
609 A167 2.40s slate blue 3.00 .50

Symbolic of Austria's Joining the UN — A168

1956, Feb. 20
610 A168 2.40s chocolate 9.00 1.10

Austria's admission to the UN.

Globe Showing Energy of the Earth A169

1956, May 8 *Perf. 13½x14*
611 A169 2.40s deep blue 8.50 1.40

Fifth Intl. Power Conf., Vienna, June 17-23.

Map of Europe and City Maps — A170

Photo. and Typo.

1956, June 8 *Perf. 14x13½*
612 A170 1.45s lt grn blk & red 2.25 .50

23rd Intl. Housing and Town Planning Congress, Vienna, July 22-28.

J.B. Fischer von Erlach, Architect, 300th Birth Anniv. — A171

1956, July 20 **Engr.**
613 A171 1.50s brown 1.00 .90

Körner Type of 1953

1957, Jan. 11
614 A155 1.50s gray black 1.10 1.00

Death of Pres. Theodor Körner.

Dr. Julius Wagner-Jauregg, Psychiatrist, Birth Cent. — A172

1957, Mar. 7 *Perf. 14x13½*
615 A172 2.40s brn violet 3.00 1.25

Anton Wildgans, Poet, 25th Death Anniv. — A173

1957, May 3 **Unwmk.**
616 A173 1s violet blue .30 .20

Old and New Postal Motor Coach A174

1957, June 14 *Perf. 13½x14*
617 A174 1s black, *yellow* .30 .20

Austrian Postal Motor Coach Service, 50th anniv.

Gasherbrum II and Glacier A175

1957, July 27
618 A175 1.50s gray blue .35 .20

Austrian Karakorum Expedition, which climbed Mount Gasherbrum II on July 7, 1956.

A176

A177

Designs: 20g, Farmhouse at Mörbisch. 50g, Heiligenstadt, Vienna. 1s, Mariazell. 1.40s, County seat, Klagenfurt. 1.50s, Rabenhof Building, Erdberg, Vienna. 1.80s, The Mint, Hall, Tyrol. 2s, Christkindl Church. 3.40s, Steiner Gate, Krems. 4s, Vienna Gate, Hainburg. 4.50s, Schwechat Airport, Vienna. 5.50s, Chur Gate, Feldkirch. 6s, County seat, Graz. 6.40s, "Golden Roof," Innsbruck. 10s, Heidenreichstein Castle.

1957-61 **Litho.** *Perf. 14x13½*

Size: 20x25mm

618A A176 20g violet blk ('61) .20 .20
619 A176 50g bluish blk ('59) .20 .20

Engr.

620 A176 1s chocolate 1.25 .20

Typo.

621 A176 1s chocolate 1.50 .20

Litho.

622 A176 1s choc ('59) .75 .20
622A A176 1.40s brt greenish bl ('60) .30 .20
623 A176 1.50s rose lake ('58) .40 .20
624 A176 1.80s brt ultra ('60) .30 .20
625 A176 2s dull blue ('58) 4.00 .20
626 A176 3.40s yel grn ('60) .90 .75
627 A176 4s brt red lil ('60) .75 .20
627A A176 4.50s dl green ('60) 1.00 .40
628 A176 5.50s grnsh gray ('60) 1.00 .20
629 A176 6s brt vio ('60) 1.10 .20
629A A176 6.40s brt blue ('60) 1.25 .90

Engr.

Size: 22x28mm

630 A177 10s dk bl grn 2.50 .45
Nos. 618A-630 (16) 17.40 4.90

Of the three 1s stamps above, Nos. 620 and 621 have two names in imprint (designer H. Strohofer, engraver G. Wimmer). No. 622 has only Strohofer's name.

Values for Nos. 618A-624, 626-630 are for stamps on white paper. Most denominations also come on grayish paper with yellowish gum.

See Nos. 688-702.

1960-65 **Photo.** *Perf. 14½x14*

Size: 17x21mm

630A A176 50g slate ('64) .20 .20

Size: 18x21½mm

630B A176 1s chocolate .20 .20

Size: 17x21mm

630C A176 1.50s dk car ('65) .20 .20
Nos. 630A-630C (3) .60 .60

Nos. 630A-630C issued in sheets and coils.

Graukogel, Badgastein A180

1958, Feb. 1 **Engr.** *Perf. 14x13½*
631 A180 1.50s dark blue .20 .20

Intl. Ski Federation Alpine championships, Badgastein, Feb. 2-7.

Plane over Map of Austria A181

1958, Mar. 27 *Perf. 13½x14*
632 A181 4s red .55 .25

Re-opening of Austrian Airlines.

Mother and Daughter — A182

1958, May 8 **Unwmk.** *Perf. 14x13½*
633 A182 1.50s dark blue .20 .20

Issued for Mother's Day.

Walther von der Vogelweide A183

1958, July 17 **Litho. and Engr.**
634 A183 1.50s multicolored .20 .20

3rd Austrian Song Festival, Vienna, 7/17-20.

Oswald Redlich (1858-1944), Historian — A184

1958, Sept. 17 **Engr.**
635 A184 2.40s ultramarine .40 .20

Renner Type of 1948

1958, Nov. 12
636 A136 1.50s deep green .45 .35

Austrian Republic, 40th anniv.

Giant "E" on Map — A185

1959, Mar. 9
637 A185 2.40s emerald .35 .20

Idea of a United Europe.

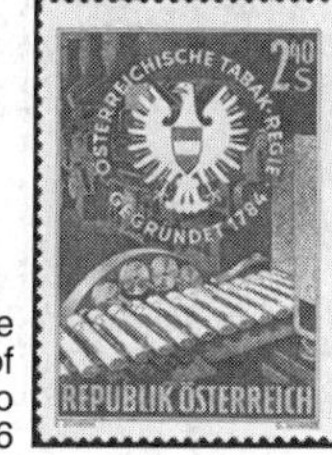

Cigarette Machine and Trademark of Tobacco Monopoly — A186

1959, May 8 Unwmk. *Perf. 13½*
638 A186 2.40s dark olive bister .25 .20

Austrian tobacco monopoly, 175th anniv.

Archduke Johann — A187

1959, May 11 *Perf. 14x13½*
639 A187 1.50s deep green .25 .20

Archduke Johann of Austria, military leader and humanitarian, death cent.

Capercaillie A188

Animals: 1.50s, Roe buck. 2.40s, Wild boar. 3.50s, Red deer, doe and fawn.

1959, May 20 Engr.

640	A188	1s	rose violet	.20	.20
641	A188	1.50s	blue violet	.35	.20
642	A188	2.40s	dk bl green	.50	.45
643	A188	3.50s	dark brown	.30	.25
			Nos. 640-643 (4)	1.35	1.10

Congress of the Intl. Hunting Council, Vienna, May 20-24.

Joseph Haydn (1732-1809), Composer A189

1959, May 30 Unwmk.
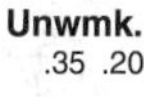
644 A189 1.50s violet brown .35 .20

Coat of Arms, Tyrol — A190

1959, June 13 *Perf. 14x13½*
645 A190 1.50s rose red .20 .20

Fight for liberation of Tyrol, 150th anniv.

Antenna, Zugspitze — A191

1959, June 19 *Perf. 13½*
646 A191 2.40s dk bl grn .25 .20

Inauguration of Austria's relay system.

Field Ball Player — A192

1s, Runner. 1.80s, Gymnast on vaulting horse. 2s, Woman hurdler. 2.20s, Hammer thrower.

1959-70 Engr. *Perf. 14x13½*

647	A192	1s	lilac	.20	.20
648	A192	1.50s	blue green	.40	.25
648A	A192	1.80s	carmine ('62)	.25	.25
648B	A192	2s	rose lake ('70)	.20	.20
648C	A192	2.20s	bluish blk ('67)	.20	.20
			Nos. 647-648C (5)	1.25	1.10

Orchestral Instruments A193

Litho. and Engr.

1959, Aug. 19 *Perf. 14x13½*
649 A193 2.40s dull bl & blk .25 .20

World tour of the Vienna Philharmonic Orchestra.

Family Fleeing over Mountains A194

1960, Apr. 7 Engr. *Perf. 13½x14*
650 A194 3s Prussian green .50 .25

WRY, July 1, 1959-June 30, 1960.

President Adolf Schärf — A195

1960, Apr. 20 *Perf. 14x13½*
651 A195 1.50s gray olive .50 .20

Pres. Adolf Scharf, 70th birthday.

Young Hikers and Hostel A196

1960, May 20 *Perf. 13½x14*
652 A196 1s carmine rose .20 .20

Youth hiking; youth hostel movement.

Anton Eiselsberg, Surgeon, Birth Cent. — A197

Litho. and Engr.

1960, June 20 *Perf. 14x13½*
653 A197 1.50s buff & dk brn .50 .20

Gustav Mahler (1860-1911), Composer A198

1960, July 7 Engr.
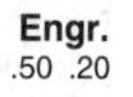
654 A198 1.50s chocolate .50 .20

Jakob Prandtauer, Architect, 300th Birth Anniv. — A199

1960, July 16 Unwmk.
655 A199 1.50s Melk Abbey .50 .20

Gross Glockner Mountain Road, 25th Anniv. — A200

1960, Aug. 3
656 A200 1.80s dark blue .60 .50

Ionic Capital — A201

1960, Aug. 29 *Perf. 14x13½*
657 A201 3s black 1.00 .75

Europa: Idea of a United Europe.

Griffen, Carinthia A202

1960, Oct. 10 Engr. *Perf. 13½x14*
658 A202 1.50s slate green .30 .20

40th anniv. of the plebiscite which kept Carinthia with Austria.

Flame and Broken Chain — A203

1961, May 8 Unwmk. *Perf. 14x13½*
659 A203 1.50s scarlet .25 .20

Victims in Austria's fight for freedom.

First Austrian Mail Plane, 1918 A204

1961, May 15 *Perf. 13½x14*
660 A204 5s violet blue .60 .30

Airmail Phil. Exhib., LUPOSTA 1961, Vienna, May.

Transportation by Road, Rail and Waterway A205

Engraved and Typographed

1961, May 29 *Perf. 13½*
661 A205 3s rose red & olive .40 .30

13th European Conference of Transportation ministers, Vienna, May 29-31.

Society of Creative Artists, Künstlerhaus, Vienna, Cent. — A206

Designs: 1s, Mountain Mower, by Albin Egger-Lienz. 1.50s, The Kiss, by August von Pettenkofen. 3s, Girl, by Anton Romako. 5s, Ariadne's Triumph, by Hans Makart.

1961, June 12 Engr. *Perf. 13½x14*

Inscriptions in Red Brown

662	A206	1s	rose lake	.20	.20
663	A206	1.50s	dull violet	.25	.25
664	A206	3s	olive green	.65	.60
665	A206	5s	blue violet	.45	.40
			Nos. 662-665 (4)	1.55	1.45

Sonnblick Mountain and Observatory A207

Mercury and Globe — A208

1961, Sept. 1 ***Perf. 14x13½***

666	A207	1.80s violet blue	.30	.25

Sonnblick meteorological observatory, 75th anniv.

1961, Sept. 18

667	A208	3s black	.55	.40

Intl. Banking Congress, Vienna, Sept. 1961. English inscription listing UN financial groups.

Coal Mine Shaft — A209

Designs: 1.50s, Generator. 1.80s, Iron blast furnace. 3s, Pouring steel. 5s, Oil refinery.

1961, Sept. 15 **Engr.** ***Perf. 14x13½***

668	A209	1s black	.20	.20
669	A209	1.50s green	.25	.20
670	A209	1.80s dark car rose	.50	.40
671	A209	3s bright lilac	.60	.50
672	A209	5s blue	.80	.60
		Nos. 668-672 (5)	2.35	1.90

15th anniversary of nationalized industry.

Arms of Burgenland A210

1961, Oct. 9 **Engr. and Litho.**

673	A210	1.50s blk, yel & dk red	.30	.20

Burgenland as part of the Austrian Republic, 40th anniv.

Franz Liszt (1811-86), Composer A211

1961, Oct. 20 **Engr.**

674	A211	3s dark brown	.50	.35

Parliament A212

1961, Dec. 18 ***Perf. 13½x14***

675	A212	1s brown	.20	.20

Austrian Bureau of Budget, 200th anniv.

Kaprun-Mooserboden Reservoir — A213

Hydroelectric Power Plants: 1.50s, Ybbs-Persenbeug dam and locks. 1.80s, Lünersee dam and reservoir. 3s, Grossraming dam. 4s, Bisamberg transformer plant. 6.40s, St. Andrä power plant.

1962, Mar. 26 **Unwmk.**

676	A213	1s violet blue	.20	.20
677	A213	1.50s red lilac	.25	.20
678	A213	1.80s green	.50	.45
679	A213	3s brown	.40	.35
680	A213	4s rose red	.40	.35
681	A213	6.40s gray	1.10	1.00
		Nos. 676-681 (6)	2.85	2.55

Nationalization of the electric power industry, 15th anniv.

Johann Nestroy — A214

1962, May 25 ***Perf. 14x13½***

682	A214	1s violet	.20	.20

Johann Nepomuk Nestroy, Viennese playwright, author and actor, death cent.

Friedrich Gauermann (1807-1862), Landscape Painter — A215

1962, July 6 **Engr.**

683	A215	1.50s intense blue	.20	.20

Scout Emblem and Handshake A216

1962, Oct. 5

684	A216	1.50s dark green	.35	.20

Austria's Boy Scouts, 50th anniv.

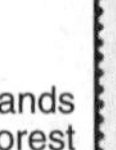

Lowlands Forest A217

1.50s, Deciduous forest. 3s, Fir & larch forest.

1962, Oct. 12 ***Perf. 13½x14***

685	A217	1s greenish gray	.20	.20
686	A217	1.50s reddish brown	.20	.20
687	A217	3s dk slate green	.80	.70
		Nos. 685-687 (3)	1.20	1.10

Buildings Types of 1957-61

Designs: 30g, City Hall, Vienna. 40g, Porcia Castle, Spittal on the Drau. 60g, Tanners' Tower, Wels. 70g, Residenz Fountain, Salzburg. 80g, Old farmhouse, Pinzgau. 1s, Romanesque columns, Millstatt Abbey. 1.20s, Kornmesser House, Bruck on the Mur. 1.30s, Schatten Castle, Feldkirch, Vorarlberg. 2s, Dragon Fountain, Klagenfurt. 2.20s, Beethoven House, Vienna. 2.50s, Danube Bridge, Linz. 3s, Swiss Gate, Vienna. 3.50s, Esterhazy Palace, Eisenstadt. 8s, City Hall, Steyr. 20s, Melk Abbey.

1962-70 **Litho.** ***Perf. 14x13½***
Size: 20x25mm

688	A176	30g greenish gray	.20	.20
689	A176	40g rose red	.20	.20
690	A176	60g violet brown	.20	.20
691	A176	70g dark blue	.20	.20
692	A176	80g yellow brown	.20	.20
693	A176	1s brown ('70)	.20	.20
694	A176	1.20s red lilac	.30	.20
695	A176	1.30s green ('67)	.20	.20
696	A176	2s dk blue ('68)	.25	.20
697	A176	2.20s green	.80	.20
698	A176	2.50s violet	.80	.20
699	A176	3s bright blue	.65	.20
700	A176	3.50s rose carmine	.65	.20
701	A176	8s claret ('65)	1.10	.20

Perf. 13½
Engr.
Size: 28x36½mm

702	A177	20s rose claret ('63)	2.50	.35
		Nos. 688-702 (15)	8.45	3.15

Values for Nos. 688-702 are for stamps on white paper. Some denominations also come on grayish paper with yellowish gum.

Electric Locomotive and Train of 1837 — A218

Lithographed and Engraved

1962, Nov. 9 ***Perf. 13½x14***

703	A218	3s buff & black	.80	.45

125th anniversary of Austrian railroads.

Postilions and Postal Clerk, 1863 — A219

1963, May 7 **Photo.** ***Perf. 14x13½***

704	A219	3s dk brn & citron	.60	.40

First Intl. Postal Conference, Paris, cent.

Hermann Bahr, Poet, Birth Cent. — A220

Lithographed and Envraved

1963, July 19 ***Perf. 14x13½***

705	A220	1.50s blue & black	.20	.20

St. Florian Statue, Kefermarkt, Contemporary and Old Fire Engines — A221

1963, Aug. 30 **Unwmk.**

706	A221	1.50s brt rose & blk	.35	.20

Austrian volunteer fire brigades, cent.

Factory, Flag and "ÖGB" on Map of Austria A222

1963, Sept. 23 **Litho.** ***Perf. 13½x14***

707	A222	1.50s gray, red & dk brn	.20	.20

5th Congress of the Austrian Trade Union Federation (ÖGB), Sept. 23-28.

Arms of Austria and Tyrol A223

1963, Sept. 27 **Unwmk.**

708	A223	1.50s tan, blk, red & yel	.20	.20

Tyrol's union with Austria, 600th anniv.

Prince Eugene of Savoy (1663-1736), Austrian General — A224

1963, Oct. 18 **Engr.** ***Perf. 14x13½***

709	A224	1.50s violet	.20	.20

Intl. Red Cross, Cent. — A225

1963, Oct. 25 **Engr. and Photo.**

710	A225	3s blk, sil & red	.45	.25

Slalom A226

Sports: 1.20s, Biathlon (skier with rifle). 1.50s, Ski jump. 1.80s, Women's figure skating. 2.20s, Ice hockey. 3s, Tobogganing. 4s, Bobsledding.

Photo. and Engr.

1963, Nov. 11 ***Perf. 13½x14***

711 A226	1s multi		.20	.20
712 A226	1.20s multi		.20	.20
713 A226	1.50s multi		.20	.20
714 A226	1.80s multi		.20	.20
715 A226	2.20s multi		.40	.30
716 A226	3s multi		.25	.25
717 A226	4s multi		.55	.40
	Nos. 711-717 (7)		2.00	1.75

9th Winter Olympic Games, Innsbruck, Jan. 29-Feb. 9, 1964.

Baroque Creche by Josef Thaddäus Stammel — A227

1963, Nov. 29 **Engr.** ***Perf. 14x13½***

718 A227 2s dark Prus green .20 .20

Flowers A228

1964, Apr. 17 **Litho.** ***Perf. 14***

719 A228	1s	Nasturtium	.20	.20
720 A228	1.50s	Peony	.20	.20
721 A228	1.80s	Clematis	.20	.20
722 A228	2.20s	Dahlia	.20	.20
723 A228	3s	Morning glory	.40	.25
724 A228	4s	Hollyhock	.50	.35
	Nos. 719-724 (6)		1.70	1.40

Vienna Intl. Garden Show, Apr. 16-Oct. 11.

St. Mary Magdalene and Apostle — A229

1964, May 21 **Engr.** ***Perf. 13½***

725 A229 1.50s bluish black .20 .20

Romanesque art in Austria. The 12th century stained-glass window is from the Weitensfeld Church, the bust of the Apostle from the portal of St. Stephen's Cathedral, Vienna.

Pallas Athena and National Council Chamber — A230

Engr. and Litho.

1964, May 25 ***Perf. 14x13½***

726 A230 1.80s black & emer .25 .20

2nd Parliamentary and Scientific Conf., Vienna.

The Kiss, by Gustav Klimt A231

1964, June 5 **Litho.** ***Perf. 13½***

727 A231 3s multicolored .35 .25

Re-opening of the Vienna Secession, a museum devoted to early 20th century art (art nouveau).

Brother of Mercy and Patient — A232

1964, June 11 **Engr.** ***Perf. 14x13½***

728 A232 1.50s dark blue .20 .20

Brothers of Mercy in Austria, 350th anniv.

"Bringing the News of Victory at Kunersdorf" by Bernardo Bellotto — A233

"The Post in Art": 1.20s, Changing Horses at Relay Station, by Julius Hörmann. 1.50s, The Honeymoon Trip, by Moritz von Schwind. 1.80s, After the Rain, by Ignaz Raffalt. 2.20s, Mailcoach in the Mountains, by Adam Klein. 3s, Changing Horses at Bavarian Border, by Friedrich Gauermann. 4s, Postal Sleigh (Truck) in the Mountains, by Adalbert Pilch. 6.40s, Saalbach Post Office, by Adalbert Pilch.

1964, June 15 ***Perf. 13½x14***

729 A233	1s	rose claret	.20	.20
730 A233	1.20s	sepia	.20	.20
731 A233	1.50s	violet blue	.20	.20
732 A233	1.80s	brt violet	.20	.20
733 A233	2.20s	black	.30	.30
734 A233	3s	dl car rose	.25	.25
735 A233	4s	slate green	.40	.35
736 A233	6.40s	dull claret	.90	.80
	Nos. 729-736 (8)		2.65	2.50

15th UPU Cong., Vienna, May-June 1964.

Workers — A234

1964, Sept. 4 ***Perf. 14x13½***

737 A234 1s black .20 .20

Centenary of Austrian Labor Movement.

Common Design Types pictured following the introduction.

Europa Issue, 1964

Common Design Type

1964, Sept. 14 **Litho.** ***Perf. 12***

Size: 21x36mm

738 CD7 3s dark blue .40 .25

Emblem of Radio Austria and Transistor Radio Panel A235

1964, Oct. 1 **Photo.** ***Perf. 13½***

739 A235 1s black brn & red .20 .20

Forty years of Radio Austria.

6th Congress of the Intl. Graphic Federation, Vienna, Oct. 12-17 — A236

Litho. and Engr.

1964, Oct. 12 ***Perf. 14x13½***

740 A236 1.50s Old printing press .20 .20

Dr. Adolf Schärf (1890-1965), Pres. of Austria (1957-65) A237

Pres. Adolf Schärf, Schärf Student Center.

Typo. and Engr.

1965, Apr. 20 ***Perf. 12***

741 A237 1.50s bluish black .20 .20

Ruins and New Buildings — A238

1965, Apr. 27 **Engr.** ***Perf. 14x13½***

742 A238 1.80s carmine lake .20 .20

Twenty years of reconstruction.

Oldest Seal of Vienna University — A239

Photo. and Engr.

1965, May 10 ***Perf. 14x13½***

743 A239 3s gold & red .35 .25

University of Vienna, 600th anniv.

St. George, 16th Century Wood Sculpture A240

1965, May 17 **Engr.**

744 A240 1.80s bluish black .25 .20

Art of the Danube Art School, 1490-1540, exhibition, May-Oct. 1965. The stamp background shows an engraving by Albrecht Altdorfer.

ITU Emblem, Telegraph Key and TV Antenna — A241

1965, May 17 **Unwmk.**

745 A241 3s violet blue .30 .25

ITU, cent.

Ferdinand Raimund — A242

Portraits: No. 746, Dr. Ignaz Philipp Semmelweis. No. 747, Bertha von Suttner. No. 749, Ferdinand Georg Waldmüller.

1965 **Engr.** ***Perf. 14x13½***

746 A242	1.50s	violet	.25	.20
747 A242	1.50s	bluish black	.25	.20
748 A242	3s	dark brown	.40	.20
749 A242	3s	greenish blk	.40	.25
	Nos. 746-749 (4)		1.30	.85

Semmelweis (1818-65), who discovered the cause of puerperal fever and introduced antisepsis into obstetrics (#746). 60th anniv. of the awarding of the Nobel Prize for Peace to von Suttner (1843-1914), pacifist and author (#747). Raimund (1790-1836), actor and playwright (#748). Waldmüller (1793-1865), painter (#749).

Issue dates: No. 746, Aug. 13; No. 747, Dec. 1; No. 748, June 1; No. 749, Aug. 23.

4th Gymnaestrada, Intl. Athletic Meet, Vienna, July 20-24 — A243

1.50s, Male gymnasts with practice bars. 3s, Dancers with tambourines.

1965, July 20 **Photo. and Engr.**

750 A243	1.50s	gray & black	.20	.20
751 A243	3s	bister & blk	.25	.25

Red Cross and Strip of Gauze — A244

1965, Oct. 1 Litho. *Perf. 14x13½*

752 A244 3s black & red .35 .20

20th Intl. Red Cross Conference, Vienna.

Austrian Flag and Eagle with Mural Crown — A245

1965, Oct. 7 Photo. and Engr.

753 A245 1.50s gold, red & blk .20 .20

50th anniv. of the Union of Austrian Towns.

Austrian Flag, UN Headquarters and Emblem A246

Lithographed and Engraved

1965, Oct. 25 Unwmk. *Perf. 12*

754 A246 3s blk, brt bl & red .40 .25

Austria's admission to the UN, 10th anniv.

University of Technology, Vienna A247

1965, Nov. 8 Engr. *Perf. 13½x14*

755 A247 1.50s violet .20 .20

Vienna University of Technology, 150th anniv.

Map of Austria with Postal Zone Numbers — A248

1966, Jan. 14 Photo. *Perf. 12*

756 A248 1.50s yel, red & blk .20 .20

Introduction of postal zone numbers, 1/1/66.

PTT Building, Emblem and Churches of Sts. Maria Rotunda and Barbara — A249

Lithographed and Engraved

1966, Mar. 4 *Perf. 14x13½*

757 A249 1.50s blk, *dull yellow* .20 .20

Headquarters of the Post and Telegraph Administration, cent.

Maria von Ebner Eschenbach (1830-1916), Novelist, Poet — A250

1966, Mar. 11 Engr.

758 A250 3s plum .30 .20

Ferris Wheel, Prater — A251

1966, Apr. 19 Engr. *Perf. 14x13½*

759 A251 1.50s slate green .20 .20

Opening of the Prater (park), Vienna, to the public by Emperor Joseph II, 200th anniv.

Josef Hoffmann (1870-1956), Architect A252

1966, May 6 Unwmk. *Perf. 12*

760 A252 3s dark brown .30 .20

Wiener Neustadt Arms — A253

Photo. and Engr.

1966, May 27 *Perf. 14*

761 A253 1.50s multicolored .20 .20

Wiener Neustadt Art Exhib., centered around the time and person of Frederick III (1440-93).

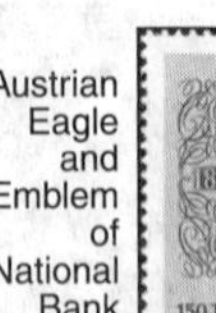

Austrian Eagle and Emblem of National Bank A254

1966, May 27 *Perf. 14*

762 A254 3s gray grn, dk brn & dk green .30 .20

Austrian National Bank, 150th anniv.

Puppy — A255

Litho. and Engr.

1966, June 16 *Perf. 12*

763 A255 1.80s yellow & black .25 .20

120th anniv. of the Vienna Humane Society.

Alpine Flowers — A256

1.50s, Columbine. 1.80s, Turk's cap. 2.20s, Wulfenia carinthiaca. 3s, Globeflowers. 4s, Fire lily. 5s, Pasqueflower.

1966, Aug. 17 Litho. *Perf. 13½*

Flowers in Natural Colors

764	A256	1.50s dark blue	.20	.20
765	A256	1.80s dark blue	.20	.20
766	A256	2.20s dark blue	.25	.20
767	A256	3s dark blue	.30	.30
768	A256	4s dark blue	.45	.35
769	A256	5s dark blue	.50	.40
		Nos. 764-769 (6)	1.90	1.65

Fair Building A257

1966, Aug. 26 Engr. *Perf. 13½x13*

770 A257 3s violet blue .30 .20

First International Fair at Wels.

Peter Anich (1723-1766), Tirolean Cartographer and Books — A258

1966, Sept. 1 *Perf. 14x13½*

771 A258 1.80s black .20 .20

Sick Worker and Health Emblem — A259

1966, Sept. 19 Engr. and Litho.

772 A259 3s black & vermilion .30 .20

15th Occupational Medicine Congress, Vienna, Sept. 19-24.

Theater Collection: "Eunuchus" by Terence from a 1496 Edition A260

Designs: 1.80s, Map Collection: Title page of Geographia Blavania (Cronus, Hercules and celestial sphere). 2.20s, Picture Archive and Portrait Collection: View of Old Vienna after a watercolor by Anton Stutzinger. 3s, Manuscript Collection: Illustration from the 15th century "Livre du Cuer d'Amours Espris" of the Duke René d'Anjou.

Photogravure and Engraved

1966, Sept. 28 *Perf. 13½x14*

773	A260	1.50s multicolored	.20	.20
774	A260	1.80s multicolored	.20	.20
775	A260	2.20s multicolored	.30	.20
776	A260	3s multicolored	.30	.25
		Nos. 773-776 (4)	1.00	.85

Austrian National Library.

Young Girl A261

Strawberries A262

Litho. and Engr.

1966, Oct. 3 *Perf. 14x13½*

777 A261 3s light blue & black .30 .20

"Save the Child" society, 10th anniv.

1966, Nov. 25 Photo. *Perf. 13½x13*

778	A262	50g shown	.20	.20
779	A262	1s Grapes	.20	.20
780	A262	1.50s Apple	.20	.20
781	A262	1.80s Blackberries	.25	.20
782	A262	2.20s Apricots	.30	.25
783	A262	3s Cherries	.30	.25
		Nos. 778-783 (6)	1.45	1.30

Coat of Arms of University of Linz — A263

Photo. and Engr.

1966, Dec. 9 *Perf. 14x13½*

784 A263 3s multi .30 .20

Inauguration of the Universary of Linz, Oct. 8, 1966.

Vienna Ice Skating Club, Cent. — A264

Photo. and Engr.

1967, Feb. 3 *Perf. 14x13½*

785 A264 3s Skater, 1866 .35 .20

Ballet Dancer — A265

1967, Feb. 15 Engr. *Perf. 11½x12*

786	A265	3s deep claret	.35	.20
a.		Perf. 12	1.00	.90

"Blue Danube" waltz by Johann Strauss, cent.

Dr. Karl Schönherr (1867-1943), Poet, Playwright and Physician — A266

1967, Feb. 24 Engr. ***Perf. 14x13½***
787 A266 3s gray brown .35 .20

Ice Hockey Goalkeeper A267

Photogravure and Engraved

1967, Mar. 17 ***Perf. 13½x14***
788 A267 3s pale grn & dk bl .35 .20

Ice Hockey Championships, Vienna, Mar. 18-29.

Violin, Organ and Laurel — A268

1967, Mar. 28 Engr. ***Perf. 13½***
789 A268 3.50s indigo .35 .20

Vienna Philharmonic Orchestra, 125th anniv.

Motherhood, Watercolor by Peter Fendi — A269

1967, Apr. 28 Litho. ***Perf. 14***
790 A269 2s multicolored .25 .20

Mother's Day.

Gothic Mantle Madonna A270

1967, May 19 Engr. ***Perf. 13½x14***
791 A270 3s slate .30 .20

"Austrian Gothic," art exhibition, Krems, 1967. The Gothic wood carving is from Frauenstein in Upper Austria.

Medieval Gold Cross A271

Swan, Tapestry by Oscar Kokoschka A272

Litho. and Engr.

1967, June 9 ***Perf. 13½***
792 A271 3.50s Prus grn & multi .35 .20

Salzburg Treasure Chamber; exhibition at Salzburg Cathedral, June 12-Sept. 15.

1967, June 9 Photo.
793 A272 2s multicolored .25 .20

Nibelungen District Art Exhibition, Pöchlarn, celebrating the 700th anniversary of Pöchlarn as a city. The design is from the border of the Amor and Psyche tapestry in the Salzburg Festival Theater.

View and Arms of Vienna A273

Engraved and Photogravure

1967, June 12 ***Perf. 13x13½***
794 A273 3s black & red .35 .20

10th Europa Talks, "Science and Society in Europe," Vienna, June 13-17.

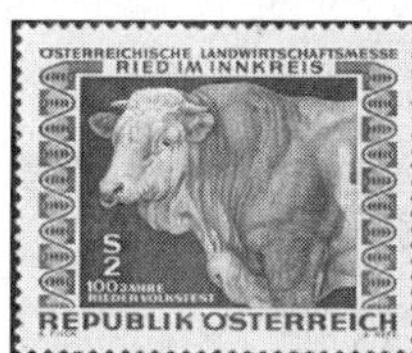

Prize Bull "Mucki" A274

1967, Aug. 28 Engr. ***Perf. 13½***
795 A274 2s deep claret .25 .20

Centenary of the Ried Festival and the Agricultural Fair.

Potato Beetle A275

Engraved and Photogravure

1967, Aug. 29 ***Perf. 13½x14***
796 A275 3s black & multi .35 .20

6th Intl. Congress for Plant Protection, Vienna.

First Locomotive Used on Brenner Pass A276

1967, Sept. 23 Photo. ***Perf. 12***
797 A276 3.50s tan & slate grn .45 .20

Centenary of railroad over Brenner Pass.

Christ in Glory — A277

1967, Oct. 9 ***Perf. 13½***
798 A277 2s multicolored .25 .20

Restoration of the Romanesque (11th century) frescoes in the Lambach monastery church.

Main Gate to Fair, Prater, Vienna A278

1967, Oct. 24 Photo. ***Perf. 13½x14***
799 A278 2s choc & buff .25 .20

Congress of Intl. Trade Fairs, Vienna, Oct., 1967.

Medal Showing Minerva and Art Symbols — A279

Litho. & Engr.

1967, Oct. 25 ***Perf. 13½***
800 A279 2s dk brn, dk bl & yel .25 .20

Vienna Academy of Fine Arts, 275th anniv. The medal was designed by Georg Raphael Donner (1693-1741) and is awarded as an artist's prize.

Frankfurt Medal for Reformation, 1717 — A280

1967, Oct. 31 Engr. ***Perf. 14x13½***
801 A280 3.50s blue black .35 .20

450th anniversary of the Reformation.

Mountain Range and Stone Pines A281

1967, Nov. 7 ***Perf. 13½***
802 A281 3.50s green .55 .25

Centenary of academic study of forestry.

Land Survey Monument, 1770 — A282

1967, Nov. 7 Photo.
803 A282 2s olive black .25 .20

150th anniversary of official land records.

St. Leopold, Window, Heiligenkreuz Abbey — A283

1967, Nov. 15 Engr. & Photo.
804 A283 1.80s multicolored .25 .20

Margrave Leopold III (1075-1136), patron saint of Austria.

Tragic Mask and Violin — A284

1967, Nov. 17 ***Perf. 13½***
805 A284 3.50s bluish lil & blk .40 .20

Academy of Music and Dramatic Art, 150th anniv.

Nativity from 15th Century Altar — A285

1967, Nov. 27 Engr. ***Perf. 14x13½***
806 A285 2s green .25 .20

Christmas.

The design shows the late Gothic carved center panel of the altar in St. John's Chapel in Nonnberg Convent, Salzburg.

Innsbruck Stadium, Alps and FISU Emblem — A286

1968, Jan. 22 Engr. ***Perf. 13½***
807 A286 2s dark blue .25 .20

Winter University Games under the auspices of FISU (Fédération Internationale du Sport Universitaire), Innsbruck, Jan. 21-28.

Camillo Sitte (1843-1903), Architect, City Planner — A287

1968, Apr. 17 *Perf. 13½*
808 A287 2s black brown .25 .20

Mother and Child — A288

1968, May 7
809 A288 2s slate green .25 .20

Mother's Day.

Cup and Serpent Emblem — A289

1968, May 7 **Photo.**
810 A289 3.50s dp plum, gray & gold .35 .20

Bicentenary of the Veterinary College.

Bride with Lace Veil — A290

1968, May 24 **Engr.** *Perf. 12*
811 A290 3.50s blue black .40 .20

Embroidery industry of Vorarlberg, cent.

Horse Race A291

1968, June 4 *Perf. 13½*
812 A291 3.50s sepia .40 .20

Centenary of horse racing at Freudenau, Vienna.

Dr. Karl Landsteiner A292

1968, June 14 *Perf. 14x13½*
813 A292 3.50s dark blue .40 .20

Birth cent. of Dr. Karl Landsteiner (1868-1943), pathologist, discoverer of the four main human blood types.

Peter Rosegger (1843-1918), Poet and Writer — A293

1968, June 26
814 A293 2s slate green .25 .20

Angelica Kauffmann, Self-portrait A294

1968, July 15 **Engr.** *Perf. 14x13½*
815 A294 2s intense black .30 .20

"Angelica Kauffmann and her Contemporaries," art exhibitions, Bregenz, July 28-Oct. 13, and Vienna, Oct. 22, 1968-Jan. 6, 1969.

Bronze Statue of Young Man, 1st Century B.C. — A295

1968, July 15 **Litho. & Engr.**
816 A295 2s grnsh gray & blk .25 .20

20 years of excavations on Magdalene Mountain, Carinthia.

Bishop, Romanesque Bas-relief — A296

1968, Sept. 20 **Engr.** *Perf. 14x13½*
817 A296 2s blue gray .25 .20

Graz-Seckau Bishopric, 750th anniv.

Koloman Moser (1868-1918), Stamp Designer, Painter — A297

Engr. & Photo.

1968, Oct. 18 *Perf. 12*
818 A297 2s black brn & ver .25 .20

Intl. Human Rights Year — A298

1968, Oct. 18 **Photo.** *Perf. 14x13½*
819 A298 1.50s gray, dp car & dk green .35 .20

Republic of Austria, 50th Anniv. — A299

#820, Pres. Karl Renner and States' arms. #821, Coats of arms of Austria and Austrian states. #822, Article I of Austrian Constitution and States' coats of arms.

Engr. & Photo.

1968, Nov. 11 *Perf. 13½*
820 A299 2s black & multi .25 .25
821 A299 2s black & multi .25 .25
822 A299 2s black & multi .25 .25
Nos. 820-822 (3) .75 .75

Hymn "Silent Night, Holy Night," 150th Anniv. — A300

Crèche, Memorial Chapel, Oberndorf-Salzburg.

1968, Nov. 29 **Engr.** *Perf. 14x13½*
823 A300 2s slate green .25 .20

Christmas.

Angels, from Last Judgment by Troger (Röhrenbach-Greillenstein Chapel) — A301

Baroque Frescoes: No. 825, Vanquished Demons, by Paul Troger, Altenburg Abbey. No. 826, Sts. Peter and Paul, by Troger, Melk Abbey. No. 827, The Glorification of Mary, by Franz Anton Maulpertsch, Maria Treu Church, Vienna. No. 828, St. Leopold Carried into Heaven, by Maulpertsch, Ebenfurth Castle Chapel. No. 829, Symbolic figures from The Triumph of Apollo, by Maulpertsch, Halbthurn Castle.

Engr. & Photo.

1968, Dec. 11 *Perf. 13½x14*
824 A301 2s multicolored .25 .25
825 A301 2s multicolored .25 .25
826 A301 2s multicolored .25 .25
827 A301 2s multicolored .25 .25
828 A301 2s multicolored .25 .25
829 A301 2s multicolored .25 .25
Nos. 824-829 (6) 1.50 1.50

St. Stephen — A302

Statues in St. Stephen's Cathedral, Vienna: No. 831, St. Paul. No. 832, Mantle Madonna. No. 833, St. Christopher. No. 834, St. George and the Dragon. No. 835, St. Sebastian.

1969, Jan. 28 **Engr.** *Perf. 13½*
830 A302 2s black .25 .25
831 A302 2s rose claret .25 .25
832 A302 2s gray violet .25 .25
833 A302 2s slate blue .25 .25
834 A302 2s slate green .25 .25
835 A302 2s dk red brn .25 .25
Nos. 830-835 (6) 1.50 1.50

500th anniversary of Diocese of Vienna.

Parliament and Pallas Athena Fountain, Vienna A303

1969, Apr. 8 **Engr.** *Perf. 13½*
836 A303 2s greenish black .25 .20

Interparliamentary Union Conf., Vienna, 4/7-13.

Europa Issue, 1969

Common Design Type

1969, Apr. 28 **Photo.** *Perf. 12*
837 CD12 2s gray grn, brick red & blue .25 .20

Council of Europe Emblem A304

1969, May 5
838 A304 3.50s gray, ultra, blk & yel .45 .25

20th anniversary of Council of Europe.

Frontier Guards — A305

Engr. & Photo.

1969, May 14 *Perf. 12*
839 A305 2s sepia & red .25 .20

Austrian Federal Army.

Don Giovanni, by Mozart A306

Cent. of Vienna Opera House: a, Don Giovanni, Mozart. b, Magic Flute, Mozart. c, Fidelio, Beethoven. d, Lohengrin, Wagner. e, Don Carlos, Verdi. f, Carmen, Bizet. g, Rosencavalier, Richard Strauss. h, Swan Lake, Ballet by Tchaikovsky.

1969, May 23 *Perf. 13½*
840 A306 Sheet of 8 3.75 3.75
a.-h. 2s, any single .35 .35

Centenary of Vienna Opera House.
No. 840 contains 8 stamps arranged around gold and red center label showing Opera House. Printed in sheets containing 4 Nos. 840 with wide gutters between.

Emperor Maximilian I Exhibition, Innsbruck, May 30-Oct. 5 — A307

Gothic armor of Maximilian I.

1969, June 4 **Engr.**
841 A307 2s bluish black .25 .20

19th Cong. of the Intl. Org. of Municipalities, Vienna — A308

1969, June 16 **Photo.** *Perf. 13½*
Oldest Municipal Seal of Vienna.
842 A308 2s tan, red & black .25 .20

SOS Children's Villages in Austria, 20th Anniv. — A309

Girl's head and village house.

Engraved and Photogravure
1969, June 16 *Perf. 13½x14*
843 A309 2s yel grn & sepia .25 .20

ILO, 50th Anniv. — A310

1969, Aug. 22 **Photo.** *Perf. 13x13½*
Hands holding wrench, and UN emblem.
844 A310 2s deep green .25 .20

Year of Austrians Living Abroad, 1969 — A311

Austria's flag and shield circling the world.

Engraved and Lithographed
1969, Aug. 22 *Perf. 14x13½*
845 A311 3.50s slate & red .40 .20

Etching Collection in the Albertina, Vienna, Bicent. — A312

Etchings: No. 846, Young Hare, by Dürer. No. 847, El Cid Killing a Bull, by Francisco de Goya. No. 848, Madonna with the Pomegranate, by Raphael. No. 849, The Painter, by Peter Brueghel. No. 850, Rubens' Son Nicolas, by Rubens. No. 851, Self-portrait, by Rembrandt. No. 852, Lady Reading, by Francois Guerin. No. 853, Wife of the Artist, by Egon Schiele.

Engraved and Photogravure
1969, Sept. 26 *Perf. 13½*
Gray Frame, Buff Background

846	A312 2s black & brown	.25	.25
847	A312 2s black	.25	.25
848	A312 2s black	.25	.25
849	A312 2s black	.25	.25
850	A312 2s black & salmon	.25	.25
851	A312 2s black	.25	.25
852	A312 2s black & salmon	.25	.25
853	A312 2s black	.25	.25
	Nos. 846-853 (8)	2.00	2.00

President Franz Jonas — A313

1969, Oct. 3
854 A313 2s gray & vio blue .25 .20

70th birthday of Franz Jonas, Austrian Pres.

Post Horn, Globe and Lightning A314

1969, Oct. 17 *Perf. 13½x14*
855 A314 2s multicolored .25 .20

Union of Postal and Telegraph employees, 50th anniv.

Savings Box, about 1450 — A315

1969, Oct. 31 **Photo.** *Perf. 13x13½*
856 A315 2s silver & slate green .25 .20

The importance of savings.

Madonna, by Albin Egger-Lienz A316

Engr. & Photo.
1969, Nov. 24 *Perf. 12*
857 A316 2s dp claret & pale yel .25 .20

Christmas.

Josef Schöffel — A317

1970, Feb. 6 **Engr.** *Perf. 14x13½*
858 A317 2s dull purple .25 .20

60th death anniv. of Josef Schöffel, (1832-1910), who saved the Vienna Woods.

St. Klemens M. Hofbauer — A318

Engraved and Photogravure
1970, Mar. 13 *Perf. 14x13½*
859 A318 2s dk brn & lt tan .25 .20

150th death anniv. St. Klemens Maria Hofbauer (1751-1820); Redemptorist preacher in Poland and Austria, canonized in 1909.

Chancellor Leopold Figl — A319

Belvedere Palace, Vienna — A320

1970, Apr. 27 **Engr.** *Perf. 13½*
860 A319 2s dark olive gray .25 .20
861 A320 2s dark rose brown .25 .20

25th anniversary of Second Republic.

European Nature Conservation Year, 1970 — A321

1970, May 19 **Engr.** *Perf. 13½*
862 A321 2s Krimml waterfalls .30 .20

Leopold Franzens University, Innsbruck, 300th Anniv. — A322

Litho. & Engr.
1970, June 5 *Perf. 13½*
St. Leopold on oldest seal of Innsbruck University.
863 A322 2s red & black .25 .20

Organ, Great Hall, Music Academy — A323

Photo. & Engr.
1970, June 5 *Perf. 14*
864 A323 2s gold & deep claret .25 .20

Vienna Music Academy Building, cent.

Tower Clock, 1450-1550 A324

Old Clocks from Vienna Horological Museum: #866, Lyre clock, 1790-1815. #867, Pendant clock 1600-50. #868, Pendant watch, 1800-30. #869, Bracket clock, 1720-60. #870, French column clock, 1820-50.

1970

865	A324 1.50s buff & sepia	.20	.20
866	A324 1.50s greenish & grn	.20	.20
867	A324 2s pale bl & dk bl	.25	.25
868	A324 2s pale rose & lake	.25	.25
869	A324 3.50s buff & brown	.45	.45
870	A324 3.50s pale lil & brn vio	.45	.45
	Nos. 865-870 (6)	1.80	1.80

Issued: #865, 867, 869, 6/22; others, 10/23.

The Beggar Student, by Carl Millöcker — A325

Operettas: No. 872, Fledermaus, by Johann Strauss. No. 873, The Dream Waltz, by Oscar Strauss. No. 874, The Bird Seller, by Carl Zeller. No. 875, The Merry Widow, by Franz Lehar. No. 876, Two Hearts in Three-quarter Time, by Robert Stolz.

1970 Photo & Engr. *Perf. 13½*

871 A325 1.50s pale grn & grn .20 .20
872 A325 1.50s yel & vio blue .20 .20
873 A325 2s pale rose & vio brn .25 .25
874 A325 2s pale grn & sep .25 .25
875 A325 3.50s pale bl & ind .45 .45
876 A325 3.50s beige & slate .45 .45
Nos. 871-876 (6) 1.80 1.80

Issued: #871, 873, 875, 7/3; others 9/11.

Bregenz Festival Stage — A326

1970, July 23 Photo.

877 A326 3.50s dark blue & buff .40 .30

25th anniversary of Bregenz Festival.

Salzburg Festival Emblem — A327

1970, July 27 *Perf. 14*

878 A327 3.50s blk, red, gold & gray .40 .30

50th anniversary of Salzburg Festival.

A328

1970, Aug. 31 Engr.

879 A328 3.50s dark gray .40 .25

13th General Assembly of the World Veterans Federation, Aug. 28-Sept. 4. The head of St. John is from a sculpture showing the Agony in the Garden in the chapel of the Parish Church in Ried. It is attributed to Thomas Schwanthaler (1634-1702).

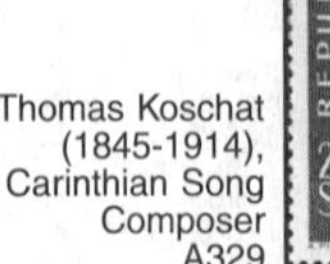

Thomas Koschat (1845-1914), Carinthian Song Composer A329

1970, Sept. 16 *Perf. 14x13½*

880 A329 2s chocolate .25 .20

Mountain Scene A330

1970, Sept. 16 Photo. *Perf. 14x13½*

881 A330 2s vio bl & pink .25 .20

Hiking and mountaineering in Austria.

Alfred Cossmann (1870-1951), Engraver — A331

1970, Oct. 2 Engr. *Perf. 14x13½*

882 A331 2s dark brown .25 .20

Arms of Carinthia — A332

Photo. & Engr.

1970, Oct. 2 *Perf. 14*

883 A332 2s ol, red, gold, blk & sil .25 .20

Carinthian plebiscite, 50th anniversary.

UN Emblem A333

1970, Oct. 23 Litho. *Perf. 14x13½*

884 A333 3.50s lt blue & blk .45 .25

25th anniversary of the United Nations.

Adoration of the Shepherds, Carving from Garsten Vicarage A334

1970, Nov. 27 Engr. *Perf. 13½x14*

885 A334 2s dk violet blue .25 .20

Christmas.

Karl Renner (1870-1950), Austrian Pres. — A335

1970, Dec. 14 Engr. *Perf. 14x13½*

886 A335 2s deep claret .25 .20

Beethoven, by Georg Waldmüller A336

Photo. & Engr.

1970, Dec. 16 *Perf. 13½*

887 A336 3.50s black & buff .40 .30

Ludwig van Beethoven (1770-1827), composer, birth bicentenary.

Enrica Handel-Mazzetti (1871-1955), Novelist, Poet — A337

1971, Jan. 11 Engr. *Perf. 14x13½*

888 A337 2s sepia .25 .20

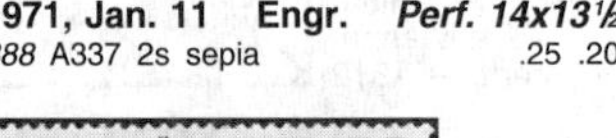

"Watch Out for Children!" A338

1971, Feb. 18 Photo. *Perf. 13½*

889 A338 2s blk, red brn & brt grn .25 .20

Traffic safety.

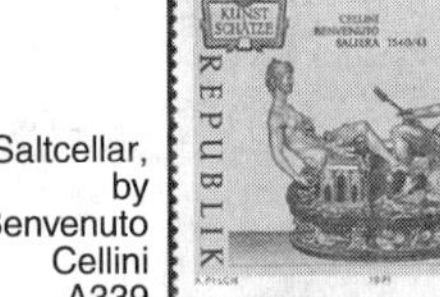

Saltcellar, by Benvenuto Cellini A339

Art Treasures: 1.50s, Covered vessel, made of prase, gold and precious stones, Florentine, 1580. 2s, Emperor Joseph I, ivory statue by Matthias Steinle, 1693.

Photo. & Engr.

1971, Mar. 22 *Perf. 14*

890 A339 1.50s gray & slate grn .20 .20
891 A339 2s gray & dp plum .25 .25
892 A339 3.50s gray, blk & bister .45 .45
Nos. 890-892 (3) .90 .90

Emblem of Austrian Wholesalers' Organization A340

1971, Apr. 16 Photo. *Perf. 13½*

893 A340 3.50s multicolored .40 .25

Intl. Chamber of Commerce, 23rd Congress, Vienna, Apr. 17-23.

Jacopo de Strada, by Titian — A341

Paintings in Vienna Museum: 2s, Village Feast, by Peter Brueghel, the Elder. 3.50s, Young Venetian Woman, by Albrecht Dürer.

1971, May 6 Engr. *Perf. 13½*

894 A341 1.50s rose lake .20 .20
895 A341 2s greenish black .25 .25
896 A341 3.50s deep brown .45 .45
Nos. 894-896 (3) .90 .90

Seal of Paulus of Franchenfordia, 1380 — A342

Photo. & Engr.

1971, May 6 *Perf. 13½x14*

897 A342 3.50s dk brn & bister .40 .25

Congress commemorating the centenary of the Austrian Notaries' Statute, May 5-8.

St. Matthew — A343 August Neilreich — A344

1971, May 27 *Perf. 12½x13½*

898 A343 2s brt rose lil & brn .25 .20

Exhibition of "1000 Years of Art in Krems." The statue of St. Matthew is from the Lentl Altar, created about 1520 by the Master of the Pulkau Altar.

1971, June 1 Engr. *Perf. 14x13½*

899 A344 2s brown .25 .20

August Neilreich (1803-71), botanist.

Singer with Lyre — A345

Photo. & Engr.

1971, July 1 *Perf. 13½x14*

900 A345 4s lt bl, vio bl & gold .45 .30

Intl. Choir Festival, Vienna, July 1-4.

Coat of Arms of Kitzbuhel — A346

1971, Aug. 23 ***Perf. 14***

901 A346 2.50s gold & multi .25 .20

700th anniversary of the town of Kitzbuhel.

Vienna Stock Exchange — A347

1971, Sept. 1 Engr. ***Perf. 13½x14***

902 A347 4s reddish brown .45 .25

Bicentenary of the Vienna Stock Exchange.

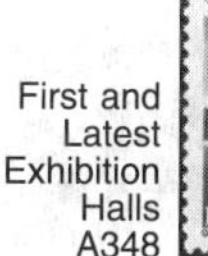

First and Latest Exhibition Halls A348

1971, Sept. 6 Photo. ***Perf. 13½x13***

903 A348 2.50s dp rose lilac .30 .20

Vienna Intl. Fair, 50th anniv.

Trade Union Emblem — A349

1971, Sept. 20 ***Perf. 14x13½***

904 A349 2s gray, buff & red .25 .20

Austrian Trade Union Assoc., 25th anniv.

Arms of Burgenland A350

1971, Oct. 1

905 A350 2s dk bl, gold, red & blk .25 .20

50th anniv. of Burgenland joining Austria.

Marcus Car — A351

Photo. & Engr.

1971, Oct. 1 ***Perf. 14***

906 A351 4s pale green & blk .45 .25

Austrian Automobile, Motorcycle and Touring Club, 75th anniv.

Europa Bridge — A352

1971, Oct. 8 Engr. ***Perf. 14x13½***

907 A352 4s violet blue .45 .25

Opening of highway over Brenner Pass.

Styria's Iron Mountain A353

Designs: 2s, Austrian Nitrogen Products, Ltd., Linz. 4s, United Austrian Iron and Steel Works, Ltd. (VÖEST), Linz Harbor.

1971, Oct. 15 ***Perf. 13½***

908	A353	1.50s reddish brown	.20	.20
909	A353	2s bluish black	.20	.20
910	A353	4s dk slate grn	.50	.40
		Nos. 908-910 (3)	.90	.80

25 years of nationalized industry.

High-speed Train on Semmering A354

1971, Oct. 21 ***Perf. 14***

911 A354 2s claret .25 .20

Inter-city rapid train service.

Trout Fisherman A355

1971, Nov. 15 ***Perf. 13½***

912 A355 2s dark red brn .25 .20

Dr. Erich Tschermak-Seysenegg (1871-1962), Botanist — A356

Photo. & Engr.

1971, Nov. 15 ***Perf. 14x13½***

913 A356 2s pale ol & dk pur .25 .20

Infant Jesus as Savior, by Dürer — A357

1971, Nov. 26 ***Perf. 13½***

914 A357 2s gold & multi .25 .20

Christmas.

Franz Grillparzer, by Moritz Daffinger — A358

Litho. & Engr.

1972, Jan. 21 ***Perf. 14x13½***

915 A358 2s buff, gold & blk .30 .20

Death cent. of Franz Grillparzer (1791-1872), dramatic poet.

Fountain, Main Square, Friesach — A359

Designs: 2s, Fountain, Heiligenkreuz Abbey. 2.50s, Leopold Fountain, Innsbruck.

1972, Feb. 23 Engr. ***Perf. 14x13½***

916	A359	1.50s rose lilac	.25	.20
917	A359	2s brown	.25	.20
918	A359	2.50s olive	.30	.25
		Nos. 916-918 (3)	.80	.65

Cardiac Patient and Monitor A360

1972, Apr. 11 ***Perf. 13½x14***

919 A360 4s violet brown .55 .25

World Health Day.

Conference of European Post and Telecommunications Ministers, Vienna, Apr. 11-14 — A361

St. Michael's Gate, Royal Palace, Vienna.

1972, Apr. 11 ***Perf. 14x13½***

920 A361 4s violet blue .55 .25

Gurk (Carinthia) Diocese, 900th Anniv. — A362

Photo. & Engr.

1972, May 5 ***Perf. 14***

921 A362 2s Sculpture, Gurk Cathedral .30 .20

. The design is after the central column supporting the sarcophagus of St. Hemma in Gurk Cathedral.

City Hall, Congress Emblem A363

1972, May 23 Litho. & Engr.

922 A363 4s red, blk & yel .55 .20

9th Intl. Congress of Public and Cooperative Economy, Vienna, May 23-25.

Power Line in Carnic Alps — A364

2.50s, Power Station, Semmering. 4s, Zemm Power Station (lake in Zillertaler Alps).

1972, June 28 ***Perf. 13½x14***

923	A364	70g gray & violet	.20	.20
924	A364	2.50s gray & red brn	.30	.30
925	A364	4s gray & slate	.50	.50
		Nos. 923-925 (3)	1.00	1.00

Nationalization of the power industry, 25th anniv.

Runner with Olympic Torch — A365

Engr. & Photo.

1972, Aug. 21 ***Perf. 14x13½***

926 A365 2s sepia & red .25 .20

Olympic torch relay from Olympia, Greece, to Munich, Germany, passing through Austria.

St. Hermes, by Conrad Laib — A366

1972, Aug. 21 Engr.

927 A366 2s violet brown .25 .20

Exhibition of Late Gothic Art, Salzburg.

Pears A367

1972, Sept. ***Perf. 14***
928 A367 2.50s dk blue & multi .30 .20

World Congress of small plot Gardeners, Vienna, Sept. 7-10.

Souvenir Sheet

Spanish Riding School, Vienna, 400th Anniv. — A368

1972, Sept. 12 ***Perf. 13½***
929 Sheet of 6 2.75 2.75
a. A368 2s Spanish walk .25 .25
b. A368 2s Piaffe .25 .25
c. A368 2.50s Levade .30 .30
d. A368 2.50s On long rein .30 .30
e. A368 4s Capriole .50 .50
f. A368 4s Courbette .50 .50

Arms of University of Agriculture A369

Photo. & Engr.

1972, Oct. 17 ***Perf. 14x13½***
930 A369 2s black & multi .25 .20

University of Agriculture, Vienna, cent.

Church and Old University — A370

1972, Nov. 7 **Engr.**
931 A370 4s red brown .55 .20

Paris Lodron University, Salzburg, 350th anniv.

Carl Michael Ziehrer — A371

1972, Nov. 14
932 A371 2s rose claret .25 .20

50th death anniv. of Carl Michael Ziehrer (1843-1922), composer.

Virgin and Child, Wood, 1420-30 A372

Photo. & Engr.

1972, Dec. 1 ***Perf. 13½***
933 A372 2s olive & chocolate .25 .20

Christmas.

Racing Sleigh, 1750 A373

Designs: 2s, Coronation landau, 1824. 2.50s, Imperial state coach, 1763.

1972, Dec. 12
934 A373 1.50s pale gray & brn .20 .20
935 A373 2s pale gray & sl grn .30 .20
936 A373 2.50s pale gray & plum .35 .25
Nos. 934-936 (3) .85 .65

Collection of historic state coaches and carriages in Schönbrunn Palace.

Map of Austrian Telephone System A374

1972, Dec. 14 **Photo.** ***Perf. 14***
937 A374 2s yellow & blk .25 .20

Completion of automation of Austrian telephone system.

"Drugs are Death" A375

1973, Jan. 26 **Photo.** ***Perf. 13½x14***
938 A375 2s scarlet & multi 1.50 .45

Fight against drug abuse.

Alfons Petzold (1882-1923), Poet — A376

1973, Jan. 26 **Engr.** ***Perf. 14x13½***
939 A376 2s reddish brn .25 .20

Theodor Körner (1873-1957), Austrian Pres. — A377

Photo. & Engr.

1973, Apr. 24 ***Perf. 14x13½***
940 A377 2s gray & deep claret .25 .20

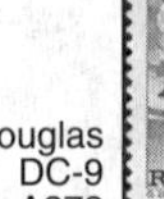

Douglas DC-9 A378

1973, May 14 ***Perf. 13½x14***
941 A378 2s vio bl & rose red .30 .20

First intl. airmail service, Vienna to Kiev, Mar. 31, 1918, 55th anniv.; Austrian Aviation Corporation, 50th anniv.; Austrian Airlines, 15th anniv.

Otto Loewi (1873-1961), Pharmacologist, Nobel Laureate — A379

1973, June 4 **Engr.** ***Perf. 14x13½***
942 A379 4s deep violet .55 .20

"Support" — A380

1973, June 25
943 A380 2s dark blue .25 .20

Federation of Austrian Social Insurance Institutes, 25th anniv.

Europa Issue 1973

Post Horn and Telephone A381

1973, July 9 **Photo.** ***Perf. 14***
944 A381 2.50s ocher, blk & yel .30 .20

Dornbirn Fair Emblem A382

1973, July 27 ***Perf. 13½x14***
945 A382 2s multicolored .30 .20

Dornbirn Trade Fair, 25th anniversary.

23rd Intl. Military Pentathlon Championships, Wiener Neustadt, Aug. 13-18 — A383

1973, Aug. 13 **Engr.** ***Perf. 14x13½***
946 A383 4s Hurdles .50 .20

Leo Slezak (1873-1946), Operatic Tenor — A384

1973, Aug. 17 ***Perf. 14***
947 A384 4s dark brown .50 .20

Gate, Vienna Hofburg, and ISI Emblem — A385

Photogravure and Engraved

1973, Aug. 20 ***Perf. 14x13½***
948 A385 2s gray, dk brn & ver .25 .20

39th Congress of Intl. Statistical Institute, Vienna, Aug. 20-30.

Tegetthoff off Franz Josef Land, by Julius Prayer A386

1973, Aug. 30 **Engr.** ***Perf. 13½x14***
949 A386 2.50s Prussian grn .30 .20

Discovery of Franz Josef Land by an Austrian North Pole expedition, cent.

Academy of Science, by Canaletto A387

1973, Sept. 4
950 A387 2.50s violet .30 .20

Intl. meteorological cooperation, cent.

Arms of Viennese Tanners — A388

Photo. & Engr.

1973, Sept. 4 ***Perf. 14***
951 A388 4s red & multi .55 .20

13th Congress of the Intl. Union of Leather Chemists' Societies, Vienna, Sept. 1-7.

Max Reinhardt (1873-1943), Theatrical Director — A389

1973, Sept. 7 **Engr.** ***Perf. 13x13½***
952 A389 2s rose magenta .25 .20

Trotter
A390

1973, Sept. 28 ***Perf. 13½***
953 A390 2s green .30 .20

Centenary of Vienna Trotting Association.

Ferdinand Hanusch (1866-1923), Secretary of State — A391

1973, Sept. 28 ***Perf. 14x13½***
954 A391 2s rose brown .25 .20

Police Radio Operator
A392

1973, Oct. 2 ***Perf. 13½x14***
955 A392 4s violet blue .50 .20

50th anniv. of Intl. Criminal Police Org. (INTERPOL).

Josef Petzval's Photographic Lens — A393

Litho. & Engr.

1973, Oct. 8 ***Perf. 14***
956 A393 2.50s blue & multi .30 .20

EUROPHOT Photographic Cong., Vienna.

Emperor's Spring, Hell Valley
A394

Photo. & Engr.

1973, Oct. 23 ***Perf. 13½x14***
957 A394 2s sepia, blue & red .25 .20

Vienna's first mountain spring water supply system, cent.

Almsee, Upper Austria — A395

Hofburg and Prince Eugene Statue, Vienna — A395a

Designs: 50g, Farmhouses, Zillertal, Tirol. 1s, Kahlenbergerdorf. 1.50s, Bludenz, Vorarlberg. 2s, Inn Bridge, Alt Finstermunz. 2.50s, Murau, Styria. 3s, Bischofsmütze, Salzburg. 3.50s, Easter Church, Oberwart. 4.50s, Windmill, Retz. 5s, Aggstein Castle, Lower Austria. 6s, Lindauer Hut, Vorarlberg. 6.50s, Holy Cross Church, Villach, Carinthia. 7s, Falkenstein Castle, Carinthia. 7.50s, Hohensalzburg. 8s, Votive column, Reiteregg, Styria. 10s, Lake Neusiedl, Burgenland. 11s, Old Town, Enns. 16s, Openair Museum, Bad Tatzmannsdorf. 20s, Myra waterfalls.

Photo. & Engr.

1973-78 ***Perf. 13½x14***

Size: 23x29mm

958	A395	50g gray & slate green	.20	.20
959	A395	1s brn & dk brown	.20	.20
960	A395	1.50s rose & brown	.25	.20
961	A395	2s gray bl & dk blue	.30	.20
962	A395	2.50s vio & dp violet	.35	.20
963	A395	3s lt ultra & vio blue	.45	.20
963A	A395	3.50s dl org & brown	.50	.20
964	A395	4s brt lil & pur	.55	.20
965	A395	4.50s brt grn & bl green	.60	.20
966	A395	5s lilac & vio	.65	.20
967	A395	6s dp rose & dk violet	.80	.20
968	A395	6.50s bl grn & indigo	.90	.20
969	A395	7s sage grn & sl green	.95	.20
970	A395	7.50s lil rose & claret	1.00	.25
971	A395	8s dl red & dp brown	1.10	.20
972	A395	10s gray grn & dk green	1.40	.20
973	A395	11s ver & dk carmine	1.60	.20
974	A395	16s bister & brown	2.25	.60
975	A395	20s ol bis & ol grn	2.75	1.25
976	A395a	50s gray vio & vio bl	6.75	2.50
		Nos. 958-976 (20)	23.55	7.80

Issued: #960-963, 1974; #958-959, 967, 976, 1975; #965, 971, 973, 1976; #968, 970, 974-975, 1977; #963A, 1978. See #1100-1109.

Nativity — A396

1973, Nov. 30 ***Perf. 14***
977 A396 2s multicolored .30 .20

Christmas. Design from 14th century stained-glass window.

Pregl — A397

1973, Dec. 12 **Engr.** ***Perf. 14x13½***
978 A397 4s deep blue .50 .20

50th anniv. of the awarding of the Nobel prize for chemistry to Fritz Pregl (1869-1930).

Radio Austria, 50th Anniv. — A398

1974, Jan. 14 **Photo.** ***Perf. 14x13½***
979 A398 2.50s Telex Machine .30 .20

Hugo Hofmannsthal (1874-1929), Poet and Playwright
A399

1974, Feb. 1 **Engr.** ***Perf. 14***
980 A399 4s violet blue .50 .20

Anton Bruckner and Bruckner House
A400

1974, Mar. 22 **Engr.** ***Perf. 14***
981 A400 4s brown .50 .20

Founding of Anton Bruckner House (concert hall), Linz, and birth of Anton Bruckner (1824-1896), composer, 150th anniv.

Vegetables
A401

Photo. & Engr.

1974, Apr. 18 ***Perf. 14***
982 A401 2s shown .30 .20
983 A401 2.50s Fruits .35 .30
984 A401 4s Flowers .50 .50
Nos. 982-984 (3) 1.15 1.00

Intl. Garden Show, Vienna, Apr. 18-Oct. 14.

Seal of Judenburg
A402

1974, Apr. 24 **Photo.** ***Perf. 14x13½***
985 A402 2s plum & multi .30 .20

750th anniversary of Judenburg.

Karl Kraus (1874-1936), Poet and Satirist — A403

1974, Apr. 6 **Engr.**
986 A403 4s dark red .50 .20

St. Michael, by Thomas Schwanthaler
A404

1974, May 3
987 A404 2.50s slate green .30 .20

Exhibition of the works by the Schwanthaler Family of sculptors, (1633-1848), Reichersberg am Inn, May 3-Oct. 13.

A405

Europa: King Arthur, from tomb of Maximilian I

1974, May 8 ***Perf. 13½***
988 A405 2.50s ocher & slate blue .30 .20

Austrian Automobile Assoc., 75th Anniv. — A406

De Dion Bouton motor tricycle.

Photo. & Engr.

1974, May 17 ***Perf. 14x13½***
989 A406 2s gray & vio brn .30 .20

Satyr's Head, Terracotta
A407

1974, May 22 ***Perf. 13½x14***
990 A407 2s org brn, gold & blk .30 .20

Exhibition, "Renaissance in Austria," Schallaburg Castle, May 22-Nov. 14.

Road Transport Union Emblem — A408

1974, May 24 **Photo.** ***Perf. 14x13½***
991 A408 4s deep orange & blk .50 .20

14th Congress of the Intl. Road Transport Union, Innsbruck.

Franz Anton Maulbertsch (1724-96), Painter — A409

1974, June 7 Engr. ***Perf. 14x13½***
992 A409 2s Self-portrait .25 .20

Gendarmes, 1824 and 1974 A410

1974, June 7 Photo. ***Perf. 13½x14***
993 A410 2s red & multi .25 .20

125th anniversary of Austrian gendarmery.

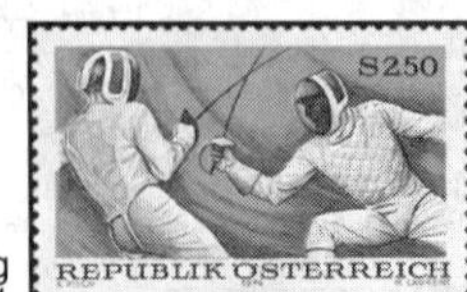

Fencing A411

Photo. & Engr.
1974, June 14 ***Perf. 13½***
994 A411 2.50s red org & blk .30 .20

Transportation Symbols — A412

1974, June 18 Photo. ***Perf. 14x13½***
995 A412 4s lt ultra & multi .50 .20

European Conference of Transportation Ministers, Vienna, June 18-21.

St. Virgil, Sculpture from Nonntal Church — A413

1974, June 28 Engr. ***Perf. 13½x14***
996 A413 2s violet blue .25 .20

Consecration of the Cathedral of Salzburg by Scotch-Irish Bishop Feirgil (St. Virgil), 1200th anniv. Salzburg was a center of Christianization in the 8th century.

Franz Jonas and Austrian Eagle — A414

1974, June 28
997 A414 2s black .25 .20

Jonas (1899-1974), Austrian Pres., 1965-1974.

Franz Stelzhamer A415 Diver A416

1974, July 12 Engr. ***Perf. 14x13½***
998 A415 2s indigo .25 .20

Franz Stelzhamer (1802-1874), poet who wrote in Upper Austrian vernacular, death cent.

Photo. & Engr.
1974, Aug. 16 ***Perf. 13x13½***
999 A416 4s blue & sepia .50 .20

13th European Swimming, Diving and Water Polo Championships, Vienna, Aug. 18-25.

Ferdinand Ritter von Hebra — A417

1974, Sept. 10 Engr. ***Perf. 14x13½***
1000 A417 4s brown .50 .20

30th Meeting of the Assoc. of German-speaking Dermatologists, Graz, Sept. 10-14. Dr. von Hebra (1816-1880) was a founder of modern dermatology.

Arnold Schonberg A418

1974, Sept. 13 ***Perf. 13½x14***
1001 A418 2.50s purple .30 .20

Schönberg (1874-1951), composer.

Radio Station, Salzburg A419

1974, Oct. 1 Photo. ***Perf. 13½x14***
1002 A419 2s multicolored .25 .20

50th anniversary of Austrian broadcasting.

Edmund Eysler (1874-1949), Composer A420

1974, Oct. 4 Engr. ***Perf. 14x13½***
1003 A420 2s dark olive .25 .20

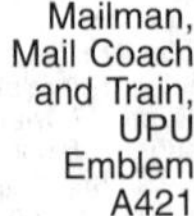

Mailman, Mail Coach and Train, UPU Emblem A421

4s, Mailman, jet, truck, 1974, & UPU emblem.

1974, Oct. 9 Photo. ***Perf. 13½***
1004 A421 2s deep claret & lil .25 .20
1005 A421 4s dark blue & gray .50 .20

Centenary of Universal Postal Union.

Gauntlet Protecting Rose A422

1974, Oct. 23 Photo. ***Perf. 13½x14***
1006 A422 2s multicolored .25 .20

Environment protection.

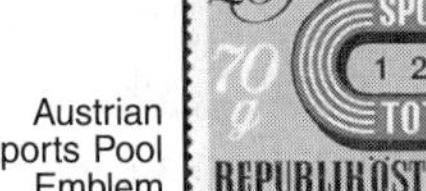

Austrian Sports Pool Emblem A423

1974, Oct. 23 Photo. ***Perf. 13½x14***
1007 A423 70g multicolored .20 .20

Austrian Sports Pool (lottery), 25th anniv.

Carl Ditters von Dittersdorf (1739-1799), Composer A424

1974, Oct. 24 Engr. ***Perf. 14x13½***
1008 A424 2s Prussian green .25 .20

Virgin and Child, Wood, c. 1600 — A425

1974, Nov. 29 **Photo. & Engr.**
1009 A425 2s brown & gold .35 .20

Christmas.

Franz Schmidt (1874-1939), Composer A426

1974, Dec. 18
1010 A426 4s gray & black .55 .20

European Architectural Heritage Year — A427

Photo. & Engr.
1975, Jan. 24 ***Perf. 13½***
1011 A427 2.50s St. Christopher .40 .20

The design shows part of a wooden figure from central panel of the retable in the Kefermarkt Church, 1490-1497.

Safety Belt and Skeleton Arms — A428

1975, Apr. 1 Photo. ***Perf. 14x13½***
1012 A428 70g violet & multi .20 .20

Introduction of obligatory use of automobile safety belts.

Stained Glass Window, Vienna City Hall — A429

1975, Apr. 2 ***Perf. 14***
1013 A429 2.50s multicolored .30 .20

11th meeting of the Council of European Municipalities, Vienna, Apr. 2-5.

Austria as Mediator A430

1975, May 2 Litho. ***Perf. 14***
1014 A430 2s blk & bister .30 .20

2nd Republic of Austria, 30th anniv.

National Forests, 50th Anniv. — A431

1975, May 6 **Engr.**
1015 A431 2s green .35 .20

High Priest, by Michael Pacher — A432

Europa Issue 1975

Photo. & Engr.

1975, May 27 ***Perf. 14x13½***

1016 A432 2.50s black & multi .40 .20

Design is detail from painting "The Marriage of Joseph and Mary," by Michael Pacher (c. 1450-1500).

Gosaukamm Funicular — A433

1975, June 23 ***Perf. 14x13½***

1017 A433 2s slate & red .30 .20

4th Intl. Funicular Cong., Vienna, 6/23-27.

Josef Misson and Mühlbach am Manhartsberg — A434

1975, June 27 ***Perf. 13½x14***

1018 A434 2s choc & redsh brn .25 .20

Josef Misson (1803-1875), poet who wrote in Lower Austrian vernacular, death cent.

Setting Sun and "P" — A435

1975, Aug. 27 Litho. ***Perf. 14x13½***

1019 A435 1.50s org, blk & bl .20 .20

Austrian Assoc. of Pensioners 25th anniv. meeting, Vienna, Aug. 1975.

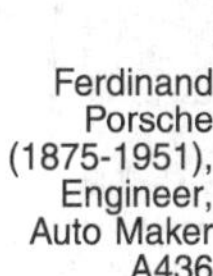

Ferdinand Porsche (1875-1951), Engineer, Auto Maker A436

Photo. & Engr.

1975, Sept. 3 ***Perf. 13½x14***

1020 A436 1.50s gray & purple .25 .20

Leo Fall (1873-1925), Composer A437

1975, Sept. 16 Engr. ***Perf. 14x13½***

1021 A437 2s violet .25 .20

10th World Judo Championships, Vienna — A438

1975, Oct. 20 Photo. ***Perf. 14x13½***

1022 A438 2.50s Judo Throw .30 .20

Heinrich Angeli (1840-1925), Painter — A439

1975, Oct. 21 Engr. ***Perf. 14x13½***

1023 A439 2s rose lake .30 .20

Johann Strauss and Dancers A440

Photo. & Engr.

1975, Oct. 24 ***Perf. 13½x14***

1024 A440 4s ocher & sepia .55 .20

Johann Strauss (1825-1899), composer.

Stylized Musician Playing a Viol — A441

1975, Oct. 30 ***Perf. 14x13½***

1025 A441 2.50s silver & vio bl .35 .20

Vienna Symphony Orchestra, 75th anniv.

Symbolic House — A442

1975, Oct. 31 **Photo.**

1026 A442 2s multicolored .25 .20

Austrian building savings societies, 50th anniv.

Fan with "Hanswurst" Scene, 18th Century A443

1975, Nov. 14 Photo. ***Perf. 13½x14***

1027 A443 1.50s green & multi .20 .20

Salzburg Theater bicentenary.

Virgin and Child, from 15th Century Altar — A444

Photo. & Engr.

1975, Nov. 28 ***Perf. 13x13½***

1028 A444 2s gold & dull purple .25 .20

Christmas.

"The Spiral Tree," by Hundertwasser A445

Photo., Engr. & Typo.

1975, Dec. 11 ***Perf. 13½x14***

1029 A445 4s multicolored .65 .25

Austrian modern art. Friedenstreich Hundertwasser is the pseudonym of Friedrich Stowasser (1928-2000).

Old Burgtheater A446

#1030b, Grand staircase, new Burgtheater.

Perf. 14 (pane), 13½x14 (stamps)

1976, Apr. 8 **Engr.**

1030 Pane of 2 + label 1.10 1.10

a. A446 3s violet blue .30 .30

b. A446 3s deep brown .30 .30

Bicentenary of Vienna Burgtheater. Label (head of Pan) and inscription in vermilion.

Dr. Robert Barany (1876-1936), Winner of Nobel Prize for Medicine, 1914 — A447

Photo. & Engr.

1976, Apr. 22 ***Perf. 14x13½***

1031 A447 3s blue & brown .45 .20

Ammonite A448

1976, Apr. 30 Photo. ***Perf. 13½x14***

1032 A448 3s red & multi .45 .20

Vienna Museum of Natural History, Centenary Exhibition.

Carinthian Dukes' Coronation Chair — A449

Photo. & Engr.

1976, May 6 ***Perf. 14x13½***

1033 A449 3s grnsh blk & org .45 .20

Millennium of Carinthia.

Siege of Linz, 17th Century Etching — A450

1976, May 14

1034 A450 4s blk & gray grn .55 .20

Upper Austrian Peasants' War, 350th anniv.

Skittles A451

1976, May 14 ***Perf. 13½x14***

1035 A451 4s black & org .55 .20

11th World Skittles Championships, Vienna.

Duke Heinrich II, Stained-glass Window — A452

1976, May 14 ***Perf. 14***

1036 A452 3s multicolored .45 .20

Babenberg Exhibition, Lilienfeld.

St. Wolfgang, from Pacher Altar — A453

1976, May 26 Engr. ***Perf. 13½***

1037 A453 6s bright violet .75 .40

Intl. Art Exhibition at St. Wolfgang.

Europa Issue 1976

Tassilo Cup, Kremsmunster, 777 — A454

Photo. & Engr.

1976, Aug. 13 ***Perf. 14x13½***

1038 A454 4s ultra & multi .60 .20

Timber Fair Emblem — A455

1976, Aug. 13 **Photo.**

1039 A455 3s green & multi .35 .20

Austrian Timber Fair, Klagenfurt, 25th anniv.

Constantin Economo, M.D. (1876-1931), Neurologist A456

1976, Aug. 23 **Engr.**

1040 A456 3s dark red brown .35 .20

Administrative Court, by Salomon Klein — A457

1976, Oct. 25 **Engr.** ***Perf. 13½x14***

1041 A457 6s deep brown .80 .30

Austrian Central Administrative Court, cent.

Souvenir Sheet

Coats of Arms of Austrian Provinces — A458

Millennium of Austria: a, Lower Austria. b, Upper Austria. c, Styria. d, Carinthia. e, Tyrol. f, Voralberg. g, Salzburg. h, Burgenland. i, Vienna.

Photo. & Engr.

1976, Oct. 25 ***Perf. 14***

1042 Sheet of 9 3.00 3.00
a.-i. A458 2s any single .30 .30

"Cancer" A459

1976, Nov. 17 **Photo.** ***Perf. 14x13½***

1043 A459 2.50s multicolored .35 .20

Fight against cancer.

UN Emblem and Bridge — A460

1976, Nov. 17

1044 A460 3s blue & gold .45 .20

UN Industrial Development Org. (UNIDO), 10th anniv.

Punched Tape, Map of Europe A461

1976, Nov. 17 ***Perf. 14***

1045 A461 1.50s multicolored .20 .20

Austrian Press Agency (APA), 30th anniv.

Viktor Kaplan, Kaplan Turbine A462

Photo. & Engr.

1976, Nov. 26 ***Perf. 13½x14***

1046 A462 2.50s multicolored .35 .20

Viktor Kaplan (1876-1934), inventor of Kaplan turbine, birth centenary.

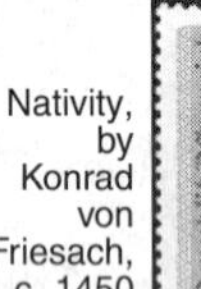

Nativity, by Konrad von Friesach, c. 1450 A463

1976, Nov. 26 ***Perf. 13½***

1047 A463 3s multicolored .40 .20

Christmas.

Augustin, the Piper — A464

Photo. & Engr.

1976, Dec. 29 ***Perf. 13½***

1048 A464 6s multicolored .75 .25

Modern Austrian art.

Rainer Maria Rilke (1875-1926), Poet — A465

Vienna City Synagogue — A466

1976, Dec. 29 **Engr.** ***Perf. 14x13½***

1049 A465 3s deep violet .40 .20

1976, Dec. 29 **Photo.** ***Perf. 13½***

1050 A466 1.50s multicolored .20 .20

Sesquicentennial of Vienna City Synagogue.

Nikolaus Joseph von Jacquin (1727-1817), Botanist — A467

1977, Feb. 16 **Engr.** ***Perf. 14x13½***

1051 A467 4s chocolate .55 .20

Oswald von Wolkenstein (1377-1445), Poet — A468

Photo. & Engr.

1977, Feb. 16 ***Perf. 14***

1052 A468 3s multicolored .35 .20

Handball A469

1977, Feb. 25 **Photo.** ***Perf. 13½x14***

1053 A469 1.50s multicolored .20 .20

World Indoor Handball Championships, Austria, Feb. 5-Mar. 6.

Alfred Kubin (1877-1959), Illustrator and Writer — A470

1977, Apr. 12 **Engr.** ***Perf. 14x13½***

1054 A470 6s dk violet blue .70 .25

Great Spire, St. Stephen's Cathedral A471

Designs: 3s, Heathen Tower and Frederick's Gable. 4s, Interior view with Albertinian Choir.

1977, Apr. 22 **Engr.** ***Perf. 13½***

1055 A471 2.50s dark brown .35 .20
1056 A471 3s dark blue .40 .25
1057 A471 4s rose lake .50 .35
Nos. 1055-1057 (3) 1.25 .80

Restoration and re-opening of St. Stephen's Cathedral, Vienna, 25th anniversary.

Fritz Hermanovsky-Orlando (1877-1954), Poet and Artist — A472

Photo. & Engr.

1977, Apr. 29 ***Perf. 13½x14***

1058 A472 6s Prus green & gold .70 .25

Intl. Atomic Energy Agency (IAEA), 20th Anniv. — A473

1977, May 2 **Photo.** ***Perf. 14***

1059 A473 3s IAEA Emblem .35 .20

Schwanenstadt, 350th Anniv. — A474

1977, June 10 **Photo.** ***Perf. 14x13½***

1060 A474 3s Town arms .35 .20

Europa Issue 1977

Attersee, Upper Austria — A475

1977, June 10 **Engr.** ***Perf. 14***

1061 A475 6s olive green .90 .30

Globe, by Vincenzo Coronelli, 1688 — A476

Photo. & Engr.

1977, June 29 *Perf. 14*

1062 A476 3s black & buff .35 .20

5th Intl. Symposium of the Coronelli World Fed. of Friends of the Globe, Austria, June 29-July 3.

Kayak Race A477

1977, July 15 Photo. *Perf. 13½x14*

1063 A477 4s multicolored .50 .20

3rd Kayak Slalom White Water Race on Lieser River, Spittal.

The Good Samaritan, by Francesco Bassano A478

1977, Sept. 16 Photo. & Engr.

1064 A478 1.50s brown & red .20 .20

Workers' Good Samaritan Org., 50th anniv.

Papermakers' Coat of Arms — A479

1977, Oct. 10 *Perf. 14x13½*

1065 A479 3s multicolored .35 .20

17th Conf. of the European Committee of Pulp and Paper Technology (EUCEPA), Vienna.

Man with Austrian Flag Lifting Barbed Wire — A480

1977, Nov. 3 *Perf. 14*

1066 A480 2.50s slate & red .35 .20

Honoring the martyrs for Austria's freedom.

"Austria," First Steam Locomotive in Austria — A481

Designs: 2.50s, Steam locomotive 214. 3s, Electric locomotive 1044.

Photo. & Engr.

1977, Nov. 17 *Perf. 13½*

1067 A481 1.50s multicolored .20 .20
1068 A481 2.50s multicolored .35 .20
1069 A481 3s multicolored .45 .20
Nos. 1067-1069 (3) 1.00 .60

140th anniversary of Austrian railroads.

Christmas — A482

Virgin and Child, wood statue, Mariastein, Tyrol.

1977, Nov. 25 *Perf. 14x13½*

1070 A482 3s multicolored .30 .20

Modern Austrian Art — A483

1977, Dec. 2 *Perf. 13½x14*

The Danube Maiden, by Wolfgang Hutter.

1071 A483 6s multicolored .75 .20

Egon Friedell (1878-1938), Writer and Historian A484

1978, Jan. 23 Photo. & Engr.

1072 A484 3s lt blue & blk .40 .20

Subway Train A485

1978, Feb. 24 Photo. *Perf. 13½x14*

1073 A485 3s multicolored .45 .20

New Vienna subway system.

Biathlon Competition A486

1978, Feb. 28 Photo. & Engr.

1074 A486 4s multicolored .45 .20

Biathlon World Championships, Hochfilzen, Tyrol, Feb. 28-Mar. 5.

Leopold Kunschak (1871-1953), Political Leader — A487

1978, Mar. 13 Engr. *Perf. 14x13½*

1075 A487 3s violet blue .40 .20

Coyote, Aztec Feather Shield A488

1978, Mar. 13 Photo. *Perf. 13½x14*

1076 A488 3s multicolored .40 .20

Ethnographical Museum, 50th anniv. exhibition.

Alpine Farm, Woodcut by Suitbert Lobisser — A489

1978, Mar. 23 Engr. *Perf. 13½*

1077 A489 3s dark brown, *buff* .40 .20

Lobisser (1878-1943), graphic artist.

Capercaillie, Hunting Bag, 1730, and Rifle, 1655 — A490

Photo. & Engr.

1978, Apr. 28 *Perf. 13½*

1078 A490 6s multicolored .75 .35

Intl. Hunting Exhibition, Marchegg.

Europa Issue 1978

Riegersburg, Styria — A491

1978, May 3 Engr.

1079 A491 6s deep rose lilac .75 .35

Parliament, Vienna, and Map of Europe — A492

1978, May 3 Photo. *Perf. 14x13½*

1080 A492 4s multicolored .45 .20

3rd Interparliamentary Conference for European Cooperation and Security, Vienna.

Admont Pietà, c. 1410 — A493

1978, May 26 Photo. & Engr.

1081 A493 2.50s ocher & black .25 .20

Gothic Art in Styria Exhibition, St. Lambrecht, 1978.

Ort Castle, Gmunden — A494

1978, June 9

1082 A494 3s multicolored .30 .20

700th anniversary of Gmunden City.

Child with Flowers and Fruit — A495

Photo. & Engr.

1978, June 30 *Perf. 14x13½*

1083 A495 6s gold & multi .85 .35

25 years of Social Tourism.

Lehar and his Home, Bad Ischl — A496

1978, July 14 Engr. *Perf. 14x13½*

1084 A496 6s slate .75 .30

International Lehar Congress, Bad Ischl. Franz Lehar (1870-1948), operetta composer.

Congress Emblem A497

1978, Aug. 21 Photo. *Perf. 13½x14*

1085 A497 1.50s black, red & yel .20 .20

Cong. of Intl. Fed. of Building Construction and Wood Workers, Vienna, Aug. 20-24.

Ottokar of Bohemia and Rudolf of Hapsburg A498

1978, Aug. 25 Photo. & Engr.

1086 A498 3s multicolored .35 .20

Battle of Durnkrut and Jedenspeigen (Marchfeld), which established Hapsburg rule in Austria, 700th anniversary.

First Documentary Reference to Villach, "ad pontem uillah" — A499

1978, Sept. 8 Litho. *Perf. 13½x14*
1087 A499 3s multicolored .35 .20

1100th anniversary of Villach, Carinthia.

Seal of Graz, 1440 — A500

Photo. & Engr.

1978, Sept. 13 *Perf. 14x13½*
1088 A500 4s multicolored .50 .25

850th anniversary of Graz.

Emperor Maximilian Fishing — A501

1978, Sept. 15 *Perf. 14x13½*
1089 A501 4s multicolored .50 .20

World Fishing Championships, Vienna, Sept. 1978.

"Aid to the Handicapped" — A502

1978, Oct. 2 Photo. *Perf. 13½x14*
1090 A502 6s orange brn & blk .75 .30

Symbolic Column — A503

1978, Oct. 9 Photo. *Perf. 13½*
1091 A503 2.50s orange, blk & gray .30 .20

9th Intl. Congress of Concrete and Prefabrication Industries, Vienna, Oct. 8-13.

Grace, by Albin Egger-Lienz A504

1978, Oct. 27 *Perf. 13½x14*
1092 A504 6s multicolored .75 .30

European Family Congress, Vienna, Oct. 26-29.

Lise Meitner (1878-1968), Physicist, and Atom Symbol — A505

1978, Nov. 7 Engr. *Perf. 14x13½*
1093 A505 6s dark violet .75 .30

Viktor Adler, by Anton Hanak A506

Photo. & Engr.

1978, Nov. 10 *Perf. 13½x14*
1094 A506 3s vermilion & black .40 .20

Viktor Adler (1852-1918), leader of Social Democratic Party, 60th death anniversary.

Franz Schubert, by Josef Kriehuber A507

1978, Nov. 17 Engr. *Perf. 14*
1095 A507 6s reddish brown .65 .35

Franz Schubert (1797-1828), composer.

Virgin and Child, Wilhering Church — A508

Photo. & Engr.

1978, Dec. 1 *Perf. 12½x13½*
1096 A508 3s multicolored .35 .20

Christmas.

Archduke Johann Shelter, Grossglockner — A509

1978, Dec. 6 *Perf. 13½x14*
1097 A509 1.50s gold & dk vio bl .20 .20

Austrian Alpine Club, centenary.

Modern Austrian Art — A510

Adam, by Rudolf Hausner.

1978, Dec. 6 Photo. *Perf. 13½x14*
1098 A510 6s multicolored .75 .35

Universal Declaration of Human Rights, 30th Anniv. — A511

1978, Dec. 6 *Perf. 14x13½*
1099 A511 6s Bound Hands .75 .30

Type of 1973

Designs: 20g, Freistadt, Upper Austria. 3s, Bishofsmutze, Salzburg. 4.20s, Hirschegg, Kleinwalsertal. 5.50s, Peace Chapel, Stoderzinken. 5.60s, Riezlern, Kleinwalsertal. 9s, Asten Carinthia. 12s, Kufstein Fortress. 14s, Weiszsee, Salzburg.

Photo. & Engr.

1978-83 *Perf. 13½x14*

Size: 23x29mm

1100 A395 20g vio bl & dk bl .20 .20

Size: 17x21mm

1102 A395 3s lt ultra & vio bl .45 .20

Size: 23x29mm

1104 A395 4.20s blk & grysh bl .55 .20
1105 A395 5.50s lilac & pur .75 .20
1106 A395 5.60s yel grn & ol grn .75 .20
1107 A395 9s rose & car 1.25 .45
1108 A395 12s ocher & vio brn 1.75 .20
1109 A395 14s lt green & green 2.00 .20
Nos. 1100-1109 (8) 7.70 1.85

Issued: 3s, 12/7/78; 4.20s, 6/22/79; 20g, 6/27/80; 12s, 10/3/80; 14s, 1/27/82; 5.50s, 5.60s, 7/1/82; 9s, 2/9/83.

Child and IYC Emblem A512

Photo. & Engr.

1979, Jan. 16 *Perf. 14*
1110 A512 2.50s dk blue, blk & brn .30 .20

International Year of the Child.

CCIR Emblem A513

1979, Jan. 16 Photo. *Perf. 13½x14*
1111 A513 6s multicolored .75 .30

Intl. Radio Consultative Committee (CCIR) of the ITU, 50th anniv.

Air Rifle, Air Pistol and Club Emblem A514

Photo. & Engr.

1979, Mar. 7 *Perf. 13½*
1112 A514 6s multicolored .75 .30

Austrian Shooting Club, cent., and European Air Rifle and Air Pistol Championships, Graz.

Figure Skater — A515

1979, Mar. 7 Photo. *Perf. 14x13½*
1113 A515 4s multicolored .55 .25

World Ice Skating Championships, Vienna.

Steamer Franz I A516

Designs: 2.50s, Tugboat Linz. 3s, Passenger ship Theodor Körner.

1979, Mar. 13 Engr. *Perf. 13½*
1114 A516 1.50s violet blue .20 .20
1115 A516 2.50s sepia .30 .20
1116 A516 3s magenta .35 .20
Nos. 1114-1116 (3) .85 .60

1st Danube Steamship Company, 150th anniv.

Fashion Design, by Theo Zasche, 1900 — A517

Photo. & Engr.

1979, Mar. 26 *Perf. 13x13½*
1117 A517 2.50s multicolored .30 .20

50th Intl. Fashion Week, Vienna.

Wiener Neustadt Cathedral, 700th Anniv. — A518

1979, Mar. 27 Engr. *Perf. 13½*
1118 A518 4s violet blue .50 .25

Teacher and Pupils, by Franz A. Zauner — A519

Photo. & Engr.

1979, Mar. 30 *Perf. 14x13½*
1119 A519 2.50s multicolored .30 .20

Education of the deaf in Austria, 200th anniv.

Population Chart and Baroque Angel — A520

1979, Apr. 6
1120 A520 2.50s multicolored .30 .20

Austrian Central Statistical Bureau, 150th anniv.

Laurenz Koschier — A521

Europa Issue, 1979

1979, May 4
1121 A521 6s ocher & purple .80 .30

Diesel Motor — A522

1979, May 4 **Photo.**
1122 A522 4s multicolored .45 .20

13th CIMAC Congress (Intl. Org. for Internal Combustion Machines).

Arms of Ried, Schärding and Braunau — A523

Photo. & Engr.

1979, June 1 ***Perf. 14x13½***
1123 A523 3s multicolored .30 .20

200th anniversary of Innviertel District.

Flood and City — A524

1979, June 1 ***Perf. 13½x14***
1124 A524 2.50s multicolored .30 .20

Control and eliminate water pollution.

Arms of Rottenmann A525

Photo. & Engr.

1979, June 22 ***Perf. 14x13½***
1125 A525 3s multicolored .30 .20

700th anniversary of Rottenmann.

Jodok Fink (1853-1929), Governor of Vorarlberg A526

1979, June 29 **Engr.** ***Perf. 14***
1126 A526 3s brown carmine .40 .20

Arms of Wels, Returnees' Emblem, "Europa Sail" — A527

1979, July 6 **Photo.** ***Perf. 14x13½***
1127 A527 4s yellow grn & blk .45 .20

5th European Meeting of the Intl. Confederation of Former Prisoners of War, Wels, July 6-8.

Symbolic Flower, Conference Emblem — A528

1979, Aug. 20 **Litho.** ***Perf. 14x13½***
1128 A528 4s turq blue .45 .20

UN Conf. for Science and Technology, Vienna, Aug. 20-31.

Donaupark, UNIDO and IAEA Emblems A529

1979, Aug. 24 **Engr.** ***Perf. 13½x14***
1129 A529 6s grayish blue .75 .30

Opening of the Donaupark Intl. Center in Vienna, seat of the UN Industrial Development Org. (UNIDO) and the Intl. Atomic Energy Agency (IAEA).

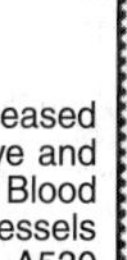

Diseased Eye and Blood Vessels A530

1979, Sept. 10 **Photo.** ***Perf. 14***
1130 A530 2.50s multicolored .35 .20

10th World Congress of Intl. Diabetes Federation, Vienna, Sept. 9-14.

View of Stanz Valley through East Portal of Arlberg Tunnel A531

1979, Sept. 14 **Photo. & Engr.**
1131 A531 4s multicolored .45 .20

16th World Road Cong., Vienna, 9/16-21.

Steam Printing Press A532

Photo. & Engr.

1979, Sept. 18 ***Perf. 13½x14***
1132 A532 3s multicolored .40 .20

Austrian Government Printing Office, 175th anniv.

Richard Zsigmondy (1865-1929), Chemist — A533

1979, Sept. 21 **Engr.** ***Perf. 14x13½***
1133 A533 6s multicolored .75 .30

"Save Energy" A534

1979, Oct. 1 **Photo.** ***Perf. 14x13½***
1134 A534 2.50s multicolored .30 .20

Festival and Convention Center, Bregenz (Model) — A535

1979, Oct. 1 **Engr.** ***Perf. 14***
1135 A535 2.50s purple .30 .20

Lions International Emblem A536

1979, Oct. 11 **Photo. & Engr.**
1136 A536 4s multicolored .45 .25

25th Lions Europa Forum, Vienna, 10/11-13.

A537

Photo. & Engr.

1979, Oct. 19 ***Perf. 13½x14***
1137 A537 2.50s Wilhelm Exner .30 .20

Centenary of Technological Handicraft Museum, founded by Wilhelm Exner.

Modern Austrian Art — A538

1979, Oct. 23 **Litho.** ***Perf. 13½x14***

The Compassionate Christ, by Hans Fronius.

1138 A538 4s olive & ol blk .50 .25

Locomotive and Arms — A539

1979, Oct. 24 **Photo.** ***Perf. 13½x14***
1139 A539 2.50s multicolored .30 .20

Raab-Odenburg-Ebenfurt railroad, cent.

August Musger — A540

Photo. & Engr.

1979, Oct. 30 ***Perf. 14x13½***
1140 A540 2.50s bl gray & blk .30 .20

August Musger (1868-1929), developer of slow-motion film technique.

Nativity, St. Barbara's Church A541

1979, Nov. 30 ***Perf. 13½x14***
1141 A541 4s multicolored .45 .25

Christmas.

Arms of Baden — A542

1980, Jan. 25 ***Perf. 14***
1142 A542 4s multicolored .45 .25

Baden, 500th anniversary.

Fight Rheumatism A543

1980, Feb. 21 ***Perf. 13½***
1143 A543 2.50s red & aqua .30 .20

Austrian Exports — A544

1980, Feb. 21 Photo. ***Perf. 14x13½***
1144 A544 4s dark blue & red .45 .25

Austrian Red Cross Centenary A545

1980, Mar. 14 Photo. ***Perf. 13½x14***
1145 A545 2.50s multicolored .30 .20

Rudolph Kirchschlager A546

Photo. & Engr.

1980, Mar. 20 ***Perf. 14x13½***
1146 A546 4s sepia & red .45 .25

Robert Hamerling (1830-1889), Poet — A547

1980, Mar. 24 Engr. ***Perf. 13½x14***
1147 A547 2.50s olive green .35 .20

Seal of Hallein — A548

Photo. & Engr.

1980, Apr. 30 ***Perf. 14x13½***
1148 A548 4s red & black .45 .25

Hallein, 750th anniversary.

Empress Maria Theresa (1717-80) A549

Paintings by: 2.50s, Andreas Moller. 4s, Martin van Meytens. 6s, Josef Ducreux.

1980, May 13 Engr. ***Perf. 13½***
1149 A549 2.50s violet brown .30 .25
1150 A549 4s dark blue .45 .40
1151 A549 6s rose lake .65 .65
Nos. 1149-1151 (3) 1.40 1.30

Flags of Austria and Four Powers A550

1980, May 14 Photo. ***Perf. 13½x14***
1152 A550 4s multicolored .45 .25

State Treaty, 25th anniversary.

St. Benedict, by Meinrad Guggenbichler A551

1980, May 16 Engr. ***Perf. 14½***
1153 A551 2.50s olive green .30 .20

Congress of Benedictine Order of Austria.

Hygeia by Gustav Klimt — A552

1980, May 20 Photo. ***Perf. 14***
1154 A552 4s multicolored .45 .25

Academic teaching of hygiene, 175th anniv.

Aflenz Ground Satellite Receiving Station Inauguration A553

1980, May 30 Photo. ***Perf. 14***
1155 A553 6s multicolored .85 .30

Steyr, Etching, 1693 A554

Photo. & Engr.

1980, June 4 ***Perf. 13½***
1156 A554 4s multicolored .45 .25

Millennium of Steyr.

Worker, Oil Drill Head — A555

1980, June 12
1157 A555 2.50s multicolored .30 .20

Austrian oil production, 25th anniversary.

Seal of Innsbruck, 1267 A556

1980, June 23 ***Perf. 13½x14½***
1158 A556 2.50s multicolored .35 .20

Innsbruck, 800th anniversary.

Duchy of Styria, 800th Anniv. — A557

Perf. 14½x13½

1980, June 23 **Photo.**
1159 A557 4s Duke's hat .45 .20

Leo Ascher (1880-1942), Composer A558

1980, Aug. 18 Engr. ***Perf. 14***
1160 A558 3s dark purple .45 .20

Bible Illustration, Book of Genesis — A559

1980, Aug. 25 ***Perf. 13½***
1161 A559 4s multicolored .45 .25

10th Intl. Cong. of the Org. for Old Testament Studies.

Europa Issue 1980

Robert Stolz (1880-1975), Composer A560

1980, Aug. 25 Engr. ***Perf. 14x13½***
1162 A560 6s red brown .85 .30

Old and Modern Bridges A561

1980, Sept. 1 Photo. ***Perf. 13½***
1163 A561 4s multicolored .45 .25

11th Congress of the Intl. Assoc. for Bridge and Structural Engineering, Vienna.

Moon Figure, by Karl Brandstätter A562

Photo. & Engr.

1980, Oct. 10 ***Perf. 14x13½***
1164 A562 4s multicolored .45 .25

Customs Service, Sesquicentennial A563

1980, Oct. 13 **Photo.**
1165 A563 2.50s multicolored .30 .20

Gazette Masthead, 1810 A564

1980, Oct. 23 Photo. ***Perf. 13½***
1166 A564 2.50s multicolored .30 .20

Official Gazette of Linz, 350th anniversary.

Waidhofen Town Book Title Page, 14th Century — A565

Photo. & Engr.

1980, Oct. 24 ***Perf. 14***
1167 A565 2.50s multicolored .30 .20

Waidhofen on Thaya, 750th anniversary.

Federal Austrian Army, 25th Anniversary A566

1980, Oct. 24 Photo. *Perf. 13½x14*
1168 A566 2.50s grnsh black & red .30 .20

Alfred Wegener A567

1980, Oct. 31 Engr.
1169 A567 4s violet blue .55 .25

Alfred Wegener (1880-1930), scientist, formulated theory of continental drift.

Robert Musil (1880-1942), Poet — A568

1980, Nov. 6 *Perf. 14x13½*
1170 A568 4s dark red brown .55 .25

Christmas — A569

Nativity, stained glass window, Klagenfurt.

Photo. & Engr.

1980, Nov. 28 *Perf. 13½*
1171 A569 4s multicolored .55 .25

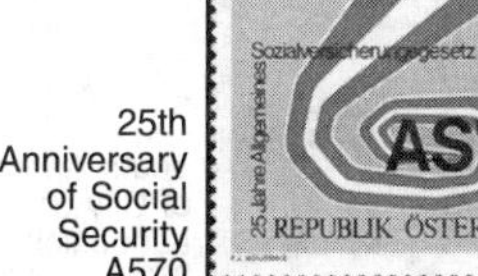

25th Anniversary of Social Security A570

1981, Jan. 19 Litho. *Perf. 13½x14*
1172 A570 2.50s multicolored .30 .20

Niebelungen Saga, 1926, by Dachauer — A571

1981, Apr. 6 Engr. *Perf. 14x13½*
1173 A571 3s sepia .40 .20

Wilhelm Dachauer (1881-1951), artist and engraver.

Machinist in Wheelchair A572

1981, Apr. 6 Photo. & Engr.
1174 A572 6s multicolored .75 .35

Rehabilitation Intl., 3rd European Regional Conf.

Sigmund Freud (1856-1939), Psychoanalyst A573

1981, May 6 Engr.
1175 A573 3s rose violet .40 .20

Heating Engineers Union Congress, Vienna — A574

1981, May 11 Photo.
1176 A574 4s multicolored .55 .25

Kuenringer Exhibition, Zwettl Monastery A575

Azzo (founder of House of Kuenringer) and his followers, bear-skin manuscript.

1981, May 15 Photo. & Engr.
1177 A575 3s multicolored .35 .20

Europa — A576

1981, May 22 Photo.
1178 A576 6s Maypole .80 .35

Telephone Service Centenary A577

Photo. and Engr.

1981 May 29 *Perf. 13½x14*
1179 A577 4s multicolored .45 .25

Seibersdorf Research Center, 25th Anniv. — A578

1981, June 29 Photo. *Perf. 13½*
1180 A578 4s multicolored .45 .25

The Frog King (Child's Drawing) A579

1981, June 29 *Perf. 13½x14*
1181 A579 3s multicolored .35 .20

Town Hall and Town Seal of 1250 A580

Photo. & Engr.

1981, July 17 *Perf. 13½x14*
1182 A580 4s multicolored .45 .25

St. Veit an der Glan, 800th anniv.

Johann Florian Heller (1813-1871), Pioneer of Urinalysis — A581

1981, Aug. 31 *Perf. 14x13½*
1183 A581 6s red brown .75 .35

11th Intl. Clinical Chemistry Congress.

Ludwig Boltzmann (1844-1906), Physicist — A582

1981, Sept. 4 Engr. *Perf. 14x13½*
1184 A582 3s dark green .45 .20

Intl. Pharmaceutical Federation World Congress, Vienna — A583

Photo. & Engr.

1981, Sept. 7 *Perf. 14*
1185 A583 6s Scale .75 .35

Otto Bauer, Politician, Birth Centenary A584

1981, Sept. 7 Photo. *Perf. 14x13½*
1186 A584 4s multicolored .45 .25

Escher's Impossible Cube — A585

1981, Sept. 14
1187 A585 4s dk blue & brt blue .45 .25

10th Intl. Mathematicians' Cong., Innsbruck.

Kneeling Virgin, Detail of Coronation of Mary Altarpiece, St. Wolfgang, 500th Anniv. — A586

1981, Sept. 25 Engr. *Perf. 14x13½*
1188 A586 3s dark blue .35 .20

South-East Fair, Graz, 75th Anniv. A587

1981, Sept. 25 Photo. *Perf. 13½x14*
1189 A587 4s multicolored .45 .25

Holy Trinity, 12th Cent. Byzantine Miniature A588

1981, Oct. 5
1190 A588 6s multicolored .75 .35

16th Intl. Byzantine Congress.

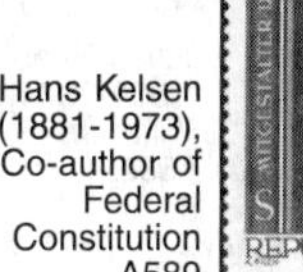

Hans Kelsen (1881-1973), Co-author of Federal Constitution A589

1981, Oct. 9 Engr.
1191 A589 3s dark carmine .35 .20

Edict of Tolerance Bicen. — A590

Photo. & Engr.

1981, Oct. 9 ***Perf. 14***
1192 A590 4s Joseph II .45 .25

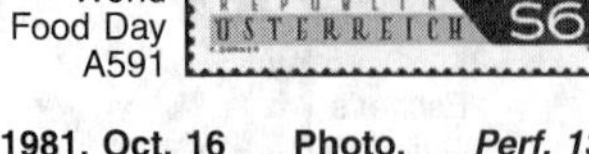

World Food Day A591

1981, Oct. 16 Photo. ***Perf. 13½***
1193 A591 6s multicolored .75 .35

Between the Times, by Oscar Asboth A592

1981, Oct. 22 Litho. ***Perf. 13½x14***
1194 A592 4s multicolored .55 .25

Intl. Catholic Workers' Day — A593

Photo. & Engr.

1981, Oct. 23 ***Perf. 14x13½***
1195 A593 3s multicolored .35 .20

Baron Josef Hammer-Purgstall, Founder of Oriental Studies, 125th Death Anniv. — A594

Photo. & Engr.

1981, Nov. 23 ***Perf. 14***
1196 A594 3s multicolored .35 .20

Julius Raab (1891-1964), Politician A595

1981, Nov. 27 Engr. ***Perf. 13½***
1197 A595 6s rose lake .75 .35

Nativity, Corn Straw Figures A596

1981, Nov. 27 Photo. & Engr.
1198 A596 4s multicolored .50 .20

Christmas.

Stefan Zweig (1881-1942), Poet — A597

1981, Nov. 27 Engr. ***Perf. 14x13½***
1199 A597 4s dull violet .50 .20

800th Anniv. of St. Nikola on the Danube A598

1981, Dec. 4 Photo. & Engr.
1200 A598 4s multicolored .55 .20

Vienna Emergency Medical Service Centenary A599

1981, Dec. 9 Photo. ***Perf. 13½x14***
1201 A599 3s multicolored .35 .20

Schladming-Haus Alpine World Skiing Championship — A600

1982, Jan. 27 ***Perf. 14***
1202 A600 4s multicolored .45 .20

Dorotheum (State Auction Gallery), 275th Anniv. — A601

Photo. & Engr.

1982, Mar. 12 ***Perf. 14***
1203 A601 4s multicolored .45 .20

Water Rescue Service, 25th Anniv. — A602

1982, Mar. 19 Photo. ***Perf. 14x13½***
1204 A602 5s multicolored .60 .30

St. Severin and the End of the Roman Era Exhibition — A603

Photo. & Engr.

1982, Apr. 23 ***Perf. 14x13½***
1205 A603 3s St. Severin .35 .20

Intl. Kneipp Hydropathy Congress, Vienna — A604

1982, May 4 ***Perf. 14***
1206 A604 4s multicolored .55 .20

Printing in Austria, 500th Anniv. — A605

1982, May 7
1207 A605 4s Printers' guild arms .55 .20

5th European Urology Soc. Cong., Vienna — A606

Design: Urine analysis, Canone di Avicenna manuscript.

1982, May 12 **Photo.**
1208 A606 6s multicolored .75 .35

St. Francis of Assisi, 800th Birth Anniv. — A607

1982, May 14 Photo. & Engr.
1209 A607 3s multicolored .35 .20

Haydn and His Time Exhibition, Rohrau — A608

1982, May 19 Engr. ***Perf. 13½***
1210 A608 3s olive green .35 .20

25th World Milk Day — A609

1982, May 25 Photo. ***Perf. 14x13½***
1211 A609 7s multicolored .90 .40

800th Anniv of Gfohl (Market Town) — A610

Photo. & Engr.

1982, May 28 ***Perf. 14***
1212 A610 4s multicolored .45 .20

Tennis Player and Austrian Tennis Federation Emblem — A611

1982, June 11
1213 A611 3s multicolored .35 .20

900th Anniv. of City of Langenlois A612

Photo. & Engr.

1982, June 11 ***Perf. 13½x14***
1214 A612 4s multicolored .45 .20

800th Anniv. of City of Weiz — A613

1982, June 18 Photo. ***Perf. 14x13½***
1215 A613 4s Arms .45 .20

Ignaz Seipel (1876-1932), Statesman A614

1982, July 30 Engr. *Perf. 14x13½*
1216 A614 3s brown violet .35 .20

Europa Issue 1982

Sesquicentennial of Linz-Freistadt-Budweis Horse-drawn Railroad — A615

1982, July 30 *Perf. 13½*
1217 A615 6s brown .90 .35

Mail Bus Service, 75th Anniv. — A616

1982, Aug. 6 Photo. *Perf. 14x13½*
1218 A616 4s multicolored .50 .20

Rocket Lift-off — A617

1982, Aug. 9 *Perf. 14*
1219 A617 4s multicolored .50 .20

2nd UN Conference on Peaceful Uses of Outer Space, Vienna, Aug. 9-21.

Geodesists' Day — A618

Photo. & Engr.
1982, Sept. 1 *Perf. 13½x14*
1220 A618 3s Tower, Office of Standards .35 .20

Protection of Endangered Species — A619

1982, Sept. 9 *Perf. 14*
1221 A619 3s Bustard .50 .25
1222 A619 4s Beaver .60 .30
1223 A619 6s Capercaillie .90 .45
Nos. 1221-1223 (3) 2.00 1.00

10th Anniv. of Intl. Institute for Applied Systems Analysis, Vienna A620

1982, Oct. 4 Photo.
1224 A620 3s Laxenburg Castle .35 .20

St. Apollonia (Patron Saint of Dentists) A621

1982, Oct. 11 Photo. & Engr.
1225 A621 4s multicolored .45 .20

70th Annual World Congress of Dentists.

Emmerich Kalman (1882-1953), Composer A622

1982, Oct. 22 Engr. *Perf. 13½*
1226 A622 3s dark blue .35 .20

Max Mell (1882-1971), Poet — A623

1982, Nov. 10 Photo. *Perf. 14x13½*
1227 A623 3s multicolored .35 .20

Christmas A624

Design: Christmas crib, Damuls Church, Vorarlberg, 1630.

Photo. & Engr.
1982, Nov. 25 *Perf. 13½*
1228 A624 4s multicolored .45 .20

Centenary of St. George's College, Istanbul — A625

1982, Nov. 26 Litho. *Perf. 14*
1229 A625 4s Bosporus .45 .20

Portrait of a Girl, by Ernst Fuchs — A626

1982, Dec. 10 Photo. & Engr.
1230 A626 4s multicolored .45 .20

Postal Savings Bank Centenary A627

Photo. & Engr.
1983, Jan. 12 *Perf. 14*
1231 A627 4s Bank .55 .20

Hildegard Burjan (1883-1933), Founder of Caritas Socialis A628

1983, Jan. 28 Engr.
1232 A628 4s rose lake .55 .20

World Communications Year — A629

1983, Feb. 18 Photo. *Perf. 13½x14*
1233 A629 7s multicolored .95 .40

75th Anniv. Children's Friends Org. — A630

Photo. & Engr.
1983, Feb. 23 *Perf. 14x13½*
1234 A630 4s multicolored .55 .20

Josef Matthias Hauer (1883-1959), Composer A631

1983, Mar. 18 Engr. *Perf. 14*
1235 A631 3s deep lilac rose .40 .20

25th Anniv. of Austrian Airlines A632

1983, Mar. 31 Photo. *Perf. 13½x14*
1236 A632 6s multicolored .85 .35

Work Inspection Centenary A633

1983, Apr. 8 Photo. *Perf. 13½*
1237 A633 4s multicolored .55 .20

Upper Austria Millennium Provincial Exhibition — A634

1983, Apr. 28 Photo. *Perf. 13½*
1238 A634 3s Wels Castle, by Mat- thaus Merian .40 .20

Gottweig Monastery, 900th Anniv. — A635

Photo. & Engr.
1983, Apr. 29 *Perf. 13½*
1239 A635 3s multicolored .40 .20

7th World Pacemakers Symposium A636

1983, Apr. 29 Photo. *Perf. 14x13½*
1240 A636 4s multicolored .55 .20

Catholic Students' Org. A637

1983, May 20 Photo. *Perf. 14*
1241 A637 4s multicolored .55 .20

Weitra, 800th Anniv. A638

Photo. & Engr.

1983, May 20 *Perf. 13½*
1242 A638 4s multicolored .55 .20

Granting of Town Rights to Hohenems, 650th Anniv. — A639

1983, May 27 **Photo.** *Perf. 14*
1243 A639 4s multicolored .55 .20

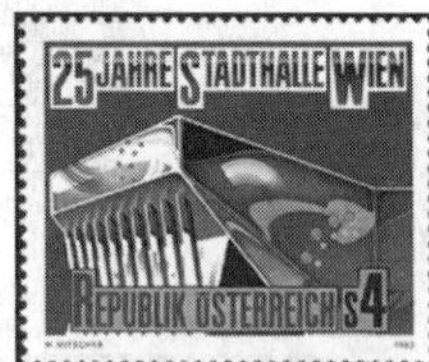

25th Anniv. of Stadthall, Vienna A640

1983, June 24 **Photo.** *Perf. 14*
1244 A640 4s multicolored .55 .20

Viktor Franz Hess (1883-1964), 1936 Nobel Prize Winner in Physics — A641

1983, June 24 **Engr.** *Perf. 14x13½*
1245 A641 6s dark green .95 .35

Europa.

Kiwanis Intl. Convention, Vienna — A642

1983, July 1 **Photo.** *Perf. 13½*
1246 A642 5s multicolored .70 .30

7th World Congress of Psychiatry, Vienna — A643

1983, July 11 **Photo.** *Perf. 14*
1247 A643 4s Emblem, St. Stephen's Cathedral .55 .20

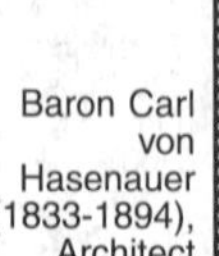

Baron Carl von Hasenauer (1833-1894), Architect A644

1983, July 20 **Engr.** *Perf. 13½x14*
1248 A644 3s Natural History Museum, Vienna .45 .20

27th Intl. Chamber of Commerce Professional Competition, Linz — A645

1983, Aug. 16 **Photo.**
1249 A645 4s Chamber building .55 .20

13th Intl. Chemotherapy Congress, Vienna, Aug. 28-Sept. 2 — A646

1983, Aug. 26
1250 A646 5s Penicillin test on cancer .70 .30

Catholics' Day — A647

1983, Sept. 9 **Photo.** *Perf. 14x13½*
1251 A647 3s multicolored .40 .20

Visit of Pope John Paul II — A648

Photo. & Engr.

1983, Sept. 9 *Perf. 13½*
1252 A648 6s multicolored .90 .35

Souvenir Sheet

Battle of 1683 to Relieve Vienna, by Frans Geffel — A649

1983, Sept. 9 *Perf. 14*
1253 A649 6s multicolored .95 .50

300th anniv. of Vienna's rescue from Turkey.

Vienna Rathaus Centenary A650

1983, Sept. 23 *Perf. 13½x14*
1254 A650 4s multicolored .55 .20

Karl von Terzaghi (1883-1963), Founder of Scientific Subterranean Engineering A651

1983, Oct. 3 **Engr.**
1255 A651 3s dark blue .40 .20

10th Trade Unions Federal Congress, Oct. 3-8 A652

1983, Oct. 3 **Photo.** *Perf. 13½*
1256 A652 3s black & red .40 .20

Evening Sun in Burgenland, by Gottfried Kumpf — A653

Photo. & Engr.

1983, Oct. 7 *Perf. 13½x14*
1257 A653 4s multicolored .55 .20

Modling-Hinterbruhl Electric Railroad Centenary — A654

1983, Oct. 21 **Photo.**
1258 A654 3s multicolored .40 .20

Provincial Museum of Upper Austria Sesquicentennial — A655

1983, Nov. 4 **Photo. & Engr.**
1259 A655 4s Francisco-Carolinum Museum .55 .20

Creche, St. Andreas Parish Church, Kitzbuhel A656

1983, Nov. 25 *Perf. 14*
1260 A656 4s multicolored .55 .20

Christmas.

Parliament Bldg. Vienna, 100th Anniv. — A657

1983, Dec. 2 **Engr.**
1261 A657 4s slate blue .55 .20

Altar Ppicture, St. Nikola/Pram Church — A658

1983, Dec. 6 **Photo.** *Perf. 14x13½*
1262 A658 3s multicolored .40 .20

Wolfgang Pauli (1900-58), Physicist, Nobel Laureate — A659

1983, Dec. 15 **Engr.** *Perf. 14½x13½*
1263 A659 6s dark red brn .90 .35

Gregor Mendel (1822-1884), Genetics Founder — A660

Photo. & Engr.

1984, Jan. 5 *Perf. 13½*
1264 A660 4s multicolored .55 .20

Anton Hanak (1875-1934), Sculptor — A661

1984, Jan. 5
1265 A661 3s red brown & blk .40 .20

50th Anniv. of 1934 Uprising — A662

1984, Feb. 10 **Photo.** *Perf. 14*
1266 A662 4.50s Memorial, Woellersdorf .65 .30

Wernher von Reichersberg Family, Bas-relief, 15th Cent. — A663

Photo. & Engr.

1984, Apr. 25 ***Perf. 14x13½***
1267 A663 3.50s brown & blue .50 .25

900th anniv. of Reichersberg Monastery.

Tobacco Monopoly Bicentenary A665

1984, May 4 ***Perf. 13½***
1269 A665 4.50s Cigar wrapper, tobacco plant .65 .30

1200th Anniv. of Kostendorf Municipality A666

1984, May 4
1270 A666 4.50s View, arms .65 .30

Automobile Engineers World Congress A667

1984, May 4 **Photo.** ***Perf. 13½x14***
1271 A667 5s Wheel bearing cross-section .70 .30

Europa (1959-1984) A668

1984, May 4 ***Perf. 13½***
1272 A668 6s multicolored .90 .35

Archduke Johann (1782-1859), by S. von Carolsfeld A669

Photo. & Engr.

1984, May 11 ***Perf. 14***
1273 A669 4.50s multicolored .65 .30

Ore and Iron Provincial Exhibition A670

1984, May 11 ***Perf. 13½***
1274 A670 3.50s Aragonite .50 .20

Era of Emperor Francis Joseph Exhibition A671

Design: Cover of Viribus Unitis, publ. by Max Herzig, 1898.

1984, May 18
1275 A671 3.50s red & gold .50 .20

City of Vocklabruck, 850th Anniv. — A672

Photo. & Engr.

1984, May 30 ***Perf. 14x13½***
1276 A672 4.50s Tower, arms .65 .30

Museum of Carinthia, Cent. — A673

1984, June 1 ***Perf. 13½***

Dionysius, Virinum mosaic.

1277 A673 3.50s multicolored .50 .20

Erosion Prevention Systems Centenary A674

1984, June 5 **Engr.** ***Perf. 14***
1278 A674 4.50s Stone reinforcement wall .65 .30

Tyrol Provincial Celebration, 1809-1984 A675

Art Exhibition: Meeting of Imperial Troops with South Tyrolean Reserves under Andreas Hofer near Sterzing in April 1809, by Ludwig Schnorr von Carolsfeld, 1830.

Photo. & Engr.

1984, June 5 ***Perf. 14x13½***
1279 A675 3.50s multicolored .50 .20

Ralph Benatzky (1884-1957), Composer A676

1984, June 5 **Engr.**
1280 A676 4s violet brown .55 .25

Christian von Ehrenfels (1859-1932), Philosopher A677

1984, June 22 **Photo.** ***Perf. 14***
1281 A677 3.50s multicolored .50 .20

25th Anniv. of Minimundus (Model City) A678

1984, June 22 ***Perf. 13½x14***
1282 A678 4s Eiffel Tower, Tower of Pisa, ferris wheel .55 .25

Blockheide Eibenstein Nature Park A679

1984 **Photo. & Engr.**
1283 A679 4s shown .55 .25
1284 A679 4s Lake Neusiedl .55 .25

Issued: #1283, June 29; #1284, Aug. 13.
See #1349-1354, 1492-1496, 1744, 1777, 1813, 1843.

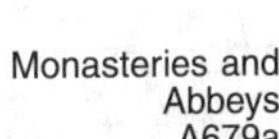

Monasteries and Abbeys A679a

Designs: 3.50s, Geras Monastery, Lower Austria. 4s, Stams. 4.50s, Schlagl. 5s, Benedictine Abbey of St. Paul Levanttal. 6s, Rein-Hohenfurth.

1984-85 ***Perf. 14***

1285	A679a	3.50s	multicolored	.50	.20
1286	A679a	4s	multicolored	.50	.20
1287	A679a	4.50s	multicolored	.65	.30
1288	A679a	5s	multicolored	.65	.30
1288A	A679a	6s	multicolored	.90	.35
	Nos. 1285-1288A (5)			3.20	1.35

Issued: 3.50s, 4/27/84; 4s, 9/28/84; 4.50s, 5/18/84; 5s, 9/27/85; 6s, 10/4/84.
See Nos. 1361-1365, 1464A-1468.

Schanatobel Railroad Bridge — A680

Railroad Anniversaries: 3.50s, Arlberg centenary. 4.50s, Tauern, 75th.

1984, July 6 ***Perf. 14***
1289 A680 3.50s shown .50 .20
1290 A680 4.50s Falkenstein Bridge .65 .20

Balloon Flight in Austria Bicent. — A681

1984, July 6 **Photo.**
1291 A681 6s Johan Stuwer's balloon .90 .35

Intl. Lawyers' Congress, Vienna — A682

1984, Aug. 31 **Photo. & Engr.**
1292 A682 7s Vienna Palace of Justice, emblem .95 .45

7th European Anatomy Congress, Innsbruck — A683

1984, Sept. 3 **Photo.**
1293 A683 6s Josef Hyrtl, anatomist .90 .35

A684

1984, Oct. 12
1294 A684 4s Window, by Karl Korab .55 .20

Johannes of Gmunden, Mathematician, 600th Birth Anniv. — A685

1984, Oct. 18
1295 A685 3.50s Clock (Immset Uhr), 1555 .50 .20

Concordia Press Club, 125th Anniv. — A686

1984, Nov. 9 Photo. *Perf. 13½*
1296 A686 4.50s Quill .65 .30

Fanny Eissler, Dancer, Death Centenary — A687

1984, Nov. 23 Photo. & Engr.
1297 A687 4s multicolored .55 .30

Christmas A688

Design: Christ is Born, Aggsbacher Altar, Herzogenburg Monastery.

1984, Nov. 30 *Perf. 14*
1298 A688 4.50s multicolored .65 .20

Karl Franzens University, Graz, 400th Anniv. — A689

1985, Jan. 4 *Perf. 14x13½*
1299 A689 3.50s Seal .50 .20

Dr. Lorenz Bohler, Surgeon, Birth Cent. — A690

1985, Jan. 15 Engr.
1300 A690 4.50s dk rose lake .60 .20

Nordic Events, Ski Championships, Seefeld — A691

1985, Jan. 17 Photo. *Perf. 13½*
1301 A691 4s Ski jumper, cross country racer .55 .20

Linz Diocese Bicentenary A692

1985, Jan. 25
1302 A692 4.50s Linz Cathedral interior .60 .20

Alban Berg (1885-1935), Composer A693

1985, Feb. 8 Engr.
1303 A693 6s bluish black .80 .25

Vocational Training Inst., 25th Anniv. A694

1985, Feb. 15 Photo. *Perf. 13½x14*
1304 A694 4.50s multicolored .60 .20

City of Bregenz, Bimillennium A695

1985, Feb. 22 *Perf. 14x13½*
1305 A695 4s multicolored .55 .20

Austrian Registration Labels Cent. A696

1985, Mar. 15 *Perf. 13½x14*
1306 A696 4.50s Label, 1885 .60 .20

Josef Stefan (1835-1893), Physicist — A697

Photo. & Engr.
1985, Mar. 22 *Perf. 14x13½*
1307 A697 6s buff, dl red brn & dk brn .80 .25

St. Leopold Exhibition, Klosterneuberg A698

St. Leopold 16th-17th cent. embroidery.

1985, Mar. 29
1308 A698 3.50s multicolored .50 .20

Liberation From German Occupation, 40th Anniv. — A699

1985, Apr. 26 Photo.
1309 A699 4.50s multicolored .60 .20

Painter Franz von Defregger (1835-1921) A700

1985, Apr. 26
1310 A700 3.50s Fairy tale teller .50 .20

Europa Issue 1985

Johann Joseph Fux (1660-1741), Composer, Violin and Trombone A701

Photo. & Engr.
1985, May 3 *Perf. 13½*
1311 A701 6s lil gray & dk brn .90 .25

Boheimkirchen (Market Town) Millennium — A702

1985, May 10 *Perf. 14*
1312 A702 4.50s View, coat of arms .60 .20

European Free Trade Assoc., 25th Anniv. — A703

Mercury staff, flags of member and affiliate nations.

1985, May 10 Photo. *Perf. 13½*
1313 A703 4s multicolored .55 .20

St. Polten Diocese, Bicent. — A704

1985, May 15 Photo. & Engr.

Episcopal residence gate, St. Polten diocese arms.

1314 A704 4.50s multicolored .60 .20

The Gumpp Family of Builders, Innsbruck — A705

Perf. 14½x13½
1985, May 17 Photo.
1315 A705 3.50s multicolored .50 .20

Garsten Market Town Millennium A706

Design: 17th century engraving by George Matthaus Fischer (1628-1696).

Photo. & Engr.
1985, June 7 *Perf. 13½x14*
1316 A706 4.50s multicolored .60 .20

UN, 40th Anniv. A707

Perf. 13½x14½
1985, June 26 Photo.
1317 A707 4s multicolored .55 .20

Austrian membership, 30th anniv.

Intl. Assoc. for the Prevention of Suicide, 13th Congress A708

Photo. & Engr.
1985, June 28 *Perf. 14*
1318 A708 5s brn, lt ap grn & yel .70 .30

Souvenir Sheet

Year of the Forest — A709

1985, June 28 ***Perf. 13½***
1319 A709 6s Healthy and damaged woodland 1.00 .35

Kurhaus, Bad Ischl Operetta Activities Emblem A710

1985, July 5 ***Perf. 14***
1320 A710 3.50s multicolored .50 .20

Bad Ischl Festival, 25th anniv.

Intl. Competition of Fire Brigades, Vocklabruck A711

1985, July 18 **Photo.** ***Perf. 14x13½***
1321 A711 4.50s Fireman, emblem .60 .20

Grossglockner Alpine Motorway, 50th Anniv. — A712

Photo. & Engr.

1985, Aug. 2 ***Perf. 13½***
1322 A712 4s View of Fuschertorl .55 .20

World Chess Federation Congress, Graz — A713

1985, Aug. 28 **Photo.** ***Perf. 13½***
1323 A713 4s Checkered globe, emblem .55 .20

The Legendary Foundation of Konigstetten by Charlemagne, by Auguste Stephan, c. 1870 — A714

Photo. & Engr.

1985, Aug. 30 ***Perf. 14***
1324 A714 4.50s multicolored .60 .20

Konigstetten millennium.

Hofkirchen-Taufkirchen-Weibern Municipalities, 1200th Anniv. — A715

1985, Aug. 30 ***Perf. 13½x14***
1325 A715 4.50s View of Weiburn, municipal arms .60 .20

Dr. Adam Politzer (1835-1923), Physician A716

1985, Sept. 12 **Engr.** ***Perf. 14***
1326 A716 3.50s blue violet .50 .20

Politzer pioneered aural therapy for auditory disorders.

Intl. Assoc. of Forwarding Agents, World Congress, Vienna — A717

1985, Oct. 7 **Photo.** ***Perf. 13½***
1327 A717 6s multicolored .85 .35

Carnival Figures Riding High Bicycles, By Paul Flora A718

Photo. & Engr.

1985, Oct. 25 ***Perf. 14***
1328 A718 4s multicolored .55 .20

St. Martin on Horseback A719

1985, Nov. 8 **Photo.**
1329 A719 4.50s multicolored .60 .30

Eisenstadt Diocese, 25th anniv.

Creche, Marble Bas-relief, Salzburg — A720

Photo. & Engr.

1985, Nov. 29 ***Perf. 13½***
1330 A720 4.50s gold, dl vio & buff .60 .30

Christmas.

Hanns Horbiger (1860-1931), Inventor A721

1985, Nov. 29 ***Perf. 14***
1331 A721 3.50s gold & sepia .50 .20

Aqueduct, Hundsau Brook, Near Gostling A722

1985, Nov. 29 ***Perf. 13½x14½***
1332 A722 3.50s red, bluish blk & brt ultra .50 .20

Vienna Aqueduct, 75th anniv.

Chateau de la Muette, Paris Headquarters — A723

1985, Dec. 13
1333 A723 4s sep, rose lil & gold .55 .25

Org. for Economic Cooperation and Development, 25th anniv.

Johann Bohm (1886-1959), Pres. Austrian Trade Fed. — A724

1986, Jan. 24 **Photo.** ***Perf. 14***
1334 A724 4.50s blk, ver & grayish black .65 .30

Intl. Peace Year — A725

Perf. 13½x14½

1986, Jan. 24 **Photo.**
1335 A725 6s multicolored .85 .35

Digital Telephone Service Introduction A726

1986, Jan. 29 **Photo.**
1336 A726 5s Push-button keyboard .75 .30

Johann Georg Albrechtsberger (b. 1736), Composer — A727

Photo. & Engr.

1986, Jan. 31 ***Perf. 13½x14½***
1337 A727 3.50s Klosterneuberg organ .50 .20

Korneuberg, 850th Anniv. — A728

1986, Feb. 7 **Photo.** ***Perf. 14***
1338 A728 5s multicolored .75 .30

Self-portrait, by Oskar Kokoschka (b.1886) — A729

Perf. 14½x13½

1986, Feb. 28 **Photo.**
1339 A729 4s multicolored .60 .30

Admission to Council of Europe, 30th Anniv. — A730

1986, Feb. 28 **Photo.** ***Perf. 13x13½***
1340 A730 6s multicolored .85 .35

Clemens Holzmeister (b. 1886), Architect, Salzburg Festival Theater, 1926 — A731

Photo. & Engr.

1986, Mar. 27 ***Perf. 13½***
1341 A731 4s sepia & redsh brn .60 .30

3rd Intl. Geotextile Congress, Vienna A732

1986, Apr. 7 **Photo.** ***Perf. 13½x14½***
1342 A732 5s multicolored .75 .30

Prince Eugen and Schlosshof Castle A733

Photo. & Engr.

1986, Apr. 21 ***Perf. 14***

1343 A733 4s multicolored .60 .30

Prince Eugen Exhibition, Schlosshof and Niederweiden.

St. Florian Monastery, Upper Austria A734

1986, Apr. 24

1344 A734 4s multicolored .60 .30

The World of Baroque provincial exhibition, St. Florian.

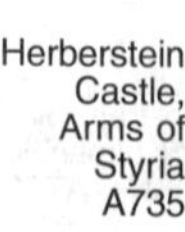

Herberstein Castle, Arms of Styria A735

1986, May 2 ***Perf. 13½x14½***

1345 A735 4s multicolored .60 .30

Europa 1986 — A736

1986, May 2 ***Perf. 13½***

1346 A736 6s Pasque flower .85 .45

Wagner, Scene from Opera Lohengrin — A737

1986, May 21

1347 A737 4s multicolored .60 .30

Intl. Richard Wagner Congress, Vienna.

Antimonite A738

1986, May 23 ***Perf. 13½x14½***

1348 A738 4s multicolored .60 .30

Burgenland Provincial Minerals Exhibition.

Scenery Type of 1984

1986-89 Photo. & Engr. ***Perf. 14***

1349 A679 5s Martinswall, Tyrol .65 .35

1350 A679 5s Tschauko Falls, Carinthia .65 .35

1351 A679 5s Dachstein Ice Caves .80 .45

1352 A679 5s Gauertal, Montafon .80 .45

1353 A679 5s Krimmler Waterfalls .80 .60

1354 A679 5s Lusthauswasser .80 .60

Nos. 1349-1354 (6) 4.50 2.80

Issued: #1351, 6/11/87; #1352, 8/21/87; #1353, 8/19/88; #1354, 9/1/89.

Waidhofen on Ybbs Township, 800th Anniv. — A739

1986, June 20 Photo. ***Perf. 13½***

1355 A739 4s multicolored .50 .30

Salzburg Local Railway, Cent. A740

1986, Aug. 8 Photo. ***Perf. 14***

1356 A740 4s multicolored .55 .30

Seals of Dukes Leopold Of Austria, Otakar of Styria, and Georgenberg Church — A741

1986, Aug. 14 Photo. & Engr.

1357 A741 5s multicolored .70 .30

Georgenberg Treaty, 800th anniv.

Julius Tandler (1869-1936), Social Reformer A742

1986, Aug. 22

1358 A742 4s multicolored .60 .30

Sonnblick Observatory, Cent. A743

Photo. & Engr.

1986, Aug. 27 ***Perf. 13½x14½***

1359 A743 4s Observatory, 1886 .60 .30

Discovery of Mandrake Root — A744

1986, Aug. 27 ***Perf. 14½x13½***

1360 A744 5s multicolored .75 .30

European Assoc. for Anesthesiology, 7th cong.

Monasteries and Abbeys Type of 1984

Designs: 5.50s, St. Gerold's Provostry, Vorarlberg. 7s, Loretto Monastery, Burgenland. 7.50s, Dominican Convent, Vienna. 8s, Zwettl Monastery. 10s, Wilten Monastery.

1986-88 Photo. & Engr. ***Perf. 14***

1361 A679a 5.50s multicolored .80 .60

1362 A679a 7s multicolored 1.10 .90

1363 A679a 7.50s multicolored 1.10 .85

1364 A679a 8s multicolored 1.40 1.00

1365 A679a 10s multicolored 1.75 1.25

Nos. 1361-1365 (5) 6.15 4.60

Issued: 5.50s, 9/12/86; 7.50s, 10/3; 7s, 8/14/87; 8s, 5/27/88; 10s, 3/18/88.

Otto Stoessl (d. 1936), Writer — A745

Photo. & Engr.

1986, Sept. 3 ***Perf. 14***

1366 A745 4s multicolored .60 .30

Vienna Fire Brigade, 300th Anniv. — A746

1986, Sept. 3 **Photo.**

1367 A746 4s Fireman, 1686 .60 .30

Silk Viennese Hunting Tapestry A747

Photo. & Engr.

1986, Sept. 3 ***Perf. 14***

1368 A747 5s multicolored .75 .40

Intl. conf. on Oriental Carpets, Vienna, Budapest.

A748

Photo. & Engr.

1986, Oct. 10 ***Perf. 14***

1369 A748 5s Minister at pulpit .70 .40

Protestant Act, 25th anniv., and Protestant Patent of Franz Josef I ensuring religious equality, 125th anniv.

Disintegration, by Walter Schmogner A749

1986, Oct. 17 ***Perf. 13½x14***

1370 A749 4s multicolored .60 .30

Franz Liszt, Composer, and Birthplace, Burgenland A750

1986, Oct. 17 ***Perf. 13½***

1371 A750 5s green & sepia .70 .40

Souvenir Sheet

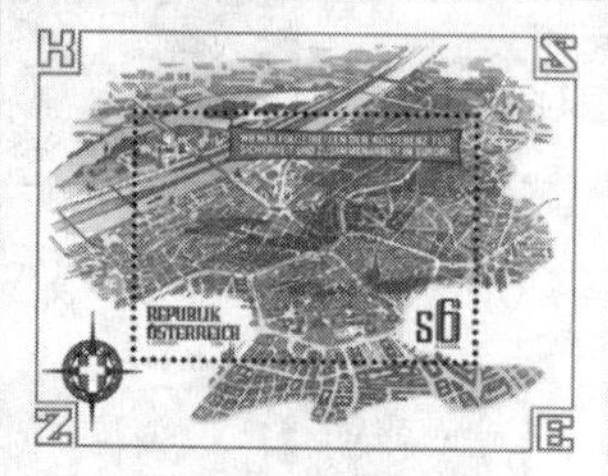

European Security Conference, Vienna — A751

Illustration reduced.

1986, Nov. 4 ***Perf. 13½x14***

1372 A751 6s Vienna .95 .65

Strettweg Cart, 7th Cent. B.C. A752

Photo. & Engr.

1986, Nov. 26 ***Perf. 14***

1373 A752 4s multicolored .65 .30

Joanneum Styrian Land Museum, 175th anniv.

Christmas A753

Design: The Little Crib, bas-relief by Schwanthaler (1740-1810), Schlierbach Monastery.

1986, Nov. 28

1374 A753 5s gold & rose lake .80 .40

Federal Chamber of Commerce, 40th Anniv. — A754

1986, Dec. 2 **Photo.**
1375 A754 5s multicolored .80 .40

Industry A755

1986-91 ***Perf. 14x13½***

1376	A755	4s Steel workers	.80	.30
1377	A755	4s Office worker, computer	.80	.35
1378	A755	4s Lab assistant	.80	.30
1378A	A755	4.50s Textile worker	.80	.60
1379	A755	5s Bricklayer	.80	.60
		Nos. 1376-1379 (5)	4.00	2.15

Issued: #1376, 12/4/86; #1377, 10/5/87; #1378, 10/21/88; 5s, 10/10/89; 4.50s, 10/11/91.

This is an expanding set. Numbers will change if necessary.

The Educated Eye, by Arnulf Rainer — A756

1987, Jan. 13 **Photo.** ***Perf. 13½x14***
1386 A756 5s multicolored .80 .40

Adult education in Vienna, cent.

The Large Blue Madonna, by Anton Faistauer (1887-1970) — A757

Paintings: 6s, Self-portrait, 1922, by A. Paris Gutersloh (1887-1973).

1987, Jan. 29 ***Perf. 14***
1387 A757 4s multicolored .55 .20
1388 A757 6s multicolored .90 .40

Europa 1987 — A758

Photo. & Engr.

1987, Apr. 6 ***Perf. 13½x14***
1389 A758 6s Hundertwasser House .95 .55

World Ice Hockey Championships, Vienna — A759

Perf. 13½x14½

1987, Apr. 17 **Photo.**
1390 A759 5s multicolored .80 .60

Opening of the Austria Center, Vienna A760

1987, Apr. 22
1391 A760 5s multicolored .80 .60

Salzburg City Charter, 700th Anniv. A761

1987, Apr. 24
1392 A761 5s multicolored .80 .60

Work-Men-Machines, Provincial Exhibition, Upper Austria — A762

Photo. & Engr.

1987, Apr. 29 ***Perf. 14***
1393 A762 4s Factory, 1920 .65 .50

Equal Rights for Men and Women — A763

1987, Apr. 29 **Photo.** ***Perf. 13½***
1394 A763 5s multicolored .80 .60

Adele Block-Bauer I, Abstract by Gustav Klimt — A764

Photo. & Engr.

1987, May 8 ***Perf. 13½***
1395 A764 4s multicolored .65 .50

The Era of Emperor Franz Joseph, provincial exhibition, Lower Austria.

Arthur Schnitzler (1862-1931), Poet — A765

1987, May 15 ***Perf. 14½x13½***
1396 A765 6s multicolored 1.00 .75

Von Raitenau, View of Salzburg A766

1987, May 15 ***Perf. 14***
1397 A766 4s multicolored .65 .50

Prince Archbishop Wolf Dietrich von Raitenau, patron of baroque architecture in Salzburg, provincial exhibition.

Lace, Lustenau Municipal Arms A767

1987, May 22
1398 A767 5s multicolored .80 .60

Lustenau, 1100th anniv.

Souvenir Sheet

Austrian Railways Sesquicentenary — A768

1987, June 5 **Photo.** ***Perf. 13½***
1399 A768 6s multicolored 1.00 .75

8th Intl. Congress of Engravers, Vienna A769

Photo. & Engr.

1987, June 17 ***Perf. 14***
1400 A769 5s gray, gray brn & dull rose .80 .60

Dr. Karl Josef Bayer (1847-1904), Chemist — A770

1987, June 22 ***Perf. 14x13½***
1401 A770 5s multicolored .80 .60

Eighth Intl. Light Metals Congress, June 22-26, Leoben and Vienna; Bayer Technique for producing aluminum oxide from bauxite, cent.

Shipping on Achensee, Cent. — A771

1987, June 26 **Photo.**
1402 A771 4s multicolored .65 .50

Ombudsmen's Office, 10th Anniv. — A772

1987, July 1
1403 A772 5s Palais Rottal, Vienna .80 .60

Dr. Erwin Schrodinger (1887-1961), 1933 Nobel Laureate in Physics — A773

1987, Aug. 11 **Photo. & Engr.**
1404 A773 5s dull olive bister, choc & buff .80 .60

Freistadt Exhibitions, 125th Anniv. A774

1987, Aug. 11 ***Perf. 14x14½***
1405 A774 5s multicolored .80 .60

Arbing, 850th Anniv. — A775

1987, Aug. 21 ***Perf. 13½***
1406 A775 5s multicolored .80 .60

1987 World Cycling Championships, Villach to Vienna — A776

1987, Aug. 25 ***Perf. 14***
1407 A776 5s multicolored .80 .60

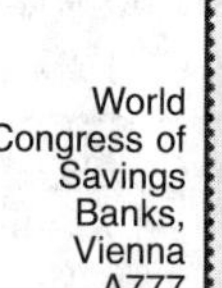

World Congress of Savings Banks, Vienna A777

Perf. 13½x14½
1987, Sept. 9 **Photo.**
1408 A777 5s multicolored .80 .60

Johann Michael Haydn (1737-1806), Composer A778

Perf. 13½x14½
1987, Sept. 14 **Engr.**
1409 A778 4s dull violet .65 .50

Paul Hofhaymer (1459-1537), Composer A779

Photo. & Engr.
1987, Sept. 11 ***Perf. 14***
1410 A779 4s gold, blk & ultra .65 .50

Bearded Vulture — A780

1987, Sept. 25
1411 A780 4s multicolored .65 .50

Innsbruck Zoo, 25th anniv.

Baumgottinnen, by Arnulf Neuwirth — A781

1987, Oct. 9 ***Perf. 14x13½***
1412 A781 5s multicolored .80 .60

Modern Art.

Gambling Monopoly, 200th Anniv. — A782

Perf. 14½x13½
1987, Oct. 30 **Photo.**
1413 A782 5s Lottery drum .80 .60

Christoph Willibald Gluck (1714-1787), Composer A784

Photo. & Engr.
1987, Nov. 13 ***Perf. 14***
1415 A784 5s cream & blk .90 .65

Oskar Helmer (b. 1887), Politician — A785

1987, Nov. 13
1416 A785 4s multicolored .70 .50

Joseph Mohr (1792-1848) and Franz Gruber (1787-1863), Opening Bars of "Silent Night, Holy Night" — A786

1987, Nov. 27
1417 A786 5s multicolored .90 .65

Christmas.

Intl. Education Congress of Salesian Fathers — A787

Photo. & Engr.
1988, Jan. 12 ***Perf. 13½***
1418 A787 5s St. John Bosco, children .90 .65

Ernst Mach (1838-1916), Physicist — A788

Photo. & Engr.
1988, Feb. 19 ***Perf. 14½x13½***
1419 A788 6s multicolored 1.10 .80

Village with Bridge (1904), by Franz von Zulow (1883-1963), Painter — A789

1988, Feb. 25 **Photo.** ***Perf. 14½x14***
1420 A789 4s multicolored .70 .50

Biedermeier Provincial Exhibition, Vormarz in Vienna — A790

Painting: Confiscation, by Ferdinand Georg Waldmuller (1793-1865).

Photo. & Engr.
1988, Mar. 11 ***Perf. 14***
1421 A790 4s multicolored .70 .50

Anschluss of March 11, 1938 — A791

1988, Mar. 11 **Photo.** ***Perf. 13½***
1422 A791 5s gray olive, brn blk & ver .85 .65

No. 2 Aigen Steam Locomotive, 1887 A792

1988, Mar. 22 ***Perf. 13½x14½***
1423 A792 4s shown .70 .50
1424 A792 5s Electric train, Josepsplatz .85 .65

Muhlkreis Railway, cent. (4s); Vienna Local Railway, cent. (5s).

World Wildlife Fund — A793

Photo. & Engr.
1988, Apr. 15 ***Perf. 13½x14***
1425 A793 5s Bee eater .90 .65

Styrian Provincial Exhibition on Glass and Coal, Barnbach A794

1988, Apr. 29 ***Perf. 13½***
1426 A794 4s Frosted glass .70 .50

Intl. Red Cross, 125th Anniv. — A795

1988, May 6 **Photo.** ***Perf. 14***
1427 A795 12s grn, brt red & blk 2.25 1.75

Gothic Silver Censer — A796

1988, May 6 **Photo. & Engr.**
1428 A796 4s multicolored .70 .50

Art and Monasticism at the Birth of Austria, lower Austrian provincial exhibition, Seitenstetten.

Europa 1988 A797

Communication and transportation.

1988, May 13 **Photo.**
1429 A797 6s multicolored 1.10 .80

Mattsee Monastery and Lion of Alz — A798

1988, May 18 **Photo. & Engr.**
1430 A798 4s multicolored .70 .50

Provincial exhibition at Mattsee Monastery: Bavarian Tribes in Salzburg.

Weinberg Castle A799

Perf. 13½x14½
1988, May 20 **Photo.**
1431 A799 4s multicolored .70 .50

Upper Austrian provincial exhibition: Weinberg Castle.

Odon von Horwath (1901-1938), Dramatist — A800

Photo. & Engr.

1988, June 1 ***Perf. 14½x13½***
1432 A800 6s olive bis & slate grn 1.10 .80

Stockerau Festival, 25th Anniv. — A801

1988, June 17 ***Perf. 14***
1433 A801 5s Stockerau Town Hall .80 .60

Tauern Motorway Opening — A802

1988, June 24 Photo. ***Perf. 13½x14***
1434 A802 4s multicolored .65 .50

Brixlegg, 1200th Anniv. A803

Photo. & Engr.

1988, July 1 ***Perf. 13½x14½***
1435 A803 5s multicolored .80 .60

View of Klagenfurt, Engraving by Matthaus Merian (1593-1650) — A804

Photo. & Engr.

1988, Aug. 12 ***Perf. 14***
1436 A804 5s multicolored .80 .60

Carinthian Postal Service, 400th Anniv.

Brixen-im-Thale, 1200th Anniv. — A805

1988, Aug. 12
1437 A805 5s multicolored .80 .60

Feldkirchen, 1100th Anniv. — A806

1988, Sept. 2 ***Perf. 13½***
1438 A806 5s multicolored .80 .60

Feldbach, 800th Anniv. A807

1988, Sept. 15 Photo. & Engr.
1439 A807 5s multicolored .80 .60

Ansfelden, 1200th Anniv. — A808

1988, Sept. 23 ***Perf. 14***
1440 A808 5s multicolored .80 .60

Exports A809

1988, Oct. 18 Photo. ***Perf. 14x13½***
1441 A809 8s multicolored 3.50 3.00

No. 1441 has a holographic image. Soaking in water may affect the hologram.

Vienna Concert Hall, 75th Anniv. A810

Photo. & Engr.

1988, Oct. 19 ***Perf. 13½***
1442 A810 5s multicolored .80 .60

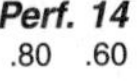
The Watchmen, by Giselbert Hoke — A811

1988, Oct. 21 ***Perf. 14***
1443 A811 5s multicolored .80 .60

Social Democrats Unification Party Congress, Cent. — A812

1988, Nov. 11 Photo. ***Perf. 14½x14***
1444 A812 4s multicolored .65 .50

Leopold Schonbauer (1888-1963), Physician — A813

Photo. & Engr.

1988, Nov. 11 ***Perf. 14½x13½***
1445 A813 4s multicolored .65 .50

Christmas A814

Nativity painting from St. Barbara's Church.

1988, Nov. 25 ***Perf. 14***
1446 A814 5s multicolored .80 .60

Benedictine Monastery, Melk, 900th Anniv. — A815

Design: Fresco by Paul Troger.

1989, Mar. 17 Photo. & Engr.
1447 A815 5s multicolored .80 .60

Madonna and Child, by Lucas Cranach (1472-1553) A816

1989, Mar. 17 ***Perf. 14½x13½***
1448 A816 4s multicolored .60 .50

Diocese of Innsbruck, 25th anniv.

Marianne Hainisch (1839-1936), Women's Rights Activist — A817

1989, Mar. 24 ***Perf. 14x13½***
1449 A817 6s multicolored .95 .70

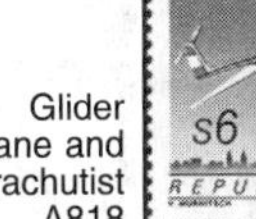
Glider Plane and Parachutist A818

1989, Mar. 31 Photo. ***Perf. 14***
1450 A818 6s multicolored 1.00 .75

World Gliding Championships, Wiener Neustadt, and World Parachuting Championships, Damuls.

Bruck an der Leitha Commune, 750th Anniv. — A819

Painting by Georg Matthaus Vischer (1628-1696).

1989, Apr. 21
1451 A819 5s multicolored .85 .60

Die Malerei, 1904, by Rudolf Jettmar (1869-1939) A820

Perf. 14½x13½

1989, Apr. 21 Photo.
1452 A820 5s multicolored .85 .60

Holy Trinity Church, Stadl-Paura A821

1989, Apr. 26 Photo. & Engr.
1453 A821 5s multicolored .85 .60

Michael Prunner (1669-1739), baroque architect.

Eduard Suess (1831-1914), Structural Geologist and Map — A822

Portrait by J. Krieher (1800-1876).

1989, Apr. 26
1454 A822 6s multicolored 1.00 .75

Ludwig Wittgenstein (1889-1951), Philosopher A823

1989, Apr. 26
1455 A823 5s multicolored .85 .60

Styrian Provincial Exhibition, Judenburg A824

Design: Judenberg, 17th cent., an engraving by Georg Matthaus Vischer.

1989, Apr. 28 ***Perf. 14x13½***
1456 A824 4s multicolored .70 .50

Industrial Technology Exhibition, Pottenstein — A825

1989, Apr. 28 Photo. ***Perf. 13½***
1457 A825 4s Steam engine .70 .50

Radstadt Township, 700th Anniv. A826

1989, May 3 Photo. ***Perf. 13½x14½***
1458 A826 5s multicolored .85 .60

Europa 1989 A827

1989, May 5
1459 A827 6s Toy boat 1.00 .75

Monastery Church at Lambach, 900th Anniv. — A828

Photo. & Engr.

1989, May 19 ***Perf. 14***
1460 A828 4s multicolored .70 .50

Paddle Steamer *Gisela* A829

1989, May 19 Photo. ***Perf. 13½***
1461 A829 5s multicolored .85 .60

Shipping on the Traunsee, 150th anniv.

St. Andra im Lavanttal, 650th Anniv. A830

Period cityscape by Matthaus Merian.

1989, May 26 **Photo. & Engr.**
1462 A830 5s multicolored .85 .60

Richard Strauss (1864-1949), Composer A831

Photo. & Engr.

1989, June 1 ***Perf. 14½x13½***
1463 A831 6s dark brn, gold & red brn 1.00 .75

Achensee Railway, Cent. A832

1989, June 8 Photo. ***Perf. 13½***
1464 A832 5s multicolored .85 .60

Monastery Type of 1984

Design: 50g, Vorau Abbey, Styria. 1s, Monastery of Mehrerau, Vorarlberg. 1.50s, Monastery of the German Order in Vienna. 2s, Bendictine Monastery, Michaelbeuern. 11s, Engelszell Abbey. 12s, Monastery of the Hospitalers, Eisenstadt. 17s, St. Peter, Salzburg. 20s, Wernberg Monastery.

1989-92 Photo. & Engr. ***Perf. 14***

1464A	A679a	50g	multi	.20	.20
1465	A679a	1s	multi	.20	.20
1465A	A679a	1.50s	multi	.30	.20
1466	A679a	2s	multi	.35	.25
1467	A679a	11s	multi	1.90	1.40
1467A	A679a	12s	multi	2.25	1.75
1468	A679a	17s	multi	2.75	2.00
1469	A679a	20s	multi	2.75	2.00
	Nos. 1464A-1469 (8)			10.70	8.00

Issued: 1s, 9/1/89; 17s, 6/29/89; 11s, 3/9/90; 50g, 10/12/90; 20s, 5/3/91; 2s, 9/27/91; 1.50s, 10/23/92; 12s, 6/17/92.

This is an expanding set. Numbers will change if necessary.

Interparliamentary Union, Cent. — A833

Photo. & Engr.

1989, June 30 ***Perf. 14***
1475 A833 6s Parliament, Vienna 1.00 .75

Social Security in Austria, Cent. — A834

1989, Aug. 1 **Photo.**
1476 A834 5s multicolored .70 .50

UN Offices in Vienna, 10th Anniv. A835

1989, Aug. 23
1477 A835 8s multicolored 1.10 .85

Wildalpen, 850th Anniv. A836

Photo. & Engr.

1989, Sept. 15 ***Perf. 13½x14***
1478 A836 5s Foundry, coat of arms .80 .60

33rd Congress of the Association for Quality Assurance (EOQC) — A837

1989, Sept. 18 Photo. ***Perf. 14x13½***
1479 A837 6s multicolored .90 .70

14th World Congress of the Soc. for Criminal Law (AIDP) A838

Photo. & Engr.

1989, Oct. 2 ***Perf. 13½***
1480 A838 6s Justice Palace, Vienna .90 .70

Lebensbaum, by Ernst Steiner — A839

1989, Oct. 10 ***Perf. 13½x14***
1481 A839 5s multicolored .80 .60

Georg Trakl (1887-1914), Expressionist Poet — A840

1989, Nov. 6 Photo. ***Perf. 14½x13½***
1482 A840 4s Trakl .60 .45
1483 A840 4s Anzengruber .60 .45

Ludwig Anzengruber (1839-1889), playwright and novelist.

Alfred Fried (1864-1921), Pacifist, Publisher and 1911 Nobel Laureate — A841

1989, Nov. 10 **Photo. & Engr.**
1484 A841 6s multicolored .90 .70

Parish Church Christ Child, by Johann Carl Reslfeld A842

1989, Dec. 1 ***Perf. 13½x14½***
1485 A842 5s multicolored .75 .60

Christmas.

Postal Communications in Europe, 500th Anniv. — A843

The Young Post Rider, an Engraving by Albrecht Durer

Photo. & Engr.

1990, Jan. 12 ***Perf. 14***
1486 A843 5s multicolored .80 .60

See Belgium No. 1332, Germany No. 1592, Berlin No. 9N584 and German Democratic Republic No. 2791.

Hahnenkamm Alpine Competition, Kitzbuhel, 50th Anniv. — A844

Perf. 13½x14½

1990, Jan. 12 **Photo.**
1487 A844 5s multicolored .80 .60

Salomon Sulzer (1804-90), Cantor and Composer A845

Perf. 14½x13½

1990, Jan. 17 **Photo.**
1488 A845 4.50s multicolored .70 .55

Friedrich Emich (1860-1940), Chemist — A846

1990, Jan. 22 **Photo. & Engr.**
1489 A846 6s claret & pale green .95 .70

Miniature from the *Market Book of Grein*, by Ulrich Schreier, c. 1490 A847

1990, Mar. 9 ***Perf. 14***
1490 A847 5s sepia, buff & gray .80 .60

City of Linz, 500th anniv.

University Seals — A848

1990, Apr. 6
1491 A848 5s multicolored .85 .65

625th Anniv. of Vienna University and 175th anniv. of Vienna Technical University.

Scenery Type of 1984

1990-97 ***Perf. 14***

1492	A679	5s	Styrian Vineyards	.85	.65
1493	A679	5s	Obir Caverns	.95	.70
1494	A679	5s	Natural Bridge, Vorarlberg	.90	.75
1495	A679	6s	Wilder Kaiser Mountain, Tyrol	1.25	.95
1496	A679	6s	Peggau Cave, Styria	1.00	.80
1497	A679	6s	Moorland, swamp, Heidenreichstein	1.25	1.00
1498	A679	6s	Hohe Tauern Natl. Park	1.25	1.00
1499	A679	6s	Nussberg Vineyards	1.00	.80
			Nos. 1492-1499 (8)	8.45	6.65

Issued: #1492, 4/27; #1493, 3/26/91; #1494, 2/5/92; #1495, 2/19/93; #1496, 4/29/94; #1497, 5/19/95; #1498, 3/29/96; #1499, 2/21/97.

Anthering, 1200th Anniv. — A849

Church and municipal arms.

1990, Apr. 27 **Photo.** ***Perf. 14x13½***
1500 A849 7s multicolored 1.25 1.00

Labor Day, Cent. — A850

1990, Apr. 30 **Photo.** ***Perf. 13½***
1501 A850 4.50s multicolored .80 .60

Seckau Abbey, 850th Anniv. — A851

1990, May 4 **Engr.** ***Perf. 14x13½***
1502 A851 4.50s bluish black .80 .60

Ebene Reichenau Post Office A852

1990, May 4 **Photo.** ***Perf. 13½x14***
1503 A852 7s multicolored 1.25 1.00

Hans Makart (1840-84), Self-Portrait A853

Self Portrait: 5s, Egon Schiele (1890-1918).

Photo. & Engr.

1990, May 29 ***Perf. 14***
1504 A853 4.50s multicolored .80 .60
1505 A853 5s multicolored .85 .65

Ferdinand Raimund (1790-1836), Actor — A854

1990, June 1 **Photo.** ***Perf. 14x13½***
1506 A854 4.50s multicolored .80 .60

Christ Healing the Sick by Rembrandt A855

Photo. & Engr.

1990, June 5 ***Perf. 14***
1507 A855 7s multicolored 1.25 1.00

2nd Intl. Christus Medicus Cong., Bad Ischl.

Hardegg, 700th Anniv. — A856

Photo. & Engr.

1990, June 8 ***Perf. 13½x14***
1508 A856 4.50s multicolored .80 .60

Oberdrauburg, 750th Anniv. — A857

1990, June 8 **Photo.**
1509 A857 5s multicolored .85 .65

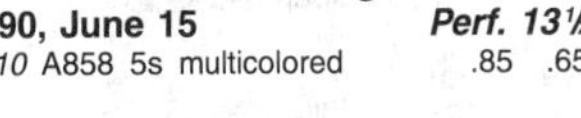

Gumpoldskirchen, 850th Anniv. — A858

Photo. & Engr.

1990, June 15 ***Perf. 13½***
1510 A858 5s multicolored .85 .65

Mathias Zdarsky (1856-1940), Alpine Skier — A859

1990, June 20 ***Perf. 14x13½***
1511 A859 5s multicolored .85 .65

Telegraph, 1880, Anton Tschechow, 1978 — A860

1990, June 28 **Photo.** ***Perf. 14***
1512 A860 9s multicolored 1.50 1.10

Modern shipbuilding in Austria, 150th anniv.

Joseph Friedrich Perkonig (1890-1959), Poet — A861

Photo. & Engr.

1990, Aug. 3 ***Perf. 14x13½***
1513 A861 5s gold & brown .85 .65

Herr des Regenbogens, by Robert Zeppel-Sperl A862

Photo. & Engr.

1990, Aug. 30 ***Perf. 13½x14***
1514 A862 5s gold & brown .85 .65

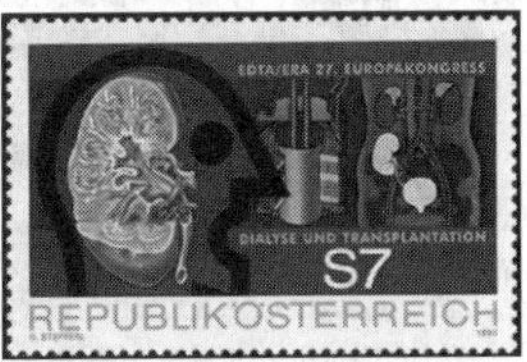

European Dialysis and Transplantation Society, 27th Congress — A863

1990, Sept. 4 **Photo.** ***Perf. 14***
1515 A863 7s multicolored 1.25 1.00

Franz Werfel (1890-1945), Writer — A864

Photo. & Engr.

1990, Sept. 11 ***Perf. 14x13½***
1516 A864 5s multicolored .95 .70

Austrian Forces in UN Peace Keeping Forces, 30th Anniv. A865

1990, Sept. 20 **Photo.** ***Perf. 13½***
1517 A865 7s multicolored 1.25 1.00

Federal and State Arms A866

1990, Sept. 24 **Photo. & Engr.**
1518 A866 5s multicolored .95 .70

Federalism in Austria.

Mining Univ., Leoben, 150th Anniv. — A867

Photo & Engr.

1990, Oct. 22 ***Perf. 14***
1519 A867 4.50s blk, bl grn & red .85 .65

Karl Freiherr von Vogelsang (1818-90), Politician — A868

Photo. & Engr.

1990, Nov. 8 ***Perf. 14x13½***
1520 A868 4.50s multicolored .85 .65

Metalworkers and Miners Trade Union, Cent. — A869

1990, Nov. 16 ***Perf. 14***
1521 A869 5s multicolored .95 .70

3rd World Curling Championships A870

1990, Nov. 23 Photo. ***Perf. 14x13½***
1522 A870 7s multicolored 1.40 1.00

Palmhouse at Schonbrunn — A871

1990, Nov. 30 ***Perf. 14***
1523 A871 5s multicolored .95 .70

Christmas A872

Altar in Klosterneuburg Abbey by the Master from Verdun.

Photo. & Engr.

1990, Nov. 23 ***Perf. 13½***
1524 A872 5s multicolored .95 .70

Franz Grillparzer (1791-1872), Dramatic Poet — A873

Photo. & Engr.

1991, Jan. 15 ***Perf. 14x13½***
1525 A873 4.50s multicolored .85 .65

Alpine Skiing World Championship, Saalbach-Hinterglemm — A874

1991, Jan. 21 ***Perf. 13½***
1526 A874 5s multicolored .95 .70

Bruno Kreisky (1911-90), Chancellor A875

1991, Jan. 21 Photo. ***Perf. 14x13½***
1527 A875 5s multicolored .95 .70

Friedrich Freiherr von Schmidt (1825-1891), Architect — A876

1991, Jan. 21 ***Perf. 14***
1528 A876 7s multicolored 1.40 1.00

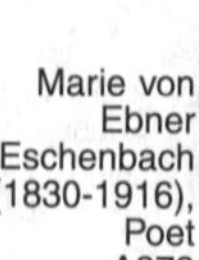

Visual Arts A877

Designs: 4.50s, Donner Fountain, Vienna, by Raphael Donner (1693-1741), sculptor. 5s, Kitzbuhel in Winter, by Alfons Walde (1891-1958), painter. 7s, Vienna Stock Exchange, Theophil Hansen (1813-1891), architect.

1991, Feb. 8
1529 A877 4.50s multicolored .85 .65
1530 A877 5s multicolored .95 .70
1531 A877 7s multicolored 1.40 1.00
Nos. 1529-1531 (3) 3.20 2.35

See No. 1543.

Marie von Ebner Eschenbach (1830-1916), Poet A878

1991, Mar. 12 Engr. ***Perf. 13½x14½***
1532 A878 4.50s rose violet .85 .65

Miniature Sheet

Wolfgang Amadeus Mozart (1756-1791), Composer A879

Design: b, Magic Flute Fountain, Vienna.

1991, Mar. 22 ***Perf. 13½***
1533 Sheet of 2 + label 1.75 1.25
a.-b. A879 5s any single .80 .60

Spittal an der Drau, 800th Anniv. A880

1991, Apr. 11 ***Perf. 14***
1534 A880 4.50s multicolored .75 .60

Europa A881

1991, May 3 Photo. ***Perf. 14***
1535 A881 7s ERS-1 satellite 1.10 .80

Garden Banquet by Anthony Bays A882

1991, May 10 Photo. ***Perf. 13½***
1536 A882 5s multicolored .75 .60

Vorarlberg Provincial Exhibition, Hohenems.

Museum of Military History, Cent. A883

7s, Interior of Museum of Art History.

Photo. & Engr.

1991, May 24 ***Perf. 13½***
1537 A883 5s multicolored .95 .80
1538 A883 7s multicolored 1.25 1.00

Museum of Art History, Cent. (#1538).

Grein, 500th Anniv. A884

1991, May 24 Photo. ***Perf. 14***
1539 A884 4.50s multicolored .90 .45

Tulln, 1200th Anniv. A885

1991, May 24 ***Perf. 13½x14***
1540 A885 5s multicolored .95 .80

Completion of Karawanken Tunnels — A886

1991, May 31 ***Perf. 14x13½***
1541 A886 7s multicolored 1.25 1.00

5th Anniv. of St. Polten as Provincial Capital of Lower Austria A887

1991, July 5 Photo. ***Perf. 14***
1542 A887 5s multicolored .80 .65

Visual Arts Type of 1991

Design: 4.50s, Karlsplatz Station of Vienna Subway by Otto Wagner (1841-1918), Architect.

1991, July 12 Photo. & Engr.
1543 A877 4.50s multicolored .75 .60

Rowing and Junior Canoeing World Championships, Vienna — A888

1991, Aug. 20 Photo. ***Perf. 13½x14***
1544 A888 5s multicolored .85 .70

European Congress of Radiologists — A889

1991, Sept. 13 ***Perf. 14***
1545 A889 7s multicolored 1.10 .95

Paracelsus (1493-1541), Physician — A890

1991, Sept. 27 ***Perf. 14x13½***
1546 A890 4.50s multicolored .75 .60

Joint Austrian-Soviet Space Mission
A891

1991, Oct. 2 ***Perf. 14***
1547 A891 9s multicolored 1.50 1.25

Austrian Folk Festivals
A892

4.50s, Almabtrieb, Tyrol. 5s, Winzerkrone, Vienna. 7s, Ernte-Monstranz, Styria.

1991, Oct. 4 **Photo. & Engr.**
1548 A892 4.50s multicolored .75 .60
1549 A892 5s multicolored .85 .70
1550 A892 7s multicolored 1.10 .95
Nos. 1548-1550 (3) 2.70 2.25

See #1577-1579, 1619-1621, 1633-1635, 1671-1673, 1694, 1705-1706, 1714, 1730, 1741, 1752-1753, 1762, 1778, 1799-1800, 1805-1806, 1824, 1836-1838.

The General by Rudolph Pointner
A893

Photo. & Engr.
1991, Oct. 11 ***Perf. 13½x14***
1551 A893 5s multicolored .85 .70

Birth of Christ, Baumgartenberg Church — A894

1991, Nov. 29
1552 A894 5s multicolored .85 .70

Christmas.

Julius Raab, Politician, Birth Cent. — A895

1991, Nov. 29 ***Perf. 14x13½***
1553 A895 4.50s red brn & brn .75 .60

1992 Winter and Summer Olympic Games
A897

1992, Jan. 14 **Photo.** ***Perf. 14***
1555 A897 7s multicolored 1.25 1.00

Trade Union of Clerks in Private Enterprises, Cent. — A898

1992, Jan. 14
1556 A898 5.50s multicolored .95 .80

8th Natural Run Toboggan World Championships
A899

1992, Jan. 29 ***Perf. 14x13½***
1557 A899 5s multicolored .90 .75

George Saiko, Poet, Birth Cent. — A900

1992, Feb. 5 **Engr.** ***Perf. 14x13½***
1558 A900 5.50s brown .95 .80

Worker's Sports, Cent. — A901

1992, Feb. 5 **Photo.** ***Perf. 14***
1559 A901 5.50s multicolored .95 .80

Souvenir Sheet

Vienna Philharmonic Orchestra, 150th Anniv. — A902

Photo. & Engr.
1992, Mar. 27 ***Perf. 14***
1560 A902 5.50s multicolored .95 .80

Scientists
A903

Designs: 5s, Franz Joseph Muller von Reichenstein (1742-1825), discoverer of tellurium. 5.50s, Dr. Paul Kitaibel (1757-1817), botanist. 6s, Christian Johann Doppler (1803-1853), physicist. 7s, Richard Kuhn (1900-1967), chemist.

1992, Mar. 27 **Photo.**
1561 A903 5s multicolored .80 .70
1562 A903 5.50s multicolored .95 .80
1563 A903 6s multicolored 1.00 .85
1564 A903 7s multicolored 1.25 .95
Nos. 1561-1564 (4) 4.00 3.30

Railway Workers Union, Cent.
A904

1992, Apr. 2 ***Perf. 14x13½***
1565 A904 5.50s black & red .95 .80

Norbert Hanrieder (1842-1913), Poet — A905

Photo. & Engr.
1992, Apr. 30 ***Perf. 14x13½***
1566 A905 5.50s purple & buff .95 .80

Carl Zeller (1842-1898) and Karl Millocker (1842-1899), Operetta Composers
A906

Photo. & Engr.
1992, Apr. 30 ***Perf. 14***
1567 A906 6s multicolored 1.00 .85

LD Steel Mill, 40th Anniv.
A907

1992, May 8 **Photo.** ***Perf. 14x13½***
1568 A907 5s multicolored .85 .70

Discovery of America, 500th Anniv.
A908

Photo. & Engr.
1992, May 8 ***Perf. 14***
1569 A908 7s multicolored 1.25 .95

Europa.

Austro-Swiss Treaty on Regulation of Rhine River, Cent. — A909

1992, May 8 **Photo.** ***Perf. 13½x14***
1570 A909 7s multicolored 1.25 .95

Protection of the Alps — A910

1992, May 22 ***Perf. 14x13½***
1571 A910 5.50s multicolored .95 .80

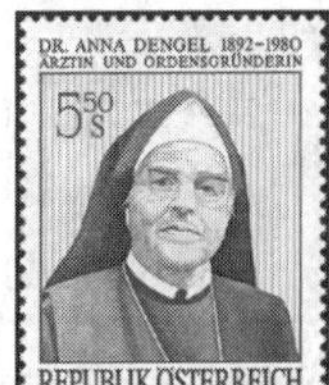
Dr. Anna Dengel (1892-1980), Physician — A911

1992, May 22 **Photo. & Engr.**
1572 A911 5.50s multicolored .95 .80

Sebastian Rieger (1867-1953), Poet — A912

1992, May 22 **Engr.**
1573 A912 5s red brown .85 .70

Lienz, 750th Anniv.
A913

1992, June 17 **Photo.** ***Perf. 14x13½***
1574 A913 5s Town Hall .90 .70

Intl. Congress of Austrian Society of Surgeons A914

Photo. & Engr.

1992, June 17 ***Perf. 14***

1575 A914 6s multicolored 1.10 .90

Dr. Kurt Waldheim, President of Austria, 1986-92 — A915

1992, June 22 ***Perf. 14x13½***

1576 A915 5.50s multicolored .95 .75

Folk Festivals Type of 1991

Designs: 5s, Marksman's target, Lower Austria. 5.50s, Peasant's chest, Carinthia. 7s, Votive icon, Vorarlberg.

Photo. & Engr.

1992, Sept. 18 ***Perf. 14***

1577 A892 5s multicolored .90 .70
1578 A892 5.50s multicolored .95 .75
1579 A892 7s multicolored 1.25 1.00
Nos. 1577-1579 (3) 3.10 2.45

Marchfeld Canal — A917

1992, Oct. 9 **Photo.** ***Perf. 13½x14***

1580 A917 5s multicolored .90 .70

5th Intl. Ombudsman Conference, Vienna — A918

Photo & Engr.

1992, Oct. 9 ***Perf. 14***

1581 A918 5.50s multicolored .95 .75

The Clearance of Seawater, by Peter Pongratz A919

1992, Oct. 9

1582 A919 5.50s multicolored .95 .75

Academy of Fine Arts, 300th Anniv. — A920

Photo. & Engr.

1992, Oct. 23 ***Perf. 14***

1583 A920 5s red & blue 1.00 .85

Birth of Christ, by Johann Georg Schmidt A921

1992, Nov. 27 ***Perf. 14x13½***

1584 A921 5.50s multicolored 1.10 .90

Christmas.

Veit Koniger, Sculptor, Death Bicent. A922

Photo. & Engr.

1992, Nov. 27 ***Perf. 14***

1585 A922 5s multicolored 1.00 .80

Herman Potocnik, Theoretician of Geosynchronous Satellite Orbit, Birth Cent. — A923

1992, Nov. 27 **Photo.**

1586 A923 10s multicolored 2.00 1.60

Famous Buildings A924

5s, Statues & dome of Imperial Palace, Vienna, designed by Joseph Emanuel Fischer von Erlach. 5.50s, Kinsky Palace, designed by Lukas von Hildebrandt. 7s, Vienna State Opera, designed by Eduard van der Null & August Siccard von Siccardsburg.

1993, Jan. 22 **Photo. & Engr.**

1587 A924 5s multicolored 1.00 .80
1588 A924 5.50s multicolored 1.10 .90
1589 A924 7s multicolored 1.40 1.10
Nos. 1587-1589 (3) 3.50 2.80

Joseph Emanuel Fischer von Erlach, 300th birth anniv. (#1587). Johann Lukas von Hildebrandt, 325th birth anniv. (#1588). Eduard van der Null, August Siccard von Siccardsburg, 125th death anniv. (#1589).

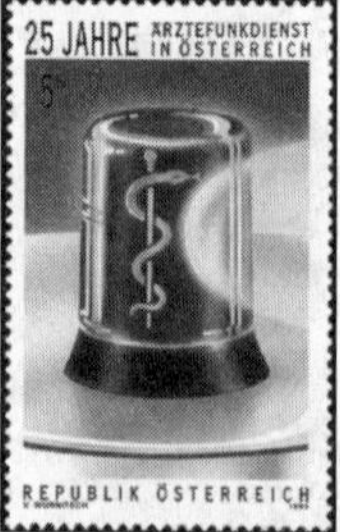

Radio Dispatched Medical Service, 25th Anniv. — A925

1993, Feb. 19 **Photo.**

1590 A925 5s multicolored 1.00 .80

Typewriter Made by Peter Mitterhofer (1822-1893) A926

1993, Feb. 19 ***Perf. 13½x14***

1591 A926 17s multicolored 3.50 2.75

Popular Entertainers — A927

Strada del Sole, by Rainhard Fendrich.

1993, Mar. 19 **Photo.** ***Perf. 14***

1592 A927 5.50s multicolored 1.00 .80

See Nos. 1626, 1639.

Charles Sealsfield (1793-1864), Writer A928

Photo. & Engr.

1993, Mar. 19 ***Perf. 13½x14***

1593 A928 10s multicolored 1.75 1.40

Rights of the Child — A930

1993, Apr. 16 **Photo.** ***Perf. 13½x14***

1595 A930 7s multicolored 1.25 1.00

Flying Harlequin, by Paul Flora A931

1993, Apr. 16 **Photo. & Engr.**

1596 A931 7s multicolored 1.25 1.00

Europa.

Monastery of Admont — A932

Designs: 1s, Detail of abbesse's crosier, St. Gabriel Abbey, Styria. 5.50s, Death, wooden statue by Josef Stammel (1695-1765). 6s, Stained glass, Mariastern-Gwiggen Monastery. 7s, Marble lion, Franciscan Monastery, Salzburg. 8s, Gothic entry, Wilhering Monastery, Upper Austria. 7.50s, Cupola fresco, by Paul Troger, Monastery of Altenburg. 10s, Altarpiece, St. Peregrinus praying, Maria Luggau Monastery. 20s, Crosier, Fiecht Monastery. 26s, Sculpture of Mater Dolorosa, Franciscan Monastery, Schwaz, Tirol. 30s, Madonna of Scottish Order, Schottenstift Monastery, Vienna.

Perf. 14x13½, 13½x14 (8s, 26s), 14 (1s, 30s)

1993-95 **Photo. & Engr.**

1599 A932 1s multicolored .20 .20
1600 A932 5.50s multicolored 1.00 .75

Perf. 14

1601 A932 6s multicolored 1.10 .90
1602 A932 7s multicolored 1.25 1.00
1603 A932 7.50s multicolored 1.25 1.00
1604 A932 8s multicolored 1.60 1.25
1605 A932 10s multicolored 1.75 1.40
1606 A932 20s multicolored 3.50 1.75
1607 A932 26s multicolored 5.25 4.25
1608 A932 30s multicolored 5.50 4.50
Nos. 1599-1608 (10) 22.40 17.00

Issued: 5.50s, 4/16; 6s, 9/17; 20s, 10/8; 7.50s, 4/4/94; 10s, 8/26/94; 30s, 10/7/94; 7s, 11/18/94; 8s, 9/15/95; 26s, 10/6/95; 1s, 4/28/95.

Peter Rosegger (1843-1918), Writer — A933

1993, May 5 **Photo.** ***Perf. 14x13½***

1617 A933 5.50s green & black 1.00 .80

Lake Constance Steamer Hohentwiel A934

1993, May 5 **Photo.** ***Perf. 14***

1618 A934 6s multicolored 1.10 .85

See Germany #1786, Switzerland #931.

Folk Festivals Type of 1991

Designs: 5s, Corpus Christi Day Procession, Upper Austria. 5.50s, Blockdrawing, Burgenland. 7s, Cracking whip when snow is melting, Salzburg.

Photo. & Engr.

1993, June 11 ***Perf. 14***

1619 A892 5s multicolored .90 .70
1620 A892 5.50s multicolored 1.00 .80
1621 A892 7s multicolored 1.25 1.00
Nos. 1619-1621 (3) 3.15 2.50

UN Conference on Human Rights, Vienna A935

1993, June 11 **Photo.**

1622 A935 10s multicolored 1.75 1.40

Franz Jagerstatter (1907-1943), Resistance Fighter — A936

1993, Aug. 6 Photo. *Perf. 14x13½*
1623 A936 5.50s multicolored 1.00 .80

Schafberg Railway, Cent. A937

1993, Aug. 6 *Perf. 13½x14*
1624 A937 6s multicolored 1.10 .90

Self-portrait with Puppet, by Rudolf Wacker (1893-1939) A938

Photo. & Engr.

1993, Aug. 6 *Perf. 14*
1625 A938 6s multicolored 1.10 .90

Popular Entertainers Type of 1993

Design: 5.50s, Granny, by Ludwig Hirsch.

1993, Sept. 3 Photo. *Perf. 14*
1626 A927 5.50s multicolored 1.00 .80

Vienna Mens' Choral Society, 150th Anniv. A940

1993, Sept. 17 Photo. *Perf. 14*
1627 A940 5s multicolored .90 .75

Easter, by Max Weiler — A941

Photo. & Engr.

1993, Oct. 8 *Perf. 13½x14*
1628 A941 5.50s multicolored 1.00 .80

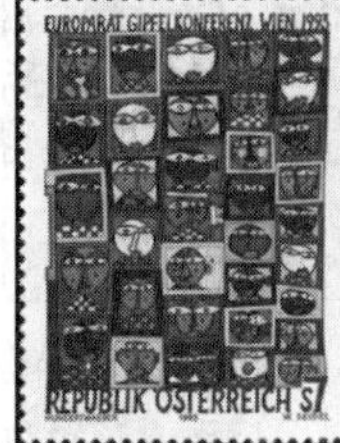

99 Heads, by Hundertwasser A942

1993, Oct. 8
1629 A942 7s multicolored 1.25 1.00

Council of Europe Conference, Vienna.

Austrian Republic, 75th Anniv. — A943

Design: 5.50s, Statue of Pallas Athena.

Photo. & Engr.

1993, Nov. 12 *Perf. 13½x14*
1630 A943 5.50s multicolored 1.00 .80

Trade Unions in Austria, Cent. A944

1993, Nov. 12 Photo. *Perf. 14*
1631 A944 5.50s multicolored 1.00 .80

Birth of Christ, by Master of the Krainburger Altar — A945

Photo. & Engr.

1993, Nov. 26 *Perf. 13½x14*
1632 A945 5.50s multicolored 1.00 .80

Christmas.

Folklore and Customs Type of 1991

Antiques: 5.50s, Dolls, cradle, Vorarlberg. 6s, Sled, Steiermark. 7s, Godparent's bowl, Upper Austria.

Photo. & Engr.

1994, Jan. 28 *Perf. 14*
1633 A892 5.50s multicolored 1.00 .80
1634 A892 6s multicolored 1.10 .90
1635 A892 7s multicolored 1.25 1.00
Nos. 1633-1635 (3) 3.35 2.70

1994 Winter Olympics, Lillehammer, Norway — A946

1994, Feb. 9
1636 A946 7s multicolored 1.25 1.00

Vienna Mint, 800th Anniv. A947

1994, Feb. 18
1637 A947 6s multicolored 1.10 .90

Lying Lady, by Herbert Boeckl (1894-1966) — A948

1994, Mar. 18 Photo. *Perf. 14x13½*
1638 A948 5.50s multicolored .95 .70

Popular Entertainers Type of 1993

Design: 6s, Rock Me Amadeus, by Falco.

1994, Mar. 18 *Perf. 14*
1639 A927 6s multicolored 1.00 .80

Wiener Neustadt, 800th Anniv. — A949

1994, Mar. 18
1640 A949 6s multicolored 1.00 .80

Lake Rudolph, Teleki-Hohnel Expedition — A950

Photo. & Engr.

1994, May 27 *Perf. 14x13½*
1641 A950 7s multicolored 1.25 1.00

Europa.

Daniel Gran, 300th Birth Anniv. A951

Fresco: 20s, Allegory of Theology, Jurisprudence and Medicine.

1994, May 27
1642 A951 20s multicolored 3.50 2.75

Carinthian Summer Festival, 25th Anniv. — A952

Design: 5.50s, Scene from The Prodigal Son.

Photo. & Engr.

1994, June 17 *Perf. 14*
1643 A952 5.50s lake & gold .95 .75

Railway Centennials — A953

1994 Photo. & Engr. *Perf. 14*
1647 A953 5.50s Gailtal .95 .75
1648 A953 6s Murtal 1.00 .80

Issued: 5.50s, 6s, 6/17/94.

Hermann Gmeiner, 75th Birth Anniv. — A954

1994, June 17 *Perf. 14x13½*
1656 A954 7s multicolored 1.25 1.00

Karl Seitz (1869-1950) Politician A955

1994, Aug. 12 Photo. *Perf. 14*
1657 A955 5.50s multicolored 1.00 .80

Karl Bohm (1894-1981), Conductor A956

Photo. & Engr.

1994, Aug. 26 *Perf. 14x13½*
1658 A956 7s gold & dk blue 1.25 1.00

Ethnic Minorities in Austria A957

1994, Sept. 9 Photo. *Perf. 13½*
1659 A957 5.50s multicolored 1.00 .80

Franz Theodor Csokor (1885-1969), Writer — A958

7s, Joseph Roth (1894-1939), writer.

1994, Sept. 9 ***Perf. 14x13½***

1660 A958 6s multicolored 1.00 .80
1661 A958 7s multicolored 1.25 1.00

Savings Banks in Austria, 175th Anniv. — A959

Photo. & Engr.

1994, Oct. 7 ***Perf. 14x13½***

1662 A959 7s Coin bank 1.25 1.00

Modern Art — A960

1994, Oct. 7 ***Perf. 13½x14***

Design: 6s, "Head," by Franz Ringel.

1663 A960 6s multicolored 1.10 .90

Austrian Working Environment — A961

1994, Nov. 18 **Photo.** ***Perf. 14***

1664 A961 6s Stewardess, child 1.10 .90

See Nos. 1690, 1703, 1736, 1773, 1828, 1859.

Richard Coudenhove Kalergi, Founder of PanEuropean Union, Birth Cent. — A962

Photo. & Engr.

1994, Nov. 18 ***Perf. 13½***

1665 A962 10s multicolored 1.90 1.50

Birth of Christ, by Anton Wollenek A963

1994, Nov. 25 ***Perf. 14***

1666 A963 6s multicolored 1.10 .90

Christmas.

Membership in European Union — A964

1995, Jan. 13 **Photo.** ***Perf. 14***

1667 A964 7s multicolored 1.25 1.00

Adolf Loos (1870-1933), Architect A965

1995, Jan. 13

1668 A965 10s House, Vienna 1.90 1.50

Official Representation for Workers, 75th Anniv. — A966

1995, Feb. 24 ***Perf. 14x13½***

1669 A966 6s multicolored 1.10 .90

Austrian Gymnastics and Sports Assoc., 50th Anniv. — A967

1995, Feb. 24

1670 A967 6s multicolored 1.10 .90

Folklore and Customs Type of 1991

Designs: 5.50s, Belt, Gailtal, Carinthia. 6s, Vineyard watchman's costume, Vienna. 7s, Bonnet, Wachau, Lower Austria.

Photo. & Engr.

1995, Mar. 24 ***Perf. 14***

1671 A892 5.50s multicolored 1.10 .90
1672 A892 6s multicolored 1.25 1.00
1673 A892 7s multicolored 1.40 1.10
Nos. 1671-1673 (3) 3.75 3.00

Second Republic, 50th Anniv. — A968

1995, Apr. 27

1674 A968 6s State seal 1.25 1.00

History of Mining & Industry A969

Design: Blast furnaces, old Heft ironworks.

1995, Apr. 28 ***Perf. 13½x14***

1675 A969 5.50s multicolored 1.10 .90

Carinthian Provincial Exhibition.

Nature Lovers Club, Cent. — A970

1995, Apr. 28 ***Perf. 14***

1676 A970 5.50s multicolored 1.10 .90

Europa — A971

1995, May 19 ***Perf. 14***

1677 A971 7s multicolored 1.50 1.25

1995 Conference of Ministers of Transportation, Vienna — A972

1995, May 26 **Photo.** ***Perf. 14***

1678 A972 7s multicolored 1.40 1.25

Bregenz Festival, 50th Anniv. A973

1995, June 9

1679 A973 6s multicolored 1.25 1.00

St. Gebhard (949-995) A974

Stained glass window, by Martin Hausle.

1995, June 9

1680 A974 7.50s multicolored 1.50 1.25

UN, 50th Anniv. — A975

1995, June 26 **Photo.** ***Perf. 14***

1681 A975 10s multicolored 2.00 2.00

Josef Loschmidt (1821-95), Chemist — A976

Photo. & Engr.

1995, June 26 ***Perf. 14x13½***

1682 A976 20s multicolored 4.00 4.00

Salzburg Festival, 75th Anniv. — A977

Photo. & Engr.

1995, Aug. 18 ***Perf. 13½x14***

1683 A977 6s multicolored 1.25 1.00

Kathe Leichter, Resistance Member, Birth Cent. — A978

1995, Aug. 18 ***Perf. 14x13½***

1684 A978 6s buff, black & red 1.25 1.00

Europaisches Landschaftsbild, by Adolf Frohner — A979

1995, Aug. 18

1685 A979 6s multicolored 1.25 1.00

Operetta Composers A980

Designs: 6s, Franz von Suppe (1819-95), scene from "The Beautiful Galathea." 7s, Nico Dostal (b. 1895), scene from "The Hungarian Wedding."

1995, Sept. 15 ***Perf. 14***

1686 A980 6s multicolored 1.25 1.00
1687 A980 7s multicolored 1.40 1.10

See Croatia No. 253.

University of Klagenfurt, 25th Anniv. — A981

1995, Oct. 6 **Photo.** ***Perf. 14***

1688 A981 5.50s multicolored 1.10 .90

Carinthian Referendum, 75th Anniv. — A982

1995, Oct. 6 **Photo. & Engr.**

1689 A982 6s multicolored 1.25 1.00

Austria Working Environment Type of 1994

1995, Oct. 20

1690 A961 6s Post office official 1.25 1.00

Composers A983

6s, Anton von Webern (1883-1945). 7s, Ludwig van Beethoven (1770-1827).

1995, Oct. 20 ***Perf. 13½x14***

1691 A983 6s orange & blue 1.25 1.00

1692 A983 7s orange & red 1.40 1.10

Christmas A984

Photo. & Engr.

1995, Dec. 1 ***Perf. 13½***

1693 A984 6s Christ Child 1.25 1.00

Folklore and Customs Type of 1991

Design: Roller and Scheller in "Procession of Masked Groups in Imst," Tyrol.

Photo. & Engr.

1996, Feb. 9 ***Perf. 14***

1694 A892 6s multicolored 1.25 1.00

Maria Theresa Academy, 250th Anniv. — A985

1996, Feb. 9

1695 A985 6s multicolored 1.25 1.00

1996 World Ski Jumping Championships A986

1996, Feb. 9 **Photo.**

1696 A986 7s multicolored 1.40 1.10

New Western Pier, Vienna Intl. Airport A987

1996, Mar. 28 **Photo.** ***Perf. 14***

1697 A987 7s multicolored 1.40 1.10

A988

6s, Mother with Child, by Peter Fendi (1796-1842). 7s, Self-portrait, by Leopold Kupelwieser (1795-1862).

1996, Mar. 29

1698 A988 6s multicolored 1.25 1.00

1699 A988 7s multicolored 1.40 1.10

Anton Bruckner (1824-96), Composer, Organist A989

Photo. & Engr.

1996, Apr. 26 ***Perf. 14***

1700 A989 5.50s Organ, music 1.10 .90

Georg Matthäus Vischer, 300th Death Anniv. A990

1996, Apr. 26

1701 A990 10s Kollmitz Castle 2.00 1.50

City of Klagenfurt, 800th Anniv. — A991

1996, May 3

1702 A991 6s Ancient square 1.25 1.00

Austrian Working Environment Type of 1994

1996, May 17

1703 A961 6s Chef, waitress 1.25 1.00

Paula von Preradovic, Author A992

1996, May 17 ***Perf. 13½x14***

1704 A992 7s black, gray & buff 1.40 1.10

Europa.

Folklore and Customs Type of 1991

Designs: 5.50s, Corpus Christi poles, Salzburg. 7s, Tyrolian riflemen.

Photo. & Engr.

1996, June 21 ***Perf. 14***

1705 A892 5.50s multicolored 1.00 .80

1706 A892 7s multicolored 1.25 1.00

1996 Summer Olympic Games, Atlanta — A993

1996, June 21

1707 A993 10s multicolored 1.90 1.50

Burgenland Province, 75th Anniv. — A994

1996, Sept. 20

1708 A994 6s multicolored 1.10 .90

Austrian Mountain Rescue Service, Cent. — A995

1996, Sept. 27

1709 A995 6s multicolored 1.10 .90

Austria Millenium A996

Designs: a, Deed by Otto III. b, Empress Maria Theresa, Josef II. c, Duke Henry II. d, 1848 Revolution. e, Rudolf IV. f, Dr. Karl Renner, 1st Republic. g, Emperor Maximilian I. h, State Treaty of 1955, 2nd Republic. i, Imperial Crown of Rudolf II. j, Austria, Europe.

Photo. & Engr.

1996, Oct. 25 ***Perf. 14***

1710 Sheet of 10 19.00 19.00

a.-b. A996 6s any single 1.10 1.10

c.-f. A996 7s any single 1.25 1.25

g.-h. A996 10s any single 1.90 1.90

i.-j. A996 20s any single 3.80 3.80

Power Station, by Reinhard Artberg A997

1996, Nov. 22

1711 A997 7s multicolored 1.25 1.25

UNICEF, 50th Anniv. — A998

1996, Nov. 22 **Photo.**

1712 A998 10s multicolored 1.90 1.90

Christmas A999

1996, Nov. 29 **Photo. & Engr.**

1713 A999 6s multicolored 1.25 1.00

Folklore and Customs Type of 1991

Epiphany Carol Singers, Burgenland.

Photo. & Engr.

1997, Jan. 17 ***Perf. 14***

1714 A892 7s multicolored 1.25 1.00

Theodor Kramer, Poet, Birth Cent. — A1000

1997, Jan. 17

1715 A1000 5.50s deep blue 1.00 .80

Austrian Academy of Sciences, 150th Anniv. — A1001

1997, Feb. 21 **Photo.** ***Perf. 14***

1716 A1001 10s multicolored 1.75 1.40

Austrian Electricity Board, 50th Anniv. A1002

1997, Mar. 21
1717 A1002 6s multicolored 1.00 .80

The Cruel Lady of Forchtenstein Castle, Burgenland A1003

Photo. & Engr.

1997, Mar. 21 ***Perf. 14***
1718 A1003 7s multicolored 1.10 .95

See #1731, 1733, 1745-1746, 1763, 1775, 1794, 1802, 1804, 1810-1811.

Erich Wolfgang Korngold (1897-1957), Composer A1004

1997, Mar. 21

Design: Scene from opera, "The Dead City."

1719 A1004 20s bl, blk & gold 3.25 1.60

Vienna Rapid, Austrian Soccer Champions — A1005

1997, Apr. 25 **Photo.** ***Perf. 14***
1720 A1005 7s multicolored 1.25 1.00

See #1754, 1779, 1807, 1839.

Deer Feeding in Wintertime A1006

1997, Apr. 25
1721 A1006 7s multicolored 1.25 1.00

See #1747, 1782, 1808, 1835.

St. Peter Canisius (1521-97) A1007

1997, Apr. 25 ***Photo. & Engr.***
1722 A1007 7.50s Canisius Altar, Innsbruck 1.25 1.10

Composers — A1008

Designs: 6s, Johannes Brahms (1833-1897). 10s, Franz Schubert (1797-1828).

1997, May 9
1723 A1008 6s gold & vio bl 1.00 .80
1724 A1008 10s purple & gold 1.75 1.40

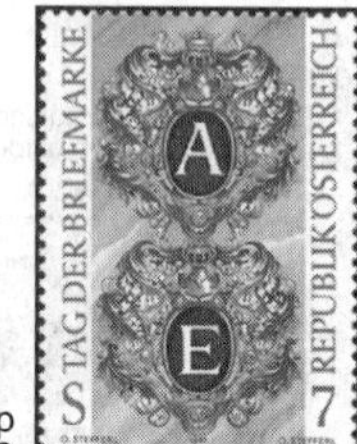

Stamp Day — A1009

1997, May 9 ***Perf. 13½***
1725 A1009 7s "A" and "E" 1.25 1.00

See #B357-B362, 1765, 1791, 1818. The 1st letters spell "Briefmarke," the 2nd "Philatelie."

Child's View of "Town Band of Bremen" A1010

1997, May 23 **Photo.**
1726 A1010 7s multicolored 1.25 1.00

Europa.

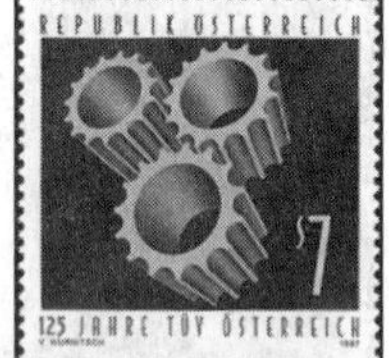

Technical Surveyance Assoc., 125th Anniv. A1011

1997, June 13 **Photo.** ***Perf. 14***
1727 A1011 7s multicolored 1.40 1.10

Railways A1012

Designs: 6s, Hochschneeberg Cog Railway. 7.50s, Wiener Neustadt-Odenburg Railway.

1997, June 13 **Photo. & Engr.**
1728 A1012 6s multicolored 1.25 .95
1729 A1012 7.50s multicolored 1.50 1.25

Folklore and Customs Type of 1991

Photo. & Engr.

1997, July 11 ***Perf. 14***
1730 A892 6.50s Marching band, Tyrol 1.25 1.00

Stories and Legends Type

Design: Dragon of Klagenfurt.

1997, July 11
1731 A1003 6.50s multicolored 1.25 1.00

Karl Heinrich Waggerl, Birth Cent. — A1013

1997, July 11
1732 A1013 7s multicolored 1.40 1.00

Stories and Legends Type of 1997

Design: Danube water nymph rescuing ferryman, Upper Austria.

Photo. & Engr.

1997, Sept. 19 ***Perf. 14***
1733 A1003 14s multicolored 2.75 2.10

1997 Orthopedics Congress, Vienna — A1014

1997, Sept. 19 **Photo.** ***Perf. 14***
1734 A1014 8s Adolph Lorenz 1.60 1.25

Vienna Agricultural University, 125th Anniv. A1015

1997, Sept. 19
1735 A1015 9s multicolored 1.75 1.40

Austrian Working Environment Type of 1994

Photo. & Engr.

1997, Oct. 17 ***Perf. 14***
1736 A961 6.50s Nurse, patient 1.25 1.00

"House in Wind," by Helmut Schickhofer — A1016

1997, Oct. 17
1737 A1016 7s multicolored 1.40 1.00

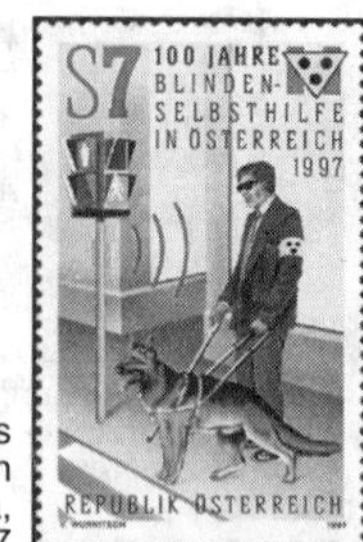

Blind Persons Assocs. in Austria, Cent. — A1017

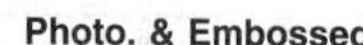

Photo. & Embossed

1997, Oct. 17
1738 A1017 7s multicolored 1.40 1.00

#1738 has embossed Braille inscription.

Dr. Thomas Klestil, Pres. of Austria, 65th birthday — A1018

Photo. & Engr.

1997, Oct. 31 ***Perf. 14x13½***
1739 A1018 7s multicolored 1.40 1.00

Oskar Werner (1922-84), Actor — A1019

1997, Oct. 31 ***Perf. 14***
1740 A1019 7s multicolored 1.40 1.00

Folklore and Customs Type of 1991

Upper Austria tower wind players, Steyr.

Photo. & Engr.

1997, Nov. 21 ***Perf. 14***
1741 A892 6.50s multicolored 1.25 1.00

Light For All Relief Organization, 25th Anniv. — A1020

1997, Nov. 28 **Photo.** ***Perf. 14***
1742 A1020 7s multicolored 1.40 1.00

Christmas A1021

Photo. & Engr.

1997, Nov. 28 ***Perf. 14***
1743 A1021 7s Mariazell Madonna 1.40 1.00

Scenery Type of 1984

Kalkalpen Natl. Park, Upper Austria.

Photo. & Engr.

1998, Jan. 23 ***Perf. 14***
1744 A679 7s multicolored 1.10 .85

Stories and Legends Type of 1997

Designs: 9s, The Charming Augustin. 13s, Pied Piper from Korneuburg.

1998, Jan. 23
1745 A1003 9s multicolored 1.40 1.00
1746 A1003 13s multicolored 2.00 1.50

Hunting and Environment Type

1998, Feb. 6 **Photo.**
1747 A1006 9s Black cocks 1.40 1.00

1998 Winter Olympic Games, Nagano — A1022

1998, Feb. 6 Photo. & Engr.
1748 A1022 14s multicolored 2.25 1.60

Lithographic Printing, Bicent. A1023

Portrait of Aloys Senefelder (1771-1834), inventor of lithography, on printing stone.

1998, Mar. 13 Litho. *Perf. 13½*
1749 A1023 7s multicolored 1.40 1.00

Joseph Binder (1898-1972), Graphic Artist — A1024

1998, Mar. 13 Photo. *Perf. 14*
1750 A1024 7s Poster 1.40 1.00

Wiener Secession, Cent. (Assoc. of Artists in Austria-Viennese Secession) A1025

1998, Mar. 13 Photo. & Engr.
1751 A1025 8s multicolored 1.60 1.25

Folklore and Customs Type of 1991

6.50s, Fiacre, Vienna. 7s, Samson figure, Palm Sunday Donkey Procession, Tyrol.

1998, Apr. 3
1752 A892 6.50s multicolored 1.25 .95
1753 A892 7s multicolored 1.40 1.00

Soccer Champions Type of 1997

1998, Apr. 17 Photo.
1754 A1005 7s Austria-Memphis Club 1.40 1.00

Salzburg Archdiocese, 1200th Anniv. A1026

1998, Apr. 17 Photo. & Engr.
1755 A1026 7s multicolored 1.40 1.00

St. Florian, Patron Saint of Fire Brigades A1027

1998, Apr. 17 Photo.
1756 A1027 7s multicolored 1.40 1.00

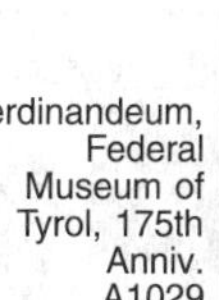

Railway Centennials A1028

No. 1757, Ybbs Railway. No. 1758, Pöstlingberg Railway. No. 1759, Pinzgau Railway.

1998 Photo. & Engr. *Perf. 14*
1757 A1028 6.50s multicolored 1.25 1.00
1758 A1028 6.50s multicolored 1.25 1.00
1759 A1028 6.50s multicolored 1.25 1.00
Nos. 1757-1759 (3) 3.75 3.00

Issued: #1757, 5/15; #1758, 6/12; #1759, 7/17.

Ferdinandeum, Federal Museum of Tyrol, 175th Anniv. A1029

1998, May 15
1760 A1029 7s multicolored 1.40 1.00

Vienna Festival Weeks — A1030

1998, May 15
1761 A1030 7s Townhall 1.40 1.00

Europa.

Folklore and Customs Type of 1991

Samson figure & the Zwergin, Lungau district, Salzburg.

1998, June 5
1762 A892 6.50s multicolored 1.25 1.00

Stories and Legends Type of 1997

Design: 25s, Saint Konrad collecting spring water in his handkerchief, Ems Castle.

1998, June 5
1763 A1003 25s multicolored 5.00 3.75

Christine Lavant, Poet, 25th Death Anniv. A1031

1998, June 5 Photo.
1764 A1031 7s multicolored 1.40 1.00

Stamp Day Type of 1997

Photo. & Engr.

1998, June 12 *Perf. 13½*
1765 A1009 7s "R" and "L" 1.40 1.00

See #1725, 1791,1818, B357-B362. The 1st letters spell "Briefmarke," the 2nd "Philatelie."

Austrian Presidency of the European Union — A1032

1998, July 1 Photo. *Perf. 13½x14*
1766 A1032 7s multicolored 1.40 1.00

The People's Opera, Vienna, 50th Anniv. & Franz Lehar (1870-1948), Composer — A1033

1998, Sept. 10 Photo. *Perf. 14*
1767 A1033 6.50s multicolored 1.25 .85

Elizabeth, Empress of Austria (1837-98) A1034

1998, Sept. 10 Photo. & Engr.
1768 A1034 7s multicolored 1.40 .90

Vienna University for Commercial Sudies, Cent. — A1035

1998, Sept. 10 Photo.
1769 A1035 7s multicolored 1.40 .90

Hans Kudlich, Emancipator of Peasants, 175th Birth Anniv. A1036

Photo. & Engr.

1998, Oct. 23 *Perf. 14*
1770 A1036 6.50s multicolored 1.25 .90

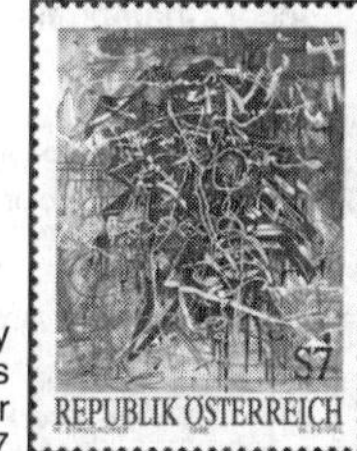

"My Garden," by Hans Staudacher A1037

1998, Oct. 23
1771 A1037 7s multicolored 1.25 .90

City of Eisenstadt, 350th Anniv. — A1038

1998, Oct. 23
1772 A1038 7s multicolored 1.25 .90

Austrian Working Environment Type of 1994

Photo. & Engr.

1998, Nov. 6 *Perf. 14*
1773 A961 6.50s Reporter, photographer 1.10 .85

Christmas A1039

1423 Fresco from Tainach/Tinje Church, Carinthia.

1998, Nov. 27
1774 A1039 7s multicolored 1.25 .85

Stories and Legends Type of 1997

The Dark Maiden of Hardegg Castle.

Photo. & Engr.

1999, Feb. 19 *Perf. 14*
1775 A1003 8s multicolored 1.25 .85

1999 Nordic Skiing World Championships, Mt. Dachstein, Ramsau A1040

1999, Feb. 19
1776 A1040 7s multicolored 1.10 .85

Scenery Type of 1984

Bohemian Forest, Upper Austria.

Photo. & Engr.

1999, Mar. 19 *Perf. 14*
1777 A679 7s multicolored 1.10 .85

Folklore and Customs Type of 1991

Traditional walking pilgrimage to Mariazell.

1999, Mar. 19
1778 A892 6.50s multicolored 1.00 .75

Soccer Champions Type of 1997

Design: Soccer Club SK Puntigamer Sturm Graz.

1999, Apr. 16 Photo. *Perf. 14*
1779 A1005 7s multicolored 1.10 .85

Schönnbrun Palace, UNESCO World Heritage Site — A1041

Photo. & Engr.

1999, Apr. 16 *Perf. 14*
1780 A1041 13s multicolored 2.00 1.50

See No. 1845.

Austrian Patent Office, Cent. — A1042

1999, Apr. 16
1781 A1042 7s multicolored 1.10 .85

Hunting and Environment Type of 1997

1999, May 7 Litho. *Perf. 14*
1782 A1006 6.50s Partridges 1.00 .75

Austrian General Sport Federation, 50th Anniv. A1043

1999, May 7 Engr. *Perf. 14*
1783 A1043 7s multicolored 1.10 .80

Council of Europe, 50th Anniv. A1044

1999, May 7 Photo. *Perf. 13½x14*
1784 A1044 14s multicolored 2.25 1.60

Karl Jenschke (1899-1969), Automobile Designer A1045

1999, May 28
1785 A1045 7s Steyr automobile 1.10 .80

Marble Relief of St. Martin A1046

Photo. & Engr.

1999, May 28 *Perf. 14*
1786 A1046 8s multicolored 1.25 .95

See Nos. 1787, 1817, 1830, 1851-1852.

Religious Art Type

Design: 9s, St. Anne, Mary and Jesus.

Photo. & Engr.

1999, Sept. 17 *Perf. 13¾*
1787 A1046 9s multicolored 1.40 1.10

Austrian Social Welfare Service, 125th Anniv. A1047

1999, June 4 Litho. *Perf. 13¾*
1788 A1047 7s multicolored 1.10 .80

Johann Strauss, the Younger (1825-99), Composer A1048

8s, Johann Strauss, the Elder (1804-49).

1999, June 4 Photo. & Engr.
1789 A1048 7s multicolored 1.10 .80
1790 A1048 8s multicolored 1.25 .95

Stamp Day Type of 1997

1999, June 18 *Perf. 13½*
1791 A1009 7s "K" and "I" 1.10 .80

See #1725, 1765, 1818, B357-B362. The 1st letters spell "Briefmarke," the 2nd "Philatelie."

Donau-Auen Natl. Park — A1049

1999, June 18 *Perf. 13¾*
1792 A1049 7s multicolored 1.10 .80

Europa.

Natl. Gendarmery, 150th Anniv. — A1050

1999, June 18
1793 A1050 7s multicolored 1.10 .80

Stories and Legends Type of 1997

Design: The Holy Notburga.

Photo. & Engr.

1999, Aug. 27 *Perf. 13¾x14*
1794 A1003 20s multicolored 3.25 2.50

Graz Opera House, 100th Anniv. — A1051

Photo. & Engr.

1999, Sept. 17 *Perf. 13¾*
1795 A1051 6.50s multicolored 1.00 .75

International Year of Older Persons — A1052

1999, Sept. 17 *Perf. 13¾*
1796 A1052 7s multicolored 1.10 .85

Federation of Austrian Trade Unions, 14th Congress A1053

1999, Oct. 15 Litho. *Perf. 13¾*
1797 A1053 6.50s multicolored 1.00 .75

"Caffee Girardi," by Wolfgang Herzig — A1054

Photo. & Engr.

1999, Oct. 22 *Perf. 13¾x14*
1798 A1054 7s multicolored 1.10 .85

Folklore & Customs Type of 1991

7s, The Pummerin, Bell in St. Stephen's Cathedral, Vienna. 8s, Pumpkin Festival, Lower Austria.

1999 Photo. & Engr. *Perf. 13¾*
1799 A892 7s multicolored 1.10 .85
1800 A892 8s multicolored 1.25 .95

Issued: 8s, 10/22; 7s, 11/12.

National Institute of Geology, 150th Anniv. A1055

Photo. & Engr.

1999, Nov. 12 *Perf. 13¾x14*
1801 A1055 7s multicolored 1.10 .85

Stories & Legends Type of 1997

Design: 32s, Discovery of Erzberg.

Photo. & Engr.

1999, Nov. 12 *Perf. 13¾x14*
1802 A1003 32s multicolored 5.00 3.75

Christmas A1056

Photo. & Engr.

1999, Nov. 26 *Perf. 13¾*
1803 A1056 7s Pinkafeld creche 1.10 .85

Stories & Legends Type of 1997

Design: 10s, House of the Basilisk, Vienna.

Photo. & Engr.

2000, Jan. 21 *Perf. 13¾x14*
1804 A1003 10s multi 1.40 1.00
a. Souvenir sheet of 1 13.00 9.50

No. 1804a was sold only with the purchase of an 80s ticket to the Vienna Intl. Philatelic Exhibition.

Folklore & Customs Type of 1991

Designs: 6.50s, Schleicherlaufen Festival, Telfs. 7s, Carrying miniature churches, Bad Eisenkappel.

2000 Photo. & Engr. *Perf. 13¾*
1805 A892 6.50s multi .90 .65
1806 A892 7s multi 1.00 .75

Issued: 6.50s, 1/21; 7s, 2/11.

Soccer Champions Type of 1997

Design: Tirol Soccer Club.

2000, Mar. 3 Photo. *Perf. 13¾*
1807 A1005 7s multi 1.00 .75

Hunting and Environment Type of 1997

2000, Mar. 3 *Perf. 14x14¼*
1808 A1006 7s Ibex 1.00 .75

Intl. Gardening Exhibition, Graz — A1057

Photo. & Embossed

2000, Mar. 3 *Perf. 13½x13¾*
1809 A1057 7s multi 1.00 .75

Stories & Legends Type of 1997

Designs: 22s, The Witch's Ride. 23s, The Bread Loaf Monument.

2000 Photo. & Engr. *Perf. 13¾x14*
1810 A1003 22s multi 3.00 2.25
1811 A1003 23s multi 3.00 2.25

Issued: 22s, 4/28. 23s, 6/16.

First Ascent of Grossglockner, Bicent. A1058

2000, Apr. 28 *Perf. 13¾*
1812 A1058 7s multi .95 .70

Scenery Type of 1984

Design: Sonnblick Glacier, Granatspitze, Weisssee, Salzburg.

2000, May 9 **Perf. 13¾x14**
1813 A679 7s multi .95 .70

Europa, 2000
Common Design Type

2000, May 9 Photo. Perf. 14¼x13½
1814 CD17 7s multi .95 .70

Klagenfurt Airport, 75th Anniv. A1059

2000, May 19 **Perf. 13¾**
1815 A1059 7s multi .95 .70

Protection of Historical Monuments, 150th Anniv. — A1060

Photo. & Engr.

2000, May 19 **Perf. 14x13¼**
1816 A1060 8s multi 1.10 .80

Religious Art Type of 1999

Design: 9s, Illustration of St. Malachy from book, *The Life of Bishop Malachy.*

2000, May 19 **Perf. 13¾**
1817 A1046 9s multi 1.25 .90

Stamp Day Type of 1997

2000, May 30 **Perf. 13½**
1818 A1009 7s "E" and "E" .95 .70

See #1725, 1765, 1791, B357-B362. The 1st letters spell "Briefmarke," the 2nd "Philatelie."

Austrian Postage Stamps, 150th Anniv. A1061

2000, May 30 **Perf. 13¾**
1819 A1061 7s Nos. 5, 1818 .95 .70

Children's Television Character, Confetti A1062

2000, May 31
1820 A1062 7s multi .95 .70

See No. 1841.

Blue Blues, by Friedensreich Hundertwasser (1928-2000), Artist — A1063

Colors of seven solid vertical panels at top: a, Silver. b, Red. c, Red violet. d, Black.

2000, June 2
1821 Sheet of 4 4.00 3.00
a.-d. A1063 7s Any single .95 .70

Discovery of Human Blood Types, Cent. A1064

Perf. 13¾x13½

2000, June 16 **Photo.**
1822 A1064 8s multi 1.10 .80

Scheduled Motorized Vehicle Passenger Transportation, Cent. — A1065

Photo. & Engr.

2000, June 16 **Perf. 14**
1823 A1065 9s multi 1.25 .90

Folklore & Customs Type of 1991

7s, Intl. meeting of rafters, Carinthia.

Photo. & Engr.

2000, Aug. 25 **Perf. 13¾**
1824 A892 7s multi .85 .65

Vienna Philharmonic Orchestra, Cent. — A1066

2000, Sept. 15
1825 A1066 7s multi .85 .65

Hallstatt-Dachstein and Salzkammergut World Heritage Site — A1067

World Heritage Site Type of 1999

Hallstatt-Dachstein and Salzkammergut

2000, Sept. 15
1826 A1067 7s multi .85 .65

2000 Summer Olympics, Sydney — A1068

2000, Sept. 15 **Perf. 14x13¾**
1827 A1068 9s multi 1.10 .80

Working Environment Type of 1994

2000, Sept. 29
1828 A961 6.50s Papermaker, printer .80 .60

Turf Turkey, by Ida Szigethy A1069

2000, Oct. 13 **Perf. 13¾**
1829 A1069 7s multi .85 .65

Religious Art Type of 1999

Design: 8s, Illuminated text, Codex 965.

2000, Oct. 13
1830 A1046 8s multi 1.00 .75

Association of Austrian Adult Education Centers, 50th Anniv. A1070

Photo. & Engr.

2000, Nov. 24 **Perf. 13¾**
1831 A1070 7s multi .95 .75

Vaccinations in Austria, Bicent. — A1071

2000, Nov. 24 **Perf. 14¼x13½**
1832 A1071 7s multi .95 .75

Christmas A1072

Altar sidewing, St. Martin's Church, Ludesch.

2000, Dec. 1 **Perf. 13¾**
1833 A1072 7s multi .95 .75

2001 Alpine Skiing World Championships, St. Anton am Arlberg — A1073

2000, Dec. 15 **Perf. 14x13¾**
1834 A1073 7s multi .95 .75

Hunting & Environment Type of 1997

2001, Feb. 16 Photo. Perf. 14x14¼
1835 A1006 7s Ducks .90 .65

Folklore & Customs Type of 1991

Designs: No. 1836, Lenten altar cloths, Eastern Tyrol. No. 1837, Water disk shooting, Prebersee. No. 1838, Boat Mill, Mureck.

Photo. & Engr.

2001, May 4 **Perf. 13¾**
1836 A892 7s multi .90 .65
1837 A892 7s multi .95 .65
1838 A892 8s multi 1.10 .85

Issued: No. 1836, 5/4/01. No. 1838, 3/30/01. No. 1837, 8/24/01.

Soccer Champions Type of 1997

2001, Mar. 30 Photo. Perf. 13¾
1839 A1005 7s Wustenrot Salzburg .90 .65

Zillertal Railway, Cent. A1074

Photo. & Engr.

2001, Mar. 30 **Perf. 13¾**
1840 A1074 7s multi .90 .65

Children's Television Character Type of 2000

2001, Apr. 20 Photo. Perf. 13¾
1841 A1062 7s Rolf Rüdiger .90 .65

Salzburg Airport, 75th Anniv. A1075

Photo. & Engr.

2001, Apr. 20 **Perf. 13½x14¼**
1842 A1075 14s multi 1.90 1.40

Scenery Type of 1984

Design: Bärenschützkamm, Styria.

Photo. & Engr.

2001, May 4 **Perf. 13¾**
1843 A679 7s multi .90 .65

Europa A1076

2001, May 18 Photo. Perf. 13¾
1844 A1076 15s multi 1.90 1.40

UNESCO World Heritage Type of 1999

Design: Semmering Railway.

Photo. & Engr.

2001, June 8 ***Perf. 13¾***
1845 A1041 35s multi 4.50 3.50

Austrian Aero Club, Cent. — A1077

2001, June 8 ***Perf. 13¾x14***
1846 A1077 7s multi .90 .65

UN High Commissioner for Refugees, 50th Anniv. — A1078

2001, June 8 ***Perf. 14x13¾***
1847 A1078 21s multi 2.60 2.00

7th IVV Hiking Olympics A1079

2001, June 22 **Photo.** ***Perf. 13¾***
1848 A1079 7s multi .90 .65

Military Post Offices Abroad A1080

2001, June 22
1849 A1080 7s multi .90 .65

Conversion of East-West Railway to Four Tracks A1081

Photo. & Engr.

2001, Aug. 31 ***Perf. 13¾***
1850 A1081 7s multi .95 .65

Religious Art Type of 1999

Designs: 7s, Church vestment cut from Turkish tent, 1683. 10s, Pluvial.

2001 **Photo. & Engr.** ***Perf. 13¾***
1851 A1046 7s multi .95 .65
1852 A1046 10s multi 1.40 .95

Issued: 7s, 10/5; 10s, 9/14.

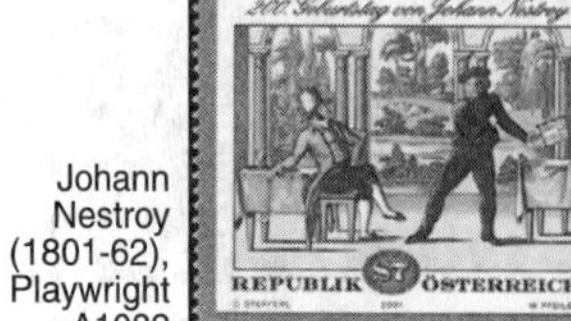

Johann Nestroy (1801-62), Playwright A1082

2001, Sept. 14
1853 A1082 7s multi .95 .65

The Continents (Detail), by Helmut Leherb — A1083

2001, Sept. 14
1854 A1083 7s multi .95 .65

Joseph Ritter von Führich (1800-76), Painter — A1084

2001, Sept. 14 ***Perf. 14***
1855 A1084 8s multi 1.10 .75

Leopold Ludwig Döbler (1801-64), Magician A1085

2001, Oct. 5
1856 A1085 7s multi .95 .65

Meteorology and Geodynamics Institute, 150th Anniv. — A1086

2001, Oct. 5
1857 A1086 12s multi 1.60 1.10

Cat King, by Manfred Deix — A1087

2001, Oct. 5 ***Perf. 13¾***
1858 A1087 19s multi 2.50 1.60

Working Environment Type of 1994

2001, Oct. 16 ***Perf. 14***
1859 A961 7s Public servants .95 .65

Christmas A1088

Photo. & Engr.

2001, Nov. 30 ***Perf. 14***
1860 A1088 7s multi .90 .65

100 Cents = 1 Euro (")

Introduction of the Euro — A1089

Photo. & Embossed with Foil Application

2002, Jan. 1 ***Perf. 13½x13¾***
1861 A1089 "3.27 multi 5.75 4.00

Austrian Scenes — A1090

Designs: 51c, Schönlaterngasse, Vienna. 58c, Street, Hadres. 73c, Farmhouse, Salzburg Province. 87c, Cow in pasture, Tyrol Province. "2.03, Stations of the Cross, Lower Austria Province.

2002, Jan. 1 **Photo.** ***Perf. 13¾x14***
1867 A1090 51c multi .90 .65
1869 A1090 58c multi 1.00 .70
1872 A1090 73c multi 1.25 .90
1875 A1090 87c multi 1.50 1.10
1879 A1090 "2.03 multi 3.50 2.50
Nos. 1867-1879 (5) 8.15 5.85

This is an expanding set. Numbers may change.

2002 Winter Olympics, Salt Lake City — A1091

Photo. & Engr.

2002, Feb. 8 ***Perf. 14x13¾***
1882 A1091 73c multi 1.25 .90

Love — A1092

2002, Feb. 14 **Photo.** ***Perf. 14¼x14***
1883 A1092 87c multi 1.50 1.10

Intl. Women's Day — A1093

2002, Mar. 8 ***Perf. 13¾***
1884 A1093 51c multi .90 .65

Promotion of Youth Philately — A1094

Cartoon characters: No. 1885, Girls Mel and Lucy. No. 1886, Sisco and Mauritius (boy and dog). No. 1887, Edison and Gogo (girl and boy).

2002 **Photo.** ***Perf. 14x13¾***
1885 A1094 58c multi 1.00 .70
1886 A1094 58c multi 1.10 .75
1887 A1094 58c multi 1.25 .85
Nos. 1885-1887 (3) 3.35 2.30

Issued: No. 1885, 4/5. No. 1886, 5/10. No. 1887, 11/22.

Roses — A1095

2002, Apr. 5 **Photo.** ***Perf. 14x13¾***
1888 A1095 58c multi 1.00 .70

80th Anniversary of Marianneum, by Alfred Kubin — A1096

2002, Apr. 10 ***Perf. 13½x13¾***
1889 A1096 87c black & buff 1.50 1.10

Caritas — A1097

2002, Apr. 26
1890 A1097 51c multi .95 .70

Europa A1098

2002, May 3 ***Perf. 13¾***
1891 A1098 87c multi 1.60 1.10

Lilienfeld Monastery, 800th Anniv. A1099

Photo. & Engr.

2002, May 17 ***Perf. 13¾***
1892 A1099 " 2.03 multi 3.75 2.60

Children's Television Character Type of 2000

2002, May 23 Photo. ***Perf. 13¾***
1893 A1062 51c Mimi .95 .70

Souvenir Sheet

Schönnbrunn Zoo, 250th Anniv. — A1100

No. 1894: a, Orangutan, leopard, lioness, zebras. b, Various birds. c, Lion, antelope, turtle, crocodile, jellyfish. d, Antelope, elephant, birds, jellyfish, fish, ray.

Photo. & Engr.

2002, June 3 ***Perf. 13½x14¼***
1894 A1100 Sheet of 4 6.25 4.50
a. 51c multi .95 .70
b. 58c multi 1.10 .75
c. 87c multi 1.60 1.10
d. " 1.38 multi 2.60 1.90

Teddy Bears, Cent. — A1101

2002, June 4 Photo. ***Perf. 14¼x14***
1895 A1101 51c multi .95 .70

Crystal Cup from Innsbruck Glassworks A1102

Photo. & Engr.

2002, June 21 ***Perf. 13¾***
1896 A1102 " 1.60 multi 3.25 2.25

Traditional arts and crafts.

Chair by Michael Thonet, 1860 — A1103

2002, June 21 **Photo.**
1897 A1103 " 1.38 multi 2.75 1.90

Austrian design.

Museum of Contemporary Art, Vienna — A1104

2002, Sept. 4 Photo. ***Perf. 14x13¾***
1898 A1104 58c multi 1.10 .85

Austrians Living Abroad — A1105

Photo. & Engr.

2002, Sept. 5 ***Perf. 13¾x14***
1899 A1105 " 2.47 multi 4.75 3.50

Clown Doctor A1106

2002, Sept. 10 Photo. ***Perf. 13¾***
1900 A1106 51c multi 1.00 .75

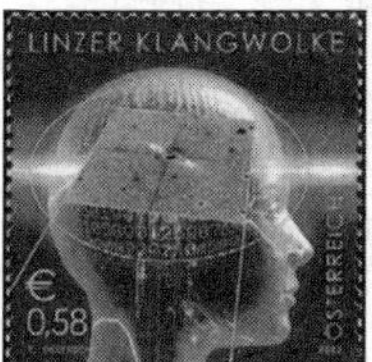

Linz "Sound Cloud" A1107

2002, Sept. 13
1901 A1107 58c multi 1.10 .85

OAF Gräf & Stift Type 40/45 Automobile A1108

2002, Sept. 27
1902 A1108 51c multi 1.00 .75

Pet Type of 2001

Design: Dog King, by Manfred Deix.

2002, Oct. 4 Photo. ***Perf. 13¾***
1903 A1087 51c multi 1.00 .75

Train at Vienna South Railway Station A1109

2002, Oct. 4 **Photo. & Engr.**
1904 A1109 51c multi 1.00 .75

Schützenhaus, by Otto Wagner — A1110

2002, Oct. 11
1905 A1110 51c multi 1.00 .75

Souvenir Sheet

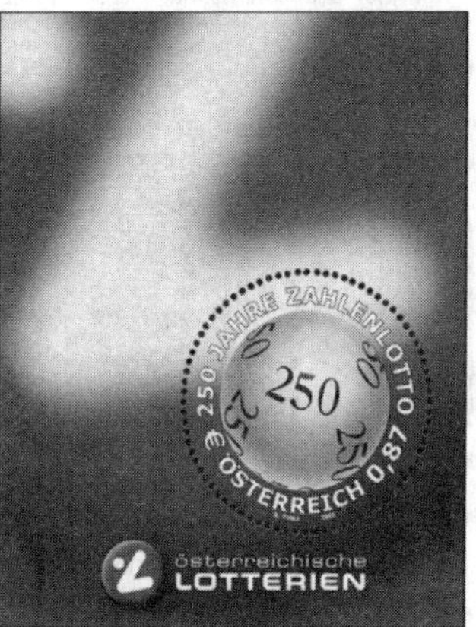

National Lottery, 250th Anniv. — A1111

2002, Oct. 17 Photo. ***Perf.***
1906 A1111 87c multi 1.75 1.40

Thayatal Natl. Park A1112

Photo. & Engr.

2002, Oct. 25 ***Perf. 13¾***
1907 A1112 58c multi 1.10 .85

Puch 175 SV Motorcycle A1113

2002, Nov. 8 Photo. ***Perf. 14x13¾***
1908 A1113 58c multi 1.25 .85

One Eye, by Wolfgang Homola A1114

2002, Nov. 15 ***Perf. 13¾***
1909 A1114 " 1.38 multi 2.75 1.90

Austrian design.

Christmas A1115

Photo. & Engr.

2002, Nov. 29 ***Perf. 14x14¼***
1910 A1115 51c multi 1.00 .70

SEMI-POSTAL STAMPS

Issues of the Monarchy

Emperor Franz Josef — SP1

Perf. 12½

1914, Oct. 4 Typo. Unwmk.
B1 SP1 5h green .20 *.30*
B2 SP1 10h rose .20 *.35*
Set, never hinged 1.10

Nos. B1-B2 were sold at an advance of 2h each over face value. Exist imperf.; value, set $50.

The Firing Step — SP2

1915, May 1

Designs: 5h+2h, Cavalry. 10h+2h, Siege gun. 20h+3h, Battleship. 35h+3h, Airplane.

B3 SP2 3h + 1h violet brn .20 *.40*
B4 SP2 5h + 2h green .20 .20
B5 SP2 10h + 2h deep rose .20 .20
B6 SP2 20h + 3h Prus blue .45 *2.10*
B7 SP2 35h + 3h ultra 2.10 *4.25*
Nos. B3-B7 (5) 3.15 *7.15*
Set, never hinged 9.00

Exist imperf. Value, set $110.

Issues of the Republic

Types of Austria, 1919-20, Overprinted in Black

1920, Sept. 16 ***Perf. 12½***
B11 A44 5h gray, *yellow* .45 *1.25*
B12 A44 10h red, *pink* .35 *1.00*
B13 A43 15h bister, *yel* .25 *.75*
B14 A45 20h dark grn, *bl* .25 *.60*
B15 A43 25h violet, *pink* .25 *.65*
B16 A45 30h brown, *buff* 1.25 *2.50*
B17 A45 40h carmine, *yel* .25 *.70*
B18 A45 50h dark bl, *blue* .25 *.55*

B19	A43	60h ol grn, *azure*	1.25	*2.50*
B20	A47	80h red	.30	*.65*
B21	A47	1k orange brown	.35	*.75*
B22	A47	2k pale blue	.35	*.75*

Granite Paper

Imperf

B23	A46	2½k brown red	.35	*.90*
B24	A46	3k dk blue & green	.45	*1.10*
B25	A46	4k carmine & violet	.55	*1.40*
B26	A46	5k blue	.60	*1.10*
B27	A46	7½k yellow green	.60	*1.10*
B28	A46	10k gray grn & red	.60	*1.25*
B29	A46	20k lilac & orange	.65	*1.75*
		Nos. B11-B29 (19)	9.35	*21.25*
		Set, never hinged	19.00	

Carinthia Plebiscite. Sold at three times face value for the benefit of the Plebiscite Propaganda Fund.

Nos. B11-B19 exist imperf. Values, set unused hinged $120, never hinged $150.

Types of Regular Issues of 1919-21 Overprinted

1921, Mar. 1 ***Perf. 12½***

B30	A44	5h gray, *yellow*	.25	*.45*
B31	A44	10h orange brown	.25	*.45*
B32	A43	15h gray	.25	*.45*
B33	A45	20h green, *yellow*	.25	*.45*
B34	A43	25h blue, *yellow*	.25	*.45*
B35	A45	30h violet, *bl*	.45	*.90*
B36	A45	40h org brn, *pink*	.50	*1.25*
B37	A45	50h green, *blue*	1.10	*2.10*
B38	A43	60h lilac, *yellow*	.35	*.90*
B39	A47	80h pale blue	.40	*.80*
B40	A47	1k red org, *blue*	.35	*.75*
B41	A47	1½k green, *yellow*	.20	*.40*
B42	A47	2k lilac brown	.20	*.40*

Overprinted

B43	A46	2½k light blue	.25	*.45*
B44	A46	3k ol grn & brn red	.25	*.45*
B45	A46	4k lilac & orange	.70	*1.50*
B46	A46	5k olive green	.25	*.55*
B47	A46	7½k brown red	.25	*.65*
B48	A46	10k blue & olive grn	.25	*.65*
B49	A46	20k car rose & vio	.45	*1.00*
		Nos. B30-B49 (20)	7.20	*15.00*
		Set, never hinged	13.00	

Nos. B30-B49 were sold at three times face value, the excess going to help flood victims.

Exists imperf. Values, set unused hinged $175, never hinged $225.

Franz Joseph Haydn — SP9

Musicians: 5k, Mozart. 7½k, Beethoven. 10k, Schubert. 25k, Anton Bruckner. 50k, Johann Strauss (son). 100k, Hugo Wolf.

1922, Apr. 24 **Engr.** ***Perf. 12½***

B50	SP9	2½k brown, perf. 11½	6.00	*10.50*
a.		Perf. 12½	7.25	*12.00*
		Never hinged	17.50	
B51	SP9	5k dark blue	1.10	*1.50*
B52	SP9	7½k black	1.40	*2.50*
a.		Perf. 11½	90.00	*140.00*
		Never hinged	150.00	
B53	SP9	10k dark violet	1.90	*3.00*
a.		Perf. 11½	2.50	*5.25*
		Never hinged	5.50	
B54	SP9	25k dark green	3.75	*6.50*
a.		Perf. 11½	4.25	*8.25*
		Never hinged	10.50	
B55	SP9	50k claret	2.10	*3.00*
B56	SP9	100k brown olive	7.00	*8.75*
a.		Perf. 11½	8.00	*17.50*
		Never hinged	21.00	
		Nos. B50-B56 (7)	23.25	*35.75*
		Set, never hinged	47.50	

These stamps were sold at 10 times face value, the excess being given to needy musicians.

All values exist imperf. on both regular and handmade papers. Values, set unused hinged $350, never hinged $425.

A 1969 souvenir sheet without postal validity contains reprints of the 5k in black, 7½k in claret and 50k in dark blue, each overprinted "NEUDRUCK" in black at top. It was issued for the Vienna State Opera Centenary Exhibition.

View of Bregenz — SP16

Designs: 120k, Mirabelle Gardens, Salzburg. 160k, Church at Eisenstadt. 180k, Assembly House, Klagenfurt. 200k, "Golden Roof," Innsbruck. 240k, Main Square, Linz. 400k, Castle Hill, Graz. 600k, Abbey at Melk. 1000k, Upper Belvedere, Vienna.

1923, May 22 ***Perf. 12½***

Various Frames

B57	SP16	100k dk green	2.75	*5.50*
B58	SP16	120k deep blue	2.50	*5.00*
B59	SP16	160k dk violet	2.50	*5.00*
B60	SP16	180k red violet	2.50	*5.00*
B61	SP16	200k lake	2.50	*5.00*
B62	SP16	240k red brown	2.50	*5.00*
B63	SP16	400k dark brown	2.50	*5.00*
B64	SP16	600k olive brn	2.75	*7.00*
B65	SP16	1000k black	4.00	*8.75*
		Nos. B57-B65 (9)	24.50	*51.25*
		Set, never hinged	55.00	

Nos. B57-B65 were sold at five times face value, the excess going to needy artists.

All values exist imperf. on both regular and handmade papers. Values, set hinged $325, never hinged $400.

Feebleness SP25

Siegfried Slays the Dragon SP30

Designs: 300k+900k, Aid to industry. 500k+1500k, Orphans and widow. 600k+1800k, Indigent old man. 1000k+3000k, Alleviation of hunger.

1924, Sept. 6 **Photo.**

B66	SP25	100k + 300k yel green	3.25	*6.25*
B67	SP25	300k + 900k red brn	4.50	*8.25*
B68	SP25	500k + 1500k brn vio	4.50	*8.25*
B69	SP25	600k + 1800k pck bl	4.50	*13.00*
B70	SP25	1000k + 3000k brn org	7.50	*14.50*
		Nos. B66-B70 (5)	24.25	*50.25*
		Set, never hinged	45.00	

The surtax was for child welfare and anti-tuberculosis work. Set exists imperf. Values, set unused hinged $350, never hinged $425.

1926, Mar. 8 **Engr.**

Designs: 8g+2g, Gunther's voyage to Iceland. 15g+5g, Brunhild accusing Kriemhild. 20g+5g, Nymphs telling Hagen the future. 24g+6g, Rudiger von Bechelaren welcomes the Nibelungen. 40g+10g, Dietrich von Bern vanquishes Hagen.

B71	SP30	3g + 2g olive blk	1.10	*.65*
B72	SP30	8g + 2g indigo	.30	*.35*
B73	SP30	15g + 5g dk claret	.30	*.35*
B74	SP30	20g + 5g olive grn	.45	*.75*
B75	SP30	24g + 6g dk violet	.45	*.75*
B76	SP30	40g + 10g red brn	3.00	*3.75*
		Nos. B71-B76 (6)	5.60	*6.60*
		Set, never hinged	12.00	

Nibelungen issue.

Nos. B71-B76 were printed in two sizes: 27½x28½mm and 28½x27½mm.

The surtax was for child welfare. Set exists imperf. Values, set unused hinged $250, never hinged $325.

Pres. Michael Hainisch SP36

Pres. Wilhelm Miklas SP37

1928, Nov. 5

B77	SP36	10g dark brown	5.00	*9.00*
B78	SP36	15g red brown	5.00	*9.00*
B79	SP36	30g black	5.00	*9.00*
B80	SP36	40g indigo	5.00	*9.00*
		Nos. B77-B80 (4)	20.00	*36.00*
		Set, never hinged	30.00	

Tenth anniversary of Austrian Republic. Sold at double face value, the premium aiding war orphans and children of war invalids.

Set exists imperf. Values, set unused hinged $250, never hinged $325.

1930, Oct. 4

B81	SP37	10g light brown	7.50	*14.50*
B82	SP37	20g red	7.50	*14.50*
B83	SP37	30g brown violet	7.50	*14.50*
B84	SP37	40g indigo	7.50	*14.50*
B85	SP37	50g dark green	7.50	*14.50*
B86	SP37	1s black brown	7.50	*14.50*
		Nos. B81-B86 (6)	45.00	*87.00*
		Set, never hinged	80.00	

Nos. B81-B86 were sold at double face value. The excess aided the anti-tuberculosis campaign and the building of sanatoria in Carinthia.

Set exists imperf. Values, set unused hinged $450, never hinged $550.

Regular Issue of 1929-30 Overprinted in Various Colors

1931, June 20

B87	A56	10g bister (Bl)	32.50	*42.50*
B88	A56	20g dk gray (R)	32.50	*42.50*
B89	A56	30g dk violet (Gl)	32.50	*42.50*
B90	A56	40g dk blue (Gl)	32.50	*42.50*
B91	A56	50g gray vio (O)	32.50	*42.50*
B92	A57	1s black brn (Bk)	32.50	*42.50*
		Nos. B87-B92 (6)	195.00	*255.00*
		Set, never hinged	475.00	

Rotary convention, Vienna.

Nos. B87 to B92 were sold at double their face values. The excess was added to the beneficent funds of Rotary International.

Exists imperf.

Ferdinand Raimund — SP38

Poets: 20g, Franz Grillparzer. 30g, Johann Nestroy. 40g, Adalbert Stifter. 50g, Ludwig Anzengruber. 1s, Peter Rosegger.

1931, Sept. 12

B93	SP38	10g dark violet	12.00	*21.00*
B94	SP38	20g gray black	12.00	*21.00*
B95	SP38	30g orange red	12.00	*21.00*
B96	SP38	40g dull blue	12.00	*21.00*
B97	SP38	50g gray green	12.00	*21.00*
B98	SP38	1s yellow brown	12.00	*21.00*
		Nos. B93-B98 (6)	72.00	*126.00*
		Set, never hinged	110.00	

Nos. B93-B98 were sold at double face value. The surtax aided unemployed young people.

Set exists imperf. Values, set unused hinged $450, never hinged $550.

Chancellor Ignaz Seipel SP44

Ferdinand Georg Waldmüller SP45

1932, Oct. 12 ***Perf. 13***

B99	SP44	50g ultra	9.00	*17.50*
		Never hinged	16.00	

Msgr. Ignaz Seipel, Chancellor of Austria, 1922-29. Sold at double face value, the excess aiding wounded veterans of World War I.

Exists imperf. Values, unused hinged $150, never hinged $200.

1932, Nov. 21

Artists: 24g, Moritz von Schwind. 30g, Rudolf von Alt. 40g, Hans Makart. 64g, Gustav Klimt. 1s, Albin Egger-Lienz.

B100	SP45	12g slate green	17.00	*30.00*
B101	SP45	24g dp violet	17.00	*30.00*
B102	SP45	30g dark red	17.00	*30.00*
B103	SP45	40g dark gray	17.00	*30.00*
B104	SP45	64g dark brown	17.00	*30.00*
B105	SP45	1s claret	17.00	*30.00*
		Nos. B100-B105 (6)	102.00	*180.00*
		Set, never hinged	160.00	

Nos. B100 to B105 were sold at double their face values. The surtax was for the assistance of charitable institutions.

Set exists imperf. Values, set unused hinged $575, never hinged $725.

Mountain Climbing SP51

Designs: 24g, Ski gliding. 30g, Walking on skis. 50g, Ski jumping.

1933, Jan. 9 **Photo.** ***Perf. 12½***

B106	SP51	12g dark green	7.00	*11.50*
B107	SP51	24g dark violet	67.50	*95.00*
B108	SP51	30g brown red	12.50	*17.50*
B109	SP51	50g dark blue	67.50	*95.00*
		Nos. B106-B109 (4)	154.50	*219.00*
		Set, never hinged	300.00	

Meeting of the Intl. Ski Federation, Innsbruck, Feb. 8-13.

These stamps were sold at double their face value. The surtax was for the benefit of "Youth in Distress."

#B106-B109 exist imperf. Values, set unused hinged $1,200, never hinged $1,500.

Stagecoach, after Painting by Moritz von Schwind — SP55

1933, June 23 **Engr.** ***Perf. 12½***

Ordinary Paper

B110	SP55	50g deep ultra	150.00	*190.00*
		Never hinged	225.00	
a.		Granite paper	300.00	*425.00*
		Never hinged	450.00	

Sheets of 25.

Nos. B110 and B110a exist imperf. Values, unused hinged $675 and $1,350, never hinged $825 and $1,600.

Souvenir Sheet

Perf. 12

Granite Paper

B111		Sheet of 4	2,000.	*2,750.*
		Never hinged	2,500.	
a.		SP55 50g deep ultra	400.	*550.*
		Never hinged	525.	

Intl. Phil. Exhib., Vienna, 1933. In addition to the postal value of 50g the stamp was sold at a premium of 50g for charity and of 1.60s for the admission fee to the exhibition.

Size of No. B111: 126x103mm.

A 50g dark red in souvenir sheet, with dark blue overprint ("NEUDRUCK WIPA 1965"), had no postal validity.

Even though the margins No. B111 have no gum, the sheet sells for a premium when definitely never hinged.

No. B111 exists imperf. Value, unused $12,500.

St. Stephen's Cathedral in 1683 — SP56

Marco d'Aviano, Papal Legate — SP57

Designs: 30g, Count Ernst Rudiger von Starhemberg. 40g, John III Sobieski, King of Poland. 50g, Karl V, Duke of Lorraine. 64g, Burgomaster Johann Andreas von Liebenberg.

1933, Sept. 6 Photo. *Perf. 12½*

B112 SP56 12g dark green 21.00 *27.50*
B113 SP57 24g dark violet 19.00 *26.00*
B114 SP57 30g brown red 19.00 *26.00*
B115 SP57 40g blue black 27.50 *42.50*
B116 SP57 50g dark blue 19.00 *26.00*
B117 SP57 64g olive brown 24.00 *37.50*
Nos. B112-B117 (6) 129.50 *185.50*
Set, never hinged 240.00

Deliverance of Vienna from the Turks, 250th anniv., and Pan-German Catholic Congress, Sept. 6, 1933.

The stamps were sold at double their face value, the excess being for the aid of Catholic works of charity.

Set exists imperf. Values, set unused hinged $850, never hinged $1,050.

Types of Regular Issue of 1925-30 Surcharged:

a

b

c

1933, Dec. 15

B118 A52(a) 5g + 2g ol grn .25 *.55*
B119 A56(b) 12g + 3g lt blue .25 *.70*
B120 A56(b) 24g + 6g brn org .25 *.60*
B121 A57(c) 1s + 50g org red 25.00 *40.00*
Nos. B118-B121 (4) 25.75 *41.85*
Set, never hinged 42.50

Winterhelp. Exists imperf. Values, set unused hinged $525, never hinged $650.

Anton Pilgram — SP62

Architects: 24g, J. B. Fischer von Erlach. 30g, Jakob Prandtauer. 40g, A. von Siccardsburg & E. van der Null. 60g, Heinrich von Ferstel. 64g, Otto Wagner.

1934, Dec. 2 Engr. *Perf. 12½*

Thick Yellowish Paper

B122 SP62 12g black 9.00 *15.00*
B123 SP62 24g dull violet 9.00 *15.00*
B124 SP62 30g carmine 9.00 *15.00*
B125 SP62 40g brown 9.00 *15.00*
B126 SP62 60g blue 9.00 *15.00*
B127 SP62 64g dull green 9.00 *15.00*
Nos. B122-B127 (6) 54.00 *90.00*
Set, never hinged 85.00

Exist imperf. Values, set unused hinged $450, never hinged $550.

Nos. B124-B127 exist in horiz. pairs imperf. between. Value, each $160.

These stamps were sold at double their face value. The surtax on this and the following issues was devoted to general charity.

Types of Regular Issue of 1934 Surcharged in Black:

a

b

1935, Nov. 11 *Perf. 12, 12½*

B128 A67(a) 5g + 2g emerald .45 *.90*
B129 A67(a) 12g + 3g blue .75 *1.00*
B130 A67(a) 24g + 6g lt brown .45 *.90*
B131 A68(b) 1s + 50g ver 24.00 *35.00*
Nos. B128-B131 (4) 25.65 *37.80*
Set, never hinged 45.00

Winterhelp. Set exists imperf. Values, set unused hinged $125, never hinged $190.

Set without surcharge unused hinged $140, never hinged $190.

Prince Eugene of Savoy — SP68

Slalom Turn — SP74

Military Leaders: 24g, Field Marshal Laudon. 30g, Archduke Karl. 40g, Field Marshal Josef Radetzky. 60g, Admiral Wilhelm Tegetthoff. 64g, Field Marshal Franz Conrad Hotzendorff.

1935, Dec. 1 *Perf. 12½*

B132 SP68 12g brown 8.50 *15.00*
B133 SP68 24g dark green 8.50 *15.00*
B134 SP68 30g claret 8.50 *15.00*
B135 SP68 40g slate 8.50 *15.00*
B136 SP68 60g deep ultra 8.50 *15.00*
B137 SP68 64g dark violet 8.50 *15.00*
Nos. B132-B137 (6) 51.00 *90.00*
Set, never hinged 85.00

These stamps were sold at double their face value. Set exists imperf. Values, set unused hinged $450, never hinged $550.

1936, Feb. 20 Photo.

Designs: 24g, Jumper taking off. 35g, Slalom turn. 60g, Innsbruck view.

B138 SP74 12g Prus green 2.50 *3.00*
B139 SP74 24g dp violet 4.50 *4.50*
B140 SP74 35g rose car 22.50 *37.50*
B141 SP74 60g sapphire 22.50 *37.50*
Nos. B138-B141 (4) 52.00 *82.50*
Set, never hinged 90.00

Ski concourse issue. These stamps were sold at twice face value. Set exists imperf. Values, set unused hinged $450, never hinged $550.

St. Martin of Tours — SP78

Designs: 12g+3g, Medical clinic. 24g+6g, St. Elizabeth of Hungary. 1s+1s, "Flame of Charity."

1936, Nov. 2 Unwmk.

B142 SP78 5g + 2g dp green .25 *.40*
B143 SP78 12g + 3g dp violet .25 *.40*
B144 SP78 24g + 6g dp blue .25 *.40*
B145 SP78 1s + 1s dk car 5.50 *11.00*
Nos. B142-B145 (4) 6.25 *12.20*
Set, never hinged 10.50

Winterhelp. Set exists imperf. Values, set unused hinged $175, never hinged $200.

Josef Ressel — SP82

Nurse and Infant — SP88

Inventors: 24g, Karl von Ghega. 30g, Josef Werndl. 40g, Carl Auer von Welsbach. 60g, Robert von Lieben. 64g, Viktor Kaplan.

1936, Dec. 6 Engr.

B146 SP82 12g dk brown 2.10 *4.50*
B147 SP82 24g dk violet 2.10 *4.50*
B148 SP82 30g dp claret 2.10 *4.50*
B149 SP82 40g gray violet 2.10 *4.50*
B150 SP82 60g vio blue 2.10 *4.50*
B151 SP82 64g dk slate green 2.10 *4.50*
Nos. B146-B151 (6) 12.60 *27.00*
Set, never hinged 24.00

These stamps were sold at double their face value. Exists imperf. Values, set unused hinged $350, never hinged $450.

1937, Oct. 18 Photo.

12g+3g, Mother and child. 24g+6g, Nursing the aged. 1s+1s, Sister of Mercy with patient.

B152 SP88 5g + 2g dk green .20 *.35*
B153 SP88 12g + 3g dk brown .20 *.35*
B154 SP88 24g + 6g dk blue .20 *.35*
B155 SP88 1s + 1s dk carmine 3.00 *6.75*
Nos. B152-B155 (4) 3.60 *7.80*
Set, never hinged 6.25

Winterhelp. Set exists imperf. Values, set unused hinged $90, never hinged $110.

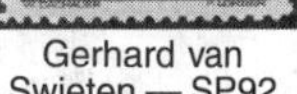

Gerhard van Swieten — SP92

The Dawn of Peace — SP101

Physicians: 8g, Leopold Auenbrugger von Auenbrugg. 12g, Karl von Rokitansky. 20g, Joseph Skoda. 24g, Ferdinand von Hebra. 30g, Ferdinand von Arlt. 40g, Joseph Hyrtl. 60g, Theodor Billroth. 64g, Theodor Meynert.

1937, Dec. 5 Engr. *Perf. 12½*

B156 SP92 5g choc 1.90 *4.00*
B157 SP92 8g dk red 1.90 *4.00*
B158 SP92 12g brown blk 1.90 *4.00*
B159 SP92 20g dk green 1.90 *4.00*
B160 SP92 24g dk violet 1.90 *4.00*
B161 SP92 30g brown car 1.90 *4.00*
B162 SP92 40g dp olive grn 1.90 *4.00*
B163 SP92 60g indigo 1.90 *4.00*
B164 SP92 64g brown vio 1.90 *4.00*
Nos. B156-B164 (9) 17.10 *36.00*
Set, never hinged 29.00

These stamps were sold at double their face value. Set exists imperf. Values, set unused hinged $550, never hinged $725.

Catalogue values for unused stamps in this section, from this point to the end of the section, are for Never Hinged items.

1945, Sept. 10 Photo. *Perf. 14*

B165 SP101 1s + 10s dk green .85 *1.40*

No. 467 Surcharged in Black

1946, June 25

B166 A110 30g + 20g dk red 3.00 *5.00*

First anniversary of United Nations.

Pres. Karl Renner SP102

1946 Engr. *Perf. 13½x14*

B167 SP102 1s + 1s dk slate grn 2.00 *4.00*
B168 SP102 2s + 2s dk blue vio 2.00 *4.00*
B169 SP102 3s + 3s dk purple 2.00 *4.00*
B170 SP102 5s + 5s dk vio brn 2.00 *4.00*
Nos. B167-B170 (4) 8.00 *16.00*

See Nos. B185-B188.

Nazi Sword Piercing Austria — SP103

Sweeping Away Fascist Symbols — SP104

Designs: 8g+6g, St. Stephen's Cathedral in Flames. 12g+12g, Pleading hand in concentration camp. 30g+30g, Hand choking Nazi serpent. 42g+42g, Hammer breaking Nazi pillar. 1s+1s, Oath of allegiance. 2s+2s, Austrian eagle and burning swastika.

Unwmk.

1946, Sept. 16 Photo. *Perf. 14*

B171 SP103 5g + (3g) dk brown .45 *.65*
B172 SP104 6g + (4g) dk slate grn .30 *.55*
B173 SP104 8g + (6g) orange red .30 *.55*
B174 SP104 12g + (12g) slate blk .30 *.55*
B175 SP104 30g + (30g) violet .30 *.55*
B176 SP104 42g + (42g) dull brn .30 *.55*
B177 SP104 1s + 1s dk red .45 *.65*
B178 SP104 2s + 2s dk car rose .60 *.65*
Nos. B171-B178 (8) 3.00 *4.70*

Anti-fascist propaganda.

Race Horse with Foal SP111

Various Race Horses.

1946, Oct. 20 Engr. *Perf. 13½x14*

B179 SP111 16g + 16g rose brown 2.00 3.00
B180 SP111 24g + 24g dk purple 2.00 3.00
B181 SP111 60g + 60g dk green 2.00 3.00
B182 SP111 1s + 1s dk blue gray 2.00 3.00
B183 SP111 2s + 2s yel brown 2.00 3.00
Nos. B179-B183 (5) 10.00 15.00

Austria Prize race, Vienna.

St. Ruprecht's Church, Vienna — SP116

1946, Oct. 30 *Perf. 14x13½*

B184 SP116 30g + 70g dark red .35 .70

Founding of Austria, 950th anniv. The surtax aided the Stamp Day celebration.

Renner Type of 1946
Souvenir Sheets

1946, Sept. 5 *Imperf.*

B185 Sheet of 8 500.00 900.00
a. SP102 1s+1s dk slate grn 55.00 100.00
B186 Sheet of 8 500.00 900.00
a. SP102 2s+2s dk blue vio 55.00 100.00
B187 Sheet of 8 500.00 900.00
a. SP102 3s+3s dark purple 55.00 100.00
B188 Sheet of 8 500.00 900.00
a. SP102 5s+5s dk vio brown 55.00 100.00

1st anniv. of Austria's liberation. Sheets of 8 plus center label showing arms.

Statue of Rudolf IV the Founder — SP118

Designs: 5g+20g, Tomb of Frederick III. 6g+24g, Main pulpit. 8g+32g, Statue of St. Stephen. 10g+40g, Madonna of the Domestics statue. 12g+48g, High altar. 30g+1.20s, Organ, destroyed in 1945. 50g+1.80s, Anton Pilgram statue. 1s+5s, Cathedral from northeast. 2s+10s, Southwest corner of cathedral.

1946, Dec. 12 Engr. *Perf. 14x13½*

B189 SP118 3g + 12g brown .25 .50
B190 SP118 5g + 20g dk vio brown .25 .50
B191 SP118 6g + 24g dk blue .25 .50
B192 SP118 8g + 32g dk grn .25 .50
B193 SP118 10g + 40g dp blue .40 .75
B194 SP118 12g + 48g dk vio .45 .80
B195 SP118 30g + 1.20s car 1.10 1.90
B196 SP118 50g + 1.80s dk bl 1.25 2.00
B197 SP118 1s + 5s brn vio 1.75 3.25
B198 SP118 2s + 10s vio brn 3.50 7.50
Nos. B189-B198 (10) 9.45 18.20

The surtax aided reconstruction of St. Stephen's Cathedral, Vienna.

Reaping Wheat — SP128

Designs: 8g+2g, Log raft. 10g+5g, Cement factory. 12g+8g, Coal mine. 18g+12g, Oil derricks. 30g+10g, Textile machinery. 35g+15g, Iron furnace. 60g+20g, Electric power lines.

1947, Mar. 23 *Perf. 14x13½*

B199 SP128 3g + 2g yel brown .40 .50
B200 SP128 8g + 2g dk bl grn .40 .50
B201 SP128 10g + 5g slate blk .40 .50
B202 SP128 12g + 8g dark pur .40 .50
B203 SP128 18g + 12g ol green .40 .50
B204 SP128 30g + 10g deep cl .40 .50
B205 SP128 35g + 15g crimson .40 .50
B206 SP128 60g + 20g dk blue .40 .50
Nos. B199-B206 (8) 3.20 4.00

Vienna International Sample Fair, 1947.

Race Horse and Jockey SP136

1947, June 29 *Perf. 13½x14*

B207 SP136 60g + 20g deep blue, *pale pink* .20 .20

Cup of Corvinus SP137

Prisoner of War — SP147

Designs: 8g+2g, Statue of Providence, Vienna. 10g+5g, Abbey at Melk. 12g+8g, Picture of a Woman, by Kriehuber. 18g+12g, Children at the Window, by Waldmuller. 20g+10g, Entrance, Upper Belvedere Palace. 30g+10g, Nymph Egeria, Schönbrunn Castle. 35g+15g, National Library, Vienna. 48g+12g, "Workshop of a Printer of Engravings," by Schmutzer. 60g+20g, Girl with Straw Hat, by Amerling.

1947, June 20 *Perf. 14x13½*

B208 SP137 3g + 2g brown .30 .40
B209 SP137 8g + 2g dk blue grn .30 .40
B210 SP137 10g + 5g dp claret .30 .40
B211 SP137 12g + 8g dk purple .30 .40
B212 SP137 18g + 12g golden brn .30 .40
B213 SP137 20g + 10g sepia .30 .40
B214 SP137 30g + 10g dk yel grn .30 .40
B215 SP137 35g + 15g deep car .30 .40
B216 SP137 48g + 12g dk brn vio .30 .40
B217 SP137 60g + 20g dp blue .30 .40
Nos. B208-B217 (10) 3.00 4.00

1947, Aug. 30

12g+8g, Prisoners' Mail, 18g+12g, Prison camp visitor. 35g+15g, Family reunion. 60g+20g, "Industry" beckoning. 1s+40g, Sower.

B218 SP147 8g + 2g dk green .20 .30
B219 SP147 12g + 8g dk vio brn .20 .30
B220 SP147 18g + 12g black brn .20 .30
B221 SP147 35g + 15g rose brn .20 .30
B222 SP147 60g + 20g dp blue .20 .30
B223 SP147 1s + 40g redsh brn .20 .30
Nos. B218-B223 (6) 1.20 1.80

Olympic Flame and Emblem — SP153

1948, Jan. 16 Engr.

B224 SP153 1s + 50g dark blue .35 .35

The surtax was used to help defray expenses of Austria's 1948 Olympics team.

Laabenbach Bridge Neulengbach SP154

Designs: 20g+10g, Dam, Vermunt Lake. 30g+10g, Danube Port, Vienna. 40g+20g, Mining, Erzberg. 45g+20g, Tracks, Southern Railway Station, Vienna. 60g+30g, Communal housing project, Vienna. 75g+35g, Gas Works, Vienna. 80g+40g, Oil refinery. 1s+50g, Gesäuse Highway, Styria. 1.40s+70g, Parliament Building, Vienna.

1948, Feb. 18 *Perf. 14x13½*

B225 SP154 10g + 5g slate blk .20 .20
B226 SP154 20g + 10g lilac .20 .20
B227 SP154 30g + 10g dull grn .50 .50
B228 SP154 40g + 20g ol brn .20 .20
B229 SP154 45g + 20g dk blue .20 .20
B230 SP154 60g + 30g dk red .20 .20
B231 SP154 75g + 35g dk vio brn .20 .20
B232 SP154 80g + 40g vio brn .20 .20
B233 SP154 1s + 50g dp blue .20 .20
B234 SP154 1.40s + 70g dp car .50 .50
Nos. B225-B234 (10) 2.60 2.60

The surtax was for the Reconstruction Fund.

Violet — SP155

Hans Makart — SP156

Designs: 20g+10g, Anemone. 30g+10g, Crocus. 40g+20g, Yellow primrose. 45g+20g, Pasqueflower. 60g+30g, Rhododendron. 75g+35g, Dogrose. 80g+40g, Cyclamen. 1s+50g, Alpine Gentian. 1.40s+70g, Edelweiss.

1948, May 14 Engr. & Typo.

B235 SP155 10g + 5g multi .35 .25
B236 SP155 20g + 10g multi .20 .20
B237 SP155 30g + 10g multi 2.50 2.00
B238 SP155 40g + 20g multi .50 .25
B239 SP155 45g + 20g multi .20 .20
B240 SP155 60g + 30g multi .20 .20
B241 SP155 75g + 35g multi .20 .20
B242 SP155 80g + 40g multi .30 .20
B243 SP155 1s + 50g multi .40 .30
B244 SP155 1.40s + 70g multi .65 .55
Nos. B235-B244 (10) 5.50 4.35

1948, June 15 Unwmk. Engr.

Designs: 20g+10g, Künstlerhaus, Vienna. 40g+20g, Carl Kundmann. 50g+25g, A. S. von Siccardsburg. 60g+30g, Hans Cannon. 1s+50g, William Unger. 1.40s+70g, Friedrich von Schmidt.

B245 SP156 20g + 10g dp yel green 6.25 5.00
B246 SP156 30g + 15g dark brown 3.00 1.90
B247 SP156 40g + 20g ind 3.00 1.90
B248 SP156 50g + 25g dk vio 3.50 2.75
B249 SP156 60g + 30g dk red 3.50 2.75
B250 SP156 1s + 50g dk blue 6.25 5.00
B251 SP156 1.40s + 70g red brown 8.50 7.50
Nos. B245-B251 (7) 34.00 26.80

Kunstlerhaus, home of the leading Austrian Artists Association, 80th anniv.

St. Rupert — SP157

Easter — SP158

Designs: 30g+15g, Cathedral and Fountain. 40g+20g, Facade of Cathedral. 50g+25g, Cathedral from South. 60g+30g, Abbey of St. Peter. 80g+40g, Inside Cathedral. 1s+50g, Salzburg Cathedral and Castle. 1.40s+70g, Madonna by Michael Pacher.

1948, Aug. 6 *Perf. 14x13½*

B252 SP157 20g + 10g dp grn 6.00 5.50
B253 SP157 30g + 15g red brn 2.50 2.50
B254 SP157 40g + 20g sl blk 1.90 1.75
B255 SP157 50g + 25g choc .40 .40
B256 SP157 60g + 30g dk red .40 .40
B257 SP157 80g + 40g dk brn vio .40 .40
B258 SP157 1s + 50g dp blue .75 .50
B259 SP157 1.40s + 70g dk grn 1.50 1.25
Nos. B252-B259 (8) 13.85 12.70

The surtax was to aid in the reconstruction of Salzburg Cathedral.

1949, Apr. 13 Unwmk.

Designs: 60g+20g, St. Nicholas Day. 1s+25g, Birthday. 1.40s+35g, Christmas.

Inscribed: "Gluckliche Kindheit"

B260 SP158 40g + 10g brn vio 17.00 12.50
B261 SP158 60g + 20g brn red 17.00 12.50
B262 SP158 1s + 25g dp ultra 17.00 12.50
B263 SP158 1.40s + 35g dk grn 17.00 12.50
Nos. B260-B263 (4) 68.00 50.00

The surtax was for Child Welfare.

Arms of Austria, 1230 — SP159

SP160

1949, Aug. 17 Engr. & Photo.

B264 SP159 40g + 10g 1230 7.00 6.00

Engraved and Typographed

B265 SP159 60g + 15g 1450 7.00 6.00
B266 SP159 1s + 25g 1600 7.00 6.00
B267 SP159 1.60s + 40g 1945 7.00 6.00
Nos. B264-B267 (4) 28.00 24.00

Surtax was for returned prisoners of war.

1949, Dec. 3 **Engr.**

Laurel Branch, Stamps and Magnifier

B268 SP160 60g + 15g dark red 2.25 1.50

Stamp Day, Dec. 3-4.

Arms of Austria and Carinthia SP161

Carinthian with Austrian Flag — SP162

Design: 1.70s+40g, Casting ballot.

1950, Oct. 10 **Photo.** ***Perf. 14x13½***

B269	SP161	60g + 15g	25.00	18.00
B270	SP162	1s + 25g	35.00	20.00
B271	SP162	1.70s + 40g	40.00	30.00
	Nos. B269-B271 (3)		100.00	68.00

Plebiscite in Carinthia, 30th anniv.

Collector Examining Cover — SP163

Miner and Mine — SP164

1950, Dec. 2 **Engr.**

B272 SP163 60g + 15g blue grn 8.50 6.00

Stamp Day.

1951, Mar. 10 **Unwmk.**

60g+15g, Mason holding brick and trowel. 1s+25g, Bridge builder with hook and chain. 1.70s+40g, Electrician, pole and insulators.

B273	SP164	40g + 10g dark brown	13.00	11.00
B274	SP164	60g + 15g dk grn	13.00	11.00
B275	SP164	1s + 25g red brown	13.00	11.00
B276	SP164	1.70s + 40g vio bl	13.00	11.00
	Nos. B273-B276 (4)		52.00	44.00

Issued to publicize Austrian reconstruction.

Laurel Branch and Olympic Circles SP165

1952, Jan. 26 ***Perf. 13½x14***

B277 SP165 2.40s + 60g grnsh black 15.00 13.00

The surtax was used to help defray expenses of Austria's athletes in the 1952 Olympic Games.

Cupid as Postman SP166

1952, Mar. 10 ***Perf. 14x13½***

B278 SP166 1.50s + 35g dark brn car 17.50 16.00

Stamp Day.

Sculpture, "Christ, The Almighty" SP167

1952, Sept. 6 ***Perf. 13½x14***

B279 SP167 1s + 25g grnsh gray 11.00 9.00

Austrian Catholic Conv., Vienna, 9/11-14.

Type of 1945-46 Overprinted in Gold

1953, Aug. 29 **Unwmk.**

B280 A124 1s + 25g on 5s dl bl 2.50 2.00

60th anniv. of labor unions in Austria.

Bummerlhaus Steyr — SP168

Globe and Philatelic Accessories SP169

Designs: 1s+25g, Johannes Kepler. 1.50s+40g, Lutheran Bible, 1st edition. 2.40s+60g, Theophil von Hansen. 3s+75g, Reconstructed Lutheran School, Vienna.

1953, Nov. 5 **Engr.** ***Perf. 14x13½***

B281	SP168	70g + 15g vio brn	.30	.30
B282	SP168	1s + 25g dk gray blue	.30	.30
B283	SP168	1.50s + 40g choc	.90	.90
B284	SP168	2.40s + 60g dk grn	2.50	2.25
B285	SP168	3s + 75g dk pur	6.00	5.75
	Nos. B281-B285 (5)		10.00	9.50

The surtax was used toward reconstruction of the Lutheran School, Vienna.

1953, Dec. 5

B286 SP169 1s + 25g chocolate 5.00 3.75

Stamp Day.

Type of 1945-46 with Denomination Replaced by Asterisks

Overprinted in Brown

1954, Feb. 19 ***Perf. 13½x14***

B287 A124 1s + 20g blue gray .20 .20

Surtax for aid to avalanche victims.

Patient Under Sun Lamp — SP170

Designs: 70g+15g, Physician using microscope. 1s+25g, Mother and children. 1.45s+35g, Operating room. 1.50s+35g, Baby on scale. 2.40s+60g, Nurse.

1954 **Engr.** ***Perf. 14x13½***

B288	SP170	30g + 10g pur	1.50	1.10
B289	SP170	70g + 15g dk brn	.25	.25
B290	SP170	1s + 25g dk bl	.30	.25
B291	SP170	1.45s + 35g dk bl green	.45	.40
B292	SP170	1.50s + 35g dk red	5.00	4.50
B293	SP170	2.40s + 60g dk red brown	6.00	5.50
	Nos. B288-B293 (6)		13.50	12.00

The surtax was for social welfare.

Early Vienna-Ulm Ferryboat SP171

1954, Dec. 4 ***Perf. 13½x14***

B294 SP171 1s + 25g dk gray grn 4.50 4.00

Stamp Day.

"Industry" Welcoming Returned Prisoner of War SP172

1955, June 29

B295 SP172 1s + 25g red brn 2.00 1.50

Surtax for returned prisoners of war and relatives of prisoners not yet released.

Collector Looking at Album — SP173

1955, Dec. 3 ***Perf. 14x13½***

B296 SP173 1s + 25g vio brn 3.00 2.75

Stamp Day. The surtax was for the promotion of Austrian philately.

Ornamental Shield and Letter — SP174

1956, Dec. 1 **Engr.**

B297 SP174 1s + 25g scarlet 2.75 2.50

Stamp Day. See note after No. B296.

Arms of Austria, 1945 — SP175

Engr. & Typo.

1956, Dec. 21 ***Perf. 14x13½***

B298 SP175 1.50s + 50g on 1.60s + 40g gray & red .25 .20

The surtax was for Hungarian refugees.

New Post Office, Linz 2 SP176

Design: 2.40s+60g, Post office, Kitzbuhel.

1957-58 **Engr.** ***Perf. 13½x14***

B299	SP176	1s + 25g dk sl grn	2.75	2.50
B300	SP176	2.40s + 60g blue	.65	.60

Stamp Day. See note after B296. Issue dates: 1s, Nov. 30, 1957. 2.40s, Dec. 6, 1957. See No. B303.

Roman Carriage from Tomb at Maria Saal SP177

Litho. & Engr.

1959, Dec. 5 ***Perf. 13½x14***

B301 SP177 2.40s + 60g pale lil & blk .55 .50

Stamp Day.

Progressive Die Proof under Magnifying Glass SP178

1960, Dec. 2 **Engr.** ***Perf. 13½x14***

B302 SP178 3s + 70g vio brn .85 .70

Stamp Day.

Post Office Type of 1957

Design: 3s+70g, Post Office, Rust.

1961, Dec. 1 **Unwmk.** ***Perf. 13½***

B303 SP176 3s + 70g dk bl grn .90 .70

Stamp Day. See note after No. B296.

Hands of Stamp Engraver at Work SP179

1962, Nov. 30 ***Perf. 13½x14***

B304 SP179 3s + 70g dull pur 1.25 .90

Stamp Day.

Railroad Exit, Post Office Vienna 101 SP180

1963, Nov. 29 **Litho. & Engr.**

B305 SP180 3s + 70g tan & blk .80 .80

Stamp Day.

View of Vienna, North SP181

Designs: Various view of Vienna with compass indicating direction.

1964, July 20 **Litho.** ***Perf. 13½x14***

B306 SP181 1.50s + 30g ("N") .20 .20
B307 SP181 1.50s + 30g ("NO") .20 .20
B308 SP181 1.50s + 30g ("O") .20 .20
B309 SP181 1.50s + 30g ("SO") .20 .20
B310 SP181 1.50s + 30g ("S") .20 .20
B311 SP181 1.50s + 30g ("SW") .20 .20
B312 SP181 1.50s + 30g ("W") .20 .20
B313 SP181 1.50s + 30g ("NW") .20 .20
Nos. B306-B313 (8) 1.60 1.60

Vienna Intl. Phil. Exhib. (WIPA 1965).

Post Bus Terminal, St. Gilgen, Wolfgangsee — SP182

1964, Dec. 4 **Unwmk.** ***Perf. 13½***

B314 SP182 3s + 70g multi .45 .45

Stamp Day.

Wall Painting, Tomb at Thebes — SP183

Development of Writing: 1.80s+50g, Cuneiform writing on stone tablet and man's head from Assyrian palace. 2.20s+60g, Wax tablet with Latin writing, Corinthian column. 3s+80g, Gothic writing on sealed letter, Gothic window from Munster Cathedral. 4s+1s, Letter with seal and postmark and upright desk. 5s+1.20s, Typewriter.

Litho. & Engr.

1965, June 4 ***Perf. 14x13½***

B315 SP183 1.50s + 40g multi .20 .20
B316 SP183 1.80s + 50g multi .20 .20
B317 SP183 2.20s + 60g multi .35 .35
B318 SP183 3s + 80g multi .20 .20
B319 SP183 4s + 1s multi .45 .45
B320 SP183 5s + 1.20s multi .60 .60
Nos. B315-B320 (6) 2.00 2.00

Vienna Intl. Phil. Exhib., WIPA, June 4-13.

Mailman Distributing Mail SP184

1965, Dec. 3 **Engr.** ***Perf. 13½x14***

B321 SP184 3s + 70g blue grn .40 .35

Stamp Day.

Letter Carrier, 16th Century — SP185

Litho. & Engr.

1966, Dec. 2 ***Perf. 13½***

B322 SP185 3s + 70g multi .40 .35

Stamp Day. Design is from Ambras Heroes' Book, Austrian National Library.

Letter Carrier, 16th Century Playing Card — SP186

Engr. & Photo.

1967, Dec. 1 ***Perf. 13x13½***

B323 SP186 3.50s + 80g multi .40 .35

Stamp Day.

Mercury, Bas-relief from Purkersdorf SP187

1968, Nov. 29 **Engr.** ***Perf. 13½***

B324 SP187 3.50s + 80g slate green .40 .35

Stamp Day.

Unken Post Station Sign, 1710 — SP188

Engr. & Photo.

1969, Dec. 5 ***Perf. 12***

B325 SP188 3.50s + 80g tan, red & blk .40 .35

Stamp Day. Design is from a watercolor by Friedrich Zeller.

Saddle, Bag, Harness and Post Horn — SP189

Engr. & Litho.

1970, Dec. 4 ***Perf. 13½x14***

B326 SP189 3.50s + 80g gray blk & yel .40 .35

Stamp Day.

"50 Years" SP190

Engr. & Photo.

1971, Dec. 3 ***Perf. 13½***

B327 SP190 4s + 1.50s gold & red brn .60 .45

50th anniversary of the Federation of Austrian Philatelic Societies.

Local Post Carrier — SP191

1972, Dec. 1 **Engr.** ***Perf. 14x13½***

B328 SP191 4s + 1s olive green .60 .45

Stamp Day.

Gabriel, by Lorenz Luchsperger, 15th Century — SP192

1973, Nov. 30

B329 SP192 4s + 1s maroon .60 .45

Stamp Day.

Mail Coach Leaving Old PTT Building — SP193

1974, Nov. 29 **Engr.** ***Perf. 14x13½***

B330 SP193 4s + 2s violet blue .70 .70

Stamp Day.

Alpine Skiing, Women's SP194

Designs: 1.50s+70g, Ice hockey. 2s+90g, Ski jump. 4s+1.90s, Bobsledding.

1975, Mar. 14 **Photo.** ***Perf. 13½x14***

B331 SP194 1s + 50g multi .25 .25
B332 SP194 1.50s + 70g multi .30 .30
B333 SP194 2s + 90g multi .35 .35
B334 SP194 4s + 1.90s multi .70 .70
Nos. B331-B334 (4) 1.60 1.60

1975, Nov. 14

Designs: 70g+30g, Figure skating, pair. 2s+1s, Cross-country skiing. 2.50s+1s, Luge. 4s+2s, Biathlon.

B335 SP194 70g + 30g multi .20 .20
B336 SP194 2s + 1s multi .30 .30
B337 SP194 2.50s + 1s multi .40 .40
B338 SP194 4s + 2s multi .70 .70
Nos. B335-B338 (4) 1.60 1.60

12th Winter Olympic Games, Innsbruck, Feb. 4-15, 1976.

Austria Nos. 5, 250, 455 — SP195

Photo. & Engr.

1975, Nov. 28 ***Perf. 14***

B339 SP195 4s + 2s multi .65 .65

Stamp Day; 125th anniv. of Austrian stamps.

Postilion's Gala Hat and Horn SP196

1976, Dec. 3 ***Perf. 13½x14***

B340 SP196 6s + 2s blk & lt vio .80 .80

Stamp Day.

Emanuel Herrmann SP197

1977, Dec. 2 ***Perf. 14x13½***

B341 SP197 6s + 2s multi .80 .80

Stamp Day. Emanuel Herrmann (1839-1902), economist, invented postal card. Austria issued first postal card in 1869.

Post Bus, 1913 SP198

1978, Dec. 1 **Photo.** ***Perf. 13½x14***

B342 SP198 10s + 5s multi 1.40 1.40

Stamp Day.

Heroes' Square, Vienna SP199

Photo. & Engr.

1979, Nov. 30 ***Perf. 13½***

B343 SP199 16s + 8s multi 2.75 2.50

No. B343 Inscribed "2. Phase"

1980, Nov. 21
B344 SP199 16s + 8s multi 2.75 2.50

Souvenir Sheet

1981, Feb. 20
B345 SP199 16s + 8s multi 3.00 2.50

WIPA 1981 Phil. Exhib., Vienna, May 22-31. No. B345 contains one stamp without inscription.

Mainz-Weber Mailbox, 1870 — SP200

1982, Nov. 26 Photo. & Engr.
B346 SP200 6s + 3s multi 1.00 1.00

Stamp Day.

Boy Examining Cover SP201

Photo. & Engr.

1983, Oct. 21 ***Perf. 14***
B347 SP201 6s + 3s multi 1.10 1.10

Stamp Day. See Nos. B349-B352, B354-B355.

World Winter Games for the Handicapped — SP202

1984, Jan. 5 Photo. ***Perf. 13½x13***
B348 SP202 4s + 2s Downhill skier .75 .75

Stamp Day Type of 1983

Designs: No. B349, Seschemnofer III burial chamber detail, pyramid of Cheops, Gizeh. No. B350, Roman messenger on horseback. No. B351, Nuremberg messenger, 16th cent. No. B352, *The Postmaster* (detail), 1841, lithograph by Carl Schuster.

1984-87 Photo. & Engr. ***Perf. 14***
B349 SP201 6s + 3s multi 1.25 1.25
B350 SP201 6s + 3s multi 1.25 1.25
B351 SP201 6s + 3s multi 1.25 1.25
B352 SP201 6s + 3s multi 1.40 1.40
Nos. B349-B352 (4) 5.15 5.15

Issue: #B349, 11/30/84; #B350, 11/28/85; #B351, 11/28/86; #B352, 11/19/87.

4th World Winter Sports Championships for the Disabled, Innsbruck — SP203

1988, Jan. 15 Photo. ***Perf. 13½***
B353 SP203 5s + 2.50s multi 1.10 1.10

Stamp Day Type of 1983

Designs: No. B354, Railway mail car. No. B355, Hansa-Brandenburg CI mail plane.

1988-89 Photo. & Engr. ***Perf. 14***
B354 SP201 6s +3s multi 1.40 1.40
B355 SP201 6s +3s multi 1.40 1.40

Issued: #B354, Nov. 17; #B355, May 24, 1989.

Stamp Day — SP204

1990, May 25 Photo. ***Perf. 13½***
B356 SP204 7s +3s multi 1.75 1.75

SP205

SP205a

1991, May 29 Photo. & Engr.
B357 SP205 7s +3s B & P 1.75 1.75

1992, May 22
B358 SP205 7s +3s R & H 1.75 1.75

1993, May 5
B359 SP205 7s +3s I & I 1.75 1.75

1994, May 27
B360 SP205 7s +3s E & L 1.75 1.75

1995, May 26
B361 SP205a 10s +5s F & A 3.00 3.00

1996, May 17
B362 SP205a 10s +5s M & T 3.00 3.00
Nos. B357-B362,1725,1765,1791 (9) 16.75 15.80

Stamp Day. The 1st letters spell "Briefmarke," the 2nd "Philatelie."

For "A" & "E," see #1725; "R" & "L," #1765; "K" & "I," #1791; "E" & "E," #1818.

Special Olympics Winter Games SP206

1993, Mar. 19 Photo. ***Perf. 13½x14***
B367 SP206 6s +3s multi 1.75 1.75

Vienna Intl. Postage Stamp Exhibition (WIPA), 2000 — SP207

#B368, #5, postman on bicycle. #B369, #339, early mail truck. #B370, #525, airplane, service vehicles.

1997-2000 Photo. & Engr. ***Perf. 14***
B368 SP207 27s +13s multi 6.75 6.75
B369 SP207 32s +13s multi 7.50 7.50
B370 SP207 32s +16s multi 7.50 7.50
a. Souvenir sheet, #B368-B370 + label 19.00 19.00
Nos. B368-B370 (3) 21.75 21.75

Stamps from #B370a are dated "2000."

Issued: #B368, 5/23; #B369, 11/6/98; #B370, 9/17/99. #B370a, 2000.

Stamp Day — SP208

Illustration reduced.

Photo. & Engr.

2001, May 18 ***Perf. 13¾***
B371 SP208 20s +10s multi + label 4.00 4.00

Design: 1919 Mail car.

Photo. & Engr.

2002, May 24 ***Perf. 13¾***
B372 SP208 € 1.60 +80c multi + label 4.50 4.50

AIR POST STAMPS

Issues of the Monarchy

Types of Regular Issue of 1916 Surcharged

1918, Mar. 30 Unwmk. ***Perf. 12½***
C1 A40 1.50k on 2k lilac 2.00 *3.75*
C2 A40 2.50k on 3k ocher 10.00 *22.50*
a. Inverted surcharge *1,100.*
Never hinged —
b. Perf. 11½ 325.00 *425.00*
Never hinged 600.00
c. Perf. 12½x11½ 27.50 *45.00*
Never hinged 52.50

Overprinted

C3 A40 4k gray 5.25 *11.00*
Nos. C1-C3 (3) 17.25 *37.25*
Set, never hinged 32.50

Set exists imperf. Values, set unused hinged $200, never hinged $325.

Nos. C1-C3 also exist without surcharge or overprint. Values, set perf unused hinged $300, never hinged $625. Values, set imperf, unused hinged $275, never hinged $625..

Nos. C1-C3 were printed on grayish and on white paper.

A 7k on 10k red brown was prepared but not regularly issued. Value, perf. or imperf., $300.

Issues of the Republic

Hawk — AP1

Wilhelm Kress — AP2

1922-24 Typo. ***Perf. 12½***
C4 AP1 300k claret .30 *1.25*
C5 AP1 400k green ('24) 4.50 *12.50*
C6 AP1 600k bister .20 *.90*
C7 AP1 900k brn orange .20 *.90*

Engr.

C8 AP2 1200k brn violet .20 *.90*
C9 AP2 2400k slate .20 *.90*
C10 AP2 3000k dp brn ('23) 2.50 *7.00*
C11 AP2 4800k dark bl ('23) 2.50 *7.00*
Nos. C4-C11 (8) 10.60 *31.35*
Set, never hinged 22.50

Set exists imperf. Values, set unused hinged $250, never hinged $300.

Plane and Pilot's Head — AP3

Airplane Passing Crane — AP4

1925-30 Typo. ***Perf. 12½***
C12 AP3 2g gray brown .35 *.90*
C13 AP3 5g red .20 *.25*
a. Horiz. pair, imperf. btwn. 250.00
Never hinged 300.00
C14 AP3 6g dark blue .80 *1.40*
C15 AP3 8g yel green .90 *1.60*
C16 AP3 10g dp org ('26) .90 *1.60*
a. Horiz. pair, imperf. btwn. 250.00
Never hinged 300.00
C17 AP3 15g red vio ('26) .35 *.80*
a. Horiz. pair, imperf. btwn. 300.00
Never hinged 375.00
C18 AP3 20g org brn ('30) 10.00 6.25
C19 AP3 25g blk vio ('30) 4.00 *7.75*
C20 AP3 30g bister ('26) 7.00 *8.25*
C21 AP3 50g bl gray ('26) 12.50 12.50
C22 AP3 80g dk grn ('30) 1.90 *3.50*

Photo.

C23 AP4 10g orange red .80 *2.50*
a. Horiz. pair, imperf. btwn. 250.00
Never hinged 300.00
C24 AP4 15g claret .55 *1.40*
C25 AP4 30g brn violet .70 *2.50*
C26 AP4 50g gray black .75 *2.75*
C27 AP4 1s deep blue 6.00 *6.25*
C28 AP4 2s dark green 1.50 *3.50*
a. Vertical pair, imperf. btwn. 250.00
Never hinged 300.00
C29 AP4 3s red brn ('26) 42.50 *52.50*
C30 AP4 5s indigo ('26) 11.50 *22.50*

Size: 25½x32mm

C31 AP4 10s blk brown, *gray* ('26) 9.00 *17.50*
Nos. C12-C31 (20) 112.20 *156.20*
Set, never hinged 225.00

Exists imperf. Values, set unused hinged $800, never hinged $1,000.

Airplane over Güssing Castle — AP5

Airplane over the Danube — AP6

Designs (each includes plane): 10g, Maria-Worth. 15g, Durnstein. 20g, Hallstatt. 25g, Salzburg. 30g, Upper Dachstein and Schladminger Glacier. 40g, Lake Wetter. 50g, Arlberg. 60g, St. Stephen's Cathedral. 80g, Church of the Minorites. 2s, Railroad viaduct, Carinthia. 3s, Gross Glockner mountain. 5s, Aerial railway. 10s, Seaplane and yachts.

1935, Aug. 16 Engr. ***Perf. 12½***
C32 AP5 5g rose violet .20 *.40*
C33 AP5 10g red orange .20 *.20*
C34 AP5 15g yel green .60 *1.25*
C35 AP5 20g gray blue .20 *.30*
C36 AP5 25g violet brn .20 *.30*
C37 AP5 30g brn orange .20 *.35*
C38 AP5 40g gray green .20 *.35*
C39 AP5 50g light sl bl .20 *.45*

No.	Type	Description	Unused	Used
C40	AP5	60g black brn	.30	*.65*
C41	AP5	80g light brown	.35	*.80*
C42	AP6	1s rose red	.30	*.70*
C43	AP6	2s olive green	1.75	*4.00*
C44	AP6	3s yellow brn	7.00	*15.00*
C45	AP6	5s dark green	4.50	*11.00*
C46	AP6	10s slate blue	42.50	*80.00*
		Nos. C32-C46 (15)	58.70	*115.75*
		Set, never hinged	87.50	

Set exists imperf. Values, set unused hinged $275, never hinged $325.

Catalogue values for unused stamps in this section, from this point to the end of the section, are for Never Hinged items.

Windmill, Neusiedler Lake Shore — AP20

1s, Roman arch, Carnuntum. 2s, Town Hall, Gmund. 3s, Schieder Lake, Hinterstoder. 4s, Praegraten, Eastern Tyrol. 5s, Torsäule, Salzburg. 10s, St. Charles Church, Vienna.

1947 Unwmk. *Perf. 14x13½*

No.	Type	Description	Unused	Used
C47	AP20	50g black brown	.20	.20
C48	AP20	1s dark brn vio	.30	.25
C49	AP20	2s dark green	.35	*.40*
C50	AP20	3s chocolate	2.25	*2.75*
C51	AP20	4s dark green	1.40	*2.00*
C52	AP20	5s dark blue	1.40	*2.00*
C53	AP20	10s dark blue	.75	*1.50*
		Nos. C47-C53 (7)	6.65	*9.10*

Rooks AP27

Birds: 1s, Barn swallows. 2s, Blackheaded gulls. 3s, Great cormorants. 5s, Buzzard. 10s, Gray heron. 20s, Golden eagle.

1950-53 *Perf. 13½x14*

No.	Type	Description	Unused	Used
C54	AP27	60g dark bl vio	2.50	1.10
C55	AP27	1s dark vio blue ('53)	17.50	15.00
C56	AP27	2s dark blue	15.00	6.00
C57	AP27	3s dk slate green ('53)	100.00	65.00
C58	AP27	5s red brn ('53)	100.00	65.00
C59	AP27	10s gray vio ('53)	45.00	30.00
C60	AP27	20s brn blk ('52)	10.00	4.00
		Nos. C54-C60 (7)	290.00	186.10
		Set, hinged	180.00	

Value at lower left on Nos. C59 and C60. No. C60 exists imperf.

Etrich "Dove" AP28

Designs: 3.50s, Twin-engine jet airliner. 5s, Four-engine jet airliner.

1968, May 31 Engr. *Perf. 13½x14*

No.	Type	Description	Unused	Used
C61	AP28	2s olive bister	.30	.25
C62	AP28	3.50s slate green	.50	.40
C63	AP28	5s dark blue	.75	.60
		Nos. C61-C63 (3)	1.55	1.25

IFA WIEN 1968 (International Air Post Exhibition), Vienna, May 30-June 4.

POSTAGE DUE STAMPS

Issues of the Monarchy

D1

D2

Perf. 10 to 13½

1894-95 Typo. Wmk. 91

No.	Type	Description	Unused	Used
J1	D1	1kr brown	1.90	1.00
a.		Perf. 13½	45.00	*37.50*
b.		Half used as ½kr on cover		*65.00*
J2	D1	2kr brown ('95)	2.50	1.90
a.		Pair, imperf. btwn.	200.00	*275.00*
b.		Half used as 1kr on cover		*150.00*
J3	D1	3kr brown	3.00	1.00
a.		Half used as 1½kr on cover		*110.00*
J4	D1	5kr brown	3.00	.90
a.		Perf. 13½	25.00	15.00
b.		Pair, imperf. btwn.	160.00	*190.00*
J5	D1	6kr brown ('95)	2.50	*5.00*
a.		Half used as 3kr on cover		*95.00*
J6	D1	7kr brown ('95)	1.25	*4.50*
a.		Vert. pair, imperf. btwn.	275.00	—
b.		Horiz. pair, imperf. btwn.	275.00	425.00
J7	D1	10kr brown	2.50	.50
a.		Half used as 5kr on cover		*110.00*
J8	D1	20kr brown	1.25	*4.50*
J9	D1	50kr brown	27.50	*55.00*
		Nos. J1-J9 (9)	45.40	*74.30*

Values for Nos. J1-J9 are for stamps that do not show the watermark. Stamps showing the watermark often sell for more.

See Nos. J204-J231.

1899-1900 *Imperf.*

No.	Type	Description	Unused	Used
J10	D2	1h brown	.25	*.30*
J11	D2	2h brown	.25	*.55*
J12	D2	3h brown ('00)	.25	*.30*
J13	D2	4h brown	1.75	1.50
J14	D2	5h brown ('00)	2.00	1.10
J15	D2	6h brown	.30	*.60*
J16	D2	10h brown	.25	*.55*
J17	D2	12h brown	.50	*1.75*
J18	D2	15h brown	.45	*1.10*
J19	D2	20h brown	16.00	3.50
J20	D2	40h brown	2.50	*1.40*
J21	D2	100h brown	3.75	2.50
		Nos. J10-J21 (12)	28.25	*15.15*

Perf. 10½, 12½, 13½ and Compound

No.	Type	Description	Unused	Used
J22	D2	1h brown	.45	.20
J23	D2	2h brown	.35	.20
J24	D2	3h brown ('00)	.30	.20
J25	D2	4h brown	.35	.20
J26	D2	5h brown ('00)	.45	.20
J27	D2	6h brown	.35	.20
J28	D2	10h brown	.35	.20
J29	D2	12h brown	.60	*.65*
J30	D2	15h brown	.75	*.80*
J31	D2	20h brown	1.00	.25
J32	D2	40h brown	1.75	.45
J33	D2	100h brown	15.00	1.50
		Nos. J22-J33 (12)	21.70	5.05

Nos. J10-J33 exist on unwmkd. paper.

For surcharges see Offices in the Turkish Empire Nos. J1-J5.

D3

1908-13 Unwmk. *Perf. 12½*

No.	Type	Description	Unused	Used
J34	D3	1h carmine	.80	1.25
J35	D3	2h carmine	.25	.25
d.		Half used as 1h on cover		77.50
J36	D3	4h carmine	.20	.20
c.		Half used as 2h on cover		77.50
J37	D3	6h carmine	.20	.20
J38	D3	10h carmine	.25	.20
c.		Half used as 5h on cover		37.50
J39	D3	14h carmine ('13)	3.25	1.75
J40	D3	20h carmine	5.50	.20
c.		Half used as 10h on cover		77.50
J41	D3	25h carmine ('10)	6.75	4.00
J42	D3	30h carmine	5.50	.25
J43	D3	50h carmine	7.50	.25
J44	D3	100h carmine	10.50	.45
		Nos. J34-J44 (11)	40.70	9.00

All values exist on ordinary paper, #J34-J38, J40, J42-J44 on chalky paper and #J34-J38, J40, J44 on thin ordinary paper. In most cases, values are for the least expensive stamp of the types. Some of the expensive types sell for considerably more.

All values exist imperf.

See Offices in the Turkish Empire type D3.

1911, July 16

No.	Type	Description	Unused	Used
J45	D3	5k violet	50.00	11.50
J46	D3	10k violet	190.00	3.00

Nos. J45-J46 exist imperf. Value, set unused hinged $900.

Regular Issue of 1908 Overprinted or Surcharged in Carmine or Black:

1916, Oct. 21

No.	Type	Description	Unused	Used
J47	A22	1h gray (C)	.20	.20
a.		Pair, one without overprint	125.00	
		Never hinged	200.00	
J48	A22	15h on 2h vio (Bk)	.20	*.60*
a.		Inverted surcharge	325.00	
		Never hinged	625.00	
		Set, never hinged	.60	

D4

D5

1916, Oct. 1

No.	Type	Description	Unused	Used
J49	D4	5h rose red	.20	.20
J50	D4	10h rose red	.20	.20
J51	D4	15h rose red	.20	.20
J52	D4	20h rose red	.20	.20
J53	D4	25h rose red	.20	*.65*
J54	D4	30h rose red	.20	*.25*
J55	D4	40h rose red	.20	.30
J56	D4	50h rose red	.50	*1.60*
J57	D5	1k ultramarine	.20	.20
a.		Horiz. pair, imperf. btwn.	190.00	400.00
		Never hinged	425.00	
J58	D5	5k ultramarine	1.90	2.40
J59	D5	10k ultramarine	2.00	1.25
		Nos. J49-J59 (11)	6.00	*7.45*
		Set, never hinged	19.00	

Exists imperf. Value, set $225.

For overprints see J64-J74, Western Ukraine Nos. 54-55, NJ1-NJ6, Poland Nos. J1-J10.

Type of Regular Issue of 1916 Surcharged

1917

No.	Type	Description	Unused	Used
J60	A38	10h on 24h blue	1.10	.40
J61	A38	15h on 36h violet	.30	.20
J62	A38	20h on 54h orange	.20	*.30*
J63	A38	50h on 42h chocolate	.20	.20
		Nos. J60-J63 (4)	1.80	1.10
		Set, never hinged	5.00	

All values of this issue are known imperforate, also without surcharge, perforated and imperforate. Values, set imperf unused hinged $140, never hinged $200. Value of set without surcharge imperf unused hinged $110, never hinged $200. Same values for set without surcharge, perf 12½.

For overprints see Western Ukraine Nos. 57-58.

Issues of the Republic

Postage Due Stamps of 1916 Overprinted

1919

No.	Type	Description	Unused	Used
J64	D4	5h rose red	.20	.20
a.		Inverted overprint	225.00	225.00
J65	D4	10h rose red	.20	.20
J66	D4	15h rose red	.25	*.35*
J67	D4	20h rose red	.25	*.35*
J68	D4	25h rose red	8.75	*13.50*
J69	D4	30h rose red	.20	*.25*
J70	D4	40h rose red	.25	*.60*
J71	D4	50h rose red	.30	*1.25*
J72	D5	1k ultramarine	3.50	*8.00*
J73	D5	5k ultramarine	8.00	*10.50*
J74	D5	10k ultramarine	7.25	3.50
		Nos. J64-J74 (11)	29.15	*38.70*
		Set, never hinged	67.50	

#J64, J65, J67, J70 exist imperf.

D6

D7

1920-21 *Perf. 12½*

No.	Type	Description	Unused	Used
J75	D6	5h bright red	.20	*.30*
J76	D6	10h bright red	.20	.20
J77	D6	15h bright red	.20	*1.10*
J78	D6	20h bright red	.20	.20
J79	D6	25h bright red	.20	*.90*
J80	D6	30h bright red	.20	*.25*
J81	D6	40h bright red	.20	*.20*
J82	D6	50h bright red	.20	*.20*
J83	D6	80h bright red	.20	*.25*
J84	D7	1k ultramarine	.20	.20
J85	D7	1½k ultra ('21)	.20	.20
J86	D7	2k ultra ('21)	.20	.20
J87	D7	3k ultra ('21)	.20	*.50*
J88	D7	4k ultra ('21)	.20	*.30*
J89	D7	5k ultramarine	.20	.20
J90	D7	8k ultra ('21)	.20	*.50*
J91	D7	10k ultramarine	.20	*.25*
J92	D7	20k ultra ('21)	.20	*.75*
		Nos. J75-J92 (18)		*6.70*
		Set, never hinged	3.50	

Nos. J84 to J92 exist on white paper and on grayish white paper. Values are for the cheaper varieties. See the Scott Classic Specialized Catalogue for detailed listings.

Nos. J84 to J92 also exist imperf. Values, set unused hinged $85, never hinged $115.

Imperf

No.	Type	Description	Unused	Used
J93	D6	5h bright red	.20	*.35*
J94	D6	10h bright red	.20	*.20*
J95	D6	15h bright red	.20	*.90*
J96	D6	20h bright red	.20	*.20*
J97	D6	25h bright red	.20	*.90*
J98	D6	30h bright red	.20	*.60*
J99	D6	40h bright red	.20	*.35*
J100	D6	50h bright red	.20	*.60*
J101	D6	80h bright red	.20	*.35*
		Nos. J93-J101 (9)		*4.45*
		Set, never hinged	1.40	

No. 207a Surcharged in Dark Blue

1921, Dec. *Perf. 12½*

No.	Type	Description	Unused	Used
J102	A43	7½k on 15h bister	.20	.20
		Never hinged	.20	
a.		Inverted surcharge	250.00	*350.00*
		Never hinged	350.00	

D8

D9

D10

1922

No.	Type	Description	Unused	Used
J103	D8	1k reddish buff	.20	*.25*
J104	D8	2k reddish buff	.20	*.25*
J105	D8	4k reddish buff	.20	*.50*
J106	D8	5k reddish buff	.20	*.25*
J107	D8	7½k reddish buff	.20	*.65*

J108 D8 10k blue green .20 .25
J109 D8 15k blue green .20 .50
J110 D8 20k blue green .20 .35
J111 D8 25k blue green .20 .80
J112 D8 40k blue green .20 .30
J113 D8 50k blue green .20 .90
Nos. J103-J113 (11) 5.00
Set, never hinged 1.75

Issue date: Nos. J108-J113, June 2.

1922-24

J114 D9 10k cobalt blue .20 .30
J115 D9 15k cobalt blue .20 .35
J116 D9 20k cobalt blue .20 .45
J117 D9 50k cobalt blue .20 .35
J118 D10 100k plum .20 .20
J119 D10 150k plum .20 .20
J120 D10 200k plum .20 .20
J121 D10 400k plum .20 .20
J122 D10 600k plum ('23) .20 .35
J123 D10 800k plum .20 .20
J124 D10 1,000k plum ('23) .20 .20
J125 D10 1,200k plum ('23) .20 2.50
J126 D10 1,500k plum ('24) .20 .25
J127 D10 1,800k plum ('24) 1.50 5.25
J128 D10 2,000k plum ('23) .30 .85
J129 D10 3,000k plum ('24) 5.75 12.00
J130 D10 4,000k plum ('24) 3.75 9.75
J131 D10 6,000k plum ('24) 6.75 16.00
Nos. J114-J131 (18) 20.65 49.60
Set, never hinged 40.00

J103-J131 sets exist imperf. Values, both sets unused hinged $240, never hinged $300.

D11

D12

1925-34 *Perf. 12½*

J132 D11 1g red .20 .20
J133 D11 2g red .20 .20
J134 D11 3g red .20 .20
J135 D11 4g red .20 .20
J136 D11 5g red ('27) .20 .20
J137 D11 6g red .20 .45
J138 D11 8g red .20 .20
J139 D11 10g dark blue .20 .20
J140 D11 12g dark blue .20 .20
J141 D11 14g dark blue ('27) .20 .20
J142 D11 15g dark blue .20 .20
J143 D11 16g dark blue ('29) .20 .20
J144 D11 18g dark blue ('34) 1.10 3.50
J145 D11 20g dark blue .20 .20
J146 D11 23g dark blue .25 .20
J147 D11 24g dark blue ('32) 1.10 .20
J148 D11 28g dark blue ('27) .90 .30
J149 D11 30g dark blue .20 .20
J150 D11 31g dark blue ('29) 1.10 .25
J151 D11 35g dark blue ('30) 1.10 .20
J152 D11 39g dark blue ('32) 1.40 .20
J153 D11 40g dark blue 1.25 1.75
J154 D11 60g dark blue .85 1.10
J155 D12 1s dark green 5.50 1.10
J156 D12 2s dark green 27.50 3.50
J157 D12 5s dark green 77.50 32.50
J158 D12 10s dark green 45.00 4.25
Nos. J132-J158 (27) 167.35 52.10
Set, never hinged 425.00

Issues of 1925-27 exist imperf. Values, set of 18 unused hinged $450, never hinged $550.

Issued: 3g, 2s-10s, Dec; 5g, 28g, 1/1; 14g, June; 31g, 2/1; 35g, Jan; 24g, 39g, Sept; 16g, May; 18g, 6/25; others, 6/1.

Coat of Arms
D13 D14

1935, June 1

J159 D13 1g red .20 .20
J160 D13 2g red .20 .20
J161 D13 3g red .20 .20
J162 D13 5g red .20 .20
J163 D13 10g blue .20 .20
J164 D13 12g blue .20 .20
J165 D13 15g blue .20 .40
J166 D13 20g blue .20 .20
J167 D13 24g blue .20 .20
J168 D13 30g blue .20 .20
J169 D13 39g blue .20 .20
J170 D13 60g blue .75 .90
J171 D14 1s green .75 .30
J172 D14 2s green 1.25 .70
J173 D14 5s green 2.75 2.50
J174 D14 10s green 3.75 .60
Nos. J159-J174 (16) 11.45 7.40
Set, never hinged 42.50

On #J163-J170, background lines are horiz.

Nos. J159-J174 exist imperf. Values, set unused hinged $200, never hinged $275.

Catalogue values for unused stamps in this section, from this point to the end of the section, are for Never Hinged items.

D15

1945 Unwmk. Typo. *Perf. 10½*

J175 D15 1g vermilion .20 .20
J176 D15 2g vermilion .20 .20
J177 D15 3g vermilion .20 .20
J178 D15 5g vermilion .20 .20
J179 D15 10g vermilion .20 .20
J180 D15 12g vermilion .20 .20
J181 D15 20g vermilion .20 .20
J182 D15 24g vermilion .20 .20
J183 D15 30g vermilion .20 .20
J184 D15 60g vermilion .20 .20
J185 D15 1s violet .20 .35
J186 D15 2s violet .20 .45
J187 D15 5s violet .20 .20
J188 D15 10s violet .20 .20
Nos. J175-J188 (14) 2.80 3.20

Issued: 1g-60g, Sept. 10; 1s-10s, Sept. 24.

Occupation Stamps of the Allied Military Government Overprinted in Black

1946 *Perf. 11*

J189 OS1 3g deep orange .35 .30
J190 OS1 5g bright green .35 .30
J191 OS1 6g red violet .35 .30
J192 OS1 8g rose pink .35 .30
J193 OS1 10g light gray .35 .30
J194 OS1 12g pale buff brown .40 .30
J195 OS1 15g rose red .40 .30
J196 OS1 20g copper brown .40 .30
J197 OS1 25g deep blue .40 .30
J198 OS1 30g bright violet .40 .30
J199 OS1 40g light ultra .40 .30
J200 OS1 60g light olive grn .40 .30
J201 OS1 1s dark violet .50 .40
J202 OS1 2s yellow .50 .40
J203 OS1 5s deep ultra .70 .60
Nos. J189-J203 (15) 6.25 5.00

Nos. J189-J203 were issued by the Renner Government. Inverted overprints exist on about half of the denominations.

Issued: 3g-60g, Apr. 23; 1s-5s, May 20.

Type of 1894-95
Inscribed "Republik Osterreich"

1947 Typo. *Perf. 14*

J204 D1 1g chocolate .20 .20
J205 D1 2g chocolate .20 .20
J206 D1 3g chocolate .20 .20
J207 D1 5g chocolate .20 .20
J208 D1 8g chocolate .20 .20
J209 D1 10g chocolate .20 .20
J210 D1 12g chocolate .20 .20
J211 D1 15g chocolate .20 .20
J212 D1 16g chocolate .20 .40
J213 D1 17g chocolate .20 .40
J214 D1 18g chocolate .20 .40
J215 D1 20g chocolate .50 .20
J216 D1 24g chocolate .30 .30
J217 D1 30g chocolate .20 .20
J218 D1 36g chocolate .50 .60
J219 D1 40g chocolate .20 .20
J220 D1 42g chocolate .50 .60
J221 D1 48g chocolate .50 .60
J222 D1 50g chocolate .55 .20
J223 D1 60g chocolate .20 .20
J224 D1 70g chocolate .20 .20
J225 D1 80g chocolate 3.75 1.75
J226 D1 1s blue .20 .20
J227 D1 1.15s blue 2.50 .30
J228 D1 1.20s blue 3.00 1.00
J229 D1 2s blue .40 .40
J230 D1 5s blue .40 .40
J231 D1 10s blue .40 .40
Nos. J204-J231 (28) 16.50 10.55

Issue dates: 1g, 20g, 50g, 80g, 1.15s, 1.20s, Sept. 25, others, Aug. 14.

D16

D17

1949-57

J232 D16 1g carmine .20 .20
J233 D16 2g carmine .20 .20
J234 D16 4g carmine ('51) 1.00 .20
J235 D16 5g carmine 2.25 .25
J236 D16 8g carmine ('51) 2.75 1.50
J237 D16 10g carmine .20 .20
J238 D16 20g carmine .20 .20
J239 D16 30g carmine .20 .20
J240 D16 40g carmine .20 .20
J241 D16 50g carmine .20 .20
J242 D16 60g carmine ('50) 7.50 .20
J243 D16 63g carmine ('57) 4.75 4.00
J244 D16 70g carmine .20 .20
J245 D16 80g carmine .20 .20
J246 D16 90g carmine ('50) .20 .20
J247 D16 1s purple .20 .20
J248 D16 1.20s purple .35 .20
J249 D16 1.35s purple .30 .20
J250 D16 1.40s purple ('51) .45 .20
J251 D16 1.50s purple ('53) .20 .20
J252 D16 1.65s purple ('50) .40 .20
J253 D16 1.70s purple .40 .20
J254 D16 2s purple .35 .20
J255 D16 2.50s purple ('51) .45 .20
J256 D16 3s purple ('51) 1.00 .20
J257 D16 4s purple ('51) 1.00 .45
J258 D16 5s purple 1.75 .20
J259 D16 10s purple 2.75 .20
Nos. J232-J259 (28) 29.85 11.00

Issued: 60g, 90g, 1.65s, 8/7; 4g, 8g, 1.40s, 2.50s-4s, 12/4; 1.50s, 2/18; 63g, 4/30; others, 11/17.

1985-89 Photo. *Perf. 14*
Background Color

J260 D17 10g brt yel ('86) .20 .20
J261 D17 20g pink ('86) .20 .20
J262 D17 50g orange ('86) .20 .20
J263 D17 1s lt blue ('86) .20 .20
J264 D17 2s pale brn ('86) .30 .20
J265 D17 3s violet ('86) .40 .30
J266 D17 5s ocher .60 .40
J267 D17 10s pale grn ('89) 1.50 1.10
Nos. J260-J267 (8) 3.60 2.80

Issue dates: 5s, Dec. 12. 20g, 1s, 3s, Mar. 19. 10g, 50g, 2s, Oct. 3. 10s, June 30.

MILITARY STAMPS

Issues of the Austro-Hungarian Military Authorities for the Occupied Territories in World War I

See Bosnia and Herzegovina for similar designs inscribed "MILITARPOST" instead of "FELDPOST."

Stamps of Bosnia of 1912-14 Overprinted

1915 Unwmk. *Perf. 12½*

M1 A23 1h olive green .20 .45
M2 A23 2h bright blue .20 .35
M3 A23 3h claret .20 .35
M4 A23 5h green .20 .20
M5 A23 6h dark gray .20 .35
M6 A23 10h rose carmine .20 .20
M7 A23 12h deep ol grn .20 .45
M8 A23 20h orange brn .20 .60
M9 A23 25h ultramarine .20 .45
M10 A23 30h orange red 1.90 4.50
M11 A24 35h myrtle grn 1.50 3.75
M12 A24 40h dark violet 1.50 3.75
M13 A24 45h olive brown 1.50 3.75
M14 A24 50h slate blue 1.50 3.75
M15 A24 60h brn violet .25 1.00
M16 A24 72h dark blue 1.50 3.75
M17 A25 1k brn vio, *straw* 1.60 4.00
M18 A25 2k dk gray, *blue* 1.60 4.00
M19 A26 3k car, *green* 19.00 37.50
M20 A26 5k dk vio, *gray* 17.00 27.50
M21 A25 10k dk ultra, *gray* 125.00 210.00
Nos. M1-M21 (21) 175.65 310.65
Set, never hinged 350.00

Exists imperf. Values, set unused hinged $225, never hinged $450.

Nos. M1-M21 also exist with overprint double, inverted and in red. These varieties were made by order of an official but were not regularly issued.

M1

M2
Emperor Franz Josef

Perf. 11½, 12½ and Compound

1915-17 Engr.

M22 M1 1h olive green .20 .20
M23 M1 2h dull blue .20 .25
M24 M1 3h claret .20 .20
M25 M1 5h green .20 .20
a. Perf. 11½ 62.50 80.00
Never hinged 110.00
b. Perf. 11½x12½ 92.50 125.00
Never hinged 175.00
c. Perf. 12½x11½ 110.00 175.00
Never hinged 210.00
M26 M1 6h dark gray .20 .25
M27 M1 10h rose carmine .20 .20
M28 M1 10h gray bl ('17) .20 .25
M29 M1 12h dp olive grn .20 .30
M30 M1 15h car rose ('17) .20 .20
a. Perf. 11½ 7.75 17.00
Never hinged 14.00
M31 M1 20h orange brn .25 .35
M32 M1 20h ol green ('17) .25 .35
M33 M1 25h ultramarine .20 .25
M34 M1 30h vermilion .20 .35
M35 M1 35h dark green .25 .55
M36 M1 40h dark violet .25 .55
M37 M1 45h olive brown .25 .55
M38 M1 50h myrtle green .25 .55
M39 M1 60h brown violet .25 .55
M40 M1 72h dark blue .25 .55
M41 M1 80h org brn ('17) .25 .25
M42 M1 90h magenta ('17) .70 1.00
M43 M2 1k brn vio, *straw* 1.25 1.90
M44 M2 2k dk gray, *blue* .75 1.00
M45 M2 3k car, *green* .70 2.00
M46 M2 4k dark violet, *gray* ('17) .60 3.25
M47 M2 5k dk vio, *gray* 16.00 27.50
M48 M2 10k dk ultra, *gray* 3.00 7.50
Nos. M22-M48 (27) 27.45 51.05
Set, never hinged 75.00

#M22-M48 exist imperf. Values, set unused hinged $140, never hinged $275.

Emperor Karl I
M3 M4

1917-18 *Perf. 12½*

M49 M3 1h grnsh blue ('18) .20 .20
a. Perf. 11½ 4.75 7.75
Never hinged 8.75
M50 M3 2h red org ('18) .20 .20
M51 M3 3h olive gray .20 .20
a. Perf. 11½ 15.00 27.50
Never hinged 32.50
b. Perf. 11½x12½ 27.50 52.50
Never hinged 55.00
M52 M3 5h olive green .20 .20
M53 M3 6h violet .20 .20
M54 M3 10h orange brn .20 .20
M55 M3 12h blue .20 .20
a. Perf. 11½ 3.00 5.50
Never hinged 6.25
M56 M3 15h bright rose .20 .20
M57 M3 20h red brown .20 .20
M58 M3 25h ultramarine .20 .25
M59 M3 30h slate .20 .20
M60 M3 40h olive bister .20 .20
a. Perf. 11½ 1.90 3.00
Never hinged 3.75
M61 M3 50h deep green .20 .20
a. Perf. 11½ 7.75 14.00
Never hinged 15.00
M62 M3 60h car rose .20 .20
M63 M3 80h dull blue .20 .20
M64 M3 90h dk violet .25 .45
M65 M4 2k rose, *straw* .20 .25
a. Perf. 11½ 2.75 5.00
Never hinged 5.50
M66 M4 3k green, *blue* .85 2.10
M67 M4 4k rose, *green* 13.50 17.00
a. Perf. 11½ 26.00 50.00
Never hinged 52.50
M68 M4 10k dl vio, *gray* 1.00 5.00
a. Perf. 11½ 12.50 25.00
Never hinged 25.00
Nos. M49-M68 (20) 18.80 27.85
Set, never hinged 47.50

Nos. M49-M68 exist imperf. Values, set unused hinged $90, never hinged $175.

See No. M82. For surcharges and overprints see Italy Nos. N1-N19, Poland Nos. 30-40, Romania Nos. 1N1-1N17, Western Ukraine Nos. 34-53, 75-81.

Emperor Karl I — M5

1918 Typo. *Perf. 12½*

No.	Type	Value	Color	Unused
M69	M5	1h	grnsh blue	16.00
M70	M5	2h	orange	6.25
M71	M5	3h	olive gray	6.25
M72	M5	5h	yellow green	.20
M73	M5	10h	dark brown	.20
M74	M5	20h	red	.55
M75	M5	25h	blue	.55
M76	M5	30h	bister	67.50
M77	M5	45h	dark slate	80.00
M78	M5	50h	deep green	42.50
M79	M5	60h	violet	90.00
M80	M5	80h	rose	52.50
M81	M5	90h	brown violet	1.60
		Engr.		
M82	M4	1k	ol bister, *blue*	.20
		Nos. M69-M82 (14)		364.30
		Set, never hinged		800.00

Nos. M69-M82 were on sale at the Vienna post office for a few days before the Armistice signing. They were never issued at the Army Post Offices. They exist imperf. Values, set unused hinged $675, never hinged $1,150.

For surcharges see Italy Nos. N20-N33.

MILITARY SEMI-POSTAL STAMPS

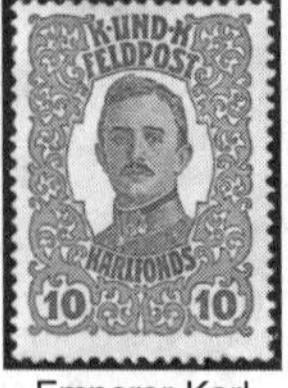
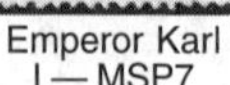

Emperor Karl I — MSP7 Empress Zita — MSP8

Perf. 12½x13

1918, July 20 Unwmk. Typo.

No.	Type	Value	Color	Unused	Used
MB1	MSP7	10h	gray green	.25	.55
MB2	MSP8	20h	magenta	.25	.55
MB3	MSP7	45h	blue	.25	.55
		Nos. MB1-MB3 (3)		.75	1.65
		Set, never hinged		2.10	

Nos. M69-M82 were on sale at the Vienna post office for a few days before the Armistice signing. They were never issued at the Army Post Offices. They exist imperf. Values, set unused hinged $675, never hinged $1,150.

These stamps were sold at a premium of 10h each over face value. The surtax was for "Karl's Fund."

For overprints see Poland Nos. 27-29, Western Ukraine Nos. 31-33.

Exist imperf. Values, set hinged unused $25, never hinged $55.

MILITARY NEWSPAPER STAMPS

Mercury — MN1

1916 Unwmk. Typo. *Perf. 12½*

No.	Type	Value	Color	Unused	Used
MP1	MN1	2h	blue	.20	*.20*
a.			Perf. 11½	1.40	*1.60*
			Never hinged	1.75	
b.			Perf. 12½x11½	150.00	*200.00*
			Never hinged	250.00	
MP2	MN1	6h	orange	.50	*.80*
MP3	MN1	10h	carmine	.60	*.80*
MP4	MN1	20h	brown	.40	*.80*
a.			Perf. 11½	1.90	*5.00*
			Never hinged	5.00	
		Nos. MP1-MP4 (4)		1.70	*2.60*
		Set, never hinged		2.10	

Exist imperf. Values, Nos. MP2-MP3, unused hinged each $3.50, never hinged $4.50; Nos. MP1, MP4, unused hinged each $19, never hinged $45.

For surcharges see Italy Nos. NP1-NP4.

NEWSPAPER STAMPS

From 1851 to 1866, the Austrian Newspaper Stamps were also used in Lombardy-Venetia.

Values for unused stamps 1851-67 are for fine copies with original gum. Specimens without gum sell for about a third or less of the figures quoted.

Issues of the Monarchy

Mercury — N1

Three Types

Type I - The "G" has no crossbar.

Type II - The "G" has a crossbar.

Type IIa - as type II but the rosette is deformed. Two spots of color in the "G."

1851-56 Unwmk. Typo. *Imperf.*

Machine-made Paper

No.	Type	Value	Description	Unused	Used
P1	N1	(0.6kr)	bl, type IIa	175.00	75.00
a.			Blue, type I	250.00	110.00
b.			Ribbed paper	625.00	160.00
c.			Blue, type II	600.00	250.00
P2	N1	(6kr)	yel, type I	—	*7,000.*
P3	N1	(30kr)	rose, type I	—	*9,000.*
P4	N1	(6kr)	scar, type II ('56)	*67,500.*	*40,000.*

From 1852 No. P3 and from 1856 No. P2 were used as 0.6 kreuzer values.

Values for Nos. P2-P3 unused are for stamps without gum. Pale shades sell at considerably lower values.

Originals of Nos. P2-P3 are usually in pale colors and poorly printed. Values are for stamps clearly printed and in bright colors. Numerous reprints of Nos. P1-P4 were made between 1866 and 1904. Those of Nos. P2-P3 are always well printed and in much deeper colors. All reprints are in type I, but occasionally show faint traces of a crossbar on "G" of "ZEITUNGS."

N2

N3

Two Types of the 1858-59 Issue

Type I - Loops of the bow at the back of the head broken.

Type II - Loops complete. Wreath projects further at top of head.

1858-59 Embossed

No.	Type	Value	Description	Unused	Used
P5	N2	(1kr)	blue, type I	650.00	550.00
P6	N2	(1kr)	lilac, type II ('59)	875.00	275.00

1861

No.	Type	Value	Description	Unused	Used
P7	N3	(1kr)	gray	175.00	125.00
a.		(1kr)	gray lilac	625.00	175.00
b.		(1kr)	deep lilac	2,500.	575.00

The embossing on the reprints of the 1858-59 and 1861 issues is not as sharp as on the originals.

N4

Wmk. 91, or, before July 1864, Unwmkd.

1863

No.	Type	Value	Description	Unused	Used
P8	N4	(1.05kr)	gray	45.00	15.00
a.			Tete beche pair	*125,000.*	
b.		(1.05kr)	gray lilac	75.00	17.50

Values are for stamps that do not show the watermark. Stamps showing the watermark often sell for more.

The embossing of the reprints is not as sharp as on the originals.

N5

Mercury — N6

Three Types

Type I - Helmet not defined at back, more or less blurred. Two thick short lines in front of wing of helmet. Shadow on front of face not separated from hair.

Type II - Helmet distinctly defined. Four thin short lines in front of wing. Shadow on front of face clearly defined from hair.

Type III - Outer white circle around head is open at top (closed on types I and II). Greek border at top and bottom is wider than on types I and II.

1867-73 Typo. Wmk. 91

Coarse Print

No.	Type	Value	Description	Unused	Used
P9	N5	(1kr)	vio, type I	37.50	4.00
a.		(1kr)	violet, type II ('73)	125.00	18.00

1874-76

Fine Print

No.	Type	Value	Description	Unused	Used
P9B	N5	(1kr)	violet, type III ('76)	.55	.20
c.		(1kr)	gray lilac, type I ('76)	90.00	25.00
d.		(1kr)	violet, type II	27.50	5.00
e.			Double impression, type III		175.00

Stamps of this issue, except No. P9c, exist in many shades, from gray to lilac brown and deep violet. Stamps in type III exist also privately perforated or rouletted.

1880

No.	Type	Value	Description	Unused	Used
P10	N6	½kr	blue green	4.50	.85

Nos. P9B and P10 also exist on thicker paper without sheet watermark and No. P10 exists with unofficial perforation.

N7

1899 Unwmk. *Imperf.*

Without Varnish Bars

No.	Type	Value	Color	Unused	Used
P11	N7	2h	dark blue	.20	.20
P12	N7	6h	orange	2.00	1.75
P13	N7	10h	brown	.80	.75
P14	N7	20h	rose	1.75	1.75
		Nos. P11-P14 (4)		4.75	4.45

1901

With Varnish Bars

No.	Type	Value	Color	Unused	Used
P11a	N7	2h	dark blue	.60	.20
P12a	N7	6h	orange	8.50	*11.50*
P13a	N7	10h	brown	10.50	6.75
P14a	N7	20h	rose	19.00	*26.00*
		Nos. P11a-P14a (4)		38.60	*44.45*

Nos. P11 to P14 were re-issued in 1905.

N8

Mercury N9

1908 *Imperf.*

No.	Type	Value	Color	Unused	Used
P15	N8	2h	dark blue	1.40	.20
a.			Tete beche pair	250.00	*300.00*
P16	N8	6h	orange	2.50	.30
P17	N8	10h	carmine	2.50	.30
P18	N8	20h	brown	2.75	.25
		Nos. P15-P18 (4)		9.15	1.05

All values are found on chalky, regular and thin ordinary paper. They exist privately perforated.

1916 *Imperf.*

No.	Type	Value	Color	Unused	Used
P19	N9	2h	brown	.20	.20
P20	N9	4h	green	.30	*.85*
P21	N9	6h	dark blue	.25	*.70*
P22	N9	10h	orange	.35	*.85*
P23	N9	30h	claret	.30	*.80*
		Nos. P19-P23 (5)		1.40	*3.40*
		Set, never hinged		2.75	

Issues of the Republic

Newspaper Stamps of 1916 Overprinted

1919

No.	Type	Value	Color	Unused	Used
P24	N9	2h	brown	.20	.20
P25	N9	4h	green	.25	*.70*
P26	N9	6h	dark blue	.20	*.70*
P27	N9	10h	orange	.25	*.90*
P28	N9	30h	claret	.20	*.50*
		Nos. P24-P28 (5)		1.10	*3.00*
		Set, never hinged		1.75	

Mercury
N10 N11

1920-21 *Imperf.*

No.	Type	Value	Color	Unused	Used
P29	N10	2h	violet	.20	.20
P30	N10	4h	brown	.20	*.20*
P31	N10	5h	slate	.20	.20
P32	N10	6h	turq blue	.20	.20
P33	N10	8h	green	.20	*.30*
P34	N10	9h	yellow ('21)	.20	.20
P35	N10	10h	red	.20	.20
P36	N10	12h	blue	.20	*.30*
P37	N10	15h	lilac ('21)	.20	.20
P38	N10	18h	blue grn ('21)	.20	*.25*
P39	N10	20h	orange	.20	*.25*
P40	N10	30h	yellow brn ('21)	.20	.20
P41	N10	45h	green ('21)	.20	*.35*
P42	N10	60h	claret	.20	.20
P43	N10	72h	chocolate ('21)	.20	*.45*
P44	N10	90h	violet ('21)	.20	*.55*
P45	N10	1.20k	red ('21)	.20	*.65*
P46	N10	2.40k	yellow grn ('21)	.20	*.55*
P47	N10	3k	gray ('21)	.20	*.40*
		Nos. P29-P47 (19)		3.80	*5.85*
		Set, never hinged		4.00	

Nos. P37-P40, P42, P44 and P47 exist also on thick grayish paper. Values are for the cheaper varieties. See the Scott Classic Specialized Catalogue for detailed listings.

1921-22

No.	Type	Value	Color	Unused	Used
P48	N11	45h	gray	.20	*.25*
P49	N11	75h	brown org ('22)	.20	*.35*
P50	N11	1.50k	ol bister ('22)	.20	*.50*
P51	N11	1.80k	gray blue ('22)	.20	*.55*
P52	N11	2.25k	light brown	.20	*.75*
P53	N11	3k	dull green ('22)	.20	*.55*
P54	N11	6k	claret ('22)	.20	*.65*
P55	N11	7.50k	bister	.20	*.85*
		Nos. P48-P55 (8)		1.60	*4.45*
		Set, never hinged		1.75	

Nos. P24-P55 exist privately perforated.

NEWSPAPER TAX STAMPS

Values for unused stamps 1853-59 are for copies in fine condition with gum. Specimens without gum sell for about one-third or less of the figures quoted.

Issues of the Monarchy

NT1

NT2

Unwmk.

1853, Mar. 1 Typo. *Imperf.*

No.	Type	Value	Color	Unused	Used
PR1	NT1	2kr	green	1,450.	50.00

The reprints are in finer print than the more coarsely printed originals, and on a smooth toned paper.

Values for Nos. PR2-PR9 are for stamps that do not show the watermark. Stamps showing the watermark often sell for more.

Wmk. 91, or, before July 1864, Unwmkd.

1858-59

Two Types.

Type I - The banderol on the Crown of the left eagle touches the beak of the eagle.

Type II - The banderol does not touch the beak.

PR2 NT2 1kr blue, type II ('59) 30.00 5.50
a. 1kr blue, type I 675.00 140.00
b. Printed on both sides, type II —
PR3 NT2 2kr brown, type II ('59) 22.50 6.75
a. 2kr red brown, type II 350.00 150.00
PR4 NT2 4kr brn, type I 400.00 *850.00*

Nos. PR2a, PR3a, and PR4 were printed only on unwatermarked paper. Nos. PR2 and PR3 exist on unwatermarked and watermarked paper.

Nos. PR2 and PR3 exist in coarse and (after 1874) in fine print, like the contemporary postage stamps.

The reprints of the 4kr brown are of type II and on a smooth toned paper.

Issue date: 4kr, Nov. 1.

See Lombardy-Venetia for the 1kr in black and the 2kr, 4fk in red.

NT3

NT4

1877 **Redrawn**

PR5 NT3 1kr blue 12.50 1.40
a. 1kr pale ultramarine *1,600.*
PR6 NT3 2kr brown 14.00 6.75

In the redrawn stamps the shield is larger and the vertical bar has eight lines above the white square and nine below, instead of five.

Nos. PR5 and PR6 exist also watermarked "WECHSEL" instead of "ZEITUNGS-MARKEN."

1890, June 1

PR7 NT4 1kr brown 9.00 1.00
PR8 NT4 2kr green 10.00 1.60

#PR5-PR8 exist with private perforation.

NT5

Perf. 13, 12½

1890, June 1 **Wmk. 91**

PR9 NT5 25kr carmine 90.00 *200.00*

Nos. PR1-PR9 did not pay postage, but were a fiscal tax, collected by the postal authorities on newspapers.

SPECIAL HANDLING STAMPS

(For Printed Matter Only) Issues of the Monarchy

Mercury SH1

1916 **Unwmk.** ***Perf. 12½***

QE1 SH1 2h claret, *yel* .60 *1.60*
QE2 SH1 5h dp green, *yel* .60 *1.60*
Set, never hinged 3.50

SH2

1917 ***Perf. 12½***

QE3 SH2 2h claret, *yel* .20 *.30*
a. Pair, imperf. between 175.00 *275.00*
Never hinged 200.00
b. Perf. 11½x12½ 55.00 *95.00*
Never hinged 110.00
c. Perf. 12½x11½ 80.00 *150.00*
Never hinged 160.00
d. Perf. 11½ 1.25 *2.50*
Never hinged 2.50
QE4 SH2 5h dp green, *yel* .20 *.30*
a. Pair, imperf. between 160.00 *250.00*
Never hinged 175.00
b. Perf. 11½x12½ 45.00 *87.50*
Never hinged 95.00
c. Perf. 12½x11½ 70.00 *140.00*
Never hinged 140.00
d. Perf. 11½ 1.25 *2.50*
Never hinged 2.50
Set, never hinged .60

Nos. QE1-QE4 exist imperforate.

Issues of the Republic

Nos. QE3 and QE4 Overprinted

1919

QE5 SH2 2h claret, *yel* .20 .20
a. Inverted overprint 325.00
Never hinged 375.00
b. Perf. 11½x12½ 5.25 *10.50*
Never hinged 8.00
c. Perf. 12½x11½ 65.00 *160.00*
Never hinged 125.00
d. Perf. 11½ .30 *1.10*
Never hinged .65
QE6 SH2 5h deep green, *yel* .20 .20
a. Perf. 11½x12½ 2.25 *3.75*
Never hinged 2.75
b. Perf. 12½x11½ 25.00 *45.00*
Never hinged 37.50
c. Perf. 11½ .20 *.70*
Never hinged .45
Set, never hinged .40

Nos. QE5 and QE6 exist imperforate. Value, set unused hinged $100.

SH3

Dark Blue Surcharge

1921

QE7 SH3 50h on 2h claret, *yel* .20 *.20*
Never hinged .20

SH4

1922 ***Perf. 12½***

QE8 SH4 50h lilac, *yel* .20 *1.75*
Never hinged .20

#QE5-QE8 exist in vertical pairs, imperf between. No. QE8 exists imperf. Value, unused hinged $110.

OCCUPATION STAMPS

Issued under Italian Occupation

Issued in Trieste

Austrian Stamps of 1916-18 Overprinted

1918 **Unwmk.** ***Perf. 12½***

N1 A37 3h bright vio 1.00 1.00
a. Double overprint 30.00 30.00
b. Inverted overprint 30.00 30.00
N2 A37 5h light grn 1.00 1.00
a. Inverted overprint 30.00 30.00
c. Double overprint 30.00
N3 A37 6h dp orange 1.40 1.40
N4 A37 10h magenta 4.00 2.50
a. Inverted overprint 30.00 30.00
N5 A37 12h light bl 2.00 2.00
a. Double overprint 30.00 30.00
N6 A42 15h dull red 1.00 1.00
a. Inverted overprint 30.00 30.00
b. Double overprint 30.00 30.00
N7 A42 20h dark green 1.00 1.00
a. Inverted overprint 30.00 30.00
c. Double overprint 67.50
N8 A42 25h deep blue 6.75 6.75
a. Inverted overprint 125.00 125.00
N9 A42 30h dl violet 2.00 2.00
N10 A39 40h olive grn 85.00 85.00
N11 A39 50h dark green 7.00 6.75
N12 A39 60h deep blue 19.00 18.00
N13 A39 80h orange brn 11.00 12.00
a. Inverted overprint —
N14 A39 1k car, *yel* 11.00 12.00
a. Double overprint 67.50
N15 A40 2k light bl 200.00 200.00
Never hinged 400.00
N16 A40 4k yellow grn 400.00 400.00
Never hinged 800.00

Handstamped

N17 A40 10k dp violet *25,000.* *25,000.*
Never hinged *27,500.*

Granite Paper

N18 A40 2k light blue 300.00
Never hinged 600.00
N19 A40 3k car rose 250.00 250.00
Never hinged 500.00
Nos. N1-N14 (14) 153.15 152.40
Set, never hinged, #N1-N14 300.00

Some authorities question the authenticity of No. N18. Counterfeits of Nos. N10, N15-N19 are plentiful.

Italian Stamps of 1901-18 Overprinted

Wmk. 140 ***Perf. 14***

N20 A42 1c brown 1.50 *2.00*
a. Inverted overprint 20.00 20.00
N21 A43 2c orange brn 1.50 *2.00*
a. Inverted overprint 17.00 *17.00*
N22 A48 5c green .70 *1.00*
a. Inverted overprint 35.00 *35.00*
b. Double overprint 85.00
N23 A48 10c claret .70 *1.00*
a. Inverted overprint 47.50 *47.50*
b. Double overprint 85.00
N24 A50 20c brn orange .90 *1.25*
a. Inverted overprint 67.50 *67.50*
b. Double overprint 85.00 *85.00*
N25 A49 25c blue 1.00 *1.75*
a. Double overprint —
b. Inverted overprint 85.00 *85.00*
N26 A49 40c brown 8.00 *10.00*
a. Inverted overprint —
N27 A45 45c olive grn 2.50 *3.50*
a. Inverted overprint 95.00 *95.00*
N28 A49 50c violet 3.50 *4.75*
N29 A49 60c brown car 42.50 *55.00*
a. Inverted overprint —
b. Double overprint 190.00
N30 A46 1 l brn & green 14.50 *21.00*
a. Inverted overprint —
Nos. N20-N30 (11) 77.30 *103.25*
Set, never hinged 150.00

Italian Stamps of 1901-18 Surcharged

N31 A48 5h on 5c green 1.00 *1.50*
Never hinged 2.00
a. "5" omitted 85.00 *85.00*
b. Inverted surcharge 85.00 *85.00*
N32 A50 20h on 20c brn org 1.00 1.50
Never hinged 2.00
a. Double surcharge 85.00 *85.00*

Issued in the Trentino

Austrian Stamps of 1916-18 Overprinted

1918 **Unwmk.** ***Perf. 12½***

N33 A37 3h bright vio 4.00 3.00
a. Double overprint 67.50 *67.50*
b. Inverted overprint 55.00 *55.00*
N34 A37 5h light grn 3.50 1.75
a. "8 nov. 1918" *1,750.*
b. Inverted overprint 55.00 *55.00*
N35 A37 6h dp orange 50.00 40.00
N36 A37 10h magenta 3.50 2.00
a. "8 nov. 1918" 95.00 95.00
N37 A37 12h light blue 140.00 110.00
N38 A42 15h dull red 4.00 3.00
N39 A42 20h dark green 2.00 2.00
a. "8 nov. 1918" 110.00 *110.00*
b. Double overprint 67.50 67.50
c. Inverted overprint 22.50 22.50
N40 A42 25h deep blue 35.00 30.00
N41 A42 30h dl violet 12.00 10.00
N42 A39 40h olive grn 45.00 40.00
N43 A39 50h dark green 27.50 22.50
a. Inverted overprint 110.00 110.00
N44 A39 60h deep blue 40.00 35.00
a. Double overprint 110.00 *110.00*
N45 A39 80h orange brn 55.00 45.00
N46 A39 90h red violet 1,250. 1,000.
N47 A39 1k car, *yel* 55.00 45.00
N48 A40 2k light blue 375.00 290.00
N49 A40 4k yel green *1,750.* *1,500.*
N50 A40 10k dp violet —

Granite Paper

N51 A40 2k light blue *475.00*
Never hinged 675.00

Counterfeits of Nos. N33-N51 are plentiful.

Italian Stamps of 1901-18 Overprinted

Wmk. 140 ***Perf. 14***

N52 A42 1c brown 1.00 *3.50*
a. Inverted overprint 55.00 55.00
b. Double overprint 55.00
N53 A43 2c orange brn 1.00 *3.50*
a. Inverted overprint 55.00 55.00
N54 A48 5c green 1.00 *3.50*
a. Inverted overprint 55.00 55.00
b. Double overprint 55.00 55.00
N55 A48 10c claret 1.00 *3.50*
a. Inverted overprint 75.00 75.00
b. Double overprint 55.00 55.00
N56 A50 20c brn orange 1.00 *3.50*
a. Inverted overprint 75.00 75.00
N57 A49 40c brown 55.00 35.00
N58 A45 45c olive grn 25.00 *35.00*
a. Double overprint 140.00 140.00
N59 A49 50c violet 25.00 *35.00*
N60 A46 1 l brn & green 25.00 35.00
a. Double overprint 140.00 140.00
Nos. N52-N60 (9) 135.00 *157.50*

Italian Stamps of 1906-18 Surcharged

N61 A48 5h on 5c green 1.00 *1.75*
N62 A48 10h on 10c claret 1.00 *1.75*
a. Inverted surcharge 67.50 *67.50*
N63 A50 20h on 20c brn org 1.00 *1.75*
a. Double surcharge 67.50 *67.50*
Nos. N61-N63 (3) 3.00 *5.25*

General Issue

Italian Stamps of 1901-18 Surcharged

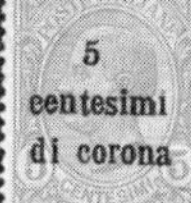

1919

N64 A42 1c on 1c brown .90 *1.25*
a. Inverted surcharge 17.00 17.50
N65 A43 2c on 2c org brn .90 *1.25*
a. Double surcharge 175.00
b. Inverted surcharge 13.50 13.50
N66 A48 5c on 5c green .85 .45
a. Inverted surcharge 40.00 40.00
b. Double surcharge 67.50
N67 A48 10c on 10c claret .90 .45
a. Inverted surcharge 40.00 40.00
b. Double surcharge 67.50 *67.50*
N68 A50 20c on 20c brn org .90 .45
a. Double surcharge 87.50 *87.50*
N69 A49 25c on 25c blue .85 *1.00*
a. Double surcharge 87.50
N70 A49 40c on 40c brown .90 *2.00*
a. "ccrona" 100.00 *100.00*
N71 A45 45c on 45c ol grn .90 *2.00*
a. Inverted surcharge 110.00 110.00
N72 A49 50c on 50c violet .90 *2.00*
N73 A49 60c on 60c brn car .90 *3.00*
a. "00" for "60" 125.00 *125.00*

Surcharged

N74 A46 1cor on 1 l brn & grn 1.75 3.00
Nos. N64-N74 (11) 10.65 16.85

Surcharges similar to these but differing in style or arrangement of type were used in Dalmatia.

Surcharged

N74 A46 1cor on 1 l brn & grn 1.75 3.00
Nos. N64-N74 (11) 10.65 16.85

Surcharges similar to these but differing in style or arrangement of type were used in Dalmatia.

OCCUPATION SPECIAL DELIVERY STAMPS

Issued in Trieste

Special Delivery Stamp of Italy of 1903 Overprinted

1918 Wmk. 140 *Perf. 14*

NE1 SD1 25c rose red 30.00 37.50
Never hinged 60.00
a. Inverted overprint 125.00 125.00

General Issue

Special Delivery Stamps of Italy of 1903-09 Surcharged

1919

NE2 SD1 25c on 25c rose 1.10 *1.75*
a. Double surcharge 67.50 *67.50*
NE3 SD2 30c on 30c bl & rose 1.50 *2.40*

OCCUPATION POSTAGE DUE STAMPS

Issued in Trieste

Postage Due Stamps of Italy, 1870-94, Overprinted

1918 Wmk. 140 *Perf. 14*

NJ1 D3 5c buff & mag .25 .45
a. Inverted overprint 13.50 13.50
b. Double overprint 150.00
NJ2 D3 10c buff & mag .35 *.50*
a. Inverted overprint 67.50 *67.50*
NJ3 D3 20c buff & mag .75 *1.10*
a. Double overprint 150.00
b. Inverted overprint 67.50 *67.50*
NJ4 D3 30c buff & mag 2.00 *3.00*
NJ5 D3 40c buff & mag 22.50 *30.00*
a. Inverted overprint 200.00 *200.00*
NJ6 D3 50c buff & mag 50.00 *67.50*
a. Inverted overprint 240.00 *250.00*
NJ7 D3 1 l bl & mag 150.00 200.00
Nos. NJ1-NJ7 (7) 225.85 *302.55*

General Issue

Postage Due Stamps of Italy, 1870-1903 Surcharged

1919

Buff & Magenta

NJ8 D3 5c on 5c .50 *.70*
a. Inverted overprint 19.00 19.00
NJ9 D3 10c on 10c .50 *.70*
a. Center and surcharge invtd. 125.00 *125.00*
NJ10 D3 20c on 20c .70 *1.00*
a. Double overprint 140.00 *140.00*
NJ11 D3 30c on 30c .85 *1.50*
NJ12 D3 40c on 40c .85 *1.50*
NJ13 D3 50c on 50c .85 *1.50*

Surcharged

NJ14 D3 1cor on 1 l bl & mag .85 *1.50*
NJ15 D3 2cor on 2 l bl & mag 45.00 *80.00*
NJ16 D3 5cor on 5 l bl & mag 45.00 *80.00*
Nos. NJ8-NJ16 (9) 95.10 *168.40*

A. M. G. ISSUE FOR AUSTRIA

Catalogue values for unused stamps in this section are for Never Hinged items.

Issued jointly by the Allied Military Government of the US and Great Britain, for civilian use in areas under American, British and French occupation. (Upper Austria, Salzburg, Tyrol, Vorarlberg, Styria and Carinthia).

OS1

1945 Unwmk. Litho. *Perf. 11*

4N1 OS1 1g aquamarine .25 *.35*
4N2 OS1 3g deep orange .25 *.35*
4N3 OS1 4g buff .25 *.35*
4N4 OS1 5g bright green .25 *.35*
4N5 OS1 6g red violet .35 *.35*
4N6 OS1 8g rose pink .25 *.35*
4N7 OS1 10g light gray .35 .35
4N8 OS1 12g pale buff brown .35 .35
4N9 OS1 15g rose red .35 .35
4N10 OS1 20g copper brown .35 .35
4N11 OS1 25g deep blue .25 *.35*
4N12 OS1 30g bright violet .25 *.35*
4N13 OS1 40g light ultra .25 *.35*
4N14 OS1 60g light olive grn .35 .35
4N15 OS1 1s dark violet .35 *.45*
4N16 OS1 2s yellow .35 *.55*
4N17 OS1 5s deep ultra .55 *.75*

For Nos. 4N2, 4N4-4N17 overprinted "PORTO" see Nos. J189-J203.

AUSTRIAN OFFICES ABROAD

These stamps were on sale and usable at all Austrian post-offices in Crete and in the Turkish Empire.

100 Centimes = 1 Franc

OFFICES IN CRETE

Used values are italicized for stamps often found with false cancellations.

Stamps of Austria of 1899-1901 Issue, Surcharged in Black:

a

b

c

d

1903-04 Unwmk. *Perf. 12½, 13½*

On Nos. 73a, 75a, 77a, 81a

Granite Paper

With Varnish Bars

1 A15(a) 5c on 5h blue green 1.40 *3.50*
2 A16(b) 10c on 10h rose .80 *4.00*
3 A16(b) 25c on 25h ultra 30.00 22.50
4 A17(c) 50c on 50h gray blue 7.50 *110.00*

On Nos. 83, 83a, 84, 85

Without Varnish Bars

5 A18(d) 1fr on 1k car rose 2.00 *100.00*
a. 1fr on 1k carmine 4.00 —
b. Horiz. or vert. pair, imperf. between 175.00
6 A18(d) 2fr on 2k ('04) 8.50 *225.00*
7 A18(d) 4fr on 4k ('04) 10.50 *4.50*
Nos. 1-7 (7) 60.70

Surcharged on Austrian Stamps of 1904-05

1905

On Nos. 89, 97

Without Varnish Bars

8a A19(a) 5c on 5h blue green 35.00 35.00
9 A20(b) 10c on 10h car .70 *9.00*

On Nos. 89a, 97a, 99a, 103a

With Varnish Bars

8 A19(a) 5c on 5h bl grn 3.50 5.25
9a A20(b) 10c on 10h carmine 18.00 22.50
10 A20(b) 25c on 25h ultra .90 *90.00*
11 A21(b) 50c on 50h dl bl .90 *375.00*

Surcharged on Austrian Stamps and Type of 1906-07

1907 *Perf. 12½, 13½*

Without Varnish Bars

12 A19(b) 5c on 5h yel green (#90) .70 *3.50*
13 A20(b) 10c on 10h car (#92) 1.00 *27.50*
14 A20(b) 15c on 15h vio 1.10 *26.00*
Nos. 12-14 (3) 2.80 *57.00*

A5

A6

1908 Typo. *Perf. 12½*

15 A5 5c green, *yellow* .30 *.60*
16 A5 10c scarlet, *rose* .35 *.80*
17 A5 15c brown, *buff* .45 *4.50*
18 A5 25c dp blue, *blue* 10.50 5.00

Engr.

19 A6 50c lake, *yellow* 1.60 *21.00*
20 A6 1fr brown, *gray* 2.25 *32.50*
a. Vert pair, imperf. btwn. 200.00
Nos. 15-20 (6) 15.45 *64.40*

Nos. 15-18 are on paper colored on the surface only. All values exist imperforate.

60th year of the reign of Emperor Franz Josef, for permanent use.

Paper Colored Through

1914 Typo.

21 A5 10c rose, *rose* 1.50 *900.00*
22 A5 25c ultra, *blue* .60 *125.00*

Nos. 21 and 22 exist imperforate.

OFFICES IN THE TURKISH EMPIRE

From 1863 to 1867 the stamps of Lombardy-Venetia (Nos. 15 to 24) were used at the Austrian Offices in the Turkish Empire.

100 Soldi = 1 Florin
40 Paras = 1 Piaster

Values for unused stamps are for copies with gum. Specimens without gum sell for about one-third or less of the figures quoted.

Used values are italicized for stamps often found with false cancellations.

For similar designs in Kreuzers, see early Austria.

A1

A2

Two different printing methods were used, as in the 1867-74 issues of Austria. They may be distinguished by the coarse or fine lines of the hair and whiskers and by the paper, which is more transparent on the later issue.

1867 Typo. Wmk. 91 *Perf. 9½*

Coarse Print

1 A1 2sld orange 1.75 *22.50*
a. 2sld yellow 50.00 27.50
2 A1 3sld green 100.00 40.00
a. 3sld dark green 125.00 70.00
3 A1 5sld red 90.00 11.00
a. 5sld carmine 110.00 14.50
4 A1 10sld blue 95.00 1.75
a. 10sld light blue 110.00 2.50
b. 10sld dark blue 100.00 3.00
5 A1 15sld brown 16.00 6.50
a. 15sld dark brown 50.00 21.00
b. 15sld reddish brown 17.50 10.00
c. 15sld gray brown 45.00 9.00
6 A1 25sld violet 12.50 *30.00*
a. 25sld brown violet 16.00 *35.00*
b. 25sld gray lilac 50.00 *35.00*
7 A2 50sld brn, perf. 10½ 1.00 *42.50*
a. Perf. 12 80.00 *65.00*
b. Perf. 13 250.00
k. Perf. 9 25.00 *50.00*
l. 50sld pale red brn, perf. 12 55.00 60.00
m. Vert. pair, imperf. btwn. 300.00 *650.00*
n. Horiz. pair, imperf. btwn. 300.00 *750.00*
o. Perf. 10½x9 60.00 100.00

Perf. 9, 9½, 10½ and Compound

1876-83

Fine Print

7C A1 2sld yellow ('83) .20 *1,300.*
7D A1 3sld green ('78) 1.00 *20.00*
7E A1 5sld red ('78) .40 *15.00*
7F A1 10sld blue 65.00 1.00
7I A1 15sld org brn ('81) 9.00 *125.00*
7J A1 25sld gray lilac ('83) .50 *275.00*
Nos. 7C-7J (6) 76.10

The 10 soldi has been reprinted in deep dull blue, perforated 10½.

A3

1883 *Perf. 9½, 10, 10½*

8 A3 2sld brown .20 *110.00*
9 A3 3sld green 1.00 *25.00*
10 A3 5sld rose .20 *16.00*
11 A3 10sld blue .75 *.50*
12 A3 20sld gray, perf. 10 1.00 *60.00*
a. Perf. 9½ 5.00 6.75
13 A3 50sld red lilac 1.40 *16.00*
Nos. 8-13 (6) 4.55

No. 9 Surcharged

10 PARAS ON 3 SOLDI:

Type I - Surcharge 16½mm across. "PARA" about ½mm above bottom of "10." 2mm space between "10" and "P"; 1½mm between "A" and "10." Perf. 9½ only.

Type II - Surcharge 15¼ to 16mm across. "PARA" on same line with figures or slightly higher or lower. 1½mm space between "10" and "P"; 1mm between "A" and "10." Perf. 9½ and 10.

1886 *Perf. 9½ and 10*

14 A3 10pa on 3sld green, type II .30 *5.50*
a. Surcharge type I 175.00 325.00
b. Inverted surcharge, type I *1,850.*

Surcharge on Austria #42-46

1888

15 A11 10pa on 3kr grn 3.00 7.50
a. "01 PARA 10" *400.00*
16 A11 20pa on 5kr rose .50 *7.25*
17 A11 1pi on 10kr blue 45.00 1.10
a. Perf. 13½ 225.00
b. Double surcharge 275.00
18 A11 2pi on 20kr gray 1.50 4.00
19 A11 5pi on 50kr vio 2.00 *15.00*
Nos. 15-19 (5) 52.00 *34.85*

Austria Nos. 52-55, 58, 61 Surcharged

1890-92 Unwmk. *Perf. 9 to 13½*

Granite Paper

20 A12 8pa on 2kr brn ('92) .20 *.50*
 a. Perf. 9½ 10.00 *13.50*
21 A12 10pa on 3kr green .65 .50
22 A12 20pa on 5kr rose .25 *.50*
23 A12 1pi on 10kr ultra .35 .20
24 A12 2pi on 20kr ol grn 5.50 *25.00*
25 A12 5pi on 50kr violet 11.00 *60.00*
 Nos. 20-25 (6) 17.95 *86.70*

See note after Austria No. 65 on missing numerals, etc.

Austria Nos. 66, 69 Surcharged

1891 *Perf. 10 to 13½*

26 A14 2pi on 20kr green 4.25 1.25
 a. Perf. 9½ 110.00 70.00
27 A14 5pi on 50kr violet 2.50 2.50

Two types of the surcharge on No. 26 exist.

Austria Nos. 62-65 Surcharged

1892 *Perf. 10½, 11½*

28 A13 10pi on 1gld blue 10.00 22.50
29 A13 20pi on 2gld car 12.00 35.00
 a. Double surcharge

1896 *Perf. 10½, 11½, 12½*

30 A13 10pi on 1gld pale lilac 12.00 19.00
31 A13 20pi on 2gld gray grn 37.50 60.00

Austria Nos. 73, 75, 77, 81, 83-85 Surcharged

#32-35

#36-38

Perf. 10½, 12½, 13½ and Compound

1900

Without Varnish Bars

32 A15 10pa on 5h bl grn 4.00 .80
33 A16 20pa on 10h rose 5.00 .75
 b. Perf. 12½x10½ 250.00 85.00
34 A16 1pi on 25h ultra 3.00 .25
35 A17 2pi on 50h gray bl 7.25 3.25
36 A18 5pi on 1k car rose 1.00 .30
 a. 5pi on 1k carmine 1.10 .90
 b. Horiz. or vert. pair, imperf. btwn. 110.00
37 A18 10pi on 2k gray lil 2.50 2.25
38 A18 20pi on 4k gray grn 2.00 *6.00*
 Nos. 32-38 (7) 24.75 *13.60*

In the surcharge on Nos. 37 and 38 "piaster" is printed "PIAST."

1901

With Varnish Bars

32a A15 10pa on 5h blue green 1.75 2.25
33a A16 20pa on 10h rose 2.25 *160.00*
34a A16 1pi on 25h ultra 1.50 .45
35a A17 2pi on 50h gray blue 3.25 5.25
 Nos. 32a-35a (4) 8.75

A4

A5

A6

1906 *Perf. 12½ to 13½*

Without Varnish Bars

39 A4 10pa dark green 11.00 2.50
40 A5 20pa rose .80 .65
41 A5 1pi ultra .35 .25
42 A6 2pi gray blue .80 .65
 Nos. 39-42 (4) 12.95 4.05

1903 With Varnish Bars

39a A4 10pa dark green 4.25 1.50
40a A5 20pa rose 2.25 .40
41a A5 1pi ultra 1.60 .25
42a A6 2pi gray blue 125.00 2.25

1907

Without Varnish Bars

43 A4 10pa yellow green .50 *1.40*
45 A5 30pa violet .50 *2.75*

A7

A8

1908 Typo. *Perf. 12½*

46 A7 10pa green, *yellow* .20 *.25*
47 A7 20pa scarlet, *rose* .25 .25
48 A7 30pa brown, *buff* .30 *.50*
49 A7 1pi deep bl, *blue* 11.00 .20
50 A7 60pa vio, *bluish* .55 *3.00*

Engr.

51 A8 2pi lake, *yellow* .35 .20
52 A8 5pi brown, *gray* .60 *.80*
53 A8 10pi green, *yellow* .80 *1.50*
54 A8 20pi blue, *gray* 1.50 *3.50*
 Nos. 46-54 (9) 15.55 *10.20*

Nos. 46-50 are on paper colored on the surface only. 60th year of the reign of Emperor Franz Josef I, for permanent use. All values exist imperforate.

1913-14 Typo.

Paper Colored Through

57 A7 20pa rose, *rose* ('14) .70 *325.00*
58 A7 1pi ultra, *blue* .35 *.45*

Nos. 57 and 58 exist imperforate.

POSTAGE DUE STAMPS

Type of Austria D2 Surcharged

Black Surcharge

1902 Unwmk. *Perf. 12½, 13½*

J1 D2 10pa on 5h green 1.10 *2.75*
J2 D2 20pa on 10h green 1.10 *2.75*
J3 D2 1pi on 20h green 1.75 *3.25*
J4 D2 2pi on 40h green 1.75 *3.25*
J5 D2 5pi on 100h green 2.75 *2.75*
 Nos. J1-J5 (5) 8.45 *14.75*

Shades of Nos. J1-J5 exist, varying from yellowish green to dark green.

D3

1908 Typo. *Perf. 12½*

J6 D3 ¼pi green 3.00 *5.50*
J7 D3 ½pi green 1.50 *5.50*
J8 D3 1pi green 2.00 *5.50*
J9 D3 1½pi green .80 *12.50*
J10 D3 2pi green 2.00 *13.50*
J11 D3 5pi green 2.00 *8.00*
J12 D3 10pi green 16.00 *100.00*
J13 D3 20pi green 16.00 *110.00*
J14 D3 30pi green 13.00 11.50
 Nos. J6-J14 (9) 56.30 *272.00*

Nos. J6-J14 exist in distinct shades of green and on thick chalky, regular and thin ordinary paper. Values are for the least expensive variety. For comprehensive listings, see Scott Classic Specialized Catalogue.

No. J6-J14 exist imperforate.

Forgeries exist.

LOMBARDY-VENETIA

Formerly a kingdom in the north of Italy forming part of the Austrian Empire. Milan and Venice were the two principal cities. Lombardy was annexed to Sardinia in 1859, and Venetia to the kingdom of Italy in 1866.

100 Centesimi = 1 Lira
100 Soldi = 1 Florin (1858)

Unused examples without gum of Nos. 1-24 are worth approximately 20% of the values given, which are for stamps with original gum as defined in the catalogue introduction.

For similar designs in Kreuzers, see early Austria.

Coat of Arms — A1

15 CENTESIMI:

Type I- "5" is on a level with the "1." One heavy line around coat of arms center.

Type II- As type I, but "5" is a trifle sideways and is higher than the "1."

Type III- As type II, but two, thinner, lines around center.

45 CENTESIMI:

Type I- Lower part of "45" is lower than "Centes." One heavy line around coat of arms center. "45" varies in height and distance from "Centes."

Type II- One heavy line around coat of arms center. Lower part of "45" is on a level with lower part of "Centes."

Type III- As type II, but two, thinner, lines around center.

Wmk. K.K.H.M. in Sheet or Unwmkd.

1850 Typo. *Imperf.*

Thick to Thin Paper

1 A1 5c buff 2,500. 125.00
 a. Printed on both sides *8,500.* 225.00
 b. 5c yellow *5,000.* 575.00
 c. 5c orange 2,750. 225.00
 d. 5c lemon yellow *1,500.*
3 A1 10c black 2,500. 125.00
 a. 10c gray black 2,650. 125.00
4 A1 15c red, type III 1,200. 5.00
 b. 15c red, type I *2,500.* 20.00
 c. Ribbed paper, type II — 750.00
 d. Ribbed paper, type I *12,500.* 190.00
 f. 15c red, type II *1,300.* 29.00
5 A1 30c brown 3,100. 12.00
 a. Ribbed paper 4,900. 125.00
6 A1 45c blue, type III *10,500.* 30.00
 a. 45c blue, type I *11,000.* 50.00
 b. Ribbed paper, type I — 375.00
 c. 45c blue, type II — 90.00

1854

Machine-made Paper, Type III

3c A1 10c black *6,000.* 225.00
4g A1 15c pale red *700.* 3.50
5b A1 30c brown *3,100.* 10.00
6d A1 45c blue *8,000.* 42.50

See note about the paper of the 1850 issue of Austria. *The reprints are type III, in brighter colors.*

A2

A3

A4

A5

A6

Two Types of Each Value.

Type I- Loops of the bow at the back of the head broken.

Type II- Loops complete. Wreath projects further at top of head.

1858-62 Embossed *Perf. 14½*

7 A2 2s yel, type II 650. 110.00
 a. 2s yellow, type I 3,900. 525.00
8 A3 3s black, type II 6,500. 140.00
 a. 3s black, type I 2,600. 275.00
 b. Perf. 16, type I 1,000.
 c. Perf. 15x16 or 16x15, type I *4,600.* 400.00
9 A3 3s grn, type II ('62) 500. 90.00
10 A4 5s red, type II 275. 5.00
 a. 5s red, type I 875. 12.50
 b. Printed on both sides, type II *6,000.*
11 A5 10s brown, type II 2,250. 10.00
 a. 10s brown, type I 500. 42.50

12	A6	15s blue, type II	2,500.	24.00
a.		15s blue, type I	3,900.	90.00
b.		Printed on both sides, type II		*15,000.*

The reprints are of type II and are perforated 10½, 11, 11½, 12, 12½ and 13. There are also imperforate reprints of Nos. 7-9.

A7

A8

1861-62 ***Perf. 14***

13	A7	5s red	2,750.	3.50
14	A7	10s brown ('62)	4,150.	32.50

The reprints are perforated 9, 9 ½, 10½, 11, 12, 12½ and 13. There are also imperforate reprints of the 2 and 3s.

The 2, 3 and 15s of this type exist only as reprints.

1863

15	A8	2s yellow	160.00	150.00
16	A8	3s green	2,250.	90.00
17	A8	5s rose	2,750.	15.00
18	A8	10s blue	5,250.	75.00
19	A8	15s yellow brown	3,500.	175.00

1864-65 **Wmk. 91** ***Perf. 9½***

20	A8	2s yellow ('65)	210.00	*450.00*
21	A8	3s green	32.50	22.50
22	A8	5s rose	4.75	3.50
23	A8	10s blue	30.00	11.00
24	A8	15s yellow brown	350.00	100.00

Nos. 15-24 reprints are perforated 10½ and 13. There are also imperforate reprints of the 2s and 3s.

NEWSPAPER TAX STAMPS

From 1853 to 1858 the Austrian Newspaper Tax Stamp 2kr green (No. PR1) was also used in Lombardy-Venetia, at the value of 10 centesimi.

NT1

Type I - The banderol of the left eagle touches the beak of the eagle.

Type II - The banderol does not touch the beak.

1858-59 **Unwmk.** **Typo.** ***Imperf.***

PR1	NT1	1kr black, type I ('59)	3,250.	*2,900.*
PR2	NT1	2kr red, type II ('59)	325.00	55.00
a.		Watermark 91	400.00	100.00
PR3	NT1	4kr red, type I	*100,000.*	*3,250.*

The reprints are on a smooth toned paper and are all of type II.

AZERBAIJAN

ˌa-zər-ˌbī-ˈjän

(Azerbaidjan)

LOCATION — Southernmost part of Russia in Eastern Europe, bounded by Georgia, Dagestan, Caspian Sea, Iran and Armenia

GOVT. — A Soviet Socialist Republic

AREA — 33,430 sq. mi.

POP. — 7,908,224 (1999 est)

CAPITAL — Baku

With Armenia and Georgia, Azerbaijan made up the Transcaucasian Federation of Soviet Republics.

Stamps of Azerbaijan were replaced in 1923 by those of Transcaucasian Federated Republics.

With the breakup of the Soviet Union on Dec. 26, 1991, Azerbaijan and ten former Soviet republics established the Commonwealth of Independent States.

100 Kopecks = 1 Ruble

100 Giapiks = 1 Manat (1992)

Catalogue values for unused stamps in this country are for Never Hinged items, beginning with Scott 350 in the regular postage section, and Scott C1 in the air post section.

National Republic

Standard Bearer — A1

Farmer at Sunset — A2

Baku — A3

Temple of Eternal Fires — A4

1919 **Unwmk.** **Litho.** ***Imperf.***

1	A1	10k multicolored	.20	*.30*
2	A1	20k multicolored	.20	*.30*
3	A2	40k green, yellow & blk	.20	*.30*
4	A2	60k red, yellow & blk	.25	*.35*
5	A2	1r blue, yellow & blk	.35	*.50*
6	A3	2r red, bister & blk	.35	*.50*
7	A3	5r blue, bister & blk	.45	*.85*
8	A3	10r olive grn, bis & blk	.65	*.95*
9	A4	25r blue, red & black	1.10	*12.50*
10	A4	50r ol grn, red & black	1.40	*1.75*
		Nos. 1-10 (10)	5.15	*18.30*

The two printings of Nos. 1-10 are distinguished by the grayish or thin white paper. Both have yellowish gum. White paper copies are worth five times the above values.

For surcharges see Nos. 57-64, 75-80.

Soviet Socialist Republic

Symbols of Labor — A5

Oil Well — A6

Bibi Eibatt Oil Field — A7

Khan's Palace, Baku — A8

Globe and Workers — A9

Maiden's Tower, Baku — A10

Goukasoff House — A11

Blacksmiths — A12

Hall of Judgment, Baku — A13

1922

15	A5	1r gray green	.20	*.35*
16	A6	2r olive black	.50	*.50*
17	A7	5r gray brown	.20	*.35*
18	A8	10r gray	.50	*.65*
19	A9	25r orange brown	.20	*.40*
20	A10	50r violet	.20	*.40*
21	A11	100r dull red	.35	*.50*
22	A12	150r blue	.35	*.50*
23	A9	250r violet & buff	.35	*.50*
24	A13	400r dark blue	.35	*.50*
25	A12	500r gray vio & blk	.35	*.50*
26	A13	1000r dk blue & rose	.35	*.60*
27	A8	2000r blue & black	.35	*.50*
28	A7	3000r brown & blue	.35	*.50*
a.		Tete beche pair	15.00	15.00
29	A11	5000r black, *ol grn*	.60	*.75*
		Nos. 15-29 (15)	5.20	*7.50*

Counterfeits exist of Nos. 1-29. They generally sell for more than genuine copies.

For overprints and surcharges see Nos. 32-41, 43, 45-55, 65-72, 300-304, 307-333.

Nos. 15, 17, 23, 28, 27 Handstamped from Metal Dies in a Numbering Machine

1922

32	A5	10,000r on 1r	9.25	9.25
33	A7	15,000r on 5r	11.00	*11.50*
34	A9	33,000r on 250r	5.75	5.75
35	A7	50,000r on 3000r	5.75	5.75
36	A8	66,000r on 2000r	12.50	11.50
		Nos. 32-36 (5)	44.25	43.75

Same Surcharges on Regular Issue and Semi-Postal Stamps of 1922

1922-23

36A	A7	500r on 5r	100.00	*100.00*
37	A6	1000r on 2r	20.00	15.00
38	A8	2000r on 10r	10.00	4.00
39	A8	5000r on 2000r	7.50	3.00
40	A11	15,000r on 5000r	12.00	10.00
41	A5	20,000r on 1r	15.00	9.00
42	SP1	25,000r on 500r	35.00	
43	A7	50,000r on 5r	30.00	12.50
44	SP2	50,000r on 1000r	26.00	
45	A11	50,000r on 5000r	5.00	4.50
45A	A8	60,000r on 2000r	30.00	*14.00*
46	A11	70,000r on 5000r	20.00	20.00
47	A6	100,000r on 2r	15.00	15.00
48	A8	200,000r on 10r	10.00	10.00
49	A9	200,000r on 25r	15.00	15.00
50	A7	300,000r on 3000r	20.00	5.00
51	A8	500,000r on 2000r	15.00	10.00

Revalued

52	A7	500r on #33	*250.00*	*250.00*
53	A11	15,000r on #46	*250.00*	*250.00*
54	A7	300,000r on #35	*250.00*	*250.00*
55	A8	500,000r on #36	*250.00*	*250.00*

The surcharged semi-postal stamps were used for regular postage.

Same Surcharges on Stamps of 1919

57	A1	25,000r on 10k	.70	*1.00*
58	A1	50,000r on 20k	.70	*1.00*
59	A2	75,000r on 40k	1.75	*2.50*
60	A2	100,000r on 60k	.70	*.95*
61	A2	200,000r on 1r	.70	*.95*
62	A3	300,000r on 2r	.95	*1.10*
63	A3	500,000r on 5r	1.00	*1.10*
64	A2	750,000r on 40k	3.50	2.75
		Nos. 57-64 (8)	10.00	*11.35*

Handstamped from Settings of Rubber Type in Black or Violet

100000 — Nos. 65-66, 71-80

200.000 — Nos. 67-70

On Stamps of 1922

65	A6	100,000r on 2r	12.00	12.00
66	A8	200,000r on 10r	13.00	*14.00*
67	A8	200,000r on 10r (V)	25.00	20.00
68	A9	200,000r on 25r (V)	25.00	20.00
a.		Black surcharge	26.00	*27.50*
69	A7	300,000r on 3000r (V)	25.00	25.00
70	A8	500,000r on 2000r (V)	20.00	20.00
a.		Black surcharge	27.50	*29.00*
72	A11	1,500,000r on 5000r (V)	16.00	15.00
a.		Black surcharge	16.00	15.00

On Stamps of 1919

75	A1	50,000r on 20k	2.50	
76	A2	75,000r on 40k	2.50	
77	A2	100,000r on 60k	2.50	
78	A2	200,000r on 1r	2.50	.20
79	A3	300,000r on 2r	2.50	
80	A3	500,000r on 5r	2.50	
		Nos. 75-80 (6)	15.00	*.20*

Inverted and double surcharges of Nos. 32-80 sell for twice the normal price.

Counterfeits exist of Nos. 32-80.

Baku Province

Regular and Semi-Postal Stamps of 1922 Handstamped in Violet or Black

БАКИНСКОИ П. К.

The overprint reads "Bakinskoi P(ochtovoy) K(ontory)," meaning Baku Post Office.

1922 **Unwmk.** ***Imperf.***

300	A5	1r gray green	*50.00*
301	A7	5r gray brown	*50.00*
302	A12	150r blue	*50.00*
303	A9	250r violet & buff	*50.00*
304	A13	400r dark blue	*50.00*
305	SP1	500r bl & pale bl	*50.00*
306	SP2	1000r brown & bis	*50.00*
307	A8	2000r blue & black	*50.00*
308	A7	3000r brown & blue	*50.00*
309	A11	5000r black, *ol grn*	*50.00*
		Nos. 300-309 (10)	*500.00*

Stamps of 1922 Handstamped in Violet

БАКИНСКАГО Г-П-Т.О.№1

Ovpt. reads: Baku Post, Telegraph Office No. 1.

1924

Overprint 24x2mm

312	A12	150r blue	*50.00*
313	A9	250r violet & buff	*50.00*
314	A13	400r dark blue	*50.00*
317	A8	2000r blue & black	*50.00*
318	A7	3000r brn & blue	*50.00*
319	A11	5000r black, *ol grn*	*50.00*

Overprint 30x3½mm

323	A12	150r blue	*50.00*
324	A9	250r violet & buff	*50.00*
325	A13	400r dark blue	*50.00*
328	A8	2000r blue & black	*50.00*
329	A7	3000r brn & blue	*50.00*
330	A11	5000r black, *ol grn*	*50.00*

Overprinted on Nos. 32-33, 35

331	A5	10,000r on 1r	*50.00*
332	A7	15,000r on 5r	*50.00*
333	A7	50,000r on 3000r	*50.00*
		Nos. 312-333 (15)	*750.00*

The overprinted semipostal stamps were used for regular postage.

A 24x2mm handstamp on #17, B1-B2, and 30x3½mm on #15, 17, B1-B2, was of private origin.

Catalogue values for unused stamps in this section, from this point to the end of the section, are for Never Hinged items.

Flag, Map — A20

Unwmk.

1992, Mar. 26		**Litho.**	***Perf. 14***	
350	A20	35k multicolored	*1.25*	1.25

For surcharge, see No. 733.

Caspian Sea — A21

1992, May 7			***Perf. 12***	
351	A21	25g on 15k multi	.30	.30
a.		Booklet pane of 12	2.50	
		Complete booklet, #351a	6.00	
352	A21	35g on 15k multi	.30	.30
353	A21	50g on 15k multi	.40	.40
354	A21	1.50m on 15k multi	1.25	1.25
355	A21	2.50m on 15k multi	2.25	2.25
		Nos. 351-355 (5)	4.50	4.50

Nos. 351-355 are overprinted or sucharged on a National Park series prepared for the Soviet Union with one stamp for each republic. Not issued without surcharge. Value, $4.

For additional surcharges see Nos. 435, 501-504.

Iran-Azerbaijan Telecommunications — A21a

1992		**Photo.**	***Perf. 13x13½***	
355A	A21a	15g multicolored	1.25	1.25

See Iran No. 2544.

For surcharges see Nos. 403-406.

Horses A22

1993, Feb. 1		**Litho.**	***Perf. 13***	
356	A22	20g shown	.20	.20
357	A22	30g Kabarda	.20	.20
358	A22	50g Qarabair	.20	.20
359	A22	1m Don	.20	.20
360	A22	2.50m Yakut	.45	.45
361	A22	5m Orlov	.75	.75
362	A22	10m Diliboz	1.75	1.75
		Nos. 356-362 (7)	3.75	3.75

Perf. 12½

Souvenir Sheet

362A	A22	8m Qarabag	1.25	1.25

For overprints see Nos. 629-636.

Maiden's Tower — A23

Government Building — A24

1992-93		**Litho.**	***Perf. 12½x12***	
363	A23	10g blk & blue grn	.20	.20
365	A23	20g black & red	.20	.20
367	A23	50g black & blue grn	.20	.20
368	A23	50g black & yellow	.35	.35
370	A23	1m black & rose lilac	.20	.20
372	A23	1.50m black & blue	1.00	1.00
373	A23	2.50m black & yellow	.35	.35
374	A23	5m black & green	.65	.65
		Nos. 363-374 (8)	3.15	3.15

Issued: 10g, 20g, 1.50m, #367, Dec. 20; #368, 1m, 2.50m, 5m, June 20, 1993.

For surcharges see Nos. 550-557.

This is an expanding set. Numbers may change.

1993, Oct. 12		**Litho.**	***Perf. 12½***	
375	A24	25g yellow & black	.20	.20
376	A24	30g green & black	.20	.20
377	A24	50g blue & black	.25	.25
378	A24	1m red & black	.50	.50
		Nos. 375-378 (4)	1.15	1.15

For surcharges see No. 407-414.

Flowers — A25

1993, Aug. 12		**Litho.**	***Perf. 12½***	
379	A25	25g Tulipa eichleri	.20	.20
380	A25	50g Puschkinia scilloides	.20	.20
381	A25	1m Iris elegantissima	.20	.20
382	A25	1.50m Iris acutiloba	.25	.25
383	A25	5m Tulipa florenskyii	.80	.80
384	A25	10m Iris reticulata	1.50	1.50
		Nos. 379-384 (6)	3.15	3.15

Souvenir Sheet

Perf. 13

385	A25	10m Muscari elecostomum	1.50	1.50

No. 385 contains one 32x40mm stamp.

Fish A26

25g, Acipenser guldenstadti. 50g, Acipenser stellatus. 1m, Rutilus frisii kutum. 1.50m, Rutilus rutilus caspicus. 5m, Salmo trutta caspius. No. 391, Alosa kessleri. #392, Huso huso.

1993, Aug. 27			***Perf. 12½***	
386	A26	25g multicolored	.20	.20
387	A26	50g multicolored	.20	.20
388	A26	1m multicolored	.20	.20
389	A26	1.50m multicolored	.25	.25
390	A26	5m multicolored	.80	.80
391	A26	10m multicolored	1.50	1.50
		Nos. 386-391 (6)	3.15	3.15

Souvenir Sheet

Perf. 13

392	A26	10m multicolored	1.50	1.50

No. 392 contains one 40x32mm stamp.

Pres. Heydar A. Aliyev — A27

Design: No. 394, Map of Nakhichevan.

1993, Sept. 12		**Litho.**	***Perf. 12½x13***	
393	A27	25m multicolored	1.25	1.25
394	A27	25m multicolored	1.25	1.25
a.		Pair, #393-394	2.50	2.50
b.		Souv. sheet, #393-394, perf. 12	*32.50*	
c.		Souv. sheet, #393-394, perf. 12	5.50	

Name on map spelled "Naxcivan" on #394c. It is spelled "Haxcivan" on #394-394b.

No. 394c issued Sept. 20, 1993.

Historic Buildings, Baku — A28

Style of tombs: 2m, Fortress, 13th-14th cent. 4m, Moorish gate, 15th cent. 8m, Oriental-style columns, 15th cent.

1994, Jan. 17		**Litho.**	***Perf. 11***	
395	A28	2m red, silver & black	.20	.20
396	A28	4m green, silver & black	.35	.35
397	A28	8m blue, silver & black	.75	.75
		Nos. 395-397 (3)	1.30	1.30

A29

1994, Jan. 17			***Perf. 12½***	
398	A29	5m Natl. Colors, Star, Crescent	.35	.35
399	A29	8m Natl. coat of arms	.65	.65

A30

1994, Jan. 17			***Perf. 12½***	
400	A30	10m multi + label	.60	.60

Mohammed Fizuli (1494-1556), poet.

Mammed Amin Rasulzade (1884-1955), 1st President — A31

Jalil Mamedkulizade, Writer, 125th Birth Anniv. — A32

1994, May 21			***Perf. 12½, 13 (#402)***	
401	A31	15m blk, yel & brown	1.00	1.00
402	A32	20m black, blue & gold	1.00	1.00

No. 402 printed se-tenant with label.

No. 355A Surcharged

1994, Jan. 18		**Photo.**	***Perf. 13x13½***	
403	A21a	2m on 15g	.20	.20
404	A21a	20m on 15g	.35	.35
405	A21a	25m on 15g	.45	.45
406	A21a	50m on 15g	1.00	1.00
		Nos. 403-406 (4)	2.00	2.00

5 m.

Nos. 375-378 Surcharged

1994, Feb. 22		**Litho.**	***Perf. 12½***	
407	A24	5m on 1m #375	.20	.20
408	A24	10m on 30g #377	.20	.20
409	A24	15m on 30g #377	.20	.20
a.		Pair, #408-409	.30	.30
410	A24	20m on 50g #378	.25	.25
411	A24	25m on 1m #375	.30	.30
a.		Pair, #407, 411	.45	.45
412	A24	40m on 50g #378	.40	.40
a.		Pair, #410, 412	.65	.65
413	A24	50m on 25g #376	.45	.45
414	A24	100m on 25g #376	1.00	1.00
a.		Pair, #413-414	1.50	1.50
		Nos. 407-414 (8)	3.00	3.00

Baku Oil Fields — A33

Designs: 15m, Temple of Eternal Fires. 20m, Oil derricks. 25m, Early tanker. 50m, Ludwig Nobel, Robert Nobel, Petr Bilderling, Alfred Nobel.

1994, June 10 Photo. *Perf. 13*

415 A33 15m multicolored .30 .30
416 A33 20m multicolored .40 .40
417 A33 25m multicolored .45 .45
418 A33 50m multicolored 1.00 1.00
a. Souvenir sheet of 1 1.00 1.00
Nos. 415-418 (4) 2.15 2.15

See Turkmenistan Nos. 39-43.

Minerals — A34

Posthorn — A35

1994, June 15 Litho. *Perf. 13*

419 A34 5m Laumontite .30 .30
420 A34 10m Epidot calcite .55 .55
421 A34 15m Andradite .80 .80
422 A34 20m Amethyst 1.10 1.10
a. Souvenir sheet, #420-423 + 2 labels, perf. 12 2.50 2.50
Nos. 419-422 (4) 2.75 2.75

1994, June 28 Litho. *Perf. 12½*

426 A35 5m black & red .20 .20
427 A35 10m black & green .20 .20
428 A35 20m black & blue .20 .20
429 A35 25m black & yellow .25 .25
431 A35 40m black & brown .40 .40
Nos. 426-431 (5) 1.25 1.25

For surcharges see Nos. 487-489A.

No. 351 Surcharged

Unwmk.

1994, Oct. 17 Litho. *Perf. 12*

435 A21 400m on 25g multi .70 .70

Souvenir Sheet

Pres. Heydar A. Aliyev — A36

Illustration reduced.

1994, Oct. 28 Litho. *Perf. 14*

436 A36 150m multicolored 2.25 2.25

Ships of the Caspian Sea A37

Designs: a, Tugboat, "Captain Racebov." b, "Azerbaijan." c, Balt Ro Ro line, "Merkuri I." d, Tanker, "Tovuz." e, Tanker.

1994, Oct. 28

437 A37 50m Strip of 5, #a.-e. 1.75 1.75

Issued in sheets of 15 stamps. The background of the sheet shows a nautical chart, giving each stamp a different background.

1994 World Cup Soccer Championships, US — A38

Various soccer plays. Denominations: 5m, 10m, 20m, 25m, 30m, 50m, 80m.

1994, June 17 Litho. *Perf. 13*

438-444 A38 Set of 7 3.00 3.00

Souvenir Sheet

445 A38 100m multicolored 1.50 1.50

No. 445 contains one 32x40mm stamp and is a continuous design.

Dinosaurs — A39

Designs: 5m, Coelophysis, segisaurus. 10m, Pentaceratops, tyrannosaurids. 20m, Segnosaurus, oviraptor. 25m, Albertosaurus, corythosaurus. 30m, Iguanodons. 50m, Stegosaurus, allosaurus. 80m, Tyrannosaurus, saurolophus.
100m, Phobetor.

1994, Sept. 15

446-452 A39 Set of 7 3.00 3.00

Souvenir Sheet

Perf. 12½

453 A39 100m multicolored 1.50 1.50

No. 453 contains one 40x32mm stamp and is a continuous design.

Lyrurus Mlokosiewickzi — A40

a, 50m, Female on nest. b, 80m, Female on mountain cliff. c, 100m, 2 males. d, 120m, Male.

1994, Dec. 15 Litho. *Perf. 12½*

454 A40 Block of 4, #a.-d. 2.75 2.75

World Wildlife Fund.

Raptors A41

10m, Haliaeetus albicilla. 15m, Aguila heliaca. 20m, Aguila rapax. 25m, Gypaetus barbatus, vert. 50m, Falco cherrug, vert.
100m, Aguila chrysaetos.

1994, Nov. 15 Litho. *Perf. 13*

458-462 A41 Set of 5 3.00 3.00

Souvenir Sheet

Perf. 12½

463 A41 100m multicolored 1.50 1.50

No. 463 contains one 40x32mm stamp and is a continuous design.

Cats A42

Designs: 10m, Felis libica, vert. 15m, Felis otocolobus, vert. 20m, Felis lyns, vert. 25m, Felis pardus. 50m, Panthera tigrus.
100m, Panthera tigrus adult and cub, vert.

1994, Dec. 14 *Perf. 13*

464-468 A42 Set of 5 3.00 3.00

Souvenir Sheet

469 A42 100m multicolored 1.50 1.50

No. 469 contains one 32x40mm stamp and is a continuous design.
For overprints see Nos. 637-642.

Butterflies A43

Designs: 10m, Parnassius apollo. 25m, Zegris menestho. 50m, Manduca atropos. 60m, Pararge adrastoides.

1995, Jan. 23 Litho. *Perf. 14*

470 A43 10m multicolored .20 .20
471 A43 25m multicolored .40 .40
472 A43 50m multicolored .80 .80
473 A43 60m multicolored 1.00 1.00
a. Souvenir sheet of 4, #470-473 2.50 2.50
Nos. 470-473 (4) 2.40 2.40

Intl. Olympic Committee, Cent. — A44

Designs: No. 474, Pierre de Coubertin. No. 475, Discus. No. 476, Javelin.

1994, Dec. 15 Litho. *Perf. 12*

474-476 A44 100m Set of 3 2.00 2.00

A45

A46

1994 Winter Olympic medalists, Lillehammer: 10m, Aleksei Urnamov, Russia, figure skating, 25, Nancy Kerrigan, US, figure skating. 40m Bonnie Blair, US, speed skating, horiz. 50m, Takanori Kano, Japan, ski jumping, horiz. 80m, Philip LaRouche, Canada, freestyle skiing. 100m, Four-man bobsled, Germany.
200m, Katja Seizinger, skiing, Germany, vert.

1995, Feb. 10 Litho. *Perf. 14*

478-483 A45 Set of 6 2.00 2.00

Souvenir Sheet

484 A45 200m multicolored 1.75 1.75

1995, Feb. 21

Women in space - #485: a, Mary Kliv, US. b, Valentina Tereshkova, Russia. c, Tamara Cernigan, US. d, Wendy Lourens, US.
#486: a, Mae Jemison, US. b, Kitty Coleman, US. c, Ellen Sulman, US. d, M.I. Weber, US.

Miniature Sheets of 4

485-486 A46 100m each, #a.-d. 2.50

First manned moon landing, 25th anniv. (in 1994).

Nos. 426-428 Surcharged

1995 Litho. *Perf. 12½*

487 A35 100m on 5m #426 .20 .20
488 A35 250m on 10m #427 .40 .40
488A A35 400m on 25m No. 429 .50 .50
489 A35 500m on 20m #428 .65 .65
489A A35 900m on 40m No. 431 1.10 1.10
Nos. 487-489A (5) 2.85 2.85

Issued: #488A, 7/7; #487-488, 489, 2/28.

Mushrooms — A47

Designs: 100m, Gymnopilus spectabilis. 250m, Fly agaris. 300m, Lepiota procera. 400m, Hygrophorus spectosus.
500m, Fly agaris, diff.

1995, Sept. 1 Litho. *Perf. 14*

490-493 A47 Set of 4 3.50 3.50

Souvenir Sheet

494 A47 500m multicolored 1.50 1.50

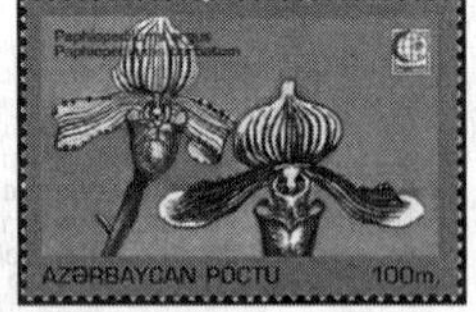

Singapore '95 — A48

Orchids: 100m, Paphiopedilum argus, paphiopedilum barbatum. 250m, Maxillaria picta. 300m, Laeliocattleya. 400m, Dendrobium nobile.
500m, Cattleya gloriette.

1995, Sept. 1

495-498 A48 Set of 4 3.50 3.50

Souvenir Sheet

499 A48 500m multicolored 1.50 1.50

UN, 50th Anniv. A49

Design: 250m, Azerbaijan Pres. Heydar A. Aliyev, UN Sec. Gen. Boutros Boutros-Ghali.

1995, Sept. 15

500 A49 250m multicolored 2.00 2.00

Nos. 352-355 Surcharged

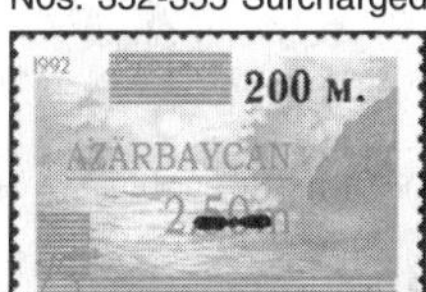

1995 Litho. *Perf. 12*

501 A21 200m on 2.50m #355 .30 .30
502 A21 600m on 35g #352 .85 .85
503 A21 800m on 50q #353 1.10 1.10
504 A21 1000m on 1.50m #354 1.40 1.40
Nos. 501-504 (4) 3.65 3.65

Uzeyir Hacibeyov (1885-1948) A50

400m, Oglu Iskenderov (1895-1965).

1995, June 30 Litho. *Perf. 12x12½*

505 A50 250m silver gray & black .60 .60
506 A50 400m gold bister & brn .90 .90

Balloons and Airships A51

100m, First hydrogen balloon, 1784. 150m, 1st motorized balloon, 1883. 250m, First elliptical balloon, 1784. 300m, 1st Scott Baldwin dirigible, 1904. 400m, US Marine balloon, 1917. 500m, Pedal-powered dirigible, 1909.
800m, 1st rigid dirigible designed by Hugo Eckener, 1924.

1995, July 20 Litho. *Perf. 13*

507 A51 100m multi, vert. .20 .20
508 A51 150m multi, vert. .30 .30
509 A51 250m multi .45 .45
510 A51 300m multi .55 .55
511 A51 400m multi .75 .75
512 A51 500m multi .90 .90
Nos. 507-512 (6) 3.15 3.15

Souvenir Sheet

513 A51 800m multicolored 1.50 1.50

Marine Life A52

50m, Loligo vulgaris. 100m, Orchistoma pileus. 150m, Pegea confoederata. 250m, Polyorchis karafutoensis. 300m, Agalma okeni.
500m, Corolla spectabillis.

1995, June 2 Litho. *Perf. 13*

514 A52 50m multi .20 .20
515 A52 100m multi .40 .40
516 A52 150m multi .50 .50
517 A52 250m multi, vert. .90 .90
518 A52 300m multi, vert. 1.10 1.10
Nos. 514-518 (5) 3.10 3.10

Souvenir Sheet

519 A52 500m multicolored 1.50 1.50

Turtles A53

Designs: 50m, Chelus fimbriatus. 100m, Caretta caretta. 150m, Geochelone pardalis. 250m, Geochelone elegans. 300m, Testudo hermanni.
500m, Macroclemys temmincki.

1995, June 12 Litho. *Perf. 13*

520 A53 50m multicolored .20 .20
521 A53 100m multicolored .40 .40
522 A53 150m multicolored .50 .50
523 A53 250m multicolored .90 .90
524 A53 300m multicolored 1.10 1.10
Nos. 520-524 (5) 3.10 3.10

Souvenir Sheet

525 A53 500m multicolored 1.50 1.50

1998 World Cup Soccer Championships, France — A54

Various soccer plays.

1995, Sept. 30 Litho. *Perf. 12½*

526 A54 100m orange & multi .40 .40
527 A54 150m green & multi .60 .60
528 A54 250m yel org & multi .90 .90
529 A54 300m yellow & multi 1.10 1.10
530 A54 400m blue & multi 1.50 1.50
Nos. 526-530 (5) 4.50 4.50

Souvenir Sheet

Perf. 13

531 A54 600m multicolored 2.25 2.25

Domestic Cats — A55

1995, Oct. 30 *Perf. 12½*

532 A55 100m Persian .20 .20
533 A55 150m Chartreux .30 .30
534 A55 250m Somali .45 .45
535 A55 300m Longhair Scottish fold .55 .55
536 A55 400m Cumric .75 .75
537 A55 500m Turkish angora .90 .90
Nos. 532-537 (6) 3.15 3.15

Souvenir Sheet

538 A55 800m Birman 1.50 1.50

No. 538 contains one 32x40mm stamp.

Fauna and Flora — A56

Designs: 100m, Horse. 200m, Muscari elecostomum, vert. 250m, Huso huso. 300m, Aquila chrysaetos. 400m, Panthera tigrus. 500m, Lyrurus miokosiewickzi, facing right. 1000m, Lyrurus miokosiewickzi, facing left.

1995, Nov. 30

539 A56 100m multicolored .20 .20
540 A56 200m multicolored .30 .30
541 A56 250m multicolored .30 .30
542 A56 300m multicolored .40 .40
543 A56 400m multicolored .50 .50
544 A56 500m multicolored .60 .60
545 A56 1000m multicolored 1.50 1.50
Nos. 539-545 (7) 3.80 3.80

John Lennon (1940-80) A57

1995, Dec. 8 *Perf. 14½*

546 A57 500m multicolored .60 .60

Issued in sheet of 16 plus label.

Miniature Sheet

Locomotives — A58

Designs: No. 547a, 4-4-0, America. b, J3 Hudson, US. c, 2-8-2. d, 2-6-2, Germany. e, 2-8-2, Germany. f, 2-6-2, Italy. g, G-C5, Japan. h, 2-10-2 QJ, China. i, 0-10-0, China.
500m, Electric passenger train, vert.

1996, Feb. 1 *Perf. 14*

547 A58 100m Sheet of 9, #a.-i. 6.00 6.00

Souvenir Sheet

548 A58 500m multicolored 3.00 3.00

Dr. M. Topcubasov, Surgeon — A59

1996, Feb. 1

549 A59 300m multicolored 1.50 1.50

Nos. 363, 365, 367-368, 370, 372-374 Surcharged

1995, Jan. 4 Litho. *Perf. 12½x12*

550 A23 250m on 10g #363 .40 .40
551 A23 250m on 20g #365 .40 .40
552 A23 250m on 50g #368 .40 .40
553 A23 250m on 1.50m #372 .40 .40
554 A23 500m on 50g #367 .75 .75
555 A23 500m on 1m #370 .75 .75
556 A23 500m on 2.50m #373 .75 .75
557 A23 500m on 5m #374 .75 .75
Nos. 550-557 (8) 4.60 4.60

1996 Olympic Games, Atlanta A60

1996, Apr. 9 Litho. *Perf. 14*

568 A60 50m Carl Lewis .20 .20
569 A60 100m Muhammed Ali .40 .40
570 A60 150m Li Ning .60 .60
571 A60 200m Said Aouita .80 .80
572 A60 250m Olga Korbut 1.00 1.00
573 A60 300m Nadia Comaneci 1.25 1.25
574 A60 400m Greg Louganis 1.50 1.50
Nos. 568-574 (7) 5.75 5.75

Souvenir Sheet

575 A60 500m Nazim Hüseynov, vert. 2.00 2.00

Husein Aliyev (1911-91), Artist A61

Paintings: 100m, Water bird, swamp. 200m, Landscape.

1996, Apr. 16 Litho. *Perf. 14*

576 A61 100m multicolored .75 .75
577 A61 200m multicolored 1.50 1.50
a. Pair, #576-577 + label 2.25 2.25

No. 577a issued in sheets of 6 stamps.

Resid Behbudov (1915-89), Singer — A62

1996, Apr. 22 *Perf. 12½*

578 A62 100m multicolored 1.25 1.25

A63

1996, Mar. 20

579 A63 250m multicolored 1.25 1.25

Novruz Bayrami, natl. holiday.

A64

1996, May 28 Litho. *Perf. 14*

580 A64 250m multicolored 1.25 1.25

Independence, 5th anniv.

A65

1996, Apr. 22 Litho. *Perf. 12½*

581 A65 100m multicolored 1.25 1.25

Yusif Memmedeliyev (1905-95), chemist.

A66

1996, June 7 *Perf. 14*

Jerusalem, 3000th Anniv.: a, 100m, Wailing Wall. b, 250m, Inside cathedral. c, 300m, Dome of the Rock.
500m, Windmill.

582 A66 Sheet of 3, #a.-c. 3.50 3.50

Souvenir Sheet

583 A66 500m multicolored 3.00 3.00

For overprints see Nos. 643-644.

Dogs A67

Designs: 50m, German shepherd. 100m, Basset hound. 150m, Collie. 200m, Bull terrier. 300m, Boxer. 400m, Cocker spaniel.
500m, Sharpei.

1996, June 18 *Perf. 13*

584-589 A67 Set of 6 5.00 5.00

Souvenir Sheet

590 A67 500m multicolored 2.50 2.50

Birds — A68

Designs: 50m, Tetraenura regia. 100m, Coliuspasser macrourus. 150m, Oriolus xanthornus. 200m, Oriolus oriolus. 300m, Sturnus vulgaris. 400m, Serinus mozambicus.
500m, Merops apiaster.

1996, June 19 *Perf. 13*

591-596 A68 Set of 6 5.00 5.00

Souvenir Sheet

597 A68 500m multicolored 2.50 2.50

Roses — A69

Designs: 50m, Burgundy. 100m, Virgo. 150m, Rose gaujard. 200m, Luna. 300m, Lady rose. 400m, Landora.
500m, Lougsor, horiz.

1996, June 19

598-603 A69 Set of 6 5.00 5.00

Souvenir Sheet

604 A69 500m multicolored 2.50 2.50

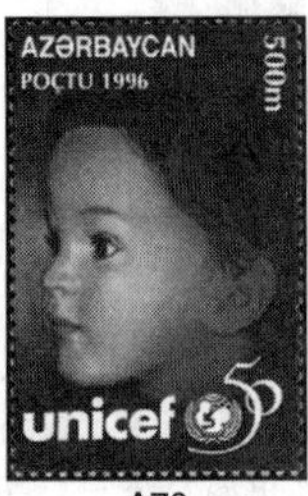

A70 A71

1996, July 8 **Litho.** *Perf. 14*

605 A70 500m multicolored 1.25 1.25

UNICEF, 50th anniv.

1996, July 22

Competing teams: 100m, Spain, Bulgaria. 150m, Romania, France. 200m, Czech Republic, Germany. 250m, England, Israel. 300m, Croatia, Turkey. 400m, Italy, Russia.
500m, Trophy cup.

606-611 A71 Set of 6 3.25 3.25

Souvenir Sheet

612 A71 500m multicolored 1.50 1.50

Euro '96, European Soccer Championships, Great Britain.

Ships A72

Ship, home country: 100m, Chinese junk. 150m, Danmark, Denmark. 200m, Nippon Maru, Japan. 250m, Mircea, Romania. 300m, Kruzenshtern, Russia. 400m, Ariadne, Germany.
500m, Tovarishch, Russia, vert.

1996, Aug. 26 **Litho.** *Perf. 14*

613-618 A72 Set of 6 4.00 4.00

Souvenir Sheet

619 A72 500m multicolored 3.00 3.00

For overprints see Nos. 645-651.

Baxram Gur Kills a Dragon, Sculpture — A73

1997, Mar. 6 **Litho.** *Perf. 13½x13*

620 A73 250m black & yellow .45 .45
621 A73 400m black & vermilion .60 .60
622 A73 500m black & green .75 .75
623 A73 1000m black & purple 1.50 1.50
Nos. 620-623 (4) 3.30 3.30

See No. 671.

Famous Personalities — A74

#624, Mamed-Kerim Ogli Aliyev (1897-1962), politician. #625, Illyas Efendiyev (1914-96), writer. #626, Fatali Xan-Xoyskiy (1875-1920), politician. #627, Nariman Narimanov (1870-1925), politician, writer.

1997, Mar. 25 **Litho.** *Perf. 14*

Background Color

624 A74 250m tan 1.10 1.10
625 A74 250m gray blue 1.10 1.10
626 A74 250m pale red 1.10 1.10
627 A74 250m pale olive 1.10 1.10
Nos. 624-627 (4) 4.40 4.40

Qobustan Prehistoric Art — A75

Rock carvings: a, Oxen. b, Large horned animals. c, Six figures.

1997, May 19 **Litho.** *Perf. 14*

628 A75 500m Sheet of 3, #a.-c. 4.25 4.25

For overprint see No. 674.

#356-362A, 464-469 Ovptd. in Red

1997, June 2 **Litho.** *Perf. 13*

Denominations as Before

629-635 A22 Set of 7 *8.00 8.00*

Souvenir Sheet

636 A22 8m multicolored *5.00 5.00*

Location of overprint varies. No. 636 is ovptd. both on stamp and in sheet margin.

1997, June 2

Denominations as Before

637-641 A42 Set of 5 *6.00 6.00*

Souvenir Sheet

642 A42 100m multicolored *5.00 5.00*

Location of overprint varies. No. 642 is ovptd. both on stamp and in sheet margin.

Nos. 582-583, 613-619 Ovptd.

1997, June 2 *Perf. 14*

643 A66 Sheet of 3, #a.-c. *5.00 5.00*

Souvenir Sheet

644 A66 500m multicolored *5.00 5.00*

Size and location of overprint varies. Overprint appears both on stamp and in sheet margin.

1997, June 2 *Perf. 14*

Denominations as Before

645-650 A72 Set of 6 *5.00 5.00*

Souvenir Sheet

651 A72 500m multicolored *5.00 5.00*

Location of overprint varies. No. 651 is ovptd. both on stamp and in sheet margin.

Grimm's Fairy Tales — A76

Bremen Musical: No. 652: a, Dog. b, Dancing horse, cat. c, Rooster.
500m, Animals looking through window at treaure chest, man.

1997, July 1 *Perf. 13½x14*

652 A76 250m Sheet of 3, #a.-c. 2.00 2.00

Souvenir Sheet

653 A76 500m multicolored 1.40 1.40

Caspian Seals A77

Designs: a, Seal looking right. b, Mountain top, seal looking forward. c, Seal, seagull. d, Seal looking left. e, Seal looking forward. f, Small seal.
500m, Mother nursing pup.

1997, July 1

654 A77 250m Sheet of 6, #a.-f. 4.25 4.25

Souvenir Sheet

655 A77 500m multicolored 1.40 1.40

Traditional Musical Instruments — A77a

1997, Aug. 4 **Litho.** *Perf. 14*

656 A77a 250m Qaval .75 .75
657 A77a 250m Tanbur .75 .75
658 A77a 500m Cenq 1.50 1.50
Nos. 656-658 (3) 3.00 3.00

A78 A79

Azerbaijan Oil Industry: a, Early oil derricks, building. b, Off-shore oil drilling platform.

1997, Aug. 18 *Perf. 14½*

Souvenir Sheet

659 A78 500m Sheet of 2, #a.-b. 3.00 3.00

1997, Sept. 12 *Perf. 14x13½*

660 A79 250m Hagani Shirvany, poet 1.00 1.00

Issued in sheets of 4 + 5 labels.

Mosques A80

#661, Ashaqi mechet Qovqar-agi, Shusha, 1874-75. #662, Momuna-Zatun, Naxcivan, 1187. #663, Taza-pir, Baku (1905-14).

1997, Sept. 18 **Litho.** *Perf. 14*

661 A80 250m multicolored .85 .85
662 A80 250m multicolored .85 .85
663 A80 250m multicolored .85 .85
Nos. 661-663 (3) 2.55 2.55

H.C. Rasul Beyov (1917-1984), Communications Official — A81

1997, Oct. 6 Litho. *Perf. 14*
664 A81 250m multicolored 2.00 2.00

1998 World Cup Soccer Championships, France — A82

Winning team photos: No. 665: a, Italy, 1938. b, Argentina, 1986. c, Uruguay, 1980. d, Brazil, 1994. e, England, 1966. f, Germany, 1990.
1500m, Tofiq Bahramov, "Golden Whistle" prize winner, 1966, vert.

1997, Oct. 15
665 A82 250m Sheet of 6, #a.-f. 5.00 5.00

Souvenir Sheet

666 A82 1500m multicolored 4.00 4.00

A83 A84

Figure skaters: No. 667: a, Katarina Witt, Germany. b, Elvis Stojko, Canada. c, Midori Ito, Japan. d, Silhouettes of various winter sports against natl. flag. e, Hand holding Olympic torch. f, Kristi Yamaguchi, US. g, John Curry, England. h, Lu Chen, China.
No. 668, Gordeyeva and Grinkov, Russia.

1997 Litho. *Perf. 14*
667 A83 250m Sheet of 8, #a.-h. 2.50 2.50

Souvenir Sheet

668 A83 500m multicolored .65 .65

1998 Winter Olympic Games, Nagano.

1998, Feb. 4 *Perf. 13½*

Diana, Princess of Wales (1961-97): No. 669, Wearing black turtleneck. No. 670, Wearing violet dress.

669 A84 400m multicolored .50 .50
670 A84 400m multicolored .50 .50

#669-670 were each issued in sheets of 6.

Sculpture Type of 1997

1998, Mar. 23 Litho. *Perf. 13½x13*
671 A73 100m blk & bright pink 1.00 1.00

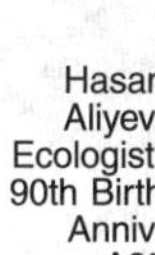

Hasan Aliyev, Ecologist, 90th Birth Anniv. A85

1998, Apr. 3 *Perf. 14*
672 A85 500m multicolored 1.00 1.00

Souvenir Sheet

Pres. Heydar Aliyev, 75th Birthday — A86

Illustration reduced.

1998, May 10 *Perf. 13½*
673 A86 500m multicolored 2.00 2.00

No. 628 Ovptd.

1998, May 13 *Perf. 14*
674 A75 500m Sheet of 3, #a.-c. 4.00 4.00

Additional inscription in sheet margin reads "ISRAEL 98 - WORLD STAMP EXHIBITION / TEL-AVIV 13-21 MAY 1998."

Musicians A87

#675, Gara Garayev. #676, Ashig Hasgar. #677, Sayid Mohammadhusein.

1998, June 7 Litho. *Perf. 14*
675 A87 250m multicolored .50 .50
676 A87 250m multicolored .50 .50
677 A87 250m multicolored .50 .50
Nos. 675-677 (3) 1.50 1.50

Bul-Bul, Singer, Birth Cent. — A88

1998, July 7
678 A88 500m multicolored 1.00 1.00

Disney Characters at World Rapid Chess Championship — A89

250m, Minnie, Mickey.
No. 679: a, Minnie, Mickey. b, Goofy. c, Donald. d, Pluto. e, Minnie. f, Daisy. g, Goofy, Donald. h, Mickey.
#680, Donald, Mickey. #681, Minnie, Mickey.

1998 *Perf. 13½*
678A A89 250m multicolored .50 .50

Perf. 13½x14

679 A89 500m Sheet of 8, #a.-h. 8.00 8.00

Souvenir Sheets

680-681 A89 4000m each 8.00 8.00

Issued: 250m, 12/28; others, 11/13.

New Year Holiday A90

Europa: 1000m, Woman rolling dough. 3000m, Men performing at holiday festival.

1998, Dec. 29 Litho. *Perf. 13x12½*
682 A90 1000m multicolored .50 .50
683 A90 3000m multicolored 1.50 1.50

Nos. 682-683 Ovptd.

1999, Apr. 27 Litho. *Perf. 13x12½*
684 A90 1000m on #682 .50 .50
685 A90 3000m on #683 1.50 1.50

A91 A92

Europa: 1000m, Rose flamingo, Gizilagach Natl. Park. 3000m, Deer, Girkan Natl. Park.

1999, Apr. 28 *Perf. 12½x12¾*
686 A91 1000m multicolored .50 .50
687 A91 3000m multicolored 1.50 1.50

1999, Aug. 3 Litho. *Perf. 11¼x11¾*

Towers: 1000m, Dord Kundge, 14th cent. 3000m, Danravy, 13th cent.

688 A92 1000m black & blue .45 .45
689 A92 3000m black & red 1.40 1.40

See Nos. 701-702, 717-718.

A93 A95

A94

Naxçivan Autonomous Republic, 75th anniv.: a, Pres. Heydar Aliyev, flag. b, Map of Naxçivan.

1999, Oct. 9 *Perf. 12*
690 A93 1000m Pair, #a.-b. .90 .90
c. Souvenir sheet, pair, #a.-b. .90 .90

1999, Oct. 20 *Perf. 12½x12*
691 A94 250m multicolored .20 .20

Gafar Gabbarli (1899-1934), playwright.

Souvenir Sheet

Perf. 14¾x14½ (a), 14½x13¾ (b-d)

1999, Oct. 30

80th anniv. of Azerbaijan postage stamps: a, #1. b, #3. c, #7. d, #10. b-d horiz.

692 A95 500m Sheet of 4, #a.-d. 1.00 1.00

A96 A98

A97

Baku Caravansary: No. 693, Inner courtyard. No. 694, Facade, camels.

1999, Dec. 29 Litho. *Perf. 13*
693-694 A96 500m Set of 2 2.10 2.10

1999, Dec. 29 *Perf. 12*
695 A97 1000m multi 1.10 1.10

Council of Europe, 50th anniv.

1999, Dec. 29

Azerbaijan flag, UPU emblem and: a, 250m, Dove. b, 3000m, Computer, satellite.

696 A98 Pair, #a.-b. 2.25 2.25

UPU, 125th anniv.

Souvenir Sheet

Epic Legend Kitabi Dede Gorgud, 1300th Anniv. A99

Designs: a, Beyrek fights with camel. b, Wounded Tural on horseback. c, Gazan Khan sleeping, horse.

1999, Dec. 29 *Perf. 12¼x11¾*
697 A99 1000m Sheet of 3, #a.-c. 2.50 2.50

Europa, 2000

Common Design Type

2000, Feb. 7 Litho. *Perf. 12¾x13*
698 CD17 1000m multi 1.00 1.00
699 CD17 3000m multi 3.00 3.00

Souvenir Sheet

Baku Transportation — A100

Designs: a, Phaeton. b, Horse-drawn tram. c, Electric tram. d, Trolleybus.
Illustration reduced.

2000, Feb. 15 Litho. ***Perf. 12½x12***
700 A100 500m Sheet of 4, #a-d 2.75 2.75

Tower Type of 1999

100m, Ramany Castle, 14th cent, horiz. 250m, Nardaran Castle, 14th cent., horiz.

2000, May 5 Litho. ***Perf. 11¾x11¼***
701 A92 100m black & orange .25 .25
702 A92 250m black & green .65 .65

World Meteorological Organization, 50th Anniv. — A101

2000, May 5 ***Perf. 12***
703 A101 1000m multi 1.00 1.00

Worldwide Fund for Nature — A102

Aythya nyroca: a, One in flight. b, Two on rocks, three in water. c, One on rocks, three in water. d, One in water, three in flight.
Illustration reduced.

2000, May 5 ***Perf. 12½x12***
704 A102 500m Block of 4, #a-d 2.00 2.00

2000 Summer Olympics, Sydney — A103

Designs: a, Wrestling. b, Weight lifting. c, Boxing. d, Running.
Illustration reduced.

2000, May 5 ***Perf. 12x12½***
705 A103 500m Block of 4, #a-d 2.00 2.00

Souvenir Sheet

Phasianus Colchicus — A104

Illustration reduced.

2000, June 21 Litho. ***Perf. 13½x13***
706 A104 2000m multi 3.25 3.25

Fruit A105

No. 707: a, Cydonia oblonga. b, Punica granatum. c, Persica L. d, Ficus carica.

2000, June 21 ***Perf. 13x13¼***
707 Sheet of 4 3.25 3.25
a.-d. A105 500m Any single .80 .80

Rasul Rza (1911-81), Poet A106

2000, Sept. 28 Litho. ***Perf. 13x13¼***
708 A106 250m multi .40 .40

Reptiles A107

No. 709: a, Vipera lebetina. b, Laserta saxcola. c, Vipera xanthina. d, Phrynocephalus mystaceus.
No. 710, Natrix tessellata, Phrynocephalus helioscopus, vert.

2000, Sept. 28 ***Perf. 13½x13***
709 Sheet of 4 3.25 3.25
a.-d. A107 500m Any single .80 .80

Souvenir Sheet
Perf. 13x13½
710 A107 500m multi .80 .80

Sabit Rahman (1910-70), Writer A108

2000, Nov. 17 ***Perf. 13x13¼***
711 A108 1000m multi 1.60 1.60

Intl. Year for the Culture of Peace — A109

2000, Nov. 17 ***Perf. 13¼x13***
712 A109 3000m multi 4.75 4.75

Souvenir Sheet

2000 Olympic Medalists — A110

No. 713: a, Namig Abdullaev, 54kg freestyle wrestling gold medalist. b, Zemfira Meftahaddinova, women's skeet shooting gold medalist. c, Vugar Alakbarov, middleweight boxing bronze medalist.

2001, Jan. 26 Litho. ***Perf. 13½x13¾***
713 A110 1000m Sheet of 3, #a-c 2.60 2.60

Dated 2000.

Europa — A111

Caspian Sea and: 1000m, Seal. 3000m, Sturgeon, crab, jellyfish.

Perf. 13½x13¼
2001, Mar. 28 Litho.
714-715 A111 Set of 2 5.00 5.00
715a Pane, 4 each #714-715 20.00

Stamps in the middle two columns of No. 715a are tete beche. No. 715a was sold with booklet cover, but unattached to it.

Admission of Azerbaijan to Council of Europe A112

2001, Apr. 25 ***Perf. 13¼x13½***
716 A112 1000m multi 1.10 1.10

Tower Type of 1999

Designs: 100m, Sheki, 18th cent., horiz. 250m, Sheki, 12th-13th cent., horiz.

2001, July 27 ***Perf. 14x13¾***
717 A92 100m black & lilac .30 .30
718 A92 250m black & yellow .80 .80

Souvenir Sheet

UN High Commissioner for Refugees, 50th Anniv. — A113

2001, Aug. 22 ***Perf. 13¼x13½***
719 A113 3000m multi 2.25 2.25

Souvenir Sheet

Nasir ad-Din at-Tusi (1201-74), Scientist — A114

2001, Sept. 7 ***Perf. 13¼***
720 A114 3000m multi 2.25 2.25

Commonwealth of Independent States, 10th Anniv. — A115

2001, Oct. 8 Litho. ***Perf. 13½x13¼***
721 A115 1000m multi .90 .90

Souvenir Sheet

First Manned Space Flight, 40th Anniv. — A116

2001, Nov. 6 ***Perf. 13¼x13½***
722 A116 3000m multi 2.25 2.25

Independence, 10th Anniv. — A117

Litho. & Embossed with Foil Application

2001, Dec. 1 ***Perf. 13¼***
723 A117 5000m gold & multi 9.00 9.00

Owls — A118

No. 724: a, Asio flammeus. b, Strix aluco. c, Otus scops. d, Asio otus. e, Bubo bubo, wings at side. f, Athene noctua.
No. 725, Bubo bubo, wings extended.

2001, Dec. 1 Litho. *Perf. 13¼x13*

724 A118 1000m Sheet of 6, #a-f *5.25* 5.25

Souvenir Sheet

725 A118 1000m shown .90 .90

Visit of Russian Pres. Vladimir Putin A119

2001, Dec. 20 *Perf. 13*

726 A119 1000m multi .90 .90

Natl. Olympic Committee, 10th Anniv. — A120

2002, Mar. 6 *Perf. 13¼x13½*

727 A120 3000m multi 2.10 2.10

Europa — A121

Designs: 1000m, Tight rope walker, musicians, strong man, acrobat. 3000m, Trapeze artist, juggler, horse trainer.

2002, Mar. 11 *Perf. 13½x13¼*

728-729 A121 Set of 2 4.50 4.50

Azerbaijan - People's Republic of China Diplomatic Relations, 10th Anniv. A122

2002, Mar. 28 Litho. *Perf. 12*

730 A122 1000m multi .90 .90

Towers Type of 1999

Designs: 100m, Molla Panah Vagif Mausoleum, Shusha. 250m, Mosque, Agdam.

2002, Apr. 23 *Perf. 13½x14*

731 A92 100m blk & ol grn .20 .20

732 A92 250m blk & tan .45 .45

No. 350 Surcharged in Red

Method & Perf. As Before

2002, May 8

733 A20 1000m on 35k multi .90 .90

New Azerbaijan Party, 10th Anniv. — A123

2002, June 1 *Perf. 13½*

734 A123 3000m multi *1.75* 1.75

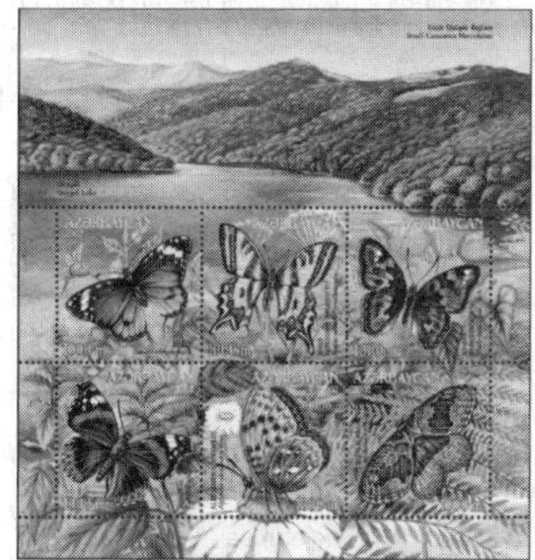

Butterflies — A124

No. 735: a, Danaus chrysippus. b, Papilio orientalis. c, Thaleropis jonia. d, Vanessa atalanta. e, Argynnis alexandra. f, Brahmaea christophi.

2002, June 19 *Perf. 13*

735 A124 1000m Sheet of 6, #a-f *4.50* 4.50

In Remembrance of Sept. 11, 2001 Terrorist Attacks — A125

2002, Sept. 18 *Perf. 13½x13¼*

736 A125 1500m multi .85 .85

Printed in sheets of 3.

Baku Telegraph Office, 70th Anniv. — A126

2002, Sept. 18 *Perf. 14¼x14*

737 A126 3000m multi 1.75 1.75

Rauf Gadjiev, Composer, 80th Anniv. of Birth A127

2002, Sept. 18 *Perf. 14x14¼*

738 A127 5000m multi 2.10 2.10

Souvenir Sheet

Visit of Pope John Paul II — A128

2002, Sept. 18 *Perf. 13¼x13½*

739 A128 1500m multi 1.75 1.75

Souvenir Sheet

European Junior Chess Championships — A129

Baku skyline and stylized chess pieces: a, King, queen, pawns. b, Knights, pawn. c, Two elephants, rook, pawn. d, King, queen, rook, pawn.

2002, Sept. 18 *Perf. 12¾x13¼*

740 A129 1500m Sheet of 4, #a-d *4.50* 4.50

Souvenir Sheet

Turkey's Third Place Finish in 2002 World Cup Soccer Championships — A130

2002, Oct. 16 *Perf. 13¼x13*

741 A130 5000m multi 2.10 2.10

Women for Peace — A131

2002, Nov. 1 *Perf. 14¼x14*

742 A131 3000m multi 1.75 1.75

SEMI-POSTAL STAMPS

Carrying Food to Sufferers SP1

1922 Unwmk. *Imperf.*

B1 SP1 500r blue & pale blue .40 .75

For overprint and surcharge see Nos. 42, 305.

Widow and Orphans — SP2

1922

B2 SP2 1000r brown & bister .50 *1.25*

Counterfeits exist.

For overprint and surcharge see #44, 306.

Russian stamps of 1909-18 were privately overprinted as above in red, blue or black by a group of Entente officers working with Russian soldiers returning from Persia. Azerbaijan was not occupied by the Allies. There is evidence that existing covers (some seemingly postmarked at Baku, dated Oct. 19, 1917, and at Tabriz, Russian Consulate, Apr. 25, 1917) are fakes.

AIR POST STAMP

Catalogue values for all stamps in this section are for never hinged items.

Eagle — AP1

1995, Oct. 16 Litho. *Perf. 14*

C1 AP1 2200m multicolored 1.50 1.50

AZORES

'ā-,zōrz

LOCATION — Group of islands in the North Atlantic Ocean, due west of Portugal
AREA — 922 sq. mi.
POP. — 253,935 (1930)
CAPITAL — Ponta Delgada

Azores stamps were supplanted by those of Portugal in 1931.

In 1934-45, #RA5-RA11, RAJ1-RAJ4, and many stamps between #155-223 were used for regular postage in Portugal.

The Azores were declared an autonomous, or self-governing, region of Portugal in 1976. See Portugal for issues since 1980.

1000 Reis = 1 Milreis
100 Centavos = 1 Escudo (1912)

Stamps of Portugal Overprinted in Black or Carmine

a

A second type of this overprint has a broad "O" and open "S."

1868 Unwmk. *Imperf.*

1	A14	5r black	*3,150.*	*1,600.*
2	A14	10r yellow	*13,000.*	*7,750.*
3	A14	20r bister	175.00	125.00
4	A14	50r green	175.00	125.00
5	A14	80r orange	200.00	140.00
6	A14	100r lilac	200.00	140.00

The reprints are on thick chalky white wove paper, ungummed, and on thin ivory paper with shiny white gum. Value $20 each.

1868-70 *Perf. 12½*

5 REIS:
Type I - The "5" at the right is 1mm from end of label.
Type II - The "5" is 1½mm from end of label.

7	A14	5r black (C)	65.00	50.00
8	A14	10r yellow	87.50	50.00
a.		Inverted overprint	*250.00*	—
9	A14	20r bister	65.00	45.00
10	A14	25r rose	65.00	8.00
a.		Inverted overprint	—	—
11	A14	50r green	190.00	140.00
12	A14	80r orange	190.00	140.00
13	A14	100r lilac	190.00	140.00
14	A14	120r blue	160.00	90.00
15	A14	240r violet	575.00	300.00

The reprints are on thick chalky white paper ungummed, perf 13½, and on thin ivory paper with shiny white gum, perf 13½. Value $15 each.

1871-75 *Perf. 12½, 13½*

21	A15	5r black (C)	12.00	6.50
a.		Inverted overprint	*45.00*	—
23	A15	10r yellow	26.00	15.00
a.		Inverted overprint	—	—
b.		Double overprint	*60.00*	—
24	A15	20r bister	25.00	15.00
25	A15	25r rose	15.00	3.00
a.		Inverted overprint	—	—
b.		Double overprint	*35.00*	
c.		Perf. 14	150.00	60.00
d.		Dbl. impression of stamp	—	—
26	A15	50r green	80.00	35.00
27	A15	80r orange	100.00	50.00
28	A15	100r lilac	80.00	40.00
a.		Perf. 14	160.00	100.00
29	A15	120r blue	150.00	82.50
a.		Inverted overprint	—	—
30	A15	240r violet	800.00	500.00

Nos. 21-29 exist with overprint "b."

The reprints are of type "b." They are on thick chalky white paper ungummed, perf 13½, and also on thin white paper with shiny white gum and perforated 13½.

Overprinted in Black

b

1875-80

15 REIS:
Type I - The figures of value, 1 and 5, at the right in upper label are close together.
Type II - The figures of value at the right in upper label are spaced.

31	A15	10r blue green	150.00	100.00
32	A15	10r yellow green	100.00	60.00
33	A15	15r lilac brown	15.00	11.50
a.		Inverted overprint	*125.00*	
34	A15	50r blue	140.00	60.00
35	A15	150r blue	160.00	100.00
36	A15	150r yellow	190.00	125.00
37	A15	300r violet	80.00	50.00

The reprints have the same papers, gum and perforations as those of the preceding issue.

Black Overprint

1880 *Perf. 12½, 13½*

38	A17	25r gray	125.00	30.00
39	A18	25r red lilac	47.50	6.00
a.		25r gray	47.50	6.00
b.		Double overprint	—	—

Overprinted in Carmine or Black

1881-82

40	A16	5r black (C)	21.00	7.50
41	A23	25r brown ('82)	45.00	5.00
a.		Double overprint		
42	A19	50r blue	150.00	30.00
		Nos. 40-42 (3)	216.00	42.50

Reprints of Nos. 38, 39, 39a, 40 and 42 have the same papers, gum and perforations as those of preceding issues.

Overprinted in Red or Black

c

1882-85 *Perf. 11½, 12½, 13½*

15, 20 REIS
Type I - The figures of value are some distance apart and close to the end of the label.
Type II - The figures are closer together and farther from the end of the label. On the 15 reis this is particularly apparent in the upper right figures.

43	A16	5r black (R)	25.00	10.00
44	A21	5r slate	15.00	3.00
a.		Double overprint	—	—
c.		Inverted overprint	—	—
45	A15	10r green	75.00	50.00
a.		Inverted overprint	—	—
46	A22	10r green	25.00	10.00
a.		Double overprint	—	—
47	A15	15r lilac brn	60.00	35.00
b.		Inverted overprint	—	—
48	A15	20r bister	90.00	50.00
a.		Inverted overprint	—	—
49	A15	20r carmine	110.00	80.00
a.		Double overprint	160.00	—
50	A23	25r brown	19.00	3.00
51	A15	50r blue	*1,000.*	*750.00*
52	A24	50r blue	24.00	3.00
a.		Double overprint	—	—
53	A15	80r yellow	55.00	37.50
a.		80r orange	67.50	42.50
b.		Double overprint	—	—
54	A15	100r lilac	100.00	62.50
55	A15	150r blue	*900.00*	*600.00*
56b	A15	150r yellow	55.00	37.50
57b	A15	300r violet	75.00	52.50

This set was issued on both ordinary and enamel surfaced papers. Nos. 51 and 55 exist only on ordinary paper, Nos. 44, 46, 49 and 53 only on surfaced paper, and the other values on both types of paper. Values for Nos. 56b and 57b are for copies printed on surfaced paper. Copies on ordinary paper are worth more.

For specialized listings of this issue and other early Azores stamps, see the *Scott Classic Specialized Catalogue.*

Reprints of the 1882-85 issues have the same papers, gum and perforations as those of preceding issues.

Red Overprint

58	A21	5r slate	20.00	4.00
59	A24a	500r black	160.00	110.00
60	A15	1000r black	110.00	82.50

1887 Black Overprint

61	A25	20r pink	25.00	10.00
a.		Inverted overprint	—	—
b.		Double overprint	—	—
62	A26	25r lilac rose	25.00	2.00
a.		Inverted overprint	—	—
b.		Double ovpt., one invtd.	—	—
63	A26	25r red violet	25.00	2.00
a.		Double overprint	—	—
64	A24a	500r red violet	125.00	75.00
a.		Perf. 13½	400.00	200.00
		Nos. 61-64 (4)	200.00	89.00

Nos. 58-64 inclusive have been reprinted on thin white paper with shiny white gum and perforated 13½.

Prince Henry the Navigator Issue

Portugal Nos. 97-109 Overprinted

1894, Mar. 4 *Perf. 14*

65	A46	5r orange yel	2.75	2.00
a.		Inverted overprint	*45.00*	*45.00*
66	A46	10r violet rose	2.75	2.00
a.		Double overprint	—	—
b.		Inverted overprint	—	—
67	A46	15r brown	3.25	2.50
68	A46	20r violet	3.50	2.50
a.		Double overprint	—	—
69	A47	25r green	4.00	3.00
a.		Double overprint	*50.00*	*50.00*
b.		Inverted overprint	*50.00*	*50.00*
70	A47	50r blue	10.00	4.25
71	A47	75r dp carmine	19.00	6.00
72	A47	80r yellow grn	21.00	6.00
73	A47	100r lt brn, *pale buff*	21.00	5.00
a.		Double overprint	—	—
74	A48	150r lt car, *pale rose*	30.00	10.00
75	A48	300r dk bl, *sal buff*	32.50	17.50
76	A48	500r brn vio, *pale lil*	60.00	25.00
77	A48	1000r gray blk, *yelsh*	110.00	45.00
a.		Double overprint	500.00	400.00
		Nos. 65-77 (13)	319.75	130.75

St. Anthony of Padua Issue

Portugal Nos. 132-146 Overprinted in Red or Black

1895, June 13 *Perf. 12*

78	A50	2½r black (R)	2.50	1.10
79	A51	5r brown yel	7.50	2.50
80	A51	10r red lilac	7.75	3.50
81	A51	15r red brown	11.50	5.00
82	A51	20r gray lilac	12.50	6.50
83	A51	25r green & vio	8.00	2.50
84	A52	50r blue & brn	25.00	12.00
85	A52	75r rose & brn	35.00	27.50
86	A52	80r lt grn & brn	40.00	30.00
87	A52	100r choc & blk	42.50	29.00
88	A53	150r vio rose & bis	80.00	80.00
89	A53	200r blue & bis	97.50	70.00
90	A53	300r slate & bis	110.00	82.50
91	A53	500r vio brn & grn	175.00	110.00
92	A53	1000r violet & grn	275.00	190.00
		Nos. 78-92 (15)	929.75	652.10

7th cent. of the birth of Saint Anthony of Padua.

Common Design Types pictured following the introduction.

Vasco da Gama Issue

Common Design Types

1898, Apr. 1 *Perf. 14, 15*

93	CD20	2½r blue green	2.75	1.00
94	CD21	5r red	2.75	1.10
95	CD22	10r gray lilac	5.00	2.00
96	CD23	25r yellow green	5.00	2.00
97	CD24	50r dark blue	8.00	6.00
98	CD25	75r violet brown	16.00	9.50
99	CD26	100r bister brown	20.00	9.50
100	CD27	150r bister	32.50	20.00
		Nos. 93-100 (8)	92.00	51.10

For overprints and surcharges see Nos. 141-148.

King Carlos — A28

King Manuel II — A29

1906 Typo. *Perf. 11½x12*

101	A28	2½r gray	.35	.30
a.		Inverted overprint	*25.00*	*25.00*
102	A28	5r orange yel	.35	.30
a.		Inverted overprint	*25.00*	*25.00*
103	A28	10r yellow grn	.35	.30
104	A28	20r gray vio	.50	.45
105	A28	25r carmine	.50	.30
106	A28	50r ultra	4.50	3.00
107	A28	75r brown, *straw*	1.50	*.80*
108	A28	100r dk blue, *bl*	1.50	*.90*
109	A28	200r red lilac, *pnksh*	1.60	*.90*
110	A28	300r dk blue, *rose*	5.00	*3.25*
111	A28	500r black, *blue*	11.00	9.00
		Nos. 101-111 (11)	27.15	19.50

"Acores" and letters and figures in the corners are in red on the 2½, 10, 20, 75 and 500r and in black on the other values.

1910, Apr. 1 *Perf. 14x15*

112	A29	2½r violet	.40	.30
113	A29	5r black	.40	.35
114	A29	10r dk green	.70	.50
115	A29	15r lilac brn	.70	.50
116	A29	20r carmine	.90	.75
117	A29	25r violet brn	.40	.35
a.		Perf. 11½	2.40	1.10
118	A29	50r blue	2.40	1.00
119	A29	75r bister brn	2.40	1.00
120	A29	80r slate	2.40	2.00
121	A29	100r brown, *lt grn*	3.00	2.50
122	A29	200r green, *sal*	3.00	2.50
123	A29	300r black, *blue*	2.40	2.00
124	A29	500r olive & brown	7.00	6.00
125	A29	1000r blue & black	15.00	12.00
		Nos. 112-125 (14)	41.10	31.75

The errors of color 10r black, 15r dark green, 25r black and 50r carmine are considered to be proofs.

Stamps of 1910 Overprinted in Carmine or Green

1910

126	A29	2½r violet	.30	.25
a.		Inverted overprint	9.00	9.00
127	A29	5r black	.25	.25
a.		Inverted overprint	9.00	9.00
128	A29	10r dk green	.30	.25
a.		Inverted overprint	9.00	9.00
129	A29	15r lilac brn	1.25	.90
a.		Inverted overprint	9.00	9.00
130	A29	20r carmine (G)	1.25	.90
a.		Inverted overprint	16.00	16.00
b.		Double overprint	16.00	16.00
131	A29	25r violet brn	.25	.25
a.		Perf. 11½	50.00	42.50
132	A29	50r blue	1.00	.80
133	A29	75r bister brn	1.00	.70
a.		Double overprint	9.00	9.00
134	A29	80r slate	1.00	.70
135	A29	100r brown, *grn*	.90	.70
136	A29	200r green, *sal*	.90	*.70*
137	A29	300r black, *blue*	2.50	1.40
138	A29	500r olive & brn	3.25	*1.75*
139	A29	1000r blue & blk	7.50	*4.00*
		Nos. 126-139 (14)	21.65	*13.55*

Vasco da Gama Issue Overprinted or Surcharged in Black:

d

e

f

1911 *Perf. 14, 15*

141 CD20(d) 2½r bl grn .50 .35
142 CD21(e) 15r on 5r red .50 .35
143 CD23(d) 25r yellow grn .50 .35
144 CD24(d) 50r dk blue 1.50 1.00
145 CD25(d) 75r violet brn 1.25 1.10
146 CD27(e) 80r on 150r bister 1.25 1.10
147 CD26(d) 100r yellow brn 1.40 1.25
a. Double surcharge 21.00 21.00
148 CD22(f) 1000r on 10r lil 14.00 9.00
Nos. 141-148 (8) 20.90 14.50

Postage Due Stamps of Portugal Overprinted or Surcharged in Black "ACORES" and

g

h

1911 *Perf. 12*

149 D1 5r black 1.00 .75
150 D1 10r magenta 2.00 .75
a. "Acores" double 16.00 12.00
151 D1 20r orange 3.50 2.00
152 D1 200r brn, *buff* 16.00 14.00
a. "Acores" inverted
153 D1 300r on 50r slate 15.00 12.50
154 D1 500r on 100r car, *pink* 15.00 12.50
Nos. 149-154 (6) 52.50 42.50

Ceres Issue of Portugal Overprinted in Black or Carmine

With Imprint

1912-31 *Perf. 12x11½, 15x14*

155 A64 ¼c olive brown .35 .25
a. Inverted overprint 9.00 7.00
156 A64 ½c black (C) .35 .25
157 A64 1c deep green .70 .50
a. Inverted overprint 9.00
158 A64 1c dp brn ('18) .35 .25
a. Inverted overprint 12.00
159 A64 1½c choc ('13) .70 .50
a. Inverted overprint 9.00
160 A64 1½c dp grn ('18) .35 .25
a. Inverted overprint 12.00
161 A64 2c carmine .50 .35
a. Inverted overprint 14.00
162 A64 2c orange ('18) .35 .30
a. Inverted overprint 18.00
163 A64 2½c violet .35 .30
164 A64 3c rose ('18) .35 .30
165 A64 3c dull ultra ('25) .35 .20
166 A64 3½c lt grn ('18) .35 .30
167 A64 4c lt grn ('19) .35 .30
168 A64 4c orange ('30) .65 .45
169 A64 5c dp blue .35 .30
170 A64 5c yel brn ('18) .50 .30
171 A64 5c ol brn ('23) .35 .30
172 A64 5c blk brn ('30) 2.40 1.75
173 A64 6c dull rose ('20) .35 .30
174 A64 6c choc ('25) .35 .30
175 A64 6c red brn ('31) .25 .20
176 A64 7½c yel brn 4.75 2.00
177 A64 7½c dp bl ('18) 1.25 .75
178 A64 8c slate ('13) .50 .40
179 A64 8c bl grn ('22) .50 .30
180 A64 8c orange ('25) .75 .55
181 A64 10c org brn .85 .50
182 A64 12c bl gray ('20) 1.90 1.00
183 A64 12c dp grn ('22) .65 .50
184 A64 13½c chlky bl ('20) 1.90 1.00
185 A64 14c dk bl, *yel* ('20) 1.75 1.00
186 A64 15c plum ('13) 12.00 3.50
187 A64 15c blk (R) ('23) .35 .30
188 A64 16c brt ultra ('24) .75 .50
189 A64 16c dp bl ('30) 2.00 1.50
190 A64 20c vio brn, *grn* ('13) 8.00 4.00
191 A64 20c choc ('20) .60 .45
192 A64 20c dp grn ('23) .80 .60
a. Double overprint 15.00 15.00
193 A64 20c gray ('24) .55 .35
194 A64 24c grnsh bl ('21) .60 .30
195 A64 25c salmon ('23) .40 .30
196 A64 30c brn, *pink* ('13) 45.00 30.00
197 A64 30c brn, *yel* ('19) 1.75 1.00
198 A64 30c gray brn ('21) 1.25 1.00
199 A64 32c dp grn ('25) 3.25 2.00
200 A64 36c red ('21) .60 .30
201 A64 40c dp blue ('23) .75 .50
202 A64 40c blk brn ('24) 1.40 .60
203 A64 40c brt grn ('30) 1.10 .50
204 A64 48c brt rose ('24) 2.50 1.00
205 A64 48c dull pink ('31) 6.25 6.00
206 A64 50c org, *sal* ('13) 5.25 1.00
207 A64 50c yellow ('23) 1.25 1.00
208 A64 50c bister ('30) 2.50 1.75
209 A64 50c red brn ('31) 2.00 1.50
210 A64 60c blue ('21) 1.00 .70
211 A64 64c pale ultra ('24) 3.00 1.00
212 A64 64c brown rose ('31) 45.00 45.00
213 A64 75c dull rose ('23) 6.00 4.00
214 A64 75c car rose ('30) 2.00 1.25
215 A64 80c dull rose ('21) 1.25 .65
216 A64 80c violet ('24) 1.25 .90
217 A64 80c dk grn ('31) 1.50 1.25
218 A64 90c chlky bl ('21) 2.00 .75
219 A64 96c dp rose ('26) 8.25 4.50
220 A64 1e dp grn, *bl* 4.75 1.50
221 A64 1e violet ('21) 2.00 .75
222 A64 1e gray vio ('24) 2.00 1.00
223 A64 1e brn lake ('30) 12.50 10.00
224 A64 1.10e yel brn ('21) 2.00 1.25
225 A64 1.20e yel grn ('21) 2.50 1.00
226 A64 1.20e buff ('24) 5.00 1.75
227 A64 1.25e dk blue ('30) 1.50 .75
228 A64 1.50e blk vio ('23) 3.00 1.75
229 A64 1.50e lilac ('25) 8.00 1.75
230 A64 1.60e dp bl ('25) 2.75 1.75
231 A64 2e slate grn ('21) 4.25 2.00
232 A64 2.40e apple grn ('26) 80.00 50.00
233 A64 3e lil pink ('26) 80.00 55.00
234 A64 3.20e gray grn ('25) 10.00 4.50
235 A64 5e emer ('24) 20.00 12.00
236 A64 10e pink ('24) 40.00 20.00
237 A64 20e pale turq ('25) 125.00 75.00
Nos. 155-237 (83) 602.70 377.65

For same overprint on surcharged stamps see Nos. 300-306. For same design without imprint see Nos. 307-313.

Castello-Branco Issue

Stamps of Portugal, 1925, Overprinted in Black or Red

1925, Mar. 29 *Perf. 12½*

238 A73 2c orange .20 .20
239 A73 3c green .20 .20
240 A73 4c ultra (R) .20 .20
241 A73 5c scarlet .20 .20
242 A74 10c pale blue .20 .20
243 A74 16c red orange .25 .25
244 A75 25c car rose .25 .25
245 A74 32c green .45 .40
246 A75 40c grn & blk (R) .45 .40
247 A74 48c red brn 1.00 .90
248 A76 50c blue green 1.00 .75
249 A76 64c orange brn 1.00 .75
250 A76 75c gray blk (R) 1.00 .75
251 A75 80c brown 1.00 .75
252 A76 96c car rose 1.10 .90
253 A77 1.50e dk bl, *bl* (R) 1.10 .90
254 A75 1.60e indigo (R) 1.25 1.00
255 A77 2e dk grn, *grn* (R) 1.90 1.50
256 A77 2.40e red, *org* 2.40 1.60
257 A77 3.20e blk, *grn* (R) 4.50 3.50
Nos. 238-257 (20) 19.65 15.60

First Independence Issue

Stamps of Portugal, 1926, Overprinted in Red

1926, Aug. 13 *Perf. 14, 14½*

Center in Black

258 A79 2c orange .25 .25
259 A80 3c ultra .25 .25
260 A79 4c yellow grn .25 .25
261 A80 5c black brn .25 .25
262 A79 6c ocher .25 .25
263 A80 15c dk green .50 .50
264 A81 20c dull violet .50 .50
265 A82 25c scarlet .50 .50
266 A81 32c deep green .50 .50
267 A82 40c yellow brn .50 .50
268 A82 50c olive bis 1.25 1.10
269 A82 75c red brown 1.40 1.25
270 A83 1e black violet 1.75 1.50
271 A84 4.50e olive green 6.00 5.00
Nos. 258-271 (14) 14.15 12.60

The use of these stamps instead of those of the regular issue was obligatory on Aug. 13th and 14th, Nov. 30th and Dec. 1st, 1926.

Second Independence Issue

Same Overprint on Stamps of Portugal, 1927, in Red

1927, Nov. 29

Center in Black

272 A86 2c lt brown .25 .25
273 A87 3c ultra .25 .25
274 A86 4c orange .25 .25
275 A88 5c dk brown .25 .25
276 A89 6c orange brn .25 .25
277 A87 15c black brn .25 .25
278 A86 25c gray 1.00 .90
279 A89 32c blue grn 1.00 .90
280 A90 40c yellow grn .60 .50
281 A90 96c red 2.50 2.00
282 A88 1.60e myrtle grn 2.50 2.10
283 A91 4.50e bister 6.50 5.00
Nos. 272-283 (12) 15.60 12.90

Third Independence Issue

Same Overprint on Stamps of Portugal, 1928, in Red

1928, Nov. 27

Center in Black

284 A93 2c lt blue .25 .25
285 A94 3c lt green .25 .25
286 A95 4c lake .25 .25
287 A96 5c olive grn .25 .25
288 A97 6c orange brn .25 .25
289 A94 15c slate .50 .40
290 A95 16c dk violet .65 .50
291 A93 25c ultra .65 .50
292 A97 32c dk green .65 .55
293 A96 40c olive brn .65 .55
294 A95 50c red orange 1.25 1.10
295 A94 80c lt gray 1.25 1.10
296 A97 96c carmine 2.25 1.75
297 A96 1e claret 2.25 1.75
298 A93 1.60e dk blue 2.25 1.75
299 A98 4.50e yellow 6.00 5.00
Nos. 284-299 (16) 19.60 16.20

A31

A32

1929-30 *Perf. 12x11½, 15x14*

300 A31 4c on 25c pink ('30) .60 .50
301 A31 4c on 60c dp blue 1.10 .80
302 A31 10c on 25c pink 1.10 .80
303 A31 12c on 25c pink 1.10 .80
304 A31 15c on 25c pink 1.10 .80
305 A31 20c on 25c pink 1.75 1.50
306 A31 40c on 1.10e yel brn 4.00 3.00
Nos. 300-306 (7) 10.75 8.20

Black or Red Overprint

1930 *Perf. 14*

Without Imprint at Foot

307 A32 4c orange .65 .40
308 A32 5c dp brown 2.10 1.75
309 A32 10c vermilion 1.10 .75
310 A32 15c black (R) 1.10 .75
311 A32 40c brt green 1.10 .60
312 A32 80c violet 11.00 8.75
313 A32 1.60e dk blue 3.00 1.10
Nos. 307-313 (7) 20.05 14.10

POSTAGE DUE STAMPS

D2

D3

Portugal Nos. J7-J13 Overprinted in Black

1904 **Unwmk.** *Perf. 12*

J1 D2 5r brown .80 .55
J2 D2 10r orange .90 .55
J3 D2 20r lilac 1.40 .90
J4 D2 30r gray green 1.40 .90
a. Double overprint
J5 D2 40r gray violet 2.40 1.25
J6 D2 50r carmine 4.00 2.25
J7 D2 100r dull blue 5.00 3.75
Nos. J1-J7 (7) 15.90 10.15

Same Overprinted in Carmine or Green (Portugal Nos. J14-J20)

1911

J8 D2 5r brown .50 .40
J9 D2 10r orange .50 .40
J10 D2 20r lilac .75 .50
J11 D2 30r gray green .75 .50
J12 D2 40r gray violet 1.25 1.00
J13 D2 50r carmine (G) 6.00 5.00
J14 D2 100r dull blue 2.50 2.00
Nos. J8-J14 (7) 12.25 9.80

Portugal Nos. J21-J27 Overprinted in Black

1918

J15 D3 ½c brown .45 .20
a. Inverted overprint 4.00
b. Double overprint 4.00
J16 D3 1c orange .45 .20
a. Inverted overprint 4.00
b. Double overprint 4.00
J17 D3 2c red lilac .45 .20
a. Inverted overprint 4.00
b. Double overprint 4.00
J18 D3 3c green .45 .20
a. Inverted overprint 4.00
b. Double overprint 4.00
J19 D3 4c gray .45 .20
a. Inverted overprint 4.00
b. Double overprint 4.00
J20 D3 5c rose .45 .20
b. Double overprint 4.00
J21 D3 10c dark blue .45 .20
Nos. J15-J21 (7) 3.15 1.40

Stamps and Type of Portugal Postage Dues, 1921-27, Overprinted in Black

1922-24 *Perf. 11½x12*

J30 D3 ½c gray green ('23) .25 .20
J31 D3 1c gray green ('23) .35 .25
J32 D3 2c gray green ('23) .35 .25
J33 D3 3c gray green ('24) .55 .25
J34 D3 8c gray green ('24) .55 .25
J35 D3 10c gray green ('24) .55 .25
J36 D3 12c gray green ('24) .55 .25
J37 D3 16c gray green ('24) .60 .25
J38 D3 20c gray green .60 .25
J39 D3 24c gray green .60 .25
J40 D3 32c gray green ('24) .60 .25
J41 D3 36c gray green .60 .30
J42 D3 40c gray green ('24) .60 .30
J43 D3 48c gray green ('24) .60 .30
J44 D3 50c gray green .60 .30
J45 D3 60c gray green .65 .30
J46 D3 72c gray green .65 .30
J47 D3 80c gray green ('24) 3.25 2.00
J48 D3 1.20e gray green 3.25 2.00
Nos. J30-J48 (19) 15.75 8.50

NEWSPAPER STAMPS

Newspaper Stamps of Portugal, Nos. P1, P1a, Overprinted Types b & c in Black or Red and:

N3

Perf. 11½, 12½ and 13½

1876-88 **Unwmk.**

P1 N1 2½r (a) olive 9.00 3.50
a. Inverted overprint
P2 N1 2½r (b) olive ('82) 3.00 1.00
a. Inverted overprint — —
b. Double overprint — —
P3 N3 2r black ('85) 3.00 2.00
a. Inverted overprint —
b. Double overprint, one inverted —

P4 N1 2½r (b) bister ('82) 3.00 1.00
a. Double overprint 5.00
P5 N3 2r black (R) ('88) 10.00 6.00
Nos. P1-P5 (5) 28.00 13.50

Reprints of the newspaper stamps have the same papers, gum and perforations as reprints of the regular issues. Value $2 each.

PARCEL POST STAMPS

Portugal Nos. Q1-Q17 Overprinted Like Nos. 155-237 in Black or Red

1921-22 Unwmk. *Perf. 12*
Q1 PP1 1c lilac brown .35 .25
a. Inverted overprint 4.00
Q2 PP1 2c orange .35 .25
a. Inverted overprint 4.00
Q3 PP1 5c light brown .35 .25
a. Inverted overprint 5.00
b. Double overprint 5.00
Q4 PP1 10c red brown .45 .25
a. Inverted overprint 5.00
b. Double overprint 5.00
Q5 PP1 20c gray blue .45 .25
a. Inverted overprint 5.00
b. Double overprint 5.00
Q6 PP1 40c carmine .45 .25
a. Double overprint 6.50
Q7 PP1 50c black (R) .65 .50
Q8 PP1 60c dark blue (R) .65 .50
Q9 PP1 70c gray brown 2.10 1.10
a. Double overprint 5.00
Q10 PP1 80c ultra 2.10 1.10
Q11 PP1 90c light violet 2.10 1.10
Q12 PP1 1e light green 2.10 1.10
Q13 PP1 2e pale lilac 3.50 2.00
Q14 PP1 3e olive 6.25 2.10
Q15 PP1 4e ultra 7.50 2.10
Q16 PP1 5e gray 7.50 4.00
Q17 PP1 10e chocolate 24.00 11.50
Nos. Q1-Q17 (17) 60.85 28.60

POSTAL TAX STAMPS

These stamps represent a special fee for the delivery of postal matter on certain days in the year. The money derived from their sale is applied to works of public charity.

Nos. 114 and 157 Overprinted in Carmine

1911-13 Unwmk. *Perf. 14x15*
RA1 A29 10r dark green 1.00 .55

The 20r of this type was for use on telegrams.

Perf. 15x14
RA2 A30 1c deep green 3.00 1.90

The 2c of this type was for use on telegrams.

Postal Tax Stamp of Portugal, No. RA4, Overprinted Like Nos. 155-237 in Black

1915 *Perf. 12*
RA3 PT2 1c carmine .40 .25

The 2c of this type was for use on telegrams.

Postal Tax Stamp of 1915 Surcharged

1924
RA4 PT1 15c on 1c rose .70 *.45*

Comrades of the Great War Issue

Postal Tax Stamps of Portugal, 1925, Overprinted

1925, Apr. 8 *Perf. 11*
RA5 PT3 10c brown .75 .55
RA6 PT3 10c green .75 .55
RA7 PT3 10c rose .75 .55
RA8 PT3 10c ultra .75 .55
Nos. RA5-RA8 (4) 3.00 2.20

The use of Nos. RA5-RA11 in addition to the regular postage was compulsory on certain days. If the tax represented by these stamps was not prepaid, it was collected by means of Postal Tax Due Stamps.

Pombal Issue
Common Design Types

1925 *Perf. 12½*
RA9 CD28 20c dp grn & blk .75 .55
RA10 CD29 20c dp grn & blk .75 .55
RA11 CD30 20c dp grn & blk .75 .55
Nos. RA9-RA11 (3) 2.25 1.65

POSTAL TAX DUE STAMPS

Postal Tax Due Stamp of Portugal Overprinted like Nos. RA5-RA8

1925, Apr. 8 Unwmk. *Perf. 11x11½*
RAJ1 PTD1 20c brown orange .75 .45

See note after No. RA8.

Pombal Issue
Common Design Types

1925, May 8 *Perf. 12½*
RAJ2 CD28 40c dp grn & blk .75 *.55*
RAJ3 CD29 40c dp grn & blk .75 *.55*
RAJ4 CD30 40c dp grn & blk .75 *.55*
Nos. RAJ2-RAJ4 (3) 2.25 *1.65*

See note after No. RA8.

BAHAMAS

bə-ˈhä-məs

LOCATION — A group of about 700 islands and 2,000 rocks in the West Indies, off the coast of Florida. Only 30 islands are inhabited.
GOVT. — Independent state in British Commonwealth
AREA — 5,382 sq. mi.
POP. — 283,705 (1999 est.)
CAPITAL — Nassau

The principal island, on which the capital is located, is New Providence. The Bahamas obtained internal self-government on January 7, 1964, and independence on July 10, 1973.

12 Pence = 1 Shilling
20 Shillings = 1 Pound
100 Cents = 1 Dollar (1966)

Catalogue values for unused stamps in this country are for Never Hinged items, beginning with Scott 130, and Scott C1 in the air post section.

Values for unused stamps are for examples with original gum as defined in the catalogue introduction. Very fine examples of Nos. 2-26 will have perforations touching the design or frameline on at least one side due to the narrow spacing of the stamps on the plates. Stamps with perfs clear of the design or framelines on all four sides are extremely scarce and will command higher prices.

Pen cancellations usually indicate revenue use. Such stamps sell for much less than postally canceled copies. Beware of stamps with revenue or pen cancellations removed and forged postal cancellations added.

Queen Victoria
A1 A2

1859-60 Unwmk. Engr. *Imperf.*
1 A1 1p dull lake ('60) 50. *1,400.*
a. 1p reddish lake *4,500. 2,000.*
b. 1p brownish lake *4,500. 2,250.*

Most unused copies of #1 are remainders, and false cancellations are plentiful. #1a and 1b are on thicker paper than #1.

1861 *Rough Perf. 14 to 16*
2 A1 1p lake 800. 300.
a. Clean-cut perf. ('60) 3,250. 700.
3 A2 4p dull rose 1,400. 450.
a. Imperf. between, pair *22,500.*
4 A2 6p gray lilac 3,250. 575.
a. Pale lilac 3,000. 500.

1862 Engr. *Perf. 11½, 12*
5 A1 1p lake 1,050. 175.
a. Pair, imperf. between *4,750.*
6 A2 4p dull rose 3,000. 375.
7 A2 6p gray violet 9,000. 475.

No. 5a was not issued in the Bahamas. It is unique and faulty.

Nos. 5-7 exist with perf. 11½ or 12 compound with 11.

Perf. 13
8 A1 1p brown lake 700. 125.
a. 1p carmine lake 850. 150.
9 A2 4p rose 2,750. 325.
10 A2 6p gray violet 3,250. 425.
a. 6p dull violet 2,900. 500.

Queen Victoria — A3

1863-65 Typo. Wmk. 1 *Perf. 12½*
11 A1 1p lake 85.00 60.00
a. 1p brown lake 80.00 60.00
b. 1p rose lake 80.00 60.00
12 A1 1p vermilion 60.00 45.00
a. 1p rose red 57.50 45.00
b. 1p red 57.50 45.00
13 A2 4p rose 375.00 60.00
a. 4p rose lake 400.00 80.00
b. 4p bright rose 250.00 67.50
14 A2 6p dk violet 160.00 65.00
a. 6p violet 250.00 85.00
b. 6p rose lilac 5,250. *3,500.*
c. 6p lilac 350.00 65.00
15 A3 1sh green ('65) 2,500. 300.00

For surcharge see No. 26.

1863-81 *Perf. 14*
16 A1 1p vermilion 60.00 22.50
17 A1 1p car lake (anil.) 1,500.
18 A2 4p rose 375.00 50.00
a. 4p deep rose ('76) 350.00 50.00
b. 4p dull rose 1,500. 50.00
19 A3 1sh green ('80) 8.00 7.50
a. 1shp dark green 175.00 50.00

Some copies of No. 16 show a light aniline appearance and care should be taken not to confuse these with No. 17. All known used copies of No. 17 bear fiscal cancels.

1882-98 Wmk. 2
20 A1 1p vermilion 400.00 60.00
21 A2 4p rose 800.00 60.00
22 A3 1sh green 32.50 15.00
23 A3 1sh blue grn ('98) 37.50 22.50

Perf. 12
24 A1 1p vermilion 42.50 25.00
25 A2 4p rose 525.00 50.00

No. 14a Surcharged in Black

1883 Wmk. 1 *Perf. 12½*
26 A2 4p on 6p violet 500. 400.
a. Inverted surcharge *12,000. 7,250.*

The surcharge, being handstamped, is found in various positions. Counterfeit overprints exist.

Queen Victoria — A5 Queen's Staircase — A6

1884-90 Typo. Wmk. 2 *Perf. 14*
27 A5 1p carmine rose 6.50 2.00
a. 1p pale rose 50.00 10.00
b. 1p car (aniline) 2.50 *6.00*
28 A5 2½p ultra 9.25 2.00
a. 2½p dull blue 55.00 15.00
29 A5 4p yellow 9.25 3.50
30 A5 6p violet 5.75 *25.00*
31 A5 5sh olive green 67.50 *67.50*
32 A5 £1 brown 275.00 *200.00*
Revenue cancellation *55.00*
Nos. 27-32 (6) 373.25 *300.00*

Cleaned fiscally used copies of No. 32 are often found with postmarks of small post offices added. Dangerous forged postmarks exist, especially dated "AU 29 94."

1901-03 Engr. Wmk. 1
33 A6 1p carmine & blk 5.00 *2.50*
34 A6 5p org & blk ('03) 6.50 *40.00*
35 A6 2sh ultra & blk ('03) 21.00 *42.50*
36 A6 3sh green & blk ('03) 27.50 *50.00*
Nos. 33-36 (4) 60.00 *135.00*

See Nos. 48, 58-62, 71, 78, 81-82.

Edward VII A7 George V A8

1902 Wmk. 2 Typo.
37 A7 1p carmine rose 1.50 2.00
38 A7 2½p ultra 6.50 1.00
39 A7 4p orange 14.50 *47.50*
40 A7 6p bister brn 3.50 *14.50*
41 A7 1sh gray blk & car 20.00 *40.00*
42 A7 5sh violet & ultra 60.00 *70.00*
43 A7 £1 green & blk 250.00 *275.00*
Nos. 37-43 (7) 356.00 *450.00*

Beware of forged postmarks, especially dated "2 MAR 10."

1906-11 Wmk. 3
44 A7 ½p green 5.00 2.00
45 A7 1p car rose 24.00 1.75
46 A7 2½p ultra ('07) 24.00 *22.50*
47 A7 6p bister brn ('11) 17.00 *50.00*
Nos. 44-47 (4) 70.00 *76.25*

1911-16 Engr.
48 A6 1p red & gray blk ('16) 4.50 2.50
a. 1p carmine & black 15.00 3.00

For overprints see Nos. B1-B2.

1912-19 Typo.
49 A8 ½p green .95 *6.00*
50 A8 1p car rose (aniline) 4.00 .45
50A A8 2p gray ('19) 2.75 *2.75*
51 A8 2½p ultra 5.50 *16.00*
52 A8 4p orange 2.75 *11.00*
53 A8 6p bister brn 2.10 *3.75*

Chalky Paper
54 A8 1sh black & car 2.10 *8.00*
55 A8 5sh violet & ultra 47.50 *57.50*
56 A8 £1 dull grn & blk 175.00 *260.00*
Nos. 49-56 (9) 242.65 *365.45*

1917-19 Engr.
58 A6 3p reddish pur, *buff* 4.50 *4.25*
59 A6 3p brown & blk ('19) 2.00 *5.00*
60 A6 5p violet & blk 2.50 *9.00*
61 A6 2sh ultra & black 26.00 *42.50*
62 A6 3sh green & black 50.00 *108.25*
Nos. 58-62 (5) 85.00 *108.25*

Peace Commemorative Issue

King George V and Seal of Bahamas — A9

1920, Mar. 1 Engr. *Perf. 14*

65 A9 ½p gray green 1.25 *3.75*
66 A9 1p deep red 3.50 1.00
67 A9 2p gray 3.50 *6.25*
68 A9 3p brown 3.50 *7.50*
69 A9 1sh dark green 16.00 *29.00*
Nos. 65-69 (5) 27.75 *47.50*

Types of 1901-12

Typo., Engr. (A6)

1921-34 Wmk. 4

70 A8 ½p green ('24) .50 .30
71 A6 1p car & black .80 *1.00*
72 A8 1p car rose 1.00 .20
73 A8 1½p fawn ('34) 3.00 *.90*
74 A8 2p gray ('27) 1.25 *2.50*
75 A8 2½p ultra ('22) 1.00 *2.50*
76 A8 3p violet, *yel* ('31) 6.50 *14.50*
77 A8 4p yellow ('24) 1.50 *4.50*
78 A6 5p red vio & gray blk ('29) 4.00 *35.00*
79 A8 6p bister brn ('22) .70 *1.10*
80 A8 1sh blk & red ('26) 2.75 *5.00*
81 A6 2sh ultra & blk ('22) 17.00 *20.00*
82 A6 3sh grn & blk ('24) 40.00 *57.50*
83 A8 5sh vio & ultra ('24) 35.00 *60.00*
84 A8 £1 grn & blk ('26) 160.00 *275.00*
Nos. 70-84 (15) 275.00 *480.00*

The 3p, 1sh, 5sh and £1 are on chalky paper.

Seal of Bahamas — A10

1930, Jan. 2 Engr. *Perf. 12*

85 A10 1p red & black 1.90 *2.50*
86 A10 3p dp brown & blk 3.50 *13.50*
87 A10 5p dk vio & blk 3.50 *13.50*
88 A10 2sh ultra & black 20.00 *40.00*
89 A10 3sh dp green & blk 37.50 *70.00*
Nos. 85-89 (5) 66.40 *139.50*

The dates on the stamps commemorate important events in the history of the colony. The 1st British occupation was in 1629. The Bahamas were ceded to Great Britain in 1729 and a treaty of peace was signed by that country, France and Spain.

Type of 1930 Issue
Without Dates at Top

1931-46

90 A10 2sh ultra & black ('43) 5.75 2.50
a. 2sh ultra & slate purple 19.00 *22.50*
91 A10 3sh dp green & blk ('46) 5.50 2.25
a. 3sh deep grn & slate purple 27.50 22.50

Nos. 90a-91a are on thick paper with yellowish gum, Nos. 90-91 are on thin white paper with colorless gum.

For overprints see Nos. 126-127.

Common Design Types pictured following the introduction.

Silver Jubilee Issue

Common Design Type

1935, May 6 *Perf. 13½x14*

92 CD301 1½p car & blue 1.00 *2.00*
93 CD301 2½p blue & brn 4.50 *7.00*
94 CD301 6p ol grn & lt bl 6.25 *10.00*
95 CD301 1sh brt vio & ind 6.50 *8.25*
Nos. 92-95 (4) 18.25 *27.25*
Set, never hinged 26.00

Flamingos in Flight A11

1935, May 22 *Perf. 12½*

96 A11 8p car & ultra 6.00 2.50
Never hinged 10.00

Coronation Issue

Common Design Type

1937, May 12 *Perf. 13½x14*

97 CD302 ½p dp green .20 .20
98 CD302 1½p brown .30 .65
99 CD302 2½p brt ultra .50 .70
Nos. 97-99 (3) 1.00 1.55
Set, never hinged 1.50

George VI — A12

Sea Gardens, Nassau A13

Fort Charlotte A14

Flamingos in Flight A15

1938-46 Typo. Wmk. 4 *Perf. 14*

100 A12 ½p green .20 *1.00*
101 A12 1p carmine 5.25 3.50
101A A12 1p gray ('41) 2.00 *2.75*
102 A12 1½p red brown 1.00 1.00
103 A12 2p gray 11.00 5.00
103B A12 2p carmine ('41) .65 .60
c. "TWO PENCE" double *4,500.*
104 A12 2½p ultra 2.00 *1.60*
104A A12 2½p lt violet ('43) .80 .75
b. "2½ PENNY" double 2,000. —
Never hinged 2,500.
105 A12 3p lt violet 10.00 3.50
105A A12 3p ultra ('43) .35 *1.00*

Engr.

Perf. 12½

106 A13 4p red org & bl .65 *.80*
107 A14 6p blue & ol grn .35 *.80*
108 A15 8p car & ultra 4.25 1.90

Typo.

Perf. 14

109 A12 10p yel org ('46) 1.25 .20
110 A12 1sh blk & brt red 5.75 .60
112 A12 5sh pur & ultra 17.00 12.50
113 A12 £1 bl grn & blk 37.50 37.50
Nos. 100-113 (17) 100.00 *75.00*
Set, never hinged 140.00

#110-113 printed on chalky & ordinary paper.

See the Classic Specialized Catalogue for listings of shades.

See Nos. 154-156. For overprints see Nos. 116-125, 128-129.

No. 104 Surcharged in Black

1940, Nov. 28 *Perf. 14*

115 A12 3p on 2½p ultra .60 .75
Never hinged 1.00

Stamps of 1931-42 Overprinted in Black

1942, Oct. 12 *Perf. 14, 12½, 12*

116 A12 ½p green .20 .55
117 A12 1p gray .20 .55
118 A12 1½p red brown .20 .55
119 A12 2p carmine .20 .60
120 A12 2½p ultra .20 .60
121 A12 3p ultra .20 .60
122 A13 4p red org & blue .25 .80
123 A14 6p blue & ol grn .35 1.60
124 A15 8p car & ultra .50 .65
125 A12 1sh black & car 2.25 3.50
126 A10 2sh dk ultra & blk 5.50 *9.50*
127 A10 3sh dp grn & sl pur 3.00 *8.00*
128 A12 5sh lilac & ultra 8.50 *12.50*
129 A12 £1 green & black 20.00 *25.00*
Nos. 116-129 (14) 41.55 *65.00*
Set, never hinged 64.50

450th anniv. of the discovery of America by Columbus.

Nos. 125, 128-129 printed on chalky and ordinary paper.

Two printings of the basic stamps were overprinted, the first with dark gum, the second with white gum.

For shades, see the *Scott Classic Catalogue.*

Catalogue values for unused stamps in this section, from this point to the end of the section, are for Never Hinged items.

Peace Issue

Common Design Type

Perf. 13½x14

1946, Nov. 11 Engr. Wmk. 4

130 CD303 1½p brown .20 .35
131 CD303 3p deep blue .20 .35

Infant Welfare Clinic A16

Designs: 1p, Modern agriculture. 1½p, Sisal. 2p, Native straw work. 2½p, Modern dairying. 3p, Fishing fleet. 4p, Out island settlement. 6p, Tuna fishing. 8p, Paradise Beach. 10p, Modern hotel. 1sh, Yacht racing. 2sh, Water skiing. 3sh, Shipbuilding. 5sh, Modern transportation. 10sh, Modern salt production. £1, Parliament Building.

1948, Oct. 11 Unwmk. *Perf. 12*

132 A16 ½p orange .30 .80
133 A16 1p olive green .30 .30
134 A16 1½p olive bister .35 .70
135 A16 2p vermilion .30 .35
136 A16 2½p red brown .60 .65
137 A16 3p brt ultra .75 .75
138 A16 4p gray black .55 .75
139 A16 6p emerald 1.60 .75
140 A16 8p violet .65 .75
141 A16 10p rose car .70 .65
142 A16 1sh olive brn 1.25 1.00
143 A16 2sh claret 5.25 7.50
144 A16 3sh brt blue 7.00 7.50
145 A16 5sh purple 7.50 *5.50*
146 A16 10sh dk gray 8.75 *8.00*
147 A16 £1 red orange 10.00 *12.50*
Nos. 132-147 (16) 45.85 *48.45*

300th anniv., in 1947, of the settlement of the colony.

Silver Wedding Issue

Common Design Type

Perf. 14x14½

1948, Dec. 1 Wmk. 4 Photo.

148 CD304 1½p red brown .20 .20

Engr.; Name Typo.

Perf. 11½x11

149 CD305 £1 gray green 30.00 *35.00*

UPU Issue

Common Design Types

Engr.; Name Typo. on #151 & 152

1949, Oct. 10 *Perf. 13½, 11x11½*

150 CD306 2½p violet .30 .35
151 CD307 3p indigo 1.25 1.50
152 CD308 6p blue gray .90 1.25
153 CD309 1sh rose car 1.50 1.50
Nos. 150-153 (4) 3.95 4.60

George VI Type of 1938

Perf. 13½x14

1951-52 Wmk. 4 Typo.

154 A12 ½p claret ('52) .80 2.25
a. Wmk. 4a (error) *2,000.*
155 A12 2p green .90 .75
156 A12 3p rose red ('52) .70 *2.75*
Nos. 154-156 (3) 2.40 *5.75*

Coronation Issue

Common Design Type

1953, June 3 Engr. *Perf. 13½x13*

157 CD312 6p blue & black .60 .60

Infant Welfare Clinic A17

Designs: 1p, Modern Agriculture. 1½p, Out island settlement. 2p, Native strawwork. 3p, Fishing fleet. 4p, Water skiing. 5p, Modern dairying. 6p, Modern transportation. 8p, Paradise Beach. 10p, Modern hotels. 1sh, Yacht racing. 2sh, Sisal. 2sh6p, Shipbuilding. 5sh, Tuna fishing. 10sh, Modern salt production. £1, Parliament Building.

1954, Jan. 1 *Perf. 11x11½*

158 A17 ½p red org & blk .20 *1.40*
159 A17 1p org brn & ol grn .20 *.30*
a. Booklet pane of 4 .55
160 A17 1½p black & blue .20 *.55*
a. Booklet pane of 4 .70
161 A17 2p dk grn & brn org .20 *.30*
a. Booklet pane of 4 .70
162 A17 3p dp car & blk .45 *.70*
163 A17 4p lil rose & bl green .25 .25
a. Booklet pane of 4 1.75
164 A17 5p dp ultra & brn 1.00 *2.10*
165 A17 6p blk & aqua 1.25 .20
a. Booklet pane of 4 5.50
166 A17 8p rose vio & blk .50 .35
a. Booklet pane of 4 2.50
167 A17 10p ultra & blk .25 .20
168 A17 1sh ol brn & ultra .50 .20
169 A17 2sh blk & brn org 1.40 .50
170 A17 2sh6p dp bl & blk 2.50 1.90
171 A17 5sh dp org & emer 13.00 .70
172 A17 10sh grnsh blk & black 14.00 2.40
173 A17 £1 vio & grnsh black 14.50 6.25
Nos. 158-173 (16) 50.40 18.30

See No. 203. For types overprinted or surcharged see Nos. 181-182, 185-200, 202.

Queen Elizabeth II — A18

Wmk. 314

1959, June 10 Engr. *Perf. 13*

174 A18 1p dk red & black .20 .20
175 A18 2p green & black .20 .20
176 A18 6p blue & black .30 .30
177 A18 10p brown & black .55 .55
Nos. 174-177 (4) 1.25 1.25

Cent. of the 1st postage stamp of Bahamas.

Christ Church Cathedral, Nassau — A19

Perf. 14x13

1962, Jan. 30 Photo. Unwmk.

178 A19 8p shown .45 .45
179 A19 10p Public library .45 .45

Centenary of the city of Nassau.

Freedom from Hunger Issue

Common Design Type

Perf. 14x14½

1963, June 4 Wmk. 314

180 CD314 8p sepia 1.00 1.00
a. "8d," "BAHAMAS" omitted 875.00

Nos. 166-167 Overprinted: "BAHAMAS TALKS/ 1962"

Perf. 11x11½

1963, July 15 Engr. Wmk. 4

181 A17 8p rose vio & black .75 .75
182 A17 10p ultra & black 1.50 1.50

Meeting of Pres. Kennedy and Prime Minister Harold Macmillan, Dec. 1962.

Red Cross Centenary Issue
Common Design Type
Wmk. 314
1963, Sept. 2 Litho. *Perf. 13*
183 CD315 1p black & red .20 .20
184 CD315 10p ultra & red 2.00 2.25

Type of 1954 Overprinted: "NEW CONSTITUTION/ 1964"

Designs as Before

Perf. 11x11½
1964, Jan. 7 Engr. Wmk. 314
185 A17 ½p red org & blk .20 *.75*
186 A17 1p org brn & ol green .20 .20
187 A17 1½p black & blue .55 *.75*
188 A17 2p dk grn & brn org .20 .20
189 A17 3p dp car & blk 1.10 1.00
190 A17 4p lil rose & bl green .30 *.45*
191 A17 5p dp ultra & brn .30 *1.25*
192 A17 6p blk & aqua 1.50 .25
193 A17 8p rose vio & blk .55 .25
194 A17 10p ultra & black .25 .20
195 A17 1sh ol brn & ultra 1.00 .20
196 A17 2sh blk & brn org 1.10 *1.40*
197 A17 2sh6p dp bl & blk 2.25 2.25
198 A17 5sh dp org & emer 5.00 2.50
199 A17 10sh grnsh blk & black 5.25 4.25
200 A17 £1 vio & grnsh black 6.25 *14.50*
Nos. 185-200 (16) 26.00 30.40

Shakespeare Issue
Common Design Type
Perf. 14x14½
1964, Apr. 23 Photo. Wmk. 314
201 CD316 6p greenish blue .35 .30

Type of 1954 Surcharged with Olympic Rings, New Value and Bars
Perf. 11x11½
1964, Oct. 1 Engr. Wmk. 314
202 A17 8p on 1sh ol brn & ultra .45 .45

18th Olympic Games, Tokyo, Oct. 10-25.

Queen Type of 1954
1964, Oct. 6 Wmk. 314
203 A17 2p dk grn & brn org .50 .50

Out Island Regatta A21

Designs: ½p, Colony badge. 1½p, Princess Margaret Hospital. 2p, High School. 3p, Flamingo. 4p, Liner "Queen Elizabeth." 6p, Island development. 8p, Yachting. 10p, Public Square, Nassau. 1sh, Sea Garden, Nassau. 2sh, Cannons at Fort Charlotte. 2sh6p, Sea plane and jetliner. 5sh, 1914 Williamson film project and 1939 underwater post office. 10sh, Conch shell. £1, Columbus' flagship.

Engr. and Litho.
1965, Jan. 7 *Perf. 13½x13*
204 A21 ½p multi, *bluish* .20 *1.00*
205 A21 1p multi .20 *.65*
a. Booklet pane of 4 .40
206 A21 1½p multi .20 *1.40*
a. Booklet pane of 4 .45
207 A21 2p multi .20 .20
a. Booklet pane of 4 .55
208 A21 3p multi 1.40 .20
209 A21 4p multi 1.90 1.50
a. Booklet pane of 4 2.50
210 A21 6p multi .20 .20
a. Booklet pane of 4 1.25
211 A21 8p multi .30 .25
a. Booklet pane of 4 1.75
212 A21 10p multi .20 .20
213 A21 1sh multi, *grnsh* .30 .20
214 A21 2sh multi, *grnsh* .65 *1.00*
215 A21 2sh6p multi 1.50 *2.40*
216 A21 5sh multi 1.75 .80
217 A21 10sh multi 10.00 2.75
218 A21 £1 multi 11.00 7.25
Nos. 204-218 (15) 30.00 20.00

Booklet panes were issued Mar. 23, 1965.
See Nos. 252-266. For surcharges see Nos. 221, 230-244.

ITU Issue
Common Design Type
Perf. 11x11½
1965, May 17 Litho. Wmk. 314
219 CD317 1p emerald & org .20 .20
220 CD317 2sh lilac & olive 1.40 1.40

No. 211 Surcharged

Engr. & Litho.
1965, July 12 *Perf. 13½x13*
221 A21 9p on 8p multi .40 .30

Intl. Cooperation Year Issue
Common Design Type
Wmk. 314
1965, Oct. 25 Litho. *Perf. 14½*
222 CD318 ½p blue grn & claret .20 .20
223 CD318 1sh lt violet & grn .50 .75

Churchill Memorial Issue
Common Design Type
1966, Jan. 24 Photo. *Perf. 14*
224 CD319 ½p multicolored .20 .20
225 CD319 2p multicolored .40 .20
226 CD319 10p multicolored .75 *1.00*
227 CD319 1sh multicolored .75 *1.50*
Nos. 224-227 (4) 2.10 2.90

Royal Visit Issue
Common Design Type Inscribed "Royal Visit / 1966"
1966, Feb. 4 Litho. *Perf. 11x12*
228 CD320 6p violet blue .65 .65
229 CD320 1sh dk car rose 1.75 1.75

Nos. 204-218 Surcharged

Engr. & Litho.
Perf. 13½x13
1966, May 25 Wmk. 314
230 A21 1c on ½p multi .20 .20
231 A21 2c on 1p multi .20 .20
232 A21 3c on 2p multi .20 .20
233 A21 4c on 3p multi .20 .20
234 A21 5c on 4p multi .20 .20
a. Surch. omitted, vert. strip of 7-10 *2,700.*
235 A21 8c on 6p multi .20 .20
236 A21 10c on 8p multi .25 .25
237 A21 11c on 1½p multi .35 .25
238 A21 12c on 10p multi .40 .30
239 A21 15c on 1sh multi .50 .35
240 A21 22c on 2sh multi .65 .40
241 A21 50c on 2sh6p multi 1.40 1.25
242 A21 $1 on 5sh multi 2.50 2.50
243 A21 $2 on 10sh multi 5.50 5.00
244 A21 $3 on £1 multi 8.00 7.50
Nos. 230-244 (15) 20.75 19.00

The denominations are next to the bars instead of below on Nos. 232, 235-240; the length of the bars varies to cover old denomination.

No. 234a, if single, is identical with No. 209, but distinguishable if in vertical strip of 7 to 10. No. 234 was printed in sheets of 100 (10x10); No. 209 in sheets of 60 (10x6).

World Cup Soccer Issue
Common Design Type
1966, July 1 Litho. *Perf. 14*
245 CD321 8c multicolored .25 .25
246 CD321 15c multicolored .40 .40

WHO Headquarters Issue
Common Design Type
1966, Sept. 20 Litho. *Perf. 14*
247 CD322 11c multicolored .40 .40
248 CD322 15c multicolored .60 .60

UNESCO Anniversary Issue
Common Design Type
1966, Dec. 1 Litho. *Perf. 14*
249 CD323 3c "Education" .20 .20
250 CD323 15c "Science" .45 .45
251 CD323 $1 "Culture" 2.10 2.10
Nos. 249-251 (3) 2.75 2.75

Type of 1965
Values in Cents and Dollars
Engr. & Litho.
1967, May 25 *Perf. 13½x13*

1c, Colony badge. 2c, Out Island Regatta. 3c, High School. 4c, Flamingo. 5c, Liner "Oceanic." 8c, Island development. 10c, Yachting. 11c, Princess Margaret Hospital. 12c, Public Square, Nassau. 15c, Sea Garden, Nassau. 22c, Cannon at Fort Charlotte. 50c, Sea plane, jetliner. $1, 1914 Williamson film project, 1939 underwater post office. $2, Conch shell. $3, Columbus' flagship.

252 A21 1c brown & multi .20 *2.50*
253 A21 2c grn, slate & bl .20 *.65*
254 A21 3c grn, indigo & vio .20 .20
255 A21 4c ultra, blue & red 3.75 .50
256 A21 5c pur, bl & indigo .85 *3.00*
257 A21 8c dk brn, bl & dl grn .20 .20
258 A21 10c car rose, bl & pur .25 *.75*
259 A21 11c bl, grn & rose red .20 *.85*
260 A21 12c ol grn, bl & lt brn .20 .20
261 A21 15c rose & multi .50 .20
262 A21 22c rose red, brn & bl .60 *.70*
263 A21 50c emer, ol & bl 1.75 .80
264 A21 $1 sep, brn org & dk blue 1.75 .65
265 A21 $2 green & multi 11.50 3.25
266 A21 $3 pur, bl & brn org 3.25 2.10
Nos. 252-266 (15) 25.40 16.55

Nos. 252-266 are on toned paper. Printings on very white, untinted paper appeared between late 1969 and May, 1971. Value, set $500.

Seal of Bahamas, Queen Elizabeth II and Lord Baden-Powell — A22

60th anniv. of world Scouting: 15c, Scout emblem and portraits as on 3c.

Perf. 14x13½
1967, Sept. 1 Photo. Wmk. 314
267 A22 3c multicolored .25 .20
268 A22 15c multicolored .70 .20

Human Rights Flame and Globe A23

Intl. Human Rights Year: 12c, Human rights flame and scales of justice. $1, Human rights flame and Seal of Bahamas.

1968, May 13 Litho. *Perf. 14*
269 A23 3c multicolored .20 .20
270 A23 12c multicolored .40 .40
271 A23 $1 multicolored 1.40 1.40
Nos. 269-271 (3) 2.00 2.00

Golf — A24

Tourist Publicity: 11c, Yachting. 15c, Horse racing. 50c, Water skiing.

1968, Aug. 20 Unwmk. *Perf. 13½*
272 A24 5c multicolored 1.40 1.40
273 A24 11c multicolored .95 .95
274 A24 15c multicolored 1.40 1.40
275 A24 50c multicolored 2.00 2.00
Nos. 272-275 (4) 5.75 5.75

Olympic Monument and Sailboat — A25

Olympic Monument, San Salvador Island, Bahamas, and: 11c, Long jump. 50c, Running. $1, Sailing.

1968, Sept. 30 Photo. *Perf. 14½x14*
276 A25 5c multicolored .40 .40
277 A25 11c multicolored .60 .60
278 A25 50c multicolored .85 .85
279 A25 $1 multicolored 2.40 2.40
Nos. 276-279 (4) 4.25 4.25

19th Olympic Games, Mexico City, 10/12-27.

Legislative Building — A26

Designs: 10c, Bahamas mace and Big Ben, London, vert. 12c, Local straw market, vert. 15c, Horse-drawn surrey.

Perf. 14½
1968, Nov. 1 Unwmk. Litho.
280 A26 3c brt blue & multi .20 .20
281 A26 10c yel, blk & blue .25 .25
282 A26 12c brt rose & multi .25 .25
283 A26 15c green & multi .30 .30
Nos. 280-283 (4) 1.00 1.00

14th Commonwealth Parliamentary Conf., Nassau, Nov. 1-8.

$100 Coin with Queen Elizabeth II and Landing of Columbus — A27

Gold Coins with Elizabeth II on Obverse: 12c, $50 coin and Santa Maria flagship. 15c, $20 coin and Nassau Harbor Lighthouse. $1, $10 coin and Fort.

Engr. on Gold Paper
1968, Dec. 2 Unwmk. *Perf. 13½*
284 A27 3c dark red .50 .50
285 A27 12c dark green .75 .75
286 A27 15c lilac .90 .90
287 A27 $1 black 2.25 2.25
Nos. 284-287 (4) 4.40 4.40

First gold coinage in the Bahamas.

Bahamas Postal Card and Airplane Wing — A28

Design: 15c, Seaplane, 1929.

Perf. 14½x14
1969, Jan. 30 Litho. Unwmk.
288 A28 12c multicolored .80 .80
289 A28 15c multicolored .95 .95

50th anniv. of the 1st flight from Nassau, Bahamas, to Miami, Fla., Jan. 30, 1919.

Game Fishing Boats A29

Designs: 11c, Paradise Beach. 12c, Sunfish sailboats. 15c, Parade on Rawson Square.

1969, Aug. 26 Litho. Wmk. 314

290 A29	3c multicolored		.20	.20
291 A29	11c multicolored		.60	.60
292 A29	12c multicolored		.65	.65
293 A29	15c multicolored		.80	.80
a.	Souvenir sheet of 4, #290-293		3.50	3.50
	Nos. 290-293 (4)		2.25	2.25

Tourist publicity.

Holy Family, by Nicolas Poussin — A30

Paintings: 3c, Adoration of the Shepherds, by Louis Le Nain. 12c, Adoration of the Kings, by Gerard David. 15c, Adoration of the Kings, by Vincenzo Foppa.

1969, Oct. 15 Photo. *Perf. 12*

294 A30	3c red & multi	.25	.25
295 A30	11c emerald & multi	.35	.35
296 A30	12c ultra & multi	.40	.40
297 A30	15c multicolored	.50	.50
	Nos. 294-297 (4)	1.50	1.50

Christmas.

Girl Guides, Globe and Flags A31

Designs: 12c, Yellow elder and Brownie emblem. 15c, Ranger emblem.

1970, Feb. 23 Wmk. 314 *Perf. 14½*

298 A31	3c vio blue, yel & red	.20	.20
299 A31	12c dk brn, grn & yel	.60	.60
300 A31	15c vio bl, bluish grn & yel	.80	.80
	Nos. 298-300 (3)	1.60	1.60

60th anniversary of the Girl Guides.

Opening of UPU Headquarters, Bern — A32

1970, May 20 Litho. *Perf. 14½*

301 A32	3c vermilion & multi	.20	.20
302 A32	15c orange & multi	.55	.55

Bus and Globe A33

Globe and: 11c, Train. 12c, Sailboat and ship. 15c, Plane.

1970, July 14 *Perf. 13½x13*

303 A33	3c orange & multi	.50	.50
304 A33	11c emerald & multi	1.50	1.50
305 A33	12c multicolored	1.50	1.50
306 A33	15c blue & multi	1.50	1.50
a.	Souvenir sheet of 4, #303-306	9.00	9.00
	Nos. 303-306 (4)	5.00	5.00

Issued to promote good will through world-wide travel and tourism.

People, Palms and Flamingo — A34

15c, Red Cross Headquarters, Nassau & marlin.

1970, Aug. 18 *Perf. 14x14½*

307 A34	3c multicolored	.75	.50
308 A34	15c multicolored	.75	*1.00*

Centenary of British Red Cross Society.

Nativity by G. B. Pittoni — A35

Christmas: 11c, Holy Family, by Anton Raphael Mengs. 12c, Adoration of the Shepherds, by Giorgione. 15c, Adoration of the Shepherds, School of Seville.

Perf. 12½x13

1970, Nov. 3 Litho. Wmk. 314

309 A35	3c multicolored	.25	.25
310 A35	11c red org & multi	.35	.35
311 A35	12c emerald & multi	.35	.35
312 A35	15c blue & multi	.55	.55
a.	Souv. sheet of 4, #309-312 + 3 labels	2.00	2.00
	Nos. 309-312 (4)	1.50	1.50

International Airport A36

2c, Breadfruit. 3c, Straw market. 4c, 6c, Hawksbill turtle. 5c, Grouper. 8c, Yellow elder. 10c, Bahamian sponge boat. 11c, Flamingos. 7c, 12c, Hibiscus. 15c, Bonefish. 18c, 22c, Royal poinciana. 50c, Post office, Nassau. $1, Pineapple, vert. $2, Crayfish, vert. $3, "Junkanoo" (costumed drummer), vert.

Wmk. 314 Upright (Sideways on $1, $2, $3)

1971 *Perf. 14½x14, 14x14½*

313 A36	1c blue & multi	.20	.20
314 A36	2c red & multi	.20	.20
315 A36	3c lilac & multi	.20	.20
316 A36	4c brown & multi	1.50	*5.25*
317 A36	5c dp org & multi	.60	.40
318 A36	6c brown & multi	.40	.80
319 A36	7c green & multi	1.75	*2.50*
320 A36	8c yel & multi	.55	*.95*
321 A36	10c red & multi	.50	.20
322 A36	11c red & multi	2.25	1.75
323 A36	12c green & multi	1.75	*1.90*
324 A36	15c gray & multi	.50	.35
325 A36	18c multicolored	.60	.40
326 A36	22c green & multi	2.50	*7.50*
327 A36	50c multicolored	1.25	*1.40*
328 A36	$1 red & multi	5.75	1.50
329 A36	$2 blue & multi	4.00	3.25
330 A36	$3 vio bl & multi	3.50	*6.25*
	Nos. 313-330 (18)	28.00	35.00

See Nos. 398-401, 426-443.

Wmk. 314 Sideways (Upright on $1, $2, $3)

1973

317a A36	5c	9.75	9.75
320a A36	8c	2.75	2.75
327a A36	50c	2.00	2.00
328a A36	$1	2.00	2.00
329a A36	$2	2.00	2.00
330a A36	$3	3.00	3.00
	Nos. 317a-330a (6)	21.50	21.50

1976 Wmk. 373

313a A36	1c	.20	.20
314a A36	2c	.20	.20
315a A36	3c	.20	.20
317b A36	5c	.20	.20
320b A36	8c	.20	.20
321a A36	10c	.20	.20
327b A36	50c	1.25	1.25
328b A36	$1	2.50	2.50
329b A36	$2	4.75	4.75
330b A36	$3	7.50	7.50
	Nos. 313a-330b (10)	17.20	17.20

Snowflake with Peace Signs A37

Christmas: 11c, "Peace on Earth" with doves. 15c, Christmas wreath around old Bahamas coat of arms. 18c, Star of Bethlehem over palms.

Perf. 14x14½

1971 Photo. Wmk. 314

331 A37	3c dp lil rose, gold & org	.20	.20
332 A37	11c violet & gold	.35	.35
333 A37	15c gold embossed & multi	.35	.35
334 A37	18c brt bl, gold & vio bl	.40	.40
a.	Souv. sheet, #331-334, perf 15	2.00	2.00
	Nos. 331-334 (4)	1.30	1.30

High Jump, Arms of Bahamas — A38

Olympic Rings, Compass, Arms of Bahamas and: 11c, Bicycling. 15c, Running. 18c, Sailing.

1972, June 27 Litho. *Perf. 13x13½*

335 A38	10c lt violet & multi	.40	.40
336 A38	11c ocher & multi	.50	.50
337 A38	15c yel green & multi	.70	.70
338 A38	18c blue & multi	.95	.95
a.	Souvenir sheet of 4, #335-338	3.25	*3.25*
	Nos. 335-338 (4)	2.55	2.55

20th Olympic Games, Munich, 8/26-9/10.

Shepherd and Star of Bethlehem — A39

Designs: 6c, Bells. 15c, Holly and monstrance. 20c, Poinsettia.

1972, Oct. 3 Wmk. 314 *Perf. 14*

339 A39	3c gold & multi	.20	.20
340 A39	6c black & multi	.20	.20
341 A39	15c black & multi	.30	.30
342 A39	20c gold & multi	.55	.55
a.	Souvenir sheet of 4, #339-342	2.00	*2.50*
	Nos. 339-342 (4)	1.25	1.25

Christmas. Gold on 15c is embossed.

Souvenir Sheet

Map of Bahama Islands — A40

1972, Nov. 1 Litho. *Perf. 15*

343 A40	Sheet of 4	3.75	*4.75*
a.	11c blue & multi	.35	.35
b.	15c blue & multi	.45	.45
c.	18c blue & multi	.55	.55
d.	50c blue & multi	1.50	1.50

Tourism Year of the Americas.

Silver Wedding Issue, 1972

Common Design Type

Design: Queen Elizabeth II, Prince Philip, mace and galleon.

Perf. 14x14½

1972, Nov. 13 Photo. Wmk. 314

344 CD324	11c car rose & multi	.25	.25
345 CD324	18c violet & multi	.45	.45

Weather Satellite, WMO Emblem A41

1973, Apr. 3 Litho. *Perf. 14*

346 A41	15c shown	.60	.40
347 A41	18c Weather radar	.80	.60

Intl. meteorological cooperation, cent.

Clarence A. Bain — A42

Virgin in Prayer, by Sassoferrato A43

Independence: 11c, New Bahamian coat of arms. 15c, New flag and Government House. $1, Milo B. Butler, Sr.

1973 Wmk. 314 *Perf. 14½x14*

348 A42	3c lilac & multi	.20	.20
349 A42	11c lt blue & multi	.30	.30
350 A42	15c lt green & multi	.50	.50
351 A42	$1 yel & multi	1.25	1.25
a.	Souvenir sheet of 4, #348-351	2.75	*2.75*
	Nos. 348-351 (4)	2.25	2.25

Issued: #348-350, 7/10; #351, 351a, 8/1.

1973, Oct. 16 Litho. *Perf. 14*

Christmas: 11c, Virgin and Child with St. John, by Filippino Lippi. 15c, Choir of Angels, by Marmion. 18c, The Two Trinities, by Murillo.

352 A43	3c blue & multi	.20	.20
353 A43	11c multicolored	.35	.35
354 A43	15c gray grn & multi	.35	.35
355 A43	18c lil rose & multi	.55	.55
a.	Souvenir sheet of 4, #352-355	1.75	*2.00*
	Nos. 352-355 (4)	1.45	1.45

Agriculture, Science and Medicine — A44

18c, Symbols of engineering, art, and law.

1974, Feb. 5 Litho. *Perf. 13½x14*

356 A44 15c dull grn & multi .40 .40
357 A44 18c multicolored .60 .60

University of the West Indies, 25th anniv.

UPU Emblem A45

Designs: 13c, UPU emblem, vert. 14c, UPU emblem. 18c, UPU monument, Bern, vert.

1974, Apr. 23 *Perf. 14*

358 A45 3c multicolored .20 .20
359 A45 13c multicolored .35 .35
360 A45 14c olive bis & multi .35 .35
361 A45 18c multicolored .40 .40
a. Souvenir sheet of 4, #358-361 1.50 *2.00*
Nos. 358-361 (4) 1.30 1.30

Centenary of Universal Postal Union.

Roseate Spoonbills, Trust Emblem — A46

Protected Birds (National Trust Emblem and): 14c, White-crowned pigeons. 21c, White-tailed tropic birds. 36c, Bahamian parrot.

1974, Sept. 10 Litho. *Perf. 14*

362 A46 13c multicolored 1.25 .60
363 A46 14c multicolored 1.25 .50
364 A46 21c multicolored 1.50 .90
365 A46 36c multicolored 1.90 *3.75*
a. Souvenir sheet of 4, #362-365 8.50 *10.00*
Nos. 362-365 (4) 5.90 5.75

Bahamas National Trust, 15th anniv.

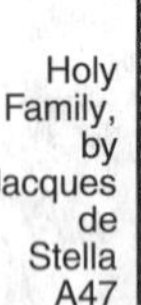

Holy Family, by Jacques de Stella A47

Christmas: 10c, Virgin and Child, by Girolamo Romanino. 12c, Virgin and Child with St. John and St. Catherine, by Andrea Previtali. 21c, Virgin and Child with Angels, by Previtali.

1974, Oct. 29 Wmk. 314 *Perf. 13*

366 A47 8c black & multi .25 .25
367 A47 10c green & multi .35 .35
368 A47 12c red & multi .35 .35
369 A47 21c ultra & multi .55 .55
a. Souvenir sheet of 4, #366-369 2.00 *2.25*
Nos. 366-369 (4) 1.50 1.50

Anteos Maerula A48

1975, Feb. 4 Litho. *Perf. 14x13½*

370 A48 3c shown .25 .25
371 A48 14c Eurema nicippe 1.00 .70
372 A48 18c Papilio andraemon 1.25 1.00
373 A48 21c Euptoieta hegesia 1.50 1.40
a. Souvenir sheet of 4, #370-373 7.00 6.00
Nos. 370-373 (4) 4.00 3.35

Sheep Raising A49

Designs: 14c, Electric reel fishing, vert. 18c, Growing food. 21c, Crude oil refinery, vert.

Unwmk.

1975, May 27 Litho. *Perf. 14*

374 A49 3c dull grn & multi .20 .20
375 A49 14c green & multi .20 .20
376 A49 18c brown & multi .30 .25
377 A49 21c vio bl & multi .90 .45
a. Souvenir sheet of 4, #374-377 1.50 1.50
Nos. 374-377 (4) 1.60 1.10

Economic diversification.

Rowena Rand, Staff and Chrismon — A50

Plant and IWY Emblem — A51

Wmk. 373

1975, July 22 Litho. *Perf. 14*

378 A50 14c multicolored .35 *.40*
379 A51 18c multicolored .40 *.60*

International Women's Year.

Adoration of the Shepherds, by Perugino — A52

Christmas: 8c, 18c, Adoration of the Kings, by Ghirlandaio. 21c, like 3c.

1975, Dec. 2 Litho. *Perf. 13½*

380 A52 3c dk green & multi .20 .20
381 A52 8c dk violet & multi .20 .20
382 A52 18c purple & multi .55 .55
383 A52 21c maroon & multi .60 .60
a. Souvenir sheet of 4, #380-383 2.25 *2.50*
Nos. 380-383 (4) 1.55 1.55

Telephones, 1876 and 1976 — A53

Designs: 16c, Radio-telephone link, Deleporte, Nassau (radar). 21c, Alexander Graham Bell. 25c, Communications satellite.

1976, Mar. 23 Litho. *Perf. 14*

384 A53 3c multicolored .20 .20
385 A53 16c multicolored .40 .40
386 A53 21c multicolored .50 .50
387 A53 25c multicolored .65 .65
Nos. 384-387 (4) 1.75 1.75

Centenary of first telephone call by Alexander Graham Bell, Mar. 10, 1876.

Bicycling and Olympic Rings — A54

Olympic Rings and: 16c, Long jump. 25c, Sailing. 40c, Boxing.

1976, July 13 Litho. *Perf. 14*

388 A54 8c magenta & blue .25 .25
389 A54 16c orange & brn .40 .40
390 A54 25c magenta & blue .60 .60
391 A54 40c orange & brn 1.10 1.10
a. Souvenir sheet of 4, #388-391 2.75 2.75
Nos. 388-391 (4) 2.35 2.35

21st Olympic Games, Montreal, Canada, July 17-Aug. 1.

John Murray, Earl of Dunmore A55

Design: 16c, Map of US and Bahamas.

1976, June 1 Wmk. 373 *Perf. 14*

392 A55 16c multicolored .50 .50
393 A55 $1 multicolored 2.00 2.00
a. Souvenir sheet of 4, #393 8.00 *9.00*

American Bicentennial.

Virgin and Child, Filippo Lippi — A56

Christmas: 21c, Adoration of the Shepherds, School of Seville. 25c, Adoration of the Kings, by Vincenzo Foppa. 40c, Virgin and Child, by Vivarini.

1976, Oct. 19 Litho. *Perf. 14½x14*

394 A56 3c brt blue & multi .20 .20
395 A56 21c dp org & multi .30 .30
396 A56 25c emerald & multi .30 .30
397 A56 40c red lilac & multi .50 .50
a. Souvenir sheet of 4, #394-397 1.75 1.75
Nos. 394-397 (4) 1.30 1.30

Type of 1971

16c, Hibiscus. 21c, Breadfruit. 25c, Hawksbill turtle. 40c, Bahamian sponge boat.

1976, Nov. 2 Litho. Wmk. 373

398 A36 16c emerald & multi .55 .40
399 A36 21c vermilion & multi .65 *1.00*
400 A36 25c brown & multi .75 .50
401 A36 40c vermilion & multi 2.50 .75
Nos. 398-401 (4) 4.45 2.65

Elizabeth II Seated under Gold Canopy — A57

16c, Coronation. 21c, Taking and signing of oath. 40c, Queen holding orb and scepter.

1977, Feb. 7 *Perf. 12*

402 A57 8c silver & multi .20 .20
403 A57 16c silver & multi .30 .30
404 A57 21c silver & multi .30 .30
405 A57 40c silver & multi .45 .45
a. Souvenir sheet of 4, #402-405 2.05 *2.55*
Nos. 402-405 (4) 1.25 1.25

Reign of Queen Elizabeth II, 25th anniv. For surcharges see Nos. 412-415. \

Featherduster — A58

Marine Life: 8c, Porkfish. 16c, Elkhorn coral. 21c, Soft coral and sponge.

1977, May 24 Litho. *Perf. 13½*

406 A58 3c multicolored .20 .20
407 A58 8c multicolored .30 .30
408 A58 16c multicolored .80 .80
409 A58 21c multicolored 1.00 1.00
a. Souv. sheet, #406-409, perf 14½ 3.00 *4.25*
Nos. 406-409 (4) 2.30 2.30

Campfire and Shower A59

1977, Sept. 27 Litho. Wmk. 373

410 A59 16c shown .60 .40
411 A59 21c Boating .75 .50

6th Caribbean Jamboree, Kingston, Jamaica, Aug. 5-14.

Nos. 402-405a Overprinted: "Royal Visit / October 1977"

1977, Oct. 19 Litho. *Perf. 12*

412 A57 8c silver & multi .20 .20
413 A57 16c silver & multi .20 .20
414 A57 21c silver & multi .25 .25
415 A57 40c silver & multi .35 .35
a. Souvenir sheet of 4 1.75 *2.25*
Nos. 412-415 (4) 1.00 1.00

Caribbean visit of Queen Elizabeth II, Oct. 19-20.

Virgin and Child — A60

Crèche Figurines: 16c, Three Kings. 21c, Adoration of the Kings. 25c, Three Kings.

1977, Oct. 25 Litho. *Perf. 13½*

416 A60 3c gold & multi .20 .20
417 A60 16c gold & multi .20 .20
418 A60 21c gold & multi .25 .25
419 A60 25c gold & multi .30 .30
a. Souv. sheet, #416-419, perf 14½ 1.00 *2.00*
Nos. 416-419 (4) .95 .95

Christmas.

Nassau Public Library — A61

Litho.

Perf. 14½x14

1978, Mar. 28

Architectural Heritage: 8c, St. Matthew's Church. 16c, Government House. 18c, The Hermitage, Cat Island.

420 A61 3c black & yel green .20 .20
421 A61 8c black & lt blue .20 .20
422 A61 16c black & lilac rose .20 .20
423 A61 18c black & salmon .25 .25
a. Souvenir sheet of 4, #420-423 1.00 *1.50*
Nos. 420-423 (4) .85 .85

Scepter, St. Edward's Crown, Orb — A62

Perf. 14x13½

1978, June 27 Litho. Wmk. 373

424 A62 16c shown .20 .20
425 A62 $1 Elizabeth II .55 .55
a. Souvenir sheet of 2, #424-425 1.40 1.40

Coronation of Queen Elizabeth II, 25th anniv.

Type of 1971

Designs as before and: 16c, Hibiscus. 25c, Hawksbill turtle.

Perf. 14½x14, 14x14½

1978, June Unwmk.

426 A36 1c blue & multi .60 .60
430 A36 5c dp org & multi .90 .90
436 A36 16c brt grn & multi 1.25 1.25
439 A36 25c brown & multi 5.75 5.75
440 A36 50c lemon & multi 2.25 2.25
441 A36 $1 lemon & multi 2.25 2.25
442 A36 $2 blue & multi 4.00 4.00
443 A36 $3 vio bl & multi 4.00 4.00
Nos. 426-443 (8) 21.00 21.00

Angels and Palms A63

Christmas: 5c, Coat of arms within wreath, and sailing ships.

Perf. 14x14½

1978, Nov. 14 Litho. Wmk. 373

444 A63 5c car, pink & gold .20 .20
445 A63 21c ultra, dk bl & gold .30 .30
a. Souvenir sheet of 2, #444-445 *2.25* *4.00*

Baby Walking, IYC Emblem — A64

IYC Emblem and: 16c, Children playing leapfrog. 21c, Girl skipping rope. 25c, Building blocks with "IYC" and emblem.

Perf. 13½x13

1979, May 15 Litho. Wmk. 373

446 A64 5c multicolored .20 .20
447 A64 16c multicolored .25 .25
448 A64 21c multicolored .35 .35
449 A64 25c multicolored .40 .40
a. Souv. sheet, #446-449, perf 14 1.50 1.50
Nos. 446-449 (4) 1.20 1.20

International Year of the Child.

Rowland Hill and Penny Black — A65

21c, Stamp printing press, 1840, Bahamas #7. 25c, Great Britain #27 with 1850's Nassau cancellation, Great Britain #29. 40c, Early mailboat, Bahamas #1.

1979, Aug. 14 ***Perf. 13½x14***

450 A65 10c multicolored .20 .20
451 A65 21c multicolored .40 .40
452 A65 25c multicolored .40 .40
453 A65 40c multicolored .75 .75
a. Souvenir sheet of 4, #450-453 2.25 2.25
Nos. 450-453 (4) 1.75 1.75

Sir Rowland Hill (1795-1879), originator of penny postage.

Commonwealth Plaque over Map of Bahamas — A66

Designs: 21c, Parliament buildings. 25c, Legislative chamber. $1, Senate chamber.

1979, Sept. 27 Litho. ***Perf. 13½***

454 A66 16c multicolored .35 .35
455 A66 21c multicolored .40 .40
456 A66 25c multicolored .40 .40
457 A66 $1 multicolored .85 .85
a. Souvenir sheet of 4, #454-457 2.50 2.50
Nos. 454-457 (4) 2.00 2.00

Parliament of Bahamas, 250th anniv.

Headdress A67

Christmas: Goombay Carnival costumes.

1979, Nov. 6 Litho. ***Perf. 13***

458 A67 5c multicolored .20 .20
459 A67 10c multicolored .20 .20
460 A67 16c multicolored .20 .20
461 A67 21c multicolored .20 .20
462 A67 25c multicolored .20 .20
463 A67 40c multicolored .25 .25
a. Souv. sheet, 458-463, perf 13½ 2.00 *2.75*
Nos. 458-463 (6) 1.25 1.25

Columbus' Landing, 1492 A68

1980, July 9 Litho. ***Perf. 15***

464 A68 1c shown 1.40 1.40
465 A68 3c Blackbeard .30 .30
466 A68 5c Articles, 1647, Eleuthera map .30 .30
467 A68 10c Ceremonial mace .20 .20
468 A68 12c Col. Andrew Deveaux .30 .30
469 A68 15c Slave trading, Vendue House 5.50 5.50
470 A68 16c Shipwreck salvage, 19th cent. 1.50 1.50
471 A68 18c Blockade runner, 1860s 1.50 1.50
472 A68 21c Bootlegging, 1919-1929 .45 .45
473 A68 25c Pineapple cultivation .45 .45
474 A68 40c Sponge clipping 1.10 1.10
475 A68 50c Victoria & Colonial Hotels 1.10 1.10
476 A68 $1 Modern agriculture 1.25 1.25
477 A68 $2 Ship, jet 4.25 4.25
478 A68 $3 Central Bank, Arms 1.40 1.40
479 A68 $5 Prince Charles, Prime Minister Pindling 1.50 1.50
Nos. 464-479 (16) 22.50 22.50

For overprints and surcharges see Nos. 496-499, 532-535.

1985, Nov. 6 Wmk. 384

464a A68 1c 1.75 1.75
465a A68 3c 2.25 2.25
467a A68 10c 2.75 2.75
473a A68 25c 6.25 6.25
Nos. 464a-473a (4) 13.00 13.00

Virgin and Child, Straw Figures — A69

1980, Oct. 28 Litho. ***Perf. 14½***

480 A69 5c shown .20 .20
481 A69 21c Three kings .30 .30
482 A69 25c Angel .30 .20
483 A69 $1 Christmas tree 1.00 .90
a. Souvenir sheet of 4, #480-483 1.75 *2.50*
Nos. 480-483 (4) 1.80 1.60

Christmas.

Man with Crutch, Sun Rays A70

1981, Feb. 10 Litho. ***Perf. 14½***

484 A70 5c shown .20 .20
485 A70 $1 Man in wheelchair 1.25 1.25
a. Souvenir sheet of 2, #484-485 1.50 *2.00*

International Year of the Disabled.

Grand Bahama Tracking Station A71

Satellite Views: 20c, Bahamas. 25c, Eleuthera. 50c, Andros and New Providence.

Wmk. 373

1981, Apr. 21 Litho. ***Perf. 13½***

486 A71 10c multi .20 .20
487 A71 20c multi, vert. .35 .35
488 A71 25c multi .45 .45
489 A71 50c multi, vert. .90 .90
a. Souvenir sheet of 4, #486-489 2.25 2.25
Nos. 486-489 (4) 1.90 1.90

Prince Charles and Lady Diana — A72

Wmk. 373

1981, July 22 Litho. ***Perf. 14½***

490 A72 30c shown .50 .25
491 A72 $2 Charles, Prime Minister 3.50 1.50
a. Souvenir sheet of 2, #490-491 6.00 3.00

Royal wedding.

Bahama Ducks A73

Wmk. 373

1981, Aug. 25 Litho. ***Perf. 14***

492 A73 5c shown 1.25 1.25
493 A73 20c Reddish egrets 1.75 1.75
494 A73 25c Brown boobies 1.75 1.75
495 A73 $1 West Indian tree ducks 3.25 3.25
a. Souvenir sheet of 4, #492-495 8.00 8.00
Nos. 492-495 (4) 8.00 8.00

See Nos. 514-517.

Nos. 466-467, 473, 475 Overprinted: "COMMONWEALTH FINANCE MINISTERS' MEETING 21-23 SEPTEMBER 1981"

1981, Sept. Litho. ***Perf. 15***

496 A68 5c multicolored .20 .20
497 A68 10c multicolored .20 .20
498 A68 25c multicolored .35 .35
499 A68 50c multicolored .75 .75
Nos. 496-499 (4) 1.50 1.50

World Food Day A74

Perf. 13x13½

1981, Oct. 16 Wmk. 373

500 A74 5c Chickens .20 .20
501 A74 20c Sheep .30 .30
502 A74 30c Lobster .50 .50
503 A74 50c Pigs 1.00 1.00
a. Souvenir sheet of 4, #500-503 2.25 *2.75*
Nos. 500-503 (4) 2.00 2.00

Christmas — A75

Wmk. 373

1981, Nov. 23 Litho. ***Perf. 14***

504 Sheet of 9 5.00 5.00
a. A75 5c Father Christmas .20 .20
b. A75 5c shown .20 .20
c. A75 5c St. Nicholas, Holland .20 .20
d. A75 25c Lussibruden, Sweden .40 .40
e. A75 25c Mother and child .40 .40
f. A75 25c King Wenceslas, Czechoslovakia .40 .40
g. A75 30c Mother and child .45 .45
h. A75 30c Mother and child standing .45 .45
i. A75 $1 Christkindl angel, Germany 1.75 1.75

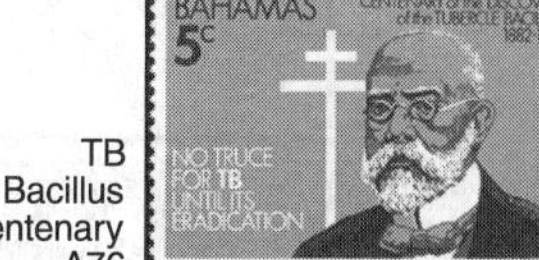

TB Bacillus Centenary A76

1982, Feb. 3 Litho. ***Perf. 14***

505 A76 5c Koch .65 .65
506 A76 16c X-ray 1.10 1.10
507 A76 21c Microscopes 1.25 1.25
508 A76 $1 Mantoux test 2.50 2.50
a. Souv. sheet, #505-508, perf 14½ 6.00 *7.00*
Nos. 505-508 (4) 5.50 5.50

Flamingoes A77

Designs: a, Females. b, Males. c, Nesting. d, Juvenile birds. e, Immature birds. No. 509 in continuous design.

Wmk. 373

1982, Apr. 28 Litho. *Perf. 14*

509 Strip of 5, multicolored 7.00 7.00
a.-e. A77 25c any single 1.40 1.40

Princess Diana Issue
Common Design Type

1982, July 1 Litho. *Perf. 14*

510 CD333 16c Arms .25 .25
511 CD333 25c Diana .40 .40
512 CD333 40c Wedding .60 .60
513 CD333 $1 Portrait 1.50 1.50
Nos. 510-513 (4) 2.75 2.75

Bird Type of 1981
Wmk. 373

1982, Aug. 18 Litho. *Perf. 14*

514 A73 10c Bat .75 .75
515 A73 16c Hutia .90 .90
516 A73 21c Racoon 1.10 1.10
517 A73 $1 Dolphins 2.50 2.50
a. Souvenir sheet of 4, #514-517 5.50 5.50
Nos. 514-517 (4) 5.25 5.25

28th Commonwealth Parliamentary Conference A78

Perf. 14x13½

1982, Oct. 16 Litho. Wmk. 373

518 A78 5c Plaque .20 .20
519 A78 25c Assoc. arms .50 .50
520 A78 40c Natl. arms .80 .80
521 A78 50c House of Assembly 1.00 1.00
Nos. 518-521 (4) 2.50 2.50

Christmas A79

Designs: 5c, Wesley Methodist Church, Baillou Hill Road. 12c, Centerville Seventh Day Adventist Church. 15c, Church of God of Prophecy, East Street. 21c, Bethel Baptist Church, Meeting Street. 25c, St. Francis Xavier Catholic Church, West Hill Street. $1, Holy Cross Anglican Church, Highbury Park.

1982, Nov. 3 *Perf. 14*

522 A79 5c multicolored .20 .20
523 A79 12c multicolored .20 .20
524 A79 15c multicolored .30 .30
525 A79 21c multicolored .35 .35
526 A79 25c multicolored .35 .35
527 A79 $1 multicolored 1.10 1.10
Nos. 522-527 (6) 2.50 2.50

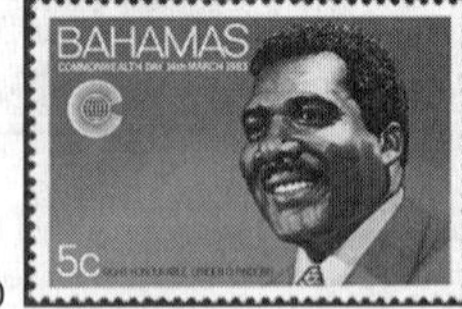

A80

1983, Mar. 14 Litho.

528 A80 5c Lynden O. Pindling .20 .20
529 A80 25c Flags .45 .45
530 A80 35c Map .45 .45
531 A80 $1 Ocean liner 1.25 1.25
Nos. 528-531 (4) 2.35 2.35

Commonwealth Day.

Nos. 469-472 Surcharged

1983, Apr. 5 Litho. *Perf. 15*

532 A68 20c on 15c multi .45 .45
533 A68 31c on 21c multi .55 .55
534 A68 35c on 16c multi 1.10 1.10
535 A68 80c on 18c multi 1.40 1.40
Nos. 532-535 (4) 3.50 3.50

30th Anniv. of Customs Cooperation Council — A81

Perf. 14x13½

1983, May 31 Wmk. 373

536 A81 31c Officers, ship .50 .50
537 A81 $1 Officers, jet 1.60 1.60

10th Anniv. of Independence A82

1983, July 6 Litho. *Perf. 14*

538 A82 $1 Flag raising 1.50 1.50
a. Souvenir sheet, perf. 12 1.50 1.50

Local Butterflies A83

1983, Aug. 24 *Perf. 14½x14*

539 A83 5c Carters skipper .25 .25
540 A83 25c Giant southern white .90 .90
541 A83 31c Large orange sulphur 1.10 1.10
542 A83 50c Flambeau 1.75 1.75
a. Souvenir sheet of 4 4.25 4.25
Nos. 539-542 (4) 4.00 4.00

No. 542a contains Nos. 539-542, perf. 14 and perf. 14½x14.

American Loyalists Arrival Bicentenary — A84

Paintings by Alton Lowe.

1983, Sept. 28 *Perf. 14*

543 A84 5c Loyalist Dreams .20 .20
544 A84 31c New Plymouth, Abaco .55 .55
545 A84 35c New Plymouth Hotel .60 .60
546 A84 50c Island Hope .90 .90
a. Souvenir sheet of 4, #543-546 2.25 2.25
Nos. 543-546 (4) 2.25 2.25

Christmas — A85

125th Anniv. of Bahamas Stamps — A86

Children's designs: 5c, Christmas Bells, by Monica Pinder. 20c, The Flamingo by Cory Bullard. 25c, The Yellow Hibiscus with Christmas Candle by Monique A. Bailey. 31c, Santa goes a Sailing by Sabrina Seiler, horiz. 35c, Silhouette scene with palm trees by James Blake. 50c, Silhouette scene with Pelicans, by Erik Russell, horiz.

1983, Nov. 1 *Perf. 14*

547 A85 5c multicolored .20 .20
548 A85 20c multicolored .30 .30
549 A85 25c multicolored .40 .40
550 A85 31c multicolored .50 .50
551 A85 35c multicolored .60 .60
552 A85 50c multicolored .80 .80
Nos. 547-552 (6) 2.80 2.80

1984, Feb. 22 Litho. *Perf. 14*

553 A86 5c No. 3 .20 .20
554 A86 $1 No. 1 1.60 1.60

Lloyd's List Issue
Common Design Type
Wmk. 373

1984, Apr. 25 Litho. *Perf. 14½*

555 CD335 5c Trent .20 .20
556 CD335 31c Orinoco .55 .55
557 CD335 35c Nassau Harbor .60 .60
558 CD335 50c Container ship Oropesa .85 .85
Nos. 555-558 (4) 2.20 2.20

1984 Summer Olympics A87

1984, June 20 Litho. *Perf. 14x14½*

559 A87 5c Running .20 .20
560 A87 25c Discus .40 .40
561 A87 31c Boxing .50 .50
562 A87 $1 Basketball 1.60 1.60
a. Souvenir sheet of 4, #559-562 2.75 2.75
Nos. 559-562 (4) 2.70 2.70

Flags of Bahamas and Caribbean Community — A88

Wmk. 373

1984, July 4 Litho. *Perf. 14*

563 A88 50c multicolored .90 .90

Conference of Heads of Government of Caribbean Community, 5th Meeting.

Allen's Cay Iguana A89

1984, Aug. 15 *Perf. 14*

564 A89 5c shown .20 .20
565 A89 25c Curly-tailed lizard .60 .60
566 A89 35c Greenhouse frog .80 .80
567 A89 50c Atlantic green turtle 1.00 1.00
a. Souvenir sheet of 4, #564-567 3.00 3.00
Nos. 564-567 (4) 2.60 2.60

25th Anniv. of Natl. Trust — A90

Christmas — A91

Wildlife: a, Calliphlox evelynae. b, Megaceryle alcyon, Eleutherodactylus planirostris. c, Phoebis sennae, Phoenicopterus ruber, Himantopus himantopus, Phoebus sennae. d, Urbanus proteus, Chelonia mydas. e, Pandion haliaetus.
Continuous design.

1984, Aug. 15 Litho. *Perf. 14*

568 Strip of 5 5.25 5.25
a.-e. A90 31c any single 1.10 1.10

1984, Nov. 7 Litho. *Perf. 13½x13*

Madonna and Child Paintings.

569 A91 5c Titian .20 .20
570 A91 31c Anais Colin .55 .55
571 A91 35c Elena Caula .60 .60
a. Souvenir sheet of 3, #569-571 1.40 1.40
Nos. 569-571 (3) 1.35 1.35

Girl Guides, 75th Anniv., Intl. Youth Year A92

1985, Feb. 22 Litho. *Perf. 14*

572 A92 5c Brownies .20 .20
573 A92 25c Camping .35 .35
574 A92 31c Girl Guides .50 .50
575 A92 35c Rangers .55 .55
a. Souvenir sheet of 4, #572-575 1.60 1.60
Nos. 572-575 (4) 1.60 1.60

Audubon Birth Bicentenary — A93

Wmk. 373

1985, Apr. 24 Litho. *Perf. 14*

576 A93 5c Killdeer .20 .20
577 A93 31c Mourning dove, vert. .85 .85
578 A93 35c Mourning doves, diff., vert. .90 .90
579 A93 $1 Killdeers, diff. 2.50 2.50
Nos. 576-579 (4) 4.45 4.45

Queen Mother 85th Birthday
Common Design Type
Perf. 14½x14

1985, June 7 Litho. Wmk. 384

580 CD336 5c Portrait, 1927 .20 .20
581 CD336 25c At christening of Peter Phillips .40 .40
582 CD336 35c Portrait, 1985 .60 .60
583 CD336 50c Holding Prince Henry .80 .80
Nos. 580-583 (4) 2.00 2.00

Souvenir Sheet

584 CD336 $1.25 In a pony and trap 2.00 2.00

UN and UN Food and Agriculture Org., 40th Annivs. — A94

Wmk. 373

1985, Aug. 26 Litho. *Perf. 14*

585 A94 25c Wheat, emblems .40 .40

Commonwealth Heads of Government Meeting, 1985 — A95

1985, Oct. 16 Wmk. 373 *Perf. 14½*

586 A95 31c Queen Elizabeth II .50 .50
587 A95 35c Flag, Commonwealth emblem .55 .55

Christmas A96

Paintings by Alton Roland Lowe: 5c, Grandma's Christmas Bouquet. 25c, Junkanoo Romeo and Juliet, vert. 31c, Bunce Girl, vert. 35c, Home for Christmas.

1985, Nov. 5 *Perf. 13*

588 A96 5c multicolored .20 .20
589 A96 25c multicolored .50 .50
590 A96 31c multicolored .60 .60
591 A96 35c multicolored .70 .70
a. Souv. sheet, #588-591, perf 14 2.00 2.00
Nos. 588-591 (4) 2.00 2.00

Queen Elizabeth II 60th Birthday

Common Design Type

Designs: 10c, Age 1, 1927. 25c, Coronation, Westminster Abbey, 1953. 35c, Giving speech, royal visit, Bahamas. 40c, At Djakova, Yugoslavia, state visit, 1972. $1, Visiting Crown Agents, 1983.

1986, Apr. 21 Wmk. 384 *Perf. 14½*

592 CD337 10c scar, blk & sil .20 *.25*
593 CD337 25c ultra & multi .35 *.45*
594 CD337 35c green & multi .45 *.60*
595 CD337 40c violet & multi .55 *.65*
596 CD337 $1 rose vio & multi 1.25 *1.75*
Nos. 592-596 (5) 2.80 *3.70*

AMERIPEX '86 — A97

1986, May 19 *Perf. 14*

597 A97 5c Nos. 464, 471 .20 .20
598 A97 25c Nos. 288-289 .45 .45
599 A97 31c No. 392 .55 .55
600 A97 50c No. 489a .90 .90
601 A97 $1 Statue of Liberty, vert. 1.75 1.75
a. Souvenir sheet of one 1.75 1.75
Nos. 597-601 (5) 3.85 3.85

Statue of Liberty, cent.

Royal Wedding Issue, 1986

Common Design Type

Designs: 10c, Formal engagement. $1, Andrew in dress uniform.

1986, July 23 *Perf. 14½x14*

602 CD338 10c multicolored .20 .20
603 CD338 $1 multicolored 1.60 1.60

Fish A98

1986-87 Wmk. 384 *Perf. 14*

604 A98 5c Rock beauty .20 .20
605 A98 10c Stoplight parrotfish .20 .20
606 A98 15c Jacknife fish .25 .25
607 A98 20c Flamefish .30 .30
608 A98 25c Swissguard basslet .35 .35
609 A98 30c Spotfin butterflyfish .40 .40
610 A98 35c Queen triggerfish .50 .50
611 A98 40c Four-eyed butterflyfish .55 .55
612 A98 45c Fairy basslet .65 .65
613 A98 50c Queen angelfish .70 .70
614 A98 60c Blue chromis .85 .85
615 A98 $1 Spanish hogfish 1.40 1.40
616 A98 $2 Harlequin bass 7.00 7.00
617 A98 $3 Blackbar soldierfish 6.50 6.50
618 A98 $5 Pygmy angelfish 7.25 7.25
618A A99 $10 Red hind ('87) 16.00 16.00
Nos. 604-618A (16) 43.10 43.10

Nos. 605, 608, 611-613, 615, 617-618 exist inscribed "1990." Nos. 611, 615, 616 "1988." Issue dates: $10, Jan. 2, others, Aug. 5.

1987, June 25 Wmk. 373

604a 5c .20 .20
605a 10c .20 .20
606a 15c .25 .25
611a 40c .55 .55
612a 45c .65 .65
613a 50c .70 .70
614a 60c .85 .85
615a $1 1.40 1.40
616a $2 2.75 2.75
Nos. 604a-616a (9) 7.55 7.55

Nos. 604a-616a dated 1987. No. 605a "1988." No. 604a "1989."

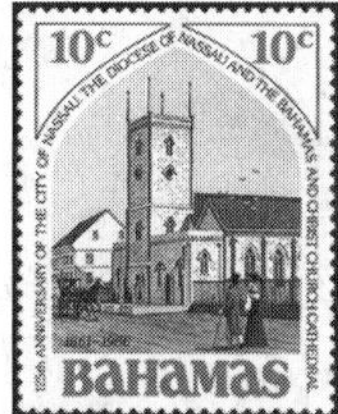

Christ Church Cathedral — A99

Wmk. 373

1986, Sept. 16 Litho. *Perf. 14½*

619 A99 10c View, 19th cent. .20 .20
620 A99 40c View, 1986 .65 .65
a. Souvenir sheet of 2, #619-620 .85 .85

City of Nassau, Diocese of Nassau and the Bahamas and Christ Church, 125th anniv.

Christmas, Intl. Peace Year A100

Wmk. 384

1986, Nov. 4 Litho. *Perf. 14*

621 A100 10c Nativity .20 .20
622 A100 40c Flight to Egypt .65 .65
623 A100 45c Children praying .75 .75
624 A100 50c Exchanging gifts .80 .80
a. Souvenir sheet of 4, #621-624 2.50 2.50
Nos. 621-624 (4) 2.40 2.40

Pirates of the Caribbean — A101

A102

Wmk. 373

1987, June 2 Litho. *Perf. 14½*

625 A101 10c Anne Bonney .25 .25
626 A101 40c Blackbeard (d. 1718) .90 .90
627 A101 45c Capt. Edward England 1.00 1.00
628 A101 50c Capt. Woodes Rogers (c. 1679-1732) 1.25 1.25
Nos. 625-628 (4) 3.40 3.40

Souvenir Sheet

629 A102 $1.25 Map of the Bahamas 2.75 2.75

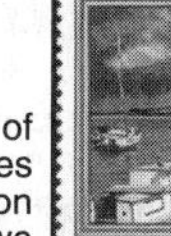

Paintings of Lighthouses by Alton Roland Lowe A103

1987, Mar. 31 Wmk. 384

630 A103 10c Great Isaac .30 .30
631 A103 40c Bird Rock 1.25 1.25
632 A103 45c Castle Is. 1.50 1.50
633 A103 $1 Hole in the Wall 3.25 3.25
Nos. 630-633 (4) 6.30 6.30

Tourist Transportation A104

Ships: No. 634a, Cruise ship, sailboat. b, Cruise ships, tugboat, speedboat. c, Pleasure boat leaving harbor, sailboat. d, Pleasure boat docked, sailboats. e, Sailboats.

Aircraft: No. 635a, Bahamasair plane. b, Bahamasair and Pan Am aircraft. c, Aircraft, radar tower. d, Control tower, aircraft. e, Helicopter, planes.

1987, Aug. 26 Wmk. 373 *Perf. 14*

634 Strip of 5 3.75 3.75
a.-e. A104 40c any single .75 .75
635 Strip of 5 3.75 3.75
a.-e. A104 40c any single .75 .75

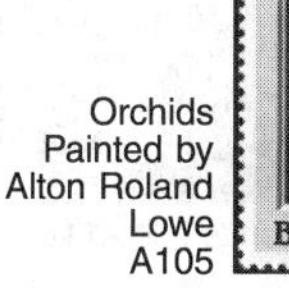

Orchids Painted by Alton Roland Lowe A105

1987, Oct. 20 Wmk. 384 *Perf. 14½*

636 A105 10c Cattleyopis lindenii .20 .20
637 A105 40c Encyclia lucayana .65 .65
638 A105 45c Encyclia hodgeana .75 .75
639 A105 50c Encyclia lleidae .80 .80
a. Souvenir sheet of 4, #636-639 2.50 2.50
Nos. 636-639 (4) 2.40 2.40

Christmas.

Discovery of America, 500th Anniv. (in 1992) — A106

10c, Ferdinand & Isabella. 40c, Columbus before the Talavera Committee. 45c, Lucayan village. 50c, Lucayan potters. $1.50, Map, c. 1500.

Perf. 14x14½

1988, Feb. 23 Litho. Wmk. 373

640 A106 10c multicolored .20 .20
641 A106 40c multicolored .65 .65
642 A106 45c multicolored .75 .75
643 A106 50c multicolored .80 .80
Nos. 640-643 (4) 2.40 2.40

Souvenir Sheet

644 A106 $1.50 multicolored 3.00 3.00

See #663-667, 688-692, 725-729, 749-753, 762.

World Wildlife Fund A107

Whistling ducks, Dendrocygna arborea.

1988, Apr. 29 *Perf. 14½*

645 A107 5c Ducks in flight .75 .25
646 A107 10c Among marine plants 1.50 .50
647 A107 20c Adults, ducklings 3.00 1.00
648 A107 45c Wading 6.25 2.25
Nos. 645-648 (4) 11.50 4.00

Abolition of Slavery, 150th Anniv. A108

1988, Aug. 9 *Perf. 14*

649 A108 10c African hut .20 .20
650 A108 40c Basket weavers in hut, Grantstown .80 .80

1988 Summer Olympics, Seoul A109

Games emblem and details of painting by James Martin: 10c, Olympic flame, high jump, hammer throw, basketball and gymnastics. 40c, Swimming, boxing, weight lifting, fencing and running. 45c, Gymnastics, shot put and javelin. $1, Running, cycling and gymnastics.

Wmk. 384

1988, Aug. 30 Litho. *Perf. 14*

651 A109 10c multicolored .20 .20
652 A109 40c multicolored .80 .80
653 A109 45c multicolored .90 .90
654 A109 $1 multicolored 2.00 2.00
a. Souvenir sheet of 4, #651-654 4.00 4.00
Nos. 651-654 (4) 3.90 3.90

Lloyds of London, 300th Anniv.

Common Design Type

Designs: 10c, Lloyds List No. 560, 1740. 40c, Freeport Harbor, horiz. 45c, Space shuttle over the Bahamas, horiz. $1, Supply ship Yarmouth Castle on fire.

1988, Oct. 4 Wmk. 373

655 CD341 10c multicolored .20 .20
656 CD341 40c multicolored .80 .80
657 CD341 45c multicolored .90 .90
658 CD341 $1 multicolored 2.00 2.00
Nos. 655-658 (4) 3.90 3.90

Christmas Carols — A110

Designs: 10c, O' Little Town of Bethlehem. 40c, Little Donkey. 45c, Silent Night. 50c, Hark! The Herald Angels Sing.

1988, Nov. 21 Wmk. 384 *Perf. 14½*

659 A110 10c multicolored .20 .20
660 A110 40c multicolored .80 .80
661 A110 45c multicolored .90 .90
662 A110 50c multicolored 1.00 1.00
a. Souvenir sheet of 4, #659-662 2.90 2.90
Nos. 659-662 (4) 2.90 2.90

Discovery of America Type

Design: 10c, Columbus as chartmaker. 40c, Development of the caravel. 45c, Navigational tools. 50c, Arawak artifacts. $1.50, Caravel under construction, an illumination from the Nuremburg Chronicles, 15th cent.

Perf. 14½x14

1989, Jan. 25 Litho. Wmk. 373

663 A106 10c multicolored .20 .20
664 A106 40c multicolored .80 .80
665 A106 45c multicolored .90 .90
666 A106 50c multicolored 1.00 1.00
Nos. 663-666 (4) 2.90 2.90

Souvenir Sheet

667 A106 $1.50 multicolored 3.00 3.00

Hummingbirds A111

Wmk. 384

1989, Mar. 29 Litho. *Perf. 14½*

668 A111 10c Cuban emerald .20 .20
669 A111 40c Ruby-throated .80 .80
670 A111 45c Bahama woodstar .90 .90
671 A111 50c Rufous 1.00 1.00
Nos. 668-671 (4) 2.90 2.90

Intl. Red Cross and Red Crescent Organizations, 125th Annivs. — A112

1989, May 31 *Perf. 14x14½*

672 A112 10c Water safety .20 .20
673 A112 $1 Dunant, Battle of Solferino 2.00 2.00

Moon Landing, 20th Anniv.
Common Design Type

Apollo 8: 10c, Apollo Communications System, Grand Bahama Is. 40c, James Lovell Jr., William Anders and Frank Borman. 45c, Mission emblem. $1, The Rising Earth (photograph). $2, Astronaut practicing lunar surface activities at Manned Spacecraft Center, Houston, in training for Apollo 11 mission.

1989, July 20 *Perf. 14x13½*
Size of Nos. 674-675: 29x29mm

674 CD342 10c multicolored .20 .20
675 CD342 40c multicolored .80 .80
676 CD342 45c multicolored .90 .90
677 CD342 $1 multicolored 2.00 2.00
Nos. 674-677 (4) 3.90 3.90

Souvenir Sheet

678 CD342 $2 multicolored 4.00 4.00

Christmas A113

Designs: 10c, Church of the Nativity, Bethlehem. 40c, Basilica of the Annunciation, Nazareth. 45c, By the Sea of Galilee, Tabgha. $1, Church of the Holy Sepulcher, Jerusalem.

Perf. 14½x14

1989, Oct. 16 Wmk. 373

679 A113 10c multicolored .20 .20
680 A113 40c multicolored .80 .80
681 A113 45c multicolored .90 .90
682 A113 $1 multicolored 2.00 2.00
a. Souvenir sheet of 4, #679-682 4.00 4.00
Nos. 679-682 (4) 3.90 3.90

World Stamp Expo '89 A114

Expo emblem and: 10c, Earth, #359. 40c, UPU Headquarters, #301. 45c, US Capitol, #601. $1, Passenger jet, #150. $2, Washington, DC, on map.

1989, Nov. 17 Wmk. 384 *Perf. 14*

683 A114 10c multicolored .20 .20
684 A114 40c multicolored .80 .80
685 A114 45c multicolored .90 .90
686 A114 $1 multicolored 2.00 2.00
Nos. 683-686 (4) 3.90 3.90

Souvenir Sheet
Perf. 14½x14

687 A114 $2 multicolored 4.00 4.00

No. 687 contains one 31x38mm stamp.

Discovery of America Type of 1988

10c, Caravel launch. 40c, Provisioning ships. 45c, Shortening sails. 50c, Lucayan fishermen. $1.50, Columbus's fleet departing from Cadiz.

Perf. 14½x14

1990, Jan. 24 Litho. Wmk. 373

688 A106 10c multicolored .30 .25
689 A106 40c multicolored 1.25 1.00
690 A106 45c multicolored 1.50 1.25
691 A106 50c multicolored 1.75 1.50
Nos. 688-691 (4) 4.80 4.00

Souvenir Sheet

692 A106 $1.50 multicolored 5.00 5.00

Organization of American States, Cent. — A115

1990, Mar. 14 Wmk. 384 *Perf. 14*

693 A115 40c multicolored .80 .80

Souvenir Sheet

Stamp World London '90 — A116

Aircraft: a, Spitfire I. b, Hurricane IIc.

1990, May 3 Wmk. 384

694 A116 Sheet of 2 4.00 4.00
a.-b. $1 any single 2.00 2.00

For surcharge see No. B3.

Intl. Literacy Year A117

10c, Teacher helping student. 40c, Children reading to each other. 50c, Children reading aloud.

1990, June 27 Wmk. 384 *Perf. 14*

695 A117 10c multicolored .20 .20
696 A117 40c multicolored .80 .80
697 A117 50c multicolored 1.00 1.00
Nos. 695-697 (3) 2.00 2.00

Queen Mother, 90th Birthday
Common Design Types

1990, Aug. 4 *Perf. 14x15*

698 CD343 40c Portrait, c. 1938 .80 .80

Perf. 14½

699 CD344 $1.50 At garden party, 1938 3.00 3.00

Bahamian Parrot — A118

1990, Sept. 26 Wmk. 373 *Perf. 14*

700 A118 10c shown .30 .25
701 A118 40c In flight 1.25 1.00
702 A118 45c Head 1.50 1.25
703 A118 50c On branch 1.75 1.50
Nos. 700-703 (4) 4.80 4.00

Souvenir Sheet

704 A118 $1.50 On branch, diff. 4.50 4.50

Christmas A119

Birds — A120

Wmk. 373

1990, Nov. 5 Litho. *Perf. 13½*

705 A119 10c Angel appears to Mary .20 .20
706 A119 40c Nativity .80 .80
707 A119 45c Angel appears to shepherds .90 .90
708 A119 $1 Three kings 2.00 2.00
a. Souvenir sheet of 4, #705-708 3.90 3.90
Nos. 705-708 (4) 3.90 3.90

Wmk. 384

1991, Feb. 4 Litho. *Perf. 14*

709 A120 5c Green heron .20 .20
710 A120 10c Turkey vulture .20 .20
711 A120 15c Osprey .30 .30
712 A120 20c Clapper rail .40 .40
713 A120 25c Royal tern .50 .50
714 A120 30c Key West quail dove .60 .60
715 A120 40c Smooth-billed ani .80 .80
716 A120 45c Burrowing owl .90 .90
717 A120 50c Hairy woodpecker 1.00 1.00
718 A120 55c Mangrove cuckoo 1.10 1.10
719 A120 60c Bahama mockingbird 1.25 1.25
720 A120 70c Red-winged blackbird 1.40 1.40
721 A120 $1 Thick-billed vireo 2.00 2.00
722 A120 $2 Bahama yellowthroat 4.00 4.00
723 A120 $5 Stripe-headed tanager 10.00 10.00
724 A120 $10 Greater Antillean bullfinch 20.00 20.00
Nos. 709-724 (16) 44.65 44.65

Issued: $10, July 1; others, Feb. 4.

1993 Wmk. 373

710a 10c .20 .20
713a 25c .50 .50
714a 30c .60 .60
715a 40c .80 .80
718a 55c 1.10 1.10
723a $5 10.00 10.00
Nos. 710a-723a (6) 13.20 13.20

Nos. 710a-723a dated 1993. 40c, 55c exist dated 1995.
Issued: 40c, 12/31/93; others, 9/23/93.

Discovery of America Type

Designs: 15c, Columbus practices celestial navigation. 40c, The fleet in rough seas. 55c, Natives on the beach. 60c, Map of voyage. $1.50, Pinta's crew sights land.

Perf. 14½x14

1991, Apr. 9 Litho. Wmk. 384

725 A106 15c multicolored .30 .30
726 A106 40c multicolored .80 .80
727 A106 55c multicolored 1.10 1.10
728 A106 60c multicolored 1.25 1.25
Nos. 725-728 (4) 3.45 3.45

Souvenir Sheet

729 A106 $1.50 multicolored 3.00 3.00

Elizabeth & Philip, Birthdays
Common Design Types
Wmk. 384

1991, June 17 Litho. *Perf. 14½*

730 CD346 15c multicolored .30 .30
731 CD345 $1 multicolored 2.00 2.00
a. Pair, #730-731 + label 2.30 2.30

Hurricane Awareness — A121

Designs: 15c, Weather radar image of Hurricane Hugo. 40c, Anatomy of hurricane rotating around eye. 55c, Flooding caused by Hurricane David. 60c, Lockheed WP-3D Orion.

1991, Aug. 28 *Perf. 14*

732 A121 15c multicolored .30 .30
733 A121 40c multicolored .80 .80
734 A121 55c multicolored 1.10 1.10
735 A121 60c multicolored 1.25 1.25
Nos. 732-735 (4) 3.45 3.45

Christmas A122

Designs: 15c, The Annunciation. 55c, Mary and Joseph traveling to Bethlehem. 60c, Angel appearing to shepherds. $1, Adoration of the Magi.

1991, Oct. 28 Wmk. 373 *Perf. 14*

736 A122 15c multicolored .30 .30
737 A122 55c multicolored 1.10 1.10
738 A122 60c multicolored 1.25 1.25
739 A122 $1 multicolored 2.00 2.00
a. Souvenir sheet of 4, #736-739 4.75 4.75
Nos. 736-739 (4) 4.65 4.65

Majority Rule, 25th Anniv. A123

Designs: 15c, First Progressive Liberal Party cabinet. 40c, Signing of Independence Constitution. 55c, Handing over constitutional instrument, vert. 60c, First Bahamian Governor-General, Sir Milo Butler, vert.

Wmk. 373

1992, Jan. 10 Litho. *Perf. 14*

740 A123 15c multicolored .35 .35
741 A123 40c multicolored 1.00 1.00
742 A123 55c multicolored 1.25 1.25
743 A123 60c multicolored 1.50 1.50
Nos. 740-743 (4) 4.10 4.10

Queen Elizabeth II's Accession to the Throne, 40th Anniv.
Common Design Type
Wmk. 373

1992, Feb. 6 Litho. *Perf. 14*

744 CD349 15c multicolored .30 .30
745 CD349 40c multicolored .70 .70
746 CD349 55c multicolored 1.00 1.00
747 CD349 60c multicolored 1.10 1.10
748 CD349 $1 multicolored 1.90 1.90
Nos. 744-748 (5) 5.00 5.00

Discovery of America Type

Designs: 15c, Lucayans first sight of fleet. 40c, Approaching Bahamas coastline. 55c, Lucayans about to meet Columbus. 60c, Columbus gives thanks for safe arrival. $1.50, Monument to Columbus' landing.

Perf. 14½x14

1992, Mar. 17 Litho. Wmk. 384

749 A106 15c multicolored .30 .30
750 A106 40c multicolored .75 .75
751 A106 55c multicolored 1.00 1.00
752 A106 60c multicolored 1.10 1.10
Nos. 749-752 (4) 3.15 3.15

Souvenir Sheet

753 A106 $1.50 multicolored 2.75 2.75

Templeton, Galbraith and Hansberger Ltd. Building — A124

Wmk. 384

1992, Apr. 22 Litho. *Perf. 14½*

754 A124 55c multicolored 1.00 1.00

Templeton Prize for Progress in Religion, 20th Anniv.

1992 Summer Olympics, Barcelona A125

Perf. 14½x14

1992, June 2 Wmk. 373

755 A125 15c Pole vault .30 .30
756 A125 40c Javelin .75 .75
757 A125 55c Hurdling 1.00 1.00
758 A125 60c Basketball 1.10 1.10
Nos. 755-758 (4) 3.15 3.15

Souvenir Sheet

759 A125 $2 Sailing 3.75 3.75

Intl. Conference on Nutrition — A126

15c, Drought-affected earth, starving child. 55c, Hand holding plant, stalks of grain.

Perf. 14½x13

1992, Aug. 11 Litho. Wmk. 373

760 A126 15c multicolored .30 .30
761 A126 55c multicolored 1.00 1.00

Discovery of America Type

Souvenir Sheet

Perf. 14x13½

1992, Oct. 12 Litho. Wmk. 384

762 A106 $2 Coming ashore 3.75 3.75

Christmas A127

1992, Nov. 2 Wmk. 373 *Perf. 14*

763 A127 15c The Annunciation .30 .30
764 A127 55c Nativity Scene 1.00 1.00
765 A127 60c Angel, shepherds 1.10 1.10
766 A127 70c The Magi 1.25 1.25
a. Souvenir sheet of 4, #763-766 3.75 3.75
Nos. 763-766 (4) 3.65 3.65

The Contract, Farm Labor Program, 50th Anniv. A128

Bahamian, American flags and: 15c, Silhouette of worker's head. 55c, Onions. 60c, Citrus fruits. 70c, Apples.

Perf. 14x14½

1993, Mar. 16 Litho. Wmk. 384

767 A128 15c multicolored .30 .30
768 A128 55c multicolored 1.00 1.00
769 A128 60c multicolored 1.10 1.10
770 A128 70c multicolored 1.25 1.25
Nos. 767-770 (4) 3.65 3.65

Royal Air Force, 75th Anniv.

Common Design Type

Designs: 15c, Westland Wapiti. 40c, Gloster Gladiator. 55c, DeHavilland Vampire. 70c, English Electric Lightning.

No. 775a, Avro Shackleton. b, Fairey Battle. c, Douglas Boston. d, DeHavilland DH9a.

Wmk. 373

1993, Apr. 1 Litho. *Perf. 14*

771 CD350 15c multicolored .25 .25
772 CD350 40c multicolored .70 .70
773 CD350 55c multicolored .95 .95
774 CD350 70c multicolored 1.25 1.25
Nos. 771-774 (4) 3.15 3.15

Souvenir Sheet of 4

775 CD350 60c #a.-d. 4.50 4.50

Coronation of Queen Elizabeth II, 40th Anniv. A129

Wmk. 373

1993, June 2 Litho. *Perf. 13½*

776 A129 15c Nos. 424-425 .30 .30
777 A129 55c No. 157 1.00 1.00
778 A129 60c Nos. 402-403 1.10 1.10
779 A129 70c Nos. 404-405 1.25 1.25
Nos. 776-779 (4) 3.65 3.65

A130

Natl. symbols: 15c, Lignum vitae. 55c, Yellow elder. 60c, Blue marlin. 70c, Flamingo.

1993, July 8 Litho. *Perf. 14*

780 A130 15c multicolored .30 .30
781 A130 55c multicolored 1.00 1.00
782 A130 60c multicolored 1.10 1.10
783 A130 70c multicolored 1.25 1.25
Nos. 780-783 (4) 3.65 3.65

Independence, 20th anniv.

A131

1993, Sept. 8 Litho. *Perf. 14*

Wildflowers.

784 A131 15c Cordia .25 .25
785 A131 55c Seaside morning glory 1.10 1.10
786 A131 60c Poinciana 1.25 1.25
787 A131 70c Spider lily 1.40 1.40
Nos. 784-787 (4) 4.00 4.00

Christmas A132

1993, Nov. 1 Litho. *Perf. 14*

788 A132 15c Angel, Mary .30 .30
789 A132 55c Shepherds, angel 1.00 1.00
790 A132 60c Holy family 1.10 1.10
791 A132 70c Three wise men 1.25 1.25
Nos. 788-791 (4) 3.65 3.65

Souvenir Sheet

792 A132 $1 Madonna and Child 1.90 1.90

Intl. Year of the Family A133

Wmk. 384

1994, Feb. 18 Litho. *Perf. 13½*

793 A133 15c shown .30 .30
794 A133 55c Children studying 1.00 1.00
795 A133 60c Son, father fishing 1.10 1.10
796 A133 70c Children, grandmother 1.25 1.25
Nos. 793-796 (4) 3.65 3.65

Hong Kong '94.

Royal Visit — A134

Designs: 15c, Bahamas, United Kingdom flags. 55c, Royal Yacht Britannia. 60c, Queen Elizabeth II. 70c, Prince Philip, Queen.

Perf. 14x13½

1994, Mar. 7 Wmk. 373

797 A134 15c multicolored .30 .30
798 A134 55c multicolored 1.00 1.00
799 A134 60c multicolored 1.10 1.10
800 A134 70c multicolored 1.25 1.25
Nos. 797-800 (4) 3.65 3.65

Natl. Family Island Regatta, 40th Anniv. A135

Designs: 15c, 55c, 60c, 70c, Various sailing boats at sea. $2, Beached yacht, vert.

Wmk. 373

1994, Apr. 27 Litho. *Perf. 14*

801 A135 15c multicolored .30 .30
802 A135 55c multicolored 1.00 1.00
803 A135 60c multicolored 1.10 1.10
804 A135 70c multicolored 1.25 1.25
Nos. 801-804 (4) 3.65 3.65

Souvenir Sheet

805 A135 $2 multicolored 3.75 3.75

Intl. Olympic Committee, Cent. — A136

Flag, Olympic rings, and: 15c, Nos. 276-279, horiz. 55c, Nos. 388-391. 60c, Nos. 559-562, horiz. 70c, Nos. 755-758.

Wmk. 373

1994, May 31 Litho. *Perf. 14*

806 A136 15c multicolored .30 .30
807 A136 55c multicolored 1.00 1.00
808 A136 60c multicolored 1.10 1.10
809 A136 70c multicolored 1.25 1.25
Nos. 806-809 (4) 3.65 3.65

Souvenir Sheet

First Recipients of the Order of the Caribbean Community — A137

Illustration reduced.

Perf. 13x14

1994, July 5 Litho. Wmk. 373

810 A137 $2 multicolored 4.00 4.00

A138

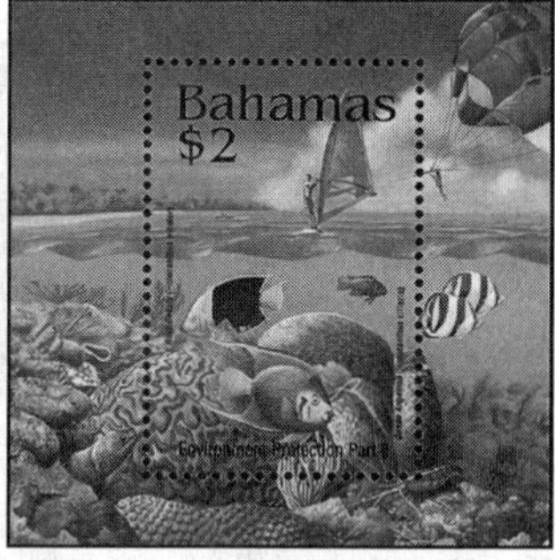

A139

Butterfly, flower: 15c, Canna skipper, canna. 55c, Cloudless sulphur, cassia. 60c, White peacock, passion flower. 70c, Devillier's swallowtail, calico flower.

1994, Aug. 16 Litho. *Perf. 14*

811 A138 15c multicolored .25 .25
812 A138 55c multicolored 1.10 1.10
813 A138 60c multicolored 1.25 1.25
814 A138 70c multicolored 1.40 1.40
Nos. 811-814 (4) 4.00 4.00

1994, Sept. 13 *Perf. 13½x14*

Marine Life: a, Cuban hogfish, Spanish hogfish. b, Tomate, squirrelfish. c, French angelfish. d, Queen angelfish. e, Rock beauty.

$2, Rock beauty, queen angelfish.

815 A139 40c Strip of 5, #a.-e. 4.00 4.00

Souvenir Sheet

816 A139 $2 multicolored 4.00 4.00

Christmas — A140

Wmk. 384

1994, Oct. 31 Litho. *Perf. 14*

817 A140 15c Angel .25 .25
818 A140 55c Holy family 1.10 1.10
819 A140 60c Shepherds 1.25 1.25
820 A140 70c Magi 1.40 1.40
Nos. 817-820 (4) 4.00 4.00

Souvenir Sheet

821 A140 $2 Christ Child, vert. 3.75 3.75

College of the Bahamas, 20th Anniv. — A141

Designs: 15c, Lion. 70c, Queen Elizabeth II, college facade.

Wmk. 373

1995, Feb. 8 Litho. *Perf. 14*

822 A141 15c multicolored .30 .30
823 A141 70c multicolored 1.40 1.40

End of World War II, 50th Anniv.

Common Design Types

Designs: 15c, Bahamian soldiers on parade. 55c, Neutrality patrols flown by PBY-5A flying boats. 60c, Bahamian women in all three services. 70c, B-24 Liberator, Bahamians in RAF.
$2, Reverse of War Medal 1939-45.

Wmk. 373

1995, May 8 Litho. *Perf. 13½*

824 CD351 15c multicolored .25 .25
825 CD351 55c multicolored 1.10 1.10
826 CD351 60c multicolored 1.25 1.25
827 CD351 70c multicolored 1.40 1.40
Nos. 824-827 (4) 4.00 4.00

Souvenir Sheet

Perf. 14

828 CD352 $2 multicolored 4.00 4.00

Kirtland's Warbler — A142

#829: a, 25c, Female feeding young. b, 25c Immature bird feeding, prior to migration. c, 15c, Female at nest. d, 15c, Singing male.
$2, Female on branch overlooking lake.

Wmk. 373

1995, June 7 Litho. *Perf. 13½*

829 A142 Strip of 4, #a.-d. 1.90 1.90

Souvenir Sheet

Perf. 13

830 A142 $2 multicolored 4.00 4.00

World Wildlife Fund (#829). No. 830 contains one 42x28mm stamp and has continuous design.

Tourism A143

Designs: 15c, Eleuthera Cliffs. 55c, Clarence Town, Long Island. 60c, Albert Lowe Museum. 70c, Yachting.

Wmk. 384

1995, July 18 Litho. *Perf. 14½*

831 A143 15c multicolored .25 .25
832 A143 55c multicolored 1.10 1.10
833 A143 60c multicolored 1.25 1.25
834 A143 70c multicolored 1.40 1.40
Nos. 831-834 (4) 4.00 4.00

FAO, 50th Anniv. A144

Designs: 15c, Pig, poultry farming. 55c, Horticultural methods. 60c, Healthy eating. 70c, Sustainable fishing.

Perf. 13½x13

1995, Sept. 5 Litho. Wmk. 373

835 A144 15c multicolored .25 .25
836 A144 55c multicolored 1.10 1.10
837 A144 60c multicolored 1.25 1.25
838 A144 70c multicolored 1.40 1.40
Nos. 835-838 (4) 4.00 4.00

UN, 50th Anniv.

Common Design Type

Designs: 15c, Sikorsky S-55, UNEF, Sinai, 1957. 55c, Ferret armored car, UNEF, Sinai, 1957. 60c, Fokker F-27, UNAMIC/UNTAC, Cambodia, 1991-93. 70c, Lockheed Hercules.

Wmk. 373

1995, Oct. 25 Litho. *Perf. 14*

839 CD353 15c multicolored .25 .25
840 CD353 55c multicolored 1.10 1.10
841 CD353 60c multicolored 1.25 1.25
842 CD353 70c multicolored 1.40 1.40
Nos. 839-842 (4) 4.00 4.00

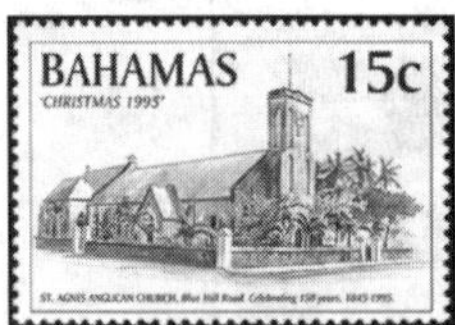

Christmas — A145

Designs: 15c, St. Agnes Anglican Church. 55c, Church of God. 60c, Sacred Heart Roman Catholic Church. 70c, Salem Union Baptist Church.

1995, Nov. 17

843 A145 15c multicolored .25 .25
844 A145 55c multicolored 1.10 1.10
845 A145 60c multicolored 1.25 1.25
846 A145 70c multicolored 1.40 1.40
Nos. 843-846 (4) 4.00 4.00

World AIDS Day A146

1995, Dec. 1

847 A146 25c Virus in blood .50 .50
848 A146 70c Scientific research 1.40 1.40

Shells A147

Designs: 5c, Sunrise tellin. 10c, Queen conch. 15c, Angular triton. 20c, True tulip. 25c, Reticulated cowrie-helmet. 30c, Sand dollar. 40c, Lace short-frond murex. 45c, Inflated sea biscuit. 50c, West Indian top shell (magpie). 55c, Spiny oyster. 60c, King helmet. 70c, Lion's paw. $1, Crown cone. $2, Atlantic partridge tun. $5, Wide-mouthed purpura. $10, Triton's trumpet.

1996 Litho. Wmk. 373 *Perf. 14*

849 A147 5c multicolored .20 .20
850 A147 10c multicolored .20 .20
851 A147 15c multicolored .30 .30
852 A147 20c multicolored .40 .40
853 A147 25c multicolored .50 .50
854 A147 30c multicolored .60 .60
855 A147 40c multicolored .80 .80
856 A147 45c multicolored .90 .90
857 A147 50c multicolored 1.00 1.00
858 A147 55c multicolored 1.10 1.10
859 A147 60c multicolored 1.25 1.25
860 A147 70c multicolored 1.40 1.40
a. Souvenir sheet of 1 1.40 1.40
861 A147 $1 multicolored 2.00 2.00
a. Souvenir sheet of 1 2.00 2.00
862 A147 $2 multicolored 4.00 4.00
863 A147 $5 multicolored 10.00 10.00
864 A147 $10 multicolored 20.00 20.00
Nos. 849-864 (16) 44.65 44.65

No. 860a issued 6/20/97 for return of Hong Kong to China.
No. 861a issued 2/3/97 for Hong Kong '97.
Nos. 849-864 exist dated "1997."
Nos. 849-853, 855, 857, 859, 861-864 exist dated "1999."
Issued: $10, 7/1; others, 1/2.
See Nos. 962-964.

Radio, Cent. A148

Designs: 15c, East Goodwin Lightship, Marconi apparatus suspended from masthead. 55c, Arrest of Dr. Crippen, newspaper headline telling of wireless message from SS Montrose. 60c, SS Philadelphia, first readable transatlantic messages. 70c, Yacht Elettra, Guglielmo Marconi.
$2, SS Titantic, SS Carpathia.

1996, Feb. 4 Litho. *Perf. 13½*

865 A148 15c multicolored .25 .25
866 A148 55c multicolored 1.10 1.10
867 A148 60c multicolored 1.25 1.25
868 A148 70c multicolored 1.40 1.40
Nos. 865-868 (4) 4.00 4.00

Souvenir Sheet

869 A148 $2 multicolored 4.00 4.00

A149 A150

Wmk. 384

1996, June 25 Litho. *Perf. 13½*

870 A149 15c Swimming .25 .25
871 A149 55c Track 1.10 1.10
872 A149 60c Basketball 1.25 1.25
873 A149 70c Long jump 1.40 1.40
Nos. 870-873 (4) 4.00 4.00

Souvenir Sheet

874 A149 $2 Javelin, 1896 4.00 4.00

Modern Olympic Games, cent.

Wmk. 384

1996, Sept. 3 Litho. *Perf. 14*

Reptiles: 15c, Green anole. 55c, Fowl snake. 60c, Inagua freshwater turtle. 70c, Acklins rock iguana.

875 A150 15c multicolored .25 .25
876 A150 55c multicolored 1.10 1.10
877 A150 60c multicolored 1.25 1.25
878 A150 70c multicolored 1.40 1.40
a. Souvenir sheet, #875-878 4.00 4.00
Nos. 875-878 (4) 4.00 4.00

Environmental protection.

Christmas A151

Designs: 15c, Angel Gabriel and Mary. 55c, Mary and Joseph. 60c, Shepherds. 70c, Magi.
$2, Presentation at the Temple.

Wmk. 373

1996, Nov. 4 Litho. *Perf. 14*

879 A151 15c multicolored .25 .25
880 A151 55c multicolored 1.10 1.10
881 A151 60c multicolored 1.25 1.25
882 A151 70c multicolored 1.40 1.40
Nos. 879-882 (4) 4.00 4.00

Souvenir Sheet

883 A151 $2 multicolored 4.00 4.00

Archives Dept., 25th Anniv. — A152

Perf. 14½x14

1996, Dec. 9 Litho. Wmk. 384

884 A152 55c shown 1.10 1.10

Souvenir Sheet

Perf. 14x13½

885 A152 $2 Building, horiz. 4.00 4.00

Queen Elizabeth II and Prince Philip, 50th Wedding Anniv. — A153

Designs: No. 886, Queen. No. 887, Grenadier Guards. No. 888, Prince Philip. No. 889, Queen reviewing Grenadier Guards. No. 890, Prince holding trophy, Queen opening jewel box. No. 891, Prince on polo pony.
$2, Queen, Prince riding in open carriage, horiz.

Wmk. 373

1997, July 9 Litho. *Perf. 13*

886 A153 50c multicolored 1.00 1.00
887 A153 50c multicolored 1.00 1.00
a. Pair, #886-887 2.00 2.00
888 A153 60c multicolored 1.25 1.25
889 A153 60c multicolored 1.25 1.25
a. Pair, #888-889 2.50 2.50
890 A153 70c multicolored 1.40 1.40
891 A153 70c multicolored 1.40 1.40
a. Pair, #890-891 2.80 2.80
Nos. 886-891 (6) 7.30 7.30

Souvenir Sheet

892 A153 $2 multicolored 4.00 4.00

Intl. Year of the Reefs A154

Various pictures of marine life and coral.

Perf. 14x14½

1997, Sept. 3 Litho. Wmk. 384

893 A154 15c multicolored .25 .25
894 A154 55c multicolored 1.10 1.10
895 A154 60c multicolored 1.25 1.25
896 A154 70c multicolored 1.40 1.40
Nos. 893-896 (4) 4.00 4.00

Christmas — A155

Perf. 13x13½

1997, Oct. 6 Litho. Wmk. 373

897 A155 15c Angel	.25	.25
898 A155 55c Madonna & Child	1.10	1.10
899 A155 60c Shepherd	1.25	1.25
900 A155 70c Magi	1.40	1.40
Nos. 897-900 (4)	4.00	4.00

Souvenir Sheet

901 A155 $2 Christ Child	4.00	4.00

Diana, Princess of Wales (1961-97)

Common Design Type

Various portraits: 902: a, 55c. b, 60c. c, 70c.

Perf. 14½x14

1998, Mar. 31 Litho. Wmk. 373

901A CD355 15c multicolored	.30	.30

Sheet of 4

902 CD355 #a.-c., 901A	4.00	4.00

Organization of American States, 50th Anniv. — A156

Map of North and South America, national flags, and: 15c, "New Vision" paper. 55c, Building.

1998, Apr. 14 ***Perf. 13½x14***

903 A156 15c multicolored	.30	.30
904 A156 55c multicolored	1.10	1.10

University of the West Indies, 50th Anniv. — A157

1998, Apr. 14

905 A157 55c multicolored	1.10	1.10

Universal Declaration of Human Rights, 50th Anniv. — A158

1998, Apr. 14

906 A158 55c multicolored	1.10	1.10

Royal Air Force, 80th Anniv.

Common Design Type of 1993 Re-Inscribed

Designs: 15c, Handley Page Hyderabad. 55c, Hawker Demon. 60c, Gloster Meteor F.8. 70c, Lockheed Neptune MR.1.

No. 911: a, Sopwith Camel. b, Short 184. c, Supermarine Spitfire PR.19. d, North American Mitchell III.

1998, Apr. 1

907 CD350 15c multicolored	.25	.25
908 CD350 55c multicolored	1.10	1.10
909 CD350 60c multicolored	1.25	1.25
910 CD350 70c multicolored	1.40	1.40
Nos. 907-910 (4)	4.00	4.00

Souvenir Sheet

911 CD350 50c Sheet of 4, #a.-d.	4.00	4.00

Independence, 25th Anniv. — A159

15c, Supreme Court Building. 55c, Nassau Library. 60c, Government House. 70c, Gregory Arch.

$2, Exuma-Family Island Regatta, George Town.

Wmk. 373

1998, July 10 Litho. ***Perf. 13½***

912 A159 15c multicolored	.25	.25
913 A159 55c multicolored	1.10	1.10
914 A159 60c multicolored	1.25	1.25
915 A159 70c multicolored	1.40	1.40
Nos. 912-915 (4)	4.00	4.00

Souvenir Sheet

916 A159 $2 multicolored	4.00	4.00

Castaway Cay, Disney Cruise Lines A160

1998, Aug. 1 ***Perf. 14***

917 A160 55c Daytime	1.10	1.10
918 A160 55c Nighttime	1.10	1.10
a. Pair, #917-918	2.25	2.25
b. Bklt. pane, 5 each #917-918	11.00	
Complete booklet, #918b	11.00	

MS Ryndam, Half Moon Cay — A161

1998, Aug. 19 ***Perf. 13½x13***

919 A161 55c multicolored	1.10	1.10

Roses A162

Wmk. 373

1998, Sept. 8 Litho. ***Perf. 14***

920 A162 55c Yellow cream	1.10	1.10
921 A162 55c Big red	1.10	1.10
922 A162 55c Seven sisters	1.10	1.10
923 A162 55c Barrel pink	1.10	1.10
924 A162 55c Island beauty	1.10	1.10
a. Bklt. pane, 2 each #920-924	11.00	
Complete booklet, #924a	11.00	
Nos. 920-924 (5)	5.50	5.50

Souvenir Sheet

925 A162 55c like #924	1.10	1.10

No. 925 has parts of other roses extending into center left and upper left area of stamp.

Intl. Year of the Ocean — A163

Wmk. 373

1998, Nov. 24 Litho. ***Perf. 14***

926 A163 15c Killer whale	.30	.30
927 A163 55c Tropical fish	1.10	1.10

Christmas A164

1998, Dec. 11

928 A164 15c The Annunciation	.25	.25
929 A164 55c Shepherds, star	1.10	1.10
930 A164 60c Magi	1.25	1.25
931 A164 70c Flight into Egypt	1.40	1.40
Nos. 928-931 (4)	4.00	4.00

Souvenir Sheet

932 A164 $2 Nativity scene	4.00	4.00

Timothy Gibson, Composer of Natl. Anthem A165

1998 Litho. Wmk. 373 ***Perf. 13½***

933 A165 60c multicolored	1.25	1.25

Independence, 25th anniv.

National Trust, 40th Anniv. — A166

Flamingos on the beach: a, One chick, adults. b, Two chicks, adults. c, One chick spreading wings, adults. d, Six in flight over others. e, Three ascending into flight.

Wmk. 384

1999, Feb. 9 Litho. ***Perf. 14***

934 A166 55c Strip of 5, #a.-e.	5.50	5.50

No. 934 is a continuous design.

See Nos. 940, 961, 969.

Australia '99, World Stamp Expo A167

Maritime history: 15c, Arawak Indians. 55c, Santa Maria. 60c, Blackbeard's ship, Queen Anne's Revenge. 70c, Banshee running Union blockade, US Civil War.

$2, American invasion of Fort Nassau, 1776.

Perf. 14x14½

1999, Mar. 9 Wmk. 373

935 A167 15c multicolored	.25	.25
936 A167 55c multicolored	1.10	1.10
937 A167 60c multicolored	1.25	1.25
938 A167 70c multicolored	1.40	1.40
Nos. 935-938 (4)	4.00	4.00

Souvenir Sheet

939 A167 $2 multicolored	4.00	4.00

National Trust, 40th Anniv. Type

Marine life: a, Dolphin. b, Large fish, four in background. c, Several fish, coral. d, Turtle, fish, coral. e, Lobster, coral.

Wmk. 384

1999, Apr. 6 Litho. ***Perf. 14***

940 A166 55c Strip of 5, #a.-e.	5.50	5.50

No. 940 is a continuous design.

Bahamas Historical Society, 40th Anniv. A168

1999, June 9 Litho. ***Perf. 13***

941 A168 $1 multicolored	2.00	2.00

1st Manned Moon Landing, 30th Anniv.

Common Design Type

15c, Ascent module in assembly area. 65c, Apollo command & service module. 70c, Descent stage. 80c, Module turns to dock with service module.

$2, Looking at earth from moon.

Perf. 14x13¾

1999, July 20 Litho. Wmk. 384

942 CD357 15c multicolored	.30	.30
943 CD357 65c multicolored	1.25	1.25
944 CD357 70c multicolored	1.40	1.40
945 CD357 80c multicolored	1.60	1.60
Nos. 942-945 (4)	4.55	4.55

Souvenir Sheet

Perf. 14

946 CD357 $2 multicolored	4.00	4.00

No. 946 contains one 40mm circular stamp 40mm.

UPU, 125th Anniv. A170

Wmk. 384

1999, Aug. 17 Litho. ***Perf. 13½***

947 A170 15c Mail Packet Delaware	.30	.30
948 A170 65c S.S. Atlantis	1.25	1.25
949 A170 70c M.V. Queen of Bermuda	1.40	1.40
950 A170 80c USS Saufley	1.60	1.60
Nos. 947-950 (4)	4.55	4.55

Queen Mother's Century

Common Design Type

Queen Mother: 15c, At Hertfordshire Hospital. 65c, With Princess Elizabeth. 70c, With Prince Andrew. 80c, With Irish Guards.

$2, With brother David and 1966 British World Cup team members.

Wmk. 373

1999, Aug. Litho. ***Perf. 13½***

951 CD358 15c multicolored	.30	.30
952 CD358 65c multicolored	1.25	1.25
953 CD358 70c multicolored	1.40	1.40
954 CD358 80c multicolored	1.60	1.60
Nos. 951-954 (4)	4.55	4.55

Souvenir Sheet

955 CD358 $2 multicolored	4.00	4.00

Environmental Protection — A171

15c, Turtle pond. 65c, Green turtles, limestone cliffs. 70c, Barracudas. 80c, Sea fans on reef.

$2, Atlantic bottlenose dolphin.

Wmk. 373

1999, Sept. 21 Litho. ***Perf. 13¾***

956 A171 15c multicolored	.30	.30
957 A171 65c multicolored	1.25	1.25
958 A171 70c multicolored	1.40	1.40
959 A171 80c multicolored	1.60	1.60
Nos. 956-959 (4)	4.55	4.55

Souvenir Sheet

960 A171 $2 multicolored	4.00	4.00

National Trust Type of 1999

Designs: a, Tern. b, Heron, c, Hummingbird, orange flower. d, Duck. e, Parrot.

Wmk. 384

1999, Oct. 8 Litho. *Perf. 14¼*
961 A166 65c Strip of 5, #a.-e. 6.50 6.50

Shell Type of 1996

1999 Litho. Wmk. 373 *Perf. 14*
962 A147 35c Like #854 .70 .70
963 A147 65c Like #856 1.25 1.25
964 A147 80c Like #858 1.60 1.60
Nos. 962-964 (3) 3.55 3.55

Christmas A172

People in various Junkanoo costumes.

Perf. 14½x14¼
1999, Oct. 25 Litho. Wmk. 373
965 A172 15c multicolored .30 .30
966 A172 65c multicolored 1.25 1.25
967 A172 70c multicolored 1.40 1.40
968 A172 80c multicolored 1.60 1.60
Nos. 965-968 (4) 4.55 4.55

National Trust Type of 1999

Designs: a, Orchid. b, Rodent. c, Hummingbird, red flowers. d, Lizard. e, Hibiscus.

Wmk. 384

1999, Oct. 8 Litho. *Perf. 14¼*
969 A166 65c Strip of 5, #a.-e. 6.50 6.50

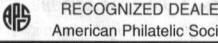

Historic Fishing Villages A173

15c, New Plymouth. 65c, Cherokee Sound. 70c, Hope Town. 80c, Spanish Wells.

Perf. 13¼x13
2000, Jan. 25 Litho. Wmk. 373
970 A173 15c multi .30 .30
971 A173 65c multi 1.25 1.25
972 A173 70c multi 1.40 1.40
973 A173 80c multi 1.60 1.60
Nos. 970-973 (4) 4.55 4.55

Souvenir Sheet

1999 World Champions in Women's 4x100-Meter Relay Race — A174

Illustration reduced.

Wmk. 373

2000, Feb. 22 Litho. *Perf. 14½*
974 A174 $2 multi 4.00 4.00

Bush Medicine Plants A175

Perf. 14¼x14½
2000, May 2 Litho. Wmk. 373
975 A175 15c Prickly pear .30 .30
976 A175 65c Buttercup 1.25 1.25
977 A175 70c Shepherd's needle 1.40 1.40
978 A175 80c Five fingers 1.60 1.60
Nos. 975-978 (4) 4.55 4.55

The Stamp Show 2000, London A176

Battle of Britain, 60th anniv.: 15c, Quick turnaround, rearm and refuel. 65c, Squadron leader R. Stanford-Tuck in Hurricane 1. 70c, Melee. 80c, Tally ho.
$2, Airplanes in flight.

2000, May 22 *Perf. 13¼x13½*
979 A176 15c multi .30 .30
980 A176 65c multi 1.25 1.25
981 A176 70c multi 1.40 1.40
982 A176 80c multi 1.60 1.60
Nos. 979-982 (4) 4.55 4.55

Souvenir Sheet

983 A176 $2 multi 4.00 4.00

Souvenir Sheet

Bahamas Cooperatives — A177

Illustration reduced.

2000, June 27 Litho. *Perf. 14*
984 A177 $2 multi 4.00 4.00

2000 Summer Olympics, Sydney A178

15c, Swimming. 65c, Triple jump. 70c, Women's 4x100 meter relay. 80c, Yachting.

2000, July 17 *Perf. 14¼x14½*
985-988 A178 Set of 4 4.50 4.50

Christmas A179

Orchids: 15c, Cockle-shell orchid. 65c, Pleated encyclia. 70c, Pine pink. 80c, Graceful encyclia.

2000, Nov. 7 *Perf. 14½x14¼*
989-992 A179 Set of 4 4.50 4.50

Bahamas Humane Society, 76th Anniv. A180

Designs: 15c, Education. 65c, Fund raising. 70c, Veterinary care. 80c, Animal rescue.

Wmk. 373

2000, Dec. 12 Litho. *Perf. 14*
993-996 A180 Set of 4 4.75 4.75

Early Settlements A181

Designs: 15c, Meadow St., Inagua. 65c, Bain Town. 70c, Hope Town, Abaco. 80c, The Blue Hills.

Wmk. 373

2001, Feb. 6 Litho. *Perf. 14¼*
997-1000 A181 Set of 4 4.75 4.75

Sir Lynden Pindling (1930-2000), Prime Minister — A182

Pindling and: 15c, Microphone. 65c, Flag.

2001, Mar. 22 *Perf. 14½x14¼*
1001-1002 A182 Set of 2 1.60 1.60
1001a Inscribed "10th July, 1973" .30 .30

No. 1001 is inscribed "10th July, 1972." Issued: No. 1001a, 8/6/01.

Edible Wild Fruits A183

Designs: 15c, Cocoplum. 65c, Guana berry. 70c, Mastic. 80c, Seagrape.

2001, May 15 *Perf. 14¼x14½*
1003-1006 A183 Set of 4 4.75 4.75

Birds and Eggs A184

Designs: 5c, Reddish egret. 10c, Purple gallinule. 15c, Antillean nighthawk. 20c, Wilson's plover. 25c, Killdeer. 30c, Bahama woodstar. 40c, Bahama swallow. 50c, Bahama mockingbird. 60c, Black-cowled oriole. 65c, Great lizard cuckoo. 70c, Audubon's shearwater. 80c, Gray kingbird. $1, Bananaquit. $2, Yellow warbler. $5, Antillean bullfinch. $10, Roseate spoonbill.

Wmk. 373

2001, July 1 Litho. *Perf. 14*
1007 A184 5c multi .20 .20
1008 A184 10c multi .20 .20
1009 A184 15c multi .30 .30
1010 A184 20c multi .40 .40
1011 A184 25c multi .50 .50
1012 A184 30c multi .60 .60
1013 A184 40c multi .80 .80
1014 A184 50c multi 1.00 1.00
1015 A184 60c multi 1.25 1.25
1016 A184 65c multi 1.25 1.25
1017 A184 70c multi 1.40 1.40
1018 A184 80c multi 1.60 1.60
1019 A184 $1 multi 2.00 2.00
1020 A184 $2 multi 4.00 4.00
1021 A184 $5 multi 10.00 10.00
1022 A184 $10 multi 20.00 20.00
Nos. 1007-1022 (16) 45.50 45.50

Visits of Royal Navy Ships A185

HMS: 15c, Norfolk, 1933. 25c, Scarborough, 1930s. 50c, Bahamas, 1944. 65c, Battleaxe, 1979. 70c, Invincible, 1997. 80c, Norfolk, 2000.

Wmk. 373

2001, Aug. 21 Litho. *Perf. 14*
1023-1028 A185 Set of 6 6.25 6.25

Christmas — A186

Paintings: 15c, The Adoration of the Shepherds, by Peter Paul Rubens. 65c, Adoration of the Magi, by Rubens and Anthony Van Dyck. 70c, The Holy Virgin in the Wreath of Flowers, by Rubens and Jan Breughel. 80c, The Holy Virgin Adored by Angels, by Rubens.

2001, Nov. 6
1029-1032 A186 Set of 4 4.75 4.75

Reign Of Queen Elizabeth II, 50th Anniv. Issue

Common Design Type

Designs: Nos. 1033, 1037a, 15c, Princess Elizabeth, 1946. Nos. 1034, 1037b, 65c, In 1992. Nos. 1035, 1037c, 70c, With Prince Edward, 1965. Nos. 1036, 1037d, 80c, In 1996. No. 1037e, $2, 1955 portrait by Annigoni (38x50mm).

Perf. 14¼x14½, 13¾ (#1037e)
2002, Feb. 6 Litho. Wmk. 373

With Gold Frames

1033-1036 CD360 Set of 4 4.75 4.75

Souvenir Sheet

Without Gold Frames

1037 CD360 Sheet of 5, #a-e 8.75 8.75

Souvenir Sheet

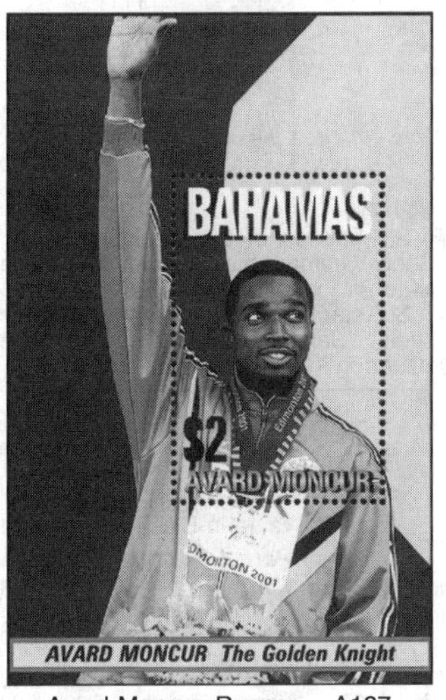

Avard Moncur, Runner — A187

Perf. 14x13¾

2002, Apr. 16 Litho. Wmk. 373

1038 A187 $2 multi 4.00 4.00

In Remembrance of Sept. 11, 2001 Terrorist Attacks — A188

Wmk. 373

2002, May 14 Litho. *Perf. 13¾*

1039 A188 $1 multi 2.00 2.00

Printed in sheets of four.

Bush Medicine Plants Type of 2000

Designs: 15c, Wild sage (lantana). 65c, Seaside maho. 70c, Sea ox-eye. 80c, Mexican poppy thistle.

Perf. 14¼x14½

2002, July 2 Litho. Wmk. 373

1040-1043 A175 Set of 4 4.75 4.75

Queen Mother Elizabeth (1900-2002)

Common Design Type

Designs: 15c, Wearing hat and maple leaf brooch. 65c, Wearing black hat.

No. 1046: a, 70c, Wearing flowered hat. b, £1, Wearing blue hat.

Wmk. 373

2002, Aug. 5 Litho. *Perf. 14¼*

With Purple Frames

1044-1045 CD361 Set of 2 1.60 1.60

Souvenir Sheet

Without Purple Frames

Perf. 14½x14¼

1046 CD361 Sheet of 2, #a-b 3.00 3.00

Flora and Fauna — A189

Plates from *The Natural History of Carolina, Florida and the Bahama Islands,* by Mark Catesby: 15c, Rice birds and rice. 25c, Alligator and red mangrove. 50c, Parrotfish. 65c, Ilatehera duck and sea oxeye. 70c, Flamingo and gorgonian coral. 80c, Crested bittern and inkberry.

Wmk. 373

2002, Oct. 1 Litho. *Perf. 14¼*

1047-1052 A189 Set of 6 6.25 6.25

Christmas A190

Carols: 15c, While Shepherds Watched Their Flocks. 65c, We Three Kings of Orient Are. 70c, Once in Royal David's City. 80c, I Saw Three Ships.

2002, Oct. 29 *Perf. 14¼x14½*

1053-1056 A190 Set of 4 4.75 4.75

SEMI-POSTAL STAMPS

No. 48 Overprinted in Red

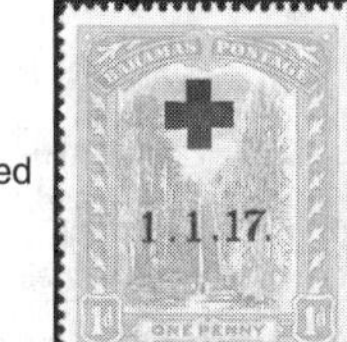

1917, May 18 Wmk. 3 *Perf. 14*

B1 A6 1p car & black .40 *1.60*

Type of 1911 Overprinted in Red

1919, Jan. 1

B2 A6 1p red & black .40 *2.25*
- **a.** Double overprint *1,600.*

This stamp was originally scheduled for release in 1918.

Souvenir Sheet

No. 694 Surcharged **HURRICANE RELIEF +$1**

Wmk. 384

1992, Nov. 16 Litho. *Perf. 14*

B3 A116 Sheet of 2, #a.-b. 8.00 8.00

AIR POST STAMPS

Catalogue values for all unused stamps in this section are for Never Hinged items.

Manned Flight Bicentenary — AP1

Airplanes.

Wmk. 373

1983, Oct. 13 Litho. *Perf. 14*

C1 AP1 10c Consolidated Catalina .50 .20
- **a.** Without emblem ('85) .20 .20
- **b.** Without emblem, wmk. 384 ('86) .20 .20

C2 AP1 25c Avro Tudor IV .65 .40
- **a.** Without emblem ('85) .45 .45
- **b.** Without emblem, wmk. 384 ('86) .45 .45

C3 AP1 31c Avro Lancastrian .75 .55
- **a.** Without emblem ('85) .55 .55

C4 AP1 35c Consolidated Commodore .60 .60
- **a.** Without emblem ('85) .85 .65

Nos. C1-C4 (4) 2.50 1.75

Aircraft AP2

1987, July 7

C5 AP2 15c Bahamasair Boeing 737 1.50 .90

C6 AP2 40c Eastern Boeing 757 2.10 1.50

C7 AP2 45c Pan Am Airbus A300 B4 2.10 1.50

C8 AP2 50c British Airways Boeing 747 2.10 1.50

Nos. C5-C8 (4) 7.80 5.40

SPECIAL DELIVERY STAMPS

No. 34 Overprinted

1916 Wmk. 1 *Perf. 14*

E1 A6 5p orange & black 6.50 *27.50*
- **a.** Double overprint *750.00* *1,000.*
- **b.** Inverted overprint *1,100.* *1,250.*
- **c.** Double ovpt., one invtd. *1,250.* *1,250.*
- **d.** Pair, one without overprint *18,000.* *27,500.*

The No. E1 overprint exists in two types. Type I (illustrated) is much scarcer. Type II shows "SPECIAL" farther right, so that the letter "I" is slightly right of the vertical line of the "E" below it.

Type of Regular Issue of 1903 Overprinted

1917, July 2 Wmk. 3

E2 A6 5p orange & black .80 *5.00*

No. 60 Overprinted in Red

1918

E3 A6 5p violet & black .60 *1.75*

WAR TAX STAMPS

Stamps of 1912-18 Overprinted

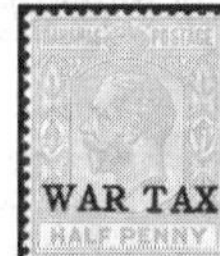

1918, Feb. 21 Wmk. 3 *Perf. 14*

MR1 A8 ½p green 8.00 *30.00*
- **a.** Double overprint 1,600. 1,100.
- **b.** Inverted overprint 1,850. *1,300.*

MR2 A8 1p car rose .80 *.90*
- **a.** Double overprint 2,000. 1,250.
- **b.** Inverted overprint 1,250. *1,300.*

MR3 A6 3p brown, *yel* 3.75 *3.50*
- **a.** Inverted overprint *1,750.* *1,100.*
- **b.** Double overprint 1,400. *1,400.*

MR4 A8 1sh black & red 75.00 *110.00*
- **a.** Double overprint 7,500. —

Nos. MR1-MR4 (4) 87.55 *144.40*

Same Overprint on No. 48a

1918, July 10

MR5 A6 1p car & black 3.50 *5.50*
- **a.** Double overprint 1,500. *1,600.*
- **b.** Double ovpt., one invtd. 1,500.
- **c.** Inverted overprint *1,600.* *1,350.*

Nos. 49-50, 54 Overprinted in Black or Red

MR6 A8 ½p green 1.60 1.60

MR7 A8 1p car rose .65 .30
- **a.** Watermarked sideways 600.00

MR8 A8 1sh black & red (R) 7.00 2.50

Nos. MR6-MR8 (3) 9.25 4.40

Nos. 58-59 Overprinted

1918-19

MR9 A6 3p brown, *yel* .90 *3.25*

MR10 A6 3p brown & blk ('19) .90 *3.75*

Nos. 49-50, 54 Overprinted in Red or Black

1919, July 14

MR11 A8 ½p green (R) .30 *1.25*

MR12 A8 1p car rose 1.10 *1.40*

MR13 A8 1sh black & red (R) 10.00 *24.00*

Nos. MR11-MR13 (3) 11.40 *26.65*

No. 59 Overprinted

MR14 A6 3p brown & black .80 *5.75*

BAHRAIN

bä-ˈrān

LOCATION — An archipelago in the Persian Gulf, including the islands of Bahrain, Muharraq, Sitra, Nebi Saleh, Kasasifeh and Arad.
GOVT. — Independent sheikdom
AREA — 255 sq. mi.
POP. — 629,090 (1999 est.)
CAPITAL — Manama

Bahrain was a British-protected territory until it became an independent state on August 15, 1971.

12 Pies = 1 Anna
16 Annas = 1 Rupee
100 Naye Paise = 1 Rupee (1957)
1000 Fils = 1 Dinar (1966)

Catalogue values for unused stamps in this country are for Never Hinged items, beginning with Scott 62 in the regular postage section and Scott MR2 in the postal tax section.

Indian Postal Administration

Stamps of India, 1926-32, Overprinted in Black

a

Wmk. Multiple Stars (196)

1933, Aug. 10 *Perf. 14*

No.	Type	Description	Unused	Used
1	A46	3p gray	2.50	.40
2	A47	½a green	7.00	3.00
3	A68	9p dark green	3.50	.85
4	A48	1a dark brown	6.50	2.25
5	A69	1a3p violet	3.50	.65
6	A60	2a vermilion	9.25	7.00
7	A51	3a blue	17.50	35.00
8	A70	3a6p deep blue	3.50	.50
9	A61	4a olive green	17.00	35.00
10	A54	8a red violet	5.25	.90
11	A55	12a claret	7.00	1.50

Overprinted in Black

b

No.	Type	Description	Unused	Used
12	A56	1r green & brown	15.00	7.50
13	A56	2r brn org & car rose	30.00	35.00
14	A56	5r dk violet & ultra	85.00	110.00
		Nos. 1-14 (14)	212.50	239.55

Stamps of India, 1926-32, Overprinted Type "a" in Black

1934

No.	Type	Description	Unused	Used
15	A72	1a dark brown	8.00	.30
16	A51	3a carmine rose	4.50	.35
17	A52	4a olive green	3.60	.35
		Nos. 15-17 (3)	16.10	1.00

India Nos. 138, 111, 111a Overprinted Type "a" in Black

1935-37 *Perf. 13½x14, 14*

No.	Type	Description	Unused	Used
18	A71	½a green	3.75	.50
19	A49	2a vermilion	32.50	7.00
a.		Small die ('37)	42.50	.25

India Stamps of 1937 Overprinted Type "a" in Black

1938-41 Wmk. 196 *Perf. 13½x14*

No.	Type	Description	Unused	Used
20	A80	3p slate	7.25	2.50
21	A80	½a brown	3.75	.20
22	A80	9p green	3.50	2.00
23	A80	1a carmine	3.00	.20
24	A81	2a scarlet	5.50	.90
26	A81	3a yel grn ('41)	8.50	4.25
27	A81	3a6p ultra	3.50	2.50
28	A81	4a dk brn ('41)	95.00	50.00
30	A81	8a bl vio ('40)	125.00	35.00
31	A81	12a car lake ('40)	85.00	42.50

Overprinted Type "b" in Black

No.	Type	Description	Unused	Used
32	A82	1r brn & slate	2.50	1.25
33	A82	2r dk brn & dk vio	11.00	2.50
34	A82	5r dp ultra & dk grn	14.00	13.00
35	A82	10r rose car & dk vio ('41)	55.00	25.00
36	A82	15r dk grn & dk brn ('41)	47.50	42.50
37	A82	25r dk vio & bl vio ('41)	80.00	70.00
		Nos. 20-37 (16)	550.00	294.30
		Set, never hinged	700.00	

India Stamps of 1941-43 Overprinted Type "a" in Black

1942-44 Wmk. 196 *Perf. 13½x14*

No.	Type	Description	Unused	Used
38	A83	3p slate	.90	.55
39	A83	½a rose vio ('44)	3.25	.85
40	A83	9p lt green ('43)	10.00	10.00
41	A83	1a car rose ('44)	3.25	.45
42	A84	1a3p bister ('43)	7.50	11.25
43	A84	1½a dk pur ('43)	4.50	3.25
45	A84	2a scarlet ('43)	3.25	1.40
46	A84	3a violet ('43)	12.25	3.75
47	A84	3½a ultra	3.25	11.25
48	A85	4a chocolate	1.75	1.25
49	A85	6a peacock blue	9.00	7.50
50	A85	8a blue vio ('43)	3.00	1.75
51	A85	12a car lake	4.50	3.25
		Nos. 38-51 (13)	66.40	56.50
		Set, never hinged	100.00	

British Postal Administration

See Oman (Muscat) for similar stamps with surcharge of new value only.

Great Britain Nos. 258 to 263, 243 and 248 Surcharged in Black

c

1948-49 Wmk. 251 *Perf. 14½x14*

No.	Type	Description	Unused	Used
52	A101	½a on ½p green	.35	.60
53	A101	1a on 1p vermilion	.35	.75
54	A101	1½a on 1½p lt red brn	.35	.80
55	A101	2a on 2p lt orange	.35	.20
56	A101	2½a on 2½p ultra	.45	1.75
57	A101	3a on 3p violet	.35	.20
58	A102	6a on 6p rose lilac	.35	.20
59	A103	1r on 1sh brown	1.40	.50

Great Britain Nos. 249A, 250 and 251A Surcharged in Black

Wmk. 259 *Perf. 14*

No.	Type	Description	Unused	Used
60	A104	2r on 2sh6p yel grn	4.50	4.25
61	A104	5r on 5sh dull red	6.50	6.00
61A	A105	10r on 10sh ultra	55.00	37.50
		Nos. 52-61A (11)	69.95	52.75
		Set, never hinged	100.00	

Surcharge bars at bottom on No. 61A.
Issued: 10r, 7/4/49; others, 4/1/48.

Catalogue values for unused stamps in this section, from this point to the end of the section, are for Never Hinged items.

Silver Wedding Issue

Great Britain Nos. 267 and 268 Surcharged in Black

Perf. 14½x14, 14x14½

1948, Apr. 26 Wmk. 251

No.	Type	Description	Unused	Used
62	A109	2½a on 2½p	.45	.25
63	A110	15r on £1	37.50	45.00

Three bars obliterate the original denomination on No. 63.

Olympic Issue

Great Britain Nos. 271 to 274 Surcharged "BAHRAIN" and New Value in Black

1948, July 29 *Perf. 14½x14*

No.	Type	Description	Unused	Used
64	A113	2½a on 2½p brt ultra	.50	.90
a.		Double surcharge	750.00	1,250.
65	A114	3a on 3p dp vio	.50	1.60
66	A115	6a on 6p red vio	1.40	2.00
67	A116	1r on 1sh dk brn	1.40	2.00
		Nos. 64-67 (4)	3.80	6.50

A square of dots obliterates the original denomination on No. 67.

UPU Issue

Great Britain Nos. 276 to 279 Surcharged "BAHRAIN," New Value and Square of Dots in Black

1949, Oct. 10 Photo. *Perf. 14½x14*

No.	Type	Description	Unused	Used
68	A117	2½a on 2½p brt ultra	.50	1.60
69	A118	3a on 3p brt vio	.80	2.25
70	A119	6a on 6p red vio	.75	2.50
71	A120	1r on 1sh brown	1.90	1.40
		Nos. 68-71 (4)	3.95	7.75

Great Britain Nos. 280-285 Surcharged Type "c" in Black

1950-51 Wmk. 251

No.	Type	Description	Unused	Used
72	A101	½a on ½p lt org	.55	.55
73	A101	1a on 1p ultra	1.40	.30
74	A101	1½a on 1½p green	1.40	7.50
75	A101	2a on 2p lt red brn	.55	.30
76	A101	2½a on 2½p ver	1.40	7.50
77	A102	4a on 4p ultra	1.40	1.40

Great Britain Nos. 286-288 Surcharged in Black

Three types of surcharge on No. 78: Type I, "2" level with "RUPEES;" Type II, "2" raised higher than "RUPEES," 15mm between "BAHRAIN" and "2 RUPEES;" Type III, as type II, but 16mm between "BAHRAIN" and "2 RUPEES."

Perf. 11x12

Wmk. 259

No.	Type	Description	Unused	Used
78	A121	2r on 2sh6p green, type I ('51)	20.00	5.25
a.		2r on 2sh6p, type II ('53)	60.00	30.00
b.		2r on 2sh6p, type III ('55)	675.00	70.00
79	A121	5r on 5sh dl red	15.00	7.00
80	A122	10r on 10sh ultra	25.00	
		Nos. 72-80 (9)	66.70	29.80

Longer bars, at lower right, on No. 80.
Issued: 4a, Nov. 2, 1950; others, May 3, 1951.

Stamps of Great Britain, 1952-54, Surcharged "BAHRAIN" and New Value in Black or Dark Blue

1952-54 Wmk. 298 *Perf. 14½x14*

No.	Type	Description	Unused	Used
81	A126	½a on ½p red org ('53)	.25	.25
a.		"½" omitted	175.00	200.00
82	A126	1a on 1p ultra	.25	.20
83	A126	1½a on 1½p grn	.25	.25
84	A126	2a on 2p red brn	.25	.25
85	A127	2½a on 2½p scar	.55	1.00
86	A127	3a on 3p dk pur (Dk Bl)	1.00	.25
87	A128	4a on 4p ultra	5.00	.50
88	A129	6a on 6p lil rose	3.50	.45
89	A132	12a on 1sh3p dk grn	3.50	.75
90	A131	1r on 1sh6p dk bl	3.50	1.00
		Nos. 81-90 (10)	18.05	4.90

Issued: #83, 85, 12/5; #81-82, 84, 8/31/53; #87, 89-90, 11/2/53; #86, 88, 1/18/54.

Six stamps of this design picturing Sheik Sulman bin Hamad Al Kalifah were for local use in 1953-57.

Six stamps of similar design (same sheik, "Bahrain" vertical at left) were issued in 1961 for local use.

Coronation Issue

Great Britain Nos. 313-316 Surcharged "BAHRAIN" and New Value in Black

Perf. 14½x14

1953, June 3 Wmk. 298

No.	Type	Description	Unused	Used
92	A134	2½a on 2½p scar	1.00	1.00
93	A135	4a on 4p brt ultra	1.75	2.50
94	A136	12a on 1sh3p dk grn	2.50	3.00
95	A137	1r on 1sh6p dk bl	6.00	3.00
		Nos. 92-95 (4)	11.25	9.50

Squares of dots obliterate the original denominations on Nos. 94-95.

Great Britain Nos. 309-311 Surcharged "BAHRAIN" and New Value in Black

1955 Wmk. 308 Engr. *Perf. 11x12*

No.	Type	Description	Unused	Used
96	A133	2r on 2sh6p dk brn	3.00	1.25
97	A133	5r on 5sh crimson	9.50	3.50
98	A133	10r on 10sh brt ultra	20.00	5.00
		Nos. 96-98 (3)	32.50	9.75

Three slightly different types of surcharge are found on the 2r; two on 5r and 10r.

Great Britain Nos. 317, 323, 325, 332-333 Surcharged "BAHRAIN" and New Value

Perf. 14½x14

1956-57 Wmk. 308 Photo.

No.	Type	Description	Unused	Used
99	A126	½a on ½p red org	.20	.20
100	A128	4a on 4p ultra	5.00	13.00
101	A129	6a on 6p lil rose	.45	.40
102	A132	12a on 1sh3p dk green	6.75	8.50
103	A131	1r on 1sh6p dk bl ('57)	7.50	.20
		Nos. 99-103 (5)	19.90	22.30

Great Britain Nos. 317-325, 328, 332 Surcharged "BAHRAIN" and New Value

1957, Apr. 1

No.	Type	Description	Unused	Used
104	A129	1np on 5p lt brown	.20	.20
105	A126	3np on ½p red org	.25	1.10
106	A126	6np on 1p ultra	.25	1.10
107	A126	9np on 1½p green	.25	1.10
108	A126	12np on 2p red brn	.30	.40
109	A127	15np on 2½p scar, type I	.35	.20
a.		Type II	.40	1.25
110	A127	20np on 3p dk pur	.25	.20
111	A128	25np on 4p ultra	.65	1.25
112	A129	40np on 6p lil rose	.65	.20
113	A130	50np on 9p dp ol grn	3.00	2.75
114	A132	75np on 1sh3p dk grn	1.75	.30
		Nos. 104-114 (11)	7.90	8.80

The arrangement of the surcharge varies on different values: there are three bars through value on No. 113.

Jubilee Jamboree Issue

Great Britain Nos. 334-336 Surcharged "BAHRAIN," New Value and Square of Dots in Black

Perf. 14½x14

1957, Aug. 1 Photo. Wmk. 308

No.	Type	Description	Unused	Used
115	A138	15np on 2½p scar	.20	.30
116	A138	25np on 4p ultra	.30	.30
117	A138	75np on 1sh3p dk grn	.40	.40
		Nos. 115-117 (3)	.90	1.00

Great Britain No. 357 Surcharged "BAHRAIN/ NP 15 NP" in Black

1960 Wmk. 322 *Perf. 14½x14*

No.	Type	Description	Unused	Used
118	A127	15np on 2½p scar, type II	3.00	9.00

A1

Sheik Sulman bin Hamad Al Khalifah — A2

Perf. 14½x14

1960, July 1 Photo. Unwmk.

119	A1	5np lt ultra	.20	.20
120	A1	15np orange	.20	.20
121	A1	20np lt violet	.20	.20
122	A1	30np olive bister	.20	.20
123	A1	40np gray	.20	.20
124	A1	50np emerald	.20	.20
125	A1	75np red brown	.30	.20

Engr.

Perf. 13x13½

126	A2	1r gray	1.50	.25
127	A2	2r carmine	2.75	1.60
128	A2	5r ultra	4.50	2.25
129	A2	10r olive green	11.00	3.50
		Nos. 119-129 (11)	21.25	9.00

Sheik Isa bin Sulman Al Khalifah A3

Bahrain Airport A4

Designs: 5r, 10r, Deep water jetty.

1964, Feb. 22 Photo. *Perf. 14½x14*

130	A3	5np ultra	.20	.20
131	A3	15np orange	.20	.20
132	A3	20np brt purple	.20	.20
133	A3	30np brown olive	.20	.20
134	A3	40np slate	.20	.20
135	A3	50np emerald	.30	.20
136	A3	75np chestnut	.60	.25

Engr.

Perf. 13½x13

137	A4	1r black	4.00	1.00
138	A4	2r rose red	6.00	1.00
139	A4	5r violet blue	9.00	6.00
140	A4	10r dull green	11.00	6.00
		Nos. 130-140 (11)	31.90	15.45

Bahrain Postal Administration

Sheik Isa bin Sulman Al Khalifah — A5

Sheik and Bahrain International Airport — A6

Pearl Divers — A7

Bab al Bahrain, Suq Al-Khamis Mosque, Sheik, Emblem, etc. — A8

Designs: 50f, 75f, Pier, Mina Sulman harbor. 200f, Falcon and horse race. 500f, "Hospitality," pouring coffee and Sheik's Palace.

Perf. 14½x14

1966, Jan. 1 Photo. Unwmk.

141	A5	5f green	.20	.20
142	A5	10f dark red	.20	.20
143	A5	15f ultra	.20	.20
144	A5	20f magenta	.20	.20

Perf. 13½x14

145	A6	30f green & black	.20	.20
146	A6	40f blue & black	.30	.20
147	A6	50f dp car rose & blk	.40	.20
148	A6	75f violet & black	.50	.25

Perf. 14½x14

149	A7	100f dk blue & yel	1.75	.75
150	A7	200f dk green & org	7.75	1.50
151	A7	500f red brown & yel	5.75	2.50
152	A8	1d multicolored	11.00	6.00
		Nos. 141-152 (12)	28.45	12.40

Produce, Date Palm, Ship, Truck and Plane — A9

Map of Bahrain and WHO Emblem — A10

1966, Mar. 28 Litho. *Perf. 13x13½*

153	A9	10f red & blue green	.30	.30
154	A9	20f green & vio	.65	.65
155	A9	40f olive bis & lt bl	1.25	1.25
156	A9	200f vio blue & pink	6.25	6.25
		Nos. 153-156 (4)	8.45	8.45

6th Bahrain Trade Fair & Agricultural Show.

1968, June Unwmk. *Perf. 13½x14*

157	A10	20f gray & black	.50	.50
158	A10	40f blue grn & black	2.00	1.40
159	A10	150f dp rose & black	7.50	5.50
		Nos. 157-159 (3)	10.00	7.40

20th anniv. of the WHO.

Isa Town A11

1968, Nov. 18 Litho. *Perf. 14½*

160	A11	50f shown	1.60	1.60
161	A11	80f Market	2.50	2.50
162	A11	120f Stadium	4.25	4.25
163	A11	150f Mosque	6.75	6.75
		Nos. 160-163 (4)	15.10	15.10

Education Symbol — A12

1969, Apr. Litho. *Perf. 13*

164	A12	40f multicolored	1.25	1.25
165	A12	60f multicolored	2.50	2.00
166	A12	150f multicolored	6.25	4.25
		Nos. 164-166 (3)	10.00	7.50

50th anniversary of education in Bahrain.

Map of Arabian Gulf, Radar and Emblem A13

Designs: 40f, 150f, Radar installation and emblem of Cable & Wireless Ltd., vert.

Perf. 14x13½, 13½x14

1969, July 14 Litho.

167	A13	20f lt green & multi	1.75	1.00
168	A13	40f vio blue & multi	3.75	2.25
169	A13	100f ocher & multi	8.50	5.25
170	A13	150f rose lilac & multi	13.50	9.00
		Nos. 167-170 (4)	27.50	17.50

Opening of the satellite earth station (connected through the Indian Ocean satellite Intelsat III) at Ras Abu Jarjur, July 14.

Municipal Building, Arms and Map of Bahrain A14

1970, Feb. 23 Litho. *Perf. 12x12½*

171	A14	30f blue & multi	2.75	2.75
172	A14	150f multicolored	10.00	10.00

2nd Conf. of the Arab Cities' Org.

Copper Bull's Head A15

Conf. Emblem and: 80f, Gateway to Qalat al Bahrain, 7th cent. B.C. 120f, Aerial view of grave mounds, Bahrain. 150f, Dilmun seal, 2000 B.C.

1970, Mar. 1 Photo. *Perf. 14½*

173	A15	60f multicolored	3.50	2.00
174	A15	80f multicolored	5.00	2.25
175	A15	120f multicolored	6.50	3.50
176	A15	150f multicolored	8.00	4.25
		Nos. 173-176 (4)	23.00	12.00

3rd Intl. Asian Archaeological Conf., Bahrain.

Vickers VC 10, Big Ben and Minaret A16

1970, Apr. 5 Litho. *Perf. 14½x14*

177	A16	30f multicolored	1.40	.85
178	A16	60f multicolored	3.00	1.90
179	A16	120f multicolored	5.50	6.25
		Nos. 177-179 (3)	9.90	9.00

1st flight to London from the Arabian Gulf Area by Gulf Aviation Company.

Intl. Education Year Emblem A17

120f, Education Year emblem & students.

1970, Nov. 1 Litho. *Perf. 14½x14*

180	A17	60f blk, blue & org	3.00	3.00
181	A17	120f multicolored	6.00	6.00

Independent State

Government House, Manama — A18

UN Emblem and Sails — A19

Designs: 30f, "Freedom" with dove and torch, and globe. 120f, 150f, Bahrain coat of arms.

1971, Oct. 2 Photo. *Perf. 14½x14*

182	A18	30f gold & multi	1.60	1.60
183	A18	60f gold & multi	3.25	3.25
184	A18	120f gold & multi	6.50	6.50
185	A18	150f gold & multi	8.25	8.25
		Nos. 182-185 (4)	19.60	19.60

Declaration of Bahrain independence, Aug. 15, 1971.

Perf. 14x14½, 14½x14

1972, Feb. 1 Litho.

30f, 60f, Dhow with sails showing UN and Arab League emblems, horiz. 150f, as 120f.

186	A19	30f multicolored	4.50	4.50
187	A19	60f red, gray & multi	7.75	7.75
188	A19	120f dull blue & multi	10.00	10.00
189	A19	150f multicolored	19.00	19.00
		Nos. 186-189 (4)	41.25	41.25

Bahrain's admission to the Arab League and the United Nations.

"Your Heart is your Health" — A20

1972, Apr. 7 Litho. *Perf. 14½x14*

190	A20	30f black & multi	3.75	3.75
191	A20	60f gray & multi	7.50	7.50

World Health Day.

UN and FAO Emblems A21

1973, May 12 Litho. *Perf. 12½x13*

192 A21 30f org red, pur & grn 3.75 3.75
193 A21 60f ocher, brn & grn 6.50 6.50

World Food Programs, 10th anniversary.

People of Various Races, Human Rights Flame — A22

1973, Nov. Litho. *Perf. 14x14½*

194 A22 30f blue, blk & brn 4.00 4.00
195 A22 60f lake, blk & brn 7.75 7.75

25th anniversary of the Universal Declaration of Human Rights.

Flour Mill A23

60f, Intl. Airport. 120f, Sulmaniya Medical Center. 150f, ALBA aluminum smelting plant.

1973, Dec. 16 Photo. *Perf. 14½*

196 A23 30f multicolored 1.00 1.00
197 A23 60f multicolored 1.75 1.75
198 A23 120f multicolored 3.50 3.50
199 A23 150f multicolored 4.25 4.25
Nos. 196-199 (4) 10.50 10.50

National Day.

Letters and UPU Emblem — A24

Carrier Pigeon and UPU Emblem A25

60f, UPU emblem & letters. 150f, Like 120f.

1974, Feb. 4 Litho. *Perf. 13½*

200 A24 30f blue & multi 1.00 1.00
201 A24 60f emerald & multi 1.75 1.75

Perf. 12½x13½

202 A25 120f ultra & multi 3.00 3.00
203 A25 150f yellow & multi 4.25 4.25
Nos. 200-203 (4) 10.00 10.00

Bahrain's admission to UPU.

Traffic Signals — A26

1974, May 4 Litho. *Perf. 14½*

204 A26 30f org brown & multi 2.75 2.75
205 A26 60f brt blue & multi 6.25 6.25

International Traffic Day.

Jet, Globe, Mail Coach and UPU Emblem — A27

1974, Sept. 1 Photo. *Perf. 14x14½*

206 A27 30f multicolored .75 .75
207 A27 60f multicolored 1.50 1.50
208 A27 120f multicolored 3.25 3.25
209 A27 150f multicolored 4.00 4.00
Nos. 206-209 (4) 9.50 9.50

Centenary of Universal Postal Union.

National Day Emblem, Sitra Power Station — A28

National Day: 120f, 150f, Bahrain dry dock.

1974, Dec. 16 Litho. *Perf. 14½*

210 A28 30f blue & multi .85 .85
211 A28 60f green & multi 1.40 1.40
212 A28 120f lil rose & multi 3.50 3.50
213 A28 150f ver & multi 4.25 4.25
Nos. 210-213 (4) 10.00 10.00

Woman's Silk Gown — A29

Photo.; Gold Embossed

1975, Feb. 1 *Perf. 14½x14*

Design: Various women's costumes.

214 A29 30f blue grn & multi .65 .65
215 A29 60f vio blue & multi 1.10 1.10
216 A29 120f rose red & multi 2.75 2.75
217 A29 150f multicolored 3.50 3.50
Nos. 214-217 (4) 8.00 8.00

Pendant — A30

Designs: Various jewelry.

1975, Apr. 1 Photo. *Perf. 14½x14*

218 A30 30f olive & multi .60 .60
219 A30 60f dp pur & multi 1.40 1.40
220 A30 120f dp car & multi 2.75 2.75
221 A30 150f dp blue & multi 3.50 3.50
Nos. 218-221 (4) 8.25 8.25

Woman Planting Flower, IWY Emblem — A31

1975, July 28 Litho. *Perf. 14½*

60f, Educated woman holding IWY emblem.

222 A31 30f multicolored 1.50 1.50
223 A31 60f multicolored 3.50 3.50

International Women's Year.

Miniature Sheet

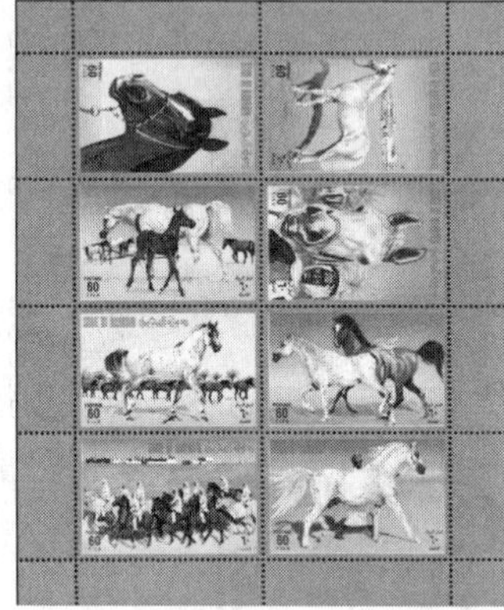

Arabian Stallion — A32

Arabian horses: a, Brown head. b, White mare. c, Mare and foal. d, White head. e, White mare. f, Mare and stallion. g, Bedouins on horseback. #224a, 224b, 224d are vert.

Perf. 14x14½, 14½x14

1975, Sept. 1 Photo.

224 Sheet of 8 52.50 32.50
a.-h. A32 60f any single 5.25 3.50

Flag of Bahrain — A33

Map of Bahrain — A34

Sheik Isa — A35

1976-80 Litho. *Perf. 14½*

225 A33 5f red & ultra .20 .20
226 A33 10f red & green .20 .20
227 A33 15f red & black .20 .20
228 A33 20f red & brown .30 .20
228A A34 25f gray & blk ('79) .40 .20
229 A34 40f blue & black .40 .25
229A A34 50f yel grn & blk ('79) .40 .30
230 A34 60f dl grn & blk ('77) .65 .35
231 A34 80f rose lil & blk 1.00 .45
232 A34 100f lt red brn & blk ('77) 1.00 .55
233 A34 150f org & black 1.90 .85
234 A34 200f yel & black 2.25 1.10

Engr.

Perf. 12x12½

235 A35 300f lt grn & grn 3.25 1.60
236 A35 400f pink & red brn 4.25 2.25
237 A35 500f lt bl & dk bl 5.25 2.75
238 A35 1d gray & sepia 9.50 5.00
239 A35 2d rose & vio ('80) 18.00 9.25
240 A35 3d buff & brn ('80) 27.50 14.00
Nos. 225-240 (18) 76.65 39.70

A later printing of the 100f-200f, and possibly others, has a larger printer's imprint at bottom.

Concorde at London Airport — A36

#245, Concorde at Bahrain Airport. #246, Concorde over London to Bahrain map. #247, Concorde on runway at night.

1976, Jan. 22 Photo. *Perf. 13x14*

244 A36 80f gold & multi 2.25 2.25
245 A36 80f gold & multi 2.25 2.25
246 A36 80f gold & multi 2.25 2.25
247 A36 80f gold & multi 2.25 2.25
a. Souvenir sheet of 4 10.00 10.00
b. Block of 4, #244-247 9.00 9.00

1st commercial flight of supersonic jet Concorde, London to Bahrain, Jan. 21. No. 247a contains 4 stamps with simulated perfs.

Soldier, Flag and Arms of Bahrain — A37

1976, Feb. 5 Litho. *Perf. 14½*

248 A37 40f yellow & multi 3.50 3.50
249 A37 80f lt blue & multi 6.50 6.50

Defense Force Day.

Sheik Isa, King Khalid, Bahrain and Saudi Flags A38

1976, Mar. 23 Litho. *Perf. 14½*

250 A38 40f gold & multi 1.75 1.75
251 A38 80f silver & multi 3.00 3.00

Visit of King Khalid of Saudi Arabia.

New Housing, Housing Ministry's Seal — A39

1976, Dec. 16 Litho. *Perf. 14½*

252 A39 40f rose & multi 1.60 1.60
253 A39 80f blue & multi 3.25 3.25

National Day.

APU Emblem A40

1977, Apr. 12 Litho. *Perf. 14½*
254 A40 40f silver & multi 1.50 1.50
255 A40 80f rose & multi 3.00 3.00

Arab Postal Union, 25th anniversary.

Miniature Sheet

Dogs on Beach and Dhow A41

Saluki dogs: b, Dog and camels. c, Dog and gazelles. d, Dog and Ruler's Palace. e, Dog's head. f, Heads of two dogs. g, Dog in dunes. h, Playing dogs.

1977, July Photo. *Perf. 14x14½*
256 Sheet of 8 28.00 28.00
a.-h. A41 80f any single 2.75 2.75

Students and Candle A42

1977, Sept. 8 Litho. *Perf. 14½*
257 A42 40f multicolored 1.50 1.50
258 A42 80f multicolored 30.00 30.00

International Literacy Day.

Shipyard and Flags A43

1977, Dec. 16 Litho. *Perf. 14½*
259 A43 40f multicolored 1.50 1.50
260 A43 80f multicolored 3.00 3.00

Inauguration of Arab Shipbuilding and Repair Yard Co.

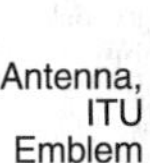

Antenna, ITU Emblem A44

1978, May 17 Litho. *Perf. 14½*
261 A44 40f yellow & multi 1.50 1.50
262 A44 80f silver & multi 3.00 3.00

10th World Telecommunications Day.

Ghanja Dhow — A45

Dhows of the Arabian Gulf. #267-270 vertical.

Perf. 14x14½, 14½x14
1979, June 16 Photo.
263 A45 100f shown 5.50 5.50
264 A45 100f Zarook 5.50 5.50
265 A45 100f Shu'ai 5.50 5.50
266 A45 100f Jaliboot 5.50 5.50
267 A45 100f Baghla 5.50 5.50
268 A45 100f Sambuk 5.50 5.50
269 A45 100f Boom 5.50 5.50
270 A45 100f Kotia 5.50 5.50
a. Block of 8, #263-270 67.50 67.50

Learning to Walk — A46

IYC Emblem and: 100f, Hands surrounding girl, UN emblem.

1979 Litho. *Perf. 14½*
271 A46 50f multicolored 1.50 1.50
272 A46 100f multicolored 3.00 3.00

International Year of the Child.

Hegira, 1,500th Anniv. — A47

1980 Photo. *Perf. 13x13½*
273 A47 50f multicolored .65 .65
274 A47 100f multicolored 1.25 1.25
a. Miniature sheet of 1 6.00 6.00
275 A47 150f multicolored 2.00 2.00
276 A47 200f multicolored 2.75 2.75
Nos. 273-276 (4) 6.65 6.65

Falcon A48

Designs: Falcons.

Perf. 13½x14, 14x13½
1980, Nov. 1 Photo.
277 Block of 8 17.50 15.00
a.-h. A48 100f any single 1.75 1.75

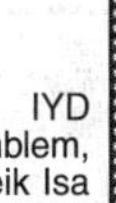

IYD Emblem, Sheik Isa A49

1981, Mar. 21 Litho. *Perf. 14½*
278 A49 50f multicolored 1.60 1.60
279 A49 100f multicolored 3.25 3.25

International Year of the Disabled.

50th Anniversary of Electricity in Bahrain — A50

1981, Apr. 26 Litho. *Perf. 14½*
280 A50 50f multicolored 1.50 1.50
281 A50 100f multicolored 2.75 2.75

Stone Cutting — A51

1981, July 1 Photo. *Perf. 14x13½*
282 A51 50f shown .75 .75
283 A51 100f Pottery 1.25 1.25
284 A51 150f Weaving 2.75 2.75
285 A51 200f Basket making 3.00 3.00
Nos. 282-285 (4) 7.75 7.75

Hegira (Pilgrimage Year) — A52

Designs: Various mosques.

1981, Oct. 1 Photo. *Perf. 14x13½*
286 A52 50f multicolored .80 .80
287 A52 100f multicolored 1.60 1.60
288 A52 150f multicolored 2.25 2.25
289 A52 200f multicolored 3.25 3.25
Nos. 286-289 (4) 7.90 7.90

Sheik Isa, 20th Anniv. of Coronation A53

1981, Dec. 16 Photo. *Perf. 14x13½*
290 A53 15f multicolored .45 .45
291 A53 50f multicolored .90 .90
292 A53 100f multicolored 1.50 1.50
293 A53 150f multicolored 2.40 2.40
294 A53 200f multicolored 2.75 2.75
Nos. 290-294 (5) 8.00 8.00

Wildlife in al Areen Park — A54

Designs: a, Gazelle. b, Oryx. c, Dhub lizard. d, Arabian hares. e, Oryxes. f, Reems.

1982, Mar. 1 Photo. *Perf. 13½x14*
295 Sheet of 6 14.00 14.00
a.-f. A54 100f any single 2.25 2.25

3rd Session of Gulf Supreme Council, Nov. — A55

1982, Nov. 9 Litho. *Perf. 14½*
296 A55 50f blue & multi .85 .85
297 A55 100f green & multi 2.25 2.25

Opening of Madinat Hamad Housing Development — A56

1983, Dec. 1 Litho. *Perf. 14½*
298 A56 50f multicolored 1.00 1.00
299 A56 100f multicolored 2.75 2.75

Al Khalifa Dynasty Bicentenary — A57

Sheiks or Emblems: a, 500fr, Isa bin Sulman. b, Emblem (tan & multi). c, Isa bin Ali, 1869-1932. d, Hamad bin Isa, 1932-42. e, Sulman bin Hamad, 1942-61. f, Emblem (pale green & multi). g, Emblem (lemon & multi). h, Emblem (light blue & multi). i, Emblem (gray & multi).

1983, Dec. 16 Litho. *Perf. 14½*
300 Sheet of 9 8.50 8.50
a.-i. A57 100f any single .80 .80

Souvenir Sheet

301 A57 500f multicolored 8.50 8.50

No. 301 contains one stamp 60x38mm.

Gulf Co-operation Council Traffic Week — A58

1984, Apr. 30 Litho. *Perf. 14½*
302 A58 15f multicolored .30 .30
303 A58 50f multicolored 1.00 1.00
304 A58 100f multicolored 2.00 2.00
Nos. 302-304 (3) 3.30 3.30

1984 Summer Olympics A59

1984, Sept. 15 *Perf. 14½*
305 A59 15f Hurdles .25 .25
306 A59 50f Equestrian .80 .80
307 A59 100f Diving 1.60 1.60
308 A59 150f Fencing 2.00 2.00
309 A59 200f Shooting 3.50 3.50
Nos. 305-309 (5) 8.15 8.15

Postal Service Cent. A60

1984, Dec. 8 Photo. *Perf. 12x11½*
310 A60 15f multicolored .40 .40
311 A60 50f multicolored 1.25 1.25
312 A60 100f multicolored 2.25 2.25
Nos. 310-312 (3) 3.90 3.90

Miniature Sheet

Coastal Fish — A61

1985, Feb. 10 Photo. *Perf. 13½x14*

313 Sheet of 10 10.00 10.00
a.-j. A61 100f any single 1.25 1.25

1st Arab Gulf States Week for Social Work A62

1985, Oct. 15 Litho. *Perf. 14½*

314 A62 15f multicolored .25 .25
315 A62 50f multicolored .85 .85
316 A62 100f multicolored 1.90 1.90
Nos. 314-316 (3) 3.00 3.00

Intl. Youth Year A63

1985, Nov. 16

317 A63 15f multicolored .25 .25
318 A63 50f multicolored .85 .85
319 A63 100f multicolored 1.90 1.90
Nos. 317-319 (3) 3.00 3.00

Bahrain-Saudi Arabia Causeway Opening — A64

1986, Nov. Litho. *Perf. 14½*

320 A64 15f Causeway, aerial view .30 .30
321 A64 50f Island .80 .80
322 A64 100f Causeway 1.40 1.40
Nos. 320-322 (3) 2.50 2.50

Sheik Isa, 25th Anniv. as the Emir — A65

1986, Dec. 16

323 A65 15f multicolored .30 .30
324 A65 50f multicolored .80 .80
325 A65 100f multicolored 1.40 1.40
a. Souvenir sheet of 3, #323-325 6.00 5.50
Nos. 323-325 (3) 2.50 2.50

WHO, 40th Anniv. A66

1988, Apr. 30 Litho. *Perf. 14½*

326 A66 50f multicolored .50 .50
327 A66 150f multicolored 1.40 1.40

Opening of Ahmed Al Fateh Islamic Center A67

1988, June 2 Litho. *Perf. 14½*

328 A67 50f multicolored .50 .50
329 A67 150f multicolored 1.40 1.40

1988 Summer Olympics, Seoul — A68

1988, Sept. 17 Litho. *Perf. 14½*

330 A68 50f Running .25 .25
331 A68 80f Equestrian .45 .45
332 A68 150f Fencing .80 .80
333 A68 200f Soccer 1.50 1.50
Nos. 330-333 (4) 3.00 3.00

Gulf Cooperation Council Supreme Council 9th Regular Session, Bahrain — A69

1988, Dec. 19 Litho. *Perf. 14½*

334 A69 50f multicolored .50 .50
335 A69 150f multicolored 1.40 1.40

Miniature Sheets

Camels — A70

No. 336: a, Close-up of head, rider in background. b, Camel kneeling at rest. c, Two adults, calf. d, Three adults. e, Camel facing right. f, Mount and rider (facing left).

No. 337: a, Man walking in front of camel, oil well. b, Man walking in front of camel. c, Oil well, camel's head. d, Mount and rider (facing forward). e, Mount and rider (facing right). f, Two dromedaries at a run.

Nos. 337a-337f vert.

Perf. 13½x14, 14x13½

1989, June 15

336 Sheet of 6 6.00 6.00
a.-f. A70 150f any single 1.00 1.00
337 Sheet of 6 6.00 6.00
a.-f. A70 150f any single 1.00 1.00

Sheik Isa — A71

1989, Dec. 16 Litho. *Perf. 13½x14*

338 A71 25f multicolored .20 .20
339 A71 40f multicolored .25 .25
340 A71 50f multicolored .30 .30
341 A71 60f multicolored .35 .35
342 A71 75f multicolored .45 .45
343 A71 80f multicolored .50 .50
344 A71 100f multicolored .60 .60
345 A71 120f multicolored .75 .75
346 A71 150f multicolored .85 .85
347 A71 200f multicolored 1.25 1.25
a. Souv. sheet of 10, #338-347 5.50 5.50
Nos. 338-347 (10) 5.50 5.50

Houbara (Bustard) — A72

Designs: a, Two birds facing right. b, Two birds facing each other. c, Chicks. d, Adult, chick. e, Adult, facing right, vert. f, In flight. g, Adult facing right. h, Chick, facing left, vert. i, Adult facing left. j, Adult male, close-up. k, Courtship display. l, Two birds facing left.

1990, Feb. 17 Photo. *Perf. 14*

348 Sheet of 12 10.00 10.00
a.-l. A72 150f any single .85 .85

Gulf Air, 40th Anniv. A73

1990, Mar. 24 Litho. *Perf. 14½*

360 A73 50f multicolored .30 .30
361 A73 80f multicolored .50 .50
362 A73 150f multicolored .95 .95
363 A73 200f multicolored 1.25 1.25
Nos. 360-363 (4) 3.00 3.00

Chamber of Commerce, 50th Anniv. — A74

1990, May 26

364 A74 50f multicolored .30 .30
365 A74 80f multicolored .50 .50
366 A74 150f multicolored .95 .95
367 A74 200f multicolored 1.25 1.25
Nos. 364-367 (4) 3.00 3.00

Intl. Literacy Year A75

1990, Sept. 8 Litho. *Perf. 14½*

368 A75 50f multicolored .30 .30
369 A75 80f multicolored .50 .50
370 A75 150f multicolored .95 .95
371 A75 200f multicolored 1.25 1.25
Nos. 368-371 (4) 3.00 3.00

Miniature Sheet

Indigenous Birds — A76

a, Galerida cristata. b, Upupa epops. c, Pycnonotus leucogenys. d, Streptopelia turtur. e, Streptopelia decaocto. f, Falco tinnunculus. g, Passer domesticus, horiz. h, Lanius excubitor, horiz. i, Psittacula krameri.

1991, Sept. 15 Litho. *Perf. 14½*

372 Sheet of 9 9.00 9.00
a.-i. A76 150f any single 1.10 1.10

See Nos. 382, 407.

Coronation of Sheik Isa, 30th Anniv. — A77

Design: Nos. 374, 376, 378, 380, 381a, Portrait at left, leaves.

Litho. & Embossed

1991, Dec. 16 *Perf. 14½*

373 A77 50f multicolored .35 .35
374 A77 50f multicolored .35 .35
375 A77 80f multicolored .55 .55
376 A77 80f multicolored .55 .55
377 A77 150f multicolored 1.10 1.10
378 A77 150f multicolored 1.10 1.10
379 A77 200f multicolored 1.50 1.50
380 A77 200f multicolored 1.50 1.50
Nos. 373-380 (8) 7.00 7.00

Souvenir Sheet

Perf. 14x14½

381 Sheet of 2 7.00 7.00
a.-b. A77 500f any single 3.50 3.50

No. 381 contains 41x31mm stamps.

Indigenous Birds Type of 1991

Miniature Sheet

#382: a, Ciconia ciconia. b, Merops apiaster. c, Sturnus vulgaris. d, Hypocolius ampelinus. e, Cuculus canorus. f, Turdus viscivorus. g, Coracias garrulus. h, Carduelis carduelis. i, Lanius collurio. j, Turdus iliacus, horiz. k, Motacilla alba, horiz. l, Oriolus oriolus, horiz. m, Erithacus rubecula. n, Luscinia luscinia. o, Muscicapa striata. p, Hirundo rustica.

1992, Mar. 21 Litho. *Perf. 14½*

382 Sheet of 16 13.50 13.50
a.-p. A76 150f any single .80 .80

Miniature Sheet

Horse Racing A78

Designs: No. 383a, Horses leaving starting gate. b, Trainers leading horses. c, Horses racing around turn. d, Horses in stretch racing by flags. e, Two horses racing by grandstand. f, Five horses galloping. g, Two brown horses racing. h, Black horse, gray horse racing.

1992, May 22

383 Sheet of 8 7.25 7.25
a.-h. A78 150f any single .90 .90

1992 Summer Olympics, Barcelona — A79

1992, July 25 Litho. *Perf. 14½*

384 A79 50f Equestrian .30 .30
385 A79 80f Running .55 .55
386 A79 150f Judo 1.00 1.00
387 A79 200f Cycling 1.40 1.40
Nos. 384-387 (4) 3.25 3.25

Bahrain Intl. Airport, 60th Anniv. A80

1992, Oct. 27 Litho. *Perf. 14½*

388 A80 50f multicolored	.30	.30
389 A80 80f multicolored	.55	.55
390 A80 150f multicolored	1.00	1.00
391 A80 200f multicolored	1.40	1.40
Nos. 388-391 (4)	3.25	3.25

Children's Art — A81

Designs: 50f, Girl jumping rope, vert. 80f, Women in traditional dress, vert. 150f, Women stirring kettle. 200f, Fishermen.

1992, Nov. 28 Litho. *Perf. 14½*

392 A81 50f multicolored	.30	.30
393 A81 80f multicolored	.55	.55
394 A81 150f multicolored	1.00	1.00
395 A81 200f multicolored	1.40	1.40
Nos. 392-395 (4)	3.25	3.25

Inauguration of Expansion of Aluminum Bahrain — A82

50f, Ore funicular. 80f, Smelting pot. 150f, Mill. 200f, Cylindrical aluminum ingots.

1992, Dec. 16

396 A82 50f multicolored	.30	.30
397 A82 80f multicolored	.55	.55
398 A82 150f multicolored	1.00	1.00
399 A82 200f multicolored	1.40	1.40
Nos. 396-399 (4)	3.25	3.25

Bahrain Defense Force, 25th Anniv. A83

Designs: 50f, Artillery forces, vert. 80f, Fighters, tanks, and ship, vert. 150f, Frigate. 200f, Jet fighter.

Perf. 13½x13, 13x13½

1993, Feb. 5 Litho.

400 A83 50f multicolored	.30	.30
401 A83 80f multicolored	.50	.50
402 A83 150f multicolored	.95	.95
403 A83 200f multicolored	1.25	1.25
Nos. 400-403 (4)	3.00	3.00

World Meteorology Day — A84

Designs: 50f, Satellite image of Bahrain, vert. 150f, Infrared satellite map of world. 200f, Earth, seen from space, vert.

1993, Mar. 23 Litho. *Perf. 14½*

404 A84 50f multicolored	.40	.40
405 A84 150f multicolored	1.00	1.00
406 A84 200f multicolored	1.60	1.60
Nos. 404-406 (3)	3.00	3.00

Bird Type of 1991

Miniature Sheet

Designs: a, Ardea purpurea. b, Gallinula chloropus. c, Phalacrocorax nigrogularis. d, Dromas ardeola. e, Alcedo atthis. f, Vanellus vanellus. g, Haematopus ostralegus, horiz. h, Nycticorax nycticorax. i, Sterna caspia, horiz. j, Arenaria interpres, horiz. k, Rallus aquaticus, horiz. l, Anas platyrhychos, horia. m, Larus fuscus, horiz.

1993, May 22 Litho. *Perf. 14½*

407 Sheet of 13 + 2 labels	12.50	12.50
a.-m. A76 150f any single	1.00	1.00

Gazella Subgutturosa Marica — A85

1993, July 24 Litho. *Perf. 14½*

408 A85 25f Calf	.55	.55
409 A85 50f Female standing	1.10	1.10
410 A85 50f Female walking	1.10	1.10
411 A85 150f Male	3.25	3.25
Nos. 408-411 (4)	6.00	6.00

World Wildlife Federation.

Wild Flowers — A86

Designs: a, Lycium shawii. b, Alhagi maurorum. c, Caparis spinosa. d, Cistanche phelypae. e, Asphodelus tenuifolius. f, Limonium axillare. g, Cynomorium coccineum. h, Calligonum polygonoides.

1993, Oct. 16 Litho. *Perf. 13½x13*

412 A86 150f Sheet of 8, #a.-h.	6.50	6.50

A87

1994, Jan. 22 Litho. *Perf. 14½*

Background Color

413 A87 50f yellow	.30	.30
414 A87 80f blue green	.50	.50
415 A87 150f purple	.95	.95
416 A87 200f blue	1.25	1.25
Nos. 413-416 (4)	3.00	3.00

Intl. Year of the Family.

A88

Butterflies: No. 417a, Lepidochrysops arabicus. b, Ypthima bolanica. c, Eurema brigitta. d, Precis limnoria. e, Aglais urticae. f, Colotis protomedia. g, Salamis anacardii. h, Byblia ilithyia.

No. 418a, Papilio machaon. b, Agrodiaetus loewii. c, Vanessa cardui. d, Papilio demoleus. e, Hamanumida daedalus. f, Funonia orithya. g, Funonia chorimine. h, Colias croceus.

Perf. 13½x13, 13x13½

1994, Mar. 21 Litho.

417 A88 50f Sheet of 8, #a.-h.	2.50	2.50
418 A88 150f Sheet of 8, #a.-h.	7.50	7.50

No. 418 is horiz.

A89

1994, May 8 Litho. *Perf. 14½*

419 A89 50f lilac & multi	.30	.30
420 A89 80f yellow & multi	.50	.50
421 A89 150f salmon & multi	.95	.95
422 A89 200f green blue & multi	1.25	1.25
Nos. 419-422 (4)	3.00	3.00

Intl. Red Cross & Red Crescent Societies, 75th anniv.

1994 World Cup Soccer Championships, US — A90

Designs: 50f, Goalkeeper. 80f, Heading ball. 150f, Dribbling ball. 200f, Slide tackle.

1994, June 17 Litho. *Perf. 14*

423 A90 50f multicolored	.30	.30
424 A90 80f multicolored	.50	.50
425 A90 150f multicolored	.95	.95
426 A90 200f multicolored	1.25	1.25
Nos. 423-426 (4)	3.00	3.00

Bahrain's First Satellite Earth Station, 25th Anniv. — A91

1994, July 14

427 A91 50f blue & multi	.30	.30
428 A91 80f yellow & multi	.50	.50
429 A91 150f violet & multi	.95	.95
430 A91 200f pink, yellow & multi	1.25	1.25
Nos. 427-430 (4)	3.00	3.00

Education in Bahrain, 75th Anniv. — A92

1994, Nov. 19 Litho. *Perf. 14½*

431 A92 50f yellow & multi	.30	.30
432 A92 80f buff & multi	.50	.50
433 A92 150f salmon & multi	.95	.95
434 A92 200f pink & multi	1.25	1.25
Nos. 431-434 (4)	3.00	3.00

Gulf Cooperation Council Supreme Council, 15th Regular Session, Bahrain — A93

1994, Dec. 19 *Perf. 14*

435 A93 50f blue green & multi	.30	.30
436 A93 80f brown & multi	.50	.50
437 A93 150f lilac rose & multi	.95	.95
438 A93 200f blue & multi	1.25	1.25
Nos. 435-438 (4)	3.00	3.00

Date Palm A94

Designs: 80f, Flowering stage. 100f, Dates beginning to ripen. 200f, Dates up close. 250f, Trees from distance.

500f, Pitcher, basket of dates.

1995, Mar. 21 Litho. *Perf. 14*

439 A94 80f multicolored	.50	.50
440 A94 100f multicolored	.60	.60
441 A94 200f multicolored	1.25	1.25
442 A94 250f multicolored	1.50	1.50
Nos. 439-442 (4)	3.85	3.85

Souvenir Sheet

443 A94 500f multicolored	3.00	3.00

No. 443 contains one 65x48mm stamp.

Fight Against Polio A95

1995, Apr. 22 Litho. *Perf. 13x13½*

444 A95 80f pink & multi	.40	.40
445 A95 200f blue & multi	1.00	1.00
446 A95 250f lt brown & multi	1.40	1.40
Nos. 444-446 (3)	2.80	2.80

World Health Day.

1st Natl. Industries Exhibition A96

1995, May 15

447 A96 80f blue green & multi	.40	.40
448 A96 200f lilac & multi	1.00	1.00
449 A96 250f lt brown & multi	1.40	1.40
Nos. 447-449 (3)	2.80	2.80

FAO, 50th Anniv. A97

Fields of various crops.

1995, June 17 Litho. *Perf. 14*

450 A97 80f lilac & multi	.40	.40
451 A97 200f blue & multi	1.00	1.00
452 A97 250f lt pink & multi	1.40	1.40
Nos. 450-452 (3)	2.80	2.80

Arab League, 50th Anniv. — A98

1995, Sept. 14 Litho. *Perf. 14½*

453 A98	80f pink & multi	.40	.40
454 A98	200f blue & multi	1.10	1.10
455 A98	250f yellow & multi	1.40	1.40
	Nos. 453-455 (3)	2.90	2.90

UN, 50th Anniv. A99

1995, Oct. 24 Litho. *Perf. 14½*

456 A99	80f yellow & multi	.40	.40
457 A99	100f green & multi	.55	.55
458 A99	200f pink & multi	1.10	1.10
459 A99	250f blue & multi	1.40	1.40
	Nos. 456-459 (4)	3.45	3.45

Miniature Sheet

Traditional Architecture — A100

Example of architecture, detail: a, Tower with balcony. b, Arched windows behind balcony. c, Double doors under arch. d, Four rows of square windows above row of arched windows. e, Door flanked by two windows. f, Three windows.

1995, Nov. 20 Litho. *Perf. 14½*

460 A100 200f Sheet of 6, #a.-f. 6.50 6.50

National Day — A101

1995, Dec. 16 Litho. *Perf. 14½*

461 A101	80f blue & multi	.40	.40
462 A101	100f green & multi	.55	.55
463 A101	200f violet & multi	1.10	1.10
464 A101	250f blue grn & multi	1.40	1.40
	Nos. 461-464 (4)	3.45	3.45

Public Library, 50th Anniv. — A102

1996, Mar. 23 Litho. *Perf. 14*

465 A102	80f pink & multi	.40	.40
466 A102	200f green & multi	1.10	1.10
467 A102	250f blue & multi	1.40	1.40
	Nos. 465-467 (3)	2.90	2.90

Pearl Diving — A103

Designs: 80f, Group of divers on ship, three in water. 100f, Five divers in water, ship. 200f, Diver underneath water. 250f, Diver being pulled up, underwater scene.

500f, Lantern, weight, scales, pearls, knife. Illustration reduced.

1996, May 8 Litho. *Perf. 14*

468 A103	80f multicolored	.40	.40
469 A103	100f multicolored	.55	.55
470 A103	200f multicolored	1.10	1.10
471 A103	250f multicolored	1.40	1.40
	Nos. 468-471 (4)	3.45	3.45

Souvenir Sheet

Perf. 14½

472 A103 500f multicolored 2.75 2.75

No. 472 contains one 70x70mm stamp.

1996 Summer Olympics, Atlanta — A104

1996, July 19 Litho. *Perf. 14*

473 A104	80f olive & multi	.40	.40
474 A104	100f pink & multi	.55	.55
475 A104	200f blue grn & multi	1.10	1.10
476 A104	250f orange & multi	1.40	1.40
	Nos. 473-476 (4)	3.45	3.45

Interpol, Intl. Criminal Police Organization — A105

1996, Sept. 25 Litho. *Perf. 14*

477 A105	80f blue & multi	.40	.40
478 A105	100f yellow & multi	.55	.55
479 A105	200f pink & multi	1.10	1.10
480 A105	250f green & multi	1.40	1.40
	Nos. 477-480 (4)	3.45	3.45

Aluminum Production in Bahrain, 25th Anniv. — A106

1996, Nov. 20 Litho. *Perf. 14*

481 A106	80f bister & multi	.40	.40
482 A106	100f orange & multi	.55	.55
483 A106	200f blue & multi	1.10	1.10
484 A106	250f green & multi	1.40	1.40
	Nos. 481-484 (4)	3.45	3.45

Accession to the Throne by Sheik Isa Bin Salman Al Khalifa, 35th Anniv. — A107

1996, Dec. 16

485 A107	80f gray & multi	.40	.40
486 A107	100f green & multi	.55	.55
487 A107	200f pink & multi	1.10	1.10
488 A107	250f blue & multi	1.40	1.40
	Nos. 485-488 (4)	3.45	3.45

Bahrain Refinery, 60th Anniv. — A108

1997, Jan. 15 Litho. *Perf. 14*

489 A108	80f red & multi	.45	.45
490 A108	200f blue & multi	1.10	1.10
491 A108	250f yellow & multi	1.25	1.25
	Nos. 489-491 (3)	2.80	2.80

Pure Strains of Arabian Horses, Amiri Stud A109

Designs: a, Musannaan, Al-Jellabieh, Rabdaan. b, Kuheilaan weld umm zorayr. c, Al-Jellaby. d, Musannaan. e, Kuheilaan aladiyat. f, Kuheilaan aafas. g, Al-Dhahma. h, Mlolshaan. i, Al-Kray. j, Krush. k, Al Hamdaany. l, Hadhfaan. m, Rabda. n, Al-Suwaitieh. o, Al-Obeyah. p, Al-Shuwaimeh. q, Al-Ma'anaghieh. r, Al-Tuwaisah. s, Wadhna. t, Al-Saqlawieh. u, Al-Shawafah.

1997, Apr. 23 Litho. *Perf. 14x14½*

492 A109 200f Sheet of 21, #a.-u. 22.50 22.50

9th Men's Junior World Volleyball Championship — A110

1997, Aug. 21 Litho. *Perf. 14x14½*

493 A110	80f brown & multi	.45	.45
494 A110	100f green & multi	.55	.55
495 A110	200f gray brn & multi	1.10	1.10
496 A110	250f blue & multi	1.25	1.25
	Nos. 493-496 (4)	3.35	3.35

Montreal Protocol on Substances that Deplete Ozone Layer, 10th Anniv. — A111

1997, Sept. 16 Litho. *Perf. 14½*

497 A111	80f yellow & multi	.45	.45
498 A111	100f purple & multi	.55	.55
499 A111	200f red & multi	1.10	1.10
500 A111	250f green & multi	1.25	1.25
	Nos. 497-500 (4)	3.35	3.35

Sheikh Isa Bin Salman Bridge A112

Designs: 80f, Pylon, supports. 200f, Center of bridge. 250f, 500f, Entire span.

1997, Dec. 28 Litho. *Perf. 13x13½*

501 A112	80f multicolored	.45	.45
502 A112	200f multicolored	1.10	1.10

Size: 76x26mm

503 A112	250f multicolored	1.25	1.25
	Nos. 501-503 (3)	2.80	2.80

Souvenir Sheet

504 A112 500f multicolored 2.75 2.75

Inauguration of Urea Plant, GPIC (Refinery) Complex — A113

Designs: 80f, View of plant from Persian Gulf. 200f, Plant facilities. 250f, Aerial view.

1998, Mar. 3 Litho. *Perf. 13x13½*

505 A113	80f multicolored	.45	.45
506 A113	200f multicolored	1.10	1.10
507 A113	250f multicolored	1.25	1.25
	Nos. 505-507 (3)	2.80	2.80

World Health Organization, 50th Anniv. — A114

1998, May 11 Litho. *Perf. 14*

508 A114	80f orange & multi	.45	.45
509 A114	200f green & multi	1.10	1.10
510 A114	250f gray & multi	1.25	1.25
	Nos. 508-510 (3)	2.80	2.80

1998 World Cup Soccer Championships, France — A115

Designs: 200f, Soccer balls, world maps, vert. 250f, Players, globe, vert.

1998, June 10

511 A115	80f multicolored	.45	.45
512 A115	200f multicolored	1.10	1.10
513 A115	250f multicolored	1.25	1.25
	Nos. 511-513 (3)	2.80	2.80

14th Arabian Gulf Soccer Cup, Bahrain A116

Design: 200f, 250f, Soccer ball.

1998, Oct. 30 Litho. *Perf. 14*

514 A116	80f shown	.45	.45
515 A116	200f pale violet & multi	1.10	1.10
516 A116	250f bister & multi	1.25	1.25
	Nos. 514-516 (3)	2.80	2.80

Grand Competition for Holy Koran Recitation A117

1999, Jan. 9 Litho. *Perf. 14*

517 A117 100f gray olive & multi .55 .55
518 A117 200f yellow & multi 1.10 1.10
519 A117 250f green & multi 1.25 1.25
Nos. 517-519 (3) 2.90 2.90

Isa Bin Salman Al-Khalifa (1933-99), Emir of Bahrain — A118

Natl. flag, map and: 100f, 500f, Emir holding sword, vert. 250f, Portrait up close, vert.

Perf. 13¼ (#520, 522), 14¼ (#521)

1999, June 5 Litho.

520 A118 100f multicolored .55 .55
521 A118 200f multicolored 1.10 1.10
522 A118 250f multicolored 1.25 1.25
Nos. 520-522 (3) 2.90 2.90

Souvenir Sheet

Perf. 14½x13

523 A118 500f multicolored 3.00 3.00

Nos. 520, 522 are 31x50mm. No. 523 contains one 67x102mm stamp.

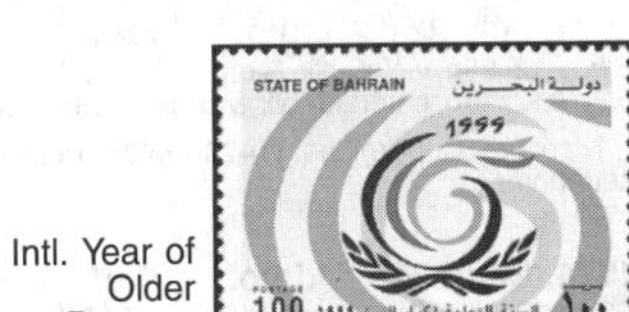

Intl. Year of Older Persons A119

1999, Oct. 9 Litho. *Perf. 13x13½*

524 A119 100f multi .55 .55
525 A119 200f multi, diff. 1.10 1.10
526 A119 250f multi, diff. 1.25 1.25
Nos. 524-526 (3) 2.90 2.90

Bahrain Stock Exchange, 10th Anniv. — A120

1999, Nov. 24 Litho. *Perf. 14¼*

527 A120 100f shown .55 .55
528 A120 200f Statues 1.10 1.10
529 A120 250f Globe 1.25 1.25
Nos. 527-529 (3) 2.90 2.90

Hamad Bin Isa Al-Khalifa, Emir of Bahrain — A121

Emir Hamad: 100f, 500f, Receiving flag from late Emir. 200f, And flag. 250f, And map.

1999, Dec. 16 Litho. *Perf. 14½*

531 A121 100f multi .55 .55
532 A121 200f multi 1.10 1.10
533 A121 250f multi 1.25 1.25
Nos. 531-533 (3) 2.90 2.90

Souvenir Sheet

Perf. 13¼x12¾

534 A121 500f multi 2.50 2.50

Dilmun Culture Exhibition A122

Map of Bahrain and: 100f, Bull's head, seal. 200f, Bull's head. 250f, Seal.

2000, Feb. 26 Litho. *Perf. 14¼*

535 A122 100f multi .55 .55
536 A122 200f multi 1.10 1.10
537 A122 250f multi 1.25 1.25
Nos. 535-537 (3) 2.90 2.90

Gulf Air, 50th Anniv. A123

Map of Bahrain and: 100f, Emblem, world map. 200f, Emblem. 250f, Birds.

2000, Mar. 24

538 A123 100f multi .55 .55
539 A123 200f multi 1.10 1.10
540 A123 250f multi 1.25 1.25
Nos. 538-540 (3) 2.90 2.90

Made in Bahrain Exhibition — A124

2000, May 9 *Perf. 14½*

541 A124 100f shown .55 .55
542 A124 200f Emblem, diff. 1.10 1.10
543 A124 250f Oil refinery 1.25 1.25
Nos. 541-543 (3) 2.90 2.90

Souvenir Sheet

Passage Through Time A125

Designs: a, Minarets, fort, flag on dhow's stern. b, Dhows, oil refinery. c, Minaret, date picker. d, Satellite dishes, fort, flag. e, Bridge, pool. f, Woman, jar, dhows. g, Dhows, coffee pot. h, Man with falcon, horse and rider. i, Pearl divers. j, Oyster shuckers. k, Men casting nets. l, Men repairing nets.

Litho. with Foil Application

2000, Oct. 9 *Perf. 14¼*

544 Sheet of 12 12.00 12.00
a.-d. A125 100f Any single .50 .50
e.-h. A125 200f Any single 1.10 1.10
i.-l. A125 250f Any single 1.40 1.40

21st Supreme Council Session of the Gulf Co-operation Council — A126

Designs: 100f, Emblem. 200f, Flags.

2000, Dec. 30 Litho. *Perf. 14¼*

545-546 A126 Set of 2 1.60 1.60

Beit al-Quran, Manama — A127

Designs: 100f, Stained-glass window. 200f, Building illuminated at dusk. 250f, Building during day.

500f, Building during day, stained-glass window, building illuminated at dusk.

2001, Feb. 18 Litho. *Perf. 14¼*

547-549 A127 Set of 3 3.00 3.00

Size: 170x80mm

Imperf

550 A127 500f multi 2.60 2.60

Housing and Agriculture Ministry, 25th Anniv. — A128

Various buildings: 100f, 150f, 200f, 250f.

2001, Apr. 28 *Perf. 14¼*

551-554 A128 Set of 4 3.75 3.75

Intl. Volunteers Year — A129

Emblem and: 100f, Stylized people with arms raised, vert. 150f, Clasped hands. 200f, Stars. 250f, Stylized people holding hands.

2001, Sept. 29 Litho. *Perf. 14¼*

555-558 A129 Set of 4 3.75 3.75

Day of the Arab Woman — A130

Designs: 100f, Emblem. 200f, Emblem and rings. 250f, Women, horiz.

2002, Feb. 1 Litho. *Perf. 14¼*

559-561 A130 Set of 3 3.00 3.00

Souvenir Sheet

2002 World Cup Soccer Championships, Japan and Korea — A131

No. 562: a, 100f. b, 200f, c, 250f.

2002, May 31

562 A131 Sheet of 3, #a-c 3.00 3.00

World Teachers' Day — A133

Background color: 100f, Gray green. 200f, Gray.

2002, Oct. 5 Litho. *Perf. 13¼x13*

579-580 A133 Set of 2 1.60 1.60

Parliamentary Elections — A134

Designs: 100f, Flag. 200f, Hand placing ballot in box, vert.

2002, Oct. 24 *Perf. 13x13¼, 13¼x13*

581-582 A134 Set of 2 1.60 1.60

WAR TAX STAMPS

WT1 WT2

1973, Oct. 21 Litho. *Perf. 14½*

MR1 WT1 5f sky blue *125.00 85.00*

Catalogue values for all unused stamps in this section, from this point to the end of the section, are for Never Hinged items.

1974 Litho. *Perf. 14½*

MR2 WT2 5f light blue 1.75 .25
a. Perf. 14½x13½ 2.50

No. MR2a was issued around 1988.

BANGKOK

'baŋ,käk

LOCATION — Capital of Siam (Thailand)

Stamps were issued by Great Britain under rights obtained in the treaty of 1855. These were in use until July 1, 1885, when the stamps of Siam were designated as the only official postage stamps to be used in the kingdom.

100 Cents = 1 Dollar

Excellent counterfeits of Nos. 1-22 are plentiful.

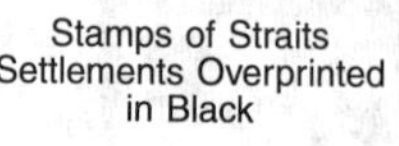
Stamps of Straits Settlements Overprinted in Black

1882 Wmk. 1 *Perf. 14*

1	A2	2c brown	*2,400.*	*1,250.*
2	A2	4c rose	*2,000.*	*1,200.*
b.		Double overprint		*6,750.*
3	A6	5c brown violet	*240.00*	*275.00*
4	A2	6c violet	*225.00*	*125.00*
5	A3	8c yel orange	*1,800.*	175.00
6	A7	10c slate	*325.00*	*175.00*
7	A3	12c blue	*800.00*	*425.00*
8	A3	24c green	*750.00*	*140.00*
9	A4	30c claret	*35,000.*	*22,500.*
10	A5	96c olive gray	*4,400.*	*2,450.*

See note after No. 20.

1882-83 Wmk. 2

11	A2	2c brown	*500.00*	*400.00*
12	A2	2c rose ('83)	*60.00*	*40.00*
a.		Inverted overprint	*18,000.*	*9,000.*
b.		Double overprint	*2,400.*	*2,400.*
c.		Triple overprint	*9,000.*	
13	A2	4c rose	*450.00*	*275.00*
14	A2	4c brown ('83)	*67.50*	*65.00*
a.		Double overprint	*3,150.*	
15	A6	5c ultra ('83)	*250.00*	*150.00*
16	A2	6c violet ('83)	*160.00*	*100.00*
17	A3	8c yel orange	*125.00*	*60.00*
a.		Inverted overprint	*16,000.*	*9,000.*
18	A7	10c slate	*140.00*	*80.00*
19	A3	12c violet brn ('83)	*275.00*	*175.00*
20	A3	24c green	*3,500.*	*2,250.*

Double overprints must have two clear impressions. Partial double overprints exist on a number of values of these issues. They sell for a modest premium over catalogue value depending on how much of the impression is present.

1883 Wmk. 1

21	A5	2c on 32c pale red	*2,000.*	*2,000.*

On Straits Settlements No. 9

1885 Wmk. 38

22	A7	32c on 2a yel (B+B)	*36,000.*	*45,000.*

BANGLADESH

,bäŋ-glə-'desh

LOCATION — In southern, central Asia, touching India, Burma, and the Bay of Bengal

GOVT. — Republic in the British Commonwealth

AREA — 55,598 sq. mi.

POP. — 127,117,967 (1999 est.)

CAPITAL — Dhaka (Dacca)

Bangladesh, formerly East Pakistan, broke away from Pakistan in April 1971, proclaiming its independence. It consists of 14 former eastern districts of Bengal and the former Sylhet district of Assam province of India.

100 Paisas = 1 Rupee

100 Paisas (Poishas) = 1 Taka (1972)

Catalogue values for all unused stamps in this country are for Never Hinged items.

Various stamps of Pakistan were handstamped locally for use in Bangladesh from March 26, 1971 until April 30, 1973.

Map of Bangladesh A1

Sheik Mujibur Rahman A2

Designs: 20p, "Dacca University Massacre." 50p, "A Nation of 75 Million People." 1r, Flag of Independence (showing map). 2r, Ballot box. 3r, Broken chain. 10r, "Support Bangladesh" and map.

Perf. 14x14½

1971, July 29 Litho. Unwmk.

1	A1	10p red, dk pur & lt bl	.20	.20
2	A1	20p bl, grn, red & yel	.20	.20
3	A1	50p dp org, gray & brn	.20	.20
4	A1	1r red, emer & yel	.25	.20
5	A1	2r lil rose, lt & dk bl	.40	.30
6	A1	3r blue, emer & grn	.50	.40
7	A2	5r dp org, tan & blk	.75	.75
8	A1	10r gold, dk bl & lil rose	1.00	1.50
		Nos. 1-8 (8)	3.50	3.75

A set of 15 stamps of types A1 and A2 in new paisa-taka values and colors was rejected by Bangladesh officials and not issued. Bangladesh representatives in England released these stamps, which were not valid, on Feb. 1, 1972.

Imperfs of Nos. 1-8 were in the Format International liquidation. They are not errors.

Nos. 1-8 Overprinted in Black or Red — BANGLADESH LIBERATED বাংলাদেশের মুক্তি

1971, Dec. 20

9	A1	10p multicolored	.20	.20
10	A1	20p multicolored	.20	
11	A1	50p multicolored	.25	
12	A1	1r multicolored	.50	
13	A1	2r multicolored	.75	
14	A1	3r multicolored	1.10	
15	A2	5r multicolored (R)	1.50	1.25
16	A1	10r multicolored	2.50	2.50
		Nos. 9-16 (8)	7.00	

Liberation of Bangladesh.

The 10p, 5r and 10r were issued in Dacca, but Nos. 10-14 were not put on sale in Bangladesh.

Monument — A3

1972, Feb. 21 Litho. *Perf. 13*

32	A3	20p green & rose	.50	.35

Language Movement Martyrs.

"Independence" A4

1972, Mar. 26 Photo. *Perf. 13*

33	A4	20p maroon & red	.20	.20
34	A4	60p dark blue & red	.25	.35
35	A4	75p purple & red	.30	.45
		Nos. 33-35 (3)	.75	1.00

First anniversary of independence.

Doves of Peace — A5

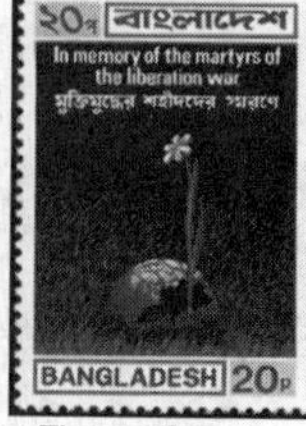

Flower Growing from Ruin — A6

1972, Dec. 16 Litho. *Perf. 13*

36	A5	20p ocher & multi	.20	.20
37	A5	60p lilac & multi	.25	.40
38	A5	75p yellow green & multi	.30	.40
		Nos. 36-38 (3)	.75	1.00

Victory Day, Dec. 16.

1973, Mar. 25 Litho. *Perf. 13*

39	A6	20p ocher & multi	.20	.20
40	A6	60p brown & multi	.40	.40
41	A6	1.35t violet blue & multi	.75	*1.10*
		Nos. 39-41 (3)	1.35	1.70

Martyrs of the war of liberation.

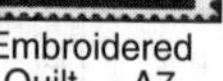
Embroidered Quilt — A7

Hilsa — A8

Court of Justice — A9

Designs: 3p, Jute field. 5p, Jack fruit. 10p, Farmer plowing with ox team. 20p, Hibiscus rosenensis. 25p, Tiger. 60p, Bamboo and water lilies. 75p, Women picking tea. 90p, Handicrafts. 2t, Collecting date palm juice, vert. 5t, Net fishing. 10t, Sixty-dome Mosque.

Perf. 14x14½, 14½x14

1973, Apr. 30 Litho.

Size: 21x28mm, 28x21mm

42	A7	2p black	.20	.20
43	A7	3p bright green	.20	.20
44	A7	5p light brown	.20	.20
45	A7	10p black	.20	.20
46	A7	20p olive	.70	.30
47	A7	25p red lilac	1.90	.60
48	A8	50p rose lilac	1.50	.50
49	A7	60p gray	.70	.25
50	A7	75p orange	1.25	.45
51	A7	90p red brown	1.25	.45

Taka Expressed as "TA"

Size: 35x22mm

52	A9	1t violet	3.50	1.25
53	A9	2t greenish gray	4.50	1.50
54	A9	5t grayish blue	6.00	2.00
55	A9	10t rose	6.50	2.25
		Nos. 42-55 (14)	28.60	10.35

See Nos. 82-85, 95-106, 165-176, 356. For overprints see Nos. O1-O10, O13.

Human Rights Flame A10

Family, Chart, Map of Bangladesh A11

1973, Dec. 10 Litho. *Perf. 13x13½*

56	A10	10p blue & multi	.20	.20
57	A10	1.25t violet & multi	.40	.40

25th anniversary of the Universal Declaration of Human Rights.

1974, Feb. 10 Litho. *Perf. 13½*

58	A11	20p blue grn & multi	.20	.20
59	A11	25p brt blue & multi	.20	.20
60	A11	75p red & multi	.45	.45
		Nos. 58-60 (3)	.85	.85

First census in Bangladesh.

For overprints see Nos. 194-196.

Copernicus, Heliocentric System — A12

Flag and UN Headquarters A13

1974, July 22 Litho. *Perf. 13½*

61	A12	25p violet, blk & org	.20	.20
62	A12	75p emerald, blk & org	.60	.60

Nicolaus Copernicus (1473-1543), Polish astronomer.

1974, Sept. 25 Litho. *Perf. 13½*

63	A13	25p lilac & multi	.20	.20
64	A13	1t blue & multi	.50	.50

Admission of Bangladesh to the UN.

A14

A15

Designs: 25p, 1.75t, UPU emblem. 1.25t, 5t, Mail runner. 25p, 1.25t, country and denomination appear on a yellow background, 1.75t, 5t, blue background.

1974, Oct. 9 *Perf. 13½*

65	A14	25p multicolored	.20	.20
66	A14	1.25t multicolored	.20	.20
67	A14	1.75t multicolored	.30	.25
68	A14	5t multicolored	.85	*1.10*
a.		Souv. sheet of 4, #65-68, imperf.	*60.00*	
		Nos. 65-68 (4)	1.55	*1.75*

1974, Nov. 4 Litho.

69	A15	25p Royal bengal tiger	.50	.25
70	A15	50p Tiger cub	1.25	.75
71	A15	2t Swimming tiger	2.75	*3.00*
		Nos. 69-71 (3)	4.50	*4.00*

"Save the Tiger," World Wildlife Fund.

Type of 1973

Taka Expressed in Bengali

1974-75 *Perf. 14½x14, 14x14½*

Size: 35x22mm

82	A9	1t violet	1.50	.20
83	A9	2t grayish green	2.50	1.00
84	A9	5t grayish blue ('75)	5.00	.80
85	A9	10t rose ('75)	11.00	7.50
		Nos. 82-85 (4)	20.00	9.50

See Nos. 350-356. For overprints see Nos. O11-O12, O14.

Family — A16

Children — A17

Family A18

1974, Dec. 30 Litho. *Perf. 14*

86 A16 25p ocher & multi .20 .20
87 A17 70p claret & multi .30 .30
88 A18 1.25t multicolored .50 .50
Nos. 86-88 (3) 1.00 1.00

Family planning. The numerals on No. 87 look like "90" but mean "70."

Betbunia Satellite Earth Station — A19

1975, June 14 Litho. *Perf. 14*

89 A19 25p red, black & silver .20 .20
90 A19 1t vio blue, blk & silver .60 .60

Opening of Betbunia Satellite Earth Station.

Allegory, IWY Emblem A20

1975, Dec. 31 Litho. *Perf. 15*

91 A20 50p rose & multi .20 .20
92 A20 2t lt lilac & multi .70 .70

International Women's Year.

Types of 1973 Redrawn

1976-77 Litho. *Perf. 15x14½*

Size: 18x23mm, 23x18mm

95 A7 5p green .20 .20
96 A7 10p black .20 .20
97 A7 20p olive green .50 .20
98 A7 25p rose lilac 1.00 .20
99 A8 50p rose lilac 1.00 .20
100 A7 60p gray .50 .25
101 A7 75p olive .80 *1.00*
102 A7 90p red brown .50 .25

Taka Expressed in Bengali

Size: 32x20mm, 20x32mm

103 A9 1t violet 1.25 .20
104 A9 2t greenish gray 6.50 .30
105 A9 5t grayish blue 4.00 2.00
106 A9 10t rose ('77) 9.00 2.00
Nos. 95-106 (12) 25.45 7.00

For overprints see Nos. O16-O25.

Telephones, 1876 and 1976 — A21

Alexander Graham Bell — A22

1976, Mar. 10 Litho. *Perf. 15*

107 A21 2.25t multicolored .25 .25
108 A22 5t multicolored .75 .75

Centenary of first telephone call by Alexander Graham Bell, Mar. 10, 1876.

Eye and Healthful Food A23

1976, Apr. 7 Litho. *Perf. 15*

109 A23 30p yellow & multi .35 .35
110 A23 2.25t orange & multi 1.60 1.60

World Health Day: Foresight prevents blindness.

Liberty Bell A24

Designs: 2.25t, Statue of Liberty, New York Skyline. 5t, Mayflower. 10t, Mt. Rushmore, presidents' heads.

1976, May 29 Photo. *Perf. 13½x14*

111 A24 30p multicolored .20 .20
112 A24 2.25t multicolored .25 .25
113 A24 5t multicolored .75 .75
114 A24 10t multicolored .75 .75
a. Souv. sheet, #111-114, perf 13 3.50 3.50
Nos. 111-114 (4) 1.95 1.95

American Bicentennial. Sheet exists imperf.

Weaver, Chemist, Farmer, Student and Emblem — A25

1976, July 29 Litho. *Perf. 15*

115 A25 30p multicolored .20 .20
116 A25 2.25t multicolored .40 .40

25th anniversary of Colombo Plan.
For overprint see No. 252.

Hurdles — A26

Montreal Olympic Emblem and: 30p, Running, horiz. 1t, High jump. 2.25t, Swimming, horiz. 3.50t, Gymnastics. 5t, Soccer.

1976, Nov. 29 Litho. *Perf. 15*

117 A26 25p multicolored .20 .20
118 A26 30p multicolored .20 .20
119 A26 1t multicolored .20 .20
120 A26 2.25t multicolored .35 .35
121 A26 3.50t multicolored .60 .60
122 A26 5t multicolored 1.10 1.10
Nos. 117-122 (6) 2.65 2.65

21st Olympic Games, Montreal, Canada, July 17-Aug. 1.

Coronation Ceremony — A27

Designs: 2.25t, Queen Elizabeth II. 10t, Queen and Prince Philip.

1977, Feb. 7 *Perf. 14x15*

123 A27 30p multicolored .20 .20
124 A27 2.25t multicolored .20 .20
125 A27 10t multicolored .55 .55
a. Souv. sheet, #123-125, perf 14½ 1.00 *1.50*
Nos. 123-125 (3) .95 .95

25th anniv. of the reign of Elizabeth II.

Qazi Nazrul Islam — A28

Nazrul A29

1977, Aug. 29 Litho. *Perf. 14*

126 A28 40p lt green & black .20 .20
127 A29 2.25t multicolored .35 .35

Qazi Nazrul Islam (1899-1976), natl. poet.

Pigeon Carrying Letter A30

1977, Sept. 29 Litho. *Perf. 14*

128 A30 30p multicolored .20 .20
129 A30 2.25t multicolored .25 .25

Asian-Oceanic Postal Union (AOPU), 15th anniversary.

Leopard A31

40p and 1t are vert.

1977, Nov. 9 Litho. *Perf. 13*

130 A31 40p Asiatic black bear .20 .20
131 A31 1t Axis deer .35 .20
132 A31 2.25t shown .70 .20
133 A31 3.50t Gayal .75 .35
134 A31 4t Elephant 1.40 .50
135 A31 5t Bengal tiger 1.60 .75
Nos. 130-135 (6) 5.00 2.20

Campfire, Tent, Scout Emblem — A32

Designs: 3.50t, Emblem, first aid, signaling, horiz. 5t, Scout emblem and oath.

1978, Jan. 22 Litho. *Perf. 13*

136 A32 40p multicolored .25 .25
137 A32 3.50t multicolored 1.00 1.00
138 A32 5t multicolored 1.75 1.75
Nos. 136-138 (3) 3.00 3.00

1st National Boy Scout Jamboree, Jan. 22.
For overprint see No. 269.

Champac — A33

Flowers and Flowering Trees: 1t, Pudding pipe tree. 2.25t, Flamboyant tree. 3.50t, Water lilies. 4t, Butea. 5t, Anthocephalus indicus.

1978, Mar. 31 Litho. *Perf. 13*

139 A33 40p multicolored .20 .20
140 A33 1t multicolored .50 .50
141 A33 2.25t multicolored .85 .85
142 A33 3.50t multicolored 1.10 1.10
143 A33 4t multicolored 1.25 1.25
144 A33 5t multicolored 1.40 1.40
Nos. 139-144 (6) 5.30 5.30

For overprints see Nos. 259A-259F.

Crown, Scepter and Staff of State — A34

Designs: 3.50t, Royal family on balcony. 5t, Queen Elizabeth II and Prince Philip. 10t, Queen in coronation regalia, Westminster Abbey.

1978, May 20 *Perf. 14*

145 A34 40p multicolored .20 .20
146 A34 3.50t multicolored .20 .20
147 A34 5t multicolored .25 .30
148 A34 10t multicolored .50 .65
a. Souv. sheet, #145-148, perf 14½ 1.40 1.40
Nos. 145-148 (4) 1.15 1.35

Coronation of Queen Elizabeth II, 25th anniv.
For overprint see No. 228B.

Alan Cobham's DH50, 1926 — A35

Planes: 2.25t, Capt. Hans Bertram's Junkers W33 Atlantis, 1932-33. 3.50t, Wright brothers' plane. 5t, Concorde.

1978, June 15 Litho. *Perf. 13*

149 A35 40p multicolored .20 .20
150 A35 2.25t multicolored 1.00 .90
151 A35 3.50t multicolored 1.50 1.25
152 A35 5t multicolored 3.00 2.50
Nos. 149-152 (4) 5.70 4.85

75th anniversary of powered flight.

Holy Kaaba, Mecca — A37

Design: 3.50t, Pilgrims at Mt. Arafat, horiz.

1978, Nov. 9 Litho. *Perf. 13*

154 A37 40p multicolored .20 .20
155 A37 3.50t multicolored .75 .75

Pilgrimage to Mecca.

Jasim Uddin, Poet A38

1979, Mar. 14 Litho. *Perf. 14*

156 A38 40p multicolored .30 .40

Rowland Hill — A39

Moulana Bhashani — A40

Hill and Stamps of Bangladesh: 3.50t, No. 1, horiz. 10t, No. 66, horiz.

1979, Aug. 27 Litho. *Perf. 14*

157 A39 40p multicolored .20 .20
158 A39 3.50t multicolored .35 .35
159 A39 10t multicolored 1.10 1.10
a. Souvenir sheet of 3, #157-159 2.75 2.75
Nos. 157-159 (3) 1.65 1.65

Sir Rowland Hill (1795-1879), originator of penny postage.

1979, Nov. 17 *Perf. 12½*

160 A40 40p multicolored .55 .55

Moulana Abdul Hamid Khan Bhashani (1880-1976), philosopher and statesman.

A41

IYC Emblem and: 40p, Boys and Hoops. 3.50t, Boys flying kites. 5t, Children jumping.

1979, Dec. 17 Litho. *Perf. 14x14½*

161 A41 40p multicolored .20 .20
162 A41 3.50t multicolored .45 .45
163 A41 5t multicolored .65 .65
a. Souv. sheet, #161-163, perf 14½ 2.50 2.50
Nos. 161-163 (3) 1.30 1.30

International Year of the Child.

Type of 1973

Designs: 5p, Lalbag Fort. 10p, Fenchungan Fertilizer Factory, vert. 15p, Pineapple. 20p, Gas well. 25p, Jute on boat. 30p, Banana tree. 40p, Baitul Mukarram Mosque. 50p, Baitul Mukarram Mosque. 80p, Garh excavations. 1ta, Dotara (musical instrument.) 2t, Karnaphuli Dam.

1979-82 Photo. *Perf. 14½*
Size: 18x23mm, 23x18mm

165 A7 5p brown ('79) .20 .20
166 A7 10p Prus blue .20 .20
167 A7 15p yellow org ('81) .20 .20
168 A7 20p dk carmine ('79) .30 .20
169 A7 25p dk blue ('82) .35 .20
170 A7 30p lt olive grn ('80) 1.25 .20
171 A8 40p rose magenta ('79) .45 .20
172 A9 50p black & gray ('81) 2.50 1.00
173 A7 80p dk brown ('80) .25 .20
174 A7 1t red lilac ('81) 3.50 .25
175 A7 2t brt ultra ('81) .75 1.25
Nos. 165-175 (11) 9.95 4.10

For overprints see Nos. O27-O36.

A42

1980, Feb. 23 Litho. *Perf. 14*

Rotary Intl., 75th Anniv.: 40p, Rotary emblem, diff.

179 A42 40p multicolored .20 .20
180 A42 5t ultra & gold .90 .90

For overprints see Nos. 285-286.

Canal Digging A43

1980, Mar. 27 Litho. *Perf. 14*

181 A43 40p multicolored .40 .30

Sher-e-Bangla A.K. Fazlul Huq (1873-1962), Natl. Leader — A44

1980, Apr. 27 Litho. *Perf. 14*

182 A44 40p multicolored .30 .30

Early Mail Transport, London 1980 Emblem — A45

1980, May 5

183 A45 1t shown .20 .20
184 A45 10t Modern mail transport 1.40 1.40
a. Souvenir sheet of 2, #183-184 1.50 *2.00*

London 80 Intl. Stamp Exhib., May 6-14.

Dome of the Rock — A46

Adult Education — A47

1980, Aug. 21 Litho. *Perf. 14½*

185 A46 50p violet rose .75 .30

For the families of Palestinians.

1980, Aug. 23 *Perf. 13½*

186 A47 50p multicolored .35 .30

Beach Scene A48

1980, Sept. 27 Litho. *Perf. 14*

187 A48 50p shown .20 .20
188 A48 5t Beach scene, diff. .80 *1.00*
a. Souvenir sheet of 2, #187-188 1.25 *1.50*
b. Pair, #187-188 1.25 1.25

World Tourism Conference, Manila, Sept. 27. No. 188b has continuous design.
For overprints see Nos. 243-244.

Hegira (Pilgrimage Year) — A49

1980, Nov. 11 Photo. *Perf. 14*

189 A49 50p multicolored .25 .25

A50

Design: Deer and Boy Scout emblem.

1981, Jan. 1 Litho. *Perf. 14*

190 A50 50p multicolored .20 .20
191 A50 5t multicolored 1.40 *1.90*

5th Asia-Pacific and 2nd Bangladesh Scout Jamboree, 1980-1981.

A51

1980, Dec. 9 Litho. *Perf. 14*

192 A51 50p multicolored .20 .20
193 A51 2t multicolored .35 .20

Begum Roquiah (1880-1932), educator.

Nos. 58-60 Overprinted: 2nd / CENSUS / 1981

1981, Mar. 6 *Perf. 13½*

194 A11 20p multicolored .20 .20
195 A11 25p multicolored .20 .20
196 A11 75p multicolored .20 .20
Nos. 194-196 (3) .60 .60

A52

1981, Mar. 16 Litho. *Perf. 14*

197 A52 1t multicolored .20 .20
198 A52 15t multicolored 2.10 *2.50*
a. Souvenir sheet of 2, #197-198 3.25 3.25

Queen Mother Elizabeth, 80th birthday (1980).

A53

1981, Mar. 26

199 A53 50p Citizen Holding Rifle & Flag .20 .20
200 A53 2t People, map .40 .40

10th anniversary of independence.
For overprint on 199, see No. 210A.

UN Conference on Least-developed Countries, Paris — A54

1981, Sept. 1 Litho. *Perf. 14x13½*

201 A54 50p multicolored .40 .20

Birth Centenary of Kemal Ataturk (First President of Turkey) — A55

1981, Nov. 10 Litho. *Perf. 14*

202 A55 50p Portrait .50 .50
203 A55 1t Portrait, diff. .70 .70

Intl. Year of the Disabled A56

1981, Dec. 26 Litho. *Perf. 14*

204 A56 50p Sign language, vert. .40 .40
205 A56 2t Amputee 1.25 1.25

World Food Day, Oct. 16 — A57

1981, Dec. 31 Litho. *Perf. 13½x14*

206 A57 50p multicolored .50 *.65*

A58

1982, May 22 Litho. *Perf. 13½x14*

207 A58 50p Boat hauling rice straw .50 *.65*

10th Anniv. of UN Conf. on Human Environment.
For overprint see No. 281.

A59

1982, Oct. 9

208 A59 50p multicolored .60 *.75*

Dr. Kazi Motahar Hossain, educator and statistician.

Scouting Year A60

1982, Oct. 21 Litho. *Perf. 14*

209 A60 50p Emblem, knots .75 .50
210 A60 2t Baden-Powell, vert. 2.75 3.25

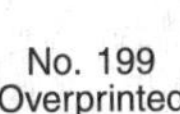
No. 199 Overprinted

1982, Nov. 21 Litho. *Perf. 14*

210A A53 50p multi — —

Armed Forces Day.

Capt. Mohiuddin Jahangir A61

Liberation Heroes (Tablet Color): b, Sepoy Hamidur Rahman (pale green). c, Sepoy Mohammed Mustafa Kamal (rose claret). d, Mohammad Ruhul Amin (yellow). e, M. Matiur Rahman (olive bister). f, Lance-Naik Munshi Abdur Rob (brown orange). g, Lance-Naik Nur Mouhammad (bright yellow green).

1982, Dec. 16 Litho. *Perf. 14*

211 Strip of 7 2.00 *2.25*
a.-g. A61 50p multicolored .30 .30

Metric System A62

1983, Jan. 10 Litho. *Perf. 14*

212 A62 50p Mail scale, vert. .50 .50
213 A62 2t Weights, measures 1.75 1.75

TB Bacillus Centenary A63

1983, Feb. 20 Litho. *Perf. 14*

214 A63 50p Koch 1.25 1.25
215 A63 1t Slides, microscope 2.25 2.25

A64

1983, Mar. 14 Litho. *Perf. 14*

216 A64 1t Open stage theater .20 .20
217 A64 3t Boat race .20 .20
218 A64 10t Snake dance .60 .60
219 A64 15t Tea garden 1.00 1.00
Nos. 216-219 (4) 2.00 2.00

Commonwealth Day.

Jnantapash Shahidullah (1885-1969), Educator and Linguist — A65

1983, July 10 Litho. *Perf. 14*

220 A65 50p multicolored .75 .75

Birds A66

1983, Aug. 17 Litho. *Perf. 14*

221 A66 50p Copsychus saulari .75 .50
222 A66 2t Halcyon smyrnensis, vert. 1.75 1.75
223 A66 3.75t Dinopium benghalense, vert. 2.00 2.00
224 A66 5t Carina scutulota 2.25 2.25
a. Souvenir sheet of 4, #221-224 9.50 9.50
Nos. 221-224 (4) 6.75 6.50

No. 224a sold for 13t.

Local Fish A67

1983, Oct. 31 Litho. *Perf. 14*

225 A67 50p Macrobrachium rosengergii .75 .25
226 A67 2t Stromateus cinereus 1.40 1.40
227 A67 3.75t Labeo rohita 1.60 1.60
228 A67 5t Anabas testudineus 2.00 2.00
a. Souv. sheet of 4, #225-228, imperf. 6.00 6.00
Nos. 225-228 (4) 5.75 5.25

No. 228a sold for 13t.

No. 148 Ovptd. "Nov. '83/Visit of Queen" in Red

1983, Nov. 14 Litho. *Perf. 14*

228B A34 10t multicolored 4.25 4.25

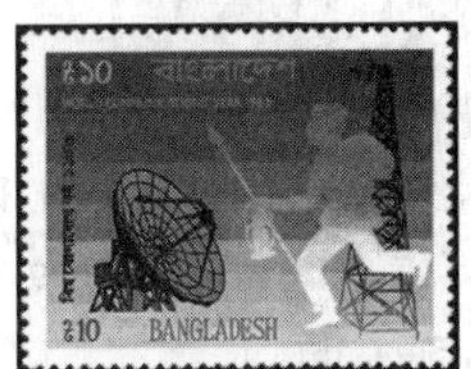

World Communications Year — A68

1983, Dec. 21 Litho. *Perf. 14*

229 A68 50p Messenger, vert. .25 .20
230 A68 5t Jet, train, ship, vert. 1.75 1.50
231 A68 10t Dish antenna, messenger 2.50 2.50
Nos. 229-231 (3) 4.50 4.20

Hall A69

1983, Dec. 5 Litho. *Perf. 14*

232 A69 50p Sangsad Bhaban .20 .20
233 A69 5t Shait Gumbaz 2.00 2.00

14th Islamic Foreign Ministers Conference.

A70

Perf. 11½x12½, 12½x11½

1983, Dec. 21

234 A70 5p Mailboat .20 .20
235 A70 10p Dacca P.O. counter .20 .20
236 A70 15p IWTA Terminal .40 .20
237 A70 20p Sorting mail .50 .20
238 A70 25p Mail delivery .20 .20
239 A70 30p Postman at mailbox .20 .20
240 A70 50p Mobile post office .20 .20

Size: 30½x18½mm

Perf. 12x11½

241 A70 1t Kamalapur Railway Station .50 .25
242 A70 2t Zia Intl. Airport .50 .50
242A A70 5t Khulna P.O. 1.10 1.10
Nos. 234-242A (10) 4.00 3.25

Nos. 235-237, 239-242A horiz.
Nos. 234-240 reprinted on cream paper.
See #270-271. For overprints see #O37-O46, O48, O51-O52.

No. 188b Overprinted in Red in English

or Bengali

1984, Feb. 1 Litho. *Perf. 14*

243 A48 50p Beach Scene .25 .25
244 A48 5t Beach Scene, diff. 2.25 2.25
a. Pair, #243-244 2.50 2.50

1st Bangladesh Natl. Philatelic Exhibition, 1984. No. 244a has continuous design.

A71

1984, May 17 *Perf. 14½*

245 50p Girl examining stamp album .25 .25
246 7.50t Boy updating collection 1.75 1.75
a. Souvenir sheet of 2, #245-246 4.25 4.25
b. A71 Pair, #245-246 1.75 1.75
c. As "a," overprinted *9.25 9.25*

#246a sold for 10t.
Overprint in sheet margin of No. 246c reads: "SILVER JUBILEE / BANGLADESH POSTAGE STAMPS 1971-96."

Dacca Zoo — A72

1984, July 17 Litho. *Perf. 14*

247 A72 1t Sarus crane, gavial 1.50 1.50
248 A72 2t Peafowl, royal Bengal tiger 3.00 3.00

Postal Life Insurance, Cent. — A73

1984, Dec. 3

249 A73	1t Chicken hawk, hen		.40	.40
250 A73	5t Beneficiaries		1.90	1.90

Abbasudin Ahmad, Bengali Singer — A74

1984, Dec. 24

251 A74	3t multicolored	.90	.90

No. 116 Ovptd. for KHULNAPEX '84 Stamp Exhibition

1984, Dec. 29 Litho. *Perf. 15*

252 A25	2.25t multicolored	1.25	1.25

1984 Summer Olympics, Los Angeles A75

1984, Dec. 31 *Perf. 14*

253 A75	1t Bicycling	1.25	.25
254 A75	5t Field hockey	2.50	2.50
255 A75	10t Volleyball	3.50	3.50
	Nos. 253-255 (3)	7.25	6.25

Islamic Development Bank, 9th Annual Congress, Dacca — A76

1985, Feb. 2

256 A76	1t Farmer	.35	.35
257 A76	5t Four Asian races	1.40	1.40

UN Child Survival Campaign A77

1985, Mar. 14

258 A77	1t Breastfeeding	.25	.25
259 A77	10t Growth monitoring	2.50	2.50

Nos. 139-144 Ovptd. in Bengali for Local Elections

1985, May 16 Litho. *Perf. 13*

259A	A33	40p multicolored	.20	.20
259B	A33	1t multicolored	.20	.20
259C	A33	2.25t multicolored	.25	.25
259D	A33	3.50t multicolored	.35	.35
259E	A33	4t multicolored	.45	.45
259F	A33	5t multicolored	.55	.55
		Nos. 259A-259F (6)	2.00	2.00

UN Decade for Women — A78

1985, July 18 *Perf. 14*

260 A78	1t shown	.20	.20
261 A78	10t Technology	1.40	1.40

UN, 40th Anniv. A79

1985, Sept. 15

262 A79	1t UN building	.20	.20
263 A79	10t World map, natl. flag	1.10	1.10

11th anniv. of UN admission.

Intl. Youth Year — A80

1985, Nov. 2 Litho. *Perf. 14*

264 A80	1t Scissors, pencil	.20	.20
265 A80	5t Hammer, wrenches	.50	.50

Seven Doves, Council Emblem — A81

1985, Dec. 8 Litho. *Perf. 14*

266 A81	1t shown	.20	.20
267 A81	5t Flags, lotus blossom	.50	.50

1st South Asian Regional Council Summit, SARC, Dacca.

Shilpacharya Zainul Abedin (1914-1976), Founder, Dacca College of Art — A82

1985, Dec. 28

268 A82	3t multicolored	.75	.50

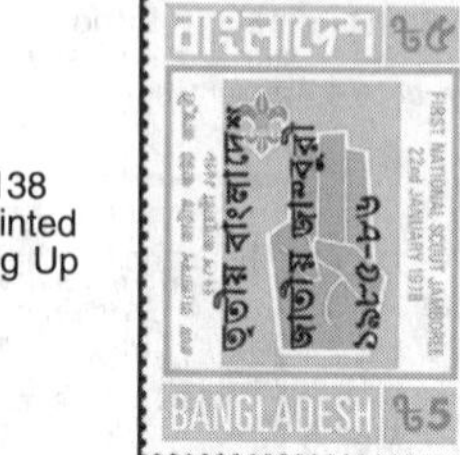

No. 138 Overprinted Reading Up

1985, Dec. 29 *Perf. 13*

269 A32	5t multicolored	2.75	2.25

3rd Natl. Scout Jamboree.
The overprint comes in two types.

Postal Services Type of 1983-84

1986-93 Litho. *Perf. 12x11½*

Size: 30½x19mm

270 A70	3t Sorting machine	.30	.30

Perf. 12x12½

Size: 33½x22½mm

271 A70	4t Chittagong Port	.55	.55

Issued: 3t, Jan. 11, 1986; 4t, Apr. 22, 1993.
For overprint see No. O46.
This is an expanding set. Numbers will change if necessary.

Fishing Net, by Safiuddin Ahmed A83

Paintings by Bengali artists: 5t, Happy Return, by Quamrul Hassan. 10t, Levelling the Plowed Field, by Zainul Abedin.

1986, Apr. 6 Litho. *Perf. 14*

275 A83	1t multicolored	.20	.20
276 A83	5t multicolored	.55	.55
277 A83	10t multicolored	1.10	1.10
	Nos. 275-277 (3)	1.85	1.85

1986 World Cup Soccer Championships, Mexico — A84

1986, June 29 *Perf. 15x14*

278 A84	1t Stealing the ball	.30	.30
279 A84	10t Goal	3.00	3.00

Souvenir Sheet

Imperf

279A A84	20t multicolored	5.25	5.25

No. 279A contains one stamp 62x45mm with simulated perfs.

Gen. M.A.G. Osmani (1918-1984), Liberation Forces Commander-in-Chief — A85

1986, Sept. 10 Litho. *Perf. 14*

280 A85	3t multicolored	1.50	1.50

No. 207 Ovptd.

1986, Dec. 3 Litho. *Perf. 13½x14*

281 A58	50p on #207	*1.75*	*2.00*

Intl. Peace Year — A86

A87

1986, Dec. 25 Litho. *Perf. 12x12½*

282 A86	1t shown	.50	.25
283 A86	10t City ruins, flower	4.00	4.00

Souvenir Sheet

284 A87	20t shown	2.00	2.00

Nos. 179-180 Ovptd. or Surcharged "CONFERENCE FOR DEVELOPMENT '87"

1987, Jan. 12 *Perf. 14*

285 A42	1t on 40p multicolored	.20	.20
286 A42	5t multicolored	.65	.65

Language Movement, 35th Anniv. — A88

Illustration reduced.

1987, Feb. 21 *Perf. 12½x12*

287	3t Protestors	1.00	1.00
288	3t Memorial	1.00	1.00
a.	A88 Pair, Nos. 287-288	2.00	2.00

World Health Day — A89

Bengali New Year — A90

1987, Apr. 7 ***Perf. 11½x12***

289 A89 1t Child immunization *2.50 2.50*

See No. 318.

1987, Apr. 16 ***Perf. 12x12½***

290 A90 1t Bengali script, embroidery .20 .20
291 A90 10t shown .40 .40

Jute Carpet A91

Exports: 1t, Jute shika (wall hanging, bowl-holder and mats), vert. 10t, Table lamp and shade, vert.

Perf. 12x12½, 12½x12

1987, May 18 **Litho.**

292 A91 1t multicolored .20 .20
293 A91 5t shown .25 .25
294 A91 10t multicolored .55 .55
Nos. 292-294 (3) 1.00 1.00

Ustad Ayet Ali Khan (1884-1967), Composer, and Surbahar A92

1987, Sept. 8 ***Perf. 12x12½***

295 A92 5t multicolored .90 .90

Palanquin A93

Transportation.

1987, Oct. 24 **Litho.** ***Perf. 12½x12***

296 A93 2t shown .20 .20
297 A93 3t Bicycle rickshaw .35 .20
298 A93 5t Paddle steamer .70 .35
299 A93 7t Train 1.75 .50
300 A93 10t Ox cart .50 .50
Nos. 296-300 (5) 3.50 1.75

For overprint see No. 424.

Hossain Shahid Suhrawardy (1893-1963), Politician — A94

1987, Dec. 5 **Litho.** ***Perf. 12x12½***

301 A94 3t multicolored .25 .25

Intl. Year of Shelter for the Homeless — A95

Illustration reduced.

1987, Dec. 15 ***Perf. 12½x12***

302 5t Homeless people .30 .30
303 5t Prosperous community .30 .30
a. A95 Pair, Nos. 302-303 .60 .60

Natl. Democracy, 1st Anniv. — A96

Design: Pres. Hossain Mohammed Ershad addressing parliament.

1987, Dec. 31

304 A96 10t multicolored 1.40 1.40

Woman Tending Crop A97

1988, Jan. 26

305 A97 3t shown .35 .35
306 A97 5t Milking cow, village .50 .50

Intl. Fund for Agricultural Development (IFAD) Seminar on Loans for Women in Rural Areas.

1988 Summer Olympics, Seoul — A98

1988 Summer Games emblem and Sports: a, Basketball. b, Weight lifting. c, Women's tennis. d, Shooting. e, Boxing.

1988, Sept. 29 **Litho.** ***Perf. 11½***

307 Strip of 5 3.00 2.50
a.-e. A98 5t any single .60 .50

Historical Sites A99

Designs: 1t, Shait Gumbaz Mosque (interior), Bagerhat. 4t, Paharpur Monastery. 5t, Kantanagar Temple, Dinajpur. 10t, Lalbag Fort, Dacca.

1988, Oct. 9 ***Perf. 12½x12***

308 A99 1t multicolored .20 .20
309 A99 4t multicolored .20 .20
310 A99 5t multicolored .25 .25
311 A99 10t multicolored .50 .35
Nos. 308-311 (4) 1.15 1.00

Qudrat-i-Khuda (1900-1977), Scientist — A100

1988, Nov. 3 ***Perf. 12x12½***

312 A100 5t multicolored .55 .55

Asia Cup Cricket — A101

1988, Nov. 27

313 Strip of 3 3.25 3.25
a. A101 1t Wicketkeeper .20 .20
b. A101 5t Batsman .95 .95
c. A101 10t Bowler 2.00 2.00

Intl. Red Cross and Red Crescent Organizations, 125th Annivs. — A102

1988, Oct. 26 **Litho.** ***Perf. 12x12½***

314 A102 5t Emblems, Dunant .60 .60
315 A102 10t Blood donation 1.25 1.25

Dacca G.P.O., 25th Anniv. — A103

1988, Dec. 6 ***Perf. 12***

316 A103 1t Exterior .20 .20
317 A103 5t Sales counter .55 .55

World Health Day Type of 1987

1988, Jan. 16 **Litho.** ***Perf. 11½x12***

318 A89 25p Oral rehydration .60 .60

32nd Meeting of the Colombo Plan Consultative Committee, Dacca — A104

1988, Nov. 29 ***Perf. 12x12½***

319 A104 3t multicolored .20 .20
320 A104 10t multicolored .50 .50

No. 191 Ovptd.

1988, Dec. 29 **Litho.** ***Perf. 14***

321 A50 5t multicolored 1.50 1.25

5th Natl. Rover Moot (Scouting).

No. 277 Overprinted

1989, Mar. 1

322 A83 10t multicolored 1.10 1.10

4th Asiatic Exposition.

A106

1989, Mar. 13 **Litho.** ***Perf. 12x12½***

324 A106 10t multicolored .75 .75

Police academy, Sardah, 75th anniv.

A107

1989, Mar. 7 **Litho.** ***Perf. 12x12½***

Modernizing water supply services.

325 A107 10t multicolored .75 .75

12th Natl. Science & Technology Week.

A108

French Revolution, Bicent. — A109

Scenes from the revolution: 5t, Close-up of revolutionaries destroying the Bastille, vert. No. 326b, Liberty guiding the people. No. 326c, Women's march on Versailles, vert. No. 327a, Celebration of the Federation on the Champ de Mars. No. 327b, Storming of the Bastille. 25t, Montage of scenes, #326a-326c.

1989, July 12 ***Perf. 14***

326 Sheet of 3 + label 2.00 2.00
- *a.* A108 5t multicolored .45 .45
- *b.-c.* A108 10t any single .70 .70

Perf. 14x15

327 Strip of 2 + label 1.40 1.40
- *a.-b.* A109 17t any single .70 .70

Size: 152x88mm

Imperf

328 A108 25t multicolored 2.00 2.00
Nos. 326-328 (3) 5.40 5.40

Labels picture the revolution anniv. emblem.

Rural Development in Asia and the Pacific (CIRDAP), 10th Anniv. — A110

Illustration reduced.

1989, Aug. 10 Litho. ***Perf. 12½x12***

329 5t multi .40 .40
330 10t multi .85 .85
- *a.* Pair, Nos. 329-330 1.25 1.25

Child Survival A111

1989, Aug. 22

331 A111 1t shown .20 .20
332 A111 10t Women and children, diff. .55 .55

SOS Children's Village, 40th anniv.

Involvement of the Bangladesh Army in UN Peace-keeping Operations, 1st Anniv. — A112

1989, Sept. 12 ***Perf. 12x12½***

333 A112 4t shown .50 .50
334 A112 10t Camp, two soldiers 1.50 1.50

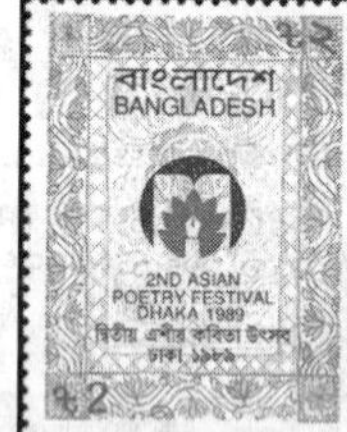

2nd Asian Poetry Festival, Dacca — A113

1989, Nov. 17 Litho. ***Perf. 12x12½***

335 A113 2t multicolored .20 .20
336 A113 10t multicolored .90 .90

State Printing Office A114

1989, Dec. 7 ***Perf. 13½***

337 A114 10t multicolored 1.25 1.25

Bangladesh Television, 25th Anniv. — A115

1989, Dec. 25 Litho. ***Perf. 12½x12***

338 A115 5t shown .50 .50
339 A115 10t Emblem, flowers, diff. 1.00 1.00

World Wildlife Fund A116

Various gavials, *(Gavialis gangeticus)*.

1990, Jan. 31 Litho. ***Perf. 14***

340 A116 50p shown .90 .50
341 A116 2t Reptile's jaws 1.10 .55
342 A116 4t 4 reptiles 1.50 .75
343 A116 10t 2 reptiles resting 2.00 1.00
- *a.* Block of 4, #340-343 5.50 5.50

A117

1990, Feb. 2 ***Perf. 14***

344 A117 6t multicolored .75 .75

Natl. Population Day.

A118

1990, May 6 ***Perf. 14***

345 A118 7t shown 1.60 1.60
346 A118 10t Penny Black, No. 230 2.50 2.50

Penny Black, 150th anniv.

Justice Syed Mahbub Murshed, (1911-1979) — A119

1990, Apr. 3 Litho. ***Perf. 12½x12***

347 A119 5t multicolored 1.10 1.10

Intl. Literacy Year — A120

Design: 10t, Boy teaching girl to write.

1990, Apr. 10 ***Perf. 12x12½***

348 A120 6t multicolored 1.40 1.40
349 A120 10t multicolored 2.00 2.00

Type of 1973 Redrawn and:

Loading Cargo Plane — A121

Curzon Hall — A122

Fertilizer Plant — A123

Postal Academy, Rajshahi A124

Salimullah Hall — A125

Bangla Academy — A126

Designs: No. 356, Sixty-dome Mosque (English inscription at LR).

1989-99 ***Perf. 12x11½, 12, 12x12½***

350 A121 3t multicolored .20 .20
- *a.* Perf. 14¼x14 .20 .20

351 A122 5t gray blk & red brn .25 .25
- *a.* Perf. 14¼ .25 .25

352 A123 10t carmine .50 .50
353 A124 20t multicolored 1.10 1.10

Perf. 14½x14

354 A125 6t blue gray & yel .55 .55

Perf. 14x14½

355 A126 2t brown & green .20 .20

Perf. 14¼

Size: 35x22 mm

Taka Expressed in Bengali

356 A9 10t rose .50 .50
Nos. 350-356 (7) 3.30 3.30

Issued: 5t, 3/31; 3t, 4/30; 10t, 20t, 7/8; 6t, 1/30/91; 2t, 12/3/93; No. 356, 3/18/99; #351a, 8/31/99.

No. 356 is very similar to No. 85 but differs in several ways: the inscription "Sixty-Dome Mosque" has been enlarged and moved from the upper left of the vignette to the lower right; a Bengali inscription has been added in its place at upper left; and the entire design has been lightened condiderably, especially in the skyline of the mosque.

For overprints see Nos. O47A-O47B, O50.

This is an expanding set. Numbers will change.

World Cup Soccer Championships, Italy — A133

1990, June 12 Litho. ***Perf. 14***

362 A133 8t shown 2.00 2.00
363 A133 10t Soccer player, diff. 3.50 3.50

Size: 115x79mm

Imperf

364 A133 25t Colosseum, soccer ball 7.50 7.50
Nos. 362-364 (3) 13.00 13.00

Fruits — A134

1990, July 16 ***Perf. 12x12½***

365 A134 1t Mangifera indica .20 .20
366 A134 2t Psidium guayava .35 .35
367 A134 3t Citrullus vulgaris .50 .50
368 A134 4t Carica papaya .70 .70
369 A134 5t Artocarpus heterophyllus .90 .90
370 A134 10t Averrhoa carambola 1.75 1.75
Nos. 365-370 (6) 4.40 4.40

UN Conference on Least Developed Nations, Paris — A135

1990, Sept. 3 Litho. ***Perf. 14***

371 A135 10t multicolored 1.90 1.90

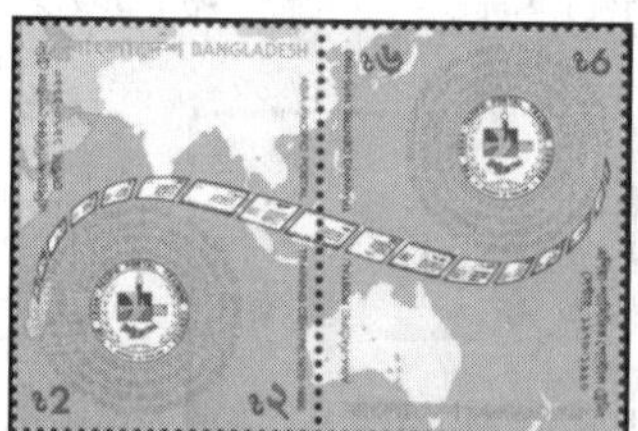

Asia-Pacific Postal Training Center, 20th Anniv. — A136

Illustration reduced.

1990, Sept. 10 ***Perf. 13½x14***

372 2t multicolored .50 .50
373 6t multicolored 1.50 1.50
- *a.* A136 Pair, #372-373 2.00 2.00

No. 373a has continuous design.

11th Asian Games, Beijing A137

1990, Sept. 22 ***Perf. 14***

374 A137 2t Rowing .40 .40
375 A137 4t Kabaddi .85 .85
376 A137 8t Wrestling 1.75 1.75
377 A137 10t Badminton 2.00 2.00
Nos. 374-377 (4) 5.00 5.00

Lalan Shah, Poet — A138

1990, Oct. 17 Litho. *Perf. 14*
378 A138 6t multicolored 1.40 1.40

UN Development Program, 40th Anniv. — A139

1990, Oct. 24 Litho. *Perf. 14*
379 A139 6t multicolored 1.25 1.25

A139a A140

1990, Nov. 29 Litho. *Perf. 14½x14*
379A A139a 2t brown .40 .40

Immunization program. See No. 560.
For surcharge see O47.

1990, Dec. 24 Litho. *Perf. 13½x12*

Butterflies.

380 A140 6t Danaus chrysippus 1.50 1.50
381 A140 6t Precis almana 1.50 1.50
382 A140 10t Ixias pyrene 2.50 2.50
383 A140 10t Danaus plexippus 2.50 2.50
a. Block of 4, #380-383 8.00 8.00

UN Decade Against Drugs A141

1991, Jan 1 Litho. *Perf. 14x13½*
384 A141 2t Drugs, map .75 .75
385 A141 4t shown 1.50 1.50

Third National Census — A142

1991, Mar. 12 Litho. *Perf. 14*
386 A142 4t multicolored .80 .80

Independence, 20th Anniv. — A143

Designs: a, Invincible Bangla statue. b, Freedom Fighter statue. c, Mujibnagar Memorial. d, Eternal flame. e, National Martyrs' Memorial.

1991, Mar. 26 *Perf. 13½*
387 A143 4t Strip of 5, #a.-e. 2.75 2.75

No. 387 printed in continuous design.

A144

Pres. Ziaur Rahman, 10th Death Anniv. — A145

1991, May 30 *Perf. 14*
388 A144 50p multicolored .20 .20
389 A145 2t multicolored .90 .90
a. Souvenir sheet of 2, #388-389 1.75 1.75

No. 389a sold for 10t.

Endangered Animals — A146

1991, June 16 *Perf. 12*
390 A146 2t Petaurista petaurista .40 .40
391 A146 4t Presbytis entellus, vert. .75 .75
392 A146 6t Buceros bicornis, vert. 1.10 1.10
a. Pair, #391-392 1.85 1.85
393 A146 10t Manis crassicaudata 1.75 1.75
a. Pair, #390, 393 2.15 2.15
Nos. 390-393 (4) 4.00 4.00

Kaikobad (1857-1951), Poet — A147

1991, July 21 Litho. *Perf. 14*
394 A147 6t multicolored .85 .85

Rabindranath Tagore, Poet, 50th Anniv. of Death — A148

1991, Aug. 7
395 A148 4t multicolored .85 .85

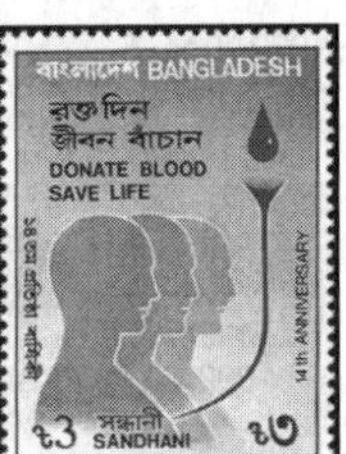

Blood and Eye Donations A149

1991, Sept. 19
396 A149 3t shown 1.00 .60
397 A149 5t Blind man and eye 1.50 1.25

Sandhani, Medical Students Association, 14th anniversary.

Shahid Naziruddin, Leader of Democratic Movement, 1st Anniv. of Death — A150

1991, Oct. 10
398 A150 2t multicolored .80 .80

Shaheed Noor Hossain, 4th Death Anniv. — A151

1991, Nov. 10 Litho. *Perf. 14*
399 A151 2t multicolored .80 .80

Archaeological Treasures of Mainamati — A152

Designs: a, Bronze Stupa with images of Buddha. b, Bowl and pitcher. c, Ruins of Salban Vihara Monastery. d, Gold coins. e, Terra-cotta plaque.

1991, Nov. 26 Litho. *Perf. 13½*
400 A152 4t Strip of 5, #a.-e. 5.00 5.00

Mass Uprising, First Anniv. A153

1991, Dec. 6 *Perf. 14*
401 A153 4t multicolored .80 .80

Miniature Sheets

Independence, 20th Anniv. — A154

Martyred intellectuals who died in 1971 - No. 402: a, A.N.M. Munier Chowdhury. b, Ghyasuddin Ahmad. c, S.M.A. Rashidul Hasan. d, Muhammad Anwar Pasha. e, Dr. Md. Mortaza. f, Shahid Saber. g, Fazlur Rahman Khan. h, Ranada Prasad Saha. i, Adhyaksha Joges Chandra Ghose. j, Santosh Chandra Bhattacharyya.

No. 403: a, Dr. Gobinda Chandra Deb. b, A.N.M. Muniruzzaman. c, Mufazzal Haider Chaudhury. d, Dr. Abdul Alim Choudhury. e, Sirajuddin Hossain. f, Shahidulla Kaiser. g, Altaf Mahmud. h, Dr. Jyotirmay Guha Thakurta. i, Dr. Md. Abul Khair. j, Dr. Serajul Haque Khan.

No. 404: a, Dr. Mohammad Fazle Rabbi. b, Mir Abdul Quyyum. c, A.N.M. Golam Mostafa. d, Dhirendranath Dutta. e, S.A. Mannan (Ladu Bhai). f, Nizamuddin Ahmad. g, Abul Bashar Chowdhury. h, Selina Parveen. i, Dr. Abul Kalam Azad. j, Saidul Hassan.

No. 404K: l, LCDR. Moazzam Hussain. m, Muhammad Habibur Rahman. n, Khandoker Abu Taleb. o, Moshiur Rahman. p, Md. Abdul Muktadir. q, Nutan Chandra Sinha. r, Syed Nazmul Haque. s, Dr. Mohammed Amin Uddin. t, Dr. N.A.M. Faizul Mohee. u, Sukha Ranjan Somaddar.

1991-93 Litho. *Perf. 13½*
Sheets of 10

402 A154 2t #a.-j. + 5 labels 1.90 1.90
403 A154 2t #a.-j. + 5 labels 1.90 1.90
404 A154 2t #a.-j. + 5 labels 1.90 1.90

Perf. 14½

404K A154 2t #l.-u. + 5 labels 3.00 3.00

Issued: #402-404, 12/14/91; #404K, 12/14/93.

See Nos. 470-471, 499-500, 534-535, 558-559, 568-569, 595, 627-628.

Shrimp — A155

Illustration reduced.

1991, Dec. 31 *Perf. 14*
405 6t Penaeus monodon 1.25 1.25
406 6t Metapenaeus monoceros 1.25 1.25
a. A155 Pair, #405-406 2.50 2.50

Shaheed Mirze Abu Raihan Jaglu, 5th Death Anniv. A156

1992, Feb. 8 Litho. *Perf. 14x13½*
407 A156 2t multicolored .95 .95

World Environment Day — A157

Design: 4t, Scenes of environmental protection and pollution control, vert.

1992, June 5 Litho. *Perf. 14*
408 A157 4t multicolored .45 .45
409 A157 10t multicolored 1.10 1.10

Nawab Sirajuddaulah of Bengal (1733-1757) A158

1992, July 2 Litho. *Perf. 14*
410 A158 10t multicolored 1.00 1.00

Syed Ismail Hossain Sirajee (1880-1931), Social Reformer A159

1992, July 17
411 A159 4t multicolored .80 .80

Tree Week — A160

1992, July 17 Litho. *Perf. 14*
412 A160 2t Couple planting tree, horiz. .50 .50
413 A160 4t Birds, trees 1.00 1.00

1992 Summer Olympics, Barcelona — A161

Olympic rings and: a, 4t, Rowing. b, 6t, Hands holding Olympic torch. c, 10t, Peace doves. d, 10t, Clasped hands.

1992, July 25 Litho. *Perf. 14*
414 A161 Block of 4, #a.-d. 2.75 2.75

The Star Mosque, 18th Cent. A162

1992, Oct. 29 Litho. *Perf. 14½x14*
415 A162 10t multicolored 1.10 1.10

Masnad-E-Ala Isa Khan, 393rd Anniv. of Death — A163

1992, Sept. 15 *Perf. 14x14½*
416 A163 4t multicolored .80 .80

7th SAARC Summit, Dacca — A164

1992, Dec. 5
417 A164 6t Flags of members .50 .50
418 A164 10t Emblem .85 .85

1992 Bangladesh Natl. Philatelic Exhibition — A165

Designs: No. 419a, Elephant and mahout, ivory work, 19th cent. b, Post rider, mail box and postman delivering mail to villager.

1992, Sept. 26 *Perf. 14½x14*
419 A165 10t Pair, #a.-b. + label 2.50 2.50
c. Souv. sheet, imperf. *2.75 2.75*

No. 419c contains one strip of No. 419 with simulated perforations and sold for 25t.

1992 Intl. Conference on Nutrition, Rome — A166

1992, Dec. 5
420 A166 4t multicolored .55 .55

Meer Nisar Ali Titumeer (1782-1831) — A167

1992, Nov. 19 Litho. *Perf. 14½x14*
421 A167 10t multicolored 1.00 1.00

Archaeological Relics, Mahasthan — A168

Relics from 3rd century B.C.-15th century A.D.: No. 422a, Terracotta seal and head. b, Terracotta hamsa. c, Terracotta Surya image. d, Gupta stone columns.

1992, Nov. 30 Litho. *Perf. 14½x14*
422 A168 10t Strip of 4, #a.-d. 4.00 4.00

Canal Digging — A169

a, Workers digging canal. b, Completed project.
Illustration reduced.

1993, Mar. 31 Litho. *Perf. 14½x14*
423 A169 2t Pair, #a.-b. 1.40 1.40

No. 300 Overprinted

1992, Aug. 18 Litho. *Perf. 12½x12*
424 A93 10t multicolored 1.10 1.10

Syed Abdus Samad (1895-1964), Soccer Player — A170

1993, Feb. 2 *Perf. 14x14½*
425 A170 2t multicolored .80 .80

A171

1993, Apr. 14
426 A171 2t multicolored .70 .70

Completion of 14th cent. Bengali era.

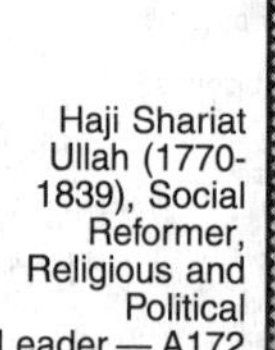

Haji Shariat Ullah (1770-1839), Social Reformer, Religious and Political Leader — A172

1993, Mar. 10 Litho. *Perf. 14x14½*
427 A172 2t multicolored .70 .70

World Health Day A173

1993, Apr. 7 *Perf. 14½x14, 14x14½*
428 A173 6t Prevent accidents 1.25 .75
429 A173 10t Prevent violence, vert. 1.50 1.50

Compulsory Primary Education — A174

1993, May 26
430 A174 2t Slate, chalk, books .40 .40
431 A174 2t Hand writing, children, vert. .40 .40

Nawab Sir Salimullah (1871-1915), Social Reformer — A175

1993, June 7 Litho. *Perf. 14½x14*
432 A175 4t multicolored .55 .55

Fishing Industry A176

1993, Aug. 15 Litho. *Perf. 14½x14*
433 A176 2t multicolored .55 .55

Tomb of Sultan Ghiyasuddin Azam Shah — A177

1993, Dec. 30 Litho. *Perf. 14½x14*
434 A177 10t multicolored 1.10 1.10

Scenic Views A178

Designs: No. 435, Sunderban. No. 436, Madhabkunda Waterfall, vert. No. 437, River, mountains, vert. No. 438, Beach, Kuakata.

1993, Oct. 30 *Perf. 14½x14, 14x14½*
435 A178 10t multicolored 1.25 1.25
436 A178 10t multicolored 1.25 1.25
437 A178 10t multicolored 1.25 1.25
438 A178 10t multicolored 1.25 1.25
a. Souv. sheet, #435-438, imperf 5.00 5.00
Nos. 435-438 (4) 5.00 5.00

#438a sold for 50t and has simulated perfs.

6th Asian Art Biennial, Bangladesh A179

1993, Nov. 7 Litho. *Perf. 14x14½*
439 A179 10t multicolored .85 .85

Foy's Lake A180

1993, Nov. 6 *Perf. 14½x14*
440 A180 10t multicolored 1.10 1.10

Tourism month.

14th Asian Pacific, 5th Bangladesh Natl. Scout Jamboree A181

1994, Jan. 5 ***Perf. 14x14½***
441 A181 2t multicolored .55 .55

Oral Rehydration Solution, 25th Anniv. — A182

1994, Feb. 5 Litho. ***Perf. 13½x14***
442 A182 2t multicolored .55 .55

6th SAF Games, Dhaka A183

1993, Dec. 6 ***Perf. 14x13½, 13½x14***
443 A183 2t Shot put .30 .30
444 A183 4t Runners, vert. .65 .65

Mosques A184

Mosques: 4t, Interior, Chhota Sona, Nawabgonj. No. 446, Exterior, Chhota Sona. No. 447, Exterior, Baba Adam's, Munshigonj.

1994, Mar. 30 Litho. ***Perf. 14x13½***
445 A184 4t multicolored .30 .30
446 A184 6t multicolored .50 .50
447 A184 6t multicolored .50 .50
Nos. 445-447 (3) 1.30 1.30

For overprint see No. 509.

ILO, 75th Anniv. A185

Designs: 4t, People, oxen working in fields. 10t, Man rotating gearwheel, vert.

Perf. 14x13½, 13½x14
1994, Apr. 11 Litho.
448 A185 4t multicolored .40 .40
449 A185 10t multicolored 1.00 1.00

Bangla Era, 15th Cent. — A186

1994, Apr. 14 ***Perf. 13½x14***
450 A186 2t multicolored .55 .55

Traditional Festivals A187

1994, May 12 ***Perf. 14x13½***
451 A187 4t Folk Festival .40 .40
452 A187 4t Baishakhi Festival .40 .40

Intl. Year of the Family — A188

1994, May 15 ***Perf. 13½x14***
453 A188 10t multicolored 1.50 1.50

Tree Planting Campaign A189

1994, June 15 Litho. ***Perf. 13½x14***
454 A189 4t Family planting trees .55 .55
455 A189 6t Hands, seedlings .80 .80

1994 World Cup Soccer Championships, US — A190

Soccer player's uniform colors: a, Red, yellow & blue. b, Yellow, green, & red.

1994, June 17 Litho. ***Perf. 14½***
456 A190 20t Pair, #a.-b. + label 4.25 4.25
Complete booklet, #456 11.50

Jamuna Multi-Purpose Bridge — A191

1994, July 24 ***Perf. 14½x14***
457 A191 4t multicolored .40 .40

Birds — A192

Designs: 4t, Oriolus xanthornus. No. 459, Gallus gallus. No. 460, Dicrurus paradiseus. No. 461, Dendrocitta vagabunda.

1994, Aug. 31 ***Perf. 14x14½***
458 A192 4t multicolored .50 .50
459 A192 6t multicolored .75 .75
460 A192 6t multicolored .75 .75
461 A192 6t multicolored .75 .75
a. Souvenir sheet, #458-461 2.75 2.75
Nos. 458-461 (4) 2.75 2.75

No. 461a sold for 25t.

Dr. Mohammad Ibrahim (1911-89), Pioneer in Treatment of Diabetes — A193

1994, Sept. 6 Litho. ***Perf. 14½x14***
462 A193 2t multicolored .40 .40

Nawab Faizunnessa Chowdhurani (1834-1903), Social Reformer A194

1994, Sept. 23 ***Perf. 14x14½***
463 A194 2t multicolored .40 .40

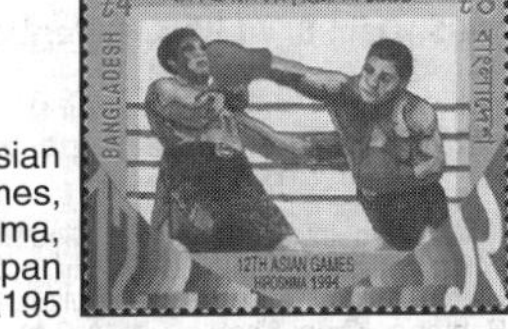
12th Asian Games, Hiroshima, Japan A195

1994, Oct. 2 ***Perf. 14½x14***
464 A195 4t multicolored .55 .55

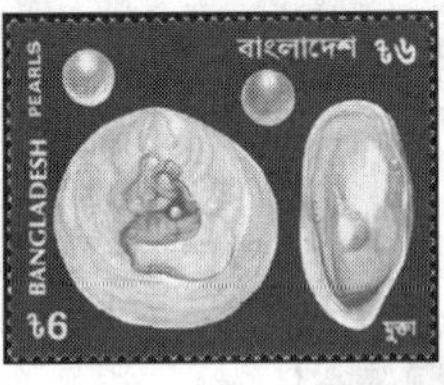
Shells A196

Designs: No. 465, White, pink pearls, oysters. No. 466, Snail, three other shells. No. 467, Scallop, other shells. No. 468, Spiral shaped shells, vert.

Perf. 14½x14, 14x14½
1994, Oct. 30 Litho.
465 A196 6t multicolored .60 .60
466 A196 6t multicolored .60 .60
467 A196 6t multicolored .60 .60
468 A196 6t multicolored .60 .60
Nos. 465-468 (4) 2.40 2.40

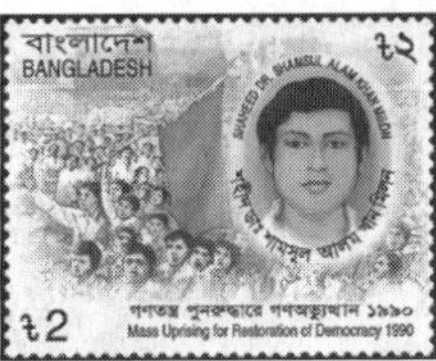
Democracy Demonstration, Death of Dr. Shamsul Alam Khan Milon, 4th Anniv. — A197

1994, Nov. 27 ***Perf. 14½x14***
469 A197 2t multicolored .40 .40

Martyred Intellectual Type of 1991
Miniature Sheets of 8

Martyred intellectuals who died in 1971: No. 470: a, Dr. Harinath Dey. b, Dr. Lt. Col. A.F. Ziaur Rahman. c, Mamum Mahmud. d, Mohsin Ali Dewan. e, Dr. Lt. Col. N.A.M. Jahangir. f, Shah Abdul Majid. g, Muhammad Akhter. h, Meherunnesa.

No. 471: a, Dr. Kasiruddin Talukder. b, Fazlul Haque Choudhury. c, Md. Shamsuzzaman. d, A.K.M. Shamsuddin. e, Lt. Mohammad Anwarul Azim. f, Nurul Amin Khan. g, Mohammad Sadeque. h, Md. Araz Ali.

1994, Dec. 14 ***Perf. 14½***
470 A154 2t #a.-h. + 4 labels 1.25 1.25
471 A154 2t #a.-h. + 4 lables 1.25 1.25

Vegetables A199

1994, Dec. 24 ***Perf. 14x14½, 14½x14***
472 A199 4t Diplazium esculentum .25 .25
473 A199 4t Momordica charantia .25 .25
474 A199 6t Lagenaria siceraria .50 .50
475 A199 6t Trichosanthes dioica .50 .50
476 A199 10t Solanum melongena .85 .85
477 A199 10t Cucurbita maxima .85 .85
Nos. 472-477 (6) 3.20 3.20

Nos. 472-476 are vert.

World Tourism Organization, 20th Anniv. — A200

1995, Jan. 2 ***Perf. 14½x14***
478 A200 10t multicolored .95 .95

Intl. Trade Fair, Dhaka A201

Designs: 4t, Trade products. 6t, Factories, emblems of industry.

1995, Jan. 7 Litho. ***Perf. 14x14½***
479 A201 4t multicolored .30 .30
480 A201 6t multicolored .60 .60

Bangladesh Rifles, Bicent. — A202

1995, Jan. 10 Litho. *Perf. 14½x14*

481 A202 2t shown .30 .30
482 A202 4t Building, battalion .60 .60

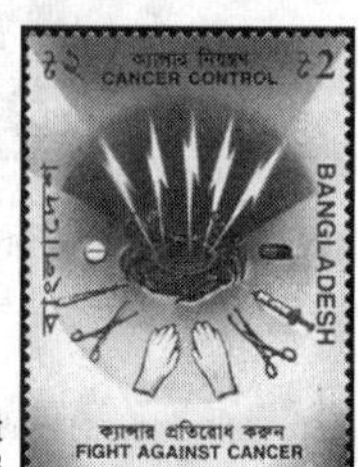

Fight Against Cancer — A203

1995, Apr. 7 Litho. *Perf. 14x14½*

483 A203 2t multicolored .40 .40

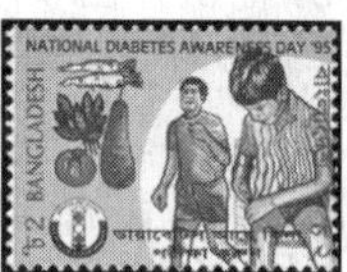

Natl. Diabetes Awareness Day — A204

1995, Feb. 28 *Perf. 14*

484 A204 2t multicolored .55 .55

For overprint see No. O49.

Munshi Mohammad Meherullah (1861-1907), Educator A205

1995, June 7 Litho. *Perf. 14x14½*

485 A205 2t multicolored .55 .55

FAO, 50th Anniv. — A206

1995, Oct. 16 Litho. *Perf. 14*

486 A206 10t multicolored .90 .90

UN, 50th Anniv. A207

UN emblem, "50," and: 2t, Dove of peace, UN headquarters. No. 488, "1945," earth from space, "1995." No. 489, Hands of different nationalities clasping, UN headquarters.

1995, Oct. 24 *Perf. 14½x14*

487 A207 2t multicolored .20 .20
488 A207 10t multicolored 1.00 1.00
489 A207 10t multicolored 1.00 1.00
Nos. 487-489 (3) 2.20 2.20

Flowers — A208

#490, Bombax ceiba. #491, Lagerstroemia speciosa. #492, Gloriosa superba. #493, Canna indica. #494, Bauhinia purpurea. #495, Passiflora incarnata.

1995, Oct. 9 *Perf. 14½x14, 14x14½*

490 A208 6t multicolored .65 .65
491 A208 6t multi, vert. .65 .65
492 A208 10t multi, vert. .85 .85
493 A208 10t multi, vert. .85 .85
494 A208 10t multi, vert. .85 .85
495 A208 10t multi, vert. .85 .85
Nos. 490-495 (6) 4.70 4.70

Shaheed Khandaker Mosharraf Hossain A208a

1995, Oct. 16 Litho. *Perf. 13¾x14¼*

496 A208a 2t multi — —

No. 496 was removed from sale shortly after release.

18th Eastern Regional Conference on Tuberculosis and Respiratory Diseases, Dhaka — A209

1995, Oct. 29 Litho. *Perf. 14½x14*

497 A209 6t multicolored .55 .55

South Asian Assoc. for Regional Cooperation (SAARC), 10th Anniv. — A210

1995, Dec. 8 Litho. *Perf. 14x14½*

498 A210 2t multicolored .70 .70

Martyred Intellectual Type of 1991

Sheets of 8

Martyred intellectuals who died in 1971 - #499: a, Shaikh Habibur Rahman. b, Dr. Major Naimul Islam. c, Md. Shahidullah. d, Ataur Rahman Khan Khadim. e, A.B.M. Ashraful Islam Bhuiyan. f, Dr. Md. Sadat Ali. g, Sarafat Ali. h, M.A. Sayeed.

No. 500: a, Abdul Ahad. b, Lt. Col. Mohammad Abdul Qadir. c, Mozammel Hoque Chowdhury. d, Rafiqul Haider Chowdhury. e, Dr. Azharul Haque. f, A.K. Shamsuddin. g, Anudwaipayan Bhattacharjee. h, Lutfunnahar Helena.

1995, Dec. 14 Litho. *Perf. 14½x14*

499 A154 2t #a.-h. + 4 labels 1.50 1.50
500 A154 2t #a.-h. + 4 labels 1.50 1.50

Second Asian Pacific Community Development Scout Camp — A211

1995, Dec. 18 Litho. *Perf. 14x14½*

501 A211 2t multicolored .55 .55

Volleyball, Cent. — A212

1995, Dec. 25

502 A212 6t multicolored .55 .55

Traditional Costumes — A213

Designs: No. 503, Man in punjabi and lungi, vert. No. 504, Woman in sari, vert. No. 505, Christian bride and groom, vert. No. 506, Muslim bridal couple, vert. No. 507, Hindu bridal couple. No. 508, Buddhist bridal couple.

1995, Dec. 25 *Perf. 14x14½, 14½x14*

503 A213 6t multicolored .60 .60
504 A213 6t multicolored .60 .60
505 A213 10t multicolored 1.00 1.00
506 A213 10t multicolored 1.00 1.00
507 A213 10t multicolored 1.00 1.00
508 A213 10t multicolored 1.00 1.00
Nos. 503-508 (6) 5.20 5.20

No. 446 Ovptd. in Red

1995 Litho. *Perf. 14x13½*

509 A184 6t multicolored 1.50 1.50

Shaheed Amanullah Mohammad Asaduzzaman (1942-69) A214

1996, Jan. 20 *Perf. 14x14½*

510 A214 2t multicolored .50 .50

1996 World Cup Cricket Championships — A215

1996, Feb. 14 *Perf. 14x14½, 14½x14*

511 A215 4t Pitching, vert. .60 .60
512 A215 6t At bat, vert. .85 .85
513 A215 10t shown 1.40 1.40
Nos. 511-513 (3) 2.85 2.85

Independence, 25th Anniv. — A216

Designs: No. 514, Natl. Martrys' Memorial. No. 515, Industrial development. No. 516, 1971 Destruction of war. No. 517, Educational development. No. 518, Development in communication. No. 519, Development in health.

1996, Mar. 26 Litho. *Perf. 14x14½*

514 A216 4t multicolored .35 .35
515 A216 4t multicolored .35 .35
516 A216 4t multicolored .35 .35
517 A216 4t multicolored .35 .35
518 A216 4t multicolored .35 .35
519 A216 4t multicolored .35 .35
Nos. 514-519 (6) 2.10 2.10

Michael Madhusudan Dutt (1824-73), Writer — A217

1996, June 29 Litho. *Perf. 14x14½*

520 A217 4t multicolored .60 .60

1996 Summer Olympic Games, Atlanta A218

1996, July 19 Litho. *Perf. 14*

521 A218 4t Gymnast, vert. .60 .60
522 A218 6t Judo, vert. .90 .90
523 A218 10t High jumper 1.40 1.40
524 A218 10t Runners 1.40 1.40
a. Souvenir sheet, #521-524 7.00 7.00
Nos. 521-524 (4) 4.30 4.30

No. 524a sold for 50t.

Sheikh Mujibur Rahman (1920-75), Prime Minister — A219

Design: No. 527, Maulana Mohammad Akrum Khan (1868-1968).

1996 Litho. *Perf. 14x14½*

526 A219 4t multicolored .60 .60
527 A219 4t multicolored .60 .60

Issued: No. 526, 8/15/96, No. 527, 8/18/96.

Ustad Alauddin Khan (1862-1972), Musician A220

1996, Sept. 6 Litho. *Perf. 14x14½*

528 A220 4t multicolored .20 .20

Children's Paintings A221

Perf. 14x14½, 14½x14

1996, Oct. 9 **Litho.**

529 A221 2t Kingfisher, vert. *.45 .45*
530 A221 4t River Crossing *.95 .95*

Jailed, 21st Death Anniv. — A222

a, Syed Nazrul Islam. b, Tajuddin Ahmad. c, M. Monsoor Ali. d, A.H.M. Quamaruzzaman.

1996, Nov. 3 **Litho.** ***Perf. 14x14½***

531 A222 4t Block of 4, #a.-d. *2.00 2.00*

UNICEF, 50th Anniv. — A223

Designs: 4t, Children receiving food, medicine, aid. 10t, Mother holding infant.

1996, Dec. 11

532 A223 4t multicolored *.65 .65*
533 A223 10t multicolored *1.60 1.60*

Martyred Intellectual Type of 1991

Martyred intellectuals who died in 1971: No. 534: a, Dr. Jekrul Haque. b, Munshi Kabiruddin Ahmed. c, Md. Abdul Jabbar. d, Mohammad Amir. e, A.K.M. Shamsul Huq Khan. f, Dr. Siddique Ahmed. g, Dr. Soleman Khan. h, S.B.M. Mizanur Rahman.

No. 535: a, Aminuddin. b, Md. Nazrul Islam. c, Zahirul Islam. d, A.K. Lutfor Rahman. e, Afsar Hossain. f, Abul Hashem Mian. g, A.T.M. Alamgir. h, Baser Ali.

1996, Dec. 14 **Litho.** ***Perf. 14½x14***
Sheets of 8

534 A154 2t #a.-h. + 4 labels *2.25 2.25*
535 A154 2t #a.-h. + 4 labels *2.25 2.25*

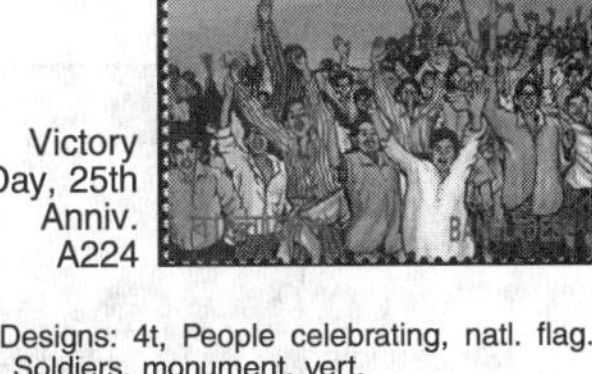

Victory Day, 25th Anniv. A224

Designs: 4t, People celebrating, natl. flag. 6t, Soldiers, monument, vert.

1996, Dec. 16 ***Perf. 14½x14, 14x14½***

536 A224 4t multicolored *.65 .65*
537 A224 6t multicolored *1.00 1.00*

Paul Harris (1868-1947), Founder of Rotary Intl. — A225

1997, Feb. 18 **Litho.** ***Perf. 14x14½***

538 A225 4t multicolored *.40 .40*

Sheikh Mujibur Rahman's Mar. 7 Speech, 26th Anniv. — A226

1997, Mar. 7 ***Perf. 12½***

539 A226 4t multicolored *.40 .40*

Sheikh Mujibur Rahman (1920-75) A227

1997, Mar. 17 ***Perf. 14x14½***

540 A227 4t multicolored *.40 .40*

Independence, 25th Anniv. (in 1996) — A228

1997, Mar. 26 **Litho.** ***Perf. 12½***

541 A228 4t multi *.40 .40*

Heinrich von Stephan (1831-97) A229

1997, Apr. 8 **Litho.** ***Perf. 14x14½***

542 A229 4t multicolored *.40 .40*

Livestock A230

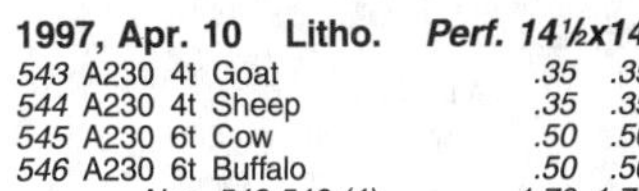

1997, Apr. 10 **Litho.** ***Perf. 14½x14***

543 A230 4t Goat *.35 .35*
544 A230 4t Sheep *.35 .35*
545 A230 6t Cow *.50 .50*
546 A230 6t Buffalo *.50 .50*
Nos. 543-546 (4) *1.70 1.70*

Paintings — A231

Designs: 6t, "Tilling the Field-2," by S.M. Sultan (1923-94). 10t, "Three Women," by Quamrul Hassan (1921-88).

1997, June 26 **Litho.** ***Perf. 12½***

547 A231 6t multicolored *.60 .60*
548 A231 10t multicolored *.95 .95*

6th Intl. Cricket Council Trophy Championship, Malaysia — A232

1997, Sept. 4

549 A232 10t multicolored *1.00 1.00*

Ancient Mosques A233

Designs: 4t, Kusumba Mosque, Naogaon, 1558. 6t, Atiya Mosque, Tangail, 1609. 10t, Bagha Mosque, Rajshahi, 1523.

1997, Sept. 4 **Litho.** ***Perf. 14½x14***

550 A233 4t multicolored *.25 .25*
551 A233 6t multicolored *.35 .35*
552 A233 10t multicolored *.60 .60*
Nos. 550-552 (3) *1.20 1.20*

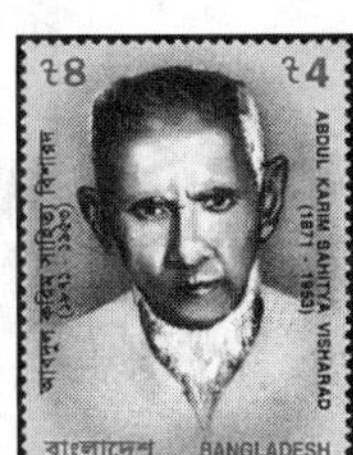

Abdul Karim Sahitya Visharad (1871-1953), Scholar — A234

1997, Oct. 11 ***Perf. 14x14½***

553 A234 4t multicolored *.25 .25*

9th Asia-Pacific, 7th Bangladesh Rover Moot '97 — A235

1997, Oct. 25 ***Perf. 14x14½***

554 A235 2t multicolored *.35 .35*

Armed Forces, 25th Anniv. A236

1997, Nov. 11 ***Perf. 14½x14***

555 A236 2t multicolored *.20 .20*

East Bengal Regiment, 50th Anniv. A237

1998, Feb. 15

556 A237 2t multicolored *.20 .20*

Mohammad Mansooruddin (1904-87) A238

1998, Feb. 4 ***Perf. 14x14½***

557 A238 4t multicolored *.25 .25*

Martyred Intellectual Type of 1991
Sheets of 8 + 4 Labels

Martyred intellectuals who died in 1971: No. 558: a, Dr. Shamsuddin Ahmed. b, Mohammad Salimullah. c, Mohiuddin Haider. d, Abdur Rahim. e, Nitya Nanda Paul. f, Abdul Jabber. g, Dr. Humayun Kabir. h, Khaja Nizamuddin Bhuiyan.

No. 559: a, Gulam Hossain. b, Ali Karim. c, Md. Moazzem Hossain. d, Rafiqul Islam. e, M. Nur Hussain. f, Captain Mahmood Hossain Akonda. g, Abdul Wahab Talukder. h, Dr. Hasimoy Hazra.

1997, Dec. 14

558-559 A154 2t #a.-h., each *1.00 1.00*

Immunization Type of 1990

1998, Jan. 22 ***Perf. 14½x14***

560 A139a 1t green *.20 .20*

For overprint see No. O53.

Bulbul Chowdhury (1919-54), Dancer — A239

1998, May 17 ***Perf. 14x14½***

561 A239 4t multicolored *.25 .25*

Opening of the Bangabandhu Bridge — A240

Designs: 4t, East approach road. 6t, West approach road. 8t, River training works. 10t, Bangabandhu Bridge.

1998, June 23 ***Perf. 14***

562 A240 4t multicolored *.25 .25*
563 A240 6t multicolored *.35 .35*
564 A240 8t multicolored *.45 .45*
565 A240 10t multicolored *.55 .55*
Nos. 562-565 (4) *1.60 1.60*

1998 World Cup Soccer Championships, France — A241

1998, June 10

566 A241	6t Trophy	*.35*	*.35*
567 A241	18t Player, trophy	*1.00*	*1.00*

Martyred Intellectural Type of 1991

Sheets of 8 + 4 Labels

Martyred intellectuals who died in 1971 - No. 568: a, Md. Khorshed Ali Sarker. b, Abu Yakub Mahfuz. c, S.M. Nurul Huda. d, Nazmul Hoque Sarker. e, Md. Taslim Uddin. f, Gulam Mostafa. g, A. H. Nurul Alam. h, Timir Kanti Dev.

No. 569: a, Altaf Hossain. b, Aminul Hoque. c, S.M. Fazlul Hoque. d, Mozammel Ali. e, Syed Akbar Hossain. f, Sk. Abdus Salam. g, Abdur Rahman. h, Dr. Shyamal Kanti Lala.

1998, Dec. 14 Litho. *Perf. 14½x14*

568-569 A154 2t #a.-h., set of 2 *1.75 1.75*

Princess Diana (1961-97) — A242

Diana: a, 8t, In hat. b, 18t, In black dress. c, 22t, In blue dress.

Illustration reduced.

1998, June 6 Litho. *Perf. 14¼*

570 A242 Horiz. strip of 3, #a-c *2.25 2.25*

World Solar Program, 1996-2005 A243

Perf. 13¾x14¼

1998, Sept. 24 Litho.

571 A243 10t multi *.55 .55*

World Habitat Day — A244

1998, Oct. 5

572 A244 4t multi *.65 .65*

Intl. Fund for Agricultural Development, 20th Anniv. — A245

Sunflower and: 6t, Farmers, "20." 10t, Vegetables, pickers.

1998, Oct. 17

573 A245	6t multi	*.35*	*.35*
574 A245	10t multi	*.55*	*.55*

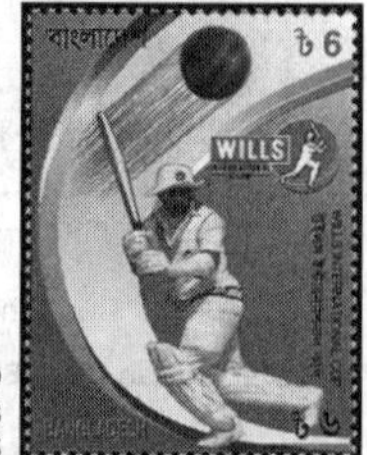

Wills Intl. Cup Cricket Matches A246

1998, Oct. 28

575 A246 6t multi *.35 .35*

Begum Rokeya (1880-1932), Author, Educator — A247

1998, Dec. 9 Litho. *Perf. 14¼x13¾*

576 A247 4t multi *.20 .20*

Universal Declaration of Human Rights, 50th Anniv. — A248

1998, Dec. 10 *Perf. 13¾x14¼*

577 A248 10t multi *.50 .50*

UN Peacekeeping, 50th Anniv. — A249

1998, Dec. 30 *Perf. 13¾x14¼*

578 A249 10t multi *.50 .50*

Qazi Nazrul Islam (1899-1976), Poet — A250

1998, Dec. 31 *Perf. 14¼*

579 A250 6t multi *.35 .35*

Sixth National Scout Jamboree A251

1999, Feb. 6 *Perf. 13¾x14¼*

580 A251 2t multi *.20 .20*

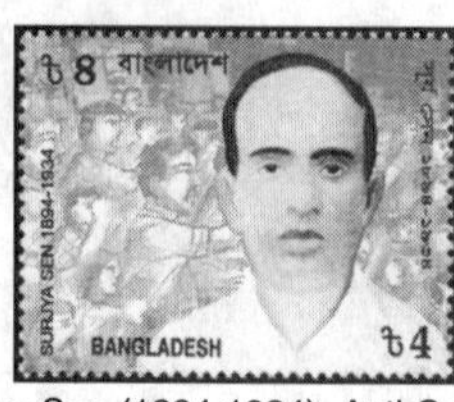

Surjya Sen (1894-1934), Anti-Colonial Leader — A252

1999, Mar. 22 *Perf. 14¼x13¾*

581 A252 4t multi *.20 .20*

Dr. Fazlur Rahman Khan (1929-82), Architect of Sears Tower, Chicago — A253

1999, Apr. 13 *Perf. 13¾x14¼*

582 A253 4t multi *.20 .20*

ICC Cricket World Cup, England — A254

Designs: 8t, Emblems. 10t, Bangladesh flag, cricket ball, tiger.

1999, May 11 *Perf. 13¾x14¼*

583 A254	8t multi	*.45*	*.45*
584 A254	10t multi	*.55*	*.55*
a.	Souv. sheet, #583-584, perf 14¼	*1.75*	*1.75*

No. 584a sold for 30t.

Mother Teresa (1910-97) A255

1999, Sept. 5 *Perf. 13¾x14¼*

585 A255 4t multi *.25 .25*

Admission to UN, 25th Anniv. — A256

1999, Sept. 13

586 A256 8t multi *.40 .40*

Shaheed Mohammad Maizuddin (1930-84) A257

1999, Sept. 27

587 A257 2t multi *.20 .20*

Intl. Year of Older Persons — A258

1999, Oct. 1

588 A258 6t multi *.30 .30*

World Habitat Day A259

1999, Oct. 4 *Perf. 14¼x13¾*

589 A259 4t multi *.20 .20*

UPU, 125th Anniv. A260

1999, Oct. 9 *Perf. 14¼x13¾*

590 A260	4t Truck	*.20*	*.20*
591 A260	4t Motorcycle	*.20*	*.20*
592 A260	6t Boat	*.35*	*.35*
593 A260	6t Airplanes	*.35*	*.35*
a.	Souv. sheet, #590-593, perf 14¼	*1.40*	*1.40*
	Nos. 590-593 (4)	*1.10*	*1.10*

No. 593a sold for 25t.

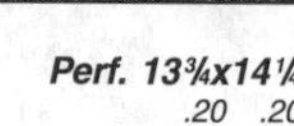

Sir Jagadis Chandra Bose (1858-1937), Physicist A261

1999 *Perf. 13¾x14¼*

594 A261 4t multi *.20 .20*

Martyred Intellectual Type of 1991

Martyred intellectuals who died in 1971 - No. 595: a, Dr. Mohammad Shafi. b, Maulana Kasimuddin Ahmed. c, Quazi Ali Imam. d, Sultanuddin Ahmed. e, A. S. M. Ershadullah. f, Mohammad Fazlur Rahman. g, Dr. Capt. A. K. M. Farooq. h, Mohammad Latafot Hossain Joarder.

1999, Dec. 14 Litho. *Perf. 14¼*
595 A154 2t Sheet of 8, #a-d, + 4 labels *1.90 1.90*

A number has been reserved for an additional sheet in this set.

Millennium — A262

Designs: 4t, Natl. Martyr's Memorial, flag. 6t, Satellite, computer, satellite dish, Bangabandhu Bridge, vert.

Perf. 14¼x13¾, 13¾x14¼
2000, Jan. 1 Litho.
597-598 A262 Set of 2 *.50 .50*

Fifth Cub Camporee A263

2000, Feb. 13 *Perf. 13¾x14¼*
599 A263 2t multi *.20 .20*

Jibanananda Das (1899-1954), Poet — A264

2000, Feb. 17
600 A264 4t multi *.20 .20*

Dr. Muhammad Shamsuzzoha (1934-69), Educator A265

2000, Feb. 18
601 A265 4t multi *.20 .20*

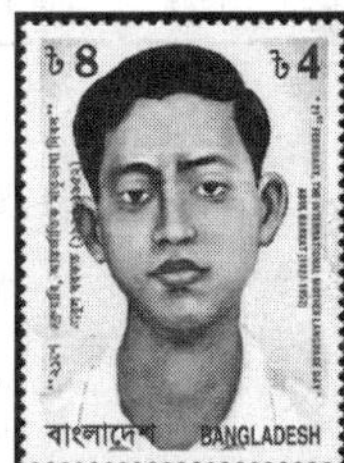

Intl. Mother Language Day — A266

Martyrs: #602, Abul Barkat (1927-52). #603, Abdul Jabbar (1919-52). #604, Shafiur Rahman (1918-52). #605, Rafiq Uddin Ahmad (1926-52).

2000, Feb. 21
602-605 A266 4t Set of 4 *.80 .80*

World Meteorological Organization, 50th Anniv. — A267

2000, Mar. 23
606 A267 10t multi *.50 .50*

ICC Cricketnext.com Cricket Week — A268

2000, Apr. 8
607 A268 6t multi *.30 .30*

Insects — A269

Designs: 2t, Wasp. 4t, Grasshopper. 6t, Apis indica. 10t, Bombyx mori.

2000, May 18 *Perf. 14¼*
608-611 A269 Set of 4 *1.10 1.10*

Fauna A270

Designs: No. 612, 4t, Gekko gecko. No. 613, 4t, Hystrix indica. No. 615, 6t, Python molurus. No. 616, 6t, Varanus bengalensis.

2000, May 18 *Perf. 14¼x13¾*
612-615 A270 Set of 4 *1.00 1.00*

7th Pepsi Asia Cricket Cup — A271

2000, May 28 *Perf. 13¾x14¼*
616 A271 6t multi *.30 .30*

Birds A272

#617, 4t, Amaurornis phoenicurus. #618, 4t, Gallicrex cinerea. #619, 6t, Phalacrocorax niger, vert. #620, 6t, Ardeola grayii, vert.

Perf. 14¼x13¾, 13¾x14¼
2000, July 15
617-620 A272 Set of 4 *1.00 1.00*

2000 Summer Olympics, Sydney — A273

Shot putters: 6t, Woman. 10t, Man.

2000, Sept. 18 *Perf. 13¾x14¼*
621-622 A273 Set of 2 *.80 .80*

Bangladesh - People's Republic of China Diplomatic Relations, 25th Anniv. — A274

2000, Oct. 4 Litho. *Perf. 12½*
623 A274 6t multi *.30 .30*

Idrakpur Fort, Munshigonj — A275

Vajrasattva Bhojavihara Mainamati, Comilla — A276

Perf. 14¼x13¾, 13¾x14¼
2000, Nov. 5 Litho.
624 A275 4t multi *.20 .20*
625 A276 6t multi *.35 .35*

Intl. Volunteers Year (in 2001) — A277

2000, Dec. 5 Litho. *Perf. 13¾x14¼*
626 A277 6t multi *.30 .30*

Martyred Intellectuals Type of 1991

Martyred intellectuals who died in 1971 - No. 627, 2t: a, M. A. Gofur. b, Faizur Rahman Ahmed. c, Muslimuddin Miah. d, Sgt. Shamsul Karim Khan. e, Bhikku Zinananda. f, Abdul Jabber. g, Sekander Hayat Chowdhury. h, Chishty Shah Helalur Rahman.

No. 628, 2t: a, Birendra Nath Sarker. b, A. K. M. Nurul Haque. c, Sibendra Nath Mukherjee. d, Zahir Raihan. e, Ferdous Dowla Bablu. f, Capt. A. K. M. Nurul Absur. g, Mizanur Rahman Miju. h, Dr. Shamshad Ali.

2000 Litho. *Perf. 12½*
Sheets of 8, #a-h, + 4 labels
627-628 A154 Set of 2 *1.75 1.75*

Hason Raza (1854-1922) A278

2000 ? *Perf. 13¾x14¼*
629 A278 6t multi *.35 .35*

2001 Census — A279

2001, Jan. 23 Litho. *Perf. 13¾x14¼*
630 A279 4t multi *.25 .25*

UN High Commissioner for Refugees, 50th Anniv. (in 2001) — A280

Perf. 13¾x14¼
2000, Dec. 14 Litho.
631 A280 10t multi *.45 .45*

Hunger-Free Bangladesh — A281

Perf. 14¼x13¾
2001, Mar. 17 Litho.
632 A281 6t multi *.40 .40*

Peasant Women, by Rashid Chowdhury A282

2001, Apr. 1 Litho. *Perf. 13¾x14¼*
633 A282 10t multi *.45 .45*

Houses of Worship — A283

No. 634: a, Lalbagh Kella Mosque. b, Uttara Ganabhavan, Natore. c, Armenian Church, Armanitola. d, Panam Nagar, Sonargaon.
Illustration reduced.

2001, Apr. 30 ***Perf. 14¼x13¾***

634	A283	6t Block of 4, #a-d	*2.75*	*2.75*

World No Tobacco Day A284

2001, May 31 Litho. ***Perf. 14¼x13¾***

635	A284	10t multi	*.70*	*.70*

Artists — A285

No. 636: a, Ustad Gul Mohammad Khan (1876-1979). b, Ustad Khadem Hossain Khan (1923-91). c, Gouhar Jamil (1928-80). d, Abdul Alim (1931-74).
Illustration reduced.

2001, May 31 ***Perf. 13¾x14¼***

636	A285	6t Block of 4, #a-d	*1.60*	*1.60*

Begum Sufia Kamal (1911-99), Poet — A286

2001, June 20

637	A286	4t multi	*.25*	*.25*

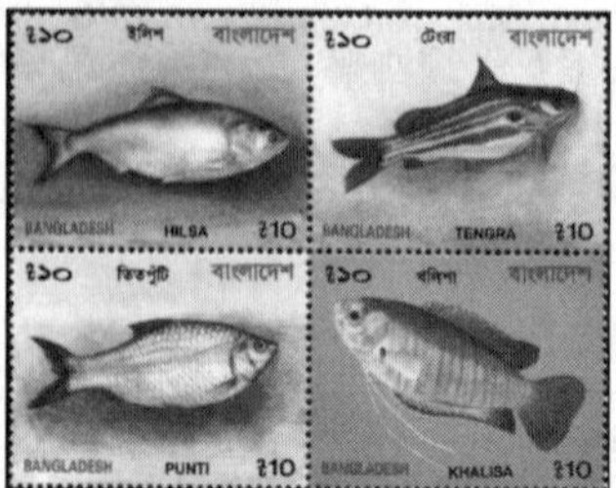

Fish — A287

No. 638: a, Hilsa. b, Tengra. c, Punti. d, Khalisa.
Illustration reduced.

2001, July 9 ***Perf. 14¼x13¾***

638	A287	10t Block of 4, #a-d	*2.75*	*2.75*

First Completion of Parliamentary Term — A288

2001, July 13

639	A288	10t multi	*.70*	*.70*

8th Parliamentary Elections — A289

2001, Sept. 30

640	A289	2t multi	.20	.20

Year of Dialogue Among Civilizations A290

2001, Oct. 24 ***Perf. 14¼***

641	A290	10t multi	*.70*	*.70*
a.		Souvenir sheet of 1	2.10	2.10

No. 641a sold for 30t.

Meer Mosharraf Hossain (1847-1912) A291

2001, Nov. 13 ***Perf. 13¾x14¼***

642	A291	4t multi	*.25*	*.25*

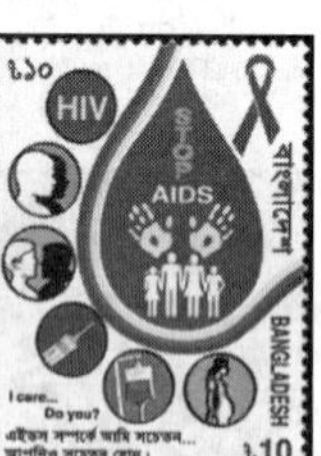

World AIDS Day — A292

2001, Dec. 1

643	A292	10t multi	*.70*	*.70*

Victory in War of Independence, 30th Anniv. — A293

Medals: a, Bir Bikram. b, Bir Protik. c, Bir Sreshto. d, Bir Uttom.

2001, Dec. 16

644		Horiz. strip of 4	*2.80*	*2.80*
a.-d.	A293	10t Any single	*.70*	*.70*

OFFICIAL STAMPS

Nos. 42-47, 49-50, 52, 82-84 and 54 Overprinted in Black or Red

Perf. 14x14½, 14½x14

1973-75 **Litho.**

O1	A7	2p black (R)	.20	.20
O2	A7	3p brt green	.20	.20
O3	A7	5p lt brown	.20	.20
O4	A7	10p black (R)	.20	.20
O5	A7	20p olive	1.10	.20
O6	A7	25p red lilac	3.00	.20
O8	A7	60p gray (R)	3.00	.20
O9	A7	75p orange ('74)	1.10	.25
O10	A9	1t violet (#52)	12.00	3.25
O11	A9	1t violet (#82)	2.25	.35
O12	A9	2t grayish grn ('74)	3.75	1.25
O13	A9	5t gray blue (#54)	5.25	4.50
O14	A9	5t grysh bl (#84) ('75)	6.50	5.00
		Nos. O1-O14 (13)	38.75	16.00

Issue date: Apr. 30, 1973.

Nos. 95-101, 103-105 Overprinted "SERVICE" in Black or Red

1976 Litho. ***Perf. 15x14½, 14½x15***

O16	A7	5p green	.30	.30
O17	A7	10p black (R)	.30	.30
O18	A7	20p olive	.30	.30
O19	A7	25p rose	.30	.30
O20	A8	50p rose lilac	.40	.40
O21	A7	60p gray (R)	.50	.50
O22	A7	75p olive	.55	.55

Perf. 15

O23	A9	1t violet	.85	.85
O24	A9	2t greenish gray	1.60	1.60
O25	A9	5t grayish blue	4.25	4.25
		Nos. O16-O25 (10)	9.35	9.35

Nos. 165-169, 171-175 Ovptd. "SERVICE"

1979-82 **Photo.** ***Perf. 14½***

O27	A7	5p brown	.20	.20
O28	A7	10p Prussian blue	.20	.20
O29	A7	15p yellow orange	.20	.20
O30	A7	20p dk carmine	.20	.20
O31	A7	25p dk blue ('82)	.25	.25
O32	A9	40p rose magenta	.45	.45
O33	A9	50p gray ('81)	.55	.55
O34	A7	80p dark brown	.80	.80
O35	A7	1t red lilac ('81)	1.10	1.10
O36	A7	2t brt ultra ('81)	1.90	1.90
		Nos. O27-O36 (10)	5.85	5.85

#234-242, 271 Ovptd. "Service" in Red, Diagonally Up on #O43A, 1t, 2t, 4t

1983-93 ***Perf. 11½x12½, 12½x11½***

O37	A70	5p bluish green	.20	.20
O38	A70	10p deep magenta	.20	.20
O39	A70	15p blue	.20	.20
O40	A70	20p dark gray	.20	.20
O41	A70	25p slate	.20	.20
O42	A70	30p gray brown	.20	.20
O43	A70	50p yellow brown	.20	.20
O43A	A70	50p yellow brown	.20	.20

Size: 30½x28½mm

Perf. 12x11½

O44	A70	1t ultramarine	.30	.30
O45	A70	2t Prussian blue	.60	.60

Perf. 12

O46	A70	4t blue	1.40	1.40
		Nos. O37-O46 (11)	3.90	3.90

Issued: 4t, 7/27/92; #O43A, 1993(?); others, 12/21/83.

No. 379A Ovptd. in Red

1990 **Litho.** ***Perf. 14½x14***

O47	A139a	2t brown		

No. 350 Ovptd. "Service" Diagonally in Red

1994, July 16 Litho. ***Perf. 12x11½***

O47A	A122	3t multicolored	*11.50*	*11.50*

No. 354 Ovptd. in Red

1992, Nov. 22 Litho. ***Perf. 14½x14***

O47B	A125	6t blue gray & yel	*6.75*	*6.75*

No. 241 Ovptd. in Red

1992, Sept. 16 Litho. ***Perf. 12x11½***

O48	A70	1t ultramarine	.20	.20

No. 484 Ovptd. in Red

1996 **Litho.** ***Perf. 14***

O49	A204	2t multicolored	*2.75*	*2.75*

No. 351 Ovptd. in Blue

1997? **Litho.** ***Perf. 12***

O50	A122	5t multicolored	*.30*	*.30*

Bengali overprint reads from top to bottom.

Nos. 235, 237 Ovptd. in Black or Red সার্ভিস

1997? ***Perf. 12½x11½***

O51	A70	10p on #235	*.65*	*.65*
O52	A70	20p on #237 (R)	*1.25*	*1.25*

No. 560 Ovptd. in Red

1998 **Litho.** ***Perf. 14½x14***

O53	A139a	1t green	*.20*	*.20*

BARBADOS

bär-ˈbā-ˌdōs

LOCATION — A West Indies island east of the Windwards
GOVT. — Independent state in the British Commonwealth
AREA — 166 sq. mi.
POP. — 266,100 (1997 est.)
CAPITAL — Bridgetown

The British colony of Barbados became an independent state on November 30, 1966.

4 Farthings = 1 Penny
12 Pence = 1 Shilling
20 Shillings = 1 Pound
100 Cents = 1 Dollar (1950)

Catalogue values for unused stamps in this country are for Never Hinged items, beginning with Scott 207 in the regular postage section, Scott B2 in the semi-postal section and Scott J1 in the postage due section.

Watermarks

Wmk. 5- Small Star

Wmk. 6- Large Star

Values for unused stamps are for examples with original gum as defined in the catalogue introduction. Very fine examples of Nos. 10-42a, 44-59a will have perforations touching the design on at least one side due to the narrow spacing of the stamps on the plates and imperfect perforation methods. Stamps with perfs clear of the design on all four sides are extremely scarce and will command higher prices.

Britannia
A1 A2

1852-55 Unwmk. Engr. *Imperf.*
Blued Paper

1	A1	(½p) deep green	100.00	*300.00*
a.		(½p) yellow green	*9,000.*	700.00
2	A1	(1p) dark blue	16.50	*65.00*
a.		(1p) blue	25.00	*175.00*
3	A1	(2p) slate blue	15.00	
a.		(2p) grayish slate	200.00	*1,100.*
b.		As "a," vert. half used as 1p on cover		*6,750.*
4	A1	(4p) brn red ('55)	62.50	*275.00*
		Nos. 1-4 (4)	194.00	

No. 3 was not placed in use. Beware of color changelings of Nos. 2-3 that may resemble No. 3a. Certificates of authenticity are required for Nos. 3a and 3b.

Use of #3b was authorized from 8/4-9/21/1854.

1855-58
White Paper

5	A1	(½p) deep green ('58)	85.50	*175.00*
a.		(½p) yellow green ('57)	400.00	100.00
6	A1	(1p) blue	20.00	*50.00*
a.		(1p) pale blue	55.00	*60.00*

It is believed that the (4p) brownish red on white paper exists only as No. 17b.

1859

8	A2	6p rose red	625.00	100.00
9	A2	1sh black	150.00	60.00

Pin-perf. 14

10	A1	(½p) pale yel grn	2,250.	350.00
11	A1	(1p) blue	2,250.	140.00

Pin-perf. 12½

12	A1	(½p) pale yel grn	*5,500.*	550.
12A	A1	(1p) blue	*16,000.*	1,250.

Pin-perf. 14x12½

12B	A1	(½p) pale yel grn	—	*3,250.*

1861 *Clean-Cut Perf. 14 to 16*

13	A1	(½p) dark blue grn	65.00	9.00
14	A1	(1p) pale blue	575.00	45.00
a.		(1p) blue	650.00	45.00
b.		Half used as ½p on cover		*3,150.*

Rough Perf. 14 to 16

15	A1	(½p) green	10.50	8.00
a.		(½p) blue green	60.00	75.00
b.		Imperf., pair	450.00	
16	A1	(1p) blue	24.00	3.00
a.		Diagonal half used as ½p on cover		*1,750.*
b.		Imperf., pair	500.00	450.00
17	A1	(4p) rose red	62.50	27.50
a.		(4p) brown red	90.00	35.00
b.		As "a," imperf., pair	850.00	
c.		(4p) rose red, imperf., pair	675.00	
18	A1	(4p) vermilion	175.00	60.00
a.		Imperf., pair	800.00	
19	A2	6p rose red	175.00	11.00
20	A2	6p orange ver	55.00	15.00
a.		6p vermilion	67.50	12.00
b.		Imperf., pair	400.00	*800.00*
21	A2	1sh brownish black	45.00	3.75
b.		Horiz. pair, imperf. btwn.	*5,250.*	
c.		1sh blue (error)	*13,500.*	

No. 21c was never placed in use. All copies are pen-marked (some have been removed) and have clipped perfs on one or more sides.

Use of #14b, 16a was authorized from 4/63-11/66.

Perf. 11 to 13

22	A1	(½p) deep green	*6,500.*	
23	A1	(1p) blue	*2,000.*	

Nos. 22 and 23 were never placed in use.

1870 Wmk. 6 *Rough Perf. 14 to 16*

24	A1	(½p) green	80.00	10.00
a.		Imperf., pair (#24)	750.00	
b.		(½p) yellow green	110.00	40.00
25	A1	(1p) blue	1,200.	40.00
a.		Imperf., pair	*1,500.*	
26	A1	(4p) dull red	700.00	80.00
27	A2	6p vermilion	650.00	50.00
28	A2	1sh black	250.00	17.50

1871 Wmk. 5

29	A1	(1p) blue	90.00	3.00
30	A1	(4p) rose red	750.00	30.00
31	A2	6p vermilion	400.00	22.50
32	A2	1sh black	125.00	10.00

Clean-Cut Perf. 14½ to 16

33	A1	(1p) blue	190.00	3.00
a.		Diagonal half used as ½p on cover		*1,500.*
34	A2	6p vermilion	600.00	50.00
35	A2	1sh black	120.00	9.00

Perf. 11 to 13x14½ to 16

36	A1	(½p) blue green	225.00	27.50
37	A1	(4p) vermilion	475.00	80.00

1873 *Perf. 14*

38	A2	3p claret	475.00	110.00

Wmk. 6
Clean-Cut Perf. 14½ to 16

39	A1	(½p) blue green	190.00	17.50
40	A1	(4p) rose red	800.00	140.00
41	A2	6p vermilion	575.00	60.00
a.		Imperf., pair	75.00	*1,500.*
b.		Horiz. pair, imperf. btwn.	*4,500.*	
42	A2	1sh black	100.00	12.00
a.		Horiz. pair, imperf. btwn.	*4,250.*	

Britannia — A3

1873 Wmk. 5 *Perf. 15½x15*

43	A3	5sh dull rose	1,000.	375.00

For surcharged bisects see Nos. 57-59.

1874 Wmk. 6 *Perf. 14*

44	A2	½p blue green	22.50	7.50
45	A2	1p blue	67.50	3.50

Clean-Cut Perf. 14½ to 16

45A	A2	1p blue		*12,000.*

1875 Wmk. 1 *Perf. 12½*

46	A2	½p yellow green	35.00	3.00
47	A2	4p scarlet	175.00	9.00
48	A2	6p orange	550.00	70.00
49	A2	1sh purple	425.00	15.00
		Nos. 46-49 (4)	1,185.	97.00

1875-78 *Perf. 14*

50	A2	½p yel green ('76)	8.00	2.00
51	A2	1p ultramarine	45.00	.75
a.		1p gray blue	45.00	.75
b.		Half used as ½p on cover		1,400.
c.		Watermarked sideways		1,500.
52	A2	3p violet ('78)	85.00	9.00
53	A2	4p rose red	85.00	8.00
a.		4p scarlet	140.00	6.00
b.		As "a," perf. 14x12½	*4,750.*	
54	A2	4p lake	450.00	5.00
55	A2	6p chrome yel	95.00	3.25
a.		6p yellow	300.00	16.00
56	A2	1sh purple ('76)	125.00	5.00
a.		1sh violet	2,500.	40.00
b.		1sh dull mauve	350.00	4.50
c.		Half used as 6p on cover		*4,500.*

#48, 49, 55, 56 have the watermark sideways.

No. 53b was never placed in use.

A4

A5

Large Surcharge, ("1" 7mm High, "D" 2¾mm High)

1878 Wmk. 5 *Perf. 15½x15*
Slanting Serif

57	A4	1p on half of 5sh	*4,000.*	650.
a.		Unsevered pair	*16,000.*	*2,250.*
b.		Unsevered horiz. pair, #57 + 58		*3,500.*
d.		Unsevered horiz. pair, #57 + 58, imperf. between		—
e.		Unsevered horiz. pair, #57 + 59, imperf. between	*25,000.*	*8,500.*

Straight Serif

58	A4	1p on half of 5sh	*4,500.*	*950.*
a.		Unsevered pair		*3,750.*

Small Surcharge, ("1" 6mm, "D" 2½mm High)

59	A5	1p on half of 5sh	*5,250.*	*950.00*
a.		Unsevered pair	*17,000.*	*3,750.*

On Nos. 57, 58 and 59 the surcharge is found reading upwards or downwards.

The perforation, which divides the stamp into halves, measures 11½ to 13.

The old denomination has been cut off the bottom of the stamps.

Queen Victoria — A6

1882-85 Typo. Wmk. 2 *Perf. 14*

60	A6	½p green	5.25	.80
61	A6	1p carmine rose	4.75	.50
a.		1p rose	47.50	1.75
b.		Half used as ½p on cover		900.00
62	A6	2½p dull blue	52.50	.75
a.		2½p ultramarine	70.00	1.50
63	A6	3p magenta	3.00	*8.75*
a.		3p lilac	85.00	26.00
64	A6	4p slate	175.00	2.00
65	A6	4p brown ('85)	2.75	1.00
66	A6	6p olive gray	52.50	25.00
67	A6	1sh orange brown	17.00	18.00
68	A6	5sh bister	125.00	*175.00*
		Nos. 60-68 (9)	437.75	*231.80*

No. 65 Surcharged in Black

1892

69	A6	½p on 4p brown	1.75	2.50
a.		Without hyphen	9.00	*15.00*
b.		Double surcharge		
c.		Double surch., red & black	500.00	*1,050.*
d.		As "c," without hyphen	1,350.	1,350.

A8

Badge of Colony — A9

1892-1903 Wmk. 2

70	A8	1f sl & car ('96)	1.60	.20
71	A8	½p green	1.90	.20
72	A8	1p carmine rose	3.50	.20
73	A8	2p sl & org ('99)	6.00	.70
74	A8	2½p ultramarine	12.50	.20
75	A8	5p olive brn	5.25	3.50
76	A8	6p vio & car	9.50	1.50
77	A8	8p org & ultra	2.75	*15.00*
78	A8	10p bl grn & car	6.00	*5.00*
79	A8	2sh6p slate & org	35.00	35.00
80	A8	2sh6p pur & grn ('03)	55.00	*97.50*
		Nos. 70-80 (11)	139.00	*159.00*

See Nos. 90-101. For surcharge see No B1.

Victoria Jubilee Issue

1897 **Wmk. 1**

No.	Type	Description	Unused	Used
81	A9	1f gray & car	1.25	.30
82	A9	½p gray green	1.75	.30
83	A9	1p carmine rose	2.00	.35
84	A9	2½p ultra	4.25	.70
85	A9	5p dk olive brn	8.50	*9.25*
86	A9	6p vio & car	12.00	*14.00*
87	A9	8p org & ultra	7.00	*15.00*
88	A9	10p bl grn & car	30.00	*35.00*
89	A9	2sh6p slate & org	35.00	*42.50*
		Nos. 81-89 (9)	101.75	*117.40*

Bluish Paper

No.	Type	Description	Unused	Used
81a	A9	1f gray & car	24.00	*27.50*
82a	A9	½p gray green	25.00	*27.50*
83a	A9	1p carmine rose	32.50	*35.00*
84a	A9	2½p ultra	35.00	*40.00*
85a	A9	5p dk olive brn	210.00	*225.00*
86a	A9	6p vio & car	125.00	125.00
87a	A9	8p org & ultra	125.00	*140.00*
88a	A9	10p bl grn & car	175.00	*200.00*
89a	A9	2sh6p slate & org	*100.00*	*110.00*
		Nos. 81a-89a (9)	851.50	*930.00*

Badge Type of 1892-1903

1904-10 **Wmk. 3**

No.	Type	Description	Unused	Used
90	A8	1f gray & car	5.50	1.25
91	A8	1f brown ('09)	3.25	.25
92	A8	½p green	9.50	.20
93	A8	1p carmine rose	9.25	.20
94	A8	1p carmine ('09)	8.75	.20
95	A8	2p gray ('09)	5.00	*7.75*
96	A8	2½p ultramarine	8.00	.40
97	A8	6p vio & car	8.00	*12.50*
98	A8	6p dl vio & vio ('10)	6.25	*12.00*
99	A8	8p org & ultra	52.50	*27.50*
100	A8	1sh blk, *grn* ('10)	6.50	*12.00*
101	A8	2sh6p pur & green	27.50	*55.00*
		Nos. 90-101 (12)	150.00	*129.25*

Nelson Centenary Issue

Lord Nelson Monument — A10

1906 **Engr.** **Wmk. 1**

No.	Type	Description	Unused	Used
102	A10	1f gray & black	2.00	.60
103	A10	½p green & black	3.00	.40
104	A10	1p car & black	3.50	.25
105	A10	2p org & black	4.00	4.25
106	A10	2½p ultra & black	5.00	4.00
107	A10	6p lilac & black	15.00	*19.00*
108	A10	1sh rose & black	17.50	*32.50*
		Nos. 102-108 (7)	50.00	*61.00*

See Nos. 110-112.

The "Olive Blossom" A11

1906, Aug. 15 **Wmk. 3**

No.	Type	Description	Unused	Used
109	A11	1p blk, green & blue	9.00	1.00

Tercentenary of the 1st British landing.

Nelson Type of 1906

1907, July 6 **Wmk. 3**

No.	Type	Description	Unused	Used
110	A10	1f gray & black	4.25	2.25
111	A10	2p org & black	15.00	*17.00*
112	A10	2½p ultra & black	8.25	*16.00*
a.		2½p indigo & black	750.00	*1,000.*
		Nos. 110-112 (3)	27.50	*35.25*

A12

A13

King George V — A14

1912 **Typo.**

No.	Type	Description	Unused	Used
116	A12	¼p brown	.40	*.85*
117	A12	½p green	1.50	.20
a.		Booklet pane of 6		
118	A12	1p carmine	3.00	.20
a.		1p scarlet	12.50	2.00
b.		Booklet pane of 6		
119	A12	2p gray	1.60	*8.25*
120	A12	2½p ultramarine	1.00	.25
121	A13	3p violet, *yel*	1.00	*8.25*
122	A13	4p blk & scar, *yel*	1.00	*9.50*
123	A13	6p vio & red vio	6.00	*7.00*
124	A14	1sh black, *green*	4.00	*6.50*
125	A14	2sh vio & ultra, *bl*	24.00	*26.00*
126	A14	3sh grn & violet	47.50	*52.50*
		Nos. 116-126 (11)	91.00	119.50

Seal of the Colony — A15

1916-18 **Engr.**

No.	Type	Description	Unused	Used
127	A15	¼p brown	.30	.25
128	A15	½p green	.75	.20
129	A15	1p red	1.00	.20
130	A15	2p gray	3.50	*10.00*
131	A15	2½p ultramarine	.85	.75
132	A15	3p violet, *yel*	2.25	*2.50*
133	A15	4p red, *yel*	.60	*5.00*
134	A15	4p red & blk ('18)	.85	*2.50*
135	A15	6p claret	1.50	*2.25*
136	A15	1sh black, *green*	3.50	*5.00*
137	A15	2sh violet, *blue*	15.00	8.50
138	A15	3sh dark violet	32.50	*70.00*
139	A15	3sh dk vio & grn ('18)	15.00	*30.00*
a.		3sh bright vio & grn ('18)	150.00	*175.00*
		Nos. 127-139 (13)	77.60	*137.15*

Nos. 134 and 139 are from a re-engraved die. The central medallion is not surrounded by a line and there are various other small alterations.

Victory Issue

A16

A17

Victory

1920, Sept. 9 **Wmk. 3**

No.	Type	Description	Unused	Used
140	A16	¼p bister & black	.25	*.55*
141	A16	½p yel green & blk	.80	.20
a.		Booklet pane of 2		
142	A16	1p org red & blk	2.25	.20
a.		Booklet pane of 2		
143	A16	2p gray & black	2.00	*4.25*
144	A16	2½p ultra & dk bl	2.40	*6.50*
145	A16	3p red lilac & blk	2.40	*3.25*
146	A16	4p gray grn & blk	2.40	*3.50*
147	A16	6p orange & blk	3.00	*6.50*
148	A17	1sh yel green & blk	7.50	*14.00*
149	A17	2sh brown & blk	17.00	*18.00*
150	A17	3sh orange & blk	20.00	*22.00*
		Nos. 140-150 (11)	60.00	*78.95*

1921, Aug. 22 **Wmk. 4**

No.	Type	Description	Unused	Used
151	A16	1p orange red & blk	14.00	.20
		Nos. 140-151 (12)	74.00	*79.15*

A18

A19

1921-24 **Wmk. 4**

No.	Type	Description	Unused	Used
152	A18	¼p brown	.20	.20
153	A18	½p green	.35	.20
154	A18	1p carmine	.30	.20
155	A18	2p gray	1.25	.20
156	A18	2½p ultramarine	.95	*4.00*
158	A18	6p claret	1.50	*3.50*
159	A18	1sh blk, *emer* ('24)	30.00	*55.00*
160	A18	2sh dk vio, *blue*	13.00	12.50
161	A18	3sh dark violet	13.00	*30.00*

Wmk. 3

No.	Type	Description	Unused	Used
162	A18	3p violet, *yel*	.75	*4.00*
163	A18	4p red, *yel*	.70	*7.75*
164	A18	1sh black, *green*	4.00	*7.00*
		Nos. 152-164 (12)	66.00	*124.55*

1925-35 **Wmk. 4** ***Perf. 14***

No.	Type	Description	Unused	Used
165	A19	¼p brown	.20	.20
166	A19	½p green	.20	.20
a.		Perf. 13½x12½ ('32)	5.00	.20
b.		Booklet pane of 10		
167	A19	1p carmine	.20	.20
a.		Perf. 13½x12½ ('32)	4.50	.30
b.		Booklet pane of 10		
168	A19	1½p org, perf. 13½x12½ ('32)	.75	.60
a.		Booklet pane of 6		
b.		Perf. 14	3.50	.80
169	A19	2p gray	.50	*1.25*
170	A19	2½p ultramarine	.50	.50
a.		Perf. 13½x12½ ('32)	4.50	2.00
171	A19	3p vio brn, *yel*	.60	.45
172	A19	3p red brn, *yel* ('35)	6.00	6.00
173	A19	4p red, *yel*	.80	.80
174	A19	6p claret	.80	.80
175	A19	1sh blk, *emerald*	1.50	*2.50*
a.		Perf. 13½x12½ ('32)	37.50	22.50
176	A19	1sh brn blk, *yel grn* ('32)	4.25	*7.50*
177	A19	2sh violet, *bl*	5.00	4.00
178	A19	2sh6p car, *blue* ('32)	15.00	*17.50*
179	A19	3sh dark violet	8.00	*12.50*
		Nos. 165-179 (15)	44.30	*55.00*

Charles I and George V — A20

1927, Feb. 17 ***Perf. 12½***

No.	Type	Description	Unused	Used
180	A20	1p carmine lake	1.25	.75

Tercentenary of the settlement of Barbados.

Common Design Types pictured following the introduction.

Silver Jubilee Issue

Common Design Type

1935, May 6 ***Perf. 11x12***

No.	Type	Description	Unused	Used
186	CD301	1p car & dk bl	.25	.25
187	CD301	1½p blk & ultra	1.25	*3.25*
188	CD301	2½p ultra & brn	1.00	*2.00*
189	CD301	1sh brn vio & ind	6.50	9.50
		Nos. 186-189 (4)	9.00	15.00
		Set, never hinged	20.00	

Coronation Issue

Common Design Type

1937, May 14 ***Perf. 13½x14***

No.	Type	Description	Unused	Used
190	CD302	1p carmine	.20	.20
191	CD302	1½p brown	.20	.20
192	CD302	2½p bright ultra	.40	.40
		Nos. 190-192 (3)	.80	.80
		Set, never hinged	1.25	

A21

1938-47 ***Perf. 13-14 & Compound***

No.	Type	Description	Unused	Used
193	A21	½p green	3.00	.20
b.		Perf. 14	45.00	1.40
c.		Booklet pane of 10		
193A	A21	½p bister ('42)	.20	.20
194	A21	1p carmine	7.75	.20
b.		Perf. 13½x13	150.00	3.00
c.		Booklet pane of 10		
194A	A21	1p green ('42)	.20	.20
d.		Perf. 13½x13	2.00	.50
195	A21	1½p red orange	.20	.20
c.		Perf. 14	3.50	.50
d.		Booklet pane of 6		
195A	A21	2p rose lake ('41)	.20	*2.25*
195B	A21	2p bright rose red ('43)	.20	*.35*
e.		Perf. 14	.20	*1.00*
196	A21	2½p ultramarine	.25	*.35*
197	A21	3p brown	.20	1.10
b.		Perf. 14	.25	.20
197A	A21	3p deep bl ('47)	.20	*1.00*
198	A21	4p black	.20	.20
a.		Perf. 14	.30	.30
199	A21	6p violet	.40	.20
199A	A21	8p red vio ('46)	.25	*1.10*
200	A21	1sh brn olive	.50	.20
a.		1sh olive green	7.50	1.40
201	A21	2sh6p brown vio	3.25	.80
201A	A21	5sh indigo ('41)	1.50	3.00
		Nos. 193-201A (16)	18.50	11.55
		Set, never hinged	30.00	

For surcharge see No. 209.

Kings Charles I, George VI Assembly Chamber and Mace A22

Perf. 13½x14

1939, June 27 **Engr.** **Wmk. 4**

No.	Type	Description	Unused	Used
202	A22	½p deep green	1.40	.35
203	A22	1p scarlet	1.40	.20
204	A22	1½p deep orange	1.40	.45
205	A22	2½p ultramarine	1.40	*2.50*
206	A22	3p yellow brown	1.40	*1.50*
		Nos. 202-206 (5)	7.00	*5.00*
		Set, never hinged	10.00	

Tercentenary of the General Assembly.

Catalogue values for unused stamps in this section, from this point to the end of the section, are for Never Hinged items.

Peace Issue

Common Design Type

1946, Sept. 18

No.	Type	Description	Unused	Used
207	CD303	1½p deep orange	.20	.20
208	CD303	3p brown	.20	.20

Nos. 195e, 195B, Surcharged in Black

1947, Apr. 21 ***Perf. 14***

No.	Type	Description	Unused	Used
209	A21	1p on 2p brt rose red	1.00	1.00
a.		Double surcharge		
b.		Perf. 13½x13	2.00	2.00

The existence of No. 209a has been questioned by specialists. The editors would like to see authenticated evidence of its existence.

Silver Wedding Issue

Common Design Types

Perf. 14x14½

1948, Nov. 24 **Photo.** **Wmk. 4**

No.	Type	Description	Unused	Used
210	CD304	1½p orange	.20	.20

Engraved; Name Typographed

Perf. 11½x11

No.	Type	Description	Unused	Used
211	CD305	5sh dark blue	10.00	8.00

UPU Issue

Common Design Types

1949, Oct. 10 ***Perf. 13½, 11x11½***

No.	Type	Description	Unused	Used
212	CD306	1½p red orange	.35	.35
213	CD307	3p indigo	.55	.55
214	CD308	4p gray	1.00	1.00
215	CD309	1sh olive	1.40	1.40
		Nos. 212-215 (4)	3.30	3.30

Dover Fort — A23

Admiral Nelson Statue — A24

Designs: 2c, Sugar cane breeding. 3c, Public buildings. 6c, Casting net. 8c, Intercolonial schooner. 12c, Flying Fish. 24c, Old Main Guard Garrison. 48c, Cathedral. 60c, Careenage. $1.20, Map. $2.40, Great Seal, 1660.

Perf. 11x11½ (A23), 13x13½ (A24)

1950, May 1 Engr. Wmk. 4

216 A23 1c slate .20 .20
217 A23 2c emerald .20 .20
218 A23 3c slate & brown .20 .20
219 A24 4c carmine .30 .30
220 A23 6c blue .35 .30
221 A23 8c choc & blue .60 .40
222 A23 12c olive & aqua 1.25 .75
223 A23 24c gray & red 1.40 1.00
224 A24 48c violet 4.00 2.75
225 A23 60c brn car & bl grn 2.50 *3.00*
226 A24 $1.20 olive & car 9.00 5.25
227 A23 $2.40 gray 21.00 13.00
Nos. 216-227 (12) 41.00 27.35

University Issue

Common Design Types

1951, Feb. 16 *Perf. 14x14½*

228 CD310 3c turq bl & choc .25 .20
229 CD311 12c ol brn & turq bl 1.00 .75

Stamp of 1852 A25

Perf. 13½

1952, Apr. 15 Wmk. 4 Engr.

230 A25 3c slate bl & dp grn .20 .20
231 A25 4c rose pink & bl .25 *.60*
232 A25 12c emer & slate bl .30 *.60*
233 A25 24c gray blk & red brn .50 .50
Nos. 230-233 (4) 1.25 *1.90*

Centenary of Barbados postage stamps.

Coronation Issue

Common Design Type

1953, June 4 *Perf. 13½x13*

234 CD312 4c red orange & black .30 .20

Harbor Police A26

Designs as in 1950 with portrait of Queen Elizabeth II. $2.40, Great Seal, 1660 ("E II R").

Perf. 11x11½ (horiz.), 13x13½ (vert.)

1953-57 Engr.

235 A23 1c slate ('53) .20 *.65*
236 A23 2c grnsh blue & deep org .20 *.35*
237 A23 3c emerald & blk .80 .45
238 A24 4c orange & gray .20 .20
239 A26 5c dp car & dp bl .70 .35
240 A23 6c red brown .40 .35
241 A23 8c brt blue & blk 1.60 .35
242 A23 12c brn ol & aqua .80 .20
243 A23 24c gray & red ('56) .35 .20
244 A24 48c violet ('56) 4.00 .90
245 A23 60c brown car & blue grn ('56) 15.00 4.50
246 A24 $1.20 ol & car ('56) 14.50 2.25
247 A23 $2.40 gray ('57) 5.75 1.10
Nos. 235-247 (13) 44.50 11.85

See Nos. 257-264.

West Indies Federation

Common Design Type

Perf. 11½x11

1958, Apr. 23 Wmk. 314

248 CD313 3c green .20 .20
249 CD313 6c blue .40 *1.00*
250 CD313 12c carmine rose .50 .40
Nos. 248-250 (3) 1.10 *1.60*

Deep Water Harbor, Bridgetown A27

1961, May 6 Engr. *Perf. 11x11½*

251 A27 4c orange & black .25 .30
252 A27 8c ultra & black .30 .50
253 A27 24c black & pink .45 .50
Nos. 251-253 (3) 1.00 1.30

Deep Water Harbor at Bridgetown opening.

Scout Emblem and Map of Barbados — A28

Perf. 11½x11

1962, Mar. 9 Wmk. 314

254 A28 4c orange & black .30 .20
255 A28 12c gray & blue .75 .25
256 A28 $1.20 greenish gray & carmine rose 1.25 *2.25*
Nos. 254-256 (3) 2.30 *2.70*

50th anniv. of the founding of the Boy Scouts of Barbados.

Queen Types of 1953-57

Perf. 11x11½, 13x13½

1964-65 Engr. Wmk. 314

257 A23 1c slate .25 *1.75*
258 A24 4c orange & gray .35 *.45*
259 A23 8c brt bl & blk ('65) .50 .30
260 A23 12c brn ol & aqua ('65) .60
261 A23 24c gray & red .60 .45
262 A24 48c violet 2.50 1.75
263 A23 60c brn car & bl grn 6.50 3.50
264 A23 $2.40 gray ('65) 4.00 2.00
Nos. 257-264 (8) 15.30
Nos. 257-259,261-264 (7) 10.20

The 12c was never put on sale in Barbados.

ITU Issue

Common Design Type

Perf. 11x11½

1965, May 17 Litho. Wmk. 314

265 CD317 2c lilac & ver .20 .20
266 CD317 48c yellow & gray 1.50 1.50

Sea Horse A29

Designs: 1c, Deep sea coral. 2c, Lobster. 4c, Sea urchin. 5c, Staghorn coral. 6c, Butterflyfish. 8c, File shell. 12c, Balloonfish. 15c, Angelfish. 25c, Brain coral. 35c, Brittle star. 50c, Flyingfish. $1, Queen conch shell. $2.50, Fiddler crab.

Wmk. 314 Upright

1965, July 15 Photo. *Perf. 14x13½*

267 A29 1c dk blue, pink & black .25 .25
268 A29 2c car rose, sepia & orange .20 .20
269 A29 3c org, brn & sep *("Hippocanpus")* .50 .65
270 A29 4c ol grn & dk bl .20 .20
a. Imperf., pair *300.00* 150.00
271 A29 5c lil, brn & pink .35 .35
272 A29 6c greenish bl, yel & blk .50 .25
273 A29 8c ultra, orange, red & black .30 .20
274 A29 12c rose lil, yel & blk .40 .20
275 A29 15c red, yel & blk .90 .55
276 A29 25c yel brn & ultra 1.10 .55
277 A29 35c grn, rose brn & blk 1.75 .20
278 A29 50c yel grn & ultra 2.25 .45
279 A29 $1 gray & multi 3.25 1.40
280 A29 $2.50 lt bl & multi 3.25 2.50
Nos. 267-280 (14) 15.20 7.95

1966-69 Wmk. 314 Sideways

Design: $5, "Dolphin" (coryphaena hippurus).

267a A29 1c .20 .20
268a A29 2c ('67) .25 *.70*
269A A29 3c *("Hippocampus")* ('67) .25 *2.40*
270b A29 4c .40 .20
271a A29 5c .35 .20
272a A29 6c ('67) .55 .20
273a A29 8c ('67) .55 .20
274a A29 12c ('67) .40 .20
275a A29 15c 1.75 .20
276a A29 25c 1.75 .35
277a A29 35c 1.90 .55
278a A29 50c 1.40 *2.75*
279a A29 $1 4.50 .85
280a A29 $2.50 5.25 2.50
280B A29 $5 dk ol & multi ('69) 10.50 7.00
Nos. 267a-280B (15) 30.00 18.50

For surcharge see No. 327.

Churchill Memorial Issue

Common Design Type

1966, Jan. 24 Wmk. 314 *Perf. 14*

281 CD319 1c multicolored .20 *1.50*
282 CD319 4c multicolored .30 .25
283 CD319 25c multicolored .80 .80
284 CD319 35c multicolored .95 .95
Nos. 281-284 (4) 2.25 3.50

Royal Visit Issue

Common Design Type

1966, Feb. 4 Litho. *Perf. 11x12*

285 CD320 3c violet blue .25 .20
286 CD320 35c dark car rose 2.00 1.75

UNESCO Anniversary Issue

Common Design Type

1967, Jan. 6 Litho. *Perf. 14*

287 CD323 4c "Education" .20 .20
288 CD323 12c "Science" .55 .55
289 CD323 25c "Culture" 1.40 1.40
Nos. 287-289 (3) 2.15 2.15

Arms of Barbados — A30

Policeman and Anchor Monument — A31

Designs: 25c, Hilton Hotel, horiz. 35c, Garfield Sobers, captain of Barbados and West Indies Cricket Team. 50c, Pine Hill Dairy, horiz.

1966, Dec. 2 Unwmk. Photo.

290 A30 4c multicolored .20 .20
291 A30 25c multicolored .20 .20
292 A30 35c multicolored 1.40 .50
293 A30 50c multicolored .70 .70
Nos. 290-293 (4) 2.50 1.60

Barbados' independence, Nov. 30, 1966.

1967, Oct. 16 Litho. *Perf. 13½x14*

Designs: 25c, Policeman with telescope. 35c, Police motor launch, horiz. 50c, Policemen at Harbor Gate.

294 A31 4c multicolored .20 .20
295 A31 25c multicolored .25 .25
296 A31 35c multicolored .40 .40
297 A31 50c multicolored .70 .70
Nos. 294-297 (4) 1.55 1.55

Centenary of Bridgetown Harbor Police.
For surcharge see No. 322.

Independence Arch — A32

1st Anniv. of Independence: 4c, Sir Winston Scott, Governor-General, vert. 35c, Treasury Building. 50c, Parliament Building.

Perf. 14½x14, 14x14½

1967, Dec. 4 Photo. Unwmk.

298 A32 4c multicolored .20 .20
299 A32 25c multicolored .20 .20
300 A32 35c multicolored .25 .25
301 A32 50c multicolored .35 .35
Nos. 298-301 (4) 1.00 1.00

UN Building, Santiago, Chile — A33

1968, Feb. 27 *Perf. 14½x14*

302 A33 15c multicolored .20 .20

20th anniv. of the UN Economic Commission for Latin America.

Radar Antenna on Top of Old Sugar Mill, Sugar Cane — A34

Designs: 25c, Caribbean Meteorological Institute, Barbados, horiz. 50c, HARP gun used in High Altitude Research Program, at Paragon in Christ Church, Barbados.

Perf. 14x14½, 14½x14

1968, June 4 Photo. Unwmk.

303	A34	3c violet & multi	.20	.20
304	A34	25c vermilion & multi	.25	.25
305	A34	50c orange & multi	.40	.40
		Nos. 303-305 (3)	.85	.85

World Meteorological Day.

Girl Scout at Campfire, Lady Baden-Powell and Queen Elizabeth II — A35

Lady Baden-Powell, Queen Elizabeth II and: 25c, Pax Hill Headquarters. 35c, Girl Scout badge.

Perf. 14x14½

1968, Aug. 29 Photo. Unwmk.

306	A35	3c dp ultra, blk & gold	.20	.20
307	A35	25c bluish green, black & gold	.35	.35
308	A35	35c org yel, blk & gold	.70	.70
		Nos. 306-308 (3)	1.25	1.25

Barbados Girl Scouts' 50th anniv.

Human Rights Flame and Escape to Freedom A36

Designs: 4c, Human Rights flame, hands, and broken chain. 25c, Human Rights flame, family and broken chain.

Perf. 11x11½

1968, Dec. 10 Litho. Unwmk.

309	A36	4c violet, gray grn & red brown	.20	.20
310	A36	25c org, blk & blue	.20	.20
311	A36	35c greenish blue, blue, blk & org	.20	.20
		Nos. 309-311 (3)	.60	.60

International Human Rights Year.

In the Paddock A37

Horse Racing: 25c, "They're off!" 35c, On the flat. 50c, The Finish.

1969, Mar. 15 Litho. *Perf. 14½*

312	A37	4c multicolored	.20	.20
313	A37	25c multicolored	.20	.20
314	A37	35c multicolored	.25	.25
315	A37	50c multicolored	.35	.35
a.		Souvenir sheet of 4, #312-315	2.25	2.75
		Nos. 312-315 (4)	1.00	1.00

Map of Caribbean — A38

Design: 12c, 50c, "Strength in Unity," horiz.

Perf. 14x14½, 14½x14

1969, May 6 Photo. Wmk. 314

316	A38	5c brown & multi	.20	.20
317	A38	12c ultra & multi	.20	.20
318	A38	25c green & multi	.20	.20
319	A38	50c magenta & multi	.30	.30
		Nos. 316-319 (4)	.90	.90

1st anniv. of CARIFTA (Caribbean Free Trade Area).

ILO Emblem A39

Perf. 14x13

1969, Aug. 5 Litho. Unwmk.

320	A39	4c bl grn, brt grn & blk	.20	.20
321	A39	25c red brn, brt mag & red	.20	.20

50th anniv. of the ILO.

No. 294 Surcharged

1969, Aug. 30 *Perf. 13½x14*

322	A31	1c on 4c multicolored	.20	.20

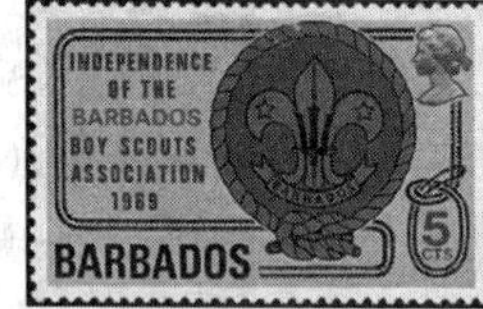

Barbados Boy Scout Emblem — A40

Designs: 25c, Sea Scouts rowing in Bridgetown harbor. 35c, Campfire. 50c, Various Scouts in front of National Headquarters and Training Center, Hazelwood.

Perf. 13½x13

1969, Dec. 16 Litho. Unwmk.

323	A40	5c multicolored	.20	.20
324	A40	25c multicolored	.50	.50
325	A40	35c multicolored	.65	.65
326	A40	50c multicolored	1.00	1.00
a.		Souvenir sheet of 4, #323-326	11.00	11.00
		Nos. 323-326 (4)	2.35	2.35

Attainment of independence by the Barbados Boy Scout Assoc.

No. 271a Surcharged

Wmk. 314 Sideways

1970, Mar. 11 Photo. *Perf. 14x13½*

327	A29	4c on 5c multicolored	.20	.20

This locally applied surcharge exists in several variations: double, triple, on back, in pair with one missing, etc.

Lion at Gun Hill — A41

Barbados Museum A42

2c, Trafalgar Fountain. 3c, Montefiore Drinking Fountain. 4c, St. James' Monument. 5c, St. Ann's Fort. 6c, Old Sugar Mill, Morgan Lewis. 8c, Cenotaph. 10c, South Point Lighthouse. 15c, Sharon Moravian Church. 25c, George Washington House. 35c, St. Nicholas Abbey. 50c, Bowmanston Pumping Station. $1, Queen Elizabeth Hospital. $2.50, Modern sugar factory. $5, Seawell Intl. Airport.

Wmk. 314 Upright (A41), Sideways (A42)

Perf. 12½x13, 13x12½

1970, May 4 Photo.

328	A41	1c bl grn & multi	.20	.20
329	A41	2c crimson & multi	.25	.20
330	A41	3c blue & multi	.20	.20
331	A41	4c yellow & multi	.85	.20
332	A41	5c dp org & multi	.20	.20
333	A41	6c dull yel & multi	.30	.30
334	A41	8c dp blue & multi	.20	.20
335	A41	10c red & multi	2.25	.50
336	A42	12c ultra & multi	1.00	.20
337	A42	15c yellow & multi	.25	.25
338	A42	25c orange & multi	.20	.20
339	A42	35c pink & multi	.25	.25
340	A42	50c bl grn & multi	.30	.30
341	A42	$1 emerald & multi	.55	.55
342	A42	$2.50 ver & multi	1.25	1.25
343	A42	$5 yellow & multi	4.75	4.75
		Nos. 328-343 (16)	13.00	9.75

Nos. 328-332, 334-343 were reissued in 1971 on glazed paper.

Wmk. 314 Sideways (A41), Upright (A42)

1972-74

331a	A41	4c	1.50	1.50
332a	A41	5c	1.25	1.25
333a	A41	6c	3.75	3.75
334a	A41	8c	1.50	1.50
335a	A41	10c ('74)	3.00	3.00
336a	A42	12c	1.75	1.75
337a	A42	15c	.75	.75
338a	A42	25c	2.50	2.50
339a	A42	35c	2.00	2.00
340a	A42	50c	3.00	3.00
341a	A42	$1	6.00	6.00
342a	A42	$2.50 ('73)	4.00	4.00
343a	A42	$5 ('73)	4.00	4.00
		Nos. 331a-343a (13)	35.00	35.00

For surcharge, see No. 391.

Primary Education, UN and Education Year Emblems — A43

UN and Education Year Emblems and: 5c, Secondary education (student with microscope). 25c, Technical education (men working with power drill). 50c, University building.

1970, June 26 Litho. *Perf. 14*

344	A43	4c multicolored	.20	.20
345	A43	5c multicolored	.20	.20
346	A43	25c multicolored	.30	.30
347	A43	50c multicolored	.40	.40
		Nos. 344-347 (4)	1.10	1.10

UN, 25th anniv., and Intl. Education Year.

Minnie Root A44

Flowers: 1c, Barbados Easter lily, vert. 10c, Eyelash orchid. 25c, Pride of Barbados, vert. 35c, Christmas hope.

1970, Aug. 24 Litho. Wmk. 314

Flowers in Natural Colors

348	A44	1c green	.20	.20
349	A44	5c deep magenta	.35	.20
350	A44	10c dark blue	1.90	.25
351	A44	25c brt orange brown	1.40	.75
352	A44	35c blue	1.40	.75
a.		Souvenir sheet of 5	3.50	3.50
		Nos. 348-352 (5)	5.25	2.15

No. 352a contains 5 imperf. stamps similar to Nos. 348-352 with simulated perforations.

Christ Carrying Cross — A45

Easter: 10c, 50c, Resurrection, by Benjamin West, St. George's Anglican Church. 35c like 4c, Window from St. Margaret's Anglican Church, St. John.

1971, Apr. 7 Wmk. 314 *Perf. 14*

353	A45	4c purple & multi	.20	.20
354	A45	10c silver & multi	.20	.20
355	A45	35c brt blue & multi	.25	.25
356	A45	50c gold & multi	.35	.35
		Nos. 353-356 (4)	1.00	1.00

Sailfish Craft A46

Tourism: 5c, Tennis. 12c, Horseback riding. 25c, Water-skiing. 50c, Scuba diving.

1971, Aug. 17 *Perf. 14x14½*

357	A46	1c multicolored	.20	.20
358	A46	5c multicolored	.30	.20
359	A46	12c multicolored	.50	.20
360	A46	25c multicolored	.35	.20
361	A46	50c multicolored	.45	.45
		Nos. 357-361 (5)	1.80	1.25

Samuel Jackman Prescod — A47

1971, Sept. 26 *Perf. 14*

362	A47	3c orange & multi	.20	.20
363	A47	35c ultra & multi	.40	.40

Samuel Jackman Prescod (1806-1871), 1st black member of Barbados Assembly.

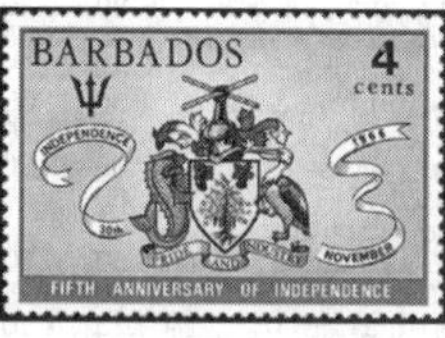

Coat of Arms A48

15c, 50c, Flag and map of Barbados.

1971, Nov. 23

364	A48	4c light blue & multi	.25	.25
365	A48	15c multicolored	.50	.50
366	A48	25c yel green & multi	.50	.50
367	A48	50c blue & multi	1.00	1.00
		Nos. 364-367 (4)	2.25	2.25

5th anniv. of independence.

Telegraphy, 1872 and 1972 — A49

Designs: 10c, "Stanley Angwin" off St. Lawrence Coast. 35c, Earth station and Intelsat 4. 50c, Mt. Misery tropospheric scatter station.

1972, Mar. 28 Litho. *Perf. 14*

368	A49	4c	purple & multi	.20	.20
369	A49	10c	emerald & multi	.25	.25
370	A49	35c	red & multi	.45	.45
371	A49	50c	orange & multi	.60	.60
			Nos. 368-371 (4)	1.50	1.50

Centenary of telecommunications to and from Barbados.

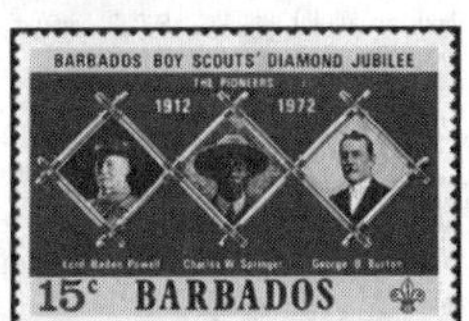

Lord Baden-Powell, Charles W. Springer, George B. Burton — A50

5c, Map of Barbados and Combermere School, vert. 25c, Photograph of 1922 troop. 50c, Flags of various Boy Scout troops.

1972, Aug. 1

372	A50	5c	ultra & multi	.20	.20
373	A50	15c	ultra & multi	.20	.20
374	A50	25c	ultra & multi	.45	.45
375	A50	50c	ultra & multi	.90	.90
			Nos. 372-375 (4)	1.75	1.75

60th anniv. of Barbados Boy Scouts and 4th Caribbean Jamboree.

Bookmobile, Open Book — A51

Intl. Book Year: 15c, Visual aids truck. 25c, Central Library, Bridgetown. $1, Codrington College.

1972, Oct. 31 Litho. Wmk. 314

376	A51	4c	brt pink & multi	.20	.20
377	A51	15c	dull org & multi	.30	.30
378	A51	25c	buff & multi	.35	.35
379	A51	$1	lt violet & multi	1.40	1.40
			Nos. 376-379 (4)	2.25	2.25

Pottery Wheels A52

Barbados pottery industry: 15c, Kiln. 25c, Finished pottery, Chalky Mount. $1, Pottery on sale at market.

1973, Mar. 1 Wmk. 314 *Perf. 14*

380	A52	5c	dull red & multi	.20	.20
381	A52	15c	olive grn & multi	.25	.20
382	A52	25c	gray & multi	.30	.20
383	A52	$1	yellow & multi	1.10	1.10
			Nos. 380-383 (4)	1.85	1.70

First Flight in Barbados, Wright Box Kite, 1911 — A53

Aircraft: 15c, First flight to Barbados, De Havilland biplane, 1928. 25c, Passenger plane, 1939. 50c, Vickers VC-10 over control tower, 1973.

1973, July 25 *Perf. 12½x12*

384	A53	5c	blue & multi	.35	.20
385	A53	15c	vio blue & multi	.90	.20
386	A53	25c	multicolored	1.25	.20
387	A53	50c	blue & multi	2.00	2.00
			Nos. 384-387 (4)	4.50	2.60

Chancellor Sir Hugh Wooding — A54

Designs: 25c, Sherlock Hall, Cave Hill Campus. 35c, Cave Hill Campus.

1973, Dec. 11 *Perf. 13x14*

388	A54	5c	dp orange & multi	.20	.20
389	A54	25c	red brown & multi	.30	.30
390	A54	35c	multicolored	.35	.35
			Nos. 388-390 (3)	.85	.85

25th anniv. of the Univ. of the West Indies.

No. 338a Surcharged

1974, Apr. 30 Photo. *Perf. 13x12½*

391	A42	4c	on 25c multi	.20	.20
a.			"4c." omitted	16.00	

Old Sailboat A55

Designs: 35c, Rowboat. 50c, Motor-powered fishing boat. $1, Trawler "Calamar."

1974, June 11 Wmk. 314 *Perf. 14*

392	A55	15c	blue & multi	.25	.25
393	A55	35c	multicolored	.50	.50
394	A55	50c	vio blue & multi	.70	.70
395	A55	$1	blue & multi	1.40	1.40
a.			Souvenir sheet of 4, #392-395	3.75	3.75
			Nos. 392-395 (4)	2.85	2.85

Fishing boats of Barbados.

Fire Orchid — A56

Orchids. 1c, 20c, 25c, $2.50, $5 horizontal.

Wmk. 314 Sideways; Upright (1c, 20c, 25c, $1, $10)

1974-77 Photo. *Perf. 14*

396	A56	1c	Cattleya gaskelliana alba	.20	.20
397	A56	2c	shown	.20	.20
398	A56	3c	Rose Marie	.20	.20
399	A56	4c	Fiery red orchid	.20	.20
400	A56	5c	Schomburgkia humboltii	.20	.20
401	A56	8c	Dancing dolls	.20	.20
402	A56	10c	Spider orchids	.20	.20
403	A56	12c	Dendrobium aggregatum	.25	.20
404	A56	15c	Lady slippers	.40	.35
404C	A56	20c	Spathoglottis	.45	.40
405	A56	25c	Eyelash	.75	.55
406	A56	35c	Bletia patula	.80	.65
406B	A56	45c	Sunset Glow	1.10	.85
407	A56	50c	Sunset Glow	1.10	.85

Perf. 14½x14, 14x14½

408	A56	$1	Ascocenda red gem	2.00	1.50
409	A56	$2.50	Brassolaelio-cattleya nugget	4.75	3.75
410	A56	$5	Caularthron bicornutum	9.50	8.00
411	A56	$10	Moon orchid	17.50	15.00
			Nos. 396-411 (18)	40.00	33.50

Issued: 20c, 45c, 5/3/77; others, 9/16/74.

For surcharge see No. B2.

Wmk. 314 Upright; Sideways (1c, 25c, $1)

1976 *Perf. 14*

396a	A56	1c	multicolored	.50	*3.00*
397a	A56	2c	multicolored	.65	*3.00*
398a	A56	3c	multicolored	.75	*3.25*
399a	A56	4c	multicolored	.50	*3.75*
402a	A56	10c	multicolored	1.00	*3.25*
404a	A56	15c	multicolored	.85	*1.10*
405a	A56	25c	multicolored	1.75	1.10
406a	A56	35c	multicolored	2.25	1.60

Perf. 14½x14

408a	A56	$1	multicolored	5.75	5.00
			Nos. 396a-408a (9)	14.00	25.05

1975 Wmk. 373 *Perf. 14*

396b	A56	1c	multicolored	.20	*1.00*
397b	A56	2c	multicolored	.20	*1.00*
398b	A56	3c	multicolored	.20	*1.00*
399b	A56	4c	multicolored	.50	*2.50*
400b	A56	5c	multicolored	.35	.20
402b	A56	10c	multicolored	.35	.20
403b	A56	12c	multicolored	7.50	.20
404b	A56	15c	multicolored	.65	.20
406c	A56	45c	multicolored	.55	.20

Perf. 14½x14, 14x14½

408b	A56	$1	multicolored	8.00	*11.00*
409b	A56	$2.50	multicolored	8.00	3.75
410b	A56	$5	multicolored	8.00	6.00
411b	A56	$10	multicolored	10.50	10.50
			Nos. 396b-411b (13)	45.00	37.75

UPU Emblem, Barbados No. 64 — A57

Cent. of the UPU: 35c, Letters encircling globe. 50c, Barbados coat of arms. $1, Map of Barbados, sailing ship and jet.

1974, Oct. 9 Litho. *Perf. 14½*

412	A57	8c	brt rose, org & gray	.20	.20
413	A57	35c	red, blk, & ocher	.35	.35
414	A57	50c	vio blue, bl & sil	.45	.45
415	A57	$1	ultra, blk & brn	1.00	1.00
a.			Souvenir sheet of 4, #412-415	2.25	2.25
			Nos. 412-415 (4)	2.00	2.00

Yacht Britannia off Barbados — A58

Royal Visit, Feb. 1975: 35c, $1, Palms and sunset.

1975, Feb. 18

416	A58	8c	brown & multi	.20	.20
417	A58	25c	blue & multi	.40	.40
418	A58	35c	purple & multi	.60	.60
419	A58	$1	violet & multi	1.60	1.60
			Nos. 416-419 (4)	2.80	2.80

St. Michael's Cathedral — A59

Designs: 15c, Bishop Coleridge. 50c, All Saint's Church. $1, St. Michael, stained glass window, St. Michael's Cathedral.

Wmk. 314

1975, July 29 Litho. *Perf. 14*

420	A59	5c	blue & multi	.20	.20
421	A59	15c	lilac & multi	.20	.20
422	A59	50c	green & multi	.60	.60
423	A59	$1	multicolored	1.00	1.00
a.			Souvenir sheet of 4, #420-423	1.75	*2.00*
			Nos. 420-423 (4)	2.00	2.00

Anglican Diocese in Barbados, sesquicentennial.

Pony Float A60

Designs: 25c, Stiltsman (band and masqueraders). 35c, Maypole dancing. 50c, Cuban dancers.

1975, Nov. 18 Litho. Wmk. 373

424	A60	8c	yellow & multi	.20	.20
425	A60	25c	buff & multi	.20	.20
426	A60	35c	ultra & multi	.20	.20
427	A60	50c	orange & multi	.40	.40
a.			Souvenir sheet of 4, #424-427	1.25	1.25
			Nos. 424-427 (4)	1.00	1.00

Crop-over (harvest) festival.

Sailing Ship, 17th Cent. — A61

Coat of Arms — A62

350th Anniv. of 1st Settlement: 10c, Bearded fig tree and fruit. 25c, Ogilvy's 17th cent. map. $1, Capt. John Powell.

1975, Dec. 17 Wmk. 373 *Perf. 13½*

428	A61	4c	lt blue & multi	.20	.20
429	A61	10c	lt blue & multi	.20	.20
430	A61	25c	yellow & multi	.55	.50
431	A61	$1	dk red & multi	1.90	1.60
a.			Souvenir sheet of 4, #428-431	3.25	*5.50*
			Nos. 428-431 (4)	2.85	2.50

Coil Stamps

1975, Dec. Unwmk. *Perf. 15x14*

432	A62	5c	light blue	.25	*.75*
433	A62	25c	violet	.35	*1.00*

Map of West Indies, Bats, Wicket and Ball A63

Prudential Cup — A64

1976, July 7 Litho. *Perf. 14*

438	A63	25c	lt blue & multi	1.00	1.00
439	A64	45c	lilac rose & black	1.50	1.50

World Cricket Cup, won by West Indies Team, 1975.

Map of South Carolina settled by Barbadians — A65

American Bicentennial: 25c, George Washington and map of Bridge Town area. 50c, Declaration of Independence. $1, Masonic emblem and Prince Hall, founder and Grand Master of African Grand Lodge, Boston, 1790-1807.

1976, Aug. 17 Wmk. 373 *Perf. 13½*

440 A65 15c multicolored .20 .20
441 A65 25c multicolored .35 .35
442 A65 50c multicolored .75 .75
443 A65 $1 multicolored 1.50 1.50
Nos. 440-443 (4) 2.80 2.80

Mailman with Bicycle A66

PO Act, 125th anniv.: 35c, Mailman on motor scooter. 50c, Cover with Barbados No. 2. $1, Mail truck.

1976, Oct. 19 Litho. *Perf. 14*

444 A66 8c rose red, blk & bis .20 .20
445 A66 35c multicolored .25 .20
446 A66 50c vio blue & multi .35 .35
447 A66 $1 red & multi .55 *1.10*
Nos. 444-447 (4) 1.35 1.85

Coast Guard Vessels A67

Designs: 15c, Bank note, reverse, showing Barbados Parliament. 25c, National anthem by Van Roland Edwards (music) and Irvine Burgie (lyrics). $1, Independence Day parade.

1976, Nov. 30 *Perf. 13x13½*

448 A67 5c multicolored .20 .20
449 A67 15c multicolored .20 .20
450 A67 25c yel, brown & blk .25 .25
451 A67 $1 multicolored 1.00 1.00
a. Souvenir sheet of 4, #448-451 2.00 2.00
Nos. 448-451 (4) 1.65 1.65

10th anniv. of independence.

Queen Knighting Garfield Sobers, 1957 Visit — A68

Designs: 50c, Queen arriving at Westminster Abbey. $1, Queen leaving coach.

1977, Feb. 7 *Perf. 14x13½*

452 A68 15c silver & multi .20 .20
453 A68 50c silver & multi .30 .30
454 A68 $1 silver & multi .50 .50
Nos. 452-454 (3) 1.00 1.00

25th anniv. of the reign of Queen Elizabeth II. See Nos. 467-469.

Underwater Park — A69

Beauty of Barbados: 35c, Royal palms, vert. 50c, Underwater caves. $1, Stalagmite in Harrison's Cave, vert.

1977, May 3 Wmk. 373 *Perf. 14*

455 A69 5c multicolored .25 .20
456 A69 35c multicolored .45 .20
457 A69 50c multicolored .60 .60
458 A69 $1 multicolored 1.10 1.10
a. Souvenir sheet of 4, #455-458 3.50 *4.00*
Nos. 455-458 (4) 2.40 2.10

House of Commons Maces — A70

Charles I Handing Charter to Carlisle — A71

Designs: 25c, Speaker's chair. 50c, Senate Chamber. $1, Sam Lord's Castle, horiz.

1977, Aug. 2 Litho. *Perf. 13½*

459 A70 10c red brown & yel .20 .20
460 A70 25c slate grn & org .20 .20
461 A70 50c dk green, grn & yel .30 .30
462 A70 $1 dk & lt blue & org .80 .80
Nos. 459-462 (4) 1.50 1.50

13th Regional Conference of Commonwealth Parliamentary Association.

Perf. 13½x13, 13x13½

1977, Oct. 11 Litho. Wmk. 373

Designs: 12c, Charter scroll. 45c, Charles I and Earl of Carlisle, horiz. $1, Map of Barbados, by Richard Ligon, 1657, horiz.

463 A71 12c buff & multi .20 .20
464 A71 25c buff & multi .20 .20
465 A71 45c buff & multi .40 .40
466 A71 $1 buff & multi .70 .70
Nos. 463-466 (4) 1.50 1.50

350th anniv. of charter granting Barbados to the Earl of Carlisle.

Silver Jubilee Type, 1977, Inscribed: "ROYAL VISIT"

1977, Oct. 31 Unwmk. *Roulette 5*
Self-adhesive

467 A68 15c silver & multi .60 .60
468 A68 50c silver & multi .35 .35
469 A68 $1 silver & multi .45 *.80*
Nos. 467-469 (3) 1.40 1.75

Caribbean visit of Queen Elizabeth II. Printed on peelable paper backing inscribed in ultramarine multiple rows: "SILVER JUBILEE ROYAL VISIT BARBADOS." Printed with die-cut label inscribed in black "BEND & PEEL" attached at left of stamp. Sheets of 50 stamps and 50 labels.

Gibson's Map of Bridgetown, 1766 — A72

25c, Bridgetown, engraving by S. Copens, 1695. 45c, Trafalgar Square, Bridgetown, drawing by J. M. Carter, 1835. $1, The Bridges, 1978.

Wmk. 373

1978, Mar. 1 Litho. *Perf. 14½*

470 A72 12c gold & multi .25 .20
471 A72 25c gold & multi .25 .25
472 A72 45c gold & multi .35 .35
473 A72 $1 gold & multi .55 .55
Nos. 470-473 (4) 1.40 1.35

350th anniv. of founding of Bridgetown.

Elizabeth II Coronation Anniv. Issue
Souvenir Sheet
Common Design Types

1978, Apr. 21 Unwmk. *Perf. 15*

474 Sheet of 6 3.00 3.00
a. CD326 50c Griffin of Edward III .50 .50
b. CD327 50c Elizabeth II .50 .50
c. CD328 50c Pelican .50 .50

No. 474 contains 2 se-tenant strips of Nos. 474a-474c, separated by horizontal gutter with commemorative and descriptive inscriptions and showing central part of coronation with coach.

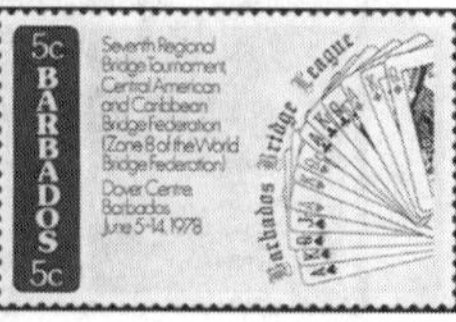

Freak Bridge Hand A73

10c, World Bridge Fed. emblem. 45c, Central American and Caribbean Bridge Fed. emblem. $1, Map of Caribbean, cards.

Wmk. 373

1978, June 6 Litho. *Perf. 14½*

475 A73 5c multicolored .20 .20
476 A73 10c multicolored .20 .20
477 A73 45c multicolored .50 .50
478 A73 $1 multicolored 1.00 1.00
a. Souvenir sheet of 4, #475-478 1.50 1.50
Nos. 475-478 (4) 1.90 1.90

7th Regional Bridge Tournament, Dover Centre, Barbados, June 5-14.

Girl Guides' Camp — A74

Designs: 28c, Girl Guides helping children and handicapped. 50c, Badge with "60," vert. $1, Badge with initials, vert.

1978, Aug. 1 Litho. *Perf. 13½*

479 A74 12c multicolored .20 .20
480 A74 28c multicolored .30 .30
481 A74 50c multicolored .50 .50
482 A74 $1 multicolored 1.00 1.00
Nos. 479-482 (4) 2.00 2.00

Girl Guides of Barbados, 60th anniv.

Garment Industry A75

Industries of Barbados: 28c, Cooper, vert. 45c, Blacksmith, vert. 50c, Wrought iron industry.

1978, Nov. 14 Litho. *Perf. 14*

483 A75 12c multicolored .20 .20
484 A75 28c multicolored .30 .30
485 A75 45c multicolored .40 .40
486 A75 50c multicolored .50 .50
Nos. 483-486 (4) 1.40 1.40

Early Mail Steamer A76

Ships: 25c, Q.E.II in Deep Water Harbour. 50c, Ra II (raft) nearing Barbados. $1, Early mail steamer.

1979, Feb. 8 Litho. *Perf. 13x13½*

487 A76 12c multicolored .20 .20
488 A76 25c multicolored .30 .30
489 A76 50c multicolored .50 .50
490 A76 $1 multicolored 1.00 1.00
Nos. 487-490 (4) 2.00 2.00

Barbados No. 235 A77

28c, Barbados #430, vert. 45c, Penny Black and Maltese postmark, vert. 50c, Barbados #21b.

Wmk. 373

1979, May 8 Litho. *Perf. 14*

491 A77 12c multicolored .20 .20
492 A77 28c multicolored .20 .20
493 A77 45c multicolored .30 .30
Nos. 491-493 (3) .70 .70

Souvenir Sheet

494 A77 50c multicolored .40 .40

Sir Rowland Hill (1795-1879), originator of penny postage.

Birds — A78

Launcher Transported through Barbados — A79

1979-81 Photo. Wmk. 373 *Perf. 14*

495 A78 1c Grass canaries .20 *.60*
496 A78 2c Rain birds .20 *.60*
497 A78 5c Sparrows .20 *.60*
498 A78 8c Frigate birds .20 *1.40*
499 A78 10c Cattle egrets .20 *.35*
500 A78 12c Green gaulins .55 *.75*
501 A78 20c Hummingbirds .25 *.45*
502 A78 25c Ground doves .25 *.50*
503 A78 28c Blackbirds 1.75 1.40
504 A78 35c Green-throated caribs .30 *.60*
505 A78 45c Wood doves 1.50 .75
506 A78 50c Ramiers 1.75 1.25
506A A78 55c Black-breasted plover ('81) 4.75 3.00
507 A78 70c Yellow breasts 1.75 2.50
508 A78 $1 Pee whistlers 1.75 1.25
509 A78 $2.50 Christmas birds 2.40 *5.00*
510 A78 $5 Kingfishers 3.75 *7.50*
511 A78 $10 Red-seal coot 7.25 *11.50*
Nos. 495-511 (18) 29.00 40.00

Issue dates: 55c, Sept. 1; others, Aug. 7.
See #570-572. For surcharges see #563-565.

1979, Oct. 9 Photo.

Designs: 10c, Gun on landing craft, Foul Bay, horiz. 20c, Firing of 16-inch launcher by day. 28c, Bath Earth Station and Intelsat IV-A, horiz. 45c, ITOS/NOAA over Caribbean, horiz. 50c, Intelsat IV-A over Atlantic, and globe. $1, Lunar landing module, horiz.

512 A79 10c multicolored .20 .20
513 A79 12c multicolored .20 .20
514 A79 20c multicolored .20 .20
515 A79 28c multicolored .20 .20
516 A79 45c multicolored .30 .30
517 A79 50c multicolored .35 .35
Nos. 512-517 (6) 1.45 1.45

Souvenir Sheet

518 A79 $1 multicolored .85 .85

Space exploration. No. 518 commemorates 10th anniversary of first moon landing.
No. 516 is incorrectly inscribed "Intelsat."

Family, IYC Emblem — A80

IYC Emblem and: 28c, Children holding hands and map of Barbados. 45c, Boy and teacher. 50c, Children playing. $1, Boy and girl flying kite.

1979, Nov. 27 Litho. *Perf. 14*

519 A80 12c multicolored .20 .20
520 A80 28c multicolored .20 .20
521 A80 45c multicolored .30 .30
522 A80 50c multicolored .35 .35
523 A80 $1 multicolored .65 .65
Nos. 519-523 (5) 1.70 1.70

Map of Barbados, Anniversary Emblem — A81

Rotary Intl., 75th Anniv.: 28c, Map of district 404. 50c, 75th anniv. emblem. $1, Paul P. Harris, founder.

1980, Feb. 19 Litho. *Perf. 13½*

524 A81	12c multicolored	.20	.20
525 A81	28c multicolored	.20	.20
526 A81	50c multicolored	.35	.35
527 A81	$1 multicolored	.65	.65
	Nos. 524-527 (4)	1.40	1.40

A82

A83

12c, Regiment volunteer, artillery company, 1909. 35c, Drum major. 50c, Sovereign's, regimental flags. $1, e, Women's corps.

Wmk. 373

1980, Apr. 8 Litho. *Perf. 14½*

528 A82	12c multicolored	.20	.20
529 A82	35c multicolored	.20	.20
530 A82	50c multicolored	.35	.35
531 A82	$1 multicolored	.65	.65
	Nos. 528-531 (4)	1.40	1.40

Barbados Regiment, 75th anniv.

Souvenir Sheets

Wmk. 373

1980, May 6 Litho. *Perf. 14*

Early mailman, London 1980 emblem. The vignette is a different color for each stamp.

532	Sheet of 6	1.10	1.10
a.-f.	A83 28c any single	.20	.20
533	Sheet of 6	2.25	2.25
a.-f.	A83 50c any single	.35	.35

London 80 Intl. Stamp Exhib., May 6-14.

Underwater Scenes — A84

1980, Sept. 30 Litho. *Perf. 13½*

534 A84	12c multicolored	.20	.20
535 A84	28c multicolored	.25	.25
536 A84	50c multicolored	.40	.40
537 A84	$1 multicolored	.75	.75
a.	Souvenir sheet of 4, #534-537	1.50	1.50
	Nos. 534-537 (4)	1.60	1.60

Bathsheba Railroad Station — A85

1981, Jan. 13 Litho. *Perf. 14½*

538 A85	12c shown	.20	.20
539 A85	28c Cab stand, The Green	.20	.20
540 A85	45c Mule-drawn tram	.30	.30
541 A85	70c Horse-drawn bus	.50	.50
542 A85	$1 Fairchild St. railroad station	.65	.65
	Nos. 538-542 (5)	1.85	1.85

See Nos. 577-580.

Visually Handicapped Girl at Typewriter — A86

1981, May 19 Litho. *Perf. 14*

543 A86	10c shown	.20	.20
544 A86	25c Sign language alphabet, vert.	.20	.20
545 A86	45c Blind people crossing street, vert.	.30	.30
546 A86	$2.50 Baseball game	1.60	1.60
	Nos. 543-546 (4)	2.30	2.30

International Year of the Disabled.

Royal Wedding Issue

Common Design Type

Wmk. 373

1981, July 22 Litho. *Perf. 13½*

547 CD331	28c Bouquet	.20	.20
548 CD331	50c Charles	.35	.35
549 CD331	$2.50 Couple	1.60	1.60
	Nos. 547-549 (3)	2.15	2.15

4th Caribbean Arts Festival (CARIFESTA), July 19-Aug. 3 — A87

1981, Aug. 11 Litho. *Perf. 14½*

550 A87	15c Landship maneuver	.20	.20
551 A87	20c Yoruba dancer	.20	.20
552 A87	40c Tuk band	.30	.30
553 A87	55c Frank Collymore (sculpture)	.40	.40
554 A87	$1 Barbados Harbor (painting)	.75	.75
	Nos. 550-554 (5)	1.85	1.85

Hurricane Gladys, View from Apollo A88

1981, Sept. 29 Litho. *Perf. 14*

555 A88	35c Satellite view over Barbados	.30	.30
556 A88	50c shown	.40	.40
557 A88	60c Police watch	.50	.50
558 A88	$1 Spotter plane	.80	.80
	Nos. 555-558 (4)	2.00	2.00

Harrison's Cave — A89

Perf. 14x14½

1981, Dec. 1 Litho. Wmk. 373

559 A89	10c Twin Falls	.20	.20
560 A89	20c Rotunda Room Stream	.20	.20
561 A89	55c Rotunda Room formation	.35	.35
562 A89	$2.50 Cascade Pool	1.60	1.60
	Nos. 559-562 (4)	2.35	2.35

Nos. 503, 505, 507 Surcharged

1981, Sept. 1 Photo. *Perf. 14*

563 A78	15c on 28c multi	.20	.20
564 A78	40c on 45c multi	.40	.40
565 A78	60c on 70c multi	.60	.60
	Nos. 563-565 (3)	1.20	1.20

Black Belly Sheep A90

1982, Feb. 9 Litho.

566 A90	40c Ram	.40	.40
567 A90	50c Ewe	.50	.50
568 A90	60c Ewe, lambs	.60	.60
569 A90	$1 Pair, map	1.00	1.00
	Nos. 566-569 (4)	2.50	2.50

Bird Type of 1979

Wmk. 373

1982, Mar. 1 Photo. *Perf. 14*

570 A78	15c like #503	.20	.20
571 A78	40c like #506	.40	.40
572 A78	60c like #507	.60	.60
	Nos. 570-572 (3)	1.20	1.20

Transportation Type

1982, Apr. 6 Litho. *Perf. 14½*

577 A85	20c Lighter	.20	.20
578 A85	35c Rowboat	.35	.35
579 A85	55c Speightstown schooner	.55	.55
580 A85	$2.50 Inter-colonial schooner	2.50	2.50
	Nos. 577-580 (4)	3.60	3.60

Early marine transport.

Visit of Pres. Ronald Reagan — A92

1982, Apr. 8 Litho. *Perf. 14*

581 A92	20c Barbados Flag, arms	.20	.20
582 A92	20c US Flag, arms	.20	.20
a.	Pair, Nos. 581-582	.40	.40
583 A92	55c like #581	.55	.50
584 A92	55c like #582	.55	.50
a.	Pair, Nos. 583-584	1.10	1.10
	Nos. 581-584 (4)	1.50	1.40

Printed in sheets of 8 with gutter showing Pres. Reagan and Prime Minister Tom Adams.

Princess Diana Issue

Common Design Type

1982, July 1 Litho. *Perf. 14½*

585 CD333	20c Arms	.20	.20
586 CD333	60c Diana	.45	.45
587 CD333	$1.20 Wedding	.90	.90
588 CD333	$2.50 Portrait	1.75	1.75
	Nos. 585-588 (4)	3.30	3.30

Scouting Year — A93

Washington's 250th Birth Anniv. — A94

1982, Sept. 7 Wmk. 373 *Perf. 14*

589 A93	15c Helping woman	.20	.20
590 A93	40c Sign, emblem, flag, horiz.	.45	.45
591 A93	55c Religious service, horiz.	.55	.55
592 A93	$1 Flags	1.00	1.00
	Nos. 589-592 (4)	2.20	2.20

Souvenir Sheet

593 A93	$1.50 Laws	1.60	1.60

1982, Nov. 2 *Perf. 13½x13*

594 A94	10c Arms	.20	.20
595 A94	55c Washington's house, Barbados	.55	.55
596 A94	60c Taking command	.60	.60
597 A94	$2.50 Taking oath	2.50	2.50
	Nos. 594-597 (4)	3.85	3.85

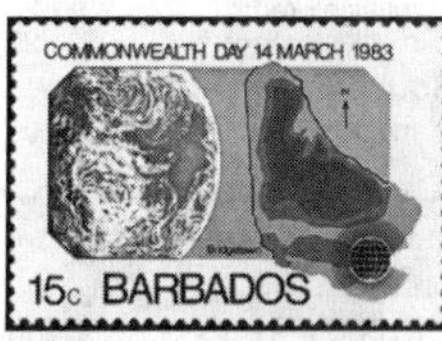

A95

1983, Mar. 14 Litho. *Perf. 14*

598 A95	15c Map, globe	.20	.20
599 A95	40c Beach	.40	.40
600 A95	60c Sugar cane harvest	.60	.60
601 A95	$1 Cricket game	1.00	1.00
	Nos. 598-601 (4)	2.20	2.20

Commonwealth day.

Gulf Fritillary A96

Perf. 13½x13

1983, Feb. 8 Litho. Wmk. 373

602 A96	20c shown	.25	.25
603 A96	40c Monarch	.45	.45
604 A96	55c Mimic	.60	.60
605 A96	$2.50 Hanno Blue	3.00	3.00
	Nos. 602-605 (4)	4.30	4.30

Manned Flight Bicentenary — A97

1983, June 14 Litho. *Perf. 14*

606 A97	20c US Navy dirigible	.30	.30
607 A97	40c Douglas DC-3	.85	.85
608 A97	55c Vickers Viscount	1.25	1.25
609 A97	$1 Lockheed TriStar	2.50	2.50
	Nos. 606-609 (4)	4.90	4.90

Nash 600, 1941 A98

1983, Aug. 9 Litho. *Perf. 14*

610 A98 25c shown .25 .25
611 A98 45c Dodge, 1938 .50 .50
612 A98 75c Ford Model AA, 1930 .75 .75
613 A98 $2.50 Dodge Four, 1918 2.50 2.50
Nos. 610-613 (4) 4.00 4.00

A99

A100

1983, Aug. 30 Litho. *Perf. 14*

614 A99 20c Players .20 .20
615 A99 65c Emblem, map .65 .65
616 A99 $1 Cup 1.00 1.00
Nos. 614-616 (3) 1.85 1.85

World Cup Table Tennis Championship.

1983, Nov. 1 *Perf. 14*

Christmas: 10c, 25c, Angel with lute, painting details. $2, The Virgin and Child, by Masaccio.

617 A100 10c multicolored .20 .20
618 A100 25c multicolored .25 .25

Souvenir Sheet

619 A100 $2 multicolored 2.00 2.00

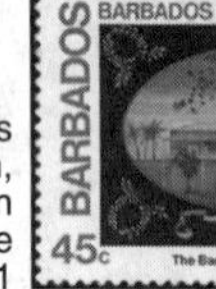
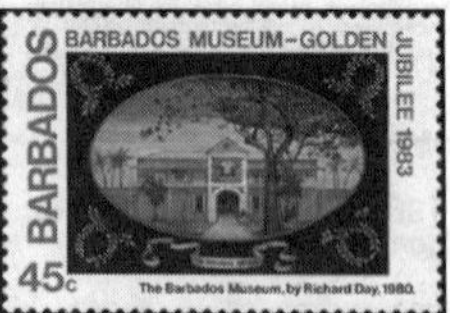

Barbados Museum, Golden Jubilee A101

Museum Paintings: 45c, by Richard Day. 75c, St. Ann's Garrison in Barbados by W.S. Hedges. $2.50, Needham's Point, Carlisle Bay.

1983, Nov. 1 *Perf. 14*

620 A101 45c multicolored .45 .45
621 A101 75c multicolored .75 .75
622 A101 $2.50 multicolored 2.50 2.50
Nos. 620-622 (3) 3.70 3.70

1984 Olympics, Los Angeles A102

1984, Apr. 3 Litho. *Perf. 14*

623 A102 50c Track & field .50 .50
624 A102 65c Shooting .65 .65
625 A102 75c Sailing .75 .75
626 A102 $1 Bicycling 1.00 1.00
a. Souvenir sheet of 4, #623-626 3.00 3.00
Nos. 623-626 (4) 2.90 2.90

Lloyd's List Issue

Common Design Type

1984, Apr. 25 Litho. *Perf. 14½*

627 CD335 45c World map .45 .45
628 CD335 50c Bridgetown Harbor .50 .50
629 CD335 75c Philosopher .75 .75
630 CD335 $1 Sea Princess 1.00 1.00
Nos. 627-630 (4) 2.70 2.70

Souvenir Sheet

1984 UPU Congress — A103

Illustration reduced.

1984, June 6 Litho. *Perf. 13½*

631 A103 $2 #213, UPU emblem 2.00 2.00

World Chess Fed., 60th Anniv. A104

1984, Aug. 8 *Perf. 14x14½*

632 A104 25c Junior match .30 .30
633 A104 45c Knights .50 .50
634 A104 65c Queens .75 .75
635 A104 $2 Rooks 2.25 2.25
Nos. 632-635 (4) 3.80 3.80

Christmas — A105

1984, Oct. 24 Litho. *Perf. 14*

636 A105 50c Poinsettia .50 .50
637 A105 65c Snow-on-the-mountain .65 .65
638 A105 75c Christmas candle .75 .75
639 A105 $1 Christmas hope 1.00 1.00
Nos. 636-639 (4) 2.90 2.90

Marine Life A106

1985 Litho. Wmk. 373 *Perf. 14*

640 A106 1c Bristle worm .20 .20
641 A106 2c Spotted trunk fish .20 .20
642 A106 5c Coney fish .20 .20
643 A106 10c Pink-tipped anemone .20 .20
645 A106 20c Christmas tree worm .30 .30
646 A106 25c Hermit crab .35 .35
648 A106 35c Animal flower .50 .50
649 A106 40c Vase sponge .60 .60
650 A106 45c Spotted moray .65 .65
651 A106 50c Ghost crab .75 .75
653 A106 65c Flaming tongue snail .95 .95
654 A106 75c Sergeant major fish 1.10 1.10
656 A106 $1 Caribbean warty anemone 1.50 1.50
657 A106 $2.50 Green turtle 3.75 3.75
658 A106 $5 Rock beauty 7.25 7.25
659 A106 $10 Elkhorn coral 15.00 15.00
Nos. 640-659 (16) 33.50 33.50

Issued: 10c, 20c, 25c, 50c, $2.50, $5, 2/26; 5c, 35c, 40c, 65c, $10, 4/9; 1c, 2c, 45c, 75c, $1, 5/7.

Exist inscribed "1987," etc.

1986 (?) Wmk. 384

640a A106 1c .20 .20
641a A106 2c .20 .20
642a A106 5c .20 .20
643a A106 10c .20 .20
645a A106 20c .30 .30
646a A106 25c .35 .35
648a A106 35c .45 .45
649a A106 40c .60 .60
650a A106 45c .65 .65
651a A106 50c .75 .75
653a A106 65c .95 .95
654a A106 75c 1.10 1.10
656a A106 $1 1.50 1.50
657a A106 $2.50 3.75 3.75
658a A106 $5 7.25 7.25
659a A106 $10 15.00 15.00
Nos. 640a-659a (16) 33.45 33.45

Some inscribed "1986." Also exist with "1987," "1988," and with no date.

Queen Mother 85th Birthday

Common Design Type

Perf. 14½x14

1985, June 7 Litho. Wmk. 384

660 CD336 25c At Buckingham Palace, 1930 .25 .25
661 CD336 65c With Lady Diana, 1981 .65 .65
662 CD336 75c At the docks .75 .75
663 CD336 $1 Holding Prince Henry 1.00 1.00
Nos. 660-663 (4) 2.65 2.65

Souvenir Sheet

664 CD336 $2 Opening the Garden Center, Syon House 2.00 2.00

Audubon Birth Bicentenary — A107

Illustrations of North American bird species. Nos. 666-668 vert.

Wmk. 373

1985, Aug. 6 Litho. *Perf. 14*

665 A107 45c Falco peregrinus .60 .60
666 A107 65c Dendroica discolor .90 .90
667 A107 75c Ardea herodias 1.10 1.10
668 A107 $1 Dendroica petechia 1.40 1.40
Nos. 665-668 (4) 4.00 4.00

Satellite Orbiting Earth A108

1985, Sept. 10

669 A108 75c multicolored .75 .75

INTELSAT, Intl. Telecommunications Satellite Consortium, 20th anniv.

Royal Barbados Police, 150th Anniv. — A109

1985, Nov. 19

670 A109 25c Traffic Dept. .25 .25
671 A109 50c Police Band .50 .50
672 A109 65c Dog Force .65 .65
673 A109 $1 Mounted Police 1.00 1.00
Nos. 670-673 (4) 2.40 2.40

Souvenir Sheet

674 A109 $2 Band on parade, horiz. 2.00 2.00

Queen Elizabeth II 60th Birthday

Common Design Type

Designs: 25c, Age 2. 50c, Senate House opening, University College of the West Indies, Jamaica, 1953. 65c, With Prince Philip, Caribbean Tour, 1985. 75c, Banquet, state visit to Sao Paulo, Brazil, 1968. $2, Visiting Crown Agents, 1983.

Perf. 14x14½

1986, Apr. 21 Litho. Wmk. 384

675 CD337 25c scar, blk & sil .20 .20
676 CD337 50c ultra & multi .45 .45
677 CD337 65c green & multi .60 .60
678 CD337 75c violet & multi .70 .70
679 CD337 $2 rose vio & multi 1.90 1.90
Nos. 675-679 (5) 3.85 3.85

EXPO '86, Vancouver — A110

1986, May 2 *Perf. 14*

680 A110 50c Trans-Canada North Star .50 .50
681 A110 $2.50 Lady Nelson 2.50 2.50

AMERIPEX '86 — A111

1986, May 22 Wmk. 373

682 A111 45c No. 441 .45 .45
683 A111 50c No. 442 .50 .50
684 A111 65c No. 558 .65 .65
685 A111 $1 Nos. 583-584 1.00 1.00
Nos. 682-685 (4) 2.60 2.60

Souvenir Sheet

686 A111 $2 Statue of Liberty, NY Harbor 2.00 2.00

Statue of Liberty, cent.

Royal Wedding Issue, 1986

Common Design Type

Designs: 45c, Informal portrait. $1, Andrew in navy uniform.

Perf. 14½x14

1986, July 23 Litho. Wmk. 384

687 CD338 45c multicolored .45 .45
688 CD338 $1 multicolored 1.00 1.00

Electrification of Barbados, 75th Anniv. A112

10c, Transporting utility poles, 1923. 25c, Heathfield ladder, 1935. 65c, Transport fleet, 1941. $2, Bucket truck, 1986.

Wmk. 384

1986, Sept. 16 Litho. *Perf. 14*

689 A112 10c multi .20 .20
690 A112 25c multi, vert. .25 .25
691 A112 65c multi .65 .65
692 A112 $2 multi, vert. 2.00 2.00
Nos. 689-692 (4) 3.10 3.10

Christmas — A113

Church windows and flowers.

1986, Oct. 28 Wmk. 373

693 A113 25c Alpinia purpurata .25 .25
694 A113 50c Anthurium andraeanum .50 .50
695 A113 75c Heliconia rostrata .75 .75
696 A113 $2 Heliconia psittacorum 2.00 2.00
Nos. 693-696 (4) 3.50 3.50

Natl. Special Olympics, 10th Anniv. A114

1987, Mar. 27 Wmk. 373 Perf. 14

697	A114 15c Shot put	.20	.20
698	A114 45c Wheelchair race	.45	.45
699	A114 65c Girl's long jump	.65	.65
700	A114 $2 Emblem, creed	2.00	2.00
	Nos. 697-700 (4)	3.30	3.30

CAPEX '87 — A115

1987, June 12

701	A115 25c Barn swallow	.35	.35
702	A115 50c Yellow warbler	.75	.75
703	A115 65c Audubon's shear-water	.90	.90
704	A115 75c Black-whiskered vireo	1.10	1.10
705	A115 $1 Scarlet tanager	1.50	1.50
	Nos. 701-705 (5)	4.60	4.60

Natl. Scouting Movement, 75th Anniv. — A116

1987, July 24 Perf. 14x14½

706	A116 10c Scout sign	.20	.20
707	A116 25c Campfire	.25	.25
708	A116 65c Merit badges, etc.	.65	.65
709	A116 $2 Marching band	2.00	2.00
	Nos. 706-709 (4)	3.10	3.10

Bridgetown Synagogue Restoration A117

1987, Oct. 6 Wmk. 384 Perf. 14½

710	A117 50c Exterior	.65	.65
711	A117 65c Interior	.85	.85
712	A117 75c Ten Commandments, vert.	1.00	1.00
713	A117 $1 Marble laver, vert.	1.40	1.40
	Nos. 710-713 (4)	3.90	3.90

Natl. Independence, 21st Anniv. — A118

E.W. Barrow (1920-87), Father of Independence — A119

25c, Coat of arms, seal of the colony. 45c, Natl. flag, Union Jack. 65c, Silver dollar, penny. $2, Old and new regimental flags, Queen Elizabeth's colors.

1987, Nov. 24 Litho. Perf. 14½

714	A118 25c multicolored	.25	.25
715	A118 45c multicolored	.45	.45
716	A118 65c multicolored	.65	.65
717	A118 $2 multicolored	2.00	2.00
	Nos. 714-717 (4)	3.35	3.35

Souvenir Sheet

718	A119 $1.50 multicolored	1.50	1.50

Cricket A120

Bat, wicket posts, ball, 18th cent. belt buckle and batters: 15c, E.A. "Manny" Martindale. 45c, George Challenor. 50c, Herman C. Griffith. 75c, Harold Austin. $2, Frank Worrell.

1988 Litho. Wmk. 373 Perf. 14

719	A120 15c multicolored	.20	.20
720	A120 45c multicolored	.45	.45
720A	A120 50c multicolored	.50	.50
721	A120 75c multicolored	.75	.75
722	A120 $2 multicolored	2.00	2.00
	Nos. 719-722 (5)	3.90	3.90

The 50c was originally printed with the wrong photograph but was not issued. Copies of the error have appeared on the market.

Issued: No. 720A, July 11; others, June 6.

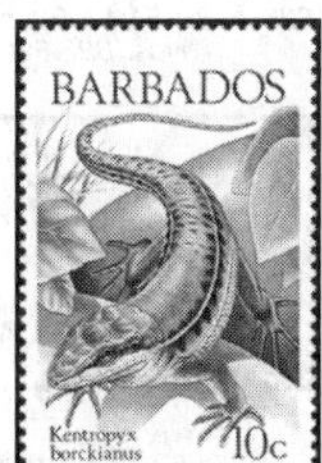
Lizards — A121

1988, June 13

723	A121 10c Kentropyx borckianus	.20	.20
724	A121 50c Hemidactylus mabouia	.60	.60
725	A121 65c Anolis extremus	.75	.75
726	A121 $2 Gymnophthalmus underwoodii	2.25	2.25
	Nos. 723-726 (4)	3.80	3.80

1988 Summer Olympics, Seoul — A122

Wmk. 373

1988, Aug. 2 Litho. Perf. 14½

727	A122 25c Cycling	.25	.25
728	A122 45c Running	.45	.45
729	A122 75c Swimming	.75	.75
730	A122 $2 Yachting	2.00	2.00
a.	Souvenir sheet of 4, #727-730	3.50	3.50
	Nos. 727-730 (4)	3.45	3.45

Lloyds of London, 300th Anniv.

Common Design Type

40c, Royal Exchange, 1774. 50c, Sugar mill (windmill), horiz. 65c, Container ship Author, horiz. $2, Sinking of the Titanic, 1912.

1988, Oct. 18 Litho. Perf. 14

731	CD341 40c multicolored	.40	.40
732	CD341 50c multicolored	.50	.50
733	CD341 65c multicolored	.65	.65
734	CD341 $2 multicolored	2.00	2.00
	Nos. 731-734 (4)	3.55	3.55

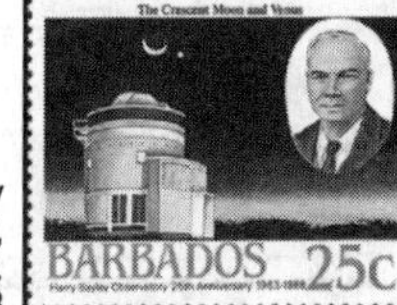
Harry Bayley Observatory, 25th Anniv. A123

Designs: 25c, Observatory, crescent Moon, Venus and Harry Bayley. 65c, Observatory and constellations. 75c, Andromeda Galaxy and telescope. $2, Orion Constellation.

1988, Nov. 28 Wmk. 384 Perf. 14½

735	A123 25c multicolored	.25	.25
736	A123 65c multicolored	.65	.65
737	A123 75c multicolored	.75	.75
738	A123 $2 multicolored	2.00	2.00
	Nos. 735-738 (4)	3.65	3.65

Commercial Aviation, 50th Anniv. — A124

Designs: 25c, Caribbean Airline Liat BAe748. 65c, Pan American DC-8. 75c, Two British Airways Concordes, Grantley Adams Intl. Airport. $2, Two Caribbean Air Cargo Boeing 707-351c.

1989, Mar. 20 Litho. Perf. 14

739	A124 25c multicolored	.25	.25
740	A124 65c multicolored	.65	.65
741	A124 75c multicolored	.75	.75
742	A124 $2 multicolored	2.00	2.00
	Nos. 739-742 (4)	3.65	3.65

Parliament, 350th Anniv. A125

1989, July 19 Litho. Perf. 13½

743	A125 25c Assembly chamber	.25	.25
744	A125 50c The Speaker	.50	.50
745	A125 75c Parliament, c. 1882	.75	.75
746	A125 $2.50 Queen in Parliament	2.50	2.50
	Nos. 743-746 (4)	4.00	4.00

See No. 752.

Wildlife Preservation — A126

1989, Aug. 1 Perf. 14x13½

747	A126 10c Wild hare, vert.	.20	.20
748	A126 50c Red-footed tortoise	.80	.80
749	A126 65c Green monkey, vert.	1.00	1.00
750	A126 $2 Toad	3.00	3.00
	Nos. 747-750 (4)	5.00	5.00

Souvenir Sheet

751	A126 $1 Mongoose, vert.	2.00	2.00

Parliament Anniv. Type of 1989

Souvenir Sheet

1989, Oct. 9 Wmk. 373 Perf. 13½

752	A125 $1 The Mace	1.00	1.00

35th Commonwealth Parliamentary Conf.

Wild Plants — A127

World Stamp Expo '89, Washington, DC — A128

1989-92 Wmk. 373 Perf. 14½

753	A127	2c Bread'n cheese	.20	.20
754	A127	5c Scarlet cordia	.20	.20
755	A127	10c Columnar cactus	.20	.20
756	A127	20c Spiderlily	.20	.20
757	A127	25c Rock balsam	.25	.25
758	A127	30c Hollyhock	.30	.30
758A	A127	35c Red sage	.35	.35
759	A127	45c Yellow shak-shak	.45	.45
760	A127	50c Whitewood	.50	.50
761	A127	55c Bluebell	.55	.55
762	A127	65c Prickly sage	.65	.65
763	A127	70c Seaside samphire	.70	.70
764	A127	80c Flat-hand dildo	.80	.80
764A	A127	90c Herringbone	.90	.90
765	A127	$1.10 Lent tree	1.10	1.10
766	A127	$2.50 Rodwood	2.50	2.50
767	A127	$5 Cowitch	5.00	5.00
768	A127	$10 Maypole	10.00	10.00
		Nos. 753-768 (18)	24.85	24.85

Issued: 35c, 90c, June 9, 1992 (inscribed 1991); others, Nov. 1.

Nos. 754-756, 763, 765 exist inscribed "1991."

For overprints see Nos. 788-790.

1990 Litho. Wmk. 384

753a	A127	2c	.20	.20
754a	A127	5c	.20	.20
755a	A127	10c	.20	.20
756a	A127	20c	.20	.20
757a	A127	25c	.25	.25
759a	A127	45c	.40	.40
760a	A127	50c	.45	.45
762a	A127	65c	.60	.60
766a	A127	$2.50	2.25	2.25
767a	A127	$5	4.50	4.50
768a	A127	$10	9.00	9.00
		Nos. 753a-768a (11)	18.25	18.25

Inscribed 1990.

1989, Nov. 17 Wmk. 384 Perf. 14

Water sports.

769	A128 25c Water skiing	.25	.25
770	A128 50c Yachting	.50	.50
771	A128 65c Scuba diving	.65	.65
772	A128 $2.50 Surfing	2.50	2.50
	Nos. 769-772 (4)	3.90	3.90

Horse Racing A129

Wmk. 373

1990, May 3 Litho. Perf. 14

773	A129 25c Bugler, jockeys	.25	.25
774	A129 45c Parade ring	.45	.45
775	A129 75c In the straight	.75	.75
776	A129 $2 Winner, vert.	2.00	2.00
	Nos. 773-776 (4)	3.45	3.45

Barbados No. 2 — A130

Stamps on stamps: No. 778, Barbados #61. 65c, Barbados #73. $2.50, Barbados #121.

No. 781a, Great Britain #1. No. 781b, Barbados #108.

1990, May 3

777 A130 25c shown .25 .25
778 A130 50c multicolored .50 .50
779 A130 65c multicolored .65 .65
780 A130 $2.50 multicolored 2.50 2.50
Nos. 777-780 (4) 3.90 3.90

Souvenir Sheet

781 Sheet of 2 1.00 1.00
a.-b. A130 50c any single .50 .50

Stamp World London '90.

Queen Mother, 90th Birthday

Common Design Types

1990, Aug. 8 Wmk. 384 *Perf. 14x15*

782 CD343 75c At age 23 .75 .75

Perf. 14½

783 CD344 $2.50 Engagement portrait, 1923 2.50 2.50

Insects A131

Wmk. 373

1990, Oct. 16 Litho. *Perf. 14*

784 A131 50c Dragonfly .50 .50
785 A131 65c Black hardback beetle .65 .65
786 A131 75c Green grasshopper .75 .75
787 A131 $2 God-horse 2.00 2.00
Nos. 784-787 (4) 3.90 3.90

Nos. 757, 764 and 766 Overprinted

1990, Nov. 21 *Perf. 14½*

788 A127 25c on No. 757 .25 .25
789 A127 80c on No. 764 .80 .80
790 A127 $2.50 on No. 766 2.50 2.50
Nos. 788-790 (3) 3.55 3.55

Christmas — A132

1990, Dec. 4 *Perf. 14*

791 A132 20c Christmas star .20 .20
792 A132 50c Nativity scene .50 .50
793 A132 $1 Stained glass window 1.00 1.00
794 A132 $2 Angel 2.00 2.00
Nos. 791-794 (4) 3.70 3.70

Yellow Warbler A133

1991, Mar. 4

795 A133 10c shown .25 .25
796 A133 20c Male, female, nest .55 .55
797 A133 45c Female, chicks 1.25 1.25
798 A133 $1 Male, fledgling 2.75 2.75
Nos. 795-798 (4) 4.80 4.80

World Wildlife Fund.

Fishing A134

Perf. 13½x14, 14x13½

1991, June 18 Litho. Wmk. 373

799 A134 5c Daily catch, vert. .20 .20
800 A134 50c Line fishing .50 .50
801 A134 75c Cleaning fish .80 .80
802 A134 $2.50 Game fishing, vert. 2.50 2.50
Nos. 799-802 (4) 4.00 4.00

Freemasonry in Barbados, 250th Anniv. — A135

Designs: 25c, Masonic Building, Bridgetown. 65c, Compass and square. 75c, Royal arch jewel. $2.50, Columns, apron and centenary badge.

1991, Sept. 17 *Perf. 14*

803 A135 25c multicolored .25 .25
804 A135 65c multicolored .65 .65
805 A135 75c multicolored .75 .75
806 A135 $2.50 multicolored 2.50 2.50
Nos. 803-806 (4) 4.15 4.15

Butterflies A136

1991, Nov. 15 Wmk. 384

807 A136 20c Polydamus swallowtail .25 .25
808 A136 50c Long-tailed skipper, vert. .65 .65
809 A136 65c Cloudless sulphur .85 .85
810 A136 $2.50 Caribbean buckeye, vert. 3.25 3.25
Nos. 807-810 (4) 5.00 5.00

Souvenir Sheet

811 A136 $4 Painted lady 6.00 6.00

Phila Nippon '91.

Independence, 25th Anniv. — A137

Governor-General Dame Nita Barrow and: 10c, Students in classrom. 25c, Barbados Workers Union headquarters. 65c, Building industry. 75c, Agriculture. $1, Inoculations given at health clinic. $2.50, Gordon Greenidge, Desmond Haynes, cricket players (no portrait).

1991, Nov. 20 Wmk. 373

812 A137 10c multicolored .20 .20
813 A137 25c multicolored .25 .25
814 A137 65c multicolored .65 .65
815 A137 75c multicolored .75 .75
816 A137 $1 multicolored 1.00 1.00
Nos. 812-816 (5) 2.85 2.85

Souvenir Sheet

817 A137 $2.50 multi, vert. 2.40 2.50

Easter — A138

Wmk. 384

1992, Apr. 7 Litho. *Perf. 14*

818 A138 35c Christ carrying cross .35 .35
819 A138 70c Christ on cross .70 .70
820 A138 90c Christ taken down from cross .95 .95
821 A138 $3 Christ risen 3.00 3.00
Nos. 818-821 (4) 5.00 5.00

Flowering Trees — A139

Perf. 14x13½

1992, June 9 Litho. Wmk. 373

822 A139 10c Cannon ball .20 .20
823 A139 30c Golden shower .30 .30
824 A139 80c Frangipani .80 .80
825 A139 $1.10 Flamboyant 1.10 1.10
Nos. 822-825 (4) 2.40 2.40

Orchids A140

Designs: 55c, Epidendrum "Costa Rica." 65c, Cattleya guttaca. 70c, Laeliacattleya "Splashing Around." $1.40, Phalaenopsis "Kathy Saegert."

1992, Sept. 8 *Perf. 13½x14*

826 A140 55c multicolored .55 .55
827 A140 65c multicolored .65 .65
828 A140 70c multicolored .70 .70
829 A140 $1.40 multicolored 1.40 1.40
Nos. 826-829 (4) 3.30 3.30

For overprints see Nos. 838-841.

Transport and Tourism A141

Designs: 5c, Mini Moke, Gun Hill Signal Station, St. George. 35c, Tour bus, Bathsheba Beach, St. Joseph. 90c, BWIA McDonnell Douglas MD 83, Grantley Adams Airport. $2, Cruise ship Festivale, deep water harbor, Bridgetown.

Wmk. 373

1992, Dec. 15 Litho. *Perf. 14½*

830 A141 5c multicolored .20 .20
831 A141 35c multicolored .35 .35
832 A141 90c multicolored .90 .90
833 A141 $2 multicolored 2.00 2.00
Nos. 830-833 (4) 3.45 3.45

Cacti and Succulents A142

Wmk. 373

1993, Feb. 9 Litho. *Perf. 14*

834 A142 10c Barbados gooseberry .20 .20
835 A142 35c Night-blooming cereus .40 .40
836 A142 $1.40 Aloe 1.40 1.40
837 A142 $2 Scrunchineel 2.00 2.00
Nos. 834-837 (4) 4.00 4.00

Nos. 826-829 Ovptd. "WORLD ORCHID CONFERENCE 1993" on 2 or 4 lines

Perf. 13½x14

1993, Apr. 1 Litho. Wmk. 373

838 A140 55c on #826 multi .55 .55
839 A140 65c on #827 multi .65 .65
840 A140 70c on #828 multi .70 .70
841 A140 $1.40 on #829 multi 1.40 1.40
Nos. 838-841 (4) 3.30 3.30

Royal Air Force, 75th Anniv.

Common Design Type

Designs: 10c, Hawker Hunter. 30c, Handley Page Victor. 70c, Hawker Typhoon. $3, Hawker Hurricane.

No. 846a, Armstrong Whitworth Siskin 3a. b, Supermarine S.6B. c, Supermarine Walrus. d, Hawker Hart.

1993, Apr. 1 *Perf. 14*

842 CD350 10c multicolored .20 .20
843 CD350 30c multicolored .30 .30
844 CD350 70c multicolored .70 .70
845 CD350 $3 multicolored 3.00 3.00
Nos. 842-845 (4) 4.20 4.20

Souvenir Sheet

846 CD350 50c Sheet of 4, #a.-d. 2.00 2.00

Cannon A143

Designs: 5c, 18-pounder Culverin, 1625, Denmark Fort. 45c, 6-pounder Commonwealth gun, 1649-1660, St. Ann's Fort. $1, 9-pounder Demi-culverin, 1691, The Main Guard. $2.50, 32-pounder Demi-cannon, 1693-94, Charles Fort.

Wmk. 373

1993, June 8 Litho. *Perf. 13*

847 A143 5c multicolored .20 .20
848 A143 45c multicolored .45 .45
849 A143 $1 multicolored 1.00 1.00
850 A143 $2.50 multicolored 2.50 2.50
Nos. 847-850 (4) 4.15 4.15

Barbados Museum, 60th Anniv. — A144

Designs: 10c, Shell box, carved figure. 75c, Map, print of three people. 90c, Silver cup, print of soldier. $1.10, Map.

Wmk. 373

1993, Sept. 14 Litho. *Perf. 14*

851 A144 10c multicolored .20 .20
852 A144 75c multicolored .75 .75
853 A144 90c multicolored .95 .95
854 A144 $1.10 multicolored 1.10 1.10
Nos. 851-854 (4) 3.00 3.00

A145

Prehistoric Aquatic Reptiles: a, Plesiosaurus. b, Ichthyosaurus. c, Elasmosaurus. d, Mosasaurus. e, Archelon. Continuous design.

Wmk. 373

1993, Oct. 28 Litho. *Perf. 13*

855 A145 90c Strip of 5, #a.-e. 5.00 5.00

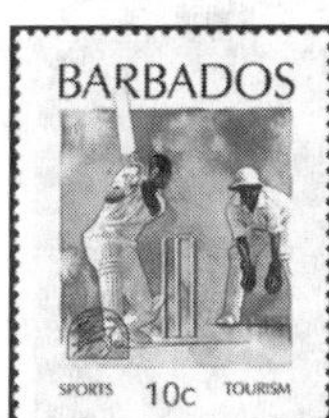

A146

Wmk. 384

1994, Jan. 11 Litho. *Perf. 14*

856 A146 10c Cricket .20 .20
857 A146 35c Motor racing .35 .35
858 A146 50c Golf .50 .50
859 A146 70c Run Barbados 10k .70 .70
860 A146 $1.40 Swimming 1.40 1.40
Nos. 856-860 (5) 3.15 3.15

Sports & tourism.

No. 822 exists inscribed "1996"; Nos. 872-877, 880, 885 "1997."

Migratory Birds A147

Wmk. 373

1994, Feb. 18 Litho. *Perf. 14*

861 A147 10c Whimbrel .20 .20
862 A147 35c American golden plover .35 .35
863 A147 70c Ruddy turnstone .70 .70
864 A147 $3 Tricolored heron 3.00 3.00
Nos. 861-864 (4) 4.25 4.25

Hong Kong '94.

1st UN Conference of Small Island Developing States — A148

1994, Apr. 25 *Perf. 14x14½*

865 A148 10c Bathsheba .20 .20
866 A148 65c Pico Teneriffe .65 .65
867 A148 90c Ragged Point Lighthouse .90 .90
868 A148 $2.50 Consett Bay 2.50 2.50
Nos. 865-868 (4) 4.25 4.25

Order of the Caribbean Community A149

First award recipients: No. 869, Sir Shridath Ramphal, statesman, Guyana. No. 870, Derek Walcott, writer, Nobel Laureate, St. Lucia. No. 871, William Demas, economist, Trinidad and Tobago.

Wmk. 373

1994, July 4 Litho. *Perf. 14*

869 A149 70c multicolored .70 .70
870 A149 70c multicolored .70 .70
871 A149 70c multicolored .70 .70
Nos. 869-871 (3) 2.10 2.10

Ships A150

Designs: 5c, Dutch Flyut, 1695. 10c, Geestport, 1994. 25c, HMS Victory, 1805. 30c, Royal Viking Queen, 1994. 35c, HMS Barbados, 1945. 45c, Faraday, 1924. 50c, USCG Hamilton, 1974. 65c, HMCS Saguenay, 1939. 70c, Inanda, 1928. 80c, HMS Rodney, 1944. 90c, USS John F. Kennedy, 1982. $1.10, William & John, 1627. $5, USCG Champlain, 1931. $10, Artist, 1877.

Wmk. 373

1994, Aug. 16 Litho. *Perf. 14*

872 A150 5c multicolored .20 .20
873 A150 10c multicolored .20 .20
874 A150 25c multicolored .25 .25
875 A150 30c multicolored .30 .30
876 A150 35c multicolored .35 .35
877 A150 45c multicolored .45 .45
878 A150 50c multicolored .50 .50
879 A150 65c multicolored .65 .65
880 A150 70c multicolored .70 .70
881 A150 80c multicolored .80 .80
882 A150 90c multicolored .90 .90
883 A150 $1.10 multicolored 1.10 1.10
884 A150 $5 multicolored 5.00 5.00
885 A150 $10 multicolored 10.00 10.00
Nos. 872-885 (14) 21.40 21.40

Nos. 872-885 are not dated. Nos. 872-877, 880, 882, 885 exist inscribed "1997." Nos. 872-873, 877, 880 exist inscribed "1998." Nos. 873, 877, 885 exist inscribed "1999."

1996 Wmk. 384

872a A150 5c .20 .20
873a A150 10c .20 .20
875a A150 30c .30 .30
876a A150 35c .35 .35
877a A150 45c .45 .45
878a A150 50c .50 .50
879a A150 65c .65 .65
880a A150 70c .70 .70
881a A150 80c .80 .80
882a A150 90c .90 .90
883a A150 $1.10 1.10 1.10
884a A150 $5 5.00 5.00
Nos. 872a-884a (12) 11.15 11.15

Inscribed (1996."

Issued: Nos. 875a-877a, 879a-882a, 9/1/96; others, May.

West India Regiment, Bicent. — A151

Designs: 30c, 2nd Regiment, 1860. 50c, 4th Regiment, Light Company, 1795. 70c, 3rd Regiment, drum major, 1860. $1, 5th Regiment, undress, working dress, 1815. $1.10, 1st, 2nd Regiments, Review Order, 1874.

Perf. 15x14

1995, Feb. 21 Litho. Wmk. 373

886 A151 30c multicolored .30 .30
887 A151 50c multicolored .50 .50
888 A151 70c multicolored .70 .70
889 A151 $1 multicolored 1.00 1.00
890 A151 $1.10 multicolored 1.10 1.10
Nos. 886-890 (5) 3.60 3.60

End of World War II

Common Design Type

10c, Barbadians serving in the Middle East. 35c, Lancaster bomber. 55c, Spitfire fighter. $2.50, SS Davisian sunk off Barbados, July 10, 1940.

$2, Reverse of War Medal 1939-45.

Wmk. 373

1995, May 8 Litho. *Perf. 14*

891 CD351 10c multicolored .20 .20
892 CD351 35c multicolored .30 .30
893 CD351 55c multicolored .55 .55
894 CD351 $2.50 multicolored 2.50 2.50
Nos. 891-894 (4) 3.55 3.55

Souvenir Sheet

895 CD352 $2 multicolored 2.50 2.50

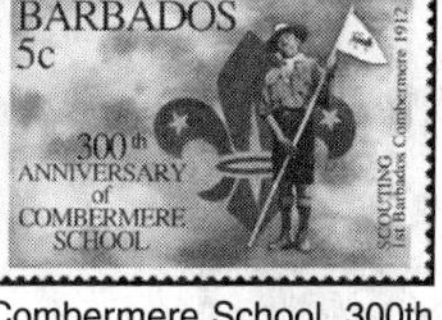

Combermere School, 300th Anniv. — A152

Designs: 5c, Scouting, Combermere 1st Barbados, 1912. 20c, Violin, sheet music. 35c, Cricket, Sir Frank Worrell, vert. 90c, Frank Collymore, #553. $3, Landscape.

Wmk. 373

1995, July 25 Litho. *Perf. 14*

896 A152 5c multicolored .20 .20
897 A152 20c multicolored .20 .20
898 A152 35c multicolored .35 .35
899 A152 $3 multicolored 3.00 3.00
Nos. 896-899 (4) 3.75 3.75

Souvenir Sheet

900 Sheet of 5, #896-899, 900a 4.50 4.50
a. A152 90c multicolored .90 .90

UN, 50th Anniv.

Common Design Type

Designs: 30c, Douglas C-124 Globemaster, Korea 1950-53. 45c, Royal Navy Sea King helicopter. $1.40, Wessex helicopter, UNFICYP, Cyprus 1964. $2, Gazelle helicopter, UNFICYP, Cyprus 1964.

Wmk. 373

1995, Oct. 24 Litho. *Perf. 14*

901 CD353 30c multicolored .30 .30
902 CD353 45c multicolored .45 .45
903 CD353 $1.40 multicolored 1.40 1.40
904 CD353 $2 multicolored 2.00 2.00
Nos. 901-904 (4) 4.15 4.15

Water Lilies — A153

Wmk. 373

1995, Dec. 19 Litho. *Perf. 14*

905 A153 10c Blue beauty .20 .20
906 A153 65c White water lily .65 .65
907 A153 70c Sacred lotus .70 .70
908 A153 $3 Water hyacinth 3.00 3.00
Nos. 905-908 (4) 4.55 4.55

Barbados Philatelic Society, Cent. A154

Magnifiying glass, tongs, and: 10c, #70. 55c, #109. $1.10, #148. $1.40, #192.

Wmk. 373

1996, Jan. 30 Litho. *Perf. 14*

909 A154 10c multicolored .20 .20
910 A154 55c multicolored .55 .55
911 A154 $1.10 multicolored 1.10 1.10
912 A154 $1.40 multicolored 1.40 1.40
Nos. 909-912 (4) 3.25 3.25

A155

Modern Olympic Games, Cent. — A156

1996, Apr. 2 Litho. *Perf. 14*

913 A155 20c Soccer .20 .20
914 A155 30c Relay race .30 .30
915 A155 55c Basketball .55 .55
916 A155 $3 Rhythmic gymnastics 3.00 3.00
Nos. 913-916 (4) 4.05 4.05

Souvenir Sheet

917 A156 $2.50 Discus thrower 2.50 2.50

Olymphilex '96 (No. 917).

CAPEX '96 A157

Transportation links with Canada: 10c, Canadian Airlines DC10. 90c, Air Canada Boeing 767. $1, Air Canada 320 Airbus. $1.40, Canadian Airlines Boeing 767.

Wmk. 373

1996, June 7 Litho. *Perf. 14*

918 A157 10c multicolored .20 .20
919 A157 90c multicolored .90 .90
920 A157 $1 multicolored 1.00 1.00
921 A157 $1.40 multicolored 1.40 1.40
Nos. 918-921 (4) 3.50 3.50

Chattel Houses A158

House features: 35c, Shed roof, lattice work. 70c, Pedimented porch, carved wooden trim. $1.10, Decorative, elegant porch. $2, Hip roof, bell pelmet window hoods.

1996, June 7

922 A158 35c multicolored .35 .35
923 A158 70c multicolored .70 .70
924 A158 $1.10 multicolored 1.10 1.10
925 A158 $2 multicolored 2.00 2.00
Nos. 922-925 (4) 4.15 4.15

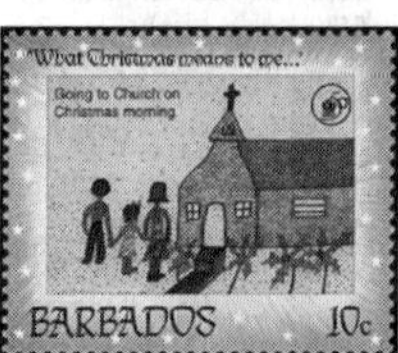

Christmas A159

Children's paintings: 10c, Going to Church on Christmas morning. 30c, The Tuk Band. 55c, Caroling on Christmas. $2.50, Decorated houses.

Wmk. 373

1996, Nov. 12 Litho. *Perf. 14½*

926 A159 10c multicolored .20 .20
927 A159 30c multicolored .30 .30
928 A159 55c multicolored .55 .55
929 A159 $2.50 multicolored 2.50 2.50
Nos. 926-929 (4) 3.55 3.55

UNICEF, 50th anniv.

Hong Kong '97 — A160

Dogs: 10c, Doberman pinscher. 30c, German shepherd. 90c, Japanese akita. $3, Irish red setter.

Perf. 14x14½

1997, Feb. 12 Litho. Wmk. 373

930 A160 10c multicolored .20 .20
931 A160 30c multicolored .30 .30
932 A160 90c multicolored .90 .90
933 A160 $3 multicolored 3.00 3.00
Nos. 930-933 (4) 4.40 4.40

Visit of US Pres. Clinton to Barbados, May 1997 A161

35c, Barbados flag, arms. 90c, US flag, arms.

1997, May 9 Litho. *Perf. 14*

934 A161 35c multicolored .35 .35
935 A161 90c multicolored .90 .90
a. Pair, #934-935 1.25 1.25

Issued in sheets of 8 stamps + 2 labels.

Shells — A162

5c, Measled cowry. 35c, Trumpet triton. 90c, Scotch bonnet. $2, West Indian murex.
$2.50, Sea bottom with miscellaneous shells.

1997, July 29 Litho. *Perf. 14*

936 A162 5c multicolored .20 .20
937 A162 35c multicolored .35 .35
938 A162 90c multicolored .90 .90
939 A162 $2 multicolored 1.90 1.90
Nos. 936-939 (4) 3.35 3.35

Souvenir Sheet

940 A162 $2.50 multicolored 2.40 2.40

Public Library, 150th Anniv. A163

Designs: 10c, Lucas manuscripts. 30c, Storytelling to children. 70c, Bookmobile. $3, Information technology.

1997, Oct. 1 Litho. *Perf. 14*

941 A163 10c multicolored .20 .20
942 A163 30c multicolored .30 .30
943 A163 70c multicolored .70 .70
944 A163 $3 multicolored 3.10 3.10
Nos. 941-944 (4) 4.30 4.30

Fruit — A164

1997, Dec. 16 Litho. *Perf. 14½*

945 A164 35c Barbados cherry .35 .35
946 A164 40c Sugar apple .40 .40
947 A164 $1.15 Soursop 1.10 1.10
948 A164 $1.70 Papaya 1.60 1.60
Nos. 945-948 (4) 3.45 3.45

Souvenir Sheet

Sir Grantley Adams, Birth Cent. — A165

a, Natl. Arms. b, Grantley Adams. c, Natl. flag.

1998, Apr. 27 Litho. *Perf. 13*

949 A165 $1 Sheet of 3, #a.-c. 3.00 3.00

Diana, Princess of Wales (1961-97)

Common Design Type of 1998

Portraits wearing: a, Blue hat. b, Red suit jacket. c, Tiara. d, Black and white.

1998, May *Perf. 14½x14*

950 CD355 $1.15 Sheet of 4, #a.-d. 6.50 6.50

Organization of American States, 50th Anniv. — A166

Designs: 15c, Beach during storm, beach during sunny day. $1, Dancers in native costumes. $2.50, Judge reading at podium, statue of justice.

1998, June 30 Litho. *Perf. 14*

951 A166 15c multicolored .20 .20
952 A166 $1 multicolored .95 .95
953 A166 $2.50 multicolored 2.50 2.50
Nos. 951-953 (3) 3.65 3.65

University of West Indies, 50th Anniv. A167

1998, July 20 *Perf. 14½*

954 A167 40c Frank Worrell Hall .40 .40
955 A167 $1.15 Graduation 1.10 1.10
956 A167 $1.40 Plaque, hummingbird 1.40 1.40
957 A167 $1.75 Quadrangle 1.75 1.75
Nos. 954-957 (4) 4.65 4.65

Tourism A168

1998, Dec. 1 Litho. *Perf. 14*

958 A168 10c Catamaran, vert. .20 .20
959 A168 45c Jolly Roger .45 .45
960 A168 70c Atlantis submarine .70 .70
961 A168 $2 MV Harbor Master, vert. 2.00 2.00
Nos. 958-961 (4) 3.35 3.35

Australia '99, World Stamp Expo — A169

Illustration reduced.

1999, Mar. 19 Litho. *Perf. 14*

962 A169 $4 Sailboat 3.50 3.50

Piping Plover A170

World Wildlife Fund: 10c, Juvenile in shallow water. 45c, Female with eggs. 50c, Fledglings in nest, male, female. 70c, Male.

1999, Apr. 27 Litho. *Perf. 14*

963 A170 10c multicolored .20 .20
964 A170 45c multicolored .45 .45
965 A170 50c multicolored .50 .50
966 A170 70c multicolored .70 .70
Nos. 963-966 (4) 1.85 1.85

1st Manned Moon Landing, 30th Anniv.

Common Design Type

Designs: 40c, Astronaut training. 45c, First stage separation. $1.15, Lunar module. $1.40, Docking with service module.
$2.50, Looking at earth from moon.

Perf. 14x13¾

1999, July 20 Litho. Wmk. 384

967 CD357 40c multicolored .40 .40
968 CD357 45c multicolored .45 .45
969 CD357 $1.15 multicolored 1.10 1.10
970 CD357 $1.40 multicolored 1.40 1.40
Nos. 967-970 (4) 3.35 3.35

Souvenir Sheet

Perf. 14

971 CD357 $2.50 multicolored 2.50 2.50

No. 971 contains one 40mm circular stamp.

Rabbits A171

Designs: a, Rabbit running. b, Rabbit profile. c, Rabbit nursing young. d, Two rabbits leaping. e, Two rabbits at rest.

Perf. 14x14½

1999, Aug. 21 Litho. Wmk. 373

972 A171 70c Strip of 5, #a.-e. 3.50 3.50

China 1999 World Philatelic Exhibition.

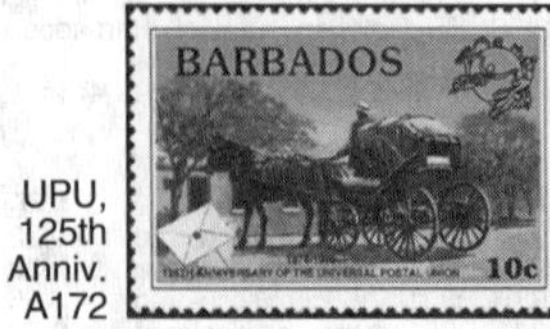
UPU, 125th Anniv. A172

1999, Oct. 11 Litho. *Perf. 14*

973 A172 10c Mail coach .20 .20
974 A172 45c Mail van .45 .45
975 A172 $1.75 Airplane 1.75 1.75
976 A172 $2 Computers 2.00 2.00
Nos. 973-976 (4) 4.40 4.40

Souvenir Sheet

Millennium — A173

Illustration reduced.

Wmk. 373

2000, Feb. 8 Litho. *Perf. 14*

977 A173 $3 multi 3.00 3.00

100th Test Cricket Match at Lord's Ground — A174

Designs: 45c, Sir Conrad Hunte. 90c, Malcolm Marshall. $2, Sir Garfield St. A. Sobers.
$2.50, Lord's Ground, horiz.

Wmk. 373

2000, May 22 Litho. *Perf. 14*

978 A174 45c multi .45 .45
979 A174 90c multi .90 .90
980 A174 $2 multi 2.00 2.00
Nos. 978-980 (3) 3.35 3.35

Souvenir Sheet

981 A174 $2.50 multi 2.50 2.50

The Stamp Show 2000, London (#981).

Sites in Barbados A175

5c, Drax Hall House. 10c, Reaping sugar cane. 40c, Needham's Point Lighthouse. 45c, Port St. Charles. 65c, Synagogue. 70c, Bridgetown port (boats point right). No. 987A, 70c, Bridgetown port (boats point left). 90c, Harrison's Cave. $1.15, Villa Nova. $1.40, Cricket at Kensington Oval. $1.75, Sunbury House. $2, Bethel Methodist Church. $3, Barbados Wildlife Reserve. $5, Royal Westmoreland golf course. $10, Grantley Adams Intl. Airport.

Wmk. 373

2000, May 22 Litho. *Perf. 14*

982 A175 5c multi .20 .20
983 A175 10c multi, vert. .20 .20
984 A175 40c multi, vert. .40 .40
985 A175 45c multi .45 .45
986 A175 65c multi .65 .65
987 A175 70c multi .70 .70
987A A175 70c multi .70 .70
988 A175 90c multi .90 .90
989 A175 $1.15 multi 1.10 1.10
990 A175 $1.40 multi 1.40 1.40
991 A175 $1.75 multi 1.75 1.75
992 A175 $2 multi 2.00 2.00
993 A175 $3 multi, vert. 3.00 3.00
994 A175 $5 multi, vert. 5.00 5.00
995 A175 $10 multi 10.00 10.00
Nos. 982-995 (15) 28.45 28.45

Nos. 982-987, 988-995 issued 5/22.
No. 983 exists dated 2002.

World Stamp Expo 2000, Anaheim — A176

25c, Golf equipment. 40c, Golfer on golf ball. $1.40, Golfer at tee. $2, Golfer putting.

Perf. 14½x14¼

2000, July 7 Litho. Wmk. 373

996-999 A176 Set of 4 4.00 4.00

Vintage Cars A177

Designs: 10c, 1947 Bentley Mk VI. 30c, Vanden Plas Princess. 90c, 1952 Austin Atlantic. $3, 1950 Bentley Special.

Perf. 14¼x14½

2000, Nov. 7 Wmk. 373

1000-1003 A177 Set of 4 4.25 4.25

Souvenir Sheet

Hong Kong 2001 Stamp Exhibition — A178

Wmk. 373

2001, Feb. 1 Litho. *Perf. 13¼*

1004 A178 $3 Thread snake 3.00 3.00

Deep Sea Creatures — A179

No. 1005: a, Lizard fish. b, Goldentail moray. c, Blackbar soldierfish. d, Golden zoanthid. e, Sponge brittle star. f, Magnificent feather duster. g, Bearded fireworm. h, Lima shell. i, Yellow tube sponge.

Wmk. 373

2001, May 31 Litho. *Perf. 13½*

1005 A179 45c Sheet of 9, #a-i 4.00 4.00

Phila Nippon '01, Japan A180

Various kites: 10c, 65c, $1.40, $1.75.

2001, Aug. 1 *Perf. 14*

1006-1009 A180 Set of 4 4.00 4.00

George Washington's Visit to Barbados, 250th Anniv. — A181

Designs: 45c, Washington, ship, trunk, dockworker. 50c, Washington, ship, palm trees. $1.15, Washington, Declaration of Independence. $2.50, Fort at Needham's Point. $3, Portrait of Washington.

Wmk. 373

2001, Nov. 2 Litho. *Perf. 13¼*

1010-1013 A181 Set of 4 4.75 4.75

Souvenir Sheet

1014 A181 $3 multi 3.00 3.00

Independence, 35th Anniv. — A182

Designs: 25c, Bank Holiday Bear. 45c, Tuk band. $1, Landship Movement Maypole dance. $2, National anthem, saxophone and guitar.

2001, Nov. 29 Litho. *Perf. 14*

1015-1018 A182 Set of 4 3.75 3.75

Reign Of Queen Elizabeth II, 50th Anniv. Issue

Common Design Type

Designs: Nos. 1019, 1023a, 10c, Princess Elizabeth. Nos. 1020, 1023b, 70c, Wearing red hat. Nos. 1021, 1023c, $1, Wearing crown. Nos. 1022, 1023d, $1.40, Wearing purple hat. No. 1023e, $3, 1955 portrait by Annigoni (38x50mm).

Perf. 14¼x14½, 13¾ (#1023e)

2002, Feb. 6 Wmk. 373

With Gold Frames

1019-1022 CD360 Set of 4 3.25 3.25

Souvenir Sheet

Without Gold Frames

1023 CD360 Sheet of 5, #a-e 6.25 6.25

Inland Post, 150th Anniv. A183

Map of Barbados and: 10c, #1. 45c, Early postman. $1.15, Steam packet R.M.S. Esk. $2, BWIA Tristar.

2002, Apr. 15 *Perf. 14*

1024-1027 A183 Set of 4 3.75 3.75

Flowers — A184

Designs: 10c, Red ginger, vert. 40c, Heliconia caribaea, vert. $1.40, Tube rose. $2.50, Anthurium.

Perf. 14¾x14, 14x14¾

2002, May 30 Litho.

1028-1031 A184 Set of 4 4.50 4.50

First Settlement, 375th Anniv. — A185

Designs: 10c, Drax Hall, St. George. 45c, Donkey cart truck. $1.15, Remains of cattle mill, Gibbons. $3, Morgan Lewis, St. Andrew.

Wmk. 373

2002, Sept. 6 Litho. *Perf. 14*

1032-1035 A185 Set of 4 4.75 4.75

Christmas A186

Designs: 45c, Traditional Christmas fare. $1.15, Christmas morning in the park. $1.40, Nativity scene.

2002, Nov. 11

1036-1038 A186 Set of 3 3.00 3.00

Pan-American Health Organization, Cent. — A187

Designs: 10c, AIDS awareness. 70c, Health and longevity. $1.15, Director General Sir George Alleyne. $2, Women's health.

Wmk. 373

2002, Dec. 2 Litho. *Perf. 14*

1039-1042 A187 Set of 4 4.00 4.00

SEMI-POSTAL STAMPS

No. 73 Surcharged in Red

Perf. 14

1907, Jan. 25 Typo. Wmk. 2

B1	A8	1p on 2p sl & org	1.75	*2.50*
a.		No period after 1d	15.00	*17.50*
b.		Inverted surcharge	1.75	*2.50*
c.		Inverted surcharge, no period after 1d	15.00	*17.50*
d.		Double surcharge	600.00	650.00
e.		Dbl. surch., both invtd.	600.00	

Catalogue values for unused stamps in this section, from this point to the end of the section, are for Never Hinged items.

No. 406 Surcharged

1979, May 29 Photo. Wmk. 314

B2 A56 28c + 4c on 35c multi .30 .30

The surtax was for victims of the eruption of Mt. Soufrière.

POSTAGE DUE STAMPS

Catalogue values for unused stamps in this section are for Never Hinged items.

D1

1934-47 Typo. Wmk. 4 *Perf. 14*

J1	D1	½p green ('35)	.75	.75
J2	D1	1p black	1.40	1.40
a.		Half used as ½p on cover		*750.00*
J3	D1	3p dk car rose ('47)	22.50	22.50
		Nos. J1-J3 (3)	24.65	24.65

A 2nd die of the 1p was introduced in 1947.

Use of #J2a was authorized from Mar. 1934 through Feb. 1935. Some examples have "½d" written on the bisect in black or red ink.

1950

J4	D1	1c green	.20	.20
J5	D1	2c black	.40	.40
J6	D1	6c carmine rose	1.50	*1.75*
		Nos. J4-J6 (3)	2.10	*2.35*

Values are for 1953 chalky paper printing.

Wmk. 4a (error)

J4a	D1	1c green	140.00
J5a	D1	2c black	190.00
J6a	D1	6c carmine rose	110.00
		Nos. J4a-J6a (3)	440.00

1965, Aug. 3 Wmk. 314 *Perf. 14*

J7	D1	1c green	.30	.30
J8	D1	2c black	.35	.35
J9	D1	6c carmine rose	.65	.65
a.		Wmk. sideways, perf 14x13½	2.25	2.25
		Nos. J7-J9 (3)	1.30	1.30

Issued: No. J9a, 2/4/74.

Wmk. 314 Sideways

1974, Dec. 4 *Perf. 13x13½*

J8b	D1	2c	1.50	1.50
J9b	D1	6c	1.50	1.50

D2

Designs: Each stamp shows different stylized flower in background.

Perf. 13½x14

1976, May 12 Litho. Wmk. 373

J10	D2	1c brt pink & mag	.20	.20
J11	D2	2c lt & dk vio blue	.20	.20
J12	D2	5c yellow & brown	.20	.20
J13	D2	10c lilac & purple	.20	.20
J14	D2	25c yel green & dk grn	.30	.30
J15	D2	$1 rose & red	.90	.90
		Nos. J10-J15 (6)	2.00	2.00

1985, July *Perf. 15x14*

J10a	D2	1c	.20	.20
J11a	D2	2c	.20	.20
J12a	D2	5c	.20	.20
J13a	D2	10c	.20	.20
J14a	D2	25c	.20	.20
		Nos. J10a-J14a (5)	1.00	1.00

WAR TAX STAMP

No. 118 Overprinted

1917	Wmk. 3		*Perf. 14*
MR1	A12 1p carmine	.20	.20
a.	Imperf., pair	*4,000.*	

BARBUDA

bär-'büd-ə

LOCATION — Northernmost of the Leeward Islands, West Indies
GOVT. — Dependency of Antigua
AREA — 63 sq. mi.
POP. — 1,500 (1995 est.)
See Antigua.

12 Pence = 1 Shilling

Catalogue values for unused stamps in this country are for Never Hinged items, beginning with Scott 12 in the regular postage section, and Scott B1 in the semi-postal section.

Watermark

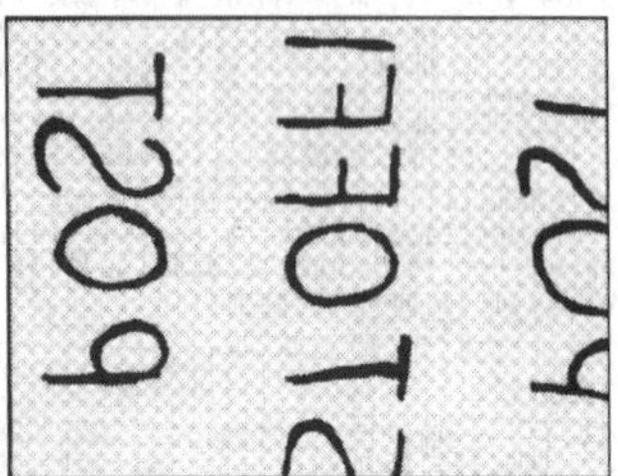

Wmk. 380- "POST OFFICE"

Leeward Islands Stamps and Types of 1912-22 Overprinted in Black or Red

Die II

For description of dies I and II, see back of this section of the Catalogue.

1922, July 13	Wmk. 4		*Perf. 14*
1	A5 ½p green	1.50	*7.00*
2	A5 1p rose red	1.50	*7.00*
3	A5 2p gray	1.60	*6.50*
4	A5 2½p ultramarine	1.60	*7.00*
5	A5 6p vio & red vio	3.00	*15.00*
6	A5 2sh vio & ultra, *bl*	13.50	*45.00*
7	A5 3sh green & violet	30.00	*67.50*
8	A5 4sh blk & scar (R)	35.00	*67.50*
	Wmk. 3		
9	A5 3p violet, *yel*	1.50	*9.00*
10	A5 1sh blk, *emer*(R)	3.00	*7.50*
11	A5 5sh grn & red, *yel*	85.00	*125.00*
	Nos. 1-11 (11)	177.20	*364.00*

Catalogue values for unused stamps in this section, from this point to the end of the section, are for Never Hinged items.

Map — B1

Fish — B2

1968-70	Litho. Unwmk.		*Perf. 14*
12	B1 ½c blk, salmon pink & red brn	.20	.20
13	B1 1c blk, org & brt org	.20	.20
14	B1 2c blk, brt pink & brt rose	.20	.20
15	B1 3c blk, yel & org yel	.20	.20
16	B1 4c blk, lt grn & brt grn	.20	.20
17	B1 5c blk, bl grn & brt bl grn	.20	.20
18	B1 6c blk, lt lil & red lil	.20	.20
19	B1 10c blk, lt bl & dk bl	.20	.20
20	B1 15c blk, dl grn & grn	.20	.20
21	B2 20c Great barracuda	.75	*1.25*
22	B2 25c Great amberjack	.30	.25
23	B2 35c French angelfish	.40	.40
24	B2 50c Porkfish	.55	.55
25	B2 75c Striped parrotfish	.80	.80
26	B2 $1 Longspine squirrelfish	1.10	1.10
27	B2 $2.50 Catalufa	2.75	2.75
28	B2 $5 Blue chromis	5.00	*6.00*
	Nos. 12-28 (17)	13.45	14.90

Issued: ½c-15c, 11/19/68; 20c, 7/22/70; 25c-75c, 2/5/69; others, 3/6/69.

For surcharge see No. 80.

1968 Summer Olympics, Mexico City — B3

Designs: 25c, Running, Aztec calendar stone. 35c, High jumping, Aztec statue. 75c, Yachting, Aztec lion mask. $1, Soccer, Aztec carved stone.

1968, Dec. 20			
29	B3 25c multicolored	.40	.20
30	B3 35c multicolored	.50	.25
31	B3 75c multicolored	.75	.40
	Nos. 29-31 (3)	1.65	.85

Souvenir Sheet

32	B3 $1 multicolored	2.50	*3.00*

The Ascension, by Orcagna — B4

1969, Mar. 24			
33	B4 25c blue & black	.20	.25
34	B4 35c dp carmine & blk	.20	.35
35	B4 75c violet & black	.25	.40
	Nos. 33-35 (3)	.65	1.00

Easter.

3rd Caribbean Boy Scout Jamboree — B5

1969, Aug. 7			
36	B5 25c Flag ceremony	.40	.45
37	B5 35c Campfire	.50	.60
38	B5 75c Rowing	.65	.75
	Nos. 36-38 (3)	1.55	1.80

The Sistine Madonna, by Raphael — B6

1969, Oct. 20			
39	B6 ½c multicolored	.20	.20
40	B6 25c multicolored	.20	.20
41	B6 35c multicolored	.20	.20
42	B6 75c multicolored	.20	.25
	Nos. 39-42 (4)	.80	.85

Christmas.

English Monarchs — B7

#43, William I. #44, William II. #45, Henry I. #46, Stephen. #47, Henry II. #48, Richard I. #49, John. #50, Henry III. #51, Edward I. #52, Edward II. #53, Edward III. #54, Richard II. #55, Henry IV. #56, Henry V. #57, Henry VI. #58, Edward IV. #59, Edward V. #60, Richard III. #61, Henry VII. #62, Henry VIII. #63, Edward VI. #64, Lady Jane Grey. #65, Mary I. #66, Elizabeth I. #67, James I. #68, Charles I. #69, Charles II. #70, James II. #71, William III. #72, Mary II. #73, Anne. #74, George I. #75, George II. #76, George III. #77, George IV. #78, William IV. #79, Victoria.

1970-71			*Perf. 14½x14*
43-79	B7 35c Set of 37	3.75	*4.50*

Issued: 1970, #43, 2/16; #44, 3/2; #45, 3/16; #46, 4/4; #47, 4/15; #48, 5/1; #49, 5/15; #50, 6/1; #51, 6/15; #52, 7/1; #53, 7/15; #54, 8/1; #55, 8/15; #56, 9/1; #57, 9/15; #58, 10/1; #59, 10/15; #60, 11/2; #61, 11/16; #62, 12/1; #63, 12/15.

1971; #64, 1/2; #65, 1/15; #66, 2/1; #67, 2/15; #68, 3/1; #69, 3/15; #70, 4/1; #71, 4/15; #72, 5/1; #73, 5/15; #74, 6/1; #75, 6/15; #76, 7/1; #77, 7/15; #78, 8/2; #79, 8/16.

See Nos. 622-627 for other Monarchs.

No. 12 Surcharged

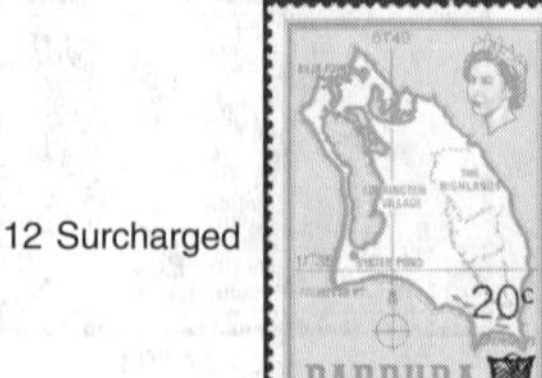

1970, Feb. 26			*Perf. 14*
80	B1 20c on 1/2c multicolored	.25	.25

Easter — B8

1970, Mar. 16			
81	B8 25c Carrying Cross	.20	.20
82	B8 35c Descent from cross	.20	.25
83	B8 75c Crucifixion	.20	.30
a.	Strip of 3, #81-83	.70	.70

Charles Dickens B9

1970, July 10			
84	B9 20c Oliver Twist	.20	.20
85	B9 75c Old Curiosity Shop	.35	.40

Christmas — B10

Designs: 20c, Madonna of the Meadow, by Giovanni Bellini. 50c, Madonna, Child and Angels from Wilton Diptych. 75c, Nativity, by Piero della Francesca.

1970, Oct. 15			
86	B10 20c multicolored	.20	.20
87	B10 50c multicolored	.20	.20
88	B10 75c multicolored	.20	.25
	Nos. 86-88 (3)	.60	.65

British Red Cross, Cent. B11

1970, Dec. 21			
89	B11 20c Patient in wheelchair, vert.	.20	*.25*
90	B11 35c shown	.25	*.35*
91	B11 75c Child care	.35	*.60*
	Nos. 89-91 (3)	.80	*1.20*

Easter — B12

Details from the Mond Crucifixion, by Raphael.

1971, Apr. 7			
92	B12 35c Angel	.20	*.40*
93	B12 50c Crucifixion	.20	*.50*
94	B12 75c Angel, diff.	.25	*.60*
a.	Strip of 3, #92-94	.75	*1.50*

Martello Tower B13

1971, May 10
95 B13 20c shown .20 .20
96 B13 25c Sailboats .20 .20
97 B13 50c Hotel bungalows .20 .20
98 B13 75c Government House, mystery stone .20 .20
Nos. 95-98 (4) .80 .80

Christmas — B14

Paintings: ½c, The Granduca Madonna, by Raphael. 35c, The Ansidei Madonna, by Raphael. 50c, The Virgin and Child, by Botticelli. 75c, The Madonna of the Trees, by Bellini.

1971, Oct. 4
99 B14 ½c multicolored .20 .20
100 B14 35c multicolored .20 .20
101 B14 50c multicolored .20 .20
102 B14 75c multicolored .25 .25
Nos. 99-102 (4) .85 .85

A set of four stamps for Durer (20c, 35c, 50c, 75c) was not authorized.

All stamps are types of Antigua or overprinted on stamps of Antigua unless otherwise specified. Many of the "BARBUDA" overprints are vertical.

Nos. 321-322 Ovptd. "BARBUDA"

1973, Nov. 14 ***Perf. 13½***
103 A65 35c multicolored 7.25 7.25
104 A65 $2 multicolored 2.25 2.25

Nos. 313-315a Ovptd. in Red "BARBUDA"

1973, Nov. 26 ***Perf. 13½x14***
105 A63 20c multicolored .20 .25
106 A63 35c multicolored .30 .50
107 A63 75c multicolored .40 .75
Nos. 105-107 (3) .90 1.50

Souvenir Sheet

108 Sheet of 4, #105-107, 108a 1.75 1.75
a. A63 5c multicolored

Carnival, 1973.

Nos. 307, 309, 311, 311a Ovptd. "BARBUDA"

Perf. 14x13½

1973, Nov. 26 **Wmk. 314**
109 A53 ½c multicolored .20 .20
110 A53 20c multicolored .20 .20
111 A53 75c multicolored .45 .25
Nos. 109-111 (3) .85 .65

Souvenir Sheet

112 Sheet of 5, #109-111, 112a-112b + label 2.75 2.75
a. A53 10c multicolored
b. A53 35c multicolored

Nos. 241a, 242-243, 244a, 245-248, 249a, 250-254, 255a, 256, 256a, 257 Ovptd. "BARBUDA"

Wmk. 314 Sideways, Upright

1973-74 ***Perf. 14***
113 A51 ½c multicolored .20 .20
114 A51 1c multicolored .20 .25
115 A51 2c multicolored .25 .25
116 A51 3c multicolored .25 .20
117 A51 4c multicolored .30 .25
118 A51 5c multicolored .40 .35
119 A51 6c multicolored .40 .35
120 A51 10c multicolored .45 .40
121 A51 15c multicolored .45 .40
122 A51 20c multicolored .55 .50
123 A51 25c multicolored .55 .50
124 A51 35c multicolored .55 .60
125 A51 50c multicolored .55 .60
126 A51 75c multicolored .55 .60
127 A51 $1 multicolored .55 .60
128 A51 $2.50 multicolored 1.25 1.25
a. Wmk. upright 9.25 10.00
129 A51 $5 multicolored 1.25 2.25
Nos. 113-129 (17) 8.70 9.55

Issue dates: ½c, 3c, 15c, $1, $2.50, Feb. 18, 1974. Others, Nov. 26.

Nos. 316-320a Ovptd. in Silver or Red "BARBUDA"

Perf. 14½

1973, Dec. 11 **Photo.** **Unwmk.**
130 A64 3c multicolored .20 .20
131 A64 5c multicolored .20 .20
132 A64 20c multicolored .20 .20
133 A64 35c multicolored (R) .20 .20
134 A64 $1 multicolored (R) .20 .20
Nos. 130-134 (5) 1.00 1.00

Souvenir Sheet

135 Sheet of 5 + label 6.50 7.50
a. A64 35c multicolored (S)
b. A64 $1 multicolored (S)

No. 135 contains Nos. 130-132, 135a-135b.

Nos. 323-324a Ovptd. "BARBUDA"

1973, Dec. 16 **Litho.** ***Perf. 13½***
136 A65 35c multicolored .25 .25
137 A65 $2 multicolored 1.25 1.25
a. Souvenir sheet of 2, #136-137 5.25 6.25

Nos. 325-328 Ovptd. "BARBUDA"

1974, Feb. 18 **Wmk. 314**
138 A66 5c multicolored .20 .20
139 A66 20c multicolored .20 .20
140 A66 35c multicolored .20 .20
141 A66 75c multicolored .20 .20
Nos. 138-141 (4) .80 .80

Nos. 329-333 Ovptd. "BARBUDA"

1974, May 1 ***Perf. 14x13½***
142 A53 ½c multicolored .20 .20
143 A53 10c multicolored .20 .20
144 A53 20c multicolored .25 .20
145 A53 35c multicolored .35 .25
146 A53 75c multicolored .50 .40
Nos. 142-146 (5) 1.50 1.25

No. 333a exists with overprint.

Nos. 334-340 Ovptd. Type "a" or "b" and No. 340 "BARBUDA" in Red

a & b

1974, July 15 **Unwmk.** ***Perf. 14½***

Se-tenant Pairs Overprinted Type "a" on Left Stamp, Type "b" on Right Stamp

148 A67 ½c multicolored .20 .20
149 A67 1c multicolored .20 .20
150 A67 2c multicolored .20 .20
151 A67 5c multicolored .40 .40
152 A67 20c multicolored 1.25 1.25
153 A67 35c multicolored 2.25 2.25
154 A67 $1 multicolored 6.50 6.50
Nos. 148-154 (7) 11.00 11.00

Souvenir Sheet

Perf. 13

155 Sheet of 7 + label 7.00 7.00
a. A67 ½c multicolored .20 .20
b. A67 1c multicolored .20 .20
c. A67 2c multicolored .20 .20
d. A67 5c multicolored .20 .20
e. A67 20c multicolored 1.00 1.00
f. A67 35c multicolored 1.50 2.00
g. A67 $1 multicolored 3.50 3.50

UPU, cent.

Nos. 341-344a Ovptd. "BARBUDA"

1974, Aug. 14 **Wmk. 314** ***Perf. 14***
156 A68 5c multicolored .20 .20
157 A68 20c multicolored .20 .20
158 A68 35c multicolored .20 .20
159 A68 75c multicolored .20 .20
a. Souvenir sheet of 4, #156-159 1.00 1.00
Nos. 156-159 (4) .80 .80

Nos. 345-348a Ovptd. "BARBUDA" and

World Cup Soccer Championships — B16

Various soccer plays.

1974, Sept. 2 **Unwmk.** ***Perf. 15, 14***
160 A69 5c multicolored .20 .20
161 A69 35c multicolored .20 .20
162 B16 35c multicolored .20 .20
163 A69 75c multicolored .20 .20
164 A69 $1 multicolored .25 .25
a. Souv. sheet of 4, #160-161, 163-164 + 2 labels, perf. 13½ 1.25 1.25
165 B16 $1.20 multicolored .25 .25
166 B16 $2.50 multicolored .35 .45
a. Souv. sheet of 3, #162, 165-166 1.25 1.25
Nos. 160-166 (7) 1.65 1.75

UPU, Cent. — B17

1974, Sept. 30 ***Perf. 14x13½***
167 B17 35c Ship letter, 1833 .20 .20
168 B17 $1.20 #1, 2 on FDC .25 .30
169 B17 $2.50 Airplane, map .40 .50
a. Souvenir sheet of 3, #167-169 1.75 1.75
Nos. 167-169 (3) .85 1.00

Greater Amberjack B18

1974-75 ***Perf. 14x14½, 14½x14***
170 B18 ½c Oleander, rose bay .20 .55
171 B18 1c Blue petrea .30 .55
172 B18 2c Poinsettia .30 .55
173 B18 3c Cassia tree .30 .55
174 B18 4c shown 2.75 .55
175 B18 5c Holy Trinity School .30 .20
176 B18 6c Snorkeling .30 .40
177 B18 10c Pilgrim Holiness Church .30 .25
178 B18 15c New Cottage Hospital .30 .25
179 B18 20c Post Office & Treasury .30 .25
180 B18 25c Island jetty & boats .60 .40
181 B18 35c Martello Tower .60 .40

Size: 39x25mm

Perf. 14

182 B18 50c Warden's House .60 .40
183 B18 75c Inter-island air service 2.00 1.40
184 B18 $1 Tortoise 1.40 1.10

Size: 45x29mm

Perf. 13½x14

185 B18 $2.50 Spiny lobster 1.60 *2.40*
186 B18 $5 Frigate birds 7.00 3.50
a. Perf. 14x15 12.00 17.50

Size: 34x47mm

187 B18 $10 Hibiscus 4.00 *6.25*
Nos. 170-187 (18) 23.15 *19.95*

Nos. 170-173, 180, 187 vert.

Issued: 4c, 5c, 6c, 10c, 15c, 20c, 25c, 35c, 75c, 10/15/74; ½c, 1c, 2c, 3c, 50c, $1, $2.50, #186, 1/6/75; #186a, 7/24/75; $10, 9/19/75.

For overprints see Nos. 213-214.

Nos. 349-352a Ovptd. "BARBUDA" in Red and

Winston Churchill, Birth Cent. — B19

1974 ***Perf. 14½, 13½x14***
188 A70 5c multicolored .20 .20
189 B19 5c Making broadcast .20 .20
190 A70 35c multicolored .30 .20
191 B19 35c Portrait .20 .20
192 A70 75c multicolored .50 .50
193 B19 75c Painting .25 .25
194 A70 $1 multicolored .75 .70
a. Souv. sheet of 4, #188, 190, 192, 194 7.50 9.00
195 B19 $1 Victory sign .35 .30
a. Souv. sheet of 4, #189, 191, 193, 195 1.25 1.75
Nos. 188-195 (8) 2.75 2.55

Issue dates: Nos. 188, 190, 192, 194, Oct. 15, others, Nov. 20. For overprints see Nos. 213-214.

Nos. 353-360a Ovptd. "BARBUDA"

1974, Nov. 25 ***Perf. 14½***
196 A71 ½c multicolored .20 .20
197 A71 1c multicolored .20 .20
198 A71 2c multicolored .20 .20
199 A71 3c multicolored .20 .20
200 A71 5c multicolored .20 .20
201 A71 20c multicolored .20 .20
202 A71 35c multicolored .20 .20
203 A71 75c multicolored .20 .20
a. Souv. sheet, #200-203, perf 13½ 1.00 1.25
Nos. 196-203 (8) 1.60 1.60

Nos. 369-373a Ovptd. "BARBUDA"

1975, Mar. 17
204 A72 5c multicolored .20 .20
205 A72 15c multicolored .35 .25
206 A72 35c multicolored .50 .35
207 A72 50c multicolored .70 .60
208 A72 $1 multicolored .75 .70
a. Souv. sheet of 5, #204-208 + label, perf. 13½x14 2.50 *3.00*
Nos. 204-208 (5) 2.50 2.10

Stamps from No. 208a are 43x28mm.

Battle of the Saints B20

1975, May 30 ***Perf. 13½x14***
209 B20 35c shown 1.00 .75
210 B20 50c Two ships 1.25 1.25
211 B20 75c Ships firing 1.50 1.50
212 B20 95c Sailors abandoning ship 1.75 2.00
Nos. 209-212 (4) 5.50 5.50

Barbuda No. 186a Ovptd.

a

b

1975, July 2 ***Perf. 14x15***
213 B18 (a) $5 multicolored 6.50 6.50
214 B18 (b) $5 multicolored 6.50 6.50

Overprint "a" is in 1st and 3rd vertical rows, "b" 2nd and 4th. The 5th row has no overprint. This can be collected se-tenant either as Nos. 213, 214 or 213, 214 and 186a.

Military Uniforms — B21

Designs: 35c, Officer of 65th Foot, 1763. 50c, Grenadier, 27th Foot, 1701-1710. 75c, Officer of 21st Foot, 1793-1796. 95c, Officer, Royal Regiment of Artillery, 1800.

1975, Sept. 17 ***Perf. 14***
215 B21 35c multicolored .50 .50
216 B21 50c multicolored .75 .75
217 B21 75c multicolored 1.25 1.25
218 B21 95c multicolored 1.50 1.50
Nos. 215-218 (4) 4.00 4.00

Barbuda Nos. 189, 191, 193, 195 Ovptd. "30th ANNIVERSARY / UNITED NATIONS / 1945 - 1975"

1975, Oct. 24 ***Perf. 13½x14***
219 B19 5c multicolored .20 .20
220 B19 35c multicolored .20 .20
221 B19 75c multicolored .20 .20
222 B19 $1 multicolored .20 .25
Nos. 219-222 (4) .80 .85

Nos. 394-401a Ovptd. "BARBUDA"

1975, Nov. 17 ***Perf. 14***
223 A77 ½c multicolored .20 .20
224 A77 1c multicolored .20 .20
225 A77 2c multicolored .20 .20
226 A77 3c multicolored .20 .20
227 A77 5c multicolored .20 .20
228 A77 10c multicolored .20 .20
229 A77 35c multicolored .20 .20
230 A77 $2 multicolored .20 .20
a. Souvenir sheet of 4, #227-230 1.75 2.00
Nos. 223-230 (8) 1.60 1.60

Nos. 402-404 Ovptd. "BARBUDA"

1975, Dec. 15 ***Perf. 14***
231 A78 5c multicolored 1.10 1.10
232 A78 35c multicolored 2.25 2.25
233 A78 $2 multicolored 4.25 4.25
Nos. 231-233 (3) 7.60 7.60

American Revolution, Bicent. B22

Details from Surrender of Cornwallis at Yorktown, by Trumbull: No. 234a, British officers. b, Gen. Benjamin Lincoln. c, Washington, Allied officers.
The Battle of Princeton: No. 235a, Infantry. b, Battle. c, Cannon fire.
Surrender of Burgoyne at Saratoga by Trumbull: No. 236a, Mounted officer. b, Washington, Burgoyne. c, American officers.
Signing the Declaration of Independence, by Trumbull: No. 237a, Delegates to Continental Congress. b, Adams, Sherman, Livingston, Jefferson and Franklin. c, Hancock, Thomson, Read, Dickinson, and Rutledge. Strips of 3 have continuous designs.

1976, Mar. 8 ***Perf. 13½x13***
234 B22 15c Strip of 3, #a.-c. .30 .30
235 B22 35c Strip of 3, #a.-c. 1.00 1.00
d. Souvenir sheet, #234-235 1.50 1.50
236 B22 $1 Strip of 3, #a.-c. 1.25 1.25
237 B22 $2 Strip of 3, #a.-c. 2.25 2.25
d. Souvenir sheet, #236-237 3.75 3.75

See Nos. 244-247.

Birds B23

1976, June 30 ***Perf. 13½x14***
238 B23 35c Bananaquits 1.10 .60
239 B23 50c Blue-hooded euphonia 1.10 .70
240 B23 75c Royal tern 1.50 .90
241 B23 95c Killdeer 1.75 1.00
242 B23 $1.25 Glossy cowbird 1.75 1.00
243 B23 $2 Purple gallinule 1.75 1.25
Nos. 238-243 (6) 8.95 5.45

Barbuda #234-237 With Inscription Added at Top Across the Three Stamps in Blue
"H.M. Queen Elizabeth" "Royal Visit 6th July 1976" "H.R.H. Duke of Edinburgh"

1976, Aug. 12 ***Perf. 13½x14***
Size: 38x31mm
244 B22 15c Strip of 3, #a.-c. .30 .30
245 B22 35c Strip of 3, #a.-c. .50 .50
d. Souvenir sheet of 2, #244-245 1.25 1.25
246 B22 $1 Strip of 3, #a.-c. .75 .75
247 B22 $2 Strip of 3, #a.-c. 1.25 1.25
d. Souvenir sheet, #246-247 3.00 3.00

Nos. 244-247 are perforated on outside edges; imperf. vertically within.

Nos. 448-452 Ovptd. "BARBUDA"

1976, Dec. 2 ***Perf. 14***
248 A85 8c multicolored .20 .20
249 A85 10c multicolored .20 .20
250 A85 15c multicolored .20 .20
251 A85 50c multicolored .20 .20
252 A85 $1 multicolored .20 .20
Nos. 248-252 (5) 1.00 1.00

Nos. 431-437 Ovptd. "BARBUDA"

1976, Dec. 28 ***Perf. 15***
253 A82 ½c yellow & multi .20 .20
254 A82 1c purple & multi .20 .20
255 A82 2c emerald & multi .20 .20
256 A82 15c brt blue & multi .20 .20
257 A82 30c olive & multi .20 .20
258 A82 $1 orange & multi .20 .20
259 A82 $2 red & multi .20 .20
a. Souv. sheet, #256-259, perf 13½ 2.25 2.25
Nos. 253-259 (7) 1.40 1.40

Telephone, Cent. — B24

1977, Jan. 31 ***Perf. 14***
260 B24 75c shown .20 .20
261 B24 $1.25 Satellite dish, television .25 .35
262 B24 $2 Satellites in earth orbit .40 .60
a. Souv. sheet, #260-262, perf 15 1.25 1.50
Nos. 260-262 (3) .85 1.15

Coronation of Queen Elizabeth II, 25th Anniv. — B25

Designs: Nos. 263a, St. Margaret's Church, Westminster. b, Westminster Abbey entrance. c, Westminster Abbey.
Nos. 264a, Riders on horseback. b, Coronation coach. c, Team of horses. Strips of 3 have continuous designs.

1977, Feb. 7 ***Perf. 13½x13***
263 B25 75c Strip of 3, #a.-c. .45 .45
264 B25 $1.25 Strip of 3, #a.-c. .60 .60

Souvenir Sheet

265 B25 Sheet of 6 1.25 1.25

Nos. 263a-264c se-tenant with labels. No. 265 contains Nos. 263a-264c with silver borders.

Nos. 405-422 Ovptd. "BARBUDA"

1977, Apr. 4 ***Perf. 15***
266 A79 ½c multicolored .20 .20
267 A79 1c multicolored .30 .20
268 A79 2c multicolored .30 .20
269 A79 3c multicolored .30 .20
270 A79 4c multicolored .30 .20
271 A79 5c multicolored .30 .20
272 A79 6c multicolored .30 .20
273 A79 10c multicolored .30 .20
274 A79 15c multicolored .30 .20
275 A79 20c multicolored .30 .25
276 A79 25c multicolored .30 .25
277 A79 35c multicolored .35 .30
278 A79 50c multicolored .40 .35
279 A79 75c multicolored .40 .40
280 A79 $1 multicolored .50 .50

Perf. 13½x14
281 A80 $2.50 multicolored 1.25 1.40
282 A80 $5 multicolored 2.25 2.50
283 A80 $10 multicolored 5.50 6.00
Nos. 266-283 (18) 13.85 13.80

For overprints see Nos. 506-516.

Nos. 459-464 Ovptd. "BARBUDA"

1977, Apr. 4 ***Perf. 13½x14, 12***
284 A87 10c multicolored .20 .20
285 A87 30c multicolored .20 .20
286 A87 50c multicolored .20 .25
287 A87 90c multicolored .25 .35
288 A87 $2.50 multicolored .50 1.00
Nos. 284-288 (5) 1.35 2.00

Souvenir Sheet

289 A87 $5 multicolored 1.40 1.50

A booklet of self-adhesive stamps contains one pane of six rouletted and die cut 50c stamps in design of 90c (silver overprint), and one pane of one die cut $5 (gold overprint) in changed colors. Panes have marginal inscriptions.
For overprints see Nos. 312-317.

Nos. 465-471a Ovptd. "BARBUDA"

1977, June 13 ***Perf. 14***
290 A88 ½c multicolored .20 .20
291 A88 1c multicolored .20 .20
292 A88 2c multicolored .20 .20
293 A88 10c multicolored .20 .20
294 A88 30c multicolroed .45 .45
295 A88 50c multicolored .75 .75
296 A88 $2 multicolored 1.50 1.50
a. Souvenir sheet of 3, #294-296 4.00 4.00
Nos. 290-296 (7) 3.50 3.50

Overprint is slightly smaller on No. 296a.

Nos. 472-476a Ovptd. "BARBUDA"

1977, Aug. 12
297 A89 10c multicolored .20 .20
298 A89 30c multicolored .20 .20
299 A89 50c multicolored .20 .20
300 A89 90c multicolored .20 .20
301 A89 $1 multicolored .20 .30
a. Souvenir sheet of 4, #298-301 1.75 1.75
Nos. 297-301 (5) 1.00 1.10

Royal Visit B26

1977, Oct. 27 ***Perf. 14½***
302 B26 50c Royal yacht Britannia .20 .20
303 B26 $1.50 Jubliee emblem .20 .25
304 B26 $2.50 Flags .30 .40
a. Souvenir sheet of 3, #302-304 2.00 2.00
Nos. 302-304 (3) .70 .85

Nos. 483-489 Ovptd. "BARBUDA"

1977, Nov. 15 ***Perf. 14***
305 A90 ½c multicolored .20 .20
306 A90 1c multicolored .20 .20
307 A90 2c multicolored .20 .20
308 A90 8c multicolored .20 .20
309 A90 10c multicolored .20 .20
310 A90 25c multicolored .20 .20
311 A90 $2 multicolored .20 .20
a. Souvenir sheet of 4, #308-311 1.60 1.60
Nos. 305-311 (7) 1.40 1.40

Nos. 477-482 Ovptd. "BARBUDA" in Black

1977, Dec. 20 ***Perf. 12***
312 A87 10c multicolored .20 .20
313 A87 30c multicolored .20 .20
314 A87 50c multicolored .20 .20
315 A87 90c multicolored .25 .25
316 A87 $2.50 multicolored .40 .40
Nos. 312-316 (5) 1.25 1.25

Nos. 312-316 exist with blue overprint.

1977, Nov. 28 ***Perf. 13½x14***
312a A87 10c multicolored .20 .20
313a A87 30c multicolored .20 .20
314a A87 50c multicolored .20 .20
315a A87 90c multicolored .25 .25
316a A87 $2.50 multicolored .40 .40
Nos. 312a-316a (5) 1.25 1.25

Souvenir Sheet

317 A87 $5 multicolored 2.00 2.00

Overprint of Nos. 312a-316a differs from that on Nos. 312-316.

Anniversaries — B27

First navigable airships, 75th anniv: No. 318a, Zeppelin LZ1. b, German Naval airship L31. c, Graf Zeppelin. d, Gondola on military airship.
Soviet space program, 20th anniv: No. 319a, Sputnik, 1957. b, Vostok rocket, 1961. c, Voskhod rocket, 1964. d, Space walk, 1965.
Lindbergh's Atlantic crossing, 50th anniv: No. 320a, Fueling for flight. b, New York take-off. c, Spirit of St. Louis. d, Welcome in England.
Coronation of Queen Elizabeth II, 25th anniv: No. 321a, Lion of England. b, Unicorn of Scotland. c, Yale of Beaufort. d, Falcon of Plantagenets.
Rubens, 400th birth anniv: No. 322a, Two lions. b, Daniel in the Lion's Den. c, Two lions lying down. d, Lion at Daniel's feet. Block of 4 has continuous design.

1977, Dec. 29 ***Perf. 14½x14***
Blocks of 4
318 B27 75c #a.-d. 1.25 1.25
319 B27 95c #a.-d. 1.50 1.50
320 B27 $1.25 #a.-d. 1.60 1.60
321 B27 $2 #a.-d. 2.00 2.00
322 B27 $5 #a.-d. 2.00 2.00
e. Min. sheet, #318-322 + 4 labels 8.00 8.00
Nos. 318-322 (5) 8.35 8.35

Nos. 490-494a Ovptd. "BARBUDA"

1978, Feb. 15 ***Perf. 13x13½***
323 A91 10c multicolored .20 .20
324 A91 15c multicolored .20 .20
325 A91 50c multicolored .25 .25
326 A91 90c multicolored .35 .35
327 A91 $2 multicolored .50 .50
a. Souv. sheet, #324-327, perf 14 4.75 3.50
Nos. 323-327 (5) 1.50 1.50

Pieta, by Michelangelo — B28

Works by Michelangelo: 95c, Holy Family. $1.25, Libyan Sibyl. $2, The Flood.

1978, Mar. 23 ***Perf. 13½x14***
328 B28 75c multicolored .20 .20
329 B28 95c multicolored .20 .20
330 B28 $1.25 multicolored .20 .20
331 B28 $2 multicolored .20 .20
a. Souvenir sheet of 4, #328-331 2.25 2.25
Nos. 328-331 (4) .80 .80

Nos. 495-502 Ovptd. "BARBUDA"

1978, Mar. 23 ***Perf. 14***
332 A92 ½c multicolored .20 .20
333 A92 1c multicolored .20 .20
334 A92 2c multicolored .20 .20
335 A92 10c multicolored .20 .20
336 A92 50c multicolored .35 .35
337 A92 90c multicolored .40 .40
338 A92 $2 multicolored 1.00 1.00
Nos. 332-338 (7) 2.55 2.55

Souvenir Sheet

339 A92 $2.50 multicolored 1.75 1.75

Nos. 503-507 Ovptd. "BARBUDA"

1978, May 22 ***Perf. 14½***
340 A93 10c multicolored .20 .20
341 A93 50c multicolored .40 .40
342 A93 90c multicolored .70 .70
343 A93 $2 multicolored 1.25 1.25
Nos. 340-343 (4) 2.55 2.55

Souvenir Sheet

344 A93 $2.50 multicolored 2.25 2.25

Coronation of Queen Elizabeth II, 25th Anniv. — B29

Crowns: No. 345a, St. Edward's. b, Imperial State. No. 346a, Queen Mary's. b, Queen Mother's. No. 347a, Queen Consort's. b, Queen Victoria's.

1978, June 2 *Perf. 15*

Miniature Sheets of Two Each Plus Two Labels

345 B29 75c Sheet of 4 1.00 1.00
346 B29 $1.50 Sheet of 4 1.50 1.50
347 B29 $2.50 Sheet of 4 2.50 2.50

Souvenir Sheet

Perf. 14½

348 B29 Sheet of 6, #345a-347b 2.50 2.50

Nos. 508-514 Ovptd. in Black or Deep Rose Lilac "BARBUDA"

1978 *Perf. 14*
349 A94 10c multicolored .20 .20
350 A94 30c multicolored .20 .20
351 A94 50c multicolored .25 .25
352 A94 90c multicolored .40 .40
353 A94 $2.50 multicolored .95 .95
Nos. 349-353 (5) 2.00 2.00

Souvenir Sheet

354 A94 $5 multicolored 2.00 2.00

Self-adhesive

355 Souvenir booklet 7.50 7.50
a. A95 Bklt. pane, 3 each 25c and 50c, die cut, rouletted (DRL) 2.00 2.00
b. A95 $5 Bklt. pane of 1, die cut 5.00 5.00

Issued: #349-354, June 2; #355, Oct. 12.

Nos. 515-518 Ovptd. "BARBUDA"

1978, Sept. 12 *Perf. 15*
356 A96 10c multicolored .20 .20
357 A96 15c multicolored .20 .20
358 A96 $3 multicolored 1.00 1.00
Nos. 356-358 (3) 1.40 1.40

Souvenir Sheet

359 Sheet of 4 1.50 1.50
a. A96 25c multicolored .20 .20
b. A96 30c multicolored .20 .20
c. A96 50c multicolored .25 .25
d. A96 $2 multicolored .75 .75

Nos. 519-523 Ovptd. "BARBUDA"

1978, Nov. 20 *Perf. 14*
360 A97 25c multicolored .35 .35
361 A97 50c multicolored .55 .55
362 A97 90c multicolored .80 .80
363 A97 $2 multicolored 1.40 1.40
Nos. 360-363 (4) 3.10 3.10

Souvenir Sheet

364 A97 $2.50 multicolored 2.75 2.75

Flora and Fauna B30

1978, Nov. 20 *Perf. 15*
365 B30 25c Blackbar soldierfish 2.25 2.25
366 B30 50c Painted lady 3.75 3.75
367 B30 75c Dwarf poinciana 2.75 2.75
368 B30 95c Zebra butterfly 3.75 3.75
369 B30 $1.25 Bougainvillea 2.50 2.50
Nos. 365-369 (5) 15.00 15.00

Nos. 524-527 Ovptd. in Silver "BARBUDA"

1978, Nov. 20 *Perf. 14*
370 A98 8c multicolored .20 .20
371 A98 25c multicolored .20 .20
372 A98 $2 multicolored .85 .85
Nos. 370-372 (3) 1.25 1.25

Souvenir Sheet

373 A98 $4 multicolored 2.50 2.50

Events and Annivs. B31

Designs: 75c, 1978 World Cup Soccer Championships, vert. 95c, Wright Brothers 1st powered flight, 75th anniv. $1.25, First Trans-Atlantic balloon flight, Aug. 1978. $2, Coronation of Elizabeth II, 25th anniv., vert.

1978, Dec. 20 *Perf. 14*
374 B31 75c multicolored .40 .40
375 B31 95c multicolored .50 .50
376 B31 $1.25 multicolored .75 .75
377 B31 $2 multicolored .90 .90
a. Souv. sheet, #374-377, imperf 5.00 5.00
Nos. 374-377 (4) 2.55 2.55

No. 377a has simulated perfs.

Nos. 528-532 Ovptd. in Bright Blue "BARBUDA" and

Sir Rowland Hill, Death Cent. B32

1979, Apr. 4
378 A99 25c multicolored .20 .20
379 A99 50c multicolored .35 .35
380 B32 75c Sir Rowland Hill, vert. .40 .40
381 B32 95c Mail coach, 1840 .50 .50
382 A99 $1 multicolored .65 .65
383 B32 $1.25 London's first pillar box, 1855 .70 .70
384 B32 $2 St. Martin's Post Office, London, vert. 1.10 1.10
a. Souvenir sheet of 4, #380-381, 383-384, imperf. 2.75 2.75
385 A99 $2 multicolored 1.40 1.40
Nos. 378-385 (8) 5.30 5.30

Souvenir Sheet

386 A99 $2.50 multicolored 2.00 2.00

No. 384a has simulated perfs.
For overprints see Nos. 423-426.

Nos. 533-536 Ovptd. "BARBUDA"

1979, Apr. 16
387 A100 10c multicolored .20 .20
388 A100 50c multicolored .30 .30
389 A100 $4 multicolored .90 .90
Nos. 387-389 (3) 1.40 1.40

Souvenir Sheet

390 A100 $2.50 multicolored 1.00 1.00

Intl. Civil Aviation Organization, 30th Anniv. — B33

1979, May 24 *Perf. 13½x14*
391 B33 75c Passengers leaving 747 .30 .40
392 B33 95c Air traffic controllers .40 .50
393 B33 $1.25 Plane on runway .50 .60
a. Block of 3, #391-393 + label 1.50 1.50

Nos. 537-541 Ovptd. "BARBUDA"

1979, May 24 *Perf. 14*
394 A101 25c multicolored .30 .30
395 A101 50c multicolored .50 .50
396 A101 90c multicolored 1.00 1.00
397 A101 $2 multicolored 1.50 1.50
Nos. 394-397 (4) 3.30 3.30

Souvenir Sheet

398 A101 $5 multicolored 2.75 2.75

Nos. 542-546 Ovptd. "BARBUDA"

1979, Aug. 1 *Perf. 14½*
399 A102 30c multicolored .30 .25
400 A102 50c multicolored .40 .40
401 A102 90c multicolored .55 .55
402 A102 $3 multicolored 1.50 1.50
Nos. 399-402 (4) 2.75 2.70

Souvenir Sheet

403 A102 $2.50 multicolored 1.60 1.60

Nos. 547-551 Ovptd. "BARBUDA"

1979, Aug. 1 *Perf. 14*
404 A103 25c multicolored .40 .40
405 A103 50c multicolored 1.10 .50
406 A103 90c multicolored 1.10 .65
407 A103 $3 multicolored 2.25 1.75
Nos. 404-407 (4) 4.85 3.30

Souvenir Sheet

408 A103 $2.50 multicolored 2.50 2.50

Intl. Year of the Child — B34

Details of the Christ Child from various paintings by Durer: 25c, 1512. 50c, 1516. 75c, 1526. $1.25, 1502.

1979, Sept. 24 *Perf. 14x13½*
409 B34 25c multicolored .20 .20
410 B34 50c multicolored .20 .20
411 B34 75c multicolored .25 .25
412 B34 $1.25 multicolored .35 .35
a. Souvenir sheet of 4, #409-412 1.50 1.50
Nos. 409-412 (4) 1.00 1.00

Nos. 552-556 Ovptd. "BARBUDA"

1979, Nov. 21 *Perf. 14*
413 A104 8c multicolored .20 .20
414 A104 25c multicolored .25 .20
415 A104 50c multicolored .40 .25
416 A104 $4 multicolored 1.40 1.40
Nos. 413-416 (4) 2.25 2.05

Souvenir Sheet

Perf. 12x12½

417 A104 $3 multicolored 1.40 1.40

Nos. 557-561 Ovptd. "BARBUDA"

1980, Mar. 18
418 A105 10c multicolored .20 .20
419 A105 25c multicolroed .20 .20
420 A105 $1 multicolored .30 .30
421 A105 $2 multicolored .45 .45
Nos. 418-421 (4) 1.15 1.15

Souvenir Sheet

422 A105 $3 multicolored 1.50 2.00

Nos. 571A-571D Overprinted "BARBUDA" in Dark Blue

1980, May 6 *Perf. 12*
423 A99 25c multicolored .30 .20
424 A99 50c multicolored .35 .40
425 A99 $1 multicolored .70 .75
426 A99 $2 multicolored 2.25 1.65
Nos. 423-426 (4) 3.60 3.00

First Moon Landing, 10th Anniv. — B35

1980, May 21 *Perf. 13½x14*
427 B35 75c Crew badge .45 .45
428 B35 95c Plaque left on moon .50 .50
429 B35 $1.25 Lunar, command modules .60 .60
430 B35 $2 Lunar module .95 .95
a. Souvenir sheet of 4, #427-430 2.75 2.75
Nos. 427-430 (4) 2.50 2.50

American Widgeon B36

1980, June 16 *Perf. 14½x14*
431 B36 1c shown .55 .40
432 B36 2c Snowy plover .55 .40
433 B36 4c Rose-breasted grosbeak .65 .40
434 B36 6c Mangrove cuckoo .65 .40
435 B36 10c Adelaide's warbler .65 .40
436 B36 15c Scaly-breasted thrasher .65 .40
437 B36 20c Yellow-crowned night heron .75 .40
438 B36 25c Bridled quail dove .75 .40
439 B36 35c Carib grackle .75 .40
440 B36 50c Northern pintail .75 .40
441 B36 75c Black-whiskered vireo .75 .45
442 B36 $1 Blue-winged teal 1.10 .75

Perf. 14x14½

443 B36 $1.50 Green-throated carib 1.40 1.00
444 B36 $2 Red-necked pigeon 2.00 1.40
445 B36 $2.50 Stolid flycatcher 2.75 1.60
446 B36 $5 Yellow-bellied sapsucker 3.25 3.25
447 B36 $7.50 Caribbean elaenia 4.75 4.75
448 B36 $10 Great egret 6.50 6.50
Nos. 431-448 (18) 29.20 23.70

Nos. 443-448 vert.

Nos. 572-578 Ovptd. "BARBUDA"

1980, July 29 ***Perf. 13½x14, 14x13½***
449 A106a 10c multicolored .20 .20
450 A106a 30c multicolored .20 .20
451 A106a 50c multicolored .35 .35
452 A106a 90c multicolored .50 .50
453 A106a $1 multicolored .50 .50
454 A106a $4 multicolored 2.25 2.25
Nos. 449-454 (6) 4.00 4.00

Souvenir Sheet

Perf. 14

455 A106a $5 multicolored 3.50 3.50

Nos. 579-583 Ovptd. "BARBUDA"

1980, Sept. 8 *Perf. 14*
456 A107 30c multicolored .20 .20
457 A107 50c multicolored .25 .25
458 A107 90c multicolored .30 .30
459 A107 $3 multicolored .75 .75
Nos. 456-459 (4) 1.50 1.50

Souvenir Sheet

460 A107 $5 multicolored 2.00 2.00

Nos. 584-586 Optd. "BARBUDA"

1980, Oct. 6
461 A108 10c multicolored .25 .25
462 A108 $2.50 multicolored 1.75 1.75

Souvenir Sheet

Perf. 12

463 A108 $3 multicolored 2.50 2.50

Nos. 587-591 Ovptd. "BARBUDA"

1980, Dec. 8 *Perf. 14*
464 A109 10c multicolored 2.00 .90
465 A109 30c multicolored 2.50 1.00
466 A109 $1 multicolored 3.50 2.50
467 A109 $2 multicolored 4.00 4.75
Nos. 464-467 (4) 12.00 9.15

Souvenir Sheet

468 A109 $2.50 multicolored 5.50 5.50

Nos. 602-606 Ovptd. "BARBUDA"

1981, Jan. 26
469 A111 25c multicolored 1.00 .25
470 A111 50c multicolored 1.25 .35
471 A111 90c multicolored 1.75 .50
472 A111 $3 multicolored 3.25 1.00
Nos. 469-472 (4) 7.25 2.10

Souvenir Sheet

473 A111 $2.50 multicolored 2.25 2.25

Famous Women — B37

1981, Mar. 9 *Perf. 14x13½*
474 B37 50c Florence Nightingale .25 .25
475 B37 90c Marie Curie .60 .60
476 B37 $1 Amy Johnson .55 .55
477 B37 $4 Eleanor Roosevelt .75 .75
Nos. 474-477 (4) 2.15 2.15

Walt Disney Characters at Sea — B38

1981, May 15 *Perf. 13½x14*

478	B38	10c Goofy	1.25	.35
479	B38	20c Donald Duck	1.50	.45
480	B38	25c Mickey Mouse	1.90	.65
481	B38	30c Goofy fishing	1.90	.75
482	B38	35c Goofy sailing	1.90	.75
483	B38	40c Mickey fishing	2.10	1.00
484	B38	75c Donald Duck boating	2.25	1.25
485	B38	$1 Minnie Mouse	2.50	1.75
486	B38	$2 Chip 'n Dale	4.00	2.50
		Nos. 478-486 (9)	19.30	9.45

Souvenir Sheet

487	B38	$2.50 Donald Duck, diff.	15.00	15.00

Nos. 618-622 Ovptd. "BARBUDA"

1981, June 9 *Perf. 14*

488	A112	10c multicolored	.20	.20
489	A112	50c multicolored	.50	.50
490	A112	90c multicolored	1.00	1.00
491	A112	$4 multicolored	2.75	2.75
		Nos. 488-491 (4)	4.45	4.45

Souvenir Sheet

Perf. 14x14½

492	A112	$5 multicolored	5.00	5.00

Miniature Sheets

Royal Wedding — B39

a-b, $1, L & R sides of Buckingham Palace.
c-d, $1.50, L & R sides of Caernarvon Castle.
e-f, $4, L & R sides of Highgrove House.

1981, July 27 *Perf. 11x11½*

Sheets of 6, #a-f

493	B39	blk & salmon	4.00	4.00
494	B39	blk & purple	4.00	4.00
495	B39	blk & gray grn	4.00	4.00

Souvenir Sheet

Perf. 11½x11

496	B39	$5 St. Paul's Cathedral, vert.	1.25	1.25

Stamps of same denomination have continuous design. For surcharges see #592-594.

Common Design Types pictured following the introduction.

Nos. 623-627 Ovptd. in Black or Silver "BARBUDA"

1981, Aug. 14 *Perf. 14*

497	CD331	25c multicolored	.20	.20
498	CD331	50c multicolored	.25	.25
499	CD331	$4 multicolored	.80	.80
		Nos. 497-499 (3)	1.25	1.25

Souvenir Sheet

500	CD331	$5 multicolored	1.50	1.50

Self-adhesive

501	CD331	Booklet	10.00	10.00
a.		Pane of 6 (2x25c, 2x$1, 2x$2), Charles, die cut, rouletted (S)	5.00	5.00
b.		Pane of 1, $5 Couple, die cut (S)	5.00	5.00

Issued: #497-500, Aug. 24; #501, Oct. 12.
For surcharge see No. B1.

Intl. Year of the Disabled B40

1981, Sept. 14 *Perf. 14*

502	B40	50c Travel	.45	.45
503	B40	90c Braille, sign language	.45	.45
504	B40	$1 Helping hands	.55	.55
505	B40	$4 Mobility aids	.80	.80
		Nos. 502-505 (4)	2.25	2.25

Nos. 607-617 Ovptd. "BARBUDA"

1981, Nov. 1 *Perf. 15*

506	A79	6c multicolored	.20	.20
507	A79	10c multicolored	.20	.20
508	A79	20c multicolored	.20	.20
509	A79	25c multicolored	.25	.20
510	A79	35c multicolored	.40	.30
511	A79	50c multicolored	.50	.40
512	A79	75c multicolored	.75	.60
513	A79	$1 multicolored	1.00	.75

Perf. 13½x14

514	A80	$2.50 multicolored	2.50	1.90
515	A80	$5 multicolored	5.00	3.75
516	A80	$10 multicolored	9.50	7.50
		Nos. 506-516 (11)	20.50	16.00

Nos. 628-632 Ovptd. "BARBUDA"

1981, Dec. 14 *Perf. 15*

517	A113	10c multicolored	.60	.20
518	A113	50c multicolored	1.25	.50
519	A113	90c multicolored	1.90	.90
520	A113	$2.50 multicolored	3.25	2.50
		Nos. 517-520 (4)	7.00	4.10

Souvenir Sheet

521	A113	$5 multicolored	4.50	4.50

Nos. 643-647 Ovptd. "BARBUDA"

1981, Dec. 14

522	A116	10c multicolored	.20	.20
523	A116	50c multicolored	.55	.55
524	A116	90c multicolored	1.00	1.00
525	A116	$2 multicolored	2.25	2.25
		Nos. 522-525 (4)	4.00	4.00

Souvenir Sheet

526	A116	$4 multicolored	3.00	3.00

Nos. 638-642 Ovptd. in Black or Silver "BARBUDA"

1981, Dec. 22

527	A115	8c multi	.20	.20
528	A115	30c multi	.25	.25
529	A115	$1 multi (S)	.50	.50
530	A115	$3 multi	1.40	1.40
		Nos. 527-530 (4)	2.35	2.35

Souvenir Sheet

531	A115	$5 multi	2.25	2.25

Birth of Prince William — B41

Various portraits.

1982, June 21 **Wmk. 380** *Perf. 14*

532	B41	$1 buff & multi	.65	.65
533	B41	$2.50 lt pink & multi	1.25	1.25
534	B41	$5 lt lilac & multi	2.75	2.75
		Nos. 532-534 (3)	4.65	4.65

Souvenir Sheet

535	B41	$5 Couple	4.00	4.00

See Nos. 540-543.

The overprint on stamps of Antigua, from here on, read "BARBUDA MAIL" in one or two lines.

#672-675 Ovptd. in Black or Silver

Perf. 14½x14

1982, Oct. 12 **Unwmk.**

536	CD332	90c multi	.65	.65
537	CD332	$1 multi (S)	.75	.75
538	CD332	$4 multi (S)	3.00	3.00
		Nos. 536-538 (3)	4.40	4.40

Souvenir Sheet

539	CD332	$5 multi	4.25	4.25

Barbuda Nos. 532-535 Inscribed "Twenty First Birthday Greetings to H.R.H. The Princess of Wales"

Various portraits.

Perf. 14x14½

1982, July 1 **Wmk. 380**

540	B41	$1 lt grn & multi	1.25	.50
541	B41	$2.50 pale sal & multi	2.00	1.50
542	B41	$5 lt bl & multi	3.25	3.00
		Nos. 540-542 (3)	6.50	5.00

Souvenir Sheet

543	B41	$4 Couple	3.50	3.50

#663-666 Ovptd. in Black or Silver

Perf. 14½x14

1982, Aug. 30 **Unwmk.**

544	CD332	90c multi	.75	.75
545	CD332	$1 multi (S)	.85	.85
546	CD332	$4 multi	3.25	3.25
		Nos. 544-546 (3)	4.85	4.85

Souvenir Sheet

547	CD332	$5 multi	6.00	6.00

Nos. 676-683 Overprinted

1982, Dec. 6 *Perf. 15*

551	A121	10c multicolored	.20	.20
552	A121	25c multicolored	.25	.25
553	A121	45c multicolored	1.00	1.00
554	A121	60c multicolored	.35	.35
555	A121	$1 multicolored	1.10	1.10
556	A121	$3 multicolored	1.10	1.10
		Nos. 551-556 (6)	4.00	4.00

Souvenir Sheets

557	A121	$4 on #682	2.75	2.75
558	A121	$4 on #683	2.75	2.75

Nos. 684-688 Overprinted

1982, Dec. 6 *Perf. 14*

559	A122	10c multicolored	.20	.20
560	A122	30c multicolored	.30	.30
561	A122	$1 multicolored	.75	.75
562	A122	$4 multicolored	1.75	1.75
		Nos. 559-562 (4)	3.00	3.00

Souvenir Sheet

563	A122	$5 multicolored	3.00	3.00

Nos. 689-693 Overprinted

1983, Mar. 14 *Perf. 14½*

564	A123	45c multicolored	.25	.25
565	A123	50c multicolored	.35	.35
566	A123	60c multicolored	.40	.40
567	A123	$4 multicolored	3.00	3.00
		Nos. 564-567 (4)	4.00	4.00

Souvenir Sheet

568	A123	$5 multicolored	4.00	4.00

Nos. 694-697 Overprinted

1983, Mar. 14 *Perf. 14*

569	A124	25c multicolored	.55	.55
570	A124	45c multicolored	.70	.70
571	A124	60c multicolored	1.00	1.00
572	A124	$3 multicolored	3.25	3.25
		Nos. 569-572 (4)	5.50	5.50

Nos. 698-702 Overprinted

1983, Apr. 12

573	A125	15c multicolored	1.00	1.00
574	A125	50c multicolored	2.50	2.50
575	A125	60c multicolored	2.00	2.00
576	A125	$3 multicolored	3.75	3.75
		Nos. 573-576 (4)	9.25	9.25

Souvenir Sheet

577	A125	$5 multicolored	4.00	4.00

First Manned Balloon Flight, Bicent. — B43

1983, June 13

578	B43	$1 Vincenzo Lunardi, 1785	.50	.50
579	B43	$1.50 Montgolfier brothers, 1783	.75	.75
580	B43	$2.50 Blanchard & Jeffries, 1785	1.25	1.25
		Nos. 578-580 (3)	2.50	2.50

Souvenir Sheet

581	B43	$5 Graf Zeppelin, 1928	3.25	3.25

Nos. 703-707 Overprinted

1983, July 4 *Perf. 15*

582	A126	15c multicolored	1.00	.35
583	A126	50c multicolored	4.00	1.50
584	A126	60c multicolored	4.50	1.60
585	A126	$3 multicolored	5.00	4.00
		Nos. 582-585 (4)	14.50	7.45

Souvenir Sheet

586	A126	$5 multicolored	8.50	8.50

Nos. 726-730 Overprinted

1983, Sept. 12

587	A128	30c multicolored	1.00	1.00
588	A128	50c multicolored	1.25	1.25
589	A128	60c multicolored	1.50	1.50
590	A128	$4 multicolored	5.25	5.25
		Nos. 587-590 (4)	9.00	9.00

Souvenir Sheet

591	A128	$5 multicolored	6.50	6.50

Barbuda Nos. 493-495 Surcharged 45c on $1, 50c on $1.50, or 60c on $4

1983, Oct. 21 *Perf. 11½x11*

592	B39	Sheet of 6, #493	7.50	7.50
593	B39	Sheet of 6, #494	7.50	7.50
594	B39	Sheet of 6, #495	7.50	7.50

Nos. 708-725 Overprinted

1983, Oct. 28 *Perf. 14*

595	A127	1c multicolored	.20	.20
596	A127	2c multicolored	.20	.20
597	A127	3c multicolored	.20	.20
598	A127	5c multicolored	.20	.20
599	A127	10c multicolored	.25	.25
600	A127	15c multicolored	.50	.50
601	A127	20c multicolored	.60	.60
602	A127	25c multicolored	.60	.60
603	A127	30c multicolored	.75	.75
604	A127	40c multicolored	.85	.85
605	A127	45c multicolored	.95	.95
606	A127	50c multicolored	1.10	1.10
607	A127	60c multicolored	1.10	1.10
608	A127	$1 multicolored	1.50	1.50
609	A127	$2 multicolored	2.25	2.25
610	A127	$2.50 multicolored	2.75	2.75
611	A127	$5 multicolored	4.00	4.00
612	A127	$10 multicolored	6.00	6.00
		Nos. 595-612 (18)	24.00	24.00

Nos. 731-735 Overprinted

1983, Oct. 28 *Perf. 14*

613	A129	10c multicolored	.20	.20
614	A129	30c multicolored	.20	.20
615	A129	$1 multicolored	.75	.75
616	A129	$4 multicolored	3.00	3.00
		Nos. 613-616 (4)	4.15	4.15

Souvenir Sheet

617	A129	$5 multicolored	4.50	4.50

#736-739 Ovptd. in Black or Silver

1983, Dec. 14 *Perf. 14*

618	A130	15c multicolored (S)	.20	.20
619	A130	50c multicolored (S)	.45	.45
620	A130	60c multicolored	.50	.50
621	A130	$3 multicolored	2.75	2.75
		Nos. 618-621 (4)	3.90	3.90

Members of Royal Family — B44

1984, Feb. 14 *Perf. 14½x14*

622	B44	$1 Edward VII	.75	*1.00*
623	B44	$1 George V	.75	*1.00*
624	B44	$1 George VI	.75	*1.00*
625	B44	$1 Elizabeth II	.75	*1.00*
626	B44	$1 Prince Charles	.75	*1.00*
627	B44	$1 Prince William	.75	*1.00*
		Nos. 622-627 (6)	4.50	6.00

Nos. 740-744 Overprinted and

1984 Summer Olympics, Los Angeles B45

1984 ***Perf. 15, 13½ (B45)***
628 A131 25c multicolored .20 .20
629 A131 50c multicolored .40 .40
630 A131 90c multicolored .45 .45
631 B45 $1.50 Olympic Stadium, Athens 1.10 1.10
632 B45 $2.50 Olympic Stadium, Los Angeles 1.90 1.90
633 A131 $3 multicolored 2.50 2.50
634 B45 $5 Torch bearer 4.00 4.00
a. Souv. sheet of 1, perf. 15 3.75 3.75
Nos. 628-634 (7) 10.55 10.55

Souvenir Sheet
635 A131 $5 multicolored 3.75 3.75

Issue dates: A131, Apr. 26, B45, July 27.

Nos. 755-759 Overprinted

1984, July 12 ***Perf. 15***
636 A133 15c multicolored .80 .80
637 A133 50c multicolored 1.00 1.00
638 A133 60c multicolored 1.25 1.25
639 A133 $3 multicolored 2.50 2.50
Nos. 636-639 (4) 5.55 5.55

Souvenir Sheet
640 A133 $5 multicolored 5.00 5.00

Nos. 745-749 Overprinted

1984, July 12
641 A132 45c multicolored 1.50 .40
642 A132 50c multicolored 1.50 .45
643 A132 60c multicolored 1.75 .50
644 A132 $4 multicolored 4.25 3.50
Nos. 641-644 (4) 9.00 4.85

Souvenir Sheet
645 A132 $5 multicolored 6.50 6.50

#760-767 Ovptd. in Black or Silver

1984, Oct. 1 ***Perf. 14***
646 A134 10c multicolored (S) .20 .20
647 A134 20c multicolored .20 .20
648 A134 30c multicolored .25 .25
649 A134 40c multicolored .30 .30
650 A134 90c multicolored (S) .70 .70
651 A134 $1.10 multicolored (S) .90 .90
652 A134 $1.50 multicolored (S) 1.25 1.25
653 A134 $2 multicolored 1.60 1.60
Nos. 646-653 (8) 5.40 5.40

Nos. 768-772 Overprinted

1984, Oct. 1
654 A135 40c multicolored .35 .35
655 A135 50c multicolored .40 .40
656 A135 60c multicolored .50 .50
657 A135 $3 multicolored 2.75 2.75
Nos. 654-657 (4) 4.00 4.00

Souvenir Sheet
658 A135 $5 multicolored 4.25 4.25

Nos. 773-778 Overprinted

1984, Nov. 21 ***Perf. 15***
659 A136 40c multicolored 2.00 .40
660 A136 50c multicolored 2.10 .50
661 A136 60c multicolored 2.25 .60
662 A136 $2 multicolored 4.00 2.00
663 A136 $3 multicolored 4.25 3.00
Nos. 659-663 (5) 14.60 6.50

Souvenir Sheet
664 A136 $5 multicolored 10.00 10.00

Nos. 782-791 Overprinted in Silver

1984 ***Perf. 15***
665 A137a 15c multicolored .20 .20
666 A137a 25c multicolored .30 .30
667 A137a 50c multicolored .60 .40
668 A137a 60c multicolored .80 .80
669 A137a 70c multicolored 1.00 1.00
670 A137a 90c multicolored 1.10 1.10
671 A137a $3 multicolored 2.50 2.50
672 A137a $4 multicolored 3.50 3.50
Nos. 665-672 (8) 10.00 9.80

Souvenir Sheets
673 A137a $5 #790 4.50 4.50
674 A137a $5 #791, horiz 5.50 5.50

Issued: Correggio, 11/21; Degas, 11/30.

Nos. 779-781 Overprinted

1984, Nov. 30
675 A137 $1 multicolored .75 .75
676 A137 $5 multicolored 4.75 4.75

Souvenir Sheet
677 A137 $5 multicolored 5.25 5.25

Nos. 819-827 Overprinted

1985, Feb. 18
678 A139 60c multicolored 2.75 2.75
679 A139 60c multicolored 2.75 2.75
680 A139 60c multicolored 2.75 2.75
681 A139 60c multicolored 2.75 2.75
682 A139 $1 multicolored 3.25 3.25
683 A139 $1 multicolored 3.25 3.25
684 A139 $1 multicolored 3.25 3.25
685 A139 $1 multicolored 3.25 3.25
Nos. 678-685 (8) 24.00 24.00

Souvenir Sheet
686 A139 $5 multicolored 6.00 6.00

Queen Mother (Lady Elizabeth Bowes-Lyon), 1907 — B46

1985, Feb. 26 ***Perf. 14x14½***
687 B46 15c shown .40 .40
688 B46 45c Duchess of York, 1926 .50 .50
689 B46 50c Coronation, 1937 .50 .50
690 B46 60c Queen Mother .50 .50
691 B46 90c Wearing tiara .60 .60
692 B46 $2 Wearing blue hat 1.00 1.00
693 B46 $3 With children 1.40 1.40
Nos. 687-693 (7) 4.90 4.90

For overprints see Nos. 724-728, 733, 735.

Nos. 828-834 Overprinted

1985, May 10 ***Perf. 15***
694 A140 25c multicolored .35 .35
695 A140 30c multicolored .50 .50
696 A140 50c multicolored .50 .50
697 A140 90c multicolored .90 .90
698 A140 $1 multicolored 1.00 1.00
699 A140 $3 multicolored 2.75 2.75
Nos. 694-699 (6) 6.00 6.00

Souvenir Sheet
700 A140 $5 multicolored 6.00 6.00

Audubon, Birth Bicentenary — B47

1985, Apr. 4 ***Perf. 14***
701 B47 45c Roseate tern .40 .40
702 B47 50c Mangrove cuckoo .45 .45
703 B47 60c Yellow-crowned night heron .55 .55
704 B47 $5 Brown pelican 4.50 4.50
Nos. 701-704 (4) 5.90 5.90

Nos. 845-849, 910-913 Ovptd. in Black or Silver

1985-86 ***Perf. 15, 12½x12***
705 A143 60c on #910 (S) 3.25 3.25
706 A143 90c on #845 4.00 4.00
707 A143 90c on #911 (S) 4.00 4.00
708 A143 $1 on #846 4.00 4.00
709 A143 $1.50 on #847 5.00 5.00
710 A143 $1.50 on #912 5.50 5.50
711 A143 $3 on #848 6.75 6.75
712 A143 $3 on #913 7.50 7.50
Nos. 705-712 (8) 40.00 40.00

Souvenir Sheet
713 A143 $5 on #849 24.00 24.00

Issue dates: Nos. 706, 708-709, 711, 713, July 18, 1985. Others, Dec. 1986.

Nos. 850-854 Overprinted

1985, July 18 ***Perf. 14***
714 A144 25c multicolored 4.50 4.50
715 A144 60c multicolored 6.25 6.25
716 A144 95c multicolored 7.75 7.75
717 A144 $4 multicolored 14.00 14.00
Nos. 714-717 (4) 32.50 32.50

Souvenir Sheet
718 A144 $5 multicolored 24.00 24.00

Nos. 840-844 Overprinted

1985, Aug. 2
719 A142 10c multicolored .65 .65
720 A142 30c multicolored 1.10 1.10
721 A142 60c multicolored 1.75 1.75
722 A142 $4 multicolored 5.25 5.25
Nos. 719-722 (4) 8.75 8.75

Souvenir Sheet
723 A142 $5 multicolored 7.50 7.50

Barbuda Nos. 687-693 Ovptd. "4TH AUG 1900-1985" and Antigua Nos. 866A-870 Ovptd. "BARBUDA / MAIL" in Silver or Black

Perf. 14, 12x12½ (#729, 731, 736)
1985-86
724 B46 15c multi .20 .20
725 B46 45c multi .35 .35
726 B46 50c multi .40 .40
727 B46 60c multi .50 .50
728 B46 90c multi .70 .70
729 A148 90c multi .70 .70
730 A148 $1 multi (S) .80 .80
731 A148 $1 like #730 .80 .80
732 A148 $1.50 multi (S) 1.25 1.25
733 B46 $2 multi 1.60 1.60
734 A148 $2.50 multi 2.00 2.00
735 B46 $3 multi 2.50 2.50
736 A148 $3 multi 2.50 2.50
Nos. 724-736 (13) 14.30 14.30

Souvenir Sheet
737 A148 $5 multi 10.00 10.00

Queen Mother's 85th birthday.
Issue dates: 15c, 45c, 50c, 60c, No. 728, $2, No. 735, Aug. 2. No. 730, $1.50, $2.50, Nov. 8. Others, Dec. 1986. Nos. 729, 731, 736 issued in sheets of 5 plus label.

Nos. 835-839 Overprinted

1985, Aug. 30 ***Perf. 15***
738 A141 15c multicolored .20 .20
739 A141 50c multicolored .40 .40
740 A141 60c multicolored .45 .45
741 A141 $3 multicolored 2.50 2.50
Nos. 738-741 (4) 3.55 3.55

Souvenir Sheet
742 A141 $5 multicolored 4.00 4.00

Nos. 855-859 Overprinted

1985, Aug. 30 ***Perf. 14***
743 A145 30c multicolored 1.40 1.40
744 A145 90c multicolored 2.25 2.25
745 A145 $1.50 multicolored 2.75 2.75
746 A145 $3 multicolored 4.00 4.00
Nos. 743-746 (4) 10.40 10.40

Souvenir Sheet
747 A145 $5 multicolored 4.25 4.25

Nos. 860-861 Overprinted

1985, Nov. 25 ***Perf. 14***
748 A146 $2 yellow green 6.75 6.75

Souvenir Sheet
749 A146 $5 deep brown 5.50 5.50

#871-875 Ovptd. in Black or Silver

1985, Nov. 25
750 A149 15c multi (S) 3.50 3.50
751 A149 45c multi 3.50 3.50
752 A149 60c multi 3.50 3.50
753 A149 $3 multi (S) 7.25 7.25
Nos. 750-753 (4) 17.75 17.75

Souvenir Sheet
754 A149 $5 multi 12.50 12.50

Nos. 862-866 Overprinted

1986, Feb. 17
755 A147 25c multicolored .20 .20
756 A147 50c multicolored .40 .40
757 A147 60c multicolored .50 .50
758 A147 $3 multicolored 2.50 2.50
Nos. 755-758 (4) 3.60 3.60

Souvenir Sheet
759 A147 $5 multicolored 4.00 4.00

Nos. 886-889 Overprinted

1986, Feb. 17 ***Perf. 14½***
760 A152 60c multicolored 2.00 2.00
761 A152 $1 multicolored 2.00 2.00
762 A152 $4 multicolored 6.00 6.00
Nos. 760-762 (3) 10.00 10.00

Souvenir Sheet
763 A152 $5 multicolored 8.00 8.00

Nos. 876-880 Overprinted

1986, Mar. 10 ***Perf. 14***
764 A150 25c multicolored 2.75 2.75
765 A150 50c multicolored 2.75 2.75
766 A150 $1 multicolored 3.75 3.75
767 A140 $3 multicolored 6.75 6.75
Nos. 764-767 (4) 16.00 16.00

Souvenir Sheet
768 A150 $5 multicolored 21.00 21.00

Nos. 881-885 Overprinted

1986, Mar. 10 ***Perf. 14***
769 A151 15c multicolored 1.40 1.40
770 A151 45c multicolored 2.50 2.50
771 A151 60c multicolored 2.50 2.50
772 A151 $3 multicolored 7.00 7.00
Nos. 769-772 (4) 13.40 13.40

Souvenir Sheet
773 A151 $5 multicolored 22.50 22.50

Nos. 905-909 Overprinted

1986, Apr. 4 ***Perf. 15***
774 A156 10c multicolored .50 .50
775 A156 25c multicolored 1.00 1.00
776 A156 60c multicolored 1.75 1.75
777 A156 $4 multicolored 4.75 4.75
Nos. 774-777 (4) 8.00 8.00

Souvenir Sheet
778 A156 $5 multicolored 4.00 4.00

B48

1986, Apr. 21
779 B48 $1 Shaking hands .90 .90
780 B48 $2 Talking with woman 1.00 1.00
781 B48 $2.50 With officer 1.00 1.00
Nos. 779-781 (3) 2.90 2.90

Souvenir Sheet
Perf. 13½x14
782 B48 $5 Portraits 6.50 6.50

No. 782 contains one 34x27mm stamp.

Nos. 925-928 Overprinted in Silver or Black

1986, Aug. 12
783 CD339 60c multi .50 .50
784 CD339 $1 multi .80 .80
785 CD339 $4 multi 3.25 3.25
Nos. 783-785 (3) 4.55 4.55

Souvenir Sheet
786 CD339 $5 multi (Bk) 4.00 4.00

Nos. 920-924 Overprinted and

Halley's Comet B49

1986 ***Perf. 14, 15 (B49)***
787 A158 5c multicolored 1.00 1.00
788 A158 10c multicolored 1.00 1.00
789 A158 60c multicolored 2.50 2.50
790 B49 $1 shown .65 .65
791 B49 $2.50 Early telescope, dish antenna, vert. 1.00 1.00
792 A158 $4 multicolored 8.25 8.25
793 B49 $5 World map, comet 1.60 1.60
Nos. 787-793 (7) 16.00 16.00

Souvenir Sheet
794 A159 $5 multicolored 4.50 4.50

Issued: #790-791, 793, 7/10; others, 9/22.

Nos. 901-904 Overprinted

1986, Aug. 12 ***Perf. 13½x14***
795 A155 40c multicolored 1.90 1.90
796 A155 $1 multicolored 3.00 3.00
797 A155 $3 multicolored 5.00 5.00
Nos. 795-797 (3) 9.90 9.90

Souvenir Sheet
Perf. 14x13½
798 A155 $5 multicolored 14.00 14.00

Nos. 915-919 Overprinted

1986, Aug. 28 ***Perf. 14***

799 A157 30c multicolored 2.75 2.75
800 A157 60c multicolored 4.25 4.25
801 A157 $1 multicolored 4.50 4.50
802 A157 $4 multicolored 8.50 8.50
Nos. 799-802 (4) 20.00 20.00

Souvenir Sheet

803 A157 $5 multicolored 18.00 18.00

See Nos. 848-851.

Nos. 934-938 Overprinted

1986, Aug. 28 Litho. ***Perf. 15***

804 A161 25c multicolored 2.10 2.10
805 A161 50c multicolored 2.75 2.75
806 A161 $1 multicolored 3.75 3.75
807 A161 $3 multicolored 6.25 6.25
Nos. 804-807 (4) 14.85 14.85

Souvenir Sheet

808 A161 $5 multicolored 5.00 5.00

Nos. 939-942 Ovptd. in Silver

1986, Sept. 22 ***Perf. 14***

809 CD340 45c multicolored .40 .40
810 CD340 60c multicolored .60 .60
811 CD340 $4 multicolored 4.00 4.00
Nos. 809-811 (3) 5.00 5.00

Souvenir Sheet

812 CD340 $5 multicolored 7.00 7.00

Nos. 943-947 Overprinted in Silver or Black

1986, Nov. 10 ***Perf. 15***

813 A162 15c multicolored 2.40 2.40
814 A162 45c multicolored 2.50 2.50
815 A162 60c multicolored 3.50 3.50
816 A162 $3 multicolored 7.25 7.25
Nos. 813-816 (4) 15.65 15.65

Souvenir Sheet

817 A162 $5 multi (Bk) 21.00 21.00

Nos. 948-957 Overprinted

1986, Nov. 10

818 A163 10c multicolored .20 .20
819 A163 15c multicolored .20 .20
820 A163 50c multicolored .40 .40
821 A163 60c multicolored .45 .45
822 A163 70c multicolored .50 .50
823 A163 $1 multicolored .75 .75
824 A163 $3 multicolored 2.25 2.25
825 A163 $4 multicolored 3.00 3.00
Nos. 818-825 (8) 7.75 7.75

Souvenir Sheets

826 A163 $4 multicolored 7.50 7.50
827 A163 $5 multicolored 7.50 7.50

Nos. 958-962 Overprinted

1986, Nov. 28

828 A164 10c multicolored .75 .75
829 A164 50c multicolored 3.00 3.00
830 A164 $1 multicolored 4.50 4.50
831 A164 $4 multicolored 8.75 8.75
Nos. 828-831 (4) 17.00 17.00

Souvenir Sheet

832 A164 $5 multicolored 20.00 20.00

Nos. 929-933 Overprinted

1987, Jan. 12 ***Perf. 14***

833 A160 30c multicolored .30 .30
834 A160 60c multicolored .55 .55
835 A160 $1 multicolored .90 .90
836 A160 $3 multicolored 2.75 2.75
Nos. 833-836 (4) 4.50 4.50

Souvenir Sheet

837 A160 $5 multicolored 4.00 4.00

Nos. 968-972A Overprinted

1987, Jan. 12

838 A165 10c multicolored .20 .20
839 A165 15c multicolored .20 .20
840 A165 50c multicolored .40 .40
841 A165 60c multicolored .50 .50
842 A165 70c multicolored .55 .55
843 A165 $1 multicolored .80 .80
844 A165 $3 multicolored 2.50 2.50
845 A165 $4 multicolored 3.25 3.25
Nos. 838-845 (8) 8.40 8.40

Souvenir Sheets

846 A165 $5 multi (#972) 4.00 4.00
847 A165 $5 multi (#972A) 4.00 4.00

Automobile, cent.

Nos. 963-966 Overprinted

1987, Mar. 10

848 A157 30c multicolored .25 .25
849 A157 60c multicolored .45 .45
850 A157 $1 multicolored .75 .75
851 A157 $4 multicolored 3.00 3.00
Nos. 848-851 (4) 4.45 4.45

See Nos. 799-802.

Nos. 1000-1004 Overprinted

1987, Apr. 23 ***Perf. 15***

852 A170 30c multicolored .25 .25
853 A170 60c multicolored .45 .45
854 A170 $1 multicolored .75 .75
855 A170 $3 multicolored 2.25 2.25
Nos. 852-855 (4) 3.70 3.70

Souvenir Sheet

856 A171 $5 multicolored 5.00 5.00

Nos. 1005-1014 Overprinted

1987, July 1 ***Perf. 14***

857 A172 15c multicolored .20 .20
858 A173 30c multicolored .25 .25
859 A172 40c multicolored .30 .30
860 A173 50c multicolored .40 .40
861 A172 60c multicolored .45 .45
862 A172 $1 multicolored .75 .75
863 A173 $2 multicolored 1.50 1.50
864 A173 $3 multicolored 2.25 2.25
Nos. 857-864 (8) 6.10 6.10

Souvenir Sheets

865 A172 $5 multicolored 4.00 4.00
866 A173 $5 multicolored 4.00 4.00

Nos. 1025-1034 Overprinted

1987, July 28 ***Perf. 15***

867 A175 10c multicolored .20 .20
868 A175 15c multicolored .20 .20
869 A175 30c multicolored .25 .25
870 A175 50c multicolored .40 .40
871 A175 60c multicolored .50 .50
872 A175 70c multicolored .55 .55
873 A175 90c multicolored .70 .70
874 A175 $1.50 multicolored 1.25 1.25
875 A175 $2 multicolored 1.60 1.60
876 A175 $3 multicolored 2.25 2.25
Nos. 867-876 (10) 7.90 7.90

SHORE CRAB BARBUDA 5c

Marine Life B50

1987, July 28

877 B50 5c Shore crab .20 .20
878 B50 10c Sea cucumber .20 .20
879 B50 15c Stop light parrotfish .20 .20
880 B50 25c Banded coral shrimp .20 .20
881 B50 35c Spotted drum .25 .25
882 B50 60c Thorny star-fish .45 .45
883 B50 75c Atlantic trumpet triton .55 .55
884 B50 90c Feather-star, yellow beaker sponge .65 .65
885 B50 $1 Blue gorgonian, vert. .75 .75
886 B50 $1.25 Slender filefish, vert. .90 .90
887 B50 $5 Barred hamlet, vert. 3.75 3.75
888 B50 $7.50 Fairy basslet, vert. 5.50 5.50
889 B50 $10 Fire coral, butterfly fish, vert. 7.50 7.50
Nos. 877-889 (13) 21.10 21.10

For surcharges see Nos. 1133-1134.

#1048-1052 Ovptd. in Silver or Black

1987, Oct. 12 ***Perf. 14***

890 A178 10c multicolored .20 .20
891 A178 60c multicolored .50 .50
892 A178 $1 multicolored .80 .80
893 A178 $3 multicolored 2.25 2.25
Nos. 890-893 (4) 3.75 3.75

Souvenir Sheet

894 A178 $5 multi (Bk) 4.00 4.00

1988 Summer Olympics, Seoul.

#990-999 Ovptd. in Black or Silver

1987, Oct. 12 ***Perf. 13½x14***

895 A169 10c multicolored .20 .20
896 A169 30c multicolored .25 .25
897 A169 40c multicolored .30 .30
898 A169 60c multicolored .50 .50
899 A169 90c multicolored .70 .70
900 A169 $1 multicolored (S) .80 .80
901 A169 $3 multicolored 2.25 2.25
902 A169 $4 multicolored 3.00 3.00
Nos. 895-902 (8) 8.00 8.00

Size: 110x95mm

Imperf

903 A169 $5 multicolored 4.00 4.00
904 A169 $5 multicolored (S) 4.00 4.00

#1015-1024 Ovptd. in Silver or Black

1987, Nov. 5 ***Perf. 14***

905 A174 15c multicolored .20 .20
906 A174 30c multicolored .25 .25
907 A174 45c multicolored .35 .35
908 A174 50c multicolored (Bk) .40 .40
909 A174 60c multicolored .50 .50
910 A174 90c multicolored .70 .70
911 A174 $1 multicolored .80 .80
912 A174 $2 multicolored 1.60 1.60
913 A174 $3 multicolored (Bk) 2.25 2.25
914 A174 $5 multicolored 4.00 4.00
Nos. 905-914 (10) 11.05 11.05

#1040-1047 Ovptd. in Black or Silver

1987, Nov. 5

915 A177 15c multicolored .45 .30
916 A177 30c multicolored 1.00 .60
917 A177 45c multicolored .50 .40
918 A177 50c multicolored .55 .45
919 A177 60c multicolored 1.50 1.00
920 A177 $1 multicolored 1.00 .75
921 A177 $2 multicolored 1.50 1.25
922 A177 $3 multicolored (S) 3.50 3.00
Nos. 915-922 (8) 10.00 7.75

Nos. 1035-1039 Overprinted

1987, Dec. 8

923 A176 30c multicolored .25 .25
924 A176 60c multicolored .50 .50
925 A176 $1 multicolored .80 .80
926 A176 $3 multicolored 2.25 2.25
Nos. 923-926 (4) 3.80 3.80

Souvenir Sheet

927 A176 $5 multicolored 4.00 4.00

Nos. 1063-1067 Overprinted

1988, Jan. 12

928 A181 45c multicolored .30 .30
929 A181 60c multicolored .45 .45
930 A181 $1 multicolored .75 .75
931 A181 $4 multicolored 3.00 3.00
Nos. 928-931 (4) 4.50 4.50

Souvenir Sheet

932 A181 $5 multicolored 4.00 4.00

Nos. 1083-1091 Overprinted

1988, Mar. 25

933 A184 25c multicolored .20 .20
934 A184 30c multicolored .25 .25
935 A184 40c multicolored .30 .30
936 A184 45c multicolored .35 .35
937 A184 50c multicolored .40 .40
938 A184 60c multicolored .50 .50
939 A184 $1 multicolored .80 .80
940 A184 $2 multicolored 1.60 1.60
Nos. 933-940 (8) 4.40 4.40

Souvenir Sheet

941 A184 $5 multicolored 4.00 4.00

Nos. 1058-1062 Ovptd. in Silver

1988, May 6

942 A180 15c multicolored .20 .20
943 A180 45c multicolored .35 .35
944 A180 60c multicolored .50 .50
945 A180 $4 multicolored 3.25 3.25
Nos. 942-945 (4) 4.30 4.30

Souvenir Sheet

946 A180 $5 multicolored 4.00 4.00

Nos. 1068-1072 Overprinted

1988, July 4

947 A182 25c multicolored .20 .20
948 A182 60c multicolored .50 .50
949 A182 $2 multicolored 1.60 1.60
950 A182 $3 multicolored 2.25 2.25
Nos. 947-950 (4) 4.55 4.55

Souvenir Sheet

951 A182 $5 multicolored 4.00 4.00

Nos. 1073-1082 Overprinted

1988, July 4

952 A183 10c multicolored .20 .20
953 A183 15c multicolored .20 .20
954 A183 50c multicolored .40 .40
955 A183 60c multicolored .50 .50
956 A183 70c multicolored .55 .55
957 A183 $1 multicolored .80 .80
958 A183 $3 multicolored 2.25 2.25
959 A183 $4 multicolored 3.25 3.25
Nos. 952-959 (8) 8.15 8.15

Souvenir Sheets

960 A183 $5 multi (#1081) 4.00 4.00
961 A183 $5 multi (#1082) 4.00 4.00

Nos. 1092-1101 Overprinted

1988, July 25

962 A185 10c multicolored .20 .20
963 A185 30c multicolored .25 .25
964 A185 45c multicolored .40 .40
965 A185 60c multicolored .55 .55
966 A185 90c multicolored .75 .75
967 A185 $1 multicolored .85 .85
968 A185 $3 multicolored 2.50 2.50
969 A185 $4 multicolored 3.50 3.50
Nos. 962-969 (8) 9.00 9.00

Souvenir Sheets

970 A185 $5 multi (#1100) 4.00 4.00
971 A185 $5 multi (#1101) 4.00 4.00

Nos. 1102-1111 Overprinted

1988, July 25 ***Perf. 13½x14***

972 A187 30c multicolored .25 .25
973 A187 40c multicolored .30 .30
974 A187 45c multicolored .35 .35
975 A187 50c multicolored .40 .40
976 A187 $1 multicolored .80 .80
977 A187 $2 multicolored 1.60 1.60
978 A187 $3 multicolored 2.25 2.25
979 A187 $4 multicolored 3.25 3.25
Nos. 972-979 (8) 9.20 9.20

Souvenir Sheets

980 A187 $5 multi (#1110) 4.00 4.00
981 A187 $5 multi (#1111) 4.00 4.00

Nos. 1053-1057 Overprinted

1988, Aug. 25 ***Perf. 15***

982 A179 10c multicolored .20 .20
983 A179 60c multicolored .45 .45
984 A179 $1 multicolored .75 .75
985 A179 $3 multicolored 2.25 2.25
Nos. 982-985 (4) 3.65 3.65

Souvenir Sheet

986 A179 $5 multicolored 4.00 4.00

Nos. 1112-1116 Overprinted

1988, Aug. 25

987 A188 30c multicolored .25 .25
988 A188 60c multicolored .50 .50
989 A188 $1 multicolored .80 .80
990 A188 $3 multicolored 2.25 2.25
Nos. 987-990 (4) 3.80 3.80

Souvenir Sheet

991 A188 $5 multicolored 4.00 4.00

Nos. 1127-1136 Overprinted

1988, Sept. 16 ***Perf. 14***

992 A190 10c multicolored .20 .20
993 A190 30c multicolored .25 .25
994 A190 50c multicolored .40 .40
995 A190 90c multicolored .60 .60
996 A190 $1 multicolored .75 .75
997 A190 $2 multicolored 1.60 1.60
998 A190 $3 multicolored 2.25 2.25
999 A190 $4 multicolored 3.00 3.00
Nos. 992-999 (8) 9.05 9.05

Souvenir Sheets

1000 A191 $5 multi (#1135) 4.00 4.00
1001 A191 $5 multi (#1136) 4.00 4.00

Nos. 1140-1144 Overprinted

1988, Sept. 16

1002 A192 40c multicolored .30 .30
1003 A192 60c multicolored .50 .50
1004 A192 $1 multicolored .80 .80
1005 A192 $3 multicolored 2.25 2.25
Nos. 1002-1005 (4) 3.85 3.85

Souvenir Sheet

1006 A192 $5 multicolored 4.00 4.00

Nos. 1145-1162 Overprinted

1988-90

1007 A193 1c multicolored .20 .20
1008 A193 2c multicolored .20 .20
1009 A193 3c multicolored .20 .20
1010 A193 5c multicolored .20 .20
1011 A193 10c multicolored .20 .20
1012 A193 15c multicolored .20 .20
1013 A193 20c multicolored .20 .20
1014 A193 25c multicolored .20 .20
1015 A193 30c multicolored .25 .25
1016 A193 40c multicolored .30 .30
1017 A193 45c multicolored .35 .35
1018 A193 50c multicolored .40 .40
1019 A193 60c multicolored .50 .50
1020 A193 $1 multicolored .80 .80
1021 A193 $2 multicolored 1.60 1.60
1022 A193 $2.50 multicolored 2.00 2.00
1023 A193 $5 multicolored 4.00 4.00
1024 A193 $10 multicolored 8.00 8.00
1025 A193 $20 multi ('90) 16.00 16.00
Nos. 1007-1025 (19) 35.80 35.80

Issue dates: $20, May 4, others Dec. 8.

Nos. 1162A-1167 Overprinted

1989, Apr. 28

1026 A194 1c multicolored .20 .20
1027 A194 2c multicolored .20 .20
1028 A194 3c multicolored .20 .20
1029 A194 4c multicolored .20 .20
1030 A194 30c multicolored .25 .25
1031 A194 60c multicolored .50 .50
1032 A194 $1 multicolored .80 .80
1033 A194 $4 multicolored 3.25 3.25
Nos. 1026-1033 (8) 5.60 5.60

Souvenir Sheet

1034 A194 $5 multicolored 4.00 4.00

Nos. 1175-1176 Overprinted

1989, May 24
1035 A196 $1.50 Strip of 4, #a.-d. 4.75 4.75

Souvenir Sheet
1036 A196 $6 multicolored 4.75 4.75

Nos. 1177-1186 Overprinted

1989, May 29
1037 A197 10c multicolored .20 .20
1038 A197 30c multicolored .35 .35
1039 A197 40c multicolored .50 .50
1040 A197 60c multicolored .70 .70
1041 A197 $1 multicolored 1.25 1.25
1042 A197 $2 multicolored 2.25 2.25
1043 A197 $3 multicolored 3.50 3.50
1044 A197 $4 multicolored 4.75 4.75
Nos. 1037-1044 (8) 13.50 13.50

Souvenir Sheets
1045 A197 $7 multi (#1185) 5.50 5.50
1046 A197 $7 multi (#1186) 5.50 5.50

Nos. 1187-1196 Overprinted

1989, Sept. 18
1047 A198 25c multicolored .20 .20
1048 A198 45c multicolored .30 .30
1049 A198 50c multicolored .40 .40
1050 A198 60c multicolored .45 .45
1051 A198 75c multicolored .55 .55
1052 A198 90c multicolored .65 .65
1053 A198 $3 multicolored 2.25 2.25
1054 A198 $4 multicolored 3.00 3.00
Nos. 1047-1054 (8) 7.80 7.80

Souvenir Sheets
1055 A198 $6 multi (#1195) 4.50 4.50
1056 A198 $6 multi (#1196) 4.50 4.50

Nos. 1197-1206 Overprinted

1989, Dec. 14 ***Perf. 14x13½***
1057 A199 25c multicolored .20 .20
1058 A199 45c multicolored .30 .30
1059 A199 50c multicolored .40 .40
1060 A199 60c multicolored .45 .45
1061 A199 $1 multicolored .75 .75
1062 A199 $2 multicolored 1.50 1.50
1063 A199 $3 multicolored 2.25 2.25
1064 A199 $4 multicolored 3.00 3.00
Nos. 1057-1064 (8) 8.85 8.85

Souvenir Sheets
1065 A199 $5 multi (#1205) 3.75 3.75
1066 A199 $5 multi (#1206) 3.75 3.75

Nos. 1217-1222 Overprinted

1989, Dec. 20 ***Perf. 14***
1067 A201 15c multicolored .20 .20
1068 A201 25c multicolored .20 .20
1069 A201 $1 multicolored .75 .75
1070 A201 $4 multicolored 3.00 3.00
Nos. 1067-1070 (4) 4.15 4.15

Souvenir Sheets
1071 A201 $5 multi (#1221) 3.75 3.75
1072 A201 $5 multi (#1222) 3.75 3.75

Nos. 1264-1273 Overprinted

1989, Dec. 20
1073 A208 10c multicolored .20 .20
1074 A208 25c multicolored .20 .20
1075 A208 30c multicolored .25 .25
1076 A208 50c multicolored .40 .40
1077 A208 60c multicolored .45 .45
1078 A208 70c multicolored .50 .50
1079 A208 $4 multicolored 3.00 3.00
1080 A208 $5 multicolored 3.75 3.75
Nos. 1073-1080 (8) 8.75 8.75

Souvenir Sheets
1081 A208 $5 multi (#1272) 3.75 3.75
1082 A208 $5 multi (#1273) 3.75 3.75

Nos. 1223-1232 Overprinted

1990, Feb. 21
1083 A202 10c multicolored .20 .20
1084 A202 25c multicolored .20 .20
1085 A202 50c multicolored .40 .40
1086 A202 60c multicolored .45 .45
1087 A202 75c multicolored .55 .55
1088 A202 $1 multicolored .75 .75
1089 A202 $3 multicolored 2.25 2.25
1090 A202 $4 multicolored 3.00 3.00
Nos. 1083-1090 (8) 7.80 7.80

Souvenir Sheets
1091 A202 $6 multi (#1231) 4.50 4.50
1092 A202 $6 multi (#1232) 4.50 4.50

Nos. 1233-1237 Overprinted

1990, Mar. 30
1093 A203 25c multicolored .20 .20
1094 A203 45c multicolored .30 .30
1095 A203 60c multicolored .45 .45
1096 A203 $4 multicolored 3.00 3.00
Nos. 1093-1096 (4) 3.95 3.95

Souvenir Sheet
1097 A203 $5 multicolored 3.75 3.75

Nos. 1258-1262 Overprinted

1990, Mar. 30
1098 A206 10c multicolored .20 .20
1099 A206 45c multicolored .30 .30
1100 A206 $1 multicolored .75 .75
1101 A206 $4 multicolored 3.00 3.00
Nos. 1098-1101 (4) 4.25 4.25

Souvenir Sheet
1102 A206 $5 multicolored 3.75 3.75

Nos. 1275-1284 Overprinted

1990, June 6
1103 A210 10c multicolored .20 .20
1104 A210 20c multicolored .20 .20
1105 A210 25c multicolored .20 .20
1106 A210 45c multicolored .30 .30
1107 A210 60c multicolored .45 .45
1108 A210 $2 multicolored 1.50 1.50
1109 A210 $3 multicolored 2.25 2.25
1110 A210 $4 multicolored 3.00 3.00
Nos. 1103-1110 (8) 8.10 8.10

Souvenir Sheets
1111 A210 $5 multi (#1283) 3.75 3.75
1112 A210 $5 multi (#1284) 3.75 3.75

Nos. 1285-1294 Overprinted

1990, July 12
1113 A211 15c multicolored .20 .20
1114 A211 45c multicolored .30 .30
1115 A211 50c multicolored .40 .40
1116 A211 60c multicolored .45 .45
1117 A211 $1 multicolored .75 .75
1118 A211 $2 multicolored 1.50 1.50
1119 A211 $3 multicolored 2.25 2.25
1120 A211 $5 multicolored 3.75 3.75
Nos. 1113-1120 (8) 9.60 9.60

Souvenir Sheets
1121 A211 $6 multi (#1293) 4.50 4.50
1122 A211 $6 multi (#1294) 4.50 4.50

Nos. 1295-1304 Overprinted

1990, Aug. 14
1123 A212 10c multicolored .20 .20
1124 A212 15c multicolored .20 .20
1125 A212 50c multicolored .40 .40
1126 A212 60c multicolored .45 .45
1127 A212 $1 multicolored .75 .75
1128 A212 $2 multicolored 1.50 1.50
1129 A212 $3 multicolored 2.25 2.25
1130 A212 $4 multicolored 3.00 3.00
Nos. 1123-1130 (8) 8.75 8.75

Souvenir Sheets
1131 A212 $5 multi (#1303) 3.75 3.75
1132 A212 $5 multi (#1304) 3.75 3.75

Barbuda Nos. 888-889 Surcharged "1st Anniversary / Hurricane Hugo / 16th September, 1989-1990"

1990, Sept. 17 ***Perf. 15***
1133 A50 $5 on $7.50 3.75 3.75
1134 A50 $7.50 on $10 5.50 5.50

Nos. 1324-1328 Overprinted

1990, Oct. 12 ***Perf. 14***
1135 A217 15c multicolored .20 .20
1136 A217 35c multicolored .30 .30
1137 A217 75c multicolored .55 .55
1138 A217 $3 multicolored 2.25 2.25
Nos. 1135-1138 (4) 3.30 3.30

Souvenir Sheet
1139 A217 $6 multicolored 4.50 4.50

No. 1313 Ovptd. in Silver
Miniature Sheet

1990, Dec. 14
1140 A215 45c Sheet of 20, #a.-t. 6.75 6.75

Nos. 1360-1369 Overprinted

1990, Dec. 14 ***Perf. 14x13½, 13½x14***
1141 A221 25c multicolored .20 .20
1142 A221 30c multicolored .25 .25
1143 A221 40c multicolored .30 .30
1144 A221 60c multicolored .45 .45
1145 A221 $1 multicolored .75 .75
1146 A221 $2 multicolored 1.50 1.50
1147 A221 $4 multicolored 3.00 3.00
1148 A221 $5 multicolored 3.75 3.75
Nos. 1141-1148 (8) 10.20 10.20

Souvenir Sheets
1149 A221 $6 multi (#1368) 4.50 4.50
1150 A221 $6 multi (#1369) 4.50 4.50

Nos. 1305-1308 Overprinted

1991, Feb. 4 ***Perf. 15x14***
1151 A213 45c green .35 .35
1152 A213 60c bright rose .45 .45
1153 A213 $5 bright ultra 3.75 3.75
Nos. 1151-1153 (3) 4.55 4.55

Souvenir Sheet
1154 A213 $6 black 4.50 4.50

Nos. 1309-1312 Overprinted

1991, Feb. 4 ***Perf. 13½***
1155 A214 50c red & deep grn .40 .40
1156 A214 75c red & vio brn .60 .60
1157 A214 $4 red & brt ultra 3.00 3.00
Nos. 1155-1157 (3) 4.00 4.00

Souvenir Sheet
1158 A214 $6 red & black 4.50 4.50

Birds — B52

1991, Mar. 25 **Litho.** ***Perf. 14***
1164 B52 60c Troupial .45 .45
1168 B52 $2 Christmas bird 1.50 1.50
1169 B52 $4 Rose-breasted grosbeak 3.00 3.00
1171 B52 $7 Stolid flycatcher 5.25 5.25
Nos. 1164-1171 (4) 10.20 10.20

This is an expanding set. Numbers will change.

Nos. 1329-1333 Overprinted

1991, Apr. 23 **Litho.** ***Perf. 14***
1173 A218 50c multicolored .40 .40
1174 A218 75c multicolored .55 .55
1175 A218 $1 multicolored .75 .75
1176 A218 $5 multicolored 3.75 3.75
Nos. 1173-1176 (4) 5.45 5.45

Souvenir Sheet
1177 A218 $6 multicolored 4.50 4.50

Nos. 1350-1359 Overprinted

1991, Apr. 23
1178 A220 10c multicolored .20 .20
1179 A220 25c multicolored .20 .20
1180 A220 50c multicolored .40 .40
1181 A220 60c multicolored .45 .45
1182 A220 $1 multicolored .75 .75
1183 A220 $2 multicolored 1.50 1.50
1184 A220 $3 multicolored 2.25 2.25
1185 A220 $4 multicolored 3.00 3.00
Nos. 1178-1185 (8) 8.75 8.75

Souvenir Sheets
1186 A220 $6 multi (#1358) 4.50 4.50
1187 A220 $6 multi (#1359) 4.50 4.50

Nos. 1370-1379 Overprinted

1991, June 21 ***Perf. 14x13½***
1188 A222 25c multicolored .20 .20
1189 A222 45c multicolored .35 .35
1190 A222 50c multicolored .40 .40
1191 A222 60c multicolored .45 .45
1192 A222 $1 multicolored .75 .75
1193 A222 $2 multicolored 1.50 1.50
1194 A222 $3 multicolored 2.25 2.25
1195 A222 $4 multicolored 3.00 3.00
Nos. 1188-1195 (8) 8.90 8.90

Souvenir Sheets
1196 A222 $6 multi (#1378) 4.50 4.50
1197 A222 $6 multi (#1379) 4.50 4.50

Nos. 1380-1390 Overprinted

1991, July 25 **Litho.** ***Perf. 14***
1198 A223 10c multicolored .20 .20
1199 A223 15c multicolored .20 .20
1200 A223 25c multicolored .20 .20
1201 A223 45c multicolored .35 .35
1202 A223 50c multicolored .40 .40
1203 A223 $1 multicolored .75 .75
1204 A223 $2 multicolored 1.50 1.50
1205 A223 $4 multicolored 3.00 3.00
1206 A223 $5 multicolored 3.75 3.75
Nos. 1198-1206 (9) 10.35 10.35

Souvenir Sheets
1207 A223 $6 multi (#1389) 4.50 4.50
1208 A223 $6 multi (#1390) 4.50 4.50

Nos. 1411-1420 Overprinted

1991, Aug. 26 **Litho.** ***Perf. 14***
1209 A226 10c multicolored .20 .20
1210 A226 15c multicolored .20 .20
1211 A226 45c multicolored .35 .35
1212 A226 60c multicolored .45 .45
1213 A226 $1 multicolored .75 .75
1214 A226 $2 multicolored 1.50 1.50
1215 A226 $4 multicolored 3.00 3.00
1216 A226 $5 multicolored 3.75 3.75
Nos. 1209-1216 (8) 10.20 10.20

Souvenir Sheets
1217 A226 $6 multi (#1419) 4.50 4.50
1218 A226 $6 multi (#1420) 4.50 4.50

Nos. 1401-1410 Overprinted

1991, Oct. 18
1219 A225 10c multicolored .20 .20
1220 A225 35c multicolored .25 .25
1221 A225 50c multicolored .40 .40
1222 A225 75c multicolored .55 .55
1223 A225 $1 multicolored .75 .75
1224 A225 $2 multicolored 1.50 1.50
1225 A225 $4 multicolored 3.00 3.00
1226 A225 $5 multicolored 3.75 3.75
Nos. 1219-1226 (8) 10.40 10.40

Souvenir Sheets
1227 A225 $6 multi (#1409) 4.50 4.50
1228 A225 $6 multi (#1410) 4.50 4.50

Nos. 1446-1455 Overprinted

1991, Nov. 18
1229 CD347 10c multicolored .20 .20
1230 CD347 15c multicolored .20 .20
1231 CD347 20c multicolored .20 .20
1232 CD347 40c multicolored .30 .30
1233 CD347 $1 multicolored .85 .85
1234 CD347 $2 multicolored 1.50 1.50
1235 CD347 $4 multicolored 3.00 3.00
1236 CD347 $5 multicolored 3.75 3.75
Nos. 1229-1236 (8) 10.00 10.00

Souvenir Sheets
1237 CD347 $4 multi (#1454) 3.00 3.00
1238 CD347 $4 multi (#1455) 3.00 3.00

Nos. 1503-1510 Overprinted

1991, Dec. 24 ***Perf. 12***
1239 A238 10c multicolored .20 .20
1240 A238 30c multicolored .25 .25
1241 A238 40c multicolored .30 .30
1242 A238 60c multicolored .45 .45
1243 A238 $1 multicolored .80 .80
1244 A238 $3 multicolored 2.25 2.25
1245 A238 $4 multicolored 3.00 3.00
1246 A238 $5 multicolored 3.75 3.75
Nos. 1239-1246 (8) 11.00 11.00

Nos. 1421-1435 Overprinted

1992, Feb. 20 ***Perf. 13½***
1249 A227 5c multicolored .20 .20
1250 A227 10c multicolored .20 .20
1251 A227 15c multicolored .20 .20
1252 A227 25c multicolored .20 .20
1253 A227 30c multicolored .25 .25
1254 A227 40c multicolored .30 .30
1255 A227 50c multicolored .40 .40
1256 A227 75c multicolored .55 .55
1257 A227 $2 multicolored 1.50 1.50
1258 A227 $3 multicolored 2.25 2.25
1259 A227 $4 multicolored 3.00 3.00
1260 A227 $5 multicolored 3.75 3.75
Nos. 1249-1260 (12) 12.80 12.80

Size: 102x76mm

Imperf
1261 A227 $5 multi (#1433) 3.75 3.75
1262 A227 $5 multi (#1434) 3.75 3.75
1263 A227 $6 multi 4.50 4.50

Nos. 1476-1483 Overprinted

1992, Apr. 7 **Litho.** ***Perf. 14***
1264 A231 10c multi .20 .20
1265 A231 15c multi, vert. .20 .20
1266 A231 45c multi, vert. .35 .35
1267 A231 60c multi, vert. .45 .45
1268 A231 $1 multi .75 .75
1269 A231 $2 multi 1.50 1.50
1270 A231 $4 multi 3.00 3.00
1271 A231 $5 multi, vert. 3.75 3.75
Nos. 1264-1271 (8) 10.20 10.20

Nos. 1484-1485 Overprinted

1992, Apr. 7 **Litho.** ***Perf. 14***

Souvenir Sheets
1272 A231 $6 multi (#1484) 5.00 5.00
1273 A231 $6 multi (#1485) 5.00 5.00

Nos. 1551-1560 Overprinted

1992, Apr. 16 **Litho.** ***Perf. 14x13½***
1274 A242 10c multicolored .20 .20
1275 A242 15c multicolored .20 .20
1276 A242 30c multicolored .25 .25
1277 A242 40c multicolored .35 .35
1278 A242 $1 multicolored .85 .85
1279 A242 $2 multicolored 1.60 1.60
1280 A242 $4 multicolored 3.25 3.25
1281 A242 $5 multicolored 4.25 4.25
Nos. 1274-1281 (8) 10.95 10.95

Souvenir Sheets
1282 A242 $6 multi (#1559) 5.00 5.00
1283 A242 $6 multi (#1560) 5.00 5.00

Nos. 1489-1492 Overprinted

1992, June 19 **Litho.** ***Perf. 14***
1284 A234 75c multi .55 .55
1285 A234 $2 multi, vert. 1.50 1.50
1286 A234 $3.50 multi 2.75 2.75
Nos. 1284-1286 (3) 4.80 4.80

Souvenir Sheet
1287 A234 $5 multi, vert. 4.25 4.25

Nos. 1493-1494 Overprinted

1992, June 19
1288 A235 $1.50 multi 1.10 1.10
1289 A235 $4 multi 3.00 3.00

Nos. 1495-1496 Overprinted

1992, June 19
1290 A236 $2 multi 1.50 1.50
1291 A236 $2.50 multi, vert. 1.90 1.90

Nos. 1499-1502 Overprinted

1992, June 19
1292 A237 25c multicolored .20 .20
1293 A237 $2 multicolored 1.50 1.50
1294 A237 $3 multicolored 2.25 2.25
1295 A237 $4 multicolored 3.50 3.50
Nos. 1292-1295 (4) 7.45 7.45

Nos. 1571-1578 Overprinted

1992, Oct. 12 Litho. *Perf. 14*
1296 A244 15c multicolored .20 .20
1297 A244 30c multicolored .25 .25
1298 A244 40c multicolored .30 .30
1299 A244 $1 multicolored .75 .75
1300 A244 $2 multicolored 1.50 1.50
1301 A244 $4 multicolored 3.00 3.00
Nos. 1296-1301 (6) 6.00 6.00

Souvenir Sheets

1302 A244 $6 multicolored 4.50 4.50
1303 A244 $6 multicolored 4.50 4.50

Nos. 1599-1600 Overprinted

1992, Oct. 12 *Perf. 14½*
1304 A247 $1 multicolored .75 .75
1305 A247 $2 multicolored 1.50 1.50

Nos. 1513-1518 Overprinted

1992, Nov. 3 *Perf. 14*
1306 CD348 10c multicolored .20 .20
1307 CD348 30c multicolored .25 .25
1308 CD348 $1 multicolored .80 .80
1309 CD348 $5 multicolored 3.75 3.75
Nos. 1306-1309 (4) 5.00 5.00

Souvenir Sheets

1310 CD348 $6 multi (#1517) 4.50 4.50
1311 CD348 $6 multi (#1518) 4.50 4.50

Nos. 1541-1550 Ovptd. "BARBUDA / MAIL"

1992, Dec. 8
1312 A241 10c multicolored .20 .20
1313 A241 15c multicolored .20 .20
1314 A241 30c multicolored .25 .25
1315 A241 50c multicolored .40 .40
1316 A241 $1 multicolored .75 .75
1317 A241 $2 multicolored 1.50 1.50
1318 A241 $4 multicolored 3.00 3.00
1319 A241 $5 multicolored 3.75 3.75
Nos. 1312-1319 (8) 10.05 10.05

Souvenir Sheets

1320 A241 $6 multi (#1549) 5.50 5.50
1321 A241 $6 multi (#1550) 5.50 5.50

Nos. 1609-1618 Ovptd. "BARBUDA MAIL"

1992, Dec. 8 Litho. *Perf. 13½x14*
1322 A251 10c multicolored .20 .20
1323 A251 25c multicolored .20 .20
1324 A251 30c multicolored .25 .25
1325 A251 40c multicolored .30 .30
1326 A251 60c multicolored .45 .45
1327 A251 $1 multicolored .75 .75
1328 A251 $4 multicolored 3.00 3.00
1329 A251 $5 multicolored 3.75 3.75
Nos. 1322-1329 (8) 8.90 8.90

Souvenir Sheets

1330 A251 $6 multi (#1616) 5.50 5.50
1331 A251 $6 multi (#1617) 5.50 5.50

No. 1601 Ovptd. "BARBUDA MAIL"

1992 Litho. *Perf. 14*

Souvenir Sheet

1332 A248 $6 multicolored 4.50 4.50

Nos. 1519-1528 Ovptd.

1993, Jan. 25 Litho. *Perf. 14*
1333 A239 10c multicolored .20 .20
1334 A239 15c multicolored .20 .20
1335 A239 30c multicolored .30 .30
1336 A239 40c multicolored .35 .35
1337 A239 $1 multicolored .90 .90
1338 A239 $2 multicolored 1.75 1.75
1339 A239 $4 multicolored 3.50 3.50
1340 A239 $5 multicolored 4.50 4.50
Nos. 1332-1339 (8) 11.70 11.70

Souvenir Sheets

1341 A239 $6 multi (#1527) 5.50 5.50
1342 A239 $6 multi (#1528) 5.50 5.50

Nos. 1561-1570 Ovptd.

1993, Mar. 22 Litho. *Perf. 13*
1343 A243 10c multicolored .20 .20
1344 A243 15c multicolored .20 .20
1345 A243 30c multicolored .25 .25
1346 A243 40c multicolored .30 .30
1347 A243 $1 multicolored .80 .80
1348 A243 $2 multicolored 1.50 1.50
1349 A243 $4 multicolored 3.00 3.00
1350 A243 $5 multicolored 3.75 3.75
Nos. 1343-1350 (8) 10.00 10.00

Imperf

Size: 120x95mm

1351 A243 $6 multi (#1569) 5.50 5.50
1352 A243 $6 multi (#1570) 5.50 5.50

Nos. 1589-1598 Ovptd.

1993, May 10 Litho. *Perf. 14*
1353 A246 10c multicolored .20 .20
1354 A246 25c multicolored .20 .20
1355 A246 45c multicolored .35 .35
1356 A246 60c multicolored .45 .45
1357 A246 $1 multicolored .75 .75
1358 A246 $2 multicolored 1.50 1.50
1359 A246 $4 multicolored 3.00 3.00
1360 A246 $5 multicolored 3.75 3.75
Nos. 1353-1360 (8) 10.20 10.20

Souvenir Sheets

1361 A246 $6 multi (#1597) 5.50 5.50
1362 A246 $6 multi (#1598) 5.50 5.50

Nos. 1603-1608 Ovptd.

1993, June 29 Litho. *Perf. 14*
1363 A250 10c multicolored .20 .20
1364 A250 25c multicolored .25 .25
1365 A250 30c multicolored .30 .30
1366 A250 40c multicolored .35 .35
1367 A250 60c multicolored .55 .55
1368 A250 $1 multicolored .90 .90
1369 A250 $4 multicolored 3.50 3.50
1370 A250 $5 multicolored 4.50 4.50
Nos. 1363-1370 (8) 10.55 10.55

Souvenir Sheets

1371 A250 $6 multi (#1607) 5.50 5.50
1372 A250 $6 multi (#1608) 5.50 5.50

Nos. 1619-1632 Ovptd.

1993, Aug. 16 Litho. *Perf. 14*
1373 A252 10c multicolored .20 .20
1374 A252 40c multicolored .30 .30
1375 A253 45c multicolored .35 .35
1376 A252 75c multicolored .60 .60
1377 A252 $1 multicolored .75 .75
1378 A252 $1.50 multicolored 1.10 1.10
1379 A252 $2 multicolored 1.50 1.50
1380 A253 $2 multi (#1626) 1.50 1.50
1381 A253 $2 multi (#1627) 1.50 1.50
1382 A252 $2.25 multicolored 1.75 1.75
1383 A252 $3 multicolored 2.25 2.25
1384 A252 $4 multi (#1630) 3.00 3.00
1385 A252 $4 multi (#1631) 3.00 3.00
1386 A252 $6 multicolored 4.50 4.50
Nos. 1373-1386 (14) 22.30 22.30

Numbers have been reserved for four souvenir sheets in this set.

Nos. 1650-1659 Ovptd.

1993, Sept. 21 Litho. *Perf. 14*
1391 A256 15c multicolored .20 .20
1392 A256 25c multicolored .20 .20
1393 A256 30c multicolored .25 .25
1394 A256 40c multicolored .35 .35
1395 A256 $1 multicolored .75 .75
1396 A256 $2 multicolored 1.50 1.50
1397 A256 $4 multicolored 3.00 3.00
1398 A256 $5 multicolored 3.75 3.75
Nos. 1391-1398 (8) 10.00 10.00

Souvenir Sheets

1399 A256 $6 multi (#1658) 6.50 6.50
1400 A256 $6 multi (#1659) 6.50 6.50

No. 1660 Ovptd.

1993, Nov. 11 Litho. *Perf. 14*
1401 A257 $1 Sheet of 12, #a.-l. 9.00 9.00

Numbers have been reserved for two souvenir sheets in this set.

Nos. 1697-1710 Ovptd.

1994, Mar. 3 Litho. *Perf. 14*
1404-1415 A267 $2 Set of 12 18.00 18.00

Souvenir Sheets

1416-1417 A267 $6 each 4.50 4.50

Nos. 1676-1678 Ovptd.

1994, Apr. 21 Litho. *Perf. 14*
1418 A260 40c multicolored .30 .30
1419 A260 $3 multicolored 2.25 2.25

Souvenir Sheet

1420 A260 $6 multicolored 4.50 4.50

Nos. 1679-1682 Ovptd.

1994, Apr. 21
1421-1423 A261 Set of 3 4.50 4.50

Souvenir Sheet

1424 A261 $6 multicolored 4.50 4.50

Nos. 1683-1685 Ovptd.

1994, Apr. 21
1425 A262 40c multicolored .30 .30
1426 A262 $4 multicolored 3.25 3.25

Souvenir Sheet

1427 A262 $5 multicolored 3.75 3.75

Nos. 1686-1688 Ovptd.

1994, Apr. 21
1428 A263 30c multicolored .25 .25
1429 A263 $4 multicolored 3.25 3.25

Souvenir Sheet

1430 A263 $6 multicolored 4.50 4.50

Nos. 1692-1693 Ovptd.

1994, Apr. 21
1431 A265 $5 multicolored 4.00 4.00

Souvenir Sheet

1432 A265 $6 multicolored 4.50 4.50

Nos. 1694-1696 Ovptd.

1994, Apr. 21
1433 A266 15c multicolored .20 .20
1434 A266 $5 multicolored 4.00 4.00

Souvenir Sheet

1435 A266 $6 multicolored 4.50 4.50

Nos. 1732-1735 Ovptd.

1994, Apr. 21
1436-1439 A270 Set of 4 1.10 1.10

Nos. 1711-1720 Ovptd.

1994, June 15
1440-1446 A268 Set of 7 12.00 12.00

Souvenir Sheets

1447-1449 A268 $6 each 4.50 4.50

Nos. 1736-1741 Ovptd.

1994, June 15
1450-1453 A271 30c Set of 4 7.25 7.25

Souvenir Sheets

1454-1455 A271 $6 each 4.50 4.50

Nos. 1689-1691 Ovptd.

1994, Sept. 21 Litho. *Perf. 14*
1456 A264 $1 multicolored .75 .75
1457 A264 $3 multicolored 2.25 2.25

Souvenir Sheet

1458 A264 $6 multicolored 4.50 4.50

Nos. 1786-1795 Ovptd.

1994, Sept. 21 Litho. *Perf. 14*
1459-1466 A279 Set of 8 10.00 10.00

Souvenir Sheets

1467-1468 A279 $6 each 4.50 4.50

Nos. 1776-1779 Ovptd.

1994, Nov. 3 Litho. *Perf. 14*
1469 A277 $1.50 multi (#1776) 9.00 9.00
1470 A277 $1.50 multi (#1777) 9.00 9.00

Souvenir Sheets

1471 A277 $1.50 multi (#1778) 1.10 1.10
1472 A277 $1.50 multi (#1779) 1.10 1.10

Nos. 1835-1842 Ovptd.

1995, Jan. 12 Litho. *Perf. 14*
1473-1478 A291 Set of 6 8.50 8.50

Souvenir Sheets

1479 A291 $6 multi (#1841) 4.50 4.50
1480 A291 $6 multi (#1842) 4.50 4.50

Nos. 1857-1866 Ovptd.

1995, Jan. 12 Litho. *Perf. 14*
1481-1488 A295 Set of 8 6.75 6.75

Souvenir Sheets

Perf. 13½x14

1489 A295 $6 multi (#1865) 4.50 4.50
1490 A295 $6 multi (#1866) 4.50 4.50

Nos. 1829-1834 Ovptd.

1996, Feb. 14 Litho. *Perf. 14*
1491 A290 75c multi (#1829) 5.50 5.50
1492 A290 75c multi (#1830) 5.50 5.50
1493 A290 75c multi (#1831) 5.50 5.50

Souvenir Sheets

1494 A290 $6 multi (#1832) 5.50 5.50
1495 A290 $6 multi (#1833) 5.50 5.50
1496 A290 $6 multi (#1834) 5.50 5.50

Nos. 1867-1881 Ovptd.

1995 Litho. *Perf. 14½x14*
1497 A296 15c multi (#1867) .20 .20
1498 A296 25c multi (#1868) .20 .20
1499 A296 35c multi (#1869) .30 .30
1500 A296 40c multi (#1870) .35 .35
1501 A296 45c multi (#1871) .40 .40
1502 A296 60c multi (#1872) .55 .55
1503 A296 65c multi (#1873) .60 .60
1504 A296 70c multi (#1873) .65 .65
1505 A296 75c multi (#1874) .70 .70
1506 A296 90c multi (#1875) .80 .80
1507 A296 $1.20 multi (#1876) 1.10 1.10
1508 A296 $2 multi (#1877) 1.75 1.75
1509 A296 $5 multi (#1878) 4.50 4.50
1510 A296 $10 multi (#1879) 9.00 9.00
1511 A296 $20 multi (#1880) 18.00 18.00
Nos. 1497-1511 (15) 39.10 39.10

Nos. 1806-1808 Ovptd.

1996, Jan. 22 Litho. *Perf. 14*
1512 A281 50c Sheet of 9, #a.-i. 3.50 3.50

Souvenir Sheets

1513 A281 $6 multi (#1807) 4.50 4.50
1514 A281 $6 multi (#1808) 4.50 4.50

Nos. 1949-1956 Ovptd.

1996, Jan. 22 *Perf. 13½x14*
1515-1520 A314 Set of 6 6.75 6.75

Souvenir Sheets

1521 A314 $5 multi (#1955) 3.75 3.75
1522 A314 $6 multi (#1956) 4.50 4.50

Nos. 1810-1813 Ovptd.

1995, Sept. 29 Litho. *Perf. 14*
1546-1548 A283 Set of 3 4.00 4.00

Souvenir Sheet

1549 A283 $6 multi (on #1813) 5.50 5.50

End of World War II, 50th Anniv. — B53

Design: German bombers over St. Paul's Cathedral, London.

1995, Nov. 13 Litho. *Perf. 13*
1550 B53 $8 multicolored 6.00 6.00

For overprints and surcharges see #1639, B3.

Queen Elizabeth, the Queen Mother, 95th Birthday B54

1995, Nov. 20
1551 B54 $7.50 multicolored 5.50 5.50

For overprints and surcharges see #1638, B2.

United Nations, 50th Anniv. — B55

1995, Nov. 27
1552 B55 $8 New York City 6.00 6.00

For surcharge see #B4.

Nos. 1848, 1851, 1854-1856 Ovptd.

1996, Feb. 14 Litho. *Perf. 14*

1553 A294 15c multi (#1848) .20 .20
1554 A294 $1 multi (#1851) .75 .75
1555 A294 $4 multi (#1854) 3.00 3.00
Nos. 1553-1555 (3) 3.95 3.95

Souvenir Sheets

1556 A294 $6 multi (#1855) 4.50 4.50
1557 A294 $6 multi (#1856) 4.50 4.50

Nos. 1882-1890 Ovptd.

1996, June 13 Litho. *Perf. 14*

1558-1563 A297 Set of 6 7.50 7.50
1564 A297 75c Sheet of 12, #a-l 8.25 8.25

Souvenir Sheets

1565 A297 $6 multi (#1889) 5.50 5.50
1566 A297 $6 multi (#1890) 5.50 5.50

Nos. 1891-1898 Ovptd.

1996, July 16 Litho. *Perf. 14*

1567-1572 A298 Set of 6 7.00 7.00

Souvenir Sheets

1573 A298 $6 multi (#1897) 5.00 5.00
1574 A298 $6 multi (#1898) 5.00 5.00

Nos. 1930-1933 Ovptd.

1996, Sept. 10

1575-1576 A310 Strip of 3, #a.-c., each 3.00 3.00

Souvenir Sheets

1577 A310 $6 multi (#1932) 5.00 5.00
1578 A310 $6 multi (#1933) 5.00 5.00

Nos. 1945-1948 Ovptd.

1996, Oct. 25 Litho. *Perf. 14*

1579 A313 $1 Sheet of 9, #a.-i. (#1945) 8.00 8.00
1580 A313 $1 Sheet of 9, #a.-i. (#1946) 8.00 8.00

Souvenir Sheets

1581 A313 $6 multi (#1947) 5.25 5.25
1582 A313 $6 multi (#1948) 5.25 5.25

Nos. 2001-2002 Ovptd.

1996, Nov. 14 *Perf. 13½x14*

1583 A323 $2 Strip of 3, #a.-c. 5.25 5.25

Souvenir Sheet

1584 A323 $6 multicolored 5.25 5.25

Nos. 2018-2025 Ovptd.

1997, Jan. 28 Litho. *Perf. 13½x14*

1585-1590 A328 Set of 6 6.50 6.50

Souvenir Sheets

1591 A328 $6 multi (#2024) 5.50 5.50
1592 A328 $6 multi (#2025) 5.50 5.50

Nos. 1905-1906 Ovptd.

1997, Feb. 24 *Perf. 14*

1593 A301 Strip of 3, #a.-c. 2.50 2.50

Souvenir Sheet

1594 A301 $6 multicolored 5.50 5.50

Nos. 1907-1908 Ovptd.

1997, Feb. 24

1595 A302 $5 multicolored 4.50 4.50

Souvenir Sheet

1596 A302 $6 multicolored 5.50 5.50

Nos. 1899-1902 Ovptd.
Sheets of 6 or 8 + Label

1997, Apr. 4 Litho. *Perf. 14*

1597 A299 $1.20 #a.-f. 6.50 6.50
1598 A299 $1.20 #a.-h. 8.50 8.50

Souvenir Sheets

1599 A299 $3 multicolored 2.75 2.75
1600 A299 $6 multicolored 5.50 5.50

Nos. 1903-1904 Ovptd.

1997 Litho. *Perf. 14*

1601 A300 Strip of 3, #a.-c. 2.50 2.50

Souvenir Sheet

1602 A300 $6 multicolored 5.50 5.50

Nos. 1909-1910 Ovptd.

1997 *Perf. 13½x14*

1603 A303 $1.50 Strip or block of 4, #a.-d. 5.50 5.50

Souvenir Sheet

1604 A303 $6 multicolored 5.50 5.50

Nos. 1913-1917 Ovptd.

1997 Litho. *Perf. 14*

1605-1608 A305 Set of 4 5.00 5.00

Souvenir Sheet

1609 A305 $6 multicolored 5.50 5.50

Nos. 1918-1919 Ovptd.

1997

1610 A306 45c Sheet of 12, #a-l 4.75 4.75

Souvenir Sheet

1611 A306 $6 multicolored 5.50 5.50

Nos. 1928-1929 Ovptd.

1997

1612 A309 75c Sheet of 12, #a-l 8.00 8.00

Souvenir Sheet

1613 A309 $6 multicolored 5.50 5.50

Nos. 1934-1942 Ovptd.

1997, May 30 Litho. *Perf. 14*

1614-1619 A311 Set of 6 7.50 7.50

Sheet of 9

1620 A311 $1.20 #a.-i. 8.25 8.25

Souvenir Sheets

1621 A311 $6 multi (#1941) 4.50 4.50
1621A A311 $6 multi (#1942) 4.50 4.50

Nos. 1911-1912 Ovptd.

1997 Litho. *Perf. 14*

1622 A304 75c Sheet of 12, #a-l 8.00 8.00

Souvenir Sheet

1623 A304 $6 multicolored 5.50 5.50

Nos. 1943-1944 Ovptd.

1997

1624 A312 75c Sheet of 12, #a-l 8.00 8.00

Souvenir Sheet

1625 A312 $6 multicolored 5.50 5.50

Nos. 1967-1970 Ovptd.

1997

1626-1627 A317 75c Strips of 4, #a.-d., each 2.75 2.75

Souvenir Sheets

1628 A317 $6 multi (#1969) 5.50 5.50
1629 A317 $6 multi (#1970) 5.50 5.50

Nos. 1970A-1974 Ovptd.

1997, Nov. 3 Litho. *Perf. 14*

1629A-1629F A318 Set of 6 2.50 2.50

Sheets of 6

1629G A318 $1.20 #k.-p. (#1971) 5.50 5.50
1629H A318 $1.50 #q.-v. (#1972) 6.75 6.75

Souvenir Sheets

1629I A318 $6 multi (#1973) 4.50 4.50
1629J A318 $6 multi (#1974) 4.50 4.50

Nos. 2111-2118 Ovptd.

1997 Litho. *Perf. 14*

1630-1635 A345 Set of 6 5.25 5.25

Souvenir Sheets

1636 A345 $6 multi (#2117) 4.50 4.50
1637 A345 $6 multi (#2118) 4.50 4.50

Nos. 2069-2070 Ovptd.

1997, Nov. 3 Litho. *Perf. 14*

Sheet of 6

1637A A337 $1 #c.-h. (#2069) 4.50 4.50

Souvenir Sheet

1637B A337 $6 multi (#2070) 4.50 4.50

Nos. 1550-1551 Ovptd. in Gold
"Golden Wedding of
H.M. Queen Elizabeth II
and H.R.H. Prince Phillip
1947-1997"

1997, July 25 Litho. *Perf. 13*

1638 B54 $7.50 on #1551 5.50 5.50
1639 B53 $8 on #1550 6.00 6.00

Nos. 1983-1986 Ovptd.

1998 Litho. *Perf. 14*

1640 A320 75c Vert. strip, #a.-d. (#1983) 2.75 2.75
1641 A320 75c Vert. strip, #a.-d. (#1984) 2.75 2.75

Souvenir Sheets

1643 A320 $5 multicolored 4.50 4.50
1644 A320 $6 multicolored 5.50 5.50

Nos. 2003-2004 Ovptd.

1998 Litho. *Perf. 14*

1645 A324 60c Block of 4, #a.-d. 2.00 2.00

Souvenir Sheet

1646 A324 $6 multi 5.25 5.25

Nos. 2094-2102 Ovptd.

1998

1647-1652 A342 Set of 6 5.75 5.75
1653 A342 $1 Sheet of 8 + label 6.75 6.75

Souvenir Sheets

1654 A342 $6 multi (#2101) 5.25 5.25
1655 A342 $6 multi (#2102) 5.25 5.25

Nos. 2005-2008 Ovptd.

1998 Litho. *Perf. 14*

1656-1658 A325 Set of 3 2.50 2.50

Souvenir Sheet

1659 A325 $6 multicolored 5.25 5.25

Nos. 2009-2012 Ovptd.

1998

1660-1662 A326 Set of 3 2.50 2.50

Souvenir Sheet

1663 A326 $6 multicolored 5.25 5.25

Nos. 2119-2122 Ovptd.

1998 Litho. *Perf. 14*

Sheets of 6

1664 A346 $1.65 #a.-f. (#2119) 8.50 8.50
1665 A346 $1.65 #a.-f. (#2120) 8.50 8.50

Souvenir Sheets

1666 A346 $6 multi (#2121) 5.25 5.25
1667 A346 $6 multi (#2122) 5.25 5.25

Nos. 2037-2038 Ovptd.

1998 Litho. *Perf. 14*

Sheet of 9

1668 A330 $1 #a.-i. (#2037) 7.75 7.75

Souvenir Sheet

1669 A330 $6 multi (#2038) 5.25 5.25

Nos. 2063-2064 Ovtpd.

1998

Sheet of 9

1670 A334 $1 #a.-i. (#2063) 7.75 7.75

Souvenir Sheet

1671 A334 $6 multi (#2064) 5.25 5.25

Nos. 2039-2047 Ovptd.

1998 Litho. *Perf. 14*

1672-1675 A331 Set of 4 4.75 4.75

Sheets of 9

1676 A331 $1.10 #a.-i. (#2043) 8.50 8.50
1677 A331 $1.10 #a.-i. (#2044) 8.50 8.50

Souvenir Sheets

1678-1680 A331 $6 each (#2045-2047) 5.25 5.25

Nos. 2140-2148 Ovptd.

1998

1681-1688 A349 Set of 8 6.50 6.50

Souvenir Sheet

1689 A349 $6 multi (#2148) 5.25 5.25

Nos. 2211-2219 Ovptd.

1998

1690-1696 A366 Set of 7 5.00 5.00

Souvenir Sheets

1697 A366 $6 multi (#2218) 5.25 5.25
1698 A366 $6 multi (#2219) 5.25 5.25

Nos. 2058-2062 Ovptd.

1998 Litho. *Perf. 14*

Sheets of 6

1699 A333 $1.20 #a.-f. (#2058) 5.50 5.50
1700 A333 $1.65 #a.-f. (#2059) 7.50 7.50

Souvenir Sheets

1701-1703 A333 $6 each (#2060-2062) 4.50 4.50

Nos. 2067-2068 Ovptd.

1999 Litho. *Perf. 14*

1704 A336 $1.75 Sheet of 3, #a.-c. 5.50 5.50

Souvenir Sheet

1705 A336 $6 multi (#2068) 6.50 6.50

Nos. 2071-2072 Ovptd.

1999 *Perf. 13½x14*

1706 A338 $1.75 Sheet of 3, #a.-c. 4.25 4.25

Souvenir Sheet

1707 A338 $6 multi (#2072) 4.75 4.75

Nos. 2084-2093 Ovptd.

1999 Litho. *Perf. 14*

1708-1713 A341 Set of 6 4.25 4.25

Sheets of 8

1714 A341 $1.65 #a.-h. (#2090) 5.00 5.00
1715 A341 $1.65 #a.-h.,(#2091) 5.00 5.00

Souvenir Sheets

1716-1717 A341 $6 each (#2092-2093) 4.50 4.50

Nos. 2065-2066 Ovptd.

1999 Litho. *Perf. 14*

1718 A335 $1.75 multicolored 1.40 1.40

Souvenir Sheet

1719 A335 $6 multicolored 4.75 4.75

Nos. 2075-2083 Ovptd.

1999

1720-1725 A340 Set of 6 4.00 4.00

Sheet of 6

1726 A340 $1.75 #a.-f. 8.00 8.00

Souvenir Sheets

1727 A340 $6 multi (#2082) 4.50 4.50
1728 A340 $6 multi (#2083) 4.50 4.50

No. 2184 Ovptd.

1999

1729 A358 $1.20 multicolored .90 .90

Nos. 2107-2110 Ovptd.

1999 Litho. *Perf. 14*

Sheets of 6

1730 A344 $1.65 #a.-f. (#2107) 7.50 7.50
1731 A344 $1.65 #a.-f. (#2108) 7.50 7.50

Souvenir Sheets

1732 A344 $6 brown (#2109) 4.50 4.50
1733 A344 $6 brown (#2110) 4.50 4.50

Nos. 2133-2139 Ovptd.

1999

1734-1739 A348 Set of 6 4.25 4.25

Souvenir Sheet

1740 A348 $6 multi (#2139) 4.50 4.50

Nos. 2155-2161 Ovptd.

1999

1741-1746 A351 Set of 6 3.25 3.25

Souvenir Sheet

1747 A351 $6 multi (#2161) 4.50 4.50

Nos. 2295-2301 Ovptd.

1999 *Perf. 13¾*

1748-1753 A383 Set of 6 5.50 5.50

Souvenir Sheet

1754 A383 $6 multi (#2301) 4.50 4.50

Nos. 2103-2106 Ovptd.

2000 Litho. *Perf. 14*

Sheets of 6

1755 A343 $1.65 #a-f (#2103) 7.50 7.50
1756 A343 $1.65 #a-f (#2104) 7.50 7.50

Souvenir Sheets

1757 A343 $6 multi (#2105) 4.50 4.50
1758 A343 $6 multi (#2106) 4.50 4.50

Nos. 2123-2132 Ovptd.

2000

1759-1764 A347 Set of 6 5.50 5.50

Sheets of 6

1765 A347 $1.65 #a-f (#2129) 7.50 7.50
1766 A347 $1.65 #a-f (#2130) 7.50 7.50

Souvenir Sheets

1767 A347 $6 multi (#2131) 4.50 4.50
1768 A347 $6 multi (#2132) 4.50 4.50

Nos. 2166-2170 Ovptd.

2000 Litho. *Perf. 14x14½*

Sheets of 3

1769 A353 $1.75 #a-c (#2166) 4.00 4.00
1770 A353 $1.75 #a-c (#2167) 4.00 4.00

Souvenir Sheets

1771 A353 $6 multi (#2168) 4.50 4.50
1772 A353 $6 multi (#2169) 4.50 4.50
1773 A353 $6 multi (#2170) 4.50 4.50

Nos. 2172-2175 Ovptd.

2000 *Perf. 14*

Sheets of 6

1774 A355 $1.65 #a-f (#2172) 7.50 7.50
1775 A355 $1.65 #a-f (#2173) 7.50 7.50

Souvenir Sheets

1776 A355 $6 multi (#2174) 4.50 4.50
1777 A355 $6 multi (#2175) 4.50 4.50

Nos. 2194-2197 Ovptd.

2000
1778-1780 A361 Set of 3 2.50 2.50

Souvenir Sheet

1781 A361 $6 multi 4.50 4.50

No. 2198 Ovptd.

2000 *Perf. 13½*
1782 A362 $1 multi .75 .75

SEMI-POSTAL STAMP

Catalogue values for unused stamps in this section are for Never Hinged items.

Barbuda No. 501 Crudely Surcharged

1982, June 28

Self-Adhesive

B1 CD331 Booklet 16.00

Nos. 1550-1552 Surcharged "HURRICANE RELIEF" in Silver

1995, Nov. Litho. *Perf. 13*
B2 B54 $7.50 +$1 on #1551 6.25 6.25
B3 B53 $8 +$1 on #1550 6.75 6.75
B4 B55 $8 +$1 on #1552 6.75 6.75
Nos. B2-B4 (3) 19.75 19.75

BASUTOLAND

bə-ˈsü-tə-ˌland

LOCATION — An enclave in the state of South Africa
GOVT. — British Crown Colony
AREA — 11,716 sq. mi.
POP. — 733,000 (est. 1964)
CAPITAL — Maseru

The Colony, a former independent native state, was annexed to the Cape Colony in 1871. In 1883 control was transferred directly to the British Crown. Stamps of the Cape of Good Hope were used from 1871 to 1910 and those of the Union of South Africa from 1910 to 1933. Basutoland became the independent state of Lesotho on Oct. 4, 1966.

12 Pence = 1 Shilling
100 Cents = 1 Rand (1961)

Catalogue values for unused stamps in this country are for Never Hinged items, beginning with Scott 29 in the regular postage section and Scott J1 in the postage due section.

George V — A1

George VI — A2

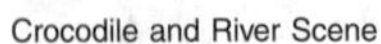
Crocodile and River Scene

Perf. 12½

1933, Dec. 1 Engr. Wmk. 4
1 A1 ½p emerald .60 *2.25*
2 A1 1p carmine .70 *1.50*
3 A1 2p red violet .90 *1.00*
4 A1 3p ultra .80 *1.25*
5 A1 4p slate 1.90 *8.25*
6 A1 6p yellow 2.10 *2.25*
7 A1 1sh red orange 2.25 *6.00*
8 A1 2sh6p dk brown 18.00 *57.50*
9 A1 5sh violet 50.00 *85.00*
10 A1 10sh olive green 100.00 *160.00*
Nos. 1-10 (10) 177.25 *325.00*
Set, never hinged 325.00

Common Design Types pictured following the introduction.

Silver Jubilee Issue

Common Design Type

1935, May 4 *Perf. 13½x14*
11 CD301 1p car & blue .60 .50
12 CD301 2p gray blk & ultra .90 *1.25*
13 CD301 3p blue & brown 3.25 *4.50*
14 CD301 6p brt vio & indigo 3.25 *4.50*
Nos. 11-14 (4) 8.00 *10.75*
Set, never hinged 16.00

Coronation Issue

Common Design Type

1937, May 12 *Perf. 13½x14*
15 CD302 1p carmine .35 .30
16 CD302 2p rose violet .50 .55
17 CD302 3p bright ultra .60 .55
Nos. 15-17 (3) 1.45 1.40
Set, never hinged 1.90

1938, Apr. 1 *Perf. 12½*
18 A2 ½p emerald .20 *1.75*
19 A2 1p rose car .35 *1.00*
20 A2 1½p light blue .25 *.65*
21 A2 2p rose lilac .20 *.80*
22 A2 3p ultra .20 *1.40*
23 A2 4p gray 1.00 *4.75*
24 A2 6p yel ocher .40 *1.75*
25 A2 1sh red orange .40 *1.40*
26 A2 2sh6p black brown 5.50 *11.00*
27 A2 5sh violet 14.50 *13.00*
28 A2 10sh olive green 14.50 *22.50*
Nos. 18-28 (11) 37.50 *60.00*
Set, never hinged 70.00

Catalogue values for unused stamps in this section, from this point to the end of the section, are for Never Hinged items.

Peace Issue

South Africa Nos. 100-102 Overprinted

Basic stamps inscribed alternately in English and Afrikaans.

1945, Dec. 3 Wmk. 201 *Perf. 14*
29 A42 1p rose pink & choc, pair .35 .35
a. Single, English .20 .20
b. Single, Afrikaans .20 .20
30 A43 2p vio & slate blue, pair .35 .35
a. Single, English .20 .20
b. Single, Afrikaans .20 .20
31 A43 3p ultra & dp ultra, pair .40 .40
a. Single, English .20 .20
b. Single, Afrikaans .20 .20
Nos. 29-31 (3) 1.10 1.10

King George VI — A3

King George VI and Queen Elizabeth A4

Princess Margaret Rose and Princess Elizabeth A5

Royal British Family A6

Perf. 12½

1947, Feb. 17 Wmk. 4 Engr.
35 A3 1p red .20 .20
36 A4 2p green .20 .20
37 A5 3p ultra .20 .20
38 A6 1sh dark violet .20 .20
Nos. 35-38 (4) .80 .80

Visit of the British Royal Family, 3/11-12/47.

Silver Wedding Issue

Common Design Types

1948, Dec. 1 Photo. *Perf. 14x14½*
39 CD304 1½p brt ultra .20 .20

Engr.; Name Typo.

Perf. 11½

40 CD305 10sh dk brn ol 45.00 *35.00*

UPU Issue

Common Design Types

Engr.; Name Typo. on 3p, 6p

Perf. 13½, 11x11½

1949, Oct. 10 Wmk. 4
41 CD306 1½p blue .50 *1.25*
42 CD307 3p indigo 1.00 *2.50*
43 CD308 6p orange yel 1.25 *2.50*
44 CD309 1sh red brown 1.25 1.25
Nos. 41-44 (4) 4.00 7.50

Coronation Issue

Common Design Type

1953, June 3 Engr. *Perf. 13½x13*
45 CD312 2p red violet & black .50 .60

Qiloane Hill — A7

Shearing Angora Goats — A8

Designs: 1p, Orange River. 2p, Mosotho horseman. 3p, Basuto household. 4½p, Maletsunyane falls. 6p, Herdboy with lesiba. 1sh, Pastoral scene. 1sh3p, Plane at Lancers Gap. 2sh6p, Old Fort Leribe. 5sh, Mission cave house.

1954, Oct. 18 Wmk. 4 *Perf. 13½*
46 A7 ½p dk brown & gray .20 .20
47 A7 1p dp grn & gray blk .20 .20
48 A7 2p org & dp blue .65 .20
49 A7 3p car & ol green .90 .25
50 A7 4½p dp blue & ind .80 .20
51 A7 6p dk grn & org brn 1.25 .20
52 A7 1sh rose vio & dk ol green 1.25 .25
53 A7 1sh3p aqua & brown 17.00 4.25
54 A7 2sh6p lilac rose & dp ultra 13.50 4.75
55 A7 5sh dp car & black 5.25 *7.75*
56 A8 10sh dp cl & black 19.00 *22.50*
Nos. 46-56 (11) 60.00 40.75

See Nos. 72-82, 87-91. For surcharges see Nos. 57, 61-71.

No. 48 Surcharged

1959, Aug. 1
57 A7 ½p on 2p org & dp blue .20 .20

Chief Moshoeshoe (Moshesh) — A9

Designs: 1sh, Council chamber. 1sh3p, Mosotho on horseback.

Perf. 13x13½

1959, Dec. 15 Wmk. 314
58 A9 3p lt yel, grn & blk .35 .20
59 A9 1sh green & pink .35 .20
60 A9 1sh3p orange & ultra .55 .30
Nos. 58-60 (3) 1.25 .70

Institution of the Basutoland National Council.

Nos. 46-56 Surcharged with New Value

2½c (I) 2½c (II) 3½c (I) 3½c (II)
5c (I) 5c (II) 10c (I) 10c (II)
12½c (I) 12½c (II)
25c (I) 25c (II) 25c (III)
50c (I) 50c (II) R1 (I) R1 (II) R1 (III)

1961, Feb. 14 Wmk. 4 *Perf. 13½*
61 A7 ½c on ½p .20 .20
a. Double surcharge *400.00*
62 A7 1c on 1p .20 .20
63 A7 2c on 2p .20 .20
a. Inverted surcharge *100.00*
64 A7 2½c on 3p (II) .20 .20
a. Type I .20 .20
b. Inverted surcharge (II) *1,750.* *1,400.*
65 A7 3½c on 4½p (I) .20 .20
a. Type II 3.00 *4.50*
66 A7 5c on 6p (II) .20 .20
a. Type I .20 .20
67 A7 10c on 1sh (I) .20 .20
a. Type II 100.00 *110.00*
68 A7 12½c on 1sh3p (II) .40 .20
a. Type I 1.00 .50
69 A7 25c on 2sh6p (I) .20 .20
a. Type II 25.00 10.00
b. Type III .65 .65
70 A7 50c on 5sh (II) .75 *1.40*
a. Type I 1.50 *2.00*
71 A8 1r on 10sh (III) 6.00 6.00
a. Type I 26.00 11.00
b. Type II 9.00 *20.00*
Nos. 61-71 (11) 8.75 9.20

Surcharge types on Nos. 64-71 are numbered chronologically.

Types of 1954

Value in Cents and Rands

Designs: ½c, Qiloane Hill. 1c, Orange River. 2c, Mosotho horseman. 2½c, Basuto household. 3½c, Maletsunyane Falls. 5c, Herdboy with lesiba. 10c, Pastoral scene. 12½c, Plane at Lancers Gap. 25c, Old Fort Leribe. 50c, Mission cave house. 1r, Shearing Angora goats.

1961-63 Wmk. 4 Engr. *Perf. 13½*
72 A7 ½c dk brn & gray ('62) .20 .20
73 A7 1c dp grn & gray blk ('62) .20 *.35*
74 A7 2c org & dp bl ('62) .50 *1.60*
75 A7 2½c car & ol grn .85 .20
76 A7 3½c dp bl & ind ('62) .30 *1.25*
77 A7 5c dk grn & org brn ('62) .40 *.55*
78 A7 10c rose vio & dk ol ('62) .40 .35
79 A7 12½c aqua & brn ('62) 20.00 10.50
80 A7 25c lilac rose & dp ultra ('62) 6.00 5.50
81 A7 50c dp car & blk ('62) 9.75 *10.00*

Perf. 11½

82 A8 1r dp cl & blk ('63) 19.00 11.00
Nos. 72-82 (11) 57.60 41.50

See Nos. 87-91. For overprints on stamps and types see Lesotho Nos. 5-14, 20a.

Freedom from Hunger Issue
Common Design Type
Perf. 14x14½

1963, June 4 Photo. Wmk. 314
83 CD314 12½c lilac .50 .40

Red Cross Centenary Issue
Common Design Type

1963, Sept. 2 Litho. *Perf. 13*
84 CD315 2½c black & red .20 .20
85 CD315 12½c ultra & red .70 .70

Queen Type of 1961-63

1964 Engr. *Perf. 13½*
87 A7 1c grn & gray blk .20 .20
88 A7 2½c car & ol green .20 .20
89 A7 5c dk green & org brn .35 .35
90 A7 12½c aqua & brown 3.00 1.75
91 A7 50c dp car & black 7.25 *10.00*
Nos. 87-91 (5) 11.00 12.50

Mosotho Woman and Child — A10

Designs: 3½c, Maseru border post. 5c, Mountains. 12½c, Legislative Building.

Perf. 14x13½

1965, May 10 Photo. Wmk. 314
97 A10 2½c ultra & multi .20 .20
98 A10 3½c blue & bister .20 .20
99 A10 5c blue & ocher .20 .20
100 A10 12½c lt blue, blk & buff .40 .40
Nos. 97-100 (4) 1.00 1.00

Attainment of self-government.

ITU Issue
Common Design Type

1965, May 17 Litho. *Perf. 11x11½*
101 CD317 1c ver & red lilac .20 .20
102 CD317 20c grnsh bl & org brn .85 .65

Intl. Cooperation Year Issue
Common Design Type

1965, Oct. 25 Wmk. 314 *Perf. 14½*
103 CD318 ½c blue grn & cl .20 .20
104 CD318 12½c lt vio & green .90 .70

Churchill Memorial Issue
Common Design Type

1966, Jan. 24 Photo. *Perf. 14*
Design in Black, Gold and Carmine Rose
105 CD319 1c bright blue .30 .20
106 CD319 2½c green .60 .20
107 CD319 10c brown .75 .50
108 CD319 22½c violet 1.10 1.10
Nos. 105-108 (4) 2.75 2.00

POSTAGE DUE STAMPS

Catalogue values for all unused stamps in this section are for Never Hinged items.

D1

1933-38 Wmk. 4 Typo. *Perf. 14*
J1 D1 1p dark red ('38) .40 *1.00*
a. 1p dark carmine 1.00 *1.50*
b. Wmk. 4a (error) 67.50
J2 D1 2p lt violet .30 *1.00*
a. Wmk. 4a (error) 67.50

Nos. J1-J2 valued on chalky paper.
For surcharge see No. J7.

Coat of Arms — D2

1956, Dec. 1
J3 D2 1p carmine .35 *3.75*
J4 D2 2p dark purple .35 *7.00*

Nos. J2-J4 Surcharged with New Value

1961
J5 D2 1c on 1p carmine .20 .20
J6 D2 1c on 2p dk purple .20 .20
J7 D1 5c on 2p lt violet 3.00 3.00
a. Wmk. 4a (error) 275.00
J8 D2 5c on 2p dark pur ("5" 7½mm high) .20 .20
a. "5" 3½mm high 17.50 *35.00*
Nos. J5-J8 (4) 3.60 3.60

Value in Cents

1964 Wmk. 314 *Perf. 14*
J9 D2 1c carmine *2.25 17.00*
J10 D2 5c dark purple *2.25 17.00*

For overprints see Lesotho Nos. J1-J2.

OFFICIAL STAMPS

Nos. 1-3 and 6 Overprinted "OFFICIAL"

1934 Wmk. 4 Engr. *Perf. 12½*
O1 A1 ½p emerald *3,500. 3,500.*
O2 A1 1p carmine *1,400. 1,000.*
O3 A1 2p red violet *850.00 500.00*
O4 A1 6p yellow *9,000. 4,500.*

Counterfeits exist.

BATUM

LOCATION — A seaport on the Black Sea

Batum is the capital of Adzhar, a territory which, in 1921, became an autonomous republic of the Georgian Soviet Socialist Republic.

Stamps of Batum were issued under the administration of British forces which occupied Batum and environs between December, 1918, and July, 1920, following the Treaty of Versailles.

100 Kopecks = 1 Ruble

Counterfeits of Nos. 1-65 abound.

A1

1919 Unwmk. Litho. *Imperf.*
1 A1 5k green 4.00 *5.50*
2 A1 10k ultramarine 4.00 *5.50*
3 A1 50k yellow 1.50 *2.00*
4 A1 1r red brown 1.75 *2.50*
5 A1 3r violet 6.50 *7.50*
6 A1 5r brown 7.50 *9.00*
Nos. 1-6 (6) 25.25 *32.00*

For overprints and surcharges see #13-20, 51-65.

Nos. 7-12, 21-50: numbers in parentheses are those of the basic Russian stamps.

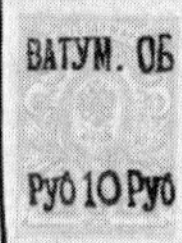

Russian Stamps of 1909-17 Surcharged

On Stamps of 1917

1919
7 10r on 1k orange (#119) 25.00 *27.50*
8 10r on 3k red (#121) 12.50 *15.00*

On Stamp of 1909-12
Perf. 14x14½
9 10r on 5k claret (#77) 225.00 225.00

On Stamp of 1917
10 10r on 10k on 7k light blue (#117) 200.00 200.00
Nos. 7-10 (4) 462.50 467.50

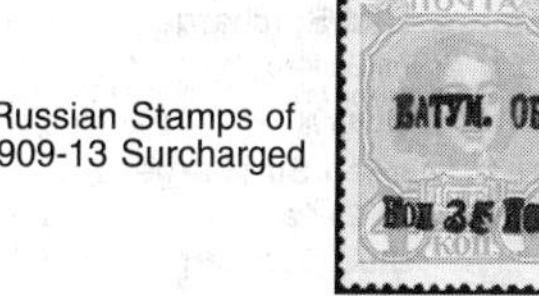

Russian Stamps of 1909-13 Surcharged

1919
11 35k on 4k carmine (#76) *1,650. 2,900.*
12 35k on 4k dull red (#91) *6,500. 7,750.*

This surcharge was intended for postal cards. A few cards which bore adhesive stamps were also surcharged.

Values are for stamps off card and without gum.

Type of 1919 Issue Overprinted

1919 Unwmk. *Imperf.*
13 A1 5k green 5.75 *6.00*
14 A1 10k dark blue 5.75 *6.00*
15 A1 25k orange 5.75 *6.00*
16 A1 1r pale blue 2.75 *5.00*
17 A1 2r salmon pink .80 *.90*
18 A1 3r violet .80 *.90*
19 A1 5r brown 1.25 *1.25*
a. "CCUPATION" *225.00 250.00*
20 A1 7r dull red 2.50 *3.50*
Nos. 13-20 (8) 25.35 *29.55*

Russian Stamps of 1909-17 Surcharged in Various Colors:

10r & 50r

BATYMЪ BRITISH P. 15 P. OCCUPATION ОБЛ.
15r

On Stamps of 1917

1919-20 *Imperf.*
21 10r on 3k red (#121) 22.50 20.00
22 15r on 1k org (R) (#119) 45.00 40.00
23 15r on 1k org (Bk) (#119) 67.50 60.00
24 15r on 1k org (V) (#119) 45.00 40.00
25 50r on 1k org (#119) 275.00 275.00
26 50r on 2k green (#120) 350.00 350.00

On Stamps of 1909-17
Perf. 14x14½
27 50r on 2k green (#74) 400.00 375.00
28 50r on 3k red (#75) 850.00 825.00
29 50r on 4k car (#76) 600.00 575.00
30 50r on 5k claret (#77) 375.00 350.00
31 50r on 10k dk blue (R) (#79) 950.00 900.00
32 50r on 15k red brn & blue (#81) 375.00 375.00

Surcharged

On Stamps of 1909-17
33 25r on 5k cl (Bk) (#77) 45.00 45.00
34 25r on 5k cl (Bl) (#77) 45.00 45.00
35 25r on 10k on 7k lt blue (Bk) (#117) 80.00 80.00
36 25r on 10k on 7k lt blue (Bl) (#117) 45.00 45.00
37 25r on 20k on 14k bl & rose (Bk) (#118) 67.50 67.50
38 25r on 20k on 14k bl & rose (Bl) (#118) 50.00 45.00
39 25r on 25k grn & gray vio (Bk) (#83) 100.00 90.00
40 25r on 25k grn & gray vio (Bl) (#83) 100.00 90.00
41 25r on 50k vio & green (Bk) (#85a) 45.00 45.00
42 25r on 50k vio & green (Bl) (#85a) 50.00 50.00
43 50r on 2k green (#74) 70.00 70.00
44 50r on 3k red (#75) 70.00 70.00
45 50r on 4k car (#76) 100.00 90.00
46 50r on 5k claret (#77) 100.00 90.00

On Stamps of 1917
Imperf
47 50r on 2k green (#120) 250.00 240.00
48 50r on 3k red (#121) 325.00 325.00
49 50r on 5k claret (#123) *950.00 900.00*

On Stamp of 1913
Perf. 13½
50 50r on 4k dull red (Bl) (#91) 67.50 67.50

Nos. 3, 13 and 15 Surcharged in Black or Blue:

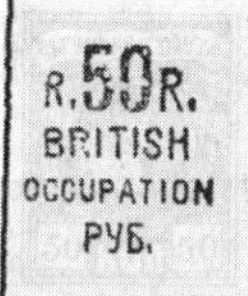

1920 *Imperf.*
51 A1 25r on 5k green 24.00 24.00
52 A1 25r on 5k grn (Bl) 30.00 30.00
53 A1 25r on 25k orange 17.00 17.00
54 A1 25r on 25k org (Bl) *65.00 65.00*
55 A1 50r on 50k yellow 15.00 15.00
56 A1 50r on 50k yel (Bl) *60.00 60.00*
Nos. 51-56 (6) *211.00 211.00*

The surcharges on Nos. 21-56 inclusive are handstamped and are known double, inverted, etc.

Tree Type of 1919 Overprinted Like Nos. 13-20

1920
57 A1 1r orange brown .60 *3.25*
58 A1 2r gray blue .65 *3.25*
59 A1 3r rose .75 *3.25*
60 A1 5r black brown .65 *3.25*
61 A1 7r yellow .65 *3.25*
62 A1 10r dark green .60 *3.25*
63 A1 15r violet .80 *4.25*
64 A1 25r vermilion .75 *4.00*
65 A1 50r dark blue .90 *6.25*
Nos. 57-65 (9) 6.35 *34.00*

The variety "BPITISH" occurs on #57-65.

BECHUANALAND

ˌbech-ˈwä-nə-ˌland

(British Bechuanaland)

LOCATION — Southern Africa
GOVT. — A British Crown Colony, annexed in 1895 to the Cape of Good Hope Colony which became a province in the Union of South Africa.
AREA — 51,424 sq. mi.
POP. — 84,210 (1904)
CAPITAL — Mafeking

12 Pence = 1 Shilling
20 Shillings = 1 Pound

Watermarks

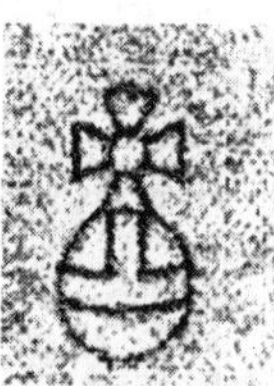
Wmk. 29- Orb

Wmk. 14- VR in Italics

Cape of Good Hope Stamps of 1871-85 Overprinted

British
Bechuanaland

1885-87 Wmk. 1 *Perf. 14*

Black Overprint

1 A6 4p blue ('86) 50.00 *57.50*

Wmk. 2

Black Overprint

3 A6 3p claret 30.00 37.50

Red Overprint

4 A6 ½p black 10.00 14.50
- *a.* Double overprint in red & blk 850.00

Wmk. Anchor (16)

Black Overprint

5 A6 ½p black ('87) 6.50 *10.00*
- *a.* "ritish" 1,800. *1,800.*
- *b.* Double overprint 2,500.

6 A6 1p rose 9.00 8.50
- *a.* "ritish" 2,100. *1,600.*
- *b.* Double overprint *2,000.*

7 A6 2p bister 27.50 10.00
- *a.* "ritish" 4,500. *4,000.*
- *b.* Double overprint 1,500.

8 A3 6p violet 70.00 35.00

9 A3 1sh green ('86) 210.00 140.00
- *a.* "ritish" *11,500.* *8,500.*

There is no period after Bechuanaland in the genuine stamps.

Black Ovpt. on Great Britain #111

1887 Wmk. 30

10 A54 ½p vermilion 1.10 *1.25*
- *a.* Double overprint 2,250.

For overprints see Bechuanaland Protectorate Nos. 51-53.

A1

A2

A3

1887 Typo. Wmk. 29

Country Name in Black

11 A1 1p lilac 16.00 3.50
12 A1 2p lilac 75.00 1.75
13 A1 3p lilac 3.25 *7.00*
14 A1 4p lilac 42.50 2.50
15 A1 6p lilac 60.00 14.50

Wmk. 14

16 A2 1sh green 35.00 5.00
17 A2 2sh green 50.00 35.00
18 A2 2sh6p green 65.00 57.50
19 A2 5sh green 90.00 175.00
- Pen cancellation 4.00

20 A2 10sh green 200.00 *375.00*
- Pen cancellation 22.50

Wmk. 29

21 A3 £1 lilac 1,100. 1,000.
- Pen cancellation 37.50

22 A3 £5 lilac 3,500. 1,750.
- Pen cancellation 175.00

The corner designs and central oval differs on No. 22.

For overprints see Bechuanaland Protectorate Nos. 54-58, 60-66. For surcharges see Nos. 23-28, 30, Cape of Good Hope No. 171.

Nos. 11-12, 14-16 Surcharged

1888

Country Name in Black

Black Surcharge

23 A1 1p on 1p lilac 8.00 7.00
- *a.* Double surcharge

24 A1 6p on 6p lilac 80.00 12.00

Red Surcharge

25 A1 2p on 2p lilac 20.00 3.00
- *a.* "2" with curved tail 190.00 150.00

26 A1 4p on 4p lilac 225.00 *325.00*

Green Surcharge

27 A1 2p on 2p lilac *3,250.*

Blue Surcharge

27A A1 6p on 6p lilac *8,000.*

Wmk. 14

Black Surcharge

28 A2 1sh on 1sh green 150.00 90.00

No. 29

One Half-Penny

No. 30

Green Ovpt. on Cape of Good Hope #41

1889 Wmk. 16

29 A4 ½p black 4.75 *25.00*

Vertical overprint, double overprints one inverted or double, and varieties such as "British" omitted probably are from printers waste.

Wmk. 29

Black Surcharge on No. 13

30 A1 ½p on 3p lilac & blk 750.00 *160.00*

Cape of Good Hope Nos. 43-44 Overprinted in Black

1891 Wmk. 16

31 A4 1p rose 13.00 9.00
- *a.* Horiz. pair, one without overprint *1,750.*
- *b.* "British" omitted — 1,000.
- *c.* "Bechuanaland" omitted 1,050.

32 A4 2p bister 4.00 3.00
- *a.* Without period 200.00 250.00

See Nos. 38-39.

Stamps of Great Britain Overprinted in Black

1891-94 Wmk. 30

33 A40 1p lilac 8.00 2.00
34 A56 2p green & car 9.75 6.00
35 A59 4p brown & green 3.25 .75
36 A62 6p violet, *rose* 4.00 2.75
37 A65 1sh green ('94) 17.50 *21.00*
Nos. 33-37 (5) 42.50 *32.50*

For surcharges see Cape of Good Hope Nos. 172, 176-177.

Cape of Good Hope Nos. 43-44 Overprinted Like Nos. 31-32 but Reading Down

1893-95 Wmk. 16

38 A6 1p rose 2.50 *2.75*
- *a.* No dots over the "i's" of "British" 75.00 75.00
- *b.* "British" omitted 1,000.
- *c.* As "a," reading up 1,275.
- *d.* Pair, one without overprint

39 A6 2p bister ('95) 4.75 2.75
- *a.* Double overprint 900.00 800.00
- *b.* No dots over the "i's" of "British" 125.00 110.00
- *c.* "British" omitted 425.00 425.00
- *d.* As "b," reading up

Cape of Good Hope No. 42 Overprinted

"BECHUANALAND" 16mm Long Overprint Lines 13mm Apart

1897

40 A6 ½p light green 3.00 *10.00*

"BECHUANALAND" 15mm Long Overprint Lines 10½mm Apart

41 A6 ½p light green 10.00 *50.00*

"BECHUANALAND" 15mm Long Overprint Lines 13½mm Apart

42 A6 ½p light green 25.00 *90.00*
Nos. 40-42 (3) 38.00 *150.00*

BECHUANALAND PROTECTORATE

ˌbech-ˈwä-nə-ˌland prə-ˈtek-tˌə-ˌrət

LOCATION — In central South Africa, north of the Republic of South Africa, east of South-West Africa and bounded on the north by the Caprivi Strip of Southwest Africa and on the east by Southern Rhodesia

GOVT. — British Protectorate

AREA — 222,000 sq. mi.

POP. — 540,400 (1964)

Bechuanaland Protectorate became the independent republic of Botswana, Sept. 30, 1966.

12 Pence = 1 Shilling
20 Shillings = 1 Pound
100 Cents = 1 Rand (1961)

Catalogue values for unused stamps in this country are for Never Hinged items, beginning with Scott 137 in the regular postage section and Scott J7 in the postage due section.

Additional Overprint in Black on Bechuanaland No. 10

Protectorate

a

b

Protectorate

c

1888-90 Wmk. 30 *Perf. 14*

51 A54(a) ½p vermilion 175.00 *225.00*
- *a.* Double overprint 725.00

52 A54(b) ½p ver ('89) 3.00 *25.00*
- *a.* Double overprint *300.00*

53 A54(c) ½p vermilion 150.00 175.00
- *a.* Inverted overprint 65.00 *85.00*
- *b.* Double overprint 80.00 *110.00*
- *c.* As "a," double 500.00 500.00

For surcharge see No. 68.

Bechuanaland Nos. 16-20 Overprinted Type "b" in Black

Wmk. 14

Country Name in Black

54 A2 1sh green 80.00 60.00
- *a.* First "o" omitted 3,250. 3,000.

55 A2 2sh green 700.00 *900.00*
- *a.* First "o" omitted 7,500. —

56 A2 2sh6p green 700.00 *800.00*
- *a.* First "o" omitted 7,500. —

57 A2 5sh green 1,400. *2,250.*
- *a.* First "o" omitted 10,000. —

58 A2 10sh green 4,000. *6,500.*
- *a.* First "o" omitted 15,000. —

Bechuanaland Nos. 11-15 Overprinted Type "b" and Surcharged in Black

1888 Wmk. 29

Country Name in Black

60 A1 1p on 1p lilac 7.00 *14.00*
- *a.* Short "1" 300.00 *325.00*

61 A1 2p on 2p lilac 22.50 17.50
- *a.* "2" with curved tail 450.00 400.00

63 A1 3p on 3p lilac 100.00 *160.00*

64 A1 4p on 4p lilac 275.00 275.00
- *a.* Small "4" 2,500. 2,400.

65 A1 6p on 6p lilac 62.50 42.50

In #60 the "1" is 2½mm high; in #60a, 2mm.

Value Surcharged in Red

66 A1 4p on 4p lilac 65.00 37.50

Cape of Good Hope Type of 1886 Overprinted in Green

1889 Wmk. 16

67 A6 ½p black 3.75 *40.00*
- *a.* Double overprint 400.00 *500.00*
- *b.* "Bechuanaland" omitted 725.00

Black Surcharge on Bechuanaland Protectorate No. 52

Wmk. 30

68 A54 4p on ½p ver 17.50 3.50
- *a.* Inverted surcharge *4,500.*

Stamps of Great Britain 1881-87, Overprinted in Black

1897, Oct.

69 A54 ½p vermilion 1.00 *2.00*
70 A40 1p lilac 4.00 *.50*
71 A56 2p green & car 3.00 5.50
72 A58 3p violet, *yel* 6.00 *10.00*
73 A59 4p brown & green 15.00 12.50
74 A62 6p violet, *rose* 25.00 12.50
Nos. 69-74 (6) 54.00 43.00

For surcharges see Cape of Good Hope Nos. 167-170, 173-175.

Same on Great Britain No. 125

1902, Feb. 25

75 A54 ½p blue green 1.50 *2.00*

Stamps of Great Britain, 1902, Overprinted in Black

1904-12

76 A66 ½p gray green ('06) 1.75 *2.50*
77 A66 1p car ('05) 7.50 .65
78 A66 2½p ultra 7.25 6.75
79 A74 1sh scar & grn ('12) 40.00 *125.00*
Nos. 76-79 (4) 56.50 *134.90*

Same on Great Britain No. 143

1908

80 A66 ½p pale yel green 3.25 *4.00*

Transvaal No. 274 Overprinted

1910 Wmk. 3

81 A27 6p brn org & blk 175.00 *325.00*

This stamp was issued for fiscal use, although it is known postally used.

Great Britain No. 154 Overprinted Like Nos. 76-79

1912, Sept. Wmk. 30 *Perf. 15x14*

82 A81 1p scarlet 1.10 .90

Great Britain Stamps of 1912-13 Overprinted Like Nos. 76-79

Wmk. Crown and GvR (33)

1914-24

83 A82 ½p green 1.50 *1.90*
84 A83 1p scarlet 3.00 .85
85 A84 1½p red brn ('20) 2.75 *3.25*
86 A85 2p orange (I) 3.00 4.50
a. 2p orange (II) ('24) 32.50 5.50
87 A86 2½p ultra 3.75 *22.50*
88 A87 3p bluish violet 6.50 *13.00*
89 A88 4p slate green 7.00 *15.00*
90 A89 6p dull violet 7.50 *18.00*
91 A90 1sh bister 10.00 *21.00*
Nos. 83-91 (9) 45.00 *100.00*

The dies of No. 86 are the same as in Great Britain 1912-13 issue.

Overprinted **BECHUANALAND PROTECTORATE**

Wmk. 34 ***Perf. 11x12***

92 A91 2sh6p dk brown 140.00 *300.00*
a. 2sh6p light brown ('16) 125.00 *300.00*
93 A91 5sh rose car 175.00 *450.00*
a. 5sh carmine ('20) 350.00 *500.00*

Nos. 92, 93 were printed by Waterlow Bros. & Layton; Nos. 92a, 93a were printed by Thomas De La Rue & Co.

Same Overprint On Retouched Stamps of 1919

1920-23

94 A91 2sh6p gray brown 100.00 *200.00*
95 A91 5sh car rose 140.00 *325.00*

Great Britain Stamps of 1924 Overprinted like Nos. 76-79

Wmk. Crown and Block GvR Multiple (35)

1925-26 ***Perf. 15x14***

96 A82 ½p green 1.50 *2.00*
97 A83 1p scarlet 2.00 1.00
99 A85 2p deep org (II) 2.50 1.25
101 A87 3p violet 5.00 *21.00*
102 A88 4p slate green 4.25 *40.00*
103 A89 6p dull violet 35.00 *70.00*
104 A90 1sh bister 11.00 *30.00*
Nos. 96-104 (7) 61.25 *165.25*

George V A11

George VI, Cattle and Baobab Tree A12

Perf. 12½

1932, Dec. 12 Engr. Wmk. 4

105 A11 ½p green .85 .20
106 A11 1p carmine .85 .20
107 A11 2p red brown .85 .20
108 A11 3p ultra .85 .50
109 A11 4p orange 1.25 *4.25*
110 A11 6p red violet 2.50 2.00
111 A11 1sh blk & ol grn 6.00 3.50
112 A11 2sh black & org 26.00 *21.00*
113 A11 2sh6p black & car 26.00 *32.50*
114 A11 3sh black & red vio 42.50 *45.00*
115 A11 5sh black & ultra 55.00 55.00
116 A11 10sh blk & red brown 77.50 110.00
Nos. 105-116 (12) 241.65 *274.35*

Common Design Types pictured following the introduction.

Silver Jubilee Issue

Common Design Type

1935, May 4 ***Perf. 11x12***

117 CD301 1p car & blue .25 *3.00*
118 CD301 2p black & ultra 1.00 *3.00*
119 CD301 3p ultra & brown 2.50 *3.00*
120 CD301 6p brown vio & ind 4.25 *3.00*
Nos. 117-120 (4) 8.00 12.00
Set, never hinged 20.00

Coronation Issue

Common Design Type

1937, May 12 ***Perf. 13½x14***

121 CD302 1p carmine .30 *.40*
122 CD302 2p brown .30 *1.10*
123 CD302 3p bright ultra .40 *1.50*
Nos. 121-123 (3) 1.00 3.00
Set, never hinged 1.50

1938, Apr. 1 ***Perf. 12½***

124 A12 ½p green 1.50 *2.50*
125 A12 1p rose car .50 .60
126 A12 1½p light blue 6.25 2.25
127 A12 2p brown .50 *.65*
128 A12 3p ultra .50 *2.50*
129 A12 4p orange 1.50 *3.75*
130 A12 6p rose violet 3.25 3.25
131 A12 1sh blk & ol grn 3.00 *4.50*
133 A12 2sh6p black & car 10.00 *14.00*
135 A12 5sh black & ultra 22.50 16.00
136 A12 10sh black & brn 10.50 *20.00*
Nos. 124-136 (11) 60.00 *70.00*
Set, never hinged 80.00

Catalogue values for unused stamps in this section, from this point to the end of the section, are for Never Hinged items.

Peace Issue

South Africa Nos. 100-102 Overprinted

Basic stamps inscribed alternately in English and Afrikaans.

1945, Dec. 3 Wmk. 201 ***Perf. 14***

137 A42 1p rose pink & choc, pair .30 .30
a. Single, English .20 .20
b. Single, Afrikaans .20 .20
138 A43 2p vio & slate blue, pair .40 .40
a. Single, English .20 .20
b. Single, Afrikaans .20 .20
139 A43 3p ultra & dp ultra, pair .50 .50
a. Single, English .25 .25
b. Single, Afrikaans .25 .25
Nos. 137-139 (3) 1.20 1.20

World War II victory of the Allies.

Royal Visit Issue

Types of Basutoland, 1947

Perf. 12½

1947, Feb. 17 Wmk. 4 Engr.

143 A3 1p red .20 .20
144 A4 2p green .20 .20
145 A5 3p ultra .20 .20
146 A6 1sh dark violet .30 .30
Nos. 143-146 (4) .90 .90

Visit of the British Royal Family, 4/17/47.

Silver Wedding Issue

Common Design Types

1948, Dec. 1 Photo. ***Perf. 14x14½***

147 CD304 1½p brt ultra .20 .20

Engr.; Name Typo.

Perf. 11½x11

148 CD305 10sh gray black 32.50 *40.00*

UPU Issue

Common Design Types

Engr.; Name Typo. on 3p and 6p

1949, Oct. 10 ***Perf. 13½, 11x11½***

149 CD306 1½p blue .25 .25
150 CD307 3p indigo .35 .35
151 CD308 6p red lilac .80 .80
152 CD309 1sh olive 1.50 1.50
Nos. 149-152 (4) 2.90 2.90

Coronation Issue

Common Design Type

1953, June 3 Engr. ***Perf. 13½x13***

153 CD312 2p brown & black .30 .30

Elizabeth II — A13

Victoria, Elizabeth II and Water Hole — A14

1955-58 ***Perf. 13x13½***

154 A13 ½p green .55 .25
155 A13 1p rose car .90 .25
156 A13 2p brown 1.40 .25
157 A13 3p ultra 3.25 .35
158 A13 4p orange ('58) *6.50* *4.25*
159 A13 4½p indigo 1.60 1.25
160 A13 6p rose violet 1.40 .90
161 A13 1sh blk & ol grn 1.40 *1.50*
162 A13 1sh3p blk & rose vio 15.00 6.50
163 A13 2sh6p black & car 11.00 10.50
164 A13 5sh black & ultra 16.00 16.00
165 A13 10sh black & brn 26.00 *30.00*
Nos. 154-165 (12) 85.00 *72.00*

For surcharges see Nos. 169-179.

Perf. 14½x14

1960, Jan. 21 Photo. Wmk. 314

166 A14 1p brown & black .40 *.50*
167 A14 3p car rose & black .40 *.50*
168 A14 6p ultra & black .40 *.50*
Nos. 166-168 (3) 1.20 1.50

Proclamation of the Protectorate, 75th anniv.

Nos. 155-165 Surcharged

1c 1c 3½c 3½c 3½c
I II I II III

5c 5c R1 R1
I II I II

Perf. 13x13½

1961, Feb. 14 Wmk. 4 Engr.

169 1c on 1p (I) .20 .20
a. Type II .20 .20
170 2c on 2p .20 .20
171 2½c on 2p .20 .20
a. Pair, one without surcharge 700.00
172 2½c on 3p 2.25 *3.75*
173 3½c on 4p (III) .20 .20
a. Type I .50 .50
b. Type II 1.60 1.60
174 5c on 6p (II) .25 .25
a. Type I .75 .75
175 10c on 1sh .30 .30
a. Pair, one without surcharge 700.00
176 12½c on 1sh3p ("12½c" 11¼mm wide) .55 .55
a. "12½c" 12½mm wide .75 .75
177 25c on 2sh6p 2.50 .80
178 50c on 5sh 3.75 1.90
179 1r on 10sh (II, "R1" at lower center) 4.50 4.50
a. Type II, "R1" at lower left 6.50 6.50
b. Type I 350.00 125.00
Nos. 169-179 (11) 14.90 12.85

Nos. 173a and 173b are found in the same sheet; each comes with "3½c" in both wide and narrow settings.

Surch. types are numbered chronologically.

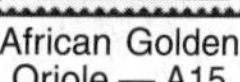

African Golden Oriole — A15

Baobab Tree — A16

Designs: 2c, African hoopoe. 2½c, Scarlet-chested sunbird. 3½c, Cape widow bird (Yellow bishop). 5c, Swallow-tailed bee-eater. 7½c, Gray hornbill. 10c, Red-headed weaver. 12½c, Brown-hooded kingfisher. 20c, Woman musician. 35c, Woman grinding corn. 50c, Bechuana ox. 1r, Lion. 2r, Police camel patrol.

Perf. 14x14½, 14½x14

1961, Oct. 2 Photo. Wmk. 314

180 A15 1c lilac, blk & yel 1.75 .55
181 A15 2c pale ol, blk & org 2.00 *3.25*
182 A15 2½c bis, blk, grn & dp car 1.75 .20
183 A15 3½c pink, blk & yel 2.25 1.75
184 A15 5c dl org, blk, grn & bl 3.75 1.10
185 A15 7½c yel grn, blk, red & brn 2.25 *2.75*
186 A15 10c aqua & multi 2.25 .70
187 A15 12½c gray, yel, red & blue 20.00 6.50
188 A15 20c gray & brn 1.10 1.10
189 A16 25c yel & dk brn 1.40 1.10
190 A15 35c dp org & ultra 1.00 *2.75*
191 A16 50c lt ol grn & sep 1.00 *2.75*
192 A15 1r ocher & black 3.50 3.00
193 A15 2r blue & brn 21.00 10.50
Nos. 180-193 (14) 65.00 38.00

Freedom from Hunger Issue

Common Design Type

1963, June 4 ***Perf. 14x14½***

194 CD314 12½c green .50 .50

Red Cross Centenary Issue

Common Design Type

1963, Sept. 2 Litho. ***Perf. 13***

195 CD315 2½c black & red .20 .20
196 CD315 12½c ultra & red .80 .80

Shakespeare Issue

Common Design Type

1964, Apr. 23 Photo. ***Perf. 14x14½***

197 CD316 12½c red brown .30 .30

Notwani River Dam, Gaberones Water Supply — A17

Wmk. 314

1965, Mar. 1 Photo. ***Perf. 14½***

198 A17 2½c dark red & gold .20 .20
199 A17 5c deep ultra & gold .20 .20
200 A17 12½c brown & gold .25 .30
201 A17 25c emerald & gold .35 .55
Nos. 198-201 (4) 1.00 1.25

Internal self-government, Mar. 1, 1965.

ITU Issue

Common Design Type

Perf. 11x11½

1965, May 17 Litho. Wmk. 314

202 CD317 2½c ver & dl yel .20 .20
203 CD317 12½c red lil & pale brn .70 .70

Intl. Cooperation Year Issue

Common Design Type

1965, Oct. 25 ***Perf. 14½***

204 CD318 1c bl grn & claret .20 .20
205 CD318 12½c lt vio & grn .75 .75

Churchill Memorial Issue

Common Design Type

1966, Jan. 24 Photo. ***Perf. 14***

Design in Black, Gold and Carmine Rose

206 CD319 1c bright blue .20 *.50*
207 CD319 2½c green .45 .20
208 CD319 12½c brown .90 .50
209 CD319 20c violet .95 .80
Nos. 206-209 (4) 2.50 2.00

Haslar Smoke Generator — A18

Wmk. 314

1966, June 1 Photo. ***Perf. 14½***

210 A18 2½c shown .20 .20
211 A18 5c Bugler .20 .20
212 A18 15c Gun site .40 .40
213 A18 35c Regimental cap badge .85 .85
Nos. 210-213 (4) 1.65 1.65

25th anniv. of the Bechuanaland Pioneers and Gunners.

POSTAGE DUE STAMPS

Postage Due Stamps of Great Britain Overprinted

On Stamp of 1914-22

1926 Wmk. 33 *Perf. 14x14½*

J1 D1 1p carmine 4.75 *60.00*

On Stamps of 1924-30

Wmk. 35

J2 D1 ½p emerald 4.75 *90.00*

Overprinted

J3 D1 2p black brown 8.50 *100.00*
Nos. J1-J3 (3) 18.00 *250.00*
Set, never hinged 30.00

D2

1932 Wmk. 4 Typo. *Perf. 14½*

J4 D2 ½p olive green 7.00 *42.50*
J5 D2 1p carmine rose 8.50 *11.00*
J6 D2 2p dull violet 10.50 *47.50*
Nos. J4-J6 (3) 26.00 *101.00*
Set, never hinged 30.00

Catalogue values for unused stamps in this section, from this point to the end of the section, are for Never Hinged items.

Nos. J4-J6 Surcharged

Type I

Type II

1961, Feb. 14

J7 D2 1c on 1p car rose, II .20 *1.75*
a. Type I .30 *.60*
b. Double surcharge, II 140.00
J8 D2 2c on 2p dull vio, II .30 *2.00*
a. Type I .35 *1.75*
J9 D2 5c on ½p ol green, I .50 *.75*
Nos. J7-J9 (3) 1.00 4.50

Nos. J7, J7a, J8 and J8a are on chalky paper. Nos. J7 and J8 printed on ordinary paper sell for much more.

Denominations in Cents

1961 Wmk. 4 *Perf. 14*

J10 D2 1c carmine rose .20 *2.00*
J11 D2 2c dull violet .20 *1.00*
J12 D2 5c olive green .40 *1.25*
Nos. J10-J12 (3) .80 *4.25*

BELARUS

ˌbē-lə-ˈrüs

(Byelorussia)

(White Russia)

LOCATION — Eastern Europe, bounded by Russia, Latvia, Lithuania and Poland
GOVT. — Independent republic, member of the Commonwealth of Independent States
AREA — 80,134 sq. mi.
POP. — 10,401,784 (1999 est.)
CAPITAL — Minsk

With the breakup of the Soviet Union on Dec. 26, 1991, Belarus and ten former Soviet republics established the Commonwealth of Independent States.

100 Kopecks = 1 Ruble

Catalogue values for all unused stamps in this country are for Never Hinged items.

Five denominations, perf and imperf, of this design produced in 1920 were not put in use. Forgeries abound.

Cross of Ephrosinia of Polotsk — A1

1992, Mar. 20 Litho. *Perf. 12x12½*

1 A1 1r multicolored .35 .20

For surcharge see No. 230.

R.R. Schurma (1892-1978), Composer A2

1992, Apr. 10 Photo. *Perf. 12x11½*

2 A2 20k blue & black .25 .20

For surcharge see No. 203.

Arms of Polotsk — A3

Designs: No. 13, Stag jumping fence. No. 14, Man's head, sword.

1992-94 Photo. *Perf. 12x11½*

11 A3 2r shown .20 .20

Perf. 12x12½

12 A3 25r Minsk .20 .20
13 A3 700r Grodno .20 .20
14 A3 700r Vitebsk .20 .20
Nos. 11-14 (4) .80 .80

Issued: 2r, 6/9/92; 25r, 11/11/93; #13, 14, 10/17/94.

This is an expanding set. Numbers will change if necessary.

National Symbols A4

No. 15, Natl. arms. No. 16, Map, flag.

1992, Aug. 31 Litho. *Perf. 12x12½*

15 A4 5r black, red & yellow .50 .40
16 A4 5r multicolored .50 .40

For surcharges see Nos. 55-58, 61-64.

No. 1 Overprinted

Cross of Ephrosinia of Polotsk — A5

A5 illustration reduced.

1992, Sept. 25 Litho. *Perf. 12x12½*

17 A1 1r on #1 multi .20 .20

Souvenir Sheet

Perf. 12

18 A5 5r multicolored .90 .75

Orthodox Church in Belarus, 1000th anniv.
No. 18, imperf, was issued Feb. 15, 1993.
For surcharges see Nos. 59-60, 65-66.

Buildings A6

Designs: No. 19, Church of Boris Gleb, Grodno, 12th cent. No. 20, World Castle, 16th cent. No. 21, Nyasvizh Castle, 16th-19th cent. No. 22, Kamyanets Tower, 12th-13th cent, vert. No. 23, Church of Ephrosinia of Polotsk, 12th cent., vert. No. 24, Calvinist Church, Zaslaw, 16th cent., vert.

1992, Oct. 15 Litho. *Perf. 12*

19 A6 2r multicolored .20 .20
20 A6 2r multicolored .20 .20
21 A6 2r multicolored .20 .20
22 A6 2r multicolored .20 .20
23 A6 2r multicolored .20 .20
24 A6 2r multicolored .20 .20
Nos. 19-24 (6) 1.20 1.20

Centuries of construction are in Roman numerals.

Natl. Arms — A7

1992-94 Litho. *Perf. 12x12½*

25 A7 30k light blue .20 .20
26 A7 45k olive green .20 .20
27 A7 50k green .20 .20
28 A7 1r brown .20 .20
29 A7 2r red brown .20 .20
30 A7 3r org yellow .20 .20
31 A7 5r blue .20 .20
32 A7 10r red .35 .25
33 A7 15r violet .25 .25
34 A7 25r yellow green .40 .30
35 A7 50r bright pink .20 .20
36 A7 100r henna brown .25 .25
37 A7 150r plum .40 .40
38 A7 200r blue green .20 .20
39 A7 300r salmon pink .20 .20
40 A7 600r light lilac .20 .20
40A A7 1000r rose carmine .25 .25
40B A7 3000r gray blue .40 .30
Nos. 25-40B (18) 4.50 4.20

Issued: 30k, 45k, 50k, 11/10; 1r-3r, 10r, 1/4/93; 5r, 15r, 25r, 2/9/93; 50r, 100r, 150r, 6/16/93; 200r-3,000r, 12/28/94; others, 1992.

For surcharges see #141-142, 211A-212.

Ceramics A8

Designs: No. 41, Pitcher and bowl. No. 42, Four pieces on tree branches. No. 43, Two large pitchers. No. 44, One large pitcher.

1992, Dec. 24 Litho. *Perf. 11½*

41 A8 1r multicolored .20 .20
42 A8 1r multicolored .20 .20
43 A8 1r multicolored .20 .20
44 A8 1r multicolored .20 .20
Nos. 41-44 (4) .80 .80

M. I. Garetzky (1893-1938), Writer — A9

1993, June 22 Photo. *Perf. 12x11½*

45 A9 50r magenta .25 .25

Straw Figures A10

Designs: 5r, Chickens. 10r, Child, mother, vert. 15r, Woman, vert. 25r, Man with scythe, woman with rake, vert.

Perf. 12x11½, 11½x12

1993, Apr. 22 Litho.

47 A10 5r multicolored .20 .20
48 A10 10r multicolored .25 .20
49 A10 15r multicolored .25 .20
50 A10 25r multicolored .30 .20
Nos. 47-50 (4) 1.00 .80

First World Congress of White Russians — A11

1993, July 8 Litho. *Perf. 12*

51 A11 50r multicolored .90 .90

Europa — A12

Paintings by Chagall: No. 52, Promenade, vert. No. 53, Man Over Vitebsk. 2500r, Allegory.

1993, Oct. 12 Litho. *Perf. 14*

52 A12 1500r multicolored *2.75 2.75*
53 A12 1500r multicolored *2.75 2.75*
a. Pair, #52-53 *6.00 6.00*

Souvenir Sheet

54 A12 2500r multicolored *45.00 45.00*

Nos. 15-16, 18 Surcharged

a

"b" overprint is the same as "a," but with "WINTER PRE-OLYMPICS GAMES LILLEHAMMER, NORWAY" in five lines at top. Size and location of surcharge varies.

1993, Oct. 15 Litho. *Perf. 12x12½*

55 A4(a) 1500r on 5r #15 *2.50 2.50*
56 A4(b) 1500r on 5r #15 *2.50 2.50*
a. Pair, #55-56 *5.00 5.00*
57 A4(a) 1500r on 5r #16 *2.50 2.50*
58 A4(b) 1500r on 5r #16 *2.50 2.50*
a. Pair, #57-58 *5.00 5.00*
Nos. 55-58 (4) *10.00 10.00*

Souvenir Sheets

Perf. 12

59 A5(a) 1500r on 5r #18 *2.00 2.00*
60 A5(b) 1500r on 5r #18 *2.00 2.00*

No. 59 exists imperf. The status of No. 60 is in question.

Nos. 15-16, 18 Surcharged

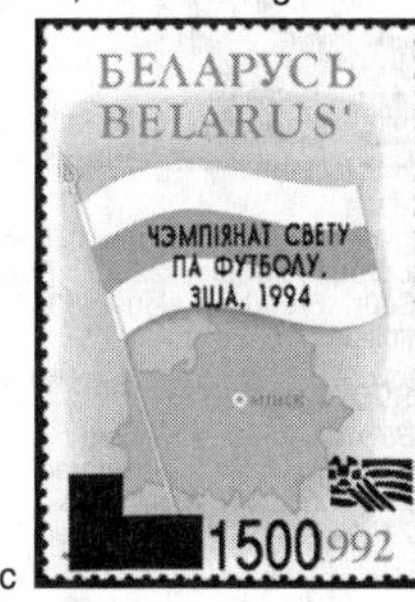

c

"d" overprint is the same as "c," but with "WORLD CUP/USA 94" at top. Size and location of surcharge varies.

1993, Oct. 15 Litho. *Perf. 12x12½*

61 A4(c) 1500r on 5r #15 *2.50 2.50*
62 A4(d) 1500r on 5r #15 *2.50 2.50*
a. Pair, #61-62 *5.00 5.00*
63 A4(c) 1500r on 5r #16 *2.50 2.50*
64 A4(d) 1500r on 5r #16 *2.50 2.50*
a. Pair, #63-64 *5.00 5.00*
Nos. 61-64 (4) *10.00 10.00*

Souvenir Sheets

Perf. 12

65 A5(c) 1500r on 5r #18 *2.00 2.00*
66 A5(d) 1500r on 5r #18 *2.00 2.00*

The status of Nos. 65-66 are in question.

Stansilavski Church A13

1993, Nov. 24 Litho. *Perf. 12*

67 A13 150r multicolored .35 .35

For surcharge see No. 242.

Famous People A14

Designs: 50r, Kastus Kalinovsky, led 1863 independence movement. No. 69, Prince Rogvold of Polotsk, map of Polotsk. No. 70, Princess Rogneda, daughter of Rogvold, fortress. 100r, Statue of Simon Budny (1530-93), writer and printer, vert.

1993 *Perf. 12x12½, 12½x12*

68 A14 50r multicolored .20 .20
69 A14 75r multicolored .20 .20
70 A14 75r multicolored .20 .20
71 A14 100r multicolored .25 .25
Nos. 68-71 (4) .85 .85

Issued: 50r, 12/29; 75r, 12/30; 100r, 12/31.

Nos. 27, 29, 30 Surcharged

1994, Feb. 1 Photo. *Perf. 12x12½*

72 A7 15r on 30k light green .20 .20
73 A7 25r on 45k olive green .20 .20
74 A7 50r on 50k green .20 .20
Nos. 72-74 (3) .60 .60

Birds — A15

1994, Jan. 19 Litho. *Perf. 11½*

75 A15 20r Aguila chrysaetos .20 .20
76 A15 40r Cygnus olor .20 .20
77 A15 40r Alcedo atthis .20 .20
a. Block of 3, #75-77 + label .60 .60

See #87-89. For surcharge see #303.

Six World Wildlife Fund labels with 1000r denominations depicting 3 different animals and 3 different birds exist. They were not valid for postage.

Liberation of Soviet Areas, 50th Anniv. A16

Battle maps and: a, Katyusha rockets, liberation of Russia. b, Fighter planes, liberation of Ukraine. c, Combined offensive, liberation of Belarus.

1994, July 3 Litho. *Perf. 12*

78 A16 500r Block of 3 + label .80 .75

See Russia No. 6213, Ukraine No. 195.

1994 Winter Olympics, Lillehammer A17

1994, Aug. 30 Litho. *Perf. 12x12½*

79 A17 1000r Speed skating .20 .20
80 A17 1000r Women's figure skating .20 .20
81 A17 1000r Hockey .20 .20
82 A17 1000r Cross-country skiing .20 .20
83 A17 1000r Biathlon .20 .20
Nos. 79-83 (5) 1.00 1.00

Painters — A18

Designs: No. 84, Farmer, oxen in field, by Ferdinand Rushchyts. No. 85, Knight on horseback, by Jasev Drazdovich. No. 86, Couple walking up path, by Petra Sergievich. Illustration reduced

1994, July 18 Litho. *Perf. 12*

84 A18 300r multicolored .20 .20
85 A18 300r multicolored .20 .20
86 A18 300r multicolored .20 .20
Nos. 84-86 (3) .60 .60

For overprint see No. 127.

Bird Type of 1994

1994, Sept. 30 *Perf. 11½*

87 A15 300r like #75 .20 .20
88 A15 400r like #76 .20 .20
89 A15 400r like #77 .20 .20
Nos. 87-89 (3) .60 .60

Ilya Yefimovich Repin (1844-1930), Ukrainian Painter — A19

#90, Self-portrait. #91, Repin Museum.

1994, Oct. 31 Litho. *Perf. 12x12½*

90 1000r multicolored .30 .30
91 1000r multicolored .30 .30
a. A19 Pair, #90-91 .60 .60

Churches A20

Designs: No. 92, Sacred Consolidated Church, Sinkavitsch, 16th cent. No. 93, Sts. Peter and Paul Cathedral, Gomel, 19th cent.

1994, Oct. 20 Litho. *Perf. 12*

92 A20 700r multicolored .20 .20
93 A20 700r multicolored .20 .20

Kosciuszko Uprising, Bicent. (in 1994) — A21

Battle scene and: No. 94, Tomasz Vaishetcki (1754-1816). No. 95, Jakov Jasinski (1761-94). No. 96, Tadeusz Kosziuszko (1746-1817). No. 97, Mikhail K. Aginski (1765-1833).

1995, Jan. 11 *Perf. 12½x12*

94 A21 600r multicolored .20 .20
95 A21 600r multicolored .20 .20
96 A21 1000r multicolored .20 .20
97 A21 1000r multicolored .20 .20
Nos. 94-97 (4) .80 .80

End of World War II, 50th Anniv. — A22

1995, May 4 Litho. *Perf. 13½*

98 A22 180r multicolored .20 .20
99 A22 600r multicolored .20 .20

A23

A24

1995, May 7 *Perf. 14*

100 A23 600r A Popov .20 .20

Radio, cent. Exists imperf.

1995-96 Litho. *Perf. 13x14*

102 A24 180r olive brown & red .20 .20
103 A24 200r gray green & bister .20 .20
105 A24 280r green & blue .20 .20
109 A24 600r plum & bister .20 .20
Nos. 102-109 (4) .80 .80

No. 102 exists imperf.

Issued: 180r, 5/10/95; 280r, 5/18/95; 600r, 8/29/95; 200r, 1/30/96.

This is an expanding set. Numbers may change.

Ivan Chersky (1845-92), Geographer A25

1995, May 15 Litho. *Perf. 13½x14*

113 A25 600r multicolored .20 .20

Exists imperf.

A26

Traditional Costumes: 600r, Woman wearing shawl, coat, ankle length skirt, man with long coat. 1200r, Woman wearing shawl & apron holding child, man wearing vest, knickers.

1995, July 13 Litho. *Perf. 14½x14*

114 A26 180r multicolored .20 .20
115 A26 600r multicolored .20 .20
116 A26 1200r multicolored .25 .25
Nos. 114-116 (3) .65 .65

See Nos. 164-167, 214-216.

A27

1995, July 20 *Perf. 12*

World Wildlife Fund: Various pictures of a beaver.

117 A27 300r multi .20 .20
118 A27 450r multi .20 .20
119 A27 450r multi, horiz. .20 .20
120 A27 800r multi, horiz. .40 .40
Nos. 117-120 (4) 1.00 1.00

A28

A29

1995, Aug. 29 Litho. *Perf. 14*

121 A28 600r Book Fair .20 .20

Exists imperf.

1995, Oct. 3 Litho. *Perf. 14*

122 A29 600r Natl. arms .20 .20
123 A29 600r Flag .20 .20

New national symbols. Exist imperf.

UN, 50th Anniv. — A30

1995, Oct. 24 Litho. *Perf. 13½x14*

124 A30 600r bister, black & blue .20 .20

Exists imperf.

Churches A31

Designs: No. 125, Mstislav, 17th-19th cent. No. 126, Kamai, 17th cent.

1995, Nov. 21 *Perf. 14*

125 A31 600r multicolored .20 .20
126 A31 600r multicolored .20 .20

No. 84 Ovptd.

1995, Dec. 27 Litho. *Perf. 12*

127 A18 300r multicolored .20 .20

P. V. Sukhi (1895-1975), Airplane Designer A32

1995, Dec. 27 *Perf. 13½*

128 A32 600r multicolored .20 .20

Wildlife A33

1000r, Lynx lynx. #130, Capreolus capreolus. #131, Ursus arctos. 3000r, Alces alcest. 5000r, Bison bonasus.
10,000r, Cervus elaphus, vert.

1995-96 Litho. *Perf. 14*

129 A33 1000r multi .20 .20
130 A33 2000r multi, vert. .30 .30
131 A33 2000r multi .30 .30
132 A33 3000r multi, vert. .45 .45
133 A33 5000r multi .75 .75
Nos. 129-133 (5) 2.00 2.00

Souvenir Sheet

Imperf

134 A33 10,000r multicolored 1.50 1.50

Issued: #129-133, 2/6/96; #134, 12/29/95.

Famous People — A34

Designs: 600r, L. Sapega (1557-1633), statesman. 1200r, K. Semyanovitch (1600-51), military scholar. 1800r, S. Polotzki (1629-80), writer. Illustration reduced.

1995, Dec. 30 Litho. *Perf. 12*

135 A34 600r multicolored .20 .20
136 A34 1200r multicolored .20 .20
137 A34 1800r multicolored .30 .30
Nos. 135-137 (3) .70 .70

Miniature Sheet

Butterflies — A35

Designs: No. 138a, Apatura iris. b, Lopinga achine. c, Callimorpha dominula. d, Catocala fraxini. e, Papilio machaon. f, Parnassius apollo. g, Ammobiota hebe. h, Colias palaeno.
No. 139, Proserpinus proserpina. No. 140, Vacciniina optilete.

1996, Mar. 29 Litho. *Perf. 14*

138 A35 300r Sheet of 8, #a.-h. 6.50 6.50

Souvenir Sheets

139-140 A35 1000r each 4.00 4.00

Inscribed 1995.

Nos. 28, 34 Surcharged in Green or Red

1996 Litho. *Perf. 12x12½*

141 A7 (B) on 1r #28 (G) .20 .20
142 A7 (A) on 25r #34 (R) .20 .20

Nos. 141-142 were valued at 200r and 400r, respectively, on day of issue.
Issued: #141, 2/28/96; #142, 3/13/96.

Souvenir Sheet

Beaver — A36

Illustration reduced.

1996, Mar. 26 Litho. *Perf. 12½x12*

143 A36 1200r multicolored .25 .25

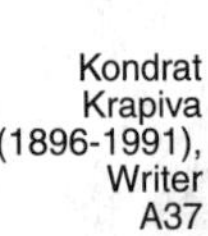

Kondrat Krapiva (1896-1991), Writer A37

1996, Mar. 5 Litho. *Perf. 14x14½*

144 A37 1000r multicolored .20 .20

Chernobyl Disaster, 10th Anniv. A38

Radiation symbol and: a, Eye. b, Leaf showing contamination. c, Boarded-up window.

1996, Apr. 10 Litho. *Perf. 14*

145 A38 1000r Block of 3, #a.-c. + label .50 .50

Coat of Arms — A39

1996, May 6 Litho. *Perf. 13½*

146 A39 100r blue & black .20 .20
147 A39 500r green & black .20 .20
148 A39 600r ver & black .20 .20
149 A39 1000r org & black .20 .20
150 A39 1500r dp lil rose & blk .20 .20
151 A39 1800r violet & black .20 .20
152 A39 2200r rose vio & blk .20 .20
153 A39 3300r yellow & blk .25 .20
154 A39 5000r grn bl & blk .35 .25
155 A39 10,000r ap grn & blk .75 .50
156 A39 30,000r brn & black 2.25 1.50
157 A39 50,000r red brn & blk 3.75 2.50
Nos. 146-157 (12) 8.75 6.35

See Nos. 182, 196-201.

Agreement with Russia A40

1996, June 14 *Perf. 13½x14*

158 A40 1500r multicolored .25 .25

1996 Summer Olympic Games, Atlanta A41

1996, July 15 Litho. *Perf. 14*

159 A41 3000r Rhythmic gymnastics .30 .30
160 A41 3000r Discus .30 .30
161 A41 3000r Wrestling .30 .30
162 A41 3000r Weight lifting .30 .30
Nos. 159-162 (4) 1.20 1.20

Souvenir Sheet

Imperf

163 A41 5000r Shooting, vert. .65 .65

No. 163 has simulated perforations.

Regional Costume Type of 1995

Couples in traditional 19th cent. costumes: 1800r, Kapilska-Kletzky region. 2200r, David-Gorodok-Turai region. 3300r, Kobrin region. 5000r, Naralyan region.

1996, Aug. 13 Litho. *Perf. 14*

164 A26 1800r multicolored .20 .20
165 A26 2200r multicolored .25 .25
166 A26 3300r multicolored .30 .30
Nos. 164-166 (3) .75 .75

Souvenir Sheet

Imperf

167 A26 5000r multicolored .75 .75

Medicinal Plants — A42

No. 168, Sanguisorba officinaus. No. 169, Acorus calamus. 2200r, Potentilla erecta. 3300r, Frangula alnus. 5000r, Menyanthes trifoliata.

1996, Aug. 15 *Perf. 14x13½*

168 A42 1500r multicolored .20 .20
169 A42 1500r multicolored .20 .20
170 A42 2200r multicolored .20 .20
171 A42 3300r multicolored .30 .30
Nos. 168-171 (4) .90 .90

Souvenir Sheet

Imperf

172 A42 5000r multicolored .75 .75

Birds A44

No. 173: a, Ardea cinerea. b, Ciconia nigra. c, Phalacrocorax caroo. d, Ciconia ciconia. e, Larus ridibundus. f, Gallinago gallinago. g, Chlidonias leucopterus. h, Remiz pendulinus. i, Botaurus stellaris. j, Fulica atra. k, Ixobrychus minutus. l, Alcedo atthts.

No. 174: a, Anas crecca. b, Anas strepera. c, Anas acuta. d, Anas platyrhynchos. e, Aythya marila. f, Clangula hyemalis. g, Anas clypeata. h, Anas querquedula. i, Anas penelope. j, Arthya nyroca. k, Bucephala clangula.

l, Mergus merganser. m, Mergus albellus. n, Aythya fuligula. o, Mergus serrator. p, Aythya ferina.
No. 175, Aythya ferina, diff. No. 176, Gallinago gallinago, diff.

1996, Sept. 10 Litho. *Perf. 14*
173 A44 400r Sheet of 12, #a.-l. 4.00 4.00
174 A44 400r Sheet of 16, #a.-p. 4.00 4.00

Souvenir Sheets

175-176 A44 1000r each 3.25 3.25

Grammar Book, 1596 — A45

1996, Sept. 19 Litho. *Perf. 14x13½*
177 A45 1500r multicolored .25 .25

Churches A46

1996, Sept. 24 *Perf. 14x14½*
178 A46 3300r Pinsk .35 .35
179 A46 3300r Mogilev, 17th cent. .35 .35

Mikola Shchakatskin (1896-1940), Art Critic — A47

1996, Oct. 16
180 A47 2000r multicolored .25 .25

Minsk Telephone Station, Cent. A48

1996, Nov. 14
181 A48 2000r multicolored .25 .25

Natl. Arms Type of 1996

1996, Nov. 21 Litho. *Perf. 13½x14*
182 A39 200r gray green & black .20 .20

Pres. Aleksandr G. Lukashenka, Natl. Flag — A49

1996, Dec. 6 Litho. *Perf. 13½*
183 A49 2500r multicolored .25 .25

Famous Men — A50

Designs: No. 184, Kyril Turovski (1130-81), Bishop of Turov. No. 185, Mikola Gusovski (1470-1533), writer. No. 186, Mikolaj Radziwil (1515-65), chancellor of Lithuania.

1996, Dec. 17 *Perf. 13½*
184 A50 3000r multicolored .30 .30
185 A50 3000r multicolored .30 .30
186 A50 3000r multicolored .30 .30
Nos. 184-186 (3) .90 .90

New Year — A51

1500r, Christmas tree, buildings in Minsk.

1996, Dec. 21 *Perf. 14*
187 A51 1500r multicolored .20 .20
188 A51 2000r multicolored, vert. .20 .20

Natl. Museum of Art, Minsk — A52

Icons: No. 189, Madonna and Child, Smolensk, 16th cent. No. 190, Paraskeva, 16th cent. No. 191, Ilya, 17th cent. No. 192, Three saints, 18th cent.
5000r, Birth of Christ, by Peter Yacijevitsch, 1649.

1996, Dec. 26 *Perf. 13½*
189 A52 3500r multicolored .35 .35
190 A52 3500r multicolored .35 .35
191 A52 3500r multicolored .35 .35
192 A52 3500r multicolored .35 .35
Nos. 189-192 (4) 1.40 1.40

Souvenir Sheet

Imperf

193 A46 5000r multicolored .60 .60

Georgi K. Zhukov (1896-1974), Soviet Marshal A53

1997, Jan. 3 *Perf. 13½*
194 A53 2000r multicolored .30 .30

Kupala Natl. Theater, Minsk — A54

1997, Jan. 3 *Perf. 13½x14*
195 A54 3500r multicolored .40 .40

Coat of Arms Type of 1996

1997 Litho. *Perf. 13½x14*
196 A39 400r lt brown & black .20 .20
197 A39 800r dull blue & black .20 .20
198 A39 1500r brt blue & black .45 .45
199 A39 2000r apple green & black .60 .60
200 A39 2500r dk blue & black
201 A39 3000r brown & black .45 .45

Issued: 400r, 2000r, 1/9; 1500r, 1/16; 800r, 2500r, 3000r, 9/22.

V.K. Byalynitsky-Birulya (1872-1957), Painter — A55

1997, Feb. 26 *Perf. 14*
202 A55 2000r multicolored .30 .30

No. 2 Surcharged in Gray

1997, Mar. 10 Photo. *Perf. 12x11½*
203 A2 3500r on 20k bl & blk .50 .50

Fish — A56

2000r, Salmo trutta. 3000r, Vimba vimba. #206, Thymallus thymallus. #207, Barbus barbus.
5000r, Acipenser ruthenus.

1997, Apr. 10 Litho. *Perf. 13½x14*
204 A56 2000r multicolored .25 .25
205 A56 3000r multicolored .30 .30
206 A56 4500r multicolored .50 .50
207 A56 4500r multicolored .50 .50
Nos. 204-207 (4) 1.55 1.55

Souvenir Sheet

208 A56 5000r multicolored .75 .75

Intl. Conference on Sustainable Development of Countries with Economies in Transition — A57

Designs: 3000r, Earth with "SOS" formed in atmosphere. 4500r, Hand above flora and fauna.

1997, Apr. 16 *Perf. 14x14½*
209 A57 3000r multicolored .40 .40
210 A57 4500r multicolored .60 .60
a. Pair, #209-210 + label 1.00 1.00

Entry into UPU, 50th Anniv. — A58

1997, May 13 *Perf. 14½x14*
211 A58 3000r multicolored .50 .50

Nos. 28-29 Surcharged in Violet Blue

1997 Litho. *Perf. 12x12½*
211A A7 100r on 1r brown *5.00 5.00*
212 A7 100r on 2r red brown .20 .20

Issued: 2r, 5/22.

World War II Liberation Day, July 3 — A59

1997, June 26 *Perf. 14½x14*
213 A59 3000r multicolored .90 .90

Traditional Costume Type

Men and women in 19th cent. costumes, regions: 2000r, Dzisna. 3000r, Navagrudak. 4500r, Byhau.

1997, July 10
214 A26 2000r multicolored .55 .55
215 A26 3000r multicolored .85 .85
216 A26 4500r multicolored 1.25 1.25
Nos. 214-216 (3) 2.65 2.65

Book Printing in Belarus, 480th Anniv. — A60

#217, Text, Vilnius period. #218, Text, Prague period. 4000r, F. Skorina (1488-1535), Polatsk period. 7500r, F. Skorina, Krakow period.

1997, Sept. 7 *Perf. 13½*
217 A60 3000r shown .85 .85
218 A60 3000r gray, black & red .85 .85
219 A60 4000r gray, black & red 1.10 1.10
220 A60 7500r gray, black & red 2.00 2.00
Nos. 217-220 (4) *4.80* 4.80

Pinsk Jesuit College A61

1997, Sept. 13 *Perf. 14x14½*
221 A61 3000r multicolored .85 .85

National Library, 75th Anniv. A62

1997, Sept. 15
222 A62 3000r multicolored .90 .90

Belarus School for the Blind, Cent. A63

1997, Sept. 28 Litho. *Perf. 14x14¼*
223 A63 3000r multicolored .45 .45

Intl. Children's Day — A64

1997, Sept. 28 Litho. *Perf. 14x14½*
224 A64 3000r multicolored .85 .85

Fight Against AIDS — A65

1997, Oct. 14 *Perf. 14½x14*
225 A65 4000r multicolored 1.10 1.10

Farm Tractors A66

3300r, Belarus "1221." 4400r, First wheel tractor, 1953. #228, Belarus "952." #229, Belarus "680."

1997, Oct. 16 *Perf. 14x14½*
226 A66 3300r multicolored 1.00 1.00
227 A66 4400r multicolored 1.25 1.25
228 A66 7500r multicolored 2.00 2.00
229 A66 7500r multicolored 2.00 2.00
a. Sheet, 2 ea #226-229 + label 13.00 13.00
Nos. 226-229 (4) 6.25 6.25

No. 1 Surcharged

1997, Dec. 8 Litho. *Perf. 12x12½*
230 A1 3000r on 1r multi .45 .45

Holiday Greetings A68

1997, Dec. 23 Litho. *Perf. 14x14¼*
231 A68 1400r New Year .20 .20
232 A68 4400r Christmas .50 .50

1998 Winter Olympic Games, Nagano — A69

Designs: a, 2000r, Cross country skiing. b, 3300r, Ice hockey. c, 4400r, Biathlon. d, 7500r, Freestyle skiing.

1998, Feb. 3 Litho. *Perf. 13½*
233 A69 Block of 4, #a.-d. 2.50

P.M. Mascherov (1918-80), Author — A70

1998, Feb. 12 Litho. *Perf. 13½*
234 A70 2500r multicolored .30 .30

Minsk Automobile Plant — A71

Dump trucks: 1400r, 1947 MAZ-205. 2000r, 1968 MAZ-503B. 3000r, 1977 MAZ-5549. 4400r, 1985 MAZ-5551. 7500r, 1994 MAZ-5516.

1998, Apr. 23 Litho. *Perf. 13½*
235 A71 1400r multicolored .20 .20
236 A71 2000r multicolored .25 .25
237 A71 3000r multicolored .40 .40
238 A71 4400r multicolored .55 .55
239 A71 7500r multicolored .95 .95
a. Souvenir sheet, #235-239 + label 2.50 2.50
Nos. 235-239 (5) 2.35 2.35

A72 A73

1998, May 5 Litho. *Perf. 14*
240 A72 15,000r multicolored 1.00 1.00

Europa. Town of Nesvizh, 775th Anniv.

1998, May 20 Litho. *Perf. 14*
241 A73 8600r multicolored 1.10 1.10

Adam Mickiewicz (1798-1855), poet.

No. 67 Surcharged in Silver with Post Horn, New Value and Cyrillic Text

1998, May 22 *Perf. 12*
242 A13 8600r on 150r multi 1.10 1.10

St. Petersburt-Mahilyou Post Route, 225th anniv.

A74 A75

Songbirds from Red Book of Belarus: 1500r, Luscinia svecica. 3200r, Remiz pendulinus. 3800r, Acrocephalus paludicola. 5300r, Locustella luscinioides. 8600r, Parus cyanus.

1998, May 29 *Perf. 14*
243 A74 1500r multicolored .20 .20
244 A74 3200r multicolored .40 .40
245 A74 3800r multicolored .50 .50
246 A74 5300r multicolored .65 .65
247 A74 8600r multicolored 1.10 1.10
a. Sheet, 2 each #243-247 5.75 5.75
Nos. 243-247 (5) 2.85 2.85

1998 *Perf. 13½x14*

Mills, Musical Instruments: 100r, Water-powered mill. 200r, Windmill. 500r, Stork. 1000r, Bison. 2000r, Christmas Star. 3200r, Dulcimer. 5000r, Church, Synkovichy. 5300r, Hurdy-gurdy. 10,000r, Flaming wheel.

248 A75 100r green & black .20 .20
249 A75 200r brown & black .20 .20
250 A75 500r bl, lt blu & blk .20 .20
251 A75 1000r grn, lt grn & blk .20 .20
252 A75 2000r bl, lt bl & blk .20 .20
253 A75 3200r ap grn & blk *1.00 1.00*
254 A75 5000r bl, lt bl & blk .20 .20
255 A75 5300r bis, blk & buff *1.75 1.75*
256 A75 10,000r org, lt org & blk .30 .30
Nos. 248-256 (9) *4.25 4.25*

Issued: 100r, 200r, 7/1; 3200r, 5300r, 6/23; 2000r, 10,000r, 8/5;
See Nos. 282-288, 331-335, 338-339, 361.

Belarussian Auto Works (BelAZ), 50th Anniv. — A76

Designs: 1500r, Front end loader.
Large quarry truck models: 3200r, #75131. 3800r, #75303. 5300r, #75483. 8600r, #755.

1998, Aug. 12 *Perf. 14x14½*
259 A76 1500r multicolored .20 .20
260 A76 3200r multicolored .20 .20
261 A76 3800r multicolored .20 .20
262 A76 5300r multicolored .20 .20
263 A76 8600r multicolored .20 .20
a. Sheet of 5, #259-263 + label .80 .80

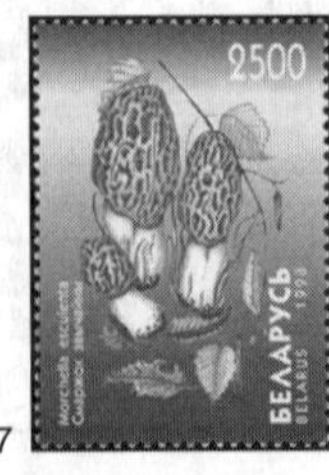

A77

Mushrooms: 2500r, Morchella esculenta. 3800r, Morchella conica. 4600r, Macrolepiota rhacodes. 5800r, Marcrolepiota procera. 9400r, Coprinus comatus.

1998, Sept. 10 Litho. *Perf. 14¼x14*
264 A77 2500r multicolored .20 .20
265 A77 3800r multicolored .20 .20
266 A77 4600r multicolored .20 .20
267 A77 5800r multicolored .20 .20
268 A77 9400r multicolored .25 .25
Nos. 264-268 (5) 1.05 1.05

Tete beche pairs

264a A77 2500r .20 .20
265a A77 3800r .20 .20
266a A77 4600r .20 .20
267a A77 5800r .30 .30
268a A77 9400r .50 .50

See Nos. 316-320.

A78

1998, Oct. 6 *Perf. 13½*

Wooden Sculptures: 3400r, Naversha, 12-13th cent. 3800r, Archangel Michael, 1470-1480. 5800r, Prophet Zacharias, 1642-1646. 9400r, Madonna and Child, 16th cent.

269 A78 3400r multicolored .20 .20
270 A78 3800r multicolored .20 .20
271 A78 5800r multicolored .20 .20
272 A78 9400r multicolored .25 .25
Nos. 269-272 (4) .85 .85

World Stamp Day — A79

1998, Oct. 9 *Perf. 14x14½*
273 A79 5500r multicolored .20 .20

Paintings from Natl. Art Museum — A80

3000r, "Kalozha" (church), by V.K. Tsvirko (1913-93). 3500r, "Corner Living Room," by S.U. Zhukovsky (1875-1944). 5000r, "Winter Dream," by V.K. Byalynitsky-Birulya (1872-1957). 5500r, "Portrait of a Girl," by I.I. Alyashkevich (1777-1830). 10,000r, "Woman with a Bowl of Fruit," by I.F. Hrutski (1810-85).

1998, Oct. 20 *Perf. 13½*
274 A80 3000r multi .20 .20
275 A80 3500r multi .20 .20
276 A80 5000r multi .20 .20
277 A80 5500r multi, vert. .20 .20
278 A80 10,000r multi, vert. .30 .20
Nos. 274-278 (5) 1.10 1.00

A81 A82

1998, Nov. 25 *Perf. 14½x14*
279 A81 7100r multicolored .20 .20

Universal Declaration of Human Rights, 50th anniv.

1998, Nov. 30

Christmas and New Year: No. 280, Girl wearing short yellow coat, rabbit, log cabin.

No. 281, Rabbit, girl wearing long fur-trimmed pink coat, hat.

280 A82 5500r multicolored .20 .20
281 A82 5500r multicolored .20 .20
a. Pair, #280-281 .20 .20

Type of 1998

Designs: 800r, Church. 1500r, Dulcimer. 3000r, Hurdy-gurdy. 30,000r, Water-powered mill. 50,000r, Windmill. 100,000r, Exhibition center, Minsk, horiz. 500,000r, Dancers.

Perf. 13½x14, 14x13½

1998-99 Litho.

282 A75 800r red lil, pale lil & blk .20 .20
283 A75 1500r golden brn, buff & blk .20 .20
284 A75 3000r yel, pale yel & blk .20 .20
285 A75 30,000r Prus bl, lt bl & blk .25 .25
286 A75 50,000r org, pale org & blk .40 .40
287 A75 100,000r brt pink & blk .80 .80
288 A75 500,000r brn & blk 3.50 3.50
Nos. 282-288 (7) 5.55 5.55

Issued: 800r, 2/5/99; 1500r, 3000r, 12/22/98; 30,000r, 50,000r, 4/14/99; 100,000r, 4/22/99; 500,000r, 6/25/99.

Statues of Aleksander Pushkin and Adam Mickiewicz, St. Petersburg — A95

1999, Jan. 20 Litho. *Perf. 13½*

294 A95 15,300r multi .20 .20

Trucks Made In Minsk — A96

10,000r, Model 8007. 15,000r, Model 543M rocket launcher. No. 297, Model 7907. No. 298, Model 543m with radar.

No. 299: a, 50,000r, Model 7917. b, 150,000r, Model 74135.

1999, Feb. 23

295 A96 10,000r multi .20 .20
296 A96 15,000r multi .20 .20
297 A96 30,000r multi .30 .30
298 A96 30,000r multi .30 .30
Nos. 295-298 (4) 1.00 1.00

Souvenir Sheet

299 A96 Sheet of 6, #295-298, 299a, 299b + 3 labels 3.25 3.25

No. 295 printed in sheets of 8.
See Nos. 322-323.

Glassware in National History and Culture Museum A97

1999, Mar. 4

300 A97 30,000r Goblet .30 .30
301 A97 30,000r Three pieces .30 .30
302 A97 100,000r Lamp .90 .90
Nos. 300-302 (3) 1.50 1.50

No. 77a Surcharged in Red

1999, Apr. 26 Litho. *Perf. 11½*

303 A15 150,000r on No. 77a 1.40 1.40

Europa — A98

Nature Reserves: No. 304, Berezina, 1925. No. 305, Belovezhskaya Forest, 1939.

1999, Apr. 27 Litho. *Perf. 13½*

304 A98 150,000r multicolored 1.25 1.25
305 A98 150,000r multicolored 1.25 1.25

Regional Architecture — A99

1999, June 10 Litho. *Perf. 13½*

306 A99 50,000r Well .40 .40
307 A99 50,000r House .40 .40
308 A99 100,000r Windmill .80 .80
Nos. 306-308 (3) 1.60 1.60

No. 306 printed in sheets of 8.

Paintings A100

30,000r, Portrait of Y. M. Pen, by A. M. Brazer. 60,000r, St. Anthony's Church, Vitebsk, by S. B. Yudovin. No. 311, Street in Vitebsk, by Y. M. Pen. No. 312, House in Vitebsk, by M. P. Michalap, horiz.

200,000r, Etching by Marc Chagall.

1999, July 2

309 A100 30,000r multi .20 .20
310 A100 60,000r multi .45 .45
311 A100 100,000r multi .70 .70
312 A100 100,000r multi .70 .70
Nos. 309-312 (4) 2.05 2.05

Souvenir Sheet

313 A100 200,000r multi 1.40 1.40

V. M. Karvat (1958-96), Hero — A101

1999, Aug. 12

314 A101 25,000r multi .20 .20

UPU, 125th Anniv. — A102

Designs: a, Minsk post office, 1954. b, First Minsk post office, 1800.

1999, Aug. 20

315 A102 150,000r Pair, #a.-b. 2.10 2.10

Mushroom Type of 1998

Designs: 30,000r, Flammulina velutipes. 50,000r, Kuehneromyces mutabilis. 75,000r, Lyophyllum connatum. 100,000r, Lyophyllum decastes.

150,000r, Armillariella mellea.

1999, Aug. 21 *Perf. 14¼x14*

316 A77 30,000r multi .20 .20
a. Tete beche pair .40 .40
317 A77 50,000r multi .35 .35
a. Tete beche pair .70 .70
318 A77 75,000r multi .55 .55
a. Tete beche pair 1.10 1.10
319 A77 100,000r multi .70 .70
a. Tete beche pair 1.40 1.40
Nos. 316-319 (4) 1.80 1.80

Souvenir Sheet

320 A77 150,000r multi 1.10 1.10
a. Tete beche pair 2.25 2.25

Left margin of No. 320 is perforated, and sheet contains two labels.

Re-annexation of Western Belarus from Poland, 60th Anniv. — A103

1999, Sept. 17 Litho. *Perf. 13½x14*

321 A103 29,000r multi *.20 .20*

Truck Type of 1999

51,000r, MAZ-6430. 86,000r, MAZ-4370.

1999, Nov. 15 Litho. *Perf. 13½*

322 A96 51,000r multi *.20 .20*
323 A96 86,000r multi *.35 .35*

Children's Art — A104

1999, Nov. 25

324 A104 32,000r shown *.20 .20*
325 A104 59,000r Girl, vert. *.25 .25*

New Year A105

No. 326: a, Bear, snow-covered trees. b, People, snowman.

1999, Nov. 30 *Perf. 14x14¼*

326 A105 30,000r Pair, #a-b, + central label *.25 .25*

Christianity, 2000th Anniv. — A106

Designs: 50r, Spaso-Preobrazhenskaya Church, Polotsk. 75r, St. Atistratig Cathedral, Slutsk. 100r, Rev, Serafim Sorovsky Church, Beloozersk.

2000, Jan. 1 *Perf. 14¼x14*

327 A106 50r multi *.20 .20*
328 A106 75r multi *.30 .30*
329 A106 100r multi *.40 .40*
Nos. 327-329 (3) *.90 .90*

Souvenir Sheet

Christianity, 2000th Anniversary — A107

Designs: a, Mother of God mosaic, St. Sofia, Cathedral, Kiev, 11th cent. b, Christ Pantocrator fresco, Church of the Savoior's Transfiguration, Polotsk, 12th cent. c, Volodymyr Madonna, Tretiakov Gallery, Moscow, 12th cent.

2000, Jan. 5 *Perf. 12x12¼*

330 A107 100r Sheet of 3, #a-c *1.25 1.25*

See Ukraine No. 370, Russia No. 6568.

Type of 1998 and

Kryzhachok Dancers — A108

2000 Litho. *Perf. 13½x14*

331 A75 1r Bison *.20 .20*
332 A75 2r Christmas star *.20 .20*
333 A75 3r Hurdy-gurdy *.20 .20*
334 A75 5r Church, Synkovichy *.20 .20*
335 A75 10r Flaming wheel *.20 .20*
336 A108 A Kupala folk holiday *.20 .20*
337 A108 20r Kryzhachok dancers *.20 .20*
338 A75 30r Water-powered mill *.20 .20*
339 A75 50r Windmill *.20 .20*
Nos. 332-339 (8) *1.60 1.60*

Booklet Stamp

Self-Adhesive

Serpentine Die Cut 5¾

340 A108 20r red & black *.20 .20*
a. Booklet pane of 18 *1.50*
Booklet, #340a *1.50*

No. 336 sold for 19r on day of issue.

No. 340 has a line below the country name. Nos. 337 and 364 have lines of microprinting below the country name.

See Nos. 364-368.

Issued: 1r, 5r, 10r, 1/6; #340, 1/14; 2r, 30r, 1/29: 3r, A, #337, 3/10; 50r, 4/6.

Sukhoi Fighter Aircraft A109

Designs: Nos. 341, 344a, Su-24. Nos. 342, 344b, Su-25. Nos. 343, 344c, Su-27.

2000, Feb. 23 Litho. *Perf. 14x14¼*

341 A109 50r multicolored .25 .25
342 A109 50r multicolored .25 .25
343 A109 50r multicolored .25 .25
Nos. 341-343 (3) .75 .75

Souvenir Sheet

344 Sheet of 3 + label 2.25 2.25
a.-c. A109 150r Any single .75 .75

Birds — A110

Designs: No. 345, Mergellus albelius. No. 346, Burhinus oedicnemus. 75r, Lagopus lagopus. 100r, Aquila pomarina, vert.

Perf. 13½x13¾, 13¾x13½

2000, Mar. 22

345 A110 50r multi .25 .25
346 A110 50r multi .25 .25
347 A110 75r multi .35 .35
348 A110 100r multi .50 .50
Nos. 345-348 (4) 1.35 1.35

Partisan Madonna of Minsk, by M. Savitsky — A111

2000, Apr. 27 *Perf. 13½*

349 A111 100r multi .45 .45

End of World War II, 55th anniv.

Europa, 2000

Common Design Type

2000, May 9 *Perf. 14x13½*

350 CD17 250r multi .85 .85
a. Tete beche pair 1.70 1.70

Ballet — A112

Designs: 100r, Male dancer lifting female dancer. 150r, Dancer with crown.

2000, May 25 Litho. *Perf. 13¾x13½*

351 A112 100r multi .45 .45

Souvenir Sheet

352 A112 150r multi + label .70 .70

UN High Commissioner for Refugees, 50th Anniv. — A113

2000, Aug. 23 Litho. *Perf. 13½x14*

353 A113 50r multi .25 .25

Worldwide Fund for Nature (WWF) — A114

Lynx lynx: No. 354, 100r, Close-up of head. No. 355, 100r, On tree. No. 356, 150r, On snow. No. 357, 150r, Adult and young.

2000, Aug. 25 *Perf. 14x13½*

354-357 A114 Block of 4 1.75 1.75
357a Sheet, 2 each #354-357 3.75 3.75

Intl. Year of Culture of Peace A115

2000, Sept. 5 Litho. *Perf. 13½x14*

358 A115 100r multi .30 .30

2000 Summer Olympics, Sydney — A116

No. 359: a, Gymnast on rings. b, Kayak. c, Rhythmic gymnastics.

Illustration reduced.

2000, Sept. 10 Litho. *Perf. 14x13½*

359 A116 100r Strip of 3, #a-c 1.00 1.00

Souvenir Sheet

360 A116 400r Runner + label 1.40 1.40

Compare Nos. 360 and 382.

Type of 2000

Designs: 20r, Kryzhachok dancers. 30r, Water-powered mill. B, Dazhynki Crop Festival. A, Kupala folk holiday. 50r, Windmill. 100r, Exhibition center, Minsk, horiz. 200r, Vitebsk Town Hall. 500r, Dancers.

13¼x14, 14x13¼ (#361), Serpentine Die Cut 5¾ (#364-370)

2000-01 Litho.

361 A75 100rbrt pink & blk .30 .30
362 A108 200ryel grn & blk ('01) .40 .40
363 A75 500rbrn & blk ('01) .95 .95

Self-Adhesive

364 A108 20r red & black .20 .20
365 A108 30r green & black .20 .20
366 A108 B yel & black .20 .20
367 A108 A blue & black .20 .20
368 A108 50r brown & black .20 .20
369 A108 100rbrt pink & blk ('01) .20 .20
370 A108 200ryel grn & blk ('01) .40 .40
Nos. 361-370 (10) 3.25 3.25

Issued: 20r, 30r, B, A, 50r, 11/8/00. No. 362, 500r, 3/19/01; No. 361, 10/18/00; No. 370, 3/29/01.

No. 364 has a line of microprinting below country name, No. 340 has hairline. Nos. 366-367 sold for 34r and 39r respectively on day of issue. Nos. 364-368 each issued in sheets of 24.

Amber — A117

Halite — A118

Flint — A119

Sylvite — A120

2000, Nov. 22 Litho. *Perf. 14x14¼*

371 A117 200r multi .60 .60
372 A118 200r multi .60 .60
373 A119 200r multi .60 .60
374 A120 200r multi .60 .60
Nos. 371-374 (4) 2.40 2.40

New Year 2001 — A121

2000, Nov. 28 Litho. *Perf. 14x13½*

375 A121 200r multi .60 .60

Christmas — A122

2000, Dec. 5

376 A122 100r multi .30 .30

A123

Children's Art Contest Winners A124

2000, Dec. 26 *Perf. 13½*

377 A123 100r multi .30 .30
378 A124 100r multi .30 .30

St. Euphrosyne of Polotsk, 900th Anniv. of Birth — A125

Illustration reduced.

2001, Jan. 5 Litho. *Imperf.*

379 A125 500r multi 1.40 1.40

Brest Arms — A126

Gomel Arms — A127

2001, Jan. 10 *Perf. 14¼x14*

380 A126 200r multi .55 .55
381 A127 200r multi .55 .55

Souvenir Sheet

Medal Count From 2000 Summer Olympics, Sydney — A128

Perf. 13¾x13½

2001, Feb. 22 Litho.

382 A128 1000r multi + label 1.90 1.90

Sukhoi Airplane Type of 2000

Designs: No. 383, 250r, RD (ANT-25), 1933. No. 384, 250r, Rodina (ANT-37), 1936.

2001, Feb. 23 Litho. *Perf. 14x14¼*

383-384 A109 Set of 2 1.00 1.00

Flowers — A131

Designs: 200r, Nymphaea alba. 400r, Cypripedium calceolus.

2001, Apr. 25 Litho. *Perf. 14x14¼*

386-387 A131 Set of 2 1.10 1.10
a. Booklet pane of 12, 6 each #386-387 6.75 —
Booklet, #387a 6.75

The two center vertical pairs in No. 387a are tete beche.

Europa — A132

Chernobyl Nuclear Disaster, 15th Anniv. — A133

National Parks : 400r, Prypyatski. 1000r, Narachanski.

2001, May 4 *Perf. 13¾x13½*

388-389 A132	Set of 2		*2.10*	*2.10*

2001, June 9

390 A133 50r multi		*.20*	*.20*

Native Costumes — A134

Designs: 200r, Woman and children, Slutsk, 19th cent. 1000r, Man, woman and child, Pinsk, 19th cent.

2001, June 15 *Perf. 14¼x14*

391-392 A134	Set of 2	*2.10*	*2.10*
**Booklet pane of 6, 3 each #391-392*		*6.50*	*—*
Booklet, #392a		*6.50*	

BELGIAN CONGO

'bel-jən 'käŋ-ˌgō

LOCATION — Central Africa
GOVT. — Belgian colony
AREA — 902,082 sq. mi. (estimated)
POP. — 12,660,000 (1956)
CAPITAL — Léopoldville

Congo was an independent state, founded by Leopold II of Belgium, until 1908 when it was annexed to Belgium as a colony. In 1960 it became the independent Republic of the Congo. See Congo Democratic Republic and Zaire.

100 Centimes = 1 Franc

Catalogue values for unused stamps in this country are for Never Hinged items, beginning with Scott 187 in the regular postage section, Scott B32 in the semi-postal section, Scott C17 in the airpost section, and Scott J8 in the postage due section.

Independent State

A1

A2

King Leopold II — A3

1886 **Unwmk.** **Typo.** *Perf. 15*

1	A1	5c green	8.50	*21.00*
2	A1	10c rose	4.00	*5.00*
3	A2	25c blue	42.50	35.00
4	A3	50c olive green	6.50	6.50
5	A1	5fr lilac	325.00	260.00
a.		Perf. 14	825.00	
b.		5fr deep lilac	725.00	475.00

Counterfeits exist.
For surcharge see No. Q1.

King Leopold II — A4

1887-94

6	A4	5c grn ('89)	.75	.75
7	A4	10c rose ('89)	1.25	1.25
8	A4	25c blue ('89)	1.25	1.25
9	A4	50c reddish brown	45.00	21.00
10	A4	50c gray ('94)	2.50	*16.00*
11	A4	5fr violet	900.00	375.00
12	A4	5fr gray ('92)	110.00	95.00
13	A4	10fr buff ('91)	400.00	275.00

The 25fr and 50fr in gray were not issued. Values, each $20.

Counterfeits exist of Nos. 10-13, 25fr and 50fr, unused, used, genuine stamps with faked cancels and counterfeit stamps with genuine cancels.

For surcharges see Nos. Q3-Q6.

Port Matadi — A5

River Scene on the Congo, Stanley Falls — A6

Inkissi Falls — A7

Railroad Bridge on M'pozo River — A8

Hunting Elephants A9

Bangala Chief and Wife — A10

1894-1901 **Engr.** *Perf. 12½ to 15*

14	A5	5c pale bl & blk	13.00	13.00
15	A5	5c red brn & blk ('95)	3.25	1.40
16	A5	5c grn & blk ('00)	1.75	.50
17	A6	10c red brn & blk	13.00	13.00
18	A6	10c grnsh bl & blk ('95)	1.50	1.40
a.		Center inverted	*1,850.*	*2,250.*
19	A6	10c car & blk ('00)	3.25	.75
20	A7	25c yel org & blk	3.50	2.40
21	A7	25c lt bl & blk ('00)	3.00	1.40
22	A8	50c grn & blk	1.40	1.40
23	A8	50c ol & blk ('00)	3.00	.75
24	A9	1fr lilac & blk	20.00	12.00
a.		1fr rose lilac & black	240.00	24.00
25	A9	1fr car & blk ('01)	210.00	5.00
26	A10	5fr lake & blk	40.00	25.00
a.		5fr carmine rose & black	87.50	37.50
		Nos. 14-26 (13)	316.65	78.00

For overprints see #31-32, 34, 36-37, 39.

Climbing Oil Palms — A11

Congo Canoe A12

1896

27	A11	15c ocher & blk	3.75	.75
28	A12	40c bluish grn & blk	3.75	3.00

For overprints see Nos. 33, 35.

Congo Village A13

River Steamer on the Congo A14

1898

29	A13	3.50fr red & blk	140.00	85.00
a.		Perf. 14x12	360.00	240.00
30	A14	10fr yel grn & blk	90.00	24.00
a.		Center inverted	*27,500.*	
b.		Perf. 12	525.00	25.00
c.		Perf. 12x14	325.00	—
		As "c," pen canceled		14.50

For overprints see Nos. 38, 40.

Belgian Congo

Overprinted

1908

31	A5	5c green & blk	7.25	7.25
a.		Handstamped	2.50	1.75
32	A6	10c car & blk	12.00	12.00
a.		Handstamped	2.50	1.75
33	A11	15c ocher & blk	7.25	7.25
a.		Handstamped	5.50	3.50
34	A7	25c lt blue & blk	3.75	2.50
a.		Handstamped	7.25	3.50
c.		Double overprint (#34)	190.00	
35	A12	40c bluish grn & blk	2.50	2.50
a.		Handstamped	7.25	5.50
36	A8	50c olive & blk	4.25	2.50
a.		Handstamped	4.25	3.50
b.		Inverted overprint (#36)	500.00	
37	A9	1fr car & blk	20.00	2.50
a.		Handstamped	26.00	7.25
38	A13	3.50fr red & blk	25.00	20.00
a.		Handstamped	160.00	110.00
39	A10	5fr car & blk	42.50	24.00
a.		Handstamped	60.00	42.50
40	A14	10fr yel grn & blk	85.00	21.00
a.		Perf. 14½	240.00	—
b.		Handstamped	125.00	47.50
c.		Handstamped, perf. 14½	290.00	225.00
		Nos. 31-40 (10)	209.50	101.50

Most of the above handstamps are also found inverted and double.

There are two types of handstamped overprints, those applied in Brussels and those applied locally. There are eight types of each overprint. Values listed are the lowest for each stamp.

Counterfeits of the handstamped overprints exist.

Port Matadi A15

River Scene on the Congo, Stanley Falls — A16

Climbing Oil Palms — A17

Railroad Bridge on M'pozo River — A18

1909 *Perf. 14*

41	A15	5c green & blk	.75	.75
42	A16	10c carmine & blk	.75	.50
43	A17	15c ocher & blk	25.00	15.00
44	A18	50c olive & blk	3.00	2.50
		Nos. 41-44 (4)	29.50	18.75

Port Matadi A19

River Scene on the Congo, Stanley Falls — A20

Climbing Oil Palms — A21

Inkissi Falls — A22

Congo Canoe A23

Railroad Bridge on M'pozo River — A24

Hunting Elephants A25

Congo Village A26

Bangala Chief and Wife — A27

River Steamer on the Congo A28

1910-15 Engr. *Perf. 14, 15*

45 A19 5c green & blk .75 .25
46 A20 10c carmine & blk .60 .25
47 A21 15c ocher & blk .50 .25
48 A21 15c grn & blk ('15) .35 .25
a. Booklet pane of 10 14.00
49 A22 25c blue & blk 1.50 .35
50 A23 40c bluish grn & blk 2.25 2.25
51 A23 40c brn red & blk ('15) 4.25 2.40
52 A24 50c olive & blk 3.50 2.00
53 A24 50c brn lake & blk ('15) 6.00 2.40
54 A25 1fr carmine & blk 3.50 2.75
55 A25 1fr ol bis & blk ('15) 2.25 .85
56 A26 3fr red & blk 16.00 12.00
57 A27 5fr carmine & blk 24.00 24.00
58 A27 5fr ocher & blk ('15) 1.75 .85
59 A28 10fr green & blk 20.00 20.00
Nos. 45-59 (15) 87.20 70.85

Nos. 48, 51, 53, 55 and 58 exist imperforate.

For overprints and surcharges see Nos. 64-76, 81-86, B5-B9.

Port Matadi A29

Stanley Falls, Congo River — A30

Inkissi Falls — A31

TEN CENTIMES.

Type I - Large white space at top of picture and two small white spots at lower edge. Vignette does not fill frame.

Type II - Vignette completely fills frame.

1915

60 A29 5c green & blk .20 .20
a. Booklet pane of 10 6.00
61 A30 10c car & blk (II) .20 .20
a. 10c carmine & black (I) .20 .20
d. Booklet pane of 10 (II) 8.50
62 A31 25c blue & blk .85 .25
a. Booklet pane of 10 50.00
Nos. 60-62 (3) 1.25 .65

Nos. 60 to 62 exist imperforate.

For surcharges see Nos. 77-80, 87, B1-B4.

Stamps of 1910 Issue Surcharged in Red or Black

1921

64 A23 5c on 40c bluish grn & blk (R) .25 .25
65 A19 10c on 5c grn & blk (R) .25 .25
66 A24 15c on 50c ol & blk (R) .25 .25
67 A21 25c on 15c ocher & blk (R) 1.50 1.00
68 A20 30c on 10c car & blk .35 .35
69 A22 50c on 25c bl & blk (R) 1.50 .90
Nos. 64-69 (6) 4.10 3.00

The position of the new value and the bars varies on Nos. 64 to 69.

Overprinted

1921

70 A25 1fr carmine & blk .80 .80
a. Double overprint 20.00
71 A26 3fr red & blk 2.50 2.50
72 A27 5fr carmine & blk 6.50 6.50
73 A28 10fr green & blk (R) 4.50 3.00
Nos. 70-73 (4) 14.30 12.80

Belgian Surcharges

Nos. 51, 53, 60-62 Surcharged in Black or Red

1922

74 A24 5c on 50c .35 .30
75 A29 10c on 5c (R) .35 .25
76 A23 25c on 40c (R) 2.00 .30
77 A30 30c on 10c (II) .20 .20
a. 30c on 10c (I) .20 .20
b. Double surcharge 4.75 4.75
78 A31 50c on 25c (R) .40 .25
Nos. 74-78 (5) 3.30 1.30

No. 74 has the surcharge at each side.

Congo Surcharges

Nos. 60, 51 Surcharged in Red or Black:

a

b

1922

80 A29 10c on 5c (R) .55 .55
a. Inverted surcharge 20.00 20.00
b. Double surcharge 4.75
c. Double surch., one invtd. 40.00
d. Pair, one without surcharge 42.50
e. On No. 45 125.00 125.00
81 A23 25c on 40c .70 .35
a. Inverted surcharge 20.00 20.00
b. Double surcharge 5.50
c. "25c" double
d. 25c on 5c, No. 60 100.00 100.00

Nos. 55, 58 Surcharged with vertical bars over original values

1922

84 A25 10c on 1fr (R) .55 .55
a. Double surcharge 14.00
b. Inverted surcharge 20.00 20.00
85 A27 25c on 5fr 1.50 1.50

Nos. 68, 77 Handstamped

86 A20 25c on 30c on 10c 7.50 7.50
87 A30 25c on 30c on 10c (II) 7.50 7.50

Nos. 86-87 exist with handstamp surcharge inverted.

Counterfeit handstamped surcharges exist.

Ubangi Woman — A32

Watusi Cattle — A44

Designs: 10c, Baluba woman. 15c, Babuende woman. No. 90, 40c, 1.25fr, 1.50fr, 1.75fr, Ubangi man. 25c, Basketmaking. 30c, 35c, Nos. 101, 102, Carving wood. 50c, Archer. Nos. 92, 100, Weaving. 1fr, Making pottery. 3fr, Working rubber. 5fr, Making palm oil. 10fr, African elephant.

1923-27 Engr. *Perf. 12*

88 A32 5c yellow .20 .20
89 A32 10c green .20 .20
90 A32 15c olive brn .20 .20
91 A32 20c olive grn ('24) .20 .20
92 A44 20c green ('26) .20 .20
93 A44 25c red brown .25 .20
94 A44 30c rose red ('24) .45 .45
95 A44 30c olive grn ('25) .20 .20
96 A44 35c green ('27) .45 .35
97 A32 40c violet ('25) .20 .20
98 A44 50c gray blue .25 .20
99 A44 50c buff ('25) .30 .20
100 A44 75c red orange .25 .20
101 A44 75c gray bl ('25) .40 .25
102 A44 75c salmon red ('26) .20 .20
103 A44 1fr bister brn .55 .25
104 A44 1fr dl blue ('25) .35 .20
105 A44 1fr rose red ('27) .85 .20
106 A32 1.25fr dl blue ('26) .30 .20
107 A32 1.50fr dl blue ('26) .30 .20
108 A32 1.75fr dl blue ('27) 3.50 3.25
109 A44 3fr gray brn ('24) 3.75 2.00
110 A44 5fr gray ('24) 10.00 4.25
111 A44 10fr gray blk ('24) 18.00 8.50

1925-26

112 A44 45c dk vio ('26) .45 .25
113 A44 60c carmine rose .45 .20
Nos. 88-113 (26) 42.45 22.95

For surcharges see Nos. 114, 136-138, 157.

No. 107 Surcharged

1927, June 14

114 A32 1.75fr on 1.50fr dl bl .60 .60

Sir Henry Morton Stanley — A45

1928, June 30 *Perf. 14*

115 A45 5c gray blk .20 .20
116 A45 10c dp violet .20 .20
117 A45 20c orange red .35 .25
118 A45 35c green .75 .75
119 A45 40c red brown .25 .20
120 A45 60c black brn .25 .20
121 A45 1fr carmine .25 .20
122 A45 1.60fr dk gray 5.00 3.50
123 A45 1.75fr dp blue 1.00 .50
124 A45 2fr dk brown .60 .30
125 A45 2.75fr red violet 5.00 .45
126 A45 3.50fr rose lake .75 .35
127 A45 5fr slate grn .60 .30
128 A45 10fr violet blue 1.00 .75
129 A45 20fr claret 4.50 2.50
Nos. 115-129 (15) 20.70 10.65

Sir Henry M. Stanley (1841-1904), explorer.

Nos. 118, 121-123, 125-126 Surcharged in Red, Blue or Black

1931, Jan. 15

130 A45 40c on 35c .50 .40
131 A45 1.25fr on 1fr (Bl) .40 .20
132 A45 2fr on 1.60fr .80 .30
133 A45 2fr on 1.75fr .75 .30
134 A45 3.25fr on 2.75fr (Bk) 2.25 2.00
135 A45 3.25fr on 3.25fr (Bk) 3.00 2.10

Nos. 96, 108, 112 Surcharged in Red

Perf. 12½, 12

136 A44 40c on 35c grn 3.25 3.00
137 A44 50c on 45c dk vio 2.00 1.10

Surcharged

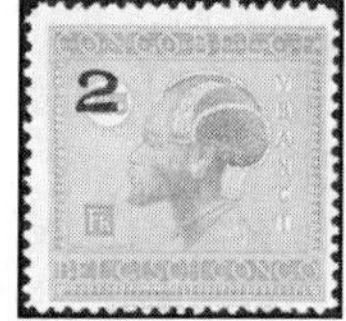

138	A32	2(fr) on 1.75fr dl bl	8.50	7.50
		Nos. 130-138 (9)	21.45	16.90

View of Sankuru River — A46

Flute Players — A50

Designs: 15c, Kivu Kraal. 20c, Sankuru River rapids. 25c, Uele hut. 50c, Musicians of Lake Leopold II. 60c, Batetelas drummers. 75c, Mangbetu woman. 1fr, Domesticated elephant of Api. 1.25fr, Mangbetu chief. 1.50fr, 2fr, Village of Mondimbi. 2.50fr, 3.25fr, Okapi. 4fr, Canoes at Stanleyville. 5fr, Woman preparing cassava. 10fr, Baluba chief. 20fr, Young woman of Irumu.

1931-37 Engr. *Perf. 11½*

139	A46	10c gray brn ('32)	.20	.20
140	A46	15c gray ('32)	.20	.20
141	A46	20c brn lil ('32)	.20	.20
142	A46	25c dp blue ('32)	.20	.20
143	A50	40c dp grn ('32)	.20	.20
144	A46	50c violet ('32)	.20	.20
b.		Booklet pane of 8	6.25	
145	A50	60c vio brn ('32)	.20	.20
146	A50	75c rose ('32)	.20	.20
b.		Booklet pane of 8	1.25	
147	A50	1fr rose red ('32)	.20	.20
148	A50	1.25fr red brown	.20	.20
b.		Booklet pane of 8	1.25	
149	A46	1.50fr dk ol gray ('37)	.20	.20
b.		Booklet pane of 8	6.00	
150	A46	2fr ultra ('32)	.20	.20
151	A46	2.50fr dp blue ('37)	.30	.20
b.		Booklet pane of 8	8.50	
152	A46	3.25fr gray blk ('32)	.45	.30
153	A46	4fr dl vio ('32)	.20	.20
154	A50	5fr dp vio ('32)	.50	.25
155	A50	10fr red ('32)	.50	.40
156	A50	20fr blk brn ('32)	1.50	1.25
		Nos. 139-156 (18)	5.85	5.00

No. 109 Surcharged in Red

1932, Mar. 15 *Perf. 12*

157	A44	3.25fr on 3fr gray brn	2.75	2.25

King Albert Memorial Issue

King Albert — A62

1934, May 7 Photo. *Perf. 11½*

158	A62	1.50fr black	.65	.35

No. 158 exists imperf. Value, $25.

Leopold I, Leopold II, Albert I, Leopold III A63

1935, Aug. 15 Engr. *Perf. 12½x12*

159	A63	50c green	.70	.40
160	A63	1.25fr dk carmine	.70	.20
161	A63	1.50fr brown vio	.70	.20
162	A63	2.40fr brown org	1.75	1.60
163	A63	2.50fr lt blue	1.75	.80
164	A63	4fr brt violet	1.75	1.10
165	A63	5fr black brn	1.75	1.25
		Nos. 159-165 (7)	9.10	5.55

Founding of Congo Free State, 50th anniv.
Nos. 159-165 exist impef. Value set, $1,750.
For surcharges see Nos. B21-B22.

Molindi River — A64

Bamboos — A65

Suza River — A66

Rutshuru River — A67

Karisimbi A68

Mitumba Forest A69

1937-38 Photo. *Perf. 11½*

166	A64	5c purple & blk	.20	.20
167	A65	90c car & brn	.40	.30
168	A66	1.50fr dp red brn & blk	.20	.20
169	A67	2.40fr ol blk & brn	.20	.20
170	A68	2.50fr dp ultra & blk	.30	.20
171	A69	4.50fr dk grn & brn	.30	.20
172	A69	4.50fr car & sep	.20	.20
		Nos. 166-172 (7)	1.80	1.50

National Parks.
No. 172 was issued in sheets of four measuring 140x111mm. It was sold by subscription, the subscription closing Oct. 20, 1937. Value, $1.60.
Nos. 166-171 were issued Mar. 1, 1938.
See #B26. For surcharges see #184, 186.

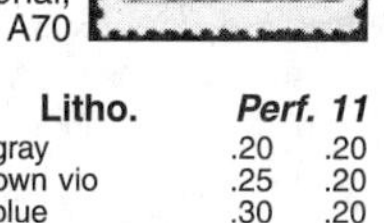

King Albert Memorial, Leopoldville — A70

1941, Feb. 7 Litho. *Perf. 11*

173	A70	10c lt gray	.20	.20
174	A70	15c brown vio	.25	.20
175	A70	25c lt blue	.30	.20
176	A70	50c lt violet	.25	.20
177	A70	75c rose pink	.95	.30
178	A70	1.25fr gray	.30	.20
179	A70	1.75fr orange	.95	.45
180	A70	2.50fr carmine	.65	.20
181	A70	2.75fr vio blue	.95	.60
182	A70	5fr lt olive grn	4.00	1.50
183	A70	10fr rose red	2.75	1.75
		Nos. 173-183 (11)	11.55	5.80

Exist imperforate.
For surcharge see No. 185.

Nos. 168, 179, 169 Surcharged in Blue or Black

Nos. 184, 186

No. 185

1941-42 *Perf. 11½, 11*

184	A66	5c on 1.50fr (Bl)	.20	.20
a.		Inverted surcharge	14.00	14.00
185	A70	75c on 1.75fr ('42)	.35	.35
a.		Inverted surcharge	14.00	14.00
186	A67	2.50(fr) on 2.40fr ('42)	.85	.70
a.		Double surcharge	27.50	27.50
b.		Inverted surcharge	14.00	14.00
		Nos. 184-186 (3)	1.40	1.25

Catalogue values for unused stamps in this section, from this point to the end of the section, are for Never Hinged items.

A71

Oil Palms — A72

Congo Woman — A73

Askari — A75

Leopard A74

Okapi A76

Inscribed "Congo Belge Belgisch Congo"

1942, May 23 Engr. *Perf. 12½*

187	A71	5c red	.20	.20
188	A72	10c olive grn	.20	.20
189	A72	15c brown car	.20	.20
190	A72	20c dp ultra	.20	.20
191	A72	25c brown vio	.20	.20
192	A72	30c blue	.20	.20
193	A72	50c dp green	.20	.20
194	A72	60c chestnut	.20	.20
195	A73	75c dl lil & blk	.20	.20
196	A73	1fr dk brn & blk	.20	.20
197	A73	1.25fr rose red & blk	.20	.20
198	A74	1.75fr dk gray brn	.75	.35
199	A74	2fr ocher	.75	.20
200	A74	2.50fr carmine	.75	.20
201	A75	3.50fr dk ol grn	.35	.20
202	A75	5fr orange	.70	.20
203	A75	6fr brt ultra	.50	.20
204	A75	7fr black	.60	.20
205	A75	10fr dp brown	.75	.20
206	A76	20fr plum & blk	8.00	.65
		Nos. 187-206 (20)	15.35	4.60

Same Inscribed "Belgisch Congo Congo Belge"

207	A72	10c olive grn	.20	.20
208	A72	15c brown car	.20	.20
209	A72	20c dp ultra	.20	.20
210	A72	25c brown vio	.20	.20
211	A72	30c blue	.20	.20
212	A72	50c dp green	.20	.20
213	A72	60c chestnut	.20	.20
214	A73	75c dl lil & blk	.20	.20
215	A73	1fr dk brn & blk	.20	.20
216	A73	1.25fr rose red & blk	.20	.20
217	A74	1.75fr dk gray brn	.75	.35
218	A74	2fr ocher	.75	.20
219	A74	2.50fr carmine	.75	.20
220	A75	3.50fr dk ol grn	.30	.20
221	A75	5fr orange	.55	.20
222	A75	6fr brt ultra	.55	.20
223	A75	7fr black	.55	.20
224	A75	10fr dp brown	.65	.20
225	A76	20fr plum & blk	7.00	.65
		Nos. 207-225 (19)	13.85	4.40

Miniature sheets of Nos. 193, 194, 197, 200, 211, 214, 217 and 219 were printed in 1944 by the Belgian Government in London and given to the Belgian political review, Message, which distributed them to its subscribers, one a month. Value per sheet, about $12.50.

Remainders of these eight miniature sheets received marginal overprints in various colors in 1950, specifying a surtax of 100fr per sheet and paying tribute to the UPU. These sheets, together with four of Ruanda-Urundi, were sold by the Committee of Cultural Works (and not at post offices) in sets of 12 for 1,217.15 francs. Set value, $400.

Nos. 187-227 imperforate had no franking value.

For surcharges see Nos. B34-B37.

Congo Woman — A77

Askari — A78

1943, Jan. 1

226	A77	50fr ultra & blk	6.50	.40
227	A78	100fr car & blk	7.50	.60

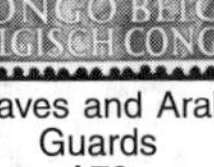

Slaves and Arab Guards A79

Auguste Lambermont A80

Design: 10fr, Leopold II.

Perf. 13x11½, 12½x12

1947 Engr. Unwmk.

228 A79 1.25fr black brown .25 .20
229 A80 3.50fr dark blue .40 .20
230 A80 10fr red orange .75 .20
Nos. 228-230 (3) 1.40 .60

50th anniv. of the abolition of slavery in Belgian Congo. See Nos. 261-262.

Baluba Carving of Former King — A82

Carved Figures and Masks of Baluba Tribe: 10c, 50c, 2fr, "Ndoha," figure of tribal king. 15c, 70c, 1.20fr, 2.50fr, "Tshimanyi," an idol. 20c, 75c, 1.60fr, 3.50fr, "Buangakokoma," statue of kneeling beggar. 25c, 1fr, 2.40fr, 5fr, "Mbuta," sacred double cup, carved with two faces, Man and Woman. 40c, 1.25fr, 6fr, 8fr, "Ngadimuashi," female mask. 1.50fr, 3fr, 10fr, 50fr, "Buadi-Muadi," mask with squared features. 6.50fr, 20fr, 100fr, "Mbowa," executioner's mask with buffalo horns.

1947-50 *Perf. 12½*

231 A82 10c dp org ('48) .20 .20
232 A82 15c ultra ('48) .20 .20
233 A82 20c brt bl ('48) .20 .20
234 A82 25c rose car ('48) .20 .20
235 A82 40c violet ('48) .20 .20
236 A82 50c olive brn .20 .20
237 A82 70c yel grn ('48) .20 .20
238 A82 75c magenta ('48) .20 .20
239 A82 1fr yel org & dk vio 1.50 .20
240 A82 1.20fr gray & brn ('50) .20 .20
241 A82 1.25fr lt bl grn & mag ('48) .30 .20
242 A82 1.50fr ol & mag ('50) 14.00 1.10
243 A82 1.60fr bl gray & brt bl ('50) .40 .20
244 A82 2fr org & mag ('48) .20 .20
245 A82 2.40fr bl grn & dk grn ('50) .30 .20
246 A82 2.50fr brn red & bl grn .30 .20
247 A82 3fr lt ultra & ind ('49) 4.25 .20
248 A82 3.50fr lt bl & blk ('48) 3.50 .20
249 A82 5fr bis & mag ('48) 1.25 .20
250 A82 6fr brn org & ind ('48) 1.40 .20
251 A82 6.50fr red org & red brn ('49) 1.90 .20
252 A82 8fr gray bl & dk grn ('50) 1.25 .20
253 A82 10fr pale vio & red brn ('48) 4.00 .20
254 A82 20fr red org & vio brn ('48) 1.90 .20
255 A82 50fr dp org & blk ('48) 3.75 .20
256 A82 100fr crim & blk brn ('48) 4.00 .30
Nos. 231-256 (26) 46.00 6.20

Railroad Train and Map — A83

1948, July 1 Unwmk. *Perf. 13½*

257 A83 2.50fr dp bl & grn 1.00 .20

50th anniv. of railway service in the Congo.

Globe and Ship A84

1949, Nov. 21 *Perf. 11½*

Granite Paper

258 A84 4fr violet blue .85 .20

75th anniv. of the UPU.

Allegorical Figure and Map — A85

1950, Aug. 12 *Perf. 12x12½*

259 A85 3fr blue & indigo 1.75 .20
260 A85 6.50fr car rose & blk brn 2.00 .25

Establishment of Katanga Province, 50th anniv.

Portrait Type of 1947

1.50fr, Cardinal Lavigerie. 3fr, Baron Dhanis.

Perf. 12½x12

1951, June 25 Unwmk.

261 A80 1.50fr purple 2.00 .25
262 A80 3fr black brown 2.00 .20

Littonia — A86

St. Francis Xavier — A86a

1952-53 Photo. *Perf. 11½*

Granite Paper

Flowers in Natural Colors

Size: 21x25½mm

263 A86 10c Dissotis .20 .20
264 A86 15c Protea .20 .20
265 A86 20c Vellozia .20 .20
266 A86 25c shown .20 .20
267 A86 40c Ipomoea .20 .20
268 A86 50c Angraecum .20 .20
269 A86 60c Euphorbia .20 .20
270 A86 75c Ochna .20 .20
271 A86 1fr Hibiscus .20 .20
272 A86 1.25fr Protea ('53) .65 .45
273 A86 1.50fr Schrizoglossum .20 .20
274 A86 2fr Ansellia .25 .20
275 A86 3fr Costus .25 .20
276 A86 4fr Nymphaea .30 .20
277 A86 5fr Thunbergia .45 .20
278 A86 6.50fr Thonningia .55 .20
279 A86 7fr Gerbera .55 .20
280 A86 8fr Gloriosa ('53) .90 .20
281 A86 10fr Silene ('53) 1.60 .20
282 A86 20fr Aristolochia 1.40 .20

Size: 22x32mm

283 A86 50fr Eulophia ('53) 7.00 .45
284 A86 100fr Crytosepalum ('53) 11.00 1.00
Nos. 263-284 (22) 26.90 5.70

Nos. 264, 269 and 270 with additional surcharges are varieties of Congo Democratic Republic Nos. 324, 327 and 328.

1953, Jan. 5 Engr. *Perf. 12½x13*

285 A86a 1.50fr ultra & gray blk .50 .30

400th death anniv. of St. Francis Xavier.

Canoe on Lake Kivu — A87

1953, Jan. 5 *Perf. 14*

286 A87 3fr car & blk 1.25 .20
287 A87 7fr dp bl & brn org 1.25 .25

Issued to publicize the Kivu Festival, 1953.

Royal Colonial Institute Jubilee Medal A88

Design: 6.50fr, Same with altered background and transposed inscriptions.

1954, Dec. 27 Photo. *Perf. 13½*

288 A88 4.50fr indigo & gray 1.10 .30
289 A88 6.50fr dk grn & brn .90 .20

25th anniv. of the founding of the Belgian Royal Colonial Institute.

King Baudouin and Tropical Scene A89

Designs: King and various views.

Inscribed "Congo Belge-Belgisch Congo"

Engr.; Portrait Photo.

1955, Feb. 15 Unwmk. *Perf. 11½*

Portrait in Black

290 A89 1.50fr rose car 5.25 .90
291 A89 3fr green 3.50 .80
292 A89 4.50fr ultra 3.50 .55
293 A89 6.50fr dp claret 5.25 .25

Inscribed "Belgisch Congo-Congo Belge"

294 A89 1.50fr rose car 5.25 .90
295 A89 3fr green 3.50 .80
296 A89 4.50fr ultra 3.50 .55
297 A89 6.50fr deep claret 5.25 .25
Nos. 290-297 (8) 35.00 5.00

Map of Africa and Emblem of Royal Touring Club — A90

1955, July 26 Engr. *Perf. 11½*

Inscription in French

298 A90 6.50fr vio blue 3.25 .25

Inscription in Flemish

299 A90 6.50fr vio blue 3.25 .25

5th International Congress of African Tourism, Elisabethville, July 26-Aug. 4. Nos. 298-299 printed in alternate rows.

Kings of Belgium A91

1958, July 1 Unwmk. *Perf. 12½*

300 A91 1fr rose vio .25 .20
301 A91 1.50fr ultra .25 .20
302 A91 3fr rose car .25 .20
303 A91 5fr green .70 .30
304 A91 6.50fr brn red .45 .20
305 A91 10fr dl vio .65 .20
Nos. 300-305 (6) 2.55 1.30

Belgium's annexation of Congo, 50th anniv.

Roan Antelope — A92

Black Buffaloes A93

20c, White rhinoceros. 40c, Giraffe. 50c, Thick-tailed bushbaby. 1fr, Gorilla. 2fr, Black-and-white colobus (monkey). 3fr, Elephants. 5fr, Okapis. 6.50fr, Impala. 8fr, Giant pangolin. 10fr, Eland and zebras.

1959, Oct. 15 Photo. *Perf. 11½*

Granite Paper

306 A92 10c bl & brn .20 .20
307 A93 20c red org & slate .20 .20
308 A92 40c brn & bl .20 .20
309 A93 50c brt ultra, red & sep .20 .20
310 A92 1fr brn, grn & blk .20 .20
311 A93 1.50fr blk & org yel .20 .20
312 A92 2fr crim, blk & brn .20 .20
313 A93 3fr blk, gray & lil rose .25 .20
314 A92 5fr brn, dk brn & brt grn .40 .20
315 A93 6.50fr bl, brn & org yel .45 .20
316 A92 8fr org brn, ol bis & lil .50 .30
317 A93 10fr multi .60 .20
Nos. 306-317 (12) 3.60 2.50

Madonna and Child — A94

1959, Dec. 1 Unwmk. *Perf. 11½*

318 A94 50c golden brn, ocher & red brn .20 .20
319 A94 1fr dk bl, pur & red brn .20 .20
320 A94 2fr gray, brt bl & red brn .20 .20
Nos. 318-320 (3) .60 .60

Map of Africa and Symbolic Honeycomb A95

1960, Feb. 19 Unwmk. *Perf. 11½*

Inscription in French

321 A95 3fr gray & red .25 .20

Inscription in Flemish

322 A95 3fr gray & red .25 .20

Commission for Technical Co-operation in Africa South of the Sahara (C. C. T. A.), 10th anniv.

SEMI-POSTAL STAMPS

Types of 1910-15 Issues Surcharged in Red

1918, May 15 Unwmk. *Perf. 14, 15*

B1 A29 5c + 10c grn & bl .20 *.20*
B2 A30 10c + 15c car & bl (I) .20 *.20*
B3 A21 15c + 20c bl grn & bl .20 *.20*
B4 A31 25c + 25c dp bl & pale bl .20 *.25*

B5	A23	40c + 40c brn red & bl	.35	*.45*
B6	A24	50c + 50c brn lake & bl	.35	*.45*
B7	A25	1fr + 1fr ol bis & bl	1.50	*2.00*
B8	A27	5fr + 5fr och & bl	8.25	*11.00*
B9	A28	10fr + 10fr grn & bl	77.50	*105.00*
		Nos. B1-B9 (9)	88.75	*119.75*

The position of the cross and the added value varies on the different stamps.

Perf 15 stamps are worth approximately twice the values shown.

Nos. B1-B9 exist imperforate.

SP1

Design: #B11 inscribed "Belgisch Congo."

1925, July 8 ***Perf. 12½***

B10	SP1	25c + 25c carmine & blk	.20	*.25*
B11	SP1	25c + 25c carmine & blk	.20	*.25*
a.		Pair, Nos. B10-B11	.40	*.50*

Colonial campaigns in 1914-1918.

The surtax helped erect at Kinshasa a monument to those who died in World War I.

Nurse Weighing Child — SP3

First Aid Station SP5

20c+10c, Missionary & Child. 60c+30c, Congo hospital. 1fr+50c, Dispensary service. 1.75fr+75c, Convalescent area. 3.50fr+1.50fr, Instruction on bathing infant. 5fr+2.50fr, Operating room. 10fr+5fr, Students.

1930, Jan. 16 **Engr.** ***Perf. 11½***

B12	SP3	10c + 5c ver	.30	.30
B13	SP3	20c + 10c dp brn	.40	.40
B14	SP5	35c + 15c dp grn	.70	.70
B15	SP5	60c + 30c dl vio	.85	.85
B16	SP3	1fr + 50c dk car	1.40	1.40
B17	SP5	1.75fr + 75c dp bl	2.10	2.10
B18	SP5	3.50fr + 1.50fr rose lake	5.00	5.00
B19	SP5	5fr + 2.50fr red brn	4.25	4.25
B20	SP5	10fr + 5fr gray blk	5.00	5.00
		Nos. B12-B20 (9)	20.00	20.00

The surtax was intended to aid welfare work among the natives, especially the children.

Nos. 161, 163 Surcharged "+50c" in Blue or Red

1936, May 15 ***Perf. 12½x12***

B21	A63	1.50fr + 50c (Bl)	2.50	*3.00*
B22	A63	2.50fr + 50c (R)	2.00	2.00

Surtax was for the King Albert Memorial Fund.

Queen Astrid with Congolese Children — SP12

1936, Aug. 29 **Photo.** ***Perf. 12½***

B23	SP12	1.25fr + 5c dark brown	.40	.35
B24	SP12	1.50fr + 10c dull rose	.40	.35
B25	SP12	2.50fr + 25c dark blue	.60	.60
		Nos. B23-B25 (3)	1.40	1.30

Issued in memory of Queen Astrid. The surtax was for the aid of the National League for Protection of Native Children.

National Park Type of 1937-38
Souvenir Sheet

1938, Oct. 3 ***Perf. 11½***

Star in Yellow

B26	Sheet of 6	18.00	18.00
a.	A64 5c ultra & light brown	3.00	3.00
b.	A65 90c ultra & light brown	3.00	3.00
c.	A66 1.50fr ultra & light brown	3.00	3.00
d.	A67 2.40fr ultra & light brown	3.00	3.00
e.	A68 2.50fr ultra & light brown	3.00	3.00
f.	A69 4.50fr ultra & light brown	3.00	3.00

Intl. Tourist Cong. A surtax of 3.15fr was for the benefit of the Congo Tourist Service.

Marabou Storks and Vultures — SP14

Buffon's Kob — SP15

Designs: 1.50fr+1.50fr, Pygmy chimpanzees. 4.50fr+4.50fr, Dwarf crocodiles. 5fr+5fr, Lioness.

1939, June 6 **Photo.** ***Perf. 14***

B27	SP14	1fr + 1fr dp cl	5.50	5.50
B28	SP15	1.25fr + 1.25fr car	5.50	5.50
B29	SP15	1.50fr + 1.50fr brt pur	7.50	7.50
B30	SP14	4.50fr + 4.50fr sl grn	5.50	5.50
B31	SP15	5fr + 5fr brown	6.00	6.00
		Nos. B27-B31 (5)	30.00	30.00

Surtax for the Leopoldville Zoological Gardens.

Sold in full sets by subscription.

Catalogue values for unused stamps in this section, from this point to the end of the section, are for Never Hinged items.

Lion of Belgium and Inscription "Belgium Shall Rise Again" — SP19

1942, Feb. 17 **Engr.** ***Perf. 12½***

B32	SP19	10fr + 40fr brt grn	1.50	*1.75*
B33	SP19	10fr + 40fr vio bl	1.50	*1.75*

Nos. 193, 216, 198 and 220 Surcharged in Red

a

b

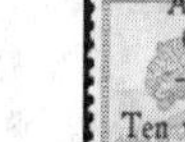

c

1945

B34	A72 (a)	50c + 50fr	2.00	*3.25*
B35	A73 (b)	1.25fr + 100fr	2.00	*3.25*
B36	A74 (c)	1.75fr + 100fr	2.00	*3.50*
B37	A75 (b)	3.50fr + 100fr	2.00	*3.50*
		Nos. B34-B37 (4)	8.00	*13.50*

The surtax was for the Red Cross.

Sold in full sets by subscription.

Mozart at Age 7 — SP20

Queen Elisabeth and Sonata by Mozart — SP21

Perf. 11½

1956, Oct. 10 **Unwmk.** **Engr.**

B38	SP20	4.50fr + 1.50fr brt lil	2.00	2.00
B39	SP21	6.50fr + 2.50fr ultra	3.00	3.00

200th anniv. of the birth of Wolfgang Amadeus Mozart.

The surtax was for the Pro-Mozart Committee.

Nurse and Children SP22

4.50fr+50c, Patient receiving injection. 6.50fr+40c, Patient being bandaged.

1957, Dec. 10 **Photo.** ***Perf. 13x10½***

Cross in Carmine

B40	SP22	3fr + 50c dk bl	.90	.85
B41	SP22	4.50fr + 50c dk grn	.80	.75
B42	SP22	6.50fr + 50c red brn	1.00	.95
		Nos. B40-B42 (3)	2.70	2.55

The surtax was for the Red Cross.

High Jump SP23

1960, May 2 **Unwmk.** ***Perf. 13½***

B43	SP23	50c + 25c shown	.20	*.25*
B44	SP23	1.50fr + 50c Hurdles	.20	*.25*
B45	SP23	2fr + 1fr Soccer	.20	*.30*
B46	SP23	3fr + 1.25fr Javelin	.75	*.90*
B47	SP23	6.50fr + 3.50fr Discus	1.00	*1.25*
		Nos. B43-B47 (5)	2.35	*2.95*

17th Olympic Games, Rome, Aug. 25-Sept. 11. The surtax was for the youth of Congo.

AIR POST STAMPS

Wharf on Congo River AP1

Congo "Country Store" AP2

View of Congo River AP3

Stronghold in the Interior — AP4

Unwmk.

1920, July 1 **Engr.** ***Perf. 12***

C1	AP1	50c orange & blk	.20	.20
C2	AP2	1fr dull vio & blk	.20	.20
C3	AP3	2fr blue & blk	.50	.20
C4	AP4	5fr green & blk	.90	.40
		Nos. C1-C4 (4)	1.80	1.00

Kraal AP5

Porters on Safari AP6

1930, Apr. 2

C5	AP5	15fr dk brn & blk	1.90	.75
C6	AP6	30fr brn vio & blk	2.25	.75

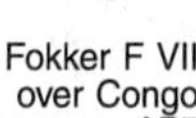

Fokker F VII over Congo AP7

1934, Jan. 22 ***Perf. 13½x14***

C7	AP7	50c gray black	.20	.20
C8	AP7	1fr dk carmine	.20	.20
a.		Booklet pane of 8	5.25	
C9	AP7	1.50fr green	.20	.20
C10	AP7	3fr brown	.20	.20
C11	AP7	4.50fr brt ultra	.25	.20
a.		Booklet pane of 8	10.00	
C12	AP7	5fr red brown	.20	.20
C13	AP7	15fr brown vio	.40	.25
C14	AP7	30fr red orange	.70	.60
C15	AP7	50fr violet	2.00	.95
		Nos. C7-C15 (9)	4.35	3.00

The 1fr, 3fr, 4.50fr, 5fr, 15fr exist imperf.

No. C10 Surcharged in Blue with New Value and Bars

1936, Mar. 25

C16 AP7 3.50fr on 3fr brown .20 .20

Catalogue values for unused stamps in this section, from this point to the end of the section, are for Never Hinged items.

No. C9 Surcharged in Black

1942, Apr. 27

C17 AP7 50c on 1.50fr green .35 .20
 a. Inverted surcharge 6.50 6.50

POSTAGE DUE STAMPS

In 1908-23 regular postage stamps handstamped "TAXES" or "TAX," usually boxed, were used in lieu of postage due stamps.

D1

1923-29(?) Typo. Unwmk. *Perf. 14*

J1	D1	5c black brown	.20	.20
J2	D1	10c rose red	.20	.20
J3	D1	15c violet	.20	.20
J4	D1	30c green	.25	.20
J5	D1	50c ultramarine	.30	.30
J6	D1	50c blue	.30	.30
J7	D1	1fr gray	.45	.25
		Nos. J1-J7 (7)	1.90	1.65

Catalogue values for unused stamps in this section, from this point to the end of the section, are for Never Hinged items.

D2

D3

1943 *Perf. 14x14½*

J8	D2	10c olive green	.20	.20
J9	D2	20c dark ultramarine	.20	.20
J10	D2	50c green	.20	.20
J11	D2	1fr dark brown	.20	.20
J12	D2	2fr yellow orange	.20	.20
		Nos. J8-J12 (5)	1.00	1.00

1943 *Perf. 12½*

J8a	D2	10c olive green	.30	.30
J9a	D2	20c dark ultramarine	.30	.30
J10a	D2	50c green	.30	.30
J11a	D2	1fr dark brown	.45	.45
J12a	D2	2fr yellow orange	.45	.45
		Nos. J8a-J12a (5)	1.80	1.80

1957 Engr. *Perf. 11½*

J13	D3	10c olive brown	.20	.20
J14	D3	20c claret	.20	.20
J15	D3	50c green	.20	.20
J16	D3	1fr light blue	.30	.25
J17	D3	2fr vermilion	.40	.25
J18	D3	4fr purple	.60	.35
J19	D3	6fr violet blue	.75	.45
		Nos. J13-J19 (7)	2.65	1.90

PARCEL POST STAMPS

PP1

PP2

PP3

Handstamped Surcharges on Nos. 5, 11-12

1887-93 Unwmk. *Perf. 15*

Blue-Black Surcharge

Q1 PP1 3.50fr on 5fr lilac 1,000. 750.00

Black Surcharge

Q3 PP2 3.50fr on 5fr vio 850.00 500.00
Q4 PP3 3.50fr on 5fr vio ('88) 575.00 325.00
 a. Blue surcharge 625.00 375.00
Q6 PP3 3.50fr on 5fr gray ('93) 95.00 72.50
 Never hinged 125.00

Nos. Q1, Q3-Q4, Q4a and Q6 are known with inverted surcharge, No. Q1 with double surcharge and No. Q6 in pair with unsurcharged stamp. These varieties sell for somewhat more than the normal surcharges.

Genuine stamps with counterfeit surcharges, counterfeit stamps with counterfeit surcharges, and both with counterfeit cancels exist.

BELGIUM

'bel-jəm

LOCATION — Western Europe, bordering the North Sea
GOVT. — Constitutional Monarchy
AREA — 11,778 sq. mi.
POP. — 10,192,264 (1998 est.)
CAPITAL — Brussels

100 Centimes = 1 Franc
100 Cents = 1 Euro (2002)

Catalogue values for unused stamps in this country are for Never Hinged items, beginning with Scott 322 in the regular postage section, Scott B370 in the semi-postal section, Scott C8 in the airpost section, Scott CB1 in the airpost semi-postal section, Scott J40 in the postage due section, Scott M1 in the military stamp section, Scott O36 in the officials section, and Scott Q267 in the parcel post section.

Watermark

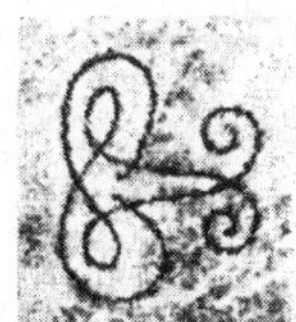

Wmk. 96 (No Frame)

King Leopold I
A1 A2

Wmk. Two "L's" Framed (96)

1849 Engr. *Imperf.*

1 A1 10c brown *2,250.* 75.00
a. 10c red brown *3,500.* 475.00
b. 10c bister brown *2,500.* 125.00
2 A1 20c blue *2,850.* 57.50
a. 20c milky blue *3,250.* 160.00
b. 20c greenish blue *3,500.* 290.00

The reprints are on thick and thin wove and thick laid paper unwatermarked.

A pale blue shade exists that is often confused with the milky blue.

A souvenir sheet containing reproductions of the 10c, 20c and 40c of 1849-51 with black burelage on back was issued Oct. 17, 1949, for the cent. of the 1st Belgian stamps. It was sold at BEPITEC 1949, an intl. stamp exhib. at Brussels, and was not valid. Value, $15.

1849-50

3 A2 10c brown ('50) *2,000.* 90.00
4 A2 20c blue ('50) *1,750.* 52.50
5 A2 40c carmine rose *1,650.* 425.00

Nos. 3-5 were printed on both thick and thin paper and sell for about the same prices.

Wmk. Two "L's" Without Frame (96)

1851-54

6 A2 10c brown 525.00 9.00
a. Ribbed paper ('54) 900.00 50.00
7 A2 20c blue 575.00 8.50
a. Ribbed paper ('54) 900.00 47.50
8 A2 40c car rose *2,850.* 100.00
a. Ribbed paper ('54) *3,500.* 260.00

Nos. 6-8 were printed on both thin and thick paper and sell for about the same prices.

Nos. 6a, 7a, 8a must have regular and parallel ribs covering the whole stamp.

1858-61 Unwmk.

9 A2 1c green ('61) *225.00* 125.00
10 A2 10c brown 375.00 7.50
11 A2 20c blue 400.00 7.50
12 A2 40c vermilion *2,400.* 70.00

Nos. 9 and 13 were valid for postage on newspapers and printed matter only.

Nos. 10-12 were printed in two sizes: 21mm high (with a 16½mm high oval) and 22mm high (with a 17¼mm high oval). The 22mm high stamps were issued in 1861. The 21mm high stamps sell for more.

Reprints of Nos. 9 to 12 are on thin wove paper. The colors are brighter than those of the originals. They were made from the dies and show lines outside the stamps.

1863-65 *Perf. 14½*

13 A2 1c green ('65) 35.00 25.00
14 A2 10c brown ('65) 47.50 3.25
15 A2 20c blue ('65) 50.00 3.25
16 A2 40c car rose ('65) 325.00 25.00
Nos. 13-16 (4) 457.50 56.50

Values for Nos. 13-16 are for copies with perfs cutting into design.

Nos. 13-16 also come perf 12½ and 12½x13, which were issued in 1863. Values differ. See the Scott Classic Specialized Catalogue.

A3

King Leopold I—A3a

A4

A4a

A5

London Print

1865 Typo. *Perf. 14*

17 A5 1fr pale violet 1,300. 110.00

Brussels Print

Thick or Thin Paper

1865-67 *Perf. 15*

18 A3 10c slate ('67) 125.00 1.50
b. Pair, imperf. between —
19 A3a 20c blue ('67) 175.00 1.50
20 A4 30c brown ('67) 425.00 11.00
b. Pair, imperf. between *1,100.*
21 A4a 40c rose ('67) 450.00 20.00
22 A5 1fr violet 1,200. 90.00

Nos. 18-22 also come perf. 14½x14, issued in 1865-66. Values differ. See the Scott Classic Specialized Catalogue. Nos. 18b and 20b are from the earlier printings.

The reprints are on thin paper, imperforate and ungummed.

Coat of Arms — A6

1866-67 *Imperf.*

23 A6 1c gray 250.00 150.00

Perf. 15, 14½x14

24 A6 1c gray 45.00 16.00
25 A6 2c blue ('67) 140.00 90.00
26 A6 5c brown 150.00 90.00
Nos. 23-26 (4) 585.00 346.00

Nos. 23-26 were valid for postage on newspapers and printed matter only.

Values are for perf. 15 stamps. Values for 14½x14 differ. See the Scott Classic Specialized Catalogue.

Counterfeits exist.

Reprints of Nos. 24-26 are on thin paper, imperforate and with or without gum.

Imperf. varieties of 1869-1912 (between Nos. 28-105) generally are without gum.

A7 A8

A9 A10

A11 A12

A13 A14

King Leopold II — A15

1869-70 *Perf. 15*

28 A7 1c green 6.50 .30
29 A7 2c ultra ('70) 20.00 1.50
30 A7 5c buff ('70) 45.00 .75
31 A7 8c lilac ('70) 80.00 50.00
32 A8 10c green 20.00 .40
33 A9 20c lt ultra ('70) 140.00 .90
34 A10 30c buff ('70) 80.00 4.00
35 A11 40c brt rose ('70) 110.00 6.00
36 A12 1fr dull lilac ('70) 350.00 17.00
a. 1fr rose lilac 350.00 20.00
Nos. 28-36 (9) 851.50 80.85

The frames and inscriptions of Nos. 30, 31 and 42 differ slightly from the illustration.

Minor "broken letter" varieties exist on several values.

Nos. 28-30, 32-33, 35-38 also were printed in aniline colors. These are not valued separately.

See Nos. 40-43, 49-51, 55.

1875-78

37 A13 25c olive bister 140.00 1.25
a. 25c ocher 140.00 1.50
38 A14 50c gray 210.00 8.50
Roller cancel 12.50
a. 50c gray black 325.00 55.00
b. 50c deep black 1,750. 225.00
39 A15 5fr dp red brown *1,500.* 1,250.
Roller cancel 575.00
a. 5fr pale brown ('78) *3,750.* 1,250.
Roller cancel 575.00

Dangerous counterfeits of No. 39 exist.

Printed in Aniline Colors

1881 *Perf. 14*

40 A7 1c gray green 20.00 .60
41 A7 2c lt ultra 17.50 2.50
42 A7 5c orange buff 57.50 1.10
a. 5c red orange 57.50 1.10
43 A8 10c gray green 30.00 .80
44 A13 25c olive bister 75.00 2.50
Nos. 40-44 (5) 200.00 7.50

See note following No. 36.

A16

A17

A18 A19

1883

45 A16 10c carmine 27.50 2.50
46 A17 20c gray 150.00 7.75
47 A18 25c blue 260.00 35.00
Roller cancel 15.00
48 A19 50c violet 260.00 35.00
Roller cancel 15.00
Nos. 45-48 (4) 697.50 80.25

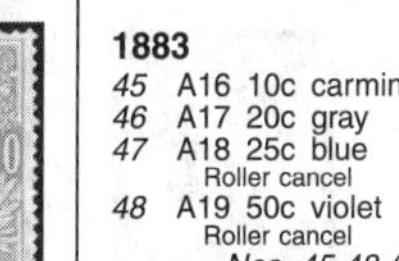

A20

A21

A22

1884-85 *Perf. 14*

49 A7 1c olive green 13.50 .85
50 A7 1c gray 4.00 .30
51 A7 5c green 32.50 .40
52 A20 10c rose, *bluish* 10.00 .40
a. Grayish paper 11.00 .50
c. Yellowish paper *200.00* 35.00
53 A21 25c blue, *pink* ('85) 11.00 .75
54 A22 1fr brown, *grnsh* *600.00* 17.50

The frame and inscription of No. 51 differ slightly from the illustration.

See note after No. 36.

A23

A24

A25

A26

1886-91

No.	Type	Description	Unused	Used
55	A7	2c purple brn ('88)	12.50	1.50
56	A23	20c olive, *grnsh*	140.00	1.25
57	A24	35c vio brn, *brnsh* ('91)	18.00	3.00
58	A25	50c bister, *yelsh*	9.50	2.25
59	A26	2fr violet, *pale lil*	90.00	40.00
		Roller cancel		6.00
		Nos. 55-59 (5)	270.00	48.00

Values quoted for Nos. 60-107 are for stamps with label attached. Stamps without label sell for much less.

Coat of Arms A27

King Leopold A28

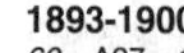

1893-1900

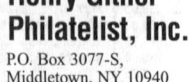

No.	Type	Description	Unused	Used
60	A27	1c gray	1.10	.20
61	A27	2c yellow	1.25	1.10
a.		Wmkd. coat of arms in sheet ('95)	—	—
62	A27	2c violet brn ('94)	1.60	.30
63	A27	2c red brown ('98)	3.25	.50
64	A27	5c yellow grn	7.75	.30
65	A28	10c orange brn	5.00	.30
66	A28	10c brt rose ('00)	3.50	.40
67	A28	20c olive green	22.50	.60
68	A28	25c ultra	20.00	.50
a.		No ball to "5" in upper left corner	32.50	12.50
69	A28	35c violet brn	25.00	1.50
a.		35c red brown	42.50	2.40
70	A28	50c bister	62.50	20.00
71	A28	50c gray ('97)	57.50	2.50
72	A28	1fr car, *lt grn*	75.00	20.00
73	A28	1fr orange ('00)	90.00	5.00
74	A28	2fr lilac, *rose*	90.00	70.00
75	A28	2fr lilac ('00)	150.00	13.50
		Nos. 60-75 (16)	615.95	136.70

Antwerp Exhibition Issue

Arms of Antwerp — A29

1894

No.	Type	Description	Unused	Used
76	A29	5c green, *rose*	4.75	3.25
77	A29	10c carmine, *bluish*	3.75	2.50
78	A29	25c blue, *rose*	1.00	1.00
		Nos. 76-78 (3)	9.50	6.75

Brussels Exhibition Issue

St. Michael and Satan
A30 A31

1896-97 ***Perf. 14x14½***

No.	Type	Description	Unused	Used
79	A30	5c deep violet	1.00	.60
80	A31	10c orange brown	8.50	3.50
81	A31	10c lilac brown	.50	.35
		Nos. 79-81 (3)	10.00	4.45

A32

A33

A34

A35

A36

A37

A38

A39

Two types of 1c:
I - Periods after "Dimanche" and "Zondag" in label.
II - No period after "Dimanche." Period often missing after "Zondag."

1905-11 ***Perf. 14***

No.	Type	Description	Unused	Used
82	A32	1c gray (I) ('07)	1.50	.20
a.		Type II ('08)	2.00	.60
83	A32	2c red brown ('07)	14.50	5.75
84	A32	5c green ('07)	11.50	.60
85	A33	10c dull rose	1.75	.60
86	A34	20c olive grn	26.00	1.00
87	A35	25c ultra	12.00	.85
a.		25c deep blue '11)	13.50	2.00
88	A36	35c red brn	27.50	2.40
89	A37	50c bluish gray	95.00	4.00
90	A38	1fr yellow orange	110.00	8.00
91	A39	2fr violet	75.00	22.50
		Bar cancellation		5.00
		Nos. 82-91 (10)	374.75	45.90

A40

A41

Lion of Belgium — A42

A43

King Albert I — A44

1912

No.	Type	Description	Unused	Used
92	A40	1c orange	.20	.20
93	A41	2c orange brn	.25	.45
94	A42	5c green	.20	.20
95	A43	10c red	.75	.40
96	A43	20c olive grn	16.00	4.00
97	A43	35c bister brn	1.00	.70
98	A43	40c green	16.00	14.50
99	A43	50c gray	1.00	.80
100	A43	1fr orange	4.00	3.00
101	A43	2fr violet	17.50	17.50
102	A44	5fr plum	80.00	25.00
		Nos. 92-102 (11)	136.90	66.75

Counterfeits exist of Nos. 97-102. Those of No. 102 are common.
For overprints see Nos. Q49-Q50, Q52, Q55-Q55A, Q57-Q60.

A45

1912-13

Larger Head

No.	Type	Description	Unused	Used
103	A45	10c red	.40	.20
a.		Without engraver's name	.20	*.25*
104	A45	20c olive grn ('13)	.40	.40
a.		Without engraver's name	2.00	2.00
105	A45	25c ultra	.25	*.40*
a.		With engraver's name	4.25	3.00
107	A45	40c green ('13)	.50	*.60*
		Nos. 103-107 (4)	1.55	1.60

For overprints see #Q51, Q53-Q54, Q56.

Albert I A46

Cloth Hall of Ypres A47

Bridge of Dinant — A48

Library of Louvain — A49

Scheldt River at Antwerp A50

Anti-slavery Campaign in the Congo A51

King Albert I at Furnes A52

Kings of Belgium Leopold I, Albert I, Leopold II A53

1915-20 **Typo.** ***Perf. 14, 15***

No.	Type	Description	Unused	Used
108	A46	1c orange	.20	.20
109	A46	2c chocolate	.20	.20
110	A46	3c gray blk ('20)	.30	.20
111	A46	5c green	1.00	.20
112	A46	10c carmine	.90	.20
113	A46	15c purple	1.50	.20
114	A46	20c red violet	3.00	.20
115	A46	25c blue	.50	.40
		Engr.		
116	A47	35c brn org & blk	.50	.30
117	A48	40c green & black	1.00	.30
a.		Vert. pair, imperf. btwn.		
118	A49	50c car rose & blk	4.50	.30
119	A50	1fr violet	32.50	1.00
120	A51	2fr slate	21.00	2.00
121	A52	5fr deep blue	275.00	125.00
		Telegraph or railroad cancel		55.00
122	A53	10fr brown	20.00	20.00
		Nos. 108-122 (15)	362.10	150.70

Two types each of the 1c, 10c and 20c; three of the 2c and 15c; four of the 5c, differing in the top left corner.
See No. 138. For surcharges see Nos. B34-B47.

Perron of Liege (Fountain) A54

King Albert in Trench Helmet A55

1919 *Perf. 11½*
123 A54 25c blue 2.40 .35
a. Sheet of 10 5,500. 5,750.
b. 25c deep blue 3.00 .45

No. 123b was the first printing of this stamp. Size 18½x28mm. No. 123 is the second printing. Size 18¼x28½mm. No. 123a is from the first printing but in the blue shade of the second printing.

Issue dates: Nos. 123a, 123b, 7/19. No. 123, 7/25.

Perf. 11, 11½, 11½x11, 11x11½

1919

Size: 18½x22mm
124 A55 1c lilac brn .20 .20
125 A55 2c olive .20 .20

Size: 22x26
126 A55 5c green .20 .20
127 A55 10c carmine, 22x26¾mm .25 .25
a. Size: 22½x26mm 1.00 .60
128 A55 15c gray vio, 22x26¾mm .30 .30
a. Size: 22½x26mm 2.40 .60
129 A55 20c olive blk 1.10 1.10
130 A55 25c deep blue 1.60 1.60
131 A55 35c bister brn 3.00 3.00
132 A55 40c red 5.00 5.00
133 A55 50c red brn 9.50 10.00
134 A55 1fr lt orange 40.00 40.00
135 A55 2fr violet 375.00 375.00

Size: 28x33½mm
136 A55 5fr car lake 100.00 100.00
137 A55 10fr claret 110.00 110.00
Nos. 124-137 (14) 646.35 646.85
Set, never hinged 1,150.

Type of 1915 Inscribed: "FRANK" instead of "FRANKEN"

1919, Dec. *Perf. 14, 15*
138 A52 5fr deep blue 1.75 1.25
Never hinged 3.00

Town Hall at Termonde — A56

1920 *Perf. 11½*
139 A56 65c cl & blk, 27x22mm .75 .20
Never hinged 1.50
a. Center inverted 57,500.
b. Size: 26¼x22½mm 5.75 2.40
Never hinged 13.50

For surcharge see No. 143.

Nos. B48-B50 Surcharged in Red or Black

1921 *Perf. 12*
140 SP6 20c on 5c + 5c (R) .60 .25
a. Inverted surcharge 525.00 525.00
Never hinged 1,000.
141 SP7 20c on 10c + 5c .40 .25
142 SP8 20c on 15c + 15c (R) .60 .25
a. Inverted surcharge 525.00 525.00
Never hinged 1,000.

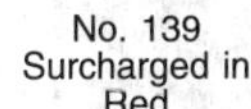

No. 139 Surcharged in Red

143 A56 55c on 65c cl & blk 1.50 .35
a. Pair, one without surcharge 2.25 .85
Nos. 140-143 (4) 3.10 1.10
Set, never hinged 8.50

A58

A59

1922-27 **Typo.** *Perf. 14*
144 A58 1c orange .20 .20
145 A58 2c olive ('26) .20 .20
146 A58 3c fawn .20 .20
147 A58 5c gray .20 .20
148 A58 10c blue grn .20 .20
149 A58 15c plum ('23) .20 .20
150 A58 20c black brn .20 .20
151 A58 25c magenta .20 .20
a. 25c dull violet ('23) .50 .20
152 A58 30c vermilion .50 .20
153 A58 30c rose ('25) .35 .20
154 A58 35c red brown .35 .30
155 A58 35c blue grn ('27) .80 .35
156 A58 40c rose .50 .20
157 A58 50c bister ('25) .50 .20
158 A58 60c olive brn ('27) 3.00 .20
159 A58 1.25fr dp blue ('26) 1.10 1.10
160 A58 1.50fr brt blue ('26) 1.60 .45
161 A58 1.75fr ultra ('27) 1.40 .20
a. Tete beche pair 5.00 5.00
c. Bklt. pane of 4 + 2 labels 40.00
Nos. 144-161 (18) 11.70 5.00
Set, never hinged 27.50

See Nos. 185-190. For overprints and surcharges see #191-195, 197, B56, O1-O6.

1921-25 **Engr.**

11, 11x11½, 11½, 11½x11, 11½x12, 11½x12½, 12½
162 A59 50c dull blue .30 .20
163 A59 75c scarlet ('22) .25 .25
164 A59 75c ultra ('24) .45 .20
165 A59 1fr black brn ('22) .80 .20
166 A59 1fr dk blue ('25) .60 .20
167 A59 2fr dk green ('22) .90 .25
168 A59 5fr brown vio ('23) 13.50 *15.00*
169 A59 10fr magenta ('22) 9.00 6.50
Nos. 162-169 (8) 25.80 *22.80*
Set, never hinged 52.50

No. 162 measures 18x20¾mm and was printed in sheets of 100.

Philatelic Exhibition Issues

1921, May 26 *Perf. 11½*
170 A59 50c dark blue 3.50 3.50
Never hinged 4.75
a. Sheet of 25 200.00 175.00
Never hinged 225.00

No. 170 measures 17½x21¼mm, was printed in sheets of 25 and sold at the Philatelic Exhibition at Brussels.

The sheet normally has pin holes and a cancellation-like marking in the margin. These are considered unused and the condition valued here.

Souvenir Sheet

1924, May 24 *Perf. 11½*
171 Sheet of 4 140.00 140.00
Never hinged 260.00
a. A59 5fr red brown 10.00 10.00
Never hinged 12.00

Sold only at the Intl. Phil. Exhib., Brussels. Sheet size: 130x145mm.

The sheet normally has pin holes and a cancellation-like marking in the margin. These are considered unused and the condition valued here.

Kings Leopold I and Albert I — A60

1925, June 1 *Perf. 14*
172 A60 10c dp green 7.25 *7.25*
173 A60 15c dull vio 3.75 *4.50*
174 A60 20c red brown 3.75 *4.50*
175 A60 25c grnsh black 3.75 *4.50*
176 A60 30c vermilion 3.75 *4.50*
177 A60 35c lt blue 3.75 *4.50*
178 A60 40c brnsh blk 3.75 *4.50*
179 A60 50c yellow brn 3.75 *4.50*
180 A60 75c dk blue 3.75 *4.50*
181 A60 1fr dk violet 6.50 6.50
182 A60 2fr ultra 4.00 4.00
183 A60 5fr blue blk 3.75 *4.50*
184 A60 10fr dp rose 6.50 *8.00*
Nos. 172-184 (13) 58.00 *66.25*
Set, never hinged 125.00

75th anniv. of Belgian postage stamps.

Nos. 172-184 were sold only in sets and only by The Administration of Posts, not at post offices.

A61

1926-27 **Typo.**
185 A61 75c dk violet .75 .70
186 A61 1fr pale yellow .60 .35
187 A61 1fr rose red ('27) 1.00 .20
a. Tete beche pair 7.50 4.50
c. Bklt. pane 4 + 2 labels 25.00
188 A61 2fr Prus blue 2.50 .45
189 A61 5fr emerald ('27) 27.50 1.60
190 A61 10fr dk brown ('27) 60.00 7.75
Nos. 185-190 (6) 92.35 11.05
Set, never hinged 250.00

For overprints and surcharge see Nos. 196, Q174-Q175.

Stamps of 1921-27 Surcharged in Carmine, Red or Blue

1927
191 A58 3c on 2c olive .20 .20
192 A58 10c on 15c plum (R) .20 .20
193 A58 35c on 40c rose (Bl) .45 .20
194 A58 1.75fr on 1.50fr brt bl 2.25 .80
Nos. 191-194 (4) 3.10 1.40
Set, never hinged 3.75

Nos. 153, 185 and 159 Surcharged in Black

1929, Jan. 1
195 A58 5c on 30c rose .20 .20
196 A61 5c on 75c dk violet .20 .20
197 A58 5c on 1.25fr dp blue .20 .20
Nos. 195-197 (3) .60 .60
Set, never hinged .65

The surcharge on Nos. 195-197 is a precancelation which alters the value of the stamp to which it is applied.

Values for precanceled stamps in unused column are for those which have not been through the post and have original gum. Values in second column are for postally used, gumless stamps.

A63

A64

1929-32 **Typo.** *Perf. 14*
198 A63 1c orange .20 .20
199 A63 2c emerald ('31) .45 .45
200 A63 3c red brown .20 .20
201 A63 5c slate .20 .20
c. Bklt. pane of 4 + 2 labels 8.25
202 A63 10c olive grn .20 .20
c. Bklt. pane of 4 + 2 labels 4.50
203 A63 20c brt violet 1.00 .25
204 A63 25c rose red .45 .20
c. Bklt. pane of 4 + 2 labels 8.25
205 A63 35c green .60 .20
c. Bklt. pane of 4 + 2 labels 9.75
206 A63 40c red vio ('30) .30 .20
c. Bklt. pane of 4 + 2 labels 9.75
207 A63 50c dp blue .45 .20
c. Bklt. pane of 4 + 2 labels 8.25
208 A63 60c rose ('30) 2.00 .20
c. Bklt. pane of 4 + 2 labels 30.00
209 A63 70c org brn ('30) 1.10 .20
c. Bklt. pane of 4 + 2 labels 22.50
210 A63 75c dk blue ('30) 2.00 .20
211 A63 75c dp brown ('32) 6.00 .20
b. Bklt. pane of 4 + 2 labels 100.00
Nos. 198-211 (14) 15.15 3.10
Set, never hinged 55.00

For overprints and surcharges see Nos. 225-226, 240-241, 254-256, 309, O7-O15.

Tete Beche Pairs

201a	A63	5c	.60	.60
202a	A63	10c	.30	.30
204a	A63	25c	1.75	1.75
205a	A63	35c	2.75	2.75
206a	A63	40c	2.75	2.75
207a	A63	50c	2.25	2.25
208a	A63	60c	8.00	7.50
209a	A63	70c	6.00	5.00
210a	A63	75c	9.00	8.50
211a	A63	75c	27.50	25.00
		Nos. 201a-211a (10)	60.90	56.40
		Set, never hinged	110.00	

Tete-beche gutter pairs also exist.

Perf. 14½, 14x14½

1929, Jan. 25 **Engr.**
212 A64 10fr dk brown 15.00 4.00
213 A64 20fr dk green 85.00 20.00
214 A64 50fr red violet 13.50 13.50
a. Perf. 14½ 37.50 40.00
215 A64 100fr brownish lake 13.50 13.50
a. Perf. 14½ 37.50 40.00
Nos. 212-215 (4) 127.00 51.00
Set, never hinged 275.00

Peter Paul Rubens — A65

Zenobe Gramme — A66

1930, Apr. 26 **Photo.** *Perf. 12½x12*
216 A65 35c blue green .40 .20
217 A66 35c blue green .40 .20
Set, never hinged 2.10

No. 216 issued for the Antwerp Exhibition, No. 217 the Liege Exhibition.

Leopold I, by Jacques de Winn3 — A67

Leopold II, by Joseph Lempoels — A68

Design: 1.75fr, Albert I.

1930, July 1 **Engr.** *Perf. 11½*
218 A67 60c brown violet .20 .20
219 A68 1fr carmine 1.10 1.10
220 A68 1.75fr dk blue 2.75 1.25
Nos. 218-220 (3) 4.05 2.55
Set, never hinged 10.00

Centenary of Belgian independence.
For overprints see Nos. 222-224.

Antwerp Exhibition Issue

Souvenir Sheet

Arms of Antwerp A70

1930, Aug. 9 ***Perf. 11½***

221 A70 4fr Sheet of 1 87.50 87.50
Never hinged 140.00
a. Single stamp 55.00 40.00

Size: 142x141mm. Inscription in lower margin "ATELIER DU TIMBRE-1930-ZEGELFABRIEK." Each purchaser of a ticket to the Antwerp Phil. Exhib., Aug. 9-15, was allowed to purchase one stamp. The ticket cost 6 francs.

The sheet normally has pin holes and a cancellation-like marking in the margin. These are considered unused and the condition valued here.

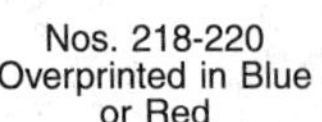

Nos. 218-220 Overprinted in Blue or Red

1930, Oct.

222 A67 60c brown vio (Bl) 2.00 2.00
223 A68 1fr carmine (Bl) 8.25 7.75
224 A68 1.75fr dk blue (R) 14.50 14.50
Nos. 222-224 (3) 24.75 24.25
Set, never hinged 55.00

50th meeting of the administrative council of the Intl. Labor Bureau at Brussels.

The names of the painters and the initials of the engraver have been added at the foot of these stamps.

Stamps of 1929-30 Surcharged in Blue or Black:

1931, Feb. 20 ***Perf. 14***

225 A63 2c on 3c red brown (Bl) .20 .20
226 A63 10c on 60c rose (Bk) .50 .20
Set, never hinged 3.75

The surcharge on No. 226 is a precancelation which alters the denomination. See note after No. 197.

King Albert
A71 A71a

1931, June 15 **Photo.**

227 A71 1fr brown carmine .50 .20
Never hinged 1.00

1932, June 1

228 A71a 75c bister brown 1.25 .20
Never hinged 5.00
a. Tete beche pair 6.75 6.75
Never hinged 17.50
c. Bklt. pane 4 + 2 labels 27.50

See No. 257. For overprint see No. O18.

A72

1931-32 **Engr.**

229 A72 1.25fr gray black .75 .50
230 A72 1.50fr brown vio 1.25 .50
231 A72 1.75fr dp blue .80 .20
232 A72 2fr red brown 1.10 .20
233 A72 2.45fr dp violet 1.90 .40
234 A72 2.50fr black brn ('32) 10.00 .50
235 A72 5fr dp green 18.00 1.10
236 A72 10fr claret 45.00 12.50
Nos. 229-236 (8) 78.80 15.90
Set, never hinged 250.00

Nos. 206 and 209 Surcharged as No. 226, but dated "1932"

1932, Jan. 1

240 A63 10c on 40c red vio 2.50 .30
241 A63 10c on 70c org brn 2.00 .20
Set, never hinged 13.50

See note after No. 197.

Gleaner A73 Mercury A74

1932, June 1 **Typo.** ***Perf. 13½x14***

245 A73 2c pale green .35 .35
246 A74 5c dp orange .20 .20
247 A73 10c olive grn .25 .20
a. Tete beche pair 4.00 4.00
Never hinged 5.75
c. Bklt. pane 4 + 2 labels 15.00
248 A74 20c brt violet 1.00 .20
249 A73 25c deep red .60 .20
a. Tete beche pair 3.50 3.50
Never hinged 5.00
c. Bklt. pane 4 + 2 labels 15.00
250 A74 35c dp green 2.40 .20
Nos. 245-250 (6) 4.80 1.35
Set, never hinged 14.50

For overprints see Nos. O16-O17.

Auguste Piccard's Balloon — A75

1932, Nov. 26 **Engr.** ***Perf. 11½***

251 A75 75c red brown 3.50 .30
252 A75 1.75fr dk blue 13.50 2.10
253 A75 2.50fr dk violet 17.00 11.50
Nos. 251-253 (3) 34.00 13.90
Set, never hinged 97.50

Issued in commemoration of Prof. Auguste Piccard's two ascents to the stratosphere.

Nos. 206 and 209 Surcharged as No. 226, but dated "1933"

1933, Nov. ***Perf. 14***

254 A63 10c on 40c red vio 14.00 4.00
255 A63 10c on 70c org brn 12.50 1.50
Set, never hinged 65.00

No. 206 Surcharged as No. 226, but dated "1934"

1934, Feb.

256 A63 10c on 40c red vio 12.50 1.50
Never hinged 35.00

For Nos. 254 to 256 see note after No. 197. Regummed copies of Nos. 254-256 abound.

King Albert Memorial Issue

Type of 1932 with Black Margins

1934, Mar. 10 **Photo.**

257 A71a 75c black .30 .20
Never hinged .60

Congo Pavilion — A76

Designs: 1fr, Brussels pavilion. 1.50fr, "Old Brussels." 1.75fr, Belgian pavilion.

1934, July 1 ***Perf. 14x13½***

258 A76 35c green .75 .30
259 A76 1fr dk carmine 1.25 .40
260 A76 1.50fr brown 5.00 .80
261 A76 1.75fr blue 5.00 .30
Nos. 258-261 (4) 12.00 1.80
Set, never hinged 45.00

Brussels Intl. Exhib. of 1935.

King Leopold III
A80 A81

1934-35 ***Perf. 13½x14***

262 A80 70c olive blk ('35) .35 .20
a. Tete beche pair 1.50 1.00
c. Bklt. pane 4 + 2 labels 6.25
263 A80 75c brown .65 .25

Perf. 14x13½

264 A81 1fr rose car ('35) 3.25 .35
Nos. 262-264 (3) 4.25 .80
Set, never hinged 10.00

For overprint see No. O19.

Coat of Arms — A82

1935-48 **Typo.** ***Perf. 14***

265 A82 2c green ('37) .20 .20
266 A82 5c orange .20 .20
267 A82 10c olive bister .20 .20
a. Tete beche pair .30 .25
Never hinged .50
b. Bklt. pane 4 + 2 labels 4.50
268 A82 15c dk violet .20 .20
269 A82 20c lilac .20 .20
270 A82 25c carmine rose .20 .20
a. Tete beche pair .30 .40
Never hinged .55
c. Bklt. pane 4 + 2 labels 4.50
271 A82 25c yel org ('46) .20 .20
272 A82 30c brown .20 .20
273 A82 35c green .20 .20
a. Tete beche pair .30 .30
Never hinged .50
c. Bklt. pane 4 + 2 labels 3.00
274 A82 40c red vio ('38) .20 .20
275 A82 50c blue .40 .20
276 A82 60c slate ('41) .20 .20
277 A82 65c red lilac ('46) .25 .20
278 A82 70c lt blue grn ('45) .25 .25
279 A82 75c lilac rose ('45) .25 .20
280 A82 80c green ('48) 3.50 .40
281 A82 90c dull vio ('46) .20 .20
282 A82 1fr red brown ('45) .20 .20
Nos. 265-282 (18) 7.25 3.85
Set, never hinged 17.00

Several stamps of type A82 exist in various shades.

Nos. 265, 361 were privately overprinted and surcharged "+10FR." by the Association Belgo-Americaine for the dedication of the Bastogne Memorial, July 16, 1950. The overprint is in six types.

See design O1. For overprints and surcharges see Nos. 312-313, 361-364, 390-394, O20-O22, O24, O26-O28, O33.

A83 A83a

Perf. 14, 14x13½, 11½

1936-51 **Photo.**

Size: 17½x21¾mm

283 A83 70c brown .30 .20
a. Tete beche pair .80 .80
Never hinged 1.40
c. Bklt. pane 4 + 2 labels 7.50

Size: 20¾x24mm

284 A83a 1fr rose car .30 .20
285 A83a 1.20fr dk brown ('51) .80 .20
286 A83a 1.50fr brt red vio ('43) .40 .30
287 A83a 1.75fr dp ultra ('43) .20 .20
288 A83a 1.75fr dk car ('50) .20 .20
289 A83a 2fr dk pur ('43) 1.00 1.00
290 A83a 2.25fr grnsh blk ('43) .25 .20
291 A83a 2.50fr org red ('51) 1.75 .30
292 A83a 3.25fr chestnut ('43) .20 .20
293 A83a 5fr dp green ('43) 1.00 .40
Nos. 283-293 (11) 6.40 3.40
Set, never hinged 17.00

Nos. 287-288, 290-291, 293 inscribed "Belgie-Belgique."

See designs A85, A91. For overprints and surcharges see #314, O23, O25, O29, O31, O34.

A84 A85

1936-51 **Engr.** ***Perf. 14x13½***

294 A84 1.50fr rose lilac .60 .35
295 A84 1.75fr dull blue .20 .20
296 A84 2fr dull vio .40 .30
297 A84 2.25fr gray vio ('41) .25 .25
298 A84 2.45fr black 32.50 .70
299 A84 2.50fr ol blk ('40) 2.00 .25
300 A84 3.25fr org brn ('41) .30 .20
301 A84 5fr dull green 2.40 .50
302 A84 10fr vio brn .60 .20
a. 10fr light brown 1.00 .20
Never hinged 3.00
303 A84 20fr vermilion 1.00 .30

Perf. 11½

304 A84 3fr yel brn ('51) .55 .20
305 A84 4fr bl, *bluish* ('50) 4.75 .20
a. White paper ('51) 5.50 .20
306 A84 6fr brt rose car ('51) 2.75 .20
307 A84 10fr brn vio ('51) .55 .20
308 A84 20fr red ('51) 1.10 .20
Nos. 294-308 (15) 49.95 4.25
Set, never hinged 150.00

See No. 1159. For overprint and surcharges see Nos. 316-317, O32.

No. 206 Surcharged as No. 226, but dated "1937"

1937 **Unwmk.** ***Perf. 14***

309 A63 10c on 40c red vio .20 .20
Never hinged .30

See note after No. 197.

1938-41 **Photo.** ***Perf. 13½x14***

310 A85 75c olive gray .25 .20
a. Tete beche pair .75 .80
Never hinged 1.50
c. Bklt. pane 4 + 2 labels 6.75
311 A85 1fr rose pink ('41) .20 .20
a. Tete beche pair .25 .25
Never hinged .40
b. Booklet pane of 6 2.25
c. Bklt. pane 4 + 2 labels 2.25
Set, never hinged .80

For overprints and surcharges see Nos. 315, O25, O30, O35.

Nos. 272, 274, 283, 310, 299, 298 Surcharged in Blue, Black, Carmine or Red

a

b

c

1938-42

312 A82 (a) 10c on 30c (Bl) .20 .20
313 A82 (a) 10c on 40c (Bl) .20 .20
314 A83 (b) 10c on 70c (Bk) .20 .20
315 A85 (b) 50c on 75c (C) .20 .20
316 A84 (c) 2.25fr on 2.50fr (C) .45 .45
317 A84 (c) 2.50fr on 2.45fr (R) 11.00 .20
Nos. 312-317 (6) 12.25 1.45
Set, never hinged 26.00

Issue date: No. 317, Oct. 31, 1938.

Basilica and Bell Tower — A86

Water Exhibition Buildings — A87

Designs: 1.50fr, Albert Canal and Park. 1.75fr, Eygenbilsen Cut in Albert Canal.

1938, Oct. 31 ***Perf. 14x13½, 13½x14***

318	A86	35c dk blue grn	.20	.20
319	A87	1fr rose red	.45	.30
320	A87	1.50fr vio brn	1.10	.60
321	A87	1.75fr ultra	1.25	.20
		Nos. 318-321 (4)	3.00	1.30
		Set, never hinged	11.00	

Intl. Water Exhibition, Liège, 1939.

Catalogue values for unused stamps in this section, from this point to the end of the section, are for Never Hinged items.

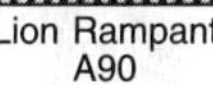

Lion Rampant A90

Leopold III, Crown and V A91

1944 Unwmk. Photo. ***Perf. 12½***

Inscribed: "Belgique-Belgie"

322	A90	5c chocolate	.20	.20
323	A90	10c green	.20	.20
324	A90	25c lt blue	.20	.20
325	A90	35c brown	.20	.20
326	A90	50c lt bl grn	.20	.20
327	A90	75c purple	.20	.20
328	A90	1fr vermilion	.20	.20
329	A90	1.25fr chestnut	.20	.20
330	A90	1.50fr orange	.45	.40
331	A90	1.75fr brt ultra	.20	.20
332	A90	2fr aqua	3.75	1.90
333	A90	2.75fr dp mag	.20	.20
334	A90	3fr claret	.75	.60
335	A90	3.50fr sl blk	.75	.60
336	A90	5fr dk olive	6.75	4.75
337	A90	10fr black	1.25	1.10
		Nos. 322-337 (16)	15.70	11.35

Inscribed: "Belgie-Belgique"

338	A90	5c chocolate	.20	.20
339	A90	10c green	.20	.20
340	A90	25c lt bl	.20	.20
341	A90	35c brown	.20	.20
342	A90	50c lt bl grn	.20	.20
343	A90	75c purple	.20	.20
344	A90	1fr vermilion	.20	.20
345	A90	1.25fr chestnut	.20	.20
346	A90	1.50fr orange	.30	*.45*
347	A90	1.75fr brt ultra	.20	.20
348	A90	2fr aqua	2.00	2.00
349	A90	2.75fr dp magenta	.20	.20
350	A90	3fr claret	.65	*.75*
351	A90	3.50fr slate blk	.65	*.75*
352	A90	5fr dark olive	5.75	5.00
353	A90	10fr black	1.00	*1.25*
		Nos. 338-353 (16)	12.35	12.20

1944-57 ***Perf. 14x13½***

354	A91	1fr brt rose red	.35	.20
355	A91	1.50fr magenta	.50	.20
356	A91	1.75fr dp ultra	.50	.55
357	A91	2fr dp vio	1.50	.20
358	A91	2.25fr grnsh blk	.55	.65
359	A91	3.25fr chnt brn	.75	.20
360	A91	5fr dk bl grn	3.00	.20
a.		Perf. 11½ ('57)	75.00	.20
		Nos. 354-360 (7)	7.15	2.20

Nos. 355, 357, 359 inscribed "Belgique-Belgie."

For surcharges see Nos. 365-367 and footnote following No. 367.

Stamps of 1935-41 Overprinted in Red

1944 ***Perf. 14***

361	A82	2c pale green	.20	.20
362	A82	15c indigo	.20	.20
363	A82	20c brt violet	.20	.20
364	A82	60c slate	.25	.20
		Nos. 361-364 (4)	.85	.80

See note following No. 282.

-10%

Nos. 355, 357, and 360 Surcharged Typographically in Black or Carmine

1946 ***Perf. 14x13½***

365	A91	On 1.50fr magenta	.40	.20
366	A91	On 2fr dp vio (C)	1.50	.45
367	A91	On 5fr dk bl grn (C)	2.00	.30
		Nos. 365-367 (3)	3.90	.95

To provide denominations created by a reduction in postal rates, the Government produced #365-367 by typographed surcharge. Also, each post office was authorized on May 20, 1946, to surcharge its stock of 1.50fr, 2fr and 5fr stamps "-10 percent." Hundreds of types and sizes of this surcharge exist, both hand-stamped and typographed. These include the "1,35," "1,80" and "4,50" applied at Ghislenghien.

M. S. Prince Baudouin — A92

2.25fr, S.S. Marie Henriette. 3.15fr, S.S. Diamant.

Perf. 14x13½, 13½x14

1946, June 15 Photo. Unwmk.

368	A92	1.35fr brt bluish grn	.20	.20
369	A92	2.25fr slate green	.30	.20
370	A92	3.15fr slate black	.30	.20
		Nos. 368-370 (3)	.80	.60

Centenary of the steamship line between Ostend and Dover.

#368 exists in two sizes: 21¼x18¼mm and 21x17mm. #369-370 are 24½x20mm.

Capt. Adrien de Gerlache — A95

Belgica and Explorers A96

1947, June ***Perf. 14x13½, 11½***

371	A95	1.35fr crimson rose	.45	.20
372	A96	2.25fr gray black	2.75	2.00

50th anniv. of Capt. Adrien de Gerlache's Antarctic Expedition.

Joseph A. F. Plateau — A97

1947, June ***Perf. 14x13½***

373	A97	3.15fr deep blue	.80	.20

Issued to mark the World Film and Fine Arts Festival, Brussels, June, 1947.

Chemical Industry — A98

Industrial Arts — A99

Agriculture A100

Textile Industry A102

Communications Center — A101

Iron Manufacture A103

Photogravure (#374-376, 378), Typographed (#377, 380), Engraved

1948 Unwmk. ***Perf. 11½***

374	A98	60c blue grn	.85	.20
375	A98	1.20fr brown	2.25	.20
376	A99	1.35fr red brown	.85	.20
377	A100	1.75fr brt red	1.60	.20
378	A99	1.75fr dk gray grn	1.10	.20
379	A101	2.25fr gray blue	2.00	1.75
380	A100	2.50fr dk car rose	6.75	.20
381	A101	3fr brt red vio	9.00	.30
382	A102	3.15fr deep blue	2.00	.20
383	A102	4fr brt ultra	8.25	.20
384	A103	6fr blue green	13.00	.20
385	A103	6.30fr brt red vio	4.00	3.75
		Nos. 374-385 (12)	51.65	7.60

See Nos. O42-O46.

Leopold I — A104

1949, July 1 Engr. ***Perf. 14x13½***

386	A104	90c dk green	1.10	.55
387	A104	1.75fr brown	.90	.20
388	A104	3fr red	3.50	3.00
389	A104	4fr deep blue	5.00	1.25
		Nos. 386-389 (4)	10.50	5.00

Cent. of Belgium's 1st postage stamps. See note on souvenir sheet below No. 2.

Stamps of 1935-45 Precanceled and Surcharged in Black

1949 ***Perf. 14***

390	A82	5c on 15c dk vio	.20	.20
391	A82	5c on 30c brown	.20	.20
392	A82	5c on 40c red vio	.20	.20
393	A82	20c on 70c lt bl grn	.30	.35
394	A82	20c on 75c lil rose	.20	.20

Similar Surcharge and Precancellation in Black on Nos. B455-B458

Perf. 14x13½

395	SP251	10c on #B455	3.50	3.00
396	SP251	40c on #B456	1.10	.85
397	SP251	80c on #B457	.65	.50
398	SP251	1.20fr on #B458	2.25	1.50
		Nos. 390-398 (9)	8.60	7.00

See note after No. 197.

St. Mary Magdalene, from Painting by Gerard David — A105

1949, July 15 Photo. ***Perf. 11***

399	A105	1.75fr dark brown	.70	.35

Gerard David Exhibition at Bruges, 1949.

Allegory of UPU A106

1949, Oct. 1 Engr. ***Perf. 11½***

400	A106	4fr deep blue	4.50	2.50

75th anniv. of the UPU.

Symbolical of Pension Fund A107

Lion Rampant A108

Perf. 11½

1950, May 1 Unwmk. Photo.

401	A107	1.75fr dark brown	.50	.25

General Pension Fund founding, cent.

1951, Feb. 15 Engr. ***Perf. 11½***

402	A108	20c blue	.25	.20

1951-75 Typo. ***Perf. 13½x14***

Size: 17½x21mm

403	A108	2c org brn ('60)	.20	.20
404	A108	3c brt lil ('60)	.20	.20
405	A108	5c pale violet	.20	.20
406	A108	5c brt pink ('74)	.20	.20
407	A108	10c red orange	.20	.20
408	A108	15c brt pink ('59)	.20	.20
409	A108	20c claret	.20	.20
410	A108	25c green	1.75	.25
411	A108	25c lt bl grn ('66)	.20	.20
412	A108	30c gray grn ('57)	.20	.20
413	A108	40c brown olive	.20	.20
414	A108	50c ultra	.20	.20
a.		50c light blue	.20	.20
415	A108	60c lilac rose	.20	.20
416	A108	65c violet brn	12.50	.55
417	A108	75c bluish lilac	.20	.20
418	A108	80c emerald	.75	.20
419	A108	90c deep blue	.75	.20
420	A108	1fr rose	.20	.20
421	A108	2fr emerald ('73)	.20	.20
422	A108	2.50fr brown ('70)	.20	.20
423	A108	3fr brt pink ('70)	.20	.20
424	A108	4fr brt rose lil ('74)	.25	.20
425	A108	4.50fr blue ('74)	.30	.20
426	A108	5fr brt lilac ('75)	.30	.20

Size: 17x20½mm

427	A108	1.50fr dk sl grn ('69)	.20	.20

Perf. 13½x13

428	A108	2fr emerald ('68)	.20	.20

Photo. ***Perf. 11½***

Size: 20½x24mm

429	A108	50c light blue ('61)	.45	.20
430	A108	60c lilac rose ('66)	1.10	.70
431	A108	1fr carmine rose ('59)	.20	.20

Perf. 13½x12½

Size: 17½x22mm

432	A108	50c lt blue ('75)	.20	.20
a.		Booklet pane of 4 (#432, 784 and 2 #785) + labels	1.00	
b.		Booklet pane of 4 (#432 and 3 #787) + labels	1.50	

433 A108 1fr rose ('69) 2.00 .90
434 A108 2fr emerald ('72) .50 .30
e. Booklet pane of 6 (4 #434 + 2 #475) 5.50
f. Booklet pane of 5 (#434, 4 #476 + label) 8.00
Nos. 403-434 (32) 24.85 8.10

Counterfeits exist of No. 416. Nos. 429, 431 also issued in coils with black control number on back of every fifth stamp. Nos. 432-434 issued in booklet panes only. No. 432 has one straightedge, and stamps in the pane are tete-beche. Each pane has 2 labels showing Belgian postal emblem and a large selvage with postal code instructions.

Nos. 433-434 have 1 or 2 straight-edges. Panes have a large selvage with inscription or map of Belgium showing postal zones.

See designs A386, O5. For surcharges see Nos. 477-478, 563-567.

Francois de Tassis (Franz von Taxis) — A109

Portraits: 1.75fr, Jean-Baptiste of Thurn & Taxis. 2fr, Baron Leonard I. 2.50fr, Count Lamoral I. 3fr, Count Leonard II. 4fr, Count Lamoral II. 5fr, Prince Eugene Alexander. 5.75fr, Prince Anselme Francois. 8fr, Prince Alexander Ferdinand. 10fr, Prince Charles Anselme. 20fr, Prince Charles Alexander.

1952, May 14 Engr. *Perf. 11½*

Laid Paper

435 A109 80c olive grn .75 .30
436 A109 1.75fr red org .75 .30
437 A109 2fr violet brn 1.50 .40
438 A109 2.50fr carmine 2.25 1.65
439 A109 3fr olive bis 2.00 1.00
440 A109 4fr ultra 3.00 .85
441 A109 5fr red brn 4.00 1.75
442 A109 5.75fr blue vio 6.75 2.25
443 A109 8fr gray 12.50 2.75
444 A109 10fr rose vio 22.50 4.50
445 A109 20fr brown 60.00 22.50
Nos. 435-445,B514 (12) 291.00 213.25

13th UPU Cong., Brussels, 1952.

King Baudouin
A110 A111

1952-58 Engr. *Perf. 11½*

Size: 21x24mm

446 A110 1.50fr gray green .55 .20
447 A110 2fr crimson .40 .20
448 A110 4fr ultra 3.50 .20

Size: 24½x35mm

449 A110 50fr gray brn 1.75 .20
a. 50fr violet brown 35.00 .60
450 A110 100fr rose red ('58) 5.00 .25

1953-72 Photo. *Perf. 11½*

451 A111 1.50fr gray .25 .20
452 A111 2fr rose carmine 6.75 .20
453 A111 2fr green .25 .20
454 A111 2.50fr red brn ('57) .60 .20
a. 2.50fr orange brown ('70) .25 .20
455 A111 3fr rose lil ('58) .40 .20
456 A111 3.50fr brt yel grn ('58) .75 .20
457 A111 4fr brt ultra .50 .20
458 A111 4.50fr dk red brn ('62) 3.00 .20
459 A111 5fr violet ('57) 1.25 .20
460 A111 6fr dp pink ('58) .75 .20
461 A111 6.50fr gray ('60) 62.50 13.00
462 A111 7fr blue ('60) .90 .20
463 A111 7.50fr grysh brn ('58) 47.50 12.50
464 A111 8fr bluish gray ('58) 1.25 .20
465 A111 8.50fr claret ('58) 15.00 .30
466 A111 9fr gray ('58) 47.50 .75
467 A111 12fr lt bl grn ('66) .90 .25
468 A111 30fr red org ('58) 5.50 .20

Redrawn

469 A111 2.50fr org brn ('71) .35 .20
470 A111 4.50fr brown ('72) 2.25 .60
471 A111 7fr blue ('71) .60 .20

Perf. 13½x12½

Size: 17½x22mm

472 A111 1.50fr gray ('70) .60 .30
b. Bklt. pane of 10 6.50
c. Bklt. pane, 3 #472, 3 #475 15.00
473 A111 2.50fr org brn ('70) 5.00 4.00
h. Bklt. pane, 1 #473, 5 #475 16.00
474 A111 3fr lilac rose ('69) .60 .20
a. Bklt. pane of 5 + label 25.00
b. Bklt. pane, 2 #433, 6 #474 18.00
475 A111 3.50fr brt yel grn ('70) .60 .25
476 A111 4.50fr dull red brn ('72) .60 .35
Nos. 446-476 (31) 217.35 36.55

Nos. 451, 453, 454a, 455, 456, 458 also issued in coils with black control number on back of every fifth stamp. These coils, except for No. 451, are on luminescent paper.

On Nos. 469-471, the 2, 4 and 7 are 3mm high. The background around the head is white. On Nos. 454, 458, 462 the 2, 4 and 7 are 2½mm high and the background is tinted.

Nos. 472-476 issued in booklets only and have 1 or 2 straight-edges. All panes have a large selvage with inscription or map.

See designs M1, O3.

Luminescent Paper

Stamps issued on both ordinary and luminescent paper include: Nos. 307-308, 430-431, 449-451, 453-460, 462, 464, 467-468, 472, 643-644, 650-651, 837, Q385, Q410.

Stamps issued only on luminescent paper include: Nos. 433, 454a, 472b, 473-474, 649, 652-658, 664-670, 679-682, 688-690, 694-696, 698-703, 705-711, 713-726, 729-747, 751-754, 756-757, 759, 761-762, 764, 766, 769, 772, 774, 778, 789, 791-793, 795, 797-799, 801-807, 809-811, 814-818, 820-834, 836, 838-848.

See note after No. 857.

Nos. 416 and 419 Surcharged and Precanceled in Black

1954, Jan. 1 Unwmk. *Perf. 13½x14*

477 A108 20c on 65c vio brn 1.75 .30
478 A108 20c on 90c dp blue 1.75 .20

See note after No. 197.

Map and Rotary Emblem A112

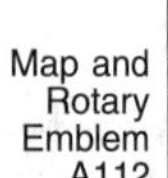

80c, Mermaid and Mercury holding emblem. 4fr, Rotary emblem and two globes.

1954, Sept. 10 Engr. *Perf. 11½*

479 A112 20c red .25 .20
480 A112 80c dark green .65 .30
481 A112 4fr ultra 1.40 .50
Nos. 479-481 (3) 2.30 1.00

5th regional conf. of Rotary Intl. at Ostend. No. 481 for Rotary 50th Anniv. (in 1955).

A souv. sheet containing one each, imperf., was sold for 500 francs. It was not valid for postage. Value, $200.

The Rabot and Begonia — A113

Designs: 2.50fr, The Oudeburg and azalea. 4fr, "Three Towers" and orchid.

1955, Feb. 15 Photo.

482 A113 80c brt carmine .85 .35
483 A113 2.50fr black brn 5.25 2.75
484 A113 4fr dk rose brn 5.00 .90
Nos. 482-484 (3) 11.10 4.00

Ghent Intl. Flower Exhibition, 1955.

Homage to Charles V as a Child, by Albrecht de Vriendt A114

Charles V, by Titian — A115

4fr, Abdication of Charles V, by Louis Gallait.

1955, Mar. 25 Unwmk. *Perf. 11½*

485 A114 20c rose red .25 .20
486 A115 2fr dk gray green 1.90 .20
487 A114 4fr blue 5.00 1.25
Nos. 485-487 (3) 7.15 1.65

Charles V Exhibition, Ghent, 1955.

Emile Verhaeren, by Montald Constant — A116

1955, May 11 Engr.

488 A116 20c dark gray .20 .20

Birth cent. of Verhaeren, poet.

Allegory of Textile Manufacture A117

1955, May 11

489 A117 2fr violet brown 1.00 .20

2nd Intl. Textile Exhibition, Brussels, June 1955.

"The Foolish Virgin" by Rik Wouters — A118

1955, June 10

490 A118 1.20fr olive green 1.10 1.10
491 A118 2fr violet 1.60 .20

3rd biennial exhibition of sculpture, Antwerp, June 11-Sept. 10, 1955.

"Departure of Volunteers from Liege, 1830" by Charles Soubre — A119

1955, Sept. 10 Photo.

492 A119 20c grnsh slate .20 .20
493 A119 2fr chocolate .90 .20

Exhibition "The Romantic Movement in Liege Province," Sept. 10-Oct. 31, 1955; and 125th anniv. of Belgium's independence from the Netherlands.

Pelican Giving Blood to Young — A120

1956, Jan. 14 Engr.

494 A120 2fr brt carmine .35 .20

Blood donor service of the Belgian Red Cross.

Buildings of Tournai, Ghent and Antwerp — A121

1956, July 14 Photo.

495 A121 2fr brt ultra .30 .20

The Scheldt exhibition (Scaldis) at Tournai, Ghent and Antwerp, July-Sept. 1956.

Europa Issue

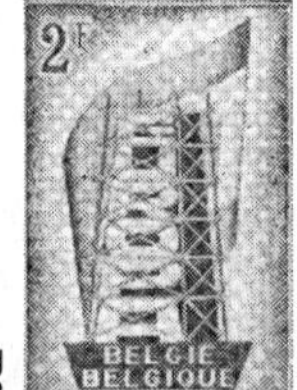

"Rebuilding Europe" — A122

1956, Sept. 15 Engr.

496 A122 2fr lt green 1.50 .20
497 A122 4fr purple 9.00 .50

Issued to symbolize the cooperation among the six countries comprising the Coal and Steel Community.

Train on Map of Belgium and Luxembourg A123

1956, Sept. 29

498 A123 2fr dark blue .45 .20

Issued to mark the electrification of the Brussels-Luxembourg railroad.

Edouard Anseele — A124

1956, Oct. 27

499 A124 20c violet brown .20 .20

Cent. of the birth of Edouard Anseele, statesman, and in connection with an exhibition held in his honor at Ghent.

"The Atom" and Exposition Emblem — A125

1957-58 **Unwmk.**

500 A125	2fr carmine rose	.25	.20
501 A125	2.50fr green ('58)	.40	.20
502 A125	4fr brt violet blue	.95	.20
503 A125	5fr claret ('58)	.85	.50
	Nos. 500-503 (4)	2.45	1.10

1958 World's Fair at Brussels.

Emperor Maximilian I Receiving Letter — A126

1957, May 19

504 A126 2fr claret .40 .20

Day of the Stamp, May 19, 1957.

Sikorsky S-58 Helicopter A127

1957, June 15

505 A127 4fr gray grn & brt bl .80 .45

100,000th passenger carried by Sabena helicopter service, June 15, 1957.

Zeebrugge Harbor A128

1957, July 6

506 A128 2fr dark blue .40 .20

50th anniv. of the completion of the port of Zeebrugge-Bruges.

Leopold I Entering Brussels, 1831 — A129

Leopold I Arriving at Belgian Border A130

1957, July 17 **Photo.**

507 A129 20c dk gray grn .20 .20
508 A130 2fr lilac .50 .20

126th anniv. of the arrival in Belgium of King Leopold I.

Boy Scout and Girl Scout Emblems A131

Design: 4fr, Robert Lord Baden-Powell, painted by David Jaggers, vert.

Perf. 11½

1957, July 29 **Unwmk.** **Engr.**

509 A131 80c gray .25 .20
510 A131 4fr light green 1.00 .45

Cent. of the birth of Lord Baden-Powell, founder of the Boy Scout movement.

"Kneeling Woman" by Lehmbruck — A132

1957, Aug. 20 **Photo.**

511 A132 2.50fr dk blue grn 1.10 .85

4th Biennial Exposition of Sculpture, Antwerp, May 25-Sept. 15.

"United Europe" — A133

1957, Sept. 16 **Engr.** ***Perf. 11½***

512 A133 2fr dk violet brn .75 .20
513 A133 4fr dark blue 2.00 .35

Europa: United Europe for peace and prosperity.

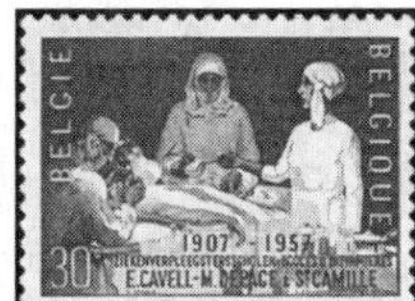

Queen Elisabeth Assisting at Operation, by Allard L'Olivier A134

Perf. 11½

1957, Nov. 23 **Unwmk.** **Engr.**

514 A134 30c rose lilac .20 .20

50th anniv. of the founding of the Edith Cavell-Marie Depage and St. Camille schools of nursing.

Post Horn and Historic Postal Insignia A135

1958, Mar. 16 **Photo.** ***Perf. 11½***

515 A135 2.50fr gray .25 .20

Postal Museum Day.

United Nations Issue

International Labor Organization A136

Allegory of UN — A137

Designs: 1fr, FAO. 2fr, World Bank. 2.50fr, UNESCO. 3fr, UN Pavilion. 5fr, ITU. 8fr, Intl. Monetary Fund. 11fr, WHO. 20fr, UPU.

Perf. 11½

1958, Apr. 17 **Unwmk.** **Engr.**

516 A136	50c gray	.90	*1.40*
517 A136	1fr claret	.30	*.45*
518 A137	1.50fr dp ultra	.30	*.45*
519 A137	2fr gray brown	.85	*1.25*
520 A136	2.50fr olive grn	.30	*.45*
521 A136	3fr grnsh blue	.85	*1.25*
522 A137	5fr rose lilac	.55	*.90*
523 A136	8fr red brown	1.00	*1.60*
524 A136	11fr dull lilac	1.25	*2.00*
525 A136	20fr car rose	1.60	*2.50*
	Nos. 516-525,C15-C20 (16)	10.20	*14.70*

World's Fair, Brussels, Apr. 17-Oct. 19.

Postally valid only from the UN pavilion at the Brussels Fair. Proceeds went toward financing the UN exhibits.

Eugène Ysaye A138

1958, Sept. 1

526 A138 30c dk blue & plum .20 .20

Ysaye (1858-1931), violinist, composer.

Common Design Types pictured in section at front of book.

Europa Issue, 1958

Common Design Type

1958, Sept. 13 **Photo.**

Size: 24½x35mm

527 CD1 2.50fr brt red & blue .60 .20
528 CD1 5fr brt blue & red 1.10 .35

Issued to show the European Postal Union at the service of European integration.

Universal Declaration of Human Rights, 10th Anniv. — A140

Infant and UN Emblem.

1958, Dec. 10 **Engr.**

529 A140 2.50fr blue gray .30 .20

Charles V , Jean-Baptiste of Thurn and Taxis — A141

1959, Mar. 15 **Unwmk.**

530 A141 2.50fr green .35 .20

Issued for the Day of the Stamp. Design from painting by J.-E. van den Bussche.

NATO Emblem — A142

1959, Apr. 3 **Photo.** ***Perf. 11½***

531 A142 2.50fr dp red & dk bl .45 .20
532 A142 5fr emerald & dk bl 1.25 *1.40*

10th anniv. of NATO. See No. 720.

City Hall, Audenarde — A143

1959, Aug. 17 **Engr.**

533 A143 2.50fr deep claret .30 .20

Pope Adrian VI, by Jan van Scorel — A144

1959, Aug. 31 ***Perf. 11½***

534 A144 2.50fr dark red .20 .20
535 A144 5fr Prus blue .55 .55

500th anniv. of the birth of Pope Adrian VI.

Europa Issue, 1959

Common Design Type

1959, Sept. 19 **Photo.**

Size: 24x35½mm

536 CD2 2.50fr dark red .25 .20
537 CD2 5fr brt grnsh blue .55 .35

Boeing 707 A146

Engraved and Photogravure

1959, Dec. 1 ***Perf. 11½***

538 A146 6fr dk bl gray & car 1.75 .80

Inauguration of jet flights by Sabena Airlines.

Countess of Taxis — A147

1960, Mar. 21 **Engr.** ***Perf. 11½***

539 A147 3fr dark blue .85 .20

Alexandrine de Rye, Countess of Taxis, Grand Mistress of the Netherlands Posts, 1628-1645, and day of the stamp, Mar. 21, 1960. The painting of the Countess is by Nicholas van der Eggermans.

24th Ghent Intl. Flower Exhibition — A148

1960, Mar. 28 **Unwmk.**

540 A148 40c Indian azalea .20 .20
541 A148 3fr Begonia .90 .20
542 A148 6fr Anthurium, bromelia 1.00 .90
Nos. 540-542 (3) 2.10 1.30

Steel Workers, by Constantin Meunier — A149

Design: 3fr, The sower, field and dock workers, from "Monument to Labor," Brussels, by Constantin Meunier, horiz.

Engraved and Photogravure

1960, Apr. 30 ***Perf. 11½***

543 A149 40c claret & brt red .20 .20
544 A149 3fr brown & brt red .85 .25

Socialist Party of Belgium, 75th anniv.

Congo River Boat Pilot — A150

Designs: 40c, Medical team. 1fr, Planting tree. 2fr, Sculptors. 2.50fr, Shot put. 3fr, Congolese officials. 6fr, Congolese and Belgian girls playing with doll. 8fr, Boy pointing on globe to independent Congo.

1960, June 30 **Photo.** ***Perf. 11½***

Size: 35x24mm

545 A150 10c bright red .30 .20
546 A150 40c rose claret .45 .20
547 A150 1fr brt lilac .85 .75
548 A150 2fr gray green .95 .85
549 A150 2.50fr blue .85 .75
550 A150 3fr dk bl gray 1.00 .45

Size: 51x35mm

551 A150 6fr violet bl 3.00 1.90
552 A150 8fr dk brown 5.00 4.00
Nos. 545-552 (8) 12.40 9.10

Independence of Congo.

Europa Issue, 1960

Common Design Type

1960, Sept. 17

Size: 35x24½mm

553 CD3 3fr claret .45 .20
554 CD3 6fr gray .90 .35

Children Examining Stamp and Globe — A152

1960, Oct. 1 **Photo.** ***Perf. 11½***

555 A152 40c bis & blk + label .20 .20

Promoting stamp collecting among children.

H. J. W. Frère-Orban A153

Engraved and Photogravure

1960, Oct. 17 **Unwmk.**

Portrait in Brown

556 A153 10c orange yel .20 .20
557 A153 40c blue grn .20 .20
558 A153 1.50fr brt violet .70 .70
559 A153 3fr red 1.10 .20
Nos. 556-559 (4) 2.20 1.30

Centenary of Communal Credit Society.

King Baudouin and Queen Fabiola A154

1960, Dec. 13 **Photo.** ***Perf. 11½***

Portraits in Dark Brown

560 A154 40c green .20 .20
561 A154 3fr red lilac .30 .20
562 A154 6fr dull blue 1.25 .60
Nos. 560-562 (3) 1.75 1.00

Wedding of King Baudouin and Dona Fabiola de Mora y Aragon, Dec. 15, 1960.

Nos. 412, 414 Surcharged

1961-68 **Typo.** ***Perf. 13½x14***

563 A108 15c on 30c gray grn .20 .20
564 A108 15c on 50c blue ('68) .20 .20
565 A108 20c on 30c gray grn .20 .20
Nos. 563-565 (3) .60 .60

No. 412 Surcharged and Precanceled

1961

566 A108 15c on 30c gray grn .90 .20
567 A108 20c on 30c gray grn 1.90 1.40

See note after No. 197.

Nicolaus Rockox, by Anthony Van Dyck — A155

Engraved and Photogravure

1961, Mar. 18 ***Perf. 11½***

568 A155 3fr bister, blk & brn .35 .20

400th anniv. of the birth of Nicolaus Rockox, mayor of Antwerp.

Seal of Jan Bode, Alderman of Antwerp, 1264 — A156

1961, Apr. 16 **Photo.**

569 A156 3fr buff & brown .35 .20

Issued for Stamp Day, April 16.

Senate Building, Brussels, Laurel and Sword A157

Engraved and Photogravure

1961, Sept. 14 **Unwmk.** ***Perf. 11½***

570 A157 3fr brn & Prus grn .30 .20
571 A157 6fr dk brn & dk car 2.75 1.00

50th Conference of the Interparliamentary Union, Brussels, Sept. 14-22.

Europa Issue, 1961

Common Design Type

1961, Sept. 16 **Photo.**

572 CD4 3fr yel grn & dk grn .20 .20
573 CD4 6fr org brn & blk .25 .20

Atomic Reactor Plant, BR2, Mol — A159

Designs: 3fr, Atomic Reactor BR3, vert. 6fr, Atomic Reactor plant BR3.

1961, Nov. 8 **Unwmk.** ***Perf. 11½***

574 A159 40c dk blue grn .20 .20
575 A159 3fr red lilac .20 .20
576 A159 6fr bright blue .35 .25
Nos. 574-576 (3) .75 .65

Atomic nuclear research center at Mol.

Horta Museum — A160

1962, Feb. 15 **Engr.**

577 A160 3fr red brown .25 .20

Baron Victor Horta (1861-1947), architect.

Postrider, 16th Century A161

Engraved and Photogravure

1962, Mar. 25 ***Perf. 11½***

Chalky Paper

578 A161 3fr brn & slate grn .30 .20

Stamp Day. See No. 677.

Gerard Mercator (Gerhard Kremer, 1512-1594), Cartographer A162

Engraved and Photogravure

1962, Apr. 14 **Unwmk.**

579 A162 3fr sepia & gray .30 .20

Bro. Alexis-Marie Gochet (1835-1910), Geographer, Educator — A163

1962, May 19 **Engr.** ***Perf. 11½***

Portrait: 3fr, Canon Pierre-Joseph Triest (1760-1836), educator and founder of hospitals and orphanages.

580 A163 2fr dark blue .30 .20
581 A163 3fr golden brown .30 .20

Europa Issue, 1962

Common Design Type

1962, Sept. 15 **Photo.**

582 CD5 3fr dp car, citron & blk .20 .20
583 CD5 6fr olive, citron & blk .30 .30

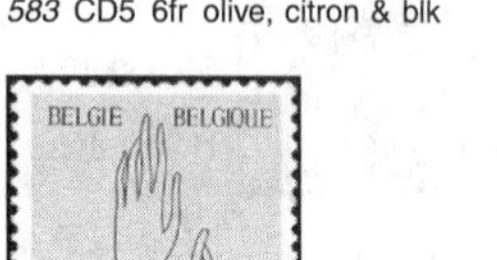

Hand with Barbed Wire and Freed Hand — A165

1962, Sept. 16 **Engr. & Photo.**

584 A165 40c lt blue & blk .20 .20

Issued in memory of concentration camp victims.

Adam, by Michelangelo, Broken Chain and UN Emblem — A166

1962, Nov. 24 ***Perf. 11½***

585 A166 3fr gray & blk .25 .20
586 A166 6fr lt redsh brn & dk brn .40 .30

UN Declaration of Human Rights.

Henri Pirenne (1862-1935), Historian — A167

1963, Jan. 15 **Engr.**

587 A167 3fr ultramarine .35 .20

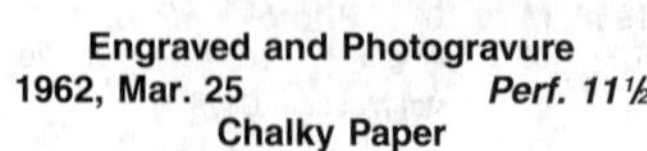

Swordsmen and Ghent Belfry A168

3fr, Modern fencers. 6fr, Arms of the Royal and Knightly Guild of St. Michael, vert.

Engraved and Photogravure

1963, Mar. 23 Unwmk. *Perf. 11½*

588 A168 1fr brn red & pale bl .20 .20
589 A168 3fr dk vio & yel grn .20 .20
590 A168 6fr gray, blk, red, bl & gold .30 .25
Nos. 588-590 (3) .70 .65

350th anniv. of the granting of a charter to the Ghent guild of fencers.

Stagecoach A169

1963, Apr. 7

591 A169 3fr gray & ocher .25 .20

Stamp Day. See No. 678.

Hotel des Postes, Paris, Stagecoach and Stamp, 1863 A170

Perf. 11½

1963, May 7 Unwmk. Engr.

592 A170 6fr dk brn, gray & yel grn .40 .35

Cent. of the 1st Intl. Postal Conf., Paris, 1863.

"Peace," Child in Rye Field — A171

1963, May 8 Engr. & Photo.

593 A171 3fr grn, blk, yel & brn .20 .20
594 A171 6fr buff, blk, brn & org .35 .25

May 8th Movement for Peace. (On May 8, 1945, World War II ended in Europe).

Allegory and Shields of 17 Member Nations A172

1963, June 13 Unwmk. *Perf. 11½*

595 A172 6fr blue & black .40 .25

10th anniversary of the Conference of European Transport Ministers.

Seal of Union of Belgian Towns — A173

1963, June 17

596 A173 6fr grn, red, blk & gold .40 .35

Intl. Union of Municipalities, 50th anniv.

Caravelle over Brussels National Airport A174

Photogravure and Engraved

1963, Sept. 1 Unwmk. *Perf. 11½*

597 A174 3fr green & gray .25 .20

40th anniversary of SABENA airline.

Europa Issue, 1963

Common Design Type

1963, Sept. 14 Photo.

Size: 35x24mm

598 CD6 3fr blk, dl red & lt brn .75 .20
599 CD6 6fr blk, lt bl & lt brn 1.00 .30

Jules Destrée A176

Design: No. 601, Henry Van de Velde.

Perf. 11½

1963, Nov. 16 Unwmk. Engr.

600 A176 1fr rose lilac .20 .20
601 A176 1fr green .20 .20

Jules Destrée (1863-1936), statesman and founder of the Royal Academy of French Language and Literature, and of Henry Van de Velde (1863-1957), architect.

No. 600 incorrectly inscribed "1864."

Development of the Mail, Bas-relief — A177

1963, Nov. 23 Engr. & Photo.

602 A177 50c dl red, slate & blk .20 .20

Postal checking service, 50th anniv.

Dr. Armauer G. Hansen A178

Fight Against Leprosy: 2fr, Leprosarium. 5fr, Father Joseph Damien.

1964, Jan. 25 Unwmk. *Perf. 11½*

603 A178 1fr brown org & blk .20 .20
604 A178 2fr brown org & blk .20 .20
605 A178 5fr brown org & blk .25 .20
a. Souvenir sheet of 3, #603-605 1.90 1.90
Nos. 603-605 (3) .65 .60

No. 605a sold for 12fr.

Andreas Vesalius (1514-64), Anatomist — A179

Jules Boulvin (1855-1920), Mechanical Engineer A180

Design: 2fr, Henri Jaspar (1870-1939), statesman and lawyer.

Engraved and Photogravure

1964, Mar. 2 Unwmk. *Perf. 11½*

606 A179 50c pale grn & blk .20 .20
607 A180 1fr pale grn & blk .20 .20
608 A180 2fr pale grn & blk .20 .20
Nos. 606-608 (3) .60 .60

Postilion of Liege, 1830-40 — A181

1964, Apr. 5 Engr. *Perf. 11½*

609 A181 3fr black .20 .20

Issued for Stamp Day 1964.

Arms of Ostend A182

1964, May 16 Photo.

610 A182 3fr ultra, ver, gold & blk .20 .20

Millennium of Ostend.

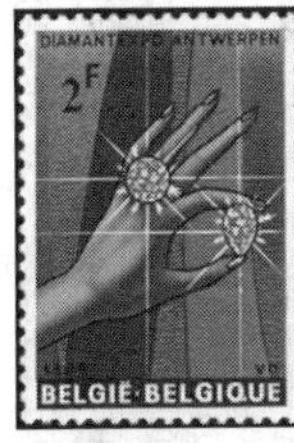

Flame, Hammer and Globe — A183

1fr, "SI" and globe. 2fr, Flame over wavy lines.

1964, July 18 Unwmk. *Perf. 11½*

611 A183 50c dark blue & red .20 .20
612 A183 1fr dark blue & red .20 .20
613 A183 2fr dark blue & red .20 .20
Nos. 611-613 (3) .60 .60

Centenary of the First Socialist International, founded in London, Sept. 28, 1864.

Europa Issue, 1964

Common Design Type

1964, Sept. 12 Photo. *Perf. 11½*

Size: 24x35½mm

614 CD7 3fr yel grn, dk car & gray .20 .20
615 CD7 6fr car rose, yel grn & bl .40 .35

Benelux Issue

King Baudouin, Queen Juliana and Grand Duchess Charlotte — A185

1964, Oct. 12

616 A185 3fr olive, lt grn & mar .20 .20

20th anniv. of the customs union of Belgium, Netherlands and Luxembourg.

Hand, Round & Pear-shaped Diamonds — A186

1965, Jan. 23 Unwmk. *Perf. 11½*

617 A186 2fr ultra, dp car & blk .20 .20

Diamond Exhibition "Diamantexpo," Antwerp, July 10-28, 1965.

Symbols of Textile Industry — A187

1965, Jan. 25 Photo.

618 A187 1fr blue, red & blk .20 .20

Eighth textile industry exhibition "Textirama," Ghent, Jan. 29-Feb. 2, 1965.

Vriesia — A188

Designs: 2fr, Echinocactus. 3fr, Stapelia.

1965, Feb. 13 Engr. & Photo.

619 A188 1fr multicolored .20 .20
620 A188 2fr multicolored .20 .20
621 A188 3fr multicolored .20 .20
a. Souvenir sheet of 3, #619-621 1.75 1.75
Nos. 619-621 (3) .60 .60

25th Ghent International Flower Exhibition, Apr. 24-May 3, 1965.

#621a was issued Apr. 26 and sold for 20fr.

Paul Hymans (1865-1941), Belgian Foreign Minister, First President of the League of Nations — A189

1965, Feb. 24 Engr. *Perf. 11½*

622 A189 1fr dull purple .20 .20

Peter Paul Rubens — A190

2fr, Frans Snyders. 3fr, Adam van Noort. 6fr, Anthony Van Dyck. 8fr, Jacob Jordaens.

1965, Mar. 15 **Photo. & Engr.**

Portraits in Sepia

623 A190 1fr carmine rose .20 .20
624 A190 2fr blue green .20 .20
625 A190 3fr plum .20 .20
626 A190 6fr deep carmine .25 .20
627 A190 8fr dark blue .35 .35
Nos. 623-627 (5) 1.20 1.15

Issued to commemorate the founding of the General Savings and Pensions Bank.

Sir Rowland Hill as Philatelist — A191

1965, Mar. 27 **Engr.** ***Perf. 11½***
628 A191 50c blue green .20 .20

Issued to publicize youth philately. The design is from a mural by J. E. Van den Bussche in the General Post Office, Brussels.

Postmaster, c. 1833 — A192

1965, Apr. 26 **Unwmk.** ***Perf. 11½***
629 A192 3fr emerald .20 .20

Issued for Stamp Day.

Telephone, Globe and Teletype Paper — A193

1965, May 8 **Photo.**
630 A193 2fr dull purple & blk .20 .20

Cent. of the ITU.

Staircase, Affligem Abbey — A194

1965, May 27 **Engr.**
631 A194 1fr gray blue .20 .20

St. Jean Berchmans and his Birthplace A195

1965, May 27 **Engr. & Photo.**
632 A195 2fr dk brn & red brn .20 .20

Issued to honor St. Jean Berchmans (1599-1621), Jesuit "Saint of the Daily Life."

TOC H Lamp and Arms of Poperinge — A196

1965, June 19 **Photo.** ***Perf. 11½***
633 A196 3fr ol bis, blk & car .20 .20

50th anniv. of the founding of Talbot House in Poperinge, which served British soldiers in World War I, and where the TOC H Movement began (Christian Social Service; TOC H is army code for Poperinge Center).

Belgian Farmers' Association (Boerenbond), 75th Anniv. — A197

50c, Farmer with tractor. 3fr, Farmer with horse-drawn roller.

Engraved and Photogravure

1965, July 17 **Unwmk.** ***Perf. 11½***
634 A197 50c bl, ol, bis brn & blk .20 .20
635 A197 3fr bl, ol grn, ol & blk .20 .20

Europa Issue, 1965

Common Design Type

1965, Sept. 25 ***Perf. 11½***

Size: 35½x24mm

636 CD8 1fr dl rose & blk .20 .20
637 CD8 3fr grnsh gray & blk .20 .20

Leopold I (1790-1865) A199

1965, Nov. 13 **Engr.**
638 A199 3fr sepia .20 .20
639 A199 6fr bright violet .25 .25

The designs of the vignettes are similar to A4 and A5.

Joseph Lebeau(1794-1865), Foreign Minister — A200

1965, Nov. 13 **Photo.**
640 A200 1fr multicolored .20 .20

Tourist Issue

Grapes and Houses, Hoeilaart A201

Bridge and Castle, Huy A202

#643, British War Memorial, Ypres. #644, Castle Spontin. #645, City Hall, Louvain. #646, Ourthe Valley. #647, Romanesque Cathedral, gothic fountain, Nivalles. #648, Water mill, Kasterlee. #649, City Hall, Cloth Guild and Statue of Margarethe of Austria, Malines. #650, Town Hall, Lier. #651, Castle Bouillon. #652, Fountain and Kursaal Spa. #653, Windmill, Bokrijk. #654, Mountain road, Vielsalm. #655, View of Furnes. #656, City Hall and Belfry, Mons. #657, St. Martin's Church, Aalst. #658, Abbey and fountain, St. Hubert.

1965-71 **Engr.** ***Perf. 11½***
641 A201 50c vio bl, lt bl & yel grn .20 .20
642 A202 50c sl grn, lt bl & red brn .20 .20
643 A202 1fr grn, lt bl, sal & brn .20 .20
644 A202 1fr ind, lt bl & ol .20 .20
645 A201 1fr brt rose lil, lt bl & blk .20 .20
646 A202 1fr blk, grnsh bl & ol .20 .20
647 A201 1.50fr sl, sky bl & bis .20 .20
648 A202 1.50fr blk, bl & ol .20 .20
649 A202 1.50fr dk bl & buff .20 .20
650 A201 2fr brn, lt bl & ind .20 .20
651 A202 2fr dk brn, grn & ocher .20 .20
652 A202 2fr bl, brt grn & blk .20 .20
653 A202 2fr blk, lt bl & yel .20 .20
654 A202 2fr blk, lt bl & yel grn .20 .20
655 A202 2fr car, lt bl & dk brn .20 .20
656 A201 2.50fr vio, buff & blk .20 .20
657 A201 2.50fr vio, lt bl, blk & ol .25 .20
658 A201 2.50fr vio bl & yel .25 .20
Nos. 641-658 (18) 3.70 3.60

Issued: #641-642, 11/13/65; #643-644, 7/15/67; #645-646, 12/16/68; #647-648, 7/6/70; #649, 656, 12/11/71; #650-651, 11/11/66; #652-653, 6/24/68; #654-655, 9/6/69; #657-658, 9/11/71.

Queen Elisabeth Type of Semi-Postal Issue, 1956

1965, Dec. 23 **Photo.** ***Perf. 11½***
659 SP305 3fr dark gray .22 .20

Queen Elisabeth (1876-1965).

A dark frame has been added in design of No. 659; 1956 date has been changed to 1965; inscription in bottom panel is Koningin Elisabeth Reine Elisabeth 3F.

"Peace on Earth" A203

Arms of Pope Paul VI — A204

1fr, "Looking toward a Better Future" (family, new buildings, sun & landscape).

1966, Feb. 12 **Photo.** ***Perf. 11½***
660 A203 50c multicolored .20 .20
661 A203 1fr ocher, blk & bl .20 .20
662 A204 3fr gray, gold, car & blk .20 .20
Nos. 660-662 (3) .60 .60

75th anniv. of the encyclical by Pope Leo XIII "Rerum Novarum," which proclaimed the general principles for the organization of modern industrial society.

Rural Mailman, 19th Century — A205

1966, Apr. 17 **Photo.** **Unwmk.**
663 A205 3fr blk, dl yel & pale lil .20 .20

Stamp Day. For overprint see No. 673.

Iguanodon, Natural Science Institute A206

Arend-Roland Comet, Observatory A207

Designs: No. 665, Ancestral head and spiral pattern, Kasai; Central Africa Museum. No. 666, Snowflakes, Meteorological Institute. No. 667, Seal of Charles V, Royal Archives. No. 668, Medieval scholar, Royal Library. 8fr, Satellite and rocket, Space Aeronautics Institute.

1966, May 28 **Engr. & Photo.**
664 A206 1fr green & blk .20 .20
665 A206 2fr gray, blk & brn org .20 .20
666 A206 2fr blue, blk & yel .20 .20
667 A207 3fr dp rose, blk & gold .20 .20
668 A207 3fr multicolored .20 .20
669 A207 6fr ultra, yel & blk .25 .20
670 A207 8fr multicolored .30 .30
Nos. 664-670 (7) 1.55 1.50

National scientific heritage.

Atom Symbol and Retort — A208

Engraved and Photogravure

1966, July 9 **Unwmk.** ***Perf. 11½***
671 A208 6fr gray, blk & red .30 .20

Issued to publicize the European chemical plant, EUROCHEMIC, at Mol.

August Kekulé, Benzene Ring — A209

1966, July 9
672 A209 3fr brt blue & blk .20 .20

August Friedrich Kekule (1829-96), chemistry professor at University of Ghent (1858-67).

No. 663 Overprinted with Red and Blue Emblem

1966, July 11 **Photo.**
673 A205 3fr multicolored .20 .20

19th Intl. P.T.T. Cong., Brussels, July 11-15.

Rik Wouters (1882-1916), Self-portrait A210

1966, Sept. 6 **Photo.** ***Perf. 11½***
674 A210 60c multicolored .20 .20

Europa Issue, 1966
Common Design Type

1966, Sept. 24 **Engr.** ***Perf. 11½***
Size: 24x34mm
675 CD9 3fr brt green .20 .20
676 CD9 6fr brt rose lilac .25 .25

Types of 1962-1963 Overprinted in Black and Red

1966, Nov. 11 **Engr. & Photo.**
677 A161 60c sepia & grnsh gray .20 .20
678 A169 3fr sepia & pale bister .20 .20

75th anniv., Royal Fed. of Phil. Circles of Belgium. Overprint shows emblem of F.I.P.

Lions Emblem — A214

1967, Jan. 14 ***Perf. 11½***
679 A214 3fr gray, blk & bl .20 .20
680 A214 6fr lt green, blk & vio .30 .20

Lions Club Intl., 50th anniv.

Pistol by Leonhard Cleuter A215

1967, Feb. 11 **Photo.**
681 A215 2fr dp car, blk & cream .20 .20

Fire Arms Museum in Liege.

International Tourist Year Emblem A216

1967, Feb. 11
682 A216 6fr ver, ultra & blk .30 .20

International Tourist Year, 1967.

Birches and Trientalis A217

Design: No. 684, Dunes, beach grass, privet and blue thistles.

1967, Mar. 11 **Photo.** ***Perf. 11½***
683 A217 1fr multicolored .20 .20
684 A217 1fr multicolored .20 .20

Issued to publicize the nature preserves at Hautes Fagnes and Westhoek.

Paul Emile Janson(1872-1944), Lawyer, Statesman — A218

1967, Apr. 15 **Engr.** ***Perf. 11½***
685 A218 10fr blue .35 .20

Postilion A219

1967, Apr. 16 **Photo. & Engr.**
686 A219 3fr rose red & claret .20 .20

Issued for Stamp Day, 1967.

Inscribed: "FITCE"

1967, June 24 ***Perf. 11½***
687 A219 10fr ultra, sep & emer .40 .30

Issued to commemorate the meeting of the Federation of Common Market Telecommunications Engineers, Brussels, July 3-8.

Europa Issue, 1967
Common Design Type

1967, May 2 **Photo.**
Size: 24x35mm
688 CD10 3fr blk, lt bl & red .20 .20
689 CD10 6fr blk, grnsh gray & yel .30 .30

Flax, Shuttle and Mills — A221

1967, June 3 **Photo.** ***Perf. 11½***
690 A221 6fr tan & multi .30 .20

Belgian linen industry.

Old Kursaal, Ostend — A222

1967, June 3 **Engr. & Photo.**
691 A222 2fr dk brn, lt bl & yel .20 .20

700th anniversary of Ostend as a city.

Charles Plisnier and Lodewijk de Raet Foundations A223

Designs: #692, Caesar Crossing Rubicon, 15th Century Tapestry. #693, Emperor Maximilian Killing a Boar, 16th cent. tapestry.

1967, Sept. 2 **Photo.** ***Perf. 11½***
692 A223 1fr multicolored .20 .20
693 A223 1fr multicolored .20 .20

Universities of Ghent and Liège, 150th Anniv. — A224

Arms of Universities: #694, Ghent. #695, Liege.

Engraved and Photogravure

1967, Sept. 30 ***Perf. 11½***
694 A224 3fr gray & multi .20 .20
695 A224 3fr gray & multi .20 .20

Princess Margaret of York — A225

1967, Sept. 30 **Photo.**
696 A225 6fr multicolored .30 .25

British Week, Sept. 28-Oct. 2.

"Virga Jesse," Hasselt — A226

1967, Nov. 11 **Engr.** ***Perf. 11½***
697 A226 1fr slate blue .20 .20

Christmas, 1967.

Hand Guarding Worker — A227

1968, Feb. 3 **Photo.** ***Perf. 11½***
698 A227 3fr multicolored .20 .20

Issued to publicize industrial safety.

Military Mailman, 1916, by James Thiriar — A228

Engraved and Photogravure

1968, Mar. 17 ***Perf. 11½***
699 A228 3fr sepia, lt bl & brn .20 .20

Issued for Stamp Day, 1968.

View of Grammont and Seal of Baudouin VI — A229

Historic Sites: 3fr, Theux-Franchimont fortress, sword and seal. 6fr, Neolithic cave and artifacts, Spiennes. 10fr, Roman oil lamp and St. Medard's Church, Wervik.

1968, Apr. 13 **Photo.** ***Perf. 11½***
700 A229 2fr bl, blk, lil & rose .20 .20
701 A229 3fr orange, blk & car .20 .20
702 A229 6fr ultra, ind & bis .25 .20
703 A229 10fr tan, blk, yel & gray .35 .30
Nos. 700-703 (4) 1.00 .90

Stamp of 1866, No. 23 — A230

1968, Apr. 13 **Engr.** ***Perf. 13***
704 A230 1fr black .20 .20

Centenary of the Malines Stamp Printery.

Europa Issue, 1968
Common Design Type

1968, Apr. 27 Photo. *Perf. 11½*
Size: 35x24mm

705 CD11 3fr dl grn, gold & blk	.20	.20
706 CD11 6fr carmine, sil & blk	.25	.25

St. Laurent Abbey, Liège — A232

Designs: 3fr, Gothic Church, Lisseweghe. No. 709. Barges in Zandvliet locks. No. 710, Ship in Neuzen lock, Ghent Canal. 10fr, Ronquieres canal ship lift.

Engraved and Photogravure

1968, Sept. 7 *Perf. 11½*

707 A232 2fr ultra, gray ol & sep	.20	.20
708 A232 3fr ol bis, gray & sep	.20	.20
709 A232 6fr ind, brt bl & sep	.30	.20
710 A232 6fr black, grnsh bl & ol	.25	.20
711 A232 10fr bister, brt bl & sep	.50	.30
Nos. 707-711 (5)	1.45	1.10

No. 710 issued Dec. 14 for opening of lock at Neuzen, Netherlands.

Christmas Candle — A233

1968, Dec. 7 *Perf. 11½*

712 A233 1fr multicolored	.20	.20

Christmas, 1968.

St. Albertus Magnus — A234

1969, Feb. 15 Engr. *Perf. 11½*

713 A234 2fr sepia	.20	.20

The Church of St. Paul in Antwerp (16th century) was destroyed by fire in Apr. 1968.

Ruins of Aulne Abbey, Gozee — A235

1969, Feb. 15 Engr. & Photo.

714 A235 3fr brt pink & blk	.20	.20

Aulne Abbey was destroyed in 1794 during the French Revolution.

The Travelers, Roman Sculpture — A236

1969, Mar. 15 Engr. *Perf. 11½*

715 A236 2fr violet brown	.20	.20

2,000th anniversary of city of Arlon.

Broodjes Chapel, Antwerp — A237

1969, Mar. 15 Engr. & Photo.

716 A237 3fr gray & blk	.20	.20

150th anniv. of public education in Antwerp.

Post Office Train — A238

1969, Apr. 13 Photo. *Perf. 11½*

717 A238 3fr multicolored	.20	.20

Issued for Stamp Day.

Europa Issue, 1969
Common Design Type

1969, Apr. 26
Size: 35x24mm

718 CD12 3fr lt grn, brn & blk	.20	.20
719 CD12 6fr sal, rose car & blk	.30	.25

NATO Type of 1959 Redrawn and Dated "1949-1969"

1969, May 31 Photo. *Perf. 11½*

720 A142 6fr org brn & ultra	.30	.30

20th anniv. of NATO. No. 720 inscribed Belgique-Belgie and OTAN-NAVO.

Construction Workers, by F. Leger — A240

1969, May 31

721 A240 3fr multicolored	.20	.20

50th anniversary of the ILO.

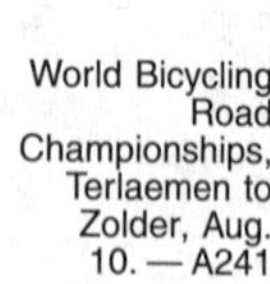

World Bicycling Road Championships, Terlaemen to Zolder, Aug. 10. — A241

1969, July 5 Photo. *Perf. 11½*

722 A241 6fr Bicyclist	.30	.25

Ribbon in Benelux Colors — A242

1969, Sept. 6 Photo. *Perf. 11½*

723 A242 3fr blk, red, ultra & yel	.20	.20

Signing of the customs union of Belgium, Netherlands & Luxembourg, 25th anniv.

Annevoie Garden and Pascali Rose A243

No. 725, Lochristi Garden and begonia.

1969, Sept. 6

724 A243 2fr multicolored	.20	.20
725 A243 2fr multicolored	.20	.20

Armstrong, Collins, Aldrin and Map Showing Tranquillity Base — A245

1969, Sept. 20 Photo.

726 A245 6fr black	.30	.25

See note after Algeria #427. See #B846.

Wounded Veteran — A246

1969, Oct. 11 Engr. *Perf. 11½*

727 A246 1fr blue gray	.20	.20

Natl. war veterans' aid organization (O.N.I.G.). The design is similar to type SP10.

Mailman — A247

1969, Oct. 18 Photo.

728 A247 1fr deep rose & multi	.20	.20

Issued to publicize youth philately. Design by Danielle Saintenoy, 14.

Kennedy Tunnel Under the Schelde, Antwerp A248

6fr, Three highways crossing near Loncin.

1969, Nov. 8 Engr. *Perf. 11½*

729 A248 3fr multicolored	.25	.20
730 A248 6fr multicolored	.30	.30

Issued to publicize the John F. Kennedy Tunnel under the Schelde and the Walloon auto route and interchange near Loncin.

Henry Carton de Wiart, by Gaston Geleyn — A249

1969, Nov. 8

731 A249 6fr sepia	.30	.20

Count de Wiart (1869-1951), statesman.

The Census at Bethlehem (detail), by Peter Brueghel A250

1969, Dec. 13 Photo.

732 A250 1.50fr multicolored	.20	.20

Christmas, 1969.

Symbols of Bank's Activity, 100fr Coin A251

1969, Dec. 13 Engr. & Photo.

733 A251 3.50fr lt ultra, blk & sil	.20	.20

50th anniv. of the Industrial Credit Bank (Societe nationale de credit a l'industrie).

Camellia — A252

1970, Jan. 31 Photo. *Perf. 11½*

734 A252 1.50fr shown	.20	.20
735 A252 2.50fr Water lily	.20	.20
736 A252 3.50fr Azalea	.20	.20
a. Souvenir sheet of 3, #734-736	2.00	2.00
Nos. 734-736 (3)	.60	.60

Ghent Int'l Flower Exhibition. No. 736a was issued Apr. 25 and sold for 25fr.

Beeches in Botanical Garden — A253

1970, Mar. 7 Engr. & Photo.

737 A253 3.50fr shown	.20	.20
738 A253 7fr Birches	.30	.30

European Nature Conservation Year.

Youth Stamp Day — A254

1970, Apr. 4 Photo.

739 A254 1.50fr Mailman	.20	.20

New UPU Headquarters and Monument, Bern — A255

1970, Apr. 12 Engr. & Photo.

740 A255 3.50fr grn & lt grn .30 .20

Opening of the new UPU Headquarters, Bern.

Europa Issue, 1970
Common Design Type

1970, May 1 Photo. *Perf. 11½*
Size: 35x24mm

741 CD13 3.50fr rose cl, yel & blk .20 .20
742 CD13 7fr ultra, pink & blk .40 .25

Cooperative Alliance Emblem — A257

1970, June 27 Photo. *Perf. 11½*

743 A257 7fr black & org .30 .20

Intl. Cooperative Alliance, 75th anniv.

Ship in Ghent Terneuzen Lock, Zelzate A258

Design: No. 745, Clock Tower, Virton, vert.

1970, June 27 Engr. & Photo.

744 A258 2.50fr indigo & lt bl .20 .20
745 A258 2.50fr dk pur & ocher .20 .20

King Baudouin — A259

1970-80 Engr. *Perf. 11½*

746 A259 1.75fr green ('71) .25 .20
747 A259 2.25fr gray grn ('72) .35 .20
748 A259 2.50fr gray grn ('74) .20 .20
749 A259 3fr emerald ('73) .20 .20
750 A259 3.25fr violet brn ('75) .20 .20
751 A259 3.50fr orange brn .25 .20
752 A259 3.50fr brown ('71) .25 .20
753 A259 4fr blue ('72) .35 .20
754 A259 4.50fr brown ('72) .25 .20
755 A259 4.50fr grnsh bl ('74) .25 .20
756 A259 5fr lilac ('72) .25 .20
757 A259 6fr rose car ('72) .30 .20
758 A259 6.50fr vio blk ('74) .35 .20
759 A259 7fr ver ('71) .35 .20
760 A259 7.50fr brt pink ('75) .35 .20
761 A259 8fr black ('72) .35 .20
762 A259 9fr ol bis ('71) .60 .20
763 A259 9fr red brn ('80) .45 .20
764 A259 10fr rose car ('71) .50 .20
765 A259 11fr gray ('76) .50 .20
766 A259 12fr Prus bl ('72) .60 .20
767 A259 13fr slate ('75) .70 .20
768 A259 14fr gray grn ('76) .65 .20
769 A259 15fr lt vio ('71) .70 .20
770 A259 16fr green ('77) .70 .20
771 A259 17fr dull mag ('75) .80 .20
772 A259 18fr steel bl ('71) 1.00 .20
773 A259 18fr grnsh bl ('80) .90 .20
774 A259 20fr vio bl ('71) 1.00 .20
775 A259 22fr black ('74) 1.40 1.10
776 A259 22fr lt grn ('79) 1.10 .20
777 A259 25fr lilac ('75) 1.25 .20
778 A259 30fr ocher ('72) 1.50 .20
779 A259 35fr emer ('80) 1.50 .20
780 A259 40fr dk blue ('77) 2.00 .20
781 A259 45fr brown ('80) 2.25 .20

Perf. 12½x13½
Photo.
Size: 22x17mm

782 A259 3fr emerald ('73) 1.00 .75
a. Booklet pane of 4 (#782 and 3 #783) + labels 10.00
783 A259 4fr blue ('73) .60 .50
784 A259 4.50fr grnsh bl ('75) .40 .30
785 A259 5fr lilac ('73) .25 .20
a. Booklet pane of 4 + labels 2.75
786 A259 6fr carmine ('78) .30 .20
787 A259 6.50fr dull pur ('75) .45 .20
788 A259 8fr gray ('78) .35 .20
Nos. 746-788 (43) 27.95 10.45

No. 751 issued Sept. 7, 1970, King Baudouin's 40th birthday, and is inscribed "1930-1970." Dates are omitted on other stamps of type A259.

Nos. 754, 756 also issued in coils in 1973 and Nos. 757, 761 in 1978, with black control number on back of every fifth stamp.

Nos. 782-788 issued in booklets only. Nos. 782, 784 have one straight-edge, Nos. 786, 788 have two. The rest have one or two. Stamps in the panes are tete-beche. Each pane has two labels showing Belgian Postal emblem with a large selvage with postal code instructions. Nos. 786, 788 not luminescent.

See designs M2, O4. See Nos. 432a, 432b, 977a, 977b.

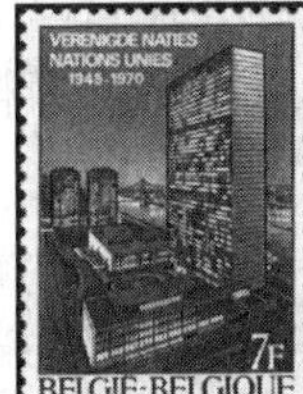

UN Headquarters, NY — A260

1970, Sept. 12 Engr. & Photo.

789 A260 7fr dk brn & Prus bl .30 .20

25th anniversary of the United Nations.

25th International Fair at Ghent, Sept. 12-27 — A261

1970, Sept. 19

790 A261 1.50fr Fair emblem .20 .20

Queen Fabiola — A262

1970, Sept. 19

791 A262 3.50fr lt blue & blk .20 .20

Issued to publicize the Queen Fabiola Foundation for Mental Health.

The Mason, by Georges Minne — A263

1970, Oct. 17 *Perf. 11½*

792 A263 3.50fr dull yel & sep .20 .20

50th anniv. of the National Housing Society.

Man, Woman and City — A264

1970, Oct. 17 Photo.

793 A264 2.50fr black & multi .20 .20

Social Security System, 25th anniv.

Madonna with the Grapes, by Jean Gossaert — A265

1970, Nov. 14 Engr. *Perf. 11½*

794 A265 1.50fr dark brown .20 .20

Christmas 1970.

Arms of Eupen, Malmédy and Saint-Vith A266

Engraved and Photogravure

1970, Dec. 12 *Perf. 11½*

795 A266 7fr sepia & dk brn .30 .20

The 50th anniversary of the return of the districts of Eupen, Malmédy and Saint-Vith.

Automatic Telephone — A267

1971, Jan. 16 Photo. *Perf. 11½*

796 A267 1.50fr multicolored .20 .20

Automatization of Belgian telephone system.

50th Automobile Show, Brussels, Jan. 19-31 A268

1971, Jan. 16

797 A268 2.50fr "Auto" .20 .20

Belgian Touring Club, 75th Anniv. — A269

1971, Feb. 13

798 A269 3.50fr Club emblem .20 .20

Tournai Cathedral A270

1971, Feb. 13 Engr.

799 A270 7fr bright blue .30 .20

Cathedral of Tournai, 8th centenary.

"The Letter Box," by T. Lobrichon — A271

1971, Mar. 13 Engr. *Perf. 11½*

800 A271 1.50fr dark brown .20 .20

Youth philately.

Albert I, Jules Destrée and Academy — A272

Engraved and Photogravure

1971, Apr. 17 *Perf. 11½*

801 A272 7fr gray & blk .30 .20

Founding of the Royal Academy of Language and French Literature, 50th anniv.

Stamp Day — A273

1971, Apr. 25

802 A273 3.50fr Mailman .20 .20

Europa Issue, 1971
Common Design Type

1971, May 1 Photo.
Size: 35x24mm

803 CD14 3.50fr olive & blk .25 .20
804 CD14 7fr dk ol grn & blk .35 .25

Radar Ground Station A275

1971, May 15 Photo. *Perf. 11½*

805 A275 7fr multicolored .30 .20

3rd World Telecommunications Day.

Antarctic Explorer, Ship and Penguins — A276

1971, June 19 Photo. *Perf. 11½*
806 A276 10fr multicolored .50 .50

Tenth anniversary of the Antarctic Treaty pledging peaceful uses of and scientific cooperation in Antarctica.

Abbey of Notre Dame, Orval, 900th Anniv. — A277

1971, June 26 Engr. *Perf. 11½*
807 A277 2.50fr Orval Abbey .20 .20

Georges Hubin (1863-1947), Socialist Leader, Minister of State — A278

1971, June 26 Engr. & Photo.
808 A278 1.50fr vio bl & blk .20 .20

Mr. and Mrs. Goliath, the Giants of Ath — A279

View of Ghent A280

1971, Aug. 7 Photo.
809 A279 2.50fr multicolored .20 .20

Engr.
810 A280 2.50fr gray brown .20 .20

Test Tubes and Insulin Molecular Diagram — A281

1971, Aug. 7 Photo.
811 A281 10fr lt gray & multi .40 .30

50th anniversary of the discovery of insulin.

Family and "50" — A283

1971, Sept. 11 Photo.
812 A283 1.50fr green & multi .20 .20

Belgian Large Families League, 50th anniv.

Achaemenidaen Tomb, Buzpar, and Persian Coat of Arms — A284

Engraved and Photogravure

1971, Oct. 2 *Perf. 11½*
813 A284 7fr multicolored .30 .20

2500th anniversary of the founding of the Persian empire by Cyrus the Great.

Dr. Jules Bordet (1870-1945), Serologist, Immunologist A285

Portrait: No. 815, Stijn Streuvels(1871-1945), Novelist (pen name Frank Lateur).

1971, Oct. 2 Engr.
814 A285 3.50fr slate green .20 .20
815 A285 3.50fr dark brown .20 .20

Flight into Egypt, Anonymous A286

1971, Nov. 13 Photo.
816 A286 1.50fr multicolored .20 .20

Christmas 1971.

Federation of Belgian Industries (FIB), 25th Anniv. — A287

1971, Nov. 13
817 A287 3.50fr black, ultra & gold .20 .20

International Book Year 1972 — A288

1972, Feb. 19
818 A288 7fr bister, blk & bl .30 .20

Coins of Belgium and Luxembourg A289

1972, Feb. 19 Engr. & Photo.
819 A289 1.50fr orange, blk & sil .20 .20

Economic Union of Belgium and Luxembourg, 50th anniversary.

Traffic Signal and Road Signs — A290

1972, Feb. 19 Photo.
820 A290 3.50fr blue & multi .20 .20

Via Secura (road safety), 25th anniversary.

Belgica '72 Emblem A291

1972, Mar. 27
821 A291 3.50fr choc, bl & lil .20 .20

International Philatelic Exhibition, Brussels, June 24-July 9.

"Your Heart is your Health" — A292

1972, Mar. 27
822 A292 7fr blk, gray, red & bl .25 .20

World Health Day.

Auguste Vermeylen (1872-1945), Flemish Writer, Educator — A293

Portrait, by Isidore Opsomer.

1972, Mar. 27
823 A293 2.50fr multicolored .20 .20

Stamp Day 1972 — A294

1972, Apr. 23
824 A294 3.50fr Astronaut on Moon .20 .20

Europa Issue 1972

Common Design Type

1972, Apr. 29

Size: 24x35mm
825 CD15 3.50fr light blue & multi .20 .20
826 CD15 7fr rose & multi .45 .30

"Freedom of the Press" — A296

1972, May 13 Photo. *Perf. 11½*
827 A296 2.50fr multicolored .20 .20

50th anniv. of the BELGA news information agency and 25th Congress of the Intl. Federation of Newspaper Editors (F.I.E.J.), Brussels, May 15-19.

Freight Cars with Automatic Coupling A297

1972, June 3
828 A297 7fr blue & multi .30 .20

Intl. Railroad Union, 50th anniv.

View of Couvin — A298

No. 830, Aldeneik Church, Maaseik, vert.

1972, June 24 Engr. *Perf. 13½x14*
829 A298 2.50fr bl, vio brn & sl grn .20 .20
830 A298 2.50fr dk brown & bl .20 .20

Beatrice, by Gustave de Smet — A299

1972, Sept. 9 Photo. *Perf. 11½*
831 A299 3fr multicolored .20 .20

Youth philately.

Radar Station, Intelsat 4 — A300

1972, Sept. 16
832 A300 3.50fr lt bl, sil & blk .20 .20

Opening of the Lessive satellite earth station.

Frans Masereel(1889-1972), Wood Engraver — A301

1972, Oct. 21
833 A301 4.50fr Self-portrait .20 .20

Adoration of the Kings, by Felix Timmermans A302

1972, Nov. 11 Photo. *Perf. 11½*
834 A302 3.50fr black & multi .20 .20

Christmas 1972.

Maria Theresa, Anonymous A303

1972, Dec. 16 Photo. *Perf. 11½*
835 A303 2fr multicolored .20 .20

200th anniversary of the Belgian Academy of Science, Literature and Art, founded by Empress Maria Theresa.

WMO Emblem, Meteorological Institute, Ukkel — A304

1973, Mar. 24 Photo. *Perf. 11½*
836 A304 9fr blue & multi .40 .20

Cent. of intl. meteorological cooperation.

Natl. Industrial Fire Prevention Campaign — A305

1973, Mar. 24
837 A305 2fr "Fire" .20 .20

Man and WHO Emblem — A306

1973, Apr. 7
838 A306 8fr dk red, ocher & blk .30 .25

25th anniv. of WHO.

Europa Issue 1973
Common Design Type

1973, Apr. 28
Size: 35x24mm
839 CD16 4.50fr org brn, vio bl & yel .25 .20
840 CD16 8fr olive, dk bl & yel .50 .40

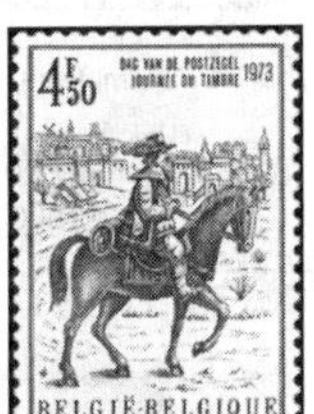

Thurn and Taxis Courier — A308

Engraved and Photogravure
1973, Apr. 28 *Perf. 11½*
841 A308 4.50fr black & red brn .20 .20

Stamp Day.

Arrows Circling Globe — A309

1973, May 12 Photo.
842 A309 3.50fr dp ocher & multi .20 .20

5th International Telecommunications Day.

Workers' Sports Exhibition Poster, Ghent, 1913 A310

1973, May 12
843 A310 4.50fr multicolored .20 .20

60th anniversary of the International Workers' Sports Movement.

Fair Emblem A311

1973, May 12 Photo. *Perf. 11½*
844 A311 4.50fr multicolored .20 .20

25th International Fair, Liege, May 12-27.

DC-10 and 1923 Biplane over Brussels Airport — A312

Design: 10fr, Tips biplane, 1908.

1973, May 19 Engr. & Photo.
845 A312 8fr gray bl, blk & ultra .30 .20
846 A312 10fr grn, lt bl & blk .45 .35

50th anniv. of SABENA, Belgian airline (8fr) and 25th anniv. of the "Vieilles Tiges" Belgian flying pioneers' society (10fr).

Adolphe Sax and Tenor Saxophone A313

1973, Sept. 15 Photo.
847 A313 9fr green, blk & bl .40 .20

Adolphe Sax (1814-1894), inventor of saxophone.

Fresco from Bathhouse, Ostend — A314

1973, Sept. 15
848 A314 4.50fr multicolored .25 .20

Year of the Spa.

St. Nicholas Church, Eupen — A315

#850, Town Hall, Leau. #851, Aarshot Church. #852, Chimay Castle. #853, Gemmenich Border: Belgium, Germany, Netherlands. #854, St. Monan and church, Nassogne. #855, Church tower, Dottignes. #856, Grand-Place, Sint-Truiden.

1973-75 Engr. *Perf. 13*
849 A315 2fr plum, sep & lt vio .20 .20
850 A315 3fr black, lt bl & mar .50 .20
851 A315 3fr brn blk & yel .30 .20
852 A315 4fr grnsh blk & grnsh bl .35 .20
853 A315 4fr grnsh blk & bl .40 .20
854 A315 4fr grnsh blk & bl .40 .20
855 A315 4.50fr multicolored .50 .20
856 A315 5fr multicolored .50 .20
Nos. 849-856 (8) 3.15 1.60

Nos. 851, 855 not luminescent. Nos. 850, 852-854, 856 horiz.

Charley, by Henri Evenepoel — A316

1973, Oct. 13 Photo. *Perf. 11½*
857 A316 3fr multicolored .20 .20

Youth philately.

Luminescent Paper

Starting with No. 858, all stamps are on luminescent paper unless otherwise noted.

Jean-Baptiste Moens — A317

1973, Oct. 13 Engr. & Photo.
858 A317 10fr multi + label .40 .20

50th anniversary of the Belgian Stamp Dealers' Association. Printed in sheets of 12 stamps and 12 labels showing association emblem.

Adoration of the Shepherds, by Hugo van der Goes — A318

1973, Nov. 17 Engr. *Perf. 11½*
859 A318 4fr blue .20 .20

Christmas 1973.

Louis Pierard, by M. I. Ianchelevici A319

1973, Nov. 17 Engr. & Photo.
860 A319 4fr vermilion & buff .25 .20

Louis Pierard (1886-1952), journalist, member of Parliament.

Highway, Automobile Club Emblem A320

1973, Nov. 17 **Photo.**
861 A320 5fr yellow & multi .25 .20

Flemish Automobile Club, 50th anniv.

Early Microphone, Emblem of Radio Belgium — A321

1973, Nov. 24 **Engr. & Photo.**
862 A321 4fr blue & black .20 .20

50th anniversary of Radio Belgium.

Felicien Rops (1833-1898), Painter, Engraver A323

Engraved and Photogravure

1973, Dec. 8 ***Perf. 11½***
863 A323 7fr Self-portrait .30 .20

King Albert, (1875-1934) A324

1974, Feb. 16 **Photo.** ***Perf. 11½***
864 A324 4fr Prus green & blk .25 .20

Sun, Bird, Flowers and Girl — A325

1974, Mar. 25 **Photo.** ***Perf. 11½***
865 A325 3fr violet & multi .20 .20

Protection of the environment.

NATO Emblem A326

1974, Apr. 20 **Photo.** ***Perf. 11½***
866 A326 10fr dp to lt blue .45 .25

25th anniversary of the signing of the North Atlantic Treaty.

Hubert Krains — A327

1974, Apr. 27 **Engr. & Photo.**
867 A327 5fr black & gray .20 .20

Stamp Day.

Europa Issue 1974

"Destroyed City," by Ossip Zadkine — A328

Design: 10fr, Solidarity, by Georges Minne.

1974, May 4
868 A328 5fr black & red .25 .20
869 A328 10fr black & ultra .60 .25

Children A329

1974, May 18 **Photo.** ***Perf. 11½***
870 A329 4fr lt blue & multi .20 .20

10th Lay Youth Festival.

Planetarium, Brussels A330

Soleilmont Abbey Ruins — A331

4fr, Pillory, Braine-le-Chateau. 7fr, Fountain, Ghent (procession symbolic of Chamber of Rhetoric). 10fr, Belfry, Bruges, vert.

Engr. and Photo.

1974, June 22 ***Perf. 11½***
871 A330 3fr sky blue & blk .20 .20
872 A330 4fr lilac rose & blk .20 .20
873 A331 5fr lt green & blk .30 .20
874 A331 7fr dull yellow & blk .35 .20
875 A330 10fr black, blue & brn .45 .20
Nos. 871-875 (5) 1.50 1.00

Historic buildings and monuments.

"BENELUX" A332

1974, Sept. 7 **Photo.** ***Perf. 11½***
876 A332 5fr bl grn, dk grn & lt bl .25 .20

30th anniversary of the signing of the customs union of Belgium, Netherlands and Luxembourg.

Jan Vekemans, by Cornelis de Vos — A333

1974, Sept. 14
877 A333 3fr multicolored .20 .20

Youth philately.

Leon Tresignies, Willebroek Canal Bridge A334

1974, Sept. 28 **Engr. & Photo.**
878 A334 4fr brn & ol grn .20 .20

60th death anniversary of Corporal Leon Tresignies (1886-1914), hero of World War I.

Montgomery Blair, UPU Emblem A335

10fr, Heinrich von Stephan, UPU emblem.

1974, Oct. 5 ***Perf. 11½***
879 A335 5fr green & blk .20 .20
880 A335 10fr brick red & blk .40 .30

Centenary of Universal Postal Union.

Symbolic Chart — A336

1974, Oct. 12 **Photo.** ***Perf. 11½***
881 A336 7fr multicolored .30 .20

Central Economic Council, 25th anniv.

Rotary Emblem A337

1974, Oct. 19
882 A337 10fr multicolored .40 .20

Rotary International of Belgium.

Wild Boar (Regimental Emblem) — A338

1974, Oct. 26
883 A338 3fr multicolored .20 .20

Granting of the colors to the Ardennes Chasseurs Regiment, 40th anniversary.

Angel, by Van Eyck Brothers — A341

1974, Nov. 16 ***Perf. 11½***
884 A341 4fr rose lilac .20 .20

Christmas 1974. The Angel shown is from the triptyque "The Mystical Lamb" in the Saint-Bavon Cathedral, Ghent.

Adolphe Quetelet, by J. Odevaere — A342

1974, Dec. 14 **Engr. & Photo.**
885 A342 10fr black & buff .40 .20

Death centenary of Adolphe Quetelet (1796-1874), statistician, astronomer and Secretary of Royal Academy of Brussels.

Themabelga, International Thematic Stamp Exhibition, Brussels, Dec. 13-21, 1975 — A343

1975, Feb. 15 **Photo.** ***Perf. 11½***
912 A343 6.50fr Themabelga emblem .30 .20

Ghent Intl. Flower Exhib., Apr. 26-May 5 — A344

1975, Feb. 22
913 A344 4.50fr Neoregelia carolinae .25 .20

Photogravure and Engraved

914 A344 5fr Coltsfoot .25 .20
915 A344 6.50fr Azalea .30 .20
Nos. 913-915 (3) .80 .60

Charles Buls Normal School for Boys, Brussels, Cent. — A345

1975, Mar. 15 ***Perf. 11½***

School emblem, man Leading boy.

916 A345 4.50fr black & multi .20 .20

Davids Foundation Emblem A346

1975, Mar. 22 **Photo.**
917 A346 5fr yellow & multi .25 .20

Centenary of the Davids Foundation, a Catholic organization for the promotion of Flemish through education and books.

King Albert (1875-1934) A347

1975, Apr. 5 **Engr. & Photo.**
918 A347 10fr black & maroon .45 .25

Mailman, 1840, by James Thiriar — A348

1975, Apr. 19 **Engr.** ***Perf. 11½***
919 A348 6.50fr dull magenta .30 .20

Stamp Day 1975.

St. John, from Last Supper, by Bouts — A349

Europa: 10fr, Woman's Head, detail from "Trial by Fire," by Dirk Bouts.

1975, Apr. 26 **Engr. & Photo.**
920 A349 6.50fr black, grn & blue .35 .20
921 A349 10fr black, ocher & red .60 .30

Liberation of Concentration Camps, 30th Anniv. — A350

Concentration Camp Symbols: "B" denoted political prisoners, "KG" prisoners of war.

1975, May 3 **Photo.**
922 A350 4.50fr multicolored .20 .20

Hospice of St. John, Bruges A351

Church of St. Loup, Namur — A352

Design: 10fr, Martyrs' Square, Brussels.

1975, May 12 **Engr.** ***Perf. 11½***
926 A351 4.50fr deep rose lilac .25 .20
927 A352 5fr slate green .25 .20
928 A351 10fr bright blue .50 .25
Nos. 926-928 (3) 1.00 .65

European Architectural Heritage Year.

Library, Louvain University, Ryckmans and Cerfaux A355

1975, June 7 **Photo.** ***Perf. 11½***
931 A355 10fr dull blue & sepia .40 .20

25th anniversary of Louvain Bible Colloquium, founded by Professors Gonzague Ryckmans (1887-1969) and Lucien Cerfaux (1883-1968).

"Metamorphose" by Pol Mara — A356

1975, June 14
932 A356 7fr multicolored .30 .20

Queen Fabiola Mental Health Foundation.

Marie Popelin, Palace of Justice, Brussels — A357

1975, June 21 **Engr. & Photo.**
933 A357 6.50fr green & claret .30 .20

International Women's Year 1975. Marie Popelin (1846-1913), first Belgian woman doctor of law.

Assia, by Charles Despiau — A358

1975, Sept. 6 ***Perf. 11½***
934 A358 5fr yellow grn & blk .25 .20

Middelheim Outdoor Museum, 25th anniv.

Cornelia Vekemans, by Cornelis de Vos — A359

1975, Sept. 20 **Photo.**
935 A359 4.50fr multicolored .20 .20

Youth philately.

Map of Schelde-Rhine Canal — A360

1975, Sept. 20
936 A360 10fr multicolored .45 .25

Opening of connection between the Schelde and Rhine, Sept. 23, 1975.

National Bank, W. F. Orban, Founder A361

Photogravure and Engraved

1975, Oct. 11 ***Perf. 12½x13***
937 A361 25fr multicolored 1.00 .30

Natl. Bank of Belgium, 125th anniv.

Edmond Thieffry and Plane, 1925 A362

1975, Oct. 18 ***Perf. 11½***
938 A362 7fr black & lilac .30 .20

First flight Brussels to Kinshasa, Congo, 50th anniversary.

"Seat of Wisdom" St. Peter's, Louvain — A363

1975, Nov. 8 ***Perf. 11½***
939 A363 6.50fr blue, blk & grn .30 .20

University of Louvain, 550th anniversary.

Angels, by Rogier van der Weyden A364

1975, Nov. 15
940 A364 5fr multicolored .25 .20

Christmas 1975.

Willemsfonds Emblem — A365

1976, Feb. 21 **Photo.** ***Perf. 11½***
941 A365 5fr multicolored .25 .20

Willems Foundation, which supports Flemish language and literature, 125th anniv.

American Bicentennial Emblem — A366

1976, Mar. 13 **Photo.** ***Perf. 11½***
942 A366 14fr multi+label .60 .30

American Bicentennial. Black engraved inscription on labels commemorates arrival of first Walloon settlers in Nieu Nederland.

Cardinal Mercier — A367

1976, Mar. 20 **Engr.**
943 A367 4.50fr brt rose lilac .20 .20

Desire Joseph Cardinal Mercier (1851-1926), professor at Louvain University, spiritual and patriotic leader during World War I.

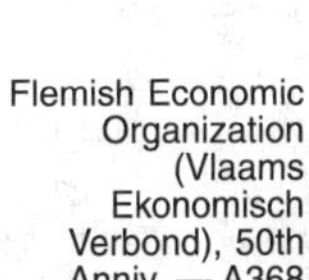

Flemish Economic Organization (Vlaams Ekonomisch Verbond), 50th Anniv. — A368

1976, Apr. 3 **Photo.** ***Perf. 11½***
944 A368 6.50fr multicolored .30 .20

General Post Office, Brussels A369

1976, Apr. 24 **Engr.** ***Perf. 11½***
945 A369 6.50fr sepia .30 .20

Stamp Day.

Potter's Hands A370

Europa: 6.50fr, Basket maker, vert.

1976, May 8 **Photo.**
946 A370 6.50fr multicolored .30 .20
947 A370 14fr multicolored .70 .30

Truck on Road
A371

1976, May 8
948 A371 14fr black, yel & red .65 .35

15th Intl. Road Union Cong., Brussels, May 9-13.

Queen Elisabeth
(1876-1965)
A372

1976, May 24 ***Perf. 11½***
949 A372 14fr green .60 .30

Ardennes Draft Horses
A373

1976, June 19
950 A373 5fr multicolored .25 .20

Ardennes Draft Horses Assoc., 50th anniv.

Souvenir Sheets

King Baudouin — A374

1976, June 26
951 A374 Sheet of 3 2.50 .50
a. 4.50fr gray .70 .70
b. 6.50fr ocher .70 .70
c. 10fr brick red .70 .70
952 A374 Sheet of 2 3.50 3.50
a. 20fr yellow green .85 .85
b. 30fr Prussian blue .85 .85

25th anniv. of the reign of King Baudouin. No. 951 sold for 30fr, No. 952 for 70fr. The surtax went to a new foundation for the improvement of living conditions in honor of the King.

Electric Train and Society Emblem — A375

1976, Sept. 11 **Photo.** ***Perf. 11½***
953 A375 6.50fr multi .30 .20

Natl. Belgian Railroad Soc., 50th anniv.

William of Nassau, Prince of Orange — A376

1976, Sept. 11 **Engr.**
954 A376 10fr slate green .40 .20

400th anniv. of the pacification of Ghent.

New Subway Train
A377

1976, Sept. 18 **Photo.**
955 A377 6.50fr multi .30 .20

Opening of first line of Brussels subway.

Young Musician, by W. C. Duyster — A378

1976, Oct. 2 **Photo.** ***Perf. 11½***
956 A378 4.50fr multi .20 .20

Young musicians and youth philately.

Charles Bernard — A379

St. Jerome in the Mountains, by Le Patinier — A380

Blind Leading the Blind, by Breughel the Elder
A381

#958, Fernand Victor Toussaint van Boelaere. #959, St. Jerome in the Mountains, by Le Patinier, vert.

1976, Oct. 16 **Engr.**
957 A379 5fr violet .20 .20
958 A379 5fr red brn & sepia .20 .20
959 A381 6.50fr dark brown .30 .20
960 A381 6.50fr slate green .30 .20
Nos. 957-960 (4) 1.00 .80

Charles Bernard (1875-1961), French-speaking journalist; Toussaint van Boelaere (1875-1947), Flemish journalist; No. 959, Charles Plisnier Belgian-French Cultural Society. No. 960, Assoc. for Language Promotion.

Remouchamps Caves — A382

Hunnegem Priory, Gramont, and Madonna
A383

Designs: No. 963, River Lys and St. Martin's Church. No. 964, Ham-sur-Heure Castle.

1976, Oct. 23 **Engr.** ***Perf. 13***
961 A382 4.50fr multi .20 .20
962 A383 4.50fr multi .20 .20
963 A383 5fr multi .25 .20
964 A383 5fr multi .25 .20
Nos. 961-964 (4) .90 .80

Tourism. #961-962 are not luminescent.

Nativity, by Master of Flemalle — A384

1976, Nov. 20 ***Perf. 11½***
965 A384 5fr violet .25 .20

Christmas 1976.

Rubens' Monogram — A385

1977, Feb. 12 **Photo. & Engr.**
966 A385 6.50fr lilac & blk .30 .20

Peter Paul Rubens (1577-1640), painter.

Heraldic Lion — A386

1977-85 **Typo.** ***Perf. 13½x14***
Size: 17x20mm
967 A386 50c brn ('80) .20 .20
a. 50c orange brown ('85) .20 .20
968 A386 1fr brt lil .20 .20
a. 1fr bright rose lilac ('84) .20 .20
969 A386 1.50fr gray ('78) .20 .20
970 A386 2fr yel ('78) .20 .20
970A A386 2.50fr yel grn ('81) .20 .20
971 A386 2.75fr Prus bl ('80) .30 .20
972 A386 3fr vio ('78) .30 .20
a. 3fr dull violet ('84) .20 .20
973 A386 4fr red brn ('80) .25 .20
a. 4fr rose brown ('85) .25 .20
974 A386 4.50fr lt ultra .30 .20
975 A386 5fr grn ('80) .30 .20
a. 5fr emerald green ('84) .20 .20
976 A386 6fr dl red brn .35 .20
a. 6fr light red brown ('85) .35 .20
Nos. 967-976 (11) 2.80 2.20

1978, Aug. **Photo.** ***Perf. 13½x12½***
Size: 17x22mm
Booklet Stamps
977 A386 1fr brt lilac .20 .20
a. Bklt. pane, #977-978, 2 #786 1.50
b. Bklt. pane, #977, 979, 2 #788 2.00
978 A386 2fr yellow .30 .30
979 A386 3fr violet .50 .50
Nos. 977-979 (3) 1.00 1.00

Each pane has 2 labels showing Belgian Postal emblem, also a large selvage with zip code instructions. No. 977-979 not luminescent.

See Nos. 1084-1088, design O5.

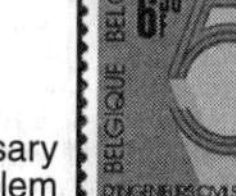

Anniversary Emblem
A387

1977, Mar. 14 **Photo.** ***Perf. 11½***
982 A387 6.50fr sil & multi .30 .20

Royal Belgian Association of Civil and Agricultural Engineers, 50th anniversary.

Birds and Lions Emblem
A388

1977, Mar. 28
983 A388 14fr multi .60 .30

Belgian District #112 of Lions Intl., 25th anniv.

Pillar Box, 1852 — A389

1977, Apr. 23 **Engr.**
984 A389 6.50fr slate green .45 .20

Stamp Day 1977.

Gileppe Dam, Jalhay
A390

Europa: 14fr, War Memorial, Yser at Nieuport.

1977, May 7 **Photo.** ***Perf. 11½***
985 A390 6.50fr multi .40 .20
986 A390 14fr multi .80 .25

Mars and Mercury Association Emblem — A391

1977, May 14
987 A391 5fr multi .25 .20

Mars and Mercury Association of Reserve and Retired Officers, 50th anniversary.

Prince de Hornes Coat of Arms — A392

Conversion of St. Hubertus — A394

Battle of the Golden Spur, from Oxford Chest — A393

Designs: 6.50fr, Froissart writing book, vert.

1977, June 11 Engr. *Perf. 11½*

988 A392 4.50fr violet .30 .20
989 A393 5fr red .35 .20
990 A393 6.50fr dark brown .40 .25
991 A393 14fr slate green .75 .35
Nos. 988-991 (4) 1.80 1.00

300th anniv. of the Principality of Overijse (4.50fr); 675th anniv. of the Battle of the Golden Spur (5f); 600th anniv. of publication of 1st volume of the Chronicles of Jehan Froissart (6.50fr); 1250th anniv. of the death of St. Hubertus (14fr).

Rubens, Self-portrait A395

1977, June 25 Photo.

992 A395 5fr multi .25 .20
a. Souvenir sheet of 3 1.25 .90

Peter Paul Rubens (1577-1640), painter. Stamps in #992a are 37¼mm high, #992, 35¼mm. #992a sold for 20fr.

Open Book, from The Lamb of God, by Van Eyck Brothers — A396

1977, Sept. 3 Photo. *Perf. 11½*

993 A396 10fr multi .45 .25

Intl. Federation of Library Associations (IFLA), 50th Anniv. Cong., Brussels, Sept. 5-10.

Gymnast and Soccer Player — A397

6.50fr, Fencers in wheelchairs, horiz. 10fr, Basketball players. 14fr, Hockey players.

1977, Sept. 10

994 A397 4.50fr multi .25 .20
995 A397 6.50fr multi .35 .20
996 A397 10fr multi .60 .20
997 A397 14fr multi .80 .30
Nos. 994-997 (4) 2.00 .90

Workers' Gymnastics and Sports Center, 50th anniversary (4.50fr); sport for the Handicapped (6.50fr); 20th European Basketball Championships (10fr); First World Hockey Cup (14fr).

Europalia 77 Emblem — A398

1977, Sept. 17

998 A398 5fr gray & multi .25 .20

5th Europalia Arts Festival, featuring German Federal Republic, Belgium, Oct.-Nov. 1977.

The Egg Farmer, by Gustave De Smet — A399

1977, Oct. 8 Engr. & Photo.

999 A399 4.50fr bister & blk .25 .20

Publicity for Belgian eggs.

Mother and Daughter with Album, by Constant Cap A400

1977, Oct. 15 Engr.

1000 A400 4.50fr dark brown .25 .20

Youth Philately.

Bailiff's House, Gembloux — A401

Market Square, St. Nicholas A402

#1002, St. Aldegonde Church & Cultural Center. #1004, Statue and bridge, Liège.

1977, Oct. 22

1001 A401 4.50fr multi .25 .20
1002 A401 4.50fr multi .25 .20
1003 A402 5fr multi .25 .20
1004 A402 5fr multi .25 .20
Nos. 1001-1004 (4) 1.00 .80

Tourism. Nos. 1001-1004 not luminescent.
See Nos. 1017-1018, 1037-1040.

Nativity, by Rogier van der Weyden — A403

1977, Nov. 11 Engr.

1005 A403 5fr rose red .30 .20

Christmas 1977.

Symbols of Transportation and Map — A404

Campidoglio Palace, Rome, and Map — A406

Designs: #1007, European Parliament, Strasbourg, Emblem, vert. #1009, Paul-Henri Spaak and map of 19 European member countries.

1978, Mar. 18 Photo. *Perf. 11½*

1006 A404 10fr blue & multi .60 .20
1007 A404 10fr blue & multi 1.10 .20
1008 A406 14fr blue & multi .65 .55
1009 A406 14fr blue & multi .65 .55
Nos. 1006-1009 (4) 3.00 1.50

European Action: 25th anniversary of the European Transport Ministers' Conference; 1st general elections for European Parliament; 20th anniversary of the signing of the Treaty of Rome; Paul Henri Spaak (1899-1972), Belgian statesman who worked for the establishment of European Community.

Grimbergen Abbey — A407

1978, Apr. 1 Engr.

1010 A407 4.50fr red brown .25 .20

850th anniversary of the Premonstratensian Abbey at Grimbergen.

Ostend Chamber of Commerce and Industry, 175th Anniv. — A408

1978, Apr. 8 Photo.

1011 A408 8fr Emblem .50 .20

No. 39 with First Day Cancel — A409

1978, Apr. 15

1012 A409 8fr multicolored .35 .20

Stamp Day.

Europa Issue

Pont des Trous, Tournai A410

8fr, Antwerp Cathedral, by Vaclav Hollar.

Photogravure and Engraved

1978, May 6 *Perf. 11½*

1013 A410 8fr multi, vert. .50 .20
1014 A410 14fr multi .70 .25

Virgin of Ghent, Porcelain Plaque — A411

Paul Pastur Workers' University, Charleroi — A412

1978, Sept. 16 Photo. *Perf. 11½*

1015 A411 6fr multicolored .40 .20
1016 A412 8fr multicolored .55 .20

Municipal education in Ghent, 150th anniversary; Paul Pastur Workers' University, Charleroi, 75th anniv. #1015-1016 are not luminescent.

Types of 1977 and

Tourist Guide, Brussels A413

#1017, Jonathas House, Enghien. #1018, View of Wetteren and couple in local costume. #1020, Prince Carnival, Eupen-St. Vith.

1978, Sept. 25 Photo. & Engr.

1017 A401 4.50fr multi .20 .20
1018 A402 4.50fr multi .20 .20
1019 A413 6fr multi .25 .20
1020 A413 6fr multi .25 .20
Nos. 1017-1020 (4) .90 .80

Tourism. #1017-1020 are not luminescent.

Royal Flemish Engineer's Organization, 50th Anniv. — A414

1978, Oct. 7 Photo.

1021 A414 8fr Emblem .35 .20

Young Philatelist A415

1978, Oct. 14 Engr. *Perf. 11½*

1022 A415 4.50fr dk violet .25 .20

Youth philately.

Nativity, Notre Dame, Huy — A416

1978, Nov. 18 Engr. *Perf. 11½*

1023 A416 6fr black .30 .20

Christmas 1978.

Tyll Eulenspiegel, Lay Action Emblem — A417

1979, Mar. 3 **Photo.** ***Perf. 11½***

1024 A417 4.50fr multi .30 .20

10th anniversary of Lay Action Centers.

European Parliament Emblem — A418

1979, Mar. 3

1025 A418 8fr multicolored .50 .20

European Parliament, first direct elections, June 7-10.

St. Michael Banishing Lucifer — A419

1979, Mar. 17 **Photo. & Engr.**

1026 A419 4.50fr rose red & blk .20 .20
1027 A419 8fr brt green & blk .30 .20

Millennium of Brussels.

NATO Emblem and Monument A420

1979, Mar. 31 **Photo.**

1028 A420 3fr multicolored 1.75 .45

NATO, 30th anniv.

Prisoner's Head — A421

1979, Apr. 7 **Photo. & Engr.**

1029 A421 6fr orange & blk .25 .20

25th anniversary of the National Political Prisoners' Monument at Breendonk.

Belgium No. Q2 — A422

1979, Apr. 21 **Photo.** ***Perf. 11½***

1030 A422 8fr multicolored .50 .20

Stamp Day 1979.

Mail Coach and Truck A423

Europa: 14fr, Chappe's heliograph, Intelsat satellite and dish antenna.

1979, Apr. 28 **Photo. & Engr.**

1031 A423 8fr multicolored .40 .20
1032 A423 14fr multicolored .80 .30

Chamber of Commerce Emblem — A424

1979, May 19 **Photo.** ***Perf. 11½***

1033 A424 8fr multicolored .35 .20

Verviers Chamber of Commerce and Industry, 175th anniversary.

"50" Emblem A425

1979, June 9 **Photo.** ***Perf. 11½***

1034 A425 4.50fr gold & ultra .30 .20

Natl. Fund for Professional Credit, 50th anniv.

Merchants, Roman Bas-relief A426

1979, June 9

1035 A426 10fr multicolored .60 .20

Belgian Chamber of Trade and Commerce, 50th anniversary.

"Tintin" as Philatelist A427

1979, Sept. 29 **Photo.** ***Perf. 11½***

1036 A427 8fr multicolored 1.10 .20

Youth philately.

Tourism Types of 1977

Designs: No. 1037, Belfry, Thuin. No. 1038, Royal Museum of Central Africa, Tervuren. No. 1039, St. Nicholas Church and cattle, Ciney. No. 1040, St. John's Church and statue of Our Lady, Poperinge.

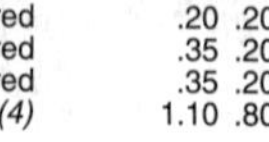

Perf. 11½ (A401), 13 (A402)

1979, Oct. 22 **Photo. & Engr.**

1037 A401 5fr multicolored .20 .20
1038 A402 5fr multicolored .20 .20
1039 A401 6fr multicolored .35 .20
1040 A402 6fr multicolored .35 .20
Nos. 1037-1040 (4) 1.10 .80

Francois Auguste Gevaert A429

Piano, String Instruments A430

Design: 6fr, Emmanuel Durlet.

1979, Nov. 3 ***Perf. 11½***

1041 A429 5fr brown .35 .20
1042 A429 6fr brown .40 .20
1043 A430 14fr brown .90 .35
Nos. 1041-1043 (3) 1.65 .75

Francois Auguste Gevaert (1828-1908), musicologist and composer; Emmanuel Durlet (1893-1977), pianist; Queen Elisabeth Musical Chapel Foundation, 40th anniv.

Virgin and Child, Notre Dame, Foy — A431

1979, Nov. 24 **Photo. & Engr.**

1044 A431 6fr lt grnsh blue .30 .20

Christmas 1979.

Independence, 150th Anniversary — A432

1980, Jan. 26 **Photo.** ***Perf. 11½***

1045 A432 9fr purple .40 .20

Frans van Cauwelaert (1880-1961), Minister of State — A433

1980, Feb. 25 **Engr.**

1046 A433 5fr gray .25 .20

Ghent Flower Show, Apr. 19-27 — A434

1980, Mar. 10 **Photo.**

1047 A434 5fr Spring flowers .25 .20
1048 A434 6.50fr Summer flowers .30 .20
1049 A434 9fr Autumn flowers .45 .20
Nos. 1047-1049 (3) 1.00 .60

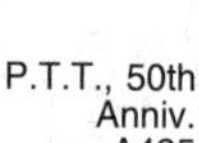

P.T.T., 50th Anniv. A435

1980, Apr. 14 **Photo.** ***Perf. 11½***

1050 A435 10fr multicolored .45 .25

Belgium No. C4 — A436

1980, Apr. 21

1051 A436 9fr multicolored .50 .20

Stamp Day.

Europa — A437

9fr, St. Benedict, by Hans Memling. 14fr, Margaret of Austria (1480-1530).

1980, Apr. 28

1052 A437 9fr multicolored .45 .20
1053 A437 14fr multicolored .65 .25

4th Interparliamentary Conf. for European Cooperation & Security, Brussels, May 12-18 — A438

1980, May 10 **Photo.** ***Perf. 11½***

1054 A438 5fr Palais des Nations, Brussels .25 .20

Golden Carriage, 1780, Mons A439

Tourism: #1056, Canal landscape, Damme.

1980, May 17

1055 A439 6.50fr multi .30 .20
1056 A439 6.50fr multi .30 .20

Souvenir Sheet

Royal Mint Theater, Brussels — A440

Photo. & Engr.

1980, May 31 ***Perf. 11½***

1057 A440 50fr black 3.25 3.25

150th anniv. of independence. Sold for 75fr.

King Baudouin, 50th Birthday — A441

1980, Sept. 6 Photo. *Perf. 11½*
1058 A441 9fr rose claret .40 .20

View of Chiny A442

Portal and Court, Diest — A443

1980 Engr. *Perf. 13*
1059 A442 5fr multicolored .25 .20
1060 A443 5fr multicolored .25 .20

Tourism. #1059-1060 are not luminescent. Issued: #1059, 9/27; #1060, 12/13.
See #1072-1075, 1120-1125.

Emblem of Belgian Heart League A444

1980, Oct. 4 Photo. *Perf. 11½*
1061 A444 14fr blue & magenta .55 .25

Heart Week, Oct. 20-25.

Rodenbach Statue, Roulers — A445

1980, Oct. 11
1062 A445 9fr multicolored .40 .20

Albrecht Rodenbach (1856-1880), poet.

Youth Philately — A446

1980, Oct. 27 Photo. *Perf. 11½*
1063 A446 5fr multicolored .25 .20

National Broadcasting Service, 50th Anniversary A447

1980, Nov. 10
1064 A447 10fr gray & blk .45 .25

Garland and Nativity, by Daniel Seghers, 17th Century A448

1980, Nov. 17
1065 A448 6.50fr multicolored .40 .20

Christmas 1980.

Baron de Gerlache, by F.J. Navez — A449

Leopold I, By Geefs A450

9fr, Baron de Stassart, by F.J. Navez.

1981, Mar. 16 Photo. *Perf. 11½*
1066 A449 6fr multicolored .35 .20
1067 A449 9fr multicolored .55 .20

Photogravure and Engraved
1068 A450 50fr multicolored 3.00 .55

Sesquicentennial of Chamber of Deputies, Senate and Dynasty.

Tchantchès and Op-Signoorke, Puppets — A451

Photogravure and Engraved
1981, May 4 *Perf. 11½*
1069 A451 9fr shown .40 .20
1070 A451 14fr d'Artagnan and Woltje .65 .30

Europa.

Impression of M.A. de Cock (Founder of Post Museum) — A452

1981, May 18 Photo.
1071 A452 9fr multicolored .40 .20

Stamp Day.

Tourism Types of 1980

#1072, Virgin and Child statue, Our Lady's Church, Tongre-Notre Dame. #1073, Egmont Castle, Zottegem. #1074, Eau d'Heure River. #1075, Tongerlo Abbey, Antwerp.

1981, June 15 Engr. *Perf. 11½*
1072 A442 6fr multi .35 .20
1073 A442 6fr multi .35 .20
1074 A443 6.50fr multi .35 .20
1075 A443 6.50fr multi .35 .20
Nos. 1072-1075 (4) 1.40 .80

Soccer Player — A453

1981, Sept. 5 Photo. *Perf. 11½*
1076 A453 6fr multicolored .35 .20

Soccer in Belgium centenary; Royal Antwerp Soccer Club.

E. Remouchamps, Founder — A454

1981, Sept. 5 Photo. & Engr.
1077 A454 6.50fr multi .40 .20

Walloon Language and Literature Club 125th anniv.

Audit Office Sesquicentennial — A455

1981, Sept. 12 Engr.
1078 A455 10fr tan & dk brn .60 .25

French Horn A456

1981, Sept. 12 Photo.
1079 A456 6.50fr multi .40 .20

Vredekring (Peace Circle) Band of Antwerp centenary.

Souvenir Sheet

Pieta, by Ben Genaux — A457

1981, Sept. 19 Photo. *Perf. 11½*
1080 A457 20fr multicolored 1.75 1.40

Mining disaster at Marcinelle, 25th anniv. Sold for 30fr.

Mausoleum of Marie of Burgundy and Charles the Bold, Bruges — A458

1981, Oct. 10 Photo. & Engr.
1081 A458 50fr multi 2.75 .60

Youth Philately — A459

1981, Oct. 24 Photo.
1082 A459 6fr multi .30 .20

Type of 1977 and

A459a

A460

King Baudouin A460a

Photo. and Engr.; Photo.
1980-86 *Perf. 13½x14, 11½*

1084	A386	65c	brt rose	.20	.20
1085	A386	1fr	on 5fr grn	.20	.20
1086	A386	7fr	brt rose	.30	.20
1087	A386	8fr	grnsh bl	.35	.20
1088	A386	9fr	dl org	.50	.20
1089	A459a	10fr	blue	.40	.20
1090	A459a	11fr	dl red	.45	.20
1091	A459a	12fr	grn	.65	.20
1092	A459a	13fr	scar	.55	.20
1093	A459a	15fr	red org	1.25	.25
1094	A459a	20fr	dk bl	.85	.20
1095	A459a	22fr	lilac	1.60	.60
1096	A459a	23fr	gray grn	1.25	.30
1097	A459a	30fr	brown	1.25	.20
1098	A459a	40fr	red org	1.75	.20
1099	A460	50fr	lt grnsh bl & bl	2.10	.20
1100	A460a	50fr	tan & dk brn	2.10	.20
1101	A460	65fr	pale lil & blk	2.75	.60

1102 A460 100fr lt bis brn & dk bl 4.25 .40
1103 A460a 100fr lt bl & dk bl 4.25 .25
Nos. 1084-1103 (20) 27.00 5.20

Issued: 65c, 4/14/80; 1fr, 5/3/82; 7fr, 5/17/82; 8fr, 5/9/83; 9fr, 2/11/85; 65fr, No. 1099, 1102, 11/5/81; 10fr, 11/15/82; 11fr, 4/5/83; 12fr, 1/23/84; 15fr, 22fr, 30fr, No. 1100, 3/26/84; 20fr, 40fr, No. 1103, 6/12/84; 23fr, 2/25/85; 13fr, 3/10/86. See #1231-1234.

Max Waller, Movement Founder — A461

Designs: 6.50fr, The Spirit Drinkers, by Gustave van de Woestyne. 9fr, Fernand Severin, poet, 50th death anniv. 10fr, Jan van Ruusbroec, Flemish mystic, 500th birth anniv. 14fr, Thought and Man TV series, 25th anniv.

1981, Nov. 7

1104 A461 6fr multi .30 .20
1105 A461 6.50fr multi .35 .20
1106 A461 9fr multi .50 .20
1107 A461 10fr multi .80 .25
1108 A461 14fr multi .75 .35
Nos. 1104-1108 (5) 2.70 1.20

La Jeune Belgique cultural movement cent. (6fr).

Nativity, 16th Cent. Engraving — A466

1981, Nov. 21

1109 A466 6.50fr multi .30 .20

Christmas 1981.

Royal Conservatory of Music Sesquicentennial — A467

Design: 9fr, Judiciary sesquicentennial.

1982, Jan. 25 Photo. *Perf. 11½*

1110 A467 6.50fr multi .30 .20
1111 A467 9fr multi .40 .20

A468

1982, Mar. 1

1112 A468 6fr Cyclotron .35 .20
1113 A468 14fr Galaxy, telescope .85 .35
1114 A468 50fr Koch 3.00 .65
Nos. 1112-1114 (3) 4.20 1.20

Radio-isotope production, Natl. Radio-elements Institute, Fleurus (6fr); Royal Belgian Observatory (14fr); centenary of TB bacillus discovery (50fr).

Joseph Lemaire (1882-1966), Minister of State — A469

1982, Apr. 17 Photo. *Perf. 11½*

1115 A469 6.50fr multi .30 .20

Europa 1982 A470

1982, May 1

1116 A470 10fr Universal suffrage .50 .20
1117 A470 17fr Edict of Tolerance, 1781 .80 .30

Stamp Day — A471

1982, May 22 Photo. & Engr.

1118 A471 10fr multi .50 .20

67th World Esperanto Congress, Anvers A472

1982, June 7 Photo. *Perf. 11½*

1119 A472 12fr Tower of Babel .60 .30

Tourism Type of 1980

Designs: No. 1120, Tower of Gosselies. No. 1121, Zwijveke Abbey, Dendermonde. No. 1122, Stavelot Abbey. No. 1123, Villers-la-Ville Abbey ruins. No. 1124, Geraardsbergen Abbey entrance. No. 1125, Beveren Pillory.

1982, June 21 Photo. & Engr.

1120 A443 7fr lt bl & blk .50 .20
1121 A443 7fr lt grn & blk .50 .20
1122 A442 7.50fr tan & dk brn .55 .25
1123 A442 7.50fr lt vio & pur .55 .25
1124 A443 7.50fr slate & blk .55 .25
1125 A443 7.50fr beige & blk .55 .25
Nos. 1120-1125 (6) 3.20 1.40

Self Portrait, by L.P. Boon (b. 1912) — A473

Designs: 10fr, Adoration of the Shepherds, by Hugo van der Goes (1440-1482). 12fr, The King on His Throne, carving by M. de Ghelderode (1898-1962). 17fr, Madonna and Child, by Pieter Paulus (1881-1959).

1982, Sept. 13 Photo. *Perf. 11½*

1126 A473 7fr multicolored .50 .20
1127 A473 10fr multicolored .60 .20
1128 A473 12fr multicolored .70 .35
1129 A473 17fr multicolored 1.00 .35
Nos. 1126-1129 (4) 2.80 1.10

Abraham Hans, Writer (1882-1932) A474

1982, Sept. 27

1130 A474 17fr multicolored 1.10 .35

Youth Philately and Scouting A475

1982, Oct. 2 Photo. *Perf. 11½*

1131 A475 7fr multicolored .50 .20

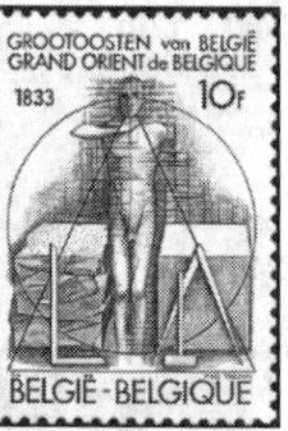

Grand Orient Lodge of Belgium Sesquicentennial A476

1982, Oct. 16 Photo. & Engr.

1132 A476 10fr Man taking oath .60 .20

Cardinal Joseph Cardijn (1882-1967) A477

1982, Nov. 13 Photo.

1133 A477 10fr multicolored .50 .20

St. Francis of Assisi (1182-1226) A478

1982, Nov. 27

1134 A478 20fr multicolored .90 .30

Horse-drawn Trolley A479

1983, Feb. 12 Photo. *Perf. 11½*

1135 A479 7.50fr shown .40 .25
1136 A479 10fr Electric trolley .50 .25
1137 A479 50fr Trolley, diff. 2.50 .50
Nos. 1135-1137 (3) 3.40 1.00

Intl. Fed. for Periodical Press, 24th World Congress, Brussels, May 11-13 A480

1983, Mar. 19 Photo. *Perf. 11½*

1138 A480 20fr multicolored 1.00 .25

Homage to Women A481

1983, Apr. 16

1139 A481 8fr Operator .45 .20
1140 A481 11fr Homemaker .55 .20
1141 A481 20fr Executive 1.00 .25
Nos. 1139-1141 (3) 2.00 .65

Stamp Day — A482

1983, Apr. 23

1142 A482 11fr multicolored .60 .20

Procession of the Precious Blood, Bruges A483

1983, Apr. 30 Photo. *Perf. 11½*

1143 A483 8fr multi .60 .20

Europa 1983 — A484

Paintings by P. Delvaux. 11fr vert.

1983, May 14

1144 A484 11fr Common Man .65 .20
1145 A484 20fr Night Train 1.10 .35

Manned Flight Bicentenary A485

1983, June 11 Photo. *Perf. 11½*

1146 A485 11fr Balloon over city .65 .20
1147 A485 22fr Country 1.40 .45

Our Lady's Church, Hastiere A486

1983, June 25

1148 A486 8fr shown .40 .20
1149 A486 8fr Landen .40 .20
1150 A486 8fr Park, Mouscron .40 .20
1151 A486 8fr Wijnendale Castle, Torhout .40 .20
Nos. 1148-1151 (4) 1.60 .80

Tineke Festival, Heule — A487

1983, Sept. 10 **Photo.**
1152 A487 8fr multi .40 .20

Enterprise Year Emblem A488

1983, Sept. 24
1153 A488 11fr multicolored .55 .20

European year for small and medium-sized enterprises and craft industry.

Youth Philately — A489

1983, Oct. 10 **Photo.** ***Perf. 11½***
1154 A489 8fr multicolored .40 .20

Belgian Exports A490

1983, Oct. 24 ***Perf. 11½***
1155 A490 10fr Diamond industry .55 .20
1156 A490 10fr Metallurgy .55 .20
1157 A490 10fr Textile industry .55 .20
Nos. 1155-1157 (3) 1.65 .60

See Nos. 1161-1164.

Hendrik Conscience (1812-1883), Novelist — A491

1983, Nov. 7
1158 A491 20fr multicolored 1.00 .25

Leopold III Type of 1936

1983, Dec. 12 **Engr.** ***Perf. 12x11½***
1159 A84 11fr black .55 .20

Leopold III memorial (1901-1983), King 1934-1951.

Free University of Brussels, Sesqui. — A492

Photogravure and Engraved

1984, Jan. 14 ***Perf. 11½***
1160 A492 11fr multicolored .55 .20

Exports Type of 1983

1984, Jan. 28 **Photo.**
1161 A490 11fr Chemicals .55 .20
1162 A490 11fr Food .55 .20
1163 A490 11fr Transportation equipment .55 .20
1164 A490 11fr Technology .55 .20
Nos. 1161-1164 (4) 2.20 .80

King Albert I, 50th Death Anniv. — A494

1984, Feb. 11 **Photo. & Engr.**
1165 A494 8fr tan & dk brn .40 .20

1984 Summer Olympic Games — A495

1984, Mar. 3 **Photo.**

Souvenir Sheet

1166 Sheet of 2 2.00 2.00
a. A495 10fr Archery .55 .55
b. A495 24fr Dressage 1.40 1.40

See Nos. B1029-B1030.

Family, Globe, Birds — A496

1984, Mar. 24 **Photo.** ***Perf. 11½***
1167 A496 12fr multicolored .60 .20

"Movement without a Name" peace org.

St. John Bosco Canonization A497

1984, Apr. 7
1168 A497 8fr multicolored .40 .20

Europa (1959-84) A498

1984, May 5 **Photo.** ***Perf. 11½***
1169 A498 12fr black & red .90 .20
1170 A498 22fr black & ultra 1.60 .25

Stamp Day — A499

1984, May 19
1171 A499 12fr No. 52 .60 .20

2nd European Parliament Elections A500

1984, May 26
1172 A500 12fr multicolored .60 .20

Royal Military School, 150th Anniv. — A501

1984, June 9 **Photo.** ***Perf. 11½***
1173 A501 22fr Hat 1.10 .25

Notre-Dame de la Chappelle, Brussels A502

Churches: No. 1175, St. Martin's, Montignyle-Tilleul. No. 1176, Tielt, vert.

Perf. 11½x12, 12x11½

1984, June 23 **Photo. & Engr.**
1174 A502 10fr multicolored .55 .20
1175 A502 10fr multicolored .55 .20
1176 A502 10fr multicolored .55 .20
Nos. 1174-1176 (3) 1.65 .60

50th Anniv. of Chirojeugd (Christian Youth Movement) A503

1984, Sept. 15 **Photo.** ***Perf. 11½***
1177 A503 10fr Emblem .50 .20

Affligem Abbey A504

1984, Oct. 6 **Photo. & Engr.**
1178 A504 8fr Averbode, vert. .40 .25
1179 A504 22fr Chimay, vert. 1.25 .25
1180 A504 24fr Rochefort, vert. 1.25 .40
1181 A504 50fr shown 2.50 .50
Nos. 1178-1181 (4) 5.40 1.40

Youth Philately A505

1984, Oct. 20 **Photo.**
1182 A505 8fr Postman smurf .45 .20

Arthur Meulemans (1884-1966), Composer — A506

1984, Nov. 17 **Photo. & Engr.**
1183 A506 12fr multi .60 .20

St. Norbert, 850th Death Anniv. — A507

1985, Jan. 14 **Photo. & Engr.**
1184 A507 22fr sepia & beige 1.10 .30

Europalia '85 — A508

1985, Jan. 21 **Photo.**
1185 A508 12fr Virgin of Louvain .65 .20

Belgian Assoc. of Professional Journalists, Cent. A509

1985, Feb. 11 **Photo.**
1186 A509 9fr multicolored .40 .20

Ghent Flower Festival, Orchids — A510

Photogravure and Engraved

1985, Mar. 18 ***Perf. 11½***
1187 A510 12fr Vanda coerules .70 .20
1188 A510 12fr Phalaenopsis .70 .20
1189 A510 12fr Suphrolaelio cattlea riffe .70 .20
Nos. 1187-1189 (3) 2.10 .60

Visit of Pope John Paul II A511

1985, Apr. 1 **Photo.**
1190 A511 12fr multicolored .60 .20

Belgian Worker's Party Cent.
A512

1985, Apr. 15 **Photo.**

1191 A512 9fr Chained factory gate .40 .20
1192 A512 12fr Broken wall, red flag .60 .20

Jean de Bast (1883-1975), Engraver
A513

1985, Apr. 22 **Engr.**

1193 A513 12fr blue black .60 .20

Stamp Day.

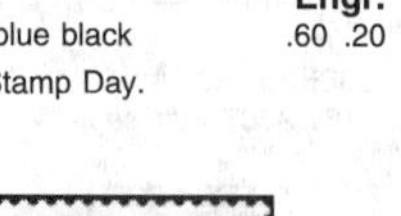

Public Transportation Year — A514

Design: 9fr, Steam tram locomotive Type 18, 1896. 12fr, Locomotive Elephant and tender, 1835. 23fr, Type 23 tank engine, 1904. 24fr, Type I Pacific locomotive, 1935. 50fr, Type 27 electric locomotive, 1975.

1985, May 6 **Photo.**

1194 A514 9fr multicolored .35 .20
1195 A514 12fr multicolored .50 .20
1196 A514 23fr multicolored .85 .35
1197 A514 24fr multicolored 1.10 .40
Nos. 1194-1197 (4) 2.80 1.15

Souvenir Sheet

1198 A514 50fr multicolored 2.75 2.00

Europa 1985
A515

1985, May 13 **Photo.**

1199 A515 12fr Cesar Franck at organ, 1887 .80 .20
1200 A515 23fr Folk figures 1.50 .25

26th Navigation Congress, Brussels
A516

1985, June 10 **Photo.** ***Perf. 11½***

1201 A516 23fr Zeebruge Harbor 1.25 .25
1202 A516 23fr Projected lock at Strepy-Thieu 1.25 .25

St. Martin's Church, Marcinelle
A517

Tourism: No. 1203, Church of the Assumption of Our Lady, Avernas-le-Baudouin, vert. No. 1204, Church of the Old Beguinage, Tongres, vert. No. 1206, Private residence, Puyenbroeck.

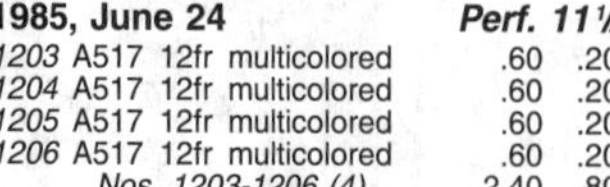

1985, June 24 ***Perf. 11½***

1203 A517 12fr multicolored .60 .20
1204 A517 12fr multicolored .60 .20
1205 A517 12fr multicolored .60 .20
1206 A517 12fr multicolored .60 .20
Nos. 1203-1206 (4) 2.40 .80

Queen Astrid (1905-1935)
A518

1985, Sept. 2 ***Perf. 11½***

1207 A518 12fr brown .60 .20

Baking Pies for the Mattetart of Geraardsbergen
A519

Folk events: 24fr, Children dancing, centenary of the St. Lambert de Hermalle-Argenteau Les Rouges youth organization.

1985, Sept. 16

1208 A519 12fr multicolored .60 .20
1209 A519 24fr multicolored .95 .30

Liberation from German Occupation, 40th Anniv. — A520

Allegories: 9fr, Dove, liberation of concentration camps. 23fr, Battle of Ardennes. 24fr, Destroyer, liberation of the River Scheldt estuary.

1985, Sept. 30 **Photo.** ***Perf. 11½***

1210 A520 9fr multicolored .50 .25
1211 A520 23fr multicolored 1.25 .65
1212 A520 24fr multicolored 1.25 .70
Nos. 1210-1212 (3) 3.00 1.60

Ernest Claes (1885-1968), Author
A521

1985, Oct. 7

1213 A521 9fr Portrait, book character .50 .25

Intl. Youth Year — A522

1985, Oct. 21

1214 A522 9fr Nude in repose, angel .50 .25

King Baudouin & Queen Fabiola, 25th Wedding Anniv. — A523

1985, Dec. 9

1215 A523 12fr multicolored .50 .40

Birds — A524

Photo. (50c-2fr, No. 1220, 4.50fr-6fr, No. 1229, 10fr), Typo. (Others)

1985-91 ***Perf. 11½***

1216 A524 50c Roitelet huppe .20 .20
1217 A524 1fr Pic epeichette .20 .20
1218 A524 2fr Moineau friquet .20 .20
1219 A524 3fr Gros bec .20 .20
1220 A524 3fr Bruant des roseax .25 .20
1221 A524 3.50fr Rouge gorge .20 .20
1222 A524 4fr Gorge bleue .25 .20
1223 A524 4.50fr Traquet Patre .35 .20
1224 A524 5fr Sittele torchepot .35 .20
1225 A524 6fr Bouvreuil .40 .20
1226 A524 7fr Mesange bleue .45 .20
1227 A524 8fr Martin-pechuer .45 .20
1228 A524 9fr Chardonneret .35 .20
1229 A524 9fr Grive musicienne .65 .20
1230 A524 10fr Pinson .65 .20
Nos. 1216-1230 (15) 5.15 3.00

Issued: 7fr, 9/7/87; 5fr, 6fr, 9/12/88; 4fr, 4/17/89; 2fr, 12/4/89; 1fr, 1/8/90; 10fr, 1/15/90; 50c, #1220, 1229, 9/30/91; others, 9/30/85.

See #1432-1447, 1627, 1641, 1645, 1651, 1660, 1676, 1696, 1700, 1702-1703, 1714-1715. For stamps denominated in Francs and Euros, see Nos. 1785-1790A, 1836-1840..

King Type of 1981

1986-90 **Photo.** ***Perf. 11½***

1231 A459a 14fr black .80 .20
1232 A459a 24fr dk grysh green 1.10 .30
1233 A459a 25fr blue black 1.40 .25
1234 A460a 200fr sage grn & dl gray grn 9.00 .75
Nos. 1231-1234 (4) 12.30 1.50

Issued: 24fr, 4/7/86; 200fr, 11/3/86; 14fr, 1/15/90; 25fr, 2/19/90.

Congo Stamp Cent. — A525

1986, Jan. 27 **Photo.** ***Perf. 11½***

1236 A525 10fr Belgian Congo #3 .40 .20

See Zaire No. 1230.

Carnival Cities of Aalst and Binche
A526

Folklore: masks, giants.

1986, Feb. 3

1237 A526 9fr Aalst Belfry .50 .20
1238 A526 12fr Binche Gilles .60 .20

Intl. Peace Year — A527

1986, Mar. 10

1239 A527 23fr Emblem, dove 1.25 .35

Stamp Day — A528

1986, Apr. 21 **Photo.** ***Perf. 11½***

1240 A528 13fr Artifacts .65 .40

Europa 1986
A529

1986, May 5

1241 A529 13fr Fish .65 .20
1242 A529 24fr Flora 1.40 .30

Dogs — A530

1986, May 26 **Photo.** ***Perf. 11½***

1243 A530 9fr Malines sheepdog .65 .30
1244 A530 13fr Tervueren sheepdog .85 .45
1245 A530 24fr Groenendael sheepdog 1.60 .80
1246 A530 26fr Flemish cattle dog 1.60 .85
Nos. 1243-1246 (4) 4.70 2.40

St. Ludger's Church, Zele — A531

#1248, Waver Town Hall. #1249, Nederzwalm Canal. #1250, Chapel of Our Lady of the Dunes, Bredene. #1251, Licot Castle, Viroinval. #1252, Eynenbourg Castle, La Calamine.

1986, June 30 **Photo. & Engr.**

1247 A531 9fr multi .60 .30
1248 A531 9fr multi .60 .30
1249 A531 13fr multi, horiz. .80 .45
1250 A531 13fr multi .80 .45
1251 A531 13fr multi, horiz. .80 .45
1252 A531 13fr multi, horiz. .80 .45
Nos. 1247-1252 (6) 4.40 2.40

Youth Philately
A532

1986, Sept. 1 Photo. *Perf. 11½*

1253 A532 9fr dl ol grn, blk & dk red .50 .30

Cartoon Exhibition, Knokke.

Famous Men — A533

Designs: 9fr, Constant Permeke, painter, sculptor. 13fr, Baron Michel-Edmond de Selys Longchamps, scientist. 24fr, Felix Timmermans, writer. 26fr, Maurice Careme, poet.

1986, Sept. 29

1254 A533 9fr multicolored .50 .30
1255 A533 13fr multicolored .75 .45
1256 A533 24fr multicolored 1.40 .80
1257 A533 26fr multicolored 1.50 .90
Nos. 1254-1257 (4) 4.15 2.45

Royal Academy for Dutch Language and Literature, Cent. A534

1986, Oct. 6 Engr.

1258 A534 9fr dark blue .50 .30

Natl. Beer Industry A535

Perf. 12½x11½

1986, Oct. 13 Photo.

1259 A535 13fr Glass, barley, hops .70 .50

Provincial Law and Councils, 150th Anniv. A536

1986, Oct. 27 *Perf. 11½*

1260 A536 13fr Stylized map .70 .50

Christian Trade Union, Cent. A537

1986, Dec. 13 Photo. *Perf. 11½*

1261 A537 9fr shown .45 .35
1262 A537 13fr design reversed .65 .50

Flanders Technology Intl. — A538

1987, Mar. 2 Photo.

1263 A538 13fr multi .70 .50

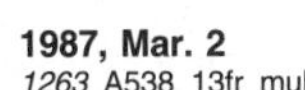

EUROPALIA '87, Austrian Cultural Events — A539

Design: Woman, detail of a fresco by Gustav Klimt, Palais Stoclet, Brussels.

1987, Apr. 4 Photo. *Perf. 11½*

1264 A539 13fr multicolored .70 .50

Stamp Day 1987 — A540

Portrait: Jakob Wiener (1815-1899), 1st engraver of Belgian stamps.

1987, Apr. 11 Photo. & Engr.

1265 A540 13fr lt greenish blue & sage grn .70 .50

Folklore A541

1987, Apr. 25 Photo.

1266 A541 9fr Penitents procession, Veurne .45 .35
1267 A541 13fr Play of John and Alice, Wavre .65 .50

Europa 1987 — A542

Modern architecture: 13fr, Louvain-la-Neuve Church. 24fr, Regional Housing Assoc. Tower, St. Maartensdal at Louvain.

1987, May 9 Photo.

1268 A542 13fr multicolored .85 .20
1269 A542 24fr multicolored 1.50 .40

Statue of Andre-Ernest Gretry (1741-1813), French Composer A543

1987, May 23

1270 A543 24fr multicolored 1.50 1.00

Wallonie Royal Opera, Liege, 20th anniv.

Tourism — A544

#1271, Statues of Jan Breydel and Pieter de Conin, Bruges. #1272, Boondael Chapel, Brussels. #1273, Windmill, Keerbergen. #1274, St. Christopher's Church, Racour. #1275, Virelles Lake, Chimay.

1987, June 13

1271 A544 13fr multicolored 1.00 .55
1272 A544 13fr multicolored 1.00 .55
1273 A544 13fr multicolored 1.00 .55
1274 A544 13fr multicolored 1.00 .55
1275 A544 13fr multicolored 1.00 .55
Nos. 1271-1275 (5) 5.00 2.75

Royal Belgian Rowing Assoc., Cent. — A545

European Volleyball Championships A546

1987, Sept. 5

1276 A545 9fr multicolored .50 .40
1277 A546 13fr multicolored .75 .55

Foreign Trade Year — A547

1987, Sept. 12

1278 A547 13fr multi .75 .55

Belgian Social Reform, Cent. A548

1987, Sept. 19

1279 A548 26fr Leisure, by P. Paulus 1.40 1.10

Youth Philately A549

1987, Oct. 3

1280 A549 9fr multi .50 .40

Newspaper Centennials A550

1987, Dec. 12

1281 A550 9fr Le Soir .55 .40
1282 A550 9fr Hett Lattste Nieuws, vert. .55 .40

The Sea — A551

Designs: a, Lighthouse, trawler, rider and mount. b, Trawler, youths playing volleyball on beach. c, Cruise ship, sailboat, beach and cabana. d, Shore, birds.

1988, Feb. 6 Photo. *Perf. 11½*

1283 Strip of 4 + label 2.50 1.75
a.-d. A551 10fr any single .60 .45

No. 1283 has a continuous design.

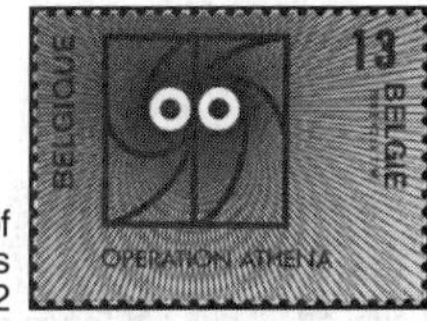

Dynamism of the Regions A552

1988, Mar. 5 Photo. *Perf. 11½*

1284 A552 13fr Operation Athena .80 .60
1285 A552 13fr Flanders Alive Campaign .80 .60

Stamp Day — A553

Painting: 19th Cent. Postman, by James Thiriar.

1988, Apr. 16 Photo. & Engr.

1286 A553 13fr buff & sepia .80 .60

Europa 1988 — A554

1988, May 9 Photo. *Perf. 11½*

Transport and communication.

1287 A554 13fr Satellite dish 1.10 .20
1288 A554 24fr Non-polluting combustion engine 1.90 1.00

Tourism A555

Designs: No. 1289, Romanesque watchtower, ca. 12th-13th cent., Amay, vert. No. 1290, Our Lady of Hanswijk Basilica, 988, Mechelen, vert. No. 1291, St. Sernin's Church, 16th cent., Waimes. No. 1292, Old Town Hall, 1637, and village water pump, 1761, Peer, vert. No. 1293, Our Lady of Bon-Secours Basilica, 1892, Peruwelz.

Photo. & Engr.

1988, June 20 *Perf. 11½*

1289 A555 9fr beige & blk .50 .40
1290 A555 9fr lt blue & blk .50 .40
1291 A555 9fr pale blue grn & blk .50 .40

1292 A555 13fr pale pink & blk .75 .55
1293 A555 13fr pale gray & blk .75 .55
Nos. 1289-1293 (5) 3.00 2.30

Our Lady of Hanswijk Basilica millennium (No. 1290); Waimes village, 1100th anniv. (No. 1291).

Jean Monnet (1888-1979), French Economist — A556

1988, Sept. 12 ***Perf. 11½***

1294 A556 13fr black .70 .50

Tapestry in the Hall of the Royal Academy of Medicine — A557

Academies building and: No. 1296, Lyre, quill pen, open book and atomic symbols.

1988, Sept. 17 **Photo.**

1295 A557 9fr shown .50 .40
1296 A557 9fr multi .50 .40

Royal Academy of Medicine (#1295); Royal Academy of Science, Literature and Fine Arts (#1296).

Cultural Heritage A558

Artifacts: 9fr, Statue and mask in the Antwerp Ethnographical Museum. 13fr, Sarcophagus, St. Martin's Church, Trazegnies. 24fr, Church organ, Geraardsbergen. 26fr, Shrine, St. Hadelin's Church, Vise.

1988, Sept. 24

1297 A558 9fr multi .50 .40
1298 A558 13fr multi .70 .50
1299 A558 24fr multi 1.25 1.00
1300 A558 26fr multi 1.40 1.00
Nos. 1297-1300 (4) 3.85 2.90

Youth Philately A559

1988, Oct. 10

1301 A559 9fr multi .50 .40

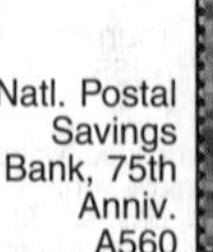

Natl. Postal Savings Bank, 75th Anniv. A560

1988, Nov. 7

1302 A560 13fr multi .70 .50

Christmas 1988 and New Year 1989 A561

1988, Nov. 21

1303 A561 9fr Winter landscape .50 .40

Royal Mounted Guard, 50th Anniv. A562

1988, Dec. 12

1304 A562 13fr multi .75 .55

Printing Presses A563

9fr, J. Moretus I, Antwerp Museum, vert. 24fr, Stanhope, Printing Museum, Brussels, vert. 26fr, Litho Krause, Royal Museum, Mariemont.

1988, Dec. 19 **Engr.**

1305 A563 9fr bl blk & blk .50 .40
1306 A563 24fr dark red brn 1.40 1.10
1307 A563 26fr grn & slate grn 1.50 1.25
Nos. 1305-1307 (3) 3.40 2.75

Lace A564

1989, Mar. 20 **Photo.**

1308 A564 9fr Marche-en-Famenne .50 .40
1309 A564 13fr Brussels .70 .50
1310 A564 13fr Brugge .70 .50
Nos. 1308-1310 (3) 1.90 1.40

Stamp Day A565

1989, Apr. 24 **Photo. & Engr.**

1311 A565 13fr Mail coach, post chaise .75 .55

Europa 1989 — A566

Children's toys.

1989, May 8 **Photo.**

1312 A566 13fr Marbles, horiz. .75 .25
1313 A566 24fr Jumping-jack 1.40 .90

Royal Academy of Fine Arts, Antwerp, 325th Anniv. — A567

1989, May 22 ***Perf. 11½***

1314 A567 13fr multi .75 .50

European Parliament 3rd Elections — A568

Illustration reduced.

1989, June 5 **Photo.**

1315 A568 13fr Brussels .75 .50

Declaration of Rights of Man and the Citizen, Bicent. — A569

1989, June 12 ***Perf. 11½***

1316 A569 13fr multi + label .75 .50

Tourism A570

#1317, St. Tillo's Church, Izegem. #1318, Logne Castle, Ferrieres. #1319, St. Laurentius's Church, Lokeren. #1320, Antoing Castle, Antoing.

1989, June 26 **Photo. & Engr.**

1317 A570 9fr multi .50 .40
1318 A570 9fr multi, vert. .50 .40
1319 A570 13fr multi, vert. .75 .50
1320 A570 13fr multi, vert. .75 .50
Nos. 1317-1320 (4) 2.50 1.80

Ducks — A571

1989, Sept. 4 **Photo.** ***Perf. 12***

Booklet Stamps

1321 A571 13fr Mallard (8a) 1.10 .50
1322 A571 13fr Winter teal (8b) 1.10 .50
1323 A571 13fr Shoveller (8c) 1.10 .50
1324 A571 13fr Pintail (8d) 1.10 .50
a. Bklt. pane of 4, #1321-1324 4.50
Complete booklet, #1324a 4.50

Shigefusa Uesugi, a Seated Japanese Warrior, 13th Cent. A572

1989, Sept. 18 ***Perf. 11½***

1325 A572 24fr multicolored 1.50 .50

Europalia.

Education League, 125th Anniv. — A573

1989, Sept. 25

1326 A573 13fr multicolored .80 .20

Treaty of London, 150th Anniv. — A574

1989, Oct. 2 **Photo.**

1327 A574 13fr Map of Limburg Provinces .80 .20

See Netherlands No. 750.

Mr. Nibbs — A575

1989, Oct. 9 ***Perf. 11½***

1328 A575 9fr multicolored .60 .20

Youth philately promotion.

Christmas, New Year 1990 A576

1989, Nov. 20 **Photo.**

1329 A576 9fr Salvation Army band .60 .20

Fr. Damien (1840-89), Missionary, Molokai Is. Leper Colony, Hawaii A577

1989, Nov. 27 **Photo.**

1330 A577 24fr multicolored 1.50 .50

Father Adolf Daens — A578

1989, Dec. 11 **Photo. & Engr.**
1331 A578 9fr pale & dk grn .55 .20

The Young Post Rider, an Engraving by Albrecht Durer — A579

Ghent Flower Festival — A580

1990, Jan. 12 **Photo. & Engr.**
1332 A579 14fr buff & red blk .75 .55

Postal communications in Europe, 500th anniv.

See Austria No. 1486, Germany No. 1592, Berlin No. 9N584 and German Democratic Republic No. 2791.

1990, Mar. 3 **Photo.**
1333 A580 10fr *Iris florentina* .50 .40
1334 A580 14fr *Cattleya harrisoniana* .75 .55
1335 A580 14fr *Lilium bulbiferum* .75 .55
Nos. 1333-1335 (3) 2.00 1.50

Intl. Women's Day — A581

1990, Mar. 12 **Photo.** ***Perf. 11½***
1336 A581 25fr Emilienne Brunfaut 1.45 1.00

Wheelchair Basketball — A582

Sports.

1990, Mar. 19
1337 A582 10fr multicolored .60 .40
1338 A582 14fr multicolored .80 .60
1339 A582 25fr shown 1.40 1.00
Nos. 1337-1339 (3) 2.80 2.00

Special Olympics (10fr); and 1990 World Cup Soccer Championships, Italy (14fr).

Natl. Water Supply Soc., 75th Anniv. A583

1990, Apr. 2
1340 A583 14fr Water means life .80 .60

Postman Roulin, by Van Gogh — A584

1990, Apr. 9
1341 A584 14fr multicolored .80 .60

Stamp Day.

Labor Day, Cent. A585

1990, Apr. 30
1342 A585 25fr multicolored 1.40 1.00

Europa 1990 A586

Post offices.

1990, May 7 **Photo. & Engr.**
1343 A586 14fr Ostend 1 .75 .20
1344 A586 25fr Liege 1, vert. 1.50 .90

18-Day Campaign, 1940 — A587

1990, May 14 **Photo.** ***Perf. 11½***
1345 A587 14fr Lys Monument, Courtrai .80 .60

Resistance of German occupation.

Stamp Collecting Promotion Type of 1988

Souvenir Sheet

Various flowers from *Sixty Roses for a Queen,* by P.J. Redoute (1759-1840): a, *Rose tricolore.* b, Belle Rubaree. c, *Mycrophylla.* d, Amelie rose. e, Adelaide rose. f, Helene rose.

1990, June 2 **Photo. & Engr.**
1346 Sheet of 6 30.00 30.00
a.-c. SP487 14fr any single 2.00 2.00
d.-f. SP487 25fr any single 2.50 2.50

BELGICA '90, Brussels, June 2-10. sold for 220fr.

Battle of Waterloo, 1815 — A588

Design: Marshal Ney leading the French cavalry. Illustration reduced.

1990, June 18 **Photo.**
1352 A588 25fr multi + label 1.60 1.10

Tourism A589

1990, July 9
1353 A589 10fr Antwerp .60 .45
1354 A589 10fr Dendermonde .60 .45
1355 A589 14fr Gerpinnes, vert. .80 .60
1356 A589 14fr Lommel .80 .60
1357 A589 14fr Watermael .80 .60
Nos. 1353-1357 (5) 3.60 2.70

A590

A590a

King Baudouin A590b

1990-92 **Photo.** ***Perf. 11½***
1364 A590 14fr multicolored .80 .20
1365 A590a 15fr rose car .75 .20
1366 A590a 28fr blue green 1.75 .40
1367 A590b 100fr slate green 5.00 .40
Nos. 1364-1367 (4) 8.30 1.20

Issue dates: 14fr, Sept. 7; 15fr, Apr. 1; 28fr, Aug. 3, 1992; 100fr, Sept. 14, 1992.

Fish A591

Designs: No. 1383, Perch (Perche). No. 1384, Minnow (Vairon). No. 1385, Bitterling (Bouviere). No. 1386, Stickleback (Epinoche).

1990, Sept. 8 ***Perf. 12***
1383 A591 14fr multicolored 1.25 .60
1384 A591 14fr multicolored 1.25 .60
1385 A591 14fr multicolored 1.25 .60
1386 A591 14fr multicolored 1.25 .60
a. Bklt. pane of 4, #1383-1386 5.00
Complete booklet, #1386a 5.00

Youth Philately A592

1990, Oct. 13 ***Perf. 11½***
1387 A592 10fr multicolored .60 .45

St. Bernard, 900th Birth Anniv. — A593

1990, Nov. 5 **Photo & Engr.**
1388 A593 25fr black & buff 1.50 1.10

Winter Scene by Jozef Lucas A594

1990, Nov. 12 **Photo.**
1389 A594 10fr .60 .40

Christmas.

Self-Portrait A595

Paintings by David Teniers (1610-1690).

1990, Dec. 3
1390 A595 10fr shown .60 .40
1391 A595 14fr Dancers .80 .60
1392 A595 25fr Bowlers 1.40 1.10
Nos. 1390-1392 (3) 2.80 2.10

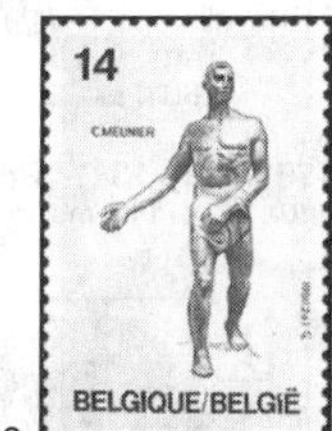
A596

Designs: 14fr, The Sower by Constantin Meunier (1831-1905). 25fr, Brabo Fountain by Jef Lambeaux (1852-1908).

Photo. & Engr.

1991, Mar. 18 ***Perf. 11½***
1393 A596 14fr buff & blk .80 .60
1394 A596 25fr lt bl & dk bl 1.50 1.10

A597

1991, Apr. 8 **Photo.** ***Perf. 11½***
1395 A597 10fr Rhythmic gymnastics .65 .50
1396 A597 10fr Korfball .65 .50

No. 1395, European Youth Olympics. No. 1396, Korfball World Championships.

Stamp Printing Office, Mechlin — A598

1991, Apr. 22
1397 A598 14fr multicolored .90 .65

Stamp Day.

Liberal Trade Union, Cent. A599

1991, Apr. 29
1398 A599 25fr blue & lt blue 1.50 1.10

Europa A600

1991, May 6
1399 A600 14fr Olympus-1 satellite 1.10 .25
1400 A600 25fr Hermes space shuttle 1.60 1.00

Rerum Novarum Encyclical, Cent. A601

1991, May 13 Photo. *Perf. 11½*
1401 A601 14fr multicolored .85 .65

Princess Isabel & Philip le Bon — A602

1991, May 27 Photo. *Perf. 11½*
1402 A602 14fr multicolored .85 .65

Europalia '91. See Portugal No. 1861.

Tourism A603

Designs: No. 1403, Neptune's Grotto, Couvin. No. 1404, Dieleghem Abbey, Jette. No. 1405, Town Hall, Niel, vert. No. 1406, Nature Reserve, Hautes Fagnes. No. 1407, Legend of giant Rolarius, Roeselare, vert.

1991, June 17 Photo. & Engr.
1403 A603 14fr multicolored .85 .65
1404 A603 14fr multicolored .85 .65
1405 A603 14fr multicolored .85 .65
1406 A603 14fr multicolored .85 .65
1407 A603 14fr multicolored .85 .65
Nos. 1403-1407 (5) 4.25 3.25

King Baudouin, Coronation, 40th Anniv. and 60th Birthday A604

1991, June 24 Photo.
1408 A604 14fr multicolored .85 .65

Royal Academy of Medicine, 150th Anniv. — A605

Photo. & Engr.
1991, Sept. 2 *Perf. 11½*
1409 A605 10fr multicolored .65 .50

The English Coast at Dover by Alfred W. Finch (1854-1930) A606

1991, Sept. 9 Photo.
1410 A606 25fr multicolored 1.50 1.10

See Finland Nos. 868-869.

Mushrooms — A607

#1411, Amanita phalloides (13A). #1412, Amanita rubescens (13B). #1413, Boletus erythropus (13C). #1414, Hygrocybe persistens (13D).

1991, Sept. 16 Photo. *Perf. 12*
Booklet Stamps
1411 A607 14fr multicolored 1.25 .75
1412 A607 14fr multicolored 1.25 .75
1413 A607 14fr multicolored 1.25 .75
1414 A607 14fr multicolored 1.25 .75
a. Bklt. pane of 4, #1411-1414 5.00
Complete booklet, #1414a 5.00

Doctors Without Borders A608

Design: No. 1415, Amnesty Intl.

1991, Sept. 23 *Perf. 11½*
1415 A608 25fr multicolored 1.50 1.10
1416 A608 25fr multicolored 1.50 1.10

Telecom '91 — A609

1991, Oct. 7 Photo. *Perf. 11½*
1417 A609 14fr multicolored .90 .70

6th World Forum and Exposition on Telecommunications, Geneva, Switzerland.

Youth Philately — A610

Cartoon characters: No. 1418, Blake and Mortimer, by Edgar P. Jacobs (16a). No. 1419, Cori the ship boy, by Bob De Moor (16b). No. 1420, Cities of the Fantastic, by Francois Schuiten (16c). No. 1421, Boule and Bill, by Jean Roba (16d).

1991, Oct. 14 *Perf. 12*
Booklet Stamps
1418 A610 14fr multicolored 1.25 .90
1419 A610 14fr multicolored 1.25 .90
1420 A610 14fr multicolored 1.25 .90
1421 A610 14fr multicolored 1.25 .90
a. Bklt. pane of 4, #1418-1421 5.00
Complete booklet, #1421a 5.00

Belgian Newspapers, Cent. — A611

1991, Nov. 4 Photo. *Perf. 11½*
1422 A611 10fr Gazet Van Antwerpen .65 .50
1423 A611 10fr Het Volk .65 .50

Icon of Madonna and Child, Chevetogne Abbey A612

1991, Nov. 25 Photo. *Perf. 11½*
1424 A612 10fr multicolored .65 .50

Christmas.

Wolfgang Amadeus Mozart, Death Bicent. — A613

1991, Dec. 2 Photo. *Perf. 11½*
1425 A613 25fr multicolored 1.75 1.25

A614

1992, Feb. 10 Photo. *Perf. 11½*
1426 A614 14fr Fire fighting .80 .60

Belgian Resistance in WWII — A615

1992, Feb. 24
1427 A615 14fr multicolored .80 .60

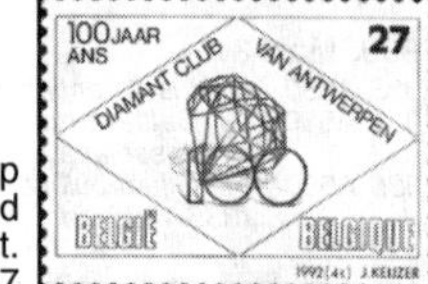

Belgian Carpet Industry — A616

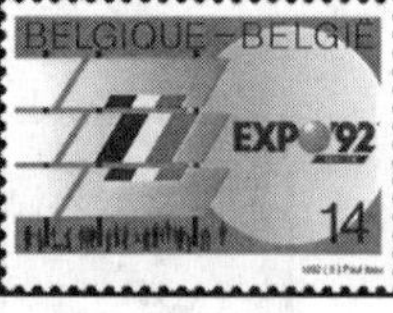

Antwerp Diamond Club, Cent. A617

Design: 14fr, Chef's hat, cutlery.

1992, Mar. 9
1428 A616 10fr multicolored .55 .40
1429 A616 14fr multicolored .80 .60
1430 A617 27fr multicolored 1.50 1.10
Nos. 1428-1430 (3) 2.85 2.10

Belgian Association of Master Chefs.

Expo '92, Seville A618

1992, Mar. 23
1431 A618 14fr multicolored .80 .60

Bird Type of 1985

1992-96 Photo. *Perf. 11½*
1432 A524 1fr Sizerin flamme .20 .20
1433 A524 2fr Merle noir .20 .20
1434 A524 2fr Grive mauvis .20 .20
1435 A524 4fr Gobe mouche noir .30 .25
1436 A524 4fr Bergeronette grise .25 .20
1437 A524 5fr Etourneau sansonnet .35 .20
1438 A524 5fr Hirondelle de cheminee .30 .20
1439 A524 5.50fr Geai des chenes .30 .25
1440 A524 6fr Cincle plongeur .35 .20
1441 A524 6.50fr Phragmite des jongs .45 .30
1442 A524 7fr Loriot .45 .20
1443 A524 8fr Mesange charbonniere .45 .20
1444 A524 10fr Verdier .60 .20
1445 A524 11fr Troglodyte mignon .65 .20
1446 A524 13fr Moineau domestique .70 .20

1446A A524 14fr Pouillot fitis .95 .25
1447 A524 16fr Jaseur boreal .90 .25
Nos. 1432-1447 (17) 7.60 3.70

Issued: 11fr, 4/1/92; 1fr, 2fr, 6fr, 8fr, 10fr, 6/92; 4fr, 5fr, 7fr, 9/7/92; 5.50fr, 9/27/93; 13fr, 16fr, 1/3/94; 6.50fr, 10/3/94; 14fr, 12/18/95; #1435A, 5/6/96; #1433A, 1434, 7/1/96.

See No. 1838 for similar stamp with additional Euro denomination.

Jean Van Noten (1903-1982), Stamp Designer — A619

Photo. & Engr.

1992, Apr. 13 ***Perf. 11½***
1448 A619 15fr ver & black .90 .70

Stamp Day.

Abstract Painting by Jo Delahaut — A620

#1449, Witte Magie No. 6, by Roger Raveel.

1992, Apr. 27 Photo. ***Perf. 11½***
1449 A620 15fr multi, vert. .85 .65
1450 A620 15fr multi .85 .65

Discovery of America, 500th Anniv. — A621

1992, May 4
1451 A621 15fr shown 1.00 .30
1452 A621 28fr 500, globe, astrolabe 1.75 1.10

Europa.

Fight Racism — A622

1992, May 18 Photo. ***Perf. 11½***
1453 A622 15fr black, gray & pink .90 .70

Paintings from Orsay Museum, Paris — A623

Paintings by Belgian artists: 11fr, The Hamlet, by Jacob Smits. 15fr, The Bath, by Alfred Stevens. 30fr, The Man at the Helm, by Theo Van Rysselberghe.

1992, June 15 Photo. ***Perf. 11½***
1454 A623 11fr multicolored .65 .50
1455 A623 15fr multicolored .90 .70
1456 A623 30fr multicolored 1.75 1.40
Nos. 1454-1456 (3) 3.30 2.60

Tourism — A624

Designs: No. 1457, Manneken Pis Fountain, Brussels. No. 1458, Landcommander Castle Alden Biesen, Bilzen, horiz. No. 1459, Building facade, Andenne. No. 1460, Fools' Monday Carnival, Renaix, horiz. No. 1461, Great Procession, Tournai, horiz.

Photo. & Engr.

1992, July 6 ***Perf. 11½***
1457 A624 15fr multicolored .90 .70
1458 A624 15fr multicolored .90 .70
1459 A624 15fr multicolored .90 .70
1460 A624 15fr multicolored .90 .70
1461 A624 15fr multicolored .90 .70
Nos. 1457-1461 (5) 4.50 3.50

Village of Andenne, 1300th anniv. (#1459). Grand Procession of Tournai, 900th anniv. (#1461).

Animals — A625

1992, Sept. 7 Photo. ***Perf. 12***
Booklet Stamps
1462 A625 15fr Polecat (13a) 1.10 .80
1463 A625 15fr Squirrel (13b) 1.10 .80
1464 A625 15fr Hedgehog (13c) 1.10 .80
1465 A625 15fr Dormouse (13d) 1.10 .80
a. Bklt. pane of 4, #1462-1465 4.50
Complete booklet, #1465a 4.50

Brabant Revolution — A626

Design: 15fr, Troops fighting and Henri Van der Noot, Jean Andre Van der Meersch, and Jean Francois Vonck, rebel leaders.

Photo. & Engr.

1992, Sept. 21 ***Perf. 11½***
1466 A626 15fr multicolored .90 .70

Arms of Thurn and Taxis — A627

1992, Oct. 5 Photo. ***Perf. 11½***
1467 A627 15fr multicolored .90 .70

Gaston Lagaffe, by Andre Franquin A628

1992, Oct. 12
1468 A628 15fr multicolored .90 .70

Youth philately.

Single European Market — A629

1992, Oct. 26
1469 A629 15fr multicolored .90 .70

Antwerp Zoo, 150th Anniv. — A630

1992, Nov. 16
1470 A630 15fr Okapi .90 .70
1471 A630 30fr Tamarin 1.75 1.75

The Brussels Place Royale in Winter, by Luc De Decker A631

1992, Nov. 23
1472 A631 11fr multicolored .70 .50

Christmas.

History A632

Designs: 11fr, Council of Leptines, 1250th anniv. 15fr, 28fr, Missale Romanum of Matthias Corvinus (Matyas Hunyadi, King of Hungary) (diff. details). 30fr, Battles of Neerwinden (1693, 1793).

1993, Mar. 15 Photo. ***Perf. 11½***
1473 A632 11fr multicolored .65 .50
1474 A632 15fr multicolored .90 .70
1475 A632 30fr multicolored 1.75 1.40
Nos. 1473-1475 (3) 3.30 2.60

Souvenir Sheet
1476 A632 28fr multicolored 1.75 1.25

Size of No. 1474, 80x28mm. No. 1476 contains one 55x40mm stamp.

See Hungary No. 3385-3386.

A633

A634

Antwerp, Cultural City of Europe A635

Designs: No. 1477, Panoramic view of Antwerp (illustration reduced). No. 1478, Antwerp Town Hall, designed by Cornelis Floris. No. 1479, Woman's Head and Warrior's Torso, by Jacob Jordaens. No. 1480, St. Job's Altar (detail), Schoonbroek. No. 1481, Angels on stained glass window, Mater Dei Chapel of Institut Marie-Josee, by Eugeen Yoors, vert.

1993, Mar. 22
1477 A633 15fr multicolored .90 .70
1478 A634 15fr multicolored .90 .70
1479 A635 15fr gray & multi .90 .70
1480 A635 15fr green & multi .90 .70
1481 A635 15fr blue & multi .90 .70
Nos. 1477-1481 (5) 4.50 3.50

Antwerp '93.

Stamp Day — A636

1993, Apr. 5
1482 A636 15fr No. 74 .90 .70

Contemporary Paintings — A637

Europa: 15fr, Florence 1960, by Gaston Bertrand. 28fr, De Sjees, by Constant Permeke.

1993, Apr. 26 Photo. ***Perf. 11½***
1483 A637 15fr multicolored .75 .20
1484 A637 28fr multicolored 1.50 1.00

Butterflies — A638

1993, May 10
1485 A638 15fr Vanessa atalanta .90 .70
1486 A638 15fr Apatura iris .90 .70
1487 A638 15fr Inachis io .90 .70
1488 A638 15fr Aglais urticae .90 .70
Nos. 1485-1488 (4) 3.60 2.80

Alumni Assoc. (UAE), Free University of Brussels, 150th Anniv. A639

1993, May 17

1489 A639 15fr blue & black .90 .70

Europalia '93 — A640

1993, May 24

1490 A640 15fr Mayan statuette .90 .70

Folklore A641

Designs: 11fr, Ommegang Procession, Brussels. 15fr, Royal Moncrabeau Folk Group, Namur. 28fr, Stilt walkers of Merchtem, vert.

1993, June 7 Photo. *Perf. 11½*

1491 A641 11fr multicolored .65 .50
1492 A641 15fr multicolored .90 .70
1493 A641 28fr multicolored 1.60 1.25
Nos. 1491-1493 (3) 3.15 2.45

Tourism A642

Castles: No. 1494, La Hulpe. No. 1495, Cortewalle (Beveren). No. 1496, Jehay. No. 1497, Arenberg (Heverlee), vert. No. 1498, Raeren.

Photo. & Engr.

1993, June 21 *Perf. 11½*

1494 A642 15fr pale green & blk .90 .70
1495 A642 15fr pale lilac & black .90 .70
1496 A642 15fr pale blue & black .90 .70
1497 A642 15fr pale brn & black .90 .70
1498 A642 15fr pale olive & blk .90 .70
Nos. 1494-1498 (5) 4.50 3.50

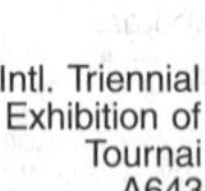

Intl. Triennial Exhibition of Tournai A643

1993, July 5 Photo. *Perf. 11½*

1499 A643 15fr black, blue & red .90 .70

Belgian Presidency of European Community Council A644

1993, Aug. 9 Photo. *Perf. 11½*

1500 A644 15fr multicolored .90 .70

Rene Magritte (1898-1967), Artist — A645

1993, Aug. 9

1501 A645 30fr multicolored 1.75 1.40

King Baudouin (1930-1993) — A646

1993, Aug. 17 Photo. *Perf. 11½*

1502 A646 15fr black & gray .90 .70

European House Cats — A647

1993, Sept. 6 Photo. *Perf. 12*

Booklet Stamps

1503 A647 15fr Brown & white (10a) 1.00 .70
1504 A647 15fr Black & white (10b) 1.00 .70
1505 A647 15fr Gray tabby (10c) 1.00 .70
1506 A647 15fr Calico (10d) 1.00 .70
a. Booklet pane of 4, #1503-1506 4.00
Complete booklet, #1506a 4.00

Publication of De Humani Corporis Fabrica, by Andreas Vesalius, 1543 — A648

1993, Oct. 4 Photo. *Perf. 11½*

1507 A648 15fr multicolored .90 .70

Air Hostess Natacha, by Francois Walthery — A649

1993, Oct. 18

1508 A649 15fr multicolored .85 .65

Youth philately.

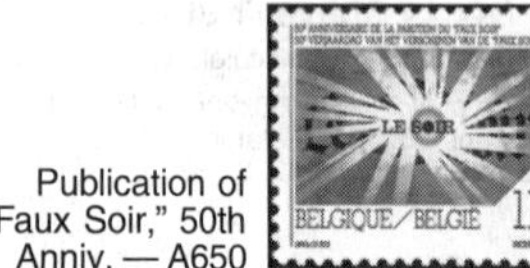

Publication of "Faux Soir," 50th Anniv. — A650

1993, Nov. 8 Photo. *Perf. 11½*

1509 A650 11fr multicolored .60 .45

Notre-Dame de la Chapelle, Brussels A651

1993, Nov. 22 Photo. *Perf. 11½*

1510 A651 11fr multicolored .65 .50

Christmas, New Year.

Children, Future Decisionmakers — A652

1993, Dec. 13 Photo. *Perf. 11½*

1511 A652 15fr multicolored .90 .70

A653

A654

King Albert II

A655 A655a

1993-98 Photo. *Perf. 11½*

1519	A653	16fr	lt gray & multi	.65	.20
1520	A653	16fr	lt & dk bl grn	.70	.20
1521	A655	16fr	multi	.75	.20
1521A	A655	16fr	blue	.75	.20
1521B	A655	17fr	blue	.75	.20
1521C	A655	18fr	olive black	.75	.25
1521D	A655	19fr	dp gray vio	.75	.30
1522	A653	20fr	cream & brn	1.00	.40
1522A	A655	20fr	brown	.90	.30
1523	A655	25fr	sepia	1.00	.25
1524	A655	28fr	claret	1.00	.30
1526	A653	30fr	red lilac	1.10	.25
1526A	A655	32fr	violet blue	1.25	.25
1527	A653	32fr	cream & org brn	1.25	.25
1527A	A655	34fr	dk bl gray	1.40	.40
1527B	A655	36fr	dk sl bl	1.50	.30
1528	A653	40fr	pink & car	1.75	.30
1529	A653	50fr	green	2.25	.35
1530	A655	50fr	green	2.50	.40
1533	A654	100fr	multi	4.50	.50
1535	A654	200fr	multi	10.00	2.50
	Nos. 1519-1535 (21)			36.50	8.30

Coil Stamp

1536	A655a	19fr	deep gray vio	1.25	.30

Issued: #1519, 12/15/93; #1520, 1/17/94; 30fr, 2/4/94; #1527, 3/7/94; 50fr, 4/18/94; #1522, 6/6/94; 40fr, 6/20/94; 100fr, 10/3/94; 200fr, 5/2/95; #1521, 6/6/96; #1521A, 1530, 28fr, 9/2/96; 17fr, 12/16/96; 34fr, 36fr, 2/10/97; 18fr, 4/7/97; #1521D, 7/7/97; 25fr, 4/20/98; #1536, 8/10/98; #1522A, 10/19/98; #1526a, 11/9/98.

This is an expanding set. Numbers will change.

Paintings A656

Designs: No. 1537, The Malleable Darkness, by Octave Landuyt. No. 1538, Ma Toute Belle, by Serge Vandercam, vert.

1994, Jan. 31 Photo. *Perf. 11½*

1537 A656 16fr multicolored .90 .70
1538 A656 16fr multicolored .90 .70

Airplanes A657

13fr, Hanriot-Dupont HD-1. 15fr, Spad XIII. 30fr, Schreck FBA-H. 32fr, Stampe-Vertongen SV-4B.

1994, Feb. 28

1539 A657 13fr multicolored .70 .50
1540 A657 15fr multicolored .85 .65
1541 A657 30fr multicolored 1.60 1.25
1542 A657 32fr multicolored 1.75 1.40
Nos. 1539-1542 (4) 4.90 3.80

Daily Newspapers — A658

No. 1543, "Le Jour-Le Courier," cent., vert. No. 1544, "La Wallonie," 75th anniv.

1994, Mar. 21 Photo. *Perf. 11½*

1543 A658 16fr multicolored .95 .70
1544 A658 16fr multicolored .95 .70

Fall of the Golden Calf (Detail), by Fernand Allard l'Olivier — A659

1994, Mar. 28

1545 A659 16fr multicolored .95 .70

Charter of Quaregnon, cent.

Stamp Day — A660

1994, Apr. 11 Photo. *Perf. 11½*

1546 A660 16fr No. 102 .95 .70

History A661

Scenes from Brabantse Yeesten, 15th cent. illuminated manuscript: 13fr, Reconciliation between John I and Arnold, squire of

Wezemaal. 16fr, Tournament at wedding of Charles the Bold and Margaret of York. 30fr, Battle of Woeringen.

1994, Apr. 25

1547	A661	13fr multicolored	.75	.55
1548	A661	16fr multicolored	.95	.70
1549	A661	30fr multicolored	1.75	1.25
		Nos. 1547-1549 (3)	3.45	2.50

No. 1549 is 81x28mm.

Europa — A662

Designs: 16fr, Abbe Georges Lemaitre (1894-1966), proposed "big-bang" theory of origins of universe. 30fr, Gerardus Mercator (1512-94), cartographer, astronomer.

1994, May 9 Photo. *Perf. 11½*

1550	A662	16fr multicolored	.85	.25
1551	A662	30fr multicolored	1.60	1.10

Papal Visit A663

#1552, Father Damien (1840-89). #1553, St. Mutien-Marie (1841-1917), Christian educator.

1994, May 16 *Perf. 11½x12*

1552	A663	16fr multicolored	.95	.70
1553	A663	16fr multicolored	.95	.70

Tourism A664

Churches: No. 1554, St. Peter's, Bertem. No. 1555, St. Bavo's, Kanegem, vert. No. 1556, Royal St. Mary's, Schaarbeek. No. 1557, St. Gery's, Aubechies. No. 1558, Sts. Peter and Paul, Saint-Severin, Condroz, vert.

1994, June 13 Photo. *Perf. 11½*

1554	A664	16fr multicolored	.95	.70
1555	A664	16fr multicolored	.95	.70
1556	A664	16fr multicolored	.95	.70
1557	A664	16fr multicolored	.95	.70
1558	A664	16fr multicolored	.95	.70
		Nos. 1554-1558 (5)	4.75	3.50

Guillaume Lekeu (1870-94), Composer A665

Design: No. 1560, Detail of painting by Hans Memling (c.1430-94).

1994, Aug. 16 Photo. *Perf. 11½*

1559	A665	16fr multicolored	1.10	.75
1560	A665	16fr multicolored	1.10	.75

Liberation of Belgium, 50th Anniv. — A666

Design: 16fr, General Crerar, Field Marshal Montgomery, Gen. Bradley, Belgium landscape. Illustration reduced.

1994, Sept. 5 Photo. *Perf. 11x11½*

1561	A666	16fr multicolored	.95	.70

Wildflowers — A667

Designs: No. 1562, Caltha palustris. No. 1563, Cephalanthera damasonium. No. 1564, Calystegia soldanella. No. 1565, Epipactis helleborine.

1994, Sept. 26 Photo. *Perf. 12*
Booklet Stamps

1562	A667	16fr multi (14a)	1.10	.75
1563	A667	16fr multi (14b)	1.10	.75
1564	A667	16fr multi (14c)	1.10	.75
1565	A667	16fr multi (14d)	1.10	.75
a.		Booklet pane of 4, #1562-1565	4.50	
		Complete booklet, #1565a	4.50	

Cubitus the Dog, by Luc Dupanloup — A668

1994, Oct. 10 *Perf. 11½*

1566	A668	16fr multicolored	1.10	.75

Youth philately.

Georges Simenon (1903-89), Writer A669

Photo. & Engr.

1994, Oct. 17 *Perf. 11½*

1567	A669	16fr multicolored	1.10	.75

See France No. 2443, Switzerland No. 948.

Christmas A670

1994, Dec. 5 Photo. *Perf. 11½*

1568	A670	13fr multicolored	.85	.65

Anniversaries and Events — A671

#1569, August Vermeylen Fund, 50th anniv. #1570, Belgian Touring Club, cent. #1571, Assoc. of Belgian Enterprises, cent. #1572, Dept. of Social Security, 50th anniv.

1995, Feb. 13 Photo. *Perf. 11½*

1569	A671	16fr multicolored	1.10	.75
1570	A671	16fr multicolored	1.10	.75
1571	A671	16fr multicolored	1.10	.75
1572	A671	16fr multicolored	1.10	.75
		Nos. 1569-1572 (4)	4.40	3.00

Flowers of Ghent A672

1995, Mar. 6

1573	A672	13fr Hibiscus rosa-sinensis	.95	.65
1574	A672	16fr Rhododendron simsii	1.10	.75
1575	A672	30fr Fuchsia hybrida	2.25	1.60
		Nos. 1573-1575 (3)	4.30	3.00

Games — A673

1995, Mar. 20

1576	A673	13fr Crossword puzzles	.95	.70
1577	A673	16fr Chess	1.10	.75
1578	A673	30fr Scrabble	2.25	1.60
1579	A673	34fr Cards	2.50	1.75
		Nos. 1576-1579 (4)	6.80	4.80

Stamp Day — A674

1995, Apr. 10 Photo. & Engr.

1580	A674	16fr Frans de Troyer	1.10	.75

Peace & Freedom A675

Europa: 16fr, Broken barbed wire, prison guard tower. 30fr, Mushroom cloud, "Never again."

1995, Apr. 24 Photo. *Perf. 11½*

1581	A675	16fr multicolored	1.00	.25
1582	A675	30fr multicolored	1.75	1.10

Liberation of concentration camps, 50th anniv. (#1581). Nuclear Non-Proliferation Treaty, 25th anniv. (#1582).

Battle of Fontenoy, 250th Anniv. — A676

16fr, Irish soldiers, Cross of Fontenoy.

1995, May 15 Photo. *Perf. 11½*

1583	A676	16fr multicolored	1.10	.75

See Ireland No. 967.

UN, 50th Anniv. A677

1995, May 22 Photo. *Perf. 11½*

1584	A677	16fr multicolored	1.10	.75

"Sauvagemont, Maransart," by Pierre Alechinsky — A678

No. 1586: "Telegram-style," by Pol Mara.

1995, June 6

1585	A678	16fr multicolored	1.10	.75
1586	A678	16fr multicolored	1.10	.75

Tourism A679

Architectural designs: No. 1587, Cauchie house, Brussels, by Paul Cauchie (1875-1952). No. 1588, De Viif Werelddelen, corner building, Antwerp, by Frans Smet-Verhas (1851-1925). No. 1589, House, Liege, by Paul Jaspar (1859-1945).

1995, June 26

1587	A679	16fr multicolored	1.10	.75
1588	A679	16fr multicolored	1.10	.75
1589	A679	16fr multicolored	1.10	.75
		Nos. 1587-1589 (3)	3.30	2.25

Sailing Ships — A680

1995, Aug. 21 Photo. *Perf. 12*
Booklet Stamps

1590	A680	16fr Mercator	1.00	.70
1591	A680	16fr Kruzenstern	1.00	.70
1592	A680	16fr Sagres II	1.00	.70
1593	A680	16fr Amerigo Vespucci	1.00	.70
a.		Booklet pane of 4, #1590-1593	4.00	
		Complete booklet, #1593a	4.00	

Classic Motorcycles A681

1995, Sept. 25 Photo. *Perf. 11½*

1594	A681	13fr 1908 Minerva	.90	.65
1595	A681	16fr 1913 FN, vert.	1.10	.80
1596	A681	30fr 1929 La Mondiale	2.00	1.50
1597	A681	32fr 1937 Gillet, vert.	2.25	1.60
		Nos. 1594-1597 (4)	6.25	4.55

Comic Character, Sammy, by Arthur Berckmans
A682

1995, Oct. 9 Photo. *Perf. 11½*

1598 A682 16fr multicolored 1.10 .80

Youth philately.

King's Day
A683

16fr, King Albert II and Queen Paola.

1995, Nov. 15 Photo. *Perf. 11½*

1599 A683 16fr multicolored 1.10 .80

Christmas — A684

13fr, Nativity scene from "Breviary," book of devotions, c. 1500.

1995, Nov. 20

1600 A684 13fr multicolored .90 .70

Liberal Party, 150th Anniv. — A685

1996, Mar. 4 Photo. *Perf. 11½*

1601 A685 16fr multicolored 1.10 .80

Portrait of Emile Mayrisch (1862-1928), by Théo Van Rysselberghe (1862-1926) — A686

1996, Mar. 2

1602 A686 (A) multicolored 1.10 .80

No. 1602 was valued at 16fr on day of issue.
See Luxembourg No. 939.

Oscar Bonnevalle, Stamp Designer — A687

1996, Apr. 1

1603 A687 16fr multicolored 1.10 .80

Stamp Day.

Insects
A688

#1604, Sympetrum sanguineum. #1605, Bombus terrestris. #1606, Lucanus cervus. #1607, Melolontha melolontha. #1608, Gryllus campestris. #1609, Coccinella septempunctata.

1996, Apr. 1 Photo. *Perf. 12*

Booklet Stamps

1604 A688 16fr multicolored 1.10 .80
1605 A688 16fr multicolored 1.10 .80
1606 A688 16fr multicolored 1.10 .80
1607 A688 16fr multicolored 1.10 .80
1608 A688 16fr multicolored 1.10 .80
1609 A688 16fr multicolored 1.10 .80
a. Booklet pane, #1604-1609 6.60
Complete booklet, #1609a 6.60

Famous Women
A689

Europa: 16fr, Yvonne Nevejean (1900-87), saved Jewish children during World War II. 30fr, Marie Gevers (1883-1975), poet.

1996, May 6 Photo. *Perf. 11½*

1610 A689 16fr multicolored .85 .25
1611 A689 30fr multicolored 1.75 1.10

Tourism — A690

Designs: No. 1612, Grotto of Han-Sur-Lesse, horiz. No. 1613, Village of Begijnendijk as separate community, bicent.

1996, June 10 Photo. *Perf. 11½*

1612 A690 16fr multicolored 1.10 .80
1613 A690 16fr multicolored 1.10 .80

Architecture in Brussels — A691

#1614, La Maison du Roi (Grand Place). #1615, Galeries Royales Saint-Hubert. #1616, Le Palais d'Egmont, Le Petit Sablon, horiz. #1617, Le Cinquantenaire, horiz.

1996, June 10

1614 A691 16fr multi (7a) 1.10 .80
1615 A691 16fr multi (7b) 1.10 .80
1616 A691 16fr multi (7c) 1.10 .80
1617 A691 16fr multi (7d) 1.10 .80
Nos. 1614-1617 (4) 4.40 3.20

Auto Races at Spa, Cent.
A692

1996, July 1

1618 A692 16fr 1900 German 6CV 1.10 .80
1619 A692 16fr 1925 Alfa Romeo P2 1.10 .80
1620 A692 16fr 1939 Mercedes Benz W154 1.10 .80
1621 A692 16fr 1967 Ferrari 330P 1.10 .80
Nos. 1618-1621 (4) 4.40 3.20

Paintings of Historical Figures — A693

Portraits from town hall triptych, Zierikzee, Netherlands: No. 1622, Philip I, the Handsome (1478-1506). No. 1623, Juana of Castile, the Mad (1479-1555).

1996, Sept. 2 Photo. *Perf. 11½*

1622 A693 16fr multicolored 1.10 .80
1623 A693 16fr multicolored 1.10 .80

Paintings from National Gallery, London — A694

14fr, Reading Man, by Rogier Van Der Weyden (1399-1464). 16fr, Susanna Fourment, by Peter Paul Rubens (1577-1640). 30fr, A Man in a Turban, by Jan Van Eyck (1390-1441).

1996, Sept. 2

1624 A694 14fr multicolored .90 .70
1625 A694 16fr multicolored 1.10 .80
1626 A694 30fr multicolored 2.00 1.50
Nos. 1624-1626 (3) 4.00 3.00

Bird Type of 1985

1996, Oct. 7 Photo. *Perf. 11½*

1627 A524 6fr Tarin des aulnes .40 .20

Comic Character, Cloro, by Raymond Macherot — A695

1996, Oct. 7

1628 A695 16fr multicolored 1.10 .80

Youth Philately.

Almanac of Mons, by Fr. Charles Letellier, 150th Anniv.
A696

1996, Oct. 7

1629 A696 16fr multicolored 1.10 .80

Music and Literature
A697

#1630, Arthur Grumiaux (1921-86), violinist. #1631, Flor Peeters (1903-86), organist. #1632, Christian Dotremont (1922-79), poet, artist. #1633, Paul Van Ostaijen (1896-1928), writer.

Photo. & Engr.

1996, Oct. 28 *Perf. 11½*

1630 A697 16fr multicolored 1.10 .80
1631 A697 16fr multicolored 1.10 .80
1632 A697 16fr multicolored 1.10 .80
1633 A697 16fr multicolored 1.10 .80
Nos. 1630-1633 (4) 4.40 3.20

Christmas and New Year — A698

Scenes from Christmas Market: a, Decorated trees, rooftops. b, Lighted greeting signs. c, Church. d, Selling desert items. e, Selling Nativity scenes. f, Selling meat. g, Santa ringing bell. h, Man smoking pipe, people with presents. i, People shopping.

1996, Nov. 18 Photo. *Perf. 11½*

1634 A698 Sheet of 9, #a.-i. 8.25 6.25
a.-i. 14fr Any single .90 .70

Catholic Faculty University, Mons, Cent.
A699

1997, Jan. 20 Photo. *Perf. 11½*

1635 A699 17fr multicolored 1.10 .80

Opera at Theatre Royal de la Monnaie, Brussels — A700

#1636, Marie Sasse (1834-1907), soprano. #1637, Ernest Van Dijck (1861-1923), tenor. #1638, Hector Dufranne (1870-1951), baritone. #1639, Clara Clairbert (1899-1970), soprano.

1997, Feb. 10

1636 A700 17fr multicolored 1.00 .75
1637 A700 17fr multicolored 1.00 .75
1638 A700 17fr multicolored 1.00 .75
1639 A700 17fr multicolored 1.00 .75
Nos. 1636-1639 (4) 4.00 3.00

Eastern Cantons — A701

Illustration reduced.

1997, Feb. 10 Photo. Perf. 11½

1640 A701 17fr multicolored 1.00 .75

Bird Type of 1985

1997, Mar. 10

1641 A524 15fr Mesange boreale .90 .25

UN Peace-Keeping Forces — A702

1997, Mar. 10

1642 A702 17fr multicolored 1.00 .75

Stories and Legends A703

Europa: 17fr, "De Bokkenrijders" (The Goat Riders). 30fr, Jean de Berneau.

1997, Mar. 10 Photo. Perf. 11½

1643 A703 17fr multicolored .90 .25
1644 A703 30fr multicolored 1.50 1.10

Bird Type of 1985

1997, Apr. 7

Size: 35x25mm

1645 A524 150fr Pie bavarde, horiz. 7.50 2.50

See No. 1840 for similar stamp with additional Euro denomination.

Constant Spinoy (1924-93), Stamp Engraver — A704

1997, Apr. 7 Photo. & Engr.

1646 A704 17fr multicolored 1.00 .75

Stamp Day.

Intl. Flower Show, Liege — A705

1997, Apr. 21 Photo.

1647 A705 17fr multicolored 1.00 .75

Paintings by Paul Delvaux (1897-1994) A706

Details or entire paintings: 15fr, Woman with garland of leaves in hair. 17fr, Nude, horiz. 32fr, Woman wearing hat, trolley.

1997, Apr. 21

1648 A706 15fr multicolored .85 .65
1649 A706 17fr multicolored 1.00 .75
1650 A706 32fr multicolored 1.75 1.40
Nos. 1648-1650 (3) 3.60 2.80

Bird Type of 1985

1997, May 7 Photo. Perf. 11½

1651 A524 3fr Alouette des champs .25 .20

Queen Paola, 60th Birthday A707

1997, May 26

1652 A707 17fr Belvedere Castle 1.00 .75

See Italy No. 2147.

Cartoon Character, "Jommeke," by Jef Nys — A708

1997, May 26

1653 A708 17fr multicolored 1.00 .75

World Congress of Rose Societies — A709

Roses: No. 1654, Rosa damascena coccinea. No. 1655, Rosa sulfurea. No. 1656, Rosa centifolia.

1997, July 7 Photo. Perf. 11½

1654 A709 17fr multicolored 1.25 .90
1655 A709 17fr multicolored 1.25 .90
1656 A709 17fr multicolored 1.25 .90
Nos. 1654-1656 (3) 3.75 2.70

Churches — A710

No. 1657, Basilica of St. Martin, Halle. No. 1658, Notre Dame Church, Laeken, horiz. No. 1659, Basilica of St. Martin, Liège.

1997, July 7 Photo. & Engr.

1657 A710 17fr multicolored 1.25 .90
1658 A710 17fr multicolored 1.25 .90
1659 A710 17fr multicolored 1.25 .90
Nos. 1657-1659 (3) 3.75 2.70

Bird Type of 1985

1997, Sept. 1 Photo. Perf. 11½

1660 A525 7fr Bergeronnette printaniere .40 .30

Bees and Apiculture — A711

#1661, Queen, workers. #1662, Development of the larvae. #1663, Bee exiting cell. #1664, Bee collecting nectar. #1665, Two bees. #1666, Two bees on honeycomb.

1997, Sept. 1 Photo. Perf. 12

Booklet Stamps

1661 A711 17fr multi (15a) 1.00 .75
1662 A711 17fr multi (15b) 1.00 .75
1663 A711 17fr multi (15c) 1.00 .75
1664 A711 17fr multi (15d) 1.00 .75
1665 A711 17fr multi (15e) 1.00 .75
1666 A711 17fr multi (15f) 1.00 .75
a. Booklet pane of 6, #1661-1666 6.00
Complete booklet, #1666a 6.00

Craftsmen A712

1997, Sept. 1 Perf. 11½

1667 A712 17fr Stone cutter .75 .60
1668 A712 17fr Mason .75 .60
1669 A712 17fr Carpenter .75 .60
1670 A712 17fr Blacksmith .75 .60
Nos. 1667-1670 (4) 3.00 2.40

Antarctic Expedition by the Belgica, Cent. — A713

1997, Sept. 22 Photo. Perf. 11½

1671 A713 17fr multicolored 1.00 .75

Royal Museum of Central Africa, Cent. — A714

No. 1672, Mask, Shaba, Congo. No. 1673, Outside view of museum, horiz. 34fr, Dish Bearer sculpture, Buli area, Congo.

1997, Sept. 22 Photo. Perf. 11½

1672 A714 17fr multicolored 1.00 .75
1673 A714 17fr multicolored 1.00 .75
1674 A714 34fr multicolored 2.00 1.50
Nos. 1672-1674 (3) 4.00 3.00

No. 1673 is 25x73mm.

"Fairon," by Pierre Grahame — A715

1997, Oct. 25 Photo. Perf. 11½

Christmas.

1675 A715 15fr multicolored .90 .70

Bird Type of 1985

1997, Dec. 1 Photo. Perf. 11½

1676 A524 15fr Mesange boreale, horiz. .90 .25

No. 1676 issued in coil rolls with every fifth stamp numbered on reverse.

Rhododendron A716

Serpentine Die Cut 13½ on 2 or 3 Sides

1997, Dec. 1

Booklet Stamp

Self-Adhesive

1677 A716 (17fr) multicolored 1.00 .25
a. Booklet pane of 10 10.00

By its nature, No. 1677a is a complete booklet. The peelable backing serves as a booklet cover.

Compare with design A757.

"Thalys" High Speed Train — A717

1998, Jan. 19 Photo. Perf. 11½

1678 A717 17fr multicolored 1.00 .75

Woman Suffrage in Belgium, 50th Anniv. — A718

1998, Jan. 19

1679 A718 17fr multicolored 1.00 .75

Gerard Walschap (1898-1989), Poet, Playwright — A719

#1681, Norge (1898-1990), writer

1998, Feb. 16 Photo. Perf. 11½

1680 A719 17fr multicolored .95 .70
1681 A719 17fr multicolored .95 .70

Paintings, by René Magritte (1898-1967) — A720

#1682, "La Magie Noire (Black Magic)," nude woman. #1683, "La Corde Sensible (Heartstring)," cloud over champagne glass. #1684, "Le Chateau des Pyrenees (Castle of the Pyranees)," castle atop floating rock.

1998, Mar. 9 Photo. *Perf. 11½*

1682 A720 17fr multi, vert. .95 .70
1683 A720 17fr multi .95 .70
1684 A720 17fr multi, vert. .95 .70
Nos. 1682-1684 (3) 2.85 2.10

Belgian Artists — A721

Details or entire paintings: No. 1685, "La Foire aux Amours," by Félicien Rops (1833-98). No. 1686, "Hospitality for the Strangers," by Gustave van de Woestijne (1881-1947). No. 1687, Self-portrait, "The Man with the Beard," by Felix de Boeck (1898-1995). No. 1688, "Black Writing Mixed with Colors," by Karel Appel & Christian Cotremont of COBRA.

1998, Mar. 9 *Perf. 12*

Booklet Stamps

1685 A721 17fr multicolored .95 .70
1686 A721 17fr multicolored .95 .70
1687 A721 17fr multicolored .95 .70
1688 A721 17fr multicolored .95 .70
a. Booklet pane, #1685-1688 3.80
Complete booklet, #1688a 3.80

Museum of Fine Arts, Ghent, bicent. (#1686). COBRA art movement of painters and poets, 50th anniv. (#1688).

Sabena Airlines, 75th Anniv. — A722

1998, Apr. 20 Photo. *Perf. 11½*

1689 A722 17fr multicolored .95 .70

Belgian Stamp Dealers' Assoc., 75th Anniv. A723

1998, Apr. 20

1690 A723 17fr multicolored .95 .70

"The Return," by René Magritte (1898-1967) — A724

1998, Apr. 20

1691 A724 17fr multicolored .95 .70

See France No. 2637.

Wildlife A725

1998, Apr. 20

1692 A725 17fr Vulpes vulpes .95 .70
1693 A725 17fr Cervus elaphus .95 .70
1694 A725 17fr Sus scrofa .95 .70
1695 A725 17fr Capreolus capreolus .95 .70
Nos. 1692-1695 (4) 3.80 2.80

"Souvenir Sheets"

Starting in 1998, items looking like souvenir sheets have appeared in the market. The 1998 item is similar to No. 1695. The 1999 item is similar to No. 1725. The 2000 item is similar to No. 1811. These have no postal value.

Bird Type of 1985

1998, May 4 Photo. *Perf. 11½*

1696 A524 1fr Mesange huppee .20 .20

Edmund Struyf (1911-96), Founder of Pro-Post, Assoc. for Promotion of Philately — A726

1998, May 4 Photo. & Engr.

1697 A726 17fr multicolored .95 .70

Stamp Day.

Natl. Festivals A727

1998, May 4 Photo. *Perf. 11½*

1698 A727 17fr Torhout & Werchter Rock Festival .95 .70
1699 A727 17fr Wallonia Festival .95 .70

Europa.

Bird Type of 1985

1998, July 6 Photo. *Perf. 11½*

1700 A524 7.50fr Pie-grieche grise .45 .20

See No. 1837 for similar stamp with additional Euro denomination.

European Heritage Days — A728

a, Logo. b, Bourla Theatre, Antwerp. c, La Halle, Durbuy. d, Halletoren, Kortrijk. e, Louvain Town Hall. f, Perron, Liège. g, Royal Theatre, Namur. h, Aspremont-Lynden Castle, Rekem. i, Neo-Gothic kiosk, Sint-Niklaas. j, Chapelle Saint Vincent, Tournai. k, Villers-la-Ville Abbey. l, Saint Gilles Town Hall, Brussels.

1998, July 6

1701 A728 17fr Sheet of 12, #a.-l. 11.00 8.50

Bird Type of 1985

1998 Photo. *Perf. 11½*

1702 A524 9fr Pic vert .50 .20
1703 A524 10fr Turtle dove .60 .20

Issued: 9fr, 8/10; 10fr, 9/28/98.

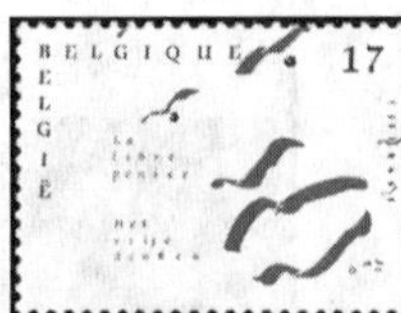

Free Thinking A729

1998, Aug. 10 Photo. *Perf. 11½*

1704 A729 17fr multicolored 1.00 .75

Philips van Marnix van Sint-Aldegonde (1540-98), Author — A730

1998, Aug. 10

1705 A730 17fr multicolored 1.00 .75

Mniszech Palace (Belgian Embassy), Warsaw, Bicent. A731

Photo. & Engr.

1998, Sept. 28 *Perf. 11½*

1706 A731 17fr multicolored 1.00 .75

See Poland No. 3420.

Contemporary Belgium Films — A732

1998, Sept. 28 Photo.

1707 A732 17fr "Le Huitieme Jour" 1.00 .75
1708 A732 17fr "Daens" 1.00 .75

Cartoon Characters, "Chick Bill" and "Ric Hochet" — A733

1998, Oct. 19 Photo. *Perf. 11½*

1709 A733 17fr multicolored 1.00 .75

Youth philately.

Assoc. of Space Explorers, 14th World Congress, Brussels — A734

1998, Oct. 19

1710 A734 17fr multicolored 1.00 .75

World Post Day A735

1998, Oct. 19 Photo. *Perf. 11½*

1711 A735 34fr blue & dark blue 2.00 1.50

World Assoc. for the Development of Philately.

FGTB-ABVV Trade Union, Cent. — A736

Center panel of triptych by Constant Draz (1875-)

1998, Nov. 9 Photo. *Perf. 11½*

1712 A736 17fr multicolored 1.00 .75

Christmas and New Year — A737

1998, Nov. 9

1713 A737 (17fr) multicolored 1.00 .75

Bird Type of 1985

1998-99 Photo. *Perf. 11½*

1714 A524 16fr Mesange noire .85 .65
1715 A524 21fr Grive litorne, horiz. 1.10 .85

No. 1715 also issued in coils with number on reverse of every 5th stamp.

Issued: 16fr, 1/25/99; 21fr, 12/14/98.

See No. 1839 for similar stamp with additional Euro denomination.

A738

A739

Greetings Stamps: No. 1716, Burning candle. No. 1717, Stork carrying a heart. No. 1718, Wristwatch. No. 1719, Four leaf clover with one leaf a heart. No. 1720, Two doves. No. 1721, Heart with arrow through it. No. 1722, Heart-shaped head on woman. No. 1723, Heart-shaped head on man.

1999, Jan. 25 Photo. *Perf. 12*

Booklet Stamps

1716 A738 (17fr) multicolored 1.00 .75
1717 A738 (17fr) multicolored 1.00 .75
1718 A738 (17fr) multicolored 1.00 .75
1719 A738 (17fr) multicolored 1.00 .75
1720 A738 (17fr) multicolored 1.00 .75
1721 A738 (17fr) multicolored 1.00 .75
1722 A738 (17fr) multicolored 1.00 .75
1723 A738 (17fr) multicolored 1.00 .75
a. Booklet pane, #1716-1723 8.00
Complete booklet, #1723a 8.00

Nos. 1716-1717, 1719-1720 each also issued in sheets of 20 on July 1.

1999, Feb. 22 Photo. *Perf. 11½*

Owls.

1724 A739 17fr Tyto alba .90 .70
1725 A739 17fr Athene noctua .90 .70
1726 A739 17fr Strix aluco .90 .70
1727 A739 17fr Asio otus .90 .70
Nos. 1724-1727 (4) 3.60 2.80

NATO, 50th Anniv. A740

1999, Mar. 15

1728 A740 17fr Leopard tank .90 .70
1729 A740 17fr F16 fighter .90 .70
1730 A740 17fr Frigate Wandelaar .90 .70
1731 A740 17fr Hospital tent .90 .70
1732 A740 17fr General staff .90 .70
Nos. 1728-1732 (5) 4.50 3.50

UPU, 125th Anniv. A741

1999, Mar. 15

1733 A741 34fr multicolored 1.90 1.40

National Parks and Nature Reserves A742

Europa: No. 1734, De Bunt, near town of Hamme. No. 1735, Harchies-Hensies-Pommeroeul.

1999, Apr. 12

1734 A742 17fr multicolored .90 .70
1735 A742 17fr multicolored .90 .70

First Belgian Postage Stamps, 150th Anniv. A743

Photo. & Engr.

1999, Apr. 26 *Perf. 11½*

1736 A743 17fr No. 1 .95 .70
1737 A743 17fr No. 2 .95 .70
a. Pair, #1736-1737 1.80 1.40

Painting, "My Favorite Room," by James Ensor (1860-1949) — A744

Designs: No. 1739, Woman Eating Oysters, vert. 30fr, Triumph Over Death, vert. 32fr, Old Lady With Masks, vert.

1999, May 17 Photo. *Perf. 11½*

1738 A744 17fr multicolored .95 .70
1739 A744 17fr multicolored .95 .70
1740 A744 30fr multicolored 1.75 1.40
1741 A744 32fr multicolored 1.90 1.50
Nos. 1738-1741 (4) 5.55 4.30

See Israel No. 1365A.
Issued: #1738, 5/17; #1739-1741, 9/11.

Tourism — A745

#1742, Giants at Geraardsbergen Fair, vert. #1743, Cart d'Or procession of the Confrérie de la Miséracordie, Mons.

1999, June 7 Photo. *Perf. 11½*

1742 A745 17fr multi (10a) .95 .70
1743 A745 17fr multi (10b) .95 .70

Belgian Chocolate A746

1999, June 7

1744 A746 17fr Bean picker .95 .70
1745 A746 17fr Candy maker .95 .70
1746 A746 17fr Consumer .95 .70
Nos. 1744-1746 (3) 2.85 2.10

King Albert and Queen Paola, 40th Wedding Anniv. — A747

1999, July 2 Photo. *Perf. 11½*

1747 A747 17fr multicolored .95 .70

Royalty Type of Semi-Postal Stamps

Souvenir Sheet

Kings: a, 50fr, Leopold I. b, 32fr, Leopold II. c, 17fr, Albert I. d, 17fr, Leopold III. e, 32fr, Baudouin. f, 50fr, Albert II.

Photo. & Engr.

1999, Sept. 29 *Perf. 11½*

1748 SP514 Sheet of 6, #a.-f. 15.00 15.00

Bruphila '99. No. 1748 sold for 300fr.

Nobel Laureates in Peace — A750

Designs: 17fr, Henri La Fontaine (1854-1943). 21fr, Auguste Beernaert (1829-1912).

Photo. & Engr.

1999, Sept. 30 *Perf. 11½*

1749 A750 17fr red & gold .90 .70
1750 A750 21fr blue & gold 1.10 .85

See Sweden Nos. 2357-2358.

A751 A752

A753

King Albert II — A754

1999-2001 Photo. *Perf. 11¾x11½*

1752 A751 17fr multicolored .90 .25
1753 A751 17fr prus blue .80 .25
1754 A751 19fr blue .95 .25
1755 A751 20fr yel brown .90 .25
1756 A752 23fr violet 1.00 .25
1757 A751 25fr brown 1.10 .30
1758 A751 30fr vio black 1.40 .35
1759 A751 32fr green 1.50 .30
1760 A751 34fr gray blue 1.50 .35
1761 A751 36fr brown 1.60 .40
Nos. 1752-1761 (10) 11.65 2.95

Engr.

Perf. 11½

1766 A753 50fr blue 2.25 .55

Photo. *Perf. 11½*

1768 A754 100fr multi 4.50 1.10

Engr.

1769 A753 200fr claret 8.75 2.25
Nos. 1752-1769 (13) 27.15 6.85

No. 1756 issued in coils.

Issued: 17fr, 10/4; 19fr, 1/24/00; 30fr, 4/3/00; 32fr, 6/19/00; 23fr, 9/4/00; 50fr, 9/11/00; No. 1753, 11/18/00; 36fr, 12/4/00; ; 20fr, 25fr, 34fr, 100fr, 200fr, 3/26/01.

This is an expanding set. Numbers may change.

Youth Philately — A756

Comic strips: a, Corentin, by Paul Cuvelier (16a). b, Jerry Spring, by Jijé (16b). c, Gil Jourdan, by Maurice Tillieux (16c). d, La Patrouille des Castors, by Mitacq (16d). e, Entrance hall of Belgian Comic Strip Museum (16e). f, Hassan & Kadour, by Jacques Laudy (16f). g, Buck Danny, by Victor Hubinon (16g). h, Tif et Tondu, by Fernand Dineur (16h). i, Les Timour, by Sirius (16i).

1999, Oct. 2 Photo. *Perf. 11½*

1771 A756 Sheet of 9, #a.-i. 7.75 6.00
a.-i. 17fr Any single .90 .60

Geranium — A757 Tulip — A758

Die Cut 10x9¾ on 2 or 3 sides

1999-2000 Photo.

Self-Adhesive

Booklet Stamps

1772 A757 (17fr) multi .85 .20
a. Complete booklet, 10 #1772 8.50
1773 A758 (21fr) multi 1.00 .25
a. Booklet, 10 #1773 10.00

Die Cut Perf. 11¼

Coil Stamps

1774 A757 (17fr) multi .85 .20

Photo.

Serpentine Die Cut 14

1775 A758 (21fr) multi 1.00 .25

Nos. 1774-1775 are on a waxed backing paper larger than the stamp.

Issued: No. 1773, 4/17/00; others, 11/22/99.

Christmas — A762

1999, Nov. 8 Photo. *Perf. 11½*

1776 A762 17fr multi .85 .65

Wedding of Prince Philippe and Mathilde d'Udekem d'Acoz, Dec. 4 — A763

1999, Nov. 29

1777 A763 17fr shown .85 .65

Souvenir Sheet

1778 A763 21fr Couple, diff. 1.00 .80

The 20th Century

A764

A764a

A764b

A764c

No. 1779: a, Pope John XXIII. b, King Baudouin. c, Willy Brandt. d, John F. Kennedy. e, Mahatma Gandhi. f, Dr. Martin Luther King, Jr. g, Lenin. h, Che Guevara. i, Golda Meir. j, Nelson Mandela. k, Jesse Owens, Modern Olympic Games. l, Soccer. m, Tour de France. n, Edith Piaf. o, The Beatles. p, Charlie Chaplin. q, Tourism. r, Youth movements. s, Tinitin comic strips. t, Philately.

No. 1780: a, Yser front, World War I. b, Concentration camps. c, First atomic bomb. d, Yalta Conference. e, United Nations. f,

Decolonization. g, Vietnam War. h, Collapse of the Berlin Wall. i, Peace movements. j, Middle East conflict. k, Rene Magritte, artist. l, Le Corbusier, architect. m, Bertolt Brecht, dramatist. n, James Joyce, novelist. o, Anne Teresa de Keersmaeker, choreographer. p, Bela Bartók, composer. q, Andy Warhol, artist. r, Maria Callas, opera singer. s, Henry Moore, sculptor. t, Toots Thielemans, Charlie Parker, jazz musicians.

No. 1781: a, Ovide Decroly, pedagogue. b, Alternative energy. c, Aviation. d, Sigmund Freud, psychologist. e, Space travel. f, Claude Lévi-Strauss, anthropologist. g, Genetics. h, Pierre Teilhard de Chardin, theologist. i, Max Weber, sociologist, j, Albert Einstein, physicist. k, Penicillin. l, Ilya Prigogine, chemist. m, Roland Barthes, semiotician. n, Simone de Beauvoir, feminist. o, Information. p, John Maynard Keynes, economist. q, Marc Bloch, historian. r, Atomic energy, J. Robert Oppenheimer, physicist. s, Pierre and Marie Curie, physicists. t, Ludwig Josef Wittgenstein, philosopher.

No. 1782: a, Social housing policy. b, May 1968 student protests. c, Telecommunications. d, Wealth and poverty. e, Secularization (laicisation). f, Urbanization. g, Universal suffrage. h, Social security. i, Education (enseignement). j, Aging of the population (vieillissement de la population). k, European Union. l, Universal Declaration of Human Rights. m, Consumer society. n, Women's liberation. o, Deindustrialization. p, Oil crises. q, Mobility. r, Contraception. s, Radio and television. t, Home appliances (appareils menagers).

1999-2002 Photo. *Perf. 11½*

1779	Sheet of 20	17.00	17.00
a.-t.	A764 17fr Any single	.85	.65
1780	Sheet of 20	16.00	16.00
a.-t.	A764a 17fr Any single	.80	.50
1781	Sheet of 20	15.00	15.00
a.-t.	A764b 17fr Any single	.75	.75
1782	Sheet of 20	17.00	17.00
a.-t.	A764c 41c Any single	.85	.65
	Nos. 1779-1782 (4)	65.00	65.00

Issued: No. 1779, 12/6/99. No. 1780, 11/20/00. No. 1781, 10/22/01. No. 1782, 10/28/02.

Denominations on No. 1782 are in euros.

Year 2000
A765

2000, Jan. 3 Photo. *Perf. 11¾x11½*

1783	A765 17fr multi	.85	.65

Brussels, 2000 European City of Culture — A766

Brussels skyline and: a, Seven people. b, Harmonica player, dancer. c, Airplane, train, ships.

2000, Jan. 24 Photo. *Perf. 11½*

1784	Strip of 3 + 2 labels	2.60	2.00
a.-c.	A766 17fr any single	.85	.65

Bird Type of 1985
Without "F" and
With Euro denomination

2000 Photo. *Perf. 11¾*

1785	A524	1fr Beccroisé des sapins	.20	.20
1786	A524	2fr Grimpereau des jardins	.20	.20
1787	A524	3fr Pipit parlouse	.20	.20
1788	A524	5fr Pinson du nord	.20	.20
1789	A524	10fr Pouillot siffleur	.45	.20
1790	A524	16fr Pie grièche écorcheur	.80	.20
1790A	A524	16fr Pie grièche écoucheur, horiz.	.70	.20
		Nos. 1785-1790A (7)	2.75	1.40

No. 1790A issued in coils.

Issued: #1790, 1/24; 1fr, 2fr, 3fr, 5fr, 5/8; 10fr, 9/11; #1790A, 9/4.

Holy Roman Emperor Charles V (1500-58)
A767

2000, Feb. 21 Photo. *Perf. 11½*

1791	A767 17fr shown	.80	.60
1792	A767 21fr At age 40	1.00	.75

Souvenir Sheet

1793	A767 34fr In armor	1.60	1.25
a.	Ovptd. in margin	1.60	1.25

No. 1793a was issued 10/6/00 and overprint in margin reads "ESPANA 2000 / Exposición Mundial de Filatelia / Madrid 6-14/X/2000."

See Spain Nos. 3026-3028.

World Mathematics Year — A768

2000, Feb. 21

1794	A768 17fr multi	.80	.60

Stampin' The Future Children's Stamp Design Contest Winner — A769

2000, Feb. 21

1795	A769 17fr multi	.80	.60

European Soccer Championships, Belgium and Netherlands — A770

Illustration reduced.

2000, Mar. 27

1796	A770 Pair + label	1.75	1.25
a.	17fr Players	.80	.60
b.	21fr Ball	.95	.65

Serpentine Die Cut 10x9¾ on 3 sides

Booklet Stamp
Self-Adhesive
Size: 21x27mm

1797	A770 (17fr) Players, diff.	.80	.60
a.	Booklet, 10 #1797	8.00	

Worldwide Fund for Nature — A771

Endangered amphibians and reptiles: No. 1798, Vipera berus. No. 1799, Lacerta agilis, vert. No. 1800, Hyla arborea, vert. No. 1801, Salamandra salamandra.

Perf. 11¾x11½, 11½x11¾

2000, Mar. 27 Photo.

1798	A771 17fr multi	.80	.60
1799	A771 17fr multi	.80	.60
1800	A771 17fr multi	.80	.60
1801	A771 17fr multi	.80	.60
	Nos. 1798-1801 (4)	3.20	2.40

Stamp Day — A772

2000, Apr. 3 Photo. *Perf. 11½*

1802	A772 17fr multi	.80	.60

Franz von Taxis — A773

Illustration reduced.

2000, Apr. 3

1803	A773 17fr multi + label	.80	.60

Postal system in Europe, 500th anniv., Belgica 2001 Stamp Exhibition.

Ghent Flower Show
A774

Designs: 16fr, Iris spuria. 17fr, Rhododendron, horiz. 21fr, Begonia.

2000, Apr. 17

1804	A774 16fr multi	.75	.55
1805	A774 17fr multi	.80	.60
1806	A774 21fr multi	.95	.70
	Nos. 1804-1806 (3)	2.50	1.85

Prince Philippe's Fund
A775

2000, Apr. 17

1807	A775 17fr multi	.80	.60

2000 Summer Olympics and Paralympics, Sydney
A776

Designs: 17fr, Belgian Olympic team emblem. No. 1809, Taekwondo. No. 1810, Wheelchair racer, horiz.

30fr+7fr, Swimmer in triathlon, horiz.

2000, May 8

1808	A776 17fr multi	.80	.60
1809	A776 17fr +4fr multi	.95	.95
1810	A776 17fr +4fr multi	.95	.95
	Nos. 1808-1810 (3)	2.70	2.50

Souvenir Sheet

1811	A776 30fr +7fr multi	1.60	1.60

Olymphilex 2000 (No. 1811).

Opening of Musical Instrument Museum, Brussels — A777

No. 1812, Harpsichord (15a). No. 1813, Violin (15b). No. 1814, Lutes (15c). No. 1815, Treble viol (15d). No. 1816, Trumpets (15e). No. 1817, Johann Sebastian Bach (15f).

2000, May 8 Photo. *Perf. 11¾*

Booklet Stamps

1812	A777 (17fr) multi	.80	.60
1813	A777 (17fr) multi	.80	.60
1814	A777 (17fr) multi	.80	.60
1815	A777 (17fr) multi	.80	.60
1816	A777 (17fr) multi	.80	.60
1817	A777 (17fr) multi	.80	.60
a.	Booklet pane, #1812-1817	5.00	
	Booklet, #1817a	5.00	

Europa, 2000
Common Design Type

2000, May 9 *Perf. 11½*

1818	CD17 (21fr) multi	1.00	.75

UNESCO World Heritage Sites
A778

Designs: No. 1819, Flemish Béguinages. No. 1820, Grand-Place, Brussels. No. 1821, Boat lifts, Canal du Centre.

2000, June 19 *Perf. 11½x11¾*

1819	A778 17fr multi	.80	.60
1820	A778 17fr multi	.80	.60
1821	A778 17fr multi	.80	.60
	Nos. 1819-1821 (3)	2.40	1.80

Tourism
A779

Churches and their organs: No. 1822, Norbertine Abbey Church, Grimbergen. No. 1823, Collégiale Sainte Waudru, Mons. No. 1824, O.-L.-V. Hemelvaartkerk, Ninove. No. 1825, St. Peter's Church, Bastogne.

2000, June 19 *Perf. 11½*

1822	A779 17fr multi	.80	.60
1823	A779 17fr multi	.80	.60
1824	A779 17fr multi	.80	.60
1825	A779 17fr multi	.80	.60
	Nos. 1822-1825 (4)	3.20	2.40

A780

2000, Sept. 4 Photo. *Perf. 11¾*

1826 A780 17fr multi .75 .50

European Postal Services, 500th Anniv., Belgica 2001 Stamp Exhibition. #1826 issued in coils.

Youth Philately — A781

2000, Sept. 11 *Perf. 11¾x11½*

1827 A781 17fr multi .75 .50

Hainault Flower Show A782

2000, Sept. 11 *Perf. 11½x11¾*

1828 A782 17fr multi .75 .50

Violets — A783

Die Cut Perf. 10x9¾ on 2 or 3 Sides

2000, Sept. 11 Photo.

Booklet Stamp

Self-Adhesive

1829 A783 (17fr) multi .80 .25
a. Booklet, 10 #1829 8.00

Contemporary Art — A784

#1831, Bing of the Ferro Lusto X, by Panamarenko. #1832, Construction, by Anne-Mie Van Kerckhoven. #1833, Belgique Eternelle, by J. & L. Charlier. #1834, Roses from series "Les Belles de Nuit," by Marie-Jo Lafontaine.

Perf. 11½x11¾, 11¾x11½

2000, Oct. 16 Photo.

1831 A784 17fr multi (21a) .75 .50
1832 A784 17fr multi (21b), vert. .75 .50
1833 A784 17fr multi (21c) .75 .50
1834 A784 17fr multi (21d) .75 .50
Nos. 1831-1834 (4) 3.00 2.00

Christmas — A785

2000, Nov. 20 Photo. *Perf. 11½*

1835 A785 17fr multi .80 .50

Bird Type of 1985

Without F and With Euro Denomination

2000-2001 Photo. *Perf. 11¾*

1836	A524	50c Roitelet huppe	.20	.20
1837	A524	7.50fr Pie-grieche grise	.35	.20
1838	A524	8fr Mesange charbonniere	.40	.20
1838A	A524	16fr Sterne pierregarin	.70	.20
1839	A524	21fr Grive litorne, horiz.	.95	.25

Perf. 11½x11¾

Size: 35x25mm

1840	A524	150fr Pie bavarde, horiz.	6.75	1.75
		Nos. 1836-1840 (6)	9.35	2.80

Issued: 8fr, 12/4/00. 50c, 7.50fr, 21fr, 150fr, 3/26/01; 16fr, 6/9/01. Numbers have been reserved for additional stamps in this set.

Holy Year 2000 — A786

Illustration reduced.

Photo. & Engr.

2000, Dec. 27 *Perf. 11½*

1841 A786 17fr multi+ label .80 .50

Royalty Type of Semi-Postal Stamps

Souvenir Sheet

Queens: a, 50fr, Louise-Marie. b, 32fr, Marie-Henriette. c, 17fr, Elisabeth. d, 17fr, Astrid. e, 32fr, Fabiola. f, 50fr, Paola.

Photo. & Engr.

2001, Feb. 12 *Perf. 11½*

1842 SP514 Sheet of 6, #a-f 14.00 14.00

No. 1842 sold for 300fr.

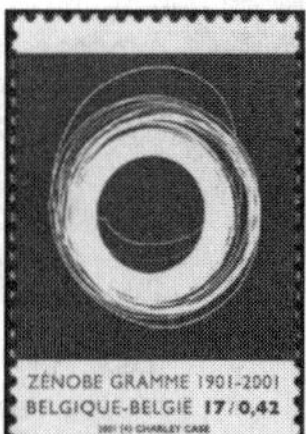
Zénobe Gramme (1826-1901), Electrical Engineer — A787

2001, Mar. 19 Photo.

1843 A787 17fr multi .80 .50

Catholic University of Louvain, 575th Anniv. — A788

2001, Mar. 19

1844 A788 17fr multi .80 .50

Europa — A789

2001, Apr. 23 Photo. *Perf. 11½*

1845 A789 21fr multi .95 .70

Musical and Literary Personalities — A790

Designs: No. 1846, Willem Elsschot (1882-1960), writer. No. 1847, Albert Ayguesparse (1900-96), writer.

21fr, Queen Elisabeth (1876-1965), patron of Queen Elisabeth Intl. Music Competition, horiz.

2001, Apr. 23 Photo. *Perf. 11½*

1846 A790 17fr multi .80 .50
1847 A790 17fr multi .80 .50

Souvenir Sheet

1848 A790 21fr multi .95 .70

Queen Elisabeth Intl. Music Competition, 50th anniv. (No. 1848).

Belgian Natl. Railway Company, 75th Anniv. — 790A

No. 1848A: b, 1938 Type 12 locomotive No. 12004. c, 1971 Series 06 dual engine No. 671. d, 1991 Series 03 threefold engine No. 328.

2001, May 7 Photo. *Perf. 11¾x11½*

1848A Horiz. strip of 3 + 2 labels 2.25 1.50
b.-d. A790A 17fr Any single .75 .50

A791

European Posts, 500th Anniv. — A792

Designs: No. 1849, Franz von Taxis, 16th cent. postrider. No. 1850, 17th cent. postman on road near Brussels. No. 1851, 18th cent. postman, quill pen, postal notice. No. 1852, 19th cent. postman, train, Belgium #2 on cover. No. 1853, 20th cent. postman, motorcycle, airplanes, mailboxes.

Illustration A791 reduced.

Perf. 11¾x11½

2001, June 9 Photo.

Stamp + label

1849 A791 17fr multi .75 .50
1850 A792 17fr multi .75 .50
1851 A792 17fr multi .75 .50
1852 A792 17fr multi .75 .50
1853 A792 17fr multi .75 .50
Nos. 1849-1853 (5) 3.75 2.50

Souvenir Sheet

Design: 150fr, 21st cent. postwoman, Belgica 2001 emblem.

1854 A792 150frmulti 13.00 13.00

Nos. 1849 printed in sheets of 10 stamps + 10 labels. For Nos. 1850-1853, each is printed in sheets of 12 stamps + 12 labels.

No. 1854 contains one 38x48mm stamp without an attached label, and sold for 300fr, with the surtax going to Pro Post for the promotion of philately.

Houses of Worship — A793

Designs: 17fr, Hassan II Mosque, Casablanca, Morocco. 34fr, Koekelberg Basilica.

2001, June 10 Photo. *Perf. 11½*

1855 A793 17fr multi .75 .50
1856 A793 34fr multi 1.50 1.10

See Morocco Nos. 897-898.

Musées Royaux des Beaux Arts, Brussels, 200th Anniv. — A794

No. 1857: a, Winter Landscape With Skaters, by Pieter Breughel the Elder. b, Study of a Negro's Head, by Peter Paul Rubens. c, Sunday, by Frits Van den Berghe. d, Mussel Triumph II, by Marcel Broodthaers.

2001, June 11 Photo. *Perf. 12*

1857 Booklet pane of 4 3.00
a.-d. A794 17fr Any single .75 .50
Booklet, #1857 3.00

Ancient Chinese Receptacles
A795

Designs: 17fr, Earthenware vase. 34fr, Porcelain coffee pot.

2001, June 12 Photo. *Perf. 11½*

1858 A795 17fr multi .75 .50
1859 A795 34fr multi 1.50 1.10

See People's Republic of China Nos. 3108-3109.

Youth Philately — A796

2001, June 13

1860 A796 17fr multi .75 .50

Belgian Chairmanship of European Union
A797

2001, June 15

1861 A797 17fr multi .75 .50

Tourism — A798

Town hall belfries: No. 1862, Binche. No. 1863, Dixmude.

2001, Aug. 6 *Perf. 11½x11¾*

1862 A798 17fr multi .80 .50
1863 A798 17fr multi .80 .50

Farmsteads — A799

2001, Aug. 6 *Perf. 11¾x11½*

1864 A799 17fr Damme .80 .50
1865 A799 17fr Beauvechain .80 .50
1866 A799 17fr Leuven .80 .50
1867 A799 17fr Honnelles .80 .50
1868 A799 17fr Hasselt .80 .50
Nos. 1864-1868 (5) 4.00 2.50

Stam and Pilou, Mascots of Stampilou Youth Philatelic Club — A800

2001, Oct. 8 Photo. *Die Cut*
Self-Adhesive
Booklet Stamp

1869 A800 (17fr) multi .75 .50
a. Booklet of 5 + 5 labels 3.75

Stamp Day.

Christmas
A801

2001, Nov. 12 Photo. *Perf. 11½*

1870 A801 15fr multi .70 .50

Tulips — A804

Die Cut Perf. 9¾ on 3 Sides
2001, Dec. 10 Photo.
Self-Adhesive
Booklet Stamp

1873 A804 (21fr) multi .95 .25
a. Booklet pane of 10 9.50

Death Announcement Stamp — A805

2001, Dec. 10 Photo. *Perf. 11½*

1874 A805 (17fr) multi .75 .55

Tintin in Africa — A806

Tintin: 17fr, In jungle. 34fr, In automobile.

2001, Dec. 31

1875 A806 17fr multi .75 .55

Souvenir Sheet

1876 A806 34fr multi 1.50 1.50

No. 1876 contains one 48x37mm stamp. See Democratic Republic of Congo No.

100 Cents = 1 Euro (")

King Albert II — A807

2002 Photo. *Perf. 11½*

1879 A807 42c red .75 .20
1881 A807 47c dark green .85 .20
1883 A807 52c blue .90 .25
Nos. 1879-1883 (3) 2.50 .65

Issued: 42c, 52c, 1/1. 47c, 5/6. This is an expanding set.

World Cyclo-Cross and Road Bicycling Championships
A811

Royal Belgian Tennis Federation, Cent. — A812

No. 1897: a, Rider looking back. b, Rider with fist in air.

No. 1898: a, Women's tennis. b, Men's tennis.

Illustration A812 reduced.

2002, Jan. 21 Photo. *Perf. 11½*

1897 A811 Vert. pair 1.50 1.10
a.-b. 42c Any single .75 .55
1898 A812 Horiz. pair 1.50 1.10
a.-b. 42c Any single .75 .55

University of Antwerp, 150th Anniv. A813

2002, Feb. 11 **Photo. & Engr.**

1899 A813 42c multi		.75	.55

Bruges, 2002 European Capital of Culture A814

Designs: No. 1900, Restorations and new architecture (4a). No. 1901, Classical and contemporary music (4b). No. 1902, Classical exhibitions and contemporary art (4c).

2002, Mar. 4 **Photo.**

1900 A814 42c multi	.75	.55
1901 A814 42c multi	.75	.55
1902 A814 42c multi	.75	.55
Nos. 1900-1902 (3)	2.25	1.65

Anna Bijns (1494-1575), Poet — A815

Anna Boch (1848-1936), Painter — A816

2002, Mar. 4

1903 A815 42c multi	.75	.55
1904 A816 84c multi	1.50	1.10

Stamp Day — A817

2002, Apr. 22 **Photo.** ***Perf. 11½***

1905 A817 47c multi	.85	.60

Belgian Dog Breeds — A818

Designs: No. 1906, Schipperke. No. 1907, Bouvier des Ardennes. No. 1908, Saint-Hubert. No. 1909, Brussels griffon. No. 1910, Papillon.

Illustration reduced.

2002, Apr. 22 **Photo.** ***Perf. 11½***

Stamp + Label

1906 A818 42c multi	.80	.60
1907 A818 42c multi	.80	.60
1908 A818 42c multi	.80	.60
1909 A818 42c multi	.80	.60
1910 A818 42c multi	.80	.60
a. Vert. strip of 5, #1906-1910, + 5 labels	4.00	3.00

Europa A819

2002, May 6

1911 A819 52c multi	.95	.70

Bird Type of 1985 With Euro Denominations Only

2002 **Photo.** ***Perf. 11¾***

1912 A524 7c Pigeon colombin	.20	.20
1914 A524 25c Huitrier pie	.50	.20

Issued: 7c, 5/6. 25c, 7/15. This is an expanding set.

Leffe Abbey, 850th Anniv. — A820

Illustration reduced.

2002, June 10 **Photo.** ***Perf. 11½***

1917 A820 42c multi + label	.80	.60

Castles — A821

No. 1918: a, Chimay. b, Alden Biesen. c, Wissekerke. d, Corroy-le-Château. e, Reinhardstein. f, Loppem. g, Horst. h, Ecaussinnes-Lalaing. i, Ooidonk. j, Modave. Nos. 1918a-1918f are 45x24mm; Nos. 1918g-1918j are 52x21mm.

2002, June 10

1918 A821 Sheet of 10	8.00	6.00
a.-j. 42c Any single	.80	.60

Horses A822

Designs: 40c, Jumping. 42c, Driving, vert. 52c, St. Paul's Horse Procession, Opwijk, cent., vert.

2002, July 1 **Photo.** ***Perf. 11½***

1919 A822 40c multi	.80	.60
1920 A822 42c multi	.85	.65

Souvenir Sheet

1921 A822 52c multi	1.00	1.00

No. 1921 contains one 38x49mm stamp.

Battle of the Courtrai, 700th Anniv. — A823

Designs: 42c, Golden spurs of defeated French knights. 52c, Castle.
57c, Battle scene, horiz.

2002, July 15

1922 A823 42c multi	.85	.65
1923 A823 52c multi	1.00	.75

Souvenir Sheet

1924 A823 57c multi	1.10	1.10

No. 1924 contains one 49x38mm stamp.

Youth Philately A826

2002, July 15 **Photo.** ***Perf. 11½***

1929 A826 42c multi	1.00	.75

Windmills A824

Lace A825

Designs: 42c, Onze-Lieve-Vrouw-Lombeek windmill, Belgium. 52c, Ilha do Faial windmill, Azores.

2002, July 15 **Photo.** ***Perf. 11½***

1925 A824 42c multi	.85	.65
1926 A824 52c multi	1.00	.75

See Portugal Azores Nos. 471-472.

2002, July 15

Lace from: 42c, Liedekerke, Belgium. 74c, Pag Island, Croatia.

1927 A825 42c multi	.85	.65
1928 A825 74c multi	1.40	1.10

See Croatia Nos. 497-498.

Rights of the Child — A827

2002, Sept. 30 **Photo.** ***Perf. 11½***

1930 A827 42c multi	.85	.60

Jean Rey (1902-83), Politician — A828

2002, Sept. 30 **Photo. & Engr.**

1931 A828 52c dk bl & lt bl	1.00	.75

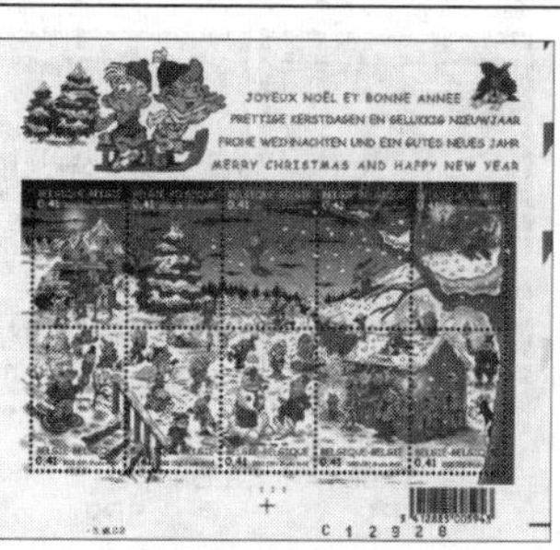
Christmas — A829

No. 1932: a, Family at ice cream truck. b, Ski jumper in Christmas tree. c, Sledder in air, skier in snow. d, Skier on hillside. e, Skiers with torches. f, Boy with ice cream cone. g, Children in snowball fight. h, Children, man and snowman. i, People at snack stand. j, Cow, policeman and burglars.

2002, Oct. 28 **Photo.**

1932 A829 Sheet of 10	8.25	6.25
a.-j. 41c Any single	.80	.60

SEMI-POSTAL STAMPS

Values quoted for Nos. B1-B24 are for stamps with label attached. Copies without label sell for one-tenth or less.

St. Martin of Tours Dividing His Cloak with a Beggar
SP1 SP2

Unwmk.

1910, June 1 Typo. *Perf. 14*

B1 SP1 1c gray .75 .75
B2 SP1 2c purple brn 6.50 6.50
B3 SP1 5c peacock blue 1.90 1.90
B4 SP1 10c brown red 1.90 1.90
B5 SP2 1c gray green 1.90 1.90
B6 SP2 2c violet brn 5.00 5.00
B7 SP2 5c peacock blue 2.25 2.25
B8 SP2 10c carmine 2.25 2.25
Nos. B1-B8 (8) 22.45 22.45
Set, never hinged 65.00

Overprinted "1911" in Black

1911, Apr. 1

B9 SP1 1c gray 20.00 16.00
a. Inverted overprint
B10 SP1 2c purple brn 57.50 42.50
B11 SP1 5c peacock blue 6.50 5.25
B12 SP1 10c brown red 6.50 5.25
B13 SP2 1c gray green 30.00 24.00
B14 SP2 2c violet brn 25.00 21.00
B15 SP2 5c peacock blue 6.50 5.25
B16 SP2 10c carmine 6.50 5.25
Nos. B9-B16 (8) 158.50 124.50
Set, never hinged 600.00

Overprinted "CHARLEROI-1911"

1911, June

B17 SP1 1c gray 3.50 2.50
B18 SP1 2c purple brn 11.00 10.00
B19 SP1 5c peacock blue 6.50 6.50
B20 SP1 10c brown red 6.50 6.50
B21 SP2 1c gray green 3.50 2.50
B22 SP2 2c violet brn 11.00 9.00
B23 SP2 5c peacock blue 6.50 6.50
B24 SP2 10c carmine 6.50 6.50
Nos. B17-B24 (8) 55.00 50.00
Set, never hinged 175.00

Nos. B1-B24 were sold at double face value, except the 10c denominations which were sold for 15c. The surtax benefited the national anti-tuberculosis organization.

King Albert I — SP3

1914, Oct. 3 Litho.

B25 SP3 5c green & red *15.00 15.00*
B26 SP3 10c red *1.50 1.50*
B27 SP3 20c violet & red *45.00 45.00*
Nos. B25-B27 (3) *61.50 61.50*
Set, never hinged *125.00*

Counterfeits of Nos. B25-B27 abound. Probably as many as 90% of the stamps on the market are counterfeits. Values are for genuine examples.

Merode Monument — SP4

1914, Oct. 3

B28 SP4 5c green & red *4.50 3.00*
B29 SP4 10c red *5.00 5.00*
B30 SP4 20c violet & red *75.00 75.00*
Nos. B28-B30 (3) *84.50 83.00*
Set, never hinged *175.00*

Counterfeits of Nos. B28-B30 abound. Probably as many as 90% of the stamps on the market are counterfeits. Values are for genuine examples.

King Albert I — SP5

1915, Jan. 1 *Perf. 12, 14*

B31 SP5 5c green & red 5.00 3.00
a. Perf. 12x14 16.00 12.00
B32 SP5 10c rose & red 20.00 6.00
B33 SP5 20c violet & red 25.00 14.00
a. Perf. 14x12 500.00 250.00
b. Perf. 12 50.00 32.50
Nos. B31-B33 (3) 50.00 23.00
Set, never hinged 150.00

Nos. B25-B33 were sold at double face value. The surtax benefited the Red Cross.

Types of Regular Issue of 1915 Surcharged in Red:

Nos. B34-B40

Nos. B41-B43

Nos. B44-B47

1918, Jan. 15 Typo. *Perf. 14*

B34 A46 1c + 1c dp orange .50 .50
B35 A46 2c + 2c brown .60 .60
B36 A46 5c + 5c blue grn 1.40 1.40
B37 A46 10c + 10c red 2.25 2.25
B38 A46 15c + 15c brt violet 3.25 3.25
B39 A46 20c + 20c plum 7.50 7.50
B40 A46 25c + 25c ultra 7.50 7.50

Engr.

B41 A47 35c + 35c lt vio & blk 10.00 10.00
B42 A48 40c + 40c dull red & blk 10.00 10.00
B43 A49 50c + 50c turq blue & blk 12.00 12.00
B44 A50 1fr + 1fr bluish slate 35.00 35.00
B45 A51 2fr + 2fr dp gray grn 100.00 100.00
B46 A52 5fr + 5fr brown 250.00 250.00
B47 A53 10fr + 10fr dp blue 500.00 500.00
Nos. B34-B47 (14) 940.00 940.00
Set, never hinged 2,000.

Discus Thrower — SP6

Racing Chariot — SP7

Runner — SP8

1920, May 20 Engr. *Perf. 12*

B48 SP6 5c + 5c dp green 1.40 1.40
B49 SP7 10c + 5c carmine 1.40 1.40
B50 SP8 15c + 15c dk brown 3.00 3.00
Nos. B48-B50 (3) 5.80 5.80
Set, never hinged 17.00

7th Olympic Games, 1920. Surtax benefited wounded soldiers.

For surcharges see Nos. 140-142.

Allegory: Asking Alms from the Crown
SP9

Wounded Veteran
SP10

1922, May 20

B51 SP9 20c + 20c brown 1.40 1.40

1923, July 5

B52 SP10 20c + 20c slate gray 1.75 1.75

Surtax on #B51-B52 was to aid wounded veterans.

SP11

SP12

St. Martin, by Van Dyck
SP13 SP14

1925, Dec. 15 Typo. *Perf. 14*

B53 SP11 15c + 5c dull vio & red .50 .20
B54 SP11 30c + 5c gray & red .25 .20
B55 SP11 1fr + 10c chalky blue & red 1.25 1.40
Nos. B53-B55 (3) 2.00 1.80

Surtax for the Natl. Anti-Tuberculosis League.

1926, Feb. 10

B56 SP12 30c + 30c bluish grn (red surch.) .50 .50
B57 SP13 1fr + 1fr lt blue 7.25 7.25
B58 SP14 1fr + 1fr lt blue 1.10 1.25
Nos. B56-B58 (3) 8.85 9.00

The surtax aided victims of the Meuse flood.

Lion and Cross of Lorraine — SP15

Queen Elisabeth and King Albert
SP16

1926, Dec. 6 Typo. *Perf. 14*

B59 SP15 5c + 5c dk brown .25 .20
B60 SP15 20c + 5c red brown .45 .40
B61 SP15 50c + 5c dull violet .30 .20

Engr. *Perf. 11½*

B62 SP16 1.50fr + 25c dk blue .75 .70
B63 SP16 5fr + 1fr rose red 6.50 6.00
Nos. B59-B63 (5) 8.25 7.50

Surtax was used to benefit tubercular war veterans.

Boat Adrift
SP17

1927, Dec. 15 Engr. *Perf. 11½, 14*

B64 SP17 25c + 10c dk brn .70 .70
B65 SP17 35c + 10c yel grn .70 .70
B66 SP17 60c + 10c dp violet .60 .40
B67 SP17 1.75fr + 25c dk blue 1.50 *2.00*
B68 SP17 5fr + 1fr plum 4.50 *4.75*
Nos. B64-B68 (5) 8.00 *8.55*

The surtax on these stamps was divided among several charitable associations.

Ogives of Orval Abbey — SP18

Monk Carving Capital of Column — SP19

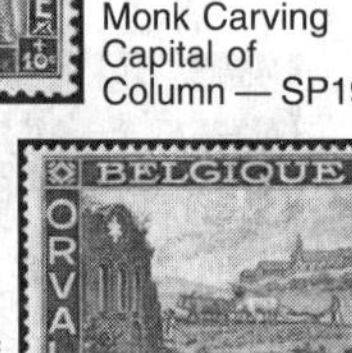

Ruins of Orval Abbey
SP20

Design: 60c+15c, 1.75fr+25c, 3fr+1fr, Countess Matilda recovering her ring.

1928, Sept. 15 Photo. *Perf. 11½*

B69 SP18 5c + 5c red & gold .20 .20
B70 SP18 25c + 5c dk vio & gold .25 .25

Engr.

B71 SP19 35c + 10c dp grn .70 .70
B72 SP19 60c + 15c red brn .45 .20
B73 SP19 1.75fr + 25c dk blue 1.90 1.25
B74 SP19 2fr + 40c dp vio 15.00 12.50
B75 SP19 3fr + 1fr red 13.50 12.00

Perf. 14

B76 SP20 5fr + 5fr rose lake 9.00 9.00
B77 SP20 10fr + 10fr blk brn 9.00 9.00
Nos. B69-B77 (9) 50.00 45.10

Surtax for the restoration of the ruined Orval Abbey.

St. Waudru, Mons — SP22

St. Rombaut, Malines — SP23

Designs: 25c + 15c, Cathedral of Tournai. 60c + 15c, St. Bavon, Ghent. 1.75fr + 25c, St. Gudule, Brussels. 5fr + 5fr, Louvain Library.

1928, Dec. 1 Photo. *Perf. 14, 11½*

B78 SP22 5c + 5c carmine .20 .20
B79 SP22 25c + 15c ol brn .25 .25

Engr.

B80 SP23 35c + 10c dp grn 1.00 1.00
B81 SP23 60c + 15c red brn .30 .30
B82 SP23 1.75fr + 25c vio bl 7.00 7.00
B83 SP23 5fr + 5fr red vio 14.00 14.00
Nos. B78-B83 (6) 22.75 22.75

The surtax was for anti-tuberculosis work.

Nos. B69-B77 with this overprint in blue or red were privately produced. They were for the laying of the 1st stone toward the restoration of the ruined Abbey of Orval. Value, set, $650.

Forgeries of the overprint exist.

Waterfall at Coo — SP28

Bayard Rock, Dinant — SP29

Designs: 35c+10c, Menin Gate, Ypres. 60c+15c, Promenade d'Orleans, Spa. 1.75fr+25c, Antwerp Harbor. 5fr+5fr, Quai Vert, Bruges.

1929, Dec. 2 Engr. *Perf. 11½*

B93 SP28 5c + 5c red brn .20 .25
B94 SP29 25c + 15c gray blk .65 .60
B95 SP28 35c + 10c green .80 .95
B96 SP28 60c + 15c rose lake .55 .50
B97 SP28 1.75fr + 25c dp blue 4.50 4.50

Perf. 14

B98 SP29 5fr + 5fr dl vio 27.50 27.50
Nos. B93-B98 (6) 34.20 34.30

Bornhem — SP34

Beloeil — SP35

Gaesbeek SP36

25c + 15c, Wynendaele. 70c + 15c, Oydonck. 1fr + 25c, Ghent. 1.75fr + 25c, Bouillon.

1930, Dec. 1 Photo. *Perf. 14*

B99 SP34 10c + 5c violet .25 *.30*
B100 SP34 25c + 15c olive brn .60 .60

Engr.

B101 SP35 40c + 10c brn vio .80 *1.00*
B102 SP35 70c + 15c gray blk .55 .55
B103 SP35 1fr + 25c rose lake 3.50 3.50
B104 SP35 1.75fr + 25c dp bl 4.50 2.75
B105 SP36 5fr + 5fr gray grn 27.50 *32.50*
Nos. B99-B105 (7) 37.70 *41.20*

Prince Leopold SP41

Queen Elisabeth SP42

Philatelic Exhibition Issue

Souvenir Sheet

1931, July 18 Photo. *Perf. 14*

B106 SP41 2.45fr + 55c car brn 140.00 140.00
Never hinged 250.00
a. Single stamp 60.00

Sold exclusively at the Brussels Phil. Exhib., July 18-21, 1931. Size: 122x159mm. Surtax for the Veterans' Relief Fund.

The sheet normally has pin holes and a cancellation-like marking in the margin. These are considered unused and the condition valued here.

1931, Dec. 1 Engr.

B107 SP42 10c + 5c red brn .30 *.50*
B108 SP42 25c + 15c dk vio 1.10 *1.25*
B109 SP42 50c + 10c dk grn .95 *1.10*
B110 SP42 75c + 15c blk brn .90 .70
B111 SP42 1fr + 25c rose lake 6.75 6.00
B112 SP42 1.75fr + 25c ultra 4.75 4.00
B113 SP42 5fr + 5fr brn vio 55.00 55.00
Nos. B107-B113 (7) 69.75 68.55

The surtax was for the National Anti-Tuberculosis League.

Désiré Cardinal Mercier — SP43

Mercier Protecting Children and Aged at Malines — SP44

Mercier as Professor at Louvain University — SP45

Mercier in Full Canonicals, Giving His Blessing SP46

1932, June 10 Photo. *Perf. 14½x14*

B114 SP43 10c + 10c dk violet .40 *.60*
B115 SP43 50c + 30c brt violet 2.25 *2.50*
B116 SP43 75c + 25c olive brn 2.25 2.25
B117 SP43 1fr + 2fr brown red 6.00 6.00

Engr. *Perf. 11½*

B118 SP44 1.75fr + 75c dp blue 70.00 *82.50*
B119 SP45 2.50fr + 2.50fr dk brn 70.00 70.00
B120 SP44 3fr + 4.50fr dull grn 70.00 70.00
B121 SP45 5fr + 20fr vio brn 80.00 *82.50*
B122 SP46 10fr + 40fr brn lake 175.00 *210.00*
Nos. B114-B122 (9) 475.90 *526.35*

Honoring Cardinal Mercier and to obtain funds to erect a monument to his memory.

Exist with privately produced black overprint "Braine-L'Alleud 17-7-33 Collegio Card. Mercier." Value, set, $850.

Belgian Infantryman SP47

Sanatorium at Waterloo SP48

1932, Aug. 4 *Perf. 14½x14*

B123 SP47 75c + 3.25fr red brn 55.00 55.00
B124 SP47 1.75fr + 4.25fr dk blue 55.00 55.00

Honoring Belgian soldiers who fought in WWI and to obtain funds to erect a natl. monument to their glory.

1932, Dec. 1 Photo. *Perf. 13½x14*

B125 SP48 10c + 5c dk vio .30 *.90*
B126 SP48 25c + 15c red vio 1.00 *1.25*
B127 SP48 50c + 10c red brn 1.00 *1.25*
B128 SP48 75c + 15c ol brn 1.00 .80
B129 SP48 1fr + 25c dp red 13.00 10.50
B130 SP48 1.75fr + 25c dp blue 10.50 9.25
B131 SP48 5fr + 5fr gray grn 85.00 *90.00*
Nos. B125-B131 (7) 111.80 *113.95*

Surtax for the assistance of the Natl. Anti-Tuberculosis Society at Waterloo.

View of Old Abbey SP49

Ruins of Old Abbey — SP50

Count de Chiny Presenting First Abbey to Countess Matilda SP56

Restoration of Abbey in XVI and XVII Centuries SP57

Abbey in XVIII Century, Maria Theresa and Charles V — SP58

Madonna and Arms of Seven Abbeys SP60

Designs: 25c+15c, Guests, courtyard, 50c+25c, Transept. 75c+50c, Bell Tower. 1fr+1.25fr, Fountain. 1.25fr+1.75fr, Cloisters. 5fr+20fr, Duke of Brabant placing 1st stone of new abbey.

1933, Oct. 15 *Perf. 14*

B132 SP49 5c + 5c dull grn 35.00 *40.00*
B133 SP50 10c + 15c ol grn 32.50 *35.00*
B134 SP49 25c + 15c dk brn 32.50 *35.00*
B135 SP50 50c + 25c red brn 32.50 *35.00*
B136 SP50 75c + 50c dp grn 32.50 *35.00*
B137 SP50 1fr + 1.25fr cop red 32.50 *35.00*
B138 SP49 1.25fr + 1.75fr gray blk 32.50 *35.00*
B139 SP56 1.75fr + 2.75fr blue 37.50 *40.00*
B140 SP57 2fr + 3fr mag 37.50 *40.00*
B141 SP58 2.50fr + 5fr dull brn 37.50 *40.00*
B142 SP56 5fr + 20fr vio 40.00 *40.00*

Perf. 11½

B143 SP60 10fr + 40fr bl 225.00 *225.00*
Nos. B132-B143 (12) 607.50 *635.00*

The surtax was for a fund to aid in the restoration of Orval Abbey. Counterfeits exist.

"Tuberculosis Society" SP61

Peter Benoit SP62

1933, Dec. 1 Engr. *Perf. 14x13½*

B144 SP61 10c + 5c blk .85 .85
B145 SP61 25c + 15c vio 3.00 3.00
B146 SP61 50c + 10c red brn 2.25 2.25
B147 SP61 75c + 15c blk brn 9.25 9.00
B148 SP61 1fr + 25c cl 10.50 10.50
B149 SP61 1.75fr + 25c vio bl 12.50 12.50
B150 SP61 5fr + 5fr lilac 115.00 115.00
Nos. B144-B150 (7) 153.35 153.10

The surtax was for anti-tuberculosis work.

1934, June 1 Photo.

B151 SP62 75c + 25c olive brn 5.50 5.50

The surtax was to raise funds for the Peter Benoit Memorial.

King Leopold III
SP63 SP64

1934, Sept. 15

B152 SP63 75c + 25c ol blk 18.00 17.00
a. Sheet of 20 750.00 750.00
B153 SP64 1fr + 25c red vio 17.00 16.00
a. Sheet of 20 750.00 750.00

The surtax aided the National War Veterans' Fund. Sold for 4.50fr a set at the Exhibition of War Postmarks 1914-18, held at Brussels by the Royal Philatelic Club of Veterans. The price included an exhibition ticket. Sold at Brussels post office Sept. 18-22. No. B152 printed in sheets of 20 (4x5) and 100 (10x10). No. B153 printed in sheets of 20 (4x5) and 150 (10x15).

1934, Sept. 24

B154 SP63 75c + 25c violet 1.25 1.25
B155 SP64 1fr + 25c red brn 7.00 7.00

The surtax aided the National War Veterans' Fund. No. B154 printed in sheets of 100 (10x10); No. B155 in sheets of 150 (10x15). These stamps remained in use one year.

Crusader SP65

1934, Nov. 17 Engr. *Perf. 13½x14*
Cross in Red

B156 SP65 10c + 5c blk 1.25 1.25
B157 SP65 25c + 15c brn 1.75 1.75
B158 SP65 50c + 10c dull grn 1.75 1.75
B159 SP65 75c + 15c vio brn .85 .85
B160 SP65 1fr + 25c rose 8.50 8.50
B161 SP65 1.75fr + 25c ultra 7.50 7.50
B162 SP65 5fr + 5fr brn vio 105.00 105.00
Nos. B156-B162 (7) 126.60 126.60

The surtax was for anti-tuberculosis work.

Prince Baudouin, Princess Josephine and Prince Albert SP66

1935, Apr. 10 Photo.

B163 SP66 35c + 15c dk grn .85 .75
B164 SP66 70c + 30c red brn .85 .60
B165 SP66 1.75fr + 50c dk blue 3.00 *3.50*
Nos. B163-B165 (3) 4.70 *4.85*

Surtax was for Child Welfare Society.

Stagecoach — SP67

Franz von Taxis — SP68

Queen Astrid — SP69

1935, Apr. 27

B166 SP67 10c + 10c ol blk .60 .65
B167 SP67 25c + 25c bis brn 1.90 1.75
B168 SP67 35c + 25c dk green 2.50 2.25
Nos. B166-B168 (3) 5.00 4.65

Printed in sheets of 10. Value, set of 3, $175.

Souvenir Sheet

1935, May 25 Engr. *Perf. 14*

B169 SP68 5fr + 5fr grnsh blk 125.00 125.00
a. Single stamp 65.00

Sheets measure 91½x117mm.

Nos. B166-B169 were issued for the Brussels Philatelic Exhibition (SITEB).

The sheet normally has pin holes and a cancellation-like marking in the margin. These are considered unused and the condition valued here.

1935 Photo. *Perf. 11½*
Borders in Black

B170 SP69 10c + 5c ol blk .20 .20
B171 SP69 25c + 15c brown .20 *.30*
B172 SP69 35c + 5c dk green .20 *.25*
B173 SP69 50c + 10c rose lil .65 .55
B174 SP69 70c + 5c gray blk .20 .20
B175 SP69 1fr + 25c red .90 .70
B176 SP69 1.75fr + 25c blue 2.00 1.50
B177 SP69 2.45fr + 55c dk vio 2.50 *2.75*
Nos. B170-B177 (8) 6.85 6.45

Queen Astrid Memorial issue. The surtax was divided among several charitable organizations.

Issued: #B174, 10/31; others, 12/1.

Borgerhout Philatelic Exhibition Issue

Souvenir Sheet

Town Hall, Borgerhout — SP70

1936, Oct. 3

B178 SP70 70c + 30c pur brn 50.00 35.00
a. Single stamp 25.00

Sheet measures 115x126mm.

The sheet normally has pin holes and a cancellation-like marking in the margin. These are considered unused and the condition valued here.

Town Hall and Belfry of Charleroi SP71

Prince Baudouin SP72

Charleroi Youth Exhibition

Souvenir Sheet

1936, Oct. 18 Engr.

B179 SP71 2.45fr + 55c gray blue 42.50 40.00
a. Single stamp 25.00

Sheet measures 95x120mm.

The sheet normally has pin holes and a cancellation-like marking in the margin. These are considered unused and the condition valued here.

1936, Dec. 1 Photo. *Perf. 14x13½*

B180 SP72 10c + 5c dk brown .20 .20
B181 SP72 25c + 5c violet .20 *.25*
B182 SP72 35c + 5c dk green .20 *.25*
B183 SP72 50c + 5c vio brn .30 *.35*
B184 SP72 70c + 5c ol grn .20 .20
B185 SP72 1fr + 25c cerise .65 .45
B186 SP72 1.75fr + 25c ultra 1.10 .65
B187 SP72 2.45fr + 2.55fr vio rose 3.00 *4.00*
Nos. B180-B187 (8) 5.85 *6.35*

The surtax was for the assistance of the National Anti-Tuberculosis Society.

1937, Jan. 10

B188 SP72 2.45fr + 2.55fr slate 1.50 1.50

Intl. Stamp Day. Surtax for the benefit of the Brussels Postal Museum, the Royal Belgian Phil. Fed. and the Anti-Tuberculosis Soc.

Queen Astrid and Prince Baudouin SP73

Queen Mother Elisabeth SP74

1937, Apr. 15 *Perf. 11½*

B189 SP73 10c + 5c magenta .20 .20
B190 SP73 25c + 5c ol blk .20 *.25*
B191 SP73 35c + 5c dk grn .20 *.25*
B192 SP73 50c + 5c violet .50 *.55*
B193 SP73 70c + 5c slate .20 *.30*
B194 SP73 1fr + 25c dk car .65 .60
B195 SP73 1.75fr + 25c dp ultra 1.10 1.10
B196 SP73 2.45fr + 1.55fr dk brn 2.75 2.75
Nos. B189-B196 (8) 5.80 6.00

The surtax was to raise funds for Public Utility Works.

1937, Sept. 15 *Perf. 14x13½*

B197 SP74 70c + 5c int black .30 .30
B198 SP74 1.75fr + 25c brt ultra .70 .70

Souvenir Sheet
Perf. 11½

B199 Sheet of 4 26.00 15.00
a. SP74 1.50fr+2.50fr red brn 3.75 3.25
b. SP74 2.45fr+3.55fr red vio 3.25 2.00

Issued for the benefit of the Queen Elisabeth Music Foundation in connection with the Eugene Ysaye intl. competition.

No. B199 contains two se-tenant pairs of Nos. B199a and B199b. Size: 111x145mm. On sale one day, Sept. 15, at Brussels.

The sheet normally has pin holes and a cancellation-like marking in the margin. These are considered unused and the condition valued here.

Princess Josephine-Charlotte SP75

1937, Dec. 1 *Perf. 14x13½*

B200 SP75 10c + 5c sl grn .20 .20
B201 SP75 25c + 5c lt brn .20 .20
B202 SP75 35c + 5c yel grn .20 .20
B203 SP75 50c + 5c ol gray .40 .35
B204 SP75 70c + 5c brn red .20 .20
B205 SP75 1fr + 25c red .70 .55
B206 SP75 1.75fr + 25c vio bl .85 .70
B207 SP75 2.45fr + 2.55fr mag 3.25 *3.50*
Nos. B200-B207 (8) 6.00 *5.90*

King Albert Memorial Issue

Souvenir Sheet

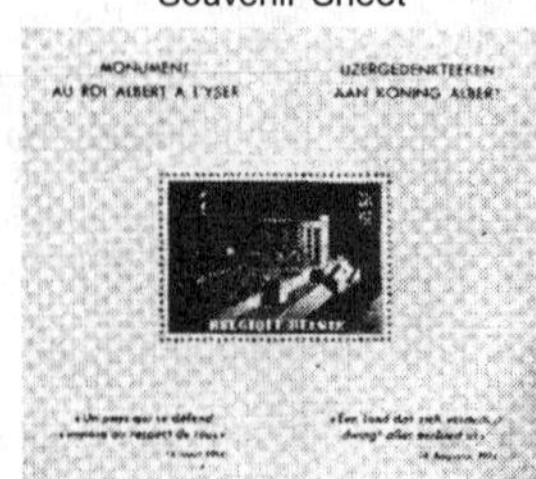
King Albert Memorial — SP76

1938, Feb. 17 *Perf. 11½*

B208 SP76 2.45fr + 7.55fr brn vio 13.00 11.00

Dedication of the monument to King Albert.

The sheet normally has pin holes and a cancellation-like marking in the margin. These are considered unused and the condition valued here.

King Leopold III in Military Plane SP77

1938, Mar. 15

B209 SP77 10c + 5c car brn .20 *.30*
B210 SP77 35c + 5c dp grn .35 *.90*
B211 SP77 70c + 5c gray blk .65 .50
B212 SP77 1.75fr + 25c ultra 1.50 1.40
B213 SP77 2.45fr + 2.55fr pur 3.50 3.00
Nos. B209-B213 (5) 6.20 6.10

The surtax was for the benefit of the National Fund for Aeronautical Propaganda.

Basilica of Koekelberg SP78

Interior View of the Basilica of Koekelberg SP79

1938, June 1 Photo.

B214 SP78 10c + 5c lt brn .20 .20
B215 SP78 35c + 5c grn .20 .20
B216 SP78 70c + 5c gray grn .20 .20
B217 SP78 1fr + 25c car .65 .55
B218 SP78 1.75fr + 25c ultra .65 .65
B219 SP78 2.45fr + 2.55fr brn vio 2.75 *3.50*

Engr.

B220 SP79 5fr + 5fr dl grn 11.00 10.50
Nos. B214-B220 (7) 15.65 15.80

Souvenir Sheet

1938, July 21 Engr. *Perf. 14*

B221 SP79 5fr + 5fr lt vio 14.00 14.00

The surtax was for a fund to aid in completing the National Basilica of the Sacred Heart at Koekelberg.

Nos. B214, B216 and B218 are different views of the exterior of the Basilica.

The sheet normally has pin holes and a cancellation-like marking in the margin. These are considered unused and the condition valued here.

Stamps of 1938 Surcharged in Black:

Nos. B222-B223

No. B224

1938, Nov. 10 *Perf. 11½*

B222 SP78 40c on 35c+5c grn .35 *.40*
B223 SP78 75c on 70c+5c gray grn .50 *.60*

B224	SP78	2.50 +2.50fr on 2.45+2.55fr	4.50	5.00
		Nos. B222-B224 (3)	5.35	6.00

Prince Albert of Liege — SP81

1938, Dec. 10 Photo. *Perf. 14x13½*

B225	SP81	10c + 5c brown	.20	.20
B226	SP81	30c + 5c mag	.20	.30
B227	SP81	40c + 5c olive gray	.20	.30
B228	SP81	75c + 5c slate grn	.20	.20
B229	SP81	1fr + 25c dk car	.55	.75
B230	SP81	1.75fr + 25c ultra	.55	.75
B231	SP81	2.50fr + 2.50fr dp grn	3.50	5.50
B232	SP81	5fr + 5fr brn lake	11.00	8.50
		Nos. B225-B232 (8)	16.40	16.50

Henri Dunant SP82

Florence Nightingale SP83

Queen Mother Elisabeth and Royal Children — SP84

Queen Astrid — SP86

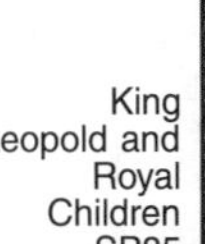

King Leopold and Royal Children SP85

Queen Mother Elisabeth and Wounded Soldier — SP87

1939, Apr. 1 Photo. *Perf. 11½*

Cross in Carmine

B233	SP82	10c + 5c brn	.20	.20
B234	SP83	30c + 5c brn car	.30	.30
B235	SP84	40c + 5c ol gray	.20	.30
B236	SP85	75c + 5c slate blk	.40	.20
B237	SP84	1fr + 25c brt rose	1.90	1.10
B238	SP85	1.75fr + 25c brt ultra	.60	.80
B239	SP86	2.50fr + 2.50fr dl vio	1.25	1.60
B240	SP87	5fr + 5fr gray grn	4.25	5.50
		Nos. B233-B240 (8)	9.10	10.00

75th anniversary of the founding of the International Red Cross Society.

In 1941, No. B240 was privately overprinted with a circular red cross overprint and 1941 date. Value, $75.

Rubens' House, Antwerp SP88

"Albert and Nicolas Rubens" — SP89

Arcade, Rubens' House SP90

"Helena Fourment and Her Children" — SP91

Rubens and Isabelle Brandt — SP92

Peter Paul Rubens — SP93

"The Velvet Hat" — SP94

"Descent from the Cross" SP95

1939, July 1

B241	SP88	10c + 5c brn	.20	.20
B242	SP89	40c + 5c brn car	.20	.20
B243	SP90	75c + 5c ol blk	.35	.35
B244	SP91	1fr + 25c rose	1.40	1.40
B245	SP92	1.50fr + 25c sep	1.60	1.60
B246	SP93	1.75fr + 25c dp ultra	2.50	2.50
B247	SP94	2.50fr + 2.50fr brt red vio	8.25	8.25
B248	SP95	5fr + 5fr slate gray	10.50	10.50
		Nos. B241-B248 (8)	25.00	25.00

Issued to honor Peter Paul Rubens. The surtax was used to restore Rubens' home in Antwerp.

"Martin van Nieuwenhove" by Hans Memling (1430?-1495), Flemish Painter — SP96

1939, July 1

B249	SP96	75c + 75c olive blk	2.75	2.75

Twelfth Century Monks at Work — SP97

Reconstructed Tower Seen through Cloister — SP98

Monks Laboring in the Fields SP99

Orval Abbey, Aerial View SP100

Bishop Heylen of Namur, Madonna and Abbot General Smets of the Trappists — SP101

King Albert I and King Leopold III and Shrine — SP102

1939, July 20

B250	SP97	75c + 75c ol blk	2.50	2.75
B251	SP98	1fr + 1fr rose red	1.60	1.60
B252	SP99	1.50fr + 1.50fr dl brn	1.60	1.60
B253	SP100	1.75fr + 1.75fr saph	1.60	1.60
B254	SP101	2.50fr + 2.50fr brt red vio	7.25	6.50
B255	SP102	5fr + 5fr brn car	7.25	7.25
		Nos. B250-B255 (6)	21.80	21.30

The surtax was used for the restoration of the Abbey of Orval.

Bruges SP103

Furnes SP104

Belfries: 30c+5c, Thuin. 40c+5c, Lierre. 75c+5c, Mons. 1.75fr+25c, Namur. 2.50fr+2.50fr, Alost. 5fr+5fr, Tournai.

1939, Dec. 1 Photo. *Perf. 14x13½*

B256	SP103	10c + 5c ol gray	.20	.25
B257	SP103	30c + 5c brn org	.25	.35
B258	SP103	40c + 5c brt red vio	.40	.45
B259	SP103	75c + 5c olive blk	.20	.25

Engr.

B260	SP104	1fr + 25c rose car	1.00	1.25
B261	SP104	1.75fr + 25c dk blue	1.00	1.25
B262	SP104	2.50fr + 2.50fr dp red brn	7.25	8.00
B263	SP104	5fr + 5fr pur	10.00	11.00
		Nos. B256-B263 (8)	20.30	22.80

Mons SP111

Ghent SP112

Coats of Arms: 40c+10c, Arel. 50c+10c, Bruges. 75c+15c, Namur. 1fr+25c, Hasselt. 1.75fr+50c, Brussels. 2.50fr+2.50fr, Antwerp. 5fr+5fr, Liege.

1940-41 Typo. *Perf. 14x13½*

B264	SP111	10c + 5c multi	.20	.20
B265	SP112	30c + 5c multi	.20	.20
B266	SP111	40c + 10c multi	.20	.20
B267	SP112	50c + 10c multi	.20	.20
B268	SP111	75c + 15c multi	.20	.20
B269	SP112	1fr + 25c multi	.30	.30
B270	SP111	1.75fr + 50c multi	.45	.40
B271	SP112	2.50fr + 2.50fr multi	1.25	1.25
B272	SP111	5fr + 5fr multi	1.50	1.50
		Nos. B264-B272 (9)	4.50	4.45

Nos. B264, B269-B272 issued in 1941. Surtax for winter relief. See No. B279.

Queen Elisabeth Music Chapel SP120

Bust of Prince Albert of Liege — SP121

1940, Nov. Photo. *Perf. 11½*

B273	SP120	75c + 75c slate	1.25	1.25
B274	SP120	1fr + 1fr rose red	1.25	1.25
B275	SP121	1.50fr + 1.50fr Prus grn	1.25	1.25
B276	SP121	1.75fr + 1.75fr ultra	1.25	1.25
B277	SP120	2.50fr + 2.50fr brn org	2.50	2.50
B278	SP121	5fr + 5fr red vio	3.00	3.00
		Nos. B273-B278 (6)	10.50	10.50

The surtax was for the Queen Elisabeth Music Foundation. Nos. B273-B278 were not authorized for postal use, but were sold to advance subscribers either mint or canceled to order. See Nos. B317-B318.

Arms Types of 1940-41
Souvenir Sheets
Perf. 14x13½, Imperf.

1941, May **Typo.**
Cross and City Name in Carmine
Arms in Color of Stamp

B279 Sheet of 9 13.00 13.00
a. SP111 10c + 5c slate 1.10 *1.25*
b. SP112 30c + 5c emerald 1.10 *1.25*
c. SP111 40c + 10c chocolate 1.10 *1.25*
d. SP112 50c + 10c light violet 1.10 *1.25*
e. SP111 75c + 15c dull purple 1.10 *1.25*
f. SP112 1fr + 25c carmine 1.10 *1.25*
g. SP111 1.75fr + 50c dull blue 1.10 *1.25*
h. SP112 2.50fr + 2.50fr ol gray 1.10 *1.25*
i. SP111 5fr + 5fr dull violet 4.00 *4.25*

The sheets measure 106x148mm. The surtax was used for relief work.

Painting
SP123

Sculpture
SP124

Monks Studying Plans of Orval Abbey — SP128

Designs: 40c+60c, 2fr+3.50fr, Monk carrying candle. 50c+65c, 1.75fr+2.50fr, Monk praying. 75c+1fr, 3fr+5fr, Two monks singing.

1941, June **Photo.** ***Perf. 11½***
B281 SP123 10c + 15c brn org .35 *.40*
B282 SP124 30c + 30c ol gray .35 *.40*
B283 SP123 40c + 60c dp brn .35 *.40*
B284 SP124 50c + 65c vio .35 *.40*
B285 SP124 75c + 1fr brt red vio .35 *.40*
B286 SP124 1fr + 1.50fr rose red .35 *.40*
B287 SP123 1.25fr + 1.75fr dp yel grn .35 *.40*
B288 SP123 1.75fr + 2.50fr dp ultra .35 *.40*
B289 SP123 2fr + 3.50fr red vio .35 *.40*
B290 SP124 2.50fr + 4.50fr dl red brn .35 *.40*
B291 SP124 3fr + 5fr dk ol grn .35 *.40*
B292 SP128 5fr + 10fr grnsh blk 1.25 1.25
Nos. B281-B292 (12) 5.10 *5.65*

The surtax was used for the restoration of the Abbey of Orval.

Maria Theresa
SP129

Charles the Bold
SP130

Portraits (in various frames): 35c+5c, Charles of Lorraine. 50c+10c, Margaret of Parma. 60c+10c, Charles V. 1fr+15c, Johanna of Castile. 1.50fr+1fr, Philip the Good. 1.75fr+1.75fr, Margaret of Austria. 3.25fr+3.25fr, Archduke Albert. 5fr+5fr, Archduchess Isabella.

1941-42 **Photo.**
B293 SP129 10c + 5c ol blk .20 .20
B294 SP129 35c + 5c dl grn .20 .20
B295 SP129 50c + 10c brn .20 .20
B296 SP129 60c + 10c pur .20 .20
B297 SP129 1fr + 15c brt car rose .20 .20
B298 SP129 1.50fr + 1fr red vio .20 .20
B299 SP129 1.75fr + 1.75fr ryl bl .20 .20
B300 SP130 2.25fr + 2.25fr dl red brn .30 .30
B301 SP129 3.25fr + 3.25fr lt brn .35 *.45*
B302 SP129 5fr + 5fr sl grn .40 *.45*
Nos. B293-B302 (10) 2.45 2.60

Souvenir Sheet

Archduke Albert and Archduchess Isabella — SP139

B302A SP139 Sheet of 2 ('42) 6.00 6.00
b. 3.25fr+6.75fr turquoise blue 2.25 2.25
c. 5fr+10fr dark carmine 2.25 2.25

The surtax was for the benefit of National Social Service Work among soldiers' families.

Souvenir Sheets

Monks Studying Plans of Orval Abbey — SP140

1941, Oct. **Photo.** ***Perf. 11½***
Inscribed "Belgie-Belgique"
B303 SP140 5fr + 15fr ultra 7.00 7.00
Inscribed "Belgique-Belgie"
Imperf
B304 SP140 5fr + 15fr ultra 7.00 7.00

Surtax for the restoration of Orval Abbey.
No. B304 exists perforated.
In 1942 these sheets were privately trimmed and overprinted "1142 1942" and ornament.

St. Martin Statue, Church of Dinant
SP141

Lennik, Saint-Quentin
SP142

St. Martin's Church, Saint-Trond
SP146

Statues of St. Martin: 50c+10c, 3.25fr+3.25fr, Beck, Limburg. 60c+10c, 2.25fr+2.25fr, Dave on the Meuse. 1.75fr+50c, Hal, Brabant.

1941-42 **Photo.** ***Perf. 11½***
B305 SP141 10c + 5c chest .20 .20
B306 SP142 35c + 5c dk bl grn .20 .20
B307 SP142 50c + 10c vio .20 .20
B308 SP142 60c + 10c dp brn .20 .20
B309 SP142 1fr + 15c car .20 .20
B310 SP141 1.50fr + 25c sl grn .20 .20
B311 SP142 1.75fr + 50c dk ultra .30 .30
B312 SP142 2.25fr + 2.25fr red vio .30 .30
B313 SP142 3.25fr + 3.25fr brn vio .30 .30
B314 SP146 5fr + 5fr dk ol grn .45 .45
Nos. B305-B314 (10) 2.55 2.55

Souvenir Sheets
Inscribed "Belgie-Belgique"
B315 SP146 5fr + 20fr vio brn ('42) 12.50 12.50
Inscribed "Belgique-Belgie"
Imperf
B316 SP146 5fr + 20fr vio brn ('42) 12.50 12.50

In 1956, the Bureau Europeen de la Jeunesse et de l'Enfance privately overprinted Nos. B315-B316: "Congres Europeen de l'education 7-12 Mai 1956," in dark red and dark green respectively. A black bar obliterates "Winterhulp-Secours d'Hiver."

Souvenir Sheets

Queen Elisabeth Music Chapel — SP147

1941, Dec. 1 **Photo.** ***Perf. 11½***
Inscribed "Belgique-Belgie"
B317 SP147 10fr + 15fr ol blk 4.50 4.00
Inscribed "Belgie-Belique"
B318 SP147 10fr + 15fr ol blk 4.50 4.00

The surtax was for the Queen Elisabeth Music Foundation. These sheets were perforated with the monogram of Queen Elisabeth in 1942.
In 1954 Nos. B317-B318 were overprinted to for the birth cent. of Edgar Tinel, composer. These overprinted sheets were not postally valid.

Jean Bollandus
SP148

Christophe Plantin
SP156

Designs: 35c+5c, Andreas Vesalius. 50c+10c, Simon Stevinus. 60c+10c, Jean Van Helmont. 1fr+15c, Rembert Dodoens. 1.75fr+50c, Gerardus Mercator. 3.25fr+3.25fr, Abraham Ortelius. 5fr+5fr, Justus Lipsius.

1942, May 15 **Photo.** ***Perf. 14x13½***
B319 SP148 10c + 5c dl brn .20 .20
B320 SP148 35c + 5c gray grn .20 .20
B321 SP148 50c + 10c fawn .20 .20
B322 SP148 60c + 10c grnsh blk .20 .20

Engr.
B323 SP148 1fr + 15c brt rose .20 .20
B324 SP148 1.75fr + 50c dl bl .20 .20
B325 SP148 3.25fr + 3.25fr lil rose .20 .20
B326 SP148 5fr + 5fr vio .25 .25

Perf. 13½x14
B327 SP156 10fr + 30fr red org .95 1.00
Nos. B319-B327 (9) 2.60 2.65

The surtax was used to help fight tuberculosis.
No. B327 was sold by subscription at the Brussels Post Office, July 1-10, 1942.

Belgian Prisoner — SP158

1942, Oct. 1 ***Perf. 11½***
B331 SP158 5fr + 45fr olive gray 5.50 5.50

The surtax was for prisoners of war. Value includes a brown inscribed label which alternates with the stamps in the sheet.

SP159

SP164

SP162

SP168

Various Statues of St. Martin.

1942-43
B332 SP159 10c + 5c org .20 .20
B333 SP159 35c + 5c dk bl grn .20 .20
B334 SP159 50c + 10c dp brn .20 .20
B335 SP162 60c + 10c blk .20 .20
B336 SP159 1fr + 15c brt rose .20 .20
B337 SP164 1.50fr + 25c grnsh blk .20 .20
B338 SP164 1.75fr + 50c dk bl .20 .20
B339 SP162 2.25fr + 2.25fr brn .30 .25
B340 SP162 3.25fr + 3.25fr brt red vio .35 .30
B341 SP168 5fr + 10fr hn brn .50 .45
B342 SP168 10fr + 20fr rose brn & vio brn ('43) .65 .65

Inscribed "Belgique-Belgie"
B343 SP168 10fr + 20fr gldn brn & vio brn ('43) .65 .65
Nos. B332-B343 (12) 3.85 3.70

The surtax was for winter relief.
Issue dates: Nos. B332-B341, Nov. 12, 1942; Nos. B342-B343, Apr. 3, 1943.

Prisoners of War — SP170

#B345, 2 prisoners with package from home.

1943, May **Photo.** ***Perf. 11½***

B344	SP170	1fr + 30fr ver	2.50	2.50
B345	SP170	1fr + 30fr brn rose	2.50	2.50

The surtax was used for prisoners of war.

Roof Tiler SP172 — Coppersmith SP173

Statues in Petit Sablon Park, Brussels: 35c+5c, Blacksmith. 60c+10c, Gunsmith. 1fr+15c, Armsmith. 1.75fr+75c, Goldsmith. 3.25fr+3.25fr, Fishdealer. 5fr+25fr, Watchmaker.

1943, June 1

B346	SP172	10c + 5c chnt brn	.20	.20
B347	SP172	35c + 5c grn	.20	.20
B348	SP173	50c + 10c dk brn	.20	.20
B349	SP173	60c + 10c slate	.20	.20
B350	SP173	1fr + 15c dl rose brn	.20	.20
B351	SP173	1.75fr + 75c ultra	.20	.20
B352	SP173	3.25fr + 3.25fr brt red vio	.30	.40
B353	SP173	5fr + 25fr dk pur	.50	.55
		Nos. B346-B353 (8)	2.00	2.15

Surtax for the control of tuberculosis.

"O" SP180

"ORVAL" — SP185

1943, Oct. 9

B354	SP180	50c + 1fr "O"	.50	.50
B355	SP180	60c + 1.90fr "R"	.30	.25
B356	SP180	1fr + 3fr "V"	.30	.25
B357	SP180	1.75fr + 5.25fr "A"	.30	.25
B358	SP180	3.25fr + 16.75fr "L"	.40	.40
B359	SP185	5fr + 30fr dp brn	.75	.75
		Nos. B354-B359 (6)	2.55	2.40

Surtax aided restoration of Orval Abbey.

St. Leonard Church, Leau SP186

St. Martin Church, Courtrai — SP190

Basilica of St. Martin, Angre — SP191

Notre Dame, Hal — SP193

St. Martin SP194

35c+5c, St. Martin Church, Dion-le-Val. 50c+15c, St. Martin Church, Alost. 60c+20c, St. Martin Church, Liege. 3.25fr+11.75fr, St. Martin Church, Loppem. No. B369, St. Martin, beggar & Meuse landscape.

1943-44

B360	SP186	10c + 5c dp brn	.20	.20
B361	SP186	35c + 5c dk bl grn	.20	.20
B362	SP186	50c + 15c ol blk	.30	.30
B363	SP186	60c + 20c brt red vio	.30	.40
B364	SP190	1fr + 1fr rose brn	.40	.40
B365	SP191	1.75fr + 4.25fr dp ultra	.90	.60
B366	SP186	3.25fr + 11.75fr red lil	.90	.65
B367	SP193	5fr + 25fr dk bl	1.25	1.25
B368	SP194	10fr + 30fr gray grn ('44)	.90	.90
B369	SP194	10fr + 30fr blk brn ('44)	.90	.90
		Nos. B360-B369 (10)	6.25	5.80

Surtax for winter relief.

Catalogue values for unused stamps in this section, from this point to the end of the section, are for Never Hinged items.

"Daedalus and Icarus" SP196

Sir Anthony Van Dyck, Self-portrait SP200

Paintings by Van Dyck: 50c+2.50fr, "The Good Samaritan." 60c+3.40fr, Detail of "Christ Healing the Paralytic." 1fr+5fr, "Madonna and Child." 5fr+30fr, "St. Sebastian."

1944, Apr. 16 **Photo.** ***Perf. 11½***
Crosses in Carmine

B370	SP196	35c + 1.65fr dk sl grn	.40	.30
B371	SP196	50c + 2.50fr grnsh blk	.40	.30
B372	SP196	60c + 3.40fr blk brn	.40	.30
B373	SP196	1fr + 5fr dk car	.60	.45
B374	SP200	1.75fr + 8.25fr int bl	.75	.60
B375	SP196	5fr + 30fr cop brn	.75	.60
		Nos. B370-B375 (6)	3.30	2.55

The surtax was for the Belgian Red Cross.

Jan van Eyck — SP202

Godfrey of Bouillon — SP203

Designs: 50c+25c, Jacob van Maerlant. 60c+40c, Jean Joses de Dinant. 1fr+50c, Jacob van Artevelde. 1.75fr+4.25fr, Charles Joseph de Ligne. 2.25fr+8.25fr, Andre Gretry. 3.25fr+11.25fr, Jan Moretus-Plantin. 5fr+35fr, Jan van Ruysbroeck.

1944, May 31

B376	SP202	10c + 15c dk pur	.40	.25
B377	SP203	35c + 15c green	.40	.25
B378	SP203	50c + 25c chnt brn	.40	.25
B379	SP203	60c + 40c ol blk	.40	.25
B380	SP203	1fr + 50c rose brn	.40	.25
B381	SP203	1.75fr + 4.25fr ultra	.40	.25
B382	SP203	2.25fr + 8.25fr grnsh blk	1.00	.55
B383	SP203	3.25fr + 11.25fr dk brn	.40	.25
B384	SP203	5fr + 35fr sl bl	.70	.70
		Nos. B376-B384 (9)	4.50	3.00

The surtax was for prisoners of war.

Sons of Aymon Astride Bayard SP211

Brabo Slaying the Giant Antigoon SP212

Till Eulenspiegel Singing to Nele SP214

50c+10c, St. Hubert converted by stag with crucifix. 1fr+15fr, St. George slaying the dragon. 1.75fr+5.25fr, Genevieve of Brabant with son & roe-deer. 3.25fr+11.75fr, Tchantches wrestling with the Saracen. 5fr+25fr, St. Gertrude rescuing the knight with the cards.

1944, June 25

B385	SP211	10c + 5c choc	.20	.20
B386	SP212	35c + 5c dk bl grn	.20	.20
B387	SP211	50c + 10c dl vio	.20	.20
B388	SP214	60c + 10c blk brn	.20	.20
B389	SP214	1fr + 15c rose brn	.20	.20
B390	SP214	1.75fr + 5.25fr ultra	.20	*.30*
B391	SP211	3.25fr + 11.75fr grnsh blk	.35	*.50*
B392	SP211	5fr + 25fr dk bl	.45	*.70*
		Nos. B385-B392 (8)	2.00	*2.50*

The surtax was for the control of tuberculosis.

Nos. B385-B389 were overprinted "Breendonk+10fr." in 1946 by the Union Royale Philatelique for an exhibition at Brussels. They had no postal validity.

Union of the Flemish and Walloon Peoples in their Sorrow — SP219

Union in Reconstruction — SP220

Perf. 11½
1945, May 1 **Unwmk.** **Photo.**

B395	SP219	1fr + 30fr carmine	1.25	.90
B396	SP220	1¾fr + 30fr brt ultra	1.25	.90

1945, July 21
Size: 34½x23½mm

B397	SP219	1fr + 9fr scarlet	.25	.20
B398	SP220	1fr + 9fr car rose	.25	.20
		Nos. B395-B398 (4)	3.00	2.20

Surtax for the postal employees' relief fund.

Prisoner of War SP221

Reunion SP222

Awaiting Execution SP223

Symbolical Figures "Recovery of Freedom" SP225

Design: 70c+30c, 3.50fr+3.50fr, Member of Resistance Movement.

1945, Sept. 10

B399	SP221	10c + 15c orange	.20	.20
B400	SP222	20c + 20c dp pur	.20	.20
B401	SP223	60c + 25c sepia	.20	.20
B402	SP221	70c + 30c dp yel grn	.20	.20
B403	SP221	75c + 50c org brn	.20	.20
B404	SP222	1fr + 75c brt bl grn	.25	.20
B405	SP223	1.50fr + 1fr brt red	.25	.20
B406	SP221	3.50fr + 3.50fr brt bl	1.10	1.00
B407	SP225	5fr + 40fr brown	.90	.90
		Nos. B399-B407 (9)	3.50	3.30

The surtax was for the benefit of prisoners of war, displaced persons, families of executed victims and members of the Resistance Movement.

Arms of West Flanders — SP226

Arms of Provinces: 20c+20c, Luxembourg. 60c+25c, East Flanders. 70c+30c, Namur. 75c+50c, Limburg. 1fr+75c, Hainaut. 1.50fr+1fr, Antwerp. 3.50fr+1.50fr, Liege. 5fr+45fr, Brabant.

1945, Dec. 1

B408 SP226 10c + 15c sl blk & sl gray .20 .20
B409 SP226 20c + 20c rose car & rose .20 .20
B410 SP226 60c + 25c dk brn & pale brn .20 .20
B411 SP226 70c + 30c dk grn & lt grn .20 .20
B412 SP226 75c + 50c org brn & pale org brn .25 .20
B413 SP226 1fr + 75c pur & lt pur .20 .20
B414 SP226 1.50fr + 1fr car & rose .20 .20
B415 SP226 3.50fr + 1.50fr dp bl & gray bl .30 .20
B416 SP226 5fr + 45fr dp mag & cer 2.25 1.90
Nos. B408-B416 (9) 4.00 3.50

The surtax was for tuberculosis prevention.

Father Joseph Damien — SP227

Father Damien Comforting Leper — SP229

Leper Colony, Molokai Island, Hawaii SP228

Perf. 11½

1946, July 15 Unwmk. Photo.

B417 SP227 65c + 75c dk blue 1.00 .65
B418 SP228 1.35fr + 2fr brown 1.00 .65
B419 SP229 1.75fr + 18fr rose brn 1.60 1.10

The surtax was for the erection of a museum in Louvain.

Symbols of Wisdom and Patriotism SP230

"In Memoriam" SP232

François Bovesse SP231

1946, July 15

B420 SP230 65c + 75c violet 1.00 .65
B421 SP231 1.35fr + 2fr dk org brn 1.40 .80
B422 SP232 1.75fr + 18fr car rose 1.90 1.10

The surtax was for the erection of a "House of the Fine Arts" at Namur.

Emile Vandervelde SP233

Sower SP235

Vandervelde, Laborer and Family — SP234

1946, July 15

B423 SP233 65c + 75c dk sl grn 1.25 .65
B424 SP234 1.35fr + 2fr dk vio bl 1.40 .80
B425 SP235 1.75fr + 18fr dp car 1.90 1.10
Nos. B417-B425 (9) 12.45 7.50

The surtax was for the Emile Vanderveide Institute, to promote social, economic and cultural activities.

For surcharges see Nos. CB4-CB12.

Pepin of Herstal — SP236

Malines — SP241

1fr+50c, Charlemagne. 1.50fr+1fr, Godfrey of Bouillon. 3.50fr+1.50fr, Robert of Jerusalem. #B430-B431, Baldwin of Constantinople.

1946, Sept. 15 Engr. *Perf. 11½x11*

B426 SP236 75c + 25c grn .60 .35
B427 SP236 1fr + 50c vio .90 .50
B428 SP236 1.50fr + 1fr plum 1.25 .65
B429 SP236 3.50fr + 1.50fr brt bl 1.50 .75
B430 SP236 5fr + 45fr red vio 12.00 7.00
B431 SP236 5fr + 45fr red org 15.00 7.75
Nos. B426-B431 (6) 31.25 17.00

The surtax on Nos. B426-B429 was for the benefit of former prisoners of war, displaced persons, the families of executed patriots, and former members of the Resistance Movement.

The surtax on Nos. B430-B431 was divided among several welfare, national celebration and educational organizations.

Issue dates: Nos. B426-B429, Apr. 15; No. B430, Sept. 15; No. B431, Nov. 15.

See Nos. B437-B441, B465-B466, B472-B476.

1946, Dec. 2 *Perf. 11½*

Coats of Arms: 90c+60c, Dinant. 1.35fr+1.15fr, Ostend. 3.15fr+1.85fr, Verviers. 4.50fr+45.50fr, Louvain.

B432 SP241 65c + 35c rose car .50 .50
B433 SP241 90c + 60c lem .50 .50
B434 SP241 1.35fr + 1.15fr dp grn .50 .50
B435 SP241 3.15fr + 1.85fr bl 1.50 1.25
B436 SP241 4.50fr + 45.50fr dk vio brn 13.00 12.00
Nos. B432-B436 (5) 16.00 14.75

The surtax was for anti-tuberculosis work. See Nos. B442-B446.

Type of 1946

Designs: 65c+35c, John II, Duke of Brabant. 90c+60c, Count Philip of Alsace. 1.35fr+1.15fr, William the Good. 3.15fr+1.85fr, Bishop Notger of Liege. 20fr+20fr, Philip the Noble.

1947, Sept. 25 Engr. *Perf. 11½x11*

B437 SP236 65c + 35c Prus grn .60 .50
B438 SP236 90c + 60c yel grn 1.00 .75
B439 SP236 1.35fr + 1.15fr car 1.40 1.10
B440 SP236 3.15fr + 1.85fr ultra 2.00 1.60
B441 SP236 20fr + 20fr red vio 52.50 42.50
Nos. B437-B441 (5) 57.50 46.45

The surtax was for victims of World War II.

Arms Type of 1946 Dated "1947"

Coats of Arms: 65c+35c, Nivelles. 90c+60c, St. Trond. 1.35fr+1.15fr, Charleroi. 3.15fr+1.85fr, St. Nicolas. 20fr+20fr, Bouillon.

1947, Dec. 15 *Perf. 11½*

B442 SP241 65c + 35c org .80 .65
B443 SP241 90c + 60c dp cl .70 .65
B444 SP241 1.35fr + 1.15fr dk brn 1.00 .70
B445 SP241 3.15fr + 1.85fr dp bl 2.50 1.75
B446 SP241 20fr + 20fr dk grn 20.00 12.50
Nos. B442-B446 (5) 25.00 16.25

The surtax was for anti-tuberculosis work.

St. Benedict and King Totila — SP247

Achel Abbey SP248

3.15fr+2.85fr, St. Benedict, legislator & builder. 10fr+10fr, Death of St. Benedict.

1948, Apr. 5 Photo.

B447 SP247 65c + 65c red brn 1.25 .55
B448 SP248 1.35fr + 1.35fr gray 1.75 .55
B449 SP247 3.15fr + 2.85fr dp ultra 2.50 1.90
B450 SP247 10fr + 10fr brt red vio 12.50 10.00
Nos. B447-B450 (4) 18.00 13.00

The surtax was to aid the Abbey of the Trappist Fathers at Achel.

St. Begga and Chevremont Castle — SP249

Chevremont Basilica and Convent SP250

3.15fr+2.85fr, Madonna of Chevremont & Chapel. 10fr+10fr, Madonna of Mt. Carmel.

1948, Apr. 5 Unwmk.

B451 SP249 65c + 65c bl grn 1.00 .55
B452 SP250 1.35fr + 1.35fr dk car rose 1.60 .55
B453 SP249 3.15fr + 2.85fr dp bl 2.25 1.90
B454 SP249 10fr + 10fr dp brn 12.00 10.00
Nos. B451-B454 (4) 16.85 13.00

The surtax was to aid the Basilica of the Carmelite Fathers of Chèvremont.

Anseele Monument Showing French Inscription — SP251

90c+60c, View of Ghent. 1.35fr+1.15fr, Van Artevelde monument, Ghent. 3.15fr+1.85fr. Anseele Monument, Flemish inscription.

1948, June 21 *Perf. 14x13½*

B455 SP251 65c + 35c rose red 2.75 1.10
B456 SP251 90c + 60c gray 3.50 1.90
B457 SP251 1.35fr + 1.15fr hn brn 2.25 1.50
B458 SP251 3.15fr + 1.85fr brt bl 8.50 5.00
a. Souv. sheet, #B455-B458 140.00 55.00
Nos. B455-B458 (4) 17.00 9.50

Issued to honor Edouard Anseele, statesman, founder of the Belgian Socialist Party.

No. B458a sold for 50fr.

For surcharges see Nos. 395-398.

Statue "The Unloader" SP252

Underground Fighter SP253

1948, Sept. 4 *Perf. 11½x11*

B460 SP252 10fr + 10fr gray grn 35.00 19.00
B461 SP253 10fr + 10fr red brn 20.00 11.00

The surtax was used toward erection of monuments at Antwerp and Liege.

Portrait Type of 1946 and

Double Barred Cross — SP254

Designs: 4fr+3.25fr, Isabella of Austria. 20fr+20fr, Archduke Albert of Austria.

1948, Dec. 15 Photo. *Perf. 13½x14*

B462 SP254 20c + 5c dk sl grn .50 .20
B463 SP254 1.20fr + 30c mag 1.25 .70
B464 SP254 1.75fr + 25c red 1.75 .60

Engr. *Perf. 11½x11*

B465 SP236 4fr + 3.25fr ultra 9.50 6.50
B466 SP236 20fr + 20fr Prus grn 42.50 30.00
Nos. B462-B466 (5) 55.50 38.00

The surtax was divided among several charities.

Souvenir Sheets

Rogier van der Weyden Paintings — SP255

Paintings by van der Weyden (No. B466A): 90c, Virgin and Child. 1.75fr, Christ on the Cross. 4fr, Mary Magdalene.

Paintings by Jordaens (No. B466B): 90c, Woman Reading. 1.75fr, The Flutist. 4fr, Old Woman Reading Letter.

1949, Apr. 1 Photo. *Perf. 11½*

B466A	SP255	Sheet of 3	125.00	110.00
c.		90c deep brown	37.50	32.50
d.		1.75fr deep rose lilac	37.50	32.50
e.		4fr dark violet blue	37.50	32.50
B466B	SP255	Sheet of 3	125.00	110.00
f.		90c dark violet	37.50	32.50
g.		1.75fr red	37.50	32.50
h.		4fr blue	37.50	32.50

The surtax went to various cultural and philanthropic organizations. Sheets sold for 50fr each.

Gum on Nos. B466A-B466B is irregularly applied.

Guido Gezelle — SP256

1949, Nov. 15 Photo. *Perf. 14x13½*

B467	SP256	1.75fr + 75c dk Prus grn	2.50	1.75

50th anniversary of the death of Guido Gezelle, poet. The surtax was for the Guido Gezelle Museum, Bruges.

Portrait Type of 1946 and

Arnica — SP257

Designs: 65c+10c, Sand grass. 90c+10c, Wood myrtle. 1.20fr+30c, Field poppy. 1.75fr+25c, Philip the Good. 3fr+1.50fr, Charles V. 4fr+2fr, Maria-Christina. 6fr+3fr, Charles of Lorraine. 8fr+4fr, Maria-Theresa.

1949, Dec. 20 Typo. *Perf. 13½x14*

B468	SP257	20c + 5c multi	.50	.50
B469	SP257	65c + 10c multi	1.25	1.10
B470	SP257	90c + 10c multi	2.00	1.50
B471	SP257	1.20fr + 30c multi	2.50	1.75

Engr. *Perf. 11½x11*

B472	SP236	1.75fr + 25c red org	1.40	.80
B473	SP236	3fr + 1.50fr dp claret	10.00	6.75
B474	SP236	4fr + 2fr ultra	10.00	8.00
B475	SP236	6fr + 3fr choc	16.00	11.00
B476	SP236	8fr + 4fr dl grn	16.00	8.75
		Nos. B468-B476 (9)	59.65	40.15

The surtax was apportioned among several welfare organizations.

Arms of Belgium and Great Britain — SP258

British Memorial — SP260

Design: 2.50fr+50c, British tanks at Hertain.

Perf. 13½x14, 11½

1950, Mar. 15 Engr.

B477	SP258	80c + 20c grn	1.50	1.00
B478	SP258	2.50fr + 50c red	5.00	3.75
B479	SP260	4fr + 2fr dp bl	9.25	6.25
		Nos. B477-B479 (3)	15.75	11.00

6th anniv. of the liberation of Belgian territory by the British army.

Hurdling SP261

Relay Race SP262

Designs: 90c+10c, Javelin throwing. 4fr+2fr, Pole vault. 8fr+4fr, Foot race.

Perf. 14x13½, 13½x14

1950, July 1 Engr. Unwmk.

B480	SP261	20c + 5c brt grn	.40	.20
B481	SP261	90c + 10c vio brn	2.75	1.50
B482	SP262	1.75fr + 25c car	5.25	1.75
a.		Souvenir sheet of 1	45.00	35.00
B483	SP261	4fr + 2fr lt bl	27.50	17.00
B484	SP261	8fr + 4fr dp grn	29.00	18.00
		Nos. B480-B484 (5)	64.90	38.45

Issued to publicize the European Athletic Games, Brussels, August 1950.

The margins of No. B482a were trimmed in April, 1951, and an overprint ("25 Francs pour le Fonds Sportif-25e Foire Internationale Bruxelles") was added in red in French and in black in Flemish by a private committee. These pairs of altered sheets were sold at the Brussels Fair. Value of the altered sheet, $25.

Gentian — SP263

Sijsele Sanatorium SP264

Tombeek Sanatorium SP265

Designs: 65c+10c, Cotton Grass. 90c+10c, Foxglove. 1.20fr+30c, Limonia. 4fr+2fr, Jauche Sanatorium.

1950, Dec. 20 Typo. *Perf. 14x13½*

B485	SP263	20c + 5c multi	.80	.40
B486	SP263	65c + 10c multi	1.50	.85
B487	SP263	90c + 10c multi	1.60	1.10
B488	SP263	1.20fr + 30c multi	2.75	2.25

Perf. 11½

Engr.

Cross in Red

B489	SP264	1.75fr + 25c car	2.50	1.40
B490	SP264	4fr + 2fr blue	13.00	7.00
B491	SP265	8fr + 4fr bl grn	21.00	15.00
		Nos. B485-B491 (7)	43.15	28.00

The surtax was for tuberculosis prevention and other charitable purposes.

Chemist SP266

Allegory of Peace SP268

Colonial Instructor and Class SP267

1951, Mar. 27 Unwmk.

B492	SP266	80c + 20c grn	1.40	1.00
B493	SP267	2.50fr + 50c vio brn	9.50	5.00
B494	SP268	4fr + 2fr dp bl	10.50	6.00
		Nos. B492-B494 (3)	21.40	12.00

Surtax for the reconstruction fund of the UNESCO.

Monument to Political Prisoners — SP269

Fort of Breendonk SP270

8fr+4fr, Monument: profile of figure on pedestal.

1951, Aug. 20 Photo. *Perf. 11½*

B495	SP269	1.75fr + 25c blk brn	2.50	1.75
B496	SP270	4fr + 2fr bl & sl gray	17.00	14.00
B497	SP269	8fr + 4fr dk bl grn	22.50	17.00
		Nos. B495-B497 (3)	42.00	32.75

The surtax was for the erection of a national monument.

Queen Elisabeth — SP271

1951, Sept. 22

B498	SP271	90c + 10c grnsh gray	1.75	.75
B499	SP271	1.75fr + 25c plum	2.25	1.50
B500	SP271	3fr + 1fr green	21.00	9.25
B501	SP271	4fr + 2fr gray bl	24.00	12.00
B502	SP271	8fr + 4fr sepia	30.00	14.00
		Nos. B498-B502 (5)	79.00	37.50

The surtax was for the Queen Elisabeth Medical Foundation.

Cross, Sun Rays and Dragon — SP272

Beersel Castle SP273

Horst Castle — SP274

Castles: 4fr+2fr, Lavaux St. Anne. 8fr+4fr, Veves.

1951, Dec. 17 Engr. Unwmk.

B503	SP272	20c + 5c red	.25	.20
B504	SP272	65c + 10c dp ultra	.85	.60
B505	SP272	90c + 10c sep	.90	.80
B506	SP272	1.20fr + 30c rose vio	1.25	.90
B507	SP273	1.75fr + 75c red brn	1.75	1.50
B508	SP274	3fr + 1fr yel grn	12.00	7.50
B509	SP273	4fr + 2fr blue	14.00	8.50
B510	SP274	8fr + 4fr gray	19.00	11.00
		Nos. B503-B510 (8)	50.00	31.00

The surtax was for anti-tuberculosis work.

See Nos. B523-B526, B547-B550.

Main Altar SP275

Basilica of the Sacred Heart Koekelberg SP276

Procession Bearing Relics of St. Albert of Louvain — SP277

1952, Mar. 1 Photo. *Perf. 11½*

B511	SP275	1.75fr + 25c blk brn	1.50	1.25
B512	SP276	4fr + 2fr indigo	11.00	7.50

Engr.

B513	SP277	8fr + 4fr vio brn	15.00	9.25
a.		Souv. sheet, #B511-B513	250.00	125.00
		Nos. B511-B513 (3)	27.50	18.00

25th anniv. of the Cardinalate of J. E. Van Roey, Primate of Belgium. The surtax was for the Basilica. No. B513a sold for 30fr.

Beaulieu Castle, Malines SP278

August Vermeylen SP279

1952, May 14 **Engr.**

Laid Paper

B514 SP278 40fr + 10fr lt grnsh bl 175.00 175.00

Issued on the occasion of the 13th Universal Postal Union Congress, Brussels, 1952.

Perf. 11½

1952, Oct. 24 **Unwmk.** **Photo.**

Portraits: 80c+40c, Karel Van de Woestijne. 90c+45c, Charles de Coster. 1.75fr+75c, M. Maeterlinck. 4fr+2fr, Emile Verhaeren. 8fr+4fr, Hendrik Conscience.

B515 SP279 65c + 30c pur 1.75 .90
B516 SP279 80c + 40c dk grn 3.75 1.10
B517 SP279 90c + 45c sepia 2.75 1.25
B518 SP279 1.75fr + 75c cer 3.75 1.75
B519 SP279 4fr + 2fr bl vio 30.00 19.00
B520 SP279 8fr + 4fr dk brn 30.00 21.00
Nos. B515-B520 (6) 72.00 45.00

1952, Nov. 15

4fr, Emile Verhaeren. 8fr, Hendrik Conscience.

B521 SP279 4fr (+ 9fr) blue 100.00 67.50
B522 SP279 8fr (+ 9fr) dk car rose 100.00 67.50

On Nos. B521-B522, the denomination is repeated at either side of the stamp. The surtax is expressed on se-tenant labels bearing quotations of Verhaeren (in French) and Conscience (in Flemish). Value is for stamp with label.

A 9-line black overprint was privately applied to these labels: "Conference Internationale de la Musique Bruxelles UNESCO International Music Conference Brussels 1953*" Value, $100.

Type of 1951 Dated "1952," and

Arms of Malmédy — SP281

Castle Ruins, Burgreuland SP282

Designs: 4fr+2fr, Vesdre Dam, Eupen. 8fr+4fr, St. Vitus, patron saint of Saint-Vith.

1952, Dec. 15 **Engr.**

B523 SP272 20c + 5c red brn .40 .40
B524 SP272 80c + 20c grn .85 .60
B525 SP272 1.20fr + 30c lil rose 1.75 1.00
B526 SP272 1.50fr + 50c ol brn 1.75 1.00
B527 SP281 2fr + 75c car 3.25 2.25
B528 SP282 3fr + 1.50fr choc 14.00 8.75
B529 SP281 4fr + 2fr blue 12.00 8.00
B530 SP281 8fr + 4fr vio brn 21.00 11.00
Nos. B523-B530 (8) 55.00 33.00

The surtax on Nos. B523-B530 was for anti-tuberculosis and other charitable works.

Walthère Dewé SP283

Princess Josephine-Charlotte SP284

1953, Feb. 16 **Photo.**

B531 SP283 2fr + 1fr brn car 3.25 1.75

The surtax was for the construction of a memorial to Walthère Dewé, Underground leader in World War II.

1953, Mar. 14 **Cross in Red**

B532 SP284 80c + 20c ol grn 1.25 .70
B533 SP284 1.20fr + 30c brn 1.75 .80
B534 SP284 2fr + 50c rose lake 1.25 1.25
a. Booklet pane of 8 80.00 65.00
B535 SP284 2.50fr + 50c crim 14.00 6.75
B536 SP284 4fr + 1fr brt blue 9.25 5.25
B537 SP284 5fr + 2fr sl grn 11.00 6.75
Nos. B532-B537 (6) 38.50 21.50

The surtax was for the Belgian Red Cross.

The selvage of No. B534a is inscribed in French. Value for selvage inscribed in Dutch, $150.

Boats at Dock SP285

Bridge and Citadel, Namur — SP286

Allegory — SP287

Designs: 1.20fr+30c, Bridge at Bouillon. 2fr+50c, Antwerp waterfront. 4fr+2fr, Wharf at Ghent. 8fr+4fr, Meuse River at Freyr.

1953, June 22 **Unwmk.** ***Perf. 11½***

B538 SP285 80c + 20c grn 1.00 .90
B539 SP285 1.20fr + 30c redsh brn 1.75 1.60
B540 SP285 2fr + 50c sep 2.25 2.00
B541 SP286 2.50fr + 50c dp mag 11.00 8.50
B542 SP286 4fr + 2fr vio bl 16.00 8.50
B543 SP286 8fr + 4fr gray blk 20.00 8.50
Nos. B538-B543 (6) 52.00 30.00

The surtax was used to promote tourism in the Ardenne-Meuse region and for various cultural works.

1953, Oct. 26 **Engr.**

B544 SP287 80c + 20c grn 3.50 2.50
B545 SP287 2.50fr + 1fr rose car 32.50 24.00
B546 SP287 4fr + 1.50fr blue 37.50 30.00
Nos. B544-B546 (3) 73.50 56.50

The surtax was for the European Bureau of Childhood and Youth.

Type of 1951 Dated "1953," and

Ernest Malvoz — SP288

Robert Koch SP289

Portraits: 3fr+1.50fr, Carlo Forlanini. 4fr+2fr, Leon Charles Albert Calmette.

1953, Dec. 15

B547 SP272 20c + 5c blue .50 .50
B548 SP272 80c + 20c rose vio 1.00 .60
B549 SP272 1.20fr + 30c choc 1.25 .80
B550 SP272 1.50fr + 50c dk gray 1.75 1.00
B551 SP288 2fr + 75c dk grn 3.00 1.60
B552 SP288 3fr + 1.50fr dk red 13.00 8.50
B553 SP288 4fr + 2fr ultra 11.00 7.00
B554 SP289 8fr + 4fr choc 17.50 10.00
Nos. B547-B554 (8) 49.00 30.00

The surtax was for anti-tuberculosis and other charitable works.

King Albert I Statue — SP290

Albert I Monument, Namur SP291

9fr+4.50fr, Cliffs of Marche-les-Dames.

1954, Feb. 17 **Photo.**

B555 SP290 2fr + 50c chnt brn 2.50 1.75
B556 SP291 4fr + 2fr blue 15.00 11.00
B557 SP290 9fr + 4.50fr ol blk 22.50 12.00
Nos. B555-B557 (3) 40.00 24.75

20th anniv. of the death of King Albert I. The surtax aided in the erection of the monument pictured on #B556.

Political Prisoners' Monument SP292

Camp and Fort, Breendonk SP293

Design: 9fr+4.50fr, Political prisoners' monument (profile).

1954, Apr. 1 **Unwmk.** ***Perf. 11½***

B558 SP292 2fr + 1fr red 12.50 7.00
B559 SP293 4fr + 2fr dk brn 30.00 17.50
B560 SP292 9fr + 4.50fr ol grn 32.50 17.50
Nos. B558-B560 (3) 75.00 42.00

The surtax was used toward the creation of a monument to political prisoners.

Gatehouse and Gateway SP294

Nuns in Courtyard SP295

Our Lady of the Vine SP296

2fr+1fr, Swans in stream. 7fr+3.50fr Nuns at well. 8fr+4fr, Statue above door.

1954, May 15

B561 SP294 80c + 20c dk bl grn 1.00 .75
B562 SP294 2fr + 1fr crim 11.00 1.50
B563 SP295 4fr + 2fr violet 16.00 9.25
B564 SP295 7fr + 3.50fr lil rose 35.00 22.50
B565 SP295 8fr + 4fr brown 32.50 19.00
B566 SP296 9fr + 4.50fr gray bl 55.00 30.00
Nos. B561-B566 (6) 150.50 83.00

The surtax was for the Friends of the Beguinage of Bruges.

Child's Head — SP297

"The Blind Man and the Paralytic," by Antoine Carte SP298

1954, Dec. 1 **Engr.**

B567 SP297 20c + 5c dk grn .50 .50
B568 SP297 80c + 20c dk gray 1.00 .90
B569 SP297 1.20fr + 30c org brn 1.50 1.00
B570 SP297 1.50fr + 50c pur 1.75 1.60
B571 SP298 2fr + 75c rose car 7.25 3.50
B572 SP298 4fr + 1fr brt blue 16.00 9.50
Nos. B567-B572 (6) 28.00 17.00

The surtax was for anti-tuberculosis work.

Ernest Solvay SP299

Jean-Jacques Dony — SP300

Portraits: 1.20fr+30c, Egide Walschaerts. 25fr+50c, Leo H. Baekeland. 3fr+1fr, Jean-Etienne Lenoir. 4fr+2fr, Emile Fourcault and Emile Gobbe.

Perf. 11½

1955, Oct. 22 Unwmk. Photo.

B573	SP299	20c + 5c brn & dk brn	.40	.35
B574	SP300	80c + 20c vio	1.00	.50
B575	SP299	1.20fr + 30c ind	1.10	.65
B576	SP300	2fr + 50c dp car	4.00	2.50
B577	SP300	3fr + 1fr dk grn	12.50	6.25
B578	SP299	4fr + 2fr brown	12.50	6.25
	Nos. B573-B578 (6)		31.50	16.50

Issued in honor of Belgian scientists.

The surtax was for the benefit of various cultural organizations.

"The Joys of Spring" by E. Canneel SP301

Einar Holböll SP302

Portraits: 4fr+2fr, John D. Rockefeller. 8fr+4fr, Sir Robert W. Philip.

1955, Dec. 5 Unwmk. *Perf. 11½*

B579	SP301	20c + 5c red lil	.70	.30
B580	SP301	80c + 20c green	1.00	.65
B581	SP301	1.20fr + 30c redsh brn	1.40	.80
B582	SP301	1.50fr + 50c vio bl	1.40	1.00
B583	SP302	2fr + 50c car	8.50	4.75
B584	SP302	4fr + 2fr ultra	17.50	10.00
B585	SP302	8fr + 4fr ol gray	21.00	12.50
	Nos. B579-B585 (7)		51.50	30.00

The surtax was for anti-tuberculosis work.

Palace of Charles of Lorraine — SP303

Queen Elisabeth and Sonata by Mozart — SP304

Design: 2fr+1fr, Mozart at age 7.

1956, Mar. 5 Engr.

B586	SP303	80c + 20c steel bl	1.00	1.00
B587	SP303	2fr + 1fr rose lake	4.25	3.00
B588	SP304	4fr + 2fr dull pur	6.75	3.75
	Nos. B586-B588 (3)		12.00	7.75

200th anniversary of the birth of Wolfgang Amadeus Mozart, composer.

The surtax was for the benefit of the Pro-Mozart Committee in Belgium.

Queen Elisabeth — SP305

1956, Aug. 16 Photo.

B589	SP305	80c + 20c slate grn	1.00	1.00
B590	SP305	2fr + 1fr deep plum	2.75	1.50
B591	SP305	4fr + 2fr brown	4.25	2.50
	Nos. B589-B591 (3)		8.00	5.00

Issued in honor of the 80th birthday of Queen Elisabeth. The surtax went to the Queen Elisabeth Foundation. See No. 659.

Ship with Cross — SP306

Infant on Scales SP307

Rehabilitation SP308

Design: 4fr+2fr, X-Ray examination.

1956, Dec. 17 Engr.

B592	SP306	20c + 5c redsh brn	.35	.30
B593	SP306	80c + 20c grn	.75	.60
B594	SP306	1.20fr + 30c dl lil	.90	.60
B595	SP306	1.5fr + 50c lt sl bl	.95	.90
B596	SP307	2fr + 50c ol grn	2.25	1.60
B597	SP307	4fr + 2fr dl pur	11.00	6.25
B598	SP308	8fr + 4fr dp car	11.00	7.25
	Nos. B592-B598 (7)		27.20	17.50

The surtax was for anti-tuberculosis work.

Charles Plisnier and Albrecht Rodenbach SP309

80c+20c, Emiel Vliebergh & Maurice Wilmotte. 1.20fr+30c, Paul Pastur & Julius Hoste. 2fr+50c, Lodewijk de Raet & Jules Destree. 3fr+1fr, Constantin Meunier & Constant Permeke. 4fr+2fr, Lieven Gevaert & Edouard Empain.

Perf. 11½

1957, June 8 Unwmk. Photo.

B599	SP309	20c + 5c brt vio	.40	.35
B600	SP309	80c + 20c lt red brn	.55	.35
B601	SP309	1.20f + 30c blk brn	.65	.60
B602	SP309	2fr + 50c claret	1.60	.95
B603	SP309	3fr + 1fr dk ol grn	2.25	1.75
B604	SP309	4fr + 2fr vio bl	3.25	2.50
	Nos. B599-B604 (6)		8.70	6.50

The surtax was for the benefit of various cultural organizations.

Dogs and Antarctic Camp SP310

1957, Oct. 18 Engr. *Perf. 11½*

B605	SP310	5fr + 2.50fr gray, org & vio brn	3.00	2.25
a.		Sheet of 4, #B605b	140.00	125.00
b.		Blue, slate & red brown	30.00	25.00

Surtax for Belgian Antarctic Expedition, 1957-58.

Gen. Patton's Grave and Flag SP311

Gen. George S. Patton, Jr. — SP312

Designs: 2.50fr+50c, Memorial, Bastogne. 3fr+1fr, Gen. Patton decorating Brig. Gen. Anthony C. McAuliffe. 6fr+3fr, Tanks of 1918 and 1944.

1957, Oct. 28 Photo.

Size: 36x25mm, 25x36mm

B606	SP311	1fr + 50c dk gray	1.25	.90
B607	SP311	2.50fr + 50c ol grn	1.75	1.50
B608	SP311	3fr + 1fr red brn	2.75	1.60
B609	SP312	5fr + 2.50fr grysh bl	6.25	5.00

Size: 53x35mm

B610	SP311	6fr + 3fr pale brn car	10.00	6.00
	Nos. B606-B610 (5)		22.00	15.00

The surtax was for the General Patton Memorial Committee and Patriotic Societies.

Adolphe Max — SP313

1957, Nov. 10 Engr.

B611	SP313	2.50fr + 1fr ultra	1.25	.75

18th anniversary of the death of Adolphe Max, mayor of Brussels. The surtax was for the national "Adolphe Max" fund.

"Chinels," Fosses SP314

"Op Signoorken," Malines SP315

Infanta Isabella Shooting Crossbow SP316

Legends: 1.50fr+50c, St. Remacle and the wolf. 2fr+1fr, Longman and the pea soup. 5fr+2fr, The Virgin with Inkwell, vert. 6fr+2.50fr, "Gilles" (clowns), Binche.

1957, Dec. 14 Engr. & Photo.

B612	SP314	30c + 20c	.20	.30
B613	SP315	1fr + 50c	.40	.30
B614	SP314	1.50fr + 50c	.80	.50
B615	SP315	2fr + 1fr	1.10	1.00
B616	SP316	2.50fr + 1fr	1.25	.90
B617	SP316	5fr + 2fr	3.25	2.25
B618	SP316	6fr + 2.50fr	4.50	3.25
	Nos. B612-B618 (7)		11.50	8.50

The surtax was for anti-tuberculosis work. See Nos. B631-B637.

Benelux Gate SP317

Designs: 1fr+50c, Civil Engineering Pavilion. 1.50fr+50c, Ruanda-Urundi Pavilion. 2.50fr+1fr, Belgium 1900. 3fr+1.50fr, Atomium. 5fr+3fr, Telexpo Pavilion.

Perf. 11½

1958, Apr. 15 Unwmk. Engr.

Size: 35½x24½mm

B619	SP317	30c + 20c multi	.20	.20
B620	SP317	1fr + 50c multi	.20	.20
B621	SP317	1.50fr + 50c multi	.25	.25
B622	SP317	2.50fr + 1fr multi	.45	.45
B623	SP317	3fr + 1.50fr multi	.90	.50

Size: 49x33mm

B624	SP317	5fr + 3fr multi	1.10	.50
	Nos. B619-B624 (6)		3.10	2.10

World's Fair, Brussels, Apr. 17-Oct. 19.

Marguerite van Eyck by Jan van Eyck — SP318

Christ Carrying Cross, by Hieronymus Bosch SP319

Paintings: 1.50fr+50c, St. Donatien, Jan Gossart. 2.50fr+1fr, Self-portrait, Lambert Lombard. 3fr+1.50fr, The Rower, James Ensor. 5fr+3fr, Henriette, Henri Evenepoel.

1958, Oct. 30 Photo. *Perf. 11½*

Various Frames in Ocher and Brown

B625	SP318	30c + 20c dk ol grn	.25	.30
B626	SP319	1fr + 50c mar	.75	.70
B627	SP318	1.50fr + 50c vio bl	1.00	.75
B628	SP318	2.50fr + 1fr dk brn	2.00	1.25
B629	SP319	3fr + 1.50fr dl red	2.75	2.00
B630	SP318	5fr + 3fr brt bl	5.25	5.00
	Nos. B625-B630 (6)		12.00	10.00

The surtax was for the benefit of various cultural organizations.

Type of 1957

Legends: 40c+10c, Elizabeth, Countess of Hoogstraten. 1fr+50c, Jean de Nivelles. 1.50fr+50c, St. Evermare play, Russon. 2fr+1fr, The Penitents of Furnes. 2.50fr+1fr, Manger and "Pax." 5fr+2fr, Sambre-Meuse procession. 6fr+2.50fr, Our Lady of Peace and "Pax," vert.

Engraved and Photogravure

1958, Dec. 6 Unwmk. Perf. 11½

No.	Type	Description	Unused	Used
B631	SP314	40c + 10c ultra & brt grn	.30	.20
B632	SP315	1fr + 50c gray brn & org	.40	.30
B633	SP315	1.50fr + 50c cl & brt grn	.60	.35
B634	SP314	2fr + 1fr brn & red	.70	.50
B635	SP316	2.50fr + 1fr vio brn & bl grn	2.50	1.90
B636	SP316	5fr + 2fr cl & bl	3.75	3.00
B637	SP316	6fr + 2.50fr bl & rose red	4.75	4.50
		Nos. B631-B637 (7)	13.00	10.75

The surtax was for anti-tuberculosis work.

"Europe of the Heart" SP320

1959, Feb. 25 Photo. Unwmk.

No.	Type	Description	Unused	Used
B638	SP320	1fr + 50c red lil	.55	.30
B639	SP320	2.50fr + 1fr dk grn	.95	.90
B640	SP320	5fr + 2.50fr dp brn	1.25	1.10
		Nos. B638-B640 (3)	2.75	2.30

The surtax was for aid for displaced persons.

Allegory of Blood Transfusion SP321

Henri Dunant and Battlefield at Solferino — SP322

Design: 2.50fr+1fr, 3fr+1.50fr, Red Cross, broken sword and drop of blood, horiz.

1959, June 10 Photo. Perf. 11½

No.	Type	Description	Unused	Used
B641	SP321	40c + 10c	.60	.30
B642	SP321	1fr + 50c	1.10	.45
B643	SP321	1.50fr + 50c	1.40	.60
B644	SP321	2.50fr + 1fr	1.90	1.10
B645	SP321	3fr + 1.50fr	4.75	2.50
B646	SP322	5fr + 3fr	7.25	3.25
		Nos. B641-B646 (6)	17.00	8.20

Cent. of the Intl. Red Cross idea. Surtax for the Red Cross and patriotic organizations.

Philip the Good — SP323

Arms of Philip the Good SP324

Designs: 1fr+50c, Charles the Bold. 1.50fr+50c, Emperor Maximilian of Austria. 2.50fr+1fr, Philip the Fair. 3fr+1.50fr, Charles V. Portraits from miniatures by Simon Bening (c. 1483-1561).

1959, July 4 Engr.

No.	Type	Description	Unused	Used
B647	SP323	40c + 10c multi	.50	.35
B648	SP323	1fr + 50c multi	.80	.50
B649	SP323	1.50fr + 50c multi	.95	.75
B650	SP323	2.50fr + 1fr multi	1.25	1.40
B651	SP323	3fr + 1.50fr multi	3.25	3.00
B652	SP324	5fr + 3fr multi	5.25	4.00
		Nos. B647-B652 (6)	12.00	10.00

The surtax was for the Royal Library, Brussels.

Portraits show Grand Masters of the Order of the Golden Fleece.

Whale, Antwerp SP325

Carnival, Stavelot SP326

Designs: 1fr+50c, Dragon, Mons. 2fr+50c, Prince Carnival, Eupen. 3fr+1fr, Jester and cats, Ypres. 6fr+2fr, Holy Family, horiz. 7fr+3fr, Madonna, Liége, horiz.

Engraved and Photogravure

1959, Dec. 5 Perf. 11½

No.	Type	Description	Unused	Used
B653	SP325	40c + 10c cit, Prus bl & red	.45	.40
B654	SP325	1fr + 50c ol & grn	.75	.60
B655	SP325	2fr + 50c lt brn, org & cl	.50	.40
B656	SP326	2.50fr + 1fr gray, pur & ultra	.80	.60
B657	SP326	3fr + 1fr gray, mar & yel	1.75	1.25
B658	SP326	6fr + 2fr ol, brt bl & hn brn	3.25	2.50
B659	SP326	7fr + 3fr chlky bl & org yel	5.00	4.25
		Nos. B653-B659 (7)	12.50	10.00

The surtax was for anti-tuberculosis work.

Child Refugee — SP327

Designs: 3fr+1.50fr, Man. 6fr+3fr, Woman.

1960, Apr. 7 Engr.

No.	Type	Description	Unused	Used
B660	SP327	40c + 10c rose claret	.20	.20
B661	SP327	3fr + 1.50fr gray brn	.65	.50
B662	SP327	6fr + 3fr dk bl	1.60	1.10
a.		Souvenir sheet of 3	50.00	45.00
		Nos. B660-B662 (3)	2.45	1.80

World Refugee Year, 7/1/59-6/30/60.

No. B662a contains Nos. B660-B662 with colors changed: 40c+10c, dull purple; 3fr+1.50fr, red brown; 6fr+3fr, henna brown.

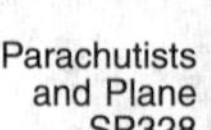

Parachutists and Plane SP328

Designs: 2fr+50c, 2.50fr+1fr, Parachutists coming in for landing, vert 3fr+1fr, 6fr+2fr, Parachutist walking with parachute.

Photogravure and Engraved

1960, June 13 Perf. 11½

Multicolored

No.	Type	Description	Unused	Used
B663	SP328	40c + 10c	.20	.20
B664	SP328	1fr + 50c	.80	.55
B665	SP328	2fr + 50c	2.75	1.25
B666	SP328	2.50fr + 1fr	3.00	2.00
B667	SP328	3fr + 1fr	3.00	2.00
B668	SP328	6fr + 2fr	6.25	4.00
		Nos. B663-B668 (6)	16.00	10.00

The surtax was for various patriotic and cultural organizations.

Mother and Child, Planes and Rainbow SP329

Designs: 40c+10c, Brussels Airport, planes and rainbow. 6fr+3fr, Rainbow connecting Congo and Belgium, and planes, vert

Perf. 11½

1960, Aug. 3 Unwmk. Photo.

Size: 35x24mm

No.	Type	Description	Unused	Used
B669	SP329	40c + 10c grnsh blue	.20	.20
B670	SP329	3fr + 1.50fr brt red	2.50	2.25

Size: 35x52mm

No.	Type	Description	Unused	Used
B671	SP329	6fr + 3fr violet	3.75	3.00
		Nos. B669-B671 (3)	6.45	5.45

The surtax was for refugees from Congo.

Infant, Milk Bottle and Mug — SP330

UNICEF: 1fr+50c, Nurse and children of 3 races. 2fr+50c, Refugee woman carrying gift clothes. 2.50fr+1fr, Negro nurse weighing infant. 3fr+1fr, Children of various races dancing. 6fr+2fr, Refugee boys.

Photogravure and Engraved

1960, Oct. 8 Perf. 11½

No.	Type	Description	Unused	Used
B672	SP330	40c + 10c gldn brn, yel & bl grn	.20	.20
B673	SP330	1fr + 50c ol gray, mar & slate	1.40	.75
B674	SP330	2fr + 50c vio, pale brn & brt grn	1.50	1.10
B675	SP330	2.50fr + 1fr dk red, sep & lt bl	1.75	1.40
B676	SP330	3fr + 1fr bl grn, red org & dl vio	.95	.85
B677	SP330	6fr + 2fr ultra, emer & brn	3.75	3.25
		Nos. B672-B677 (6)	9.55	7.55

Tapestry SP331

Belgian handicrafts: 1fr+50c, Cut crystal vases, vert. 2fr+50c, Lace, vert. 2.50fr+1fr, Metal plate & jug. 3fr+1fr, Diamonds. 6fr+2fr, Ceramics.

1960, Dec. 5 Perf. 11½

Multicolored

No.	Type	Description	Unused	Used
B678	SP331	40c + 10c	.25	.25
B679	SP331	1fr + 50c	1.00	1.00
B680	SP331	2fr + 50c	2.00	1.50
B681	SP331	2.50fr + 1fr	2.50	2.25
B682	SP331	3fr + 1fr	1.25	1.00
B683	SP331	6fr + 2fr	5.00	4.00
		Nos. B678-B683 (6)	12.00	10.00

The surtax was for anti-tuberculosis work.

Jacob Kats and Abbe Nicolas Pietkin SP332

Portraits: 1fr+50c, Albert Mockel and J. F. Willems. 2fr+50c, Jan van Rijswijck and Xavier M. Neujean. 2.50fr+1fr, Joseph Demarteau and A. Van de Perre. 3fr+1fr, Canon Jan-Baptist David and Albert du Bois. 6fr+2fr, Henri Vieuxtemps and Willem de Mol.

1961, Apr. 22 Unwmk. Perf. 11½

Multicolored

Portraits in Gray Brown

No.	Type	Description	Unused	Used
B684	SP332	40c + 10c	.25	.25
B685	SP332	1fr + 50c	1.50	1.00
B686	SP332	2fr + 50c	1.75	1.50
B687	SP332	2.50fr + 1fr	2.75	1.50
B688	SP332	3fr + 1fr	2.75	2.50
B689	SP332	6fr + 2fr	5.00	4.25
		Nos. B684-B689 (6)	14.00	11.00

The surtax was for the benefit of various cultural organizations.

White Rhinoceros SP333

Animals: 1fr+50c, Przewalski horses. 2fr+50c, Okapi. 2.50fr+1fr, Giraffe, horiz. 3fr+1fr, Lesser panda, horiz. 6fr+2fr, European elk, horiz.

Perf. 11½

1961, June 5 Unwmk. Photo.

Multicolored

No.	Type	Description	Unused	Used
B690	SP333	40c + 10c	.20	.25
B691	SP333	1fr + 50c	.90	.90
B692	SP333	2fr + 50c	1.40	1.25
B693	SP333	2.50fr + 1fr	1.10	1.10
B694	SP333	3fr + 1fr	1.00	1.00
B695	SP333	6fr + 2fr	2.25	1.50
		Nos. B690-B695 (6)	6.85	6.00

The surtax was for various philanthropic organizations.

Antonius Cardinal Perrenot de Granvelle — SP334

Designs: 3fr+1.50fr, Arms of Cardinal de Granvelle. 6fr+3fr, Tower and crosier, symbolic of collaboration between Malines and the Archbishopric.

1961, July 29 Engr.

No.	Type	Description	Unused	Used
B696	SP334	40c + 10c mag, car & brn	.20	.20
B697	SP334	3fr + 1.50fr multi	.65	.50
B698	SP334	6fr + 3fr mag pur & bis	1.25	1.10
		Nos. B696-B698 (3)	2.10	1.80

400th anniv. of Malines as an Archbishopric.

Mother and Child by Pierre Paulus — SP335

Plaintings: 1fr+50c, Mother Love, Francois-Joseph Navez. 2fr+50c, Motherhood, Constant Permeke. 2.50fr+1fr, Madonna and Child, Rogier van der Weyden. 3fr+1fr, Madonna with Apple, Hans Memling. 6fr+2fr, Madonna of the Forget-me-not, Peter Paul Rubens.

1961, Dec. 2 Photo. *Perf. 11½*

Gold Frame

B699	SP335	40c + 10c dp brn	.20	.20
B700	SP335	1fr + 50c brt bl	.40	.30
B701	SP335	2fr + 50c rose red	.60	.40
B702	SP335	2.50fr + 1fr mag	.85	.75
B703	SP335	3fr + 1fr vio bl	1.00	.85
B704	SP335	6fr + 2fr dk sl grn	1.75	1.50
		Nos. B699-B704 (6)	4.80	4.00

The surtax was for anti-tuberculosis work.

Castle of the Counts of Male — SP336

Designs: 90c+10c, Royal library, horiz. 1fr+50c, Church of Our Lady, Tongres. 2fr+50c, Collegiate Church, Soignies, horiz. 2.50fr+1fr, Church of Our Lady, Malines. 3fr+1fr, St. Denis Abbey, Broqueroi. 6fr+2fr, Cloth Hall, Ypres, horiz.

1962, Mar. 12 Engr. *Perf. 11½*

B705	SP336	40c + 10c brt grn	.20	.20
B706	SP336	90c + 10c lil rose	.20	.20
B707	SP336	1fr + 50c dl vio	.40	.45
B708	SP336	2fr + 50c violet	.70	.60
B709	SP336	2.50fr + 1fr red brn	1.00	.85
B710	SP336	3fr + 1fr bl grn	1.00	.85
B711	SP336	6fr + 2fr car rose	1.50	1.40
		Nos. B705-B711 (7)	5.00	4.55

The surtax was for various cultural and philanthropic organizations.

Andean Cock of the Rock — SP337

Birds: 1fr+50c, Red lory. 2fr+50c, Guinea touraco. 2.50fr+1fr, Keel-billed toucan. 3fr+1fr, Great bird of paradise. 6fr+2fr, Congolese peacock.

Engraved and Photogravure

1962, June 23 Unwmk. *Perf. 11½*

B712	SP337	40c + 10c multi	.20	.20
B713	SP337	1fr + 50c multi	.45	.25
B714	SP337	2fr + 50c multi	.50	.40
B715	SP337	2.50fr + 1fr multi	.55	.45
B716	SP337	3fr + 1fr multi	1.10	.95
B717	SP337	6fr + 2fr multi	2.00	1.75
		Nos. B712-B717 (6)	4.80	4.00

The surtax was for various philanthropic organizations.

Handicapped Child — SP338

Handicapped Children: 40c+10c, Reading Braille. 2fr+50c, Deaf-mute girl with earphones and electronic equipment, horiz. 2.50fr+1fr, Child with ball (cerebral palsy). 3fr+1fr, Girl with crutches (polio). 6fr+2fr, Sitting boys playing ball, horiz.

1962, Sept. 22 Photo.

B718	SP338	40c + 10c choc	.20	.20
B719	SP338	1fr + 50c rose red	.30	.30
B720	SP338	2fr + 50c brt lil	.55	.60
B721	SP338	2.50fr + 1fr dl grn	.65	.65
B722	SP338	3fr + 1fr dk blue	.80	.80
B723	SP338	6fr + 2fr dk brn	1.50	1.25
		Nos. B718-B723 (6)	4.00	3.80

The surtax was for various institutions for handicapped children.

Queen Louise-Marie SP339

Belgian Queens: No. B725, like No. B724 with "ML" initials. 1fr+50c, Marie-Henriette. 2fr+1fr, Elisabeth. 3fr+1.50fr, Astrid. 8fr+2.50fr, Fabiola.

1962, Dec. 8 Photo. & Engr.

Gray, Black & Gold

B724	SP339	40c + 10c ("L")	.20	.20
B725	SP339	40c + 10c ("ML")	.20	.20
B726	SP339	1fr + 50c	.50	.50
B727	SP339	2fr + 1fr	.85	.85
B728	SP339	3fr + 1.50fr	.95	.85
B729	SP339	8fr + 2.50fr	1.40	1.00
		Nos. B724-B729 (6)	4.10	3.60

The surtax was for anti-tuberculosis work.

British War Memorial (Porte de Menin), Ypres SP340

1962, Dec. 26 Engr. *Perf. 11½*

B730	SP340	1fr + 50c multi	.50	.50

Millennium of the city of Ypres. Issued in sheets of eight.

Peace Bell Ringing over Globe — SP341

Engraved and Photogravure

1963, Feb. 18 Unwmk. *Perf. 11½*

B731	SP341	3fr +1.50fr multi	1.50	1.50
a.		Sheet of 4	7.25	7.25
B732	SP341	6fr +3fr multi	.75	.75

The surtax was for the installation of the Peace Bell (Bourdon de la Paix) at Koekelberg Basilica and for the benefit of various cultural organizations.

#B731 was issued in sheets of 4, #B732 in sheets of 30.

The Sower by Brueghel — SP342

Designs: 3fr+1fr, The Harvest, by Brueghel, horiz. 6fr+2fr, "Bread," by Anton Carte, horiz.

1963, Mar. 21 *Perf. 11½*

B733	SP342	2fr +1fr multi	.20	.20
B734	SP342	3fr +1fr multi	.40	.30
B735	SP342	6fr +2fr multi	.55	.50
		Nos. B733-B735 (3)	1.15	1.00

FAO "Freedom from Hunger" campaign.

Speed Racing — SP343

2fr+1fr, Bicyclists at check point, horiz. 3fr+1.50fr, Team racing, horiz. 6fr+3fr, Pace setters.

Perf. 11½

1963, July 13 Unwmk. Engr.

B736	SP343	1fr + 50c multi	.20	.20
B737	SP343	2fr + 1fr bl, car, blk & ol gray	.20	.20
B738	SP343	3fr + 1.50fr multi	.35	.35
B739	SP343	6fr + 3fr multi	.50	.50
		Nos. B736-B739 (4)	1.25	1.25

80th anniversary of the founding of the Belgian Bicycle League. The surtax was for athletes at the 1964 Olympic Games.

Princess Paola with Princess Astrid — SP344

Prince Albert and Family — SP345

Designs: 40c+10c, Prince Philippe. 2fr+50c, Princess Astrid. 2.50fr+1fr, Princess Paola. 6fr+2fr, Prince Albert.

1963, Sept. 28 Photo.

B740	SP344	40c + 10c	.20	.20
B741	SP344	1fr + 50c	.35	.30
B742	SP344	2fr + 50c	.45	.40
B743	SP344	2.50fr + 1fr	.45	.40
B744	SP345	3fr + 1fr brn & multi	.45	.45
B745	SP345	3fr + 1fr yel grn & multi	1.50	1.40
a.		Booklet pane of 8	17.00	17.00
B746	SP344	6fr + 2fr	.90	.85
		Nos. B740-B746 (7)	4.30	4.00

Cent. of the Intl, Red Cross. No. B745 issued in booklet panes of 8, which are in two forms: French and Flemish inscriptions in top and bottom margins transposed. Value the same.

Daughter of Balthazar Gerbier, Painted by Rubens — SP346

Jesus, St. John and Cherubs by Rubens — SP347

Portraits (Rubens' sons): 1fr+40c, Nicolas, 2 yrs. old. 2fr+50c, Franz. 2.50fr+1fr, Nicolas, 6 yrs. old. 3fr+1fr, Albert.

Photogravure and Engraved

1963, Dec. 7 Unwmk. *Perf. 11½*

B747	SP346	50c + 10c	.20	.20
B748	SP346	1fr + 40c	.20	.20
B749	SP346	2fr + 50c	.20	.20
B750	SP346	2.50fr + 1fr	.45	.45
B751	SP346	3fr + 1fr	.35	.35
B752	SP347	6fr + 2fr	.45	.45
		Nos. B747-B752 (6)	1.85	1.85

The surtax was for anti-tuberculosis work. See No. B771.

John Quincy Adams and Lord Gambier Signing Treaty of Ghent, by Amédée Forestier — SP348

1964, May 16 Photo. *Perf. 11½*

B753	SP348	6fr + 3fr dk blue	.75	.75

Signing of the Treaty of Ghent between the US and Great Britain, Dec. 24, 1814.

Philip van Marnix — SP349

Portraits: 3fr+1.50fr, Ida de Bure Calvin. 6fr+3fr, Jacob Jordaens.

1964, May 30 Engr.

B754	SP349	1fr + 50c blue gray	.20	.20
B755	SP349	3fr + 1.50fr rose pink	.25	.25
B756	SP349	6fr + 3fr redsh brn	.45	.45
		Nos. B754-B756 (3)	.90	.90

Issued to honor Protestantism in Belgium. The surtax was for the erection of a Protestant church.

Foot Soldier, 1918 — SP350

Designs: 2fr+1fr, Flag bearer, Guides Regiment, 1914. 3fr+1.50fr, Trumpeter of the Grenadiers and drummers, 1914.

1964, Aug. 1 Photo. *Perf. 11½*

B757 SP350 1fr + 50c multi .20 .20
B758 SP350 2fr + 1fr multi .25 .25
B759 SP350 3fr + 1.50fr multi .25 .25
Nos. B757-B759 (3) .70 .70

50th anniversary of the German aggression against Belgium in 1914. The surtax aided patriotic undertakings.

Battle of Bastogne — SP351

6fr+3fr, Liberation of the estuary of the Escaut.

1964, Aug. 1 Unwmk.

B760 SP351 3fr + 1fr multi .20 .20
B761 SP351 6fr + 3fr multi .30 .30

Belgium's Resistance and liberation of World War II. The surtax was to help found an International Student Center at Antwerp and to aid cultural undertakings.

Souvenir Sheets

Rogier van der Weyden Paintings — SP352

Descent From the Cross — SP353

1964, Sept. 19 Photo. *Perf. 11½*

B762 SP352 Sheet of 3 2.25 2.25
a. 1fr Philip the Good .50 .50
b. 2fr Portrait of a Lady .50 .50
c. 3fr Man with Arrow .50 .50

Engr.

B763 SP353 8fr red brown 2.25 2.25

Rogier van der Weyden (Roger de La Pasture, 1400-64). The surtax went to various cultural organizations. #B762 sold for 14fr, #B763 for 16fr.

Ancient View of the Pand — SP354

3fr+1fr, Present view of the Pand from Lys River.

1964, Oct. 10 Photo.

B764 SP354 2fr + 1fr blk, grnsh bl & ultra .40 .40
B765 SP354 3fr + 1fr lil rose, bl & dk brn .40 .40

The surtax was for the restoration of the Pand Dominican Abbey in Ghent.

Type of 1963 and

Child of Charles I, Painted by Van Dyck — SP355

Designs: 1fr+40c, William of Orange with his bride, by Van Dyck. 2fr+1fr, Portrait of a small boy with dogs by Erasmus Quellin and Jan Fyt. 3fr+1fr, Alexander Farnese by Antonio Moro. 4fr+2fr, William II, Prince of Orange by Van Dyck. 6fr+3fr, Artist's children by Cornelis De Vos.

1964, Dec. 5 Engr. *Perf. 11½*

B766 SP355 50c + 10c rose claret .20 .20
B767 SP355 1fr + 40c car rose .20 .20
B768 SP355 2fr + 1fr vio brn .20 .20
B769 SP355 3fr + 1fr gray .20 .20
B770 SP355 4fr + 2fr vio bl .25 .25
B771 SP347 6fr + 3fr brt pur .25 .25
Nos. B766-B771 (6) 1.30 1.30

The surtax was for anti-tuberculosis work.

Liberator, Shaking Prisoner's Hand, Concentration Camp — SP356

Designs: 1fr+50c, Prisoner's hand reaching for the sun. 3fr+1.50fr, Searchlights and tank breaking down barbed wire, horiz. 8fr+5fr, Rose growing amid the ruins, horiz.

Engraved and Photogravure

1965, May 8 Unwmk. *Perf. 11½*

B772 SP356 50c + 50c tan, blk & buff .20 .20
B773 SP356 1fr + 50c multi .20 .20
B774 SP356 3fr + 1.50fr dl lil & blk .25 .25
B775 SP356 8fr + 5fr multi .35 .35
Nos. B772-B775 (4) 1.00 1.00

20th anniv. of the liberation of the concentration camps for political prisoners and prisoners of war.

Stoclet House, Brussels SP357

Stoclet House: 6fr+3fr, Hall with marble foundation, vert. 8fr+4fr, View of house from garden.

1965, June 21

B776 SP357 3fr + 1fr slate & tan .25 .25
B777 SP357 6fr + 3fr sepia .30 .30
B778 SP357 8fr + 4fr vio brn & tan .45 .45
Nos. B776-B778 (3) 1.00 1.00

Austrian architect Josef Hoffmann (1870-1956), builder of the art nouveau residence of Adolphe Stoclet, engineer and financier.

Jackson's Chameleon SP358

Animals from Antwerp Zoo: 2fr+1fr, Common iguanas. 3fr+1.50fr, African monitor. 6fr+3fr, Komodo monitor. 8fr+4fr, Nile softshell turtle.

1965, Oct. 16 Photo. *Perf. 11½*

B779 SP358 1fr + 50c multi .20 .20
B780 SP358 2fr + 1fr multi .20 .20
B781 SP358 3fr + 1.50fr multi .25 .25
B782 SP358 6fr + 3fr multi .45 .45
Nos. B779-B782 (4) 1.10 1.10

Miniature Sheet

B783 SP358 8fr + 4fr multi 1.75 1.75

The surtax was for various cultural and philanthropic organizations. No. B783 contains one stamp, size: 52x35mm.

Boatmen's and Archers' Guild Halls SP359

Buildings on Grand-Place, Brussels: 1fr+40c, Brewers' Hall. 2fr+1fr, "King of Spain." 3fr+1.50fr, "Dukes of Brabant." 10fr+4.50fr, Tower of City Hall and St. Michael.

1965, Dec. 4 Engr. *Perf. 11½*

Size: 35x24mm

B784 SP359 50c + 10c ultra .20 .20
B785 SP359 1fr + 40c bl grn .20 .20
B786 SP359 2fr + 1fr rose cl .20 .20
B787 SP359 3fr + 1.50fr violet .20 .20

Size: 24x44mm

B788 SP359 10fr + 4.50fr sep & gray .30 .30
Nos. B784-B788 (5) 1.10 1.10

The surtax was for anti-tuberculosis work.

Souvenir Sheets

Queen Elisabeth — SP360

Design: No. B790, Types of 1931 and 1956.

1966, Apr. 16 Photo. *Perf. 11½*

B789 SP360 Sheet of 2 + label 1.50 1.50
a. SP74 3fr dk brn & gray grn .60 .60
b. SP87 3fr dk brn, yel grn & gold .60 .60
B790 SP360 Sheet of 2 + label 1.50 1.50
a. SP42 3fr dk brn & dl bl .60 .60
b. SP304 3fr dk brn & gray .60 .60

The surtax went to various cultural organizations.

Each sheet sold for 20fr.

Luminescent Paper

was used in printing Nos. B789-B790, B801-B806, B808-B809, B811-B823, B825-B831, B833-B835, B837-B840, B842-B846, B848-B850, B852-B854, B856-B863, and from B865 onward unless otherwise noted. In many cases the low value of the set is not on luminescent paper. This will not be noted.

Diver — SP361

Design: 10fr+4fr, Swimmer at start.

1966, May 9 Engr.

B791 SP361 60c + 40c Prus grn, ol & org brn .20 .20
B792 SP361 10fr + 4fr ol grn, org brn & mag .40 .40

Issued to publicize the importance of swimming instruction.

Minorites' Convent, Liège — SP362

Designs: 1fr+50c, Val-Dieu Abbey, Aubel. 2fr+1fr, View and seal of Huy. 10fr+4.50fr, Statue of Ambiorix by Jules Bertin, and tower, Tongeren.

1966, Aug. 27 Engr. *Perf. 11½*

B793 SP362 60c + 40c multi .20 .20
B794 SP362 1fr + 50c multi .20 .20
B795 SP362 2fr + 1fr multi .20 .20
B796 SP362 10fr + 4.50fr multi .40 .40
Nos. B793-B796 (4) 1.00 1.00

The surtax was for various patriotic and cultural organizations.

Surveyor and Dog Team SP363

3fr+1.50fr, Adrien de Gerlache, "Belgica." 6fr+3fr, Surveyor, weather balloon, ship. 10fr+5fr, Penguins, "Magga Dan" (ship used for 1964, 1965 & 1966 expeditions).

1966, Oct. 8 Engr. *Perf. 11½*

B797 SP363 1fr + 50c bl grn .20 .20
B798 SP363 3fr + 1.50fr pale vio .20 .20
B799 SP363 6fr + 3fr dk car .35 .35
Nos. B797-B799 (3) .75 .75

Souvenir Sheet

Engraved and Photogravure

B800 SP363 10fr + 5fr dk gray, sky bl & dk red .70 .70

Belgian Antarctic expeditions. #B800 contains one 52x35mm stamp.

Boy with Ball and Dog — SP364

Designs: 2fr+1fr, Girl skipping rope. 3fr+1.50fr, Girl and boy blowing soap bubbles. 6fr+3fr, Girl and boy rolling hoops, horiz. 8fr+3.50fr, Four children at play and cat, horiz.

1966, Dec. 3 *Perf. 11½*

B801 SP364 1fr + 1fr pink & blk .20 .20
B802 SP364 2fr + 1fr lt bluish grn & blk .20 .20
B803 SP364 3fr + 1.50fr lt vio & blk .20 .20
B804 SP364 6fr + 3fr pale sal & dk brn .25 .25
B805 SP364 8fr + 3.50fr lt yel grn & dk brn .30 .30
Nos. B801-B805 (5) 1.15 1.15

The surtax was for anti-tuberculosis work.

Souvenir Sheet

Refugees — SP365

1fr, Boy receiving clothes. 2fr, Tibetan children. 3fr, African mother and children.

1967, Mar. 11 Photo. *Perf. 11½*

B806 SP365 Sheet of 3	1.25	1.25
a. 1fr black & yellow	.30	.30
b. 2fr black & blue	.30	.30
c. 3fr black & orange	.40	.40

Issued to help refugees around the world. Sheet has black border with Belgian P.T.T. and UN Refugee emblems. Sold for 20fr.

Robert Schuman SP366

Colonial Brotherhood Emblem SP368

Kongolo Memorial, Gentinnes SP367

1967, June 24 Engr. *Perf. 11½*

B807 SP366 2fr + 1fr gray blue .25 .25

Engraved and Photogravure

B808 SP367 5fr + 2fr brn & olive .30 .30
B809 SP368 10fr + 5fr multi .45 .35

Robert Schuman (1886-1963), French statesman, one of the founders of European Steel and Coal Community, 1st pres. of European Parliament (2fr+1fr); Kongolo Memorial, erected in memory of missionary and civilian victims in the Congo (5fr+2fr); a memorial for African Troops, Brussels (10fr+5fr).

Preaching Fool from "Praise of Folly" by Erasmus SP369

Erasmus, by Quentin Massys SP370

Designs: 2fr+1fr, Exhorting Fool from Praise of Folly. 5fr+2fr, Thomas More's Family, by Hans Holbein, horiz. 6fr+3fr, Pierre Gilles (Aegidius), by Quentin Massys.

Photogravure and Engraved (SP369); Photogravure (SP370)

1967, Sept. 2 Unwmk. *Perf. 11*

B810 SP369 1fr + 50c tan, blk, bl & car .20 .20
B811 SP369 2fr + 1fr tan, blk & car .20 .20
B812 SP370 3fr + 1.50fr multi .20 .20
B813 SP369 5fr + 2fr tan, blk & car .20 .20
B814 SP370 6fr + 3fr multi .20 .20
Nos. B810-B814 (5) 1.00 1.00

Issued to commemorate Erasmus (1466(?)-1536), Dutch scholar and his era.

Souvenir Sheet

Pro-Post Association Emblem — SP371

Engraved and Photogravure

1967, Oct. 21 *Perf. 11½*

B815 SP371 10fr + 5fr multi .75 .75

Issued to publicize the POSTPHILA Philatelic Exhibition, Brussels, Oct. 21-29.

Detail from Brueghel's "Children's Games" SP372

Designs: Various Children's Games. Singles of Nos. B816-B821 arranged in 2 rows of 3 show complete painting by Pieter Brueghel.

1967, Dec. 9 Photo. *Perf. 11½*

B816 SP372 1fr + 50c multi .20 .20
B817 SP372 2fr + 50c multi .20 .20
B818 SP372 3fr + 1fr multi .20 .20
B819 SP372 6fr + 3fr multi .30 .30
B820 SP372 10fr + 4fr multi .40 .40
B821 SP372 13fr + 6fr multi .60 .60
Nos. B816-B821 (6) 1.90 1.90

Queen Fabiola Holding Refugee Child from Congo — SP373

6fr+3fr, Queen Elisabeth & Dr. Depage.

1968, Apr. 27 Photo. *Perf. 11½*

Cross in Red

B822 SP373 6fr + 3fr sepia & gray .25 .25
B823 SP373 10fr + 5fr sepia & gray .45 .45

The surtax was for the Red Cross.

Woman Gymnast and Calendar Stone SP374

Yachting and "The Swimmer" by Andrien — SP375

Designs: 2fr+1fr, Weight lifter and Mayan motif. 3fr+1.50fr, Hurdler, colossus of Tula and animal head from Kukulkan. 6fr+2fr, Bicyclists and Chichen Itza Temple.

Engraved and Photogravure

1968, May 27 *Perf. 11½*

B824 SP374 1fr + 50c multi .20 .20
B825 SP374 2fr + 1fr multi .20 .20
B826 SP374 3fr + 1.50fr multi .20 .20
B827 SP374 6fr + 2fr multi .25 .25

Photo.

B828 SP375 13fr + 5fr multi .50 .50
Nos. B824-B828 (5) 1.35 1.35

Issued to publicize the 19th Olympic Games, Mexico City, Oct. 12-27.

"Explosion" SP376

Designs (Paintings by Pol Mara): 12fr+5fr, "Fire." 13fr+5fr, "Tornado."

1968, June 22 Photo.

B829 SP376 10fr + 5fr multi .40 .40
B830 SP376 12fr + 5fr multi .65 .65
B831 SP376 13fr + 5fr multi .70 .70
Nos. B829-B831 (3) 1.75 1.75

The surtax was for disaster victims.

Undulate Triggerfish SP377

Tropical Fish: 3fr+1.50fr, Angelfish. 6fr+3fr, Turkeyfish (Pterois volitans). 10fr+5fr, Orange butterflyfish.

1968, Oct. 19 Engr. & Photo.

B832 SP377 1fr + 50c multi .20 .20
B833 SP377 3fr + 1.50fr multi .20 .20
B834 SP377 6fr + 3fr multi .30 .30
B835 SP377 10fr + 5fr multi .40 .40
Nos. B832-B835 (4) 1.10 1.10

King Albert and Queen Elisabeth Entering Brussels SP378

Tomb of the Unknown Soldier and Eternal Flame, Brussels — SP379

Designs: 1fr+50c, King Albert, Queen Elisabeth and Crown Prince Leopold on balcony, Bruges, vert. 6fr+3fr, King and Queen entering Liège.

1968, Nov. 9 Photo. *Perf. 11½*

B836 SP378 1fr + 50c multi .20 .20
B837 SP378 3fr + 1.50fr multi .20 .20
B838 SP378 6fr + 3fr multi .30 .30

Engraved and Photogravure

B839 SP379 10fr + 5fr multi .40 .40
Nos. B836-B839 (4) 1.10 1.10

50th anniv. of the victory in World War I.

Souvenir Sheet

The Painter and the Amateur, by Peter Brueghel — SP380

1969, May 10 Engr. *Perf. 11½*

B840 SP380 10fr + 5fr sepia 1.10 1.10

Issued to publicize the POSTPHILA 1969 Philatelic Exhibition, Brussels, May 10-18.

Huts, by Ivanka D. Pancheva, Bulgaria — SP381

Children's Drawings and UNICEF Emblem: 3fr+1.50fr, "My Art" (Santa Claus), by Claes Patric, Belgium. 6fr+3fr, "In the Sun" (young boy), by Helena Rejchlova, Czechoslovakia. 10fr+5fr, "Out for a Walk" by Phillis Sporn, US, horiz.

1969, May 31 Photo. *Perf. 11½*

B841 SP381 1fr + 50c multi .20 .20
B842 SP381 3fr + 1.50fr multi .20 .20
B843 SP381 6fr + 3fr multi .35 .35
B844 SP381 10fr + 5fr multi .50 .50
Nos. B841-B844 (4) 1.25 1.25

The surtax was for philanthropic purposes.

Msgr. Victor Scheppers SP382

1969, July 5 Engr.

B845 SP382 6fr + 3fr rose claret .45 .45

Msgr. Victor Scheppers (1802-77), prison reformer and founder of the Brothers of Mechlin (Scheppers).

Moon Landing Type of 1969

Souvenir Sheet

Design: 20fr+10fr, Armstrong, Collins and Aldrin and moon with Tranquillity Base, vert.

1969, Sept. 20 Photo. *Perf. 11½*

B846 A245 20fr + 10fr indigo 3.00 3.00

See note after No. 726.

Heads from Alexander the Great Tapestry, 15th Century — SP383

Designs from Tapestries: 3fr+1.50fr, Fiddler from "The Feast," c. 1700. 10fr+4fr, Head of beggar from "The Healing of the Paralytic," 16th century.

1969, Sept. 20

B847	SP383	1fr + 50c multi	.20	.20
B848	SP383	3fr + 1.50fr multi	.20	.20
B849	SP383	10fr + 4fr multi	.45	.45
		Nos. B847-B849 (3)	.85	.85

The surtax was for philanthropic purposes.

Bearded Antwerp Bantam SP384

1969, Nov. 8 Engr. & Photo.

B850	SP384	10fr + 5fr multi	.70	.70

Angel Playing Lute — SP385

Designs from Stained Glass Windows: 1.50fr+50c, Angel with trumpet, St. Waudru's, Mons. 7fr+3fr, Angel with viol, St. Jacques', Liege. 9fr+4fr, King with bagpipes, Royal Art Museum, Brussels.

1969, Dec. 13 Photo.

Size: 24x35mm

B851	SP385	1.50fr + 50c multi	.20	.20
B852	SP385	3.50fr + 1.50fr multi	.20	.20
B853	SP385	7fr + 3fr multi	.35	.35

Size: 35x52mm

B854	SP386	9fr + 4fr multi	.50	.50
		Nos. B851-B854 (4)	1.25	1.25

The surtax was for philanthropic purposes.

Farm and Windmill, Open-air Museum, Bokrijk SP386

Belgian Museums: 3.50fr+1.50fr, Stage Coach Inn, Courcelles. 7fr+3fr, "The Thresher of Trevires," Gallo-Roman sculpture, Gaumais Museum, Virton. 9fr+4fr, "The Sovereigns," by Henry Moore, Middelheim Museum, Antwerp.

Engraved and Photogravure

1970, May 30 ***Perf. 11½***

B855	SP386	1.50fr + 50c multi	.20	.20
B856	SP386	3.50fr + 1.50fr multi	.25	.25
B857	SP386	7fr + 3fr multi	.35	.35
B858	SP386	9fr + 4fr multi	.40	.40
		Nos. B855-B858 (4)	1.20	1.20

The surtax went to various culture organizations.

"Resistance" SP387

Design: 7fr+3fr, "Liberation of Camps." The designs were originally used as book covers.

1970, July 4 Photo. ***Perf. 11½***

B859	SP387	3.50fr + 1.50fr blk, gray grn & dp car	.20	.20
B860	SP387	7fr + 3fr blk, lil & dp car	.40	.40

Honoring the Resistance Movement and 25th anniv. of the liberation of concentration camps.

Fishing Rod and Reel SP388

Design: 9fr+4fr, Hockey stick and puck, vert.

1970, Sept. 19 Engr. & Photo.

B861	SP388	3.50fr + 1.50fr multi	.30	.30
B862	SP388	9fr + 4fr multi	.50	.50

Souvenir Sheet

Belgium Nos. 31, 36, 39 — SP389

1970, Oct. 10 ***Perf. 11½***

B863	SP389	Sheet of 3	4.75	4.75
	a.	1.50fr + 50c black & dull lilac	1.40	1.40
	b.	3.50fr + 1.50fr black & lilac	1.40	1.40
	c.	9fr + 4fr black & red brown	1.40	1.40

BELGICA 72 International Philatelic Exhibition, Brussels, June 24-July 9.

Camille Huysmans (1871-1968) SP390

3.50fr+1.50fr, Joseph Cardinal Cardijn (1882-1967). 7fr+3fr, Maria Baers (1883-1959). 9fr+4fr, Paul Pastur (1866-1938).

1970, Nov. 14 ***Perf. 11½***

Portraits in Sepia

B864	SP390	1.50fr + 50c car rose	.20	.20
B865	SP390	3.50fr + 1.50fr lilac	.20	.20
B866	SP390	7fr + 3fr green	.40	.40
B867	SP390	9fr + 4fr blue	.50	.50
		Nos. B864-B867 (4)	1.30	1.30

"Anxious City" (Detail) by Paul Delvaux — SP391

7fr+3fr, "The Memory," by Rene Magritte.

1970, Dec. 12 Photo.

B868	SP391	3.50fr + 1.50fr multi	.20	.20
B869	SP391	7fr + 3fr multi	.40	.40

Notre Dame du Vivier, Marche-les-Dames — SP392

7fr+3fr, Turnhout Beguinage and Beguine.

1971, Mar. 13 ***Perf. 11½***

B870	SP392	3.50fr + 1.50fr multi	.20	.20
B871	SP392	7fr + 3fr multi	.40	.40

The surtax was for philanthropic purposes.

Red Cross — SP393

1971, May 22 Photo. ***Perf. 11½***

B872	SP393	10fr + 5fr crim & blk	.75	.75

Belgian Red Cross.

Discobolus and Munich Cathedral — SP394

1971, June 19 Engr. & Photo.

B873	SP394	7fr + 3fr bl & blk	.40	.40

Publicity for the 20th Summer Olympic Games, Munich 1972.

Festival of Flanders — SP395

1971, Sept. 11 Photo. ***Perf. 11½***

Design: 7fr+3fr, Wallonia Festival.

B874	SP395	3.50fr + 1.50fr multi	.20	.20
B875	SP395	7fr + 3fr multi	.40	.40

Attre Palace — SP396

Steen Palace, Elewijt — SP397

Design: 10fr+5fr, Royal Palace, Brussels.

1971, Oct. 23 Engr.

B876	SP396	3.50fr + 1.50fr sl grn	.30	.30
B877	SP397	7fr + 3fr red brn	.50	.50
B878	SP396	10fr + 5fr vio bl	.70	.70
		Nos. B876-B878 (3)	1.50	1.50

Surtax was for BELGICA 72, International Philatelic Exposition.

Ox Fly, tabanus bromius SP398

Insects: 1.50fr+50c, Luna moth, vert. 7fr+3fr, Wasp, polistes gallicus. 9fr+4fr, Tiger beetle, vert.

1971, Dec. 11 Photo. ***Perf. 11½***

B879	SP398	1.50fr + 50c multi	.20	.20
B880	SP398	3.50fr + 1.50fr multi	.20	.20
B881	SP398	7fr + 3fr multi	.40	.40
B882	SP398	9fr + 4fr multi	.60	.60
		Nos. B879-B882 (4)	1.40	1.40

Surtax was for philanthropic purposes.

Leopold I on #1 — SP399

2fr+1fr, Leopold I on #5. 2.50fr+1fr, Leopold II on #45. 3.50fr+1.50fr, Leopold II on #48. 6fr+3fr, Albert I on #135. 7fr+3fr, Albert I on #214. 10fr+5fr, Albert I on #231. 15fr+7.50fr, Leopold III on #290. 20fr+10fr, King Baudouin on #718.

Engraved and Photogravure

1972, June 24 ***Perf. 11½***

B883	SP399	1.50fr + 50c	.20	.20
B884	SP399	2fr + 1fr	.20	.20
B885	SP399	2.50 + 1fr	.20	.20
B886	SP399	3.50fr + 1.50fr	.30	.30
B887	SP399	6fr + 3fr	.50	.50
B888	SP399	7fr + 3fr	.70	.70
B889	SP399	10fr + 5fr	.90	.90
B890	SP399	15fr + 7fr	1.10	1.10
B891	SP399	20fr + 10fr	2.00	2.00
		Nos. B883-B891 (9)	6.10	6.10

Belgica 72, Intl. Philatelic Exhibition, Brussels, June 24-July 9. Nos. B883-B891 issued in sheets of 10 and of 20 (2 tete beche sheets with gutter between). Sold in complete sets.

Epilepsy Emblem — SP400

1972, Sept. 9 Photo. ***Perf. 11½***

B892	SP400	10fr + 5fr multi	.55	.55

The surtax was for the William Lennox Center for epilepsy research and treatment.

Gray Lag Goose — SP401

Designs: 4.50fr+2fr, Lapwing. 8fr+4fr, Stork. 9fr+4.50fr, Kestrel, horiz.

1972, Dec. 16 Photo. *Perf. 11½*

B893	SP401	2fr + 1fr multi	.25	.25
B894	SP401	4.50fr + 2fr multi	.30	.30
B895	SP401	8fr + 4fr multi	.60	.60
B896	SP401	9fr + 4.50fr multi	.60	.60
		Nos. B893-B896 (4)	1.75	1.75

Bijloke Abbey, Ghent — SP402

4.50fr+2fr, St. Ursmer Collegiate Church, Lobbes. 8fr+4fr, Park Abbey, Heverle. 9fr+4.50fr, Abbey, Floreffe.

1973, Mar. 24 Engr. *Perf. 11½*

B897	SP402	2fr + 1fr sl grn	.20	.20
B898	SP402	4.50fr + 2fr brown	.25	.25
B899	SP402	8fr + 4fr rose lil	.50	.50
B900	SP402	9fr + 4.50fr brt bl	.60	.60
		Nos. B897-B900 (4)	1.55	1.55

Basketball SP403

1973, Apr. 7 Photo. & Engr.

B901	SP403	10fr + 5fr multi	.60	.60

First World Basketball Championships of the Handicapped, Bruges, Apr. 16-21.

Dirk Martens' Printing Press — SP404

Lady Talbot, by Petrus Christus — SP405

Hadrian and Marcus Aurelius Coins SP406

Council of Malines, by Coussaert — SP407

Designs: 3.50fr+1.50fr, Head of Amon and Tutankhamen's cartouche. 10fr+5fr, Three-master of Ostend Merchant Company.

Photogravure and Engraved; Photogravure (#B906)

1973, June 23 *Perf. 11½*

B902	SP404	2fr + 1fr multi	.20	.20
B903	SP404	3.50fr + 1.50fr multi	.20	.20
B904	SP405	4.50fr + 2fr multi	.20	.20
B905	SP406	8fr + 4fr multi	.60	.60
B906	SP407	9fr + 4.50fr multi	.85	.85
B907	SP407	10fr + 5fr multi	1.50	1.50
		Nos. B902-B907 (6)	3.55	3.55

500th anniv. of 1st book printed in Belgium (#B902); 50th anniv. of Queen Elisabeth Egyptological Foundation (#B903); 500th anniv. of death of painter Petrus Christus (#B904); Discovery of Roman treasure at Luttre-Liberchies (#B905); 500th anniv. of Great Council of Malines (#B906); 250th anniv. of the Ostend Merchant Company (#B907).

No. B902 is not luminescent.

Queen of Hearts — SP408

Old Playing Cards: #B909, King of Clubs. #B910, Jack of Diamonds. #B911, King of Spades.

1973, Dec. 8 Photo. *Perf. 11½*

B908	SP408	5fr + 2.50fr multi	.40	.40
B909	SP408	5fr + 2.50fr multi	.40	.40
B910	SP408	5fr + 2.50fr multi	.40	.40
B911	SP408	5fr + 2.50fr multi	.40	.40
a.		Strip of 4, #B908-B911	1.60	1.60

Surtax was for philanthropic purposes.

Symbol of Blood Donations SP409

Design: 10fr+5fr, Traffic lights, Red Cross (symbolic of road accidents).

1974, Feb. 23 Photo. *Perf. 11½*

B912	SP409	4fr + 2fr multi	.25	.25
B913	SP409	10fr + 5fr multi	.55	.55

The Red Cross as blood collector and aid to accident victims.

Armand Jamar, Self-portrait SP410

Designs: 5fr+2.50fr, Anton Bergmann and view of Lierre. 7fr+3.50fr, Henri Vieuxtemps and view of Verviers. 10fr+5fr, James Ensor, self-portrait, and masks.

1974, Apr. 6 Photo. *Perf. 11½*

Size: 24x35mm

B914	SP410	4fr + 2fr multi	.25	.25
B915	SP410	5fr + 2.50fr multi	.30	.30
B916	SP410	7fr + 3.50fr multi	.40	.40

Size: 35x52mm

B917	SP410	10fr + 5fr multi	.65	.65
		Nos. B914-B917 (4)	1.60	1.60

Van Gogh, Self-portrait and House at Cuesmes — SP411

1974, Sept. 21 Photo. *Perf. 11½*

B918	SP411	10fr + 5fr multi	.55	.55

Opening of Vincent van Gogh House at Cuesmes, where he worked as teacher.

Gentian — SP412

Spotted Cat's Ear — SP414

Badger SP413

Design: 7fr+3.50fr, Beetle.

1974, Dec. 8 Photo. *Perf. 11½*

B919	SP412	4fr + 2fr multi	.25	.25
B920	SP413	5fr + 2.50fr multi	.30	.30
B921	SP413	7fr + 3.50fr multi	.40	.40
B922	SP414	10fr + 5fr multi	.60	.60
		Nos. B919-B922 (4)	1.55	1.55

Pesaro Palace, Venice SP415

St. Bavon Abbey, Ghent SP416

Virgin and Child, by Michelangelo SP417

1975, Apr. 12 Engr. *Perf. 11½*

B923	SP415	6.50fr + 2.50fr brn	.35	.35
B924	SP416	10fr + 4.50 vio brn	.60	.60
B925	SP417	15fr + 6.50fr brt bl	.80	.80
		Nos. B923-B925 (3)	1.75	1.75

Surtax was for various cultural organizations.

Frans Hemerijckx and Leprosarium, Kasai — SP418

1975, Sept. 13 Photo. *Perf. 11½*

B926	SP418	20fr + 10fr multi	1.40	1.40

Dr. Frans Hemerijckx (1902-1969), tropical medicine and leprosy expert.

Emile Moyson SP419

Beheading of St. Dympna SP420a

Hand Reading Braille SP420

#B928, Dr. Ferdinand Augustin Snellaert.

1975, Nov. 22 Engr. *Perf. 11½*

B927	SP419	4.50fr + 2fr lilac	.25	.25
B928	SP419	6.50fr + 3fr green	.35	.35

Engraved and Photogravure

B929	SP420	10fr + 5fr multi	.50	.50

Photo.

B930	SP420a	13fr + 6fr multi	.70	.70
		Nos. B927-B930 (4)	1.80	1.80

Emile Moyson (1838-1868), freedom fighter for the rights of Flemings and Walloons; Dr. Snellaert (1809-1872), physician and Flemish patriot; Louis Braille (1809-1852), sesquicentennial of invention of Braille system of writing for the blind; St. Dympna, patron saint of Geel, famous for treatment of mentally ill.

The Cheese Vendor — SP421

Designs (THEMABELGA Emblem and): No. B932, Potato vendor. No. B933, Basket carrier. No. B934, Shrimp fisherman with horse, horiz. No. B935, Knife grinder, horiz. No. B936, Milk vendor with dog cart, horiz.

1975, Dec. 13 Engr. & Photo.

B931	SP421	4.50fr + 1.50fr multi	.20	.20
B932	SP421	6.50fr + 3fr multi	.30	.30
B933	SP421	6.50fr + 3fr multi	.30	.30
B934	SP421	10fr + 5fr multi	.45	.45
B935	SP421	10fr + 5fr multi	.45	.45
B936	SP421	30fr + 15fr multi	1.50	1.50
		Nos. B931-B936 (6)	3.20	3.20

THEMABELGA Intl. Topical Philatelic Exhib., Brussels, Dec. 13-21. Issued in sheets of 10 (5x2).

Blackface Fund Collector — SP422

1976, Feb. 14 Photo. *Perf. 11½*

B937 SP422 10fr + 5fr multi .55 .55

"Conservatoire Africain" philanthropic soc., cent., and to publicize the Princess Paola creches.

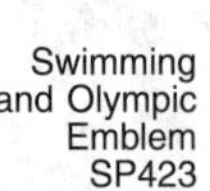

Swimming and Olympic Emblem SP423

Montreal Olympic Games Emblem and: 5fr+2fr, Running, vert. 6.50fr+2.50fr, Equestrian.

1976, Apr. 10 Photo. *Perf. 11½*

B938	SP423	4.50fr + 1.50fr multi	.20	.20
B939	SP423	5fr + 2fr multi	.25	.25
B940	SP423	6.50fr + 2.50fr multi	.45	.45
		Nos. B938-B940 (3)	.90	.90

21st Olympic Games, Montreal, Canada, July 17-Aug. 1.

Queen Elisabeth Playing Violin SP424

1976, May 1 Engr. and *Perf. 11½* Photo.

B941 SP424 14fr + 6fr blk & cl .95 .95

Queen Elisabeth International Music Competition, 25th anniversary.

Souvenir Sheet

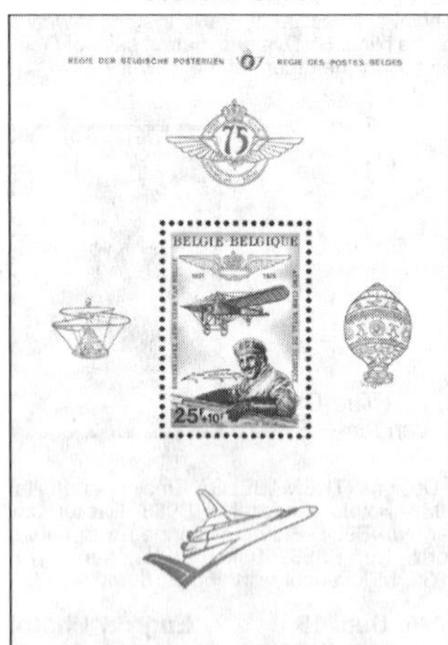

Jan Olieslagers, Bleriot Monoplane, Aero Club Emblem — SP425

Engraved and Photogravure

1976, June 12 *Perf. 11½*

B942 SP425 25fr + 10fr multi 2.25 2.25

Royal Belgian Aero Club, 75th anniversary, and Jan Olieslagers (1883-1942), aviation pioneer.

Adoration of the Shepherds (detail), by Rubens — SP426

Rubens Paintings (Details): 4.50fr, Descent from the Cross. No. B945, The Virgin with the Parrot. No. B946, Adoration of the Kings. No. B947, Last Communion of St. Francis. 30fr+15fr, Virgin and Child.

1976, Sept. 4 Photo. *Perf. 11½*

Size: 35x52mm

B943	SP426	4.50fr + 1.50fr multi	.35	.35

Size: 24x35mm

B944	SP426	6.50fr + 3fr multi	.55	.55
B945	SP426	6.50fr + 3fr multi	.55	.55
B946	SP426	10fr + 5fr multi	.85	.85
B947	SP426	10fr + 5fr multi	.85	.85

Size: 35x52mm

B948	SP426	30fr + 15fr multi	1.75	1.75
		Nos. B943-B948 (6)	4.90	4.90

Peter Paul Rubens (1577-1640), Flemish painter, 400th birth anniversary.

Dwarf, by Velazquez SP427

1976, Nov. 6 Photo. *Perf. 11½*

B949 SP427 14fr + 6fr multi .80 .80

Surtax was for the National Association for the Mentally Handicapped.

Dr. Albert Hustin SP428

Red Cross and Rheumatism Year Emblem SP429

1977, Feb. 19 Photo. *Perf. 11½*

B950	SP428	6.50fr + 2.50 multi	.40	.40
B951	SP429	14fr + 7fr multi	.75	.75

Belgian Red Cross.

Bordet Atheneum, Empress Maria Theresa SP430

Conductor and Orchestra, by E. Tytgat SP431

Lucien Van Obbergh, Stage SP432

Humanistic Society Emblem SP433

Camille Lemonnier SP434

Design: No. B953, Marie-Therese College, Herve, and coat of arms.

1977, Mar. 21 Photo. *Perf. 11½*

B952	SP430	4.50fr + 1fr multi	.20	.20
B953	SP430	4.50fr + 1fr multi	.20	.20
B954	SP431	5fr + 2fr multi	.25	.25
B955	SP432	6.50fr + 2fr multi	.30	.30
B956	SP433	6.50fr + 2fr blk & red	.30	.30

Engr.

B957	SP434	10fr + 5fr slate bl	.50	.50
		Nos. B952-B957 (6)	1.75	1.75

Bicentenaries of the Jules Bordet Atheneum, Brussels, and the Marie-Therese College, Herve (#B952-B953); 50th anniv. of the Brussels Philharmonic Soc., and Artists' Union (#B954-B955); 25th anniv. of the Flemish Humanistic Organization (#B956); 75th anniv. of the French-speaking Belgian writers' organization (#957).

Young Soccer Players — SP435

1977, Apr. 18 Photo.

B958 SP435 10fr + 5fr multi .55 .55

30th Intl. Junior Soccer Tournament.

Albert-Edouard Janssen, Financier — SP436

Famous Men: No. B960, Joseph Wauters (1875-1929), editor of Le Peuple, and newspaper. No. B961, Jean Capart (1877-1947), Egyptologist, and hieroglyph. No. B962, August de Boeck (1865-1937), composer, and score.

1977, Dec. 3 Engr. *Perf. 11½*

B959	SP436	5fr + 2.50fr brown	.30	.30
B960	SP436	5fr + 2.50fr red	.30	.30
B961	SP436	10fr + 5fr magenta	.55	.55
B962	SP436	10fr + 5fr blue gray	.55	.55
		Nos. B959-B962 (4)	1.70	1.70

Abandoned Child SP437

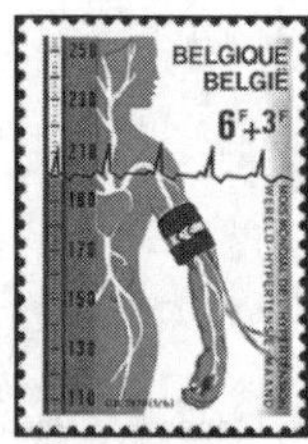

Checking Blood Pressure SP438

De Mick Sanatorium, Brasschaat — SP439

1978, Feb. 18 Photo. *Perf. 11½*

B963	SP437	4.50fr + 1.50fr multi	.20	.20
B964	SP438	6fr + 3fr multi	.40	.40
B965	SP439	10fr + 5fr multi	.60	.60
		Nos. B963-B965 (3)	1.20	1.20

Help for abandoned children (No. B963); fight against hypertension (No. B964); fight against tuberculosis (No. B965).

Actors and Theater SP440

Karel van de Woestijne SP441

Designs: No. B967, Harquebusier, Harquebusier Palace and coat of arms. 10fr+5fr, John of Austria and his signature.

Engraved and Photogravure

1978, June 17 *Perf. 11½*

B966	SP440	6fr + 3fr multi	.40	.40
B967	SP440	6fr + 3fr multi	.40	.40

Engr.

B968	SP441	8fr + 4fr black	.45	.45
B969	SP441	10fr + 5fr black	.55	.55
		Nos. B966-B969 (4)	1.80	1.80

Cent. of Royal Flemish Theater, Brussels (#B966); 400th anniv. of Harquebusiers' Guild of Vise, Liege (#967); Karel van de Woestijne (1878-1929), poet (#B968); 400th anniv. of signing of Perpetual Edict by John of Austria (#969).

Lake Placid '80 and Belgian Olympic Emblems — SP442

Moscow '80 Emblem and: 8fr+3.50fr, Kremlin Towers, Belgian Olympic Committee emblem. 7fr+3fr, Runners from Greek vase, Lake Placid '80 emblem, Olympic rings. 14fr+6fr, Olympic flame, Lake Placid '80, Belgian emblems, Olympic rings.

1978, Nov. 4 Photo. *Perf. 11½*

B970	SP442	6fr + 2.50fr multi	.30	.30
B971	SP442	8fr + 3.50fr multi	.45	.45

Souvenir Sheet

B972		Sheet of 2	1.50	1.50
a.		SP442 7fr + 3fr multi	.55	.55
b.		SP442 14fr + 6fr multi	.90	.90

Surtax was for 1980 Olympic Games.

Great Synagogue, Brussels — SP443

Dancers SP444

Father Pire, African Village SP445

1978, Dec. 2 Engr. *Perf. 11½*

B973 SP443 6fr + 2fr sepia	.45	.45

Photo.

B974 SP444 8fr + 3fr multi	.35	.35
B975 SP445 14fr + 7fr multi	.65	.65
Nos. B973-B975 (3)	1.45	1.45

Centenary of Great Synagogue of Brussels; Flemish Catholic Youth Action Organization, 50th anniversary; Nobel Peace Prize awarded to Father Dominique Pire for his "Heart Open to the World" movement, 20th anniversary.

Young People Giving First Aid — SP446

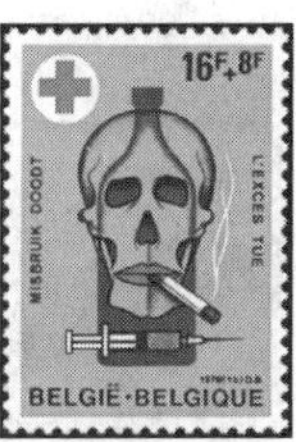
Skull with Bottle, Cigarette, Syringe — SP447

1979, Feb. 10 Photo. *Perf. 11½*

B976 SP446 8fr + 3fr multi	.35	.35
B977 SP447 16fr + 8fr multi	.85	.85

Belgian Red Cross.

Beatrice Soetkens with Statue of Virgin Mary SP448

Details from Tapestries, 1516-1518, Showing Legend of Our Lady of Sand: 8fr+3fr, Francois de Tassis accepting letter from Emperor Frederick III (beginning of postal service). 14fr+7fr, Arrival of statue, Francois de Tassis and Philip the Fair. No. B981, Statue carried in procession by future Emperor Charles V and his brother Ferdinand. No. B982, Ship carrying Beatrice Soetkens with statue to Brussels, horiz.

1979, May 5 Photo. *Perf. 11½*

B978 SP448 6fr + 2fr multi	.25	.25
B979 SP448 8fr + 3fr multi	.40	.40
B980 SP448 14fr + 7fr multi	.65	.65
B981 SP448 20fr + 10fr multi	1.10	1.10
Nos. B978-B981 (4)	2.40	2.40

Souvenir Sheet

B982 SP448 20fr + 10fr multi	.90	.90

The surtax was for festivities in connection with the millennium of Brussels.

Notre Dame Abbey, Brussels — SP449

Designs: 8fr+3fr, Beauvoorde Castle. 14fr+7fr, 1st issue of "Courrier de L'Escaut" and Barthelemy Dumortier, founder. 20fr+10fr, Shrine of St. Hermes, Renaix.

Engraved and Photogravure

1979, Sept. 15 *Perf. 11½*

B983 SP449 6fr + 2fr multi	.35	.35
B984 SP449 8fr + 3fr multi	.50	.50
B985 SP449 14fr + 7fr multi	.60	.60
B986 SP449 20fr + 10fr multi	1.10	1.10
Nos. B983-B986 (4)	2.55	2.55

50th anniv. of restoration of Notre Dame de la Cambre Abbey; historic Beauvoorde Castle, 15th cent. sesquicentennial of the regional newspaper "Le Courrier de L'Escaut"; 850th anniv. of the consecration of the Collegiate Church of St. Hermes, Renaix.

Grand-Hornu Coal Mine — SP450

1979, Oct. 22 Engr. *Perf. 11½*

B987 SP450 10fr + 5fr blk	.55	.55

Henry Heyman SP451

Veterans Organization Medal SP452

Boy and IYC Emblem — SP453

1979, Dec. 8 Photo. *Perf. 11½*

B988 SP451 8fr + 3fr multi	.45	.45
B989 SP452 10fr + 5fr multi	.55	.55
B990 SP453 16fr + 8fr multi	.75	.75
Nos. B988-B990 (3)	1.75	1.75

Henri Heyman (1879-1958), Minister of State; Disabled Veterans' Organization, 50th anniv.; Intl. Year of the Child.

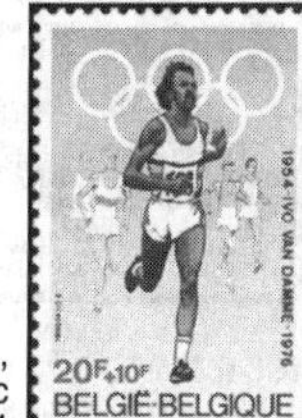
Ivo Van Damme, Olympic Rings — SP454

1980, May 3 Photo. *Perf. 11½*

B991 SP454 20fr + 10fr multi	1.10	1.10

Ivo Van Damme (1954-1976), silver medalist, 800-meter race, Montreal Olympics, 1976. Surtax was for Van Damme Memorial Foundation.

Queen Louis-Marie, King Leopold I — SP455

150th Anniversary of Independence (Queens and Kings): 9fr+3fr, Marie Henriette. Leopold II. 14fr+6fr, Elisabeth, Albert I. 17fr+8fr, Astrid, Leopold III. 25fr+10fr, Fabiola, Baudouin.

Photogravure and Engraved

1980, May 31 *Perf. 11½*

B992 SP455 6.50 + 1.50fr multi	.30	.30
B993 SP455 9 + 3fr multi	.50	.50
B994 SP455 14 + 6fr multi	.70	.70
B995 SP455 17 + 8fr multi	1.00	1.00
B996 SP455 25 + 10fr multi	1.25	1.25
Nos. B992-B996 (5)	3.75	3.75

Miner, by Constantine Meunier SP456

Seal of Bishop Notger, First Prince-Bishop — SP457

9fr+3fr, Brewer, 16th century, from St. Lambert's reliquary, vert. 25fr+10fr, Virgin and Child, 13th century, St. John's Collegiate Church, Liege.

1980, Sept. 13 Photo. *Perf. 11½*

B997 SP456 9 + 3fr multi	.35	.35
B998 SP456 17 + 6fr multi	.70	.70
B999 SP456 25 + 10fr multi	1.10	1.10
Nos. B997-B999 (3)	2.15	2.15

Souvenir Sheet

B1000 SP457 20 + 10fr multi	1.25	1.25

Millennium of the Principality of Liege.

Visual and Oral Handicaps SP458

Intl. Year of the Disabled: 10fr+5fr, Cerebral handicap, vert.

1981, Feb. 9 Photo. *Perf. 11½*

B1001 SP458 10 + 5fr multi	.70	.70
B1002 SP458 25 + 10fr multi	1.60	1.60

Dove with Red Cross Carrying Globe SP459

Design: 10fr+5fr, Atomic model, vert.

1981, Apr. 6 Photo. *Perf. 11½*

B1003 SP459 10 + 5fr multi	.70	.70
B1004 SP459 25 + 10fr multi	1.60	1.60

Red Cross and: 15th Intl. Radiology Congress, Brussels, June 24-July 1 (#B1003); intl. disaster relief (#B1004).

Ovide Decroly SP460

1981, June 1 Photo. *Perf. 11½*

B1005 SP460 35 + 15fr multi	2.00	2.00

Ovide Decroly (1871-1932), developer of educational psychology.

Mounted Police Officer — SP461

Anniversaries: 9fr+4fr, Gendarmerie (State Police Force), 150th. 20fr+7fr, Carabineers Regiment, 150th. 40fr+20fr, Guides Regiment.

1981, Dec. 7 Photo. *Perf. 11½*

B1006 SP461 9 + 4fr multi	.60	.60
B1007 SP461 20 + 7fr multi	1.25	1.25
B1008 SP461 40 + 20fr multi	2.75	2.75
Nos. B1006-B1008 (3)	4.60	4.60

Billiards — SP462

1982, Mar. 29 Photo. *Perf. 11½*

B1009 SP462 6 + 2fr shown	.40	.40
B1010 SP462 9 + 4fr Cycling	.60	.60
B1011 SP462 10 + 5fr Soccer	.70	.70
B1012 SP462 50 + 14fr Yachting	3.00	3.00
Nos. B1009-B1012 (4)	4.70	4.70

Souvenir Sheet

B1013 Sheet of 4	5.00	5.00
a. SP462 25fr like #B1009	1.40	1.40
b. SP462 25fr like #B1010	1.40	1.40
c. SP462 25fr like #B1011	1.40	1.40
d. SP462 25fr like #B1012	1.40	1.40

#B1013 shows designs in changed colors.

Christmas SP463

1982, Nov. 6

B1014 SP463 10 + 1fr multi	.60	.45

Surtax was for tuberculosis research.

Belgica '82 Intl. Stamp Exhibition, Brussels, Dec. 11-19 SP464

Messengers (Prints). #B1016-B1018 vert.

Photogravure and Engraved

1982, Dec. 11 ***Perf. 11½***

B1015 SP464 7 + 2fr multi .40 .40
B1016 SP464 7.50 + 2.50fr multi .45 .45
B1017 SP464 10 + 3fr multi .55 .55
B1018 SP464 17 + 7fr multi 1.10 1.10
B1019 SP464 20 + 9fr multi 1.25 1.25
B1020 SP464 25 + 10fr multi 1.50 1.50
Nos. B1015-B1020 (6) 5.25 5.25

Souvenir Sheet

B1021 SP464 50 + 25fr multi 6.00 6.00

No. B1021 contains one 48x37mm stamp.

50th Anniv. of Catholic Charities — SP465

1983, Jan. 22 **Photo.** ***Perf. 11½***

B1022 SP465 10 + 2fr multi .65 .65

Mountain Climbing — SP466

1983, Mar. 7 **Photo.**

B1023 SP466 12 + 3fr shown .80 .80
B1024 SP466 20 + 5fr Hiking 1.25 1.25

Surtax was for Red Cross.

Madonna by Jef Wauters — SP467

1983, Nov. 21 **Photo.** ***Perf. 11½***

B1025 SP467 11 + 1fr multi .60 .60

Rifles Uniform — SP468

1983, Dec. 5 **Photo.** ***Perf. 11½***

B1026 SP468 8 + 2fr shown .50 .50
B1027 SP468 11 + 2fr Lancers uniform .75 .75
B1028 SP468 50 + 12fr Grenadiers uniform 3.50 3.50
Nos. B1026-B1028 (3) 4.75 4.75

Type of 1984

1984, Mar. 3 **Photo.** ***Perf. 11½***

B1029 A495 8 + 2fr Judo, horiz. .55 .55
B1030 A495 12 + 3fr Wind surfing .85 .85

50th Anniv. of Natl. Lottery SP469

1984, Mar. 31 **Photo.** ***Perf. 11½***

B1031 SP469 12 + 3fr multi .75 .75

Brussels Modern Art Museum Opening SP470

Paintings: 8fr+2fr, Les Masques Singuliers, by James Ensor. 12fr+3fr, Empire des Lumieres, by Rene Magritte. 22fr+5fr, The End, by Jan Cox. 50fr+13fr, Rhythm No. 6, by Jo Delahaut.

1984, Sept. 1 **Photo.**

B1032 SP470 8 + 2fr multi .60 .60
B1033 SP470 12 + 3fr multi .90 .90
B1034 SP470 22 + 5fr multi 1.60 1.60
B1035 SP470 50 + 13fr multi 3.75 3.75
Nos. B1032-B1035 (4) 6.85 6.85

Child with Parents — SP471

1984, Nov. 3 **Photo.**

B1036 SP471 10 + 2fr shown .60 .60
B1037 SP471 12 + 3fr Siblings .75 .75
B1038 SP471 15 + 3fr Merry-go-round .85 .85
Nos. B1036-B1038 (3) 2.20 2.20

Surtax was for children's programs.

Christmas 1984 SP472

1984, Dec. 1

B1039 SP472 12 + 1fr Three Kings .75 .75

Belgian Red Cross Blood Transfusion Service, 50th Anniv. — SP473

1985, Mar. 4 **Photo.** ***Perf. 11½***

B1040 SP473 9 + 2fr Tree .60 .60
B1041 SP473 23 + 5fr Hearts 1.40 1.40

Surtax was for the Belgian Red Cross.

Solidarity SP474

Castles.

1985, Nov. 4 **Photo. & Engr.**

B1042 SP474 9 + 2fr Trazegnies .60 .60
B1043 SP474 12 + 3fr Laarne .80 .80
B1044 SP474 23 + 5fr Turnhout 1.40 1.40
B1045 SP474 50 + 12fr Colonster 3.50 3.50
Nos. B1042-B1045 (4) 6.30 6.30

Christmas 1985, New Year 1986 — SP475

Painting: Miniature from the Book of Hours, by Jean duc de Berry.

1985, Nov. 25 **Photo.**

B1046 SP475 12 + 1fr multi .70 .70

King Baudouin Foundation SP476

1986, Mar. 24 **Photo.**

B1047 SP476 12 + 3fr Emblem .80 .80

Surtax for the foundation.

Madonna SP477

Adoration of the Mystic Lamb, St. Bavon Cathedral Altarpiece, Ghent — SP478

Paintings by Hubert van Eyck (c. 1370-1426).

1986, Apr. 5 **Photo.** ***Perf. 11½***

B1048 SP477 9 + 2fr shown .65 .65
B1049 SP477 13 + 3fr Christ in Majesty .95 .95
B1050 SP477 24 + 6fr St. John the Baptist 1.75 1.75
Nos. B1048-B1050 (3) 3.35 3.35

Souvenir Sheet

B1051 SP478 50 + 12fr multi 5.25 5.25

Surtax for cultural organizations.

Antique Automobiles SP479

1986, Nov. 3 **Photo.**

B1052 SP479 9 + 2fr Lenoir, 1863 .65 .65
B1053 SP479 13 + 3fr Pipe de Tourisme, 1911 .90 .90
B1054 SP479 24 + 6fr Minerva 22 HP, 1930 1.75 1.75
B1055 SP479 26 + 6fr FN 8 Cylinder, 1931 1.90 1.90
Nos. B1052-B1055 (4) 5.20 5.20

Christmas 1986, New Year 1987 SP480

1986, Nov. 24 **Photo.**

B1056 SP480 13 + 1fr Village in winter .75 .75

Natl. Red Cross — SP482

Nobel Prize winners for physiology (1938) and medicine (1974): No. B1058, Corneille Heymans (1892-1968). No. B1059, A. Claude (1899-1983).

Photogravure and Engraved

1987, Feb. 16 ***Perf. 11½***

B1058 SP482 13 + 3fr dk brn & red .90 .90
B1059 SP482 24 + 6fr dk brn & red 1.60 1.60

European Conservation Year — SP483

1987, Mar. 16 **Photo.**

B1060 SP483 9 + 2fr Bee orchid .65 .65
B1061 SP483 24 + 6fr Horse-shoe bat 1.60 1.60
B1062 SP483 26 + 6fr Peregrine falcon 1.75 1.75
Nos. B1060-B1062 (3) 4.00 4.00

Castles — SP484

1987, Oct. 17 **Photo. & Engr.**

B1063 SP484 9 + 2fr Rixensart .60 .60
B1064 SP484 13 + 3fr Westerlo .90 .90
B1065 SP484 26 + 5fr Fallais 1.75 1.75
B1066 SP484 50 + 12fr Gaasbeek 3.50 3.50
Nos. B1063-B1066 (4) 6.75 6.75

Christmas 1987 — SP485

Painting: Holy Family, by Rev. Father Lens.

1987, Nov. 14 Photo.
B1067 SP485 13 + 1fr multi .85 .85

White and Yellow Cross of Belgium, 50th Anniv. — SP486

1987, Dec. 5
B1068 SP486 9 + 2fr multi .70 .70

Promote Philately — SP487

Various flowers from Sixty Roses for a Queen, by P. J. Redoute (1759-1840).

1988, Apr. 25 Photo. *Perf. 11½*
B1069 SP487 13 + 3fr shown 1.00 1.00
B1070 SP487 24 + 6fr multi, diff. 1.75 1.75

Souvenir Sheet

B1071 SP487 50 + 12fr multi, diff. 3.75 3.75

See #B1081-B1083, B1089-B1091, 1346.

1988 Summer Olympics, Seoul — SP488

1988, June 6 Photo. *Perf. 11½*
B1072 SP488 9fr + 2fr Table tennis .65 .65
B1073 SP488 13fr + 3fr Cycling .95 .95

Souvenir Sheet

B1074 SP488 50fr + 12fr Marathon runners 3.70 3.70

Solidarity — SP489

1988, Oct. 24 Photo. *Perf. 12x11½*
B1075 SP489 9fr + 2fr Jacques Brel .60 .60
B1076 SP489 13fr + 3fr Jef Denyn .90 .90
B1077 SP489 26fr + 6fr Fr. Ferdinand Verbiest 1.75 1.75
Nos. B1075-B1077 (3) 3.25 3.25

Belgian Red Cross SP490

Paintings: No. B1078, *Crucifixion of Christ,* by Rogier van der Weyden (c. 1399-1464). No. B1079, *Virgin and Child,* by David (c. 1460-1523). B1089, *The Good Samaritan,* by Denis van Alsloot.

1989, Feb. 20 Photo. *Perf. 11½*
B1078 SP490 9fr + 2fr multi .60 .60
B1079 SP490 13fr + 3fr multi .90 .90
B1080 SP490 24fr + 6fr multi 1.60 1.60
Nos. B1078-B1080 (3) 3.10 3.10

Stamp Collecting Promotion Type of 1988

Various flowers from *Sixty Roses for a Queen,* by P.J. Redoute (1759-1840) and inscriptions: No. B1081, "Centfeuille unique melee de rouge." No. B1082, "Bengale a grandes feuilles." No. B1083, Aeme vibere (tea roses).

1989, Apr. 17
B1081 SP487 13fr + 5fr multi 1.00 1.00
B1082 SP487 24fr + 6fr multi 1.60 1.60

Souvenir Sheet

B1083 SP487 50fr + 17fr multi 3.75 3.75

Solidarity SP491

Royal Greenhouses of Laeken.

1989, Oct. 23
B1084 SP491 9fr + 3fr Exterior .60 .60
B1085 SP491 13fr + 4fr Interior, vert. .85 .85
B1086 SP491 24fr + 5fr Dome exterior, vert. 1.40 1.40
B1087 SP491 26fr + 6fr Dome interior, vert. 1.50 1.50
Nos. B1084-B1087 (4) 4.35 4.35

Queen Elisabeth Chapelle Musicale, 50th Anniv. — SP492

1989, Nov. 6
B1088 SP492 24fr + 6fr G clef 1.50 1.50

Stamp Collecting Promotion Type of 1988

Various flowers from *Sixty Roses for a Queen,* by P.J. Redoute (1759-1840): No. B1089, *Bengale desprez.* No. B1090, *Bengale philippe.* No. B1091, *Maria leonida.*

1990, Feb. 5
B1089 SP487 14fr + 7fr multi 1.10 1.10
B1090 SP487 25fr + 12fr multi 2.00 2.00

Souvenir Sheet

B1091 SP487 50fr + 20fr multi 3.75 3.75

Youth and Music — SP493

14fr+3fr, Beethoven & Lamoraal, Count of Egmont (1522-1568). 25fr+6fr, Joseph Cantre (1890-1957), drawing & sculpture.

1990, Oct. 6
B1092 SP493 10fr + 2fr multi .70 .70
B1093 SP493 14fr + 3fr multi 1.00 1.00
B1094 SP493 25fr + 6fr multi 1.75 1.75
Nos. B1092-B1094 (3) 3.45 3.45

King Baudouin & Queen Fabiola, 30th Wedding Anniv. — SP494

1990, Dec. 10
B1095 SP494 50fr +15fr multi 4.25 4.25

Belgian Red Cross SP495

Details from paintings: No. B1096, The Temptation of St. Anthony by Hieronymus Bosch. No. B1097, The Annunciation by Dirk Bouts.

1991, Feb. 25, Photo. *Perf. 11½*
B1096 SP495 14fr +3fr multi 1.10 1.10
B1097 SP495 25fr +6fr multi 2.00 2.00

Belgian Film Personalities — SP496

10fr+2fr, Charles Dekeukeleire (1905-71), producer. 14fr+3fr, Jacques Ledoux (1921-88), film conservationist. 25fr+6fr, Jacques Feyder (1899-1948), director.

1991, Oct. 28 Photo. *Perf. 11½*
B1098 SP496 10fr +2fr multi .75 .75
B1099 SP496 14fr +3fr multi 1.10 1.10
B1100 SP496 25fr +6fr multi 1.90 1.90
Nos. B1098-B1100 (3) 3.75 3.75

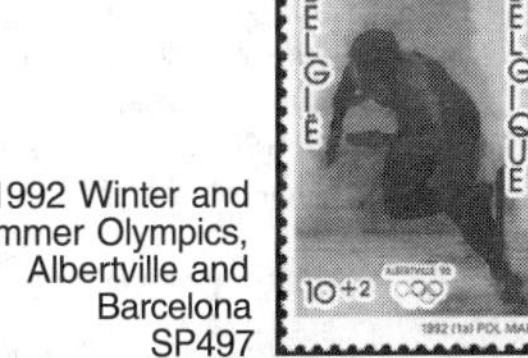

1992 Winter and Summer Olympics, Albertville and Barcelona SP497

1992, Jan. 20 Photo. *Perf. 11½*
B1101 SP497 10fr +2fr Speed skating .75 .75
B1102 SP497 10fr +2fr Baseball .75 .75
B1103 SP497 14fr +3fr Women's tennis, horiz. 1.10 1.10
B1104 SP497 25fr +6fr Skeet shooting 1.90 1.90
Nos. B1101-B1104 (4) 4.50 4.50

Folk Legends SP498

11fr + 2fr, Proud Margaret. 15fr + 3fr, Gustine Maca & the Witches. 28fr + 6fr, Reynard the Fox.

1992, June 22 Photo. *Perf. 11½*
B1105 SP498 11fr +2fr multi .80 .80
B1106 SP498 15fr +3fr multi 1.10 1.10
B1107 SP498 28fr +6fr multi 2.00 2.00
Nos. B1105-B1107 (3) 3.90 3.90

Belgian Red Cross SP499

Paintings: 15fr + 3fr, Man with the Pointed Hat, by Adriaen Brouwer (1605-1638). 28fr + 7fr, Nereid and Triton, by Peter Paul Rubens, horiz.

1993, Feb. 15 Photo. *Perf. 11½*
B1108 SP499 15fr +3fr multi 1.10 1.10
B1109 SP499 28fr +7fr multi 2.10 2.10

Fight Against Cancer SP500

1993, Sept. 20 Photo. *Perf. 11½*
B1110 SP500 15fr +3fr multi 1.10 1.10

Intl. Olympic Committee, Cent. — SP501

#B1112, Soccer players. #B1113, Figure skater.

1994, Feb. 14 Photo. *Perf. 11½*
B1111 SP501 16fr +3fr multi 1.00 1.00
B1112 SP501 16fr +3fr multi 1.00 1.00
B1113 SP501 16fr +3fr multi 1.00 1.00
Nos. B1111-B1113 (3) 3.00 3.00

1994 World Cup Soccer Championships, Los Angeles (#B1112). 1994 Winter Olympics, Lillehammer, Norway (#B1113).

Porcelain — SP502

Designs: No. B1114, Tournai plate, Museum of Mariemont-Morlanweiz. No. B1115, Etterbeek cup, saucer, Municipal Museum, Louvain. 50fr+11fr, Delft earthenware jars, Pharmacy Museum of Maaseik.

1994, June 27 Photo. *Perf. 11½*
B1114 SP502 16fr +3fr multi 1.10 1.10
B1115 SP502 16fr +3fr multi 1.10 1.10

Souvenir Sheet

B1116 SP502 50fr +11fr multi 3.50 3.50

No. B1116 contains one 49x38mm stamp.

Solidarity SP503

Design: 16fr+3fr, Hearing-impaired person.

1994, Nov. 14 Photo. *Perf. 11½*
B1117 SP503 16fr +3fr multi 1.25 1.25

Museums — SP504

#B1118, Natl. Flax Museum, Kortrijk. #B1119, Natl. Water & Fountain Museum, Genval.
34fr+6fr, Intl. Carnival and Mask Museum, Binche.

1995, Jan. 30 Photo. *Perf. 11½*

B1118 SP504 16fr +3fr multi 1.25 1.25
B1119 SP504 16fr +3fr multi 1.25 1.25

Souvenir Sheet

B1120 SP504 34fr +6fr multi 2.75 2.75

Surtax for promotion of philately.

"Souvenir Sheets"

Beginning in 1995 items looking like souvenir sheets have appeared in the market. The 1995 one has the design used for No. B1120. The 1996 one has the design similar to the one used for No. B1128. The 1997 one has the design used for No. B1131. These have no postal value.

Royal Belgian Soccer Assoc., Cent. SP505

1995, Aug. 21 Photo. *Perf. 11½*

B1121 SP505 16fr +4fr multi 1.40 1.40

Belgian Red Cross SP506

#B1122, Princess Astrid, chairwoman of Belgian Red Cross. #B1123, Wilhelm C. Röntgen (1845-1923), discoverer of the X-ray. #B1124, Louis Pasteur (1822-95), scientist.

1995, Sept. 11

B1122 SP506 16fr +3fr multi 1.25 1.25
B1123 SP506 16fr +3fr multi 1.25 1.25
B1124 SP506 16fr +3fr multi 1.25 1.25
Nos. B1122-B1124 (3) 3.75 3.75

Solidarity — SP507

1995, Nov. 6 Photo. *Perf. 11½*

B1125 SP507 16fr +4fr multi 1.25 1.25

Surtax for fight against AIDS.

Museums — SP508

#B1126, Museum of Walloon Life, Liège. #B1127, Natl. Gin Museum, Hasselt.
34fr+6fr, Butchers' Guild Hall Museum, Antwerp.

1996, Feb. 19 Photo. *Perf. 11½*

B1126 SP508 16fr +4fr multi 1.25 1.25
B1127 SP508 16fr +4fr multi 1.25 1.25

Souvenir Sheet

B1128 SP508 34fr +6fr multi 2.50 2.50

Modern Olympic Games, Cent. SP509

1996, July 1 Photo. *Perf. 11½*

B1129 SP509 16fr +4fr Table tennis 1.25 1.25
B1130 SP509 16fr +4fr Swimming 1.25 1.25

Souvenir Sheet

B1131 SP509 34fr +6fr High jump 2.50 2.50

No. B1131 contains one 49x38mm stamp.

UNICEF, 50th Anniv. SP510

1996, Nov. 18 Photo. *Perf. 11½*

B1132 SP510 16fr +4fr multi 1.40 1.40

Museums SP511

#B1133, Deportation and Resistance Museum, Mechlin. #B1134, Iron Museum, Saint Hubert.
41fr+9fr, Horta Museum, Saint Gilles.

1997, Jan. 20 Photo. *Perf. 11½*

B1133 SP511 17fr +4fr multi 1.25 1.25
B1134 SP511 17fr +4fr multi 1.25 1.25

Souvenir Sheet

B1135 SP511 41fr +9fr multi 3.00 3.00

Surtax for "Pro-Post" association.

Judo — SP512

1997, May 5 Photo. *Perf. 11½*

B1136 SP512 17fr +4fr Men's (10a) 1.25 1.25
B1137 SP512 17fr +4fr Women's (10b) 1.25 1.25

Surtax for Belgian Olympic Committee.

Solidarity — SP513

1997, Oct. 25

B1138 SP513 17fr +4fr multi 1.25 1.25

Surtax for Multiple Sclerosis research.

King Leopold III — SP514

32fr+15fr, King Baudouin I. 50fr+25fr, King Albert II.

1998, Feb. 16 Engr. *Perf. 11½*

B1139 SP514 17fr +8fr dk grn 1.50 1.50
B1140 SP514 32fr +15fr dk brn blk 2.75 2.75

Souvenir Sheet

B1141 SP514 50fr +25fr dk vio brn 4.50 4.50

See #B1146-B1148, 1748, B1154-B1156, 1842, B1158-B1160.

Sports SP515

1998, June 8 Photo. *Perf. 11½*

B1142 SP515 17fr +4fr Pelota 1.25 1.25
B1143 SP515 17fr +4fr Handball 1.25 1.25

Souvenir Sheet

B1144 SP515 30fr +7fr Soccer 2.00 2.00

1998 World Cup Soccer Championships, France (#B1144).

Assist the Blind — SP516

Photo. & Embossed

1998, Nov. 9 *Perf. 11½*

B1145 SP516 17fr +4fr multi 1.25 1.25

Face value is indicated in Braille.

Royalty Type of 1998

Designs: 17fr+8fr, King Albert I. 32fr+15fr, King Leopold II. 50fr+25fr, King Leopold I.

1999, Jan. 25 Engr. *Perf. 11½*

B1146 SP514 17fr +8fr deep green 1.50 1.50
B1147 SP514 32fr +15fr black 2.75 2.75

Souvenir Sheet

B1148 SP514 50fr +25fr deep brown 4.50 4.50

Motorcycles — SP517

1999, May 17 Photo. *Perf. 11½*

B1149 SP517 17fr +4fr Speed race 1.10 1.10
B1150 SP517 17fr +4fr Trial, vert. 1.10 1.10

Souvenir Sheet

B1151 SP517 30fr +7fr Motocross, vert. 2.00 2.00

Solidarity SP518

#1152, First aid. #1153, Dental care, vert.

1999, Nov. 8 Photo. *Perf. 11½*

B1152 SP518 17fr +4fr multi 1.00 1.00
B1153 SP518 17fr +4fr multi 1.00 1.00

Royalty Type of 1998

Queens: 17fr + 8fr, Astrid (1905-35). 32fr +15fr, Fabiola (b. 1928). 50fr +25fr, Paola (b. 1937).

Photo. & Engr.

2000, Jan. 24 *Perf. 11½*

B1154 SP514 17fr +8fr green 1.25 1.25
B1155 SP514 32fr +15fr black 2.25 2.25

Souvenir Sheet

B1156 SP514 50fr +25fr claret 3.75 3.75

Red Cross/Red Crescent SP519

2000, Mar. 27 Photo. *Perf. 11½*

B1157 SP519 17fr +4fr multi .95 .95

Royalty Type of 1998

Queens: 17fr+8fr, Elisabeth (1876-1965). 32fr+15fr, Marie-Henriette (1836-1902).
50fr+25fr, Louise-Marie (1812-50).

Photo. & Engr.

2001, Feb. 12 *Perf. 11½*

B1158 SP514 17fr +8fr green 1.10 1.10
B1159 SP514 32fr +15fr black 2.25 2.25

Souvenir Sheet

B1160 SP514 50fr +25fr brown 3.50 3.50

Sports SP520

World championship meets: No. B1161, Cycle track racing, Antwerp. No. B1162, Artistic gymnastics, Ghent.

2001, June 14 Photo. *Perf. 11½*

B1161 SP520 17fr +4fr multi .90 .90
B1162 SP520 17fr +4fr multi .90 .90

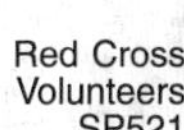

Red Cross Volunteers SP521

2001, Sept. 10

B1163 SP521 17fr +4fr multi	.95	.95

Winning Drawing in Belgica 2001 Children's Stamp Design Contest SP522

2002, Feb. 11 Photo. *Perf. 11½*

B1164 SP522 42c +10c multi	.90	.90

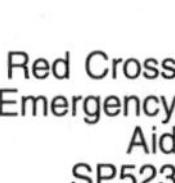

Red Cross Emergency Aid SP523

2002, June 5 Photo. *Perf. 11½*

B1165 SP523 84c +12c multi	1.90	1.90

AIR POST STAMPS

Fokker FVII/3m over Ostend AP1

Designs: 1.50fr, Plane over St. Hubert. 2fr, over Namur. 5fr, over Brussels.

Perf. 11½

1930, Apr. 30 Unwmk. Photo.

C1 AP1 50c blue	.40	.40
C2 AP1 1.50fr black brn	2.25	2.50
C3 AP1 2fr deep green	2.00	.55
C4 AP1 5fr brown lake	1.75	.95
Nos. C1-C4 (4)	6.40	4.40
Set, never hinged	20.00	

Exist imperf.

1930, Dec. 5

C5 AP1 5fr dark violet	25.00	25.00
Never hinged	45.00	

Issued for use on a mail carrying flight from Brussels to Leopoldville, Belgian Congo, starting Dec. 7.

Exists imperf.

#C2, C4 Surcharged in Carmine or Blue

1935, May 23

C6 AP1 1fr on 1.50fr (C)	.55	.40
C7 AP1 4fr on 5fr (Bl)	7.50	7.00
Set, never hinged	25.00	

Catalogue values for unused stamps in this section, from this point to the end of the section, are for Never Hinged items.

DC-4 Skymaster, Sabena Airline AP5

1946, Apr. 20 Engr. *Perf. 11½*

C8 AP5 6fr blue	.75	.25
C9 AP5 8.50fr violet brn	1.00	.35
C10 AP5 50fr yellow grn	5.00	.60
a. Perf. 12x11½ ('54)	325.00	1.00
C11 AP5 100fr gray	8.25	.80
a. Perf. 12x11½ ('54)	65.00	1.10
Nos. C8-C11 (4)	15.00	2.00

Evolution of Postal Transportation — AP6

1949, July 1

C12 AP6 50fr dark brown	42.50	15.00

Centenary of Belgian postage stamps.

Glider — AP7

Design: 7fr, "Tipsy" plane.

1951, June 18 Photo. *Perf. 13½*

C12A Strip of 2 + label	60.00	40.00
b. AP7 6fr dark blue	20.00	14.00
c. AP7 7fr carmine rose	20.00	14.00

For the 50th anniv. of the Aero Club of Belgium. The strip sold for 50fr.

1951, July 25 *Perf. 13½*

C13 AP7 6fr sepia	4.50	.20
C14 AP7 7fr Prus green	3.50	.95

UN Types of Regular Issue, 1958

Designs: 5fr, ICAO. 6fr, World Meteorological Organization. 7.50fr, Protection of Refugees. 8fr, General Agreement on Tariffs and Trade. 9fr, UNICEF. 10fr, Atomic Energy Agency.

Perf. 11½

1958, Apr. 17 Unwmk. Engr.

C15 A137 5fr dull blue	.25	.30
C16 A136 6fr yellow grn	.30	.45
C17 A137 7.50fr lilac	.30	.30
C18 A136 8fr sepia	.30	.30
C19 A137 9fr carmine	.40	.50
C20 A136 10fr redsh brown	.75	.60
Nos. C15-C20 (6)	2.30	2.45

World's Fair, Brussels, Apr. 17-Oct. 19. See note after No. 476.

AIR POST SEMI-POSTAL STAMPS

Catalogue values for unused stamps in this section are for Never Hinged items.

American Soldier in Combat — SPAP1

Perf. 11x11½

1946, June 15 Unwmk. Engr.

CB1 SPAP1 17.50fr + 62.50fr dl brn	2.00	.90
CB2 SPAP1 17.50fr + 62.50fr dl gray grn	2.00	.90

Surtax for an American memorial at Bastogne.

An overprint, "Hommage a Roosevelt," was privately applied to Nos. CB1-CB2 in 1947 by the Association Belgo-Americaine.

In 1950 another private overprint was applied, in red, to Nos. CB1-CB2. It consists of "16-12-1944, 25-1-1945, Dedication July 16, 1950" and outlines of the American eagle emblem and the Bastogne Memorial. Similar overprints were applied to Nos. 265 and 345.

Flight Allegory SPAP2

1946, Sept. 7 *Perf. 11½*

CB3 SPAP2 2fr + 8fr brt vio	.60	*1.00*

The surtax was for the benefit of aviation.

Nos. B417-B425 Surcharged in Various Arrangements in Red or Dark Blue

Type I

Type II

Type I- Top line "POSTE AERIENNE"
Type II- Top line "LUCHTPOST"

1947, May 18 Photo. *Perf. 11½*

Type I

CB4 SP227 1fr + 2fr (R)	.60	*.90*
CB5 SP228 1.50fr + 2.50fr	.60	*.90*
CB6 SP229 2fr + 45fr	.60	*.90*
CB7 SP230 1fr + 2fr (R)	.60	*.90*
CB8 SP231 1.50fr + 2.50fr	.60	*.90*
CB9 SP232 2fr + 45fr	.60	*.90*
CB10 SP233 1fr + 2fr (R)	.60	*.90*
CB11 SP234 1.50fr + 2.50fr (R)	.60	*.90*
CB12 SP235 2fr + 45fr	.60	*.90*

Type II

CB4A SP227 1fr + 2fr (R)	.60	*.90*
CB5A SP228 1.50fr + 2.50fr	.60	*.90*
CB6A SP229 2fr + 45fr	.60	*.90*
CB7A SP230 1fr + 2fr (R)	.60	*.90*
CB8A SP231 1.50fr + 2.50fr	.60	*.90*
CB9A SP232 2fr + 45fr	.60	*.90*
CB10A SP233 1fr + 2fr (R)	.60	*.90*
CB11A SP234 1.50fr + 2.50fr (R)	.60	*.90*
CB12A SP235 2fr + 45fr	.60	*.90*
Nos. CB4-CB12A (18)	10.80	*16.20*

Issued for CIPEX, NYC. In 1948 Nos. CB4-CB12 and CB4A-CB12A were punched with the letters "IMABA," and the inscription "Imaba du 21 au 29 aout 1948" was applied to the backs. Value $20.

Helicopter Leaving Airport SPAP3

1950, Aug. 7

CB13 SPAP3 7fr + 3fr blue	9.00	5.25

Surtax for the Natl. Aeronautical Committee.

SPECIAL DELIVERY STAMPS

From 1874 to 1903 certain hexagonal telegraph stamps were used as special delivery stamps.

Town Hall, Brussels — SD1

Eupen — SD2

2.35fr, Street in Ghent. 3.50fr, Bishop's Palace, Liege. 5.25fr, Notre Dame Cathedral, Antwerp.

1929 Unwmk. Photo. *Perf. 11½*

E1 SD1 1.75fr dark blue	.80	.30
E2 SD1 2.35fr carmine	1.50	.45
E3 SD1 3.50fr dark violet	10.00	9.00
E4 SD1 5.25fr olive green	5.50	5.25

1931

E5 SD2 2.45fr dark green	11.00	2.50
Nos. E1-E5 (5)	28.80	17.50
E Set, never hinged		
E	60.00	

No. E5 Surcharged in Red

1932

E6 SD2 2.50fr on 2.45fr dk grn	9.00	1.25
Never hinged	25.00	

POSTAGE DUE STAMPS

D1

D2

1870 Unwmk. Typo. *Perf. 15*

J1 D1 10c green	3.75	2.00
J2 D1 20c ultra, thin paper	30.00	3.75

In 1909 many bisects of Nos. J1-J2 were created. The 10c bisect used as 5c on piece sells for $3.50.

No. J2 was also printed on thicker paper and in aniline ink on thin paper.

1895-09 *Perf. 14*

J3 D2 5c yellow grn	.20	.20
J4 D2 10c orange brn	17.50	1.75
J5 D2 10c carmine ('00)	.20	.20
J6 D2 20c olive green	.20	.20
J7 D2 30c pale blue ('09)	.30	.25
J8 D2 50c yellow brn	17.50	5.00
J9 D2 50c gray ('00)	.75	.45
J10 D2 1fr carmine	20.00	11.50
J11 D2 1fr ocher ('00)	6.50	5.00
Nos. J3-J11 (9)	63.15	24.55

1916 Redrawn

J12 D2 5c blue grn	25.00	7.00
J13 D2 10c carmine	42.50	11.00
J14 D2 20c dp gray grn	42.50	15.00
J15 D2 30c brt blue	6.00	5.00
J16 D2 50c gray	125.00	60.00
Nos. J12-J16 (5)	241.00	98.00

In the redrawn stamps the lions have a heavy, colored outline. There is a thick vertical line at the outer edge of the design on each side.

D3

D4

1919 *Perf. 14*

J17 D3 5c green .40 .50
J18 D3 10c carmine .95 .35
J19 D3 20c gray green 7.25 1.25
J20 D3 30c bright blue 1.40 .40
J21 D3 50c gray 2.75 .50
Nos. J17-J21 (5) 12.75 3.00

The 5c, 10c, 20c and 50c values also exist perf 14x15.

1922-32 *Perf. 14x13½*

J22 D4 5c dk gray .20 .20
J23 D4 10c green .20 .20
J24 D4 20c deep brown .20 .20
J25 D4 30c ver ('24) .65 .20
a. 30c rose red 1.00 .45
J26 D4 40c red brn ('25) .25 .20
J27 D4 50c ultra 1.90 .20
J28 D4 70c red brn ('29) .30 .20
J29 D4 1fr violet ('25) .45 .20
J30 D4 1fr rose lilac ('32) .55 .20
J31 D4 1.20fr ol grn ('29) .65 .45
J32 D4 1.50fr ol grn ('32) .65 .45
J33 D4 2fr violet ('29) .75 .20
J34 D4 3.50fr dp blue ('29) 1.00 .25
Nos. J22-J34 (13) 7.75 3.15

1934-46 *Perf. 14x13½*

J35 D4 35c green ('35) .40 *.45*
J36 D4 50c slate .20 .20
J37 D4 60c carmine ('38) .40 .30
J38 D4 80c slate ('38) .30 .20
J39 D4 1.40fr gray ('35) .65 .45
J39A D4 3fr org brn ('46) 1.50 .60
J39B D4 7fr brt red vio ('46) 2.25 *3.25*
Nos. J35-J39B (7) 5.70 *5.45*

See Nos. J54-J61.

Catalogue values for unused stamps in this section, from this point to the end of the section, are for Never Hinged items.

D5 D6

1945 **Typo.** *Perf. 12½*

Inscribed "TE BETALEN" at Top

J40 D5 10c gray olive .20 .20
J41 D5 20c ultramarine .20 .20
J42 D5 30c carmine .20 .20
J43 D5 40c black violet .20 .20
J44 D5 50c dl bl grn .20 .20
J45 D5 1fr sepia .20 .20
J46 D5 2fr red orange .20 .20

Inscribed "A PAYER" at Top

J47 D5 10c gray olive .20 .20
J48 D5 20c ultramarine .20 .20
J49 D5 30c carmine .20 .20
J50 D5 40c black vio .20 .20
J51 D5 50c dl bl grn .20 .20
J52 D5 1fr sepia .20 .20
J53 D5 2fr red orange .20 .20
Nos. J40-J53 (14) 2.80 2.80

Type of 1922-32

1949-53 **Typo.** *Perf. 14x13½*

J54 D4 65c emerald 7.00 3.75
J55 D4 1.60fr lilac rose ('53) 14.00 6.50
J56 D4 1.80fr red 15.00 6.50
J57 D4 2.40fr gray lilac ('53) 9.00 4.00
J58 D4 4fr deep blue ('53) 11.00 .50
J59 D4 5fr red brown 3.50 .40
J60 D4 8fr lilac rose 7.25 3.75
J61 D4 10fr dark violet 7.25 3.75
Nos. J54-J61 (8) 74.00 29.15

Numerals 6½mm or More High

1966-70 **Photo.**

J62 D6 1fr brt pink .20 .20
J63 D6 2fr blue green .20 .20
J64 D6 3fr blue .20 .20
J65 D6 5fr purple .25 .20
J66 D6 6fr bister brn .40 .25
J67 D6 7fr red org ('70) .45 .30
J68 D6 20fr slate grn 1.50 1.00
Nos. J62-J68 (7) 3.20 2.35

Printed on various papers.

Numerals 4½-5½mm High

1985-87 **Photo.** *Perf. 14x13½*

J69 D6 1fr lilac rose .20 .20
J70 D6 2fr dull blue grn .20 .20
J71 D6 3fr greenish blue .20 .20
J72 D6 4fr green .20 .20
J73 D6 5fr lt violet .25 .20
J73A D6 6fr brown — —
J74 D6 7fr brt orange .35 .30
J75 D6 8fr pale gray .40 .30
J76 D6 9fr rose lake .45 .35
J77 D6 10fr lt red brown .50 .40
J78 D6 20fr lt olive grn 1.10 1.10
Nos. J69-J78 (10) 3.85 3.45

Printed on various papers.

Issue dates: 3fr, 4fr, 8fr-10fr, Mar. 25, 1985. 6fr, 9/5/86. 20fr, 9/8/86. 2fr, 11/12/86. 6fr, 9/5/86. 1fr, 5fr, 7fr, 1987.

This is an expanding set. Numbers will change again if necessary.

MILITARY STAMPS

Catalogue values for unused stamps in this section are for Never Hinged items.

King Baudouin
M1 M2

Unwmk.

1967, July 17 **Photo.** *Perf. 11*

M1 M1 1.50fr greenish gray .25 .25

1971-75 **Engr.** *Perf. 11½*

M2 M2 1.75fr green .50 .45
M3 M2 2.25fr gray green ('72) .30 .30
M4 M2 2.50fr gray green ('74) .20 .20
M5 M2 3.25fr vio brown ('75) .25 .20
Nos. M2-M5 (4) 1.25 1.15

#M1-M3 are luminescent, #M4-M5 are not.

MILITARY PARCEL POST STAMP

Type of Parcel Post Stamp of 1938 Surcharged with New Value and "M" in Blue.

1939 **Unwmk.** *Perf. 13½*

MQ1 PP19 3fr on 5.50fr copper red .30 .20
Never hinged .60

OFFICIAL STAMPS

For franking the official correspondence of the Administration of the Belgian National Railways.

Most examples of Nos. O1-O25 in the marketplace are counterfeits. Values are for genuine examples.

Regular Issue of 1921-27 Overprinted in Black

1929-30 **Unwmk.** *Perf. 14*

O1 A58 5c gray .20 .20
O2 A58 10c blue green .30 .40
O3 A58 35c blue green .40 .30
O4 A58 60c olive green .45 .30
O5 A58 1.50fr brt blue 8.00 6.25
O6 A58 1.75fr ultra ('30) 1.75 2.00
Nos. O1-O6 (6) 11.10 9.45

Same Overprint, in Red or Black, on Regular Issues of 1929-30

1929-31

O7 A63 5c slate (R) .25 .35
O8 A63 10c olive grn (R) .50 .40
O9 A63 25c rose red (Bk) 1.50 .85
O10 A63 35c dp green (R) 1.75 .50
O11 A63 40c red vio (Bk) 1.25 .45
O12 A63 50c dp blue (R) ('31) .80 .35
O13 A63 60c rose (Bk) 6.00 6.00
O14 A63 70c orange brn (Bk) 4.25 1.25
O15 A63 75c black vio (R) ('31) 4.00 .85
Nos. O7-O15 (9) 20.30 11.00

Overprinted on Regular Issue of 1932

1932

O16 A73 10c olive grn (R) .50 .60
O17 A74 35c dp green 9.00 .75
O18 A71a 75c bister brn (R) 1.50 .30
Nos. O16-O18 (3) 11.00 1.65

Overprinted on No. 262 in Red

1935 *Perf. 13½x14*

O19 A80 70c olive black 2.75 .25

Regular Stamps of 1935-36 Overprinted in Red

1936-38 *Perf. 13½, 13½x14, 14*

O20 A82 10c olive bister .20 *.35*
O21 A82 35c green .25 *.40*
O22 A82 50c dark blue .45 .35
O23 A83 70c brown 1.50 .65

Overprinted in Black or Red on Regular Issue of 1938

Perf. 13½x14

O24 A82 40c red violet (Bk) .30 *.35*
O25 A85 75c olive gray (R) .65 .30
Nos. O20-O25 (6) 3.35 2.40

Regular Issues of 1935-41 Overprinted in Red or Dark Blue

1941-44 *Perf. 14, 14x13½, 13½x14*

O26 A82 10c olive bister .20 .20
a. Inverted overprint *40.00*
O27 A82 40c red violet .55 *.75*
O28 A82 50c dark blue .20 .20
a. Inverted overprint
O29 A83a 1fr rose car (Bl) .45 .35
O30 A85 1fr rose pink (Bl) .20 .20
O31 A83a 2.25fr grnsh blk ('44) .30 *.50*
O32 A84 2.25fr gray violet .45 *.70*
Nos. O26-O32 (7) 2.35 *2.90*

Nos. O21, O23 and O25 Surcharged with New Values in Black or Red

1942

O33 A82 10c on 35c green .20 *.35*
O34 A83 50c on 70c brown .20 .20
O35 A85 50c on 75c ol gray (R) .20 .20
Nos. O33-O35 (3) .60 .75

Counterfeits exist of Nos. O26-O35.

Catalogue values for unused stamps in this section, from this point to the end of the section, are for Never Hinged items.

O1 O2

1946-48 **Unwmk.** *Perf. 14*

O36 O1 10c olive bister .25 .20
O37 O1 20c brt violet 2.00 .50
O38 O1 50c dk blue .25 .20
O39 O1 65c red lilac ('48) 3.25 .75
O40 O1 75c lilac rose .25 .20
O41 O1 90c brown violet 4.25 .35
Nos. O36-O41 (6) 10.25 2.20

Types A99, A101 and A102 with "B" Emblem Added to Design

1948 *Perf. 11½*

O42 A99 1.35fr red brown 4.25 .75
O43 A99 1.75fr dk gray green 4.75 .25
O44 A101 3fr brt red violet 25.00 3.50
O45 A102 3.15fr deep blue 11.00 7.00
O46 A102 4fr brt ultra 20.00 13.00
Nos. O42-O46 (5) 65.00 24.50

1953-66 **Typo.** *Perf. 13½x14*

O47 O2 10c orange .65 .20
O48 O2 20c red lilac .80 .25
O49 O2 30c gray green ('58) .80 .55
O50 O2 40c olive gray .50 .20
O51 O2 50c light blue .75 .20
O51A O2 60c lilac rose ('66) 1.10 .55
O52 O2 65c red lilac 27.50 21.00
O53 O2 80c emerald 4.50 .70
O54 O2 90c deep blue 6.00 .85
O55 O2 1fr rose .40 .20
Nos. O47-O55 (10) 43.00 24.70

See Nos. O66, O68.

King Baudouin
O3 O4

1954-70 **Photo.** *Perf. 11½*

O56 O3 1.50fr gray .30 .20
O57 O3 2fr rose red 37.50 .25
O58 O3 2fr blue grn ('59) .30 .20
O59 O3 2.50fr red brown ('58) 27.50 .75
O60 O3 3fr red lilac ('58) 1.25 .20
O61 O3 3.50fr yel green ('70) .75 .20
O62 O3 4fr brt blue .90 .25
O63 O3 6fr car rose ('58) 1.50 .60
Nos. O56-O63 (8) 70.00 2.65

Type of 1953-66 Redrawn

1970-75 **Typo.** *Perf. 13½x14*

O66 O2 1.50fr grnsh gray ('75) .20 .20
O68 O2 2.50fr brown .20 .20

1971-73 **Engr.** *Perf. 11½*

O71 O4 3.50fr org brn ('73) .25 .25
O72 O4 4.50fr brown ('73) .25 .25
O73 O4 7fr red .40 .50
O74 O4 15fr violet .75 .30
Nos. O71-O74 (4) 1.65 1.30

Nos. O71-O74 are on luminescent paper.

1974-80

O75 O4 3fr yellow grn 1.50 1.00
O76 O4 4fr blue 1.50 .50
O77 O4 4.50fr grnsh bl ('75) .30 .20
O78 O4 5fr lilac .30 .20
O79 O4 6fr carmine ('78) .35 .20
O80 O4 6.50fr black ('76) .40 .35
O81 O4 8fr bluish blk ('78) .50 .25
O82 O4 9fr lt red brn ('80) .55 .25
O83 O4 10fr rose carmine .60 .25
O84 O4 25fr lilac ('76) 1.50 .50
O85 O4 30fr org brn ('78) 1.75 .50
Nos. O75-O85 (11) 9.25 4.20

Heraldic Lion — O5

1977-82 **Typo.** *Perf. 13½x14*

O87 O5 50c brown ('82) .20 .20
O92 O5 1fr lilac ('82) .20 .20
O94 O5 2fr orange ('82) .20 .20
O95 O5 4fr red brown .25 .20
O96 O5 5fr green ('80) .25 .20
Nos. O87-O96 (5) 1.10 1.00

NEWSPAPER STAMPS

Most examples of Nos. P1-P40 in the marketplace are counterfeits. Values are for genuine examples.

Parcel Post Stamps of 1923-27 Overprinted

Perf. 14½x14, 14x14½

1928 **Unwmk.**

P1 PP12 10c vermilion .25 *.40*
P2 PP12 20c turq blue .25 *.40*
P3 PP12 40c olive grn .25 *.40*
P4 PP12 60c orange .70 *.90*
P5 PP12 70c dk brown .45 .40
P6 PP12 80c violet .60 *.70*
P7 PP12 90c slate 2.25 2.00
P8 PP13 1fr brt blue .90 .60
a. 1fr ultramarine 12.00 5.00
P10 PP13 2fr olive grn 1.50 .60
P11 PP13 3fr orange red 1.60 .90
P12 PP13 4fr rose 2.25 1.10
P13 PP13 5fr violet 2.25 1.00
P14 PP13 6fr bister brn 4.50 1.75
P15 PP13 7fr orange 5.00 2.25
P16 PP13 8fr dk brown 6.00 2.75

P17 PP13 9fr red violet 10.00 3.00
P18 PP13 10fr blue green 9.00 2.75
P19 PP13 20fr magenta 15.00 7.00
Nos. P1-P8,P10-P19 (18) 62.75 28.90

Parcel Post Stamps of 1923-28 Overprinted

1929-31

P20 PP12 10c vermilion .25 .20
P21 PP12 20c turq blue .25 .20
P22 PP12 40c olive green .30 .20
a. Inverted overprint
P23 PP12 60c orange .55 .35
P24 PP12 70c dk brown .55 .20
P25 PP12 80c violet .60 .25
P26 PP12 90c gray 2.00 1.00
P27 PP13 1fr ultra .60 .25
a. 1fr bright blue 4.00 2.50
P28 PP13 1.10fr org brn ('31) 6.25 1.40
P29 PP13 1.50fr gray vio ('31) 6.25 1.90
P30 PP13 2fr olive green 2.00 .25
P31 PP13 2.10fr sl gray ('31) 17.00 12.00
P32 PP13 3fr orange red 2.25 .45
P33 PP13 4fr rose 2.25 .70
P34 PP13 5fr violet 3.00 .55
P35 PP13 6fr bister brn 3.75 1.00
P36 PP13 7fr orange 3.75 1.00
P37 PP13 8fr dk brown 3.75 1.00
P38 PP13 9fr red violet 5.25 1.50
P39 PP13 10fr blue green 3.75 1.10
P40 PP13 20fr magenta 13.00 4.50
Nos. P20-P40 (21) 77.35 30.00

PARCEL POST AND RAILWAY STAMPS

Values for used Railway Stamps (Chemins de Fer) stamps are for copies with railway cancellations. Railway Stamps with postal cancellations sell for twice as much.

Coat of Arms — PP1

1879-82 Unwmk. Typo. *Perf. 14*

Q1 PP1 10c violet brown 57.50 5.75
Q2 PP1 20c blue 175.00 17.50
Q3 PP1 25c green ('81) 225.00 10.00
Q4 PP1 50c carmine 1,250. 10.00
Q5 PP1 80c yellow 1,350. 57.50
Q6 PP1 1fr gray ('82) 175.00 16.00

Used copies of Nos. Q1-Q6 with pinholes, a normal state, sell for approximately one third the values given.

Most of the stamps of 1882-1902 (Nos. Q7 to Q28) are without watermark. Twice in each sheet of 100 stamps they have one of three watermarks: (1) A winged wheel and "Chemins de Fer de l'Etat Belge," (2) Coat of Arms of Belgium and "Royaume de Belgique," (3) Larger Coat of Arms, without inscription.

PP2

1882-94 *Perf. 15½x14¼*

Q7 PP2 10c brown ('86) 20.00 1.50
Q8 PP2 15c gray ('94) 8.75 7.25
Q9 PP2 20c blue ('86) 65.00 7.00
Q10 PP2 25c yel grn ('91) 72.50 4.25
Q11 PP2 50c carmine 72.50 2.50
Q12 PP2 80c brnsh buff 72.50 .90
Q13 PP2 80c lemon 75.00 1.60
Q14 PP2 1fr lavender 350.00 3.00
Q15 PP2 2fr yel buff ('94) 210.00 67.50

Counterfeits exist.

PP3

Name of engraver below frame

1895-97

Numerals in Black, except 1fr, 2fr

Q16 PP3 10c red brown ('96) 11.00 .60
Q17 PP3 15c gray 11.00 7.00
Q18 PP3 20c blue 17.50 1.00
Q19 PP3 25c green 17.50 1.25
Q20 PP3 50c carmine 25.00 .80
Q21 PP3 60c violet ('96) 50.00 1.00
Q22 PP3 80c ol yel ('96) 50.00 1.40
Q23 PP3 1fr lilac brown 175.00 3.00
Q24 PP3 2fr yel buff ('97) 200.00 15.00

Counterfeits exist.

1901-02

Numerals in Black

Q25 PP3 30c orange 21.00 2.00
Q26 PP3 40c green 26.00 1.75
Q27 PP3 70c blue 50.00 1.40
a. Numerals omitted 750.00
b. Numerals printed on reverse 750.00
Q28 PP3 90c red 65.00 2.00
Nos. Q25-Q28 (4) 162.00 7.15

Winged Wheel PP4

Without engraver's name

1902-14 *Perf. 15*

Q29 PP3 10c yel brn & slate .20 .20
Q30 PP3 15c slate & vio .20 .20
Q31 PP3 20c ultra & yel brn .20 .20
Q32 PP3 25c yel grn & red .20 .20
Q33 PP3 30c orange & bl grn .20 .20
Q34 PP3 35c bister & bl grn ('12) .35 .20
Q35 PP3 40c blue grn & vio .20 .20
Q36 PP3 50c pale rose & vio .20 .20
Q37 PP3 55c lilac brn & ultra ('14) .35 .20
Q38 PP3 60c violet & red .20 .20
Q39 PP3 70c blue & red .20 .20
Q40 PP3 80c lemon & vio brn .20 .20
Q41 PP3 90c red & yel grn .20 .20
Q42 PP4 1fr vio brn & org .20 .20
Q43 PP4 1.10fr rose & blk ('06) .20 .20
Q44 PP4 2fr ocher & bl grn .20 .20
Q45 PP4 3fr black & ultra .35 .20
Q46 PP4 4fr yel grn & red ('13) 1.25 .70
Q47 PP4 5fr org & bl grn ('13) .55 .55
Q48 PP4 10fr ol yel & brn vio ('13) .90 .55
Nos. Q29-Q48 (20) 6.55 5.20

Regular Issues of 1912-13 Handstamped in Violet

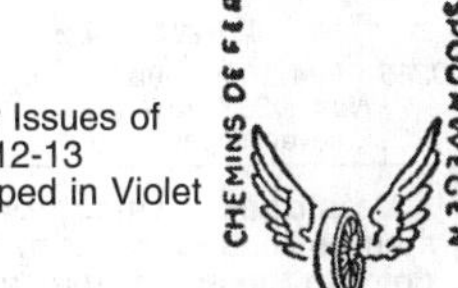

1915 *Perf. 14*

Q49 A42 5c green 160.00 160.00
Q50 A43 10c red 800.00 800.00
Q51 A45 10c red 175.00 175.00
a. With engraver's name 750.00 750.00
Q52 A43 20c olive grn *1,200. 1,200.*
Q53 A45 20c olive grn 200.00 200.00
a. With engraver's name 750.00 750.00
Q54 A45 25c ultra 200.00 200.00
a. With engraver's name 750.00 750.00
Q55 A43 35c bister brn 250.00 250.00
Q55A A43 40c green *1,750. 1,750.*
Q56 A45 40c green 250.00 250.00
Q57 A43 50c gray 250.00 250.00
Q58 A43 1fr orange 200.00 200.00
Q59 A43 2fr violet *1,650. 1,650.*
Q60 A44 5fr plum *3,500. 3,500.*

Excellent forgeries of this overprint exist.

PP5

PP6

1916 Litho. *Perf. 13½*

Q61 PP5 10c pale blue 1.10 .20
Q62 PP5 15c olive grn 1.40 .50
Q63 PP5 20c red 2.25 .50
Q64 PP5 25c lt brown 2.25 .50
Q65 PP5 30c lilac 1.40 .50
Q66 PP5 35c gray 1.40 .45
Q67 PP5 40c orange yel 3.00 1.50
Q68 PP5 50c bister 2.25 .45
Q69 PP5 55c brown 3.00 2.25
Q70 PP5 60c gray vio 2.25 .45
Q71 PP5 70c green 2.25 .45
Q72 PP5 80c red brown 2.25 .45
Q73 PP5 90c blue 2.25 .45
Q74 PP6 1fr gray 2.25 .45
Q75 PP6 1.10fr ultra *(Franken)* 27.50 21.00
Q76 PP6 2fr red 25.00 .45
Q77 PP6 3fr violet 25.00 .45
Q78 PP6 4fr emerald 45.00 1.50
Q79 PP6 5fr brown 45.00 3.00
Q80 PP6 10fr orange 45.00 1.50
Nos. Q61-Q80 (20) 241.80 37.00

Type of 1916 Inscribed "FRANK" instead of "FRANKEN"

1920

Q81 PP6 1.10fr ultra 2.00 .45

PP7

PP8

1920 *Perf. 14*

Q82 PP7 10c blue grn 1.75 .75
Q83 PP7 15c olive grn 1.75 1.10
Q84 PP7 20c red 1.75 .75
Q85 PP7 25c gray brn 2.50 .75
Q86 PP7 30c red vio 27.00 22.50
Q87 PP7 40c pale org 11.00 .75
Q88 PP7 50c bister 9.00 .75
Q89 PP7 55c pale brown 5.50 4.50
Q90 PP7 60c dk violet 10.00 .75
Q91 PP7 70c green 18.00 1.10
Q92 PP7 80c red brown 40.00 1.50
Q93 PP7 90c dull blue 10.00 .75
Q94 PP8 1fr gray 85.00 1.50
Q95 PP8 1.10fr ultra 26.00 2.00
Q96 PP8 1.20fr dk green 11.00 .75
Q97 PP8 1.40fr black brn 11.00 .75
Q98 PP8 2fr vermilion 110.00 1.25
Q99 PP8 3fr red vio 125.00 .85
Q100 PP8 4fr yel grn 125.00 .75
Q101 PP8 5fr bister brn 125.00 .75
Q102 PP8 10fr brown org 125.00 .75
Nos. Q82-Q102 (21) 881.25 45.30

PP9

PP10

Types PP7 and PP9 differ in the position of the wheel and the tablet above it.

Types PP8 and PP10 differ in the bars below "FR".

There are many other variations in the designs.

1920-21 Typo.

Q103 PP9 10c carmine .30 .20
Q104 PP9 15c yel grn .30 .20
Q105 PP9 20c blue grn .70 .20

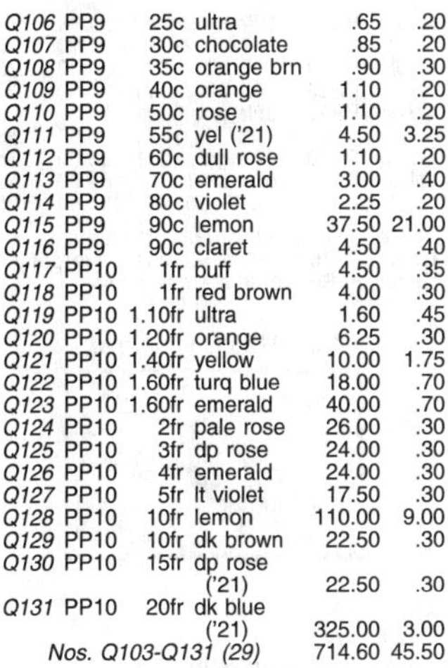

Q106 PP9 25c ultra .65 .20
Q107 PP9 30c chocolate .85 .20
Q108 PP9 35c orange brn .90 .30
Q109 PP9 40c orange 1.10 .20
Q110 PP9 50c rose 1.10 .20
Q111 PP9 55c yel ('21) 4.50 3.25
Q112 PP9 60c dull rose 1.10 .20
Q113 PP9 70c emerald 3.00 .40
Q114 PP9 80c violet 2.25 .20
Q115 PP9 90c lemon 37.50 21.00
Q116 PP9 90c claret 4.50 .40
Q117 PP10 1fr buff 4.50 .35
Q118 PP10 1fr red brown 4.00 .30
Q119 PP10 1.10fr ultra 1.60 .45
Q120 PP10 1.20fr orange 6.25 .30
Q121 PP10 1.40fr yellow 10.00 1.75
Q122 PP10 1.60fr turq blue 18.00 .70
Q123 PP10 1.60fr emerald 40.00 .70
Q124 PP10 2fr pale rose 26.00 .30
Q125 PP10 3fr dp rose 24.00 .30
Q126 PP10 4fr emerald 24.00 .30
Q127 PP10 5fr lt violet 17.50 .30
Q128 PP10 10fr lemon 110.00 9.00
Q129 PP10 10fr dk brown 22.50 .30
Q130 PP10 15fr dp rose ('21) 22.50 .30
Q131 PP10 20fr dk blue ('21) 325.00 3.00
Nos. Q103-Q131 (29) 714.60 45.50

PP11

1922 Engr. *Perf. 11½*

Q132 PP11 2fr black 4.00 .20
Q133 PP11 3fr brown 37.50 .20
Q134 PP11 4fr green 9.00 .20
Q135 PP11 5r claret 9.00 .20
Q136 PP11 10fr yel brown 10.00 .20
Q137 PP11 15fr rose red 10.00 .25
Q138 PP11 20fr blue 67.50 .25
Nos. Q132-Q138 (7) 147.00 1.50

PP12

PP13

Perf. 14x13½, 13½x14

1923-40 Typo.

Q139 PP12 5c red brn .20 .25
Q140 PP12 10c vermilion .20 .20
Q141 PP12 15c ultra .20 .30
Q142 PP12 20c turq blue .20 .20
Q143 PP12 30c brn vio ('27) .20 .20
Q144 PP12 40c olive grn .20 .20
Q145 PP12 50c mag ('27) .20 .20
Q146 PP12 60c orange .25 .20
Q147 PP12 70c dk brn ('24) .20 .20
Q148 PP12 80c violet .20 .20
Q149 PP12 90c sl ('27) 1.25 .20
Q150 PP13 1fr ultra .35 .20
Q151 PP13 1fr brt blue ('28) .55 .20
Q152 PP13 1.10fr orange 3.00 .30
Q153 PP13 1.50fr turq blue 3.25 .30
Q154 PP13 1.70fr dp brown ('31) .75 .60
Q155 PP13 1.80fr claret 4.25 .60
Q156 PP13 2fr olive grn ('24) .35 .20
Q157 PP13 2.10fr gray grn 7.50 .85
Q158 PP13 2.40fr dp violet 4.00 .85
Q159 PP13 2.70fr gray ('24) 12.00 .75
Q160 PP13 3fr org red .45 .20
Q161 PP13 3.30fr brn ('24) 12.50 .75
Q162 PP13 4fr rose ('24) .55 .20
Q163 PP13 5fr vio ('24) .90 .20
Q163A PP13 5fr brn vio ('40) .45 .30
Q164 PP13 6fr bis brn ('27) .50 .20
Q165 PP13 7fr org ('27) .90 .20
Q166 PP13 8fr dp brown ('27) .75 .20
Q167 PP13 9fr red vio ('27) 2.50 .20

Q168 PP13 10fr blue grn ('27) 1.10 .20
Q168A PP13 10fr blk ('40) 4.00 3.75
Q169 PP13 20fr mag ('27) 1.90 .20
Q170 PP13 30fr turq grn ('31) 6.00 .40
Q171 PP13 40fr gray ('31) 55.00 .75
Q172 PP13 50fr bis ('27) 9.00 .30
Nos. Q139-Q172 (36) 135.80 15.25

See Nos. Q239-Q262. For overprints see Nos. Q216-Q238. Stamps overprinted "Bagages Reisgoed" are revenues.

No. Q158 Surcharged

1924

Green Surcharge

Q173 PP13 2.30fr on 2.40fr violet 3.00 .50
Never hinged 12.00
a. Inverted surcharge 57.50

Type of Regular Issue of 1926-27 Overprinted

1928 ***Perf. 14***

Q174 A61 4fr buff 6.50 .90
Q175 A61 5fr bister 6.50 1.10
Set, never hinged 40.00

Central P.O., Brussels PP15

1929-30 Engr. *Perf. 11½*

Q176 PP15 3fr black brn 1.40 .20
Q177 PP15 4fr gray 1.40 .20
Q178 PP15 5fr carmine 1.40 .20
Q179 PP15 6fr vio brn ('30) 22.50 25.00
Nos. Q176-Q179 (4) 26.70 25.60
Set, never hinged 100.00

No. Q179 Surcharged in Blue

1933

Q180 PP15 4(fr) on 6fr vio brn 25.00 .25
Never hinged 90.00

Modern Locomotive PP16

1934 Photo. *Perf. 13½x14*

Q181 PP16 3fr dk green 10.00 2.50
Q182 PP16 4fr red violet 3.00 .20
Q183 PP16 5fr dp rose 9.50 .20
Nos. Q181-Q183 (3) 22.50 2.90
Set, never hinged 120.00

Modern Railroad Train — PP17

Old Railroad Train — PP18

1935 Engr. *Perf. 14x13½, 13½x14*

Q184 PP17 10c rose car .30 .20
Q185 PP17 20c violet .35 .20
Q186 PP17 30c black brn .45 .30
Q187 PP17 40c dk blue .55 .20
Q188 PP17 50c orange red .55 .20
Q189 PP17 60c green .65 .20
Q190 PP17 70c ultra .70 .20
Q191 PP17 80c olive blk .65 .20
Q192 PP17 90c rose lake .85 .45
Q193 PP18 1fr brown vio .85 .20
Q194 PP18 2fr gray blk 2.00 .20
Q195 PP18 3fr red org 2.50 .20
Q196 PP18 4fr violet brn 3.00 .20
Q197 PP18 5fr plum 3.25 .20
Q198 PP18 6fr dp green 3.50 .20
Q199 PP18 7fr dp violet 17.00 .20
Q200 PP18 8fr olive blk 17.00 .20
Q201 PP18 9fr dk blue 17.00 .20
Q202 PP18 10fr car lake 17.00 .20
Q203 PP18 20fr green 90.00 .20
Q204 PP18 30fr violet 90.00 2.00
Q205 PP18 40fr black brn 90.00 2.50
Q206 PP18 50fr rose car 100.00 2.00
Q207 PP18 100fr ultra 250.00 45.00
Nos. Q184-Q207 (24) 708.15 55.85
Set, never hinged 1,750.

Centenary of Belgian State Railway.

Winged Wheel PP19

Surcharge in Red or Blue

1938 Photo. *Perf. 13½*

Q208 PP19 5fr on 3.50fr dk grn 6.50 .45
Q209 PP19 5fr on 4.50fr rose vio (Bl) .20 .20
Q210 PP19 6fr on 5.50fr cop red (Bl) .30 .20
a. Half used as 3fr on piece 8.00
Nos. Q208-Q210 (3) 7.00 .85
Set, never hinged 50.00

Nos. Q208-Q210 exist without surcharge. Value, set, $550.

See Nos. MQ1, Q297-Q299.

Symbolizing Unity Achieved Through Railroads PP20

1939 Engr. *Perf. 13½x14*

Q211 PP20 20c redsh brn 3.50 *3.75*
Q212 PP20 50c vio bl 3.50 *3.75*
Q213 PP20 2fr rose red 3.50 *3.75*
Q214 PP20 9fr slate grn 3.50 *3.75*
Q215 PP20 10fr dk vio 3.50 *3.75*
Nos. Q211-Q215 (5) 17.50 *18.75*
Set, never hinged 22.50

Railroad Exposition and Cong. held at Brussels.

Parcel Post Stamps of 1925-27 Overprinted in Blue or Carmine

Perf. 14½x14, 14x14½

1940 Unwmk.

Q216 PP12 10c vermilion .20 .20
Q217 PP12 20c turq bl (C) .20 .20
Q218 PP12 30c brn vio .20 .20
Q219 PP12 40c ol grn (C) .20 .20
Q220 PP12 50c magenta .20 .20
Q221 PP12 60c orange .20 *.25*
Q222 PP12 70c dk brn .20 .20
Q223 PP12 80c vio (C) .20 .20
Q224 PP12 90c slate (C) .25 .25
Q225 PP13 1fr ultra (C) .25 .20
Q226 PP13 2fr ol grn (C) .25 .20
Q227 PP13 3fr org red .25 .20
Q228 PP13 4fr rose .25 .20
Q229 PP13 5fr vio (C) .25 .20
Q230 PP13 6fr bis brn .35 .25
Q231 PP13 7fr orange .35 .20
Q232 PP13 8fr dp brn .35 .20
Q233 PP13 9fr red vio .35 .20
Q234 PP13 10fr bl grn (C) .35 .25
Q235 PP13 20fr magenta .60 .25
Q236 PP13 30fr turq grn (C) 1.10 .75
Q237 PP13 40fr gray (C) 1.40 *2.00*
Q238 PP13 50fr bister 1.60 1.10
Nos. Q216-Q238 (23) 9.55 8.10
Set, never hinged 16.00

Types of 1923-40

1941

Q239 PP12 10c dl olive .20 .20
Q240 PP12 20c lt vio .20 .20
Q241 PP12 30c fawn .20 .20
Q242 PP12 40c dull blue .20 .20
Q243 PP12 50c lt grn .20 .20
Q244 PP12 60c gray .20 .20
Q245 PP12 70c chalky grn .20 .20
Q246 PP12 80c orange .20 .20
Q247 PP12 90c rose lilac .20 .20
Q248 PP13 1fr lt yel grn .20 .20
Q249 PP13 2fr vio brn .40 .20
Q250 PP13 3fr slate .45 .20
Q251 PP13 4fr dl olive .50 .20
Q252 PP13 5fr rose lilac .50 .20
Q253 PP13 5fr black .85 .30
Q254 PP13 6fr org ver .75 .30
Q255 PP13 7fr lilac .75 .20
Q256 PP13 8fr chalky grn .75 .20
Q257 PP13 9fr blue .90 .20
Q258 PP13 10fr rose lilac .90 .20
Q259 PP13 20fr milky blue 2.00 .20
Q260 PP13 30fr orange 4.50 .35
Q261 PP13 40fr rose 5.00 .35
Q262 PP13 50fr brt red vio 6.75 .20
Nos. Q239-Q262 (24) 27.00 5.30
Set, never hinged 90.00

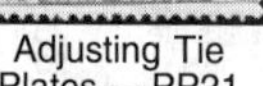

Adjusting Tie Plates — PP21

Engineer at Throttle — PP22

Freight Station Interior — PP23

Signal and Electric Train — PP24

1942 Engr. *Perf. 14x13½*

Q263 PP21 9.20fr red org .60 *.85*
Q264 PP22 12.30fr dp grn .60 *.90*
Q265 PP23 14.30fr dk car .80 *1.25*

Perf. 11½

Q266 PP24 100fr ultra 20.00 17.00
Nos. Q263-Q266 (4) 22.00 20.00
Set, never hinged 25.00

Catalogue values for unused stamps in this section, from this point to the end of the section, are for Never Hinged items.

PP25

PP26

PP27

1945-46 Photo. Unwmk.

Q267 PP25 10c ol blk ('46) .30 .20
Q268 PP25 20c dp vio .30 .20
Q269 PP25 30c chnt brn ('46) .30 .20
Q270 PP25 40c dp bl ('46) .30 .20
Q271 PP25 50c peacock grn .30 .20
Q272 PP25 60c blk ('46) .30 .20
Q273 PP25 70c emer ('46) .45 .25
Q274 PP25 80c orange .75 .20
Q275 PP25 90c brn vio ('46) .30 .25
Q276 PP26 1fr bl grn ('46) .30 .20
Q277 PP26 2fr blk brn .30 .20
Q278 PP26 3fr grnsh blk ('46) 2.00 .20
Q279 PP26 4fr dark blue .45 .20
Q280 PP26 5fr sepia .50 .20
Q281 PP26 6fr dk ol grn ('46) 2.25 .20
Q282 PP26 7fr dk vio ('46) .75 .25
Q283 PP26 8fr red org .75 .20
Q284 PP26 9fr dp bl ('46) .90 .20
Q285 PP27 10fr dk red ('46) 3.25 .20
Q286 PP27 10fr sepia ('46) 1.60 .25
Q287 PP27 20fr dk yel grn ('46) .75 .20
Q288 PP27 30fr dp vio 1.00 .20
Q289 PP27 40fr rose pink .90 .20
Q290 PP27 50fr brt bl ('46) 12.00 .20
Nos. Q267-Q290 (24) 31.00 5.00

Mercury — PP28

1945-46 *Perf. 13½x13*

Q291 PP28 3fr emer ('46) .25 .25
Q292 PP28 5fr ultra .20 .20
Q293 PP28 6fr red .20 .20

Inscribed "Belgique-Belgie"

Q294 PP28 3fr emer ('46) .25 .25
Q295 PP28 5fr ultra .20 .20
Q296 PP28 6fr red .20 .20
Nos. Q291-Q296 (6) 1.30 1.30

Winged Wheel Type of 1938 Carmine Surcharge

1946 *Perf. 13½x14*

Q297 PP19 8fr on 5.50fr brn .65 .20
Q298 PP19 10fr on 5.50fr dk bl .75 .20
Q299 PP19 12fr on 5.50fr vio 1.10 .20
Nos. Q297-Q299 (3) 2.50 .60

Railway Crossing PP29

1947 Engr. *Perf. 12½*

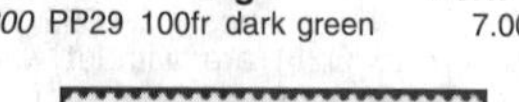

Q300 PP29 100fr dark green 7.00 .25

Crossbowman with Train — PP30

1947 Photo. *Perf. 11½*

Q301 PP30 8fr dark olive brn 1.00 .20
Q302 PP30 10fr gray & blue 1.10 .25
Q303 PP30 12fr dark violet 1.60 .45
Nos. Q301-Q303 (3) 3.70 .90

Surcharged with New Value and Bars in Carmine

1948

Q304 PP30 9fr on 8fr 1.25 .20
Q305 PP30 11fr on 10fr 1.25 .25
Q306 PP30 13.50fr on 12fr 2.00 .25
Nos. Q304-Q306 (3) 4.50 .70

Delivery of Parcel — PP31

1948

Q307 PP31 9fr chocolate 6.50 .20
Q308 PP31 11fr brown car 7.00 .20
Q309 PP31 13.50fr gray 10.50 .25
Nos. Q307-Q309 (3) 24.00 .65

Locomotive of 1835 PP32

Various Locomotives.

Lathe Work in Frame Differs

1949 Engr. *Perf. 12½*

Q310 PP32 ½fr dark brown .60 .20
Q311 PP32 1fr carmine rose .70 .20
Q312 PP32 2fr deep ultra .95 .20
Q313 PP32 3fr dp magenta 2.00 .20
Q314 PP32 4fr blue green 2.75 .20
Q315 PP32 5fr orange red 2.75 .20
Q316 PP32 6fr brown vio 3.00 .25
Q317 PP32 7fr yellow grn 4.00 .20
Q318 PP32 8fr grnsh blue 5.00 .20
Q319 PP32 9fr yellow brn 6.00 .25
Q320 PP32 10fr citron 7.25 .20
Q321 PP32 20fr orange 11.00 .20
Q322 PP32 30fr blue 15.00 .20
Q323 PP32 40fr lilac rose 21.00 .25
Q324 PP32 50fr violet 21.00 .30
Q325 PP32 100fr red 65.00 .25

Engraved; Center Typographed

Q326 PP32 10fr car rose & blk 9.00 .80
Nos. Q310-Q326 (17) 177.00 4.30

See No. Q337.

1949 Engr.

Design: Electric locomotive.

Q327 PP32 60fr black brown 20.00 .20

Opening of Charleroi-Brussels electric railway line, Oct. 15, 1949.

Mailing Parcel Post PP33

Sorting PP34

Loading PP35

1950-52 *Perf. 12, 12½*

Q328 PP33 11fr red orange 6.00 .20
Q329 PP33 12fr red vio ('51) 20.00 1.50
Q330 PP34 13fr dk blue grn 6.00 .20
Q331 PP34 15fr ultra ('51) 15.00 .30
Q332 PP35 16fr gray 6.00 .20
Q333 PP33 17fr brown ('52) 8.00 .20
Q334 PP35 18fr brt car ('51) 16.00 .45
Q335 PP35 20fr brn org ('52) 8.00 .20
Nos. Q328-Q335 (8) 85.00 3.25

For surcharges see Nos. Q338-Q340.

Mercury and Winged Wheel — PP36

1951

Q336 PP36 25fr dark blue 10.00 8.50

25th anniv. of the founding of the Natl. Soc. of Belgian Railroads.

Type of 1949

Design: Electric locomotive.

1952 Unwmk. *Perf. 11½*

Q337 PP32 300fr red violet 150.00 .50

Nos. Q331, Q328 and Q334 Surcharged with New Value and "X" in Red, Blue or Green

1953 *Perf. 12*

Q338 PP34 13fr on 15fr (R) 60.00 3.00
Q339 PP33 17fr on 11fr (Bl) 35.00 2.25
Q340 PP35 20fr on 18fr (G) 30.00 2.50
Nos. Q338-Q340 (3) 125.00 7.75

Electric Train, 1952 PP37

1953 Engr.

Q341 PP37 200fr dk yel grn & vio brn 250.00 4.00
Q342 PP37 200fr dk green 225.00 1.00

No. Q341 was issued to commemorate the opening of the railway link connecting Brussels North and South Stations, Oct. 4, 1952.

New North Station, Brussels — PP38

Chapelle Station, Brussels PP39

Designs: No. Q348, 15fr, Congress Station. 10fr, 20fr, 30fr, 40fr, 50fr, South Station. 100fr, 200fr, 300fr, Central Station.

1953-57 Unwmk. *Perf. 11½*

Q343 PP38 1fr bister .30 .20
Q344 PP38 2fr slate .40 .20
Q345 PP38 3fr blue grn .60 .20
Q346 PP38 4fr orange .80 .20
Q347 PP38 5fr red brn .80 .20
Q348 PP38 5fr dk red brn 10.00 .25
Q349 PP38 6fr rose vio 1.10 .20
Q350 PP38 7fr brt green 1.10 .20
Q351 PP38 8fr rose red 1.40 .20
Q352 PP38 9fr brt grnsh bl 2.00 .20
Q353 PP38 10fr lt grn 2.25 .20
Q354 PP38 15fr dl red 13.00 .20
Q355 PP38 20fr blue 4.00 .20
Q356 PP38 30fr purple 6.25 .20
Q357 PP38 40fr brt purple 8.00 .20
Q358 PP38 50fr lilac rose 10.00 .20
Q359 PP39 60fr brt purple 20.00 .20
Q360 PP39 80fr brown vio 30.00 .20
Q361 PP39 100fr emerald 18.00 .20
Q361A PP39 200fr brt vio bl 95.00 1.60
Q361B PP39 300fr lilac rose 175.00 2.25
Nos. Q343-Q361B (21) 400.00 7.70

Issued: #Q347, 20fr, 30fr, 1953; 80fr, 1955; 200fr, 1956; 300fr, 1957; others, 1954.

See Nos. Q407, Q431-Q432.

Electric Train — PP40

1954

Q362 PP40 13fr chocolate 14.00 .20
Q363 PP40 18fr dark blue 17.00 .20
Q364 PP40 21fr lilac rose 18.00 .45
Nos. Q362-Q364 (3) 49.00 .85

Nos. Q362-Q364 Surcharged with New Value and "X" in Blue, Red or Green

1956

Q365 PP40 14fr on 13fr (B) 8.00 .20
Q366 PP40 19fr on 18fr (R) 8.25 .25
Q367 PP40 22fr on 21fr (G) 8.75 .45
Nos. Q365-Q367 (3) 25.00 .90

Mercury and Winged Wheel — PP41

1957 Engr. *Perf. 11½*

Q368 PP41 14fr brt green 7.75 .20
Q369 PP41 19fr olive gray 8.00 .20
Q370 PP41 22fr carmine rose 8.75 .30
Nos. Q368-Q370 (3) 24.50 .70

Nos. Q369-Q370 Surcharged with New Value and "X" in Pink or Green

1959

Q371 PP41 20fr on 19fr (P) 22.50 .35
Q372 PP41 20fr on 22fr (G) 27.50 .55

Old North Station, Brussels PP42

1959 Engr. *Perf. 11½*

Q373 PP42 20fr olive green 12.50 .20

See Nos. Q381, Q383. For surcharges see Nos. Q378, Q382, Q384.

Diesel and Electric Locomotives and Association Emblem PP43

1960 Unwmk. *Perf. 11½*

Q374 PP43 20fr red 42.50 30.00
Q375 PP43 50fr dark blue 42.50 30.00
Q376 PP43 60fr red lilac 42.50 30.00
Q377 PP43 70fr emerald 42.50 30.00
Nos. Q374-Q377 (4) 170.00 120.00

Intl. Assoc. of Railway Congresses, 75th anniv.

No. Q373 Surcharged with New Value and "X" in Red

1961

Q378 PP42 24fr on 20fr ol grn 60.00 .25

South Station, Brussels — PP44

1962 Unwmk. *Perf. 11½*

Q379 PP44 24fr dull red 6.25 .25

No. Q379 Surcharged with New Value and "X" in Light Green

1963

Q380 PP44 26fr on 24fr dl red 6.50 .25

Type of 1959

Design: 26fr, Central Station, Antwerp.

1963 Engr. *Perf. 11½*

Q381 PP42 26fr blue 6.25 1.75

No. Q381 Surcharged in Red

1964, Apr. 20

Q382 PP42 28fr on 26fr blue 6.25 .25

Type of 1959

Design: 28fr, St. Peter's Station, Ghent.

1965 Engr. *Perf. 11½*

Q383 PP42 28fr red lilac 6.25 1.40

Nos. Q383 Surcharged with New Value and "X" in Green

1966

Q384 PP42 35fr on 28fr red lil 6.25 .20

Arlon Railroad Station PP45

Perf. 11½

1967, Aug. Unwmk. Engr.

Q385 PP45 25fr bister 10.00 .20
Q386 PP45 30fr blue green 5.00 .20
Q387 PP45 35fr deep blue 7.00 .35
Nos. Q385-Q387 (3) 22.00 .75

See #Q408. For surcharges see #Q410-Q412.

Electric Train PP46

Designs: 2fr, 3fr, 4fr, 5fr, 6fr, 7fr, 8fr, 9fr, like 1fr. 10fr, 20fr, 30fr, 40fr, Train going right. 50fr, 60fr, 70fr, 80fr, 90fr, Train going left. 100fr, 200fr, 300fr, Diesel train.

1968-73 Engr. *Perf. 11½*

Q388 PP46 1fr olive bis .20 .20
Q389 PP46 2fr slate .25 .20
Q390 PP46 3fr blue green .55 .20
Q391 PP46 4fr orange .55 .20
Q392 PP46 5fr brown .65 .20
Q393 PP46 6fr plum .55 .20
Q394 PP46 7fr brt green .65 .20
Q395 PP46 8fr carmine .85 .20
Q396 PP46 9fr blue 1.40 .20
Q397 PP46 10fr green 2.75 .20
Q398 PP46 20fr dk blue 1.60 .20
Q399 PP46 30fr dk purple 4.00 .20
Q400 PP46 40fr brt lilac 5.50 .20
Q401 PP46 50fr brt pink 6.75 .20
Q402 PP46 60fr brt violet 8.25 .30
Q402A PP46 70fr dp bister ('73) 6.75 .30
Q403 PP46 80fr dk brown 6.75 .20
Q403A PP46 90fr yel grn ('73) 5.50 .30
Q404 PP46 100fr emerald 11.00 .25
Q405 PP46 200fr violet blue 13.00 .50
Q406 PP46 300fr lilac rose 22.50 1.25
Nos. Q388-Q406 (21) 100.00 5.90

See No. Q409.

Types of 1953-68

10fr, Congress Station, Brussels. 40fr, Arlon Station. 500fr, Electric train going left.

1968, June Engr. *Perf. 11½*

Q407	PP38	10fr gray	1.50	.20
Q408	PP45	40fr vermilion	22.50	.20
Q409	PP46	500fr yellow	30.00	1.90
		Nos. Q407-Q409 (3)	54.00	2.30

Nos. Q385, Q387 and Q408 Surcharged with New Value and "X"

1970, Dec.

Q410	PP45	37fr on 25fr bister	45.00	3.00
Q411	PP45	48fr on 35fr dp bl	13.00	5.00
Q412	PP45	53fr on 40fr ver	15.00	6.00
		Nos. Q410-Q412 (3)	73.00	14.00

Ostend Station PP47

1971, Mar. Engr. *Perf. 11½*

Q413	PP47	32fr bis & blk	2.50	2.25
Q414	PP47	37fr gray & blk	2.50	2.50
Q415	PP47	42fr bl & blk	4.00	3.00
Q416	PP47	44fr brt rose & blk	4.50	3.00
Q417	PP47	46fr vio & blk	4.50	3.00
Q418	PP47	50fr brick red & blk	5.25	3.25
Q419	PP47	52fr sep & blk	5.25	3.25
Q420	PP47	54fr yel grn & blk	5.75	3.25
Q421	PP47	61fr grnsh bl & blk	5.75	4.00
		Nos. Q413-Q421 (9)	40.00	27.50

Nos. Q413-Q416, Q419-Q421 Surcharged with New Value and "X"

1971, Dec. 15

Denomination in Black

Q422	PP47	34fr on 32fr bister	2.00	.55
Q423	PP47	40fr on 37fr gray	2.50	.70
Q424	PP47	47fr on 44fr brt rose	2.75	.80
Q425	PP47	53fr on 42fr blue	3.25	.85
Q426	PP47	56fr on 52fr sepia	3.25	1.00
Q427	PP47	59fr on 54fr yel grn	3.25	1.00
Q428	PP47	66fr on 61fr grnsh blue	4.00	1.10
		Nos. Q422-Q428 (7)	21.00	6.00

Track, Underpinning of Railroad Car and Emblems — PP48

1972, Mar. Photo.

Q429	PP48	100fr emer, red & blk	10.00	1.10

Centenary of International Railroad Union.

Congress Emblem PP49

1974, Apr. Photo. *Perf. 11½*

Q430	PP49	100fr yel, blk & red	8.00	1.25

4th International Symposium on Railroad Cybernetics, Washington, DC, Apr. 1974.

Type of 1953-1957

1975, June 1 Engr. *Perf. 11½*

Q431	PP38	20fr emerald	1.75	.20
Q432	PP38	50fr blue	3.75	.55

Railroad Tracks PP50

1976, June 10 Photo. *Perf. 11½*

Q433	PP50	20fr ultra & multi	3.00	.20
Q434	PP50	50fr brt grn & multi	1.75	.50
Q435	PP50	100fr dp org & multi	4.00	1.00
Q436	PP50	150fr brt lil & multi	6.25	1.75
		Nos. Q433-Q436 (4)	15.00	3.45

Railroad Station — PP51

1977 Photo. *Perf. 11½*

Q437	PP51	1000fr multi	40.00	10.00

See note following No. Q465.

Freight Car — PP52

Designs: 1fr-9fr, Freight car. 10fr-40fr, Hopper car. 50fr-90fr, Maintenance car. 100fr-500fr, Liquid fuel car.

1980, Dec. 16 Engr. *Perf. 11½*

Q438	PP52	1fr bis brn & blk	.20	.20
Q439	PP52	2fr claret & blk	.20	.20
Q440	PP52	3fr brt bl & blk	.20	.20
Q441	PP52	4fr grnsh blk & blk	.20	.20
Q442	PP52	5fr sepia & blk	.20	.20
Q443	PP52	6fr dp org & blk	.35	.20
Q444	PP52	7fr purple & blk	.40	.20
Q445	PP52	8fr black	.40	.20
Q446	PP52	9fr green & blk	.45	.20
Q447	PP52	10fr yel bis & blk	.50	.20
Q448	PP52	20fr grnsh bl & blk	1.10	.20
Q449	PP52	30fr bister & blk	2.25	.35
Q450	PP52	40fr lt lil & blk	2.50	.40
Q451	PP52	50fr dk brn & blk	2.75	.55
Q452	PP52	60fr olive & blk	2.75	.70
Q453	PP52	70fr vio bl & blk	3.50	.75
Q454	PP52	80fr vio brn & blk	4.00	.85
Q455	PP52	90fr lil rose & blk	5.00	.95
Q456	PP52	100fr crim rose & blk	5.25	1.00
Q457	PP52	200fr brn & blk	10.00	2.00
Q458	PP52	300fr ol gray & blk	14.00	3.00
Q459	PP52	500fr dl pur & blk	25.00	5.25
		Nos. Q438-Q459 (22)	81.20	18.00

Train in Station — PP53

1982 Engr. *Perf. 11½*

Q460	PP53	10fr red & blk	1.75	.25
Q461	PP53	20fr green & blk	1.25	.50
Q462	PP53	50fr sepia & blk	4.25	.75
Q463	PP53	100fr blue & blk	7.25	2.75
		Nos. Q460-Q463 (4)	14.50	4.25

Electric Locomotives PP54

1985, May 3 Photo. *Perf. 11½*

Q464	PP54	250fr BB-150	11.00	2.00
Q465	PP54	500fr BB-120	24.00	10.00

Seven limited edition souvenir sheets exist. These include souvenir sheets of 4 of #Q437, Q464-Q465 with French or Flemish inscriptions, and a bilingual sheet with one each of #Q437, Q464-Q465.

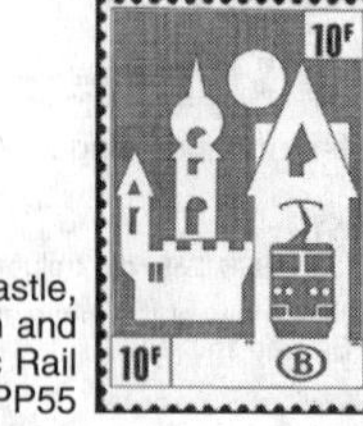

Stylized Castle, Gabled Station and Electric Rail Car — PP55

1987, Oct. 12 Engr. *Perf. 11½*

Q466	PP55	10fr dk red & blk	.50	.40
Q467	PP55	20fr dk grn & blk	1.00	.75
Q468	PP55	50fr dk brn & blk	2.50	1.90
Q469	PP55	100fr dk lil & blk	5.25	3.75
Q470	PP55	150fr dark olive bister & blk	7.75	5.75
		Nos. Q466-Q470 (5)	17.00	12.55

High Speed Trains PP56

1996, June 2 Litho. *Perf. 11½*

Q471	PP56	100fr shown	6.00	4.50
Q472	PP56	300fr Train going left	18.50	13.50

Electric Trains PP57

Designs: 50fr, Passenger railcars. 100fr, End car. 200fr, Front car.

1997, Oct. 14 Photo. *Perf. 11½*

Q473	PP57	50fr multicolored	2.75	2.10
Q474	PP57	100fr multicolored	5.50	4.25
Q475	PP57	200fr multicolored	11.00	8.50
		Nos. Q473-Q475 (3)	19.25	14.85

Electric Trains PP58

Designs: No. Q476, Eurostar (yellow & white train). No. Q477, Thalys (red & white train). 160fr, Eurostar, Thalys side by side.

1998 Photo. *Perf. 11½*

Q476	PP58	80fr multicolored	4.75	3.50
Q477	PP58	80fr multicolored	4.75	3.50
Q478	PP58	160fr multicolored	9.50	7.25
		Nos. Q476-Q478 (3)	19.00	14.25

Agents — PP59

50fr, Male agent. 75fr, Female agent. 100fr, Female agent on platform, man in train. 125fr, Male agent on platform, woman in train.

Perf. 11¾x11½

1999, Sept. 25 Photo.

Q479	PP59	50fr multi	2.40	1.75
Q480	PP59	75fr multi	3.75	2.75
Q481	PP59	100fr multi	5.00	3.75
Q482	PP59	125fr multi	6.00	4.50
		Nos. Q479-Q482 (4)	17.15	12.75

A 1000fr limited edition souvenir sheet exists, picturing the Ottignies Station, issued in January, 2000. Value, $200.

Train Cars — PP60

Designs: 20fr, Gray tanker. 30fr, Red tanker. 50fr, Silver and blue tanker. 150fr, Locomotive, horiz.

2000, Oct. 20 Photo. *Perf. 11½*

Q483	PP60	20fr multi	.85	.65
Q484	PP60	30fr multi	1.25	.95
Q485	PP60	50fr multi	2.10	1.60
		Nos. Q483-Q485 (3)	4.20	3.20

Souvenir Sheet

Q486	PP60	150fr multi	6.25	6.25

Miniature Sheet

Trains and Stations — PP62

No. Q488: a, 4fr, AM 96 train. b, 8fr, Ostend railway station. c, 12fr, AR41 train. d, 16fr, Type 16 engine. e, 20fr, Type 13 engine. f, 24fr, Repainted Type 16 engine. g, I28fr, -11 rail car. h, 32fr, Eurostar. i, 36fr, Charleroi railway station. j, 40fr, Thalys. k, 121fr, Gare du Luxembourg, Brussels (39x54mm).

2001, Oct. 8 Photo. *Perf. 11½*

Q488	PP62	Sheet of 11, #a-k	15.00	15.00

ISSUED UNDER GERMAN OCCUPATION

German Stamps of 1906-11 Surcharged

Nos. N1-N6

Nos. N7-N9

Wmk. Lozenges (125)

1914-15 *Perf. 14, 14½*

N1	A16	3c on 3pf brown	.45	.20
N2	A16	5c on 5pf green	.40	.20
N3	A16	10c on 10pf car	.50	.20
N4	A16	25c on 20pf ultra	.50	.25
N5	A16	50c on 40pf lake & blk	2.50	1.25

N6 A16 75c on 60pf mag .90 *1.25*
N7 A16 1fr on 80pf lake & blk, *rose* 2.50 1.75
N8 A17 1fr25c on 1m car 20.00 12.50
N9 A21 2fr50c on 2m gray bl 18.00 15.00
Nos. N1-N9 (9) 45.75 32.60
Set, never hinged 160.00

German Stamps of 1906-18 Surcharged

Nos. N10-N21

No. N22

Nos. N23-N25

1916-18

N10 A22 2c on 2pf drab .25 .25
N11 A16 3c on 3pf brn .35 .25
N12 A16 5c on 5pf grn .35 .25
N13 A22 8c on 7½pf org .65 .35
N14 A16 10c on 10pf car .25 .25
N15 A22 15c on 15pf yel brn .65 .25
N16 A22 15c on 15pf dk vio .65 .45
N17 A16 20c on 25pf org & blk, *yel* .35 .35
N18 A16 25c on 20pf ultra .35 .25
a. 25c on 20pf blue .40 .25
N19 A16 40c on 30pf org & blk, *buff* .40 .30
N20 A16 50c on 40pf lake & blk .35 .30
N21 A16 75c on 60pf mag 1.00 *12.50*
N22 A16 1fr on 80pf lake & blk, *rose* 2.00 *2.50*
N23 A17 1fr25c on 1m car 2.00 2.00
N24 A21 2fr50c on 2m gray bl 27.50 25.00
a. 2fr50c on 1m car (error) *3,500.*
N25 A20 6fr25c on 5m sl & car 40.00 37.50
Nos. N10-N25 (16) 77.10 82.75
Set, never hinged 145.00

A similar series of stamps without "Belgien" was used in parts of Belgium and France while occupied by German forces. See France Nos. N15-N26.

BELIZE

bə-ˈlēz

LOCATION — Central America bordering on Caribbean Sea to east, Mexico to north, Guatemala to west
GOVT. — Independent state
AREA — 8,867 sq. mi.
POP. — 219,296 (1996 est.)
CAPITAL — Belmopan

Belize was known as British Honduras until 1973. The former British colony achieved independence in September 1981.

100 Cents = 1 Dollar

Catalogue values for all unused stamps in this country are for Never Hinged items.

Fish-Animal Type of British Honduras Regular Issue 1968-72 Overprinted in Black on Silver Panel

Wmk. 314 (½c, 5c, $5), Unwmkd.
1973, June 1 Litho. *Perf. 13x12½*

312 A37 ½c multi (#235) .20 .20
313 A37 1c multi (#214) .20 .20
314 A37 2c multi (#215) .20 .20
315 A37 3c multi (#216) .20 .20
316 A37 4c multi (#217) .20 .20
317 A37 5c multi (#238) .20 .20
318 A37 10c multi (#219) .20 .20
319 A37 15c multi (#220) .20 .20
320 A37 25c multi (#221) .30 .30
321 A37 50c multi (#222) .50 .65
322 A37 $1 multi (#223) .90 *1.25*
323 A37 $2 multi (#224) 2.00 *2.40*
324 A37 $5 multi (#240) 5.50 *4.00*
Nos. 312-324 (13) 10.80 *10.20*

No. 315 with silver panel omitted exists canceled. Nos. 313 and 319 exist with silver panel double.

Common Design Types pictured following the introduction.

Princess Anne's Wedding Issue
Common Design Type

1973, Nov. 14 Wmk. 314 *Perf. 14*

325 CD325 26c blue grn & multi .20 .25
326 CD325 50c ocher & multi .35 *.50*

Crana A50

1974, Jan. 1 Litho. *Perf. 13½*

327 A50 ½c shown .20 .20
328 A50 1c Jewfish .20 .20
329 A50 2c White-lipped peccary .20 .20
330 A50 3c Grouper .20 .20
331 A50 4c Collared anteater .20 .20
332 A50 5c Bonefish .20 .20
333 A50 10c Paca .20 .20
334 A50 15c Dolphinfish .20 .20
335 A50 25c Kinkajou .25 .25
336 A50 50c Muttonfish .55 .55
337 A50 $1 Tayra 1.00 1.00
338 A50 $2 Great barracudas 2.00 2.00
339 A50 $5 Mountain lion 5.25 5.25
Nos. 327-339 (13) 10.65 10.65

Stag, Mayan Pottery A51

Designs: Mayan pottery decorations.

1974, May 1 *Perf. 14½*

340 A51 3c shown .20 .20
341 A51 6c Fire snake .20 .20
342 A51 16c Mouse .20 .20
343 A51 26c Eagle .30 .30
344 A51 50c Parrot .65 .65
Nos. 340-344 (5) 1.55 1.55

Parides Arcas A52

Designs: Butterflies of Belize.

Wmk. 314 Sideways
1974-77 *Perf. 14*

345 A52 ½c shown .20 .20
346 A52 1c Thecla regalis .20 .20
347 A52 2c Colobura dirce .20 .20
348 A52 3c Catonephele numilia .20 .20
349 A52 4c Battus belus .20 .20
350 A52 5c Callicore patelina .35 .20
351 A52 10c Callicore astala .70 .35

Perf. 14x15; 14 (26, 35c)

352 A52 15c Nessaea aglaura .80 .50
a. Watermark upright ('75) .70 .40
353 A52 16c Prepona pseudojoiceyi .45 .25
354 A52 25c Papilio thoas 1.10 .65
a. Watermark upright ('77) .80 .45
355 A52 26c Hamadryas arethusa 7.00 *7.50*
356 A52 50c Thecla bathildis 2.25 1.25
a. Watermark upright ('77) 1.00 .60
357 A52 $1 Caligo uranus 2.25 1.25
358 A52 $2 Heliconius sapho 4.25 2.40
359 A52 $5 Eurytides philolaus 13.00 7.50
a. Watermark upright ('75) 11.00 6.00
360 A52 $10 Philaethria dido 21.00 12.00
Nos. 345-360 (16) 54.15 34.85

Issue dates: No. 355A, July 25, 1977; No. 360, Jan. 2, 1975; others Sept. 2, 1974.
For surcharges & overprint see #380, 386, 395.

1975-78 Wmk. 373

345a A52 ½c multicolored .20 .20
347a A52 2c multi ('77) .20 .20
348a A52 3c multi ('77) .20 .20
349a A52 4c multi ('77) .25 .25
350a A52 5c multi ('77) .30 .30
351a A52 10c multicolored .65 .65
352b A52 15c multi ('77) .90 .90
354b A52 25c multi ('78) 1.25 1.25
355A A52 35c Parides arcas ('77) 2.00 2.00
Nos. 345a-355A (9) 5.95 5.95

For overprints and surcharges see Nos. 395-396, 424, 426-427.

Churchill and Coronation Coach of Queen Elizabeth II — A53

$1, Churchill & Williamsburg, VA Liberty Bell.

Wmk. 373
1974, Nov. 30 Litho. *Perf. 14*

363 A53 50c multicolored .20 .20
364 A53 $1 multicolored .35 .35

Sir Winston Churchill (1874-1965).

Mayan Urn — A54

Designs: Various Mayan vessels.

1975, June 2 Wmk. 314 *Perf. 14*

365 A54 3c lt green & multi .20 .20
366 A54 6c lt blue & multi .20 .20
367 A54 16c dull yel & multi .20 .20
368 A54 26c lilac & multi .25 .25
369 A54 50c lt brown & multi .50 .50
Nos. 365-369 (5) 1.35 1.35

Musicians A55

Christmas: 26c, Nativity (Thatched hut and children). 50c, Drummers, vert. $1, Map of Belize, star, fleeing family, vert.

Perf. 14x14½, 14½x14
1975, Nov. 17 Litho. Wmk. 314

370 A55 6c multicolored .20 .20
371 A55 26c multicolored .20 .20
372 A55 50c multicolored .30 .30
373 A55 $1 multicolored .60 .60
Nos. 370-373 (4) 1.30 1.30

William Wrigley, Jr., Sapodilla Tree — A56

Bicentennial Emblem and: 35c, Charles Lindbergh and "Spirit of St. Louis." $1, John Lloyd Stephens and Mayan temple.

1976, Mar. 29 Wmk. 373 *Perf. 14½*

374 A56 10c multicolored .20 .20
375 A56 35c multicolored .25 .25
376 A56 $1 multicolored .65 .65
Nos. 374-376 (3) 1.10 1.10

American Bicentennial.

Bicycling A57

Wmk. 373
1976, July 17 Litho. *Perf. 14½*

377 A57 35c shown .20 .20
378 A57 45c Running .20 .20
379 A57 $1 Shooting .45 .45
Nos. 377-379 (3) .85 .85

21st Olympic Games, Montreal, Canada, July 17-Aug. 1.

No. 355 Surcharged with New Value and Bar

Wmk. 314
1976, Aug. 30 Litho. *Perf. 14*

380 A52 20c on 26c multi 2.00 1.10

Map of West Indies, Bats, Wicket and Ball A57a

Prudential Cup — A57b

Unwmk.
1976, Oct. 18 Litho. *Perf. 14*

381 A57a 35c lt blue & multi .60 .60
382 A57b $1 lilac rose & blk 1.40 1.40

World Cricket Cup, won by West Indies Team, 1975.

Royal Visit, 1975 A58

Designs: 35c, Rose window and Queen's head. $2, Queen surrounded by bishops.

1977, Feb. 7 Litho. *Perf. 13½x14*

383 A58 10c multicolored .20 .20
384 A58 35c multicolored .20 .20
385 A58 $2 multicolored .60 .60
Nos. 383-385 (3) 1.00 1.00

25th anniv. of the reign of Elizabeth II.

No. 352 Surcharged with New Value and Bar

1977 Wmk. 314 *Perf. 14x15*

386 A52 5c on 15c multi 1.90 1.90

The first setting has the "5c" close to the the right edge of the block (varies). The second, and more common, setting has about 7mm from the right edge to the "5c."

Red-capped Manakin — A59

Designs: Birds of Belize.

Wmk. 373

1977, Sept. 3 Litho. *Perf. 14½*

387 A59 8c shown .85 .60
388 A59 10c Hooded oriole .75 .30
389 A59 25c Blue-crowned motmot 1.40 .60
390 A59 35c Slaty-breasted tinamou 1.75 .75
391 A59 45c Ocellated turkey 2.00 1.25
392 A59 $1 White hawk 3.25 *5.50*
a. Souvenir sheet of 6, #387-392 10.00 *12.50*
Nos. 387-392 (6) 10.00 9.00

See Nos. 398-403, 416-421, 500-501. For overprints and surcharges see No. 502.

Medical Laboratory A60

Design: $1, Mobile medical unit and children receiving treatment.

1977, Dec. 2 *Perf. 13½*

393 A60 35c multicolored .25 .25
394 A60 $1 multicolored .65 .65
a. Souvenir sheet of 2, #393-394 1.10 *1.50*

Pan American Health Org., 75th anniv.

Nos. 351 and 355A Overprinted in Gold: "BELIZE DEFENCE FORCE / 1ST JANUARY 1978"

Wmk. 314, 373

1978, Feb. 15 Litho. *Perf. 14*

395 A52 10c multicolored .60 .60
396 A52 35c multicolored 1.25 1.25

Elizabeth II Coronation Anniversary Issue

Common Design Types

Souvenir Sheet

1978, Apr. 21 Unwmk. *Perf. 15*

397 Sheet of 6 1.25 1.25
a. CD326 75c White lion of Mortimer .20 .20
b. CD327 75c Elizabeth II .20 .20
c. CD328 75c Jaguar (Maya god) .20 .20

No. 397 contains 2 se-tenant strips of Nos. 397a-397c, separated by horizontal gutter with commemorative and descriptive inscriptions and showing central part of coronation procession with coach.

Bird Type of 1977

Wmk. 373

1978, July 31 Litho. *Perf. 14½*

398 A59 10c White-crowned parrot .65 .65
399 A59 25c Crimson-collared tanager 1.00 1.00
400 A59 35c Citreoline trogon 1.50 1.50
401 A59 45c Sungrebe 1.60 1.60
402 A59 50c Muscovy duck 1.75 1.75
403 A59 $1 King vulture 2.50 2.50
a. Souvenir sheet of 6, #398-403 9.00 *11.00*
Nos. 398-403 (6) 9.00 9.00

Russelia Sarmentosa A61

Wild Flowers and Ferns: 15c, Lygodium polymorphum. 35c, Heliconia aurantiaca. 45c, Adiantum tetraphyllum. 50c, Angelonia ciliaris. $1, Thelypteris obliterata.

1978, Oct. 16 Litho. *Perf. 14x13½*

404 A61 10c multicolored .30 .30
405 A61 15c multicolored .35 .35
406 A61 35c multicolored .35 .35
407 A61 45c multicolored .35 .35
408 A61 50c multicolored .35 .35
409 A61 $1 multicolored .70 .70
Nos. 404-409 (6) 2.40 2.40

Christmas.

Internal Airmail Service, 1937 — A62

Mail Service: 10c, MV Heron, 1949. 35c, Dugout canoe on river, 1920. 45c, Stann Creek railroad, 1910. 50c, Mounted courier, 1882. $2, RMS Eagle, 1856, and "paid" cancel.

Perf. 13½x14

1979, Jan. 15 Litho. Wmk. 373

410 A62 5c multicolored .30 .30
411 A62 10c multicolored .30 .30
412 A62 35c multicolored .30 .30
413 A62 45c multicolored .45 .45
414 A62 50c multicolored .45 .45
415 A62 $2 multicolored 1.75 1.75
Nos. 410-415 (6) 3.55 3.55

Centenary of membership in UPU.

Bird Type of 1977

1979, Apr. 16 Unwmk. *Perf. 14½*

416 A59 10c Boat-billed heron .25 .25
417 A59 25c Gray-necked wood rail .70 .70
418 A59 35c Lineated woodpecker .80 .80
419 A59 45c Blue gray tanager 1.00 1.00
420 A59 50c Laughing falcon 1.25 1.25
421 A59 $1 Long-tailed hermit 2.50 2.50
a. Souvenir sheet of 6, #416-421 6.50 6.50
Nos. 416-421 (6) 6.50 6.50

Nos. 477, 354b, 595, 355A, 599, 651 Surcharged with New Value and Bar

1979-83 Litho. *Perf. 14*

422 A67 10c on 15c multi 4.00 4.00
423 A67 10c on 15c multi — —
424 A52 10c on 25c multi *2.00* 1.50
424A A67 10c on 35c multi *30.00*
b. Round obliterator *30.00*
425 A76 10c on 35c multi
426 A52 15c on 35c multi *50.00*
427 A52 15c on 35c multi 2.00 2.00
428 A76 $1.25 on $2 multi 6.00 4.00
429 A81 $1.25 on $2 multi 5.00 3.00

No. 422 has a square the width of the "10c" obliterating the old value. No. 423 has a rectangle that is wider than the "10c."

No. 424A has a square obliterator.

No. 426 has "15c" at top of stamp, No. 427 has "15c" at right of rectangle. Type differs.

No. 429 has rectangular obliterator with new value at top of stamp.

Many errors exist from printer's waste.

Issued: #426, 3/79; #427, 6/79; #424, 3/31/80; #422, 8/22/81; #423, 1/28/83; #425, 4/15/83; #428-429, 6/9/83.

Used Stamps

Postally used copies are valued the same as unused. CTO's are of minimal value. Most used stamps from No. 430-679 exist CTO. Most of these appeared on the market after the contract was canceled and were not authorized. The cancellations are printed and the paper differs from the issued stamps.

Imperforate Stamps

Stamps from No. 430-679 exist imperforate in small quantities.

Queen Elizabeth II, 25th Anniv. of Coronation — A63

Designs: 25c, No. 439, Paslow Bldg., #397c. 50c, Parliament, London, #397a. 75c, Coronation coach. $1, Queen on horseback, vert. $2, Prince of Wales, vert. $3, Queen and Prince Philip, vert. $4, Queen Elizabeth II, portrait, vert. No. 437, St. Edward's Crown, vert. No. 438a, $5, Princess Anne on horseback, Montreal Olympics, vert. No. 438b, $10, Queen, Montreal Olympics, vert.

Unwmk.

1979, May 31 Litho. *Perf. 14*

430 A63 25c multicolored 1.25
431 A63 50c multicolored 1.75
432 A63 75c multicolored 2.40
433 A63 $1 multicolored 3.00
434 A63 $2 multicolored 3.25
435 A63 $3 multicolored 3.25
436 A63 $4 multicolored 3.50
437 A63 $5 multicolored 4.00
Nos. 430-437 (8) 22.40

Souvenir Sheets

438 A63 Sheet of 2, #a.-b. 15.00
439 A63 $15 multicolored 15.00

Powered Flight, 75th Anniv. — A64

1979, July 30

440 A64 4c Safety, 1909 .50
441 A64 25c Boeing 707 1.50
442 A64 50c Concorde 3.75
443 A64 75c Handley Page W8b, 1922 2.10
444 A64 $1 AVRO F, 1912 2.10
445 A64 $1.50 Cody, 1910 3.00
446 A64 $2 Triplane Roe II, 1909 3.00
447 A64 $3 Santos-Dumont, 1906 3.00
448 A64 $4 Wright Brothers Flyer, 1903 3.75
Nos. 440-448 (9) 22.70

Souvenir Sheets

Perf. 14½

449 Sheet of 2 15.00
a. A64 $5 Dunne D.5, 1910 7.50
b. A64 $5 Great Britain #581 7.50
450 A64 $10 Belize Airways Jet 15.00

Sir Rowland Hill, death cent., "75th anniv." of ICAO.

1980 Summer Olympics, Moscow — A65

1979, Oct. 10 *Perf. 14*

451 A65 25c Handball .60
452 A65 50c Weight lifting .85
453 A65 75c Track 1.25
454 A65 $1 Soccer 1.60
455 A65 $2 Sailing 2.25
456 A65 $3 Swimming 2.50
457 A65 $4 Boxing 3.25
458 A65 $5 Cycling 6.50
Nos. 451-458 (8) 18.80

Souvenir Sheets

Perf. 14½

459 Sheet of 2 12.00
a. A65 $5 Track, diff. 4.00
b. A65 $10 Boxing, diff. 8.00
460 A65 $15 Cycling, diff. 12.00

1980 Winter Olympics, Lake Placid — A66

1979, Dec. 4 *Perf. 14*

461 A66 25c Torch .20
462 A66 50c Slalom skiing .40
463 A66 75c Figure skating .65
464 A66 $1 Downhill skiing .85
465 A66 $2 Speed skating 1.75
466 A66 $3 Cross country skiing 2.50
467 A66 $4 Biathlon 3.50
468 A66 $5 Olympic medals 4.25
Nos. 461-468 (8) 14.10

Souvenir Sheets

Perf. 14½

469 Sheet of 2 10.50
a. A66 $5 Torch bearers 3.50
b. A66 $10 Medals, diff. 7.00
470 A66 $15 Torch, diff. 10.50

See Nos. 503-512.

Cypraea Zebra A67

1980, Jan. 7 Litho. *Perf. 14*

471 A67 1c shown .65 .20
472 A67 2c Macrocallista maculata .80 .20
473 A67 3c Arca zebra, vert. .95 .20
474 A67 4c Chama macerophylla, vert. .95 .20
475 A67 5c Latirus cariniferus .95 .20
476 A67 10c Conus spurius, vert. 1.10 .20
477 A67 15c Murex cabritii, vert. 1.60 .20
478 A67 20c Atrina rigida 1.75 .20
479 A67 25c Chlamys imbricata, vert. 1.75 .20
480 A67 35c Conus granulatus 2.00 .20
481 A67 45c Tellina radiata, vert. 2.25 .20

482 A67 50c Leucozonia nassa 2.25 .20
483 A67 85c Tripterotyphis triangularis 3.50 .20
484 A67 $1 Strombus gigas, vert. 3.75 .20
485 A67 $2 Strombus gallus, vert. 5.75 .30
486 A67 $5 Fasciolaria tulipa 8.75 .75
487 A67 $10 Arene cruentata 11.00 1.25
Nos. 471-487 (17) 49.75 5.10

Souvenir Sheets

488 A67 Sheet of 2, 85c, $5 15.00 10.00
489 A67 Sheet of 2, $2, $10 30.00 20.00

Stamps in Nos. 488-489 have different color border and are of a slightly different size than the sheet stamps.

The 10c, 50c, 85c, $1 exist dated 1981.

For overprints and surcharges see Nos. 422-423, 424A, 572-589, 592-593.

Intl. Year of the Child — A68

Various children. No. 498a, Three children. No. 498b, Madonna and Child by Durer. No. 499, Children before Christmas tree.

1980, Mar. 15 Litho. *Perf. 14*

490 A68 25c multicolored .50
491 A68 50c multicolored .80
492 A68 75c multicolored 1.10
493 A68 $1 multicolored 1.10
494 A68 $1.50 multicolored 1.75
495 A68 $2 multicolored 2.00
496 A68 $3 multicolored 2.50
497 A68 $4 multicolored 2.75
Nos. 490-497 (8) 12.50

Souvenir Sheets

Perf. 13½

498 A68 $5 Sheet of 2, #a.-b. 10.00
499 A68 $10 multicolored 10.00

No. 498 contains two 35x54mm stamps. No. 499 contains one 73x110mm stamp.

Bird Type of 1977

Souvenir Sheets

1980, June 16 Unwmk. *Perf. 13½*

500 Sheet of 6 42.50 25.00
a. A59 10c Jabiru 6.00 3.75
b. A59 25c Barred antshrike 6.75 3.75
c. A59 35c Royal flycatcher 7.25 3.75
d. A59 45c White-necked puffbird 7.25 4.00
e. A59 50c Ornate hawk-eagle 7.25 4.00
f. A59 $1 Golden-masked tanager 7.75 5.25
g. Sheet of 12 85.00 70.00
501 Sheet of 2 30.00 30.00
a. A59 $2 Jabiru 12.50 12.50
b. A59 $3 Golden-masked tanager 17.50 17.50

No. 500g contains 2 each Nos. 500a-500f with gutter between; inscribed "Protection of Environment" and "Wildlife Protection."

No. 500 Overprinted or Surcharged with Exhibition Emblem

1980, Oct. 3 Litho. *Perf. 13½*

502 Sheet of 6 37.50 37.50
a. A59 10c multicolored 5.50 2.75
b. A59 25c multicolored 6.00 3.00
c. A59 35c multicolored 6.00 3.00
d. A59 40c on 45c multi 6.50 3.25
e. A59 40c on 50c multi 6.50 3.25
f. A59 40c on $1 multi 6.50 3.25

ESPAMER '80 Stamp Exhibition, Madrid, Spain, Oct. 3-12.

1980 Winter Olympics, Lake Placid — A69

Events and winning country: 25c, Men's speed skating, US. 50c, Ice hockey, US. 75c, No. 512, Men's figure skating, Great Britain. $1, Alpine skiing, Austria. $1.50, Women's giant slalom, Germany. $2, Women's speed skating, Netherlands. $3, Cross country skiing, Sweden. $5, Men's giant slalom, Sweden. Nos. 511a ($5), 511b ($10), Speed skating, US.

1980, Aug. 20 Litho. *Perf. 14*

503 A69 25c multi + label .25
504 A69 50c multi + label .50
505 A69 75c multi + label .75
506 A69 $1 multi + label .95
507 A69 $1.50 multi + label 1.50
508 A69 $2 multi + label 1.90
509 A69 $3 multi + label 3.00
510 A69 $5 multi + label 4.75
Nos. 503-510 (8) 13.60

Souvenir Sheets

Perf. 14½

511 A69 Sheet of 2, #a.-b. 6.50
512 A69 $10 multicolored 13.00

Nos. 503-510 issued with se-tenant label.

Intl. Year of the Child — A70

Nos. 513-521: Scenes from Sleeping Beauty. $8, Detail from Paumgartner Family Altarpiece by Albrecht Durer.

1980, Nov. 24 *Perf. 14*

513 A70 35c multicolored 1.25
514 A70 40c multicolored 1.50
515 A70 50c multicolored 1.75
516 A70 75c multicolored 1.90
517 A70 $1 multicolored 2.10
518 A70 $1.50 multicolored 3.00
519 A70 $3 multicolored 4.25
520 A70 $4 multicolored 4.25
Nos. 513-520 (8) 20.00

Souvenir Sheets

Perf. 14½

521 Sheet of 2 14.00
a. A70 $5 Marriage 7.00
b. A70 $5 Couple on horseback 7.00
522 A70 $8 multicolored 11.00

Nos. 513-520 issued with se-tenent label.

Queen Mother Elizabeth, 80th Birthday — A71

1980, Dec. 12

523 A71 $1 multicolored 3.50

Souvenir Sheet

Perf. 14½

524 A71 $5 multicolored 11.00

No. 524 contains one 46x31mm stamp. No. 523 issued in sheet of 6.

Christmas — A72

1980, Dec. 30 Litho. *Perf. 14*

525 A72 25c Annunciation .60
526 A72 50c Bethlehem .95
527 A72 75c Holy Family 1.25
528 A72 $1 Nativity 1.40
529 A72 $1.50 Flight into Egypt 1.90
530 A72 $2 Shepards 2.25
531 A72 $3 With angel 2.75
532 A72 $4 Adoration 3.00
Nos. 525-532 (8) 14.10

Souvenir Sheets

Perf. 14½

533 A72 $5 Nativity 6.50
534 A72 $10 Madonna & Child 13.00

Nos. 525-532 each issued in sheets of 20 + 10 labels. The 2nd and 5th vertical rows consist of labels.

Nos. 529, 532, 534 Surcharged $2

1981, May 22

535 A72 $1 on $1.50 multi 3.00
536 A72 $2 on $4 multi 3.50

Souvenir Sheet

Perf. 14½

537 A72 $2 on $10 multi 4.50

Location of overprint and surcharge varies.

Intl. Rotary Club — A73

Designs: 25c, Paul P. Harris, founder. 50c, No. 546, Rotary, project emblem. $1, No. 545b, 75th anniv. emblem. $1.50 Diploma, horiz. $2, No. 545a, Project Hippocrates. $3, 75th anniv. project emblems, horiz. No. 544, Hands reach out, horiz.

1981, May 26 *Perf. 14*

538 A73 25c multicolored 1.25
539 A73 50c multicolored 2.00
540 A73 $1 multicolored 2.75
541 A73 $1.50 multicolored 4.00
542 A73 $2 multicolored 4.75
543 A73 $3 multicolored 5.50
544 A73 $5 multicolored 7.00
Nos. 538-544 (7) 27.25

Souvenir Sheets

Perf. 14½

545 Sheet of 2 25.00
a. A73 $5 multicolored 8.00
b. A73 $10 multicolored 16.00
546 A73 $10 multicolored 17.50

Originally scheduled to be issued Mar. 30, the set was postponed and issued without a 75c stamp. Supposedly some of the 75c were sold to the public.

For overprints and surcharges see Nos. 563-571, 590-591.

Royal Wedding of Prince Charles and Lady Diana — A74

1981, July 16 *Perf. 13½x14*

548 A74 50c Coat of Arms .50
549 A74 $1 Prince Charles 1.00
550 A74 $1.50 Couple 1.50

Size: 25x43mm

Perf. 13½

551 A74 50c like No. 548 .50
552 A74 $1 like No. 549 1.00
553 A74 $1.50 like No. 550 1.50
Nos. 548-553 (6) 6.00

Miniature Sheet

Perf. 14½

554 Sheet of 3, #554a-554c 3.00
a. A74 $3 like No. 550 1.00
b. A74 $3 like No. 548 1.00
c. A74 $3 like No. 549 1.00

Nos. 551-553 issued in sheets of 6 + 3 labels. No. 554 contains three 35x50mm stamps.

For overprints see Nos. 659-665.

1984 Olympics A75

1981, Sept. 14 *Perf. 14*

555 A75 85c Track 1.75
556 A75 $1 Cycling 4.50
557 A75 $1.50 Boxing 3.00
558 A75 $2 Emblems 3.50
559 A75 $3 Baron Coubertin 4.50
560 A75 $5 Torch, emblems 5.25
Nos. 555-560 (6) 22.50

Souvenir Sheets

Perf. 13½

561 Sheet of 2 24.00
a. A75 $5 like No. 559 8.00
b. A75 $10 like No. 560 16.00

Perf. 14½

562 A75 $15 like No. 558 24.00

No. 561 contains two 35x54mm stamps. No. 562 contains one 46x68mm stamp.

Nos. 561-562 exist with gold background.

Nos. 538-546 Overprinted in Black or Gold

1981, Sept. 21 *Perf. 14*

563 A73 25c multicolored (G) 1.40
564 A73 50c multicolored 1.75
565 A73 $1 multicolored 2.10
566 A73 $1.50 multicolored 2.75
567 A73 $2 multicolored (G) 3.25

568 A73 $3 multicolored 3.75
569 A73 $5 multicolored 5.00
Nos. 563-569 (7) 20.00

Souvenir Sheets

Perf. 14½

570 A73 Sheet of 2, #a.-b. (G) 15.00
571 A73 $10 multicolored 15.00

Size of overprint varies.

Nos. 471-483, 485-489 Overprinted

1981, Sept. 21

572 A67 1c multicolored .70
573 A67 2c multicolored .70
574 A67 3c multicolored .90
575 A67 4c multicolored .90
576 A67 5c multicolored .90
577 A67 10c multicolored 1.10
578 A67 15c multicolored 1.75
579 A67 20c multicolored 1.75
580 A67 25c multicolored 2.00
581 A67 35c multicolored 2.00
582 A67 45c multicolored 2.40
583 A67 50c mulitcolored 2.40
584 A67 85c multicolored 3.50
585 A67 $2 multicolored 6.25
586 A67 $5 multicolored 7.25
587 A67 $10 multicolored 10.50
Nos. 572-587 (16) 45.00

Souvenir Sheets

588 A67 Sheet of 2, #488 17.50
589 A67 Sheet of 2, #489 17.50

Size and style of overprint varies, italic on horiz. stamps, upright on vert. stamps and upright capitals on souvenir sheets.

The 10c is dated 1981. Less than 16 sheets dated 1980 were also overprinted.

Nos. 541, 545 Surcharged

1981, Nov. 13 ***Perf. 14***

590 A73 $1 on $1.50 multi 5.00

Souvenir Sheet

Perf. 14½

591 Sheet of 2 8.00
a. A73 $1 on $5 multicolored 4.00
b. A73 $1 on $10 multicolored 4.00

Espamer '81.

Nos. 488, 489 Surcharged in Red

1981, Nov. 14 ***Perf. 14½***

Souvenir Sheets

592 Sheet of 2 10.00
a. A67 $1 on 85c 5.00
b. A67 $1 on $5 5.00
593 Sheet of 2 10.00
a. A67 $1 on $2 5.00
b. A67 $1 on $10 5.00

Independence — A76

1981-82 ***Perf. 14***

594 A76 10c Flag 1.50
595 A76 35c Map, vert. 3.00
596 A76 50c Black orchid, vert. 8.00
597 A76 85c Tapir 2.50
598 A76 $1 Mahogany tree, vert. 2.50
599 A76 $2 Keel-billed toucan 11.50
Nos. 594-599 (6) 29.00

Souvenir Sheet

Perf. 14½

600 A76 $5 like 10c 16.00

Issued: 50c-$2, 12/18; 10c, 35c, $5, 2/10/82.

For surcharges see Nos. 425, 428, 616.

1982 World Cup Soccer Championships, Spain — A77

1981, Dec. 28 ***Perf. 14***

601 A77 10c Uruguay '30, '50 1.00
602 A77 25c Italy '34, '38 1.75
603 A77 50c Germany '54, '74 2.25
604 A77 $1 Brazil '58, '62, '70 2.75
605 A77 $1.50 Argentina '78 3.50
606 A77 $2 England '66 3.75
Nos. 601-606 (6) 15.00

Souvenir Sheets

Perf. 14½

607 A77 $2 Emblem 5.00
608 A77 $3 Player 5.00

No. 608 contains one 46x78mm stamp.

For surcharge see No. 617.

Sailing Ships — A78

1982, Mar. 15 ***Perf. 14***

609 A78 10c Man of war, 19th cent. 2.50
610 A78 25c Madagascar, 1837 3.75
611 A78 35c Whitby, 1838 4.25
612 A78 50c China, 1838 4.75
613 A78 85c Swiftsure, 1850 6.00
614 A78 $2 Windsor Castle, 1857 8.75
Nos. 609-614 (6) 30.00

Souvenir Sheet

Perf. 14½

615 A78 $5 19th cent. ships 30.00

Nos. 599 and 606 Surcharged

1982, Apr. 28

616 A76 $1 on $2 multi 4.00
617 A77 $1 on $2 multi 4.00

Essen '82 Philatelic Exhibition.

Princess of Wales, 21st Birthday — A79

Various portraits.

1982, May 20 ***Perf. 13½x14***

618 A79 50c multicolored .50
619 A79 $1 multicolored 1.00
620 A79 $1.50 multicolored 1.50

Size: 25x42mm

Perf. 13½

621 A79 50c like No. 618 .50
622 A79 $1 like No. 619 1.00
623 A79 $1.50 like No. 620 1.50
Nos. 618-623 (6) 6.00

Souvenir Sheet

Stamp Size: 31x47mm

Perf. 14½

624 A79 $3 Sheet of 3, #a.-c. like #618-620 4.00

Nos. 618-620 also exist with gold borders, size: 30x45mm.

Overprinted in Silver

1982, Oct. 21 ***Perf. 13½x14***

628 A79 50c multicolored .35
629 A79 $1 multicolored .45
630 A79 $1.50 multicolored .60

Size: 25x42mm

Perf. 13½

631 A79 50c multicolored .35
632 A79 $1 multicolored .45
633 A79 $1.50 multicolored .60
Nos. 628-633 (6) 2.80

Souvenir Sheet

Perf. 14½

634 A79 $3 Sheet of 3, #a.-c. 8.50

Size of overprint varies. The overprint exists on the gold bordered stamps. No. 634 exists with a second type of overprint.

Boy Scouts — A80

1982, Aug. 31 ***Perf. 14***

638 A80 10c Building camp fire .95
639 A80 25c Bird watching 1.75
640 A80 35c Playing guitar 1.40
641 A80 50c Hiking 1.50
642 A80 85c Flag, scouts 2.00
643 A80 $2 Salute 2.40
Nos. 638-643 (6) 10.00

Souvenir Sheets

Perf. 14½

644 A80 $2 Scout holding flag, vert. 6.00
645 A80 $3 Lord Baden Powell, vert. 6.00

Scouting, 75th anniv. and Lord Baden Powell, 125th birth anniv.

For overprints see Nos. 653-658.

Marine Life — A81

1982, Sept. 20 ***Perf. 14***

646 A81 10c Gorgonia ventalina 2.25
647 A81 35c Carpilius corallinus 3.75
648 A81 50c Plexaura flexuosa 4.25
649 A81 85c Condylactis gigantea 4.50
650 A81 $1 Stenopus hispidus 5.75
651 A81 $2 Abudefduf saxatilis 7.00
Nos. 646-651 (6) 27.50

Souvenir Sheet

Perf. 14½

652 A81 $5 Scyllarides aequinoctialis 32.50

For surcharge see No. 429.

Nos. 638-643 Ovptd. in Gold: BELGICA 82 INT. YEAR OF THE CHILD SIR ROWLAND HILL 1795 1879 Picasso CENTENARY OF BIRTH and Emblems

1982, Oct. 1 ***Perf. 14***

653 A80 10c Building camp fire 2.50
654 A80 25c Bird watching 4.25
655 A80 35c Playing guitar 3.75
656 A80 50c Hiking 4.25
657 A80 85c Flag, scouts 6.75
658 A80 $2 Salute 11.00
Nos. 653-658 (6) 32.50

Overprint is different on Nos. 654-655.

Sheets include labels with native Christmas themes.

Nos. 548-554 Overprinted in Gold Similar to Nos. 628-634

1982, Oct. 25 ***Perf. 13½x14***

659 A74 50c Coat of Arms 1.40
660 A74 $1 Prince Charles 2.75
661 A74 $1.50 Couple 4.25

Size: 25x43mm

Perf. 13½

662 A74 50c like No. 659 1.40
663 A74 $1 like No. 660 2.75
664 A74 $1.50 like No. 661 4.25
Nos. 659-664 (6) 16.80

Miniature Sheet

Perf. 14½

665 Sheet of 3, #665a-665c 10.00
a. A74 $3 like No. 661 2.75
b. A74 $3 like No. 659 2.75
c. A74 $3 like No. 660 2.75

Nos. 662-664 issued in sheets of 6 plus 3 labels. No. 665 contains three 35x50mm stamps. Size and style of overprint varies.

Visit by Pope John Paul II — A82

1983, Mar. 7 ***Perf. 13½***

666 A82 50c Belize Cathedral 2.50

Souvenir Sheet

Perf. 14½

667 A82 $2.50 Pope John Paul II 10.00

No. 667 contains one 30x47mm stamp.

No. 666 issued in sheet of 6.

Commonwealth Day — A83

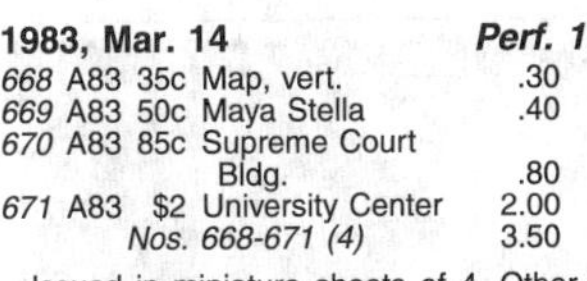

1983, Mar. 14 *Perf. 13½*

668 A83 35c Map, vert. .30
669 A83 50c Maya Stella .40
670 A83 85c Supreme Court Bldg. .80
671 A83 $2 University Center 2.00
Nos. 668-671 (4) 3.50

Issued in miniature sheets of 4. Other formats are suspect.

First Manned Flight, Bicent. — A84

1983, May 16 *Perf. 14*

672 A84 10c Flying boat, 1670 1.50
673 A84 25c Flying machine, 1709 2.00
674 A84 50c Airship Guyton de Morveau 2.25
675 A84 85c Dirigible 2.75
676 A84 $1 Clement Bayard 3.00
677 A84 $1.50 Great Britain R-34 3.25
Nos. 672-677 (6) 14.75

Souvenir Sheets

Perf. 14½

678 A84 $3 Nassau Balloon 8.00
679 A84 $3 Montgolfier Brothers balloon, vert. 8.00

"Errors"

Many "errors," including imperforates, exist of Nos. 680-898. These unauthorized varieties were printed without the knowledge of the Belize postal service. There may be large quantities of them.

Mayan Monuments — A85

1983, Nov. 14 Litho. *Perf. 13½x14*

680 A85 10c Altun Ha .20 .20
681 A85 15c Xunantunich .20 .20
682 A85 75c Cerros .50 .50
683 A85 $2 Lamanai 1.10 1.10
Nos. 680-683 (4) 2.00 2.00

Souvenir Sheet

684 A85 $3 Xunantunich, diff. 2.25 2.25

World Communications Year — A86

1983, Nov. 28 *Perf. 14*

685 A86 10c Belmopan Earth Station .20 .20
686 A86 15c Telstar 2 .20 .20
687 A86 75c UPU monument .75 .75
688 A86 $2 Mail boat 2.00 2.00
Nos. 685-688 (4) 3.15 3.15

Jaguar, World Wildlife Fund Emblem A87

1983, Dec. 9

689 A87 5c Sitting .35 .35
690 A87 10c Standing .40 .40
691 A87 85c Swimming 2.00 2.00
692 A87 $1 Walking 2.25 2.25
Nos. 689-692 (4) 5.00 5.00

Souvenir Sheet

693 A87 $3 Sitting in tree 3.25 3.25

No. 693 contains one stamp 45x28mm.

Christmas — A88

Scenes from mass celebrated by Pope John Paul II during visit, Mar.

1983, Dec. 22

694 A88 10c multicolored .50 .50
695 A88 15c multicolored .50 .50
696 A88 75c multicolored 1.00 1.00
697 A88 $2 multicolored 1.75 1.75
Nos. 694-697 (4) 3.75 3.75

Souvenir Sheet

698 A88 $3 multicolored 3.25 3.25

Foureye Butterflyfish — A89

1984, Feb. 27 *Perf. 15*

699 A89 1c shown .20 .20
700 A89 2c Cushion star .20 .20
701 A89 3c Flower coral .20 .20
702 A89 4c Fairy basslets .20 .20
703 A89 5c Spanish hogfish .20 .20
704 A89 6c Star-eyed hermit crab .20 .20
705 A89 10c Sea fans, fire sponge .20 .20
706 A89 15c Blueheads .20 .20
707 A89 25c Blue-striped grunt .25 .25
708 A89 50c Coral crab .50 .50
709 A89 60c Tube sponge .60 .60
710 A89 75c Brain coral .75 .75
711 A89 $1 Yellow-tail snapper 1.00 1.00
712 A89 $2 Common lettuce slug 2.00 2.00
713 A89 $5 Yellow damselfish 5.00 5.00
714 A89 $10 Rock beauty 10.00 10.00
Nos. 699-714 (16) 21.70 21.70

For overprints and surcharge see Nos. 715-716, 762A-762C, 922.

The 50c, 60c, 75c, $1 exist inscribed "1986."

1988, July *Perf. 13½*

705a A89 10c .45 .45
706a A89 15c .65 .65
707a A89 25c .95 .95
708a A89 50c 1.40 1.40
709a A89 60c 1.40 1.40
711a A89 $1 1.40 1.40
Nos. 705a-711a (6) 6.25 6.25

Nos. 705, 708 Overprinted: "VISIT OF THE LORD / ARCHBISHOP OF CANTERBURY / 8th-11th MARCH 1984"

1984, Mar. 8

715 A89 10c multicolored 1.25 1.25
716 A89 50c multicolored 2.25 2.25

1984 Summer Olympics — A90

1984, Apr. 30 *Perf. 13½x14*

717 A90 25c Shooting .25 .25
718 A90 75c Boxing .75 .75
719 A90 $1 Running 1.10 1.10
720 A90 $2 Bicycling 1.90 1.90
Nos. 717-720 (4) 4.00 4.00

Souvenir Sheet

721 A90 $3 Discus 2.75 2.75

1984 Summer Olympics — A91

1984, Apr. 30 Litho. *Perf. 14½*

Booklet Stamps

722 A91 5c Running .20 .20
a. Booklet pane of 4 .30
723 A91 20c Javelin .25 .25
a. Booklet pane of 4 1.10
724 A91 25c Shot put .35 .35
a. Booklet pane of 4 1.50
725 A91 $2 Torch 2.50 2.50
a. Booklet pane of 4 5.00
Nos. 722-725 (4) 3.30 3.30

Ausipex '84 — A92

1984, Sept. 26 Litho. *Perf. 15*

726 A92 15c Br. Honduras #3 .20 .20
727 A92 30c Bath-Bristol mail coach, 1784 .30 .30
728 A92 65c Penny Black, Rowland Hill .65 .65
729 A92 75c Railroad Pier, Commerce Bight .75 .75

Perf. 14

730 A92 $2 Royal Exhibition Bldgs. 1.60 1.60
Nos. 726-730 (5) 3.50 3.50

Souvenir Sheet

731 A92 $3 Australia #132, Br. Hond. #3 1.50 1.50

House of Tudor, 500th Anniv. — A93

White-fronted Parrot — A94

1984, Oct. 15 *Perf. 14*

732 A93 50c Queen Victoria .35 .35
733 A93 50c Prince Albert .35 .35
a. Sheet of 4, 2 each, #732-733 1.50
734 A93 75c King George VI .55 .55
735 A93 75c Queen Elizabeth .55 .55
a. Sheet of 4, 2 each, #734-735 2.25
736 A93 $1 Prince Charles .75 .75
737 A93 $1 Princess Diana .75 .75
a. Sheet of 4, 2 each, #736-737 3.00
Nos. 732-737 (6) 3.30 3.30

Souvenir Sheet

738 Sheet of 2 2.00 2.00
a. A93 $1.50 Prince Philip 1.00 1.00
b. A93 $1.50 Queen Elizabeth II 1.00 1.00

1984, Nov. 1 *Perf. 11*

Parrots: b, White-capped. c, Red-lored. d, Mealy. b, d, horiz.

739 Block of 4 8.00 8.00
a.-d. A94 $1 any single 2.00 2.00

Miniature Sheet

Perf. 14

740 A94 $3 Scarlet macaw 4.50 4.50

No. 740 contains one 48x32mm stamp.

Mayan Artifacts — A95

1984, Nov. 30 *Perf. 15*

741 A95 25c Incense holder, 1450 .25 .25
742 A95 75c Cylindrical vase, 675 .75 .75
743 A95 $1 Tripod vase, 500 1.00 1.00
744 A95 $2 Kinich Ahau (sun god) 2.00 2.00
Nos. 741-744 (4) 4.00 4.00

Girl Guides 75th Anniv., Intl. Youth Year A96

1985, Mar. 15 Litho. *Perf. 15*

745 A96 25c Gov.-Gen. Gordon .40 .40
746 A96 50c Camping .60 .60
747 A96 90c Map reading .80 .80
748 A96 $1.25 Students in laboratory .95 .95
749 A96 $2 Lady Baden-Powell 1.25 1.25
Nos. 745-749 (5) 4.00 4.00

Each stamp shows the scouting and IYY emblems.

For overprints see Nos. 777-781.

Audubon Birth Bicentenary — A97

Illustrations by Audubon. 10c, 25c, 75c, $1, $5 vert.

Perf. 14, 15 ($1)

1985, May 30-1988 Litho.

750 A97 10c White-tailed kite .75 .75
751 A97 15c Cuvier's kinglet 1.00 1.00
752 A97 25c Painted bunting 1.10 1.10
752A A97 60c like #752 ('88)
753 A97 75c Belted kingfisher 1.10 1.10
754 A97 $1 Northern cardinal 1.10 1.10
755 A97 $3 Long-billed curlew 1.60 1.60
Nos. 750-752,753-755 (6) 6.65 6.65

Souvenir Sheet

Perf. 13½x14

756 A97 $5 Portrait of Audubon, 1826, by John Syme 5.00 5.00

No. 756 contains one 38x51mm stamp.

Queen Mother, 85th Birthday — A98

Designs: 10c, The Queen Consort and Princess Elizabeth, 1928. 15c, Queen Mother, Elizabeth. 75c, Queen Mother waving a greeting. No. 760, Royal family photograph, christening of Prince Henry. $2, Holding the infant Prince Henry. No. 762, Queen Mother, diff.

1985, June 20

757 A98 10c shown .20 .20
758 A98 15c multicolored .20 .20
759 A98 75c multicolored .85 .85
760 A98 $5 multicolored 3.25 3.25
Nos. 757-760 (4) 4.50 4.50

Souvenir Sheets

761 A98 $2 multicolored 1.75 1.75
762 A98 $5 multicolored 4.25 4.25

Nos. 761-762 contain one 38x51mm stamp. For overprints see Nos. 771-776.

Nos. 705-706, 708 Ovptd.: INAUGURATION OF NEW GOVERNMENT 21st. DECEMBER 1984

1985, June 24 ***Perf. 15***

762A A89 10c multicolored .80 .80
762B A89 15c multicolored .95 .95
762C A89 50c multicolored 1.25 1.25
Nos. 762A-762C (3) 3.00 3.00

Miniature Sheet

Commonwealth Stamp Omnibus, 50th Anniv. — A99

British Honduras Nos. 111-112, 127, 129, 143, 194, 307 and Belize Nos. 326, 385 and 397b on: a, George V and Queen Mary in an open carriage. b, George VI and Queen Consort Elizabeth crowned. c, Civilians celebrating the end of WWII. d, George VI and Queen Consort at mass service. e, Elizabeth II wearing robes of state and the imperial crown. f, Winston Churchill, WWII fighter planes. g, Bridal photograph of Elizabeth II and Prince Philip. h, Bridal photograph of Princess Anne and Capt. Mark Phillips. i, Elizabeth II. j, Imperial crown.

1985, July 25 ***Perf. 14½x14***

763 Sheet of 10 5.00 5.00
a.-j. A99 50c any single .50 .50

Souvenir Sheet

Perf. 14

764 A99 $5 Elizabeth II coronation photograph 5.00 5.00

No. 764 contains one 38x51mm stamp. For overprints see Nos. 796-797.

British Post Office, 350th Anniv. A100

1985, Aug. 1 ***Perf. 15***

765 A100 10c Postboy, letters .40 .40
766 A100 15c Packet, privateer .55 .55
767 A100 25c Duke of Marlborough .70 .70
768 A100 75c Diana 1.25 1.25
769 A100 $1 Falmouth P.O. packet 1.25 1.25
770 A100 $3 S. S. Conway 2.25 2.25
Nos. 765-770 (6) 6.40 6.40

Nos. 757-762 Ovptd. in Silver "COMMONWEALTH SUMMIT / CONFERENCE, BAHAMAS / 16th-22nd OCTOBER 1985"

1985, Sept. 5 Litho. ***Perf. 15***

771 A98 10c multicolored .40 .40
772 A98 15c multicolored .60 .60
773 A98 75c multicolored 1.25 1.25
774 A98 $5 multicolored 3.00 3.00
Nos. 771-774 (4) 5.25 5.25

Souvenir Sheets

775 A98 $2 multicolored 1.50 1.50
776 A98 $5 multicolored 4.50 4.50

Nos. 745-749 Ovptd. "80th ANNIVERSARY OF / ROTARY INTERNATIONAL"

1985, Sept. 25 ***Perf. 15***

777 A96 25c multicolored .45 .45
778 A96 50c multicolored .75 .75
779 A96 90c multicolored 1.10 1.10
780 A96 $1.25 multicolored 1.60 1.60
781 A96 $2 multicolored 2.10 2.10
Nos. 777-781 (5) 6.00 6.00

Royal Visit — A101

1985, Oct. 9 ***Perf. 15x14½***

782 A101 25c Royal and natl. flags .25 .25
783 A101 75c Elizabeth II .75 .75

Size: 81x38mm

784 A101 $4 Britannia 5.00 5.00
a. Strip of 3, #782-784 5.00
Nos. 782-784 (3) 6.00 6.00

Souvenir Sheet

Perf. 13½x14

785 A101 $5 Elizabeth II, diff. 4.50 4.50

No. 785 contains one 38x51mm stamp.

Disneyland, 30th Anniv. A102

Characters from "It's a Small World."

1985, Nov. 1 ***Perf. 11***

786 A102 1c Royal Canadian Mounted Police .20 .20
787 A102 2c American Indian .20 .20
788 A102 3c Inca of the Andes .20 .20
789 A102 4c Africa .20 .20
790 A102 5c Far East .20 .20
791 A102 6c Belize .20 .20
792 A102 50c Balkans .80 .80
793 A102 $1.50 Saudi Arabia 1.75 1.75
794 A102 $3 Japan 3.25 3.25
Nos. 786-794 (9) 7.00 7.00

Souvenir Sheet

Perf. 14

795 A102 $4 Montage 6.00 6.00

Christmas.

Nos. 763-764 Ovptd. "PRE 'WORLD CUP FOOTBALL' / MEXICO 1986"

1985, Dec. 20 ***Perf. 14½x14***

796 Sheet of 10 7.00 7.00
a.-j. A99 50c, any single .60 .60

Souvenir Sheet

797 A99 $5 multicolored 5.50 5.50

Women in Folk Costumes — A103

1986, Jan. 15 ***Perf. 15***

798 A103 5c India .60 .60
799 A103 10c Maya .65 .65
800 A103 15c Garifuna .80 .80
801 A103 25c Creole 1.00 1.00
802 A103 50c China 1.40 1.40
803 A103 75c Lebanon 1.60 1.60
804 A103 $1 Europe 1.60 1.60
805 A103 $2 South America 2.25 2.25
Nos. 798-805 (8) 9.90 9.90

Souvenir Sheet

Perf. 14

806 A103 $5 Maya, So. America 6.25 6.25

No. 806 contains one 38x51mm stamp.

Miniature Sheet

A104

Easter — A105

Papal arms, crucifix and: a, Pius X. b, Benedict XV. c, Pius XI. d, Pius XII. e, John XXIII. f, Paul VI. g, John Paul I. h, John Paul II. No. 573, John Paul II saying mass in Belize.

1986, Apr. 15 Litho. ***Perf. 11***

807 Sheet of 8 + label 7.00 7.00
a.-h. A104 50c, any single 1.00 1.00

Souvenir Sheet

Perf. 14

808 A105 $4 multi 8.50 8.50

No. 807 contains center label picturing the Vatican, and papal crest.

Queen Elizabeth II, 60th Birthday — A106

A107

1986, Apr. 21 ***Perf. 14***

809 Strip of 3 1.50 1.50
a. A106 25c Age 2 .25 .25
b. A106 50c Coronation .50 .50
c. A106 75c Riding horse .75 .75
810 A106 $3 Wearing crown jewels 3.00 3.00

Souvenir Sheet

811 A107 $4 Portrait 3.25 3.25

A108

Halley's Comet — A109

1986, Apr. 30

812 Strip of 3 .75 .75
a. A108 10c Planet-A probe .20 .20
b. A108 15c Sighting, 1910 .20 .20
c. A108 50c Giotto probe .50 .50
813 Strip of 3 3.75 3.75
a. A108 75c Weather bureau .75 .75
b. A108 $1 US space telescope, shuttle 1.00 1.00
c. A108 $2 Edmond Halley 2.00 2.00

Souvenir Sheet

814 A109 $4 Computer graphics 5.00 5.00

Miniature Sheet

A110

US Presidents — A111

1986, May ***Perf. 11***

815 Sheet of 6 + 3 labels 3.75 3.75
a. A110 10c George Washington .20 .20
b. A110 20c John Adams .20 .20
c. A110 30c Thomas Jefferson .25 .25
d. A110 50c James Madison .40 .40
e. A110 $1.50 James Monroe 1.10 1.10
f. A110 $2 John Quincy Adams 1.60 1.60

Souvenir Sheet

Perf. 14

816 A111 $4 Washington 4.00 4.00

No. 815 contains 3 center labels picturing the great seal of the US.

Issue dates: #815, May 5; #816, May 7.

A112

Statue of Liberty, Cent. — A113

Designs: 25c, Bartholdi, statue. 50c, Statue, US centennial celebration, Philadelphia, 1876. 75c, Statue close-up, flags, 1886 unveiling. $3, Flags, statue close-up. $4, Statue, New York City skyline.

1986, May 15 *Perf. 14*

817 Strip of 3 4.00 4.00
- *a.* A112 25c multicolored .25 .25
- *b.* A112 75c multicolored .75 .75
- *c.* A112 $3 multicolored 3.00 3.00

818 A112 50c multicolored .50 .50

Souvenir Sheet

819 A113 $4 multicolored 4.00 4.00

A114

AMERIPEX '86, Chicago, May 22-June 1 — A115

1986, May 22

820 Strip of 3 .75 .75
- *a.* A114 10c British Honduras No. 3 .20 .20
- *b.* A114 15c Stamp of 1981 .20 .20
- *c.* A114 50c US No. C3a .50 .50

821 Strip of 3 3.75 3.75
- *a.* A114 75c USS Constitution .75 .75
- *b.* A114 $1 Liberty Bell 1.00 1.00
- *c.* A114 $2 White House 2.00 2.00

Souvenir Sheet

822 A115 $4 Capitol Building 3.50 3.50

For overprints see Nos. 835-837.

1986 World Cup Soccer Championships, Mexico — A116

Designs: 25c, England vs. Brazil. 50c, Mexican player, Mayan statues. 75c, Belize players. $3, Aztec calendar stone, Mexico. $4, Flags composing soccer balls.

1986, June 16 Litho. *Perf. 11*

823 A116 25c multicolored 1.25 1.25
824 A116 50c multicolored 1.50 1.50
825 A116 75c multicolored 1.75 1.75
826 A116 $3 multicolored 2.00 2.00
Nos. 823-826 (4) 6.50 6.50

Souvenir Sheet

Perf. 14

827 A116 $4 multicolored 5.00 5.00

Nos. 823-826 printed in sheets of 8 plus label picturing Azteca Stadium, 2 each value per sheet.

Nos. 823-827 Overprinted "ARGENTINA - /WINNERS 1986"

1986, Aug. 15

828 A116 25c multicolored .25 .25
829 A116 50c multicolored .50 .50
830 A116 75c multicolored .75 .75
831 A116 $3 multicolored 3.00 3.00
Nos. 828-831 (4) 4.50 4.50

Souvenir Sheet

832 A116 $4 multicolored 4.00 4.00

A117

Wedding of Prince Andrew and Sarah Ferguson A118

1986, July 23 *Perf. 14x14½*

833 Strip of 3 3.25 3.25
- *a.* A117 25c Sarah .20 .20
- *b.* A117 75c Andrew .60 .60
- *c.* A117 $3 Couple 2.25 2.25

Souvenir Sheet

Perf. 14½

834 Sheet of 2 4.00 4.00
- *a.* A118 $1 Sarah, diff. 1.00 1.00
- *b.* A118 $3 Andrew, diff. 3.00 3.00

Size of No. 833c: 92x41mm.

Nos. 820-822 Ovptd. with STOCKHOLMIA '86 Emblems

1986, Aug. 28 Litho. *Perf. 14*

835 Strip of 3 .75 .75
- *a.* A114 10c multicolored .20 .20
- *b.* A114 15c multicolored .20 .20
- *c.* A114 50c multicolored .50 .50

836 Strip of 3 3.75 3.75
- *a.* A114 75c multicolored .75 .75
- *b.* A114 $1 multicolored 1.00 1.00
- *c.* A114 $2 multicolored 2.00 2.00

Souvenir Sheet

837 A115 $4 multicolored 4.00 4.00

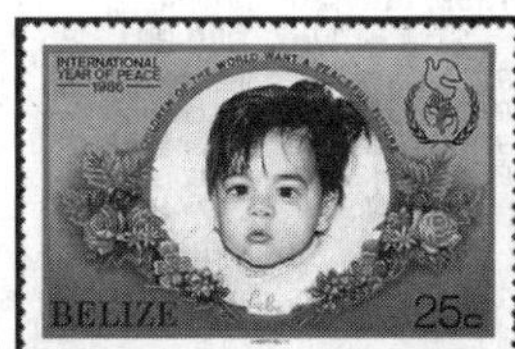

A119

Intl. Peace Year — A120

Children.

1986, Oct. 3 Litho. *Perf. 14*

838 A119 25c Infant .25 .25
839 A119 50c Caucasians .50 .50
840 A119 75c Oriental .75 .75
841 A119 $3 Indian, caucasian 3.00 3.00
Nos. 838-841 (4) 4.50 4.50

Souvenir Sheet

842 A120 $4 shown 4.00 4.00

Nos. 838-841 printed se-tenant in sheets of 8 (2 each) plus center label.

Fungi — A121

Toucans — A122

1986, Oct. 30 *Perf. 14*

843 A121 5c Amanita lilloi .20 .20
844 A122 10c Keel-billed toucan .20 .20
845 A121 20c Boletellus cubensis .30 .30
846 A122 25c Collared aracari .40 .40
847 A121 75c Psilocybe caerulescens 1.25 1.25
848 A122 $1 Emerald toucanet 1.50 1.50
849 A122 $1.25 Crimson-rumped toucan 1.75 1.75
850 A121 $2 Russula puiggarii 3.00 3.00
Nos. 843-850 (8) 8.60 8.60

Stamps of the same design printed in sheets of 8 plus center label picturing Audubon Society emblem.

Christmas A123

Disney characters.

1986, Nov. 14 *Perf. 11*

851 Sheet of 9 6.50 6.50
- *a.* A123 2c Jose Carioca .20 .20
- *b.* A123 3c Carioca, Panchito, Donald .20 .20
- *c.* A123 4c Daisy .20 .20
- *d.* A123 5c Mickey, Minnie .20 .20
- *e.* A123 6c Carioca playing music .20 .20
- *f.* A123 50c Panchito, Donald .65 .65
- *g.* A123 65c Donald, Carioca .90 .90
- *h.* A123 $1.35 Donald 1.75 1.75
- *i.* A123 $2 Goofy 2.75 2.75

Souvenir Sheet

Perf. 14

852 A123 $4 Donald 6.00 6.00

Marriage of Queen Elizabeth II and the Duke of Edinburgh, 40th Anniv. — A124

A125

1987, Oct. 7 Litho. *Perf. 15*

853 A124 25c Elizabeth, 1947 .20 .20
854 A124 75c Couple, c. 1980 .55 .55
855 A124 $1 Elizabeth, 1986 .75 .75
856 A124 $4 Wearing robes of Order of the Garter 3.00 3.00
Nos. 853-856 (4) 4.50 4.50

Souvenir Sheet

Perf. 14

857 A125 $6 shown 6.00 6.00

A126

America's Cup 1986-87 — A127

Yachts that competed in the 1987 finals.

1987, Oct. 21 *Perf. 15*

858 A126 25c America II .25 .25
859 A126 75c Stars and Stripes .75 .75
860 A126 $1 Australia II 1.00 1.00
861 A126 $4 White Crusader 4.00 4.00
Nos. 858-861 (4) 6.00 6.00

Souvenir Sheet

Perf. 14

862 A127 $6 Australia II sails 6.00 6.00

Woodcarvings by Sir George Gabb (b. 1928) — A128

A129

1987, Nov. 4 *Perf. 15*

863 A128 25c Mother and Child .20 .20
864 A128 75c Standing Form .60 .60
865 A128 $1 Love-Doves .80 .80
866 A128 $4 Depiction of Music 3.25 3.25
Nos. 863-866 (4) 4.85 4.85

Souvenir Sheet

Perf. 14

867 A129 $6 African Heritage 4.50 4.50

A130

Indigenous Primates — A131

1987, Nov. 11 ***Perf. 15***

868 A130 25c Black spider monkey .25 .25
869 A130 75c Male black howler .75 .75
870 A130 $1 Spider monkeys 1.00 1.00
871 A130 $4 Howler monkeys 4.00 4.00
Nos. 868-871 (4) 6.00 6.00

Souvenir Sheet

Perf. 14

872 A131 $6 Black spider, diff. 6.00 6.00

Natl. Girl Guides Movement, 50th Anniv. — A132

Lady Olave Baden-Powell, Founder — A133

1987, Nov. 25 ***Perf. 15***

873 A132 25c Flag-bearers .25 .25
874 A132 75c Camping .75 .75
875 A132 $1 On parade, camp 1.00 1.00
876 A132 $4 Olave Baden-Powell 4.00 4.00
Nos. 873-876 (4) 6.00 6.00

Souvenir Sheet

Perf. 14

877 A133 $6 Lady Olave, diff. 6.00 6.00

Intl. Year of Shelter for the Homeless A134

1987, Dec. 3 ***Perf. 15***

878 A134 25c Tent dwellings .25 .25
879 A134 75c Urban slum .75 .75
880 A134 $1 Tents, diff. 1.00 1.00
881 A134 $4 Construction 4.00 4.00
Nos. 878-881 (4) 6.00 6.00

Orchids A135

Illustrations from Reichenbachia, published by Henry F. Sander in 1886: 1c, Laelia euspatha. 2c, Cattleya citrina. 3c, Masdevallia bachousiana. 4c, Cypripedium tautzianum. 5c, Trichopilia suavis alba. 6c, Odontoglossum hebraicum. 7c, Cattleya trianaei schroederiana. 10c, Saccolabium giganteum. 30c, Cattleya warscewiczii. 50c, Chysis bractescens. 70c, Cattleya rochellensis. $1, Laelia elegans schilleriana. $1.50, Laelia anceps percivaliana. #895, $3, Laelia gouldiana.

#896, $3, Odontoglossum roezlii. $5, Cattleya dowiana aurea.

1987, Dec. 16 Litho. ***Perf. 14***

882-895 A135 Set of 14 11.00 11.00

Miniature Sheets

896-897 A135 Set of 2 8.00 8.00

Nos. 882-887 and 889-894 printed in blocks of six. Sheets of 14 contain 2 blocks of Nos. 882-887 plus 2 No. 888 and center label or 2 blocks of Nos. 889-894 plus center strip containing 2 No. 895 and center label. Center labels picture various illustrations from Reichenbachia.

Nos. 896-897 contain one 44x51mm stamp.

Miniature Sheet

Easter A136

Stations of the Cross (in sequential order): a, Jesus condemned to death. b, Carries the cross. c, Falls the first time. d, Meets his mother, Mary. e, Cyrenean takes up the cross. f, Veronica wipes Jesus's face. g, Falls the second time. h, Consoles the women of Jerusalem. i, Falls the third time. j, Stripped of his robes. k, Nailed to the cross. l, Dies. m, Taken down from the cross. n, Laid in the sepulcher.

1988, Mar. 21 ***Perf. 14***

898 Sheet of 14 + label 5.75 5.75
a.-n. A136 40c, any single .40 .40

A $6 souvenir sheet was prepared but not issued.

1988 Summer Olympics, Seoul — A137

1988, Aug. 15 Litho. ***Perf. 14***

899 A137 10c Basketball .20 .20
900 A137 25c Volleyball .25 .25
901 A137 60c Table tennis .60 .60
902 A137 75c Diving .75 .75
903 A137 $1 Judo 1.00 1.00
904 A137 $2 Field hockey 2.00 2.00
Nos. 899-904 (6) 4.80 4.80

Souvenir Sheet

905 A137 $3 Women's gymnastics 3.00 3.00

Intl. Red Cross, 125th Anniv. A138

1988, Nov. 18 Litho. ***Perf. 14***

906 A138 60c Travelling nurse, 1912 .60 .60
907 A138 75c Hospital ship, ambulance boat, 1937 .75 .75
908 A138 $1 Ambulance, 1956 1.00 1.00
909 A138 $2 Ambulance plane, 1940 2.00 2.00
Nos. 906-909 (4) 4.35 4.35

Indigenous Small Animals — A139

1989 Litho. Wmk. 384 ***Perf. 14***

910 A139 10c Gibnut (agouti) .25 .25

Unwmk.

911 A139 25c Four-eyed opossum, vert. .65 .65
a. Wmk. 384 .65 .65
912 A139 50c Ant bear 1.40 1.40
913 A139 60c like 10c 1.60 1.60
914 A139 75c Antelope 2.00 2.00
915 A139 $2 Peccary 5.50 5.50
Nos. 910-915 (6) 11.40 11.40

Issued: 10c, 7/23; #911a, 12/6; others, 2/24.

Moon Landing, 20th Anniv.

Common Design Type

Apollo 9: 25c, Command service and lunar modules docked in space. 50c, Command service module. 75c, Mission emblem. $1, First manned lunar module in space. $5, Apollo 11 command service module.

Perf. 14x13½

1989, July 20 Wmk. 384

Size of Nos. 680-681: 29x29mm

916 CD342 25c multicolored .20 .20
917 CD342 50c multicolored .45 .45
918 CD342 75c multicolored .65 .65
919 CD342 $1 multicolored .90 .90
Nos. 916-919 (4) 2.20 2.20

Souvenir Sheet

920 CD342 $5 multi 5.00 5.00

No. 920 Overprinted

WORLD STAMP EXPO '89™
United States Postal Service
Nov. 17 — 20 and
Nov. 24 — Dec. 3, 1989
Washington Convention Center
Washington, DC

1989, Nov. 17 ***Perf. 14x13½***

921 CD342 $5 multicolored 5.00 5.00

World Stamp Expo '89.

5c

No. 704 Surcharged

1989, Nov. 15 ***Perf. 15***

922 A89 5c on 6c multi *2.00*

Christmas A140

Old churches.

Wmk. 384

1989, Dec. 13 Litho. ***Perf. 14***

927 A140 10c Wesley .20 .20
928 A140 25c Baptist .25 .25
929 A140 60c St. John's Cathedral .60 .60
930 A140 75c St. Andrew's Presbyterian .75 .75
931 A140 $1 Holy Redeemer Cathedral 1.00 1.00
Nos. 927-931 (5) 2.80 2.80

A141

Wmk. 373

1990, Mar. 1 Litho. ***Perf. 14***

Birds and Butterflies: 5c, *Piranga leucoptera, Catonephele numilia* female. 10c, *Ramphastos sulfuratus, Nessaea aglaura.* 15c, *Fregata magnificens, Eurytides philolaus.* 25c, *Jabiru mycteria, Heliconius sapho.* 30c, *Ardea herodias, Colobura dirce.* 50c, *Icterus galbula, Hamadryas arethusia.* 60c, *Ara macao, Thecla regalis.* 75c, *Cyanerpes cyaneus, Callicore patelina.* $1, *Pulsatrix perspicillata, Caligo uranus.* $2, *Cyanocorax yncas, Philaethria dido.* $5, *Cathartes aura, Battus belus.* $10, *Pandion haliaetus, Papilio thoas.*

932 A141 5c multicolored .20 .20
933 A141 10c multicolored .20 .20
934 A141 15c multicolored .20 .20
935 A141 25c multicolored .25 .25
936 A141 30c multicolored .30 .30
937 A141 50c multicolored .50 .50
938 A141 60c multicolored .60 .60
939 A141 75c multicolored .75 .75
940 A141 $1 multicolored 1.00 1.00
941 A141 $2 multicolored 2.00 2.00
942 A141 $5 multicolored 5.00 5.00
943 A141 $10 multicolored 10.00 10.00
Nos. 932-943 (12) 21.00 21.00

The 10c exists inscribed "1993."

For overprints and surcharge see Nos. 944, 1021, 1030.

No. 940 Overprinted in Gold: "FIRST DOLLAR / COIN / 1990"

1990, Mar. 1

944 A141 $1 multicolored 1.00 1.00

Turtles A142

Wmk. 373

1990, Aug. 8 Litho. ***Perf. 14***

945 A142 10c Green .20 .20
946 A142 25c Hawksbill .25 .25
947 A142 60c Loggerhead .60 .60
948 A142 75c Loggerhead, diff. .75 .75
949 A142 $1 Bocatora 1.00 1.00
950 A142 $2 Hicatee 2.00 2.00
Nos. 945-950 (6) 4.80 4.80

Battle of Britain, 50th Anniv. A143

Aircraft.

1990, Sept. 15 Wmk. 384 *Perf. 13½*

951 A143 10c Fairey Battle .20 .20
952 A143 25c Bristol Beaufort .25 .25
953 A143 60c Bristol Blenheim .60 .60
954 A143 75c Armstrong-Whitworth Whitley .75 .75
955 A143 $1 Vickers-Armstrong Wellington 1.00 1.00
956 A143 $2 Handley-Page Hampden 2.00 2.00
Nos. 951-956 (6) 4.80 4.80

Orchids — A144

1990, Nov. 1 Wmk. 384 *Perf. 14*

957 A144 25c Cattleya bowringiana .25 .25
958 A144 50c Rhyncholaelia digbyana .50 .50
959 A144 60c Sobralia macrantha .60 .60
960 A144 75c Chysis bractescens .75 .75
961 A144 $1 Vanilla planifolia 1.00 1.00
962 A144 $2 Epidendrum polyanthum 2.00 2.00
Nos. 957-962 (6) 5.10 5.10

Christmas.

Indigenous Fauna — A145

1991, Apr. 10

963 A145 25c Iguana .25 .25
964 A145 50c Crocodile .50 .50
965 A145 60c Manatee .60 .60
966 A145 75c Boa constrictor .75 .75
967 A145 $1 Tapir 1.00 1.00
968 A145 $2 Jaguar 2.00 2.00
Nos. 963-968 (6) 5.10 5.10

Elizabeth & Philip, Birthdays
Common Design Types

1991, June 17 *Perf. 14½*

969 CD345 $1 multicolored 1.00 1.00
970 CD346 $1 multicolored 1.00 1.00
a. Pair, #969-970 + label 2.00 2.00

Hurricanes — A146

1991, July 31 Wmk. 373 *Perf. 14*

971 A146 60c Weather radar .60 .60
972 A146 75c Weather observation station .75 .75
973 A146 $1 Scene after hurricane 1.00 1.00
974 A146 $2 Hurricane Gilbert 2.00 2.00
Nos. 971-974 (4) 4.35 4.35

Independence, 10th Anniv. — A147

Famous Men: 25c, Thomas V. Ramos (1887-1955). 60c, Sir Isaiah Morter (1860-1924). 75c, Antonio Soberanis (1897-1975). $1, Santiago Ricalde (1920-1975).

1991, Sept. 4 Wmk. 384

975 A147 25c multicolored .30 .30
976 A147 60c multicolored .65 .65
977 A147 75c multicolored .80 .80
978 A147 $1 multicolored 1.10 1.10
Nos. 975-978 (4) 2.85 2.85

Folktales A148

Christmas.

Wmk. 373

1991, Nov. 6 Litho. *Perf. 14*

979 A148 25c Anansi .30 .30
980 A148 50c Jack-O-Lantern .55 .55
981 A148 60c Tata Duende, vert. .65 .65
982 A148 75c Xtabai .80 .80
983 A148 $1 Warrie Massa, vert. 1.10 1.10
984 A148 $2 Old Heg 2.25 2.25
Nos. 979-984 (6) 5.65 5.65

See Nos. 999-1002.

Orchids — A149

Easter: 25c, Gongora quinquenervis. 50c, Oncidium sphacelatum. 60c, Encyclia bractescens. 75c, Epidendrum ciliare. $1, Psygmorchis pusilla. $2, Galeandra batemanii.

1992, Apr. 1

985 A149 25c multicolored .30 .30
986 A149 50c multicolored .55 .55
987 A149 60c multicolored .65 .65
988 A149 75c multicolored .80 .80
989 A149 $1 multicolored 1.10 1.10
990 A149 $2 multicolored 2.25 2.25
Nos. 985-990 (6) 5.65 5.65

Famous Belizeans A150

Designs: 25c, Gwendolyn Lizarraga, MBE (1901-75). 60c, Rafael Fonseca, CMG, OBE (1921-78). 75c, Vivian Seay, MBE (1881-1971). $1, Samuel A. Haynes (1898-1971).

1992, Aug. 26 *Perf. 13x12½*

991 A150 25c multicolored .30 .30
992 A150 60c multicolored .65 .65
993 A150 75c multicolored .80 .80
994 A150 $1 multicolored 1.10 1.10
Nos. 991-994 (4) 2.85 2.85

See Nos. 1013-1016.

Discovery of America, 500th Anniv. — A151

Mayan ruins, modern buildings: 25c, Xunantunich, National Assembly. 60c, Altun Ha, Supreme Court Building. 75c, Santa Rita, Tower Hill Sugar Factory. $5, Lamanai, The Citrus Company.

Perf. 13½x14

1992, Oct. 1 Litho. Wmk. 384

995 A151 25c multicolored .30 .30
996 A151 60c multicolored .65 .65
997 A151 75c multicolored .80 .80
998 A151 $5 multicolored 5.50 5.50
Nos. 995-998 (4) 7.25 7.25

Folklore Type of 1991

Christmas.

Perf. 13x12½

1992, Nov. 16 Litho. Wmk. 373

999 A148 25c Hashishi Pampi .25 .25
1000 A148 60c Cadejo .60 .60
1001 A148 $1 La Sucia, vert. 1.00 1.00
1002 A148 $5 Sisimito 5.00 5.00
Nos. 999-1002 (4) 6.85 6.85

Royal Air Force, 75th Anniv.
Common Design Type

Designs: 25c, Aerospatiale Puma. 50c, British Aerospace Harrier. 60c, DeHavilland Mosquito. 75c, Avro Lancaster. $1, Consolidated Liberator. $3, Short Stirling.

Wmk. 373

1993, Apr. 1 Litho. *Perf. 14*

1003 CD350 25c multicolored .25 .25
1004 CD350 50c multicolored .50 .50
1005 CD350 60c multicolored .65 .65
1006 CD350 75c multicolored .80 .80
1007 CD350 $1 multicolored 1.00 1.00
1008 CD350 $3 multicolored 3.25 3.25
Nos. 1003-1008 (6) 6.45 6.45

1993 World Orchid Conference, Glasgow — A152

Perf. 14½x14

1993, Apr. 24 Litho. Wmk. 384

1009 A152 25c Lycaste aromatica .30 .30
1010 A152 60c Sobralia decora .65 .65
1011 A152 $1 Maxillaria alba 1.10 1.10
1012 A152 $2 Brassavola nodosa 2.25 2.25
Nos. 1009-1012 (4) 4.30 4.30

Famous Belizeans Type of 1992

Designs: 25c, Herbert Watkin Beaumont (1880-1978). 60c, Dr. Selvyn Walford Young (1899-1977). 75c, Cleopatra White (1898-1987). $1, Dr. Karl Heusner (1872-1960).

Wmk. 384

1993, Aug. 11 Litho. *Perf. 14*

1013 A150 25c multicolored .30 .30
1014 A150 60c multicolored .65 .65
1015 A150 75c multicolored .85 .65
1016 A150 $1 multicolored 1.10 1.10
Nos. 1013-1016 (4) 2.90 2.70

Christmas — A153

Wmk. 373

1993, Nov. 3 Litho. *Perf. 14*

1017 A153 25c Boom and chime band .30 .30
1018 A153 60c John Canoe dance .65 .65
1019 A153 75c Cortez dance .80 .80
1020 A153 $2 Maya Musical Group 2.25 2.25
Nos. 1017-1020 (4) 4.00 4.00

No. 940 Ovptd. with Hong Kong '94 Emblem

Wmk. 373

1994, Feb. 18 Litho. *Perf. 14*

1021 A141 $1 multicolored 1.10 1.10

Royal Visit — A154

Designs: 25c, Belize, United Kingdom Flags. 60c, Queen Elizabeth II wearing hat. 75c, Queen. $1, Queen, Prince Philip.

Perf. 14½x14

1994, Feb. 24 Litho. Wmk. 373

1022 A154 25c multicolored .30 .30
1023 A154 60c multicolored .65 .65
1024 A154 75c multicolored .80 .80
1025 A154 $1 multicolored 1.10 1.10
Nos. 1022-1025 (4) 2.85 2.85

Bats A155

Wmk. 384

1994, May 30 Litho. *Perf. 14*

1026 A155 25c Insect feeder .25 .25
1027 A155 60c Fruit feeder .60 .60
1028 A155 75c Fish feeder .75 .75
1029 A155 $2 Common vampire 2.00 2.00
Nos. 1026-1029 (4) 3.60 3.60

No. 939 Surcharged

Wmk. 373

1994, Aug. 18 Litho. *Perf. 14*

1030 A141 10c on 75c multi .20 .20

Christmas A156

Orchids: 25c, Cycnoches chlorochilon. 60c, Brassavolas cucullata. 75c, Sobralia mucronata. $1, Nidema Boothii.

1994, Nov. 7 Wmk. 384

1031 A156 25c multicolored .25 .25
1032 A156 60c multicolored .60 .60
1033 A156 75c multicolored .75 .75
1034 A156 $1 multicolored 1.00 1.00
Nos. 1031-1034 (4) 2.60 2.60

For overprints see Nos. 1051-1054.

Insects A157

Wmk. 373

1995, Jan. 11 Litho. *Perf. 14*

1035 A157 5c Ground beetle .20 .20
1036 A157 10c Harlequin beetle .20 .20
1037 A157 15c Giant water bug .20 .20
1038 A157 25c Peanut-head bug .25 .25
1039 A157 30c Coconut weevil .30 .30
1040 A157 50c Mantis .50 .50
1041 A157 60c Tarantula wasp .60 .60
1042 A157 75c Rhinoceros beetle .75 .75
1043 A157 $1 Metallic wood borer 1.00 1.00
1044 A157 $2 Dobson fly 2.00 2.00
1045 A157 $5 Click beetle 5.00 5.00

1046	A157	$10 Long-horned beetle	10.00	10.00
		Nos. 1035-1046 (12)	21.00	21.00

Nos. 1035-1046 exist inscribed "1996."
For overprints see Nos. 1063-1066.

End of World War II, 50th Anniv.
Common Design Type

Designs: 25c, War Memorial Cenotaph. 60c, Remembrance Sunday. 75c, British Honduras Forestry Unit. $1, Wellington Bomber.

Wmk. 373

1995, May 8 Litho. *Perf. 13½*

1047	CD351	25c multicolored	.30	.30
1048	CD351	60c multicolored	.65	.65
1049	CD351	75c multicolored	.80	.80
1050	CD351	$1 multicolored	1.10	1.10
		Nos. 1047-1050 (4)	2.85	2.85

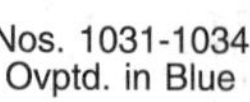

Nos. 1031-1034 Ovptd. in Blue

1995, Sept. 1 Wmk. 384 *Perf. 14*

1051	A156	25c on No. 1031	.25	.25
1052	A156	60c on No. 1032	.60	.60
1053	A156	75c on No. 1033	.75	.75
1054	A156	$1 on No. 1034	1.00	1.00
		Nos. 1051-1054 (4)	2.60	2.60

UN, 50th Anniv.
Common Design Type

Designs: 25c, M113 Light reconnaissance vehicle. 60c, Sultan, armored command vehicle. 75c, Leyland/DAF 8x4 "Drops" vehicle. $2, Warrior infantry combat vehicle.

Wmk. 384

1995, Oct. 24 Litho. *Perf. 14*

1055	CD353	25c multicolored	.25	.25
1056	CD353	60c multicolored	.60	.60
1057	CD353	75c multicolored	.75	.75
1058	CD353	$2 multicolored	2.00	2.00
		Nos. 1055-1058 (4)	3.60	3.60

Christmas A158

Doves: 25c, Blue ground. 60c, White-fronted. 75c, Ruddy ground. $1, White-winged.

1995, Nov. 6 Wmk. 373

1059	A158	25c multicolored	.25	.25
1060	A158	60c multicolored	.60	.60
1061	A158	75c multicolored	.75	.75
1062	A158	$1 multicolored	1.00	1.00
		Nos. 1059-1062 (4)	2.60	2.60

Nos. 1037, 1039-1040, 1044 Ovptd.

Wmk. 373

1996, May 17 Litho. *Perf. 14*

1063	A157	15c on #1037	.20	.20
1064	A157	30c on #1039	.30	.30
1065	A157	50c on #1040	.50	.50
1066	A157	$2 on #1044	2.00	2.00
		Nos. 1063-1066 (4)	3.00	3.00

CAPEX '96 A159

Trains: 25c, Unloading banana train onto freighter, Commerce Bight Pier. 60c, Engine No. 1, Stann Creek Station. 75c, Mahogany log train, Hunslet 0-6-0 Side Tank Engine No. 4. $3, LMS Jubilee Class 4-6-0 Locomotive No. 5602 "British Honduras."

Perf. 13½x13

1996, June 6 Litho. Wmk. 373

1067	A159	25c multicolored	.25	.25
1068	A159	60c multicolored	.60	.60
1069	A159	75c multicolored	.75	.75
1070	A159	$3 multicolored	3.00	3.00
		Nos. 1067-1070 (4)	4.60	4.60

Christmas — A160

Orchids: 25c, Epidendrum stamfordianum. 60c, Oncidium carthagenense. 75c, Oerstedella verrucosa. $1, Coryanthes speciosa.

Wmk. 373

1996, Nov. 6 Litho. *Perf. 14*

1071	A160	25c multicolored	.25	.25
1072	A160	60c multicolored	.60	.60
1073	A160	75c multicolored	.75	.75
1074	A160	$1 multicolored	1.00	1.00
		Nos. 1071-1074 (4)	2.60	2.60

Hong Kong '97 A161

Cattle: 25c, Red poll. 60c, Brahman. 75c, Longhorn. $1, Charbray.

Wmk. 373

1997, Feb. 12 Litho. *Perf. 14*

1075	A161	25c multicolored	.30	.30
1076	A161	60c multicolored	.70	.70
1077	A161	75c multicolored	.85	.85
1078	A161	$1 multicolored	1.10	1.10
		Nos. 1075-1078 (4)	2.95	2.95

Snakes — A162

Howler Monkeys — A163

25c, Coral snake. 60c, Green vine snake. 75c, Yellow-jawed tommygoff. $1, Speckled racer.

Wmk. 373

1997, May 28 Litho. *Perf. 14*

1079	A162	25c multicolored	.30	.30
1080	A162	60c multicolored	.65	.65
1081	A162	75c multicolored	.80	.80
1082	A162	$1 multicolored	1.10	1.10
		Nos. 1079-1082 (4)	2.85	2.85

Wmk. 373

1997, Aug. 13 Litho. *Perf. 14*

World Wildlife Fund: 10c, Adult male. 25c, Female feeding. 60c, Female with infant. 75c, Juvenile feeding.

1083	A163	10c multicolored	.20	.20
1084	A163	25c multicolored	.25	.25
1085	A163	60c multicolored	.60	.60
1086	A163	75c multicolored	.75	.75
		Nos. 1083-1086 (4)	1.80	1.80

Christmas A164

Orchids: 25c, Maxillaria elatior. 60c, Dimerandra emarginata. 75c, Macradenia brassavolae. $1, Ornithocephalus gladiatus.

Wmk. 373

1997, Nov. 21 Litho. *Perf. 14*

1087	A164	25c multicolored	.25	.25
1088	A164	60c multicolored	.65	.65
1089	A164	75c multicolored	.80	.80
1090	A164	$1 multicolored	1.10	1.10
		Nos. 1087-1090 (4)	2.80	2.80

Diana, Princess of Wales (1961-97)
Common Design Type

Designs: a, Up close portrait, smiling. b, Wearing evening dress. c, Up close portrait, serious. d, Holding bouquet of flowers.

Perf. 14½x14

1998, Mar. 31 Litho. Wmk. 373

1091	CD355	$1 Sheet of 4, #a.-d.	4.50	4.50

University of West Indies, 50th Anniv. A165

Wmk. 373

1998, July 22 Litho. *Perf. 13*

1092	A165	$1 multicolored	1.00	1.00

Organization of American States, 50th Anniv. A166

Designs: 25c, Children working computers, connecting high schools to the internet. $1, Map of Central America, Inter American Drug Abuse Control Commission.

1998, July 22

1093	A166	25c multicolored	.25	.25
1094	A166	$1 multicolored	1.00	1.00

Battle of St. George's Cay, Bicent. A167

Views of Old Belize from St. George, vert: No. 1095, Woman, child beside small boat. No. 1096, Soldiers at dock, cannon. No. 1097, Cannon balls, cannon, boats in water.

25c, Bayman gun flats. 60c, Bayman sloops. 75c, Schooners. $1, HMS Merlin. $2, Spanish flagship.

1998, Aug. 5 *Perf. 13½*

1095	A167	10c multicolored	.20	.20
1096	A167	10c multicolored	.20	.20
1097	A167	10c multicolored	.20	.20
	a.	Strip of 3, #1095-1097	.30	.30
1098	A167	25c multicolored	.25	.25
1099	A167	60c multicolored	.60	.60
1100	A167	75c multicolored	.75	.75
1101	A167	$1 multicolored	1.00	1.00
1102	A167	$2 multicolored	2.00	2.00
		Nos. 1095-1102 (8)	5.20	5.20

A168

Christmas - Flowers: 25c, Brassia maculata. 60c, Encyclia radiata. 75c, Stanhopea ecornuta. $1, Isochilius carnosiflorus.

1998, Nov. 4 *Perf. 14*

1103	A168	25c multicolored	.25	.25
1104	A168	60c multicolored	.60	.60
1105	A168	75c multicolored	.75	.75
1106	A168	$1 multicolored	1.00	1.00
		Nos. 1103-1106 (4)	2.60	2.60

A169

1999, Mar. 17 *Perf. 13*

Easter - Orchids: 10c, Eucharis grandiflora. 25c, Hippeastrum puniceum. 60c, Zephyranthes citrina. $1, Hymenocallis littoralis.

1107	A169	10c multicolored	.15	.15
1108	A169	25c multicolored	.25	.25
1109	A169	60c multicolored	.60	.60
1110	A169	$1 multicolored	1.00	1.00
		Nos. 1107-1110 (4)	2.00	2.00

UPU, 125th Anniv. A170

1999, Oct. 18 *Perf. 13¼*

1111	A170	25c Bicycle	.25	.25
1112	A170	60c Truck	.60	.60
1113	A170	75c Mailship "Dee"	.75	.75
1114	A170	$1 Airplane	1.00	1.00
		Nos. 1111-1114 (4)	2.60	2.60

Christmas — A171

Designs: 25c, Holy Family with Jesus and St. John, by school of Peter Paul Rubens. 60c, The Holy Family with St. John, by unknown artist. 75c, Madonna with Child, St. John and Angel, by unknown artist. $1, Madonna with Child and St. John by Andrea da Salerno.

1999, Dec. 6 *Perf. 14*

1115	A171	25c multicolored	.25	.25
1116	A171	60c multicolored	.60	.60
1117	A171	75c multicolored	.75	.75
1118	A171	$1 multicolored	1.00	1.00
		Nos. 1115-1118 (4)	2.60	2.60

Fauna
A172

Wmk. 373

2000, Feb. 15 Litho. *Perf. 14*

1119	A172	5c Iguana	.20	.20
1120	A172	10c Gibnut	.20	.20
1121	A172	15c Howler monkey	.20	.20
1122	A172	25c Ant bear	.25	.25
1123	A172	30c Hawksbill turtle	.30	.30
1124	A172	50c Antelope	.50	.50
1125	A172	60c Jaguar	.60	.60
1126	A172	75c Manatee	.75	.75
1127	A172	$1 Crocodile	1.00	1.00
1128	A172	$2 Tapir	2.00	2.00
1129	A172	$5 Collared peccary	5.00	5.00
1130	A172	$10 Boa constrictor	10.00	10.00
		Nos. 1119-1130 (12)	21.00	21.00

Fruits
A173

Wmk. 373

2000, Apr. 19 Litho. *Perf. 14*

1131	A173	25c Mango	.25	.25
1132	A173	60c Cashew	.60	.60
1133	A173	75c Papaya	.75	.75
1134	A173	$1 Banana	1.00	1.00
		Nos. 1131-1134 (4)	2.60	2.60

People's United Party, 50th Anniv.
A174

10c, Birth of party politics, 9/29/50. 25c, People gain voting rights, 4/28/54. 60c, Self-government, 1/1/64. 75c, Building the new capital Belmopan, 1967-70. $1, Independence, 9/21/81.

Perf. 13¼x13¾

2000, Sept. 18 Litho. Wmk. 373

1135-1139 A174 Set of 5 3.00 3.00

Christmas
A175

Orchids: 25c, Bletia purpurea. 60c, Cyrtopodium punctata. 75c, Cycnoches egertonianum. $1, Catasetum integerrimum.

Perf. 14¼x14¼

2000 Litho. Wmk. 373

1140-1143 A175 Set of 4 2.60 2.60

Independence, 20th Anniv. — A176

Designs: 25c, Education. 60c, Shrimp farming. 75c, Privassion Cascade, vert. $2, Map, vert.

Wmk. 373

2001, Oct. 3 Litho. *Perf. 14*

1144-1147 A176 Set of 4 3.75 3.75

Christmas
A177

Orchids: 25c, Sobralia fragrans. 60c, Encyclia cordigera. 75c, Maxillaria fulgens. $1, Epidendrum nocturnum.

Wmk. 373

2001, Dec. 28 Litho. *Perf. 14*

1148-1151 A177 Set of 4 2.60 2.60

Reign Of Queen Elizabeth II, 50th Anniv. Issue

Common Design Type

Designs: Nos. 1152, 1156a, 25c, Princess Elizabeth, 1943. Nos. 1153, 1156b, 60c, In 1952. Nos. 1154, 1156c, 75c, With Prince Charles and Princess Anne. Nos. 1155, 1156d, $1, In 1995. No. 1156e, $5, 1955 portrait by Annigoni (38x50mm).

Perf. 14¼x14½, 13¾ (#1156e)

2002, Feb. 6 Litho. Wmk. 373

With Gold Frames

1152-1155 CD360 Set of 4 2.60 2.60

Souvenir Sheet

Without Gold Frames

1156 CD360 Sheet of 5, #a-e 7.75 7.75

Christmas — A178

Orchids: 25c, Dichaea neglecta. 50c, Epidendrum hawkesii. 60c, Encyclia belizensis. 75c, Eriopsis biloba. $1, Harbenaria monorrhiza. $2, Mormodes buccinator.

Wmk. 373

2002, Dec. 12 Litho. *Perf. 14*

1157-1162 A178 Set of 6 5.25 5.25

SEMI-POSTAL STAMPS

World Cup Soccer Championship — SP1

Designs: 20c+10c, 30c+15c, Scotland vs. New Zealand (diff.). 40c+20c, Kuwait vs. France. 60c+30c, Italy vs. Brazil. No. B5, France vs. Northern Ireland. $1.50+75c, Austria vs. Chile. No. B7, Italy vs. Germany, vert. $2+$1, England vs. France, vert.

1982, Dec. 10 Litho. *Perf. 14*

B1	SP1	20c +10c multi	.25	.25
B2	SP1	30c +15c multi	.35	.35
B3	SP1	40c +20c multi	.45	.45
B4	SP1	60c +30c multi	.75	.75
B5	SP1	$1 +50c multi	3.00	3.00
B6	SP1	$1.50 +75c multi	5.00	5.00
		Nos. B1-B6 (6)	9.80	9.80

Souvenir Sheets

Perf. 14½

B7	SP1	$1 +50c multi	3.50	3.50
B8	SP1	$2 +$1 multi	6.00	6.00

Nos. B7-B8 each contain one 50x70mm stamp.

POSTAGE DUE STAMPS

Numeral — D2

Each denomination has different border.

1976, July 1 Litho. Wmk. 373

J6	D2	1c green & red	.20	.20
J7	D2	2c violet & rose lil	.20	.20
J8	D2	5c ocher & brt grn	.20	.20
J9	D2	15c brown org & yel grn	.30	.30
J10	D2	25c slate grn & org	.50	.50
		Nos. J6-J10 (5)	1.40	1.40

CAYES OF BELIZE

Catalogue values for all unused stamps in this country are for Never Hinged items.

Spiny Lobster
A1

Perf. 14½x14, 14x14½

1984, May 30 Litho. Unwmk.

1	A1	1c shown	.20	.20
2	A1	2c Blue crab	.20	.20
3	A1	5c Red-footed booby	.20	.20
4	A1	10c Brown pelican	.20	.20
5	A1	15c White-tailed deer	.20	.20
6	A1	25c Lighthouse, English Caye	.20	.20
7	A1	75c Spanish galleon, Santa Yaga, c. 1750	.55	.55
8	A1	$3 Map of Ambergris Caye, vert.	2.25	2.25
a.		Souvenir booklet	7.50	
9	A1	$5 Jetty, windsurfers	3.75	3.75
		Nos. 1-9 (9)	7.75	7.75

No. 8a contains four panes. One has one $3 stamp, one has a block of four 25c stamps, two have blocks of four 75c stamps but different text. The stamps are larger than Nos. 6-8, have slightly different colors and are perf. 14½.

The $1 stamp was not issued. Eighteen sheets of 40 were sold for postage by accident.

Lloyd's List Issue

Common Design Type

1984, June 6 *Perf. 14½x14*

10	CD335	25c Queen Elizabeth 2	.20	.20
11	CD335	75c Lutine Bell	.55	.55
12	CD335	$1 Loss of the Fishburn	.75	.75
13	CD335	$2 Trafalgar Sword	1.50	1.50
		Nos. 10-13 (4)	3.00	3.00

1984 Summer Olympics, Los Angeles — A2

1984, Oct. 5 *Perf. 15*

14	A2	10c Yachting	.20	.20
15	A2	15c Windsurfing	.20	.20
16	A2	75c Swimming	.75	.75
17	A2	$2 Kayaking	2.00	2.00
		Nos. 14-17 (4)	3.15	3.15

No. 17 inscribed Canoeing.

First Cayes Stamps, 90th Anniv.
A3

1984, Nov. 5

18	A3	10c 1895 cover	.20	.20
19	A3	15c Sydney Cuthbert	.20	.20
20	A3	75c Cuthbert's steam yacht	.55	.55
21	A3	$2 British Honduras #133	1.50	1.50
		Nos. 18-21 (4)	2.45	2.45

Audubon Birth Bicentenary — A4

Illustrations by Audubon.

1985, May 20 *Perf. 14*

22	A4	25c Blue-winged teal	.20	.20
23	A4	75c Semipalmated sandpiper	.55	.55
24	A4	$1 Yellow-crowned night heron, vert.	.75	.75
25	A4	$3 Common gallinule	2.25	2.25
		Nos. 22-25 (4)	3.75	3.75

Shipwrecks — A5

a, Oxford, c. 1675. b, Santa Yaga, 1780. c, No. 27, Comet, 1822. d, Yeldham, 1800.

1985, June 5 *Perf. 15*

26 A5 $1 Strip of 4+label, #a.-d. 4.00 4.00

Souvenir Sheet

Perf. 13½x14

27 A5 $5 multicolored 5.00 5.00

No. 27 contains one 38x51mm stamp. No. 26 has continuous design.

BENIN

bə-'nin

French Colony

LOCATION — West Coast of Africa
GOVT. — French Possession
AREA — 8,627 sq. mi.
POP. — 493,000 (approx.)
CAPITAL — Benin

In 1895 the French possessions known as Benin were incorporated into the colony of Dahomey and postage stamps of Dahomey superseded those of Benin. Dahomey took the name Benin when it became a republic in 1975.

100 Centimes = 1 Franc

Catalogue values for unused stamps in this country are for Never Hinged items, beginning with Scott 342 in the regular postage section, Scott C240 in the airpost section, Scott J44 in the postage due section, and Scott Q8 in the parcel post section.

Watermark

Wmk. 385

Handstamped on Stamps of French Colonies

1892 Unwmk. *Perf. 14x13½*

Black Overprint

1	A9	1c blk, *bluish*	110.00	95.00
2	A9	2c brn, *buff*	90.00	75.00
3	A9	4c claret, *lav*	35.00	30.00
4	A9	5c grn, *grnsh*	13.00	12.00
5	A9	10c blk, *lavender*	57.50	45.00
6	A9	15c blue	20.00	9.00
7	A9	20c red, *grn*	160.00	150.00
8	A9	25c blk, *rose*	70.00	40.00
9	A9	30c brn, *yelsh*	140.00	100.00
10	A9	35c blk, *orange*	140.00	100.00
11	A9	40c red, *straw*	110.00	90.00
12	A9	75c car, *rose*	275.00	225.00
13	A9	1fr brnz grn, *straw*	300.00	275.00

Red Overprint

14	A9	15c blue	70.00	45.00

Blue Overprint

15	A9	5c grn, *grnsh*	1,750.	750.00
15A	A9	15c blue	1,750.	750.00

For inverted and double overprints see the *Scott Classic Specialized Catalogue.* The overprints of Nos. 1-15A are of four types, three without accent mark on "E." They exist diagonal.

Counterfeits exist of Nos. 1-19.

Additional Surcharge in Red or Black

1892

16	A9	01c on 5c grn, *grnsh*	225.	175.
a.		Double surcharge	600.	600.
17	A9	40c on 15c blue	140.	60.
a.		Double surcharge		2,500.
18	A9	75c on 15c blue	625.	425.
19	A9	75c on 15c bl (Bk)	2,500.	1,900.

Counterfeits exist.

Navigation and Commerce
A3 A4

1893 Typo. *Perf. 14x13½*

Name of Colony in Blue or Carmine

20	A3	1c blk, *bluish*	2.00	1.75
21	A3	2c brn, *buff*	2.75	2.10
22	A3	4c claret, *lav*	2.75	2.50
23	A3	5c grn, *grnsh*	4.00	3.00
24	A3	10c blk, *lavender*	4.50	3.00
25	A3	15c blue, quadrille paper	22.50	14.00
26	A3	20c red, *grn*	11.00	8.00
27	A3	25c blk, *rose*	29.00	18.00
28	A3	30c brn, *bis*	12.50	11.00
29	A3	40c red, *straw*	3.75	3.00
30	A3	50c car, *rose*	3.50	2.50
31	A3	75c vio, *org*	7.00	6.00
32	A3	1fr brnz grn, *straw*	42.50	35.00
		Nos. 20-32 (13)	147.75	109.85

Perf. 13½x14 stamps are counterfeits.

1894 *Perf. 14x13½*

33	A4	1c blk, *bluish*	2.00	1.50
34	A4	2c brn, *buff*	2.00	1.50
35	A4	4c claret, *lav*	2.00	1.50
36	A4	5c grn, *grnsh*	2.50	1.50
37	A4	10c blk, *lavender*	3.50	2.50
38	A4	15c bl, quadrille paper	5.50	2.50
39	A4	20c red, *grn*	5.00	4.00
40	A4	25c blk, *rose*	6.50	3.00
41	A4	30c brn, *bis*	4.00	3.50
42	A4	40c red, *straw*	12.00	7.00
43	A4	50c car, *rose*	16.00	8.00
44	A4	75c vio, *org*	10.00	8.00
45	A4	1fr brnz grn, *straw*	3.00	2.00
		Nos. 33-45 (13)	74.00	46.50

Perf. 13½x14 stamps are counterfeits.

PEOPLE'S REPUBLIC OF BENIN

LOCATION — West Coast of Africa
GOVT. — Republic.
AREA — 43,483 sq. mi.
POP. — 6,305,567 (1999 est.)
CAPITAL — Porto Novo (Cotonou is the seat of government)

The Republic of Dahomey proclaimed itself the People's Republic of Benin on Nov. 30, 1975. See Dahomey for stamps issued before then.

Catalogue values for unused stamps in this section are for Never Hinged items.

Allamanda Cathartica — A83

Flowers: 35fr, Ixora coccinea. 45fr, Hibiscus, 60fr, Phaemeria magnifica.

Unwmk.

1975, Dec. 8 Photo. *Perf. 13*

342	A83	10fr lilac & multi	.20	.20
343	A83	35fr gray & multi	.25	.20
344	A83	45fr multi	.35	.25
345	A83	60fr blue & multi	.40	.30
		Nos. 342-345 (4)	1.20	.95

For surcharges see Nos. 612, 618, 719, 723, 788.

Flag Bearers, Arms of Benin — A84

1976, Apr. 30 Litho. *Perf. 12*

Design: 60fr, Speaker, wall with "PRPB," flag and arms of Benin. 100fr, Flag and arms of Benin.

346	A84	50fr ocher & multi	.30	.20
347	A84	60fr ocher & multi	.40	.20
348	A84	100fr multi	.70	.40
		Nos. 346-348 (3)	1.40	.80

Proclamation of the People's Republic of Benin. Nov. 30, 1975.

A.G. Bell, Satellite and 1876 Telephone — A85

1976, July 9 Litho. *Perf. 13*

349	A85	200fr lilac, red & brn	1.25	.75

Centenary of first telephone call by Alexander Graham Bell, Mar. 10, 1876.

Dahomey Nos. 277-278 Surcharged

1976, July 19 Photo. *Perf. 12½x13*

350	A57	50fr on 1fr multi	.30	.20
351	A57	60fr on 2fr multi	.40	.20

For overprint & surcharge see #654A, 711.

African Jamboree, Nigeria 1976 — A86

1976, Aug. 16 Litho. *Perf. 12½x13*

352	A86	50fr Scouts Cooking	.35	.20
353	A86	70fr Three scouts	.45	.30

Blood Bank, Cotonou — A87

Designs: 50fr, Accident and first aid station. 60fr, Blood donation.

1976, Sept. 24 Litho. *Perf. 13*

354	A87	5fr multicolored	.20	.20
355	A87	50fr multicolored	.30	.20
356	A87	60fr multicolored	.35	.25
		Nos. 354-356 (3)	.85	.65

National Blood Donors Day.

A88

A89

1976, Oct. 4 Litho. *Perf. 13x12½*

357	A88	20fr Manioc	.30	.20
358	A88	50fr Corn	.40	.20
359	A88	60fr Cacao	.55	.20
360	A88	150fr Cotton	1.25	.40
		Nos. 357-360 (4)	2.50	1.00

Natl. agricultural production campaign.
For surcharge see No. 565.

1976, Oct. 25

361	A89	50fr Classroom	.45	.25

Third anniversary of KPARO newspaper, used in local language studies.

Roan Antelope — A90

Flags, Wall, Broken Chains — A91

Penhari National Park: 30fr, Buffalo. 50fr, Hippopotamus, horiz. 70fr, Lion.

1976, Nov. 8 Photo.

362	A90	10fr multicolored	.25	.20
363	A90	30fr multicolored	.45	.25
364	A90	50fr multicolored	.85	.35
365	A90	70fr multicolored	.95	.55
		Nos. 362-365 (4)	2.50	1.35

1976, Nov. 30 Litho. *Perf. 12½*

150fr, Corn, raised hands with weapons.

366	A91	40fr multicolored	.20	.20
367	A91	150fr multicolored	.80	.60

First anniversary of proclamation of the People's Republic of Benin.

Table Tennis, Map of Africa (Games' Emblem) — A92

Design: 50fr, Stadium, Cotonou.

1976, Dec. 26 Litho. *Perf. 13*

368 A92 10fr multi .20 .20
369 A92 50fr multi .30 .20

West African University Games, Cotonou, Dec. 26-31.

Europafrica Issue

Planes over Africa and Europe — A93

1977, May 13 Litho. *Perf. 13*

370 A93 200fr multi 1.50 .85

For surcharge see No. 590.

Snake A94

1977, June 13 Litho. *Perf. 13x13½*

371 A94 2fr shown .20 .20
372 A94 3fr Tortoise .20 .20
373 A94 5fr Zebus .20 .20
374 A94 10fr Cats .20 .20
Nos. 371-374 (4) .80 .80

Patients at Clinic A95

1977, Aug. 2 Litho. *Perf. 12½*

375 A95 100fr multi .70 .40

World Rheumatism Year.

Karate, Map of Africa — A96

Designs: 100fr, Javelin, map of Africa, Benin Flag, horiz. 150fr, Hurdles.

1977, Aug. 30 Litho. *Perf. 12½*

376 A96 90fr multi .65 .30
377 A96 100fr multi .75 .40
378 A96 150fr multi 1.10 .60
a. Souvenir sheet of 3, #376-378 3.00 3.00
Nos. 376-378 (3) 2.50 1.30

2nd West African Games, Lagos, Nigeria.
For surcharge see No. 925.

Chairman Mao — A97

Lister and Vaporizer — A98

1977, Sept. 9 Litho. *Perf. 13x12½*

379 A97 100fr multicolored .50 .40

Mao Tse-tung (1893-1976), Chinese communist leader.

1977, Sept. 20 Engr. *Perf. 13*

Designs: 150fr, Scalpels and flames, symbols of antisepsis, and Red Cross.

380 A98 150fr multi .75 .60
381 A98 210fr multi 1.25 .80

Joseph Lister (1827-1912), surgeon, founder of antiseptic surgery.
For surcharges see Nos. 560, 566, 919.

Guelege Mask, Ethnographic Museum, Porto Novo — A99

Designs: 50fr, Jar, symbol of unity, emblem of King Ghezo, Historical Museum, Abomey, vert. 210fr, Abomey Museum.

1977, Oct. 17 *Perf. 13*

382 A99 50fr red & multi .30 .20
383 A99 60fr blk, bl & bister .50 .25
384 A99 210fr multi 1.40 .80
Nos. 382-384 (3) 2.20 1.25

For surcharge see Nos. 562, 920.

Atacora Falls — A100

Mother and Child, Owl of Wisdom — A101

Tourist Publicity: 60fr, Pile houses, Ganvie, horiz. 150fr, Round huts, Savalou.

1977, Oct. 24 Litho. *Perf. 12½*

385 A100 50fr multi .30 .25
386 A100 60fr multi .40 .25
387 A100 150fr multi 1.00 .70
a. Souvenir sheet of 3, #385-387 2.00 2.00
Nos. 385-387 (3) 1.70 1.20

Perf. 12½x13, 13x12½

1977, Dec. 3 Photo.

150fr, Chopping down magical tree, horiz.

388 A101 60fr multi .60 .25
389 A101 150fr multi 1.25 .60

Campaign against witchcraft.
For surcharge see No. 576.

Battle Scene — A102

1978, Jan. 16 Litho. *Perf. 12½*

390 A102 50fr multi .60 .20

Victory of people of Benin over imperialist forces.

Map, People and Houses of Benin — A103

1978, Feb. 1

391 A103 50fr multi .45 .20

General population and dwelling census.

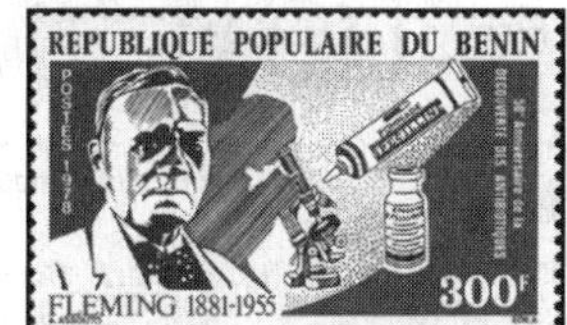

Alexander Fleming, Microscope and Penicillin — A104

1978, Mar. 12 Litho. *Perf. 13*

392 A104 300fr multi 2.00 1.10

Alexnader Fleming (1881-1955), 50th anniversary of discovery of penicillin.

Abdoulaye Issa, Weapons and Fighters A105

1978, Apr. 1 *Perf. 12½x13*

393 A105 100fr red, blk & gold .60 .30

First anniversary of death of Abdoulaye Issa and National Day of Benin's Youth.

Ed Hadj Omar and Horseback Rider — A106

Design: 90fr, L'Almamy Samory Toure (1830-1900) and horseback riders.

1976, Apr. 10 *Perf. 13x12½*

394 A106 90fr red & multi .60 .20
395 A106 100fr multi .65 .30

African heroes of resistance against colonialism.

ITU Emblem, Satellite, Landscape — A107

1978, May 17 Litho. *Perf. 13*

396 A107 100fr multi .65 .40

10th World Telecommunications Day.

Soccer Player, Stadium, Argentina '78 Emblem — A108

Designs (Argentina '78 Emblem and): 300fr, Soccer players and ball, vert. 500fr, Soccer player, globe with ball on map.

1978, June 1 Litho. *Perf. 12½*

397 A108 200fr multi 1.25 .70
398 A108 300fr multi 1.60 1.10
399 A108 500fr multi 2.75 1.75
a. Souvenir sheet of 3 7.00 7.00
Nos. 397-399 (3) 5.60 3.55

11th World Cup Soccer Championship, Argentina, June 1-25. No. 399a contains 3 stamps similar to Nos. 397-399 in changed colors.
For surcharges see #591, 593, 595.

Nos. 397-399a Overprinted in Red Brown:
a. FINALE / ARGENTINE: 3 / HOLLANDE: 1
b. CHAMPION / 1978 / ARGENTINE
c. 3e BRESIL / 4e ITALIE

1978, June 25 Litho. *Perf. 12½*

400 A108 (a) 200fr multi 1.25 .75
401 A108 (b) 300fr multi 1.60 1.10
402 A108 (c) 500fr multi 2.75 1.75
a. Souvenir sheet of 3 7.00 7.00
Nos. 400-402 (3) 5.60 3.60

Argentina's victory in 1978 Soccer Championship.
For surcharge, see #596.

Games' Flag over Africa, Basketball Players — A109

Designs: 60fr, Map of Africa, volleyball players. 80fr, Map of Benin, bicyclists.

1978, July 13 *Perf. 13x12½*

403 A109 50fr lt bl & multi .35 .20
404 A109 60fr ultra & multi .40 .25
405 A109 80fr multi .55 .35
a. Souvenir sheet of 3 2.00 2.00
Nos. 403-405 (3) 1.30 .80

3rd African Games, Algiers, July 13-28. No. 405a contains 3 stamps in changed colors similar to Nos. 403-405.

Martin Luther King, Jr. — A110

1978, July 30 ***Perf. 12½***

406 A110 300fr multi 2.00 1.10

Martin Luther King, Jr. (1929-1968), American civil rights leader.

For surcharge see No. 592.

Kanna Taxi, Oueme A111

60fr Leatherworker & goods. 70fr, Drummer & tom-toms. 100fr, Metalworker & calabashes.

1978, Aug. 26

407 A111 50fr multi .60 .20
408 A111 60fr multi .55 .20
409 A111 70fr multi .60 .30
410 A111 100fr multi .75 .40
Nos. 407-410 (4) 2.50 1.10

Getting to know Benin through its provinces.

Map of Italy and Exhibition Poster — A112

1978, Aug. 26 **Litho.** ***Perf. 13***

411 A112 200fr multi 1.25 .50

Riccione 1978 Philatelic Exhibition.

For overprint see No. 537.

Poultry Breeding — A113

1978 Oct. 5 **Photo.** ***Perf. 12½x13***

412 A113 10fr Turkeys .20 .20
413 A113 20fr Ducks .25 .20
414 A113 50fr Chicken .65 .25
415 A113 60fr Guinea fowl .65 .35
Nos. 412-415 (4) 1.75 1.00

Royal Messenger, UPU Emblem — A114

UPU Emblem and: 60fr, Boatsman, ship & car. 90fr, Special messenger & plane.

1978, Oct. 16 ***Perf. 13x12½, 12½x13***

416 A114 50fr multi .35 .20
417 A114 60fr multi, vert. .40 .20
418 A114 90fr multi, vert. .60 .35
Nos. 416-418 (3) 1.35 .75

Centenary of change of "General Postal Union" to "Universal Postal Union."

For surcharge see No. 1009.

Raoul Follereau A115

1978, Dec. 17 **Litho.** ***Perf. 12½***

419 A115 200fr multi 1.00 .50

Raoul Follereau (1903-1977), apostle to the lepers and educator of the blind.

IYC Emblem A116

Intl. Year of the Child: 20fr, Glove as balloon carrying childern. 50fr, Children of various races surrounding globe.

1979, Feb. 20 **Litho.** ***Perf. 12x13***

420 A116 10fr multi .20 .20
421 A116 20fr multi .20 .20
422 A116 50fr multi .35 .35
Nos. 420-422 (3) .75 .75

Hydrangea — A117

Flowers: 25fr, Assangokan. 30fr, Geranium. 40fr, Water lilies, horiz.

Perf. 13x12½, 12½x13

1979, Feb. 28 **Litho.**

423 A117 20fr multi .20 .20
424 A117 25fr multi .20 .20
425 A117 30fr multi .20 .20
426 A117 40fr multi .25 .25
Nos. 423-426 (4) .85 .85

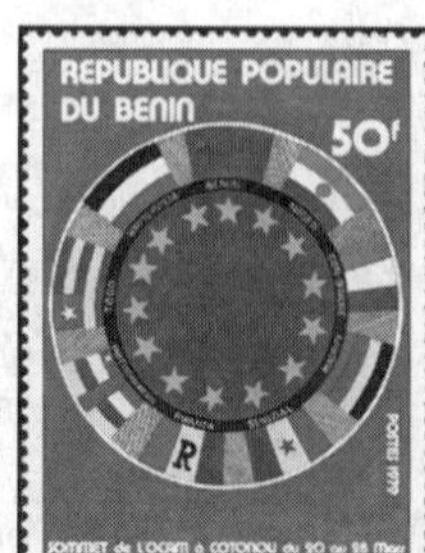

Emblem: Map of Africa and Members' Flags A118

60fr, Map of Benin & flags. 80fr, OCAM flag & map of Africa showing member states.

1979, Mar. 20 **Litho.** ***Perf. 12x13***

427 A118 50fr multi .30 .25
428 A118 60fr multi .40 .25
429 A118 80fr multi .65 .35
Nos. 427-429 (3) 1.35 .85

OCAM Summit Conf., Cotonou, Mar. 20-28.

For overprints see Nos. 434-436.

Tower, Waves, Satellite, ITU Emblem A119

1979, May 17 **Litho.** ***Perf. 12½***

430 A119 50fr multi .40 .20

World Telecommunications Day.

Bank Building and Sculpture A120

1979, May 26 **Litho.**

431 A120 50fr multi .40 .20

Opening of Headquarters of West African Savings Bank in Dakar.

Guelede Mask, Abomey Tapestry, Malaconotus Bird — A121

Design: 50fr, Jet, canoe, satellite, UPU and exhibition emblems.

1979, June 8 **Litho.** ***Perf. 13***

432 A121 15fr multi .30 .20

Engr.

433 A121 50fr multi .60 .35

Philexafrique II, Libreville, Gabon, June 8-17. Nos. 432, 433 each printed in sheets of 10 with 5 labels showing exhibition emblem.

Nos. 427-429 Overprinted: "26 au 28 juin 1979" and Dots

1979, June 26

434 A118 50fr multi .45 .25
435 A118 60fr multi .50 .25
436 A118 80fr multi .65 .30
Nos. 434-436 (3) 1.60 .80

2nd OCAM Summit Conf., June 26-28.

Olympic Flame, and Emblems A122

Pre-Olympic Year: 50fr, High jump.

1979, July 1 **Litho.**

437 A122 10fr multi .20 .20
438 A122 50fr multi .35 .35

Antelope A123

Animals: 10fr, Giraffes, map of Benin, vert 20fr, Chimpanzee. 50fr, Elephants, map of Benin, vert.

1979, Oct. 1 **Litho.** ***Perf. 13***

439 A123 5fr multi .20 .20
440 A123 10fr multi .20 .20
441 A123 20fr multi .35 .25
442 A123 50fr multi .65 .35
Nos. 439-442 (4) 1.40 1.00

Map of Africa, Emblem and Jet — A124

1979, Dec. 12 **Litho.** ***Perf. 12½***

443 A124 50fr multi .25 .20
444 A124 60fr multi .35 .20

ASECNA (Air Safety Board), 20th anniv.

Mail Services A125

50fr, Post Office and headquarters, vert.

1979, Dec. 19 **Litho.** ***Perf. 13***

445 A125 50fr multi .25 .20
446 A125 60fr multi .35 .20

Office of Posts and Telecommunications, 20th anniversary.

Lenin and Globe — A126

1980, Apr. 22 **Litho.** ***Perf. 12½***

447 A126 50fr shown .35 .20
448 A126 150fr Lenin in library 1.00 .50

Lenin, 110th birth anniversary.

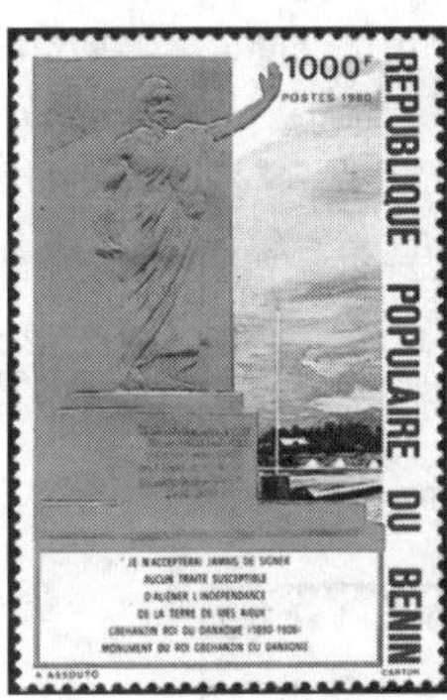

Monument to King Behanzin A126a

Litho. & Embossed

1980, May 31 *Perf. 12½*
448A A126a 1000fr gold & multi 6.25 5.50

For overprint see No. Q10A.

Cotonou Club Emlem — A127

1980, Feb. 23 **Litho.** *Perf. 12½*
449 A127 90fr shown .50 .30
450 A127 200fr Rotary emblem on globe, horiz. 1.25 .60

Rotary International, 75th anniversary.
For surcharge see No. 915.

Galileo, Astrolabe — A128

1980, Apr. 2
451 A128 70fr shown .45 .25
452 A128 100fr Copernicus, solar system .65 .35

Discovery of Pluto, 50th anniversary.

Abu Simbel, UNESCO Emblem — A129

1980, Apr. 15 *Perf. 13*
453 A129 50fr Column, vert. .35 .25
454 A129 60fr Ramses II, vert. .40 .35
455 A129 150fr shown .75 .50
Nos. 453-455 (3) 1.50 1.10

UNESCO campaign to save Nubian monuments, 20h anniversary.

Monument, Martyrs' Square, Cotonou A130

Designs: Various monuments in Martyrs' Square. Cotonou. 60fr, 70fr, 100fr, horiz.

1980, May 2 *Perf. 12½x13, 13x12½*
456 A130 50fr multi .35 .20
457 A130 60fr multi .40 .30
458 A130 70fr multi .45 .30
459 A130 100fr multi .65 .40
Nos. 456-459 (4) 1.85 1.20

For surcharge see No. 539.

Musical Instruments — A131

1980, May 20 *Perf. 12½*
460 A131 5fr Assan, vert. .20 .20
461 A131 10fr Tinbo .20 .20
462 A131 15fr Tam-tam sato, vert. .20 .20
463 A131 20fr Kora .20 .20
464 A131 30fr Gangan .20 .20
465 A131 50fr Sinhoun .35 .35
Nos. 460-465 (6) 1.35 1.35

First Non-stop Flight, Paris-New York — A132

1980, June 2 **Litho.** *Perf. 12½*
466 A132 90fr shown .60 .30
467 A132 100fr Dieudonne Coste, Maurice Bellonte .65 .30

For surcharges see Nos. 564, 926.

Lunokhod I on the Moon — A133

1980, June 15 **Engr.** *Perf. 13*
468 A133 90fr multi .40 .30

Lunokhod I Soviet unmanned moon mission, 10th anniv. See #C290.

Olympic Flame and Mischa, Moscow '80 Emblem — A134

1980, July 16 **Litho.** *Perf. 12½*
469 A134 50fr shown .25 .20
470 A134 60fr Equestrian, vert. .30 .25
471 A134 70fr Judo .45 .25
472 A134 200fr Flag, sports, globe, vert. 1.00 .45
473 A134 300fr Weight lifting, vert. 1.50 .75
Nos. 469-473 (5) 3.50 1.90

22nd Summer Olympic Games, Moscow, July 19-Aug. 3.
For surcharges see Nos. 559, 561.

Telephone and Rising Sun A135

World Telecommunications Day: 50fr, Farmer on telephone, vert.

1980, May 17 **Litho.** *Perf. 12½*
474 A135 50fr multi .20 .20
475 A135 60fr multi .30 .25

Cotonou West African Community Village A136

Designs: View of Cotonou.

1980, July 26 *Perf. 13x13½*
476 A136 50fr multi .35 .20
477 A136 60fr multi .40 .20
478 A136 70fr multi .45 .25
Nos. 476-478 (3) 1.20 .65

For surcharge see No. 540.

Agbadja Dancers — A137

Designs: Dancers and muscians.

1980, Aug. 1 *Perf. 12½*
479 A137 30fr multi .30 .20
480 A137 50fr multi .40 .20
481 A137 60fr multi .55 .30
Nos. 479-481 (3) 1.25 .70

Fisherman A138

Philippines under Magnifier A139

Designs: 5fr, Throwing net. 15fr, Canoe and shore fishing. 20fr, Basket traps. 50fr, Hauling net. 60fr, River fishing. All horiz.

1980, Sept. 1
482 A138 5fr multi .20 .20
483 A138 10fr multi .20 .20
484 A138 15fr multi .20 .20
485 A138 20fr multi .20 .20
486 A138 50fr multi .35 .25
487 A138 60fr multi .40 .25
Nos. 482-487 (6) 1.55 1.30

For surcharge see No. 535.

Perf. 13x13½, 13x½x13

1980, Sept. 27

World Tourism Conference, Manila, Sept. 27: 60fr, Emblem on flag, hand pointing to Manila on globe, horiz.

488 A139 50fr multi .35 .35
489 A139 60fr multi .40 .40

For surcharge see No. 557.

A140

1980, Oct. 1 *Perf. 12½*
490 A140 40fr Othreis materna .40 .20
491 A140 50fr Othreis fullonia .60 .20
492 A140 200fr Oryctes sp. 2.00 .75
Nos. 490-492 (3) 3.00 1.15

A141

Photo.
Perf. 13½

1980, Oct. 24
493 A141 75fr multi .40 .20

African Postal Union, 5th Anniv.

A142

1980, Nov. 4 *Perf. 12½x13*
494 A142 30fr shown .25 .20
495 A142 50fr Freed prisoner .35 .25
496 A142 60fr Man holding torch .40 .25
Nos. 494-496 (3) 1.00 .70

Declaration of human rights, 30th anniv.

A143

1980, Dec. 1 **Litho.** *Perf. 13*

Self-portrait, by Vincent van Gogh, 1888.

497 A143 100fr shown .75 .50
498 A143 300fr Facteur Roulin 2.25 1.25

Vincent van Gogh (1853-1890), artist.
For surcharge see No. 579.

Offenbach and Scene from Orpheus in the Underworld — A144

1980, Dec. 15 **Engr.**

499 A144 50fr shown		.40	.25
500 A144 60fr Paris Life		.60	.35

Jacques Offenbach (1819-1880), composer.

Kepler and Satellites — A145

1980, Dec. 20

501 A145 50fr Kepler, diagram, vert.	.35	.20
502 A145 60fr shown	.50	.30

Johannes Kepler (1571-1630), astronomer.

Intl. Year of the Disabled — A146

1981, Apr. 10 **Litho.** ***Perf. 12½***

503 A146 115fr multi	.70	.25

For surcharge see No. 582.

20th Anniv. of Manned Space Flight — A147

1981, May 30 ***Perf. 13***

504 A147 500fr multi	3.00	1.50

For surcharges see Nos. 580, 790.

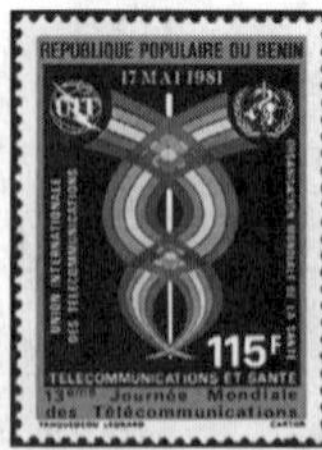

13th World Telecommunications Day — A148

1981, May 30 **Litho.** ***Perf. 12½***

505 A148 115fr multi	.50	.25

For surcharge see No. 583.

Amaryllis A149

1981, June 20 ***Perf. 12½***

506 A149 10fr shown	.20	.20
507 A149 20fr Eischornia crassipes, vert.	.25	.25
508 A149 80fr Parkia biglobosa, vert.	.55	.35
Nos. 506-508 (3)	1.00	.80

For surcharge see No. 542.

Benin Sheraton Hotel A150

1981, July

509 A150 100fr multi	.50	.25

For surcharge see No. 541.

Guinea Pig — A151

1981, July 31 ***Perf. 13x13½***

510 A151 5fr shown	.20	.20
511 A151 60fr Cat	.40	.30
512 A151 80fr Dogs	.55	.40
Nos. 510-512 (3)	1.15	.90

For surcharges see Nos. 536, 543, 563.

World UPU Day — A152

1981, Oct. 9 **Engr.** ***Perf. 13***

513 A152 100fr red brn & blk	.60	.30

25th Intl. Letter Writing Week, Oct. 6-12 — A153

1981, Oct. 15

514 A153 100fr dk bl & pur	.50	.25

For surcharge see No. 558.

West African Economic Community A154

1981, Nov. 20 **Litho.** ***Perf. 12½***

515 A154 60fr multi	.40	.20

West African Rice Development Assoc. 10th Anniv. — A155

1981, Dec. 10 ***Perf. 13x13½***

516 A155 60fr multi	.40	.20

TB Bacillus Centenary A156

1982, Mar. 1 **Litho.** ***Perf. 13***

517 A156 115fr multi	1.00	.50

For surcharge see No. 584.

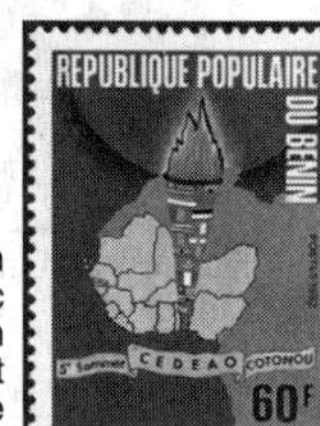

West African Economic Community, 5th Summit Conference A157

1982, May 27 ***Perf. 12½***

518 A157 60fr multi	.40	.25

1982 World Cup — A158

1982, June 1 ***Perf. 13***

519 A158 90fr Players	.55	.35
520 A158 300fr Flags on leg	1.75	.90

For overprints and surcharges see #523-524, 594, 789.

France No. B349 Magnified, Map of France — A159

1982, June 11

521 A159 90fr multi	.60	.30

For surcharge see No. 916.

PHILEXFRANCE '82 Stamp Exhibition, Paris, June 11-21.

George Washington — A160

1982, Mar. 10 **Litho.** ***Perf. 14***

522 A160 200fr Washington, flag, map	1.25	1.00

For surcharge see No. 577.

Nos. 519-520 Overprinted with Finalists Names

1982, Aug. 16 ***Perf. 12½***

523 A158 90fr multi	.60	.60
524 A158 300fr multi	2.00	2.00

Italy's victory in 1982 World Cup.
For surcharge see No. 811.

Bluethroat A161

1982, Sept. 1 ***Perf. 14x14½, 14½x14***

525 A161 5fr Daoelo gigas, vert.	.20	.20
526 A161 10fr shown	.20	.20
527 A161 15fr Swallow, vert.	.20	.20
528 A161 20fr Kingfisher, weaver bird, vert.	.30	.25
529 A161 30fr Great sedge warbler	.30	.25
530 A161 60fr Common warbler	.65	.35
531 A161 80fr Owl, vert.	1.00	.50
532 A161 100fr Cockatoo, vert.	1.25	.80
Nos. 525-532 (8)	4.10	2.75

ITU Plenipotentiaries Conference, Nairobi, Sept. — A162

1982, Sept. 26 ***Perf. 13***

533 A162 200fr Map	1.10	.50

For surcharge see No. 585.

13th World UPU Day — A163

1982, Oct. 9 **Engr.** ***Perf. 13***

534 A163 100fr Monument	.60	.30

Nos. 482, 510, 411 Overprinted in Red or Blue:
#535 "Croix Rouge / 8 Mai 1982"
#536 "UAPT 1982"
#537 "RICCONE 1982"

Perf. 13, 12½, 13x13½

1982, Nov. **Litho.**

535 A138 60fr on 5fr multi	.40	.25
536 A151 60fr on 5fr multi	.40	.25
537 A112 200fr multi (Bl)	1.10	.50
Nos. 535-537 (3)	1.90	1.00

Visit of French Pres. Francois Mitterand A164

1983, Jan. 15 **Litho.** ***Perf. 12½x13***

538 A164 90fr multi	.85	.50

For surcharge see No. 917.

Nos. 458, 476, 508-509, 512 Surcharged

Perf. 13x12½, 13x13½, 12½

1983 **Litho.**

539	A130	60fr on 70fr multi	.40	.25
540	A136	60fr on 50fr multi	.40	.25
541	A150	60fr on 100fr multi	.40	.25
542	A149	75fr on 80fr multi	.50	.25
543	A151	75fr on 80fr multi	.50	.35
		Nos. 539-543 (5)	2.20	1.35

Seme Oil Rig — A165

1983, Apr. 28 **Litho.** ***Perf. 13x12½***

544 A165 125fr multi .80 .80

World Communications Year — A166

1983, May 17 **Litho.** ***Perf. 13***

545 A166 185fr multi 1.00 1.00

For surcharge see No. 898.

Riccione '83, Stamp Show — A167

1983, Aug. 27 **Litho.** ***Perf. 13***

546 A167 500fr multi 3.25 3.25

For surcharge see No. 922.

Benin Red Cross, 20th Anniv. A168

1983, Sept. 5 **Photo.** ***Perf. 13***

547 A168 105fr multi .70 .70

For surcharge see No. 581.

Handicrafts A169

Designs: 75fr, Handcarved lion chairs and table. 90fr, Natural tree table and stools. 200fr, Monkeys holding jar.

1983, Sept. 18 **Litho.** ***Perf. 13***

548	A169	75fr multi	.40	.40
549	A169	90fr multi	.50	.50
550	A169	200fr multi	1.10	1.10
		Nos. 548-550 (3)	2.00	2.00

For surcharge see No. 578.

14th UPU Day — A170

1983, Oct. 9 **Engr.** ***Perf. 13***

551 A170 125fr multi .80 .80

For surcharge see No. 575.

Religious Movements A171

1983, Oct. 31 **Litho.** ***Perf. 14x15***

552	A171	75fr Zangbeto	.35	.35
553	A171	75fr Egoun	.35	.35

Plaited Hair Styles — A172

1983, Nov. 14

554	A172	30fr Rockcoco	.25	.25
555	A172	75fr Serpent	.35	.35
556	A172	90fr Songas	.40	.40
		Nos. 554-556 (3)	1.00	1.00

Stamps of 1976-81 Surcharged

1983, Nov.

557	A139	5fr on 50fr #488	.20	.20
558	A153	10fr on 100fr #514	.20	.20
559	A134	15fr on 200fr #472	.20	.20
560	A98	15fr on 210fr #381	.20	.20
561	A134	25fr on 70fr #471	.20	.20
562	A99	25fr on 210fr #384	.20	.20
563	A151	75fr on 5fr #510	.35	.35
564	A132	75fr on 100fr #467	.35	.35
565	A88	75fr on 150fr #360	.35	.35
566	A98	75fr on 150fr #380	.35	.35
		Nos. 557-566 (10)	2.60	2.60

Alfred Nobel (1833-96) A173

1983, Dec. 19 **Litho.** ***Perf. 15x14***

567 A173 300fr multi 1.40 1.40

For surcharge see No. 923.

Council of Unity — A174

1984, May 29 **Litho.** ***Perf. 12***

568	A174	75fr multi	.35	.35
569	A174	90fr multi	.40	.40

For surcharge see No. 918.

1984 UPU Congress A175

1984, June 18 **Litho.** ***Perf. 13***

570 A175 90fr multi .40 .40

Abomey Calavi Earth Station A176

1984, June 29 **Litho.** ***Perf. 12½x13***

571 A176 75fr Satellite dish .35 .35

Traditional Costumes A177

1984, July 2 **Litho.** ***Perf. 13½x13***

572	A177	5fr Koumboro	.20	.20
573	A177	10fr Taka	.20	.20
574	A177	20fr Toko	.20	.20
		Nos. 572-574 (3)	.60	.60

Nos. 389, 498, 503-505, 517, 522, 533, 547, 550 and 551 Surcharged

1984, Sept.

575	A170	5fr on 125fr #551	.20	.20
576	A101	5fr on 150fr #389	.20	.20
577	A160	10fr on 200fr #522	.20	.20
578	A169	10fr on 200fr #550	.20	.20
579	A143	15fr on 300fr #498	.20	.20
580	A147	40fr on 500fr #504	.25	.25
581	A168	75fr on 105fr #547	.35	.35
582	A146	75fr on 115fr #503	.35	.35
583	A148	75fr on 115fr #505	.35	.35
584	A156	75fr on 115fr #517	.35	.35
585	A162	75fr on 200fr #533	.35	.35
		Nos. 575-585 (11)	3.00	3.00

World Food Day — A178

1984, Oct. 16 **Litho.** ***Perf. 12½***

586 A178 100fr Malnourished child .30 .30

Dinosaurs A179

1984, Dec. 14 **Litho.** ***Perf. 13½***

587	A179	75fr Anatosaurus	.25	.25
588	A179	90fr Brontosaurus	.25	.25

Cultural & Technical Cooperation Agency, 15th Anniv. — A180

1985, Mar 20 **Litho.** ***Perf. 13***

589 A180 300fr Emblem, globe, hands, book .90 .90

Stamps of 1977-82 Surcharged

1985, Mar.

590	A93	75fr on 200fr No. 370	.20	.20
591	A108	75fr on 200fr No. 397	.20	.20
592	A110	75fr on 300fr No. 406	.20	.20
593	A108	75fr on 300fr No. 398	.20	.20
594	A158	90fr on 300fr No. 520	.25	.25
595	A108	90fr on 500fr No. 399	.25	.25
596	A108	90fr on 500fr No. 402	.25	.25
		Nos. 590-596 (7)	1.55	1.55

End of World War II, 40th Anniv. — A180a

1985, May **Litho.** ***Perf. 12***

596A A180a 100fr multicolored

Traditional Dances A181

1985, June 1 **Litho.** ***Perf. 15x14½***

597	A181	75fr Teke, Borgou Tribe	.20	.20
598	A181	100fr Tipen'ti, L'Atacora Tribe	.30	.30

Intl. Youth Year — A182

1985, July 16 ***Perf. 13½***

599 A182 150fr multi .45 .45

1986 World Cup Soccer Championships, Mexico — A183

1985, July 22 ***Perf. 13x12½***

600 A183 200fr multi .60 .60

Beginning with Scott 601, Benin again surcharged stamps of Dahomey with a variety of surcharges. While the listings that follow contain more than 80 surcharged stamps, the Scott editors still need to examine more than 60 other stamps, in order to list all of those that are currently known to exist.

The size and location of the surcharge varies from stamp to stamp. The type face used in the surcharge may also vary from issue to issue.

a

b

c

55 f

République
Populaire
du Bénin

d

e

DU BENIN

5 F.

f

g

h

i

j

Dahomey No. 336 Surcharged with Black Bars and New Value

1985, Aug. ***Perf. 12½***

601 A78(a) 15fr on 40fr multi .20 .20

ASECNA Airlines, 25th Anniv. — A184

1985, Sept. 16 ***Perf. 13***

602 A184 150fr multi .45 .45

UN 40th Anniv. A185

1985, Oct. 24 ***Perf. 12½***

603 A185 250fr multi .90 .90

Benin UN membership, 25th anniv.

ITALIA'85, Rome A186

1985, Oct. 25 ***Perf. 13½***

604 A186 200fr multi .75 .75

PHILEXAFRICA '85, Lome — A187

1985, Nov. 16 ***Perf. 13***

605 A187 250fr #569, labor emblem .90 .90
606 A187 250fr #C252, Gabon #366, magnified stamp .90 .90
a. Pair, Nos. 605-606 + label 1.80 1.80

Audubon Birth Bicent. — A188

1985, Oct. 17 **Litho.** ***Perf. 14x15***

607 A188 150fr Skua gull .55 .55
608 A188 300fr Oyster catcher 1.10 1.10

Mushrooms and Toadstools A189

1985, Oct. 17

609 A189 35fr Boletus edible .20 .20
610 A189 40fr Amanite phalloide .20 .20
611 A189 100fr Brown chanterelle .40 .40
Nos. 609-611 (3) .80 .80

Dahomey #282, 292, Benin #343 Surcharged

1986, Mar. **Photo.**

612 A83(b) 75fr on 35fr #343 .25 .25
613 A57(c) 90fr on 70fr #282 .35 .35
614 A60(b) 90fr on 140fr #292 .40 .40
Nos. 612-614 (3) 1.00 1.00

African Parliamentary Union, 10th Anniv. — A190

1986, May 8 **Litho.** ***Perf. 13x12½***

615 A190 100fr multi .40 .40

9th Conference, Cotonou, May 8-10.

Halley's Comet — A191

1986, May 30 ***Perf. 12½x12***

616 A191 205fr multi 1.50 1.50

For surcharge see No. 809.

Dahomey No. 283, Benin No. 344 Surcharged

Engraved, Photogravure

1986, June ***Perf. 13***

617 A58(b) 100fr on 40fr #283 .40 .40
618 A83(b) 150fr on 45fr #344 .55 .55

1986 World Cup Soccer Championships, Mexico — A192

1986, June 29 **Litho.**

619 A192 500fr multi 1.75 1.75

For surcharge see No. 792.

Fight against Desert Encroachment — A193

1986, July 16 ***Perf. 13½***

620 A193 150fr multi .55 .55

King Behanzin A194

Amazon A194a

1986-88 **Engr.** ***Perf. 13***

621 A194 40fr black .20 .20
622 A194a 100fr brt blue .40 .40
623 A194 125fr maroon .60 .60
624 A194a 150fr violet .60 .60
625 A194 190fr dark ultra .90 .90
627 A194 220fr dark grn 1.00 1.00
Nos. 621-627 (6) 3.70 3.70

Issued: 100fr, 150fr, 8/1; others, 10/1/88.

See No. 636. For surcharge see No. 787.

Flowers — A195

Perf. 13x12½, 12½x13

1986, Sept. 1 **Litho.**

631 A195 100fr Haemanthus .40 .40
632 A195 205fr Hemerocalle, horiz. .90 .90

For surcharge see No. 1061F.

Butterflies A196

1986, Sept. 15

#633, Day peacock, little tortoiseshell, morio. #634, Aurora, machaon and fair lady.

633 A196 150fr shown .60 .60
634 A196 150fr multi .60 .60

Dahomey Nos. 290, 307 Overprinted

1985, Oct. 15

Perfs. & Printing Methods as Before

634A A67(b) 50fr on #307
634B A60(d) 150fr on 100fr #290

Statue of Liberty, Cent. — A197

1986, Oct. 28 Litho. *Perf. 12½*

635 A197 250fr multi .90 .90

King Behanzin — A198

1986, Oct. 30 *Perf. 13½*

636 A198 440fr multi 1.60 1.60

Behanzin, leader of resistance movement against French occupation (1886-1894).
For surcharge see No. 921.

Brazilian Cultural Week, Cotonou — A200

1987, Jan. 17 *Perf. 12½*

638 A200 150fr multi .90 .90

Rotary Intl. District 910 Conference, Cotonou, Apr. 23-25 — A201

1987, Apr. 23 Litho. *Perf. 13½*

639 A201 300fr Center for the Blind, Cotonou 1.75 1.75

Automobile Cent. — A202

Modern car and: 150fr, Steam tricycle, by De Dion-Bouton and Trepardoux, 1887. 300fr, Gas-driven Victoria, by Daimler, 1886.

1987, July 1 *Perf. 12½*

640 A202 150fr multi .90 .90
641 A202 300fr multi 1.75 1.75

For surcharge see No. 679B.

Snake Temple Baptism — A203

1987, July 20 *Perf. 13½*

642 A203 100fr multi .55 .55

Shellfish A204

1987, July 24 *Perf. 12½*

643 A204 100fr crayfish .55 .55
644 A204 150fr crab .90 .90

G. Hansen, R. Follerau — A205

1987, Sept. 4 *Perf. 13*

645 A205 200fr Cure Leprosy 1.10 1.10

Beginning of Benin Revolution, 15th Anniv. — A205a

1987, Oct. 28 Litho. *Perf. 12x12½*

645A A205a 100fr multicolored

Locust Control A206

1987, Dec. 7 Litho. *Perf. 12½x13*

646 A206 100fr multi .70 .70

Christmas 1987 A207

1987, Dec. 21 *Perf. 13*

647 A207 150fr multi 1.10 1.10

Dahomey Nos. 268, 284 Ovptd. or Surchd.

1987 Engr. *Perf. 13*

647A A58(b) 15fr on 100fr #284
647B A53(b) 40fr on #268

See Nos. C362, C369.

Intl. Red Cross and Red Crescent Organizations, 125th Anniv. — A208

1988, May 25 Litho. *Perf. 13½*

648 A208 200fr multi 1.25 1.25

A209

1988, July 11 *Perf. 12½*

649 A209 200fr multi 1.25 1.25

Martin Luther King, Jr. (1929-68), American civil rights leader.

A210

1988, May 25 Litho. *Perf. 13½*

650 A210 125fr multi .90 .90

Organization of African Unity, 25th anniv.

WHO, 40th Anniv. — A211

1988, Sept. 1 Litho. *Perf. 13x12½*

651 A211 175fr multi 1.10 1.10

Alma Ata Declaration, 10th anniv.; Health Care for All on Earth by the Year 2000.
For surcharge see No. 786.

Ganvie Lake Village — A212

1988, Sept. 4 *Perf. 13½*

652 A212 125fr shown .85 .85
653 A212 190fr Boatman, village, diff. 1.25 1.25

A213

1988, Aug. 14 *Perf. 12½*

654 A213 125fr multi .90 .90

1st Benin Scout Jamboree, Aug. 12-19.

Benin No. 351, Dahomey Nos. 296, 328 Surcharged

1988

Printing Method & Perfs as Before

654A A57(d) 10fr on 60fr on 2fr #351
654B A62(d) 10fr on 65fr #296
654E A74(d) 150fr on 200fr #328

A214

1988, Dec. 30 Litho. *Perf. 13*

Ritual Offering to Hebiesso, God of Thunder and Lightning.

655 A214 125fr multicolored .80 .80

Dahomey Nos. 161, 247, 302, 333, 339, 341 Surcharged

1988 Photo. *Perf. 12½x13*

655A A19(d) 5fr on 3fr #161
655C A82(d) 30fr on 150fr #341
655D A76(d) 25fr on 100fr #333
655E A45(b) 50fr on 45fr #247
655F A81(d) 55fr on 200fr #339
655G A65(b) 65fr on 85fr #302

These are part of a set of 10. Another set of 19 surcharges also is known to exist. The editors need to see the rest of these stamps before listings can be created.

Rural Development Council, 30th Anniv. — A214a

1989, May 29 Litho. *Perf. 15x14*

655K A214a 75fr multicolored

World Wildlife Fund — A216

Roseate terns, *Sterna dougalli.*

1989, Jan. 30 Litho. *Perf. 13*

657 A216 10fr Three terns 1.25 .75
658 A216 15fr Feeding on fish 1.25 .75
659 A216 50fr Perched 2.50 2.00
660 A216 125fr In flight 5.00 3.75
Nos. 657-660 (4) 10.00 7.25

Eiffel Tower Cent. — A217

1989, Apr. 24 Litho. *Perf. 13x12½*

661 A217 190fr multi 1.10 1.10

PHILEXFRANCE '89, French Revolution Bicent. — A218

Design: Bastille, emblems, Declaration of Human Rights and Citizenship, France No. B252-B253.

1989, July 7 *Perf. 13*

662 A218 190fr multicolored 1.10 1.10

Electric Corp. of Benin, 20th Anniv. A219

1989, Oct. Litho. *Perf. 12½x13*

663 A219 125fr multicolored .80 .80

Fish A220

1989, Sept. 22 *Perf. 13½*

664 A220 125fr Lote .80 .80
665 A220 190fr Pike, salmon 1.25 1.25

Death of King Glele, Cent. — A221

1989, Dec. 16 Litho. *Perf. 13½*

666 A221 190fr multicolored 1.25 1.25

Christmas A222

1989, Dec. 25 *Perf. 13*

667 A222 200fr Holy family 1.40 1.40

Benin Posts & Telecommunications, Cent. — A223

1990, Jan. 1 *Perf. 13½*

668 A223 125fr multicolored .80 .80

Fruits and Flora A224

1990, Jan. 23 Litho. *Perf. 11½*

669 A224 60fr Oranges .40 .40
670 A224 190fr Kaufmann Tulips, vert. 1.40 1.40
671 A224 250fr Cashews, vert. 1.75 1.75
Nos. 669-671 (3) 3.55 3.55

Dated 1989.

No. 669 exists with "Populaire" obliterated by black marker.

Moon Landing, 20th Anniv. A225

1990, Jan. 23

672 A225 190fr multicolored 1.40 1.40

Dated 1989.

World Cup Soccer Championships, Italy — A226

1990, June 8 Litho. *Perf. 12½*

673 A226 125fr shown 1.00 1.00
674 A226 190fr Character trade-mark, vert. 1.50 1.50

For overprint see No. 676.

Post, Telephone & Telegraph Administration in Benin, Cent. — A227

1990, July 1 *Perf. 13*

675 A227 150fr multicolored 1.25 1.25

No. 673 Overprinted

1990 Litho. *Perf. 12½*

676 A226 125fr multicolored 1.00 1.00

Charles de Gaulle (1890-1970) — A228

1990, Nov. 22 Litho. *Perf. 13*

677 A228 190fr multicolored 1.50 1.50

See No. 689.

Galileo Probe and Jupiter A229

1990, Dec. 1

678 A229 100fr multicolored .75 .75

For overprint see No. 681.

A230

1990, Dec. 25 Litho. *Perf. 12½x13*

679 A230 200fr multicolored 1.75 1.75

Christmas.

Benin No. 641 Surcharged

1990

Perf. & Printing Method as Before

679B A202(e) 190fr on 300fr #641

A230a

A231

1990 Litho. *Perf. 11½x12*

679C A230a 125fr multicolored

National People's Congress.

1991, Sept. 3 Litho. *Perf. 13½*

680 A231 125fr multicolored 1.00 1.00

Independence, 31st anniv.

No. 678 Ovptd. in Red

1991 *Perf. 13*

681 A229 100fr multicolored .85 .85

French Open Tennis Championships, Cent. — A232

1991 *Perf. 13½*

682 A232 125fr multicolored 1.00 1.00

African Tourism Year — A233

1991

683 A233 190fr multicolored 1.60 1.60

Christmas A234

1991, Dec. 2 Litho. *Perf. 13½*

684 A234 125fr multicolored 1.00 1.00

Dancer of Guelede — A235

1991, Dec. 2

685 A235 190fr multicolored 1.60 1.60

Wolfgang Amadeus Mozart, Death Bicent. — A236

1991, Dec. 2

686 A236 1000fr multicolored 6.00 6.00

For surcharge see No. 793.

Discovery of America, 500th Anniv. A237

1000fr, Columbus coming ashore, horiz.

1992, Apr. 24 Litho. *Perf. 13*

687 A237 500fr blk, blue & brn 3.00 3.00
688 A237 1000fr multicolored 6.00 6.00
a. Souvenir sheet, #687-688 9.00 9.00

De Gaulle Type of 1990

1992 Litho. *Perf. 13*

689 A228 300fr like #677 2.25 2.25

Intl. Conference on Nutrition, Rome — A238

1992, Dec. 5 Litho. *Perf. 13*

690 A238 190fr multicolored 1.60 1.60

For surcharge see 928.

Dahomey Nos. 160, 266, 303, 311, 327, 334, 338, C161 Surcharged or Overprinted (#690A)

1992

Perfs. & Printing Methods as Before

690A A66(e) 5fr on #303
690E A80(f) 35fr on #338
690F A19(e) 125fr on 2fr #160
690G AP54(f) 125fr on 65fr #C161
690H A77(f) 125fr on 65fr #334 (G)
690I CD137(e) 125fr on 100fr #311
690J A52(f) 190fr on 45fr #266
690K A74(f) 125fr on 100fr #327

Visit of Pope John Paul II, Feb. 3-5 — A239

Ouidah 92, First Festival of Voodoo Culture — A240

1993, Feb. 3 Litho. *Perf. 13x12½*

691 A239 190fr multicolored 1.50 1.50

1993, Feb. 8 *Perf. 13½*

692 A240 125fr multicolored 1.00 1.00

Well of Possotome, Eurystome A241

1993, May 25 Litho. *Perf. 12½*

693 A241 125fr multicolored 1.00 1.00

OAU, 30th Anniv. A242

1993, June 7 Litho. *Perf. 13½*

694 A242 125fr multicolored 1.00 1.00

John F. Kennedy — A243

1993, June 24 *Perf. 13*

695 A243 190fr shown 1.50 1.50
696 A243 190fr Martin Luther King, vert. 1.50 1.50

Assassinations of Kennedy, 30th anniv. (#695), and King, 25th anniv. (#696).

Dahomey Nos. 161, 173, 175, 277, 335 Overprinted or Surcharged

1993

Perfs. & Printing Methods as Before

697 A21(e) 5fr on #175
700 A19(f) 10fr on 3fr #161
701 A77(f) 10fr on 100fr #335
703 A57(f) 20fr on 1fr #277
704 A21(f) 25fr on 1fr #173

Benin Nos. 343, 345, 350, Dahomey Nos. 169, 226-227, 249, 276, 295, 283, 286, 319, 333 Surcharged or Overprinted (#711, 713)

1994-95

707 A38(f) 5fr on 1fr #226
709 A71(f) 25fr on #319
710 A59(e) 40fr on #286
711 A57(e) 50fr on 1fr #350
712 A58(e) 80fr on 40fr #283
713 A76(g) 100fr on #333
715 A38(f) 135fr on 3fr #227
718 A62(e) 135fr on 30fr #295
719 A83(g) 135fr on 35fr #343
720 A56(h) 135fr on 40fr multi
722 A20(e) 135fr on 60fr #169
723 A83(g) 135fr on 60fr #345
725 A45(e) 200fr on 100fr #249

UNESCO Conference on The Slave Route — A244

1994 Litho. *Perf. 13x13½*

729 A244 200fr multicolored
730 A244 300fr multicolored

Natitingou Scout Encampment A245

1994 *Perf. 12¾x12½*

731 A245 135fr multi

Intl. Year of the Family A246

1994 Litho. *Perf. 12½*

732 A246 200fr multicolored

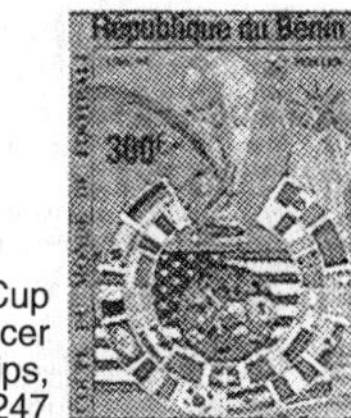

1994 World Cup Soccer Championships, US — A247

1994 Litho. *Perf. 13x13½*

733 A247 300fr multicolored

1996 Summer Olympics, Atlanta — A248

Perf. 12½x13, 13x12½

1995, Apr. 30 Litho.

734 A248 45fr Water polo .35 .35
735 A248 50fr Javelin .40 .40
736 A248 75fr Weight lifting .60 .60
737 A248 100fr Tennis .75 .75
738 A248 135fr Baseball 1.10 1.10
739 A248 200fr Synchronized swimming 1.50 1.50
Nos. 734-739 (6) 4.70 4.70

Souvenir Sheet

740 A248 300fr Diving *3.50 3.50*

Nos. 735-740 are vert. No. 740 contains one 32x40mm stamp.

Dogs A249

1995, Aug. 23 Litho. *Perf. 12½*

741 A249 40fr German shepherd .30 .30
742 A249 50fr Beagle .40 .40
743 A249 75fr Great dane .55 .55
744 A249 100fr Boxer .75 .75
745 A249 135fr Pointer 1.10 1.10
746 A249 200fr Fox terrier 1.50 1.50
Nos. 741-746 (6) 4.60 4.60

Souvenir Sheet

747 A249 300fr Schnauzer *5.00 5.00*

Ships A250

Designs: 40fr, Steam driven paddle boat, 1788. 50fr, Paddle steamer Charlotte, 1802. 75fr, Transatlantic steamship, Citta de Catania. 100fr, Hovercraft Mountbatten SR-N4. 135fr, QE II. 200fr, Japanese experimental atomic energy ship, Mutsu-NEF.
300fr, Paddle-steamer Savannah, 1819.

1995, May 20

748 A250 40fr multicolored .30 .30
749 A250 50fr multicolored .40 .40
750 A250 75fr multicolored .55 .55
751 A250 100fr multicolored .75 .75
752 A250 135fr multicolored 1.10 1.10
753 A250 200fr multicolored 1.50 1.50
Nos. 748-753 (6) 4.60 4.60

Souvenir Sheet

754 A250 300fr multicolored *3.50 3.50*

No. 754 contains one 40x32mm stamp.

Primates A251

1995, June 30

755 A251 50fr Pan troglodytes .40 .40
756 A251 75fr Mandrillus sphinx .55 .55
757 A251 100fr Colobus .75 .75
758 A251 135fr Macaca sylvanus 1.10 1.10
759 A251 200fr Comopithecus hamadryas 1.50 1.50
Nos. 755-759 (5) 4.30 4.30

Souvenir Sheet

760 A251 300fr Papio cynocephalus *3.50 3.50*

No. 760 contains one 32x40mm stamp.
For surcharge on No. 757, see No. 1260.

Domestic Cats A252

1995, July 30 Litho. *Perf. 12½x13*

761 A252 40fr Shorthair tabby .30 .30
762 A252 50fr Ruddy red .40 .40
763 A252 75fr White longhair .55 .55
764 A252 100fr Seal color point .75 .75
765 A252 135fr Tabby point 1.10 1.10
766 A252 200fr Black shorthair 1.50 1.50
Nos. 761-766 (6) 4.60 4.60

Souvenir Sheet

767 A252 300fr Cat in basket *3.50 3.50*

No. 767 contains one 40x32mm stamp.

Flowers — A253

Designs: 40fr, Dracunculus vulgaris. 50fr, Narcissus watieri. 75fr, Amaryllis belladonna. 100fr, Nymphaea capensis. 135fr, Chrysanthemum carinatum. 200fr, Iris tingitana.

1995, Oct. 15 Litho. *Perf. 12½*

768 A253 40fr multicolored .30 .30
769 A253 50fr multicolored .40 .40
770 A253 75fr multicolored .60 .60
771 A253 100fr multicolored .85 .85
772 A253 135fr multicolored 1.10 1.10
773 A253 200fr multicolored 1.75 1.75
Nos. 768-773 (6) 5.00 5.00

Wild Animals A254

50fr, Panthera leo. 75fr, Syncerus caffer. 100fr, Pan troglodytes. 135fr, Aepyceros melampus. 200fr, Geosciurus inaurus.
300fr, Loxodonta, vert.

Perf. 13x12½, 12½x13

1995, Sept. 20

774 A254 50fr multicolored .40 .40
775 A254 75fr multicolored .60 .60
776 A254 100fr multicolored .85 .85
777 A254 135fr multicolored 1.10 1.10
778 A254 200fr multicolored 1.75 1.75
Nos. 774-778 (5) 4.70 4.70

Souvenir Sheet

779 A254 300fr multicolored *3.50 3.50*

Nos. 774-777 are vert. No. 779 contains one 32x40mm stamp.

Birds Feeding Their Chicks — A255

Designs: 40fr, Cocothraustes cocothraustes. 50fr, Streptopelia chinensis. 75fr, Falco peregrinus. 100fr, Dendroica fusca. 135fr, Larus ridibundus. 200fr, Pelecanus onocrotalus.

1995, Aug. 28 *Perf. 12½x13*

780 A255 40fr multicolored .30 .30
781 A255 50fr multicolored .40 .40
782 A255 75fr multicolored .60 .60
783 A255 100fr multicolored .85 .85
784 A255 135fr multicolored 1.10 1.10
785 A255 200fr multicolored 1.75 1.75
Nos. 780-785 (6) 5.00 5.00

Benin Nos. 344, 504, 520, 619, 627, 651, 686 and Dahomey No. 291 Surcharged

1994-95

Printing Method and Perfs as Before

786 A211 25fr on 175fr #651
787 A194 50fr on 220fr #627
788 A83(h) 150fr on 45fr #344
789 A158 150fr on 90fr #519
790 A147 150fr on 500fr #504
791 A60(f) 200fr on 135fr #291
792 A192 200fr on 500fr #619
793 A236 250fr on 1000fr #686

Natl. Arms — A256

1995 Litho. *Perf. 12½*

793A A256 135fr yellow & multi 1.00 1.00
793B A256 150fr yel grn & multi 1.10 1.10
794 A256 200fr multicolored

See Nos. 948-951. For surcharge see No. 1021A

Orchids — A257

Designs: 40fr, Angraecum sesquipedale. 50fr, Polystachya virginea. 75fr, Disa uniflora. 100fr, Ansellia africana. 135fr, Angraecum eichlerianum. 200fr, Jumellea confusa.

1995, Nov. 10 Litho. *Perf. 12½*

795 A257 40fr multicolored .30 .30
796 A257 50fr multicolored .40 .40
797 A257 75fr multicolored .55 .55
798 A257 100fr multicolored .75 .75
799 A257 135fr multicolored 1.00 1.00
800 A257 200fr multicolored 1.50 1.50
Nos. 795-800 (6) 4.50 4.50

Butterflies A258

Designs: 40fr, Graphium policenes. 50fr, Vanessa atalanta. 75fr, Polymmatus icarus. 100fr, Danaus chrysipus. 135fr, Cynthia cardui. 200fr, Argus celbulina.
1000fr, Charaxes jasius.

1996, Mar. 10

801 A258 40fr multicolored .30 .30
802 A258 50fr multicolored .40 .40
803 A258 75fr multicolored .55 .55
804 A258 100fr multicolored .75 .75
805 A258 135fr multicolored 1.10 1.10
806 A258 200fr multicolored 1.50 1.50
Nos. 801-806 (6) 4.60 4.60

Souvenir Sheet

807 A258 1000fr multicolored *4.50 4.50*

CHINA '96, Beijing A259

Designs: a, 40fr, Dancer in traditional Chinese costume. b, 50fr, Exhibition emblem. c, 75fr, Water lily. d, 100fr, Temple of Heaven.

1996, Apr. 8

808 A259 Block of 4, #a.-d. *3.75 3.75*

Benin Nos. 523, 616 and Dahomey No. 306 Surcharged or Overprinted (#810)

1996?

Perfs. & Printing Methods as Before

809 A191 5fr on 205fr #616
810 A67(g) 35fr on #306
811 A158 150fr on 90fr #523

15th Lions Intl. District Convention — A260

1996 Litho. *Perf. 12½*

811A A260 100fr multicolored .35 .35
811B A260 135fr green & multi 1.10 1.10
812 A260 150fr yellow & multi 1.10 1.10
813 A260 200fr red & multi 1.50 1.50
Nos. 811A-813 (4) 4.05 4.05

For surcharge see No. 1021B.
Issued: #811A, 12/27; others, 5/2.

La Francoponie Conference A261

1995, Dec. 2 Litho. *Perf. 12½*

814 A261 150fr pink & multi .90 .90
815 A261 200fr blue & multi 1.25 1.25

Cats — A262

1995, Nov. 2 Litho. *Perf. 13*

816 A262 40fr Lynx lynx .30 .30
817 A262 50fr Felis concolor .40 .40
818 A262 75fr Acinonyx jubatus .50 .50
819 A262 100fr Panthera pardus .70 .70
820 A262 135fr Panthera tigris .95 .95
821 A262 200fr Panthera leo 1.40 1.40
Nos. 816-821 (6) 4.25 4.25

1998 World Cup Soccer Championships, France — A263

Various soccer players.

1996, Feb. 10 Litho. *Perf. 13*

822 A263 40fr multicolored .30 .30
823 A263 50fr multicolored .40 .40
824 A263 75fr multicolored .55 .55
825 A263 100fr multicolored .75 .75
826 A263 135fr multicolored 1.10 1.10
827 A263 200fr multicolored 1.50 1.50
Nos. 822-827 (6) 4.60 4.60

Souvenir Sheet

Perf. 12½

828 A263 1000fr multicolored *4.50 4.50*

No. 828 contains one 32x40mm stamp.

1996 Summer Olympic Games, Atlanta — A264

1996, Jan. 28 Litho. *Perf. 13*

829 A264 40fr Diving .30 .30
830 A264 50fr Tennis .40 .40
831 A264 75fr Running .55 .55
832 A264 100fr Gymnastics .75 .75
833 A264 135fr Weight lifting 1.10 1.10
834 A264 200fr Shooting 1.50 1.50
Nos. 829-834 (6) 4.60 4.60

Souvenir Sheet

835 A264 1000fr Water polo *4.50 4.50*

No. 835 contains one 32x40mm stamp.

Christmas Paintings — A265

Entire paintings or details: 40fr, Holy Family Under the Oak Tree, by Raphael. 50fr, The Holy Family, by Raphael. 75fr, St. John the Baptist as a Child, by Murillo. 100fr, The Virgin of Balances, by Leonardo da Vinci. 135fr, The Virgin and the Infant, by Gerard David. 200fr, Adoration of the Magi, by Juan Batista Mayno.
1000fr, Rest on the Flight into Egypt, by Murillo.

1996, May 5 Litho. *Perf. 13*

836 A265 40fr multicolored .30 .30
837 A265 50fr multicolored .40 .40
838 A265 75fr multicolored .60 .60
839 A265 100fr multicolored .75 .75
840 A265 135fr multicolored 1.10 1.10
841 A265 200fr multicolored 1.60 1.60
Nos. 836-841 (6) 4.75 4.75

Souvenir Sheet

842 A265 1000fr multicolored *4.75 4.75*

No. 842 contains one 40x32mm stamp.

Wild Cats — A266

Designs: 40fr, Leptailurus serval. 50fr, Profelis temmincki. 75fr, Leopardus pardalis. 100fr, Lynx rufus. 135fr, Prionailurus bengalensis. 200fr, Felis euphtilura.
1000fr, Neofelis nebulosa.

1996, June 10 Litho. *Perf. 12x12½*

843 A266 40fr multicolored .30 .30
844 A266 50fr multicolored .40 .40
845 A266 75fr multicolored .60 .60

846 A266 100fr multicolored .75 .75
847 A266 135fr multicolored 1.10 1.10
848 A266 200fr multicolored 1.60 1.60
Nos. 843-848 (6) 4.75 4.75

Souvenir Sheet

Perf. 12½

849 A266 1000fr multicolored 4.75 4.75

No. 849 contains one 32x40mm stamp.

Sailing Ships A267

1996, May 27 ***Perf. 13x12½***
850 A267 40fr Thermopylae .30 .30
851 A267 50fr 5-masted bark .40 .40
852 A267 75fr Nightingale .60 .60
853 A267 100fr Opium clipper .75 .75
854 A267 135fr The Torrens 1.10 1.10
855 A267 200fr English clipper 1.60 1.60
Nos. 850-855 (6) 4.75 4.75

Souvenir Sheet

Perf. 13

856 A267 1000fr Opium clipper, diff. 4.75 4.75

No. 856 contains one 32x40mm stamp.
For No. 850 surcharge see No. 1209.

Olymphilex '96 — A268

1996, July 2 ***Perf. 13***
857 A268 40fr Running .30 .30
858 A268 50fr Kayaking .40 .40
859 A268 75fr Gymnastics .60 .60
860 A268 100fr Soccer .75 .75
861 A268 135fr Tennis 1.10 1.10
862 A268 200fr Baseball 1.50 1.50
Nos. 857-862 (6) 4.65 4.65

Souvenir Sheet

863 A268 1000fr Basketball 4.75 4.75

No. 863 contains one 32x40mm stamp.
For surcharge on No. 860, see No. 1270.

Modern Olympic Games, Cent. — A269

a, 40fr, Gold medal, woman hurdler. b, 50fr, Runner, Olympic flame. c, 75fr, Pierre de Coubertin, map of US. d, 100fr, Map of US, "1996."

1996, June 20
864 A269 Block of 4, #a.-d. 4.00 4.00

No. 864 is a continuous design.

Horses A270

Various horses.

1996, Aug. 10 **Litho.** ***Perf. 13***
865 A270 40fr multi, vert. .30 .30
866 A270 50fr multi, vert. .40 .40
867 A270 75fr multi, vert. .55 .55
868 A270 100fr multi, vert. .75 .75
869 A270 135fr multi, vert. 1.10 1.10
870 A270 200fr multicolored 1.50 1.50
Nos. 865-870 (6) 4.60 4.60

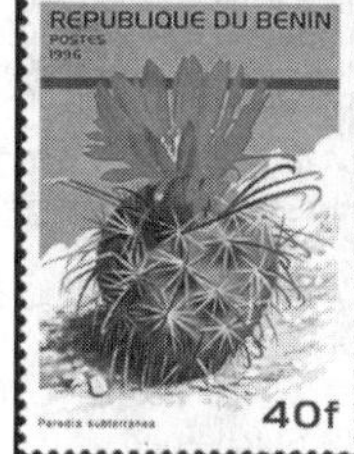
Flowering Cacti — A271

40fr, Parodia subterranea. 50fr, Astrophytum senile. 75fr, Echinocereus melanocentrus. 100fr, Turbinicarpus kinkerianus. 135fr, Astrophytum capricorne. 200fr, Neloydia grandiflora.

1996, July 25
871 A271 40fr multicolored .30 .30
872 A271 50fr multicolored .40 .40
873 A271 75fr multicolored .55 .55
874 A271 100fr multicolored .75 .75
875 A271 135fr multicolored 1.10 1.10
876 A271 200fr multicolored 1.50 1.50
Nos. 871-876 (6) 4.60 4.60

For No. 873 surcharge see No. 1210. For No. 874 surcharge see No. 1272.

Mushrooms A272

Designs: 40fr, Stropharia cubensis. 50fr, Psilocybe zapotecorum. 75fr, Psilocybe mexicana. 100fr, Conocybe siligineoides. 135fr, Psilocybe caerulescens mazatecorum. 200fr, Psilocybe caerulescens nigripes.
1000fr, Psilocybe aztecorum, horiz.

1996, Sept. 30
877 A272 40fr multicolored .30 .30
878 A272 50fr multicolored .40 .40
879 A272 75fr multicolored .55 .55
880 A272 100fr multicolored .75 .75
881 A272 135fr multicolored 1.10 1.10
882 A272 200fr multicolored 1.50 1.50
Nos. 877-882 (6) 4.60 4.60

Souvenir Sheet

Perf. 12½

883 A272 1000fr multicolored 4.50 4.50

No. 883 contains one 40x32mm stamp.

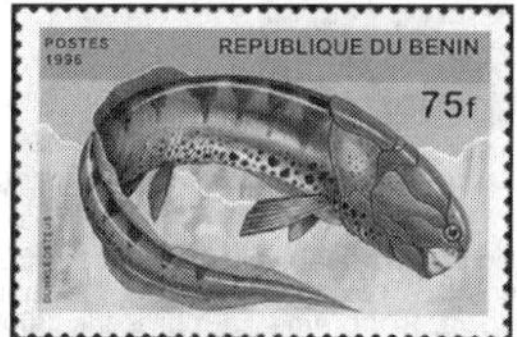
Prehistoric Animals — A273

1996, Aug. 30 ***Perf. 12½***
884 A273 40fr Longisquama, vert. .30 .30
885 A273 50fr Dimophodon, vert. .40 .40
886 A273 75fr Dunkleosteus .55 .55
887 A273 100fr Eryops .75 .75
888 A273 135fr Peloneustes 1.10 1.10
889 A273 200fr Deinonychus 1.50 1.50
Nos. 884-889 (6) 4.60 4.60

Birds — A274

Designs: 40fr, Campephilus principalis. 50fr, Picathartes oreas. 75fr, Strigops habroptilus. 100fr, Amazona vittata. 135fr, Nipponia nippon. 200fr, Gymnogyps californianus.
1000fr, Paradisea rudolphi.

1996, Sept. 10
890 A274 40fr multicolored .30 .30
891 A274 50fr multicolored .40 .40
892 A274 75fr multicolored .55 .55
893 A274 100fr multicolored .75 .75
894 A274 135fr multicolored 1.10 1.10
895 A274 200fr multicolored 1.50 1.50
Nos. 890-895 (6) 4.60 4.60

Souvenir Sheet

896 A274 1000fr multicolored 4.50 4.50

No. 896 contains one 32x40mm stamp.

Dahomey No. 235 Overprinted
Benin No. 545 Surcharged

199?
Perfs. & Printing Methods as Before
897 A40(e) 30fr on #235
898 A166 75fr on 185fr #545

Dahomey Nos. 208, 239-241, 257-258, 261, 269, 274, 283, 320, 326, 334-336, 337 Surcharged or Overprinted (#899)

1996?
Perfs. & Printing Methods as Before
899 A77(f) 100fr on #335
900 A79(e) 125fr on 150fr #337
901 A77(h) 135fr on 65fr #334
902 A42(e) 150fr on 30fr #239
903 A43(h) 150fr on 30fr #241
904 A48(h) 150fr on 30fr #257
905 A50(h) 150fr on 30fr #261
906 CD132(h) 150fr on 40fr #269
907 A58(h) 150fr on 40fr #283
908 A71(e) 150fr on 40fr #320
909 A74(e) 150fr on 40fr #326
910 A78(e) 150fr on 40fr #336
911 A32(e) 150fr on 50fr #208
912 A42(e) 150fr on 70fr #240
913 A48(h) 150fr on 70fr #258
914 A55(h) 150fr on 200fr #274

Benin Nos. 381, 384, 449, 521, 538, 546, 567, 569, 636, Surcharged

1996?
Perfs. & Printing Methods as Before
915 A127 10fr on 90fr #449
916 A159 10fr on 90fr #521
917 A164 10fr on 90fr #538
918 A174 10fr on 90fr #569
919 A98 40fr on 210fr #381
920 A99 40fr on 210fr #384
921 A198 75fr on 440fr #636
922 A167 100fr on 500fr #546
923 A173 125r on 300fr #567

Obliterator on No. 922 has either one or two bars. Pairs of No. 922 exist with each stamp having a different obliterator.

Nos. 376, 466, 690 Surcharged

1995 **Method and Perf. as Before**
925 A96 10fr on 90fr #376 — —
926 A132 10fr on 90fr #466
928 A238 150fr on 190fr #690

Ungulates — A275

Designs: 40fr, Aepyceros melampus. 50fr, Kobus ellipsiprymnus. 75fr, Caffer caffer. 100fr, Connochaetes taurinus. 135fr, Okapia johnstoni. 200fr, Tragelaphus strepsiceros.

1996, Oct. 15 **Litho.** ***Perf. 12½x12***
930 A275 40fr multicolored .30 .30
931 A275 50fr multicolored .40 .40
932 A275 75fr multicolored .55 .55
933 A275 100fr multicolored .75 .75
934 A275 135fr multicolored 1.10 1.10
935 A275 200fr multicolored 1.50 1.50
Nos. 930-935 (6) 4.60 4.60

Marine Mammals — A276

Designs: 40fr, Delphinapterus leucas. 50fr, Tursiops truncatus. 75fr, Belaenoptera musculus. 100fr, Eubalaena australis. 135fr, Gramphidelphis griseus. 200fr, Orcinus orca.

1996, Nov. 5 ***Perf. 13***
936 A276 40fr multicolored .30 .30
937 A276 50fr multicolored .40 .40
938 A276 75fr multicolored .55 .55
939 A276 100fr multicolored .75 .75
940 A276 135fr multicolored 1.10 1.10
941 A276 200fr multicolored 1.50 1.50
Nos. 936-941 (6) 4.60 4.60

For No. 938 surcharge, see No. 1255.

Fish A277

1996, Dec. 4 **Litho.** ***Perf. 12½***
942 A277 50fr Pomacanthidae, vert. .40 .40
943 A277 75fr Acanthuridae .55 .55
944 A277 100fr Carangidae .75 .75
945 A277 135fr Chaetodontidae 1.10 1.10
946 A277 200fr Chaetodontidae, diff. 1.50 1.50
Nos. 942-946 (5) 4.30 4.30

Souvenir Sheet

947 A277 1000fr Scaridae 4.50 4.50

No. 947 contains one 40x32mm stamp.

Coat of Arms Type of 1995

1996-97 ***Perf. 12½***
948 A256 100fr multicolored .45 .45
949 A256 135fr lt yellow & multi .55 .55
950 A256 150fr lt bl grn & multi .60 .60
951 A256 200fr lt orange & multi .85 .85
Nos. 948-951 (4) 2.45 2.45

#949-951 have "Republique du Benin" at bottom.
Issued: 100fr, 12/27/96; 135fr, 150fr, 200fr, 5/15/97.
For surcharge see No. 1021A.

Military Uniforms — A278

Regiments of European infantry: 135fr, Grenadier, Glassenapp. 150fr, Officer, Von Groben. 200fr, Musketeer, Comte Dohna. 270fr, Bombardier. 300fr, Gendarme. 400fr, Dragoon, Mollendorf.
1000fr, Soldiers, flag, horses, vert.

1997, Feb. 20
952 A278 135fr multicolored .55 .55
953 A278 150fr multicolored .60 .60
954 A278 200fr multicolored .80 .80
955 A278 270fr multicolored 1.10 1.10

956 A278 300fr multicolored 1.25 1.25
957 A278 400fr multicolored 1.60 1.60
Nos. 952-957 (6) 5.90 5.90

Souvenir Sheet

Perf. 13

958 A278 1000fr multicolored 4.00 4.00

No. 958 contains one 32x40mm stamp.

Trains A279

135fr, Steam turbine, Reid Maclead, 1920. 150fr, Experimental high speed, 1935. 200fr, Renard Argent, 1935. 270fr, Class No. 21-C-6, 1941. 300fr, Diesel, 1960. 400fr, Diesel, 1960, diff.

1000fr, Coronation Scot, 1937.

1997, Mar. 26 Litho. *Perf. 13*

959 A279 135fr multicolored .50 .50
960 A279 150fr multicolored .55 .55
961 A279 200fr multicolored .75 .75
962 A279 270fr multicolored 1.00 1.00
963 A279 300fr multicolored 1.10 1.10
964 A279 400fr multicolored 1.50 1.50
Nos. 959-964 (6) 5.40 5.40

Souvenir Sheet

965 A279 1000fr multicolored 3.75 3.75

No. 965 contains one 40x32mm stamp.

1998 World Cup Soccer Championship, France — A280

Various soccer plays.

1997, Apr. 9 *Perf. 12½x13*

966 A280 135fr multicolored .50 .50
967 A280 150fr multicolored .55 .55
968 A280 200fr multicolored .75 .75
969 A280 270fr multicolored 1.00 1.00
970 A280 300fr multi, horiz. 1.10 1.10
971 A280 400fr multi, horiz. 1.50 1.50
Nos. 966-971 (6) 5.40 5.40

Souvenir Sheet

972 A280 1000fr multicolored 3.75 3.75

No. 972 contains one 40x32mm stamp.

For No. 969 surcharge, see No. 1277.

Orchids — A281

Phalaenopsis: 135fr, Penetrate. 150fr, Golden sands. 200fr, Sun spots. 270fr, Fuscata. 300fr, Christi floyd. 400fr, Cayanne.

1000fr, Janet kuhn.

1997, June 9 Litho. *Perf. 12½x13*

973 A281 135fr multicolored .50 .50
974 A281 150fr multicolored .55 .55
975 A281 200fr multicolored .70 .70
976 A281 270fr multicolored 1.00 1.00
977 A281 300fr multicolored 1.10 1.10
978 A281 400fr multicolored 1.40 1.40
Nos. 973-978 (6) 5.25 5.25

Souvenir Sheet

Perf. 12½

979 A281 1000fr multicolored 3.60 3.60

No. 979 contains one 32x40mm stamp.

Dogs — A282

Designs: 135fr, Irish setter. 150fr, Saluki. 200fr, Doberman pinscher. 270fr, Siberian husky. 300fr, Basenji. 400fr, Boxer.

1000fr, Rhodesian ridgeback.

1997, May 30 *Perf. 13*

980 A282 135fr multicolored .50 .50
981 A282 150fr multicolored .55 .55
982 A282 200fr multicolored .70 .70
983 A282 270fr multicolored 1.00 1.00
984 A282 300fr multicolored 1.10 1.10
985 A282 400fr multicolored 1.40 1.40
Nos. 980-985 (6) 5.25 5.25

Souvenir Sheet

Perf. 12½

986 A282 1000fr multicolored 3.60 3.60

No. 986 contains one 32x40mm stamp.

Antique Automobiles — A283

1997, July 5 Litho. *Perf. 13x12½*

987 A283 135fr 1905 Buick .45 .45
988 A283 150fr 1903 Ford .50 .50
989 A283 200fr 1913 Stanley .70 .70
990 A283 270fr 1911 Stoddar-Dayton .90 .90
991 A283 300fr 1934 Cadillac 1.00 1.00
992 A283 400fr 1931 Cadillac 1.40 1.40
Nos. 987-992 (6) 4.95 4.95

Souvenir Sheet

Perf. 13

993 A283 1000fr 1928 Ford 3.40 3.40

No. 993 contains one 40x32mm stamp.

Songbirds — A284

Designs: 135fr, Pyrrhula pyrrhula. 150fr, Carduelis spinus. 200fr, Turdus torquatus. 270fr, Parus cristatus. 300fr, Nucifraga caryocatactes. 400fr, Luscinia megarhynchos.

1000fr, Motacilla flava.

1997, July 30 *Perf. 13x12½*

994 A284 135fr multicolored .45 .45
995 A284 150fr multicolored .50 .50
996 A284 200fr multicolored .70 .70
997 A284 270fr multicolored .90 .90
998 A284 300fr multicolored 1.00 1.00
999 A284 400fr multicolored 1.40 1.40
Nos. 994-999 (6) 4.95 4.95

Souvenir Sheet

Perf. 12½

1000 A284 1000fr multicolored 3.40 3.40

No. 1000 contains one 32x40mm stamp.

Flowering Cactus — A285

Designs: 135fr, Faucaria lupina. 150fr, Conophytum bilobun. 200fr, Lithops aucampiae. 270fr, Lithops helmutii. 300fr, Stapelia grandiflora. 400fr, Lithops fulviceps.

1000fr, Pleiospilos willowmorensis.

1997, Aug. 30 Litho. *Perf. 13x12½*

1001 A285 135fr multicolored .45 .45
1002 A285 150fr multicolored .50 .50
1003 A285 200fr multicolored .70 .70
1004 A285 270fr multicolored .90 .90
1005 A285 300fr multicolored 1.00 1.00
1006 A285 400fr multicolored 1.25 1.25
Nos. 1001-1006 (6) 4.80 4.80

Souvenir Sheet

Perf. 12½

1007 A285 1000fr multicolored 3.40 3.40

No. 1007 contains one 32x40mm stamp.

Benin No. 418 Surcharged

1995

Perfs. & Printing Methods as Before

1009 A114 10fr on 90fr #418

Benin Nos. 813, 948 Surcharged

Printing Methods and Perfs as before

1997-99 (?)

1021A A256 135fr on 100fr #948
1021B A260 135fr on 200fr #813

Early Locomotives — A286

Designs: 135fr, Puffing Billy, 1813. 150fr, La Fusée, 1829. 200fr, Royal George, 1827. 270fr, Nouveauté, 1829. 300fr, Locomotion, 1825, vert. 400fr, Sans Pareil, 1829, vert.

1000fr, Trevithick locomotive.

1997, Dec. 3 Litho. *Perf. 13*

1022 A286 135fr multicolored .45 .45
1023 A286 150fr multicolored .50 .50
1024 A286 200fr multicolored .70 .70
1025 A286 270fr multicolored .95 .95
1026 A286 300fr multicolored 1.00 1.00
1027 A286 400fr multicolored 1.40 1.40
Nos. 1022-1027 (6) 5.00 5.00

Souvenir Sheet

1028 A286 1000fr multicolored 3.50 3.50

No. 1028 contains one 40x32mm stamp.

Mushrooms A287

Designs: 135fr, Amanita caesarea. 150fr, Cortinarius collinitus. 200fr, Amanita bisporigera. 270fr, Amanita rubescens. 300fr, Russula virescens. 400fr, Amanita inaurata.

1000fr, Amanita muscaria.

1997, Nov. 5 Litho. *Perf. 13*

1029 A287 135fr multicolored .40 .40
1030 A287 150fr multicolored .55 .55
1031 A287 200fr multicolored .70 .70
1032 A287 270fr multicolored .95 .95

1033 A287 300fr multicolored 1.00 1.00
1034 A287 400fr multicolored 1.40 1.40
Nos. 1029-1034 (6) 5.00 5.00

Souvenir Sheet

1035 A287 1000fr multicolored 3.50 3.50

No. 1035 contains one 32x40mm stamp.

Assoc. of African Petroleum Producers, 10th Anniv. — A288

1997, Oct. 20 Litho. *Perf. 13*

1036 A288 135fr green & multi
1037 A288 200fr orange & multi
1038 A288 300fr blue & multi
1039 A288 500fr yellow & multi 1.75 1.75

Old Sailing Vessels — A289

Designs: 135fr, Egyptian. 150fr, Greek. 200fr, Assyrian-Phoenician. 270fr, Roman. 300fr, Norman. 400fr, Mediterranean.

1000fr, English.

1997, Sept. 10 Litho. *Perf. 12½*

1040 A289 135fr multicolored .50 .50
1041 A289 150fr multicolored .55 .55
1042 A289 200fr multicolored .75 .75
1043 A289 270fr multicolored 1.00 1.00
1044 A289 300fr multicolored 1.10 1.10
1045 A289 400fr multicolored 1.50 1.50
Nos. 1040-1045 (6) 5.40 5.40

Souvenir Sheet

1046 A289 1000fr multicolored 3.75 3.75

No. 1046 contains one 32x40mm stamp.

Fish A290

Designs: 135fr, Epinephelus fasciatus. 150fr, Apogon victoriae. 200fr, Scarus gibbus. 270fr, Pygoplites diacanthus. 300fr, Cirrhilabrus punctatus. 400fr, Cirrhitichthys oxycephalus.

1000fr, Bodianus bilunulatus.

1997, Sept. 15 Litho. *Perf. 12½*

1047 A290 135fr multicolored .50 .50
1048 A290 150fr multicolored .55 .55
1049 A290 200fr multicolored .75 .75
1050 A290 270fr multicolored 1.00 1.00
1051 A290 300fr multicolored 1.10 1.10
1052 A290 400fr multicolored 1.50 1.50
Nos. 1047-1052 (6) 5.40 5.40

Souvenir Sheet

Perf. 13

1053 A290 1000fr multicolored 3.75 3.75

No. 1053 contains one 40x32mm stamp.

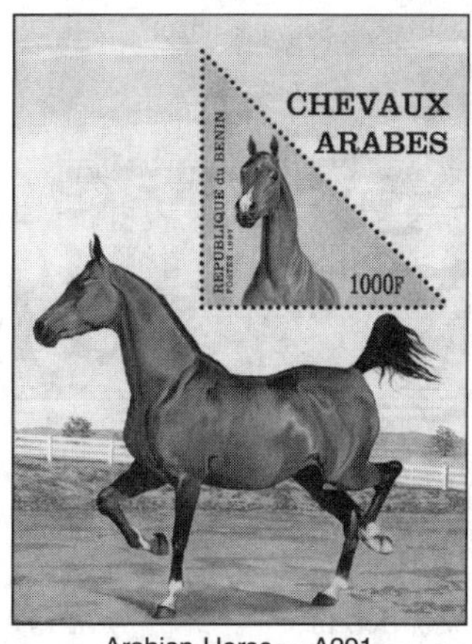
Arabian Horse — A291

Various horses. Denominations and background colors: d, 135fr, green. e, 150fr, red brown. f, 200fr, yellow. g, 270fr, orange brown. h, 300fr, tan. i, 400fr, olive green.

1997, May 25 Litho. *Perf. 12½*

1053A	A291	Pair, #d.-e.	1.00	1.00
1053B	A291	Pair, #f.-g.	1.60	1.60
1053C	A291	Pair, #h.-i.	2.50	2.50
		Nos. 1053A-1053C (3)	5.10	5.10

Souvenir Sheet

1054	A291	1000fr multicolored	3.50	3.50

Mushrooms A292

135fr, Tephrocybe carbonaria. 150fr, Suillus luteus. 200fr, Pleurotus ostreatus. 270fr, Hohenbuehelia geogenia. 300fr, Tylopilus felleus. 400fr, Lepiota leucothites.
1000fr, Gymnopilus junonius.

1998, Apr. 28 Litho. *Perf. 12½*

1055	A292	135fr multicolored	.45	.45
1056	A292	150fr multicolored	.50	.50
1057	A292	200fr multicolored	.65	.65
1058	A292	270fr multicolored	.90	.90
1059	A292	300fr multicolored	1.00	1.00
1060	A292	400fr multicolored	1.40	1.40
		Nos. 1055-1060 (6)	4.90	4.90

Souvenir Sheet

1061	A292	1000fr multicolored	3.50	3.50

No. 632 Surcharged

1998 Method and Perf. as Before

1061F A195(h) 150fr on 205fr #632

Fire Fighting Apparatus — A293

135fr, Philadelphia Double Deck, 1885. 150fr, Veteran, 1850. 200fr, Merry Weather, 1894. 270fr, Horse-drawn wagon, 19th cent. 300fr, 1948 Jeep. 400fr, Chevrolet 6400.
1000fr, 1952 American-La France-Foamite Corp.

1998, Apr. 30 Litho. *Perf. 12¾*

1062	A293	135fr multicolored	.45	.45
1063	A293	150fr multicolored	.50	.50
1064	A293	200fr multicolored	.65	.65
1065	A293	270fr multicolored	.90	.90
1066	A293	300fr multicolored	1.00	1.00
1067	A293	400fr multicolored	1.40	1.40
		Nos. 1062-1067 (6)	4.90	4.90

Souvenir Sheet

1068	A293	1000fr multicolored	3.50	3.50

No. 1068 contains one 40x32mm stamp.

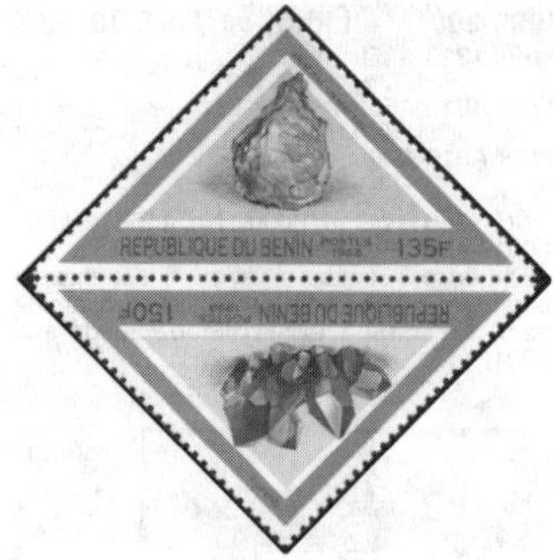
Minerals — A294

#1069a, 135fr, Uranifere. #1069b, 150fr, Quartz. #1070a, 200fr, Aragonite. #1070b, 270fr, Malachite. #1071a, 300fr, Turquoise. #1071b, 400fr, Corundum.
1000fr, Marble.

1998, June 5 Litho. *Perf. 12½*

1069	A294	Pair, #a.-b.	1.00	1.00
1070	A294	Pair, #a.-b.	1.60	1.60
1071	A294	Pair, #a.-b.	2.50	2.50
		Nos. 1069-1071 (3)	5.10	5.10

Souvenir Sheet

1072	A294	1000fr multicolored	3.50	3.50

Locomotives — A295

Designs: 135fr, Red 0-6-0. 150fr, 0-4-4. 200fr, Brown 0-6-0. 270fr, Purple 0-6-0. 300fr, Blue 0-6-0. 400fr, "Helvetia" 0-6-0.
1000fr, "Shelby Steel" 0-6-0.

1998, June 30 Litho. *Perf. 12¾*

1073	A295	135fr multicolored	.45	.45
1074	A295	150fr multicolored	.50	.50
1075	A295	200fr multicolored	.65	.65
1076	A295	270fr multicolored	.90	.90
1077	A295	300fr multicolored	1.00	1.00
1078	A295	400fr multicolored	1.40	1.40
		Nos. 1073-1078 (6)	4.90	4.90

Souvenir Sheet

Perf. 13

1079	A295	1000fr multicolored	3.50	3.50

No. 1079 contains one 40x32mm stamp.

Diana, Princess of Wales (1961-97) — A296

Portraits: a, 135fr. b, 150fr. c, 200fr. d, 270fr. e, 300fr. f, 400fr. g, 500fr. h, 600fr. i, 700fr.

1998, July 10 Litho. *Perf. 12½*

1083	A296	Sheet of 9, #a.-i.	11.50	11.50

Dahomey No. 302 Surcharged

1997?

Perfs. & Printing Method as Before

1084 A65(h) 35fr on 85fr #302

Dinosaurs — A297

No. 1085: a, 135fr, Sordes. b, 150fr, Scaphognatus. c, 200fr, Dsungaripterus. d, 270fr, Brontosaurus. e, 300fr, Diplodocus. f, 400fr, Coelurus, Baryonyx. g, 500fr, Kronosaurus, Ichthyosaurus. h, 600fr, Ceratosaurus. i, 700fr, Yangchuansaurus.

1998, July 25 Litho. *Perf. 12¾*

1085	A297	Sheet of 9, #a-i	9.50	9.50

Python Regius A298

Various views of python: a, 135fr. b, 150fr. c, 200fr. d, 2000fr.

1999, Apr. 27 Litho. *Perf. 13*

1086	A298	Strip of 4, #a.-d.	8.75	8.75

World Wildlife Fund.

Dogs — A299

1998, July 31 Litho. *Perf. 12¾*

1087	A299	135fr Beagle	.40	.40
1088	A299	150fr Dalmatian	.45	.45
1089	A299	200fr Dachshund	.60	.60
1090	A299	270fr Cairn terrier	.80	.80
1091	A299	300fr Shih Tzu	.85	.85
1092	A299	400fr Pug	1.10	1.10
		Nos. 1087-1092 (6)	4.20	4.20

Souvenir Sheet

Perf. 13

1093	A299	1000fr Springer spaniel, horiz.	3.00	3.00

No. 1093 contains one 40x32mm stamp.

Cats A300

135fr, Abyssinian. 150fr, Striped shorthair. 200fr, Siamese. 270fr, Red striped cat. 300fr, Gray cat with black stripes. 400fr, Manx.
1000fr, Cat with orange, black and white fur.

Perf. 12¼x12½, 12½x12¼

1998, Aug. 10 Litho.

1094	A300	135fr multi, vert.	.45	.45
1095	A300	150fr multi, vert.	.50	.50
1096	A300	200fr multi, vert.	.65	.65
1097	A300	270fr multi	.90	.90
1098	A300	300fr multi	1.00	1.00
1099	A300	400fr multi	1.25	1.25
		Nos. 1094-1099 (6)	4.75	4.75

Souvenir Sheet

Perf. 13

1100	A300	1000fr multicolored	3.25	3.25

No. 1100 contains one 40x32mm stamp.

Antique Automobiles - 301

Designs: 135fr, 1910 Bugatti 13. 150fr, 1903 Clément. 200fr, 1914 Stutz Bearcat. 270fr, 1907 Darracq. 300fr, 1913 Napier. 400fr, 1911 Pierce-Arrow.
1000fr, 1904 Piccolo, vert.

1998, Oct. 12 Litho. *Perf. 12¾*

1101	A301	135fr multi	.40	.40
1102	A301	150fr multi	.45	.45
1103	A301	200fr multi	.60	.60
1104	A301	270fr multi	.80	.80
1105	A301	300fr multi	.85	.85
1106	A301	400fr multi	1.10	1.10
		Nos. 1101-1106 (6)	4.20	4.20

Souvenir Sheet

Perf. 12¾x12½

1107	A301	1000fr multi	3.00	3.00

No. 1107 contains one 32x40mm stamp.

Butterflies A301a

Designs: 135fr, Parnassius apollo. 150fr, Anthocharis cardamines. 200fr, Nymphalis antiopa. 250fr, Parage aegeria. 300fr, Palaeochrysophanus hippothoe. 400fr, Carterocephalus palaemon.
1000fr, Aglais urticae.

1998, Dec. 10 Litho. *Perf. 12¾*

1107A-1107F	A301a	Set of 6	3.75	3.75

Souvenir Sheet

Perf. 13

1107G	A301a	1000fr multi	2.50	2.50

No. 1107G contains one 40x32mm stamp.

African Wildlife — A302

Designs: 50fr, Ceratotherium simun. 100fr, Hipotragus niger. No. 1110, Phacochoerus aethiopicus. No. 1111, Hyaena brunnea. No. 1112, Colobus guereza. No. 1113, Hippopotamus amphibius. No. 1114, Cyncerus caffer caffer. No. 1115, Equus zebra. No. 1116, Acinonyx jubatus. No. 1117, Panthera leo leo. 400fr, Lycaon pictus. 500fr, Perodicticus potto.

Perf. 12¼x12½

1999, Mar. 10 Litho.

1108	A302	50fr gray	.20	.20
1109	A302	100fr brt violet	.35	.35
1110	A302	135fr gray green	.45	.45
1111	A302	135fr black	.45	.45
1112	A302	150fr gray blue	.50	.50
1113	A302	150fr emerald	.50	.50
1114	A302	200fr dull brown	.65	.65
1115	A302	200fr blue	.65	.65
1116	A302	300fr henna brown	1.00	1.00
1117	A302	300fr brown	1.00	1.00
1118	A302	400fr red brown	1.40	1.40
1119	A302	500fr deep bister	1.60	1.60
		Nos. 1108-1119 (12)	8.75	8.75

Birds — A303

Designs: 135fr, Chloebia gouldiae. 150fr, Sicalis flaveola. 200fr, Quelea quelea. 270fr, Euplectes afer. 300fr, Paroaria coronata. 400fr, Emberiza flaviventris.
1000fr, Mandingoa nitidula.

1999, Jan. 30 Litho. *Perf. 12¾*
1120-1125 A303 Set of 6 3.75 3.75

Souvenir Sheet
Perf. 12½
1126 A303 1000fr multi 2.60 2.60

No. 1126 contains one 32x40mm stamp.
For No. 1123 surcharge, see No. 1293.

Orchids A304

Designs: 50fr, Brassocattleya cliftonii. 100fr, Wilsonara. 150fr, Cypripedium paeony. 300fr, Cymbidium babylon. 400fr, Cattleya. 500fr, Miltonia minx.

1999, Apr. 25 Litho. *Perf. 12¾*

1127	A304	50fr multi	.20	.20
1128	A304	100fr multi	.35	.35
1129	A304	150fr multi	.50	.50
1130	A304	300fr multi	1.00	1.00
1131	A304	400fr multi	1.40	1.40
1132	A304	500fr multi	1.60	1.60
		Nos. 1127-1132 (6)	5.05	5.05

Souvenir Sheet
Perf. 13
1133 A304 1000fr Miltonia (isis) 3.25 3.25

No. 1133 contains one 28x36mm stamp.

Chess Players A305

Designs: 135fr, Mikhail Tal. 150fr, Emanuel Lasker. 200fr, José Raul Capablanca. 270fr, Alexander Alekhine. 300fr, Max Euwe. 400fr, Mikhail Botvinnik.
1000fr, Wilhelm Steinitz.

1999, Mar. 28 Litho. *Perf. 12¾*
1134-1139 A305 Set of 6 3.75 3.75

Souvenir Sheet
Perf. 13
1140 A305 1000fr multi 2.60 2.60

No. 1140 contains one 32x40mm stamp.

Ancient Sailing Ships A306

Designs: 135fr, Ceylonese canot. 150fr, Tanka-tim. 200fr, Sampan. 270fr, Polynesian canot. 300fr, Japanese junk. 400fr, Dacca-pulwar.
1000fr, Chinese junk.

1999, Feb. 15 Litho. *Perf. 12¾*
1141-1146 A306 Set of 6 3.75 3.75

Souvenir Sheet
Perf. 12½
1147 A306 1000fr multi 2.50 2.50

No. 1147 contains one 40x32mm stamp.

Fish - A307

Designs: 135fr, Notopterus chitala. 150fr, Puntius filamentosus. 200fr, Epaizeorhynchos bicolor. 270fr, Rasbora maculata. 300fr, Pristolepis fasciatus. 400fr, Betta splendens.
1000fr, Trichogaster trichopterus.

1999, May 10 Litho. *Perf. 12½x12¼*

1148	A307	135fr multi
1149	A307	150fr multi
1150	A307	200fr multi
1151	A307	270fr multi
1152	A307	300fr multi
1153	A307	400fr multi

Souvenir Sheet
Perf. 13x13¼
1154 A307 1000fr multi

No. 1154 contains one 40x32mm stamp.

Grand Prix de l'Amitie — A308

1999 Litho. *Perf. 13½x13*

1154A	A308	135fr multi	— —
1155	A308	150fr multi	
1156	A308	200fr multi	
1157	A308	300fr multi	
1157A	A308	500fr multi	

The editors would like to examine any additional stamps that may have been issued in this set.

Grand Prix de l'Amitie Type of 1999

1999 Litho. *Perf. 13½x13*
1158 A308 1000fr multi

Numbers have been reserved for two additional stamps in this set. The editors would like to examine any examples.

Early Steam Vehicles A309

Designs: 135fr, 1786 tricycle made by A. Murdock. 150fr, 1800 locomotive made by Richard Trevithick. 200fr, 1803 locomotive made by Trevithick. 270fr, 1811 locomotive made by John Blenkinsop. 300fr, 1829 locomotive, Stourbridge Lion. 400fr, 1830 locomotive, Tom Thumb.
1000fr, 1760 locomotive made by Isaac Newton, horiz.

1999, June 18 Litho. *Perf. 12¾*
1159-1164 A309 Set of 6 3.75 3.75

Souvenir Sheet
Perf. 13
1165 A309 1000fr multi 2.50 2.50

No. 1165 contains one 40x32 mm stamp.

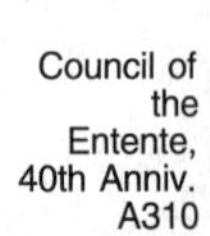

Council of the Entente, 40th Anniv. A310

1999-2001 Litho. *Perf. 13x13½*

1166	A310	135fr multi	— —
	a.	Perf. 13½, dated "2000"	— —
1167	A310	150fr multi	
	a.	Perf. 13½x13	— —
1168	A310	200fr multi	
	a.	Perf. 13x13¼, dated 1999	— —

No. 1166 is dated "2000." No. 1168 is dated "2001." Nos. 1167 exists dated "2000."
The editors suspect other stamps in this set have been issued and would like to examine them. No. 1168a exists dated "2000" and "2001."

block>

Snakes A311

Designs: 135fr, Elaphe longissima. 150fr, Pituophis melanoleucus. 200fr, Natrix natrix. 270fr, Oxybelis fulgidus. 300fr, Epicrates subflavus. 400fr, Crotalus atrox.
1000fr, Vipera berus.

1999, July 18 Litho. *Perf. 12¾*
1170-1175 A311 Set of 6 3.75 3.75

Souvenir Sheet
Perf. 13
1176 A311 1000fr multi 2.60 2.60

No. 1176 contains one 40x32mm stamp.

China 1999 World Philatelic Exhibition — A312

No. 1177: a, 50fr, Rocket testing, 14th cent. b, 100fr, Jiuquan space launch center. c, 135fr, DFH-3 communications satellite. d, 150fr, Launch of a foreign satellite. e, 200fr, Long March rocket CZ-2C. f, 300fr, Ship Yuan Wang. g, 400fr, Satellite dish. h, 500fr, Cacheted stamped covers.

1999, Aug. 22 *Perf. 12½*
1177 A312 Sheet of 8, #a-h 5.75 5.75

SOS Children's Villages, 50th Anniv. — A313

Denominations and panel colors: 135fr, Light green. 200fr, Pink. 300fr, Light blue. 500fr, Yellow.

1999, Oct. 15 Litho. *Perf. 12¾*
1178-1181 A313 Set of 4 3.50 3.50

For No. 1180 surcharge see No. 1208.

Souvenir Sheet

Manchester United, 1999 English Soccer Champions — A314

No. 1182: a, 135fr, Players celebrating on platform. b, 200fr, Players in action. c, 300fr, Players celebrating. d, 400fr, Stadium. e, 500fr, Trophies. f, 1000fr, Player with trophy.

1999, Oct. 15 *Perf. 13¼*
1182 A314 Sheet of 6, #a-f 7.75 7.75

The sets formerly listed as Nos. 1183-1189 (New Year 2000 - Year of the Dragon) and 1211-1217 (Dogs) were apparently prepared but not issued. These and two other sets, depicting insects (5 stamps and a souvenir sheet) and songbirds (12 stamps) were not sold in Benin, and they were not valid for postage.

Wild Cats A316

Designs: 135fr, Acinonyx jubatus. 150fr, Panthera onca. 200fr, Panthera uncia. 270fr, Panthera pardus. 300fr, Felis concolor. 400fr, Panthera tigris.
1000fr, Panthera leo.

Perf. 12½x12¼
1999, Sept. 28 Litho.
1190-1195 A316 Set of 6 3.75 3.75

Souvenir Sheet
1196 A316 1000fr multi 2.60 2.60

Cacti — A317

Designs: 135fr, Mammillaria lenta. 150fr, Oehmea nelsonii. 200fr, Neobesseya rosiflora. 270fr, Opuntia gosseliniana. 300fr, Parodia nivosa. 400fr, Rebutia senilis.
1000fr, Opuntia retrorsa, vert.
Illustration reduced.

1999, Oct. 10 Litho. *Perf. 12¼*
1197-1202 A317 Set of 6 3.75 3.75

Souvenir Sheet
Perf. 12½
1203 A317 1000fr multi 2.50 2.50

No. 1203 contains one 32x40mm rectangular stamp.

Birds A318

No. 1204: a, 135fr, Estrilda locustella. b, 150fr, Estrilda melanotis.
No. 1205: a, 200fr, Pytelia melba. b, 270fr, Uraeginthus bengalensis.
No. 1206: a, 300fr, Pyromelana orix. b, 400fr, Ploceus cucullatus.
1000fr, Steganura paradisea.

1999, Dec. 7 Litho. *Perf. 12¼*
Pairs, #a-b

1204-1206 A318 Set of 3 3.75 3.75

Souvenir Sheet

1207 A318 1000fr multi 2.60 2.60

No. 1180 Surcharged Method and Perf. as Before

2000 ?

1208 A313 135fr on 300fr #1180

Nos. 850, 873 Surcharged Methods and Perfs. as Before

2000 ?

1209 A267 135fr on 40fr #850
1210 A271 150fr on 75fr #873

Abdus Salam, 1979 Nobel Physics Laureate — A320

Man and Building A321

2001 Litho. *Perf. 13¼x13*

1218 A320 135fr multi — —
1219 A321 150fr multi — —

Edward Bouchet Abdus Salam Institute Intl. Conference on Physics and High Technology for the Development of Africa, Cotonou. The editors suspect there may be additional stamps in this set and would like to examine any examples. Numbers may change.

Nos. 757, 860, 874, 938, 969, 1123 Surcharged Methods and Perfs As Before

2000

1255 A276 150fr on 75fr #938 — —
1260 A251 150fr on 100fr #757 — —
1270 A268 150fr on 100fr #860 — —
1272 A271 150fr on 100fr #874 — —
1277 A280 150fr on 270fr #969 — —
1293 A303 150fr on 270fr #1123 — —

AIR POST STAMPS

PEOPLE'S REPUBLIC

Catalogue values for unused stamps in this section are for Never Hinged items.

Nativity, by Aert van Leyden — AP84

Christmas: 85fr, Adoration of the Kings, by Rubens, vert. 140fr, Adoration of the Shepherds, by Charles Lebrun. 300fr, The Virgin with the Blue Diadem, by Raphael, vert.

1975, Dec. 19 Litho. *Perf. 13*

C240 AP84 40fr gold & multi .20 .20
C241 AP84 85fr gold & multi .40 .20
C242 AP84 140fr gold & multi .60 .25
C243 AP84 300fr gold & multi 1.40 .65
Nos. C240-C243 (4) 2.60 1.30

For surcharges see Nos. C362, C367, C407, C432.

Slalom, Innsbruck Olympic Emblem — AP85

Innsbruck Olympic Games Emblem and: 150fr, Bobsledding, vert. 300fr, Figure skating, pairs.

1976, June 28 Litho. *Perf. 12½*

C244 AP85 60fr multi .65 .40
C245 AP85 150fr multi 1.10 .65
C246 AP85 300fr multi 2.25 1.25
Nos. C244-C246 (3) 4.00 2.30

12th Winter Olympic Games, Innsbruck, Austria, Feb. 4-15.

Dahomey Nos. C263-C265 Overprinted or Surcharged: "POPULAIRE / DU BENIN" and Bars

1976, July 4 Engr. *Perf. 13*

C247 AP86 135fr multi .55 .25
C248 AP86 210fr on 300fr multi .90 .35
C249 AP86 380fr on 500fr multi 1.50 .65
Nos. C247-C249 (3) 2.95 1.25

The overprint includes a bar covering "DU DAHOMEY" in shades of brown; "POPULAIRE DU BENIN" is blue on Nos. C247-C248, red on No. C249. The surcharge and bars over old value are blue on No. C248, red, brown on No. C249.

Long Jump AP86

Designs (Olympic Rings and): 150fr, Basketball, vert. 200fr, Hurdles.

1976, July 16 Photo. *Perf. 13*

C250 AP86 60fr multi .30 .20
C251 AP86 150fr multi .85 .30
C252 AP86 200fr multi 1.25 .45
a. Souv. sheet of 3, #C250-C252 3.00 3.00
Nos. C250-C252 (3) 2.40 .95

21st Olympic Games, Montreal, Canada, July 17-Aug 1.

Konrad Adenauer and Cologne Cathedral — AP87

Design: 90fr, Konrad Adenauer, vert.

1976, Aug. 27 Engr. *Perf. 13*

C253 AP87 90fr multi .60 .25
C254 AP87 250fr multi 1.75 .70

Konrad Adenauer (1876-1967), German Chancellor, birth centenary.
For surcharge see No. C289B.

Children's Heads and Flying Fish (Dahomey Type A32) — AP88

210fr, Lion cub's head, Benin design A3, vert.

1976, Sept. 13

C255 AP88 60fr Prus bl & vio bl .50 .25
C256 AP88 210fr multi 1.50 .75

JUVAROUEN 76, Intl. Youth Phil. Exhib., Rouen, France, Apr. 25-May 2.
For surcharges see Nos. C300, C494.

Apollo 14 Emblem and Blast-off — AP89

270fr, Landing craft and man on moon.

1976, Oct. 18 Engr. *Perf. 13*

C257 AP89 130fr multi .75 .30
C258 AP89 270fr multi 1.50 .65

Apollo 14 Moon Mission, 5th anniversary.
For surcharges see Nos. C312, C454.

Annunciation, by Master of Jativa — AP90

Christmas: 60fr, Nativity, by Gerard David. 270fr, Adoration of the Kings, Dutch School. 300fr, Flight into Egypt, by Gentile Fabriano, horiz.

1976, Dec. 20 Litho. *Perf. 12½*

C259 AP90 50fr gold & multi .25 .20
C260 AP90 60fr gold & multi .35 .20
C261 AP90 270fr gold & multi 1.50 .60
C262 AP90 300fr gold & multi 1.60 1.00
Nos. C259-C262 (4) 3.70 2.00

For surcharges see Nos. C310, C321, C484.

Gamblers and Lottery Emblem — AP91

1977, Mar. 13 Litho. *Perf. 13*

C263 AP91 50fr multi .50 .25

National lottery, 10th anniversary.

Sassenage Castle, Grenoble — AP92

1977, May 16 *Perf. 12½*

C264 AP92 200fr multi 1.25 .60

10th anniv. of Intl. French Language Council.
For surcharge see No. C334.

Concorde, Supersonic Plane — AP93

Designs: 150fr, Zeppelin. 300fr, Charles A. Lindbergh and Spirit of St. Louis. 500fr, Charles Nungesser and François Coli, French aviators lost over Atlantic, 1927.

1977, July 25 Engr. *Perf. 13*

C265 AP93 80fr ultra & red .50 .25
C266 AP93 150fr multi 1.00 .60
C267 AP93 300fr multi 1.50 .90
C268 AP93 500fr multi 3.00 2.00
Nos. C265-C268 (4) 6.00 3.75

Aviation history.
For overprint and surcharges see Nos. C274, C316, C336.

Soccer Player — AP94

200fr, Soccer players and Games' emblem.

1977, July 28 Litho. *Perf. 12½x12*

C269 AP94 60fr multi .35 .20
C270 AP94 200fr multi 1.10 .80

World Soccer Cup elimination games.
For surcharges see Nos. C289A, C308.

Miss Haverfield, by Gainsborough — AP95

Designs: 150fr, Self-portrait, by Rubens. 200fr, Anguish, man's head by Da Vinci.

1977, Oct. 3 Engr. *Perf. 13*

C271 AP95 100fr sl grn & mar 1.00 .40
C272 AP95 150fr red brn & dk brn 1.50 .60
C273 AP95 200fr brn & red 2.00 .80
Nos. C271-C273 (3) 4.50 1.80

For surcharges see Nos. C309, C317.

No. C265 Overprinted: "1er VOL COMMERCIAL / 22.11.77 PARIS NEW-YORK"

1977, Nov. 22 Engr. *Perf. 13*

C274 AP93 80fr ultra & red .75 .35

Concorde, 1st commercial flight, Paris to NY.

Viking on Mars — AP96

150fr, Isaac Newton, apple globe, stars. 200fr, Vladimir M. Komarov, spacecraft and earth. 500fr, Dog Laika, rocket and space.

1977, Nov. 28 Engr. *Perf. 13*

C275 AP96 100fr multi .50 .30
C276 AP96 150fr multi .90 .50
C277 AP96 200fr multi 1.40 .60
C278 AP96 500fr multi 3.25 2.00
Nos. C275-C278 (4) 6.05 3.40

Operation Viking on Mars; Isaac Newton (1642-1727); 10th death anniv. of Russian cosmonaut Vladimir M. Komarov; 20th anniv. of 1st living creature in space.

For surcharges see Nos. C301, C314, C497.

Monument, Red Star Place, Cotonou AP97

Lithographed; Gold Embossed

1977 Nov. 30 *Perf. 12½*

C279 AP97 500fr multi 3.50 1.50

Suzanne Fourment, by Rubens AP98

380fr, Nicholas Rubens, by Rubens.

1977, Dec. 12 Engr. *Perf. 13*

C280 AP98 200fr multi 1.60 .80
C281 AP98 380fr claret & ocher 2.60 1.40

For surcharges see Nos. C311, C313, C483.

Parthenon and UNESCO Emblem — AP99

Designs: 70fr, Acropolis and frieze showing Pan-Athenaic procession, vert. 250fr, Parthenon and frieze showing horsemen, vert.

1978, Sept. 22 Litho. *Perf. 12½x12*

C282 AP99 70fr multi .35 .20
C283 AP99 250fr multi 1.25 .80
C284 AP99 500fr multi 2.75 1.50
Nos. C282-C284 (3) 4.35 2.50

Save the Parthenon in Athens campaign.
For surcharge see No. C338.

Philexafrique II—Essen Issue

Common Design Types

Designs: No. C285, Buffalo and Dahomey #C33. No. C286, Wild ducks and Baden #1.

1978, Nov. 1 Litho. *Perf. 12½*

C285 CD138 100fr multi 1.75 .75
C286 CD139 100fr multi 1.75 .75
a. Pair, #C285-C286 3.50 1.50

Wilbur and Orville Wright and Flyer — AP100

1978, Dec. 28 Engr. *Perf. 13*

C287 AP100 500fr multi 3.50 2.00

75th anniversary of 1st powered flight.
For surcharge see No. C339.

Cook's Ships, Hawaii, World Map — AP101

Design: 50fr, Battle at Kowrowa.

1979, June 1 Engr. *Perf. 13*

C288 AP101 20fr multi .45 .20
C289 AP101 50fr multi .55 .25

Capt. James Cook (1728-1779), explorer.

No. C253, C269 Surcharged

1979

Perfs. & Printing Method as Before

C289A AP94 50fr on 60fr #C269
C289B AP87 50fr on 90fr multi

Lunokhod Type of 1980

1980, June 15 Engr. *Perf. 13*

Size: 27x48mm

C290 A133 210fr multi 1.40 .75

For surcharges see Nos. C305, C450.

Soccer Players — AP102

1981, Mar. 31 Litho. *Perf. 13*

C291 AP102 200fr Ball, globe .90 .90
C292 AP102 500fr shown 2.50 2.50

ESPANA '82 World Soccer Cup eliminations.
For surcharges see Nos. C335, C455, Q10B.

Prince Charles and Lady Diana, London Bridge — AP103

1981, July 29 Litho. *Perf. 12½*

C293 AP103 500fr multi 3.00 3.00

Royal wedding.
For surcharges see Nos. C323, C500.

Three Musicians, by Pablo Picasso (1881-1973) — AP104

Perf. 12½x13, 13x12½

1981, Nov. 2 Litho.

C294 AP104 300fr Dance, vert. 2.00 2.00
C295 AP104 500fr shown 3.50 3.50

For surcharges see Nos. C320, C340.

1300th Anniv. of Bulgaria AP105

1981, Dec. 2 Litho. *Perf. 13*

C296 AP105 100fr multi .60 .60

Visit of Pope John Paul II — AP106

1982, Feb. 17 Litho. *Perf. 13*

C297 AP106 80fr multi .55 .55

20th Anniv. of John Glenn's Flight — AP107

1982, Feb. 21 Litho. *Perf. 13*

C298 AP107 500fr multi 3.00 3.00

For surcharge see No. C315.

Scouting Year AP108

1982, June 1 *Perf. 12½*

C299 AP108 105fr multi .70 .70

For surcharge see No. C324.

Nos. C256, C275 Surcharged

1982, Nov. Engr. *Perf. 13*

C300 AP88 50fr on 210fr multi .35 .35
C301 AP96 50fr on 100fr multi .35 .35

Monet in Boat, by Claude Monet (1832-1883) — AP109

1982, Dec. 6 Litho. *Perf. 13x12½*

C302 AP109 300fr multi 2.00 2.00

For surcharge see No. C326.

Christmas 1982 AP110

Virgin and Child Paintings.

1982, Dec. 20 *Perf. 12½x13*

C303 AP110 200fr Matthias Grunewald 1.25 1.25
C304 AP110 300fr Correggio 1.75 1.75

For surcharges see Nos. C325, C337.

No. C290 Surcharged

1983 Engr. *Perf. 13*
C305 A133 75fr on 210fr multi .50 .50

Bangkok '83 Stamp Exhibition AP111

1983, Aug. 4 Photo. *Perf. 13*
C306 AP111 300fr multi 1.50 1.50

For surcharge see No. C322.

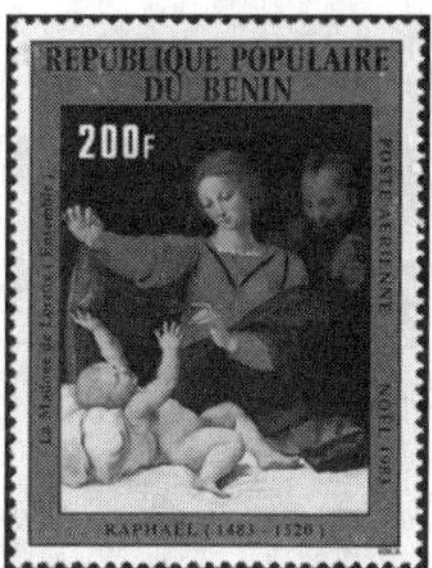

Christmas 1983 AP112

1983, Dec. 26 Litho. *Perf. 12½x13*
C307 AP112 200fr Loretto Madonna, by Raphael .65 .65

For surcharge see No. C319.

Types of 1976-82 Surcharged

1983, Nov.
C308 AP94 10fr on 200fr C270 .20 .20
C309 AP95 15fr on 200fr C273 .20 .20
C310 AP90 15fr on 270fr C261 .20 .20
C311 AP98 20fr on 200fr C280 .20 .20
C312 AP89 25fr on 270fr C258 .20 .20
C313 AP98 25fr on 380fr C281 .20 .20
C314 AP96 30fr on 200fr C277 .20 .20
C315 AP107 40fr on 500fr C298 .20 .20
C316 AP93 75fr on 150fr C266 .40 .40
C317 AP95 75fr on 150fr C272 .40 .40
Nos. C308-C317 (10) 2.40 2.40

Summer Olympics — AP113

1984, July 16 Litho. *Perf. 13x13½*
C318 AP113 300fr Sam the Eagle, mascot 1.00 1.00

Nos. C262, C293-C294, C299, C302-C303, C306-C307 Surcharged

1984, Sept.
C319 AP112 15fr on 200fr multi .20 .20
C320 AP104 15fr on 300fr multi .20 .20
C321 AP90 25fr on 300fr multi .20 .20
C322 AP111 25fr on 300fr multi .20 .20
C323 AP103 40fr on 500fr multi .20 .20
C324 AP108 75fr on 105fr multi .25 .25
C325 AP110 90fr on 200fr multi .30 .30
C326 AP109 90fr on 300fr multi .30 .30
Nos. C319-C326 (8) 1.85 1.85

Christmas 1984 AP114

1984, Dec. 17 Litho. *Perf. 12½x13*
C327 AP114 500fr Virgin and Child, by Murillo 1.50 1.50

For surcharge see No. C486

Ships — AP115

1984, Dec. 28 Litho. *Perf. 13*
C328 AP115 90fr Sidon merchant ship .30 .30
C329 AP115 125fr Wavertree, vert. .40 .40

Benin-S.O.M. Postal Convention AP116

Wmk. 385

1985, Apr. 15 Litho. *Perf. 13½*
C330 AP116 75fr Benin arms .25 .25
C331 AP116 75fr Sovereign Order of Malta .25 .25
a. Pair, #C330-C331 .45 .45

PHILEXAFRICA III, Lome — AP117

1985, June 24 *Perf. 13*
C332 AP117 200fr Oil platform .60 .60
C333 AP117 200fr Soccer players .60 .60
a. Pair, #C332-C333 + label 1.25 1.25

For surcharges see Nos. C485-C485A.

Stamps of 1977-82 Surcharged

1985, Mar.
C334 AP92 75fr on 200fr #C264 .20 .20
C335 AP102 75fr on 200fr #C291 .20 .20
C336 AP93 75fr on 300fr #C267 .20 .20
C337 AP110 75fr on 300fr #C304 .20 .20
C338 AP99 90fr on 500fr #C284 .25 .25
C339 AP100 90fr on 500fr #C287 .25 .25
C340 AP104 90fr on 500fr #C295 .25 .25
Nos. C334-C340 (7) 1.55 1.55

Dahomey Stamps of 1971-75 Surcharged

1985, Aug.
C341 AP87(i) 25fr on 40fr #C266 .20 .20
C342 AP49(a) 40fr #C142 .20 .20
C343 AP56(i) 75fr on 85fr #C164 .20 .20
C344 AP60(a) 75fr on 100fr #C173 .20 .20
C345 AP64(i) 75fr on 125fr #C186 .20 .20
C346 AP56(i) 90fr on 20fr #C163 .25 .25
C347 A61(i) 90fr on 150fr #C153 .25 .25
C348 AP49(a) 90fr on 200fr #C143 .25 .25
C349 AP78(j) 90fr on 200fr #C237 .25 .25
C350 AP78(j) 150fr #C236 .45 .45
Nos. C341-C350 (10) 2.45 2.45

Christmas — AP118

1985, Dec. 20 Litho. *Perf. 13x12½*
C351 AP118 500fr multi 1.75 1.75

For surcharge see No. C449.

Dahomey Nos. C34-C37, C84, C131 Surcharged or Overprinted

1986 Photo. Perfs. as before
C352 AP33(b) 75fr on 70fr #C84 .25 .25
C353 AP14(b) 75fr on 100fr #C34 .25 .25
C354 AP15(b) 75fr on 200fr #C35 .25 .25
C355 AP15(b) 90fr on 250fr #C36 .35 .35
C356 AP45(b) 100fr #C131 .40 .40
C357 AP14(b) 150fr on 500fr #C37 .50 .50
Nos. C352-C357 (6) 2.00 2.00

Issued: 75fr, 90fr, Mar; 100fr, 150fr, June.

Dahomey Nos. C82, C139, C141, C146 Surcharged

1986

Perfs. & Printing Methods as Before
C357A AP33(d) 15fr on 45fr #C82
C357B AP48(d) 25fr on 200fr #C141 (S)
C357D AP48(d) 100fr on #C139
C357E CD135(d) 100fr on #C146

Christmas — AP119

1986, Dec. 24 Litho. *Perf. 13x12½*
C358 AP119 300fr multi 1.25 1.25

Air Africa, 25th Anniv. AP120

1986, Dec. 30 *Perf. 12½*
C359 AP120 100fr multi .40 .40

Intl. Agricultural Development Fund (FIDA), 10th Anniv. — AP121

1987, Dec. 14 Litho. *Perf. 13½*
C360 AP121 500fr multi 3.50 3.50

Christmas — AP122

1988, Dec. 23 Litho. *Perf. 13x12½*
C361 AP122 500fr Adoration of the Magi, storyteller 3.25 3.25

No. C241 Surcharged

1989, Apr. 24 Litho. *Perf. 13*
C362 AP84(b) 15fr on 85fr multi .20 .20

Dahomey Nos. C37, C53, C152, C156, C165, C175, C182, C234 Benin No. C242 Surcharged or Overprinted

République Populaire du Bénin

1987

Perfs. & Printing Methods as Before
C363 AP77 20fr on 250fr #C234
C364 AP48(b) 25fr on 150fr #C175 (S&B)
C365 AP63(b) 40fr on 15fr #C182
C366 AP48(b) 40fr on 100fr #C152
C367 AP84(b) 50fr on 140fr #C242
C368 AP14(b) 50fr on 500fr #C37
C369 AP22(b) 80fr on #C53
C370 AP56(b) 80fr on 150fr #C165
C373 AP52(b) 100fr on #C156

Dahomey Nos. C140, C144, C158, C166, C177, C185, C188 C191, C195, C207, C262 Surcharged

1988

Perfs. & Printing Methods as Before
C374 AP50(d) 10fr on 50fr #C144
C375 AP64(d) 10fr on 65fr #C185
C376 AP72(d) 15fr on 150fr #C207
C377 AP67(d) 25fr on 200fr #C191
C378 AP61(d) 40fr on 35fr #C195
C380 AP53(d) 70fr on 250fr #C158
C381 AP48(d) 100fr on #C140
C382 AP65(d) 100fr on #C188
C384 AP61(f) 125fr on #C177
C385 AP86(d) 125fr on 75fr #C262
C386 AP57(d) 150fr on 100fr #C166

Dahomey Nos. C181, C196, C208 Surcharged

1988

Perfs. & Printing Methods as Before
C388 AP61(d) 25fr on 100fr #C196
C390 AP62 40fr on 100fr #C181
C391 AP73(d) 40fr on 150fr #C208

Dahomey Nos. C108, C147-C148, C162, C167, C178, C187, C194

1992

Perfs. & Printing Methods as Before
C394 AP51(f) 70fr on #C148
C395 AP55(e) 100fr on #C162
C396 AP68(g) 100fr on #C194
C397 AP51(e) 125fr on 40fr #C147
C398 A52(f) 125fr on 70fr #C108
C400 AP64a(e) 125fr on 100fr #C187
C401 AP61(f) 190fr on 140fr #C178
C402 AP58(f) 190fr on 150fr #C167

Dahomey Nos. C145, C149-C150, C182, C189, C198, C257, C264-C265 Surcharged Benin No. C241 Surcharged

1993

Perfs. & Printing Methods as Before
C403 AP51(e) 5fr on 100fr #C149
C404 AP50(f) 10fr on 100fr #C145
C405 AP51(f) 20fr on 200fr #C150
C406 AP83(f) 20fr on 500fr #C257

C407 AP84(e) 25fr on 85fr #C241
C409 AP63(f) 30fr on 15fr #C182
C410 AP61(f) 30fr on 200fr #C198
C411 AP66(b) 35fr on #C189
C412 AP86(g) 300fr on #C264

Dahomey Nos. C14, C31, C34, C54, C101, C110, C128, C144, C151, C153, C155, C197, C222, C234, C250, C254-C256, C261, Benin C242 Surcharged or Overprinted

1994-95?
Perfs. & Printing Methods as Before

C414 AP52(e) 15fr on 40fr #C155
C415 AP83(f) 25fr on 200fr #C256
C416 AP83(f) 35fr on #C255
C417 AP49(g) 50fr on #C101
C418 AP48(g) 75fr on 40fr #C151
C419 AP4(g) 100fr on #C14
C420 AP22(h) 100fr #C54
C421 AP50(g) 125fr on 50fr #C144
C422 AP75(e) 125fr on 65fr #C222
C425 AP21(f) 135fr on 45fr #C110
C429 AP43(e) 135fr on 70fr #C128
C430 AP81(f) 135fr on 250fr #C250
C432 AP84(f) 150fr on 140fr #C242
C433 A61(b) 150fr on #C153
C434 AP61(f) 150fr on #C197
C435 AP13(e) 200fr on 100fr #C31
C436 AP14(e) 200fr on 100fr #C34
C439 AP61(e) 200fr on 100fr #C253 — —
C445 AP61(e) 200fr on 250fr #C234
C446 AP61(e) 200fr on 250fr #C254
C447 AP85(f) 300fr on #C261

Dahomey No. C37, Benin No. C351 Surcharged

1994-95
Printing Method and Perfs as Before

C449 AP118 200fr on 500fr #C351

Benin No. C290 Surcharged
Dahomey Nos. C206, C257 Surcharged

1996?
Perfs. & Printing Methods as Before

C450 A133 40fr on 210fr #C290
C451 AP83(f) 200fr on 500fr #C257
C452 AP72(f) 1000fr on 150fr #C206

Dahomey No. C265 Surcharged
Benin Nos. C258, C292 Surcharged

1996?
Perfs. & Printing Methods as Before

C453 AP86(g) 25fr on 500fr #C265
C454 AP89 35fr on 270fr #C258
C455 AP102 100fr on 500fr #C292

Dahomey Nos. C61, C74, C85, C88, C94, C106, C109, C111, C113, C115, C120, C124-C125, C130, C135-C136, C138, C142-C143, C150, C157, C204-C205, C207-C208, C260, C263 Surcharged

1996?
Perfs. & Printing Methods as Before

C456 AP48(e) 70fr on 100fr #C138
C457 AP34(h) 150fr on #C88
C458 AP21(e) 150fr on #C115
C459 AP72(e) 150fr on #C207
C460 AP73(h) 150fr on #C208
C461 AP34(e) 150fr on 30fr #C85
C462 AP31(h) 150fr on 30fr #C74
C463 AP21(e) 150fr on 30fr #C109
C464 AP40(e) 150fr on 40fr on 30fr #C120
C465 AP47(e) 150fr on 40fr #C136
C466 AP49(e) 150fr on 40fr #C142
C467 CD128(h) 150fr on 50fr #C94
C468 AP38(h) 150fr on 50fr #C106
C469 AP71(e) 150fr on 50fr #C204
C470 AP54(h) 150fr on 70fr #C124
C471 CD124(h) 150fr on 100fr #C61
C472 AP21(e) 150fr on 100fr #C113
C473 AP53(h) 150fr on 100fr #C157
C474 AP84(h) 150fr on 100fr #C260
C475 AP21(h) 150fr on 110fr #C111
C476 AP44(h) 150fr on 110fr #C130
C477 AP54(h) 150fr on 120fr #C125
C478 AP86(g) 150fr on 135fr #C263
C479 AP46(h) 150fr on 200fr #C135
C480 AP49(e) 150fr on 200fr #C143
C481 AP51(h) 150fr on 200fr #C150
C482 AP71(e) 150fr on 200fr #C205

Benin Nos. C261, C281, C327, C332-C333 Surcharged
Dahomey Nos. C201, C127, C175 Surcharged

1996-97?
Perfs. & Printing Methods as Before

C483 AP98 30fr on 380fr #C281
C484 AP90 35fr on 270fr #C261
C485 AP117 125fr on 200fr #C332
C485A AP117 125fr on 200fr #C333
C486 AP114 200fr on 500fr #C327
C488 AP43(h) 150fr on 40fr #C127
C489 AP70(f) 150fr on 50fr #C201
C490 AP48(e) 200fr on 150fr #C175

No. C256, 278 Surcharged
Method and Perf. as Before

1995-96 ?

C494 AP88 40fr on 210fr #C256 ('96)
C497 AP96 150fron 500fr #C278 — —

Benin #C293 Surcharged
Dahomey #C147, C250 Surcharged Type f

1995-97?
Perf. & Printing Methods as Before

C500 AP103 150fr on 500fr #C293
C503 AP51(e) 135fr on 40fr #C147
C509 AP81(f) 150fr on 250fr #C250

Dahomey Nos. #C86, C126, C70 Surcharged

1995-99?
Perfs. & Printing Methods as Before

C513 AP34(h) 35fr on 45fr #C86
C515 AP42(h) 35fr on 100fr on 200fr #C126
C516 AP29(h) 35fr on 100fr #C70

Dahomey No. C105 Surcharged
Method and Perf. as Before

1997 ?

C523 A51(h) 35fr on 100fr #C105

POSTAGE DUE STAMPS

French Colony

Handstamped in Black on Postage Due Stamps of French Colonies

BENIN

1894		Unwmk.	Imperf.	
J1	D1	5c black	125.00	45.00
J2	D1	10c black	125.00	45.00
J3	D1	20c black	125.00	45.00
J4	D1	30c black	125.00	45.00
		Nos. J1-J4 (4)	500.00	180.00

Nos. J1-J4 exist with overprint in various positions.

Catalogue values for unused stamps in this section are for Never Hinged items.

People's Republic

Pineapples
D6

Mail Delivery
D7

Designs: 20fr, Cashew, vert. 40fr, Oranges. 50fr, Akee. 80fr, Mail delivery by boat.

1978, Sept. 5		**Photo.**	***Perf. 13***	
J44	D6	10fr multicolored	.20	.20
J45	D6	20fr multicolored	.20	.20
J46	D6	40fr multicolored	.30	.20
J47	D6	50fr multicolored	.45	.25
		Engr.		
J48	D7	60fr multi	.30	.25
J49	D7	80fr multi	.45	.30
		Nos. J44-J49 (6)	1.90	1.40

PARCEL POST STAMPS

Catalogue values for unused stamps in this section are for Never Hinged items.

Nos. 448-448A, 459, 473, C292 Overprinted or Surcharged "Colis Postaux"

Perfs. and Printing Methods as Before

1982, Nov.				
Q8	A126	100fr on 150fr	.40	.20
Q9	A130	100fr multi	.40	.20
Q10	A134	300fr multi	1.25	.60
Q10A	A126a	1000fr multi	5.50	5.50
Q10B	AP102	5000fr on 500fr	27.50	27.50
		Nos. Q8-Q10B (5)	35.05	34.00

Dahomey No. C205 Surcharged

1989	**Photo.**	***Perf. 12½x13***	
Q11 AP71	500fr on 200fr multi	3.25	3.25

BERMUDA

bər-ˈmyü-də

LOCATION — A group of about 150 small islands of which only 20 are inhabited, lying in the Atlantic Ocean about 580 miles southeast of Cape Hatteras.
GOVT. — British Crown Colony
AREA — 20.5 sq. mi.
POP. — 62,471 (1999 est.)
CAPITAL — Hamilton

Bermuda achieved internal self-government in 1968.

4 Farthings = 1 Penny
12 Pence = 1 Shilling
20 Shillings = 1 Pound
100 Cents = 1 Dollar (1970)

Catalogue values for unused stamps in this country are for Never Hinged items, beginning with Scott 131.

POSTMASTER STAMPS

PM1

1848-54	**Unwmk.**	***Imperf.***
X1 PM1 1p blk, *bluish* (1848)		*125,000.*
a. Dated 1849		*135,000.*
X2 PM1 1p red, *bluish* (1856)		*175,000.*
a. Dated 1854		*225,000.*
X3 PM1 1p red (1853)		*160,000.*

PM2

1860	
X4 PM2 (1p) red, *yellowish*	*100,000.*

Same inscribed "HAMILTON"

1861	
X5 PM2 (1p) red, *bluish*	*130,000.*

Nos. X1-X3 were produced and used by Postmaster William B. Perot of Hamilton. No. X4 is attributed to Postmaster James H. Thies of St. George's.

Only a few of each stamp exist. Values reflect actual sales figures for stamps in the condition in which they are found.

GENERAL ISSUES

Values for unused stamps are for examples with original gum as defined in the catalogue introduction. Very fine examples of Nos. 1-1a, 2-15b will have perforations touching the design (or framelines where applicable) on at least one side due to the narrow spacing of the stamps on the plates. Stamps with perfs clear of the design on all four sides are scarce and will command higher prices.

Queen Victoria
A1 A2

A3

A4

A5

1865-74		**Typo.**	**Wmk. 1**	***Perf. 14***
1	A1	1p rose red	80.00	2.50
b.		Imperf.	*22,500.*	*13,750.*
2	A2	2p blue ('66)	225.00	17.50
3	A3	3p buff ('73)	425.00	60.00
4	A4	6p brown lilac	900.	100.00
5	A4	6p lilac ('74)	21.00	16.00
6	A5	1sh green	250.00	42.50
		Nos. 1-6 (6)	1,901.	238.50

See Nos. 7-9, 19-21, 23, 25. For surcharges see Nos. 10-15.
No. 1b is a proof.

1882-1903 **Perf. 14x12½**

7 A3 3p buff 160.00 55.00
8 A4 6p violet ('03) 15.00 20.00
9 A5 1sh green ('94) 20.00 110.00
 a. Vert. strip of 3, perf. all around & imperf. btwn. 13,000. 15,000.
 Nos. 7-9 (3) 195.00 185.00

Handstamped Diagonally

1874 **Perf. 14**

10 A5 3p on 1sh green 1,400. 950.

Handstamped Diagonally

11 A1 3p on 1p rose 12,500. —
12 A5 3p on 1sh green 2,250. 900.
 a. "P" with top like "R" 2,250. 1,100.

No. 11 is stated to be an essay, but a few copies are known used. Nos. 10-12 are found with double or partly double surcharges.

Surcharged in Black

1875

13 A2 1p on 2p blue 700.00 375.00
 a. Without period 11,000. 7,250.
14 A3 1p on 3p buff 450.00 350.00
15 A5 1p on 1sh green 500.00 300.00
 a. Inverted surcharge — 17,500.
 b. Without period 13,750. 8,750.

A6 A7

1880 **Wmk. 1**

16 A6 ½p brown 2.25 3.75
17 A7 4p orange 15.00 2.50

See Nos. 18, 24.

A8 A9

1883-1904 **Wmk. 2**

18 A6 ½p dp gray grn ('93) 2.50 2.50
 a. ½p green ('92) 2.25 .75
19 A1 1p aniline car ('89) 7.50 .30
 a. 1p dull rose 125.00 4.00
 b. 1p rose red 70.00 3.00
 c. 1p carmine rose ('86) 45.00 .90
20 A2 2p blue ('86) 50.00 3.50
21 A2 2p brn pur ('98) 3.00 2.50
 a. 2p aniline pur ('93) 11.00 4.00
22 A8 2½p ultra ('84) 6.00 .50
 a. 2½p deep ultra 12.00 2.25
23 A3 3p gray ('86) 20.00 6.00
24 A7 4p brown org ('04) 27.50 55.00
25 A5 1sh olive bister ('93) 16.00 15.00
 a. 1sh yellow brown 15.00 14.00
 Nos. 18-25 (8) 132.50 85.30

Black Surcharge

1901

26 A9 1f on 1sh gray .80 .50

Dry Dock — A10

1902-03

28 A10 ½p gray grn & blk ('03) 8.00 2.25
29 A10 1p car rose & brown 7.00 .35
30 A10 3p ol grn & violet 2.50 3.50
 Nos. 28-30 (3) 17.50 6.10

1906-10 **Wmk. 3**

31 A10 ¼p pur & brn ('08) 1.40 1.40
32 A10 ½p gray grn & blk 16.00 1.50
33 A10 ½p green ('09) 10.00 2.25
34 A10 1p car rose & brn 20.00 .20
35 A10 1p carmine ('08) 16.00 .90
36 A10 2p orange & gray 6.75 10.00
37 A10 2½p blue & brown 12.50 11.50
38 A10 2½p ultra ('10) 11.00 8.50
39 A10 4p vio brn & blue ('09) 2.75 14.00
 Nos. 31-39 (9) 96.40 50.25

Caravel A11

King George V A12

1910-20 **Engr.** **Perf. 14**

40 A11 ¼p brown 1.40 2.25
41 A11 ½p yel green 1.10 .30
 a. ½p dark green 5.75 1.25
42 A11 1p rose red (I) 12.50 .35
 a. 1p carmine (I) 42.50 7.00
43 A11 2p gray 2.75 7.00
44 A11 2½p ultra (I) 3.25 .55
45 A11 3p violet, yel 1.60 5.50
46 A11 4p red, yellow 4.25 10.00
47 A11 6p claret 10.00 7.00
48 A11 1sh blk, green 3.50 4.50
 a. 1sh black, olive 4.00 11.50

Typographed

Chalky Paper

49 A12 2sh ultra & dl vio, bl ('20) 16.00 45.00
50 A12 2sh6p red & blk, bl 25.00 65.00
51 A12 4sh car & black ('20) 55.00 125.00
52 A12 5sh red & grn, yellow 45.00 75.00
53 A12 10sh red & grn, green 140.00 300.00
54 A12 £1 black & vio, red 350.00 500.00
 Nos. 40-54 (15) 671.35 1,147.

Types I of 1p and 2½p are illustrated above Nos. 81-97.

The 1p was printed from two plates, the 2nd of which, #42a, exists only in carmine on opaque paper with a bluish tinge. Compare #MR1 (as #42) and MR2 (as #42a).

Revenue cancellations are found on Nos. 52-54.

See Nos. 81-97.

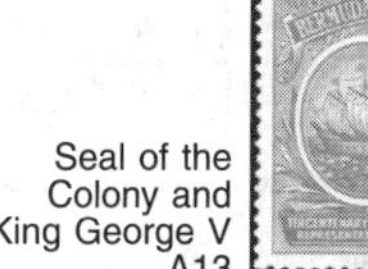

Seal of the Colony and King George V A13

1920-21 **Wmk. 3** **Ordinary Paper**

55 A13 ¼p brown 2.25 12.00
56 A13 ½p green 2.25 6.25
57 A13 2p gray 9.25 27.50

Chalky Paper

58 A13 3p vio & dl vio, yel 8.50 24.00
59 A13 4p red & blk, yellow 9.25 24.00
60 A13 1sh blk, gray grn 12.50 37.50

Ordinary Paper

Wmk. 4

67 A13 1p rose red 2.75 .25
68 A13 2½p ultra 9.25 8.50

Chalky Paper

69 A13 6p red vio & dl vio 19.00 50.00
 Nos. 55-60,67-69 (9) 75.00 190.00

Issued: 6p, 1/19/21; others, 11/11/20.

King George V A14

1921, May 12 **Engr.**

71 A14 ¼p brown .45 2.75
72 A14 ½p green 3.50 4.50
73 A14 1p carmine 2.50 .25

Wmk. 3

74 A14 2p gray 6.00 20.00
75 A14 2½p ultra 6.00 2.25
76 A14 3p vio, orange 4.25 11.50
77 A14 4p scarlet, org 8.00 15.00
78 A14 6p claret 8.50 32.50
79 A14 1sh blk, green 16.00 35.00
 Nos. 71-79 (9) 55.20 123.75

Tercentenary of "Local Representative Institutions" (Nos. 55-79).

Types of 1910-20 Issue

Types of 1p: 1d (I) 1d (II) 1d (III)

Types of 2½p: 2½d (I) 2½d (II)

Three types of the 1d value: type I, figure "1" has pointed serifs, scroll at top left very weak; type II, thick "1" with square serifs, scroll weak; type III, thinner "1" with long square serifs, scroll complete with strong line. Two types of the 2½d value: type I, small "d," short, thick figures of value; type II, larger "d," taller, thinner figures of value.

1922-34 **Wmk. 4**

81 A11 ¼p brown ('28) .30 .75
82 A11 ½p green .20 .20
83 A11 1p car, III ('28) 7.50 .30
 a. 1p carmine, II ('26) 17.50 1.00
 b. 1p carmine, I 15.00 .60
84 A11 1½p red brown ('34) 3.00 .30
85 A11 2p gray ('23) 1.00 1.00
86 A11 2½p ap grn ('23) 1.00 1.00
87 A11 2½p ultra, II ('32) 2.00 .35
 a. 2½p ultra, I ('26) 2.25 .50
88 A11 3p ultra ('24) 14.00 20.00
89 A11 3p vio, yellow ('26) .80 .60
90 A11 4p red, yellow ('24) 1.00 1.00
91 A11 6p claret ('24) .80 .80
92 A11 1sh blk, emer ('27) 5.00 5.00
93 A11 1sh brn blk, yel grn ('34) 30.00 40.00

Chalky Paper

94 A12 2sh ultra & vio, bl ('27) 30.00 40.00
 a. 2sh bl & dp vio, dp bl ('31) 40.00 50.00
95 A12 2sh 6p red & blk, bl ('27) 40.00 37.50
 a. 2sh6p pale org ver & blk, gray bl ('30) 2,750. 2,250.
 b. 2sh6p dp ver & blk, deep blue ('31) 70.00 80.00
96 A12 10sh red & grn, emer ('24) 150.00 175.00
 a. 10sh dp red & pale grn, dp emer ('31) 125.00 200.00
97 A12 12sh 6p ocher & gray blk ('32) 300.00 350.00
 Nos. 81-97 (17) 586.60 673.80

Revenue cancellations are found on Nos. 94-97.

For the 12sh6p with "Revenue" on both sides, see #AR1.

Common Design Types pictured following the introduction.

Silver Jubilee Issue

Common Design Type

1935, May 6 *Perf. 11x12*

No.	Type	Denom.	Color	Unused	Used
100	CD301	1p	car & dk bl	.40	.35
101	CD301	1½p	blk & ultra	.60	*1.10*
102	CD301	2½p	ultra & brn	1.00	.55
103	CD301	1sh	brn vio & ind	10.50	*13.00*
			Nos. 100-103 (4)	12.50	*15.00*
			Set, never hinged	14.00	

Hamilton Harbor — A15

Yacht "Lucie" — A17

South Shore — A16

Grape Bay — A18

Typical Cottage — A19

Scene at Par-la-Ville — A20

1936-40 *Perf. 12*

No.	Type	Denom.	Color	Unused	Used
105	A15	½p	blue green	.20	.20
106	A16	1p	car & black	.20	.20
107	A16	1½p	choc & black	.65	.40
108	A17	2p	lt bl & blk	3.00	2.00
109	A17	2p	brn blk & turq bl ('38)	29.00	8.75
109A	A17	2p	red & ultra ('40)	1.00	1.00
110	A18	2½p	dk bl & lt bl	.65	.25
111	A19	3p	car & black	1.75	1.25
112	A20	6p	vio & rose lake	.50	.20
113	A18	1sh	deep green	2.75	*8.25*
114	A15	1sh6p	brown	.30	.25
			Nos. 105-114 (11)	40.00	22.75
			Set, never hinged	65.00	

No. 108, blue border and black center.
No. 109, black border, blue center.

Coronation Issue

Common Design Type

1937, May 14 *Perf. 13½x14*

No.	Type	Denom.	Color	Unused	Used
115	CD302	1p	carmine	.25	.20
116	CD302	1½p	brown	.30	.20
117	CD302	2½p	bright ultra	.55	.35
			Nos. 115-117 (3)	1.10	.75
			Set, never hinged	1.50	

Hamilton Harbor — A21

Grape Bay — A22

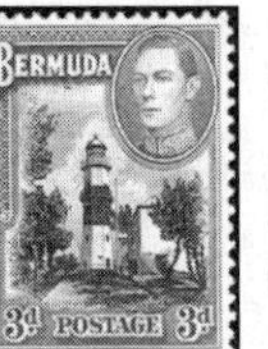

St. David's Lighthouse A23

King George VI A25

Bermudian Water Scene and Yellow-billed Tropic Bird — A24

1938-51 **Wmk. 4** *Perf. 12*

No.	Type	Denom.	Color	Unused	Used
118	A21	1p	red & black ('40)	.40	.20
a.			1p rose red & black	12.00	1.00
119	A21	1½p	vio brn & bl	3.25	.85
a.			1½p dl vio brn & bl ('43)	2.00	.20
120	A22	2½p	blue & lt bl	6.25	.70
120A	A22	2½p	ol brn & lt bl ('41)	1.75	.85
b.			2½p dk ol blk & pale blue ('43)	2.00	1.00
121	A23	3p	car & blk	10.00	1.40
121A	A23	3p	dp ultra & blk ('42)	1.00	.20
c.			3p brt ultra & blk ('41)	.25	.20
121D	A24	7½p	yel grn, bl & blk ('41)	3.75	1.40
122	A22	1sh	green	1.10	.30

Typo.

Perf. 13

No.	Type	Denom.	Color	Unused	Used
123	A25	2sh	ultra & red vio, *bl* ('50)	9.50	8.50
a.			2sh ultra & vio, *bl*, perf. 14	6.75	2.50
b.			2sh ultra & dl vio, *bl* (mottled paper), perf. 14 ('42)	6.75	2.50
124	A25	2sh 6p	red & blk, *bl*	10.50	6.25
a.			Perf. 14	20.00	6.50
125	A25	5sh	red & grn, *yel*	12.50	11.50
a.			Perf. 14	45.00	15.00
126	A25	10sh	red & grn, *grn* ('51)	30.00	*24.00*
a.			10sh brn lake & grn, *grn*, perf. 14	100.00	75.00
b.			10sh red & grn, *grn*, perf. 14 ('39)	175.00	150.00
127	A25	12sh 6p	org & gray blk	65.00	55.00
a.			12sh 6p org & gray, perf. 14	85.00	45.00
b.			12sh 6p yel & gray, perf. 14 ('47)	550.00	450.00
c.			12sh 6p brn org & gray, perf. 14	200.00	80.00

Wmk. 3

No.	Type	Denom.	Color	Unused	Used
128	A25	£1	blk & vio, *red* ('51)	40.00	*47.50*
a.			£1 blk & pur, *red*, perf. 14	225.00	100.00
b.			£1 blk & dk vio, *salmon*, perf. 14 ('42)	65.00	50.00
			Nos. 118-128 (14)	195.00	158.65
			Set, never hinged	250.00	

No. 127b is the so-called "lemon yellow" shade.

Revenue cancellations are found on Nos. 123-128. Copies with removed revenue cancellations and forged postmarks are abundant.

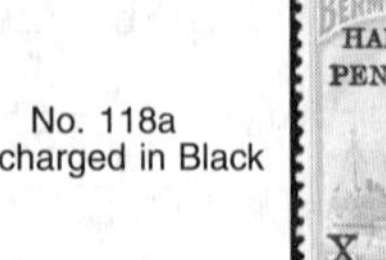

No. 118a Surcharged in Black

1940, Dec. 20 **Wmk. 4** *Perf. 12*

No.	Type	Denom.	Color	Unused	Used
129	A21	½p on 1p	rose red & blk	.30	.30
			Never hinged	.50	

Catalogue values for unused stamps in this section, from this point to the end of the section, are for Never Hinged items.

Peace Issue

Common Design Type

Perf. 13½x14

1946, Nov. 6 **Engr.** **Wmk. 4**

No.	Type	Denom.	Color	Unused	Used
131	CD303	1½p	brown	.20	.20
132	CD303	3p	deep blue	.30	.30

Silver Wedding Issue

Common Design Types

1948, Dec. 1 **Photo.** *Perf. 14x14½*

No.	Type	Denom.	Color	Unused	Used
133	CD304	1½p	red brown	.20	.20

Engr.; Name Typo.

Perf. 11½x11

No.	Type	Denom.	Color	Unused	Used
134	CD305	£1	rose carmine	47.50	47.50

Postmaster Stamp of 1848 — A26

1949, Apr. 11 **Engr.** *Perf. 13x13½*

No.	Type	Denom.	Color	Unused	Used
135	A26	2½p	dk brown & dp bl	.20	.20
136	A26	3p	dp blue & black	.20	.20
137	A26	6p	green & rose vio	.45	.45
			Nos. 135-137 (3)	.85	.85

No. 137 shows a different floral arrangement.
Bermuda's first postage stamp, cent.

UPU Issue

Common Design Types

Engr.; Name Typo.

1949, Oct. 10 *Perf. 13½, 11x11½*

No.	Type	Denom.	Color	Unused	Used
138	CD306	2½p	slate	.50	.50
139	CD307	3p	indigo	.65	.65
140	CD308	6p	rose violet	1.10	1.10
141	CD309	1sh	blue green	2.25	2.25
			Nos. 138-141 (4)	4.50	4.50

Coronation Issue

Common Design Type

1953, June 4 **Engr.** *Perf. 13½x13*

No.	Type	Denom.	Color	Unused	Used
142	CD312	1½p	dk blue & blk	.40	.20

A27

Easter Lilies — A28

Designs: 1p, 4p, Perot stamp. 2p, Racing dinghy. 2½p, Sir George Somers and "Sea Venture." 3p, 1sh3p, Map. 4½p, 9p, "Sea Venture," boat, hog coin and Perot stamp. 6p, 8p, Yellow-billed tropic bird. 1sh, Hog coins. 2sh, Arms of St. George. 2sh6p, Warwick Fort. 5sh, Hog coin. 10sh, Earliest hog coin. £1, Arms of Bermuda.

1953-58 *Perf. 13½x13, 13x13½*

No.	Type	Denom.	Color	Unused	Used
143	A27	½p	olive green	.40	.20
144	A27	1p	rose red & blk	1.00	.20
145	A28	1½p	dull green	.20	.20
146	A27	2p	red & ultra	.30	.20
147	A27	2½p	carmine rose	1.25	.20
148	A27	3p	vio *(Sandy's)*	.20	.20
149	A27	3p	violet *(Sandys)* ('57)	.65	.20
150	A27	4p	dp ultra & blk	.20	.20
151	A27	4½p	green	.65	.60
152	A27	6p	dk bluish grn & blk	3.50	.30
153	A27	8p	red & blk ('55)	1.60	.35
154	A27	9p	violet ('58)	5.00	.95
155	A27	1sh	orange	.30	.20
156	A27	1sh3p	blue *(Sandy's)*	2.25	.35
157	A27	1sh3p	blue *(Sandys)* ('57)	4.50	.50
158	A27	2sh	yellow brown	2.50	.65
159	A28	2sh6p	scarlet	3.00	1.25
160	A27	5sh	dp car rose	12.50	2.00
161	A27	10sh	deep ultra	8.50	4.50

Engr. and Typo.

No.	Type	Denom.	Color	Unused	Used
162	A27	£1	dp ol grn & multi	16.00	*17.50*
			Nos. 143-162 (20)	64.50	30.75

For overprints, see Nos. 164-167.

Type of 1953 Inscribed "ROYAL VISIT 1953"

Design: 6p, Yellow-billed tropic bird.

1953, Nov. 26 **Engr.**

No.	Type	Denom.	Color	Unused	Used
163	A27	6p	dk bluish grn & blk	.40	.35

Visit of Queen Elizabeth II and the Duke of Edinburgh, 1953.

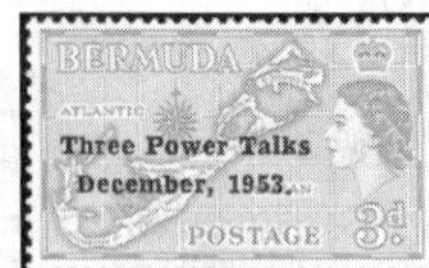

Nos. 148 and 156 Overprinted in Violet Blue or Red

1953, Dec. 8 *Perf. 13½x13*

No.	Type	Denom.	Color	Unused	Used
164	A27	3p	violet	.20	.20
165	A27	1sh3p	blue (R)	.45	.40

Three Power Conference, Tucker's Town, December 1953.

Nos. 153 and 156 Overprinted in Black or Red

1956, June 22

No.	Type	Denom.	Color	Unused	Used
166	A27	8p	red & black	.25	.30
167	A27	1sh3p	blue (R)	.35	.50

Newport-Bermuda Yacht Race, 50th anniv.

Perot Post Office, Hamilton A29

Perf. 13½x13

1959, Jan. 1 **Engr.** **Wmk. 4**

No.	Type	Denom.	Color	Unused	Used
168	A29	6p	lilac & black	.50	.30

Restoration and reopening of the post office operated at Hamilton by W. B. Perot in the mid-nineteenth century.

Arms of James I and Elizabeth II — A30

Engr. and Litho.

1959, July 29 **Wmk. 314** *Perf. 13*

Coats of Arms in Blue, Yellow & Red

No.	Type	Denom.	Color	Unused	Used
169	A30	1½p	dark blue	.35	.35
170	A30	3p	gray	.40	.40
171	A30	4p	rose violet	.50	.50
172	A30	8p	violet gray	.50	.50
173	A30	9p	olive green	.50	.50
174	A30	1sh3p	orange brown	.50	.50
			Nos. 169-174 (6)	2.75	2.75

350th anniv. of the shipwreck of the "Sea Venture" which resulted in the first permanent settlement of Bermuda.

The Old Rectory, St. George's, 1730 A31

Designs: 2p, Church of St. Peter. 3p, Government House. 4p, Cathedral, Hamilton. 5p, No. 185A, H.M. Dockyard. 6p, Perot's Post Office, 1848. 8p, General Post Office, 1869.

9p, Library and Historical Society. 1sh, Christ Church, Warwick, 1719. 1sh3p, City Hall, Hamilton. 10p, No. 185, Bermuda Cottage, 1705. 2sh, Town of St. George. 2sh3p, Bermuda House, 1710. 2sh6p, Bermuda House, 18th century. 5sh, Colonial Secretariat, 1833. 10sh, Old Post Office, Somerset, 1890. £1, House of Assembly, 1815.

Wmk. 314 Upright

1962-65 Photo. *Perf. 12½*

175 A31 1p org, lil & blk .20 *.45*
176 A31 2p sl, lt vio, grn & yel .25 .20
a. Light vio omitted *800.00* 650.00
b. Green omitted 2,500.
d. Imperf., pair *1,250.*
177 A31 3p lt bl & yel brn .20 .20
a. Yellow brown omitted *3,750.*
178 A31 4p car rose & red brn .20 *.30*
179 A31 5p dk bl & pink 1.25 *2.25*
180 A31 6p emer, lt & dk bl .20 .20
181 A31 8p grn, dp org & ultra .25 .25
182 A31 9p org brn & grnsh bl .20 *.25*
182A A31 10p brt vio & bis ('65) 6.75 1.25
183 A31 1sh multi .20 .20
184 A31 1sh3p sl, lem & rose car .65 .25
185 A31 1sh6p brt vio & bis 1.10 1.00
186 A31 2sh brn & org 2.50 1.00
187 A31 2sh3p brn & brt yel grn 1.25 *5.00*
188 A31 2sh6p grn, yel & sep .45 .40
189 A31 5sh choc & brt grn 1.10 *1.25*
190 A31 10sh dl grn, buff & rose car 3.75 *4.50*
191 A31 £1 cit, bis, blk & org 12.00 11.00
Nos. 175-191 (18) 32.50 29.95

See #252a. For surcharges see #238-254.

1966-69 Wmk. 314 Sideways

Unnamed Colors as in 1962-65 Issue

176c A31 2p ('69) 5.00 *5.50*
181a A31 8p ('67) .50 *1.40*
182b A31 10p .70 .55
183a A31 1sh ('67) .60 *1.25*
185A A31 1sh6p indigo & rose 2.10 *.45*
186a A31 2sh ('67) 2.10 .85
Nos. 176c-186a (6) 11.00 10.00

For surcharges see #239, 245-246, 248-249.

Freedom from Hunger Issue

Common Design Type

1963, June 4 *Perf. 14x14½*

192 CD314 1sh3p sepia 2.25 2.00

Red Cross Centenary Issue

Common Design Type

Wmk. 314

1963, Sept. 2 Litho. *Perf. 13*

193 CD315 3p black & red .50 .30
194 CD315 1sh3p ultra & red 4.00 4.00

Finn Boat — A32

Wmk. 314

1964, Sept. 28 Photo. *Perf. 13½*

195 A32 3p blue, vio & red .25 .25

18th Olympic Games, Tokyo, Oct. 10-25.

ITU Issue

Common Design Type

Perf. 11x11½

1965, May 17 Litho. Wmk. 314

196 CD317 3p blue & emerald .50 .50
197 CD317 2sh yel & vio blue 2.25 2.25

Scout Badge and Royal Cipher A33

1965, July 24 Photo. *Perf. 12½*

198 A33 2sh multicolored .65 .65

50th anniversary of Scouting in Bermuda.

Intl. Cooperation Year Issue

Common Design Type

1965, Oct. 25 Litho. *Perf. 14½*

199 CD318 4p blue grn & cl .40 .20
200 CD318 2sh6p lt violet & grn 1.60 1.25

Churchill Memorial Issue

Common Design Type

1966, Jan. 24 Photo. *Perf. 14*

Design in Black, Gold and Carmine Rose

201 CD319 3p bright blue .55 .55
202 CD319 6p green .85 .85
203 CD319 10p brown 1.10 1.10
204 CD319 1sh3p violet 1.50 1.50
Nos. 201-204 (4) 4.00 4.00

World Cup Soccer Issue

Common Design Type

1966, July 1 Litho. *Perf. 14*

205 CD321 10p multicolored .50 .50
206 CD321 2sh6p multicolored 1.50 1.50

UNESCO Anniversary Issue

Common Design Type

1966, Dec. 1 Litho. *Perf. 14*

207 CD323 4p "Education" .40 .40
208 CD323 1sh3p "Science" 1.50 1.50
209 CD323 2sh "Culture" 2.50 2.50
Nos. 207-209 (3) 4.40 4.40

Post Office, Hamilton A34

Wmk. 314

1967, June 23 Photo. *Perf. 14½*

210 A34 3p vio blue & multi .30 .30
211 A34 1sh orange & multi .30 .30
212 A34 1sh6p green & multi .60 .60
213 A34 2sh6p red & multi .60 .60
Nos. 210-213 (4) 1.80 1.80

Opening of the new GPO, Hamilton.

Cable Ship Mercury A35

Designs: 1sh, Map of Bermuda and Virgin Islands, telephone and microphone. 1sh6p, Radio tower, television set, telephone and cable. 2sh6p, Cable at sea bottom and ship.

1967, Sept. 14 Photo. Wmk. 314

214 A35 3p multicolored .20 .20
215 A35 1sh multicolored .35 .35
216 A35 1sh6p multicolored .35 .35
217 A35 2sh6p multicolored .60 .60
Nos. 214-217 (4) 1.50 1.50

Completion of the Bermuda-Tortola, Virgin Islands, telephone link.

Human Rights Flame, Globe and Doves A36

1968, Feb. 1 Litho. *Perf. 14x14½*

218 A36 3p indigo, lt grn & bl .35 .35
219 A36 1sh brown, lt bl & bl .35 .35
220 A36 1sh6p black, pink & blue .35 .35
221 A36 2sh6p green, yellow & bl .45 .45
Nos. 218-221 (4) 1.50 1.50

International Human Rights Year.

Mace A37

#224-225, House of Assembly, Bermuda, Parliament, London & royal cipher.

1968, July 1 Photo. *Perf. 14½*

222 A37 3p rose red & multi .35 .35
223 A37 1sh ultra & multi .35 .35
224 A37 1sh6p yellow & multi .35 .35
225 A37 2sh6p multicolored .45 .45
Nos. 222-225 (4) 1.50 1.50

New constitution.

Olympic Sports and Rings A38

1968, Sept. 24 Wmk. 314 *Perf. 12½*

226 A38 3p lilac & multi .20 .20
a. Rose brown omitted ("3d BERMUDA") *2,500.*
227 A38 1sh multicolored .30 .30
228 A38 1sh6p multicolored .50 .50
229 A38 2sh6p multicolored .50 .50
Nos. 226-229 (4) 1.50 1.50

19th Olympic Games, Mexico City, 10/12-27.

Girl Guides A39

Designs: 1sh, Like 3p. 1sh6p, 2sh6p, Girl Guides and arms of Bermuda.

1969, Feb. 17 Litho. *Perf. 14*

230 A39 3p lilac & multi .20 .20
231 A39 1sh green & multi .40 .40
232 A39 1sh6p gray & multi .50 .50
233 A39 2sh6p red & multi .65 .65
Nos. 230-233 (4) 1.75 1.75

Bermuda Girl Guides, 50th anniv.

Gold and Emerald Cross — A40

Design: 4p, 2sh, Different background.

1969, Sept. 29 Photo. *Perf. 14½x14*

Cross in Yellow, Brown and Emerald

234 A40 4p violet .25 .25
235 A40 1sh3p green .75 .75
236 A40 2sh black 1.10 1.10
237 A40 2sh6p carmine rose 1.40 1.25
Nos. 234-237 (4) 3.50 3.35

Treasures salvaged off the coast of Bermuda. The cross shown is from the Tucker treasure from the 16th century Spanish galleon San Pedro.

Buildings Issue and Type of 1962-69 Surcharged with New Value and Bar in Black or Brown

1970, Feb. 6 Wmk. 314 *Perf. 12½*

238 A31 1c on 1p multi .20 *1.50*
239 A31 2c on 2p multi .20 .20
a. Watermark upright 1.00 *2.25*
b. Light violet omitted *700.00*
c. Pair, one without surch. *3,000.*
240 A31 3c on 3p multi .20 .20
241 A31 4c on 4p multi (Br) .20 .20
242 A31 5c on 8p multi .20 *1.50*
243 A31 6c on 6p multi .20 *.60*
244 A31 9c on 9p multi (Br) .25 *1.75*
245 A31 10c on 10p multi .30 *.25*
246 A31 12c on 1sh multi .35 *.45*
247 A31 15c on 1sh3p multi .70 *.85*
248 A31 18c on 1sh6p multi .70 *.55*
249 A31 24c on 2sh multi .85 *.75*
250 A31 30c on 2sh6p multi 1.00 *2.10*
251 A31 36c on 2sh3p multi 1.25 *5.25*
252 A31 60c on 5sh multi 2.00 *2.50*
a. Surcharge omitted *700.00*
253 A31 $1.20 on 10sh multi 4.00 *13.00*
254 A31 $2.40 on £1 multi 8.00 *16.00*
Nos. 238-254 (17) 20.60 *47.65*

Watermark upright on 1c, 3c to 9c and 36c; sideways on others. Watermark is sideways on No. 252a, upright on No. 189.

Spathiphyllum — A41

Flowers: 2c, Bottlebrush. 3c, Oleander, vert. 4c, Bermudiana. 5c, Poinsettia. 6c, Hibiscus. 9c, Cereus. 10c, Bougainvillea, vert. 12c, Jacaranda. 15c, Passion flower. 18c, Coralita. 24c, Morning glory. 30c, Tecoma. 36c, Angel's trumpet. 60c, Plumbago. $1.20, Bird of paradise. $2.40, Chalice cup.

Wmk. 314, Sideways on Horiz. Stamps

1970, July 6 ***Perf. 14***

255 A41 1c lt grn & multi .20 .20
256 A41 2c pale bl & multi .35 .20
257 A41 3c yellow & multi .20 .20
258 A41 4c buff & multi .20 .20
259 A41 5c pink & multi .55 .25
a. Imperf., pair 1,500.
260 A41 6c org & multi .55 .30
261 A41 9c lt grn & multi .35 .20
262 A41 10c pale sal & multi .35 .20
263 A41 12c pale yel & multi 1.40 .85
264 A41 15c buff & multi 1.60 .70
265 A41 18c pale sal & multi 4.00 1.10
266 A41 24c pink & multi 2.75 .75
267 A41 30c plum & multi 1.75 .75
268 A41 36c dk gray & multi 2.25 1.10
269 A41 60c gray & multi 3.00 1.75
270 A41 $1.20 blue & multi 4.75 3.50
271 A41 $2.40 multicolored 9.75 8.25
Nos. 255-271 (17) 34.00 20.50

See #322-328. For overprints see #288-291.

1974-76 **Wmk. 314 Upright**

259b A41 5c multicolored 1.00 1.00
260a A41 6c multicolored 2.25 2.25
263a A41 12c multicolored 1.60 1.60
267a A41 30c multicolored ('76) 3.00 3.00
Nos. 259b-267a (4) 7.85 7.85

Issued: 30c, June 11; others, June 13.

1975-76 **Wmk. 373**

256a A41 2c multicolored 1.00 1.00
260b A41 6c multicolored 5.75 5.75

Issued: 2c, Dec. 8; 6c, June 11, 1976.

State House, St. George's, 1622-1815 — A42

Designs: 15c, The Sessions House, Hamilton, 1893. 18c, First Assembly House, St. Peter's Church, St. George's. 24c, Temporary Assembly House, Hamilton, 1815-26.

1970, Oct. 12 **Litho.** ***Perf. 14***

272 A42 4c multicolored .20 .20
273 A42 15c multicolored .45 .45
274 A42 18c multicolored .65 .65
275 A42 24c multicolored 1.10 1.10
a. Souvenir sheet of 4, #272-275 3.00 *4.25*
Nos. 272-275 (4) 2.40 2.40

350th anniv. of Bermuda's Parliament.

Street in St. George's A43

"Keep Bermuda Beautiful": 15c, Horseshoe Bay. 18c, Gibb's Hill Lighthouse. 24c, View of Hamilton Harbor.

1971, Feb. 8 **Wmk. 314** ***Perf. 14***

276 A43 4c multicolored .25 .25
277 A43 15c multicolored .70 .70
278 A43 18c multicolored .90 .90
279 A43 24c multicolored 1.50 1.50
Nos. 276-279 (4) 3.35 3.35

Building of "Deliverance" — A44

Designs: 15c, "Deliverance" and "Patience" arriving in Jamestown, Va., 1610, vert. 18c, Wreck of "Sea Venture," vert. 24c, "Deliverance" and "Patience" under sail, 1610.

1971, May 10 **Litho.** **Wmk. 314**

280 A44 4c multicolored .35 .35
281 A44 15c brown & multi 1.40 1.40
282 A44 18c purple & multi 1.75 1.75
283 A44 24c blue & multi 2.50 2.50
Nos. 280-283 (4) 6.00 6.00

Voyage of Sir George Somers to Jamestown, Va., from Bermuda, 1610.

Ocean View Golf Course A45

Golf Courses: 15c, Port Royal. 18c, Castle Harbour. 24c, Belmont.

1971, Nov. 1 ***Perf. 13***

284 A45 4c multicolored .55 .55
285 A45 15c multicolored 1.10 1.10
286 A45 18c multicolored 1.10 1.10
287 A45 24c multicolored 1.25 1.25
Nos. 284-287 (4) 4.00 4.00

Golfing in Bermuda.

Nos. 258, 264-266 Overprinted: "HEATH-NIXON / DECEMBER 1971"

1971, Dec. 20 **Photo.** ***Perf. 14***

288 A41 4c buff & multi .25 .25
289 A41 15c buff & multi .25 .25
290 A41 18c pale sal & multi .40 .40
291 A41 24c pink & multi .50 .50
Nos. 288-291 (4) 1.40 1.40

Meeting of President Richard M. Nixon and Prime Minister Edward Heath of Great Britain, at Hamilton, Dec. 20-21, 1971.

Bonefish A46

1972, Aug. 7 **Litho.** ***Perf. 13½x14***

292 A46 4c shown .20 .20
293 A46 15c Wahoo .70 .70
294 A46 18c Yellowfin tuna .85 .85
295 A46 24c Greater amberjack 1.25 1.25
Nos. 292-295 (4) 3.00 3.00

World fishing records.

Silver Wedding Issue, 1972
Common Design Type

Design: Queen Elizabeth II, Prince Philip, Admiralty oar and mace.

1972, Nov. 20 **Photo.** ***Perf. 14x14½***

296 CD324 4c violet & multi .20 .20
297 CD324 15c car rose & multi .30 .30

Palmettos — A47

1973, Sept. 3 **Wmk. 314** ***Perf. 14***

298 A47 4c shown .25 .25
299 A47 15c Olivewood .75 .75
a. Brown (Queen's head, "15c") omitted 1,000.
300 A47 18c Bermuda cedar 1.00 1.00
301 A47 24c Mahogany 1.25 1.25
Nos. 298-301 (4) 3.25 3.25

Bermuda National Trust, and "Plant a Tree" campaign.

Princess Anne's Wedding Issue
Common Design Type

1973, Nov. 21 **Litho.**

302 CD325 15c lilac & multi .25 .25
303 CD325 18c slate & multi .35 .35

National Tennis Stadium, Pembroke, 1973 — A48

15c, Bermuda's 1st tennis court, Pembroke, 1873. 18c, Britain's 1st tennis court, Leamington Spa, 1872. 24c, 1t US tennis club, Staten Island, 1874.

1973, Dec. 17 **Wmk. 314**

304 A48 4c black & multi .20 .20
305 A48 15c black & multi .55 .55
306 A48 18c black & multi .75 .75
307 A48 24c black & multi 1.00 1.00
Nos. 304-307 (4) 2.50 2.50

Centenary of tennis in Bermuda.

Rotary Emblem, Weather Vane, City Hall, Hamilton A49

Rotary Emblem and: 17c, St. Peter's Church, St. George's. 20c, Somerset Drawbridge, Somerset. 25c, Map of Bermuda on globe, 1626.

1974, June 24 ***Perf. 14***

308 A49 5c emerald & multi .25 .25
309 A49 17c blue & multi .55 .55
310 A49 20c yel org & multi .75 .75
311 A49 25c lt violet & multi 1.00 1.00
Nos. 308-311 (4) 2.55 2.55

50th anniv. of Rotary Intl. in Bermuda.

Jack of Clubs and a Good Bridge Hand — A50

Bermuda Bowl and: 17c, Queen of diamonds. 20c, King of hearts. 25c, Ace of spades.

1975, Jan. 27 **Litho.** **Wmk. 314**

312 A50 5c blue & multi .25 .25
313 A50 17c dull yel & multi .75 .75
314 A50 20c ver & multi .80 .80
315 A50 25c lilac & multi 1.10 1.10
Nos. 312-315 (4) 2.90 2.90

World Bridge Championship, Bermuda, Jan. 1975.

Queen Elizabeth II and Prince Philip — A51

Perf. 14x14½

1975, Feb. 17 **Photo.** **Wmk. 373**

316 A51 17c multicolored .50 .50
317 A51 20c dk blue & multi .75 .75

Royal Visit, Feb. 16-18, 1975.

British Cavalier Flying Boat, 1937 A52

17c, US Navy airship "Los Angeles," 1925, flying from Lakehurst, NJ to Hamilton, Bermuda. 20c, Constellation over Kindley Field, 1946. 25c, Boeing 747 on tarmac, 1970.

1975, Apr. 28 **Litho.** ***Perf. 14***

318 A52 5c lt green & multi .40 .40
319 A52 17c lt ultra & multi 1.25 1.25
320 A52 20c multicolored 1.75 1.75
321 A52 25c rose lil & multi 2.00 2.00
a. Souvenir sheet of 4, #318-321 9.00 *10.00*
Nos. 318-321 (4) 5.40 5.40

Airmail service to Bermuda, 50th anniv.

Flower Type of 1970

1975, June 2 **Photo.** **Wmk. 314**

322 A41 17c Passion flower 1.90 1.90
323 A41 20c Coralita 1.90 1.90
324 A41 25c Morning glory 1.90 1.90
325 A41 40c Angel's trumpet 1.90 1.90
326 A41 $1 Plumbago 2.25 2.25
327 A41 $2 Bird-of-paradise flower 3.75 3.75
328 A41 $3 Chalice cup 6.75 6.75
Nos. 322-328 (7) 20.35 20.35

Royal Magazine Break-in A54

17c, Sympathizers rowing towards magazine. 20c, Loading gun powder barrels onto ships. 25c, Gun powder barrels on beach.

Perf. 13x13½

1975, Oct. 27 **Litho.** **Wmk. 373**

329 A54 5c multicolored .30 .30
330 A54 17c multicolored .60 .60
331 A54 20c multicolored .65 .65
332 A54 25c multicolored .70 .70
a. Souv. sheet, #329-332, perf 14 3.25 *5.00*
Nos. 329-332 (4) 2.25 2.25

Gunpowder Plot, 1775, American War of Independence.

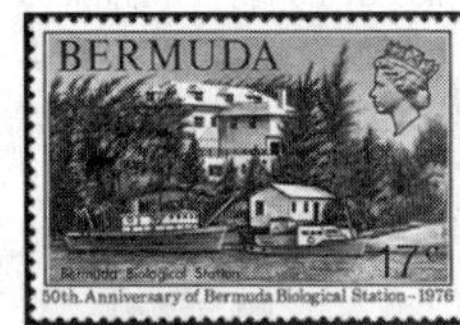

Bermuda Biological Station A55

Designs: 5c, Launching of bathysphere from "Ready," vert. 20c, Sailing ship Challenger, 1873. 25c, Descent of Beebe's bathysphere, 1934, and marine life, vert.

1976, Mar. 29 **Litho.** ***Perf. 14***

333 A55 5c multicolored .30 .30
334 A55 17c multicolored .70 .70
335 A55 20c multicolored .85 .85
336 A55 25c multicolored 1.00 1.00
Nos. 333-336 (4) 2.85 2.85

Bermuda Biological Station, 50th anniv.

Christian Radich, Norway A56

Tall Ships: 12c, Juan Sebastian de Elcano, Spain. 17c, Eagle, US. 20c, Sir Winston Churchill, Great Britain. 40c, Kruzenshtern, USSR. $1, Cutty Sark (silver trophy).

1976, June 15 Litho. *Perf. 13*

337 A56 5c lt green & multi .95 .95
338 A56 12c violet & multi 1.00 1.00
339 A56 17c ultra & multi 1.00 1.00
340 A56 20c blue & multi 1.00 1.00
341 A56 40c yellow & multi 1.25 1.25
342 A56 $1 sl grn & multi 1.60 1.60
Nos. 337-342 (6) 6.80 6.80

Trans-Atlantic Cutty Sark International Tall Ships Race, Plymouth, England-New York City (Operation Sail '76).

Silver Cup Trophy and Crossed Club Flags A57

Designs: 17c, St. George's Cricket Club and emblem. 20c, Somerset Cricket Club and emblem. 25c, Cricket match.

1976, Aug. 16 Wmk. 373 *Perf. 14½*

343 A57 5c multicolored .25 .25
344 A57 17c multicolored .85 .85
345 A57 20c multicolored .95 .95
346 A57 25c multicolored 1.40 1.40
Nos. 343-346 (4) 3.45 3.45

St. George's and Somerset Cricket Club matches, 75th anniversary.

Queen's Visit to Bermuda, 1975 — A58

Designs: 20c, St. Edward's Crown. $1, Queen seated in Chair of Estate.

1977, Feb. 7 Litho. *Perf. 14x13½*

347 A58 5c silver & multi .30 .30
348 A58 20c silver & multi .45 .45
349 A58 $1 silver & multi 1.25 1.25
Nos. 347-349 (3) 2.00 2.00

Reign of Queen Elizabeth II, 25th anniv.

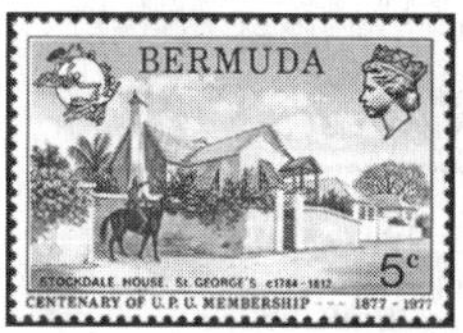

Stockdale House, St. George's A59

UPU Emblem and: 15c, Perot Post Office and Perot Stamp. 17c, St. George's Post Office, c. 1860. 20c, Old GPO, Hamilton, c. 1935. 40c, New GPO, Hamilton, 1967.

1977, June 20 Litho. *Perf. 13x13½*

350 A59 5c multicolored .20 .20
351 A59 15c multicolored .35 .35
352 A59 17c multicolored .35 .35
353 A59 20c multicolored .45 .45
354 A59 40c multicolored .65 .65
Nos. 350-354 (5) 2.00 2.00

Bermuda's UPU membership, cent.

Sailing Ship, 17th Century, Approaching Castle Island — A60

Designs: 15c, King's pilot leaving 18th century naval ship at Murray's Anchorage. 17c, Pilot gigs racing to meet steamship, early 19th century. 20c, Harvest Queen, late 19th century. 40c, Pilot cutter and Queen Elizabeth II off St. David's Lighthouse.

Perf. 13½x14

1977, Sept. 26 Wmk. 373

355 A60 5c multicolored .40 .40
356 A60 15c multicolored .65 .65
357 A60 17c multicolored .70 .70
358 A60 20c multicolored .75 .75
359 A60 40c multicolored 1.25 1.25
Nos. 355-359 (5) 3.75 3.75

Piloting in Bermuda waters.

Elizabeth II A61

Designs: 8c, Great Seal of Elizabeth I. 50c, Great Seal of Elizabeth II.

1978, Aug. 28 Litho. *Perf. 14x13½*

360 A61 8c gold & multi .20 .20
361 A61 50c gold & multi .85 .85
362 A61 $1 gold & multi 1.75 1.75
Nos. 360-362 (3) 2.80 2.80

25th anniv. of coronation of Elizabeth II.

White-tailed Tropicbird — A62

Perf. 14; 14x14½ (4c, 5c, $2, $3, $5)

1978-79 Photo. Wmk. 373

363 A62 3c shown .20 .20
364 A62 4c White-eyed vireo .20 .20
365 A62 5c Eastern bluebird .20 .20
366 A62 7c Whistling tree frog .20 .20
367 A62 8c Cardinal .20 .20
368 A62 10c Spiny lobster .20 .20
369 A62 12c Land crab .20 .20
370 A62 15c Skink .25 .25
371 A62 20c Four-eyed butterflyfish .35 .35
372 A62 25c Red hind .45 .45
  a. Greenish blue (background) omitted 2,500.
373 A62 30c Monarch butterfly .50 .50
374 A62 40c Rock beauty .70 .70
375 A62 50c Banded butterflyfish 1.00 1.00
376 A62 $1 Blue angelfish 2.00 2.00
377 A62 $2 Humpback whale 4.25 4.25
378 A62 $3 Green turtle 6.25 6.25
379 A62 $5 Bermuda Petrel 10.50 10.50
Nos. 363-379 (17) 27.65 27.65

Issued: 3c, 4c, 5c, 8c, $5, 1978; others, 1979.

For surcharge see No. 509.

Map of Bermuda, by George Somers, 1609 — A63

Old Maps of Bermuda: 15c, by John Seller, 1685. 20c, by Herman Moll, 1729, vert. 25c, by Desbruslins, 1740. 50c, by John Speed, 1626.

1979, May 14 Litho. *Perf. 13½*

380 A63 8c multicolored .20 .20
381 A63 15c multicolored .30 .30
382 A63 20c multicolored .40 .40
383 A63 25c multicolored .45 .45
384 A63 50c multicolored .95 .95
Nos. 380-384 (5) 2.30 2.30

Bermuda Police Centenary — A64

20c, Traffic direction, horiz. 25c, Water patrol, horiz. 50c, Motorbike and patrol car.

1979, Nov. 26 Wmk. 373 *Perf. 14*

385 A64 8c multicolored .25 .25
386 A64 20c multicolored .45 .45
387 A64 25c multicolored .55 .55
388 A64 50c multicolored 1.00 1.00
Nos. 385-388 (4) 2.25 2.25

Bermuda No. X1, Penny Black — A65

Bermuda #X1 and: 20c, Hill. 25c, "Paid 1" marking on cover. 50c, "Paid 1" marking.

1980, Feb. 25 Litho. *Perf. 13½x14*

389 A65 8c multicolored .20 .20
390 A65 20c multicolored .40 .40
391 A65 25c multicolored .50 .50
392 A65 50c multicolored 1.00 1.00
Nos. 389-392 (4) 2.10 2.10

Sir Rowland Hill (1795-1879), originator of penny postage.

Tristar-500, London 1980 Emblem — A66

1980, May 6 Litho. *Perf. 13x14*

393 A66 25c shown .35 .35
394 A66 50c "Orduna," 1926 .70 .70
395 A66 $1 "Delta," 1856 1.50 1.50
396 A66 $2 "Lord Sidmouth," 1818 3.00 3.00
Nos. 393-396 (4) 5.55 5.55

London 1980 Intl. Stamp Exhib., May 6-14.

Gina Swainson, Miss World, 1979-80, Arms of Bermuda — A67

1980, May 8 *Perf. 14*

397 A67 8c shown .20 .20
398 A67 20c After crowning ceremony .35 .35
399 A67 50c Welcome home party .90 .90
400 A67 $1 In carriage 1.75 1.75
Nos. 397-400 (4) 3.20 3.20

Queen Mother Elizabeth Birthday Issue

Common Design Type

1980, Aug. 4 Wmk. 373 *Perf. 14*

401 CD330 25c multicolored .45 .45

Camden, Prime Minister's House A68

1980, Sept. 24 Litho. *Perf. 14*

402 A68 8c View from satellite .20 .20
403 A68 20c shown .40 .40
404 A68 25c Princess Hotel, Hamilton .50 .50
405 A68 50c Government House 1.00 1.00
Nos. 402-405 (4) 2.10 2.10

Commonwealth Finance Ministers Meeting, Bermuda, Sept.

18th Century Kitchen A69

1981, May 21 Wmk. 373 *Perf. 14*

406 A69 8c shown .20 .20
407 A69 25c Gathering Easter lilies .40 .40
408 A69 30c Fisherman .50 .50
409 A69 40c Stone cutting, 19th cent. .70 .70
410 A69 50c Onion shipping, 19th cent. .85 .85
411 A69 $1 Ships, 17th cent. 1.75 1.75
Nos. 406-411 (6) 4.40 4.40

Royal Wedding Issue

Common Design Type

1981, July 22 Wmk. 373 *Perf. 14*

412 CD331 30c Bouquet .50 .50
413 CD331 50c Charles .90 .90
414 CD331 $1 Couple 1.75 1.75
Nos. 412-414 (3) 3.15 3.15

Girl Helping Blind Man Cross Street — A70

1981, Sept. 28 Litho. *Perf. 14*

415 A70 10c shown .20 .20
416 A70 25c Kayaking, Paget Island .50 .50
417 A70 30c Mountain climbing, St. David's Island .55 .55
418 A70 $1 Duke of Edinburgh 1.90 1.90
Nos. 415-418 (4) 3.15 3.15

Duke of Edinburgh's Awards, 25th anniv.

Conus Species A71

1982, May 13 Wmk. 373 *Perf. 14*

419 A71 10c shown .20 .20
420 A71 25c Bursa finlayi .50 .50
421 A71 30c Sconsia striata .60 .60
422 A71 $1 Murex pterynotus lightbourni 1.90 1.90
Nos. 419-422 (4) 3.20 3.20

Bermuda Regiment A72

1982, June 17 Litho. Wmk. 373

423 A72 10c Color guard .20 .20
424 A72 25c Queen's birthday parade .40 .40

No.	Type	Value	Description	Unused	Used
425	A72	30c	Governor inspecting honor guard	.60	.60
426	A72	40c	Beating the retreat	.80	.80
427	A72	50c	Ceremonial gunners	1.00	1.00
428	A72	$1	Royal visit, 1975	2.00	2.00
			Nos. 423-428 (6)	5.00	5.00

Southampton Fort — A73

1982, Nov. 18 Litho. Wmk. 373

No.	Type	Value	Description	Unused	Used
429	A73	10c	Charles Fort, vert.	.20	.20
430	A73	25c	Pembroks Fort, vert.	.50	.50
431	A73	30c	shown	.60	.60
432	A73	$1	Smiths and Pagets Forts	1.90	1.90
			Nos. 429-432 (4)	3.20	3.20

Arms of Sir Edwin Sandys (1561-1629) A74

Coats of Arms: 25c, Bermuda Company. 50c, William Herbert, 3rd Earl of Pembroke (1584-1630). $1, Sir George Somers (1554-1610).

1983, Apr. 14 Litho. Perf. 13½

No.	Type	Value	Description	Unused	Used
433	A74	10c	multicolored	.20	.20
434	A74	25c	multicolored	.45	.45
435	A74	50c	multicolored	.90	.90
436	A74	$1	multicolored	1.75	1.75
			Nos. 433-436 (4)	3.30	3.30

See Nos. 457-460, 474-477.

Fitted Dinghies — A75

1983, July 21 Wmk. 373 Perf. 14

Old and modern boats.

No.	Type	Value	Description	Unused	Used
437	A75	12c	multicolored	.25	.25
438	A75	30c	multicolored	.55	.55
439	A75	40c	multicolored	.70	.70
440	A75	$1	multicolored	1.75	1.75
			Nos. 437-440 (4)	3.25	3.25

Manned Flight Bicentenary — A76

Designs: 12c, Curtiss Jenny, 1919 (first flight over Bermuda). 30c, Stinson Pilot Radio, 1930 (first completed US-Bermuda flight). 40c, Cavalier, 1937 (first scheduled passenger flight). $1, USS Los Angeles airship moored to USS Patoka, 1925.

1983, Oct. 13 Litho. Perf. 14

No.	Type	Value	Description	Unused	Used
441	A76	12c	multicolored	.30	.30
442	A76	30c	multicolored	.65	.65
443	A76	40c	multicolored	.90	.90
444	A76	$1	multicolored	1.75	1.75
			Nos. 441-444 (4)	3.60	3.60

Newspaper and Postal Services, 200th Anniv. — A77

1984, Jan. 26 Litho. Perf. 14

No.	Type	Value	Description	Unused	Used
445	A77	12c	Joseph Stockdale	.25	.25
446	A77	30c	First Newspaper	.55	.55
447	A77	40c	Stockdale's Postal Service, horiz.	.70	.70
448	A77	$1	"Lady Hammond," horiz.	1.75	1.75
			Nos. 445-448 (4)	3.25	3.25

375th Anniv. of Bermuda Settlement — A78

Designs: 12c, Thomas Gates, George Somers. 30c, Jamestown, Virginia, US. 40c, Sea Venture shipwreck. $1, Fleet leaving Plymouth, England.

1984, May 3 Litho. Wmk. 373

No.	Type	Value	Description	Unused	Used
449	A78	12c	multicolored	.25	.25
450	A78	30c	multicolored	.55	.55
451	A78	40c	multicolored	.70	.70
452	A78	$1	multicolored	1.75	1.75
a.			Souv. sheet of 2, #450, 452	5.00	5.00
			Nos. 449-452 (4)	3.25	3.25

1984 Summer Olympics A79

1984, July 19 Litho. Perf. 14

No.	Type	Value	Description	Unused	Used
453	A79	12c	Swimming, vert.	.20	.20
454	A79	30c	Track & field	.50	.50
455	A79	40c	Equestrian, vert.	.70	.70
456	A79	$1	Sailing	1.60	1.60
			Nos. 453-456 (4)	3.00	3.00

Arms Type of 1983

1984, Sept. 27 Litho. Perf. 13½

No.	Type	Value	Description	Unused	Used
457	A74	12c	Southampton	.20	.20
458	A74	30c	Smith	.60	.60
459	A74	40c	Devonshire	.75	.75
460	A74	$1	St. George	1.60	1.60
			Nos. 457-460 (4)	3.15	3.15

Architecture, Buttery — A80

1985, Jan. 24 Litho. Perf. 13½x13

No.	Type	Value	Description	Unused	Used
461	A80	12c	shown	.35	.35
462	A80	30c	Rooftops	.75	.75
463	A80	40c	Chimneys	1.00	1.00
464	A80	$1.50	Archway	3.50	3.50
			Nos. 461-464 (4)	5.60	5.60

Audubon Birth Bicentenary — A81

1985, Mar. 21 Wmk. 373 Perf. 14

No.	Type	Value	Description	Unused	Used
465	A81	12c	Osprey, vert.	.30	.30
466	A81	30c	Yellow-crowned night heron, vert.	.75	.75
467	A81	40c	Great egret	1.00	1.00
468	A81	$1.50	Bluebird, vert.	3.50	3.50
			Nos. 465-468 (4)	5.55	5.55

Queen Mother 85th Birthday Issue

Common Design Type

Designs: 12c, Queen Consort, 1937. 30c, With grandchildren, 80th birthday. 40c, At Clarence House, 83rd birthday. $1.50, Holding Prince Henry. No. 473, In coach with Prince Charles.

Perf. 14½x14

1985, June 7 Wmk. 384

No.	Type	Value	Description	Unused	Used
469	CD336	12c	gray, bl & blk	.35	.35
470	CD336	30c	multicolored	.75	.75
471	CD336	40c	multicolored	1.00	1.00
472	CD336	$1.50	multicolored	3.50	3.50
			Nos. 469-472 (4)	5.60	5.60

Souvenir Sheet

No.	Type	Value	Description	Unused	Used
473	CD336	$1	multicolored	4.50	4.50

Arms Type of 1983

Coats of Arms: 12c, James Hamilton, 2nd Marquess of Hamilton (1589-1625). 30c, William Paget, 4th Lord Paget (1572-1629). 40c, Robert Rich, 2nd Earl of Warwick (1587-1658). $1.50, Hamilton, 1957.

1985, Sept. 19 Litho. Perf. 13½

No.	Type	Value	Description	Unused	Used
474	A74	12c	multicolored	.30	.30
475	A74	30c	multicolored	.75	.75
476	A74	40c	multicolored	1.00	1.00
477	A74	$1.50	multicolored	3.75	3.75
			Nos. 474-477 (4)	5.80	5.80

Halley's Comet A82

1985, Nov. 21 Wmk. 384 Perf. 14½

No.	Type	Value	Description	Unused	Used
478	A82	15c	Bermuda Archipelago	.40	.40
479	A82	40c	Nuremberg Chronicles, 1493	1.00	1.00
480	A82	50c	Peter Apian woodcut, 1532	1.25	1.25
481	A82	$1.50	Painting by Samuel Scott (c.1702-72)	3.75	3.75
			Nos. 478-481 (4)	6.40	6.40

Shipwrecks — A83

1986 Wmk. 384 Perf. 14

No.	Type	Value	Description	Unused	Used
482	A83	3c	Constellation, 1943	.20	.20
483	A83	5c	Early Riser, 1876	.20	.20
484	A83	7c	Madiana, 1903	.20	.20
485	A83	10c	Curlew, 1856	.20	.20
486	A83	12c	Warwick, 1619	.20	.20
487	A83	15c	HMS Vixen, 1890	.30	.30
488	A83	20c	San Pedro, 1594	.35	.35
489	A83	25c	Alert, 1877	.50	.50
490	A83	40c	North Carolina, 1880	.75	.75
491	A83	50c	Mark Antonie, 1777	1.00	1.00
492	A83	60c	Mary Celestia, 1864	1.10	1.10
493	A83	$1	L'Herminie, 1839	1.75	1.75
494	A83	$1.50	Caesar, 1818	2.75	2.75
495	A83	$2	Lord Amherst, 1778	3.50	3.50
496	A83	$3	Minerva, 1849	5.50	5.50
497	A83	$5	Caraquet, 1923	9.00	9.00
498	A83	$8	HMS Pallas, 1783	14.50	14.50
			Nos. 482-498 (17)	42.00	42.00

Nos. 493, 495-496 exist inscribed "1989." Nos. 482, 488, "1990."

See #545-546. For surcharges see #598-600.

Inscribed "1992"

1992 Litho. Wmk. 373 Perf. 14

No.	Type	Value	Description	Unused	Used
485a	A83	10c		.20	.20
487a	A83	15c		.30	.30
488a	A83	20c		.35	.35
489a	A83	25c		.45	.45
492a	A83	60c		1.10	1.10
497a	A83	$5		9.25	9.25
498a	A83	$8		14.75	14.75
			Nos. 485a-498a (7)	26.40	26.40

Queen Elizabeth II 60th Birthday

Common Design Type

15c, Age 3. 40c, With the Earl of Rosebury, Oaks May Meeting, Epsom, 1954. 50c, With Prince Philip, state visit,1979. 60c, At the British embassy in Paris, state visit, 1972. $1.50, Visiting Crown Agents' offices, 1983.

1986, Apr. 21 Wmk. 384 Perf. 14½

No.	Type	Value	Description	Unused	Used
499	CD337	15c	scar, blk & sil	.25	.25
500	CD337	40c	ultra & multi	.65	.65
501	CD337	50c	green & multi	.80	.80
502	CD337	60c	violet & multi	.95	.95
503	CD337	$1.50	rose vio & multi	2.50	2.50
			Nos. 499-503 (5)	5.15	5.15

AMERIPEX '86 — A84

1986, May 22 Perf. 14

No.	Type	Value	Description	Unused	Used
504	A84	15c	No. 452a	.25	.25
505	A84	40c	No. 307	.65	.65
506	A84	50c	No. 441	.80	.80
507	A84	$1	No. 339	1.60	1.60
			Nos. 504-507 (4)	3.30	3.30

Souvenir Sheet

No.	Type	Value	Description	Unused	Used
508	A84	1.50	Statue of Liberty, S.S. Queen of Bermuda	4.50	4.50

Statue of Liberty, cent.

No. 378 Surcharged

Perf. 14x14½

1986, Dec. 4 Photo. Wmk. 373

No.	Type	Value	Description	Unused	Used
509	A62	90c	on $3 multi	3.00	3.00

Exists with double surcharge.

Transport Railway, c. 1931-1947 — A85

Wmk. 373

1987, Jan. 22 Litho. Perf. 14

No.	Type	Value	Description	Unused	Used
510	A85	15c	Front Street, c. 1940	.25	.25
511	A85	40c	Springfield Trestle	.65	.65
512	A85	50c	No. 101, Bailey's Bay Sta.	.80	.80
513	A85	$1.50	No. 31, ship Prince David	2.50	2.50
			Nos. 510-513 (4)	4.20	4.20

Paintings by Winslow Homer (1836-1910) A86

1987, Apr. 30 Perf. 14½

No.	Type	Value	Description	Unused	Used
514	A86	15c	Bermuda Settlers, 1901	.30	.30
515	A86	30c	Bermuda, 1900	.55	.55
516	A86	40c	Bermuda Landscape, 1901	.75	.75
517	A86	50c	Inland Water, 1901	.95	.95
518	A86	$1.50	Salt Kettle, 1899	3.00	3.00
			Nos. 514-518 (5)	5.55	5.55

Booklet Stamps

No.	Type	Value	Description	Unused	Used
519	A86	40c	like 15c	.65	.65
520	A86	40c	like 30c	.65	.65
521	A86	40c	like No. 516	.65	.65

522 A86 40c like 50c .65 .65
523 A86 40c like $1.50 .65 .65
a. Bklt. pane, 2 each #519-523 6.50

Nos. 519-523 printed in strips of 5 within pane. "ER" at lower left.

Intl. Flights Inauguration — A87

1987, June 18 ***Perf. 14***
524 A87 15c Sikorsky S-42B, 1937 .50 .50
525 A87 40c Shorts S-23 Cavalier 1.40 1.40
526 A87 50c S-42B Bermuda Clipper 1.60 1.60
527 A87 $1.50 Cavalier, Bermuda Clipper 5.00 5.00
Nos. 524-527 (4) 8.50 8.50

Bermuda Telephone Company, Cent. — A88

1987, Oct. 1 Litho. Wmk. 384
528 A88 15c Telephone poles on wagon .25 .25
529 A88 40c Operators .70 .70
530 A88 50c Telephones .85 .85
531 A88 $1.50 Satellite, fiber optics, world 2.50 2.50
Nos. 528-531 (4) 4.30 4.30

Horse-drawn Commercial Vehicles — A89

1988, Mar. 3 Litho. ***Perf. 14***
532 A89 15c Mail wagon, c. 1869 .30 .30
533 A89 40c Open cart, c. 1823 .75 .75
534 A89 50c Closed cart, c. 1823 .95 .95
535 A89 $1.50 Two-wheel wagon, c. 1930 2.75 2.75
Nos. 532-535 (4) 4.75 4.75

Old Garden Roses A90

1988, Apr. 21 Wmk. 373
536 A90 15c Old blush .25 .25
537 A90 30c Anna Olivier .50 .50
538 A90 40c Rosa chinensis semperflorens, vert. .70 .70
539 A90 50c Archduke Charles .90 .90
540 A90 $1.50 Rosa chinensis viridiflora, vert. 2.75 2.75
Nos. 536-540 (5) 5.10 5.10

See Nos. 561-575.

Lloyds of London, 300th Anniv.
Common Design Type

18c, Loss of the H.M.S. Lutine, 1799. 50c, Cable ship Sentinel. 60c, The Bermuda, Hamilton, 1931. $2, Valerian, lost during a hurricane, 1926.

1988, Oct. 13 Litho. Wmk. 384
541 CD341 18c multi .30 .30
542 CD341 50c multi, horiz. .90 .90
543 CD341 60c multi, horiz. 1.10 1.10
544 CD341 $2 multi 3.50 3.50
Nos. 541-544 (4) 5.80 5.80

Shipwreck Type of 1986

1988 Litho. Wmk. 384 ***Perf. 14***
545 A83 18c like 7c .35 .35
546 A83 70c like $1.50 1.40 1.40

Issue dates: 18c, Sept. 22; 70c, Oct. 27.

Military Uniforms — A91

18c, Devonshire Parish Militia, 1812. 50c, 71st Regiment Highlander, 1831-34. 60c, Cameron Highlander, 1942. $2, Troop of Horse, 1774.

1988, Nov. 10 Wmk. 373 ***Perf. 14½***
547 A91 18c multicolored .30 .30
548 A91 50c multicolored .85 .85
549 A91 60c multicolored 1.00 1.00
550 A91 $2 multicolored 3.50 3.50
Nos. 547-550 (4) 5.65 5.65

Ferry Service A92

1989 Litho. Wmk. 384 ***Perf. 14***
551 A92 18c Corona .30 .30
552 A92 50c Rowboat ferry .85 .85
553 A92 60c St. George's Ferry 1.00 1.00
554 A92 $2 Laconia 3.50 3.50
Nos. 551-554 (4) 5.65 5.65

Photography, Sesquicent. A93

Perf. 14x14½

1989, May 11 Litho. Wmk. 373
555 A93 18c Morgan's Is. .35 .35
556 A93 30c Front Street, Hamilton (cannon in square) .60 .60
557 A93 50c Front Street (seascape) 1.00 1.00
558 A93 60c Crow Lane, Hamilton Harbor 1.25 1.25
559 A93 70c Hamilton Harbor (shipbuilding) 1.40 1.40
560 A93 $1 Dockyard 2.00 2.00
Nos. 555-560 (6) 6.60 6.60

Old Garden Roses Type of 1988

1989, July 13 ***Perf. 14***
561 A90 18c Agrippina .35 .35
562 A90 30c Smith's Parish .60 .60
563 A90 50c Champney's pink cluster 1.00 1.00
564 A90 60c Rosette delizy 1.25 1.25
565 A90 $1.50 Rosa bracteata 3.00 3.00
Nos. 561-565 (5) 6.20 6.20

Nos. 561-562 vert.

Old Garden Roses Type of 1988 with Royal Cipher Instead of Queen's Silhouette

1989, July 13 Booklet Stamps
566 A90 50c like No. 562 1.00 1.00
567 A90 50c like No. 540 1.00 1.00
568 A90 50c like No. 561 1.00 1.00
569 A90 50c like No. 538 1.00 1.00
570 A90 50c like No. 563 1.00 1.00
571 A90 50c like No. 536 1.00 1.00
572 A90 50c like No. 564 1.00 1.00
573 A90 50c like No. 537 1.00 1.00
574 A90 50c like No. 565 1.00 1.00
575 A90 50c like No. 539 1.00 1.00
a. Bklt. pane of 10, #566-575 10.00

Bermuda Library, 150th Anniv. A94

1989, Sept. 14 ***Perf. 13½x14***
576 A94 18c Hamilton Main Library .30 .30
577 A94 50c St. George's, The Old Rectory .85 .85
578 A94 60c Springfield, Somerset Library 1.00 1.00
579 A94 $2 Cabinet Building 3.50 3.50
Nos. 576-579 (4) 5.65 5.65

Commonwealth Postal Conference — A95

1989, Nov. 3 Wmk. 384 ***Perf. 14***
580 A95 18c No. 1 .30 .30
581 A95 50c No. 2 .85 .85
582 A95 60c Type A4 1.00 1.00
583 A95 $2 No. 6 3.50 3.50
Nos. 580-583 (4) 5.65 5.65

For overprints see Nos. 594-597.

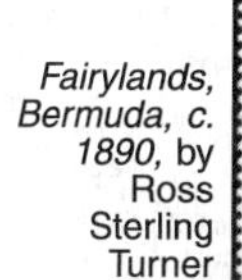

Fairylands, Bermuda, c. 1890, by Ross Sterling Turner A96

Paintings: 50c, *Shinebone Alley, c. 1953,* by Ogden M. Pleissner. 60c, *Salt Kettle, 1916,* by Prosper Senate. $2, *St. George's, 1934,* by Jack Bush.

1990, Apr. 19
590 A96 18c multicolored .30 .30
591 A96 50c multicolored .85 .85
592 A96 60c multicolored 1.00 1.00
593 A96 $2 multicolored 3.50 3.50
Nos. 590-593 (4) 5.65 5.65

Nos. 580-583 Overprinted

1990, May 3
594 A95 18c multicolored .35 .35
595 A95 50c multicolored 1.00 1.00
596 A95 60c multicolored 1.25 1.25
597 A95 $2 multicolored 4.00 4.00
Nos. 594-597 (4) 6.60 6.60

Stamp World London '90.

Nos. 486, 491, 494 Surcharged

1990, Aug. 13
598 A83 30c on 12c No. 486 .50 .50
599 A83 55c on 50c No. 491 1.00 1.00
600 A83 80c on $1.50 No. 494 1.50 1.50
Nos. 598-600 (3) 3.00 3.00

Nova Scotia-Bermuda Cable, Cent. — A97

1990, Oct. 18 Litho. Unwmk.
601 A97 20c Office .35 .35
602 A97 55c Cableship SS Westmeath 1.00 1.00
603 A97 70c Radio station, 1928 1.25 1.25
604 A97 $2 Cableship Sir Eric Sharp 3.50 3.50
Nos. 601-604 (4) 6.10 6.10

Nos. 601-602 with Added Inscription: "BUSH-MAJOR / 16 MARCH 1991"

1991, Mar. Unwmk. ***Perf. 14***
605 A97 20c like #601 .40 .40
606 A97 55c like #602 1.10 1.10

Carriages A98

Designs: 20c, Two-seat pony cart, c. 1805. 30c, Varnished rockaway, c. 1830. 55c, Vis-a-Vis Victoria, c. 1895. 70c, Semi-formal phaeton, c. 1900. 80c, Pony runabout, c. 1905. $1, Ladies' phaeton, c. 1910.

Perf. 14x14½

1991, Mar. 21 Litho. Wmk. 373
607 A98 20c green & multi .40 .40
608 A98 30c bl gray & multi .60 .60
609 A98 55c dk car & multi 1.10 1.10
610 A98 70c blue & multi 1.40 1.40
611 A98 80c yel org & multi 1.60 1.60
612 A98 $1 dk gray & multi 2.00 2.00
Nos. 607-612 (6) 7.10 7.10

Paintings A99

Designs: 20c, Bermuda by Prosper Senat, vert. 55c, Bermuda Cottage by Frank Allison. 70c, Old Maid's Lane by Jack Bush, vert. $2, St. George's by Ogden M. Pleissner.

Perf. 14x13½

1991, May 16 Litho. Wmk. 373
613 A99 20c multicolored .40 .40
614 A99 55c multicolored 1.10 1.10
615 A99 70c multicolored 1.40 1.40
616 A99 $2 multicolored 4.00 4.00
Nos. 613-616 (4) 6.90 6.90

Elizabeth & Philip, Birthdays
Common Design Types

1991, June 20 Wmk. 384 ***Perf. 14½***
617 CD346 55c multicolored 1.10 1.10
618 CD345 70c multicolored 1.40 1.40
a. Pair, #617-618 + label 2.50 2.50

Bermuda in World War II A100

Designs: 20c, Floating drydock. 55c, Kindley Air Field. 70c, Trans-atlantic air route, Boeing 314. $2, Censored trans-atlantic mail.

1991, Sept. 19 Wmk. 373 ***Perf. 14***
619 A100 20c multicolored .40 .40
620 A100 55c multicolored 1.10 1.10
621 A100 70c multicolored 1.40 1.40
622 A100 $2 multicolored 4.00 4.00
Nos. 619-622 (4) 6.90 6.90

Queen Elizabeth II's Accession to the Throne, 40th Anniv.
Common Design Type

1992, Feb. 6
623 CD349 20c multicolored .40 .40
624 CD349 30c multicolored .60 .60
625 CD349 55c multicolored 1.10 1.10
626 CD349 70c multicolored 1.40 1.40
627 CD349 $1 multicolored 2.00 2.00
Nos. 623-627 (5) 5.50 5.50

Age of Exploration — A101

Artifacts: 25c, Rings, medallion. 35c, Ink wells. 60c, Gold pieces. 75c, Bishop button, crucifix. 85c, Pearl earrings and buttons. $1, 8-real coin, jug and measuring cups.

1992, July 23 ***Perf. 13½***
628 A101 25c multicolored .50 .50
629 A101 35c multicolored .70 .70
630 A101 60c multicolored 1.25 1.25
631 A101 75c multicolored 1.50 1.50
632 A101 85c multicolored 1.75 1.75
633 A101 $1 multicolored 2.00 2.00
Nos. 628-633 (6) 7.70 7.70

Stained Glass Windows — A102

Designs: 25c, Ship wreck. 60c, Birds in tree. 75c, St. Francis feeding bird. $2, Seashells.

1992, Sept. 24 ***Perf. 14***
634 A102 25c multicolored .50 .50
635 A102 60c multicolored 1.25 1.25
636 A102 75c multicolored 1.50 1.50
637 A102 $2 multicolored 4.00 4.00
Nos. 634-637 (4) 7.25 7.25

7th World Congress of Kennel Clubs A103

Perf. 13½x14, 14x13½
1992, Nov. 12 Litho. Wmk. 373
638 A103 25c German shepherd .50 .50
639 A103 35c Irish setter .65 .65
640 A103 60c Whippet, vert. 1.10 1.10
641 A103 75c Border terrier, vert. 1.40 1.40
642 A103 85c Pomeranian, vert. 1.60 1.60
643 A103 $1 Schipperke, vert. 1.90 1.90
Nos. 638-643 (6) 7.15 7.15

A104

Tourist Posters — A105

1993, Feb. 25 Wmk. 373 *Perf. 14*
644 A104 25c Cyclist, carriage, ship .50 .50
645 A105 60c Golf course 1.10 1.10
646 A105 75c Coastline 1.40 1.40
647 A104 $2 Dancers 3.75 3.75
Nos. 644-647 (4) 6.75 6.75

Royal Air Force, 75th Anniv.
Common Design Type

Designs: 25c, Consolidated Catalina. 60c, Supermarine Spitfire. 75c, Bristol Beaufighter. $2, Handley Page Halifax.

1993, Apr. 1
648 CD350 25c multicolored .50 .50
649 CD350 60c multicolored 1.10 1.10
650 CD350 75c multicolored 1.40 1.40
651 CD350 $2 multicolored 3.75 3.75
Nos. 648-651 (4) 6.75 6.75

Duchesse de Brabant Rose, Bee — A106

1993, Apr. 1 Wmk. 384
Booklet Stamps
652 A106 10c green & multi .20 .20
653 A106 25c violet & multi .50 .50
a. Booklet pane of 5 2.50
654 A106 50c sepia & multi 1.00 1.00
a. Booklet pane, 2 #652, 3 #654 3.50
655 A106 60c vermilion & multi 1.10 1.10
a. Booklet pane of 5 5.50
Nos. 652-655 (4) 2.80 2.80

Hamilton, Bicent. — A107

Designs: 25c, Modern skyline. 60c, Front Street, ships at left. 75c, Front Street, horse carts. $2, Hamilton Harbor, 1823.

Wmk. 373
1993, Sept. 16 Litho. *Perf. 14½*
656 A107 25c multicolored .50 .50
657 A107 60c multicolored 1.10 1.10
658 A107 75c multicolored 1.40 1.40
659 A107 $2 multicolored 3.75 3.75
Nos. 656-659 (4) 6.75 6.75

Furness Lines — A108

25c, Furness Liv-Aboard Bermuda cruises, vert. 60c, SS Queen of Bermuda entering port. 75c, SS Queen of Bermuda, SS Ocean Monarch. $2, Starlit night aboard ship, vert.

Perf. 15x14, 14x15
1994, Jan. 20 Litho. Wmk. 373
660 A108 25c multicolored .50 .50
661 A108 60c multicolored 1.10 1.10
662 A108 75c multicolored 1.40 1.40
663 A108 $2 multicolored 3.75 3.75
Nos. 660-663 (4) 6.75 6.75

Royal Visit — A109

25c, Queen Elizabeth II. 60c, Queen Elizabeth II, Duke of Edinburgh. 75c, Royal yacht Britannia.

Wmk. 373
1994, Mar. 9 Litho. *Perf. 13½*
664 A109 25c multicolored .50 .50
665 A109 60c multicolored 1.10 1.10
666 A109 75c multicolored 1.50 1.50
Nos. 664-666 (3) 3.10 3.10

Flowering Fruits A110

1994-95 Litho. Wmk. 373 *Perf. 14*
668 A110 5c Peach .20 .20
669 A110 7c Fig .20 .20
670 A110 10c Calabash, vert .20 .20
671 A110 15c Natal plum .30 .30
672 A110 18c Locust & wild honey .35 .35
673 A110 20c Pomegranate .40 .40
674 A110 25c Mulberry, vert. .50 .50
675 A110 35c Grape, vert. .70 .70
676 A110 55c Orange, vert. 1.10 1.10
677 A110 60c Surinam cherry 1.25 1.25
678 A110 75c Loquat 1.50 1.50
679 A110 90c Sugar apple 1.75 1.75
680 A110 $1 Prickly pear, vert. 2.00 2.00
681 A110 $2 Paw paw 4.00 4.00
682 A110 $3 Bay grape 6.00 6.00
683 A110 $5 Banana, vert. 10.00 10.00
684 A110 $8 Lemon 16.00 16.00
Nos. 668-684 (17) 46.45 46.45

No. 672 exists dated "1996." Nos. 668, 671-674, 678-680 dated "1998."
Issued: 5c, 7c, 15c, 20c, $8, 7/14/94; 10c, 25c, 35c, 55c, $1, $5, 10/6/94; 18c, 60c, 75c, 90c, $2, $3, 3/23/95.

1996-98 Wmk. 384
668a A110 5c .20 .20
671a A110 15c .30 .30
672a A110 18c .35 .35
673a A110 20c .40 .40
674a A110 25c .50 .50
678a A110 75c 1.50 1.50
679a A110 90c 1.75 1.75
680a A110 $1 2.00 2.00
Nos. 668a-680a (8) 7.00 7.00

#672a exists dated "1998."
Issued: #668a, 671a, 673a-674a, 678a-680a, 9/1/98; #672a, 9/1/96.

Hospital Care, Cent. — A111

1994, Sept. 15 *Perf. 15x14*
685 A111 25c Child birth .50 .50
686 A111 60c Dialysis 1.10 1.10
687 A111 75c Emergency 1.50 1.50
688 A111 $2 Therapy 4.00 4.00
Nos. 685-688 (4) 7.10 7.10

Christmas — A112

1994, Nov. 10 *Perf. 14x15*
689 A112 25c Gombey dancers .50 .50
690 A112 60c Carollers 1.10 1.10
691 A112 75c Marching band 1.50 1.50
692 A112 $2 Natl. dance group 4.00 4.00
Nos. 689-692 (4) 7.10 7.10

Decimalization, 25th Anniv. — A113

Stamps, 1970 coins: 25c, #255, one cent. 60c, #259, five cents. 75c, #262, ten cents. $2, #324, twenty-five cents.

Wmk. 373
1995, Feb. 6 Litho. *Perf. 14*
693 A113 25c multicolored .50 .50
694 A113 60c multicolored 1.10 1.10
695 A113 75c multicolored 1.50 1.50
696 A113 $2 multicolored 4.00 4.00
Nos. 693-696 (4) 7.10 7.10

Outdoor Celebrations — A114

Perf. 14x15
1995, May 30 Litho. Wmk. 373
697 A114 25c Kite flying .50 .50
698 A114 60c Majorettes 1.10 1.10
699 A114 75c Portuguese dancers 1.50 1.50
700 A114 $2 Floral float 4.00 4.00
Nos. 697-700 (4) 7.10 7.10

Parliament, 375th Anniv. — A115

Designs: 25c, $1, Bermuda coat of arms.

Perf. 14x13½
1995, Nov. 3 Litho. Wmk. 373
701 A115 25c blue & multi .50 .50
702 A115 $1 green & multi 2.00 2.00

See No. 731.

Military Bases A116

Force insignia and: 20c, Ordnance Island Submarine Base. 25c, Royal Naval Dockyard. 60c, Fort Bell and Kindley Field. 75c, Darrell's Island. 90c, US Navy Operating Base. $1, Canadian Forces Station, Daniel's Head.

1995, Dec. 4 *Perf. 14*
703 A116 20c multicolored .40 .40
704 A116 25c multicolored .50 .50
705 A116 60c multicolored 1.25 1.25

706 A116 75c multicolored 1.50 1.50
707 A116 90c multicolored 1.75 1.75
708 A116 $1 multicolored 2.00 2.00
Nos. 703-708 (6) 7.40 7.40

Modern Olympic Games, Cent. — A117

Wmk. 384

1996, May 21 Litho. *Perf. 14*
709 A117 25c Track & field .50 .50
710 A117 30c Cycling .65 .65
711 A117 65c Sailing 1.25 1.25
712 A117 80c Equestrian 1.60 1.60
Nos. 709-712 (4) 4.00 4.00

CAPEX '96 A118

Methods of transportation: 25c, Sommerset Express, c. 1900. 60c, Bermuda Railway, 1930's. 75c, First bus, 1946. $2, Early sightseeing bus, c.1947.

Perf. 13½x14

1996, June 7 Litho. Wmk. 373
713 A118 25c multicolored .50 .50
714 A118 60c multicolored 1.25 1.25
715 A118 75c multicolored 1.50 1.50
716 A118 $2 multicolored 4.00 4.00
Nos. 713-716 (4) 7.25 7.25

Panoramas of Hamilton and St. George's, by E. J. Holland, 1933 A119

Hamilton, looking across water from Bostock Hill: No. 717, Palm trees, Furness Line ship coming through Two Rock Passage. No. 718, House, buildings on other side. No. 719, Sailboats on water, Princess Hotel. No. 720, Island, Bermudiana Hotel, Cathedral. No. 721, Coral roads on hillside, city of Hamilton.

St. George's, looking across water from St. David's: No. 722, Island, harbor. No. 723, Sailboat, buildings along shore. No. 724, Sailboat, St. George's Hotel, buildings. No. 725, Hillside, ship. No. 726, Homes on hill top, passage out of harbor.

Perf. 14x14½

1996, May 21 Wmk. 373

Booklet Stamps
717 A119 60c multicolored 1.25 1.25
718 A119 60c multicolored 1.25 1.25
719 A119 60c multicolored 1.25 1.25
720 A119 60c multicolored 1.25 1.25
721 A119 60c multicolored 1.25 1.25
a. Strip of 5, #717-721 6.25 6.25
722 A119 60c multicolored 1.25 1.25
723 A119 60c multicolored 1.25 1.25
724 A119 60c multicolored 1.25 1.25
725 A119 60c multicolored 1.25 1.25
726 A119 60c multicolored 1.25 1.25
a. Strip of 5, #722-726 6.25 6.25
b. Booklet pane, #721a, 726a 12.50
Complete booklet, #726b 12.50

Lighthouses A120

Designs: 30c, Hog Fish Beacon. 65c, Gibbs Hill Lighthouse. 80c, St. David's Lighthouse. $2, North Rock Beacon.

Perf. 14x13½

1996, Aug. 15 Litho. Wmk. 373
727 A120 30c multicolored .60 .60
728 A120 65c multicolored 1.25 1.25
729 A120 80c multicolored 1.60 1.60
730 A120 $2 multicolored 4.00 4.00
Nos. 727-730 (4) 7.45 7.45

See Nos. 737-740.

Bermuda Coat of Arms Type of 1995 Inscribed "Commonwealth Finance Ministers Meeting"

Perf. 14x13½

1996, Sept. 24 Litho. Wmk. 373
731 A115 $1 red & multi 2.00 2.00

Queen Elizabeth II — A121

1996, Nov. 7
732 A121 $22 blue & org brn 44.00 44.00

Architectural Heritage — A122

Wmk. 384

1996, Nov. 28 Litho. *Perf. 14*
733 A122 30c Waterville .60 .60
734 A122 65c Bridge House 1.25 1.25
735 A122 80c Fannie Fox's Cottage 1.60 1.60
736 A122 $2.50 Palmetto House 5.00 5.00
Nos. 733-736 (4) 8.45 8.45

Lighthouse Type of 1996 Redrawn

Wmk. 373

1997, Feb. 12 Litho. *Perf. 14*
737 A120 30c Like #727 .60 .60
738 A120 65c Like #728 1.25 1.25
739 A120 80c Like #729 1.60 1.60
740 A120 $2.50 Like #730 5.00 5.00
Nos. 737-740 (4) 8.45 8.45

Nos. 737-740 each have Hong Kong '97 emblem. No. 738 inscribed "Gibbs Hill Lighthouse c. 1900." No. 739 inscribed "St. David's Lighthouse c. 1900."

Birds A123

Designs: 30c, White-tailed tropicbird. 60c, White-tailed tropicbird, adult, chick, vert. 80c, Cahow, adult, chick, vert. $2.50, Cahow.

Wmk. 384

1997, Apr. 17 Litho. *Perf. 14*
741 A123 30c multicolored .60 .60
742 A123 60c multicolored 1.25 1.25
743 A123 80c multicolored 1.60 1.60
744 A123 $2.50 multicolored 5.00 5.00
Nos. 741-744 (4) 8.45 8.45

See Nos. 798-801.

Queen Elizabeth II and Prince Philip, 50th Wedding Anniv. A124

Perf. 14x14½

1997, Oct. 9 Litho. Wmk. 373
745 A124 30c Queen, crowd .60 .60
746 A124 $2 Queen, Prince 4.00 4.00
a. Souvenir sheet of 2, #745-746 4.60 4.60

Education in Bermuda A125

Designs: 30c, Man, children using blocks. 40c, Teacher, students with map. 60c, Boys holding sports trophy. 65c, Students in front of Berkeley Institute. 80c, Students working in lab. 90c, Students in graduation gowns.

Wmk. 384

1997, Dec. 18 Litho. *Perf. 14*
747 A125 30c multicolored .60 .60
748 A125 40c multicolored .80 .80
749 A125 60c multicolored 1.25 1.25
750 A125 65c multicolored 1.25 1.25
751 A125 80c multicolored 1.60 1.60
752 A125 90c multicolored 1.75 1.75
Nos. 747-752 (6) 7.25 7.25

Diana, Princess of Wales (1961-97)

Common Design Type

Various portraits: a. 30c. b, 40c. c, 65c. d, 80c.

Perf. 14x14½

1998, Mar. 31 Litho. Wmk. 373
753 CD355 Sheet of 4, #a.-d. 4.75 4.75

No. 753 sold for $2.15 + 25c, with surtax from international sales being donated to the Princess Diana Memorial Fund and surtax from national sales being donated to designated local charity.

Paintings of the Islands A126

Designs: 30c, Fox's Cottage, St. David's. 40c, East Side, Somerset. 65c, Long Bay Road, Somerset. $2, Flatts Village.

1998, June 4 *Perf. 13½x14*
754 A126 30c multicolored .60 .60
755 A126 40c multicolored .80 .80
756 A126 65c multicolored 1.25 1.25
757 A126 $2 multicolored 4.00 4.00
Nos. 754-757 (4) 6.65 6.65

Hospitality for Tourists in Bermuda — A127

Designs: 25c, Carriage ride. 30c, Golfer at registration desk. 65c, Maid leaving flowers on hotel bed. 75c, Chefs preparing food. 80c, Waiter serving couple. 90c, Singer, bartender, guests.

Wmk. 384

1998, Sept. 24 Litho. *Perf. 14½*
758 A127 25c multicolored .50 .50
759 A127 30c multicolored .60 .60
760 A127 65c multicolored 1.25 1.25
761 A127 75c multicolored 1.50 1.50
762 A127 80c multicolored 1.60 1.60
763 A127 90c multicolored 1.75 1.75
Nos. 758-763 (6) 7.20 7.20

Bermuda's Botantical Gardens, Cent. — A128

Wmk. 373

1998, Oct. 15 Litho. *Perf. 14*
764 A128 30c Agave attenuata .60 .60
765 A128 65c Bermuda palmetto tree 1.25 1.25
766 A128 $1 Banyan tree 2.00 2.00
767 A128 $2 Cedar tree 4.00 4.00
Nos. 764-767 (4) 7.85 7.85

Christmas A129

Children's paintings: 25c, Lizard in Santa hat stringing Christmas lights, vert. 40c, Stairway, wreath on door.

Wmk. 373

1998, Nov. 26 Litho. *Perf. 14*
768 A129 25c multicolored .50 .50
769 A129 40c multicolored .75 .75

Beaches — A130

Wmk. 373

1999, Apr. 29 Litho. *Perf. 13½*
770 A130 30c Shelly Bay .60 .60
771 A130 60c Catherine's Bay 1.25 1.25
772 A130 65c Jobson's Cove 1.25 1.25
773 A130 $2 Warwick Long Bay 4.00 4.00
Nos. 770-773 (4) 7.10 7.10

Common Design Type and:

First Manned Moon Landing, 30th Anniv. A131

Wmk. 373

1999, July 20 Litho. *Perf. 13*
774 A131 30c Ground station .60 .60
775 A131 60c Lift-off, vert. 1.25 1.25
776 A131 75c Aerial view of ground station 1.50 1.50
777 A131 $2 Moon walk, vert. 4.00 4.00
Nos. 774-777 (4) 7.35 7.35

Souvenir Sheet

Wmk. 384

Perf. 14
778 CD357 65c Looking at earth from moon 1.25 1.25

No. 778 contains one 40mm circular stamp.

Mapmaking — A132

Wmk. 373

1999, Aug. 19 Litho. *Perf. 14*
779 A132 30c Somerset Is., theodolite .60 .60
780 A132 65c 1901 street map 1.25 1.25
781 A132 80c Aerial photo, modern street map 1.60 1.60
782 A132 $1 Satellite, island 2.00 2.00
Nos. 779-782 (4) 5.45 5.45

Mail Boxes and Stamps — A133

Wmk. 373

1999, Oct. 5 Litho. *Perf. 14¼*

783 A133 30c Victoria era, #6 .60 .60
784 A133 75c George V era, #49 1.50 1.50
785 A133 95c George VI era, #121 1.90 1.90
786 A133 $1 Elizabeth II era, #142 2.00 2.00
Nos. 783-786 (4) 6.00 6.00

Pioneers of Progress — A134

No. 787: a, Dr. E. F. Gordon, labor leader. b, Sir Henry Tucker, banker. c, Gladys Morrell, suffragist.
Illustration reduced.

Perf. 13½x13¼

2000, May 1 Litho. Wmk. 373

787 A134 30c Horiz. strip of 3, #a-c 1.90 1.90

Sailing Ships — A135

Designs: 30c, Amerigo Vespucci. 60c, Europa. 80c Juan Sebastian de Elcano.

2000, May 23 *Perf. 14*

788 A135 30c multi .60 .60
789 A135 60c multi 1.25 1.25
790 A135 80c multi 1.60 1.60
Nos. 788-790 (3) 3.45 3.45

Royal Family Birthdays — A136

35c, Prince William, 18th. 40c, Prince Andrew, 40th. 50c, Princess Anne, 50th. 70c, Princess Margaret, 70th. $1, Queen Mother, 100th.

2000, Aug. 7

791 A136 35c multi .70 .70
792 A136 40c multi .80 .80
793 A136 50c multi 1.00 1.00
794 A136 70c multi 1.40 1.40
795 A136 $1 multi 2.00 2.00
  a. Souvenir sheet, #791-795 6.00 6.00
Nos. 791-795 (5) 5.90 5.90

Christmas A137

Children's art: 30c, Santa Claus and Bermuda onion, by Meghan Jones. 45c, Christmas tree, by Carlita Lodge.

Wmk. 384

2000, Sept. 26 Litho. *Perf. 13¾*

796-797 A137 Set of 2 1.40 1.40

Bird Type of 1997 Redrawn with WWF Emblem

Designs: No. 798, 15c, White-tailed tropic bird. No. 799, 15c, Cahow. No. 800, 20c, Cahow, vert. No. 801, 20c, White-tailed tropic bird, vert.

Wmk. 373

2001, Feb. 1 Litho. *Perf. 14*

798-801 A123 Set of 4 1.40 1.40
801a Miniature sheet, 4 each #798-801 5.75

Hong Kong 2001 Stamp Exhibition (No. 801a).

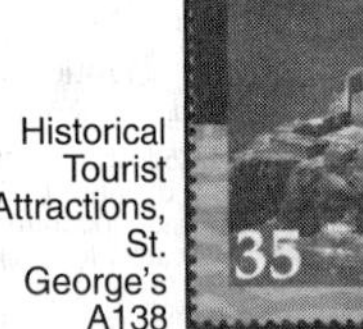

Historical Tourist Attractions, St. George's A138

Designs: 35c, King's Castle. 50c, Bridge House. 55c, Whitehall. 70c, Fort Cunningham. 85c, St. Peter's Church. 95c, Water Street.

2001, May 1 *Perf. 13¾*

802-807 A138 Set of 6 7.75 7.75

Boer War, Cent. — A139

Designs: 35c, Crowded boat, plow. 50c, Men, boot last. 70c, Man with children, rings and pin. 95c, Men and women, stamped cover.

2001, June 28 *Perf. 14*

808-811 A139 Set of 4 5.00 5.00

Aquarium, Museum and Zoo, 75th Anniv. — A140

Designs: 35c, Child, sea urchins, starfish, vert. 50c, Child, museum display. 55c, Child, tortoise. 70c, Aquarium. 80c, Diver in aquarium tank, vert. 95c, Turtle, vert.

Perf. 14¾x14¼, 14¼x14¾

2001, Aug. 9 Litho. Wmk. 373

812-817 A140 Set of 6 7.75 7.75

Paintings by Charles Lloyd Tucker — A141

Various paintings: 35c, 70c, 85c, $1.

2001, Oct. 9 *Perf. 14¼x14¾*

818-821 A141 Set of 4 6.00 6.00

Reign Of Queen Elizabeth II, 50th Anniv. Issue

Common Design Type

Designs: Nos. 822, 826a, 10c, Princess Elizabeth with dog, 1952. Nos. 823, 826b, 35c, In 1965. Nos. 824, 826c, 70c, Waving. Nos. 825, 826d, 85c, In 1991. No. 826e, $1, 1955 portrait by Annigoni (38x50mm).

Perf. 14¼x14½, 13¾ (#826e)

2002, Feb. 6 Litho. Wmk. 373

With Gold Frames

822-825 CD360 Set of 4 4.00 4.00

Souvenir Sheet

Without Gold Frames

826 CD360 Sheet of 5, #a-e 6.00 6.00

Caves A142

Designs: 35c, Fantasy Cave. 70c, Crystal Cave. 80c, Prospero's Cave. $1, Cathedral Cave.

Wmk. 373

2002, May 1 Litho. *Perf. 14*

827-830 A142 Set of 4 5.75 5.75

Cricket Cup Match, Cent. — A143

Details from "One Hundred Up," by Robert D. Bassett: No. 831, 35c, Umpire and fielder. No. 832, 35c, Batsman and wicketkeeper.
$1, Entire painting, horiz.

Wmk. 373

2002, July 4 Litho. *Perf. 14*

831-832 A143 Set of 2 1.40 1.40

Souvenir Sheet

833 A143 $1 multi 2.00 2.00

Queen Mother Elizabeth (1900-2002)

Common Design Type

Designs: Nos. 834, 836a, 30c, Without hat (sepia photograph). Nos. 835, 836b, $1.25, Wearing blue hat.

Perf. 13¾x14¼

2002, Aug. 5 Litho. Wmk. 373

With Purple Frames

834-835 CD361 Set of 2 3.25 3.25

Souvenir Sheet

Without Purple Frames

Perf. 14½x14¼

836 CD361 Sheet of 2, #a-b 3.25 3.25

Shells — A144

Designs: 5c, Slit worm-shell. 10c, Netted olive. 35c, Noble wentletrap. 45c, Zigzag scallop. 50c, Bermuda cone. $8, Sunrise tellin.

Wmk. 373

2002, Sept. 10 Litho. *Perf. 14*

837 A144 5c multi .20 .20
838 A144 10c multi .20 .20
842 A144 35c multi .70 .70
844 A144 45c multi .90 .90
845 A144 50c multi 1.00 1.00
854 A144 $8 multi 16.00 16.00
Nos. 837-854 (6) 19.00 19.00

This is an expanding set.

World Peace Day — A145

Dove facing: 35c, Right. 70c, Left.

Wmk. 373

2002, Nov. 7 Litho. *Perf. 14¼*

855-856 A145 Set of 2 2.10 2.10

POSTAL-FISCAL STAMP

"Revenue Revenue" PF1

1936 Typo. Wmk. 4 *Perf. 14*

Chalky Paper

AR1 PF1 12sh6p org & grayish blk 1,200. *2,250.*
Revenue cancel 75.00

#AR1 was authorized for postal use from Feb. 1 through May, 1937 and during Nov. and Dec. 1937. Used values are for examples with dated postal cancels indicating usage during the authorized periods. Beware of bogus and improperly dated favor cancels

WAR TAX STAMPS

No. 42 Overprinted

1918 Wmk. 3 *Perf. 14*

MR1 A11 1p rose red .50 .40

No. 42a Overprinted

1920

MR2	A11	1p carmine	.45	*.80*

BHUTAN

bü-'tän

LOCATION — Eastern Himalayas
GOVT. — Kingdom
AREA — 18,000 sq. mi.
POP. — 1,951,965(?) (1999 est.)
CAPITAL — Thimphu

100 Chetrum = 1 Ngultrum or Rupee

Catalogue values for all unused stamps in this country are for Never Hinged items.

Postal Runner — A1

Designs: 3ch, 70ch, Archer. 5ch, 1.30nu, Yak. 15ch, Map of Bhutan, portrait of Druk Gyalpo (Dragon King) Ugyen Wangchuk (1867-1902) and Paro Dzong (fortress-monastery). 33ch, Postal runner. All horiz. except 2ch and 33ch.

Perf. 14x14½, 14½x14

1962 Litho. Unwmk.

1	A1	2ch red & gray	.20	.20
2	A1	3ch red & ultra	.20	.20
3	A1	5ch green & brown	.85	.85
4	A1	15ch red, blk & org yel	.20	.20
5	A1	33ch blue grn & lil	.20	.20
6	A1	70ch dp ultra & lt blue	.50	.50
7	A1	1.30nu blue & black	1.10	1.00
		Nos. 1-7 (7)	3.25	3.15

Nos. 1-7 were issued for inland use in April, 1962, and became valid for international mail on Oct. 10, 1962.

For overprint & surcharges see #42, 72-73.

Refugee Year Emblem and Arms of Bhutan A2

1962, Oct. 10 ***Perf. 14½x14***

8	A2	1nu dk blue & dk car rose	.75	.75
9	A2	2nu yel grn & red lilac	2.25	2.25

World Refugee Year. For surcharges see #68-69.

Equipment of Ancient Warrior — A3

Boy Filling Grain Box and Wheat Emblem — A4

1963 Unwmk. ***Perf. 14x14½***

10	A3	33ch multicolored	.20	.20
11	A3	70ch multicolored	.40	.40
12	A3	1.30nu multicolored	.75	.75
		Nos. 10-12 (3)	1.35	1.35

Bhutan's membership in Colombo Plan.

1963, July 15 ***Perf. 13½x14***

13	A4	20ch lt blue, yel & red brn	.20	.20
14	A4	1.50nu rose lil, bl & red brn	.65	.65

FAO "Freedom from Hunger" campaign.

For surcharge see No. 117M.

Masked Dancer — A5

Various Bhutanese Dancers (Five Designs; 2ch, 5ch, 20ch, 1nu, 1.30nu vert.)

1964, Apr. 16 ***Perf. 14½x14, 14x14½***

15	A5	2ch multicolored	.20	.20
16	A5	3ch multicolored	.20	.20
17	A5	5ch multicolored	.20	.20
18	A5	20ch multicolored	.20	.20
19	A5	33ch multicolored	.20	.20
20	A5	70ch multicolored	.20	.20
21	A5	1nu multicolored	.35	.35
22	A5	1.30nu multicolored	.40	.40
23	A5	2nu multicolored	.65	.65
		Nos. 15-23 (9)	2.60	2.60

For surcharges & overprints see #70-71, 74-75, 129A, 129G, C1-C3, C11-C13.

Stone Throwing A6

Sport: 5ch, 33ch, Boxing. 1nu, 3nu, Archery. 2nu, Soccer.

1964, Oct. 10 Litho. ***Perf. 14½***

24	A6	2ch emerald & multi	.20	.20
25	A6	5ch orange & multi	.20	.20
26	A6	15ch brt citron & multi	.20	.20
27	A6	33ch rose lil & multi	.20	.20
28	A6	1nu multicolored	.40	.40
29	A6	2nu rose lilac & multi	.60	.60
30	A6	3nu lt blue & multi	.90	.90
		Nos. 24-30 (7)	2.70	2.70

18th Olympic Games, Tokyo, Oct. 10-25. See No. B4.

Nos. 24-30 exist imperf. Value $8.

Flags of the World at Half-mast — A7

1964, Nov. 22 Unwmk. ***Perf. 14½***

Flags in Original Colors

31	A7	33ch steel gray	.20	.20
32	A7	1nu silver	.45	.45
33	A7	3nu gold	1.10	1.10
a.		Souv. sheet, perf. 13½ or imperf.	3.50	3.50
		Nos. 31-33 (3)	1.75	1.75

Issued in memory of those who died in the service of their country. Nos. 31-33 exist imperf.

No. 33a contains 2 stamps similar to Nos. 32-33.

For overprints see Nos. 44, 46.

Flowers — A8

1965, Jan. 6 Litho. ***Perf. 13***

34	A8	2ch Primrose	.20	.20
35	A8	5ch Gentian	.20	.20
36	A8	15ch Primrose	.20	.20
37	A8	33ch Gentian	.20	.20
38	A8	50ch Rhododendron	.20	.20
39	A8	75ch Peony	.20	.20
40	A8	1nu Rhododendron	.20	.20
41	A8	2nu Peony	.40	.40
		Nos. 34-41 (8)	1.80	1.80

For overprints see #43, 45, C4-C5, C14-C15.

Nos. 5, 40, 32, 41 and 33 Overprinted: "WINSTON CHURCHILL 1874-1965"

1965, Feb. 27

42	A1	33ch bl grn & lilac	.35	.35
43	A8	1nu pink, grn & dk gray	.60	.60
44	A7	1nu silver & multi	.50	.50
45	A8	2nu sepia, yel & grn	.70	.70
46	A7	3nu gold & multi	.85	.85
		Nos. 42-46 (5)	3.00	3.00

Issued in memory of Sir Winston Churchill (1874-1965), British statesman. The overprint is in three lines on Nos. 42-43 and 45; in two lines on Nos. 43 and 46.

#44, 46 exist imperf. Value, both, $4.50.

Skyscraper, Pagoda and World's Fair Emblem — A9

Designs: 10ch, 2nu, Pieta by Michelangelo and statue of Khmer Buddha. 20ch, Skyline of NYC and Bhutanese village. 33ch, George Washington Bridge, NY, and foot bridge, Bhutan.

1965, Apr. 21 Litho. ***Perf. 14½***

47	A9	1ch blue & multi	.20	.20
48	A9	10ch green & multi	.20	.20
49	A9	20ch rose lilac & multi	.20	.20
50	A9	33ch bister & multi	.20	.20
51	A9	1.50nu bister & multi	.45	.45
52	A9	2nu multicolored	.60	.60
a.		Souv. sheet, perf. 13½ or imperf.	2.75	2.75
		Nos. 47-52 (6)	1.85	1.85

Nos. 47-52 exist imperf.; value $3.50.

No. 52a contains two stamps similar to Nos. 51-52.

For overprints see #87-87B, C6-C10, C16-C20.

Telstar, Short-wave Radio and ITU Emblem — A10

Designs (ITU Emblem and): 2nu, Telstar and Morse key. 3nu, Syncom and ear phones.

1966, Mar. 2 Litho. ***Perf. 14½***

53	A10	35ch multicolored	.20	.20
54	A10	2nu multicolored	.55	.55
55	A10	3nu multicolored	.75	.75
		Nos. 53-55 (3)	1.50	1.50

Cent. (in 1965) of the ITU. Souvenir sheets exist containing two stamps similar to Nos. 54-55, perf. 13½ and imperf. Value, 2 sheets, $5.

Leopard — A11

Animals: 1ch, 4nu, Asiatic black bear. 4ch, 2nu, Pigmy hog. 8ch, 75ch, Tiger. 10ch, 1.50nu, Dhole (Asiatic hunting dog). 1nu, 5nu, Takin (goat).

1966, Mar. 24 Litho. ***Perf. 13***

56	A11	1ch yellow & blk	.20	.20
57	A11	2ch pale grn & blk	.20	.20
58	A11	4ch lt citron & blk	.20	.20
59	A11	8ch lt blue & blk	.20	.20
60	A11	10ch lt lilac & blk	.20	.20
61	A11	75ch lt yel grn & blk	.20	.20
62	A11	1nu lt green & blk	.50	.50
63	A11	1.50nu lt bl grn & blk	.40	.40
64	A11	2nu dull org & blk	.50	.50
65	A11	3nu bluish lil & blk	.75	.75
66	A11	4nu lt green & blk	1.00	1.00
67	A11	5nu pink & black	1.40	1.40
		Nos. 56-67 (12)	5.75	5.75

For surcharges see Nos. 115C, 115E, 115I, 117N, 117P, 129B, 129J.

Nos. 6-9, 20-23 Surcharged

10 CH

1965(?) ***Perf. 14½x14, 14x14½***

68	A2	5ch on 1nu	*26.00*	*26.00*
69	A2	5ch on 2nu	*26.00*	*26.00*
70	A5	10ch on 70ch	*4.25*	*4.25*
71	A5	10ch on 2nu	*4.25*	*4.25*
72	A1	15ch on 70ch	*6.25*	*6.25*
73	A1	15ch on 1.30nu	*6.25*	*6.25*
74	A5	20ch on 1nu	*8.25*	*8.25*
75	A5	20ch on 1.30nu	*8.25*	*8.25*
		Nos. 68-75 (8)	*89.50*	*89.50*

The surcharges on Nos. 68-69 contain two bars at left and right obliterating the denomination on both sides of the design. Four bars on Nos. 72-73.

Simtokha Dzong A12

Tashichho Dzong — A13

Daga Dzong A14

Designs: 5ch, Rinpung Dzong. 50ch, Tongsa Dzong. 1nu, Lhuntsi Dzong.

Perf. 14½x14 (A12), 13½ (A13, A14)

1966-70 Photo.

76	A12	5ch orange brn ('67)	.20	.20
77	A13	10ch dk grn & rose vio ('68)	.20	.20
78	A12	15ch brown	.20	.20
79	A12	20ch green	.20	.20
80	A13	50ch blue grn ('68)	.25	.20
81	A14	75ch dk bl & ol gray ('70)	.25	.25
82	A14	1nu dk vio & vio bl ('70)	.40	.40
		Nos. 76-82 (7)	1.70	1.65

Sizes: 5ch, 15ch, 20ch, 37x20½mm. 10ch, 53½x28½mm. 50ch, 35½x25½mm.

King Jigme Wangchuk — A14a

Coins: 1.30nu, 3nu, 5nu, reverse.

Litho. & Embossed on Gold Foil

1966, July 8 Die Cut *Imperf.*

No.	Design	Value	Color	Unused	Used
83	A14a	10ch	green	.20	.20
83A	A14a	25ch	green	.20	.20
83B	A14a	50ch	green	.35	.35
83C	A14a	1nu	red	.60	.60
83D	A14a	1.30nu	red	.80	.80
83E	A14a	2nu	red	1.10	1.10
83F	A14a	3nu	red	1.75	1.75
83G	A14a	4nu	red	2.50	2.50
83H	A14a	5nu	red	3.00	3.00
			Nos. 83-83H (9)	10.50	10.50

See Nos. 98-98B.

Abominable Snowman — A14b

1966 Photo. *Perf. 13½*

No.	Design	Value	Description	Unused	Used
84	A14b	1ch	multicolored	.20	.20
84A	A14b	2ch	multi, diff.	.20	.20
84B	A14b	3ch	multi, diff.	.20	.20
84C	A14b	4ch	multi, diff.	.20	.20
84D	A14b	5ch	multi, diff.	.20	.20
84E	A14b	15ch	like #84	.20	.20
84F	A14b	30ch	like #84A	.20	.20
84G	A14b	40ch	like #84B	.20	.20
84H	A14b	50ch	like #84C	.20	.20
84I	A14b	1.25nu	like #84D	.30	.30
84J	A14b	2.50nu	like #84	.65	.65
84K	A14b	3nu	like #84A	.75	.75
84L	A14b	5nu	like #84B	1.25	1.25
84M	A14b	6nu	like #84C	1.25	1.25
84N	A14b	7nu	like #84D	1.25	1.25
			Nos. 84-84N (15)	7.25	7.25

Issue dates: 1ch, 2ch, 3ch, 4ch, 5ch, 15ch, 30ch, 40ch, 50ch, Oct. 12; others, Nov. 15. Exist imperf.

For overprints see Nos. 93-93G. For surcharges see Nos. 115D, 115K, 115O, 115P, 117I, 117S.

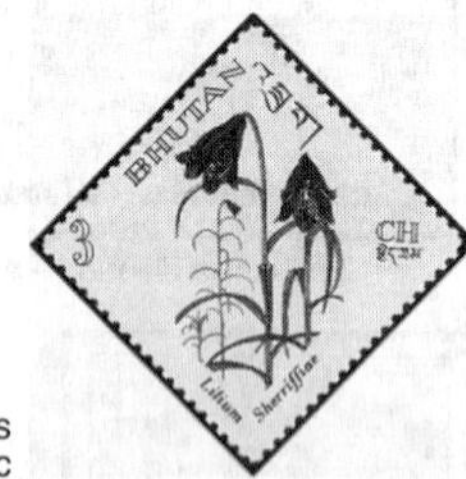

Flowers A14c

Designs: 3ch, 50ch, Lilium sherriffiae. 5ch, 1nu, Meconopsis dhwoju. 7ch, 2.50nu, Rhododendron chaetomallum. 10ch, 4nu, Pleione hookeriana. 5nu, Rhododendron giganteum.

1967, Feb. 9 Litho. *Perf. 13*

No.	Design	Value	Description	Unused	Used
85	A14c	3ch	multicolored	.20	.20
85A	A14c	5ch	multicolored	.20	.20
85B	A14c	7ch	multicolored	.20	.20
85C	A14c	10ch	multicolored	.20	.20

Gray Background

No.	Design	Value	Description	Unused	Used
85D	A14c	50ch	multicolored	.20	.20
85E	A14c	1nu	multicolored	.30	.30
85F	A14c	2.50nu	multicolored	.75	.75
85G	A14c	4nu	multicolored	1.25	1.25
85H	A14c	5nu	multicolored	1.50	1.50
			Nos. 85-85H (9)	4.80	4.80

For surcharges see Nos. 115F, 115L.

Boy Scouts — A14d

1967, Mar. 28 Photo. *Perf. 13½*

No.	Design	Value	Description	Unused	Used
86	A14d	5ch	Planting tree	.20	.20
86A	A14d	10ch	Cooking	.20	.20
86B	A14d	15ch	Mountain climbing	.20	.20

Emblem, Border in Gold

No.	Design	Value	Description	Unused	Used
86C	A14d	50ch	like #86	.20	.20
86D	A14d	1.25nu	like #86A	.60	.60
86E	A14d	4nu	like #86B	1.75	1.75
f.			Souv. sheet of 2, #86D, 86E	6.00	6.00
			Nos. 86-86E (6)	3.15	3.15

Exist imperf. Value, $6.

See Nos. 89-89E for overprints. For surcharges see Nos. 115G, 117J, 129K.

Nos. 50-52, 52a Ovptd.

Perfs. as Before

1967, May 25 Litho.

No.	Design	Value	Description	Unused	Used
87	A9	33ch	on #50	.20	.20
87A	A9	1.50nu	on #51	.45	.45
87B	A9	2nu	on #52	.60	.60
c.			Souv. sheet of 2, on #52a	1.50	1.50
			Nos. 87-87B (3)	1.25	1.25

Nos. 87-87B exist imperf.

Airplanes — A14f

1967, June 26 Litho. *Perf. 13½*

No.	Design	Value	Description	Unused	Used
88	A14f	45ch	Lancaster	.20	.20
88A	A14f	2nu	Spitfire	.45	.45
88B	A14f	4nu	Hurricane	.95	.95
c.			Souv. sheet of 2, #88A, 88B	2.00	2.00
			Nos. 88-88B (3)	1.60	1.60

Churchill and Battle of Britain. Exist imperf.

For surcharges see Nos. 117Q, 117T.

Nos. 86-86D, 86e Overprinted "WORLD JAMBOREE / IDAHO, U.S.A. / AUG. 1-9,/67"

1967, Aug. 8 Photo. *Perf. 13½*

No.	Design	Value	Description	Unused	Used
89	A14d	5ch	Planting tree	.20	.20
89A	A14d	10ch	Cookout	.20	.20
89B	A14d	15ch	Mountain climbing	.20	.20
89C	A14d	50ch	like #89	.20	.20
89D	A14d	1.25nu	like #89A	.55	.55
89E	A14d	4nu	like #89B	1.90	1.90
f.			Souv. sheet of 2, #89D, 89E	3.25	3.25
			Nos. 89-89E (6)	3.25	3.25

No. 89Ef sold for 6.25nu. Exist imperf.

Girl Scouts — A14g

1967, Sept. 28 Photo. *Perf. 13½*

No.	Design	Value	Description	Unused	Used
90	A14g	5ch	Painting	.20	.20
90A	A14g	10ch	Making music	.20	.20
90B	A14g	15ch	Picking fruit	.20	.20

Emblem, Border in Gold

No.	Design	Value	Description	Unused	Used
90C	A14g	1.50nu	like #90	.50	.50
90D	A14g	2.50nu	like #90A	1.00	1.00
90E	A14g	5nu	like #90B	2.10	2.10
f.			Souv. sheet of 2, #90A, 90B	5.00	5.00
			Nos. 90-90E (6)	4.20	4.20

Exist imperf. Value, $8.50.

For surcharge see No. 266.

Astronaut, Space Capsule — A14h

Astronaut walking in space and: 5ch, 30ch, 4nu, Orbiter, Lunar modules docked. 7ch, 50ch, 5nu, Lunar module. 10ch, 1.25nu, 9nu, Other astronauts.

1967, Oct. 30 Litho. *Imperf.*

No.	Design	Value	Description	Unused	Used
91	A14h	3ch	multi	.20	.20
91A	A14h	5ch	multi	.20	.20
91B	A14h	7ch	multi	.20	.20
91C	A14h	10ch	multi	.25	.25
m.			Souv. sheet of 4, #91-91C	2.25	2.25
91D	A14h	15ch	multi	.35	.35
91E	A14h	30ch	multi	.75	.75
91F	A14h	50ch	multi	1.25	1.25
91G	A14h	1.25nu	multi	3.00	3.00
n.			Souv. sheet of 4, #91D-91G	5.00	5.00
91H	A14h	2.50nu	multi	1.75	1.75
91I	A14h	4nu	multi	3.00	3.00
91J	A14h	5nu	multi	3.75	3.75
91K	A14h	9nu	multi	6.50	6.50
o.			Souv. sheet of 4, #91H-91K	15.00	15.00
			Nos. 91-91K (12)	21.20	21.20

Nos. 91H-91K are airmail. Simulated 3-dimensions using a plastic overlay.

For other space issues see designs A15a, A15e.

Pheasants — A14i

Designs: 1ch, 2nu, Tragopan satyra. 2ch, 4nu, Lophophorus sclareti. 4ch, 5nu, Lophophorus impeyanus. 8ch, 7nu, Lophura leucomelana. 15ch, 9nu, Crossoptilon crossoptilon.

1968 Photo. *Perf. 13½*

No.	Design	Value	Description	Unused	Used
92	A14i	1ch	multicolored	.20	.20
92A	A14i	2ch	multicolored	.20	.20
92B	A14i	4ch	multicolored	.20	.20
92C	A14i	8ch	multicolored	.20	.20
92D	A14i	15ch	multicolored	.20	.20

Border in Gold

No.	Design	Value	Description	Unused	Used
92E	A14i	2nu	multicolored	.40	.40
92F	A14i	4nu	multicolored	.80	.80
92G	A14i	5nu	multicolored	1.00	1.00
92H	A14i	7nu	multicolored	1.40	1.40
92I	A14i	9nu	multicolored	1.90	1.90
			Nos. 92-92I (10)	6.50	6.50

Issue dates: 1ch, 2ch, 4ch, 8ch, 15ch, 2nu, 4nu, 7nu, Jan 20; 5nu, 9nu, Apr. 23.

Unauthorized imperfs exist. Value, $10.

For surcharges see Nos. 115H, 117R, 117V, 129D, 129L.

Nos. 84G, 84I, 84K, 84M Ovptd. in Black on Silver

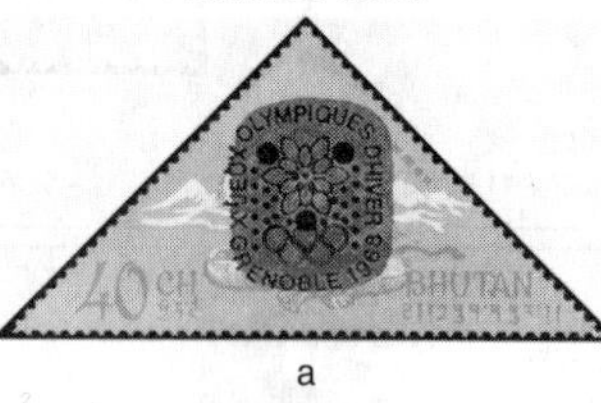

a

b

Perfs. as Before

1968, Feb. 16 Photo.

Overprint Type "a"

No.	Design	Value	Description	Unused	Used
93	A14b	40ch	on #84G	.20	.20
93A	A14b	1.25nu	on #84I	.20	.20
93B	A14b	3nu	on #84K	.50	.50
93C	A14b	6nu	on #84M	1.00	1.00

Overprint Type "b"

No.	Design	Value	Description	Unused	Used
93D	A14b	40ch	on #84G	.20	.20
93E	A14b	1.25nu	on #84I	.20	.20
93F	A14b	3nu	on #84K	.50	.50
93G	A14b	6nu	on #84M	1.00	1.00
			Nos. 93-93G (8)	3.80	3.80

Exist imperf. Value, $20.

Snow Lion — A14j

1968, Mar. 14 Photo. *Perf. 12½*

No.	Design	Value	Description	Unused	Used
94	A14j	2ch	Elephant	.20	.20
94A	A14j	3ch	Garuda	.20	.20
94B	A14j	4ch	Monastery Tiger	.20	.20
94C	A14j	5ch	Wind Horse	.20	.20
94D	A14j	15ch	Snow Lion	.20	.20
94E	A14j	20ch	like #94	.20	.20
94F	A14j	30ch	like #94A	.20	.20
94G	A14j	50ch	like #94B	.20	.20
94H	A14j	1.25nu	like #94C	.20	.20
94I	A14j	1.50nu	like #94	.20	.20
94J	A14j	2nu	like #94D	.30	.30
94K	A14j	2.50nu	like #94A	.30	.30
94L	A14j	4nu	like #94B	.55	.55
94M	A14j	5nu	like #94C	.75	.75
94N	A14j	10nu	like #94D	1.40	1.40
			Nos. 94-94N (15)	5.30	5.30

Nos. 94I, 94K-94N are airmail. All exist imperf.

For surcharges see Nos. 115, 115M, 115Q, 117-117E, 129C, C35-C36.

Butterflies A14k

Designs: 15ch, Catagramma sorana. 50ch, Delias hyparete. 1.25nu, Anteos maerula. 2nu, Ornithoptera priamus urvilleanus. 3nu, Euploea mulciber. 4nu, Morpho rhetenor. 5nu, Papilio androgeous. 6nu, Troides magellanus.

1968, May 20 Litho. *Imperf.*

95 A14k 15ch multi .45 .45
95A A14k 50ch multi .65 .65
95B A14k 1.25nu multi 1.25 1.25
95C A14k 2nu multi 1.90 1.90
h. Souv. sheet of 4, #95-95C 8.00 8.00
95D A14k 3nu multi 2.00 2.00
95E A14k 4nu multi 2.75 2.75
95F A14k 5nu multi 2.00 2.00
95G A14k 6nu multi 3.00 3.00
i. Souv. sheet of 4, #95D-95G 11.00 11.00
Nos. 95-95G (8) 14.00 14.00

Souv. sheets issued Oct. 23. Nos. 95D-95G, 95Gi are airmail. Simulated 3-dimensions using a plastic overlay.

Paintings — A14m

1968 Litho. & Embossed *Imperf.*

96 A14m 2ch Van Gogh .20 .20
96A A14m 4ch Millet .20 .20
96B A14m 5ch Monet .20 .20
96C A14m 10ch Corot .20 .20
p. Souv. sheet of 4, #96-96C .80 .80
96D A14m 45ch like #96 .20 .20
96E A14m 80ch like #96A .35 .35
96F A14m 1.05nu like #96B .45 .45
96G A14m 1.40nu like #96C .60 .60
q. Souv. sheet of 4, #96D-96G 1.60 1.60
96H A14m 1.50nu like #96 .65 .65
96I A14m 2nu like #96 .85 .85
96J A14m 2.50nu like #96A 1.10 1.10
96K A14m 3nu like #96A 1.25 1.25
96L A14m 4nu like #96B 1.10 1.10
96M A14m 5nu like #96C 1.40 1.40
r. Souv. sheet of 4, #96I, 96K-96M 2.50 2.50
96N A14m 6nu like #96B 1.75 1.75
96O A14m 8nu like #96C 2.25 2.25
s. Souv. sheet of 4, #96H, 96J, 96N-96O 5.00 5.00
Nos. 96-96O (16) 12.75 12.75

Issued: #96-96G, 96I, 96K-96M, 7/8; #96Cp, 96Gq, 96Mr, 8/5; others, 8/28.
Nos. 96H, 96J, 96N-96O are airmail.
See Nos. 114-114O, 144-144G.

Summer Olympics, Mexico, 1968 — A14n

1968, Oct. 1 Photo. *Perf. 13½*

97 A14n 5ch Discus .20 .20
97A A14n 45ch Basketball .20 .20
97B A14n 60ch Javelin .20 .20
97C A14n 80ch Shooting .20 .20
97D A14n 1.05nu like #97 .20 .20
97E A14n 2nu like #97B .20 .20
97F A14n 3nu like #97C .35 .35
97G A14n 5nu Soccer .60 .60
h. Souv. sheet of 4, #97D, 97G 2.25 2.25
Nos. 97-97G (8) 2.15 2.15

Exist imperf.
For surcharges see Nos. 129E, B5-B7.

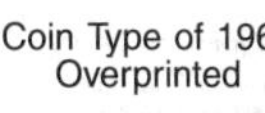

Coin Type of 1966 Overprinted

Embossed on Gold Foil

1968, Nov. 12 Die Cut *Imperf.*

98 A14a 15ch green .20 .20
98A A14a 33ch green .25 .25
98B A14a 9nu green 4.75 4.75
Nos. 98-98B (3) 5.20 5.20

Human Rights Year.

Birds — A14p

2ch, 20ch, 1.50nu, Crimson-winged laughing thrush. 3ch, 30ch, 2.50nu, Ward's trogon. 4ch, 50ch, 4nu, Grey peacock-pheasant. 5ch, 1.25nu, 5nu, Rufous necked hornbill. 15ch, 2nu, 10nu, Myzornis.

1968-69 Photo. *Perf. 12½*

99 A14p 2ch multi .20 .20
99A A14p 3ch multi, vert. .20 .20
99B A14p 4ch multi .20 .20
99C A14p 5ch multi, vert. .20 .20
99D A14p 15ch multi .25 .25
99E A14p 20ch multi .30 .30
99F A14p 30ch multi, vert. .35 .35
99G A14p 50ch multi .35 .35
99H A14p 1.25nu multi, vert. .50 .50
99I A14p 1.50nu multi .60 .60
99J A14p 2nu multi .80 .80
99K A14p 2.50nu multi, vert. .80 .80
99L A14p 4nu multi 1.25 1.25
99M A14p 5nu multi, vert. 1.75 1.75
99N A14p 10nu multi 3.25 3.25
Nos. 99-99N (15) 11.00 11.00

Issued: 2c-5ch, 15ch, 30ch, 50ch, 12/7; 20ch, 1.25nu, 2nu, 12/28; others, 1/29/69.
1.50nu, 2.50nu, 4nu, 5nu, 10nu are airmail.
Exist imperf.
For surcharges see Nos. 115A-115B, 115I, 115M, 115R, 117F-117G, 117K, 117O, 129H.

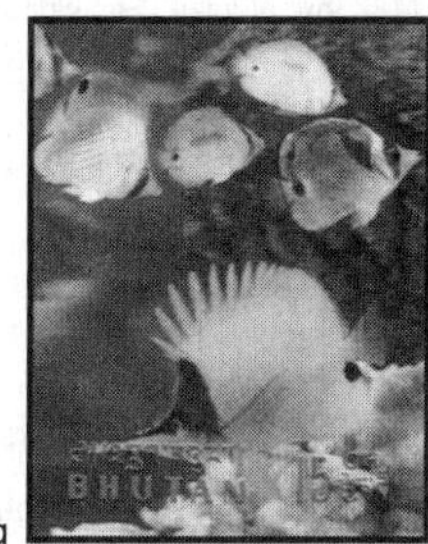

Fish — A14q

1969, Feb. 27 Litho. *Imperf.*

100 A14q 15ch multicolored .75 .75
100A A14q 20ch multi, diff. 1.00 1.00
100B A14q 30ch multi, diff. 1.50 1.50
100C A14q 5nu multi, diff. 2.00 2.00
100D A14q 6nu multi, diff. 2.50 2.50
100E A14q 7nu multi, diff. 3.00 3.00
f. Souv. sheet, #100B-100E 12.50 12.50
Nos. 100-100E (6) 10.75 10.75

Nos. 100C-100E are airmail. Simulated 3-dimensions using a plastic overlay.

Insects — A14r

1969, Apr. 10 Litho. *Imperf.*

101 A14r 10ch multicolored .55 .55
101A A14r 75ch multi, diff. .90 .90
101B A14r 1.25nu multi, diff. 1.25 1.25
101C A14r 2nu multi, diff. 2.40 2.40
h. Souv. sheet, #101-101C 17.50 17.50
101D A14r 3nu multi, diff. 3.00 3.00
101E A14r 4nu multi, diff. 1.75 1.75
101F A14r 5nu multi, diff. 2.40 2.40
101G A14r 6nu multi, diff. 3.00 3.00
i. Souv. sheet, #101D-101G 9.00 9.00
Nos. 101-101G (8) 15.25 15.25

Nos. 101D-101G, 101i are airmail. Stamps from souvenir sheets have inscription at lower right. Simulated 3-dimensions using a plastic overlay.

Admission to UPU — A14s

Illustration reduced.

1969, May 2 Photo. *Perf. 13*

102 A14s 5ch multicolored .20 .20
102A A14s 10ch multicolored .20 .20
102B A14s 15ch multicolored .20 .20
102C A14s 45ch multicolored .20 .20
102D A14s 60ch multicolored .20 .20
102E A14s 1.05nu multicolored .25 .25
102F A14s 1.40nu multicolored .35 .35
102G A14s 4nu multicolored 1.00 1.00
Nos. 102-102G (8) 2.60 2.60

Exist imperf.
For surcharges see #117H, 117L, 117U, 129.

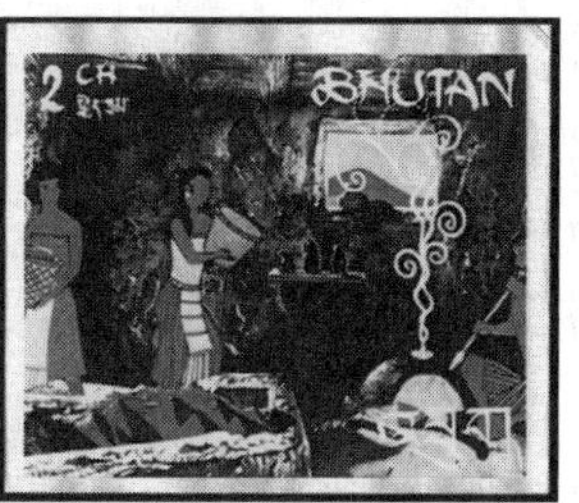

History of Steel Making — A14t

Designs: 2ch, Pre-biblical. 5ch, Damascus sword. 15ch, 3nu, Saugus Mill. 45ch, Beehive coke ovens. 75ch, 4nu, Bessemer converter. 1.50nu, 5nu, Rolling mill. 1.75nu, Steel mill. 2nu, 6nu, Future applications.

Litho. on Steel Foil

1969, June 2 *Imperf.*

Without Gum

103 A14t 2ch multicolored .20 .20
103A A14t 5ch multicolored .20 .20
103B A14t 15ch multicolored .20 .20
m. Souv. sheet, #103A-103B .60 .60
103C A14t 45ch multicolored .20 .20
n. Souv. sheet, #103, 103C .60 .60
103D A14t 75ch multicolored .20 .20
103E A14t 1.50nu multicolored .45 .45
103F A14t 1.75nu multicolored .50 .50
o. Souv. sheet, #103E-103F .60 .60
103G A14t 2nu multicolored .60 .60
p. Souv. sheet, #103D, 103G .60 .60
103H A14t 3nu multicolored .85 .85
103I A14t 4nu multicolored 1.10 1.10
103J A14t 5nu multicolored 1.40 1.40
q. Souv. sheet, #103I-103J 3.75 3.75
103K A14t 6nu multicolored 1.60 1.60
r. Souv. sheet, #103H,103K 3.75 3.75
Nos. 103-103K (12) 7.50 7.50

Nos. 103H-103K, 103q, 103r are airmail. Souv. sheets issued June 30.

Birds A14u

1969, Aug. 5 Litho. *Imperf.*

104 A14u 15ch Owl 3.50 3.50
104A A14u 50ch Red birds 3.50 3.50
104B A14u 1.25nu Hawk 3.50 3.50
104C A14u 2nu Penguin 3.50 3.50
h. Souv. sheet, #104-104C 22.50 22.50
104D A14u 3nu Macaws 3.50 3.50
104E A14u 4nu Bird of paradise 2.00 2.00
104F A14u 5nu Duck 2.25 2.25
104G A14u 6nu Pheasant 2.50 2.50
i. Souv. sheet, #104D-104G 22.50 22.50
Nos. 104-104G (8) 24.25 24.25

Nos. 104D-104G, 104Gi are airmail. Simulated 3-dimensions using a plastic overlay. Souv. sheets issued Aug. 28.

Buddhist Prayer Banners — A14v

Litho. on Cloth

1969, Sep. 30 *Imperf.*

Self-adhesive

Sizes: 15ch, 75ch, 2nu, 57x57mm, 5nu, 6nu, 70x37mm

105 A14v 15ch multicolored .20 .20
105A A14v 75ch multi, diff. .25 .25
105B A14v 2nu multi, diff. .70 .70
105C A14v 5nu multi, diff. 1.75 1.75
105D A14v 6nu multi, diff. 2.25 2.25
Nos. 105-105D (5) 5.15 5.15

Souvenir Sheet

105E Sheet of 3 5.00 5.00

No. 105E shows denominations of 75ch, 5nu, 6nu with design elements of Nos. 105A, 105C, 105D with gray frame. Exists perf. 13½.

Mahatma Gandhi — A15

1969, Oct. 2 Litho. *Perf. 13x13½*

106 A15 20ch light blue & brn .20 .20
107 A15 2nu lemon & brn olive .75 .75

Mohandas K. Gandhi (1869-1948), leader in India's struggle for independence.

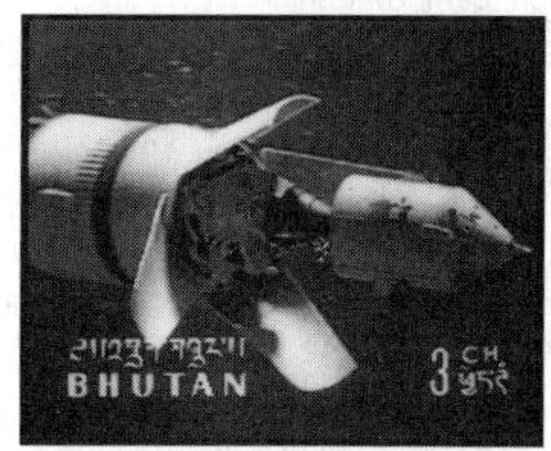

Apollo 11 Moon Landing — A15a

Designs: 3ch, Separation from third stage. 5ch, Entering lunar orbit. 15ch, Lunar module separating from orbiter. 20ch, 3nu, Astronaut standing on lunar module's foot pad. 25ch, Astronaut, lunar module on moon. 45ch, Astronaut, flag. 50ch, 4nu, Setting up experiments. 1.75nu, Lunar module docking with orbiter. 5nu, Lift-off from Cape Canaveral. 6nu, Recovery at sea.

1969 Litho. *Imperf.*

108 A15a 3ch multi .20 .20
108A A15a 5ch multi .20 .20
108B A15a 15ch multi .20 .20
108C A15a 20ch multi .25 .25
m. Souv. sheet, #108-108C 4.00 4.00
108D A15a 25ch multi .30 .30
108E A15a 45ch multi .50 .50
108F A15a 50ch multi .55 .55
108G A15a 1.75nu multi 1.75 1.75
n. Souv. sheet, #108D-108G 8.00 8.00
108H A15a 3nu multi 1.50 1.50
108I A15a 4nu multi 2.00 2.00
108J A15a 5nu multi 2.50 2.50
108K A15a 6nu multi 3.00 3.00
o. Souv. sheet, #108H-108K 21.00 21.00
Nos. 108-108K (12) 12.95 12.95

Nos. 108H-108K, 108Ko are airmail. Simulated 3-dimensions using a plastic overlay.
"Aldrin" misspelled on No. 108o.
Issue dates: Nos. 108-108G, Nov. 3; Nos. 108H-108K, Nov. 20; Souv. sheets, Dec. 20.

Paintings
A15b

1970, Jan. 19 Litho. *Imperf.*

109 A15b 5ch Clouet .20 .20
109A A15b 10ch van Eyck .20 .20
109B A15b 15ch David .20 .20
109C A15b 2.75nu Rubens .75 .75
h. Souv. sheet, #109-109C 4.00 4.00
109D A15b 3nu Homer 1.00 1.00
109E A15b 4nu Gentileschi 1.40 1.40
109F A15b 5nu Raphael 1.75 1.75
109G A15b 6nu Ghirlandaio 2.25 2.25
i. Souv. sheet, #109D-109G 4.00 4.00
Nos. 109-109G (8) 7.75 7.75

Nos. 109D-109G, 109Gi are airmail. Simulated 3-dimensions using a plastic overlay. Souv. sheets issued Feb. 25.

Various Forms of Mail Transport, UPU Headquarters, Bern — A15c

1970, Feb. 27 Photo. *Perf. 13½*

110 A15c 3ch ol grn & gold .20 .20
111 A15c 10ch red brn & gold .20 .20
112 A15c 20ch Prus bl & gold .20 .20
113 A15c 2.50nu dp mag & gold .65 .65
Nos. 110-113 (4) 1.25 1.25

New Headquarters of Universal Postal Union, Bern, Switzerland.
Exist imperf. Value $5.
For surcharge see No. 129I.

Painting Type of 1968

Paintings of flowers.

Litho. & Embossed

1970, May 6 *Imperf.*

114 A14m 2ch Van Gogh .20 .20
114A A14m 3ch Redon .20 .20
114B A14m 5ch Kuroda .20 .20
114C A14m 10ch Renoir .25 .25
p. Souv. sheet, #114-114C .75 .75
114D A14m 15ch Renoir, diff. .25 .25
114E A14m 75ch Monet .25 .25
114F A14m 80ch like #114 .50 .50
114G A14m 90ch like #114A .50 .50
114H A14m 1nu La Tour .25 .25
114I A14m 1.10nu like #114B .50 .50
114J A14m 1.40nu Oudot .50 .50
q. Souv. sheet, #114D, 114E, 114H, 114J 1.90 1.90
114K A14m 1.40nu like #114C .50 .50
r. Souv. sheet, #114F, 114G, 114I, 114K 1.25 1.25
114L A14m 1.60nu like #114D .60 .60
114M A14m 1.70nu like #114E .75 .75
114N A14m 3nu like #114H .90 .90
114O A14m 3.50nu like #114J 1.40 1.40
s. Souv. sheet, #114L-114O 2.75 2.75
Nos. 114-114O (16) 7.75 7.75

#114F-114G, 114I, 114K-114O are airmail.

Stamps of 1966-69 Surcharged

1970, June 19

115 A14j 20ch on 2nu, #94J 2.50 2.50
115A A14p 20ch on 2nu, #99J 2.50 2.50
115B A14p 20ch on 2.50nu, #99K 2.50 2.50
115C A11 20ch on 3nu, #65 2.50 2.50
115D A14b 20ch on 3nu, #84K 2.50 2.50
115E A11 20ch on 4nu, #66 2.50 2.50
115F A14c 20ch on 4nu, #85G 2.50 2.50
115G A14d 20ch on 4nu, #86E 2.50 2.50
115H A14i 20ch on 4nu, #92F 2.50 2.50
115I A14p 20ch on 4nu, #99L 2.50 2.50
115J A11 20ch on 5nu, #67 2.50 2.50
115K A14b 20ch on 5nu, #84L 2.50 2.50
115L A14c 20ch on 5nu, #85H 2.50 2.50
115M A14j 20ch on 5nu, #94M 2.50 2.50
115N A14p 20ch on 5nu, #99M 2.50 2.50
115O A14b 20ch on 6nu, #84M 2.50 2.50
115P A14b 20ch on 7nu, #84N 2.50 2.50
115Q A14j 20ch on 10nu, #94N 2.50 2.50
115R A14p 20ch on 10nu, #99N 2.50 2.50
Nos. 115-115R (19) 47.50 47.50

Nos. 115B, 115I, 115M-115N, 115Q-115R are airmail.

Animals — A15d

1970, Oct. 15 Litho. *Imperf.*

116 A15d 5ch African elephant .55 .55
116A A15d 10ch Leopard .55 .55
116B A15d 20ch Ibex .80 .80
116C A15d 25ch Tiger .80 .80
116D A15d 30ch Abominable snowman .80 .80
116E A15d 40ch Water buffalo .80 .80
116F A15d 65ch Rhinoceros 1.90 1.90
116G A15d 75ch Giant pandas 1.90 1.90
116H A15d 85ch Snow leopard 2.40 2.40
116I A15d 2nu Young deer 2.75 2.75
116J A15d 3nu Wild boar, vert. 3.25 3.25
116K A15d 4nu Collared bear, vert. 1.50 1.50
116L A15d 5nu Takin 2.00 2.00
Nos. 116-116L (13) 20.00 20.00

Nos. 116I-116L are airmail. Simulated 3-dimensions using a plastic overlay.

Stamps of 1963-69 Surcharged

1970, Nov. 2

117 A14j 5ch on 30ch, #94F .60 .60
117A A14j 5ch on 50ch, #94G .60 .60
117B A14j 5ch on 1.25nu, #94H .60 .60
117C A14j 5ch on 1.50nu, #94I .60 .60
117D A14j 5ch on 2nu, #94J .60 .60
117E A14j 5ch on 2.50nu, #94K .60 .60
117F A14p 20ch on 30ch, #99F 2.50 2.50
117G A14p 20ch on 50ch, #99G 2.50 2.50
117H A14s 20ch on 1.05nu, #102E 2.50 2.50
117I A14b 20ch on 1.25nu, #84I 2.50 2.50
117J A14d 20ch on 1.25nu, #86D 2.50 2.50
117K A14p 20ch on 1.25nu, #99H 2.50 2.50
117L A14s 20ch on 1.40nu, #102F 2.50 2.50
117M A4 20ch on 1.50nu, #14 2.50 2.50
117N A11 20ch on 1.50nu, #63 2.50 2.50
117O A14p 20ch on 1.50nu, #99I 2.50 2.50
117P A11 20ch on 2nu, #64 2.50 2.50
117Q A14f 20ch on 2nu, #88A 2.50 2.50
117R A14i 20ch on 2nu, #92E 2.50 2.50
117S A14b 20ch on 2.50nu, #84J 2.50 2.50
117T A14f 20ch on 4nu, #88B 2.50 2.50
117U A14s 20ch on 4nu, #102G 2.50 2.50
117V A14i 20ch on 7nu, #92H 2.50 2.50
Nos. 117-117V (23) 46.10 46.10

Nos. 117C, 117E, 117O are airmail.

Conquest of Space — A15e

Designs: 2ch, Jules Verne's "From the Earth to the Moon." 5ch, V-2 rocket. 15ch, Vostok. 25ch, Mariner 2. 30ch, Gemini 7. 50ch, Lift-off. 75ch, Edward White during space walk. 1.50nu, Apollo 13. 2nu, View of Earth from moon. 3nu, Another galaxy. 6nu, Moon, Earth, Sun, Mars, Jupiter. 7nu, Future space station.

1970 Litho. *Imperf.*

118 A15e 2ch multi .20 .20
118A A15e 5ch multi .20 .20
118B A15e 15ch multi .20 .20
118C A15e 25ch multi .20 .20
m. Souv. sheet, #118-118C .60 .60
118D A15e 30ch multi 3.00 3.00
118E A15e 50ch multi .35 .35
118F A15e 75ch multi .55 .55
118G A15e 1.50nu multi 1.10 1.10
n. Souv. sheet, #118D-118G 4.00 4.00
118H A15e 2nu multi .70 .70
118I A15e 3nu multi 1.00 1.00
118J A15e 6nu multi 2.00 2.00
118K A15e 7nu multi 2.25 2.25
o. Souv. sheet, #118H-118K 12.50 12.50
Nos. 118-118K (12) 11.75 11.75

Issued: #118-118G, 11/9; #118H-118K, 11/30. Souv. sheets, Dec. 18. Nos. 118H-118K are airmail. Simulated 3-dimensions using a plastic overlay.
See #127-127C. For surcharge see #129F.

Wangdiphodrang Dzong and Bridge — A15f

1971-72 Photo. *Perf. 13½*

119 A15f 2ch gray .20 .20
120 A15f 3ch deep red lilac .20 .20
121 A15f 4ch violet .20 .20
122 A15f 5ch dark green .20 .20
123 A15f 10ch orange brown .20 .20
124 A15f 15ch deep blue .20 .20
125 A15f 20ch deep plum .20 .20
Nos. 119-125 (7) 1.40 1.40

Issued: 5ch-20ch, 2/22; 2ch-4ch, 4/72.

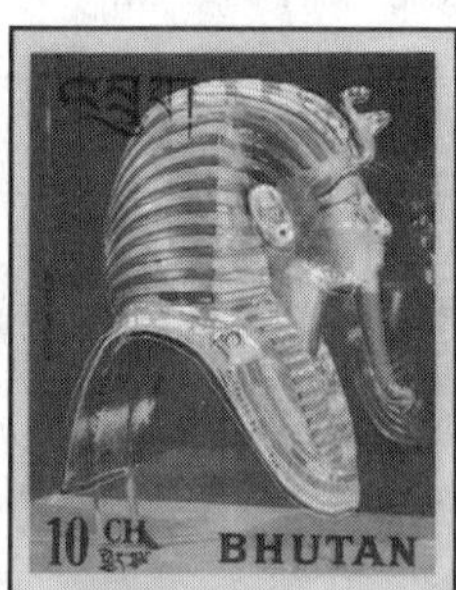

Funeral Mask of King Tutankhamen — A15g

History of Sculpture: 75ch, Winged Bull. 1.25nu, Head of Zeus. 2nu, She-wolf Suckling Romulus and Remus, horiz. 3nu, Head of Cicero. 4nu, Head of David, by Michaelangelo. 5nu, Age of Bronze, by Rodin. 6nu, Head of Woman, by Modigliani.

1971, Feb. 27 Litho. *Imperf.*

Self-adhesive

126 A15g 10ch multicolored .20 .20
126A A15g 75ch multicolored .25 .25
126B A15g 1.25nu multicolored .50 .50
126C A15g 2nu multicolored .90 .90
h. Souv. sheet, #126-126C 2.50 2.50
126D A15g 3nu multicolored 1.40 1.40
126E A15g 4nu multicolored 1.75 1.75
126F A15g 5nu multicolored 2.25 2.25
126G A15g 6nu multicolored 1.75 1.75
i. Souv. sheet, #126D-126G 6.00 6.00
Nos. 126-126G (8) 9.00 9.00

Stamps are plastic heat molded into three dimensions. Nos. 126D-126G are airmail.

Conquest of Space Type of 1970

Designs: 10ch, 2.50nu, Lunokhod 1. 1.70nu, 4nu, Apollo 15.

1971, Mar. 20 Litho. *Imperf.*

127 A15e 10ch multicolored .25 .25
127A A15e 1.70nu multicolored 1.75 1.75
127B A15e 2.50nu multicolored 2.50 2.50
127C A15e 4nu multicolored 4.00 4.00
d. Souv. sheet of 4, #127-127C 14.00 14.00
Nos. 127-127C (4) 8.50 8.50

Nos. 127B-127C are airmail. Simulated 3-dimensions using a plastic overlay.

Antique Automobiles — A15h

2ch, Mercedes Benz, Germany. 5ch, Ford, US. 10ch, Alfa Romeo, Italy. 15ch, Cord, US. 20ch, Hispano Suiza, Spain. 30ch, Invicta, Britain. 60ch, Renault, France. 75ch, Talbot, Britain. 85ch, Mercer, US. 1nu, Sunbeam, Britain. 1.20nu, Austrian Daimler. 1.55nu, Bugatti, Italy. 1.80nu, Simplex, US. 2nu, Amilcar, France. 2.50nu, Bentley, Britain. 4nu, Morris Garage, Britain. 6nu, Duesenberg, US. 7nu, Aston Martin, Britain. 9nu, Packard, US. 10nu, Rolls Royce, Britain.

1971 Litho. *Imperf.*

128-128S A15h Set of 20 17.50 17.50

Issued: #128-128F, 5/20; #128G-128N, 6/10; #128O-128S, 7/5. Nos. 128O-128S are airmail. Simulated 3-dimensions using a plastic overlay.
"Romeo" misspelled.

Stamps of 1964-71 Surcharged

1971, July 1

129 A14s 55ch on 60ch, #102D 1.00 1.00
129A A5 55ch on 1.30nu, #22 1.00 1.00
129B A11 55ch on 3nu, #65 1.00 1.00
129C A14j 55ch on 4nu, #94L .60 .60
129D A14i 55ch on 5nu, #92G 3.25 3.25
129E A14n 90ch on 1.05nu, #97D 1.50 1.50
129F A15e 90ch on 1.70nu, #127A 1.00 1.00
129G A5 90ch on 2nu, #23 1.00 1.00
129H A14p 90ch on 2nu, #99J 3.25 3.25
129I A15c 90ch on 2.50nu, #113 6.50 6.50
129J A11 90ch on 4nu, #66 1.00 1.00
129K A14d 90ch on 4nu, #86E 1.00 1.00
129L A14i 90ch on 9nu, #92I 3.25 3.25
Nos. 129-129L (13) 25.35 25.35

No. 129C is airmail. No. 129F comes with lines 8mm or 18mm long.

UN Emblem and Bhutan Flag — A16

Designs (Bhutan Flag and): 10ch, UN Headquarters, NY. 20ch, Security Council

Chamber and mural by Per Krohg. 3nu, General Assembly Hall.

1971, Sept. 21 Photo. *Perf. 13½*

130	A16	5ch gold, bl & multi	.20	.20
131	A16	10ch gold & multi	.20	.20
132	A16	20ch gold & multi	.20	.20
133	A16	3nu gold & multi	.60	.60
		Nos. 130-133,C21-C23 (7)	3.50	3.50

Bhutan's admission to the UN. Exist imperf.

For overprints see Nos. 140-143. For surcharge see No. 252.

Boy Scout Crossing Stream in Rope Sling — A17

Emblem & Boy Scouts: 20ch, 2nu, mountaineering. 50ch, 6nu, reading map. 75ch, as 10ch.

1971, Nov. 30 Litho. *Perf. 13½*

134	A17	10ch gold & multi	.20	.20
135	A17	20ch gold & multi	.20	.20
136	A17	50ch gold & multi	.20	.20
137	A17	75ch silver & multi	.20	.20
138	A17	2nu silver & multi	.20	.20
139	A17	6nu silver & multi	1.00	1.00
a.		Souv. sheet of 2, #138-139 + 2 labels	2.50	2.50
		Nos. 134-139 (6)	2.00	2.00

60th anniv. of the Boy Scouts. Exist imperf.

For overprint and surcharge see #253, 383.

Nos. 130-133 Overprinted in Gold

1971, Dec. 23

140	A16	5ch gold & multi	.30	.30
141	A16	10ch gold & multi	.30	.30
142	A16	20ch gold & multi	.30	.30
143	A16	3nu gold & multi	.60	.60
		Nos. 140-143,C24-C26 (7)	4.50	4.50

World Refugee Year. Exist imperf.

The Bathing Girl by Renoir — A17a

Designs: 20ch, A Bar at the Follies, by Monet, horiz. 90ch, Mona Lisa, by da Vinci. 1.70nu, Cart of Father Junier, by Rousseau, horiz. 2.50nu, The Gleaners, by Millet, horiz. 4.60nu, White Horse, by Gaugin. 5.40nu, The Dancing Lesson, by Degas. 6nu, After the Rain, by Gaillauman, horiz.

1972 Litho. & Embossed *Imperf.*

144	A17a	15ch multicolored	.30	.30
144A	A17a	20ch multicolored	.30	.30
144B	A17a	90ch multicolored	.35	.35
144C	A17a	1.70nu multicolored	.50	.50
144D	A17a	2.50nu multicolored	1.00	1.00
h.		Souv. sheet of 4, #144-144B, 144D	3.50	3.50
144E	A17a	4.60nu multicolored	1.40	1.40
144F	A17a	5.40nu multicolored	1.60	1.60
144G	A17a	6nu multicolored	1.90	1.90
i.		Souv. sheet of 4, #144C, 144E-144G	5.00	5.00
		Nos. 144-144G (8)	7.35	7.35

Issued: #144-144B, 144D, 1/29; others, 2/28.

Nos. 144C, 144E-144G are airmail.

Famous Men A17b

1972, Apr. 17 Litho. *Imperf.*

Self-adhesive

145	A17b	10ch John F. Kennedy	.20	.20
145A	A17b	15ch Gandhi	.20	.20
145B	A17b	55ch Churchill	.45	.45
145C	A17b	2nu De Gaulle	.50	.50
145D	A17b	6nu Pope John XVIII	1.50	1.50
145E	A17b	8nu Eisenhower	2.00	2.00
f.		Souv. sheet, #145B-145E	5.25	5.25
		Nos. 145-145E (6)	4.85	4.85

Nos. 145C-145E are airmail. Stamps are plastic heat molded into three dimensions.

Book Year Emblem A17c

1972, May 15 Photo. *Perf. 13½x13*

146	A17c	2ch multicolored	.20	.20
146A	A17c	3ch multicolored	.20	.20
146B	A17c	5ch multicolored	.20	.20
146C	A17c	20ch multicolored	.20	.20
		Nos. 146-146C (4)	.80	.80

International Book Year.

1972 Summer Olympics, Munich — A17d

1972, June 6 Photo. *Perf. 13½*

147	A17d	10ch Handball	.20	.20
147A	A17d	15ch Archery	.20	.20
147B	A17d	20ch Boxing	.20	.20
147C	A17d	30ch Discus	.20	.20
147D	A17d	35ch Javelin	.20	.20
147E	A17d	45ch Shooting	.20	.20
147F	A17d	1.35nu like #147A	.70	.70
147G	A17d	7nu like #147	1.10	1.10
h.		Souv. sheet of 3, #147D, 147F-147G	2.50	2.50
		Nos. 147-147G (8)	3.00	3.00

Nos. 147D, 147F-147G are airmail and have a gold border.

Exist imperf.

For overprint see No. 384.

Apollo 11 Type of 1969

Apollo 16: 15ch, Lift-off, vert. 20ch, Achieving lunar orbit. 90ch, Astronauts Young, Mattingly, Duke, vert. 1.70nu, Lunar module. 2.50nu, Walking on moon. 4.60nu, Gathering rock samples. 5.40nu, Apollo 16 on launch pad, vert. 6nu, Looking at earth, vert.

1972, Sept. 1 Litho. *Imperf.*

148	A15a	15ch multicolored	.25	.25
148A	A15a	20ch multicolored	.25	.25
148B	A15a	90ch multicolored	.25	.25
148C	A15a	1.70nu multicolored	.45	.45
148D	A15a	2.50nu multicolored	.65	.65
h.		Souv. sheet of 4, #148-148B, 148D	7.00	7.00
148E	A15a	4.60nu multicolored	1.25	1.25
148F	A15a	5.40nu multicolored	1.40	1.40
148G	A15a	6nu multicolored	1.75	1.75
i.		Souv. sheet of 4, #148C, 148E-148G	10.50	10.50
		Nos. 148-148G (8)	6.25	6.25

Nos. 148C, 148E-148G are airmail. Simulated 3-dimensions using a plastic overlay.

Dogs A17f

1972-73 Photo. *Perf. 13½*

149	A17f	2ch Pointer	.20	.20
149A	A17f	3ch Irish Setter	.20	.20
149B	A17f	5ch Lhasa Apso, vert	.20	.20
149C	A17f	10ch Dochi	.20	.20
149D	A17f	15ch Damci	.20	.20
149E	A17f	15ch Collie	.20	.20
149F	A17f	20ch Basset hound	.20	.20
149G	A17f	25ch Damci, diff	.20	.20
149H	A17f	30ch Fox terrier	.20	.20
149I	A17f	55ch Lhasa Apso, diff.	.20	.20
149J	A17f	99ch Boxer	.25	.25
149K	A17f	2.50nu St. Bernard	.50	.50
149L	A17f	4nu Cocker Spaniel	1.00	1.00
o.		Souv. sheet of 3, #149J-149L, perf. 14	3.00	3.00
149M	A17f	8nu Damci, diff.	1.50	1.50
p.		Souv. sheet of 2, #149I, 149M, perf. 14	4.00	4.00
		Nos. 149-149M (14)	5.25	5.25

Souvenir Sheet

Perf. 14

149N	A17f	18nu Poodle	3.75	3.75

Issued: #149B-149D, 149G, 149I, 149M, 149p, 10/5; #149-149A, 149E-149F, 149H, 149J-149L, 149o, 1/1/73; #149N, 1/15/73. No. 149N is airmail. All exist imperf.

For surcharges & overprints see #268-269, 385.

Roses — A17g

1973, Jan. 30 Photo. *Perf. 13½*

Scented Paper

150	A17g	15ch Wendy Cussons	.20	.20
150A	A17g	25ch Iceberg	.20	.20
150B	A17g	30ch Marchioness of Urquio	.20	.20
150C	A17g	3nu Pink parfait	.70	.70
150D	A17g	6nu Roslyn	1.40	1.40
150E	A17g	7nu Blue moon	1.60	1.60
f.		Souv. sheet, #150D-150E	2.75	2.75
		Nos. 150-150E (6)	4.30	4.30

#150D-150E are airmail. Exist imperf.

Apollo 11 Type of 1969

Apollo 17: 10ch, Taking photographs on moon. 15ch, Setting up experiments. 55ch, Earth. 2nu, Driving lunar rover. 7nu, Satellite. 9nu, Astronauts Cernan, Evans, Schmitt.

1973, Feb. 28 Litho. *Imperf.*

Size: 50x49mm

151	A15a	10ch multicolored	.20	.20
151A	A15a	15ch multicolored	.20	.20
151B	A15a	55ch multicolored	.20	.20
151C	A15a	2nu multicolored	.70	.70
f.		Souv. sheet of 4, #151-151C	2.50	2.50
151D	A15a	7nu multicolored	2.25	2.25
151E	A15a	9nu multicolored	3.25	3.25
g.		Souv. sheet of 2, #151D-151E	8.00	8.00
		Nos. 151-151E (6)	6.80	6.80

Simulated 3-dimensions using a plastic overlay. Nos. 151D-151E are airmail. No. 151g is circular, 160mm in diameter.

Phonograph Records

A17h

Recordings: 10ch, Bhutanese History. 25ch, Royal Bhutan Anthem. 1.25nu, Bhutanese History (English). 3nu, Bhutanese History (Bhutanese), Folk Song #1. 7nu, Folk Song #1. 8nu, Folk Song #2. 9nu, History in English, Folk Songs #1 & 2.

1973, Apr. 15

Self-adhesive

Diameter: #152-152B, 152D-152E, 69mm, #152C, 152F, 100mm

152	A17h	10ch yel on red	*6.50*	*6.50*
152A	A17h	25ch gold on grn	*9.00*	*9.00*
152B	A17h	1.25nu sil on bl	*13.50*	*13.50*
152C	A17h	3nu sil on pur	*42.50*	*42.50*
152D	A17h	7nu sil on blk	*16.00*	*16.00*
152E	A17h	8nu red on white	*35.00*	*35.00*
152F	A17h	9nu blk on yel	*52.50*	*52.50*
		Nos. 152-152F (7)	*175.00*	*175.00*

Nos. 152C, 152F are airmail.

King Jigme Dorji Wangchuk (d. 1972) — A17i

Embossed on Gold Foil

1973, May 2 Die Cut *Imperf.*

153	A17i	10ch orange	.20	.20
153A	A17i	25ch red	.20	.20
153B	A17i	3nu green	.45	.45
153C	A17i	6nu blue	.90	.90
153D	A17i	8nu purple	1.25	1.25
e.		Souv. sheet of 2, #153C-153D	4.50	4.50
		Nos. 153-153D (5)	3.00	3.00

Nos. 153C-153D are airmail.

Mushrooms — A17j

Different mushrooms.

1973, Sept. 25 Litho. *Imperf.*

154 A17j 15ch multicolored *.20 .20*
154A A17j 25ch multicolored *.20 .20*
154B A17j 30ch multicolored *.25 .25*
154C A17j 3nu multicolored *2.50 2.50*
f. Souv. sheet, #154-154C *7.50 7.50*
154D A17j 6nu multicolored *5.75 5.75*
154E A17j 7nu multicolored *6.75 6.75*
g. Souv. sheet, #154D-154E *35.00 35.00*
Nos. 154-154E (6) *15.65 15.65*

Simulated 3-dimensions using a plastic overlay. Nos. 154D-154E are airmail.

Bhutanese Mail Service — A17k

Designs: 5ch, 6nu, Letter carrier at mail box. 10ch, 5nu, Postmaster, letter carrier. 15ch, Sacking mail. 25ch, Mailtruck. 1.25nu, Sorting mail. 3nu, Hand-delivered mail.

1973, Nov. 14 Photo. *Perf. 13½*

155 A17k 5ch multicolored .20 .20
155A A17k 10ch multicolored .20 .20
155B A17k 15ch multicolored .20 .20
155C A17k 25ch multicolored .20 .20
155D A17k 1.25nu multicolored .20 .20
155E A17k 3nu multicolored .50 .50
155F A17k 5nu multicolored 1.00 1.00
155G A17k 6nu multicolored 1.25 1.25
h. Souv. sheet, #155F-155G 5.00 5.00
Nos. 155-155G (8) 3.75 3.75

Indipex '73. Nos. 155F-155G are airmail. All exist imperf.

For surcharges and overprint see Nos. 267, 382, C37-C38.

A set of 15 stamps plus souvenir sheet of 3 showing paintings with reading and writing themes was not authorized.

King Jigme Singye Wangchuk and Royal Crest — A18

Designs (King and): 25ch, 90ch, Flag of Bhutan. 1.25nu, Wheel with 8 good luck signs. 2nu, 4nu, Punakha Dzong, former winter capital. 3nu, 5nu, Crown. 5ch, same as 10ch.

1974, June 2 Litho. *Perf. 13½*

157 A18 10ch maroon & multi .20 .20
158 A18 25ch gold & multi .20 .20
159 A18 1.25nu multi .25 .25
160 A18 2nu gold & multi .50 .50
161 A18 3nu multi .70 .70
Nos. 157-161 (5) 1.85 1.85

Souvenir Sheets

Perf. 13½, Imperf.

162 Sheet of 2 2.50 2.50
a. A18 5ch maroon & multi .20
b. A18 5nu red orange & multi 2.25
163 Sheet of 2 2.50 2.50
a. A18 90ch gold & multi .75
b. A18 4nu gold & multi 2.00

Coronation of King Jigme Singye Wangchuk, June 2, 1974.

Mailman on Horseback
A19

Old and New Locomotives
A20

Designs (UPU Emblem, Carrier Pigeon and): 3ch, Sailing and steam ships. 4ch, Old biplane and jet. 25ch, Mail runner and jeep.

1974, Oct. 9 Litho. *Perf. 14½*

164 A19 1ch grn & multi .20 .20
165 A20 2ch lilac & multi .20 .20
166 A20 3ch ocher & multi .20 .20
167 A20 4ch yel grn & multi .20 .20
168 A20 25ch salmon & multi .20 .20
Nos. 164-168,C27-C29 (8) 2.15 2.15

Centenary of Universal Postal Union. Issued in sheets of 50 and sheets of 5 plus label with multicolored margin. Exist imperf.

Family and WPY Emblem — A21

1974, Dec. 17 *Perf. 13½*

169 A21 25ch bl & multi .20 .20
170 A21 50ch org & multi .20 .20
171 A21 90ch ver & multi .30 .30
172 A21 2.50nu brn & multi .65 .65
a. Souvenir sheet, 10nu 2.25 2.25
Nos. 169-172 (4) 1.35 1.35

For surcharge see No. 254.

Sephisa Chandra — A22

Designs: Indigenous butterflies.

1975, Sept. 15 Litho. *Perf. 14½*

173 A22 1ch *shown* .20 .20
174 A22 2ch *Lethe kansa* .20 .20
175 A22 3ch *Neope bhadra* .20 .20
176 A22 4ch *Euthalia duda* .20 .20
177 A22 5ch *Vindula erota* .20 .20
178 A22 10ch *Bhutanitis Lidderdale* .20 .20
179 A22 3nu *Limenitis zayla* .60 .60
180 A22 5nu *Delis thysbe* 1.40 1.40
Nos. 173-180 (8) 3.20 3.20

Souvenir Sheet

Perf. 13

181 A22 10nu *Dabasa gyas* 2.50 2.50

For surcharges see Nos. 255-256.

Apollo and Apollo-Soyuz Emblem — A23

Design: No. 183, Soyuz and emblem.

1975, Dec. 1 Litho. *Perf. 14x13½*

182 A23 10nu multicolored 2.50 2.50
183 A23 10nu multicolored 2.50 2.50
a. Souvenir sheet of 2, 15nu 7.00 7.00

Apollo Soyuz link-up in space, July 17. Nos. 182-183 printed se-tenant in sheets of 10. No. 183a contains two 15nu stamps similar to Nos 182-183. Exist imperf.

For surcharges see Nos. 257-258.

Jewelry — A24

Designs: 2ch, Coffee pot, bell and sugar cup. 3ch, Container and drinking horn. 4ch, Pendants and box cover. 5ch, Painter. 15ch, Silversmith. 20ch, Wood carver with tools. 1.50nu, Mat maker. 5nu, 10nu, Printer.

1975, Dec. 17 *Perf. 14½*

184 A24 1ch multicolored .20 .20
185 A24 2ch multicolored .20 .20
186 A24 3ch multicolored .20 .20
187 A24 4ch multicolored .20 .20
188 A24 5ch multicolored .20 .20
189 A24 15ch multicolored .20 .20
190 A24 20ch multicolored .20 .20
191 A24 1.50nu multicolored .25 .25
192 A24 10nu multicolored 2.00 2.00
Nos. 184-192 (9) 3.65 3.65

Souvenir Sheet

Perf. 13

193 A24 5nu multicolored 2.50 2.50

Handicrafts and craftsmen.

For surcharges see No. 259, 381.

King Jigme Singye Wangchuk
A25

Designs: 25ch, 90ch, 1nu, 2nu, 4nu, like 15ch. 1.30nu, 3nu, 5nu, Coat of arms. Sizes (Diameter): 15ch, 1nu, 1.30nu, 38mm. 25ch, 2nu, 3nu, 49mm. 90ch, 4nu, 5nu, 63mm.

Lithographed, Embossed on Gold Foil

1975, Nov. 11 *Imperf.*

194 A25 15ch emerald .20 .20
195 A25 25ch emerald .20 .20
196 A25 90ch emerald .35 .35
197 A25 1nu bright carmine .40 .40
198 A25 1.30nu bright carmine .45 .45
199 A25 2nu bright carmine .65 .65
200 A25 3nu bright carmine 1.00 1.00
201 A25 4nu bright carmine 1.60 1.60
202 A25 5nu bright carmine 2.00 2.00
Nos. 194-202 (9) 6.85 6.85

King Jigme Singye Wangchuk's 20th birthday.

Rhododendron Cinnabarinum
A28

Rhododendron: 2ch, Campanulatum. 3ch, Fortunei. 4ch, Red arboreum. 5ch, Pink arboreum. 1nu, Falconeri. 3nu, Hodgsonii. 5nu, Keysii. 10nu, Cinnabarinum.

1976, Feb. 15 Litho. *Perf. 15*

203 A28 1ch rose & multi .20 .20
204 A28 2ch lt grn & multi .20 .20
205 A28 3ch gray & multi .20 .20
206 A28 4ch lil & multi .20 .20
207 A28 5ch ol gray & multi .20 .20
208 A28 1nu brn org & multi .25 .25
209 A28 3nu ultra & multi .75 .75
210 A28 5nu gray & multi 1.25 1.25
Nos. 203-210 (8) 3.25 3.25

Souvenir Sheet

Perf. 13½

211 A28 10nu multicolored 3.00 3.00

For surcharge see No. 260.

Slalom and Olympic Games Emblem — A29

Olympic Games Emblem and: 2ch, 4-men bobsled. 3ch, Ice hockey. 4ch, Cross-country skiing. 5ch, Figure skating, women's. 2nu, Downhill skiing. 4nu, Speed skating. 6nu, Ski jump. 10nu, Figure skating, pairs.

1976, Mar. 29 Litho. *Perf. 13½*

212 A29 1ch multicolored .20 .20
213 A29 2ch multicolored .20 .20
214 A29 3ch multicolored .20 .20
215 A29 4ch multicolored .20 .20
216 A29 5ch multicolored .20 .20
217 A29 2nu multicolored .40 .35
218 A29 4nu multicolored .90 .75
219 A29 10nu multicolored 2.50 1.75
Nos. 212-219 (8) 4.80 3.85

Souvenir Sheet

220 A29 6nu multicolored 2.00 2.00

12th Winter Olympic Games, Innsbruck, Austria, Feb. 4-15.

For surcharges see Nos. 261-262.

Ceremonial Masks
A29a

Various masks.

1976, Apr. 23 Litho. *Imperf.*

220A A29a 5ch multicolored .20 .20
220B A29a 10ch multicolored .20 .20
220C A29a 15ch multicolored .20 .20
220D A29a 20ch multicolored .20 .20
220E A29a 25ch multi, horiz. .20 .20
220F A29a 30ch multi, horiz. .20 .20
220G A29a 35ch multi, horiz. .20 .20
220H A29a 1nu multi, horiz. .30 .30
220I A29a 2nu multi, horiz. .55 .55
220J A29a 2.50nu multi, horiz. .70 .70
220K A29a 3nu multi, horiz. .80 .80
Nos. 220A-220K (11) 3.75 3.75

Souvenir Sheets

220L A29a 5nu like #220C 1.60 1.60
220M A29a 10nu like #220F 6.00 6.00

Simulated 3-dimensions using a plastic overlay. Nos. 220H-220M are airmail.

Sizes of stamps: No. 220L, 59x70mm, No. 220M, 69x57mm.

Orchid A30

Designs: Various flowers.

1976, May 29 Litho. *Perf. 14½*

221	A30	1ch multicolored		.20	.20
222	A30	2ch multicolored		.20	.20
223	A30	3ch multicolored		.20	.20
224	A30	4ch multicolored		.20	.20
225	A30	5ch multicolored		.20	.20
226	A30	2nu multicolored		.45	.45
227	A30	4nu multicolored		.80	.80
228	A30	6nu multicolored		1.25	1.25
		Nos. 221-228 (8)		3.50	3.50

Souvenir Sheet

Perf. 13½

229	A30	10nu multicolored	3.50	3.50

For surcharges see Nos. 263-264.

Double Carp Design A31

Designs: Various symbolic designs and Colombo Plan emblem.

1976, July 1 Litho. *Perf. 14½*

230	A31	3ch red & multi	.20	.20
231	A31	4ch ver & multi	.20	.20
232	A31	5ch multicolored	.20	.20
233	A31	25ch bl & multi	.20	.20
234	A31	1.25nu multicolored	.35	.30
235	A31	2nu yel & multi	.60	.50
236	A31	2.50nu vio & multi	.75	.60
237	A31	3nu multicolored	.90	.80
		Nos. 230-237 (8)	3.40	3.00

Colombo Plan, 25th anniversary.
For surcharge see No. 265.

Bandaranaike Conference Hall — A32

1976, Aug. 16 Litho. *Perf. 13½*

238	A32	1.25nu multicolored	.35	.25
239	A32	2.50nu multicolored	.65	.45

5th Summit Conference of Non-aligned Countries, Colombo, Sri Lanka, Aug. 9-19.

Elizabeth II — A33

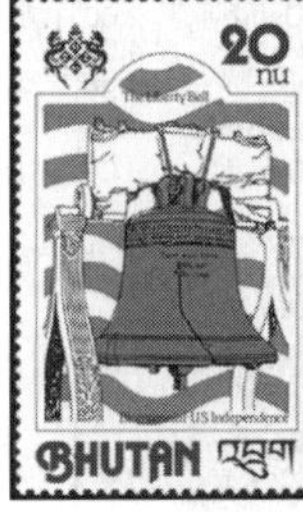
Liberty Bell — A34

Spirit of St. Louis — A35

Bhutanese Archer, Olympic Rings — A36

Designs: No. 242, Alexander Graham Bell. No. 245, LZ 3 Zeppelin docking, 1907. No. 246, Alfred B. Nobel.

1978, Nov. 15 Litho. *Perf. 14½*

240	A33	20nu multicolored	4.00	4.00
241	A34	20nu multicolored	4.00	4.00
242	A33	20nu multicolored	4.00	4.00
243	A35	20nu multicolored	4.00	4.00
244	A36	20nu multicolored	4.00	4.00
245	A35	20nu multicolored	4.00	4.00
246	A33	20nu multicolored	4.00	4.00
		Nos. 240-246 (7)	28.00	28.00

25th anniv. of coronation of Elizabeth II; American Bicentennial; cent. of 1st telephone call by Alexander Graham Bell; Charles A. Lindbergh crossing the Atlantic, 50th anniv.; Olympic Games; 75th anniv. of the Zeppelin; 75th anniv. of Nobel Prize. Seven souvenir sheets exist, each 25nu, commemorating same events with different designs. Size: 103x80mm.

Issues of 1967-1976 Surcharged with New Value and Bars

Perforations and Printing as Before

1978

252	A16	25ch on 3nu (#133)		
253	A17	25ch on 6nu (#139)		
254	A21	25ch on 2.50nu (#172)		
255	A22	25ch on 3nu (#179)		
256	A22	25ch on 5nu (#180)		
257	A23	25ch on 10nu (#182)		
258	A23	25ch on 10nu (#183)		
259	A24	25ch on 10nu (#192)		
260	A28	25ch on 5nu (#210)		
261	A29	25ch on 4nu (#218)		
262	A29	25ch on 10nu (#219)		
263	A30	25ch on 4nu (#227)		
264	A30	25ch on 6nu (#228)		
265	A31	25ch on 2.50nu (#236)		
266	A14g	25ch on 5nu (#90E)		
267	A17k	25ch on 3nu (#155E)		
268	A17f	25ch on 4nu (#149L)		
269	A17f	25ch on 8nu (#149M)		
		Nos. 252-269, C31-C38 (26)	*80.00*	*80.00*

Mother and Child, IYC Emblem — A37

IYC Emblem and: 5nu, Mother and two children. 10nu, Boys with blackboards and stylus.

1979, June Litho. *Perf. 14x13½*

289	A37	2nu multicolored	.50	.40
290	A37	5nu multicolored	1.40	1.00
291	A37	10nu multicolored	2.50	2.00
a.		Souv. sheet of 3, #289-291 + label, perf. 15x13½	4.25	3.25
		Nos. 289-291 (3)	4.40	3.40

International Year of the Child.
For overprints see Nos. 761-763.

Conference Emblem and Dove — A38

10nu, Emblem and Bhutanese symbols.

1979, Sept. 3 Litho. *Perf. 14x13½*

292	A38	25ch multicolored	.20	.20
293	A38	10nu multicolored	3.25	2.50

6th Non-Aligned Summit Conference, Havana, August 1979.

Silver Rattle, Dorji A39

Antiques: 10ch, Silver handell, Dilbu, vert. 15ch, Cylindrical jar, Jadum, vert. 25ch, Ornamental teapot, Jamjee. 1nu, Leather container, Kem, vert. 1.25nu, Brass teapot, Jamjee. 1.70nu, Vessel with elephant-head legs, Sangphor, vert. 2nu, Teapot with ornamental spout, Jamjee, vert. 3nu, Metal pot on claw-shaped feet, Yangtho, vert. 4nu, Dish inlaid with precious stones, Battha. 5nu, Metal circular flask, Chhap, vert.

1979, Dec. 17 Photo. *Perf. 14*

294	A39	5ch multicolored	.20	.20
295	A39	10ch multicolored	.20	.20
296	A39	15ch multicolored	.20	.20
297	A39	25ch multicolored	.20	.20
298	A39	1nu multicolored	.45	.40
299	A39	1.25nu multicolored	.50	.50
300	A39	1.70nu multicolored	.70	.70
301	A39	2nu multicolored	.90	.75
302	A39	3nu multicolored	1.25	1.10
303	A39	4nu multicolored	1.60	1.50
304	A39	5nu multicolored	2.25	1.90
		Nos. 294-304 (11)	8.45	7.65

Hill, Rinpiang Dzong — A40

Hill Statue, Stamps of Bhutan and: 2nu, Dzong. 5nu, Ounsti Dzong. 10nu, Lingzi Dzong, Gt. Britain Type 81. 20nu, Rope bridge, Penny Black.

1980, May 6 Litho. *Perf. 14x13½*

305	A40	1nu multicolored	.30	.25
306	A40	2nu multicolored	.60	.50
307	A40	5nu multicolored	1.60	1.25
308	A40	10nu multicolored	3.00	2.50
		Nos. 305-308 (4)	5.50	4.50

Souvenir Sheet

309	A40	20nu multicolored	5.75	4.25

Sir Rowland Hill (1795-1879), originator of penny postage.

Kichu Lhakhang Monastery, Phari — A41

Guru Padma Sambhava's Birthday: Monasteries.

1981, July 11 Litho. *Perf. 14*

310	A41	1nu Dungtse, Phari, vert	.25	.20
311	A41	2nu shown	.50	.40
312	A41	2.25nu Kurjey	.65	.45
313	A41	3nu Tangu, Thimphu	.75	.60
314	A41	4nu Cheri, Thimphu	1.00	.75
315	A41	5nu Chorten, Kora	1.50	1.00
316	A41	7nu Tak-Tsang, Phari, vert	2.00	1.50
		Nos. 310-316 (7)	6.65	4.90

Prince Charles and Lady Diana — A42

Orange-bellied Chloropsis — A43

1981, Sept. 10 Litho. *Perf. 14½*

317	A42	1nu St. Paul's Cathedral	.20	.20
318	A42	5nu like #317	1.00	.65
319	A42	20nu shown	4.00	2.50
320	A42	25nu like #319	4.50	3.50
		Nos. 317-320 (4)	9.70	6.85

Souvenir Sheet

321	A42	20nu Wedding procession	5.00	4.00

Royal wedding. Nos. 318-319 issued in sheets of 5 plus label.
For surcharges see Nos. 471-475.

1982, Apr. 19 Litho. *Perf. 14*

322	A43	2nu shown	.55	.40
323	A43	3nu Monal pheasant	.80	.60
324	A43	5nu Ward's trogon	1.40	1.00
325	A43	10nu Mrs. Gould's sunbird	2.50	2.00
		Nos. 322-325 (4)	5.25	4.00

Souvenir Sheet

326	A43	25nu Maroon oriole	7.00	5.00

1982 World Cup — A44

Designs: Various soccer players.

1982, June 25 Litho. *Perf. 14½x14*

327 A44 1nu multicolored .25 .20
328 A44 2nu multicolored .55 .40
329 A44 3nu multicolored .80 .60
330 A44 20nu multicolored 5.25 4.00
Nos. 327-330 (4) 6.85 5.20

Souvenir Sheets

331 A44 25nu multicolored 12.00 7.50

Nos. 331 have margins continuing design and listing finalists (Algeria, etc. or Hungary, etc.).

For surcharges see Nos. 481-485.

21st Birthday of Princess Diana — A45

1982, Aug.

332 A45 1nu St. James' Palace .25 .20
332A A45 10nu Diana, Charles 2.50 1.75
332B A45 15nu Windsor Castle 4.00 4.50
333 A45 25nu Wedding 6.50 4.50
Nos. 332-333 (4) 13.25 10.95

Souvenir Sheet

334 A45 20nu Diana 5.50 4.00

10nu-15nu issued only in sheets of 5 + label.

For overprints and surcharges see Nos. 361-363, 455-459, 476-480.

Scouting Year A46

1982, Aug. 23 Litho. *Perf. 14*

335 A46 3nu Baden-Powell, vert. .65 .50
336 A46 5nu Eating around fire 1.10 .85
337 A46 15nu Reading map 3.50 2.50
338 A46 20nu Pitching tents 4.50 3.50
Nos. 335-338 (4) 9.75 7.35

Souvenir Sheet

339 A46 25nu Mountain climbing 6.00 4.50

For surcharges see Nos. 450-454, 559-563..

Rama and Cubs with Mowgli — A47

Scenes from Disney's The Jungle Book.

1982, Sept. 1 *Perf. 11*

340 A47 1ch multicolored .20 .20
341 A47 2ch multicolored .20 .20
342 A47 3ch multicolored .20 .20
343 A47 4ch multicolored .20 .20
344 A47 5ch multicolored .20 .20
345 A47 10ch multicolored .20 .20
346 A47 30ch multicolored .20 .20
347 A47 2nu multicolored .50 .35
348 A47 20nu multicolored 5.50 4.25
Nos. 340-348 (9) 7.40 6.00

Souvenir Sheets

Perf. 13½

349 A47 20nu Baloo and Mowgli in forest 5.25 4.00
350 A47 20nu Baloo and Mowgli floating 5.25 4.00

George Washington Surveying — A48

1982, Nov. 15 Litho. *Perf. 15*

351 A48 50ch shown .20 .20
352 A48 1nu FDR, Harvard .20 .20
353 A48 2nu Washington at Valley Forge .30 .25
354 A48 3nu FDR, family .50 .40
355 A48 4nu Washington, Battle of Monmouth .65 .50
356 A48 5nu FDR, White House .85 .65
357 A48 15nu Washington, Mt. Vernon 2.50 2.00
358 A48 20nu FDR, Churchill, Stalin 3.25 2.50
Nos. 351-358 (8) 8.45 6.70

Souvenir Sheets

359 A48 25nu Washington, vert. 4.25 3.25
360 A48 25nu FDR, vert. 4.25 3.25

Washington and Franklin D. Roosevelt.

Nos. 332-334 Overprinted: "ROYAL BABY / 21.6.82"

1982, Nov. 19 *Perf. 14½x14*

361 A45 1nu multicolored .25 .25
361A A45 10nu multicolored 2.50 1.75
361B A45 15nu multicolored 3.75 3.00
362 A45 25nu multicolored 6.25 4.75
Nos. 361-362 (4) 12.75 9.75

Souvenir Sheet

363 A45 20nu multicolored 5.25 4.25

Birth of Prince William of Wales, June 21.

500th Birth Anniv. of Raphael A51

Portraits.

1983, Mar. 23 *Perf. 13½*

375 A51 1nu Angelo Doni .25 .20
376 A51 4nu Maddalena Doni 1.00 .75
377 A51 5nu Baldassare Castiglione 1.25 .90
378 A51 20nu La Donna Velata 5.00 3.75
Nos. 375-378 (4) 7.50 5.60

Souvenir Sheets

379 A51 25nu Expulsion of Heliodorus 6.25 4.75
380 A51 25nu Mass of Bolsena 6.25 4.75

Nos. 184, 155F, 139, 184, 147G, 149M Surchd. or Ovptd.: "Druk Air"

1983, Feb. 11

381 A24 30ch on 1ch multi .20 .20
382 A17k 5nu multicolored 2.00 1.25
383 A17 6nu multicolored 2.25 1.50
384 A17d 7nu multicolored 2.50 1.50
385 A17f 8nu multicolored 2.50 1.75
Nos. 381-385 (5) 9.45 6.20

Druk Air Service inauguration. Overprint of 8nu all caps. Nos. 382, 384 air mail.

Manned Flight Bicentenary — A52

1983, Aug. 15 Litho. *Perf. 15*

386 A52 50ch Dornier Wal .20 .20
387 A52 3nu Savoia-Marchetti S-66 .75 .55
388 A52 10nu Hawker Osprey 2.00 1.75
389 A52 20nu Ville de Paris 4.00 3.75
Nos. 386-389 (4) 6.95 6.25

Souvenir Sheet

390 A52 25nu Balloon Captif 5.00 3.75

Buddhist Symbols — A53

1983, Aug. 11 Litho. *Perf. 13½*

391 A53 25ch Sacred vase .20 .20
392 A53 50ch Five Sensory Symbols .20 .20
393 A53 2nu Seven Treasures .35 .30
394 A53 3nu Five Sensory Organs .60 .45
395 A53 8nu Five Fleshes 1.50 1.10
396 A53 9nu Sacrificial cake 1.75 1.25
a. Souv. sheet of 6, #391-396 4.50 3.50
Nos. 391-396 (6) 4.60 3.50

Size of Nos. 393, 396: 45x40mm.

World Communications Year (1983) — A54

Various Disney characters and history of communications.

1984, Apr. 10 Litho. *Perf. 14½x14*

397 A54 4ch multicolored .20 .20
398 A54 5ch multicolored .20 .20
399 A54 10ch multicolored .20 .20
400 A54 20ch multicolored .20 .20
401 A54 25ch multicolored .20 .20
402 A54 50ch multicolored .20 .20
403 A54 1nu multicolored .30 .25
404 A54 5nu multicolored 1.10 .95
405 A54 20nu multicolored 4.25 3.75
Nos. 397-405 (9) 6.85 6.15

Souvenir Sheets

Perf. 14x14½

406 A54 20nu Donald Duck on phone, horiz. 4.75 4.00
407 A54 20nu Mickey Mouse on TV 4.75 4.00

1984 Winter Olympics — A55

1984, June 16 *Perf. 14*

408 A55 50ch Skiing .20 .20
409 A55 1nu Cross-country skiing .25 .20
410 A55 3nu Speed skating .60 .45
411 A55 20nu Bobsledding 3.75 3.00
Nos. 408-411 (4) 4.80 3.85

Souvenir Sheet

412 A55 25nu Hockey 5.00 3.25

Golden Langur A56 Locomotives A57

1984, June 10 Litho. *Perf. 14½*

413 A56 50ch shown .20 .20
414 A56 1nu Group in tree, horiz. .20 .20
415 A56 2nu Family, horiz. .40 .30
416 A56 4nu Group walking .80 .60
Nos. 413-416 (4) 1.60 1.30

Souvenir Sheets

417 A56 20nu Snow leopard 4.00 2.00
418 A56 25nu Yak 4.00 2.00
419 A56 25nu Blue sheep, horiz. 4.00 2.00

1984, July 16

420 A57 50ch Sans Pareil, 1829 .20 .20
421 A57 1nu Planet, 1830 .20 .20
422 A57 3nu Experiment, 1832 .60 .45
423 A57 4nu Black Hawk, 1835 .80 .60
424 A57 5.50nu Jenny Lind, 1847 1.10 .85
425 A57 8nu Semmering-Bavaria, 1851 1.60 1.25
426 A57 10nu Great Northern #1, 1870 2.00 1.50
427 A57 25nu German Natl. Tinder, 1880 5.00 3.75
Nos. 420-427 (8) 11.50 8.80

Souvenir Sheets

428 A57 20nu Darjeeling Himalayan Railway, 1984 4.00 3.00
429 A57 20nu Sondermann Freight, 1896 4.00 3.00
430 A57 20nu Crampton's locomotive, 1846 4.00 3.00
431 A57 20nu Erzsebet, 1870 4.00 3.00

Nos. 424-427 horiz.

Classic Cars A58

1984, Aug. 29 Litho. *Perf. 14*

432 A58 50ch Riley Sprite, 1936 .20 .20
433 A58 1nu Lanchester, 1919 .20 .20
434 A58 3nu Itala, 1907 .65 .45
435 A58 4nu Morris Oxford Bullnose, 1913 .90 .60
436 A58 5.50nu Lagonda LG6, 1939 1.25 .85
437 A58 6nu Wolseley, 1903 1.40 .90
438 A58 8nu Buick Super, 1952 1.75 1.25
439 A58 20nu Maybach Zeppelin, 1933 4.50 3.00
Nos. 432-439 (8) 10.85 7.45

Souvenir Sheets

440 A58 25nu Simplex, 1912 2.50 1.50
441 A58 25nu Renault, 1901 2.50 1.50

For surcharges see Nos. 537-544.

Summer Olympic Games — A59

1984, Oct. 27 Litho.

442 A59 15ch Women's archery .20 .20
443 A59 25ch Men's archery .20 .20

444 A59 2nu Table tennis .40 .30
445 A59 2.25nu Basketball .45 .35
446 A59 5.50nu Boxing 1.10 .85
447 A59 6nu Running 1.25 .90
448 A59 8nu Tennis 1.60 1.25
Nos. 442-448 (7) 5.20 4.05

Souvenir Sheet

449 A59 25nu Archery 5.00 3.50

For overprints see Nos. 537-544.

Nos. 335-339 Surcharged with New Values and Bars in Black or Silver

1985 Litho. *Perf. 14*

450 A46 10nu on 3nu multi 2.00 1.50
451 A46 10nu on 5nu multi 2.00 1.50
452 A46 10nu on 15nu multi 2.00 1.50
453 A46 10nu on 20nu multi 2.00 1.50
Nos. 450-453 (4) 8.00 6.00

Souvenir Sheet

454 A46 20nu on 25nu multi 4.00 3.00

Nos. 332, 332A, 332B, 333-334 Surcharged with New Values and Bars

1985, Feb. 28

455 A45 5nu on 1nu multi 1.00 .70
456 A45 5nu on 10nu multi 1.00 .70
457 A45 5nu on 15nu multi 1.00 .70
458 A45 40nu on 25nu multi 8.00 5.25
Nos. 455-458 (4) 11.00 7.35

Souvenir Sheet

459 A45 25nu on 20nu multi 5.00 4.00

50th Anniv. of Donald Duck — A60

1984, Dec. 10 Litho. *Perf. 13½x14*

460 A60 4ch Magician Mickey .20 .20
461 A60 5ch Slide, Donald, Slide .20 .20
462 A60 10ch Donald's Golf Game .20 .20
463 A60 20ch Mr. Duck Steps Out .20 .20
464 A60 25ch Lion Around .20 .20
465 A60 50ch Alpine Climbers .20 .20
466 A60 1nu Flying Jalopy .20 .20
467 A60 5nu Frank Duck 1.10 .75
468 A60 20nu Good Scouts 4.50 3.25
Nos. 460-468 (9) 7.00 5.40

Souvenir Sheets

469 A60 20nu Three Caballeros 4.50 3.25
470 A60 20nu Sea Scouts 4.50 3.25

Nos. 317-321 Surcharged with New Values and Bars

1985, Feb. 28 Litho. *Perf. 14½*

471 A42 10nu on 1nu multi 2.00 1.50
472 A42 10nu on 5nu multi 2.00 1.50
473 A42 10nu on 20nu multi 2.00 1.50
474 A42 10nu on 25nu multi 2.00 1.50
Nos. 471-474 (4) 8.00 6.00

Souvenir Sheet

475 A42 30nu on 20nu multi 6.00 5.00

Nos. 361, 361A, 361B, 362-363 Surcharged with New Values and Bars

1985, Feb. 28 *Perf. 14½x14*

476 A45 5nu on 1nu multi .75 .75
477 A45 5nu on 10nu multi .75 .55
478 A45 5nu on 15nu multi .75 .55
479 A45 40nu on 25nu multi 7.50 5.50
Nos. 476-479 (4) 9.75 7.35

Souvenir Sheet

480 A45 25nu on 20nu multi 5.00 3.75

Nos. 327-331 Surcharged with New Values and Bars in Black or Silver

1985, June

481 A44 5nu on 1nu multi 1.50 1.10
482 A44 5nu on 2nu multi 1.50 1.10
483 A44 5nu on 3nu multi 1.50 1.10
484 A44 5nu on 20nu multi 1.50 1.10
Nos. 481-484 (4) 6.00 4.40

Souvenir Sheets

485 A44 20nu on 25nu multi 7.50 5.50

Mask Dance of the Judgement of Death — A61

1985, Apr. 27 *Perf. 13½*

486 A61 5ch Shinje Choegyel .20 .20
487 A61 35ch Raksh Lango .20 .20
488 A61 50ch Druelgo .20 .20
489 A61 2.50nu Pago .45 .35
490 A61 3nu Telgo .55 .40
491 A61 4nu Due Nakcung .75 .60
492 A61 5nu Lha Karpo .90 .70
a. Souv. sheet, #486-487, 491-492 1.90 1.50
493 A61 5.50nu Nyalbum 1.00 .75
494 A61 6nu Khimda Pelkyi 1.10 .85
Nos. 486-494 (9) 5.35 4.25

For overprints see Nos. 764-772.

Monasteries A62

1984, Dec. 1 Litho. *Perf. 12*

495 A62 10ch Domkhar .20 .20
496 A62 25ch Shemgang .20 .20
497 A62 50ch Chapcha .20 .20
498 A62 1nu Tashigang .20 .20
499 A62 2nu Pungthang Chhug .30 .30
500 A62 5nu Dechhenphoda .70 .70
Nos. 495-500 (6) 1.80 1.80

Veteran's War Memorial Building, San Francisco A63

1985, Oct. 24 Litho. *Perf. 14*

502 A63 50ch Flags of Bhutan, UN, vert. .20 .20
503 A63 15nu Headquarters, NY, vert. 2.75 2.00
504 A63 20nu shown 3.75 2.75
Nos. 502-504 (3) 6.70 4.95

Souvenir Sheet

505 A63 25nu UN Human Rights Declaration 4.25 3.00

UN, 40th anniv.

Audubon Birth Bicentenary — A64

Illustrations of North American bird species by Audubon.

1985

506 A64 50ch Anas breweri .20 .20
507 A64 1nu Lagopus lagopus .20 .20
508 A64 2nu Charadrius montanus .35 .25
509 A64 3nu Cavia stellata .50 .40
510 A64 4nu Canachites canadensis .70 .50
511 A64 5nu Mergus cucullatus .85 .60
512 A64 15nu Olor buccinator 2.50 1.75
513 A64 20nu Bucephala clangula 3.50 2.50
Nos. 506-513 (8) 8.80 6.40

Souvenir Sheets

514 A64 25nu Accipiter striatus 3.75 2.25
515 A64 25nu Parus bicolor 3.75 2.25

Issued: #507, 510-511, 514, 11/15; #506, 508-509, 513, 515, 12/6.

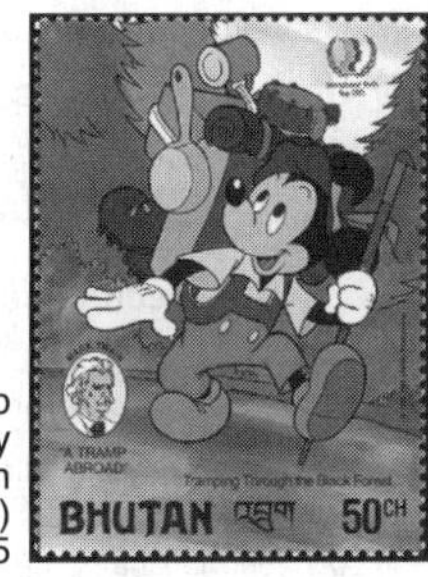

A Tramp Abroad, by Mark Twain (1835-1910) A65

Walt Disney animated characters.

1985, Nov. 15

516 A65 50ch multicolored .20 .20
517 A65 2nu multicolored .35 .25
518 A65 5nu multicolored .85 .60
519 A65 9nu multicolored 1.50 1.10
520 A65 20nu multicolored 3.50 2.50
Nos. 516-520 (5) 6.40 4.65

Souvenir Sheet

521 A65 25nu Goofy, Mickey Mouse 5.00 3.50

Intl. Youth Year.
For overprints see Nos. 554, 556-557.

Rapunzel, by Jacob and Wilhelm Grimm A66

Walt Disney animated characters.

1985, Nov. 15

522 A66 1nu multicolored .20 .20
523 A66 4nu multicolored .70 .50
524 A66 7nu multicolored 1.25 .95
525 A66 8nu multicolored 1.40 1.00
526 A66 15nu multicolored 2.50 1.75
Nos. 522-526 (5) 6.05 4.40

Souvenir Sheet

527 A66 25nu multicolored 5.00 4.00

No. 525 printed in sheets of 8.
For overprints see Nos. 553, 555, 558.

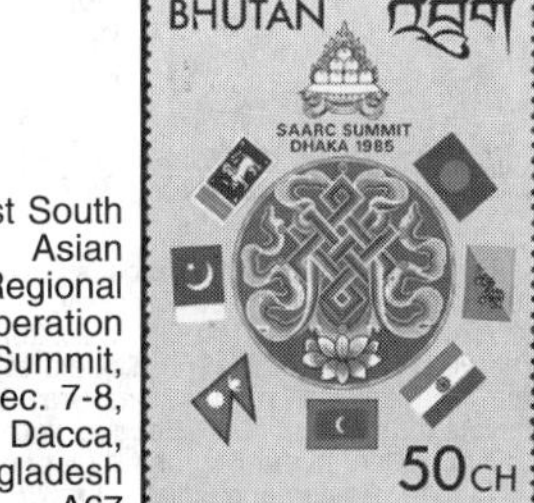

First South Asian Regional Cooperation Summit, Dec. 7-8, Dacca, Bangladesh A67

1985, Dec. 8 *Perf. 14*

528 A67 50ch multicolored .20 .20
529 A67 5nu multicolored .85 .60

Seven Precious Attributes of the Universal King — A68

1986, Feb. 12 Litho. *Perf. 13x12½*

530 A68 30ch Wheel .20 .20
531 A68 50ch Gem .20 .20
532 A68 1.25nu Queen .20 .20
533 A68 2nu Minister .30 .30
534 A68 4nu Elephant .55 .55
535 A68 6nu Horse .85 .85
536 A68 8nu General 1.10 1.10
Nos. 530-536 (7) 3.40 3.40

Nos. 442-443, 445-449 Ovptd. with Medal, Winners' Names and Countries. No. 449 Ovptd. for Men's and Women's Events

1986, May 5 Litho. *Perf. 14*

537 A59 15ch Hyang Soon Seo, So. Korea .20 .20
538 A59 25ch Darrell Pace, US .20 .20
539 A59 2.25nu US .30 .30
540 A59 5.50nu Mark Breland, US .80 .80
541 A59 6nu Daley Thompson, Britain .85 .85
542 A59 8nu Stefan Edberg, Sweden 1.10 1.10
Nos. 537-542 (6) 3.45 3.45

Souvenir Sheets

543 A59 25nu Hyang Soon Seo 3.50 3.50
544 A59 25nu Darrel Pace 3.50 3.50

Kilkhor Mandalas, Deities — A69

Religious art: 10ch, 1nu, Phurpa, ritual dagger. 25ch, 3nu, Amitayus in wrath. 50ch, 5nu, Overpowering Deities. 75ch, 7nu, Great Wrathful One, Guru Rinpoche.

1986, June 17 *Perf. 13½*

545 A69 10ch multicolored .20 .20
546 A69 25ch multicolored .20 .20
547 A69 50ch multicolored .20 .20
548 A69 75ch multicolored .20 .20
549 A69 1nu multicolored .20 .20
550 A69 3nu multicolored .40 .40
551 A69 5nu multicolored .70 .70
552 A69 7nu multicolored 1.00 1.00
Nos. 545-552 (8) 3.10 3.10

Nos. 525, 519, 526, 520, 521 and 527 Ovptd. with AMERIPEX '86 Emblem

1986, June 16 Litho. *Perf. 14*

553 A66 8nu multi 1.40 1.00
554 A65 9nu multi 1.50 1.10
555 A66 15nu multi 2.50 1.75
556 A65 20nu multi 3.50 2.50
Nos. 553-556 (4) 8.90 6.35

Souvenir Sheets

557 A65 25nu #521 4.25 3.00
558 A66 25nu #527 4.25 3.00

Nos. 335-339 Overprinted

1986, July 23 Litho. *Perf. 14*

559 A46 3nu multi — —
560 A46 5nu multi — —
561 A46 15nu multi — —
562 A46 20nu multi — —

Souvenir Sheet

563 A46 25nu multi — —

A70

A71

Halley's Comet — A72

Designs: 50ch, Babylonian tablet fragments, 2349 B.C. sighting. 1nu, 17th cent. print, A.D. 66 sighting. 2nu, French silhouette art, 1835 sighting. 3nu, Bayeux Tapestry, 1066 sighting. 4nu, Woodblock, 684 sighting. 5nu, Illustration from Bybel Printen, 1650. 15nu, 1456 Sighting, Cancer constellation. 20nu, Delft plate, 1910 sighting. No. 572, Comet over Himalayas. No. 573, Comet over domed temple Dug-gye Jong.

1986, Nov. 4 Litho. *Perf. 15*

564 A70 50ch multicolored .20 .20
565 A70 1nu multicolored .20 .20
566 A71 2nu multicolored .35 .30
567 A70 3nu multicolored .50 .35
568 A70 4nu multicolored .70 .50
569 A71 5nu multicolored .85 .65
570 A70 15nu multicolored 2.50 2.00
571 A70 20nu multicolored 3.50 2.50
Nos. 564-571 (8) 8.80 6.70

Souvenir Sheets

572 A72 25nu multicolored 4.25 3.00
573 A72 25nu multicolored 4.25 3.00

A73

Statue of Liberty, Cent. — A74

Statue and ships: 50ch, Mircea, Romania. 1nu, Shalom, Israel. 2nu, Leonardo da Vinci, Italy. 3nu, Libertad, Argentina. 4nu, France, France. 5nu, SS United States, US. 15nu, Queen Elizabeth II, England. 20nu, Europa, West Germany. No. 582, Statue. No. 583, Statue, World Trade Center.

1986, Nov. 4

574 A73 50ch multicolored .20 .20
575 A73 1nu multicolored .20 .20
576 A73 2nu multicolored .35 .30
577 A73 3nu multicolored .50 .35
578 A73 4nu multicolored .65 .50
579 A73 5nu multicolored .85 .65
580 A73 15nu multicolored 2.50 1.90
581 A73 20nu multicolored 3.50 2.50
Nos. 574-581 (8) 8.75 6.60

Souvenir Sheets

582 A74 25nu multicolored 4.25 3.00
583 A74 25nu multi, diff. 4.25 3.00

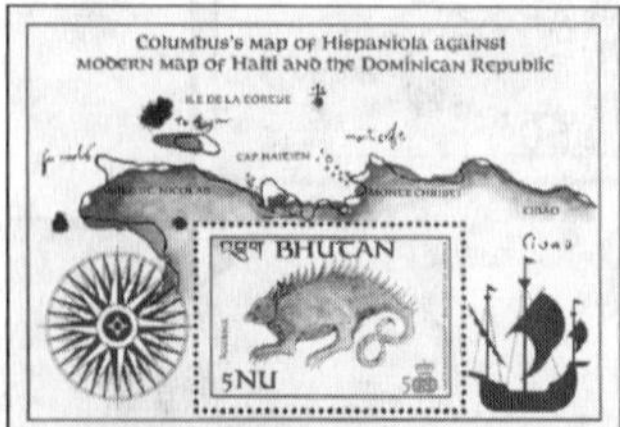

Discovery of America, 500th Anniv. — A75

1987, May 25 Litho. *Perf. 14*

584 A75 20ch Santa Maria .40 .40
585 A75 25ch Queen Isabella .40 .40
586 A75 50ch Ship, flying fish .40 .40
587 A75 1nu Columbus's coat of arms .75 .60
588 A75 2nu Christopher Columbus 1.40 1.00
589 A75 3nu Landing in the New World 2.00 2.00
a. Miniature sheet of 6, #584-589 5.00 5.00
Nos. 584-589 (6) 5.35 4.80

Souvenir Sheets

590 A75 20ch Pineapple
591 A75 25ch Indian hammock
592 A75 50ch Tobacco plant
593 A75 1nu Flamingo
594 A75 2nu Navigator, astrolabe, 15th cent.
595 A75 3nu Lizard
596 A75 5nu Iguana 1.25 .95

All stamps are vertical except those contained in Nos. 591, 595 and 596. Stamps from No. 589a have white background.

CAPEX '87 — A76

Locomotives.

1987, June 15

597 A76 50ch Canadian Natl. U1-f .20 .20
598 A76 1nu Via Rail L.R.C. .20 .20
599 A76 2nu Canadian Natl. GM GF-30t .35 .25
600 A76 3nu Canadian Natl. 4-8-4 .50 .35
601 A76 8nu Canadian Pacific 4-6-2 1.40 1.00
602 A76 10nu Via Express passenger train 1.75 1.25
603 A76 15nu Canadian Nat. Turbotrain 2.50 1.90
604 A76 20nu Canadian Pacific Diesel-Electric Express 3.25 2.50
Nos. 597-604 (8) 10.15 7.65

Souvenir Sheet

605 A76 25nu Royal Hudson 4-6-4 4.25 3.00
606 A76 25nu Canadian Natl. 4-8-4, diff. 4.25 3.00

Two Faces, Sculpture by Marc Chagall (1887-1984) A77

Paintings: 1nu, At the Barber's. 2nu, Old Jew with Torah. 3nu, Red Maternity. 4nu, Eve of Yom Kippur. 5nu, The Old Musician. 6nu, The Rabbi of Vitebsk. 7nu, Couple at Dusk. 9nu, The Artistes. 10nu, Moses Breaking the Tablets of the Law. 12nu, Bouquet with Flying Lovers. 20nu, In the Sky of the Opera.

No. 619, Romeo and Juliet. No. 620, Magician of Paris. No. 621, Maternity. No. 622, The Carnival for Aleko: Scene II. No. 623, Visit to the Grandparents. No. 624, The Smolensk Newspaper. No. 625, The Concert. No. 626, Composition with Goat. No. 627, Still Life. No. 628. The Red Gateway. No. 629, Cow with Parasol. No. 630, Russian Village.

1987, Dec. 17 Litho. *Perf. 14*

607-618 A77 Set of 12 12.75 12.75

Size: 110x95mm

Imperf

619-630 A77 25nu Set of 12 48.00 36.00

1988 Winter Olympics, Calgary — A78

Emblem and Disney animated characters as competitors in Olympic events.

1988, Feb. 15 Litho. *Perf. 14*

631 A78 50ch Slalom .20 .20
632 A78 1nu Downhill skiing .20 .20
633 A78 2nu Ice hockey .30 .25
634 A78 4nu Biathlon .65 .50
635 A78 7nu Speed skating 1.10 .85
636 A78 8nu Figure skating 1.25 .95
637 A78 9nu Figure skating, diff. 1.50 1.10
638 A78 20nu Bobsled 3.25 2.50
Nos. 631-638 (8) 8.45 6.55

Souvenir Sheets

639 A78 25nu Ski jumping 4.00 4.00
640 A78 25nu Ice dancing 4.00 4.00

Transportation Innovations — A79

1988, Mar. 31

641 A79 50ch Pullman Pioneer, 1865 .20 .20
642 A79 1nu Stephenson's Rocket, 1829 .20 .20
643 A79 2nu Pierre L'Allement's Velocipede, 1866 .30 .25
644 A79 3nu Benz Velocipede, 1886 .50 .35
645 A79 4nu Volkswagen Beetle, c. 1960 .65 .50
646 A79 5nu Natchez Vs. Robert E. Lee, 1870 .80 .60
647 A79 6nu American La France, 1910 1.00 .75
648 A79 7nu USS Constitution, 1787, vert. 1.10 .80
649 A79 9nu Bell Rocket Belt, 1961, vert. 1.50 1.10
650 A79 10nu Trevithick Locomotive, 1804 1.60 1.25
Nos. 641-650 (10) 7.85 6.00

Souvenir Sheets

651 A79 25nu Concorde jet 4.00 4.00
652 A79 25nu Mallard, 1938, vert. 4.00 4.00
653 A79 25nu Shinkansen 4.00 4.00
654 A79 25nu TGV, 1981 4.00 4.00

1988 Summer Olympics, Seoul A80

7nu-20nu vert.

1989, Feb. 15 Litho.

655 A80 50ch Women's gymnastics .20 .20
656 A80 1nu Tae kwon do .20 .20
657 A80 2nu Shot put .30 .25
658 A80 4nu Women's volleyball .65 .50
659 A80 7nu Basketball 1.10 .85
660 A80 8nu Soccer 1.25 .95
661 A80 9nu Women's high jump 1.50 1.10
662 A80 20nu Running 3.25 2.50
Nos. 655-662 (8) 8.45 6.55

Souvenir Sheets

663 A80 25nu Archery, vert. 4.00 4.00
664 A80 25nu Fencing 4.00 4.00

Paintings by Titian — A81

Designs: 50ch, *Gentleman with a Book.* 1nu, *Venus and Cupid, with a Lute Player.* 2nu, *Diana and Actaeon.* 3nu, *Cardinal Ippolito dei Medici.* 4nu, *Sleeping Venus.* 5nu, *Venus Risen from the Waves.* 6nu, *Worship of Venus.* 7nu, *Fete Champetre.* 10nu, *Perseus and Andromeda.* 15nu, *Danae.* 20nu, *Venus at the Mirror.* 25nu, *Venus and the Organ Player.* No. 677, *The Pardo Venus,* horiz. No. 678, *Venus and Cupid, with an Organist.* No. 679, *Miracle of the Irascible Son.* No. 680, *Diana and Callisto.* No. 681, *Saint John the Almsgiver.* No. 682, *Danae with the Shower of Gold,* horiz. No. 683, *Bacchus and Ariadne.* No. 684, *Venus Blindfolding Cupid.* No. 685, *Portrait of Laura Dianti.* No. 686, *Venus of Urbino.* No. 687, *Portrait of Johann Friedrich.* No. 688, *Mater Dolorosa with Raised Hands.*

Perf. 13½x14, 14x13½

1989, Feb. 15 Litho.

665 A81 50ch multicolored .20 .20
666 A81 1nu multicolored .20 .20
667 A81 2nu multicolored .30 .25
668 A81 3nu multicolored .50 .35
669 A81 4nu multicolored .65 .50
670 A81 5nu multicolored .80 .60
671 A81 6nu multicolored .90 .75
672 A81 7nu multicolored 1.10 .85
673 A81 10nu multicolored 1.60 1.25
674 A81 15nu multicolored 2.50 1.75
675 A81 20nu multicolored 3.25 2.50
676 A81 25nu multicolored 4.00 3.00
Nos. 665-676 (12) 16.00 12.20

Souvenir Sheets

677-688 A81 25nu Set of 12 48.00 48.00

Mickey Mouse, 60th Anniv. (in 1988) — A82

Movie posters: 1ch, Mickey Mouse, 1930s. 2ch, *Barnyard Olympics,* 1932. 3ch, *Society Dog Show,* 1939. 4ch, *Fantasia,* 1980s re-release. 5ch, *The Mad Dog,* 1932. 10ch, *A Gentleman's Gentleman,* 1941. 50ch, *Symphony hour,* 1942. 10nu, *The Moose Hunt,* 1931. 15nu, *Wild Waves,* 1929. 20nu, *Mickey in Arabia,* 1932. 25nu, *Tugboat Mickey,* 1940. 30nu, *Building a Building,* 1933.

#701, *The Mad Doctor,* 1933. #702, *The Meller Drammer,* 1933. #703, *Ye Olden Days,* 1933. #704, *Mickey's Good Deed,* 1932. #705, *Mickey's Pal Pluto,* 1933. #706, *Trader Mickey,* 1932. #707, *Touchdown Mickey,* 1932. #708, *Steamboat Willie,* 1928. #709, *The Whoopee Party,* 1932. #710, *Mickey's Nightmare,* 1932. #711, *The Klondike Kid,* 1932. #712, *The Wayward Canary,* 1932.

1989, June 20 Litho. *Perf. 13½x14*

689-700 A82 Set of 12 16.00 13.00

Souvenir Sheets

701-712 A82 25nu Set of 12 48.00 48.00

Mushrooms — A83

1989, Aug. 22 Litho. *Perf. 14*

713 A83 50ch *Tricholoma pardalotum* .20 .20
714 A83 1nu *Suillus placidus* .20 .20

715 A83 2nu *Boletus regius* .30 .25
716 A83 3nu *Gomphidius glutinosus* .50 .35
717 A83 4nu *Boletus calopus* .65 .50
718 A83 5nu *Suillus grevillei* .80 .60
719 A83 6nu *Boletus appendiculatus* .90 .70
720 A83 7nu *Lactarius torminosus* 1.10 .80
721 A83 10nu *Macrolepiota rhacodes* 1.60 1.25
722 A83 15nu *Amanita rubescens* 2.50 1.75
723 A83 20nu *Amanita phalloides* 3.25 2.50
724 A83 25nu *Amanita citrina* 4.00 3.00
Nos. 713-724 (12) 16.00 12.10

Souvenir Sheets

725 A83 25nu *Russula aurata* 4.00 4.00
726 A83 25nu *Gyroporus castaneus* 4.00 4.00
727 A83 25nu *Cantharellus cibarius* 4.00 4.00
728 A83 25nu *Boletus rhodoxanthus* 4.00 4.00
729 A83 25nu *Paxillus involutus* 4.00 4.00
730 A83 25nu *Gyroporus cyanescens* 4.00 4.00
731 A83 25nu *Lepista nuda* 4.00 4.00
732 A83 25nu *Dentinum repandum* 4.00 4.00
733 A83 25nu *Lepista saeva* 4.00 4.00
734 A83 25nu *Hydnum imbricatum* 4.00 4.00
735 A83 25nu *Xerocomus subtomentosus* 4.00 4.00
736 A83 25nu *Russula olivacea* 4.00 4.00

Intl. Maritime Organization, 30th Anniv. — A84

Ships: 50ch, Spanish galleon *La Reale*, 1680. 1 nu, Submersible *Turtle*, 1776. 2nu, *Charlote Dundas*, 1802. 3nu, *Great Eastern*, c. 1858. 4nu, HMS *Warrior*, 1862. 5nu, Mississippi steamer, 1884. 6nu, *Preussen*, 1902. 7nu, USS *Arizona*, 1915. 10nu, *Bluenose*, 1921. 15nu, Steam trawler, 1925. 20nu, American liberty ship, 1943. No. 748, S.S. *United States*, 1952. No. 749, Moran tug, c. 1950. No. 750, Sinking of the *Titanic*, 1912. No. 751, U-boat, c. 1942. No. 752, Japanese warship *Yamato*, 1944. No. 753, HMS *Dreadnought*. No. 754, S.S. *Normandie*, c. 1933, and a Chinese junk. No. 755, HMS *Victory*, 1805. No. 756, USS *Monitor*, 1862. No. 757, *Cutty Sark*, 1869. No. 758, USS *Constitution*. No. 759, HMS *Resolution*. No. 760, Chinese junk.

1989, Aug. 24 Litho. *Perf. 14*

737 A84 50ch multicolored .20 .20
738 A84 1nu multicolored .20 .20
739 A84 2nu multicolored .30 .25
740 A84 3nu multicolored .50 .35
741 A84 4nu multicolored .65 .50
742 A84 5nu multicolored .80 .60
743 A84 6nu multicolored .90 .70
744 A84 7nu multicolored 1.10 .80
745 A84 10nu multicolored 1.60 1.25
746 A84 15nu multicolored 2.50 1.75
747 A84 20nu multicolored 3.25 2.50
748 A84 25nu multicolored 4.00 3.00
Nos. 737-748 (12) 16.00 12.10

Souvenir Sheets

749-760 A84 25nu each 4.00 4.00

Nos. 289-291 Overprinted: WORLD / AIDS DAY

1988, Dec. 1 Litho. *Perf. 14x13½*

761 A37 2nu multicolored .45 .35
762 A37 5nu multicolored 1.10 .90
763 A37 10nu multicolored 2.25 1.75
Nos. 761-763 (3) 3.80 3.00

Nos. 486-494 Ovptd. in Silver: ASIA-PACIFIC EXPOSITION FUKUOKA '89

1989, Mar. 17 *Perf. 13½*

764 A61 5ch multicolored .20 .20
765 A61 35ch multicolored .20 .20
766 A61 50ch multicolored .20 .20
767 A61 2.50nu multicolored .40 .30
768 A61 3nu multicolored .50 .35
769 A61 4nu multicolored .65 .50
770 A61 5nu multicolored .80 .60
771 A61 5.50nu multicolored .90 .65
772 A61 6nu multicolored 1.00 .80
Nos. 764-772 (9) 4.85 3.80

This set exists overprinted in Japanese.

Chhukha Hydroelectric Project — A85

1988, Oct. 21 Litho. *Perf. 13½*

773 A85 50ch multicolored .20 .20

Jawaharlal Nehru (1889-1964), Indian Prime Minister A85a

1989, Nov. 14 Photo. *Perf. 14*

773A A85a 100ch olive brown .20 .20

Denomination is shown as 1.00ch in error.

Birds A86

Designs: 50ch, Larger goldenbacked woodpecker. 1nu, Black-naped monarch. 2nu, White-crested laughing thrush. 3nu, Bloodpheasant. 4nu, Blossom-headed parakeet. 5nu, Rosy minivet. 6nu, Chestnut-headed tit babbler. 7nu, Blue pitta. 10nu, Black-naped oriole. 15nu, Green magpie. 20nu, Indian three-toed kingfisher. No. 785, Ibisbill. No. 786, Great pied hornbill. No. 787, Himalayan redbreasted falconet. No. 788, Lammergeier. No. 789, Large racket-tailed drongo. No. 790, Fire-tailed sunbird. No. 791, Indian crested swift. No. 792, White-eared pheasant. No. 793, Satyr tragopan. No. 794, Wallcreeper. No. 795, Fairy bluebird. No. 796, Little spiderhunter. No. 797, Spotted forktail. Nos. 774-779 vert.

1989, Nov. 22 Litho. *Perf. 14*

774 A86 50ch multicolored .20 .20
775 A86 1nu multicolored .20 .20
776 A86 2nu multicolored .30 .25
777 A86 3nu multicolored .50 .35
778 A86 4nu multicolored .65 .50
779 A86 5nu multicolored .80 .60
780 A86 6nu multicolored .90 .70
781 A86 7nu multicolored 1.10 .80
782 A86 10nu multicolored 1.60 1.25
783 A86 15nu multicolored 2.50 1.75
784 A86 20nu multicolored 3.25 2.50
785 A86 25nu multicolored 4.00 3.00
Nos. 774-785 (12) 16.00 12.10

Souvenir Sheets

786-797 A86 25nu each 4.00 4.00

Steam Locomotives — A87

Designs: 50ch, *Best Friend of Charleston*, 1830, US 1nu, Class U, 1949, France. 2nu, *Consolidation*, 1866, US. 3nu, *Luggage Engine*, 1843, Great Britain. 4nu, Class 60-3 Shay, 1913, US. 5nu, *John Bull*, 1831, US. 6nu, *Hercules*, 1837, US. 7nu, Eight-wheel tank engine, 1874, Great Britain. 10nu, *The Illinois*, 1852, US. 15nu, German State 4-6-4, 1935. 20nu, American Standard, 1865. No. 809, Class Ps-4, 1926, US. No. 810, *Puffing Billy*, 1814, Great Britain. No. 811, Stephenson's *Rocket*, 1829, Great Britain. No. 812, *Cumberland*, 1845, US, vert. No. 813, *John Stevens*, 1849, US, vert. No. 814, No. 22 Baldwin Locomotive Works, 1873, US, No. 815, *Ariel*, 1877, US. No. 816, 1899 *No. 1301* Webb Compound Engine, Great Britain. No. 817, 1893 *No. 999* Empire State Express, US. No. 818, 1923 Class K-36, US. No. 819, 1935 Class A4, Great Britain. No. 820, 1935 Class A, US. No. 821, 1943 Class P-1, US.

1990, Jan. 30

798 A87 50ch multi .20 .20
799 A87 1nu multi .20 .20
800 A87 2nu multi .30 .25
801 A87 3nu multi .50 .35
802 A87 4nu multi .65 .50
803 A87 5nu multi .80 .60
804 A87 6nu multi .90 .70
805 A87 7nu multi 1.10 .80
806 A87 10nu multi 1.60 1.25
807 A87 15nu multi 2.50 1.75
808 A87 20nu multi 3.25 2.50
809 A87 25nu multi 4.00 3.00
Nos. 798-809 (12) 16.00 12.10

Souvenir Sheets

810-821 A87 25nu each 4.00 4.00

Butterflies A88

1990, Jan. 30 Litho. *Perf. 14*

822 A88 50ch *Charaxes harmodius* .20 .20
823 A88 1nu *Prioneris thestylis* .20 .20
824 A88 2nu *Sephisa chandra* .30 .25
825 A88 3nu *Penthema usarda* .50 .35
826 A88 4nu *Troides aecus* .65 .50
827 A88 5nu *Polyura eudamippus* .80 .60
828 A88 6nu *Polyura dolon* .90 .70
829 A88 7nu *Neope bhadra* 1.10 .80
830 A88 10nu *Delias descombesi* 1.60 1.25
831 A88 15nu *Childreni childrena* 2.50 1.75
832 A88 20nu *Kallima inachus* 3.25 2.50
833 A88 25nu *Elymnias malelas* 4.00 3.00
Nos. 822-833 (12) 16.00 12.10

Souvenir Sheets

834 A88 25nu Red lacewing 4.00 4.00
835 A88 25nu Bhutan glory 4.00 4.00
836 A88 25nu Great eggfly 4.00 4.00
837 A88 25nu Kaiser-I-Hind 4.00 4.00
838 A88 25nu Chestnut tiger 4.00 4.00
839 A88 25nu Common map 4.00 4.00
840 A88 25nu Swallowtail 4.00 4.00
841 A88 25nu Jungle glory 4.00 4.00
842 A88 25nu Checkered swallowtail 4.00 4.00
843 A88 25nu Common birdwing 4.00 4.00
844 A88 25nu Blue banded peacock 4.00 4.00
845 A88 25nu Camberwell beauty 4.00 4.00

Nos. 822-824, 826-827, 830-831, 834-835, 844-845 are vert.

Paintings by Hiroshige A89

10ch, Plum Estate, Kameido. 20ch, Yatsumi Bridge. 50ch, Ayase River and Kanegafuchi. 75ch, View of Shiba Coast. 1nu, Grandpa's Teahouse, Meguro. 2nu, Kameido Tenjin Shrine. 6nu, Yoroi Ferry, Koami-cho. 7nu, Sakasai Ferry. 10nu, Fukagawa Lumberyards. 15nu, Suido Bridge & Surugadai. 20nu, Meguro Drum Bridge, Sunset Hill. #857, Atagoshita & Yabu Lane. #858, Towboats Along the Yotsugi-dori Canal. #859, Minowa, Kanasugi, Mikawashima. #860, Horikiri Iris Garden. #861, Fukagawa Susaki & Jumantsubo. #862, Suijin Shrine & Massaki on the Sumida River. #863, New Year's Eve Foxfires at the Changing Tree, Oji. #864, Nihonbashi, Clearing After Snow. #865, View to the North from Asukayama. #866, Komakata Hall & Azuma Bridge. #867, The City Flourishing, Tanabata Festival. #868, Suruga-cho. #869, Sudden Shower over Shin-Ohashi Bridge & Atake.

1990, May 21 Litho. *Perf. 13½*

846 A89 10ch multicolored .20 .20
847 A89 20ch multicolored .20 .20
848 A89 50ch multicolored .20 .20
849 A89 75ch multicolored .20 .20
850 A89 1nu multicolored .20 .20
851 A89 2nu multicolored .30 .25
852 A89 6nu multicolored .95 .70
853 A89 7nu multicolored 1.10 .85
854 A89 10nu multicolored 1.60 1.25
855 A89 15nu multicolored 2.50 1.75
856 A89 20nu multicolored 3.25 2.50
857 A89 25nu multicolored 4.00 3.00
Nos. 846-857 (12) 14.70 11.30

Souvenir Sheets

858-869 A89 25nu each 4.00 3.00

Hirohito (1901-1989) and enthronement of Akihito as emperor of Japan.

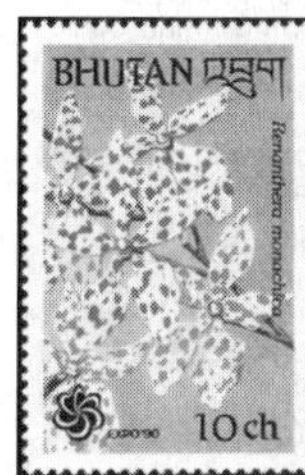

Orchids — A90

1990, Apr. 6 Litho. *Perf. 14*

870 A90 10ch *Renanthera monachica* .20 .20
871 A90 50ch *Vanda coerulea* .20 .20
872 A90 1nu *Phalaenopsis violacea* .20 .20
873 A90 2nu *Dendrobium nobile* .30 .20
874 A90 5nu *Vandopsis lissochiloides* .80 .60
875 A90 6nu *Paphiopedilum rothschildianum* .95 .70
876 A90 7nu *Phalaenopsis schilleriana* 1.10 .80
877 A90 9nu *Paphiopedilum insigne* 1.50 1.10
878 A90 10nu *Paphiopedilum bellatulum* 1.60 1.25
879 A90 20nu *Doritis pulcherrima* 3.25 2.50
880 A90 25nu *Cymbidium giganteum* 4.00 3.00
881 A90 35nu *Phalaenopsis mariae* 5.50 4.25
Nos. 870-881 (12) 19.60 15.00

Souvenir Sheets

882 A90 30nu *Vanda coerulescens* 4.75 4.75
883 A90 30nu *Vandopsis parishi* 4.75 4.75
884 A90 30nu *Dendrobium aphyllum* 4.75 4.75
885 A90 30nu *Phalaenopsis amabilis* 4.75 4.75
886 A90 30nu *Paphiopedilum haynaldianum* 4.75 4.75
887 A90 30nu *Dendrobium lodgigesii* 4.75 4.75
888 A90 30nu *Vanda alpina* 4.75 4.75
889 A90 30nu *Phalaenopsis equestris* 4.75 4.75
890 A90 30nu *Vanda cristata* 4.75 4.75
891 A90 30nu *Phalaenopsis cornu cervi* 4.75 4.75
892 A90 30nu *Paphiopedilum niveum* 4.75 4.75
893 A90 30nu *Dendrobium margaritaceum* 4.75 4.75

EXPO '90 Intl. Garden and Greenery Exposition, Osaka, Apr. 1-Dec. 31.

G.P.O., Thimphu — A90a

1990, May 29 Photo. *Perf. 14*

893A A90a 1nu multicolored .20 .20

Penny Black, 150th Anniv. A90b

Penny Black and: 50ch, Bhutan #1. 1nu, Oldenburg #1. 2nu, Bergedorf #3. 4nu, German Democratic Republic #48. 5nu, Brunswick #1. 6nu, Basel #3L1. 8nu, Geneva #2L1. 10nu, Zurich #1L1. No. 902, France #3. 20nu, Vatican City #1. 25nu, Israel #1. No. 905, Japan #1.

Penny Black and: No. 906a, Mecklenburg-Schwerin #1. b, Mecklenburg-Strelitz #1. No. 907a, Germany #5, #9. b, Prussia #2. No. 908a, Hamburg #1. b, North German Confederation #1, #7. No. 909a, Baden #1. b, Wurttemberg #1. No. 910a, Heligoland #1. b, Hanover #1. No. 911a, Thurn & Taxis #3. b, Thurn & Taxis #42. No. 912a, Schleswig-Holstein #1. b, Lubeck #5. No. 913, Saxony #1. No. 914, Berlin #9N1. No. 915, No other stamp. No. 916, US #1. No. 917, Bavaria #1.

1990, Oct. 9 ***Perf. 14***

894	A90b	50ch multicolored	.20	.20
895	A90b	1nu multicolored	.20	.20
896	A90b	2nu multicolored	.30	.25
897	A90b	4nu multicolored	.65	.50
898	A90b	5nu multicolored	.80	.60
899	A90b	6nu multicolored	1.00	.75
900	A90b	8nu multicolored	1.25	1.00
901	A90b	10nu multicolored	1.60	1.25
902	A90b	15nu multicolored	2.50	1.75
903	A90b	20nu multicolored	3.25	2.50
904	A90b	25nu multicolored	4.00	3.00
905	A90b	30nu multicolored	4.75	3.50
		Nos. 894-905 (12)	20.50	15.50

Souvenir Sheets

Sheets of 2 (#906-912) or 1

906-912	A90b	15nu each	4.75	4.75
913-917	A90b	30nu each	4.75	4.75

Stamp World London '90.

Giant Pandas A91

Tiger A92

Endangered wildlife of Asia.

1990 ***Perf. 14***

918	A91	50ch multi, diff.	.20	.20
919	A91	1nu multi, diff.	.20	.20
920	A91	2nu multi, diff.	.30	.25
921	A91	3nu shown	.50	.35
922	A91	4nu multi, diff.	.65	.50
923	A92	5nu shown	.80	.60
924	A91	6nu multi, diff.	.90	.70
925	A91	7nu multi, diff.	1.10	.80
926	A92	10nu Elephant	1.60	1.25
927	A91	15nu multi, diff.	2.50	1.75
928	A92	20nu Barking deer	3.25	2.50
929	A92	25nu Snow leopard	4.00	3.00
		Nos. 918-929 (12)	16.00	12.10

Souvenir Sheets

930	A92	25nu Rhinoceros	4.00	4.00
931	A92	25nu Clouded leopard	4.00	4.00
932	A92	25nu Asiatic wild dog	4.00	4.00
933	A92	25nu Himalayan shou	4.00	4.00
934	A92	25nu Golden cat	4.00	4.00
935	A92	25nu Himalayan musk deer	4.00	4.00
936	A91	25nu multi, diff.	4.00	4.00
937	A92	25nu Asiatic black bear	4.00	4.00
938	A92	25nu Gaur	4.00	4.00
939	A92	25nu Pygmy hog	4.00	4.00
940	A92	25nu Wolf	4.00	4.00
941	A92	25nu Sloth bear	4.00	4.00

Nos. 919-920 and 927 vert.

Buddhist Musical Instruments — A93

1990, Sept. 29 Litho. ***Perf. 13½x13***

942	A93	10ch Dungchen	.20	.20
943	A93	20ch Dungkar	.20	.20
944	A93	30ch Roim	.20	.20
945	A93	50ch Tinchag	.20	.20
946	A93	1nu Dradu & drilbu	.20	.20
947	A93	2nu Gya-ling	.30	.25
948	A93	2.50nu Nga	.40	.30
a.		Souv. sheet, #943, 945, 947-948	.85	.65
949	A93	3.50nu Kang-dung	.55	.45
a.		Souv. sheet, #942, 944, 946, 949	.85	.65
		Nos. 942-949 (8)	2.25	2.00

Year of the Girl Child — A94

1990, Dec. 8

950	A94	50ch shown	.20	.20
951	A94	20nu Young girl	3.25	2.50

Wonders of the World — A95

Walt Disney characters viewing: 1ch, Temple of Artemis, Ephesus. 2ch, Statue of Zeus, Olympia. 3ch, Egyptian pyramids. 4ch, Lighthouse, Alexandria. 5ch, Mausoleum at Halicarnassus. 10ch, Colossus of Rhodes. 50ch, Hanging gardens of Babylon. 5nu, Mauna Loa volcano, Hawaii. 6nu, Carlsbad Caverns, New Mexico. 10nu, Rainbow Bridge, Utah. 15nu, Grand Canyon of the Colorado, Arizona. 20nu, Old Faithful geyser, Wyoming. 25nu, Giant sequoias, California. 30nu, Crater Lake and Wizard Island, Oregon. 5nu, 6nu, 10nu, 15nu, 20nu, 25nu, 30nu are horiz.

Walt Disney characters viewing: No. 966, Great Wall of China, horiz. No. 967, Mosque of St. Sophia, Istanbul, Turkey. No. 968, The Leaning Tower of Pisa, Italy. No. 969, Colosseum, Rome. No. 970, Stonehenge, England. No. 971, Catacombs of Alexandria, Egypt. No. 972, Porcelain Tower, Nanking, China, horiz. No. 973, The Panama Canal, horiz. No. 974, Golden Gate Bridge, San Francisco, horiz. No. 975, Sears Tower, Chicago, horiz. No. 976, Gateway Arch, St. Louis. No. 977, Alcan Highway, Alaska and Canada, horiz. No. 978, Hoover Dam, Nevada. No. 979, Empire State Building, New York.

1991, Feb. 2 Litho. ***Perf. 14***

952	A95	1ch multicolored	.20	.20
953	A95	2ch multicolored	.20	.20
954	A95	3ch multicolored	.20	.20
955	A95	4ch multicolored	.20	.20
956	A95	5ch multicolored	.20	.20
957	A95	10ch multicolored	.20	.20
958	A95	50ch multicolored	.20	.20
959	A95	5nu multicolored	.80	.60
960	A95	6nu multicolored	.95	.70
961	A95	10nu multicolored	1.60	1.25
962	A95	15nu multicolored	2.50	1.75
963	A95	20nu multicolored	3.25	2.50
964	A95	25nu multicolored	4.00	3.00
965	A95	30nu multicolored	4.75	3.50
		Nos. 952-965 (14)	19.25	14.70

Souvenir Sheets

Perf. 14x13½, 13½x14

966-979	A95	25nu each	4.00	4.00

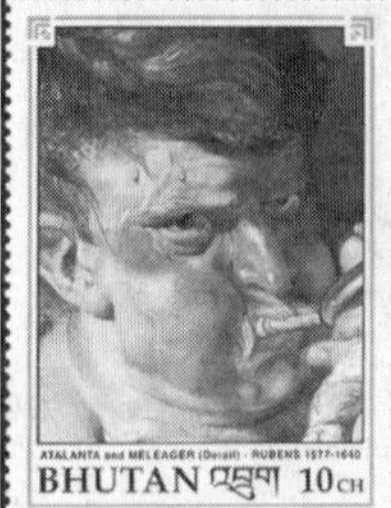

Peter Paul Rubens (1577-1640), Painter A96

Entire paintings or different details from: 10ch, 5nu, 6nu, 10nu, No. 992, Atalanta and Meleager. 50ch, Fall of Phaethon. 1nu, No. 993, Feast of Venus Verticordia. 2nu, Achilles Slaying Hector. 3nu, No. 994, Arachne Punished by Minerva. 4nu, No. 995, Jupiter Receives Psyche on Olympus. 7nu, Venus in Vulcan's Furnace. 20nu, No. 996, Briseis Returned to Achilles. 30nu, No. 997, Mars and Rhea Sylvia. No. 998, Venus Shivering. No. 999, Ganymede and the Eagle. No. 1000, Origin of the Milky Way. No. 1001, Adonis and Venus. No. 1002, Hero and Leander. No. 1003, Fall of the Titans.

Nos. 994, 996-997, 1000-1003 are horiz.

1991, Feb. 2

980	A96	10ch multicolored	.20	.20
981	A96	50ch multicolored	.20	.20
982	A96	1nu multicolored	.20	.20
983	A96	2nu multicolored	.30	.20
984	A96	3nu multicolored	.50	.20
985	A96	4nu multicolored	.65	.20
986	A96	5nu multicolored	.80	.60
987	A96	6nu multicolored	.95	.70
988	A96	7nu multicolored	1.10	.85
989	A96	10nu multicolored	1.60	1.25
990	A96	20nu multicolored	3.25	2.50
991	A96	30nu multicolored	4.75	3.50
		Nos. 980-991 (12)	14.50	10.60

Souvenir Sheets

992-1003	A96	25nu each	4.00	4.00

Vincent Van Gogh (1853-1890), Painter — A97

Paintings: 10ch, Cottages, Reminiscence of the North. 50ch, Head of a Peasant Woman with Dark Cap. 1nu, Portrait of a Woman in Blue. 2nu, The Midwife. 8nu, Vase with Hollyhocks. 10nu, Portrait of a Man with a Skull Cap. 12nu, Agostina Segatori Sitting in the Cafe du Tambourin. 15nu, Vase with Daisies and Anemones. 18nu, Fritillaries in a Copper Vase. 20nu, Woman Sitting in the Grass. 25nu, On the Outskirts of Paris, horiz. 30nu, Chrysanthemums and Wild Flowers in a Vase.

No. 1016, Le Moulin de la Galette. No. 1017, Bowl with Sunflowers, Roses and Other Flowers, horiz. No. 1018, Poppies and Butterflies. No. 1019, Trees in the Garden of Saint-Paul Hospital. No. 1020, Le Moulin de Blute Fin. No. 1021, Le Moulin de la Galette, diff. No. 1022, Vase with Peonies. No. 1023, Vase with Zinnias. No. 1024, Fishing in the Spring, Pont de Clichy, horiz. No. 1025, Village Street in Auvers, horiz. No. 1026, Vase with Zinnias and Other Flowers, horiz. No. 1027, Vase with Red Poppies.

1991, July 22 Litho. ***Perf. 13½***

1004	A97	10ch multicolored	.20	.20
1005	A97	50ch multicolored	.20	.20
1006	A97	1nu multicolored	.20	.20
1007	A97	2nu multicolored	.30	.20
1008	A97	8nu multicolored	1.25	1.00
1009	A97	10nu multicolored	1.60	1.25
1010	A97	12nu multicolored	2.00	1.50
1011	A97	15nu multicolored	2.50	1.75
1012	A97	18nu multicolored	3.00	2.25
1013	A97	20nu multicolored	3.25	2.50
1014	A97	25nu multicolored	4.00	3.00
1015	A97	30nu multicolored	4.75	3.50
		Nos. 1004-1015 (12)	23.25	17.55

Size: 76x102mm, 102x76mm

Imperf

1016-1027	A97	30nu each	4.75	4.75

History of World Cup Soccer — A98

Winning team pictures, plays or possible future site: 50ch, Uruguay, 1930. 1nu, Italy, 1934. 2nu, Italy, 1938. 3nu, Uruguay, 1950. 5nu, West Germany, 1954. 10nu, Brazil, 1958. 20nu, Brazil, 1962. 25nu, England, 1966. 29nu, Brazil, 1970. 30nu, West Germany, 1974. 31nu, Argentina, 1978. 32nu, Italy, 1982. 33nu, Argentina, 1986. 34nu, West Germany, 1990. 35nu, Los Angeles Coliseum, 1994.

Players: No. 1043, Claudio Caniggia, Argentina, vert. No. 1044, Salvatore Schillaci, Italy, vert. No. 1045, Roberto Baggio, Italy, vert. No. 1046, Peter Shilton, England, vert. No. 1047, Lothar Matthaus, West Germany, vert. No. 1048, Paul Gascoigne, England, vert.

1991, Aug. 1 Litho. ***Perf. 13½***

1028	A98	50ch multicolored	.20	.20
1029	A98	1nu multicolored	.20	.20
1030	A98	2nu multicolored	.30	.20
1031	A98	3nu multicolored	.50	.20
1032	A98	5nu multicolored	.80	.60
1033	A98	10nu multicolored	1.60	1.25
1034	A98	20nu multicolored	3.25	2.50
1035	A98	25nu multicolored	4.00	3.00
1036	A98	29nu multicolored	4.75	3.50
1037	A98	30nu multicolored	4.75	3.50
1038	A98	31nu multicolored	5.00	3.75
1039	A98	32nu multicolored	5.25	4.00
1040	A98	33nu multicolored	5.50	4.00
1041	A98	34nu multicolored	5.50	4.25
1042	A98	35nu multicolored	5.75	4.25
		Nos. 1028-1042 (15)	47.35	35.40

Souvenir Sheets

1043-1048	A98	30nu each	4.75	4.75

Phila Nippon '91 — A99

1991, Nov. 16 ***Perf. 13***

1049	A99	15nu multicolored	2.50	1.50

Education in Bhutan A100

1992, Mar. 5 Photo. ***Perf. 13½***

1050	A100	1nu multicolored	.20	.20

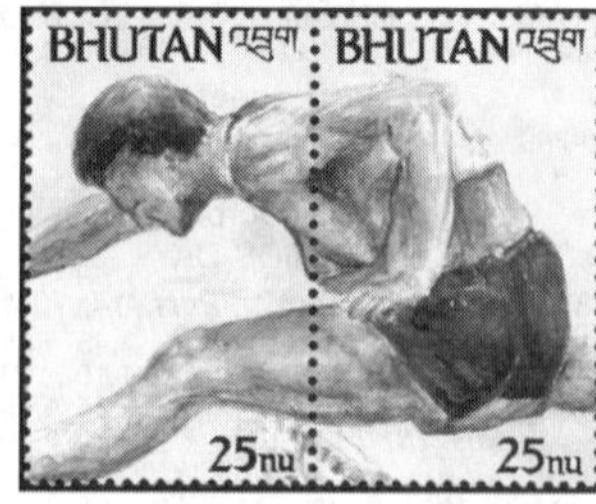

A101

1992 Summer Olympics, Barcelona — A102

1992, July 24 Litho. *Perf. 12*

1051 A101 25nu Pair, #a.-b. 8.25 8.25

Souvenir Sheet

1052 A102 25nu Archer 4.00 4.00

German Reunification — A103

1992, Oct. 3 Litho. *Perf. 12*

1053 A103 25nu multicolored 2.00 2.00

Souvenir Sheet

1054 A103 25nu multicolored 2.00 2.00

Stamp from No. 1054 does not have white inscription or border.

Bhutan Postal Service, 30th Anniv. A104

Designs: 1nu, Mail truck, plane. 3nu, Letter carrier approaching village. 5nu, Letter carrier emptying mail box.

1992, Oct. 9

1055 A104 1nu multicolored .20 .20
1056 A104 3nu multicolored .25 .25
1057 A104 5nu multicolored .40 .40
Nos. 1055-1057 (3) .85 .85

Environmental Protection — A105

Designs: a, 7nu, Red panda. b, 20nu, Takin. c, 15nu, Black-necked crane, blue poppy. d, 10nu, One-horned rhinoceros.

1993, July 1 Litho. *Perf. 14*

1058 A105 Sheet of 4, #b.-e.

No. 1058 was delayed from its originally scheduled release in 1992, although some copies were made available to the trade at that time.

A106 A107

1992, Sept. 18 *Perf. 12*

1059 A106 15nu Ship 1.25 1.25
1060 A106 20nu Portrait 1.60 1.60

Souvenir Sheet

1061 A106 25nu like #1060 2.00 2.00

Discovery of America, 500th anniv.
Stamp from No. 1061 does not have silver inscription or white border.

1992, Nov. 11 Litho. *Perf. 12*

Reign of King Jigme Singye Wangchuk, 20th Anniv.: a, 1nu, Man tilling field, factory. b, 5nu, Airplane. c, 10nu, House, well. d, 15nu, King.
20nu, People, flag, King, horiz.

1062 A107 Block of 4, #a.-d. 2.50 2.50

Souvenir Sheet

1063 A107 20nu multicolored 1.75 1.75

Intl. Volunteer Day — A108

a, 1.50nu, White inscription. b, 9nu, Green inscription. c, 15nu, Red inscription.

1992, Dec. 5 Litho. *Perf. 14*

1067 A108 Block of 4, #a.-c. + label 2.00 2.00

Medicinal Plants — A109

1993, Jan. 1 Litho. *Perf. 12*

1068 A109 1.50nu Meconopsis grandis prain .20 .20
1069 A109 7nu Meconopsis sp. .60 .60
1070 A109 10nu Meconopsis wallichii .80 .80
1071 A109 12nu Meconopsis horridula 1.00 1.00
1072 A109 20nu Meconopsis discigera 1.75 1.75
Nos. 1068-1072 (5) 4.35 4.35

Souvenir Sheet

1073 A109 25nu Meconopsis horridula, diff. 2.00 2.00

Miniature Sheet

Lunar New Year — A110

1993, Feb. 22 Litho. *Perf. 14*

1074 A110 25nu multicolored 2.00 2.00

No. 1074 Surcharged "TAIPEI '93" in Silver and Black

1993, Aug. 14 Litho. *Perf. 14*

1075 A110 30nu on 25nu 2.50 2.50

Door Gods — A112

1993, Dec. 17 Litho. *Perf. 12*

1091 A112 1.50nu Namtheo-Say .20 .20
1092 A112 5nu Pha-Ke-Po .50 .50
1093 A112 10nu Chen-Mi-Jang 1.00 1.00
1094 A112 15nu Yul-Khor-Sung 1.50 1.50
Nos. 1091-1094 (4) 3.20 3.20

Flowers — A113

1993, Jan. 1 *Perf. 13*

Designs: No. 1095a, 1nu, Rhododendron mucronatum. b, 1.5nu. Anemone rupicola. c, 2nu, Polemonium coeruleum. d, 2.5nu, Rosa marophylla. e, 4nu, Paraquilegia microphylla. f, 5nu, Aquilegia nivalis. g, 6nu, Geranium wallichianum. h, 7nu, Rhodendron campanulatum. i, 9nu, Viola suavis. j, 10nu, Cyananthus lobatus.
13nu, Red flower, horiz.

1095 A113 Strip of 10, #a.-j. 4.75 4.75

Souvenir Sheet

1096 A113 13nu multicolored 1.40 1.40

New Year 1994 (Year of the Dog) — A114

1994, Feb. 11 Litho. *Perf. 14*

1097 A114 11.50nu multicolored .80 .80

Souvenir Sheet

1098 A114 20nu like #1097 1.40 1.40

Hong Kong '94.

Stamp Cards — A115

Designs: 16nu, Tagtshang Monastery. 20nu, Map of Bhutan. Illustration reduced.

Rouletted 26 on 2 or 3 Sides

1994, Aug. 15 Litho.

Self-Adhesive

Cards of 6 + 6 labels

1099 A115 16nu #a.-f. 6.25 6.25
1100 A115 20nu #a.-f. 7.75 7.75

Individual stamps measure 70x9mm and have a card backing. Se-tenant labels inscribed "AIR MAIL."

Souvenir Sheet

First Manned Moon Landing, 25th Anniv. — A116

a, 30nu, Astronaut on moon. b, 36nu, Space shuttle, earth, moon. Illustration reduced.

1994, Nov. 11 Litho. *Perf. 14x14½*

1101 A116 Sheet of 2, #a.-b. 4.25 4.25

Nos. 1101a, 1101b have holographic images. Soaking in water may affect the holograms.

Souvenir Sheet

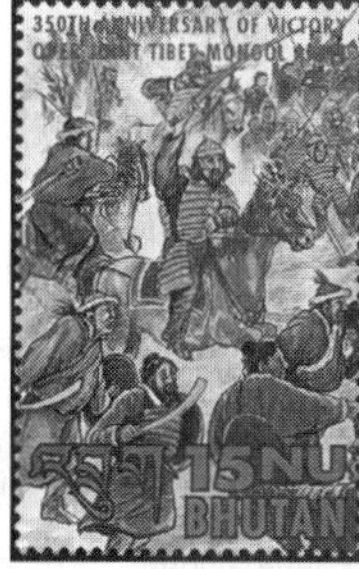

Victory Over Tibet-Mongol Army, 350th Anniv. — A117

Battle scene: a, Mounted officer. b, Hand to hand combat, soldiers in yellow or blue armor. c, Soldier on gray horse. d, Soldiers in red, drummer, horn player.

1994, Dec. 17 Litho. *Perf. 12½*

Granite Paper

1102 A117 15nu Sheet of 4, #a.-d. 4.00 4.00

Souvenir Sheet

Bridges A118

a, 15nu, Tower Bridge, London, cent. b, 16nu, Wangdue Bridge, Bhutan, 250th anniv.

1994, Nov. 11 *Perf. 12*

1103 A118 Sheet of 2, #a.-b. 2.00 2.00

1994 World Cup Soccer Championships, US — A119

1994, July 17 Litho. *Perf. 12*
1104 A119 15nu multicolored 1.00 1.00

Souvenir Sheet

World Tourism Year A120

Scenes of Bhutan: a, 1.50nu, Paro Valley. b, 5nu, Chorten Kora. c, 10nu, Thimphu Tshechu. d, 15nu, Wangdue Tshechu.

1995, Apr. 2 Litho. *Perf. 12*
1105 A120 Sheet of 4, #a.-d. 2.00 2.00

Miniature Sheet of 12

New Year 1995 (Year of the Boar) A121

Symbols of Chinese Lunar New Year: a, 10ch, Rat. b, 20ch, Ox. c, 30ch, Tiger. d, 40ch, Rabbit. e, 1nu, Dragon. f, 2nu, Snake. g, 3nu, Horse. h, 4nu, Sheep. i, 5nu, Monkey. j, 7nu, Rooster. k, 8nu, Dog. l, 9nu, Boar.
10nu, Wood Hog.

1995, Mar. 2
1106 A121 #a.-l. 2.50 2.50

Souvenir Sheet

1107 A121 10nu multicolored .65 .65

No. 1107 is a continuous design.

A122

Flowers: 9nu, Pleione praecox. 10nu, Primula calderina. 16nu, Primula whitei. 18nu, Notholirion macrophyllum.

1995, May 2 Litho. *Perf. 12*
1108-1111 A122 Set of 4 3.50 3.50

A123

1995, June 26 *Perf. 14*

UN, 50th Anniv.: a, 1.5nu, Human resources development. b, 9nu, Health & population. c, 10nu, Water & sanitation. d, 5nu, Transport & communications. e, 16nu, Forestry & environment. f, 18nu, Peace & security. g, 11.5nu, UN in Bhutan.

1112 A123 Strip of 7 4.75 4.75

Miniature Sheet of 6

Singapore '95 — A124

Birds - #1113: a, 1nu, Himalayan pied kingfisher. b, 2nu, Blyth's tragopan. c, 3nu, Long-tailed minivet. d, 10nu, Red junglefowl. e, 15nu, Black-capped sibia. f, 20nu, Red-billed chough.
No. 1114, Black-neck crane.

1995, June 2 Litho. *Perf. 12*
1113 A124 #a.-f. + 3 labels 3.50 3.50

Souvenir Sheet

1114 A124 20nu multicolored 1.40 1.40

Traditional Crafts — A125

1nu, Drying parchment. 2nu, Making tapestry. 3nu, Restoring archaeological finds. 10nu, Weaving textiles. 15nu, Sewing garments. No. 1120, 20nu, Carving wooden vessels.
No. 1121, Mosaic.

1995, Aug. 15 Litho. *Perf. 14*
1115-1120 A125 Set of 6 2.50 2.50

Souvenir Sheet

1121 A125 20nu multicolored 1.40 1.40

New Year 1996 (Year of the Rat) — A126

Designs: a, Monkey. b, Rat, fire. c, Dragon.

1996, Jan. 1 Litho. *Perf. 14*
1122 A126 10nu Sheet of 3, #a.-c. 2.00 2.00

Butterflies A127

a, 2nu, Blue pansy. b, 3nu, Blue peacock. c, 5nu, Great Mormon. d, 10nu, Fritillary. e, 15nu, Blue duke. f, 25nu, Brown Gorgon.
No. 1124, Xanthomelas. No. 1124A, Fivebar swordtail.

1996, May 2 Litho. *Perf. 14*
1123 A127 Sheet of 6, #a.-f. 4.00 4.00

Souvenir Sheets

1124-1124A A127 30nu each 2.00 2.00

1996 Summer Olympic Games, Atlanta A128

5nu, Silver 300n coin, soccer. 7nu, Silver 300n coin, basketball. 10nu, Gold 5s coin, judo. 15nu, Archery.

1996, June 15 Litho. *Perf. 14*
1125-1127 A128 Set of 3 1.50 1.50

Souvenir Sheet

1128 A128 15nu multicolored 1.00 1.00

Olymphilex '96.

Folktales — A129

Designs: a, 1nu, The White Bird. b, 2nu, Sing Sing Lhamo and the Moon. c, 3nu, The Hoopoe. d, 5nu, The Cloud Fairies. e, 10nu, The Three Wishes. f, 20nu, The Abominable Snowman.

1996, Apr. 15 *Perf. 12*
1129 A129 Sheet of 6, #a.-f. 3.00 3.00

Souvenir Sheet

1130 A129 25nu like #1129d 1.75 1.75

Locomotives — A130

No. 1131: a, 0-6-4 Tank engine (Chile). b, First Pacific locomotive in Europe (France). c, 4-6-0 Passenger engine (Norway). d, Atlantic type express (Germany). e, 4-Cylinder 4-6-0 express (Belgium). f, Standard type "4" diesel-electric (England).
No. 1132: a, Standard 0-6-0 Goods engine (India). b, Main-line 1,900 horsepower diesel-electric (Finland). c, 0-8-0 Shunting tank engine (Russia). d, Alco "PA-1" diesel-electric (US). e, "C11" Class 2-6-4 branch passenger tank engine (Japan). f, "Settebello" deluxe high-speed electric train (Italy).
No. 1133, Class "KD" 0-6-0 Goods locomotive, 1900 (Sweden). No. 1134, Shinkansen "New Railway" series 200 (Japan).

1996, Nov. 25 Litho. *Perf. 14*

Sheets of 6, #a-f

1131-1132 A130 20nu Set of 2 16.00 16.00

Souvenir Sheets

1133-1134 A130 70nu each 4.75 4.75

Penny Black — A131

Litho. & Embossed

1996, Dec. 17 *Perf. 13½*
1135 A131 140nu black & gold 9.50 9.50

A132

Winter Olympic Medalists: 10nu, Vegard Ulvang, cross-country skiing, 1992. 15nu, Kristi Yamaguchi, figure skating, 1992. 25nu, Markus Wasmeier, giant slalom, 1994. 30nu, Georg Hackl, luge, 1992.
No. 1140: a, Andreas Ostler, 2-man bobsled, 1952. b, Wolfgang Hoppe, 4-man bobsled, 1984. c, Stein Eriksen, giant slalom, 1952. d, Alberto Tomba, giant slalom, 1988.
No. 1141, Henri Oreiller, downhill, 1948. No. 1142, Eduard Scherrer, 4-man bobsled, 1924.

1997, Jan. 1 *Perf. 14*
1136-1139 A132 Set of 4 5.50 5.50
1140 A132 15nu Strip of 4, #a.-d. 4.00 4.00

Souvenir Sheets

1141-1142 A132 70nu each 4.50 4.50

No. 1140 was issued in sheets of 8 stamps.

A133

1997, Jan. 15 *Perf. 13*

Insects and Arachnids: a, 1ch, Apis laboriosa smith. b, 2ch, Neptunides polychromus. c, 3ch, Conocephalus maculctus. d, 4ch, Blattidae. e, 5ch, Dytiscus marginalis. f, 10ch, Dynastes hercules. g, 15ch, Hippodamia. h, 20ch, Sarcophaga haemorrhoidalis. i, 25ch, Lucanus cervus. j, 30ch, Caterpillar. k, 35ch, Lycia hirtaria. l, 40ch, Clytarlus pennatus. m, 45ch, Ephemera denica. n, 50ch, Gryllus campestris. o, 60ch, Deilephila elpenor. p, 65ch, Gerris. q, 70ch, Agrion splendens. r, 80ch, Tachyta nana. s, 90ch, Eurydema pulchra. t, 1nu, Hadrurus hirsutus. u, 1.50nu, Vespa germanica. v, 2nu, Pyrops. w, 2.50nu, Mantis religiosa. x, 3nu, Araneus diadematus. y, 3.50nu, Atrophaneura.
15nu, Melolontha.

1143 A133 Sheet of 25, #a.-y. 1.40 1.40

Souvenir Sheet

1144 A133 15nu multicolored 1.00 1.00

Hong Kong '97 — A134

Wildlife: a, Thalarctos maritiumus. b, Phascolarctos cinereus. c, Selenarcios thibelanus. d, Ailurus fulgens.
20nu, Ailuropoda melanoleuca.

1997, Feb. 1 Litho. *Perf. 14*
1145 A134 10nu Sheet of 4, #a.-d. 2.75 2.75

Souvenir Sheet

1146 A134 20nu multicolored 1.40 1.40

Signs of the Chinese Zodiac — A135

No. 1147: a, 1ch, Mouse. b, 2ch, Ox. c, 3ch, Tiger. d, 4ch, Rabbit. e, 5nu, Dragon. f, 6nu, Snake. g, 7nu, Horse. h, 8nu, Sheep. i, 90ch, Monkey. j, 10nu, Rooster. k, 11nu, Dog. l, 12nu, Pig.
20nu, Ox, diff.

1997, Feb. 8 Litho. *Perf. 14*

1147 A135 Sheet of 12, #a.-l. + label 4.00 4.00

Souvenir Sheet

1148 A135 20nu multicolored 1.40 1.40

Fauna A136

Cuon alpinus: No. 1149: a, Adult, hind legs off ground. b, Adult walking right. c, Mother nursing young. d, Two seated.

Endangered species: No. 1150: a, Lynx. b, Red panda. c, Takin. d, Musk deer. e, Snow leopard. f, Golden langur. g, Tiger. h, Muntjac. i, Marmot.

No. 1151, Pseudois nayaur. No. 1152, Ursus thibetanus.

1997, Apr. 24

1149 A136 10nu Block or strip of 4, #a.-d. 2.75 2.75

1150 A136 10nu Sheet of 9, #a.-i. 6.00 6.00

Souvenir Sheets

1151-1152 A136 70nu each 4.75 4.75

World Wildlife Fund (No. 1149). No. 1149 issued in sheets of 12 stamps.

UNESCO, 50th Anniv. A137

No. 1153: a, Mount Hungshan, China. b, Mausoleum of first Qin Emperor, China. c, Imperial Bronze Dragon, China. d, Tikal Natl. Park, Guatemala. e, Evora, Portugal. f, Shirakami-Sanchi, Japan. g, Paris, France. h, Valley Below the Falls, Plitvice Lakes Natl. Park, Croatia.

Sites in Germany: No. 1154: a, Cathedral, Bamberg. b, Bamberg. c, St. Michael's Church, Hildesheim. d, Potsdam Palace. e, Potsdam Church. f, Lubeck. g, Quedlinberg. h, Benedictine Church, Lorsch.

No. 1155, Goslar, Germany, horiz. No. 1156, Cathedral, Comenzada, Portugal, horiz.

1997, May 15

Sheets of 8 + Label

1153 A137 10nu #a.-h. 5.50 5.50

1154 A137 15nu #a.-h. 8.00 8.00

Souvenir Sheets

1155-1156 A137 60nu each 4.00 4.00

Chernobyl Disaster, 10th Anniv. A138

1997, May 2 Litho. *Perf. 13½x14*

1157 A138 35nu UNESCO 2.40 2.40

Dogs — A139 Cats — A140

Designs: 10nu, Dalmatian. 15nu, Siberian husky. 20nu, Saluki. 25nu, Shar pei.

No. 1162: a, Dandie Dinmont terrier. b, Chinese crested. c, Norwich terrier. d, Basset hound. e, Cardigan welsh corgi. f, French bulldog.

60nu, Hovawart.

1997, July 15 *Perf. 14*

1158-1161 A139 Set of 4 4.75 4.75

1162 A139 20nu Sheet of 6, #a.-f. 8.00 8.00

Souvenir Sheet

1163 A139 60nu multicolored 4.00 4.00

1997, July 15

Designs: 10nu, Turkish angora. 15nu, Oriental shorthair. 20nu, British shorthair. 25nu, Burmese.

No. 1168: a, Japanese bobtail. b, Ceylon. c, Exotic. d, Rex. e, Ragdoll. f, Russian blue.

60nu, Tonkinese.

1164-1167 A140 Set of 4 4.75 4.75

1168 A140 15nu Sheet of 6, #a.-f. 6.00 6.00

Souvenir Sheet

1169 A140 60nu multicolored 4.25 4.25

1998 World Cup Soccer, France A141

English players: 5nu, Pearce. 10nu, Gascoigne. 15nu, Beckham. 20nu, McManaman. 25nu, Adams. 30nu, Ince.

World Cup captains, horiz.: No. 1176: a, Maradona, Argentina, 1986. b, Alberto, Brazil, 1970. c, Dunga, Brazil, 1994. d, Moore, England, 1966. e, Fritzwalter, Germany, 1954. f, Matthaus, Germany, 1990. g, Beckenbauer, Germany, 1974. h, Passarella, Argentina, 1978.

Winning teams, horiz.: No. 1177: a, Italy, 1938. b, W. Germany, 1954. c, Uruguay, 1958. d, England, 1966. e, Argentina, 1978. f, Brazil, 1962. g, Italy, 1934. h, Brazil, 1970. i, Uruguay, 1930.

No. 1178, Philippe Albert, Belgium. No. 1179, Salvatore (Toto) Schillaci, Italy, horiz.

Perf. 13½x14, 14x13½

1997, Oct. 9 Litho.

1170-1175 A141 Set of 6 7.00 7.00

Sheets of 8 or 9

1176 A141 10nu #a.-h. + label 5.50 5.50

1177 A141 10nu #a.-i. 6.00 6.00

Souvenir Sheets

1178-1179 A141 35nu each 3.75 3.75

Friendship Between India and Bhutan A142

3nu, Jawaharlal Nehru, King Jigme Dorji Wangchuk. 10nu, Rajiv Gandhi, King Jigme Singye Wangchuk.

20nu, Indian Pres. R. V. Venkataraman, King Jigme Singye Wangchuk.

1998 Litho. *Perf. 13x13½*

1180 A142 3nu multicolored .20 .20

1181 A142 10nu multicolored .80 .80

Souvenir Sheet

1182 A142 20nu multicolored 1.25 1.25

No. 1182 contains one 76x35mm stamp.

A143

A144

Indepex '97: No. 1183: a, 3nu, Buddha seated with legs crossed. b, 15nu, Buddha seated with legs down. c, 7nu, Gandhi with hands folded. d, 10nu, Gandhi.

No. 1184, Buddha. No. 1185, Gandhi holding staff.

1998 *Perf. 13½x13*

1183 A143 Sheet of 4, #a.-d. 2.10 2.10

Souvenir Sheets

1184-1185 A143 15nu each 1.25 1.25

India's independence, 50th anniv.

1998, Feb. 28 Litho. *Perf. 14*

New Year 1998 (Year of the Tiger): 3nu, Stylized tiger walking right.

Tigers: No. 1187: a, 5nu, Lying down. b, 15nu, Adult walking forward. c, 17nu, Cub walking over rocks.

20nu, Adult up close.

1186 A144 3nu multicolored .20 .20

1187 A144 Sheet of 4, #a.-c., #1186 2.40 2.40

Souvenir Sheet

1188 A144 20nu multicolored 1.25 1.25

WHO, 50th Anniv. A145

1998, Apr. 7 Litho. *Perf. 13½*

1189 A145 3nu multicolored .20 .20

1190 A145 10nu multicolored .60 .60

Souvenir Sheet

Perf. 14

1191 A145 15nu Mother, child .90 .90

Safe Motherhood. No. 1191 contains one 35x35mm stamp.

Mother Teresa (1910-97) A146

No. 1191A, Mother Teresa, Princess Diana.

No. 1192: a, Portrait (shown). b, Holding child. c, Holding starving infant. d, Seated among nuns. e, Looking down at sick. f, With hands folded in prayer. g, With Pope John Paul II. h, Portrait, diff.

No. 1193: a, like #1191A. b, like #1192g.

1998, May 25 Litho. *Perf. 13½*

1191A A146 10nu multi .60 .60

1192 A146 10nu Sheet of 9, #a.-h., 1191A 5.50 5.50

Souvenir Sheet of 2

1193 A146 25nu #a.-b. 3.00 3.00

No. 1193 contains two 38x43mm stamps.

Birds — A147

No. 1194: a, 10ch, Red-billed chough. b, 30ch, Great hornbill. c, 50ch, Singing lark. d, 70ch, Chestnut-flanked white-eye. e, 90ch, Magpie-robin. f, 1nu, Mrs. Gould's sunbird. g, 2nu, Tailorbird. h, 3nu, Duck. i, 5nu, Spotted cuckoo. j, 7nu, Gold crest. k, 9nu, Common mynah. l, 10nu, Green cochoa.

15nu, Turtle dove.

1998, July 28 Litho. *Perf. 13*

1194 A147 Sheet of 12, #a.-l. 2.50 2.50

Souvenir Sheet

1195 A147 15nu multicolored .90 .90

No. 1195 contains one 40x30mm stamp.

New Year 1999 (Year of the Rabbit) A148

1999, Jan. 1 Litho. *Perf. 13*

1196 A148 4nu White rabbit .25 .25

1197 A148 15nu Brown rabbit .90 .90

Souvenir Sheet

Perf. 13½

1198 A148 20nu Rabbit facing forward 1.25 1.25

No. 1198 contains one 35x35mm stamp.

King Jigme Singye Wangchuk, 25th Anniv. of Coronation — A149

Various portraits, background color - No. 1199: a, Blue. b, Yellow. c, Orange. d, Green.

No. 1200, Bright pink background.

1999, June 2 Litho. *Perf. 12¼*

1199 A149 25nu Sheet of 4, #a.-d. 5.00 5.00

Souvenir Sheet

1200 A149 25nu multicolored 1.25 1.25

Trains A150

Designs: 5nu, Early German steam. 10nu, EID 711 electric. 20nu, Steam engine. 30nu, Trans Europe Express, Germany.

No. 1205: a, Bullet train, Japan, 1964. b, 2-D-2 Class 26, South Africa, 1953. c, Super Chief, US, 1946. d, Magleus Magnet, Japan, 1991. e, The Flying Scotsman, UK, 1922. f, Kodama Train, Japan, 1958. g, Blue Train, South Africa, 1969. h, Inter-City, Germany, 1960. i, High Speed ET 403, Germany, 1973. j, US Standard 4-4-0, 1855. k, Bayer Garratt,

South Africa, 1954. l, Settebello train, Italy, 1953.

No. 1206: a, Diesel-electric, France. b, 6-4-4-6 Pennsylvania RR, US. c, 2-8-2 Steam, Germany. d, Amtrak, US. e, GS&W 2-2-2, Britain. f, Class P steam, Denmark. g, French electric. h, First Japanese locomotive. i, 2-8-2 Germany.

No. 1207: a, Pacific Class 01, Germany. b, Neptune Express, Germany. c, 4-4-0 Steam, Britain. d, Shovelnose streamliner, US. e, German electric. f, Early steam, Germany. g, Union Pacific, US. h, Borsig steam, Germany, 1881. i, Borsig 4-6-4, Germany.

No. 1208, Union Pacific electric locomotive E2 streamliner, US. No. 1209, Great Northern diesel electric streamliner, US.

1999, July 21 *Perf. 14*

1201-1204 A150 Set of 4 3.25 3.25

Sheets of 12 and 9

1205 A150 10nu Sheet of 12, #a.-l. 6.00 6.00

1206-1207 A150 15nu #a.-i., each 6.75 6.75

Souvenir Sheets

1208-1209 A150 80nu each 4.00 4.00

Paintings by Hokusai (1760-1849) A151

Details or entire paintings - No. 1210: a, Suspension Bridge Between Hida and Etchu. b, Drawings of Women (partially nude). c, Exotic Beauty. d, The Poet Nakamaro in China. e, Drawings of Women (clothed). f, Chinese Poet in Snow.

No. 1211: a, Festive Dancers (with umbrella). b, Drawings of Women (holding book). c, Festive Dancers (man wearing checked pattern). d, Festive Dancers (person wearing black outfit). e, Drawings of Women (holding baby). f, Festive Dancers (woman with scarf tied under chin).

No. 1212, horiz.: a, Mount Fuji Seen Above Mist on the Tama River. b, Mount Fuji Seen from Shichirigahama. c, Sea Life (turtle). d, Sea Life (fish). e, Mount Fuji Reflected in a Lake. f, Mount Fuji Seen Through the Piers of Mannenbashi.

No. 1213, The Lotus Pedestal. No. 1214, Kushunoki Masashige. No. 1215, Peasants Leading Oxen.

1999, July 27 *Perf. 13½x14, 14x13½*

Sheets of 6

1210-1212 A151 15nu #a.-f., each 4.50 4.50

Souvenir Sheet

1213-1215 A151 80nu each 4.00 4.00

Souvenir Sheet

IBRA '99, Nuremberg A152

a, 35nu, City view. b, 40nu, Show emblem.

1999, Apr. 27 **Litho.** *Perf. 13¾*

1216 A152 Sheet of 2, #a.-b. 3.50 3.50

Prehistoric Animals — A153

No. 1217: a, Pterodactylus, Brachiosaurus. b, Pteranodon. c, Anurognathus, Tyrannosaurus. d, Brachiosaurus. e, Corythosaurus. f, Iguanodon. g, Lesothosaurus. h, Allosaurus. i, Velociraptor. j, Triceratops. k, Stegosaurus. l, Compsognatus.

No. 1218: a, Tyrannosaurus, black inscriptions b, Dimorphodon. c, Diplodocus. d, Pterodaustro. e, Tyrannosaurus, white inscriptions. f, Edmontosaurus. g, Apatosaurus. h, Deinonychus. i, Hypsilophodon. j, Oviraptor. k, Stegosaurus, diff. l, Triceratops, diff.

No. 1219: a, Moeritherium. b, Platybelodon. c, Wooly mammoth. d, African elephant. e, Deinonychus, diff. f, Dimorphodon, diff. g, Archaeopteryx. h, Ring-necked pheasant.

No. 1220, Triceratops, vert. No. 1221, Pteranodon. No. 1222, Hoatzin, vert. No. 1223, Ichthyosaur, vert.

1999, Aug. 10 **Litho.** *Perf. 14*

Sheets of 12 and 8

1217-1218 A153 10nu a.-l., each 5.50 5.50

1219 A153 20nu a.-h. 7.50 7.50

Souvenir Sheets

1220-1223 A153 80nu each 3.75 3.75

No. 1221 is incorrectly inscribed "Triceratops" instead of "Pteranodon," and No. 1223 is "Present Day Dolphin" instead of "Ichthysoaur."

Fauna — A154

Designs: a, Musk deer. b, Takin. c, Blue sheep. d, Yak. e, Goral.

1999, Aug. 21 **Litho.** *Perf. 12¾*

1224 A154 20nu Sheet of 5, #a.-e. + label 4.75 4.75

Birds A155

No. 1225: a, Chestnut-bellied chlorophonia. b, Yellow-faced Amazon parrot. c, White ibis. d, Caique. e, Green jay. f, Tufted coquette. g, Common troupial. h, Purple gallinule. i, Copper-rumped hummingbird.

No. 1226: a, Common egret. b, Rufous-browed peppershrike. c, Glittering-throated emerald. d, Great kiskadee. e, Cuban green woodpecker. f, Scarlet ibis. g, Belted kingfisher. h, Barred antshrike. i, Caribbean parakeet.

No. 1227, vert.: a, Rufous-tailed jacamar. b, Scarlet macaw. c, Channel-billed toucan. d, Tricolored heron. e, St. Vincent parrot. f, Blue-crowned motmot. g, Horned screamer. h, Black-billed plover. i, Common meadowlark.

No. 1228, Toco toucan. No. 1229, Red-billed scythebill, vert. No. 1230, Military macaws, vert.

1999, Oct. 17 **Litho.** *Perf. 14*

Sheets of 9, #a.-i.

1225-1227 A155 15nu each 6.25 6.25

Souvenir Sheets

1228-1230 A155 80nu each 3.75 3.75

Butterflies A156

Designs: 5nu, Sara orange tip. 10nu, Pipepine swallowtail. 15nu, Longwings. No. 1234, 20nu, Viceroy. 25nu, Silver-spotted skipper, vert. 30nu, Great spangled fritillary, vert. 35nu, Little copper.

No. 1238: a, Frosted skipper. b, Fiery skipper. c, Banded hairstreak. d, Clouded sulphur. e, Milberts tortoise shell. f, Eastern tailed blue.

No. 1239: a, Zebra swallowtail. b, Colorado hairstreak. c, Pink-edged sulphur. d, Fairy yellow. e, Red-spotted purple. f, Aphrodite.

No. 1240, Checkered white. No. 1241, Gray hairstreak, vert. No. 1242, Gulf fritillary, vert. No. 1243, Monarch, vert.

1999, Oct. 4 **Litho.** *Perf. 14*

1231-1237 A156 Set of 7 6.50 6.50

Sheets of 6

1238-1239 A156 20nu #a.-f., each 5.50 5.50

Souvenir Sheets

1240-1243 A156 80nu each 3.75 3.75

First Manned Moon Landing, 30th Anniv. — A157

No. 1244: a, Neil A. Armstrong (with name patch). b, Michael Collins. c, Edwin E. Aldrin, Jr. d, Command and service modules. e, Lunar module. f, Aldrin on Moon.

No. 1245: a, X-15 rocket. b, Gemini 8. c, Apollo 11 Saturn V rocket. d, Command and service modules (docked with lunar module). e, Lunar module (docked with command and service modules). f, Aldrin on lunar module ladder.

No. 1246: a, Yuri Gagarin. b, Alan B. Shepard, Jr. c, John H. Glenn, Jr. d, Valentina Tereshkova. e, Edward H. White II. f, Armstrong (no name patch).

No. 1247, Armstrong, diff. No. 1248, Apollo 11 splashdown. No. 1249, Gemini 8 docked with Agena rocket, horiz.

1999, Nov. 1 **Litho.** *Perf. 14*

Sheets of 6

1244-1246 A157 20nu #a.-f., each 5.50 5.50

Souvenir Sheets

1247-1249 A157 80nu each 3.75 3.75

No. 1249 contains one 57x42mm stamp.

Cats, Horses, Dogs A158

Cats: No. 1250, 5nu, Tortoiseshell. No. 1251, 5nu, Woman and cat. 10nu, Chinchilla Golden Longhair.

No. 1253: a, Russian Blue. b, Birman. c, Devon Rex. d, Pewter Longhair. e, Bombay. f, Sorrel Somali. g, Red Tabby Manx. h, Blue Smoke Longhair. i, Oriental Tabby Shorthair.

70nu, Norwegian Shorthair.

1999, Nov. 15 **Litho.** *Perf. 14*

1250-1252 A158 Set of 3 .90 .90

Sheet of 9

1253 A158 12nu #a.-i. 5.00 5.00

Souvenir Sheet

1254 A158 70nu multicolored 3.25 3.25

1999, Nov. 15

Horses: 15nu, Lipizzaner. 20nu, Andalusian.

No. 1257: a, Przewalski. b, Shetland. c, Dutch Gelderlander. d, Shire. e, Arabian. f, Boulonnais. g, Falabella. h, Orlov Trotter. i, Suffolk Punch.

70nu, Connemara.

1255-1256 A158 Set of 2 1.60 1.60

Sheet of 9

1257 A158 12nu #a.-i. 5.00 5.00

Souvenir Sheet

1258 A158 70nu multicolored 3.25 3.25

1999, Nov. 15

Dogs: 25nu, Weimaraner. 30nu, German Shepherd.

No. 1261: a, Australian Silky Terrier. b, Samoyed. c, Basset Bleu de Gascogne. d, Bernese Mountain Dog. e, Pug. f, Bergamasco. g, Basenji. h, Wetterhoun. i, Drever.

70nu, Labrador Retriever.

1259-1260 A158 Set of 2 1.60 1.60

Sheet of 9

1261 A158 12nu #a.-i. 5.00 5.00

Souvenir Sheet

1262 A158 70nu multicolored 3.25 3.25

Birds, Mushrooms, Animlals A159

No. 1263: a, Crested lark. b, Ferruginous duck. c, Blood pheasant. d, Laughing thrush. e, Golden eagle. f, Siberian rubythroat.

No. 1264: a, Red-crested pochard. b, Satyr tragopan. c, Lammergeier vulture. d, Kalij pheasant. e, Great Indian hornbill. f, Stork.

No. 1265, a, Rufous-necked hornbill. b, Drongo. c, Himalayan monal pheasant. d, Black-necked crane. e, Little green bee-eater. f, Ibis.

No. 1266, Siberian rubythroat. No. 1267, Black-naped monarch. No. 1268, Mountain peacock pheasant.

1999, Dec. 17 *Perf. 13¾*

Sheets of 6. #a.-f.

1263-1265 A159 20nu each 5.50 5.50

Souvenir Sheets

1266-1268 A159 100nu each 4.50 4.50

1999, Dec. 17

No. 1269: a, Boletus frostii. b, Morchella estculenta. c, Hypomyces lactifuorum. d, Polyporus auricularius. e, Cantahrellus lateritius. f, Volvariella pusilla.

No. 1270: a, Microglossum rufum. b, Lactarius hygrophoroides. c, Lactarius speciousus complex. d, Calostoma cinnabarina. e, Clitocybe clavipes. f, Microstoma floccosa.

No. 1271: a, Mutinus elegans. b, Pholiota squarrosoides. c, Coprinus quadrifudus. d, Clavulinopsis fusiformis. e, Spathularia velutipes. f, Ganoderma lucidum.

No. 1272, Pholiota aurivella. No. 1273, Ramaria grandis. No. 1274, Oudemansiella lucidum.

Sheets of 6, #a.-f.

1269-1271 A159 20nu each 5.50 5.50

Souvenir Sheets

1272-1274 A159 100nu each 4.50 4.50

1999, Nov. 24 **Litho.** *Perf. 13¾*

No. 1275: a, Otter. b, Tibetan wolf. c, Himalayan black bear. d, Snow leopard. e, Flying squirrel. f, Red fox.

No. 1276: a, Bharal. b, Lynx. c, Rat snake. d, Elephant. e, Langur. f, Musk deer.

No. 1277: a, Ibex. b, Takin. c, Agama lizard. d, Marmot. e, Red panda. f, Leopard cat.

No. 1278, Rhinoceros. No. 1279, Cobra. No. 1280, Tiger.

Sheets of 6, #a-f

1275-1277 A159 20nu Set of 3 15.00 15.00

Souvenir Sheets

1278-1280 A159 100nu Set of 3 13.50 13.50

Millennium A160

Frame background color: 10nu, Dark blue green. 20nu, Bright violet.

1999, Dec. 15

1281-1282 A160 Set of 2 1.50 1.50

New Year 2000 (Year of the Dragon) A161

Various dragons. Denominations: 3nu, 5nu, 8nu, 12nu.
15nu, Dragon, vert.

2000

1283-1286 A161 Set of 4 1.25 1.25

Souvenir Sheet

Perf. 12¾

1287 A161 15nu multi .70 .70

No. 1287 contains one 30x40mm stamp.

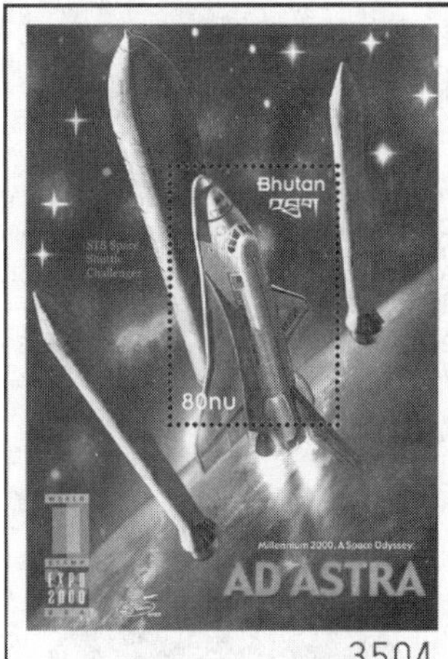

Space — A162

#1288, horiz.: a, Victor Patsayev. b, Vladislav Volkov. c, Georgi Dobrovolski. d, Virgil Grissom. e, Roger Chaffee. f, Edward White.
#1289, horiz.: a, NASA shuttle Challenger. b, X-15. c, Buran. d, Hermes. e, X-33 Venturi Star. f, Hope.
#1290, horiz.: a, Luna 3. b, Ranger 9. c, Lunar Orbiter. d, Lunar Prospector. e, Apollo 11. f, Selene.
#1291, Challenger. #1292, Buran. #1293, Astronaut on moon.
Illustration reduced.

2000, May 15 Litho. *Perf. 14*

Sheets of 6, #a-f

1288-1290 A162 25nu Set of 3 20.00 20.00

Souvenir Sheets

1291-1293 A162 80nu Set of 3 11.00 11.00

World Stamp Expo 2000, Anaheim.

First Zeppelin Flight, Cent. — A163

#1294, horiz.: a, LZ-1 and hills. b, LZ-9. c, LZ-6 in hangar. d, LZ-10. e, LZ-7. f, LZ-11.
#1295, horiz.: a, LZ-1 and sky. b, LZ-2 and treetops. c, LZ-3 and ground. d, LZ-127. e, LZ-129. f, LZ-130.
#1296, horiz.: a, LZ-1 and treetops. b, LZ-2 and mountains. c, LZ-3 and sky. d, LZ-4. e, LZ-5. f, LZ-6.
#1297, Ferdinand von Zeppelin, without hat. #1298, Zeppelin with white hat. #1299, Zeppelin with black hat.
Illustration reduced.

2000, May 15

Sheets of 6, #a-f

1294-1296 A163 25nu Set of 3 20.00 20.00

Souvenir Sheets

1297-1299 A163 80nu Set of 3 11.00 11.00

Souvenir Sheet

2000 Summer Olympics, Sydney — A164

No. 1300: a, Jesse Owens. b, Kayaking. c, Fulton County Stadium, Atlanta. d, Ancient greek broad jump.
Illustration reduced.

2000, July 24

1300 A164 20nu Sheet of 4, #a-d 3.75 3.75

British Railway System, 175th Anniv. — A165

No. 1301: a, George Stephenson's Rocket. b, London and Birmingham Railway, 1828. c, Northumbrian engine, 1825.
100nu, Stockton and Darlington Railway opening, 1825.
Illustration reduced.

2000, July 31 Litho. *Perf. 14*

1301 A165 50nu Sheet of 3, #a-c 6.50 6.50

Souvenir Sheet

1302 A165 100nu multi 4.25 4.25

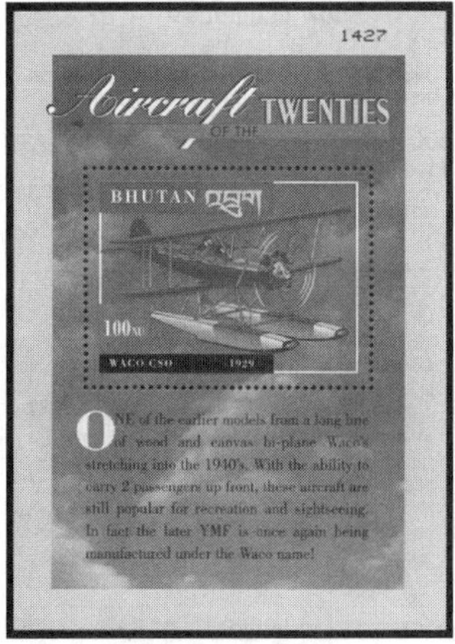

Airplanes — A166

No. 1303, 25nu: a, Laird Commercial. b, Ryan Brougham. c, Cessna AW. d, Travel Air 4000. e, Fairchild F-71. f, Command Aire.
No. 1304, 25nu: a, WACO YMF. b, Piper J4 Cub Coupe. c, Ryan ST-A. d, Spartan Executive. e, Luscombe 8. f, Stinson SR5 Reliant.
No. 1305, 25nu: a, Cessna 195. b, WACO SRE. c, Erco Ercoupe. d, Boeing Stearman. e, Beech Staggerwing. f, Republic Seabee.
No. 1306, 100nu, WACO CSO. No. 1307, 100nu, Curtiss-Wright 19W. No. 1308, 100nu, Grumman G-44 Widgeon.
Illustration reduced.

2000, Aug. 7 *Perf. 13¾*

Sheets of 6, #a-f

1303-1305 A166 Set of 3 20.00 20.00

Souvenir Sheets

1306-1308 A166 Set of 3 13.00 13.00

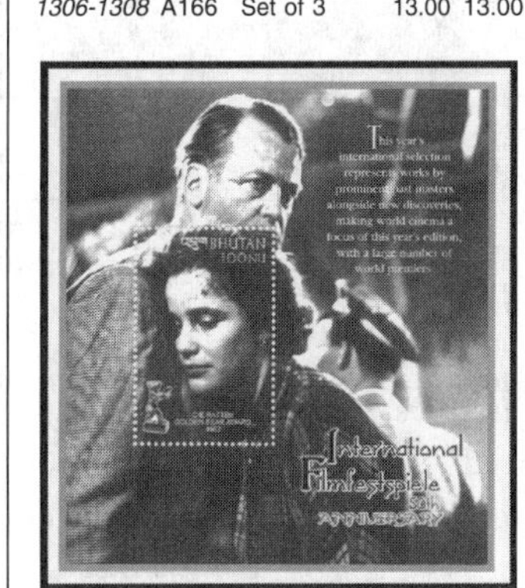

Berlin Film Festival, 50th Anniv. — A167

No. 1309: a, A Kind of Loving. b, Bushido Zankoku Monogatari. c, Hobson's Choice. d, El Lazarillo de Tormes. e, In the Name of the Father. f, Les Cousins.
100nu, Die Ratten.
Illustration reduced.

2000, Aug. 15 *Perf. 14*

1309 A167 25nu Sheet of 6, #a-f 6.50 6.50

Souvenir Sheet

1310 A167 100nu multi 4.25 4.25

Souvenir Sheet

Albert Einstein (1879-1955) — A168

Illustration reduced.

2000, Sept. 1 *Perf. 12x12¼*

1311 A168 100nu multi 4.25 4.25

Flowers — A169

No. 1312, 25nu: a, Crinum amoenum. b, Beaumontia grandiflora. c, Trachelospermum lucidum. d, Curcuma aromatica. e, Barleria cristata. f, Holmskioldia sanguinea.
No. 1313, 25nu: a, Meconopsis villosa. b, Salvia hians. c, Caltha palustris. d, Anemone polyanthes. e, Cypripedium cordigerum. f, Cryptochilus luteus.
No. 1314, 25nu: a, Androsace globifera. b, Tanacetum atkinsonii. c, Aster stracheyi. d, Arenaria glanduligera. e, Sibbaldia purpurea. f, Saxifraga parnassifolia.
No. 1315, 100nu, Dendrobium densiflorum, vert. No. 1316, 100nu, Rhododendron arboreum, vert. No. 1317, Gypsophila cerastioides.
Illustration reduced.

Perf. 14¼x14½, 14½x14¼

2000, Sept. 5

Sheets of 6, #a-f

1312-1314 A169 Set of 3 20.00 20.00

Souvenir Sheets

1315-1317 A169 Set of 3 13.00 13.00

St. Thomas Aquinas (1225-1274) A170

2000, Sept. 18 *Perf. 14x14¾*

1318 A170 25nu multi 1.10 1.10

No. 1318 printed in sheets of 4.

A171

Millennium — A172

Medical pioneers - #1319, 25nu: a, Albert Calmette. b, Camillo Golgi and Santiago Ramón y Cajal. c, Alexander Fleming. d, Jonas Salk. e, Christiaan Barnard. f, Luc Montagnier.
Olympic movement - #1320, 25nu: a, Baron Pierre de Coubertin. b, 1896 Athens Games. c, Jesse Owens. d, 1972 Munich Games. e, 2000 Sydney Games. f, 2004 Athens Games.
100nu, Paro Taktsang.
Illustrations reduced.

2000, Sept. 18 *Perf. 14*

Sheets of 6, #a-f

1319-1320 A171 Set of 2 13.00 13.00

Souvenir Sheet

1321 A172 100nu multi 4.25 4.25

Souvenir Sheets

Explorers — A173

No. 1322, Christopher Columbus. No. 1323, Capt. James Cook.
Illustration reduced.

2000, Sept. 18
1322-1323 A173 100nu Set of 2 8.50 8.50

Expo 2000, Hanover — A174

No. 1324 - Dzongs: a, 3nu, Trashigang. b, 4nu, Lhuentse. c, 6nu, Gasa. d, 7nu, Punakha. e, 10nu, Trashichhoe. f, 20nu, Paro.
No. 1325 - Flora and Fauna, 10nu: a, Snow leopard, b, Raven. c, Golden langur. d, Rhododendron. e, Black-necked crane. f, Blue poppy.
Illustration reduced.

Perf. 13x13¼ (#1324), 12¾
2000, June 1 **Litho.**
Sheets of 6, #a-f
1324-1325 A174 Set of 2 4.75 4.75
Souvenir Sheet
1326 A174 15nu Temple .65 .65

Size of stamps in #1325-1326: 40x31mm.

Paintings from the Prado — A175

No. 1327, 25nu: a, Portrait of an Old man, by Joos van Cleve. b, Mary I, by Anthonis Mor. c, Portrait of a Man, by Jan van Scorel. d, The Court Jester Pejerón, by Mor. e, Elizabeth of France, by Frans Pourbus, the Younger. f, King James I, by Paul van Somer.
No. 1328, 25nu: a, Isabella of Portugal, by Titian. b, Lucrecia di Baccia del Fede, the Painter's Wife, by Andrea del Sarto. c, Self-portrait, by Titian. d, Philip II, by Sofonisba Anguisciola. e, Portrait of a Doctor, by Lucia Anguisciola. f, Anna of Austria, by Sofonisba Anguisciola.
No. 1329, 25nu: a, Duchess. b, Child. c, Duke. d, Isidoro Maiquez, by Goya. e, Doña Juana Galarza de Goicoechea, by Goya. f, Ferdinand VII in an Encampment, by Goya. a-c from #1332.
No. 1330, 100nu, Charles V on Horseback at the Battle of Mühlberg. No. 1331, 100nu, The Relief of Genoa, by Antonio de Pereda y Salgado. No. 1332, 100nu, The Duke and Duchess of Osuna With Their Children, by Goya, horiz.
Illustration reduced.

2000, Oct. 6 ***Perf. 12x12¼, 12¼x12***
Sheets of 6, #a-f
1327-1329 A175 Set of 3 19.00 19.00
Souvenir Sheets
1330-1332 A175 Set of 3 13.00 13.00

España 2000 Intl. Philatelic Exhibition.

Indepex 2000 Philatelic Exhibition, India — A176

No. 1333: a, 5nu, Butterfly. b, 8nu, Red jungle fowl. c, 10nu, Zinnia elegans. d, 12nu, Tiger.
15nu, Spotted deer.

2000 **Litho.** ***Perf. 13¾***
1333 A176 Sheet of 4, #a-d 1.50 1.50
Souvenir Sheet
Perf. 13¼x13½
1334 A176 15nu multi .65 .65

New Year 2001 (Year of the Snake) — A177

Various snakes and flowers with panel colors of: 3nu, Light blue. No. 1337a, 10nu, Dark blue. No. 1337b, 15nu, Green. 20nu, Red.

2001 ***Perf. 12¾***
1335-1336 A177 Set of 2 .95 .95
Souvenir Sheet
1337 A177 Sheet, #a-b, 1335-1336 2.00 2.00

Souvenir Sheet

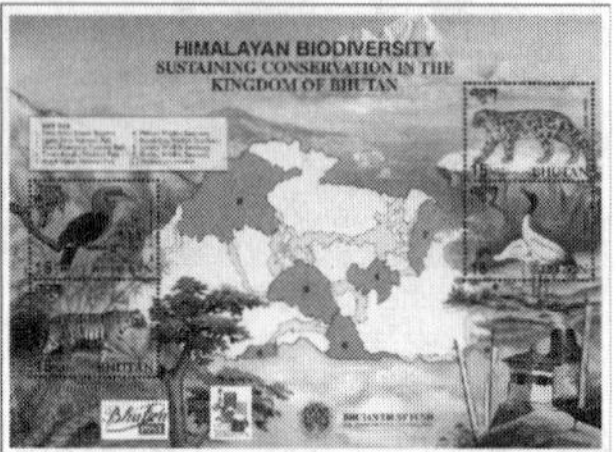

Hong Kong 2001 Stamp Exhibition — A178

No. 1338: a, Uncia uncia. b, Aceros nipalensis. c, Grus nigricollis. d, Panthera tigris.

2001
1338 A178 15nu Sheet of 4, #a-d 2.50 2.50

Intl. Volunteers Year A179

Various children's drawings: 3nu, 4nu, 10nu, 15nu.

2001
1339-1342 A179 Set of 4 1.40 1.40
a. Souvenir sheet, #1339-1342 1.40 1.40

Souvenir Sheet

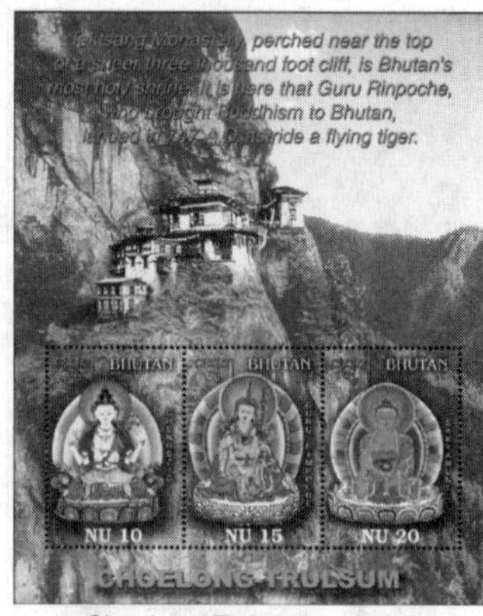

Choelong Trulsum — A180

No. 1343: a, 10nu, Chenrezig. b, 15nu, Guru Rimpoche. c, 20nu, Sakyamuni.

2001, Sept. 23 **Litho.** ***Perf. 13¼***
1343 A180 Sheet of 3, #a-c 2.00 2.00

Nos. 495-498 Surcharged

2001, Oct. 9 **Litho.** ***Perf. 11¾***
1344 A62 4nu on 10ch #495 .20 .20
1345 A62 10nu on 25ch #496 .40 .40
1346 A62 15nu on 50ch #497 .60 .60
1347 A62 20nu on 1nu #498 .85 .85
Nos. 1344-1347 (4) 2.05 2.05

Souvenir Sheet

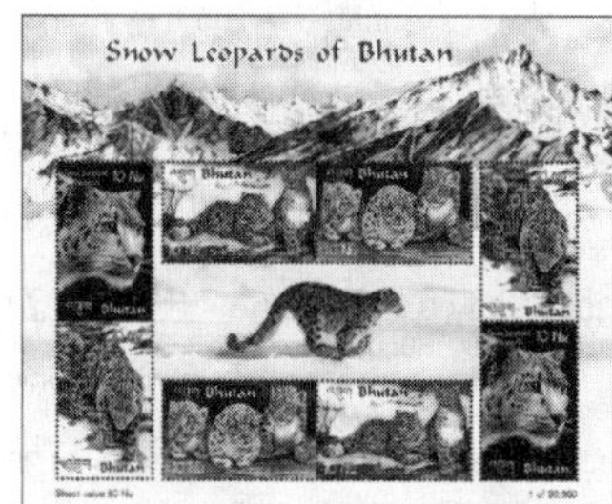

Snow Leopards — A181

No. 1348: a, Face, vert. b, Two leopards. c, Three kittens. d, Leopard walking, vert.

2001, Dec. 17 **Litho.** ***Perf. 13½***
1348 A181 10nu Sheet of 8, 2 each #a-d 3.50 3.50

Souvenir Sheet

Mountains — A182

No. 1349: a, Teri Gang. b, Tsenda Gang. c, Jomolhari. d, Gangheytag. e, Jitchudrake. f, Tse-rim Gang.

2002, Feb. 5 ***Perf. 12¾***
1349 A182 20nu Sheet of 6, #a-f 5.00 5.00

Souvenir Sheet

Orchids — A183

No. 1350: a, Rhomboda lanceolata. b, Odontochilus lanceolatus. c, Zeuxine glandulosa. d, Goodyera schlechtendaliana. e, Anoectochilus lanceolatus. f, Goodyera hipsida.

2002, Apr. 3 ***Perf. 13x13¼***
1350 A183 10nu Sheet of 6 #a-f 2.50 2.50

Souvenir Sheet

Rhododendrons — A184

No. 1351: a, Rhododendron arboreum. b, Rhododendron niveum. c, Rhododendron dalhousiae. d, Rhododendron glaucophyllum. e, Rhododendron barbatum. f, Rhododendron grande.

2002, May 1 ***Perf. 13¾***
1351 A184 15nu Sheet of 6, #a-f, + label 3.75 3.75

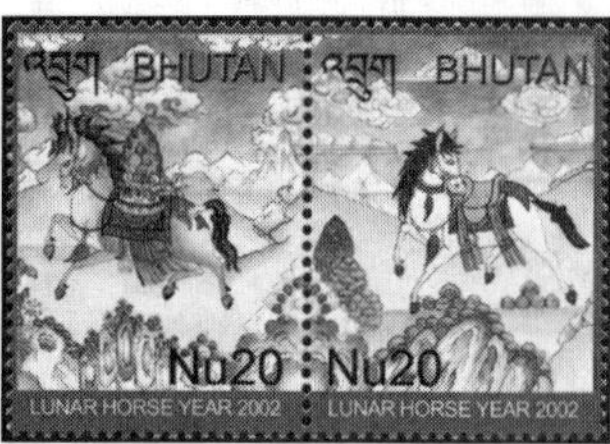

New Year 2002 (Year of the Horse) — A185

No. 1352: a, Tan horse. b, White horse.
25nu, Yellow horse, horiz.

2002, Jan. 1 ***Perf. 12¾***
1352 A185 20nu Horiz. pair, #a-b 1.60 1.60
Souvenir Sheet
1353 A185 25nu multi 1.00 1.00

Medicinal Plants — A186

Designs: No. 1354, 10nu, Bombax ceiba. No. 1355, 10nu, Brugmansia suaveolens. No. 1356, 10nu, Podophyllum hexandrum. No. 1357, 10nu, Phytolacca acinosa.

2002, June 2 **Litho.** ***Perf. 12¾***
1354-1357 A186 Set of 4 1.60 1.60
a. Souvenir sheet, #1354-1357 1.60 1.60

United We Stand — A187

2002, Sept. 16 ***Perf. 14***
1358 A187 25nu multi 1.00 1.00

Printed in sheets of 4.

Souvenir Sheet

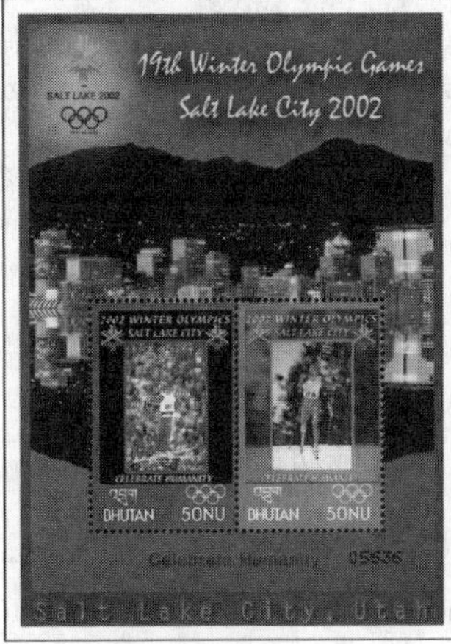

2002 Winter Olympics, Salt Lake City — A188

No. 1359: a, Ski jumper. b, Cross-country skier.

2002, Sept. 16
1359 A188 50nu Sheet of 2, #a-b 4.25 4.25

Reign of Queen Elizabeth II, 50th Anniv. — A189

No. 1360: a, Wearing blue hat. b, Wearing green and white hat. c, Wearing red violet hat. d, Wearing white hat with blue trim.
90nu, Wearing tiara.

2002, Sept. 16 ***Perf. 14¼***
1360 A189 40nu Sheet of 4, #a-d 6.75 6.75

Souvenir Sheet

1361 A189 90nu multi 3.75 3.75

Intl. Year of Ecotourism — A190

No. 1362: a, Lotus. b, Northern jungle queen butterfly. c, Bengal tiger.
90nu, Peacock.

2002, Oct. 14 ***Perf. 14***
1362 A190 50nu Sheet of 3, #a-c 6.25 6.25

Souvenir Sheet

1363 A190 90nu multi 3.75 3.75

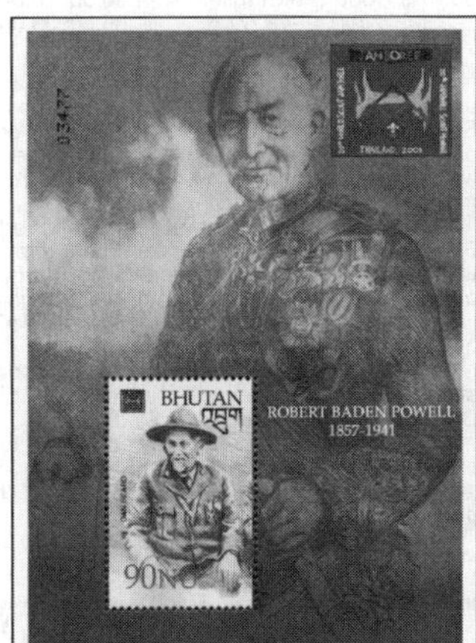

20th World Scout Jamboree, Thailand — A191

No. 1364, horiz.: a, Scout. b, Four scouts. c, Boy saluting, 1908.
90nu, Daniel Beard.

2002, Oct. 14
1364 A191 50nu Sheet of 3, #a-c 6.25 6.25

Souvenir Sheet

1365 A191 90nu multi 3.75 3.75

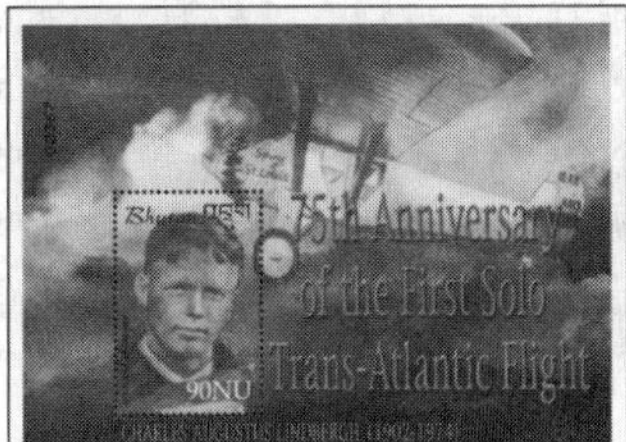

First Solo Transatlantic Flight, 75th Anniv. — A192

No. 1366: a, Charles Lindbergh and The Spirit of St. Louis. b, Lindbergh.
90nu, Lindbergh, diff.

2002, Oct. 14
1366 A192 75nu Sheet of 2, #a-b 6.25 6.25

Souvenir Sheet

1367 A192 90nu multi 3.75 3.75

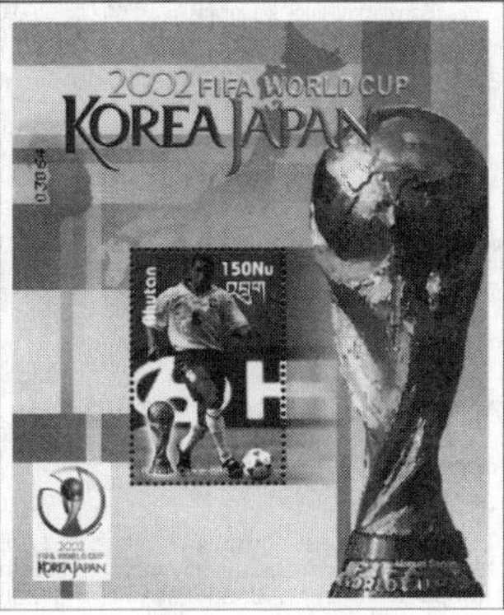

2002 World Cup Soccer Championships, Japan and Korea — A193

No. 1368: a, Zinedine Zidane. b, Michael Owen. c, Miyagi Stadium, Japan. d, Cuahutemoc Blanco. e, Gabriel Batistuta. f, Incheon Stadium, Korea.
150nu, Roberto Carlos.

2002
1368 A193 25nu Sheet of 6, #a-f 6.25 6.25

Souvenir Sheet

1369 A193 150nu multi 6.25 6.25

SEMI-POSTAL STAMPS

Nos. 10-12 Surcharged

Perf. 14x14½

1964, Mar. Litho. Unwmk.

B1	A3	33ch + 50ch multi	2.00 2.00
B2	A3	70ch + 50ch multi	2.00 2.00
B3	A3	1.30nu + 50ch multi	2.00 2.00
		Nos. B1-B3 (3)	6.00 6.00

9th Winter Olympic Games, Innsbruck, Jan. 29-Feb. 9, 1964.

Olympic Games Type of Regular Issue, 1964
Souvenir Sheet

1964, Oct. 10 ***Perf. 13½, Imperf.***

B4	A6	Sheet of 2	7.50 7.50
a.		1nu + 50ch Archery	.90 .90
b.		2nu + 50ch Soccer	2.00 2.00

18th Olympic Games, Tokyo, Oct. 10-25.

Nos. 97, 97C, 97E Surcharged

1968, Dec. 7 Photo. ***Perf. 13½***

B5	A14n	5ch +5ch	.20 .20
B6	A14n	80ch +25ch	.35 .35
B7	A14n	2nu +50ch	.85 .85
		Nos. B5-B7 (3)	1.40 1.40

AIR POST STAMPS

Nos. 19-21, 38-39, 63-67 Ovptd.

a

Perfs. as Before

1967, Jan. 10 Litho.

Overprint "a"

C1	A5	33ch on #19	.20 .20
C2	A5	70ch on #20	.30 .30
C3	A5	1nu on #21	.40 .40
C4	A8	50ch on #38	.20 .20
C5	A8	75ch on #39	.30 .30
C6	A11	1.50nu on #63	.65 .65
C7	A11	2nu on #64	.85 .85
C8	A11	3nu on #65	1.25 1.25
C9	A11	4nu on #66	1.75 1.75
C10	A11	5nu on #67	2.25 2.25

b

Overprint "b"

C11	A5	33ch on #19	.20 .20
C12	A5	70ch on #20	.30 .30
C13	A5	1nu on #21	.40 .40
C14	A8	50ch on #38	.20 .20
C15	A8	75ch on #39	.30 .30
C16	A11	1.50nu on #63	.65 .65
C17	A11	2nu on #64	.85 .85
C18	A11	3nu on #65	1.25 1.25
C19	A11	4nu on #66	1.75 1.75
C20	A11	5nu on #67	2.25 2.25
		Nos. C1-C20 (20)	16.30 16.30

UN Type of Regular Issue

Bhutan Flag and: 2.50nu, UN Headquarters, NYC. 5nu, Security Council Chamber and mural by Per Krohg. 6nu, General Assembly Hall.

1971, Sept. 21 Photo. ***Perf. 13½***

C21	A16	2.50nu silver & multi	.45 .45
C22	A16	5nu silver & multi	.85 .85
C23	A16	6nu silver & multi	1.00 1.00
		Nos. C21-C23 (3)	2.30 2.30

Bhutan's admission to the United Nations. Exist imperf.

Nos. C21-C23 Overprinted in Gold: "UNHCR / UNRWA / 1971" like Nos. 145-145C

1971, Dec. 23 Litho. ***Perf. 13½***

C24	A16	2.50nu silver & multi	.50 .50
C25	A16	5nu silver & multi	1.00 1.00
C26	A16	6nu silver & multi	1.50 1.50
		Nos. C24-C26 (3)	3.00 3.00

World Refugee Year. Exist imperf.

UPU Types of 1974

UPU Emblem, Carrier Pigeon and: 1nu, Mail runner and jeep. 1.40nu, 10nu, Old and new locomotives. 2nu, Old biplane and jet.

1974, Oct. 9 Litho. ***Perf. 14½***

C27	A19	1nu salmon & multi	.25 .25
C28	A20	1.40nu lilac & multi	.40 .40
C29	A20	2nu multicolored	.50 .50
		Nos. C27-C29 (3)	1.15 1.15

Souvenir Sheet

Perf. 13

C30 A20 10nu lilac & multi 2.75 2.75

Cent. of the UPU. Nos. C27-C29 were issued in sheets of 50 and sheets of 5 plus label with multicolored margin. Exist imperf.

Issues of 1968-1974 Surcharged 25ch and Bars

1978 Perf. & Printing as Before

C31	A16	25ch on 5nu, #C22	1.25 1.25
C32	A16	25ch on 6nu, #C23	1.25 1.25
C33	A20	25ch on 1.40nu, #C28	1.25 1.25
C34	A20	25ch on 2nu, #C29	1.25 1.25
C35	A14j	25ch on 4nu, #94L	1.25 1.25

C36 A14j 25ch on 10nu, #94N 1.25 1.25
C37 A17k 25ch on 5nu, #154F 1.25 1.25
C38 A17k 25ch on 6nu, #154G 1.25 1.25
Nos. C31-C38 (8) 10.00 10.00

BOLIVIA

bə-'li-vē-ə

LOCATION — Central South America, separated from the Pacific Ocean by Chile and Peru.
GOVT. — Republic
AREA — 424,165 sq. mi.
POP. — 7,949,933 (1998 est.)
CAPITAL — Sucre (La Paz is the actual seat of government).

100 Centavos = 1 Boliviano
100 Centavos = 1 Peso Boliviano (1963)
100 Centavos = 1 Boliviano (1987)

Catalogue values for unused stamps in this country are for Never Hinged items, beginning with Scott 308 in the regular postage section, Scott C112 in the airpost section, Scott RA5 in the postal tax section, and Scott RAC1 in airpost postal tax section.

On Feb. 21, 1863, the Bolivian Government decreed contracts for carrying the mails should be let to the highest bidder, the service to commence on the day the bid was accepted, and stamps used for the payment of postage. On Mar. 18, the contract was awarded to Sr. Justiniano Garcia and was in effect until Apr. 29, 1863, when it was rescinded. Stamps in the form illustrated above were prepared in denominations of ½, 1, 2 and 4 reales. All values exist in black and in blue. The blue are twice as scarce as the black. Value, black, $75 each.

It is said that used copies exist on covers, but the authenticity of these covers remains to be established.

Condor — A1

A2

A3

72 varieties of each of the 5c, 78 varieties of the 10c, 30 varieties of each of the 50c and 100c.

The plate of the 5c stamps was entirely reengraved 4 times and retouched at least 6 times. Various states of the plate have distinguishing characteristics, each of which is typical of most, though not all the stamps in a sheet. These characteristics (usually termed types) are found in the shading lines at the right side of the globe. a, vertical and diagonal lines. b, diagonal lines only. c, diagonal and horizontal with traces of vertical lines. d, diagonal and horizontal lines. e, horizontal lines only. f, no lines except the curved ones forming the outlines of the globe.

1867-68 Unwmk. Engr. *Imperf.*

1 A1 5c yel grn, thin paper (a, b) 5.50 *10.00*
a. 5c blue green (a) 5.50 *14.00*
b. 5c deep green (a) 5.50 *14.00*
c. 5c ol grn, thick paper (a) 35.00 25.00
d. 5c yel grn, thick paper (a) 90.00 90.00
e. 5c yel grn, thick paper (b) 90.00 90.00
f. 5c blue green (b) 5.50 *14.00*
2 A1 5c green (d) 5.00 *10.00*
a. 5c green (c) 5.00 *10.00*
b. 5c green (e) 5.00 *10.00*
c. 5c green (f) 5.00 *10.00*
3 A1 5c vio ('68) 225.00 150.00
a. 5c rose lilac ('68) 175.00 140.00
Revenue cancel 35.00
4 A3 10c brown 225.00 140.00
Revenue cancel 55.00
5 A2 50c orange 27.50
Revenue cancel 14.00
6 A2 50c blue ('68) *400.00*
a. 50c dark blue ('68) *400.00*
Revenue cancel 100.00
7 A3 100c blue 45.00
Revenue cancel 15.00
8 A3 100c green ('68) 175.00
a. 100c pale blue grn ('68) 175.00
Revenue cancel 75.00

Used values are for postally canceled copies. Pen cancellations usually indicate that the stamps have been used fiscally and such stamps sell for about one-fifth as much as those with postal cancellations.

The 500c is an essay.

Reprints of Nos. 3,4, 6 and 8 are common. Value, $10 each. Reprints of Nos. 2 and 5 are scarcer. Value, $25 each.

Coat of Arms
A4 A5

1868-69 *Perf. 12*

Nine Stars

10 A4 5c green 22.50 12.50
11 A4 10c vermilion 40.00 15.00
12 A4 50c blue 45.00 25.00
13 A4 100c orange 55.00 27.50
14 A4 500c black 750.00 750.00

Eleven Stars

15 A5 5c green 15.00 7.50
16 A5 10c vermilion 25.00 12.50
a. Half used as 5c as cover 400.00
17 A5 50c blue 40.00 22.50
18 A5 100c dp orange 42.50 22.50
19 A5 500c black *2,250.* *2,250.*

See Nos. 26-27, 31-34.

Arms and "The Law" — A6

1878 Various Frames *Perf. 12*

20 A6 5c ultra 10.00 2.00
21 A6 10c orange 10.00 2.00
a. Half used as 5c on cover 50.00
22 A6 20c green 20.00 4.00
a. Half used as 10c on cover 160.00
23 A6 50c dull carmine 110.00 20.00
Nos. 20-23 (4) 150.00 28.00

A7 (11 Stars) A8 (9 Stars)
Numerals Upright

1887 *Rouletted*

24 A7 1c rose 2.25 1.90
25 A7 2c violet 2.25 1.90
26 A5 5c blue 7.25 3.00
27 A5 10c orange 7.25 3.00
Nos. 24-27 (4) 19.00 9.80

See No. 37.

1890 *Perf. 12*

28 A8 1c rose 2.00 .80
29 A8 2c violet 3.00 2.00
30 A4 5c blue 4.50 .80
31 A4 10c orange 10.00 .95
32 A4 20c dk green 15.00 1.60
33 A4 50c red 6.25 1.60
34 A4 100c yellow 12.50 3.25
Nos. 28-34 (7) 53.25 11.00

See Nos. 35-36, 38-39.

1893 Litho. *Perf. 11*

35 A8 1c rose 5.00 2.50
a. Imperf. pair 100.00
b. Horiz. pair, imperf. vert. 20.00
c. Horiz. pair, imperf. btwn. 35.00
36 A8 2c violet 5.00 2.50
a. Block of 4 imperf. vert. and horiz. through center 50.00
b. Horiz. pair, imperf. btwn. 27.50
c. Vert. pair, imperf betwn. 27.50
37 A7 5c blue 5.00 2.00
a. Vert. pair, imperf. horiz. 27.50
b. Horiz. pair, imperf. btwn. 35.00
38 A8 10c orange 17.00 6.00
a. Horiz. pair, imperf. btwn. 50.00
39 A8 20c dark green 75.00 30.00
a. Imperf. pair, vert. or horiz. 250.00
b. Pair, imperf. btwn., vert. or horiz. 140.00
Nos. 35-39 (5) 107.00 43.00

Coat of Arms — A9

1894 Unwmk. Engr. *Perf. 14, 14½*

Thin Paper

40 A9 1c bister 1.50 1.25
41 A9 2c red orange 2.50 2.25
42 A9 5c green 1.50 1.25
43 A9 10c yellow brn 1.50 1.25
44 A9 20c dark blue 6.00 4.00
45 A9 50c claret 12.50 8.00
46 A9 100c brown rose 30.00 20.00
Nos. 40-46 (7) 55.50 38.00

Stamps of type A9 on thick paper were surreptitiously printed in Paris on the order of an official and without government authorization. Some of these stamps were substituted for part of a shipment of stamps on thin paper, which had been printed in London on government order.

When the thick paper stamps reached Bolivia they were at first repudiated but afterwards were allowed to do postal duty. A large quantity of the thick paper stamps were fraudulently canceled in Paris with a cancellation of heavy bars forming an oval.

To be legitimate, copies of the thick paper stamps must have genuine cancellations of Bolivia. Value, on cover, each $125.

The 10c blue on thick paper is not known to have been issued.

Some copies of Nos. 40-46 show part of a papermakers' watermark "1011."

For overprints see Nos. 55-59.

President Tomas Frias — A10

President Jose M. Linares — A11

Pedro Domingo Murillo A12

Bernardo Monteagudo A13

Gen. Jose Ballivian — A14

Gen. Antonio Jose de Sucre — A15

Simon Bolivar — A16 Coat of Arms — A17

1897 Litho. *Perf. 12*

47 A10 1c pale yellow grn 1.50 1.00
a. Vert. pair, imperf. horiz. 75.00
b. Vert. pair, imperf. btwn. 75.00
48 A11 2c red 2.25 1.75
49 A12 5c dk green 1.50 .60
a. Horiz. pair, imperf. btwn. 75.00
50 A13 10c brown vio 1.75 1.00
a. Vert. pair, imperf. btwn. 75.00
51 A14 20c lake & blk 3.00 1.50
a. Imperf., pair 150.00
52 A15 50c orange 4.75 2.50
53 A16 1b Prus blue 6.00 3.00
54 A17 2b red, yel, grn & blk 37.50 *50.00*
Nos. 47-54 (8) 58.25 *61.35*

Excellent forgeries of No. 54, perf and imperf, exist, some postally used.

Reprint of No. 53 has dot in numeral. Same value.

Nos. 40-44 Handstamped in Violet or Blue

1899 *Perf. 14½*

55 A9 1c yellow bis 20.00 20.00
56 A9 2c red orange 35.00 30.00
57 A9 5c green 10.50 10.50
58 A9 10c yellow brn 13.00 10.50
59 A9 20c dark blue 45.00 35.00
Nos. 55-59 (5) 123.50 106.00

The handstamp is found inverted, double, etc. Values twice the listed amounts. Forgeries of this handstamp are plentiful. "E.F." stands for Estado Federal.

The 50c and 100c (Nos. 45-46) were overprinted at a later date in Brazil.

Antonio José de Sucre — A18

Perf. 11½, 12

1899 Engr. Thin Paper

62 A18 1c gray blue 2.00 1.25
63 A18 2c brnsh red 2.00 1.25
64 A18 5c dk green 3.00 1.25
65 A18 10c yellow org 2.50 1.25
66 A18 20c rose pink 3.00 1.50
67 A18 50c bister brn 7.50 2.50
68 A18 1b gray violet 7.50 2.50
Nos. 62-68 (7) 27.50 11.50

1901

69 A18 5c dark red 1.90 .60

Col. Adolfo Ballivian A19

Eliodoro Camacho A20

President Narciso Campero
A21

Jose Ballivian
A22

Gen. Andres Santa Cruz — A23

Coat of Arms — A24

1901-02 **Engr.**

No.	Type	Description	Unused	Used
70	A19	lc claret	.55	.20
71	A20	2c green	.55	.20
73	A21	5c scarlet	.55	.20
74	A22	10c blue	1.40	.20
75	A23	20c violet & blk	.80	.20
76	A24	2b brown	3.75	2.75
		Nos. 70-71,73-76 (6)	7.60	3.75

#73-74 exist imperf. Value, pairs, each $50.
For surcharges see #95-96, 193.

1904 **Litho.**

No.	Type	Description	Unused	Used
77	A19	1c claret	2.25	.55

In No. 70 the panel above "CENTAVO" is shaded with continuous lines. In No. 77 the shading is of dots.
See Nos. 103-105, 107, 110.

Coat of Arms of Dept. of La Paz — A25

Murillo — A26

Jose Miguel Lanza — A27

Ismael Montes — A28

1909 **Litho.** ***Perf. 11***

No.	Type	Description	Unused	Used
78	A25	5c blue & blk	10.00	5.00
79	A26	10c green & blk	10.00	5.00
80	A27	20c orange & blk	10.00	5.00
81	A28	2b red & black	10.00	5.00
		Nos. 78-81 (4)	40.00	20.00

Centenary of Revolution of July, 1809.
Nos. 78-81 exist imperf. and tête bêche.
Nos. 79-81 exist with center inverted.

Miguel Betanzos
A29

Col. Ignacio Warnes
A30

Murillo
A31

Monteagudo
A32

Esteban Arce — A33

Antonio Jose de Sucre — A34

Simon Bolivar — A35

Manuel Belgrano — A36

1909 **Dated 1809-1825** ***Perf. 11½***

No.	Type	Description	Unused	Used
82	A29	1c lt brown & blk	.55	.20
83	A30	2c green & blk	.55	.40
84	A31	5c red & blk	.55	.30
85	A32	10c dull bl & blk	.55	.25
86	A33	20c violet & blk	.65	.40
87	A34	50c olive bister & blk	1.00	.50
88	A35	1b gray brn & blk	1.00	.90
89	A36	2b chocolate & blk	1.60	1.00
		Nos. 82-89 (8)	6.45	3.95

War of Independence, 1809-1825.
Exist imperf. For surcharge see #97.

Warnes
A37

Betanzos
A38

Arce — A39

Dated 1910-1825

1910 ***Perf. 13x13½***

No.	Type	Description	Unused	Used
92	A37	5c green & black	.40	.20
a.		Imperf., pair	5.00	
93	A38	10c claret & indigo	.40	.20
a.		Imperf., pair	10.00	
94	A39	20c dull blue & indigo	.65	.40
a.		Imperf., pair	5.00	
		Nos. 92-94 (3)	1.45	.80

War of Independence.
Nos. 92-94 may be found with parts of a papermaker's watermark: "A I & Co/EXTRA STRONG/9303."
Both perf and imperf exist with inverted centers.

Nos. 71 and 75 Surcharged in Black

1911 ***Perf. 11½, 12***

No.	Type	Description	Unused	Used
95	A20	5c on 2c green	.45	.20
a.		Inverted surcharge	7.50	7.50
b.		Double surcharge	7.50	
c.		Period after "1911"	3.00	1.00
d.		Blue surcharge	75.00	60.00
e.		Double dsurch., one invtd.	7.50	
96	A23	5c on 20c vio & blk	15.00	15.00
a.		Inverted surcharge	30.00	30.00
b.		Double surch., one invtd.	60.00	

No. 83 Handstamp Surcharged in Green

No.	Type	Description	Unused	Used
97	A30	20c on 2c grn & blk	*1,100.*	

This provisional was issued by local authorities at Villa Bella, a town on the Brazilian border. The 20c surcharge was applied after the stamp had been affixed to the cover. Excellent forgeries of No. 96-97 exist.

"Justice"
A40 A41

1912

Black or Dark Blue Overprint On Revenue Stamps

No.	Type	Description	Unused	Used
98	A40	2c green (Bk)	.35	.20
a.		Inverted overprint	7.50	
99	A41	10c ver (Bl)	1.10	.50
a.		Inverted overprint	7.50	

A42 A43

Red or Black Overprint

Engr.

No.	Type	Description	Unused	Used
100	A42	5c orange (R)	.45	.35
a.		Inverted overprint	7.50	
b.		Pair, one without overprint	7.50	
c.		Black overprint	40.00	

Red or Black Surcharge

No.	Type	Description	Unused	Used
101	A43	10c on 1c bl (R)	.55	.30
a.		Inverted surcharge	7.50	
b.		Double surcharge	7.50	
c.		Dbl. surcharge, one invtd.	7.50	
d.		Black surcharge	100.00	100.00
e.		As "d," inverted	*125.00*	
f.		As "d," double surcharge	*110.00*	
g.		Pair, one without black surch.	400.00	

Fakes of No. 101d are plentiful.

Revenue Stamp Surcharged "CORREOS / 10 Cts. / - 1917 -" in Red

1917 **Litho.**

No.	Description	Unused	Used
102	10c on 1c blue	*1,750.*	*1,750.*

Design similar to type A43.
Excellent forgeries exist.

Types of 1901 and

Frias-A45

Sucre-A46

Bolivar-A47

1913 **Engr.** ***Perf. 12***

No.	Type	Description	Unused	Used
103	A19	1c car rose	.40	.25
104	A20	2c vermilion	.40	.20
105	A21	5c green	.45	.20
106	A45	8c yellow	.80	.50
107	A22	10c gray	.80	.25
108	A46	50c dull violet	1.50	.55
109	A47	1b slate blue	2.25	1.40
110	A24	2b black	4.50	2.75
		Nos. 103-110 (8)	11.10	6.10

No. 107, litho., was not regularly issued.

Nine values commemorating the Guiqui-La Paz railroad were printed in 1915 but never issued. Typographed forgeries exist.

Monolith of Tiahuanacu
A48

Mt. Potosí
A49

Lake Titicaca — A50

Mt. Illimani — A51

Legislature Building — A53

FIVE CENTAVOS.
Type I - Numerals have background of vertical lines. Clouds formed of dots.
Type II - Numerals on white background. Clouds near the mountain formed of wavy lines.

1916-17 **Litho.** ***Perf. 11½***

No.	Type	Description	Unused	Used
111	A48	½c brown	.20	.20
a.		Horiz. pair, imperf. vert.	15.00	
112	A49	1c gray green	.20	.20
a.		Imperf., pair	7.50	
113	A50	2c car & blk	.25	.20
a.		Imperf., pair	2.00	
b.		Vert. pair, imperf. horiz.		
c.		Center inverted	14.00	14.00
d.		Imperf., center inverted	17.50	
114	A51	5c dk blue (I)	.50	.20
a.		Imperf., pair	7.50	
b.		Vert. pair, imperf. horiz.	7.50	
c.		Horiz. pair, imperf. vert.	7.50	
115	A51	5c dk blue (II)	.50	.20
a.		Imperf., pair	7.50	
116	A53	10c org & bl	1.00	.20
a.		Imperf., pair	7.50	
b.		No period after "Legislativo"	1.00	.20
c.		Center inverted	47.50	47.50
d.		Vertical pair, imperf. between	5.00	
		Nos. 111-116 (6)	2.65	1.20

For surcharges see Nos. 194-196.

Coat of Arms
A54 A55

Printed by the American Bank Note Co.

1919-20 **Engr.** ***Perf. 12***

No.	Type	Description	Unused	Used
118	A54	1c carmine	.25	.20
119	A54	2c dk violet	4.75	3.00
120	A54	5c dk green	.50	.20
121	A54	10c vermilion	.50	.20

122 A54 20c dk blue 1.50 .30
123 A54 22c lt blue .90 .75
124 A54 24c purple .60 .50
125 A54 50c orange 4.75 .60
126 A55 1b red brown 6.00 1.75
127 A55 2b black brn 9.00 4.50
Nos. 118-127 (10) 28.75 12.00

Printed by Perkins, Bacon & Co., Ltd.

1923-27 Re-engraved ***Perf. 13½***

128 A54 1c carmine ('27) .20 .20
129 A54 2c dk violet .30 .20
130 A54 5c dp green .80 .20
131 A54 10c vermilion 14.00 10.00
132 A54 20c slate blue 1.75 .20
135 A54 50c orange 2.75 .60
136 A55 1b red brown .70 .30
137 A55 2b black brown .50 .30
Nos. 128-137 (8) 21.00 12.00

There are many differences in the designs of the two issues but they are too minute to be illustrated or described.

Nos. 128-137 exist imperf.

See #144-146, 173-177. For surcharges see #138-143, 160, 162, 181-186, 236-237.

Stamps of 1919-20 Surcharged in Blue, Black or Red

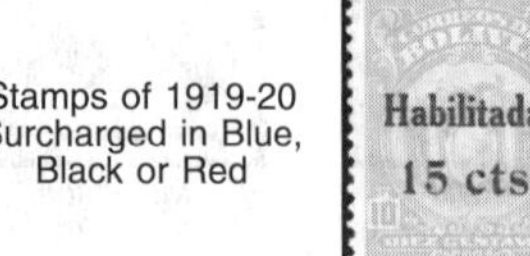

1924 ***Perf. 12***

138 A54 5c on 1c car (Bl) .40 .20
a. Inverted surcharge 6.00 6.00
b. Double surcharge 6.00 6.00
139 A54 15c on 10c ver (Bk) .70 .50
a. Inverted surcharge 6.00 6.00
140 A54 15c on 22c lt bl (Bk) .70 .30
a. Inverted surcharge 6.00 6.00
b. Double surcharge, one inverted *6.00 6.00*

No. 140 surcharged in red or blue probably are trial impressions. They appear jointly, and with black in blocks.

Same Surcharge on No. 131
Perf. 13½

142 A54 15c on 10c ver (Bk) .70 .25
a. Inverted surcharge 6.00 6.00

No. 121 Surcharged

Habilitada
15 cts.

Perf. 12

143 A54 15c on 10c ver (Bk) .90 .30
a. Inverted surcharge 6.00 6.00
b. Double surcharge 6.00 6.00
Nos. 138-143 (5) 3.40 1.55

Type of 1919-20 Issue
Printed by Waterlow & Sons
Second Re-engraving

1925 Unwmk. ***Perf. 12½***

144 A54 5c deep green .80 .20
145 A54 15c ultra .80 .20
146 A54 20c dark blue .40 .20
Nos. 144-146 (3) 2.00 .60

These stamps may be identified by the perforation.

Miner — A56

Condor Looking Toward the Sea A57

Designs: 2c, Sower. 5c, Torch of Eternal Freedom. 10c, National flower (kantuta). 15c, Pres. Bautista Saavedra. 50c, Liberty head. 1b, Archer on horse. 2b, Mercury. 5b, Gen. A. J. de Sucre.

1925 Engr. ***Perf. 14***

150 A56 1c dark green .90
151 A56 2c rose .90
152 A56 5c red, *grn* .65 .35
153 A56 10c car, *yel* .90 .75
154 A56 15c red brown .65 .25
155 A57 25c ultra 1.50 .50
156 A56 50c dp violet 1.50 .50
157 A56 1b red 3.00 1.25
158 A57 2b orange 3.50 1.75
159 A56 5b black brn 3.50 2.00
Nos. 150-159 (10) 17.00

Cent. of the Republic. The 1c and 2c were not released for general use.

Nos. 150-159 exist imperf. Value, $60 each pair.

For surcharges see Nos. C59-C62.

Stamps of 1919-27 Surcharged in Blue, Black or Red

1927

160 A54 5c on 1c car (Bl) 2.50 .90
a. Inverted surcharge 6.00 6.00
b. Black surcharge 22.50 22.50

Perf. 12

162 A54 10c on 24c pur (Bk) 2.50 1.50
a. Inverted surcharge 30.00 30.00
b. Red surcharge 22.50 22.50

Coat of Arms — A66

Printed by Waterlow & Sons

1927 Litho. ***Perf. 13½***

165 A66 2c yellow .40 .20
166 A66 3c pink .50 .50
167 A66 4c red brown .40 .40
168 A66 20c lt ol grn .65 .20
169 A66 25c deep blue .65 .30
170 A66 30c violet .80 .80
171 A66 40c orange 1.50 1.25
172 A66 50c dp brown 1.50 .50
173 A55 1b red 1.75 1.25
174 A55 2b plum 2.50 2.50
175 A55 3b olive grn 2.50 2.50
176 A55 4b claret 4.00 3.50
177 A55 5b bister brn 4.75 4.00
Nos. 165-177 (13) 21.90 17.90

For overprints and surcharges see Nos. 178-180, 208, 211-212.

Type of 1927 Issue Overprinted

1927

178 A66 5c dark green .20 .20
179 A66 10c slate .45 .20
180 A66 15c carmine .65 .25
Nos. 178-180 (3) 1.30 .65

Exist with inverted overprint. Value $20 each.

Stamps of 1919-27 Surcharged

1928 ***Perf. 12, 12½, 13½***

Red Surcharge

181 A54 15c on 20c #122 9.00 9.00
182 A54 15c on 20c #132 9.00 9.00
a. Black surcharge 30.00
183 A54 15c on 20c #146 150.00 150.00

Black Surcharge

184 A54 15c on 24c #124 1.75 .90
a. Inverted surcharge 5.00 5.00
b. Blue surcharge 50.00

185 A54 15c on 50c #125 35.00 30.00
186 A54 15c on 50c #135 1.25 .60
Nos. 181-186 (6) 206.00 199.50

No. 183 exists with inverted surcharge.

Condor — A67

Hernando Siles — A68

Map of Bolivia — A69

Printed by Perkins, Bacon & Co., Ltd.

1928 Engr. ***Perf. 13½***

189 A67 5c green 1.50 .20
190 A68 10c slate .30 .20
191 A69 15c carmine lake .60 .20
Nos. 189-191 (3) 2.40 .60

Nos. 104, 111, 113, Surcharged in Various Colors

1930 ***Perf. 12, 11½***

193 A20 1c on 2c (Bl) 1.10 .90
a. "0.10" for "0.01" 12.50 12.50
194 A50 3c on 2c (Br) 1.10 .90
195 A48 25c on ½c (Bk) 1.40 .90
196 A50 25c on 2c (V) 1.40 .90
Nos. 193-196 (4) 5.00 3.60

The lines of the surcharges were spaced to fit the various shapes of the stamps. The surcharges exist inverted, double, etc.

Trial printings were made of the surcharges on #193 and 194 in black and on #196 in brown.

Mt. Potosi — A70

Mt. Illimani — A71

Eduardo Abaroa — A72

Map of Bolivia — A73

Sucre — A74

Bolivar — A75

1931 Engr. ***Perf. 14***

197 A70 2c green 1.00 .50
198 A71 5c light blue 1.00 .20
199 A72 10c red orange 1.00 .20
200 A73 15c violet 2.75 .20
201 A73 35c carmine 1.50 .85
202 A73 45c orange 1.50 .75
203 A74 50c gray 1.25 .55
204 A75 1b brown 1.75 .55
Nos. 197-204 (8) 11.75 3.80

No. 198 exists imperf.

See #207, 241. For surcharges see #209-210.

Symbols of 1930 Revolution — A76

1931 Litho. ***Perf. 11***

205 A76 15c scarlet 2.25 .40
a. Pair, imperf. between 15.00
206 A76 50c brt violet 1.00 .70
a. Pair, imperf. between 20.00

Revolution of June 25, 1930.

For surcharges see Nos. 239-240.

Map Type of 1931
Without Imprint

1932 **Litho.**

207 A73 15c violet 2.00 .35

Stamps of 1927-31 Surcharged

1933 ***Perf. 13½, 14***

208 A66 5c on 1b red .35 .20
a. Without period after "Cts" 1.10 1.10
209 A73 15c on 35c car .35 .20
a. Inverted surcharge 20.00
210 A73 15c on 45c orange .35 .20
a. Inverted surcharge 3.00 3.00
211 A66 15c on 50c dp brn 1.50 .75
212 A66 25c on 40c orange .35 .20
Nos. 208-212 (5) 2.90 1.55

The hyphens in "13-7-33" occur in three positions.

Coat of Arms — A77

1933 Engr. ***Perf. 12***

213 A77 2c blue green .25 .20
214 A77 5c blue .25 .20
215 A77 10c red .45 .20
216 A77 15c deep violet .35 .20
217 A77 25c dark blue .70 .55
Nos. 213-217 (5) 2.00 1.35

For surcharges see Nos. 233-235, 238.

Mariano Baptista — A78

Map of Bolivia — A79

1935

218 A78 15c dull violet .45 .35

1935

219 A79 2c dark blue .20 .20
220 A79 3c yellow .20 .20
221 A79 5c vermilion .20 .20
222 A79 5c blue grn .35 .20
223 A79 10c black brn .35 .20
224 A79 15c deep rose .35 .20
225 A79 15c ultra .35 .20
226 A79 20c yellow grn .40 .20
227 A79 25c lt blue .40 .20
228 A79 30c deep rose .80 .55
229 A79 40c orange .80 .55
230 A79 50c gray violet .80 .25
231 A79 1b yellow .55 .35
232 A79 2b olive brown .80 .70
Nos. 219-232 (14) 6.55 4.20

Regular Stamps of 1925-33 Surcharged in Black

1937 *Perf. 11, 12, 13½*

233	A77	5c on 2c bl grn	.25	.25
234	A77	15c on 25c dk bl	.30	.30
235	A77	30c on 25c dk bl	.50	.50
236	A55	45c on 1b red brn	.60	.60
237	A55	1b on 2b plum	.75	.75
a.		"1" missing	7.50	7.50
238	A77	2b on 25c dk bl	.75	.75

"Comunicaciones" on one line

239	A76	3b on 50c brt vio	1.25	1.25
a.		"3" of value missing	7.00	7.00
240	A76	5b on 50c brt vio	1.25	1.25
		Nos. 233-240 (8)	5.65	5.65

Exist inverted, double, etc.

President Siles — A80

1937 **Unwmk.** *Perf. 14*

241 A80 1c yellow brown .30 .30

Native School — A81

Oil Wells — A82

Modern Factories A83

Torch of Knowledge A84

Map of the Sucre-Camiri R. R. — A85

Allegory of Free Education — A86

Allegorical Figure of Learning — A87

Symbols of Industry — A88

Modern Agriculture — A89

1938 **Litho.** *Perf. 10½, 11*

242	A81	2c dull red	.40	.40
243	A82	10c pink	.45	.25
244	A83	15c yellow grn	.60	.30
245	A84	30c yellow	.75	.35
246	A85	45c rose red	1.40	.75
247	A86	60c dk violet	1.10	.35
248	A87	75c dull blue	1.50	.35
249	A88	1b lt brown	2.25	.35
250	A89	2b bister	2.00	.75
		Nos. 242-250 (9)	10.45	3.85

For surcharge see No. 314.

Llamas — A90

Vicuna — A91

Coat of Arms — A92

Cocoi Herons — A93

Chinchilla — A94

Toco Toucan — A95

Condor — A96

Jaguar — A97

1939, Jan. 21 *Perf. 10½, 11½x10½*

251	A90	2c green	.40	.30
252	A90	4c fawn	.40	.30
253	A90	5c red violet	.40	.25
254	A91	10c black	.60	.30
255	A91	15c emerald	.60	.35
256	A91	20c dk slate grn	.60	.25
257	A92	25c lemon	.60	.25
258	A92	30c dark blue	.60	.30
259	A93	40c vermilion	1.40	.30
260	A93	45c gray	1.40	.30
261	A94	60c rose red	1.40	.55
262	A94	75c slate blue	2.75	.55
263	A95	90c orange	2.00	.55
264	A95	1b blue	2.00	.55
265	A96	2b rose lake	2.75	.55
266	A96	3b dark violet	3.50	.85
267	A97	4b brown org	4.00	1.10
268	A97	5b gray brown	5.00	1.40
		Nos. 251-268 (18)	30.40	9.00

All but 20c exist imperf.

Imperf. counterfeits with altered designs exist of some values.

For surcharges see Nos. 315-317.

Flags of 21 American Republics — A98

1940, Apr. **Litho.** *Perf. 10½*

269 A98 9b multicolored 2.25 1.10

Pan American Union, 150th anniversary.

Statue of Murillo — A99

Urns of Murillo and Sagarnaga — A100

Dream of Murillo — A101

Murillo — A102

1941, Apr. 15

270	A99	10c dull vio brn	.20	.20
271	A100	15c lt green	.20	.20
a.		Imperf., pair	7.00	
b.		Double impression	4.50	
272	A101	45c carmine rose	.20	.20
a.		Double impression	4.50	
273	A102	1.05b dk ultra	.40	.20
		Nos. 270-273 (4)	1.00	.80

130th anniv. of the execution of Pedro Domingo Murillo (1759-1810), patriot.

For surcharge see No. 333.

First Stamp of Bolivia and 1941 Airmail Stamp — A103

1942, Oct. **Litho.** *Perf. 13½*

274	A103	5c pink	.50	.50
275	A103	10c orange	.50	.40
276	A103	20c yellow grn	1.00	.65
277	A103	40c carmine rose	1.25	.80
278	A103	90c ultra	2.50	1.00
279	A103	1b violet	3.00	1.60
280	A103	10b olive bister	10.00	8.25
		Nos. 274-280 (7)	18.75	13.20

1st School Phil. Exposition held in La Paz, Oct., 1941.

Gen. Ballivian Leading Cavalry Charge, Battle of Ingavi — A104

1943 **Photo.** *Perf. 12½*

281	A104	2c lt blue grn	.20	.20
282	A104	3c orange	.20	.20
283	A104	25c deep plum	.30	.20
284	A104	45c ultra	.40	.20
285	A104	3b scarlet	.70	.35
286	A104	4b brt rose lilac	1.10	.45
287	A104	5b black brown	1.10	.55
		Nos. 281-287 (7)	4.00	2.15

Souvenir Sheets

Perf. 13, Imperf.

288	A104	Sheet of 4	3.00	3.00
289	A104	Sheet of 3	7.00	7.00

Centenary of the Battle of Ingavi, 1841. No. 288 contains 4 stamps similar to Nos. 281-284, No. 289 three stamps similar to Nos. 285-287.

Potosi A107

Quechisla A108

Miner — A109

Dam A110

Mine Interior A111

Chaquiri Dam A112

Entrance to Pulacayo Mine A113

1943 **Engr.** *Perf. 12½*

290	A107	15c red brown	.25	.20
291	A108	45c vio blue	.50	.20
292	A109	1.25b brt rose vio	.75	.30
293	A110	1.50b emerald	.75	.30
294	A111	2b brown blk	.75	.35
295	A112	2.10b lt blue	.75	.45
296	A113	3b red orange	.75	.55
		Nos. 290-296 (7)	4.50	2.35

General José Ballivián and Cathedral at Trinidad A114

1943, Nov. 18

297	A114	5c dk green & brn	.20	.20
298	A114	10c dull pur & brn	.20	.20
299	A114	30c rose red & brn	.20	.20
300	A114	45c brt ultra & brn	.25	.25
301	A114	2.10b dp org & brn	.45	.35
		Nos. 297-301,C91-C95 (10)	3.45	2.30

Department of Beni centenary.

"Honor, Work, Law" — A115

"United for the Country" — A116

1944 Litho. *Perf. 13½*

302	A115	20c orange	.20	.20
303	A115	90c ultra	.20	.20
304	A116	1b brt red vio	.20	.20
305	A116	2.40b dull brown	.20	.20

1945

306	A115	20c green	.20	.20
307	A115	90c dp rose	.20	.20
		Nos. 302-307,C96-C99 (10)	2.10	2.00

Nos. 302-307 were issued to commemorate the Revolution of Dec. 20, 1943.

Catalogue values for unused stamps in this section, from this point to the end of the section, are for Never Hinged items.

Leopold Benedetto Vincenti, Joseph Ignacio de Sanjines and Bars of Anthem — A117

1946, Aug. 21 Litho. *Perf. 10½*

308	A117	5c rose vio & blk	.20	.20
309	A117	10c ultra & blk	.20	.20
310	A117	15c blue grn & blk	.20	.20
311	A117	30c vermilion & brn	.20	.20
a.		Souv. sheet of 1, imperf.	.65	.65
312	A117	90c dk blue & brn	.20	.20
313	A117	2b black & brn	.30	.20
a.		Souv. sheet of 1, imperf.	1.25	1.25
		Nos. 308-313 (6)	1.30	1.20

Adoption of Bolivia's natl. anthem, cent. Nos. 311a and 313a sold for 4b over face.

Nos. 248 and 262 Surcharged in Carmine, Black or Orange

1947, Mar. 12 *Perf. 10½, 11*

314	A87	1.40b on 75c (C)	.20	.20
315	A94	1.40b on 75c (Bk)	.20	.20
316	A94	1.40b on 75c (C)	.20	.20
317	A94	1.40b on 75c (O)	.20	.20
		Nos. 314-317,C112 (5)	1.00	1.00

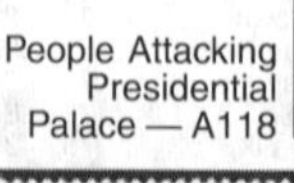
People Attacking Presidential Palace — A118

Arms of Bolivia and Argentina A119

1947, Sept. Litho. *Perf. 13½*

318	A118	20c blue grn	.20	.20
319	A118	50c lilac rose	.20	.20
320	A118	1.40b grnsh bl	.20	.20
321	A118	3.70b dull org	.20	.20
322	A118	4b violet	.20	.20
323	A118	10b olive	.40	.25
		Nos. 318-323,C113-C117 (11)	2.40	2.25

1st anniv. of the Revolution of July 21, 1946. Exist imperf.

1947, Oct. 23

324	A119	1.40b deep orange	.20	.20

Meeting of Presidents Enrique Hertzog of Bolivia and Juan D. Peron of Argentina at Yacuiba on Oct. 23, 1947. Exist imperf.

See No. C118.

Statue of Christ above La Paz — A120

2b, Child kneeling before cross of Golgotha. 3b, St. John Bosco. #328, Virgin of Copacabana. #329, Pope Pius XII blessing University of La Paz.

1948, Sept. 26 Unwmk. *Perf. 11½*

325	A120	1.40b blue & yel	.30	.20
326	A120	2b yel grn & sal	.40	.20
327	A120	3b green & gray	.60	.20
328	A120	5b violet & sal	.80	.25
329	A120	5b red brn & lt grn	1.10	.25
		Nos. 325-329,C119-C123 (10)	6.00	2.65

3rd Inter-American Cong. of Catholic Education.

Map and Emblem of Bolivia Auto Club — A125

Pres. Gregorio Pacheco, Map and Post Horn — A126

1948, Oct. 20

330	A125	5b indigo & salmon	1.50	.20

Intl. Automobile Races of South America, Sept.-Oct. 1948. See No. C124.

1950, Jan. 2 Litho. *Perf. 11½*

331	A126	1.40b violet blue	.20	.20
332	A126	4.20b red	.20	.20
		Nos. 331-332,C125-C127 (5)	1.00	1.00

75th anniv. of the UPU.

No. 273 Surcharged in Black

1950 *Perf. 10½*

333	A102	2b on 1.05b dk ultra	.20	.20

Crucifix and View of Potosi — A127

Symbols of United Nations — A128

Perf. 11½

1950, Sept. 14 Litho. Unwmk.

334	A127	20c violet	.20	.20
335	A127	30c dp orange	.20	.20
336	A127	50c lilac rose	.20	.20
337	A127	1b carmine	.20	.20
338	A127	2b blue	.30	.20
339	A127	6b chocolate	.25	.20
		Nos. 334-339 (6)	1.35	1.20

400th anniv. of the appearance of a crucifix at Potosi. Exist imperf.

1950, Oct. 24

340	A128	60c ultra	1.00	.20
341	A128	2b green	1.40	.22
		Nos. 340-341,C138-C139 (4)	3.55	.82

5th anniv. of the UN, Oct. 24, 1945.

Gate of the Sun and Llama A129

Church of San Francisco — A130

40c, Avenue Camacho. 50c, Consistorial Palace. 1b, Legislative Palace. 1.40b, Communications Bldg. 2b, Arms. 3b, La Gasca ordering Mendoza to found La Paz. 5b, Capt. Alonso de Mendoza founding La Paz. 10b, Arms; portrait of Mendoza.

1951, Mar. Engr. *Perf. 12½*

Center in Black

342	A129	20c green	.20	.20
343	A130	30c dp orange	.20	.20
344	A129	40c bister brn	.20	.20
345	A129	50c dk red	.20	.20
346	A129	1b dp purple	.20	.20
347	A129	1.40b dk vio blue	.20	.20
348	A129	2b dp purple	.20	.20
349	A129	3b red lilac	.20	.20
a.		Sheet, Nos. 345, 346, 348, 349	1.10	1.10
b.		As "a," imperf.	1.10	1.10
350	A129	5b dk red	.25	.20
a.		Sheet, Nos. 344, 347, 350	1.10	1.10
b.		As "a," imperf.	1.10	1.10
351	A129	10b sepia	.50	.25
a.		Sheet, Nos. 342, 343, 351	1.10	1.10
b.		As "a," imperf.	1.10	1.10
		Nos. 342-351,C140-C149 (20)	5.55	5.25

400th anniv. of the founding of La Paz. For surcharges see Nos. 393-402.

Boxing A131

Perf. 12½

1951, July 1 Unwmk. Engr.

352	A131	20c shown	.20	.20
353	A131	50c Tennis	.20	.20
354	A131	1b Diving	.20	.20
355	A131	1.40b Soccer	.20	.20
356	A131	2b Skiing	.40	.30
357	A131	3b Handball	.80	.80
a.		Sheet, #352-353, 356-357	2.25	1.75
b.		As "a," imperf.	2.25	1.75
358	A131	4b Cycling	1.00	1.00
a.		Sheet, #354-355, 358	2.00	1.50
b.		As "a," imperf.	2.00	1.50
		Nos. 352-358,C150-C156 (14)	8.25	6.25

The stamps were intended to commemorate the 5th athletic championship matches held at La Paz, October 1948.

Eagle and Flag of Bolivia A132

1951, Nov. 5 Litho. *Perf. 11½*

Flag in Red, Yellow and Green.

359	A132	2b aqua	.20	.20
360	A132	3.50b ultra	.20	.20
361	A132	5b purple	.20	.20
362	A132	7.50b gray	.20	.20
363	A132	15b dp car	.25	.25
364	A132	30b sepia	.50	.50
		Nos. 359-364 (6)	1.55	1.55

Cent. of the adoption of Bolivia's natl. flag.

Eduardo Abaroa — A133

Queen Isabella I — A134

1952, Mar. *Perf. 11*

365	A133	80c dk carmine	.20	.20
366	A133	1b red orange	.20	.20
367	A133	2b emerald	.20	.20
368	A133	5b ultra	.25	.20
369	A133	10b lilac rose	.50	.20
370	A133	20b dk brown	.75	.65
		Nos. 365-370,C157-C162 (12)	5.10	4.45

73rd anniv. of the death of Eduardo Abaroa.

1952, July 16 Unwmk. *Perf. 13½*

371	A134	2b vio bl	.20	.20
372	A134	6.30b carmine	.20	.20
		Nos. 371-372,C163-C164 (4)	1.40	1.00

Birth of Isabella I of Spain, 500th anniv.

Columbus Lighthouse — A135

1952, July 16 Litho.

373	A135	2b vio bl, *bl*	.20	.20
374	A135	5b car, *sal*	.50	.40
375	A135	9b emer, *grn*	.85	.60
		Nos. 373-375,C165-C168 (7)	2.55	2.00

Miner — A136

1953, Apr. 9

376	A136	2.50b vermilion	.20	.20
377	A136	8b violet	.20	.20

Nationalization of the mines.

Gualberto Villarroel, Victor Paz Estenssoro and Hernan Siles Zuazo A137

1953, Apr. 9 *Perf. 11½*

378	A137	50c rose lil	.20	.20
379	A137	1b brt rose	.20	.20
380	A137	2b vio bl	.20	.20
381	A137	3b lt grn	.20	.20
382	A137	4b yel org	.20	.20
383	A137	5b dl vio	.20	.20
		Nos. 378-383,C169-C175 (13)	2.85	2.60

Revolution of Apr. 9, 1952, 1st anniv.

Map of Bolivia and Cow's Head — A138

25b, 85b, Map and ear of wheat.

1954, Aug. 2 *Perf. 12x11½*

384 A138	5b car rose	.20	.20
385 A138	17b aqua	.20	.20
386 A138	25b chalky blue	.20	.20
387 A138	85b blk brn	.20	.20
	Nos. 384-387,C176-C181 (10)	2.95	2.10

Nos. 384-385 for the agrarian reform laws of 1953-54. Nos. 386-387 for the 1st National Congress of Agronomy. Exist imperf.

Oil Refinery A139

1955, Oct. 9 **Unwmk.** *Perf. 12x11½*

388 A139	10b ultra & lt ultra	.20	.20
389 A139	35b rose car & rose	.20	.20
390 A139	40b dk & lt yel grn	.20	.20
391 A139	50b red vio & lil rose	.20	.20
392 A139	80b brn & bis brn	.20	.20
	Nos. 388-392,C182-C186 (10)	3.50	3.25

Exist imperf.

Nos. 342-351, Surcharged with New Values and Bars in Ultramarine

1957, Feb. 14 **Engr.** *Perf. 12½*

Center in Black

393 A129	50b on 3b red lilac	.20	.20
394 A129	100b on 2b dp pur	.20	.20
395 A129	200b on 1b dp pur	.20	.20
396 A129	300b on 1.40b dk vio bl	.20	.20
397 A129	350b on 20c green	.20	.20
398 A129	400b on 40c bis brn	.20	.20
399 A130	600b on 30c dp org	.35	.20
400 A129	800b on 50c dk red	.40	.20
401 A129	1000b on 10b sepia	.40	.20
402 A129	2000b on 5b dk red	.65	.20
	Nos. 393-402 (10)	3.00	2.00

See Nos. C187-C196.

CEPAL Building, Santiago de Chile, and Meeting Hall in La Paz — A140

1957, May 15 **Litho.** *Perf. 13*

403 A140	150b gray & ultra	.20	.20
404 A140	350b bis brn & gray	.20	.20
405 A140	550b chlky bl & brn	.20	.20
406 A140	750b dp rose & grn	.30	.20
407 A140	900b grn & brn blk	.40	.20
	Nos. 403-407,C197-C201 (10)	5.10	3.60

7th session of the C. E. P. A. L. (Comision Economica para la America Latina de las Naciones Unidas), La Paz. Exist imperf.

For surcharges see Nos. 482-484.

Presidents Siles Zuazo and Aramburu A141

1957, Dec. 15 **Unwmk.** *Perf. 11½*

408 A141	50b red org	.20	.20
409 A141	350b blue	.25	.20
410 A141	1000b redsh brn	.45	.20
	Nos. 408-410,C202-C204 (6)	2.00	1.20

Opening of the Santa Cruz-Yacuiba Railroad and the meeting of the Presidents of Bolivia and Argentina. Exist imperf.

For surcharge see No. 699.

Flags of Bolivia and Mexico and Presidents Hernan Siles Zuazo and Adolfo Lopez Mateos A142

1960, Jan. 30 **Litho.** *Perf. 11½*

411 A142	350b olive	.20	.20
412 A142	600b red brown	.25	.25
413 A142	1500b black brown	.50	.50
	Nos. 411-413,C205-C207 (6)	3.10	2.25

Issued for an expected visit of Mexico's President Adolfo Lopez Mateos. On sale Jan. 30-Feb. 1, 1960.

Indians and Mt. Illimani A143

1960, Mar. 26 **Unwmk.**

414 A143	500b olive bister	.50	.20
415 A143	1000b blue	.90	.30
416 A143	2000b brown	2.00	.50
417 A143	4000b green	3.75	2.50
	Nos. 414-417,C208-C211 (8)	23.90	12.95

Refugee Children — A144

1960, Apr. 7 *Perf. 11½*

418 A144	50b brown	.20	.20
419 A144	350b claret	.20	.20
420 A144	400b steel blue	.20	.20
421 A144	1000b gray brown	.50	.50
422 A144	3000b slate green	1.00	1.00
	Nos. 418-422,C212-C216 (10)	4.40	4.35

World Refugee Year, 7/1/59-6/30/60.

For surcharges see Nos. 454-458, 529.

Jaime Laredo A145

1960, Aug. 15 **Litho.** *Perf. 11½*

423 A145	100b olive	.20	.20
424 A145	350b deep rose	.30	.25
425 A145	500b Prus green	.40	.20
426 A145	1000b brown	.50	.50
427 A145	1500b violet blue	.85	.90
428 A145	5000b gray	3.00	3.00
	Nos. 423-428,C217-C222 (12)	13.00	8.75

Issued to honor violinist Jaime Laredo.

For surcharge see No. 485.

Rotary Emblem and Nurse with Children — A146

1960, Nov. 19 *Perf. 11½*

429 A146	350b multi	.20	.20
430 A146	500b multi	.25	.20
431 A146	600b multi	.35	.35
432 A146	1000b multi	.40	.20
	Nos. 429-432,C223-C226 (8)	6.20	3.70

Issued for the Children's Hospital, sponsored by the Rotary Club of La Paz.

For surcharges see Nos. 486-487.

Designs from Gate of the Sun A147 A148

Designs: Various prehistoric gods and ornaments from Tiahuanacu excavations.

1960, Dec. 16 *Perf. 13x12, 12x13*

Gold Background

Surcharge in Black or Dark Red

Sizes: 21x23mm, 23x21mm

433 A147	50b on ½c red	.45	.30
434 A147	100b on 1c red	.35	.20
435 A147	200b on 2c blk	.75	.35
436 A147	300b on 5c grn (DR)	.25	.20
437 A147	350b on 10c grn	.25	.75
438 A148	400b on 15c ind	.35	.20
439 A148	500b on 20c red	.35	.25
440 A148	500b on 50c red	.40	.20
441 A148	600b on 22½c grn	.45	.45
442 A148	600b on 60c vio	.55	.50
443 A148	700b on 25c vio	.70	.20
444 A148	700b on 1b grn	1.00	1.00
445 A148	800b on 30c red	.60	.20
446 A148	900b on 40c grn	.45	.20
447 A148	1000b on 2b bl	.60	.50
448 A148	1800b on 3b gray	5.00	3.50

Perf. 11

Size: 49½x23mm

449 A148	4000b on 4b gray	30.00	25.00

Perf. 11x13½

Size: 49x53mm

450 A147	5000b on 5b gray	7.50	7.00
	Nos. 433-450 (18)	50.00	41.00

Nos. 433-450 were not regularly issued without surcharge. Value, set $20.

The decree for Nos. 433-450 stipulated that 7 were for air mail (500b on 50c, 600b on 60c, 700b on 1b, 1000b, 1800b, 4000b and 5000b), but the overprinting failed to include "Aereo."

The 800b surcharge also exists on the 1c red and gold. This was not listed in the decree.

For surcharges see Nos. 528, 614.

Miguel de Cervantes A149

Nuflo de Chaves A150

1961, Nov. **Photo.** *Perf. 13x12½*

451 A149	600b ocher & dl vio	.40	.20

Cervantes' appointment as Chief Magistrate of La Paz. See No. C230.

1961, Nov. **Unwmk.**

452 A150	1500b dk bl, *buff*	.75	.30

Founding of Santa Cruz de la Sierra, 400th anniv. See #468, C246. For surcharge see #533.

People below Eucharist Symbol — A151

Flowers — A152

1962, Mar. 19 **Litho.** *Perf. 10½*

453 A151	1000b gray grn, red & yel	.65	.35

4th Natl. Eucharistic Congress, Santa Cruz, 1961. See No. C231.

Nos. 418-422 Surcharged Horizontally with New Value and Bars or Greek Key Border Segment

1962, June *Perf. 11½*

454 A144	600b on 50b brown	.20	.20
455 A144	900b on 350b claret	.25	.20
456 A144	1000b on 400b steel blue	.30	.20
457 A144	2000b on 1000b gray brn	.40	.25
458 A144	3500b on 3000b slate grn	.65	.65
	Nos. 454-458,C232-C236 (10)	5.20	4.60

Old value obliterated with two short bars on No. 454; four short bars on Nos. 455-456 and Greek key border on Nos. 457-458. The Greek key obliteration comes in two positions: two full "keys" on top, and one full and two half keys on top.

1962, June 28 **Litho.** *Perf. 10½*

459 A152	200b Hibiscus	.30	.20
460 A152	400b Bicolored vanda	.45	.20
461 A152	600b Lily	.75	.20
462 A152	1000b Orchid	1.00	.20
	Nos. 459-462,C237-C240 (8)	7.50	3.45

Bolivia's Armed Forces — A153

Anti-Malaria Emblem — A154

1962, Sept. 5 *Perf. 11½*

463 A153	400b Infantry	.20	.20
464 A153	500b Cavalry	.20	.20
465 A153	600b Artillery	.20	.20
466 A153	2000b Engineers	.50	.35
	Nos. 463-466,C241-C244 (8)	4.10	2.35

1962, Oct. 4

467 A154	600b dk & lt vio & yel	.25	.25

WHO drive to eradicate malaria. See #C245.

Portrait Type of 1961

Design: 600b, Alonso de Mendoza.

1962 **Photo.** *Perf. 13x12½*

468 A150	600b rose vio, *bluish*	.25	.20

Soccer and Flags A155

Design: 1b, Goalkeeper catching ball, vert.

1963, Mar. 21 **Litho.** *Perf. 11½*

Flags in National Colors

469 A155	60c gray	.40	.40
470 A155	1b gray	.60	.20

21st South American Soccer Championships. See Nos. C247-C248.

Globe and Wheat Emblem A156

1963, Aug. 1 Unwmk. *Perf. 11½*

471 A156 60c dk bl, bl & yel .25 .25

"Freedom from Hunger" campaign of the FAO. See No. C249.

Oil Derrick and Chart — A157

Designs: 60c, Map of Bolivia. 1b, Students.

1963, Dec. 21 Litho. *Perf. 11½*

472 A157 10c green & dk brn .20 .20
473 A157 60c ocher & dk brn .25 .20
474 A157 1b dk blue, grn & yel .30 .20
Nos. 472-474,C251-C253 (6) 2.65 1.95

Revolution of Apr. 9, 1952, 10th anniv.

Flags of Bolivia and Peru A158

1966, Aug. 10 Wmk. 90 *Perf. 13½*

Flags in National Colors

475 A158 10c black & tan .20 .20
476 A158 60c black & lt grn .20 .20
477 A158 1b black & gray .40 .35
478 A158 2b black & rose .50 .50
Nos. 475-478,C254-C257 (8) 3.00 2.95

Marshal Andrés Santa Cruz (1792-1865), president of Bolivia and of Peru-Bolivian Confederation.

Children — A159

Perf. 13½

1966, Dec. 16 Unwmk. Litho.

479 A159 30c ocher & sepia .20 .20

Issued to help poor children. See No. C258.

Map and Flag of Bolivia and Generals Ovando and Barrientos A160

1966, Dec. 16 Litho. *Perf. 13½*

Flag in Red, Yellow and Green

480 A160 60c violet brn & tan .30 .20
481 A160 1b dull grn & tan .45 .20

Issued to honor Generals Rene Barrientos Ortuno and Alfredo Ovando C., co-Presidents, 1965-66. See Nos. C259-C260.

Various Issues 1957-60 and Type A161 Surcharged with New Values and Bars

A161

1966, Dec. 21

On No. 403: "Centenario de la / Cruz Roja / Internacional"

482 A140 20c on 150b gray & ultra .20 .20

On Nos. 405-406: "Homenaje a la / Generala / J. Azurduy de / Padilla"

483 A140 30c on 550b chlky bl & brn .30 .20
484 A140 2.80b on 750b dp rose & grn .75 .50

On No. 424: "CL Aniversario / Heroinas Coronilla"

485 A145 60c on 350b dp rose .50 .20

Nos. 429-430 Surcharged

486 A146 1.60b on 350b multi .75 .50
487 A146 2.40b on 500b multi 1.00 .75

Revenue Stamps of 1946 surcharged with New Value, "X" and: "XXV Aniversario / Gobierno Busch"

488 A161 20c on 5b red .20 .20

Overprinted: "XX Aniversario / Gob. Villaroel"

489 A161 60c on 2b grn .30 .20

Overprinted: "Centenario do / Rurrenabaque"

490 A161 1b on 10b brn .50 .20

Overprinted: "XXV Aniversario / Dpto. Pando"

491 A161 1.60b on 50c vio .50 .20
Nos. 482-491,C261-C272 (22) 14.50 9.30

For surcharge see No. C272.

Sower A162

"Macheteros" A163

1967, Sept. 20 Litho. *Perf. 13½x13*

492 A162 70c multicolored .35 .20

50th anniv. of Lions Intl. See #C273-C273a.

1968, June 24 *Perf. 13½x13*

Designs (Folklore characters): 60c, Chunchos. 1b, Wiphala. 2b, Diablada.

493 A163 30c gray & multi .20 .20
494 A163 60c sky bl & multi .25 .25
495 A163 1b gray & multi .40 .20
496 A163 2b gray ol & multi .65 .20
Nos. 493-496,C274-C277 (8) 4.00 1.75

Issued to publicize the 9th Congress of the Postal Union of the Americas and Spain.

A souvenir sheet exists containing 4 imperf. stamps similar to #493-496. Size: 131x81½mm.

Arms of Tarija — A164

Pres. Gualberto Villaroel — A165

1968, Oct. 29 Litho. *Perf. 13½x13*

497 A164 20c pale sal & multi .20 .20
498 A164 30c gray & multi .20 .20
499 A164 40c dl yel & multi .20 .20
500 A164 60c lt yel grn & multi .20 .20
Nos. 497-500,C278-C281 (8) 3.30 2.60

Battle of Tablada sesquicentennial.

1968, Nov. 6 Unwmk.

501 A165 20c sepia & org .30 .20
502 A165 30c sepia & dl bl grn .30 .20
503 A165 40c sepia & dl rose .30 .20
504 A165 50c sepia & yel grn .30 .20
505 A165 1b sepia & ol bister .30 .20
Nos. 501-505 (5) 1.50 1.00

4th centenary of the founding of Cochabamba. See Nos. C282-C286.

ITU Emblem A166

1968, Dec. 3 Litho. *Perf. 13x13½*

506 A166 10c gray, blk & yel .20 .20
507 A166 60c org, blk & ol .40 .40

Cent. (in 1965) of the ITU. See Nos. C287-C288.

Polychrome Painted Clay Cup, Inca Period — A167

1968, Nov. 14 *Perf. 13½x13*

508 A167 20c dk bl grn & multi .20 .20
509 A167 60c vio bl & multi .35 .35

20th anniv. (in 1966) of UNESCO. See Nos. C289-C290.

John F. Kennedy A168

1968, Nov. 22 *Perf. 13x13½*

510 A168 10c yel grn & blk .20 .20
511 A168 4b vio & blk 1.40 1.40

A souvenir sheet contains one imperf. stamp similar to No. 511. Green marginal inscription. Size: 131x81½mm.

See Nos. C291-C292.

Tennis Player — A169

1968, Dec. 10 *Perf. 13x13½*

512 A169 10c gray, blk & lt brn .25 .25
513 A169 20c yel, blk & lt brn .25 .25
514 A169 30c ultra, blk & lt brn .25 .25
Nos. 512-514 (3) .75 .75

32nd South American Tennis Championships, La Paz, 1965. See Nos. C293-C294.

A souvenir sheet exists containing 3 imperf. stamps similar to Nos. 512-514. Size: 131x81½mm.

Issue of 1863 — A170

1968, Dec. 23 Litho. *Perf. 13x13½*

515 A170 10c yel grn, brn & blk .35 .20
516 A170 30c lt bl, brn & blk .35 .35
517 A170 2b gray, brn & blk .35 .35
Nos. 515-517,C295-C297 (6) 3.55 3.40

Cent. of Bolivian postage stamps. See Nos. C295-C297.

A souvenir sheet exists containing 3 imperf. stamps similar to Nos. 515-517. Yellow green marginal inscription. Size: 131x81½mm.

Rifle Shooting A171

Sports: 50c, Equestrian. 60c, Canoeing.

1969, Oct. 29 Litho. *Perf. 13x13½*

518 A171 40c red brn, org & blk .40 .40
519 A171 50c emer, red & blk .40 .40
520 A171 60c bl, emer & blk .40 .40
Nos. 518-520,C299-C301 (6) 4.20 3.85

19th Olympic Games, Mexico City, 10/12-27/68.

A souvenir sheet exists containing 3 imperf. stamps similar to #518-520. Size: 130½x81mm.

Temenis Laothoe Violetta A172

Butterflies: 10c, Papilio crassus. 20c, Catagramma cynosura. 30c, Eunica eurota flora. 80c, Ituna phenarete.

1970, Apr. 24 Litho. *Perf. 13x13½*

521 A172 5c pale lil & multi .70 .70
522 A172 10c pink & multi 1.40 1.40
523 A172 20c gray & multi 1.40 1.40
524 A172 30c yel & multi 1.40 1.40
525 A172 80c multicolored 1.40 1.40
Nos. 521-525,C302-C306 (10) 20.20 20.20

A souvenir sheet exists containing 3 imperf. stamps similar to Nos. 521-523. Black marginal inscription. Size: 129½x80mm.

Boy Scout — A173

Design: 10c, Girl Scout planting rose bush.

1970, June 17 *Perf. 13½x13*

526 A173 5c multicolored .20 .20
527 A173 10c multicolored .20 .20
Nos. 526-527,C307-C308 (4) 1.00 1.00

Honoring the Bolivian Scout movement.

No. 437 Surcharged "EXFILCA 70 / $b. 0.30" and Two Bars in Red

1970, Dec. 6 Litho. *Perf. 13x12*

528 A147 30c on 350b on 10c .25 .25

EXFILCA 70, 2nd Interamerican Philatelic Exhib., Caracas, Venezuela, Nov. 27-Dec. 6.

Nos. 455 and 452 Surcharged in Black or Red

1970, Dec. Photo. *Perf. 11½*

529 A144 60c on 900b on 350b .25 .20
533 A150 1.20b on 1500b (R) .50 .20

Amaryllis Yungacensis A174

Bolivian Flowers: 30c, Amaryllis escobar uriae, horiz. 40c, Amaryllis evansae, horiz. 2b, Gymnocalycium chiquitanum.

Perf. 13x13½, 13½x13

1971, Aug. 9 Litho. Unwmk.

534 A174 30c gray & multi .30 .30
535 A174 40c multi .30 .30
536 A174 50c multi .40 .35
537 A174 2b multi 1.00 .60
Nos. 534-537,C310-C313 (8) 7.00 4.45

Sica Sica Church, EXFILIMA Emblem — A175

1971, Nov. 6 Perf. 14x13½

538 A175 20c red & multi .20 .20

EXFILIMA '71, 3rd Inter-American Philatelic Exhibition, Lima, Peru, Nov. 6-14.

A176

Design: Pres. Hugo Banzer Suarez.

1972, Jan. 24 Litho. Perf. 13½

539 A176 1.20b blk & multi .50 .20

Bolivia's development, 8/19/71-1/24/72.

A177

1972, Mar. 23 Litho. Perf. 13½x13

Folk Dances: 20c, Chiriwano de Achocalla. 40c, Rueda Chapaca. 60c, Kena-kena. 1b, Waca Thokori.

540 A177 20c red & multi .20 .20
541 A177 40c rose lil & multi .30 .25
542 A177 60c cream & multi .45 .20
543 A177 1b citron & multi .55 .25
Nos. 540-543,C314-C315 (6) 2.65 1.30

Madonna and Child by B. Bitti — A178

Bolivian paintings: 10c, Nativity, by Melchor Perez de Holguin. 50c, Coronation of the Virgin, by G. M. Berrio. 70c, Harquebusier, anonymous. 80c, St. Peter of Alcantara, by Holguin.

1972 Litho. Perf. 14x13½

544 A178 10c gray & multi .20 .20
545 A178 50c sal & multi .25 .20
546 A178 70c lt grn & multi .35 .20
547 A178 80c buff & multi .40 .20
548 A178 1b multi .50 .20
Nos. 544-548,C316-C319 (9) 3.45 1.80

Issue dates: 1b, Aug. 17; others, Dec. 4.

Tarija Cathedral, EXFILBRA Emblem — A179

1972, Aug. 26

549 A179 30c multi .20 .20

4th Inter-American Philatelic Exhibition, EXFILBRA, Rio de Janeiro, Brazil, 8/26-9/2.

Echinocactus Notocactus A180

Designs: Various cacti.

1973, Aug. 6 Litho. Perf. 13½

550 A180 20c crim & multi .30 .25
551 A180 40c multi .30 .25
552 A180 50c multi .30 .20
553 A180 70c multi .30 .20
Nos. 550-553,C321-C323 (7) 2.70 1.55

Power Station, Santa Isabel A181

Designs: 20c, Tin industry. 90c, Bismuth industry. 1b, Natural gas plant.

1973, Nov. 26 Litho. Perf. 13½

554 A181 10c gray & multi .20 .20
555 A181 20c tan & multi .20 .20
556 A181 90c lt grn & multi .25 .20
557 A181 1b yel & multi .25 .20
Nos. 554-557,C324-C325 (6) 1.90 1.20

Bolivia's development.

Cattleya Nobilior — A182

Orchids: 50c, Zygopetalum bolivianum. 1b, Huntleya melagris.

1974, May 15 Perf. 13½

558 A182 20c gray & multi .40 .20
559 A182 50c lt bl & multi .40 .20
560 A182 1b cit & multi .40 .20
Nos. 558-560,C327-C330 (7) 7.70 2.15

For surcharge see No. 704.

UPU and Philatelic Exposition Emblems — A183

1974, Oct. 9

561 A183 3.50b grn, blk & bl 1.00 .40

Centenary of Universal Postal Union: PRENFIL-UPU Philatelic Exhibition, Buenos Aires, Oct. 1-12; EXPO-UPU Philatelic Exhibition, Montevideo, Oct. 20-27.

Gen. Sucre, by I. Wallpher A184

1974, Dec. 9 Litho. Perf. 13½

562 A184 5b multicolored 1.10 .50

Sesquicentennial of the Battle of Ayacucho.

Lions Emblem and Steles A185

1975, Mar. Litho. Perf. 13½

563 A185 30c red & multi .35 .35

Lions Intl. in Bolivia, 25th anniv.

España 75 Emblem A186

1975, Mar.

564 A186 4.50b yel, red & blk .80 .35

Espana 75 International Philatelic Exhibition, Madrid, Apr. 4-13.

Emblem A187

1975 Litho. Perf. 13½

565 A187 2.50b lil, blk & sil .65 .25

First meeting of Postal Ministers, Quito, Ecuador, March 1974, and for the Cartagena Agreement.

Pando Coat of Arms — A188

Designs: Departmental coats of arms.

1975, July 16 Litho. Perf. 13½

566 A188 20c shown .20 .20
567 A188 2b Chuquisaca .40 .40
568 A188 3b Cochabamba .50 .50
Nos. 566-568,C336-C341 (9) 4.25 4.25

Sesquicentennial of Republic of Bolivia.

Simón Bolívar — A189

Presidents and Statesmen of Bolivia: 30c, Victor Paz Estenssoro. 60c, Tomas Frias. 1b, Ismael Montes. 2.50b, Aniceto Arce. 7b, Bautista Saavedra. 10b, Jose Manuel Pando. 15b, Jose Maria Linares. 50b, Simon Bolivar.

1975 Litho. Perf. 13½

Size: 24x32mm

569 A189 30c multi .20 .20
569A A189 60c multi .20 .20
570 A189 1b multi .30 .30
571 A189 2.50b multi .50 .50
572 A189 7b multi 1.40 .50
573 A189 10b multi 2.00 .75
574 A189 15b multi 2.50 2.50

Size: 28x39mm

575 A189 50b multi 10.00 10.00
Nos. 569-575,C346-C353 (16) 36.10 31.20

Sesquicentennial of Republic of Bolivia.

"EXFIVIA 75" A190

1975, Dec. 1 Litho. Perf. 13½

576 A190 3b multicolored .75 .60
a. Souvenir sheet 1.50 1.50

EXFIVIA 75, 1st Bolivian Philatelic Exposition. #576a contains one stamp similar to #576 with simulated perfs. Sold for 5b.

A191

Chiang Kai-shek, flags of Bolivia and China.

1976, Apr. 4 Litho. Perf. 13½

577 A191 2.50b multi, red circle 1.00 1.00
578 A191 2.50b multi, bl circle 1.00 1.00

Pres. Chiang Kai-shek of China (1887-1975).

Erroneous red of sun's circle on Chinese flag of No. 577 was corrected on No. 578 with a dark blue overlay.

A192

1976, Apr. Litho. Perf. 13½

579 A192 50c Naval insignia .40 .35

Navy anniversary.

Geological Map, Pickax and Lamp — A193

1976, May
580 A193 4b multicolored .80 .60

Bolivian Geological Institute.

Lufthansa Jet, Bolivian and German Colors A194

1976, May
581 A194 3b multicolored .80 .35

Lufthansa, 50th anniversary.

Boy Scout and Scout Emblem — A195

1976, May Litho. *Perf. 13½*
582 A195 1b multicolored .50 .50

Bolivian Boy Scouts, 60th anniversary.

Battle Scene, US Bicentennial Emblem — A196

1976, May 25
583 A196 4.50b bis & multi 1.40 .65

American Bicentennial.

A souvenir sheet contains one stamp similar to No. 583 with simulated perforations. Size: 130x80mm.

Family, Map of Bolivia — A197

Vicente Bernedo — A198

1976 *Perf. 13½*
584 A197 2.50b multicolored .50 .40

National Census 1976.

1976, Oct.
585 A198 1.50b multicolored .35 .30

Brother Vicente Bernedo de Potosi (1544-1619), missionary to the Indians.

Policeman with Dog, Rainbow over La Paz — A199

1976, Oct.
586 A199 2.50b multicolored .60 .60

Bolivian Police, 150 years of service.

Emblem, Bolivar and Sucre A200

1976, Nov. 18 Litho. *Perf. 13½*
587 A200 1.50b multicolored .60 .60

Intl. Congress of Bolivarian Societies.

Pedro Poveda, View of La Paz — A201

1976, Dec.
588 A201 1.50b multicolored .35 .25

Pedro Poveda (1874-1936), educator.

A202

Boy and Girl — A203

1976, Dec. 17 *Perf. 10½*

594	A202	20c brown	.30	.20
595	A202	1b ultra	.45	.20
596	A202	1.50b green	.75	.50
		Nos. 594-596 (3)	1.50	.90

1977, Feb. 4 Litho. *Perf. 13½*
599 A203 50c multicolored .20 .20

Christmas 1976, and for 50th anniversary of the Inter-American Children's Institute.

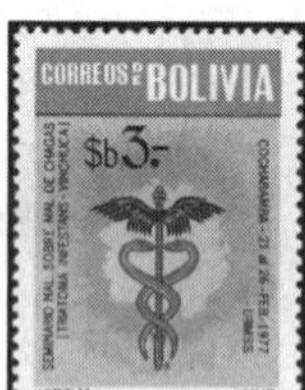

Staff of Aesculapius A204

Supreme Court, La Paz A205

1977, Mar. 18 Litho. *Perf. 13½x13*
600 A204 3b multicolored .75 .30

National Seminar on Chagas' disease, Cochabamba, Feb. 21-26.

1977, May 3

Designs: 4b, Manuel Maria Urcullu, first President of Supreme Court. 4.50b, Pantaleon Dalence, President 1883-1889.

601	A205	2.50b multi	.30	.30
602	A205	4b multi	.40	.20
603	A205	4.50b multi	.50	.20
		Nos. 601-603 (3)	1.20	.70

Sesquicentennial of Bolivian Supreme Court.

Newspaper Mastheads A206

Map of Bolivia, Tower and Flag A207

Designs: 2.50b, Alfredo Alexander and Hoy, horiz. 3b, Jose Carrasco and El Diario, horiz. 4b, Demetrio Canelas and Los Tiempos. 5.50b, Frontpage of Presencia.

1977, June Litho. *Perf. 13½*

604	A206	1.50b multi	.25	.20
605	A206	2.50b multi	.35	.30
606	A206	3b multi	.40	.25
607	A206	4b multi	.50	.35
608	A206	5.50b multi	.65	.20
		Nos. 604-608 (5)	2.15	1.30

Bolivian newspapers and their founders.

1977, June
609 A207 3b multi .50 .20

90th anniversary of Oruro Club.

Games' Poster — A208

Tin Miner and Emblem — A209

1977, Oct. 20 Litho. *Perf. 13½*
610 A208 5b blue & multi .75 .20

8th Bolivian Games, La Paz, Oct. 1977.

1977, Oct. 31 Litho. *Perf. 13*
611 A209 3b multicolored .60 .40

Bolivian Mining Corp., 25th anniv.

Miners, Globe, Tin Symbol — A210

Map of Bolivia, Radio Masts — A211

1977, Nov. 3
612 A210 6b silver & multi .80 .25

Intl. Tin Symposium, La Paz, Nov. 14-21.

1977, Nov. 11
613 A211 2.50b blue & multi .50 .35

Radio Bolivia, ASBORA, 50th anniversary.

No. 450 Surcharged with New Value, 3 Bars and "EXFIVIA-77"

1977, Nov. 25 Litho. *Perf. 11x13½*
614 A147 5b on 5000b on 5b 1.00 1.25

EXFIVIA '77 Philatelic Exhibition, Cochabamba.

Eye, Compass, Book of Law — A212

1978, May 3 Litho. *Perf. 13½x13*
615 A212 5b multi .65 .20

Audit Department, 50th anniversary.

Mt. Illimani A213

Pre-Columbian Monolith A214

Design: 1.50b, Mt. Cerro de Potosi.

Perf. 11x10½, 10½x11
1978, June 1 Litho.

616	A213	50c bl & Prus bl	.20	.20
617	A214	1b brn & lemon	.20	.20
618	A213	1.50b red & bl gray	.35	.25
		Nos. 616-618 (3)	.75	.65

Andean Countries, Staff of Aesculapius A215

Map of Americas with Bolivia A216

1978, June 1 *Perf. 10½x11*
626 A215 2b org & blk .35 .20

Health Ministers of Andean Countries, 5th meeting.

1978, June 1
627 A216 2.50b dp ultra & red .35 .20

World Rheumatism Year.

For surcharges see Nos. 697, 972.

Central Bank Building — A217

Jesus and Children — A218

1978, July 26 Litho. *Perf. 13½*
628 A217 7b multi 1.00 .25

50th anniversary of Bank of Bolivia.

1979, Feb. 20 Litho. *Perf. 13½*
629 A218 8b multicolored .90 .20

International Year of the Child.

Antofagasta Cancel — A219

Eduardo Abaroa, Chain — A220

Designs: 1b, La Chimba cancel. 1.50b, Mejillones cancel. 5.50b, View of Antofagasta, horiz. 6.50b, Woman in chains, symbolizing captive province. 8b, Map of Antofagasta Province, 1876. 10b, Arms of province.

1979, Mar. 23 Litho. *Perf. 10½*

630 A219 50e buff & blk .30 .20
631 A219 1b pink & blk .50 .25
632 A219 1.50b pale grn & blk .50 .25

Perf. 13½

633 A220 5.50b multi .60 .25
634 A220 6.50b multi .80 .30
635 A220 7b multi .80 .30
636 A220 8b multi .90 .35
637 A220 10b multi 1.10 .35
Nos. 630-637 (8) 5.50 2.25

Loss of Antofagasta coastal area to Chile, cent.
For surcharge see No. 696.

Emblem and Map of Bolivia — A221

Gymnast — A222

1979, Mar. 26 *Perf. 13½x13*

638 A221 3b multicolored .75 .50

Radio Club of Bolivia.

1979, Mar. 27 *Perf. 13x13½, 13½x13*

6.50b, Runner and Games emblem, horiz.

639 A222 6.50b multi .80 .50
640 A222 10b multi 1.10 .25

Southern Cross Sports Games, Bolivia, Nov. 3-12, 1978.
A souvenir sheet contains 1 stamp similar to No. 640 with simulated perforations. Sold for 20b. Size: 80x130mm.
For surcharge see No. 965.

Bulgaria No. 1 — A223

1979, Mar. 30 *Perf. 10½*

641 A223 2.50b multi .35 .25

PHILASERDICA '79 International Philatelic Exhibition, Sofia, Bulgaria, May 18-27.
For surcharge see No. 694.

EXFILMAR Emblem — A224

1979, Apr. 2

642 A224 2b multi .20 .20

Bolivian Maritime Philatelic Exhibition, La Paz, Nov. 18-28.
For surcharge see No. 698.

OAS Emblem, Map of Bolivia — A226

1979, Oct. 22 Litho. *Perf. 14x13½*

644 A226 6b multi .75 .25

Organization of American States, 9th Congress, La Paz, Oct.-Nov.

Franz Tamayo — A227

Bolivian and Japanese Flags, Hospital — A228

UN Emblem and Meeting — A229

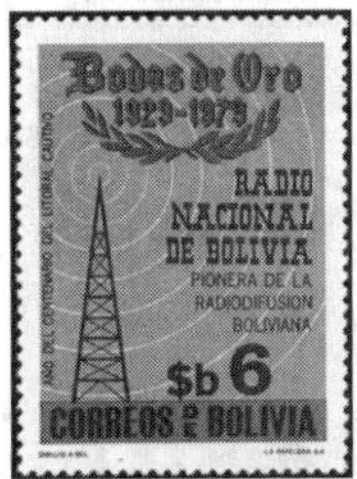

Radio Tower and Waves — A230

1979, Dec.

645 A227 2.80b blk & gray .35 .25
646 A228 5b multi .50 .35
648 A229 5b multi .50 .35
649 A230 6b multi .65 .25
Nos. 645-649 (4) 2.00 1.20

Franz Tamayo, lawyer, birth centenary; Japanese-Bolivian health care cooperation; CEPAL, 18th Congress, La Paz, Sept. 18-26; Bolivian National Radio, 50th anniversary.
For surcharge see No. 695.

Puerto Suarez Iron Ore Deposits A231

1979 Litho. *Perf. 13½x14*

650 A231 9.50b multi 1.10 .50

Bolivia No. 19, EXFILMAR Emblem, Bolivian Flag — A232

1980 Litho. *Perf. 13½*

651 A232 4b multi .55 .30

EXFILMAR, Bolivian Maritime Philatelic Exhibition, La Paz, Nov. 18-28, 1979.

Juana Azurduy on Horseback A233

1980 Litho. *Perf. 14x13½*

652 A233 4b multi .55 .30

Juana Azurduy de Padilla, independence fighter, birth bicentenary.

La Salle and World Map A234

1980 *Perf. 13½x14*

653 A234 9b multi 1.10 .60

St. Jean Baptiste de la Salle (1651-1719), educator.
For surcharge see No. 966.

"Victory" in Chariot, Madrid, Exhibition Emblem, Flags of Bolivia and Spain A235

1980, Oct. Litho. *Perf. 13½x14*

654 A235 14b multi 1.60 .75

ESPAMER '80 Stamp Exhibition, Madrid.

Map of South America, Flags of Argentina, Bolivia and Peru — A236

1980, Oct. *Perf. 14x13½*

655 A236 2b multi .25 .20

Ministers of Public Works and Transport of Argentina, Bolivia and Peru meeting.

Santa Cruz-Trinidad Railroad, Inauguration of Third Section — A237

1980, Oct.

656 A237 3b multi .35 .20

Flag on Provincial Map — A238

Parrots — A239

Perf. 14x13½, 13½x14

1981, May 11 Litho.

657 A238 1b Soldier, flag, map .20 .20
658 A238 3b Flag, map .35 .20
659 A238 40b shown 5.00 1.25
660 A238 50b Soldier, civilians, horiz. 6.00 1.25
Nos. 657-660 (4) 11.55 2.90

July 17 Revolution memorial.

1981, May 11 *Perf. 14x13½*

661 A239 4b Ara macao .50 .30
662 A239 7b Ara chloroptera .80 .50
663 A239 8b Ara ararauna 1.00 .60
664 A239 9b Ara rubrogenys 1.10 .65
665 A239 10b Ara auricollis 1.10 .65
666 A239 12b Anodorynchus hyacinthinus 1.50 .75
667 A239 15b Ara militaris 1.75 1.00
668 A239 20b Ara severa 2.25 1.25
Nos. 661-668 (8) 10.00 5.70

Christmas 1981 — A240

1981, Dec. 7 Litho. *Perf. 10½*

669 A240 1b Virgin and Child, vert. .20 .20
670 A240 2b Child, star .25 .20

American Airforces Commanders' 22nd Conference, Buenos Aires — A241

1982, Apr. 12 Litho. *Perf. 13½*

671 A241 14b multi 1.60 .50

75th Anniv. of Cobija — A242

Simon Bolivar Birth Bicentenary (1983) A243

1982, July 8 Litho. *Perf. 13½*

672 A242 28b multi .40 .25

1982, July 12

673 A243 18b multi .25 .20

1983 World Telecommunications Day — A244

1982 World Cup — A245

1982, July 15

674 A244 26b Receiving station .40 .25

1982, July 21 *Perf. 11*

675 A245 4b shown .20 .20
676 A245 100b Final Act, by Picasso 1.75 .95

For surcharge see No. 701.

Girl Playing Piano — A246

1982, July 25 *Perf. 13½*

677 A246 16b Boy playing soccer, vert. .25 .20
678 A246 20b shown .35 .20

Bolivian-Chinese Agricultural Cooperation, 1972-1982 — A247

1982, Aug. 12

679 A247 30b multi .50 .25

First Bolivian-Japanese Gastroenterology Conference, La Paz, Jan. — A248

1982, Aug. 26

680 A248 22b multi .35 .25

A249

1982, Aug. 31 Litho. *Perf. 14x13½*

681 A249 19b Stamps .35 .20

10th Anniv. of Bolivian Philatelic Federation.

A250

1982, Sept. 1

682 A250 20b tan & dk brown .30 .20

Pres. Hernando Siles, birth centenary.

Scouting Year — A251

Cochabamba Philatelic Center, 25th Anniv. — A252

1982, Sept. 3 *Perf. 11*

683 A251 5b Baden-Powell .20 .20

For surcharge see No. 703.

1982, Sept. 14

684 A252 3b multicolored .20 .20

For surcharge see No. 700.

Cochabamba Superior Court of Justice Sesquicentennial — A253

1982 Litho. *Perf. 13½*

685 A253 10b multicolored .20 .20

For surcharge see No. 970.

Enthronement of Virgin of Copacabana, 400th Anniv. — A254

1982, Nov. 15 Litho. *Perf. 13½*

686 A254 13b multicolored .25 .20

For surcharge see No. 971.

Navy Day — A255

1982, Nov. 17

687 A255 14b Port Busch Naval Base .25 .20

A256

A257

1982, Nov. 19 *Perf. 11*

688 A256 10b green & gray .20 .20

Christmas. For surcharge see No. 702.

1983, Feb. 13 Litho. *Perf. 13½*

689 A257 50b multicolored .80 .40

10th Youth Soccer Championship, Jan. 22-Feb. 13.

EXFIVIA '83 Philatelic Exhibition A258

1983, Nov. 5 Litho. *Perf. 13½*

690 A258 150b brown carmine 1.00 .50

Visit of Brazilian Pres. Joao Figueiredo, Feb. — A259

1984, Feb. 7 Litho. *Perf. 13½x14*

691 A259 150b multicolored .40 .20

Simon Bolivar Entering La Paz, by Carmen Baptista A260

Paintings of Bolivar: 50b, Riding Horse, by Mulato Gil de Quesada, vert.

Perf. 14x13½, 13½x14

1984, Mar. 30

692 A260 50b multi .20 .20
693 A260 200b multi .55 .25

Types of 1957-79 Surcharged

No. 697

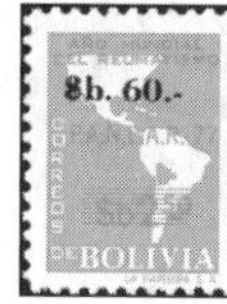

1984, Mar.

694	A223	40b on 2.50b #641	.20	.20
695	A227	40b on 2.80b #645	.20	.20
696	A219	60b on 1.50b #632	.20	.20
697	A216	60b on 2.50b #627	.20	.20
698	A224	100b on 2b #642	.30	.20
699	A141	200b on 350b #409	.60	.25
		Nos. 694-699 (6)	1.70	1.25

See #972 for surcharge similar to #697.

Nos. 675, 683-684, 688, C328 Surcharged

1984, June 27 Litho. *Perf. 11*

700	A252	500b on 3b #684	.75	.35
701	A245	1000b on 4b #675	1.50	.75
702	A256	2000b on 10b #688	3.00	1.25
703	A251	5000b on 5b #683	7.50	3.00

Perf. 13½

704	A182	10,000b on 3.80b #C328	10.00	6.00
		Nos. 700-704 (5)	22.75	11.35

Road Safety Education — A261

Cartoons.

1984, Sept. 7 Litho. *Perf. 11*

705 A261 80b Jaywalker .20 .20
706 A261 120b Motorcycle policeman, ambulance .20 .20

Jose Eustaquio Mendez, 200th Birth Anniv. — A262

Perf. 14x13½, 13½x14

1984, Sept. 19

Paintings: 300b, Birthplace, by Jorge Campos. 500b, Mendez Leading the Battle of La Tablada, by M. Villegas, horiz.

707 A262 300b multi .20 .20
708 A262 500b multi .20 .20

1983 World Cup Soccer Championships, Mexico — A263

Chasqui, Postal Runner — A264

Sponsoring shoe-manufacturers' trademarks and: 100b, 200b, Outline map of Bolivia, natl. colors. 600b, World map, soccer ball.

1984, Oct. 26 *Perf. 11*

709	A263	100b multi	.20	.20
710	A263	200b multi	.20	.20
711	A263	600b multi, horiz.	.20	.20
		Nos. 709-711 (3)	.60	.60

1985

712 A264 11000b vio bl .25 .20

For surcharge see No. 962.

Intl. Year of Professional Education A265

Intl. Anti-Polio Campaign A266

1985, Apr. 25

713 A265 2000b Natl. Manual Crafts emblem .20 .20

For surcharges see Nos. 721-722, 959.

1985, May 22

714 A266 20000b lt bl & vio .25 .20

Endangered Wildlife — A267

1985, May 22

715 A267 23000b Altiplano boliviano .20 .20
716 A267 25000b Sarcorhamphus gryphus .25 .20
717 A267 30000b Blastocaros dichotomus .30 .20
Nos. 715-717 (3) .75 .60

Nos. 716-717 vert.
For surcharge see No. 963.

Dona Vicenta Juaristi Eguino (b. 1785), Independence Heroine — A268

1985, Oct. Litho. *Perf. 13½*

718 A268 300000b multi .20 .20

UN, 40th Anniv. — A269

1985, Oct. 24 *Perf. 11*

719 A269 1000000b bl & gold .65 .30

For surcharge see No. 964.

A270

A271

1985, Nov.

720 A270 200000b multi .20 .20

Soccer Team named "The Strongest," 75th anniv.

No. 713 Surcharged

1986 Litho. *Perf. 11*

721 A265 200000b on 2000b .25 .20
722 A265 5000000b on 2000b 5.25 2.50

1986

723 A271 300000 Emblems, vert. .30 .20
724 A271 550000 Pique trademark, vert. .60 .25
725 A271 1000000 Azteca Stadium 1.00 .50
726 A271 2500000 World cup, vert. 2.75 1.25
Nos. 723-726 (4) 4.65 2.20

1986 World Cup Soccer Championships.
For surcharge see No. 961.

Intl. Youth Year
A272 A273

1986

727 A272 150000 brt car rose .20 .20
728 A272 500000 bl grn .55 .30
729 A273 3000000 multi 3.25 1.50
Nos. 727-729 (3) 4.00 2.00

Inscribed 1985.
For surcharge see No. 958.

Alfonso Sobieta Viaduct, Carretera Quillacollo, Confital A274

1986 *Perf. 13½*

730 A274 400000 int bl & gray .40 .20

Inter-American Development Bank, 25th anniv.

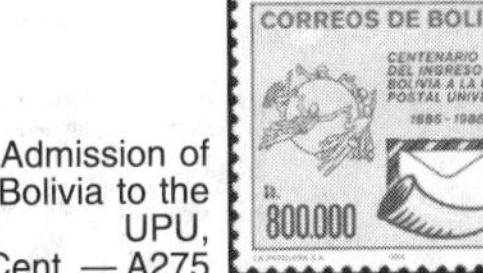

Admission of Bolivia to the UPU, Cent. — A275

1986, Apr. 3 *Perf. 11*

731 A275 800000 multi .85 .40

Postal Workers Soc., 50th Anniv. — A276

1986, Sept. 5

732 A276 2000000 brn & pale brn 2.10 1.00

For surcharge see No. 967.

Founding of Trinidad, 300th Anniv. A277

1986, May 25 *Perf. 13½x14*

733 A277 1400000 Bull and Rider, by Vaca 1.50 .75

For surcharge see No. 960.

Bolivian Philatelic Federation, 15th Anniv. — A278

1986, Nov. 28

734 A278 600000b No. 19 .60 .30

Death of a Priest, by Jose Antonio Zampa — A279

Intl. Peace Year — A280

1986, Nov. 21 *Perf. 14x13½*

735 A279 400000b multi .40 .20

1986, Sept. 16 *Perf. 11*

736 A280 200000 yel grn & pale grn .25 .20

Natl. Oil Corp. (YPBF), 50th Anniv. — A281

1986, Dec. 22 Litho. *Perf. 11*

737 A281 1000000b multi 1.50 .50

A282

Photograph of a Devil-mask Dancer, by Jimenez Cordero.

1987, Feb. 13 Litho. *Perf. 14x13½*

738 A282 20c multi .30 .20

February 10th Society, cent. (in 1985).

A283

1987, Mar. 20 Litho. *Perf. 14x13½*

739 A283 30c Crossed flags .45 .25

State Visit of Richard von Weizsacker, Pres. of Germany, Mar. 20.

State Visit of King Juan Carlos of Spain, May 20 A284

1987, May 20 *Perf. 13½x14*

740 A284 60c Natl. arms .90 .40

EXFIVIA '87 — A285

Mount Potosi, 18th cent. engraving.

1987, Oct. Litho. *Perf. 13½*

741 A285 50c multi .70 .35

See No. 750.

Wildlife Conservation A286

1987, Oct.

742 A286 20c Condor .30 .20
743 A286 20c Tapir .30 .20
744 A286 30c Vicuna .45 .25
745 A286 30c Armadillo .45 .25
746 A286 40c Spectacled bears .60 .30
747 A286 60c Toucans .90 .40
Nos. 742-747 (6) 3.00 1.60

Wildlife in danger of extinction.

ESPAMER '87, La Coruna A287

1987, Oct. Litho. *Perf. 14x13½*

748 A287 20c Nina, stern of Santa Maria .30 .20
749 A287 20c Bow of Santa Maria, Pinta .30 .20
a. Pair, #748-749 .60 .25

No. 749a has a continuous design.

EXFIVIA Type of 1987

Photograph of Mt. Potosi by Jimenez Cordero.

1987, Aug. 5 Litho. *Perf. 13½*

750 A285 40c multi .60 .30

Musical Instruments — A288

1987, Dec. 3 *Perf. 13½x14, 14x13½*

751 A288 50c Zampona and quena (wind instruments) .70 .35
752 A288 1b Charango, vert. 1.40 .70

A289

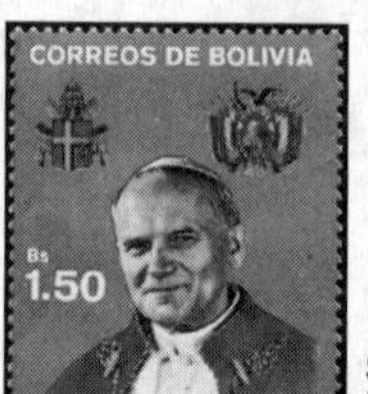

State Visit of Pope John Paul II A290

Pontiff, religious architecture and art: No. 753, Cathedral of Kings, Beni. No. 754, Carabuco Church. No. 755, Tihuanacu Church. No. 756, St. Francis's Church, Sucre. No. 757, St. Joseph's of Chiquitos Church. 40c, Cobija Chapel, vert. No. 759, Jayu Kcota Church. No. 760, Cochabamba Cathedral, vert. 60c, St. Francis's Basilica, La Paz, vert. No. 762, Christ of Machaca Church. No. 763, St. Lawrence's Church, Potosi, vert. No. 764, *The Holy Family*, by Rubens, vert. No. 765, *The Virgin of Copacabana*, statue, vert. No. 766, Vallegrande Church. No. 767, Tarija Cathedral, vert. No. 768, Concepcion Church.

1988 Litho. *Perf. 13½x14, 14x13½*

753 A289 20c multi .25 .20
754 A289 20c multi .25 .20
755 A289 20c multi .25 .20
756 A289 30c multi .40 .20
757 A289 30c multi .40 .20
758 A289 40c multi .50 .25
759 A289 50c multi .65 .30
760 A289 50c multi .65 .30
761 A289 60c multi .75 .35
762 A289 70c multi .90 .35
763 A289 70c multi .90 .35
764 A289 80c multi 1.00 .45
765 A289 80c multi 1.00 .45
766 A289 80c multi 1.00 .45
767 A289 1.30b multi 1.60 .75
768 A289 1.30b multi 1.60 .75
769 A290 1.50b shown 1.90 .90
Nos. 753-769 (17) 14.00 6.65

Issue dates: 1.50b, May 9; others, Mar. 3.

Visit of Pres. Jose Sarney of Brazil A291

1988, Aug. 2 Litho. *Perf. 13½x14*
770 A291 50c multi .60 .30

St. John Bosco (1815-1888) A292

1988, Aug. 16 *Perf. 13½*
771 A292 30c multi .40 .20

Bolivian Railways, Cent. — A293

Design: 1b, Steam locomotive from the La Paz-Beni line, made by Marca Shy Ohio, Natl. Railway Museum, Sucre.

1988, Aug. 29
772 A293 1b multi 1.25 .60

Nataniel Aguirre (b. 1888), Author — A294

Department of Pando, 50th Anniv. — A295

1988, Sept. 14 Litho. *Perf. 13½*
773 A294 1b blk & beige 1.25 .60

1988, Sept. 26 *Perf. 13½*

Designs: 40c, *Columna Porvenir*, memorial to the Battle of Bahio. 60c, Siringuero rubber production (worker sapping latex from *Hevea brasiliensis*).

774 A295 40c multi .50 .25
775 A295 60c multi .70 .35

A296

A297

1988, Sept. 27
776 A296 1.50b multi 1.90 .90

1988 Summer Olympics, Seoul.

1988

Designs: 70c, Archbishop Bernardino de Cardenas (1579-1668). 80c, Mother Rosa Gattorno (1831-1900), founder of the Sisters of Santa Ana.

777 A297 70c multi .90 .45
778 A297 80c multi 1.00 .50

Issue dates: 70c, Oct. 20, 80c, Oct. 14.

Ministry of Transportation & Communications A298

1988, Oct. 24 Litho. *Perf. 14x13½*
779 A298 2b deep car, blk & pale olive grn 2.40 1.00

Army Communications, 50th Anniv. (in 1987) — A299

1988, Nov. 29 Litho. *Perf. 13½*
780 A299 70c multi .95 .45

Bolivian Automobile Club, 50th Anniv. A300

1988, Dec. 29 Litho. *Perf. 13½*
781 A300 1.50b multi 1.50 .70

Flowering Plants and Emblems A301

50c, Orchid, BULGARIA '89 emblem. 60c, Kantuta blossoms, ITALIA '90 emblem. 70c, *Heliconia humilis*, Albertville '86 emblem. 1b, Hoffmanseggia, Barcelona '92 Games emblem. 2b, Puya raymondi, Seoul '88 Games and five-ring emblems.

1989, Feb. 17 Litho. *Perf. 13½*
782 A301 50c multi, vert. .60 .25
783 A301 60c multi .70 .30
784 A301 70c multi, vert. .80 .30
785 A301 1b multi, vert. 1.10 .45
786 A301 2b multi, vert. 2.25 .90
Nos. 782-786 (5) 5.45 2.20

Radio FIDES, 50th Anniv. A302

1989, Feb. 2
787 A302 80c multi .90 .40

Gold Quarto of 1852 A303

1989, Feb. 9 *Perf. 13½x14*
788 A303 1b multi 1.25 .50

French Revolution, Bicent. — A304

1989, June 23 Litho. *Perf. 14x13½*
789 A304 70c red, blk & blue .90 .35

Uyuni Township, Cent. — A305

1989, July 9 Litho. *Perf. 14x13½*
790 A305 30c bl, blk & gray .40 .20

Noel Kempff Mercado Natl. Park, Santa Cruz — A306

1.50b, Federico Ahlfeld Falls, Pauserna River. 3b, *Ozotoceros bezcarticus* (deer).

1989, Sept. 24 Litho. *Perf. 13½x14*
791 A306 1.50b multicolored 2.00 .75
792 A306 3b multicolored 4.00 1.50

UPAEP A306a

1989, Oct. 12 Litho. *Perf. 13½*
792A A306a 50c Metalworking .50 .20
792B A306a 1b Temple of Kalasasaya 1.00 .40

See Nos. 808-809

State Visit by Dr. Carlos Andres Perez, Pres. of Venezuela — A306b

1989, Oct. 14
792C A306b 2b multi 2.00 .80

See Nos. 825-826, 832.

City of Potosi — A306c

1989, Nov. 10 Litho. *Perf. 13½*
792D A306c 60c Cobija Arch .75 .30
792E A306c 80c Mint .85 .40
f. Pair, #792D-792E 1.60 .70

Christmas — A307

Paintings: 40c, *Andean Stillwaters*, by Arturo Borda. 60c, *The Virgin of the Roses*, anonymous. 80c, *The Conquistador*, by Jorge de la Reza. 1b, *Native Harmony*, by Juan Rimsa. 1.50b, *Woman with Jug*, by Cecilio Guzman de Rojas. 2b, *Bloom of Tenderness*, by Gil Imana. Nos. 794-798 vert.

1989, Dec. 18 *Perf. 13½x14, 14x13½*
793 A307 40c multicolored .40 .20
794 A307 60c multicolored .60 .25
795 A307 80c multicolored .80 .30
796 A307 1b multicolored 1.00 .40
797 A307 1.50b multicolored 1.50 .60
798 A307 2b multicolored 2.00 .80
Nos. 793-798 (6) 6.30 2.55

A308

1990, Jan. 23 Litho. *Perf. 13½*
799 A308 80c multicolored .85 .35

Fight against drug abuse.

A309

1990, May 13 ***Perf. 14x13½***

Great Britain #1, Sir Rowland Hill, Bolivia #1

800 A309 4b multicolored 4.00 1.75

Penny Black, 150th anniv.

World Cup Soccer Championships, Italy — A310

1990, June 16 ***Perf. 13½***

801 A310 2b Stadium, Milan 2.00 .80
802 A310 6b Game 6.00 2.40

Organization of American States, Cent. — A311

1990, Apr. 14

803 A311 80c dark bl & brt bl .80 .30

A312

1990, Apr. 16

804 A312 1.20b multi 1.25 .60

A313

1990 Litho. ***Perf. 14x13½***

805 A313 70c Telecommunications .70 .55

National Chamber of Commerce, Cent. — A314

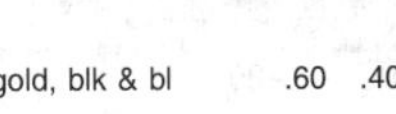

1990, June

806 A314 50c gold, blk & bl .60 .40

Cochabamba Social Club, Cent. — A315

1990, Sept. 14 Litho. ***Perf. 13½***

807 A315 40c multicolored .40 .30

UPAEP Type of 1989

Perf. 13½x14, 14x13½

1990, Oct. 12 Litho.

808 A306a 80c Huts .75 .30
809 A306a 1b Mountains, lake, vert. .95 .40

A317

1990, Oct. 19 ***Perf. 14x13½***

810 A317 1.20b multicolored 1.00 .40

Magistrate's District of Larecaja, 400th Anniv.

A318

1990, Oct. 12 ***Perf. 14x13½***

811 A318 2b multicolored 1.75 .70

Discovery of America, 500th anniv. (in 1992).

German Reunification A319

1990, Nov. 19 Litho. ***Perf. 14x13½***

812 A319 2b multicolored 1.75 .70

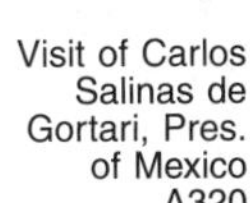

Visit of Carlos Salinas de Gortari, Pres. of Mexico A320

Design: 80c, Visit of Rodrigo Borja Cevallos, Pres. of Ecuador.

1990, Dec. 13 Litho. ***Perf. 13½***

813 A320 60c multicolored .75 .30
814 A320 80c multicolored .85 .40

4th Congress of the Andean Presidents — A321

1990, Nov. 29 ***Perf. 13½x14***

815 A321 1.50b multicolored 1.40 .55

Exfivia '90 — A322

Christmas — A323

1990, Dec. 9 ***Perf. 13½***

816 A322 40c dk blue .40 .20

1990, Nov. 20 ***Perf. 11***

817 A323 50c multicolored .45 .20

Express Mail Service A324

1990, Dec. 14 ***Perf. 13½x14***

818 A324 1b multicolored .90 .35

Bolivian Radio Club, 50th Anniv. — A325

1991, Mar. 1 Litho. ***Perf. 14x13½***

819 A325 2.40b multicolored 2.00 .80

End of Chaco War, 56th Anniv. — A326

Map of Heroes of Chaco Highway.

1991, June 14 Litho. ***Perf. 14x13½***

820 A326 60c multicolored .55 .25

National Museums — A327

1991, June 13 ***Perf. 13½***

821 A327 50c Archaeology .40 .20
822 A327 50c Art .40 .20
823 A327 1b Ethnology, Folklore .85 .35
a. Strip of 3, #821-823 1.70 .70

Espamer '91.

A328

Our Lady of Peace, Metropolitan Cathedral.

1991, July 15 Litho. ***Perf. 14x13½***

824 A328 1.20b multicolored 1.10 .45

Presidential State Visit Type of 1989

Jaime Paz Zamora, Pres. of Bolivia and: No. 825, Dr. Carlos Saul Menem, Pres. of Argentina. No. 826, Dr. Luis Alberto Lacalle, Pres. of Uruguay.

1991 ***Perf. 13½x14***

825 A306b 1b multicolored .85 .35
826 A306b 1b multicolored .85 .35

Issue dates: #825, Aug. 5; #826, Aug. 12.

A329

1991, May 31 ***Perf. 13½***

Tremarctos ornatus.

827 A329 30c Adult, 2 cubs 1.10 .20
828 A329 30c Adult's head 1.10 .20
829 A329 30c Adult on tree limb 1.10 .20
830 A329 30c Adult, cubs on tree limb 1.10 .20
Nos. 827-830 (4) 4.40 .80

World Wildlife Fund.

A330

1991, Aug. 21 Litho. ***Perf. 14x13½***

831 A330 70c multicolored .70 .30

Bolivian Philatelic Federation, 20th anniv.

Presidential State Visit Type of 1989

Design: 50c, Jaime Paz Zamora, Pres. of Bolivia and Alberto Fujimori, Pres. of Peru.

1991, Aug. 29 ***Perf. 13½x14***

832 A306b 50c multicolored .45 .20

A331

1991, Nov. 19 Litho. *Perf. 14x13½*

833 A331 50c multicolored .45 .20

National census.

America Issue — A332

UPAEP emblem and: 60c, First Discovery of Chuquiago, 1535, by Arturo Reque M. 1.20c, Founding of the City of La Paz, 1548, by J. Rimsa, vert.

1991, Oct. 12 *Perf. 13½x14, 14x13½*

834 A332 60c multicolored .60 .25
835 A332 1.20b multicolored 1.10 .45

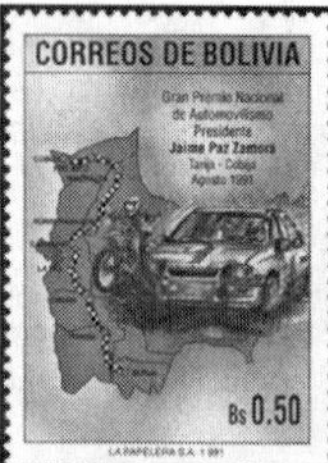
First National Grand Prix Auto and Motorcycle Race — A332a

1991, Sept. 5 Litho. *Perf. 14x13½*

835A A332a 50c multicolored .45 .20

ECOBOL, Postal Security System — A333

1991, Sept. 9 *Perf. 13½x14*

836 A333 1.40b multicolored 1.40 .50

Simon Bolivar — A334

1992, Feb. 15 Litho. *Perf. 13½*

837 A334 1.20b buff, brn & org brn 1.10 .45

Exfilbo '92.

Scouting in Bolivia, 75th Anniv. (in 1990) and 1992 Andes Jamboree A335

1992, Jan. 13 *Perf. 13½x14*

838 A335 1.20b multicolored 1.10 .45

Dated 1991.

Christmas A336

Paintings: 2b, Landscape, by Daniel Pena y Sarmiento. 5b, Woman with Fruit, by Cecilio Guzman de Rojas. 15b, Native Mother, by Crespo Gastelu.

1991, Dec.19 Litho. *Perf. 13½*

839 A336 2b multicolored 1.50 .60
840 A336 5b multicolored 3.75 1.50
841 A336 15b multicolored 11.25 4.50
Nos. 839-841 (3) 16.50 6.60

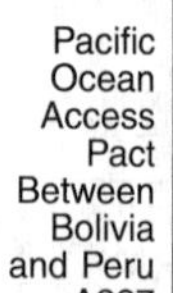

Pacific Ocean Access Pact Between Bolivia and Peru A337

Designs: 1.20b, Pres. Zamora raising flag, vert. 1.50b, Pres. Jaime Paz Zamora of Bolivia and Pres. Alberto Fujimori, Peru. 1.80b, Shoreline of access zone near Ilo, Peru.

1992, Mar. 23 *Perf. 14x13½, 13½x14*

842 A337 1.20b multicolored .95 .40
843 A337 1.50b multicolored 1.10 .50
844 A337 1.80b multicolored 1.40 .55
Nos. 842-844 (3) 3.45 1.45

Expo '92, Seville A338

1992, Apr. 15 *Perf. 13½x14*

845 A338 30c multicolored .30 .20
846 A338 50c Columbus' ships .45 .20

Miraflores Rotary Club, District 4690, Mt. Illimani A339

1992, Apr. 30 Litho. *Perf. 13½*

847 A339 90c multicolored .70 .45

Prof. Elizardo Perez, Founder of Ayllu of Warisata School, Birth Cent. — A340

1992, June 6 Litho. *Perf. 13½*

848 A340 60c multicolored .50 .25

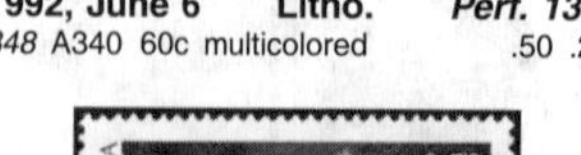

Government Palace, Sucre — A341

1992, July 10 Litho. *Perf. 13½x14*

849 A341 50c multicolored .40 .20

A342

1992, Sept. 11 *Perf. 14x13½*

850 A342 50c multicolored .40 .20

Los Tiempos Newpaper, 25th anniv.

A343

1992, Aug. 9 *Perf. 13½*

Mario Martinez Guzman, tennis player.

851 A343 1.50b multicolored 1.10 .50

1992 Summer Olympics, Barcelona.

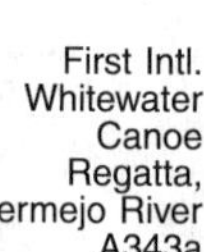

First Intl. Whitewater Canoe Regatta, Bermejo River A343a

1992, Sept. 17 Litho. *Perf. 13½*

851A A343a 1.20b multicolored 1.10 .50

1994 World Cup Soccer Championships, US — A344

1992, Oct. 2 Litho. *Perf. 13½*

852 A344 1.20b multicolored 1.90 .75

Oruro Technical University, Cent. — A345

1992, Oct. 15 *Perf. 13½x14*

853 A345 50c multicolored .40 .20

Interamerican Institute for Agricultural Cooperation, 50th Anniv. — A346

1992, Oct. 7 *Perf. 13½*

854 A346 1.20b Chenopodium quinoa 1.10 .50

Discovery of America, 500th Anniv. A347

Paintings: 60c, Columbus departing from Palos, vert. 2b, Columbus with Caribbean natives.

1992, Oct. 1 *Perf. 14x13½, 13½x14*

855 A347 60c multicolored .40 .20
856 A347 2b multicolored 1.40 .60

Battle of Ingavi, 150th Anniv. (in 1991) A348

1992, Nov. 18 Litho. *Perf. 13½x14*

857 A348 1.20b sepia & black .95 .40

12th Bolivian Games, Cochabamba and Santa Cruz — A349

1992, Nov. 13

858 A349 2b multicolored 1.50 .60

Fauna, Events A350

Event emblem and fauna: 20c, Beni Dept., sesquicentennial, caiman. 50c, Polska '93, paca. 1b, Bangkok '93, chinchilla. 2b, 1994 Winter Olympics, Lillehammer, Norway, ant-eater. 3b, Brandenburg Gate, jaguar. 4b, Brasiliana '93, hummingbird, vert. 5b, 1994 World Cup Soccer Championships, US, piranhas.

1992, Nov. 18 Litho. *Perf. 13½*

859 A350 20c multicolored .20 .20
860 A350 50c multicolored .35 .20
861 A350 1b multicolored .75 .35
862 A350 2b multicolored 1.50 .60
863 A350 3b multicolored 2.25 .90
864 A350 4b multicolored 3.00 1.25
865 A350 5b multicolored 3.75 1.50
Nos. 859-865 (7) 11.80 5.00

Christmas A350a

Designs: 1.20b, Man in canoe, star. 2.50b, Star over churches. 6b, Flowers, church, infant on hay.

1992, Dec. 1 Litho. *Perf. 13½*

865A A350a 1.20b multicolored .90 .35
865B A350a 2.50b multicolored 1.90 .75
865C A350a 6b multicolored 4.50 1.75
Nos. 865A-865C (3) 7.30 2.85

A351

A352

Nicolaus Copernicus (1473-1543), Polish Astronomer: 50c, Santa Ana Intl. astrometrical observatory, Tarija, horiz.

Perf. 13x13½, 13½x13

1993, Feb. 18 Litho.

866 A351 50c multicolored .40 .20
867 A351 2b black 1.50 .60

1993, Apr. 14 Litho. *Perf. 13½*

868 A352 60c multicolored .60 .25

Beatification of Mother Nazaria.

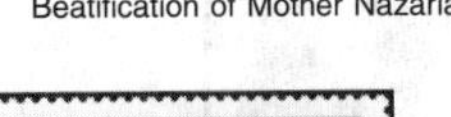

12th Bolivar Games
A353

1993, Apr. 24 *Perf. 13½x14*

869 A353 2.30b multicolored 1.60 .65

Bolivia #C240, Brazil #3
A354

1993, May 31

870 A354 2.30b multicolored 1.60 .65

First Brazilian Stamp, 150th anniv.

A355

Eternal Father, by Gaspar de la Cueva.

1993, June 9 Litho. *Perf. 13½*

871 A355 1.80b multicolored 1.25 .50

A356

1993, July 31 Litho. *Perf. 14x13½*

872 A356 50c Virgin of Urkupina .35 .20

City of Quillacollo, 400th anniv.

Pedro Domingo Murillo Industrial School
A357

1993, Aug. 4 *Perf. 13½*

873 A357 60c multicolored .40 .20

Butterflies
A358

1993, June 4 *Perf. 13½x14*

874 A358 60c Archaeoprepona demophon .55 .20
875 A358 60c Morpho sp. .55 .20
876 A358 80c Papilio sp. .70 .25
877 A358 80c Historis odius .70 .25
878 A358 80c Euptoieta hegesia .70 .25
879 A358 1.80b Morpho deidamia 1.75 .55
880 A358 1.80b Papilio thoas 1.75 .55
881 A358 1.80b Danaus plexippus 1.75 .55
882 A358 2.30b Caligo sp. 2.00 .60
883 A358 2.30b Anaea marthesia 2.00 .60
884 A358 2.30b Rothschildia sp. 2.00 .60
885 A358 2.70b Heliconius sp. 2.25 .75
886 A358 2.70b Marpesia corinna 2.25 .75
887 A358 2.70b Prepona chromus 2.25 .75
888 A358 3.50b Heliconius sp., diff. 3.00 .95
889 A358 3.50b Siproeta epaphus 3.00 .95
a. Sheet of 16, #874-889 30.00 30.00
Nos. 874-889 (16) 27.20 8.75

Pan-American Health Organization, 90th Anniv. — A359

1993, Oct. 13 Litho. *Perf. 13½*

890 A359 80c multicolored .55 .20

Archaelogical Finds — A360

Location of cave paintings: No. 891, Oruro. No. 892, Santa Cruz, vert. No. 893, Beni, vert. No. 894, Chuquisaca, vert. No. 895, Chuquisaca. No. 896, Potosi. No. 897, La Paz, vert. No. 898, Tarija, vert. No. 899, Cochabamba.

1993, Sept. 28

891 A360 80c multicolored .55 .20
892 A360 80c multicolored .55 .20
893 A360 80c multicolored .55 .20
894 A360 80c multicolored .55 .20
895 A360 80c multicolored .55 .20
896 A360 80c multicolored .55 .20
897 A360 80c multicolored .55 .20
898 A360 80c multicolored .55 .20
899 A360 80c multicolored .55 .20
Nos. 891-899 (9) 4.95 1.80

America Issue — A361

1993, Oct. 9 Litho. *Perf. 13½*

900 A361 80c Saimiri sciereus .55 .20
901 A361 2.30b Felis pordalis 1.50 .60

Famous People — A361a

Designs: 50c, Yolanda Bedregal, poet. 70c, Simon Martinic, President of Cochabamba Philatelic Center. 90c, Eugenio von Boeck, politician, President of Bolivian Philatelic Federation. 1b, Marina Nunez del Prado, sculptor.

1993, Nov. 17 Litho. *Perf. 11*

901A A361a 50c sepia .30 .20
901B A361a 70c sepia .45 .20
901C A361a 90c sepia .55 .25
901D A361a 1b sepia .60 .25
Nos. 901A-901D (4) 1.90 .90

Christmas
A361b

1993, Dec. 8 *Perf. 14x13½*

Paintings: 2.30b, Adoration of the Shepherds, by Leonardo Flores. 3.50b, Virgin with Child and Saints, by unknown artist. 6b, Virgin of the Milk, by Melchor Perez de Holguin.

901E A361b 2.30b multicolored 1.40 .55
901F A361b 3.50b multicolored 2.25 .85
901G A361b 6b multicolored 3.75 1.50
Nos. 901E-901G (3) 7.40 2.90

Town of Riberalta, Cent. — A362

1994, Feb. 3 Litho. *Perf. 13½*

902 A362 2b multicolored 1.25 .60

World Population Day — A363

1994, Feb. 17 Litho. *Perf. 13½*

903 A363 2.30b multicolored 1.50 .60

A364

1994, Feb. 21 *Perf. 13½*

904 A364 2b buff & multi 1.25 .60
905 A364 2.30b multi 1.50 .60

Inauguration of Pres. Gonzalo Sanchez de Lozada.

A365

1994, Mar. 22

1994 World Cup Soccer Championships, US: 80c, Mascot. 1.80b, Bolivia, Uruguay. 2.30b, Bolivia, Venezuela. No. 909, Part of Bolivian team, goalies in black. No. 910, Part of Bolivian team, diff. 2.70b, Bolivia, Ecuador. 3.50b, Bolivia, Brazil.

906 A365 80c multicolored .50 .20
907 A365 1.80b multicolored 1.10 .45
908 A365 2.30b multicolored 1.40 .55
909 A365 2.50b multicolored 1.50 .60
910 A365 2.50b multicolored 1.50 .60
a. Pair, #909-910 3.00 1.25
911 A365 2.70b multicolored 1.60 .65
912 A365 3.50b multicolored 2.25 .85
Nos. 906-912 (7) 9.85 3.90

SOS Children's Village, Bolivia — A366

1994, Apr. 12 Litho. *Perf. 13½*

913 A366 2.70b multicolored 1.60 .65

Catholic Archdiocese La Paz, 50th Anniv. — A367

Churches, priests: 1.80b, Church of San Pedro, Msgr. Jorge Manrique Hurtado. 2b, Archbishop Abel I. Antezana y Rojas, Church of the Sacred Heart of Mary, vert. 3.50b, Msgr. Luis Sainz Hinojosa, Church of Santo Domingo, vert.

1994, July 12 Litho. *Perf. 13½*

914 A367 1.80b multicolored 1.10 .45
915 A367 2b multicolored 1.25 .60
916 A367 3.50b multicolored 2.25 .85
Nos. 914-916 (3) 4.60 1.90

A368

Design: 2b, Pres. Victor Paz Estenssoro.

1994, Oct. 2 Litho. *Perf. 13½*

917 A368 2b multicolored 1.25 .50

A369

1994, Oct. 9

918 A369 1.80b No. 46 1.10 .45

Battle of Ft. Boqueron
A370

Col. Manuel Marzana Oroza, battle scene.

1994, Oct. 6

919 A370 80c multicolored .50 .20

San Borja, 300th Anniv. A371

1994, Oct. 14

920 A371 1.60b Erythrina fusca 1.00 .40

America Issue — A372

Old, new methods of postal transport: 1b, Streetcar, van. 5b, Airplane, ox cart.

1994, Oct. 12

921 A372 1b multicolored .65 .25
922 A372 5b multicolored 3.25 1.25

1994 Solar Eclipse — A373

1994 Oct. 21

923 A373 3.50b multicolored 2.25 .85

Environmental Protection — A374

1994, Sept. 21

Trees: 60c, Buddleja coriacea. 1.80b, Bertholletia exelsa. 2b, Schinus molle, horiz. 2.70b, Polylepis racemosa. 3, Tabebuia chrysantha. 3.50b, Erythrina falcata, horiz.

924 A374 60c multicolored .40 .20
925 A374 1.80b multicolored 1.10 .45
926 A374 2b multicolored 1.25 .50
927 A374 2.70b multicolored 1.60 .65
928 A374 3b multicolored 1.90 .75
929 A374 3.50b multicolored 2.25 .85
Nos. 924-929 (6) 8.50 3.40

Gen. Antonio Jose de Sucre (1795-1830) A375

1995, Jan. 25 Litho. *Perf. 13½*

930 A375 1.80b shown .75 .30
931 A375 3.50b diff. background 1.50 .60

A377

1994, Nov. 25 Litho. *Perf. 13½*

933 A377 2b Tarija girl 1.10 .45
934 A377 5b High plateau child 2.75 .45
935 A377 20b Eastern girl 11.00 3.75
Nos. 933-935 (3) 14.85 4.65

Christmas.

A378

1994, Nov. 28 Litho. *Perf. 13½*

936 A378 1.80b multicolored .90 .35

Pan-American Scout Jamboree, Cochabamba

Cathedral of St. Anne — A379

1995, Apr. 21 Litho. *Perf. 13½*

937 A379 1.90b black & multi 1.25 .60
938 A379 2.90b blue & multi 1.75 .90

Yacuma-Beni Province, cent.

Franciscans at Copacabana Natl. Sanctuary, Cent. — A380

1995, May 2

939 A380 60c gray & multi .40 .20
940 A380 80c bister & multi .55 .20

A381

1995 Litho. *Perf. 13½*

941 A381 2b multicolored 1.00 .40

Peace Between Bolivia and Paraguay. Dated 1994.

A382

1995, July 25

942 A382 2.40b multicolored 1.25 .50

Andes Development Corporation (CAF), 25th anniv.

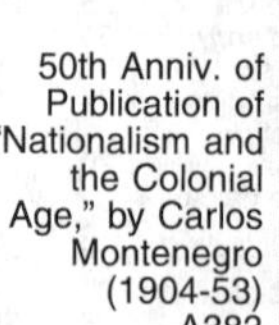

50th Anniv. of Publication of "Nationalism and the Colonial Age," by Carlos Montenegro (1904-53) A383

1995, Aug. 8

943 A383 1.20b pink & black .60 .25

A384

1995, Sept. 26

944 A384 1b multicolored .50 .20

FAO, 50th anniv.

A385

1995, Oct. 24 *Perf. 14½*

945 A385 2.90b multicolored 1.50 .60

UN, 50th anniv.

America Issue A386

1995, Nov. 21 *Perf. 14*

946 A386 5b Condor 2.50 1.00
947 A386 5b Llamas 2.50 1.00
a. Pair, #946-947 5.00 2.00

ICAO, 50th Anniv. — A387

1995, Dec. 4 *Perf. 13½x13*

948 A387 50c multicolored .25 .20

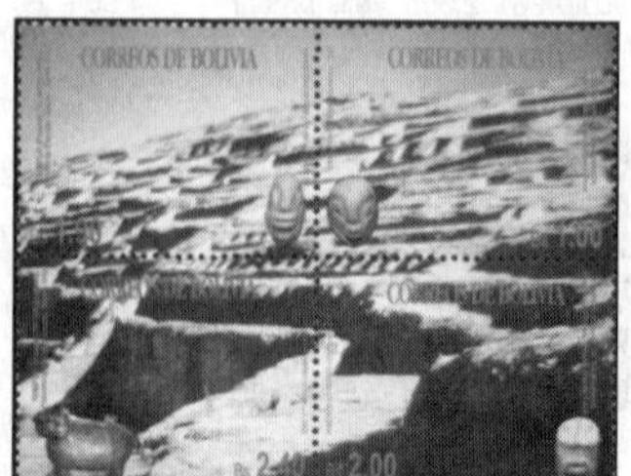

Temple of Samaipata — A388

Archaeological finds and: a, 1.90b, Top of ruins. b, 1b, Top of ruins, diff. c, 2.40b, Lower excavation. d, 2b, Floor, tiers.

1995, Dec. 4 *Perf. 13x13½*

949 A388 Block of 4, #a.-d. 3.75 1.50

No. 949 is a continuous design.

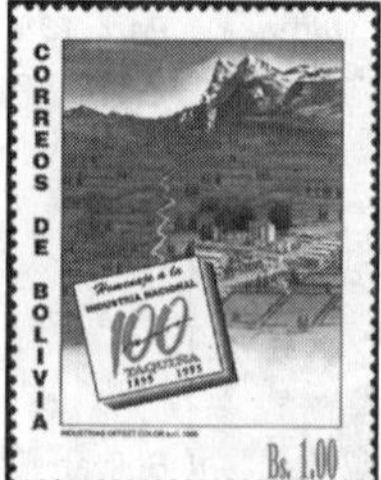

Taquiña Brewery, Cent. — A389

1995, Dec. 8 *Perf. 14*

950 A389 1b multicolored .50 .20

Christmas A390

Paintings: 1.20b, The Annunciation, by Cima da Conegliano. 3b, The Nativity, by Hans Baldung. 3.50b, Adoration of the Magi, by Rogier van der Weyden.

1995, Dec. 15 *Perf. 14x13½*

951 A390 1.20b multicolored .60 .25
952 A390 3b multicolored 1.50 .60
953 A390 3.50b multicolored 1.75 .70
Nos. 951-953 (3) 3.85 1.55

Natl. Anthem, 150th Anniv. — A391

Designs: 1b, J.I. de Sanjines, lyricist. 2b, B. Vincenti, composer.

1995, Dec. 18 Litho. *Perf. 13½*

954 A391 1b multicolored .40 .20
955 A391 2b multicolored .80 .30
a. Pair, #954-955 1.20 .45

Decree to Abolish Abuse of Indian Labor, 50th Anniv. — A392

Designs: 1.90b, Modern representations of industry, Gov. Gualberto Villarroel. 2.90, Addressing labor policies, silhouettes of people rejoicing.

1996, Jan. 26 *Perf. 14*

956 A392 1.90b multicolored .75 .30
957 A392 2.90b multicolored 1.10 .45
a. Pair, #956-957 1.90 .75

Nos. 639, 653, 685-686, 712-713, 715, 719, 726, 729, 732-733, C332, C348 Surcharged

Perfs. and Printing Methods as Before

1996

958	A273	50c on 3,000,000b #729	.20	.20
959	A265	60c on 2000b #713	.25	.20
960	A277	60c on 1,400,000b #733	.25	.20
961	A271	1b on 2,500,000b #726	.40	.20
962	A264	1.50b on 11,000b #712	.60	.25
963	A267	2.50b on 23,000b #715	1.00	.40
964	A269	3b on 1,000,000b #719	1.10	.45
965	A222	3.50b on 6.50b #639	1.40	.55
966	A234	3.50b on 9b #653	1.40	.55
967	A276	3.50b on 2,000,000b #732	1.40	.55
968	AP67	3.80b on 3.80b #C332	1.50	.60
969	A189	20b on 3.80b #C348	8.00	3.25
970	A253	20b on 10b #685	8.00	3.25
971	A254	20b on 13b #686	8.00	3.25
		Nos. 958-971 (14)	33.50	13.90

Size and location of surcharge varies.

No. 627 Surcharged

1996 Litho. *Perf. 10½*

972 A216 60c on 2.50b multi .40 .20

See No. 697 for similar surcharge.

10th Summit of the Chiefs of State and Government(Rio Group), Cochabamba A393

Designs: 2.50b, Stylized person. 3.50b, Stylized globe surrounded by lines.

1996, Sept. 4 *Perf. 14*

973	A393	2.50b multicolored	1.00	.40
974	A393	3.50b multicolored	1.40	.55

Anniversaries A394

50c, Natl. Bank of Bolivia, 125th anniv. 1b, Jose Joaquin de Lemoine (1776-1851), first postal administrator, vert.

1996, Dec. 8 Litho. *Perf. 13½*

975	A394	50c multicolored	.20	.20
976	A394	1b multicolored	.40	.20

Summit of the Americas to Sustain Development A395

1996, Dec. 8 *Perf. 14x13½*

977	A395	2.50b brown & multi	.95	.40
978	A395	5b black & multi	1.90	.75

CARE in Bolivia, 20th Anniv. — A396

1996, Dec. 19 *Perf. 13½*

979	A396	60c Family, horiz.	.25	.20
980	A396	70c shown	.25	.20

Natl. Symphony Orchestra, 50th Anniv. — A397

1996, Dec. 24

981	A397	1.50b shown	.60	.25
982	A397	2b String instruments	.75	.30
a.		Pair, #981-982	1.40	.55

No. 982a is a continuous design.

Tourism in Oruro A398

Designs: 50c, Miners' Monument, vert. 60c, Folklore costume, vert. 1b, Virgin of Socavon, vert. 1.50b, Sajama mountains. 2.50b, Chipaya child, building, vert. 3b, Raul Shaw, "Moreno."

1997, Feb. 3 Litho. *Perf. 14½*

983	A398	50c multicolored	.20	.20
984	A398	60c multicolored	.25	.20
985	A398	1b multicolored	.40	.20
986	A398	1.50b multicolored	.60	.25
987	A398	2.50b multicolored	.95	.40
988	A398	3b multicolored	1.10	.45
		Nos. 983-988 (6)	3.50	1.70

Dated 1996.

Tourism in Chuquisaca — A399

Designs: 60c, La Glorieta. 1b, Governor's Palace, vert. No. 991, Dinosaur tracks. No. 992, House of Liberty. 2b, Tarabaqueno, vert. 3b, Statue of Juana Azurduy of Padilla, vert.

1997, Jan. 30 *Perf. 13½x14, 14x13½*

989	A399	60c multicolored	.25	.20
990	A399	1b multicolored	.40	.20
991	A399	1.50b multicolored	.60	.25
992	A399	1.50b multicolored	.60	.25
993	A399	2b multicolored	.75	.30
994	A399	3b multicolored	1.10	.45
		Nos. 989-994 (6)	3.70	1.65

Dated 1996.

Tourism in Tarija A400

Designs: 50c, House of Culture, Dorada, vert. 60c, Church of Entre Rios, vert. 80c, San Luis Falls. 1b, Monument to the Chaco War. 3b, Temple, Statue of the Virgin Mary, Chaguay. 20b, Eustaquio Mendez house, monument.

1997, Jan. 24 *Perf. 14x13½, 13½x14*

995	A400	50c multicolored	.20	.20
996	A400	60c multicolored	.25	.20
997	A400	80c multicolored	.30	.20
998	A400	1b multicolored	.40	.20
999	A400	3b multicolored	1.10	.45
1000	A400	20b multicolored	7.75	3.00
		Nos. 995-1000 (6)	10.00	4.25

Dated 1996.

Visit of French Pres. Jacques Chirac A401

Design: Bolivian Pres. Gonzalo Sanchez de Lozada, Chirac.

1997, Mar. 15 *Perf. 14*

1001 A401 4b multicolored 1.50 .60

Salesian Order in Bolivia, Cent. — A402

Designs: 1.50b, St. John Bosco (1815-88), church. 2b, Statue of St. John Bosco talking with boy, church.

1997, Apr. 29 Litho. *Perf. 13½*

1002	A402	1.50b multicolored	.60	.25
1003	A402	2b multicolored	.75	.30

UNICEF, 50th Anniv. A403

Children's drawings: 50c, Houses, children on playground. 90c, Child running, cactus, rock, lake. 1b, Boys, girls arm in arm across globe. 2.50b, Girl on swing, others in background.

1997

1004	A403	50c multicolored	.20	.20
1005	A403	90c multicolored	.35	.20
1006	A403	1b multicolored	.40	.20
1007	A403	2.50b multicolored	.95	.40
		Nos. 1004-1007 (4)	1.90	1.00

Department of La Paz — A404

Tourism: 50c, Mt. Chulumani, Las Yungas, vert. 80c, Inca monolith, vert. 1.50b, City, Mt. Illimani, vert. 2b, Gate of the Sun, Tiwanacu. 2.50b, Traditional dancers, vert. 10b, Virgin of Copacabana, reed boat.

1997, May 28 Litho. *Perf. 13½*

1008	A404	50c multicolored	.20	.20
1009	A404	80c multicolored	.30	.20
1010	A404	1.50b multicolored	.60	.25
1011	A404	2b multicolored	.75	.30
1012	A404	2.50b multicolored	.95	.40
1013	A404	10b multicolored	3.75	1.50
		Nos. 1008-1013 (6)	6.55	2.85

1997 America Cup Soccer Championships, Bolivia — A405

1998 World Cup Soccer Championships, France — A406

1997, June 13

1014	A405	3b multicolored	1.25	.50
1015	A406	5b multicolored	1.90	.75

National Congress A407

1997, July 8 Litho. *Perf. 13½*

1016 A407 1b multicolored .40 .20

America Issue — A408

Women in traditional costumes: 5b, From valley region. 15b, From eastern Bolivia.

1997, July 14 Litho. *Perf. 13½*

1017	A408	5b multicolored	1.90	.75
1018	A408	15b multicolored	5.75	2.25

Mercosur (Common Market of Latin America) A409

1997, Sept. 26

1019 A409 3b multicolored 1.10 .45

See Argentina #1975, Brazil #2646, Paraguay #2565, Uruguay #1681.

Christmas A410

Paintings: 2b, Virgin del Cerro, by unknown artist. 5b, Virgin de la Leche, by unknown artist. 10b, The Holy Family, by Melchor Pérez de Holguin.

1997, Dec. 19 Litho. *Perf. 13½*

1020 A410 2b multicolored .75 .30
1021 A410 5b multicolored 1.75 .75
1022 A410 10b multicolored 3.50 1.50
Nos. 1020-1022 (3) 6.00 2.55

Diana, Princess of Wales (1961-97) A411

1997, Dec. 29

1023 A411 2b Portrait, vert. 1.25 .50
1024 A411 3b In mine field 1.75 .75

Visit of Prime Minister of Spain A412

Hugo Banzer Suarez, Pres. of Bolivia and José Maria Aznar.

1998, Mar. 16

1025 A412 6b multicolored 3.25 1.25

Bolivian Society of Engineers, 75th Anniv. A413

1998, Apr. 28

1026 A413 3.50b multicolored 1.25 .55

A414

A415

1998, Apr. 30 Litho. *Perf. 13½*

1027 A414 5b multicolored 1.75 .75

Rotary Intl. in Bolivia, 70th anniv.

1998, July 9

Letter Carriers, 1942: 3b, Postman delivering mail to woman, vert.

1028 A415 3b multicolored 1.10 .45
1029 A415 4b multicolored 1.40 .60

America Issue.

Famous Men — A416

1.50b, Werner Guttentag Tichauer, bibliographer. 2b, Dr. Martin Cardenas Hermosa, botanist. 3.50b, Adrian Patiño Carpio, composer.

1998, July 10

1030 A416 1.50b brown .55 .20
1031 A416 2b green, vert .70 .30
1032 A416 3.50b black, vert 1.25 .50
Nos. 1030-1032 (3) 2.50 1.00

Regions in Bolivia A417

Beni: 50c, Victoria regia. 1b, Callandria. 1.50b, White Tajibo tree, vert. 3.50b, Amazon mask. 5b, Nutrea. 7b, Tropical condor.

1998, Oct. 11 Litho. *Perf. 13½*

1033 A417 50c black & multi .20 .20
1034 A417 1b black & multi .35 .20
1035 A417 1.50b black & multi .55 .25
1036 A417 3.50b black & multi 1.25 .55
1037 A417 5b black & multi 1.75 .80
1038 A417 7b black & multi 2.50 1.10
Nos. 1033-1038 (6) 6.60 3.10

Pando: 50c, Acre River. 1b, Sloth climbing bamboo tree, vert. 1.50b, Bahia Arroyo, vert. 4b, Boa. 5b, Family of capybaras. 7b, Houses, palm trees, vert.

1039 A417 50c green & multi .20 .20
1040 A417 1b green & multi .35 .20
1041 A417 1.50b green & multi .55 .25
1042 A417 4b green & multi 1.40 .65
1043 A417 5b green & multi 1.75 .80
1044 A417 7b green & multi 2.50 1.10
Nos. 1039-1044 (6) 6.75 3.20
Nos. 1033-1044 (12) 13.35 6.30

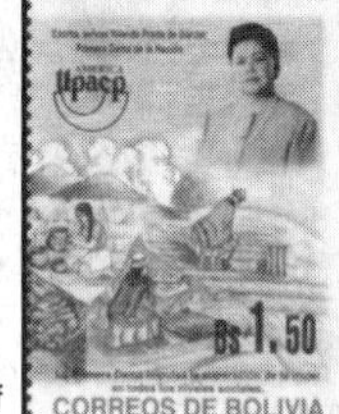

Women of Bolivia — A418

First Lady Yolanda Prada de Banzer and: 1.50b, Women working in fields, making pottery, weaving. 2b, Women working on computer, standing at blackboard.

1998, Oct. 11

1045 A418 1.50b multicolored .55 .25
1046 A418 2b multicolored .70 .30
a. Pair, #1045-1046 1.25 .55

America Issue.

City of La Paz, 450th Anniv. A419

1998, Oct. 14

1047 A419 2b Plaza de Laja Church .70 .30

A420

A422

A421

1998, Nov. 6 Litho. *Perf. 13½x13¾*

1048 A420 3.50b blue & yellow 1.25 .60

Organization of American States, 50th anniv.

1998, Nov. 12 *Perf. 13¼x13½*

1049 A421 2b multicolored .70 .35

Bolivian Philatelic Federation, 25th anniv., Espamer '98, Buenos Aires.

Perf. 13¼x13½, 13½x13¼
1998, Nov. 26

Christmas: 2b, Child's drawing of church. 6b, Pope John Paul II. 7b, John Paul II, Mother Teresa.

1050 A422 2b multi, horiz. .70 .35
1051 A422 6b multi 2.00 .95
1052 A422 7b multi 2.40 1.25
Nos. 1050-1052 (3) 5.10 2.55

UPU, 125th Anniv. A423

1999, Jan. 26 Litho. *Perf. 13½*

1053 A423 3.50b multicolored 1.25 .60

AFC Soccer Club, 75th Anniv. — A424

1999, Apr. 22 Litho. *Perf. 13½*

1054 A424 5b multicolored *4.25 2.25*

Geneva Convention and Bolivian Red Cross, 50th Anniv. A425

1999, May 18

1055 A425 5b multicolored 1.90 .95

Bernardo Guarachi, First Bolivian to Reach Summit of Mt. Everest A426

1999, May 25

1056 A426 6b multicolored 2.25 1.10

Special Olympics of Bolivia, 30th Anniv. — A427

Designs: 2b, Medalists on podium. 2.50b, Winners of swimming event, running event.

1999

1057 A427 2b multicolored .75 .35
1058 A427 2.50b multicolored .90 .45

Japanese Immigration to Bolivia, Cent. — A428

Designs: 3b, Golden Pavilion, Kyoto. 6b, Sun setting across water, vert.

1999, June 3

1059 A428 3b multicolored 1.10 .55
1060 A428 6b multicolored 2.25 1.10

Bolivian Cinema, 100th Anniv. A429

1999 Litho. *Perf. 13½*

1061 A429 50c Hacia la Gloria, 1932-33 .20 .20
1062 A429 50c Jonas y la Ballena Rosada, 1995 .20 .20
1063 A429 1b Wara Wara, 1929 .35 .20
1064 A429 1b Vuelve Sebastiana, 1953 .35 .20
1065 A429 3b La Campana del Chaco, 1933 .65 .30
1066 A429 3b La Vertiente, 1958 .65 .30
1067 A429 6b Yawar Mallku, 1969 2.00 .95
1068 A429 6b Mi Socio, 1982 2.00 .95
a. Sheet of 8, #1061-1068 6.50 3.25
Nos. 1061-1068 (8) 6.40 3.30

SOS Children's Village, 50th Anniv. — A430

1999, July 8

1069 A430 3.50b multicolored 1.25 .60

Intl. Day Against Illegal Drugs A431

Perf. 13¼x13½
1999, June 26 Litho.

1070 A431 3.50b multicolored 1.25 .60

Completion of Bolivian-Brazilian Gas Pipeline — A432

Designs: 3b, Presidents of Bolivia and Brazil, map of pipeline. 6b, Presidents, gas flame.

1999, July 1 Litho. *Perf. 13½*

1071 A432 3b multicolored 1.00 .50
1072 A432 6b multicolored 2.00 .95

La Paz Lions Club, 50th Anniv. — A433

1999 *Perf. 13½x13¼*

1073 A433 3.50b multicolored 1.25 .60

Cochabamba Tourism — A434

50c, Mt. Tunari. 1b, Cochabamba Valley. 2b, Container from Omerque culture, idol from Pachamama culture. 3b, Totora. 5b, Composer Teofilo Vargas Candia. 6b, Statue of Jesus Christ.

1999 *Perf. 13½x13¾, 13¾x13½*

1074	A434	50c multi	.20	.20
1075	A434	1b multi	.35	.20
1076	A434	2b multi, vert.	.70	.35
1077	A434	3b multi	1.10	.55
1078	A434	5b multi, vert.	1.75	.85
1079	A434	6b multi, vert.	2.10	1.00
		Nos. 1074-1079 (6)	6.20	3.15

Potosí Tourism A435

50c, Tarapaya Lake. 1b, Obverse and reverse of 1827 Bolivian coin. 2b, Mt. Chorolque. 3b, Lake, llama, birds. 5b, "Mestizo Woman with a Cigaretee Case," by Teofilo Loaiza. 6b, Alfredo Dominguez Romero, musician.

Perf. 13¾x13½, 13½x13¾

1999 **Litho.**

1080	A435	50c multi, vert.	.20	.20
1081	A435	1b multi	.35	.20
1082	A435	2b multi	.70	.35
1083	A435	3b multi	1.10	.55
1084	A435	5b multi, vert.	1.75	.90
1085	A435	6b multi, vert.	2.25	1.10
		Nos. 1080-1085 (6)	6.35	3.30

America Issue, A New Millennium Without Arms — A436

1999 *Perf. 13½x13¼*

1086	A436	3.50b shown	1.25	.60
1087	A436	3.50b Globe, flower	1.25	.60

Christmas A437

2b, Children, Christmas tree. 6b, The Birth of Jesus, by Gaspar Miguel de Berrios. 7b, Our Families of the World, by Omar Medina.

1999 *Perf. 13¼x13½, 13½x13¼*

1088	A437	2b multi	.70	.35
1089	A437	6b multi, vert.	2.10	1.00
1090	A437	7b multi, vert.	2.40	1.25
		Nos. 1088-1090 (3)	5.20	2.60

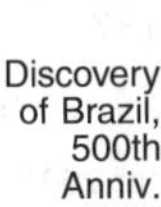

Discovery of Brazil, 500th Anniv. A438

2000 **Litho.** *Perf. 13½x13¾*

1091 A438 5b multi 1.60 .80

2000 Doble Copacabana Bicycle Race — A439

Various views of racers.

2000

1092	A439	1b multi	.35	.20
1093	A439	3b multi	1.00	.50
1094	A439	5b multi	1.60	.80
1095	A439	7b multi	2.40	1.25
		Nos. 1092-1095 (4)	5.35	2.75

Sgt. Maximiliano Paredes Military School, Cent. — A440

2000 **Litho.** *Perf. 13½x13¾*

1096 A440 2.50b multi .80 .40

Federal Republic of Germany, 50th Anniv. (in 1999) A441

2000

1097 A441 6b multi 2.00 1.00

Paintings of Cecilio Guzmán de Rojas (1900-51) — A442

Designs: 1b, Self-portrait, vert. 2.50b, Triunfo de la Naturaleza. 5b, Andina, vert. 6b, Riña de Estudiantes.

2000 *Perf. 13¾x13½, 13½x13¾*

1098-1101 A442 Set of 4 4.75 2.40

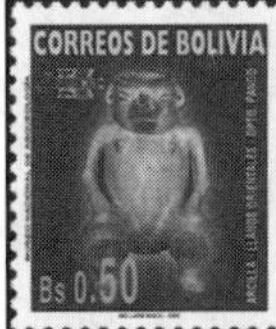

Artifacts from Natl. Archaeological Museum — A443

Artifacts from: #1102, 50c, Pando. #1103, 50c, Potosí. 70c, Beni. 90c, Tarija. #1106, 1b, Chuquisaca. #1107, 1b, Oruro. 3b, Cochabamba. 5b, Santa Cruz. 20b, La Paz.

2000 *Perf. 11¼x11*

1102-1110 A443 Set of 9 11.00 5.50

America Issue, Fight Against AIDS — A444

Designs: No. 1111, 3.50b, Symbols for male and female in whirlwind. No. 1112, 3.50b, Man, woman, clouds, brick wall.

2000 *Perf. 13¼x13½*

1111-1112 A444 Set of 2 2.25 1.10

Victor Agustin Ugarte, Soccer Player — A445

2000, Apr. 24 **Litho.** *Perf. 13½x13¼*

1113 A445 3b multi 1.00 .50

Santa Cruz Tourism A446

Designs: 50c, Fountains, Parque el Arenal. 1b, Ox cart. 2b, Writers Raúl Otero Reiche, Gabriel René Moreno, Hernando Sanabria Fernández. 3b, Virgin of Cotoca, vert. 5b, Anthropomorphic vessel, vert. 6b, Speothos venaticus.

Perf. 13½x13¾, 13¾x13½

2000, Apr. 28

1114-1119 A446 Set of 6 6.25 3.25

Millennium — A448

2000 **Litho.** *Perf. 13½x13¼*

1121 A448 5b multi 1.60 .80

Sovereign Military Order of Malta, 900th Anniv. — A449

2000 *Perf. 13¾x13½*

1122 A449 6b multi 2.00 1.00

Christmas — A450

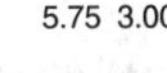
Angels from Calamarca Church: 3b, Gabriel. 5b, Angel of Virtue. 10b, Angel with spike of grain.

2000

1123-1125 A450 Set of 3 5.75 3.00

Holy Year 2000 — A451

Holy Year emblem and: 4b, Basilica de San Francisco, La Paz. 6b, Wheat stalks, barbed wire.

2000 **Litho.** *Perf. 13½x13¼*

1126-1127 A451 Set of 2 3.50 1.75

Promotion of Philately A452

National Symbols A453

Designs: 50c, Man carying first day covers up stairs. 1b, Child, six stamps. 1.50b, Stamp collector. 2b, Child, three stamps. 2.50b, Envelope in bin. 10b, Patuju bandera, current national flower. 20b, La kantuta, previous national flower. 30b, Coat of arms, 1825. 50b, Coat of arms, 1826. 100b, Coat of arms, 1851.

2001 **Litho.** *Perf. 10½*

1128	A452	50c green	.20	.20
1129	A452	1b green	.30	.20
1130	A452	1.50b green	.50	.25
1131	A452	2b green	.65	.30
1132	A452	2.50b green	.80	.40

Perf. 13¾x13½

1133	A453	10b multi	3.25	1.60
1134	A453	20b multi	6.50	3.25
1135	A453	30b multi	9.75	5.00
1136	A453	50b multi	16.00	8.00
1137	A453	100b multi	32.50	16.00
		Nos. 1128-1137 (10)	70.45	35.20

Issued: 50c, 1b, 1.50b, 2b, 2.50b, 6/12; 10b, 6/29; 20b, 6/8; 30b, 5/16; 50b, 3/16; 100b, 4/16.

Bolivia - European Union Cooperation, 25th Anniv. — A454

2001, May 8 **Litho.** *Perf. 13½x13¾*

1138 A454 6b multi 2.00 1.00

Law and Political Science Faculty of San Andres University, 171st Anniv. — A455

2001, May 18 *Perf. 13¾x13½*

1139 A455 6b multi 2.00 1.00

Muela del Diablo A457

2001, July 6 Litho. ***Perf. 13½x13¾***

1141 A457 1.50b multi .50 .25

2001 Census — A458

2001, Aug. 1 ***Perf. 11***

1142 Horiz. strip of 5 3.00 1.50
- *a.* A458 1b purple & multi .30 .20
- *b.* A458 1.50b red & multi .50 .25
- *c.* A458 1.50b green & multi .50 .25
- *d.* A458 2.50b blue & multi .80 .40
- *e.* A458 3b violet & multi .90 .45

Butterflies and Insects A459

Butterflies: No. 1143, 1b, Heliconinae. 1.50b, Philaethria dido. No. 1145, 2.50b, Diathria clymene. No. 1146, 5b, Arctiidae. No. 1147, 6b, Morpho godarti. No. 1148, 6b, Caligo idomineus.

Insects: No. 1149, 1b, Orthopteridae. No. 1150, 2.50b, Mantidae. No. 1151, 3b, Tropidacris latreillei. 4b, Dynastidae. No. 1153, 5b, Acrocinus longimanus. No. 1154, 5b, Lucanidae.

Perf. 13¼x13½

2001, Aug. 30 **Litho.**

1143-1148 A459 Set of 6 7.00 7.00

1149-1154 A459 Set of 6 6.50 6.50

21st Inter-American Scout Conference A460

2001, Sept. 13 ***Perf. 13¾x13½***

1155 A460 3.50b multi 1.10 1.10

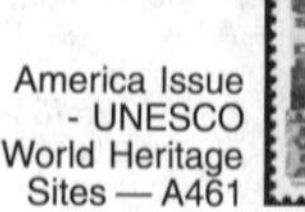

America Issue - UNESCO World Heritage Sites — A461

Designs: 1.50b, Door from Church of St. Francis, Potosi, vert. 5b, Tiwanakwu monoliths.

Perf. 13¾x13½, 13½x13¾

2001, Sept. 26

1156-1157 A461 Set of 2 2.00 2.00

Breast Cancer Prevention A462

2001, Oct. 18 Litho. ***Perf. 13¼x13½***

1158 A462 1.50b multi .50 .50

Christmas — A463

Sculptures by Gaspar de la Cueva: 3b, St. Mary Magdalene. 5b, St. Apolonia. 10b, St. Teresa of Avila.

2001, Nov. 15 ***Perf. 13½x13¼***

1159-1161 A463 Set of 3 5.50 5.50

Joaquin Gantier, Historian, and Casa de la Libertad — A464

2001, Nov. 20

1162 A464 4b multi 1.25 1.25

Bolivian - Belgian Cooperation A465

2001, Nov. 21 ***Perf. 13¼x13½***

1163 A465 6b multi 1.90 1.90

Meeting of Bolivian and Peruvian Presidents A466

Arms of Bolivia and Peru and: 50c, Dam, aerial view of Lake Titicaca. 3b, Bridge, Route from La Paz, Bolivia to Ilo, Peru.

2002, Jan. 26 ***Perf. 13¾x13½***

1164-1165 A466 Set of 2 1.10 1.10

Mauro Nuñez, Composer, Cent. of Birth — A467

No. 1166: a, 1b, Musical score and stringed instruments. b, 6b, Musical score and Nuñez. Illustration reduced.

2002, Jan. 29

1166 A467 Horiz. pair, #a-b 2.25 2.25

Naming of Oruro Carnival as UNESCO Masterpiece of Oral and Intangible Heritage of Humanity A468

Dances: 50c, Diablada. 1.50b, Morenada. 2.50b, Caporales. 5b, Tobas. No. 1171, 7b, Suri Sikuri, vert. No. 1172, 7b, Pujllay, vert.

Perf. 13¼x13½, 13½x13¼

2002, Feb. 8

1167-1172 A468 Set of 6 7.25 7.25

Butterfly and insect Type of 2001

Miniature Sheet

No. 1173: a, Urania leilus. b, Tropidacris latreillei. c, Papilio cresphontes. d, Acrocinus longimanus. e, Preponia buckleyana. f, Half of Thysannia agripyna, denomination at left. g, Half of Thysannia agripyna, denomination at right. h, Lucanidae. i, Nymphalidae. j, Dynastidae. k, Nymphalidae-heliconinae. l, Orthopteridae.

2002, Feb. 15 ***Perf. 13¼x13½***

1173 A459 3b Sheet of 12, #a-l 11.00 11.00

3rd Intl. Theater Festival, La Paz — A469

2002, Mar. 21 ***Perf. 13¾x13½***

1174 A469 3b multi .95 .95

Intl. Year of Mountains and Intl. Year of Ecotourism A470

Designs: 80c, Viscachas Mountain, Potosi Department. 1b, Tree, Cochabamba Department, vert. 1.50, Mount Huayna Potosi, La Paz Department. No. 1178, 2.50b, Mt. Sajama, Oruro Department, vert. No. 1179, 2.50b, Mt. Payachatas, Oruro Department.

Perf. 13¼x13½, 13½x13¼

2002, Apr. 2

1175-1179 A470 Set of 5 2.60 2.60

Dr. Gunnar Mendoza, Historian A471

2002, May 25 ***Perf. 13¼x13½***

1180 A471 4b multi 1.25 1.25

Gen. Germán Busch Military Aviation College, 50th Anniv. — A472

Designs: 4b, Airplane over mountains. 5b, Two airplanes, vert. 6b, Three helicopters.

Perf. 13¼x13½, 13½x13¼

2002, June 14

1181-1183 A472 Set of 3 4.75 4.75

Museo de la Recoleta, Sucre, 400th Anniv. — A473

2002, July 12 ***Perf. 13¾x13½***

1184 A473 4b multi 1.25 1.25

Birds — A474

Designs: 50c, Neochen jubata. 4b, Falco deiroleucus. 6b, Dryocopus schulzi.

2002, July 12 ***Perf. 13½x13¼***

1185-1187 A474 Set of 3 3.25 3.25

Cefilco Philatelic Co., Cochabamba (50c), Bolivian Philatelic Federation, 30th anniv. (4b), Phila Korea 2002 World Stamp Exhibition, Seoul (6b).

Art by Maria Luisa Pacheco A475

Designs: 70c, Untitled work, vert. 80c, Cordillera, 1967, vert. 5b, Cerros, 1967.

Perf. 13½x13¼, 13¼x13½

2002, July 29

1188-1190 A475 Set of 3 2.00 2.00

Armando Alba Zambrana (1901-74), Historian A477

2002 Litho. ***Perf. 13¼x13½***

1194 A477 3b multi .95 .95

Pan-American Health Organization, Cent. — A478

2002 ***Perf. 13½x13¾***

1195 A478 3b multi .95 .95

America Issue - Education A479

Students: 1b, In classroom. 2.50b, At computer.

2002 ***Perf. 13¼x13½***

1196-1197 A479 Set of 2 1.10 1.10

Alcide d'Orbigny (1802-57), Naturalist A480

Designs: 1b, D'orbigny and man and woman in native costumes, vert. 4b, D'Orbigny and boat. 6b, Portrait, vert.

2002 ***Perf. 13¾x13½, 13½x13¾***
1198-1200 A480 Set of 3 3.50 3.50

AIR POST STAMPS

Aviation School
AP1 AP2

1924, Dec. Unwmk. Engr. ***Perf. 14***

C1	AP1 10c ver & blk	.25	.30
a.	Inverted center	*800.00*	
C2	AP1 15c carmine & blk	1.50	.50
C3	AP1 25c dk bl & blk	.60	.60
C4	AP1 50c orange & blk	1.50	1.25
C5	AP2 1b red brn & blk	.90	.95
C6	AP2 2b blk brn & blk	1.75	1.75
C7	AP2 5b dk vio & blk	5.50	5.50
	Nos. C1-C7 (7)	12.00	10.85

Natl. Aviation School establishment.

These stamps were available for ordinary postage. Nos. C1, C3, C5 and C6 exist imperforate. Proofs of the 2b with inverted center exist imperforate and privately perforated.

For overprints and surcharges see Nos. C11-C23, C56-C58.

Emblem of Lloyd Aéreo Boliviano AP3

1928 Litho. ***Perf. 11***

C8	AP3 15c green	1.00	1.00
a.	Imperf., pair	50.00	
C9	AP3 20c dark blue	.25	.25
C10	AP3 35c red brown	.60	.60
	Nos. C8-C10 (3)	1.85	1.85

No. C8 exists imperf. between.
For surcharges see #C24-C26, C53-C55.

Graf Zeppelin Issues

Nos. C1-C5 Surcharged or Overprinted in Various Colors:

Nos. C11, C19

Nos. C12-C18, C20-C23

1930, May 6 ***Perf. 14***

C11	AP1 5c on 10c ver & blk (G)	9.50	9.50
C12	AP1 10c ver & blk (Bl)	9.50	9.50
C13	AP1 10c ver & blk (Br)	600.00	875.00
C14	AP1 15c car & blk (V)	9.50	9.50
C15	AP1 25c dk bl & blk (R)	9.50	9.50
C16	AP1 50c org & blk (Br)	9.50	9.50
C17	AP1 50c org & blk (R)	475.00	*600.00*
C18	AP2 1b red brn & blk (gold)	150.00	150.00

Experts consider the 50c with gold or silver overprint and 5c with black to be trial color proofs.

Nos. C11-C18 exist with the surcharges inverted, double, or double with one inverted, but the regularity of these varieties is questioned.

See notes following No. C23.

Surcharged or Overprinted in Bronze Inks of Various Colors

C19	AP1 5c on 10c ver & blk (G)	77.50	*80.00*
C20	AP1 10c ver & blk (Bl)	67.50	*67.50*
C21	AP1 15c car & blk (V)	77.50	*80.00*
C22	AP1 25c dk bl & blk (cop)	77.50	*80.00*
C23	AP2 1b red brn & blk (gold)	190.00	*200.00*
	Nos. C19-C23 (5)	490.00	*507.50*

Flight of the airship Graf Zeppelin from Europe to Brazil and return via Lakehurst, NJ.

Nos. C19 to C23 were intended for use on postal matter forwarded by the Graf Zeppelin.

No. C18 was overprinted with light gold or gilt bronze ink. No. C23 was overprinted with deep gold bronze ink. Nos. C13 and C17 were overprinted with trial colors but were sold with the regular printings. The 5c on 10c is known surcharged in black and in blue.

No. C8-C10 Surcharged

1930, May 6 ***Perf. 11***

C24	AP3 1.50b on 15c	25.00	25.00
a.	Inverted surcharge	57.50	57.50
b.	Comma instead of period after "1"	35.00	35.00
C25	AP3 3b on 20c	25.00	25.00
a.	Inverted surcharge	62.50	62.50
b.	Comma instead of period after "3"	40.00	40.00
C26	AP3 6b on 35c	37.50	*40.00*
a.	Inverted surcharge	110.00	110.00
b.	Comma instead of period after "6"	62.50	62.50
	Nos. C24-C26 (3)	87.50	90.00

Airplane and Bullock Cart — AP6

Airplane and River Boat — AP7

1930, July 24 Litho. ***Perf. 14***

C27	AP6 5c dp violet	1.25	1.00
C28	AP7 15c red	1.25	1.00
C29	AP7 20c yellow	.50	.45
C30	AP6 35c yellow grn	.40	.25
C31	AP7 50c deep blue	.40	.25
C32	AP6 1b lt brown	.40	.25
C33	AP7 2b deep rose	.40	.40
C34	AP6 3b slate	1.40	1.40
	Nos. C27-C34 (8)	6.00	5.00

Nos. C27 to C34 exist imperforate.
For surcharge see No. C52.

Air Service Emblem AP8

1932, Sept. 16 ***Perf. 11***

C35	AP8 5c ultra	.70	.55
C36	AP8 10c gray	.45	.35
C37	AP8 15c dark rose	.70	.55
C38	AP8 25c orange	.70	.55
C39	AP8 30c green	.60	.30
C40	AP8 50c violet	.60	.35
C41	AP8 1b dk brown	.60	.35
	Nos. C35-C41 (7)	4.35	3.00

Map of Bolivia — AP9

1935, Feb. 1 Engr. ***Perf. 12***

C42	AP9 5c brown red	.20	.20
C43	AP9 10c dk green	.20	.20
C44	AP9 20c dk violet	.20	.20
C45	AP9 30c ultra	.25	.20
C46	AP9 50c orange	.30	.20
C47	AP9 1b bister brn	.30	.25
C48	AP9 1½b yellow	.60	.20
C49	AP9 2b carmine	.60	.30
C50	AP9 5b green	1.10	.40
C51	AP9 10b dk brown	1.75	.75
	Nos. C42-C51 (10)	5.50	2.90

Nos. C1, C4, C10, C30 Surcharged in Red (#C52-C56) or Green (#C57-C58)

c

1937, Oct. 6 ***Perf. 11, 14***

C52	AP6 5c on 35c yel grn	.40	.30
a.	"Carreo"	12.50	
b.	Inverted surcharge		
C53	AP3 20c on 35c red brn	.50	.40
a.	Inverted surcharge		
C54	AP3 50c on 35c red brn	1.50	1.25
a.	Inverted surcharge	17.50	
C55	AP3 1b on 35c red brn	1.10	.65
a.	Inverted surcharge		
C56	AP1 2b on 50c org & blk	1.60	1.00
a.	Inverted surcharge		
C57	AP1 12b on 10c ver & blk	5.75	4.75
a.	Inverted surcharge	22.50	
C58	AP1 15b on 10c ver & blk	5.75	2.75
a.	Inverted surcharge		

Regular Postage Stamps of 1925 Surcharged in Green or Red—d

Perf. 14

C59	A56 (d) 3b on 50c dp vio (G)	1.10	1.00
C60	A56 (d) 4b on 1b red (G)	1.40	1.40
C61	A57 (c) 5b on 2b org (G)	1.90	1.60
a.	Double surcharge	90.00	
C62	A56 (d) 10b on 5b blk brn	4.50	3.25
a.	Double surcharge	35.00	
	Nos. C52-C62 (11)	25.50	18.35

No. C59-C62 exist with inverted surcharge, No. C62a with black and black and red surcharges.

Courtyard of Potosi Mint — AP10

Miner — AP11

Emancipated Woman AP12

Pincers, Torch and Good Will Principles AP15

Airplane over Field AP13

Airplanes and Liberty Monument AP14

Airplane over River AP16

Emblem of New Government AP17

Transport Planes over Map of Bolivia AP18

1938, May Litho. ***Perf. 10½***

C63	AP10 20c deep rose	.25	.25
C64	AP11 30c gray	.25	.25
C65	AP12 40c yellow	.25	.25
C66	AP13 50c yellow grn	.50	.25
C67	AP14 60c dull blue	.50	.25
C68	AP15 1b dull red	.75	.25
C69	AP16 2b bister	1.25	.25
C70	AP17 3b lt brown	1.25	.25
C71	AP18 5b dk violet	1.90	.25
	Nos. C63-C71 (9)	6.90	2.25

40c, 1b, 2b exist imperf.

Chalice — AP19

Virgin of Copacabana AP20

Jesus Christ — AP21

Church of San Francisco, La Paz AP22

St. Anthony of Padua — AP23

1939, July 19 Litho. *Perf. 13½, 10½*

No.	Type	Description	Unused	Used
C72	AP19	5c dull violet	.35	.35
a.		Pair, imperf. between	30.00	
C73	AP20	30c lt bl grn	.30	.20
C74	AP21	45c violet bl	.60	.20
a.		Vertical pair, imperf. between	42.50	
C75	AP22	60c carmine	.40	.35
C76	AP23	75c vermilion	.65	.60
C77	AP23	90c deep blue	.45	.25
C78	AP22	2b dull brown	.75	.25
C79	AP21	4b deep plum	1.00	.40
C80	AP20	5b lt blue	2.50	.25
C81	AP19	10b yellow	5.00	.25
		Nos. C72-C81 (10)	12.00	3.10

2nd National Eucharistic Congress.
For surcharge see No. C112.

Plane over Lake Titicaca — AP24

Mt. Illimani and Condor — AP25

1941, Aug. 21 *Perf. 13½*

No.	Type	Description	Unused	Used
C82	AP24	10b dull green	3.25	.40
C83	AP24	20b light ultra	3.75	.60
C84	AP25	50b rose lilac	6.50	1.00
C85	AP25	100b olive bister	16.00	6.00
		Nos. C82-C85 (4)	29.50	8.00

Counterfeits exist.

Liberty and Clasped Hands — AP26

1942, Nov. 12

No.	Type	Description	Unused	Used
C86	AP26	40c rose lake	.25	.25
C87	AP26	50c ultra	.25	.25
C88	AP26	1b orange brn	1.25	.75
C89	AP26	5b magenta	.75	.25
a.		Double impression		
C90	AP26	10b dull brn vio	2.50	1.25
		Nos. C86-C90 (5)	5.00	2.75

Conference of Chancellors, Jan. 15, 1942.

Ballivián Type of Regular Issue

General José Ballivián; old and modern transportation.

1943, Nov. 18 Engr. *Perf. 12½*

No.	Type	Description	Unused	Used
C91	A114	10c rose vio & brn	.20	.20
C92	A114	20c emerald & brn	.20	.20
C93	A114	30c rose car & brn	.20	.20
C94	A114	3b blue & brn	.75	.20
C95	A114	5b black & brn	.80	.30
		Nos. C91-C95 (5)	2.15	1.10

Condor and Sun Rising — AP28

Plane — AP29

1944, Sept. 19 Litho. *Perf. 13½*

No.	Type	Description	Unused	Used
C96	AP28	40c red violet	.20	.20
C97	AP28	1b blue violet	.20	.20
C98	AP29	1.50b yellow green	.20	.20
C99	AP29	2.50b dk gray blue	.30	.20
		Nos. C96-C99 (4)	.90	.80

Revolution of Dec. 20, 1943.

Map of Natl. Airways — AP30

Map of Bolivian Air Lines — AP31

1945, May 31 *Perf. 11*

No.	Type	Description	Unused	Used
C100	AP30	10c red	.20	.20
a.		Imperf., pair	9.00	
C101	AP30	50c yellow	.20	.20
a.		Imperf., pair	27.50	
C102	AP30	90c lt green	.25	.20
a.		Imperf., pair	30.00	
C103	AP30	5b lt ultra	.35	.20
C104	AP30	20b deep brown	1.00	.45
		Nos. C100-C104 (5)	2.00	1.25

10th anniversary of first flight, La Paz to Tacha, Peru, by Panagra Airways.
For surcharges see Nos. C128-C129.

1945, Sept. 15 *Perf. 13½*
Centers in Red and Blue

No.	Type	Description	Unused	Used
C105	AP31	20c violet	.20	.20
C106	AP31	30c orange brn	.20	.20
C107	AP31	50c brt blue grn	.20	.20
C108	AP31	90c brt violet	.20	.20
C109	AP31	2b blue	.20	.20
C110	AP31	3b magenta	.20	.20
C111	AP31	4b olive bister	.35	.20
		Nos. C105-C111 (7)	1.55	1.40

Founding of Lloyd Aéreo Boliviano, 20th anniv.

Catalogue values for unused stamps in this section, from this point to the end of the section, are for Never Hinged items.

No. C76 Surcharged in Blue

1947, Mar. 23

No.	Type	Description	Unused	Used
C112	AP23	1.40b on 75c ver	.20	.20
		Nos. 314-317,C112 (5)	2.15	1.00

Mt. Illimani AP32

L. A. B. Plane AP35

1947, Sept. 15 Litho. *Perf. 11½*

No.	Type	Description	Unused	Used
C113	AP32	1b rose car	.20	.20
C114	AP32	1.40b emerald	.20	.20
C115	AP32	2.50b blue	.20	.20
C116	AP32	3b dp orange	.20	.20
C117	AP32	4b rose lilac	.20	.20
		Nos. C113-C117 (5)	1.00	1.00
		Nos. 318-323,C113-C117 (11)	4.85	2.55

1st anniv. of the Revolution of July 21, 1946. 1.40b, 2.50b exist imperf.
For surcharge see No. C137.

Bolivia/Argentina Arms Type

1947, Oct. 23 *Perf. 13½*

No.	Type	Description	Unused	Used
C118	A119	2.90b ultra	.25	.25
a.		Imperf., pair	20.00	
b.		Perf. 10½	5.00	4.00

Statue of Christ Type

Designs: 2.50b, Statue of Christ above La Paz. 3.70b, Child kneeling before cross. No. C121, St. John Bosco. No. C122, Virgin of Copacabana. 13.60b, Pope Plus XII blessing University of La Paz.

1948, Sept. 26 *Perf. 11½*

No.	Type	Description	Unused	Used
C119	A120	2.50b ver & yellow	.45	.35
C120	A120	3.70b rose & cream	.55	.35
C121	A120	4b rose lil & gray	.55	.25
C122	A120	4b lt ultra & sal	.55	.20
C123	A120	13.60b ultra & lt grn	.70	.40
		Nos. C119-C123 (5)	2.80	1.55

Bolivia Auto Club Type

1948, Oct.

No.	Type	Description	Unused	Used
C124	A125	10b emerald & salmon	1.60	.20

Pacheco Type of Regular Issue

1950, Jan. 2 Unwmk.

No.	Type	Description	Unused	Used
C125	A126	1.40b orange brown	.20	.20
C126	A126	2.50b orange	.20	.20
C127	A126	3.30b rose violet	.20	.20
		Nos. C125-C127 (3)	.60	.60

75th anniv. of the UPU.

Nos. C100 and C104 Surcharged in Black

1950, May 31 *Perf. 11*

No.	Type	Description	Unused	Used
C128	AP30	4b on 10c red	.20	.20
a.		Inverted surcharge	17.50	17.50
C129	AP30	10b on 20b dp brn	.30	.25
a.		Inverted surcharge	17.50	17.50

Panagra air services in Bolivia, 15th anniv.

1950, Sept. 15 Litho. *Perf. 13½*

No.	Type	Description	Unused	Used
C130	AP35	20c red orange	.20	.20
C131	AP35	30c purple	.20	.20
C132	AP35	50c green	.20	.20
C133	AP35	1b orange	.20	.20
C134	AP35	3b ultra	.25	.20
C135	AP35	15b carmine	.50	.20
C136	AP35	50b chocolate	1.00	.35
		Nos. C130-C136 (7)	2.55	1.55

25th anniv. of the founding of Lloyd Aero Boliviano. 30c, 50c, 15b exist imperforate.
No. C132 exists without imprint at bottom of stamp.

No. C116 Surcharged in Black

1950, Sept. 24 *Perf. 11½*

No.	Type	Description	Unused	Used
C137	AP32	1.40b on 3b dp org	.25	.25

1st anniv. of the ending of the Civil War of Aug. 24-Sept. 24, 1949.
Exists with inverted and double surcharge.

UN Type of Regular Issue

1950, Oct. 24 Unwmk.

No.	Type	Description	Unused	Used
C138	A128	3.60b crimson rose	.50	.20
C139	A128	4.70b black brown	.65	.20

La Paz Type of Regular Issue

20c, Gate of the Sun and llama. 30c, Church of Old Ssanfrancisco. 40c, Avenue Camacho. 50c, Consistorial Palace. 1b, Legislative Palace. 2b, Communications Bldg. 3b, Arms. 4b, La Gasca ordering Mendoza to found La Paz. 5b, Capt. Alonso de Mendoza founding La Paz. 10b, Arms; portrait of Mendoza.

1951, Mar. 1 Engr. *Perf. 12½*
Center in Black

No.	Type	Description	Unused	Used
C140	A129	20c carmine	.20	.20
C141	A130	30c dk vio bl	.20	.20
C142	A129	40c dark blue	.20	.20
C143	A129	50c blue green	.20	.20
C144	A129	1b red	.20	.20
C145	A129	2b red orange	.35	.35
C146	A129	3b deep blue	.35	.35
C147	A129	4b vermilion	.45	.45
a.		Souvenir sheet of 4	1.00	1.00
b.		As "a," imperf.	1.00	1.00
C148	A129	5b dark green	.40	.40
a.		Souvenir sheet of 3	1.00	1.00
b.		As "a," imperf.	1.00	1.00
C149	A129	10b red brown	.65	.65
a.		Souvenir sheet of 3	1.00	1.00
b.		As "a," imperf.	1.00	1.00
		Nos. C140-C149 (10)	3.20	3.20
		Nos. 342-351,C140-C149 (20)	13.20	10.35

#C147a-C147b contain #C143-C145, C147; #C148a-C148b contain #C142, C146, C148; #C149a-C149b contain #C140, C141, C149.
For surcharges see Nos. C187-C196.

Athletic Type of Regular Issue

20c, Horsemanship. 30c, Baskethall. 50c, Fencing. 1b, Hurdling. 2.50b, Javelin throwing. 3b, Relay race. 5b, La Paz stadium.

1951, Aug. 23 Unwmk.
Center in Black

No.	Type	Description	Unused	Used
C150	A131	20c purple	.20	.20
C151	A131	30c rose vio	.30	.20
C152	A131	50c dp red org	.50	.20
C153	A131	1b chocolate	.50	.20
C154	A131	2.50b orange	.75	.30
C155	A131	3b black brn	1.00	.75
a.		Souv. sheet, #C153-C155	4.00	3.50
b.		As "a," imperf.	4.00	4.00
C156	A131	5b red	2.00	1.50
a.		Souv. sheet of 4, #C150-C152, C156	4.50	4.00
b.		As "a," imperf.	4.50	4.50
		Nos. C150-C156 (7)	5.25	3.35
		Nos. 352-358,C150-C156 (10)	19.75	17.85

Eduardo Abaroa Type

1952, Mar. 24 Litho. *Perf. 11*

No.	Type	Description	Unused	Used
C157	A133	70c rose red	.20	.20
C158	A133	2b orange yel	.20	.20
C159	A133	3b yellow green	.25	.20
C160	A133	5b blue	.25	.20
C161	A133	50b rose lilac	1.00	.90
C162	A133	100b gray black	1.10	1.10
a.		Perf. 14	10.00	
		Nos. C157-C162 (6)	3.00	2.80

Queen Isabella I Type

1952, July 16 *Perf. 13½*

No.	Type	Description	Unused	Used
C163	A134	50b emerald	.35	.25
C164	A134	100b brown	.65	.35

Exist imperforate.

Columbus Lighthouse Type

1952, July 16

No.	Type	Description	Unused	Used
C165	A135	2b rose lilac, *salmon*	.20	.20
C166	A135	3.70b blue grn, *bl*	.20	.20
C167	A135	4.40b orange, *salmon*	.20	.20
C168	A135	20b dk brn, *cream*	.40	.20
		Nos. C165-C168 (4)	1.00	.80

No. C168 exists imperforate.

Revolution Type and:

Soldiers — AP43

Perf. 13½ (AP43), 11½ (A137)

1953, Apr. 9 Litho.

No.	Type	Description	Unused	Used
C169	A137	3.70b chocolate	.20	.20
C170	AP43	6b red violet	.20	.20
C171	A137	9b brown rose	.20	.20
C172	A137	10b aqua	.20	.20
C173	A137	16b vermilion	.20	.20

C174 AP43 22.50b dk brown .25 .20
C175 A137 40b gray .40 .20
Nos. C169-C175 (7) 1.65 1.40
Nos. C169-C175,378-383 (13) 2.85 2.60

Nos. C169-C170 and C174 exist imperf.

Map and Peasant Type and:

Pres. Victor Paz Estenssoro Embracing Indian — AP45

1954, Aug. 2 ***Perf. 12x11½***

C176 AP45 20b orange brn .20 .20
C177 A138 27b brt pink .20 .20
C178 A138 30b red org .20 .20
C179 A138 45b violet brn .20 .20
C180 AP45 100b blue grn .35 .20
C181 A138 300b yellow grn 1.00 .30
Nos. C176-C181 (6) 2.15 1.30
Nos. C176-C181,384-387 (10) 2.95 2.10

AP45 for 3rd Inter-American Indian Cong. A138 agrarian reform laws of 1953-54.

Nos. C176-C180 exist imperf.

For surcharge see No. C261.

Oil Derricks — AP47

Map of South America and La Paz Arms — AP48

1955, Oct. 9 ***Perf. 10½***

C182 AP47 55b dk & lt grnsh bl .20 .20
C183 AP47 70b dk gray & gray .20 .20
C184 AP47 90b dk & lt grn .20 .20

Perf. 13

C185 AP47 500b red lilac .65 .40
C186 AP47 1000b blk brn & fawn 1.25 1.25
Nos. C182-C186 (5) 2.50 2.25
Nos. C182-C186,388-392 (10) 3.50 3.25

For surcharge see No. C262.

Nos. C140-C149 Surcharged with New Values and Bars in Black or Carmine

1957 **Engr.** ***Perf. 12½***
Center in Black

C187 A129 100b on 3b (C) .20 .20
C188 A129 200b on 2b .20 .20
C189 A129 500b on 4b .20 .20
C190 A129 600b on 1b .20 .20
C191 A129 700b on 20c .25 .20
C192 A129 800b on 40c (C) .35 .20
C193 A130 900b on 30c (C) .40 .20
C194 A129 1800b on 50c (C) .60 .25
C195 A129 3000b on 5b (C) 1.00 .45
C196 A129 5000b on 10b (C) 1.60 .75
Nos. C187-C196 (10) 5.00 2.85

See Nos. 393-402.

Unwmk.
1957, May 25 **Litho.** ***Perf. 12***

C197 AP48 700b lilac & vio .35 .35
C198 AP48 1200b pale brn .40 .35
C199 AP48 1350b rose car .55 .50
C200 AP48 2700b blue grn 1.10 .65
C201 AP48 4000b violet bl 1.40 .75
Nos. C197-C201 (5) 3.80 2.60
Nos. C197-C201,403-407 (10) 5.10 3.60

Exist imperf.

For surcharges see Nos. C263-C265.

Type of Regular Issue, 1957

1957, Dec. 19 ***Perf. 11½***

C202 A141 600b magenta .25 .20
C203 A141 700b violet blue .35 .20
C204 A141 900b pale green .50 .20
Nos. C202-C204 (3) 1.10 .60

Type of Regular Issue, 1960

1960, Jan. 30

C205 A142 400b rose claret .50 .30
C206 A142 800b slate blue .65 .40
C207 A142 2000b slate 1.00 .60
Nos. C205-C207 (3) 2.15 1.30

Gate of the Sun, Tiahuanacu AP49

Uprooted Oak Emblem AP50

1960, Mar. 26 **Litho.** ***Perf. 11½***

C208 AP49 3000b gray 2.00 1.10
C209 AP49 5000b orange 3.00 1.10
C210 AP49 10,000b rose cl 4.75 2.75
C211 AP49 15,000b blue violet 7.00 4.50
Nos. C208-C211 (4) 16.75 9.45
Nos. C208-C211,414-417 (8) 23.90 12.95

1960, Apr. 7 ***Perf. 11½***

C212 AP50 600b ultra .35 .35
C213 AP50 700b lt red brn .35 .35
C214 AP50 900b dk bl grn .35 .35
C215 AP50 1800b violet .60 .60
C216 AP50 2000b gray .65 .60
Nos. C212-C216 (5) 2.30 2.25
Nos. C212-C216,418-422 (10) 4.40 4.35

WRY, July 1, 1959-June 30, 1960.

No. C215 exists with "1961" overprint in dark carmine, but was not regularly issued in this form.

Jaime Laredo Type

Laredo facing left, Bolivia in color.

Perf. 11½
1960, Aug. 15 **Unwmk.** **Litho.**

C217 A145 600b rose vio .75 .45
C218 A145 700b ol gray .75 .25
C219 A145 800b vio brn .75 .25
C220 A145 900b dk bl 1.00 .25
C221 A145 1800b green 1.50 1.50
C222 A145 4000b dk gray 3.00 1.00
Nos. C217-C222 (6) 7.75 3.70

Issued to honor the violinist Jaime Laredo.

For surcharges see Nos. C266-C267.

Children's Hospital Type of 1960

1960, Nov. 21 ***Perf. 11½***

C223 A146 600b multi .40 .25
C224 A146 1000b multi .60 .25
C225 A146 1800b multi 1.00 1.00
C226 A146 5000b multi 3.00 1.25
Nos. C223-C226 (4) 5.00 2.75

For surcharges see No. C268-C269.

Pres. Paz Estenssoro and Pres. Getulio Vargas of Brazil AP52

1960, Dec. 14 **Litho.** ***Perf. 11½***

C227 AP52 1200b on 10b org & blk .70 .70

Exists with surcharge inverted.

No. C227 without surcharge was not regularly issued, although a decree authorizing its circulation was published. Value, $2.

Postally-used counterfeits of surcharge exist.

Pres. Paz Estenssoro and Pres. Frondizi of Argentina AP53

4000b, Flags of Bolivia and Argentina.

1961, May 23 ***Perf. 10½***

C228 AP53 4000b brn, red, yel, grn & bl .75 .75
C229 AP53 6000b dk grn & blk 1.50 1.50

Visit of the President of Argentina, Dr. Arturo Frondizi, to Bolivia.

For surcharge see No. C309.

Miguel de Cervantes — AP54

1961, Oct. **Photo.** ***Perf. 13***

C230 AP54 1400b pale grn & dk ol grn .60 .25

Cervantes' appointment as Chief Magistrate of La Paz. See No. 451.

Virgin of Cotoca and Symbol of Eucharist AP55

Planes and Parachutes AP56

1962, Mar. 19 **Litho.** ***Perf. 10½***

C231 AP55 1400b brn, pink & yel .65 .35

4th Natl. Eucharistic Cong., Santa Cruz, 1961.

Nos. C212-C216 Surcharged Vertically with New Value and Greek Key Border

1962, June **Unwmk.** ***Perf. 11½***

C232 AP50 1200b on 600b .55 .55
C233 AP50 1300b on 700b .50 .50
C234 AP50 1400b on 900b .55 .55
C235 AP50 2800b on 1,800b .90 .75
C236 AP50 3000b on 2,000b .90 .75
Nos. C232-C236 (5) 3.40 3.10

The overprinted segment of Greek key border on Nos. C232-C236 comes in two positions: two full "keys" on top, and one full and two half keys on top.

Flower Type of 1962

Flowers: 100b, 1800b, Cantua buxifolia. 800b, 10,000b, Cantua bicolor.

1962, June 28 **Litho.** ***Perf. 10½***
Flowers in Natural Colors

C237 A152 100b dk bl .25 .20
C238 A152 800b green .50 .20
C239 A152 1800b violet 1.00 .50
a. Souvenir sheet of 3 7.50 6.00
C240 A152 10,000b dk bl 3.25 1.75
Nos. C237-C240 (4) 5.00 2.65

No. C239a contains 3 imperf. stamps similar to Nos. C237-C239, but with the 1,800b background color changed to dark violet blue.

For surcharges see Nos. C270-C271.

1962, Sept. 5 **Litho.** ***Perf. 11½***

1200b, 5000b, Plane and oxcart. 2000b, Aerial photography (plane over South America).

Emblem in Red, Yellow & Green

C241 AP56 600b blk & bl .25 .20
C242 AP56 1200b multi .50 .20
C243 AP56 2000b multi .75 .35
C244 AP56 5000b multi 1.50 .65
Nos. C241-C244 (4) 3.00 1.40

Armed Forces of Bolivia.

Malaria Type of 1962

Design: Inscription around mosquito, laurel around globe.

1962, Oct. 4

C245 A154 2000b ind, grn & yel .80 .50

Type of Regular Issue, 1961

Design: Pedro de la Gasca (1485-1567).

1962 Unwmk. Photo. ***Perf. 13x12½***

C246 A150 1200b brn, *yel* .35 .20

Condor, Soccer Ball and Flags — AP57

Alliance for Progress Emblem — AP58

1.80b, Map of Bolivia, soccer ball, goal and flags.

1963, Mar. 21 **Litho.** ***Perf. 11½***

C247 AP57 1.40b multi 1.00 .65
C248 AP57 1.80b multi 1.00 1.00

21st South American Soccer Championships.

Freedom from Hunger Type

Design: Wheat, globe and wheat emblem.

1963, Aug. 1 **Unwmk.** ***Perf. 11½***

C249 A156 1.20b dk grn, bl & yel .75 .75

1963, Nov. 15 ***Perf. 11½***

C250 AP58 1.20b dl yel, ultra & grn .80 .75

2nd anniv. of the Alliance for Progress, which aims to stimulate economic growth and raise living standards in Latin America.

Type of Regular Issue, 1963

1.20b, Ballot box and voters. 1.40b, Map and farmer breaking chain. 2.80b, Miners.

1963, Dec. 21 ***Perf. 11½***

C251 A157 1.20b gray, dk brn & rose .40 .20
C252 A157 1.40b bister & grn .50 .25
C253 A157 2.80b slate & buff 1.00 .90
Nos. C251-C253 (3) 1.90 1.35

Andrés Santa Cruz — AP59

Perf. 13½
1966, Aug. 10 **Wmk. 90** **Litho.**

C254 AP59 20c dp bl .20 .20
C255 AP59 60c dp grn .20 .20
C256 AP59 1.20b red brn .50 .50
C257 AP59 2.80b black .80 .80
Nos. C254-C257 (4) 1.70 1.70

Cent. (in 1965) of the death of Marshal Andrés Santa Cruz (1792-1865), pres. of Bolivia and of Peru-Bolivia Confederation.

Children Type of 1966

Design: 1.40b, Mother and children.

1966, Dec. 16 **Unwmk.** ***Perf. 13½***

C258 A159 1.40b gray bl & blk 1.00 .40

Co-Presidents Type of Regular Issue

1966, Dec. 16 Litho. *Perf. 12½*
Flag in Red, Yellow and Green

C259 A160 2.80b gray & tan 1.40 1.00
C260 A160 10b sep & tan 1.60 .50
a. Souvenir sheet of 4 6.50 6.50

No. C260a contains 4 imperf. stamps similar to Nos. 480-481 and C259-C260. Dark green marginal inscription. Size: 135x82mm.

Various Issues 1954-62 Surcharged with New Values and Bars

1966, Dec. 21

On No. C177: "XII Aniversario / Reforma / Agraria"

C261 A138 10c on 27b .20 .20
a. Agraria/Agraria 10.00

On No. C182: "XXV / Aniversario Paz / del Chaco"

C262 AP47 10c on 55b .20 .20

On No. C199: "Centenario de / Tupiza"

C263 AP48 60c on 1350b .50 .20

On No. C200: "XXV / Aniversario / Automovil Club / Boliviano"

C264 AP48 2.80b on 2700b 2.00 1.60

On No. C201: "Centenario de la / Cruz Roja / Internacional"

C265 AP48 4b on 4000b 1.40 1.00

On No. C219: "CL Aniversario / Heroinas Coronilla"

C266 A145 1.20b on 800b .75 .50

On No. C222: "Centenario Himno / Paceño"

C267 A145 1.40b on 4,000b .75 .50

Nos. C224-C225 Surcharged

C268 A146 1.40b on 1,000b .60 .60
C269 A146 1.40b on 1,800b .60 .60

On Nos. C238-C239: "Aniversario / Centro Filatelico / Cochabamba"

C270 A152 1.20b on 800b 1.00 .25
C271 A152 1.20b on 1,800b 1.00 .25

Revenue Stamp of 1946 Surcharged with New Value "X" and: "XXV Aniversario / Dpto. Pando / Aéreo"

C272 A161 1.20b on 1b dk bl .50 .25
Nos. C261-C272 (12) 9.50 6.15

Lions Emblem and Pre-historic Sculptures AP60

1967, Sept. 20 Litho. *Perf. 13x13½*

C273 AP60 2b red & multi .80 .65
a. Souvenir sheet of 2 3.75 3.75

50th anniv. of Lions Intl. No. C273a contains 2 imperf. stamps similar to Nos. 492 and C273.

Folklore Type of Regular Issue

Folklore characters: 1.20p, Pujllay. 1.40p, Ujusiris. 2p, Morenada. 3p, Auki-aukis.

1968, June 24 *Perf. 13½x13*

C274 A163 1.20b lt yel grn & multi .35 .20
C275 A163 1.40b gray & multi .40 .20
C276 A163 2b dk ol bis & multi .75 .25
C277 A163 3b sky bl & multi 1.00 .25
Nos. C274-C277 (4) 2.50 .90

A souvenir sheet exists containing 4 imperf. stamps similar to Nos. C274-C277. Size: 131x81½mm.

Moto Mendez — AP61

1968, Oct. 29 Litho. *Perf. 13½x13*

C278 AP61 1b multi .35 .20
C279 AP61 1.20b multi .40 .35
C280 AP61 2b multi .75 .50
C281 AP61 4b multi 1.00 .75
Nos. C278-C281 (4) 2.50 1.80

Battle of Tablada sesquicentennial.

Pres. Gualberto Villaroel AP62

1968, Nov. 6 *Perf. 13x13½*

C282 AP62 1.40b org & blk .30 .25
C283 AP62 3b lt bl & blk .55 .30
C284 AP62 4b rose & blk .70 .40
C285 AP62 5b gray grn & blk .85 .55
C286 AP62 10b pale pur & blk 1.60 1.10
Nos. C282-C286 (5) 4.00 2.60

4th centenary of Cochabamba.

ITU Type of Regular Issue

1968, Dec. 3 Litho. *Perf. 13x13½*

C287 A166 1.20b gray, blk & yel .60 .30
C288 A166 1.40b bl, blk & gray ol .60 .20

UNESCO Emblem — AP63

1968, Nov. 14 *Perf. 13½x13*

C289 AP63 1.20b pale vio & blk .35 .35
C290 AP63 2.80b yel grn & blk .65 .65

20th anniv. (in 1966) of UNESCO.

Kennedy Type of Regular Issue

1968, Nov. 22 Unwmk.

C291 A168 1b grn & blk .25 .20
C292 A168 10b scar & blk 2.75 2.75

A souvenir sheet contains one imperf. stamp similar to No. C291. Dark violet marginal inscription. Size: 131x81½mm.

Tennis Type of Regular Issue

1968, Dec. 10 *Perf. 13x13½*

C293 A169 1.40b org, blk & lt brn .35 .35
C294 A169 2.80b sky bl, blk & lt brn .65 .65

A souvenir sheet exists containing one imperf. stamp similar to No. C293. Size: 131x81½mm.

Stamp Centenary Type

Design: 1.40b, 2.80b, 3b, Bolivia No. 1.

1968, Dec. 23 Litho. *Perf. 13x13½*

C295 A170 1.40b org, grn & blk .50 .50
C296 A170 2.80b pale rose, grn & blk 1.00 1.00
C297 A170 3b lt vio, grn & blk 1.00 1.00
Nos. C295-C297 (3) 2.50 2.50

A souvenir sheet exists containing 3 imperf. stamps similar to Nos. C295-C297. Size: 131x81½mm.

Franklin D. Roosevelt — AP64

1969, Oct. 29 Litho. *Perf. 13½x13*

C298 AP64 5b brn, blk & buff 1.75 1.10

Olympic Type of Regular Issue

Sports: 1.20b, Woman runner, vert. 2.80b, Discus thrower, vert. 5b, Hurdler.

Perf. 13½x13, 13x13½

1969, Oct. 29 Litho.

C299 A171 1.20b yel grn, bis & blk .50 .40
C300 A171 2.80b red, org & blk 1.00 .75
C301 A171 5b bl, lt bl, red & blk 1.50 1.50
Nos. C299-C301 (3) 3.00 2.65

A souvenir sheet exists containing 3 imperf. stamps similar to Nos. C299-C301. Size: 130½x81mm.

Butterfly Type of Regular Issue

1b, Metamorpha dido wernichei. 1.80b, Heliconius felix. 2.80b, Morpho casica. 3b, Papilio yuracares. 4b, Heliconius melitus.

1970, Apr. 24 Litho. *Perf. 13x13½*

C302 A172 1b sal & multi 1.40 1.40
C303 A172 1.80b lt bl & multi 2.00 2.00
C304 A172 2.80b multi 3.25 3.25
C305 A172 3b multi 3.25 3.25
C306 A172 4b multi 4.00 4.00
Nos. C302-C306 (5) 13.90 13.90

A souvenir sheet exists containing 3 imperf. stamps similar to Nos. C302-C304. Black marginal inscription. Size: 129½x80mm.

Scout Type of Regular Issue

Designs: 50c, Boy Scout building brick wall. 1.20b, Bolivian Boy Scout emblem.

1970, June 17 Litho. *Perf. 13½x13*

C307 A173 50c yel & multi .20 .20
C308 A173 1.20b multi .40 .40

No. C228 Surcharged

1970, Dec. Litho. *Perf. 10½*

C309 AP53 1.20b on 4000b multi .25 .20

Flower Type of Regular Issue

Bolivian Flowers: 1.20b, Amaryllis pseudopardina, horiz. 1.40b, Rebutia kruegeri. 2.80b, Lobivia pentlandii, horiz. 4b, Rebutia tunariensis.

Perf. 13x13½, 13½x13

1971, Aug. 9 Litho. Unwmk.

C310 A174 1.20b multi .70 .40
C311 A174 1.40b multi .80 .50
C312 A174 2.80b multi 1.50 .75
C313 A174 4b multi 2.00 1.25
Nos. C310-C313 (4) 5.00 2.90

Two souvenir sheets of 4 exist. One contains imperf. stamps similar to Nos. 534-535 and C310, C312. The other contains imperf. stamps similar to Nos. 536-537, C311, C313. Size: 130x80mm.

Folk Dance Type of Regular Issue

1972, Mar. 23 Litho. *Perf. 13½x13*

C314 A177 1.20b Kusillo .50 .20
C315 A177 1.40b Taquirari .65 .20

Two souvenir sheets of 3 exist. One contains imperf. stamps similar to Nos. 542-543, C314. The other contains imperf. stamps similar to Nos. 540-541, C315. Size: 80x129mm.

Painting Type of Regular Issue

Bolivian Paintings: 1.40b, Portrait of Chola Paceña, by Cecilio Guzman de Rojas. 1.50b, Adoration of the Kings, by G. Gamarra. 1.60b, Adoration of Pachamama (mountain), by A. Borda. 2b, The Kiss of the Idol, by Guzman de Rojas.

1972 Litho. *Perf. 13½*

C316 A178 1.40b multi .40 .20
C317 A178 1.50b multi .40 .20
C318 A178 1.60b multi .40 .20
C319 A178 2b multi .55 .20
Nos. C316-C319 (4) 1.75 .80

Two souvenir sheets of 2 exist. One contains imperf. stamps similar to Nos. 548 and C318. The other contains imperf. stamps similar to Nos. C317 and C319. Size: 129x80mm.
Issued: 1.40b, Dec. 4; others, Aug. 17.

Bolivian Coat of Arms AP65

1972, Dec. 4 *Perf. 13½x14*

C320 AP65 4b lt bl & multi 1.40 .50

Cactus Type of Regular Issue

Designs: Various cacti.

1973, Aug. 6 Litho. *Perf. 13½*

C321 A180 1.20b tan & multi .35 .20
C322 A180 1.90b org & multi .50 .20
C323 A180 2b multi .65 .25
Nos. C321-C323 (3) 1.50 .65

Development Type of Regular Issue

1.40b, Highway 1Y4. 2b, Rail car on bridge.

1973, Nov. 26 Litho. *Perf. 13½*

C324 A181 1.40b salmon & multi .40 .20
C325 A181 2b multi .60 .20

Santos-Dumont and 14-Bis Plane — AP66

1973, July 20

C326 AP66 1.40b yel & blk .65 .35

Alberto Santos-Dumont (1873-1932), Brazilian aviation pioneer.

Orchid Type of 1974

Orchids: 2.50b, Cattleya luteola, horiz. 3.80b, Stanhopaea. 4b, Catasetum, horiz. 5b, Maxillaria.

1974 Litho. *Perf. 13½*

C327 A182 2.50b multi 1.00 .25
C328 A182 3.80b rose & multi 1.50 .45
C329 A182 4b multi 1.50 .40
C330 A182 5b sal & multi 2.50 .45
Nos. C327-C330 (4) 6.50 1.55

Air Force Emblem, Plane over Map of Bolivia AP67

Designs: 3.80b, Plane over Andes. 4.50b, Triple decker and jet. 8b, Rafael Pabon and double decker. 15b, Jet and "50."

1974 Litho. *Perf. 13x13½*

C331 AP67 3b multi .65 .25
C332 AP67 3.80b multi 1.00 .25
C333 AP67 4.50b multi 1.00 .25
C334 AP67 8b multi 1.60 .40
C335 AP67 15b multi 3.50 .50
Nos. C331-C335 (5) 7.75 1.65

Bolivian Air Force, 50th anniv. Exist imperf.
For surcharge see No. 968.

Coat of Arms Type of 1975

Designs: Departmental coats of arms.

1975, July 16 Litho. *Perf. 13½*

C336 A188 20c Beni .20 .20
C337 A188 30c Tarija .20 .20
C338 A188 50c Potosi .25 .25
C339 A188 1b Oruro .50 .50
C340 A188 2.50b Santa Cruz 1.00 1.00
C341 A188 3b La Paz 1.00 1.00
Nos. C336-C341 (6) 3.15 3.15

LAB Emblem — AP68

Bolivia on Map of Americas AP69

Map of Bolivia, Plane and Kyllmann AP70

1975 Litho. *Perf. 13½*

C342 AP68 1b gold, bl & blk .40 .40
C343 AP69 1.50b multi .60 .60
C344 AP70 2b multi .75 .75
Nos. C342-C344 (3) 1.75 1.75

Lloyd Aereo Boliviano, 50th anniversary, founded by Guillermo Kyllmann.

Bolivar, Presidents Perez and Banzer, and Flags — AP71

1975, Aug. 4 Litho. *Perf. 13½*

C345 AP71 3b gold & multi .75 .65

Visit of Pres. Carlos A. Perez of Venezuela.

Bolivar Type of 1975

Presidents and Statesmen of Bolivia: 50c, Rene Barrientes O. 2b, Francisco B. O'Connor. 3.80b, Gualberto Villarroel. 4.20b, German Busch. 4.50b, Hugo Banzer Suarez. 20b, José Ballivian. 30b, Andres de Santa Cruz. 40b, Antonio Jose de Sucre.

1975 Litho. *Perf. 13½*

Size: 24x33mm

C346 A189 50c multi .25 .25
C347 A189 2b multi .50 .50
C348 A189 3.80b multi .75 .75
C349 A189 4.20b multi 1.00 .75

Size: 28x39mm

C350 A189 4.50b multi 1.00 .50

Size: 24x33mm

C351 A189 20b multi 4.00 2.00
C352 A189 30b multi 5.00 5.00
C353 A189 40b multi 6.50 6.50
Nos. C346-C353 (8) 19.00 16.25

For surcharge see No. 969.

UPU Emblem AP72

1975, Dec. 7 Litho. *Perf. 13½*

C358 AP72 25b blue & multi 3.00 3.00

Cent. of UPU (in 1974).

POSTAGE DUE STAMPS

D1

1931 Unwmk. Engr. *Perf. 14, 14½*

J1 D1 5c ultra 1.10 *1.25*
J2 D1 10c red 1.10 *1.25*
J3 D1 15c yellow 1.75 *2.00*
J4 D1 30c deep green 1.75 *2.00*
J5 D1 40c deep violet 2.75 *3.25*
J6 D1 50c black brown 4.00 *4.50*
Nos. J1-J6 (6) 12.45 *14.25*

Symbol of Youth — D2

Torch of Knowledge D3

Symbol of the Revolution of May 17, 1936 — D4

1938 Litho. *Perf. 11*

J7 D2 5c deep rose .50 .45
a. Pair, imperf. between
J8 D3 10c green .50 .45
J9 D4 30c gray blue .50 .45
Nos. J7-J9 (3) 1.50 1.35

POSTAL TAX STAMPS

Worker — PT1

Imprint: "LITO. UNIDAS LA PAZ."

Perf. 13½x10½, 10½, 13½

1939 Litho. Unwmk.

RA1 PT1 5c dull violet .70 .20
a. Double impression

Redrawn

Imprint: "TALL. OFFSET LA PAZ."

1940 *Perf. 12x11, 11*

RA2 PT1 5c violet .60 .20
a. Horizontal pair, imperf. between 2.00
b. Imperf. horiz., pair

Tax of Nos. RA1-RA2 was for the Workers' Home Building Fund.

Communications Symbols — PT2

Condor, Envelope and Post Horn — PT3

Communication Symbols — PT4

Postman Blowing Horn — PT5

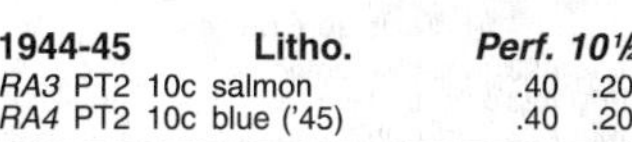

1944-45 Litho. *Perf. 10½*

RA3 PT2 10c salmon .40 .20
RA4 PT2 10c blue ('45) .40 .20

A 30c orange inscribed "Centenario de la Creacion del Departmento del Beni" was issued in 1946 and required to be affixed to all air and surface mail to and from the Department of Beni in addition to regular postage. Five higher denominations in the same scenic design were used for local revenue purposes.

Catalogue values for unused stamps in this section, from this point to the end of the section, are for Never Hinged items.

Type of 1944 Redrawn

1947-48 Unwmk. *Perf. 10½*

RA5 PT2 10c carmine .40 .20
RA6 PT2 10c org yel ('48) .35 .20
RA7 PT2 10c yel brn ('48) .35 .20
RA8 PT2 10c emerald ('48) .35 .20
Nos. RA5-RA8 (4) 1.45 .80

Post horn and envelope reduced in size.

1951-52

RA9 PT3 20c deep orange .40 .20
a. Imperf., pair 20.00
RA10 PT3 20c green ('52) .50 .20
a. Imperf., pair 20.00
RA11 PT3 20c blue ('52) .50 .20
a. Imperf., pair 20.00
Nos. RA9-RA11 (3) 1.40 .60

For surcharges see Nos. RA17-RA18.

1952-54 *Perf. 13½, 10½, 10½x12*

RA12 PT4 50c green .50 .20
RA13 PT4 50c carmine .50 .20
RA14 PT4 3b green .50 .20
RA15 PT4 3b olive bister .50 .50
RA16 PT4 5b violet ('54) .50 .50
Nos. RA12-RA16 (5) 2.50 1.60

For surcharges see Nos. RA21-RA22.

No. RA10 and Type of 1951-52 Surcharged with New Value in Black

1953 *Perf. 10½*

RA17 PT3 50c on 20c green .25 .20
RA18 PT3 50c on 20c red vio .25 .20

1954-55 Unwmk. *Perf. 10½*

RA19 PT5 1b brown .20 .20
RA20 PT5 1b car rose ('55) .20 .20

Exist imperf.

Nos. RA15 and RA14 Surcharged in Black "Bs. 5.-/D. S./21-IV-55"

1955 *Perf. 10½, 10½x12*

RA21 PT4 5b on 3b olive bister .25 .20
RA22 PT4 5b on 3b green .25 .20

Tax of Nos. RA3-RA22 was for the Communications Employees Fund.

No. RA21 is known with surcharge in thin type of different font and with comma added after "55."

Plane over Airport — PT6

Planes — PT7

Perf. 10½, 12, 13½

1955 Unwmk. Litho.

RA23 PT6 5b dp ultra .25 .20
a. Vertical pair imperf. between

Perf. 11½

RA24 PT7 10b light green .20 .20

PT8

PT9

1955 Litho. *Perf. 10½*

RA25 PT8 5b red 7.50 7.50
a. Imperf., pair 35.00

Perf. 12

RA26 PT9 20b dark brown .25 .20

Tax of Nos. RA23-RA26 was for the building of new airports.

General Alfredo Ovando and Three Men — PT10

1970, Sept. 26 Litho. *Perf. 13x13½*

RA27 PT10 20c black & red .50 .20

See No. RAC1.

Pres. German Busch PT11

1971, May 13 Litho. *Perf. 13x13½*

RA28 PT11 20c lilac & black .50 .20

AIR POST POSTAL TAX STAMPS

Catalogue values for unused stamps in this section are for Never Hinged items.

Type of Postal Tax Issue

Design: 30c, General Ovando and oil well.

1970, Sept. 26 Litho. *Perf. 13x13½*

RAC1 PT10 30c blk & grn .50 .20

Pres. Gualberto Villarroel, Refinery PTAP1

1971, May 25 Litho. *Perf. 13x13½*

RAC2 PTAP1 30c lt bl & blk .50 .20

Type of 1971 Inscribed: "XXV ANIVERSARIO DE SU GOBIERNO"

1975 Litho. *Perf. 13x13½*

RAC3 PTAP1 30c lt bl & blk 3.00 3.00

BOSNIA AND HERZEGOVINA

'bäz-nē-ə and ˌhert-sə-gō-'vē-nə

LOCATION — Dalmatia and Serbia
GOVT. — Provinces of Turkey under Austro-Hungarian occupation, 1879-1908; provinces of Austria-Hungary 1908-1918
AREA — 19,768 sq. mi.
POP. — 2,000,000 (approx. 1918)
CAPITAL — Sarajevo

Following World War I Bosnia and Herzegovina united with the kingdoms of Montenegro and Serbia, and Croatia, Dalmatia and Slovenia, to form the Kingdom of Yugoslavia (See Yugoslavia.)

100 Novcica (Neukreuzer) = 1 Florin (Gulden)

100 Heller = 1 Krone (1900)

Watermark

Wmk. 91- BRIEF-MARKEN or (from 1890) ZEITUNGS-MARKEN in Double-lined Capitals, Across the Sheet

Coat of Arms — A1

Type I - The heraldic eaglets on the right side of the escutcheon are entirely blank. The eye of the lion is indicated by a very small dot, which sometimes fails to print.

Type II - There is a colored line across the lowest eaglet. A similar line sometimes appears on the middle eaglet. The eye of the lion is formed by a large dot which touches the outline of the head above it.

Type III - The eaglets and eye of the lion are similar to type I. Each tail feather of the large eagle has two lines of shading and the lowest feather does not touch the curved line below it. In types I and II there are several shading lines in these feathers, and the lowest feather touches the curved line.

Varieties of the Numerals

2 NOVCICA:
A - The "2" has curved tail. All are type I.
B - The "2" has straight tail. All are type II.

15 NOVCICA:
C - The serif of the "1" is short and forms a wide angle with the vertical stroke.
D - The serif of the "1" forms an acute angle with the vertical stroke.

The numerals of the 5n were retouched several times and show minor differences, especially in the flag.

Other Varieties

½ NOVCICA:
There is a black dot between the curved ends of the ornaments near the lower spandrels.
G - This dot touches the curve at its right. Stamps of this (1st) printing are litho.
H - This dot stands clear of the curved lines. Stamps of this (2nd) printing are typo.

10 NOVCICA:
Ten stamps in each sheet of type II show a small cross in the upper section of the right side of the escutcheon.

Perf. 9 to 13½ and Compound

1879-94 Litho. Wmk. 91

Type I

No.	Type	Description	Unused	Used
1	A1	½n blk (type II) ('94)	6.00	17.50
2	A1	1n gray	10.00	1.60
c.		1n gray lilac		1.60
4	A1	2n yellow	12.50	.90
5	A1	3n green	15.00	1.75
6	A1	5n rose red	21.00	.40
7	A1	10n blue	85.00	.85
8	A1	15n brown	85.00	5.50
9	A1	20n gray green ('93)	340.00	8.00
10	A1	25n violet	75.00	6.25
		Nos. 1-10 (9)	649.50	42.75

No. 2c was never issued. It is usually canceled by blue pencil marks and "mint" copies generally have been cleaned.

Perf. 10½ to 13 and Compound

1894-98 Typo.

Type II

No.	Type	Description	Unused	Used
1a	A1	½n black	10.00	15.00
2a	A1	1n gray	3.75	1.00
4a	A1	2n yellow	2.75	.50
5a	A1	3n green	3.75	1.10
6a	A1	5n rose red	72.50	.35
7a	A1	10n blue	5.00	.70
8a	A1	15n brown	4.25	3.25
9a	A1	20n gray green	5.50	3.50
10a	A1	25n violet	6.25	5.75
		Nos. 1a-10a (9)	113.75	31.15

Type III

No.	Type	Description	Unused	Used
6b	A1	5n rose red ('98)	3.00	.45

All the preceding stamps exist in various shades.

Nos. 1a to 10a were reprinted in 1911 in lighter colors, on very white paper and perf. 12½. Value, set $25.

A2

A3

Perf. 10½, 12½ and Compound

1900 Typo.

No.	Type	Description	Unused	Used
11	A2	1h gray black	.20	.20
12	A2	2h gray	.20	.20
13	A2	3h yellow	.20	.20
14	A2	5h green	.20	.20
15	A2	6h brown	.25	.20
16	A2	10h red	.20	.20
17	A2	20h rose	80.00	5.50
18	A2	25h blue	.75	.30
19	A2	30h bister brown	85.00	6.50
20	A2	40h orange	110.00	10.00
21	A2	50h red lilac	.50	.35
22	A3	1k dark rose	.60	.50
23	A3	2k ultra	1.00	1.00
24	A3	5k dull blue grn	2.25	4.00
		Nos. 11-24 (14)	281.35	29.35

All values of this issue except the 3h exist on ribbed paper.

Nos. 17, 19 and 20 were reprinted in 1911. The reprints are in lighter colors and on whiter paper than the originals. Reprints of Nos. 17 and 19 are perf. 10½ and those of No. 20 are perf. 12½. Value each $1.50.

Numerals in Black

1901-04 *Perf. 12½*

No.	Type	Description	Unused	Used
25	A2	20h pink ('02)	.50	.40
26	A2	30h bister brn ('03)	.50	.40
27	A2	35h blue	.80	.50
a.		35h ultramarine	110.00	5.50
28	A2	40h orange ('03)	.80	.70
29	A2	45h grnsh blue ('04)	.70	.55
		Nos. 25-29 (5)	3.30	2.55

Nos. 11-16, 18, 21-29 exist imperf. Most of Nos. 11-29 exist perf. 6½; compound with 12½; part perf.; in pairs imperf. between. These were supplied only to some high-ranking officials and never sold at any P.O.

View of Deboj A4

The Carsija at Sarajevo — A5

Designs: 2h, View of Mostar. 3h, Pliva Gate, Jajce. 5h, Narenta Pass and Prenj River. 6h, Rama Valley. 10h, Vrbas Valley. 20h, Old Bridge, Mostar. 25h, Bey's Mosque, Sarajevo. 30h, Donkey post. 35h, Jezero and tourists' pavilion. 40h, Mail wagon. 45h, Bazaar at Sarajevo. 50h, Postal car. 2k, St. Luke's Campanile, Jajce. 5k, Emperor Franz Josef.

Perf. 6½, 9½, 10½ and 12½, also Compounds

1906 Engr. Unwmk.

No.	Type	Description	Unused	Used
30	A4	1h black	.20	.20
31	A4	2h violet	.20	.20
32	A4	3h olive	.20	.20
33	A4	5h dark green	.30	.20
34	A4	6h brown	.20	.20
a.		Perf. 13½	13.50	19.00
35	A4	10h carmine	.30	.20
36	A4	20h dark brown	.50	.20
a.		Perf. 13½	40.00	55.00
37	A4	25h deep blue	1.10	.75
38	A4	30h green	1.25	.30
39	A4	35h myrtle green	1.25	.30
40	A4	40h orange red	1.25	.30
41	A4	45h brown red	1.25	.90
42	A4	50h dull violet	1.50	.65
43	A5	1k maroon	4.00	1.75
44	A5	2k gray green	5.25	7.00
45	A5	5k dull blue	4.25	6.00
		Nos. 30-45 (16)	23.00	19.35

Nos. 30-45 exist imperf. Value, set $50 unused, $37.50 canceled.

For overprint and surcharges see #126, B1-B4.

Birthday Jubilee Issue

Designs of 1906 Issue, with "1830-1910" in Label at Bottom

1910 *Perf. 12½*

No.	Type	Description	Unused	Used
46	A4	1h black	.30	.25
47	A4	2h violet	.40	.25
48	A4	3h olive	.40	.25
49	A4	5h dark green	.45	.20
50	A4	6h orange brn	.45	.30
51	A4	10h carmine	.50	.20
52	A4	20h dark brown	1.25	1.50
53	A4	25h deep blue	2.50	2.50
54	A4	30h green	1.75	2.25
55	A4	35h myrtle grn	2.00	2.25
56	A4	40h orange red	2.00	3.00
57	A4	45h brown red	3.75	5.00
58	A4	50h dull violet	4.25	5.00
59	A5	1k maroon	4.25	5.50
60	A5	2k gray green	17.50	20.00
61	A5	5k dull blue	2.25	4.50
		Nos. 46-61 (16)	44.00	52.95

80th birthday of Emperor Franz Josef.

Scenic Type of 1906

Views: 12h, Jaice. 60h, Konjica. 72h, Vishegrad.

1912

No.	Type	Description	Unused	Used
62	A4	12h ultra	4.00	4.50
63	A4	60h dull blue	2.25	3.50
64	A4	72h carmine	8.75	16.00
		Nos. 62-64 (3)	15.00	24.00

Value, imperf. set, $75.

See Austria for similar designs inscribed "FELDPOST" instead of "MILITARPOST."

Emperor Franz Josef
A23 A24

A25

A26

1912-14

Various Frames

No.	Type	Description	Unused	Used
65	A23	1h olive green	.35	.20
66	A23	2h brt blue	.35	.20
67	A23	3h claret	.35	.20
68	A23	5h green	.35	.20
69	A23	6h dark gray	.35	.20
70	A23	10h rose car	.35	.20
71	A23	12h dp olive grn	.65	.30
72	A23	20h orange brn	2.75	.20
73	A23	25h ultra	1.50	.20
74	A23	30h orange red	1.50	.20
75	A24	35h myrtle grn	1.50	.20
76	A24	40h dk violet	4.50	.20
77	A24	45h olive brn	2.25	.20
78	A24	50h slate blue	2.25	.20
79	A24	60h brown vio	1.50	.20
80	A24	72h dark blue	3.25	3.00
81	A25	1k brn vio, *straw*	8.00	.35
82	A25	2k dk gray, *bl*	7.25	.25
83	A26	3k carmine, *grn*	8.00	9.00
84	A26	5k dk vio, *gray*	14.50	20.00
85	A25	10k dk ultra, *gray* ('14)	87.50	70.00
		Nos. 65-85 (21)	149.00	105.70

Value, imperf. set, $450.

For overprints and surcharges see #127, B5-B8, Austria M1-M21.

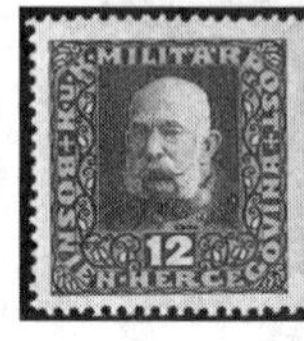

A27

A28

1916-17 *Perf. 12½*

No.	Type	Description	Unused	Used
86	A27	3h dark gray	.20	.20
87	A27	5h olive green	.20	.35
88	A27	6h violet	.20	.35
89	A27	10h bister	1.40	1.60
90	A27	12h blue gray	.20	.45
91	A27	15h car rose	.20	.20
92	A27	20h brown	.25	.45
93	A27	25h blue	.20	.35
94	A27	30h dark green	.20	.35
95	A27	40h vermilion	.20	.35
96	A27	50h green	.20	.35
97	A27	60h lake	.20	.35
98	A27	80h orange brn	1.00	.40
a.		Perf. 11½	2.00	3.75
99	A27	90h dark violet	.70	.50
a.		Perf. 11½	550.00	675.00
101	A28	2k claret, *straw*	.40	.75
102	A28	3k green, *bl*	.75	3.25
103	A28	4k carmine, *grn*	4.50	7.25
104	A28	10k dp vio, *gray*	14.00	20.00
		Nos. 86-104 (18)	25.00	37.50

Value, imperf. set, $175.

For overprints see Nos. B11-B12.

Emperor Karl I
A29 A30

1917 *Perf. 12½*

No.	Type	Description	Unused	Used
105	A29	3h olive gray	.20	.20
a.		Perf. 11½	60.00	100.00
b.		Perf. 12½x11½	13.00	29.00
106	A29	5h olive green	.20	.20
107	A29	6h violet	.30	.55
108	A29	10h orange brn	.20	.20
a.		Perf. 11½x12½	62.50	95.00
b.		Perf. 11½	62.50	
109	A29	12h blue	.50	.75
110	A29	15h brt rose	.20	.20
111	A29	20h red brown	.20	.20
112	A29	25h ultra	1.00	.50
113	A29	30h gray green	.25	.20
114	A29	40h olive bis	.25	.20
115	A29	50h dp green	.85	.50
116	A29	60h car rose	.85	.45
a.		Perf. 11½	15.00	30.00
117	A29	80h steel blue	.25	.25
118	A29	90h dull violet	1.00	1.40
119	A30	2k carmine, *straw*	.50	.45
120	A30	3k green, *bl*	13.00	16.00
121	A30	4k carmine, *grn*	5.25	7.25
122	A30	10k dp violet, *gray*	3.25	5.75
		Nos. 105-122 (18)	28.25	35.25

Value, imperf. set, $85.

Nos. 47 and 66 Overprinted in Red

1918

126 A4 2h violet .45 *.50*
b. Inverted overprint 17.50
d. Double overprint 37.50
f. Double overprint, one inverted
127 A23 2h bright blue .50 *.60*
a. Pair, one without overprint
b. Inverted overprint 15.00
c. Double overprint 15.00
d. Double overprint, one inverted

Emperor Karl I — A31

1918 Typo. *Perf. 12½, Imperf.*

128 A31 2h orange 7.00
129 A31 3h dark green 7.00
130 A31 5h lt green 7.00
131 A31 6h blue green 7.00
132 A31 10h brown 7.00
133 A31 20h brick red 7.00
134 A31 25h ultra 7.00
135 A31 45h dk slate 7.00
136 A31 50h lt bluish grn 7.00
137 A31 60h blue violet 7.00
138 A31 70h ocher 7.00
139 A31 80h rose 7.00
140 A31 90h violet brn 7.00

Engr.

141 A30 1k ol grn, *grnsh* *1,500.*
Nos. 128-140 (13) 91.00

Nos. 128-141 were prepared for use in Bosnia and Herzegovina, but were not issued there. They were sold after the Armistice at the Vienna post office for a few days.

SEMI-POSTAL STAMPS

Nos. 33 and 35 Surcharged in Red

1914 Unwmk. *Perf. 12½*

B1 A4 7h on 5h dk grn .40 .40
B2 A4 12h on 10h car .40 .40

Various minor varieties of the surcharge include "4" with open top, narrow "4" and wide "4."

Nos. B1-B2 exist with double and inverted surcharges. Value about $20 each.

#33, 35 Surcharged in Red or Blue

1915 *Perf. 12½*

B3 A4 7h on 5h (R) 9.50 9.00
a. Perf. 9½ 140.00 140.00
B4 A4 12h on 10h (Bl) .30 .30

Nos. B3-B4 exist with double and inverted surcharges. Value about $18.50 each.

#68, 70 Surcharged in Red or Blue

1915

B5 A23 7h on 5h (R) .80 .75
a. "1915" at top and bottom 30.00 *37.50*
B6 A23 12h on 10h (Bl) 1.40 *1.50*
a. Surcharged "7 Heller." 30.00 *37.50*

Nos. B5-B6 are found in three types differing in length of surcharge lines:
I- date 18mm, denomination 14mm.
II- date 16mm, denomination 14mm.
III- date 18mm, denomination 16mm.
Nos. B5-B6 exist with double and inverted surcharges. Value $25 each.
Nos. B5a and B6a exist double and inverted.

#68, 70 Surcharged in Red or Blue

1916

B7 A23 7h on 5h (R) .50 *.65*
B8 A23 12h on 10h (Bl) .50 *.65*

Nos. B7-B8 exist with double and inverted surcharges. Value $12.50 each.

Wounded Soldier — SP1

Blind Soldier — SP2

1916 Engr.

B9 SP1 5h (+ 2h) green .65 .65
B10 SP2 10h (+ 2h) magenta 1.00 1.00

Nos. B9-B10 exist imperf. Value, set $27.50.

Nos. 89, 91 Overprinted

1917

B11 A27 10h bister .20 .20
B12 A27 15h carmine rose .20 .20

Nos. B11-B12 exist imperf. Value set, $16.
Nos. B11-B12 exist with double and inverted overprint. Value $9 each.

Design for Memorial Church at Sarajevo SP3

Archduke Francis Ferdinand — SP4

Duchess Sophia and Archduke Francis Ferdinand SP5

1917 Typo. *Perf. 11½, 12½*

B13 SP3 10h violet black .20 .20
B14 SP4 15h claret .20 .20
B15 SP5 40h deep blue .20 .20
Nos. B13-B15 (3) .60 .60

Assassination of Archduke Ferdinand and Archduchess Sophia. Sold at a premium of 2h each which helped build a memorial church at Sarajevo.
Exist imperf. Value, set $2.50.

Blind Soldier — SP6

Emperor Karl I — SP8

Design: 15h, Wounded soldier.

1918 Engr. *Perf. 12½*

B16 SP6 10h (+ 10h) grnsh bl .60 .60
B17 SP6 15h (+ 10h) red brn .60 .60

#B16-B17 exist imperf. Value, set $18.50.

1918 Typo. *Perf. 12½x13*

Design: 15h, Empress Zita.

B18 SP8 10h gray green .35 *.60*
B19 SP8 15h brown red .35 *.60*
B20 SP8 40h violet .35 *.60*
Nos. B18-B20 (3) 1.05 *1.80*

Sold at a premium of 10h each which went to the "Karl's Fund."
#B18-B20 exist imperf. Value, set $22.50.

POSTAGE DUE STAMPS

D1

D2

Perf. 9½, 10½, 12½ and Compound

1904 Unwmk.

J1 D1 1h black, red & yel .45 .20
J2 D1 2h black, red & yel .45 .20
J3 D1 3h black, red & yel .50 .20
J4 D1 4h black, red & yel .50 .20
J5 D1 5h black, red & yel .50 .20
J6 D1 6h black, red & yel .20 .20
J7 D1 7h black, red & yel 2.75 2.50
J8 D1 8h black, red & yel 2.75 .50
J9 D1 10h black, red & yel .65 .20
J10 D1 15h black, red & yel .60 .20
J11 D1 20h black, red & yel 3.25 .20
J12 D1 50h black, red & yel 2.25 .20
J13 D1 200h black, red & grn 9.25 .70
Nos. J1-J13 (13) 24.10 5.70

Value, imperf. set, $150.
For overprints see Western Ukraine Nos. 61-72.

1916-18 *Perf. 12½*

J14 D2 2h red ('18) .30 *.30*
J15 D2 4h red ('18) .20 *.20*
J16 D2 5h red .30 *.30*
J17 D2 6h red ('18) .20 *.20*
J18 D2 10h red .30 *.30*
J19 D2 15h red 2.25 *2.25*
J20 D2 20h red .30 *.30*
J21 D2 25h red .90 *.90*
J22 D2 30h red .75 *.75*
J23 D2 40h red 6.25 *6.25*
J24 D2 50h red 20.00 *20.00*
J25 D2 1k dark blue 2.75 *2.75*
J26 D2 3k dark blue 11.50 *11.50*
Nos. J14-J26 (13) 46.00 *46.00*

Nos. J25-J26 have colored numerals on a white tablet.
Value, imperf. set, $110.
For surcharges see Italy Nos. NJ1-NJ7.

NEWSPAPER STAMPS

Bosnian Girl — N1

1913 Unwmk. *Imperf.*

P1 N1 2h ultra .40 .40
P2 N1 6h violet 1.75 1.50
P3 N1 10h rose 1.75 1.50
P4 N1 20h green 2.10 1.90
Nos. P1-P4 (4) 6.00 5.30

After Bosnia and Herzegovina became part of Yugoslavia stamps of type N1 perf., and imperf. copies surcharged with new values, were used as regular postage stamps. See Yugoslavia Nos. 1L21-1L22, 1L43-1L45.

SPECIAL HANDLING STAMPS

"Lightning" — SH1

1916 Unwmk. Engr. *Perf. 12½*

QE1 SH1 2h vermilion .20 .20
a. Perf. 11½x12½ 250.00 250.00
QE2 SH1 5h deep green .35 .35
a. Perf. 11½ 13.00 13.00

For surcharges see Italy Nos. NE1-NE2.

BOSNIA AND HERZEGOVINA

'bäz-nē-ə and ˌhert-sə-gō-'vē-nə

LOCATION — Between Croatia and Yugoslavia.
GOVT. — Republic
CAPITAL — Sarajevo

Formerly part of Yugoslavia. Proclamation of independence in 1992 was followed by protracted civil war that was ended by the Dayton Peace Agreement of Nov. 21, 1995.

While Dinars were the official currency until 6/22/98, a currency pegged to the German mark was in use for some time prior to that. Stamps are denominated in pfennigs and marks in 11/97.

100 Paras = 1 Dinar
100 Pfennig = 1 Mark (6/22/98)

Catalogue values for all unused stamps in this country are for Never Hinged items.

Muslim Government in Sarajevo

Natl. Arms — A50

Denominations: 100d, 500d, 1000d, 5000d, 10,000d, 20,000d, 50,000d.

1993, Oct. 27 Litho. ***Imperf.***
Booklet Stamps

200-206 A50 Set of 7 12.50 12.50

Nos. 200-206 each were available in bklts. of 50 (10 strips of 5).

1984 Winter Olympic Games, Sarajevo, 10th Anniv. — A51

#207, Games emblem. #208a, 100,000d, Four man bobsled. #208b, 200,000d, Hockey.

1994, Feb. 8

207 A51 50,000d org & blk 1.00 1.00

Souvenir Sheet

208 A51 Sheet of 2, #a.-b. 8.25 8.25

No. 208 contains 45x27mm stamps.

Souvenir Sheet

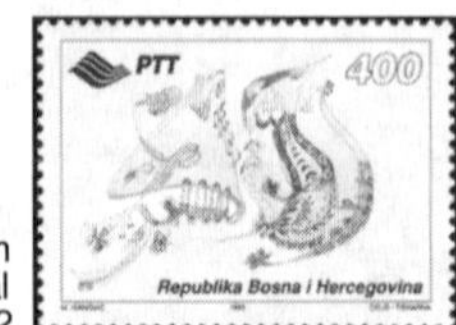

Bairam Festival A52

Various illustrations from Koran: a, 400d. b, 600d.

1995, May 12 ***Perf. 14***

209 A52 Sheet of 2, #a.-b. 10.50 10.50

Main Post Office, Sarajevo A53

Designs: 10d, Facade. 20d, 30d, Demolished interior. 35d, 50d, Pre-civil war exterior. 100d, 200d, Post-war exterior.

1995, June 12

210-216 A53 Set of 7 5.00 5.00
216a Pane of 7 6.00 6.00

No. 216a sold unattached in booklet covers.

Bosnian History A54

Designs: 35d, Historical map, 10th-15th cent. 100d, Tomb, vert. 200d, Arms, Kotromanic Dynasty, vert. 300d, Charter by Ban Kulin, 1189.

1995, Aug. 12 ***Perf. 11½***

217-220 A54 Set of 4 7.50 7.50

Peace & Freedom, Europa A55

1995, Sept. 25

221 A55 200d multicolored 2.50 2.50

A56 A57

1995, Sept. 25

222 A56 100d multicolored 1.25 1.25

World Post Day.

1995, Oct. 12

Flowers: No. 223: a, 100d, Simphyandra hofmannii. b, 200d, Lilium bosniacum.

223 A57 Pair, #a.-b. 3.50 3.50

Fish A58

No. 224: a, 100d, Aulopyge hugeli. b, 200d, Paraphoxinus alepidotus.

1995, Oct. 12

224 A58 Pair, #a.-b. 3.50 3.50

Children's Week A59

1995, Oct. 12

225 A59 100d multicolored 1.25 1.25

Electric Tram System, Sarajevo, Cent. A60

1995, Oct. 12

226 A60 200d multicolored 2.50 2.50

Bridges A61

Designs: 20d, Kozija, Sarajevo. 30d, Arslanagica, Trebinje. 35d, Latinska, Sarajevo. 50d, Old Bridge, Mostar. 100d, Visegrad.

1995, Dec. 12

227-231 A61 Set of 5 3.00 3.00

Christmas A62

Designs: 100d, Visiting friends. 200d, Madonna and Child, vert.

1995, Dec. 24

232-233 A62 Set of 2 3.50 3.50

A63 A64

Designs: 30d, Queen Jelena's tomb.

1995, Dec. 31

234 A63 30d multicolored .35 .35

1995, Dec. 31

Design: Husein Gradascevic (1802-33).

235 A64 35d multicolored .35 .35

Mirza Safvet Basagic (1870-1934) — A65

1995, Dec. 31

236 A65 100d multicolored 1.10 1.10

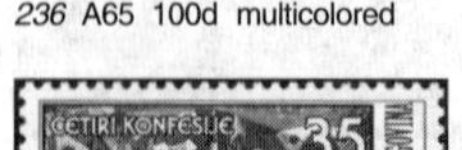

Religious Diversity A66

1995, Dec. 31

237 A66 35d multicolored .50 .50

Destruction of Olympic Stadium, Sarajevo — A67

35d, Stadium, various skaters. 100d, Stadium ablaze, vert.

1995, Dec. 31

238-239 A67 Set of 2 1.60 1.60

Famous Women — A68

Europa: 80d, Bahrija Hadzic (1904-93), opera singer. 120d, Nasiha Hadzic (1932-95), writer.

1996, Apr. 15 ***Perf. 15***

240-241 A68 Set of 2 3.50 3.50

UNICEF, 50th Anniv. — A69

Designs: a, 50d, Child stepping on land mine. b, 150d, Child's handprint.

1996, Apr. 15 ***Perf. 11½***

242 A69 Pair, #a.-b. 3.50 3.50

Bobovac Castle — A70 Bairam Festival — A71

1996, May 5 ***Perf. 11½***

243 A70 35d multicolored .30 .30

1996, May 5 ***Perf. 14***

244 A71 80d multicolored 1.10 1.10

No. 244 was issued in sheets of 2.

Sarajevo Town Hall, Cent. A72

1996, May 5 ***Perf. 11½***

245 A72 80d multicolored .60 .60

Bosnian Journalists Assoc., Cent. A73

1996, May 5
246 A73 100d multicolored .75 .75

Essen '96, Intl. Philatelic Expo A74

1996, May 25 ***Perf. 11½***
247 A74 200d multicolored 2.75 2.75

1996 Summer Olympic Games, Atlanta — A75

No. 248: a, 120d, Baron de Coubertin. b, 80d, Olympic Torch. c, 30d, Runners. d, 35d, Atlanta Games emblem.

1996, May 25
248 A75 Block of 4, #a.-d. 4.00 4.00

Background of No. 248 differs with location on sheet.

Alexander Graham Bell's Telephone, 120th Anniv. A76

1996, July 10 ***Perf. 11½***
249 A76 80d multicolored 1.10 1.10

Extension of Privleges to Dubrovnik by Ban Stepan II, 1333 A77

1996, July 10
250 A77 100d multicolored 1.40 1.40

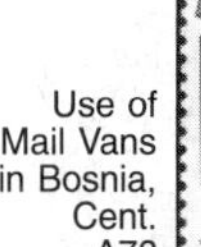

Use of Mail Vans in Bosnia, Cent. A78

1996, July 10
251 A78 120d multicolored 1.25 1.25

Flowers — A79

No. 252: a, 30d, Campanula hercegovina. b, 35d, Iris bosniaca.

1996, July 10
252 A79 Pair, #a.-b. 1.00 1.00

Printed checkerwise on the sheet.

Dogs A80

No. 253: a, 35d, Barak. b, 80d, Tornjak.

1996, July 10
253 A80 Pair, #a.-b. 2.00 2.00

Printed checkerwise on the sheet.

SOS Children's Village, Sarajevo — A81

1996, Sept. 1
254 A81 100d multicolored 1.40 1.40

A83 A84

Traditional costumes - No. 255: a, 50d, Moslem, Bjelasnice. b, 80d, Croatian. c, 100d, Moslem, Sarajevo.

Uniforms - No. 256: a, 35d, Bogomil soldier. b, 80d, Austro-Hungarian rifleman. c, 100d, Turkish light cavalry. d, 120d, Medieval Bosnian king.

1996, Sept. 20
255 A83 Strip of 3, #a.-c. + label 3.25 3.25
256 A84 Strip of 4, #a.-d. 5.00 5.00

Winter Festival, Sarajevo A85

1996, Nov. 25
257 A85 100d multicolored 1.50 1.50

Bosnia Day — A86

1996, Nov. 25
258 A86 120d Map, natl. arms 1.90 1.90

Christmas A87

1996, Dec. 21
259 A87 100d multicolored 1.50 1.50

Visit by Pope John Paul II — A88

1996, Dec. 21 ***Perf. 14***
260 A88 500d multicolored 6.50 6.50

Archaeological Finds — A89

Designs: 35d, Paleolithic rock carving, Badanj. 50d, Neolithic ceramic head, Butmir. 80d, Bronze age bird wagon, Glasinac.

Walls of Daorson, Illyria - No. 264: a, 100d, Walls, rock face at L. b, 120d, Low wall outside city wall.

1997, Mar. 31 ***Perf. 15***
261-263 A89 Set of 3 2.25 2.25

Souvenir Sheet

264 A89 Sheet of 2, #a.-b. 2.75 2.75

Children's Week — A90 Bairam Festival — A91

1997, Apr. 15 ***Perf. 11½***
265 A90 100d multicolored 1.40 1.40

1997, Apr. 15 ***Perf. 11½***
266 A91 200d Ferhad Pasha Mosque 2.50 2.50

A92

1997, Apr. 25 ***Perf. 14***
267 A92 100d multicolored 1.25 1.25

Mujaga Komadina (1839-1925), mayor of Mostar.

A93

1997, May 3 ***Perf. 11½***

Europa (Myths & Legends): 100d, Trojan warriors, map. 120d, Man on prayer mat, castle from The Miraculous Spring of Ajvatovica.

268-269 A93 Set of 2 3.00 3.00

Greenpeace, 25th Anniv. — A94

Rainbow Warrior, inscribed: a, 35d, Grace. b, 80d, Dorreboom. c, 100d, Beltra. d, 120d, Morgan.

1997, May 25
270 A94 Block or strip of 4, #a.-d. 4.25 4.25

Third Intl. Film Festival, Sarajevo A95

1997, June 15
271 A95 110d multicolored 1.50 1.50

Mediterranean Games, Bari — A96

Designs: 40d, Games emblem. 130d, Boxing, basketball, kick boxing.

1997, June 15
272-273 A96 Set of 2 2.10 2.10

Discovery of Electrons, Cent. A97

1997, June 25
274 A97 40d multicolored .65 .65

Vasco da Gama's Voyage Around Africa, 500th Anniv. — A98

1997, June 25
275 A98 110d multicolored 1.50 1.50

Stamp Day — A99

1997, June 25

276 A99 130d multicolored 1.75 1.75

Railroads in Bosnia & Herzegovina, 125th Anniv. — A100

1997, June 25

277 A100 150d multicolored 1.90 1.90

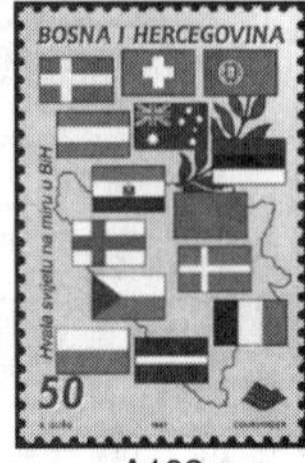
Fauna — A101 A102

No. 278: a, 40d, Dinaromys bogdanovi. b, 80d, Triturus alpestris.
No. 279: a, 40d, Oxytropis prenja. b, 110d, Dianthus freynii.

1997, Aug. 25

278 A101 Pair, #a.-b. 1.60 1.60
279 A101 Pair, #a.-b. 2.00 2.00

1997, Aug. 25

World Peace Day: a, 50d, Sweden, Switzerland, Australia & other flags. b, 60d, Flags, globe showing Europe, Africa. c, 70d, Flags, globe showing North & South America. d, 110d, US, UK, Canadian & other flags.

280 A102 Strip of 4, #a.-d. 3.75 3.75

Great Sarajevo Fire, 300th Anniv. — A103

1997, Sept. 15

281 A103 110d multicolored 1.75 1.75

Architecture — A104

Designs: 40d, House with attic. 50d, Tiled stove, door. 130d, Three-storied house.

1997, Sept. 15

282-284 A104 Set of 3 3.00 3.00

Italian Pioneer Corps Aid in Reconstruction of Sarajevo — A105

1997, Nov. 1 ***Perf. 14***

285 A105 1.40m multicolored 1.90 1.90

Famous Men A106

1.30m, Augustin Tin Ujevic (1891-1955), writer. 2m, Zaim Imamovic (1920-94), singer, vert.

1997, Nov. 1 ***Perf. 11½***

286-287 A106 Set of 2 4.25 4.25

Diana, Princess of Wales (1961-97) — A107

1997, Nov. 3 ***Perf. 14***

288 A107 2.50m multicolored 4.00 4.00

Gnijezdo, by Fikret Libovac A108

Sarajevo Library, by Nusret Pasic A109

1997, Nov. 6 ***Perf. 11½***

289-290 A108-A109 Set of 2 1.40 1.40

Samac-Sarajevo Railway, 50th Anniv. — A110

1997, Nov. 17 ***Perf. 14***

291 A110 35pf multicolored .55 .55

A111 A112

Religious Holidays: 50pf, Nativity Scene, Orthodox Christmas. No. 293, 1.10m, Wreath on door, Christmas. No. 294, 1.10m, Pupils before teacher, Hagada.

1997, Dec. 22 ***Perf. 11½***

292-294 A111 Set of 3 4.25 4.25

1998, Jan. 15 ***Perf. 14***

Designs: a, 35pf, Sports. b, 1m, Games emblem.

295 A112 Sheet of 2, #a.-b. 2.00 2.00

1998 Winter Olympic Games, Nagano.

Bairam Festival — A113

1998, Jan. 28

296 A113 1m Mosque fountain 1.50 1.50

Ahmed Muradbegovic (1898-1972), Writer — A114

1998, Mar. 20

297 A114 1.50m multicolored 2.25 2.25

Fortified Towns — A115

No. 298: a, 35pf, Zvornik. b, 70pf, Bihac. c, 1m, Pocitelj. d, 1.20m, Gradacac.

1998, Mar. 20

298 A115 Booklet pane of 4, #a.-d. 5.00 5.00
Complete booklet, #298 5.00

A116 A117

1998, May 5 ***Perf. 11½***

299 A116 1.10m multicolored 1.60 1.60

Intl. Theater Festival, Sarajevo, Europa.

1998, May 5

Former Presidents of Univ. of Arts and Science: 40pf, Branislav Durdev (1908-93). 70pf, Alojz Benac (1914-92). 1.30m, Edhem Camo (1909-96).

300-302 A117 Set of 3 3.50 3.50

A118 A119

Ciconia Ciconia - No. 303: a, 70pf, Three in water. b, 90pf, Two in flight. c, 1.10m, Two in nest. d, 1.30m, Adult, chicks.

1998, May 5

303 A118 Strip of 4, #a.-d. 4.00 4.00

1998, May 22

304 A119 2m Sheet with 2 labels 3.25 3.25

World Congress of Intl. League of Humanists, Sarajevo.

1998 World Cup Soccer Championships, France — A120

50pf, Soccer balls. 1m, Map, soccer ball. 1.50m, Asim Ferhatovic Hase (1934-87), soccer player.

1998, May 22 ***Perf. 14½***

305-307 A120 Set of 3 4.50 4.50

A121 A122

1998, July 20 ***Perf. 11½***

308 A121 1.10m multicolored 1.75 1.75

Sarajevo Tunnel, 5th anniv.

1998, July 30

Mushrooms: 50pf, Morchella esculenta. 80pf, Cantharellus cibarius. 1.10m, Boletus edulis. 1.35m, Amanita caesarea.

309-312 A122 Set of 4 6.00 6.00

Paris Subway A123

1998, Aug. 30

313 A123 2m violet blue & green 3.25 3.25

Henri Dunant — A124

1998, Sept. 14 ***Perf. 14***

314 A124 50pf multicolored .75 .75

Intl. Red Cross fight against tuberculosis.

Cities — A125

1998, Sept. 24

315 A125 5pf Travnik	.20	.20
316 A125 38pf Sarajevo	.45	.45

Chess — A126

Bosnian players - No. 317: a, 20pf, Woman at chess board. b, 40pf, Silver medal team, 31st Chess Olympiad. c, 60pf, Women's team, 32nd Chess Olympiad. d, 80pf, Men, Women's teams, 11th European Chess Championships.

1998, Sept. 24

317 A126 Sheet of 4, #a.-d.	3.25	3.25

A127 A128

1998, Oct. 9 ***Perf. 11½***

318 A127 1m multicolored	1.60	1.60

World Post Day.

1998, Oct. 23

319 A128 80pf Musical instruments	1.40	1.40

Intl. Day of Disabled Persons A129

1998, Dec. 3

320 A129 1m multicolored	1.60	1.60

Mt. Bjelasnica A130

1998, Dec. 3

321 A130 1m multicolored	1.60	1.60

Universal Declaration of Human Rights, 50th Anniv. — A131

1998, Dec. 10 ***Perf. 14½***

322 A131 1.35m multicolored	2.25	2.25

New Year A132

Christmas — A133

Designs: 1m, Child's drawing. 1.50m, Fr. Andeo Zvizdovic (1420?-98).

1998, Dec. 18 ***Perf. 11½***

323-324 A132-A133 Set of 2	4.25	4.25

School Anniversaries — A134

Designs: No. 325, 40pf, First Sarajevo High School, 120th anniv. No. 326, 40pf, Sarajevo University, 50th anniv., vert.

1999, Apr. 22 Litho. ***Perf. 11¾***

325-326 A134 Set of 2	1.10	1.10

Flora and Fauna A135

80pf, Pigeons. 1.10m, Knautia sarajevensis.

1999, Apr. 22 Litho. ***Perf. 11¾***

327-328 A135 Set of 2	2.75	2.75

First Manned Moon Landing, 30th Anniv. — A136

1999, May 20 Litho. ***Perf. 11¾***

329 A136 2m multicolored	3.00	3.00

Una River - A137

1999, May 20

330 A137 2m multicolored	3.00	3.00

Gorazde A137a

1999, June 9 Litho. ***Perf. 14x14¼***

330A A137a 40pf multi	.50	.50

World Environmental Protection Day — A138

1999, June 15 Litho. ***Perf. 11¾***

331 A138 80pf Buna River Well-spring	1.10	1.10

Philex France 99 — A139

1999, June 15

332 A139 2m multicolored	2.75	2.75

Special Olympics A140

1999, June 15

333 A140 50pf multicolored	.70	.70

Bosnia & Herzegovina Postage Stamps, 120th Anniv. — A141

1999, July 1

334 A141 1m multicolored	1.00	1.00

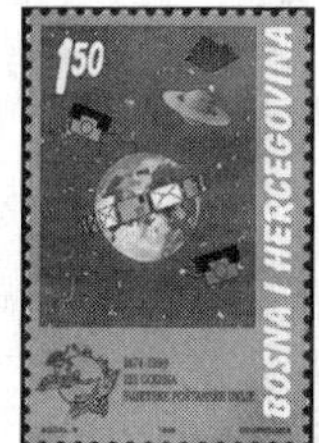

UPU, 125th Anniv. — A142

1999, July 1 Litho. ***Perf. 11¾***

335 A142 1.50m multi	1.60	1.60

Minerals A143

Designs: 40pf, Tuzlite. 60pf, Siderite. 1.20m, Hijelofan. 1.80m, Quartz, vert.

1999, July 27 Litho. ***Perf. 11¾***

336-339 A143 Set of 4	4.25	4.25

Dzuzovi Mehmed Pasha Sokolovic Koran Manuscript A144

1999, Sept. 23

340 A144 1.50m multicolored	1.60	1.60

Kursumli Medresa Library, Founded 1537 — A145

1999, Sept. 23

341 A145 1m multicolored	1.00	1.00

Radiology in Bosnia & Herzegovina, Cent. — A146

1999, Oct. 5

342 A146 90pf multicolored	.95	.95

Handija Kasevljakovic (1888-1959), Historian — A147

1999, Oct. 5

343 A147 1.30m multicolored	1.40	1.40

25th European Chess Club Cup Finals — A148

1999, Oct. 29 Litho. ***Perf. 14***

344 A148 1.10m multicolored	1.10	1.10

Hvalov Zbornik, Book in Glagolitic Text — A149

1999, Sept. 23 Litho. *Perf. 11¾*
345 A149 1.10m multicolored 1.10 1.10

Sarajevo Summit A150

1999, July 29 Litho. *Perf. 14*
346 A150 2m multi 2.10 2.10

Expo 2000, Hanover A151

1999, Nov. 9 Litho. *Perf. 11¾*
347 A151 1m multi 1.25 1.25

Painting by Afan Ramic A152

1999, Nov. 25
348 A152 1.20m multi 1.50 1.50

Birth of Six Billionth Person A153

1999, Nov. 25 *Perf. 14*
349 A153 2.50m multi 3.25 3.25

Souvenir Sheet

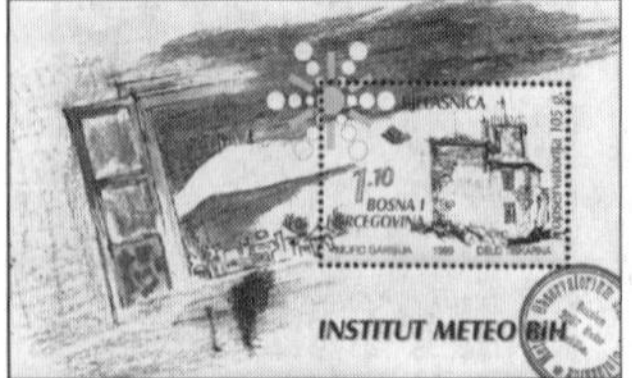
Bjelasnica Weather Observatory, 105th Anniv. — A154

1999, Dec. 15
350 A154 1.10m multi 1.40 1.40

Sarajevo Philharmonic A155

Sarajevo Intl. Music Festival A156

1999, Dec. 20
351 A155 40pf multi .50 .50
352 A156 1.10m multi 1.40 1.40

Mehmed Spaho (1883-1939), Politician — A157

2000, Mar. 15 *Perf. 11¾*
353 A157 1m multi 1.25 1.25

Bairam Festival — A158

2000, Mar. 15
354 A158 1.10m multi 1.40 1.40

Amateur Radio in Bosnia and Herzegovina, 50th Anniv. — A159

2000, Mar. 15
355 A159 1.50m multi 1.90 1.90

Oriental Institute, Sarajevo, 50th Anniv. — A160

2000, Mar. 15
356 A160 2m multi 2.50 2.50

Souvenir Sheet

2000 Summer Olympics, Sydney — A161

Emblem of Sydney Olympics and map of: a, 1.30m, Bosnia & Herzegovina. b, 1.70m, Australia.
Illustration reduced.

2000, Apr. 10 Litho. *Perf. 14¾*
357 A161 Sheet of 2, #a-b 3.75 3.75

Europa, 2000
Common Design Type

2000, May 9 *Perf. 11¾*
358 CD17 2m multi 2.40 2.40

Birds A162

1m, Gyps fulvus. 1.50m, Platalea leucorodia.

2000, May 9 Litho. *Perf. 11¾*
359-360 A162 Set of 2 3.00 3.00

Lake Boracko A163

River Una Emeralds — A164

2000, May 9
361 A163 40pf multi .50 .50
362 A164 1m multi 1.10 1.10

World Environmental Protection Day.

Souvenir Sheet

Greenpeace — A165

a, 50pf, Fish. b, 60pf, Lobster. c, 90pf, Anemones. d, 1.50m, Diver on shipwreck.
Illustration reduced.

2000, May 9 *Perf. 11¾x11½*
363 A165 Sheet of 4, #a-d 4.00 4.00

First Zeppelin Flight, Cent. A166

2000, June 10 *Perf. 11¾*
364 A166 1.50m multi 1.75 1.75

Cities — A167

2000, June 9 Litho. *Perf. 14*
365 A167 50pf Zenica .55 .55
366 A167 1m Mostar 1.10 1.10
367 A167 1.10m Bihac 1.25 1.25
368 A167 1.50m Tuzla, vert. 1.60 1.60
Nos. 365-368 (4) 4.50 4.50

Vranduk A168

Kraljeva Sutjeska A169

2000, Sept. 20 *Perf. 11¾x11½*
369 A168 1.30m multi 1.25 1.25
370 A169 1.50m multi 1.50 1.50

The Adventures of Tom Sawyer, by Mark Twain A170

2000, Sept. 20
371 A170 1.50m multi 1.50 1.50

Souvenir Sheet

Millennium — A171

2000, Sept. 20 *Perf. 11¾*
372 A171 2m multi 2.00 2.00

No. 372 contains one 29x57mm 80pf "stamp," and one 57x57mm 1.20m "stamp," but both lack the country name, which appears only in the sheet margin.

Intl. Children's Week — A172

2000, Oct. 5 *Perf. 11½x11¾*
373 A172 1.60m multi 1.60 1.60

Paintings A173

Paintings by: 60pf, J. Mujezinovic. 80pf, I. Seremet.

2000, Oct. 5 *Perf. 11¾x11½*
374-375 A173 Set of 2 1.40 1.40

UN High Commissioner for Refugees, 50th Anniv. — A174

2000, Dec. 14 ***Perf. 11¾x11½***
376 A174 1m multi 1.00 1.00

Cities — A175

2001, Mar. 22 ***Perf. 14***
377 A175 10pf Tesanj, vert. .20 .20
378 A175 20pf Bugojno .20 .20
379 A175 30pf Konjic .30 .30
380 A175 35pf Zivinice .30 .30
381 A175 2m Cazin 1.90 1.90
Nos. 377-381 (5) 2.90 2.90

Animals Type of 2001

No. 382, vert.: a, 90pf, Alcedo atthis. b, 1.10m, Bombycilla garrulus.

2001, Mar. 22 Litho. ***Perf. 11¾***
382 A176 Horiz. pair, #a-b 2.00 2.00

Animals — A176

No. 383: a, 1.10m, Equus caballus facing right. b, 1.90m, Equus caballus facing left.
Illustration reduced.

Perf. 11¾x11½
2001, Mar. 22 Litho.
383 A176 Horiz. pair, #a-b 2.50 2.50

A number has been reserved for an additional item in this set.

Walt Disney (1901-66) — A177

Perf. 11½x11¾
2001, Mar. 22 Litho.
384 A177 1.10m multi 1.10 1.10

Shell Fossils — A178

Denominations in: a, 1.30m, Blue. b, 1.80m, Black.
Illustration reduced.

2001, Mar. 22 ***Perf. 11¾x11½***
385 A178 Horiz. pair, #a-b 3.00 3.00

Souvenir Sheet

Comic Strips — A179

Inscriptions: a, Ti si moje janje. b, Ti si moj medo. c, Ti si moja maca. d, Ti si moj cvijet. e, Ti si moje pile.

2001, Mar. 22 Litho. ***Perf. 11¾***
Granite Paper
386 A179 30pf Sheet of 5, #a-e 1.25 1.25

Souvenir Sheet

Europa — A180

2001, Apr. 10 ***Perf. 11½x11¾***
387 A180 2m multi 1.75 1.75

Souvenir Sheet

Bosnia Institute, Sarajevo — A181

2001, May 25 Litho. ***Perf. 14***
388 A181 1.10m multi 1.10 1.10

Souvenir Sheet

Emir Balic, Mostar Bridge Diver — A182

2001, May 30 ***Perf. 11½x11¾***
389 A182 2m multi 2.00 2.00

14th Mediterranean Games, Tunis — A183

2001, May 30 Litho. ***Perf. 14x14¼***
390 A183 1.30m multi 1.40 1.40

Ferrari Race Cars — A184

No. 391: a, 40pf, 15954 625 F1. b, 60pf, 1970 312 B. c, 1.30m, 1978 312 T3. d, 1.70m, 1983 126 C3.
Illustration reduced.

2001, June 20 Litho. ***Perf. 14x14¼***
391 A184 Block of 4, #a-d 4.00 4.00

Zeljeznic, Soccer Champions — A185

2001, July 18
392 A185 1m multi 1.00 1.00

Nobel Prizes, Cent. A186

2001, July 18
393 A186 1.50m multi 1.50 1.50

Charlie Chaplin (1889-1977) A187

2001, July 18 ***Perf. 14x13¾***
394 A187 1.60m multi 1.60 1.60

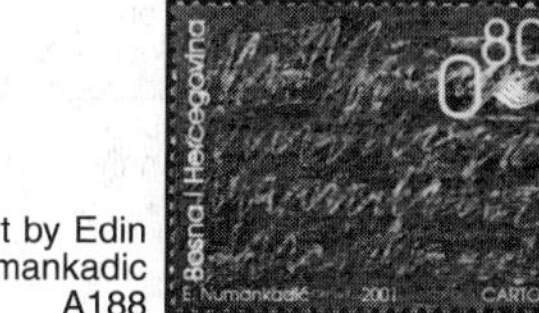

Art by Edin Numankadic A188

Perf. 12½x12¾
2001, Sept. 10 Litho.
395 A188 80pf multi .85 .85

Portions of the design were applied by a thermographic process producing a shiny, raised effect.

David, by Michelangelo, 500th Anniv. — A189

2001, Sept. 10
396 A189 2m multi 2.10 2.10

Portions of the design were applied by a thermographic process producing a shiny, raised effect.

Breastfeeding Week — A190

2001, Oct. 1 Litho. ***Perf. 14***
397 A190 1.10m multi 1.25 1.25

World Post Day — A191

2001, Oct. 9
398 A191 1.30m multi 1.40 1.40

Horse-drawn Mail Delivery Railcar — A192

2001, Oct. 30 Litho. ***Perf. 14¼x14***
399 A192 1.10m multi 1.25 1.25

Alija Bejtic (1920-81), Historian — A193

2001, Nov. 10 Litho. ***Perf. 14***
400 A193 80pf multi .85 .85

Albert Einstein A194

2001, Dec. 14
401 A194 1.50m multi 1.60 1.60

Musical Group "Indexi" A195

2002, Apr. 5 Litho. *Perf. 14*
402 A195 38pf multi .40 .40

Sarajevo's Candidacy to Host 2010 Winter Olympics — A199

2002, Apr. 15 Litho. *Perf. 13¾x14*
406 A199 1.50m multi 1.60 1.60

Bosnia & Herzegovina Scouting Organization, 80th Anniv. — A201

2002, Apr. 20 Litho. *Perf. 14x13¾*
408 A201 1m multi 1.10 1.10

Europa — A202

2002, Apr. 20 *Perf. 13¾x14*
409 A202 2.50m multi 2.75 2.75

Independence, 10th Anniv. — A203

2002, Apr. 20 *Perf. 14x13¾*
410 A203 2.50m multi 2.75 2.75

Souvenir Sheet

Sarajevo Fire Fighters — A204

2002, Apr. 20 *Perf. 13¾x14*
411 A204 2.20m multi 2.40 2.40

Butterflies — A206

Designs: 1.50m, Parnassus apollo. 2.50m, Iphiclides podalirius.

2002, Apr. 20 Litho. *Perf. 13¾x14*
414-415 A206 Set of 2 4.50 4.50

BOSNIA AND HERZEGOVINA (CROAT ADMIN.)

Bosnian Croat Administration Located In Mostar
(Herceg Bosna)

100 Paras = 1 Dinar (1993)
100 Lipa = 1 Kuna (1994)
100 pfennig = 1 Mark (6/22/98)

Catalogue values for all unused stamps in this country are for Never Hinged items.

A1

1993, May 12 Litho. *Perf. 14*
1 A1 2000d multicolored 1.60 1.60

Our Lady of Peace Shrine, Medjugorje.

A2

1993

Silvije Kranjcevic (1865-1908), poet: 500d, Waterfall, gate at Jajce. 1000d, Old bridge, Mostar, horiz.

2-4 A2 Set of 3 1.40 1.40

Issued: 200d, 5/20; 500d, 5/18; 1000d, 5/15.

Census in Bosnia & Herzegovina, 250th Anniv. — A3

1993, May 24
5 A3 100d Medieval gravestone .20 .20

Madonna of the Grand Duke, by Raphael — A4

1993, Dec. 3
6 A4 6000d multicolored 2.75 2.75

Christmas.

Paintings, by Gabrijel Jurkic (1886-1974) — A5

Europa: a, 3500d, Uplands in Bloom. b, 5000d, Wild Poppy.

1993, Dec. 6
7 A5 Pair, #a.-b. 6.75 6.75

Kravica Waterfalls A6

1993, Dec. 7
8 A6 3000d multicolored 1.50 1.50

Grand Duke Hrvoje Vukcic-Hrvatinic (1350-1416) — A7

1993, Dec. 8
9 A7 1500d multicolored .75 .75

Pleham Monastery A8

1993, Dec. 15
10 A8 2200d multicolored 1.00 1.00

Formation of Bosnian Croat Administration A9

1994, Feb. 10
11 A9 10,000d multicolored 4.25 4.25

Bronze Cross, Rama A10

1994, Nov. 28
12 A10 2.80k multicolored 1.25 1.25

Flora & Fauna — A11

a, 3.80k, Campanula hercegovina. b, 4k, Dog.

1994, Nov. 30
13 A11 Pair, #a.-b. 3.25 3.25

Hutovo Wetlands A12

1994, Dec. 2
14 A12 80 l multicolored .40 .40

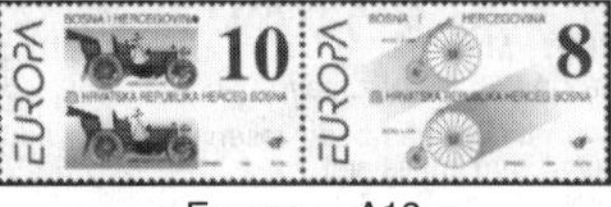
Europa — A13

Transportation: a, 8k, Bicycles, 1885. b, 10k, 1901 Mercedes.

1994, Dec. 5
15 A13 Pair, #a.-b. 7.00 7.00

City of Ljubuski, 550th Anniv. — A14

1994, Dec. 8
16 A14 1k multicolored .45 .45

Dr. Nikolic Franciscan Hospital, Nova Bila, 2nd Anniv. — A15

1994, Dec. 12
17 A15 5k multicolored 2.25 2.25

UN, 50th Anniv. — A16

1995, Oct. 24 *Rouletted*
Self-Adhesive
18 A16 1.50k Card of 10 6.75 6.75

Color ranges from pale pink at UL of card to dark rose at LR of card. Each stamp is numbered at LR.

Christmas — A17

1995, Dec. 4 *Perf. 14*
19 A17 5.40k multicolored 2.25 2.25

Kraljeva Sutjeska Monastery A18

1995, Dec. 7
20 A18 3k multicolored 1.40 1.40

Cities — A19

Europa — A20

Monasteries: 2k, Srebrenica. 4k, Mostar.

1995
21-22 A19 Set of 2 2.50 2.50

Issued: 2k, 12/20; 4k, 12/12.

1995, Dec. 28
23 A20 6.50k multicolored 2.75 2.75

A21

Europa — A22

1996, June 24
24 A21 10k multicolored 4.25 4.25
a. Booklet pane of 4 17.00
Complete booklet, #24a 17.00

Apparitions at Medugorje, 15th anniv.

1996, July 20
25 A22 2.40k multicolored 1.00 1.00

Queen Katarina Kosaca Kotromanic.

A23

A24

1996, July 23
26 A23 1.40k multicolored .60 .60

Franciscan Monastery, Siroki Brijeg, 150th anniv.

1996, Aug. 14 *Rouletted*
Self-Adhesive

Virgin Mary.

27 A24 2k multicolored .85 .85
a. Card of 10 8.50
28 A24 9k multicolored 3.75 3.75
a. Card of 5 + 5 labels 19.00

Nos. 27-28 Surcharged

1.10

1996, Oct. 21 *Rouletted*
Self-Adhesive

29 A24 1.10k on 2k multi
a. Card of 10
30 A24 1.10k on 9k multi
a. Card of 5 + 5 labels

Taipei '96 Philatelic Exhibition.

Christmas — A25

Europa — A26

1996, Dec. 8 **Litho.** *Perf. 14*
31 A25 2.20k multicolored 1.00 1.00

1997, Apr. 4

Myths & legends: a, 2k, St. George slaying the dragon. b, 5k, Zeus coming to Europa disguised as a bull.

32 A26 Pair, #a.-b. 2.75 2.75

No. 32b is 39x34mm.

A27

A28

1997, Apr. 12
33 A27 3.60k multicolored 1.50 1.50
a. Pane of 4 6.00

Visit of Pope John Paul II.

1997, Apr. 20
34 A28 1.40k Samatorje Church .65 .65

Flora & Fauna — A29

Designs: 1k, Ardea purpurea. 2.40k, Symphyandra hofmannii.

1997
35-36 A29 Set of 2 1.60 1.60

Issued: 1k, 11/19. 2.40k, 11/17.

Christmas A30

1997, Dec. 1
37 A30 1.40k multicolored .65 .65

World Animated Film Festival A31

1998, Apr. 1
38 A31 6.50k multicolored 2.75 2.75

Europa.

Hercegovina, 550th Anniv. — A32

1998, Apr. 8
39 A32 2.30k multicolored 1.00 1.00

City of Livno, 1100th Anniv. — A33

1998, Apr. 9
40 A33 1.20k multicolored .50 .50

Sibiraea Croatica — A34

Gyps Fulvus — A35

1998, Nov. 9
41 A34 1.40k multicolored .60 .60

1998, Nov. 16
42 A35 2.40m multicolored 1.00 1.00

A36

A37

1998, Dec. 2
43 A36 5.40k Christmas 2.25 2.25

1999, Mar. 26 **Litho.** *Perf. 14*
44 A37 40pf Native attire .65 .65

A. B. Simic (1898-1925) — A38

1999, Mar. 29
45 A38 30pf multi .50 .50

Bobovac Castle — A39

1999, Mar. 30
46 A39 10pf multi .20 .20

Europa — A40

1999, Mar. 31
47 A40 1.50m Blidinje Park 2.50 2.50

Dianthus Freynii — A41

1999, Oct. 11 **Litho.** *Perf. 14*
48 A41 80pf multi 1.00 1.00

Martes Martes — A42

1999, Oct. 15
49 A42 40pf multi .50 .50

Stolac Castle — A43

1999, Nov. 3
50 A43 10pf multi .20 .20

Christmas — A44

1999, Nov. 22
51 A44 30pf multi .40 .40

Nikola Sop (1904-82), Writer — A45

World Health Day — A46

2000, Apr. 5 **Litho.** *Perf. 14*
52 A45 40pf multi .45 .45

2000, Apr. 7
53 A46 40pf multi .45 .45

Europa — A47

2000, May 9
54 A47 1.80m multi 2.00 2.00

Brother Lovro Karaula (1800-75) A48

Quercus Sessilis A49

2000, May 19
55 A48 80pf multi .90 .90

2000, Aug. 16
56 A49 1.50m multi 1.75 1.75

Anguilla Anguilla — A50

2000, Aug. 18
57 A50 80pf multi .90 .90

16th European Chess Club Cup — A51

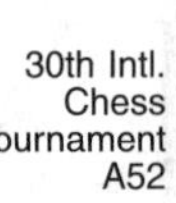

30th Intl. Chess Tournament A52

2000, Sept. 23
58 A51 80pf multi .90 .90
59 A52 80pf multi .90 .90

Tomislavgrad Monastery A53

2000, Sept. 26
60 A53 1.50m multi 1.75 1.75

Woman From Kraljeva Sutjeska — A54

2000, Sept. 27
61 A54 40pf multi .45 .45

Fight Against AIDS A55

Christmas A56

2000, Dec. 1
62 A55 80pf multi .90 .90

2000, Dec. 4
63 A56 40pf multi .45 .45

Fish — A57

Designs: 30pf, Chondrostoma phoxinus. 1.50m, Salmo marmoratus.

2001
64-65 A57 Set of 2 1.75 1.75

Europa — A58

Designs: 1.10m, Tihaljine spring. 1.80m, Plivini waterfall.

2001, Mar. 31
66-67 A58 Set of 2 3.00 3.00

Execution of Zrinski and Frankopan, 330th Anniv. — A59

No. 68: a, Petar Zrinski (1621-71). b, Fran Krsto Frankopan (1643-71).

2001, Apr. 30 Litho. ***Perf. 14***
68 A59 40pf Vert. pair, #a-b .85 .85

16th Century Galley — A60

2001, June 15
69 A60 1.80m multi 2.00 2.00

Boat From Neretva River Valley — A61

2001, June 20 ***Perf. 14x14¼***
70 A61 80pf multi .85 .85

Souvenir Sheet

Apparition of the Virgin Mary at Medjugorje, 20th Anniv. — A62

2001, June 24
71 A62 3.80m multi 4.00 4.00

Our Lady of Kondzilo — A63

2001, Aug. 15 ***Perf. 14***
72 A63 80pf multi .85 .85

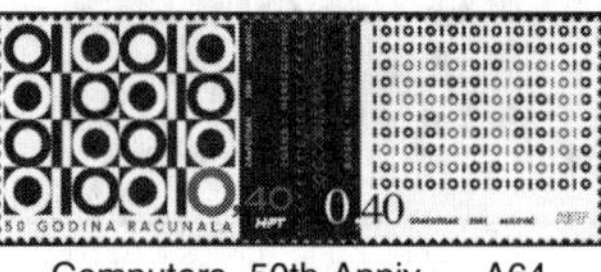
Computers, 50th Anniv. — A64

No. 73: a, Denomination in red. b, Denomination in black and white.
Illustration reduced.

2001, Sept. 9
73 A64 40pf Horiz. pair, #a-b .85 .85

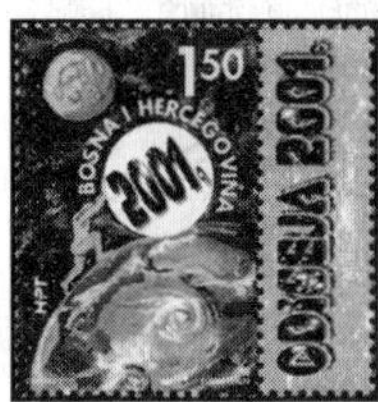
Mars Odyssey Mission — A65

2001, Sept. 9
74 A65 1.50m multi + label 1.60 1.60

Father Slavko Barbaric (1946-2000), Priest at Medjugorje — A66

2001, Nov. 24
75 A66 80pf multi .90 .90

Walt Disney (1901-66), Animated Film Producer A67

2001, Dec. 5
76 A67 1.50m multi 1.60 1.60

Christmas A68

2001, Dec. 8
77 A68 40pf multi .45 .45

2002 Winter Olympics, Salt Lake City — A70

2002, Feb. 4 Litho. ***Perf. 14***
79 A70 80pf multi .75 .75

BOSNIA AND HERZEGOVINA (SERB ADMIN.)

Bosnian Serb Administration Located In Banja Luca
(Republika Srpska)

100 Paras = 1 Dinar
100pfennig = 1 mark (6/22/98)

Catalogue values for all unused stamps in this country are for Never Hinged items.

Stamps of Yugoslavia Surcharged

100
Република
Српска

1992, Oct. 26 Litho. ***Perf. 12½***

1	A559	5d on 10p #2004	.40	.40
2	A559	30d on 3d #2015	*125.00*	*125.00*
3	A559	50d on 40p #2007a, perf. 13½	1.00	1.00
a.		Thick bars in obliterator	5.00	5.00
b.		Oon #2007, perf 12½		
4	A559	60d on 20p #2005	1.25	1.25
5	A559	60d on 30p #2006	1.25	1.25
6	A559	100d on 1d #2013	2.00	2.00
7	A559	100d on 2d #2014a, perf. 13½	2.00	2.00
a.		On #2014, perf 12½		
8	A559	100d on 3d #2015	2.00	2.00
9	A621	300d on 5d #2017a, perf. 13½	6.00	6.00
a.		On #2017, perf 12½		
10	A620	500d on 50p #2008	10.00	10.00
11	A619	500d on 60p #2009	10.00	10.00
a.		On #2009 perf. 13½	*90.00*	*90.00*
		Nos. 1-11 (11)	*160.90*	*160.90*

Obliterator on Nos. 1, 3 and 9 has thin bars.

Musical Instrument — A1

Designs: 10d, 20d, 30d, 5000d, 6000d, 10,000d, Stringed instrument. 50d, 100d, 20,000d, 30,000d, Coat of arms, vert. 500d, 50,000d, Monastery.

1993 *Perf. 13¼, 12½ (#19)*

12	A1	10d blk & org yel	.20	.20
13	A1	20d blk & blue	.30	.30
14	A1	30d blk & salmon	.45	.45
15	A1	50d blk & ver	.75	.75
16	A1	100d blk & ver	*1.50*	*1.50*
17	A1	500d blk & blue	*7.50*	*7.50*
18	A1	5000d blk & lilac	.20	.20
19	A1	6000d blk & yel	.20	.20
20	A1	10,000d blk & vio bl	.30	.30
a.		Perf. 12½		
21	A1	20,000d blk & ver	.60	.60
22	A1	30,000d blk & ver	.90	.90
23	A1	50,000d blk & lilac	1.50	1.50
		Nos. 12-23 (12)	14.40	*14.40*

Nos. 12-17 dated 1992, others dated 1993.
Issued: Nos. 12-17, 1/11; others 6/8.
For surcharges see Nos. 24-26, 34-36, 41-45, F9

Nos. 15-16 Surcharged

1993, June 15

24	A1	7500d on 50d #15	2.00	2.00
25	A1	7500d on 100d #16	2.00	2.00
26	A1	9000d on 50d #15	2.75	2.75
		Nos. 24-26 (3)	6.75	6.75

Referendum, May 15-16, 1993.

A2

A3

1993, Aug. 16 *Perf. 13¼*

Symbol of St. John, the Evangelist.

27 A2 (A) vermilion 1.00 1.00

1994, Jan. 9 *Perf. 14*

28 A3 1d Icon of St. Stefan 8.00 8.00

King Peter I Karageorge A4

1994, May 28

29 A4 80p sepia 5.00 5.00

City of Banja Luka, 500th Anniv. A5

1994, July 18

30 A5 1.20d multicolored 5.00 5.00

Nos. 31-32 have been reserved for surcharges on Nos. 13, 21. The editors would like to examine these stamps.

Madonna & Child, Cajnica Church — A6

1994, Sept. 1

33 A6 1d multicolored 5.00 5.00

Nos. 18, 20, 23 Surcharged

1994, Nov. 1 *Perf. 13¼*

34	A1	(A) on 5000d #18	1.75	1.75
35	A1	40p on 10,000d #20	1.75	1.75
a.		on #20a		
36	A1	2d on 50,000d #23	1.75	1.75
		Nos. 34-36,F9 (4)	7.00	7.00

No. 34 sold for 20p on day of issue.

Mostanica Monastery A7

Designs: 60p, Tavna Monastery, vert. 1.20d, Zitomislic Monastery, vert.

1994 *Perf. 14*

37-39 A7 Set of 3 14.50 14.50

Issued: 60p, 11/11; 1d, 12/31; 1.20d, 12/28.

Flora & Fauna A8

No. 40: a, Shore lark. b, Dinaromys bogdanovi. c, Edraianthus niveus. d, Aquilegia dinarica.

1996, Mar. 1 *Perf. 13¾*

40 A8 1.20d Block of 4, #a.-d. 7.00 7.00

Nos. 14-16, 19, 22 Surcharged

1996, July 1 *Perf. 13¼*

41	A1	70p on 30d #14	.60	.60
42	A1	1d on 100d #16	.80	.80
43	A1	2d on 30,000d #22	1.60	1.60
44	A1	3d on 50d #15	2.50	2.50
		Perf. 12½		
45	A1	5d on 6000d #19	4.50	4.50
		Nos. 41-45 (5)	10.00	10.00

Relay Station, Mt. Kozara — A9

1.20d, Drina River Bridge, Srbinje, horiz. 2d, Mt. Romanija relay station. 5d, Stolice relay station, Mt. Maljevica. 10d, Visegrad Bridge, horiz.

1996, Sept. 20 *Perf. 14*

46	A9	(A) multicolored	.20	.20
47	A9	1.20d multicolored	.70	.70
48	A9	2d multicolored	1.25	1.25
49	A9	5d multicolored	3.00	3.00
50	A9	10d multicolored	6.00	6.00
		Nos. 46-50,F10 (6)	11.70	11.70

No. 46 sold for 30p on day of issue.

Church, Bashcharsi A10

1997, July 7 *Perf. 13¾*

51 A10 2.50d multicolored 1.75 1.75

Mihailo Pupin (1848-1935), Electrical Engineer A11

1997, July 14

52 A11 2.50d multicolored 1.75 1.75

A12

A13

Flowers: No. 53, Oxytropis compestris. No. 54, Primula kitaibeliana. No. 55, Pedicularis hoermanniana. No. 56, Knautia sarajevensis.

1997, Sept. 12

53-56 A12 3.20d Set of 4 6.50 6.50

1997, Nov. 1 *Perf. 13¾*

Famous Men: A, Branko Copic (1915-85). 1.50d, Mesa Selimovic (1910-82). 3d, Aleksa Santic (1868-1924). 5d, Peter Kocic (1873-1916). 10d, Ivo Andric (1892-1975).

57	A13	A multicolored	.30	.30
58	A13	1.50d multicolored	.70	.70
59	A13	3d multicolored	1.40	1.40
60	A13	5d multicolored	2.25	2.25
61	A13	10d multicolored	4.50	4.50
		Nos. 57-61,F11 (6)	9.60	9.60

No. 57 sold for 60p on day of issue.

A14

Europa — A15

2.50d, Lutra lutra. 4.50d, Capreolus capreolus. 6.50d, Ursus arctos.

1997, Nov. 12

62-64 A14 Set of 3 7.25 7.25

1997, Nov. 12

Stories & legends: 2.50d, Two queens. 6.50d, Prince on horseback.

65-66 A15 Set of 2 6.25 6.25

Diana, Princess of Wales (1961-97) — A16

"Diana" in: a, Roman letters. b, Cyrillic letters.

1997, Dec. 22

67 A16 3.50d Pair, #a.-b. 13.00 13.00

1998 World Cup Soccer Championships, France — A17

Players, country flags - No. 68: a, Brazil. b, Morocco. c, Norway. d, Scotland. e, Italy. f, Chile. g, Austria. h, Cameroun.
No. 69: a, France. b, Saudi Arabia. c, Denmark. d, South Africa. e, Spain. f, Nigeria. g, Paraguay. h, Bulgaria.
No. 70: a, Netherlands. b, Belgium. c, Mexico. d, South Korea. e, Germany. f, US. g, Yugoslavia. h, Iran.
No. 71: a, Romania. b, England. c, Tunisia. d, Colombia. e, Argentina. f, Jamaica. g, Croatia. h, Japan.

1998, May 5
Sheets of 8 + label

68-71 A17 90p each 10.00 10.00

Europa — A18

Natl. festivals: No. 72, Instrument at R. No. 73, Instrument at L.

1998, June 9

72-73 A18 7.50d Set of 2 6.25 6.25

Icons, Chelandari Monastery A19

Various icons: 50p, 70p, 1.70d, 2d.

1998

74-77 A19 Set of 4 10.00 10.00

Buildings — A20

Designs: 15pf, Bijelina. 20pf, Sokolac. A, Banja Luca. 75pf, Prijedor. 2m, Brcko, vert. 4.50m, Zvornik, vert. 10m, Doboj.

1999, Mar. 15 **Litho.** *Perf. 13¾*

78-84 A20 Set of 7 30.00 30.00

No. 80 has black "A." It sold for 50pf on day of issue. See No. F12.

Air Srpska Airplanes A21

Airplane: No. 85, 50pf, In clouds. No. 86, 50pf, Over lake. 75pf, Over rocks. 1.50m, Over lake, diff.

1999, Mar. 26 Litho. *Perf. 13¾*
85-88 A21 Set of 4 4.50 4.50

World Table Tennis Championships, Belgrade — A22

Designs: 1m, Cracked globe as ball. 2m, Table, paddle, ball.

1999, Apr. 19
89-90 A22 Set of 2 5.50 5.50
Issued in sheets of 8 + label.

Europa — A23

Natl. Parks: 1.50m, Kozara. 2m, Peruchitsa.

1999, May 4
91-92 A23 Set of 2 6.00 6.00

Anniversaries — A24

No. 93: a, Gorazde incorporation document. b, Dobrin Monastery (denomination at UL). c, Illuminated letter. d, Zitomislic Monastery. e, Gomionica Monastery (2 steeples). f, Madonna and Child icon. g, St. Nicholas icon. h, Holy trinity icon.
Illustration reduced.

1999, May 26 Litho. *Perf. 13¾*
93 A24 50pf Sheet of 8, #a-h, + label 6.50 6.50

Dabrobosanska and Zahumskohercegovacka Archbishopric, 780th anniv., Gorazde Printing Press, 480th anniv.

Fish — A25

No. 94: a, 50pf, Salmo trutta m. fario. b, 50pf, Salmo trutta m. lacustris. c, 75pf, Hucho hucho. d, 1m, Thymallus thymallus.

1999, June 17
94 A25 Horiz. strip of 4, #a-d, + central label 5.50 5.50
Issued in sheets of 5 strips with different labels.

Man on the Moon, 30th Anniv. — A26

Designs: 1m, Equipment on moon. 2m, Astronaut, lunar module.

1999, July 21
95-96 A26 Set of 2 5.75 5.75
Issued in sheets of 8 + 1 label.

UPU, 125th Anniv. — A27

Designs: 75pf, Pencil. 1.25m, Arc and map.

1999, Sept. 9
97-98 A27 Set of 2 4.00 4.00
Issued in sheets of 8 + 1 label.

Icons — A28

No. 99: a, Madonna and Child (black denomination at UL). b, Madonna and Child (white denomination at UL). c, Madonna and Child (white denomination at LR). d, Saint with cross. e, Pieta. f, Christ enters Jerusalem (on donkey). g, St. Jovan (with scroll). h, Sts. Sava and Simeon.

1999, Oct. 29
99 A28 50pf Sheet of 8, #a-h, + label 7.75 7.75

Millennium A29

a, Egyptians, obelisk. b, Hourglass. c, Iron bell. d, Locomotive, steamship. e, Balloon, airplanes, automobiles. f, Man on the moon.

1999, Nov. 22
100 Booklet pane of 6 7.00 7.00
a.-e. A29 50pf Any single 1.00 1.00
f. A29 1m multi 2.00 2.00
Booklet, #100 7.00

See No. 126.

Postal Services in Serbian Territory, 135th Anniv. — A30

1999, Dec. 23
101 A30 50pf shown .80 .80

Souvenir Sheet
102 A30 3m Postriders on bridge *40.00 40.00*

Prince Stephen Nemanja — A31

2000, Feb. 29
103 A31 1.50m multi 2.50 2.50
Issued in sheets of 8 + 1 label.

Flora — A32

1m, Prunus domestica. 2m, Corylus avellana.

2000, Mar. 22
104-105 A32 Set of 2 5.00 5.00
Issued in sheets of 8 + 1 label.

Bridges — A33

#106, Brod (deer at left). #107, Pavlovica (horses and birds). #108, Zepce (bird at right). #109, Zvornik (bird at left).

2000, Apr. 12
106-109 A33 1m Set of 4 6.50 6.50
Issued in sheets of 8 + 1 label.

Jovan Ducic (1871-1943), Writer — A34

2000, Apr. 26 Litho. *Perf. 13¾*
110 A34 20pf multi *.40 .40*

Common Design Type and

Europa — A35

2000, May 5 Litho. *Perf. 13¾*
111 CD17 1.50m multi *13.50 13.50*
112 A35 2.50m multi *22.50 22.50*

Banja Luca Province, Cent. — A36

2000, May 26 Litho. *Perf. 13¾*
113 A36 1.50m multi *3.00 3.00*

European Soccer Championships A37

Various players. Denominations: 1m, 2m.

2000, June 14
114-115 A37 Set of 2 *6.00 6.00*

Souvenir Sheet
116 A37 6m Players, map *15.00 15.00*
No. 116 contains one 35x42mm stamp.

Nevesinje Rebellion, 125th Anniv. — A38

2000, July 12
117 A38 1.50m multi *3.00 3.00*

2000 Summer Olympics, Sydney A39

Map of Australia and: No. 118, 50pf, Handball. No. 119, 50pf, Basketball. No. 120, 50pf, Hurdles. No. 121, 50pf, Volleyball.
2m, Emu, kangaroo, Australian arms.

2000, Sept. 6
118-121 A39 Set of 4 *4.00 4.00*

Souvenir Sheet
122 A39 2m multi + label *5.00 5.00*
No. 122 contains one 42x35mm stamp.

Locomotives A40

No. 123 - Locomotive from: a, 1848. b, 1865. c, 1930. d, 1990.

2000, Oct. 4 Litho. *Perf. 13¾*
123 Horiz. strip of 4 + central label *3.75 3.75*
a.-c. A40 50pf Any single *.75 .75*
d. A40 1m multi *1.50 1.50*

Protected Species — A41

Designs: 1m, Leontopodium alpinum. 2m, Proteus anguinus, horiz.

2000, Oct. 31

124-125 A41 Set of 2 4.25 4.25

Millennium Type of 1999

No. 126: a, Ship. b, Glassblowers. c, Blacksmith. d, Printers. e, James Watt, steam engine, steam-powered vehicle. f, Satellites. g, People on shore, ships (105x55mm).

2000, Nov. 22

126 Booklet pane of 7 + label 7.50
a.-f. A29 50pf Any single .60 .60
g. A29 3m multi 3.75 3.75
Booklet, #126 7.50

Icons — A42

Icons from: No. 127, 50pf, 1577-78. No. 128, 50pf, 1607-08. No. 129, 1m, 1577-78. No. 130, 1m, Unknown year.

2000, Dec. 20

127-130 A42 Set of 4 4.25 4.25

Invention of the Telephone, 125th Anniv. — A43

2001, Feb. 27

131 A43 1m multi 1.50 1.50

Manned Space Flight, 40th Anniv. — A44

Designs: 1m, Yuri Gagarin, Vostok 1. 3m, Gagarin, Earth, rocket lift-off.

2001, Mar. 29

132 A44 1m multi 1.40 1.40

Souvenir Sheet

133 A44 3m multi 4.00 4.00

No. 133 contains one 53x35mm stamp.

Vlado Milosevic, Composer A45

Europa A46

2001, Apr. 11

134 A45 50pf multi .65 .65

2001, May 4 ***Perf. 13¾***

Designs: Nos. 135, 137a, 1m, Skakavac Waterfall. No. 136, 137b, 2m, Turjanica River.

White Border

135-136 A46 Set of 2 4.00 4.00

Light Blue Border

Perf. 13¾ Vert.

137 A46 Vert. pair, #a-b 4.00 4.00

No. 137 printed in panes of 3 pairs which were sold with a booklet cover, but unattached to it.

Butterflies — A47

Designs: No. 138, 50pf, Maniola jurtina. No. 139, 50pf, Pyrgus malvae. No. 140, 1m, Papilio machaon. No. 141, 1m, Lycaena pylaeas.

2001, June 19 ***Perf. 13¾***

138-141 A47 Set of 4 4.25 4.25

Kostanica A48

Srbinje — A49

2001, Sept. 5 Litho. ***Perf. 13¾***

142 A48 25pf multi .35 .35
143 A49 1m multi 1.40 1.40

Issued: 25pf, 9/5. 1m, 9/20.

Karate Championships A50

2001, Sept. 5

144 A50 1.50m multi 2.10 2.10

A51

A51a

Costumes

A51b A51c

2001, July 17 Litho. ***Perf. 13¾***

145 A51 50pf multi .60 .60
146 A51a 50pf multi .60 .60
147 A51b 1m multi 1.25 1.25
148 A51c 1m multi 1.25 1.25
Nos. 145-148 (4) 3.70 3.70

A52

A53

A54

A55

Caves

A56 A57

2001, Sept. 20 ***Perf. 13¾ Vert.***

149 Booklet pane of 6 3.60
a. A52 50pf Rastusha Cave .60 .60
b. A53 50pf Vaganska Cave .60 .60
c. A54 50pf Pavlova Cave .60 .60
d. A55 50pf Orlovacha Cave .60 .60
e. A56 50pf Ledana Cave .60 .60
f. A57 50pf Pod Jelikom Cave .60 .60

Building Type of 1999 with Red "A"

2001, Oct. 23 Litho. ***Perf. 13¾***

150 A20 A Banja Luka .65 .65

No. 150 sold for 50pf on day of issue. "A" on No. 80 is in black.

Nobel Prizes, Cent. — A58

Designs: 1m, Alfred Nobel (1833-96). 2m, Ivo Andric (1892-1975), 1961 Literature laureate.

2001, Oct. 23

151-152 A58 Set of 2 3.75 3.75

Each stamp printed in sheets of 8 + central label.

Bardacha-Srbac — A59

Lake Klinje — A60

2001, Nov. 15

153 A59 1m multi 1.25 1.25
154 A60 1m multi 1.25 1.25

Each stamp printed in sheets of 8 + central label.

Art A61

Designs: No. 155, 50pf, Belgrade Suburb, by Kosta Hakman (1899-1961). No. 156, 50pf, Djerdap, by Todor Shvrakic (1882-1931). No. 157, 50pf, Still Life With Parrot, by Jovan Bijelic (1884-1964), vert. No. 158, 50pf, Adela, by Miodrag Vujacic Mirski (1932-97), vert.

2001, Dec. 5

155-158 A61 Set of 4 2.40 2.40

Each stamp printed in sheets of 8 + central label.

Christmas A62

2001, Dec. 5

159 A62 1m multi 1.25 1.25

Printed in sheets of 8 + central label.

Borac Soccer Team, 75th Anniv. — A63

2001, Dec. 24

160 A63 1.50m multi 1.75 1.75

Printed in sheets of 8 + central label.

Serb Administration, 10th Anniv. — A64

Designs: 50pf, Arms, vert. 1m, Flag.

2002, Jan. 10

161-162 A64 Set of 2 1.75 1.75

Nos. 161-162 were each printed in sheets of 8 + central label. A number has been reserved for an additional item in this set.

Souvenir Sheet

Serb Administration, 10th Anniv. — A65

2002, Jan. 10 Litho. ***Perf. 13¾***

163 A65 2m multi 2.40 2.40

War on Terrorism — A66

Designs: 1m, Hand holding snake. 2m, Globe, eyes, guns.

2002, Jan. 29 Litho. *Perf. 13¾*
164 A66 1m multi *1.25 1.25*

Souvenir Sheet

165 A66 2m multi *2.40 2.40*

No. 164 printed in sheets of 8 + central label. No. 165 contains one 35x46mm stamp.

2002 Winter Olympics, Salt Lake City — A67

Designs: 50pf, Ski jumper. 1m, Bobsled.

2002, Feb. 13
166-167 A67 Set of 2 *1.75 1.75*

Each stamp printed in sheets of 8 + label.

Serbian Sarajevo — A68

Serbian Brod — A69

2002
168 A68 50pf multi *.60 .60*
169 A69 2m multi *2.40 2.40*

Issued: 50pf, 3/5. 2m, 4/18.

Education, Cent. — A70

2002, Mar. 5
170 A70 1m multi *1.25 1.25*

Printed in sheets of 8 + central label.

Charles Lindbergh's Non-stop Solo Trans-Atlantic Flight, 75th Anniv. — A71

2002, Apr. 11
171 A71 1m multi *1.25 1.25*

Printed in sheets of 8 + central label.

Europa — A72

Designs: 1m, Horses and clown. 1.50m, Elephants and clowns.

2002, Apr. 30 Litho. *Perf. 13¾*
172-173 A72 Set of 2 *3.25 3.25*

2002 World Cup Soccer Championships, Japan and Korea — A73

Designs: 50pf, Two players. 1m, Two players, diff.

2002, May 31
174-175 A73 Set of 2 *1.90 1.90*

Resorts — A74

Designs: 25pf, Banja Slatina. 50pf, Banja Mljechanica. 75pf, Banja Vilina Vlas. 1m, Banja Laktashi. 1.50m, Banja Vruchica. 5m, Banja Dvorovi.

2002, July 5
176-181 A74 Set of 6 *11.50 11.50*

Artifacts — A75

Designs: No. 182, 50pf, Greco-Illyrian helmet, 4th-5th cent. No. 183, 50pf, Glassware, 14th cent. No. 184, 1m, Silver snake heads, 4th-5th cent. No. 185, 1m, Inscriptions on stone, 12th cent.

2002, Sept. 5
182-185 A75 Set of 4 *3.75 3.75*

Mushrooms A76

No. 186: a, Boletus regius. b, Macrolepiota procera. c, Amanita caesarea. d, Craterellus cornucopioides.

2002, Oct. 17 Litho. *Perf. 13¾*
186 Horiz. strip of 4, #a=d, + central label *3.50 3.50*
a.-b. A76 50pf Any single *.60 .60*
c.-d. A76 1m Any single *1.10 1.10*

REGISTRATION STAMPS

No. 19 Surcharged

1994, Nov. 1 Litho. *Perf. 13¼*
F9 A1 (P) on 6,000d #19 1.75 1.75

No. F9 sold for 40p on day of issue.

Relay Station Type of 1996

Kraljica relay station, Mt. Ozren.

1996, Sept. 20 *Perf. 14*
F10 A9 (R) multicolored .55 .55

No. F10 sold for 90p on day of issue.

Famous Men Type of 1997

1997, Nov. 1 *Perf. 13¾*
F11 A13 (R) Jovan Ducic (1871-1943) .45 .45

No. F11 sold for 90p on day of issue.

Building Type of 1999

1999, Mar. 15 Litho. *Perf. 13¾*
F12 A20 (R) Trebinje 1.60 1.60

No. F12 sold for 1m on day of issue.

POSTAL TAX STAMPS

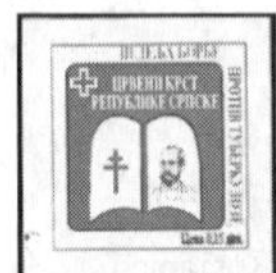

Robert Koch (1843-1910) — PT1

1997, Sept. 14 Litho. *Imperf.*

Self-Adhesive

RA1 PT1 15p red & blue 1.25 1.25

Obligatory on mail 9/14-21.

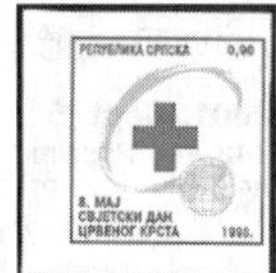

Red Cross — PT2

1998, May 5

Self-Adhesive

RA2 PT2 90p multicolored 1.50 1.50

Obligatory on mail 5/5-15.

Fight Against Tuberculosis PT3

1998, Sept. 14 *Perf. 10¾*
RA3 PT3 75pf multicolored 1.50 1.50

Obligatory on mail 9/14-21.

Red Cross — PT4

1999, May 8 Litho. *Perf. 10¾*
RA4 PT4 10pf multi *.35 .35*

Obligatory on mail 5/8-5/15.

Red Cross — PT5

1999, Sept. 14 Litho. *Perf. 10¾*
RA5 PT5 10pf multi .40 .40

Obligatory on mail 9/14-21.

Red Cross — PT6

2000, May 8 Litho. *Perf. 10¾*
RA6 PT6 10pf multi *.35 .35*

Obligatory on mail 5/8-5/15.

Red Cross — PT7

2000, Sept. 14 Litho. *Perf. 10¾*
RA7 PT7 10pf multi *.30 .30*

Obligatory on mail 9/14-21.

Red Cross — PT8

2001, May 8 Litho. *Perf. 10¾*
RA8 PT8 10pf multi .20 .20

Obligatory on mail 5/8-5/15.

Anti-Tuberculosis Week — PT9

2001, Sept. 14 Litho. *Perf. 10½*
RA9 PT9 10pf multi .20 .20

Obligatory on mail 9/14-9/21.

Red Cross — PT10

2002, May 8 Litho. *Perf. 10¾*
RA10 PT10 10pf multi .20 .20

Obligatory on mail 5/8-5/15.

Fight Against Tuberculosis — PT11

2002, Sept. 14 Litho. *Perf. 10¾*
RA11 PT11 10pf multi .20 .20

Obligatory on mail 9/14-9/21.

BOTSWANA

bä-ˈswä-nə

LOCATION — In central South Africa, north of the Republic of South Africa, east of South-West Africa and bounded on the north and east by Angola and Zimbabwe.
GOVT. — Independent republic
AREA — 222,000 sq. mi.
POP. — 1,464,167 (1999 est.)
CAPITAL — Gaborone

The former Bechuanaland Protectorate became an independent republic, September 30, 1966, taking the name Botswana.

100 Cents = 1 Rand
100 Thebe = 1 Pula (1976)

Catalogue values for all unused stamps in this country are for Never Hinged items.

National Assembly Building — A1

Designs: 5c, Abattoir, Lobatsi. 15c, Dakota plane. 35c, State House, Gaborone.

Unwmk.

1966, Sept. 30 Photo. *Perf. 14*

1 A1 2½c multicolored .20 .20
a. Imperf., pair *225.00*
2 A1 5c multicolored .30 .20
3 A1 15c multicolored .90 .25
4 A1 35c multicolored .60 .50
Nos. 1-4 (4) 2.00 1.15

Establishment of Republic of Botswana.

Bechuanaland Protectorate Nos. 180-193 Overprinted

Perf. 14x14½, 14½x14

1966, Sept. 30 Wmk. 314

5 A15 1c multicolored .20 .20
6 A15 2c multicolored .20 1.00
7 A15 2½c multicolored .20 .20
8 A15 3½c multicolored .20 .20
9 A15 5c multicolored .20 *1.50*
10 A15 7½c multicolored .20 *1.75*
11 A15 10c multicolored .25 .20
12 A15 12½c multicolored 2.50 *2.75*
13 A15 20c gray & brown .75 1.00
14 A15 25c yel & dk brn .60 *2.00*
15 A15 35c dp org & ultra .70 *2.25*
16 A15 50c lt ol grn & sep 1.25 .70
17 A15 1r ocher & black 2.25 1.25
18 A15 2r blue & brown 5.50 2.50
Nos. 5-18 (14) 15.00 17.50

European Golden Oriole — A2

Birds: 2c, African hoopoe. 3c, Groundscraper thrush. 4c, Blue waxbill. 5c, Secretary bird. 7c, Yellow-billed hornbill. 10c, Crimson-breasted shrike. 15c, Malachite kingfisher. 20c, Fish eagle. 25c, Gray lourie. 35c, Scimitar bill. 50c, Knob-billed duck. 1r, Crested barbet. 2r, Didrio cuckoo.

Perf. 14x14½

1967, Jan. 3 Photo. Unwmk.

19 A2 1c gray & multi .30 .20
20 A2 2c lt blue & multi .45 .20
21 A2 3c yel green & multi .60 .20
22 A2 4c salmon & multi .60 .25
23 A2 5c pink & multi .60 .30
24 A2 7c slate & multi .65 .45
25 A2 10c emerald & multi .65 .55
26 A2 15c lt green & multi 9.25 1.00
27 A2 20c ultra & multi 9.25 1.25
28 A2 25c green & multi 5.50 1.60
29 A2 35c multicolored 7.50 2.00
30 A2 50c dl yel & multi 3.50 3.00
31 A2 1r dl grn & multi 8.50 4.00
32 A2 2r org brn & multi 10.00 *12.00*
Nos. 19-32 (14) 57.35 27.00

University Buildings and Graduates — A3

1967, Apr. 7 *Perf. 14x14½*

33 A3 3c yel, sepia & dp blue .20 .20
34 A3 7c blue, sepia & dp bl .20 .20
35 A3 15c dull rose, sepia & dp bl .20 .20
36 A3 35c lt vio, sepia & dp bl .30 .30
Nos. 33-36 (4) .90 .90

1st conferment of degrees by the University of Botswana, Lesotho and Swaziland at Roma, Lesotho.

Chobe Bush Bucks A4

Designs: 7c, Sable antelopes. 35c, Fishing on the Chobe River.

1967, Oct. 2 Photo. *Perf. 14*

37 A4 3c multicolored .20 .20
38 A4 7c multicolored .20 .20
39 A4 35c multicolored .60 .95
Nos. 37-39 (3) 1.00 1.35

Publicity for Chobe Game Reserve.

Human Rights Flame and Arms of Botswana — A5

Design elements rearranged on 15c, 25c.

1968, Apr. 8 Litho. *Perf. 13½x13*

40 A5 3c brown red & multi .20 .20
41 A5 15c emerald & multi .25 *.35*
42 A5 25c yellow & multi .40 *.40*
Nos. 40-42 (3) .85 .95

International Human Rights Year.

Rock Painting A6

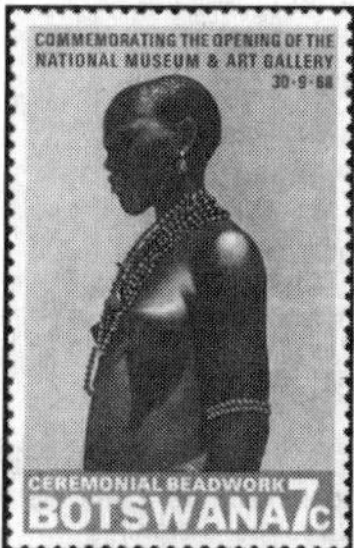

Girl Wearing Ceremonial Beads — A7

Designs: 10c, Baobab Trees, by Thomas Baines (34x25mm). 15c, National Museum and Art Gallery (71½x19mm).

Perf. 13x13½ (3c, 10c); Perf. 12½ (7c); Perf. 12½x13 (15c)

1968, Sept. 30 Litho.

43 A6 3c multicolored .30 .20
44 A7 7c multicolored .40 .35
45 A6 10c multicolored .40 .30
46 A6 15c multicolored .65 *1.40*
a. Souv. sheet of 4, #43-46, perf. 13½ 1.75 *2.50*
Nos. 43-46 (4) 1.75 2.25

Opening of the National Museum and Art Gallery, Gaborone, Sept. 30, 1968.

African Nativity Scene A8

1968, Nov. 11 Unwmk. *Perf. 13x14*

47 A8 1c car & multi .20 .20
48 A8 2c brown & multi .20 .20
49 A8 5c green & multi .20 .20
50 A8 25c dp violet & multi .25 .50
Nos. 47-50 (4) .85 1.10

Christmas.

Boy Scout, Botswana Scout Emblem and Lion — A9

Botswana Boy Scout Emblem, Lion and: 15c, Boy Scouts cooking, vert. 25c, Boy Scouts around campfire.

1969, Aug. 21 Litho. *Perf. 13½*

51 A9 3c emerald & multi .20 .20
52 A9 15c lt brown & multi .90 *1.25*
53 A9 25c dk brown & multi 1.50 *1.75*
Nos. 51-53 (3) 2.60 3.20

22nd World Scouting Conf., Helsinki, Finland, Aug. 21-27.

Mother, Child and Star of Bethlehem — A10

Diamond Treatment Plant, Orapa — A11

1969, Nov. 6 *Perf. 14½x14*

54 A10 1c dk brn & lt blue .20 .20
55 A10 2c dk brn & apple grn .20 .20
56 A10 4c dk brn & dull yel .20 .20
57 A10 35c dk brn & vio blue .30 .30
a. Souv. sheet, #54-57, perf 14½ 1.25 *1.40*
Nos. 54-57 (4) .90 .90

Christmas.

1970, Mar. 23 *Perf. 14½x14, 14x14½*

Designs: 7c, Copper and nickel mining, Selebi-Pikwe. 10c, Copper and nickel mining and metal bars, Selebi-Pikwe, horiz. 35c, Orapa diamond mine and diamonds, horiz.

58 A11 3c multicolored *.50* *.30*
59 A11 7c multicolored *1.10* *.30*
60 A11 10c multicolored *2.25* *.25*
61 A11 35c multicolored *3.50* *1.90*
Nos. 58-61 (4) 7.35 *2.75*

Botswana development program.

Mr. Micawber and Charles Dickens A12

Charles Dickens (1812-70), English novelist and: 7c, Scrooge. 15c, Fagin. 25c, Bill Sykes.

1970, July 7 Litho. *Perf. 11*

62 A12 3c gray green & multi .20 .20
63 A12 7c multicolored .30 .20
64 A12 15c brown & multi .60 .50
65 A12 25c dp violet & multi 1.00 .75
a. Souvenir sheet of 4, #62-65 4.00 4.50
Nos. 62-65 (4) 2.10 1.65

UN Headquarters, Emblem — A13

1970, Oct. 24 Litho. *Perf. 11*

66 A13 15c ultra, red & silver .70 .40

United Nations' 25th anniversary.

Toys A14

1970, Nov. 3 Litho. *Perf. 14*

67 A14 1c Crocodile .20 .20
68 A14 2c Giraffe .20 .20
69 A14 7c Elephant .20 .20
70 A14 25c Rhinoceros .75 .75
a. Souvenir sheet of 4, #67-70 2.00 2.00
Nos. 67-70 (4) 1.35 1.35

Christmas.

Sorghum A15

1971, Apr. 6 Litho. *Perf. 14*

71 A15 3c shown .20 .20
72 A15 7c Millet .20 .20
73 A15 10c Corn .25 .20
74 A15 35c Peanuts 1.00 .65
Nos. 71-74 (4) 1.65 1.25

Ox Head and Botswana Map — A16

Map of Botswana and: 4c, Cogwheels and waves. 7c, Zebra rampant. 10c, Tusk and corn. 20c, Coat of arms of Botswana.

1971, Sept. 30 *Perf. 14½x14*

75 A16 3c yel grn, blk & brn .20 .20
76 A16 4c lt blue, blk & bl .20 .20
77 A16 7c orange & blk .20 .20

78 A16 10c yellow & multi .30 .20
79 A16 20c blue & multi .60 1.75
Nos. 75-79 (5) 1.50 2.55

5th anniversary of independence.

King Bringing Gift — A17

1971, Nov. 11 ***Perf. 14***

Christmas: 2c, King bringing gift. 7c, Kneeling King with gift. 20c, Three Kings and star.

80 A17 2c brt rose & multi .20 .20
81 A17 3c lt blue & multi .20 .20
82 A17 7c brt pink & multi .20 .20
83 A17 20c vio blue & multi .30 .50
a. Souvenir sheet of 4, #80-83 1.25 2.00
Nos. 80-83 (4) .90 1.10

Constellation Orion — A18

Night Sky over Botswana: 7c, Scorpio. 10c, Centaur. 20c, Southern Cross.

1972, Apr. 24 **Litho.** ***Perf. 14***

84 A18 3c dp org, bl grn & blk .40 .40
85 A18 7c org, blue & blk .75 .75
86 A18 10c org, green & blk 1.10 1.10
87 A18 20c emer, vio bl & blk 2.25 2.25
Nos. 84-87 (4) 4.50 4.50

Gubulawayo Cancel and Map of Trail — A19

Cross, Map of Botswana, Bells — A20

Sections of Mafeking-Gubulawayo Trail and: 4c, Bechuanaland Protectorate No. 65. 7c, Mail runners. 20c, Mafeking 638 killer cancellation.

1972, Aug. 21 ***Perf. 13½x13***

88 A19 3c cream & multi .20 .20
89 A19 4c cream & multi .20 .20
90 A19 7c cream & multi .45 .45
91 A19 20c cream & multi 1.50 1.50
a. Souvenir sheet of 4 14.00 17.50
Nos. 88-91 (4) 2.35 2.35

84th anniv. of Mafeking to Gubulawayo runner post. No. 91a contains one each of Nos. 88-91, arranged vertically to show map of trail. Compare with design A89.

1972, Nov. 6 **Litho.** ***Perf. 14***

Cross, Map of Botswana and: 3c, Candle. 7c, Christmas tree. 20c, Star and holly.

92 A20 2c yellow & multi .20 .20
93 A20 3c pale lilac & multi .20 .20
94 A20 7c yel green & multi .20 .20
95 A20 20c pink & multi .50 .50
a. Souvenir sheet of 4, #92-95 2.00 2.00
Nos. 92-95 (4) 1.10 1.10

Christmas.

Chariot of the Sun, Trundholm, Denmark — A21

WMO Emblem and: 3c, Thor, Norse thunder god, vert. 7c, Ymir, Icelandic frost giant, vert. 20c, Odin on 8-legged horse Sleipnir.

1973, Mar. 23 **Litho.** ***Perf. 14***

96 A21 3c orange & multi .20 .20
97 A21 4c yellow & multi .25 .20
98 A21 7c ultra & multi .45 .20
99 A21 20c gold & multi 1.25 .90
Nos. 96-99 (4) 2.15 1.50

Intl. meteorological cooperation, cent.

Livingstone and Boat on Lake Ngwami — A22

Design: 20c, Livingstone and his meeting with Henry Stanley.

1973, Sept. 10 **Litho.** ***Perf. 13½x14***

100 A22 3c gray & multi .20 .20
101 A22 20c yel green & multi .95 .80

Dr. David Livingstone (1813-1873), medical missionary and explorer.

Shepherd and Flock — A23

Christmas: 3c, Ass and foal, African huts, vert. 7c, African mother, child and star, vert. 20c, Tribal meeting (kgotla), symbolic of Wise Men.

1973, Nov. 12 **Litho.** ***Perf. 14½***

102 A23 3c multicolored .20 .20
103 A23 4c multicolored .20 .20
104 A23 7c multicolored .20 .20
105 A23 20c multicolored .30 .40
Nos. 102-105 (4) .90 1.00

Gaborone Campus, Botswana A24

7c, Kwaluseni Campus, Swaziland. 20c, Roma Campus, Lesotho. 35c, Map and flags of Botswana, Swaziland & Lesotho.

1974, May 8 **Litho.** ***Perf. 14***

106 A24 3c lt blue & multi .20 .20
107 A24 7c yel green & multi .20 .20
108 A24 20c yel green & multi .20 .20
109 A24 35c brt blue & multi .30 .30
Nos. 106-109 (4) .90 .90

10th anniversary of the University of Botswana, Lesotho and Swaziland.

UPU Emblem, Mail Vehicles — A25

UPU Cent.: 3c, Post Office, Palapye, c. 1889. 7c, Bechuanaland police camel post, 1900. 20c, 1920 and 1974 planes.

1974, May 22 **Litho.** ***Perf. 13½x14***

110 A25 2c car & multi .60 .40
111 A25 3c green & multi .60 .40
112 A25 7c brown & multi 1.00 .70
113 A25 20c blue & multi 3.00 2.75
Nos. 110-113 (4) 5.20 4.25

Amethyst A26

Minerals, precious and semiprecious stones.

1974, July 1 **Photo.** ***Perf. 14x13***

114 A26 1c shown .55 .90
115 A26 2c Agate .55 .90
116 A26 3c Quartz .60 .70
117 A26 4c Niccolite .70 .50
118 A26 5c Moss agate .70 .90
119 A26 7c Agate .80 .55
120 A26 10c Stilbite 1.60 .55
121 A26 15c Moshaneng banded marble 2.00 2.75
122 A26 20c Gem diamonds 4.00 3.50
123 A26 25c Chrysotile 5.00 2.25
124 A26 35c Jasper 5.25 4.00
125 A26 50c Moss quartz 4.50 6.25
126 A26 1r Citrine 7.75 8.75
127 A26 2r Chalcopyrite 21.00 17.50
Nos. 114-127 (14) 55.00 50.00

For surcharges see Nos. 155-168.

Stapelia Variegata — A27

Pres. Sir Seretse Khama — A28

Flowers of Botswana: 7c, Hibiscus lunarifolius. 15c, Ceratotheca triloba. 20c, Nerine laticoma.

1974, Nov. 4 **Litho.** ***Perf. 14***

128 A27 2c multicolored .20 .45
129 A27 7c multicolored .55 .20
130 A27 15c multicolored 1.00 1.60
131 A27 20c multicolored 1.50 2.00
a. Souvenir sheet of 4, #128-131 4.00 4.75
Nos. 128-131 (4) 3.25 4.25

1975, Mar. 24 **Photo.** ***Perf. 13½x13***

132 A28 4c olive & multi .20 .20
133 A28 10c yellow & multi .20 .20
134 A28 20c ultra & multi .30 .30
135 A28 35c brown & multi .50 .50
a. Souvenir sheet of 4, #132-135 1.25 1.75
Nos. 132-135 (4) 1.20 1.20

10th anniv. of self-government.

Ostrich and Rock Painting A29

Paintings and Animals: 10c, Rhinoceros. 25c, Hyena. 35c, Scorpion.

1975, June 23 **Litho.** ***Perf. 14x14½***

136 A29 4c yel green & multi .85 .20
137 A29 10c buff & multi 1.40 .20
138 A29 25c blue & multi 2.50 .75
139 A29 35c lilac & multi 2.75 1.50
a. Souvenir sheet of 4, #136-139 10.00 2.75
Nos. 136-139 (4) 7.50 2.65

Rock paintings from Tsodilo Hills.

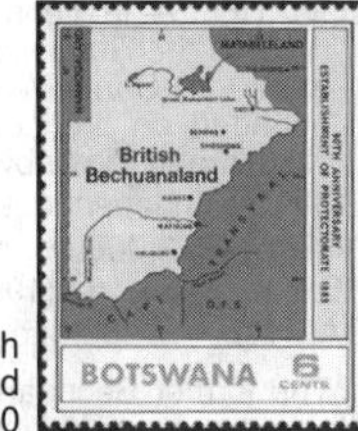

Map of British Bechuanaland A30

Chiefs Sebele, Bathoen and Khama A31

10c, Khama the Great and antelope.

Perf. 14½x14, 14x14½

1975, Oct. 31 **Litho.**

140 A30 6c buff & multi .35 .20
141 A30 10c rose & multi .45 .20
142 A31 25c lt green & multi .95 .85
Nos. 140-142 (3) 1.75 1.25

Establishment of Protectorate, 90th anniv. (6c); Khama the Great (1828-1923), centenary of his accession as chief (10c); visit of the chiefs of the Bakwena, Bangwaketse and Bamangwato tribes to London, 80th anniv. (25c).

Aloe Marlothii — A32

Christmas: 10c, Aloe lutescens. 15c, Aloe zebrina. 25c, Aloe littoralis.

1975, Nov. 3 **Litho.** ***Perf. 14½x14***

143 A32 3c multicolored .25 .20
144 A32 10c multicolored .75 .20
145 A32 15c multicolored 1.00 1.75
146 A32 25c multicolored 2.00 3.00
Nos. 143-146 (4) 4.00 5.15

Drum A33

Traditional Musical Instruments: 10c, Hand piano. 15c, Segankuru (violin). 25c, Kudu signal horn.

1976, Mar. 1 **Litho.** ***Perf. 14***

147 A33 4c yellow & multi .20 .20
148 A33 10c lilac & multi .25 .20
149 A33 15c dull yel & multi .35 .60
150 A33 25c lt blue & multi .45 1.40
Nos. 147-150 (4) 1.25 2.40

1-pula Bank Note with Seretse Khama A34

Reverse of Bank Notes: 10c, Farm workers. 15c, Antelopes. 25c, National Assembly building.

1976, June 28 **Litho.** ***Perf. 14***

151 A34 4c rose & multi .20 .20
152 A34 10c brt green & multi .20 .20
153 A34 15c yel green & multi .35 .35

154 A34 25c blue & multi .50 .50
a. Souvenir sheet of 4, #151-154 2.00 3.00
Nos. 151-154 (4) 1.25 1.25

First national currency.

Nos. 114-127 Surcharged in Black or Gold

1976, Aug. 23 Photo. Perf. 14x13

155 A26 1t on 1c multi 1.75 .60
156 A26 2t on 2c multi 1.75 .90
157 A26 3t on 3c multi (G) 1.40 .50
158 A26 4t on 4c multi 2.25 .35
159 A26 5t on 5c multi 2.25 .35
160 A26 7t on 7c multi 1.10 2.10
161 A26 10t on 10c multi 1.25 .65
162 A26 15t on 15c multi (G) 4.00 1.90
163 A26 20t on 20c multi 7.00 .65
164 A26 25t on 25c multi 4.50 1.00
165 A26 35t on 35c multi 4.00 3.75
166 A26 50t on 50c multi 6.50 7.50
167 A26 1p on 1r multi 7.25 8.00
168 A26 2p on 2r multi (G) 10.00 9.25
Nos. 155-168 (14) 55.00 37.50

Cattle Industry A35

Designs: 10t, Antelope, tourism, vert. 15t, Schoolhouse and children, education. 25t, Rural weaving, vert. 35t, Mining industry, vert.

1976, Sept. 30 Litho. Perf. 14x14½
Textured Paper

169 A35 4t multicolored .20 .20
170 A35 10t multicolored .40 .40
171 A35 15t multicolored .50 .50
172 A35 25t multicolored .75 .75
173 A35 35t multicolored 1.00 1.00
Nos. 169-173 (5) 2.85 2.85

10th anniversary of independence.

Colophospermum Mopane — A36

Trees: 4t, Baikiaea plurijuga. 10t, Sterculia rogersii. 25t, Acacia nilotica. 40t, Kigelia africana.

1976, Nov. 1 Litho. Perf. 13

174 A36 3t multicolored .20 .20
175 A36 4t multicolored .20 .20
176 A36 10t multicolored .35 .35
177 A36 25t multicolored .75 .75
178 A36 40t multicolored 1.25 1.25
Nos. 174-178 (5) 2.75 2.75

Christmas.

Pres. Seretse Khama and Elizabeth II — A37

Designs: 25t, Coronation coach in procession. 40t, Recognition scene.

1977, Feb. 7 Litho. Perf. 12

179 A37 4t multicolored .20 .20
180 A37 25t multicolored .25 .30
181 A37 40t multicolored .40 .50
Nos. 179-181 (3) .85 1.00

Reign of Queen Elizabeth II, 25th anniv.

Clawless Otter — A38

Wildlife Fund Emblem and: 4t, Serval. 10t, Bat-eared foxes. 25t, Pangolins. 40t, Brown hyena.

1977, June 6 Litho. Perf. 14

182 A38 3t multicolored 5.25 .50
183 A38 4t multicolored 5.25 1.00
184 A38 10t multicolored 6.50 1.75
185 A38 25t multicolored 15.00 4.00
186 A38 40t multicolored 18.00 9.00
Nos. 182-186 (5) 50.00 16.25

Endangered wildlife.

Khama Memorial A39

4t, Cwihaba Caves. 15t, Green's (expedition) tree. 20t, Mmajojo ruins. 25t, Ancient morabaraba board. 35t, Matsieng's footprints.

1977, Aug. 22 Litho. Perf. 14

187 A39 4t multicolored .20 .20
188 A39 5t multicolored .20 .20
189 A39 15t multicolored .45 .45
190 A39 20t multicolored .55 .55
191 A39 25t multicolored .80 .80
192 A39 35t multicolored 1.10 1.10
a. Souvenir sheet of 6, #187-192 3.50 4.00
Nos. 187-192 (6) 3.30 3.30

Historical sites and national monuments.

Hypoxis itida — A40

Black Korhaan — A41

Lilies: 5t, Haemanthus magnificus. 10t, Boophane disticha. 25t, Vellozia retinervis. 40t, Ammocharis coranica.

1977, Oct. 31 Litho. Perf. 14

193 A40 3t sepia & multi .20 .20
194 A40 5t gray & multi .20 .20
195 A40 10t multicolored .30 .30
196 A40 25t multicolored .55 .75
197 A40 40t multicolored .75 1.25
Nos. 193-197 (5) 2.00 2.70

Christmas.

1978, July 3 Photo. Perf. 14

Designs: Birds.

198 A41 1t shown .65 1.00
199 A41 2t Marabou storks .65 1.00
200 A41 3t Red-billed hoopoe .65 .75
201 A41 4t Carmine bee-eaters .65 .65
202 A41 5t African jacana .65 .35
203 A41 7t Paradise flycatcher .65 2.25
204 A41 10t Bennett's woodpecker 1.60 .50
205 A41 15t Red bishop .95 2.25
206 A41 20t Crowned plovers 1.40 1.75
207 A41 25t Giant kingfishers .65 2.25
208 A41 30t White-faced ducks .65 .60
209 A41 35t Green-backed heron .65 2.75
210 A41 45t Black-headed herons .95 2.40
211 A41 50t Spotted eagle owl 6.00 4.00
212 A41 1p Gabar goshawk 3.00 4.00
213 A41 2p Martial eagle 3.75 7.00
214 A41 5p Saddlebill storks 11.50 14.00
Nos. 198-214 (17) 35.00 47.50

For surcharges see Nos. 289-290.

Tawana Making Kaross (garment) A42

Designs: 5t, Map of Okavango Delta. 15t, Bushman collecting roots. 20t, Herero woman milking cow. 25t, Yei pulling mokoro (boat). 35t, Mbukushu fishing.

1978, Sept. 11 Litho. Perf. 14
Textured Paper

215 A42 4t multicolored .20 .20
216 A42 5t multicolored .20 .20
217 A42 15t multicolored .20 .35
218 A42 20t multicolored .30 .45
219 A42 25t multicolored .40 .50
220 A42 35t multicolored .50 1.25
a. Souvenir sheet of 6, #215-220 2.50 3.00
Nos. 215-220 (6) 1.80 2.95

People of the Okavango Delta.

Caralluma Lutea — A43

Boy at Sip Well — A44

Flowers: 10t, Hoodia lugardii. 15t, Ipomoea transvaalensis. 25t, Ansellia gigantea.

1978, Nov. 6

221 A43 5t multicolored .40 .20
222 A43 10t multicolored .60 .30
223 A43 15t multicolored 1.00 .50
224 A43 25t multicolored 1.25 .80
Nos. 221-224 (4) 3.25 1.80

Christmas.

1979, Feb. 12 Litho. Perf. 14

Water Development: 5t, Watering pit. 10t, Hand-dug well and goats. 25t, Windmill, well and cattle. 40t, Modern drilling rig.

225 A44 3t multicolored .20 .20
226 A44 5t multicolored .20 .20
227 A44 10t multicolored .20 .20
228 A44 25t multicolored .40 .40
229 A44 40t multicolored .65 .65
Nos. 225-229 (5) 1.65 1.65

Botswana Pot — A45

Handicrafts: 10t, Clay buffalo. 25t, Woven covered basket. 40t, Beaded bag.

1979, June 4 Litho. Perf. 14

230 A45 5t multicolored .20 .20
231 A45 10t multicolored .20 .20
232 A45 25t multicolored .40 .40
233 A45 40t multicolored .65 .65
a. Souvenir sheet of 4, #230-233 1.60 1.60
Nos. 230-233 (4) 1.45 1.45

Bechuanaland No. 6, Rowland Hill — A46

Sir Rowland Hill (1795-1879), originator of penny postage, and: 25t, Bechuanaland Protectorate No. 107. 45t, Botswana No. 20.

1979, Aug. 27 Litho. Perf. 13½

234 A46 5t rose & black .20 .20
235 A46 25t multicolored .35 .35
236 A46 45t multicolored .60 .60
Nos. 234-236 (3) 1.15 1.15

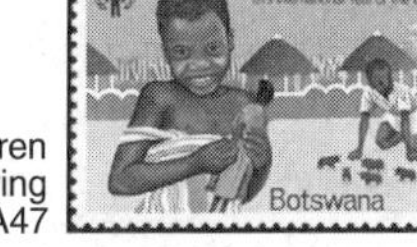

Children Playing A47

Design: 10t, Child playing with rag doll, and IYC emblem, vert.

1979, Sept. 24 Perf. 14

237 A47 5t multicolored .20 .20
238 A47 10t multicolored .25 .25

International Year of the Child.

Ximenia Caffra — A48

Christmas: 10t, Sclerocarya caffra. 15t, Hexalobus monopetalus. 25t, Ficus soldanella.

1979, Nov. 12 Litho. Perf. 14

239 A48 5t multicolored .20 .20
240 A48 10t multicolored .20 .20
241 A48 15t multicolored .30 .30
242 A48 25t multicolored .50 .50
Nos. 239-242 (4) 1.20 1.20

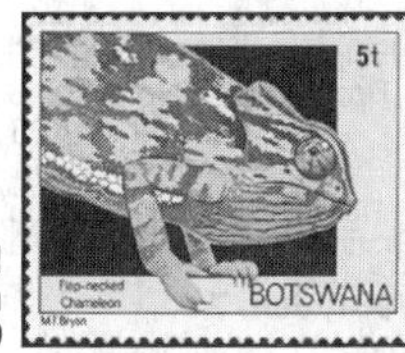

Flap-Necked Chameleon A49

1980, Mar. 3 Litho. Perf. 14

243 A49 5t shown .65 .65
244 A49 10t Leopard tortoise .65 .65
245 A49 25t Puff adder 1.10 1.10
246 A49 40t White-throated monitor 1.60 1.60
Nos. 243-246 (4) 4.00 4.00

Rock Breaking (Early Mining) A50

1980, July 7 Litho. Perf. 13½x14

247 A50 5t shown .30 .30
248 A50 10t Ore hoisting .35 .35
249 A50 15t Ore transport .85 .85
250 A50 20t Ore crushing .90 .90
251 A50 25t Smelting .95 .95
252 A50 35t Tools, products 1.25 1.25
Nos. 247-252 (6) 4.60 4.60

Chiwele and the Giant — A51

Folktales: 10t, Kgori Is Not Deceived. 30t, Nyambi's Wife and Crocodile. 45t, Clever Hare, horiz.

Perf. 14, 14½ (10t, 30t)

1980, Sept. 8

253 A51 5t multicolored .20 .20

Size: 28x36mm

254 A51 10t multicolored .20 .20
255 A51 30t multicolored .50 .50

Size: 44x26mm

256 A51 45t multicolored .80 .80
Nos. 253-256 (4) 1.70 1.70

Game Watching — A52

1980, Oct. 6 Litho. Perf. 14

257 A52 5t multicolored .20 .20

World Tourism Conf., Manila, Sept. 27.

Acacia Gerrardii — A53

Christmas: Flowering Trees.

1980, Nov. 3 Litho. *Perf. 14*

258 A53 5t shown .20 .20
259 A53 10t Acacia nilotica .25 .20
260 A53 25t Acacia erubescens .50 .30
261 A53 40t Dichrostachys cinerea .80 .45
Nos. 258-261 (4) 1.75 1.15

Heinrich von Stephan, Bechuanaland Protectorate No. 150, Botswana No. 111 — A55

Design: 20t, Von Stephan, Bechuanaland Protectorate No. 151, Botswana No. 112.

1981, Jan. 7 *Perf. 14*

266 A55 6t multicolored .75 .50
267 A55 20t multicolored 1.75 *2.50*

Von Stephan (1831-1897), founder of UPU.

Emperor Dragonfly — A56

1981, Feb. 23 Litho. *Perf. 14*

268 A56 6t shown .25 .20
269 A56 7t Praying mantis .25 .25
270 A56 10t Elegant grasshopper .30 .25
271 A56 20t Dung beetle .50 *.65*
272 A56 30t Citrus swallowtail butterfly .75 *.90*
273 A56 45t Mopane worm .95 *1.50*
a. Souv. sheet of 6, #268-273 5.00 *10.00*
Nos. 268-273 (6) 3.00 3.75

Blind Basket Weaver A57

1981, Apr. 4 Litho. *Perf. 14*

274 A57 6t Seamstress .20 .20
275 A57 20t shown .55 .30
276 A57 30t Carpenter .75 .40
Nos. 274-276 (3) 1.50 .90

International Year of the Disabled.

Woman Reading Letter (Literacy Campaign) — A58

1981, June 8

277 A58 6t shown .20 .20
278 A58 7t Man sending telegram .20 .20
279 A58 20t Boy, newspaper .70 .25
280 A58 30t Father and daughter reading .90 .35
Nos. 277-280 (4) 2.00 1.00

Pres. Seretse Khama and Flag A59

First death anniv. of Pres. Khama: Portrait and local buildings.

1981, July 13

281 A59 6t multicolored .20 .20
282 A59 10t multicolored .20 .20
283 A59 30t multicolored .40 .40
284 A59 45t multicolored .60 .60
Nos. 281-284 (4) 1.40 1.40

Cattle in Agricultural Show — A60

1981, Sept. 21 Litho. *Perf. 14½*

285 A60 6t Plowing .20 .20
286 A60 20t shown .20 .20
287 A60 30t Meat Commission .35 .35
288 A60 45t Vaccine Institute .50 .50
Nos. 285-288 (4) 1.25 1.25

Nos. 209, 204 Surcharged in Black

1981, Sept. Photo. *Perf. 14*

289 A41 25t on 35t multicolored 3.50 2.50
290 A41 30t on 10t multicolored 3.50 2.50

Christmas — A61

Designs: Water lilies.

1981, Nov. 2 Litho.

291 A61 6t Nymphaea caerulea .25 .20
292 A61 10t Nymphoides indica .35 .20
293 A61 25t Nymphaea lotus .80 .80
294 A61 40t Ottelia kunenensis 1.00 2.25
Nos. 291-294 (4) 2.40 3.45

Children's Drawings — A62

1982, Feb. 15 Litho. *Perf. 14½x14*

295 A62 6t Cattle .45 .45
296 A62 10t Kgotla meeting .55 .55
297 A62 30t Village 1.75 1.75
298 A62 45t Huts 1.75 1.75
Nos. 295-298 (4) 4.50 4.50

Traditional Houses — A63

1982, May 3 Litho. *Perf. 14*

299 A63 6t Common type .45 .20
300 A63 10t Kgatleng .55 .20
301 A63 30t Northeastern 2.25 1.10
302 A63 45t Sarwa 2.25 3.00
Nos. 299-302 (4) 5.50 4.50

Red-billed Teals — A64

Perf. 14x14½, 14½x14

1982, July 1 Photo.

303 A64 1t Masked weaver .90 *1.25*
304 A64 2t Lesser double-collared sunbirds 1.00 *1.50*
305 A64 3t White-fronted bee-eaters 1.10 *1.50*
306 A64 4t Ostriches 1.10 *1.50*
307 A64 5t Grey-headed gulls 1.10 *1.50*
308 A64 6t Pygmy geese 1.10 .40
309 A64 7t Cattle egrets 1.10 .20
310 A64 8t Lanner falcon 2.25 1.25
311 A64 10t Yellow-billed storks 1.10 .20
312 A64 15t shown 2.75 .25
313 A64 20t Barn owls 6.00 3.75
314 A64 25t Hamerkops 3.25 .75
315 A64 30t Stilts 4.00 .95
316 A64 35t Blacksmith plovers 4.00 .80
317 A64 45t Wattled plover 4.00 1.95
318 A64 50t Crowned guinea-fowl 5.50 2.75
319 A64 1p Cape vultures 9.50 *12.50*
320 A64 2p Augur bustards 11.00 *17.00*
Nos. 303-320 (18) 60.75 50.00

Nos. 303-311 vert.
For surcharges see Nos. 401-403.

Christmas — A65

Endangered Species — A67

A66

Designs: Mushrooms.

1982, Nov. 2 Litho. *Perf. 14½*

321 A65 7t Shaggy mane *1.75* *.75*
322 A65 15t Orange milk *3.00* *1.50*
323 A65 35t Panther *4.75* *3.50*
324 A65 50t King boletus *6.00* *4.75*
Nos. 321-324 (4) *15.50* *10.50*

1983, Mar. 14 Litho. *Perf. 14*

325 A66 7t Pres. Quett Masire .20 .20
326 A66 15t Dancers .20 *.25*
327 A66 35t Melbourne Conference Center .50 *.75*
328 A66 45t Heads of State meeting .60 *1.10*

Commonwealth Day.

1983, Apr. 19 Litho. *Perf. 14x14½*

329 A67 7t Wattle crane 3.00 .45
330 A67 15t Aloe lutescens 2.50 .80
331 A67 35t Roan antelope 3.00 2.75
332 A67 50t Hyphaene ventricosa 3.50 5.00
Nos. 329-332 (4) 12.00 9.00

Wooden Spoons — A68

1983, July 20 Litho. *Perf. 14*

333 A68 7t shown .25 .20
334 A68 15t Jewelry .45 .35
335 A68 35t Ox-hide milk bag 1.10 .85
336 A68 50t Decorated knives 1.25 1.00
a. Souvenir sheet of 4, #333-336 6.00 5.00
Nos. 333-336 (4) 3.05 2.40

Christmas A69

1983, Nov. 7 Litho. *Perf. 14½x14*

Designs: Dragonflies.

337 A69 6t Pantala flavescens .85 .20
338 A69 15t Anax imperator 1.90 .35
339 A69 25t Trithemis arteriosa 2.25 .70
340 A69 45t Chlorolestes elegans 3.00 3.75
Nos. 337-340 (4) 8.00 5.00

Mining Industry — A70

1984, Mar. 19 Litho. *Perf. 14½*

341 A70 7t Diamonds 2.25 2.25
342 A70 15t Lime 2.25 2.25
343 A70 35t Copper, nickel, vert. 3.75 3.75
344 A70 50t Coal, vert. 4.25 4.25
Nos. 341-344 (4) 12.50 12.50

Traditional Transport A71

1984, June 16 Litho. *Perf. 14½x14*

345 A71 7t Man riding ox .25 .25
346 A71 25t Sled .90 .90
347 A71 35t Wagon 1.10 1.10
348 A71 50t Cart 1.75 1.75
Nos. 345-348 (4) 4.00 4.00

Intl. Civil Aviation Org., 40th Anniv. — A72

1984, Oct. 8 Litho. *Perf. 14x13½*

349 A72 7t Avro 504 .85 .20
350 A72 10t Westland Wessex 1.25 .35
351 A72 15t Junkers 52-3M 1.75 .95
352 A72 25t Dragon Rapide 2.40 1.75
353 A72 35t DC-3 2.75 *3.75*
354 A72 50t F27 Fokker Friendship 3.00 *6.00*
Nos. 349-354 (6) 12.00 13.00

Christmas A73

Butterflies.

1984, Nov. 5 Litho. *Perf. 14½x14*

355 A73 7t Papilio demodocus 2.50 .25
356 A73 25t Byblia acheloia 4.00 1.75
357 A73 35t Hypolimnas missipus 4.25 3.50
358 A73 50t Graphium taboranus 5.75 *11.00*
Nos. 355-358 (4) 16.50 16.50

Traditional & Exotic Foods — A74

Bechuanaland No. 4 — A75

1985, Mar. 18 Litho. *Perf. 14½*

359 A74 7t Man preparing ses-waa .20 .20
360 A74 15t Woman preparing bogobe .20 .20
361 A74 25t Girl eating madilla .30 .30
362 A74 50t Woman collecting caterpillars .65 .65
a. Souvenir sheet of 4, #359-362 1.40 1.40
Nos. 359-362 (4) 1.35 1.35

Southern African Development Coordination Conference, 5th anniv.

1985, June 24

Postage stamp cent.: 15t, Bechuanaland Protectorate No. 72. 25t, Bechuanaland Protectorate No. 106. 35t, Bechuanaland No. 199, 50t, Botswana No. 1, horiz.

363 A75 7t multicolored .20 .20
364 A75 15t multicolored .20 .20
365 A75 25t multicolored .30 .30
366 A75 35t multicolored .40 .40
367 A75 50t multicolored .60 .60
Nos. 363-367 (5) 1.70 1.70

Police Centenary A76

7t, Bechuanaland Border Police, 1885-95. 10t, Bechuanaland Mounted Police, 1894-1902. 25t, Bechuanaland Protectorate Police, 1903-66. 50t, Botswana Motorcycle Police, 1966-85.

1985, Aug. 5 *Perf. 14½x14*

368 A76 7t multicolored .20 .20
369 A76 10t multicolored .20 .20
370 A76 25t multicolored .30 .30
371 A76 50t multicolored .60 .60
Nos. 368-371 (4) 1.30 1.30

Edible Wild Cucumbers A77

1985, Nov. 4

372 A77 7t Cucumis metuliferus .20 .20
373 A77 15t Acanthosicyos naudinianus .20 .20
374 A77 25t Coccinia sessifolia .30 .30
375 A77 50t Momordica bal-samina .60 .60
Nos. 372-375 (4) 1.30 1.30

Christmas.

Declaration of Protectorate, Cent. — A78

1985, Dec. 30 Litho. *Perf. 14x14½*

376 A78 7t Heads of state meet .20 .20
377 A78 15t Declaration reading, 1885 .20 .20
378 A78 25t Mackenzie and Khama .30 .30
379 A78 50t Map .60 .60
a. Souvenir sheet of 4, #376-379 1.25 1.25
Nos. 376-379 (4) 1.30 1.30

Halley's Comet — A79

1986, Mar. 24 *Perf. 14½x14*

380 A79 7t Comet over Serowe .20 .20
381 A79 15t Over Bobonong .20 .20
382 A79 35t Over Gomare swamps .40 .40
383 A79 50t Over Thamaga, Letlhakeng .60 .60
Nos. 380-383 (4) 1.40 1.40

Milk Containers — A80

1986, June 23 *Perf. 14½*

384 A80 8t Leather bag .20 .20
385 A80 15t Ceramic pots .20 .20
386 A80 35t Wood pot .40 .40
387 A80 50t Woman, pots .60 .60
Nos. 384-387 (4) 1.40 1.40

Souvenir Sheet

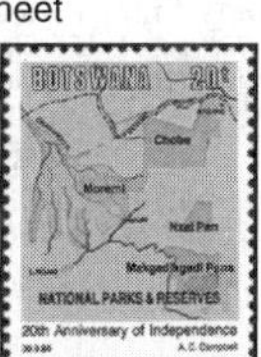

Natl. Independence, 20th Anniv. — A81

Designs: a, Map of natl. parks and reserves. b, Morupule Power Station. c, Cattle, Kgalagadi. d, Natl. Assembly.

1986, Sept. 30 Litho. *Perf. 14½x14*

388 Sheet of 4 .90 .90
a.-d. A81 20t any single .25 .25

Flowers of the Okavango Swamps — A82

1986, Nov. 3 Litho. *Perf. 14x14½*

389 A82 8t Ludwigia stogonifera .20 .20
390 A82 15t Sopubia mannii .20 .20
391 A82 35t Commelina diffusa .40 .40
392 A82 50t Hibiscus diversifolius .55 .55
Nos. 389-392 (4) 1.35 1.35

Christmas.

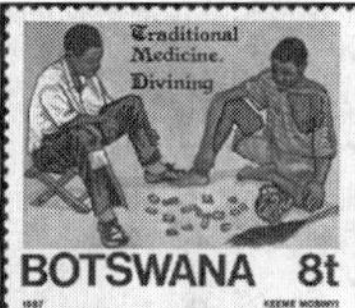

Traditional Medicine A83

1987, Mar. 2 Litho. *Perf. 14½x14*

393 A83 8t Professional diviners .20 .20
394 A83 15t Lightning prevention .20 .20
395 A83 35t Rainmaker .45 .45
396 A83 50t Bloodletting .65 .65
Nos. 393-396 (4) 1.50 1.50

UN Child Survival Campaign — A84

1987, June 1

397 A84 8t Oral rehydration therapy .20 .20
398 A84 15t Growth monitoring .20 .20
399 A84 35t Immunization .45 .45
400 A84 50t Breast-feeding .65 .65
Nos. 397-400 (4) 1.50 1.50

Nos. 308, 311 and 318 Surcharged

Perf. 14x14½,14½x14

1987, Apr. 1 Photo.

401 A64 3t on 6t No. 308 .20 .20
402 A64 5t on 10t No. 311 .20 .20
403 A64 20t on 50t No. 318 .30 .30
Nos. 401-403 (3) .70 .70

Wildlife Conservation — A85

1987, Aug. 3 *Perf. 14*

404 A85 1t Cape fox .20 .20
405 A85 2t Lechwe .20 .20
406 A85 3t Zebra .20 .20
407 A85 4t Duiker .20 .20
408 A85 5t Banded mon-goose .20 .20
409 A85 6t Rusty-spotted ge-net .20 .20
410 A85 8t Hedgehog .20 .20
411 A85 10t Scrub hare .20 .20
412 A85 12t Hippopotamus .20 .20
413 A85 15t Suricate .20 .20
414 A85 20t Caracal .25 .20
415 A85 25t Steenbok .35 .30
416 A85 30t Gemsbok .45 .35
417 A85 35t Square-lipped rhi-no .50 .45
418 A85 40t Mountain reed-buck .60 .50
419 A85 50t Rock dassie .75 .60
420 A85 1p Giraffe 1.50 1.25
421 A85 2p Tsessebe 3.00 2.50
422 A85 3p Side-striped jackal 4.75 3.75
423 A85 5p Hartebeest 8.00 6.50
Nos. 404-423 (20) 22.15 18.40

For surcharges see Nos. 480-482, 506-509.

Wetland Grasses — A86

1987, Oct. 26 *Perf. 14x14½*

424 A86 8t Cyperus articulatus .20 .20
425 A86 15t Miscanthus junceus .20 .20
426 A86 30t Cyperus alopecuroides .35 .35
427 A86 1p Typha latifolia 1.25 1.25
a. Souvenir sheet of 4, #424-427 1.90 1.90
Nos. 424-427 (4) 2.00 2.00

Christmas, preservation of the Okavango and Kuando-Chobe River wetlands.

Early Cultivation Techniques A87

1988, Mar. 14 Litho. *Perf. 14½x14*

428 A87 8t Digging stick .20 .20
429 A87 15t Iron hoe .20 .20
430 A87 35t Wooden plow .40 .40
431 A87 50t Communal planting, Lesotla .60 .60
Nos. 428-431 (4) 1.40 1.40

World Wildlife Fund — A88

Designs: WWF emblem and various red lechwe, Kobus leche.

1988, June 6 Litho. *Perf. 14½x14*

432 A88 10t Adult wading *.35 .35*
433 A88 15t Adult, sun *.50 .50*
434 A88 35t Cow, calf *1.10 1.10*
435 A88 75t Herd *2.50 1.75*
Nos. 432-435 (4) *4.45 3.70*

Runner Post, Cent. — A89

Routes and: 10t, Gubulawayo, Bechuanaland, cancellation dated Aug. 21 '88. 15t, Bechuanaland Protectorate No. 65. 30t, Pack traders. 60t, Mafeking killer cancel No. 638.

1988, Aug. 22 Litho. *Perf. 14½*

436 A89 10t multicolored .20 .20
437 A89 15t multicolored .20 .20
438 A89 30t multicolored .35 .35
439 A89 60t multicolored .65 .65
a. Souvenir sheet of 4, #436-439 1.25 1.25
Nos. 436-439 (4) 1.40 1.40

Printed in a continuous design picturing the Mafeking-Gubulawayo route and part of the Shoshong runner post route.

State Visit of Pope John Paul II, Sept. 13 — A90

Natl. Museum and Art Gallery, Gaborone, 20th Anniv. — A91

1988, Sept. 13 Litho. *Perf. 14x14½*

440 A90 10t Map, portrait .20 .20
441 A90 15t Portrait .20 .20
442 A90 30t Map, portrait, diff. .35 .35
443 A90 80t Portrait, diff. .85 .85
Nos. 440-443 (4) 1.60 1.60

1988, Sept. 30 *Perf. 14½*

444 A91 8t Museum .20 .20
445 A91 15t Pottery, c. 400-1300 .20 .20
446 A91 30t Buffalo bellows .35 .35
447 A91 60t Children, mobile mu-seum .70 .70
Nos. 444-447 (4) 1.45 1.45

A92

Flowering plants of southeastern Botswana.

1988, Oct. 11 Litho. *Perf. 14x14½*

448 A92 8t Grewia flava .20 .20
449 A92 15t Cienfuegosia digitata .20 .20
450 A92 40t Solanum seaforthi-anum .40 .40
451 A92 75t Carissa bispinosa .80 .80
Nos. 448-451 (4) 1.60 1.60

Christmas.

A93

1989, Mar. 13 Litho. *Perf. 14x14½*

Traditional grain storage.

452	A93	8t Sesigo basket granary	.20	.20
453	A93	15t Letlole daga granary	.20	.20
454	A93	30t Sefalana bisque granary	.30	.30
455	A93	60t Serala granaries	.60	.60
		Nos. 452-455 (4)	1.30	1.30

Slaty Egrets A94

1989, July 5 *Perf. 15x14*

456	A94	8t Nesting	*.20*	*.20*
457	A94	15t Young	*.45*	*.30*
458	A94	30t Adult in flight	*.75*	*.60*
459	A94	60t Two adults	*1.60*	*1.40*
a.		Souvenir sheet of 4, #456-459	*3.00*	*2.50*
		Nos. 456-459 (4)	*3.00*	*2.50*

Children's Drawings A95

1989, Sept. 4 *Perf. 14½x14, 14x14½*

460	A95	10t Ephraim Seeletso	.20	.20
461	A95	15t Neelma Bhatia, vert.	.20	.20
462	A95	30t Thabo Habana	.30	.30
463	A95	1p Thabo Olesitse	1.00	1.00
		Nos. 460-463 (4)	1.70	1.70

Star and Orchids — A96

1989, Oct. 30 Litho. *Perf. 14x14½*

464	A96	8t *Eulophia angolensis*	.20	.20
465	A96	15t *Eulophia hereroensis*	.25	.25
466	A96	30t *Eulophia speciosa*	.50	.50
467	A96	60t *Eulophia petersii*	*1.10*	*1.10*
		Nos. 464-467 (4)	*2.05*	*2.05*

Christmas.

Anniversaries — A97

8t, Bechuanaland Protectorate #201. 15t, Voter at ballot box. 30t, Map & flags of nations at SADCC conference. 60t, Great Britain #1.

1990, Mar. 5 Litho. *Perf. 14½*

468	A97	8t multicolored	.20	.20
469	A97	15t multicolored	.20	.20
470	A97	30t multicolored	.30	.30
471	A97	60t multicolored	.60	.60
		Nos. 468-471 (4)	1.30	1.30

25th anniv. of self government (8t); 1st elections, 25th anniv. (15t); Southern African Development Coordination Conference (SADCC), 10th anniv. (30t); and Penny Black, 150th anniv. (60t).

Stamp World London '90 — A98

Traditional Dress — A99

Aspects of the telecommunications industry.

1990, May 3

472	A98	8t Training	.20	.20
473	A98	15t Transmission	.20	.20
474	A98	30t Public telephone	.30	.30
475	A98	2p Testing circuitry	2.00	2.00
		Nos. 472-475 (4)	2.70	2.70

1990, Aug. 1 Litho. *Perf. 14*

476	A99	8t Children	.20	.20
477	A99	15t Young woman	.20	.20
478	A99	30t Man	.25	.25
479	A99	2p Adult woman	1.75	1.75
a.		Souvenir sheet of 4, #476-479	2.50	2.50
		Nos. 476-479 (4)	2.40	2.40

10t

Nos. 404 and 412 Surcharged

No. 409 Surcharged 20t

1990

480	A85	10t on 1t No. 404	.20	.20
481	A85	20t on 6t No. 409	.20	.20
482	A85	50t on 12t No. 412	.50	.50
		Nos. 480-482 (3)	.90	.90

Flowering Trees — A100

1990, Oct. 30 Litho. *Perf. 14*

483	A100	8t Acacia nigrescens	.20	.20
484	A100	15t Peltophorum africanum	.20	.20
485	A100	30t Burkea africana	.25	.25
486	A100	2p Pterocarpus angolensis	1.75	1.75
		Nos. 483-486 (4)	2.40	2.40

Christmas.

Natl. Road Safety Day A101

1990, Dec. 7 Litho. *Perf. 14½*

487	A101	8t Children playing on road	.20	.20
488	A101	15t Accident	.20	.20
489	A101	30t Livestock on road	.35	.35
		Nos. 487-489 (3)	.75	.75

Petroglyphs A102

Various petroglyphs.

1991, Mar. 4 Litho. *Perf. 14x14½*
Textured Paper

490	A102	8t multicolored	.20	.20
491	A102	15t multicolored	.20	.20
492	A102	30t multicolored	.30	.30
493	A102	2p multicolored	2.00	2.00
		Nos. 490-493 (4)	2.70	2.70

Natl. Census — A103

1991, June 3 Litho. *Perf. 14*

494	A103	8t Children playing	.20	.20

Perf. 14½

495	A103	15t Houses	.20	.20

Perf. 14x14½

496	A103	30t Children in schoolyard	.35	.35
497	A103	2p Children, hospital	2.40	2.40
		Nos. 494-497 (4)	3.15	3.15

African Tourism Year A104

1991, Sept. 30 Litho. *Perf. 14*

498	A104	8t Tourists, elephants	.20	.20
499	A104	15t Birds, crocodiles	.20	.20
500	A104	35t Airplane, fish eagles	.40	.40

Size 26x43mm

501	A104	2p Okavango Delta	2.40	2.40
		Nos. 498-501 (4)	3.20	3.20

No. 501 incorporates designs of #498-500.

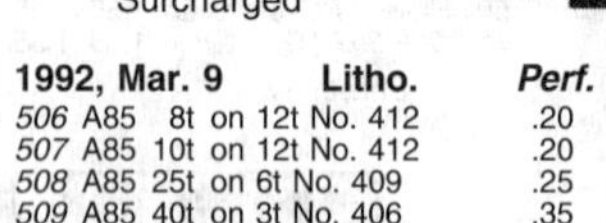

Christmas — A105

Seed pods: 8t, Harpagophytum procumbens. 15t, Tylosema esculentum. 30t, Abrus precatorius. 2p, Kigelia africana.

1991, Nov. 4 Litho. *Perf. 14*

502	A105	8t multicolored	.20	.20
503	A105	15t multicolored	.20	.20
504	A105	30t multicolored	.30	.30
505	A105	2p multicolored	2.25	2.25
		Nos. 502-505 (4)	2.95	2.95

Nos. 406, 409 & 412 Surcharged 8t

1992, Mar. 9 Litho. *Perf. 14*

506	A85	8t on 12t No. 412	.20	.20
507	A85	10t on 12t No. 412	.20	.20
508	A85	25t on 6t No. 409	.25	.25
509	A85	40t on 3t No. 406	.35	.35
		Nos. 506-509 (4)	1.00	1.00

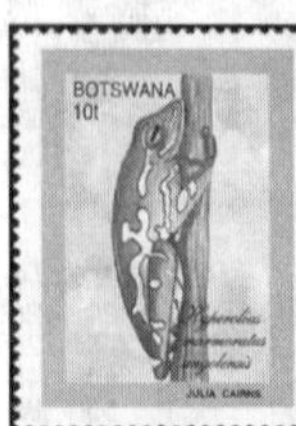

Climbing Frogs — A106

Designs: 8t, Cacosternum boettgeri, horiz. 10t, Hyperolius marmoratus angolensis. 40t, Bufo fenoulheti, horiz. 1p, Hyperolius.

1992, Mar. 23 *Perf. 14½x14, 14x14½*

510	A106	8t multicolored	.20	.20
511	A106	10t multicolored	.20	.20
512	A106	40t multicolored	.40	.40
513	A106	1p multicolored	.95	.95
		Nos. 510-513 (4)	1.75	1.75

Botswana Railways A107

10t, Deluxe air-conditioned coaches. 25t, BD1 locomotive. 40t, Deluxe coach interio. 2p, Locomotive pulling air-conditioned coaches.

1992, June 29 Litho. *Perf. 14*

514	A107	10t multi	.20	.20
515	A107	25t multi, vert.	.20	.20
516	A107	40t multi, vert.	.20	.20
517	A107	2p multi	1.00	1.00
a.		Souv. sheet of 4, #514-517 + label	1.40	1.40
		Nos. 514-517 (4)	1.60	1.60

Wild Animals A108

1992, Aug. 3 Litho. *Perf. 14½*

518	A108	1t Cheetah	.20	.20
519	A108	2t Spring hares	.20	.20
520	A108	4t Blackfooted cat	.20	.20
521	A108	5t Striped mouse	.20	.20
522	A108	10t Oribi	.20	.20
523	A108	12t Pangolin	.20	.20
524	A108	15t Aardwolf	.20	.20
525	A108	20t Warthog	.20	.20
526	A108	25t Ground squirrels	.25	.25
527	A108	35t Honey badger	.30	.30
528	A108	40t Common mole rat	.35	.35
529	A108	45t Wild dogs	.40	.40
530	A108	50t Water mongoose	.45	.45
531	A108	80t Klipspringer	.70	.70
532	A108	1p Lesser bushbaby	.90	.90
533	A108	2p Bushveld elephant shrew	1.75	1.75
534	A108	5p Zorilla	4.50	4.50
535	A108	10p Vervet monkey	9.00	9.00
		Nos. 518-535 (18)	20.20	20.20

For surcharges see Nos. 594A-597.

A109

Ferns — A110

1992, Aug. 7 *Perf. 14x15*

536	A109	10t Boxer	.20	.20
537	A109	50t Four sprinters	.45	.45
538	A109	1p Two boxers	.95	.95
539	A109	2p Three runners	1.90	1.90
a.		Souvenir sheet of 4, #536-539	3.50	3.50
		Nos. 536-539 (4)	3.50	3.50

1992 Summer Olympics, Barcelona.

1992, Nov. 23 Litho. *Perf. 14½*

540	A110	10t Adiantum incisum	.20	.20
541	A110	25t Actiniopteris radiata	.25	.25
542	A110	40t Ceratopteris cornuta	.40	.40
543	A110	1.50p Pellaea calomelanos	1.40	1.40
		Nos. 540-543 (4)	2.25	2.25

Christmas.

Organizations A111

10t, Lions Intl., conquering blindness. 15t, Red Cross Society. 25t, Ecumenical Decade, churches in solidarity with women. 35t, Round

Table supporting the deaf. 40t, Rotary Intl. 50t, Botswana Christian Council.

1993, Mar. 29 Litho. *Perf. 14*

544 A111 10t multi, vert. .20 .20
545 A111 15t multi .20 .20
546 A111 25t multi, vert. .20 .20
547 A111 35t multi .30 .30
548 A111 40t multi, vert. .40 .40
549 A111 50t multi .45 .45
Nos. 544-549 (6) 1.75 1.75

Botswana Railway, Cent. A112

Designs: 10t, Engine No. 1, 6th class 4-6-0, Bechuanaland Railways. 40t, Engine No. 317, 19th class 4-8-2. 50t, Engine No. 256, 12th class 4-8-2. 1.50p, Engine No. 71, 7th class 4-8-0, Rhodesia Railways.

1993, May 24 Litho. *Perf. 15x14*

550 A112 10t multicolored .20 .20
551 A112 40t multicolored .40 .40
552 A112 50t multicolored .50 .50
553 A112 1.50p multicolored 1.50 1.50
a. Souvenir sheet of 4, #550-553 2.50 2.50
Nos. 550-553 (4) 2.60 2.60

Eagles — A113

1993, Aug. 30 Litho. *Perf. 14½*

554 A113 10t Long crested eagle .20 .20
555 A113 25t Snake eagle .50 .50
556 A113 50t Bateleur eagle 1.00 1.00
557 A113 1.50p Secretary bird 3.00 3.00
Nos. 554-557 (4) 4.70 4.70

Christmas A114

1993, Oct. 25 Litho. *Perf. 14x14½*

558 A114 12t Aloe zebrina .20 .20
559 A114 25t Croton megalobotrys .20 .20
560 A114 50t Boophane distícha .45 .45
561 A114 1p Euphorbia davyi .90 .90
Nos. 558-561 (4) 1.75 1.75

Traditional Children's Toys A115

1994, Mar. 28 Litho. *Perf. 14½*

562 A115 10t Mantadile .20 .20
563 A115 40t Dikgomo tsa mimopa .30 .30
564 A115 50t Sefuu-fuu .40 .40
565 A115 1p Mantlwane .75 .75
Nos. 562-565 (4) 1.65 1.65

ICAO, 50th Anniv. A116

Perf. 14½x14, 14x14½

1994, June 30 Litho.

566 A116 10t Inside control tower .20 .20
567 A116 25t Fire engine .25 .25
568 A116 40t Baggage carts, vert. .40 .40
569 A116 50t Control tower, vert. .50 .50
Nos. 566-569 (4) 1.35 1.35

A117

Environmental Protection: 10t, Flamingos, Sua Pan, vert. 35t, Makgadikgadi Pan trees. 50t, Zebra, Makgadikgadi Palm trees, vert. 2p, Map of Makgadikgadi Pans.

1994, Aug. 30 Litho. *Perf. 14*

570 A117 10t multicolored .20 .20
571 A117 35t multicolored .45 .45
572 A117 50t multicolored .65 .65
573 A117 2p multicolored 2.50 2.50
Nos. 570-573 (4) 3.80 3.80

A118

1994, Oct. 24

Edible fruits: 10t, Ziziphus mucronata. 25t, Strychnos cocculoides. 40t, Bauhinia petersiana. 50t, Schinziphyton rautaneii.

574 A118 10t multicolored .20 .20
575 A118 25t multicolored .20 .20
576 A118 40t multicolored .25 .25
577 A118 50t multicolored .35 .35
Nos. 574-577 (4) 1.00 1.00

Christmas.
See Nos. 587-590.

Traditional Fishing A119

1995, Apr. 3 Litho. *Perf. 14*

578 A119 15t Spear .20 .20
579 A119 40t Hook .30 .30
580 A119 65t Net .50 .50
581 A119 80t Basket .60 .60
Nos. 578-581 (4) 1.60 1.60

UN, 50th Anniv. — A120

1995, Oct. 16 Litho. *Perf. 14*

582 A120 20t FAO .20 .20
583 A120 50t World Food Program .35 .35
584 A120 80t Development Plan .60 .60
585 A120 1p UNICEF .70 .70
Nos. 582-585 (4) 1.85 1.85

World Wildlife Fund A121

Hyaena brunnea: a, 20t, Adult walking right. b, 50t, Two young. c, 80t, Adult finding eggs. d, 1p, Two young, adult resting.

1995, Nov. 6

586 A121 Strip of 4, #a.-d. 1.75 1.75

No. 586 was issued in miniature sheets of 4 each.

Christmas Type of 1994

1995, Nov. 27 Litho. *Perf. 14*

587 A118 20t Adenia glauca .20 .20
588 A118 50t Pterodiscus ngamicus .35 .35
589 A118 80t Sesamothamnus lugardii .60 .60
590 A118 1p Fockea multiflora .70 .70
Nos. 587-590 (4) 1.85 1.85

Traditional Weapons A122

1996, Mar. 25 Litho. *Perf. 14*

591 A122 20t Spears .20 .20
592 A122 50t Axes .30 .30
593 A122 80t Shield, knob-kerries .50 .50
594 A122 1p Knives, cases .60 .60
Nos. 591-594 (4) 1.60 1.60

No. 523 Surcharged 10t

Nos. 518-520 Surcharged 20t

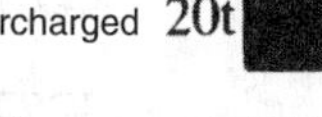

1994-96 Litho. *Perf. 14½*

594A A108 10t multicolored .20 .20
595 A108 20t on 2t No. 519 .20 .20
596 A108 30t on 1t No. 518 .20 .20
597 A108 70t on 4t No. 520 .40 .40
Nos. 595-597 (3) .80 .80

Issued: #594, 8/1/94; others, 2/12/96.

A123

Radio, Cent.: 20t, Child listening to early radio. 50t, Mobile unit, transmitter. 80t, Local police. 1p, Radio Botswana at the Kgotila.

1996, June 3 Litho. *Perf. 14*

598 A123 20t multicolored .20 .20
599 A123 50t multicolored .35 .35
600 A123 80t multicolored .60 .60
601 A123 1p multicolored .75 .75
Nos. 598-601 (4) 1.90 1.90

A124

1996, July 19 Litho. *Perf. 14*

Modern Olympic Games, Cent.: 20t, Hand holding torch, laurel wreath, Olympic rings. 50t, Pierre de Coubertin. 80t, Map, flag of Botswana, athletes. 1p, Ruins of original Olympic Stadium, Olympia.

602 A124 20t multicolored .20 .20
603 A124 50t multicolored .35 .35
604 A124 80t multicolored .60 .60
605 A124 1p multicolored .75 .75
Nos. 602-605 (4) 1.90 1.90

A125

A126

Worthy Causes: 20t, Family planning education, Welfare Association. 30t, Skills for the blind, Pudulogong Rehabilitation Center. 50t, Collection of seeds, Forestry Association. 70t, Secretarial class, YWCA. 80t, Day care center, Council of Women. 1p, SOS Children's Village, Tlokweng.

1996, Sept. 23 Litho. *Perf. 14*

606 A125 20t multicolored .20 .20
607 A125 30t multicolored .25 .25
608 A125 50t multicolored .35 .35
609 A125 70t multicolored .55 .55
610 A125 80t multicolored .60 .60
611 A125 1p multicolored .75 .75
Nos. 606-611 (6) 2.70 2.70

1996, Nov. 4 Litho. *Perf. 14*

Adansonia Digitata

612 A126 20t Leaf, flower .20 .20
613 A126 50t Fruit .35 .35
614 A126 80t Tree in leaf .60 .60
615 A126 1p Tree without leaves .75 .75
Nos. 612-615 (4) 1.90 1.90

Christmas.

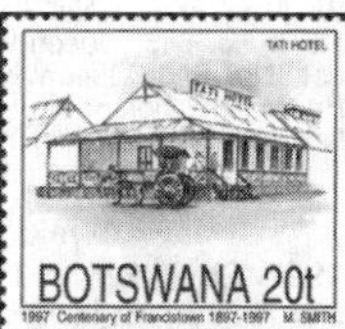

Francistown, Cent. — A127

20t, Tati Hotel. 50t, Railway station. 80t, Company manager's house. 1p, Monarch Mine.

1997, Apr. 21 Litho. *Perf. 14*

616 A127 20t multicolored .20 .20
617 A127 50t multicolored .30 .30
618 A127 80t multicolored .45 .45
619 A127 1p multicolored .55 .55
Nos. 616-619 (4) 1.50 1.50

Birds — A128

5t, Pel's fishing owl. 10t, Gymnogene. 15t, Meyers parrot. 20t, Harlequin quail. 25t, Marico sunbird. 30t, Kurrichane thrush. 40t, Redheaded finch. 50t, Buffalo weaver. 60t, Sacred ibis. 70t, Cape shoveller. 80t, Greater honeyguide. 1p, Woodland kingfisher. 1.25p, Purple heron. 1.50p, Yellowbilled oxpecker. 2p, Shafttailed whydah. 2.50p, White stork. 5p, Ovambo sparrowhawk. 10p, Spotted crake.

1997, Aug. 4 Litho. *Perf. 13½*

620 A128 5t multi, vert. .20 .20
621 A128 10t multi .20 .20
622 A128 15t multi, vert. .20 .20
623 A128 20t multi .20 .20
624 A128 25t multi .20 .20
625 A128 30t multi .20 .20
626 A128 40t multi, vert. .25 .25
627 A128 50t multi, vert. .30 .30
628 A128 60t multi .35 .35
629 A128 70t multi .40 .40
630 A128 80t multi .45 .45
631 A128 1p multi .55 .55
632 A128 1.25p multi, vert. .70 .70
633 A128 1.50p multi .85 .85
634 A128 2p multi, vert. 1.10 1.10
635 A128 2.50p multi, vert. 1.40 1.40
636 A128 5p multi, vert. 2.75 2.75
637 A128 10p multi, vert. 5.50 5.50
Nos. 620-637 (18) 15.80 15.80

Botswana Railway, Cent. — A129

Designs: 35t, Bechuanaland Rail, 1897. 50t, Elephants on the tracks. 80t, First locomotives in Bechuanaland, Cape of Good Hope 4-6-0. 1p, 4-6-4+4-6-4 Beyer Garratt. 2p, New BD3 locomotive. 2.50p, Fantuzzi Container Stacker.

1997, July 12 Litho. *Perf. 14x14½*

638 A129	35t multicolored	.20	.20
639 A129	50t multicolored	.30	.30
640 A129	80t multicolored	.50	.50
641 A129	1p multicolored	.60	.60
642 A129	2p multicolored	1.25	1.25
643 A129	2.50p multicolored	1.50	1.50
	Nos. 638-643 (6)	4.35	4.35

A130

A131

Queen Elizabeth II and Prince Philip, 50th Wedding Anniv.: No. 644, Prince in casual attire. No. 645, Queen wearing white & blue hat. No. 646, Queen with horse. No. 647, Prince with horse. No. 648, Prince, Queen. No. 649, Princess Ann in riding attire.

10p, Queen, Prince riding in open carriage.

Wmk. 373

1997, Sept. 22 Litho. *Perf. 13*

644 A130	35t multicolored	.20	.20
645 A130	35t multicolored	.20	.20
a.	Pair, #644-645	.40	.40
646 A130	2p multicolored	1.25	1.25
647 A130	2p multicolored	1.25	1.25
a.	Pair, #646-647	2.40	2.40
648 A130	2.50p multicolored	1.50	1.50
649 A130	2.50p multicolored	1.50	1.50
a.	Pair, #648-649	3.00	3.00
	Nos. 644-649 (6)	5.90	5.90

Souvenir Sheet

650 A130	10p multicolored	6.00	6.00

1997, Nov. 10 Unwmk. *Perf. 14*

Christmas (Combretum):, 35t, Zeyheri. 1p, Apiculatum. 2p, Molle. 2.50p, Imberbe.

651 A131	35t multicolored	.20	.20
652 A131	1p multicolored	.60	.60
653 A131	2p multicolored	1.25	1.25
654 A131	2.50p multicolored	1.50	1.50
	Nos. 651-654 (4)	3.55	3.55

Tourism A132

1998, Mar. 23

655 A132	35t Baobab trees	.20	.20
656 A132	1p Crocodile	.55	.55
657 A132	2p Stalactites, vert.	1.10	1.10
658 A132	2.50p Tourists, vert.	1.40	1.40
	Nos. 655-658 (4)	3.25	3.25

Diana, Princess of Wales (1961-97)

Common Design Type

Portraits: 35t, #663a, Wearing red (without hat). 1p, #663b, Wearing red with hat. 2p, #663c, Wearing white (hand on face). #662, Greeting people.

1998, June 1 Wmk. 373 *Perf. 13*

659 CD355	35t multicolored	.20	.20
660 CD355	1p multicolored	.55	.55
661 CD355	2p multicolored	1.10	1.10
662 CD355	2.50p multicolored	1.40	1.40
	Nos. 659-662 (4)	3.25	3.25

Sheet of 4

663 CD355	2.50p #a.-c. + #662	5.50	5.50

A133

A134

Textiles: 35t, Tapestry of a village. 55t, Woman arranging materials on ground. 1p, Tapestry of African map, animals, huts, people. 2p, Woman seated at loom.

2.50p, Tapestry of elephants and trees, horiz.

Perf. 14x13½

1998, Sept. 28 Litho. Unwmk.

664 A133	35t multicolored	.20	.20
665 A133	55t multicolored	.30	.30
666 A133	1p multicolored	.55	.55
667 A133	2p multicolored	1.10	1.10
	Nos. 664-667 (4)	2.15	2.15

Souvenir Sheet

Perf. 13½

668 A133	2.50p multicolored	1.40	1.40

1998 Litho. *Perf. 13x13½*

Christmas - Berries: 35t, Ficus ingens. 55t, Ficus pygmaea. 1p, Ficus abutilifolia. 2.50p, Ficus sycomorus.

669 A134	35t multicolored	.20	.20
670 A134	55t multicolored	.30	.30
671 A134	1p multicolored	.55	.55
672 A134	2.50p multicolored	1.40	1.40
	Nos. 669-672 (4)	2.45	2.45

Tourism A135

35t, Rock paintings. 55t, Salt pan. 1p, Rock paintings, diff. 2p, Baobab tree.

1999, May 24 Litho. *Perf. 13½x14*

673 A135	35t multi	.20	.20
674 A135	55t multi	.25	.25

Perf. 14x13½

675 A135	1p multi, vert.	.45	.45
676 A135	2p multi, vert.	.95	.95
	Nos. 673-676 (4)	1.85	1.85

Souvenir Sheet

Southern African Development Community Day — A136

Illustration reduced.

1999, Aug. 17 Litho. *Perf. 14¼*

677 A136	5p multi	2.00	2.00

UPU, 125th Anniv. A137

1999, Oct. 9 Litho. *Perf. 14¼*

678 A137	2p multicolored	.85	.85

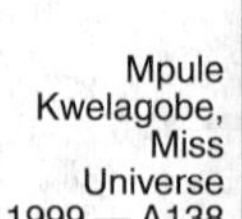

Mpule Kwelagobe, Miss Universe 1999 — A138

1999, Dec. 1 *Perf. 14½*

679 A138	35t With crown, vert.	.20	.20
680 A138	1p With headdress	.40	.40
681 A138	2p In swimsuit, vert.	.80	.80
682 A138	2.50p With Botswana sash	1.10	1.10
683 A138	15p With leopard	6.50	6.50
a.	Souvenir sheet of 5, #679-683	9.00	9.00
	Nos. 679-683 (5)	9.00	9.00

River Scenes A139

Designs: 35t, Bird over river. 1p, Hippopotami in river, vert. 2p, Bird, man in canoe. 2.50p, Elephant on shore, vert.

2000, Apr. 5 Litho. *Perf. 14*

684 A139	35t multi	.20	.20
685 A139	1p multi	.40	.40
686 A139	2p multi	.80	.80
687 A139	2.50p multi	1.00	1.00
	Nos. 684-687 (4)	2.40	2.40

Moths A140

Designs: 35t, Mopane. 70t, Wild silk. 1p, Crimson-speckled footman. 2p, African lunar. 15p, Speckled emperor.

2000, July 19 Litho. *Perf. 12½*

688-692 A140	Set of 5	7.00	7.00
692a	Souvenir sheet, #688-692	7.00	7.00

Literacy Decade A141

Designs: 35t, Mother and child. 70t, Old men learning to read. 2p, Man unaware of fire danger. 2.50p, Man at ATM machine.

2000, Aug. 23 *Perf. 12*

693-696 A141	Set of 4 + labels	2.10	2.10

Kings and Presidents A142

Designs: 35t, Sebele I of Bakwena, Bathoen I of Bangwaketse, Khama III of Bangwato (60x40mm). 1p, Sir Seretse Khama. 2p, Sir Ketumile J. Masire. 2.50p, Festus G. Mogae.

Litho. & Embossed

2000, Sept. 29 *Perf. 14*

697-700 A142	Set of 4	2.25	2.25

Botswana Flying Mission — A143

Designs: 35t, Two men, plane with yellow stripes. 1.75p, Plane, nurses, people. 2p, Plane in air, natives in boats. 2.50p, Plane, donkey cart.

2000, Nov. 3 Litho. *Perf. 13½*

701-704 A143	Set of 4	2.50	2.50
704a	Horiz. strip of 4, #701-704, + central label	2.50	2.50

Wetlands Fauna A144

Designs: 35t, Hippopotamus. 1p, Tiger fish, tilapia. 1.75p, Wattled crane, painted reed frog, vert. 2p, Vervet monkey, Pels fishing owl, vert. 2.50p, Sitatunga, Nile crocodile, red lechwe.

2000, Dec. 6 Litho. *Perf. 13¾*

705-709 A144	Set of 5	3.00	3.00
709a	Souvenir sheet, #705-709, perf. 13½	3.00	3.00
709b	As "a," with emblem of Hong Kong 2001 Stamp Exhibition in margin	3.00	3.00

Issued: No. 709b, 1/2/01.

Diamonds — A145

Cut diamond and: 35t, Uncut diamonds. 1.75p, Mine. 2p, Diamond grader. 2.50p, Pendant and ring.

Illustration reduced.

Serpemtine Die Cut 10

2001, Feb. 1 Litho.

Self-Adhesive

710-713 A145	Set of 4	2.50	2.50

Unused value is for stamps with surrounding selvage.

Kgalagadi Transfrontier Park A146

Designs: 35t, Pygmy falcons. 1p, Leopard. 2p, Gemsboks, flags of Botswana and South Africa. 2.50p, Bat-eared fox.

2001, May 12 Litho. *Perf. 13x13¼*

714-717 A146	Set of 4	2.25	2.25
717a	Souvenir sheet #715, 717	1.40	1.40

See South Africa Nos. 1252-1255.

Basketry A147

Designs: 35t, Shown. 1p, Tall basket with triangles and chevrons. 2p, Basket weaver. 2.50p, Spherical basket.

2001, July 30 ***Perf. 13¼***

718-721	A147	Set of 4	2.10	2.10
721a		Souvenir sheet, #718-721	2.10	2.10

Sky Views A148

Natives and pictures of sun on horizon: 50t, 1p, 2p, 10p.

2001, Sept. 28 ***Perf. 13½***

722-725	A148	Set of 4	4.50	4.50

Wetlands Fauna Type of 2000

Designs: 50t, Water monitor, carmine bee-eaters. 1.75p, Buffalos. 2p, Savanna baboons, vert. 2.50p, Lion, vert. 3p, African elephants.

2001, Dec. 12 Litho. ***Perf. 13¾***

726-730	A144	Set of 5	3.25	3.25
730a		Souvenir sheet, #726-730, perf. 13½	3.25	3.25

Snakes A149

Designs: 50t, Black mamba. 1.75p, Spitting cobra, vert. 2.50p, Puff adder. 3p, Boomslang, vert.

2002, Mar. 22 ***Perf. 14x13¼, 13¼x14***

731-734	A149	Set of 4	2.40	2.40

Pottery A150

Pots: 50t, Mbukushu. 2p, Sekgatla. 2.50p, Setswana. 3p, Kalanga.

2002, May 31 Litho. ***Perf. 13¾***

735-738	A150	Set of 4	2.75	2.75

Reign of Queen Elizabeth II, 50th Anniv. A151

Mammals A152

Queen Elizabeth II: 55t, Wearing crown, horiz. 2.75p, Holding flowers.

2002, July 25 ***Perf. 13x13¼, 13¼x13***

739-740	A151	Set of 2	1.10	1.10

Perf. 13½x13¼, 13¼x13½

2002, Aug. 5 Photo.

Designs: 5t, Tree squirrel. 10t, Black-backed jackal. 20t, African wild cat. 30t, Slender mongoose, horiz. 40t, African civet, horiz. 55t, Elephant. 90t, Reedbuck. 1p, Kudu. 1.45p, Waterbuck. 1.95p, Sable, horiz. 2.20p, Sitatunga, horiz. 2.75p, Porcupine, horiz. 3.30p, Serval, horiz. 4p, Antbear, horiz. 5p, Bush pig, horiz. 15p, Chakma baboon.

741	A152	5t	multi	.20	.20
742	A152	10t	multi	.20	.20
743	A152	20t	multi	.20	.20
744	A152	30t	multi	.20	.20
745	A152	40t	multi	.20	.20
746	A152	55t	multi	.20	.20
747	A152	90t	multi	.25	.25
748	A152	1p	multi	.30	.30
749	A152	1.45p	multi	.45	.45
750	A152	1.95p	multi	.60	.60
751	A152	2.20p	multi	.70	.70
752	A152	2.75p	multi	.90	.90
753	A152	3.30p	multi	1.00	1.00
754	A152	4p	multi	1.25	1.25
755	A152	5p	multi	1.60	1.60
756	A152	15p	multi	4.75	4.75
			Nos. 741-756 (16)	13.00	13.00

POSTAGE DUE STAMPS

Bechuanaland Protectorate Nos. J10-J12 Overprinted: "REPUBLIC OF / BOTSWANA"

Perf. 14

1967, Mar. 1 Wmk. 4 Typo.

J1	D2	1c carmine rose	.20	*1.00*
J2	D2	2c dull violet	.25	*1.50*
J3	D2	5c olive green	.55	*2.00*
		Nos. J1-J3 (3)	1.00	*4.50*

Elephant D1

Zebra D2

Perf. 13½

1971, June 9 Litho. Unwmk.

J4	D1	1c carmine rose	1.00	*2.25*
J5	D1	2c violet blue	1.25	*3.00*
J6	D1	6c sepia	2.00	*5.00*
J7	D1	14c green	4.00	*7.00*
		Nos. J4-J7 (4)	8.25	*17.25*

1978 ***Perf. 12½***

J8	D2	1t red orange & black	.70	.70
J9	D2	2t emerald & black	.70	.70
J10	D2	4t red & black	.70	.70
J11	D2	10t dark blue & black	.70	.70
J12	D2	16t brown & black	.70	.70
		Nos. J8-J12 (5)	3.50	*3.50*

1984 ***Perf. 14½x14***

J8a	D2	1t	.60	*.60*
J9a	D2	2t	.60	*.60*
J10a	D2	4t	.60	*.60*
J11a	D2	10t	.60	*.60*
J12a	D2	16t	.60	*.60*
		Nos. J8a-J12a (5)	3.00	*3.00*

1989, Apr. 1 ***Perf. 14½***

J8b	D2	1t	.20	.20
J9b	D2	2t	.20	.20
J10b	D2	4t	.20	.20
J11b	D2	10t	.20	.20
J12b	D2	16t	.45	.45
		Nos. J8b-J12b (5)	1.25	1.25

The design is the same size on the 1984 and 1989 issues, but the grass of Nos. J8b-J12b is lower and less defined than on previous issues. The paper is wider on the 1989 issue.

1994, Dec. 1 ***Perf. 14***

J8c	D2	1t	.20	.20
J9c	D2	2t	.20	.20
J10c	D2	4t	.20	.20
J11c	D2	10t	.20	.20
J12c	D2	16t	.20	.20
		Nos. J8c-J12c (5)	1.00	1.00

See note after No. J12b.

BRAZIL

brə-'zil

Brasil (after 1918)

LOCATION — On the north and east coasts of South America, bordering on the Atlantic Ocean.
GOVT. — Republic
AREA — 3,286,000 sq. mi.
POP. — 157,070,163 (1996)
CAPITAL — Brasilia

Brazil was an independent empire from 1822 to 1889, when a constitution was adopted and the country became officially known as The United States of Brazil.

1000 Reis = 1 Milreis
100 Centavos = 1 Cruzeiro (1942)
100 Centavos = 1 Cruzado (1986)
100 Centavos = 1 Cruzeiro (1990)
(Cruzeiro Real 8/2/93-7/1/94)

Catalogue values for unused stamps in this country are for Never Hinged items, beginning with Scott 680 in the regular postage section, Scott B12 in the semi-postal section, Scott C66 in the airpost section, Scott RA2 in the postal tax section, and Scott RAB1 in the postal tax semi-postal section.

Values for unused stamps are for examples with original gum as defined in the catalogue introduction except for Nos. 1-38 and 42-52 which are valued without gum.

Watermarks

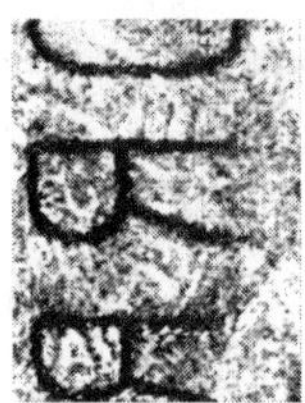

Wmk. 97- "CORREIO FEDERAL REPUBLICA DOS ESTADOS UNIDOS DO BRAZIL" in Sheet

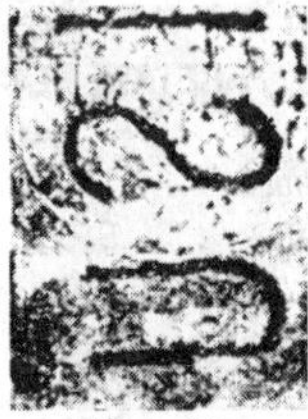

Wmk. 98- "IMPOSTO DE CONSUMO REPUBLICA DOS ESTADOS UNIDOS DO BRAZIL" in Sheet

Wmk. 99- "CORREIO"

Wmk. 100- "CASA DA MOEDA" in Sheet

Because of the spacing of this watermark, a few stamps in each sheet may show no watermark.

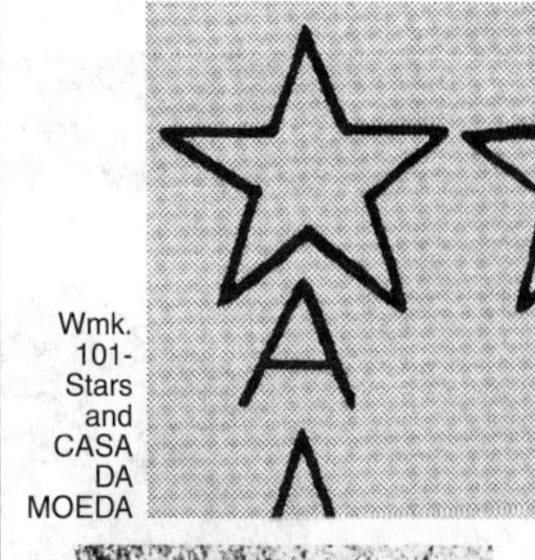

Wmk. 101- Stars and CASA DA MOEDA

Wmk. 193- ESTADOS UNIDOS DO BRASIL

Wmk. 206- Star-framed CM, Multiple

Wmk. 218- E U BRASIL Multiple, Letters 8mm High

Wmk. 221- ESTADOS UNIDOS DO BRASIL, Multiple, Letters 6mm High

Wmk. 222- CORREIO BRASIL and 5 Stars in Squared Circle

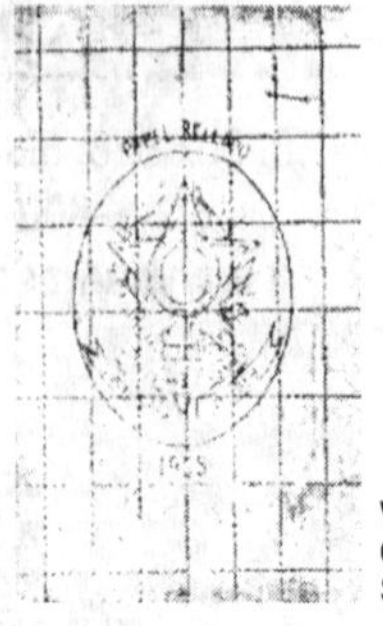

Wmk. 236- Coat of Arms in Sheet

Watermark (reduced illustration) covers 22 stamps in sheet.

Wmk. 245- Multiple "CASA DA MOEDA DO BRASIL" and Small Formee Cross

Wmk. 249- "CORREIO BRASIL" multiple

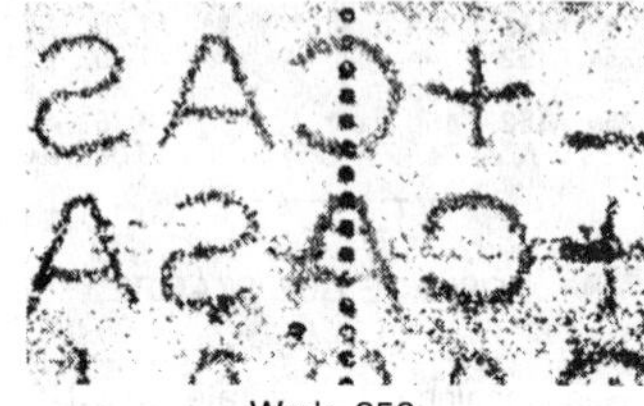

Wmk. 256- "CASA+DA+MOEDA+DO+BRAZIL" in 8mm Letters

Wmk. 264- "*CORREIO*BRASIL*" Multiple, Letters 7mm High

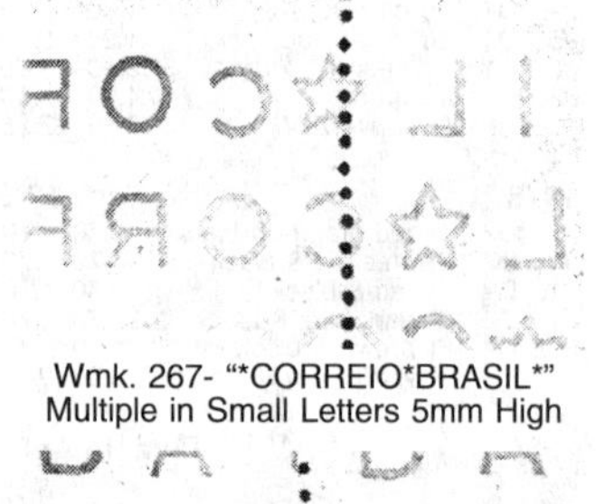

Wmk. 267- "*CORREIO*BRASIL*" Multiple in Small Letters 5mm High

Wmk. 268- "CASA+DA+MOEDA+DO+BRASIL" in 6mm Letters

Wmk. 270- Wavy Lines and Seal

Wmk. 271- Wavy Lines

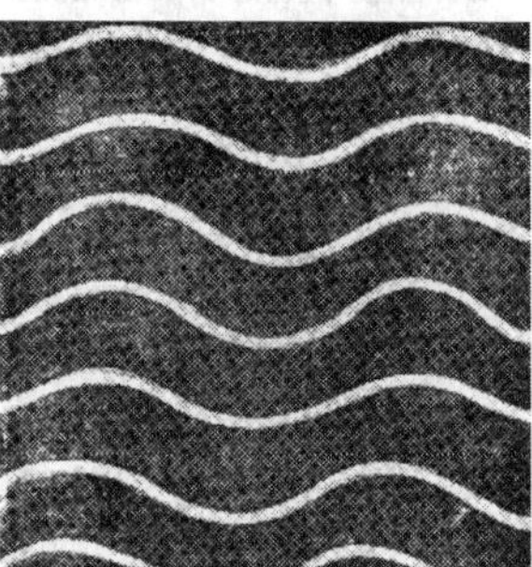

Wmk. 281- Wavy Lines

Issues of the Empire

A1

Grayish or Yellowish Paper
Fine Impressions
Unwmk.

1843, Aug. 1 Engr. *Imperf.*

1	A1 30r black	3,000.	550.
c.	Pair, #1-2		*300,000.*
2	A1 60r black	600.	240.
3	A1 90r black	3,000.	1,200.

Nos. 1-3 were issued with gum, but very few unused examples retain even a trace of their original gum. Copies with original gum command substantial premiums.

Fine impressions are true black and have background lathework complete. Intermediate impressions are grayish black and have weaker lathework in the background. These sell for somewhat less than fine impressions. Worn impressions have white areas in the background surrounding the numerals due to plate wear affecting especially the lathework. These examples sell for somewhat less than intermediate impressions.

Most examples of Nos. 1-3 also exist on white paper, usually thin and somewhat translucent. Such examples are scarce and command premiums.

A2

A3

Grayish or Yellowish Paper

1844-46

7	A2	10r black	100.00	20.00
8	A2	30r black	125.00	30.00
9	A2	60r black	100.00	20.00
10	A2	90r black	750.00	100.00
11	A2	180r black	3,500.	1,350.
12	A2	300r black	5,250.	1,800.
13	A2	600r black	5,000.	2,000.

Nos. 8, 9 and 10 exist on thick paper and are considerably scarcer.

Grayish or Yellowish Paper

1850, Jan. 1

21	A3	10r black	25.00	*35.00*
22	A3	20r black	75.00	*100.00*
23	A3	30r black	10.00	3.00
24	A3	60r black	10.00	2.50
25	A3	90r black	80.00	12.00
26	A3	180r black	80.00	55.00
27	A3	300r black	325.00	60.00
28	A3	600r black	375.00	90.00

No. 22 used is generally found precanceled with a single horizontal line in pen or blue crayon. Value precanceled without gum, $75.

All values except the 90r were reprinted in 1910 on very thick paper.

1854

37	A3	10r blue	12.00	11.50
38	A3	30r blue	32.50	*50.00*

A4

1861

39	A4	280r red	150.00	100.00
40	A4	430r yellow	225.00	140.00

Nos. 39 and 40 have been reprinted on thick white paper with white gum. They are printed in aniline inks and the colors are brighter than those of the originals.

1866 *Perf. 13½*

42	A3	10r blue	125.00	*150.00*
43	A3	20r black	900.00	400.00
44	A3	30r black	300.00	150.00
45	A3	30r blue	*675.00*	*750.00*
46	A3	60r black	125.00	25.00
47	A3	90r black	575.00	275.00
48	A3	180r black	600.00	275.00
49	A4	280r red	650.00	*675.00*
50	A3	300r black	750.00	400.00
51	A4	430r yellow	600.00	350.00
52	A3	600r black	575.00	240.00

Fraudulent perforations abound. Purchases should be accompanied by certificates of authenticity.

A 10r black is questioned.

A5

A6

A7

A8

A8a

A9

Emperor Dom Pedro — A9a

Thick or Thin White Wove Paper

1866, July 1 *Perf. 12*

53	A5	10r vermilion	12.00	5.00
54	A6	20r red lilac	20.00	3.00
a.		20r dull violet	65.00	25.00
56	A7	50r blue	30.00	2.50
57	A8	80r slate violet	75.00	5.00
58	A8a	100r blue green	30.00	1.50
a.		100r yellow green	30.00	1.50
59	A9	200r black	100.00	8.00
a.		Half used as 100r on cover		*1,500.*
60	A9a	500r orange	200.00	35.00
		Nos. 53-60 (7)	467.00	60.00

The 10r and 20r exist imperf. on both white and bluish paper. Some authorities consider them proofs.

Nos. 58 and 65 are found in three types.

Bluish Paper

53a	A5	10r	500.00	425.00
54b	A6	20r	160.00	24.00
56a	A7	50r	200.00	25.00
57a	A8	80r	240.00	27.50
58b	A8a	100r	800.00	110.00

1876-77 ***Rouletted***

61	A5	10r vermilion ('77)	60.00	35.00
62	A6	20r red lilac ('77)	70.00	27.50
63	A7	50r blue ('77)	70.00	10.00
64	A8	80r violet ('77)	175.00	20.00
65	A8a	100r green	40.00	1.25
66	A9	200r black ('77)	80.00	7.50
a.		Half used as 100r on cover		*1,100.*
67	A9a	500r orange	190.00	40.00
		Nos. 61-67 (7)	685.00	141.25

A10

A11

A12

A13

A14

A15

A16

A17

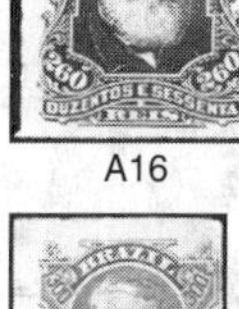

A18

A19

A20

1878-79 ***Rouletted***

68	A10	10r vermilion	12.00	3.00
69	A11	20r violet	15.00	2.50
70	A12	50r blue	24.00	2.00
71	A13	80r lake	27.50	10.00
72	A14	100r green	27.50	1.25
73	A15	200r black	140.00	17.50
a.		Half used as 100r on cover		*1,200.*
74	A16	260r dk brown	80.00	22.50
75	A18	300r bister	80.00	6.00
a.		One-third used as 100r on cover		*10,000.*
76	A19	700r red brown	160.00	85.00
77	A20	1000r gray lilac	190.00	37.50
a.		Half used as 500r on cover		*10,000.*
		Nos. 68-77 (10)	756.00	187.25

1878, Aug. 21 *Perf. 12*

78	A17	300r orange & grn	85.00	20.00

Nos. 68-78 exist imperforate.

A21 A22 A23

Small Heads
Laid Paper

Perf. 13, 13½ and Compound

1881, July 15

79	A21	50r blue	125.00	18.00
80	A22	100r olive green	500.00	30.00
81	A23	200r pale red brn	475.00	110.00
a.		Half used as 100r on cover		*1,750.*

On Nos. 79 and 80 the hair above the ear curves forward. On Nos. 83 and 88 it is drawn backward. On the stamps of the 1881 issue the beard is smaller than in the 1882-85 issues and fills less of the space between the neck and the frame at the left.

See No. 88.

A24

A25

A26

A27

Two types each of the 100 and 200 reis.

100 REIS:

Type I - Groundwork formed of diagonal crossed lines and horizontal lines.

Type II - Groundwork formed of diagonal crossed lines and vertical lines.

200 REIS:

Type I - Groundwork formed of diagonal and horizontal lines.

Type II - Groundwork formed of diagonal crossed lines.

Larger Heads
Laid Paper

Perf. 12½ to 14 and Compound

1882-84

82	A24	10r black	10.00	*20.00*
83	A25	100r ol grn, type I	37.50	3.00
b.		100r dark green, type II	200.00	12.00
84	A26	200r pale red brn, type I	85.00	22.50
a.		Half used as 100r on cover		*1,100.*
85	A27	200r pale rose, type II	45.00	4.50
a.		Diag. half used as 100r on cover		800.00
		Nos. 82-85 (4)	177.50	50.00

See No. 86.

A28

A29

A30

Three types of A29

Type I - Groundwork of horizontal lines.

Type II - Groundwork of diagonal crossed lines.

Type III - Groundwork solid.

Perf. 13, 13½, 14 and Compound

1884-85

86	A24	10r orange	2.50	2.00
87	A28	20r slate green	30.00	3.00
a.		20r olive green	30.00	3.00
b.		Half used as 10r on newspaper		*3,000.*
88	A21	50r bl, head larger	30.00	3.00
90	A29	100r lilac, type I	125.00	2.50
a.		100r lilac, type II	450.00	75.00
b.		100r lilac, type III	325.00	55.00
91	A30	100r lilac	175.00	4.00
		Nos. 86-91 (5)	362.50	14.50

A31

A32

Southern Cross
A33

Crown
A34

Perf. 13, 13½, 14 and Compound

1885

92 A31 100r lilac 100.00 2.50

Compare design A31 with A35.

1887

93 A32 50r chalky blue 27.50 4.00
94 A33 300r gray blue 200.00 25.00
95 A34 500r olive 110.00 12.00
Nos. 93-95 (3) 337.50 41.00

A35

A36

Entrance to Bay of Rio de Janeiro — A37

1888

96 A35 100r lilac 60.00 1.50
a. Imperf., pair 125.00 *160.00*
97 A36 700r violet 65.00 *100.00*
98 A37 1000r dull blue 250.00 100.00
Nos. 96-98 (3) 375.00 *201.50*

Issues of the Republic

Southern Cross — A38

Wove Paper, Thin to Thick

Perf. 12½ to 14, 11 to 11½, and 12½ to 14x11 to 11½, Rough or Clean-Cut

Engraved; Typographed (#102)

1890-91

99 A38 20r gray green 2.00 1.50
a. 20r blue green 2.00 1.50
b. 20r emerald 16.00 6.00
100 A38 50r gray green 5.00 1.50
a. 50r olive green 12.00 6.00
b. 50r yellow green 12.00 6.00
c. 50r dark slate green 7.00 3.50
d. Horiz. pair, imperf. btwn. —
101 A38 100r lilac rose 350.00 4.50
102 A38 100r red lil, redrawn 25.00 1.50
a. Tete beche pair *15,000.* *16,500.*
103 A38 200r purple 8.00 1.50
a. 200r violet 10.00 2.00
b. 200r violet blue 22.50 3.00
104 A38 300r dark violet 75.00 5.00
a. 300r gray 75.00 8.50
b. 300r gray blue 85.00 8.50
c. 300r slate violet 150.00 25.00
105 A38 500r olive bister 17.50 8.00
a. 500r olive gray 17.50 10.00
106 A38 500r slate 17.50 12.00
107 A38 700r fawn 16.00 16.00
a. 700r chocolate 20.00 *22.50*
108 A38 1000r bister 15.00 3.00
a. 1000r yellow buff 30.00 7.50
Nos. 99-108 (10) 531.00 54.50

The redrawn 100r may be distinguished by the absence of the curved lines of shading in the left side of the central oval. The pearls in the oval are not well aligned and there is less shading at right and left of "CORREIO" and "100 REIS."

A 100 reis stamp of type A38 but inscribed "BRAZIL" instead of "E. U. DO BRAZIL" was not placed in issue but postmarked copies are known. A reprint on thick paper was made in 1910.

No. 101 exists imperf., not regularly issued.

For surcharges see Nos. 151-158.

Liberty Head
A39 A40

Perf. 12½ to 14, 11 to 11½ and 12½ to 14x11 to 11½

1891, May 1 **Typo.**

109 A39 100r blue & red 32.50 1.50
a. Frame inverted 100.00 90.00
b. Tete beche pair 675.00 *750.00*
c. 100r ultra & red 32.50 1.50

Perf. 11, 11½, 13, 13½, 14 and Compound

1893, Jan. 18 **Litho.**

111 A40 100r rose 75.00 1.75

A41

Sugarloaf Mountain—A41a

A42

Liberty Head — A42a

Hermes — A43

Perf. 11 to 11½, 12½ to 14 and 12½ to 14x11 to 11½

1894-97 **Unwmk.**

112 A41 10r rose & blue 2.00 .80
113 A41a 10r rose & blue 2.00 .80
114 A41a 20r orange & bl 1.00 .30
115 A41a 50r dk bl & bl 8.00 1.25
116 A42 100r car & blk 4.00 .40
a. Vert. pair, imperf. btwn. 100.00
118 A42a 200r orange & blk 1.00 .40
a. Imperf. horiz., pair 80.00
b. Vert. pair, imperf. btwn. 80.00
119 A42a 300r green & blk 15.00 .60
120 A42a 500r blue & blk 25.00 1.75
121 A42a 700r lilac & blk 16.00 1.75
122 A43 1000r green & vio 55.00 1.75
124 A43 2000r blk & gray lil 60.00 15.00
Nos. 112-124 (11) 189.00 24.80

The head of No. 116 exists in five types. See Nos. 140-150A, 159-161, 166-171d.

Newspaper Stamps Surcharged:

a

b

c

Surcharged on 1889 Issue of type N1

1898 ***Rouletted***

Green Surcharge

125 N1 (b) 700r on 500r yel 6.75 *10.00*
126 N1 (c) 1000r on 700r yel 32.50 27.50
a. Surcharged "700r" 675.00 775.00
127 N1 (c) 2000r on 1000r yel 27.50 15.00
128 N1 (c) 2000r on 1000r brn 20.00 6.00

Violet Surcharge

129 N1 (a) 100r on 50r brn yel 2.00 *45.00*
130 N1 (c) 100r on 50r brn yel 65.00 50.00
131 N1 (c) 300r on 200r blk 3.50 1.25
a. Double surcharge 160.00 275.00

The surcharge on No. 130 is handstamped. The impression is blurred and lighter in color than on No. 129. The two surcharges differ most in the shapes and serifs of the figures "1."

Counterfeits exist of No. 126a.

Black Surcharge

132 N1 (b) 200r on 100r violet 3.50 1.25
a. Double surcharge 80.00 *175.00*
b. Inverted surcharge 80.00 *175.00*
132C N1 (b) 500r on 300r car 5.50 3.00
133 N1 (b) 700r on 500r green 8.00 2.00

Blue Surcharge

134 N1 (b) 500r on 300r car 6.50 5.50

Red Surcharge

135 N1 (c) 1000r on 700r ultra 22.50 15.00
a. Inverted surcharge 200.00 —

Surcharged on 1890-94 Issues:

d

e

Perf. 11 to 14 and Compound

Black Surcharge

136 N3(e) 20r on 10r bl 3.00 6.00
137 N2(d) 200r on 100r red lilac 20.00 15.00
a. Double surcharge 225.00 250.00

Surcharge on No. 137 comes blue to deep black.

Blue Surcharge

138 N3(e) 50r on 20r grn 8.00 10.00

Red Surcharge

139 N3(e) 100r on 50r grn 18.00 20.00
a. Blue surcharge 12.50

The surcharge on Nos. 139 and 139a exists double, inverted, one missing, etc.

Types of 1894-97

1899

Perf. 5½-7 and 11-11½x5½-7

140 A41a 10r rose & bl 4.50 *12.00*
141 A41a 20r orange & bl 7.50 7.50
142 A41a 50r dk bl & lt bl 9.00 *30.00*
143 A42 100r car & blk 16.00 4.50
144 A42a 200r org & blk 9.00 3.00
145 A42a 300r green & blk 60.00 7.50
Nos. 140-145 (6) 106.00 *64.50*

Perf. 8½-9½, 8½-9½x11-11½

146 A41a 10r rose & bl 4.50 3.00
147 A41a 20r orange & bl 15.00 3.00
147A A41a 50r dk bl & bl 125.00 30.00
148 A42 100r car & blk 30.00 1.50
149 A42a 200r org & blk 15.00 1.00
150 A42a 300r green & blk 60.00 5.00
150A A43 1000r green & vio 125.00 12.50
Nos. 146-150A (7) 374.50 56.00

Nos. 140-150A are valued with perfs just cut into the design on one or two sides. Expect some irregularity of the perforations.

Issue of 1890-93 Surcharged in Violet or Magenta

Perf. 11 to 11½, 12½ to 14 and Compound

1899, June 25

151 A38 50r on 20r gray grn 2.00 *3.00*
a. Double surcharge 125.00 125.00
152 A38 100r on 50r gray grn 2.00 *3.00*
b. Double surcharge 100.00 100.00
153 A38 300r on 200r pur 7.50 *12.00*
a. Double surcharge 250.00 —
b. Pair, one without surcharge 425.00 —
154 A38 500r on 300r ultra, perf. 13 18.00 7.50
a. 500r on 300r gray lilac 30.00 9.00
b. Pair, one without surcharge 425.00 *500.00*
c. 500r on 300r slate violet 37.50 15.00
155 A38 700r on 500r ol bis 24.00 6.00
a. Pair, one without surcharge 425.00 —
156 A38 1000r on 700r choc 17.50 6.00
157 A38 1000r on 700r fawn 17.50 6.00
a. Pair, one without surcharge 425.00 *500.00*
158 A38 2000r on 1000r bister (perf 11-11½ 30.00 4.50
a. 2000r on 1000r yel buff (perf 13) 60.00 4.50
b. Pair, one without surcharge 425.00 *500.00*
Nos. 151-158 (8) 118.50 48.00

Types of 1894-97

Perf. 11, 11½, 13 and Compound

1900

159 A41a 50r green 10.00 .60
160 A42 100r rose 20.00 .30
a. Frame around inner oval 100.00 4.00
161 A42a 200r blue 12.00 .35
Nos. 159-161 (3) 42.00 1.25

Three types exist of No. 161, all of which have the frame around inner oval.

Cabral Arrives at Brazil — A44

Independence Proclaimed — A45

"Emancipation of Slaves" — A46

Allegory, Republic of Brazil — A47

1900, Jan. 1 Litho. *Perf. 12½*

162 A44 100r red 5.50 4.50
a. Imperf., pair 400.00 500.00
163 A45 200r green & yel 5.50 4.50
164 A46 500r blue 5.50 4.50
165 A47 700r emerald 5.50 4.50
Nos. 162-165 (4) 22.00 18.00

Discovery of Brazil, 400th anniversary.

Types of 1894-97

Wmk. (97? or 98?)

1905 *Perf. 11, 11½*

166 A41a 10r rose & bl 5.75 4.00
167 A41a 20r org & bl 10.00 2.00
168 A41a 50r green 20.00 3.00
169 A42 100r rose 27.50 1.00
170 A42a 200r dark blue 16.00 1.00
171 A42a 300r grn & blk 55.00 2.00
Nos. 166-171 (6) 134.25 13.00

Positive identification of Wmk. 97 or 98 places stamp in specific watermark groups below.

Wmk. 97

166b A41a 10r rose & blue 30.00 16.00
167b A41a 20r org & blue 30.00 8.00
168b A41a 50r green 55.00 8.00
169b A42 100r rose 200.00 30.00
170b A42a 200r dark blue 125.00 4.00
171b A42a 300r green & blk 375.00 30.00
171A A43 1000r grn & vio 290.00 30.00
Nos. 166b-171A (7) 1,105. 126.00

Wmk. 98

166c A41a 10r rose & blue 40.00 40.00
167c A41a 20r org & blue 80.00 20.00
168c A41a 50r green 160.00 30.00
169c A42 100r rose 80.00 4.00
170c A42a 200r dark blue 125.00 4.00
171d A42a 300r green & blk 290.00 30.00
Nos. 166c-171d (6) 775.00 128.00

Allegory, Pan-American Congress - A48

1906, July 23 Litho. Unwmk.

172 A48 100r carmine rose 30.00 30.00
173 A48 200r blue 75.00 10.00

Third Pan-American Congress.

Aristides Lobo A48a

Benjamin Constant A49

Pedro Alvares Cabral A50

Eduardo Wandenkolk A51

Manuel Deodoro da Fonseca A52

Floriano Peixoto A53

Prudente de Moraes A54

Manuel Ferraz de Campos Salles A55

Francisco de Paula Rodrigues Alves — A56

Liberty Head — A57

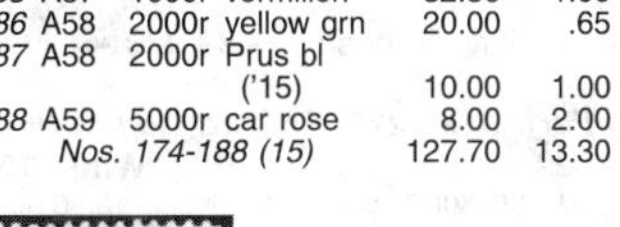
A58 A59

1906-16 Engr. *Perf. 12*

174 A48a 10r bluish slate .90 .20
175 A49 20r aniline vio .90 .20
176 A50 50r green .90 .20
a. Booklet pane of 6 ('08) 40.00 *125.00*
177 A51 100r anil rose 2.00 .20
a. Imperf. vert., coil ('16) 4.00 .35
b. Booklet pane of 6 ('08) 80.00 *125.00*
178 A52 200r blue 2.00 .20
a. Booklet pane of 6 ('08) 60.00 *125.00*
179 A52 200r ultra ('15) 2.00 .35
a. Imperf. vert., coil ('16) 2.00 .35
180 A53 300r gray blk 3.50 .65
181 A54 400r olive grn 30.00 2.00
182 A55 500r dk violet 6.00 .65
183 A54 600r ol grn ('10) 3.00 1.00
184 A56 700r red brown 6.00 3.00
185 A57 1000r vermilion 32.50 1.00
186 A58 2000r yellow grn 20.00 .65
187 A58 2000r Prus bl ('15) 10.00 1.00
188 A59 5000r car rose 8.00 2.00
Nos. 174-188 (15) 127.70 13.30

Allegorical Emblems: Liberty, Peace, Industry, etc. — A60

1908, July 14

189 A60 100r carmine 20.00 1.75

National Exhibition, Rio de Janeiro.

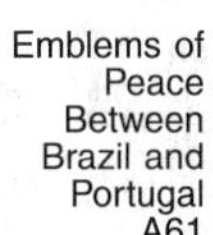

Emblems of Peace Between Brazil and Portugal A61

1908, July 14

190 A61 100r red 8.00 1.25

Opening of Brazilian ports to foreign commerce, cent. Medallions picture King Carlos I of Portugal and Pres. Affonso Penna of Brazil.

Bonifacio, Bolivar, Hidalgo, O'Higgins, San Martin, Washington — A62

1909

191 A62 200r deep blue 7.50 1.00

For surcharge see No. E1.

Nilo Peçanha A63

Baron of Rio Branco A64

1910, Nov. 15

192 A63 10,000r brown 8.00 2.00

1913-16

193 A64 1000r deep green 3.75 .35
194 A64 1000r slate ('16) 21.00 .65

Cabo Frio — A65

Perf. 11½

1915, Nov. 13 Litho. Wmk. 99

195 A65 100r dk grn, *yelsh* 4.00 3.50

Founding of the town of Cabo Frio, 300th anniversary.

Bay of Guajara A66

1916, Jan. 5

196 A66 100r carmine 7.50 4.00

City of Belem, 300th anniversary.

Revolutionary Flag — A67

1917, Mar. 6

197 A67 100r deep blue 15.00 7.50

Revolution of Pernambuco, Mar. 6, 1817.

Rodrigues Alves — A68

Unwmk.

1917, Aug. 31 Engr. *Perf. 12*

198 A68 5000r red brown 60.00 10.00

Liberty Head
A69 A70

Perf. 12½, 13, 13x13½

1918-20 Typo. Unwmk.

200 A69 10r orange brn .50 .25
201 A69 20r slate .50 .25
202 A69 25r ol gray ('20) .50 .25
203 A69 50r green 27.50 3.25
204 A70 100r rose 1.75 .25
a. Imperf., pair —
205 A70 300r red orange 19.00 3.25
206 A70 500r dull violet 19.00 3.25
Nos. 200-206 (7) 68.75 10.75

1918-20 Wmk. 100

207 A69 10r red brown 6.00 1.75
a. Imperf., pair —
207B A69 20r slate 1.50 1.50
c. Imperf., pair —
208 A69 25r ol gray ('20) .75 .50
209 A69 50r green 1.50 .50
210 A70 100r rose 47.50 .50
a. Imperf., pair —
211 A70 200r dull blue 6.00 .50
212 A70 300r orange 47.50 3.50
213 A70 500r dull violet 47.50 7.50
214 A70 600r orange 2.50 *7.50*
Nos. 207-214 (9) 160.75 23.75

Because of the spacing of this watermark, a few stamps in each sheet may show no watermark.

"Education" — A72

1918 Engr. *Perf. 11½*

215 A72 1000r blue 6.00 .25
216 A72 2000r red brown 27.50 6.00
217 A72 5000r dark violet 7.50 6.00
Nos. 215-217 (3) 41.00 12.25

Watermark note below No. 257 also applies to Nos. 215-217.

See Nos. 233-234, 283-285, 404, 406, 458, 460. For surcharge see No. C30.

Railroad A73

"Industry" A74

"Aviation" A75

Mercury A76

"Navigation" — A77

Perf. 13½x13, 13x13½

1920-22 Typo. Unwmk.

218 A73 10r red violet .75 .40
219 A73 20r olive green .75 .40
220 A74 25r brown violet .60 .40
221 A74 50r blue green .85 .40
222 A74 50r orange brn ('22) 1.40 .40
223 A75 100r rose red 2.75 .40
224 A75 100r orange ('22) 7.50 .40
225 A75 150r violet ('21) 1.40 .40
226 A75 200r blue 4.50 .40
227 A75 200r rose red ('22) 8.00 .40
228 A76 300r olive gray 12.50 .50
229 A76 400r dull blue ('22) 22.50 3.50
230 A76 500r red brown 17.50 .50
Nos. 218-230 (13) 81.00 8.50

See Nos. 236-257, 265-266, 268-271, 273-274, 276-281, 302-311, 316-322, 326-340, 357-358, 431-434, 436-441, 461-463B, 467-

470, 472-474, 488-490, 492-494. For surcharges see Nos. 356-358, 376-377.

Perf. 11, 11½

Engr. Wmk. 100

231	A77	600r red orange	2.00	.35
232	A77	1000r claret	5.00	.25
a.		Perf. 8½	37.50	7.50
233	A72	2000r dull violet	20.00	.75
234	A72	5000r brown	16.00	9.00
		Nos. 231-234 (4)	43.00	10.35

Nos. 233 and 234 are inscribed "BRASIL CORREIO." Watermark note below No. 257 also applies to Nos. 231-234.

See No. 282.

King Albert of Belgium and President Epitacio Pessoa A78

1920, Sept. 19 Engr. *Perf. 11½x11*

235	A78	100r dull red	.65	.65

Visit of the King and Queen of Belgium.

Types of 1920-22 Issue

Perf. 13x13½, 13x12½

1922-29 Typo. Wmk. 100

236	A73	10r red violet	.30	.20
237	A73	20r olive green	.30	.20
238	A75	20r gray vio ('29)	.30	.20
239	A74	25r brown violet	.35	.20
240	A74	50r blue grn	*3.25*	*35.00*
241	A74	50r org brn ('23)	.45	.35
a.		Booklet pane of 6		
242	A75	100r rose red	22.50	.40
243	A75	100r orange ('26)	.50	.20
a.		Booklet pane of 6		
244	A75	100r turq grn ('28)	.35	.20
245	A75	150r violet	2.50	.20
246	A75	200r blue	300.00	12.50
247	A75	200r rose red	.40	.20
a.		Booklet pane of 6		
248	A75	200r ol grn ('28)	2.50	3.00
249	A76	300r olive gray	1.90	.25
a.		Booklet pane of 6		
250	A76	300r rose red ('29)	.35	.25
251	A76	400r blue	1.90	.20
252	A76	400r orange ('29)	.75	.60
253	A76	500r red brown	7.50	.50
a.		Booklet pane of 6		
254	A76	500r ultra ('29)	8.50	.20
255	A76	600r brn org ('29)	7.50	3.00
256	A76	700r dull vio ('29)	7.50	1.75
257	A76	1000r turq bl ('29)	9.50	.70
		Nos. 236-257 (22)	379.10	*60.30*

Because of the spacing of the watermark, a few stamps in each sheet show no watermark.

"Agriculture" — A79

1922 Unwmk. *Perf. 13x13½*

258	A79	40r orange brown	.50	.35
259	A79	80r grnsh blue	.35	*2.50*

See Nos. 263, 267, 275.

Declaration of Ypiranga — A80

Dom Pedro I and Jose Bonifacio — A81

National Exposition and President Pessoa — A82

Unwmk.

1922, Sept. 7 Engr. *Perf. 14*

260	A80	100r ultra	5.00	.40
261	A81	200r red	6.00	.30
262	A82	300r green	6.00	.30
		Nos. 260-262 (3)	17.00	1.00

Cent. of independence and Natl. Exposition of 1922.

Agriculture Type of 1922

Perf. 13½x12

1923 Wmk. 100 Typo.

263	A79	40r orange brown	.60	*.60*

Brazilian Army Entering Bahia — A83

Unwmk.

1923, July 12 Litho. *Perf. 13*

264	A83	200r rose	7.50	5.00

Centenary of the taking of Bahia from the Portuguese.

Types of 1920-22 Issues

Perf. 13x13½

1924 Typo. Wmk. 193

265	A73	10r red violet	5.50	3.75
266	A73	20r olive green	6.00	3.75
267	A79	40r orange brown	4.25	.60
268	A74	50r orange brown	3.75	*18.00*
269	A75	100r orange	4.25	.35
270	A75	200r rose	6.00	.25
271	A76	400r blue	3.75	3.75
		Nos. 265-271 (7)	33.50	*30.45*

Arms of Equatorial Confederation, 1824 — A84

Unwmk.

1924, July 2 Litho. *Perf. 11*

272	A84	200r bl, blk, yel, & red	3.00	2.25
a.		Red omitted	275.00	275.00

Centenary of the Equatorial Confederation.

Types of 1920-22 Issues

Perf. 9½ to 13½ and Compound

1924-28 Typo. Wmk. 101

273	A73	10r red violet	.45	.30
274	A73	20r olive gray	.45	.30
275	A79	40r orange brn	.45	.30
276	A74	50r orange brn	.75	.30
277	A75	100r red orange	1.50	.30
278	A75	200r rose	.75	.30
279	A76	300r ol gray ('25)	7.00	1.00
280	A76	400r blue	4.00	.35
281	A76	500r red brown	9.00	.45

Engr.

282	A77	600r red orange ('26)	1.00	.30
283	A72	2000r dull vio ('26)	5.00	.30
284	A72	5000r brown ('26)	15.00	.70
285	A72	10,000r rose ('28)	17.50	.90
		Nos. 273-285 (13)	62.85	5.80

Nos. 283-285 are inscribed "BRASIL CORREIO."

Ruy Barbosa — A85

1925 Wmk. 100 *Perf. 11½*

286	A85	1000r claret	4.25	1.50

1926 Wmk. 101

287	A85	1000r claret	1.75	.35

"Justice" — A86

Scales of Justice and Map of Brazil — A87

Perf. 13½x13

1927, Aug. 11 Typo. Wmk. 206

288	A86	100r deep blue	.90	.50
289	A87	200r rose	.80	.35

Founding of the law courses, cent.

Liberty Holding Coffee Leaves — A88

1928, Mar. 5

290	A88	100r blue green	1.00	.60
291	A88	200r carmine	.65	.50
292	A88	300r olive black	5.00	.40
		Nos. 290-292 (3)	6.65	1.50

Introduction of the coffee tree in Brazil, bicent.

Official Stamps of 1919 Surcharged in Red or Black

Perf. 11, 11½

1928 Wmk. 100 Engr.

293	O3	700r on 500r org	2.25	1.50
a.		Inverted surcharge	175.00	175.00
294	O3	1000r on 100r rose red (Bk)	1.50	.30
295	O3	2000r on 200r dull bl	2.25	.45
296	O3	5000r on 50r grn	2.25	.55
297	O3	10,000r on 10r ol grn	11.00	.90
		Nos. 293-297 (5)	19.25	3.70

#293-297 were used for ordinary postage.

Stamps in the outer rows of the sheets are often without watermark.

Ruy Barbosa — A89

Perf. 9, 9½x11, 11, and Compound

1929 Wmk. 101

300	A89	5000r blue violet	12.50	.75

See #405, 459. For surcharge see #C29.

Types of 1920-21 Issue

Perf. 13½x12½

1929 Typo. Wmk. 218

302	A75	20r gray violet	.25	.20
303	A75	50r red brown	.25	.20
304	A75	100r turq green	.30	.20
305	A75	200r olive green	12.50	2.25
306	A76	300r rose red	.60	.20
307	A76	400r orange	.70	.25
308	A76	500r ultra	7.00	.45
309	A76	600r brown org	8.50	.60
310	A76	700r dp violet	2.25	.20
311	A76	1000r turq blue	4.00	.20
		Nos. 302-311 (10)	36.35	4.75

Wmk. 218 exists both in vertical alignment and in echelon.

Wmk. in echelon

302a	A75	20r	.25	.35
303a	A75	50r	80.00	27.50
306a	A76	300r	.65	.30
308a	A76	500r	110.00	15.00
311a	A76	1000r	6.50	6.50

Architectural Fantasies

A90 A91

Architectural Fantasy — A92

Perf. 13x13½

1930, June 20 Wmk. 206

312	A90	100r turq blue	1.25	.80
313	A91	200r olive gray	2.00	.70
314	A92	300r rose red	3.50	.80
		Nos. 312-314 (3)	6.75	2.30

Fourth Pan-American Congress of Architects and Exposition of Architecture.

Types of 1920-21 Issues

1930 Wmk. 221 *Perf. 13x12½*

316	A75	20r gray violet	.20	.20
317	A75	50r red brown	.20	.20
318	A75	100r turq blue	.25	.20
319	A75	200r olive green	3.00	.25
320	A76	300r rose red	.60	.25
321	A76	500r ultra	1.50	.25
322	A76	1000r turq blue	25.00	.65
		Nos. 316-322 (7)	30.75	2.00

Imperforates

Since 1930, imperforate or partly perforated sheets of nearly all commemorative and some definitive issues have become obtainable.

Types of 1920-29 Issue

Perf. 11, 13½x13, 13x12½

1931-34 Typo. Wmk. 222

326	A75	10r deep brown	.20	.20
327	A75	20r gray violet	.20	.20
328	A74	25r brn vio ('34)	.20	.60
330	A75	50r blue green	.20	.20
331	A75	50r red brown	.20	.20
332	A75	100r orange	.30	.20
334	A75	200r dp carmine	.45	.20
335	A76	300r olive green	.60	.20
336	A76	400r ultra	.85	.20
337	A76	500r red brown	3.50	.20
338	A76	600r brown org	3.50	.20
339	A76	700r deep violet	3.50	.20
340	A76	1000r turq blue	12.50	.20
		Nos. 326-340 (13)	26.20	3.00

Getulio Vargas and Joao Pessoa A93

Vargas and Pessoa A94

Oswaldo Aranha

A95 A96

Antonio Carlos A97

Pessoa A98

Vargas — A99

Unwmk.

1931, Apr. 29 Litho. *Perf. 14*

342	A93	10r + 10r lt bl	.20	*4.50*
343	A93	20r + 20r yel brn	.20	*3.25*
344	A95	50r + 50r bl grn, red & yel	.20	.20
a.		Red missing at left	.90	.90
345	A93	100r + 50r orange	.30	.30
346	A93	200r + 100r green	.30	.30
347	A94	300r + 150r multi	.30	.30
348	A93	400r + 200r dp rose	1.00	.65
349	A93	500r + 250r dk bl	.70	.55
350	A93	600r + 300r brn vio	.50	*6.50*
351	A94	700r + 350r multi	.90	.55
352	A96	1000r + 500r brt grn, red & yel	2.00	.25
353	A97	2000r + 1000r gray blk & red	4.00	.55
354	A98	5000r + 2500r blk & red	17.50	4.50
355	A99	10000r + 5000r brt grn & yel	42.50	10.00
		Nos. 342-355 (14)	70.60	32.40

Revolution of Oct. 3, 1930. Prepared as semi-postal stamps, Nos. 342-355 were sold as ordinary postage stamps with stated surtax ignored.

Nos. 306, 320 and 250 Surcharged

1931

200 Réis

Wmk. E U BRASIL Multiple (218)

1931, July 20 *Perf. 13½x12½*

356	A76	200r on 300r rose red	.90	.90
a.		Wmk. in echelon	17.50	17.50
b.		Inverted surcharge	40.00	

Perf. 13x12½

Wmk. 221

357	A76	200r on 300r rose red	.30	.20
a.		Inverted surcharge	45.00	45.00

Perf. 13½x12½

Wmk. 100

358	A76	200r on 300r rose red	60.00	60.00

Map of South America Showing Meridian of Tordesillas — A100

Joao Ramalho and Tibiriça A101

Martim Affonso de Souza A102

King John III of Portugal A103

Disembarkation of M. A. de Souza at Sao Vicente — A104

Wmk. 222

1932, June 3 Typo. *Perf. 13*

359	A100	20r dk violet	.20	.20
360	A101	100r black	.35	.35
361	A102	200r purple	1.00	.25
362	A103	600r red brown	1.65	1.25

Engr.

Wmk. 101

Perf. 9½, 11, 9½x11

363	A104	700r ultra	2.50	1.75
		Nos. 359-363 (5)	5.70	3.80

1st colonization of Brazil at Sao Vicente, in 1532, under the hereditary captaincy of Martim Affonso de Souza.

Revolutionary Issue

Map of Brazil — A105

Soldier and Flag — A106

Allegory: Freedom, Justice, Equality A107

Soldier's Head A108

"LEX" and Sword A109

Symbolical of Law and Order — A110

Symbolical of Justice — A111

Perf. 11½

1932, Sept. 13 Litho. Unwmk.

364	A105	100r brown org	.40	2.00
365	A106	200r dk car	.35	.70
366	A107	300r gray green	2.00	3.50
367	A108	400r dark blue	7.25	7.25
368	A105	500r blk brn	7.25	7.25
369	A107	600r red	7.25	7.25
370	A106	700r violet	3.50	*7.25*
371	A108	1000r orange	1.75	*7.25*
372	A109	2000r dark brn	14.00	20.00
373	A110	5000r yellow grn	17.50	32.50
374	A111	10000r plum	20.00	37.50
		Nos. 364-374 (11)	81.25	132.45

Issued by the revolutionary forces in the state of Sao Paulo during the revolt of September, 1932. Subsequently the stamps were recognized by the Federal Government and placed in general use.

Excellent counterfeits of Nos. 373 and 374 exist. Counterfeit cancellations abound.

City of Vassouras and Illuminated Memorial — A112

Wmk. 222

1933, Jan. 15 Typo. *Perf. 12*

375	A112	200r rose red	1.00	.90

City of Vassouras founding, cent.

Nos. 306, 320 Surcharged

Perf. 13½x12½

1933, July 28 Wmk. 218

376	A76	200r on 300r rose red	.60	.60
a.		Wmk. 218 in echelon (No. 306a)	12.50	12.50
b.		Wmk. 100 (No. 250)	87.50	87.50

Perf. 13x12½

Wmk. 221

377	A76	200r on 300r rose red	.45	.45
a.		Inverted surcharge	35.00	
b.		Double surcharge	35.00	

Religious Symbols and Inscriptions — A113

Wmk. 222

1933, Sept. 3 Typo. *Perf. 13*

378	A113	200r dark red	.90	.75

1st Natl. Eucharistic Congress in Brazil.

"Flag of the Race" A114

1933, Aug. 18

379	A114	200r deep red	.90	.75

The raising of the "Flag of the Race" and the 441st anniv. of the sailing of Columbus from Palos, Spain, Aug. 3, 1492.

Republic Figure, Flags of Brazil and Argentina — A115

Wmk. 101

1933, Oct. 7 Engr. *Perf. 11½*

380	A115	200r blue	.35	.25

Thick Laid Paper

Perf. 11, 11½

Wmk. 236

381	A115	400r green	.90	.75
382	A115	600r brt rose	3.00	3.25
383	A115	1000r lt violet	4.50	3.75
		Nos. 380-383 (4)	8.75	8.00

Visit of President Justo of the Argentina to Brazil, Oct. 2-7, 1933.

Allegory: "Faith and Energy" — A116

Allegory of Flight — A117

1933 Typo. Wmk. 222

384	A116	200r dark red	.25	.20
385	A116	200r dark violet	.30	.20

See Nos. 435, 471, 491.

Wmk. 236

1934, Apr. 15 Engr. *Perf. 12*

386	A117	200r blue	.50	.50

1st Natl. Aviation Congress at Sao Paulo.

A118

Wmk. 222

1934, May 12 Typo. *Perf. 11*

387	A118	200r dark olive	.25	.25
388	A118	400r carmine	1.50	1.50
389	A118	700r ultra	1.50	.90
390	A118	1000r orange	3.75	.60
		Nos. 387-390 (4)	7.00	3.25

7th Intl. Fair at Rio de Janeiro.

Christ of Corcovado A119

1934, Oct. 20

392	A119	300r dark red	1.90	1.90
a.		Tete beche pair	6.00	*7.25*
393	A119	700r ultra	8.00	5.00
a.		Tete beche pair	19.00	*22.50*

Visit of Eugenio Cardinal Pacelli, later Pope Pius XII, to Brazil.

The three printings of Nos. 392-393, distinguishable by shades, sell for different prices.

José de Anchieta A120

Thick Laid Paper

1934, Nov. 8 Wmk. 236 *Perf. 11, 12*

394	A120	200r yellow brown	.55	.20
395	A120	300r violet	.45	.25
396	A120	700r blue	1.75	1.40
397	A120	1000r lt green	3.50	.55
		Nos. 394-397 (4)	6.25	2.40

Jose de Anchieta, S.J. (1534-1597), Portuguese missionary and "father of Brazilian literature."

A121

"Brazil" and "Uruguay" — A122

Wmk. 222

1935, Jan. 8 Typo. *Perf. 11*

398	A121	200r orange	.65	.40
399	A122	300r yellow	.80	.50
400	A122	700r ultra	3.25	3.25
401	A121	1000r dk violet	8.00	4.00
		Nos. 398-401 (4)	12.70	8.15

Visit of President Terra of Uruguay.

View of Town of Igarassu A123

1935, July 1

402	A123	200r maroon & brn	.85	.45
403	A123	300r vio & olive brn	.85	.35

Captaincy of Pernambuco founding, 400th anniv.

Types of 1918-29
Thick Laid Paper
Perf. 9½, 11, 12, 12x11

1934-36 Engr. Wmk. 236

404	A72	2000r violet	3.75	.40
405	A89	5000r blue vio ('36)	11.00	.50
406	A72	10000r claret ('36)	8.75	.75
		Nos. 404-406 (3)	23.50	1.65

No. 404 is inscribed "BRASIL CORREIO."

Revolutionist A124

Bento Gonçalves da Silva — A125

Duke of Caxias A126

1935, Sept. 20 *Perf. 11, 12*

407	A124	200r black	.55	.45
408	A124	300r rose lake	.55	.35
409	A125	700r dull blue	2.25	2.25
410	A126	1000r light violet	2.50	1.40
		Nos. 407-410 (4)	5.85	4.45

Centenary of the "Ragged" Revolution.

Federal District Coat of Arms A127

Wmk. 222

1935, Oct. 19 Typo. *Perf. 11*

411	A127	200r blue	2.25	2.25

8th Intl. Sample Fair held at Rio de Janeiro.

Coutinho's Ship — A128

Arms of Fernandes Coutinho — A129

1935, Oct. 25

412	A128	300r maroon	2.25	1.00
413	A129	700r turq blue	3.25	2.00

400th anniversary of the establishment of the first Portuguese colony at Espirito Santo by Vasco Fernandes Coutinho.

Gavea, Rock near Rio de Janeiro A130

1935, Oct. 12 Wmk. 245 *Perf. 11*

414	A130	300r brown & vio	1.75	1.50
415	A130	300r blk & turq bl	1.75	1.50
416	A130	300r Prus bl & ultra	1.75	1.50
417	A130	300r crimson & blk	1.75	1.50
		Nos. 414-417 (4)	7.00	6.00

"Child's Day," Oct. 12.

Viscount of Cairu — A131

Perf. 11, 12x11

1936, Jan. 20 Engr. Wmk. 236

418	A131	1200r violet	6.00	2.75

Jose da Silva Lisboa, Viscount of Cairu (1756-1835).

View of Cametá A132

1936, Feb. 26 *Perf. 11, 12*

419	A132	200r brown orange	1.25	1.00
420	A132	300r green	1.25	.80

300th anniversary of the founding of the city of Cameta, Dec. 24, 1635.

Coining Press A133

Thick Laid Paper

1936, Mar. 24 *Perf. 11*

421	A133	300r pur brn, *cr*	1.25	.90

1st Numismatic Cong. at Sao Paulo, Mar., 1936.

Carlos Gomes — A134

Il Guarany" — A135

Thick Laid Paper

1936, July 11 *Perf. 11, 11x12*

422	A134	300r dull rose	.50	.35
423	A134	300r black brown	.50	.35
424	A135	700r ocher	2.00	.90
425	A135	700r blue	1.75	.90
		Nos. 422-425 (4)	4.75	2.50

Birth cent. of Antonio Carlos Gomes, who composed the opera "Il Guarany."

Scales of Justice — A136

Wmk. 222

1936, July 4 Typo. *Perf. 11*

426	A136	300r rose	1.25	.45

First National Judicial Congress.

Federal District Coat of Arms A137

1936, Nov. 13 Typo. Wmk. 249

427	A137	200r rose red	.75	.45

Ninth International Sample Fair held at Rio de Janeiro.

Eucharistic Congress Seal — A138

1936, Dec. 17 Wmk. 245 *Perf. 11½*

428	A138	300r grn, yel, bl & blk	.70	.45

2nd Natl. Eucharistic Congress in Brazil.

Botafogo Bay A139

Thick Laid Paper

Wmk. 236

1937, Jan. 2 Engr. *Perf. 11*

429	A139	700r blue	.75	.45
430	A139	700r black	.75	.45

Birth cent. of Francisco Pereira Passos, engineer who planned the modern city of Rio de Janeiro.

Types of 1920-21, 1933
Perf. 11, 11½ and Compound

1936-37 Typo. Wmk. 249

431	A75	10r deep brown	.20	.20
432	A75	20r dull violet	.20	.20
433	A75	50r blue green	.20	.20
434	A75	100r orange	.25	.20
435	A116	200r dk violet	.45	.20
436	A76	300r olive green	.25	.20
437	A76	400r ultra	.45	.20
438	A76	500r lt brown	.70	.20
439	A76	600r brn org ('37)	1.50	.20
440	A76	700r deep violet	2.75	.20
441	A76	1000r turq blue	3.00	.20
		Nos. 431-441 (11)	9.95	2.20

Massed Flags and Star of Esperanto A140

1937, Jan. 19

442	A140	300r green	1.00	.50

Ninth Brazilian Esperanto Congress.

Bay of Rio de Janeiro A141

1937, June 9 Unwmk. *Perf. 12½*

443	A141	300r orange red & blk	.50	.50
444	A141	700r blue & dk brn	1.25	.50

2nd South American Radio Communication Conf. held in Rio, June 7-19.

Globe — A142

Perf. 11, 12

1937, Sept. 4 Wmk. 249

445	A142	300r green	.85	.50

50th anniversary of Esperanto.

Monroe Palace, Rio de Janeiro A143

Botanical Garden, Rio de Janeiro — A144

1937, Sept. 30 Unwmk. *Perf. 12½*
446 A143 200r lt brn & bl .50 .35
447 A144 300r org & ol grn .50 .35
448 A143 2000r grn & cerise 3.75 5.50
449 A144 10000r lake & indigo 32.50 27.50
Nos. 446-449 (4) 37.25 33.70

Brig. Gen. Jose da Silva Paes — A145

Eagle and Shield — A146

1937, Oct. 11 Wmk. 249 *Perf. 11½*
450 A145 300r blue .75 .30

Bicentenary of Rio Grande do Sul.

1937, Dec. 2 Typo. *Perf. 11*
451 A146 400r dark blue .75 .30

150th anniversary of the US Constitution.

Bags of Brazilian Coffee A147

Frame Engraved, Center Typographed

1938, Jan. 17 Unwmk. *Perf. 12½*
452 A147 1200r multicolored 3.00 .40

Arms of Olinda A148

Perf. 11, 11x11½

1938, Jan. 24 Engr. Wmk. 249
453 A148 400r violet .50 .25

4th cent. of the founding of the city of Olinda.

Independence Memorial, Ypiranga A149

1938, Jan. 24 Typo. *Perf. 11*
454 A149 400r brown olive .60 .25

Proclamation of Brazil's independence by Dom Pedro, Sept. 7, 1822.

Iguaçu Falls — A150

Perf. 12½

1938, Jan. 10 Unwmk. Engr.
455 A150 1000r sepia & yel brn 1.50 .75
456 A150 5000r ol blk & grn 17.00 7.50

Couto de Magalhaes A151

Perf. 11, 11x11½

1938, Mar. 17 Wmk. 249
457 A151 400r dull green .50 .25

General Couto de Magalhaes (1837-1898), statesman, soldier, explorer, writer, developer.

Types of 1918-38

Perf. 11, 12x11, 12x11½, 12

1938 Engr. Wmk. 249
458 A72 2000r blue violet 6.50 .20
459 A89 5000r violet blue 24.00 .50
a. 5000r deep blue 20.00 .50
460 A72 10000r rose lake 27.50 1.00
Nos. 458-460 (3) 58.00 1.70

No. 458 is inscribed "BRASIL CORREIO."

Types of 1920-22

1938 Wmk. 245 Typo. *Perf. 11*
461 A75 50r blue green .50 .75
462 A75 100r orange .50 .75
463 A76 300r olive green .50 .20
463A A76 400r ultra 100.00 35.00
463B A76 500r red brown .50 *10.00*
Nos. 461-463B (5) 102.00 46.70

National Archives Building A152

1938, May 20 Wmk. 249
464 A152 400r brown .40 .25

Centenary of National Archives.

Souvenir Sheets

Sir Rowland Hill — A153

1938, Oct. 22 *Imperf.*
465 A153 Sheet of 10 12.50 12.50
a. 400r dull green, single stamp .75 .75

Brazilian Intl. Philatelic Exposition (Brapex). Issued in sheets measuring 106x118mm. A few perforated sheets exist.

President Vargas — A154

1938, Nov. 10 *Perf. 11*
Without Gum
466 A154 Sheet of 10 5.00 8.50
a. 400r slate blue, single stamp .40 .40

Constitution of Brazil, set up by President Vargas, Nov. 10, 1937. Size: 113x135½mm.

Types of 1920-33

1939 Typo. Wmk. 256 *Perf. 11*
467 A75 10r red brown .30 .25
468 A75 20r dull violet .30 .20
469 A75 50r blue green .30 .20
470 A75 100r yellow org .45 .20
471 A116 200r dk violet .55 .20
472 A76 400r ultra 1.00 .20
473 A76 600r dull orange 1.00 .20
474 A76 1000r turq blue 7.00 .20
Nos. 467-474 (8) 10.90 1.65

View of Rio de Janeiro — A155

View of Santos — A156

1939, June 14 Engr. Wmk. 249
475 A155 1200r dull violet 1.25 .25

1939, Aug. 23
476 A156 400r dull blue .40 .20

Centenary of founding of Santos.

Chalice Vine and Blossoms — A157

Eucharistic Congress Seal — A158

1939, Aug. 23
477 A157 400r green 1.00 .25

1st South American Botanical Congress held in January, 1938.

1939, Sept. 3
478 A158 400r rose red .40 .20

Third National Eucharistic Congress.

Duke of Caxias, Army Patron — A159

1939, Sept. 12 Photo. *Rouletted*
479 A159 400r deep ultra .40 .25

Issued for Soldiers' Day.

A159a

A159b

A159d

A159c

Designs: 400r, George Washington. 800r, Emperor Pedro II. 1200r, Grover Cleveland. 1600r, Statue of Friendship, given by US.

Unwmk.

1939, Oct. 7 Engr. *Perf. 12*
480 A159a 400r yellow orange .40 .25
481 A159b 800r dark green .25 .20
482 A159c 1200r rose car .50 .20
483 A159d 1600r dark blue .50 .25
Nos. 480-483 (4) 1.65 .90

New York World's Fair.

Benjamin Constant A160

Fonseca on Horseback A161

Manuel Deodoro da Fonseca and President Vargas A162

Wmk. 249

1939, Nov. 15 Photo. *Rouletted*

484 A160 400r deep green .30 .20
485 A162 1200r chocolate .75 .30

Engr. *Perf. 11*

486 A161 800r gray black .45 .30
Nos. 484-486 (3) 1.50 .80

Proclamation of the Republic, 50th anniv.

President Roosevelt, President Vargas and Map of the Americas A163

1940, Apr. 14

487 A163 400r slate blue .70 .40

Pan American Union, 50th anniversary.

Types of 1920-33

1940-41 Typo. Wmk. 264 *Perf. 11*

488 A75 10r red brown .20 .25
489 A75 20r dull violet .25 .25
489A A75 50r blue grn ('41) .85 *1.25*
490 A75 100r yellow org 1.00 .20
491 A116 200r violet .75 .20
492 A76 400r ultra 4.50 .20
493 A76 600r dull orange 4.50 .20
494 A76 1000r turq blue 11.00 .20
Nos. 488-494 (8) 23.05 *2.75*

Map of Brazil — A164

1940, Sept. 7 Engr.

495 A164 400r carmine .40 .20
a. Unwmkd. 50.00 30.00

9th Brazilian Congress of Geography held at Florianopolis.

Victoria Regia Water Lily — A165

President Vargas — A166

Relief Map of Brazil — A167

1940, Oct. 30 Wmk. 249 *Perf. 11*
Without Gum

496 A165 1000r dull violet .85 .85
a. Sheet of 10 8.50 *25.00*
497 A166 5000r red 6.75 5.00
a. Sheet of 10 72.50 *110.00*
498 A167 10,000r slate blue 7.50 2.50
a. Sheet of 10 100.00 110.00
Nos. 496-498 (3) 15.10 8.35

New York World's Fair.

All three sheets exist unwatermarked and also with papermaker's watermark of large globe and "AMERICA BANK" in sheet. A few imperforate sheets also exist.

Joaquim Machado de Assis — A168

Pioneers and Buildings of Porto Alegre — A169

1940, Nov. 1

499 A168 400r black .50 .20

Birth centenary of Joaquim Maria Machado de Assis, poet and novelist.

1940, Nov. 2 Wmk. 264

500 A169 400r green .40 .20

Colonization of Porto Alegre, bicent.

Proclamation of King John IV of Portugal — A173

1940, Dec. 1 Wmk. 249

501 A173 1200r blue black 1.00 .25

800th anniv. of Portuguese independence and 300th anniv. of the restoration of the monarchy.

No. 501 was also printed on paper with papermaker's watermark of large globe and "AMERICA BANK." Unwatermarked copies are from these sheets.

Brazilian Flags and Head of Liberty — A175

Wmk. 256

1940, Dec. 18 Engr. *Perf. 11*

502 A175 400r dull violet .50 .20
b. Unwmkd. 40.00 40.00

Wmk. 245

502A A175 400r dull violet 40.00 40.00

10th anniv. of the inauguration of President Vargas.

Calendar Sheet and Inscription "Day of the Fifth General Census of Brazil" — A176

Wmk. 256

1941, Jan. 14 Typo. *Perf. 11*

503 A176 400r blue & red .40 .20

Wmk. 245

504 A176 400r blue & red 3.00 .80

Fifth general census of Brazil.

King Alfonso Henriques A177

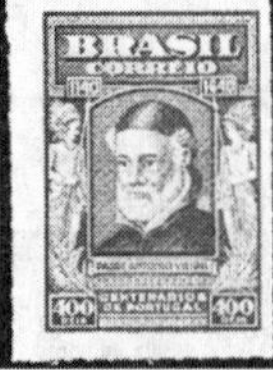

Father Antonio Vieira A178

Salvador Corrêia de Sa e Benevides — A179

President Carmona of Portugal and President Vargas A180

Wmk. 264

1940-41 Photo. *Rouletted*

504A A177 200r pink .20 .20
505 A178 400r ultra .20 .20
506 A179 800r brt violet .25 .20
506A A180 5400r slate grn 1.65 .70

Wmk. 249

507 A177 200r pink 5.25 3.25
507A A178 400r ultra 25.00 8.50
508 A180 5400r slate grn 2.50 1.25
Nos. 504A-508 (7) 35.05 14.30

Portuguese Independence, 800th anniv.
For surcharge & overprint see #C45, C47.

Jose de Anchieta A181

Amador Bueno A182

Wmk. 264

1941, Aug. 1 Engr. *Perf. 11*

509 A181 1000r gray violet 1.00 .50

Society of Jesus, 400th anniversary.

1941, Oct. 20 *Perf. 11½*

510 A182 400r black .50 .30

300th anniv. of the acclamation of Amador Bueno (1572-1648) as king of Sao Paulo.

Air Force Emblem A183

1941, Oct. 20 *Perf. 11*

511 A183 5400r slate green 3.00 2.00

Issued in connection with Aviation Week, as propaganda for the Brazilian Air Force.

Petroleum A184

Agriculture A185

Steel Industry A186

Commerce A187

Marshal Peixoto A188

Count of Porto Alegre A189

Admiral J. A. C. Maurity A190

"Armed Forces" A191

Vargas — A192

1941-42 Wmk. 264 Typo. *Perf. 11*

512 A184 10r yellow brn .20 .20
513 A184 20r olive grn .20 .20
514 A184 50r olive bis .20 .20
515 A184 100r blue grn .20 .20
516 A185 200r brown org .45 .20
517 A185 300r lilac rose .25 .20
518 A185 400r grnsh blue .65 .20
519 A185 500r salmon .30 .20
520 A186 600r violet .65 .20
521 A186 700r brt rose .30 .20
522 A186 1000r gray 1.75 .20
523 A186 1200r dl blue 3.00 .20
524 A187 2000r gray vio 2.50 .20

Engr.

525 A188 5000r blue 5.50 .20
526 A189 10,000r rose red 7.00 .20
527 A190 20,000r dp brown 7.00 .35
528 A191 50,000r red ('42) 27.50 21.00
529 A192 100,000r blue ('42) .60 *9.00*
Nos. 512-529 (18) 58.25 33.35

Nos. 512 to 527 and later issues come on thick or thin paper. The stamps on both papers also exist with three vertical green lines printed on the back, a control mark.

See Nos. 541-587, 592-593, 656-670.

Bernardino de Campos A193

Prudente de Morais A194

1942, May 25

533 A193 1000r red 1.25 .40
534 A194 1200r blue 3.00 .25

100th anniversary of the birth of Bernardino de Campos and Prudente de Morais, lawyers and statesmen of Brazil.

Head of Indo-Brazilian Bull — A195

1942, May 1 Wmk. 264 *Perf. 11½*

535 A195 200r blue .45 .25
536 A195 400r orange brn .45 .25
a. Wmk. 267 45.00 45.00

2nd Agriculture and Livestock Show of Central Brazil held at Uberaba.

Outline of Brazil and Torch of Knowledge A196

Map of Brazil Showing Goiania A197

Wmk. 264

1942, July 5 Typo. *Perf. 11*

537 A196 400r orange brn .30 .25

8th Brazilian Congress of Education.

1942, July 5

538 A197 400r lt violet .40 .30

Founding of Goiania city.

Seal of Congress A198

1942, Sept. 20 Wmk. 264

539 A198 400r olive bister .25 .20
a. Wmk. 267 25.00 12.50

4th Natl. Eucharistic Cong. at Sao Paulo.

Types of 1941-42

1942-47 Wmk. 245 *Perf. 11*

541 A184 20r olive green .20 .40
542 A184 50r olive bister .20 .20
543 A184 100r blue grn .40 .40
544 A185 200r brown org .65 .50
545 A185 400r grnsh blue .40 .20
546 A186 600r lt violet 3.00 .20
547 A186 700r brt rose .35 .80
548 A186 1200r dl blue 1.25 .20
549 A187 2000r gray vio ('47) 9.00 9.00

Engr.

550 A188 5000r blue 10.00 .40
551 A189 10,000r rose red 6.00 1.50
552 A190 20,000r dp brn ('47) 4.50 .45
553 A192 100,000r blue 3.50 8.00
Nos. 541-553 (13) 39.45 22.25

Types of 1941-42

1941-47 Typo. Wmk. 268 *Perf. 11*

554 A184 20r olive grn .20 .20
555 A184 50r ol bis ('47) .55 .55
556 A184 100r bl grn ('43) .20 .20
557 A185 200r brn org ('43) .20 .20
558 A185 300r lilac rose ('43) .20 .20
559 A185 400r grnsh bl ('42) .30 .20
560 A185 500r sal ('43) .20 .20
561 A186 600r violet .60 .20
562 A186 700r brt rose ('45) .35 *1.75*
563 A186 1000r gray .65 .20
564 A186 1200r dp bl ('44) .85 .20
565 A187 2000r gray vio ('43) 3.00 .20

Engr.

566 A188 5000r blue ('43) 4.25 .20
567 A189 10,000r rose red ('43) 8.50 .40
568 A190 20,000r dp brn ('42) 19.00 .45
569 A191 50,000r red ('42) 21.00 3.00
a. 50,000r dark brown red ('47) 15.00 8.50
570 A192 100,000r blue .55 .55
Nos. 554-570 (17) 60.60 8.90

Types of 1941-42

1942-47 Typo. Wmk. 267

573 A184 20r ol grn ('43) .20 .20
574 A184 50r ol bis ('43) .20 .20
575 A184 100r bl grn ('43) .20 .20
576 A185 200r brn org ('43) .25 .25
577 A185 400r grnsh blue .25 .20
578 A185 500r sal ('43) 70.00 10.00
579 A186 600r violet ('43) .45 .30
580 A186 700r brt rose ('47) .35 *3.50*
581 A186 1000r gray ('44) 2.10 .20
582 A186 1200r dl bl 2.50 .20
583 A187 2000r gray vio 2.50 .20

Engr.

584 A188 5000r blue 4.25 .20
585 A189 10,000r rose red ('44) 7.00 .60
586 A190 20,000r dp brn ('45) 8.50 .45
587 A191 50,000r red ('43) 25.00 5.25
Nos. 573-587 (15) 123.75 21.95

1942 Typo. Wmk. 249

592 A184 100r bl grn 4.00 2.50
593 A186 600r violet 4.00 .80

Map Showing Amazon River — A199

1943, Mar. 19 Wmk. 267 *Perf. 11*

607 A199 40c orange brown .35 .35

Discovery of the Amazon River, 400th anniv.

Reproduction of Brazil Stamp of 1866 — A200

1943, Mar. 28 Wmk. 267

608 A200 40c violet .50 .25
a. Wmk. 268 *650.00*

Centenary of city of Petropolis.

Adaptation of 1843 "Bull's-eye" A201

1943, Aug. 1 Engr. *Imperf.*

609 A201 30c black .45 .25
610 A201 60c black .55 .25
611 A201 90c black .45 .25
Nos. 609-611 (3) 1.45 .75

Cent. of the 1st postage stamp of Brazil. The 30c and 90c exist unwatermarked; values $25 and $65.

Souvenir Sheet

A202

Wmk. 281 Horizontally or Vertically

1943 Engr. *Imperf.*

Without Gum

612 A202 Sheet of 3 7.50 6.75
a. 30c black 1.90 1.90
b. 60c black 1.90 1.90
c. 90c black 1.90 1.90

Ubaldino do Amaral — A203

"Justice" — A204

Perf. 11, 12

1943, Aug. 27 Typo. Wmk. 264

613 A203 40c dull slate green .40 .20
a. Wmk. 267 20.00 15.00

Birth centenary of Ubaldino do Amaral, banker and statesman.

1943, Aug. 30 Wmk. 267

614 A204 2cr bright rose .70 .40

Centenary of Institute of Brazilian Lawyers.

Indo-Brazilian Bull — A205

1943, Aug. 30 Engr.

615 A205 40c dk red brn .70 .40

9th Livestock Show at Bahia.

José Barbosa Rodrigues — A206

1943, Nov. 13 Typo.

616 A206 40c bluish grn .40 .20

Birth cent. of Jose Barbosa Rodrigues, botanist.

Charity Hospital, Santos A207

1943, Nov. 7 Engr.

617 A207 1cr blue .40 .30

400th anniv. of Charity Hospital, Santos.

Pedro Americo de Figueirido e Melo (1843-1905), Artist-hero and Statesman — A208

Wmk. 267

1943, Dec. 16 Typo. *Perf. 11*

618 A208 40c brown orange .20 .20

Gen. A. E. Gomes Carneiro A209

1944, Feb. 9 Engr.

619 A209 1.20cr rose .50 .35

50th anniversary of the Lapa siege.

Statue of Baron of Rio Branco — A210

1944, May 13 Typo.

620 A210 1cr blue .40 .25

Statue of the Baron of Rio Branco unveiling.

Duke of Caxias A211

1944, May 13 Unwmk. *Perf. 12*

Granite Paper

621 A211 1.20cr bl grn & pale org .50 .30

Centenary of pacification of Sao Paulo and Minas Gerais in an independence movement in 1842.

YMCA Seal — A212

1944, June 7 Litho. *Perf. 11*

Granite Paper

622 A212 40c dp bl, car & yel .30 .20

Centenary of Young Men's Christian Assn.

Chamber of Commerce Rio Grande — A213

Wmk. 268

1944, Sept. 25 Engr. *Perf. 12*

623 A213 40c lt yellow brn .30 .25

Centenary of the Chamber of Commerce of Rio Grande.

Martim F. R. de Andrada A214

1945, Jan. 30 ***Perf. 11***

624 A214 40c blue .30 .25

Ccentenary of the death of Martim F. R. de Andrada, statesman.

Meeting of Duke of Caxias and David Canabarro A215

1945, Mar. 19 **Photo.**

625 A215 40c ultra .30 .20

Pacification of Rio Grande do Sul, cent.

Globe and "Esperanto" — A216

1945, Apr. 16

626 A216 40c lt blue grn .50 .25

10th Esperanto Congress, Rio, Apr. 14-22.

Baron of Rio Branco's Bookplate A217

1945, Apr. 20 **Wmk. 268** ***Perf. 11***

627 A217 40c violet .50 .25

Cent. of the birth of Jose Maria da Silva Paranhos, Baron of Rio Branco.

Tranquility A218

Glory — A219

Victory A220

Peace A221

Cooperation — A222

Rouletted 7

1945, May 8 **Engr.** **Wmk. 268**

628 A218 20c dk rose vio .20 .20
629 A219 40c dk carmine .20 .20
630 A220 1cr dull orange .35 .30
631 A221 2cr steel blue .85 .45
632 A222 5cr green 1.65 .55
Nos. 628-632 (5) 3.25 1.70

Victory of the Allied Nations in Europe.
Nos. 628-632 exist on thin card, imperf. and unwatermarked.

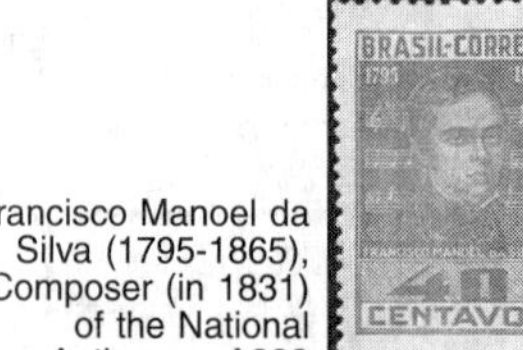

Francisco Manoel da Silva (1795-1865), Composer (in 1831) of the National Anthem — A223

Wmk. 245

1945, May 30 **Typo.** ***Perf. 12***

633 A223 40c brt rose .45 .30
a. Wmk. 268 6.75 6.75

Bahia Institute of Geography and History A224

1945, May 30 **Wmk. 268** ***Perf. 11***

634 A224 40c lt ultra .25 .20

50th anniv. of the founding of the Institute of Geography and History at Bahia.

Emblems of 5th Army and B.E.F.
A225 A226

US Flag and Shoulder Patches A227

Brazilian Flag and Shoulder Patches A228

Victory Symbol and Shoulder Patches — A229

1945, July 18 **Litho.**

635 A225 20c multicolored .20 .20
636 A226 40c multicolored .20 .20
637 A227 1cr multicolored .70 .40
638 A228 2cr multicolored 1.00 .60
639 A229 5cr multicolored 3.00 .70
Nos. 635-639 (5) 5.10 2.10

Honoring the Brazilian Expeditionary Force and the US 5th Army Battle against the Axis in Italy.

Radio Tower and Map — A230

1945, Sept. 3 **Engr.**

640 A230 1.20cr gray .45 .25

Third Inter-American Conference on Radio Communications.
No. 640 was reproduced on a souvenir card with blue background and inscriptions. Size: 145x161mm.

A 40c lilac stamp, picturing the International Bridge between Argentina and Brazil and portraits of Presidents Justo and Vargas, was prepared late in 1945. It was not issued, but later was sold, without postal value, to collectors. Value, 20 cents.

Admiral Luiz Felipe Saldanha da Gama (1846-1895) — A231

1946, Apr. 7

641 A231 40c gray black .25 .25

Princess Isabel d'Orleans-Braganca Birth Cent. — A232

1946, July 29 **Unwmk.**

642 A232 40c black .25 .25

Post Horn, V and Envelope — A233

Post Office, Rio de Janeiro A234

Bay of Rio de Janeiro and Plane A235

Wmk. 268

1946, Sept. 2 **Litho.** ***Perf. 11***

643 A233 40c blk & pale org .20 .20

Perf. 12½

Engr. **Unwmk.**

Center in Ultramarine

644 A234 2cr slate .50 .20
645 A234 5cr orange brn 2.50 .85
646 A234 10cr dk violet 2.75 .50

Center in Brown Orange

647 A235 1.30cr dk green .30 .35
648 A235 1.70cr car rose .30 .35
649 A235 2.20cr dp ultra .50 .50
Nos. 643-649 (7) 7.05 2.95

5th Postal Union Congress of the Americas and Spain.
No. 643 was reproduced on a souvenir card. Size: 188x239mm. Sold for 10cr.

Liberty — A236

Perf. 11x11½

1946, Sept. 18 **Wmk. 268**

650 A236 40c blk & gray .25 .20
a. Unwmkd. 150.00

Adoption of the Constitution of 1946.

Columbus Lighthouse, Dominican Republic — A237

1946, Sept. 14 **Litho.** ***Perf. 11***

651 A237 5cr Prus grn 4.00 1.50

Orchid — A238

Gen. A. E. Gomes Carneiro — A239

1946, Nov. 8 Wmk. 268

652 A238 40c ultra, red & yel .40 .30
a. Unwmkd. 55.00

4th National Exhibition of Orchids, Rio de Janeiro, November, 1946.

Perf. 10½x12

1946, Dec. 6 Engr. Unwmk.

653 A239 40c deep green .20 .20

Centenary of the birth of Gen. Antonio Ernesto Gomes Carneiro.

Brazilian Academy of Letters A240

1946, Dec. 14 *Perf. 11*

654 A240 40c blue .25 .20

50th anniv. of the foundation of the Brazilian Academy of Letters, Rio de Janeiro.

Antonio de Castro Alves (1847-1871), Poet — A241

1947, Mar. 14 Litho. Wmk. 267

655 A241 40c bluish green .20 .20

Types of 1941-42, Values in Centavos or Cruzeiros

1947-54 Wmk. 267 Typo. *Perf. 11*

656	A184	2c	olive	.20	.20
657	A184	5c	yellow brn	.20	.20
658	A184	10c	green	.20	.20
659	A185	20c	brown org	.20	.20
660	A185	30c	dk lil rose	.60	.20
661	A185	40c	blue	.30	.20
b.	Wmk. 268			800.00	60.00
661A	A185	50c	salmon	.60	.20
662	A186	60c	lt violet	1.00	.20
663	A186	70c	brt rose ('54)	.40	.20
664	A186	1cr	gray	1.00	.20
665	A186	1.20cr	dull blue	2.50	.20
a.	Wmk. 268			11.00	9.00
666	A187	2cr	gray violet	4.00	.20
			Engr.		
667	A188	5cr	blue	7.50	.20
668	A189	10cr	rose red	7.50	.20
			Perf. 11, 13		
669	A190	20cr	deep brn	15.00	.75
670	A191	50cr	red	30.00	.50
	Nos. 656-670 (16)			71.20	4.05

The 5, 20, 50cr also exist with perf. 12-13.

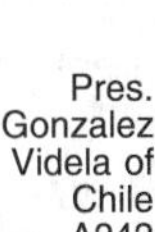

Pres. Gonzalez Videla of Chile A242

1947, June 26 Unwmk. *Perf. 12x11*

671 A242 40c dk brown orange .20 .20

Visit of President Gabriel Gonzalez Videla of Chile, June 1947.

A souvenir folder contains four impressions of No. 671, and measures 6½x8¼ inches.

"Peace" and Western Hemisphere A243

1947, Aug. 15 *Perf. 11x12*

672 A243 1.20cr blue .20 .20

Inter-American Defense Conference at Rio de Janeiro, August-September, 1947.

Pres. Harry S. Truman, Map and Statue of Liberty A244

1947, Sept. 1 Typo. *Perf. 12x11*

673 A244 40c ultra .20 .20

Visit of US President Harry S Truman to Brazil, Sept. 1947.

Pres. Eurico Gaspar Dutra — A245

Mother and Child — A246

Wmk. 268

1947, Sept. 7 Engr. *Perf. 11*

674 A245 20c green .20 .20
675 A245 40c rose carmine .20 .20
676 A245 1.20cr deep blue .25 .20
Nos. 674-676 (3) .65 .60

The souvenir sheet containing Nos. 674-676 is listed as No. C73A. See No. 679.

1947, Oct. 10 Typo. Unwmk.

677 A246 40c brt ultra .20 .20

Issued to mark Child Care Week, 1947.

Arms of Belo Horizonte — A247

Globe — A248

1947, Dec. 12 Engr. Wmk. 267

678 A247 1.20cr rose carmine .30 .20

50th anniversary of the founding of the city of Belo Horizonte.

Dutra Type of 1947

1948 Engr. Wmk. 267

679 A245 20c green 1.50 1.50

Catalogue values for unused stamps in this section, from this point to the end of the section, are for Never Hinged items.

1948, July 10 Litho.

680 A248 40c dl grn & pale lil .35 .20

International Exposition of Industry and Commerce, Petropolis, 1948.

Arms of Paranagua A249

Child Reading Book — A250

1948, July 29

681 A249 5cr bister brown 1.75 .50

300th anniversary of the founding of the city of Paranagua, July 29, 1648.

1948, Aug. 1

682 A250 40c green .25 .20

National Education Campaign.

No. 682 was reproduced on a souvenir card. Size: 124x157mm.

Tiradentes A251

Symbolical of Cancer Eradication A252

1948, Nov. 12

683 A251 40c brown orange .25 .20

200th anniversary of the birth of Joaquim José da Silva Xavier (Tiradentes).

1948, Dec. 14

684 A252 40c claret .25 .25

Anti-cancer publicity.

Adult Student A253

1949, Jan. 3 Wmk. 267 *Perf. 12x11*

685 A253 60c red vio & pink .25 .20

Campaign for adult education.

"Battle of Guararapes," by Vitor Meireles — A254

1949, Feb. 15 *Perf. 11½x12*

686 A254 60c lt blue .95 .60

2nd Battle of Guararapes, 300th anniv.

Church of Sao Francisco de Paula — A255

Manuel de Nobrega — A256

Perf. 11x12

1949, Mar. 8 Unwmk. Engr.

687 A255 60c dark brown .20 .20
a. Souvenir sheet 30.00 30.00

Bicentenary of city of Ouro Fino, state of Minas Gerais.

No. 687a contains one imperf. stamp similar to No. 687, with dates in lower margin. Size: 70x89mm.

1949, Mar. 29 *Imperf.*

688 A256 60c violet .25 .25

Founding of the City of Salvador, 400th anniv.

Emblem of Brazilian Air Force and Plane A257

1949, June 18

689 A257 60c blue violet .25 .25

Issued to honor the Brazilian Air Force.

Star and Angel — A258

1949 Wmk. 267 Litho. *Perf. 11x12*

690 A258 60c pink .20 .20

1st Ecclesiastical Cong., Salvador, Bahia.

Globe A259

1949, Oct. 31 Typo. *Perf. 12x11*

691 A259 1.50cr blue .25 .20

75th anniv. of the UPU.

Ruy Barbosa A260

Unwmk.

1949, Dec. 14 Engr. ***Perf. 12***
692 A260 1.20cr rose carmine .65 .30

Centenary of birth of Ruy Barbosa.

Joaquim Cardinal Arcoverde A. Cavalcanti, Birth Centenary — A261

Perf. 11x12

1950, Feb. 27 Litho. Wmk. 267
693 A261 60c rose .25 .20

Grapes and Factory A262

1950, Mar. 15 ***Perf. 12x11***
694 A262 60c rose lake .25 .20

75th anniversary of Italian immigration to the state of Rio Grande do Sul.

Virgin of the Globe — A263

Globe and Soccer Players — A264

1950, May 31 ***Perf. 11x12***
695 A263 60c blk & lt bl .25 .20

Establishment in Brazil of the Daughters of Charity of St. Vincent de Paul, cent.

1950, June 24
696 A264 60c ultra, bl & gray .85 .50

4th World Soccer Championship.

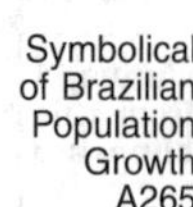

Symbolical of Brazilian Population Growth A265

1950, July 10 Typo. ***Perf. 12x11***
697 A265 60c rose lake .25 .20

Issued to publicize the 6th Brazilian census.

Dr. Oswaldo Cruz — A266

1950, Aug. 23 Litho. ***Perf. 11x12***
698 A266 60c orange brown .25 .20

5th International Congress of Microbiology.

View of Blumenau and Itajai River A267

Perf. 12x11

1950, Sept. 9 Wmk. 267
699 A267 60c bright pink .25 .20

Centenary of the founding of Blumenau.

Amazonas Theater, Manaus A268

1950, Sept. 27
700 A268 60c light brn red .20 .20

Centenary of Amazonas Province.

Arms of Juiz de Fora — A269

1950, Oct. 24 ***Perf. 11x12***
701 A269 60c carmine .25 .25

Centenary of the founding of Juiz de Fora.

Post Office at Recife A270

1951, Jan. 10 Typo. ***Perf. 12x11***
702 A270 60c carmine .20 .20
703 A270 1.20cr carmine .30 .20

Opening of the new building of the Pernambuco Post Office.

Arms of Joinville — A271

Jean-Baptiste de La Salle — A272

1951, Mar. 9 ***Perf. 11x12***
704 A271 60c orange brown .25 .20

Centenary of the founding of Joinville.

1951, Apr. 30 Litho.
705 A272 60c blue .25 .20

Birth of Jean-Baptiste de La Salle, 300th anniv.

Heart and Flowers — A273

Sylvio Romero — A274

1951, May 13 Engr.
706 A273 60c deep plum .25 .20

Mother's Day, May 14, 1951.

1951, Apr. 21 Litho.
707 A274 60c dl vio brn .20 .20

Romero (1851-1914), poet and author.

Joao Caetano, Stage and Masks A275

1951, July 9 ***Perf. 12x11***
708 A275 60c lt gray bl .25 .20

1st Brazilian Theater Cong., Rio, July 9-13, 1951.

Orville A. Derby — A276

First Mass Celebrated in Brazil — A277

1951, July 23 ***Perf. 11x12***
709 A276 2cr slate .35 .35

Centenary of the birth (in New York State) of Orville A. Derby, geologist.

1951, July 25
710 A277 60c dl brn & buff .20 .20

4th Inter-American Congress on Catholic Education, Rio de Janeiro, 1951.

Euclides Pinto Martins A278

1951, Aug. 16 ***Perf. 12x11***
711 A278 3.80cr brn & citron 1.50 .35

1st flight from NYC to Rio, 29th anniv.

Monastery of the Rock A279

1951, Sept. 8
712 A279 60c dl brn & cream .20 .20

Founding of Vitoria, 4th centenary.

Santos-Dumont and Model Plane Contest — A280

Dirigible and Eiffel Tower — A281

Perf. 11x12

1951, Oct. 19 Wmk. 267 Litho.
713 A280 60c salmon & dk brn .42 .35

Unwmk. Engr.
714 A281 3.80cr dark purple 1.25 .40

Week of the Wing and 50th anniv. of Santos-Dumont's flight around the Eiffel Tower.

In December 1951, Nos. 713 and 714 were privately overprinted: "Exposicao Filatelica Regional Distrito Federal 15-XII-1951 23-XII-1951." These were attached to souvenir sheets bearing engraved facsimiles of Nos. 38, 49 and 51, which were sold by Clube Filatelico do Brasil to mark its 20th anniversary. The overprinted stamps on the sheets were canceled, but 530 "unused" sets were sold by the club.

Farmers and Ear of Wheat — A282

1951, Nov. 10 Litho. Wmk. 267
715 A282 60c dp grn & gray .25 .25

Festival of Grain at Bage, 1951.

Map and Open Bible A283

1951, Dec. 9 ***Perf. 12x11***
716 A283 1.20cr brn org .50 .35

Issued to publicize the Day of the Bible.

Queen Isabella — A284

Henrique Oswald — A285

1952, Mar. 10 ***Perf. 11x12***
717 A284 3.80cr lt bl .60 .30

500th anniversary of the birth of Queen Isabella I of Spain.

1952, Apr. 22
718 A285 60c brown .25 .20

Oswald (1852-1931), composer.

Vicente Licinio Cardoso — A286

Map and Symbol of Labor — A287

1952, May 2
719 A286 60c gray blue .25 .20

4th Brazilian Homeopathic Congress.

1952, Apr. 30
720 A287 1.50cr brnsh pink .25 .20

5th International Labor Organization Conference for American Countries.

Gen. Polidoro da Fonseca — A288

Luiz de Albuquerque M. P. Caceres — A289

Portraits: 5cr, Baron de Capanema. 10cr, Minister Eusebio de Queiros.

Unwmk.

1952, May 11 Engr. ***Perf. 11***
721 A288 2.40cr lt car .35 .20
722 A288 5cr blue 2.25 .30
723 A288 10cr dk bl grn 2.25 .30
Nos. 721-723 (3) 4.85 .80

Centenary of telegraph in Brazil.

Perf. 11x12

1952, June 8 Litho. Wmk. 267
724 A289 1.20cr vio bl .25 .20

200th anniversary of the founding of the city of Mato Grosso.

Symbolizing the Glory of Sports — A290

1952, July 21 ***Perf. 12x11***
725 A290 1.20cr dp bl & bl .60 .40

Fluminense Soccer Club, 50th anniversary.

José Antonio Saraiva — A291

Emperor Dom Pedro — A292

1952, Aug. 16 ***Perf. 11x12***
726 A291 60c lil rose .25 .20

Centenary of the founding of Terezina, capital of Piaui State.

1952, Sept. 3 Wmk. 267
727 A292 60c lt bl & blk .25 .20

Issued for Stamp Day and the 2nd Philatelic Exhibition of Sao Paulo.

Flag-encircled Globe — A293

1952, Oct. 24 ***Perf. 13½***
728 A293 3.80cr blue .85 .50

Issued to publicize United Nations Day.

View of Sao Paulo, Sun and Compasses — A294

1952, Nov. 8 Litho. ***Perf. 12x11***
729 A294 60c dl bl, yel & gray grn .25 .20

City Planning Day.

Father Diogo Antonio Feijo — A295

1952, Nov. 9 ***Perf. 11x12***
730 A295 60c Fawn .25 .20

Rodolpho Bernardelli and His "Christ and the Adultress" A297

1952, Dec. 18 ***Perf. 12x11***
732 A297 60c gray blue .25 .20

Bernardelli, sculptor and painter, birth cent.

Map of Western Hemisphere and View of Rio de Janeiro — A298

1952, Sept. 20
733 A298 3.80cr vio brn & lt grn .80 .30

2nd Congress of American Industrial Medicine, Rio de Janeiro, 1952.

Arms and Head of Pioneer A299

Coffee, Cotton and Sugar Cane — A300

2.80cr, Jesuit monk planting tree. 3.80cr, 5.80cr, Spiral, symbolizing progress.

1953, Jan. 25 Litho. ***Perf. 11***
734 A299 1.20cr ol brn & blk brn .50 .35
735 A300 2cr olive grn & yel 1.75 .35
736 A300 2.80cr red brn & dp org 1.20 .20
737 A300 3.80cr dk brn & yel grn 1.00 .20
738 A300 5.80cr int bl & yel grn .70 .20
Nos. 734-738 (5) 5.15 1.30

400th anniversary of Sao Paulo.

Used copies of No. 734 exist with design inverted.

Ledger and Winged Cap A301

1953, Feb. 22 ***Perf. 12x11***
739 A301 1.20cr dl brn & fawn .25 .20

6th Brazilian Accounting Congress.

Joao Ramalho — A302

Wmk. 264

1953, Apr. 8 Engr. ***Perf. 11½***
740 A302 60c blue .25 .20

Founding of the city of Santo Andre, 4th cent.

Aarao Reis and Plan of Belo Horizonte A303

1953, May 6 Photo.
741 A303 1.20cr red brn .25 .20

Aarao Leal de Carvalho Reis (1853-1936), civil engineer.

A304

A305

1953, May 16

742 A304 1.50cr Almirante Saldanha .40 .25

4th globe-circling voyage of the training ship Almirante Saldanha.

1953, July 5 **Photo.**

Joaquim Jose Rodrigues Torres, Viscount of Itaborai.

743 A305 1.20cr violet .20 .20

Centenary of the Bank of Brazil.

Lamp and Rio-Petropolis Highway — A306

1953, July 14

744 A306 1.20cr gray .25 .20

10th Intl. Congress of Nursing, Petropolis, 1953.

Bay of Rio de Janeiro A307

1953, July 15

745 A307 3.80cr dk bl grn .40 .20

Issued to publicize the fourth World Congress of Baptist Youth, July 1953.

Arms of Jau and Map A308

1953, Aug. 15 **Engr.**

746 A308 1.20cr purple .25 .20

Centenary of the city of Jau.

Ministry of Health and Education Building, Rio — A309

Maria Quiteria de Jesus Medeiros — A310

1953, Aug. 1

747 A309 1.20cr dp grn .25 .20

Day of the Stamp and the first Philatelic Exhibition of National Education.

1953, Aug. 21 **Photo.**

748 A310 60c vio bl .25 .20

Centenary of the death of Maria Quiteria de Jesus Medeiros (1792-1848), independence heroine.

Pres. Odria of Peru — A311

Duke of Caxias Leading his Troops — A312

1953, Aug. 25

749 A311 1.40cr rose brn .25 .20

Issued to publicize the visit of Gen. Manuel A. Odria, President of Peru, Aug. 25, 1953.

Engr. (60c, 5.80cr); Photo.

1953, Aug. 25

1.20cr, Caxias' tomb. 1.70cr, 5.80cr, Portrait of Caxias. 3.80cr, Arms of Caxias.

750 A312	60c	dp grn	.30	.20
751 A312	1.20cr	dp claret	.40	.20
752 A312	1.70cr	slate grn	.40	.20
753 A312	3.80cr	rose brn	.65	.20
754 A312	5.80cr	gray vio	.65	.20
	Nos. 750-754 (5)		2.40	1.00

150th anniversary of the birth of Luis Alves de Lima e Silva, Duke of Caxias.

Quill Pen, Map and Tree — A313

Horacio Hora — A314

1953, Sept. 12 **Photo.**

755 A313 60c ultra .25 .20

5th National Congress of Journalism.

1953, Sept. 17 **Litho.** **Wmk. 267**

756 A314 60c org & dp plum .25 .20

Horacio Pinto de Hora (1853-1890), painter.

Pres. Somoza of Nicaragua — A315

Auguste de Saint-Hilaire A316

1953, Sept. 24 **Photo.** **Wmk. 264**

757 A315 1.40cr dk vio brn .25 .20

Issued to publicize the visit of Gen. Anastasio Somoza, president of Nicaragua.

1953, Sept. 30

758 A316 1.20cr dk brn car .25 .25

Centenary of the death of Auguste de Saint-Hilaire, explorer and botanist.

Jose Carlos do Patrocinio — A317

Clock Tower, Crato — A318

1953, Oct. 9 **Photo.**

759 A317 60c dk slate gray .25 .20

Jose Carlos do Patrocinio, (1853-1905), journalist and abolitionist.

1953, Oct. 17

760 A318 60c blue green .25 .20

Centenary of the city of Crato.

Joao Capistrano de Abreu — A319

Allegory: "Justice" — A320

1953, Oct. 23

761 A319 60c dull blue .20 .20
762 A319 5cr purple .85 .85

Joao Capistrano de Abreu (1853-1927), historian.

1953, Nov. 17

763 A320 60c indigo .25 .20
764 A320 1.20cr dp magenta .25 .20

50th anniv. of the Treaty of Petropolis.

Farm Worker in Wheat Field — A321

Teacher and Pupils — A322

1953, Nov. 29 **Photo.** ***Perf. 11½***

766 A321 60c dk green .25 .20

3rd Natl. Wheat Festival, Erechim, 1953.

1953, Dec. 14

767 A322 60c red .25 .25

First National Conference of Primary School Teachers, Salvador, 1953.

Zacarias de Gois e Vasconsellos A323

Alexandre de Gusmao — A324

5cr, Porters with trays of coffee beans.

1953-54 **Photo.**

768 A323 2cr org brn & blk, *buff* ('54) .65 .40
a. White paper 1.75 .40
769 A323 5cr dp org & blk 1.25 .40

Centenary of the state of Parana.

1954, Jan. 13

770 A324 1.20cr brn vio .25 .20

Gusmao (1695-1753), statesman, diplomat and writer.

Symbolical of Sao Paulo's Growth — A325

Arms and View of Sao Paulo A326

Designs: 2cr, Priest, settler and Indian. 2.80cr, José de Anchieta.

1954, Jan. 25 ***Perf. 11½x11***

771 A325 1.20cr dk vio brn .75 .50
a. Buff paper 1.75 1.00

Engr.

772 A325 2cr lilac rose 1.00 .60
773 A325 2.80cr pur gray 1.00 1.00

Perf. 11x11½

774 A326 3.80cr dl grn 1.25 .50
a. Buff paper 2.25 2.00
775 A326 5.80cr dl red 1.25 .60
a. Buff paper 5.00 .75
Nos. 771-775 (5) 5.25 3.20

400th anniversary of Sao Paulo.

J. Fernandes Vieira, A. Vidal de Negreiros, A. F. Camarao and H. Dias — A327

Perf. 11x11½

1954, Feb. 18 **Photo.** **Unwmk.**

776 A327 1.20cr ultra .25 .25

300th anniversary of the recovery of Pernambuco from the Dutch.

Sao Paulo and Minerva A328

1954, Feb. 24

777 A328 1.50cr dp plum .25 .25

10th International Congress of Scientific Organizations, Sao Paulo, 1954.

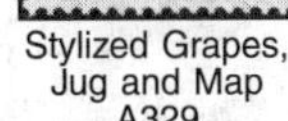

Stylized Grapes, Jug and Map A329

Monument of the Immigrants A330

1954, Feb. 27 **Photo.** ***Perf. 11½x11***

778 A329 40c dp claret .25 .20

Grape Festival, Rio Grande do Sul.

1954, Feb. 28

779 A330 60c dp vio bl .25 .20

Unveiling of the Monument to the Immigrants of Caxias do Sul.

First Brazilian Locomotive — A331

Perf. 11x11½

1954, Apr. 30 **Unwmk.**

781 A331 40c carmine .25 .20

Centenary of the first railroad engine built in Brazil.

Pres. Chamoun of Lebanon — A332

1954, May 12 **Photo.** ***Perf. 11½x11***

782 A332 1.50cr maroon .25 .25

Visit of Pres. Camille Chamoun of Lebanon.

Sao Jose College, Rio de Janeiro A333

J. B. Champagnat Marcelin — A334

Apolonia Pinto — A335

1954, June 6 ***Perf. 11x11½, 11½x11***

783 A333 60c purple .20 .20
784 A334 120cr vio blue .20 .20

50th anniversary of the founding of the Marist Brothers in Brazil.

1954, June 21 **Photo.**

785 A335 1.20cr bright green .20 .20

Apolonia Pinto (1854-1937), actress.

Adm. Margues Tamandare — A336

Portraits: 2c, 5c, 10c, Admiral Margues Tamandare. 20c, 30c, 40c, Oswaldo Cruz. 50c, 60c, 90c, Joaquim Murtinho. 1cr, 1.50cr, 2cr, Duke of Caxias. 5cr, 10cr, Ruy Barbosa. 20cr, 50cr, Jose Bonifacio.

1954-60 **Wmk. 267** ***Perf. 11x11½***

786 A336 2c vio blue .20 .20
787 A336 5c org red .20 .20
788 A336 10c brt green .20 .20
789 A336 20c magenta .20 .20
790 A336 30c dk gray grn .20 .20
791 A336 40c rose red .35 .20
792 A336 50c violet .25 .20
793 A336 60c gray grn .20 .20
794 A336 90c orange ('55) .35 .20
795 A336 1cr brown .20 .20
796 A336 1.50cr blue .20 .20
a. Wmk. 264 16.00 8.00
797 A336 2cr dk bl grn ('56) .45 .20
798 A336 5cr rose lil ('56) .35 .20
799 A336 10cr lt grn ('60) .90 .20
800 A336 20cr crim rose ('59) .90 .20
801 A336 50cr ultra ('59) 5.50 .20
Nos. 786-801 (16) 10.65 3.20

See Nos. 890, 930-933.

Boy Scout Waving Flag (Statue) — A337

Baltasar Fernandes, Explorer — A338

1954, Aug. 2 **Unwmk.** ***Perf. 11½x11***

802 A337 1.20cr vio bl .40 .25

Intl. Boy Scout Encampment, Sao Paulo.

1954, Aug. 15

803 A338 60c dk red .25 .25

300th anniversary of city of Sorocaba.

Adeodato Giovanni Cardinal Piazza — A339

Our Lady of Aparecida, Map of Brazil — A340

1954, Sept. 2

804 A339 4.20cr red org .50 .35

Visit of Adeodato Cardinal Piazza, papal legate to Brazil.

1954

Design: 1.20cr, Virgin standing on globe.

805 A340 60c claret .30 .30
806 A340 1.20cr vio bl .40 .30

No. 805 was issued for the 1st Cong. of Brazil's Patron Saint (Our Lady of Aparecida); No. 806, the cent. of the proclamation of the dogma of the Immaculate Conception. Both stamps also for the Marian Year.

Issue dates: 60c, Sept. 6; 1.20cr, Sept. 8.

Benjamin Constant and Hand Reading Braille A341

1954, Sept. 27 **Photo.** **Unwmk.**

807 A341 60c dk grn .25 .20

Centenary of the founding of the Benjamin Constant Institute.

River Battle of Riachuelo — A342

Admiral F. M. Barroso A343

Dr. Christian F. S. Hahnemann A344

1954, Oct. 6 ***Perf. 11x11½, 11½x11***

808 A342 40c redsh brown .30 .20
809 A343 60c purple .20 .20

Admiral Francisco Manoel Barroso da Silva (1804-82).

1954, Oct. 8 ***Perf. 11½x11***

810 A344 2.70cr dk green .30 .25

1st World Cong. of Homeopathic Medicine.

Nizia Floresta — A345

Ears of Wheat — A346

1954, Oct. 12

811 A345 60c lilac rose .25 .20

Reburial of the remains of Nizia Floresta (Dio Nizia Pinto Lisboa), writer and educator.

1954, Oct. 22

812 A346 60c olive green .20 .20

4th National Wheat Festival, Carazinho.

Basketball Player and Ball-Globe A347

Allegory of the Spring Games A348

1954, Oct. 23 **Photo.**

813 A347 1.40cr orange red .30 .30

Issued to publicize the second World Basketball Championship Matches, 1954.

Perf. 11½x11

1954, Nov. 6 **Wmk. 267**

814 A348 60c red brown .25 .20

Issued to publicize the 6th Spring Games.

San Francisco Hydroelectric Plant — A349

1955, Jan. 15 ***Perf. 11x11½***

815 A349 60c brown org .20 .20

Issued to publicize the inauguration of the San Francisco Hydroelectric Plant.

Itutinga Hydroelectric Plant — A350

1955, Feb. 3

816 A350 40c blue .20 .20

Issued to publicize the inauguration of the Itutinga Hydroelectric Plant at Lavras.

Rotary Emblem and Bay of Rio de Janeiro — A351

1955, Feb. 23 ***Perf. 12x11½***

817 A351 2.70cr slate gray & blk .85 .25

Rotary International, 50th anniversary.

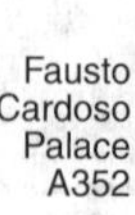

Fausto Cardoso Palace A352

1955, Mar. 17 ***Perf. 11x11½***

818 A352 40c henna brown .25 .25

Centenary of Aracaju.

Aviation Symbols A353

1955, Mar. 13 **Photo.** ***Perf. 11½***

819 A353 60c dark gray green .20 .20

Issued to publicize the third National Aviation Congress at Sao Paulo, Mar. 6-13.

Arms of Botucatu A354

1955, Apr. 14

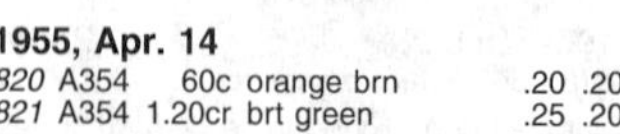

820 A354 60c orange brn .20 .20
821 A354 1.20cr brt green .25 .20

Centenary of Botucatu.

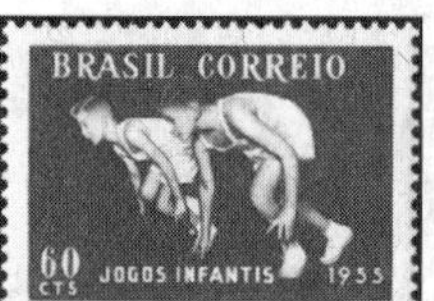

Young Racers at Starting Line A355

Perf. 11½

1955, Apr. 30 **Photo.** **Unwmk.**

823 A355 60c orange brn .25 .20

5th Children's Games.

Marshal Hermes da Fonseca — A356

Congress Altar, Sail and Sugarloaf Mountain — A357

1955, May 12 **Wmk. 267**

824 A356 60c purple .20 .20

Marshal Hermes da Fonseca, birth cent.

Engraved; Photogravure (2.70cr)

1955, July 17 **Unwmk.** ***Perf. 11½***

Designs: 2.70cr, St. Pascoal. 4.20cr, Aloisi Benedetto Cardinal Masella.

Granite Paper

825 A357 1.40cr green .20 .20
826 A357 2.70cr deep claret .25 .20
827 A357 4.20cr blue .30 .20
Nos. 825-827 (3) .75 .60

36th World Eucharistic Cong. in Rio de Janeiro.

Girl Gymnasts A358

1955, Nov. 12 **Engr.**

Granite Paper

828 A358 60c rose lilac .20 .20

Issued to publicize the 7th Spring Games.

José B. Monteiro Lobato, Author A359

1955, Dec. 8

Granite Paper

829 A359 40c dark green .20 .20

Adolfo Lutz — A360

Lt. Col. Vilagran Cabrita — A361

1955, Dec. 18

Granite Paper

830 A360 60c dk green .20 .20

Centenary of the birth of Adolfo Lutz, public health pioneer.

1955, Dec. 22 **Photo.** **Wmk. 267**

831 A361 60c violet blue .20 .20

First Battalion of Engineers, cent.

Salto Grande Hydroelectric Dam A362

1956, Jan. 15 **Unwmk.** ***Perf. 11½***

Granite Paper

832 A362 60c brick red .20 .20

Arms of Mococa — A363

"G" and Globe — A364

Wmk. 256

1956, Apr. 17 **Photo.** ***Perf. 11½***

833 A363 60c brick red .20 .20

Centenary of Mococa, Sao Paulo.

1956, Apr. 14 **Unwmk.**

Granite Paper

834 A364 1.20cr violet blue .20 .20

18th Intl. Geographic Cong., Rio, Aug. 1956.

Girls' Foot Race A365

1956, Apr. 28 **Photo.**

Granite Paper

835 A365 2.50cr brt blue .30 .20

6th Children's Games.

Plane over Map of Brazil — A366

1956, June 12 **Wmk. 267** ***Perf. 11½***

836 A366 3.30cr brt vio bl .40 .20

National Airmail Service, 25th anniv.

Fireman Rescuing Child A367

1956, July 2 **Wmk. 264**

837 A367 2.50cr crimson .40 .25
a. Buff paper 2.25 2.00

Centenary of the Fire Brigade.

Map of Brazil and Open Book A368

1956, Sept. 8 **Wmk. 267**

838 A368 2.50cr brt vio bl .30 .20

50th anniversary of the arrival of the Marist Brothers in Northern Brazil.

Church and Monument, Franca — A369

1956, Sept. 7 **Engr.**

839 A369 2.50cr dk blue .30 .20

Centenary of city of Franca, Sao Paulo.

Woman Hurdler A370

1956, Sept. 22 **Photo.** **Unwmk.**

Granite Paper

840 A370 2.50cr dk car .40 .20

Issued to publicize the 8th Spring Games.

Forest and Map of Brazil — A371

1956, Sept. 30 **Wmk. 267** ***Perf. 11½***

841 A371 2.50cr dk green .25 .20

Issued to publicize education in forestry.

Baron da Bocaina A372

1956, Oct. 8 **Engr.** **Wmk. 268**

842 A372 2.50cr reddish brown .25 .20

Centenary of the birth of Baron da Bocaina, who introduced the special delivery mail system to Brazil.

Marbleized Paper

Paper with a distinct wavy-line or marbleized watermark (which Brazilians call *marmorizado* paper) has been found on many stamps of Brazil, 1956-68, including Nos. 843-845, 847, 851-854, 858-858A, 864, 878, 880, 882, 884, 886-887, 896, 909, 918, 920-921, 925-928, 936-939, 949, 955-958, 960, 962-964, 978-979, 983, 985-987, 997-998, 1002-1003, 1005, 1009-1012, 1017, 1024, 1026, 1055, 1075, 1078, 1082, C82, C82a, C83-C87, C96, C99, C109.

Quantities are much less than those of stamps on regular paper.

Panama Stamp Showing Pres. Juscelino Kubitschek A373

1956, Oct. 12 Photo. Wmk. 267

843 A373 3.30cr green & blk .40 .20

Issued on America Day, Oct. 12, to commemorate the meeting of the Presidents and the Pan-American Conference at Panama City, July 21-22.

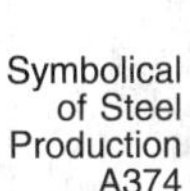

Symbolical of Steel Production A374

Wmk. 267

1957, Jan. 31 Photo. *Perf. 11½*

844 A374 2.50cr chocolate .25 .20

2nd expansion of the National Steel Company at Volta Redonda.

Joaquim E. Gomes da Silva — A375

1957, Mar. 1 Photo. Unwmk.

Granite Paper

845 A375 2.50cr dk bl grn .25 .20

Centenary of the birth (in 1856) of Joaquim E. Gomes da Silva.

Allan Kardec A376

Wmk. 268

1957, Apr. 18 Engr. *Perf. 11½*

846 A376 2.50cr dk brown .25 .20

Issued in honor of Allan Kardec, pen name of Leon Hippolyto Denizard Rivail, and for the centenary of the publication of his "Codification of Spiritism."

Boy Gymnast A377

1957, Apr. 27 Photo. Unwmk.

Granite Paper

847 A377 2.50cr lake .50 .25

7th Children's Games.

Pres. Craveiro Lopes — A378

Stamp of 1932 — A379

1957, June 7 Engr. Wmk. 267

848 A378 6.50cr blue .40 .20

Visit of Gen. Francisco Higino Craveiro Lopes, President of Portugal.

1957, July 9 Photo.

849 A379 2.50cr rose .25 .20

25th anniv. of the movement for a constitution.

St. Antonio Monastery, Pernambuco — A380

1957, Aug. 24 Engr. Wmk. 267

850 A380 2.50cr deep magenta .25 .20

300th anniv. of the emancipation of the Franciscan province of St. Antonio in Pernambuco State.

Volleyball — A381

Basketball — A382

1957, Sept. 28 Photo. *Perf. 11½*

851 A381 2.50cr dull org red .45 .25

Issued for the 9th Spring Games.

1957, Oct. 12

852 A382 3.30cr org & brt grn .45 .25

2nd Women's International Basketball Championship, Rio de Janeiro.

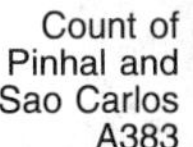

Count of Pinhal and Sao Carlos A383

1957, Nov. 4 Wmk. 267 *Perf. 11½*

853 A383 2.50cr rose .30 .25

Centenary of the city of Sao Carlos and honoring the Count of Pinhal, its founder.

Auguste Comte — A384

1957, Nov. 15

854 A384 2.50cr dk red brn .25 .20

Centenary of the death of Auguste Comte, French mathematician and philosopher.

Radio Station A385

1957, Dec. 10 Wmk. 268

855 A385 2.50cr dk green .20 .20

Opening of Sarapui Central Radio Station.

Admiral Tamandare and Warship A386

Design: 3.30cr, Aircraft carrier.

1957-58 Photo.

856 A386 2.50cr light blue .25 .20

Engr.

857 A386 3.30cr green ('58) .30 .20

150th anniversary of the birth of Admiral Joaquim Marques de Tamandare, founder of the Brazilian navy.

Coffee Plant and Symbolic "R" — A387

Wmk. 267

1957-58 Photo. *Perf. 11½*

858 A387 2.50cr magenta .50 .35

Unwmk.

Granite Paper

858A A387 2.50cr magenta ('58) .45 .35

Centenary (in 1956) of the city of Ribeirao Preto in Sao Paulo state.

Dom John VI — A388

1958, Jan. 28 Engr. Wmk. 268

859 A388 2.50cr magenta .35 .25

150th anniversary of the opening of the ports of Brazil to foreign trade.

Bugler A389

1958, Mar. 18 Wmk. 267

860 A389 2.50cr red .35 .25

Brazilian Marine Corps, 150th anniv.

Station at Rio and Locomotive of 1858 — A390

Court House — A391

Wmk. 267

1958, Mar. 29 Photo. *Perf. 11½*

861 A390 2.50cr red brn .35 .25

Central Railroad of Brazil, cent.

1958, Apr. 1 Engr. Wmk. 256

862 A391 2.50cr green .25 .20

150th anniv. of the Military Superior Court.

Emblem and Brazilian Pavilion A392

1958, Apr. 17 Wmk. 267

863 A392 2.50cr dk blue .25 .25

World's Fair, Brussels, Apr. 17-Oct. 19.

High Jump — A393

1958, Apr. 20 Photo. Unwmk.

Granite Paper

864 A393 2.50cr crimson rose .25 .20

8th Children's Games.

Marshal Mariano da Silva Rondon A394

1958, Apr. 19 Engr. Wmk. 267
865 A394 2.50cr magenta .25 .20

Issued to honor Marshal Mariano da Silva Rondon and the "Day of the Indian."

Hydroelectric Station — A395

1958, Apr. 28 Wmk. 267 *Perf. 11½*
866 A395 2.50cr magenta .25 .20

Opening of Sao Paulo State power plant.

National Printing Plant A396

1958, May 22 Photo.
867 A396 2.50cr redsh brn .20 .20

150th anniversary of the founding of the National Printing Plant.

Marshal Osorio — A397

1958, May 24
868 A397 2.50cr brt violet .20 .20

150th anniversary of the birth of Marshal Manoel Luiz Osorio.

Pres. Ramon Villeda Morales — A398

Fountain — A399

1958, June 7 Engr. *Perf. 11½*
869 A398 6.50cr dk green 1.25 .75
a. Wmk. 268 5.00 2.00

Visit of Pres. Ramon Villeda Morales of Honduras.

1958, June 13
870 A399 2.50cr dk green .25 .20

Botanical Garden, Rio de Janeiro, 150th anniv.

Symbols of Agriculture A400

Prophet Joel — A401

1958, June 18 Photo.
871 A400 2.50cr rose carmine .25 .20

50th anniv. of Japanese immigration to Brazil.

1958, June 21 Engr.
872 A401 2.50cr dk blue .25 .20

Bicentenary of the Cathedral of Bom Jesus at Matosinhos.

Stylized Globe A402

1958, July 10 Photo.
873 A402 2.50cr dk brown .20 .20

Intl. Investment Conference, Belo Horizonte.

Julio Bueno Brandao — A403

1958, Aug. 1 Wmk. 268 *Perf. 11½*
874 A403 2.50cr red brown .25 .20

Centenary of the birth of Julio Bueno Brandao, President of Minas Gerais.

Palacio Tiradentes (House of Congress) A404

1958, July 24 Engr.
875 A404 2.50cr sepia .25 .20

47th Interparliamentary Conference, Rio de Janeiro, July 24-Aug. 1.

Presidential Palace, Brasilia — A405

1958, Aug. 8 Photo. Wmk. 267
876 A405 2.50cr ultra .20 .20

Issued to publicize the construction of Brazil's new capital, Brasilia.

Freighters A406

1958, Aug. 22
877 A406 2.50cr blue .25 .20

Brazilian merchant marine.

Joaquim Caetano da Silva A407

1958, Sept. 2 Unwmk.
Granite Paper
878 A407 2.50cr redsh brn .25 .20

Joaquim Caetano da Silva, scientist & historian.

Giovanni Gronchi — A408

Archers — A409

1958, Sept. 4 Engr. Wmk. 268
879 A408 7cr dk blue .50 .20

Visit of Italy's President Giovanni Gronchi to Brazil.

Perf. 11½
1958, Sept. 21 Photo. Unwmk.
Granite Paper
880 A409 2.50cr red org .35 .20

Issued to publicize the 10th Spring Games.

Elderly Couple — A410

Machado de Assis — A411

1958, Sept. 27 Wmk. 267
881 A410 2.50cr magenta .25 .20

Day of the Old People, Sept. 27.

1958, Sept. 28 Unwmk.
882 A411 2.50cr red brn .25 .20

50th anniversary of the death of Joaquim Maria Machado de Assis, writer.

Pres. Vargas and Oil Derrick A412

1958, Oct. 6 Wmk. 268
883 A412 2.50cr blue .25 .20

5th anniv. of Pres. Getulio D. Vargas' oil law.

Globe — A413

Gen. Lauro Sodré — A414

Wmk. 267
1958, Nov. 14 Photo. *Perf. 11½*
884 A413 2.50cr blue .30 .20

7th Inter-American Congress of Municipalities.

1958, Nov. 15 Engr.
885 A414 3.30cr green .25 .20

Cent. of the birth of Gen. Lauro Sodré.

UN Emblem — A415

Soccer Player — A416

1958, Dec. 26 Photo. *Perf. 11½*
886 A415 2.50cr brt blue .20 .20

10th anniv. of the signing of the Universal Declaration of Human Rights.

1959, Jan. 20
887 A416 3.30cr emer & red brn .40 .20

World Soccer Championships of 1958.

Railroad Track and Map — A417

Pres. Sukarno of Indonesia — A418

1959, Apr. Wmk. 267 *Perf. 11½*
888 A417 2.50cr dp orange .25 .20

Centenary of the linking of Patos and Campina Grande by railroad.

1959, May 20
889 A418 2.50cr blue .25 .20

Visit of President Sukarno of Indonesia.

Dom John VI — A419

Boy Polo Players — A420

Perf. 10½x11½

1959, June 12 Wmk. 267
890 A419 2.50cr crimson .25 .20

1959, June 13 *Perf. 11½*
891 A420 2.50cr orange brn .25 .20

9th Children's Games.

Loading Freighter — A421

Organ and Emblem — A422

1959, July 10
892 A421 2.50cr dk green .25 .20

Honoring the merchant marine.

1959, July 16 Photo.
893 A422 3.30cr magenta .25 .20

Bicentenary of the Carmelite Order in Brazil.

Joachim Silverio de Souza — A423

Symbolic Road — A424

1959, July 20 *Perf. 11½*
894 A423 2.50cr red brown .25 .20

Birth centenary of Joachim Silverio de Souza, first bishop of Diamantina, Minas Gerais.

1959, Sept. 27 Wmk. 267
895 A424 3.30cr bl grn & ultra .25 .20

11th International Roadbuilding Congress.

Woman Athlete — A425

1959, Oct. 4
896 A425 2.50cr lilac rose .25 .20

11th Spring Games.

Map of Parana A426

1959, Sept. 27
897 A426 2.50cr dk green .25 .20

Founding of Londrina, Parana, 25th anniv.

Globe and Snipes — A427

Cross of Lusitania — A428

1959, Oct. 22 *Perf. 11½*
898 A427 6.50cr dull grn .20 .20

World Championship of Snipe Class Sailboats, Porto Alegre, won by Brazilian yachtsmen.

1959, Oct. 24 Engr.
899 A428 6.50cr dull blue .20 .20

4th Intl. Conf. on Brazilian-Portuguese Studies, University of Bahia, Aug. 10-20.

Factory Entrance and Order of Southern Cross — A429

Corcovado Christ, Globe and Southern Cross — A430

1959, Nov. 19 Photo.
900 A429 3.30cr orange red .20 .20

Pres. Vargas Gunpowder Factory, 50th anniv.

1959, Nov. 26 *Perf. 11½*
901 A430 2.50cr blue .20 .20

Universal Thanksgiving Day.

Burning Bush A431

1959, Dec. 24 Wmk. 267
902 A431 3.30cr lt grn .20 .20

Centenary of Presbyterian work in Brazil.

Piraja da Silva and Schistosoma Mansoni — A432

1959, Dec. 28
903 A432 2.50cr rose violet .20 .20

25th anniv. of the discovery and identification of schistosoma mansoni, a parasite of the fluke family, by Dr. Piraja da Silva.

Luiz de Matos A433

1960, Jan. 3 Photo.
904 A433 3.30cr red brown .20 .20

Birth centenary of Luiz de Matos.

Zamenhof — A434

Adél Pinto — A435

1960, Mar. 10 Wmk. 267 *Perf. 11½*
905 A434 6.50cr emerald .20 .20

Lazarus Ludwig Zamenhof (1859-1917), Polish oculist who invented Esperanto in 1887.

1960, Mar. 19 Engr. Wmk. 268
906 A435 11.50cr rose red .20 .20

Centenary of the birth of Adél Pinto, civil engineer and railroad expert.

Presidential Palace, Colonnade — A436

Design: 27cr, Plan of Brasilia (like #C98).

Perf. 11x11½

1960 Photo. Wmk. 267
907 A436 2.50cr brt green .20 .20

Size: 105x46½mm

908 A436 27cr salmon .60 .60
Nos. 907-908,C95-C98 (6) 2.15 1.60

No. 907 for the inauguration of Brazil's new capital, Brasilia, Apr. 21, 1960.
No. 908 for the birthday of Pres. Juscelino Kubitschek and has a 27cr in design of No. C98, flanked by the chief design features of Nos. 907, C95-C97, with Kubitschek signature below. Issued in sheets of 4 with wide horizontal gutter.
Issued: 2.50cr, 4/21; 27cr, 9/12.

Grain, Coffee, Cotton and Cacao — A437

Paulo de Frontin — A438

Perf. 11½x11

1960, July 28 Wmk. 267

909 A437 2.50cr brown .20 .20

Centenary of Ministry of Agriculture.

1960, Oct. 12 Wmk. 268

910 A438 2.50cr orange red .20 .20

Cent. of the birth of Paulo de Frontin, engineer.

Woman Athlete Holding Torch — A439

1960, Oct. 18 ***Perf. 11½x11***

911 A439 2.50cr blue grn .20 .20

12th Spring Games.

Volleyball and Net — A440

Locomotive Wheels — A441

Perf. 11½x11

1960, Nov. 12 Wmk. 268

912 A440 11cr blue .20 .20

International Volleyball Championships.

1960, Oct. 15 ***Perf. 11½x11***

913 A441 2.50cr ultra .20 .20

10th Pan-American Railroad Congress.

Symbols of Flight A442

1960, Dec. 16 Photo. ***Perf. 11½***

914 A442 2.50cr brn & yel .20 .20

Intl. Fair of Industry and Commerce, Rio.

Emperor Haile Selassie — A443

1961, Jan. 31 ***Perf. 11½x11***

915 A443 2.50cr dk brown .20 .20

Visit of Emperor Haile Selassie of Ethiopia to Brazil, Dec. 1960.

Map of Brazil, Open Book and Sacred Heart Emblem A444

Perf. 11x11½

1961, Mar. 13 Wmk. 268

916 A444 2.50cr blue .20 .20

50th anniv. of the operation in Brazil of the Order of the Blessed Heart of Mary.

Map of Guanabara — A445

1961, Mar. 27 Wmk. 267

917 A445 7.50cr org brn .20 .20

Promulgation of the constitution of the state of Guanabara.

Arms of Agulhas Negras — A446

Brazil and Senegal Linked on Map — A447

Design: 3.30cr, Dress helmet and sword.

Perf. 11½x11

1961, Apr. 23 Wmk. 267

918 A446 2.50cr green .20 .20

919 A446 3.30cr rose car .20 .20

Sesquicentennial of the Agulhas Negras Military Academy.

1961, Apr. 28 Photo.

920 A447 27cr ultra .25 .20

Visit of Afonso Arinos, Brazilian foreign minister, to Senegal to attend its independence ceremonies.

View of Ouro Preto, 1711 A448

1961, June 6 ***Perf. 11x11½***

921 A448 1cr orange .20 .20

250th anniversary of Ouro Preto.

War Arsenal A449

1961, June 20 Wmk. 256

924 A449 5cr dk red brn .25 .20

War Arsenal, Rio de Janeiro, 150th anniv.

Coffee Bean and Branch — A450

Rabindranath Tagore — A451

Perf. 11½x11

1961, June 26 Wmk. 267

925 A450 20cr redsh brn .80 .25

8th Directorial Committee meeting of the Intl. Coffee Convention, Rio, June 26.

1961, July 28 Photo. Wmk. 267

926 A451 10cr rose car .20 .20

Rabindranath Tagore, Indian poet, birth cent.

Stamp of 1861 and Map of English Channel A452

Design: 20cr, 430r stamp of 1861 and map of Netherlands.

1961, Aug. 1 ***Perf. 11x11½***

927 A452 10cr rose .75 .20

928 A452 20cr salmon pink 2.00 .30

Centenary of 1861 stamp issue.

Portrait Type of 1954-60

Designs as Before

1961 Wmk. 268 ***Perf. 11x11½***

930 A336 1cr brown .80 .50

931 A336 2cr dk bl grn 1.25 .50

932 A336 5cr red lilac 3.75 .30

933 A336 10cr emerald 7.25 .30

Nos. 930-933 (4) 13.05 1.60

1cr, 5cr, 10cr have patterned background.

Sun, Clouds, Rain and Weather Symbols — A453

Dedo de Deus Peak — A454

1962, Mar. 23 ***Perf. 11½x11***

936 A453 10cr red brown .75 .30

World Meteorological Day, Mar. 23.

1962, Apr. 14 Photo. Wmk. 267

937 A454 8cr emerald .20 .25

50th anniversary of the climbing of Dedo de Deus (Finger of God) peak.

Dr. Gaspar Vianna and Leishmania Protozoa — A455

1962, Apr. 24 ***Perf. 11x11½***

938 A455 8cr blue .25 .20

Discovery by Gaspar Oliveiro Vianna (1885-1914) of a cure for leishmaniasis, 50th anniv.

Henrique Dias A456

1962, June 18 Wmk. 267

939 A456 10cr dk vio brn .30 .20

300th anniversary of the death of Henrique Dias, Negro military leader who fought against the Dutch and Spaniards.

Millimeter Gauge — A457

Sailboats, Snipe Class — A458

1962, June 26 ***Perf. 11½x11***

940 A457 100cr car rose .35 .20

Centenary of the introduction of the metric system in Brazil.

1962, July 21 Photo. Wmk. 267

941 A458 8cr Prus green .20 .20

Commemorating the 13th Brazilian championships for Snipe Class sailing.

Julio Mesquita A459

1962, Aug. 18 ***Perf. 11x11½***

942 A459 8cr dull brown .20 .20

Julio Mesquita, journalist and founder of a Sao Paulo newspaper, birth cent.

Empress Leopoldina — A460

1962, Sept. 7 ***Perf. 11½x11***

943 A460 8cr rose claret .20 .20

140th anniversary of independence.

Buildings, Brasilia — A461

Perf. 11x11½

1962, Oct. 24 Wmk. 267
944 A461 10cr orange .30 .20

51st Interparliamentary Conf., Brasilia.

Pouring Ladle — A462

1962, Oct. 26 ***Perf. 11½x11***
945 A462 8cr orange .20 .20

Inauguration of the Usiminas State Iron and Steel Foundry at Belo Horizonte, Minas Gerais.

UPAE Emblem A463

1962, Nov. 19 ***Perf. 11x11½***
946 A463 8cr bright magenta .20 .20

Founding of the Postal Union of the Americas and Spain, UPAE, 50th anniv.

Chimney and Cogwheel Forming "10" — A464

1962, Nov. 26 ***Perf. 11½x11***
947 A464 10cr lt blue grn .20 .20

Natl. Economic and Development Bank, 10th anniv.

Quintino Bocaiuva A465

Soccer Player and Globe A466

Perf. 11½x11

1962, Dec. 27 Photo. Wmk. 267
948 A465 8cr brown org .20 .20

Bocaiuva, journalist, 50th death anniv.

1963, Jan. 14
949 A466 10cr blue grn .40 .20

World Soccer Championship of 1962.

Carrier Pigeon — A467

1963, Jan. Unwmk. Litho. ***Perf. 14***
950 A467 8cr yel, dk bl, red & grn .20 .20

Souvenir Sheet

Imperf

951 A467 100cr yel, dk bl, red & grn 1.25 *3.00*

300 years of Brazilian postal service. Issue dates: 8cr, Jan. 25; 100cr, Jan. 31.

Severino Neiva — A468

Perf. 10½x11½

1963, Jan. 31 Photo. Wmk. 267
952 A468 8cr brt vio .20 .20

Radar Tracking Station and Rockets — A469

"Cross of Unity" — A470

Perf. 11½x11

1963, Mar. 15 Wmk. 268
953 A469 21cr lt ultra .20 .20

International Aeronautics and Space Exhibition, Sao Paulo.

1963 Wmk. 267 ***Perf. 11½x11***
954 A470 8cr red lilac .20 .20

Vatican II, the 21st Ecumenical Council of the Roman Catholic Church.

"ABC" in Geometric Form — A471

Basketball Player — A472

1963, Apr. 22 Photo. Wmk. 267
955 A471 8cr brt bl & lt bl .20 .20

Education Week, Apr. 22-27, 3-year alphabetization program.

1963, May 15
956 A472 8cr dp lilac rose .20 .20

4th International Basketball Championships, Rio de Janeiro, May 10-25, 1963.

Games Emblem A473

"OEA" and Map of the Americas A474

1963, May 22 ***Perf. 11½x11***
957 A473 10cr car rose .30 .20

4th Pan American Games, Sao Paulo.

1963, June 6
958 A474 10cr org & dp org .30 .20

15th anniversary of the charter of the Organization of American States.

José Bonifacio de Andrada — A475

1963, June 13
959 A475 8cr dk brown .20 .20

Bicentenary of the birth of José Bonifacio de Andrada e Silva, statesman.

Wheat A476

Perf. 11x11½

1963, June 19 Photo. Wmk. 267
960 A476 10cr blue .30 .20

FAO "Freedom from Hunger" campaign.

Centenary Emblem — A477

Joao Caetano — A478

1963, Aug. 19 ***Perf. 11½x11***
961 A477 8cr yel org & red .25 .20

Centenary of International Red Cross.

1963, Aug. 24 ***Perf. 11½x11***
962 A478 8cr slate .20 .20

Death centenary of Joao Caetano, actor.

Symbols of Agriculture, Industry and Atomic Energy — A479

Hammer Thrower — A480

1963, Aug. 28
963 A479 10cr car rose .25 .20

Atomic Development Law, 1st anniv.

1963, Sept. 13
964 A480 10cr gray .40 .20

Intl. College Students' Games, Porto Alegre.

Marshal Tito — A481

Compass Rose, Map of Brazil and View of Rio — A482

1963, Sept. 19
965 A481 80cr sepia .35 .30

Visit of Marshal Tito of Yugoslavia.

1963, Sept. 20
966 A482 8cr lt blue grn .20 .20

8th International Leprology Congress.

Oil Derrick and Storage Tank A483

1963, Oct. 3 ***Perf. 11x11½***
967 A483 8cr dk slate grn .20 .20

Petrobras, the natl. oil company, 10th anniv.

"Spring Games" A484

1963, Nov. 5 Photo. Wmk. 267
968 A484 8cr yel & org .20 .20

1963 Spring Games.

Dr. Borges de Medeiros (1863-1962), Governor of Rio Grande do Sul — A485

1963, Nov. 29 ***Perf. 11½x11***
969 A485 8cr red brown .20 .20

Sao Joao del Rei A486

1963, Dec. 8 ***Perf. 11x11½***
970 A486 8cr violet blue .20 .20

250th anniversary of Sao Joao del Rei.

Dr. Alvaro Alvim A487

1963, Dec. 19
971 A487 8cr dk gray .20 .20

Alvaro Alvim (1863-1928), X-ray specialist and martyr of science.

Viscount de Mauá — A488

Mandacaru Cactus and Emblem — A489

1963, Dec. 28 ***Perf. 11½x11***
972 A488 8cr rose car .20 .20

Sesquicentennial of the birth of Viscount de Mauá, founder of first Brazilian railroad.

1964, Jan. 23 Photo. Wmk. 267
973 A489 8cr dull green .20 .20

Bank of Northeast Brazil, 10th anniv.

Coelho Netto — A490

Lauro Müller — A491

1964, Feb. 21 ***Perf. 11½x11***
974 A490 8cr brt violet .20 .20

Birth centenary of Coelho Netto, writer.

1964, Mar. 8 Wmk. 267
975 A491 8cr dp orange .20 .20

Lauro Siverino Müller, politician and member of the Brazilian Academy of Letters, birth cent.

Child Holding Spoon A492

1964, Mar. 25 ***Perf. 11x11½***
976 A492 8cr yel brn & yel .20 .20

Issued for "School Meals Week."

Chalice Rock — A493

Allan Kardec — A494

1964, Apr. 9 Engr. ***Perf. 11½x11***
977 A493 80cr red orange .20 .20

Issued for tourist publicity.

1964, Apr. 18 Photo.
978 A494 30cr slate green .45 .20

Cent. of "O Evangelho" (Gospel) of the codification of Spiritism.

Heinrich Lübke — A495

Pope John XXIII — A496

Perf. 11½x11

1964, May 8 Photo. Wmk. 267
979 A495 100cr red brown .60 .20

Visit of President Heinrich Lübke of Germany.

1964, June 29 Wmk. 267
980 A496 20cr dk car rose .20 .20
a. Unwmkd. .20 .20

Issued in memory of Pope John XXIII.

Pres. Senghor of Senegal — A497

1964, Sept. 19 Wmk. 267
981 A497 20cr dk brown .25 .20

Visit of Leopold Sedar Senghor, President of Senegal.

Botafogo Bay and Sugarloaf Mountain — A498

Designs: 100cr, Church of Our Lady of the Rock, vert. 200cr, Copacabana beach.

Perf. 11x11½, 11½x11

1964-65 Photo.

983	A498	15cr org & bl	.30	.25
984	A498	100cr brt grn & red brn, *yel*	.20	.20
985	A498	200cr black & red	1.75	.30
a.		Souvenir sheet of 3 ('65)	4.75	4.00
		Nos. 983-985 (3)	2.25	.75

4th cent. of Rio de Janeiro.

No. 985a contains three imperf. stamps similar to Nos. 983-985, but printed in brown. Sold for 320cr. Issued Dec. 30, 1965.

A souvenir card containing one lithographed facsimile of No. 984, imperf., exists, but has no franking value. Size: 100x125mm. Sold by P.O. for 250cr.

Pres. Charles de Gaulle A499

Pres. John F. Kennedy A500

1964, Oct. 13 ***Perf. 11½x11***
986 A499 100cr orange brn .35 .20

Visit of Charles de Gaulle, President of France, Oct. 13-15.

1964, Oct. 24 Photo. Wmk. 267
987 A500 100cr slate .20 .20

"Prophet" by Lisboa — A501

1964, Nov. 18 ***Perf. 11½x11***
988 A501 10cr slate .20 .20

150th death anniv. of the sculptor Antonio Francisco Lisboa, "O Aleijadinho" (The Cripple).

Antonio Goncalves Dias — A502

Designs: 30cr, Euclides da Cunha. 50cr, Prof. Angelo Moreira da Costa Lima. 200cr, Tiradentes. 500cr, Dom Pedro I. 1000cr, Dom Pedro II.

1965-66 Wmk. 267 ***Perf. 11x11½***

989	A502	30cr brt bluish grn ('66)	2.00	.25
989A	A502	50cr dull brn ('66)	1.50	.20
990	A502	100cr blue	.60	.20
991	A502	200cr brown org	2.00	.20
992	A502	500cr red brown	6.00	.50
992A	A502	1000cr sl bl ('66)	10.00	.50
		Nos. 989-992A (6)	22.10	1.85

Statue of St. Sebastian, Guanataro Bay — A503

The Arches A504

Design: 35cr, Estacio de Sa (1520-67), founder of Rio de Janeiro.

1965 Photo. ***Perf. 11½***
Size: 24x37mm
993 A503 30cr bl & rose red .30 .20

Lithographed and Engraved
Perf. 11x11½
994 A504 30cr lt bl & blk .30 .20

Photo. ***Perf. 11½***
Size: 21x39mm

995	A503	35cr blk & org	.20	.25
a.		Souvenir sheet of 3	3.25	4.00
		Nos. 993-995 (3)	.80	.65

4th cent. of Rio de Janeiro.

No. 995a contains three imperf. stamps similar to Nos. 993-995, but printed in deep orange. Size: 130x79mm. Sold for 100cr.

Issued: #993, 3/5; #994, 11/30; #995, 7/28; #995a, 12/30.

Sword and Cross — A505

1965, Apr. 15 Wmk. 267 ***Perf. 11½***
996 A505 120cr gray .30 .20

1st anniv, of the democratic revolution.

Vital Brazil — A506

Shah of Iran — A507

1965, Apr. 28 Wmk. 267 ***Perf. 11½***
997 A506 120cr deep orange .30 .20

Centenary of birth of Vital Brazil, M.D.

A souvenir card containing one impression similar to No. 997, imperf., exists, printed in dull plum. Sold by P.O. for 250cr. Size: 114x180mm.

1965, May 5 Photo.
998 A507 120cr rose claret .25 .20

Commemorating the visit of Shah Mohammed Riza Pahlavi of Iran.

Marshal Mariano da Silva Rondon — A508

Lions' Emblem — A509

1965, May 7 Engr.
999 A508 30cr claret .25 .20

Marshal Mariano da Silva Rondon (1865-1958), explorer and expert on Indians.

1965, May 14 Photo.
1000 A509 35cr pale vio & blk .20 .20

12th convention of the Lions Clubs of Brazil, Rio de Janeiro, May 11-16.

ITU Emblem, Old and New Communication Equipment — A510

1965, May 21 ***Perf. 11½***
1001 A510 120cr yellow & grn .30 .20

Centenary of the ITU.

Epitácio Pessoa — A511

Statue of Admiral Barroso — A512

1965, May 23 **Photo.**
1002 A511 35cr blue gray .20 .20

Epitácio da Silva Pessoa (1865-1942), jurist, president of Brazil, 1919-22.

1965, June 11
1003 A512 30cr blue .25 .20

Cent. of the naval battle of Riachuelo.

A souvenir card containing one lithographed facsimile of No. 1003, imperf., exists. Size: 100x139½mm.

José de Alencar and Indian Princess — A513

1965, June 24 ***Perf. 11½x11***
1004 A513 30cr deep plum .25 .20

Centenary of the publication of "Iracema" by Joséde Alencar.

A souvenir card containing one lithographed facsimile of No. 1004, printed in rose red and imperf., exists. Size: 100x141½mm.

Winston Churchill A514

1965, June 25 ***Perf. 11x11½***
1005 A514 200cr slate .50 .25

Scout Jamboree Emblem — A515

1965, July 17 **Photo.**
1006 A515 30cr dull bl grn .30 .20

1st Pan-American Boy Scout Jamboree, Fundao Island, Rio de Janeiro, July 15-25.

ICY Emblem A516

1965, Aug. 25 **Wmk. 267** ***Perf. 11½***
1007 A516 120cr dl bl & blk .25 .20

International Cooperation Year, 1965.

Leoncio Correias — A517

Emblem — A518

1965, Sept. 1 ***Perf. 11½x11***
1008 A517 35cr slate grn .25 .20

Leoncio Correias, poet, birth cent.

1965, Sept. 4
1009 A518 30cr brt rose .20 .20

Eighth Biennial Fine Arts Exhibition, Sao Paulo, Nov.-Dec., 1965.

Pres. Saragat of Italy — A519

1965, Sept. 11 **Photo.** **Wmk. 267**
1010 A519 100cr slate grn, *pink* .25 .20

Visit of Pres. Giuseppe Saragat of Italy.

Grand Duke and Duchess of Luxembourg — A520

1965, Sept. 17 ***Perf. 11x11½***
1011 A520 100cr brn olive .25 .20

Visit of Grand Duke Jean and Grand Duchess Josephine Charlotte of Luxembourg.

Biplane — A521

1965, Oct. 8 **Photo.** ***Perf. 11½x11***
1012 A521 35cr ultra .20 .20

3rd Aviation Week Philatelic Exhibition, Rio.

A souvenir card carries one impression of this 35cr, imperf. Size: 102x140mm. Sold for 100cr.

Flags of OAS Members A522

1965, Nov. 17 ***Perf. 11x11½***
1013 A522 100cr brt bl & blk .25 .20

2nd meeting of OAS Foreign Ministers, Rio.

King Baudouin and Queen Fabiola of Belgium A523

1965, Nov. 18
1014 A523 100cr gray .25 .20

Visit of King and Queen of Belgium.

"Coffee Beans" — A524

Perf. 11½x11
1965, Dec. 21 **Photo.** **Wmk. 267**
1015 A524 30cr brown .30 .20

Brazilian coffee publicity.

Conveyor and Loading Crane A525

1966, Apr. 1 ***Perf. 11x11½***
1016 A525 110cr tan & dk sl grn .25 .20

Opening of the new terminal of the Rio Doce Iron Ore Company at Tubarao.

Pouring Ladle and Steel Beam — A526

Prof. de Rocha Dissecting Cadaver — A527

Perf. 11½x11
1966, Apr. 16 **Photo.** **Wmk. 267**
1017 A526 30cr blk, *dp org* .25 .20

25th anniv. of the National Steel Company (nationalization of the steel industry).

1966, Apr. 26
1018 A527 30cr brt bluish grn .40 .20

50th anniv. of the discovery and description of Rickettsia Prowazeki, the cause of typhus fever, by Prof. Henrique de Rocha Lima.

Battle of Tuiuti A528

Perf. 11x11½
1966, May 24 **Photo.** **Wmk. 267**
1019 A528 30cr gray grn .30 .20

Centenary of the Battle of Tuiuti.

Symbolic Water Cycle — A529

Pres. Shazar of Israel — A530

1966, July 1 ***Perf. 11½x11***
1020 A529 100cr lt brn & bl .25 .20

Hydrological Decade (UNESCO), 1965-74.

1966, July 18 **Photo.** **Wmk. 267**
1021 A530 100cr ultra .30 .20

Visit of Pres. Zalman Shazar of Israel.

Imperial Academy of Fine Arts A531

Perf. 11x11½
1966, Aug. 12 **Engr.** **Wmk. 267**
1022 A531 100cr red brown .60 .20

150th anniversary of French art mission.

Military Service Emblem A532

1966, Sept. 6 **Photo.** ***Perf. 11x11½***
1023 A532 30cr yel, ultra & grn .25 .20
a. With commemorative border 3.50 3.00

New Military Service Law.

No. 1023a issued in sheets of 4. It carries at left a 30cr, design A532, in deeper tones of yellow and ultramarine, Wmk. 264. Without gum. Sold for 100cr.

Ruben Dario — A533

Perf. 11½x11

1966, Sept. 20 Photo. Wmk. 267

1024 A533 100cr brt rose lilac .25 .20

Ruben Dario (pen name of Felix Ruben Garcia Sarmiento (1867-1916), Nicaraguan poet, newspaper correspondent and diplomat.

Ceramic Candlestick from Santarém — A534

1966, Oct. 6 ***Perf. 11x11½***

1025 A534 30cr dk brn, *salmon* .25 .20

Centenary of Goeldi Museum at Belem.

Arms of Santa Cruz — A535

Perf. 11½x11

1966, Oct. 15 Photo. Wmk. 267

1026 A535 30cr slate grn .25 .20

1st Natl. Tobacco Exposition, Santa Cruz.

UNESCO Emblem A536

1966, Oct. 24 Engr. ***Perf. 11½***

1027 A536 120cr black .75 .25
a. With commemorative border 6.00 6.00

20th anniv. of UNESCO. No. 1027a issued in sheets of 4. It carries at right a design similar to No. 1027. Unwatermarked granite paper, without gum. Sold for 150cr.

Captain Antonio Correia Pinto and Map of Lages — A537

Cross of Lusitania and Southern Cross — A538

Perf. 11½x11

1966, Nov. 22 Photo. Wmk. 267

1028 A537 30cr salmon pink .25 .20

Arrival of Capt. Antonio Correia Pinto, cent.

1966, Dec. 4 ***Perf. 11½***

1029 A538 100cr blue green .30 .20

LUBRAPEX 1966 philatelic exhibition at the National Museum of Fine Arts, Rio.

Madonna and Child — A539

A540

Perf. 11½x11

1966, Dec. Photo. Wmk. 267

1030 A539 30cr blue green .25 .20

Perf. 11½

1031 A540 35cr salmon & ultra .20 .20
a. 150cr salmon & ultra 2.50 3.00

Christmas 1966.

No. 1031a measures 46x103mm and is printed in sheets of 4. It is inscribed "Pax Hominibus" (but not "Brasil Correio") and carries the Madonna shown on No. 1031. Issued without gum.

Issued: 30cr, 12/8; 35cr, 12/22; 150cr, 12/28.

Arms of Laguna A541

1967, Jan. 4 Engr. ***Perf. 11x11½***

1032 A541 60cr sepia .20 .20

Centenary of the Post and Telegraph Agency of Laguna, Santa Catarina.

Railroad Bridge A542

1967, Feb. 16 Photo. Wmk. 267

1033 A542 50cr deep orange .45 .20

Centenary of the Santos-Jundiai railroad.

Black Madonna of Czestochowa, Polish Eagle and Cross — A543

1967, Mar. 12 ***Perf. 11x11½***

1034 A543 50cr yel, bl & rose red .35 .20

Adoption of Christianity in Poland, 1,000th anniv.

Research Rocket A544

Anita Garibaldi A545

1967, Mar. 23 ***Perf. 11½x11***

1035 A544 50cr blk & brt bl .60 .30

World Meteorological Day, March 23.

Perf. 11x11½

1967-69 Photo. Wmk. 267

Portraits: 1c, Mother Joana Angelica. 2c, Marilia de Dirceu. 3c, Dr. Rita Lobato. 6c, Ana Neri. 10c, Darcy Vargas.

1036 A545	1c	dp ultra	.20	.20
1037 A545	2c	red brn	.20	.20
1038 A545	3c	brt grn	.20	.20
1039 A545	5c	black	.35	.20
1040 A545	6c	brown	.35	.20
1041 A545	10c	dk slate grn	1.10	.30
	Nos. 1036-1041 (6)		2.40	1.30

Issued: 1c, 5/3; 2c, 8/14; 3c, 6/7; 5c, 4/14; 6c, 5/14/67; 10c, 6/18/69.

VARIG Airlines — A546

Madonna and Child, by Robert Feruzzi — A548

Lions Emblem and Globes A547

1967, May 8 ***Perf. 11½x11***

1046 A546 6c brt bl & blk .30 .25

40th anniversary of VARIG Airlines.

1967, May 9 Engr. ***Perf. 11x11½***

1047 A547 6c green .30 .25
a. Souvenir sheet 2.50 *3.00*

50th anniv. of Lions Intl. No. 1047a contains one imperf. stamp similar to No. 1047. Sold for 15c.

1967, May 14 Photo. ***Perf. 11½x11***

1048 A548 5c violet .25 .20
a. 15c Souvenir sheet 2.25 *2.25*

Mother's Day. No. 1048a contains one 15c imperf. stamp in design of No. 1048.

Prince Akihito and Princess Michiko A549

1967, May 25 ***Perf. 11x11½***

1049 A549 10c black & pink .30 .20

Visit to Brazil of Crown Prince Akihito and Princess Michiko of Japan.

Carrier Pigeon and Radar Screen A550

Brother Vicente do Salvador A551

Perf. 11½x11

1967, June 20 Photo. Wmk. 267

1050 A550 10c sl & brt pink .25 .20

Commemorating the opening of the Communications Ministry in Brasilia.

1967, June 28 Engr.

1051 A551 5c brown .25 .20

400th birth anniv. of Brother Vicente do Salvador (1564-1636), founder of Franciscan convent in Rio de Janeiro, and historian.

Boy, Girl and 4-S Emblem A552

1967, July 12 Photo. ***Perf. 11½***

1052 A552 5c green & blk .25 .20

National 4-S (4-H) Day.

Möbius Strip A553

1967, July 21 ***Perf. 11x11½***

1053 A553 5c brt bl & blk .25 .20

6th Brazilian Mathematical Congress.

Fish A554

1967, Aug. 1 ***Perf. 11½***

1054 A554 5c slate .30 .20

Bicentenary of city of Piracicaba.

Golden Rose and Papal Arms — A555

1967, Aug. 15
1055 A555 20c mag & yel 1.00 .40

Offering of a golden rose by Pope Paul VI to the Virgin Mary of Fatima (Our Lady of Peace), Patroness of Brazil.

General Sampaio A556

King Olaf of Norway A557

1967, Aug. 25 Engr. *Perf. 11½x11*
1056 A556 5c blue .25 .20

Honoring General Antonio de Sampaio, hero of the Battle of Tutui.

1967, Sept. 8 Photo.
1057 A557 10c brown org .25 .20

Visit of King Olaf of Norway.

Sun over Sugar Loaf, Botafogo Bay A558

Nilo Peçanha A559

Photogravure and Embossed
1967, Sept. 25 Wmk. 267 *Perf. 11½*
1058 A558 10c blk & dp org .25 .20

22nd meeting of the Intl. Monetary Fund, Intl. Bank for Reconstruction and Development, Intl. Financial Corporation and Intl. Development Assoc.

Perf. 11½x11
1967, Oct. 1 Photo. Wmk. 267
1059 A559 5c brown violet .25 .20

Peçanha (1867-1924), Pres. of Brazil 1909-10.

Virgin of the Apparition and Basilica of Aparecida — A560

Cockerel, Festival Emblem — A561

1967, Oct. 11 *Perf. 11½*
1060 A560 5c ultra & dl yel .30 .20
a. Souvenir sheet of 2 3.25 3.25

250th anniv. of the discovery of the statue of Our Lady of the Apparition, now in the National Basilica of the Apparition at Aparecida do Norte.
No. 1060a contains imperf. 5c and 10c stamps similar to No. 1060. Issued Dec. 27, 1967, for Christmas.

Engraved and Photogravure
1967, Oct. 16 *Perf. 11½x11*
1061 A561 20c black & multi .50 .40

Second International Folksong Festival.

Balloon, Plane and Rocket A562

Perf. 11x11½
1967, Oct. 18 Photo. Unwmk.
1062 A562 10c blue .50 .30
a. 15c souvenir sheet 4.50 4.50

Week of the Wing, Oct. 18-23. No. 1062a contains one imperf. 15c stamp similar to No. 1062 and was issued Oct. 23.

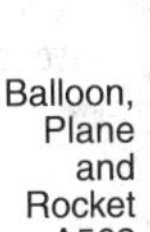
Pres. Arthur Bernardes — A563

Portraits of Brazilian Presidents: 20c, Campos Salles. 50c, Wenceslau Pereira Gomes Braz. 1cr, Washington Pereira de Souza Luiz. 2cr, Castello Branco.

Perf. 11x11½
1967-68 Photo. Wmk. 267
1063 A563 10c blue .25 .20
1064 A563 20c dk red brn .75 .20

Engr.
1065 A563 50c black ('68) 3.75 .30
1066 A563 1cr lil rose ('68) 6.00 .30
1067 A563 2cr emerald ('68) 1.10 .30
Nos. 1063-1067 (5) 11.85 1.30

Carnival of Rio — A564

Ships, Anchor and Sailor — A565

1967, Nov. 22 *Perf. 11½x11*
1070 A564 10c lem, ultra & pink .30 .20
a. 15c souvenir sheet 3.50 4.50

Issued for International Tourist Year, 1967. No. 1070a contains a 15c imperf. stamp in design of No. 1070. Issued Nov. 24.

1967, Dec. 6
1071 A565 10c ultra .30 .25

Issued for Navy Week.

Christmas Decorations A566

1967, Dec. 8 *Perf. 11½*
1072 A566 5c car, yel & bl .25 .20

Christmas 1967.

Olavo Bilac, Planes, Tank and Aircraft Carrier A567

Perf. 11x11½
1967, Dec. 16 Photo. Wmk. 267
1073 A567 5c brt blue & yel .30 .20

Issued for Reservists' Day and to honor Olavo Bilac, sponsor of compulsory military service.

Rodrigues de Carvalho — A568

1967, Dec. 18 Engr. *Perf. 11½x11*
1074 A568 10c green .25 .20

Cent. of the birth of Rodrigues de Carvalho, poet and lawyer.

Orlando Rangel A569

1968, Feb. 29 Photo. *Perf. 11x11½*
1075 A569 5c lt grnsh bl & blk .35 .25

Orlando de Fonseca Rangel, pioneer of pharmaceutical industry in Brazil, birth cent.

Virgin of Paranagua and Diver — A570

Map of Brazil Showing Manaus — A571

1968, Mar. 9 *Perf. 11½x11*
1076 A570 10c dk sl grn & brt yel grn .35 .25

250th anniversary of the first underwater explorations at Paranagua.

1968, Mar. 13 Photo. Wmk. 267
1077 A571 10c yel, grn & red .35 .25

Free port of Manaus on the Amazon River.

Human Rights Flame — A572

Paul Harris and Rotary Emblem — A573

1968, Mar. 21 *Perf. 11½x11*
1078 A572 10c blue & salmon .35 .25

International Human Rights Year.

1968, Apr. 19 Litho. Unwmk.
Without Gum
1079 A573 20c grn & org brn 1.25 .70

Paul Percy Harris (1868-1947), founder of Rotary International.

Pedro Alvares Cabral and his Fleet — A574

Design: 20c, First Mass celebrated in Brazil.

1968 Without Gum *Perf. 11½*
1080 A574 10c multicolored .55 .45
1081 A574 20c multicolored .80 .60

500th anniversary of the birth of Pedro Alvares Cabral, navigator, who took possession of Brazil for Portugal.
Issue dates: 10c, Apr. 22; 20c, July 11.

College Arms — A575

1968, Apr. 22 Photo. Wmk. 267
1082 A575 10c vio bl, red & gold .55 .35

Centenary of St. Luiz College, Sao Paulo.

Motherhood, by Henrique Bernardeli
A576

1968, May 12 Litho. Unwmk.
Without Gum

1083 A576 5c multicolored .35 .25

Issued for Mother's Day.

Harpy Eagle
A577

Photogravure and Engraved

1968, May 28 Wmk. 267

1084 A577 20c brt bl & blk 1.50 .50

Sesquicentennial of National Museum.

Brazilian and Japanese Women — A578

1968, June 28 Litho. Unwmk.
Without Gum

1085 A578 10c yellow & multi .60 .40

Commemorating the inauguration of Varig's direct Brazil-Japan airline.

Horse Race
A579

Perf. 11x11½

1968, July 16 Litho. Unwmk.
Without Gum

1086 A579 10c multicolored .35 .25

Centenary of the Jockey Club of Brazil.

Musician Wren
A580

Designs: 10c, Red-crested cardinal, vert. 50c, Royal flycatcher, vert.

Perf. 11½x11, 11x11½

1968-69 Engr. Wmk. in Sheet
Without Gum

1087 A580 10c multi ('69) .45 .30
1088 A580 20c multicolored .75 .30
1089 A580 50c multicolored 1.00 .55
Nos. 1087-1089 (3) 2.20 1.15

Some stamps in each sheet of Nos. 1087-1089 show parts of a two-line papermaker's watermark: "WESTERPOST / INDUSTRIA BRASILEIRA" with diamond-shaped emblem between last two words. Entire watermark appears in one sheet margin.

Issued: 10c, 8/20/69; 20c, 7/9/68; 50c, 8/2/68.

Mailbox and Envelope
A581

Photogravure and Engraved

1968, Aug. 1 Wmk. 267 *Perf. 11*

1091 A581 5c citron, blk & grn .20 .20

Stamp Day, 1968 and for 125th anniv. of the 1st Brazilian postage stamps.

Emilio Luiz Mallet — A582

Map of South America — A583

Perf. 11½x11

1968, Aug. 25 Engr. Wmk. 267

1092 A582 10c pale purple .20 .20

Honoring Marshal Emilio Luiz Mallet, Baron of Itapevi, patron of the marines.

1968, Sept. 5 Photo.

1093 A583 10c deep orange .20 .20

Visit of President Eduardo Frei of Chile.

Seal of Portuguese Literary School — A584

Photogravure and Engraved

1968, Sept. 10 *Perf. 11½*

1094 A584 5c pink & grn .20 .20

Centenary of Portuguese Literary School.

Map of Brazil and Telex Tape
A585

1968, Sept. Photo. *Perf. 11x11½*

1095 A585 20c citron & brt grn .50 .25

Linking of 25 Brazilian cities by teletype.

Soldiers' Heads on Medal — A586

Perf. 11½x11

1968, Sept. 24 Litho. Unwmk.
Without Gum

1096 A586 5c blue & gray .20 .25

8th American Armed Forces Conference.

Clef, Notes and Sugarloaf Mountain
A587

1968, Sept. 30 *Perf. 11½*
Without Gum

1097 A587 6c blk, yel & red .50 .30

Third International Folksong Festival.

Catalytic Cracking Plant
A588

1968, Oct. 4
Without Gum

1098 A588 6c blue & multi .50 .40

Petrobras, the natl. oil company, 15th anniv.

Child Protection — A589

Whimsical Girl — A590

5c, School boy walking toward the sun.

Perf. 11½x11, 11x11½

1968, Oct. 16 Litho. Unwmk.
Without Gum

1099 A590 5c gray & lt bl .30 .30
1100 A589 10c brt bl, dk red & blk .40 .25
1101 A590 20c multicolored .50 .25
Nos. 1099-1101 (3) 1.20 .80

22nd anniv. of UNICEF.

Children with Books
A591

1968, Oct. 23 *Perf. 11x11½*
Without Gum

1102 A591 5c multicolored .25 .25

Book Week.

UN Emblem and Flags — A592

1968, Oct. 24 *Perf. 11½x11*
Without Gum

1103 A592 20c black & multi .45 .25

20th anniv. of WHO.

Jean Baptiste Debret, Self-portrait — A593

Perf. 11x11½

1968, Oct. 30 Litho. Unwmk.
Without Gum

1104 A593 10c dk gray & pale yel .35 .25

Jean Baptiste Debret, (1768-1848), French painter who worked in Brazil (1816-31). Design includes his "Burden Bearer."

Queen Elizabeth II
A594

1968, Nov. 4 *Perf. 11½*
Without Gum

1105 A594 70c lt bl & multi 1.75 1.00

Visit of Queen Elizabeth II of Great Britain.

Francisco Braga — A595

Perf. 11½x11

1968, Nov. 19 Wmk. 267

1106 A595 5c dull red brn .40 .25

Cent. of the birth of Antonio Francisco Braga, composer of the Hymn of the Flag.

Brazilian Flag — A596

1968, Nov. 19 Unwmk. *Perf. 11½*
Without Gum
1107 A596 10c multicolored .40 .30

Issued for Flag Day.

Clasped Hands and Globe A597

Perf. 11x11½
1968, Nov. 25 Typo. Unwmk.
Without Gum
1108 A597 5c multicolored .25 .25

Issued for Voluntary Blood Donor's Day.

Old Locomotive — A598

1968, Nov. 28 Litho. *Perf. 11½*
Without Gum
1109 A598 5c multicolored 1.00 .50

Centenary of the Sao Paulo Railroad.

Bell — A599

Francisco Caldas, Jr. — A600

Design: 6c, Santa Claus and boy.

1968 Without Gum *Perf. 11½x11*
1110 A599 5c multicolored .30 .25
1111 A599 6c multicolored .30 .25

Christmas 1968.
Issue dates: 5c, Dec. 12; 6c, Dec. 20.

1968, Dec. 13
Without Gum
1112 A600 10c crimson & blk .20 .20

Cent. of the birth of Francisco Caldas, Jr., journalist and founder of Correio de Povo, newspaper.

Map of Brazil, War Memorial and Reservists' Emblem — A601

Perf. 11x11½
1968, Dec. 16 Photo. Wmk. 267
1113 A601 5c bl grn & org brn .30 .20

Issued for Reservists' Day.

Radar Antenna — A602

Viscount of Rio Branco — A603

Perf. 11½x11
1969, Feb. 28 Litho. Unwmk.
Without Gum
1114 A602 30c ultra, lt bl & blk .70 .55

Inauguration of EMBRATEL, satellite communications ground station bringing US television to Brazil via Telstar.

1969, Mar. 16
Without Gum
1115 A603 5c black & buff .25 .25

José Maria da Silva Paranhos, Viscount of Rio Branco (1819-1880), statesman.

St. Gabriel — A604

1969, Mar. 24
Without Gum
1116 A604 5c multicolored .40 .25

Honoring St. Gabriel as patron saint of telecommunications.

Shoemaker's Last and Globe — A605

Perf. 11x11½
1969, Mar. 29 Litho. Unwmk.
Without Gum
1117 A605 5c multicolored .25 .25

4th Intl. Shoe Fair, Novo Hamburgo.

Allan Kardec A606

1969, Mar. 31 Photo. Wmk. 267
1118 A606 5c brt grn & org brn .25 .25

Allan Kardec (pen name of Leon Hippolyto Denizard Rivail, 1803-1869), French physician and spiritist.

Men of 3 Races and Arms of Cuiabá A607

1969, Apr. 8 Litho. Unwmk.
Without Gum
1119 A607 5c black & multi .25 .25

250th anniversary of the founding of Cuiabá, capital of Matto Grosso.

State Mint — A608

1969, Apr. 11 *Perf. 11½*
Without Gum
1120 A608 5c olive bister & org .45 .35

Opening of the state money printing plant.

Brazilian Stamps and Emblem A609

Perf. 11x11½
1969, Apr. 30 Litho. Unwmk.
Without Gum
1121 A609 5c multicolored .25 .25

Sao Paulo Philatelic Society, 50th anniv.

St. Anne, Baroque Statue A610

1969, May 8 *Perf. 11½*
Without Gum
1122 A610 5c lemon & multi .50 .40

Issued for Mother's Day.

ILO Emblem A611

Perf. 11x11½
1969, May 13 Photo. Wmk. 267
1123 A611 5c dp rose red & gold .25 .20

50th anniv. of the ILO.

Diving Platform and Swimming Pool — A612

Mother and Child at Window — A613

Lithographed and Photogravure
Perf. 11½x11
1969, June 13 Unwmk.
Without Gum
1124 A612 20c bis brn, blk & bl grn .55 .40

40th anniversary of the Cearense Water Sports Club, Fortaleza.

1969 Litho. *Perf. 11½*

Designs: 20c, Modern sculpture by Felicia Leirner. 50c, "The Sun Sets in Brasilia," by Danilo di Prete. 1cr, Angelfish, painting by Aldemir Martins.

Size: 24x36mm
1125 A613 10c orange & multi .55 .25

Size: 33x34mm
1126 A613 20c red & multi .55 .50

Size: 33x53mm
1127 A613 50c yellow & multi 1.90 1.25

Without Gum
1128 A613 1cr gray & multi 2.50 1.25
Nos. 1125-1128 (4) 5.50 3.25

10th Biennial Art Exhibition, Sao Paulo, Sept.-Dec. 1969.

Angelfish A614

Fish — A615

Fish: 10c, Tetra. 15c, Piranha. No. 1130c, Megalamphodus megalopterus. 30c, Black tetra.

Wmk. 267
1969, July 21 Litho. *Perf. 11½*
1129 A614 20c multicolored .70 .40

Souvenir Sheet

1969, July 24 Unwmk. *Imperf.*
1130 A615 Sheet of 4 5.00 *5.00*
a. 10c yellow & multi .90 .90
b. 15c bright blue & multi .90 .90
c. 20c green & multi .90 .90
d. 30c orange & multi .90 .90

Issued to publicize the work of ACAPI, an organization devoted to the preservation and development of fish in Brazil.
#1130 contains 4 38½x21mm stamps.

L. O. Teles de Menezes A616

Mailman A617

Perf. 11½x11

1969, July 26 Photo. Wmk. 267

1131 A616 50c dp org & bl grn 1.25 1.00

Centenary of Spiritism press in Brazil.

1969, Aug. 1

1132 A617 30c blue 1.10 .90

Issued for Stamp Day.

Map of Brazil A618

Gen. Tasso Fragoso — A620

Railroad Bridge A619

Perf. 11½

1969, Aug. 25 Unwmk. Litho.

Without Gum

1133 A618 10c lt ultra, grn & yel .25 .20

Perf. 11x11½

1134 A619 20c multicolored .80 .40

Perf. 11½x11

Engr. Wmk. 267

With Gum

1135 A620 20c green .80 .50

Nos. 1133-1135 (3) 1.85 1.10

No. 1133 honors the Army as guardian of security; No. 1134, as promoter of development. No. 1135 the birth centenary of Gen. Tasso Fragoso.

Jupia Dam, Parana River A621

Perf. 11½

1969, Sept. 10 Litho. Unwmk.

Without Gum

1136 A621 20c lt blue & multi .35 .35

Inauguration of the Jupia Dam, part of the Urubupunga hydroelectric system serving Sao Paulo.

Gandhi and Spinning Wheel A622

1969, Oct. 2 *Perf. 11x11½*

1137 A622 20c yellow & blk .40 .30

Mohandas K. Gandhi (1869-1948), leader in India's fight for independence.

Santos Dumont, Eiffel Tower and Module Landing on Moon — A623

1969, Oct. 17 *Perf. 11½*

Without Gum

1138 A623 50c dk bl & multi 1.75 1.25

Man's first landing on the moon, July 20, 1969. See note after US No. C76.

Smelting Plant A624

1969, Oct. 26 Unwmk. *Perf. 11½*

Without Gum

1139 A624 20c multicolored .45 .40

Expansion of Brazil's steel industry.

Steel Furnace A625

1969, Oct. 31 Litho.

Without Gum

1140 A625 10c yellow & multi .45 .40

25th anniversary of Acesita Steel Works.

Water Vendor, by J. B. Debret — A626

Design: 30c, Street Scene, by Debret.

1969-70

Without Gum

1141 A626 20c multicolored 1.25 .50

1141A A626 30c multicolored 1.25 1.00

Jean Baptiste Debret (1768-1848), painter. Issued: 20c, 11/5/69; 30c, 5/19/70.

Exhibition Emblem — A627

1969, Nov. 15 *Perf. 11½x11*

Without Gum

1142 A627 10c multicolored .35 .20

ABUEXPO 69 Philatelic Exposition, Sao Paulo, Nov. 15-23.

Plane — A628

1969, Nov. 23

Without Gum

1143 A628 50c multicolored 2.75 1.40

Publicizing the year of the expansion of the national aviation industry.

Pelé Scoring A629

1969-70

Without Gum

1144 A629 10c multicolored .40 .30

Souvenir Sheet

Imperf

1145 A629 75c multi ('70) 4.50 3.50

Commemorating the 1,000th goal scored by Pele, Brazilian soccer player.

No. 1145 contains one imperf. stamp with simulated perforations.

Issued: 10c, 11/28/69; 75c, 1/23/70.

Madonna and Child from Villa Velha Monastery A630

Perf. 11½

1969, Dec. Unwmk. Litho.

Without Gum

1146 A630 10c gold & multi .35 .20

Souvenir Sheet

Imperf

1147 A630 75c gold & multi 12.00 *15.00*

Christmas 1969.

No. 1147 has simulated perforations.

Issue dates: 10c, Dec. 8; 75c, Dec. 18.

Destroyer and Submarine — A631

Perf. 11x11½

1969, Dec. 9 Engr. Wmk. 267

1148 A631 5c bluish gray .40 .25

Issued for Navy Day.

Dr. Herman Blumenau A632

1969, Dec. 26 *Perf. 11½*

1149 A632 20c gray grn .85 .40

Dr. Herman Blumenau (1819-1899), founder of Blumenau, Santa Catarina State.

Carnival Scene — A633

Sugarloaf Mountain, Mask, Confetti and Streamers A634

Designs: 5c, Jumping boy and 2 women, vert. 20c, Clowns. 50c, Drummer.

1969-70 Litho. Unwmk.

Without Gum

1150 A633 5c multicolored .40 .30

1151 A633 10c multicolored .40 .30

1152 A633 20c multicolored .50 .40

1153 A634 30c multicolored 3.00 3.00

1154 A634 50c multicolored 2.75 2.50

Nos. 1150-1154 (5) 7.05 6.50

Carico Carnival, Rio de Janeiro. Issued: #1150-1152, 12/29; others, 2/5/70.

Opening Bars of "Il Guarani" with Antonio Carlos Gomes Conducting A635

1970, Mar. 19 Litho. *Perf. 11½*
Without Gum

1155 A635 20c blk, yel, gray & brn .60 .40

Centenary of the opera Il Guarani, by Antonio Carlos Gomes.

Church of Penha A636

1970, Apr. 6 Unwmk. *Perf. 11½*
Without Gum

1156 A636 20c black & multi .30 .20

400th anniversary of the Church of Penha, State of Espirito Santo.

Assembly Building A637

10th anniv. of Brasilia: 50c, Reflecting Pool. 1cr, Presidential Palace.

1970, Apr. 21
Without Gum

1157	A637	20c multicolored	.90	.70
1158	A637	50c multicolored	2.25	1.75
1159	A637	1cr multicolored	2.25	1.75
		Nos. 1157-1159 (3)	5.40	4.20

Symbolic Water Design A638

1970, May 5 Unwmk. *Perf. 11½*
Without Gum

1161 A638 50c multicolored 2.50 3.00

Publicizing the Rondon Project for the development of the Amazon River basin.

Marshal Manoel Luiz Osorio and Osorio Arms — A639

1970, May 8
Without Gum

1162 A639 20c multicolored 1.50 1.00

Commemorating the inauguration of the Marshal Osorio Historical Park.

Madonna, from San Antonio Monastery, Rio de Janeiro A640

Detail from Brasilia Cathedral — A641

1970, May 10
Without Gum

1163 A640 20c multicolored .40 .40

Issued for Mother's Day.

1970, May 27 Engr. Wmk. 267

1164 A641 20c lt yellow grn .25 .25

8th National Eucharistic Congress, Brasilia.

Census Symbol — A642

Perf. 11½
1970, June 22 Unwmk. Litho.
Without Gum

1165 A642 20c green & yel .60 .60

Publicizing the 8th general census.

Soccer Cup, Maps of Brazil and Mexico A643

Swedish Flag and Player Holding Rimet Cup — A644

Designs: 2cr, Chilean flag and soccer. 3cr, Mexican flag and soccer.

1970
Without Gum

1166	A643	50c blk, lt bl & gold	.90	.90
1167	A644	1cr pink & multi	2.75	1.50
1168	A644	2cr gray & multi	5.25	1.50
1169	A644	3cr multicolored	4.50	1.00
		Nos. 1166-1169 (4)	13.40	4.90

9th World Soccer Championships for the Jules Rimet Cup, Mexico City, May 30-June 21. No. 1166 honors Brazil's victory.

Issued: #1166, 6/24; #1167-1169, 8/4.

Corcovado Christ and Map of South America A645

1970, July 18
Without Gum

1170 A645 50c brn, dk red & bl 2.50 2.50

6th World Cong. of Marist Brothers' Alumni.

Pandia Calogeras, Minister of War — A646

Perf. 11½x11
1970, Aug. 25 Photo. Unwmk.

1171 A646 20c blue green .50 .50

Brazilian Military Emblems and Map A647

Perf. 11x11½
1970, Sept. 8 Litho. Unwmk.
Without Gum

1172 A647 20c gray & multi .50 .50

25th anniv. of victory in World War II.

Annunciation (Brazilian Primitive Painting) A648

1970, Sept. 29 *Perf. 11½*
Without Gum

1173 A648 20c multicolored 1.25 1.00

Issued for St. Gabriel's (patron saint of communications) Day.

Boy in Library — A649

UN Emblem — A650

1970, Oct. 23
Without Gum

1174 A649 20c multicolored 1.25 1.00

Issued to publicize Book Week.

1970, Oct. 24
Without Gum

1175 A650 50c dk bl, lt bl & sil 1.25 1.25

25th anniversary of the United Nations.

Rio de Janeiro, 1820 — A651

Designs: 50c, LUBRAPEX 70 emblem. 1cr, Rio de Janeiro with Sugar Loaf Mountain, 1970. No. 1179, like 20c.

1970, Oct.
Without Gum

1176	A651	20c multicolored	1.75	1.00
1177	A651	50c yel brn & blk	3.50	2.00
1178	A651	1cr multicolored	3.50	3.75
		Nos. 1176-1178 (3)	8.75	6.75

Souvenir Sheet
Imperf

1179 A651 1cr multicolored 11.00 *17.00*

LUBRAPEX 70, 3rd Portuguese-Brazilian Phil. Exhib., Rio de Janeiro, Oct. 24-31.

Issued: #1176-1178, 10/27; #1179, 10/31.

Holy Family by Candido Portinari A652

1970, Dec. Litho. *Perf. 11½*
Without Gum

1180 A652 50c multicolored 1.50 1.50

Souvenir Sheet
Imperf

1181 A652 1cr multicolored 15.00 *24.00*

Christmas 1970. No. 1181 contains one stamp with simulated perforations.

Issue dates: 50c, Dec. 1; 1cr, Dec. 8.

Battleship — A653

CIH Emblem — A654

1970, Dec. 11 Litho. *Perf. 11½*
Without Gum

1182 A653 20c multicolored 1.25 .75

Navy Day.

1971, Mar. 28 Litho. *Perf. 11½*
Without Gum

1183 A654 50c black & red 1.50 1.75

3rd Inter-American Housing Cong., 3/27-4/3.

Links Around Globe — A655

1971, Mar. 31 Litho. *Perf. 12½x11*
Without Gum

1184 A655 20c grn, yel, blk & red .65 .50

Intl. year against racial discrimination.

Morpho Melacheilus — A656

Design: 1cr, Papilio thoas brasiliensis.

Perf. 11x11½
1971, Apr. 28 Litho. Unwmk.
Without Gum

1185	A656	20c multicolored	1.25	.60
1186	A656	1cr multicolored	5.50	3.25

Madonna and Child — A657

1971, May 9 Litho. *Perf. 11½*
Without Gum

1187 A657 20c multicolored .85 .40

Mother's Day, 1971.

Basketball A658

1971, May 19
Without Gum

1188 A658 70c multicolored 1.50 1.00

6th World Women's Basketball Championship.

Map of Trans-Amazon Highway — A659

Perf. 11½
1971, July 1 Unwmk. Litho.
Without Gum

1189		40c multicolored	5.50	2.75
1190		1cr multicolored	5.50	5.50
a.		'A659' Pair, #1189-1190	11.00	11.00

Trans-Amazon Highway. No. 1190a printed in sheets of 28 (4x7). Horizontal rows contain 2 No. 1190a with a label between. Each label carries different inscription.

Man's Head, by Victor Mairelles de Lima A661

Stamp Day: 1cr, Arab Violinist, by Pedro Américo.

1971, Aug. 1
Without Gum

1191	A661	40c pink & multi	1.25	.80
1192	A661	1cr gray & multi	3.25	1.65

Duke of Caxias and Map of Brazil A662

1971, Aug. 23 Photo.

1193 A662 20c yel grn & red brn .50 .60

Army Week.

Anita Garibaldi — A663

1971, Aug. 30 Litho.
Without Gum

1194 A663 20c multicolored .40 .40

Anita Garibaldi (1821-1849), heroine in liberation of Brazil.

Xavante Jet and Santos Dumont's Plane, 1910 — A664

1971, Sept. 6
Without Gum

1195 A664 40c yellow & multi 1.40 .75

First flight of Xavante jet plane.

Flags and Map of Central American Nations — A665

"71" in French Flag Colors — A666

1971, Sept. 15
Without Gum

1196 A665 40c ocher & multi 1.25 .60

Sesquicentennial of the independence of Central American nations.

1971, Sept. 16
Without Gum

1197 A666 1.30cr ultra & multi 1.25 1.10

French Exhibition.

Black Mother, by Lucilio de Albuquerque A667

Archangel Gabriel A668

1971, Sept. 28
Without Gum

1198 A667 40c multicolored .60 .50

Centenary of law guaranteeing personal freedom starting at birth.

1971, Sept. 29 *Perf. 11½x11*
Without Gum

1199 A668 40c multicolored .75 .65

St. Gabriel's Day.

Bridge over River A669

Children's Drawings: 35c, People crossing bridge. 60c, Woman with hat.

1971, Oct. 25 *Perf. 11½*
Without Gum

1200	A669	35c pink, bl & blk	.55	.45
1201	A669	45c black & multi	1.40	.45
1202	A669	60c olive & multi	.55	.45
		Nos. 1200-1202 (3)	2.50	1.35

Children's Day.

Werkhäuserii Superba — A670

1971, Nov. 16
Without Gum

1203 A670 40c blue & multi 2.00 1.00

In memory of Carlos Werkhauser, botanist.

Greek Key Pattern "25" — A671

Design: 40c, like 20c but inscribed "sesc / servicio social / do comercio."

1971, Dec. 3
Without Gum

1204	A671	20c black & blue	1.25	1.00
1205	A671	40c black & org	1.25	1.00
a.		Pair, #1204-1205	2.50	2.50

25th anniversary of SENAC (national apprenticeship system) and SESC (commercial social service).

Gunboat A672

1971, Dec. 8 *Perf. 11*
Without Gum

1206 A672 20c blue & multi .85 .50

Navy Day.

Cross and Circles — A673

Washing of Bonfim Church, Salvador, Bahia — A674

1971, Dec. 11

1207	A673	20c car & blue	.40	.40
1208	A673	75c silver & gray	.80	*3.00*
1209	A673	1.30cr blk, yel, grn & bl	4.75	2.50
		Nos. 1207-1209 (3)	5.95	*5.90*

Christmas 1971.

1972, Feb. 18 Litho. *Perf. 11½x11*

40c, Grape Festival, Rio Grande do Sul. 75c, Festival of the Virgin of Nazareth, Belém. 1.30cr, Winter Arts Festival, Ouro Preto.

Without Gum

1210	A674	20c silver & multi	1.50	.75
1211	A674	40c silver & multi	2.75	.75
1212	A674	75c silver & multi	2.75	3.00
1213	A674	1.30cr silver & multi	6.00	3.00
		Nos. 1210-1213 (4)	13.00	7.50

Pres. Lanusse and Flag of Argentina A675

1972, Mar. 13 *Perf. 11x11½*
Without Gum

1214 A675 40c blue & multi 2.00 2.50

Visit of Lt. Gen. Alejandro Agustin Lanusse, president of Argentina.

Presidents Castello Branco, Costa e Silva and Garrastazu Medici — A676

1972, Mar. 29

Without Gum

1215 A676 20c emerald & multi 1.25 .60

Anniversary of 1964 revolution.

Post Office Emblem — A677

Perf. 11½x11

1972, Apr. 10 Photo. Unwmk.

1216 A677 20c red brown 2.00 .20

No. 1216 is luminescent.

Pres. Thomas and Portuguese Flag — A678

1972, Apr. 22 Litho. *Perf. 11*

Without Gum

1217 A678 75c ol brn & multi 1.75 1.75

Visit of Pres. Americo Thomas of Portugal to Brazil, Apr. 22-27.

Soil Research (CPRM) A679

1972, May 3 *Perf. 11½*

Without Gum

1218 A679 20c shown 1.50 .50
1219 A679 40c Offshore oil rig 3.50 .85
1220 A679 75c Hydroelectric dam 1.50 1.75
1221 A679 1.30cr Iron ore production 3.50 1.40
Nos. 1218-1221 (4) 10.00 4.50

Industrial development. Stamps are inscribed with names of industrial firms.
See Nos. 1228-1229.

Souvenir Sheet

Poster for Modern Art Week 1922 — A680

1972, May 5

1222 A680 1cr black & car 26.00 26.00

50th anniversary of Modern Art Week.

Mailman, Map of Brazil and Letters A681

Designs: 45c, "Telecommunications", vert. 60c, Tropospheric scatter system. 70c, Road map of Brazil and worker.

1972, May 26

Without Gum

1223 A681 35c blue & multi 1.25 .40
1224 A681 45c silver & multi 1.50 1.50
1225 A681 60c black & multi 1.50 1.25
1226 A681 70c multicolored 1.75 1.25
Nos. 1223-1226 (4) 6.00 4.40

Unification of communications in Brazil.

Development Type and

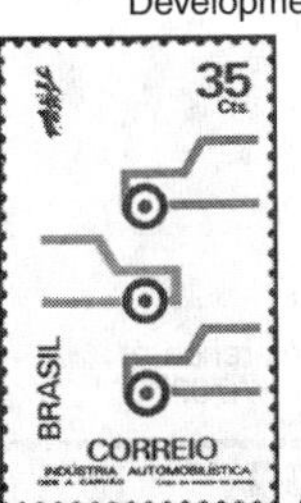

Automobiles — A682

Perf. 11x11½, 11½x11

1972, June 21 Photo.

1227 A682 35c shown 1.00 .50

Litho.

1228 A679 45c Ships 1.00 .60
1229 A679 70c Ingots 1.00 .40
Nos. 1227-1229 (3) 3.00 1.50

Industrial development. The 35c is luminescent.

Soccer — A683

75c, Folk music. 1.30cr, Plastic arts.

Perf. 11½x11

1972, July 7 Photo. Unwmk.

1230 A683 20c black & yel 1.00 .50
1231 A683 75c black & ver 2.00 3.50
1232 A683 1.30cr black & ultra 4.00 3.50
Nos. 1230-1232 (3) 7.00 7.50

150th anniv. of independence. #1230 publicizes the 1972 sports tournament, a part of independence celebrations. Luminescent.

Souvenir Sheet

Shout of Independence, by Pedro Americo de Figueiredo e Melo — A684

1972, July 19 Litho. *Perf. 11½*

Without Gum

1233 A684 1cr multicolored 4.00 *9.00*

4th Interamerican Philatelic Exhibition, EXFILBRA, Rio de Janeiro, Aug 26-Sept. 2.

Figurehead A685

Brazilian folklore: 60c, Gauchos dancing fandango. 75c, Acrobats (capoeira). 1.15cr, Karajá (ceramic) doll. 1.30cr, Mock bullfight (bumba meu boi).

1972, Aug. 6

Without Gum

1234 A685 45c multicolored .85 .35
1235 A685 60c org & multi 1.65 1.50
1236 A685 75c gray & multi .30 .30
1237 A685 1.15cr multicolored .55 .55
1238 A685 1.30cr yellow & multi 5.00 2.00
Nos. 1234-1238 (5) 8.35 4.70

Map of Brazil, by Diego Homem, 1568 A686

Designs: 1cr, Map of Americas, by Nicholas Visscher, 1652. 2cr, Map of Americas, by Lopo Homem, 1519.

1972, Aug. 26 Litho. *Perf. 11½*

Without Gum

1239 A686 70c multicolored .50 .50
1240 A686 1cr multicolored 9.00 1.00
1241 A686 2cr multicolored 4.50 1.50
Nos. 1239-1241 (3) 14.00 3.00

4th Inter-American Philatelic Exhibition, EXFILBRA, Rio de Janeiro, Aug. 26-Sept. 2.

Dom Pedro Proclaimed Emperor, by Jean Baptiste Debret — A687

Designs: 30c, Founding of Brazil (people with imperial flag), vert. 1cr, Coronation of Emperor Dom Pedro, vert. 2cr, Dom Pedro commemorative medal. 3.50cr, Independence Monument, Ipiranga.

1972, Sept. 4 Litho. *Perf. 11½x11*

1242 A687 30c yellow & grn 1.25 1.25
1243 A687 70c pink & rose lil 1.25 .80
1244 A687 1cr buff & red brn 8.00 1.25
1245 A687 2cr pale yel & blk 4.00 1.25
1246 A687 3.50cr gray & blk 7.25 4.00
Nos. 1242-1246 (5) 21.75 8.55

Sesquicentennial of independence.

Souvenir Sheet

"Automobile Race" — A688

1972, Nov. 14 *Perf. 11½*

1247 A688 2cr multicolored 10.00 15.00

Emerson Fittipaldi, Brazilian world racing champion.

Numeral and Post Office Emblem — A689

Möbius Strip A689a

Perf. 11½x11

1972-75 Unwmk. Photo.

1248 A689 5c orange .35 .20
a. Wmk. 267 .20 .20
1249 A689 10c brown ('73) .20 .20
a. Wmk. 267 4.00 .20
1250 A689 15c brt blue ('75) .20 .20
1251 A689 20c ultra .35 .20
1252 A689 25c sepia ('75) .25 .20
1253 A689 30c dp carmine .40 .20
1254 A689 40c dk grn ('73) .20 .20
1255 A689 50c olive .30 .20
1256 A689 70c red lilac ('75) .30 .20

Engr. *Perf. 11½*

1257 A689a 1cr lilac ('74) .45 .20
1258 A689a 2cr grnsh bl ('74) .65 .20
1259 A689a 4cr org & vio ('75) 1.40 .20
1260 A689a 5cr brn, car & buff ('74) 2.00 .20
1261 A689a 10cr grn, blk & buff ('74) 4.50 .30
Nos. 1248-1261 (14) 11.55 2.90

The 5cr and 10cr have beige lithographed multiple Post Office emblem underprint.
Nos. 1248-1261 are luminescent. Nos. 1248a and 1249a are not.

Hand Writing "Mobral" A690

20c, Multiracial group and population growth curve. 1cr, People and hands holding house. 2cr, People, industrial scene and upward arrow.

1972, Nov. 28 Litho. *Perf. 11½*
Without Gum

1262 A690 10c black & multi .20 *.50*
1263 A690 20c black & multi 1.00 .75
1264 A690 1cr black & multi 8.75 .30
1265 A690 2cr black & multi 2.00 .75
Nos. 1262-1265 (4) 11.95 2.30

Publicity for: "Mobral" literacy campaign (10c); Centenary of census (20c); Housing and retirement fund (1cr); Growth of gross national product (2cr).

Congress Building, Brasilia, by Oscar Niemeyer, and "Os Guerreiros," by Bruno Giorgi — A691

1972, Dec. 4
Without Gum

1266 A691 1cr blue, blk & org 10.00 6.00

Meeting of Natl. Cong., Brasilia, Dec. 4-8.

Holy Family (Clay Figurines) A692

Retirement Plan A693

1972, Dec. 13 Photo. *Perf. 11½x11*

1267 A692 20c ocher & blk .85 .50

Christmas 1972. Luminescent.

Perf. 11½x11, 11x11½
1972, Dec. 20 Litho.

#1269, School children and traffic lights, horiz. 70c, Dr. Oswaldo Cruz with Red Cross, caricature. 2cr, Produce, fish and cattle, horiz.

Without Gum

1268 A693 10c blk, bl & dl org .50 .50
1269 A693 10c orange & multi 1.00 1.00
1270 A693 70c blk, red & brn 9.00 3.75
1271 A693 2cr green & multi 15.00 6.50
Nos. 1268-1271 (4) 25.50 11.75

Publicity for: Agricultural workers' assistance program (No. 1268); highway and transportation development (No. 1269); centenary of the birth of Dr. Oswaldo Cruz (1872-1917), Director of Public Health Institute (70c); agricultural and cattle export (2cr). Nos. 1268-1271 are luminescent.

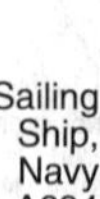

Sailing Ship, Navy A694

Designs: 10c, Monument, Brazilian Expeditionary Force. No. 1274, Plumed helmet, Army. No. 1275, Rocket, Air Force.

Lithographed and Engraved
1972, Dec. 28 *Perf. 11x11½*
Without Gum

1272 A694 10c brn, dk brn & blk 1.50 1.10
1273 A694 30c lt ultra, grn & blk 1.50 1.10
1274 A694 30c yel grn, bl grn & blk 1.50 1.10
1275 A694 30c lilac, mar & blk 1.50 1.10
a. Block of 4, #1272-1275 6.00 5.00

Armed Forces Day.

Rotary Emblem and Cogwheels A695

Perf. 11½
1973, Mar. 21 Litho. Unwmk.

1276 A695 1cr ultra, grnsh bl & yel 1.75 1.50

Rotary International serving Brazil 50 years.

Swimming — A696

#1278, Gymnastics. #1279, Volleyball, vert.

1973 Photo. *Perf. 11x11½, 11½x11*

1277 A696 40c brt bl & red brn .35 .35
1278 A696 40c green & org brn 2.75 .70
1279 A696 40c violet & org brn .70 .70
Nos. 1277-1279 (3) 3.80 1.75

Issued: #1277, 4/19; #1278, 5/22; #1279, 10/15.

Flag of Paraguay A697

Perf. 11½
1973, Apr. 27 Litho. Unwmk.

1280 A697 70c multicolored 1.75 1.25

Visit of Pres. Alfredo Stroessner of Paraguay, Apr. 25-27.

"Communications" — A698

1cr, Neptune, map of South America and Africa.

1973, May 5 *Perf. 11x11½*

1281 A698 70c multicolored .80 .70
1282 A698 1cr multicolored 4.25 3.00

Inauguration of the Ministry of Communications Building, Brasilia (70c); and of the first underwater telephone cable between South America and Europe, Bracan 1 (1cr).

Congress Emblem — A699

1973, May 19 *Perf. 11½x11*

1283 A699 1cr orange & pur 4.00 3.00

24th Congress of the International Chamber of Commerce, Rio de Janeiro, May 19-26.

Swallowtailed Manakin — A700

Birds: No. 1285, Orange-backed oriole. No. 1286, Brazilian ruby (hummingbird).

1973 Litho. *Perf. 11x11½*

1284 A700 20c multicolored .50 .20
1285 A700 20c multicolored .50 .20
1286 A700 20c multicolored .50 .20
Nos. 1284-1286 (3) 1.50 .60

Issued: #1284, 5/26; #1285, 6/6; #1286, 6/19.

Tourists A701

1973, June 28 Litho. *Perf. 11x11½*

1287 A701 70c multicolored .90 .85

National Tourism Year.

Conference at Itu — A702

Satellite and Multi-spectral Image A703

1973 *Perf. 11½x11*

1288 A702 20c shown .50 .35
1289 A702 20c Decorated wagon .50 .35
1290 A702 20c Indian .50 .35
1291 A702 20c Graciosa Road .50 .35
Nos. 1288-1291 (4) 2.00 1.40

Centenary of the Itu Convention (1288); sesquicentennial of the July 2 episode (1289); 400th anniversary of the founding of Niteroi (1290); centenary of Graciosa Road (1291). Issue dates: #1291, July 29; others July 2.

1973, July 11 *Perf. 11½*

70c, Official opening of Engineering School, 1913. 1cr, Möbius strips and "IMPA."

1292 A703 20c black & multi .25 .40
1293 A703 70c dk blue & multi 2.25 1.00
1294 A703 1cr lilac & multi 3.00 1.00
Nos. 1292-1294 (3) 5.50 2.40

Institute for Space Research (20c); School of Engineering, Itajubá, 60th anniversary (70c); Institute for Pure and Applied Mathematics (1cr).

Santos-Dumont and 14-Bis Plane — A704

Santos-Dumont and: 70c, No. 6 Balloon and Eiffel Tower. 2cr Demoiselle plane.

Lithographed and Engraved
1973, July 20 *Perf. 11x11½*

1295 A704 20c lt grn, brt grn & brn .75 .25
1296 A704 70c yel, rose red & brn 1.75 1.25
1297 A704 2cr bl, vio bl & brn 1.75 1.25
Nos. 1295-1297 (3) 4.25 2.75

Centenary of the birth of Alberto Santos-Dumont (1873-1932), aviation pioneer.

Mercator Map A705

#1299, Same, red border on top and at left.

Photogravure and Engraved
1973, Aug. 1 Wmk. 267

1298 A705 40c red & black 2.50 1.50
1299 A705 40c red & black 2.10 2.10
a. Block of 4 21.00 15.00

Stamp Day. Nos. 1298-1299 are printed se-tenant horizontally and tête bêche vertically in sheets of 55. Blocks of 4 have red border all around.

Gonçalves Dias (1823-1864), Poet — A706

Perf. 11½x11
1973, Aug. 10 Wmk. 267

1300 A706 40c violet & blk .70 .40

Souvenir Sheet

Copernicus and Sun — A707

Perf. 11x11½
1973, Aug. 15 Litho. Unwmk.

1301 A707 1cr multicolored 4.00 5.00

500th anniversary of the birth of Nicolaus Copernicus (1473-1543), Polish astronomer.

Folklore Festival Banner — A708

1973, Aug. 22 *Perf. 11½*

1302 A708 40c ultra & multi .75 .50

Folklore Day, Aug. 22.

Masonic Emblem A709

1973, Aug. 24 Photo. *Perf. 11x11½*

1303 A709 1cr Prus blue 3.00 2.00

Free Masons of Brazil, 1822-1973.

Nature Protection — A710

#1305, Fire protection. #1306, Aviation safety. #1307, Safeguarding cultural heritage.

1973, Sept. 20 Litho. *Perf. 11x11½*

1304 A710 40c brt grn & multi .75 .40
1305 A710 40c dk blue & multi .75 .40
1306 A710 40c lt blue & multi .75 .40
1307 A710 40c pink & multi .75 .40
Nos. 1304-1307 (4) 3.00 1.60

Souvenir Sheet

St. Gabriel and Proclamation of Pope Paul VI — A711

Lithographed and Engraved

1973, Sept. 29 Unwmk. *Perf. 11½*

1308 A711 1cr bister & blk 7.50 *10.00*

1st National Exhibition of Religious Philately, Rio de Janeiro, Sept. 29-Oct. 6.

St. Teresa — A712

Photogravure and Engraved

Perf. 11½x11

1973, Sept. 30 **Wmk. 267**

1309 A712 2cr dk org & brn 3.50 2.50

St. Teresa of Lisieux, the Little Flower (1873-1897), Carmelite nun.

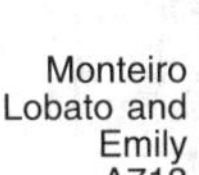

Monteiro Lobato and Emily A713

Perf. 11½

1973, Oct. 12 Litho. Unwmk.

1310 A713 40c shown .80 .50
1311 A713 40c Aunt Nastacia .80 .50
1312 A713 40c Snubnose, Peter and Rhino .80 .50
1313 A713 40c Viscount de Sabugosa .80 .50
1314 A713 40c Dona Benta .80 .50
a. Block of 5 + label 4.00 4.00

Monteiro Lobato, author of children's books.

Soapstone Sculpture of Isaiah (detail) A714

Baroque Art in Brazil: No. 1316, Arabesque, gilded wood carving, horiz. 70c, Father José Mauricio Nuñes Garcia and music score. 1cr, Church door, Salvador, Bahia. 2cr, Angels, church ceiling painting by Manoel da Costa Athayde, horiz.

1973, Nov. 5

1315 A714 40c multicolored .30 .30
1316 A714 40c multicolored .30 .30
1317 A714 70c multicolored 1.50 1.40
1318 A714 1cr multicolored 9.00 3.00
1319 A714 2cr multicolored 4.00 3.00
Nos. 1315-1319 (5) 15.10 8.00

Old and New Telephones — A715

1973, Nov. 28 *Perf. 11x11½*

1320 A715 40c multicolored .35 .30

50th anniv. of Brazilian Telephone Co.

Symbolic Angel A716

1973, Nov. 30 *Perf. 11½*

1321 A716 40c ver & multi .35 .30

Christmas 1973.

River Boats A717

1973, Nov. 30 Litho. *Perf. 11x11½*

1322 A717 40c "Gaiola" .35 .35
1323 A717 70c "Regatao" 1.05 1.05
1324 A717 1cr "Jangada" 4.50 3.00
1325 A717 2cr "Saveiro" 4.25 3.00
Nos. 1322-1325 (4) 10.15 7.40

Nos. 1322-1325 are luminescent.

Scales of Justice A718

1973, Dec. 5 *Perf. 11½*

1326 A718 40c magenta & vio .50 .30

To honor the High Federal Court, created in 1891. Luminescent.

José Placido de Castro — A719

Scarlet Ibis and Victoria Regia — A720

Lithographed and Engraved

Perf. 11½x11

1973, Dec. 12 **Wmk. 267**

1327 A719 40c lilac rose & blk .60 .35

Centenary of the birth of Jose Placido de Castro, liberator of the State of Acre.

Perf. 11½x11

1973, Dec. 28 Litho. Unwmk.

Designs: 70c, Jaguar and spathodea campanulata. 1cr, Scarlet macaw and carnauba palm. 2cr, Rhea and coral tree.

1328 A720 40c brown & multi .80 .50
1329 A720 70c brown & multi 2.25 1.50
1330 A720 1cr bister & multi 3.50 .40
1331 A720 2cr bister & multi 6.25 3.50
Nos. 1328-1331 (4) 12.80 5.90

Nos. 1328-1331 are luminescent.

Saci Perere, Mocking Goblin — A721

Characters from Brazilian Legends: 80c, Zumbi, last chief of rebellious slaves. 1cr, Chico Rei, African king. 1.30cr, Little Black Boy of the Pasture. 2.50cr, Iara, Queen of the Waters.

Perf. 11½x11

1974, Feb. 28 Litho. Unwmk.

Size: 21x39mm

1332 A721 40c multicolored .35 .25
1333 A721 80c multicolored .70 .60
1334 A721 1cr multicolored 1.65 .45

Perf. 11½

Size: 32½x33mm

1335 A721 1.30cr multicolored 2.50 .85
1336 A721 2.50cr multicolored 10.50 2.50
Nos. 1332-1336 (5) 15.70 4.65

Nos. 1332-1336 are luminescent.

Pres. Costa e Silva Bridge A722

1974, Mar. 11

1337 A722 40c multicolored .60 .30

Inauguration of the Pres. Costa e Silva Bridge, Rio Niteroi, connecting Rio de Janeiro and Guanabara State.

"The Press" A723

1974, Mar. 25 *Perf. 11½*

1338 A723 40c shown .50 .30
1339 A723 40c "Radio" .25 .25
1340 A723 40c "Television" .40 .30
Nos. 1338-1340 (3) 1.15 .85

Communications Commemorations: No. 1338, bicentenary of first Brazilian newspaper, published in London by Hipolito da Costa; No. 1339, founding of the Radio Sociedade do Rio de Janeiro by Roquette Pinto; No. 1340, installation of first Brazilian television station by Assis Chateaubriand. Luminescent.

"Reconstruction" — A724

1974, Mar. 31

1341 A724 40c multicolored .70 .45

10 years of progress. Luminescent.

Corcovado Christ, Marconi, Colors of Brazil and Italy — A725

1974, Apr. 25 Litho. *Perf. 11½*

1342 A725 2.50cr multi 6.00 3.00

Guglielmo Marconi (1874-1937), Italian physicist and inventor. Luminescent.

Stamp Printing Press, Stamp Designing A726

1974, May 6

1343 A726 80c multicolored 1.00 .50

Brazilian mint.

World Map, Indian, Caucasian and Black Men — A727

World Map and: #1345, Brazilians. #1346, Cabin & German horseback rider. #1347, Italian farm wagon. #1348, Japanese woman & torii.

1974, May 3 **Unwmk.**

1344 A727	40c multicolored	.30	.30
1345 A727	40c multicolored	.20	.20
1346 A727	2.50cr multicolored	3.25	1.50
1347 A727	2.50cr multicolored	4.75	1.50
1348 A727	2.50cr multicolored	1.25	.85
Nos. 1344-1348 (5)		9.75	4.35

Ethnic and migration influences in Brazil.

Sandstone Cliffs, Sete Cidades National Park — A728

Tourist publicity: 80c, Ruins of Cathedral of Sao Miguel das Missões.

Lithographed and Engraved

1974, June 8 ***Perf. 11x11½***

1349 A728 40c multicolored .75 .50
1350 A728 80c multicolored .75 .50

Souvenir Sheet

Soccer — A729

1974, June 20 Litho. ***Perf. 11½***

1351 A729 2.50cr multi 3.50 *6.00*

World Cup Soccer Championship, Munich, June 13-July 7.

Church and College, Caraça A730

1974, July 6 Litho. ***Perf. 11x11½***

1352 A730 40c multicolored .45 .30

College (Seminary) of Caraça, bicent.

Wave on Television Screen A731

1974, July 15 ***Perf. 11½***

1353 A731 40c black & blue .30 .40

TELEBRAS, Third Brazilian Congress of Telecommunications, Brasilia, July 15-20.

Fernao Dias Paes A732

1974, July 21 ***Perf. 11½***

1354 A732 20c green & multi .30 .30

3rd centenary of the expedition led by Fernao Dias Paes exploring Minas Gerais and the passage from South to North in Brazil.

Mexican Flag — A733

1974, July 24 Litho. ***Perf. 11½***

1355 A733 80c multicolored 2.25 1.10

Visit of Pres. Luis Echeverria Alvares of Mexico, July 24-29.

Flags of Brazil and Germany A734

1974, Aug. 5 ***Perf. 11x11½***

1356 A734 40c multicolored .50 .50

World Cup Soccer Championship, 1974, victory of German Federal Republic.

Souvenir Sheet

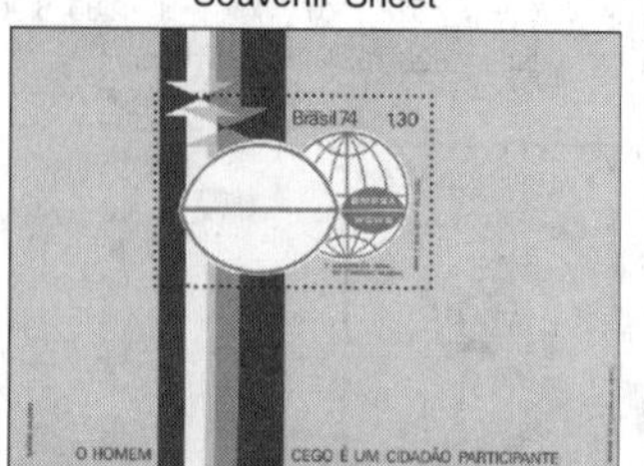

Congress Emblem — A735

1974, Aug. 7 ***Perf. 11½***

1357 A735 1.30cr multi .85 *1.75*

5th World Assembly of the World Council for the Welfare of the Blind, Sao Paulo, Aug. 7-16. Stamp and margin inscribed in Braille with name of Assembly.

Raul Pederneiras (1874-1953, Journalist, Professor of Law and Fine Arts), Caricature by J. Carlos — A736

Lithographed and Engraved

1974, Aug. 15 ***Perf. 11½x11***

1358 A736 40c buff, blk & ocher .30 .40

Society Emblem and Landscape — A737

1974, Aug. 19 Litho. ***Perf. 11x11½***

1359 A737 1.30cr multi 1.25 .90

13th Congress of the International Union of Building and Savings Societies.

Souvenir Sheet

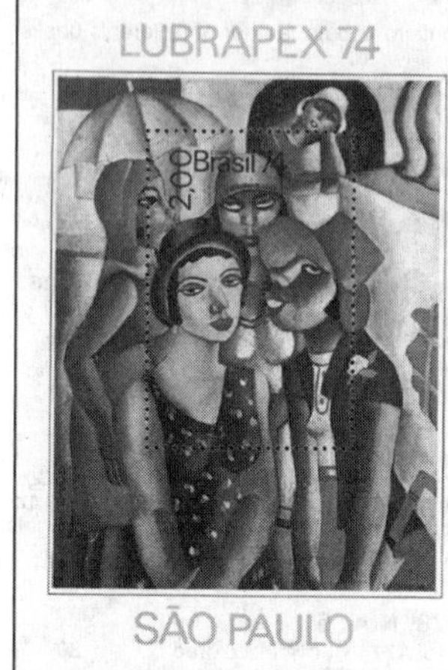

Five Women, by Di Cavalcanti — A738

1974, Aug. 26 Litho. ***Perf. 11½***

1360 A738 2cr multicolored 2.50 *6.00*

LUBRAPEX 74, 5th Portuguese-Brazilian Phil. Exhib., Sao Paulo, Nov. 26-Dec. 4.

"UPU" and World Map A739

1974, Oct. 9 Litho. ***Perf. 11½***

1361 A739 2.50cr blk & brt bl 4.50 1.75

Centenary of Universal Postal Union.

Hammock (Antillean Arawak Culture) A740

Bilro Lace — A741

Singer of "Cord" Verses — A742

Ceramic Figure by Master Vitalino — A743

1974, Oct. 16 Litho. ***Perf. 11½***

1362 A740	50c deep rose lilac	2.00	.40
1363 A741	50c lt & dk blue	2.50	.40
1364 A742	50c yel & red brn	.60	.40
1365 A743	50c brt yel & dk brn	.75	.40
Nos. 1362-1365 (4)		5.85	1.60

Popular Brazilian crafts.

Branch of Coffee A744

1974, Oct. 27 Unwmk. ***Perf. 11***

1366 A744 50c multicolored 1.00 .60

Centenary of city of Campinas.

Hornless Tabapua A745

Animals of Brazil: 1.30cr, Creole horse. 2.50cr, Brazilian mastiff.

1974, Nov. 10 ***Perf. 11½***

1367 A745	80c multi	1.10	.75
1368 A745	1.30cr multi	1.10	.75
1369 A745	2.50cr multi	7.75	2.50
Nos. 1367-1369 (3)		9.95	4.00

Christmas — A746

1974, Nov. 18 ***Perf. 11½x11***

1370 A746 50c Angel .70 .30

Solteira Island Hydroelectric Dam — A747

1974, Nov. 11 ***Perf. 11½***

1371 A747 50c black & yellow 1.40 .50

Inauguration of the Solteira Island Hydroelectric Dam over Parana River.

The Girls, by Carlos Reis — A748

1974, Nov. 26
1372 A748 1.30cr multi .70 .50

LUBRAPEX 74, 5th Portuguese-Brazilian Phil. Exhib., Sao Paulo, Nov. 26-Dec. 4.

Youths, Judge, Scales A749

1974, Dec. 20 Litho. *Perf. 11½*
1373 A749 90c yel, red & bl .30 .35

Juvenile Court of Brazil, 50th anniversary.

Long Distance Runner — A750

1974, Dec. 23
1374 A750 3.30cr multi .75 .75

Sao Silvestre long distance running, 50th anniversary.

News Vendor, 1875, Masthead, 1975 A751

1975, Jan. 4
1375 A751 50c multicolored 1.25 .75

Newspaper "O Estado de S. Paulo," cent.

Sao Paulo Industrial Park A752

Designs: 1.40cr, Natural rubber industry, Acre. 4.50cr, Manganese mining, Amapá.

1975, Jan. 24 Litho. *Perf. 11x11½*
1376 A752 50c vio bl & yel 1.25 .40
1377 A752 1.40cr yellow & brn .60 .40
1378 A752 4.50cr yellow & blk 6.00 .40
Nos. 1376-1378 (3) 7.85 1.20

Economic development.

Fort of the Holy Cross A753

Colonial forts: No. 1380, Fort of the Three Kings. No. 1381, Fort of Monteserrat. 90c, Fort of Our Lady of Help.

Litho. & Engr.

1975, Mar. 14 *Perf. 11½*
1379 A753 50c yel & red brn .25 .20
1380 A753 50c yel & red brn .40 .20
1381 A753 50c yel & red brn .80 .20
1382 A753 90c yel & red brn .25 .20
Nos. 1379-1382 (4) 1.70 .80

House on Stilts, Amazon Region A754

Designs: 50c, Modern houses and plan of Brasilia. 1.40cr, Indian hut, Rondonia. 3.30cr, German-style cottage (Enxaimel), Santa Catarina.

1975, Apr. 18 Litho. *Perf. 11½*
1383 A754 50c yel & multi 1.25 2.25
1384 A754 50c yel & multi 8.50 6.25
a. Pair, #1383-1384 10.00 8.50
1385 A754 1cr yel & multi .85 .25
1386 A754 1.40cr yel & multi 1.75 2.50
1387 A754 1.40cr yel & multi .50 .85
a. Pair, #1386-1387 2.25 3.50
1388 A754 3.30cr yel & multi .75 1.25
1389 A754 3.30cr yel & multi 3.50 4.00
a. Pair, #1388-1380 4.25 5.25
Nos. 1383-1389 (7) 17.10 17.35

Brazilian architecture. Nos. 1383, 1386, 1388 have yellow strip at right side, others at left.

Astronotus Ocellatus A755

Designs: Brazilian fresh-water fish.

1975, May 2 Litho. *Perf. 11½*
1390 A755 50c *shown* 1.40 .40
1391 A755 50c *Colomesus psitacus* .25 .25
1392 A755 50c *Phallocerus caudimaculatus* .25 .40
1393 A755 50c *Symphysodon discus* .48 .50
Nos. 1390-1393 (4) 2.38 1.55

Soldier's Head in Brazil's Colors, Plane, Rifle and Ship — A756

Brazilian Otter — A757

1975, May 8 *Perf. 11½x11*
1394 A756 50c vio bl & multi .35 .30

In honor of the veterans of World War II, on the 30th anniversary of victory.

1975, June 17 Litho. *Perf. 11½*

Nature protection: 70c, Brazilian pines, horiz. 3.30cr, Marsh cayman, horiz.

1395 A757 70c bl, grn & blk 1.05 .50
1396 A757 1cr multi 1.05 1.00
1397 A757 3.30cr multi .90 .75
Nos. 1395-1397 (3) 3.00 2.25

Petroglyphs, Stone of Ingá — A758

Marjoara Vase, Pará — A759

Vinctifer Comptoni, Petrified Fish A760

1975, July 8 Litho. *Perf. 11½*
1398 A758 70c multicolored .55 .40
1399 A759 1cr multicolored .35 .40
1400 A760 1cr multicolored .35 .40
Nos. 1398-1400 (3) 1.25 1.20

Archaeological discoveries.

Immaculate Conception, Franciscan Monastery, Vitoria — A761

Post and Telegraph Ministry — A762

1975, July 15
1401 A761 3.30cr blue & multi .95 .95

Holy Year 1975 and 300th anniv. of establishment of the Franciscan Province in Southern Brazil.

1975, Aug. 8 Engr. *Perf. 11½*
1402 A762 70c dk carmine .70 .30

Stamp Day 1975.

Sword Dance, Minas Gerais A763

Folk Dances: No. 1404, Umbrella Dance, Pernambuco. No. 1405, Warrior's Dance, Alagoas.

1975, Aug. 22 Litho. *Perf. 11½*
1403 A763 70c gray & multi .35 .35
1404 A763 70c pink & multi .35 .35
1405 A763 70c yellow & multi .35 .35
Nos. 1403-1405 (3) 1.05 1.05

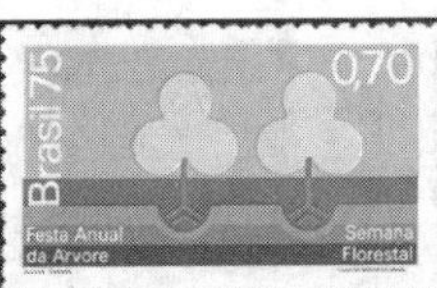

Trees A764

1975, Sept. 15 *Perf. 11x11½*
1406 A764 70c multicolored .30 .25

Annual Tree Festival.

Globe, Radar and Satellite — A765

1975, Sept. 16 *Perf. 11½*
1407 A765 3.30cr multi .70 .75

Inauguration of 2nd antenna of Tangua Earth Station, Rio de Janeiro State.

Woman Holding Flowers and Globe A766

1975, Sept. 23
1408 A766 3.30cr multi 1.00 1.00

International Women's Year 1975.

Tile, Railing and Column, Alcantara A767

Cross and Monastery, Sao Cristovao — A768

Historic cities: No. 1411, Jug and Clock Tower, Goiás, vert.

1975, Sept. 27 Litho. *Perf. 11½*
1409 A767 70c multicolored .30 .45
1410 A768 70c multicolored .60 .45
1411 A768 70c multicolored .60 .45
Nos. 1409-1411 (3) 1.50 1.35

"Books teach how to live" A769

1975, Oct. 23 Litho. *Perf. 11½*
1412 A769 70c multicolored .25 .30

Day of the Book.

ASTA Congress Emblem A770

1975, Oct. 27 *Perf. 11x11½*

1413 A770 70c multicolored .25 .30

American Society of Travel Agents, 45th World Congress, Rio, Oct. 27-Nov. 1.

Angels A771

1975, Nov. 11

1414 A771 70c red & brown .25 .20

Christmas 1975.

Map of Americas, Waves — A772

Dom Pedro II — A773

1975, Nov. 19 *Perf. 11½x12*

1415 A772 5.20cr gray & multi 2.75 2.00

2nd Interamerican Conference of Telecommunications (CITEL), Rio, Nov. 19-27.

1975, Dec. 2 **Engr.** *Perf. 12*

1416 A773 70c violet brown .75 .45

Dom Pedro II (1825-1891), emperor of Brazil, birth sesquicentennial.

People and Cross A774

1975, Nov. 27 **Litho.** *Perf. 11x11½*

1417 A774 70c lt bl & dp bl .50 .65

National Day of Thanksgiving.

Guarapari Beach, Espirito Santo A775

Tourist Publicity: #1419, Salt Stone beach, Piaui. #1420, Cliffs, Rio Grande Do Sul.

1975, Dec. 19 **Litho.** *Perf. 11½*

1418 A775 70c multicolored .30 .30
1419 A775 70c multicolored .30 .30
1420 A775 70c multicolored .30 .30
Nos. 1418-1420 (3) .90 .90

Triple Jump, Games Emblem A776

1975, Dec. 22 *Perf. 11x11½*

1421 A776 1.60cr bl grn & blk .25 .35

Triple jump world record by Joao Carlos de Oliveira in 7th Pan-American Games, Mexico City, Oct. 12-26.

UN Emblem and Headquarters — A777

1975, Dec. 29 *Perf. 11½*

1422 A777 1.30cr dp bl & vio bl .25 .30

United Nations, 30th anniversary.

Light Bulbs, House and Sun A778

Energy conservation: No. 1424, Gasoline drops, car and sun.

1976, Jan. 16

1423 A778 70c multicolored .30 .20
1424 A778 70c multicolored .30 .20

Concorde A779

1976, Jan. 21 **Litho.** *Perf. 11x11½*

1425 A779 5.20cr bluish black .50 .35

First commercial flight of supersonic jet Concorde from Paris to Rio, Jan. 21.

Souvenir Sheet

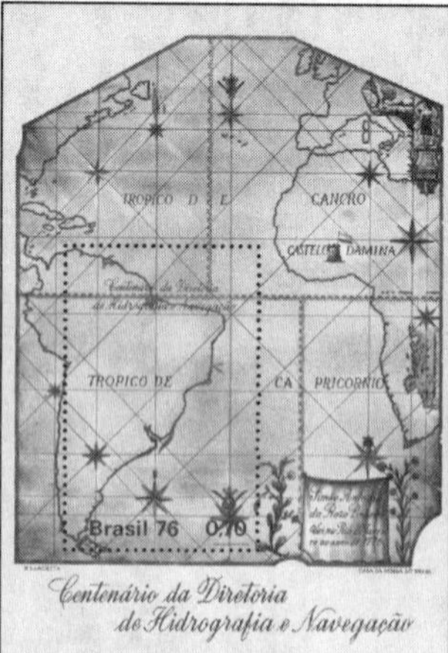

Nautical Map of South Atlantic, 1776 — A780

1976, Feb. 2 *Perf. 11½*

1426 A780 70c salmon & multi .85 *1.50*

Centenary of the Naval Hydrographic and Navigation Institute.

Telephone Lines, 1876 Telephone — A781

1976, Mar. 10 **Litho.** *Perf. 11x11½*

1427 A781 5.20cr orange & blue .65 .50

Centenary of first telephone call by Alexander Graham Bell, March 10, 1876.

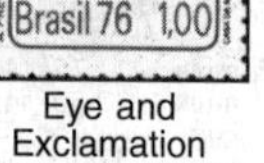

Eye and Exclamation Point — A782

Kaiapo Body Painting — A783

1976, Apr. 7 **Litho.** *Perf. 11½x11*

1428 A782 1cr vio red brn & brn .50 *.75*

World Health Day: "Foresight prevents blindness."

1976, Apr. 19 **Litho.** *Perf. 11½*

Designs: No. 1430, Bakairi ceremonial mask. No. 1431, Karajá feather headdress.

1429 A783 1cr light violet & multi .20 .20
1430 A783 1cr light violet & multi .20 .20
1431 A783 1cr light violet & multi .20 .20
Nos. 1429-1431 (3) .60 .60

Preservation of indigenous culture.

Itamaraty Palace, Brasilia A784

1976, Apr. 20

1432 A784 1cr multicolored .60 .60

Diplomats' Day. Itamaraty Palace, designed by Oscar Niemeyer, houses the Ministry of Foreign Affairs.

Watering Can over Stones, by José Tarcisio A785

Fingers and Ribbons, by Pietrina Checcacci A786

1976, May 14 **Litho.** *Perf. 11½*

1433 A785 1cr multi .25 .20
1434 A786 1.60cr multi .25 .20

Modern Brazilian art.

Basketball — A787 Orchid — A788

Designs (Olympic Rings and): 1.40cr, Yachting. 5.20cr, Judo.

1976, May 21 **Litho.** *Perf. 11½*

1435 A787 1cr emerald & blk .20 .20
1436 A787 1.40cr dk blue & blk .20 .20
1437 A787 5.20cr orange & blk .65 .50
Nos. 1435-1437 (3) 1.05 .90

21st Olympic Games, Montreal, Canada, July 17-Aug. 1.

1976, June 4 *Perf. 11½x11*

Nature protection: No. 1439, Golden-faced lion monkey.

1438 A788 1cr multicolored .25 .20
1439 A788 1cr multicolored .25 .20

Film Camera, Brazilian Colors — A789

1976, June 19

1440 A789 1cr vio bl, brt grn & yel .20 .25

Brazilian film industry.

Bahia Woman — A790

Designs: 10c, Oxcart driver, horiz. 20c, Raft fishermen, horiz. 30c, Rubber plantation worker. 40c, Cowboy, horiz. 50c, Gaucho. 80c, Gold panner. 1cr, Banana plantation worker. 1.10cr, Grape harvester. 1.30cr, Coffee picker. 1.80cr, Farmer gathering wax palms. 2cr, Potter. 5cr, Sugar cane cutter. 7cr, Salt mine worker. 10cr, Fisherman. 15cr, Coconut seller. 20cr, Lacemaker.

Perf. 11½x11, 11x11½

1976-78 **Photo.**

1441 A790 10c red brown ('77) .20 .20
1442 A790 15c brown .25 .30
1443 A790 20c violet blue .20 .20
1444 A790 30c lilac rose .20 .20
1445 A790 40c orange ('77) .20 .20
1446 A790 50c citron .20 .20
1447 A790 80c slate green .40 .20
1448 A790 1cr black .20 .20
1449 A790 1.10cr magenta ('77) .20 .20
1450 A790 1.30cr red ('77) .20 .20
1451 A790 1.80cr dk vio bl ('78) .20 .20

Engr.

1452 A790 2cr brown ('77) .25 .20
1453 A790 5cr dk pur ('77) .50 .20
1454 A790 7cr violet 1.50 .20
1455 A790 10cr yel grn ('77) .55 .20
1456 A790 15cr gray grn ('78) 1.40 .20
1457 A790 20cr blue 1.40 .20
Nos. 1441-1457 (17) 8.05 3.50

See Nos. 1653-1657.

Hyphessobrycon Innesi — A791

Designs: Brazilian fresh-water fish.

1976, July 12 Litho. *Perf. 11x11½*

1460 A791 1cr *shown* .40 .40
1461 A791 1cr *Copeina arnoldi* .40 .40
1462 A791 1cr *Prochilodus insignis* .40 .40
1463 A791 1cr *Crenicichla lepidota* .40 .40
1464 A791 1cr *Ageneiosus* .40 .40
1465 A791 1cr *Corydoras reticulatus* .40 .40
a. Block of 6, #1460-1465 2.50 2.50

Santa Marta Lighthouse A792

1976, July 29 Engr. *Perf. 12x11½*

1466 A792 1cr blue .20 .30

300th anniversary of the city of Laguna.

Children on Magic Carpet A793

1976, Aug. 1 Litho. *Perf. 11½x12*

1467 A793 1cr multicolored .20 .20

Stamp Day.

Nurse's Lamp and Head A794

1976, Aug. 12 Litho. *Perf. 11½*

1468 A794 1cr multicolored .20 .20

Brazilian Nurses' Assoc., 50th anniv.

Puppet, Soldier — A795

Winner's Medal — A796

Designs: 1.30cr, Girl's head. 1.60cr, Hand with puppet head on each finger, horiz.

1976, Aug. 20

1469 A795 1cr multi .20 .20
1470 A795 1.30cr multi .20 .20
1471 A795 1.60cr multi .20 .20
Nos. 1469-1471 (3) .60 .60

Mamulengo puppet show.

1976, Aug. 21

1472 A796 5.20cr multi .70 .50

27th International Military Athletic Championships, Rio de Janeiro, Aug. 21-28.

Family Protection — A797

1976, Sept. 12

1473 A797 1cr lt & dk blue .20 .20

National organizations SENAC and SESC helping commercial employees to improve their living standard, both commercially and socially.

Dying Tree — A798

1976, Sept. 20 Litho. *Perf. 11½*

1474 A798 1cr gray & multi .20 .20

Protection of the environment.

Atom Symbol, Electron Orbits A799

1976, Sept. 21

1475 A799 5.20cr multi .70 .50

20th General Conference of the International Atomic Energy Agency, Rio de Janeiro, Sept. 21-29.

Train in Tunnel A800

1976, Sept. 26

1476 A800 1.60cr multi .25 .25

Sao Paulo subway, 1st in Brazil.

St. Francis and Birds A801

1976, Oct. 4

1477 A801 5.20cr multi .60 .40

St. Francis of Assisi, 750th death anniv.

Ouro Preto School of Mining — A802

1976, Oct. 12 Engr. *Perf. 12x11½*

1478 A802 1cr dk vio .40 .50

Ouro Preto School of Mining, centenary.

Three Kings A803

Designs: Children's drawings.

1976, Nov. 4 Litho. *Perf. 11½*

1479 A803 80c shown .30 .30
1480 A803 80c Santa Claus on donkey .30 .30
1481 A803 80c Virgin and Child and Angels .30 .30
1482 A803 80c Angels with candle .30 .30
1483 A803 80c Nativity .30 .30
a. Strip of 5, #1479-1483 1.40 1.40

Christmas 1976.

Souvenir Sheet

30,000 Reis Banknote — A804

1976, Nov. 5 Litho. *Perf. 11½*

1484 A804 80c multicolored .40 *1.50*

Opening of 1000th branch of Bank of Brazil, Barra do Bugres, Mato Grosso.

Virgin of Monte Serrat, by Friar Agostinho A805

St. Joseph, 18th Century Wood Sculpture — A806

5.60cr, The Dance, by Rodolfo Bernadelli, 19th cent. 6.50cr, The Caravel, by Bruno Giorgi, 20th cent. abstract sculpture.

1976, Nov. 5

1485 A805 80c multi .20 .20
1486 A806 5cr multi .65 .40
1487 A805 5.60cr multi .65 .40
1488 A806 6.50cr multi .65 .40
Nos. 1485-1488 (4) 2.15 1.40

Development of Brazilian sculpture.

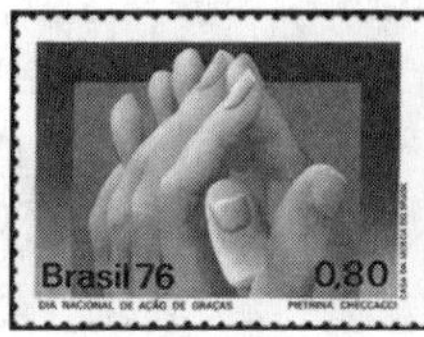

Praying Hands A807

1976, Nov. 25

1489 A807 80c multicolored .25 .25

National Day of Thanksgiving.

Sailor, 1840 — A808

Design: 2cr, Marine's uniform, 1808.

1976, Dec. 13 Litho. *Perf. 11½x11*

1490 A808 80c multicolored .25 .25
1491 A808 2cr multicolored .30 .25

Brazilian Navy.

"Natural Resources and Development" — A809

1976, Dec. 17 *Perf. 11½*

1492 A809 80c multicolored .20 .20

Brazilian Bureau of Standards, founded 1940.

Wheel of Life — A810

Designs: 5.60cr, Beggar, sculpture by Agnaldo dos Santos. 6.50cr, Benin mask.

1977, Jan. 14

1493 A810 5cr multi .55 .35
1494 A810 5.60cr multi .55 .35
1495 A810 6.50cr multi 1.10 .35
Nos. 1493-1495 (3) 2.20 1.05

FESTAC '77, 2nd World Black and African Festival, Lagos, Nigeria, Jan. 15-Feb. 12.

A811

1977, Jan. 20 Litho. *Perf. 11½*

1496 A811 6.50cr bl & yel grn .85 .65

Rio de Janeiro International Airport.

Seminar Emblem with Map of Americas — A812

Salicylate, Microphoto A813

1977, Feb. 6

1497 A812 1.10cr gray, vio bl & bl .35 .20

6th Inter-American Budget Seminar.

1977, Apr. 10 Litho. *Perf. 11½*

1498 A813 1.10cr multi .20 .20

International Rheumatism Year.

Lions International Emblem A814

1977, Apr. 16

1499 A814 1.10cr multi .20 .20

25th anniv. of Brazilian Lions Intl.

Heitor Villa Lobos A815

1977, Apr. 26 *Perf. 11x11½*

1500 A815 1.10cr shown .20 .20
1501 A815 1.10cr Chiquinha Gonzaga .20 .20
1502 A815 1.10cr Noel Rosa .20 .20
Nos. 1500-1502 (3) .60 .60

Brazilian composers.

Farmer and Worker — A816

Medicine Bottles and Flask — A817

1977, May 8 Litho. *Perf. 11½*

1503 A816 1.10cr grn & multi .20 .20
1504 A817 1.10cr lt & dk grn .20 .20

Support and security for rural and urban workers (No. 1503) and establishment in 1971 of Medicine Distribution Center (CEME) for low-cost medicines (No. 1504).

Churchyard Cross, Porto Seguro — A818

Views, Porto Seguro: 5cr, Beach and boats. 5.60cr, Our Lady of Pena Chapel. 6.50cr, Town Hall.

1977, May 25 Litho. *Perf. 11½*

1505 A818 1.10cr multi .20 .20
1506 A818 5cr multi 1.40 .35
1507 A818 5.60cr multi .55 .45
1508 A818 6.50cr multi .80 .55
Nos. 1505-1508 (4) 2.95 1.55

Cent. of Brazil's membership in UPU.

Diario de Porto Alegre A819

1977, June 1

1509 A819 1.10cr multi .20 .20

Diario de Porto Alegre, newspaper, 150th anniv.

Blue Whale A820

1977, June 3

1510 A820 1.30cr multi .20 .20

Protection of marine life.

"Life and Development" A821

1977, June 20

1511 A821 1.30cr multi .20 .20

National Development Bank, 25th anniv.

Vasum Cassiforme A823

Caduceus, Formulas for Water and Fluoride A824

Train Leaving Tunnel A822

1977, July 8 Engr. *Perf. 11½*

1512 A822 1.30cr black .20 .20

Centenary of Sao Paulo-Rio de Janeiro railroad.

Sea Shells: No. 1514, Strombus goliath. No. 1515, Murex tenuivaricosus.

1977, July 14 Litho.

1513 A823 1.30cr blue & multi .20 .20
1514 A823 1.30cr brown & multi .20 .20
1515 A823 1.30cr green & multi .20 .20
Nos. 1513-1515 (3) .60 .60

1977, July 15 *Perf. 11½x11*

1516 A824 1.30cr multi .20 .20

3rd Intl. Odontology Congress, Rio, 7/15-21.

Masonic Emblem, Map of Brazil — A825

"Stamps Don't Sink or Lose their Way" — A826

1977, July 18 *Perf. 11½*

1517 A825 1.30cr bl, lt bl & blk .20 .20

50th anniversary of the founding of the Brazilian Grand Masonic Lodge.

1977, Aug. 1

1518 A826 1.30cr multi .20 .20

Stamp Day 1977.

Dom Pedro's Proclamation A827

Horses and Bulls — A828

1977, Aug. 11 Litho. *Perf. 11½*

1519 A827 1.30cr multi .20 .20

150th anniversary of Brazilian Law School.

1977, Aug. 20 *Perf. 11½x11, 11x11½* Litho.

Brazilian folklore: No. 1521, King on horseback. No. 1522, Joust, horiz.

1520 A828 1.30cr ocher & multi .20 .20
1521 A828 1.30cr blue & multi .20 .20
1522 A828 1.30cr yel & multi .20 .20
Nos. 1520-1522 (3) .60 .60

2000-reis Doubloon A829

Brazilian Colonial Coins: No. 1524, 640r pataca. No. 1525, 20r copper "vintem."

1977, Aug. 31 *Perf. 11½*

1523 A829 1.30cr vio bl & multi .20 .20
1524 A829 1.30cr dk red & multi .20 .20
1525 A829 1.30cr yel & multi .20 .20
Nos. 1523-1525 (3) .60 .60

Pinwheel A830

Neoregelia Carolinae A831

1977, Sept. 1

1526 A830 1.30cr multi .20 .20

National Week.

1977, Sept. 21 Litho. *Perf. 11½*

1527 A831 1.30cr multi .20 .20

Nature preservation.

Pen, Pencil, Letters — A832

1977, Oct. 15 Litho. *Perf. 11½*

1528 A832 1.30cr multi .20 .20

Primary education, sesquicentennial.

Dome and Telescope A833

1977, Oct. 15

1529 A833 1.30cr multi .20 .20

National Astrophysics Observatory, Brasópolis, sesquicentennial.

"Jahu" Hydroplane (Savoia Marchetti S-55) — A834

Design: No. 1531, PAX, dirigible.

1977, Oct. 17

1530 A834 1.30cr multi .25 .25
1531 A834 1.30cr multi .25 .25

50th anniv. of crossing of South Atlantic by Joao Ribeiro de Barros, Genoa-Sao Paulo (#1530) and 75th anniv. of the PAX airship (#1531).

A835

A836

1977, Oct. 24

1532 A835 1.30cr Il'Guarani .20 .20

Book Day and to honor Jose Martiniano de Alencar, writer, jurist.

1977, Nov. 5 Litho. *Perf. 11½*

1533 A836 1.30cr Waves .20 .20

Amateur Radio Operators' Day.

Nativity A837

Christmas (folk art): 2cr, Annunciation. 5cr, Nativity.

1977, Nov. 10

1534 A837 1.30cr bister & multi .25 .20
1535 A837 2cr bister & multi .30 .20
1536 A837 5cr bister & multi .65 .25
Nos. 1534-1536 (3) 1.20 .65

A838

A839

1977, Nov. 19

1537 A838 1.30cr Emerald .20 .20
1538 A838 1.30cr Topaz .20 .20
1539 A838 1.30cr Aquamarine .20 .20
Nos. 1537-1539 (3) .60 .60

PORTUCALE 77, 2nd International Topical Exhibition, Porto, Nov. 19-20.

1977, Nov. 24 Litho. *Perf. 11½*

1540 A839 1.30cr Angel, cornucopia .20 .20

National Thanksgiving Day.

Army's Railroad Construction Battalion — A840

Civilian services of armed forces: No. 1542, Navy's Amazon flotilla. No. 1543, Air Force's postal service (plane).

1977, Dec. 5

1541 A840 1.30cr multi .20 .20
1542 A840 1.30cr multi .20 .20
1543 A840 1.30cr multi .20 .20
Nos. 1541-1543 (3) .60 .60

Varig Emblem, Jet A841

1977, Dec. *Perf. 11x11½*

1544 A841 1.30cr bl & blk .20 .20

50th anniversary of Varig Airline.

Sts. Cosme and Damiao Church, Igaracu — A842

Woman Holding Sheaf — A843

Brazilian Architecture: 7.50cr, St. Bento Monastery Church, Rio de Janeiro. 8.50cr, Church of St. Francis of Assisi, Ouro Preto. 9.50cr, St. Anthony Convent Church, Joao Pessoa.

1977, Dec. 8

1545 A842 2.70cr multi .30 .20
1546 A842 7.50cr multi .90 .35
1547 A842 8.50cr multi .90 .40
1548 A842 9.50cr multi 1.25 .45
Nos. 1545-1548 (4) 3.35 1.40

1977, Dec. 19 *Perf. 11½*

1549 A843 1.30cr multi .20 .20

Brazilian diplomacy.

Soccer Ball and Foot — A844

Designs: No. 1551, Soccer ball in net. No. 1552, Symbolic soccer player.

1978, Mar. 1 Litho. *Perf. 11½*

1550 A844 1.80cr multi .30 .20
1551 A844 1.80cr multi .30 .20
1552 A844 1.80cr multi .30 .20
Nos. 1550-1552 (3) .90 .60

11th World Cup Soccer Championship, Argentina, June 1-25.

"La Fosca" on La Scala Stage and Carlos Gomes A845

1978, Feb. 9

1553 A845 1.80cr multi .20 .20

Bicentenary of La Scala in Milan, and to honor Carlos Gomes (1836-1893), Brazilian composer.

Symbols of Postal Mechanization — A846

1978, Mar. 15 Litho. *Perf. 11½*

1554 A846 1.80cr multi .20 .20

Opening of Postal Staff College.

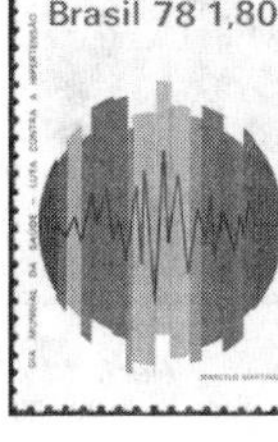

Hypertension Chart — A847

Waves from Antenna Uniting World — A848

1978, Apr. 4

1555 A847 1.80cr multi .20 .20

World Health Day, fight against hypertension.

1978, May 17 Litho. *Perf. 12x11½*

1556 A848 1.80cr multi .20 .20

10th World Telecommunications Day.

Brazilian Canary A849

Birds: 8.50cr, Cotinga. 9.50cr, Tanager fastuosa.

1978, June 5 *Perf. 11½x12*

1557 A849 7.50cr multi 1.00 .75
1558 A849 8.50cr multi 1.00 .80
1559 A849 9.50cr multi 1.00 1.00
Nos. 1557-1559 (3) 3.00 2.55

Inocencio Serzedelo Correa and Manuel Francisco Correa, 1893 — A850

1978, June 20 Litho. *Perf. 11x11½*

1560 A850 1.80cr multi .20 .20

85th anniversary of Union Court of Audit.

Post and Telegraph Building A851

1978, June 22 *Perf. 11½*

1561 A851 1.80cr multi .20 .25

Souvenir Sheet

Imperf

1562 A851 7.50cr multi .75 1.50

Inauguration of Post and Telegraph Building (ECT), Brasilia, and for BRAPEX, 3rd Brazilian Philatelic Exhibition, Brasilia, June 23-28 (No. 1562).

Ernesto Geisel, President of Brazil — A852

1978, June 22 Engr. *Perf. 11½*

1563 A852 1.80cr dull green .20 .20

Savoia-Marchetti S-64, Map of South Atlantic — A853

1978, July 3 **Litho.**
1564 A853 1.80cr multi .20 .20

50th anniv. of 1st crossing of South Atlantic by Carlos del Prete and Arturo Ferrarin.

Symbolic of Smallpox Eradication A854

Brazil No. 68 — A855

1978, July 25
1565 A854 1.80cr multi .20 .20

Eradication of smallpox.

1978, Aug. 1
1566 A855 1.80cr multi .20 .20

Stamp Day, centenary of the "Barba Branca" (white beard) issue.

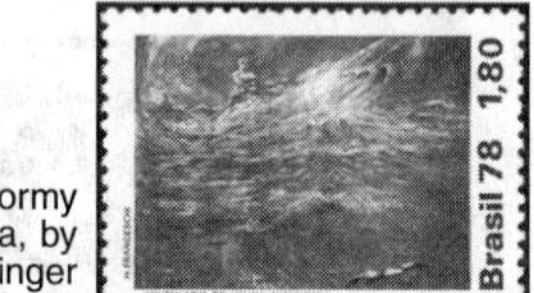

Stormy Sea, by Seelinger A856

1978, Aug. 4
1567 A856 1.80cr multi .20 .20

Helios Seelinger, painter, birth centenary.

Guitar Players A857

Musicians and Instruments: No. 1569, Flutes. No. 1570, Percussion instruments.

1978, Aug. 22 **Litho.** ***Perf. 11½***
1568 A857 1.80cr multi .20 .20
1569 A857 1.80cr multi .20 .20
1570 A857 1.80cr multi .20 .20
Nos. 1568-1570 (3) .60 .60

Children at Play A858

1978, Sept. 1 **Litho.** ***Perf. 11½***
1571 A858 1.80cr multi .20 .20

National Week.

Collegiate Church A859

1978, Sept. 6 **Engr.**
1572 A859 1.80cr red brn .20 .20

Restoration of patio of Collegiate Church, Sao Paulo.

Justice by A. Geschiatti A860

1978, Sept. 18 **Litho.**
1573 A860 1.80cr blk & olive .20 .20

Federal Supreme Court, sesquicentennial.

Iguacu Falls — A861

Design: No. 1575, Yellow ipecac.

1978, Sept. 21
1574 A861 1.80cr multi .20 .20
1575 A861 1.80cr multi .20 .20

Iguacu National Park.

Stages of Intelsat Satellite A862

1978, Oct. 9 **Litho.** ***Perf. 11½***
1576 A862 1.80cr multi .20 .20

Flag of Order of Christ A863

Brazilian Flags: No. 1578, Principality of Brazil. No. 1579, United Kingdom. No. 1580, Imperial Brazil. No. 1581, National flag (current).

1978, Oct. 13
1577 A863 1.80cr multi .65 .55
1578 A863 1.80cr multi .65 .55
1579 A863 1.80cr multi .65 .55
1580 A863 8.50cr multi .65 .55
1581 A863 8.50cr multi .65 .55
a. Block of 5, #1577-1581 + label 4.00 6.50
Nos. 1577-1581 (5) 3.25 2.75

7th LUBRAPEX Philatelic Exhibition, Porto Alegre.

Mail Street Car A864

Mail Transportation: No. 1583, Overland mail truck. No. 1584, Mail delivery truck. 7.50cr. Railroad mail car. 8.50cr, Mail coach. 9.50cr, Post riders.

1978, Oct. 21 ***Perf. 11x11½***
1582 A864 1.80cr multi .50 .40
1583 A864 1.80cr multi .50 .40
1584 A864 1.80cr multi .50 .40
1585 A864 7.50cr multi .50 .40
1586 A864 8.50cr multi .50 .40
1587 A864 9.50cr multi .50 .50
a. Block of 6, #1582-1587 3.00 3.00

18th UPU Congress, Rio de Janeiro, 1979.

Gaucho Herding Cattle, and Cactus — A865

1978, Oct. 23 ***Perf. 11½x11***
1588 A865 1.80cr multi .20 .20

Joao Guimaraes Rosa, poet and diplomat, 70th birthday.

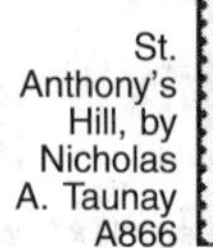

St. Anthony's Hill, by Nicholas A. Taunay A866

Landscape Paintings: No. 1590, Castle Hill, by Victor Meirelles. No. 1591, View of Sabara, by Alberto da Veiga Guignard. No. 1592, View of Pernambuco, by Frans Post.

1978, Nov. 6 **Litho.** ***Perf. 11½***
1589 A866 1.80cr multi .20 .20
1590 A866 1.80cr multi .20 .20
1591 A866 1.80cr multi .20 .20
1592 A866 1.80cr multi .20 .20
Nos. 1589-1592 (4) .80 .80

Angel with Harp — A867

Christmas: No. 1594, Angel with lute. No. 1595, Angel with oboe.

1978, Nov. 10
1593 A867 1.80cr multi .20 .20
1594 A867 1.80cr multi .20 .20
1595 A867 1.80cr multi .20 .20
Nos. 1593-1595 (3) .60 .60

Symbolic Candles — A868

1978, Nov. 23
1596 A868 1.80cr blk, gold & car .20 .20

National Thanksgiving Day.

Red Crosses and Activities A869

1978, Dec. 5 **Litho.** ***Perf. 11x11½***
1597 A869 1.80cr blk & red .20 .20

70th anniversary of Brazilian Red Cross.

Paz Theater, Belem A870

12cr, José de Alencar Theater, Portaleza. 12.50cr, Municipal Theater, Rio de Janeiro.

1978, Dec. 6 ***Perf. 11½***
1598 A870 10.50cr multi .70 .25
1599 A870 12cr multi .70 .25
1600 A870 12.50cr multi .70 .25
Nos. 1598-1600 (3) 2.10 .75

Subway Trains — A871

1979, Mar. 5 **Litho.** ***Perf. 11½***
1601 A871 2.50cr multi .20 .20

Inauguration of Rio subway system.

Old and New Post Offices A872

Designs: No. 1603, Old and new mail boxes. No. 1604, Manual and automatic mail sorting. No. 1605, Old and new planes. No. 1606, Telegraph and telex machine. No. 1607, Mailmen's uniforms.

1979, Mar. 20 **Litho.** ***Perf. 11x11½***
1602 A872 2.50cr multi .25 .20
1603 A872 2.50cr multi .25 .20
1604 A872 2.50cr multi .25 .20
1605 A872 2.50cr multi .25 .20
1606 A872 2.50cr multi .25 .20
1607 A872 2.50cr multi .25 .20
a. Block of 6, #1602-1607 1.50 1.50

10th anniv. of the new Post and Telegraph Dept., and 18th Universal Postal Union Cong., Rio de Janeiro, Sept.-Oct., 1979.

O'Day 23 Class Yacht
A873

Yachts and Stamp Outlines: 10.50cr, Penguin Class. 12cr, Hobie Cat Class. 12.50cr, Snipe Class.

1979, Apr. 18 Litho. *Perf. 11x11½*

1608 A873 2.50cr multi .30 .25
1609 A873 10.50cr multi .55 .45
1610 A873 12cr multi .55 .35
1611 A873 12.50cr multi .75 .35
Nos. 1608-1611 (4) 2.15 1.40

Brasiliana '79, 3rd World Thematic Stamp Exhibition, Sao Conrado, Sept. 15-23.

Children, IYC Emblem — A874

1979, May 30 Litho. *Perf. 11½*

1612 A874 2.50cr multi .25 .20

Intl. Year of the Child & Children's Book Day.

Giant Water Lily — A875

12cr, Amazon manatee. 12.50cr, Arrau (turtle).

1979, June 5 Litho. *Perf. 11½*

1613 A875 10.50cr multi .70 .50
1614 A875 12cr multi .90 .60
1615 A875 12.50cr multi .90 .60
Nos. 1613-1615 (3) 2.50 1.70

Amazon National Park, nature conservation.

Bank Emblem
A876

1979, June 7

1616 A876 2.50cr multi .20 .20

Northwest Bank of Brazil, 25th anniversary.

Physician Tending Patient 15th Cent. Woodcut
A877

1979, June 30

1617 A877 2.50cr multi .20 .20

Natl. Academy of Medicine, 50th anniv.

Flower made of Hearts — A878

1979, July 8 Litho. *Perf. 11½*

1618 A878 2.50cr multi .20 .20

35th Brazilian Cardiology Congress.

Souvenir Sheet

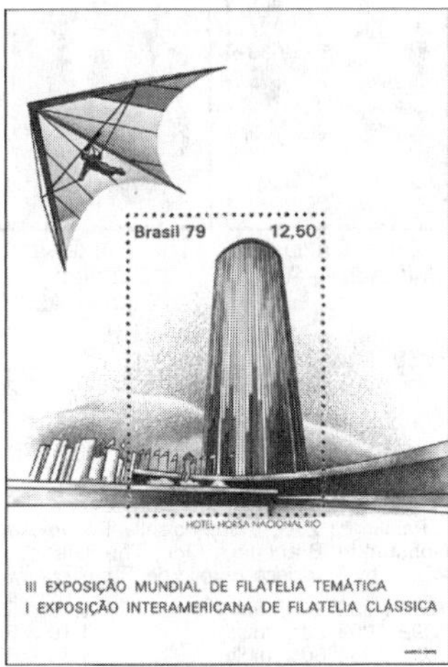

Hotel Nacional, Rio de Janeiro — A879

1979, July 16

1619 A879 12.50cr multi .75 1.50

Brasiliana '79 comprising 1st Inter-American Exhibition of Classical Philately and 3rd World Topical Exhibition, Rio de Janeiro, Sept. 15-23.

Cithaerias Aurora
A880

Moths: 10.50cr, Evenus regalis. 12cr, Caligo eurilochus. 12.50cr, Diaethria clymena janeira.

1979, Aug. 1

1620 A880 2.50cr multi .20 .20
1621 A880 10.50cr multi .60 .40
1622 A880 12cr multi .70 .50
1623 A880 12.50cr multi .70 .50
Nos. 1620-1623 (4) 2.20 1.60

Stamp Day 1979.

EMB-121 Xingo
A881

1979, Aug. 19 Litho. *Perf. 11½*

1624 A881 2.50cr vio blue .20 .20

Embraer, Brazilian aircraft comp., 10th anniv.

A882

A883

Natl. emblem over landscape.

1979, Sept. 12

1625 A882 3.20cr multi .20 .20

National Week.

1979, Sept. 8 Litho. *Perf. 11½*

1626 A883 2.50cr multi .20 .20

Statue of Our Lady of the Apparition, 75th anniversary of coronation.

"UPU," Envelope and Mail Transport
A884

"UPU" and: No. 1628, Post Office emblems. 10.50cr, Globe. 12cr, Flags of Brazil and UN. 12.50cr, UPU emblem.

1979, Sept. 12 *Perf. 11x11½*

1627 A884 2.50cr multi .20 .20
1628 A884 2.50cr multi .20 .20
1629 A884 10.50cr multi .50 .50
1630 A884 12cr multi .70 .70
1631 A884 12.50cr multi .70 .70
Nos. 1627-1631 (5) 2.30 2.30

18th UPU Cong., Rio, Sept.-Oct. 1979.

Pyramid Fountain, Rio de Janeiro — A885

Fountains: 10.50cr, Facade, Marilia, Ouro Preto, horiz. 12cr, Boa Vista, Recife.

Perf. 12x11½, 11½x12

1979, Sept. 15

1632 A885 2.50cr multi .20 .20
1633 A885 10.50cr multi .50 .50
1634 A885 12cr multi .60 .60
Nos. 1632-1634 (3) 1.30 1.30

Brasiliana '79, 1st Interamerican Exhibition of Classical Philately.

Church of the Glory
A886

Landscapes by Leandro Joaquim: 12cr, Fishing on Guanabara Bay. 12.50cr, Boqueirao Lake and Carioca Arches.

1979, Sept. 15 *Perf. 11½*

1635 A886 2.50cr multi .20 .20
1636 A886 12cr multi .60 .60
1637 A886 12.50cr multi .60 .60
Nos. 1635-1637 (3) 1.40 1.40

Brasiliana '79, 3rd World Topical Exhibition, Sao Conrado, Sept. 15-23.

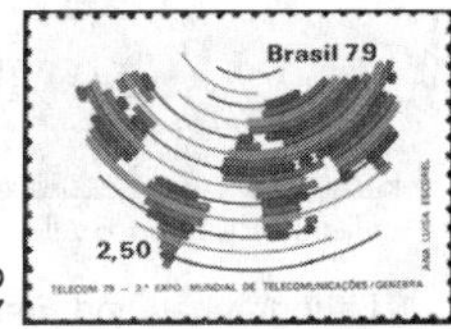

World Map
A887

1979, Sept. 20

1638 A887 2.50cr multi .20 .20

3rd World Telecommunications Exhibition, Geneva, Sept. 20-26.

"UPU" and UPU Emblem — A888

1979, Oct. 9 Litho. *Perf. 11½x11*

1639 A888 2.50cr multi .20 .20
1640 A888 10.50cr multi .55 .55
1641 A888 12cr multi .65 .65
1642 A888 12.50cr multi .65 .65
Nos. 1639-1642 (4) 2.05 2.05

Universal Postal Union Day.

IYC Emblem, Feather Toy
A889

IYC Emblem and Toys: No. 1644, Bumble bee, ragdoll. No. 1645, Flower, top. No. 1646, Wooden acrobat.

1979, Oct. 12 *Perf. 11½*

1643 A889 2.50cr multi .25 .20
1644 A889 3.20cr multi .25 .25
1645 A889 3.20cr multi .25 .25
1646 A889 3.20cr multi .25 .25
Nos. 1643-1646 (4) 1.00 .95

International Year of the Child.

Adoration of the Kings
A890

Christmas 1979: No. 1648, Nativity. No. 1649 Jesus and the Elders in the Temple.

1979, Nov. 12 Litho. *Perf. 11½*

1647 A890 3.20cr multi .20 .20
1648 A890 3.20cr multi .20 .20
1649 A890 3.20cr multi .20 .20
Nos. 1647-1649 (3) .60 .60

Souvenir Sheet

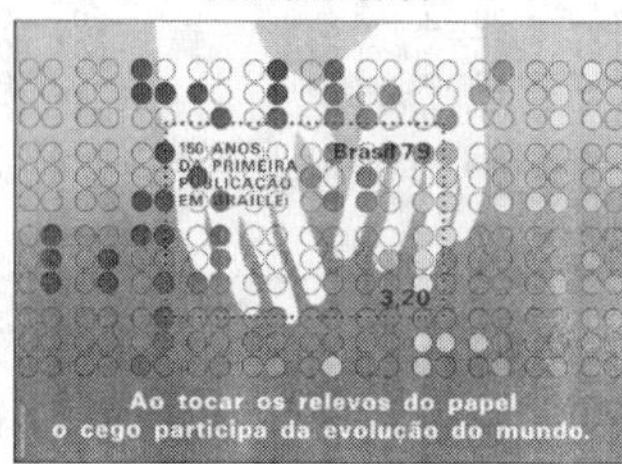

Hands Reading Braille — A891

Lithographed and Embossed

1979, Nov. 20. ***Perf. 11½***
1650 A891 3.20cr multi .50 1.25

Publication of Braille script, 150th anniversary. Margin shows extension of stamp design with Braille printed and embossed.

Wheat Harvester — A892

Steel Mill — A893

1979, Nov. 22
1651 A892 3.20cr multi .20 .20

Thanksgiving 1979.

1979, Nov. 23
1652 A893 3.20cr multi .20 .20

COSIPA Steelworks, Sao Paulo, 25th anniversary.

Type of 1976

Designs: 70c, Women grinding coconuts. 2.50cr, Basket weaver. 3.20cr, River boatman. 21cr, Harvesting ramie (China grass). 27cr, Man leading pack mule. 3.20cr, 27cr, horiz.

Photogravure, Engraved (21cr)

1979 ***Perf. 11x11½, 11½x11***
1653 A790 70c gray green .20 .20
1654 A790 2.50cr sepia .20 .20
1655 A790 3.20cr blue .20 .20
1656 A790 21cr purple .38 .20
1657 A790 27cr sepia .45 .20
Nos. 1653-1657 (5) 1.43 1.00

A894

Designs: 2cr, Coconuts. 3cr, Mangoes. 4cr, Corn. 5cr,Onions. 7cr, Oranges. 10cr, Maracuja. 12cr, Pineapple. 15cr, Bananas. 17cr, Guarana. 20cr, Sugar cane. 24cr, Beekeeping. 30cr, Silkworm. 34cr, Cacao. 38cr, Coffee. 42cr, Soybeans. 45cr, Mandioca. 50cr, Wheat. 57cr, Peanuts. 66cr, Grapes. 100cr, Cashews. 140cr, Tomatoes. 200cr, Mamona. 500cr, Cotton.

1980-83 **Photo.** ***Perf. 11½x11***
1658 A894 2cr yel brn ('82) .20 .20
1659 A894 3cr red ('82) .20 .20
1660 A894 4cr orange .20 .20
1661 A894 5cr dk pur ('82) .20 .20
1662 A894 7cr org ('81) .20 .20
1663 A894 10cr bl grn ('82) .20 .20
1664 A894 12cr dk grn ('81) .20 .20
1665 A894 15cr gldn brn ('83) .20 .20
1666 A894 17cr brn org ('82) .25 .20
1667 A894 20cr olive ('82) .25 .20
1668 A894 24cr bis ('82) .20 .20
1669 A894 30cr blk ('82) .20 .20
1670 A894 34cr brown .35 .20
1671 A894 38cr red ('83) .20 .20
1672 A894 42cr green 5.75 .50
1673 A894 45cr sepia ('83) .55 .20
1674 A894 50cr yel org ('82) .20 .20
1675 A894 57cr brn ('83) .20 .20
1676 A894 66cr pur ('81) 3.75 .20
1677 A894 100cr dk red brn ('81) 2.25 .20
1678 A894 140cr red ('82) 2.75 .20

Engr.

1678A A894 200cr grn ('82) 2.75 .20
1679 A894 500cr brn ('82) 5.75 .20
Nos. 1658-1679 (23) 27.00 4.90

See Nos. 1934-1941.

Plant Inside Raindrop — A896

Light Bulb Containing: 17cr+7cr, Sun. 20cr+8cr, Windmill. 21cr+9cr, Dam.

1980, Jan. 2 **Litho.** ***Perf. 12***
1680 A896 3.20cr multi .20 .20
1681 A896 24cr (17 + 7) 1.25 .65
1682 A896 28cr (20 + 8) 1.50 .75
1683 A896 30cr (21 + 9) 2.25 .85
Nos. 1680-1683 (4) 5.20 2.45

Anthracite Industry A897

1980, Mar. 19 **Litho.** ***Perf. 11½***
1684 A897 4cr multi .20 .20

Map of Americas, Symbols of Development — A898

1980, Apr. 14 **Litho.** ***Perf. 11x11½***
1685 A898 4cr multi .20 .20

21st Assembly of Inter-American Development Bank Governors, Rio, Apr. 14-16.

Tapirape Mask, Mato Grosso A899

1980, Apr. 18 ***Perf. 11½***
1686 A899 4cr shown .20 .20
1687 A899 4cr Tukuna mask, Amazonas, vert. .20 .20
1688 A899 4cr Kanela mask, Maranhao, vert. .20 .20
Nos. 1686-1688 (3) .60 .60

Brazilian Television, 30th Anniversary A900

1980, May 5 **Litho.** ***Perf. 11½***
1689 A900 4cr multicolored .20 .20

Duke of Caxias, by Miranda — A901

The Worker, by Candido Partinari — A902

1980, May 7
1690 A901 4cr multicolored .20 .20

Duke of Caxias, death centenary.

1980, May 18

Paintings: 28cr, Mademoiselle Pogany, by Constantin Brancusi. 30cr, The Glass of Water, by Francisco Aurelio de Figueiredo.

1691 A902 24cr multi 1.10 .55
1692 A902 28cr multi 1.10 .55
1693 A902 30cr multi 1.65 .55
Nos. 1691-1693 (3) 3.85 1.65

Graf Zeppelin, 50th Anniversary of Atlantic Crossing A903

1980, June **Litho.** ***Perf. 11x11½***
1694 A903 4cr multicolored .20 .20

Pope John Paul II, St. Peter's, Rome, Congress Emblem A904

Pope, Emblem and Brazilian Churches: No. 1696, Fortaleza, vert. 24cr, Apericida 28cr, Rio de Janeiro. 30cr, Brasilia.

1980, June 24 ***Perf. 12***
1695 A904 4cr multi .20 .20
1696 A904 4cr multi .20 .20
1697 A904 24cr multi .90 .40
1698 A904 28cr multi .90 .40
1699 A904 30cr multi 1.75 .40
Nos. 1695-1699 (5) 3.95 1.60

Visit of Pope John Paul II to Brazil, June 30-July 12; 10th National Eucharistic Congress, Fortaleza, July 9-16.

1st Airmail Flight across the South Atlantic, 50th Anniv. A905

1980, June **Litho.** ***Perf. 11x11½***
1700 A905 4cr multicolored .20 .20

Souvenir Sheet

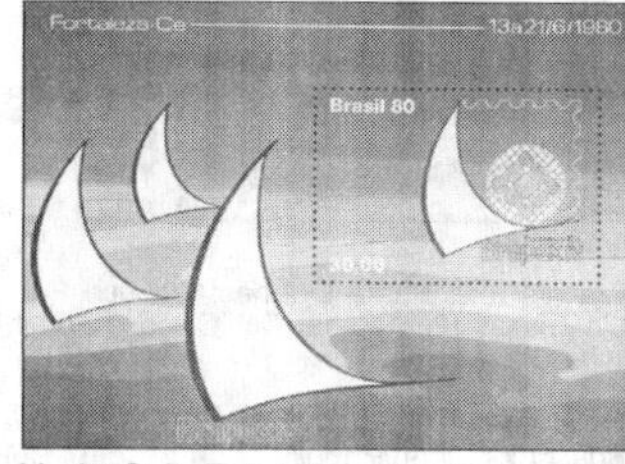

Yacht Sail, Exhibition Emblem — A906

1980, June ***Perf. 11½***
1701 A906 30cr multi 1.00 1.50

Brapex IV Stamp Exhib., Fortaleza, June 13-21.

Rowing, Moscow '80 Emblem A907

1980, June 30
1702 A907 4cr shown .20 .20
1703 A907 4cr Target shooting .20 .20
1704 A907 4cr Bicycling .20 .20
Nos. 1702-1704 (3) .60 .60

22nd Summer Olympic Games, Moscow, July 19-Aug. 3.

Rondon Community Works Project A908

1980, July 11
1705 A908 4cr multicolored .20 .20

Helen Keller and Anne Sullivan A909

1980, July 28
1706 A909 4cr multicolored .20 .20

Helen Keller (1880-1968), blind deaf writer and lecturer taught by Anne Sullivan (1867-1936).

Souvenir Sheet

Sáo Francisco River Canoe — A910

1980, Aug. 1 **Litho.** ***Perf. 11½***
1707 A910 24cr multi 1.00 1.50

Stamp Day.

Microscope, Red Cross, Insects, Brick and Tile Houses — A911

1980, Aug. 5 ***Perf. 11½x11***
1708 A911 4cr multi .25 .20

National Health Day.

Brazilian Postal Administration, 15th Anniversary — A912

1980, Sept. 16 Litho. ***Perf. 12***
1709 A912 5cr multi .25 .20

Souvenir Sheet

A913

1980, Sept. 29 ***Perf. 11½x12***
1710 A913 30cr multi 1.00 1.50

St. Gabriel World Union, 6th congress.

Cattleya Amethystoglossa — A914

1980, Oct. 3 ***Perf. 11½***
1711 A914 5cr *shown* .20 .20
1712 A914 5cr *Laelia cinnabarina* .20 .20
1713 A914 24cr *Zygopetalum crinitum* 1.10 .60
1714 A914 28cr *Laelia tenebrosa* 1.10 .60
Nos. 1711-1714 (4) 2.60 1.60

Espamer 80, American-European Philatelic Exhibition, Madrid, Oct. 3-12.

Amazona Braziliensis A915

Captain Rodrigo, Hero of Erico Verissimo's "O Continento" A916

Parrots: #1716, Amazona Vinacea. #1717, Touit melanonota. #1718, Amazona pretrei.

1980, Oct. 18 Litho. ***Perf. 12***
1715 A915 5cr multi .20 .20
1716 A915 5cr multi .20 .20
1717 A915 28cr multi 1.10 .60
1718 A915 28cr multi 1.10 .60
Nos. 1715-1718 (4) 2.60 1.60

Lubrapex '80 Stamp Exhib., Lisbon, Oct. 18-26.

1980, Oct. 23
1719 A916 5cr multi .25 .20

Book Day.

Flight into Egypt A917

1980, Nov. 5
1720 A917 5cr multi .25 .20

Christmas 1980.

Sound Waves and Oscillator Screen A918

1980, Nov. 7
1721 A918 5cr multi .25 .20

Telebras Research Center inauguration.

Carvalho Viaduct, Paranagua-Curitiba Railroad — A919

1980, Nov. 10
1722 A919 5cr multi .25 .20

Engineering Club centenary.

A920

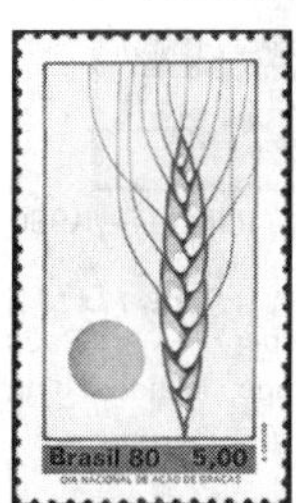

A921

1980, Nov. 18 Litho. ***Perf. 11½***
1723 A920 5cr Portable chess board .25 .50

Postal chess contest.

1980, Nov. 27 ***Perf. 11½x11***
1724 A921 5cr Sun, wheat .25 .40

Thanksgiving 1980

Father Anchieta Writing "Virgin Mary, Mother of God" on Sand of Iperoig Beach — A922

1980, Dec. 8 ***Perf. 12***
1725 A922 5cr multi .25 .20

Christ Carrying Cross, By O Aleijadinho A923

Antonio Francisco Lisboa (O Aleijadinho), 250th Birth Anniv.: Paintings of the life of Christ: a, Mount of Olives. b, Arrest in the Garden. c, Flagellation. d, Crown of Thorns. f, Crucifixion.

1980, Dec. 29
1726 Block of 6 1.60 1.60
a.-f. A923 5cr any single .25 .20

Agricultural Productivity — A924

1981, Jan. 2 Litho. ***Perf. 11x11½***
1727 A924 30cr shown 1.25 .35
1728 A924 35cr Domestic markets 1.10 .30
1729 A924 40cr Exports 1.10 .35
Nos. 1727-1729 (3) 3.45 1.00

Boy Scout and Campfire A925

1981, Jan. 22 Litho. ***Perf. 11x11½***
1730 A925 5cr shown .25 .20
1731 A925 5cr Scouts cooking .25 .20
1732 A925 5cr Scout, tents .25 .20
Nos. 1730-1732 (3) .75 .60

4th Pan-American Scout Jamboree.

Souvenir Sheet

Mailman, 1930 — A926

1981, Mar. 11 Litho. ***Perf. 11***
1733 Sheet of 3 4.00 4.00
a. A926 30cr shown 1.00 1.00
b. A926 35cr Mailman, 1981 1.00 1.00
c. A926 40cr Telegram messenger, 1930 1.00 1.00

Dept. of Posts & Telegraphs, 50th anniv.

Souvenir Sheet

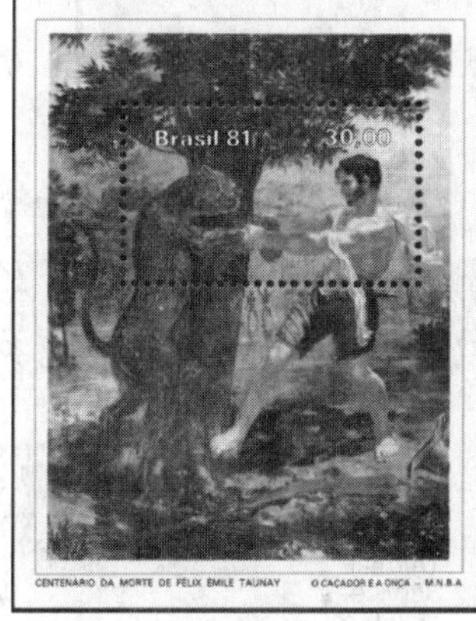

The Hunter and the Jaguar, by Felix Taunay (1795-1881) — A927

1981, Apr. 10 Litho. ***Perf. 11***
1734 A927 30cr multi 1.00 *2.00*

Lima Barreto and Rio de Janeiro, 1900 A928

1981, May 13 Litho. ***Perf. 11½***
1735 A928 7cr multi .25 .20

Lima Barreto, writer, birth centenary.

Maraca Indian Funerary Urn — A929

1981, May 18
1736 A929 7cr shown .25 .20
1737 A929 7cr Marajoara triangular jug .25 .20
1738 A929 7cr Tupi-Guarani bowl .25 .20
Nos. 1736-1738 (3) .75 .60

Lophornis Magnifica A930

Designs: Hummingbirds.

1981, May 22 ***Perf. 11½***
1739 A930 7cr shown .30 .20
1740 A930 7cr Phaethornis pretrei .30 .20
1741 A930 7cr Chrysolampis mosquitus .30 .20
1742 A930 7cr Heliactin cornuta .30 .20
Nos. 1739-1742 (4) 1.20 .80

Rotary Emblem and Faces A931

1981, May 31
1743 A931 7cr Emblem, hands .20 .20
1744 A931 35cr shown 1.00 .80

72nd Convention of Rotary Intl., Sao Paulo.

Environmental Protection — A932

1981, June 5 *Perf. 12*

1745 A932 7cr shown .25 .20
1746 A932 7cr Forest .25 .20
1747 A932 7cr Clouds (air) .25 .20
1748 A932 7cr Village (soil) .25 .20
a. Block of 4, #1745-1748 1.00 1.00

Biplane, 1931 (Airmail Service, 50th Anniv.) A933

1981, June 10 *Perf. 11½*

1749 A933 7cr multi .25 .20

Madeira-Mamore Railroad, 50th Anniv. of Nationalization — A934

1981, July 10 Litho. *Perf. 11x11½*

1750 A934 7cr multi .25 .20

66th Intl. Esperanto Congress, Brasilia A935

1981, July 26 *Perf. 12*

1751 A935 7cr green & blk .25 .20

No. 79 A936

1981, Aug. 1

1752 A936 50cr shown 1.40 .30
1753 A936 55cr No. 80 1.40 .30
1754 A936 60cr No. 81 1.40 .30
Nos. 1752-1754 (3) 4.20 .90

Stamp Day; cent. of "small head" stamps.

Institute of Military Engineering, 50th Anniv. — A937

1981, Aug. 11 Litho. *Perf. 11½*

1755 A937 12cr multi .25 .20

Reisado Dancers A938

1981, Aug. 22

1756 A938 50cr Dancers, diff. .80 .25
1757 A938 55cr Sailors .80 .25
1758 A938 60cr shown .80 .20
Nos. 1756-1758 (3) 2.40 .70

Intl. Year of the Disabled A939

1981, Sept. 17 Litho. *Perf. 11½*

1759 A939 12cr multi .25 .20

Flowers of the Central Plateau A940

1981, Sept. 21 Litho. *Perf. 12*

1760 A940 12cr Palicourea rigida .25 .20
1761 A940 12cr Dalechampia caperonioides .25 .20
1762 A940 12cr Cassia clausseni, vert. .25 .20
1763 A940 12cr Eremanthus sphaerocephalus, vert. .25 .20
Nos. 1760-1763 (4) 1.00 .80

Virgin of Nazareth Statue — A941

Christ the Redeemer Statue, Rio de Janeiro, 50th Anniv. — A942

1981, Oct. 10 Litho. *Perf. 12*

1764 A941 12cr multi .25 .20

Candle Festival of Nazareth, Belem.

1981, Oct. 12

1765 A942 12cr multi .25 .20

World Food Day A943

1981, Oct. 16

1766 A943 12c multi .25 .20

75th Anniv. of Santos-Dumont's First Flight — A944

1981, Oct. 23 Litho. *Perf. 12*

1767 A944 60cr multi 1.00 .35

Father José de Santa Rita Durao, Titlepage of his Epic Poem Caramuru, Diego Alvares Correia (Character) — A945

1981, Oct. 29

1768 A945 12cr multi .25 .20

Caramuru publication cent.; World Book Day.

Christmas 1981 A946

Designs: Creches and figurines.

1981, Nov. 10 Litho. *Perf. 12*

1769 A946 12cr multi .20 .20
1770 A946 50cr multi 1.25 .25
1771 A946 55cr multi, vert. 1.25 .25
1772 A946 60cr multi, vert. 1.25 .30
Nos. 1769-1772 (4) 3.95 1.00

State Flags A947

Designs: a, Alagoas. b, Bahia. c, Federal District. d, Pernambuco. e, Sergipe.

1981, Nov. 19

1773 Block of 5 + label 1.25 1.25
a.-e. A947 12cr, any single .20 .20

Label shows arms of Brazil.

See #1830, 1892, 1962, 2037, 2249, 2726-2727.

Thanksgiving 1981 — A948

1981, Nov. 26 Litho. *Perf. 11½*

1776 A948 12cr multi .25 .20

Ministry of Labor, 50th Anniv. A949

1981, Nov. 26

1777 A949 12cr multi .20 .20

School of Engineering, Itajuba — A950

1981, Nov. 30 *Perf. 11x11½*

1778 A950 15cr lt grn & pur .35 .20

Theodomiro C. Santiago, founder, birth centenary.

Sao Paulo State Police Sesquicentennial A951

1981, Dec. 15 Litho. *Perf. 12*

1779 A951 12cr Policeman with saxophone .20 .20
1780 A951 12cr Mounted policemen .20 .20

Army Library Centenary A952

1981, Dec. 17

1781 A952 12cr multi .20 .20

Souvenir Sheet

A953

1981, Dec. 18 *Perf. 11*

1782 A953 180cr multi 4.50 *4.50*

Philatelic Club of Brazil, 50th anniv.

Brigadier Eduardo Gomes A954

1982, Jan. 20 Litho. *Perf. 11x11½*

1783 A954 12cr blue & blk .30 .20

Birth Centenary of Henrique Lage, Industrialist — A956

1982, Mar. 14 Litho. *Perf. 11½*

1785 A956 17cr multi .50 .20

1982 World Cup Soccer A957

TB Bacillus Cent. — A958

Designs: Various soccer players.

1982, Mar. 19

1786 A957 75cr multi .75 .25
1787 A957 80cr multi .75 .30
1788 A957 85cr multi .75 .30
Nos. 1786-1788 (3) 2.25 .85

Souvenir Sheet

Imperf

1789 Sheet of 3 3.00 *6.00*
a. A957 100cr like #1786 1.00
b. A957 100cr like #1787 1.00
c. A957 100cr like #1788 1.00

1982, Mar. 24 ***Perf. 12***

1790 A958 90cr Microscope, lung 1.25 .80
1791 A958 100cr Lung, pills 1.25 .90
a. Pair, #1790-1791 2.50 2.00

Souvenir Sheet

A959

1982, Apr. 17 Litho. ***Perf. 11***

1792 A959 Sheet of 3 3.50 3.25
a. 75cr Laelia Purpurata 1.00 .50
b. 80cr Oncidium flexuosum 1.00 .50
c. 85cr Cleistes revoluta 1.25 .55

BRAPEX V Stamp Exhibition, Blumenau.

Oil Drilling Centenary A960

1982, Apr. 18 ***Perf. 11½***

1793 A960 17cr multi .25 .20

400th Birth Anniv. of St. Vincent de Paul A961

1982, Apr. 24 Litho. ***Perf. 11½***

1794 A961 17cr multi .25 .20

Seven Steps of Guaira (Waterfalls) A962

1982, Apr. 29

1795 A962 17cr Fifth Fall .20 .20
1796 A962 21cr Seventh Fall .30 .20

Ministry of Communications, 15th Anniv. — A963

1982, May 15

1797 A963 21cr multi .25 .20

Museology Course, Natl. Historical Museum, 50th Anniv. A964

1982, May 18

1798 A964 17cr blk & sal pink .20 .20

Vale de Rio Doce Mining Co. — A965

1982, June 1

1799 A965 17cr Gears .25 .20

Martin Afonso de Souza Reading Charter to Settlers A966

1982, June 3 Litho. ***Perf. 11½***

1800 A966 17cr multi .25 .20

Town of Sao Vincente, 450th anniv.

Armadillo A967

1982, June 4

1801 A967 17cr shown .55 .20
1802 A967 21cr Wolves .55 .20
1803 A967 30cr Deer 1.65 .25
Nos. 1801-1803 (3) 2.75 .65

Film Strip and Award A968

1982, June 19

1804 A968 17cr multi .25 .20

20th anniv. of Golden Palm award for The Promise Keeper, Cannes Film Festival.

Souvenir Sheet

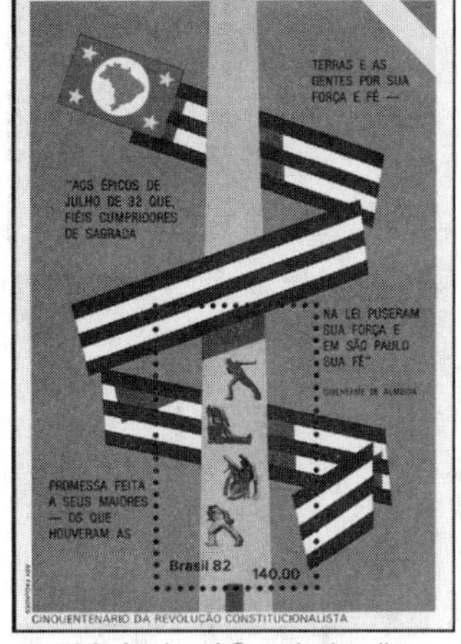

50th Anniv. of Constitutionalist Revolution — A969

1982, July 9 Litho. ***Perf. 11***

1805 A969 140cr multi 1.75 1.75

Church of Our Lady of O'Sabara — A970

St. Francis of Assisi, 800th Birth Anniv. — A971

Baroque Architecture, Minas Gerais State: No. 1807, Church of Our Lady of the Rosary, Diamantina. No. 1808, Town Square, Mariana.

1982, July 16 ***Perf. 11½***

1806 A970 17cr multi .25 .20
1807 A970 17cr multi, horiz. .25 .20
1808 A970 17cr multi, horiz. .25 .20
Nos. 1806-1808 (3) .75 .60

1982, July 24

1809 A971 21cr multi .20 .20

Stamp Day and Centenary of Pedro II "Large Head" Stamps A972

1982, Aug. 1

1810 A972 21cr No. 82 .25 .20

Port of Manaus Free Trade Zone A973

1982, Aug. 15 ***Perf. 11x11½***

1811 A973 75cr multi .65 .35

Scouting Year — A974

1982, Aug. 21 Litho. ***Perf. 11***

1812 A974 Sheet of 2 2.75 *3.75*
a. 85cr Baden-Powell 1.00 *1.10*
b. 185cr Scout 1.65 *2.00*

Orixas Folk Costumes of African Origin A975

1982, Aug. 21 ***Perf. 11½***

1813 A975 20cr Iemanja .20 .20
1814 A975 20cr Xango .20 .20
1815 A975 20cr Oxumare .20 .20
Nos. 1813-1815 (3) .60 .60

10th Anniv. of Central Bank of Brazil Currency Museum A976

1982, Aug. 31

1816 A976 25cr 12-florin coin, 1645, obverse and reverse .25 .20
1817 A976 25cr Emperor Pedro's 6.40-reis coronation coin, 1822 .25 .20

National Week A977

1982, Sept. 1

1818 A977 25cr Don Pedro proclaiming independence .38 .25

A978

A979

1982, Oct. 4

1819 A978 85cr Portrait 1.00 .60

St. Theresa of Avila (1515-1582).

1982, Oct. 15 Litho. ***Perf. 11½x11***

1820 A979 75cr Instruments .65 .40
1821 A979 80cr Dancers .65 .40
1822 A979 85cr Musicians .70 .40
a. Souv. sheet, #1820-1822, perf 11 2.75 *2.75*
Nos. 1820-1822 (3) 2.00 1.20

Lubrapex '82, 4th Portuguese-Brazilian Stamp Exhibition. Stamps in No. 1822a are without "LUBRAPEX 82."

Aviation Industry Day
A980

1982, Oct. 17 ***Perf. 12***
1823 A980 24cr Embraer EMB-312 trainer plane .25 .20

Bastos Tigre, Poet, Birth Centenary, and "Saudade" Text
A981

1982, Oct. 29
1824 A981 24cr multi .25 .20

Book Day.

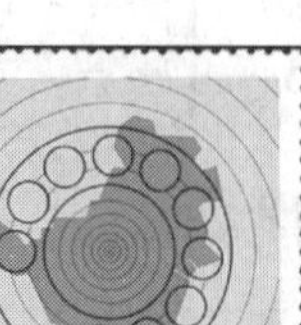
10th Anniv. of Brazilian Telecommunications Co. — A982

1982, Nov. 9 Litho. ***Perf. 11½***
1825 A982 24cr multi .25 .20

Christmas 1982
A983

Children's Drawings.

1982, Nov. 10
1826 A983 24cr Nativity .25 .20
1827 A983 24cr Angels .25 .20
1828 A983 30cr Nativity, diff. .30 .45
1829 A983 30cr Flight into Egypt .30 .45
Nos. 1826-1829 (4) 1.10 1.30

State Flags Type of 1981

Designs: a, Ceara. b, Espirito Santo. c, Paraiba. d, Grande de Norte. e, Rondonia.

1982, Nov. 19
1830 Block of 5 + label 5.25 5.25
a.-e. A947 24cr any single 1.00 .20

Thanksgiving 1982 — A985

1982, Nov. 25
1835 A985 24cr multi .25 .20

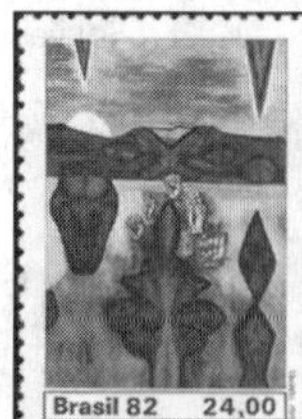
Homage to the Deaf — A986

1982, Dec. 1
1836 A986 24cr multi .25 .20

Naval Academy Bicentenary
A987

Training Ships.

1982, Dec. 14
1837 A987 24cr Brazil .35 .20
1838 A987 24cr Benjamin Constant .35 .20
1839 A987 24cr Almirante Saldanha .35 .20
Nos. 1837-1839 (3) 1.05 .60

Souvenir Sheet

No. 12 — A988

1982, Dec. 18 Litho. ***Perf. 11***
1840 A988 200cr multi 4.00 *5.00*

BRASILIANA '83 Intl. Stamp Exhibition, Rio de Janeiro, July 29-Aug. 7.

Brasiliana '83 Carnival
A989

1983, Feb. 9 Litho. ***Perf. 11½***
1841 A989 24cr Samba drummers .20 .20
1842 A989 130cr Street parade 1.40 .50
1843 A989 140cr Dancer 1.40 .50
1844 A989 150cr Male dancer 1.40 .55
Nos. 1841-1844 (4) 4.40 1.75

Antarctic Expedition
A990

1983, Feb. 20 Litho. ***Perf. 11½***
1845 A990 150cr Support ship Barano de Teffe 2.00 .55

50th Anniv. of Women's Rights — A991

1983, Mar. 8
1846 A991 130cr multi 1.25 .50

Itaipu Hydroelectric Power Station Opening — A992

1983, Mar. Litho. ***Perf. 12***
1847 A992 140cr multi 1.90 .40

Cancer Prevention
A993

Martin Luther (1483-1546)
A994

30cr, Microscope. 38cr, Antonio Prudente, Paulista Cancer Assoc. founder, Camargo Hospital.

1983, Apr. 18
1848 A993 30cr multi .30 .20
1849 A993 38cr multi .30 .20
a. Pair, #1848-1849 .65 .35

1983, Apr. 18
1850 A994 150cr pale grn & blk 1.25 .50

Agricultural Research
A995

1983, Apr. 26 Litho. ***Perf. 11½***
1851 A995 30cr Chestnut tree .20 .20
1852 A995 30cr Genetic research .20 .20
1853 A995 38cr Tropical soy beans .25 .20
Nos. 1851-1853 (3) .65 .60

Father Rogerio Neuhaus (1863-1934), Centenary of Ordination — A996

1983, May 3 ***Perf. 11½x11***
1854 A996 30cr multi .25 .20

30th Anniv. of Customs Cooperation Council — A997

1983, May 5 ***Perf. 11x11½***
1855 A997 30cr multi .25 .20

World Communications Year — A998

1983, May 17 Litho. ***Perf. 11½***
1856 A998 250cr multi 1.50 .45

Toucans
A999

1983, May 21
1857 A999 30cr Tucanucu .20 .20
1858 A999 185cr White-breasted 1.25 .40
1859 A999 205cr Green-beaked 1.25 .40
1860 A999 215cr Black-beaked 1.25 .45
Nos. 1857-1860 (4) 3.95 1.45

Souvenir Sheet

Resurrection, by Raphael (1483-1517) — A1000

1983, May 25 ***Perf. 11***
1861 A1000 250cr multi 2.50 *3.00*

Hohenzollern 980 Locomotive, 1875 — A1001

Various locomotives.

1983, June 12 Litho. *Perf. 11½*

1862 A1001 30cr shown .25 .20
1863 A1001 30cr Baldwin #1, 1881 .25 .20
1864 A1001 38cr Fowler #1, 1872 .30 .20
Nos. 1862-1864 (3) .80 .60

9th Women's Basketball World Championship A1002

1983, July 24 Litho. *Perf. 11½x11*

1865 A1002 30cr Players, front view .20 .20
1866 A1002 30cr Players, rear view .20 .20

Simon Bolivar (1783-1830) — A1003

1983, July 24 *Perf. 12*

1867 A1003 30cr multi .20 .20

Children's Polio and Measles Vaccination Campaign — A1004

1983, July 25

1868 A1004 30cr Girl, measles .20 .20
1869 A1004 30cr Boy, polio .20 .20

A1005 A1006

1983, July 28 *Perf. 11½x11*

1870 A1005 30cr Minerva (goddess of wisdom), computer tape .20 .20

20th Anniv. of Master's program in engineering.

1983, July 29 Engr.

Guanabara Bay.

1871 A1006 185cr No. 1 1.50 .40
1872 A1006 205cr No. 2 1.50 .40
1873 A1006 215cr No. 3 1.50 .45
Nos. 1871-1873 (3) 4.50 1.25

Souvenir Sheet

Perf. 11

1874 Sheet of 3 8.00 *10.00*
a. A1006 185cr No. 1 2.00 *3.00*
b. A1006 205cr No. 2 2.00 *3.00*
c. A1006 215cr No. 3 2.00 *3.00*

BRASILIANA '83 Intl. Stamp Show, Rio de Janeiro, July 29-Aug. 7.

Stamps in No. 1874 have unframed denomination at bottom of the stamps. The background scene is enlarged to cover all 3 stamps in a continuous design.

Souvenir Sheets

A set of five 2000cr souvenir sheets also exist for BRASILIANA '83. These picture early flying attempts, Ademar Ferreira da Silva, Olympic gold medal winner, Soccer, Formula 1 auto racing, and Gold medal winners in Olympic sailing.

Souvenir Sheet

The First Mass in Brazil, by Vitor Meireles (1833-1903) — A1007

1983, Aug. 18 *Perf. 11*

1875 A1007 250cr multi 3.00 1.50

EMB-120 Brasilia Passenger Plane A1008

1983, Aug. 19 *Perf. 12*

1876 A1008 30cr multi .25 .20

Vision of Don Bosco Centenary A1009

1983, Aug. 30

1877 A1009 130cr multi .75 .25

Independence Week — A1010

1983, Sept. 1 Litho. *Perf. 11½*

1878 A1010 50cr multi .25 .20

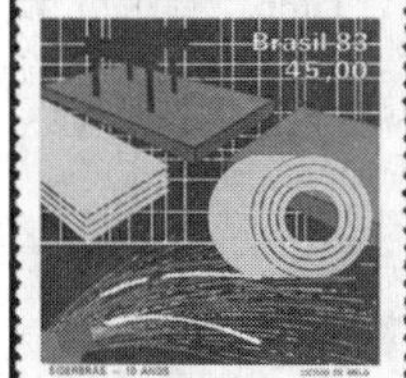

National Steel Corp., 10th Anniv. A1011

1983, Sept. 17 Litho. *Perf. 11½*

1879 A1011 45cr multi .25 .20

Cactus A1012

1983, Sept. 12 Litho. *Perf. 11½*

1880 A1012 45cr Pilosocereus gounellei .30 .20
1881 A1012 45cr Melocactus bahiensis .30 .20
1882 A1012 57cr Cereus jamacaru .40 .20
Nos. 1880-1882 (3) 1.00 .60

1st National Eucharistic Congress A1013

1983, Oct. 12 Litho. *Perf. 11½*

1883 A1013 45cr multi .25 .20

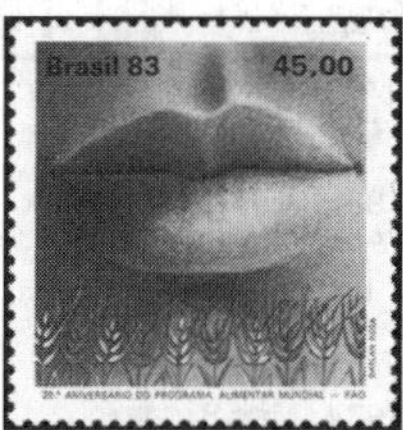

World Food Program A1014

1983, Oct. 14 Litho. *Perf. 11½*

1884 A1014 45cr Mouth, grain .30 .20
1885 A1014 57cr Fish, sailboat .40 .20

Souvenir Sheet

Louis Breguet, Death Centenary — A1015

1983, Oct. 27 Litho. *Perf. 11*

1886 A1015 376cr Telegraph transmitter 4.25 1.50

Christmas 1983 A1016

17th-18th Cent. Statues: 45cr, Our Lady of the Angels. 315cr, Our Lady of the Parturition. 335cr, Our Lady of Joy. 345cr, Our Lady of the Presentation.

1983, Nov. 10 Litho. *Perf. 11½*

1887 A1016 45cr multi .25 .20
1888 A1016 315cr multi 1.65 .60
1889 A1016 335cr multi 1.65 .65
1890 A1016 345cr multi 1.65 .70
Nos. 1887-1890 (4) 5.20 2.15

Marshal Mascarenhas Birth Centenary — A1017

1983, Nov. 13 Litho. *Perf. 11½*

1891 A1017 45cr Battle sites .20 .20

Commander of Brazilian Expeditionary Force in Italy.

State Flags Type of 1981

Designs: a, Amazonas. b, Goias. c, Rio. d, Mato Grosso Do Sol. e, Parana.

1983, Nov. 17 Litho. *Perf. 11½*

1892 Block of 5 + label 3.00 3.00
a.-e. A947 45cr any single .50 .20

Thanksgiving — A1018

1983, Nov. 24 Litho. *Perf. 12*

1896 A1018 45cr Madonna, wheat .35 .20

Manned Flight Bicentenary A1019

1983, Dec. 15 Litho. *Perf. 12*

1897 A1019 345cr Montgolfiere balloon, 1783 5.00 .50

Ethnic Groups A1020

1984, Jan. 20 Litho. *Perf. 12*

1898 A1020 45cr multi .20 .20

50th anniv. of publication of Masters and Slaves, sociological study by Gilberto Freyre.

Centenary of Crystal Palace, Petropolis A1021

1984, Feb. 2

1899 A1021 45cr multi .20 .20

Souvenir Sheet

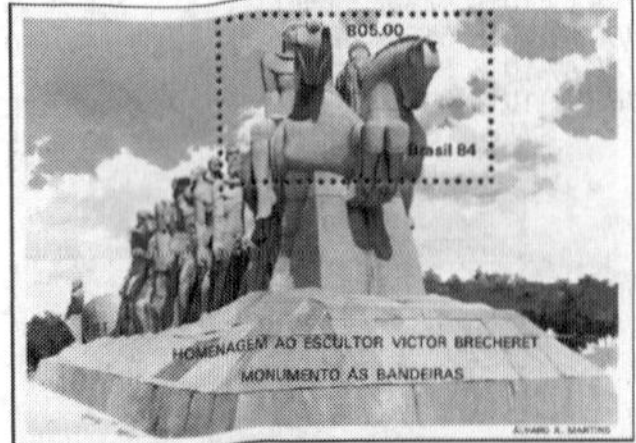

Flags (Sculpture with 40 Figures), by Victor Brecheret (b. 1894) — A1022

1984, Feb. 22 Litho. *Perf. 11*
1900 A1022 805cr multi 1.50 1.00

Naval Museum Centenary A1023

1984, Mar. 23 Litho. *Perf. 11½*
1901 A1023 620cr Figurehead, frigate, 1847 .85 .50

Slavery Abolition Centenary A1024

1984, Mar. 25
1902 A1024 585cr Broken chain, raft .85 .55
1903 A1024 610cr Freed slave .90 .60

Souvenir Sheet

Visit of King Carl XVI Gustaf of Sweden — A1025

1984, Apr. 2 *Perf. 11*
1904 A1025 2105cr multi 3.50 2.50

1984 Summer Olympics A1026

1984, Apr. 13 *Perf. 11½*
1905 A1026 65cr Long jump .20 .20
1906 A1026 65cr 100-meter race .20 .20
1907 A1026 65cr Relay race .20 .20
1908 A1026 585cr Pole vault .80 .65
1909 A1026 610cr High jump .85 .70
1910 A1026 620cr Hurdles .90 .80
a. Bklt of 6, #1905-1910 3.00 3.00

Voters Casting Ballots, Symbols of Labor A1027

Pres. Getulio Vargas Birth Centenary: Symbols of Development.

1984, Apr. 19 Litho. *Perf. 11½*
1911 A1027 65cr shown .20 .20
1912 A1027 65cr Oil rig, blast furnace .20 .20
1913 A1027 65cr High-tension towers .20 .20
Nos. 1911-1913 (3) .60 .60

Columbus, Espana '84 Emblem — A1028

1984, Apr. 27
1914 A1028 65cr Pedro Cabral .20 .20
1915 A1028 610cr shown 1.25 .70

Map of Americas, Heads — A1029

Lubrapex '84 — A1030

1984, May 7 Litho. *Perf. 11½*
1916 A1029 65cr multi .20 .20

Pan-American Association of Finance and Guarantees, 8th Assembly.

1984, May 8 *Perf. 11½x11*

18th Century Paintings, Mariana Cathedral.

1917 A1030 65cr Hunting scene .20 .20
1918 A1030 585cr Pastoral scene .75 .40
1919 A1030 610cr People under umbrellas .80 .50
1920 A1030 620cr Elephants .85 .50
Nos. 1917-1920 (4) 2.60 1.60

Souvenir Sheet

Intl. Fedn. of Soccer Associations, 80th Anniv. — A1031

1984, May 21 *Perf. 11*
1921 A1031 2115cr Globe 3.50 1.75

Matto Grosso Lowland Fauna A1032

1984, June 5 Litho. *Perf. 11½*
1922 Strip of 3 .60 .30
a. A1032 65cr Deer .20 .20
b. A1032 65cr Jaguar .20 .20
c. A1032 80cr Alligator .20 .20

First Letter Mailed in Brazil, by Guido Mondin — A1033

1984, June 8 *Perf. 12x11½*
1923 A1033 65cr multi .20 .20

Postal Union of Americas and Spain, first anniv. of new headquarters.

Brazil-Germany Air Service, 50th Anniv. — A1034

1984, June 19
1924 610cr Dornier-Wal seaplane 1.00 .70
1925 620cr Steamer Westfalen 1.05 .70
a. A1034 Pair, #1924-1925 2.05 1.50

Woolly Spider Monkey, World Wildlife Fund Emblem — A1036

1984, July 6 *Perf. 11½*
1926 A1036 65cr Mother, baby .50 .20
1927 A1036 80cr Monkey .30 .20

Agriculture Type of 1980

Designs: 65cr, Rubber tree. 80cr, Brazil nuts. 120cr, Rice. 150cr, Eucalyptus. 300cr, Pinha da Parana. 800cr, Carnauba. 1000cr, Babacu. 2000cr, Sunflower.

Photogravure (65, 80, 120, 150cr), Engraved

1984-85 *Perf. 11x11½*
1934 A894 65cr lilac .20 .20
1935 A894 80cr brn red .25 .20
1936 A894 120cr dk sl bl .35 .20
1937 A894 150cr green .20 .20
1938 A894 300cr rose mag .50 .20
1939 A894 800cr grnsh bl 1.40 .20
1940 A894 1000cr lemon 1.40 .20
1941 A894 2000cr yel org ('85) .75 .25
Nos. 1934-1941 (8) 5.05 1.65

Marajo Isld. Buffalo A1037

1984, July 9 Litho. *Perf. 12*
1942 Strip of 3 .50 .30
a. A1037 65cr Approaching stream .20 .20
b. A1037 65cr Standing on bank .20 .20
c. A1037 80cr Drinking .20 .20

Continuous design.

Banco Economico Sesquicentenary — A1038

1984, July 13 *Perf. 11½*
1943 A1038 65cr Bank, coins .20 .20

Historic Railway Stations A1039

1984, July 23 Litho. *Perf. 11½*
1944 A1039 65cr Japeri .20 .20
1945 A1039 65cr Luz, vert. .20 .20
1946 A1039 80cr Sao Joao del Rei .20 .20
Nos. 1944-1946 (3) .60 .60

A1040

A1041

1984, Aug. 13 *Perf. 11*

Souvenir Sheet

1947 A1040 585cr Girl scout 1.40 1.00

Girl Scouts in Brazil, 65th anniv.

1984, Aug. 21 Litho. *Perf. 11½*
1948 A1041 65cr Couple sheltered from rain .20 .20

Housing project bank, 20th anniv.

Independence Week — A1042

Children's Drawings.

1984, Sept. 3
1949 A1042 100cr Explorer & ship .20 .20
1950 A1042 100cr Sailing ships .20 .20
1951 A1042 100cr "BRASIL" mural .20 .20
1952 A1042 100cr Children under rainbow .20 .20
Nos. 1949-1952 (4) .80 .80

Rio de Janeiro Chamber of Commerce Sesquicentenary — A1043

1984, Sept. 10
1953 A1043 100cr Monument, worker silhouette .20 .20

Death Sesquicentenary of Don Pedro I (IV of Portugal) — A1044

1984, Sept. 23 ***Perf. 12x11½***
1954 A1044 1000cr Portrait 1.50 1.10

Local Mushrooms A1045

Book Day — A1046

1984, Oct. 22 ***Perf. 11½***
1955 A1045 120cr Pycnoporus sanguineus .20 .20
1956 A1045 1050cr Calvatia sp 1.10 1.25
1957 A1045 1080cr Pleurotus sp, horiz. 1.20 1.30
Nos. 1955-1957 (3) 2.50 2.75

1984, Oct. 23 ***Perf. 11½***
1958 A1046 120cr Girl in open book .20 .20

New State Mint Opening — A1047

1984, Nov. 1
1959 A1047 120cr multi .20 .20

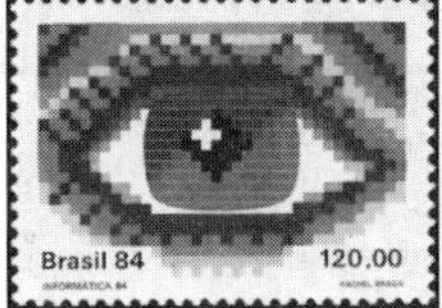

Informatics Fair & Congress A1048

1984, Nov. 5 **Litho.** ***Perf. 12***
1960 A1048 120cr Eye, computer terminal .20 .20

Org. of American States, 14th Assembly A1049

1984, Nov. 14
1961 A1049 120cr Emblem, flags .20 .20

State Flags Type of 1981

Designs: a, Maranhaio. b, Mato Grosso. c, Minas Gerais. d, Piaui. e, Santa Catarina.

1984, Nov. 19 ***Perf. 11½***
1962 Block of 5 + label 1.00 1.00
a.-e. A947 120cr, any single .20 .20

Thanksgiving 1984 — A1051

1984, Nov. 22
1963 A1051 120cr Bell tower, Brasilia .20 .20

Christmas 1984 A1052

Paintings: No. 1964, Nativity, by Djanira. No. 1965, Virgin and Child, by Glauco Rodrigues. No. 1966, Flight into Egypt, by Paul Garfunkel. No. 1967, Nativity, by Di Cavalcanti.

1984, Dec. 3 **Litho.** ***Perf. 12***
1964 A1052 120cr multi .20 .20
1965 A1052 120cr multi .20 .20
1966 A1052 1050cr multi .85 .40
1967 A1052 1080cr multi .85 .40
Nos. 1964-1967 (4) 2.10 1.20

40th Anniv., International Civil Aviation Organization — A1053

1984, Dec. 7 **Litho.** ***Perf. 12***
1968 A1053 120cr Aircraft, Earth globe .20 .20

25th Anniv., North-Eastern Development — A1054

1984, Dec. 14 **Litho.** ***Perf. 12***
1969 A1054 120cr Farmer, field .20 .20

Emilio Rouede A1055

Painting: Church of the Virgin of Safe Travels, by Rouede.

1985, Jan. 22 **Litho.** ***Perf. 12***
1970 A1055 120cr multi .20 .20

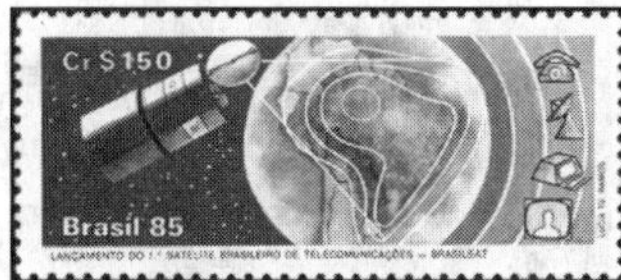

BRASILSAT — A1056

1985, Feb. 8 **Litho.** ***Perf. 11½x12***
1971 A1056 150cr Satellite, Brazil .20 .20

Metropolitan Railways — A1057

1985, Mar. 2 **Litho.** ***Perf. 11x11½***
1972 A1057 200cr Passenger trains .20 .20

Brasilia Botanical Gardens A1058

1985, Mar. 8 **Litho.** ***Perf. 11½x12***
1973 A1058 200cr Caryocar brasiliense .20 .20

40th Anniv., Brazilian Paratroops A1059

1985, Mar. 8 **Litho.** ***Perf. 11½x12***
1974 A1059 200cr Parachute drop .20 .20

Natl. Climate Awareness Program — A1060

1985, Mar. 18 **Litho.** ***Perf. 11½x12***
1975 A1060 500cr multi .20 .20

Pure Bred Horses A1061

1985, Mar. 19 **Litho.** ***Perf. 12***
1976 A1061 1000cr Campolina .40 .25
1977 A1061 1500cr Marajoara .70 .35
1978 A1061 1500cr Mangalarga marchador .70 .35
Nos. 1976-1978 (3) 1.80 .95

Ouro Preto — A1062

1985, Apr. 18 **Litho.** ***Perf. 11½x12***
1979 A1062 220cr shown .20 .20
1980 A1062 220cr St. Miguel des Missoes .20 .20
1981 A1062 220cr Olinda .20 .20
Nos. 1979-1981 (3) .60 .60

Polivolume, by Mary Vieira — A1063

1985, Apr. 20 **Litho.**
1982 A1063 220cr multi .20 .20

Rio Branco Inst., 40th anniv.

Natl. Capital, Brasilia, 25th Anniv. — A1064

1985, Apr. 22 **Litho.**
1983 A1064 220cr Natl. Theater, acoustic shell .20 .20
1984 A1064 220cr Catetinho Palace, JK Memorial .20 .20

A1065

A1065a

1985-86 **Photo.** ***Perf. 11½***
1985 A1065 50cr lake .20 .20
1986 A1065 100cr dp vio .20 .20
1987 A1065 150cr violet .20 .20
1988 A1065 200cr ultra .20 .20
1989 A1065 220cr green .20 .20
1990 A1065 300cr royal bl .20 .20
1991 A1065 500cr olive blk .30 .25
1992 A1065a 1000cr brn ol ('86) .20 .20
1993 A1065a 2000cr brt grn ('86) .30 .25
1994 A1065a 3000cr dl vio .40 .30
1995 A1065a 5000cr brown .60 .45
Nos. 1985-1995 (11) 3.00 2.65

Marshal Rondon, 120th Birth Anniv. A1066

1985, May 5 ***Perf. 11x11½***
1996 A1066 220cr multi .20 .20

Educator, protector of the Indians, building superintendent of telegraph lines.

Candido Fontoura (1885-1974) A1067

Brapex VI A1068

1985, May 14 ***Perf. 12x11½***

1997 A1067 220cr multi .20 .20

Pioneer of the Brazilian pharmaceutical industry.

1985, May 18 ***Perf. 11½x11***

Cave paintings: No. 1998, Deer, Cerca Grande. No. 1999, Lizards, Lapa do Caboclo. No. 2000, Running deer, Grande Abrigo de Santana do Riacho.

1998 A1068	300cr multi		.20	.20
1999 A1068	300cr multi		.20	.20
2000 A1068	2000cr multi		.75	.50
a.	Souvenir sheet of 3, #1998-2000, perf. 10½x11		1.00	1.00
	Nos. 1998-2000 (3)		1.15	.90

Wildlife Conservation — A1069

Birds in Marinho dos Abrolhos National Park.

1985, June 5 ***Perf. 11½x12***

2001 A1069	220cr Fregata magnificens	.20	.20
2002 A1069	220cr Sula dactylatra	.20	.20
2003 A1069	220cr Anous stolidus	.20	.20
2004 A1069	2000cr Pluvialis squatarola	.60	.25
	Nos. 2001-2004 (4)	1.20	.85

A1070

A1071

1985, June 11 ***Perf. 12x11½***

2005 A1070	220cr Mother breastfeeding infant	.20	.20
2006 A1070	220cr Hand, eyedropper, children	.20	.20
a.	Pair, #2005-2006	.25	.20

UN infant survival campaign.

1985, June 22 Litho. ***Perf. 11½x11***

Helicopter rescue, search ship, diver.

2007 A1071 220cr multi .20 .20

Sea Search & Rescue.

Souvenir Sheet

World Cup Soccer, Mexico, 1986 — A1072

1985, June 23 ***Perf. 11***

2008 A1072 2000cr Player dribbling, World Cup 4.00 .85

Intl. Youth Year — A1073

11th Natl. Eucharistic Congress A1074

1985, June 28 ***Perf. 12***

2009 A1073 220cr Circle of children .20 .20

1985, July 16 ***Perf. 12x11½***

2010 A1074 2000cr Mosaic, Priest raising host .55 .40

Director Humberto Mauro, Scene from Sangue Mineiro, 1929 — A1075

1985, July 27

2011 A1075 300cr multi .20 .20

Cataguases Studios, 60th anniv.

Escola e Sacro Museum, Convent St. Anthony, Joao Pessoa, Paraiba A1076

1985, Aug. 5 ***Perf. 11½x12***

2012 A1076 330cr multi .20 .20

Paraiba State 400th anniv.

Inconfidencia Museum A1077

Cabanagem Insurrection, 150th Anniv. — A1078

1985, Aug. 11 ***Perf. 12x11½***

2013 A1077	300cr shown	.20	.20
2014 A1077	300cr Museum of History & Diplomacy	.20	.20

1985, Aug. 14

Design: Revolutionary, detail from an oil painting by Guido Mondin.

2015 A1078 330cr multi .20 .20

AMX Subsonic Air Force Fighter Plane A1079

1985, Aug. 19 ***Perf. 11½x12***

2016 A1079 330cr multi .20 .20

AMX Project, joint program with Italy.

16th-17th Century Military Uniforms A1080

1985, Aug. 26 ***Perf. 12x11½***

2017 A1080	300cr Captain, crossbowman	.20	.20
2018 A1080	300cr Harquebusier, sergeant	.20	.20
2019 A1080	300cr Musketeer, pikeman	.20	.20
2020 A1080	300cr Fusilier, pikeman	.20	.20
	Nos. 2017-2020 (4)	.80	.80

Farrouphilha Insurrection, 150th Anniv. — A1081

Design: Bento Goncalves and insurrectionist cavalry on Southern battlefields, detail of an oil painting by Guido Mondin.

1985, Sept. 20 ***Perf. 11½x12***

2021 A1081 330cr multi .20 .20

Aparados da Serra National Park A1082

1985, Sept. 23

2022 A1082	3100cr Ravine	.65	.50
2023 A1082	3320cr Mountains	.70	.55
2024 A1082	3480cr Forest, waterfall	.75	.60
	Nos. 2022-2024 (3)	2.10	1.65

President-elect Tancredo Neves — A1083

Design: Portrait, Natl. Congress, Alvorada Palace, Federal Supreme Court.

1985, Oct. 10 Litho. ***Perf. 11x11½***

2025 A1083 330cr multi .20 .20

FEB, Postmark A1084

1985, Oct. 10 ***Perf. 11½x12***

2026 A1084 500cr multi .20 .20

Brazilian Expeditionary Force Postal Service, 41st anniv.

Rio de Janeiro-Niteroi Ferry Service, 150th Anniv. — A1085

1985, Oct. 14 ***Perf. 11½x12***

2027 A1085	500cr Segunda	.20	.20
2028 A1085	500cr Terceira	.20	.20
2029 A1085	500cr Especuladora	.20	.20
2030 A1085	500cr Urca	.20	.20
	Nos. 2027-2030 (4)	.80	.80

Muniz M-7 Inaugural Flight, 50th Anniv. — A1086

1985, Oct. 22

2031 A1086 500cr multi .20 .20

UN 40th Anniv. A1087

Natl. Press System A1088

1985, Oct. 24 ***Perf. 11½x11***

2032 A1087 500cr multi .20 .20

1985, Nov. 7

2033 A1088 500cr Newspaper masthead, reader .20 .20

Diario de Pernambuco, newspaper, 160th anniv.

Christmas 1985 A1089

1985, Nov. 11 ***Perf. 11½x12***

2034 A1089 500cr Christ in Manger .20 .20
2035 A1089 500cr Adoration of the Magi .20 .20
2036 A1089 500cr Flight to Egypt .20 .20
Nos. 2034-2036 (3) .60 .60

State Flags Type of 1981

a, Para. b, Rio Grande do Sul. c, Acre. d, Sao Paulo.

1985, Nov. 19 ***Perf. 12***

2037 Block of 4 .80 .60
a.-d. A947 500cr, any single .20 .20

Thanksgiving Day — A1091

1985, Nov. 28 ***Perf. 12x11½***

2038 A1091 500cr Child gathering wheat .20 .20

Economic Development of Serra dos Carajas Region — A1092

1985, Dec. 11 Litho. ***Perf. 11½x12***

2039 A1092 500cr multi .20 .20

Fr. Bartholomeu Lourenco de Gusmao (1685-1724), Inventor, the Aerostat — A1093

1985, Dec. 19 Litho. ***Perf. 11x11½***

2040 A1093 500cr multi .20 .20

A1094

A1095

The Trees, by Da Costa E Silva (b. 1885), poet.

1985, Dec. 20 Litho. ***Perf. 12x11½***

2041 A1094 500cr multi .20 .20

1986, Mar. 3 Litho. ***Perf. 11***

Souvenir Sheet

2042 A1095 10000cr multi 2.25 2.00

1986 World Cup Soccer Championships, Mexico. LUBRAPEX '86, philatelic exhibition.

Halley's Comet — A1096

1986, Apr. 11 Litho. ***Perf. 11½x12***

2043 A1096 50c multi .20 .20

Commander Ferraz Antarctic Station, 2nd Anniv. — A1097

1986, Apr. 25

2044 A1097 50c multi .20 .20

Labor Day — A1098

Maternity, by Henrique Bernardelli (1858-1936) A1099

1986, May 1 Litho. ***Perf. 12x11½***

2045 A1098 50c multi .20 .20

1986, May 8

2046 A1099 50c multi .20 .20

Amnesty Intl., 25th Anniv. A1100

1986, May 28 Litho. ***Perf. 11½x12***

2047 A1100 50c multi .20 .20

Butterflies A1101

1986, June 5 ***Perf. 12x11½***

2048 A1101 50c Pyrrhopyge ruficauda .20 .20
2049 A1101 50c Prepona eugenes diluta .20 .20
2050 A1101 50c Pierriballia mandel molione .20 .20
Nos. 2048-2050 (3) .60 .60

Score from Opera "Il Guarani" and Antonio Carlos Gomes (1836-1896), Composer — A1102

1986, July 11 ***Perf. 11½x12***

2051 A1102 50c multi .20 .20

Natl. Accident Prevention Campaign — A1103

1986, July 30 Litho. ***Perf. 11½x11***

2052 A1103 50c Lineman .20 .20

Souvenir Sheet

Stamp Day — A1104

1986, Aug. 1 ***Perf. 11***

2053 A1104 5cz No. 53 .85 .35

Brazilian Phil. Soc., 75th anniv., and Dom Pedro II issue, Nos. 53-60, 120th anniv.

Architecture A1105

Famous Men A1106

Designs: 10c, House of Garcia D'Avila, Nazare de Mata, Bahia. 20c, Church of Our Lady of the Assumption, Anchieta Village. 50c, Fort Reis Magos, Natal. 1cz, Pilgrim's Column, Alcantara Village, 1648. 2cz, Cloisters, St. Francis Convent, Olinda. 5cz, St. Anthony's Chapel, Sao Roque. 10cz, St. Lawrence of the Indians Church, Niteroi. 20cz, Principe da Beiro Fort, Mato Dentro. 50cz, Jesus of Matozinhos Church, vert. 100cz, Church of our Lady of Sorrow, Campanha. 200cz, Casa dos Contos, Ouro Preto. 500cz, Antiga Alfandega, Belem, Para.

Perf. 11½x11, 11x11½

1986-88 **Photo.**

2055 A1105 10c sage grn .20 .20
2057 A1105 20c brt blue .20 .20
2059 A1105 50c orange .20 .20
2064 A1105 1cz golden brn .20 .20
2065 A1105 2cz dull rose .25 .20
a. Litho., perf. 13 ('88) .20 .20
2067 A1105 5cz lt olive grn .60 .45
a. Litho., perf. 13 ('88) .20 .20
2068 A1105 10cz slate blue .50 .35
2069 A1105 20cz lt red brn .75 .60
2070 A1105 50cz brn org 2.25 1.75
2071 A1105 100cz dull grn 2.70 2.00
2072 A1105 200cz deep blue 2.50 1.85
2073 A1105 500cz dull red brn 1.30 1.00
Nos. 2055-2073 (12) 11.65 9.00

Issued: 10c, 8/11; 20c, 12/8; 50c, 8/19; 1cz, 11/19; 2cz, 11/9; 5cz, 12/30; 10cz, 6/2/87; 20cz, 50cz, 9/18/87; 100cz, 12/21/87; 200cz, 5/9/88; 500cz, 11/22/88.

This is an expanding set. Numbers will change if necessary.

1986 ***Perf. 12x11½, 11½x12***

Designs: No. 2074, Juscelino Kubitschek de Oliveira, president 1956-61, and Alvorado Palace, Brasilia. No. 2075, Octavio Mangabeira, statesman, and Itamaraty Palace, Rio de Janeiro, horiz.

2074 A1106 50c multi .20 .20
2075 A1106 50c multi .20 .20

Issued: #2074, Aug. 21; #2075, Aug. 27.

World Gastroenterology Congress, Sao Paulo — A1107

1986, Sept. 7 ***Perf. 11½x12***

2076 A1107 50c multi .20 .20

Federal Broadcasting System, 50th Anniv. — A1108

Intl. Peace Year — A1109

1986, Sept. 15 ***Perf. 12x11½***

2077 A1108 50c multi .20 .20

1986, Sept. 16

Painting (detail): War and Peace, by Candido Portinari.

2078 A1109 50c multi .20 .20

Ernesto Simoes Filho (b. 1886), Publisher of A Tarde A1110

1986, Oct. 4 Litho. *Perf. 11½x12*

2079 A1110 50c multi .20 .20

Famous Men — A1111

Federal Savings Bank, 125th Anniv. — A1112

Designs: No. 2080, Title page from manuscript, c. 1683-94, by Gregorio Mattose e Guerra (b. 1636), author. No. 2081, Manuel Bandeira (1886-1968), poet, text from I'll Go Back to Pasargada.

1986, Oct. 29 *Perf. 11½x11*

2080 A1111 50c lake & beige .20 .20
2081 A1111 50c lake & dl grn .20 .20

1986, Nov. 4 *Perf. 12x11½*

2082 A1112 50c multi .20 .20

Flowering Plants A1113

Glauber Rocha, Film Industry Pioneer A1114

Perf. 12x11½, 11½x12

1986, Sept. 23

2083 A1113 50c Urera mitis .20 .20
2084 A1113 6.50cz Couroupita guyanensis .50 .40
2085 A1113 6.90cz Bauhinia variegata, horiz. .55 .40
Nos. 2083-2085 (3) 1.25 1.00

1986, Nov. 20 *Perf. 12x11½*

2086 A1114 50c multi .20 .20

LUBRAPEX '86 — A1115

Cordel Folk Tales: No. 2087, Romance of the Mysterious Peacock. No. 2088, History of the Empress Porcina.

1986, Nov. 21 *Perf. 11x12*

2087 A1115 6.90cz multi .45 .35
2088 A1115 6.90cz multi .45 .35
a. Souvenir sheet of 2, #2087-2088, perf. 11 1.10 .85

Christmas A1116

Birds: 50c, And Christ child. 6.50cz, And tree. 7.30cz, Eating fruit.

1986, Nov. 10 *Perf. 11½x12*

2089 A1116 50c multi .20 .20
2090 A1116 6.50cz multi .65 .50
2091 A1116 7.30cz multi .75 .60
Nos. 2089-2091 (3) 1.60 1.30

Military Uniforms, c. 1930 — A1117

Bartolomeu de Gusmao Airport, 50th Anniv. — A1118

Designs: No. 2092, Navy lieutenant commander, dreadnought Minas Gerais. No. 2093, Army flight lieutenant, WACO S.C.O. biplane, Fortaleza Airport.

1986, Dec. 15 *Perf. 12x11½*

2092 A1117 50c multi .20 .20
2093 A1117 50c multi .20 .20

Fortaleza Air Base, 50th anniv. (No. 2093).

1986, Dec. 26

2094 A1118 1cz multi .20 .20

Heitor Villa Lobos (1887-1959), Conductor A1119

1987, Mar. 5 Litho. *Perf. 12x11½*

2095 A1119 1.50cz multi .20 .20

Natl. Air Force C-130 Transport Plane, Flag, the Antarctic A1120

1987, Mar. 9 *Perf. 11x11½*

2096 A1120 1cz multi .20 .20

Antarctic Project.

Special Mail Services A1121

1987, Mar. 20 *Perf. 12x11½*

2097 A1121 1cz Rural delivery .20 .20
2098 A1121 1cz Intl. express .20 .20

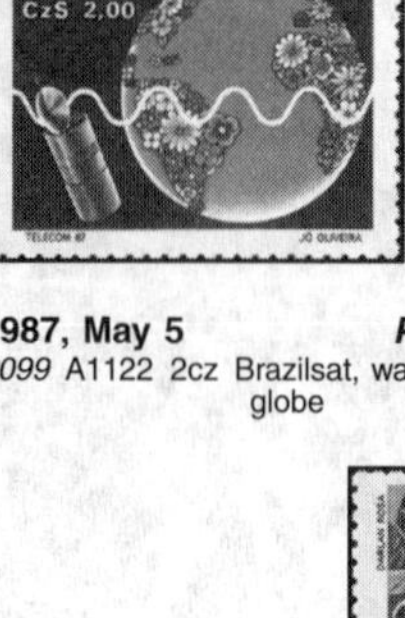

TELECOM '87, Geneva A1122

1987, May 5 *Perf. 11½x12*

2099 A1122 2cz Brazilsat, wave, globe .20 .20

10th Pan American Games, Indianapolis, Aug. 7-25 — A1123

1987, May 20 *Perf. 12x11½*

2100 A1123 18cz multi 1.00 .75

Natl. Fine Arts Museum, 150th Anniv A1124

1987, Jan. 13 *Perf. 11½x12*

2101 A1124 1cz multi .20 .20

Marine Conservation — A1125

1987, June 5

2102 A1125 2cz Eubalaena australis .20 .20
2103 A1125 2cz Eretmochelys imbricata .20 .20

Federal Court of Appeal, 40th Anniv. A1126

1987, June 15

2104 A1126 2cz multi .20 .20

Military Club, Cent. — A1127

1987, June 26 *Perf. 12x11½*

2105 A1127 3cz multi .20 .20

Agriculture Institute of Campinas, Cent. A1128

1987, June 27 *Perf. 11½x12*

2106 A1128 2cz multi .20 .20

Entomological Society, 50th Anniv. — A1129

1987, July 17

2107 A1129 3cz Zoolea lopiceps .20 .20
2108 A1129 3cz Fulgora servillei .20 .20

Natl. Tourism Year A1130

Designs: No. 2109, Monuments and Sugarloaf Mountain, Rio de Janeiro. No. 2110, Colonial church, sailboats, parrot, cashews.

1987, Aug. 4

2109 A1130 3cz multi .20 .20
2110 A1130 3cz multi .20 .20

Royal Portuguese Cabinet of Literature, 150th Anniv. — A1131

1987, Aug. 27 *Perf. 12x11½*

2111 A1131 30cz ver & brt grn 1.10 .85

Sport Club Intl. A1132

Championship soccer clubs, Brazil's Gold Cup: b, Sao Paulo. c, Guarani. d, Regatas do Flamengo.

1987, Aug. 29 *Perf. 11½x12*

2112 Block of 4 .60 .40
a.-d. A1132 3cz any single .20 .20

St. Francis Convent, 400th Anniv. A1133

1987, Oct. 4

2113 A1133 4cz multi .20 .20

Jose Americo de Almeida, Author
A1134

Design: Characters from romance novel, "A Bagaceira," 1928, and portrait of author.

1987, Oct. 23 Litho. ***Perf. 11x11½***
2114 A1134 4cz multi .20 .20

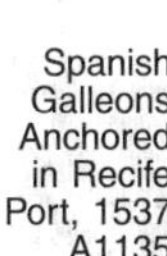

Spanish Galleons Anchored in Recife Port, 1537
A1135

1987, Nov. 12 Litho. ***Perf. 11½x12***
2115 A1135 5cz Harbor entrance .20 .20

Recife City, 450th anniv.

Thanksgiving
A1136

1987, Nov. 26 ***Perf. 12x11½***
2116 A1136 5cz multi .20 .20

Christmas 1987
A1137

1987, Nov. 30 ***Perf. 11½x12***
2117 A1137 6cz Shepherd and flock .20 .20
2118 A1137 6cz Christmas pageant .20 .20
2119 A1137 6cz Six angels .20 .20
Nos. 2117-2119 (3) .60 .60

Pedro II College, 150th Anniv. — A1138

Gold pen Emperor Pedro II used to sign edict establishing the school, and Senator Bernardo Pereira de Vasconcellos, founder.

1987, Dec. 2
2120 A1138 6cz multi .20 .20

Natl. Orchid Growers' Soc., 50th Anniv.
A1139

1987, Dec. 3
2121 A1139 6cz Laelia lobata veitch .20 .20
2122 A1139 6cz Cattleya guttata lindley .20 .20

Marian Year — A1140

Statue of Our Lady and Basilica at Fatima, Portugal.

1987, Dec. 20 ***Perf. 12x11½***
2123 A1140 50cz multi 1.10 .85

Exhibit of the Statue of Our Lady of Fatima in Brazil.

Descriptive Treatise of Brazil, by Gabriel S. de Sousa, 400th Anniv. — A1141

1987, Dec. 21 Litho. ***Perf. 11x11½***
2124 A1141 7cz multi .20 .20

Natl. Archives, 150th Anniv.
A1142

Design: Text from illuminated Gregorian canticle and computer terminal.

1988, Jan. 5 ***Perf. 11½x12***
2125 A1142 7cz multi .20 .20

Opening of Brazilian Ports to Ships of Friendly Nations, 180th Anniv.
A1143

1988, Jan. 28 ***Perf. 11x11½***
2126 A1143 7cz multi .25 .20

Souvenir Sheet

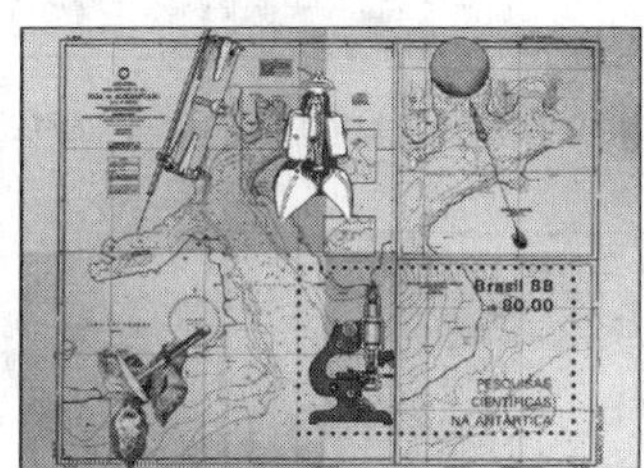

Antarctic Research — A1144

1988, Feb. 9 Litho. ***Perf. 11***
2127 A1144 80cz multi 2.00 2.00

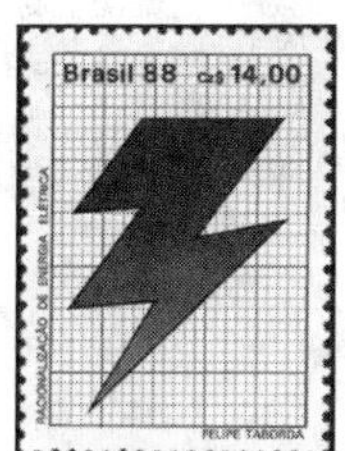

Energy Resources
A1145

1988, Mar. 15 Litho. ***Perf. 12x11½***
2128 A1145 14cz Electricity .25 .20
2129 A1145 14cz Fossil fuels .25 .20

Souvenir Sheet

Brazilians as Formula 1 World Champions in 1981, 1983, 1987 — A1146

1988, Mar. 30 ***Perf. 11***
2130 A1146 300cz multi 4.50 4.50

Jose Bonifacio, Armorial and Masonic Emblems
A1147

1988, Apr. 6 ***Perf. 12x11½***
2131 A1147 20cz multi .30 .25

Jose Bonifacio de Andrada e Silva (c. 1763-1838), geologist and prime minister under Pedro I who supported the movement for independence from Portugal and was exiled for opposing the emperor's advisors.

Abolition of Slavery, Cent. — A1148

Telecom '88 — A1149

Designs: 20cz, Declaration and quill pen. 50cz, Slave ship and maps of African coastline and slave trade route between Africa and South America.

1988, May 12 Litho. ***Perf. 12x11½***
2132 A1148 20cz multi .25 .20
2133 A1148 50cz multi .65 .50

1988, May 16 ***Perf. 11½x11***
2134 A1149 50cz multi .60 .45

Jesus of Matosinhos Sanctuary
A1150

1988, May 16 ***Perf. 11½x12***
2135 A1150 20cz shown .25 .20
2136 A1150 50cz Pilot plan of Brazilia .60 .45
2137 A1150 100cz Salvador historic district 1.20 .90
Nos. 2135-2137 (3) 2.05 1.55

LUBRAPEX '88. World heritage list.

Japanese Immigrants in Brazil, 80th Anniv. — A1151

1988, June 18 Litho. ***Perf. 11½x11***
2138 A1151 100cz multi .75 .55

A1152

A1153

1988, July 1 Photo. ***Perf. 13***
2139 A1152 (A) brt blue .25 .20

No. 2139 met the first class domestic letter postage rate (28cz).

See Nos. 2201, 2218.

1988, July 14 Litho. ***Perf. 12x11½***
2140 A1153 20cz Judo .25 .20

1988 Summer Olympics, Seoul.

Wildlife Conservation — A1154

1988, July 24 ***Perf. 11½x12***
2141 A1154 20cz Myrmecophaga tridactyla .20 .20
2142 A1154 50cz Chaetomys subspinosus .30 .25
2143 A1154 100cz Speothos venaticus .65 .50
Nos. 2141-2143 (3) 1.15 .95

Souvenir Sheet

The Motherland, 1919 by Pedro Bruno — A1155

1988, Aug. 1 Litho. ***Perf. 11***
2144 A1155 250cz multi 1.50 1.50

Stamp Day, BRASILIANA '89.

Natl. Confederation of Industries, 50th Anniv. — A1156

1988, Aug. 12 ***Perf. 11½x12***
2145 A1156 50cz multi .25 .20

Soccer Clubs A1157

No. 2146, Recife, Pernambuco. No. 2147, Coritiba, Parana. 100cz, Gremio, Porto Alegre, Rio Grando do Sul. 200cz, Fluminense, Rio de Janeiro.

1988, Sept. 29 ***Perf. 11½x12***

2146	A1157	50cz multi	.20	.20
2147	A1157	50cz multi	.20	.20
2148	A1157	100cz multi	.30	.25
2149	A1157	200cz multi	.60	.50
a.		Block of 4, #2146-2149	1.25	.95

Poems, 1888 A1158

Portraits and text: 50cz, *O Ateneu*, by Raul Pompeia. 100cz, *Poesias*, by Olavo Bilac.

1988, Oct. 28 ***Perf. 11x11½***

2150	A1158	50cz multi	.20	.20
2151	A1158	100cz multi	.25	.20

Souvenir Sheet

1988 Democratic Constitution for the Union of the People and the State — A1159

1988, Oct. 5 **Litho.** ***Perf. 11***

2152	A1159	550cz Government building	2.40	2.40

Origami Art A1160

1988, Nov. 11 **Litho.** ***Perf. 11½x12***

2153	A1160	50cz Abbey, nuns	.20	.20
2154	A1160	100cz Nativity	.25	.20
2155	A1160	200cz Santa Claus, presents	.50	.40
		Nos. 2153-2155 (3)	.95	.80

Christmas.

ARBRAFEX Philatelic Exhibition of Argentina and Brazil — A1161

1988, Nov. 26

2156	A1161	400cz multi	.85	.65

Fresh-water Fish — A1162

Designs: a, *Gasteropelecus*. b, *Osteoglossum ferreirai*. c, *Moenkhausia*. d, *Xavantei*. e, *Ancistrus hoplogenys*. f, *Brochis splendens*. Se-tenant in a continuous design. Illustration reduced.

1988, Nov. 29 **Litho.** ***Perf. 11½x12***

2157	Block of 6	.90	.70
a.-f.	A1162 55cz any single	.20	.20

Souvenir Sheet

BRAPEX '88, Ecological Preservation — A1163

1988, Dec. 10 ***Perf. 11***

2158	Sheet of 3	1.80	1.80
a.	A1163 100cz Parrot	.25	.25
b.	A1163 250cz Plant	.60	.60
c.	A1163 400cz Egret	.95	.95

Satellite Dishes — A1164

Performing Arts — A1165

1988, Dec. 20 ***Perf. 12x11½***

2159	A1164	70cz multi	.20	.20

Ansat 10-Earth satellite station communication.

1988, Dec. 21

2160	A1165	70cz multi	.20	.20

Court of Justice, Bahia, 380th Anniv. A1166

1989, Mar. 10 **Litho.** ***Perf. 11½x12***

2161	A1166	25c multi	.40	.30

Public Library Year A1167

1989, Mar. 13 ***Perf. 11½***

2162	A1167	25c Library, Bahia, 1811	.40	.30

Brazilian Post & Telegraph Enterprise, 20th Anniv. A1168

Intl. and domestic postal services: a, Facsimile transmission (Post-Grama). b, Express mail (EMS). c, Parcel post (Sedex). d, Postal savings (CEFPostal).

1989, Mar. 20 ***Perf. 11½x12***

2163	Block of 4	1.65	1.25
a.-d.	A1168 25c any single	.40	.30

Souvenir Sheet

Ayrton Senna, 1988 Formula 1 World Champion — A1169

1989, Mar. 23

2164	A1169	2cz multi	4.00	4.00

Environmental Conservation A1170

1989, Apr. 6 **Litho.** ***Perf. 12x11½***

2165	A1170	25c multi	.35	.25

Mineira Inconfidencia Independence Movement, Bicent. — A1171

Designs: a, Pyramid, hand. b, Figure of a man, houses. c, Destruction of houses.

1989, Apr. 21 ***Perf. 11½x12***

2166	Strip of 3	1.30	.95
a.-b.	A1171 30c any single	.40	.30
c.	A1171 40c multi	.50	.40

First rebellion against Portuguese dominion.

Military School, Rio de Janeiro, Cent. A1172

1989, May 6 **Litho.** ***Perf. 11½x12***

2167	A1172	50c multi	.50	.40

Flowering Plants A1173

1989, June 5 ***Perf. 11½x12, 12x11½***

2168	A1173	50c *Pavonia alnifolia*	.60	.45
2169	A1173	1cz *Worsleya rayneri*	1.25	.90
2170	A1173	1.50cz *Heliconia farinosa*	1.75	1.40
		Nos. 2168-2170 (3)	3.60	2.75

Nos. 2169-2170 vert.

Barreto and Recife Law School, Pedro II Square A1174

1989, June 7 ***Perf. 11x11½***

2171	A1174	50c multi	.65	.50

Tobias Barreto (b. 1839), advocate of Germanization of Brazil.

Cultura Broadcasting System, 20th Anniv. — A1175

1989, June 27 **Litho.** ***Perf. 11½x12***

2172	A1175	50c multi	.60	.45

Aviation A1176

1989, July 7

2173	A1176	50c Ultra-light aircraft	.50	.40
2174	A1176	1.50cz Eiffel Tower, *Demoiselle*	1.65	1.10

Flight of Santos-Dumont's *Demoiselle*, 80th anniv (1.50cz).

Indigenous Flora — A1177

1989 **Photo.** ***Perf. 11x11½, 11½x11***

2176	A1177	10c *Dichorisandra, vert.*	.20	.20
2177	A1177	20c *Quiabentia zehnteri*	.25	.20
2178	A1177	50c *Bougainvillea glabra*	.50	.40
2179	A1177	1cz *Impatiens specie*	1.00	.80
2180	A1177	2cz *Chorisia crispiflora*	.25	.20
2181	A1177	5cz *Hibiscus trilineatus*	.60	.45
		Nos. 2176-2181 (6)	2.80	2.25

Issued: 10c, July 4; 20c, June 21; 50c, June 26; 1cz, June 19; 2cz, 5cz, Dec. 4.

No. 2181 vert.

See Nos. 2259-2273.

Souvenir Sheet

Largo da Carioca, by Nicolas Antoine Taunay — A1179

1989, July 7 **Litho.** ***Perf. 11***

2197	A1179	3cz multi	3.00	3.00

PHILEXFRANCE '89, French revolution bicent.

Cut and Uncut Gemstones
A1180

1989, July 12 Litho. *Perf. 12x11½*

2198 A1180 50c Tourmaline .40 .30
2199 A1180 1.50cz Amethyst 1.20 .90

Souvenir Sheet

Paco Imperial, Rio de Janeiro, and Map — A1181

1989, July 28 *Perf. 11*

2200 A1181 5cz multi 3.75 3.75

BRASILANA '89.

Type of 1988 Redrawn

1989, July 26 Photo. *Perf. 13*

Size: 17x21mm

2201 A1152 (A) org & brt blue .20 .20

Size of type and postal emblem are smaller on No. 2201; "1e PORTE" is at lower left.

No. 2201 met the first class domestic letter postage rate (cz).

Pernambuco Commercial Assoc., 150th Anniv. — A1182

1989, Aug. 1 Litho. *Perf. 11½x12*

2202 A1182 50c multi .40 .30

Photography, 150th Anniv. — A1183

1989, Aug. 14

2203 A1183 1.50cz multi 1.10 .85

1st Hydroelecric Power Station in South America, Marmelos-o, Cent. — A1184

1989, Sept. 5 Litho. *Perf. 11½x12*

2204 A1184 50c multi .35 .25

Conchs Endemic to the Brazilian Coast
A1185

1989, Sept. 8

2205 A1185 50c *Voluta ebraea* 30 .25
2206 A1185 1cz *Morum matthewsi* .60 .45
2207 A1185 1.50cz *Agaronia travassosi* .90 .65
Nos. 2205-2207 (3) 1.80 1.35

Wildlife conservation.

America Issue
A1186

UPAE emblem and pre-Columbian stone carvings: 1cz, Muiraquita ritual statue, vert. 4cz, Ceramic brazier under three-footed votive urn.

Perf. 12x11½, 11½x12

1989, Oct. 12 Litho.

2208 A1186 1cz multicolored .50 .35
2209 A1186 4cz shown 1.85 1.40

Discovery of America 500th anniv. (in 1992).

A1187

Hologram and: a. *Lemons,* by Danilo di Prete. b. *O Indio E A Suacuapara,* by sculptor Victor Brecheret. c. Francisco Matarazzo.

1989, Oct. 14 *Perf. 11*

Souvenir Sheet

2210 A1187 Sheet of 3 3.75 3.75
a. 2cz multicolored .70 .70
b. 3cz multicolored 1.10 1.10
c. 5cz multicolored 1.75 1.75

Sao Paulo 20th intl. art biennial.

A1188

1989, Oct. 26 *Perf. 11½x11*

Writers, residences and quotes: No. 2211, Casimiro de Abreu (b. 1839). No. 2212, Cora Coralina (b. 1889). No. 2213, Joaquim Machado de Assis (b. 1839).

2211 A1188 1cz shown .55 .40
2212 A1188 1cz multicolored .55 .40
2213 A1188 1cz multicolored .55 .40
Nos. 2211-2213 (3) 1.65 1.20

Federal Police Department, 25th Anniv. — A1189

1989, Nov. 9 *Perf. 11½x12*

2214 A1189 1cz multicolored .25 .20

Christmas
A1190

Thanksgiving Day — A1191

1989, Nov. 10 *Perf. 12x11½*

2215 A1190 70c Heralding angel .20 .20
2216 A1190 1cz Holy family .25 .20

1989, Nov. 23

2217 A1191 1cz multicolored .25 .20

Type of 1988 Redrawn

1989, Nov. 6 Photo. *Perf. 13x13½*

Size: 22x26mm

2218 A1152 (B) org & dark red 2.00 1.50

Size of type and postal emblem are smaller on No. 2218; "1e PORTE" is at lower left.

No. 2218 met the first class intl. letter postage rate, initially at 9cz.

Souvenir Sheet

Proclamation of the Republic, Cent. — A1192

1989, Nov. 19 Litho. *Perf. 11*

2225 A1192 15cz multicolored 4.50 4.50

Bahia Sports Club, 58th Anniv.
A1193

1989, Nov. 30 *Perf. 11½x12*

2226 A1193 50c Soccer .20 .20

Yellow Man, by Anita Malfatti (b. 1889)
A1194

1989, Dec. 2 *Perf. 12x11½*

2227 A1194 1cz multicolored .25 .20

Bahia State Public Archives, Cent. — A1195

1990, Jan. 16 Litho. *Perf. 11½x12*

2228 A1195 2cz multicolored .30 .20

Brazilian Botanical Soc., 40th Anniv.
A1196

1990, Jan. 21

2229 A1196 2cz Sabia, Caatinga .25 .20
2230 A1196 13cz Pau, Brazil 1.40 1.10

Churches
A1197

Designs: 2cz, St. John the Baptist Cathedral, Santa Cruz do Sul, vert. 3cz, Our Lady of Victory Church, Oeiras. 5cz, Our Lady of the Rosary Church, Ouro Preto, vert.

1990, Feb. 5 *Perf. 12x11½, 11½x12*

2231 A1197 2cz multicolored .20 .20
2232 A1197 3cz multicolored .25 .20
2233 A1197 5cz multicolored .40 .30
Nos. 2231-2233 (3) .85 .70

Lloyd's of London in Brazil, Cent.
A1198

1990, Feb. 19 Litho. *Perf. 11½x12*

2234 A1198 3cz multicolored .20 .20

Souvenir Sheet

Antarctic Research Program — A1199

1990, Feb. 22 Litho. *Perf. 11*

2235 A1199 20cz Fauna, map 1.55 1.55

Vasco da Gama Soccer Club A1200

1990, Mar. 5

2236 A1200 10cz multicolored .50 .40

Lindolfo Collor (b. 1890), Syndicated Columnist, and Labor Monument A1201

1990, Mar. 7

2237 A1201 20cz multicolored .95 .70

A1202

A1203

Pres. Jose Sarney.

1990, Mar. 8 ***Perf. 12x11½***

2238 A1202 20cz chalky blue .95 .70

1990, Apr. 6 ***Perf. 12x11½***

2239 A1203 20cz multicolored .70 .50

AIDS prevention.

Souvenir Sheet

Penny Black, 150th Anniv. — A1204

Designs: 20cr, Dom Pedro, Brazil No. 1. 100cr, Queen Victoria, Great Britain No. 1.

1990, May 3 Litho. ***Perf. 11***

2240 A1204 Sheet of 2 2.35 1.75
a. 20cr multicolored
b. 100cr multicolored

Central Bank, 25th Anniv. A1205

1990, Mar. 30 Litho. ***Perf. 11½x12***

2241 A1205 20cr multicolored .70 .50

Amazon River Postal Network, 21st Anniv. A1207

1990, Apr. 20 ***Perf. 11x11½***

2243 A1207 20cr multicolored .70 .50

Souvenir Sheet

World Cup Soccer Championships, Italy — A1208

1990, May 12 Litho. ***Perf. 12x11½***

2244 A1208 120cr multicolored 3.00 3.00

22nd Congress of the Intl. Union of Highway Transportation — A1209

1990, May 14 ***Perf. 11½x12***

2245 A1209 20cr multicolored .65 .50
2246 A1209 80cr multicolored 3.00 2.25
a. Pair, #2245-2246 3.75 2.75

No. 2246a has a continuous design.

Imperial Crown, 18th Cent. — A1210

Designs: No. 2248, Our Lady of Immaculate Conception, 18th cent.

1990, May 18 ***Perf. 12x11½***

2247 A1210 20cr shown .70 .50
2248 A1210 20cr multicolored .70 .50

Imperial Museum, 50th anniv.(No. 2247). Mission Museum, 50th anniv. (No. 2248).

State Flags Type of 1981

1990, May 20 ***Perf. 11½x12***

2249 A947 20cr Tocantins .70 .50

Army Geographical Service, Cent. — A1212

1990, May 30 ***Perf. 11x11½***

2250 A1212 20cr multicolored .70 .50

Film Personalities — A1213

1990, June 19 ***Perf. 11½x12***

2251 A1213 25cr Adhemar Gonzaga .80 .60
2252 A1213 25cr Carmen Miranda .80 .60
2253 A1213 25cr Carmen Santos .80 .60
2254 A1213 25cr Oscarito .80 .60
a. Block of 4, #2251-2254 3.20 2.40

France-Brazil House, Rio de Janeiro — A1214

1990, July 14 Litho. ***Perf. 11½x11***

2255 A1214 50cr multicolored 1.50 1.10

See France No. 2226.

World Men's Volleyball Chmpships. A1215

Intl. Literacy Year A1217

CBA 123 A1216

1990, July 28 Litho. ***Perf. 12x11½***

2256 A1215 10cr multicolored .30 .25

1990, July 30 ***Perf. 11½x12***

2257 A1216 10cr multicolored .30 .25

1990, Aug. 22 ***Perf. 12x11½***

2258 A1217 10cr multicolored .30 .25

Flora Type of 1989

1cr, like #2179. 2cr, like #2180. 5cr, like #2181. 10cr, Tibouchina granulosa. 20cr, Cassia macranthera. #2264, Clitoria fairchildiana. #2265, Tibouchina mutabilis. 100cr, Erythrina crista-galli. 200cr, Jacaranda mimosifolia. 500cr, Caesalpinia peltophoroides. 1000, Pachira aquatica. 2000, Hibiscus pernambucensis. 5000, Triplaris surinamensis. 10,000, Tabebuia heptaphylla. 20,000, Erythrina speciosa.

Perf. 11x11½, 11½x11

1989-93 **Photo.**

Design A1177

2259 A1177 1cr multi .20 .20
2260 A1177 2cr multi .20 .20
2261 A1177 5cr multi .20 .20
2262 A1177 10cr multi .20 .20
2263 A1177 20cr multi .20 .20
2264 A1177 50cr multi .30 .20
2265 A1177 50cr multi .35 .35
2266 A1177 100cr multi, perf. 13 .55 .30
2267 A1177 200cr multi 1.10 .55
2268 A1177 500cr multi 2.75 1.40
2269 A1177 1000cr multi .20 .20
2270 A1177 2000cr multi .20 .20
2271 A1177 5000cr multi .85 .85
2272 A1177 10,000cr multi 1.65 1.65
2273 A1177 20,000cr multi 2.25 2.25
Nos. 2259-2273 (15) 11.20 8.95

Issued: 1cr, 11/8/90; 2cr, 11/12/90; 5cr, 11/16/90; #2264, 6/1/89; 10cr, 4/18/90; 20cr, 5/4/90; 100cr, 8/24/90; 200cr, 6/16/91; 500cr, 5/14/91; 1000cr, 9/2/92; 2000cr, 9/8/92; 5000cr, 10/16/92; 10,000cr, 11/16/92; 20,000cr, 4/25/93; #2265, 10/20/93.

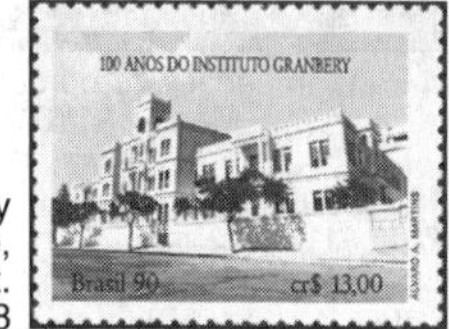

Granbery Instutute, Cent. A1218

1990, Sept. 8 Litho. ***Perf. 11½x12***

2279 A1218 13cr multicolored .40 .30

18th Panamerican Railroad Congress — A1219

1990, Sept. 9

2280 A1219 95cr multicolored 2.00 1.50

Embratel, 25th Anniv. — A1220

1990, Sept. 21

2281 A1220 13cr multicolored .40 .30

LUBRAPEX '90 A1221

Statues by Ceschiatti and Giorgi (No. 2283).

1990, Sept. 22

2282 A1221 25cr As Banhistas .60 .45
2283 A1221 25cr Os Candangos .60 .45
2284 A1221 100cr Evangelista Sao Joao 1.25 .90
2285 A1221 100cr A Justica 1.25 .90
a. Block of 4, #2282-2285 4.00 3.00
b. Souv. sheet of 4, #2282-2285 6.00 6.00

Praia Do Sul Wildlife Reserve A1222

1990, Oct. 12

2286 A1222 15cr Flowers .45 .30
2287 A1222 105cr Shoreline 2.60 1.80
a. Pair, #2286-2287 3.05 2.10

Discovery of America, 500th anniv. (in 1992).

Natl. Library, 180th Anniv. A1223

Writers: No. 2289, Guilherme de Almeida (1890-1969). No. 2290, Oswald de Andrade (1890-1954).

1990, Oct. 29 Litho. *Perf. 11x11½*

2288 A1223 15cr multicolored .40 .30
2289 A1223 15cr multicolored .40 .30
2290 A1223 15cr multicolored .40 .30
Nos. 2288-2290 (3) 1.20 .90

Natl. Tax Court, Cent. A1224

1990, Nov. 7 Litho. *Perf. 11½x12*

2291 A1224 15cr multicolored .40 .30

Christmas A1225

Architecture of Brasilia: No. 2292, National Congress. No. 2293, Television tower.

1990, Nov. 20

2292 A1225 15cr multicolored .40 .30
2293 A1225 15cr multicolored .40 .30

A1226 A1227

1990, Dec. 13 Litho. *Perf. 12x11½*

2294 A1226 15cr multicolored .20 .20

Organization of American States, cent.

1990, Dec. 14

2295 A1227 15cr multicolored .20 .20

First Flight of Nike Apache Missile, 25th anniv.

Colonization of Sergipe, Founding of Sao Cristovao, 400th Anniv. — A1228

1990, Dec. 18 Litho. *Perf. 11½x12*

2296 A1228 15cr multicolored .20 .20

World Congress of Physical Education A1229

1991, Jan. 7 *Perf. 11½x12*

2297 A1229 17cr multicolored .20 .20

Rock in Rio II — A1230

1991, Jan. 9 *Perf. 12x11½*

2298 A1230 25cr Cazuza .20 .20
2299 A1230 185cr Raul Seixas 1.65 1.00
a. Pair, #2298-2299 2.00 1.10

Printed in sheets of 12.

Ministry of Aviation, 50th Anniv. A1231

1991, Jan. 20 *Perf. 11x11½*

2300 A1231 17cr multicolored .20 .20

A1232

A1233

Carnivals.

1991, Feb. 8 Litho. *Perf. 12x11½*

2301 A1232 25cr Olinda .25 .20
2302 A1232 30cr Salvador .25 .20
2303 A1232 280cr Rio de Janeiro 2.50 2.00
Nos. 2301-2303 (3) 3.00 2.40

1991, Feb. 20

2304 A1233 300cr multicolored 3.00 2.25

Visit by Pres. Collor to Antarctica.

Hang Gliding World Championships — A1234

1991, Feb. 24 *Perf. 11½x12*

2305 A1234 36cr multicolored .35 .30

11th Pan American Games, 25th Summer Olympics A1235

1991, Mar. 30 Litho. *Perf. 11½x12*

2306 A1235 36cr Sailing .30 .25
2307 A1235 36cr Rowing .30 .25
2308 A1235 300cr Swimming 2.50 1.90
a. Block of 3, #2306-2308 + label 3.25 2.50

Fight Against Drugs — A1236

Yanomami Indian Culture — A1237

1991, Apr. 7 Litho. *Perf. 12x11½*

2309 A1236 40cr Drugs .35 .30
2310 A1236 40cr Alcohol .35 .30
2311 A1236 40cr Smoking .35 .30
Nos. 2309-2311 (3) 1.05 .90

1991, Apr. 19 *Perf. 11½x11, 11x11½*

2312 A1237 40cr shown .35 .30
2313 A1237 400cr Indian, horiz. 3.50 2.75

Journal of Brazil, Cent. A1238

1991, Apr. 8 Litho. *Perf. 11x11½*

2314 A1238 40cr multicolored .35 .30

Neochen Jubata (Orinoco Goose) — A1239

1991, June 5 Litho. *Perf. 12x11½*

2315 A1239 45cr multi .30 .25

UN Conference on Development.

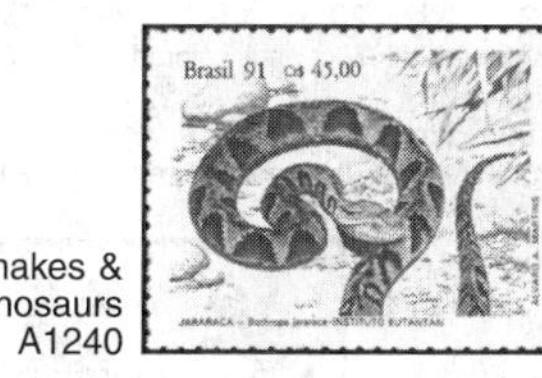

Snakes & Dinosaurs A1240

1991, June 6 *Perf. 11½x12*

2316 A1240 45cr Bothrops jararaca .30 .25
2317 A1240 45cr Corallus caninus .30 .25
a. Pair, #2316-2317 .60 .50
2318 A1240 45cr Teropods .30 .25
2319 A1240 350cr Sauropods 2.10 1.60
a. Pair, #2318-2319 2.40 1.85
Nos. 2316-2319 (4) 3.00 2.35

Flag of Brazil — A1241

1991, June 10 Photo. *Perf. 13x13½*

2320 A1241 A multicolored .25 .20

Valued at domestic letter rate (cr) on day of issue.

Exists with inscription at lower right. Same value.

Fire Pumper A1242

1991, July 2 Litho. *Perf. 11½x12*

2321 A1242 45cr multicolored .30 .25

Tourism A1243

Map location and: 45cr, Painted stones, Roraima. 350cr, Dedo de Deus Mountain, Rio De Janeiro.

1991, July 6 *Perf. 11x11½*

2322 A1243 45cr multicolored .28 .20
2323 A1243 350cr multicolored 2.00 1.50

Labor Laws, 50th Anniv. A1244

1991, Aug. 11 *Perf. 11½x12*

2324 A1244 45cr multicolored .30 .25

Leonardo Mota, Birth Cent. A1245

1991, Aug. 22

2325 A1245 45cr buff, blk & red .30 .25

Folklore Festival.

Jose Basilio da Gama (1741-1795), Poet — A1246

#2327, Fagundes Varela (b. 1841), poet. #2328, Jackson de Figueiredo (b. 1891), writer.

1991, Aug. 29

2326 A1246 45cr multicolored .25 .20
2327 A1246 50cr multicolored .30 .25
2328 A1246 50cr multicolored .30 .25
Nos. 2326-2328 (3) .85 .70

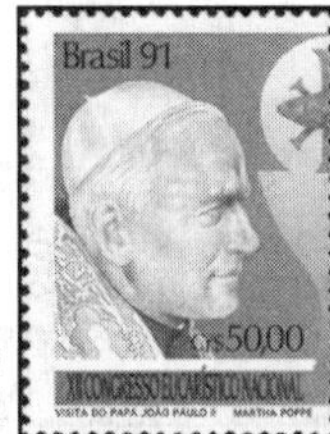

12th Natl. Eucharistic Congress A1247

1991, Oct. 6 Litho. *Perf. 12x11½*
2329 A1247 50cr Pope John Paul II .20 .20
2330 A1247 400cr Map, crosses 1.40 1.05
a. Pair, #2329-2330 1.60 1.20

Visit by Pope John Paul II.

First Brazilian Constitution, Cent. — A1248

1991, Oct. 7 *Perf. 11½x12*
2331 A1248 50cr multicolored .20 .20

Telecom '91 — A1249

1991, Oct. 8 *Perf. 12x11½*
2332 A1249 50cr multicolored .20 .20

Sixth World Forum and Exposition on Telecommunications, Geneva, Switzerland.

America Issue A1250

UPAEP emblem and explorers: 50cr, Ferdinand Magellan (c. 1480-1521). 400cr, Francisco de Orellana (c. 1490-c. 1546).

1991, Oct. 12 *Perf. 11½x12*
2333 A1250 50cr multicolored .20 .20
2334 A1250 400cr multicolored 1.40 1.05

Discovery of America, 500th anniv. (in 1992).

A1251 A1252

BRAPEX VIII (Orchids and Hummingbirds): 50cr, Colibri serrirostris, cattleya warneri. No. 2336, Chlorostilbon aureoventris, rodriguezia venusta. No. 2337, Clytolaema rubricauda, zygopetalum intermedium. No. 2338a, 50cr, Colibri serrirostris. b, 50cr, Chlorostilbon aureoventris. c, 500cr, Clytolaema rubricauda.

1991, Oct. 29 Litho. *Perf. 12x11½*
2335 A1251 50cr multicolored .20 .20
2336 A1251 65cr multicolored .20 .20
2337 A1251 65cr multicolored .20 .20
Nos. 2335-2337 (3) .60 .60

Souvenir Sheet

2338 A1251 Sheet of 3, #a.-c. 2.20 1.65

1991, Oct. 29 Litho. *Perf. 11½x11*
2339 A1252 400cr multicolored .90 .65

Lasar Segall, artist, birth cent.

Bureau of Agriculture and Provision of Sao Paulo, Cent. — A1253

1991, Nov. 11 *Perf. 12x11½*
2340 A1253 70cr multicolored .20 .20

First Civilian Presidents, Birth Sesquicentennials — A1254

1991, Nov. 14 *Perf. 11½x12*
2341 A1254 70cr Manuel de Campos Salles .20 .20
2342 A1254 90cr Prudente de Moraes Barros .25 .20
a. Pair, #2341-2342 .45 .35

Christmas A1255

Thanksgiving A1256

1991, Nov. 20 *Perf. 12x11½*
2343 A1255 70cr multicolored .20 .20

1991, Nov. 28
2344 A1256 70cr multicolored .20 .20

Military Police A1257

1991, Dec. 1 *Perf. 11½x12*
2345 A1257 80cr multicolored .25 .20

Souvenir Sheet

Emperor Dom Pedro (1825-1891) — A1258

a, 80cr, Older age. b, 800cr, Wearing crown.

Litho. & Engr.

1991, Nov. 29 *Perf. 11*
2346 A1258 Sheet of 2, #a.-b. 2.50 2.50

BRASILIANA 93.

Churches A1259

#2347, Presbyterian Church, Rio de Janeiro. #2348, First Baptist Church, Niteroi.

1992, Jan. 12 Litho. *Perf. 12x11½*
2347 A1259 250cr multicolored .30 .25
2348 A1259 250cr multicolored .30 .25

1992 Summer Olympics, Barcelona A1260

Medalists in shooting, Antwerp, 1920: 300cr, Afranio Costa, silver. 2500cr, Guihlherme Paraense, gold.

1992, Jan. 28 *Perf. 11½x12*
2349 A1260 300cr multicolored .30 .25
2350 A1260 2500cr multicolored 2.75 2.00

Port of Santos, Cent. A1261

1992, Feb. 3 Litho. *Perf. 11½*
2351 A1261 300cr multicolored .45 .35

Fauna of Fernando de Noronha Island A1262

1992, Feb. 25 Litho. *Perf. 11½x12*
2352 A1262 400cr White-tailed tropicbirds .40 .30
2353 A1262 2500cr Dolphins 2.50 1.75

Earth Summit, Rio de Janeiro.

Yellow Amaryllis — A1263

1992, Feb. 27 Photo. *Perf. 13½*
2354 A1263 (A) multicolored .25 .20

No. 2354 met the second class domestic letter postage rate of 265cr on date of issue.

ARBRAFEX '92, Argentina-Brazil Philatelic Exhibition — A1264

Designs: No. 2355, Gaucho throwing bola at rhea. No. 2356, Man playing accordion, couple dancing. No. 2357, Couple in horse-drawn cart, woman. 1000cr, Gaucho throwing lasso at steer.

No. 2358c, 250cr, like #2356. d, 500cr, like #2355. e, 1500cr, like #2358.

1992, Mar. 20 Litho. *Perf. 11½x12*
2355 A1264 250cr multicolored .20 .20
2356 A1264 250cr multicolored .20 .20
2357 A1264 250cr multicolored .20 .20
2358 A1264 1000cr multicolored .60 .60
a. Block of 4, Nos. 2355-2358 1.05 1.05

Souvenir Sheet

2358B A1264 Sheet of 4, #2357, 2358c-2358e 1.05 1.05

1992 Summer Olympics, Barcelona A1265

1992, Apr. 3 *Perf. 12x11½*
2359 A1265 300cr multicolored .20 .20

Discovery of America, 500th Anniv. A1266

1992, Apr. 24 *Perf. 11½x12*
2360 A1266 500cr Columbus' fleet .30 .30
2361 A1266 3500cr Columbus, map 2.10 2.10
a. Pair, #2360-2361 2.40 2.40

Telebras Telecommunications System — A1267

1992, May 5 *Perf. 11x11½*
2362 A1267 350cr multicolored .20 .20

Installation of 10 million telephones.

Langsdorff Expedition to Brazil, 170th Anniv. A1268

#2363, Aime-Adrien Taunay, natives. #2364, Johann Moritz Rugendas, monkey. #2365, Hercule Florence, flowering plant. 3000cr, Gregory Ivanovitch Langsdorff, map.

1992, June 2 ***Perf. 11½x12***

2363 A1268 500cr multicolored .25 .25
2364 A1268 500cr multicolored .25 .25
2365 A1268 500cr multicolored .25 .25
2366 A1268 3000cr multicolored 1.50 1.50
Nos. 2363-2366 (4) 2.25 2.25

UN Conf. on Environmental Development, Rio.

UN Conference on Environmental Development, Rio de Janeiro — A1269

Globe and: No. 2367, Flags of Sweden and Brazil. No. 2368, City, grain, mountain and tree. 3000cr, Map of Brazil, parrot, orchid.

1992, June 3 Litho. ***Perf. 11x11½***

2367 A1269 450cr multicolored .20 .20
2368 A1269 450cr multicolored .20 .20
2369 A1269 3000cr multicolored 1.50 1.50
Nos. 2367-2369 (3) 1.90 1.90

Ecology A1270

Designs: No. 2370, Flowers, waterfall, and butterflies. No. 2371, Butterflies, canoe, and hummingbirds. No. 2372, Boy taking pictures of tropical birds. No. 2373, Armadillo, girl picking fruit.

1992, June 4 ***Perf. 11½x12***

2370 A1270 500cr multicolored .25 .25
2371 A1270 500cr multicolored .25 .25
2372 A1270 500cr multicolored .25 .25
2373 A1270 500cr multicolored .25 .25
a. Strip of 4, #2370-2373 1.00 1.00

UN Conf. on Environmental Development, Rio.

Floral Paintings by Margaret Mee — A1271

1992, June 5 ***Perf. 12x11½***

2374 A1271 600cr Nidularium innocentii .35 .35
2375 A1271 600cr Canistrum exiguum .35 .35
2376 A1271 700cr Canistrum cyathiforme .40 .40
2377 A1271 700cr Nidularium rubens .40 .40
Nos. 2374-2377 (4) 1.50 1.50

UN Conf. on Environmental Development, Rio.

Souvenir Sheet

Joaquim Jose da Silva Xavier (1748-1792), Patriot — A1272

Litho. & Engr.

1992, Apr. 21 ***Perf. 11***

2378 A1272 3500cr multicolored 2.10 2.10

Souvenir Sheet

A1273

Expedition of Alexandre Rodrigues Ferreira, Bicent.: a, 500cr, Sailing ships, gray and green hulls. b, 1000cr, Sailing ships, red hulls. c, 2500cr, Sailing ship at shore.

1992, May 9 Litho. ***Perf. 11½x12***

2379 A1273 Sheet of 3, #a.-c. 2.40 2.40

Lubrapex '92.

A1274 A1275

1992, June 5 Litho. ***Perf. 12x11½***

2380 A1274 600cr Hummingbird .25 .25

Diabetes Day.

1992, July 13 Litho. ***Perf. 11½x11***

2381 A1275 550cr multicolored .25 .25

Volunteer firemen of Joinville.

A1276

A1277

Serra da Capivara National Park: No. 2382, Leopard, animals, map of park. No. 2383, Canyon, map of Brazil.

1992, July 17 ***Perf. 12x11½***

2382 A1276 550cr multicolored .25 .25
2383 A1276 550cr multicolored .25 .25
a. Pair, #2382-2383 .45 .45

1992, July 24

2384 A1277 550cr multicolored .25 .25

Financing for studies and projects.

Natl. Service for Industrial Training, 50th Anniv. — A1278

1992, Aug. 5 ***Perf. 11½x12***

2385 A1278 650cr multicolored .35 .35

Fortresses A1279

1992, Aug. 19 Litho. ***Perf. 11½x12***

2386 A1279 650cr Santa Cruz .30 .30
2387 A1279 3000cr Santo Antonio 1.25 1.25

Masonic Square, Compass and Lodge A1280

1992, Aug. 20

2388 A1280 650cr multicolored .30 .30

Brazilian Assistance Legion, 50th Anniv. — A1281

Hospital of Medicine and Orthopedics A1282

1992, Aug. 28 ***Perf. 12x11½***

2389 A1281 650cr multicolored .30 .30

1992, Sept. 11

2390 A1282 800cr multicolored .30 .30

Merry Christmas A1283

1992, Nov. 20 ***Perf. 11½***

2391 A1283 (1) multicolored .25 .25

No. 2391 met the first class domestic letter postage rate of 1090cr on day of issue.

Writers A1284

#2392, Graciliano Ramos (1892-1953). #2393, Menotti del Picchia (1892-1988). 1000cr, Assis Chateaubriand (1892-1968).

Perf. 12x11½, 11½x12

1992, Oct. 29 **Litho.**

2392 A1284 900cr multi, vert. .25 .25
2393 A1284 900cr multi, vert. .25 .25
2394 A1284 1000cr multi .30 .30

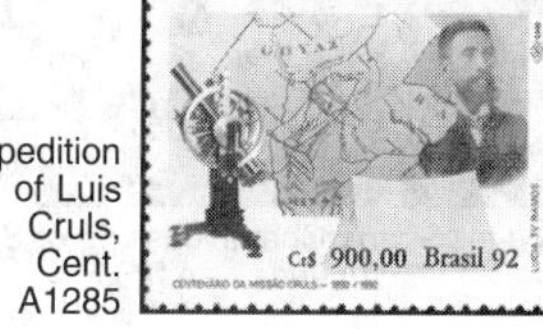

Expedition of Luis Cruls, Cent. A1285

1992, Nov. 11 ***Perf. 11½x12***

2395 A1285 900cr multicolored .25 25

Brazillian Program for Quality and Productivity A1286

1992, Nov. 12

2396 A1286 1200cr multicolored .30 .30

Souvenir Sheet

Tourism Year in the Americas — A1287

a, 1200cr, Mountains, coastline. b, 9000cr, Sugarloaf Mt., aerial tram, Rio de Janeiro.

1992, Nov. 18 Litho. ***Perf. 11½x12***

2397 A1287 Sheet of 2, #a.-b. 2.00 2.00

Brasiliana '93.

Sister Irma Dulce A1288

1993, Mar. 13 Litho. ***Perf. 11½x12***

2398 A1288 3500cr multicolored .35 .35

Souvenir Sheet

Water Sports Championships of South America — A1289

Designs: a, 3500cr, Diver. b, 3500cr, Synchronized swimmers. c, 25,000cr, Water polo.

1993, Mar. 21 Litho. *Perf. 11*
2399 A1289 Sheet of 3, #a.-c. 2.75 2.75

Curitiba, 300th Anniv. A1290

1993, Mar. 29
2400 A1290 4500cr multicolored .40 .40

Health and Preservation of Life — A1291

Pedro Americo, 150th Birth Anniv. — A1292

Red Cross emblem and: No. 2401, Bleeding heart, flowers. No. 2402, Cancer symbol, breast. No. 2403, Brain waves, rainbow emerging from head.

1993, Apr. 7 Litho. *Perf. 12x11½*
2401 A1291 4500cr multicolored .30 .30
2402 A1291 4500cr multicolored .30 .30
2403 A1291 4500cr multicolored .30 .30
a. Strip of 3, #2401-2403 .90 .90

1993, Apr. 29 *Perf. 12x11½, 11½x12*

Paintings: 5500cr, A Study of Love, 1883. No. 2405, David and Abizag, 1879, horiz. No. 2406, Seated Nude, 1882.

2404 A1292 5500cr multi .30 .30
2405 A1292 36,000cr multi 1.60 1.60
2406 A1292 36,000cr multi 1.60 1.60
Nos. 2404-2406 (3) 3.50 3.50

Natl. Flag A1292a

1993, May 26 Litho. *Die Cut*
Self-adhesive
2407 A1292a A multicolored .35 .35

No. 2407 valued at first class domestic letter rate of 9570cr on day of issue.

Beetles A1293

1993, June 5 Litho. *Perf. 11½x12*
2408 A1293 8000cr Dynastes hercules .35 .35
2409 A1293 55,000cr Batus barbicornis 2.25 2.25

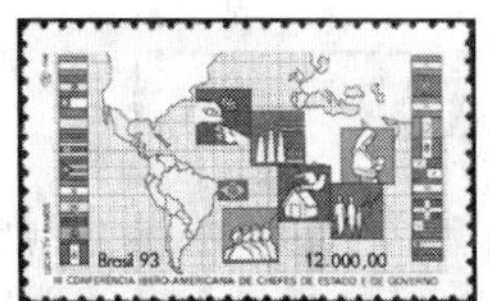

3rd Iberian-American Conference of Chiefs of State and Heads of Government, Salvador — A1294

1993, July 15 Litho. *Perf. 11x11½*
2410 A1294 12,000cr multi .20 .20

1st Brazilian Postage Stamps, 150th Anniv. — A1295

Litho. & Engr.
1993, July 30 *Perf. 12x11½*
2411 A1295 30,000cr No. 1 .30 .30
2412 A1295 60,000cr No. 2 .60 .60
2413 A1295 90,000cr No. 3 .90 .90
a. Souvenir sheet of 3, #2411-2413, wmk. 268 10.00 10.00
Nos. 2411-2413 (3) 1.80 1.80

No. 2413a sold for 200,000cr and was issued without gum. Stamps in No. 2413a do not have imprint at bottom.

Union of Portuguese Speaking Capitals A1296

a, 15,000cr, Brasilia. b, 71,000cr, Rio de Janiero.

1993, July 30 Litho. *Perf. 11½x12*
2414 A1296 Pair, #a.-b. .90 .90

No. 2414 printed in continuous design.

Monica & Friends, by Mauricio de Sousa A1297

Monica, Cebolinha, Cascao, Magali, and Bidu: a, Engraving die. b, Reading proclamation, king, No. 1. c, Writing and sending letter, No. 2. d, Receiving letter, No. 3.

1993, Aug. 1
2415 A1297 (1) Strip of 4, #a.-d. .85 .85

First Brazilian postage stamps, 150th anniv. Nos. 2415a-2415d paid the first class rate (9600cr)on day of issue.

Brazilian Post, 330th Anniv. A1298

Postal buildings: a, Imperial Post Office, Rio de Janeiro. b, Petropolis. c, Central office, Rio de Janeiro. d, Niteroi.

1993, Aug. 3 Litho. *Perf. 11½x12*
2416 A1298 20,000cr Block of 4, #a.-d. .45 .45

Brazilian Engineering Schools — A1299

Designs: No. 2417, School of Engineering, Federal University, Rio de Janeiro. No. 2418, Polytechnical School, University of Sao Paulo.

1993, Aug. 24 Litho. *Perf. 11x11½*
2417 A1299 17cr multicolored .30 .30
2418 A1299 17cr multicolored .30 .30

Preservation of Sambaquis Archaelogical Sites — A1300

1993, Sept. 19 *Perf. 12x11½*
2419 A1300 17cr Two artifacts .25 .25
2420 A1300 17cr Six artifacts .25 .25

Ulysses Guimaraes, Natl. Congress — A1301

1993, Oct. 6 Litho. *Perf. 11x11½*
2421 A1301 22cr multicolored .30 .30

A1302

A1303

1993, Oct. 8 Litho. *Perf. 12x11½*
2422 A1302 22cr multicolored .30 .30

Virgin of Nazare Religious Festival, bicent.

1993, Oct. 13 Litho. *Perf. 11½x11*

Endangered birds (America Issue): 22cr, Anodorhynchus hyacinthinus, anodorhynchus glaucus, anodorhynchus leari. 130cr, Cyanopsitta spixii.

2423 A1303 22cr multicolored .25 .25
2424 A1303 130cr multicolored 1.40 1.40

A1304

A1307

Composers.

1993, Oct. 19 Litho. *Perf. 12x11½*
2425 A1304 22cr Vinicius de Moraes .20 .20
2426 A1304 22cr Pixinguinha .20 .20

1993, Oct. 29 Litho. *Perf. 12x11½*

Poets: No. 2427, Mario de Andrade (1893-1945). No. 2428, Alceu Amoroso Lima (Tristao de Athayde) (1893-1983). No. 2429, Gilka Machado (1893-1980).

2427 A1307 30cr multicolored .30 .30
2428 A1307 30cr multicolored .30 .30
2429 A1307 30cr multicolored .30 .30
Nos. 2427-2429 (3) .90 .90

Natl. Book Day.

Brazil-Portugal Treaty of Consultation and Friendship, 40th Anniv. — A1308

1993, Nov. 3 Litho. *Perf. 11½x12*
2430 A1308 30cr multicolored .30 .30

See Portugal No. 1980.

Image of the Republic — A1309

Photo. & Engr.

1993, Nov. 3 ***Perf. 13***

2431 A1309 (B) multicolored 2.50 2.50

Valued at first class international letter rate (178.70 cr) on day of issue.

2nd Intl. Biennial of Comic Strips A1310

Cartoon drawings: No. 2432, Nho-Quim. No. 2433, Benjamin. No. 2434, Lamparina. No. 2435, Reco-Reco, Bolao, Azeitona.

1993, Nov. 11 **Litho.** ***Perf. 11½x12***

2432 A1310 (1) multicolored .40 .40
2433 A1310 (1) multicolored .40 .40
2434 A1310 (1) multicolored .40 .40
2435 A1310 (1) multicolored .40 .40
a. Block of 4, #2432-2435 1.75 1.75

Valued at first class domestic letter rate (30.20 cr) on day of issue.

Launching of First Brazilian-Built Submarine — A1311

1993, Nov. 18 ***Perf. 11½***

2436 A1311 240cr multicolored 1.75 1.75

Christmas A1312

1993, Nov. 20

2437 A1312 (1) multicolored .45 .45

Valued at first class domestic letter rate (30.20 cr) on day of issue.

First Fighter Group, 50th Anniv. A1313

1993, Dec. 18 **Litho.** ***Perf. 11½***

2438 A1313 42cr multicolored .35 .35

Convent of Merces, 340th Anniv. A1314

1994, Jan. 31 **Litho.** ***Perf. 11½x12***

2439 A1314 58cr multicolored .30 .30

Mae Menininha of Gantois, Birth Cent. — A1315

1994, Feb. 10 **Litho.** ***Perf. 11x11½***

2440 A1315 80cr multicolored .40 .40

Intl. Olympic Committee, Cent. A1316

1994, Feb. 17 ***Perf. 11½x12***

2441 A1316 (1) multicolored 2.25 2.25

No. 2441 valued at first class international letter rate (446.30 cr) on day of issue.

Natl. Flag — A1317

1994, Jan. 31 **Litho.** ***Die Cut***

Self-Adhesive

2442 A1317 (1) multicolored .40 .40

No. 2442 valued at first class domestic letter rate (55.90 cr) on day of issue.

Birds A1318

Image of the Republic A1318a

1994 **Photo.** ***Perf. 11x11½***

2443 A1318 10cr Notiochelidon cyanoleuca .20 .20
2444 A1318 20cr Buteo magnirostris .20 .20
2445 A1318 50cr Turdus rufiventris .20 .20
2446 A1318 100cr Columbina talpacoti .20 .20
2447 A1318 200cr Vanellus chilensis .20 .20
2448 A1318 500cr Zonotrichia capensis .50 .50
Nos. 2443-2448 (6) 1.50 1.50

Issued: 10cr, 3/17; 20cr, 3/9; 50cr, 3/1; 100cr, 200cr, 4/4; 500cr, 4/13.

See Nos. 2484-2494.

1994, May 10 **Litho.**

Self-Adhesive

Die Cut

2449 A1318a (1) blue .25 .25
2450 A1318a (3) claret .40 .40

Size: 25x35mm

Perf. 12x11½

2451 A1318a (4) green .85 .85
2452 A1318a (5) henna brown 1.50 1.50
Nos. 2449-2452 (4) 3.00 3.00

Nos. 2449, 2450, 2451, 2452 valued 131.37cr, 321.14cr, 452.52cr 905.05cr on day of issue.

Prince Henry the Navigator (1394-1460) — A1319

1994, Mar. 4 **Litho.** ***Perf. 11½x12***

2463 A1319 635cr multicolored 2.25 2.25

See Macao No. 719, Portugal No. 1987.

America Issue A1320

Postal vehicles: 110cr, Bicycle, country scene. 635cr, Motorcycle, city scene.

1994, Mar. 18

2464 A1320 110cr multicolored .20 .20
2465 A1320 635cr multicolored 1.10 1.10

Father Cicero Romao Batista, 150th Birth Anniv. A1321

1994, Mar. 24 ***Perf. 11x11½***

2466 A1321 (1) multicolored .35 .35

No. 2466 valued at first class domestic letter rate (98.80 cr) on day of issue.

Albert Sabin, Campaign Against Polio A1322

1994, Apr. 7 ***Perf. 11½x12***

2467 A1322 160cr multicolored .30 .30

Carlos Castello Branco, Journalist A1323

1994, Apr. 14

2468 A1323 160cr multicolored .30 .30

Karl Friedrich Phillip von Martius, Naturalist A1324

Flowers: No. 2469, Euterpe oleracea. No. 2470, Jacaranda paucifoliolata. No. 2471, Barbacernia tomentosa.

1994, Apr. 24 ***Perf. 12x11½***

2469 A1324 (1) multicolored .35 .35
2470 A1324 (1) multicolored .35 .35
2471 A1324 (1) multicolored 2.00 2.00
Nos. 2469-2471 (3) 2.70 2.70

Nos. 2469-2470 were valued at first class domestic letter rate (144 cr) on day of issue. No. 2471 valued at first class intl. letter rate (860 cr) on day of issue.

Monkeys — A1326

No. 2474, Leontopithecus rosalia. No. 2475, Saguinus imperator. No. 2476, Saguinus bicolor.

1994, May 24

2474 A1326 (1) multicolored .35 .35
2475 A1326 (1) multicolored .35 .35
2476 A1326 (1) multicolored .35 .35
Nos. 2474-2476 (3) 1.05 1.05

Nos. 2474-2476 were valued at first class domestic letter rate (207.03 cr) on day of issue.

1994 World Cup Soccer Championships, US — A1327

1994, May 19 ***Perf. 11½x12***

2477 A1327 (1) multicolored 2.00 2.00

No. 2477 was valued at first class intl. rate (1378.32 cr) on day of issue.

Soccer in Brazil, cent.

Souvenir Sheet

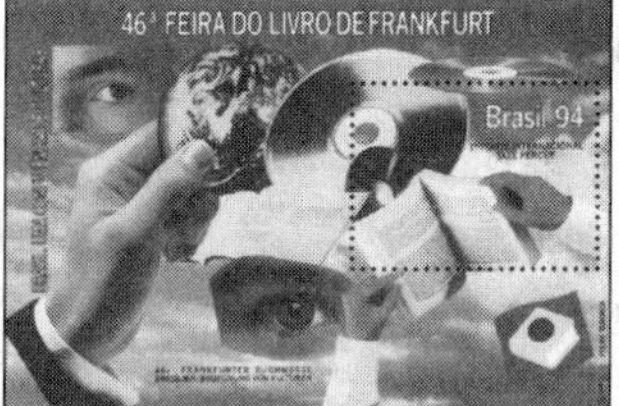

46th Frankfurt Intl. Book Fair — A1328

Illustration reduced.

1994, May 27

2478 A1328 (1) multicolored 2.00 2.00

No. 2478 was valued at first class intl. rate (1523.83 cr) on day of issue.

Natl. Literacy Program — A1329

#2479, Pencil, buildings. #2480, Pencil, people on television, people watching. #2481, Classroom, pencil. #2482, Pencils crossed over fingerprint, map of Brazil.

1994, June 3 **Litho.** ***Perf. 12x11½***

2479 A1329 (1) multicolored .30 .30
2480 A1329 (1) multicolored .30 .30
2481 A1329 (1) multicolored .30 .30
2482 A1329 (1) multicolored .30 .30
Nos. 2479-2482 (4) 1.20 1.20

Nos. 2479-2482 were valued at first class domestic letter rate (233.05 cr) on day of issue.

Souvenir Sheet

Treaty of Tordesillas, 500th Anniv. — A1330

1994, June 7

2483 A1330 (1) multicolored 2.25 2.25

No. 2483 was valued at first class intl. letter rate (1689.02 cr) on day of issue.

Bird Type of 1994 and

A1330a

Perf. 11x11½, 13 (15c), 12½13 (22c, (22c)

1994-98 Photo.

2484 A1318 1c like No. 2443 .20 .20
2485 A1318 2c like No. 2444 .20 .20
2486 A1318 5c like No. 2445 .20 .20
2487 A1318 10c like No. 2446 .20 .20
2488 A1330a 15c Sicalis flaveola .35 .35
2489 A1318 20c like No. 2447 .40 .40
2490 A1318 22c Tyrannus savana .50 .50
2491 A1318 50c like No. 2448 1.00 1.00
2494 A1318 1r Furnarius rufus 2.25 2.25
Nos. 2484-2494 (9) 5.30 5.30

Size: 21x26mm

Self-Adhesive

Serpentine Die Cut

2498 A1330a 22c Myiozetetes similis .50 .50
2499 A1330a (22c) Volatinia jacarina .50 .50

No. 2499 is inscribed "1o PORTE NATIONAL" and was valued at 22c on day of issue.

Issued: 1c, 2c, 5c, 20c, 20c, 50c, 1r, 7/1/94; 11/16/95; #2490, 10/13/97; #2498, 2/16/98; #2499, 7/22/97.

No. 2498 exists dated "1998" and "1999." No. 2499 exists dated "2000."

This is an expanding set. Numbers may change.

Prominent Brazilians A1331

Designs: No. 2504, Edgard Santos (1894-1962), surgeon, educator. No. 2505, Oswaldo Aranha (1894-1960), politician. No. 2507, Otto Lara Resende (1922-92), writer, educator.

1994, July 5 Litho. *Perf. 11½x12*

2504 A1331 (1) multicolored .30 .30
2505 A1331 (1) multicolored .30 .30
2506 A1331 (1) multicolored .30 .30
Nos. 2504-2506 (3) .90 .90

Nos. 2504-2506 were valued at first class domestic letter rate (12c) on day of issue.

A1332 A1333

1994, July 15 *Perf. 12x11½*

2507 A1332 12c multicolored .30 .30

Petrobras, 40th anniv.

Litho. & Engr.

1994, July 26 *Perf. 11½*

2508 A1333 12c multicolored .30 .30

Brazilian State Mint, 300th anniv.

Campaign Against Famine & Misery A1334

1994, July 27 Litho. *Perf. 11½x12*

2509 A1334 (1) Fish .30 .30
2510 A1334 (1) Bread .30 .30

Nos. 2509-2510 were valued at first class domestic letter rate (12c) on day of issue.

Institute of Brazilian Lawyers, 150th Anniv. A1335

1994, Aug. 11

2511 A1335 12c multicolored .30 .30

Intl. Year of the Family A1336

1994, Aug. 16 *Perf. 11½*

2512 A1336 84c multicolored 2.00 2.00

Maternity Hospital of Sao Paulo, Cent. A1337

1994, Aug. 26 *Perf. 11½x12*

2513 A1337 12c multicolored .30 .30

Vincente Celestino (1894-1968), Singer — A1338

1994, Sept. 12

2514 A1338 12c multicolored .30 .30

"Contos da Carochinha," First Brazilian Children's Book, Cent. — A1339

Fairy tales: a, Joao e Maria (Hansel & Gretel). b, Dona Baratinha. c, Puss 'n Boots. d, Tom Thumb.

1994, Oct. 5 Litho. *Perf. 11½x12*

2515 Block of 4 4.75 4.75
a.-b. A1339 12c any single .30 .30
c.-d. A1339 84c any single 2.00 2.00

Brazilian Literature A1340

Portraits: No. 2516, Tomas Antonio Gonzaga (1744-1809?), poet. No. 2517, Fernando de Azevedo (1894-1974), author.

1994, Oct. 5 *Perf. 11½*

2516 A1340 12c multicolored .30 .30
2517 A1340 12c multicolored .30 .30

St. Clare of Assisi (1194-1253) A1341

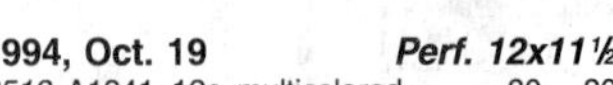

1994, Oct. 19 *Perf. 12x11½*

2518 A1341 12c multicolored .30 .30

Ayrton Senna (1960-1994), Race Car Driver — A1342

Designs: a, McClaren Formula 1 race car, Brazilian flag. b, Fans, Senna. c, Flags, race cars, Senna.

1994, Oct. 24 *Perf. 11½x12*

2519 Triptych 2.75 2.75
a.-b. A1342 12c any single .30 .30
c. A1342 84c multicolored 2.00 2.00

Institute of History & Geography of Sao Paulo, Cent. A1343

1994, Nov. 1

2520 A1343 12c multicolored .30 .30

Popular Music A1344

Designs: No. 2521, Music from "The Sea," by Dorival Caymmi. No. 2522, Adoniran Barbosa (1910-82), samba composer.

1994, Nov. 5 *Perf. 11½*

2521 A1344 12c multicolored .30 .30
2522 A1344 12c multicolored .30 .30

Christmas A1345

Folk characters: No. 2523: a, Boy wearing Santa coat, pot on head. b, Worm in apple. c, Man, animals singing. d, Shoe on tree stump, man with pipe holding pen.

1994, Dec. 1 Litho. *Perf. 11½*

2523 Block of 4 2.75 2.75
a. A1345 84c multicolored 1.90 1.90
b.-d. A1345 12c any single .30 .30
e. Booklet pane, #2523 + 4 labels *5.50*
Complete booklet, #2523a *5.50*

Souvenir Sheet

Brazil, 1994 World Cup Soccer Champions — A1346

Illustration reduced.

1994, Dec. 5 *Perf. 12x11½*

2524 A1346 2.14r multicolored 5.00 5.00

Louis Pasteur (1822-95) A1347

1995, Feb. 19 Litho. *Perf. 11½x12*

2525 A1347 84c multicolored 2.00 2.00

Historical Events A1348

Designs: No. 2526, Capture of Monte Castello, 50th anniv. No. 2527, End of the Farroupilha Revolution, 150th anniv.

1995, Feb. 21

2526 A1348 12c multicolored .30 .30
2527 A1348 12c multicolored .30 .30

Pres. Itamar Franco — A1349

FAO, 50th Anniv. — A1350

1995, Mar. 22 Litho. *Perf. 12x11½*
2528 A1349 12c multicolored .30 .30

1995, Apr. 3 *Perf. 11½x11*
2529 A1350 84c multicolored 2.00 2.00

Famous Men A1351

#2530, Alexandre de Gusmao (1695-1753), diplomat. #2531, Francisco Brandao, Viscount of Jequitinhonha (1794-1870), lawyer, abolitionist. 15c, Jose da Silva Paranhos, Jr., Baron of Rio Branco (1845-1912), politician, diplomat.

1995, Apr. 28 *Perf. 11½x12*
2530 A1351 12c multicolored .30 .30
2531 A1351 12c multicolored .30 .30
2532 A1351 15c multicolored .35 .35
Nos. 2530-2532 (3) .95 .95

Radio, Cent. A1352

Design: Guglielmo Marconi (1874-1937), transmitting equipment.

1995, May 5 Litho. *Perf. 11½x12*
2533 A1352 84c multicolored 2.00 2.00

Friendship Between Brazil & Japan A1353

1995, May 29
2534 A1353 84c multicolored 2.00 2.00

Endangered Birds — A1354

1995, June 5 *Perf. 12x11½*
2535 A1354 12c Tinamus solitarius .30 .30
2536 A1354 12c Mitu mitu .30 .30

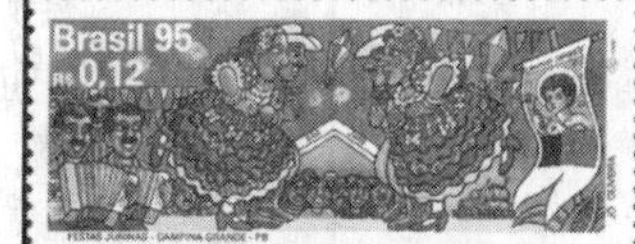
June Festivals — A1355

Designs: No. 2537, Couples dancing at Campina Grande, "Greatest St. John's Party of the World." No. 2538, Bride, bridegroom, festivities, Caruaru.

1995, June 11 *Perf. 11½x12*
2537 A1355 12c multicolored .30 .30
2538 A1355 12c multicolored .30 .30

St. Anthony of Padua (1195-1231) — A1356

1995, June 13
2539 A1356 84c multicolored 2.00 2.00

See Portugal No. 2054.

Souvenir Sheet

Motion Picture, Cent. — A1357

Louis and Auguste Lumiere, camera.

1995, June 21
2540 A1357 2.14r multicolored 4.75 4.75

New Currency, The Real, 1st Anniv. — A1358

Volleyball, Cent. — A1359

1995, July 1 Litho. *Perf. 12x11½*
2541 A1358 12c multicolored .30 .30

1995, July 8
2542 A1359 15c multicolored .35 .35

Dinosaurs A1360

1995, July 23 *Perf. 11½x12*
2543 A1360 15c Angaturama limai .35 .35
2544 A1360 1.50r Titanosaurus 3.25 3.25

Traffic Safety Program A1361

Designs: 12c, Test dummy without seat belt hitting windshield. 71c, Auto hitting alcoholic beverage glass.

1995, July 25
2545 A1361 12c multicolored .30 .30
2546 A1361 71c multicolored 1.65 1.65

Souvenir Sheet

Roberto Burle Marx, Botanist — A1362

Designs: a, 15c, Calathea burle-marxii. b, 15c, Vellozia burle-marxii. c, 1.50r, Heliconia aemygdiana. Illustration reduced.

1995, Aug. 4 Litho. *Perf. 12x11½*
2547 A1362 Sheet of 3, #a.-c. 4.50 4.50

Singapore '95.

Parachute Infantry Brigade, 50th Anniv. — A1363

1995, Aug. 23
2548 A1363 15c multicolored .35 .35

Paulista Museum, Cent. A1364

1995, Sept. 5 *Perf. 11½*
2549 A1364 15c multicolored .35 .35

Lighthouses A1365

1995, Sept. 28
2550 A1365 15c Olinda .35 .35
2551 A1365 15c Sao Joao .35 .35
2552 A1365 15c Santo Antonio da Barra .35 .35
Nos. 2550-2552 (3) 1.05 1.05

Wilhelm Röntgen (1845-1923), Discovery of the X-Ray, Cent. A1366

1995, Sept. 30
2553 A1366 84c multicolored 2.00 2.00

Lubrapex '95, 15th Brazilian-Portuguese Philatelic Exhibition — A1367

Wildlife scene along Tiete River: 15c, #2556a, Bird, otter with fish. 84c, #2556b, Birds, river boat.

1995, Sept. 30 *Perf. 12x11½*
2554 A1367 15c multicolored .35 .35
2555 A1367 84c multicolored 2.00 2.00

Souvenir Sheet

2556 A1367 1.50r Sheet of 2, #a.-b. 6.50 6.50

No. 2556 is a continuous design.

Flamengo Regatta Soccer Club — A1368

1995, Oct. 6 *Perf. 11x11½*
2557 A1368 15c multicolored .35 .35

America Issue A1369

Outdoor scenes: 15c, Trees, mushrooms, alligator, lake. 84c, Black-neck swans on lake, false swans in air.

1995, Oct. 12 Litho. *Perf. 11½x12*
2558 A1369 15c multicolored .35 .35
2559 A1369 84c multicolored 2.00 2.00
a. Pair, #2558-2559 2.35 2.35

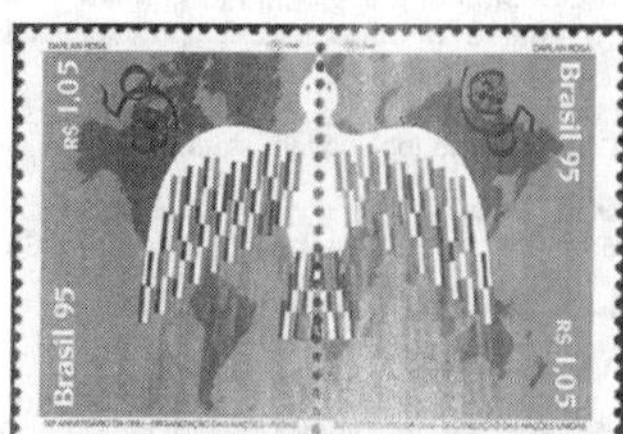
UN, 50th Anniv. — A1370

1995, Oct. 24 *Perf. 12x11½*
2560 1.05r multicolored 2.25 2.25
2561 1.05r multicolored 2.25 2.25
a. A1370 Pair, No. 2560-2561 4.50 4.50

Writers — A1372

Designs: No. 2562, Eca de Queiroz (1845-90), village. No. 2563, Rubem Braga (1913-90), beach, Rio de Janeiro. 23c, Carlos Drummond de Andrade (1902-87), letters.

1995, Oct. 27 ***Perf. 12x11***

2562 A1372 15c multicolored .35 .35
2563 A1372 15c multicolored .35 .35
2564 A1372 23c multicolored .50 .50
Nos. 2562-2564 (3) 1.20 1.20

Souvenir Sheet

Death of Zumbi Dos Palmares, Slave Resistance Leader, 300th Anniv. — A1373

Illustration reduced.

1995, Nov. 20 ***Perf. 12x11½***

2565 A1373 1.05r multicolored 2.25 2.25

2nd World Short Course Swimming Championships — A1374

Four swimmers performing different strokes: a, Freestyle. b, Backstroke. c, Butterfly. d, Breaststroke.

1995, Nov. 30 ***Perf. 11½x12***

2566 A1374 23c Block of 4, #a.-d. 2.00 2.00

Christmas A1375

Designs: a, 23c, Cherub looking right, stars. b, 15c, Cherub looking left, stars.

1995, Dec. 1 ***Perf. 11½***

2567 A1375 Pair, #a.-b.+2 labels .85 .85

Botafogo Soccer and Regatta Club A1376

1995, Dec. 8 ***Perf. 11x11½***

2568 A1376 15c multicolored .35 .35

Diário de Pernambuco Newspaper, 170th Anniv. — A1377

1995, Dec. 14 **Litho.** ***Perf. 12x11½***

2569 A1377 23c multicolored .50 .50

Souvenir Sheet

Amazon Theatre, Cent. — A1378

Illustration reduced.

1996, Feb. 27

2570 A1378 1.23r multicolored 2.50 2.50

Francisco Prestes Maia, Politician, Birth Cent. A1379

1996, Mar. 19 ***Perf. 11½x12***

2571 A1379 18c multicolored .40 .40

Irineu Bornhausen, Governor of Santa Catarina, Birth Cent. — A1380

1996, Mar. 25 ***Perf. 11x11½***

2572 A1380 27c multicolored .55 .55

Paintings A1381

Designs: No. 2573, Boat with Little Flags and Birds, by Alfredo Volpi. No. 2574, Ouro Preto Landscape, by Alberto da Veiga Guignard.

1996, Apr. 15 ***Perf. 12x11½***

2573 A1381 15c multicolored .30 .30
2574 A1381 15c multicolored .30 .30

UNICEF, 50th Anniv. A1382

1996, Apr. 16 ***Perf. 11½***

2575 A1382 23c multicolored .50 .50

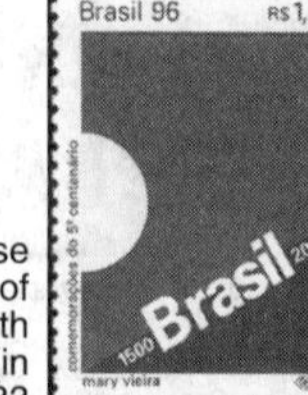

Portuguese Discovery of Brazil, 500th Anniv. (in 2000) — A1383

1996, Apr. 22 ***Perf. 12x11½***

2576 A1383 1.05r multicolored 2.10 2.10

See No. 2626.

Israel Pinheiro da Silva, Politician, Business Entrepeneur, Birth Cent. — A1384

1996, Apr. 23 ***Perf. 11½x12***

2577 A1384 18c multicolored .40 .40

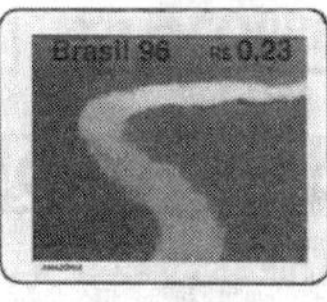

Tourism A1385

#2578, Amazon River. #2579, Swampland area. #2580, Sail boat, northeastern states. #2581, Sugarloaf, Guanabara Bay. #2582, Iguacu Falls.

1996, Apr. 24 ***Die Cut***

Self-Adhesive

2578 A1385 23c multicolored .50 .50
2579 A1385 23c multicolored .50 .50
2580 A1385 23c multicolored .50 .50
2581 A1385 23c multicolored .50 .50
2582 A1385 23c multicolored .50 .50
a. Strip of 5, #2578-2582 2.50

Hummingbirds — A1386

Espamer '96: 15c, Topaza pella. 1.05r, Stephanoxis lalandi. 1.15r, Eupetomena macroura.

1996, May 4 **Litho.** ***Perf. 11½***

2583 A1386 15c multicolored .35 .35
2584 A1386 1.05r multicolored 2.40 2.40
2585 A1386 1.15r multicolored 2.60 2.60
Nos. 2583-2585 (3) 5.35 5.35

1996 Summer Olympic Games, Atlanta A1387

1996, May 21

2586 A1387 18c Marathon .40 .40
2587 A1387 23c Gymnastics .50 .50
2588 A1387 1.05r Swimming 2.40 2.40
2589 A1387 1.05r Beach volleyball 2.40 2.40
Nos. 2586-2589 (4) 5.70 5.70

Souvenir Sheet

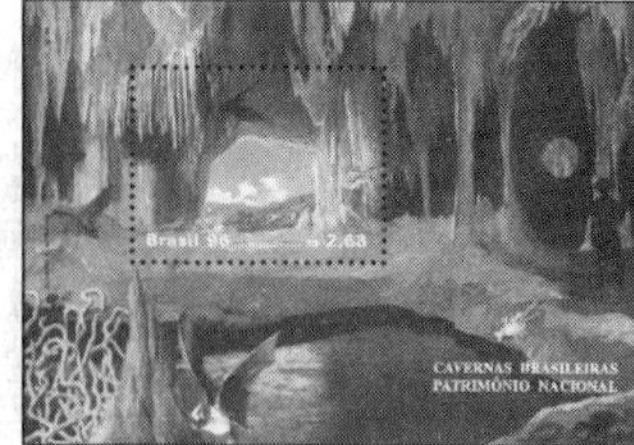
Brazilian Caverns — A1388

Illustration reduced.

1996, June 5 ***Perf. 11½x12***

2590 A1388 2.68r multicolored 6.25 6.25

Americas Telecom '96 — A1389

1996, June 10 ***Perf. 11½***

2591 A1389 1.05r multicolored 2.40 2.40

Souvenir Sheet

World Day to Fight Desertification — A1390

Illustration reduced.

1996, June 17 ***Perf. 12x11½***

2592 A1390 1.23r multicolored 2.80 2.80

Fight Against Drug Abuse A1391

1996, June 26 ***Perf. 11½x12***

2593 A1391 27c multicolored .65 .65

Year of Education A1392

1996, July 10 ***Perf. 12x11½***

2594 A1392 23c multicolored .55 .55

Princess Isabel, 150th Birth Anniv. A1393

1996, July 29 *Perf. 11½x12*

2595 A1393 18c multicolored .40 .40

Carlos Gomes (1836-96), Composer A1394

1996, Sept. 16 *Perf. 11½*

2596 A1394 50c multicolored 1.25 1.25

15th World Orchid Conference A1395

#2597, Promenaea stapelioides. #2598, Cattleya eldorado. #2599, Cattleya loddigesii.

1996, Sept. 17

2597 A1395 15c multicolored .35 .35
2598 A1395 15c multicolored .35 .35
2599 A1395 15c multicolored .35 .35
Nos. 2597-2599 (3) 1.05 1.05

Apparition of Virgin Mary at La Salette, 150th Anniv. A1396

1996, Sept. 19

2600 A1396 1r multicolored 2.30 2.30

Souvenir Sheet

Popular Legends — A1397

Designs: a, 23c, "Cuca" walking from house. b, 1.05r, "Boitatá," snake of life. c, 1.15r, "Caipora," defender of ecology.

1996, Sept. 28 *Perf. 11x10½*

2601 A1397 Sheet of 3, #a.-c. 5.60 5.60

BRAPEX '96.

23rd Sao Paulo Intl. Biennial Exhibition A1398

Designs: a, Marilyn Monroe by Andy Warhol, vert. b, The Scream, by Edvard Munch, vert. c, Abstract, by Louise Bourgeois, vert. d, Woman Drawing, by Pablo Picasso.

1996, Oct. 5 *Perf. 12x11½*

2602 A1398 55c Block of 4, #a.-d. 5.00 5.00

Traditional Costumes A1400

America issue: 50c, Man dressed as cowboy. 1r, Woman dressed in baiana clothes.

1996, Oct. 12 Litho. *Perf. 11½*

2604 A1400 50c multicolored 1.15 1.15
2605 A1400 1r multicolored 2.30 2.30

Christmas A1401

José Carlos (1884-1950), Caricaturist A1402

1996, Nov. 4 Litho. *Perf. 12x11½*

2606 A1401 1st multicolored .60 .60

No. 2606 was valued at 23c on day of issue.

1996, Nov. 22

2607 A1402 1st multicolored .60 .60

No. 2607 was valued at 23c on day of issue.

Tourism A1403

#2608, Ipiranga Monument, Sao Paulo. #2607, Hercílio Luz Bridge, Florianópolis. #2608, Natl. Congress Building, Brasília. #2609, Pelourinho, Salvador. #2610, Ver-o-Peso Market, Belém.

Serpentine Die Cut

1996, Dec. 9 **Photo.**

Self-Adhesive

2608 A1403 1st multicolored .75 .75
2609 A1403 1st multicolored .75 .75
2610 A1403 1st multicolored .75 .75
2611 A1403 1st multicolored .75 .75
2612 A1403 1st multicolored .75 .75
a. Strip of 5, #2608-2612 3.75

Nos. 2608-2612 are inscribed "1o PORTE NACIONAL," and were valued 23c on day of issue. Selvage surrounding each stamp in #2612a is rouletted.

Rio de Janeiro, Candidate for 2004 Summer Olympic Games A1404

1997, Jan. 17 Litho. *Perf. 11½*

2613 A1404 1st multicolored 2.25 2.25

No. 2613 is inscribed "1o PORTE INTERNACIONAL" and was valued at 1.05r on day of issue.

The Postman A1405

1997, Jan. 25

2614 A1405 1st multicolored .85 .85

America issue. No. 2614 is inscribed "1o PORTE NACIONAL" and was valued at 23c on day of issue.

Antonio de Castro Alves (1847-71), Poet A1406

1997, Mar. 14

2615 A1406 15c multicolored .35 .35

Marquis of Tamandaré, Naval Officer, Death Cent. — A1407

1997, Mar. 19 *Perf. 11x11½*

2616 A1407 23c multicolored .50 .50

Stamp Design Contest Winner A1408

1997, Mar. 20 *Perf. 11½x12*

2617 A1408 15c "Joy Joy" .35 .35

World Day of Water — A1409

1997, Mar. 22 *Perf. 12x11½*

2618 A1409 1.05r multicolored 2.10 2.10

Brazilian Airplanes A1410

#2619, EMB-145. #2620, AMX. #2621, EMB-312 H Super Tucano. #2622, EMB-120 Brasilia. #2623, EMB-312 Tucano.

1997, Mar. 27 Litho. ***Die Cut***

Self-Adhesive

2619 A1410 15c multicolored .25 .25
2620 A1410 15c multicolored .25 .25
2621 A1410 15c multicolored .25 .25
2622 A1410 15c multicolored .25 .25
2623 A1410 15c multicolored .25 .25
a. Strip of 5, #2619-2623 1.25

Campaign Against AIDS — A1411

1997, Apr. 7 Litho. *Perf. 12x11½*

2624 A1411 23c multicolored .50 .50

Souvenir Sheet

Indian Culture — A1412

Weapons of the Xingu Indians. Illustration reduced.

1997, Apr. 16 *Perf. 11x11½*

2625 A1412 1.15r multicolored 2.25 2.25

Portuguese Discovery of Brazil, 500th Anniv. Type

1997, Apr. 22 *Perf. 12x11½*

2626 A1383 1.05r like #2576 2.10 2.20

No. 2576 has green background and blue in lower right corner. No. 2626 has those colors reversed and is inscribed "BRASIL 97" at top.

Pixinguinha (1897-1973), Composer, Musician — A1413

1997, Apr. 23

2627 A1413 15c multicolored .35 .35

Souvenir Sheet

Brazilian Claim to Trindade Island, Cent. — A1414

Illustration reduced.

1997, May 7 ***Perf. 11½x11***
2628 A1414 1.23r multicolored 2.50 2.50

Human Rights — A1415

1997, May 13 ***Perf. 12x11½***
2629 A1415 18c multicolored .45 .45

Souvenir Sheet

Brazilian Antarctic Program — A1416

1997, May 13
2630 A1416 2.68r multicolored 5.50 5.50

Fruits and Nuts — A1417

1c, Oranges. 2c, Bananas. 5c, Papayas. 10c, Pineapple. #2635, 2636L, Cashews. #2636, 2636Q, Sugar apple. #2636A, Grapes. #2636B, 2636M, 2636R, Watermelon. 50c, Surinam cherry (pitanga), 51c, Coconuts. 80c, Apples. 82c, Lemons. 1r, Strawberries.

1997-99 Litho. *Serpentine Die Cut*
Self-Adhesive

2631 A1417 1c multi .20 .20
2632 A1417 2c multi .20 .20
2633 A1417 5c multi .20 .20
2634 A1417 10c multi, vert. .20 .20
2635 A1417 20c multi, vert. .40 .40
2636 A1417 20c multi, vert. .40 .40
2636A A1417 22c multi .40 .40
2636B A1417 (22c) multi .45 .45
2636C A1417 50c multi .55 .55
2636D A1417 51c multi, vert. 1.00 1.00
2636E A1417 80c multi, vert. 1.40 1.40
2636F A1417 82c multi, vert. 1.60 1.60
2636G A1417 1r multi, vert. 2.00 2.00
Nos. 2631-2636G (13) 9.00 9.00

Issued: (22c), 5/28; 1c, 6/97; 2c, 10c, #2635, 7/97; 5c, 8/97; 1r, 8/3; 22c, 10/3; #2636, 51c, 80c, 82c, 1/15/98; 50c, 11/26/99.

No. 2636B is inscribed "1o PORTE NATIONAL" and was valued at 22c on day of issue.

Fruits and Nuts Type of 1997-99
1998-99 Litho. *Die Cut*
Self-Adhesive

2636H A1417 1c multi .20 .20
2636I A1417 2c multi .45 .45
2636J A1417 5c multi 1.10 1.10
2636K A1417 10c multi, vert. 2.25 2.25
2636L A1417 20c multi, vert. 4.25 4.25
2636M A1417 (22c) multi 4.75 4.75
Nos. 2636H-2636M (6) 13.00 13.00

Issued: No. 2636M, 1999; others, 1998.

Fruit and Nuts Type of 1997-99
1999 Litho. *Microperfed*
Without Gum

2636N A1417 1c multi *.25 .25*
2636O A1417 5c multi *1.10 1.10*
2636P A1417 10c multi, vert. *2.25 2.25*
2636Q A1417 20c multi, vert. *4.50 4.50*
2636R A1417 (31c) multi *7.00 7.00*
2636S A1417 51c multi, vert. *11.50 11.50*
2636T A1417 80c multi, vert. *18.00 18.00*
2636U A1417 1r multi, vert. *22.50 22.50*
Nos. 2636N-2636U (8) *67.10 67.10*

Issued: Nos. 2636N-2636Q, 9/28/99; No. 2636R, 9/12/99; No. 2636S, 9/22/99; Nos. 2636T, 2636U, 9/15/99.

A1418

Amazon Flora and Fauna — A1419

Designs: No. 2637, Swietenia macropylla. No. 2638, Arapaima gigas.

1997, June 5 Litho. *Perf. 11½x12*
2637 A1418 27c multicolored .55 .55
2638 A1419 27c multicolored .55 .55

Fr. José de Anchieta (1534-97), Missionary in Brazil — A1420

Design: No. 2640, Fr. António Vieira (1608-97), missionary in Brazil, diplomat.

1997, June 9 ***Perf. 12***
2639 A1420 1.05r multicolored 2.10 2.10
2640 A1420 1.05r multicolored 2.10 2.10

See Portugal Nos. 2168-2169.

Tourism A1421

Designs: No. 2641, Parnaíba River Delta. No. 2642, Lencóis Maranhenses Park.

1997, June 20 ***Perf. 11½x12***
2641 A1421 1st multicolored 2.10 2.10
2642 A1421 1st multicolored 2.10 2.10

Nos. 2641-2642 are inscribed "1o PORTE INTERNACIONAL TAXE PERCUE" and were each valued at on day of issue.

Brazilian Academy of Literature, Cent. A1422

1997, July 20
2643 A1422 22c multicolored .50 .50

Emiliano de Cavalcanti (1897-1976), Painter A1423

1997, Sept. 16 Litho. *Perf. 11½*
2644 A1423 31c multicolored .65 .65

2nd World Meeting of the Pope with Families, Rio de Janeiro A1424

1997, Sept. 22 ***Perf. 11½x12***
2645 A1424 1.20r multicolored 2.50 2.50

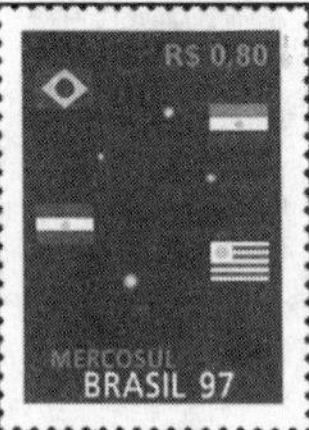

A1425

A1426

1997, Sept. 26 ***Perf. 12x11½***
2646 A1425 80c multicolored 1.60 1.60

MERCOSUR (Common Market of Latin America). See Argentina #1975, Bolivia #1019, Paraguay #2565, Uruguay #1681.

1997, Sept. 27
2647 A1426 22c multicolored .45 .45

End of Canudos War, cent.

Integration of MERCOSUR Communications by Telebras, 25th Anniv. — A1427

1997, Oct. 6 ***Perf. 11½***
2648 A1427 80c multicolored 1.60 1.60

Composers — A1428

#2649, Oscar Lorenzo Fernandez (1897-1948). #2650, Francisco Mignone (1897-1986).

1997, Oct. 7 ***Perf. 11x11½***
2649 A1428 22c multicolored .45 .45
2650 A1428 22c multicolored .45 .45

Marist Brothers Presence in Brazil, Cent. A1429

1997, Oct. 22
2651 A1429 22c multicolored .45 .45

Christmas A1430

1997, Nov. 5 ***Perf. 12x11½***
2652 A1430 22c multicolored .45 .45

Education and Citzenship — A1431

1997, Dec. 10 ***Perf. 11x11½***
2653 A1431 31c blue & yellow .65 .65

City of Belo Horizonte, Cent. A1432

1997, Dec. 12 ***Perf. 11½x12***
2654 A1432 31c multicolored .65 .65

Citzenship A1433

Map of Brazil and: No. 2655, Education, stack of books. No. 2656, Employment, worker's papers. No. 2657, Agriculture, oranges. No. 2658, Health, stethoscope, vert. No. 2659, Culture, clapboard with musical notes, artist's paint brush, vert.

1997, Dec. 20 ***Die Cut***
Self-Adhesive
Booklet Stamps

2655 A1433 22c multicolored .45 .45
2656 A1433 22c multicolored .45 .45
2657 A1433 22c multicolored .45 .45
2658 A1433 22c multicolored .45 .45
2659 A1433 22c multicolored .45 .45
a. Bklt. pane, 2 ea #2655-2659 4.50

The peelable paper backing of No. 2659a serves as a booklet cover.

Gems — A1434

1998, Jan. 22 ***Perf. 12x11½***

2660 A1434 22c Alexandrite .45 .45
2661 A1434 22c Cat's eye chrysoberyl .45 .45
2662 A1434 22c Indicolite .45 .45
a. Strip of 3, #2660-2662 1.40 1.40

Famous Brazilian Women A1435

America Issue: No. 2663, Elis Regina, singer. No. 2664, Clementina de Jesus, singer. No. 2665, Dulcina de Moraes, actress. No. 2666, Clarice Lispector, writer.

1998, Mar. 11 ***Perf. 11½***

2663 A1435 22c multicolored .45 .45
2664 A1435 22c multicolored .45 .45
2665 A1435 22c multicolored .45 .45
2666 A1435 22c multicolored .45 .45
a. Block of 4, #2663-2666 1.80 1.80

Education — A1436

1998, Mar. 19 ***Perf. 12x11½***

2667 31c Children at desks .65 .65
2668 31c Teacher at blackboard .65 .65
a. A1436 Pair, #2667-2668 1.30 1.30

Cruz e Sousa (1861-98), Poet A1437

1998, Mar. 19 **Litho.** ***Perf. 11½x12***

2669 A1437 36c multicolored .65 .65

Discovery of Brazil, 500th Anniv. — A1438

#2670, 1519 map showing natives, vegetation, fauna. #2671, Caravel from Cabral's fleet.

1998, Apr. 22 ***Perf. 12x11½***

2670 1.05r multicolored 1.75 1.75
2671 1.05r multicolored 1.75 1.75
a. A1438 Pair, #2670-2671 3.50 3.50

Volunteer Work A1439

Designs: a, Caring for sick man. b, Caring for sick child. c, Fighting forest fire. c, Child's hand holding adult's finger.

1998, May 5 ***Perf. 11½x12***

2672 A1439 31c Block of 4, #a.-d. 2.25 2.25

Brazilian Circus — A1440

Piolin the clown: a, Looking through circle. b, Standing in ring. c, With outside of tent to the left. d, With inside of tent to the right.

1998, May 18 ***Perf. 12x11½***

2673 A1440 31c Block of 4, #a.-d. 2.25 2.25

Intl. Year of the Ocean A1441

Pictures, drawings of marine life: a, Turtle. b, Tail fin of whale. c, Barracuda. d, Jellyfish, school of fish. e, School of fish, diver. f, Dolphins. g, Yellow round fish. h, Two whales. i, Two black-striped butterfly fish. j, Orange & yellow fish. k, Manatee. l, Yellow-striped fish. m, Blue & yellow fish. n, Several striped fish. o, Fish with wing-like fins. p, Manta ray. q, Two fish swimming in opposite directions. r, Long, thin fish, coral. s, Moray eel. t, Yellow & black butterfly fish, coral. u, Starfish, fish. v, Crab, coral. w, Black & orange fish, coral. x, Sea horse, coral.

1998, May 22 ***Perf. 11½x12***
Sheet of 24

2674 A1441 31c #a.-x. 12.50 12.50

Expo '98.

1998 World Cup Soccer Championships, France — A1442

Stylized paintings, by: a, Gregorio Gruber. b, Mario Gruber. c, Maciej Babinski. d, Cildo Meireles, vert. e, Claudio Tozzi, vert. f, Antonio Henrique Amaral, vert. g, Jose Roberto Aguilar. h, Nelson Leirner. i, Wesley Duke Lee. j, Mauricio Nogueira Lima. k, Zelio Alves Pinto, vert. l, Aldemir Martins, vert. m, Ivald Granato. n, Carlos Vergara. o, Joao Camara, vert. p, Roberto Magalhaes, vert. q, Guto Lacaz, vert. r, Glauco Rodrigues, vert. s, Leda Catunda. t, Tomoshige Kusuno. u, Jose Zaragoza. v, Luiz Zerbine, vert. w, Antonio Peticov, vert. x, Marcia Grostein, vert.

1998, May 28 ***Perf. 11½x12, 12x11½***

2675 A1442 22c Sheet of 24, #a.-x. 9.00 9.00

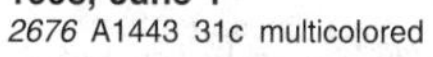
Feijoada, Traditional Cuisine A1443

1998, June 1 ***Perf. 11½***

2676 A1443 31c multicolored .55 .55

Preservation of Flora and Fauna — A1444

Designs: No. 2677, Araucaria angustifolia. No. 2678, Cyanocorax caeruleus.

1998, June 5 ***Perf. 11½x12***

2677 A1444 22c multicolored .40 .40
2678 A1444 22c multicolored .40 .40
a. Pair, #2677-2678 .80 .80

Launching of Submarine Tapajó A1445

1998, June 5

2679 A1445 51c multicolored .90 .90

Luiz de Queiroz (1849-98), Founder of Agricultural School A1446

1998, June 6 ***Perf. 11½***

2680 A1446 36c multicolored .65 .65

Benedictine Monastery, Sao Paulo, 400th Anniv. A1447

1998, July 10 **Litho.** ***Perf. 11½x12***

2681 A1447 22c multicolored .25 .25

Alberto Santos-Dumont (1873-1932), Aviation Pioneer — A1448

#2682, Balloon "Brazil." #2683, Dirigible Nr. 1, Santos-Dumont at controls.

1998, July 18

2682 A1448 31c multicolored .35 .35
2683 A1448 31c multicolored .35 .35
a. Pair, #2682-2683 .70 .70

Brazilian Cinema, Cent. (in 1997) A1449

Designs: a, Guanabara Bay, by Lumière, 1897. b, Taciana Reiss in "Limite," by Mário Peixoto, 1931. c, Actors in (Chanchada)," from "A Dupla do Barulho," by Carlos Manga, 1953. d, Films produced by Vera Cruz pictures, caricature of Mazzaropi from "The Dream Factory." e, Glauber Rocha's "New Cinema". f, International film festival awards won by Brazilian films.

1998, July 24 ***Perf. 11½***

2684 A1449 31c Block of 6, #a.-f. 2.00 2.00

Rodrigo Melo Franco de Andrade (1898-1969) — A1450

Church of Our Lady of the Rosary, Ouro Preto.

1998, Aug. 17 ***Perf. 11x11½***

2685 A1450 51c multicolored .60 .60

Luís da Camara Cascudo (1898-1986), Writer — A1451

1998, Aug. 22

2686 A1451 22c multicolored .25 .25

42nd Aeronautical Pentathlon World Championship A1452

Stylized designs: a, Fencing. b, Running. c, Swimming. d, Shooting. e, Basketball.

1998, Aug. 22 ***Perf. 12x11½***

2687 A1452 22c Strip of 5, #a.-e. 1.25 1.25

Mercosur — A1453

Design: Missionary Cross, ruins of the Church of Sao Migeul das Missoes.

1998, Sept. 17 ***Perf. 11½x12***

2688 A1453 80c multicolored .90 .90

24th Sao Paulo Art Biennial — A1454

a, Biennial emblem, by José Leonilson. b, Tapuia Dance, by Albert von Eckhout. c, The Schoolboy, by Vincent van Gogh. d, Portrait of Michel Leiris, by Francis Bacon. e, The King's Museum, by René Magritte. f, Urutu, by Tarsila do Amaral. g, Facade with Arcs, Circle and Fascia, by Alfredo Volpi. h, The Raft of the Medusa, by Asger Jorn.

1998, Sept. 22

2689 A1454 31c Block of 8, #a.-h. 2.00 2.00

Nos. 2689b, 2689h have horiz. designs placed vert. on stamps.

Child and Citizenship Stamp Design Contest Winner A1455

1998, Oct. 9

2690 A1455 22c multicolored .25 .25

Reorganization of Maritime Mail from Portugal to Brazil, Bicent. — A1456

1998, Oct. 9

2691 A1456 1.20r multicolored 1.25 1.25

See Portugal Nos. 2271-2272.

Dom Pedro I (1798-1834) A1457

1998, Oct. 13 ***Perf. 11½***

2692 A1457 22c multicolored .25 .25

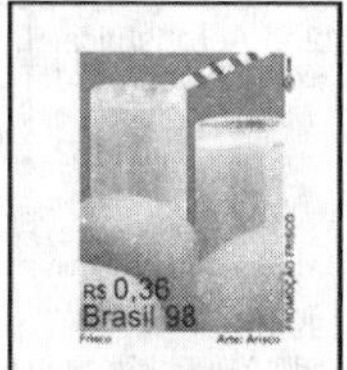

Frisco's Mango Refreshment Promotional Stamp — A1458

Serpentine Die Cut

1998, Oct. 15 **Photo.**

Self-Adhesive

2693 A1458 36c multicolored .40 .40

No. 2693 is valid on all mail, but must be used on mail entries to Frisco on Faustao's Truck raffle.

Flowers A1459

Designs: a, Solanum lycocarpum. b, Cattleya walkeriana. c, Kielmeyera coriacea.

1998, Oct. 23 **Litho.** ***Perf. 11½***

2694 A1459 31c Strip of 3, #a.-c. 1.00 1.00

Humanitarians — A1460

Designs: a, Mother Teresa (1910-97). b, Friar Galvao (1739-1822). c, Herbert José de Souza "Betinho" (b. 1935). d, Friar Damiao (1898-1997).

1998, Oct. 25

2695 A1460 31c Block of 4, #a.-d. 1.40 1.40

Natl. Telecommunications Agency (ANATEL) — A1461

Design: Sergio Motta, former Minister of Communications, ANATEL headquarters, Brasilia.

1998, Nov. 5 ***Perf. 12x11½***

2696 A1461 31c multicolored .35 .35

Christmas — A1462

Design: Athos Bulcao's tiles, Church of Our Lady of Fatima, Brasilia, outline of sanctuary.

1998, Nov. 19 ***Perf. 11½x12***

2697 A1462 22c multicolored .25 .25

Domestic Animals A1463

No. 2698, Moxotó goat. No. 2699, Brazilian donkey. No. 2700, Junqueira ox. No. 2701, Brazilian terrier. No. 2702, Brazilian shorthair cat.

1998, Nov. 20 ***Die Cut***

Booklet Stamps

Self-Adhesive

2698 A1463 22c multi .25 .25
2699 A1463 22c multi .25 .25
2700 A1463 22c multi .25 .25
2701 A1463 22c multi, vert. .25 .25
2702 A1463 22c multi, vert. .25 .25
a. Bklt. pane, 2 ea #2698-2702 2.50

No. 2702a is a complete booklet.

Universal Declaration of Human Rights, 50th Anniv. — A1464

1998, Dec. 9 ***Perf. 12x11½***

2703 A1464 1.20r multicolored 1.25 1.25

Natal, 400th Anniv. A1465

Perf. 11x11½, 11½x11

1999, Jan. 6 **Litho.**

2704 A1465 31c Wise Men's Fortress .35 .35
2705 A1465 31c Mother Luiza Lighthouse, vert. .35 .35

Program for Evaluating Resources in Brazil's Exclusive Economic Zone A1466

No. 2706: a, Satellite, St. Peter and St. Paul Archpelago. b, Bird on buoy. c, Fishing boat. d, Sea turtle. e, Dolphin. f, Diver.

1999, Mar. 5 ***Perf. 11½x12***

2706 A1466 31c Block of 6, #a.-f. 2.00 2.00

Australia '99 World Stamp Expo.

UPU, 125th Anniv. A1467

No. 2707: a, Stamp vending machines from 1940s and 1998. b, Vending machines, 1906, 1998. c, Collection boxes, 1870, 1973. d, Federal Government's 1998 Quality Award.

1999, Mar. 19 ***Perf. 11½***

2707 A1467 31c Block of 4, #a.-d. 1.40 1.40

Reorganization of Brazilian Posts and Telegraphs, 30th anniv.

City of Salvador, 450th Anniv. — A1468

1999, Mar. 29 **Litho.** ***Perf. 11½x12***

2708 A1468 1.05r multi 1.25 1.25

Dinosaurs' Valley A1469

1999, Apr. 17 **Litho.** ***Perf. 11½x12***

2709 A1469 1.05r multicolored 1.10 1.10

Fort of Santo Amaro da Barra Grande — A1470

1999, Apr. 21 **Litho.** ***Perf. 11½x12***

2710 A1470 22c multicolored .25 .25

Souvenir Sheet

Discovery of Brazil, 500th Anniv. (in 2000) — A1471

Illustration reduced.

1999, Apr. 22 **Litho.** ***Perf. 11½x11***

2711 A1471 2.68r multi 3.25 3.25

Lubrapex 2000.

6th Air Transportation Squadron, 30th Anniv. — A1472

1999, May 12 **Litho.** ***Perf. 11x11½***

2712 A1472 51c multicolored .55 .55

Holy Spirit Feast, Planaltina — A1473

1999, May 21 ***Perf. 12x11½***

2713 A1473 22c multicolored .25 .25

Historical and Cultural Heritage A1474

Views of cities: a, Ouro Preto. b, Olinda. c, Sao Luís.

1999, June 2 ***Perf. 11½x11***

2714 A1474 1.05r Sheet of 3, #a.-c. 3.25 3.25

PhilexFrance '99, World Philatelic Exhibition.

Sao Paolo State Institute for Technological Research, Cent. — A1475

1999, June 24 Litho. *Perf. 11½x12*
2715 A1475 36c multicolored .40 .40

Flight of Alberto Santos-Dumont's Dirigible No. 3, Cent. — A1476

1999, July 20
2716 A1476 1.20r multicolored 1.40 1.40

Forest Fire Prevention A1477

a, Anteater. b, Flower. c, Leaf. d, Burnt trunk.

Serpentine Die Cut 6

1999, Aug. 1 Litho.

Self-Adhesive

2717 Block of 4 2.10
a.-d. A1477 51c Any single .50 .50

No. 2717 is printed on recycled paper impregnated with burnt wood odor.

Souvenir Sheet

America Issue, A New Millennium Without Arms — A1478

Designs: a, Hands of adult and child drawing dove. b, Overturned tank.

1999, Aug. 6 Litho. *Perf. 12x11½*
2718 A1478 90c Sheet of 2, #a.-b. 1.90 1.90

Issued with rouletted tab at right showing Universal Product Code.

Political Amnesty, 20th Anniv. — A1479

1999, Aug. 18
2719 A1479 22c multicolored .25 .25

Famous Brazilians — A1480

Designs: 22c, Joaquim Nabuco (1849-1910), politician and diplomat. 31c, Ruy Barbosa (1849-1923), politician and justice for International Court.

1999, Aug. 19 Litho. *Perf. 11½x12*
2720 A1480 22c multicolored .25 .25
2721 A1480 31c multicolored .35 .35

Fish — A1481

Designs: a, 22c, Salminus maxillosus. b, 31c, Brycon microlepsus. c, 36c, Acestrorhynchus pantaneiro. d, 51c, Hyphessobrycon eques. e, 80c, Rineloricaria. f, 90c, Leporinus macrocephalus. g, 1.05r, Abramites. h, 1.20r, Ancistrus.

1999, Aug. 20 Litho. *Perf. 11½x12*
2722 A1481 Sheet of 8, #a.-h. 5.50 5.50

China 1999 World Philatelic Exhibition. No. 2722h has a holographic image. Soaking in water may affect hologram.

Mercosur Cultural Heritage Day A1482

1999, Sept. 17 Litho. *Perf. 11½x12*
2723 A1482 80c multi .90 .90

Water Resources — A1483

Designs: a, Ecological station, Aguas Emendadas. b, House on water's edge, boat. c, Cedro Dam. d, Orós Dam.

1999, Oct. 21
2724 A1483 31c Block of 4, #a.-d. 1.40 1.40

National Library of Rio de Janeiro Bookplate A1484

1999, Oct. 29 Litho. *Perf. 12x11½*
2725 A1484 22c multi .25 .25

State Flag Type of 1981

1999, Nov. 19 Litho. *Perf. 11½x12*
2726 A947 31c Amapá .35 .35
2727 A947 36c Roraima .35 .35

Antonio Carlos Jobim (1927-94), Composer A1485

1999, Nov. 22
2728 A1485 31c multi .35 .35

Christianity, 2000th Anniv. — A1486

No. 2729: a, The Annunciation. b, Birth of Jesus and adoration of the Magi. c, Presentation of Jesus in the temple. d, Baptism of Jesus by John the Baptist. e, Evangelization of Jesus and Apostles. f, Death of Jesus and resurrection.
Illustration reduced.

1999, Nov. 26 Litho. *Perf. 11½*
2729 A1486 22c Block of 6, #a-f 1.50 1.50

New Middle School Education System — A1487

1999, Dec. 2 *Perf. 11x11½*
2730 A1487 31c multi .35 .35

Itamaraty Palace, Rio A1488

Litho. & Engr.

1999, Dec. 6 *Perf. 11½x12*
2731 A1488 1.05r pale yel & brn 1.25 1.25

New Year 2000 — A1489

Illustration reduced.

2000, Jan. 1 Litho.
2732 A1489 90c multi 1.00 1.00

National School Book Program A1490

2000, Feb. 7 *Perf. 11x11½*
2733 A1490 31c multi .35 .35

Aviatrixes — A1491

No. 2734: a, Ada Rogato (1920-86). b, Thereza de Marzo (1903-86). c, Anésia Pinheiro (1904-99).

2000, Mar. 8 *Perf. 11½x12*
2734 A1491 22c Horiz. strip of 3, #a-c .75 .75

Regional Cuisine — A1492

a, Moqueca Capixaba. b, Moqueca Baiana.

2000, Mar. 21
2735 A1492 1.05r Pair, #a-b 2.40 2.40

Gilberto Freyre (1900-87), Sociologist — A1493

Illustration reduced.

2000, Mar. 24
2736 A1493 36c multi .40 .40

UIT Telecom A1494

2000, Apr. 9 Litho. *Perf. 11½*
2737 A1494 51c multi .55 .55

Discovery of Brazil, 500th anniv.

Discovery of Brazil, 500th Anniv. — A1495

No. 2738: a, Two sailors, three natives, parrot. b, Sailor, ships, four natives. c, Sailors, natives, sails. d, Sailor and natives inspecting tree.
Ilustration reduced.

2000, Apr. 11 Litho. *Perf. 11½x12*
2738 A1495 31c Block of 4, #a-d 1.40 1.40

See Portugal Nos. 2354-2357.

Discovery of Brazil, 500th Anniv. — A1496

Illustration reduced.

2000, Apr. 11 Litho. *Perf. 11½*
2739 A1496 31c multi + label .35 .35

Pritned in sheets of 9 stamps + 9 labels that could be personalized.

Discovery of Brazil, 500th Anniv. — A1497

No. 2740: a, Brazilian flag as sails of ship. b, Man with pineapple, telephone dial, horn. c, Parrot and ships. d, Ship, map of Brazil, children. e, Race car driver Ayrton Senna. f, Flora and fauna. g, Map of Brazil, compass roses. h, Dove. i, Native with decorated face. j, Stylized "500." k, Native with feathered headdress. l, Children's drawing. m, Aviator Alberto Santos Dumont. n, Ship, manuscript. o, World Cup trophies, soccer player and ball, map. p, Fiber optic cables, street lights. q, Bull with Brazilian flag. r, Parrot. s, Native masks. t, Ship, Brazil highlighted on globe.

2000, Apr. 22 Litho. *Perf. 11½*
2740 A1497 45c Sheet of 20, #a-t, + 4 labels 10.00 10.00

Brazil Trade Net Website, 2nd Anniv. A1498

2000, May 11 Litho. *Perf. 11½*
2741 A1498 27c multi .30 .30

National Coastal Management Program — A1499

2000, May 16 Litho. *Perf. 11½*
2742 A1499 40c multi .40 .40

Souvenir Sheet

Expo 2000, Hanover — A1500

No. 2743: a, Map of Western Brazil. b, Map of Eastern Brazil. c, Gold and gemstones.
Illustration reduced.

2000, May 19 Litho. *Perf. 10¾x11*
2743 A1500 1.30r #a-c 4.00 4.00

Oswaldo Cruz Foundation, Cent. — A1501

Illustration reduced.

2000, May 25 *Perf. 11½x12*
2744 A1501 40c multicolored .40 .40

Africa Day A1502

2000, May 25 *Perf. 11½*
2745 A1502 1.10r multi 1.10 1.10

Sailing Feats of Amyr Klink A1503

No. 2746: a, First crossing of South Atlantic by rowboat, 1984. b, Solo circumnavigation of Antarctica, 1999.

2000, May 27
2746 A1503 1r Vert. pair, #a-b 2.00 2.00

Juiz de Fora, 150th Anniv. — A1504

Illustration reduced.

2000, May 31 *Perf. 11½x12*
2747 A1504 60c multi .60 .60

Sports — A1505

Serpentine Die Cut 5¾
2000 Photo.
Self-Adhesive
2748 A1505 27c Hanggliding .30 .30
2749 A1505 27c Surfing .30 .30
2750 A1505 40c Mountain climbing .45 .45
2751 A1505 40c Skateboarding .45 .45
Nos. 2748-2751 (4) 1.50 1.50

Issued: Nos. 2748, 2750, 6/1; No. 2749, 8/1; No. 2751, 7/1.

Environmental Protection — A1506

No. 2752: a, Trees. b, Trees, Felis tigrina in background. c, Heads of two Felis tigrina, two white flowers. d, Felis tigrina, one white flower.
Illustration reduced.

2000, June 5 *Perf. 11½*
2752 A1506 40c Block of 4, #a-d 1.75 1.75

Ships — A1507

No. 2753: a, Cisne Branco. b, Brasil.
Illustration reduced.

2000, June 11 Litho. *Perf. 11x11½*
2753 A1507 27c Pair, #a-b .60 .60

Souvenir Sheets

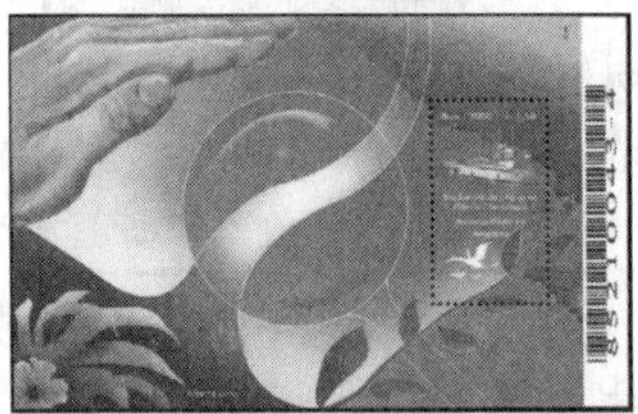

Military Presence in Amazonia — A1508

Illustration reduced.

2000, June 11 Litho. *Perf. 11½x11*
2754 A1508 1.50r multi 1.50 1.50

Barcode is separated from the sheet margin by a row of microperfs.

America Issue — A1509

No. 2755: a, Campaign against AIDS. b, Natl. anti-drug week.
Illustration reduced.

2000, June 19 *Perf. 12x11½*
2755 A1509 1.10r Sheet of 2, #a-b 2.25 2.25

Barcode is separated from the sheet margin by a row of microperfs.

Anísio Teixeira (1900-71), Educator — A1510

Illustration reduced.

2000, July 12 Litho. *Perf. 11½x12*
2756 A1510 45c multi .50 .50

Children's and Teenagers Statute, 10th Anniv. — A1511

2000, July 13 *Perf. 12x11½*
2757 A1511 27c multi .30 .30

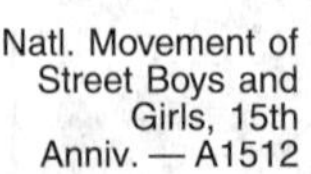

Natl. Movement of Street Boys and Girls, 15th Anniv. — A1512

2000, July 13
2758 A1512 40c multi .40 .40

Gustavo Capanema (1900-54), Politician — A1513

Illustration reduced.

2000, Aug. 10 Litho. ***Perf. 11½x12***
2759 A1513 60c multi .65 .65

Milton Campos, Politician — A1514

Illustration reduced.

2000, Aug. 16
2760 A1514 1r multi 1.10 1.10

World Ozone Layer Protection Day — A1515

2000, Sept. 16 ***Perf. 12x11½***
2761 A1515 1.45r multi 1.60 1.60

Fruit — A1516

Serpentine Die Cut 5¾

2000, Sept. 21 Litho.

Self-Adhesive

2762 A1516 27c Cupuacu .30 .30
2763 A1516 40c Soursop .45 .45

2000 Summer Olympics, Sydney — A1517

Designs: a, Pommel horse. b, Weight lifting. c, Discus. d, Men's rings. e, Sprinting. f, Javelin. g, Rhythmic gymnastics. h, Field hockey. i, Volleyball. j, Synchronized swimming. k, Judo. l, Wrestling. m, Cycling. n, Rowing. o, Parallel bars. p, Equestrian. q, Pole vault. r, Fencing. s, Shooting. t, Taekwondo.
Illustration reduced.

2000, Sept. 23 Litho. ***Perf. 11½x12***
2764 Sheet of 20 + 4 labels 8.75 8.75
a.-t. A1517 40c Any single .40 .40

Olympics Type of 2000

No. 2765: a, Archery. b, Beach volleyball. c, Boxing. d, Soccer. e, Canoeing. f, Handball. g, Diving. h, Rhythmic gymnastics. i, Badminton. j, Swimming. k, Hurdles. l, Pentathlon. m, Basketball. n, Tennis. o, Marathon. p, High jump. q, Long jump. r, Triple jump. s, Triathlon. t, Yachting.

2000, Sept. 23 Litho. ***Perf. 11½x12***
2765 Sheet of 20 + 4 labels 8.75 8.75
a.-t. A1517 40c Any single .40 .40

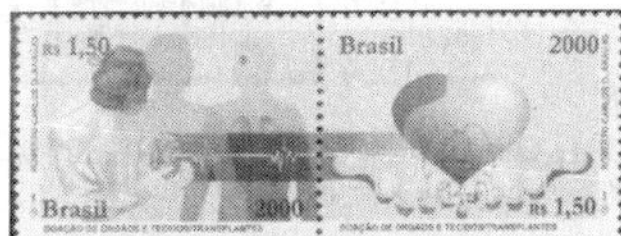

Organ Donation and Transplantation — A1519

No. 2766: a, Doctor holding heart. b, Heart, hands, body with organs outlined.
Illustration reduced.

2000, Sept. 27
2766 A1519 1.50r Horiz. pair, #a-b 3.25 3.25

Masks and Puppets A1520

Designs: No. 2767, 27c, Chinese puppet. No. 2768, 27c, Brazilian mask.

2000, Oct. 9
2767-2768 A1520 Set of 2 .60 .60

Brazil-People's Republic of China diplomatic relations, 25th anniv. See People's Republic of China Nos. 3053-3054.

Race Car Drivers A1521

Designs: 1.30r, Francisco "Chico" Landi (1907-89). 1.45r, Ayrton Senna (1960-94).

2000, Oct. 12 ***Perf. 11x11½***
2769-2770 A1521 Set of 2 3.00 3.00

Telecourse 2000 Project A1522

2000, Oct. 13 Litho. ***Perf. 11½x12***
2771 A1522 27c multi .30 .30

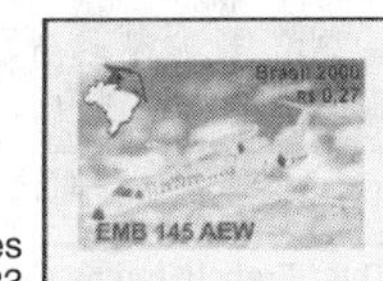

Airplanes A1523

No. 2772: a, EMB 145 AEW. b, Super Tucano. c, AMX-T. d, ERJ 135. e, ERJ 170. f, ERJ 145. g, ERJ 190. h, EMB 145 RS/MP. i, ERJ 140. j, EMB 120.

2000, Oct. 23 Litho. ***Die Cut***

Self-Adhesive

2772 Pane of 10 3.00 3.00
a.-j. A1523 27c Any single .30 .30

Christmas A1524

No. 2773: a, Hand of Jesus, star of Bethlehem. b, Mary, baby Jesus. c, Hand of Jesus, fish, boats on Sea of Galilee. d, Jesus, Sea of Galilee. e, Hand of Jesus, mountain, trees, Earth. f, Jesus, Earth.

2000, Nov. 23 ***Perf. 11½***
2773 Block of 6 1.80 1.80
a.-f. A1524 27c Any single .30 .30

Light and Sound Project — A1525

2000, Dec. 2 ***Perf. 12x11½***
2774 A1525 1.30r multi 1.40 1.40

Settlement of Brazil-French Guiana Border Dispute, Cent. — A1526

2000, Dec. 12 ***Perf. 11½x12***
2775 A1526 40c multi .45 .45

Advent of New Millennium — A1527

Designs: Nos. 2776, 2779a, 40c, Chalice and eucharist. Nos. 2777, 2779b, 1.30r, Star of David, menorah, Torah, tablets. Nos. 2778, 2779c, 1.30r, Minaret, dome of mosque, Holy Ka'aba.

2001, Jan. 1 ***Perf. 11x11½***
2776-2778 A1527 Set of 3 3.00 3.00

Souvenir Sheet

2779 A1527 Sheet of 3, #a-c 3.00 3.00

Nos. 2779a-2779c lack white border. On No. 2779, barcode is separated from sheet margin by a row of rouletting.

Pan-American Scout Jamboree, Foz do Iguaçu — A1528

No. 2780: a, Flags, map, emblems. b, Scouts in canoe, waterfall.

2001, Jan. 7 ***Perf. 12x11½***
2780 A1528 1.10r Horiz. pair, #a-b 2.25 2.25

New Year 2001 (Year of the Snake) — A1529

Illustration reduced.

Litho. & Embossed

2001, Jan. 24 ***Perf. 11½***
2781 A1529 1.45r multi 1.50 1.50

Hong Kong 2001 Stamp Exhibition.

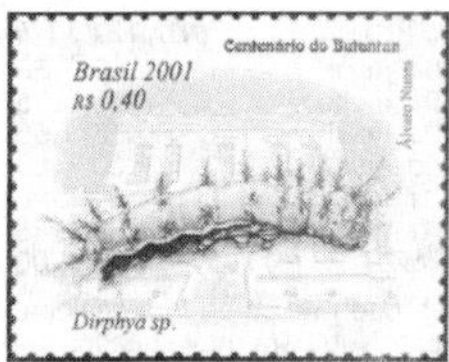

Venomous Animals A1530

No. 2782: a, Dirphya sp. b, Megalopyge sp. c, Phoneutria sp. d, Tityus bahiensis. e, Crotalus durissus. f, Micrurus corallinus. g, Lachesis muta. h, Bothrops jararaca.

2001, Feb. 23 Litho. ***Perf. 11½x12***
2782 Sheet of 8 3.25 3.25
a.-h A1530 40c Any single .40 .40

Butantan Institute, cent.

Brazilian Publishing Industry — A1531

2001, Mar. 5 ***Perf. 11x11½***
2783 A1531 27c multi .30 .30

Special Exports Program — A1532

Illustration reduced.

2001, Mar. 5 ***Perf. 11½x12***
2784 A1532 1.30r multi 1.25 1.25

National Library, 190th Anniv. — A1533

Illustration reduced.

Litho. & Engr.

2001, Mar. 26 ***Perf. 11½x12***
2785 A1533 27c multi .25 .25

Council for Scientific and Technical Development — A1534

2001, Apr. 17
2786 A1534 40c blue .35 .35

Soccer Teams — A1535

Designs: No. 2787, Regatas Vasco da Gama. No. 2788, Palmeiras. No. 2789, Gremio. No. 2790, Sao Paolo. No. 2791, Santos. No. 2792, Regatas do Flamengo.

2001 Litho. *Perf. 12x11½*

2787 A1535 70c multi .55 .55
2788 A1535 70c multi .55 .55
2789 A1535 70c multi .55 .55
2790 A1535 70c multi .60 .60
2791 A1535 1r multi .90 .90
2792 A1535 1r multi .85 .85
Nos. 2787-2792 (6) 4.00 4.00

Numbers have been reserved for additional stamps in this set. Numbers may change.
Issued: No. 2787, 8/21; No. 2788, 8/26; No. 2789, 9/10; No. 2790, 12/16; No. 2791, 4/20. No. 2792, 11/28.

Intl. Culture of Peace Year — A1536

2001, May 3 Litho. *Perf. 12x11½*
2794 A1536 1.10r multi .95 .95

Murilo Mendes (1901-75), Poet — A1537

2001, May 13 *Perf. 11x11½*
2795 A1537 40c multi .35 .35

Minas Commercial Association, Cent. A1538

2001, May 16 *Perf. 11½*
2796 A1538 40c multi .35 .35

World Tobacco-free Day — A1539

2001, May 31 *Perf. 12x11½*
2797 A1539 40c multi .35 .35

José Lins do Rego (1901-87), Writer — A1540

2001, May 31 *Perf. 11x11½*
2798 A1540 60c multi .50 .50

Souvenir Sheet

Worldwide Fund for Nature (WWF) — A1541

Parrots: a, Anodorhynchus hyacinthinus. b, Aratinga solstitialis auricapilla. c, Pyrrhura cruentata. d, Amazona xanthops.

2001, June 3 *Perf. 11½*
2799 A1541 1.30r Sheet of 4, #a-d 4.50 4.50

Barbosa Lima Sobrinho (1897-2000), Journalist A1542

2001, June 6
2800 A1542 40c multi .35 .35

Beaches A1543

No. 2801: a, Jericoacoara. b, Ponta Negra. c, Rosa.

2001, June 13 *Perf. 11x11½*
2801 Horiz. strip of 3 1.10 1.10
a.-c. A1543 40c Any single .35 .35

Issued in sheets of 25 stamps containing 10 each of Nos. 2801a-2801b and 5 of No. 2801c.

Souvenir Sheet

Automobiles — A1544

No. 2802: a, 1959 Romi Isetta. b, 1965 DKW Vemag. c, 1962 Renault Gordini. d, 1959 Volkswagen 1200. e, 1964 Simca Chambord. f, 1961 Aero-Willys.

2001, June 16 *Perf. 11½x12*
2802 A1544 1.10r Sheet of 6, #a-f 5.75 5.75

Bernardo Sayao (1901-59), Politician A1545

2001, June 18 *Perf. 11½*
2803 A1545 60c multi .50 .50

Eleazar de Carvalho (1912-96), Composer A1546

2001, July 1
2804 A1546 45c multi .35 .35

Souvenir Sheet

Third French Tennis Open Victory of Gustavo Kuerten — A1547

2001, July 10
2805 A1547 1.30r multi 1.00 1.00

Academic Qualifications Coordinating Institution, 50th Anniv. — A1548

2001, July 11 *Perf. 11x11½*
2806 A1548 40c multi .35 .35

Pedro Aleixo, Politician, Cent. of Birth A1549

2001, Aug. 1 *Perf. 11½*
2807 A1549 55c multi .45 .45

Solidarity Community Programs — A1550

No. 2808: a, Map on man. b, Man on map. Illustration reduced.

2001, Aug. 25
2808 A1550 55c Horiz. pair, #a-b .85 .85

World Conference Against Racism, Durban, South Africa — A1551

2001, Aug. 30 *Perf. 12x11½*
2809 A1551 1.30r multi .95 .95

See South Africa Nos. 1261-1262.

Musical Instruments A1552

Designs: 1c, Tambourine. 5c, Saxophone. 10c, Ukulele. 40c, Flute. 50c, Rebec. 55c, Guitar. 60c, Drum. 70c, Guitar (viola caipira). 1r, Trombone.

Serpentine Die Cut 5¾
2001, Sept. 20 Litho.
Self-Adhesive

2810 A1552 1c multi .20 .20
2811 A1552 5c multi .20 .20
2812 A1552 10c multi .20 .20
2813 A1552 40c multi .30 .30
2814 A1552 50c multi .35 .35
2815 A1552 55c multi .40 .40
2816 A1552 60c multi .40 .40
2817 A1552 70c multi .50 .50
2818 A1552 1r multi .70 .70
Nos. 2810-2818 (9) 3.25 3.25

Clóvis Beviláqua (1859-1944), Writer of Civil Law Code A1553

2001, Oct. 4 Litho. *Perf. 11½*
2819 A1553 55c multi .40 .40

Year of Dialogue Among Civilizations A1554

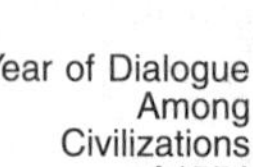

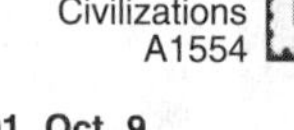

2001, Oct. 9 *Perf. 12x11½*
2820 A1554 1.30r multi .95 .95

Souvenir Sheet

Commercial Aircraft — A1555

No. 2821: a, Junkers F-13. b, Douglas C-47. c, Dornier Wal. d, Lockheed Constellation. e, Convair 340. f, Caravelle.

2001, Oct. 23 Litho. *Perf. 11½x12*
2821 A1555 55c Sheet of 6, #a-f 2.50 2.50

Barcode is separated from sheet margin by a row of rouletting.

Cecília Meireles (1901-64), Poet — A1556

2001, Nov. 7 Litho. *Perf. 11x11½*
2822 A1556 55c multi .45 .45

America Issue - Bom Jesus de Matosinhos Sanctuary, UNESCO World Heritage Site — A1557

2001, Nov. 9 *Perf. 11½x12*
2823 A1557 1.30r multi 1.00 1.00

Madalena Caramuru, First Literate Woman in Brazil A1558

2001, Nov. 14
2824 A1558 55c multi .45 .45

National Day of Black Consciousness — A1559

2001, Nov. 20
2825 A1559 40c multi .35 .35

Pantanal Flora A1560

No. 2826: a, Caiman crocodilus yacare, Plataleia ajaja. b, Anhinga anhinga. c, Ardea cocoi. d, Jabiru mycteria. e, Pseudoplatystoma fasciatum. f, Leporinus macrocephalus. g, Hydrochoerus hydrochoeris. h, Nasua nasua, Casmerodius albus. i, Eichornia crassipes. j, Porphyrula martinica.

2001, Nov. 20 *Die Cut Perf. 6¼*
Self-Adhesive
2826 Booklet of 10 4.50
a.-j. A1560 55c Any single .45 .45

See No. 2832.

Christmas A1561

2001, Nov. 23 *Perf. 11½x12*
2827 A1561 40c multi .35 .35

Souvenir Sheet

Minerals — A1562

No. 2828: a, Topaz jewelry. b, Garnet ring.

2001, Nov. 30 *Perf. 12x11½*
2828 A1562 1.30r Sheet of 2, #a-b 2.25 2.25

Intl. Day of Disabled Persons — A1563

Illustration reduced.

2001, Dec. 3 *Perf. 11½*
2829 A1563 1.45r multi 1.25 1.25

Coffee A1564

2001, Dec. 7 *Perf. 11½x12*
2830 A1564 1.30r multi 1.10 1.10

No. 2830 is impregnated with a coffee scent.

Merchant Ships — A1565

No. 2831: a, Copacabana. b, Flamengo.

2001, Dec. 13 *Perf. 11x11½*
2831 A1565 55c Horiz. pair, #a-b .95 .95

Pantanal Flora Type of 2001 With "MERCOSUL" Inscription Added

2001, Dec. 21 *Perf. 11½x12*
2832 A1560 1r Eichornia crassipes .85 .85

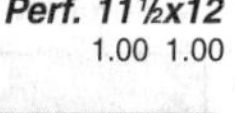

Kahal Zur Israel, First Synagogue in the Americas A1566

2001, Oct. 21 Litho. *Perf. 11½x12*
2833 A1566 1.30r multi 1.00 1.00

New Year 2002 (Year of the Horse) — A1567

Illustration reduced.

Litho. With Foil Application
2002, Jan. 25 *Perf. 11½*
2834 A1567 1.45r multi 1.25 1.25

2002 Winter Olympics, Salt Lake City — A1568

No. 2835: a, Alpine skiing. b, Cross-country skiing. c, Luge. d, Bobsled.
Illustration reduced.

2002, Feb. 4 Litho. *Perf. 11½x12*
2835 A1568 1.10r Block of 4, #a-d 3.75 3.75

Lucio Costa (1902-98), Architect A1569

2002, Feb. 27
2836 A1569 55c multi .45 .45

Intl. Women's Day — A1570

2002, Mar. 8 *Perf. 11½*
2837 A1570 40c multi .35 .35

Sao José do Rio Preto, 150th Anniv. A1571

2002, Mar. 19 *Perf. 11½x12*
2838 A1571 40c multi .35 .35

Pres. Juscelino Kubitschek (1902-76) — A1572

2002, Apr. 21 Litho.
2839 A1572 55c multi .45 .45

2002 World Cup Soccer Championships, Japan and Korea — A1573

No. 2840: a, Flags, soccer ball, and field (28mm diameter). b, Soccer players, years of Brazilian championships.
Illustration reduced.

2002, Apr. 22 Photo. *Perf. 13¾*
2840 A1573 55c Horiz. pair, #a-b .90 .90

See Argentina No. , France No. 2891, Germany No. 2163, Italy No. , and Uruguay No. .

Progress in Brazilian Education — A1574

No. 2841: a, Children in classroom, globe, letters "a-d." b, Computer, globe, letters "e-h."
Illustration reduced.

2002, Apr. 28 Litho. *Perf. 11½x12*
2841 A1574 40c Horiz. pair, #a-b .65 .65

St. Josemaría Escrivá de Balaguer (1902-75) — A1575

2002, May 1
2842 A1575 55c multi .45 .45

Souvenir Sheet

Brazilian Air Force's Esquadrilha da Fumaça Aerobatics Team — A1576

No. 2843: a, T-6 North American. b, T-24 Super Fouga Magister. c, T-25 Universal. d, Two T-27 Tucanos, one flying upside-down. e,

T-27 Tucanos, heart-shaped smoke design. f, Blue, green and yellow T-27 Tucano.

2002, May 17

2843 A1576 55c Sheet of 6, #a-f 2.75 2.75

Barcode is separated from sheet margin by a row of rouletting.

Children's Cavalhadinha of Pirenópolis — A1577

No. 2844: a, Procession of virgins and stick-pony riders. b, Stick-pony combat. c, Children wearing masks. d, Musicians and vendor. Illustration reduced.

2002, May 19 ***Perf. 11x11½***

2844 A1577 40c Block of 4, #a-d 1.25 1.25

Souvenir Sheet

Coral Reefs — A1579

No. 2846 - Coral and: a, Orange fish, school of fish. b, Seahorse. c, Orange fish. d, Orange fish, starfish.

2002, June 5 ***Perf. 11½***

2846 A1579 40c Sheet of 4, #a-d 1.25 1.25

Philakorea 2002 World Stamp Exhibition, Seoul. Barcode is separated from sheet margin by a row of rouletting.

Brazil's Fifth World Cup Soccer Championship A1581

2002, July 2 Litho. ***Perf. 12x11½***

2848 A1581 55c multi .40 .40

Fluminense Soccer Team, Cent. — A1583

2002, July 17 Litho. ***Perf. 12x11½***

2850 A1583 55c multi .40 .40

SEMI-POSTAL STAMPS

In 1980 three stamps that were intended to be semi-postals were issued as postage stamps at the total combined face value. See Nos. 1681-1683.

National Philatelic Exhibition Issue

SP1

Wmk. Coat of Arms in Sheet (236)

1934, Sept. 16 Engr. ***Imperf.***

Thick Paper

B1 SP1 200r + 100r dp cl 1.00 *2.00*
B2 SP1 300r + 100r ver 1.00 *2.00*
B3 SP1 700r + 100r brt bl 6.00 *17.50*
B4 SP1 1000r + 100r blk 6.00 *17.50*
Nos. B1-B4 (4) 14.00 *39.00*

The surtax was to help defray the expenses of the exhibition. Issued in sheets of 60, inscribed "EXPOSICAO FILATELICA NACIONAL."

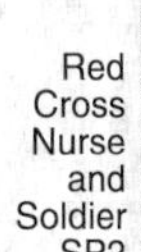

Red Cross Nurse and Soldier SP2

Wmk. 222

1935, Sept. 19 Typo. ***Perf. 11***

B5 SP2 200r + 100r pur & red 1.25 1.25
B6 SP2 300r + 100r ol brn & red 1.25 .90
B7 SP2 700r + 100r turq bl & red 8.00 7.00
Nos. B5-B7 (3) 10.50 9.15

3rd Pan-American Red Cross Conf. Exist imperf.

Three Wise Men and Star of Bethlehem — SP3

Angel and Child — SP4

Southern Cross and Child — SP5

Mother and Child — SP6

Wmk. 249

1939, Dec. 20 Litho. ***Perf. 10½***

B8 SP3 100r + 100r chlky bl & bl blk .75 .75
  a. Horiz. or vert. pair, imperf. between 35.00
B9 SP4 200r + 100r brt grnsh bl 1.00 1.00
  a. Horizontal pair, imperf. between 35.00
B10 SP5 400r + 200r ol grn & ol .80 .50
B11 SP6 1200r + 400r crim & brn red 3.25 1.50
  a. Vertical pair, imperf. between 35.00
Nos. B8-B11 (4) 5.80 3.75

Surtax for charitable institutions. For surcharges see Nos. C55-C59.

Catalogue values for unused stamps in this section, from this point to the end of the section, are for Never Hinged items.

Children and Citzenship — SP7

Designs: a, Cutouts of children forming pyramid. b, Man and woman's hands holding onto girl. c, Children going into school. d, Pregnant woman in front of house. e, Children flying paper doves. f, Parent working in garden, child writing letters, doves. g, Breastfeeding. h, Father holding birth certificate, mother holding infant. i, Disabled child on wheelchair ramp. j, Mother, father with sick child. k, Stylized child, pencil, letters. l, Hands above and below pregnant woman. m, Two families of different races. n, Small child playing large guitar. o, People looking to baby on pedestal. p, Children, book, "Statute of Children and Adolescent."

1997, Nov. 20 Litho. ***Perf. 12x11½***

B12 Sheet of 16 9.60 9.60
  a.-p. SP7 22c +8c any single .60 .60

Surcharge for Natl. Fund for Children and Adolescents.

Stampin' the Future Children's Stamp Design Contest Winners — SP8

Art by: a, Jonas Sampaio de Freitas. b, Clarissa Cazane. c, Caio Ferreira Guimaraes de Oliveira. d, Milena Karoline Ribeiro Reis. Illustration reduced.

2000, Jan. 1 Litho. ***Perf. 11½x12***

B13 SP8 22c + 8c Block of 4, #a-d 1.40 1.40

AIR POST STAMPS

Nos. O14-O29 Surcharged

1927, Dec. 28 Unwmk. ***Perf. 12***

C1 O2 50r on 10r .35 .35
  a. Inverted surcharge 325.00
  b. Top ornaments missing 75.00
C2 O2 200r on 1000r 2.25 2.75
  a. Double surcharge 325.00
C3 O2 200r on 2000r 1.40 4.75
  a. Double surcharge 750.00
  b. Double surcharge, one inverted 750.00
C4 O2 200r on 5000r 1.50 1.00
  a. Double surcharge 325.00 —
  b. Double surcharge, one inverted 350.00
  c. Triple surcharge 450.00
C5 O2 300r on 500r 1.50 2.00
C6 O2 300r on 600r .75 .90
  b. Pair, one without surch. —
C6A O2 500r on 10r 325.00 375.00
C7 O2 500r on 50r 1.50 .65
  a. Double surcharge 300.00 —
C8 O2 1000r on 20r 1.00 .35
  a. Double surcharge 300.00 —
C9 O2 2000r on 100r 2.25 1.40
  a. Pair, one without surcharge —
  b. Double surcharge 300.00
C10 O2 2000r on 200r 2.75 1.40
C11 O2 2000r on 10,000r 2.25 .50
C12 O2 5000r on 20,000r 7.50 3.00
C13 O2 5000r on 50,000r 7.50 3.00
C14 O2 5000r on 100,000r 25.00 30.00
C15 O2 10,000r on 500,000r 27.50 22.50
C16 O2 10,000r on 1,000,000r 25.00 25.00
Nos. C1-C6,C7-C16 (16) 110.00 99.55

Nos. C1, C1b, C7, C8 and C9 have small diamonds printed over the numerals in the upper corners.

Monument to de Gusmao — AP1

Santos-Dumont's Airship — AP2

Augusto Severo's Airship "Pax" — AP3

Santos-Dumont's Biplane "14 Bis" — AP4

Ribeiro de Barros's Seaplane "Jahu" — AP5

Perf. 11, 12½x13, 13x13½

1929 Typo. Wmk. 206

C17 AP1 50r blue grn .35 .20
C18 AP2 200r red 1.40 .20
C19 AP3 300r brt blue 1.75 .20
C20 AP4 500r red violet 2.50 .20
C21 AP5 1000r orange brn 9.00 .40
Nos. C17-C21 (5) 15.00 1.20

See #C32-C36. For surcharges see #C26-C27.

Bartholomeu de Gusmao AP6

Augusto Severo AP7

Alberto Santos-Dumont — AP8

Perf. 9, 11 and Compound

1929-30 Engr. Wmk. 101

C22 AP6 2000r lt green ('30) 7.50 .35
C23 AP7 5000r carmine 7.50 1.25
C24 AP8 10,000r olive grn 7.50 1.40
Nos. C22-C24 (3) 22.50 3.00

Nos. C23-C24 exist imperf.
See Nos. C37, C40.

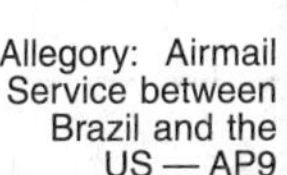

Allegory: Airmail Service between Brazil and the US — AP9

1929 Typo. Wmk. 206

C25 AP9 3000r violet 10.00 1.75

Exists imperf. See Nos. C38, C41. For surcharge see No. C28.

Nos. C18-C19 Surcharged in Blue or Red

1931, Aug. 16 Perf. 12½x13½

C26 AP2 2500r on 200r (Bl) 25.00 25.00
C27 AP3 5000r on 300r (R) 30.00 30.00

No. C25 Surcharged

1931, Sept. 2 Perf. 11

C28 AP9 2500r on 3000r vio 27.50 *27.50*
a. Inverted surcharge 160.00 —
b. Surch. on front and back 160.00

Regular Issues of 1928-29 Surcharged

1932, May Wmk. 101 Perf. 11, 11½

C29 A89 3500r on 5000r gray lil 20.00 20.00
C30 A72 7000r on 10,000r rose 20.00 20.00
b. Horiz. pair, imperf. between *750.00*

Imperforates

Since 1933, imperforate or partly perforated sheets of nearly all of the airmail issues have become available.

Flag and Airplane AP10

Wmk. 222

1933, June 7 Typo. Perf. 11

C31 AP10 3500r grn, yel & dk bl 5.00 2.00

See Nos. C39, C42.

1934 Wmk. 222

C32 AP1 50r blue grn 1.75 1.75
C33 AP2 200r red 2.25 .65
C34 AP3 300r brt blue 5.50 1.90
C35 AP4 500r red violet 2.25 .65
C36 AP5 1000r orange brn 7.50 .65
Nos. C32-C36 (5) 19.25 5.60

1934 Wmk. 236 Engr. Perf. 12x11

Thick Laid Paper

C37 AP6 2000r lt green 4.50 1.50

Types of 1929, 1933

Perf. 11, 11½, 12

1937-40 Typo. Wmk. 249

C38 AP9 3000r violet 17.50 1.75
C39 AP10 3500r grn, yel & dk bl 3.00 1.50

Engr.

C40 AP7 5000r ver ('40) 4.00 .75
Nos. C38-C40 (3) 24.50 4.00

Watermark note after #501 also applies to #C40.

Types of 1929-33

Perf. 11, 11½x12

1939-40 Typo. Wmk. 256

C41 AP9 3000r violet 1.25 .60
C42 AP10 3500r bl, dl grn & yel ('40) .90 .50

Map of the Western Hemisphere Showing Brazil — AP11

1941, Jan. 14 Engr. Perf. 11

C43 AP11 1200r dark brown 2.50 .65

5th general census of Brazil.

No. 506A Overprinted in Carmine

1941, Nov. 10 Wmk. 264 Rouletted

C45 A180 5400r slate grn 2.50 1.25
a. Overprint inverted 140.00

President Varges' new constitution, 4th anniv.

Nos. 506A and 508 Surcharged in Black

1942, Nov. 10 Wmk. 264

C47 A180 5.40cr on 5400r sl grn 2.50 1.90
a. Wmk. 249 80.00 80.00
b. Surcharge inverted 60.00 75.00

President Vargas' new constitution, 5th anniv. The status of No. C47a is questioned.

Southern Cross and Arms of Paraguay AP12

Wmk. 270

1943, May 11 Engr. Perf. 12½

C48 AP12 1.20cr lt gray blue 1.75 1.00

Issued in commemoration of the visit of President Higinio Morinigo of Paraguay.

Map of South America — AP13

1943, June 30 Wmk. 271 Perf. 12½

C49 AP13 1.20cr multi 1.75 .75

Visit of President Penaranda of Bolivia.

Numeral of Value AP14

1943, Aug. 7

C50 AP14 1cr blk & dull yel 2.00 1.50
a. Double impression 30.00
C51 AP14 2cr blk & pale grn 2.75 1.50
a. Double impression 40.00
C52 AP14 5cr blk & pink 3.25 2.00
Nos. C50-C52 (3) 8.00 5.00

Centenary of Brazil's first postage stamps.

Souvenir Sheet

AP15

Without Gum Imperf.

C53 AP15 Sheet of 3 35.00 35.00
a. 1cr black & dull yellow 10.00 10.00
b. 2cr black & pale green 10.00 10.00
c. 5cr black & pink 10.00 10.00

100th anniv. of the 1st postage stamps of Brazil and the 2nd Phil. Exposition (Brapex). Printed in panes of 6 sheets, perforated 12½ between. Each sheet is perforated on two or three sides. Size approximately 155x155mm.

Law Book — AP16

1943, Aug. 13 Perf. 12½

C54 AP16 1.20cr rose & lil rose .50 .30

2nd Inter-American Conf. of Lawyers.

No. B10 Surcharged in Red, Carmine or Black

1944, Jan. 3 Wmk. 249 Perf. 10½

C55 SP5 20c on 400r+200r (R) .85 .65
C56 SP5 40c on 400r+200r (Bk) 1.25 .65
C57 SP5 60c on 400r+200r (C) 1.25 .45
C58 SP5 1cr on 400r+200r (Bk) 1.75 .65
C59 SP5 1.20cr on 400r+200r (C) 2.25 .45
Nos. C55-C59 (5) 7.35 2.85

No. C59 is known with surcharge in black but its status is questioned.

Bartholomeu de Gusmao and the "Aerostat" — AP17

Wmk. 268

1944, Oct. 23 Engr. Perf. 12

C60 AP17 1.20cr rose carmine .35 .20

Week of the Wing.

L. L. Zamenhof AP18

1945, Apr. 16 Litho. Perf. 11

C61 AP18 1.20cr dull brown .35 .25

Esperanto Congress held in Rio, Apr. 14-22.

Map of South America — AP19

Baron of Rio Branco — AP20

1945, Apr. 20

C62 AP19 1.20cr gray brown .35 .25
C63 AP20 5cr rose lilac .95 .40

Centenary of the birth of José Maria de Silva Paranhos, Baron of Rio Branco.

Dove and Flags of American Republics AP21

Perf. 12x11

1947, Aug. 15 Engr. Unwmk.

C64 AP21 2.20cr dk blue green .30 .25

Inter-American Defense Conference at Rio de Janeiro August-September, 1947.

Santos-Dumont Monument, St. Cloud, France — AP22

Bay of Rio de Janeiro and Rotary Emblem — AP23

1947, Nov. 15 Typo. *Perf. 11x12*

C65 AP22 1.20cr org brn & ol .30 .25

Issued to commemorate the Week of the Wing and to honor the Santos-Dumont monument which was destroyed in World War II.

Catalogue values for unused stamps in this section, from this point to the end of the section, are for Never Hinged items.

1948, May 16 Engr. *Perf. 11*

C66 AP23 1.20cr deep claret .50 .40
C67 AP23 3.80cr dull violet 1.00 .40

39th convention of Rotary Intl., Rio.

Hotel Quitandinha, Petropolis — AP24

1948, July 10 Litho. Wmk. 267

C68 AP24 1.20cr org brn .25 .25
C69 AP24 3.80cr violet .50 .30

International Exposition of Industry and Commerce, Petropolis, 1948.

Musician and Singers AP25

1948, Aug. 13 Engr. Unwmk.

C70 AP25 1.20cr blue .30 .20

National School of Music, cent.

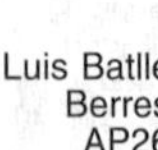

Luis Batlle Berres AP26

1948, Sept. 2 Typo.

C71 AP26 1.70cr blue .20 .20

Visit of President Luis Batlle Berres of Uruguay, September, 1948.

Merino Ram AP27

Perf. 12x11

1948, Oct. 10 Wmk. 267

C72 AP27 1.20cr dp orange .50 .30

Intl. Livestock Exposition at Bagé.

Eucharistic Congress Seal — AP28

Unwmk.

1948, Oct. 23 Engr. *Perf. 11*

C73 AP28 1.20cr dk car rose .30 .30

5th Natl. Eucharistic Cong., Porto Alegre, Oct. 24-31.

Souvenir Sheet

AP28a

1948, Dec. 14 Engr. *Imperf.*
Without Gum

C73A AP28a Sheet of 3 50.00 65.00

No. C73A contains one each of Nos. 674-676. Issued in honor of President Eurico Gasper Dutra and the armed forces. Exists both with and without number on back. Measures 130x75mm.

Church of Prazeres, Guararapes — AP29

Perf. 11½x12

1949, Feb. 15 Litho. Wmk. 267

C74 AP29 1.20cr pink 1.50 .75

Second Battle of Guararapes, 300th anniv.

Thomé de Souza Meeting Indians — AP30

Perf. 11x12

1949, Mar. 29 Engr. Unwmk.

C75 AP30 1.20cr blue .20 .20

Founding of the City of Salvador, 400th anniv.

A souvenir folder, issued with No. C75, has an engraved 20cr red brown postage stamp portraying John III printed on it, and a copy of No. C75 affixed to it and postmarked. Paper is laid, and size of folder front is 100x150mm. Value, $5.

Franklin D. Roosevelt AP31

1949, May 20 Unwmk. *Imperf.*

C76 AP31 3.80cr deep blue .60 .60
a. Souvenir sheet 12.00 15.00

No. C76a measures 85x110mm, with deep blue inscriptions in upper and lower margins. It also exists with papermaker's watermark.

Joaquim Nabuco (1849-1910), Lawyer and Writer — AP32

1949, Aug. 30 *Perf. 12*

C77 AP32 3.80cr rose lilac .40 .30
a. Wmk. 256, imperf. 25.00

Maracanã Stadium AP33

Soccer Player and Flag — AP34

Perf. 11x12, 12x11

1950, June 24 Litho. Wmk. 267

C78 AP33 1.20cr ultra & salmon .95 .40
C79 AP34 5.80cr bl, yel grn & yel 2.75 .50

4th World Soccer Championship, Rio.

AP35

AP36

Symbolical of Brazilian population growth.

1950, July 10 *Perf. 12x11*

C80 AP35 1.20cr red brown .30 .20

Issued to publicize the 6th Brazilian census.

1956, Sept. 8 Engr. *Perf. 11½*

Design: J. B. Marcelino Champagnat.

C81 AP36 3.30cr rose lilac .30 .20

50th anniversary of the arrival of the Marist Brothers in Northern Brazil.

Santos-Dumont's 1906 Plane — AP37

1956 Photo.

C82	AP37	3cr dk blue grn		.85	.30
C83	AP37	3.30cr brt ultra		.20	.20
C84	AP37	4cr dp claret		.40	.20
C85	AP37	6.50cr red brown		.20	.20
C86	AP37	11.50cr orange red		.85	.35
		Nos. C82-C86 (5)		2.50	1.25

Souvenir Sheet

C86A AP37 Sheet of 4 6.00 6.00
b. 3cr dark carmine 1.50 .90

1st flight by Santos-Dumont, 50th anniv. Issued: #C86A, 10/14; others 10/16.

Lord Baden-Powell AP38

1957, Aug. 1 Unwmk.
Granite Paper

C87 AP38 3.30cr deep red lilac .25 .20

Centenary of the birth of Lord Baden-Powell, founder of the Boy Scouts.

UN Emblem, Soldier and Map of Suez Canal Area AP39

Wmk. 267

1957, Oct. 24 Engr. *Perf. 11½*

C88 AP39 3.30cr dark blue .25 .20

Brazilian contingent of the UN Emergency Force.

Basketball Player — AP40

1959, May 30 Photo. *Perf. 11½*

C89 AP40 3.30cr brt red brn & bl .25 .20

Brazil's victory in the World Basketball Championships of 1959.

Symbol of Flight AP41

1959, Oct. 21 Wmk. 267

C90 AP41 3.30cr deep ultra .20 .20

Issued to publicize Week of the Wing.

Caravelle AP42

1959, Dec. 18 *Perf. 11½*
C91 AP42 6.50cr ultra .20 .20

Inauguration of Brazilian jet flights.

Pres. Adolfo Lopez Mateos — AP43

Pres. Dwight D. Eisenhower AP44

1960, Jan. 19 Photo. Wmk. 267
C92 AP43 6.50cr brown .20 .20

Issued to commemorate the visit of President Adolfo Lopez Mateos of Mexico.

1960, Feb. 23 *Perf. 11½*
C93 AP44 6.50cr deep orange .20 .20

Visit of Pres. Dwight D. Eisenhower.

World Refugee Year Emblem — AP45

Tower at Brasilia — AP46

1960, Apr. 7 Wmk. 268
C94 AP45 6.50cr blue .20 .20

WRY, July 1, 1959-June 30, 1960.

Type of Regular Issue and AP46

Designs: 3.30cr, Square of the Three Entities. 4cr, Cathedral. 11.50cr, Plan of Brasilia.

Perf. 11x11½, 11½x11

1960, Apr. 21 Photo. Wmk. 267

C95	A436	3.30cr violet	.20	.20
C96	A436	4cr blue	.75	.20
C97	AP46	6.50cr rose carmine	.20	.20
C98	A436	11.50cr brown	.20	.20
		Nos. C95-C98 (4)	1.35	.80

Inauguration of Brazil's new capital, Brasilia, Apr. 21, 1960.

Chrismon and Oil Lamp AP47

1960, May 16 *Perf. 11x11½*
C99 AP47 3.30cr lilac rose .20 .20

7th Natl. Eucharistic Congress at Curitiba.

Cross, Sugarloaf Mountain and Emblem — AP48

1960, July 1 Wmk. 267
C100 AP48 6.50cr brt blue .20 .20

10th Cong. of the World Baptist Alliance, Rio.

Boy Scout — AP49

Caravel — AP50

1960, July 23 *Perf. 11½x11*
C101 AP49 3.30cr orange ver .20 .20

Boy Scouts of Brazil, 50th anniversary.

1960, Aug. 5 Engr. Wmk. 268
C102 AP50 6.50cr black .20 .20

Prince Henry the Navigator, 500th birth anniv.

Maria E. Bueno AP51

1960, Dec. 15 Photo. ***Perf. 11x11½***
C103 AP51 60cr pale brown .20 .20

Victory at Wimbledon of Maria E. Bueno, women's singles tennis champion.

War Memorial, Sugarloaf Mountain and Allied Flags — AP52

1960, Dec. 22 Wmk. 268
C104 AP52 3.30cr lilac rose .20 .20

Reburial of Brazilian servicemen of WW II.

Power Line and Map — AP53

Malaria Eradication Emblem — AP54

1961, Jan. 20 *Perf. 11½x11*
C105 AP53 3.30cr lilac rose .20 .20

Inauguration of Three Marias Dam and hydroelectric station in Minas Gerais.

1962, May 24 Wmk. 267 Engr.
C106 AP54 21cr blue .20 .20

WHO drive to eradicate malaria.

F. A. de Varnhagen — AP55

1966, Feb. 17 Photo. Wmk. 267
C107 AP55 45cr red brown .20 .20

Francisco Adolfo de Varnhagen, Viscount of Porto Seguro (1816-1878), historian and diplomat.

Map of the Americas and Alliance for Progress Emblem AP56

1966, Mar. 14 *Perf. 11x11½*
C108 AP56 120cr grnsh bl & vio bl .40 .20

5th anniv. of the Alliance for Progress.

A souvenir card contains one impression of No. C108, imperf. Size: 113x160mm.

Nun and Globe — AP57

Face of Jesus from Shroud of Turin — AP58

1966, Mar. 25 Photo. *Perf. 11½x11*
C109 AP57 35cr violet .20 .20

Centenary of the arrival of the teaching Sisters of St. Dorothea.

1966, June 3 Photo. Wmk. 267
C110 AP58 45cr brown org .20 .20

Issued to commemorate Vatican II, the 21st Ecumenical Council of the Roman Catholic Church, Oct. 11, 1962-Dec. 8, 1965.

A souvenir card contains one impression of No. C110, imperf. Size: 100x39mm.

Admiral Mariz e Barros — AP59

"Youth" by Eliseu Visconti — AP60

1966, June 13 Photo. Wmk. 267
C111 AP59 35cr red brown .20 .20

Death centenary of Admiral Antonio Carlos Mariz e Barros, who died in the Battle of Itaperu.

1966, July 31 *Perf. 11½x11*
C112 AP60 120cr red brown .40 .20

Birth centenary of Eliseu Visconti, painter.

SPECIAL DELIVERY STAMPS

No. 191 Surcharged

1930 Unwmk. *Perf. 12*
E1 A62 1000r on 200r dp blue 4.00 1.75
a. Inverted surcharge 500.00

POSTAGE DUE STAMPS

D1 D2

1889 Unwmk. Typo. ***Rouletted***

J1	D1	10r carmine	2.00	1.40
J2	D1	20r carmine	2.75	2.00
J3	D1	50r carmine	5.00	4.00
J4	D1	100r carmine	2.00	1.40
J5	D1	200r carmine	55.00	15.00
J6	D1	300r carmine	6.00	*8.00*
J7	D1	500r carmine	6.00	*8.00*
J8	D1	700r carmine	10.00	*14.00*
J9	D1	1000r carmine	10.00	10.00
		Nos. J1-J9 (9)	98.75	63.80

Counterfeits are common.

1890

J10	D1	10r orange	.60	.30
J11	D1	20r ultra	.60	.30
J12	D1	50r olive	1.25	.30
J13	D1	200r magenta	6.00	.60
J14	D1	300r blue green	3.00	1.50
J15	D1	500r slate	4.00	3.00
J16	D1	700r purple	4.50	*7.50*
J17	D1	1000r dk violet	5.50	5.00
		Nos. J10-J17 (8)	25.45	18.50

Perf. 11 to 11½, 12½ to 14 and Compound

1895-1901

J18	D2	10r dk blue ('01)	2.00	1.25
J19	D2	20r yellow grn	8.00	3.00
J20	D2	50r yellow grn ('01)	10.00	5.50
J21	D2	100r brick red	6.25	1.25
J22	D2	200r violet	6.00	.60
a.		200r gray lilac ('98)	12.00	2.00
J23	D2	300r dull blue	3.50	2.25
J24	D2	2000r brown	12.00	12.00
		Nos. J18-J24 (7)	47.75	25.85

1906 Wmk. 97
J25 D2 100r brick red 8.00 3.00

Wmk. (97? or 98?)

J26	D2	200r violet	7.50	1.25
a.		Wmk. 97	275.00	85.00
b.		Wmk. 98	12.50	50.00

D3

D4

1906-10 Unwmk. Engr. *Perf. 12*

J28	D3	10r slate	.20	.20
J29	D3	20r brt violet	.20	.20
J30	D3	50r dk green	.25	.20
J31	D3	100r carmine	1.75	.60
J32	D3	200r dp blue	1.00	.30
J33	D3	300r gray blk	.40	.60
J34	D3	400r olive grn	1.00	.90
J35	D3	500r dk violet	35.00	35.00
J36	D3	600r violet ('10)	1.25	*3.00*
J37	D3	700r red brown	30.00	30.00
J38	D3	1000r red	1.50	*3.00*
J39	D3	2000r green	4.75	5.50
J40	D3	5000r choc ('10)	1.50	*14.00*
		Nos. J28-J40 (13)	78.80	93.50

Perf. 12½, 11, 11x10½

1919-23 **Typo.**
J41 D4 5r red brown .20 .25
J42 D4 10r violet .25 .25
J43 D4 20r olive gray .20 .20
J44 D4 50r green ('23) .20 .20
J45 D4 100r red 1.10 1.00
J46 D4 200r blue 5.25 1.50
J47 D4 400r brown ('23) 1.40 1.25
Nos. J41-J47 (7) 8.60 4.65

Perf. 12½, 12½x13½

1924-35 **Wmk. 100**
J48 D4 5r red brown .25 .20
J49 D4 100r red .75 .30
J50 D4 200r slate bl ('29) 1.00 .50
J51 D4 400r dp brn ('29) 1.50 1.00
J52 D4 600r dk vio ('29) 1.75 1.10
J53 D4 600r orange ('35) .75 .50
Nos. J48-J53 (6) 6.00 3.60

1924 **Wmk. 193** ***Perf. 11x10½***
J54 D4 100r red 45.00 45.00
J55 D4 200r slate blue 5.50 5.50

Perf. 11x10½, 13x13½

1925-27 **Wmk. 101**
J56 D4 20r olive gray .20 .20
J57 D4 100r red 1.05 .30
J58 D4 200r slate blue 3.25 .35
J59 D4 400r brown 1.75 1.25
J60 D4 600r dk violet 4.25 2.50
Nos. J56-J60 (5) 10.50 4.60

Wmk. E U BRASIL Multiple (218)

1929-30 ***Perf. 12½x13½***
J61 D4 100r light red .25 .20
J62 D4 200r blue black .40 .25
J63 D4 400r brown .40 .25
J64 D4 1000r myrtle green .75 .50
Nos. J61-J64 (4) 1.80 1.20

Perf. 11, 12½x13, 13

1931-36 **Wmk. 222**
J65 D4 10r lt violet ('35) .20 .20
J66 D4 20r black ('33) .20 .20
J67 D4 50r blue grn ('35) .25 .20
J68 D4 100r rose red ('35) .25 .20
J69 D4 200r sl blue ('35) .40 .30
J70 D4 400r blk brn ('35) 2.00 2.00
J71 D4 600r dk violet .35 .20
J72 D4 1000r myrtle grn .50 .35
J73 D4 2000r brown ('36) .80 .80
J74 D4 5000r indigo ('36) 1.25 1.00
Nos. J65-J74 (10) 6.20 5.45

1938 **Wmk. 249** ***Perf. 11***
J75 D4 200r slate blue 2.00 .75

1940 **Typo.** **Wmk. 256**
J76 D4 10r light violet .50 .50
J77 D4 20r black .50 .50
J79 D4 100r rose red .50 .50
J80 D4 200r myrtle green .50 .50
Nos. J76-J80 (4) 2.00 2.00

1942 **Wmk. 264**
J81 D4 10r lt violet .20 .20
J82 D4 20r olive blk .20 .20
J83 D4 50r lt blue grn .20 .20
J84 D4 100r vermilion .40 .30
J85 D4 200r gray blue .40 .30
J86 D4 400r claret .40 .30
J87 D4 600r rose vio .30 .20
J88 D4 1000r dk bl grn .30 .20
J89 D4 2000r dp yel brn .75 .50
J90 D4 5000r indigo .40 .30
Nos. J81-J90 (10) 3.55 2.70

1949 **Wmk. 268**
J91 D4 10c pale rose lilac 4.00 3.25
J92 D4 20r black 25.00 25.00

No. J92 exists in shades of gray ranging to gray olive.

OFFICIAL STAMPS

Pres. Affonso Penna
O1

Pres. Hermes da Fonseca
O2

Unwmk.

1906, Nov. 15 **Engr.** ***Perf. 12***
O1 O1 10r org & grn .75 .30
O2 O1 20r org & grn .90 .30
O3 O1 50r org & grn 1.50 .30
O4 O1 100r org & grn .75 .30
O5 O1 200r org & grn .90 .30
O6 O1 300r org & grn 2.75 .60
O7 O1 400r org & grn 6.00 1.75
O8 O1 500r org & grn 3.00 1.25
O9 O1 700r org & grn 4.50 3.00
O10 O1 1000r org & grn 4.50 1.25
O11 O1 2000r org & grn 5.00 2.25
O12 O1 5000r org & grn 10.00 .50
O13 O1 10,000r org & grn 10.00 1.25
Nos. O1-O13 (13) 50.55 13.35

The portrait is the same but the frame differs for each denomination of this issue.

1913, Nov. 15

Center in Black
O14 O2 10r gray .35 .50
O15 O2 20r ol grn .35 .50
O16 O2 50r gray .35 .50
O17 O2 100r ver 1.00 .35
O18 O2 200r blue 1.75 .35
O19 O2 500r orange 3.00 .65
O20 O2 600r violet 3.50 2.75
O21 O2 1000r blk brn 4.25 1.25
O22 O2 2000r red brn 6.50 1.25
O23 O2 5000r brown 7.50 3.00
O24 O2 10,000r black 15.00 7.50
O25 O2 20,000r blue 27.50 27.50
O26 O2 50,000r green 50.00 55.00
O27 O2 100,000r org red 175.00 200.00
O28 O2 500,000r brown 300.00 325.00
O29 O2 1,000,000r dk brn 325.00 350.00
Nos. O14-O29 (16) 921.05 976.10

The portrait is the same on all denominations of this series but there are eight types of the frame.

Pres. Wenceslau Braz — O3

Perf. 11, 11½

1919, Apr. 11 **Wmk. 100**
O30 O3 10r olive green .40 2.00
O31 O3 50r green 1.00 1.25
O32 O3 100r rose red 2.00 .85
O33 O3 200r dull blue 2.75 .85
O34 O3 500r orange 7.50 14.00
Nos. O30-O34 (5) 13.65 18.95

The official decree called for eleven stamps in this series but only five were issued.
For surcharges see Nos. 293-297.

NEWSPAPER STAMPS

N1

Rouletted

1889, Feb. 1 **Unwmk.** **Litho.**
P1 N1 10r yellow 3.00 3.00
a. Pair, imperf. between 125.00 140.00
P2 N1 20r yellow 6.00 7.50
P3 N1 50r yellow 10.00 6.00
P4 N1 100r yellow 3.75 3.00
P5 N1 200r yellow 3.00 1.50
P6 N1 300r yellow 3.00 1.50
P7 N1 500r yellow 20.00 8.00
P8 N1 700r yellow 3.00 *10.00*
P9 N1 1000r yellow 3.00 *10.00*
Nos. P1-P9 (9) 54.75 50.50

For surcharges see Nos. 125-127.

1889, May 1
P10 N1 10r olive 2.00 .50
P11 N1 20r green 2.00 .50
P12 N1 50r brn yel 2.75 1.00
P13 N1 100r violet 3.00 2.00
a. 100r deep violet 6.50 *15.00*
b. 100r lilac 12.00 10.00
P14 N1 200r black 3.00 2.00
P15 N1 300r carmine 12.00 10.00
P16 N1 500r green 50.00 50.00
P17 N1 700r pale blue 25.00 *30.00*
a. 700r ultramarine 65.00 *75.00*
b. 700r cobalt 400.00 *425.00*
P18 N1 1000r brown 12.00 *15.00*
Nos. P10-P18 (9) 111.75 111.00

For surcharges see Nos. 128-135.

N2

N3

White Wove Paper Thin to Thick

Perf. 11 to 11½, 12½ to 14 and 12½ to 14x11 to 11½

1890 **Typo.**
P19 N2 10r blue 14.00 10.00
a. 10r ultramarine 14.00 10.00
P20 N2 20r emerald 40.00 15.00
P21 N2 100r violet 16.00 14.00
Nos. P19-P21 (3) 70.00 39.00

For surcharge see No. 137.

1890-93
P22 N3 10r ultramarine 3.00 3.00
a. 10r blue 7.50 4.00
P23 N3 10r ultra, *buff* 3.00 3.00
P24 N3 20r green 10.00 3.00
a. 20r emerald 10.00 3.00
P25 N3 50r yel grn ('93) 17.50 10.00
Nos. P22-P25 (4) 33.50 19.00

For surcharges see Nos. 136, 138-139.

POSTAL TAX STAMPS

Icarus from the Santos-Dumont Monument at St. Cloud, France — PT1

Perf. 13½x12½, 11

1933, Oct. 1 **Typo.** **Wmk. 222**
RA1 PT1 100r deep brown .65 .25

Honoring the Brazilian aviator, Santos-Dumont. Its use was obligatory as a tax on all correspondence sent to countries in South America, the US and Spain. Its use on correspondence to other countries was optional. The funds obtained were used for the construction of airports throughout Brazil.

Catalogue values for unused stamps in this section, from this point to the end of the section, are for Never Hinged items.

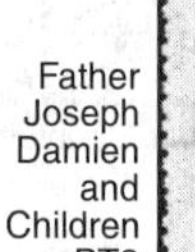

Father Joseph Damien and Children
PT2

Perf. 12x11

1952, Nov. 24 **Litho.** **Wmk. 267**
RA2 PT2 10c yellow brown .25 .20

1953, Nov. 30
RA3 PT2 10c yellow green .25 .20

Father Bento Dias Pacheco
PT3

Eunice Weaver
PT4

1954, Nov. 22 **Photo.** ***Perf. 11½***
RA4 PT3 10c violet blue .20 .20

1955-69, Nov. 24
RA5 PT3 10c dk car rose .20 .20
RA6 PT3 10c org red ('57) .20 .20
RA7 PT3 10c dp emer ('58) .20 .20
RA8 PT3 10c red lilac ('61) .20 .20
RA9 PT3 10c choc ('62) .20 .20
RA10 PT3 10c slate ('63) .20 .20
RA11 PT3 2cr dp mag ('64) .20 .20
RA12 PT3 2cr violet ('65) .20 .20
RA13 PT3 2cr orange ('66) .20 .20
RA14 PT3 5c brt yel grn ('68) 1.25 .75
RA15 PT3 5c deep plum ('69) .50 .25

Issued: 11/25, #RA14; 11/28, #RA15; others, 11/24.

1971-73, Nov. 24
RA16 PT4 10c slate green 1.00 .40
RA17 PT4 10c brt rose lil ('73) .20 .20

Father Nicodemos
PT5

Father Vicente Borgard (1888-1977)
PT6

1975, Nov. 24 **Litho.** **Unwmk.**
RA18 PT5 10c sepia .20 .20

1983, Nov. 24 **Photo.** ***Perf. 11½***
RA19 PT6 10cr brown .60 .60

Father Bento Dias Pacheco
PT7

Father Santiago Uchoa
PT8

1984, Nov. 24 **Photo.** ***Perf. 11½***
RA20 PT7 30cr deep blue .20 .20

1985, Nov. 24 **Litho.**
RA21 PT7 100cr lake .20 .20

1986, Nov. 24 **Litho.**
RA22 PT7 10c gray brown .20 .20

1987, Nov. 24 **Photo.**
RA23 PT7 30c sage green .20 .20

1988, Nov. 24 **Litho.**
RA24 PT8 1.30cz dull red brn .20 .20

See Nos. RA29-RA30.

Fr. Joseph Damien — PT9

1989-92 **Photo.** ***Perf. 11½***
RA25 PT9 2c deep lilac rose .20 .20
RA26 PT9 50c blue .20 .20

Perf. 12½
RA27 PT9 3cr green .20 .20
RA28 PT9 30cr brown .20 .20
Nos. RA25-RA28 (4) .80 .80

Issued: 2c, Nov. 24; 50c, Nov. 24, 1990; 3cr, Nov. 24, 1991; 30cr, Nov. 24, 1992.

Father Santiago Uchoa Type of 1988

1993, Nov. 24 **Photo.** ***Perf. 12½***
RA29 PT8 50c blue .20 .20

1994, Nov. 24
RA30 PT8 1c dull lake .20 .20

The tax was for the care and treatment of lepers.
Use of #RA2-RA30 was required for one week.

POSTAL TAX SEMI-POSTAL STAMP

Catalogue values for unused stamps in this section are for Never Hinged items.

Icarus — PTSP1

Wmk. 267

1947, Nov. 15 Typo. *Perf. 11*

RAB1 PTSP1 40c + 10c brt red .35 .20
a. Pair, imperf. between *350.00*

Aviation Week, November 15-22, 1947, and compulsory on all domestic correspondence during that week.

BRITISH ANTARCTIC TERRITORY

'bri-tish ˌant-'ärk-tik 'ter-ə-ˌtōr-ē

LOCATION — South Atlantic Ocean between 20-80 degrees longitude and south of 60 degrees latitude
GOVT. — British territory
POP. — About 300 scientific staff at research stations.

This territory includes Graham Land (Palmer Peninsula), South Shetland Islands and South Orkney Islands. Formerly part of Falkland Islands Dependency.

12 Pence = 1 Shilling
20 Shillings = 1 Pound
100 Pence = 1 Pound (1971)

Catalogue values for all unused stamps in this country are for Never Hinged items.

M. V. Kista Dan — A1

1p, Skiers hauling load. 1½p, Muskeg (tractor). 2p, Skiers. 2½p, Beaver seaplane. 3p, R.R.S. John Biscoe. 4p, Camp scene. 6p, H.M.S. Protector. 9p, Dog sled. 1sh, Otter skiplane. 2sh, Huskies & aurora australis. 2sh6p, Helicopter. 5sh, Snocat (truck). 10sh, R.R.S. Shackleton. £1, Map of Antarctica.

Perf. 11x11½

1963, Feb. 1 Engr. Wmk. 314

1 A1 ½p dark blue .75 1.25
2 A1 1p brown 1.00 .75
3 A1 1½p plum & red 1.00 1.25
4 A1 2p rose violet 1.00 .75
5 A1 2½p dull green 1.75 1.25
6 A1 3p Prus blue 3.00 1.25
7 A1 4p sepia 2.25 1.40
8 A1 6p dk blue & olive 3.50 1.90
9 A1 9p olive 2.75 1.90
10 A1 1sh steel blue 3.00 .65
11 A1 2sh dl vio & bis 16.00 6.75
12 A1 2sh6p blue 16.00 7.25
13 A1 5sh rose red & org 17.00 12.50
14 A1 10sh grn & vio bl 35.00 25.00
15 A1 £1 black & blue 45.00 45.00
Nos. 1-15 (15) 149.00 108.85

See No. 24. For surcharges see Nos. 25-38.

Common Design Types pictured following the introduction.

Churchill Memorial Issue
Common Design Type

1966, Jan. 24 Photo. *Perf. 14*

16 CD319 ½p bright blue .70 4.00
17 CD319 1p green 2.50 4.00
18 CD319 1sh brown 17.50 8.25
19 CD319 2sh violet 20.00 8.75
Nos. 16-19 (4) 40.70 25.00

Lemaire Channel, Iceberg and Adelie Penguins — A2

Designs: 6p, Weather sonde and operator. 1sh, Muskeg (tractor) pulling tent equipment. 2sh, Surveyors with theodolite.

1969, Feb. 6 Litho.

20 A2 3½p blue, vio bl & blk 3.75 2.50
21 A2 6p emer, blk & dp org 2.00 2.10
22 A2 1sh ultra, blk & ver 2.00 1.75
23 A2 2sh grnsh bl, blk & och 2.00 2.50
Nos. 20-23 (4) 9.75 8.85

25 years of continuous scientific work in the Antarctic.

Type of 1963

£1, H.M.S. Endurance and helicopter.

1969, Dec. 1 Engr. *Perf. 11x11½*

24 A1 £1 black & rose red 125.00 110.00

Nos. 1-14 Surcharged in Decimal Currency; Three Bars Overprinted

1971, Feb. 15 Wmk. 314

25 A1 ½p on ½p .40 *2.50*
26 A1 1p on 1p .70 .70
27 A1 1½p on 1½p .85 .60
28 A1 2p on 2p .85 .35
29 A1 2½p on 2½p 2.10 1.90
30 A1 3p on 3p 1.75 .60
31 A1 4p on 4p 1.60 .60
32 A1 5p on 6p 3.25 3.00
33 A1 6p on 9p 11.50 7.00
34 A1 7½p on 1sh 12.00 7.25
35 A1 10p on 2sh 14.00 12.00
36 A1 15p on 2sh6p 14.00 13.00
37 A1 25p on 5sh 17.00 14.50
38 A1 50p on 10sh 30.00 26.00
Nos. 25-38 (14) 110.00 90.00

Map of Antarctica, Aurora Australis, Explorers — A3

Capt. Cook and "Resolution" — A4

Map of Antarctica, Aurora Australis and: 4p, Sea gulls. 5p, Seals. 10p, Penguins.

Litho. & Engr.

1971, June 23 *Perf. 14x13*

39 A3 1½p multicolored 4.50 1.25
40 A3 4p multicolored 12.00 4.00
41 A3 5p multicolored 7.00 6.00
42 A3 10p multicolored 16.00 10.00
Nos. 39-42 (4) 39.50 21.25

10th anniv. of the Antarctic Treaty pledging peaceful uses of and scientific cooperation in Antarctica.

Silver Wedding Issue, 1972
Common Design Type

Design: Queen Elizabeth II, Prince Philip, seals and emperor penguins.

1972, Dec. 13 Photo. *Perf. 14x14½*

43 CD324 5p rose brn & multi 3.00 3.00
44 CD324 10p olive & multi 3.00 3.00

Wmk. 373

1975-80 Litho. *Perf. 14½*

Polar Explorers and their Crafts: 1p, Thaddeus von Bellingshausen and "Vostok." 1½p, James Weddell and "Jane." 2p, John Biscoe and "Tula." 2½p, J. S. C. Dumont d'Urville and "Astrolabe." 3p, James Clark Ross and "Erebus." 4p, C. A. Larsen and "Jason." 5p, Adrien de Gerlache and "Belgica." 6p, Otto Nordenskjöld and "Antarctic." 7½p, W. S. Bruce and "Scotia." 10p, Jean-Baptiste Charcot and "Pourquoi Pas?" 15p, Ernest Shackleton and "Endurance." 25p, Hubert Wilkins and airplane "San Francisco." 50p, Lincoln Ellsworth and airplane "Polar Star." £1, John Rymill and "Penola."

45 A4 ½p multi .20 .20
46 A4 1p multi ('78) .20 .20
47 A4 1½p multi ('78) .20 .20
48 A4 2p multi ('79) .20 .20
49 A4 2½p multi ('79) .20 .20
50 A4 3p multi ('79) .20 .20
52 A4 5p multi ('79) .30 .30
55 A4 10p multi ('79) .65 .65
56 A4 15p multi ('79) 1.00 1.00
57 A4 25p multi ('79) 1.60 1.60
58 A4 50p multi ('79) 3.25 3.25
59 A4 £1 multi ('78) 5.25 5.25
Nos. 45-59 (12) 13.25 13.25

1973, Feb. 14 Wmk. 314

45a A4 ½p multi *1.10* *2.00*
46a A4 1p multi *2.25* *3.25*
47a A4 1½p multi *9.75* *4.50*
48a A4 2p multi 2.00 1.75
49a A4 2½p multi 1.40 *1.75*
50a A4 3p multi .80 *1.75*
51a A4 4p multi .80 *1.75*
52a A4 5p multi .90 *1.75*
53a A4 6p multi 1.10 *1.75*
54a A4 7½p multi 1.40 *2.25*
55a A4 10p multi 2.50 *3.00*
56a A4 15p multi 5.25 4.00
57a A4 25p multi 3.25 *4.00*
58a A4 50p multi 2.25 *4.50*
59a A4 £1 multi 2.75 *7.75*
Nos. 45a-59a (15) 37.50 45.75

1980 Wmk. 373 *Perf. 12*

51 A4 4p multi .30 .30
53 A4 6p multi .40 .40
54 A4 7½p multi .50 .50
55b A4 10p multi .65 .65
56b A4 15p multi .70 .70
57b A4 25p multi 1.25 1.25
58b A4 50p multi 2.50 2.50
59b A4 £1 multi 5.00 5.00
Nos. 51-59b (8) 11.30 11.30

Princess Anne's Wedding Issue
Common Design Type

1973, Nov. 14 Wmk. 314 *Perf. 14*

60 CD325 5p ocher & multi .40 .30
61 CD325 15p blue grn & multi .85 .80

Wedding of Princess Anne and Capt. Mark Phillips, Nov. 14, 1973.

Churchill and Map of Churchill Peninsula — A5

Design: 15p, Churchill and "Trepassey" of Operation Tabarin, 1943.

1974, Nov. 30 Litho. *Perf. 14*

62 A5 5p multicolored 1.25 .80
63 A5 15p multicolored 2.50 2.50
a. Souvenir sheet of 2, #62-63 13.00 13.00

Sir Winston Churchill (1874-1965).

Humpback Whale — A6

Wmk. 373

1977, Jan. 4 Litho. *Perf. 14*

64 A6 2p Sperm whale 5.25 3.50
65 A6 8p Fin whale 6.25 4.00
66 A6 11p shown 6.50 4.00
67 A6 25p Blue whale 7.00 5.50
Nos. 64-67 (4) 25.00 17.00

Conservation of whales.

Prince Philip in Antarctica, 1956-57 — A7

Designs: 11p, Coronation oath. 33p, Queen before taking oath.

1977, Feb. 7 *Perf. 13½x14*

68 A7 6p multicolored .45 .45
69 A7 11p multicolored .55 .55
70 A7 33p multicolored 2.00 .75
Nos. 68-70 (3) 3.00 1.75

25th anniv. of the reign of Elizabeth II.

Elizabeth II Coronation Anniversary Issue
Common Design Types
Souvenir Sheet

Unwmk.

1978, June 2 Litho. *Perf. 15*

71 Sheet of 6 5.00 5.00
a. CD326 25p Black bull of Clarence .75 .75
b. CD327 25p Elizabeth II .75 .75
c. CD328 25p Emperor penguin .75 .75

No. 71 contains 2 se-tenant strips of Nos. 71a-71c, separated by horizontal gutter with commemorative and descriptive inscriptions and showing central part of coronation procession with coach.

Macaroni Penguins — A8

Perf. 13½x14

1979, Jan. 14 Litho. Wmk. 373

72 A8 3p shown *8.75* *8.75*
73 A8 8p Gentoo *2.50* *2.50*
74 A8 11p Adelie *2.75* *2.75*
75 A8 25p Emperor *3.50* *3.50*
Nos. 72-75 (4) *17.50* *17.50*

John Barrow, Tula, Society Emblem — A9

Royal Geographical Society Sesquicentennial (Past Presidents and Expedition Scenes): 7p, Clement Markham 11p, Lord Curzon. 15p, William Goodenough. 22p, James Wordie. 30p, Raymond Priestley.

Wmk. 373

1980, Dec. 1 Litho. *Perf. 13½*

76 A9 3p multicolored .20 .20
77 A9 7p multicolored .20 .20
78 A9 11p multicolored .30 .30
79 A9 15p multicolored .50 .50
80 A9 22p multicolored .75 .75
81 A9 30p multicolored .95 .95
Nos. 76-81 (6) 2.90 2.90

20th Anniv. of Antarctic Treaty — A10

1981, Dec. 1 *Perf. 13½x14*

82 A10 10p Map .25 *.65*
83 A10 13p Conservation research .40 *.75*
84 A10 25p Satellite image mapping .70 *.80*
85 A10 26p Global geophysics .75 *.80*
Nos. 82-85 (4) 2.10 3.00

Continental Drift and Climatic Change — A11

1982, Mar. 8 Litho. *Perf. 13½x14*

86 A11 3p Land, water .25 *.35*
87 A11 6p Shrubs .30 *.45*
88 A11 10p Dinosaur .30 *.55*
89 A11 13p Volcano .40 *.60*
90 A11 25p Trees .50 *.65*
91 A11 26p Penguins .50 *.65*
Nos. 86-91 (6) 2.25 3.25

Princess Diana Issue
Common Design Type

1982, July 1 Litho. *Perf. 14½x14*

92 CD333 5p Arms .20 .20
93 CD333 17p Diana, by Bryan Organ .55 .55
94 CD333 37p Wedding 1.25 1.25
95 CD333 50p Portrait 1.60 1.60
Nos. 92-95 (4) 3.60 3.60

10th Anniv. of Convention for Conservation of Antarctic Seals — A12

1982, Nov. Litho.

96 A12 5p shown .20 .20
97 A12 10p Weddell seals .30 .30
98 A12 13p Elephant seals .40 .40
99 A12 17p Fur seals .55 .55
100 A12 25p Ross seal .55 .55
101 A12 34p Crabeater seals 1.10 1.10
Nos. 96-101 (6) 3.10 3.10

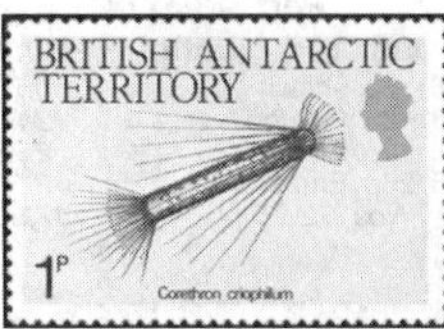

Corethron Criophilum — A13

1p, shown. 2p, Desmonema gaudichaudi. 3p, Tomopteris carpenteri. 4p, Pareuchaeta antarctica. 5p, Antarctomysis maxima. 6p, Antarcturus signiensis. 7p, Serolis comuta. 8p, Parathemisto gaudichaudii. 9p, Bovallia gigantea. 10p (#110A), Euphausia superba. 15p, Colossendeis australis. 20p, Todarodes sagittatus. 25p, Notothenia neglecta. 50p, Chaenocephalus aceratus. £1, Lobodon carcinophagus. £3, Antarctic marine food chain.

1984, Mar. 15 Litho. *Perf. 14*

102-116 A13 Set of 16 17.00 *30.00*

Manned Flight Bicentenary — A14

1983, Dec. 17 Wmk. 373

117 A14 5p De Havilland Twin Otter .20 .20
118 A14 13p De Havilland Single Otter .35 .35
119 A14 17p Consolidated Canso .55 .55
120 A14 50p Lockheed Vega 1.60 1.60
Nos. 117-120 (4) 2.70 2.70

British-Graham Land Expedition, 1934-1937 — A15

Designs: 7p, M. Y. Penola in Stella Creek. 22p, Northern base, Winter Island. 27p, D. H. Fox Moth at southern base, Barry Island. 54p, Dog team near Ablation Point, George VI Sound.

1985, Mar. 23 Litho. *Perf. 14½*

121 A15 7p multicolored .50 .50
122 A15 22p multicolored .85 .85
123 A15 27p multicolored 1.00 1.00
124 A15 54p multicolored 1.90 1.90
Nos. 121-124 (4) 4.25 4.25

A16

Naturalists, fauna and flora: 7p, Robert McCormick (1800-1890), Catharacta Skua Maccormicki. 22p, Sir Joseph Dalton Hooker (1817-1911), Deschampsea antarctica. 27p, Jean Rene C. Quoy (1790-1869), Lagenorhynchus cruciger. 54p, James Weddell (1787-1834), Leptonychotes weddelli.

1985, Nov. 4 Litho. *Perf. 14½*

125 A16 7p multicolored 1.75 1.75
126 A16 22p multicolored 2.40 2.40
127 A16 27p multicolored 2.50 2.50
128 A16 54p multicolored 3.75 3.75
Nos. 125-128 (4) 10.40 10.40

A17

1986, Jan. 6 Wmk. 373 *Perf. 14*

Halley's comet.

129 A17 7p Edmond Halley 1.00 *1.25*
130 A17 22p Halley Station 1.60 *2.10*
131 A17 27p Trajectory, 1531 1.90 *2.40*
132 A17 54p Giotto space probe 3.25 *4.25*
Nos. 129-132 (4) 7.75 10.00

Intl. Glaciological Society, 50th Anniv. — A18

Different snowflakes.

1986, Dec. 6 Wmk. 384 *Perf. 14½*

133 A18 10p dp blue & lt bl .30 .30
134 A18 24p blue grn & lt bl grn .70 .70
135 A18 29p dp rose lil & lt lil .85 .85
136 A18 58p dp vio & pale vio blue 1.75 1.75
Nos. 133-136 (4) 3.60 3.60

Capt. Robert Falcon Scott, CVO RN (1868-1912) A19

Designs: 24p, The Discovery at Hut Point, 1902-1904. 29p, Cape Evans Hut, 1911-1913. 58p, South Pole, 1912.

1987, Mar. 19 Litho. Wmk. 373

137 A19 10p multicolored .75 *.85*
138 A19 24p multicolored 1.25 *1.90*
139 A19 29p multicolored 1.50 *2.25*
140 A19 58p multicolored 2.00 *3.00*
Nos. 137-140 (4) 5.50 8.00

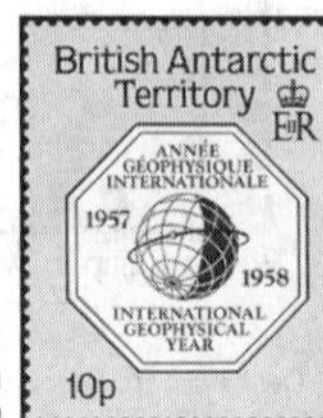

Intl. Geophysical Year, 30th Anniv. — A20

1987, Dec. 25 Wmk. 384

141 A20 10p Emblem .40 .40
142 A20 24p Port Lockroy .90 .90
143 A20 29p Argentine Islands 1.10 1.10
144 A20 58p Halley Bay 2.25 2.25
Nos. 141-144 (4) 4.65 4.65

Commonwealth Trans-Antarctic Expedition] — A21

1988, Mar. 19 *Perf. 14*

145 A21 10p Aurora over South Ice .35 .35
146 A21 24p Otter aircraft .80 .80
147 A21 29p Seismic ice-depth sounding .95 .95
148 A21 58p Sno-cat over crevasse 1.90 1.90
Nos. 145-148 (4) 4.00 4.00

Lichens A22

1989, Mar. 25 Wmk. 373

149 A22 10p Xanthoria elegans .90 .90
150 A22 24p Usnea aurantiaco-atra 1.60 1.60
151 A22 29p Cladonia chlorophaea 1.75 1.75
152 A22 58p Umbilicaria antarctica 2.75 2.75
Nos. 149-152 (4) 7.00 7.00

Fossils A23

1990, Apr. 2 Litho. Wmk. 384

153 A23 1p Archaeocyath .80 *1.00*
154 A23 2p Brachiopod .80 *1.00*
155 A23 3p Trilobite *(Triplagnostus)* .95 *1.00*
156 A23 4p Trilobite *(Lyriaspis)* .95 *1.00*
157 A23 5p Gymnosperm .95 *1.00*
158 A23 6p Fern .95 *1.10*
159 A23 7p Belemnite .95 *1.10*
160 A23 8p Ammonite *(Sanmartinoceras)* .95 *1.10*
161 A23 9p Bivalve *(Pinna)* .95 *1.10*
162 A23 10p Bivalve *(Aucellina)* .95 *1.10*
163 A23 20p Bivalve *(Trigonia)* 1.40 *1.50*
164 A23 25p Gastropod 1.40 *1.50*
165 A23 50p Ammonite *(Ainoceras)* 2.00 *2.75*
166 A23 £1 Ammonite *(Gunnarites)* 3.25 *4.25*
167 A23 £3 Crayfish 6.75 *7.50*
Nos. 153-167 (15) 24.00 28.00

Queen Mother, 90th Birthday
Common Design Types

1990, Aug. 4 Wmk. 384 *Perf. 14x15*

170 CD343 26p Wedding portrait, 1923 1.25 1.25

Perf. 14½

171 CD344 £1 Family portrait, 1940 4.00 4.00

Age of Dinosaurs A24

1991, Mar. 27 Wmk. 373 *Perf. 14*

172 A24 12p Late Cretaceous forest 1.25 1.25
173 A24 26p Hypsilophodont dinosaur 2.00 2.00
174 A24 31p Frilled shark 2.25 2.25
175 A24 62p Mosasaur, plesiosaur 3.50 3.50
Nos. 172-175 (4) 9.00 9.00

Antarctic Ozone Hole — A25

1991, Mar. 30 *Perf. 14½x14*

176 A25 12p Launching weather balloon .40 .40
177 A25 26p Measuring ozone .95 .95
178 A25 31p Ozone hole over Antarctica 1.25 1.25
179 A25 62p Airplane, chemical studies 2.40 2.40
Nos. 176-179 (4) 5.00 5.00

Antarctic Treaty, 30th Anniv. — A26

1991, June 24 *Perf. 14½*

180 A26 12p Dry valley .40 .40
181 A26 26p Mapping ice sheet .95 .95
182 A26 31p BIOMASS emblem 1.25 1.25
183 A26 62p Ross seal 2.40 2.40
Nos. 180-183 (4) 5.00 5.00

Royal Research Ship James Clark Ross — A27

Designs: 12p, HMS Erebus and Terror in Antarctic by John W. Carmichael. 26p, Launch of RRS James Clark Ross. 62p, Scientific research.

1991, Dec. 10 *Perf. 14x14½*

184 A27 12p multicolored .40 .40
185 A27 26p multicolored .95 .95
186 A27 31p shown 1.25 1.25
187 A27 62p multicolored 2.40 2.40
Nos. 184-187 (4) 5.00 5.00

Inscribed in Blue

1991, Dec. 24

188 A27 12p like #184 .40 .40
189 A27 26p like #185 .95 .95
190 A27 31p like #186 1.25 1.25
191 A27 62p like #187 2.40 2.40
Nos. 188-191 (4) 5.00 5.00

Seals and Penguins A28

1992, Oct. 20 *Perf. 13½*

192 A28 4p Ross seal .20 .20
193 A28 5p Adelie penguin .20 .20
194 A28 7p Weddell seal .30 .30

195 A28 29p Emperor penguin 1.25 1.25
196 A28 34p Crabeater seal 1.50 1.50
197 A28 68p Chinstrap penguin 3.00 3.00
Nos. 192-197 (6) 6.45 6.45

World Wildlife Fund.

Lower Atmospheric Phenomena A29

Perf. 14x14½

1992, Dec. 22 Litho. Wmk. 373

198 A29 14p Sun pillar at Faraday .50 .50
199 A29 29p Halo with iceberg 1.10 1.10
200 A29 34p Lee wave cloud 1.25 1.25
201 A29 68p Nacreous clouds 2.50 2.50
Nos. 198-201 (4) 5.35 5.35

Research Ships A30

Wmk. 373

1993, Dec. 13 Litho. *Perf. 14*

202 A30 1p SS Fitzroy .20 .20
203 A30 2p HMS William Scoresby .20 .20
204 A30 3p SS Eagle .20 .20
205 A30 4p MV Trepassey .20 .20
206 A30 5p RRS John Biscoe (I) .20 .20
207 A30 10p MV Norsel .30 .30
208 A30 20p HMS Protector .55 .55
209 A30 30p MV Oluf Sven .85 .85
210 A30 50p RRS John Biscoe (II), RRS Shackleton 1.40 1.40
a. Souvenir sheet of 1 1.75 1.75
211 A30 £1 MV Tottan 2.75 2.75
a. Souvenir sheet of 1 3.50 3.50
212 A30 £3 MV Perla Dan 8.50 8.50
213 A30 £5 HMS Endurance (I) 14.00 14.00
Nos. 202-213 (12) 29.35 29.35

No. 210a for Hong Kong '97. Issued 2/3/97.
No. 211a for return of Hong Kong to China. Issued 7/1/97.

Operation Taberin, 50th Anniv. — A31

Designs: 15p, Bransfield House and Post Office, Port Lockroy. 31p, Survey team, Hope Bay. 36p, Dog team, Hope Bay. 72p, SS Fitzroy, HMS William Scoresby at sea.

Wmk. 373

1994, Mar. 19 Litho. *Perf. 14*

214 A31 15p multicolored .45 .45
215 A31 31p multicolored .90 .90
216 A31 36p multicolored 1.10 1.10
217 A31 72p multicolored 2.25 2.25
Nos. 214-217 (4) 4.70 4.70

Old and New Transportation — A32

Designs: 15p, Huskies. 24p, DeHavilland DHC-2 Turbo Beaver, British Antarctic Survey. 31p, Dogs, cargo being taken from aircraft. 36p, DHC-6 Twin Otter, sled team. 62p, DHC-6 in flight. 72p, DHC-6 taxiing down runway.

1994, Mar. 21

218 A32 15p multicolored .45 .45
219 A32 24p multicolored .70 .70
220 A32 31p multicolored .90 .90
221 A32 36p multicolored 1.10 1.10
222 A32 62p multicolored 1.75 1.75
223 A32 72p multicolored 2.25 2.25
Nos. 218-223 (6) 7.15 7.15

Ovptd. with Hong Kong '94 Emblem

1994, Feb. 18

224 A32 15p on #218 .45 .45
225 A32 24p on #219 .70 .70
226 A32 31p on #220 .90 .90
227 A32 36p on #221 1.10 1.10
228 A32 62p on #222 1.75 1.75
229 A32 72p on #223 2.25 2.25
Nos. 224-229 (6) 7.15 7.15

Antarctic Food Chain — A33

a, Crabeater seals. b, Blue whale. c, Wandering albatross. d, Mackeral icefish. e, Krill. f, Squid.

1994, Nov. 29

230 A33 35p Sheet of 6, #a-f 6.50 6.50

Geological Structures A34

Designs: 17p, Hauberg Mountains, folded sedimentary rocks. 35p, Arrowsmith Peninsula, dikes cross-cutting granite. 40p, Colbert Mountains, columnar jointing in volcanic rocks. 76p, Succession Cliffs, flat-lying sedimentary rocks.

Perf. 14x14½

1995, Nov. 28 Litho. Wmk. 373

231 A34 17p multicolored .55 .55
232 A34 35p multicolored 1.10 1.10
233 A34 40p multicolored 1.25 1.25
234 A34 76p multicolored 2.50 2.50
Nos. 231-234 (4) 5.40 5.40

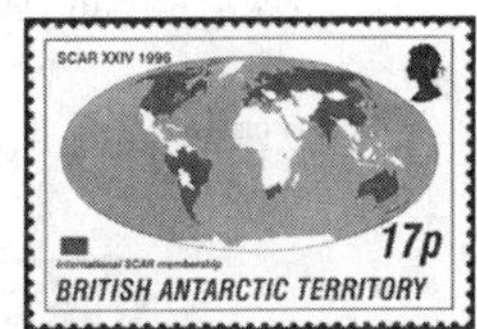

Scientific Committee on Antarctic Research (SCAR) — A35

Designs: 17p, World map showing SCAR member countries. 35p, Earth sciences. 40p, Atmospheric sciences. 76p, Life sciences. £1, Cambridge, August 1996.

Wmk. 384

1996, Mar. 23 Litho. *Perf. 14*

235 A35 17p multicolored .55 .55
236 A35 35p multicolored 1.10 1.10
237 A35 40p multicolored 1.25 1.25
238 A35 76p multicolored 2.50 2.50
Nos. 235-238 (4) 5.40 5.40

Souvenir Sheet

239 A35 £1 multicolored 3.25 3.25

Queen Elizabeth II, 70th Birthday

Common Design Type

Various portraits of Queen: 17p, Pink outfit. 35p, In formal dress, tiara. 40p, Blue outfit. 76p, Red coat.

Wmk. 384

1996, Nov. 25 Litho. *Perf. 14½*

240 CD354 17p multicolored .60 .60
241 CD354 35p multicolored 1.10 1.10
242 CD354 40p multicolored 1.40 1.40
243 CD354 76p multicolored 2.50 2.50
Nos. 240-243 (4) 5.60 5.60

Whales A36

Wmk. 373

1996, Nov. 25 Litho. *Perf. 14*

244 A36 17p Killer whale .60 .60
245 A36 35p Sperm whale 1.10 1.10
246 A36 40p Minke whale 1.40 1.40
247 A36 76p Blue whale 2.50 2.50
Nos. 244-247 (4) 5.60 5.60

Souvenir Sheet

248 A36 £1 Humpback whale 3.50 3.50

Christmas — A37

Penguins in snow: 17p, Sledding. 35p, Caroling. 40p, Throwing snowballs. 76p, Ice skating.

Wmk. 384

1997, Dec. 22 Litho. *Perf. 14½*

249 A37 17p multicolored .55 .55
250 A37 35p multicolored 1.10 1.10
251 A37 40p multicolored 1.40 1.40
252 A37 76p multicolored 2.40 2.40
Nos. 249-252 (4) 5.45 5.45

History of Mapping — A38

Maps of Antarctic and: 16p, Surveyor looking through theodolite, 1902-03. 30p, Cartographer, 1949. 35p, Man using radar rangefinder, 1964. 40p, Satellite, 1981. 65p, Tripod, hand held remote control device, 1993.

Wmk. 373

1998, Mar. 19 Litho. *Perf. 14*

253 A38 16p multicolored .55 .55
254 A38 30p multicolored 1.00 1.00
255 A38 35p multicolored 1.25 1.25
256 A38 40p multicolored 1.40 1.40
257 A38 65p multicolored 2.25 2.25
Nos. 253-257 (5) 6.45 6.45

Diana, Princess of Wales (1961-97)

Common Design Type

a, Wearing sun glasses. b, In white top. c, Up close. d, Wearing blue-green blazer.

1998, Mar. 31 *Perf. 14½x14*

258 CD355 35p Sheet of 4, #a-d 5.25 5.25

No. 258 sold for £1.40 + 20p, with surtax and 50% of profit from total sales being donated to the Princess Diana Memorial Fund.

Antarctic Clothing Through the Ages — A39

Man outfitted for cold weather: 30p, Holding shovel, sailing ship, 1843. 35p, With dog, sailing ship, 1900. 40p, With sketch pad, tripod, dog, steamer ship, 1943. 65p, Wearing red suit, penguins, ship, 1998.

Perf. 14½x14

1998, Nov. 30 Litho. Wmk. 373

259 A39 30p multicolored 1.00 1.00
260 A39 35p multicolored 1.10 1.10
261 A39 40p multicolored 1.25 1.25
262 A39 65p multicolored 2.10 2.10
Nos. 259-262 (4) 5.45 5.45

Birds A40

Designs: 1p, Sheathbill. 2p, Antarctic prion. 5p, Adelie penguin. 10p, Emperor penguin. 20p, Antarctic tern. 30p, Black bellied storm petrel. 35p, Antarctic fulmar. 40p, Blue eyed shag. 50p, McCormick's skua. £1, Kelp gull. £3, Wilson's storm petrel. £5, Brown skua.

1998 *Perf. 14*

263 A40 1p multicolored .20 .20
264 A40 2p multicolored .20 .20
265 A40 5p multicolored .20 .20
266 A40 10p multicolored .35 .35
267 A40 20p multicolored .65 .65
268 A40 30p multicolored 1.00 1.00
269 A40 35p multicolored 1.10 1.10
270 A40 40p multicolored 1.25 1.25
271 A40 50p multicolored 1.60 1.60
272 A40 £1 multicolored 3.25 3.25
273 A40 £3 multicolored 10.00 10.00
274 A40 £5 multicolored 16.00 16.00
Nos. 263-274 (12) 35.80 35.80

Fish — A41

Wmk. 373

1999, Nov. 14 Litho. *Perf. 13½*

275 A41 10p Mackerel icefish .35 .35
276 A41 20p Toothfish .65 .65
277 A41 25p Borch .80 .80
278 A41 50p Marbled notothen 1.60 1.60
279 A41 80p Bernach 2.60 2.60
Nos. 275-279 (5) 6.00 6.00

Survey Discoveries — A42

15p, Map of crustal microplates of West Antarctica. 30p, Lead levels in ice. 35p, Gigantism in marine invertebrates. 40p, Ozone hole. 70p, Electric field associated with aurora.

Wmk. 373

1999, Dec. 18 Litho. *Perf. 14*

280 A42 15p multi, vert. .45 .45
281 A42 30p multi, vert. .95 .95
282 A42 35p multi 1.10 1.10
283 A42 40p multi 1.25 1.25
284 A42 70p multi 2.25 2.25
Nos. 280-284 (5) 6.00 6.00

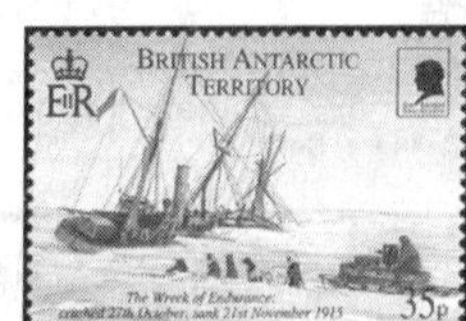

Sir Ernest Shackleton (1874-1922), Polar Explorer — A43

Designs: 35p, Wreck of the Endurance. 40p, Ocean Camp on ice floe. 65p, Launching the James Caird from Elephant Island.

2000, Feb. 10 Wmk. 373

285 A43 35p multi 1.10 1.10
286 A43 40p multi 1.25 1.25
287 A43 65p multi 2.10 2.10
Nos. 285-287 (3) 4.45 4.45

See Falkland Islands Nos. 758-760, South Georgia and South Sandwich Islands Nos. 254-256.

The Stamp Show 2000, London — A44

Commonwealth Trans-Antarctic Exhibition of 1955-58: a, Map of route. b, Expedition at South Pole, 1958. c, MV Magga Dan. d, Sno-cat repair camp. e, Sno-cat over crevasse. f, Seismic explosion.
Illustration reduced.

Perf. 13¼x13¾

2000, May 22 Litho. Wmk. 373

288 A44 37p Sheet of 6, #a-f 6.75 6.75

Survey Ships A45

Designs: 20p, RRS Bransfield unloading near Halley, vert. 33p, Supply boat Tula and RRS Ernest Shackleton, vert. 37p, RRS Bransfield. 43p, RRS Ernest Shackleton.

Wmk. 373

2000, Nov. 30 Litho. *Perf. 14*

289-292 A45 Set of 4 4.00 4.00

Composing of Antarctic Symphony, by Sir Peter Maxwell Davies — A46

Designs: No. 293, 37p, RRS James Clark Ross and track cut through ice. No. 294, 37p, Iceberg. No. 295, 43p, Camp on Jones Ice Shelf. No. 296, 43p, Iceberg, diff.

2000, Dec. 4

293-296 A46 Set of 4 4.75 4.75

Port Lockroy — A47

Designs: 33p, Visitors near building, penguins, flagpole, 2001. 37p, Visitors on rocks below building, ship in water, 2001. 43p, Port Lockroy building, 1945. 65p, Laboratory interior, 1945.

Perf. 13¾x14

2001, Nov. 29 Litho. Wmk. 373

297-300 A47 Set of 4 5.25 5.25

British National Antarctic Expedition of 1901-04, Cent. A48

Designs: 33p, Map of expedition's route, vert. 37p, Capt. Robert Falcon Scott (1868-1912), vert. 43p, First Antarctic balloon ascent, 1902. 65p, Emperor penguin chick, vert. 70p, Ernest Shackleton, Scott, Edward Adrian Wilson, sleds at southernmost point of expedition. 80p, Discovery trapped in ice.

2001, Dec. 5 Wmk. 384 *Perf. 14*

301-306 A48 Set of 6 9.25 9.25

Reign Of Queen Elizabeth II, 50th Anniv. Issue

Common Design Type

Designs: Nos. 307, 311a, 20p, Princess Elizabeth making first broadcast. Nos. 308, 311b, 37p, At Garter ceremony, 1998. Nos. 309, 311c, 43p, In 1952. Nos. 310, 311d, 50p, In 1996. No. 311e, 50p, 1955 portrait by Annigoni (38x50mm).

Perf. 14¼x14½, 13¾ (#311e)

2002, Feb. 6 Litho. Wmk. 373

With Gold Frames

307-310 CD360 Set of 4 4.25 4.25

Souvenir Sheet

Without Gold Frames

311 CD360 Sheet of 5, #a-e 5.75 5.75

Queen Mother Elizabeth (1900-2002)

Common Design Type

Designs: 40p, Without hat (sepia photograph). 45p, Wearing blue green hat.
No. 314: a, 70p, Wearing feathered hat (black and white photograph). b, 95p, Wearing dark blue hat.

Wmk. 373

2002, Aug. 5 Litho. *Perf. 14¼*

With Purple Frames

312-313 CD361 Set of 2 2.60 2.60

Souvenir Sheet

Without Purple Frames

Perf. 14½x14¼

314 CD361 Sheet of 2, #a-b 5.00 5.00

Commission for the Conservation of Antarctic Marine Living Resources, 20th Anniv. — A49

No. 315: a, Map of Antarctica, vessel monitoring satellite. b, Wandering albatross, fishing boat. c, Icefish, toothfish and crabeater seal. d, Krill and phytoplankton.

Perf. 13½x13¾

2002, Oct. 22 Litho. Wmk. 373

315	Vert. strip of 4	4.75	4.75
a.-d.	A49 37p Any single	1.10	1.10

SEMI-POSTAL STAMPS

Antarctic Heritage SP1

Designs: 17p+3p, Capt. James Cook, HMS Resolution. 35p+15p, Sir James Clark Ross, HMS Erebus, HMS Terror. 40p+10p, Capt. Robert Falcon Scott. 76p+4p, Sir Ernest Shackleton, HMS Endurance trapped in ice.

Wmk. 384

1994, Nov. 23 Litho. *Perf. 14½*

B1	SP1	17p + 3p multi	.65	.65
B2	SP1	35p + 15p multi	1.50	1.50
B3	SP1	40p + 10p multi	1.50	1.50
B4	SP1	76p + 4p multi	2.50	2.50
		Nos. B1-B4 (4)	6.15	6.15

Surtax for United Kingdom Antarctic Heritage Trust.

BRITISH CENTRAL AFRICA

'bri-tish 'sen-trəl 'a-fri-kə

LOCATION — Central Africa, on the west shore of Lake Nyassa

GOVT. — British territory, under charter to the British South Africa Company

AREA — 37,800 sq. mi.

POP. — 1,639,329

CAPITAL — Zomba

In 1907 the name was changed to Nyasaland Protectorate, and stamps so inscribed replaced those of British Central Africa.

12 Pence = 1 Shilling
20 Shillings = 1 Pound

Rhodesia Nos. 2, 4-19 Overprinted in Black

1891-95 Unwmk. *Perf. 14*

1	A1	1p black	3.25	*3.50*
2	A2	2p gray green & ver	3.25	*3.50*
3	A2	4p red brn & blk	3.50	*4.50*
4	A1	6p ultramarine	45.00	24.00
5	A1	6p dark blue	5.00	*7.50*
6	A2	8p rose & blue	12.00	*27.50*
7	A1	1sh bis brown	12.00	10.00
8	A1	2sh vermilion	22.50	*45.00*
9	A1	2sh6p gray lilac	55.00	*70.00*
10	A2	3sh brn & grn ('95)	50.00	*55.00*
11	A2	4sh gray & ver ('93)	55.00	*75.00*
12	A1	5sh yellow	55.00	*67.50*
13	A1	10sh green	110.00	*160.00*
14	A3	£1 blue	550.00	*550.00*
15	A3	£2 rose red	800.00	*900.00*
16	A3	£5 yel green	1,600.	*1,700.*
17	A3	£10 red brown	*3,250.*	*3,500.*
		Nos. 1-13 (13)	431.50	*553.00*

High values with fiscal cancellation are fairly common and can be purchased at a small fraction of the above values. This applies to subsequent issues also.
For surcharge see No. 20.

B.C.A.
THREE
SHILLINGS.

Rhodesia Nos. 13-14 Surcharged in Black

1892-93

18	A2	3sh on 4sh gray & ver ('93)	300.00	300.00
19	A1	4sh on 5sh yellow	70.00	*80.00*

No. 2 Surcharged in Black, with Bar

1895

20	A2	1p on 2p	7.50	*25.00*
a.		Double surcharge	*3,000.*	*2,400.*

A double surcharge, without period after "Penny," and measuring 16mm instead of 18mm, is from a trial printing.

A4

Coat of Arms of the Protectorate — A5

1895 Unwmk. Typo. *Perf. 14*

21	A4	1p black	11.00	6.50
22	A4	2p green & black	17.50	11.00
23	A4	4p org & black	32.50	26.00
24	A4	6p ultra & black	50.00	7.50
25	A4	1sh rose & black	55.00	22.50
26	A5	2sh6p vio & black	150.00	*225.00*
27	A5	3sh yel & black	85.00	45.00
28	A5	5sh olive & blk	125.00	150.00
29	A5	£1 org & black	800.00	375.00
30	A5	£10 ver & black	*3,750.*	*3,250.*
31	A5	£25 bl grn & blk	*6,500.*	*6,500.*
		Nos. 21-28 (8)	526.00	493.50

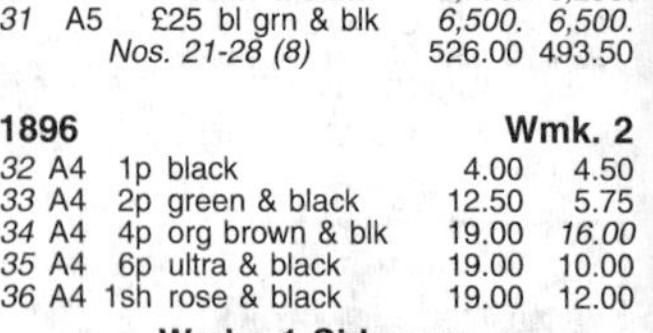

1896 Wmk. 2

32	A4	1p black	4.00	4.50
33	A4	2p green & black	12.50	5.75
34	A4	4p org brown & blk	19.00	*16.00*
35	A4	6p ultra & black	19.00	10.00
36	A4	1sh rose & black	19.00	12.00

Wmk. 1 Sideways

37	A5	2sh6p vio rose & blk	100.00	100.00
38	A5	3sh yel & black	75.00	45.00
39	A5	5sh olive & blk	110.00	*140.00*
40	A5	£1 blue & blk	800.00	475.00
41	A5	£10 ver & blk	*4,250.*	*3,250.*
42	A5	£25 bl grn & blk	*9,500.*	*9,500.*
		Nos. 32-39 (8)	358.50	333.25

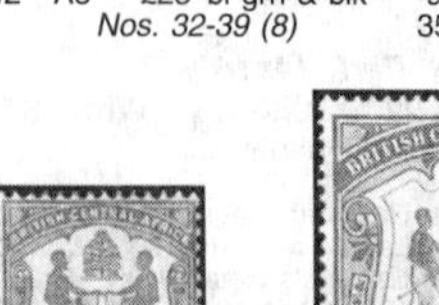

A6

A7

1897-1901 Wmk. 2

43	A6	1p ultra & black	2.25	.80
44	A6	1p rose & violet ('01)	1.75	.80
45	A6	2p yel & black	1.75	1.60
46	A6	4p car rose & blk	5.00	2.25
47	A6	4p ol grn & vio ('01)	7.00	*10.00*
48	A6	6p green & black	37.50	4.00
49	A6	6p red brn & vio ('01)	4.00	2.75
50	A6	1sh gray lilac & blk	8.50	6.25

Wmk. 1

51	A7	2sh6p ultra & blk	40.00	*37.50*
52	A7	3sh gray grn & blk	175.00	*200.00*
53	A7	4sh car rose & blk	62.50	*70.00*
54	A7	10sh olive & black	100.00	*110.00*
55	A7	£1 dp vio & blk	250.00	150.00
56	A7	£10 orange & black	*4,000.*	*1,700.*
		Nos. 43-54 (12)	445.25	*445.95*

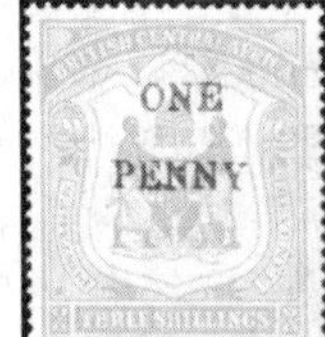

No. 52 Surcharged in Red

1897

57	A7	1p on 3s	5.00	*8.00*
a.		"PNNEY"	1,700.	1,700.
b.		"PENN"	1,150.	900.00
c.		Double surcharge	675.00	

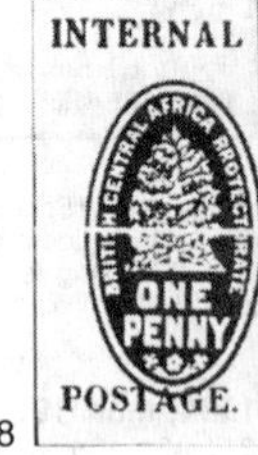

A8

Type I - The vertical framelines are not continuous between stamps.
Type II - The vertical framelines are continuous between stamps.

1898, Mar. 11 Unwmk. *Imperf.*

Type I

Control on Reverse

58	A8	1p ver & ultra	—	75.00
a.		1p ver & deep ultra	—	75.00
b.		No control on reverse	1,750.	125.00
c.		Control double		375.00
d.		Control on front	3,000.	
e.		Pair, one without oval	10,000.	

Type II

Control on Reverse

f.	1p ver & ultra	—	350.00

No Control on Reverse

i.	Oval inverted	9,500.	
j.	Oval double	—	
k.	Pair, with 3 ovals	—	

Perf. 12
Type I
Control on Reverse

59 A8 1p ver & ultra 1,750. 15.00
a. 1p ver & deep ultra — 27.50
b. Two diff. controls on reverse — 550.00

No Control on Reverse

d. 1p ver & ultra 1,800. 75.00

There are 30 types of each setting of Nos. 58-59.
No. 58 issued without gum.
Control consists of figures or letters.
See the *Scott Classic Catalogue* for additional varieties.

A9

King Edward VII — A10

1903-04 Wmk. 2

60 A9 1p car & black 4.25 1.60
61 A9 2p vio & dull vio 3.00 2.25
62 A9 4p blk & gray green 2.25 *8.00*
63 A9 6p org brn & blk 2.25 *4.00*
64 A9 1sh pale blue & blk ('04) 2.50 *8.75*

Wmk. 1

65 A10 2sh6p gray green 35.00 *57.50*
66 A10 4sh vio & dl vio 55.00 *67.50*
67 A10 10sh blk & gray green 80.00 *160.00*
68 A10 £1 scar & blk 200.00 150.00
69 A10 £10 ultra & blk *3,750. 3,000.*
Nos. 60-68 (9) 384.25 *459.60*

1907 Wmk. 3

70 A9 1p car & black 4.00 2.25
71 A9 2p vio & dull vio *8,500.*
72 A9 4p blk & gray grn *8,500.*
73 A9 6p org brn & blk 25.00 *40.00*

Nos. 71-72 were not issued.
British Central Africa stamps were replaced by those of Nyasaland Protectorate in 1908.

BRITISH EAST AFRICA

'bri-tish 'ēst 'a-fri-kə

LOCATION — Included all of the territory in East Africa under British control.

Postage stamps were issued by the British East Africa Company in 1896. Later the territory administered by this company was incorporated in the East Africa and Uganda Protectorate which, together with Kenya, became officially designated Kenya Colony.

16 Annas = 1 Rupee

Queen Victoria
A1 A2 A3

1890 Wmk. 30 Perf. 14

1 A1 ½a on 1p lilac 300.00 200.00
2 A2 1a on 2p grn & car rose 400.00 275.00
3 A3 4a on 5p lilac & bl 400.00 275.00

Sun and Crown Symbolical of "Light and Liberty"
A4 A5

1890-94 Unwmk. Litho. Perf. 14

14 A4 ½a bister brown 1.00 *4.50*
b. ½a deep brown 1.00 *3.00*
c. As "b," horiz. pair, imperf. btwn. *1,500.* 750.00
d. As "b," vert. pair, imperf. btwn. 850.00 475.00
15 A4 1a blue green 3.00 *4.25*
16 A4 2a vermilion 2.50 *3.50*
17 A4 2½a black, *yel* ('91) 4.00 5.00
b. Vert. pair, imperf. btwn. 1,200. 400.00
c. Horiz. pair, imperf. btwn. 1,200. 525.00
18 A4 3a black, *red* ('91) 1.60 *4.50*
b. Horiz. pair, imperf. btwn. 700.00 400.00
c. Vert. pair, imperf. btwn. 550.00 375.00
19 A4 4a yellow brown 2.50 *5.00*
20 A4 4½a brown vio ('91) 2.50 *12.50*
b. 4½a gray violet ('91) 32.50 12.50
c. Horiz. pair, imperf. btwn. 1,250. 1,250.
d. Vert. pair, imperf. btwn. 850.00 450.00
21 A4 5a black, *blue* ('94) 1.25 *10.00*
22 A4 7½a black ('94) 1.25 *12.00*
23 A4 8a blue 5.50 *8.00*
24 A4 8a gray 275.00 *325.00*
25 A4 1r rose 6.00 *8.50*
26 A4 1r gray 225.00 225.00
27 A5 2r brick red 12.50 *24.00*
28 A5 3r gray violet 7.50 *27.50*
29 A5 4r ultra 12.00 *30.00*
30 A5 5r gray green 35.00 *60.00*
Nos. 14-30 (17) 598.10 *769.25*

Some of the paper used for this issue had a papermaker's watermark and parts of it often can be seen on the stamps.
Values for Nos. 14c, 14d, 17b, 17c, 18b, 18c, 20c, 20d, unused, are for copies with little or no original gum. Stamps with natural straight edges are almost as common as fully perforated stamps from the early printings of Nos. 14-30, and for all printings of the rupee values. Values about the same.
For surcharges and overprints see #31-53.

1890-91 Imperf.

Values for Pairs except No. 19b.

14a A4 ½a bister brown 800. 375.
14e A4 ½a deep brown 900. 500.
15a A4 1a blue green 1,000. 500.
16a A4 2a vermilion 1,350. 550.
17a A4 2½a black, *yellow* 900. 400.
18a A4 3a black, *red* 850. 600.
19a A4 4a yel brown 1,500. 700.
19b A4 4a gray 1,400. 1,400.
20a A4 4½a dull violet 1,300. 525.
23a A4 8a blue 2,250. 650.
25a A4 1r rose 2,750. 700.

A6

A7

Handstamped Surcharges

1891 Perf. 14

31 A6 ½a on 2a ver ("A.D.") 3,750. 900.00
a. Double surcharge *3,750.*
32 A6 1a on 4a yel brn ("A.B.") 6,500. 1,500.

Nos. 31-32 are initialed in manuscript "A.D." or "A.B." See note below No. 35.

Manuscript Surcharges

1891-95

33 A6 ½a on 2a ver ("A.B.") 3,500. 725.00
a. "½ Annas" ("A.B.") 1,200.
b. Initialed "A.D." 1,750.
c. "½ Annas" ("A.D.") 2,000.
34 A6 ½a on 3a blk, *red* ("T.E.C.R.") 350.00 50.00
b. Initialed "A.B." 4,750. 1,375.
34A A6 1a on 3a blk, *red* ("V.H.M.") 4,750. 1,200.
c. Initialed "T.E.C.R." 3,750. 1,800.
35 A6 1a on 4a yel brn ("A.B.") 3,500. 1,275.

The manuscript initials on Nos. 31-35, given in parentheses, stand for Andrew Dick, Archibald Brown, Victor H. Mackenzie (1891) and T.E. C. Remington (1895).

Printed Surcharges

1894

36 A7 5a on 8a blue 52.50 *75.00*
37 A7 7½a on 1r rose 52.50 *75.00*

Stamps of 1890-94 Handstamped in Black

1895

38 A4 ½a deep brown 60.00 24.00
39 A4 1a blue green 70.00 65.00
40 A4 2a vermilion 140.00 125.00
41 A4 2½a black, *yellow* 110.00 45.00
42 A4 3a black, *red* 50.00 37.50
43 A4 4a yel brown 37.50 37.50
44 A4 4½a gray violet 125.00 85.00
a. 4½a brown violet 750.00 650.00
45 A4 5a black, *blue* 150.00 90.00
b. Inverted overprint *2,000.*
46 A4 7½a black 87.50 80.00
47 A4 8a blue 80.00 75.00
b. Inverted overprint *2,000.*
48 A4 1r rose 47.50 47.50
49 A5 2r brick red 250.00 175.00
50 A5 3r gray violet 140.00 125.00
b. Inverted overprint
51 A5 4r ultra 125.00 125.00
52 A5 5r gray green 325.00 *350.00*
Nos. 38-52 (15) 1,797. 1,486.

Double Overprints

38a A4 ½a 350. 350.
39a A4 1a 350. 350.
40a A4 2a 400. 400.
41a A4 2½a 400. 350.
43a A4 4a 375. 375.
44b A4 4½a gray violet 475. 450.
44c A4 4½a brown violet 1,500. 1,400.
45a A4 5a 700. 650.
46a A4 7½a 450. 450.
47a A4 8a 475. 475.
48a A4 1r 425. 425.
50a A5 3r 750. 750.
51a A5 4r 750. 750.
52a A5 5r 1,100. 1,100.

Surcharged in Red

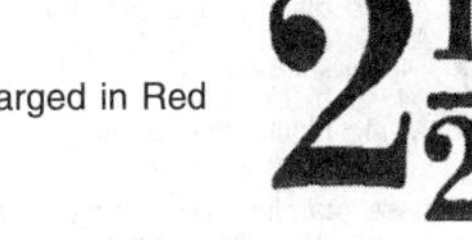

1895

53 A4 2½a on 4½a gray vio 90.00 60.00
a. Double overprint (#44b) 700.00 700.00

Stamps of India 1874-95 Overprinted or Surcharged

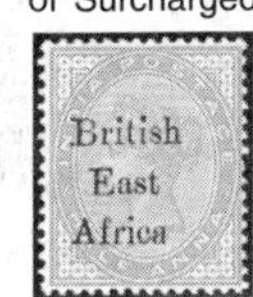

2½ 2½ 2½
a b c

1895 Wmk. Star (39)

54 A17 ½a green 4.25 *4.50*
55 A19 1a maroon 3.50 *4.25*
56 A20 1a6p bister brn 3.50 *4.00*
57 A21 2a ultra 4.25 2.50
58 A28 2a6p green 5.00 2.75
59 A20(a) 2½a on 1a6p bis brown 60.00 35.00
a. "½" without fraction line 70.00
d. As "a," "1" of "½" invtd. 775.00 600.00
62 A22 3a orange 7.00 *8.50*
63 A23 4a olive green 27.50 22.50
64 A25 8a red violet 27.50 *45.00*
a. 8a red lilac 50.00 *57.50*
65 A26 12a vio, *red* 20.00 *25.00*
66 A27 1r gray 60.00 60.00
67 A29 1r car & grn 40.00 *75.00*
a. Dbl. ovpt., one sideways 400.00 *675.00*
68 A30 2r bis & rose 60.00 *90.00*
69 A30 3r grn & brn 65.00 *110.00*
70 A30 5r vio & ultra 85.00 *125.00*
a. Double overprint 1,800.

Wmk. Elephant's Head (38)

71 A14 6a bister 25.00 *40.00*
Nos. 54-59,62-71 (16) 497.50 *654.00*

Varieties of the overprint include: "Britlsh," "Brltish," "Bpitish" and "Biitish"; "Afrlca"; "Eas" and "Easa."
No. 59 is surcharged in bright red; surcharges in brown red were prepared for the UPU, but not regularly issued as stamps. See note following No. 93.

Queen Victoria and British Lions — A8

1896-1903 Engr. Wmk. 2 Perf. 14

72 A8 ½a yel green 1.25 .70
73 A8 1a carmine 3.00 .40
a. 1a red 3.00 .40
74 A8 1a dp rose ('03) 27.50 3.75
75 A8 2a chocolate 3.75 *4.00*
76 A8 2½a dark blue 5.00 1.40
77 A8 3a gray 2.50 *5.50*
78 A8 4a deep green 6.00 3.25
79 A8 4½a orange 4.50 *12.50*
80 A8 5a dk ocher 7.00 4.00
81 A8 7½a lilac 5.00 *20.00*
82 A8 8a olive gray 2.50 *5.50*
83 A8 1r ultra 45.00 42.50
a. 1r pale blue 35.00 22.50
84 A8 2r red orange 47.50 24.00
85 A8 3r deep violet 55.00 27.50
86 A8 4r lake 55.00 55.00
87 A8 5r dark brown 50.00 40.00
Nos. 72-87 (16) 320.50 250.00

Zanzibar Nos. 38-40, 44-46 Overprinted in Black

1897 Wmk. Rosette (71)

88 A2 ½a yel grn & red 45.00 45.00
89 A2 1a indigo & red 80.00 80.00
90 A2 2a red brn & red 27.50 22.50
91 A2 4½a org & red 42.50 25.00
92 A2 5a bister & red 42.50 30.00
93 A2 7½a lilac & red 42.50 35.00
a. Ovptd. on front and back
Nos. 88-93 (6) 280.00 237.50

The 1a with red overprint, which includes a period after "Africa", was sent to the UPU, but never placed in use. Nos. 88, 90-93 and 95-100 also exist with period (in black) in sets sent to the UPU. Some experts consider these essays.

Black Ovpt. on Zanzibar #39, 42
New Value Surcharged in Red

1897

95 A2(a) 2½a on 1a 75.00 50.00
a. Black overprint double *6,500.*
96 A2(b) 2½a on 1a 160.00 90.00
97 A2(c) 2½a on 1a 85.00 55.00
a. Black overprint double *6,500.*
98 A2(a) 2½a on 3a 75.00 45.00
99 A2(b) 2½a on 3a 160.00 85.00
100 A2(c) 2½a on 3a 80.00 50.00
Nos. 95-100 (6) 635.00 375.00

A special printing of the 2½a surcharge on the 1a and 3a stamps was made for submission to the U.P.U. Stamps have a period after "Africa" in the overprint, and the surcharges included a "2" over "1" error in the fraction of the surcharge. These stamps were never placed in use. The fraction error appears on both the 1a and 3a stamps. Value, each, $1,200.

A10

1898 Wmk. 1 Engr.

102 A10 1r gray blue 40.00 22.50
a. 1r ultramarine 160.00 125.00
103 A10 2r orange 60.00 60.00
104 A10 3r dk violet 65.00 *80.00*
105 A10 4r carmine 175.00 *225.00*
106 A10 5r black brown 140.00 *190.00*
107 A10 10r bister 160.00 *225.00*
108 A10 20r yel green 575.00 *1,250.*
109 A10 50r lilac 1,900. *3,500.*
Nos. 102-107 (6) 640.00 *802.50*

The stamps of this country were superseded in 1904 by the stamps of East Africa and Uganda Protectorate.

BRITISH GUIANA

ˈbri-tish gē-ˈa-nə, -ˈä-nə

LOCATION — On the northeast coast of South America
GOVT. — British Crown Colony
AREA — 83,000 sq. mi.
POP. — 628,000 (estimated 1964)
CAPITAL — Georgetown

British Guiana became the independent state of Guyana May 26, 1966.

100 Cents = 1 Dollar

Catalogue values for unused stamps in this country are for Never Hinged items, beginning with Scott 242 in the regular postage section and Scott J1 in the postage due section.

Values for unused stamps are for copies with original gum except for Nos. 6-12 and 35-53, which are valued without gum. Very fine examples of all stamps from No. 6 on will have four clear margins. Inferior copies sell at much reduced prices, depending on the condition of the individual specimen.

A1

1850-51 Typeset Unwmk. *Imperf.*

1 A1 2c blk, *pale rose*, cut to shape ('51) 70,000.
2 A1 4c black, *orange* 24,000.
Cut to shape 3,750.
a. 4c black, *yellow* 35,000.
Cut to shape 4,250.
3 A1 4c blk, *yellow* (pelure) 42,500.
Cut to shape 4,750.
4 A1 8c black, *green* 14,000.
Cut to shape 3,000.
5 A1 12c black, *blue* 5,250.
Cut to shape 2,000.
a. 12c black, *pale blue* 11,000.
Cut to shape 3,000.
b. 12c black, *indigo* 13,000.
Cut to shape 3,000.
c. "1" of "12" omitted 35,000.

These stamps were initialed before use by the Deputy Postmaster General or by one of the clerks of the Colonial Postoffice at Georgetown. The following initials are found:—E. T. E. D(alton); E. D. W(ight); G. B. S(mith); H. A. K(illikelley); W. H. L(ortimer). As these stamps are type-set there are several types of each value.

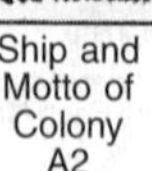

Ship and Motto of Colony
A2

Seal of the Colony
A3

1852 Litho.

6 A2 1c black, *magenta* 10,000. 5,250.
7 A2 4c black, *blue* 15,000. 5,750.

Both 1c and 4c are found in two types. Copies with paper cracked or rubbed sell for much less.

Some copies are initialed E. D. W(ight).

The reprints are on thicker paper and the colors are brighter. They are perforated 12½ and imperforate. Value $15 each.

1853-59 *Imperf.*

Without Line above Value

8 A3 1c vermilion 4,500. 1,150.

Copies in reddish brown probably are proofs.

Full or Partial White Line Above Value

9 A3 1c red 2,750. 950.
10 A3 4c blue 1,100. 450.
a. 4c dark blue 2,000. 600.
b. 4c pale blue 1,000. 375.

On No. 9, "ONE CENT" varies from 11 to 13mm in width.

No. 10 Retouched; White Line above Value Removed

11 A3 4c blue 1,650. 600.
a. 4c dark blue 2,400. 850.
b. 4c pale blue 1,600. 650.

Reprints of Nos. 8 and 10 are on thin paper, perf. 12½ or imperf. The 1c is orange red, the 4c sky blue.

1860

Numerals in Corners Framed

12 A3 4c blue 3,250. 450.

A4

1856 Typeset *Imperf.*

13 A4 1c black, *magenta* —
14 A4 4c black, *magenta* 7,500.
a. 4c black, *rose carmine* 20,000. 10,500.
15 A4 4c black, *blue* 45,000.
16 A4 4c black, *blue, paper colored through* 60,000.

These stamps were initialed before being issued and the following initials are found:—E. T. E. D.; E. D. W.; W. H. L.; C. A. W. No. 13 is unique.

A5

Wide space between value and "Cents"

1860-61 Litho. *Perf. 12*

Thick Paper

17 A5 1c brown red ('61) 350.00 100.00
18 A5 1c pink 1,100. 200.00
19 A5 2c orange 160.00 37.50
20 A5 8c rose 325.00 60.00
21 A5 12c gray 375.00 35.00
a. 12c lilac 450.00 40.00
22 A5 24c green 950.00 75.00

All denominations of type A5 above four cents are expressed in Roman numerals.

Bisects and trisects are found on covers. These were not officially authorized.

The reprints of the 1c pink are perforated 12½; the other values have not been reprinted.

Thin Paper

1862-65

23 A5 1c brown 400.00 175.00
24 A5 1c black 100.00 45.00
25 A5 2c orange 80.00 32.50
26 A5 8c rose 110.00 45.00
27 A5 12c lilac 150.00 32.50
28 A5 24c green 750.00 85.00

Perf. 12½ and 13

29 A5 1c black 60.00 25.00
30 A5 2c orange 80.00 22.50
31 A5 8c rose 225.00 75.00
32 A5 12c lilac 475.00 110.00
33 A5 24c green 550.00 75.00

Medium Paper

33A A5 1c black 50.00 27.50
33B A5 2c orange 52.50 17.00
33C A5 8c pink 150.00 50.00
33D A5 12c lilac ('65) 425.00 95.00
33E A5 24c green 160.00 65.00
f. 24c deep green 325.00 85.00

Perf. 10

34 A5 12c gray lilac 400.00 65.00

Imperfs. are proofs. See Nos. 44-62.

A6

A7

A8

A9

A10

A11

1862 Typeset *Rouletted*

35 A6 1c black, *rose* 2,000. 450.
Unsigned 225.
36 A7 1c black, *rose* 2,750. 575.
Unsigned 275.
37 A8 1c black, *rose* 4,000. 750.
Unsigned 450.
38 A6 2c black, *yellow* 2,000. 300.
Unsigned 700.
39 A7 2c black, *yellow* 2,750. 375.
Unsigned 750.
40 A8 2c black, *yellow* 4,000. 600.
Unsigned 900.
41 A9 4c black, *blue* 3,000. 600.
Unsigned 475.
42 A10 4c black, *blue* 4,000. 1,450.
Unsigned 600.
a. Without inner lines 3,000. 600.
As "a," unsigned 475.
43 A11 4c black, *blue* 2,250. 450.
Unsigned 475.

Nos. 35-43 were typeset, there being 24 types of each value. They were initialed before use "R. M. Ac. R. G.," being the initials of Robert Mather, Acting Receiver General.

The initials are in black on the 1c and in red on the 2c. An alkali was used on the 4c stamps, which, destroying the color of the paper, caused the initials to appear to be written in white.

Uninitialed stamps are remainders, few sheets having been found.

Specimens with roulette on all sides are valued higher.

Narrow space between value and "Cents"

1860 Thick Paper Litho. *Perf. 12*

44 A5 4c blue 275.00 60.00
c. 4c deep blue 375.00 75.00

Thin Paper

44A A5 4c blue 77.50 25.00

Perf. 12½ and 13

44B A5 4c blue 75.00 22.50

Medium Paper

1863-68 *Perf. 12½ and 13*

45 A5 1c black ('66) 32.50 20.00
46 A5 2c orange 35.00 5.00
47 A5 4c blue ('64) 65.00 12.50
48 A5 8c rose ('68) 150.00 15.00
49 A5 12c lilac ('67) 375.00 22.50
Nos. 45-49 (5) 657.50 75.00

1866 *Perf. 10*

50 A5 1c black 8.00 4.00
51 A5 2c orange 20.00 3.00
52 A5 4c blue 75.00 7.50
a. Half used as 2c on cover 4,000.
53 A5 8c rose 110.00 17.50
a. Diagonal half used as 4c on cover —
54 A5 12c lilac 125.00 17.50
a. Third used as 4c on cover —
Nos. 50-54 (5) 338.00 49.50

1875 *Perf. 15*

58 A5 1c black 40.00 7.50
59 A5 2c orange 125.00 8.00
60 A5 4c blue 250.00 85.00
61 A5 8c rose 250.00 80.00
62 A5 12c lilac 550.00 50.00
Nos. 58-62 (5) 1,215. 230.50

Seal of Colony
A12 A13

1863 *Perf. 12*

63 A12 24c yellow green 125.00 12.50
a. 24c green 250.00 22.50

Perf. 12½ to 13

64 A12 6c blue 85.00 40.00
65 A12 24c green 125.00 10.00
66 A12 48c deep red 200.00 45.00
a. 48c rose 250.00 45.00
Nos. 63-66 (4) 535.00 107.50

1866 *Perf. 10*

67 A12 6c blue 100.00 27.50
a. 6c ultramarine 125.00 37.50
68 A12 24c yellow green 150.00 8.00
a. 24c green 190.00 10.00
69 A12 48c rose red 275.00 27.50
Nos. 67-69 (3) 525.00 63.00

For surcharges see Nos. 83-92.

1875 *Perf. 15*

70 A12 6c ultra 400.00 80.00
71 A12 24c yellow green 525.00 35.00
a. 24c deep green 675.00 65.00

1876 Typo. Wmk. 1 *Perf. 14*

72 A13 1c slate 3.00 1.50
a. Perf. 14x12½ 200.00
73 A13 2c orange 37.50 2.00
74 A13 4c ultra 110.00 8.00
a. Perf. 12½ 1,350. 200.00
75 A13 6c chocolate 70.00 7.50
76 A13 8c rose 100.00 1.00
77 A13 12c lilac 55.00 2.50
78 A13 24c green 65.00 4.00
79 A13 48c red brown 125.00 22.50
80 A13 96c bister 475.00 275.00
Nos. 72-80 (9) 1,040. 324.00

See Nos. 107-111. For surcharges see Nos. 93-95, 98-101.

Stamps Surcharged by Brush-like Pen Lines

Surcharge Types:
Type a - Two horiz. lines.
Type b - Two lines, one horiz., one vert.
Type c - Three lines, two horiz., one vert.
Type d - One horiz. line.

On Nos. 75 and 67

1878 *Perf. 10, 14*

82 A13(a) (1c) on 6c choc 37.50 *90.00*
83 A12(b) (1c) on 6c blue 140.00 65.00
84 A13(b) (1c) on 6c choc 225.00 85.00

On Nos. O3, O8-O10

85 A13(c) (1c) on 4c ultra 175.00 85.00
a. Type b 2,500.
86 A13(c) (1c) on 6c choc 250.00 85.00
87 A5(c) (2c) on 8c rose *1,000.* 225.00
88A A13(b) (2c) on 8c rose 250.00 90.00

On Nos. O1, O3, O6-O7

89 A5(d) (1c) on 1c blk 160.00 75.00
89A A5(d) (2c) on 8c rose
90 A13(d) (1c) on 1c sl 140.00 50.00
91 A13(d) (2c) on 2c org 250.00 65.00

The provisional values of Nos. 82 to 91 were established by various official decrees. The horizontal lines crossed out the old value, "OFFICIAL," or both.

Nos. 69 and 80 Surcharged with New Values in Black

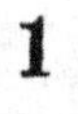

No. 92

No. 93

No. 94

No. 95

1881

92 A12 1c on 48c red 35.00 5.00
93 A13 1c on 96c bister 4.50 *5.50*
94 A13 2c on 96c bister 4.50 *10.00*
95 A13 2c on 96c bister 45.00 *70.00*
Nos. 92-95 (4) 89.00 *90.50*

Nos. O4, O5 and Unissued Official Stamps Surcharged with New Values

No. 96

No. 97

Nos. 98, 100

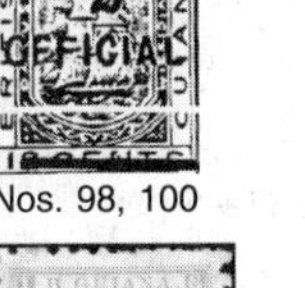

Nos. 99, 101

No. 102

1881
96 A5 1c on 12c lilac (#O4) 110.00 65.00
97 A13 1c on 48c red brn 125.00 90.00
98 A13 2c on 12c lilac 350.00 250.00
99 A13 2c on 12c lilac 60.00 25.00
a. "2" inverted
b. "2" double 750.00 475.00
100 A13 2c on 24c green 575.00 575.00
101 A13 2c on 24c green 75.00 40.00
a. "2" inverted
d. Double surcharge 800.00
102 A12 2c on 24c green (#O5) 200.00 125.00

A27

Typeset

ONE AND TWO CENTS.
Type I - Ship with three masts.
Type II - Brig with two masts.

"SPECIMEN"
Perforated Diagonally across Stamp

1882 Unwmk. *Perf. 12*
103 A27 1c black, *lil rose,* I 35.00 30.00
a. Without "Specimen" 400.00 290.00
104 A27 1c black, *lil rose,* II 35.00 30.00
a. Without "Specimen" 400.00 300.00
105 A27 2c black, *yel,* I 55.00 40.00
a. Without "Specimen" 350.00 325.00
b. Diagonal half used as 1c on cover
106 A27 2c black, *yel,* II 60.00 45.00
a. Without "Specimen" 350.00 325.00
Nos. 103-106 (4) 185.00 145.00

Nos. 103-106 were typeset, 12 to a sheet, and, to prevent fraud on the government, the word *"Specimen"* was perforated across them before they were issued. There were 2 settings of the 1c and 3 settings of the 2c, thus there are 24 types of the former and 36 of the latter.

Type of 1876

1882 Typo. Wmk. 2 *Perf. 14*
107 A13 1c slate 7.50 .35
108 A13 2c orange 20.00 .35
a. "2 CENTS" double —
109 A13 4c ultra 80.00 6.50
110 A13 6c brown 6.00 7.50
111 A13 8c rose 85.00 1.00
Nos. 107-111 (5) 198.50 15.70

A28

A29

4 CENTS and $4
Type I - Figure "4" is 3mm high.
Type II - Figure "4" is 3½mm high.
6 CENTS
Type I - Top of "6" is flat.
Type II - Top of "6" turns downward.

"INLAND REVENUE" Overprint and Surcharged in Black

1889
112 A28 1c lilac 1.75 .55
113 A28 2c lilac 1.50 .40
114 A28 3c lilac 1.00 .40
115 A28 4c lilac, I 5.00 .40
116 A28 4c lilac, II 21.00 12.50
117 A28 6c lilac, I 18.00 4.50
118 A28 6c lilac, II 5.50 3.00
119 A28 8c lilac 1.75 .65
120 A28 10c lilac 6.00 2.50
121 A28 20c lilac 17.50 10.00
122 A28 40c lilac 20.00 15.00
123 A28 72c lilac 35.00 *40.00*
124 A28 $1 green 400.00 400.00
125 A28 $2 green 175.00 175.00
126 A28 $3 green 110.00 110.00
127 A28 $4 green, I 350.00 350.00
127A A28 $4 green, II 950.00 *975.00*
128 A28 $5 green 225.00 200.00
Nos. 112-128 (18) 2,344. 2,299.

For surcharges see Nos.129, 148-151B.

No. 113 Surcharged "2" in Red

1889
129 A29 2c on 2c lilac 1.10 .40

Inverted and double surcharges of "2" were privately made.

A30

A31

1889-1903 Typo.
130 A30 1c lilac & gray 2.50 1.60
131 A30 1c green ('90) .50 .20
131A A30 1c gray grn ('00) 3.00 3.00
132 A30 2c lilac & org 1.50 .20
133 A30 2c lil & rose ('00) 3.50 .25
134 A30 2c vio & blk, *red* ('01) 1.25 .20
135 A30 4c lilac & ultra 4.00 1.50
a. 4c lilac & blue 19.00 2.25
136 A30 5c ultra ('91) 3.00 .25
137 A30 6c lilac & mar 6.00 *10.00*
a. 6c lilac & brown 32.50 11.00
138 A30 6c gray blk & ultra ('02) 6.50 *10.00*
139 A30 8c lilac & rose 11.00 .75
140 A30 8c lil & blk ('90) 3.00 2.00
141 A30 12c lilac & vio 8.00 2.00
142 A30 24c lilac & grn 7.50 2.50
143 A30 48c lilac & ver 15.00 8.50
144 A30 48c dk gray & lil brn ('01) 27.50 27.50
a. 48c gray & purple brown 50.00 35.00
145 A30 60c gray grn & car ('03) 60.00 *160.00*
146 A30 72c lil & org brn 27.50 *35.00*
a. 72c lilac & yellow brown 70.00 75.00
147 A30 96c lilac & car 70.00 *75.00*
a. 96c lilac & rose 75.00 80.00
Nos. 130-147 (19) 261.25 *340.45*

Stamps of the 1889-1903 issue with pen or revenue cancellation sell for a small fraction of the above quotations.

See Nos. 160-177.

Red Surcharge

1890
148 A31 1c on $1 grn & blk 1.25 .50
a. Double surcharge — *80.00*
149 A31 1c on $2 grn & blk .90 .60
a. Double surcharge 80.00 —
150 A31 1c on $3 grn & blk 1.50 1.25
a. Double surcharge 90.00 —
151 A31 1c on $4 grn & blk, type I 2.00 *6.00*
a. Double surcharge 80.00 —
151B A31 1c on $4 grn & blk, type II 10.00 *25.00*
c. Double surcharge
Nos. 148-151B (5) 15.65 *33.35*

Mt. Roraima A32

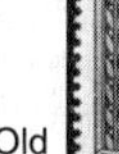

Kaieteur (Old Man's) Falls — A33

1898 Wmk. 1 Engr.
152 A32 1c car & gray blk 3.50 .90
153 A33 2c indigo & brn 12.50 1.60
a. Horiz. pair, imperf. between 4,500.
b. 2c blue & brown 16.00 2.00
154 A32 5c brown & grn 35.00 4.50
155 A33 10c red & blue blk 16.00 *20.00*
156 A32 15c blue & red brn 24.00 15.00
Nos. 152-156 (5) 91.00 42.00

60th anniv. of Queen Victoria's accession to the throne.

Nos. 154-156 Surcharged in Black

1899
157 A32 2c on 5c brn & grn 2.25 1.75
a. Without period 70.00 60.00
158 A33 2c on 10c red & bl black 1.75 *1.75*
a. "GENTS" 55.00 *75.00*
b. Inverted surcharge *325.00* *375.00*
c. Without period 25.00 *50.00*
159 A32 2c on 15c bl & red brown 1.50 1.50
a. Without period 57.50 57.50
b. Double surcharge *475.00* *650.00*
c. Inverted surcharge 350.00 *425.00*
Nos. 157-159 (3) 5.50 5.00

There are many slight errors in the setting of this surcharge, such as: small "E" in "CENTS"; no period and narrow "C"; comma between "T" and "S"; dash between "TWO" and "CENTS"; comma between "N" and "T."

Ship Type of 1889-1903

1905-10 Wmk. 3

Chalky Paper

160 A30 1c gray green 3.50 3.00
a. 1c blue green, ordinary paper ('10) 13.50 2.50
b. Booklet pane of 6
161 A30 2c vio & blk, *red* 3.25 .20
162 A30 4c lilac & ultra 10.00 *11.00*
163 A30 5c lil & blue, *bl* 7.00 6.00
164 A30 6c gray black & ultra 14.00 *37.50*
165 A30 12c lilac & vio 20.00 *37.50*
166 A30 24c lil & grn ('06) 3.50 *4.25*
167 A30 48c gray & vio brn 12.50 *17.50*
168 A30 60c gray grn & car rose 12.50 *75.00*
169 A30 72c lil & org brn ('07) 32.50 *60.00*
170 A30 96c blk & red, *yel* ('06) 35.00 *42.50*
Nos. 160-170 (11) 153.75 *294.45*

The 2c-60c exist on ordinary paper.

A34

George V — A35

Black Overprint

171 A34 $2.40 grn & vio *190.00 190.00*

Ship Type of 1889-1903
Ordinary Paper

TWO CENTS
Type I - Only the upper right corner of the flag touches the mast.
Type II - The entire right side of the flag touches the mast.

1907
172 A30 2c red, type I 3.75 .30
b. 2c red, type II 1.00 .25

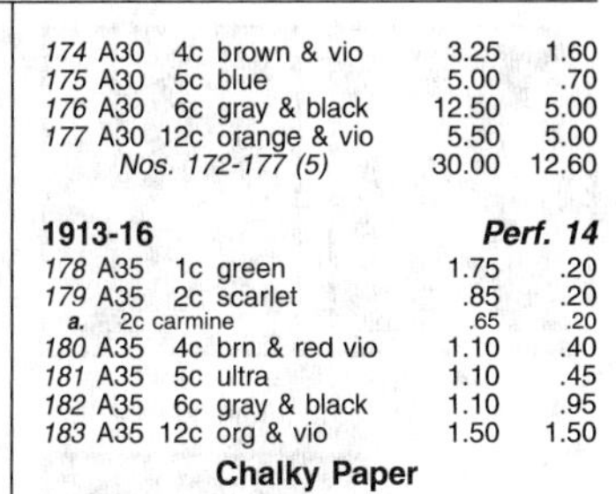

174 A30 4c brown & vio 3.25 1.60
175 A30 5c blue 5.00 .70
176 A30 6c gray & black 12.50 5.00
177 A30 12c orange & vio 5.50 5.00
Nos. 172-177 (5) 30.00 12.60

1913-16 *Perf. 14*
178 A35 1c green 1.75 .20
179 A35 2c scarlet .85 .20
a. 2c carmine .65 .20
180 A35 4c brn & red vio 1.10 .40
181 A35 5c ultra 1.10 .45
182 A35 6c gray & black 1.10 .95
183 A35 12c org & vio 1.50 1.50

Chalky Paper

184 A35 24c dl vio & grn 2.50 2.50
185 A35 48c blk & vio brn 6.00 6.00
186 A35 60c grn & car 13.00 *19.00*
187 A35 72c dl vio & org brn 24.00 *30.00*

Surface Colored Paper

188 A35 96c blk & red, *yel* 24.00 *30.00*

Paper Colored Through

189 A35 96c blk & red, *yel* ('16) 17.00 *21.00*
Nos. 178-189 (12) 93.90 *112.20*

The 72c and late printings of the 2c and 5c are from redrawn dies. The ruled lines behind the value are thin and faint, making the tablet appear lighter than before. The shading lines in other parts of the stamps are also lighter.

1921-27 Wmk. 4
191 A35 1c green 3.00 .20
192 A35 2c rose red 2.50 .20
193 A35 2c dp vio ('23) 1.75 .20
194 A35 4c brn & vio 3.25 .20
195 A35 6c ultra 1.90 .20
196 A35 12c org & vio 1.90 1.00

Chalky Paper

197 A35 24c dl vio & grn 1.40 *3.00*
198 A35 48c blk & vio brn ('26) 6.50 2.25
199 A35 60c grn & car ('26) 7.00 *30.00*
200 A35 72c dl vio & brn org 14.00 *32.50*
201 A35 96c blk & red, *yel* ('27) 12.50 *29.00*
Nos. 191-201 (11) 55.70 *98.75*

Plowing a Rice Field — A36

Indian Shooting Fish — A37

Kaieteur Falls — A38

Georgetown, Public Buildings A39

1931, July 21 Engr. *Perf. 12½*
205 A36 1c blue green 1.25 .50
206 A37 2c dk brown 1.25 .45
207 A38 4c car rose 2.75 1.75
208 A39 6c ultra 2.25 *2.50*
209 A38 $1 violet 24.00 *30.00*
Nos. 205-209 (5) 31.50 *35.20*

Cent. of the union of Berbice, Demerara and Essequibo to form the Colony of British Guiana.

A40

A41

Gold Mining — A42

Shooting Logs over Falls — A44

Kaieteur Falls — A43

Stabroek Market — A45

Sugar Cane in Punts — A46

Forest Road — A47

Victoria Regia Lilies — A48

Mt. Roraima — A49

Sir Walter Raleigh and Son — A50

Botanical Gardens A51

1934, Oct. 1 ***Perf. 12½***

210 A40 1c green .40 .25
211 A41 2c brown .75 .20
212 A42 3c carmine .30 .20
b. Perf. 12½x13½ ('43) .50 .75
c. Perf. 13x13½ ('49) .50 .20
213 A43 4c vio black 1.50 .50
a. Vert. pair, imperf. horiz. — *7,500.*
214 A44 6c dp ultra 2.00 1.75
215 A45 12c orange .20 .20
a. Perf. 13½x13 ('51) .20 *.40*
216 A46 24c rose violet 3.00 1.75
217 A47 48c black 10.50 9.25
218 A43 50c green 12.00 *15.00*
219 A48 60c brown 21.00 *24.00*
220 A49 72c rose violet 1.25 1.00
221 A50 96c black 20.00 *25.00*
222 A51 $1 violet 25.00 22.50
Nos. 210-222 (13) 97.90 *101.60*

See Nos. 236, 238, 240.

Common Design Types pictured following the introduction.

Silver Jubilee Issue

Common Design Type

1935, May 6 ***Perf. 13½x14***

223 CD301 2c gray blk & ultra .25 .20
224 CD301 6c blue & brown .75 .80
225 CD301 12c indigo & grn 2.50 4.50
226 CD301 24c brt vio & ind 3.50 4.50
Nos. 223-226 (4) 7.00 10.00
Set, Never Hinged 11.00

Coronation Issue

Common Design Type

1937, May 12 ***Perf. 13½x14***

227 CD302 2c brown .20 .20
228 CD302 4c gray black .40 .40
229 CD302 6c bright ultra .45 .45
Nos. 227-229 (3) 1.05 1.05
Set, Never Hinged 1.25

A52

A53

A54

A56

A55

A57

A58

Victoria Regia Lilies and Jacanas — A59

1938-52 **Engr.** **Wmk. 4** ***Perf. 12½***

230 A52 1c green .20 .20
b. Perf. 14x13 ('49) .20 *.65*

Perf. 13x14

231 A53 2c violet blk ('49) .20 .20
b. Perf. 12½ .45 .20
232 A54 4c black & rose ('52) .35 .20
a. Perf. 12½ .55 .20
c. Vert. pair, imperf. between *11,000.* *7,500.*
233 A55 6c dp ultra ('49) .20 .20
a. Perf. 12½ .30 .20

Perf. 12½

234 A56 24c deep green .95 .20
a. Wmk. upright 20.00 8.75
235 A53 36c purple 1.40 .20
a. Perf. 13x14 ('51) 2.50 .25
236 A47 48c orange yel .45 .35
a. Perf. 14x13 ('51) 1.25 1.10
237 A57 60c brown 8.50 3.00
238 A50 96c brown vio 1.90 *2.25*
a. Perf. 12½x13½ ('44) 4.00 *5.00*
239 A58 $1 deep violet 7.75 .30
a. Perf. 14x13 ('51) 225.00 *300.00*
240 A49 $2 rose vio ('45) 3.25 *11.00*
a. Perf. 14x13 ('50) 10.00 *12.50*
241 A59 $3 org brn ('45) 19.00 *21.00*
a. Perf. 14x13 ('52) 20.00 *37.50*
Nos. 230-241 (12) 44.15 *39.10*
Set, Never Hinged 65.00

The watermark on No. 234 is sideways.

Catalogue values for unused stamps in this section, from this point to the end of the section, are for Never Hinged items.

Peace Issue

Common Design Type

1946, Oct. 21 ***Perf. 13½x14***

242 CD303 3c carmine .20 .20
243 CD303 6c deep blue .20 .20

Silver Wedding Issue

Common Design Types

1948, Dec. 20 **Photo.** ***Perf. 14x14½***

244 CD304 3c scarlet .20 .20

Engr.

Perf. 11½x11

245 CD305 $3 orange brown 11.00 *17.00*

UPU Issue

Common Design Types

Engr.; Name Typo. on 6c and 12c

Perf. 13½, 11x11½

1949, Oct. 10 **Wmk. 4**

246 CD306 4c rose carmine .20 .20
247 CD307 6c indigo 1.40 .75
248 CD308 12c orange .20 *.75*
249 CD309 24c blue green .20 *.75*
Nos. 246-249 (4) 2.00 2.45

University Issue

Common Design Types

1951, Feb. 16 **Engr.** ***Perf. 14x14½***

250 CD310 3c carmine & black .30 .20
251 CD311 6c dp ultra & black .40 .40

Coronation Issue

Common Design Type

1953, June 2 ***Perf. 13½x13***

252 CD312 4c carmine & black .20 .20

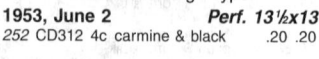

G. P. O., Georgetown A60

Indian Shooting Fish — A61

Designs: 2c, Botanical gardens. 3c, Victoria regia lilies and jacanas. 5c, Map. 6c, Rice combine. 8c, Sugar cane entering factory. 12c, Felling greenheart tree. 24c, Bauxite mining. 36c, Mt. Roraima. 48c, Kaieteur Falls. 72c, Arapaima (fish). $1, Toucan. $2, Dredging gold. $5, Coat of Arms.

Engr., Center Litho. on $1

Perf. 12½x13, 13

1954, Dec. 1 **Wmk. 4**

253 A60 1c black .20 .20
254 A60 2c dark green .20 .20
255 A60 3c red brn & ol 2.50 .20
256 A61 4c violet .20 .20
257 A60 5c black & red .20 .20
258 A60 6c yellow green .30 .20
259 A60 8c ultramarine .20 .20
260 A61 12c brown & black .50 .30
261 A60 24c orange & black 3.25 .20
262 A60 36c black & rose 2.50 1.00
263 A61 48c red brn & ultra .45 *.60*
264 A61 72c emerald & rose 8.50 2.25
265 A60 $1 blk, yel, grn & sal 14.00 2.50
266 A60 $2 magenta 13.00 4.75
267 A61 $5 black & ultra 9.00 *16.00*
Nos. 253-267 (15) 55.00 *29.00*

See Nos. 279-287.

Clasped Hands — A62

Perf. 14½x14

1961, Oct. 23 **Photo.** **Wmk. 314**

268 A62 5c sal pink & brown .20 .20
269 A62 6c lt blue grn & brown .20 .20
270 A62 30c lt orange & brown .40 .40
Nos. 268-270 (3) .80 .80

Fourth annual History and Culture Week.

Freedom from Hunger Issue

Common Design Type

1963, June 4 ***Perf. 14x14½***

271 CD314 20c lilac .40 .40

Red Cross Centenary Issue

Common Design Type

Wmk. 314

1963, Sept. 2 **Litho.** ***Perf. 13***

272 CD315 5c black & red .20 .20
273 CD315 20c ultra & red .65 .50

Queen Types of 1954

Engr.; Center Litho. on $1

Perf. 12½x13, 13

1963-65 **Wmk. 314**

279 A60 3c red brn & ol ('65) 3.25 *4.75*
280 A60 5c black & red ('64) .25 .20
281 A61 12c brown & blk ('64) .20 .20
282 A60 24c orange & black 3.50 .20
283 A60 36c black & rose .55 .20
284 A61 48c red brn & ultra 1.25 *2.00*
285 A61 72c emerald & rose 3.75 *16.00*
286 A60 $1 blk, yel, grn & sal 6.25 .75
287 A60 $2 magenta 10.00 *12.50*
Nos. 279-287 (9) 29.00 *36.80*

Weight Lifter A63

1964, Oct. 1 Photo. *Perf. 13x13½*
290 A63 5c orange .20 .20
291 A63 8c blue .20 .20
292 A63 25c carmine rose .30 .30
Nos. 290-292 (3) .70 .70

18th Olympic Games, Tokyo, Oct. 10-25.

ITU Issue
Common Design Type
Perf. 11x11½

1965, May 17 Litho. Wmk. 314
293 CD317 5c emerald & olive .20 .20
294 CD317 25c lt blue & brt pink .30 .30

Intl. Cooperation Year Issue
Common Design Type

1965, Oct. 25 Wmk. 314 *Perf. 14½*
295 CD318 5c blue grn & claret .20 .20
296 CD318 25c lt vio & green .35 .35

Winston Churchill and St. George's Cathedral, Georgetown — A64

1966, Jan. 24 Photo. *Perf. 14x14½*
297 A64 5c multicolored .50 .20
298 A64 25c dp blue, blk & gold 1.50 .50

Sir Winston Leonard Spencer Churchill (1874-1965), statesman and WWII leader.

Royal Visit Issue
Common Design Type

1966, Feb. 4 Litho. *Perf. 11x12*
299 CD320 3c violet blue .50 .20
300 CD320 25c dark car rose 1.75 .75

POSTAGE DUE STAMPS

Catalogue values for unused stamps in this section are for Never Hinged items.

D1

Perf. 13½x14

1940-52 Typo. Wmk. 4
J1 D1 1c green 1.10 7.50
a. Wmk. 4a (error) 45.00
J2 D1 2c black 1.10 3.25
a. Wmk. 4a (error) 37.50
J3 D1 4c ultra ('52) .25 *7.50*
a. Wmk. 4a (error) 37.50
J4 D1 12c carmine 5.00 *20.00*
Nos. J1-J4 (4) 7.45 *38.25*

The 2c and 12c are on chalky paper as well as ordinary paper.

WAR TAX STAMP

Regular Issue No. 179 Overprinted

1918, Jan. 4 Wmk. 3 *Perf. 14*
MR1 A35 2c scarlet .20 .20

OFFICIAL STAMPS

Counterfeit overprints exist.

No. 50 Overprinted in Red **OFFICIAL**

1875 Unwmk. *Perf. 10*
O1 A5 1c black 40.00 17.50
a. Horiz. pair, imperf btwn. 4,250.

Nos. 51, 53-54, 68 Overprinted in Black **OFFICIAL**

O2 A5 2c orange 150.00 17.50
O3 A5 8c rose 375.00 150.00
O4 A5 12c lilac 1,450. 575.00
O5 A12 24c green 875.00 275.00

For surcharges see Nos. 87, 89, 89A, 96, 102.

Nos. 72-76 Overprinted "OFFICIAL" Similar to #O2-O5

1877 Wmk. 1 *Perf. 14*
O6 A13 1c slate 250.00 95.00
a. Vert. pair, imperf btwn. 6,500.
O7 A13 2c orange 95.00 17.50
O8 A13 4c ultramarine 100.00 35.00
O9 A13 6c chocolate 3,750. 625.00
O10 A13 8c rose 2,250. 525.00

The type A13 12c lilac, 24c green and 48c red brown overprinted "OFFICIAL" were never placed in use. A few copies of the 12c and 24c have been seen but the 48c is only known surcharged with new value for provisional use in 1881. See Nos. 97-101.

For surcharges see #85-86, 88A, 90-91.

BRITISH HONDURAS

'bri-tish hän-'dur-əs

LOCATION — Central America bordering on Caribbean on east, Mexico on north and Guatemala on west.
GOVT. — British Crown Colony
AREA — 8,867 sq. mi.
POP. — 130,000 (est. 1972)
CAPITAL — Belmopan

Before British Honduras became a colony (subordinate to Jamaica) in 1862, it was a settlement under British influence. In 1884 it became an independent colony. In 1973 the colony changed its name to Belize.

12 Pence = 1 Shilling
100 Cents = 1 Dollar (1888)

Catalogue values for unused stamps in this country are for Never Hinged items, beginning with Scott 127 in the regular postage section, Scott J1 in the postage due section.

Values for unused stamps are for examples with original gum as defined in the catalogue introduction. Very fine examples of Nos. 1-37 will have perforations touching the design on at least one side due to the narrow spacing of the stamps on the plates. Stamps with perfs clear of the design on all four sides are extremely scarce and will command higher prices.

Queen Victoria — A1

1866 Unwmk. Typo. *Perf. 14*
1 A1 1p pale blue 60.00 50.00
a. Horiz. pair, imperf. btwn.
2 A1 6p rose 250.00 110.00
3 A1 1sh green 275.00 100.00
Nos. 1-3 (3) 585.00 260.00

The 6p and 1sh were printed only in a sheet with the 1p. The 1sh is known in se-tenant gutter pairs with the 1p and the 6p.

1872 Wmk. 1 *Perf. 12½*
4 A1 1p blue 60.00 17.00
5 A1 3p brown 100.00 65.00
6 A1 6p rose 190.00 30.00
7 A1 1sh green 300.00 27.50
a. Horiz. pair, imperf. btwn. *12,500.*
Nos. 4-7 (4) 650.00 139.50

For surcharges see Nos. 18-19.
No. 7a is unique and has faults.

1877-79 *Perf. 14*
8 A1 1p blue 50.00 14.00
a. Horiz. strip of 3, imperf. btwn. *4,500.*
9 A1 3p brown 90.00 17.50
10 A1 4p violet ('79) 140.00 10.00
11 A1 6p rose ('78) 275.00 175.00
12 A1 1sh green 175.00 12.50
Nos. 8-12 (5) 730.00 229.00

For surcharges see Nos. 20-21, 29.

1882-87 Wmk. 2
13 A1 1p blue ('84) 40.00 18.00
14 A1 1p rose ('84) 20.00 12.50
a. Diag. half used as ½p on cover
15 A1 4p violet 70.00 4.25
16 A1 6p yellow ('85) 250.00 175.00
17 A1 1sh gray ('87) 250.00 150.00
Nos. 13-17 (5) 630.00 359.75

For surcharges see Nos. 22-26, 28-35.

Stamps of 1872-87 Surcharged in Black

1888 Wmk. 1 *Perf. 12½*
18 A1 2c on 6p rose 140.00 100.00
19 A1 3c on 3p brown *10,000. 5,250.*

Perf. 14
20 A1 2c on 6p rose 80.00 70.00
a. Diagonal half used as 1c on cover *210.00*
b. Double surcharge 1,350. —
c. "2" with curved tail 900.00 —
21 A1 3c on 3p brown 55.00 55.00

Wmk. 2
22 A1 2c on 1p rose 9.00 *17.50*
a. Diagonal half used as 1c on cover 225.00
b. Double surcharge 1,000. 950.00
c. Inverted surcharge 1,500. 1,400.
23 A1 10c on 4p violet 40.00 15.00
a. Inverted surcharge
24 A1 20c on 6p yellow 27.50 *30.00*
25 A1 50c on 1sh gray 350.00 *500.00*

No. 25 with Additional Surcharge in Red or Black

26 A1 2c (R) on 50c on 1sh gray 40.00 *75.00*
a. "TWO" in black *8,750. 8,500.*
b. "TWO" double (Blk + R) *8,750. 8,000.*
c. Diagonal half used as 1c on cover 275.00

Stamps of 1872-87 Surcharged in Black

c

1888-89
28 A1 2c on 1p rose .45 *1.60*
a. Diagonal half used as 1c on cover 100.00
29 A1 3c on 3p brown 2.25 1.40
30 A1 10c on 4p violet 5.50 1.50
a. Double surcharge *1,400.*
31 A1 20c on 6p yel ('89) 11.00 *15.00*
32 A1 50c on 1sh gray 25.00 *65.00*
Nos. 28-32 (5) 44.20 *84.50*

For other examples of this surcharge see Nos. 36, 47. For overprint see No. 51.

No. 30 with Additional Surcharge in Black or Red

1891
33 A1 6c (Blk) on 10c on 4p .90 *3.25*
a. "6" and bar inverted *2,750. 825.*
b. "6" only inverted *2,750.*
34 A1 6c (R) on 10c on 4p .90 *2.25*
a. "6" and bar inverted *450. 450.*
b. "6" only inverted *2,750.*

Stamps similar to No. 33 but with "SIX" instead of "6," both with and without bar, were prepared but not regularly issued.
See No. 37.

No. 29 with Additional Surcharge in Black

35 A1 5c on 3c on 3p brown 1.40 *3.00*
a. Double surcharge of "Five" and bar 240.00 *275.00*

Black Surcharge, Type "c"
36 A1 6c on 3p blue 2.25 *10.00*

No. 36 with Additional Surcharge like Nos. 33-34 in Red

1891
37 A1 15c (R) on 6c on 3p blue 10.00 *21.00*
a. Double surcharge —

A8

A9

1891-98 Wmk. 2 *Perf. 14*
38 A8 1c green 1.75 1.10
39 A8 2c carmine rose 1.60 .25
40 A8 3c brown 5.00 3.00
41 A8 5c ultra ('95) 11.00 .80
42 A8 6c ultramarine 4.75 1.75
43 A8 10c vio & grn ('95) 8.00 8.00
44 A8 12c vio & green 3.50 2.50
45 A8 24c yellow & blue 5.50 *12.50*
46 A8 25c red brn & grn ('98) 47.50 *85.00*
Nos. 38-46 (9) 88.60 *114.90*

Numeral tablet on Nos. 43-46 has lined background with colorless value and "c."
For overprints see Nos. 48-50.

Type of 1866 Surcharged Type "c"

1892
47 A1 1c on 1p green .55 *1.40*

Regular Issue Overprinted in Black

1899
48 A8 5c ultramarine 8.00 2.25
a. "BEVENUE" 70.00 *80.00*
49 A8 10c lilac & green 3.50 *11.50*
a. "BEVENUE" 175.00 *225.00*
50 A8 25c red brn & grn 2.75 *27.50*
a. "BEVENUE" 125.00 *275.00*
51 A1 50c on 1sh gray (No. 32) 125.00 *250.00*
a. "BEVENUE" 2,750. —
Nos. 48-51 (4) 139.25 *291.25*

The overprint is found in two lengths: 12mm (43 to the pane) and 11mm (17 to the pane). The "U" is found in both a tall, narrow type and the more common small type.

1899-1901
52 A9 5c gray blk & ultra, *bl* ('00) 12.50 2.25
53 A9 10c vio & grn ('01) 8.00 *7.00*
54 A9 50c grn & car rose 20.00 *50.00*
55 A9 $1 grn & car rose 55.00 *90.00*
56 A9 $2 green & ultra 75.00 *110.00*
57 A9 $5 green & black 240.00 *275.00*
Nos. 52-57 (6) 410.50 *534.25*

Numeral tablet on Nos. 53-54 has lined background with colorless value and "c."

King Edward VII — A10

1902-04 Typo. Wmk. 2

58	A10	1c gray grn & grn ('04)	3.50	*19.00*
59	A10	2c vio & blk, *red*	1.75	.30
60	A10	5c gray blk & ultra, *blue*	4.50	.70
61	A10	20c dl vio & vio ('04)	4.50	*15.00*
		Nos. 58-61 (4)	14.25	*35.00*

1904-06 Chalky Paper Wmk. 3

62	A10	1c green	.60	*1.60*
63	A10	2c vio & blk, *red*	.60	.20
64	A10	5c blk & ultra, *bl* ('05)	1.60	.20
65	A10	10c vio & grn ('06)	4.50	*10.00*
67	A10	25c vio & org ('06)	6.25	*37.50*
68	A10	50c grn & car rose ('06)	13.50	*62.50*
69	A10	$1 grn & car rose ('06)	42.50	*62.50*
70	A10	$2 grn & ultra ('06)	75.00	*140.00*
71	A10	$5 grn & blk ('06)	160.00	*225.00*
		Nos. 62-71 (9)	304.55	*539.50*

The 1c and 2c exist also on ordinary paper.

1909 Ordinary Paper

72	A10	2c carmine	8.50	.20
73	A10	5c ultramarine	1.60	.20

1911

74	A10	25c black, *green*	5.50	*40.00*

Numeral tablet on #61, 65-68, 74 has lined background with colorless value and "c."

King George V
A11 A12

1913-17 Wmk. 3 *Perf. 14*

75	A11	1c green	1.00	.40
76	A11	2c scarlet	1.10	.30
a.		2c carmine	.90	.95
77	A11	3c orange ('17)	.45	.20
78	A11	5c ultra	2.25	1.25

Chalky Paper

79	A12	10c dl vio & ol grn	2.50	*5.00*
80	A12	25c blk, *gray grn*	3.75	*7.50*
a.		25c black, *emerald*	2.50	*12.50*
b.		25c blk, *bl grn,* olive back	3.25	*13.00*
81	A12	50c vio & ultra, *bl*	4.50	*9.00*
82	A11	$1 black & scar	8.00	*17.50*
83	A11	$2 grn & dull vio	32.50	*37.50*
84	A11	$5 vio & blk, *red*	225.00	*250.00*
		Nos. 75-84 (10)	281.05	*328.65*

See #91. For overprints see #MR2-MR5.

With Moire Overprint in Violet

1915

85	A11	1c green	2.00	*12.50*
86	A11	2c carmine	2.25	.40
87	A11	5c ultramarine	.25	*4.50*
		Nos. 85-87 (3)	4.50	*17.40*

For overprint see No. MR1.

Peace Commemorative Issue

Seal of Colony and George V
A13

1921, Apr. 28 Engr.

89	A13	2c carmine	2.50	1.00

Similar to A13 but without "Peace Peace"

1922 Wmk. 4

90	A13	4c dark gray	4.50	.95

Type of 1913-17

1921 Typo. Wmk. 4

91	A11	1c green	3.50	*7.50*

A14

1922-33 Typo. Wmk. 4

92	A14	1c green ('29)	.80	*1.10*
93	A14	2c dark brown	.35	.20
94	A14	2c rose red ('27)	.85	.70
95	A14	3c orange ('33)	3.50	1.00
96	A14	4c gray ('29)	1.25	.25
97	A14	5c ultramarine	1.00	.20

Chalky Paper

98	A14	10c olive grn & lil	1.25	.35
99	A14	25c black, *emerald*	1.50	*4.00*
100	A14	50c ultra & vio, *bl*	4.00	*9.00*
101	A14	$1 scarlet & blk	6.50	*12.50*
102	A14	$2 red vio & grn	22.50	*50.00*

Wmk. 3

103	A14	25c black, *emerald*	4.25	*17.50*
104	A14	$5 blk & vio, *red*	200.00	*190.00*
		Nos. 92-104 (13)	247.75	*286.80*

For surcharges see Nos. B1-B5.

Common Design Types pictured following the introduction.

Silver Jubilee Issue

Common Design Type

Perf. 11x12

1935, May 6 Engr. Wmk. 4

108	CD301	3c black & ultra	.65	.45
109	CD301	4c indigo & grn	1.10	*3.25*
110	CD301	5c ultra & brn	2.00	.75
111	CD301	25c brn vio & ind	4.00	3.75
		Nos. 108-111 (4)	7.75	*8.20*
		Set, never hinged	12.00	

Coronation Issue

Common Design Type

1937, May 12 *Perf. 13½x14*

112	CD302	3c deep orange	.20	.25
113	CD302	4c gray black	.30	.25
114	CD302	5c bright ultra	.50	1.00
		Nos. 112-114 (3)	1.00	1.50
		Set, never hinged	1.60	

Mayan Figures
A15

Chicle Tapping — A16

Cohune Palm — A17

Local Products
A18

Grapefruit Industry
A19

Mahogany Logs in River — A20

Sergeant's Cay — A21

Dory — A22

Chicle Industry
A23

Court House, Belize — A24

Mahogany Cutting — A25

Seal of Colony — A26

1938 *Perf. 11x11½, 11½x11*

115	A15	1c green & violet	.20	*.70*
116	A16	2c car & black	.20	*.70*
a.		Perf. 12 ('47)	1.10	.75
117	A17	3c brown & dk vio	.20	*.50*
118	A18	4c green & black	.20	*.50*
119	A19	5c slate bl & red vio	.40	.30
120	A20	10c brown & yel grn	.50	*.50*
121	A21	15c blue & brown	.70	.50
122	A22	25c green & ultra	1.10	.85
123	A23	50c dk vio & blk	7.00	2.50
124	A24	$1 ol green & car	12.50	5.25
125	A25	$2 rose lake & ind	14.00	13.00
126	A26	$5 brn & carmine	13.00	*19.00*
		Nos. 115-126 (12)	50.00	*44.30*
		Set, never hinged	80.00	

Issued: 3c-5c, 1/10; 1c, 2c, 10c-50c, 2/14; $1-$5, 2/28.

Catalogue values for unused stamps in this section, from this point to the end of the section, are for Never Hinged items.

Peace Issue

Common Design Type

Perf. 13½x14

1946, Sept. 9 Engr. Wmk. 4

127	CD303	3c brown	.20	.20
128	CD303	5c deep blue	.20	.20

Silver Wedding Issue

Common Design Types

1948, Oct. 1 Photo. *Perf. 14x14½*

129	CD304	4c dark green	.20	.20

Engraved; Name Typographed

Perf. 11½x11

130	CD305	$5 light brown	20.00	*30.00*

St. George's Cay — A27

H.M.S. Merlin — A28

1949, Jan. 10 Engr. *Perf. 12½*

131	A27	1c green & ultra	.20	.20
132	A27	3c yel brn & dp blue	.20	.20
133	A27	4c purple & brn ol	.30	.30
134	A28	5c dk blue & brown	.30	.30
135	A28	10c vio brn & blue grn	.50	.50
136	A28	15c ultra & emerald	.90	.90
		Nos. 131-136 (6)	2.40	2.40

Battle of St. George's Cay, 150th anniv.

UPU Issue

Common Design Types

Perf. 13½, 11x11½

1949, Oct. 10 Engr. Wmk. 4

137	CD306	4c blue green	.35	.35
138	CD307	5c indigo	.55	.55
139	CD308	10c chocolate	.90	.90
140	CD309	25c blue	1.50	1.50
		Nos. 137-140 (4)	3.30	3.30

University Issue

Common Design Types

1951, Feb. 16 Engr. *Perf. 14x14½*

141	CD310	3c choc & purple	.35	.35
142	CD311	10c choc & green	.65	.65

Coronation Issue

Common Design Type

1953, June 2 *Perf. 13½x13*

143	CD312	4c dk green & black	.40	.40

Arms — A29

Maya — A30

Designs: 2c, Tapir. 3c, Legislative Council Chamber and mace. 4c, Pine industry. 5c, Spiny lobster. 10c, Stanley Field Airport. 15c, Mayan frieze. 25c, Blue butterfly. $1, Armadillo. $2, Hawkesworth Bridge. $5, Pine Ridge orchid.

1953-57 Engr. *Perf. 13½*

144	A29	1c gray blk & green	.20	.20
145	A29	2c gray blk & brn, perf. 14 ('57)	.20	.20
a.		Perf. 13½	.35	.30
146	A29	3c mag & rose lil, perf. 14 ('57)	.20	.20
a.		Perf. 13½	.25	.20
147	A29	4c grn & dk brn	.30	.20
148	A29	5c car & ol brn, perf. 14 ('57)	.20	.20
a.		Perf. 13½	.50	.45
149	A29	10c ultra & bl gray	.20	.20
150	A29	15c vio & yel grn	.20	*.35*
151	A29	25c brown & ultra	4.25	1.75
152	A30	50c purple & brown	5.00	1.60
153	A29	$1 red brn & sl bl	3.75	3.50
154	A29	$2 gray & car	4.50	4.00
155	A30	$5 blue gray & pur	32.50	15.00
		Nos. 144-155 (12)	51.50	27.40

Issued: 5c, 5/15; 2c, 3c, 9/18, perf. 13½, 9/2.
For overprints see Nos. 159-166.

View of Belize, 1842 — A31

Designs: 10c, Public seals, 1860 and 1960. 15c, Tamarind Tree, Newtown Barracks.

Perf. 11½x11

1960, July 1 Wmk. 314

156 A31 2c green .20 .20
157 A31 10c carmine .25 .25
158 A31 15c blue .45 .45
Nos. 156-158 (3) .90 .90

Cent. of the establishment of a local PO.

Nos. 145-146 and 149-150 Overprinted: "NEW CONSTITUTION/1960"

1961, Mar. 1 Wmk. 4 *Perf. 14, 13*

159 A29 2c gray black & brn .20 .20
160 A29 3c mag & rose lilac .20 .20
161 A29 10c ultra & blue gray .35 .25
162 A29 15c violet & yel green .50 .35
Nos. 159-162 (4) 1.25 1.00

Nos. 144, 149, 151 and 152 Overprinted: "HURRICANE/HATTIE"

1962, Jan. 15 *Perf. 13*

163 A29 1c gray black & green .20 .20
164 A29 10c ultra & blue gray .20 .20
165 A29 25c brown & ultra .30 .30
166 A30 50c purple & brown .70 .70
Nos. 163-166 (4) 1.40 1.40

Hurricane Hattie struck Belize, Oct. 31, 1961.

Great Curassow A32

Birds: 2c, Red-legged honeycreeper. 3c, American jacana. 4c, Great kiskadee. 5c, Scarlet-rumped tanager. 10c, Scarlet macaw. 15c, Massena trogon. 25c, Redfooted booby. 50c, Keel-billed toucan. $1, Magnificent frigate bird. $2, Rufoustailed jacamar. $5, Montezuma oropendola.

Perf. 14x14½

1962, Apr. 2 Photo. Wmk. 314

Birds in Natural Colors; Black Inscriptions

167 A32 1c yellow .90 .70
168 A32 2c gray 1.40 .20
a. Green omitted 200.00
169 A32 3c lt yel green 1.40 .85
a. Dark grn (legs) omitted 300.00
170 A32 4c lt gray 2.75 1.25
171 A32 5c buff 1.60 .20
172 A32 10c beige 1.90 .20
a. Blue omitted 225.00
173 A32 15c pale lemon .90 .30
174 A32 25c bluish gray & pink 3.50 .25
175 A32 50c pale blue 5.00 .35
b. Blue (beak & claw) omitted —
176 A32 $1 blue 7.75 .70
177 A32 $2 pale gray 8.25 2.50
178 A32 $5 light blue 24.00 12.50
Nos. 167-178 (12) 59.35 20.00

For overprints see Nos. 182-186, 195-199.

1967 Wmk. 314 Sideways

Colors as 1962 Issue

167a A32 1c .20 .20
168b A32 2c .20 .20
170a A32 4c .30 .25
171a A32 5c .55 .30
172b A32 10c .80 .65
173a A32 15c 1.10 .90
175a A32 50c 4.25 3.50
Nos. 167a-175a (7) 7.40 6.00

Issued: 1, 4, 5, 50c, 2/16; 2, 10, 15c, 11/28.

Freedom from Hunger Issue

Common Design Type

1963, June 4 *Perf. 14x14½*

179 CD314 22c green .75 .65

Red Cross Centenary Issue

Common Design Type

Wmk. 314

1963, Sept. 2 Litho. *Perf. 13*

180 CD315 4c black & red .20 .20
181 CD315 22c ultra & red 1.10 1.10

Nos. 167, 169, 170, 172 and 174 Overprinted: "SELF GOVERNMENT / 1964"

1964 Photo. *Perf. 14x14½*

182 A32 1c multicolored .20 .20
a. Yellow omitted 90.00
183 A32 3c multicolored .30 .20
184 A32 4c multicolored .30 .20
185 A32 10c multicolored .30 .30
186 A32 25c multicolored .65 .55
Nos. 182-186 (5) 1.75 1.45

Attainment of self-government.

ITU Issue

Common Design Type

Perf. 11x11½

1965, May 17 Litho. Wmk. 314

187 CD317 2c ver & green .20 .20
188 CD317 50c yel & red lilac 1.00 1.00

Intl. Cooperation Year Issue

Common Design Type

1965, Oct. 25 *Perf. 14½*

189 CD318 1c bl grn & claret .20 .20
190 CD318 22c lt violet & green .55 .55

Churchill Memorial Issue

Common Design Type

1966, Jan. 24 Photo. *Perf. 14*

Design in Black, Gold and Carmine Rose

191 CD319 1c bright blue .20 .20
192 CD319 4c green .30 .30
193 CD319 22c brown .60 .60
194 CD319 25c violet .70 .70
Nos. 191-194 (4) 1.80 1.80

Bird Type of 1962 Overprinted: "DEDICATION OF SITE / NEW CAPITAL / 9th OCTOBER 1965"

Wmk. 314 Sideways

1966, July 1 *Perf. 14x14½*

195 A32 1c multicolored .20 .20
196 A32 3c multicolored .30 .20
197 A32 4c multicolored .30 .20
198 A32 10c multicolored .30 .25
199 A32 25c multicolored .65 .50
Nos. 195-199 (5) 1.75 1.35

Citrus Grove — A33

10c, Half Moon Cay & Lighthouse Reef. 22c, Hidden Valley Falls & Mountain Pine Ridge. 25c, Xunantunich Mayan ruins in Cayo district.

Perf. 14x14½

1966, Oct. 1 Photo. Wmk. 314

200 A33 5c multicolored .20 .20
201 A33 10c multicolored .20 .20
202 A33 22c multicolored .20 .20
203 A33 25c multicolored .20 .20
Nos. 200-203 (4) .80 .80

1st British Honduras stamp issue, cent.

International Tourist Year — A34

1967, Dec. 4 *Perf. 12½*

204 A34 5c Sailfish .20 .20
205 A34 10c Deer .20 .20
206 A34 22c Jaguar .30 .30
207 A34 25c Tarpon .30 .30
Nos. 204-207 (4) 1.00 1.00

Schomburgkia Tibicinis — A35

Belizean Patriots' Memorial, Belize City, and Human Rights Flame — A36

Orchids: 10c, Maxillaria tenuifolia. 22c, Bletia purpurea. 25c, Sobralia macrantha.

Inscribed: "20th Anniversary of E.C.L.A."

Perf. 14½x14

1968, Apr. 16 Photo. Wmk. 314

208 A35 5c violet & multi .35 .35
209 A35 10c green & multi .40 .40
210 A35 22c multicolored .50 .50
211 A35 25c olive & multi .65 .65
Nos. 208-211 (4) 1.90 1.90

20th anniv. of the Economic Commission for Latin America. See #226-229, 255-258.

Perf. 13x13½

1968, July 15 Litho. Wmk. 314

Design: 50c, Mayan motif stele, monument at new capital site and Human Rights flame.

212 A36 22c multicolored .25 .25
213 A36 50c multicolored .50 .50

International Human Rights Year.

Jewfish A37

Designs: 2c, White-lipped peccary. 3c, Grouper (sea bass). 4c, Collared anteater. 5c, Bonefish. 10c, Paca. 15c, Dolphinfish. 25c, Kinkajou. 50c, Yellow-and-green-banded muttonfish. $1, Tayra. $2, Great barracudas. $5, Mountain lion.

Perf. 13x12½

1968, Oct. 15 Litho. Unwmk.

214 A37 1c yellow & multi .20 .20
215 A37 2c brt yel & multi .20 .20
216 A37 3c pink & multi .20 .20
217 A37 4c brt grn & multi .20 .20
218 A37 5c brick red & multi .20 .20
219 A37 10c lilac & multi .20 .20
220 A37 15c org yel & multi .65 .20
221 A37 25c multicolored .25 .40
222 A37 50c bl grn & multi .65 .85
223 A37 $1 ocher & multi 2.25 1.75
224 A37 $2 violet & multi 2.25 *3.50*
225 A37 $5 ultra & multi 11.50 7.50
Nos. 214-225 (12) 18.75 15.40

See Nos. 234-240, Belize 327-339.
For overprints see Nos. 251-254, 281-282.

Orchid Type of 1968 Inscribed "Orchids of Belize"

Designs: 5c, Rhyncholaetia digbyana. 10c, Cattleya bowringiana. 22c, Lycaste cochleatum. 25c, Coryanthes speciosum.

Perf. 14½x14

1969, Apr. 9 Photo. Wmk. 314

226 A35 5c Prus blue & multi .50 .50
227 A35 10c olive bis & multi .55 .55
228 A35 22c yellow grn & multi .85 .85
229 A35 25c violet blue & multi 1.10 1.10
Nos. 226-229 (4) 3.00 3.00

Hardwood Trees — A38

Virgin and Child, by Giovanni Bellini — A39

1969, Sept. 1 Litho. *Perf. 14*

230 A38 5c Ziricote .20 .20
231 A38 10c Rosewood .20 .20
232 A38 22c Mayflower .25 .25
233 A38 25c Mahogany .35 .35
Nos. 230-233 (4) 1.00 1.00

Timber industry of British Honduras. Issued in sheets of 9 (3x3) on simulated wood background.

Fish-Animal Type of 1968

Designs: ½c, Crana (fish). Others as before.

Wmk. 314 Sideways (½c, 2c, $5), Upright (3c, 5c, 10c)

1969-72 Litho. *Perf. 13x12½*

234 A37 ½c vio bl, yel & blk .20 .20
235 A37 ½c citron, blk & bl ('71) .70 *1.00*
236 A37 2c brt yel, blk & grn ('72) 3.00 3.00
237 A37 3c pink & multi ('72) 1.00 *1.60*
a. Wmk. sideways ('72) 3.00 3.00
238 A37 5c brick red & multi ('72) 1.00 *1.60*
239 A37 10c lilac & multi ('72) 1.00 *1.60*
a. Wmk. sideways ('72) 3.50 3.50
240 A37 $5 ultra & multi ('70) 9.00 9.00
Nos. 234-240 (7) 15.90 18.00

For overprints see Nos. 251-252.

1969, Oct. 1 Litho. *Perf. 14*

Christmas: 22c, 25c, Adoration of the Kings, by Veronese.

247 A39 5c multicolored .20 .20
248 A39 15c dp orange & multi .20 .20
249 A39 22c lilac rose & multi .25 .25
250 A39 25c emerald & multi .25 .25
Nos. 247-250 (4) .90 .90

Nos. 238-239 and Type of 1968 Overprinted "POPULATION/ CENSUS 1970"

Wmk. 314 Sideways

1970, Feb. 2 Photo. *Perf. 13x12½*

251 A37 5c brick red & multi .20 .20
252 A37 10c lilac & multi .20 .20
253 A37 15c org yel & multi .20 .20
254 A37 25c multicolored .20 .20
Nos. 251-254 (4) .80 .80

Orchid Type of 1968 Inscribed: "Orchids of Belize"

Wmk. 314

1970, Apr. 2 Litho. *Perf. 14*

255 A35 5c Black .35 .20
256 A35 15c White butterfly .50 .35
257 A35 22c Swan .70 .50
258 A35 25c Butterfly .70 .60
Nos. 255-258 (4) 2.25 1.65

Santa Maria Tree and Wood (Calophyllum Brasiliense) A40

Nativity, by Arthur Hughes A41

Hardwood Trees and Woods: 15c, Nargusta (terminalia amazonia). 22c, Cedar (cedrela mexicana). 25c, Sapodilla (achras sapota).

1970, Sept. 7 *Perf. 14*

259 A40 5c multicolored .20 .20
260 A40 15c multicolored .30 .30
261 A40 22c multicolored .45 .45
262 A40 25c multicolored .45 .45
Nos. 259-262 (4) 1.40 1.40

1970, Nov. 2 *Perf. 14*

Christmas: 5c, 15c, 50c, Mystic Nativity, by Botticelli.

263 A41 ½c black & multi .20 .20
264 A41 5c brown & multi .20 .20
265 A41 10c multicolored .20 .20
266 A41 15c slate bl & multi .25 .25
267 A41 22c dk green & multi .30 .30
268 A41 50c black & multi .50 .50
Nos. 263-268 (6) 1.65 1.65

Legislative Assembly House A42

Designs: 5c, View of South Side of Belize. 10c, Government Plaza, Belmopan. 22c, Magistrates' Court. 25c, Police Headquarters. 50c, New General Post Office.

1971, Jan. 30 Litho. ***Perf. 13½x14***

Size: 59x22mm

269 A42 5c multicolored .20 .20
270 A42 10c multicolored .20 .20

Size: 37x21½mm

271 A42 15c multicolored .20 .20
272 A42 22c multicolored .25 .25
273 A42 25c multicolored .25 .25
274 A42 50c multicolored .45 .45
Nos. 269-274 (6) 1.55 1.55

New capital at Belmopan.

Tabebuia Chrysantha — A43

Flowers: 5c, 22c, Hymenocallis littoralis. 10c, 25c, Hippeastrum equestre. 15c, like ½c.

1971, Mar. 27 Litho. ***Perf. 14***

275 A43 ½c vio blue & multi .20 .20
276 A43 5c olive & multi .20 .20
277 A43 10c violet & multi .20 .20
278 A43 15c multicolored .30 .30
279 A43 22c multicolored .30 .30
280 A43 25c lt brown & multi .30 .30
Nos. 275-280 (6) 1.50 1.50

Easter.

Type of 1968 Overprinted: "RACIAL EQUALITY / YEAR—1971"

Perf. 13x12½

1971, June 14 Litho. Wmk. 314

281 A37 10c lilac & multi .25 .25
282 A37 50c blue green & multi 1.00 1.00

Intl. year against racial discrimination.

Tubroos (Enterolobium Cyclocarpum) A44

Hardwood Trees of Belize: 15c, Yemeri (Vochysia hondurensis). 26c, Billyweb (Sweetia panamensis). 50c, Logwood (Haematoxylum campechiaum).

1971, Aug. 16 ***Perf. 14***

Queen's Head in Silver

283 A44 5c green, brn & blk .45 .45
284 A44 15c multicolored .65 .65
285 A44 26c multicolored .90 .90
286 A44 50c multicolored 1.75 1.75
a. Souvenir sheet of 4, #283-286 4.75 4.75
Nos. 283-286 (4) 3.75 3.75

Verrazano-Narrows Bridge, New York, and Quebec Bridge, Canada — A45

Bridges of the World: ½c, Hawksworth Bridge connecting San Ignacio and Santa Helena and Belcan Bridge, Belize, Br. Honduras. 26c, London Bridge in 1871, and at Lake Havasu City, Ariz., in 1971. 50c, Belize-Mexico Bridge and Belize Swing Bridge.

1971, Sept. 23 Litho.

287 A45 ½c multicolored .20 .20
288 A45 5c multicolored .20 .20
289 A45 26c multicolored .50 .50
290 A45 50c multicolored 1.10 1.10
Nos. 287-290 (4) 2.00 2.00

Petrae Volubis — A46

Seated Jade Figure — A47

Wild Flowers: 15c, Vochysia hondurensis. 26c, Tabebuia pentaphylla. 50c, Erythrina americana.

1972, Feb. 28

Flowers in Natural Colors; Black Inscriptions

292 A46 6c lilac & yellow .20 .20
293 A46 15c lt blue & pale grn .40 .40
294 A46 26c pink & lt blue .50 .50
295 A46 50c orange & lt grn .90 .90
Nos. 292-295 (4) 2.00 2.00

Easter.

Perf. 14x13½, 13½x14

1972, May 22 Unwmk.

Mayan Carved Jade, 4th-8th centuries: 6c, Dancing priest. 16c, Sun god's head, horiz. 26c, Priest on throne and sun god's head. 50c, Figure and mask.

296 A47 3c rose red & multi .20 .20
297 A47 6c vio bl & multi .25 .25
298 A47 16c brown & multi .45 .45
299 A47 26c ol grn & multi .60 .60
300 A47 50c purple & multi 1.25 1.25
Nos. 296-300 (5) 2.75 2.75

Black inscription with details of designs on back of stamps.

Banak (Virola Koschnyi) — A48

Hardwood Trees of Belize: 5c, Quamwood (Schizolobium parahybum). 16c, Waika chewstick (Symphonia globulifera). 26c, Mammee-apple (Mammea americana). 50c, My lady (Aspidosperma megalocarpon).

1972, Aug. 21 Wmk. 314 ***Perf. 14***

Queen's Head in Gold

301 A48 3c brt pink & multi .20 .20
302 A48 5c gray & multi .20 .20
303 A48 16c green & multi .40 .40
304 A48 26c lemon & multi .55 .55
305 A48 50c lt violet & multi 1.40 1.40
Nos. 301-305 (5) 2.75 2.75

Silver Wedding Issue, 1972

Common Design Type

Design: Queen Elizabeth II, Prince Philip and Belize orchids.

1972, Nov. 20 Photo. ***Perf. 14x14½***

306 CD324 26c slate grn & multi .35 .35
307 CD324 50c violet & multi .55 .55

Baron Bliss Day A49

Festivals of Belize: 10c, Labor Day boat race. 26c, Carib Settlement Day dance. 50c, Pan American Day parade.

1973, Mar. 9 Litho. ***Perf. 14½***

308 A49 3c dull blue & black .20 .20
309 A49 10c red & multi .20 .20
310 A49 26c ver & multi .40 .40
311 A49 50c black & multi .75 .75
Nos. 308-311 (4) 1.55 1.55

SEMI-POSTAL STAMPS

Regular Issue of 1921-29 Surcharged in Black or Red

1932 Wmk. 4 ***Perf. 14***

B1 A14 1c + 1c green 1.50 *5.00*
B2 A14 2c + 2c rose red 1.50 *4.75*
B3 A14 3c + 3c orange 2.50 *11.00*
B4 A14 4c + 4c gray (R) 3.25 *14.50*
B5 A14 5c + 5c ultra 5.00 *10.00*
Nos. B1-B5 (5) 13.75 *45.25*

The surtax was for a fund to aid sufferers from the destruction of the city of Belize by a hurricane in Sept. 1931.

POSTAGE DUE STAMPS

Catalogue values for unused stamps in this section are for Never Hinged items.

D1

1923-64 Typo. Wmk. 4 ***Perf. 14***

J1 D1 1c black .35 *15.00*
J2 D1 2c black .35 *15.00*
J3 D1 4c black .60 *10.00*
Nos. J1-J3 (3) 1.30 *40.00*

Nos. J1-J3 were re-issued on chalky paper in 1956. Values shown are for the 1956 issue. The 1923 issue, on yellowish thin ordinary paper, sells for $5 unused, $25 used. The 1c was reprinted in 1964 on white, ordinary paper, value $8.50 unused, $25 used.

Perf. 13½x13, 13½x14

1965-72 Wmk. 314

J4 D1 2c black ('72) 1.50 *3.00*
J5 D1 4c black 1.00 *3.50*

WAR TAX STAMPS

Nos. 85, 75 and 77 Overprinted

1916-17 Wmk. 3 ***Perf. 14***

With Moire Overprint

MR1 A11 1c green .20 *.75*
a. "WAR" inverted 200.00 *225.00*

Without Moire Overprint

MR2 A11 1c green ('17) 1.25 *3.00*
MR3 A11 3c orange ('17) 3.00 4.00
a. Double overprint 350.00 *350.00*
Nos. MR1-MR3 (3) 4.45 *7.75*

Nos. 75 and 77 Overprinted

1918

MR4 A11 1c green .20 *.25*
MR5 A11 3c orange .50 *1.50*

BRITISH INDIAN OCEAN TERRITORY

ˈbri-tish ˈin-dēən ˈō-chən ˈter-ə-ˌtōr-ē

LOCATION — Indian Ocean
GOVT. — British Dependency
POP. — 0

B.I.O.T. was established Nov. 8, 1965. This island group lies 1,180 miles north of Mauritius. It consisted of Chagos Archipelago (chief island: Diego Garcia), Aldabra, Farquhar and Des Roches Islands until June 23, 1976, when the last three named islands were returned to Seychelles.

There is no permanent population on the islands. There are military personel located there.

100 Cents = 1 Rupee
100 Pence = 1 Pound (1990)

Catalogue values for all unused stamps in this country are for Never Hinged items.

Seychelles Nos. 198-202, 204-212 Overprinted

Perf. 14½x14, 14x14½

1968, Jan. 17 Photo. Wmk. 314

Size: 24x31, 31x24mm

1 A17 5c multicolored .20 .55
2 A17 10c multicolored .20 .20
3 A17 15c multicolored .20 .20
4 A17 20c multicolored .20 .20
5 A17 25c multicolored .20 .20
6 A18 40c multicolored .20 .20
7 A18 45c multicolored .20 .25
8 A17 50c multicolored .20 .25
9 A17 75c multicolored .20 .30
10 A18 1r multicolored .40 .30
11 A18 1.50r multicolored 1.75 1.40
12 A18 2.25r multicolored 3.00 3.25
13 A18 3.50r multicolored 3.00 4.00
14 A18 5r multicolored 8.75 6.75

Perf. 13x14

Size: 22½x39mm

15 A17 10r multicolored 18.50 18.00
Nos. 1-15 (15) 37.20 36.05

Lascar A1

Marine Fauna: 10c, Hammerhead shark, vert. 15c, Tiger shark. 20c, Sooty eagle ray. 25c, Butterflyfish, vert. 30c, Robber crab. 40c, Green carangue. 45c, Needlefish, vert. 50c, Barracuda. 60c, Spotted pebble crab. 75c, Parrotfish. 85c, Rainbow runner (fish). 1r, Giant hermit crab. 1.50r, Humphead. 2.25r, Rock cod. 3.50r, Black marlin. 5r, Whale shark, vert. 10r, Lionfish.

Perf. 14x13½, 13½x14; 14 (30c, 60c, 85c)

1968-73 Litho. Wmk. 314

16 A1 5c multicolored .40 .40
a. Wmk. upright ('73) .65 .65
17 A1 10c multicolored .20 .20
18 A1 15c multicolored .20 .20
19 A1 20c multicolored .20 .20
20 A1 25c multicolored .35 .35
21 A1 30c multi ('70) .40 .40
22 A1 40c multicolored .35 .35
23 A1 45c multicolored 2.75 2.75
24 A1 50c multicolored .35 .35
25 A1 60c multi ('70) .90 .90
26 A1 75c multicolored 4.00 4.00
27 A1 85c multi ('70) 1.75 1.75
28 A1 1r multicolored 1.40 1.40
29 A1 1.50r multicolored 1.75 1.75
30 A1 2.25r multicolored 14.00 14.00
31 A1 3.50r multicolored 4.00 4.00
32 A1 5r multicolored 6.00 6.00
33 A1 10r multicolored 17.00 17.00
Nos. 16-33 (18) 56.00 56.00

No. 16 has watermark sideways.

Aldabra Atoll and Sacred Ibis — A2

1969, July 10 Litho. *Perf. 13½x13*

34 A2 2.25r vio blue & multi 2.00 1.50

Outrigger Canoe — A3

75c, Beaching canoe. 1r, Merchant ship Nordvaer. 1.50r, Yacht, Isle of Farquhar.

Perf. 13½x14

1969, Dec. 15 Litho. Wmk. 314

35 A3 45c multicolored .45 *.40*
36 A3 75c multicolored .85 *.75*
37 A3 1r multicolored 1.25 *1.10*
38 A3 1.50r multicolored 2.25 *1.75*
Nos. 35-38 (4) 4.80 *4.00*

Giant Land Tortoise — A4

Designs: 75c, Aldabra lily. 1r, Aldabra tree snail. 1.50r, Dimorphic egrets.

1971, Feb. 1 Litho. Wmk. 314

39 A4 45c multicolored 2.00 2.00
40 A4 75c multicolored 2.50 2.00
41 A4 1r multicolored 5.00 2.25
42 A4 1.50r multicolored 6.50 *7.75*
Nos. 39-42 (4) 16.00 14.00

Aldabra Nature Reserve.

Society Coat of Arms and Flightless Rail — A5

1971, June 30 Litho. *Perf. 13½*

43 A5 3.50r multicolored 12.00 8.50

Opening of Royal Society Research Station at Aldabra.

Acropora Formosa A6

Corals: 60c, Goniastrea pectinata. 1r, Fungia fungites. 1.75r, Tubipora musica.

1972, Mar. 1

44 A6 40c blue & multi 3.25 3.25
45 A6 60c brt pink & multi 3.75 3.75
46 A6 1r blue & multi 3.75 3.75
47 A6 1.75r brt pink & multi 4.50 4.50
Nos. 44-47 (4) 15.25 15.25

Common Design Types pictured following the introduction.

Silver Wedding Issue, 1972

Common Design Type

Design: Queen Elizabeth II, Prince Philip, flightless rail and sacred ibis.

1972, Nov. 20 Photo. *Perf. 14x14½*

48 CD324 95c multicolored 1.00 .50
49 CD324 1.50r violet & multi 1.00 .50

Crucifixion, 17th Century — A7

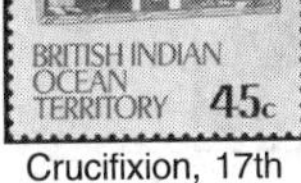

Upsidedown Jellyfish — A8

Paintings, Ethiopian Manuscripts, 17th Century: 75c, 1.50r, Joseph and Nicodemus burying Jesus. 1r, Like 45c.

1973, Apr. 9 Litho. *Perf. 14*

50 A7 45c buff & multi .30 *.40*
51 A7 75c buff & multi .45 *.55*
52 A7 1r buff & multi .65 .40
53 A7 1.50r buff & multi 1.10 .70
a. Souvenir sheet of 4, #50-53 3.00 *3.50*
Nos. 50-53 (4) 2.50 2.05

Easter.

1973, Nov. 12 Litho. Wmk. 314

54 A8 50c shown 3.25 2.75
55 A8 1r Butterflies 3.50 2.75
56 A8 1.50r Spider 3.75 2.75
Nos. 54-56 (3) 10.50 8.25

Nordvaer and July 14, 1969 Cancel — A9

1974, July 14

57 A9 85c multicolored .85 .50
58 A9 2.50r multicolored 1.40 1.50

Nordvaer traveling post office, 5th anniv.

2.50r, Nordvaer offshore and cancel.

Terebra Maculata and Terebra Subulata — A10

Sea Shells: 75c, Turbo marmoratus. 1r, Drupa rubusidaeus. 1.50r, Cassis rufa.

1974, Nov. 12 Litho. *Perf. 13½x14*

59 A10 45c multicolored 2.10 .70
60 A10 75c multicolored 2.40 1.25
61 A10 1r multicolored 2.50 1.75
62 A10 1.50r multicolored 3.00 3.00
Nos. 59-62 (4) 10.00 6.70

Aldabra Drongo — A11

Grewia Salicifolia — A12

Birds: 10c, Malagasy coucal. 20c, Red-headed forest fody. 25c, Fairy tern. 30c, Crested tern. 40c, Brown booby. 50c, Noddy tern. 60c, Gray heron. 65c, Blue-faced booby. 95c, Malagasy white-eye. 1r, Green-backed heron. 1.75r, Lesser frigate bird. 3.50r, White-tailed tropic bird. 5r, Souimanga sunbird. 10r, Malagasy turtledove. Nos. 69, 71-77 horiz.

1975, Feb. 28 Wmk. 314 *Perf. 14*

63 A11 5c buff & multi .20 *2.40*
64 A11 10c lt ultra & multi .20 *2.40*
65 A11 20c dp yel & multi .20 *2.40*
66 A11 25c ultra & multi .25 *2.40*
67 A11 30c dl yel & multi .35 *2.40*
68 A11 40c bis & multi .45 *2.50*
69 A11 50c lt blue & multi .50 *2.50*
70 A11 60c yel & multi .55 *2.50*
71 A11 65c yel grn & multi .65 *2.50*
72 A11 95c citron & multi .80 *2.50*
73 A11 1r bister & multi 1.00 *2.50*
74 A11 1.75r yel & multi 2.00 *4.25*
75 A11 3.50r blue & multi 4.00 *4.25*
76 A11 5r pale sal & multi 6.50 *4.25*
77 A11 10r brt yel & multi 10.00 *7.75*
Nos. 63-77 (15) 27.65 *47.50*

1975, July 10 Litho. Wmk. 314

Native Plants: 65c, Cassia aldabrensis. 1r, Hypoestes aldabrensis. 1.60r, Euphorbia pyrifolia.

78 A12 50c multicolored .35 *1.10*
79 A12 65c multicolored .50 *1.25*
80 A12 1r multicolored .75 *1.25*
81 A12 1.60r multicolored 1.25 *1.40*
Nos. 78-81 (4) 2.85 5.00

Nature protection.

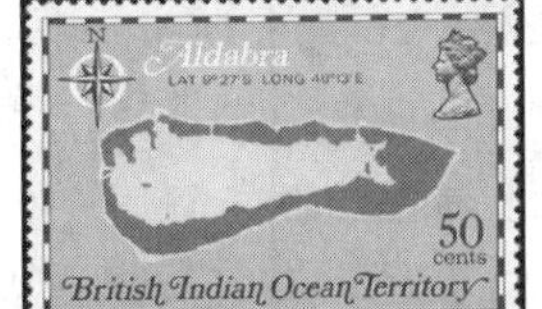

Aldabra and Compass Rose — A13

Maps of Islands: 1r, Desroches. 1.50r, Farquhar. 2r, Diego Garcia.

1975, Nov. 8 Litho. *Perf. 13½x14*

82 A13 50c blk, blue & grn .80 .80
83 A13 1r green & multi .95 .95
84 A13 1.50r blk, ultra & grn 1.10 1.10
85 A13 2r blk, lilac & grn 1.25 1.25
a. Souvenir sheet of 4, #82-85 7.50 7.50
Nos. 82-85 (4) 4.10 4.10

British Indian Ocean Territory, 10th anniv.

Crimson Speckled Moth — A14

Insects: 1.20r, Dysdercus fasciatus. 1.50r, Sphex torridus. 2r, Oryctes rhinoceros.

1976, Mar. 22 Litho. Wmk. 373

86 A14 65c multicolored .45 .40
87 A14 1.20r multicolored .70 .65
88 A14 1.50r multicolored 1.00 .90
89 A14 2r multicolored 1.50 1.40
Nos. 86-89 (4) 3.65 3.35

Exhibition Emblem and No. 37 — A15

1990, May 3 Wmk. 373 *Perf. 14*

90 A15 15p No. 62 2.50 2.00
91 A15 20p No. 89 2.75 2.25
92 A15 34p No. 85 4.00 3.25
93 A15 54p shown 5.75 5.00
Nos. 90-93 (4) 15.00 12.50

Stamp World London '90.

Birds — A16

1990, May 3 Wmk. 384 *Perf. 14*

94 A16 15p White-tailed tropic birds 1.10 *1.75*
95 A16 20p Turtle doves 1.25 *1.75*
96 A16 24p Greater frigate birds 1.40 *1.75*
97 A16 30p Little green herons 1.50 *2.00*
98 A16 34p Greater sand plovers 1.75 *2.00*
99 A16 41p Crab plovers 1.75 *2.25*
100 A16 45p Crested terns 2.00 *2.25*
101 A16 54p Lesser crested terns 2.25 *2.50*
102 A16 62p Fairy terns 2.25 *2.50*
103 A16 71p Red-footed boobies 2.25 *2.75*
104 A16 80p Indian mynahs 2.50 *3.00*
105 A16 £1 Madagascar fodies 2.50 *3.00*
Nos. 94-105 (12) 22.50 27.50

For overprints see Nos. 145-146.

Queen Mother, 90th Birthday

Common Design Types

Designs: 24p, Lady Elizabeth Bowes-Lyon, 1923. £1, Queen, Princesses Elizabeth & Margaret, 1940.

1990, Aug. 4 Wmk. 384 *Perf. 14x15*

106 CD343 24p multicolored 5.25 5.25

Perf. 14½

107 CD344 £1 brown & black 9.75 9.75

British Indian Ocean Territory, 25th Anniv. — A17

1990, Nov. 8 Litho. *Perf. 14*

108 A17 20p Flag 5.75 5.75
109 A17 24p Coat of arms 5.75 5.75

Souvenir Sheet

110 A17 £1 Map 12.00 *14.00*

Govt. Services A18

Wmk. 373

1991, June 3 Litho. *Perf. 14*

111 A18 20p Postal service 2.00 2.00
112 A18 24p Royal Marines 2.25 2.25
113 A18 34p Police station, officers 4.00 4.00
114 A18 54p Customs service 5.75 5.75
Nos. 111-114 (4) 14.00 14.00

Visiting Ships A19

1991, Nov. 8

115 A19 20p Survey ship Experiment, 1786 3.00 3.00
116 A19 24p US Brig Pickering, 1819 3.25 3.25
117 A19 34p SMS Emden, 1914 4.25 4.25
118 A19 54p HMS Edinburgh, 1988 5.50 5.50
Nos. 115-118 (4) 16.00 16.00

Queen Elizabeth II's Accession to the Throne, 40th Anniv.

Common Design Type

Wmk. 373

1992, Feb. 6 Litho. *Perf. 14*

119 CD349 15p multicolored 1.60 1.60
120 CD349 20p multicolored 1.90 1.90
121 CD349 24p multicolored 4.00 4.00
122 CD349 34p multicolored 3.25 3.25
123 CD349 54p multicolored 3.25 3.25
Nos. 119-123 (5) 14.00 14.00

Aircraft A20

Wmk. 384

1992, Oct. 23 Litho. *Perf. 14*

124 A20 20p Catalina 2.25 2.25
125 A20 24p Nimrod 2.75 2.75
126 A20 34p P-3 Orion 3.25 3.25
127 A20 54p B-52 4.25 4.25
Nos. 124-127 (4) 12.50 12.50

Christmas — A21

Paintings: 5p, The Mystical Marriage of St. Cathrin, by Correggio. 24p, Madonna and Child by unknown artist. 34p, Madonna and Child by unknown artist, diff. 54p, The Birth of Jesus, by Kaspar Jele.

1992, Nov. 27 *Perf. 14½*

128 A21 5p multicolored .75 .75
129 A21 24p multicolored 1.60 1.60
130 A21 34p multicolored 1.90 1.90
131 A21 54p multicolored 2.75 2.75
Nos. 128-131 (4) 7.00 7.00

Coconut Crab A22

Wmk. 384

1993, Mar. 3 Litho. *Perf. 14*

132 A22 10p Crab, coconut *1.25 1.25*
133 A22 10p Large crab *1.25 1.25*
134 A22 10p Two crabs *1.25 1.25*
135 A22 15p Crab on tree trunk *1.75 1.75*
Nos. 132-135 (4) *5.50 5.50*

World Wildlife Fund.

Royal Air Force, 75th Anniv.

Common Design Type

#136, Vickers Virginia. 24p, Bristol Bulldog. 34p, Short Sunderland. 54p, Bristol Blenheim IV.

#140: a, Douglas Dakota. b, Gloster Javelin. c, Blackburn Beverley. d, Vickers VC10.

1993, Apr. 1 Wmk. 373

136 CD350 20p multicolored 1.10 1.10
137 CD350 24p multicolored 1.25 1.25
138 CD350 34p multicolored 1.60 1.60
139 CD350 54p multicolored 2.50 2.50
Nos. 136-139 (4) 6.45 6.45

Souvenir Sheet of 4

140 CD350 20p #a.-d. 6.50 6.50

Flowers — A23

Christmas: 20p, Stachytarpheta urticifolia. 24p, Ipomea pes-caprae. 34p, Sida pusilla. 54p, Catharanthus roseus.

Wmk. 373

1993, Nov. 22 Litho. *Perf. 14½*

141-144 A23 Set of 4 7.50 7.50

Nos. 96, 105 Ovptd. with Hong Kong '94 Emblem

Wmk. 384

1994, Feb. 18 Litho. *Perf. 14*

145 A16 24p multicolored 2.50 2.50
146 A16 £1 multicolored 5.00 5.00

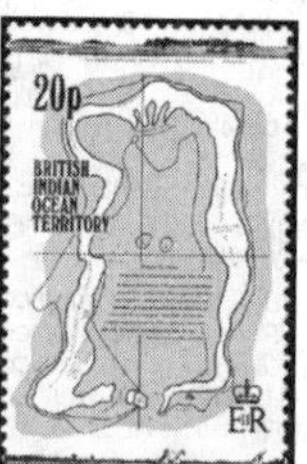

A24

Butterflies — A25

18th Cent. Maps and Charts: a, 20p, Sketch of Diego Garcia. b, 24p, Plan of harbor, Chagos Island or Diego Garcia, by Lt. Archibald Blair. c, 34p, Chart of Chagos Archipelago, by Lt. Blair. d, 44p, Plan of part of Chagos Island or Diego Garcia, from survey made by the Drake. e, 54p, Plan of Chagos Island or Diego Garcia, by M. Aa Fontaine.

1994, June 1 Wmk. 373

147 A24 Strip of 5, #a.-e. 7.00 7.00

1994, Aug. 16 Wmk. 384

148 A25 24p Junonia villida 1.90 1.90
149 A25 30p Petrelaea dana 2.40 2.40
150 A25 56p Hypolimnas misippus 4.00 4.00
Nos. 148-150 (3) 8.30 8.30

Sharks A26

1994, Nov. 1 Wmk. 373

151 A26 15p Nurse .45 .45
152 A26 20p Silver tip .60 .60
153 A26 24p Black tip reef .75 .75
154 A26 30p Oceanic white tip .95 .95
155 A26 35p Black tip 1.10 1.10
156 A26 41p Smooth hammerhead 1.25 1.25
157 A26 46p Lemon 1.40 1.40
158 A26 55p White tip reef 1.75 1.75
159 A26 65p Tiger 2.00 2.00
a. Souvenir sheet of 1 2.00 2.00
160 A26 74p Indian sand tiger 2.25 2.25
a. Souvenir sheet of 1 2.25 2.25
161 A26 80p Great hammerhead 2.50 2.50
162 A26 £1 Great white 3.00 3.00
Nos. 151-162 (12) 18.00 18.00

No. 159a for Hong Kong '97. Issued 2/3/97.
No. 160a for return of Hong Kong to China. Issued 7/1/97.

End of World War II, 50th Anniv.

Common Design Types

20p, War graves, memorial cross, Diego Garcia. 24p, 6-inch naval gun, Cannon Point. 30p, Sunderland flying boat, 230 Squadron. 56p, HMIS Clive.
£1, Reverse of War Medal 1939-45.

Wmk. 373

1995, May 8 Litho. *Perf. 14*

163 CD351 20p multicolored 1.50 1.50
164 CD351 24p multicolored 1.75 1.75
165 CD351 30p multicolored 2.00 2.00
166 CD351 56p multicolored 2.75 2.75
Nos. 163-166 (4) 8.00 8.00

Souvenir Sheet

167 CD352 £1 multicolored 3.50 3.50

Game Fish A27

1995, Oct. 6 Wmk. 384

168 A27 20p Dolphinfish 1.40 1.40
169 A27 24p Sailfish 1.50 1.50
170 A27 30p Wahoo 2.10 2.10
171 A27 56p Striped marlin 3.00 3.00
Nos. 168-171 (4) 8.00 8.00

Sea Shells A28

20p, Terebra crenulata. 24p, Bursa bufonia. 30p, Nassarius papillosus. 56p, Lopha cristagalli.

1996, Jan. 8 Wmk. 373 *Perf. 14*

172 A28 20p multicolored 1.25 1.25
173 A28 24p multicolored 1.25 1.25
174 A28 30p multicolored 1.75 1.75
175 A28 56p multicolored 2.75 2.75
Nos. 172-175 (4) 7.00 7.00

Queen Elizabeth II, 70th Birthday

Common Design Type

Various portraits of Queen, scenes of British Indian Ocean Territory: 20p, View to north from south end of lagoon. 24p, Manager's House, Peros Banhos. 30p, Wireless station, Peros Banhos. 56p, Sunset scene.
£1, Wearing crown, formal dress.

Perf. 14x14½

1996, Apr. 22 Wmk. 384

176 CD354 20p multicolored .65 .65
177 CD354 24p multicolored .85 .85
178 CD354 30p multicolored 1.00 1.00
179 CD354 56p multicolored 2.00 2.00
Nos. 176-179 (4) 4.50 4.50

Souvenir Sheet

180 CD354 £1 multicolored 3.50 3.50

Turtles A29

1996, Sept. 2 Wmk. 373

181 A29 20p Loggerhead 1.00 1.00
182 A29 24p Leatherback 1.25 1.25
183 A29 30p Hawksbill 1.50 1.50
184 A29 56p Green 2.25 2.25
Nos. 181-184 (4) 6.00 6.00

Uniforms — A30

Designs: 20p, British representative. 24p, Royal Marine officer. 30p, Royal Marine in camouflage. 56p, Police dog handler, female police officer.

1996, Dec. *Perf. 14*

185 A30 20p multicolored 1.10 1.10
186 A30 24p multicolored 1.25 1.25
187 A30 30p multicolored 1.60 1.60
188 A30 56p multicolored 2.50 2.50
Nos. 185-188 (4) 6.45 6.45

Queen Elizabeth II and Prince Philip, 50th Wedding Anniv. — A31

#189, Queen up close. #190, 4-horse team fording river. #191, Queen riding in open carriage. #192, Prince Philip up close. #193, Prince driving 4-horse team, Prince, Queen near jeep. #194, Queen on horseback, castle in distance.
£1.50, Queen, Prince riding in open carriage.

1997, July 10 *Perf. 14½x14*

189 A31 20p multicolored .65 .65
190 A31 20p multicolored .65 .65
a. Pair, #189-190 1.30 1.30
191 A31 24p multicolored .80 .80
192 A31 24p multicolored .80 .80
a. Pair, #191-192 1.60 1.60
193 A31 30p multicolored 1.00 1.00
194 A31 30p multicolored 1.00 1.00
a. Pair, #193-194 2.00 2.00
Nos. 189-194 (6) 4.90 4.90

Souvenir Sheet

195 A31 £1.50 multicolored 5.00 5.00

Ocean Wave '97, Naval Exercise — A32

Designs: a, HMS Richmond, HMS Beaver. b, HMS Illustrious. c, HMS Beaver. d, RFA Sir Percivale, HMY Britannia, HMS Beaver. e, HMY Britannia. f, HMS Richmond, HMS Beaver, HMS Gloucester. g, HMS Richmond. h, HMS Illustrious (aerial view). i, HMS Sheffield. j, RFA Diligence, HMS Trenchant. k, HMS Illustrious, RFA Fort George, HMS Gloucester. l, HMS Richmond, HMS Beaver, HMS Gloucester.

1997, Dec. 1 Litho. *Perf. 14x14½*

196 A32 24p Sheet of 12, #a.-l. 9.25 9.25

Diana, Princess of Wales (1961-97)

Common Design Type

Various portraits: a, 26p, shown. b, 26p, Close-up. c, 34p. d, 60p.

1998, Mar. 31 *Perf. 14½x14*

197 CD355 Sheet of 4, #a.-d. 5.50 5.50

No. 197 sold for £1.46 + 20p, with surtax and 50% of profits from total sale being donated to the Princess Diana Memorial Fund.

Royal Air Force, 80th Anniv.

Common Design Type of 1993

Re-inscribed

Designs: 26p, Blackburn Iris, 1930-34. 34p, Gloster Gamecock, 1926-33. 60p, North American Sabre F86, 1953-56. 80p, Avro Lincoln, 1945-55.

No. 202: a, Sopwith Baby, 1915-19. b, Martinsyde Elephant, 1916-19. c, De Havilland Tiger Moth, 1932-55. d, North American Mustang III, 1943-47.

1998, Apr. 1 Wmk. 384 *Perf. 14*

198	CD350 26p multicolored		.85	.85
199	CD350 34p multicolored		1.10	1.10
200	CD350 60p multicolored		2.00	2.00
201	CD350 80p multicolored		2.75	2.75
	Nos. 198-201 (4)		6.70	6.70

Souvenir Sheet

202 CD350 34p Sheet of 4, #a.-d. 4.50 4.50

Intl. Year of the Ocean A33

Dolphins and whales: No. 203, Striped dolphin. No. 204, Bryde's whale. No. 205, Pilot whale. No. 206, Spinner dolphin.

Wmk. 373

1998, Dec. 7 Litho. *Perf. 14*

203	A33 26p multicolored	.85	.85
204	A33 26p multicolored	.85	.85
205	A33 34p multicolored	1.10	1.10
206	A33 34p multicolored	1.10	1.10
	Nos. 203-206 (4)	3.90	3.90

Sailing Ships — A34

2p, Bark "Westminster," 1837. 15p, "Sao Cristovao," Spain, 1589. 20p, Clipper ship "Sea Witch," US, 1849. 26p, HMS "Royal George," 1778. 34p, Clipper ship "Cutty Sark," 1883. 60p, British East India Co. ship "Mentor," 1789. 80p, HM brig "Trinculo," 1809. £1, Paddle steamer "Enterprise," 1825. £1.15, Privateer "Confiance," France, 1800. £2, British East India Co. ship "Kent," 1820.

Wmk. 373

1999, Feb. 1 Litho. *Perf. 14*

207	A34 2p multicolored	.20	.20
208	A34 15p multicolored	.50	.50
209	A34 20p multicolored	.65	.65
210	A34 26p multicolored	.85	.85
211	A34 34p multicolored	1.10	1.10
212	A34 60p multicolored	1.90	1.90
213	A34 80p multicolored	2.50	2.50
214	A34 £1 multicolored	3.25	3.25
215	A34 £1.15 multicolored	3.75	3.75
216	A34 £2 multicolored	6.50	6.50
	Nos. 207-216 (10)	21.20	21.20

Tea Race, 1872 A35

a, Cutty Sark (up close). b, Thermopylae (in distance).

Wmk. 384

1999, Mar. 19 Litho. *Perf. 14*

217 A35 60p Sheet of 2, #a.-b. 3.75 3.75

Australia '99 World Stamp Expo.

The Stamp Show 2000, London — A36

Winning photos in photography contest: a, 26p, Field vole by Colin Sargent. b, 34p, Puffin, by P. J. Royal. c, 55p, Red fox, by Jim Wilson. d, £1, Robin, by Harry Smith.

Illustration reduced.

Perf. 14½x14¼

2000, May 22 Litho. Wmk. 373

218 A36 Sheet of 4, #a-d 6.50 6.50

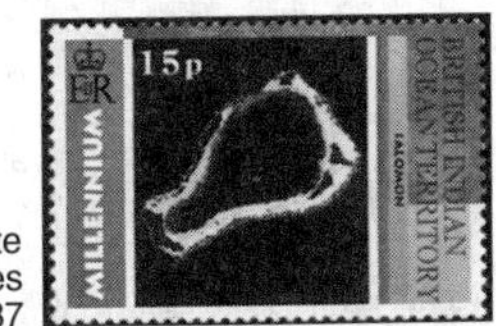

Satellite Images A37

Designs: 15p, Salomon Atoll. 20p, Egmont Atoll. 60p, Blenheim Reef. 80p, Diego Garcia.

Wmk. 373

2000, July 3 Litho. *Perf. 14*

219-222 A37 Set of 4 5.00 5.00

Queen Mother, 100th Birthday — A38

Designs: 26p, Blue hat. 34p, Blue green hat. No. 225: a, 55p, Blue hat. £1, Yellow hat.

2000, Aug. 4 Wmk. 373 *Perf. 13¾*

223-224 A38 Set of 2 1.75 1.75

Souvenir Sheet

225 A38 Sheet of 2, #a-b 4.50 4.50

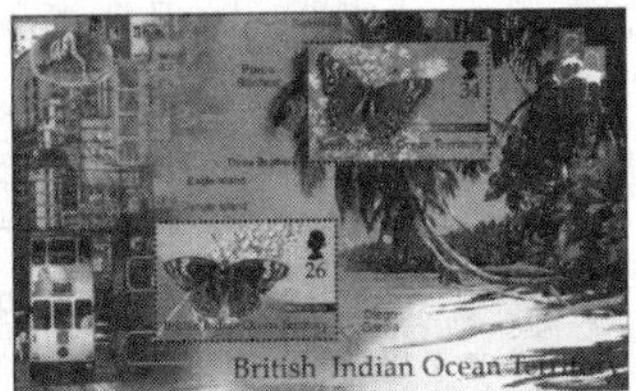

Flowers — A39

Designs: 26p, Delonix regia. 34p, Barringtonia asiatica. 60p, Zephyranthes rosea.

2000, Dec. 4 *Perf. 14½x14¼*

226-228 A39 Set of 3 3.75 3.75

Souvenir Sheet

New Year 2001 (Year of the Snake) — A40

Butterflies: a, 26p, Precis orithya. b, 34p, Junonia villida chagoensis.

Illustration reduced.

Perf. 14 ¼

2001, Feb. 1 Litho. Wmk. 373

229 A40 Sheet of 2, #a-b 1.75 1.75

Hong Kong 2001 Stamp Exhibition.

Souvenir Sheet

Royal Navy Submarines, Cent. — A41

No. 230: a, 26p, HMS Turbulent. b, 26p, HMS Churchill. c, 34p, HMS Resolution. d, 34p, HMS Vanguard. e, 60p, HMS Otter. f, 60p, HMS Oberon. Size of Nos. 230e-230f: 75x30mm.

Perf. 14¼x14½

2001, May 28 Litho. Wmk. 373

230 A41 Sheet of 6, #a-f 6.75 6.75

Worldwide Fund for Nature (WWF) A42

Starfish: 15p, Cushion star. 26p, Azure sea star. 34p, Crown-of-thorns. 56p, Banded bubble star.

Wmk. 373

2001, Aug. 1 Litho. *Perf. 13¾*

231-234	A42 Set of 4	3.75	3.75
234a	Strip, #231-234	3.75	3.75

Plants — A43

Designs: 10p, Catharanthus roseus, horiz. 26p, Scadoxus mutiflora. 34p, Striga asiatica. 60p, Argusia argentia, horiz. 70p, Euphorbia cyathophora, horiz.

2001, Sept. 24 *Perf. 13¾x14¼*

235	A43 26p multi	.75	.75
a.	Perf. 14½	.75	.75
236	A43 34p multi	1.00	1.00
a.	Perf. 14½	1.00	1.00

Souvenir Sheet

Perf. 14½

237	Sheet, #a-c, 235a, 236a	5.75	5.75
a.	A43 10p multi	.25	.25
b.	A43 60p multi	1.75	1.75
c.	A43 70p multi	2.00	2.00

Souvenir Sheet

Birdlife International World Bird Festival — A44

Crab plover: a, Resting. b, Eating crab, vert. c, Close-up of head, vert. d, In flight. e, Standing on one leg.

2001, Oct. 1 *Perf. 14½*

238 A44 50p Sheet of 5, #a-e 7.25 7.25

Reign Of Queen Elizabeth II, 50th Anniv. Issue

Common Design Type

Designs: Nos. 239, 243a, 10p, Princess Elizabeth, 1943. Nos. 240, 243b, 25p, In 1967. Nos. 241, 243c, 35p, With Prince Philip, 1947. Nos. 242, 243d, 55p, Wearing tiara. No. 243e, 75p, 1955 portrait by Annigoni (38x50mm).

Perf. 14¼x14½, 13¾ (#243e)

2002, Feb. 6 Litho. Wmk. 373

With Gold Frames

239-242 CD360 Set of 4 3.75 3.75

Souvenir Sheet

Without Gold Frames

243 CD360 Sheet of 5, #a-e 5.75 5.75

Souvenir Sheet

Red-footed Booby — A45

No. 244: a, Head of bird with brown feathers. b, Bird in flight, vert. c, Bird on nest, vert. d, Close-up of bird with white and black feathers. e, Chick.

Wmk. 373

2002, June 17 Litho. *Perf. 14½*

244 A45 50p Sheet of 5, #a-e 7.50 7.50

Queen Mother Elizabeth (1900-2002)

Common Design Type

Designs: 26p, Wearing hat (sepia photograph). No. 246, £1, Wearing blue green hat.

No. 247: a, £1, Wearing feathered hat (black and white photograph). b, £1, Wearing dark blue hat.

Wmk. 373
2002, Aug. 5 Litho. ***Perf. 14¼***
With Purple Frames
245-246 CD361 Set of 2 4.00 4.00

Souvenir Sheet
Without Purple Frames
Perf. 14½x14¼
247 CD361 Sheet of 2, #a-b 6.25 6.25

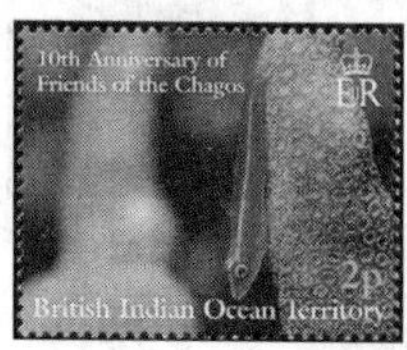

Friends of the Chagos, 10th Anniv. — A46

Various reef fish: 2p, 15p, 26p, 34p, 58p, £1. £1.90, Fish.

Perf. 14¼x14½
2002, Oct. 3 Litho. Wmk. 373
248-253 A46 Set of 6 7.50 7.50

Souvenir Sheet
254 A46 £1.90 multi 6.00 6.00

No. 254 is a parcel post stamp.

BRUNEI

'brü-ˌnī

LOCATION — On the northwest coast of Borneo
GOVT. — Independent state
AREA — 2,226 sq. mi.
POP. — 322,982 (1999 est.)
CAPITAL — Bandar Seri Begawan

Brunei became a British protectorate in 1888. A treaty between the sultan and the British Government in 1979 provided for independence in 1983.

100 Cents (Sen) = 1 Dollar

Catalogue values for unused stamps in this country are for Never Hinged items, beginning with Scott 62.

Watermarks

Wmk. 385 - CARTOR

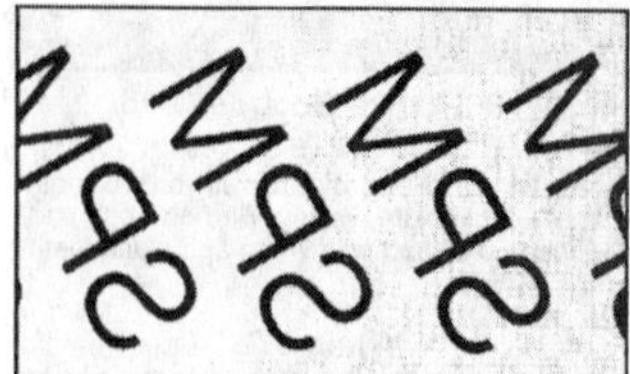

Wmk. 388- Multiple "SPM"

Syncopated Perforation

Type A (first stamp #555): On 2 longer sides, oval holes equal in width to 3 holes which are the 11th hole from the top and 10th hole from the bottom.

Labuan Stamps of 1902-03 Overprinted or Surcharged in Red:

1906 Unwmk. ***Perf. 12 to 16***
1 A38 1c violet & blk 22.50 *45.00*
 a. Black overprint *2,000. 2,750.*
2 A38 2c on 3c brn & blk 1.50 *7.50*
 a. "BRUNEI." double *4,250. 3,000.*
 b. "TWO CENTS." double *9,500.*
3 A38 2c on 8c org & blk 25.00 *70.00*
 a. "TWO CENTS." double *8,250.*
 b. "TWO CENTS." omitted, in pair with normal *9,250.*
4 A38 3c brown & blk 25.00 *70.00*
5 A38 4c on 12c yel & black 2.00 *5.00*
6 A38 5c on 16c org brn & green 37.50 *60.00*
7 A38 8c orange & blk 8.00 *25.00*
8 A38 10c on 16c org brn & green 6.50 *18.00*
9 A38 25c on 16c org brn & green 90.00 *125.00*
10 A38 30c on 16c org brn & green 85.00 *125.00*
11 A38 50c on 16c org brn & green 85.00 *125.00*
12 A38 $1 on 8c org & blk 85.00 *125.00*
 Nos. 1-12 (12) 473.00 *800.50*

The 25c surcharge reads: "25 CENTS."

Scene on Brunei River — A1

Two Types of 1908 1c, 3c:
Type I - Dots form bottom line of water shading. (Double plate.)
Type II - Dots removed. (Single plate.)

1907-21 Engr. Wmk. 3 ***Perf. 14***
13 A1 1c yel green & blk 2.00 *9.00*
14 A1 1c green (II) ('08) .55 *1.60*
 a. Type I ('19) *.75 2.10*
15 A1 2c red & black 2.40 *4.00*
16 A1 2c brn & blk ('11) 2.25 *1.50*
17 A1 3c red brn & blk 12.50 *18.00*
18 A1 3c car (I) ('08) 2.25 1.50
 a. Type II ('17) *60.00 32.50*
19 A1 4c lilac & blk 7.00 *9.00*
20 A1 4c claret ('12) 3.50 .70
21 A1 5c ultra & blk 45.00 *85.00*
22 A1 5c org & blk ('08) 6.50 6.50
23 A1 5c orange ('16) 12.00 12.00
24 A1 8c orange & blk 7.00 *20.00*
25 A1 8c blue ('08) 6.50 *10.00*
26 A1 8c ultra ('16) 4.50 *20.00*
27 A1 10c dk green & blk 4.00 *13.50*
28 A1 10c violet, *yel* ('12) 1.40 1.25
29 A1 25c yel brn & blue 27.50 *45.00*
30 A1 25c violet ('12) 3.25 *12.00*
31 A1 30c black & pur 19.00 *27.50*
32 A1 30c org & red vio ('12) 8.00 *12.50*
33 A1 50c brown & grn 17.50 *27.50*
34 A1 50c blk, *grn* ('12) 25.00 *60.00*
35 A1 50c blk, *grnsh bl* ('21) 8.00 *30.00*
36 A1 $1 slate & red 62.50 *85.00*
37 A1 $1 red & blk, *bl* ('12) 22.50 *50.00*
38 A1 $5 lake, *grn* ('08) 85.00 *140.00*
39 A1 $25 blk, *red* ('08) 450.00 *800.00*
 Nos. 13-38 (26) 397.60 *703.05*

Used value for No. 39 is for a CTO example dated before December 1941. CTOs dated later are worth about half the value given.

Stamps of 1908-21 Overprinted in Black: "MALAYA-BORNEO EXHIBITION, 1922" in Four Lines

1922
14b A1 1c green 2.25 *17.00*
16a A1 2c brown & black 5.00 *21.00*
18b A1 3c carmine 6.75 *30.00*
20a A1 4c claret 5.25 *35.00*
23a A1 5c orange 10.00 *45.00*
28a A1 10c violet, *yellow* 8.75 *45.00*
30a A1 25c violet 19.00 *67.50*
35a A1 50c greenish blue 60.00 *125.00*
37a A1 $1 red & black, *blue* 92.50 *160.00*
 Nos. 14b-37a (9) 209.50 *545.50*

Industrial fair, Singapore, Mar. 31-Apr. 15.

Type of 1907 Issue

1924-37 Wmk. 4
43 A1 1c black ('26) .55 *.35*
44 A1 2c deep brown .90 *3.75*
45 A1 2c green ('33) .55 .35
46 A1 3c green .80 *4.00*
47 A1 4c claret brown 1.60 .80
48 A1 4c orange ('29) 1.10 .50
49 A1 5c orange 3.50 *.95*
50 A1 5c lt gray ('31) 9.25 7.50
51 A1 5c brown ('33) 6.75 .30
52 A1 8c ultra ('27) 6.25 4.50
53 A1 8c gray ('33) 6.50 .50
54 A1 10c violet, *yel* ('37) 12.00 *20.00*
55 A1 25c dk violet ('31) 5.25 *9.50*
56 A1 30c org & red vio ('31) 7.50 *13.50*
57 A1 50c black, *grn* ('31) 7.50 *12.50*
58 A1 $1 red & blk, *bl* ('31) 25.00 *60.00*
 Nos. 43-58 (16) 95.00 *139.00*

For overprints see Nos. N1-N20.

Dwellings in Town of Brunei A2

1924-31
59 A2 6c black 10.50 9.25
60 A2 6c red ('31) 3.00 *10.00*
61 A2 12c blue 4.00 *8.25*
 Nos. 59-61 (3) 17.50 *27.50*

See note after Nos. N1-N19.

Catalogue values for unused stamps in this section, from this point to the end of the section, are for Never Hinged items.

Types of 1907-24

1947-51 Engr. ***Perf. 14***
62 A1 1c brown .45 *1.10*
63 A1 2c gray .85 *1.50*
 a. Perf. 14½x13½ ('50) *1.75 4.00*
64 A2 3c dark green 1.00 *3.00*
65 A1 5c deep orange .80 *1.25*
 a. Perf. 14½x13½ ('50) *4.00 12.50*
66 A2 6c gray black 1.00 *3.00*
67 A1 8c scarlet .45 *.80*
 a. Perf. 13 ('51) *.60 8.00*
68 A1 10c violet .70 .25
 a. Perf. 14½x13½ ('50) *2.25 5.00*
69 A1 15c brt ultra .45 *.60*
70 A1 25c red violet 1.00 .70
 a. Perf. 14½x13½ ('51) *1.75 7.50*
71 A1 30c dp org & gray blk .95 *1.00*
 a. Perf. 14½x13½ ('51) *1.75 11.00*
72 A1 50c black 1.60 .90
 a. Perf. 13 ('50) *3.50 14.00*
73 A1 $1 scar & gray blk 3.75 .90
74 A1 $5 red org & grn ('48) 15.00 *15.00*
75 A1 $10 dp claret & gray blk ('48) 40.00 30.00
 Nos. 62-75 (14) 68.00 *60.00*

Sultan Ahmed and Pile Dwellings A3

1949, Sept. 22 Wmk. 4 ***Perf. 13***
76 A3 8c car & black 1.25 1.25
77 A3 25c red orange & pur 1.25 *1.50*
78 A3 50c blue & black 1.50 1.50
 Nos. 76-78 (3) 4.00 4.25

25th anniv. of the reign of Sultan Ahmed Tajudin Akhazul Khair Wad-din.

Common Design Types pictured following the introduction.

UPU Issue
Common Design Types
Engr.; Name Typo. on 15c and 25c
1949, Oct. 10 ***Perf. 13½, 11x11½***
79 CD306 8c rose car 1.40 1.40
80 CD307 15c indigo 2.10 2.10
81 CD308 25c red lilac 1.60 1.60
82 CD309 50c slate 2.40 2.40
 Nos. 79-82 (4) 7.50 7.50

Sultan Omar Ali Saifuddin — A4

River Kampong A5

Perf. 13½x13
1952, Mar. 1 Engr. Wmk. 4
Center in Black
83 A4 1c black .20 .20
84 A4 2c red orange .20 .20
85 A4 3c red brown .20 .20
86 A4 4c green .20 .20
87 A4 6c gray .20 .20
88 A4 8c carmine .25 .20
89 A4 10c olive brown .20 .20
90 A4 12c violet 1.40 .20
91 A4 15c blue 1.40 .20
92 A4 25c purple 1.90 .25
93 A4 50c ultramarine 1.25 .35

Perf. 13
94 A5 $1 dull green 1.60 .60
95 A5 $2 red 8.00 1.50
96 A5 $5 deep plum 13.00 5.50
 Nos. 83-96 (14) 30.00 10.00

See Nos. 101-114.

Mosque and Sultan Omar A6

1958, Sept. 24 Wmk. 314 ***Perf. 13***
Center in Black
97 A6 8c dull green .20 *.30*
98 A6 15c carmine rose .25 .25
99 A6 35c rose violet .30 *.75*
 Nos. 97-99 (3) .75 *1.30*

Opening of the Brunei Mosque.

Freedom from Hunger Issue
Common Design Type with Portrait of Sultan Omar

1963, June 4 Photo. ***Perf. 14x14½***
100 CD314 12c sepia 2.50 1.50

Types of 1952
Wmk. 314 Upright
1964-70 Engr. ***Perf. 13½x13***
Center in Black
101 A4 1c black .20 .20
102 A4 2c red orange .20 .20
103 A4 3c red brown .20 .20
104 A4 4c green .25 .20
105 A4 6c black .60 .20
106 A4 8c dk carmine .45 .20
107 A4 10c olive brown .35 .25
108 A4 12c violet 1.00 .20
109 A4 15c blue .75 .20
110 A4 25c purple 1.50 .20
111 A4 50c ultramarine 1.75 .45

Perf. 13
112 A5 $1 dull green ('68) 7.00 2.50
113 A5 $2 red ('70) 25.00 25.00
114 A5 $5 deep plum ('70) 32.50 30.00
 Nos. 101-114 (14) 71.75 60.00

Nos. 101-112 were reissued in 1968-70 on whiter, glazed paper; the $2 and $5 are only on this paper.

Wmk. 314 Sideways
1972-73 ***Perf. 13½x13***
Center in Black
102a A4 2c red orange 1.50 .35
103a A4 3c red brown 1.75 .40
104a A4 4c green .50 .50
105a A4 6c black 2.75 .85
106a A4 8c dark carmine 1.75 1.75
107a A4 10c olive brown 1.00 .20
108a A4 12c violet 1.75 *2.25*
109a A4 15c blue 2.00 *3.00*
 Nos. 102a-109a (8) 13.00 9.30

The stamps with watermark sideways are on the whiter, glazed paper.

Issue dates: 2c, 8c, May 9, 1973, others, Nov. 17, 1972.

The following six sets are Common Design Types but with the portrait of Sultan Omar.

ITU Issue

Perf. 11x11½

1965, May 17 Litho. Wmk. 314

116 CD317 4c red lil & org brn .20 .20
117 CD317 75c orange & emer 1.40 1.40

Intl. Cooperation Year Issue

1965, Oct. 25 ***Perf. 14½***

118 CD318 4c blue grn & claret .20 .20
119 CD318 15c lt violet & grn .60 .60

Churchill Memorial Issue

1966, Jan. 24 Photo. ***Perf. 14***

120 CD319 3c multicolored .20 .20
121 CD319 10c multicolored .65 .65
122 CD319 15c multicolored 1.40 1.40
123 CD319 75c multicolored 4.50 4.50
Nos. 120-123 (4) 6.75 6.75

World Cup Soccer Issue

1966, July 4 Litho. ***Perf. 14***

124 CD321 4c multicolored .25 .25
125 CD321 75c multicolored .75 .75

WHO Headquarters Issue

1966, Sept. 20 Litho. ***Perf. 14***

126 CD322 12c multicolored .25 .20
127 CD322 25c multicolored .75 .75

UNESCO Anniversary Issue

1966, Dec. 1 Litho. Wmk. 314

128 CD323 4c "Education" .35 .35
129 CD323 15c "Science" .90 .90
130 CD323 75c "Culture" 2.50 2.50
Nos. 128-130 (3) 3.75 3.75

State Religious Building and Sultan Hassanal Bolkiah A7

1967, Dec. 19 Photo. ***Perf. 12½***

131 A7 4c violet & multi .20 .20
132 A7 10c red & multi .20 .20
133 A7 25c orange & multi .30 .30
134 A7 50c lt violet & multi .45 .45
Nos. 131-134 (4) 1.15 1.15

A three-stamp set (12c, 25c, 50c) showing views of the new Language and Communications Headquarters was prepared and announced for release in April, 1968. The Crown Agents distributed sample sets, but the stamps were not issued. Later, Nos. 144-146 were issued instead.

Sultan Hassanal Bolkiah, Brunei Mosque and Flags A8

Sultan Hassanal Bolkiah Installation: 12c, Sultan, Mosque and flags, horiz.

Perf. 13x14, 14x13

1968, July 9 Photo. Unwmk.

135 A8 4c green & multi .20 .20
136 A8 12c dp bister & multi .30 .30
137 A8 25c violet & multi .75 .75
Nos. 135-137 (3) 1.25 1.25

Sultan Hassanal Bolkiah A9

Wmk. 314

1968, July 15 Litho. ***Perf. 12***

138 A9 4c multicolored .20 .20
139 A9 12c multicolored .20 .20
140 A9 25c multicolored .40 *.50*
Nos. 138-140 (3) .80 *.90*

Sultan Hassanal Bolkiah's birthday.

Coronation of Sultan Hassanal Bolkiah, Aug. 1, 1968 — A10

1968, Aug. 1 Photo. ***Perf. 14½x14***

141 A10 4c Prus blue & multi .20 .20
142 A10 12c rose lilac & multi .25 .25
143 A10 25c multicolored .55 .55
Nos. 141-143 (3) 1.00 1.00

A11

Hall of Language and Culture — A12

Perf. 13½, 12½x13½ (A12)

1968, Sept. 29 Photo. Wmk. 314

144 A11 10c blue grn & multi .20 *.25*
145 A12 15c ocher & multi .20 *.30*
146 A12 30c ultra & multi .45 *.75*
Nos. 144-146 (3) .85 *1.30*

Opening of the Hall of Language and Culture and of the Broadcasting and Information Department Building. Nos. 144-146 are overprinted "1968" and 4 bars over the 1967 date. They were not issued without this overprint.

Human Rights Flame and Struggling Man — A13

Unwmk.

1968, Dec. 16 Litho. ***Perf. 14***

147 A13 12c green, yel & blk .20 .20
148 A13 25c ultra, yel & blk .25 .25
149 A13 75c dk plum, yel & blk .55 .55
Nos. 147-149 (3) 1.00 1.00

International Human Rights Year.

Sultan and WHO Emblem A14

1968, Dec. 19 Litho. ***Perf. 14***

150 A14 4c lt blue, org & blk .25 .25
151 A14 15c brt purple, org & blk .35 .35
152 A14 25c olive, org & blk .65 .65
Nos. 150-152 (3) 1.25 1.25

20th anniv. of the WHO.

Sultan Hassanal Bolkiah, Pengiran Shahbandar and Oil Rig — A15

Perf. 14x13

1969, July 10 Photo. Wmk. 314

153 A15 12c green & multi .40 .40
154 A15 40c dk rose brn & multi 1.00 1.00
155 A15 50c violet & multi 1.60 1.60
Nos. 153-155 (3) 3.00 3.00

Installation of Pengiran Shahbandar as Second Minister (Di-Galong Sahibol Mal).

Royal Assembly Hall and Council Chamber — A16

Design: 50c, Front view of buildings.

Unwmk.

1969, Sept. 23 Litho. ***Perf. 15***

156 A16 12c multicolored .20 .20
157 A16 25c multicolored .30 .30
158 A16 50c violet & pink .60 .60
Nos. 156-158 (3) 1.10 1.10

Opening of the Royal Assembly Hall and Council Chamber.

Youth Center — A17

1969, Dec. 20 Litho. Wmk. 314

159 A17 6c lt org, blk & dull vio .20 .20
160 A17 10c cit, blk & dl Prus grn .25 .25
161 A17 30c yel green, blk & brn .55 .55
Nos. 159-161 (3) 1.00 1.00

Opening of Youth Center, Mar. 15, 1969.

Helicopter and Emblem — A18

Designs: 10c, Soldier and emblem, vert. 75c, Patrol boat and emblem.

1971, May 31 Litho. ***Perf. 14***

162 A18 10c green & multi .55 .55
163 A18 15c Prus blue & multi .80 .80
164 A18 75c lt ultra & multi 4.00 4.00
Nos. 162-164 (3) 5.35 5.35

10th anniv. of Royal Brunei Malay Reg.

50th Anniv. of the Royal Brunei Police Force — A19

1971, Aug. 14 ***Perf. 14½***

165 A19 10c Superintendent .50 .50
166 A19 15c Constable .75 .75
167 A19 50c Traffic policeman 2.75 2.75
Nos. 165-167 (3) 4.00 4.00

Sultan, Heir Apparent and View of Brunei — A20

Portraits and: 25c, View of Brunei with Mosque. 50c, Mosque and banner.

1971, Aug. 27 Litho. Wmk. 314

168 A20 15c multicolored .40 .25
169 A20 25c multicolored .75 .55
170 A20 50c multicolored 1.40 1.10
Nos. 168-170 (3) 2.55 1.90

Installation of Sultan Hassanal Bolkiah's brother Muda Omar Ali Saifuddin as heir apparent (Perdana Wazir).

Brass and Copper Goods A21

Designs: 12c, Basketware. 15c, Leather goods. 25c, Silverware. 50c, Brunei Museum.

1972, Feb. 29 ***Perf. 13½x14***

Size: 37x21mm

Portrait in Black

171 A21 10c brn, sal & yel grn .30 .30
172 A21 12c org, yel & green .35 .35
173 A21 15c dk grn, emer & org .40 .40
174 A21 25c brown, org & slate 1.10 1.10

Size: 58x21mm

175 A21 50c dull blue & multi 2.25 2.25
Nos. 171-175 (5) 4.40 4.40

Opening of Brunei Museum.

Queen Elizabeth II, Sultan and View — A22

Queen Elizabeth II, Sultan Hassanal Bolkiah and: 15c, View of Brunei. 25c, Mosque and barge. 50c, Royal Assembly Hall.

1972, Feb. 29 Photo. ***Perf. 13x13½***

176 A22 10c lt brown & multi .30 .30
177 A22 15c lt blue & multi .60 .60
178 A22 25c lt green & multi 1.60 1.60
179 A22 50c dull purple & multi 3.00 3.00
Nos. 176-179 (4) 5.50 5.50

Visit of Queen Elizabeth II, Feb. 29.

Bangunan Secretariat (Government Buildings) — A23

Sultans Omar Ali Saifuddin and Hassanal Bolkiah: 15c, Istana Darul Hana (Sultan's residence). 25c, View of capital. 50c, View of new Mosque.

1972, Oct. 4 Litho. *Perf. 13½*

180 A23 10c org, blk & green .20 .20
181 A23 15c green & multi .30 .30
182 A23 25c ultra & multi .50 .50
183 A23 50c rose red & multi 1.00 1.00
Nos. 180-183 (4) 2.00 2.00

Change of capital's name from Brunei to Bandar Seri Begawan, Oct. 4, 1970.

Beverley Plane Landing — A24

Design: 25c, Blackburn Beverley plane dropping supplies by parachute, vert.

Perf. 14x13½, 13½x14

1972, Nov. 15 Litho.

184 A24 25c blue & multi 1.60 1.60
185 A24 75c ultra & multi 4.00 4.00

Opening of Royal Air Force Museum, Hendon, London.

Silver Wedding Issue, 1972

Common Design Type

Design: Queen Elizabeth II, Prince Philip; girl and boy with traditional gifts.

1972, Nov. 20 Photo. *Perf. 14x14½*

186 CD324 12c multi .40 .20
187 CD324 75c multi 1.25 1.25

INTERPOL Emblem and Headquarters, Paris — A25

Design: 50c, similar to 25c.

1973, Sept. 7 Litho. *Perf. 14x14½*

188 A25 25c emerald & multi .75 .75
189 A25 50c multicolored 1.50 1.50

50th anniv. of Intl. Criminal Police Org. (INTERPOL).

Princess Anne and Mark Phillips — A26

1973, Nov. 14 Litho. *Perf. 13½*

190 A26 25c vio blue & multi .20 .20
191 A26 50c red lilac & multi .40 .40

Wedding of Princess Anne and Capt. Mark Phillips, Nov. 14, 1973.

Churchill Painting Outdoors A27

Sultan Hassanal Bolkiah A28

Design: 50c, Churchill making "V" sign.

Perf. 14x13½

1973, Dec. 31 Litho. Wmk. 314

192 A27 12c car rose & multi .20 .20
193 A27 50c dk green & multi .55 .55

Winston Churchill Memorial Exhibition.

Wmk. 314 Sideways

1974, July 15 Photo. *Perf. 13x15*

194 A28 4c blue grn & multi .20 .20
195 A28 5c dull blue & multi .20 .20
196 A28 6c olive grn & multi .20 .20
197 A28 10c lt violet & multi .20 .20
b. Watermark upright ('76) .20 .20
198 A28 15c brown & multi .20 .20
199 A28 20c buff & multi .20 .20
b. Watermark upright ('76) .20 .20
200 A28 25c olive & multi .20 .20
b. Watermark upright ('76) .20 .20
201 A28 30c multicolored .25 .20
202 A28 35c gray & multi .25 .25
203 A28 40c multicolored .30 .30
204 A28 50c yel brn & multi .40 .35
205 A28 75c multicolored .60 .50
206 A28 $1 dull org & multi .75 .65
207 A28 $2 multicolored 1.60 1.40
208 A28 $5 silver & multi 3.50 3.25
209 A28 $10 gold & multi 8.25 8.25
Nos. 194-209 (16) 17.30 16.55

Issue date: Nos. 197b-200b, Apr. 12.

1975, Aug. 13 Wmk. 373

194a A28 4c .20 .20
195a A28 5c .20 .20
196a A28 6c .20 .20
197a A28 10c .20 .20
198a A28 15c .20 .20
199a A28 20c .20 .20
200a A28 25c .20 .20
201a A28 30c .25 .25
202a A28 35c .30 .30
203a A28 40c .35 .35
204a A28 50c .40 .40
205a A28 75c .60 .60
206a A28 $1 .80 .80
207a A28 $2 1.60 1.60
208a A28 $5 4.00 4.00
209a A28 $10 8.00 8.00
Nos. 194a-209a (16) 17.70 17.70

For surcharge see No. 225.

Brunei Airport A29

Design: 75c, Sultan Hassanal Bolkiah in uniform and jet over airport.

Perf. 14x14½, 12½x13 (75c)

1974, July 18 Litho. Wmk. 314

Size: 44x28mm

215 A29 50c multicolored 1.00 1.00

Size: 47x36mm

216 A29 75c multicolored 1.40 1.40

Opening of Brunei Airport.

UPU Emblem A30

1974, Oct. 28 *Perf. 14½*

217 A30 12c orange & multi .20 .20
218 A30 50c blue & multi .50 .50
219 A30 75c emerald & multi .75 .75
Nos. 217-219 (3) 1.45 1.45

Centenary of Universal Postal Union.

Winston Churchill A31

Design: 75c, Churchill smoking cigar.

1974, Nov. 30 Wmk. 373 *Perf. 14*

220 A31 12c vio blue, blue & gold .20 .20
221 A31 75c dk green, black & gold .90 .90

Sir Winston Churchill (1874-1965).

Boeing 737 Planes at Airport A32

Designs: 35c, Boeing 737 over Bandar Seri Begawan Mosque. 75c, Boeing 737 in flight. All planes with crest of Royal Brunei Airlines.

Perf. 12½x12

1975, May 14 Unwmk.

222 A32 12c multicolored .30 .25
223 A32 35c multicolored 1.00 .75
224 A32 75c multicolored 2.00 2.00
Nos. 222-224 (3) 3.30 3.00

Inauguration of Royal Brunei Airlines.

No. 196a Surcharged in Silver

Perf. 13x15

1976, Aug. 16 Photo. Wmk. 373

225 A28 10c on 6c multicolored .25 .25

British Royal Coat of Arms — A33

20c, Imperial State Crown. 75c, Elizabeth II.

Wmk. 373

1977, June 7 Litho. *Perf. 14*

226 A33 10c dk blue & multi .20 .20
227 A33 20c purple & multi .20 .20
228 A33 75c yellow & multi .60 .60
Nos. 226-228 (3) 1.00 1.00

25th anniv. of the reign of Elizabeth II.

Coronation of Elizabeth II A34

20c, Elizabeth II with coronation regalia. 75c, Departure from Westminster Abbey (coach).

1978, June 2 Litho. *Perf. 13½x13*

229 A34 10c multicolored .20 .20
230 A34 20c multicolored .20 .20
231 A34 75c multicolored .60 .60
Nos. 229-231 (3) 1.00 1.00

25th anniv. of coronation of Elizabeth II.

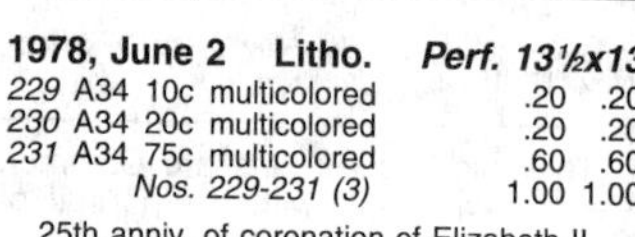

Sultan's Coat of Arms — A35

Struggling Man, Human Rights Flame — A36

Coronation of Sultan Hassanal Bolkiah, 10th Anniv.: 20c, Ceremony. 75c, Royal crown.

1978, Aug. 1 Wmk. 373 *Perf. 12*

232 A35 10c multicolored .20 .20
233 A35 20c multicolored .25 .20
234 A35 75c multicolored .90 .75
a. Souvenir sheet of 3, #232-234 8.50 6.00
Nos. 232-234 (3) 1.35 1.15

1978, Dec. 10 Litho. *Perf. 14*

235 A36 10c red, black & yel .20 .20
236 A36 20c violet, black & yel .20 .20
237 A36 75c olive, black & yel .60 .60
Nos. 235-237 (3) 1.00 1.00

Universal Declaration of Human Rights, 30th anniversary.

Children and IYC Emblem A37

1979, June 30 Wmk. 373 *Perf. 14*

238 A37 10c shown .20 .20
239 A37 $1 IYC emblem .90 .90

Telisai Earth Satellite Station A38

Designs: 20c, Radar screen and satellite. 75c, Cameraman, telex operator, telephone.

1979, Sept. 23 Litho. *Perf. 14½x14*

240 A38 10c multicolored .20 .20
241 A38 20c multicolored .20 .20
242 A38 75c multicolored .75 .75
Nos. 240-242 (3) 1.15 1.15

Hajeer Emblem — A39

1979, Nov. 21

243 A39 10c multicolored .20 .20
244 A39 20c multicolored .20 .20
245 A39 75c multicolored .75 .75
a. Souvenir sheet of 3, #243-245 2.50 2.50
Nos. 243-245 (3) 1.15 1.15

Hegira, 1400th anniversary.

A40 A41

1980 Litho. *Perf. 14*

246 A40 10c Installation ceremony .20 .20
247 A40 10c Ceremony, diff. .20 .20
248 A40 75c Jefri Bolkiah .60 .60
249 A40 75c Sufri Bolkiah .60 .60
Nos. 246-249 (4) 1.60 1.60

Installation of Jefri Bolkiah and Sufri Bolkiah as Wizars (Ministers of State for Royalty) 1st anniv. Issued: #246, 248, 11/8; others, 12/6.

1981, Jan. 19 Litho. *Perf. 12x11½*

255 A41 10c Umbrella .20 .20
256 A41 15c Dagger, shield .20 .20
257 A41 20c Spears .25 .25
258 A41 30c Gold pouch .35 .35

Size: 22½x40mm

Perf. 14x13½

259 A41 50c Headdress .60 .60
a. Souvenir sheet of 5, #255-259 2.25 2.25
Nos. 255-259 (5) 1.60 1.60

A42

A43

1981, May 17 Litho. *Perf. 13x13½*

260 A42 10c car rose & black .20 .20
261 A42 75c dp violet & black .75 .75

13th World Telecommunications Day.

Perf. 12½x12, 12 (75c)

1981, July 15 Litho.

Deep Rose Lilac Background

262 A43 10c Dagger, case .20 .20
263 A43 15c Rifle, powder pouch .20 .20
264 A43 20c Spears .20 .20
265 A43 30c Sword, tunic, shield .30 .30
266 A43 50c Horns .50 .50

Size: 28½x45mm

267 A43 75c Gold bowl, table .75 .75
Nos. 262-267 (6) 2.15 2.15

See Nos. 278-289.

Royal Wedding Issue

Common Design Type

1981, July 29 *Perf. 14*

268 CD331 10c Bouquet .20 .20
269 CD331 $1 Charles .65 .65
270 CD331 $2 Couple 1.25 1.25
Nos. 268-270 (3) 2.10 2.10

World Food Day — A44

Intl. Year of the Disabled — A45

1981, Oct. 16 Litho. *Perf. 12*

271 A44 10c Fishermen .20 .20
272 A44 $1 Produce .80 .80

1981, Dec. 16 Wmk. 373 *Perf. 12*

273 A45 10c Blind man .20 .20
274 A45 20c Sign language .20 .20
275 A45 75c Man in wheelchair .60 .60
Nos. 273-275 (3) 1.00 1.00

TB Bacillus Centenary — A46

1982, Mar. 24 *Perf. 12, 13½ (75c)*

276 A46 10c Lungs .20 .20
277 A46 75c Bacillus, microscope .60 .60

Type of 1981

1982, May 31 Litho. *Perf. 12½x12*

Deep Magenta Background

278 A43 10c shown .20 .20
279 A43 15c Pedestal urn .20 .20
280 A43 20c Silver bowl .20 .20
281 A43 30c Candle .30 .30
282 A43 50c Gold pipe .50 .50

Size: 28x44mm

Perf. 13½

283 A43 75c Silver pointer .75 .75
Nos. 278-283 (6) 2.15 2.15

1982, July 15 Litho. *Perf. 12½x12*

Violet Background

284 A43 10c Urn .20 .20
285 A43 15c Crossed banners .20 .20
286 A43 20c Golden fan .20 .20
287 A43 30c Lid .30 .30
288 A43 50c Sword, sheath .50 .50

Size: 28x44mm

Perf. 12

289 A43 75c Golden chalice pole .75 .75
Nos. 284-289 (6) 2.15 2.15

A47

1983, Mar. 14 Litho. *Perf. 13½*

290 A47 10c Flag .20 .20
291 A47 20c Natl. palace .20 .20
292 A47 75c Oil drilling .75 .75
293 A47 $2 Sultan Bolkiah 2.00 2.00
a. Block of 4, #290-293 3.00 3.00

Commonwealth Day.

World Communications Year — A48

1983, July 15 Litho. *Perf. 13½*

294 A48 10c Mail delivery .20 .20
295 A48 75c Typewriter, phone .80 .80
296 A48 $2 Dish antenna, satellite, TV 2.00 2.00
Nos. 294-296 (3) 3.00 3.00

Opening of Hassanal Bolkiah National Stadium — A49

1983, Sept. 23 Litho. *Perf. 12*

297 A49 10c Soccer, vert. .20 .20
298 A49 75c Runners, vert. 1.00 1.00
299 A49 $1 shown 1.25 1.25
Nos. 297-299 (3) 2.45 2.45

Size, Nos. 297-298: 26x33mm.

Fishing Industry — A50

1983, Sept. 23 Litho. *Perf. 13½*

300 A50 10c Shrimp, lobster .20 .20
301 A50 50c Pacific jacks .65 .65
302 A50 75c Parrotfish, flatfish .90 .90
303 A50 $1 Tuna 1.25 1.25
Nos. 300-303 (4) 3.00 3.00

State Assembly Building — A51

Map of Southeast Asia, Flag — A52

Sultan Hassanal Bolkiah — A53

1984, Jan. 1 Litho. *Perf. 13*

304 A51 10c shown .20 .20
305 A51 20c State Secretariat building .25 .25
306 A51 35c New Law Court .40 .40
307 A51 50c Liquid natural gas well .60 .60
308 A51 75c Omar Ali Saifuddin Mosque .90 .90
309 A51 $1 Sultan's Palace 1.25 1.25
310 A52 $3 shown 3.75 3.75
a. Souvenir sheet of 7, #304-310 7.25 7.25
Nos. 304-310 (7) 7.35 7.35

Souvenir Sheets

311 Sheet of 4, Constitution signing, 1959 1.25 1.25
a.-d. A53 25c any single .25 .25
312 Sheet of 4, Brunei U.K. Friendship Agreement, 1979 1.25 1.25
a.-d. A53 25c any single .25 .25

Forestry Resources — A54

1984, Apr. 21 Litho. *Perf. 13½*

313 A54 10c Forests, enrichment planting .20 .20
314 A54 50c Irrigation canal .65 .65
315 A54 75c Recreation forest .90 .90
316 A54 $1 Wildlife 1.25 1.25
Nos. 313-316 (4) 3.00 3.00

Philakorea 1984 — A55

Litho. & Engr.

1984, Oct. 22 *Perf. 13*

317 A55 10c No. 93 .20 .20
a. Souvenir sheet of 1 .20 .20
318 A55 75c No. 27 .90 .90
a. Souvenir sheet of 1 .90 .90
319 A55 $2 1895 local stamp 2.50 2.50
a. Souvenir sheet of 1 2.50 2.50
Nos. 317-319 (3) 3.60 3.60

Brunei Admission to Intl. Organizations A56

1985, Sept. 23 Litho. *Perf. 13*

320 A56 50c UN .45 .45
321 A56 50c Commonwealth .45 .45
322 A56 50c ASEAN .45 .45
323 A56 50c OIC .45 .45
a. Souv. sheet, #320-323 + label 2.00 2.00
Nos. 320-323 (4) 1.80 1.80

Intl. Youth Year A57

1985, Oct. 17 *Perf. 12*

324 A57 10c shown .20 .20
325 A57 75c Industry, education .55 .55
326 A57 $1 Public Service .70 .70
Nos. 324-326 (3) 1.45 1.45

Intl. Day of Solidarity with the Palestinian People A58

1985, Nov. 29 *Perf. 12x12½*

327 A58 10c lt blue & multi .20 .20
328 A58 50c pink & multi .55 .55
329 A58 $1 lt green & multi 1.10 1.10
Nos. 327-329 (3) 1.85 1.85

Natl. Scout Jamboree, Dec. 14-20 — A59

Sultan Hassanal Bolkiah — A60

1985, Dec. 14 *Perf. 13½*

330 A59 10c Scout handshake .20 .20
331 A59 20c Semaphore .20 .20
332 A59 $2 Jamboree emblem 1.75 1.75
Nos. 330-332 (3) 2.15 2.15

1985-86 Wmk. 233 *Perf. 13½x14½*

333 A60 10c multi .20 .20
334 A60 15c multi .20 .20
335 A60 20c multi .20 .20
336 A60 25c multi .25 .25
337 A60 35c multi ('86) .30 .30
338 A60 40c multi ('86) .35 .35
339 A60 50c multi ('86) .45 .45
340 A60 75c multi ('86) .70 .70

Size: 35x42mm

Perf. 14

341 A60 $1 multi ('86) .90 .90
342 A60 $2 multi ('86) 1.75 1.75
343 A60 $5 multi ('86) 4.50 4.50
344 A60 $10 multi ('86) 9.00 9.00
Nos. 333-344 (12) 18.80 18.80

Issued: #333-336, Dec. 23; #337-340, Jan. 15; #341-343, Feb. 23; #344, Mar. 29.

Admission to Intl. Organizations A61

Wmk. Cartor (385)

1986, Apr. 30 Litho. *Perf. 13*

345 A61 50c WMO .50 *.60*
346 A61 50c ITU .50 *.60*
347 A61 50c UPU .50 *.60*
348 A61 50c ICAO .50 *.60*
a. Souv. sheet, #345-348 + label 2.25 *2.50*
Nos. 345-348 (4) 2.00 *2.40*

Royal Brunei Armed Forces, 25th Anniv. A62

1986, May 31 Unwmk. *Perf. 13½*

349 Strip of 4 1.40 1.40
a. A62 10c In combat .20 .20
b. A62 20c Communications .20 .20
c. A62 50c Air and sea defense .45 .45
d. A62 75c On parade, Royal Palace .70 .70

Royal Ensigns — A63

#350, Tunggul charok buritan, Pisang-pisang, Alam bernaga, Sandaran. #351, Dadap, Tunggul kawan, Ambal, Payong ubor-ubor, Sapu-sapu ayeng and Rawai lidah. #352, Ula-ula besar, Payong haram, Sumbu layang. #353, Payong ubor-ubor tiga ringkat and Payong tinggi. #354, Panji-panji, Chogan istiadat, Chogan ugama. #355, Lambang duli yang maha mulia and Mahligai.

1986 Litho. *Perf. 12½*

350 A63 10c multicolored .20 .20
351 A63 10c multicolored .20 .20
352 A63 75c multicolored .70 .70
353 A63 75c multicolored .70 .70
354 A63 $2 multicolored 1.75 1.75
355 A63 $2 multicolored 1.75 1.75
Nos. 350-355 (6) 5.30 5.30

Intl. Peace Year — A64

1986, Oct. 24 Litho. *Perf. 12*

356 A64 50c Peace doves .50 .50
357 A64 75c Hands .70 .70
358 A64 $1 Peace symbols .90 .90
Nos. 356-358 (3) 2.10 2.10

Natl. Anti-Drug Campaign Posters — A65

Brass Artifacts — A66

1987, Mar. 15 Litho. *Perf. 12*

359 A65 10c Jail .20 .20
360 A65 75c Noose .65 .65
361 A65 $1 Execution .90 .90
Nos. 359-361 (3) 1.75 1.75

1987, July 15

362 A66 50c Kiri (kettle) .45 .45
363 A66 50c Langguai (bowl) .45 .45
364 A66 50c Badil (cannon) .45 .45
365 A66 50c Pelita (lamp) .45 .45
Nos. 362-365 (4) 1.80 1.80

See Nos. 388-391.

Dewan Bahasa Dan Pustaka, 25th Anniv. — A67

Illustration reduced.

1987, Sept. 29 *Perf. 13½x13*

366 A67 Strip of 3 1.75 1.75
a. 10c multicolored .20 .20
b. 50c multicolored .30 .30
c. $2 multicolored 1.25 1.25

Language and Literature Bureau.

ASEAN, 20th Anniv. — A68

1987, Aug. 8 Litho. *Perf. 14x13½*

367 A68 20c Map .20 .20
368 A68 50c Year dates .45 .45
369 A68 $1 Flags, emblem .90 .90
Nos. 367-369 (3) 1.55 1.55

World Food Day A70

Fruit: a, Artocarpus odoratissima. b, Canarium odontophyllum mig. c, Litsea garciae. d, Mangifera foetida lour.

1987, Oct. 31 *Perf. 12½*

370 Strip of 4 1.90 1.90
a.-d. A70 50c any single .45 .45

See Nos. 374, 405, 423, 457-460.

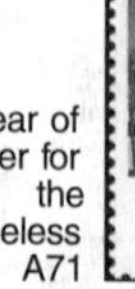

Intl. Year of Shelter for the Homeless A71

Various houses.

1987, Nov. 28 Litho. *Perf. 13*

371 A71 50c multi .50 .50
372 A71 75c multi, diff. .70 .70
373 A71 $1 multi, diff. .95 .95
Nos. 371-373 (3) 2.15 2.15

Fruit Type of 1987 Without FAO Emblem, Dated 1988

Fruit: a, Durio. b, Durio oxleyanus. c, Durio graveolens (cross section at L). d, Durio graveolens (cross section at R).

1988, Jan. 30 Litho. *Perf. 12*

374 Strip of 4 2.00 2.00
a.-d. A70 50c, any single .50 .50

Opening of Malay Technology Museum — A72

1988, Feb. 29 *Perf. 12½x12*

375 A72 10c Wooden lathe .20 .20
376 A72 75c Water wheel, buffalo .80 .80
377 A72 $1 Bird caller in blind 1.00 1.00
Nos. 375-377 (3) 2.00 2.00

Handwoven Cloth — A73

Designs: 10c, Kain Beragi Bunga Sakah-Sakah Dan Bunga Cengkih. 20c, Kain Jong Sarat. 25c, Kain Si Pugut. 40c, Kain Si Pugut Bunga Berlapis. 75c, Kain Si Lobang Bangsi Bunga Belitang Kipas.

1988, Apr. 30 Litho. *Perf. 12*

378 A73 10c multicolored .20 .20
379 A73 20c org brown & blk .20 .20
380 A73 25c multicolored .25 .25
381 A73 40c multicolored .40 .40
382 A73 75c multicolored .75 .75
a. Souvenir sheet of 5, #378-382 + label 2.00 2.00
Nos. 378-382 (5) 1.80 1.80

1988, Sept. 29 Litho. *Perf. 12*

Designs: 10c, Kain Beragi. 20c, Kain Bertabur. 25c, Kain Sukma Indra. 40c, Kain Si Pugut Bunga Bersusup. 75c, Kain Beragi Si Lobang Bangsi Bunga Cendera Kesuma.

383 A73 10c multicolored .20 .20
384 A73 20c multicolored .20 .20
385 A73 25c multicolored .25 .25
386 A73 40c multicolored .40 .40
387 A73 75c multicolored .75 .75
a. Souvenir sheet of 5, #383-387 2.00 2.00
Nos. 383-387 (5) 1.80 1.80

Brass Artifacts Type of 1987

1988, June 30 Litho. *Perf. 12*

388 A66 50c Celapa (repousse box) .50 .50
389 A66 50c Gangsa (footed plate) .50 .50
390 A66 50c Periok (lidded pot) .50 .50
391 A66 50c Lampong (candlestick) .50 .50
Nos. 388-391 (4) 2.00 2.00

Coronation of Sultan Hassanal Bolkiah, 20th Anniv. — A74

1988, Aug. 1 Litho. *Perf. 14*

392 A74 20c shown .25 .25
393 A74 75c Reading from the Koran .75 .75

Size: 26x62mm

Perf. 12½x13

394 A74 $2 In full regalia 2.00 2.00
a. Souvenir sheet of 3, #392-394 3.00 3.00
Nos. 392-394 (3) 3.00 3.00

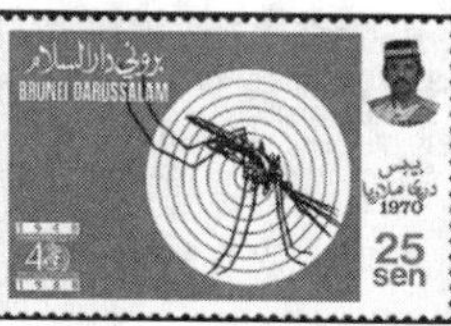

Eradicate Malaria, WHO 40th Anniv. — A75

1988, Dec. 17 Litho. *Perf. 14x13½*

395 A75 25c Mosquito .25 .25
396 A75 35c Extermination .35 .35
397 A75 $2 Microscope, infected blood cells 2.10 2.10
Nos. 395-397 (3) 2.70 2.70

Natl. Day A76

1989, Feb. 23 Litho. *Perf. 12*

Size of 60c: 22x54½mm

398 A76 20c Sultan Bolkiah, officials .20 .20
399 A76 30c Honor guard .30 .30
400 A76 60c Fireworks, palace, vert. .60 .60
401 A76 $2 Religious ceremony 2.00 2.00
a. Souvenir sheet of 4, #398-401 3.25 3.25
Nos. 398-401 (4) 3.10 3.10

Independence from Britain, 5th anniv.

Solidarity with the Palestinians — A77

1989, Apr. 1 Litho. *Perf. 13½*

402 A77 20c shown .25 .25
403 A77 75c Map, flag .75 .75
404 A77 $1 Dome of the Rock 1.00 1.00
Nos. 402-404 (3) 2.00 2.00

Fruit Type of 1987 Without FAO Emblem, Dated 1989

Designs: a, Daemonorops fissa. b, Eleiodoxa conferia. c, Salacca zalacca. d, Calamus ornatus.

1989, Oct. 31 Litho. *Perf. 12*

405 Strip of 4 2.50 2.50
a.-d. A70 60c any single .80 .80

Oil and Gas Industry, 60th Anniv. A79

1989, Dec. 28 *Perf. 13½*

406 A79 20c Drill .25 .25
407 A79 60c Tanker .65 .65
408 A79 90c Refinery 1.00 1.00
409 A79 $1 Rail transport 1.10 1.10
410 A79 $2 Offshore rig 2.25 2.25
Nos. 406-410 (5) 5.25 5.25

Brunei Museum, 25th Anniv. A80

1990, Jan. 1 Litho. *Perf. 12x12½*

411 A80 30c Exhibits .30 .30
412 A80 60c Official opening, 1965 .60 .60
413 A80 $1 Museum exterior 1.00 1.00
Nos. 411-413 (3) 1.90 1.90

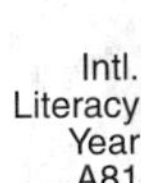

Intl. Literacy Year
A81

1990, July 15 Litho. *Perf. 12x12½*
414 A81 15c multicolored .20 .20
415 A81 90c multicolored .95 .95
416 A81 $1 multicolored 1.10 1.10
Nos. 414-416 (3) 2.25 2.25

Tarsier — A82

Fight Against AIDS — A83

1990, Sept. 29 Litho. *Perf. 12*
417 A82 20c shown .25 .25
418 A82 60c Eating leaves .75 .75
419 A82 90c Climbing tree 1.00 1.00
Nos. 417-419 (3) 2.00 2.00

1990, Dec. 1 Litho. *Perf. 13*
420 A83 20c shown .25 .25
421 A83 30c AIDS transmission .35 .35
422 A83 90c Tombstone, skulls 1.00 1.00
Nos. 420-422 (3) 1.60 1.60

Fruit Type of 1987

Without FAO Emblem, Dated 1990

Fruit: a, Willoughbea (uncut core). b, Willoughbea (core cut in half). c, Willoughbea angustifolia.

1990, Dec. 31 *Perf. 12½*
423 Strip of 3 2.10 2.10
a.-c. A70 60c any single .70 .70

Proboscis Monkey — A84

1991, Mar. 30 Litho. *Perf. 13½x14*
424 A84 15c shown .20 .20
425 A84 20c Head, facing .25 .25
426 A84 50c Sitting on branch .60 .60
427 A84 60c Adult with young .70 .70
Nos. 424-427 (4) 1.75 1.75

Teacher's Day
A85

Design: 90c, Teacher at blackboard.

1991, Sept. 23 Litho. *Perf. 13½x14*
428 A85 60c multicolored .70 .70
429 A85 90c multicolored 1.10 1.10

Brunei Beauty
A86

1991, Oct. 1 Litho. *Perf. 13*
430 A86 30c Three immature .35 .35
431 A86 60c Female .70 .70
432 A86 $1 Adult male 1.25 1.25
Nos. 430-432 (3) 2.30 2.30

Happy Family Campaign — A87

1991, Nov. 30 Litho. *Perf. 13*
433 A87 20c Family, graduating son .25 .25
434 A87 60c Mothers, children .65 .65
435 A87 90c Adults, children, heart 1.10 1.10
Nos. 433-435 (3) 2.00 2.00

World Health Day — A88

1992, Apr. 7 Litho. *Perf. 13*
436 A88 20c multicolored .25 .25
437 A88 50c multi, diff. .60 .60

Size: 48x28mm

438 A88 75c multi, diff. .90 .90
Nos. 436-438 (3) 1.75 1.75

Brunei-Singapore and Brunei-Malaysia-Philippines Fiber Optic Submarine Cables — A89

1992, Apr. 28 Litho. *Perf. 12*
439 A89 20c Map .25 .25
440 A89 30c Diagram .35 .35
441 A89 90c Submarine cable 1.10 1.10
Nos. 439-441 (3) 1.70 1.70

Visit ASEAN Year — A90

Designs: a, 20c, Sculptures. b, 60c, Judo exhibition. c, $1, Sculptures, diff.

1992, June 30 Litho. *Perf. 13½x14*
442 A90 Strip of 3, #a.-c. 2.00 2.00

ASEAN, 25th Anniv. — A91

A92

1992, Aug. 8 Litho. *Perf. 14*
443 A91 20c shown .25 .25
444 A91 60c Building .65 .65
445 A91 90c Views of member states 1.10 1.10
Nos. 443-445 (3) 2.00 2.00

1992, Oct. 5 *Perf. 14x13½*

Sultan in various forms of dress and: No. 446a, Coronation procession. b, Airport. c, New Law Court, Sultan's Palace. d, Ship and Brunei University. e, Mosque, buildings.

446 A92 25c Strip of 5, #a.-e. 1.50 1.50

Sultan Hassanal Bolkiah's Accession to the Throne, 25th Anniv.

Birds
A93

Designs: No. 447, Crested wood partridge, vert. No. 448, Long-tailed parakeet, vert. No. 449, Chestnut-breasted malkoha. No. 450, Asian paradise flycatcher, vert. No. 451, Magpie robin, vert. No. 452, White-rumped shama. No. 453, Great argus pheasant, vert. No. 454, Malay lorikeet, vert. No. 455, Black and red broadbill, vert.

Perf. 14x13½, 13½x14

1992-93 Litho.
447 A93 30c multicolored .40 .40
448 A93 30c multicolored .40 .40
449 A93 30c multicolored .40 .40
450 A93 60c multicolored .75 .75
451 A93 60c multicolored .75 .75
452 A93 60c multicolored .75 .75
453 A93 $1 multicolored 1.25 1.25
454 A93 $1 multicolored 1.25 1.25
455 A93 $1 multicolored 1.25 1.25
Nos. 447-455 (9) 7.20 7.20

Issued: #447, 450, 453, 12/30/92; #448, 451, 454, 1/27/93; others, 5/3/93.

Natl. Day, 10th Anniv. — A94

10th anniv. emblem and: a, 10c, Natl. flag. b, 20c, Hands supporting inscription. c, 30c, Natl. day emblems, 1985-93. d, 60c, Emblem with star, crossed swords.

1994, June 16 Litho. *Perf. 13*
456 A94 Strip of 4, #a.-d. 1.50 1.50

Fruit Type of 1987

Without FAO Emblem, Dated 1994

#457, Nephelium mutabile. #458, Nephelium xerospermoides. #459, Nephelium spp. #460, Nephelium macrophyllum.

1994, Aug. 8 Litho. *Perf. 13½x13*
457 A70 60c multicolored .75 .75
458 A70 60c multicolored .75 .75
459 A70 60c multicolored .75 .75
460 A70 60c multicolored .75 .75
Nos. 457-460 (4) 3.00 3.00

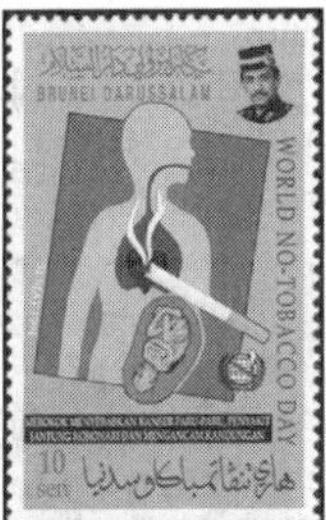

A95

A96

World Stop Smoking Day: 10c, Cigarette, lung, fetus over human figure. 15c, People throwing away tobacco, cigarettes, pipe. $2, Arms around world crushing out cigarettes.

1994, Sept. 1 Litho. *Perf. 13½x13*
461 A95 10c multicolored .20 .20
462 A95 15c multicolored .20 .20
463 A95 $2 multicolored 2.50 2.50
Nos. 461-463 (3) 2.90 2.90

1994, Oct. 7 *Perf. 13½*

Girl Guides in Brunei, 40th anniv.: a, Leader. b, Girl receiving award. c, Girl reading. d, Girls in various costumes. e, Girls camping out.

464 A96 40c Strip of 5, #a.-e. 2.50 2.50

Royal Brunei Airlines, 20th Anniv.
A97

Airplanes: 10c, Twin-engine propeller. 20c, Passenger jet attached to tow bar. $1, Passenger jet in air.

1994, Nov. 18 Litho. *Perf. 13½*
465 A97 10c multicolored .20 .20
466 A97 20c multicolored .30 .30
467 A97 $1 multicolored 1.25 1.25
Nos. 465-467 (3) 1.75 1.75

Intl. Day Against Drug Abuse — A98

Healthy people wearing traditional costumes: 20c, 60c, $1.

1994, Dec. 30 Litho. *Perf. 13½*
468 A98 Strip of 3, #a.-c. 2.25 2.25

No. 468 is a continuous design.

City of Bandar Seri Begawan, 25th Anniv.
A100

Aerial view of city: 30c, In 1970. 50c, In 1980, with details of significant buildings. $1, In 1990.

1995, Oct. 4 Litho. ***Perf. 13½***

481 A100 30c multicolored .40 .40
482 A100 50c multicolored .70 .70
483 A100 $1 multicolored 1.40 1.40
Nos. 481-483 (3) 2.50 2.50

A101

A102

UN headquarters: 20c, Delegates in General Assembly. 60c, Security Council. 90c, Exterior.

1995, Oct. 24 ***Perf. 14½x14***

484 A101 20c multicolored .30 .30
485 A101 60c multicolored .85 .85

Size: 27x44mm

486 A101 90c multicolored 1.25 1.25
Nos. 484-486 (3) 2.40 2.40

UN, 50th anniv.

1995, Oct. 28 ***Perf. 13x13½***

University of Brunei, 10th Anniv.: 30c, Students in classroom. 50c, Campus buildings. 90c, Sultan in procession.

487 A102 30c multicolored .40 .40
488 A102 50c multicolored .70 .70
489 A102 90c multicolored 1.25 1.25
Nos. 487-489 (3) 2.35 2.35

A103

A104

Royal Brunei Police, 75th Anniv.: 25c, Policemen in various uniforms. 50c, Various tasks performed by police. 75c, Sultan reviewing police.

1996, Feb. 10 Litho. ***Perf. 13½x13***

490 A103 25c multicolored .35 .35
491 A103 50c multicolored .75 .75
492 A103 75c multicolored 1.10 1.10
Nos. 490-492 (3) 2.20 2.20

1996, May 17 Litho. ***Perf. 13½***

World Telecommunications Day: 20c, Cartoon telephone, cordless telephone. 35c, Globe, telephone dial surrounded by communication devices. $1, Signals transmitting from earth, people communicating.

493 A104 20c multicolored .30 .30
494 A104 35c multicolored .50 .50
495 A104 $1 multicolored 1.40 1.40
Nos. 493-495 (3) 2.20 2.20

A105

A106

Sultan: No. 496, Among people, in black attire. No. 497, Waving, in yellow attire. No. 498, In blue shirt. No. 499, Among people, wearing cream-colored robe.
$1, Hand raised in yellow attire.

1996, July 15 Litho. ***Perf. 13***

496 A105 50c multicolored .75 .75
497 A105 50c multicolored .75 .75
498 A105 50c multicolored .75 .75
499 A105 50c multicolored .75 .75
Nos. 496-499 (4) 3.00 3.00

Souvenir Sheet

500 A105 $1 multicolored 1.40 1.40

Sultan Paduka Seri Baginda, 50th birthday.
A souvenir sheet of five $50 stamps exists.

1996, Nov. 11 Litho. ***Perf. 13½***

Terns.

501 A106 20c Black-naped tern .30 .30
502 A106 30c Roseate tern .45 .45
503 A106 $1 Bridle tern 1.40 1.40
Nos. 501-503 (3) 2.15 2.15

No. 502 is spelled "Roslate" on stamp.

Sultan Hassanal Bolkiah
A107 A108

Perf. 14x13½

1996, Oct. 9 Litho. Wmk. 387

Background Color

504 A107 10c yellow green .20 .20
505 A107 15c pale pink .20 .20
506 A107 20c lilac pink .30 .30
507 A107 30c salmon .45 .45
508 A107 50c yellow .75 .75
509 A107 60c pale green .85 .85
510 A107 75c blue 1.10 1.10
511 A107 90c lilac 1.25 1.25
512 A108 $1 pink 1.40 1.40
513 A108 $2 orange yellow 3.00 3.00
514 A108 $5 light blue 7.25 7.25
515 A108 $10 bright yellow 14.50 14.50
Nos. 504-515 (12) 31.25 31.25

Flowers
A109

1997, May 29 Litho. ***Perf. 12***

516 A109 20c Acanthus ebracteatus .30 .30
517 A109 30c Lumnitzera littorea .45 .45
518 A109 $1 Nypa fruticans 1.40 1.40
Nos. 516-518 (3) 2.15 2.15

Marine Life
A110

Designs: No. 519, Bohadschia argus. No. 520, Oxycomanthus bennetti. No. 521, Heterocentrotus mammillatus. No. 522, Linckia laevigata.

1997, Dec. 15 Litho. ***Perf. 12***

519 A110 60c multicolored .85 .85
520 A110 60c multicolored .85 .85
521 A110 60c multicolored .85 .85
522 A110 60c multicolored .85 .85
Nos. 519-522 (4) 3.40 3.40

Asian and Pacific Decade of Disabled Persons (1993-2002) — A111

Designs: 20c, Silhouettes of people, hands finger spelling "Brunei," children. 50c, Fireworks over city, blind people participating in arts, crafts, music. $1, Handicapped people playing sports.

1998, Mar. 31 Litho. ***Perf. 13x13½***

523 A111 20c multicolored .25 .25
524 A111 50c multicolored .65 .65
525 A111 $1 multicolored 1.25 1.25
Nos. 523-525 (3) 2.15 2.15

ASEAN, 30th Anniv. — A112

Designs: No. 526, Night scene of Sultan's Palace, buildings, map of Brunei. No. 527, Flags of ASEAN nations. No. 528, Daytime scenes of Sultan's Palace, transportation methods, buildings in Brunei.

1998, Aug. 8 Litho. ***Perf. 13½***

526 A112 30c multicolored .40 .40
527 A112 30c multicolored .40 .40
528 A112 30c multicolored .40 .40
Nos. 526-528 (3) 1.20 1.20

Sultan Hassanal Bolkiah, 30th Anniv. of Coronation — A113

Designs: 60c, In procession, saluting, on throne. 90c, Sultan Omar Ali Saifuddin standing, Sultan Hassanal Bolkiah on throne. $1, Procession.

1998, Aug. 1 Litho. ***Perf. 12***

529 A113 60c multicolored .65 .65
530 A113 90c multicolored 1.10 1.10
531 A113 $1 multicolored 1.25 1.25
a. Souvenir sheet, #529-531 3.00 3.00
Nos. 529-531 (3) 3.00 3.00

A114

A115

Investiture of Crown Prince Al-Muhtadee Billah: $1, Signing document. $2, Formal portrait. $3, Arms of the Crown Prince.

1998, Aug. 10

532 A114 $1 multicolored 1.25 1.25
533 A114 $2 multicolored 2.50 2.50
534 A114 $3 multicolored 3.50 3.50
a. Souvenir sheet, #532-534 7.25 7.25
Nos. 532-534 (3) 7.25 7.25

1998, Sept. 29 ***Perf. 13x13½***

30c, Hands clasped, woman, man. 60c, Dollar sign over book, arrows, "7.45AM." 90c, Silhouettes of people seated at table, standing, scales.

535 A115 30c multicolored .35 .35
536 A115 60c multicolored .70 .70
537 A115 90c multicolored 1.10 1.10
Nos. 535-537 (3) 2.15 2.15

Civil Sevice Day, 5th anniv.

A116

A117

Kingfishers.

1998, Nov. 11 Litho. ***Perf. 13½x13***

538 A116 20c Blue-eared .25 .25
539 A116 30c Common .35 .35
540 A116 60c White-collared .75 .75
541 A116 $1 Stork-billed 1.25 1.25
Nos. 538-541 (4) 2.60 2.60

1999, Feb. 23 Litho. ***Perf. 13***

National Day, 15th Anniv.: 20c, Boat docks, residential area. 60c, Methods of communications. 90c, Buildings, roadways, tower, oil rig.

542 A117 20c multicolored .25 .25
543 A117 60c multicolored .75 .75
544 A117 90c multicolored 1.10 1.10
a. Souvenir sheet, #542-544 2.25 2.25
Nos. 542-544 (3) 2.10 2.10

20th Sea Games, 1999 — A119

No. 549: a, Field hockey, cycling. b, Basketball, soccer. c, Tennis, track and field. d, Billiards. e, Bowling.
No. 550: a, Shooting. b, Golf, squash. c, Boxing. d, Kick fighting, badminton, ping pong. e, Swimming, rowing.
$1, Shooting, tennis, running, soccer, cycling, basketball.

1999, Aug. 7 Litho. *Perf. 14¼*

Strips of 5, #a.-e.

549-550 A119 20c each 2.40 2.40

Souvenir Sheet

551 A119 $1 multicolored 1.25 1.25

No. 551 contains one 35x35mm stamp.

UPU, 125th Anniv. — A120

20c, Handshake, globe, letters. 30c, Emblems of UPU, Brunei Post. 75c, Postal workers & services.

1999, Oct. 9 Litho. *Perf. 14*

552 A120 20c multicolored .25 .25
553 A120 30c multicolored .35 .35
554 A120 75c multicolored .90 .90
Nos. 552-554 (3) 1.50 1.50

Millennium A121

No. 555: a, Building with clock, children at computer. b, Building with red roof, man and woman at computer. c, Building with gray roof, mosque. d, Map of park. e, Airplane and ships. f, Satellite dishes.

Perf. 13¾x13½ Syncopated Type A

2000, Feb. 1 Litho.

555 A121 20c Strip of 6, #a-f 1.40 1.40
g. Souvenir sheet, #555 1.40 1.40

Flowers A122

Designs: 30c, Rafflesia pricei. 50c, Rhizanthes lowi. 60c, Nepenthes rafflesiana.

2000, Oct. 2 Litho. *Perf. 14¼x14*

556-558 A122 Set of 3 1.60 1.60

Asia-Pacific Economic Cooperation A123

Designs: 20c, Satellite dish, people at computers. 30c, Food processing enterprises. 60c, Eco-tourism (flower and bridge).

2000, Nov. 15 *Perf. 13½x13*

559 A123 20c multi .20 .20
a. Booklet pane of 1 .20
560 A123 30c multi .35 .35
a. Booklet pane of 1 .35
561 A123 60c multi .70 .70
a. Booklet pane of 1 .70
Booklet, #559a-561a 1.25
b. Souvenir sheet, #559-561 1.25 1.25

The 20th Century — A124

No. 562 - Scenes from: a, 1901-20. b, 1921-40. c, 1941-60. d, 1961-80. e, 1981-99.

Perf. 13¾x13½ Syncopated Type A

2000, Feb. 23 Litho.

562 Strip of 5 1.75 1.75
a.-e. A124 30c Any single .35 .35

Turtles A125

No. 563: a, Green turtle. b, Hawksbill turtle. c, Olive Ridley turtle.

2000, Nov. 16 *Perf. 13¼x13*

563 Strip of 3 1.10 1.10
a.-c. A125 30c Any single .35 .35

Sultans — A126

No. 564: a, Hashim Jalilul Alam. b, Muhammad Jamalul Alam II. c, Ahmed Tajudin. d, Haji Omar Ali Saifuddin. e, Haji Hassanal Bolkiah.

2000, July 15 Litho. *Perf. 13¾*

564 Horiz. strip of 5 3.50 3.50
a.-e. A126 60c Any single .70 .70
f. Souvenir sheet, #564, perf. 14¼x14 3.50 3.50
g. Booklet pane of 1, #564a .70
h. Booklet pane of 1, #564b .70
i. Booklet pane of 1, #564c .70
j. Booklet pane of 1, #564d .70
k. Booklet pane of 1, #564e .70
Booklet, #564g-564k 3.50

Visit Brunei Year — A127

Designs: 20c, People in boat. 30c, Houses on pilings. 60c, Shown.

2001, Mar. 14 *Perf. 14¼x13¾*

565-567 A127 Set of 3 1.25 1.25

Sultan Hassanal Bolkiah, 55th Birthday — A128

No. 568: a, Navy blue uniform. b, Light blue uniform. c, Robes. d, Camouflage uniform. e, White uniform.

No. 569, Casual shirt.

Perf. 12¼

2001, July 15 Litho. Unwmk.

568 Horiz. strip of 5 3.25 3.25
a.-e. A128 55c Any single .65 .65

Souvenir Sheet

Perf. 12

569 A128 55c multi .65 .65

No. 569 contains one 40x70mm stamp.

International Youth Camp 2001 — A129

No. 570: a, Scout, administering first aid. b, Girls, tents. c, Scouts and leader.

2001, Aug. 5 Wmk. 388 *Perf. 12¼*

570 Horiz. strip of 3 1.00 1.00
a.-c. A129 30c Any single .30 .30
d. Souvenir sheet, #570 1.00 1.00

First Intl. Islamic Expo A130

No. 571: a, Jewelry, cane. b, Mosque exterior. c, Computer, satellite dishes. d, Mosque interior.

2001, Aug. 18 Wmk. 388 *Perf. 12*

571 Horiz. strip of 4 1.00 1.00
a.-d. A130 20c Any single .25 .25

Visit Brunei Year A131

No. 572: a, Bridge. b, Waterfall. c, Aerial view of city. d, Dock.

Perf. 13¼x13½

2001, Sept. 1 Unwmk.

572 Horiz. strip of 4 1.00 1.00
a.-d. A131 20c Any single .25 .25

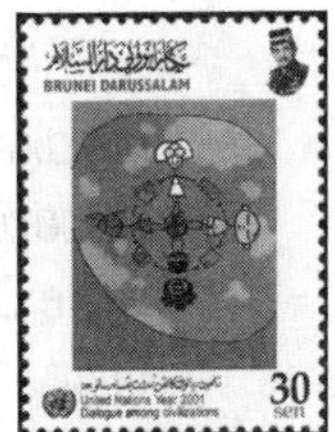

Year of Dialogue Among Civilizations A132

No. 573: a, Emblem. b, Two abstract heads. c, Cubist-style head, native. d, Multicolored leaves.

2001, Oct. 9 Unwmk. *Perf. 12*

573 Horiz. strip of 4 1.25 1.25
a.-d. A132 30c Any single .30 .30

Worldwide Fund for Nature (WWF) — A133

No. 574 - Bulwer's pheasant: a, Male and female. b, Male. c, Female and chicks. d, Female.

2001, Nov. 1 Wmk. 388 *Perf. 12*

574 Horiz. strip of 4 1.25 1.25
a.-d. A133 30c Any single .30 .30

Jabatan Telekom Brunei, 50th Anniv. — A134

No. 575: a, People, old telecommunications equipment. b, Anniversary emblem. c, Women, computer, new services.
Illustration reduced.

2002 Litho. *Perf. 12¼*

575 A134 50c Horiz. strip of 3, #a-c 1.75 1.75

Survey Department, 50th Anniv. — A135

No. 576: a, "50." b, Headquarters. c, Surveyor.

2002, July Litho. *Perf. 12¼*

576 Horiz. strip of 3 1.75 1.75
a.-c. A135 50c Any single .55 .55

Yayasan Sultan Haji Hassanal Bolkiah, 10th Anniv. — A136

No. 577: a, Stilt house community. b, Mosque. c, School and children. d, Buildings.

2002 *Perf. 12¾x12½*

577 Horiz. strip of 4 .45 .45
a.-d. A136 10c Any single .20 .20

OCCUPATION STAMPS

Issued under Japanese Occupation

Stamps and Types of 1908-37 Handstamped in Violet, Red Violet, Blue or Red

Perf. 14, 14x11½ (#N7)

1942-44 Wmk. 4

N1	A1	1c black	6.50	*24.00*
N2	A1	2c green	57.50	*110.00*
N3	A1	2c dull orange	3.00	*8.00*
N4	A1	3c green	30.00	*75.00*
N5	A1	4c orange	4.00	*14.00*
N6	A1	5c brown	4.00	*14.00*
N7	A2	6c slate gray	60.00	*200.00*
N8	A2	6c red	575.00	575.00
N9	A1	8c gray (RV)	700.00	*850.00*
N10	A2	8c carmine	5.00	*12.00*
N11	A1	10c violet, *yel*	11.00	*26.00*

N12 A2 12c blue 24.00 *26.00*
N13 A2 15c ultra 13.00 *26.00*
N14 A1 25c dk violet 24.00 *65.00*
N15 A1 30c org & red vio 100.00 *190.00*
N16 A1 50c blk, *green* 45.00 *80.00*
N17 A1 $1 red & blk, *bl* 60.00 *100.00*

Wmk. 3

N18 A1 $5 lake, *green* 900.00 *1,750.*
N19 A1 $25 black, *red* 1,000. *1,750.*

Overprints vary in shade. Nos. N3, N7, N10 and N13 without overprint are not believed to have been regularly issued.

No. 43 Surcharged in Red

1944 **Wmk. 4** ***Perf. 14***

N20 A1 $3 on 1c black *6,000. 5,500.*
a. On No. N1 *3,250. 3,250.*

BULGARIA

ˌbəl-ˈgar-ē-ə

LOCATION — Southeastern Europe bordering on the Black Sea on the east and the Danube River on the north
GOVT. — Republic
AREA — 42,855 sq. mi.
POP. — 8,194,772 (1999 est.)
CAPITAL — Sofia

In 1885 Bulgaria, then a principality under the suzerainty of the Sultan of Turkey, was joined by Eastern Rumelia. Independence from Turkey was obtained in 1908.

100 Centimes = 1 Franc
100 Stotinki = 1 Lev (1881)

Catalogue values for unused stamps in this country are for Never Hinged items, beginning with Scott 293 in the regular postage section, Scott B1 in the semi-postal section, Scott C15 in the airpost section, Scott CB1 in the airpost semi-postal section, Scott E1 in the special delivery section, Scott J47 in the postage due section, Scott O1 in the officials section, and Scott Q1 in the parcel post section.

Watermarks

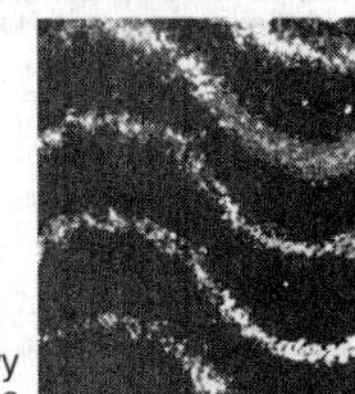

Wmk. 145- Wavy Lines

Wmk. 168- Wavy Lines and EZGV in Cyrillic

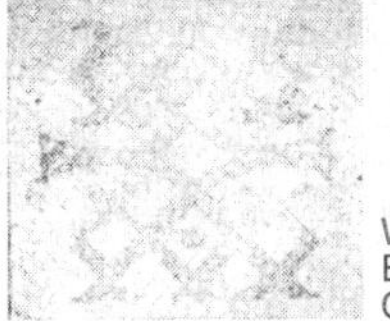

Wmk. 275- Entwined Curved Lines

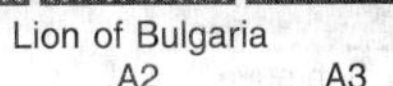

Lion of Bulgaria
A1 A2 A3

Perf. 14½x15

1879, May 1 Wmk. 168 Typo.

Laid Paper

No.	Type	Description	Unused	Used
1	A1	5c black & orange	80.00	21.00
2	A1	10c black & green	400.00	75.00
3	A1	25c black & violet	210.00	18.00
a.		Imperf.		
4	A1	50c black & blue	400.00	60.00
5	A2	1fr black & red	60.00	21.00

1881, Apr. 10

No.	Type	Description	Unused	Used
6	A3	3s red & silver	15.00	2.75
7	A3	5s black & orange	15.00	2.75
a.		Background inverted		*1,750.*
8	A3	10s black & green	75.00	8.00
9	A3	15s dp car red & green	75.00	8.00
10	A3	25s black & violet	400.00	37.50
11	A3	30s blue & fawn	21.00	8.00

1882, Dec. 4

No.	Type	Description	Unused	Used
12	A3	3s orange & yellow	1.25	.50
a.		Background inverted	*1,800.*	*1,000.*
13	A3	5s green & pale green	7.25	.60
a.		5s rose & pale rose (error)	*1,800.*	*1,800.*
14	A3	10s rose & pale rose	9.50	.90
15	A3	15s red vio & pale lil	7.25	.50
16	A3	25s blue & pale blue	7.25	.60
17	A3	30s violet & green	7.25	.90
18	A3	50s blue & pink	7.25	.90
		Nos. 12-18 (7)	47.00	4.90

See Nos. 207-210, 286.

A4 A5

Surcharged in Black, Carmine or Vermilion

1884, May 1

Typo. Surcharge

No.	Type	Description	Unused	Used
19	A4	3s on 10s rose (Bk)	125.00	37.50
20	A4	5s on 30s blue & fawn (C)	125.00	37.50
20A	A4	5s on 30s bl & fawn (Bk)	*1,750.*	*1,750.*
21	A5	15s on 25s blue (C)	175.00	50.00

On some values the surcharge may be found inverted or double.

1885, Apr. 5

Litho. Surcharge

No.	Type	Description	Unused	Used
21B	A4	3s on 10s rose (Bk)	55.00	32.50
21C	A4	5s on 30s bl & fawn (V)	60.00	42.50
21D	A5	15s on 25s blue (V)	85.00	55.00
22	A5	50s on 1fr blk & red (Bk)	225.00	150.00

Forgeries of Nos. 19-22 are plentiful.

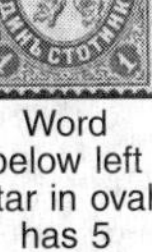

Word below left star in oval has 5 letters
A6

Third letter below left star is "A"
A7

1885, May 25

No.	Type	Description	Unused	Used
23	A6	1s gray vio & pale gray	15.00	6.00
24	A7	2s sl grn & pale gray	14.00	5.00

Word below left star has 4 letters
A8

Third letter below left star is "b" with cross-bar in upper half
A9

A10

1886-87

No.	Type	Description	Unused	Used
25	A8	1s gray vio & pale gray	1.00	.20
26	A9	2s sl grn & pale gray	1.00	.20
27	A10	1 l black & red ('87)	32.50	3.50
		Nos. 25-27 (3)	34.50	3.90

For surcharge see No. 40.

A11

Perf. 10½, 11, 11½, 13, 13½

1889 Wove Paper Unwmk.

No.	Type	Description	Unused	Used
28	A11	1s lilac	.65	.20
29	A11	2s gray	1.10	.20
30	A11	3s bister brown	.45	.20
31	A11	5s yellow green	4.50	.20
a.		Vert. pair, imperf. btwn.		
32	A11	10s rose	3.50	.20
33	A11	15s orange	10.50	.20
34	A11	25s blue	3.50	.20
35	A11	30s dk brown	6.00	.20
36	A11	50s green	.35	.30
37	A11	1 l orange red	.35	.40
		Nos. 28-37 (10)	30.90	2.30

The 10s orange is a proof.
Nos. 28-34 exist imperforate. Value, set $225.
See Nos. 39, 41-42. For overprints and surcharges see Nos. 38, 55-56, 77-81, 113.

No. 35 Surcharged in Black

1892, Jan. 26

No.	Type	Description	Unused	Used
38	A11	15s on 30s brn	12.00	1.00
a.		Inverted surcharge	*70.00*	*52.50*

1894 ***Perf. 10½, 11, 11½***

Pelure Paper

No.	Type	Description	Unused	Used
39	A11	10s red	7.00	.50
a.		Imperf.	*57.50*	

No. 26 Surcharged in Red

Wmk. Wavy Lines (168)

1895, Oct. 25 ***Perf. 14½x15***

Laid Paper

No.	Type	Description	Unused	Used
40	A9	1s on 2s	.90	.25
a.		Inverted surcharge	6.00	5.00
b.		Double surcharge	*62.50*	*62.50*
c.		Pair, one without surcharge	*125.00*	*125.00*

This surcharge on No. 24 is a proof.

Wmk. Coat of Arms in the Sheet

1896, Apr. 30 ***Perf. 11½, 13***

Wove Paper

No.	Type	Description	Unused	Used
41	A11	2 l rose & pale rose	2.50	1.75
42	A11	3 l black & buff	4.25	3.75

Coat of Arms
A14

Cherry Wood Cannon
A15

1896, Feb. 2 ***Perf. 13***

No.	Type	Description	Unused	Used
43	A14	1s blue green	.35	.20
44	A14	5s dark blue	.35	.20
45	A14	15s purple	.60	.30
46	A14	25s red	5.75	1.00
		Nos. 43-46 (4)	7.05	1.70

Baptism of Prince Boris.
Examples of Nos. 41-46 from sheet edges show no watermark.
Nos. 43, 45-46 were also printed on rough unwatermarked paper.

1901, Apr. 20 Litho. Unwmk.

No.	Type	Description	Unused	Used
53	A15	5s carmine	1.50	1.10
54	A15	15s yellow green	1.50	1.10

Insurrection of Independence in April, 1876, 25th anniversary.
Exist imperf. Forgeries exist.

Nos. 30 and 36 Surcharged in Black

1901, Mar. 24 Typo.

No.	Type	Description	Unused	Used
55	A11	5s on 3s bister brn	2.50	.90
a.		Inverted surcharge	42.50	42.50
b.		Pair, one without surcharge	*70.00*	*70.00*
56	A11	10s on 50s green	2.50	.90
a.		Inverted surcharge	50.00	50.00
b.		Pair, one without surcharge	*70.00*	*70.00*

Tsar Ferdinand
A17

Fighting at Shipka Pass
A18

ONE LEV:
Type I - The numerals in the upper corners have, at the top, a sloping serif on the left side and a short straight serif on the right.
Type II - The numerals in the upper corners are of ordinary shape without the serif at the right.

1901, Oct. 1-05 Typo. ***Perf. 12½***

No.	Type	Description	Unused	Used
57	A17	1s vio & gray blk	.20	.20
58	A17	2s brnz grn & ind	.25	.20
a.		Imperf.		
59	A17	3s orange & ind	.25	.20
60	A17	5s emerald & brn	2.25	.20
61	A17	10s rose & blk	1.50	.20
62	A17	15s claret & gray blk	.80	.20
63	A17	25s blue & blk	.80	.20
64	A17	30s bis & gray blk	18.00	.30
65	A17	50s dk blue & brn	1.00	.20
66	A17	1 l red org & brnz grn, type I	2.50	1.25
67	A17	1 l brn red & brnz grn, II ('05)	55.00	4.00
68	A17	2 l carmine & blk	5.00	.85
69	A17	3 l slate & red brn	6.00	2.25
		Nos. 57-69 (13)	93.55	10.25

For surcharges see Nos. 73, 83-85, 87-88.

1902, Aug. 29 Litho. ***Perf. 11½***

No.	Type	Description	Unused	Used
70	A18	5s lake	1.25	.45
71	A18	10s blue green	1.25	.45
72	A18	15s blue	6.25	2.00
		Nos. 70-72 (3)	8.75	2.90

Battle of Shipka Pass, 1877.
Imperf. copies are proofs.
Excellent forgeries of Nos. 70 to 72 exist.

No. 62 Surcharged in Black

1903, Oct. 1 ***Perf. 12½***

No.	Type	Description	Unused	Used
73	A17	10s on 15s	6.00	.40
a.		Inverted surcharge	*57.50*	*50.00*
b.		Double surcharge	*57.50*	*50.00*
c.		Pair, one without surcharge	*100.00*	*100.00*
d.		10s on 10s rose & black	*325.00*	*325.00*

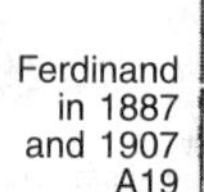

Ferdinand in 1887 and 1907
A19

1907, Aug. 12 Litho. *Perf. 11½*

74	A19	5s deep green	8.00	1.10
75	A19	10s red brown	14.00	1.10
76	A19	25s deep blue	21.00	2.10
		Nos. 74-76 (3)	43.00	4.30

Accession to the throne of Ferdinand I, 20th anniversary.

Nos. 74-76 imperf. are proofs. Nos. 74-76 exist in pairs imperforate between.

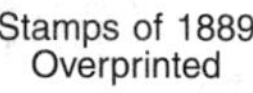

Stamps of 1889 Overprinted

1909

77	A11	1s lilac	1.25	.50
a.		Inverted overprint	21.00	17.50
b.		Double overprint, one inverted	24.00	24.00
78	A11	5s yellow green	1.25	.50
a.		Inverted overprint	25.00	25.00
b.		Double overprint	25.00	25.00

With Additional Surcharge

79	A11	5s on 30s brown (Bk)	2.00	.25
a.		"5" double		
b.		"1990" for "1909"	*700.00*	*550.00*
80	A11	10s on 15s org (Bk)	2.00	.50
a.		Inverted surcharge	17.50	17.50
b.		"1909" omitted	*27.50*	*27.50*
81	A11	10s on 50s dk grn (R)	2.00	.50
a.		"1990" for "1909"	100.00	100.00
b.		Black surcharge	52.50	52.50

Nos. 62 & 64 Surcharged with Value Only

83	A17	5s on 15s (Bl)	1.75	.60
a.		Inverted surcharge	21.00	21.00
84	A17	10s on 15s (Bl)	4.50	.40
a.		Inverted surcharge	21.00	21.00
85	A17	25s on 30s (R)	5.75	.90
a.		Double surcharge	70.00	70.00
b.		"2" of "25" omitted	87.50	87.50
c.		Blue surcharge	*275.00*	*175.00*

Nos. 59 and 62 Surcharged in Blue

1910, Oct.

87	A17	1s on 3s	4.25	.90
a.		"1910" omitted	21.00	
88	A17	5s on 15s	1.50	.60

Tsar Assen's Tower (Crown over lion)
A20

Tsar Ferdinand
A21

City of Trnovo
A22

Tsar Ferdinand
A23

Ferdinand
A24

Isker River
A25

Ferdinand
A26

Rila Monastery (Crown at UR)
A27

Tsar and Princes — A28

Ferdinand in Robes of Ancient Tsars — A29

Monastery of Holy Trinity — A30

View of Varna — A31

1911, Feb. 14 Engr. *Perf. 12*

89	A20	1s myrtle green	.20	.20
90	A21	2s car & blk	.20	.20
91	A22	3s lake & blk	.40	.20
92	A23	5s green & blk	1.00	.20
93	A24	10s dp red & blk	1.40	.20
94	A25	15s brown bister	3.00	.20
95	A26	25s ultra & blk	.50	.20
96	A27	30s blue & blk	4.00	.20
97	A28	50s ocher & blk	15.00	.25
a.		Center inverted		*2,700.*
98	A29	1 l chocolate	7.25	.20
99	A30	2 l dull pur & blk	2.00	.50
100	A31	3 l blue vio & blk	8.25	3.75
		Nos. 89-100 (12)	43.20	6.30

See Nos. 114-120, 161-162. For overprints and surcharges see Nos. 104-112, 188, B8, Greece N167-N178, N182-N187, Thrace 16-21, Romania 2N1-2N4.

Tsar Ferdinand — A32

1912, Aug. 2 Typo. *Perf. 12½*

101	A32	5s olive green	2.75	.85
a.		5s pale green	*325.00*	*150.00*
102	A32	10s claret	4.25	1.75
103	A32	25s slate	6.50	2.10
		Nos. 101-103 (3)	13.50	4.70

25th year of reign of Tsar Ferdinand.

Nos. 89-95 Overprinted in Various Colors

1913, Aug. 6 Engr.

104	A20	1s myrtle grn (C)	.20	.20
105	A21	2s car & blk (Bl)	.20	.20
107	A22	3s lake & blk (Bl Bk)	.20	.20
108	A23	5s grn & blk (R)	.20	.20
109	A24	10s dp red & blk (Bk)	.30	.20
110	A25	15s brown bis (G)	.55	.25
111	A26	25s ultra & blk (R)	2.75	.40
		Nos. 104-111 (7)	4.40	1.65

Victory over the Turks in Balkan War of 1912-1913.

No. 95 Surcharged in Red

1915, July 6

112	A26	10s on 25s	.50	.20

No. 28 Surcharged in Green

113	A11	3s on 1s lilac	3.50	4.50

Types of 1911 Re-engraved

1915, Nov. 7 *Perf. 11½, 14*

114	A20	1s dk bl grn	.20	.20
115	A23	5s grn & brn vio	1.40	.20
116	A24	10s red brn & brnsh blk	.25	.20
117	A25	15s olive green	.25	.20
118	A26	25s indigo & blk	.25	.20
119	A27	30s ol grn & red brn	.25	.20
120	A29	1 l dark brown	.30	.30
		Nos. 114-120 (7)	2.90	1.50

Widths: No. 114 is 19½mm; No. 89, 18½mm. No. 118 is 19¼mm; No. 95, 18¼mm. No. 120 is 20mm; No. 98, 19mm. The re-engraved stamps also differ from the 1911 issue in many details of design. Nos. 114-120 exist imperforate.

The 5s and 10s exist perf. 14x11½.

For Nos. 114-116 and 118 overprinted with Cyrillic characters and "1916-1917," see Romania Nos. 2N1-2N4.

Coat of Arms — A33

Peasant and Bullock — A34

Soldier and Mt. Sonichka — A35

View of Nish — A36

Town and Lake Okhrida - A37

Demir-Kapiya (Iron Gate) — A37a

View of Gevgeli — A38

Perf. 11½, 12½x13, 13x12½

1917-19 Typo.

122	A33	5s green	.30	.20
123	A34	15s slate	.20	.20
124	A35	25s blue	.20	.20
125	A36	30s orange	.20	.20
126	A37	50s violet	.50	.30
126A	A37a	2 l brn org ('19)	.50	.35
127	A38	3 l claret	1.75	1.75
		Nos. 122-127 (7)	3.65	3.20

Liberation of Macedonia. A 1 l dark green was prepared but not issued. Value $1.65.

For surcharges see Nos. B9-B10, B12.

View of Veles — A39

Monastery of St. Clement at Okhrida — A40

1918 *Perf. 13x14*

128	A39	1s gray	.20	.20
129	A40	5s green	.20	.20

Tsar Ferdinand
A41

Plowing with Oxen
A42

1918, July 1 *Perf. 12½x13*

130	A41	1s dark green	.20	.20
131	A41	2s dark brown	.20	.20
132	A41	3s indigo	.30	.20
133	A41	10s brown red	.30	.20
		Nos. 130-133 (4)	1.00	.80

Ferdinand's accession to the throne, 30th anniv.

1919 *Perf. 13½x13*

134	A42	1s gray	.20	.20

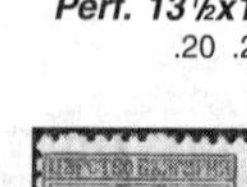

Sobranye Palace — A43

Tsar Boris III — A44

1919 *Perf. 11½x12, 12x11½*

135	A43	1s black	.20	.20
137	A43	2s olive green	.20	.20

For surcharges see Nos. 186, B1.

1919, Oct. 3

138 A44	3s orange brn	.20	.20
139 A44	5s green	.20	.20
140 A44	10s rose red	.20	.20
141 A44	15s violet	.20	.20
142 A44	25s deep blue	.20	.20
143 A44	30s chocolate	.20	.20
144 A44	50s yellow brn	.20	.20
	Nos. 138-144 (7)	1.40	1.40

1st anniv. of enthronement of Tsar Boris III.
Nos. 135-144 exist imperforate.
For surcharges see Nos. 187, B2-B7.

Birthplace of Vazov at Sopot and Cherrywood Cannon — A47

"The Bear Fighter"-a Character from "Under the Yoke" — A48

Ivan Vazov in 1870 and 1920 A49

Vazov — A50

The Monk Paisii — A52

Homes of Vazov at Plovdiv and Sofia A51

1920, Oct. 20 Photo. *Perf. 11½*

147 A47	30s brown red	.20	.20
148 A48	50s dark green	.20	.20
149 A49	1 l drab	.25	.30
150 A50	2 l light brown	.60	.60
151 A51	3 l black violet	.95	.65
152 A52	5 l deep blue	1.10	.80
	Nos. 147-152 (6)	3.30	2.75

70th birthday of Ivan Vazov (1850-1921), Bulgarian poet and novelist.
Several values of this series exist imperforate and in pairs imperforate between.

Tsar Ferdinand
A53 A54

Mt. Shar — A55

Bridge over Vardar River — A56

View of Ohrid — A57

Perf. 13x14, 14x13

1921, June 11 Typo.

153 A53	10s claret	.20	.20
154 A54	10s claret	.20	.20
155 A55	10s claret	.20	.20
156 A56	10s rose lilac	.20	.20
157 A57	20s blue	.30	.20
	Nos. 153-157 (5)	1.10	1.00

Nos. 153-157 were intended to be issued in 1915 to commemorate the liberation of Macedonia. They were not put in use until 1921. A 50s violet was prepared but never placed in use. Value $1.75.

View of Sofia — A58

"The Liberator," Monument to Alexander II A59

Monastery at Shipka Pass — A62

Tsar Boris III — A63

Harvesting Grain — A64

Tsar Assen's Tower (No crown over lion) — A65

Rila Monastery (Rosette at upper right) — A66

1921-23 Engr. *Perf. 12*

158 A58	10s blue gray	.20	.20
159 A59	20s deep green	.20	.20
160 A63	25s blue grn ('22)	.20	.20
161 A22	50s orange	.20	.20
162 A22	50s dk blue ('23)	2.50	2.50
163 A62	75s dull vio	.20	.20
164 A62	75s dp blue ('23)	.30	.20
165 A63	1 l carmine	.30	.20
166 A63	1 l dp blue ('22)	.30	.20
167 A64	2 l brown	.30	1.00
168 A65	3 l brown vio	1.40	1.10
169 A66	5 l lt blue	2.50	1.25
170 A63	10 l violet brn	6.75	2.10
	Nos. 158-170 (13)	15.35	9.55

For surcharge see No. 189.

Bourchier in Bulgarian Costume A67

James David Bourchier A68

View of Rila Monastery A69

1921, Dec. 31

171 A67	10s red orange	.20	.20
172 A67	20s orange	.20	.20
173 A68	30s dp gray	.20	.20
174 A68	50s bluish gray	.20	.20
175 A68	1 l dull vio	.20	.20
176 A69	1½ l olive grn	.20	.20
177 A69	2 l deep green	.20	.20
178 A69	3 l Prus blue	.45	.20
179 A69	5 l red brown	.85	.35
	Nos. 171-179 (9)	2.70	1.95

Death of James D. Bourchier, Balkan correspondent of the London Times.
For surcharges see Nos. B13-B16.

Postage Due Stamps of 1919-22 Surcharged

a

1924

182 D6	10s on 20s yellow	.20	.20
183 D6	20s on 5s gray grn	.20	.20
a.	20s on 5s emerald	7.00	7.00
184 D6	20s on 10s violet	.20	.20
185 D6	20s on 30s orange	.20	.20
	Nos. 182-185 (4)	.80	.80

Nos. 182 to 185 were used for ordinary postage.

Regular Issues of 1919-23 Surcharged in Blue or Red:

1 левъ
b

c

186 A43 (a)	10s on 1s black (R)	.20	.20
187 A44 (b)	1 l on 5s emer (Bl)	.20	.20
188 A22 (c)	3 l on 50s dk bl (R)	.20	.20
189 A63 (b)	6 l on 1 l car (Bl)	.60	.20
	Nos. 186-189 (4)	1.20	.80

The surcharge of No. 188 comes in three types: normal, thick and thin.
#182, 184-189 exist with inverted surcharge.

A70

Lion of Bulgaria — A71

Tsar Boris III — A72

New Sofia Cathedral — A73

Harvesting A74

1925 Typo. *Perf. 13, 11½*

191 A70	10s red & bl, *pink*	.20	.20
192 A70	15s car & org, *blue*	.20	.20
193 A70	30s blk & buff	.20	.20
a.	Cliche of 15s in plate of 30s		
194 A71	50s choc, *green*	.20	.20
195 A72	1 l dull green	.50	.20
196 A73	2 l dk grn & buff	1.10	.20
197 A74	4 l lake & yellow	1.10	.20
	Nos. 191-197 (7)	3.50	1.40

Several values of this series exist imperforate and in pairs imperforate between.
See #199, 201. For overprint see #C2.

Cathedral of Sveta Nedelya, Sofia, Ruined by Bomb — A75

1926 *Perf. 11½*

198 A75	50s gray black	.20	.20

A76 A77

Type A72 Re-engraved. (Shoulder at left does not touch frame)

1926

199 A76	1 l gray	.45	.20
a.	1 l green	.45	.20
201 A76	2 l olive brown	.50	.20

Center Embossed

202 A77	6 l dp bl & pale lemon	1.10	.20
203 A77	10 l brn blk & brn org	4.00	.75
	Nos. 199-203 (4)	6.05	1.35

For overprints see Nos. C1, C3-C4.

Christo Botev — A78

Tsar Boris III — A79

1926, June 2

204 A78	1 l olive green	.30	.20
205 A78	2 l slate violet	.90	.20
206 A78	4 l red brown	.90	.35
	Nos. 204-206 (3)	2.10	.75

Botev (1847-76), Bulgarian revolutionary, poet.

Lion Type of 1881

1927-29 *Perf. 13*

207	A3	10s dk red & drab	.20	.20
208	A3	15s blk & org ('29)	.20	.20
209	A3	30s dk bl & bis brn ('28)	.20	.20
a.		30s indigo & buff	.20	.20
210	A3	50s blk & rose red ('28)	.20	.20
		Nos. 207-210 (4)	.80	.80

1928, Oct. 3 *Perf. 11½*

211	A79	1 l olive green	.90	.20
212	A79	2 l deep brown	1.00	.20

St. Clement
A80

Konstantin Miladinov
A81

George S. Rakovski
A82

Drenovo Monastery
A83

Paisii — A84

Tsar Simeon — A85

Lyuben Karavelov
A86

Vassil Levski
A87

Georgi Benkovski
A88

Tsar Alexander II
A89

1929, May 12

213	A80	10s dk violet	.20	.20
214	A81	15s violet brn	.40	.40
215	A82	30s red	.20	.20
216	A83	50s olive grn	.25	.20
217	A84	1 l orange brn	.60	.20
218	A85	2 l dk blue	.70	.20
219	A86	3 l dull green	1.50	.45
220	A87	4 l olive brown	2.50	.25
221	A88	5 l brown	1.50	.35
222	A89	6 l Prus green	2.25	.90
		Nos. 213-222 (10)	10.10	3.35

Millenary of Tsar Simeon and 50th anniv. of the liberation of Bulgaria from the Turks.

Royal Wedding Issue

Tsar Boris and Fiancee, Princess Giovanna
A90

Queen Ioanna and Tsar Boris — A91

1930, Nov. 12 *Perf. 11½*

223	A90	1 l green	.25	.25
224	A91	2 l dull violet	.25	.30
225	A90	4 l rose red	.25	.30
226	A91	6 l dark blue	.25	.40
		Nos. 223-226 (4)	1.00	1.25

Fifty-five copies of a miniature sheet incorporating one each of Nos. 223-226 were printed and given to royal, governmental and diplomatic personages.

Tsar Boris III
A92 A93

Perf. 11½, 12x11½, 13

1931-37 **Unwmk.**

227	A92	1 l blue green	.25	.20
228	A92	2 l carmine	.40	.20
229	A92	4 l rod org ('34)	.75	.20
230	A92	4 l yel org ('37)	.20	.20
231	A92	6 l deep blue	.70	.20
232	A92	7 l dp bl ('37)	.20	.20
233	A92	10 l slate blk	8.75	.70
234	A92	12 l lt brown	.40	.20
235	A92	14 l lt brn ('37)	.30	.25
236	A93	20 l claret & org brn	1.00	.45
		Nos. 227-236 (10)	12.95	2.80

Nos. 230-233 and 235 have outer bars at top and bottom as shown on cut A92; Nos. 227-229 and 234 are without outer bars.

See Nos. 251, 279-280, 287. For surcharge see No. 252.

Balkan Games Issues

Gymnast
A95

Soccer — A96

Riding — A97

Swimmer
A100

"Victory"
A101

Designs: 6 l, Fencing. 10 l, Bicycle race.

1931, Sept. 18 *Perf. 11½*

237	A95	1 l lt green	1.75	.50
238	A96	2 l garnet	1.75	.50
239	A97	4 l carmine	4.00	.75
240	A95	6 l Prus blue	7.50	1.25
241	A95	10 l red org	20.00	3.75
242	A100	12 l dk blue	65.00	7.50
243	A101	50 l olive brn	60.00	22.50
		Nos. 237-243 (7)	160.00	36.75

1933, Jan. 5

244	A95	1 l blue grn	1.25	.95
245	A96	2 l blue	2.00	.95
246	A97	4 l brn vio	2.75	1.10
247	A95	6 l brt rose	5.00	1.60
248	A95	10 l olive brn	40.00	9.00
249	A100	12 l orange	65.00	18.00
250	A101	50 l red brown	175.00	82.50
		Nos. 244-250 (7)	291.00	114.10

Nos. 244-250 were sold only at the philatelic agency.

Boris Type of 1931
Outer Bars at Top and Bottom Removed

1933 *Perf. 13*

251	A92	6 l deep blue	.80	.20

Type of 1931 Surcharged in Blue

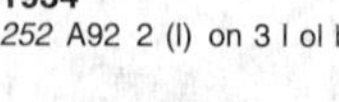

1934

252	A92	2 (l) on 3 l ol brn	4.00	.25

Soldier Defending Shipka Pass
A102

Shipka Battle Memorial
A103

Color-Bearer
A104

Veteran of the War of Liberation, 1878 — A105

Widow and Orphans — A106

Perf. 10½, 11½

1934, Aug. 26 **Wmk. 145**

253	A102	1 l green	.45	.40
254	A103	2 l pale red	.45	.25
255	A104	3 l bister brn	1.50	1.25
256	A105	4 l dk carmine	1.25	.60
257	A104	7 l dk blue	2.25	2.00
258	A106	14 l plum	6.00	5.75
		Nos. 253-258 (6)	11.90	10.25

Shipka Pass Battle memorial unveiling.

An unwatermarked miniature sheet incorporating one each of Nos. 253-258 was put on sale in 1938 in five cities at a price of 8,000 leva. Printing: 100 sheets.

1934, Sept. 21

259	A102	1 l bright green	.45	.40
260	A103	2 l dull orange	.45	.25
261	A104	3 l yellow	1.40	1.25
262	A105	4 l rose	1.25	.60
263	A104	7 l blue	2.25	2.00
264	A106	14 l olive bister	6.00	5.75
		Nos. 259-264 (6)	11.80	10.25

An unwatermarked miniature sheet incorporating one each of Nos. 259-263 was issued.

Velcho A. Djamjiyata
A108

Capt. G. S. Mamarchev
A109

1935, May 5 *Perf. 11½*

265	A108	1 l deep blue	.95	.25
266	A109	2 l maroon	.95	.30

Bulgarian uprising against the Turks, cent.

Soccer Game
A110

Cathedral of Alexander Nevski
A111

Soccer Team
A112

Symbolical of Victory
A113

Player and Trophy
A114

The Trophy
A115

1935, June 14

267	A110	1 l green	2.25	.90
268	A111	2 l blue gray	3.50	1.40
269	A112	4 l crimson	4.50	2.00
270	A113	7 l brt blue	11.00	2.50
271	A114	14 l orange	11.00	3.25
272	A115	50 l lilac brn	95.00	52.50
		Nos. 267-272 (6)	127.25	62.55

5th Balkan Soccer Tournament.

Gymnast on Parallel Bars
A116

Youth in "Yunak" Costume
A117

Girl in "Yunak" Costume
A118

Pole Vaulting
A119

Stadium, Sofia
A120

Yunak Emblem
A121

1935, July 10

No.	Type	Value	Color	Unused	Used
273	A116	1 l	green	2.10	1.10
274	A117	2 l	lt blue	3.00	1.10
275	A118	4 l	carmine	5.50	2.25
276	A119	7 l	dk blue	5.75	3.00
277	A120	14 l	dk brown	5.75	3.00
278	A121	50 l	red	67.50	42.50
			Nos. 273-278 (6)	89.60	52.95

8th tournament of the Yunak Gymnastic Organization at Sofia, July 12-14.

Boris Type of 1931

1935 Wmk. 145 *Perf. 12½, 13*

No.	Type	Value	Color	Unused	Used
279	A92	1 l	green	.30	.20
280	A92	2 l	carmine	20.00	.20

Janos Hunyadi
A122

King Ladislas Varnenchik
A123

Varna Memorial
A124

King Ladislas III — A125

Battle of Varna, 1444 — A126

1935, Aug. 4 *Perf. 10½, 11½*

No.	Type	Value	Color	Unused	Used
281	A122	1 l	brown org	1.10	.75
282	A123	2 l	maroon	1.10	.75
283	A124	4 l	vermilion	5.50	3.75
284	A125	7 l	dull blue	2.50	1.25
285	A126	14 l	green	2.50	1.25
			Nos. 281-285 (5)	12.70	7.75

Battle of Varna, and the death of the Polish King, Ladislas Varnenchik (1424-44).

Lion Type of 1881

1935 Wmk. 145 *Perf. 13*

No.	Type	Value	Color	Unused	Used
286	A3	10s	dk red & drab	.70	.20

Boris Type of 1933
Outer Bars at Top and Bottom Removed

1935

No.	Type	Value	Color	Unused	Used
287	A92	6 l	gray blue	.60	.20

Dimitr Monument
A127

Haji Dimitr — A128

Haji Dimitr and Stefan Karaja
A129

Taking the Oath — A130

Birthplace of Dimitr
A131

1935, Oct. 1 Unwmk. *Perf. 11½*

No.	Type	Value	Color	Unused	Used
288	A127	1 l	green	1.25	.35
289	A128	2 l	brown	1.75	.70
290	A129	4 l	car rose	3.50	2.50
291	A130	7 l	blue	4.50	3.50
292	A131	14 l	orange	4.50	3.50
			Nos. 288-292 (5)	15.50	10.55

67th anniv. of the death of the Bulgarian patriots, Haji Dimitr and Stefan Karaja.

Catalogue values for unused stamps in this section, from this point to the end of the section, are for Never Hinged items.

A132

A133

1936-39 *Perf. 13x12½, 13*

No.	Type	Value	Color	Unused	Used
293	A132	10s	red org ('37)	.20	.20
294	A132	15s	emerald	.20	.20
295	A133	30s	maroon	.20	.20
296	A133	30s	yel brn ('37)	.20	.20
297	A133	30s	Prus bl ('37)	.20	.20
298	A133	50s	ultra	.20	.20
299	A133	50s	dk car ('37)	.20	.20
300	A133	50s	slate grn ('39)	.20	.20
			Nos. 293-300 (8)	1.60	1.60

Meteorological Station, Mt. Moussalla
A134

Peasant Girl
A135

Town of Nessebr
A136

1936, Aug. 16 Photo. *Perf. 11½*

No.	Type	Value	Color	Unused	Used
301	A134	1 l	purple	1.40	.65
302	A135	2 l	ultra	1.40	.60
303	A136	7 l	dark blue	3.75	1.50
			Nos. 301-303 (3)	6.55	2.75

4th Geographical & Ethnographical Cong., Sofia, Aug. 1936.

Sts. Cyril and Methodius
A137

Displaying the Bible to the People
A138

1937, June 2

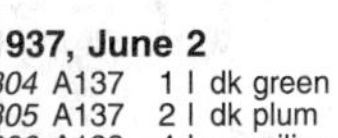

No.	Type	Value	Color	Unused	Used
304	A137	1 l	dk green	.25	.20
305	A137	2 l	dk plum	.25	.20
306	A138	4 l	vermilion	.45	.25
307	A137	7 l	dk blue	1.75	1.10
308	A138	14 l	rose red	1.75	1.10
			Nos. 304-308 (5)	4.45	2.85

Millennium of Cyrillic alphabet.

Princess Marie Louise
A139

Tsar Boris III
A140

1937, Oct. 3

No.	Type	Value	Color	Unused	Used
310	A139	1 l	yellow green	.35	.20
311	A139	2 l	brown red	.25	.20
312	A139	4 l	scarlet	.35	.20
			Nos. 310-312 (3)	.95	.60

Issued in honor of Princess Marie Louise.

1937, Oct. 3

No.	Type	Value	Color	Unused	Used
313	A140	2 l	brown red	.35	.20

19th anniv. of the accession of Tsar Boris III to the throne. See No. B11.

National Products Issue

Peasants Bundling Wheat
A141

Sunflower
A142

Wheat — A143

Chickens and Eggs — A144

Cluster of Grapes — A145

Rose and Perfume Flask — A146

Strawberries
A147

Girl Carrying Grape Clusters
A148

Rose — A149

Tobacco Leaves — A150

1938 *Perf. 13*

No.	Type	Value	Color	Unused	Used
316	A141	10s	orange	.20	.20
317	A141	10s	red org	.20	.20
318	A142	15s	brt rose	.30	.20
319	A142	15s	deep plum	.30	.20
320	A143	30s	golden brn	.20	.20
321	A143	30s	copper brn	.20	.20
322	A144	50s	black	.20	.20
323	A144	50s	indigo	.20	.20
324	A145	1 l	yel grn	.65	.20
325	A145	1 l	green	.65	.20
326	A146	2 l	rose pink	.60	.20
327	A146	2 l	rose brn	.60	.20
328	A147	3 l	dp red lil	1.25	.20
329	A147	3 l	brn lake	1.25	.20
330	A148	4 l	plum	.80	.20
331	A148	4 l	golden brn	.80	.20
332	A149	7 l	vio blue	1.50	1.50
333	A149	7 l	dp blue	1.50	1.50
334	A150	14 l	dk brown	2.25	1.90
335	A150	14 l	red brn	2.25	1.90
			Nos. 316-335 (20)	15.90	10.00

Several values of this series exist imperforate.

Crown Prince Simeon
A151 A153

Designs: 2 l, Same portrait as 1 l, value at lower left. 14 l, similar to 4 l, but no wreath.

1938, June 16

No.	Type	Value	Color	Unused	Used
336	A151	1 l	brt green	.20	.20
337	A151	2 l	rose pink	.20	.20
338	A153	4 l	dp orange	.20	.20

339	A151	7 l ultra	.80	.40
340	A153	14 l dp brown	.80	.40
		Nos. 336-340 (5)	2.20	1.40

First birthday of Prince Simeon.

Tsar Boris III
A155 A156

Various Portraits of Tsar.

1938, Oct. 3

341	A155	1 l lt green	.20	.20
342	A156	2 l rose brown	.60	.20
343	A156	4 l golden brn	.20	.20
344	A156	7 l brt ultra	1.00	1.00
345	A156	14 l deep red lilac	.35	.25
		Nos. 341-345 (5)	2.35	1.85

Reign of Tsar Boris III, 20th anniv.

Early Locomotive A160

Designs: 2 l, Modern locomotive. 4 l, Train crossing bridge. 7 l, Tsar Boris in cab.

1939, Apr. 26

346	A160	1 l yel green	.25	.20
347	A160	2 l copper brn	.25	.20
348	A160	4 l red orange	1.50	.20
349	A160	7 l dark blue	3.50	.85
		Nos. 346-349 (4)	5.50	1.45

50th anniv. of Bulgarian State Railways.

Post Horns and Arrows — A164

Central Post Office, Sofia — A165

1939, May 14 **Typo.**

350	A164	1 l yellow grn	.25	.20
351	A165	2 l brt carmine	.30	.20

Establishment of the postal system, 60th anniv.

Gymnast on Bar — A166

Yunak Emblem — A167

Discus Thrower — A168

Athletic Dancer — A169

Weight Lifter — A170

1939, July 7 **Photo.**

352	A166	1 l yel grn & pale grn	.35	.20
353	A167	2 l brt rose	.35	.20
354	A168	4 l brn & gldn brn	.50	.25
355	A169	7 l dk bl & bl	1.25	.60
356	A170	14 l plum & rose vio	5.50	2.75
		Nos. 352-356 (5)	7.95	4.00

9th tournament of the Yunak Gymnastic Organization at Sofia, July 4-8.

Tsar Boris III — A171

Bulgaria's First Stamp — A172

1940-41 **Typo.**

356A	A171	1 l dl grn ('41)	.80	.20
357	A171	2 l brt crimson	.20	.20

1940, May 19 **Photo.** ***Perf. 13***

20 l, Similar design, scroll dated "1840-1940."

358	A172	10 l olive black	1.25	.85
359	A172	20 l indigo	1.25	.85

Cent. of 1st postage stamp. Exist imperf.

Peasant Couple and Tsar Boris — A174

Flags over Wheat Field and Tsar Boris — A175

Tsar Boris and Map of Dobrudja A176

1940, Sept. 20

360	A174	1 l slate green	.20	.20
361	A175	2 l rose red	.20	.20
362	A176	4 l dark brown	.20	.20
363	A176	7 l dark blue	1.60	1.25
		Nos. 360-363 (4)	2.20	1.85

Return of Dobrudja from Romania.

Fruit A177

Bees and Flowers A178

Plowing A179

Shepherd and Sheep A180

Tsar Boris III — A181

Perf. 10, 10½x11½, 11½, 13

1940-44 **Typo.** **Unwmk.**

364	A177	10s red orange	.20	.20
365	A178	15s blue	.20	.20
366	A179	30s olive brn ('41)	.20	.20
367	A180	50s violet	.20	.20
368	A181	1 l brt green	.20	.20
369	A181	2 l rose car	.20	.20
370	A181	4 l red orange	.20	.20
371	A181	6 l red vio ('44)	.30	.20
372	A181	7 l blue	.30	.20
373	A181	10 l blue grn ('41)	.30	.20
		Nos. 364-373 (10)	2.30	2.00

See Nos. 373A-377, 440. For overprints see Nos. 455-463, C31-C32.

1940-41 **Wmk. 145** ***Perf. 13***

373A	A180	50s violet ('41)	.20	.20
374	A181	1 l brt grn	.20	.20
375	A181	2 l rose car	.20	.20
376	A181	7 l dull blue	.45	.20
377	A181	10 l blue green	.65	.20
		Nos. 373A-377 (5)	1.70	1.00

Watermarked vertically or horizontally.

P. R. Slaveikov A182

Sofronii, Bishop of Vratza A183

Saint Ivan Rilski — A184

Martin S. Drinov — A185

Monk Khrabr — A186

Kolio Ficheto — A187

1940, Sept. 23 **Photo.** **Unwmk.**

378	A182	1 l brt bl grn	.20	.20
379	A183	2 l brt carmine	.20	.20
380	A184	3 l dp red brn	.20	.20
381	A185	4 l red orange	.20	.20
382	A186	7 l deep blue	1.00	.60
383	A187	10 l dp red brn	1.50	.85
		Nos. 378-383 (6)	3.30	2.25

Liberation of Bulgaria from the Turks in 1878.

Johannes Gutenberg A188

N. Karastoyanov, 1st Bulgarian Printer A189

1940, Dec. 16

384	A188	1 l slate green	.20	.20
385	A189	2 l orange brown	.20	.20

500th anniv. of the invention of the printing press and 100th anniv. of the 1st Bulgarian printing press.

Christo Botev — A190

Monument to Botev — A192

Botev with his Insurgent Band — A191

1941, May 3

386	A190	1 l dark blue green	.20	.20
387	A191	2 l crimson rose	.20	.20
388	A192	3 l dark brown	.65	.30
		Nos. 386-388 (3)	1.05	.70

Christo Botev, patriot and poet.

Palace of Justice, Sofia — A193

20 l, Workers' hospital. 50 l, National Bank.

1941-43 **Engr.** ***Perf. 11½***

389	A193	14 l lt gray brn ('43)	.20	.20
390	A193	20 l gray grn ('43)	.40	.20
391	A193	50 l lt bl gray	1.90	1.25
		Nos. 389-391 (3)	2.50	1.65

Macedonian Woman — A196

City of Okhrida — A200

Outline of Macedonia and Tsar Boris III A197

View of Aegean Sea — A198

Poganovski Monastery A199

1941, Oct. 3 **Photo.** ***Perf. 13***

392	A196	1 l slate grn	.20	.20
393	A197	2 l crimson	.20	.20
394	A198	2 l red org	.20	.20

395 A199 4 l org brn .20 .20
396 A200 7 l dp gray bl 1.40 1.25
Nos. 392-396 (5) 2.20 2.05

Issued to commemorate the acquisition of Macedonian territory from neighboring countries.

Peasant Working in a Field — A201

Designs: 15s, Plowing. 30s, Apiary. 50s, Women harvesting fruit. 3 l, Shepherd and sheep. 5 l, Inspecting cattle.

1941-44

397 A201 10s dk violet .20 .20
398 A201 10s dk blue .20 .20
399 A201 15s Prus blue .20 .20
400 A201 15s dk ol brn .20 .20
401 A201 30s red orange .20 .20
402 A201 30s dk slate grn .20 .20
403 A201 50s blue vio .20 .20
404 A201 50s red lilac .20 .20
405 A201 3 l henna brn .40 .25
406 A201 3 l dk brn ('44) 1.40 1.10
407 A201 5 l sepia .50 .50
408 A201 5 l vio bl ('44) 1.40 1.10
Nos. 397-408 (12) 5.30 4.55

Girls Singing — A207

Boys in Camp — A208

Raising Flag — A209

Folk Dancers — A211

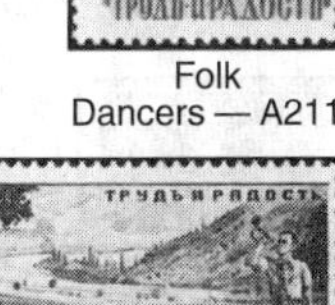
Camp Scene A210

1942, June 1 **Photo.**

409 A207 1 l dk bl grn .20 .20
410 A208 2 l scarlet .20 .20
411 A209 4 l olive gray .20 .20
412 A210 7 l deep blue .20 .20
413 A211 14 l fawn .30 .25
Nos. 409-413 (5) 1.10 1.05

National "Work and Joy" movement.

Wounded Soldier — A212

Soldier's Farewell A213

4 l, Aiding wounded soldier. 7 l, Widow & orphans at grave. 14 l, Tomb of Unknown Soldier. 20 l, Queen Ioanna visiting wounded.

1942, Sept. 7

414 A212 1 l slate grn .20 .20
415 A213 2 l brt rose .20 .20
416 A213 4 l yel org .20 .20
417 A213 7 l dark blue .20 .20
418 A213 14 l brown .20 .20
419 A213 20 l olive blk .25 .20
Nos. 414-419 (6) 1.25 1.20

Issued to aid war victims. No. 419 was printed in sheets of 50, alternating with 50 labels.

Legend of Kubrat — A218

Cavalry Charge — A219

Designs: 30s, Rider of Madara. 50s, Christening of Boris I. 1 l, School, St. Naum. 2 l, Crowning of Tsar Simeon by Boris I. 3 l, Golden era of Bulgarian literature. 4 l, Sentencing of the Bogomil Basil. 5 l, Proclamation of 2nd Bulgarian Empire. 7 l, Ivan Assen II at Trebizond. 10 l, Deporting the Patriarch Jeftimi. 14 l, Wandering minstrel. 20 l, Monk Paisii. 30 l, Monument, Shipka Pass.

1942, Oct. 12

420 A218 10s bluish blk .20 .20
421 A219 15s Prus grn .20 .20
422 A219 30s dk rose vio .20 .20
423 A219 50s indigo .20 .20
424 A219 1 l slate grn .20 .20
425 A219 2 l crimson .20 .20
426 A219 3 l brown .20 .20
427 A219 4 l orange .20 .20
428 A219 5 l grnsh blk .20 .20
429 A219 7 l dk blue .20 .20
430 A219 10 l brown blk .20 .20
431 A219 14 l olive blk .20 .20
432 A219 20 l henna brn .40 .30
433 A219 30 l black .70 .40
Nos. 420-433 (14) 3.50 3.10

Tsar Boris III A234

Designs: Various portraits of Tsar.

Perf. 13, Imperf.

1944, Feb. 28 **Photo.** **Wmk. 275**

Frames in Black

434 A234 1 l olive grn .20 .20
435 A234 2 l red brown .20 .20
436 A234 4 l brown .20 .20
437 A234 5 l gray vio .30 .20
438 A234 7 l slate blue .30 .20
Nos. 434-438 (5) 1.20 1.00

Tsar Boris III (1894-1943).

Tsar Simeon II — A239

Perf. 11½, 13

1944, June 12 **Typo.** **Unwmk.**

439 A239 3 l red orange .30 .20

Shepherd Type of 1940

1944

440 A180 50s yellow green .20 .20

Parcel Post Stamps of 1944 Overprinted in Black or Orange

1945, Jan. 25 ***Perf. 11½***

448 PP5 1 l dk carmine .20 .20
449 PP5 7 l rose lilac .20 .20
450 PP5 20 l org brn .20 .20
451 PP5 30 l dk brn car .20 .20
452 PP5 50 l red orange .25 .20
453 PP5 100 l blue (O) .60 .20

Overprint reads: "Everything for the Front."

No. 448 with Additional Surcharge of New Value in Black

454 PP5 4 l on 1 l dk car .20 .20
Nos. 448-454 (7) 1.85 1.40

Nos. 368 to 370 Overprinted in Black

1945, Mar. 15 ***Perf. 11½, 13***

455 A181 1 l brt green .25 .20
456 A181 2 l rose carmine .40 .20
457 A181 4 l red orange .60 .20

Overprint reads: "Collect old iron."

Overprinted in Black

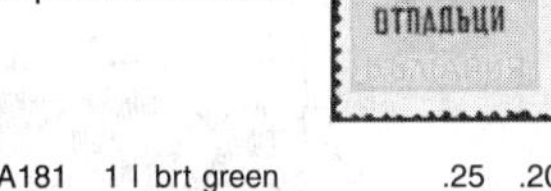

458 A181 1 l brt green .25 .20
459 A181 2 l rose carmine .40 .20
460 A181 4 l red orange .60 .20

Overprint reads: "Collect discarded paper."

Overprinted in Black

461 A181 1 l brt green .25 .20
462 A181 2 l rose carmine .40 .20
463 A181 4 l red orange .60 .20
Nos. 455-463 (9) 3.75 1.80

Overprint reads: "Collect all kinds of rags."

Oak Tree — A245

Imperf., Perf. 11½.

1945 **Litho.** **Unwmk.**

464 A245 4 l vermilion .20 .20
465 A245 10 l blue .20 .20

Imperf

466 A245 50 l brown lake .20 .20
Nos. 464-466 (3) .60 .60

Slav Congress, Sofia, March, 1945.

A246

A247

A248

A249

A251

A252

A253

A254

2 l and 4 l:
Type I. Large crown close to coat of arms.
Type II. Smaller crown standing high.

1945-46 **Photo.** ***Perf. 13***

469 A246 30s yellow grn .20 .20
470 A247 50s peacock grn .20 .20
471 A248 1 l dk green .20 .20
472 A249 2 l choc (I) .20 .20
a. Type II .20 .20
473 A249 4 l dk blue (I) .20 .20
a. Type II .20 .20
475 A251 5 l red violet .20 .20
476 A251 9 l slate gray .20 .20
477 A252 10 l Prus blue .20 .20
478 A253 15 l brown .20 .20
479 A254 20 l carmine .20 .20
480 A254 20 l gray blk .20 .20
Nos. 469-480 (11) 2.20 2.20

Breaking Chain — A255

1 Lev Coin — A256

Water Wheel — A257

Coin and Symbols of Agriculture and Industry — A258

Unwmk.

1945, June 4 Litho. *Imperf.*

Laid Paper

481 A255 50 l brn red, *pink* .20 .20
482 A255 50 l org, *pink* .20 .20
483 A256 100 l gray bl, *pink* .20 .20
484 A256 100 l brn, *pink* .20 .20
485 A257 150 l dk ol gray, *pink* .35 .20
486 A257 150 l dl car, *pink* .35 .20
487 A258 200 l dp bl, *pink* .50 .30
488 A258 200 l ol grn, *pink* .50 .30
Nos. 481-488 (8) 2.50 1.80

Souvenir Sheets

489 Sheet of 4 3.00 1.75
a. A255 50 l violet blue .30 .20
b. A256 100 l violet blue .30 .20
c. A257 150 l violet blue .30 .20
d. A258 200 l violet blue .30 .20
490 Sheet of 4 3.00 1.75
a. A255 50 l brown orange .30 .20
b. A256 100 l brown orange .30 .20
c. A257 150 l brown orange .30 .20
d. A258 200 l brown orange .30 .20

Publicizing Bulgaria's Liberty Loan.

Olive Branch — A260

1945, Sept. 1 Typo. *Perf. 13*

491 A260 10 l org brn & yel grn .20 .20
492 A260 50 l dull red & dp grn .25 .20

Victory of Allied Nations, World War II.

September 9, 1944 — A261

Numeral, Broken Chain — A262

1945, Sept. 7

493 A261 1 l gray green .20 .20
494 A261 4 l deep blue .20 .20
495 A261 5 l rose lilac .20 .20
496 A262 10 l lt blue .20 .20
497 A262 20 l brt car .20 .20
498 A261 50 l brt bl grn .40 .20
499 A261 100 l orange brn .50 .35
Nos. 493-499 (7) 1.90 1.55

1st anniv. of Bulgaria's liberation.

Old Postal Savings Emblem — A263

Child Putting Coin in Bank — A265

First Bulgarian Postal Savings Stamp A264

Postal Savings Building, Sofia — A266

1946, Apr. 12

500 A263 4 l brown org .20 .20
501 A264 10 l dk olive .20 .20
502 A265 20 l ultra .20 .20
503 A266 50 l slate gray .50 .50
Nos. 500-503 (4) 1.10 1.10

50th anniv. of Bulgarian Postal Savings.

Refugee Children A267

Nurse Assisting Wounded Soldier A269

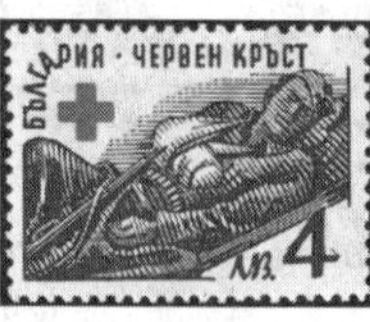

Wounded Soldier A268

35 l, 100 l, Red Cross hospital train.

1946, Apr. 4

Cross in Carmine

504 A267 2 l dk olive .20 .20
505 A268 4 l violet .20 .20
506 A267 10 l plum .20 .20
507 A268 20 l ultra .20 .20
508 A269 30 l brown org .20 .20
509 A268 35 l gray blk .20 .20
510 A269 50 l violet brn .25 .20
511 A268 100 l gray brn .70 .60
Nos. 504-511 (8) 2.15 2.00

See Nos. 553-560.

Advancing Troops A271

Grenade Thrower — A272

Attacking Planes — A274

Designs: 5 l, Horse-drawn cannon. 9 l, Engineers building pontoon bridge. 10 l, 30 l, Cavalry charge. 40 l, Horse-drawn supply column. 50 l, Motor transport column. 60 l, Infantry, tanks and planes.

1946, Aug. 9 Typo. Unwmk.

512 A271 2 l dk red vio .20 .20
513 A272 4 l dk gray .20 .20
514 A271 5 l dk org red .20 .20
515 A274 6 l black brn .20 .20
516 A271 9 l rose lilac .20 .20
517 A271 10 l dp violet .20 .20
518 A271 20 l dp blue .25 .20
519 A271 30 l red org .25 .20
520 A271 40 l dk ol bis .30 .20
521 A271 50 l dk green .30 .20
522 A271 60 l red brown .40 .30
Nos. 512-522 (11) 2.70 2.30

Bulgaria's participation in World War II.

Arms of Russia and Bulgaria A279

Lion Rampant A280

1946, May 23

523 A279 4 l red orange .20 .20
525 A279 20 l turq green .25 .20

Congress of the Bulgarian-Soviet Association, May 1946. The 4 l exists in dk car rose and 20 l in blue, value, set $7.

1946, May 25 *Imperf.*

526 A280 20 l blue .30 .25

Day of the Postage Stamp, May 26, 1946.

Alekandr Stamboliski A281

Flags of Albania, Romania, Bulgaria and Yugoslavia A282

1946, June 13 *Perf. 12*

527 A281 100 l red orange 5.00 3.00

23rd anniversary of the death of Alekandr Stamboliski, agrarian leader.

1946, July 6 *Perf. 11½*

528 A282 100 l black brown .75 .50

1946 Balkan Games.

Sheet of 100 arranged so that all stamps are tete beche vert. and horiz., except 2 center rows in left pane which provide 10 vert. pairs that are not tete beche vert.

St. Ivan Rilski — A283

A286

A284

A285

Views of Rila Monastery A287

1946, Aug. 26

529 A283 1 l red brown .20 .20
530 A284 4 l black brn .20 .20
531 A285 10 l dk green .20 .20
532 A286 20 l dp blue .20 .20
533 A287 50 l dk red .80 .50
Nos. 529-533 (5) 1.60 1.30

Millenary of Rila Monastery.

People's Republic

A288

1946, Sept. 15 Typo.

534 A288 4 l brown lake .20 .20
535 A288 20 l dull blue .20 .20
536 A288 50 l olive bister .20 .20
Nos. 534-536 (3) .60 .60

No. 535 is inscribed "BULGARIA" in Latin characters.

Referendum of Sept. 8, 1946, resulting in the establishment of the Bulgarian People's Republic.

Partisan Army — A289

Snipers — A290

Soldiers: Past and Present — A291

Design: 30 l, Partisans advancing.

1946, Dec. 2

537 A289 1 l violet brn .20 .20
538 A290 4 l dull grn .20 .20
539 A291 5 l chocolate .20 .20
540 A290 10 l crimson .20 .20
541 A289 20 l ultra .25 .20
542 A290 30 l olive bister .25 .20
543 A291 50 l black .30 .25
Nos. 537-543 (7) 1.60 1.45

Relief Worker and Children — A294

Child with Gift Parcels — A295

Waiting for Food Distribution A296

Mother and Child A297

1946, Dec. 30

545 A294 1 l dk vio brn .20 .20
546 A295 4 l brt red .20 .20
547 A295 9 l olive bis .20 .20
548 A294 10 l slate gray .20 .20
549 A296 20 l ultra .20 .20
550 A297 30 l dp brn org .20 .20
551 A296 40 l maroon .20 .20
552 A294 50 l peacock grn .30 .30
Nos. 545-552 (8) 1.70 1.70

"Bulgaria" is in Latin characters on No. 548.

Red Cross Types of 1946

1947, Jan. 31

Cross in Carmine

553 A267 2 l olive bister .20 .20
554 A268 4 l olive black .20 .20
555 A267 10 l blue grn .20 .20
556 A268 20 l brt blue .20 .20
557 A269 30 l yellow grn .30 .25
558 A268 35 l grnsh gray .30 .25
559 A269 50 l henna brn .50 .35
560 A268 100 l dark blue .70 .50
Nos. 553-560 (8) 2.60 2.15

Laurel Branch, Allied and Bulgarian Emblems A298

Dove of Peace A299

1947, Feb. 28

561 A298 4 l olive .20 .20
562 A299 10 l brown red .20 .20
563 A299 20 l deep blue .20 .20
Nos. 561-563 (3) .60 .60

Return to peace at the close of World War II. "Bulgaria" in Latin characters on No. 563.

A302

Guerrilla Fighters
A303 A304

1947, Jan. 21 ***Perf. 11½***

567 A302 10 l choc & brn org .30 .20
568 A303 20 l dk bl & bl .30 .20
569 A304 70 l dp claret & rose 20.00 20.00
Nos. 567-569 (3) 20.60 20.40

Issued to honor the anti-fascists.

Hydroelectric Station A305

Miner — A306

Symbols of Industry — A307

Tractor A308

1947, Aug. 6

570 A305 4 l olive green .20 .20
571 A306 9 l red brown .20 .20
572 A307 20 l deep blue .20 .20
573 A308 40 l olive brown .40 .30
Nos. 570-573 (4) 1.00 .90

Exhibition Building A309

Former Home of Alphonse de Lamartine A310

Symbols of Agriculture and Horticulture A311

Perf. 11x11½, 11½x11

1947, Aug. 31 **Litho.** **Unwmk.**

574 A309 4 l scarlet .20 .20
575 A310 9 l brown lake .20 .20
576 A311 20 l brt ultra .20 .20
Nos. 574-576 (3) .60 .60

Plovdiv Intl. Fair, 1947. See No. C54.

Basil Evstatiev Aprilov — A312

1947, Oct. 19 **Photo.** ***Perf. 11***

577 A312 40 l brt ultra .35 .20

Cent. of the death of Basil Evstatiev Aprilov, educator and historian. See No. 603.

Bicycle Race — A313

Basketball A314

Chess A315

Balkan Games: 20 l, Soccer players. 60 l, Four flags of participating nations.

1947, Sept. 29 **Typo.** ***Perf. 11½***

578 A313 2 l plum .20 .20
579 A314 4 l dk olive grn .20 .20
580 A315 9 l orange brn 2.00 2.00
581 A315 20 l brt ultra .80 .20
582 A315 60 l violet brn 1.60 .75
Nos. 578-582 (5) 4.80 3.35

People's Theater, Sofia A316

National Assembly A317

Central Post Office, Sofia A318

Presidential Mansion A319

1947-48 **Typo.** ***Perf. 12½***

583 A316 50s yellow grn .20 .20
584 A317 50s yellow grn .20 .20
585 A318 1 l green .20 .20
586 A319 1 l green .20 .20
587 A316 2 l brown lake .20 .20
588 A317 2 l lt brown .20 .20
589 A316 4 l deep blue .20 .20
590 A317 4 l deep blue .20 .20
591 A316 9 l carmine .35 .20
592 A317 20 l deep blue .75 .30
Nos. 583-592 (10) 2.70 2.10

On Nos. 583-592 inscription reads "Bulgarian Republic." No. 592 is inscribed in Latin characters.

Redrawn

"НАРОДНА" added to inscription

593 A318 1 l green .20 .20
594 A318 2 l brown lake .20 .20
595 A318 4 l deep blue .20 .20
Nos. 593-595 (3) .60 .60

Cyrillic inscription beneath design on Nos. 593-595 reads "Bulgarian People's Republic."

Geno Kirov — A320

Actors' Portraits: 1 l, Zlatina Nedeva. 2 l, Ivan Popov. 3 l, Athanas Kirchev. 4 l, Elena Snejina. 5 l, Stoyan Bachvarov.

Perf. 10½

1947, Dec. 8 **Unwmk.** **Litho.**

596 A320 50s bister brn .20 .20
597 A320 1 l lt blue grn .20 .20
598 A320 2 l slate green .20 .20
599 A320 3 l dp blue .20 .20
600 A320 4 l scarlet .20 .20
601 A320 5 l red brown .20 .20
Nos. 596-601,B22-B26 (11) 2.50 2.30

National Theater, 50th anniversary.

Merchant Ship "Fatherland" — A321

1947, Dec. 19

602 A321 50 l Prus bl, *cream* .45 .20

B. E. Aprilov — A322

Worker — A323

1948, Feb. 19 ***Perf. 11***

603 A322 4 l brn car, *cream* .20 .20

Centenary of the death of Basil Evstatiev Aprilov, educator and historian.

1948, Feb. 29 **Photo.** ***Perf. 11½x12***

604 A323 4 l dp blue, *cream* .20 .20

2nd Bulgarian Workers' Congress.

Self-education A324

Accordion Player — A325

Factory Recess — A326

Girl Throwing Basketball — A327

1948, Mar. 31 **Photo.**

605 A324 4 l red .20 .20
606 A325 20 l deep blue .20 .20
607 A326 40 l dull green .20 .20
608 A327 60 l brown .60 .35
Nos. 605-608 (4) 1.20 .95

Nicholas Vaptzarov — A328

Portraits: 9 l, P. K. Iavorov. 15 l, Christo Smirnenski. 20 l, Ivan Vazov. 45 l, P. R. Slaveikov.

1948, May 18 **Litho.** ***Perf. 11***

Cream Paper

611 A328 4 l brt ver .20 .20
612 A328 9 l lt brown .20 .20
613 A328 15 l claret .20 .20
614 A328 20 l deep blue .20 .20
615 A328 45 l green .30 .30
Nos. 611-615 (5) 1.10 1.10

Soviet Soldier — A329

Civilians Offering Gifts to Soldiers A330

Designs: 20 l, Soldiers, 1878 and 1944. 60 l, Stalin and Spasski Tower.

1948, July 5 **Photo.**

Cream Paper

No.	Type	Value	Color	Unused	Used
616	A329	4 l	brown org	.20	.20
617	A330	10 l	olive grn	.20	.20
618	A330	20 l	dp blue	.20	.20
619	A329	60 l	olive brn	.40	.35
			Nos. 616-619 (4)	1.00	.95

The Soviet Army.

Demeter Blagoev — A331

Monument to Bishop Andrey A332

9 l, Gabriel Genov. 60 l, Marching youths.

1948, Sept. 6 **Litho.**

Cream Paper

No.	Type	Value	Color	Unused	Used
620	A331	4 l	dk brown	.20	.20
621	A331	9 l	brown org	.20	.20
622	A332	20 l	dp blue	.20	.20
623	A332	60 l	brown	.50	.40
			Nos. 620-623 (4)	1.10	1.00

No. 623 is inscribed in Cyrillic characters.
Natl. Insurrection of 1923, 25th anniv.

Christo Smirnenski A333

Battle of Grivitza, 1877 A334

1948, Oct. 2 **Photo.** ***Perf. 11½***

Cream Paper

No.	Type	Value	Color	Unused	Used
624	A333	4 l	blue	.20	.20
625	A333	16 l	red brown	.20	.20

Christo Smirnenski, poet, 1898-1923.

1948, Nov. 1

No.	Type	Value	Color	Unused	Used
626	A334	20 l	blue	.20	.20
			Nos. 626,C56-C57 (3)	.95	.70

Romanian-Bulgarian friendship.

Bath, Gorna Banya — A335

Bath, Bankya — A336

Mineral Bath, Sofia A337

Maliovitza A338

1948-49 **Typo.** ***Perf. 12½***

No.	Type	Value	Color	Unused	Used
627	A335	2 l	red brown	.20	.20
628	A336	3 l	red orange	.20	.20
629	A337	4 l	deep blue	.20	.20
630	A338	5 l	violet brown	.20	.20
631	A336	10 l	red violet	.20	.20
632	A338	15 l	olive grn ('49)	.20	.20
633	A335	20 l	deep blue	.75	.20
			Nos. 627-633 (7)	1.95	1.40

Latin characters on No. 633. See No. 653.

Emblem of the Republic — A339

1948-50

No.	Type	Value	Color	Unused	Used
634	A339	50s	red orange	.20	.20
634A	A339	50s	org brn ('50)	.20	.20
635	A339	1 l	green	.20	.20
636	A339	9 l	black	.20	.20
			Nos. 634-636 (4)	.80	.80

Botev's Birthplace, Kalofer A340

Christo Botev — A341

Designs: 9 l, Steamer "Radetzky." 15 l, Kalofer village. 20 l, Botev in uniform. 40 l, Botev's mother. 50 l, Pen, pistol and wreath.

Perf. 11x11½, 11½

1948, Dec. 21 **Photo.**

Cream Paper

No.	Type	Value	Color	Unused	Used
638	A340	1 l	dk green	.20	.20
639	A341	4 l	violet brn	.20	.20
640	A340	9 l	violet	.20	.20
641	A340	15 l	brown	.20	.20
642	A341	20 l	blue	.20	.20
643	A340	40 l	red brown	.25	.20
644	A341	50 l	olive blk	.35	.25
			Nos. 638-644 (7)	1.60	1.45

Botev, Bulgarian natl. poet, birth cent.

Lenin — A342

Lenin Speaking — A343

1949, Jan. 24 **Unwmk.** ***Perf. 11½***

Cream Paper

No.	Type	Value	Color	Unused	Used
645	A342	4 l	brown	.25	.20
646	A343	20 l	brown red	.35	.20

25th anniversary of the death of Lenin.

Road Construction A344

Designs: 5 l, Tunnel construction. 9 l, Locomotive. 10 l, Textile worker. 20 l, Female tractor driver. 40 l, Workers in truck.

1949, Apr. 6 ***Perf. 10½***

Inscribed: "CHM"

Cream Paper

No.	Type	Value	Color	Unused	Used
647	A344	4 l	dark red	.20	.20
648	A344	5 l	dark brown	.20	.20
649	A344	9 l	dk slate grn	.25	.20
650	A344	10 l	violet	.25	.20
651	A344	20 l	dull blue	.60	.40
652	A344	40 l	brown	.95	.55
			Nos. 647-652 (6)	2.45	1.75

Honoring the Workers' Cultural Brigade.

Type of 1948
Redrawn
Country Name and "POSTA" in Latin Characters

1949 **Typo.** ***Perf. 12½***

No.	Type	Value	Color	Unused	Used
653	A337	20 l	deep blue	.55	.20

Miner — A345

1949 ***Perf. 11x11½***

No.	Type	Value	Color	Unused	Used
654	A345	4 l	dark blue	.20	.20

A347

Prime Minister George Dimitrov, 1882-1949 A348

1949, July 10 **Photo.**

No.	Type	Value	Color	Unused	Used
656	A347	4 l	red brown	.25	.20
657	A348	20 l	dark blue	.50	.20

Power Station — A349

Grain Towers — A350

Farm Machinery — A351

Tractor Parade A352

Agriculture and Industry A353

1949, Aug. 5 ***Perf. 11½x11, 11x11½***

No.	Type	Value	Color	Unused	Used
658	A349	4 l	olive green	.20	.20
659	A350	9 l	dark red	.20	.20
660	A351	15 l	purple	.20	.20
661	A352	20 l	blue	.55	.40
662	A353	50 l	orange brn	1.75	.85
			Nos. 658-662 (5)	2.90	1.85

Bulgaria's Five Year Plan.

Grenade and Javelin Throwers — A354

Hurdlers A355

Motorcycle and Tractor A356

Boy and Girl Athletes — A357

1949, Sept. 5

No.	Type	Value	Color	Unused	Used
663	A354	4 l	brown orange	.30	.20
664	A355	9 l	olive green	.60	.25
665	A356	20 l	violet blue	1.25	.65
666	A357	50 l	red brown	3.00	1.25
			Nos. 663-666 (4)	5.15	2.35

A358

Frontier Guards — A359

1949, Oct. 31

No.	Type	Value	Color	Unused	Used
667	A358	4 l	chestnut brn	.20	.20
668	A359	20 l	gray blue	.60	.25

See No. C60.

George Dimitrov — A360

Laborers of Both Sexes — A362

Allegory of Labor — A361

Workers and Flags of Bulgaria and Russia — A363

Perf. 11½

1949, Dec. 13 Photo. Unwmk.

669	A360	4 l	orange brn	.20	.20
670	A361	9 l	purple	.20	.20
671	A362	20 l	dull blue	.30	.25
672	A363	50 l	red	.65	.45
			Nos. 669-672 (4)	1.35	1.10

Joseph V. Stalin — A364

Stalin and Dove — A365

1949, Dec. 21

673	A364	4 l	deep orange	.25	.20
674	A365	40 l	rose brown	.65	.30

70th anniv. of the birth of Joseph V. Stalin.

Kharalamby Stoyanov — A366

Communications Strikers — A368

Railway Strikers A367

1950, Feb. 15

675	A366	4 l	yellow brown	.20	.20
676	A367	20 l	violet blue	.25	.20
677	A368	60 l	brown olive	.60	.40
			Nos. 675-677 (3)	1.05	.80

30th anniv. (in 1949) of the General Railway and Postal Employees' Strike of 1919.

Miner — A369

Locomotive A370

Shipbuilding — A371

Tractor A372

Stalin Central Heating Plant — A374

Textile Worker — A375

Farm Machinery A373

1950-51 *Perf. 11½, 13*

678	A369	1 l	olive	.20	.20
679	A370	2 l	gray blk	.20	.20
680	A371	3 l	gray blue	.20	.20
681	A372	4 l	dk blue grn	1.75	.50
682	A373	5 l	henna brn	.40	.20
682A	A373	9 l	gray blk ('51)	.20	.20
683	A374	10 l	dp plum ('51)	.30	.20
684	A375	15 l	dk car ('51)	.40	.20
685	A375	20 l	dk blue ('51)	.70	.40
			Nos. 678-685 (9)	4.35	2.30

No. 685 is inscribed in Latin characters. See Nos. 750-751A.

Vassil Kolarov (1877-1950) — A377

1950, Mar. 6 *Perf. 11½*

Size: 21½x31½mm

686	A377	4 l	red brown	.20	.20

Size: 27x39½mm

687	A377	20 l	violet blue	.25	.25

No. 687 has altered frame and is inscribed in Latin characters.

Stanislav Dospevski, Self-portrait A378

King Kaloyan and Desislava A379

Plowman Resting, by Christo Stanchev A380

Statue of Dimtcho Debelianov, by Ivan Lazarov — A381

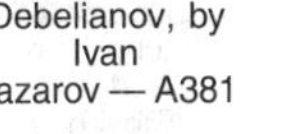
"Harvest," by V. Dimitrov — A382

Design: 9 l, Nikolai Pavlovich, self-portrait.

1950, Apr. 15 *Perf. 11½*

688	A378	1 l	dk olive grn	.30	.20
689	A379	4 l	dk red	.90	.25
690	A378	9 l	chocolate	.90	.25
691	A380	15 l	brown	1.50	.45
692	A380	20 l	deep blue	2.00	1.10
693	A381	40 l	red brown	2.75	1.50
694	A382	60 l	deep orange	4.00	2.25
			Nos. 688-694 (7)	12.35	6.00

Latin characters on No. 692.

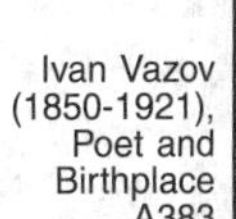

Ivan Vazov (1850-1921), Poet and Birthplace A383

1950, June 26

695	A383	4 l	olive green	.20	.20

Road Building A384

Men of Three Races and "Stalin" Flag — A385

Perf. 11½x11, 11x11½

1950, Sept. 19

696	A384	4 l	brown red	.20	.20
697	A385	20 l	violet blue	.30	.20

2nd National Peace Conference.

Molotov, Kolarov, Stalin and Dimitrov A386

Spasski Tower and Flags — A387

Russian and Bulgarian Women — A388

Loading Russian Ship — A389

Perf. 11½

1950, Oct. 10 Unwmk. Photo.

698	A386	4 l	brown	.20	.20
699	A387	9 l	rose carmine	.20	.20
700	A388	20 l	gray blue	.20	.20
701	A389	50 l	dk grnsh blue	1.10	.45
			Nos. 698-701 (4)	1.70	1.05

2nd anniversary of the Soviet-Bulgarian treaty of mutual assistance.

St. Constantine Sanatorium — A390

2 l, 10 l, Children at seashore. 5 l, Rest home.

1950 Typo.

702	A390	1 l	dark green	.20	.20
703	A390	2 l	carmine	.20	.20
704	A390	5 l	deep orange	.20	.20
705	A390	10 l	deep blue	.40	.25
			Nos. 702-705 (4)	1.00	.85

Originally prepared in 1945 as "Sunday Delivery Stamps," this issue was released for ordinary postage in 1950.

Runners — A393

1950, Aug. 21 Photo. *Perf. 11*

706	A393	4 l	shown	.25	.25
707	A393	9 l	Cycling	.35	.35
708	A393	20 l	Shot put	.45	.45
709	A393	40 l	Volleyball	.95	.95
			Nos. 706-709 (4)	2.00	2.00

Marshal Fedor I. Tolbukhin — A394

Natives Greeting Tolbukhin A395

Perf. 11½x11, 11x11½

1950, Dec. 10 Photo. Unwmk.

710 A394 4 l claret .20 .20
711 A395 20 l dk blue .35 .20

The return of Dobrich and part of the province of Dobruja from Romania to Bulgaria.

Dimitrov's Birthplace A396

George Dimitrov
A397 A398
Various Portraits, Inscribed:

Design: 2 l, Dimitrov Museum, Sofia.

1950, July 2 ***Perf. 10½***

712 A396 50s olive grn .20 .20
713 A397 50s brown .20 .20
714 A397 1 l redsh brn .25 .20
715 A396 2 l gray .25 .20
716 A397 4 l claret .45 .20
717 A397 9 l red brown .65 .25
718 A398 10 l brown red .70 .35
719 A396 15 l olive gray .70 .35
720 A396 20 l dark blue 1.75 .55
Nos. 712-720,C61 (10) 8.15 4.00

1st anniversary of the death of George Dimitrov, statesman. No. 720 is inscribed in Latin characters.

A. S. Popov — A400

1951, Feb. 10

722 A400 4 l red brown .20 .20
723 A400 20 l dark blue .55 .20

No. 723 is inscribed in Latin characters.

Arms of Bulgaria
A401 A402

1950 Unwmk. Typo. ***Perf. 13***

724 A401 2 l dk brown .20 .20
725 A401 3 l rose .20 .20
726 A402 5 l carmine .20 .20
727 A402 9 l aqua .20 .20
Nos. 724-727 (4) .80 .80

Nos. 724-727 were prepared in 1947 for official use but were issued as regular postage stamps Oct. 1, 1950.

Heroes Chankova, Antonov-Malchik, Dimitrov and Dimitrova — A403

Stanke Dimitrov-Marek A404

George Kirkov A405

George Dimitrov at Leipzig A406

Natcho Ivanov and Avr. Stoyanov A407

9 l, Anton Ivanov. 15 l, Christo Michailov.

1951, Mar. 25 Photo. ***Perf. 11½***

728 A403 1 l red violet .20 .20
729 A404 2 l dk red brn .20 .20
730 A405 4 l car rose .20 .20
731 A405 9 l orange brn .45 .20
732 A405 15 l olive brn .80 .25
733 A406 20 l dark blue 1.10 .55
734 A407 50 l olive gray 2.50 .90
Nos. 728-734 (7) 5.45 2.50

First Bulgarian Tractor A408

First Steam Roller — A409

First Truck — A410

Bulgarian Embroidery — A411

15 l, Carpet. 20 l, Tobacco & roses. 40 l, Fruits.

Perf. 11x10½

1951, Mar. 30 Photo. Unwmk.

735 A408 1 l olive brn .20 .20
736 A409 2 l violet .30 .20
737 A410 4 l red brown .50 .20
738 A411 9 l purple .70 .20
739 A409 15 l deep plum 1.00 .30
740 A411 20 l violet blue 1.50 .30
741 A410 40 l deep green 2.50 .65

Perf. 13

Size: 23x18½mm

742 A408 1 l purple .20 .20
743 A409 2 l Prus green .28 .20
744 A410 4 l red brown .28 .20
Nos. 735-744 (10) 7.46 2.65

See #894, 973. For surcharge see #973.

Turkish Attack on Mt. Zlee Dol A412

Designs: 4 l, Georgi Benkovski speaking to rebels. 9 l, Cherrywood cannon of 1876 and Russian cavalry, 1945. 20 l, Rebel, 1876 and partisan, 1944. 40 l, Benkovski and Dimitrov.

1951, May 3 ***Perf. 10½***

Cream Paper

745 A412 1 l redsh brown .20 .20
746 A412 4 l dark green .20 .20
747 A412 9 l violet brown .50 .30
748 A412 20 l deep blue .65 .50
749 A412 40 l dark red 1.00 .70
Nos. 745-749 (5) 2.55 1.90

75th anniv. of the "April" revolution.

Industrial Types of 1950

1951 ***Perf. 13***

750 A369 1 l violet .20 .20
751 A370 2 l dk brown .20 .20
751A A372 4 l dk yel grn .75 .20
Nos. 750-751A (3) 1.15 .60

Demeter Blagoev Addressing 1891 Congress at Busludja — A413

1951 Photo. ***Perf. 11***

752 A413 1 l purple .25 .20
753 A413 4 l dark green .35 .20
754 A413 9 l deep claret .65 .30
Nos. 752-754 (3) 1.25 .70

60th anniversary of the first Congress of the Bulgarian Social-Democratic Party.
See Nos. 1174-1176.

Day Nursery A414

Designs: 4 l, Model building construction. 9 l, Playground. 20 l, Children's town.

1951, Oct. 10 Unwmk.

755 A414 1 l brown .20 .20
756 A414 4 l deep plum .20 .20
757 A414 9 l blue green .60 .25
758 A414 20 l deep blue 1.00 .55
Nos. 755-758 (4) 2.00 1.20

Children's Day, Sept. 25, 1951.

Order of Labor
A415 A416

1952, Feb. 1 ***Perf. 13***

Reverse of Medal

759 A415 1 l red brown .20 .20
760 A415 4 l blue green .20 .20
761 A415 9 l dark blue .30 .20

Obverse of Medal

762 A416 1 l carmine .20 .20
763 A416 4 l green .20 .20
764 A416 9 l purple .30 .20
Nos. 759-764 (6) 1.40 1.20

No. 764 has numeral at lower left and different background.

Workers and Symbols of Industry — A417

Design: 4 l, Flags, Dimitrov, Chervenkov.

1951, Dec. 29 ***Perf. 11***

Inscribed: "16 XII 1951"

765 A417 1 l olive black .20 .20
766 A417 4 l chocolate .20 .20

Third Congress of Bulgarian General Workers' Professional Union.

Dimitrov and Chemical Works — A418

George Dimitrov and V. Chervenkov — A419

Portrait: 80s, Dimitrov.

Unwmk.

1952, June 18 Photo. ***Perf. 11***

767 A418 16s brown .35 .25
768 A419 44s brown carmine .55 .25
769 A418 80s brt blue 1.10 .50
Nos. 767-769 (3) 2.00 1.00

70th anniv. of the birth of George Dimitrov.

Vassil Kolarov Dam — A420

Republika Power Station — A421

1952, May 16 ***Perf. 13***

770 A420 4s dark green .20 .20
771 A420 12s purple .20 .20
772 A420 16s red brown .20 .20
773 A420 44s rose brown .50 .20
774 A420 80s brt blue 1.60 .20
Nos. 770-774 (5) 2.70 1.00

No. 774 is inscribed in Latin characters.

1952, June 30 ***Perf. 13, Pin Perf.***

775 A421 16s dark brown .20 .20
776 A421 44s magenta .75 .20

Nikolai I. Vapzarov A422

Designs: Various portraits.

1952, July 23 *Perf. 10½*

777 A422 16s rose brown .20 .20
778 A422 44s dk red brn .65 .20
779 A422 80s dk olive brn 1.40 .50
Nos. 777-779 (3) 2.25 .90

10th anniversary of the death of Nikolai I. Vapzarov, poet and revolutionary.

Dimitrov and Youth Conference — A423

16s, Resistance movement incident. 44s, Frontier guards & industrial scene. 80s, George Dimitrov & young workers.

1952, Sept. 1 *Perf. 11x11½*

780 A423 2s brown carmine .20 .20
781 A423 16s purple .20 .20
782 A423 44s dark green .50 .30
783 A423 80s dark brown 1.10 .60
Nos. 780-783 (4) 2.00 1.30

40th anniv. of the founding conference of the Union of Social Democratic Youth.

Assault on the Winter Palace — A424

Designs: 8s, Volga-Don Canal. 16s, Symbols of world peace. 44s, Lenin and Stalin. 80s, Himlay hydroelectric station.

Perf. 11½
1952, Nov. 6 Unwmk. Photo.
Dated: "1917-1952"

784 A424 4s red brown .20 .20
785 A424 8s dark green .20 .20
786 A424 16s dark blue .30 .20
787 A424 44s brown .45 .20
788 A424 80s olive brown .85 .35
Nos. 784-788 (5) 2.00 1.15

35th anniv. of the Russian revolution.

Vassil Levski — A425

Design: 44s, Levski and comrades.

1953, Feb. 19 *Perf. 11*
Cream Paper

789 A425 16s brown .20 .20
790 A425 44s brown blk .25 .20

80th anniv. of the death of Levski, patriot.

Ferrying Artillery and Troops into Battle A426

Soldier A427

Mother and Children A428

Designs: 44s, Victorious soldiers. 80s, Soldier welcomed. 1 l, Monuments.

1953, Mar. 3 *Perf. 10½*

791 A426 8s Prus green .20 .20
792 A427 16s dp brown .25 .20
793 A426 44s dk slate grn .40 .20
794 A426 80s dull red brn 1.50 1.25
795 A426 1 l black 1.10 .30
Nos. 791-795 (5) 3.45 2.15

Bulgaria's independence from Turkey, 75th anniv.

1953, Mar. 9

796 A428 16s slate green .20 .20
797 A428 16s bright blue .20 .20

Women's Day.

Woodcarvings at Rila Monastery
A429 A430

Designs: 12s, 16s, 28s, Woodcarvings, Rila Monastery. 44s, Carved Ceilings, Trnovo. 80s, 1 l, 4 l, Carvings, Pasardjik.

1953 Unwmk. Photo. *Perf. 13*

798 A429 2s gray brown .20 .20
799 A430 8s dk slate grn .20 .20
800 A430 12s brown .20 .20
801 A430 16s rose lake .25 .20
802 A429 28s dk olive grn .30 .20
803 A430 44s dk brown .50 .20
804 A430 80s ultra .85 .20
805 A430 1 l violet blue 1.75 .25
806 A430 4 l rose lake 3.50 .90
Nos. 798-806 (9) 7.75 2.55

For surcharge see No. 1204.

Karl Marx — A431

"Das Kapital" — A432

1953, Apr. 30 *Perf. 10½*

807 A431 16s bright blue .20 .20
808 A432 44s deep brown .30 .20

70th anniversary of the death of Karl Marx.

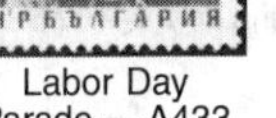

Labor Day Parade — A433

Joseph V. Stalin — A434

1953, Apr. 30 *Perf. 13*

809 A433 16s brown red .20 .20

Labor Day, May 1, 1953.

1953, May 23 *Perf. 13x13½*

810 A434 16s dark gray .25 .20
811 A434 16s dark brown .25 .20

Death of Joseph V. Stalin, Mar. 5, 1953.

Georgi Delchev — A435

Battle Scene — A436

Peasants Attacking Turkish Troops A437

1953, Aug. 8 *Perf. 13*

812 A435 16s dark brown .20 .20
813 A436 44s purple .30 .20
814 A437 1 l deep claret .45 .20
Nos. 812-814 (3) .95 .60

50th anniv. of the Ilinden Revolt (#812, 814) and the Preobrazhene Revolt (#813).

Soldier and Rebels A438

44s, Soldier guarding industrial construction.

1953, Sept. 18

815 A438 16s deep claret .20 .20
816 A438 44s greenish blue .35 .20

Army Day.

George Dimitrov and Vassil Kolarov A439

Demeter Blagoev — A440

Designs: 16s, Citizens in revolt. 44s, Attack.

1953, Sept. 22

817 A439 8s olive gray .20 .20
818 A439 16s dk red brn .20 .20
819 A439 44s cerise .45 .20
Nos. 817-819 (3) .85 .60

September Revolution, 30th anniversary.

1953, Sept. 21

Portraits: 44s, G. Dimitrov and D. Blagoev.

820 A440 16s brown .25 .20
821 A440 44s red brown .40 .20

50th anniversary of the formation of the Social Democratic Party.

Railway Viaduct A441

Pouring Molten Metal — A442

Designs: 16s, Welder and storage tanks. 80s, Harvesting machine.

1953, Oct. 17

826 A441 8s brt blue .20 .20
827 A441 16s grnsh blk .20 .20
828 A442 44s brown red .30 .20
829 A441 80s orange .45 .30
Nos. 826-829 (4) 1.15 .90

Month of Bulgarian-Russian friendship.

Belladonna A443

Kolarov Library, Sofia A444

Medicinal Flowers: 4s, Jimson weed. 8s, Sage. 12s, Dog rose. 16s, Gentian. 20s, Poppy. 28s, Peppermint. 40s, Bear grass. 44s, Coltsfoot. 80s, Cowslip. 1 l, Dandelion. 2 l, Foxglove.

1953 Unwmk. Photo. *Perf. 13*
White or Cream Paper

830 A443 2s dull blue .20 .20
831 A443 4s brown org .20 .20
832 A443 8s blue grn .20 .20
833 A443 12s brown org .20 .20
834 A443 12s blue grn .20 .20
835 A443 16s violet blue .20 .20
836 A443 16s dp red brn .25 .25
837 A443 20s car rose .20 .20
838 A443 28s dk gray grn .35 .35
839 A443 40s dark blue .40 .40
840 A443 44s brown .40 .40
841 A443 80s yellow brn .80 .80
842 A443 1 l henna brn 2.00 .50
843 A443 2 l purple 3.50 1.25
a. Souvenir sheet 27.50 25.00
Nos. 830-843 (14) 9.10 5.35

No. 843a contains 12 stamps, one of each denomination above, printed in dark green. Size: 161x172mm. Sold for 6 leva.

1953, Dec. 16

854 A444 44s brown .25 .20

75th anniversary of the founding of the Kolarov Library, Sofia.

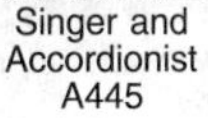

Singer and Accordionist A445

Lenin and Stalin A446

1953, Dec. 26

855 A445 16s shown .20 .20
856 A445 44s Dancers .20 .20

1954, Mar. 13

Designs: 44s, Lenin statue. 80s, Lenin mausoleum, Moscow. 1 l, Lenin.

Cream Paper

857 A446	16s brown		.20	.20
858 A446	44s rose brown		.35	.20
859 A446	80s blue		.50	.20
860 A446	1 l dp olive grn		.75	.50
	Nos. 857-860 (4)		1.80	1.10

30th anniversary of the death of Lenin.

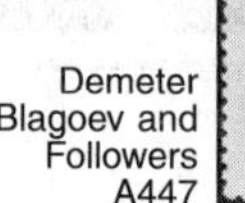

Demeter Blagoev and Followers A447

Design: 44s, Blagoev at desk.

1954, Apr. 28

Cream Paper

861 A447	16s dp red brn	.20	.20
862 A447	44s black brn	.30	.20

30th anniv. of the death of Demeter Blagoev.

George Dimitrov — A448

Dimitrov and Refinery A449

1954, June 11

863 A448	44s lake, *cream*	.25	.20
864 A449	80s brown, *cream*	.65	.20

5th anniv. of the death of George Dimitrov.

Train Leaving Tunnel — A450

1954, July 30

865 A450	44s dk grn, *cream*	.60	.20
866 A450	44s blk brn, *cream*	.60	.20

Day of the Railroads, Aug. 1, 1954.

Miner at Work — A451

1954, Aug. 19

867 A451	44s grnsh blk, *cream*	.20	.20

Miners' Day.

Academy of Science A452

1954, Oct. 27

868 A452	80s black, *cream*	.55	.20

85th anniversary of the foundation of the Bulgarian Academy of Science.

Horsemanship — A454

16s, 44s, 2 l, vert.

1954, Dec. 21

869 A454	16s Gymnastics	.50	.25
870 A454	44s Wrestling	.60	.35
871 A454	80s shown	1.25	.90
872 A454	2 l Skiing	3.00	2.75
	Nos. 869-872 (4)	5.35	4.25

Welcoming Liberators A455

Soldier's Return — A456

28s, Refinery. 44s, Dimitrov & Workers. 80s, Girl & boy. 1 l, George Dimitrov.

1954, Oct. 4

Cream Paper

873 A455	12s brown car	.20	.20
874 A456	16s dp carmine	.20	.20
875 A455	28s indigo	.20	.20
876 A455	44s redsh brn	.20	.20
877 A456	80s deep blue	.55	.25
878 A456	1 l dark green	.55	.25
	Nos. 873-878 (6)	1.90	1.30

10th anniversary of Bulgaria's liberation.

Recreation at Workers' Rest Home — A457

Metal Worker and Furnace — A458

80s, Dimitrov, Blagoev, Kirkov.

Unwmk.

1954, Dec. 28 Photo. *Perf. 13*

Cream Paper

879 A457	16s dark green	.20	.20
880 A458	44s brown orange	.20	.20
881 A457	80s dp violet blue	.40	.20
	Nos. 879-881 (3)	.80	.60

50th anniversary of Bulgaria's trade union movement.

Geese — A459

Designs: 4s, Chickens. 12s, Hogs. 16s, Sheep. 28s, Telephone building. 44s, Communist party headquarters. 80s, Apartment buildings. 1 l, St. Kiradgieff Mills.

1955-56

882 A459	2s dk blue grn	.20	.20
883 A459	4s olive green	.30	.20
884 A459	12s dk red brn	.40	.20
885 A459	16s brown orange	.65	.20
886 A459	28s violet blue	.30	.20
887 A459	44s lil red, *cream*	.60	.20
a.	44s brown red	4.50	1.00
888 A459	80s dk red brown	.75	.20
889 A459	1 l dk blue green	1.50	.20
	Nos. 882-889 (8)	4.70	1.60

Issued: #887, 4/20/56; others, 2/19/55.

Textile Worker A460

Mother and Child — A461

Design: 16s, Woman feeding calf.

1955, Mar. 5

890 A460	12s dark brown	.20	.20
891 A460	16s dark green	.20	.20
892 A461	44s dk car rose	.50	.20
893 A461	44s blue	.50	.20
	Nos. 890-893 (4)	1.40	.80

Women's Day, Mar. 8, 1955.

No. 744 Surcharged in Blue

1955, Mar. 8 *Perf. 13*

894 A410	16s on 4 l red brown	.45	.20

May Day Demonstration of Workers — A462

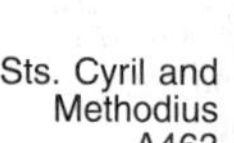

Sts. Cyril and Methodius A463

Design: 44s, Three workers and globe.

1955, Apr. 23 Photo.

895 A462	16s car rose	.20	.20
896 A462	44s blue	.30	.20

Labor Day, May 1, 1955.

1955, May 21

Designs: 8s, Paisii Hilendarski. 16s, Nicolas Karastoyanov's printing press. 28s, Christo Botev. 44s, Ivan Vazov. 80s, Demeter Blagoev and socialist papers. 2 l, Blagoev printing plant, Sofia.

Cream Paper

897 A463	4s deep blue	.20	.20
898 A463	8s olive	.20	.20
899 A463	16s black	.20	.20
900 A463	28s henna brn	.20	.20
901 A463	44s brown	.30	.20
902 A463	80s rose red	.50	.20
903 A463	2 l black	1.50	.40
	Nos. 897-903 (7)	3.10	1.60

Creation of the Cyrillic alphabet, 1100th anniv. Latin lettering at bottom on #901-903.

Sergei Rumyantzev A464

Mother and Children A465

16s, Christo Jassenov. 44s, Geo Milev.

1955, June 30 Unwmk. *Perf. 13*

Cream Paper

904 A464	12s orange brn	.20	.20
905 A464	16s lt brown	.20	.20
906 A464	44s grnsh blk	.40	.20
	Nos. 904-906 (3)	.80	.60

30th anniv. of the deaths of Sergei Rumyanchev, Christo Jassenov and Geo Milev. Latin lettering at bottom of No. 906.

1955, July 30

907 A465	44s brn car, *cream*	.30	.20

World Congress of Mothers in Lausanne, 1955.

Young People of Three Races — A466

Friedrich Engels and Book — A467

1955, July 30

908 A466	44s blue, *cream*	.30	.20

5th World Festival of Youth in Warsaw, July 31-Aug. 14.

1955, July 30

909 A467	44s brown	.30	.20

60th anniv. of the death of Friedrich Engels.

Entrance to Fair, 1892 — A468

Statuary Group at Fair, 1955 — A469

Designs: 44s, "Fruit of our Land." 80s, Woman holding Fair emblem.

1955, Aug. 31

Cream Paper

910 A468	4s deep brown	.20	.20
911 A469	16s dk car rose	.20	.20
912 A468	44s olive blk	.20	.20
913 A469	80s deep blue	.45	.20
	Nos. 910-913 (4)	1.05	.80

16th International Plovdiv Fair. Latin lettering on Nos. 912-913.

Friedrich von Schiller — A470

44s, Adam Mickiewicz. 60s, Hans Christian Andersen. 80s, Baron de Montesquieu. 1 l, Miguel de Cervantes. 2 l, Walt Whitman.

1955, Oct. 31

Cream Paper

914 A470 16s brown .25 .20
915 A470 44s brown red .50 .20
916 A470 60s Prus blue .70 .20
917 A470 80s black .85 .30
918 A470 1 l rose violet 1.60 .75
919 A470 2 l olive green 2.10 1.60
Nos. 914-919 (6) 6.00 3.25

Various anniversaries of famous writers. Nos. 918 and 919 are issued in sheets alternating with labels without franking value. The labels show title pages for Leaves of Grass and Don Quixote in English and Spanish, respectively. Latin lettering on #915-919.

A471

A472 A473

2s, Karl Marx Industrial Plant. 4s, Alekandr Stamboliski Dam. 16s, Bridge over Danube. 44s, Friendship Monument. 80s, I. V. Michurin. 1 l, Vladimir V. Mayakovsky.

1955, Dec. 1 **Unwmk.**

920 A471 2s slate blk .20 .20
921 A471 4s deep blue .20 .20
922 A471 16s dk blue grn .20 .20
923 A472 44s red brown .20 .20
924 A473 80s dark green .25 .20
925 A473 1 l gray blk .40 .20
Nos. 920-925 (6) 1.45 1.20

Russian-Bulgarian friendship.

Library Seal — A474

Krusto Pishurka A475

Portrait: 44s, Bacho Kiro.

1956, Feb. 10 ***Perf. 11x10½***

926 A474 12s car lake, *cream* .20 .20
927 A475 16s dp brn, *cream* .20 .20
928 A475 44s slate blk, *cream* .25 .20
Nos. 926-928 (3) .65 .60

100th anniversary of the National Library. Latin lettering at bottom of No. 928.

Canceled to Order

Beginning about 1956, some issues were sold in sheets canceled to order. Values in second column when much less than unused are for "CTO" copies. Postally used stamps are valued at slightly less than, or the same as, unused.

Quinces — A476

Cherrywood Cannon A477

8s, Pears. 16s, Apples. 44s, Grapes.

1956 **Photo.** ***Perf. 13***

929 A476 4s carmine .75 .20
930 A476 8s blue green .30 .20
931 A476 16s lilac rose .80 .20
932 A476 44s deep violet .80 .20
Nos. 929-932 (4) 2.65 .80

Latin lettering on #932. See #964-967. For surcharge see #1364.

1956, Apr. 28 ***Perf. 11x10½***

933 A477 16s shown .20 .20
934 A477 44s Cavalry attack .25 .20

April Uprising against Turkish rule, 80th anniv.

Demeter Blagoev (1856-1924), Writer, Birthplace A478

Cherries — A479

1956, May 30 ***Perf. 11***

935 A478 44s Prus blue .25 .20

1956 **Unwmk.** ***Perf. 13***

936 A479 2s shown .20 .20
937 A479 12s Plums .20 .20
938 A479 28s Peaches .20 .20
939 A479 80s Strawberries .55 .20
Nos. 936-939 (4) 1.15 .80

Latin lettering on No. 939.

Gymnastics A480

Pole Vaulting A481

Designs: 12s, Discus throw. 44s, Soccer, 80s, Basketball. 1 l, Boxing.

Perf. 11x10½, 10½x11

1956, Aug. 29

940 A480 4s brt ultra .25 .20
941 A480 12s brick red .35 .20
942 A481 16s yellow brn .40 .20
943 A481 44s dark green .75 .35
944 A480 80s dark red brn 1.25 .75
945 A481 1 l deep magenta 1.75 1.00
Nos. 940-945 (6) 4.75 2.70

Latin lettering on Nos. 943-945.

16th Olympic Games at Melbourne, Nov. 22-Dec. 8, 1956.

Tobacco, Rose and Distillery — A482

People's Theater A483

1956, Sept. 1 ***Perf. 13***

946 A482 44s deep carmine .75 .75
947 A482 44s olive green .75 .75

17th International Plovdiv Fair.

1956, Nov. 16 **Unwmk.**

Design: 44s, Dobri Woinikoff and Sawa Dobroplodni, dramatists.

948 A483 16s dull red brown .20 .20
949 A483 44s dark blue green .25 .20

Bulgarian Theater centenary.

Benjamin Franklin — A484

Cyclists, Palms and Pyramids — A485

Portraits: 20s, Rembrandt. 40s, Mozart. 44s, Heinrich Heine. 60s, Shaw. 80s, Dostoevski. 1 l, Ibsen. 2 l, Pierre Curie.

1956, Dec. 29

950 A484 16s dark olive grn .20 .20
951 A484 20s brown .20 .20
952 A484 40s dark car rose .20 .20
953 A484 44s dark violet brn .25 .20
954 A484 60s dark slate .30 .20
955 A484 80s dark brown .45 .20
956 A484 1 l bluish grn .80 .30
957 A484 2 l Prus green 1.75 .50
Nos. 950-957 (8) 4.15 2.00

Great personalities of the world.

1957, Mar. 6 **Photo.** ***Perf. 10½***

958 A485 80s henna brown .50 .25
959 A485 80s Prus green .50 .25

Fourth Egyptian bicycle race.

Woman Technician A486

"New Times" Review — A487

Designs: 16s, Woman and children. 44s, Woman feeding chickens.

1957, Mar. 8

960 A486 12s deep blue .20 .20
961 A486 16s henna brown .20 .20
962 A486 44s slate green .30 .20
Nos. 960-962 (3) .70 .60

Women's Day. Latin lettering on 44s.

1957, Mar. 8 **Unwmk.**

963 A487 16s deep carmine .20 .20

60th anniversary of the founding of the "New Times" review.

Fruit Type of 1956.

4s, Quinces. 8s, Pears. 16s, Apples. 44s, Grapes.

1957 **Photo.** ***Perf. 13***

964 A476 4s yellow green .20 .20
965 A476 8s brown orange .20 .20
966 A476 16s rose red .20 .20
967 A476 44s orange yellow .40 .20
Nos. 964-967 (4) 1.00 .80

Latin lettering on #967. For surcharge see #1364.

Sts. Cyril and Methodius — A488

Basketball A489

1957, May 22 ***Perf. 11***

968 A488 44s olive grn & buff .50 .20

Centenary of the first public veneration of Sts. Cyril and Methodius, inventors of the Cyrillic alphabet.

1957, June 20 **Photo.** ***Perf. 10½x11***

969 A489 44s dark green .95 .30

10th European Basketball Championship at Sofia.

Dancer and Spasski Tower, Moscow — A490

1957, July 18 ***Perf. 13***

970 A490 44s blue .30 .20

Sixth World Youth Festival in Moscow.

George Dimitrov (1882-1949) — A491

1957, July 18
971 A491 44s deep carmine .50 .20

Vassil Levski — A492

1957, July 18 ***Perf. 11***
972 A492 44s grnsh black .30 .20

120th anniversary of the birth of Vassil Levski, patriot and national hero.

No. 742 Surcharged in Carmine

1957 **Unwmk.** ***Perf. 13***
973 A408 16s on 1 l purple .20 .20

Trnovo and Lazarus L. Zamenhof A493

1957, July 27
974 A493 44s slate green .50 .20

50th anniv. of the Bulgarian Esperanto Society and the 70th anniv. of Esperanto.
For surcharge see No. 1235.

Bulgarian Veteran of 1877 War and Russian Soldier — A494

Design: 44s, Battle of Shipka Pass.

1957, Aug. 13
975 A494 16s dk blue grn .20 .20
976 A494 44s brown .30 .20

80th anniversary of Bulgaria's liberation from the Turks. Latin lettering on No. 976.

Woman Planting Tree — A495

Red Deer in Forest — A496

16s, Dam, lake and forest. 44s, Plane over forest. 80s, Fields on edge of forest.

1957, Sept. 16 **Photo.** ***Perf. 13***
977 A495 2s deep green .20 .20
978 A496 12s dark brown .20 .20
979 A496 16s Prus blue .20 .20
980 A496 44s Prus green .25 .20
981 A496 80s yellow green .40 .20
Nos. 977-981 (5) 1.25 1.00

Latin lettering on Nos. 980 and 981.

Lenin — A497

Designs: 16s, Cruiser "Aurora." 44s, Dove over map of communist area. 60s, Revolutionaries and banners. 80s, Oil refinery.

1957, Oct. 29 ***Perf. 11***
982 A497 12s chocolate .25 .20
983 A497 16s Prus green .55 .20
984 A497 44s deep blue .80 .30
985 A497 60s dk car rose 1.25 .40
986 A497 80s dark green 1.90 .55
Nos. 982-986 (5) 4.75 1.65

40th anniv. of the Communist Revolution. Latin lettering on Nos. 984-985.

Globes A498

1957, Oct. 4 ***Perf. 13***
987 A498 44s Prus blue .30 .20

4th Intl. Trade Union Cong., Leipzig, 10/4-15.

Vassil Kolarov Hotel A499

Bulgarian Health Resorts: 4s, Skis and Pirin Mountains. 8s, Old house at Koprivspitsa. 12s, Rest home at Velingrad. 44s, Momin-Prochod Hotel. 60s, Nesebr Hotel, shoreline and peninsula. 80s, Varna beach scene. 1 l, Hotel at Varna.

1958 **Photo.** ***Perf. 13***
988 A499 4s blue .20 .20
989 A499 8s orange brn .20 .20
990 A499 12s dk green .20 .20
991 A499 16s green .20 .20
992 A499 44s dk blue grn .20 .20
993 A499 60s deep blue .20 .20
994 A499 80s fawn .30 .20
995 A499 1 l dk red brn .35 .20
Nos. 988-995 (8) 1.85 1.60

Latin lettering on 44s, 60s, 80s, and 1 l.
Issue dates: #991-994, 1/20; others, 7/5.
For surcharges see Nos. 1200, 1436.

Mikhail I. Glinka — A500

Portraits: 16s, Jan A. Komensky (Comenius). 40s, Carl von Linné. 44s, William Blake. 60s, Carlo Goldoni. 80s, Auguste Comte.

1957, Dec. 30
996 A500 12s dark brown .20 .20
997 A500 16s dark green .20 .20
998 A500 40s Prus blue .20 .20
999 A500 44s maroon .20 .20
1000 A500 60s orange brown .75 .20
1001 A500 80s deep plum 2.50 .90
Nos. 996-1001 (6) 4.05 1.90

Famous men of other countries. Latin lettering on Nos. 999-1001.

Young Couple, Flag, Dimitrov — A501

People's Front Salute — A502

1957, Dec. 28 ***Perf. 11***
1002 A501 16s carmine rose .20 .20

10th anniversary of Dimitrov's Union of the People's Youth.

1957, Dec. 28
1003 A502 16s dk violet brn .20 .20

15th anniversary of the People's Front.

Hare A503

12s, Red deer (doe), vert. 16s, Red deer (stag). 44s, Chamois. 80s, Brown bear. 1 l, Wild boar.

Perf. 10½
1958, Apr. 5 **Unwmk.** **Photo.**
1004 A503 2s lt & dk ol grn .30 .20
1005 A503 12s sl grn & red brn .50 .20
1006 A503 16s bluish grn & dk red brn .75 .20
1007 A503 44s blue & brown .85 .30
1008 A503 80s bis & dk brn 1.10 .45
1009 A503 1 l stl bl & dk brn 1.25 .80
Nos. 1004-1009 (6) 4.75 2.15

Value, imperf. set $5.

Marx and Lenin A504

Designs: 16s, Marchers and flags. 44s, Lenin blast furnaces.

1958, July 2 ***Perf. 11***
1010 A504 12s dark brown .20 .20
1011 A504 16s dark carmine .20 .20
1012 A504 44s dark blue .85 .20
Nos. 1010-1012 (3) 1.25 .60

Bulgarian Communist Party, 7th Congress.

Wrestlers — A505

1958, June 20 ***Perf. 10½***
1013 A505 60s dk carmine rose 1.00 .85
1014 A505 80s deep brown 1.25 .95

World Wrestling Championship, Sofia.

Chessmen and Globe A506

Perf. 10½
1958, July 18 **Unwmk.** **Photo.**
1015 A506 80s grn & yel grn 4.00 4.00

5th World Students' Chess Games, Varna.

Conference Emblem A507

1958, Sept. 24
1016 A507 44s blue .40 .20

World Trade Union Conference of Working Youth, Prague, July 14-20.

Swimmer A508

1958 Students' Games: 28s, Dancer, vert. 44s, Volleyball, vert.

1958, Sept. 19 ***Perf. 11x10½***
1017 A508 16s bright blue .20 .20
1018 A508 28s brown orange .25 .20
1019 A508 44s bright green .30 .20
Nos. 1017-1019 (3) .75 .60

Onions — A509

Vegetables: 12s, Garlic. 16s, Peppers. 44s, Tomatoes. 80s, Cucumbers. 1 l, Eggplant.

1958, Sept. 20 ***Perf. 13***
1020 A509 2s orange brown .20 .20
1021 A509 12s Prus blue .20 .20
1022 A509 16s dark green .20 .20
1023 A509 44s deep carmine .20 .20
1024 A509 80s deep green .40 .20
1025 A509 1 l brt purple .60 .20
Nos. 1020-1025 (6) 1.80 1.20

Value, imperf. set $5.
See No. 1072. For surcharge see No. 1201.

Plovdiv Fair Building A510

1958, Sept. 14 **Unwmk.** ***Perf. 11***
1026 A510 44s deep carmine .40 .20

18th International Plovdiv Fair.

Attack — A511

44s, Fighter dragging wounded man.

1958, Sept. 23 **Photo.** ***Perf. 11***
1027 A511 16s orange ver .20 .20
1028 A511 44s lake .35 .20

35th anniv. of the September Revolution.

Emblem, Brussels Fair — A512

1958, Oct. 13 ***Perf. 11***

1029 A512 1 l blk & brt blue 5.00 5.00

Brussels World's Fair, Apr. 17-Oct. 19.
Exists imperf. Value, $8.

Runner at Finish Line — A513

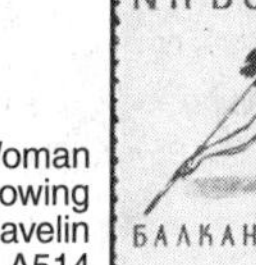

Woman Throwing Javelin A514

60s, High jumper. 80s, Hurdler. 4 l, Shot putter.

1958, Nov. 30

1030 A513 16s red brn, *pnksh* .35 .20
1031 A514 44s olive, *yelsh* .35 .25
1032 A514 60s dk bl, *bluish* .65 .30
1033 A514 80s dp grn, *grnsh* .90 .50
1034 A513 4 l dp rose cl, *pnksh* 5.75 3.25
Nos. 1030-1034 (5) 8.00 4.50

1958 Balkan Games.
Latin lettering on Nos. 1032-1033.

Christo Smirnenski A515

1958, Dec. 22

1035 A515 16s dark carmine .20 .20

Christo Smirnenski (1898-1923), poet.

Girls Harvesting — A516

Girl Tending Calves A517

16s, Boy & girl laborers. 40s, Boy pushing wheelbarrow. 44s, Headquarters building.

1959, Nov. 29 **Photo.**

1036 A516 8s dk olive green .20 .20
1037 A517 12s redsh brown .20 .20
1038 A516 16s violet brown .20 .20
1039 A517 40s Prus blue .20 .20
1040 A516 44s deep carmine .60 .20
Nos. 1036-1040 (5) 1.40 1.00

4th Congress of Dimitrov's Union of People's Youth.

UNESCO Building, Paris A518

1959, Mar. 28 **Unwmk.** ***Perf. 11***

1041 A518 2 l dp red lilac, *cream* 1.25 1.00

Opening of UNESCO Headquarters, Paris, Nov. 3, 1958. Value imperf. $2.50.

Skier — A519

Soccer Players — A520

1959, Mar. 28 ***Perf. 11***

1042 A519 1 l blue, *cream* 1.25 .70

Forty years of skiing in Bulgaria.

1959, Mar. 25

1043 A520 2 l chestnut, *cream* 1.25 .65

1959 European Youth Soccer Championship.

Russian Soldiers Installing Telegraph Wires — A521

First Bulgarian Postal Coach A522

Designs: 60s, Stamp of 1879. 80s, First Bulgarian automobile. 1 l, Television tower. 2 l, Strike of railroad and postal workers, 1919.

1959, May 4

1044 A521 12s dk grn & cit .20 .20
1045 A522 16s deep plum .25 .20
1046 A521 60s dk brn & yel .50 .30
1047 A522 80s hn brn & sal .55 .30
1048 A521 1 l blue .70 .35
1049 A522 2 l dk red brown 1.90 1.40
Nos. 1044-1049 (6) 4.10 2.75

80th anniv. of the Bulgarian post. Latin lettering on Nos. 1046-1049.

Two imperf. souvenir sheets exist with olive borders and inscriptions. One contains one copy of No. 1046 in black & ocher, and measures 92x121mm. The other sheet contains one copy each of Nos. 1044-1045 and 1047-1048 in changed colors: 12s, olive green & ocher; 16s, deep claret & ocher; 80s, dark red & ocher; 1 l, olive & ocher. Each sheet sold for 5 leva. Value, each $35.

Great Tits A523

Birds: 8s, Hoopoe. 16s, Great spotted woodpecker, vert. 45s, Gray partridge, vert. 60s, Rock partridge. 80s, European cuckoo.

1959, June 30 **Photo.**

1050 A523 2s olive & sl grn .20 .20
1051 A523 8s dp orange & blk .40 .20
1052 A523 16s chestnut & dk brn .40 .20
1053 A523 45s brown & blk .85 .35
1054 A523 60s dp blue & gray 1.75 .50
1055 A523 80s dp bl grn & gray 2.40 .80
Nos. 1050-1055 (6) 6.00 2.25

Bagpiper — A524

12s, Acrobats. 16s, Girls exercising with hoops. 20s, Male dancers. 80s, Ballet dancers. 1 l, Ceramic pitcher. 16s, 20s, 80s are horiz.

1959, Aug. 29 **Unwmk.** ***Perf. 11***

Surface-colored Paper

1056 A524 4s dk olive .20 .20
1057 A524 12s scarlet .20 .20
1058 A524 16s maroon .20 .20
1059 A524 20s dk blue .25 .20
1060 A524 80s brt green .50 .25
1061 A524 1 l brown org .95 .40
Nos. 1056-1061 (6) 2.30 1.45

7th International Youth Festival, Vienna. Latin inscriptions on Nos. 1060-1061.

Partisans in Truck A525

Designs: 16s, Partisans and soldiers shaking hands. 45s, Refinery. 60s, Tanks. 80s, Harvester. 1.25 l, Children with flag, vert.

1959, Sept. 8

1062 A525 12s red & Prus grn .20 .20
1063 A525 16s red & dk pur .20 .20
1064 A525 45s red & int bl .20 .20
1065 A525 60s red & ol grn .20 .20
1066 A525 80s red & brn .25 .20
1067 A525 1.25 l red & dp brn .65 .40
Nos. 1062-1067 (6) 1.70 1.40

15th anniversary of Bulgarian liberation.

Soccer A526

1959, Oct. 10 **Unwmk.** ***Perf. 11***

1068 A526 1.25 l dp green, *yel* 3.50 2.00

50 years of Bulgarian soccer.
Set exists imperf. in changed colors. Value $7.50 unused, $4 canceled.

Batak Defenders A527

1959, Aug. 8

1069 A527 16s deep claret .20 .20

300th anniv. of the settlement of Batak.

Post Horn and Letter — A528

Bird-shaped Lyre — A529

Design: 1.25 l, Dove and letter.

1959, Nov. 23

1070 A528 45s emerald & blk .30 .20
1071 A528 1.25 l lt blue, red & blk .50 .20

Intl. Letter Writing Week Oct. 5-11.

Type of 1958 Surcharged "45 CT." in Dark Blue

Design: Tomatoes.

1959 **Photo.** ***Perf. 13***

1072 A509 45s on 44s scarlet .55 .20

1960, Feb. 23 **Unwmk.** ***Perf. 10½***

1073 A529 80s shown .40 .20
1074 A529 1.25 l Lyre .70 .20

50th anniv. of Bulgaria's State Opera.

N. I. Vapzarov — A530

Parachute and Radio Tower — A531

1959, Dec. 14 ***Perf. 11***

1075 A530 80s yel grn & red brn .35 .20

Vapzarov, poet and patriot, 50th birth anniv.

1959, Dec. 3 **Photo.**

1076 A531 1.25 l dp grnsh bl & yel 1.25 .45

3rd Cong. of Voluntary Participants in Defense.

Cotton Picker — A532

Harvester Combine A533

Designs: 2s, Kindergarten. 4s, Woman doctor and child. 10s, Woman milking cow. 12s, Woman holding tobacco leaves. 15s, Woman working loom. 16s, Stalin textile mill, Dimitrovgrad. 25s, Rural electrification. 28s, Woman picking sunflowers. 40s, "Cold-well" hydroelectric dam. 45s, Miner. 60s, Foundry worker. 80s. Woman harvesting grapes. 1 l, Worker and peasant with cogwheel. 1.25 l, Industrial worker. 2 l, Party leader.

1959-61 Photo. *Perf. 13*

1077	A533	2s brn org ('60)	.20	.20
1077A	A532	4s gldn brn ('61)	.20	.20
1078	A532	5s dk green	.20	.20
1079	A533	10s red brn ('61)	.20	.20
1080	A532	12s red brown	.20	.20
1081	A532	15s red lil ('60)	.20	.20
1082	A533	16s dp vio ('60)	.20	.20
1083	A533	20s orange	.20	.20
1084	A532	25s brt blue ('60)	.20	.20
1085	A532	28s brt green	.20	.20
1086	A533	40s brt grnsh bl	.30	.20
1087	A532	45s choc ('60)	.25	.20
1088	A533	60s scarlet	.40	.20
1089	A532	80s olive ('60)	.50	.20
1090	A532	1 l maroon	.50	.20
1090A	A533	1.25 l dull bl ('61)	1.75	.30
1091	A532	2 l dp car ('60)	1.10	.25
		Nos. 1077-1091 (17)	6.80	3.55

Early completion of the 5-year plan (in 1959).
For surcharges see Nos. 1192-1199, 1202-1203.

L. L. Zamenhof A534

Path of Lunik 3 — A535

1959, Dec. 5 Unwmk. *Perf. 11*

1092 A534 1.25 l dk grn & yel grn .80 .40

Lazarus Ludwig Zamenhof (1859-1917), inventor of Esperanto.

1960, Mar. 28 *Perf. 11*

1093 A535 1.25 l Prus bl & brt yel 3.50 1.90

Flight of Lunik 3 around moon. Value, imperf. $5

Skier A536

1960, Apr. 15 Litho.

1094 A536 2 l ultra, blk & brn .95 .35

8th Winter Olympics, Squaw Valley, CA, Feb. 18-29. Value, imperf. $2 unused, $1 canceled.

Vela Blagoeva A537

Portraits: 28s, Anna Maimunkova. 45s, Vela Piskova. 60s, Rosa Luxemburg. 80s, Klara Zetkin. 1.25 l, N. K. Krupskaya.

1960, Apr. 27 Photo. *Perf. 11*

1095	A537	16s rose & red brn	.20	.20
1096	A537	28s citron & olive	.20	.20
1097	A537	45s ol grn & sl grn	.20	.20
1098	A537	60s lt bl & Prus bl	.20	.20
1099	A537	80s red org & dp brn	.35	.20
1100	A537	1.25 l dull yel & olive	.60	.20
		Nos. 1095-1100 (6)	1.75	1.20

International Women's Day, Mar. 8, 1960.

Lenin — A538

1960, May 12

1101	A538	16s shown	.50	.20
1102	A538	45s Lenin sitting	1.10	.20

90th anniversary of the birth of Lenin.

A539

A541

1960, June 3 *Perf. 11*

1103 A539 1.25 l yel & slate grn .85 .35

Seventh European Women's Basketball championships.

1960, June 29 Litho.

1105	A541	16s Parachutist	.55	.30
1106	A541	1.25 l Parachutes	1.50	.45

5th International Parachute Championships.

Yellow Gentian — A542

5s, Tulips. 25s, Turk's-cap lily. 45s, Rhododendron. 60s, Lady's-slipper. 80s, Violets.

1960, July 27 Photo. *Perf. 11*

1107	A542	2s beige, grn & yel	.20	.20
1108	A542	5s yel grn, grn & car rose	.20	.20
1109	A542	25s pink, grn & org	.20	.20
1110	A542	45s pale lil, grn & rose lil	.35	.20
1111	A542	60s yel, grn & org	.75	.20
1112	A542	80s gray, grn & vio bl	.90	.25
		Nos. 1107-1112 (6)	2.60	1.25

Soccer A543

12s, Wrestling. 16s, Weight lifting. 45s, Woman gymnast. 80s, Canoeing. 2 l, Runner.

1960, Aug. 29 Unwmk. *Perf. 11*
Athletes' Figures in Pink

1113	A543	8s brown	.25	.20
1114	A543	12s violet	.25	.20
1115	A543	16s Prus blue	.25	.20
1116	A543	45s deep plum	.25	.20
1117	A543	80s blue	.50	.20
1118	A543	2 l deep green	1.75	.35
		Nos. 1113-1118 (6)	3.25	1.35

17th Olympic Games, Rome, 8/25-9/11. Value, set imperf. in changed colors, $5.

Globes — A544

Unwmk.
1960, Oct. 12 Photo. *Perf. 11*

1125 A544 1.25 l blue & ultra .50 .20

15th anniversary of the World Federation of Trade Unions.

Alexander Popov A545

1960, Oct. 12

1126 A545 90s blue & blk .75 .20

Centenary of the birth of Alexander Popov, radio pioneer.

Bicyclists A546

1960, Sept. 22

1127 A546 1 l yel, red org & blk .90 .45

The 10th Tour of Bulgaria Bicycle Race.

Jaroslav Vésin A547

1960, Nov. 22 Unwmk. *Perf. 11*

1128 A547 1 l brt citron & ol grn 2.75 .65

Birth centenary of Jaroslav Vesin, painter.

UN Headquarters A548

Costume of Kyustendil A549

1961, Jan. 14 Photo. *Perf. 11*

1129	A548	1 l brown & yel	1.00	.45
a.		Souvenir sheet	5.00	5.00

15th anniv. of the UN. #1129 sold for 2 l. Value, imperf. $3.50.

No. 1129a sold for 2.50 l and contains one copy of No. 1129, imperf, in dark olive and pink.

1961, Jan. 28

Regional Costumes: 16s, Pleven. 28s, Sliven. 45s, Sofia. 60s, Rhodope. 80s, Karnobat.

1130	A549	12s sal, sl grn & yel	.20	.20
1131	A549	16s pale lil, brn vio & buff	.20	.20
1132	A549	28s pale grn, sl grn & rose	.20	.20
1133	A549	45s blue & red	.30	.20
1134	A549	60s grnsh bl, Prus bl & yel	.50	.20
1135	A549	80s yel, sl grn & pink	.60	.25
		Nos. 1130-1135 (6)	2.00	1.25

Theodor Tiro (Fresco) A550

Designs: 60s, Boyana Church. 1.25 l, Duchess of Dessislava (fresco).

1961, Jan. 28 Photo.

1136	A550	60s yel grn, blk & grn	1.10	.50
1137	A550	80s yel, sl grn & org	1.40	.65
1138	A550	1.25 l yel grn, hn brn & buff	2.00	1.10
		Nos. 1136-1138 (3)	4.50	2.25

700th anniv. of murals in Boyana Church.

Clock Tower, Vratsa — A551

Wooden Jug — A552

Designs: 12s, Clock tower, Bansko. 20s, Anguchev House, Mogilitsa. 28s, Oslekov House, Koprivspitsa, horiz. 40s, Pasha's house. Melnik, horiz. 45s, Lion sculpture. 60s, Man on horseback, Madara. 80s, Fresco, Bratchkovo monastery. 1 l, Tsar Assen coin.

1961, Feb. 25 Unwmk. *Perf. 11*
Denomination and Stars in Vermilion

1139	A551	8s olive grn	.20	.20
1140	A551	12s lt violet	.20	.20
1141	A552	16s dk red brn	.20	.20
1142	A551	20s brt blue	.20	.20
1143	A551	28s grnsh blue	.20	.20
1144	A551	40s red brown	.20	.20
1145	A552	45s olive gray	.20	.20
1146	A552	60s slate	.30	.20
1147	A552	80s dk olive gray	.55	.20
1148	A552	1 l green	.70	.20
		Nos. 1139-1148 (10)	2.95	2.00

Capercaillie A553

Birds: 4s, Dalmatian pelican. 16s, Ring-necked pheasant. 80s, Great bustard. 1 l, Lammergeier. 2 l, Hazel hen.

1961, Mar. 31

1149	A553	2s blk, sal & Prus grn	.20	.20
1150	A553	4s blk, yel grn & org	.20	.20
1151	A553	16s brn, lt grn & org	.20	.20

1152 A553 80s brn, bluish grn & yel 1.10 .55
1153 A553 1 l blk, lt bl & yel 1.25 .85
1154 A553 2 l brn, bl & yel 1.60 1.00
Nos. 1149-1153 (5) 2.95 2.00

Radio Tower and Winged Anchor A554

1961, Apr. 1 Unwmk. *Perf. 11*

1155 A554 80s brt green & blk .45 .20

50th anniv. of the Transport Workers' Union.

T. G. Shevchenko A555

Water Polo — A556

1961, Apr. 27

1156 A555 1 l olive & blk 2.50 1.75

Centenary of the death of Taras G. Shevchenko, Ukrainian poet.

1961, May 15

Designs: 5s, Tennis. 16s, Fencing. 45s, Throwing the discus. 1.25 l, Sports Palace. 2 l, Basketball. 5 l, Sports Palace, different view. 5s, 16s, 45s and 1.25 l, are horizontal.

Black Inscriptions

1157 A556 4s lt ultra .20 .20
1158 A556 5s orange ver .20 .20
1159 A556 16s olive grn .20 .20
1160 A556 45s dull blue .20 .20
1161 A556 1.25 l yellow brn .60 .20
1162 A556 2 l lilac .85 .40
Nos. 1157-1162 (6) 2.25 1.40

Souvenir Sheet

Imperf

1163 A556 5 l yel grn, dl bl & yel 7.50 6.50

1961 World University Games, Sofia, Aug. 26-Sept. 3.

Value, Nos. 1157-1162 in changed colors, imperf. $4.50.

Monk Seal A557

Black Sea Fauna: 12s, Jellyfish. 16s, Dolphin. 45s, Black Sea sea horse, vert. 1 l, Starred sturgeon. 1.25 l, Thornback ray.

1961, June 19 *Perf. 11*

1164 A557 2s green & blk .20 .20
1165 A557 12s Prus grn & pink .20 .20
1166 A557 16s ultra & vio bl .20 .20
1167 A557 45s lt blue & brn .55 .40
1168 A557 1 l yel grn & Prus grn 1.25 .85
1169 A557 1.25 l lt vio bl & red brn 1.60 1.40
Nos. 1164-1169 (6) 4.00 3.25

Hikers — A558

Designs: 4s, "Sredetz" hostel, horiz. 16s, Tents. 1.25 l, Mountain climber.

1961, Aug. 25 Litho. *Perf. 11*

1170 A558 4s yel grn, yel & blk .20 .20
1171 A558 12s lt bl, cr & blk .20 .20
1172 A558 16s green, cr & blk .20 .20
1173 A558 1.25 l bister, cr & blk .45 .20
Nos. 1170-1173 (4) 1.05 .80

"Know Your Country" campaign.

Demeter Blagoev Addressing 1891 Congress at Busludja — A559

1961, Aug. 5 Photo.

1174 A559 45s dk red & buff .20 .20
1175 A559 80s blue & pink .30 .20
1176 A559 2 l dk brn & pale cit .75 .25
Nos. 1174-1176 (3) 1.25 .65

70th anniversary of the first Congress of the Bulgarian Social-Democratic Party.

The Golden Girl A560

Fairy Tales: 8s, The Living Water. 12s, The Golden Apple. 16s, Krali-Marko, hero. 45s, Samovila-Vila, Witch. 80s, Tom Thumb.

1961, Oct. 10 Unwmk. *Perf. 11*

1177 A560 2s blue, blk & org .20 .20
1178 A560 8s rose lil, blk & gray .25 .20
1179 A560 12s bl grn, blk & pink .25 .20
1180 A560 16s red, blk, bl & gray .40 .20
1181 A560 45s ol grn, blk & pink .75 .25
1182 A560 80s ocher, blk & dk car 1.10 .30
Nos. 1177-1182 (6) 2.95 1.35

Caesar's Mushroom A561

Miladinov Brothers and Title Page — A562

Designs: Various mushrooms.

1961, Dec. 20 Photo. *Perf. 11*

Denominations in Black

1183 A561 2s lemon & red .20 .20
1184 A561 4s ol grn & red brn .20 .20
1185 A561 12s bister & red brn .20 .20
1186 A561 16s lilac & red brn .20 .20
1187 A561 45s car rose & yel .20 .20
1188 A561 80s brn org & sepia .20 .20
1189 A561 1.25 l vio & dk brn .40 .20
1190 A561 2 l org brn & brn .70 .40
Nos. 1183-1190 (8) 2.30 1.80

Value, denomination in dark grn, imperf set $5 unused or canceled.

1961, Dec. 21 Unwmk. *Perf. 10½*

1191 A562 1.25 l olive & blk .75 .30

Publication of "Collected Folksongs" by the Brothers Miladinov, Dimitri and Konstantin, cent.

Nos. 1079-1085, 1087, 992, 1023, 1090-1091 and 806 Surcharged with New Value in Black, Red or Violet

1962, Jan. 1

1192 A533 1s on 10s red brown .20 .20
1193 A532 1s on 12s red brown .20 .20
1194 A532 2s on 15s red lilac .20 .20
1195 A533 2s on 16s dp vio (R) .20 .20
1196 A533 2s on 20s orange .20 .20
a. "2 CT." on 2 lines .20 .20
1197 A532 3s on 25s brt bl (R) .20 .20
a. Black surcharge 6.00 4.00
1198 A532 3s on 28s brt grn (R) .20 .20
1199 A532 5s on 45s chocolate .20 .20
1200 A499 5s on 44s dk bl grn (R) .20 .20
1201 A509 5s on 44s dp car (V) .20 .20
1202 A532 10s on 1 l maroon .25 .20
1203 A532 20s on 2 l dp car .70 .25
1204 A430 40s on 4 l rose lake (V) 1.50 .50
Nos. 1192-1204 (13) 4.45 2.95

Freighter "Varna" A563

Designs: 5s, Tanker "Komsomoletz." 20s, Liner "G. Dimitrov."

1962, Mar. 1 Photo. *Perf. 10½*

1205 A563 1s lt grn & brt bl .20 .20
1206 A563 5s lt blue & grn .20 .20
1207 A563 20s gray bl & grnsh bl .70 .20
Nos. 1205-1207 (3) 1.10 .60

Dimitrov Working as Printer — A564

Roses — A565

13s, Griffin, emblem of state printing works.

1962, Mar. 19 Unwmk.

1208 A564 2s ver, blk & yel .20 .20
1209 A564 13s red org, blk & yel .40 .20

80th anniversary (in 1961) of the George Dimitrov state printing works.

1962, Mar. 28

Various Roses in Natural Colors

1210 A565 1s deep violet .20 .20
1211 A565 2s salmon & dk car .20 .20
1212 A565 3s gray & car .20 .20
1213 A565 4s dark green .30 .20
1214 A565 5s ultra .50 .20
1215 A565 6s bluish grn & dk car .60 .35
1216 A565 8s citron & car 1.50 .65
1217 A565 13s blue 2.50 1.75
Nos. 1210-1217 (8) 6.00 3.75

For overprint and surcharges see Nos. 1281-1283.

Malaria Eradication Emblem and Mosquito A566

Design: 20s, Malaria eradication emblem.

1962, Apr. 19

1218 A566 5s org brn, yel & blk .40 .20
1219 A566 20s emerald, yel & blk .85 .35

WHO drive to eradicate malaria.

Value, imperf. $2.50 unused, $1.50 canceled.

Lenin and First Issue of Pravda A567

1962, May 4 Unwmk. *Perf. 10*

1220 A567 5s deep rose & slate .25 .20

50th anniversary of Pravda, Russian newspaper founded by Lenin.

Blackboard and Book — A568

1962, May 21 Photo.

1221 A568 5s Prus bl, blk & yel .25 .20

The 1962 Teachers' Congress.

Soccer Player and Globe A569

1962, May 26 *Perf. 10½*

1222 A569 13s brt grn, blk & lt brn .65 .25

World Soccer Championship, Chile, May 30-June 17. Value, imperf. in changed colors, $3.25 unused or canceled.

George Dimitrov A570

1962, June 18 Photo.

1223 A570 2s dark green .20 .20
1224 A570 5s turq blue .40 .20

80th anniv. of the birth of George Dimitrov (1882-1949), communist leader and premier of the Bulgarian Peoples' Republic.

Bishop — A571

1962, July 7 Unwmk. *Perf. 10½*

1225 A571 1s shown .20 .20
1226 A571 2s Rook .20 .20
1227 A571 3s Queen .20 .20
1228 A571 13s Knight .65 .25
1229 A571 20s Pawn 1.10 .40
Nos. 1225-1229 (5) 2.35 1.25

15th Chess Olympics, Varna. Nos. 1225-1229 were also issued imperf in changed colors. Value, $5 unused.

An imperf. souvenir sheet contains one 20s horizontal stamp showing five chessmen. Size: 75x66mm. Value, $8 unused.

Rila Mountain A572

Designs: 2s, Pirin mountain. 6s, Nesebr, Black Sea. 8s, Danube. 13s, Vidin Castle. 1 l, Rhodope mountain.

1962-63 *Perf. 13*

1230 A572 1s dk blue grn .20 .20
1231 A572 2s blue .20 .20
1232 A572 6s grnsh blue .20 .20
1233 A572 8c lilac .20 .20
1234 A572 13s yellow grn .40 .20
1234A A572 1 l dp green ('63) 3.25 .80
Nos. 1230-1234A (6) 4.45 1.80

No. 974 Surcharged in Red

1962, July 14 *Perf. 13*

1235 A493 13s on 44s slate grn 2.25 1.00

25th Bulgarian Esperanto Congress, Burgas, July 14-16.

Girl and Festival Emblem A573

Design: 5s, Festival emblem.

1962, Aug. 18 Photo. *Perf. 10½*

1236 A573 5s green, lt bl & pink .20 .20
1237 A573 13s lilac, lt bl & gray .35 .20

8th Youth Festival for Peace and Friendship, Helsinki, July 28-Aug. 6, 1962.

Parnassius Apollo — A574

1962, Sept. 13
Various Butterflies in Natural Colors

1238 A574 1s pale cit & dk grn .20 .20
1239 A574 2s rose & brown .20 .20
1240 A574 3s buff & red brn .20 .20
1241 A574 4s gray & brown .20 .20
1242 A574 5s lt gray & brn .25 .20
1243 A574 6s gray & black .55 .20
1244 A574 10s pale grn & blk 1.90 .60
1245 A574 13s buff & red brn 2.50 1.50
Nos. 1238-1245 (8) 6.00 3.30

Planting Machine — A575

2s, Electric locomotive. 3s, Blast furnace. 13s, Blagoev, Dimitrov & Communist flag.

1962, Nov. 1 *Perf. 11½*

1246 A575 1s bl grn & dk ol grn .20 .20
1247 A575 2s bl & Prus bl .20 .20
1248 A575 3s carmine & brn .20 .20
1249 A575 13s plum, red & blk .55 .20
Nos. 1246-1249 (4) 1.15 .80

Bulgarian Communist Party, 8th Congress.

Title Page of "Slav-Bulgarian History" — A576

Paisii Hilendarski Writing History A577

1962, Dec. 8 Unwmk. *Perf. 10½*

1250 A576 2s olive grn & blk .20 .20
1251 A577 5s brown org & blk .20 .20

200th anniv. of "Slav-Bulgarian History."

Aleco Konstantinov (1863-1897), Writer A578

1963, Mar. 5 Photo. *Perf. 11½*

1252 A578 5s red, grn & blk .25 .20

Printed with alternating red brown and black label showing Bai Ganu, hero from Konstantinov's books.

A579

Sofia University — A580

#1255, Levski Stadium, Sofia. #1256, Arch, Nissaria. #1257, Parachutist.

1963, Feb. 20 Unwmk. *Perf. 10*

1253 A579 1s brown red .20 .20
1254 A580 1s red brown .20 .20
1255 A580 1s blue green .20 .20
1256 A580 1s dark green .20 .20
1257 A580 1s brt blue .20 .20
Nos. 1253-1257 (5) 1.00 1.00

Vassil Levski A581

Boy, Girl and Dimitrov — A582

1963, Apr. 11 Photo.

1258 A581 13s grnsh blue & buff .75 .25

90th anniversary of the death of Vassil Levski, revolutionary leader in the fight for liberation from the Turks.

1963, Apr. 25 Unwmk. *Perf. 11½*

13s, Girl with book & boy with hammer.

1259 A582 2s org, ver, red brn & blk .20 .20
1260 A582 13s bluish grn, brn & blk .40 .20

10th Congress of Dimitrov's Union of the People's Youth.

Red Squirrel — A583

Sun Coast Promenade A584

2s, Hedgehog. 3s, European polecat. 5s, Pine marten. 13s, Badger. 20s, Otter. 2s, 3s, 5s, 13s, horiz.

1963, Apr. 30
Red Numerals

1261 A583 1s grn & brn, *grnsh* .20 .20
1262 A583 2s grn & blk, *yel* .20 .20
1263 A583 3s grn & brn, *bis* .20 .20
1264 A583 5s vio & red brn, *lil* .40 .20
1265 A583 13s red brn & blk, *pink* 1.25 .45
1266 A583 20s blk & brn, *blue* 2.00 .75
Nos. 1261-1266 (6) 4.25 2.00

1963, Mar. 12 Unwmk. *Perf. 13*

Black Sea Resorts: 2s, 3s, 13s, Views of Gold Sand. 5s, 20s, Sun Coast.

1267 A584 1s blue .20 .20
1268 A584 2s vermilion .25 .20
1269 A584 2s car rose .50 .20
1270 A584 3s ocher .20 .20
1271 A584 5s lilac .20 .20
1272 A584 13s blue green .55 .20
1273 A584 20s green 1.10 .20
Nos. 1267-1273 (7) 3.00 1.40

Freestyle Wrestling A585

Design: 20s, Freestyle wrestling, horiz.

1963, May 31 *Perf. 11½*

1274 A585 5s yel bister & blk .20 .20
1275 A585 20s org brn & blk .80 .20

15th International Freestyle Wrestling Competitions, Sofia.

"Women for Peace" A586

1963, June 24 Unwmk. *Perf. 11½*

1276 A586 20s blue & blk .60 .20

World Congress of Women, Moscow, June 24-29.

Esperanto Emblem and Arms of Sofia — A587

Moon, Earth and Lunik 4 — A588

1963, June 29 Photo.

1277 A587 13s multicolored .65 .20

48th World Esperanto Congress, Sofia, Aug. 3-10.

1963, July 22

2s, Radar equipment. 3s, Satellites and moon.

1278 A588 1s ultra .20 .20
1279 A588 2s red lilac .20 .20
1280 A588 3s greenish blue .20 .20
Nos. 1278-1280 (3) .60 .60

Russia's rocket to the moon, Apr. 2, 1963.

Nos. 1211-1212 and 1215 Overprinted or Surcharged in Green, Ultramarine or Black

1963, Aug. 31 *Perf. 10½*

1281 A565 2s (G) .25 .20
1282 A565 5s on 3s (U) .40 .20
1283 A565 13s on 6s .70 .25
Nos. 1281-1283 (3) 1.35 .65

Intl. Stamp Fair, Riccione, Aug. 31.

Women's Relay Race — A589

2s, Hammer thrower. 3s, Women's long jump. 5s, Men's high jump. 13s, Discus thrower.

Perf. 11½

1963, Sept. 13 Photo. Unwmk.

Flags in National Colors

1284 A589 1s slate green .20 .20
1285 A589 2s purple .20 .20
1286 A589 3s Prus blue .20 .20
1287 A589 5s maroon .45 .30
1288 A589 13s chestnut brn 1.60 1.25
Nos. 1284-1288 (5) 2.65 2.15

Balkan Games. A multicolored, 50s, imperf. souvenir sheet shows design of women's relay race. Size: 74x70mm. Value, $3 unused.

"Slav-Bulgarian History" — A590

1963, Sept. 19 ***Perf. 10½***

1289 A590 5s sal pink, slate & yel .20 .20

5th International Slavic Congress.

Revolutionists A591

Christo Smirnenski A592

1963, Sept. 22 ***Perf. 11½***

1290 A591 2s brt red & blk .20 .20

40th anniv. of the September Revolution.

1963, Oct. 28 ***Perf. 10½***

1291 A592 13s pale lilac & indigo .45 .20

Christo Smirnenski, poet, 65th birth anniv.

Columbine A593

Horses — A594

1963, Oct. 9 Photo. ***Perf. 11½***

1292 A593 1s shown .20 .20
1293 A593 2s Edelweiss .20 .20
1294 A593 3s Primrose .20 .20
1295 A593 5s Water lily .20 .20
1296 A593 6s Tulips .20 .20
1297 A593 8s Larkspur .30 .20
1298 A593 10s Alpine clematis .70 .20
1299 A593 13s Anemone 1.25 .25
Nos. 1292-1299 (8) 3.25 1.65

1963, Dec. 28 Unwmk. ***Perf. 10½***

Designs: 2s, Charioteer and chariot. 3s, Trumpeters. 5s, Woman carrying tray with food. 13s, Man holding bowl. 20s, Woman in armchair. Designs are from a Thracian tomb at Kazanlik.

1300 A594 1s gray, org & dk red .20 .20
1301 A594 2s gray, ocher & pur .20 .20
1302 A594 3s gray, dl yel & sl grn .20 .20
1303 A594 5s pale grn, ocher & brn .20 .20
1304 A594 13s pale grn, bis & blk .40 .20
1305 A594 20s pale grn, org & dk car .75 .30
Nos. 1300-1305 (6) 1.95 1.30

World Map and Emblem A595

Designs: 2s, Blood transfusion. 3s, Nurse bandaging injured wrist. 5s, Red Cross nurse. 13s, Henri Dunant.

1964, Jan. 27 ***Perf. 10½***

1306 A595 1s lem, blk & red .20 .20
1307 A595 2s ultra, blk & red .20 .20
1308 A595 3s gray, sl, blk & red .20 .20
1309 A595 5s brt bl, blk & red .20 .20
1310 A595 13s org yel, blk & red .40 .20
Nos. 1306-1310 (5) 1.20 1.00

Centenary of International Red Cross.

Speed Skating A596

Sports: 2s, 50s, Women's figure skating. 3s, Cross-country skiing. 5s, Ski jump. 10s, Ice hockey goalkeeper. 13s, Ice hockey players.

1964, Feb. 21 Unwmk. ***Perf. 10½***

1311 A596 1s grnsh bl, ind & ocher .20 .20
1312 A596 2s brt pink, ol grn & dk sl grn .20 .20
1313 A596 3s dl grn, dk grn & brn .20 .20
1314 A596 5s bl, blk & yel brn .20 .20
1315 A596 10s gray, org & blk .40 .20
1316 A596 13s lil, blk & lil rose .70 .30
Nos. 1311-1316 (6) 1.90 1.30

Miniature Sheet

Imperf

1317 A596 50s gray, Prus grn & pink 4.00 4.00

9th Winter Olympic Games, Innsbruck, Jan. 29-Feb. 9, 1964.

Mask of Nobleman, 2nd Century A597

2s, Thracian horseman. 3s, Ceramic jug. 5s, Clasp & belt. 6s, Copper kettle. 8s, Angel. 10s, Lioness. 13s, Scrub woman, contemporary sculpture.

1964, Mar. 14 Photo. ***Perf. 10½***

Gray Frame

1318 A597 1s dp green & red .20 .20
1319 A597 2s ol gray & red .20 .20
1320 A597 3s bister & red .20 .20
1321 A597 5s indigo & red .20 .20
1322 A597 6s org brn & red .25 .20
1323 A597 8s brn red & red .40 .20
1324 A597 10s olive & red .40 .20
1325 A597 13s gray ol & red .65 .25
Nos. 1318-1325 (8) 2.50 1.65

2,500 years of Bulgarian art.

"The Unborn Maid" A598

Fairy Tales: 2s, Grandfather's Glove. 3s, The Big Turnip. 5s, The Wolf and the Seven Kids. 8s, Cunning Peter. 13s, The Wheat Cake.

1964, Apr. 17 Unwmk. ***Perf. 10½***

1326 A598 1s bl grn, red & org brn .20 .20
1327 A598 2s ultra, ocher & blk .20 .20
1328 A598 3s cit, red & blk .20 .20
1329 A598 5s dp rose, brn & blk .20 .20
1330 A598 8s yel grn, red & blk .20 .20
1331 A598 13s lt vio bl, grn & blk .70 .20
Nos. 1326-1331 (6) 1.70 1.20

Ascalaphus Otomanus A599

Insects: 2s, Nemoptera coa., vert. 3s, Saga natalia (grasshopper). 5s, Rosalia alpina, vert. 13s, Anisoplia austriaca, vert. 20s, Scolia flavitrons.

1964, May 16 Photo. ***Perf. 11½***

1332 A599 1s brn org, yel & blk .20 .20
1333 A599 2s dl bl grn, bis & blk .20 .20
1334 A599 3s gray, grn & blk .20 .20
1335 A599 5s lt ol grn, blk & vio .20 .20
1336 A599 13s vio, bis & blk .55 .20
1337 A599 20s gray bl, yel & blk .85 .30
Nos. 1332-1337 (6) 2.20 1.30

Soccer — A600

Designs: 13s, Women's volleyball. 60s, Map of Europe and European Women's Volleyball Championship Cup (rectangular, size: 60x69mm).

1964, June 8 Unwmk. ***Perf. 11½***

1338 A600 2s bl, dk bl, ocher & red .20 .20
1339 A600 13s bl, dk bl, ocher & red .50 .25

Miniature Sheet

Imperf

1340 A600 60s ultra, ocher, red & gray 3.00 2.25

Levski Physical Culture Assoc., 50th anniv.

Peter Beron and Title Page of Primer — A601

1964, June 22 ***Perf. 11½***

1341 A601 20s red brn & dk brn, *grysh* 1.00 .60

140th anniversary of the publication of the first Bulgarian primer.

Robert Stephenson's "Rocket" Locomotive, 1825 — A602

Designs: 2s, Modern steam locomotive. 3s, Diesel locomotive. 5s, Electric locomotive. 8s, Freight train on bridge. 13s, Diesel locomotive and tunnel.

1964, July 1 Photo. ***Perf. 11½***

1342 A602 1s multicolored .20 .20
1343 A602 2s multicolored .20 .20
1344 A602 3s multicolored .20 .20
1345 A602 5s multicolored .20 .20
1346 A602 8s multicolored .30 .20
1347 A602 13s multicolored .80 .20
Nos. 1342-1347 (6) 1.90 1.20

German Shepherd — A603

1964, Aug. 22 **Photo.**

1348 A603 1s shown .20 .20
1349 A603 2s Setter .20 .20
1350 A603 3s Poodle .20 .20
1351 A603 4s Pomeranian .20 .20
1352 A603 5s St. Bernard .20 .20
1353 A603 6s Terrier .25 .25
1354 A603 10s Pointer 1.40 .75
1355 A603 13s Dachshund 2.75 1.25
Nos. 1348-1355 (8) 5.40 3.25

Partisans — A604

Designs: 2s, People welcoming Soviet army. 3s, Russian aid to Bulgaria. 4s, Blast furnace, Kremikovski. 5s, Combine. 6s, Peace demonstration. 8s, Sentry. 13s, Demeter Blagoev and George Dimitrov.

1964, Sept. 9 Unwmk. ***Perf. 11½***

Flag in Red

1356 A604 1s lt & dp ultra .20 .20
1357 A604 2s ol bis & dp ol .20 .20
1358 A604 3s rose lil & mar .20 .20
1359 A604 4s lt vio & vio .20 .20
1360 A604 5s org & red brn .20 .20
1361 A604 6s bl & dp bl .20 .20
1362 A604 8s lt grn & grn .20 .20
1363 A604 13s fawn & red brn .40 .20
Nos. 1356-1363 (8) 1.80 1.60

20th anniv. of People's Government of Bulgaria.

No. 967 Surcharged

1964, Sept. 13 ***Perf. 13***

1364 A476 20s on 44s org yel 1.00 .35

International Plovdiv Fair.

Gymnast on Parallel Bars — A606

Vratcata Mountain Road — A607

Sports: 2s, Long jump. 3s, Woman diver. 5s, Soccer. 13s, Women's volleyball. 20s, Wrestling.

1964, Oct. 10 ***Perf. 11½***

1366 A606 1s pale grn, grn & red .20 .20
1367 A606 2s pale vio, vio bl & red .20 .20
1368 A606 3s bl grn, brn & red .20 .20
1369 A606 5s pink, pur & red .20 .20
1370 A606 13s bl, Prus grn & red .50 .20
1371 A606 20s yel, grn & red .90 .25
Nos. 1366-1371 (6) 2.20 1.25

18th Olympic Games, Tokyo. Oct. 10-25. See No. B27.

1964, Oct. 26 Photo. ***Perf. 12½x13***

Bulgarian Views: 2s, Ritlite mountain road. 3s, Pines, Malovica peak. 4s, Pobitite rocks. 5s, Erkupria. 6s, Rhodope mountain road.

1372 A607 1s dk slate grn .20 .20
1373 A607 2s brown .20 .20
1374 A607 3s grnsh blue .20 .20
1375 A607 4s dk red brn .20 .20
1376 A607 5s deep green .20 .20
1377 A607 6s blue violet .30 .20
Nos. 1372-1377 (6) 1.30 1.20

Mail Coach, Plane and Rocket A608

1964, Oct. 3 Unwmk. ***Perf. 11½***

1378 A608 20s greenish blue 1.25 .50

First national stamp exhibition, Sofia, Oct. 3-18. Issued in sheets of 12 stamps and 12 labels (woman's head and inscription, 5x5) arranged around one central label showing stylized bird design.

Exists imperf.

Students Holding Book — A609

1964, Dec. 30 **Photo.**

1379 A609 13s lt blue & blk .45 .25

8th Intl. Students' Congress, Sofia.

500-Year-Old Walnut Tree at Golemo Drenovo — A610

Designs: Various old trees.

1964, Dec. 28

1380 A610 1s blk, buff & cl brn .20 .20
1381 A610 2s blk, pink & dp cl .20 .20
1382 A610 3s blk, yel & dk brn .20 .20
1383 A610 4s blk, lt bl & Prus bl .20 .20
1384 A610 10s blk, pale grn & grn .25 .20
1385 A610 13s blk, pale bis & dk ol grn .40 .20
Nos. 1380-1385 (6) 1.45 1.20

Soldiers' Monument A611

1965, Jan. 1 **Unwmk.**

1386 A611 2s red & black .20 .20

Bulgarian-Soviet friendship.

Olympic Medal Inscribed "Olympic Glory" A612

1965, Jan. 27 Photo. ***Perf. 11½***

1387 A612 20s org brn, gold & blk .75 .40

Bulgarian victories in the 1964 Olympic Games.

"Victory Over Fascism" A613

13s, "Fight for Peace" (dove and globe).

1965, Apr. 16 ***Perf. 11½***

1388 A613 5s gray, blk & ol bis .20 .20
1389 A613 13s gray, blk & blue .25 .20

Victory over Fascism, 5/9/45, 20th anniv.

Vladimir M. Komarov and Section of Globe — A614

Designs: 2s, Konstantin Feoktistov. 5s, Boris B. Yegorov. 13s, Komarov, Feoktistov and Yegorov. 20s, Spaceship Voskhod.

1965, Feb. 15 **Photo.**

1390 A614 1s pale lil & dk bl .20 .20
1391 A614 2s lt bl, ind & dl vio .20 .20
1392 A614 5s pale grn, grn & ol grn .20 .20
1393 A614 13s pale pink, dp rose & mar .40 .20
1394 A614 20s lt bl, vio bl, grnsh bl & yel .75 .20
Nos. 1390-1394 (5) 1.75 1.00

Russian 3-man space flight, Oct. 12-13, 1964.

Imperfs in changed colors. Four low values se-tenant. Value, set $2 unused, $1 canceled.

Bullfinch — A615

Birds: 2s, European golden oriole. 3s, Common rock thrush. 5s, Barn swallow. 8s, European roller. 10s, European goldfinch. 13s, Rosy pastor starling. 20s, Nightingale.

1965, Apr. 20 Unwmk. ***Perf. 11½***

Birds in Natural Colors

1395 A615 1s blue green .20 .20
1396 A615 2s rose lilac .20 .20
1397 A615 3s rose .20 .20
1398 A615 5s brt blue .20 .20
1399 A615 8s citron .30 .25
1400 A615 10s gray 1.10 .35
1401 A615 13s lt vio blue 1.10 .70
1402 A615 20s emerald 2.25 1.50
Nos. 1395-1402 (8) 5.55 3.60

Black Sea Fish A616

1965, June 10 Photo. ***Perf. 11½***

Gray Frames

1403 A616 1s Sting ray .20 .20
1404 A616 2s Belted bonito .20 .20
1405 A616 3s Hogfish .20 .20
1406 A616 5s Gurnard .20 .20
1407 A616 10s Scad .75 .20
1408 A616 13s Turbot 1.10 .25
Nos. 1403-1408 (6) 2.65 1.25

Plane, Bus, Train, Ship and Whale A617

1965, Apr. 30

1409 A617 13s multicolored .50 .30

4th Intl. Conf. of Transport, Dock and Fishery Workers, Sofia, May 10-14.

ITU Emblem and Communications Symbols — A618

1965, May 17

1410 A618 20s multicolored .65 .30

Centenary of the ITU.

Col. Pavel Belyayev and Lt. Col. Alexei Leonov — A619

Design: 20s, Leonov floating in space.

1965, May 20 **Unwmk.**

1411 A619 2s gray, dull bl & dk brn .20 .20
1412 A619 20s multicolored 1.00 .45

Space flight of Voskhod 2 and the first man floating in space, Lt. Col. Alexei Leonov.

ICY Emblem A620

1965, May 15 **Photo.**

1413 A620 20s orange, olive & blk .85 .50

International Cooperation Year, 1965.

Corn — A621

Marx and Lenin — A622

1965, Apr. 1 ***Perf. 12½x13***

1414 A621 1s shown .20 .20
1415 A621 2s Wheat .20 .20
1416 A621 3s Sunflowers .20 .20
1417 A621 4s Sugar beet .20 .20
1418 A621 5s Clover .20 .20
1419 A621 10s Cotton .40 .20
1420 A621 13s Tobacco .60 .20
Nos. 1414-1420 (7) 2.00 1.40

1965, June ***Perf. 10½***

1421 A622 13s red & dk brn .65 .20

6th Conference of Postal Ministers of Communist Countries, Peking, June 21-July 15.

Film and UNESCO Emblem A623

1965, June 30

1422 A623 13s dp bl, blk & lt gray .50 .20

Balkan Film Festival, Varna.

Ballerina — A624

1965, July 10 **Photo.**

1423 A624 5s dp lil rose & blk .80 .80

2nd Intl. Ballet Competition, Varna.

Map of Balkan Peninsula and Dove with Letter
A625

Col. Pavel Belyayev and Lt. Col. Alexei Leonov — A626

2s, Sailboat and modern buildings. 3s, Fish and plants. 13s, Symbolic sun and rocket. 40s, Map of Balkan Peninsula and dove with letter (like 1s).

1965 — *Perf. 10½*

1424 A625 1s sil, dp ultra & yel .20 .20
1425 A625 2s sil, pur & yel .20 .20
1426 A625 3s gold, grn & yel .20 .20
1427 A625 13s gold, hn brn & yel .55 .50
1428 A626 20s sil, bl & brn .95 .95
Nos. 1424-1428 (5) 2.10 2.05

Miniature Sheet

Imperf

1429 A625 40s gold & brt bl 1.75 1.00

Balkanphila 1965 Philatelic Exhibition, Varna, Aug. 7-15, and visit of Russian astronauts Belyayev and Leonov.

Value, No. 1428 imperf. in changed colors, 90 cents.

Issued: 20s, 40s, 8/7; others, 7/23.

Woman Gymnast — A627

Designs: 2s, Woman gymnast on parallel bars. 3s, Weight lifter. 5s, Automobile and chart. 10s, Women basketball players. 13s, Automobile and map of rally.

1965, Aug. 14 — *Perf. 10½*

1430 A627 1s crim, brn & blk .20 .20
1431 A627 2s rose vio, dp cl & blk .20 .20
1432 A627 3s dp car, brn & blk .20 .20
1433 A627 5s fawn, red brn & blk .25 .20
1434 A627 10s dp lil rose, dp cl & blk .50 .20
1435 A627 13s lilac, claret & blk .65 .20
Nos. 1430-1435 (6) 2.00 1.20

Sports events in Bulgaria during May-June, 1965.

No. 989 Surcharged

1965, Aug. 12 — *Perf. 13*

1436 A499 2s on 8s orange brn, surcharge 36mm wide .75 .25
a. Surcharge 32mm wide 1.50 1.50

1st Natl. Folklore Competition, Aug. 12-15.

Escaping Prisoners — A628

Fruit — A629

1965, July 23 — *Perf. 10½*

1437 A628 2s slate .20 .20

40th anniversary of the escape of political prisoners from Bolshevik Island.

1965, July 1 — *Perf. 13*

1438 A629 1s Apples .20 .20
1439 A629 2s Grapes .20 .20
1440 A629 3s Pears .20 .20
1441 A629 4s Peaches .20 .20
1442 A629 5s Strawberries .20 .20
1443 A629 6s Walnuts .30 .20
Nos. 1438-1443 (6) 1.30 1.20

Horsemanship — A630

1965, Sept. 30 Unwmk. — *Perf. 10½*

1444 A630 1s Dressage .20 .20
1445 A630 2s Three-day test .20 .20
1446 A630 3s Jumping .20 .20
1447 A630 5s Race .30 .20
1448 A630 10s Steeplechase 1.50 .75
1449 A630 13s Hurdle race 1.60 1.00
Nos. 1444-1449 (6) 4.00 2.55

See No. B28.

Smiling Children — A631

Designs: 2s, Two girl Pioneers. 3s, Bugler. 5s, Pioneer with model plane. 8s, Two singing girls in national costume. 13s, Running boy.

1965, Oct. 24 — **Photo.**

1450 A631 1s dk bl grn & yel grn .20 .20
1451 A631 2s vio & deep rose .20 .20
1452 A631 3s olive & lemon .20 .20
1453 A631 5s dp blue & bister .20 .20
1454 A631 8s olive bister & org .30 .20
1455 A631 13s rose car & vio .65 .25
Nos. 1450-1455 (6) 1.75 1.25

Dimitrov Pioneer Organization.

U-52 Plane over Trnovo
A632

2s, IL-14 over Plovdiv. 3s, Mi-4 Helicopter over Dimitrovgrad. 5s, Tu-104 over Ruse. 13s, IL-18 over Varna. 20s, Tu-114 over Sofia.

1965, Nov. 25 — *Perf. 10½*

1456 A632 1s gray, blue & red .20 .20
1457 A632 2s gray, lilac & red .20 .20
1458 A632 3s gray, grnsh bl & red .20 .20
1459 A632 5s gray, orange & red .20 .20
1460 A632 13s gray, bister & red .70 .20
1461 A632 20s gray, lt grn & red 1.00 .30
Nos. 1456-1461 (6) 2.50 1.30

Development of Bulgarian Civil Air Transport.

IQSY Emblem, and Earth Radiation Zones
A633

Designs (IQSY Emblem and): 2s, Sun with corona. 13s, Solar eclipse.

1965, Dec. 15 Photo. — *Perf. 10½*

1462 A633 1s grn, yel & ultra .20 .20
1463 A633 2s yel, red lil & red .20 .20
1464 A633 13s bl, yel & blk .30 .20
Nos. 1462-1464 (3) .70 .60

International Quiet Sun Year, 1964-65.

"North and South Bulgaria"
A634

"Martenitsa" Emblem — A635

1965, Dec. 6

1465 A634 13s brt yel grn & blk .60 .40

Union of North and South Bulgaria, cent.

1966, Jan. 10 Photo. — *Perf. 10½*

"Spring" in Folklore: 2s, Drummer. 3s, Bird ornaments. 5s, Dancer "Lazarka." 8s, Vase with flowers. 13s, Bagpiper.

1466 A635 1s rose lil, vio bl & gray .20 .20
1467 A635 2s gray, blk & crim .20 .20
1468 A635 3s red, vio & gray .20 .20
1469 A635 5s lil, blk & crimson .20 .20
1470 A635 8s rose lil, brn & pur .25 .20
1471 A635 13s bl, blk & rose lilac .50 .20
Nos. 1466-1471 (6) 1.55 1.20

Church of St. John the Baptist, Nessebr
A636

Designs: 1s, Christ, fresco from Bojana Church. 2s, Ikon "Destruction of Idols," horiz. 3s, Bratchkovo Monastery. 4s, Zemen Monastery, horiz. 13s, Nativity, ikon from Arbanassi. 20s, Ikon "Virgin and Child," 1342.

1966, Feb. 25 Litho. — *Perf. 11½*

1472 A636 1s gray & multi 3.50 1.25
1473 A636 2s gray & multi .25 .20
1474 A636 3s multicolored .25 .20
1475 A636 4s multicolored .25 .20
1476 A636 5s multicolored .25 .20
1477 A636 13s gray & multi .50 .20
1478 A636 20s multicolored .95 .35
Nos. 1472-1478 (7) 5.95 2.60

2,500 years of art in Bulgaria.

Georgi Benkovski and T. Kableshkov — A637

1s, Proclamation of April Uprising, Koprivstitsa. 3s, Dedication of flag, Panaguriste. 5s, V. Petleshkov, Z. Dyustabanov. 10s, Botev landing at Kozlodui. 13s, P. Volov, Ilarion Dragostinov.

1966, Mar. 3 Photo. — *Perf. 10½*

Center in Black

1479 A637 1s red brn & gold .20 .20
1480 A637 2s brt red & gold .20 .20
1481 A637 3s ol grn & gold .20 .20
1482 A637 5s steel bl & gold .20 .20
1483 A637 10s brt rose lil & gold .20 .20
1484 A637 13s lt vio & gold .50 .20
Nos. 1479-1484 (6) 1.50 1.20

April Uprising against the Turks, 90th anniv.

Sofia Zoo Animals
A638

1966, May 23 — **Litho.**

1485 A638 1s Elephant .20 .20
1486 A638 2s Tiger .20 .20
1487 A638 3s Chimpanzee .20 .20
1488 A638 4s Siberian ibex .20 .20
1489 A638 5s Polar bear .50 .20
1490 A638 8s Lion .60 .30
1491 A638 13s Bison 1.75 .70
1492 A638 20s Kangaroo 2.25 1.00
Nos. 1485-1492 (8) 5.90 3.00

WHO Headquarters, Geneva — A639

1966, May 3 — **Photo.**

1493 A639 13s deep blue & silver .60 .25

Inauguration of the WHO Headquarters, Geneva.

Worker
A640

1966, May 9 Photo. — *Perf. 10½*

1494 A640 20s gray & rose .90 .50

Sixth Trade Union Congress.

Yantra River Bridge, Biela — A641

#1496, Maritsa River Bridge, Svilengrad. #1497, Fountain, Samokov. #1498, Ruins of Fort, Kaskovo. 8s, Old Fort, Ruse. 13s, House, Gabrovo.

1966, Feb. 10 Photo. — *Perf. 13*

1495 A641 1s Prus blue .20 .20
1496 A641 1s brt green .20 .20
1497 A641 2s olive green .20 .20
1498 A641 2s dk red brown .20 .20

1499 A641 8s red brown .25 .20
1500 A641 13s dark blue .40 .20
Nos. 1495-1500 (6) 1.45 1.20

Souvenir Sheet

Moon Allegory — A642

1966, Apr. 29 ***Imperf.***
1501 A642 60s blk, plum & sil 2.50 2.00

1st Russian soft landing on the moon by Luna 9, Feb. 3, 1966.

Steamer Radetzky and Bugler — A643

1966, May 28 ***Perf. 10½***
1502 A643 2s multicolored .20 .20

90th anniv. of the participation of the Danube steamer Radetzky in the uprising against the Turks.

Standard Bearer Nicola Simov-Kuruto A644

1966, May 30
1503 A644 5s bister, green & olive .25 .20

Hero of the Turkish War.

UNESCO Emblem A645

1966, June 8
1504 A645 20s gold, blk & ver .60 .30

20th anniv. of UNESCO.

Youth Federation Badge — A646

1966, June 6 Photo. ***Perf. 10½***
1505 A646 13s silver, bl & blk .50 .20

7th Assembly of the Intl. Youth Federation.

Soccer — A647

Various soccer scenes. 50s, Jules Rimet Cup.

1966, June 27
1506 A647 1s gray, yel brn & blk .20 .20
1507 A647 2s gray, crim & blk .20 .20
1508 A647 5s gray, ol bis & blk .20 .20
1509 A647 13s gray, ultra & blk .35 .20
1510 A647 20s gray, Prus bl & blk .60 .20
Nos. 1506-1510 (5) 1.55 1.00

Miniature Sheet

Imperf

1511 A647 50s gray, dp lil rose & gold 2.25 1.50

World Soccer Cup Championship, Wembley, England, July 11-30. Size of No. 1511: 60x64mm.

Woman Javelin Thrower — A648

No. 1513, Runner. No. 1514, Young man and woman carrying banners, vert.

1966 Photo. ***Perf. 10½***
1512 A648 2s grn, yel & ver .20 .20
1513 A648 13s dp grn, yel & sal pink .40 .20
1514 A648 13s bl, lt bl & salmon .40 .20
Nos. 1512-1514 (3) 1.00 .60

Nos. 1512-1513: 3rd Spartacist Games; issued Aug. 10. No. 1514: 3rd congress of the Bulgarian Youth Federation; issued May 25.

Wrestlers Nicolas Petrov and Dan Kolov — A649

1966, July 29
1515 A649 13s bis brn, dk brn & lt ol grn .50 .30

3rd International Wrestling Championships.

Map of Balkan Countries, Globe and UNESCO Emblem — A650

1966, Aug. 26 ***Perf. 10½x11½***
1516 A650 13s ultra, lt grn & pink .50 .20

First Congress of Balkanologists.

Children with Building Blocks A651

2s, Bunny & teddy bear with book. 3s, Children as astronauts. 13s, Children with pails & shovel.

1966, Sept. 1 ***Perf. 10½***
1517 A651 1s dk car, org & blk .20 .20
1518 A651 2s emerald, blk & red brn .20 .20
1519 A651 3s ultra, org & blk .20 .20
1520 A651 13s blue, rose & blk .60 .20
Nos. 1517-1520 (4) 1.20 .80

Children's Day.

Yuri A. Gagarin and Vostok 1 — A652

Designs: 2s, Gherman S. Titov, Vostok 2. 3s, Andrian G. Nikolayev, Pavel R. Popovich, Vostoks 3 & 4. 5s, Valentina Tereshkova, Valeri Bykovski, Vostoks 5 & 6. 8s, Vladimir M. Komarov, Boris B. Yegorov, Konstantin Feoktistov, Voskhod 1. 13s, Pavel Belyayev, Alexei Leonov, Voskhod 2.

1966, Sept. 29 Photo. ***Perf. 11½x11***
1521 A652 1s slate & gray .20 .20
1522 A652 2s plum & gray .20 .20
1523 A652 3s yel brn & gray .20 .20
1524 A652 5s brn red & gray .20 .20
1525 A652 8s ultra & gray .20 .20
1526 A652 13s Prus bl & gray .50 .20
Nos. 1521-1526,B29 (7) 2.50 1.55

Russian space explorations.

St. Clement, 14th Century Wood Sculpture A653

1966, Oct. 27 Photo. ***Perf. 11½x11***
1527 A653 5s red, buff & brown .20 .20

1050th anniversary of the birth of St. Clement of Ochrida.

Metodi Shatorov A654

Portraits: 3s, Vladimir Trichkov. 5s, Valcho Ivanov. 10s, Raiko Daskalov. 13s, General Vladimir Zaimov.

1966, Nov. 8 ***Perf. 11x11½***

Gold Frame, Black Denomination

1528 A654 2s crimson & bl vio .20 .20
1529 A654 3s magenta & blk .20 .20
1530 A654 5s car rose & dk bl .20 .20
1531 A654 10s orange & olive .30 .20
1532 A654 13s red & brown .40 .20
Nos. 1529-1532 (4) 1.10 .80

Fighters against fascism.

George Dimitrov — A655

Steel Worker — A656

1966, Nov. 14 Photo. ***Perf. 11½x11***
1533 A655 2s magenta & blk .20 .20
1534 A656 20s fawn, gray & blk .90 .20

Bulgarian Communist Party, 9th Congress.

Deer's Head Drinking Cup A667

Gold Treasure: 2s, 6s, 10s, Various Amazon's head jugs. 3s, Ram's head cup. 5s, Circular plate. 8s, Deer's head cup. 13s, Amphora. 20s, Ram drinking horn.

1966, Nov. 28 ***Perf. 12x11½***

Vessels in Gold and Brown; Black Inscriptions

1535 A667 1s gray & violet .20 .20
1536 A667 2s gray & green .20 .20
1537 A667 3s gray & dk bl .20 .20
1538 A667 5s gray & red brn .20 .20
1539 A667 6s gray & Prus bl .20 .20
1540 A667 8s gray & brn ol .85 .20
1541 A667 10s gray & sepia .85 .20
1542 A667 13s gray & dk vio bl .85 .30
1543 A667 20s gray & vio brn .95 .30
Nos. 1535-1543 (9) 4.50 2.00

The gold treasure from the 4th century B.C. was found near Panagyurishte in 1949.

Tourist House, Bansko — A668

Tourist Houses: No. 1545, Belogradchik. No. 1546, Triavna. 20s, Rila.

1966, Nov. 29 Photo. ***Perf. 11x11½***
1544 A668 1s dark blue .20 .20
1545 A668 2s dark green .20 .20
1546 A668 2s brown red .20 .20
1547 A668 20s lilac .40 .20
Nos. 1544-1547 (4) 1.00 .80

Decorated Tree A669

Design: 13s, Jug with bird design.

1966, Dec. 12 ***Perf. 11***
1548 A669 2s grn, pink & gold .20 .20
1549 A669 13s brn lake, rose, emer & gold .40 .20

New Year, 1967.

Pencho Slavikov, Author — A670

Dahlia — A671

Portraits: 2s, Dimcho Debeljanov, author. 3s, P. H. Todorov, author. 5s, Dimitri Dobrovich, painter. 8s, Ivan Markvichka, painter. 13s, Ilya Bezhkov, painter.

1966, Dec. 15 ***Perf. 10½x11***
1550 A670 1s blue, olive & org .20 .20
1551 A670 2s org, brn & gray .20 .20
1552 A670 3s olive, bl & org .20 .20
1553 A670 5s gray, red brn & org .20 .20

1554 A670 8s lilac, dk gray & bl .30 .20
1555 A670 13s blue, vio & lil .40 .20
Nos. 1550-1555 (6) 1.50 1.20

1966, Dec. 29

Flowers: No. 1557, Clematis. No. 1558, Foxglove. No. 1559, Narcissus. 3s, Snowdrop. 5s, Petunia. 13s, Tiger lily. 20s, Bellflower.

Flowers in Natural Colors

1556 A671 1s gray & lt brn .20 .20
1557 A671 1s gray & dull bl .20 .20
1558 A671 2s gray & dull lil .20 .20
1559 A671 2s gray & brown .20 .20
1560 A671 3s gray & dk grn .20 .20
1561 A671 5s gray & dp ultra .25 .20
1562 A671 13s gray & brown .60 .20
1563 A671 20s gray & ultra .95 .20
Nos. 1556-1563 (8) 2.80 1.60

Ringnecked Pheasant — A672

Game: 2s, Rock partridge. 3s, Gray partridge. 5s, Hare. 8s, Roe deer. 13s, Red deer.

1967, Jan. 28 ***Perf. 11x10½***

1564 A672 1s lt ultra, dk brn & ocher .20 .20
1565 A672 2s pale yel grn & dk grn .20 .20
1566 A672 3s lt bl, blk & cr .20 .20
1567 A672 5s lt grn & blk .50 .25
1568 A672 8s pale bl, dk brn & ocher 1.40 .50
1569 A672 13s bl & dk brn 1.50 .90
Nos. 1564-1569 (6) 4.00 2.25

Bulgaria No. 1, 1879 — A673

Thracian Coin, 6th Century, B.C. — A674

1967, Feb. 4 **Photo.** ***Perf. 10½***

1570 A673 10s emerald, blk & yel 1.00 .75

Bulgarian Philatelic Union, 10th Congress.

1967, Mar. 30 ***Perf. 11½x11***

Coins: 2s, Macedonian tetradrachma, 2nd cent. B.C. 3s, Tetradrachma of Odessus, 2nd cent. B.C. 5s, Philip II of Macedonia, 4th cent., B.C. 13s, Thracian King Seuthus VII, 4th cent., B.C., obverse and reverse. 20s, Apollonian coin, 5th cent., B.C., obverse and reverse.

Size: 25x25mm

1571 A674 1s brn, blk & sil .20 .20
1572 A674 2s red lil, blk & sil .20 .20
1573 A674 3s grn, blk & sil .20 .20
1574 A674 5s brn org, blk & sil .20 .20

Size: 37½x25mm

1575 A674 13s brt bl, blk & brnz .70 .25
1576 A674 20s vio, blk & sil 1.25 .45
Nos. 1571-1576 (6) 2.75 1.50

Partisans Listening to Radio — A675

Design: 20s, George Dimitrov addressing crowd and Bulgarian flag.

1967, Apr. 20 ***Perf. 11x11½***

1577 A675 1s red, gold, buff & sl grn .20 .20
1578 A675 20s red, gold, dl red, grn & blk .55 .20

25th anniversary of the Union of Patriotic Front Organizations.

Nikolas Kofardjiev A676

2s, Petko Napetov. 5s, Petko D. Petkov. 10s, Emil Markov. 13s, Traitcho Kostov.

1967, Apr. 24 ***Perf. 11½x11***

1579 A676 1s brn red, gray & blk .20 .20
1580 A676 2s ol grn, gray & blk .20 .20
1581 A676 5s brn, gray & blk .20 .20
1582 A676 10s dp bl, gray & blk .20 .20
1583 A676 13s mag, gray & blk .40 .20
Nos. 1579-1583 (5) 1.20 1.00

Fighters against fascism.

Symbolic Flower and Flame — A677

1967, May 18 **Photo.** ***Perf. 11x11½***

1584 A677 13s gold, yel & lt grn .45 .20

First Cultural Congress, May 18-19.

Gold Sand Beach and ITY Emblem A678

20s, Hotel, Pamporovo. 40s, Nessebr Church.

1967, June 12 **Photo.** ***Perf. 11x11½***

1585 A678 13s ultra, yel & blk .30 .20
1586 A678 20s Prus bl, blk & buff .40 .20
1587 A678 40s brt grn, blk & ocher 1.00 .30
Nos. 1585-1587 (3) 1.70 .70

International Tourist Year, 1967.

Angora Cat — A679

Cats: 2s, Siamese, horiz. 3s, Abyssinian. 5s, Black European. 13s, Persian, horiz. 20s, Striped domestic.

Perf. 11½x11, 11x11½

1967, June 19

1588 A679 1s dl vio, dk brn & buff .20 .20
1589 A679 2s ol, sl & brt bl .20 .20
1590 A679 3s dull blue & brn .25 .20
1591 A679 5s grn, blk & yel .85 .20
1592 A679 13s dl red brn, sl & org 1.00 .20
1593 A679 20s gray grn, brn & buff 1.50 .25
Nos. 1588-1593 (6) 4.00 1.25

Scene from Opera "The Master of Boyana" by K. Iliev A680

Songbird on Keyboard — A681

1967, June 19

1594 A680 5s gray, vio bl & dp car .40 .20
1595 A681 13s gray, dp car & dk bl 1.10 .20

3rd Intl. Competition for Young Opera Singers.

George Kirkov (1867-1919), Revolutionist — A682

1967, June 24 ***Perf. 11x11½***

1596 A682 2s rose red & dk brn .20 .20

Symbolic Tree and Stars — A683

1967, July 28 **Photo.** ***Perf. 11½x11***

1597 A683 13s dp bl, car & blk .50 .20

11th Congress of Dimitrov's Union of the People's Youth.

Roses and Distillery A684

Designs: No. 1599, Chick and incubator. No. 1600, Cucumbers and hothouse. No. 1601, Lamb and sheep farm. 3s, Sunflower and oil mill. 4s, Pigs and pig farm. 5s, Hops and hop farm. 6s, Corn and irrigation system. 8s, Grapes and Bolgar tractor. 10s, Apples and cultivated tree. 13s, Bees and honey. 20s, Bee, blossoms and beehives.

1967 ***Perf. 11x11½***

1598 A684 1s multicolored .20 .20
1599 A684 1s dk car, yel & blk .20 .20
1600 A684 2s vio, lt grn & blk .20 .20
1601 A684 2s brt grn, gray & blk .20 .20
1602 A684 3s yel grn, yel & blk .20 .20
1603 A684 4s brt pur, yel & blk .20 .20
1604 A684 5s ol bis, yel grn & blk .20 .20
1605 A684 6s ol, brt grn & blk .20 .20
1606 A684 8s grn, bis & blk .20 .20
1607 A684 10s multicolored .25 .20
1608 A684 13s grn, bis brn & blk .40 .20
1609 A684 20s grnsh bl, brt pink & blk .55 .20
Nos. 1598-1609 (12) 3.00 2.40

Issue dates: Nos. 1598-1601, 1607, 1609, July 15; Nos. 1602-1606, 1608, July 24.

Map of Communist Countries, Spasski Tower A685

2s, Lenin speaking to soldiers. 3s, Fighting at Wlodaja, 1918. 5s, Marx, Engels & Lenin. 13s, Oil refinery. 20s, Molniya communication satellite.

1967, Aug. 25 ***Perf. 11***

1610 A685 1s multicolored .20 .20
1611 A685 2s magenta & olive .20 .20
1612 A685 3s mag & dull vio .20 .20
1613 A685 5s magenta & red .20 .20
1614 A685 13s magenta & ultra .25 .20
1615 A685 20s magenta & blue .45 .20
Nos. 1610-1615 (6) 1.50 1.20

Russian October Revolution, 50th anniv.

Rod, "Fish" and Varna A686

1967, Aug. 29 **Photo.** ***Perf. 11***

1616 A686 10s multicolored .35 .20

7th World Angling Championships, Varna.

Skiers and Winter Olympics' Emblem — A687

Sports and Emblem: 2s, Ski jump. 3s, Biathlon. 5s, Ice hockey. 13s, Figure skating couple.

1967, Sept. 20 **Photo.** ***Perf. 11***

1617 A687 1s dk bl grn, red & blk .20 .20
1618 A687 2s ultra, blk & ol .20 .20
1619 A687 3s vio brn, bl & blk .20 .20
1620 A687 5s green, yel & blk .20 .20
1621 A687 13s vio bl, blk & buff .35 .20
Nos. 1617-1621,B31 (6) 2.25 1.30

10th Winter Olympic Games, Grenoble, France, Feb. 6-18, 1968.

Mountain Peaks — A688

1967, Sept. 25 **Engr.** ***Perf. 11½***

1622 A688 1s Bogdan .20 .20
1623 A688 2s Czerny .20 .20
1624 A688 3s Ruen, vert. .20 .20
1625 A688 5s Persenk .20 .20
1626 A688 10s Botev .20 .20
1627 A688 13s Rila, vert. .25 .20
1628 A688 20s Vihren .55 .20
Nos. 1622-1628 (7) 1.80 1.40

George Rakovski A689

1967, Oct. 20 Photo. *Perf. 11*

1629 A689 13s yellow grn & blk .50 .25

Centenary of the death of George Rakovski, revolutionary against Turkish rule.

Yuri A. Gagarin, Valentina Tereshkova and Alexei Leonov — A690

Designs: 2s, Lt. Col. John H. Glenn, Jr., and Maj. Edward H. White. 5s, Earth and Molniya 1. 10s, Gemini 6 and 7. 13s, Luna 13 moon probe. 20s, Gemini 10 and Agena rocket.

1967, Nov. 25

1630 A690 1s Prus bl, blk & yel .20 .20
1631 A690 2s dl bl, blk & dl yel .20 .20
1632 A690 5s vio bl, grnsh bl & blk .20 .20
1633 A690 10s dk bl, blk & red .35 .20
1634 A690 13s grnsh bl, brt yel & blk .55 .20
1635 A690 20s dl bl, blk & red .75 .20
Nos. 1630-1635 (6) 2.25 1.20

Achievements in space exploration.

Various Views of Trnovo A691

1967, Dec. 5 Photo. *Perf. 11*

1636 A691 1s multicolored .20 .20
1637 A691 2s multicolored .20 .20
1638 A691 3s multicolored .20 .20
1639 A691 5s multicolored .20 .20
1640 A691 13s multicolored .30 .20
1641 A691 20s multicolored .50 .20
Nos. 1636-1641 (6) 1.60 1.20

Restoration of the ancient capital Veliko Trnovo.

Ratchenitza Folk Dance, by Ivan Markvichka — A692

1967, Dec. 9

1642 A692 20s gold & gray grn 1.00 .80

Belgo-Bulgarian Philatelic Exposition, Brussels, Dec. 9-10. Printed in sheets of 8 stamps and 8 labels.

Cosmos 186 and 188 Docking — A693

40s, Venus 4 and orbits around Venus.

1968, Jan.

1643 A693 20s multi .55 .20
1644 A693 40s multi, horiz. 1.00 .25

Docking maneuvers of the Russian spaceships Cosmos 186 and Cosmos 188, Nov. 1, 1967, and the flight to Venus of Venus 4, June 12-Nov. 18, 1967.

Crossing the Danube, by Orenburgski — A694

Paintings: 2s, Flag of Samara, by J. Veschin, vert. 3s, Battle of Pleven by Orenburgski. 13s, Battle of Orlovo Gnezdo, by N. Popov, vert. 20s, Welcome for Russian Soldiers, by D. Gudienov.

1968, Jan. 25 Photo. *Perf. 11*

1645 A694 1s gold & dk green .20 .20
1646 A694 2s gold & dk blue .20 .20
1647 A694 3s gold & chocolate .20 .20
1648 A694 13s gold & dk vio .30 .20
1649 A694 20s gold & Prus grn .50 .20
Nos. 1645-1649 (5) 1.40 1.00

90th anniv. of the liberation from Turkey.

Shepherds, by Zlatyn Boyadjiev — A695

Paintings: 2s, Wedding dance, by V. Dimitrov, vert. 3s, Partisans' Song, by Ilya Petrov. 5s, Portrait of Anna Penchovich, by Nikolai Pavlovich, vert. 13s, Self-portrait, by Zachary Zograf, vert. 20s, View of Old Plovdiv, by T. Lavrenov. 60s, St. Clement of Ochrida, by A. Mitov.

1967, Dec. Litho. *Perf. 11½*

Size: 45x38mm, 38x45mm

1650 A695 1s gray & multi .20 .20
1651 A695 2s gray & multi .20 .20

Size: 55x35mm

1652 A695 3s gray & multi .25 .20

Size: 38x45mm, 45x38mm

1653 A695 5s gray & multi .40 .20
1654 A695 13s gray & multi .90 .25
1655 A695 20s gray & multi 1.25 .40
Nos. 1650-1655 (6) 3.20 1.45

Miniature Sheet

Size: 65x84mm

Imperf

1656 A695 60s multicolored 3.25 1.90

Marx Statue, Sofia — A696

Maxim Gorky — A697

1968, Feb. 20 Photo. *Perf. 11*

1657 A696 13s black & red .50 .20

150th anniversary of birth of Karl Marx.

1968, Feb. 20

1658 A697 13s ver & grnsh blk .50 .20

Maxim Gorky (1868-1936), Russian writer.

Folk Dancers — A698

5s, Runners. 13s, Doves. 20s, Festival poster, (head, flowers, birds). 40s, Globe & Bulgaria No. 1 under magnifying glass.

1968, Mar. 20

1659 A698 2s multicolored .20 .20
1660 A698 5s multicolored .20 .20
1661 A698 13s multicolored .25 .20
1662 A698 20s multicolored .50 .20
1663 A698 40s multicolored 1.10 .40
Nos. 1659-1663 (5) 2.25 1.20

9th Youth Festival for Peace and Friendship, Sofia, July 28-Aug. 6.

Bellflower — A699

1968, Apr. 25 *Perf. 11*

1664 A699 1s shown .20 .20
1665 A699 2s Gentian .20 .20
1666 A699 3s Crocus .20 .20
1667 A699 5s Iris .20 .20
1668 A699 10s Dog-tooth violet .20 .20
1669 A699 13s Sempervivum .70 .20
1670 A699 20s Dictamnus .95 .25
Nos. 1664-1670 (7) 2.65 1.45

"The Unknown Hero," Tale by Ran Bosilek A700

Design: 20s, The Witch and the Young Man (Hans Christian Andersen fairy tale.)

1968, Apr. 25 Photo. *Perf. 10½*

1671 A700 13s black & multi .35 .20
1672 A700 20s black & multi .65 .35

Bulgarian-Danish Philatelic Exhibition.

Memorial Church, Shipka — A701

1968, May 3

1673 A701 13s multi + label .70 .20

Bulgarian Stamp Exhibition in Berlin.

Show Jumping A702

Olympic Rings and: 1s, Gymnast on bar. 3s, Fencer. 10s, Boxer. 13s, Woman discus thrower.

1968, June 24 Photo. *Perf. 10½*

1674 A702 1s red & black .20 .20
1675 A702 2s gray, blk & rose brn .20 .20
1676 A702 3s mag, gray & blk .20 .20
1677 A702 10s grnsh bl, blk & lem .20 .20
1678 A702 13s vio bl, gray & pink .55 .20
Nos. 1674-1678,B33 (6) 2.35 1.30

19th Olympic Games, Mexico City, 10/12-27.

Battle of Buzluja A703

Design: 13s, Haji Dimitr and Stefan Karaja.

1968, July 1

1679 A703 2s silver & red brn .20 .20
1680 A703 13s gold & sl grn .30 .20

Centenary of the death of the patriots Haji Dimitr and Stefan Karaja.

Lakes of Smolian — A704

Sofia Zoo, Cent. — A705

Bulgarian Scenes: 2s, Ropotamo Lake. 3s, Erma-Idreloto mountain pass. 8s, Isker River dam. 10s, Slanchev Breg (sailing ship). 13s, Cape Caliacra. 40s, Old houses, Sozopol. 2 l, Chudnite Skali ("Strange Mountains").

1968 Photo. *Perf. 13*

1681 A704 1s Prus green .20 .20
1682 A704 2s dark green .20 .20
1683 A704 3s dark brown .20 .20
1684 A704 8s olive green .20 .20
1685 A704 10s redsh brown .20 .20
1686 A704 13s dk olive grn .25 .20
1687 A704 40s Prus blue .60 .25
1688 A704 2 l sepia 3.75 .85
Nos. 1681-1688 (8) 5.60 2.30

1968, July 29 ***Perf. 10½***

1689	A705	1s	Cinereous vulture	.20	.20
1690	A705	2s	Crowned crane	.20	.20
1691	A705	3s	Zebra	.20	.20
1692	A705	5s	Cheetah	.35	.20
1693	A705	13s	Indian python	1.40	.55
1694	A705	20s	African crocodile	1.90	.90
			Nos. 1689-1694 (6)	4.25	2.25

Human Rights Flame — A706

1968, July 8

1695	A706	20s	dp blue & gold	.75	.40

International Human Rights Year, 1968.

Congress Hall, Varna, and Emblem A707

1968, Sept. 17 **Photo.** ***Perf. 10½***

1696	A707	20s	bister, grn & red	.60	.20

56th International Dental Congress, Varna.

Flying Swans A708

Rose A709

Stag Beetle — A710

Designs: 2s, Jug. 20s, Five Viking ships.

1968 **Photo.** ***Perf. 10½***

1697	A709	2s	green & ocher	.75	.50
1698	A708	5s	dp blue & gray	.75	.50
1699	A709	13s	dp plum & lil rose	.75	.50
a.			Pair, #1698, 1699 + label	1.50	1.00
1700	A708	20s	dp vio & gray	.75	.50
a.			Pair, #1697, 1700 + label	1.50	1.00
			Nos. 1697-1700 (4)	3.00	2.00

Cooperation with the Scandinavian countries. Issued: 5s, 13s, Sept. 12; 2s, 20s, Nov. 22.

Perf. 12½x13, 13x12½

1968, Aug. 26

#1702, Ground beetle (Procerus scabrosus). #1703, Ground beetle (Calosoma sycophania). #1704, Scarab beetle, horiz. #1705, Saturnid moth, horiz.

1701	A710	1s	brown olive	.20	.20
1702	A710	1s	dark blue	.20	.20
1703	A710	1s	dark green	.20	.20
1704	A710	1s	orange brown	.20	.20
1705	A710	1s	magenta	.20	.20
			Nos. 1701-1705 (5)	1.00	1.00

Turks Fighting Insurgents, 1688 — A711

1968, Aug. 22 ***Perf. 10½***

1706	A711	13s	multicolored	.45	.20

280th anniversary of the Tchiprovtzi insurrection.

Christo Smirnenski (1898-1923), Poet — A712

1968, Sept. 28 **Litho.** ***Perf. 10½***

1707	A712	13s	gold, red org & blk	.50	.20

Dalmatian Pelican — A713

Birds: 2s, Little egret. 3s, Crested grebe. 5s, Common tern. 13s, European spoonbill. 20s, Glossy ibis.

1968, Oct. 28 **Photo.**

1708	A713	1s	silver & multi	.20	.20
1709	A713	2s	silver & multi	.20	.20
1710	A713	3s	silver & multi	.20	.20
1711	A713	5s	silver & multi	.20	.20
1712	A713	13s	silver & multi	.50	.20
1713	A713	20s	silver & multi	1.10	.30
			Nos. 1708-1713 (6)	2.40	1.30

Srebirna wild life reservation.

Carrier Pigeon A714

1968, Oct. 19

1714	A714	20s	emerald	.90	.60
a.			Sheet of 4 + labels	5.00	1.60

2nd Natl. Stamp Exhib. in Sofia, Oct. 25-Nov. 15. No. 1714a contains 4 No. 1714 and 5 labels.

Man and Woman from Lovech A715

Regional Costumes: 1s, Silistra. 3s, Yambol. 13s, Chirpan. 20s, Razgrad. 40s, Ihtiman.

1968, Nov. 20 **Litho.** ***Perf. 13½***

1715	A715	1s	dp org & multi	.20	.20
1716	A715	2s	Prus bl & multi	.20	.20
1717	A715	3s	multicolored	.20	.20
1718	A715	13s	multicolored	.30	.20
1719	A715	20s	multicolored	.55	.25
1720	A715	40s	green & multi	1.40	.45
			Nos. 1715-1720 (6)	2.85	1.50

St. Arsenius A716

10th cent. Murals & Icons: 2s, Procession with relics of St. Ivan Rilsky, horiz. 3s, St. Michael Torturing the Soul of the Rich Man. 13s, St. Ivan Rilski. 20s, St. John. 40s, St. George. 1 l, Procession meeting relics of St. Ivan Rilsky, horiz.

Perf. 11½x12½, 12½x11½

1968, Nov. 25 **Photo.**

1721	A716	1s	gold & multi	.20	.20
1722	A716	2s	gold & multi	.20	.20
1723	A716	3s	gold & multi	.20	.20
1724	A716	13s	gold & multi	.40	.20
1725	A716	20s	gold & multi	.95	.30
1726	A716	40s	gold & multi	1.40	.60
			Nos. 1721-1726 (6)	3.35	1.70

Souvenir Sheet

Imperf

1727	A716	1 l	gold & multi	3.75	2.75

Millenium of Rila Monastery. No. 1727 also: Sofia 1969 Intl. Phil. Exhib., May 31-June 8, 1969. No. 1727 contains one stamp, size: 57x51mm.

Medlar A717

Herbs: No. 1729, Camomile. 2s, Lily-of-the-valley. 3s, Belladonna. 5s, Mallow. 10s, Buttercup. 13s, Poppies. 20s, Thyme.

1969, Jan. 2 **Litho.** ***Perf. 10½***

1728	A717	1s	blk, grn & org red	.20	.20
1729	A717	1s	black, grn & yel	.20	.20
1730	A717	2s	blk, emer & grn	.20	.20
1731	A717	3s	black & multi	.20	.20
1732	A717	5s	black & multi	.20	.20
1733	A717	10s	black, grn & yel	.20	.20
1734	A717	13s	black & multi	.30	.20
1735	A717	20s	black, lil & grn	.65	.20
			Nos. 1728-1735 (8)	2.15	1.60

Silkworms and Spindles A718

Designs: 2s, Silkworm, cocoons and pattern. 3s, Cocoons and spinning wheel. 5s, Cocoons, woof-and-warp diagram. 13s, Silk moth, Cocoon and spinning frame. 20s, Silk moth, eggs and shuttle.

1969, Jan. 30 **Photo.** ***Perf. 10½***

1736	A718	1s	bl, grn, sil & blk	.20	.20
1737	A718	2s	dp car, sil & blk	.20	.20
1738	A718	3s	Prus bl, sil & blk	.20	.20
1739	A718	5s	pur, ver, sil & blk	.20	.20
1740	A718	13s	red lil, ocher, sil & blk	.25	.20
1741	A718	20s	grn, org, sil & blk	.45	.20
			Nos. 1736-1741 (6)	1.50	1.20

Bulgarian silk industry.

Attack and Capture of Emperor Nicephorus A719

Sts. Cyril and Methodius, Mural, Troian Monastery A720

Designs (Manasses Chronicle): No. 1742, Death of Ivan Asen. 3s, Khan Kroum feasting after victory. No. 1748, Invasion of Bulgaria by Prince Sviatoslav of Kiev. No. 1750, Russian invasion and campaigns of Emperor John I Zimisces, c. 972 A.D. 40s, Tsar Ivan Alexander, Jesus and Constantine Manasses.

Horizontal designs: No. 1743, Kings Nebuchadnezzar, Balthazar, Darius and Cyrus. No. 1745, Kings Cambyses, Gyges and Darius. 5s, King David and Tsar Ivan Alexander. No. 1749, Persecution of Byzantine army after battle of July 26, 811. No. 1751, Christening of Bulgarian Tsar Boris, 865. 60s, Arrival of Tsar Simeon in Constantinople and his succeeding surprise attack on that city.

1969 **Photo.** ***Perf. 14x13½, 13½x14***

1742	A719	1s	multicolored	.20	.20
1743	A719	1s	multicolored	.20	.20
1744	A719	2s	multicolored	.20	.20
1745	A719	2s	multicolored	.20	.20
1746	A719	3s	multicolored	.20	.20
1747	A719	5s	multicolored	.20	.20
1748	A719	13s	multicolored	.40	.20
1749	A719	13s	multicolored	.40	.20
1750	A719	20s	multicolored	.80	.20
1751	A719	20s	multicolored	.80	.20
1752	A719	40s	multicolored	1.25	.40
1753	A719	60s	multicolored	2.25	.40
			Nos. 1742-1753 (12)	7.10	2.80

1969, Mar. 23

1754	A720	28s	gold & multi	.75	.45

Post Horn — A721

Designs: 13s, Bulgaria Nos. 1 and 534. 20s, Street fighting at Stackata, 1919.

1969, Apr. 15 **Photo.** ***Perf. 10½***

1755	A721	2s	green & yel	.20	.20
1756	A721	13s	multicolored	.40	.20
1757	A721	20s	dk bl & lt bl	.50	.20
			Nos. 1755-1757 (3)	1.10	.60

Bulgarian postal administration, 90th anniv.

The Fox and the Rabbit A722

Children's Drawings: 2s, Boy reading to wolf and fox. 13s, Two birds and cat singing together.

1969, Apr. 21

1758 A722 1s emer, org & blk .20 .20
1759 A722 2s org, lt bl & blk .20 .20
1760 A722 13s lt bl, ol & blk .40 .20
Nos. 1758-1760 (3) .80 .60

Issued for Children's Week.

ILO Emblem — A723

1969, Apr. 28

1761 A723 13s dull grn & blk .35 .20

50th anniv. of the ILO.

St. George and SOFIA 69 Emblem A724

Designs: 2s, Virgin Mary and St. John Bogoslov. 3s, Archangel Michael. 5s, Three Saints. 8s, Jesus Christ. 13s, Sts. George and Dimitrie. 20s, Christ, the Almighty. 40s, St. Dimitrie. 60s, The 40 Martyrs. 80s, The Transfiguration.

1969, Apr. 30 ***Perf. 11x12***

1762 A724 1s gold & multi .20 .20
1763 A724 2s gold & multi .20 .20
1764 A724 3s gold & multi .20 .20
1765 A724 5s gold & multi .20 .20
1766 A724 8s gold & multi .20 .20
1767 A724 13s gold & multi .30 .20
1768 A724 20s gold & multi .65 .25
1769 A724 40s gold & multi 1.40 .40
a. Sheet of 4 5.75 5.00
1770 A724 60s gold & multi 1.75 .85
1771 A724 80s gold & multi 2.75 1.00
Nos. 1762-1771 (10) 7.85 3.70

Old Bulgarian art from the National Art Gallery. No. 1769a contains 4 of No. 1769 with center gutter showing Alexander Nevski Shrine. See note on SOFIA 69 after Nos. C112-C120.

St. Cyril Preaching A725

Design: 28s, St. Cyril and followers.

1969, June 20 **Litho.** ***Perf. 10½***

1772 A725 2s sil, grn & red .20 .20
1773 A725 28s sil, dk bl & red 1.00 .50

St. Cyril (827-869), apostle to the Slavs, inventor of Cyrillic alphabet. Issued in sheets of 25 with se-tenant labels; Cyrillic inscription on label of 2s, Glagolitic inscription on label of 28s.

St. Sophia Church — A726

Sofia Through the Ages: 1s, Roman coin with inscription "Ulpia Serdica." 2s, Roman coin with Aesculapius Temple. 4s, Bojana Church. 5s, Sobranic Parliament. 13s, Vasov National Theater. 20s, Alexander Nevski Shrine. 40s, Clement Ochrida University. 1 l, Coat of arms.

1969, May 25 ***Perf. 13x12½***

1774 A726 1s gold & blue .20 .20
1775 A726 2s gold & ol grn .20 .20
1776 A726 3s gold & red brn .20 .20
1777 A726 4s gold & purple .20 .20
1778 A726 5s gold & plum .20 .20
1779 A726 13s gold & brt grn .30 .20
1780 A726 20s gold & vio bl .45 .20
1781 A726 40s gold & dp car 1.10 .25
Nos. 1774-1781 (8) 2.85 1.65

Souvenir Sheet

Imperf

1782 A726 1 l grn, gold & red 2.25 2.00

Historic Sofia in connection with the International Philatelic Exhibition, Sofia, 5/31-6/8.

#1782 contains one 43½x43½mm stamp. Emblems of 8 preceding philatelic exhibitions in metallic ink in margin; gold inscription.

No. 1782 was overprinted in green "IBRA 73" and various symbols, and released May 4, 1973, for the Munich Philatelic Exhibition. The overprint also exists in gray.

St. George A727

1969, June 9 **Litho.** ***Perf. 11½***

1783 A727 40s sil, blk & pale rose 1.50 .75

38th FIP Congress, June 9-11.

Hand Planting Sapling A728

1969, Apr. 28 **Photo.** ***Perf. 11***

1784 A728 2s ol grn, blk & lilac .20 .20

25 years of the reforestation campaign.

Partisans — A729

Designs: 2s, Combine harvester. 3s, Dam. 5s, Flutist and singers. 13s, Factory. 20s, Lenin, Dimitrov, Russian and Bulgarian flags.

1969, Sept. 9

1785 A729 1s blk, pur & org .20 .20
1786 A729 2s blk, ol bis & org .20 .20
1787 A729 3s blk, bl grn & org .20 .20
1788 A729 5s blk, brn red & org .20 .20
1789 A729 13s blk, bl & org .30 .20
1790 A729 20s blk, brn & org .50 .20
Nos. 1785-1790 (6) 1.60 1.20

25th anniversary of People's Republic.

Women Gymnasts — A730

1969, Sept. **Photo.** ***Perf. 11***

1791 A730 2s shown .20 .20
1792 A730 20s Wrestlers .40 .25

Third National Spartakiad.

Tchanko Bakalov Tcherkovski, Poet. Birth Cent. — A731

1969, Sept. 6

1793 A731 13s multicolored .40 .20

Woman Gymnast A732

2s, Two women with hoops. 3s, Woman with hoop. 5s, Two women with spheres.

1969, Oct.

Gymnasts in Light Gray

1794 A732 1s green & dk blue .20 .20
1795 A732 2s blue & dk blue .20 .20
1796 A732 3s emer & sl grn .20 .20
1797 A732 5s orange & pur .20 .20
Nos. 1794-1797,B35-B36 (6) 1.90 1.30

World Championships for Artistic Gymnastics, Varna.

The Priest Rilski, by Zachary Zograf A733

Paintings from the National Art Gallery. 2s, Woman at Window, by Vasil Stoilov. 3s, Workers at Rest, by Nenko Balkanski, horiz. 4s, Woman Dressing (Nude), by Ivan Nenov. 5s, Portrait of a Woman, by N. Pavlovich. 13s, Falstaff, by Duzunov Kr. Sarafov. No. 1804, Portrait of a Woman, by N. Mihajlov, horiz. No. 1805, Workers at Mealtime, by Stojan Sotirov, horiz. 40s, Self-portrait, by Tcheno Togorov.

Perf. 11½x12, 12x11½

1969, Nov. 10

1798 A733 1s gold & multi .20 .20
1799 A733 2s gold & multi .20 .20
1800 A733 3s gold & multi .20 .20
1801 A733 4s gold & multi .20 .20
1802 A733 5s gold & multi .20 .20
1803 A733 13s gold & multi .30 .20
1804 A733 20s gold & multi .70 .25
1805 A733 20s gold & multi .70 .25
1806 A733 40s gold & multi 1.40 .60
Nos. 1798-1806 (9) 4.10 2.30

Roman Bronze Wolf — A734

Design: 2s, Roman statue of woman, found at Silistra, vert.

1969, Oct. **Photo.** ***Perf. 11***

1807 A734 2s sil, ultra & gray .20 .20
1808 A734 13s sil, dk grn & gray .60 .30

City of Silistra's 1,800th anniversary.

Worker and Factory A735

1969 ***Perf. 13***

1809 A735 6s ultra & blk .20 .20

25th anniversary of the factory militia.

European Hake — A736

Designs: No. 1811, Deep-sea fishing trawler. Fish: 2s, Atlantic horse mackerel. 3s, Pilchard. 5s, Dentex macrophthalmus. 10s, Chub mackerel. 13s, Otolithes macrognathus. 20s, Lichia vadigo.

1969 ***Perf. 11***

1810 A736 1s ol grn & blk .20 .20
1811 A736 1s ultra, ind & gray .20 .20
1812 A736 2s lilac & blk .20 .20
1813 A736 3s vio bl & blk .20 .20
1814 A736 5s rose cl, pink & blk .25 .20
1815 A736 10s gray & blk .50 .20
1816 A736 13s ver, sal & blk .70 .20
1817 A736 20s ocher & black 1.25 .20
Nos. 1810-1817 (8) 3.50 1.60

Marin Drinov A737

1969, Nov. 10 **Litho.** ***Perf. 11***

1818 A737 20s black & red org .35 .20

Centenary of the Bulgarian Academy of Science, founded by Marin Drinov.

Trapeze Artists — A738

Pavel Bania Sanatorium A739

Circus Performers: 2s, Jugglers. 3s, Jugglers with loops. 5s, Juggler and bear on bicycle. 13s, Woman and performing horse. 20s, Musical clowns.

1969 Photo. *Perf. 11*

1819 A738 1s dk blue & multi .20 .20
1820 A738 2s dk green & multi .20 .20
1821 A738 3s dk violet & multi .20 .20
1822 A738 5s multicolored .20 .20
1823 A738 13s multicolored .30 .20
1824 A738 20s multicolored .55 .20
Nos. 1819-1824 (6) 1.65 1.20

1969, Dec. Photo. *Perf. 10½-14*

Health Resorts: 5s, Chisar Sanatorium. 6s, Kotel Children's Sanatorium. 20s, Narechen Polyclinic.

1825 A739 2s blue .20 .20
1826 A739 5s ultra .20 .20
1827 A739 6s green .20 .20
1828 A739 20s emerald .30 .20
Nos. 1825-1828 (4) .90 .80

G. S. Shonin, V. N. Kubasov and Spacecraft A740

Designs: 2s, A. V. Filipchenko, V. N. Volkov, V. V. Gorbatko and spacecraft. 3s, Vladimir A. Shatalov, Alexei S. Yeliseyev and spacecraft. 28s, Three spacecraft in orbit.

1970, Jan. Photo. *Perf. 11*

1829 A740 1s rose car, ol grn & blk .20 .20
1830 A740 2s bl, dl cl & blk .20 .20
1831 A740 3s grnsh bl, vio & blk .20 .20
1832 A740 28s vio bl, lil rose & lt bl .70 .20
Nos. 1829-1832 (4) 1.30 .80

Russian space flights of Soyuz 6, 7 and 8, Oct. 11-13, 1969.

Khan Krum and Defeat of Emperor Nicephorus, 811 — A741

Bulgarian History: 1s, Khan Asparuch and Bulgars crossing the Danube (679). 3s, Conversion of Prince Boris to Christianity, 865. 5s, Tsar Simeon and battle of Akhelo, 917. 8s, Tsar Samuel defeating the Byzantines, 976. 10s, Tsar Kaloyan defeating Emperor Baldwin, 1205. 13s, Tsar Ivan Assen II defeating Greek King Theodore Komnine, 1230. 20s, Coronation of Tsar Ivailo, 1277.

1970, Feb. *Perf. 10½*

1833 A741 1s gold & multi .20 .20
1834 A741 2s gold & multi .20 .20
1835 A741 3s gold & multi .20 .20
1836 A741 5s gold & multi .20 .20
1837 A741 8s gold & multi .20 .20
1838 A741 10s gold & multi .30 .20
1839 A741 13s gold & multi .40 .20
1840 A741 20s gold & multi .70 .20
Nos. 1833-1840 (8) 2.40 1.60

See Nos. 2126-2133.

Bulgarian Pavilion, EXPO '70 — A742

1970 *Perf. 12½*

1841 A742 20s brown, sil & org .75 .50

EXPO '70 International Exposition, Osaka, Japan, Mar. 15-Sept. 13, 1970.

Soccer — A743

Designs: Various views of soccer game.

1970, Mar. 4 Photo. *Perf. 12½*

1842 A743 1s blue & multi .20 .20
1843 A743 2s rose car & multi .20 .20
1844 A743 3s ultra & multi .20 .20
1845 A743 5s green & multi .20 .20
1846 A743 20s emerald & multi .55 .20
1847 A743 40s red & multi 1.25 .30
Nos. 1842-1847 (6) 2.60 1.30

9th World Soccer Championships for the Jules Rimet Cup, Mexico City, May 30-June 21, 1970. See No. B37.

Lenin (1870-1924) — A744

1970, Apr. 22

1848 A744 2s shown .20 .20
1849 A744 13s Portrait .30 .20
1850 A744 20s Writing .70 .20
Nos. 1848-1850 (3) 1.20 .60

Tephrocactus Alexanderi V. Bruchii — A745

Cacti: 2s, Opuntia drummondii. 3s, Hatiora cilindrica. 5s, Gymnocalycium vatteri. 8s, Heliantho cereus grandiflorus. 10s, Neochilenia andreaeana. 13s, Peireskia vargasii v. longispina. 20s, Neobesseya rosiflora.

1970 Photo. *Perf. 12½*

1851 A745 1s multicolored .20 .20
1852 A745 2s dk green & multi .20 .20
1853 A745 3s multicolored .20 .20
1854 A745 5s blue & multi .20 .20
1855 A745 8s brown & multi .30 .20
1856 A745 10s vio bl & multi 1.00 .20
1857 A745 13s brn red & multi 1.00 .20
1858 A745 20s purple & multi 1.40 .30
Nos. 1851-1858 (8) 4.50 1.70

Rose — A746

Designs: Various Roses.

1970, June 5 Litho. *Perf. 13½*

1859 A746 1s gray & multi .20 .20
1860 A746 2s gray & multi .20 .20
1861 A746 3s gray & multi .20 .20
1862 A746 4s gray & multi .20 .20
1863 A746 5s gray & multi .20 .20
1864 A746 13s gray & multi .20 .20
1865 A746 20s gray & multi 1.10 .25
1866 A746 28s gray & multi 1.90 .40
Nos. 1859-1866 (8) 4.20 1.85

Gold Bowl A747

Designs: Various bowls and art objects from Gold Treasure of Thrace.

1970, June 15 Photo. *Perf. 12½*

1867 A747 1s blk, bl & gold .20 .20
1868 A747 2s blk, lt vio & gold .20 .20
1869 A747 3s blk, ver & gold .20 .20
1870 A747 5s blk, yel grn & gold .20 .20
1871 A747 13s blk, org & gold .70 .20
1872 A747 20s blk, lil & gold .85 .20
Nos. 1867-1872 (6) 2.35 1.20

EXPO Emblem, Rose and Bulgarian Woman — A748

Designs (EXPO Emblem and): 2s, Three women. 3s, Woman and fruit. 28s, Dancers. 40s, Mt. Fuji and pavilions.

1970, June 20

1873 A748 1s gold & multi .20 .20
1874 A748 2s gold & multi .20 .20
1875 A748 3s gold & multi .20 .20
1876 A748 28s gold & multi .70 .25
Nos. 1873-1876 (4) 1.30 .85

Miniature Sheet

Imperf

1877 A748 40s gold & multi 1.25 .60

EXPO '70 International Exposition, Osaka, Japan, Mar. 15-Sept. 13. No. 1877 contains one stamp with simulated perforations.

Ivan Vasov A749

1970, Aug. 1 Photo. *Perf. 12½*

1878 A749 13s violet blue .40 .20

Ivan Vasov, author, 120th birth anniv.

UN Emblem — A750

1970, Aug. 1

1879 A750 20s Prus bl & gold .50 .20

25th anniversary of the United Nations.

George Dimitrov — A751

Retriever A752

1970, June 8

1880 A751 20s blk, gold & org .60 .20

BZNC (Bulgarian Communist Party), 70th anniv.

1970 Photo. *Perf. 12½*

Dogs: 1s, Golden retriever, horiz. 3s, Great Dane. 4s, Boxer. 5s, Cocker spaniel. 13s, Doberman pinscher. 20s, Scottish terrier. 28s, Russian greyhound, horiz.

1881 A752 1s multicolored .20 .20
1882 A752 2s multicolored .20 .20
1883 A752 3s multicolored .20 .20
1884 A752 4s multicolored .20 .20
1885 A752 5s multicolored .20 .20
1886 A752 13s multicolored .50 .20
1887 A752 20s multicolored 1.10 .25
1888 A752 28s multicolored 1.60 .30
Nos. 1881-1888 (8) 4.20 1.75

Volleyball A753

#1890, Two women players. #1891, Woman player. #1892, Man player.

1970, Sept. Photo. *Perf. 12½*

1889 A753 2s dk red brn, bl & blk .20 .20
1890 A753 2s ultra, org & blk .20 .20
1891 A753 20s Prus bl, yel & blk .50 .20
1892 A753 20s grn, yel & blk .50 .20
Nos. 1889-1892 (4) 1.40 .80

World Volleyball Championships.

Enrico Caruso and "I Pagliacci" by Ruggiero Leoncavallo — A754

Opera Singers and Operas: 2s, Christina Morfova and "The Bartered Bride" by Bedrich Smetana. 3s, Peter Reitchev and "Tosca" by Giacomo Puccini. 10s, Svetana Tabakova and "The Flying Dutchman" by Richard Wagner. 13s, Katia Popova and "The Masters" by Paroshkev Hadjev. 20s, Feodor Chaliapin and "Boris Godunov" by Modest Musorgski.

1970, Oct. 15 Photo. *Perf. 14*

1893 A754 1s black & multi .20 .20
1894 A754 2s black & multi .20 .20
1895 A754 3s black & multi .20 .20
1896 A754 10s black & multi .20 .20
1897 A754 13s black & multi .30 .20
1898 A754 20s black & multi 1.00 .25
Nos. 1893-1898 (6) 2.10 1.25

Honoring opera singers in their best roles.

Ivan Assen II Coin — A755

Coins from 14th Century with Ruler's Portrait: 2s, Theodor Svetoslav. 3s, Mikhail Chichman. 13s, Ivan Alexander and Mikhail Assen. 20s, Ivan Sratsimir. 28s, Ivan Chichman (initials).

1970, Nov. ***Perf. 12½***

1899 A755 1s buff & multi .20 .20
1900 A755 2s gray & multi .20 .20
1901 A755 3s multicolored .20 .20
1902 A755 13s multicolored .25 .20
1903 A755 20s lt blue & multi .60 .20
1904 A755 28s multicolored .85 .25
Nos. 1899-1904 (6) 2.30 1.25

Fire Protection A756

1970 **Litho.** ***Perf. 12½***

1905 A756 1s Fireman .20 .20
1906 A756 3s Fire engine .20 .20

Bicyclists A757

Congress Emblem — A758

1970 **Photo.**

1907 A757 20s grn, yel & pink .50 .20

20th Bulgarian bicycle race.

1970

1908 A758 13s gold & multi .35 .20

7th World Congress of Sociology, Varna, Sept. 14-19.

Ludwig van Beethoven A759

Friedrich Engels — A760

1970

1909 A759 28s lil rose & dk bl .90 .40

Beethoven (1770-1827), composer.

1970 **Photo.** ***Perf. 12½***

1910 A760 13s ver, tan & brn .30 .20

Friedrich Engels (1820-1895), German socialist, collaborator of Karl Marx.

Miniature Sheets

Luna 16 A761

Russian moon mission: 80s, Lunokhod 1, unmanned vehicle on moon, horiz.

1970 **Photo.** ***Imperf.***

1911 A761 80s plum, sil, blk & bl 2.00 2.00
1912 A761 1 l vio bl, sil & red 4.00 2.75

No. 1911 , Lunokhod 1, Nov. 10-17. No. 1912, Luna 16 mission, Sept. 12-24.
Issue dates: 80s, Dec. 18; 1 l, Nov. 10.

Snowflake — A762

1970, Dec. 15 **Photo.** ***Perf. 12½x13***

1913 A762 2s ultra & multi .20 .20

New Year 1971.

Birds and Flowers A763

Folk Art: 2s, Bird and flowers. 3s, Flying birds. 5s, Birds and flowers. 13s, Sun. 20s, Tulips and pansies.

1971, Jan. 25 ***Perf. 12½x13½***

1914 A763 1s multicolored .20 .20
1915 A763 2s multicolored .20 .20
1916 A763 3s multicolored .20 .20
1917 A763 5s multicolored .20 .20
1918 A763 13s multicolored .20 .20
1919 A763 20s multicolored .55 .20
Nos. 1914-1919 (6) 1.55 1.20

Spring 1971.

Girl, by Zeko Spiridonov A764

Modern Bulgarian Sculpture: 2s, Third Class (people looking through train window), by Ivan Funev. 3s, Bust of Elin Pelin, by Marko Markov. 13s, Bust of Nina, by Andrej Nikolov. 20s, Monument to P. K. Yavorov (kneeling woman), by Ivan Lazarov. 28s, Engineer, by Ivan Funev. 1 l, Refugees, by Sekul Krimov, horiz.

1970, Dec. 28 ***Perf. 12½***

1920 A764 1s gold & vio .20 .20
1921 A764 2s gold & dk ol grn .20 .20
1922 A764 3s gold & rose brn .20 .20
1923 A764 13s gold & dk grn .30 .20
1924 A764 20s gold & red brn .50 .20
1925 A764 28s gold & dk brn .80 .20
Nos. 1920-1925 (6) 2.20 1.20

Souvenir Sheet

Imperf

1926 A764 1 l gold, dk brn & buff 2.00 1.75

Runner A765

Design: 20s, Woman putting the shot.

1971, Mar. 13 **Photo.** ***Perf. 12½x13***

1927 A765 2s brown & multi .20 .20
1928 A765 20s dp grn, org & blk .90 .25

2nd European Indoor Track and Field Championships.

Bulgarian Secondary School, Bolgrad — A766

Educators: 20s, Dimiter Mitev, Prince Bogoridi and Sava Radoulov.

1971, Mar. 16 ***Perf. 12½***

1929 A766 2s silver, brn & grn .20 .20
1930 A766 20s silver, brn & vio .50 .20

First Bulgarian secondary school, 1858, in Bolgrad, USSR.

Communards — A767

1971, Mar. 18 **Photo.** ***Perf. 12½x13***

1931 A767 20s rose magenta & blk .50 .20

Centenary of the Paris Commune.

Dimitrov Facing Goering, Quotation, FIR Emblem — A768

1971, Apr. 11 ***Perf. 12½***

1932 A768 2s grn, gold, blk & red .20 .20
1933 A768 13s plum, gold, blk & red .70 .20

Intl. Fed. of Resistance Fighters (FIR), 20th anniv.

George S. Rakovski (1821-1867), Revolutionary Against Turkish Rule — A769

1971, Apr. 14

1934 A769 13s olive & blk brn .30 .20

Edelweiss Hotel, Borovets A770

2s, Panorama Hotel, Pamporovo. 4s, Boats at Albena, Black Sea. 8s, Boats at Rousalka. 10s, Shtastlivetsa Hotel, Mt. Vitosha.

1971 ***Perf. 13***

1935 A770 1s brt green .20 .20
1936 A770 2s olive gray .20 .20
1937 A770 4s brt blue .20 .20
1938 A770 8s blue .20 .20
1939 A770 10s bluish green .25 .20
Nos. 1935-1939 (5) 1.05 1.00

Technological Progress — A771

Designs: 1s, Mason with banner, vert. 13s, Two men and doves, vert.

1971, Apr. 20 **Photo.** ***Perf. 12½***

1940 A771 1s gold & multi .20 .20
1941 A771 2s gray blue & multi .20 .20
1942 A771 13s lt green & multi .50 .20
Nos. 1940-1942 (3) .90 .60

10th Cong. of Bulgarian Communist Party.

Panayot Pipkov and Anthem A772

1971, May 20

1943 A772 13s sil, blk & brt grn .45 .20

Panayot Pipkov, composer, birth cent.

Mammoth A773

Prehistoric Animals: 2s, Bear, vert. 3s, Hipparion (horse). 13s, Platybelodon. 20s, Dinotherium, vert. 28s, Saber-tooth tiger.

1971, May 29 ***Perf. 12½***

1944 A773 1s dull bl & multi .20 .20
1945 A773 2s lilac & multi .20 .20
1946 A773 3s multicolored .20 .20
1947 A773 13s multicolored .50 .20
1948 A773 20s dp grn & multi .80 .20
1949 A773 28s multicolored 1.40 .30
Nos. 1944-1949 (6) 3.30 1.30

Khan Asparuch Crossing Danube, 679 A.D., by Boris Angelushev — A774

Historical Paintings: 3s, Reception at Trnovo, by Ilya Petrov. 5s, Chevartov's Troops at Benkovsky, by P. Morozov. 8s, Russian Gen. Gurko and People in Sofia, 1878, by D. Gudjenko. 28s, People Greeting Red Army, by S. Venov.

1971, Mar. 6 ***Perf. 13½x14***

1950	A774	2s gold & multi	.20	.20
1951	A774	3s gold & multi	.20	.20
1952	A774	5s gold & multi	.20	.20
1953	A774	8s gold & multi	.30	.20
a.		Souv. sheet of 4, #1950-1953	1.00	.50
1954	A774	28s gold & multi	2.75	.85
		Nos. 1950-1954 (5)	3.65	1.65

In 1973, No. 1953a was surcharged 1 lev and overprinted "Visitez la Bulgarie," airline initials and emblems, and, on the 5s stamp, "Par Avion."

Freed Black, White and Yellow Men — A775

1971, May 20 **Photo.** ***Perf. 12½***

1955	A775	13s blue, blk & yel	.35	.20

Intl. Year against Racial Discrimination.

Map of Europe, Championship Emblem — A776

"XXX" Supporting Barbell — A777

1971, June 19

1956	A776	2s lt blue & multi	.20	.20
1957	A777	13s yellow & multi	.60	.20

30th European Weight Lifting Championships, Sofia, June 19-27.

Facade, Old House, Koprivnica — A778

Designs: Decorated facades of various old houses in Koprivnica.

1971, July 10 **Photo.** ***Perf. 12½***

1958	A778	1s green & multi	.20	.20
1959	A778	2s brown & multi	.20	.20
1960	A778	6s violet & multi	.20	.20
1961	A778	13s dk red & multi	.40	.20
		Nos. 1958-1961 (4)	1.00	.80

Frontier Guard and German Shepherd A779

1971, July 31 ***Perf. 13***

1962	A779	2s green & ol grn	.20	.20

25th anniversary of the Frontier Guards.

Congress of Busludja, Bas-relief — A780

1971, July 31 ***Perf. 12½***

1963	A780	2s dk red & ol grn	.20	.20

80th anniversary of the first Congress of the Bulgarian Social Democratic party.

Young Woman, by Ivan Nenov — A781

Paintings: 2s, Lazarova in Evening Gown, by Stefan Ivanov. 3s, Performer in Dress Suit, by Kyril Zonev. 13s, Portrait of a Woman, by Detchko Uzunov. 20s, Woman from Kalotina, by Vladimir Dimitrov. 40s, Gorjanin (Mountain Man), by Stoyan Venev.

1971, Aug. 2 ***Perf. 14x13½***

1964	A781	1s green & multi	.20	.20
1965	A781	2s green & multi	.20	.20
1966	A781	3s green & multi	.20	.20
1967	A781	13s green & multi	.40	.20
1968	A781	20s green & multi	.75	.30
1969	A781	40s green & multi	1.60	.45
		Nos. 1964-1969 (6)	3.35	1.55

National Art Gallery.

Wrestlers A782

Designs: 13s, Wrestlers.

1971, Aug. 27 ***Perf. 12½***

1970	A782	2s green, blk & bl	.20	.20
1971	A782	13s red org, blk & bl	.50	.20

European Wrestling Championships.

Young Workers — A783

Post Horn Emblem A784

1971 **Photo.** ***Perf. 13***

1972	A783	2s dark blue	.20	.20

25th anniv. of the Young People's Brigade.

1971, Sept. 15 ***Perf. 12½***

1973	A784	20s dp green & gold	.45	.20

8th meeting of postal administrations of socialist countries, Varna.

FEBS Waves Emblem — A785

1971, Sept. 20

1974	A785	13s black, red & mar	.50	.20

7th Congress of European Biochemical Association (FEBS), Varna.

Statue of Republic — A786

Design: 13s, Bulgarian flag.

1971, Sept. 20 ***Perf. 13x12½***

1975	A786	2s gold, yel & dk red	.20	.20
1976	A786	13s gold, grn & red	.40	.20

Bulgarian People's Republic, 25th anniv.

Cross Country Skiing and Winter Olympics Emblem A787

Sport and Winter Olympics Emblem: 2s, Downhill skiing. 3s, Ski jump and skiing. 4s, Women's figure skating. 13s, Ice hockey. 28s, Slalom skiing. 1 l, Torch and stadium.

1971, Sept. 25 ***Perf. 12½***

1977	A787	1s dk green & multi	.20	.20
1978	A787	2s vio blue & multi	.20	.20
1979	A787	3s ultra & multi	.20	.20
1980	A787	4s dp plum & multi	.20	.20
1981	A787	13s dk blue & multi	.40	.20
1982	A787	28s multicolored	.90	.35
		Nos. 1977-1982 (6)	2.10	1.35

Miniature Sheet

Imperf

1983	A787	1 l multicolored	3.50	1.60

11th Winter Olympic Games, Sapporo, Japan, Feb. 3-13, 1972.

Factory, Botevgrad A788

Industrial Buildings: 2s, Petro-chemical works, Pleven, vert. 10s, Chemical works, Vratsa. 13s, Maritsa-Istok Power Station, Dimitrovgrad. 40s, Electronics works, Sofia.

1971 **Photo.** ***Perf. 13***

1984	A788	1s violet	.20	.20
1985	A788	2s orange	.20	.20
1986	A788	10s deep purple	.20	.20
1987	A788	13s lilac rose	.25	.20
1988	A788	40s deep brown	.70	.20
		Nos. 1984-1988 (5)	1.55	1.00

UNESCO Emblem A789

1971, Nov. 4 ***Perf. 12½***

1989	A789	20s lt bl, blk, gold & red	.45	.20

25th anniv. of UNESCO.

Soccer Player, by Kyril Zonev (1896-1971) A790

Paintings by Kyril Zonev: 2s, Landscape, horiz. 3s, Self-portrait. 13s, Lilies. 20s, Landscape, horiz. 40s, Portrait of a Young Woman.

1971, Nov. 10 ***Perf. 11x12***

1990	A790	1s gold & multi	.20	.20
1991	A790	2s gold & multi	.20	.20
1992	A790	3s gold & multi	.20	.20
1993	A790	13s gold & multi	.25	.20
1994	A790	20s gold & multi	.85	.25
1995	A790	40s gold & multi	1.25	.35
		Nos. 1990-1995 (6)	2.95	1.40

Salyut Space Station — A791

Astronauts Dobrovolsky, Volkov and Patsayev — A792

Designs: 13s, Soyuz 11 space transport. 40s, Salyut and Soyuz 11 joined.

1971, Dec. 20 ***Perf. 12½***

1996	A791	2s dk grn, yel & red	.20	.20
1997	A791	13s multicolored	.25	.20
1998	A791	40s dk blue & multi	1.25	.40
		Nos. 1996-1998 (3)	1.70	.80

Souvenir Sheet

Imperf

1999	A792	80s multicolored	2.00	1.50

Salyut-Soyuz 11 space mission, and in memory of the Russian astronauts Lt. Col. Georgi T. Dobrovolsky, Vladislav N. Volkov and Victor I. Patsayev, who died during the Soyuz 11 space mission, June 6-30, 1971.

Oil Tanker Vihren — A793

1972, Jan. 8 Photo. *Perf. 12½*

2000 A793 18s lil rose, vio & blk .75 .25

Bulgarian shipbuilding industry.

Goce Delchev A794

5s, Jan Sandanski. 13s, Damjan Gruev.

1972, Jan. 21 Photo. *Perf. 12½*

2001 A794 2s brick red & blk .20 .20
2002 A794 5s green & blk .20 .20
2003 A794 13s lemon & blk .35 .20
Nos. 2001-2003 (3) .75 .60

Centenary of the births of Bulgarian patriots Delchev (1872-1903) and Sandanski, and of Macedonian Gruev (1871-1906).

Gymnast with Hoop, Medals — A795

13s, Gymnast with ball, medals. 70s, Gymnasts with hoops, medals.

1972, Feb. 10

2004 A795 13s multicolored .40 .20
2005 A795 18s multicolored .55 .20

Miniature Sheet

Imperf

2006 A795 70s multicolored 2.50 2.00

5th World Women's Gymnastic Championships, Havana, Cuba.

View of Melnik, by Petar Mladenov — A796

Paintings from National Art Gallery: 2s, Plower, by Pencho Georgiev. 3s, Funeral, by Alexander Djendov. 13s, Husband and Wife, by Vladimir Dimitrov. 20s, Nursing Mother, by Nenko Balkanski. 40s, Paisii Hilendarski Writing History, by Koio Denchev.

1972, Feb. 20 *Perf. 13½x14*

2007 A796 1s green & multi .20 .20
2008 A796 2s green & multi .20 .20
2009 A796 3s green & multi .20 .20
2010 A796 13s green & multi .40 .20
2011 A796 20s green & multi .75 .20
2012 A796 40s green & multi 1.25 .35
Nos. 2007-2012 (6) 3.00 1.35

Paintings from National Art Gallery.

Worker — A797

1972, Mar. 7 *Perf. 12½*

2013 A797 13s silver & multi .20 .20

7th Bulgarian Trade Union Congress.

Singing Harvesters A798

Designs: Paintings by Vladimir Dimitrov.

1972, Mar. 31 *Perf. 11½x12, 12x11½*

2014 A798 1s shown .20 .20
2015 A798 2s Harvester .20 .20
2016 A798 3s Women Diggers .20 .20
2017 A798 13s Fabric Dyers .35 .20
2018 A798 20s "My Mother" .70 .20
2019 A798 40s Self-portrait 1.40 .30
Nos. 2014-2019 (6) 3.05 1.30

Vladimir Dimitrov, painter, 90th birth anniv.

"Your Heart is your Health" — A799

St. Mark's Basilica and Wave — A800

1972, Apr. 30 *Perf. 12½*

2020 A799 13s red, blk & grn .70 .30

World Health Day.

1972, May 6 *Perf. 13x12½*

Design: 13s, Ca' D'Oro and wave.

2021 A800 2s ol grn, bl grn & lt bl .20 .20
2022 A800 13s red brn, vio & lt grn .50 .20

UNESCO campaign to save Venice.

Dimitrov in Print Shop, 1901 — A801

Designs: Life of George Dimitrov.

1972, May 8 Photo. *Perf. 12½*

2023 A801 1s shown .20 .20
2024 A801 2s Dimitrov as leader of 1923 uprising .20 .20
2025 A801 3s Leipzig trial, 1933 .20 .20
2026 A801 5s As Communist functionary, 1935 .20 .20
2027 A801 13s As leader and teacher, 1948 .20 .20
2028 A801 18s Addressing youth rally, 1948 .40 .20
2029 A801 28s With Pioneers, 1948 .65 .20
2030 A801 40s Mausoleum 1.00 .30
2031 A801 80s Portrait 2.75 .45
a. Souvenir sheet 4.25 2.50
Nos. 2023-2031 (9) 5.80 2.15

90th anniversary of the birth of George Dimitrov (1882-1949), communist leader.

No. 2031a contains one imperf. stamp similar to No. 2031, but in different colors.

Value, No. 2031 imperf. in slightly changed colors, $5.

Paisii Hilendarski A802

Design: 2s, Flame and quotation.

1972, May 12

2032 A802 2s gold, grn & brn .20 .20
2033 A802 13s gold, grn & brn .50 .20

Paisii Hilendarski (1722-1798), monk, writer of Bulgarian-Slavic history.

Canoeing, Motion and Olympic Emblems — A803

Designs (Motion and Olympic emblems and): 2s, Gymnastics. 3s, Swimming, women's. 13s, Volleyball. 18s, Jumping. 40s, Wrestling. 80s, Stadium and sports.

1972, June 25

Figures of Athletes in Silver & Black

2034 A803 1s lt blue & multi .20 .20
2035 A803 2s orange & multi .20 .20
2036 A803 3s multicolored .20 .20
2037 A803 13s yellow & multi .20 .20
2038 A803 18s multicolored .40 .20
2039 A803 40s pink & multi 1.25 .30
Nos. 2034-2039 (6) 2.45 1.30

Miniature Sheet

Imperf

Size: 62x60mm

2040 A803 80s gold, ver & yel 1.75 1.00

20th Olympic Games, Munich, 8/26-9/11.

Angel Kunchev A804

1972, June 30 Photo. *Perf. 12½*

2041 A804 2s mag, dk pur & gold .20 .20

Centenary of the death of Angel Kunchev, patriot and revolutionist.

Zlatni Pyassatsi A805

1972, Sept. 16

2042 A805 1s shown .20 .20
2043 A805 2s Drouzhba .20 .20
2044 A805 3s Slunchev Bryag .20 .20
2045 A805 13s Primorsko .20 .20
2046 A805 28s Roussalka .60 .25
2047 A805 40s Albena .85 .30
Nos. 2042-2047 (6) 2.25 1.35

Bulgarian Black Sea resorts.

Bronze Medal, Olympic Emblems, Canoeing — A806

Olympic Emblems and: 2s, Silver medal, broad jump. 3s, Gold medal, boxing. 18s, Gold medal, wrestling. 40s, Gold medal, weight lifting.

1972, Sept. 29

2048 A806 1s Prus bl & multi .20 .20
2049 A806 2s dk green & multi .20 .20
2050 A806 3s orange brn & multi .20 .20
2051 A806 18s olive & multi .50 .20
2052 A806 40s multicolored 1.00 .40
Nos. 2048-2052 (5) 2.10 1.20

Bulgarian victories in 20th Olympic Games. For overprint see No. 2066.

Stoj Dimitrov — A807

Resistance Fighters: 2s, Cvetko Radoinov. 3s, Bogdan Stivrodski. 5s, Mirko Laiev. 13s, Nedelyo Nikolov.

1972, Oct. 30 Photo. *Perf. 12½x13*

2053 A807 1s olive & multi .20 .20
2054 A807 2s multicolored .20 .20
2055 A807 3s multicolored .20 .20
2056 A807 5s multicolored .20 .20
2057 A807 13s multicolored .30 .20
Nos. 2053-2057 (5) 1.10 1.00

"50 Years USSR" A808

1972, Nov. 3 Photo. *Perf. 12½x13*

2058 A808 13s gold, red & yel .25 .20

50th anniversary of Soviet Union.

Turk's-cap Lily — A809

Protected Plants: 2s, Gentian. 3s, Sea daffodil. 4s, Globe flower. 18s, Primrose. 23s, Pulsatilla vernalis. 40s, Snake's-head.

1972, Nov. 25 ***Perf. 12½***
Flowers in Natural Colors

2059 A809	1s	olive bister	.20	.20
2060 A809	2s	olive bister	.20	.20
2061 A809	3s	olive bister	.20	.20
2062 A809	4s	olive bister	.20	.20
2063 A809	18s	olive bister	.30	.20
2064 A809	23s	olive bister	.75	.20
2065 A809	40s	olive bister	1.40	.35
		Nos. 2059-2065 (7)	3.25	1.55

No. 2052 Overprinted in Red

1972, Nov. 27
2066 A806 40s multicolored .95 .25

Bulgarian weight lifting Olympic gold medalists.

Dobri Chintulov A810

1972, Nov. 28 **Photo.** ***Perf. 12½***
2067 A810 2s gray, dk & lt grn .20 .20

Chintulov, writer, 150th birth anniv.

Forehead Band — A811

Designs (14th-19th Century Jewelry): 2s, Belt buckles. 3s, Amulet. 8s, Pendant. 23s, Earrings. 40s, Necklace.

1972, Dec. 27 **Engr.** ***Perf. 14x13½***

2068 A811	1s	red brn & blk	.20	.20
2069 A811	2s	emerald & blk	.20	.20
2070 A811	3s	Prus bl & blk	.20	.20
2071 A811	8s	dk red & blk	.20	.20
2072 A811	23s	red org & multi	.50	.20
2073 A811	40s	violet & blk	1.10	.40
		Nos. 2068-2073 (6)	2.40	1.40

Skin Divers A812

Designs: 2s, Shelf-1 underwater house and divers. 18s, Diving bell and diver, vert. 40s, Elevation balloon and divers, vert.

1973, Jan. 24 **Photo.** ***Perf. 12½***

2074 A812	1s	lt bl, blk & yel	.20	.20
2075 A812	2s	blk, bl & org yel	.20	.20
2076 A812	18s	blk, Prus bl & dl org	.40	.20
2077 A812	40s	blk, ultra & bister	.95	.30
		Nos. 2074-2077 (4)	1.75	.90

Bulgarian deep-sea research in the Black Sea.

A souvenir sheet of four contains imperf. 20s stamps in designs of Nos. 2074-2077 with colors changed. Sold for 1 l. Value $3.50 unused, $3 canceled.

Execution of Levski, by Boris Angelushev A813

20s, Vassil Levski, by Georgi Danchev.

1973, Feb. 19 ***Perf. 13x12½***
2078 A813 2s dull rose & Prus grn .20 .20
2079 A813 20s dull grn & brn .90 .20

Centenary of the death of Vassil Levski (1837-1873), patriot, executed by the Turks.

Kukersky Mask, Elhovo Region A814

Nicolaus Copernicus A815

Kukersky Masks at pre-Spring Festival: 2s, Breznik. 3s, Hissar. 13s, Radomir. 20s, Karnobat. 40s, Pernik.

1973, Feb. 26 ***Perf. 12½***

2080 A814	1s	dp rose & multi	.20	.20
2081 A814	2s	emerald & multi	.20	.20
2082 A814	3s	violet & multi	.20	.20
2083 A814	13s	multicolored	.35	.20
2084 A814	20s	multicolored	.40	.20
2085 A814	40s	multicolored	2.25	1.10
		Nos. 2080-2085 (6)	3.60	2.10

1973, Mar. 21 **Photo.** ***Perf. 12½***
2086 A815 28s ocher, blk & claret 1.25 .60

500th anniversary of the birth of Nicolaus Copernicus (1473-1543), Polish astronomer.

Vietnamese Worker and Rainbow — A816

1973, Apr. 16
2087 A816 18s lt blue & multi .35 .20

Peace in Viet Nam.

A817 A818

Wild flowers.

1973, May **Photo.** ***Perf. 13***

2088 A817	1s	Poppy	.20	.20
2089 A817	2s	Daisy	.20	.20
2090 A817	3s	Peony	.20	.20
2091 A817	13s	Centaury	.25	.20
2092 A817	18s	Corn cockle	2.75	1.10
2093 A817	28s	Ranunculus	.60	.25
		Nos. 2088-2093 (6)	4.20	2.15

1973, June 2
2094 A818 2s pale grn, buff & brn .20 .20
2095 A818 18s pale brn, gray & grn .65 .40

Christo Botev (1848-1876), poet.

"Suffering Worker" — A819

1s, Asen Halachev and revolutionists.

1973, June 6 **Photo.** ***Perf. 13***
2096 A819 1s gold, red & blk .20 .20
2097 A819 2s gold, org & dk brn .20 .20

50th anniversary of Pleven uprising.

Muskrat A820

Perf. 12½x13, 13x12½
1973, June 29 **Litho.**

2098 A820	1s	shown	.20	.20
2099 A820	2s	Racoon	.20	.20
2100 A820	3s	Mouflon, vert.	.20	.20
2101 A820	12s	Fallow deer, vert.	.25	.20
2102 A820	18s	European bison	.50	.20
2103 A820	40s	Elk	2.50	1.00
		Nos. 2098-2103 (6)	3.85	2.00

Aleksandr Stamboliski A821

1973, June 14 **Photo.** ***Perf. 12½***
2104 A821 18s dp brown & org .35 .20
a. 18s orange 2.50 .75

Aleksandr Stamboliski (1879-1923), leader of Peasants' Party and premier.

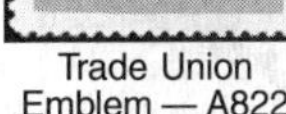

Trade Union Emblem — A822

Stylized Sun, Olympic Rings — A823

1973, Aug. 27 **Photo.** ***Perf. 12½***
2105 A822 2s yellow & multi .20 .20

8th Congress of World Federation of Trade Unions, Varna, Oct. 15-22.

1973, Aug. 29 ***Perf. 13***

28s, Emblem of Bulgarian Olympic Committee & Olympic rings. 80s, Soccer, emblems of Innsbruck & Montreal 1976 Games, horiz.

2106 A823 13s multicolored .70 .30
2107 A823 28s multicolored 1.25 .40

Souvenir Sheet

2108 A823 80s multicolored 3.25 1.75

Olympic Congress, Varna. No. 2108 contains one stamp. It also exists imperf.; also with violet margin, imperf.

Revolutionists with Communist Flag — A824

Designs: 5s, Revolutionists on flatcar blocking train. 13s, Raising Communist flag, vert. 18s, George Dimitrov and Vassil Kolarov.

1973, Sept. 22 **Photo.** ***Perf. 12½***

2109 A824	2s	magenta & multi	.20	.20
2110 A824	5s	magenta & multi	.20	.20
2111 A824	13s	magenta & multi	.30	.20
2112 A824	18s	magenta & multi	.85	.30
		Nos. 2109-2112 (4)	1.55	.90

50th anniv. of the September Revolution.

Warrior Saint A825

Murals from Boyana Church: 1s, Tsar Kaloyan and 2s, his wife Dessislava. 5s, "St. Wystratti." 10s, Tsar Constantine Assen. 13s, Deacon Laurentius. 18s, Virgin Mary. 20s, St. Ephraim. 28s, Jesus. 80s, Jesus in the Temple, horiz.

1973, Sept. 24

2113 A825	1s	gold & multi	.20	.20
2114 A825	2s	gold & multi	.20	.20
2115 A825	3s	gold & multi	.20	.20
2116 A825	5s	gold & multi	.20	.20
2117 A825	10s	gold & multi	.35	.20
2118 A825	13s	gold & multi	.45	.20
2119 A825	18s	gold & multi	.70	.20
2120 A825	20s	gold & multi	.95	.20
2121 A825	28s	gold & multi	3.50	.35
		Nos. 2113-2121 (9)	6.75	1.95

Miniature Sheet
Imperf

2122 A825 80s gold & multi 3.75 2.25

No. 2122 contains one stamp with simulated perforations.

Christo Smirnenski — A826

1973, Sept. 29 **Photo.** ***Perf. 12½***
2123 A826 1s multicolored .20 .20
2124 A826 2s vio blue & multi .20 .20

Christo Smirnenski (1898-1923), poet.

Human Rights Flame — A827

1973, Oct. 10
2125 A827 13s dk bl, red & gold .30 .20

Universal Declaration of Human Rights, 25th anniv.

Bulgarian History Type

1s, Tsar Theodor Svetoslav receiving Byzantine envoys. 2s, Tsar Mihail Shishman's army in battle with Byzantines. 3s, Tsar Ivan

Alexander's victory at Russocastro. 4s, Patriarch Euthimius at the defense of Turnovo. 5s, Tsar Ivan Shishman leading horsemen against the Turks. 13s, Momchil attacking Turks at Umour. 18s, Tsar Ivan Stratsimir meeting King Sigismund's crusaders. 28s, The Boyars Balik, Theodor & Dobrotitsa, meeting ship bringing envoys from Anne of Savoy.

1973, Oct. 23 ***Perf. 13***

Silver and Black Vignettes

2126	A741	1s olive bister	.20	.20
2127	A741	2s Prus blue	.20	.20
2128	A741	3s lilac	.20	.20
2129	A741	4s green	.20	.20
2130	A741	5s violet	.20	.20
2131	A741	13s orange & brn	.25	.20
2132	A741	18s olive green	.40	.20
2133	A741	28s yel brn & brn	1.10	.50
		Nos. 2126-2133 (8)	2.75	1.90

Finn Class — A828

Sailboats: 2s, Flying Dutchman. 3s, Soling class. 13s, Tempest class. 20s, Class 470. 40s, Tornado class.

1973, Oct. 29 **Litho.** ***Perf. 13***

2134	A828	1s ultra & multi	.20	.20
2135	A828	2s green & multi	.20	.20
2136	A828	3s dk blue & multi	.20	.20
2137	A828	13s dull vio & multi	.30	.20
2138	A828	20s gray bl & multi	.60	.30
2139	A828	40s dk blue & multi	2.50	2.00
		Nos. 2134-2139 (6)	4.00	3.10

Value, set imperf. in changed colors, $10.

Village, by Bencho Obreshkov — A829

Paintings: 2s, Mother and Child, by Stoyan Venev. 3s, Rest (woman), by Tsenko Boyadjiev. 13s, Flowers in Vase, by Sirak Skitnik. 18s, Meri Kuneva (portrait), by Ilya Petrov. 40s, Winter in Plovdiv, by Zlatyu Boyadjiev. 13s, 18s, 40s, vert.

Perf. 12½x12, 12x12½

1973, Nov. 10

2140	A829	1s gold & multi	.20	.20
2141	A829	2s gold & multi	.20	.20
2142	A829	3s gold & multi	.20	.20
2143	A829	13s gold & multi	.25	.20
2144	A829	18s gold & multi	.40	.20
2145	A829	40s gold & multi	2.25	.75
		Nos. 2140-2145 (6)	3.50	1.75

Souvenir Sheet

Paintings by Stanislav Dospevski: a, Domnica Lambreva. b, Self-portrait. Both vert.

2146	Sheet of 2	2.75	1.75
a.	A829 50s gold & multi	.70	.50
b.	A829 50s gold & multi	.70	.50

Bulgarian paintings. No. 2146 commemorates the 150th birth anniv. of Stanislav Dospevski.

Souvenir Sheet

Soccer — A830

1973, Dec. 10 **Photo.** ***Perf. 13***

2147	A830	28s multicolored	3.75	3.25

No. 2147 sold for 1 l. Exists overprinted for Argentina 78.

Angel and Ornaments A831

1s, Attendant facing right. 2s, Passover table and lamb. 3s, Attendant facing left. 8s, Abraham and ornaments. 13s, Adam and Eve. 28s, Expulsion from Garden of Eden.

1974, Jan. 21 **Photo.** ***Perf. 13***

2148	A831	1s fawn, yel & brn	.20	.20
2149	A831	2s fawn, yel & brn	.20	.20
2150	A831	3s fawn, yel & brn	.20	.20
a.		Strip of 3, #2148-2150	.25	.20
2151	A831	5s slate grn & yel	.20	.20
2152	A831	8s slate grn & yel	.20	.20
a.		Pair, #2151-2152	.30	.25
2153	A831	13s lt brown, yel & ol	.30	.25
2154	A831	28s lt brown, yel & ol	.50	.30
a.		Pair, #2153-2154	.80	.35
		Nos. 2148-2154 (7)	1.80	1.55

Woodcarvings from Rozhen Monastery, 19th century.

Lenin, by N. Mirtchev — A832

18s, Lenin visiting Workers, by W. A. Serov.

1974, Jan. 28 **Litho.** ***Perf. 12½x12***

2155	A832	2s ocher & multi	.20	.20
2156	A832	18s ocher & multi	.50	.25

50th anniversary of the death of Lenin.

1974, Jan. 28

Demeter Blagoev at Rally, by G. Kowachev.

2157	A832	2s multicolored	.20	.20

50th anniversary of the death of Demeter Blagoev, founder of Bulgarian Communist Party.

Domestic Animals A833

1974, Feb. 1 **Photo.** ***Perf. 13***

2158	A833	1s Sheep	.20	.20
2159	A833	2s Goat	.20	.20
2160	A833	3s Pig	.20	.20
2161	A833	5s Cow	.20	.20
2162	A833	13s Buffalo cow	.30	.20
2163	A833	20s Horse	.80	.30
		Nos. 2158-2163 (6)	1.90	1.30

Comecon Emblem A834

1974, Feb. 11 **Photo.** ***Perf. 13***

2164	A834	13s silver & multi	.40	.20

25th anniversary of the Council of Mutual Economic Assistance.

Soccer — A835

Designs: Various soccer action scenes.

1974, Mar. **Photo.** ***Perf. 13***

2165	A835	1s dull green & multi	.20	.20
2166	A835	2s brt green & multi	.20	.20
2167	A835	3s slate grn & multi	.20	.20
2168	A835	13s olive & multi	.20	.20
2169	A835	28s blue grn & multi	.65	.40
2170	A835	40s emerald & multi	1.50	.70
		Nos. 2165-2170 (6)	2.95	1.90

Souvenir Sheet

2171	A835	1 l green & multi	3.00	1.60

World Soccer Championship, Munich, June 13-July 7. No. 2171 exists imperf.

Salt Production A836

Children's Paintings: 1s, Cosmic Research for Peaceful Purposes. 3s, Fire Dancers. 28s, Russian-Bulgarian Friendship (train and children). 60s, Spring (birds).

1974, Apr. 15 **Photo.** ***Perf. 13***

2172	A836	1s lilac & multi	.20	.20
2173	A836	2s lt green & multi	.20	.20
2174	A836	3s blue & multi	.20	.20
2175	A836	28s slate & multi	1.75	.95
		Nos. 2172-2175 (4)	2.35	1.55

Souvenir Sheet

Imperf

2176	A836	60s blue & multi	2.25	1.75

Third World Youth Philatelic Exhibition, Sofia, May 23-30. No. 2176 contains one stamp with simulated perforations.

Folk Singers — A837

Designs: 2s, Folk dancers (men). 3s, Bagpiper and drummer. 5s, Wrestlers. 13s, Runners (women). 18s, Gymnast.

1974, Apr. 25 ***Perf. 13***

2178	A837	1s vermilion & multi	.20	.20
2179	A837	2s org brn & multi	.20	.20
2180	A837	3s brn red & multi	.20	.20
2181	A837	5s blue & multi	.20	.20
2182	A837	13s ultra & multi	.75	.25
2183	A837	18s violet bl & multi	.40	.20
		Nos. 2178-2183 (6)	1.95	1.25

4th Amateur Arts and Sports Festival

Flowers A838

1974, May **Photo.** ***Perf. 13***

2184	A838	1s Aster	.20	.20
2185	A838	2s Petunia	.20	.20
2186	A838	3s Fuchsia	.20	.20
2187	A838	18s Tulip	.30	.20
2188	A838	20s Carnation	.60	.25
2189	A838	28s Pansy	1.60	.55
		Nos. 2184-2189 (6)	3.10	1.60

Souvenir Sheet

2190	A838	80s Sunflower	1.75	.85

Automobiles and Emblems — A839

1974, May 15 **Photo.** ***Perf. 13***

2191	A839	13s multicolored	.30	.20

International Automobile Federation (FIA) Spring Congress, Sofia, May 20-24.

Old and New Buildings, UNESCO Emblem A840

1974, June 15

2192	A840	18s multicolored	.30	.20

UNESCO Executive Council, 94th Session, Varna.

Postrider A841

Designs: 18s, First Bulgarian mail coach. 28s, UPU Monument, Bern.

1974, Aug. 5

2193	A841	2s ocher, blk & vio	.20	.20
2194	A841	18s ocher, blk & grn	.40	.20

Souvenir Sheet

2195	A841	28s ocher, blk & bl	2.00	1.50

UPU cent. No. 2195 exists imperf.

Pioneer and Komsomol Girl — A842

Designs: 2s, Pioneer and birds. 60s, Emblem with portrait of George Dimitrov.

1974, Aug. 12

2196 A842 1s green & multi .20 .20
2197 A842 2s blue & multi .20 .20

Souvenir Sheet

2198 A842 60s red & multi 1.00 1.00

30th anniversary of Dimitrov Pioneer Organization, Septemvriiche.

"Bulgarian Communist Party" — A843

Symbolic Designs: 2s, Russian liberators. 5s, Industrialization. 13s, Advanced agriculture and husbandry. 18s, Scientific and technical progress.

1974, Aug. 20

2199 A843 1s blue gray & multi .20 .20
2200 A843 2s blue gray & multi .20 .20
2201 A843 5s gray & multi .20 .20
2202 A843 13s gray & multi .25 .20
2203 A843 18s gray & multi .35 .20
Nos. 2199-2203 (5) 1.20 1.00

30th anniversary of the People's Republic.

Gymnast on Parallel Bars — A844

Design: 13s, Gymnast on vaulting horse.

1974, Oct. 18 Photo. *Perf. 13*

2204 A844 2s multicolored .20 .20
2205 A844 13s multicolored .30 .20

18th Gymnastic Championships, Varna.

Souvenir Sheet

Symbols of Peace — A845

1974, Oct. 29 Photo. *Perf. 13*

2206 A845 Sheet of 4 2.50 1.10
a. 13s Doves .20 .20
b. 13s Map of Europe .20 .20
c. 13s Olive Branch .20 .20
d. 13s Inscription .20 .20

1974 European Peace Conference. "Peace" in various languages written on Nos. 2206a-2206c. Sold for 60s. Exists imperf.

Nib and Envelope — A846

1974, Nov. 20

2207 A846 2s yellow, blk & grn .20 .20

Introduction of postal zone numbers.

Flowers A847

1974, Dec. 5

2208 A847 2s emerald & multi .20 .20

St. Todor, Ceramic Icon — A848

Fruit Tree Blossoms — A849

Designs: 2s, Medallion, Veliko Turnovo. 3s, Carved capital. 5s, Silver bowl. 8s, Goblet. 13s, Lion's head finial. 18s, Gold plate with Cross. 28s, Breastplate with eagle.

1974, Dec. 18 Photo. *Perf. 13*

2209 A848 1s orange & multi .20 .20
2210 A848 2s pink & multi .20 .20
2211 A848 3s blue & multi .20 .20
2212 A848 5s lt vio & multi .20 .20
2213 A848 8s brown & multi .20 .20
2214 A848 13s multicolored .25 .20
2215 A848 18s red & multi .30 .20
2216 A848 28s ultra & multi 1.00 .60
Nos. 2209-2216 (8) 2.55 2.00

Art works from 9th-12th centuries.

1975, Jan. Photo. *Perf. 13*

2217 A849 1s Apricot .20 .20
2218 A849 2s Apple .20 .20
2219 A849 3s Cherry .20 .20
2220 A849 19s Pear .30 .20
2221 A849 28s Peach .70 .20
Nos. 2217-2221 (5) 1.60 1.00

Tree and Book A850

1975, Mar. 25 Photo. *Perf. 13*

2222 A850 2s gold & multi .20 .20

Forestry High School, 50th anniversary.

Souvenir Sheet

Farmers' Activities (Woodcuts) — A851

1975, Mar. 25

2223 A851 Sheet of 4 .80 .50
a. 2s Farmer with ax and flag
b. 5s Farmers on guard
c. 13s Dancing couple
d. 18s Woman picking fruit

Bulgarian Agrarian Peoples Union, 75th anniv.

Michelangelo, Self-portrait A852

13s, Night, horiz. 18s, Day, horiz. Both designs after sculptures from Medici Tomb, Florence.

1975

2224 A852 2s plum & dk blue .20 .20
2225 A852 13s vio bl & plum .25 .20
2226 A852 18s brown & green .50 .20
Nos. 2224-2226 (3) .95 .60

Souvenir Sheet

2227 A852 2s olive & red 1.25 1.25

Michelangelo Buonarotti (1475-1564), Italian sculptor, painter and architect. No. 2227 issued to publicize ARPHILA 75 Intl. Phil. Exhib., Paris, June 6-16. Sheet sold for 60s. Issued: #2224-2226, 3/28; #2227, 3/31.

Souvenir Sheet

Spain No. 1 and España 75 Emblem — A853

1975, Apr. 4

2228 A853 40s multicolored 3.75 3.00

Espana 75 International Philatelic Exhibition, Madrid, Apr. 4-13.

Gabrov Costume A854

Regional Costumes: 3s, Trnsk. 5s, Vidin. 13s, Gocedelchev. 18s, Risen.

1975, Apr. Photo. *Perf. 13*

2229 A854 2s blue & multi .20 .20
2230 A854 3s emerald & multi .20 .20
2231 A854 5s orange & multi .20 .20
2232 A854 13s olive & multi .35 .20
2233 A854 18s multicolored .80 .25
Nos. 2229-2233 (5) 1.75 1.05

Red Star and Arrow — A855

Standard Kilogram and Meter — A856

Design: 13s, Dove and broken sword.

1975, May 9

2234 A855 2s red, blk & gold .20 .20
2235 A855 13s blue, blk & gold .30 .20

Victory over Fascism, 30th anniversary.

1975, May 9 *Perf. 13x13½*

2236 A856 13s silver, lil & blk .35 .20

Cent. of Intl, Meter Convention, Paris, 1875.

IWY Emblem, Woman's Head — A857

Ivan Vasov — A858

1975, May 20 Photo. *Perf. 13*

2237 A857 13s multicolored .35 .20

International Women's Year 1975.

1975, May

Design: 13s, Ivan Vasov, seated.

2238 A858 2s buff & multi .20 .20
2239 A858 13s gray & multi .30 .20

125th birth anniversary of Ivan Vasov.

Nikolov and Sava Kokarechkov — A859

2s, Mitko Palaouzov, Ivan Vassilev. 5s, Nicolas Nakev, Stevtcho Kraychev. 13s, Ivanka Pachkoulova, Detelina Mintcheva.

1975, May 30

2240 A859 1s multicolored .20 .20
2241 A859 2s multicolored .20 .20
2242 A859 5s multicolored .20 .20
2243 A859 13s multicolored .30 .20
Nos. 2240-2243 (4) .90 .80

Teen-age resistance fighters, killed during World War II.

Mother Feeding Child, by John E. Millais A861

Etchings: 2s, The Dead Daughter, by Goya. 3s, Reunion, by Beshkov. 13s, Seated Nude, by Renoir. 20s, Man in a Fur Hat, by Rembrandt. 40s, The Dream, by Daumier, horiz. 1 l, Temptation, by Dürer.

Photogravure and Engraved

1975, Aug. *Perf. 12x11½, 11½x12*

2248 A861 1s yel grn & multi .20 .20
2249 A861 2s orange & multi .20 .20
2250 A861 3s lilac & multi .20 .20
2251 A861 13s lt blue & multi .25 .20
2252 A861 20s ocher & multi .40 .20
2253 A861 40s rose & multi 1.10 .30
Nos. 2248-2253 (6) 2.35 1.30

Souvenir Sheet

2254 A861 1 l emerald & multi 2.00 1.25

World Graphics Exhibition.

Letter "Z" from 12th Century Manuscript A862

Initials from Illuminated Manuscripts: 2s, "B" from 17th cent. prayerbook. 3s, "V" from 16th cent. Bouhovo Gospel. 8s, "B" from 14th cent. Turnovo collection. 13s, "V" from Dobreisho's Gospel, 13th cent. 18s, "E" from 11th cent. Enina book of the Apostles.

1975, Aug. Litho. *Perf. 11½*

2255 A862 1s multicolored .20 .20
2256 A862 2s multicolored .20 .20
2257 A862 3s multicolored .20 .20
2258 A862 8s multicolored .20 .20
2259 A862 13s multicolored .25 .20
2260 A862 18s multicolored .65 .20
Nos. 2255-2260 (6) 1.70 1.20

Bulgarian art.

Whimsical Globe — A863

1975, Aug. Photo. *Perf. 13*

2261 A863 2s multicolored .20 .20

Festival of Humor and Satire.

Lifeboat Dju IV and Gibraltar-Cuba Route — A864

1975, Aug. 5 Photo. *Perf. 13*

2262 A864 13s multicolored .25 .20

Oceanexpo 75, 1st Intl. Ocean Exhib., Okinawa, July 20, 1975-Jan. 18, 1976.

Sts. Cyril and Methodius — A865

Sts. Constantine and Helena — A866

St. Sophia Church, Sofia, Woodcut by V. Zahriev — A867

1975, Aug. 21

2263 A865 2s ver, yel & brn .20 .20
2264 A866 13s green, yel & brn .25 .20

Souvenir Sheet

2265 A867 50s orange & multi 1.25 .80

Balkanphila V, philatelic exhibition, Sofia, Sept. 27-Oct. 5.

Peace Dove and Map of Europe — A868

1975, Nov. Photo. *Perf. 13*

2266 A868 18s ultra, rose & yel .45 .25

European Security and Cooperation Conference, Helsinki, Finland, July 30-Aug. 1. No. 2266 printed in sheets of 5 stamps and 4 labels, arranged checkerwise.

Acherontia Atropos — A869

Designs: Moths.

1975 Photo. *Perf. 13*

2267 A869 1s *shown* .20 .20
2268 A869 2s *Daphnis nerii* .20 .20
2269 A869 3s *Smerinthus ocellata* .20 .20
2270 A869 10s *Deilephila nicea* .20 .20
2271 A869 13s *Choerocampa elpenor* .25 .20
2272 A869 18s *Macroglossum fuciformis* .90 .25
Nos. 2267-2272 (6) 1.95 1.25

Soccer Player — A870

1975, Sept. 21

2273 A870 2s multicolored .20 .20

8th Inter-Toto (soccer pool) Soccer Championships, Varna.

Constantine's Rebellion Against the Turks, 1403 — A871

Designs (Woodcuts): 2s, Campaign of Vladislav III, 1443-1444. 3s, Battles of Turnovo, 1598 and 1686. 10s, Battle of Liprovsko, 1688. 13s, Guerrillas, 17th century. 18s, Return of exiled peasants.

1975, Nov. 27 Photo. *Perf. 13*

2274 A871 1s bister, grn & blk .20 .20
2275 A871 2s blue, car & blk .20 .20
2276 A871 3s yellow, lil & blk .20 .20
2277 A871 10s orange, grn & blk .20 .20
2278 A871 13s green, lil & blk .25 .20
2279 A871 18s pink, grn & blk .45 .20
Nos. 2274-2279 (6) 1.50 1.20

Bulgarian history.

Red Cross and First Aid — A872

Design: 13s, Red Cross and dove.

1975, Dec. 1

2280 A872 2s red brn, red & blk .20 .20
2281 A872 13s bl grn, red & blk .25 .20

90th anniversary of Bulgarian Red Cross.

Egyptian Galley A873

Historic Ships: 2s, Phoenician galley. 3s, Greek trireme. 5s, Roman galley. 13s, Viking longship. 18s, Venetian galley.

1975, Dec. 15 Photo. *Perf. 13*

2282 A873 1s multicolored .20 .20
2283 A873 2s multicolored .20 .20
2284 A873 3s multicolored .20 .20
2285 A873 5s multicolored .20 .20
2286 A873 13s multicolored .30 .20
2287 A873 18s multicolored .60 .20
Nos. 2282-2287 (6) 1.70 1.20

See Nos. 2431-2436, 2700-2705.

Souvenir Sheet

Ethnographical Museum, Plovdiv — A874

1975, Dec. 17

2288 Sheet of 3 4.50 2.50
a. A874 80s grn, yel & dark brn 1.25 .65

European Architectural Heritage Year. No. 2288 contains 3 stamps and 3 labels showing stylized bird.

Dobri Hristov — A875

1975, Dec. ***Perf. 13***
2289 A875 5s brt green, yel & brn .20 .20

Dobri Hristov, musician, birth centenary.

United Nations Emblem — A876

1975, Dec.
2290 A876 13s gold, blk & mag .20 .20

United Nations, 30th anniversary.

Glass Ornaments — A877

13s, Peace dove, decorated ornament.

1975, Dec. 22 Photo. ***Perf. 13***
2291 A877 2s brt violet & multi .20 .20
2292 A877 13s gray & multi .20 .20

New Year 1976.

Downhill Skiing — A878

Designs (Winter Olympic Games Emblem and): 2s, Cross country skier, vert. 3s, Ski jump. 13s, Biathlon, vert. 18s, Ice hockey, vert. 23s, Speed skating, vert. 80s, Figure skating, pair, vert.

1976, Jan. 30 ***Perf. 13½***
2293 A878 1s silver & multi .20 .20
2294 A878 2s silver & multi .20 .20
2295 A878 3s silver & multi .20 .20
2296 A878 13s silver & multi .25 .20
2297 A878 18s silver & multi .30 .20
2298 A878 23s silver & multi .80 .30
Nos. 2293-2298 (6) 1.95 1.30

Souvenir Sheet

2299 A878 80s silver & multi 1.75 1.10

12th Winter Olympic Games, Innsbruck, Austria, Feb. 4-15.

Electric Streetcar, Sofia, 1976 — A879

Design: 13s, Streetcar and trailer, 1901.

1976, Jan. 12 Photo. ***Perf. 13½x13***
2300 A879 2s gray & multi .20 .20
2301 A879 13s gray & multi .40 .20

75th anniversary of Sofia streetcars.

Stylized Bird — A880

5s, Dates "1976," "1956" & star. 13s, Hammer & sickle. 50s, George Dimitrov.

1976, Mar. 1 ***Perf. 13***
2302 A880 2s gold & multi .20 .20
2303 A880 5s gold & multi .20 .20
2304 A880 13s gold & multi .25 .20
Nos. 2302-2304 (3) .65 .60

Souvenir Sheet

2305 A880 50s gold & multi .25 .45

11th Bulgarian Communist Party Congress.

A. G. Bell and Telephone, 1876 — A881

1976, Mar. 10
2306 A881 18s dk brn, yel & ocher .25 .20

Centenary of first telephone call by Alexander Graham Bell, Mar. 10, 1876.

Mute Swan — A882

Waterfowl: 2s, Ruddy shelduck. 3s, Common shelduck. 5s, Garganey teal. 13s, Mallard. 18s, Red-crested pochard.

1976, Mar. 27 Litho. ***Perf. 11½***
2307 A882 1s vio bl & multi .20 .20
2308 A882 2s yel grn & multi .20 .20
2309 A882 3s blue & multi .20 .20
2310 A882 5s multicolored .25 .20
2311 A882 13s purple & multi .65 .20
2312 A882 18s green & multi .90 .20
Nos. 2307-2312 (6) 2.40 1.20

Guerrillas — A883

Designs (Woodcuts by Stoev): 2s, Peasants with rifle and proclamation. 5s, Raina Knaginia with horse and guerrilla. 13s, Insurgents with cherrywood cannon.

1976, Apr. 5 Photo. ***Perf. 13***
2313 A883 1s multicolored .20 .20
2314 A883 2s multicolored .20 .20
2315 A883 5s multicolored .20 .20
2316 A883 13s multicolored .25 .20
Nos. 2313-2316 (4) .85 .80

Centenary of uprising against Turkey.

Guard and Dog A884

13s, Men on horseback, observation tower.

1976, May 15
2317 A884 2s multicolored .20 .20
2318 A884 13s multicolored .20 .20

30th anniversary of Border Guards.

Construction Worker — A885

1976, May 20
2319 A885 2s multicolored .20 .20

Young Workers Brigade, 30th anniversary.

Busludja, Bas-relief A886

AES Complex — A887

Design: 5s, Memorial building.

1976, May 28 Photo. ***Perf. 13***
2320 A886 2s green & multi .20 .20
2321 A886 5s violet bl & multi .20 .20

First Congress of Bulgarian Social Democratic Party, 85th anniversary.

1976, Apr. 7

8s, Factory. 10s, Apartment houses. 13s, Refinery. 20s, Hydroelectric station.

2322 A887 5s green .20 .20
2323 A887 8s maroon .20 .20
2324 A887 10s green .20 .20
2325 A887 13s violet .30 .20
2326 A887 20s brt green .40 .20
Nos. 2322-2326 (5) 1.30 1.00

Five-year plan accomplishments.

Children Playing Around Table — A888

Kindergarten Children: 2s, with doll carriage & hobby horse. 5s, playing ball. 23s, in costume.

1976, June 15
2327 A888 1s green & multi .20 .20
2328 A888 2s yellow & multi .20 .20
2329 A888 5s lilac & multi .20 .20
2330 A888 23s rose & multi .40 .20
Nos. 2327-2330 (4) 1.00 .80

Demeter Blagoev — A889

1976, May 28
2331 A889 13s bluish blk, red & gold .25 .20

Demeter Blagoev (1856-1924), writer, political leader, 120th birth anniversary.

Christo Botev — A890

1976, May 25
2332 A890 13s ocher & slate grn .25 .20

Christo Botev (1848-1876), poet, death centenary. Printed se-tenant with yellow green and ocher label, inscribed with poem.

Boxing, Montreal Olympic Emblem — A891

Belt Buckle — A892

Designs (Montreal Olympic Emblem): 1s, Wrestling, horiz. 3s, 1 l, Weight lifting. 13s, One-man kayak. 18s, Woman gymnast. 28s, Woman diver. 40s, Woman runner.

1976, June 25
2333 A891 1s orange & multi .20 .20
2334 A891 2s multicolored .20 .20
2335 A891 3s lilac & multi .20 .20
2336 A891 13s multicolored .20 .20
2337 A891 18s multicolored .30 .20
2338 A891 28s blue & multi .40 .20
2339 A891 40s lemon & multi .75 .30
Nos. 2333-2339 (7) 2.25 1.50

Souvenir Sheet

2340 A891 1 l orange & multi 1.60 1.10

21st Olympic Games, Montreal, Canada, July 17-Aug. 1.

1976, July 30 Photo. ***Perf. 13***

Thracian Art (8th-4th Centuries): 2s, Brooch. 3s, Mirror handle. 5s, Helmet cheek cover. 13s, Gold ornament. 18s, Lion's head (harness decoration). 20s, Knee guard. 28s, Jeweled pendant.

2341 A892 1s brown & multi .20 .20
2342 A892 2s blue & multi .20 .20
2343 A892 3s multicolored .20 .20
2344 A892 5s claret & multi .20 .20
2345 A892 13s purple & multi .25 .20
2346 A892 18s multicolored .30 .20
2347 A892 20s multicolored .40 .20
2348 A892 28s multicolored .60 .20
Nos. 2341-2348 (8) 2.35 1.60

Souvenir Sheet

Composite of Bulgarian Stamp Designs — A893

1976, June 5

2349 A893 50s red & multi 1.60 .65

International Federation of Philately (F.I.P.), 50th anniversary and 12th Congress.

Partisans at Night, by Ilya Petrov — A894

Paintings: 5s, Old Town, by Tsanko Lavenov. 13s, Seated Woman, by Petrov, vert. 18s, Seated Boy, by Petrov, vert. 28s, Old Plovdiv, by Lavenov, vert. 80s, Ilya Petrov, self-portrait, vert.

1976, Aug. 11 Photo. *Perf. 14*

2350 A894 2s multicolored .20 .20
2351 A894 5s multicolored .20 .20
2352 A894 13s ultra & multi .30 .20
2353 A894 18s multicolored .45 .20
2354 A894 28s multicolored .65 .20
Nos. 2350-2354 (5) 1.80 1.00

Souvenir Sheet

2354A A894 80s multicolored 1.25 .95

Souvenir Sheet

Olympic Sports and Emblems — A895

1976, Sept. 6 Photo. *Perf. 13*

2355 A895 Sheet of 4 1.60 1.00
a. 25s Weight Lifting .35 .20
b. 25s Rowing .35 .20
c. 25s Running .35 .20
d. 25s Wrestling .35 .20

Medalists, 21st Olympic Games, Montreal.

Souvenir Sheet

Fresco and UNESCO Emblem — A896

1976, Dec. 3

2356 A896 50s red & multi 1.25 .55

UNESCO, 30th anniv.

"The Pianist" by Jendov — A897

Fish and Hook — A898

Designs (Caricatures by Jendov): 5s, Imperialist "Trick or Treat." 13s, The Leader, 1931.

1976, Sept. 30 Photo. *Perf. 13*

2357 A897 2s green & multi .20 .20
2358 A897 5s purple & multi .20 .20
2359 A897 13s magenta & multi .30 .20
Nos. 2357-2359 (3) .70 .60

Alex Jendov (1901-1953), caricaturist.

1976, Sept. 21 Photo. *Perf. 13*

2360 A898 5s multicolored .20 .20

World Sport Fishing Congress, Varna.

St. Theodore A899

Frescoes: 3s, St. Paul. 5s, St. Joachim. 13s, Melchizedek. 19s, St. Porphyrius. 28s, Queen. 1 l, The Last Supper.

1976, Oct. 4 Litho. *Perf. 12x12½*

2361 A899 2s gold & multi .20 .20
2362 A899 3s gold & multi .20 .20
2363 A899 5s gold & multi .20 .20
2364 A899 13s gold & multi .30 .20
2365 A899 19s gold & multi .35 .20
2366 A899 28s gold & multi .65 .20
Nos. 2361-2366 (6) 1.90 1.20

Miniature Sheet

Perf. 12

2367 A899 1 l gold & multi 1.50 .95

Zemen Monastery frescoes, 14th cent.

Document A900

1976, Oct. 5

2368 A900 5s multicolored .20 .20

State Archives, 25th anniversary.

Cinquefoil A901

1976, Oct. 14 Photo. *Perf. 13*

2369 A901 1s Chestnut .20 .20
2370 A901 2s shown .20 .20
2371 A901 5s Holly .20 .20
2372 A901 8s Yew .20 .20
2373 A901 13s Daphne .30 .20
2374 A901 23s Judas tree .60 .20
Nos. 2369-2374 (6) 1.70 1.20

Dimitri Polianov — A902

1976, Nov. 19

2375 A902 2s dk purple & ocher .20 .20

Dimitri Polianov (1876-1953), poet.

Christo Botev, by Zlatyu Boyadjiev A903

Paintings: 2s, Partisan Carrying Cherrywood Cannon, by Ilya Petrov. 3s, "Necklace of Immortality" (man's portrait), by Detchko Uzunov. 13s, "April 1876," by Georgi Popoff. 18s, Partisans, by Stoyan Venev. 60s, The Oath, by Svetlin Ruseff.

1976, Dec. 8

2376 A903 1s bister & multi .20 .20
2377 A903 2s bister & multi .20 .20
2378 A903 3s bister & multi .20 .20
2379 A903 13s bister & multi .25 .20
2380 A903 18s bister & multi .35 .20
Nos. 2376-2380 (5) 1.20 1.00

Souvenir Sheet

Imperf

2381 A903 60s gold & multi .95 .55

Uprising against Turkish rule, centenary.

"Pollution" and Tree A904

Design: 18s, "Pollution" obscuring sun.

1976, Nov. 10 *Perf. 13*

2382 A904 2s ultra & multi .20 .20
2383 A904 18s blue & multi .30 .20

Protection of the environment.

Congress Emblem A904a

Flags — A904b

1976, Nov. 28 Photo. *Perf. 13*

2384 A904a 2s multicolored .20 .20
2384A A904b 13s multicolored .25 .20

33rd BSIS Cong. (Bulgarian Socialist Party).

Tobacco Workers, by Stajkov A905

Paintings by Stajkov: 2s, View of Melnik. 13s, Shipbuilder.

1976, Dec. 16 Photo. *Perf. 13*

2385 A905 1s multicolored .20 .20
2386 A905 2s multicolored .20 .20
2387 A905 13s multicolored .30 .20
Nos. 2385-2387 (3) .70 .60

Veselin Stajkov (1906-1970), painter.

Snowflake A906

1976, Dec. 20

2388 A906 2s silver & multi .20 .20

New Year 1977.

Zachary Stoyanov (1851-1889), Historian — A907

1976, Dec. 30
2389 A907 2s multicolored .20 .20

Bronze Coin of Septimus Severus — A908

Roman Coins: 2s, 13s, 18s, Bronze coins of Caracalla, diff. 23s, Copper coin of Diocletian.

1977, Jan. 28 Photo. *Perf. 13½x13*
2390 A908 1s gold & multi .20 .20
2391 A908 2s gold & multi .20 .20
2392 A908 13s gold & multi .20 .20
2393 A908 18s gold & multi .25 .20
2394 A908 23s gold & multi .45 .20
Nos. 2390-2394 (5) 1.30 1.00

Coins struck in Serdica (modern Sofia).

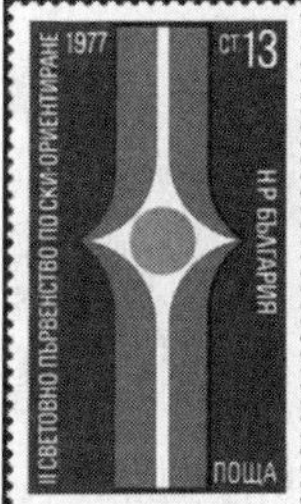
Skis and Compass — A909

Tourist Congress Emblem — A910

1977, Feb. 14 *Perf. 13*
2395 A909 13s ultra, red & lt bl .25 .20

2nd World Ski Orienteering Championships.

1977, Feb. 24 Photo. *Perf. 13*
2396 A910 2s multicolored .20 .20

5th Congress of Bulgarian Tourist Organization.

Bellflower A911

Designs: Various bellflowers.

1977, Mar. 2
2397 A911 1s yellow & multi .20 .20
2398 A911 2s rose & multi .20 .20
2399 A911 3s lt blue & multi .20 .20
2400 A911 13s multicolored .30 .20
2401 A911 43s yellow & multi 1.10 .30
Nos. 2397-2401 (5) 2.00 1.10

Vasil Kolarov — A912

Union Congress Emblem — A913

1977, Mar. 21 Photo. *Perf. 13*
2402 A912 2s blue & black .20 .20

Vasil Kolarov (1877-1950), politician.

1977, Mar. 25
2403 A913 2s multicolored .20 .20

8th Bulgarian Trade Union Cong., Apr. 4-7.

Wolf A914

Wild Animals: 2s, Red fox. 10s, Weasel. 13s, European wildcat. 23s, Jackal.

1977, May 16 Litho. *Perf. 12½x12*
2404 A914 1s multicolored .20 .20
2405 A914 2s multicolored .20 .20
2406 A914 10s multicolored .20 .20
2407 A914 13s multicolored .35 .20
2408 A914 23s multicolored .60 .20
Nos. 2404-2408 (5) 1.55 1.00

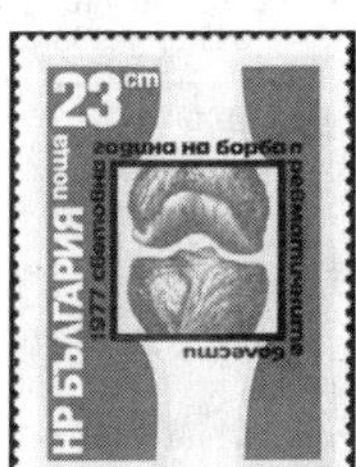
Diseased Knee — A915

1977, Mar. 31 Photo. *Perf. 13*
2409 A915 23s multicolored .40 .20

World Rheumatism Year.

Writers' Congress Emblem A916

1977, June 7
2410 A916 23s lt bl & yel grn .65 .20

International Writers Congress: "Peace, the Hope of the Planet." No. 2410 printed in sheets of 8 stamps and 4 labels with signatures of participating writers.

Old Testament Trinity, Sofia, 16th Century A917

Icons: 1s, St. Nicholas, Nessebur, 13th cent. 3s, Annunciation, Royal Gates, Veliko Turnovo, 16th cent. 5s, Christ Enthroned, Nessebur, 17th cent. 13s, St. Nicholas, Elena, 18th cent. 23s, Presentation of the Virgin, Rila Monastery, 18th cent. 35s, Virgin and Child, Tryavna, 19th cent. 40s, St. Demetrius on Horseback, Provadia, 19th cent. 1 l, The 12 Holidays, Rila Monastery, 18th cent.

1977, May 10 Photo. *Perf. 13*
2411 A917 1s black & multi .20 .20
2412 A917 2s green & multi .20 .20
2413 A917 3s brown & multi .20 .20
2414 A917 5s blue & multi .20 .20
2415 A917 13s olive & multi .30 .20
2416 A917 23s maroon & multi .50 .20
2417 A917 35s green & multi .80 .25
2418 A917 40s dp ultra & multi 1.10 .40
Nos. 2411-2418 (8) 3.50 1.85

Miniature Sheet

Imperf

2419 A917 1 l gold & multi 2.25 1.10

Bulgarian icons. See Nos. 2615-2619.

Souvenir Sheet

St. Cyril — A918

1977, June 7 Photo. *Perf. 13*
2420 A918 1 l gold & multi 1.75 .90

St. Cyril (827-869), reputed inventor of Cyrillic alphabet.

Congress Emblem — A919

1977, May 9
2421 A919 2s red, gold & grn .20 .20

13th Komsomol Congress.

Newspaper Masthead — A920

1977, June 3 Photo. *Perf. 13*
2422 A920 2s multicolored .20 .20

Cent. of Bulgarian daily press and 50th anniv. of Rabotnichesko Delo newspaper.

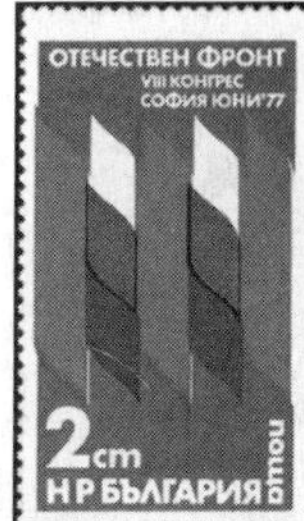
Patriotic Front Emblem — A921

Weight Lifting — A922

1977, May 26
2423 A921 2s gold & multi .20 .20

8th Congress of Patriotic Front.

1977, June 15
2424 A922 13s dp brown & multi .25 .20

European Youth Weight Lifting Championships, Sofia, June.

Women Basketball Players — A923

1977, June 15 *Perf. 13*
2425 A923 23s multicolored .50 .20

7th European Women's Basketball Championships.

Wrestling — A924

Games Emblem and: 13s, Running. 23s, Basketball. 43s, Women's gymnastics.

1977, Apr. 15
2426 A924 2s multicolored .20 .20
2427 A924 13s multicolored .20 .20
2428 A924 23s multicolored .40 .20
2429 A924 43s multicolored .70 .25
Nos. 2426-2429 (4) 1.50 .85

UNIVERSIADE '77, University Games, Sofia, Aug. 18-27.

TV Tower, Berlin — A925

1977, Aug. 12 Litho. *Perf. 13*

2430 A925 25s blue & dk blue .50 .20

SOZPHILEX 77 Philatelic Exhibition, Berlin, Aug. 19-28.

Ship Type of 1975

Historic Ships: 1s, Hansa cog. 2s, Santa Maria, caravelle. 3s, Golden Hind, frigate. 12s, Santa Catherina, carrack. 13s, La Corone, galleon. 43s, Mediterranean galleass.

1977, Aug. 29 Photo. *Perf. 13*

2431 A873 1s multicolored .20 .20
2432 A873 2s multicolored .20 .20
2433 A873 3s multicolored .20 .20
2434 A873 12s multicolored .25 .20
2435 A873 13s multicolored .25 .20
2436 A873 43s multicolored 1.00 .25
Nos. 2431-2436 (6) 2.10 1.25

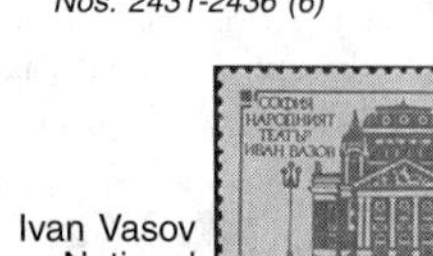

Ivan Vasov National Theater A926

Buildings, Sofia: 13s, Party Headquarters. 23s, House of the People's Army. 30s, Clement Ochrida University. 80s, National Gallery. 1 l, National Assembly.

1977, Aug. 30 Photo. *Perf. 13*

2437 A926 12s red, *gray* .20 .20
2438 A926 13s red brn, *gray* .20 .20
2439 A926 23s blue, *gray* .30 .20
2440 A926 30s olive, *gray* .40 .20
2441 A926 80s violet, *gray* 1.10 .40
2442 A926 1 l claret, *gray* 1.40 .50
Nos. 2437-2442 (6) 3.60 1.70

Map of Europe A927

1977, June 10

2443 A927 23s brown, bl & grn .40 .20

21st Congress of the European Organization for Quality Control, Varna.

Union of Earth and Water, by Rubens A928

Rubens Paintings: 23s, Venus and Adonis. 40s, Pastoral Scene (man and woman). 1 l, Portrait of a Lady in Waiting.

1977, Sept. 23 Litho. *Perf. 12*

2444 A928 13s gold & multi .50 .20
2445 A928 23s gold & multi .70 .20
2446 A928 40s gold & multi 1.10 .25
Nos. 2444-2446 (3) 2.30 .65

Souvenir Sheet

2447 A928 1 l gold & multi 2.75 1.60

Peter Paul Rubens (1577-1640).

George Dimitrov A929

1977, June 17 Photo. *Perf. 13*

2448 A929 13s red & deep claret .35 .20

George Dimitrov (1882-1947).

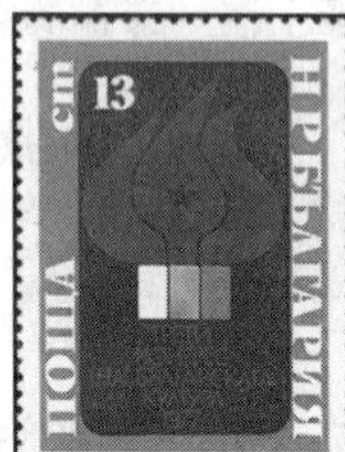

Flame with Star — A930

Smart Pete on Donkey, by Ilya Beshkov — A931

1977, May 17

2449 A930 13s gold & multi .25 .20

3rd Bulgarian Culture Congress.

1977, May 19

2450 A931 2s multicolored .20 .20

11th National Festival of Humor and Satire Gabrovo.

Elin Pelin — A932

Writers: 2s, Pelin (Dimitur Ivanov Stojanov, (1877-1949). 5s, Peju K. Jaworov (1878-1914).

Artists: 13s, Boris Angelushev (1902-1966), 23s, Ceno Todorov (Ceno Todorov Dikov, 1877-1953). Each printed with label showing scenes from authors' works or illustrations by the artists.

1977, Aug. 26 Photo. *Perf. 13*

2451 A932 2s gold & brown .20 .20
2452 A932 5s gold & gray grn .20 .20
2453 A932 13s gold & claret .25 .20
2454 A932 23s gold & blue .45 .20
Nos. 2451-2454 (4) 1.10 .80

13th Canoe World Championships — A933

1977, Sept. 1 Photo. *Perf. 13*

2455 A933 2s shown .20 .20
2456 A933 23s 2-man canoe .40 .20

Albena, Black Sea A933a

1977, Oct. 5 Photo. *Perf. 13*

2456A A933a 35s shown .65 .25
2456B A933a 43s Rila Monastery .80 .30

Sheet contains 4 each plus label.

Dr. Pirogov — A934

1977, Oct. 14 Photo. *Perf. 13*

2457 A934 13s olive, ocher & brn .25 .20

Centenary of visit by Russian physician N. J. Pirogov during war of liberation from Turkey.

Peace Decree, 1917 — A935

Old Soldier with Grandchild A936

13s, Lenin, 1917. 23s, "1917" as a flame.

1977, Oct. 21

2458 A935 2s black, buff & red .20 .20
2459 A935 13s multicolored .25 .20
2460 A935 23s multicolored .45 .20
Nos. 2458-2460 (3) .90 .60

60th anniv. of Russian October Revolution.

1977, Sept. 30

Designs (Festival Posters): 13s, "The Bugler." 23s, Liberation Monument, Sofia (detail). 25s, Samara flag.

2461 A936 2s multicolored .20 .20
2462 A936 13s multicolored .25 .20
2463 A936 23s multicolored .40 .20
2464 A936 25s multicolored .50 .25
Nos. 2461-2464 (4) 1.35 .85

Liberation from Turkish rule, centenary.

Souvenir Sheet

Games' and Sports Emblems — A937

1977, Aug. 10 Photo. *Perf. 13½x13*

2465 A937 1 l multicolored 1.50 1.25

University Games '77, Sofia.

Conference Building — A938

1977, Sept. 12 *Perf. 13½*

2466 A938 23s multicolored .40 .20

64th Interparliamentary Union Conf., Sofia.

Bulgarian Worker's Newspaper, Anniversaries A939

1977, Sept. 12 Photo. *Perf. 13*

2467 A939 2s yel grn, blk & red .20 .20

Ornament A940

New Year 1978: 13s, Different ornament.

1977, Dec. 1

2468 A940 2s gold & multi .20 .20
2469 A940 13s silver & multi .25 .20

Railroad Bridge — A941

1977, Nov. 9

2470 A941 13s green, yel & gray .30 .20

Transport Organization, 50th anniversary.

A942

1977, Nov. 15

2471 A942 8s gold & vio brn .20 .20

Petko Ratchev Slaveikov (1827-95), poet, birth sesquicentennial. No. 2471 printed in sheets of 8 stamps and 8 labels in 4 alternating vertical rows.

A943

Designs: 23s, Soccer player and Games' emblem. 50s, Soccer players.

1978, Jan. 30 Photo. *Perf. 13*

2472 A943 13s multicolored .25 .20
2473 A943 23s multicolored .45 .20

Souvenir Sheet

2474 A943 50s ultra & multi 1.00 .85

11th World Cup Soccer Championship, Argentina, June 1-25.

Todor Zhivkov and Leonid I. Brezhnev — A944

Ostankino Tower, Moscow, Bulgarian Post Emblem — A945

1977, Sept. 7 Photo. *Perf. 13*

2475 A944 18s gold, car & brn .30 .20

Bulgarian-Soviet Friendship. No. 2475 issued in sheets of 3 stamps and 3 labels.

1978, Mar. 1

2476 A945 13s multicolored .25 .20

Comecon Postal Organization (Council of Mutual Economic Assistance), 20th anniv.

Leo Tolstoy — A946

Shipka Pass Monument — A947

5s, Fedor Dostoevski. 13s, Ivan Sergeevich Turgenev. 23s, Vasili Vasilievich Vershchagin. 25s, Giuseppe Garibaldi. 35s, Victor Hugo.

1978, Mar. 28 Photo. *Perf. 13*

2477 A946 2s yellow & dk grn .20 .20
2478 A946 5s lemon & brown .20 .20
2479 A946 13s tan & sl grn .25 .20
2480 A946 23s gray & vio brn .35 .20
2481 A946 25s yel grn & blk .40 .20
2482 A946 35s lt bl & vio bl .80 .40
Nos. 2477-2482 (6) 2.20 1.40

Souvenir Sheet

2483 A947 50s multicolored .80 .60

Bulgaria's liberation from Ottoman rule, cent.

Bulgarian and Russian Colors A948

1978, Mar. 18

2484 A948 2s multicolored .20 .20

30th anniv. of Russo-Bulgarian co-operation.

Heart and WHO Emblem A949

1978, May 12

2485 A949 23s gray, red & org .30 .20

World Health Day, fight against hypertension.

Goddess A950

Ceramics (2nd-4th Cent.) & Exhibition Emblem: 5s, Mask of bearded man. 13s, Vase. 23s, Vase. 35s, Head of Silenus. 53s, Cock.

1978, Apr. 26

2486 A950 2s green & multi .20 .20
2487 A950 5s multicolored .20 .20
2488 A950 13s multicolored .25 .20
2489 A950 23s multicolored .50 .20
2490 A950 35s multicolored .75 .25
2491 A950 53s carmine & multi 1.25 .30
Nos. 2486-2491 (6) 3.15 1.35

Philaserdica Philatelic Exhibition.

Nikolai Roerich, by Svyatoslav Roerich — A951

"Mind and Matter," by Andrei Nikolov — A952

1978, Apr. 5

2492 A951 8s multicolored .20 .20
2493 A952 13s multicolored .30 .20

Nikolai K. Roerich (1874-1947) and Andrei Nikolov (1878-1959), artists.

Bulgarian Flag and Red Star — A953

1978, Apr. 18

2494 A953 2s vio blue & multi .20 .20

Bulgarian Communist Party Congress.

Young Man, by Albrecht Dürer A954

Paintings: 23s, Bathsheba at Fountain, by Rubens. 25s, Portrait of a Man, by Hans Holbein the Younger. 35s, Rembrandt and Saskia, by Rembrandt. 43s, Lady in Mourning, by Tintoretto. 60s, Old Man with Beard, by Rembrandt. 80s, Knight in Armor, by Van Dyck.

1978, June 19 Photo. *Perf. 13*

2495 A954 13s multicolored .20 .20
2496 A954 23s multicolored .30 .20
2497 A954 25s multicolored .30 .20
2498 A954 35s multicolored .45 .20
2499 A954 43s multicolored .55 .20
2500 A954 60s multicolored .85 .25
2501 A954 80s multicolored 1.10 .40
Nos. 2495-2501 (7) 3.75 1.65

Dresden Art Gallery paintings.

Doves and Festival Emblem — A955

1978, May 31

2502 A955 13s multicolored .25 .20

11th World Youth Festival, Havana, 7/28-8/5.

Fritillaria Stribrnyi — A956

Rare Flowers: 2s, Fritillaria drenovskyi. 3s, Lilium rhodopaeum. 13s, Tulipa urumoffii. 23s, Lilium jankae. 43s, Tulipa rhodopaea.

1978, June 27

2503 A956 1s multicolored .20 .20
2504 A956 2s multicolored .20 .20
2505 A956 3s multicolored .20 .20
2506 A956 13s multicolored .25 .20
2507 A956 23s multicolored .45 .20
2508 A956 43s multicolored .90 .30
Nos. 2503-2508 (6) 2.20 1.30

Yacht Cor Caroli and Map of Voyage A957

1978, May 19 Photo. *Perf. 13*

2509 A957 23s multicolored .50 .20

First Bulgarian around-the-world voyage, Capt. Georgi Georgiev, 12/20/76-12/20/77.

Market, by Naiden Petkov — A958

Views of Sofia: 5s, Street, by Emil Stoichev. 13s, Street, by Boris Ivanov. 23s, Tolbukhin Boulevard, by Nikola Tanev. 35s, National Theater, by Nikola Petrov. 53s, Market, by Anton Mitov.

1978, Aug. 28 Litho. *Perf. 12½x12*

2510 A958 2s multicolored .20 .20
2511 A958 5s multicolored .20 .20
2512 A958 13s multicolored .20 .20
2513 A958 23s multicolored .30 .20
2514 A958 35s multicolored .50 .20
2515 A958 53s multicolored .85 .30
Nos. 2510-2515 (6) 2.25 1.30

Miniature Sheet

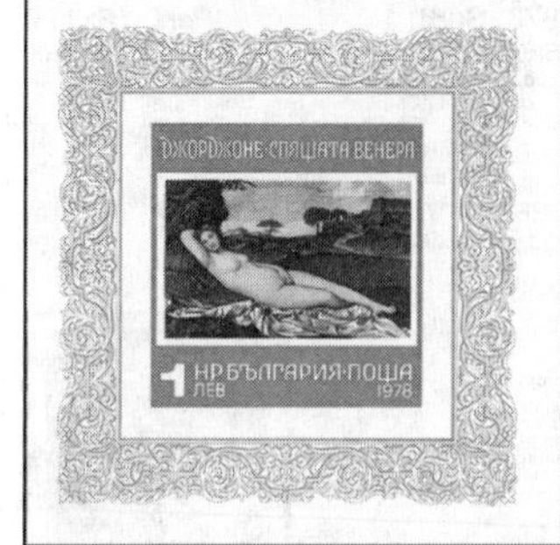

Sleeping Venus, by Giorgione — A959

1978, Aug. 7 Photo. *Imperf.*

2516 A959 1 l multicolored 2.25 .85

View of Varna — A960

1978, July 13 Photo. ***Perf. 13***

2517 A960 13s multicolored .25 .20

63rd Esperanto Cong., Varna, 7/29-8/5.

Black Woodpecker A961

Woodpeckers: 2s, Syrian. 3s, Three-toed. 13s, Middle spotted. 23s, Lesser spotted. 43s, Green.

1978, Sept. 1

2518	A961	1s multicolored	.25	.20
2519	A961	2s multicolored	.25	.20
2520	A961	3s multicolored	.25	.20
2521	A961	13s multicolored	.30	.20
2522	A961	23s multicolored	.45	.20
2523	A961	43s multicolored	1.10	.25
		Nos. 2518-2523 (6)	2.60	1.25

"September 1923" — A962

1978, Sept. 5

2524 A962 2s red & brn .25 .20

55th anniversary of September uprising.

Souvenir Sheet

National Theater, Sofia A963

Photogravure and Engraved

1978, Sept. 1 ***Perf. 12x11½***

2525	Sheet of 4	2.50	1.00
a.	A963 40s shown	.60	.20
b.	A963 40s Festival Hall, Sofia	.60	.20
c.	A963 40s Charles Bridge, Prague	.60	.20
d.	A963 40s Belvedere Palace, Prague	.60	.20

PRAGA '78 and PHILASERDICA '79 Philatelic Exhibitions.

Black and White Hands, Human Rights Emblem — A964

1978, Oct. 3 Photo. ***Perf. 13x13½***

2526 A964 13s multicolored .25 .20

Anti-Apartheid Year.

Gotse Deltchev — A965

Bulgarian Calculator — A966

1978, Aug. 1 Photo. ***Perf. 13***

2527 A965 13s multicolored .25 .20

Gotse Deltchev (1872-1903), patriot.

1978, Sept. 3

2528 A966 2s multicolored .20 .20

International Sample Fair, Plovdiv.

Guerrillas — A967

1978, Aug. 1

2529 A967 5s blk & rose red .20 .20

Ilinden and Preobrazhene revolts, 75th anniv.

"Pipe Line" and Flags A968

1978, Oct. 3

2530 A968 13s multicolored .25 .20

Construction of gas pipe line from Orenburg to Russian border.

A969

1978, Oct. 4 ***Perf. 13x13½***

2531 A969 13s Three acrobats .25 .20

3rd World Acrobatic Championships, Sofia, Oct. 6-8.

A970

1978, Sept. 18 Photo. ***Perf. 13***

2532 A970 2s dp claret & ocher .20 .20

Christo G. Danov (1828-1911), 1st Bulgarian publisher. No. 2532 printed with se-tenant label showing early printing press.

Insurgents, by Todor Panajotov — A971

1978, Sept. 20

2533 A971 2s multicolored .20 .20

Vladaja mutiny, 60th anniversary.

A972

A973

1978, Oct. 11 Photo. ***Perf. 13***

2534 A972 13s dk brn & org red .25 .20

Salvador Allende (1908-1973), president of Chile.

1978, Oct. 18

2535 A973 23s Human Rights flame .50 .20

Universal Declaration of Human Rights, 30th anniversary.

A974 A975

Burgarian Paintings: 1s, Levski and Matei Mitkaloto, by Kalina Tasseva. 2s, "Strength for my Arm" by Zlatyu Boyadjiev. 3s, Rumena, woman military leader, by Nikola Mirchev, horiz. 13s, Kolju Ficeto, by Elza Goeva. 23s, Family, National Revival Period, by Naiden Petkov.

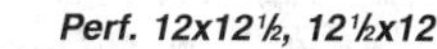

Perf. 12x12½, 12½x12

1978, Oct. 25 **Litho.**

2536	A974	1s multicolored	.20	.20
2537	A974	2s multicolored	.20	.20
2538	A974	3s multicolored	.20	.20
2539	A974	13s multicolored	.25	.20
2540	A974	23s multicolored	.40	.20
		Nos. 2536-2540 (5)	1.25	1.00

1300th anniversary of Bulgaria (in 1981).

1978, Nov. 1 Photo. ***Perf. 13***

Designs: a, Tourism building, Plovdiv. b, Chrelo Tower, Rila Cloister.

Souvenir Sheet

2541	Sheet of 5 + label	4.00	2.00
a.	A975 43s multicolored	.70	.30
b.	A975 43s multicolored	.70	.30

Conservation of European architectural heritage. No. 2541 contains 3 No. 2541a & 2 No. 2541b.

Ferry, Map of Black Sea with Route A976

1978, Nov. 1 Photo. ***Perf. 13***

2542 A976 13s multicolored .25 .20

Opening of Ilychovsk-Varna Ferry.

Bird, from Marble Floor, St. Sofia Church — A977

1978, Nov. 20

2543 A977 5s multicolored .20 .20

3rd Bulgaria '78, National Philatelic Exhibition, Sofia. Printed se-tenant with label showing emblems of Bulgaria '78 and Philaserdica '79.

Initial, 13th Century Gospel — A978

Designs: 13s, St. Cyril, miniature, 1567. 23s, Book cover, 16th century. 80s, St. Methodius, miniature, 13th century.

1978, Dec. 15 Photo. ***Perf. 13***

2544	A978	2s multicolored	.20	.20
2545	A978	13s multicolored	.20	.20
2546	A978	23s multicolored	.35	.20
		Nos. 2544-2546 (3)	.75	.60

Souvenir Sheet

2547 A978 80s multicolored 1.25 1.00

Cent. of the Cyril and Methodius Natl. Library.

Bulgaria No. 53 A979

Bulgarian Stamps: 13s, #534. 23s, #968. 35s, #1176, vert. 53s, #1223, vert. 1 l, #1.

1978, Dec. 30

2548 A979 2s ol grn & red .20 .20
2549 A979 13s ultra & rose car .20 .20
2550 A979 23s rose lil & ol grn .30 .20
2551 A979 35s brt bl & blk .50 .20
2552 A979 53s ver & sl grn .90 .30
Nos. 2548-2552 (5) 2.10 1.10

Souvenir Sheet

2553 A979 1 l multicolored 1.75 1.25

Philaserdica '79, International Philatelic Exhibition, Sofia, May 18-27, 1979, and centenary of Bulgarian stamps. No. 2553 exists imperf. See Nos. 2560-2564.

St. Clement of Ochrida — A980

1978, Dec. 8

2554 A980 2s multicolored .20 .20

Clement of Ochrida University, 90th anniv.

Ballet Dancers A981

1978, Dec. 22

2555 A981 13s multicolored .30 .20

Bulgarian ballet, 50th anniversary.

Nikola Karastojanov — A982

1978, Dec. 12

2556 A982 2s multicolored .20 .20

Nikola Karastojanov (1778-1874), printer. No. 2556 printed se-tenant with label showing printing press.

Christmas Tree Made of Birds — A983

1978, Dec. 22

2557 A983 2s shown .20 .20
2558 A983 13s Post horn .20 .20

New Year 1979.

COMECON Building, Moscow, Members' Flags — A984

1979, Jan. 25 Photo. *Perf. 13*

2559 A984 13s multicolored .25 .20

Council for Mutual Economic Aid (COMECON), 30th anniversary.

Philaserdica Type of 1978
Designs as Before

1979, Jan. 30

2560 A979 2s brt bl & red .20 .20
2561 A979 13s grn & dk car .20 .20
2562 A979 23s org brn & multi .30 .20
2563 A979 35s dl red & blk .50 .25
2564 A979 53s vio & dk ol .90 .35
Nos. 2560-2564 (5) 2.10 1.20

Philaserdica '79.

Bank Building, Commemorative Coin — A985

1979, Feb. 13

2565 A985 2s yel, gray & silver .20 .20

Centenary of Bulgarian People's Bank.

Aleksandr Stamboliski A986

1979, Feb. 28

2566 A986 2s orange & dk brn .20 .20

Aleksandr Stamboliski (1879-1923), leader of peasant's party and premier.

Flower with Child's Face, IYC Emblem — A987

1979, Mar. 8

2568 A987 23s multicolored .40 .20

International Year of the Child.

Stylized Heads, World Association Emblem — A988

1979, Mar. 20

2569 A988 13s multicolored .25 .20

8th World Cong. for the Deaf, Varna, June 20-27.

"75" and Trade Union Emblem — A989

1979, Mar. 20

2570 A989 2s slate grn & org .20 .20

75th anniversary of Bulgarian Trade Unions.

Souvenir Sheet

Sculptures in Sofia — A990

Designs: 2s, Soviet Army Monument (detail). 5s, Mother and Child, Central Railroad Station. 13s, 23s, 25s, Bas-relief from Monument of the Liberators.

1979, Apr. 2 Photo. *Perf. 13*

2571 A990 Sheet of 5 + label 1.40 .60
a. 2s multicolored .20
b. 5s multicolored .20
c. 13s multicolored .25
d. 23s multicolored .40
e. 25s multicolored .50

Centenary of Sofia as capital.

Rocket Launch, Space Flight Emblems A991

Intercosmos & Bulgarian-USSR Flight Emblems and: 25s, Link-up, horiz. 35s, Parachute descent. 1 l, Globe, emblems & orbit, horiz.

1979, Apr. 11

2572 A991 12s multicolored .20 .20
2573 A991 25s multicolored .45 .20
2574 A991 35s multicolored .60 .25
Nos. 2572-2574 (3) 1.25 .65

Souvenir Sheet

2575 A991 1 l multicolored 1.60 .75

1st Bulgarian cosmonaut on Russian space flight.

A slightly larger imperf. sheet similar to No. 2575 with control numbers at bottom and rockets at sides exists.

Nicolai Rukavishnikov — A992

Design: 13s, Rukavishnikov and Soviet cosmonaut Georgi Ivanov.

1979, May 14 Photo. *Perf. 13*

2576 A992 2s multicolored .20 .20
2577 A992 13s multicolored .30 .20

Col. Rukavishnikov, 1st Bulgarian astronaut.

Souvenir Sheet

Thracian Gold-leaf Collar — A993

1979, May 16

2578 A993 1 l multicolored 2.25 1.50

48th International Philatelic Federation Congress, Sofia, May 16-17.

Post Horn, Carrier Pigeon, Jet, Globes and UPU Emblem — A994

Designs (Post Horn, Globes and ITU Emblem): 5s, 1st Bulgarian and modern telephones. 13s, Morse key and teleprinter. 23s, Old radio transmitter and radio towers. 35s, Bulgarian TV tower and satellite. 50s, Ground receiving station

1979, May 8 *Perf. 13½x13*

2579 A994 2s multicolored .20 .20
2580 A994 5s multicolored .20 .20
2581 A994 13s multicolored .20 .20
2582 A994 23s multicolored .40 .20
2583 A994 35s multicolored .60 .25
Nos. 2579-2583 (5) 1.60 1.05

Souvenir Sheet

Perf. 13

2584 A994 50s vio, blk & gray 1.10 .65

Intl. Telecommunications Day and cent. of Bulgarian Postal & Telegraph Services. Size of stamp in #2584: 39x28mm. #2584 exists imperf.

Hotel Vitosha-New Otani — A996

1979, May 20

2586 A996 2s ultra & pink .20 .20

Philaserdica '79 Day.

Horseman Receiving Gifts, by Karellia and Boris Kuklievi — A997

1979, May 23
2587 A997 2s multicolored .20 .20

Bulgarian-Russian Friendship Day.

A998

A999

Man on Donkey, by Boris Angeloushev.

1979, May 23 Photo. *Perf. 13½*
2588 A998 2s multicolored .20 .20

12th National Festival of Humor and Satire, Gabrovo.

Lithographed and Engraved
1979, May 31 *Perf. 14x13½*

Durer Engravings: 13s, Four Women. 23s, Three Peasants. 25s, The Cook and his Wife. 35s, Portrait of Helius Eobanus Hessus. 80s, Rhinoceros, horiz.

2589 A999 13s multicolored .25 .20
2590 A999 23s multicolored .40 .20
2591 A999 25s multicolored .45 .20
2592 A999 35s multicolored .65 .20
Nos. 2589-2592 (4) 1.75 .80

Souvenir Sheet
Imperf

2593 A999 80s multicolored 2.00 1.25

Albrecht Durer (1471-1528), German engraver and painter.

R. Todorov (1879-1916) — A1000

Bulgarian Writers: #2595, Dimitri Dymov (1909-66). #2596, S. A. Kostov (1879-1939).

1979, June 26 Photo. *Perf. 13*
2594 A1000 2s multicolored .20 .20
2595 A1000 2s slate grn & yel grn .20 .20
2596 A1000 2s dp claret & yel .20 .20
Nos. 2594-2596 (3) .60 .60

Nos. 2594-2596 each printed se-tenant with label showing title page or character from writer's work.

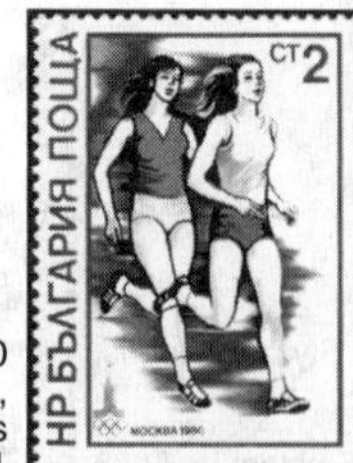

Moscow '80 Emblem, Runners A1001

Moscow '80 Emblem and: 13s, Pole vault, horiz. 25s, Discus. 35s, Hurdles, horiz. 43s, High jump, horiz. 1 l, Long jump.

1979, May 15 *Perf. 13*
2597 A1001 2s multicolored .20 .20
2598 A1001 13s multicolored .20 .20
2599 A1001 25s multicolored .40 .20
2600 A1001 35s multicolored .80 .25
2601 A1001 43s multicolored 1.00 .30
2602 A1001 1 l multicolored 2.25 .65
Nos. 2597-2602 (6) 4.85 1.80

Souvenir Sheet

2602A A1001 2 l multicolored 6.00 3.25

22nd Summer Olympic Games, Moscow, July 19-Aug. 3, 1980.

Rocket — A1002

5s, Flags of USSR and Bulgaria. 13s, "35."

1979, Sept. 4 Photo.
2603 A1002 2s multicolored .20 .20
2604 A1002 5s multicolored .20 .20
2605 A1002 13s multicolored .20 .20
Nos. 2603-2605 (3) .60 .60

35th anniversary of liberation.

Moscow '80 Emblem, Gymnast A1003

Moscow '80 Emblem & gymnasts.

1979, July 31 Photo. *Perf. 13*
2606 A1003 2s multi .20 .20
2607 A1003 13s multi, horiz. .20 .20
2608 A1003 25s multi .50 .20
2609 A1003 35s multi .75 .25
2610 A1003 43s multi 1.00 .25
2611 A1003 1 l multi 2.25 .80
Nos. 2606-2611 (6) 4.90 1.90

Souvenir Sheet

2612 A1003 2 l multicolored 6.00 3.25

22nd Summer Olympic Games, Moscow, July 19-Aug. 3, 1980.

A1004

A1005

1979, July 8 Photo. *Perf. 13*
2613 A1004 13s ultra & blk .20 .20

Theater Institute, 18th Congress.

1979, July 17
2614 A1005 8s multicolored .20 .20

Journalists' Vacation House, Varna, 20th Anniv.

Icon Type of 1977

Virgin and Child from: 13s, 23s, Nesebar, 16th cent., diff. 35s, 43s, Sozopol, 16th cent., diff. 53s, Samokov, 19th cent. Inscribed 1979.

1979, Aug. 7 Litho. *Perf. 12½*
2615 A917 13s multicolored .20 .20
2616 A917 23s multicolored .35 .20
2617 A917 35s multicolored .50 .20
2618 A917 43s multicolored .60 .20
2619 A917 53s multicolored .85 .25
Nos. 2615-2619 (5) 2.50 1.05

A1006

A1007

1979, Aug. 9 Photo. *Perf. 13x13½*
2620 A1006 2s Anton Besenschek .20 .20

Bulgarian stenography centenary.

1979, Aug. 28 *Perf. 13*
2621 A1007 2s multicolored .20 .20

Bulgarian Alpine Club, 50th anniv.

Public Health Ordinance — A1008

1979, Aug. 31 *Perf. 13½*
2622 A1008 2s multicolored .20 .20

Public Health Service centenary. No. 2622 printed with label showing Dimitar Mollov, founder.

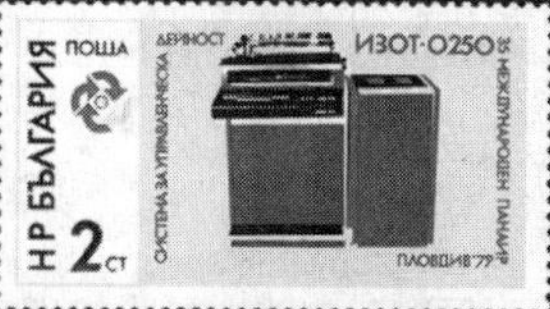

Isotope Measuring Device — A1009

1979, Sept. 8 *Perf. 13½x13*
2623 A1009 2s multicolored .20 .20

International Sample Fair, Plovdiv.

Games' Emblem A1010

1979, Sept. 20 *Perf. 13*
2624 A1010 5s multicolored .20 .20

Universiada '79, World University Games, Mexico City, Sept.

Sofia Locomotive Sports Club, 50th Anniversary — A1011

1979, Oct. 2
2625 A1011 2s blue & org red .20 .20

Ljuben Karavelov (1837-1879), Poet and Freedom Fighter — A1012

1979, Oct. 4 Photo. *Perf. 13*
2626 A1012 2s blue & slate grn .20 .20

A1013

A1014

1979, Oct. 20

2627 A1013 2s Biathlon .20 .20
2628 A1013 13s Speed skating .25 .20
2629 A1013 23s Downhill skiing .40 .20
2630 A1013 43s Luge .75 .25
Nos. 2627-2630 (4) 1.60 .85

Souvenir Sheet

Imperf

2631 A1013 1 l Slalom 1.75 1.10

13th Winter Olympic Games, Lake Placid, NY, Feb. 12-24.

1979, Oct. 31 ***Perf. 14***

Decko Uzunov, 80th Birthday: 12s, Apparition in Red. 13s, Woman from Thrace. 23s, Composition.

2632 A1014 12s multicolored .25 .20
2633 A1014 13s multicolored .25 .20
2634 A1014 23s multicolored .40 .20
Nos. 2632-2634 (3) .90 .60

Swimming, Moscow '80 Emblem — A1016

1979, Nov. 30 **Photo.** ***Perf. 13***

2636 A1016 2s Two-man kayak, vert. .20 .20
2637 A1016 13s Swimming, vert. .20 .20
2638 A1016 25s shown .40 .20
2639 A1016 35s One-man kayak .80 .20
2640 A1016 43s Diving, vert 1.00 .40
2641 A1016 1 l Diving, vert., diff. 2.25 .70
Nos. 2636-2641 (6) 4.85 1.90

Souvenir Sheet

2642 A1016 2 l Water polo, vert. 6.00 3.25

22nd Summer Olympic Games, Moscow, July 19-Aug. 3, 1980.

Nikola Vapzarov — A1017

1979, Dec. 7 **Photo.** ***Perf. 13***

2643 A1017 2s claret & rose .20 .20

Vapzarov (1909-1942), poet and freedom fighter. No. 2643 printed with label showing smokestacks.

The First Socialists, by Bojan Petrov — A1018

Paintings: 13s, Demeter Blagoev Reading Newspaper, by Demeter Gjudshenov, 1892. 25s, Workers' Party March, by Sotir Sotirov, 1917. 35s, Dawn in Plovdiv, by Johann Leviev, vert.

Perf. 12½x12, 12x12½

1979, Dec. 10 **Litho.**

2644 A1018 2s multicolored .20 .20
2645 A1018 13s multicolored .25 .20
2646 A1018 25s multicolored .40 .20
2647 A1018 35s multicolored .55 .20
Nos. 2644-2647 (4) 1.40 .80

Sharpshooting, Moscow '80 Emblem A1019

1979, Dec. 22 **Photo.** ***Perf. 13***

2648 A1019 2s shown .20 .20
2649 A1019 13s Judo, horiz. .20 .20
2650 A1019 25s Wrestling, horiz. .40 .20
2651 A1019 35s Archery .80 .25
2652 A1019 43s Fencing, horiz. 1.00 .50
2653 A1019 1 l Fencing 2.25 .90
Nos. 2648-2653 (6) 4.85 2.25

Souvenir Sheet

2654 A1019 2 l Boxing 6.00 4.00

Procession with Relics, 11th Century Fresco A1020

Frescoes of Sts. Cyril and Methodius, St. Clement's Basilica, Rome: 13s, Reception by Pope Hadrian II. 23s, Burial of Cyril the Philosopher, 18th century. 25s, St. Cyril. 35s, St. Methodius.

1979, Dec. 25

2655 A1020 2s multicolored .20 .20
2656 A1020 13s multicolored .25 .20
2657 A1020 23s multicolored .40 .20
2658 A1020 25s multicolored .45 .20
2659 A1020 35s multicolored .65 .20
Nos. 2655-2659 (5) 1.95 1.00

Bulgarian Television Emblem — A1021

1979, Dec. 29 ***Perf. 13½***

2660 A1021 5s violet bl & lt bl .20 .20

Bulgarian television, 25th anniversary. No. 2660 printed with label showing Sofia television tower.

Doves in Girl's Hair A1022

Design: 2s, Children's heads, mosaic, vert.

1979 ***Perf. 13***

2661 A1022 2s multicolored .20 .20
2662 A1022 13s multicolored .20 .20

International Year of the Child. Issue dates: 2s, July 17; 13s, Dec. 14.

Puppet on Horseback, IYC Emblem — A1023

Thracian Rider, Votive Tablet, 3rd Century — A1024

1980, Jan. 22 **Photo.** ***Perf. 13***

2663 A1023 2s multicolored .20 .20

UNIMA, Intl. Puppet Theater Organization, 50th anniv. (1979); Intl. Year of the Child (1979).

1980, Jan. 29 **Photo.** ***Perf. 13x13½***

National Archaeological Museum Centenary; 13s, Deines stele, 5th century B.C.

2664 A1024 2s brown & gold .20 .20
2665 A1024 13s multicolored .20 .20

Dimitrov Meeting Lenin in Moscow, by Alexander Poplilov A1026

1980, Mar. 28 ***Perf. 12x12½***

2667 A1026 13s multicolored .20 .20

Lenin, 110th birth anniversary.

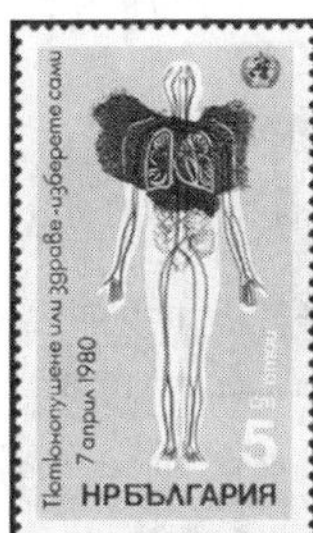

A1027

A1027a

Circulatory system, lungs enveloped in smoke.

1980, Apr. 7 ***Perf. 13***

2668 A1027 5s multicolored .20 .20

World Health Day fight against cigarette smoking.

1980, Apr. 10 **Photo.** ***Perf. 13***

2669 A1027a 2s Basketball .20 .20
2670 A1027a 13s Soccer .20 .20
2671 A1027a 25s Hockey .40 .20
2672 A1027a 35s Cycling .80 .20
2673 A1027a 43s Handball 1.00 .40
2674 A1027a 1 l Volleyball 2.25 .70
Nos. 2669-2674 (6) 4.85 1.90

Souvenir Sheet

2675 A1027a 2 l Weightlifting 6.50 4.25

Souvenir Sheet

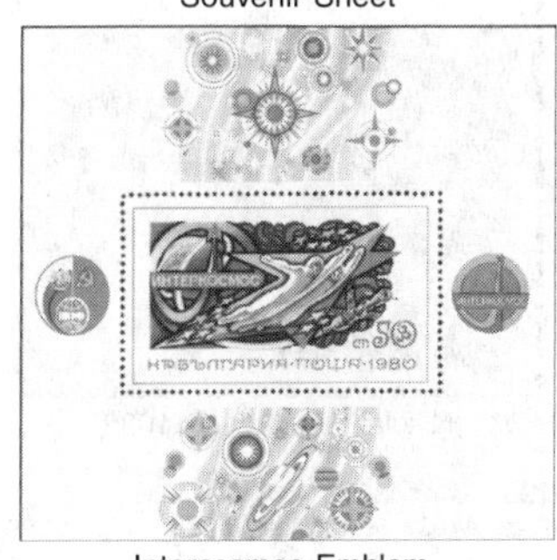

Intercosmos Emblem, Cosmonauts — A1028

1980, Apr. 22 ***Perf. 12***

2676 A1028 50s multicolored 1.00 .45

Intercosmos cooperative space program.

Penio Penev (1930-1959), Poet — A1029

1980, Apr. 22 **Photo.** ***Perf. 13***

2677 A1029 5s multicolored .20 .20

Se-tenant with label showing quote from author's work.

Penny Black — A1030

1980, Apr. 24 ***Perf. 13***

2678 A1030 25s dark red & sepia .60 .45

London 1980 International Stamp Exhibition, May 6-14; printed se-tenant with label showing Rowland Hill between every two stamps.

Demeter H. Tchorbadjiiski, Self-portrait — A1031

1980, Apr. 29

2679 A1031 5s shown .20 .20
2680 A1031 13s "Our People" .20 .20

Nikolai Giaurov — A1032

1980, Apr. 30

2681 A1032 5s multicolored .20 .20

Nikolai Giaurov (b. 1930), opera singer; printed se-tenant with label showing Boris Godunov.

Raising Red Flag Reichstag Building, Berlin — A1033

Armistice, 35th Anniversary: 13s, Soviet Army memorial, Berlin-Treptow.

1980, May 6 *Perf. 13x13½*

2682 A1033 5s multicolored .20 .20
2683 A1033 13s multicolored .20 .20

Numeral — A1034

1979 *Perf. 14*

2684 A1034 2s ultra .20 .20
2685 A1034 5s rose car .20 .20

A1034a

A1035

1980, May 12 **Photo.** *Perf. 13*

2685A A1034a 5s multicolored .20 .20

75th Anniv. of Teachers' Union.

1980, May 14 **Photo.** *Perf. 13*

2686 A1035 13s multicolored .20 .20

Warsaw Pact, 25th anniv.

A1036

A1037

Statues.

1980, June 10

2687 A1036 2s multicolored .20 .20
2688 A1036 13s multicolored .20 .20
2689 A1036 25s multicolored .40 .20
2690 A1036 35s multicolored .80 .30
2691 A1036 43s multicolored 1.00 .60
2692 A1036 1 l multicolored 2.25 1.10
Nos. 2687-2692 (6) 4.85 2.60

Souvenir Sheet

2693 A1036 2 l multicolored 6.00 3.25

22nd Summer Olympic Games, Moscow, July 19-Aug. 3.

1980, Sept. **Photo.** *Perf. 13*

2694 A1037 13s multicolored .25 .20

10th Intl. Ballet Competition, Varna.

Hotel Europa, Sofia A1038

Hotels: No. 2696, Bulgaria, Burgas, vert. No. 2697, Plovdiv, Plovdiv. No. 2698, Riga, Russe, vert. No. 2699, Varna, Djuba.

1980, July 11

2695 A1038 23s lt ultra & multi .30 .20
2696 A1038 23s orange & multi .30 .20
2697 A1038 23s gray & multi .30 .20
2698 A1038 23s blue & multi .30 .20
2699 A1038 23s yellow & multi .30 .20
Nos. 2695-2699 (5) 1.50 1.00

See No. 2766.

Ship Type of 1975

Ships of 16th, 17th Centuries: 5s, Christ of Lubeck, galleon. 8s, Roman galley. 13s, Eagle, Russian galleon. 23s, Mayflower. 35s, Maltese galley. 53s, Royal Louis, galleon.

1980, July 14

2700 A873 5s multicolored .20 .20
2701 A873 8s multicolored .20 .20
2702 A873 13s multicolored .25 .20
2703 A873 23s multicolored .45 .20
2704 A873 35s multicolored .70 .20
2705 A873 53s multicolored 1.10 .35
Nos. 2700-2705 (6) 2.90 1.35

Int'l Year of the Child, 1979 — A1040

Designs: Children's drawings and IYC emblem. 43s, Tower. 5s, 25s, 43s, vert.

1980 **Litho.** *Perf. 12½x12, 12x12½*

2708 A1040 3s multicolored .20 .20
2709 A1040 5s multicolored .20 .20
2710 A1040 8s multicolored .20 .20
2711 A1040 13s multicolored .20 .20
2712 A1040 25s multicolored .40 .20
2713 A1040 35s multicolored .50 .20
2714 A1040 43s multicolored .65 .20
Nos. 2708-2714 (7) 2.35 1.40

Helicopter, Missile Transport, Tank — A1041

1980, Sept. 23 **Photo.** *Perf. 13*

2715 A1041 3s shown .20 .20
2716 A1041 5s Jet, radar, rocket .20 .20
2717 A1041 8s Helicopter, ships .20 .20
Nos. 2715-2717 (3) .60 .60

Bulgarian People's Army, 35th anniversary.

St. Anne, by Leonardo da Vinci A1042

Da Vinci Paintings: 8s, 13s, Annunciation (diff.). 25s, Adoration of the Kings. 35s, Lady with the Ermine. 50s, Mona Lisa.

1980, Nov.

2718 A1042 5s multicolored .20 .20
2719 A1042 8s multicolored .20 .20
2720 A1042 13s multicolored .20 .20
2721 A1042 25s multicolored .40 .20
2722 A1042 35s multicolored .55 .20
Nos. 2718-2722 (5) 1.55 1.00

Souvenir Sheet

Imperf

2723 A1042 50s multicolored 1.10 .35

International Peace Conference, Sofia — A1043

1980, Sept. 4 **Photo.** *Perf. 13*

2724 A1043 25s multicolored .35 .20

Yordan Yovkov (1880-1937), Writer — A1044

1980, Sept. 19

2725 A1044 5s multicolored .20 .20

Se-tenant with label showing scene from Yovkov's work.

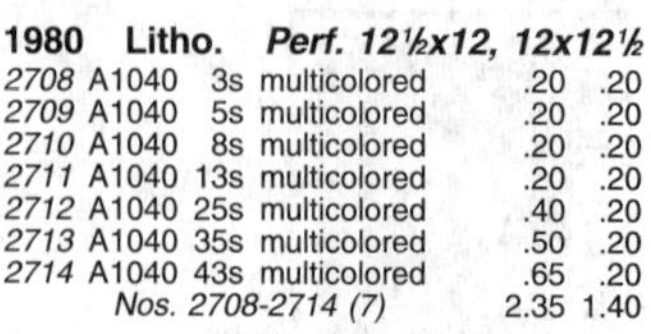

International Samples Fair, Plovdiv — A1045

1980, Sept. 24 *Perf. 13½x13*

2726 A1045 5s multicolored .20 .20

Blooming Cacti — A1045a

1980, Nov. 4 **Photo.** *Perf. 13*

2726A A1045a 5s multicolored .20 .20
2726B A1045a 13s multicolored .20 .20
2726C A1045a 25s multicolored .40 .20
2726D A1045a 35s multicolored .60 .25
2726E A1045a 53s multicolored 1.00 .30
Nos. 2726A-2726E (5) 2.40 1.15

Souvenir Sheet

25th Anniv. of Bulgarian UN Membership — A1045b

1980, Nov. 25

2726F A1045b 60s multicolored 2.40 2.10

World Ski Racing Championship, Velingrad — A1046

1981, Jan. 17 **Photo.** *Perf. 13*

2727 A1046 43s multicolored .60 .25

Hawthorn A1047

Slalom — A1048

Designs: Medicinal herbs.

1981, Jan.

2728 A1047	3s shown	.20	.20
2729 A1047	5s St. John's wort	.20	.20
2730 A1047	13s Common elder	.20	.20
2731 A1047	25s Blackberries	.40	.20
2732 A1047	35s Lime	.55	.20
2733 A1047	43s Wild briar	.65	.25
	Nos. 2728-2733 (6)	2.20	1.25

1981, Feb. 27 Photo. *Perf. 13*

2734 A1048 43s multicolored .60 .25

Evian Alpine World Ski Cup Championship, Borovets.

Nuclear Traces, Research Institute — A1049

1981, Mar. 10 *Perf. 13½x13*

2735 A1049 13s gray & blk .20 .20

Nuclear Research Institute, Dubna, USSR, 25th anniversary.

Congress Emblem — A1050

1981, Mar. 12 *Perf. 13½*

2736 A1050	5s shown	.20	.20
2737 A1050	13s Stars	.20	.20
2738 A1050	23s Teletape	.35	.20
	Nos. 2736-2738 (3)	.75	.60

Souvenir Sheet

2739 A1050 50s Demeter Blagoev, George Dimitrov .80 .50

12th Bulgarian Communist Party Congress. Nos. 2736-2738 each printed se-tenant with label.

Paintings by Zachary Zograf — A1050a

1981, Mar. 23 Photo. *Perf. 12x12½*

2739A A1050a	5s multicolored	.20	.20
2739B A1050a	13s multicolored	.25	.20
2739C A1050a	23s multicolored	.40	.20
2739D A1050a	25s multicolored	.50	.20
2739E A1050a	35s multicolored	.70	.20
	Nos. 2739A-2739E (5)	2.05	1.00

Nos. 2739A-2739C are vert.

EXPO '81, Plovdiv A1050b

1981, Apr. 7

2739F A1050b	5s multicolored	.20	.20
2739G A1050b	8s multicolored	.20	.20
2739H A1050b	13s multicolored	.25	.20
2739J A1050b	25s multicolored	.45	.20
2739K A1050b	53s multicolored	1.00	.25
	Nos. 2739F-2739K (5)	2.10	1.05

Centenary of Bulgarian Shipbuilding — A1050c

1981, Apr. 15 Photo. *Perf. 13*

2739L A1050c	35s Georgi Dimitrov, liner	.55	.20
2739M A1050c	43s 5th from RMS, freighter	.65	.25
2739N A1050c	53s Khan Asparuch, tanker	.80	.30
	Nos. 2739L-2739N (3)	2.00	.75

Arabian Horse A1051

Various breeds.

1980, Nov. 27 Litho. *Perf. 12½x12*

2740 A1051	3s multicolored	.20	.20
2741 A1051	5s multicolored	.20	.20
2742 A1051	13s multicolored	.30	.20
2743 A1051	23s multicolored	.45	.20
2744 A1051	35s multicolored	.75	.20
	Nos. 2740-2744 (5)	1.90	1.00

Vassil Stoin, Ethnologist, Birth Centenary — A1052

1980, Dec. 5 Photo. *Perf. 13½x13*

2745 A1052 5s multicolored .20 .20

12th Bulgarian Communist Party Congress — A1052a

1980, Dec. 26 Photo. *Perf. 13x13½*

2745A A1052a 5s Party symbols .20 .20

New Year A1053

1980, Dec. 8 *Perf. 13*

2746 A1053	5s shown	.20	.20
2747 A1053	13s Cup, date	.20	.20

Culture Palace, Sofia A1053a

1981, Mar. 13 Photo. *Perf. 13*

2747A A1053a 5s multicolored .20 .20

Vienna Hofburg Palace A1054

1981, May 15 Photo. *Perf. 13*

2748 A1054 35s multicolored .45 .20

WIPA 1981 Intl. Philatelic Exhibition, Vienna, May 22-31.

34th Farmers' Union Congress — A1055

1981, May 18 *Perf. 13½*

2749 A1055	5s shown	.20	.20
2750 A1055	8s Flags	.20	.20
2751 A1055	13s Flags, diff.	.20	.20
	Nos. 2749-2751 (3)	.60	.60

Wild Cat — A1056

1981, May 27

2752 A1056	5s shown	.20	.20
2753 A1056	13s Boar	.25	.20
2754 A1056	23s Mouflon	.40	.20
2755 A1056	25s Mountain goat	.45	.20
2756 A1056	35s Stag	.60	.20
2757 A1056	53s Roe deer	1.00	.25
	Nos. 2752-2757 (6)	2.90	1.25

Souvenir Sheet

Perf. 13½x13

2758 A1056 1 l Stag, diff. 1.75 .85

EXPO '81 Intl. Hunting Exhibition, Plovdiv. Nos. 2752-2757 each se-tenant with labels showing various hunting rifles. No. 2758 contains one stamp, size: 48½x39mm.

25th Anniv. of UNESCO Membership A1057

1981, June 11 *Perf. 13*

2759 A1057 13s multicolored .20 .20

Hotel Type of 1980

1981, July 13 Photo. *Perf. 13*

2766 A1038 23s Veliko Tirnovo Hotel .35 .20

Flying Figure, Sculpture by Velichko Minekov — A1059

Bulgarian Social Democratic Party Buzludja Congress, 90th Anniv. (Minkov Sculpture): 13s, Advancing Female Figure.

1981, July 16 *Perf. 13½*

2767 A1059	5s multicolored	.20	.20
2768 A1059	13s multicolored	.20	.20

Kukeri, by Georg Tschapkanov A1060

Statistics Office Centenary A1061

1981, May 28 Photo. *Perf. 13*

2769 A1060 5s multicolored .20 .20

13th Natl. Festival of Humor and Satire.

1981, June 9

2770 A1061 5s multicolored .20 .20

Gold Dish A1063

Designs: Goldsmiths' works, 7th-9th cent.

1981, July 21

2772 A1063	5s multicolored	.20	.20
2773 A1063	13s multicolored	.20	.20
2774 A1063	23s multicolored	.35	.25
2775 A1063	25s multicolored	.40	.25
2776 A1063	35s multicolored	.55	.35
2777 A1063	53s multicolored	.90	.40
	Nos. 2772-2777 (6)	2.60	1.65

35th Anniv. of Frontier Force — A1064

1981, July 28 ***Perf. 13½x13***

2778 A1064 5s multicolored .20 .20

1300th Anniv. of First Bulgarian State — A1065

Designs: No. 2779, Sts. Cyril and Methodius. No. 2780, 9th cent. bas-relief. 8s, Floor plan, Round Church, Preslav, 10th cent. 12s, Four Evangelists of King Ivan Alexander, miniature, 1356. No. 2783, King Ivan Asen II memorial column. No. 2784, Warriors on horseback. 16s, April uprising, 1876. 23s, Russian liberators, Tirnovo. 25s, Social Democratic Party founding, 1891. 35s, September uprising, 1923. 41s, Fatherland Front. 43s, Prime Minister George Dimitrov, 5th Communist Party Congress, 1948. 50s, Lion, 10th cent. bas-relief. 53s, 10th Communist Party Congress. 55s, Kremikovski Metalurgical Plant. 1 l, Brezhnev, Gen. Todor Zhivkov.

1981, Aug. 10

2779 A1065 5s multicolored .20 .20
2780 A1065 5s multicolored .20 .20
2781 A1065 8s multicolored .20 .20
2782 A1065 12s multicolored .20 .20
2783 A1065 13s multicolored .20 .20
2784 A1065 13s multicolored .20 .20
2785 A1065 16s multicolored .25 .20
2786 A1065 23s multicolored .30 .20
2787 A1065 25s multicolored .35 .20
2788 A1065 35s multicolored .50 .20
2789 A1065 41s multicolored .55 .25
2790 A1065 43s multicolored .60 .25
2791 A1065 53s multicolored .75 .30
2792 A1065 55s multicolored .75 .30
Nos. 2779-2792 (14) 5.25 3.10

Souvenir Sheets

2793 A1065 50s multicolored .90 .55
2794 A1065 1 l multicolored 1.90 1.10

European Volleyball Championship A1066

1981, Sept. 16 ***Perf. 13***

2795 A1066 13s multicolored .20 .20

Pegasus, Bronze Sculpture (Word Day) — A1067

World Food Day — A1068

1981, Oct. 2

2796 A1067 5s olive & cream .20 .20

1981, Oct. 16

2797 A1068 13s multicolored .20 .20

Professional Theater Centenary A1069

1981, Oct. 30

2798 A1069 5s multicolored .20 .20

Anti-Apartheid Year — A1070

1981, Dec. 2

2799 A1070 5s multicolored .20 .20

Espana '82 World Cup Soccer — A1071

Designs: Various soccer players.

1981, Dec.

2800 A1071 5s multicolored .20 .20
2801 A1071 13s multicolored .25 .20
2802 A1071 43s multicolored .70 .25
2803 A1071 53s multicolored .95 .35
Nos. 2800-2803 (4) 2.10 1.00

Heritage Day A1072

1981, Nov. 21 **Photo.** ***Perf. 13***

2804 A1072 13s multicolored .20 .20

Souvenir Sheet

2804A A1072 60s multicolored 5.00 1.10

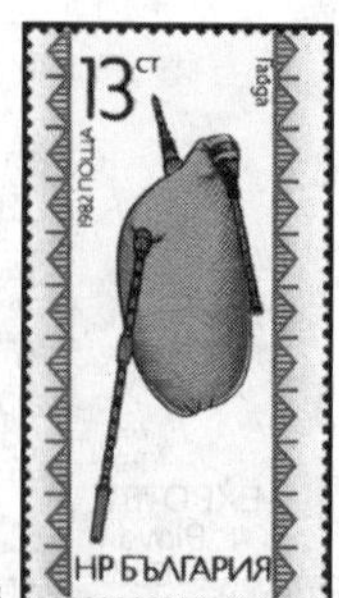

Bagpipe — A1073

Public Libraries and Reading Rooms, 125th Anniv — A1074

1982, Jan. 14

2805 A1073 13s shown .20 .20
2806 A1073 25s Flutes .40 .20
2807 A1073 30s Rebec .50 .20
2808 A1073 35s Flute, recorder .55 .25
2809 A1073 44s Mandolin .75 .30
Nos. 2805-2809 (5) 2.40 1.15

1982, Jan. 20

2810 A1074 5s dk grn .20 .20

Souvenir Sheet

Intl. Decade for Women (1975-1985) — A1075

1982, Mar. 8

2811 A1075 1 l multicolored 1.75 1.00

New Year 1982 A1076

1981, Dec. 22 **Photo.** ***Perf. 13***

2812 A1076 5s Ornament .20 .20
2813 A1076 13s Ornament, diff. .20 .20

The Sofia Plains, by Nicolas Petrov (1881-1916) — A1077

1982, Feb. 10 ***Perf. 12½***

2814 A1077 5s shown .20 .20
2815 A1077 13s Girl Embroidering .20 .20
2816 A1077 30s Fields of Peshtera .50 .20
Nos. 2814-2816 (3) .90 .60

35th Anniv. of UNICEF (1981) — A1078

Mother and Child Paintings.

1982, Feb. 25 ***Perf. 14***

2817 A1078 53s Vladimir Dimitrov .80 .30
2818 A1078 53s Basil Stoilov .80 .30
2819 A1078 53s Ivan Milev .80 .30
2820 A1078 53s Liliana Russeva .80 .30
Nos. 2817-2820 (4) 3.20 1.20

Figures, by Vladamir Dimitrov (1882-1961) — A1079

1982, Mar. 8 **Litho.**

2821 A1079 5s shown .20 .20
2822 A1079 8s Landscape .20 .20
2823 A1079 13s View of Istanbul .25 .20
2824 A1079 25s Harvesters, vert. .40 .20
2825 A1079 30s Woman in a Landscape, vert. .50 .20
2826 A1079 35s Peasant Woman, vert. .60 .25
Nos. 2821-2826 (6) 2.15 1.25

Souvenir Sheet

2827 A1079 50s Self-portrait .85 .65

No. 2827 contains one stamp, size: 54x32mm.

Trade Union Congress — A1080

1982, Apr. 8 **Photo.** ***Perf. 13½***

2828 A1080 5s Dimitrov reading union paper .20 .20
2829 A1080 5s Culture Palace .20 .20

#2828-2829 se-tenant with label showing text.

Marsh Snowdrop A1081

Designs: Medicinal plants.

1982, Apr. 10 Photo. *Perf. 13*

2830 A1081 3s shown .20 .20
2831 A1081 5s Chicory .20 .20
2832 A1081 8s Chamaenerium angustifolium .20 .20
2833 A1081 13s Solomon's seal .25 .20
2834 A1081 25s Violets .50 .20
2835 A1081 35s Centaury .70 .25
Nos. 2830-2835 (6) 2.05 1.25

Cosmonauts' Day — A1082

1982, Apr. 12 *Perf. 13½*

2836 A1082 13s Salyut-Soyuz link-up .20 .20

Se-tenant with label showing K.E. Tsiolkovsky (space pioneer).

Souvenir Sheet

SOZFILEX Stamp Exhibition — A1083

1982, May 7 *Perf. 13*

2837 A1083 50s Dimitrov, emblems 1.00 .45

14th Komsomol Congress (Youth Communists) — A1084

1982, May 25

2838 A1084 5s multicolored .20 .20

PHILEXFRANCE '82 Intl. Stamp Exhibition, Paris, June 11-21 — A1085

1982, May 28

2839 A1085 42s France #1, Bulgaria #1 .70 .25

19th Cent. Fresco A1086

Designs: Various floral pattern frescoes.

1982, June 8 *Perf. 11½*

2840 A1086 5s red & multi .20 .20
2841 A1086 13s green & multi .25 .20
2842 A1086 25s violet & multi .40 .20
2843 A1086 30s ol grn & multi .50 .20
2844 A1086 42s blue & multi .75 .25
2845 A1086 60s brown & multi 1.00 .40
Nos. 2840-2845 (6) 3.10 1.45

Souvenir Sheet

George Dimitrov (1882-1949), First Prime Minister — A1087

1982, June 15 *Perf. 13*

2846 A1087 50s multicolored 1.10 .45

9th Congress of the National Front — A1088

1982, June 21 Photo. *Perf. 13*

2847 A1088 5s Dimitrov .20 .20

35th Anniv. of Balkan Bulgarian Airline — A1089

1982, June 28 *Perf. 13½x13*

2848 A1089 42s multicolored .65 .25

A1090

A1091

1982, July 15 *Perf. 13*

2849 A1090 13s multicolored .25 .20

Nuclear disarmament.

1982, July Photo. *Perf. 13*

2850 A1091 5s multicolored .20 .20
2851 A1091 13s multicolored .20 .20

Souvenir Sheet

2852 A1091 1 l multicolored 1.25 .75

Ludmila Zhivkova (b. 1942), artist.

5th Congress of Bulgarian Painters — A1092

1982, July 27 *Perf. 13½*

2853 A1092 5s multicolored .20 .20

Se-tenant with label showing text.

Flag of Peace Youth Assembly — A1093

Various children's drawings.

1982, Aug. 10 *Perf. 14*

2853A A1093 3s multicolored .20 .20
2853B A1093 5s multicolored .20 .20
2853C A1093 8s multicolored .20 .20
2853D A1093 13s multicolored .25 .20
Nos. 2853A-2853D (4) .85 .80

Souvenir Sheet

Perf. 14, Imperf.

2853E A1093 50s In balloon 3.25 .35

See Nos. 2864-2870, 3052-3058, 3321-3327.

10th Anniv. of UN Conference on Human Environment, Stockholm — A1093a

1982, Nov. 10 *Perf. 13*

2854 A1093a 13s dk blue & grn .20 .20

A1094

A1095

Designs: No. 2855, Park Hotel Moskva, Sofia. No. 2856, Tchernomore, Varna.

1982, Oct. 20 Photo. *Perf. 13*

2855 A1094 32s lt blue & multi .40 .20
2856 A1094 32s pink & multi .40 .20

1982, Nov. 4

2857 A1095 13s Cruiser Aurora, Sputnik II .20 .20

October Revolution, 65th anniv.

60th Anniv. of Institute of Communications A1096

1982, Dec. 9

2858 A1096 5s ultra .20 .20

60th Anniv. of USSR A1097

1982, Dec. 9

2859 A1097 13s multicolored .20 .20

The Piano, by Pablo Picasso (1881-1973) A1098

Perf. 11½x12½

1982, Dec. 24 Litho.

2860 A1098 13s shown .20 .20
2861 A1098 30s Portrait of Jacqueline .40 .20
2862 A1098 42s Maternity .60 .25
Nos. 2860-2862 (3) 1.20 .65

Souvenir Sheet

2863 A1098 1 l Self-portrait 2.75 .75

Children's Drawings Type of 1982

Various children's drawings. 8s, 13s, 50s vert.

1982, Dec. 28 *Perf. 14*

2864 A1093 3s multicolored .20 .20
2865 A1093 5s multicolored .20 .20
2866 A1093 8s multicolored .20 .20
2867 A1093 13s multicolored .20 .20
2868 A1093 25s multicolored .35 .20
2869 A1093 30s multicolored .40 .20
Nos. 2864-2869 (6) 1.55 1.20

Souvenir Sheet

Perf. 14, Imperf.

2870 A1093 50s Shaking hands 2.75 .35

New Year
A1100

1982, Dec. 28 Photo. *Perf. 13*

2872	A1100	5s	multicolored	.20	.20
2873	A1100	13s	multicolored	.20	.20

A1101

A1102

1982, Dec. 28

2874	A1101	25s	Robert Koch	.40	.20
2875	A1101	30s	Simon Bolivar	.40	.20
2876	A1101	30s	Rabindranath Tagore (1861-1941)	.40	.20
	Nos. 2874-2876 (3)			1.20	.60

No. 2874 also for TB bacillus cent.

1983, Jan. 10 Photo. *Perf. 13x13½*

2877	A1102	5s	olive & brown	.25	.20

Vassil Levski (1837-73), revolutionary.

Universiade Games — A1103

1983, Feb. 15 *Perf. 13*

2878	A1103	30s	Downhill skiing	.35	.20

Fresh-water Fish — A1104

1983, Mar. 24 Photo. *Perf. 13½x13*

2879	A1104	3s	Pike	.20	.20
2880	A1104	5s	Sturgeon	.20	.20
2881	A1104	13s	Chub	.20	.20
2882	A1104	25s	Perch	.40	.20
2883	A1104	30s	Catfish	.40	.20
2884	A1104	42s	Trout	.55	.25
	Nos. 2879-2884 (6)			1.95	1.25

Karl Marx (1818-1883)
A1105

1983, Apr. 5 *Perf. 13x13½*

2885	A1105	13s	multicolored	.20	.20

Jaroslav Hasek (1883-1923) — A1106

1983, Apr. 20 Photo. *Perf. 13*

2886	A1106	13s	multicolored	.20	.20

Martin Luther (1483-1546)
A1107

1983, May 10

2887	A1107	13s	multicolored	.20	.20

55th Anniv. of Komsomol Youth Movement — A1108

1983, May 13

2888	A1108	5s	"PMC"	.20	.20

A1109

A1111

National costumes.

1983, May 17 Litho. *Perf. 14*

2889	A1109	5s	Khaskovo	.20	.20
2890	A1109	8s	Pernik	.20	.20
2891	A1109	13s	Burgas	.20	.20
2892	A1109	25s	Tolbukhin	.35	.20
2893	A1109	30s	Blagoevgrad	.40	.20
2894	A1109	42s	Topolovgrad	.50	.20
	Nos. 2889-2894 (6)			1.85	1.20

1983, May 20

6th Intl. Satire and Humor Biennial, Gabrovo: Old Man Feeding Chickens.

2900	A1111	5s	multicolored	.20	.20

Christo Smirnensky (1898-1983), Poet — A1112

1983, May 25

2901	A1112	5s	multicolored	.20	.20

17th Intl. Geodesists' Congress
A1113

1983, May 27

2902	A1113	30s	Emblem	.45	.20

Interarch '83 Architecture Exhibition, Sofia — A1114

1983, June 6

2903	A1114	30s	multicolored	.45	.20

8th European Chess Championships, Plovdiv
A1115

1983, June 20 Photo. *Perf. 13*

2904	A1115	13s	Chess pieces, map of Europe	.20	.20

Souvenir Sheet

BRASILIANA '83 Philatelic Exhibition — A1116

1983, June 24

2905	A1116	1 l	Brazilian and Bulgarian stamps	1.50	.95

Social Democratic Party Congress of Russia, 80th Anniv. — A1118

Design: Lenin addressing congress.

1983, July 29 Photo. *Perf. 13*

2907	A1118	5s	multicolored	.25	.20

Ilinden-Preobrazhensky Insurrection, 80th Anniv. — A1119

1983, July 29

2908	A1119	5s	Gun, dagger, book	.20	.20

Institute of Mining and Geology, Sofia, 30th Anniv. — A1120

1983, Aug. 10

2909	A1120	5s	multicolored	.20	.20

60th Anniv. of September 1923 Uprising — A1121

1983, Aug. 19

2910	A1121	5s	multicolored	.20	.20
2911	A1121	13s	multicolored	.20	.20

Angora Cat
A1123

1983, Sept. 26 *Perf. 13*

2917	A1123	5s	shown	.20	.20
2918	A1123	13s	Siamese	.25	.20
2919	A1123	20s	Abyssinian, vert.	.40	.20
2920	A1123	25s	Persian	.45	.20
2921	A1123	30s	European, vert.	.55	.25
2922	A1123	42s	Indochinese	.75	.30
	Nos. 2917-2922 (6)			2.60	1.35

Animated Film Festival — A1124

1983, Sept. 15 Photo. *Perf. 14x13½*
2923 A1124 5s Articulation layout .20 .20

Trevethick's Engine, 1804 — A1125

Locomotives: 13s, Blenkinsop's Prince Royal, 1810. 42s, Hedley's Puffing Billy, 1812. 60s, Adler (first German locomotive), 1835.

1983, Oct. 20 *Perf. 13*
2924 A1125 5s multicolored .20 .20
2925 A1125 13s multicolored .30 .20
2926 A1125 42s multicolored .95 .30
2927 A1125 60s multicolored 1.40 .40
Nos. 2924-2927 (4) 2.85 1.10

See Nos. 2983-2987.

Souvenir Sheet

Liberation Monument, Plovdiv — A1126

1983, Nov. 4
2928 A1126 50s multicolored 1.00 .60

Philatelic Federation, 90th anniv.

Sofia Opera, 75th Anniv. — A1127

1983, Dec. 2 *Perf. 13x13½*
2929 A1127 5s Mask, lyre, laurel .20 .20

Composers' Assoc., 50th Anniv. — A1128

Composers: 5s, Ioan Kukuzel (14th cent.) 8s, Atanasov. 13s, Petko Stainov. 20s, Veselin Stodiov. 25s, Liubomir Pipkov. 30s, Pancho Vladigerov. Se-tenant with labels showing compositions.

1983, Dec. 5
2930 A1128 5s multicolored .20 .20
2931 A1128 8s multicolored .20 .20
2932 A1128 13s multicolored .20 .20
2933 A1128 20s multicolored .30 .20
2934 A1128 25s multicolored .40 .20
2935 A1128 30s multicolored .50 .20
Nos. 2930-2935 (6) 1.80 1.20

New Year 1984 A1129

1983, Dec. 10 *Perf. 13*
2936 A1129 5s multicolored .20 .20

Angelo Donni, by Raphael A1130

1983, Dec. 22 *Perf. 14*
2937 A1130 5s shown .20 .20
2938 A1130 13s Cardinal .20 .20
2939 A1130 30s Baldassare Castiglioni .45 .20
2940 A1130 42s Donna Belata .70 .30
Nos. 2937-2940 (4) 1.55 .90

Souvenir Sheet

2941 A1130 1 l Sistine Madonna 1.75 1.25

Bat, World Wildlife Emblem — A1131

Various bats and rodents.

1983, Dec. 30 *Perf. 13*
2942 A1131 12s multicolored .30 .20
2943 A1131 13s multicolored .30 .20
2944 A1131 20s multicolored .45 .20
2945 A1131 30s multicolored .55 .25
2946 A1131 42s multicolored .75 .30
Nos. 2942-2946 (5) 2.35 1.15

Dmitri Mendeleev (1834-1907), Russian Chemist — A1132

1984, Mar. 14
2947 A1132 13s multicolored .25 .20

Ljuben Karavelov, Poet and Freedom Fighter, Birth Sesquicentenary A1133

1984, Jan. 31 *Perf. 13x13½*
2948 A1133 5s multicolored .20 .20

Tanker Gen. V.I. Zaimov A1137

1984, Mar. 22 *Perf. 13½*
2959 A1137 5s shown .20 .20
2960 A1137 13s Mesta .20 .20
2961 A1137 25s Veleka .40 .20
2962 A1137 32s Ferry .50 .20
2963 A1137 42s Cargo ship Rossen .70 .30
Nos. 2959-2963 (5) 2.00 1.10

Souvenir Sheet

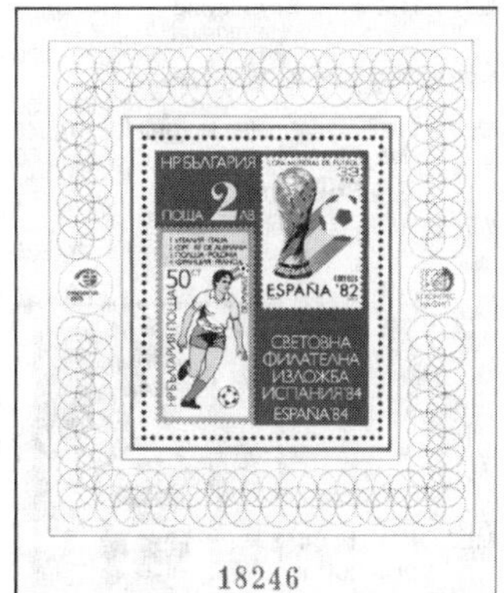

World Cup Soccer Commemorative of 1982, Spain No. 2281 — A1137a

1984, Apr. 18 Photo. *Perf. 13x13½*
2963A A1137a 2 l multicolored 3.25 2.50

ESPANA '84.

Dove with Letter over Globe — A1138

Berries — A1139

1984, Apr. 24 *Perf. 13*
2964 A1138 5s multicolored .20 .20

World Youth Stamp Exhibition, Pleven, Oct. 5-11.

1984, May 5
2965 A1139 5s Cherries .20 .20
2966 A1139 8s Strawberries .20 .20
2967 A1139 13s Blackberries .20 .20
2968 A1139 20s Raspberries .35 .20
2969 A1139 42s Currants .70 .30
Nos. 2965-2969 (5) 1.65 1.10

A1140

A1142

1984, May 23
2970 A1140 13s Athlete, doves .20 .20

6th Republican Spartikiade games,

1984, June 12
2972 A1142 5s Folk singer, drum .20 .20

6th amateur art festival.

Bulgarian-Soviet Relations, 50th Anniv. — A1143

1984, June 27
2973 A1143 13s Initialed seal .20 .20

Doves and Pigeons A1144

1984, July 6 Litho. *Perf. 14*
2974 A1144 5s Rock dove .20 .20
2975 A1144 13s Stock dove .20 .20
2976 A1144 20s Wood pigeon .35 .20
2977 A1144 30s Turtle dove .50 .20
2978 A1144 42s Domestic pigeon .70 .30
Nos. 2974-2978 (5) 1.95 1.10

1st Natl. Communist Party Congress, 60th Anniv. — A1145

1984, May 18 Photo. *Perf. 13½x13*
2979 A1145 5s multicolored .20 .20

Souvenir Sheet

Intl. Stamp Exhibition, Essen, May 26-31 — A1146

Europa Conf. stamps: a, 1980. b, 1981.

1984, May 22 ***Perf. 13x13½***

2980 A1146 Sheet of 2 *12.50 10.00*
a.-b. 1.50 l multi *6.00 5.00*

Mount Everest A1147

1984, May 31 ***Perf. 13***

2981 A1147 5s multicolored .20 .20

1st Bulgarian Everest climbing expedition, Apr. 20-May 9.

Souvenir Sheet

UPU Congress, Hamburg — A1148

1984, June 11 ***Perf. 13½x13***

2982 A1148 3 l Sailing ship *12.50 10.00*

Locomotives Type of 1983

1984, July 31 ***Perf. 13***

2983 A1125 13s Best Friend of Charleston, 1830, US .25 .20
2984 A1125 25s Saxonia, 1836, Dresden .40 .25
2985 A1125 30s Lafayette, 1837, US .50 .30
2986 A1125 42s Borsig, 1841, Germany .75 .40
2987 A1125 60s Philadelphia, 1843, Austria 1.10 .65
Nos. 2983-2987 (5) 3.00 1.80

September 9 Revolution, 40th Anniv. — A1149

1984, Aug. 4

2988 A1149 5s K, production quality emblem .20 .20
2989 A1149 20s Victory Monument, Sofia .30 .20
2990 A1149 30s Star, "9" .40 .30
Nos. 2988-2990 (3) .90 .70

Paintings by Nenko Balkanski (1907-1977) — A1150

1984, Sept. 17 ***Perf. 14***

2991 A1150 5s Boy Playing Harmonica, vert. .20 .20
2992 A1150 30s A Paris Window, vert. .55 .30
2993 A1150 42s Double Portrait .80 .40
Nos. 2991-2993 (3) 1.55 .90

Souvenir Sheet

2994 A1150 1 l Self-portrait, vert. 1.90 1.25

MLADPOST '84 International Youth Stamp Exhibition, Pleven — A1151

Buildings in Pleven: 5s, Mausoleum to Russian soldiers, 1877-78 Russo-Turkish War. 13s, Panorama Building.

1984, Sept. 20 ***Perf. 13***

2995 A1151 5s multicolored .20 .20
2996 A1151 13s multicolored .30 .20

Septembrist Young Pioneers Org., 40th Anniv. — A1152

1984, Sept. 21 **Photo.** ***Perf. 13***

2997 A1152 5s multicolored .20 .20

Nikola Vapzarov A1153

1984, Oct. 2

2998 A1153 5s maroon & pale yel .20 .20

Natl. Soccer, 75th Anniv. A1154

1984, Oct. 3

2999 A1154 42s multicolored .75 .40

Souvenir Sheet

MLADPOST '84 — A1155

1984, Oct. 5 **Photo.** ***Perf. 13***

3000 A1155 50s multicolored 1.10 .50

Bridges and Maps — A1156

1984, Oct. 5 **Photo.** ***Perf. 13½x13***

3001 A1156 5s Devil's Bridge, Arda River .20 .20
3002 A1156 13s Koljo-Fitscheto, Bjala .25 .20
3003 A1156 30s Asparuchow, Warna .60 .30
3004 A1156 42s Bebresch Highway Bridge, Botevgrad .75 .40
Nos. 3001-3004 (4) 1.80 1.10

Intl. Olympic Committee, 90th Anniv. — A1158

1984, Oct. 24 **Photo.** ***Perf. 13***

3007 A1158 13s multicolored .25 .20

A1159

A1160

Pelecanus crispus.

1984, Nov. 2

3008 A1159 5s Adult, young .25 .20
3009 A1159 13s Two adults .35 .20
3010 A1159 20s Adult in water .45 .20
3011 A1159 32s In flight .70 .30
Nos. 3008-3011 (4) 1.75 .90

World Wildlife Fund.

1984, Nov. 2

3012 A1160 5s multicolored .20 .20

Anton Ivanov (1884-1942), labor leader.

Women's Socialist Movement, 70th Anniv. — A1161

1984, Nov. 9

3013 A1161 5s multicolored .20 .20

Telecommunication Towers — A1162

1984, Nov. 23

3014 A1162 5s Snezhanka .20 .20
3015 A1162 1 l Orelek 1.90 1.00

Snowflakes, New Year 1985 — A1163

1984, Dec. 5

3016 A1163 5s Doves, posthorns .20 .20
3017 A1163 13s Doves, blossom .25 .20

Paintings by Stoyan Venev (b. 1904) — A1164

1984, Dec. 10 **Litho.**

3018 A1164 5s September Nights .20 .20
3019 A1164 30s Man with Three Medals .50 .30
3020 A1164 42s The Best .70 .40
Nos. 3018-3020 (3) 1.40 .90

Butterflies
A1165

1984, Dec. 14 *Perf. 11½*

3021 A1165 13s Inachis io .25 .20
3022 A1165 25s Papilio machaon .45 .25
3023 A1165 30s Brintesia circe .55 .30
3024 A1165 42s Anthocaris cardamines .80 .40
3025 A1165 60s Vanessa atalanta 1.10 .60
Nos. 3021-3025 (5) 3.15 1.75

Souvenir Sheet

3026 A1165 1 l Limenitis populi 2.25 1.00

A1166

A1167

1984, Dec. 18 Photo. *Perf. 13x13½*

3027 A1166 13s multicolored .25 .20

Cesar Augusto Sandino (1895-1934), Nicaraguan freedom fighter.

1984, Dec. 28 Litho. *Perf. 14*

3028 A1167 5s The Three Graces .20 .20
3029 A1167 13s Cupid and the Graces .30 .20
3030 A1167 30s Original Sin .55 .30
3031 A1167 42s La Fornarina .80 .40
Nos. 3028-3031 (4) 1.85 1.10

Souvenir Sheet

3032 A1167 1 l Galatea 2.25 1.00

Raphael, 500th birth anniv. (1983).

Cruise Ship Sofia, Maiden Voyage — A1168

1984, Dec. 29 Photo. *Perf. 13*

3033 A1168 13s blue, dk bl & yel .25 .20

Predators
A1170

1985, Jan. 17

3035 A1170 13s Conepatus leuconotus .25 .20
3036 A1170 25s Prionodon linsang .40 .25
3037 A1170 30s Ictonix striatus .50 .30
3038 A1170 42s Hemigalus derbyanus .75 .40
3039 A1170 60s Galidictis fasciata 1.00 .60
Nos. 3035-3039 (5) 2.90 1.75

Nikolai Liliev (1885-1960), Poet, UNESCO Emblem — A1171

1985, Jan. 25

3040 A1171 30s multicolored .50 .30

Zviatko Radojnov (1895-1942), Labor Leader — A1172

1985, Jan. 29

3041 A1172 5s dk red & dk brn .20 .20

Dr. Assen Zlatarov (1885-1936), Chemist
A1173

1985, Feb. 14

3042 A1173 5s multicolored .20 .20

Souvenir Sheet

Akademik, Research Vessel — A1174

1985, Mar. 1

3043 A1174 80s multicolored 1.40 .80

UNESCO Intl. Oceanographic Commission, 25th anniv.

Souvenir Sheet

Lenin — A1175

1985, Mar. 12

3044 A1175 50s multicolored .75 .50

A1176

A1177

1985, Mar. 19

3045 A1176 13s multicolored .25 .20

Warsaw Treaty Org., 30th anniv.

1985, Mar. 25

Composers.

3046 A1177 42s Bach .50 .30
3047 A1177 42s Mozart .50 .30
3048 A1177 42s Tchaikovsky .50 .30
3049 A1177 42s Mussorgsky .50 .30
3050 A1177 42s Verdi .50 .30
3051 A1177 42s Tenev .50 .30
Nos. 3046-3051 (6) 3.00 1.80

Children's Drawings Type of 1982

Inscribed 1985. Various children's drawings.

1985, Mar. 26 Litho. *Perf. 14*

3052 A1093 5s multicolored .20 .20
3053 A1093 8s multicolored .20 .20
3054 A1093 13s multicolored .20 .20
3055 A1093 20s multicolored .30 .20
3056 A1093 25s multicolored .40 .25
3057 A1093 30s multicolored .50 .30
Nos. 3052-3057 (6) 1.80 1.35

Souvenir Sheet

3058 A1093 50s Children dancing, vert. 1.10 .50

3rd Flag of Peace Intl. Assembly, Sofia. No. 3058 exists imperf. with blue control number, same value.

St. Methodius, 1100th Death Anniv. — A1179

1985, Apr. 6 Photo. *Perf. 13*

3059 A1179 13s multicolored .25 .20

Victory Parade, Moscow, 1945 — A1180

13s, 11th Infantry on parade, Sofia. 30s, Soviet soldier, orphan. 50s, Soviet flag-raising, Berlin.

1985, Apr. 30 *Perf. 13½*

3060 A1180 5s multicolored .20 .20
3061 A1180 13s multicolored .25 .20
3062 A1180 30s multicolored .50 .30
Nos. 3060-3062 (3) .95 .70

Souvenir Sheet

Perf. 13

3063 A1180 50s multicolored 1.10 .50

Defeat of Nazi Germany, end of World War II, 40th anniv. Nos. 3060-3062 printed se-tenant with labels picturing Soviet (5s, 30s) and Bulgarian medals of honor.

7th Intl. Humor and Satire Biennial — A1181

1985, Apr. 30 *Perf. 13½*

3064 A1181 13s yel, sage grn & red .25 .20

No. 3064 printed se-tenant with label picturing Gabrovo Cat emblem.

Intl. Youth Year — A1182

1985, May 21 *Perf. 13*

3065 A1182 13s multicolored .25 .20

Ivan Vasov (1850-1921), Poet — A1183

1985, May 30 *Perf. 13½*

3066 A1183 5s tan & sepia .20 .20

No. 3066 printed se-tenant with label picturing Vasov's birthplace in Sopot.

Soviet War Memorial, Haskovo City Arms A1184

1985, June 1 *Perf. 13*

3067 A1184 5s multicolored .20 .20

Haskovo millennium.

12th World Youth Festival, Moscow — A1185

1985, June 25

3068 A1185 13s multicolored .20 .20

Indira Gandhi (1917-1984), Prime Minister of India — A1186

1985, June 26

3069 A1186 30s org yel, sep & ver .60 .30

Vasil Aprilov, Founder — A1187

1985, June 30

3070 A1187 5s multicolored .20 .20

1st secular school, Gabrovo, 150th anniv.

INTERSTENO '85 — A1188

1985, June 30

3071 A1188 13s multicolored .25 .20

Congress for the Intl. Union of Stenographers and Typists, Sofia.

Alexander Nevski Cathedral A1189

1985, July 9

3072 A1189 42s multicolored .80 .40

World Tourism Org., general assembly, Sofia.

UN, 40th Anniv. A1190

1985, July 16

3073 A1190 13s multicolored .25 .20

A1191

Roses — A1192

1985, July 16

3074 A1191 13s multicolored .25 .20

Admission of Bulgaria to UN, 30th anniv.

1985, July 20 **Litho.**

3075	A1192	5s	Rosa damascena	.20	.20
3076	A1192	13s	Rosa trakijka	.25	.20
3077	A1192	20s	Rosa radiman	.35	.20
3078	A1192	30s	Rosa marista	.50	.30
3079	A1192	42s	Rosa valentina	.75	.40
3080	A1192	60s	Rosa maria	1.00	.60
a.			Min. sheet of 6, #3075-3080	3.50	2.00
			Nos. 3075-3080 (6)	3.05	1.90

Helsinki Conference, 10th Anniv. — A1193

1985, Aug. 1 **Photo.**

3081 A1193 13s multicolored .25 .20

European Swimming Championships, Sofia — A1194

1985, Aug. 2 **Litho.** *Perf. 12½*

3082	A1194	5s	Butterfly stroke	.20	.20
3083	A1194	13s	Water polo, vert.	.20	.20
3084	A1194	42s	Diving, vert.	.60	.35
3085	A1194	60s	Synchronized swimming	.75	.40
			Nos. 3082-3085 (4)	1.75	1.15

The 60s exists with central design inverted.

Natl. Tourism Assoc., 90th Anniv. A1195

1985, Aug. 15 **Photo.** *Perf. 13*

3086 A1195 5s multicolored .20 .20

1986 World Cup Soccer Championships, Mexico A1196

Various soccer plays.

1985, Aug. 29 *Perf. 13*

3087	A1196	5s	multicolored	.20	.20
3088	A1196	13s	multicolored	.20	.20
3089	A1196	30s	multicolored	.40	.20
3090	A1196	42s	multicolored	.50	.25
			Nos. 3087-3090 (4)	1.30	.85

Souvenir Sheet

3091 A1196 1 l multi, horiz. 1.25 .75

Union of Eastern Rumelia and Bulgaria, 1885 — A1197

1985, Aug. 29 *Perf. 14x13½*

3092 A1197 5s multicolored .20 .20

Computer Design Portraits — A1198

1985, Sept. 23 *Perf. 13*

3093	A1198	5s	Boy	.20	.20
3094	A1198	13s	Youth	.25	.20
3095	A1198	30s	Cosmonaut	.50	.30
			Nos. 3093-3095 (3)	.95	.70

Intl. Exhibition of the Works of Youth Inventors, Plovdiv.

St. John the Baptist Church, Nessebar A1199

Natl. restoration projects: 13s, Tyrant Hreljo Tower, Rila Monastery. 35s, Soldier, fresco, Ivanovo Rock Church. 42s, Archangel Gabriel, fresco, Bojana Church. 60s, Thracian Woman, fresco, Tomb of Kasanlak, 3rd century B.C. 1 l, The Horseman of Madara, bas-relief.

1985, Sept. 25 **Litho.** *Perf. 12½*

3096	A1199	5s	multicolored	.20	.20
3097	A1199	13s	multicolored	.25	.20
3098	A1199	35s	multicolored	.60	.30
3099	A1199	42s	multicolored	.75	.40
3100	A1199	60s	multicolored	1.10	.60
			Nos. 3096-3100 (5)	2.90	1.70

Souvenir Sheet

Imperf

3101 A1199 1 l multicolored 1.90 1.00

UNESCO, 40th anniv.

Souvenir Sheet

Ludmila Zhishkova Cultural Palace, Sofia — A1200

1985, Oct. 8 *Perf. 13*

3102 A1200 1 l multicolored 1.60 1.00

UNESCO 23rd General Assembly, Sofia.

Colosseum, Rome — A1201

1985, Oct. 15 Photo. *Perf. 13½*
3103 A1201 42s multicolored .75 .40

ITALIA '85. No. 3103 printed se-tenant with label picturing the exhibition emblem.

Souvenir Sheet

Cultural Congress, Budapest — A1202

Designs: No. 3104a, St. Cyril, patron saint of Europe. No. 3104b, Map of Europe. No. 3104c, St. Methodius, patron saint of Europe.

Perf. 13, 13 Vert. (#3104b)
1985, Oct. 22 Photo.
3104 A1202 Sheet of 3 3.00 1.50
a.-c. 50s, any single .90 .50

Helsinki Congress, 10th anniv.

Flowers — A1203

1985, Oct. 22 Photo. *Perf. 13x13½*
3105 A1203 5s Gladiolus hybridy .20 .20
3106 A1203 5s Iris germanica .20 .20
3107 A1203 5s Convolvulus tricolor .20 .20
Nos. 3105-3107 (3) .60 .60

See Nos. 3184-3186.

Historic Sailing Ships A1204

1985, Oct. 28 Photo. *Perf. 13*
3108 A1204 5s Dutch .20 .20
3109 A1204 12s Sea Sovereign, Britain .20 .20
3110 A1204 20s Mediterranean .20 .20
3111 A1204 25s Royal Prince, Britain .25 .20
3112 A1204 42s Mediterranean .50 .30
3113 A1204 60s British battleship .85 .35
Nos. 3108-3113 (6) 2.20 1.45

Souvenir Sheet

PHILATELIA '85, Cologne — A1205

Designs: a, Cologne Cathedral. b, Alexander Nevski Cathedral, Sofia.

1985, Nov. 4 *Imperf.*
3114 A1205 Sheet of 2 1.40 .65
a.-b. 30s, any single .60 .30

Conspiracy to Liberate Bulgaria from Turkish Rule, 150th Anniv. — A1206

Freedom fighters and symbols: #3115, Georgi Stojkov Rakowski (1820-76). #3116, Batscho Kiro (1835-76). #3117, Sword, Bible & hands.

1985, Nov. 6 *Perf. 13*
3115 A1206 5s multicolored .20 .20
3116 A1206 5s multicolored .20 .20
3117 A1206 13s multicolored .25 .20
Nos. 3115-3117 (3) .65 .60

Liberation from Byzantine Rule, 800th Anniv. — A1207

Paintings: 5s, The Revolt 1185, by G. Bogdanov. 13s, The Revolt 1185, by Alexander Tersiev. 30s, Battle Near Klokotnitza, by B. Grigorov and M. Ganowski. 42s, Velika Tarnovo Town Wall, by Zanko Lawrenov. 1 l, St. Dimitriev Church, 12th cent.

1985, Nov. 15 Litho.
3118 A1207 5s multicolored .20 .20
3119 A1207 13s multicolored .25 .20
3120 A1207 30s multicolored .50 .30
3121 A1207 42s multicolored .75 .40
Nos. 3118-3121 (4) 1.70 1.10

Souvenir Sheet

Imperf

3122 A1207 1 l multicolored 2.00 1.00

Souvenir Sheet

BALKANPHILA '85 — A1208

1985, Nov. 29 Photo. *Perf. 13*
3123 A1208 40s Dove, posthorn .50 .40

Intl. Post and Telecommunications Development Program — A1209

1985, Dec. 2
3124 A1209 13s multicolored .25 .20

Anton Popov (1915-1942), Freedom Fighter — A1210

1985, Dec. 11 Photo. *Perf. 13*
3125 A1210 5s lake .20 .20

New Year 1986 A1211

1985, Dec. 11 Photo. *Perf. 13*
3126 A1211 5s Doves, snowflake .20 .20
3127 A1211 13s Doves .25 .20

Hunting Dogs and Prey — A1212

5s, Pointer, partridge. 8s, Irish setter, pochard. 13s, English setter, mallard. 20s, Cocker spaniel, woodcock. 25s, German pointer, rabbit. 30s, Balkan hound, boar. 42s, Shorthaired dachshund, fox.

1985, Dec. 27 Litho. *Perf. 13x12½*
3128 A1212 5s multicolored .20 .20
3129 A1212 8s multicolored .20 .20
3130 A1212 13s multicolored .20 .20
3131 A1212 20s multicolored .20 .20
3132 A1212 25s multicolored .30 .20
3133 A1212 30s multicolored .40 .20
3134 A1212 42s multicolored .80 .30
Nos. 3128-3134 (7) 2.30 1.50

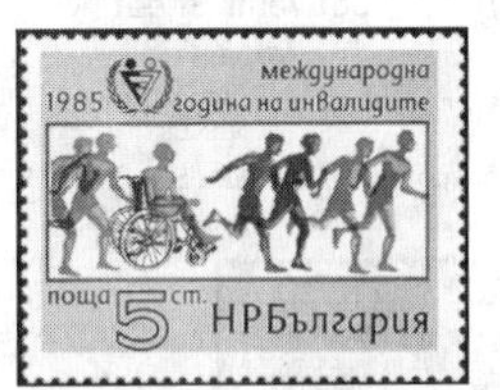

Intl. Year of the Handicapped — A1213

1985, Dec. 30 Photo. *Perf. 13*
3135 A1213 5s multicolored .20 .20

George Dimitrov (1882-1949) — A1214

1985, Dec. 30 Photo. *Perf. 13*
3136 A1214 13s brn lake .25 .20

7th Intl. Communist Congress, Moscow.

UN Child Survival Campaign — A1215

1986, Jan. 21 Photo. *Perf. 13*
3137 A1215 13s multicolored .25 .20

UNICEF, 40th anniv.

Demeter Blagoev (1856-1924) A1216

1986, Jan. 28 Photo. *Perf. 13*
3138 A1216 5s dk lake, car & dk red .20 .20

Intl. Peace Year A1217

1986, Jan. 31 *Perf. 13½*
3139 A1217 5s multicolored .20 .20

Orchids — A1218

1986, Feb. 12 Litho. *Perf. 13x12½*
3140 A1218 5s Dactylorhiza romana .20 .20
3141 A1218 13s Epipactis palustris .20 .20
3142 A1218 30s Ophrys cornuta .40 .30
3143 A1218 32s Limodorum abortivum .40 .30
3144 A1218 42s Cypripedium calceolus .50 .40
3145 A1218 60s Orchis papilionacea 1.00 .50
a. Min. sheet of 6, #3140-3145 3.25 1.50
Nos. 3140-3145 (6) 2.70 1.90

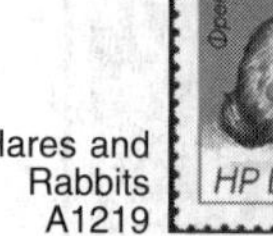

Hares and Rabbits A1219

1986, Feb. 24 ***Perf. 12½x12***

3146 A1219 5s multicolored .20 .20
3147 A1219 25s multicolored .45 .25
3148 A1219 30s multicolored .55 .30
3149 A1219 32s multicolored .60 .30
3150 A1219 42s multicolored .75 .40
3151 A1219 60s multicolored 1.00 .60
Nos. 3146-3151 (6) 3.55 2.05

Bulgarian Eagle, Newspaper, 140th Anniv. — A1220

Front page of 1st issue & Ivan Bogorov, journalist.

1986, Feb. 2 **Photo.** ***Perf. 13***

3152 A1220 5s multicolored .20 .20

Souvenir Sheet

Halley's Comet A1221

Comet's orbit in the Solar System: a, 1980. b, 1910-86. c, 1916-70. d, 1911.

1986, Mar. 7 ***Perf. 13½x13***

3153 Sheet of 4 1.90 1.25
a.-d. A1221 25s, any single .40 .30

A1222

A1223

1986, Mar. 12 ***Perf. 13x13½***

3154 A1222 5s dp bl & bl .20 .20

Vladimir Bachev (1935-1967), poet.

1986, Mar. 17 ***Perf. 13***

3155 A1223 5s Wavy lines .20 .20
3156 A1223 8s Star .20 .20
3157 A1223 13s Worker .25 .20
Nos. 3155-3157 (3) .65 .60

Souvenir Sheet

Imperf

3158 A1223 50s Scaffold, flags .70 .50

13th Natl. Communist Party Congress.

Souvenir Sheet

1st Manned Space Flight, 25th Anniv. — A1224

Designs: a, Vostok I, 1961. b, Yuri Gagarin (1934-68), Russian cosmonaut.

1986, Mar. 28 ***Perf. 13½x13***

3159 Sheet of 2 1.90 1.00
a.-b. A1224 50s, any single 1.00 .50

April Uprising against the Turks, 110th Anniv. — A1225

Monuments: 5s, 1876 Uprising monument, Panagjuriste. 13s, Christo Botev, Vraca.

1986, Mar. 30 ***Perf. 13***

3160 A1225 5s multicolored .20 .20
3161 A1225 13s multicolored .25 .20

A1225a

Levsky-Spartak Sports Club, 75th Anniv. — A1226

1986 ***Perf. 13***

3161A A1225a 5s multicolored .20 .20

Souvenir Sheet

Imperf

3162 A1226 50s Rhythmic gymnastics .90 .50

Issue dates: 5s, Dec. 50s, May 12.

A1227

A1228

1986, May 19 ***Perf. 13***

3163 A1227 5s Congress emblem .20 .20
3164 A1227 8s Emblem on globe .20 .20
3165 A1227 13s Flags .25 .20
Nos. 3163-3165 (3) .65 .60

35th Congress of Bulgarian farmers, Sofia.

1986, May 27 ***Perf. 13x13½***

3166 A1228 13s multicolored .25 .20

Conference of Transport Ministers from Socialist Countries.

17th Intl. Book Fair, Sofia — A1229

1986, May 28

3167 A1229 13s blk, brt red & grysh blk .25 .20

1986 World Cup Soccer Championships, Mexico — A1230

Various soccer plays; attached labels picture Mexican landmarks.

1986, May 30 ***Perf. 13½***

3168 A1230 5s multi, vert. .20 .20
3169 A1230 13s multicolored .25 .20
3170 A1230 20s multicolored .35 .20
3171 A1230 30s multicolored .55 .30
3172 A1230 42s multicolored .75 .40
3173 A1230 60s multi, vert. 1.10 .60
Nos. 3168-3173 (6) 3.20 1.90

Souvenir Sheet

Perf. 13

3174 A1230 1 l Azteca Stadium 2.00 1.00

Treasures of Preslav — A1231

Gold artifacts: 5s, Embossed brooch. 13s, Pendant with pearl cross, vert. 20s, Crystal and pearl pendant. 30s, Embossed shield. 42s, Pearl and enamel pendant, vert. 60s, Enamel shield.

1986, June 7 ***Perf. 13½x13, 13x13½***

3175 A1231 5s multicolored .20 .20
3176 A1231 13s multicolored .25 .20
3177 A1231 20s multicolored .35 .20
3178 A1231 30s multicolored .55 .30
3179 A1231 42s multicolored .75 .40
3180 A1231 60s multicolored 1.00 .60
Nos. 3175-3180 (6) 3.10 1.90

World Fencing Championships, Sofia, July 25-Aug. 3 — A1232

1986, July 25 **Photo.** ***Perf. 13***

3181 A1232 5s Head cut, lunge .20 .20
3182 A1232 13s Touche .25 .20
3183 A1232 25s Lunge, parry .45 .25
Nos. 3181-3183 (3) .90 .65

Flower Type of 1985

1986, July 29 ***Perf. 13x13½***

3184 A1203 8s Ipomoea tricolor .20 .20
3185 A1203 8s Anemone coronaria .20 .20
3186 A1203 32s Lilium auratum .55 .30
Nos. 3184-3186 (3) .95 .70

A1233

A1234

1986, Aug. 25

3187 A1233 42s sepia, sal brn & lake .80 .45

STOCKHOLMIA '86. No. 3187 printed in sheets of 3 + 3 labels picturing folk art.

Miniature Sheet

Environmental Conservation: a, Ciconia ciconia. b, Nuphar lutea. c, Salamandra salamandra. d, Nymphaea alba.

1986, Aug. 25 **Litho.** ***Perf. 14***

3188 Sheet of 4 + label 3.50 1.10
a.-d. A1234 30s any single .50 .25

No. 3188 contains center label picturing the oldest oak tree in Bulgaria, Granit Village.

Natl. Arms, Building of the Sobranie — A1235

1986, Sept. 13 **Photo.** ***Perf. 13***

3189 A1235 5s Prus grn, yel grn & red .20 .20

People's Republic of Bulgaria, 40th anniv.

15th Postal Union Congress — A1236

1986, Sept. 24

3190 A1236 13s multicolored .25 .20

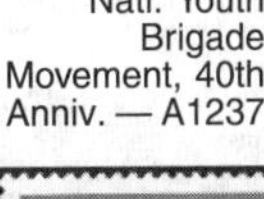

Natl. Youth Brigade Movement, 40th Anniv. — A1237

Intl. Organization of Journalists, 10th Congress A1238

1986, Oct. 4
3191 A1237 5s multicolored .20 .20

1986, Oct. 13
3192 A1238 13s blue & dark blue .25 .20

Sts. Cyril and Methodius, Disciples — A1239

1986, Oct. 23 ***Perf. 13½***
3193 A1239 13s dark brown & buff .25 .20

Sts. Cyril and Methodius in Bulgaria, 1100th anniv. No. 3193 se-tenant with inscribed label.

Telephones in Bulgaria, Cent. — A1240

1986, Nov. 5 ***Perf. 13***
3194 A1240 5s multicolored .20 .20

World Weight Lifting Championships — A1241

1986, Nov. 6
3195 A1241 13s multicolored .25 .20

Ships A1242

1986, Nov. 20
3196 A1242 5s King of Prussia .20 .20
3197 A1242 13s East Indiaman, 18th cent. .25 .20
3198 A1242 25s Shebek, 18th cent. .45 .25
3199 A1242 30s St Paul .55 .30
3200 A1242 32s Topsail schooner, 18th cent. .60 .30
3201 A1242 42s Victory .80 .40
Nos. 3196-3201 (6) 2.85 1.65

Souvenir Sheet

European Security and Cooperation Congress, Vienna — A1243

Various buildings and emblems: a, Bulgaria. b, Austria. c, Donau Park, UN.

Perf. 13, Imperf. x13 (#3202b)
1986, Nov. 27
3202 Sheet of 3 3.25 1.50
a.-c. A1243 50s any single 1.00 .50

Exists imperf. bearing control number.

Rogozen Thracian Pitchers A1244

1986, Dec. 5 ***Perf. 13***
3203 A1244 10s Facing left .20 .20
3204 A1244 10s Facing right .20 .20
a. Block, #3203-3204 + 2 labels .40 .40

Union of Bulgarian Philatelists, 14th Congress.

New Year 1987 A1245

1986, Dec. 9
3205 A1245 5s shown .20 .20
3206 A1245 13s Snow flakes .25 .20

Home Amateur Radio Operators in Bulgaria, 60th Anniv. — A1246

1986, Dec. 10
3207 A1246 13s multicolored .25 .20

Miniature Sheet

Paintings by Bulgarian Artists — A1247

a, Red Tree, by Danail Dechev (1891-1962). b, Troopers Confront Two Men, by Ilya Beshkov (1901-58). c, View of Melnik, by Veselin Stajkov (1906-70). d, View of Houses through Trees, by Kyril Zonev (1896-1961).

1986, Dec. 10 **Litho.** ***Perf. 14***
3208 A1247 Sheet of 4 2.25 1.10
a.-b. 25s any single .50 .25
c.-d. 30s any single .60 .30

Sofia Academy of Art, 90th anniv.

Augusto Cesar Sandino (1893-1934), Nicaraguan Revolutionary, and Flag — A1248

1986, Dec. 16 **Photo.** ***Perf. 13***
3209 A1248 13s multicolored .20 .20

Sandinista movement in Nicaragua, 25th anniv.

Smoyan Mihylovsky (b. 1856), Writer — A1249

Ran Bossilek (b. 1886) A1250

Title Page from Bulgarian Folk Songs of the Miladinov Brothers — A1251

Annivs. and events: No. 3211, Pentcho Slaveyckov (b. 1861), writer. No. 3212, Nickola Atanassov (b. 1886), musician.

1986, Dec. 17
3210 A1249 5s multicolored .20 .20
3211 A1249 5s multicolored .20 .20
3212 A1249 8s multicolored .20 .20
3213 A1250 8s multicolored .20 .20
3214 A1251 10s multicolored .20 .20
Nos. 3210-3214 (5) 1.00 1.00

Paintings by Titian — A1252

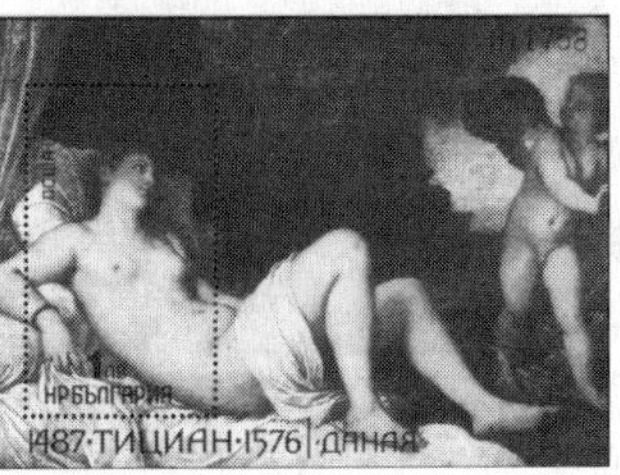

A1253

Various portraits.

1986, Dec. 23 **Litho.** ***Perf. 14***
3215 A1252 5s multicolored .20 .20
3216 A1252 13s multicolored .35 .20
3217 A1252 20s multicolored .45 .20
3218 A1252 30s multicolored .65 .30
3219 A1252 32s multicolored .75 .30
3220 A1252 42s multicolored .90 .40
a. Min. sheet of 6, #3215-3220 3.00 1.50
Nos. 3215-3220 (6) 3.30 1.60

Souvenir Sheet

3221 A1253 1 l multicolored 2.75 1.00

Rayko Daskalov (b. 1886), Politician — A1254

1986, Dec. 23 **Photo.** ***Perf. 13***
3222 A1254 5s deep claret .20 .20

Sports Cars — A1255

1986, Dec. 30 **Litho.** ***Perf. 13½***
3223 A1255 5s 1905 Fiat .20 .20
3224 A1255 10s 1928 Bugatti .20 .20
3225 A1255 25s 1936 Mercedes .40 .25
3226 A1255 32s 1952 Ferrari .50 .30
3227 A1255 40s 1985 Lotus .60 .40
3228 A1255 42s 1986 McLaren .65 .40
Nos. 3223-3228 (6) 2.55 1.75

Varna Railway Inauguration, 120th Anniv. — A1257

1987, Jan. 19 **Photo.** ***Perf. 13½***
3229 A1257 5s multicolored .20 .20
a. Perf. 11 .40 .40

Dimcho Debelianov (1887-1916), Poet — A1258

1987, Jan. 20 **Photo.** ***Perf. 13***
3230 A1258 5s blue, dull yel & dp blue .20 .20

L.L. Zamenhof, Creator of Esperanto — A1259

1987, Feb. 12

3231 A1259 13s multicolored .25 .20

Mushrooms A1260

10th Natl. Trade Unions Congress A1261

1987, Feb. 6 Litho. *Perf. 11½*

3232 A1260 5s Amanita rubescens .20 .20
3233 A1260 20s Boletus regius .35 .25
3234 A1260 30s Leccinum aurantiacum .50 .35
3235 A1260 32s Coprinus comatus .55 .40
3236 A1260 40s Russula vesca .75 .50
3237 A1260 60s Cantharellus cibarius 1.00 .60
a. Min. sheet of 6, #3232-3237 5.25
Nos. 3232-3237 (6) 3.35 2.30

1987, Mar. 20 Photo. *Perf. 13*

3238 A1261 5s dark red & violet .20 .20

Rogozen Thracian Treasure A1262

Embossed and gilded silver artifacts: 5s, Plate, Priestess Auge approaching Heracles. 8s, Pitcher, lioness attacking stag. 20s, Plate, floral pattern. 30s, Pitcher, warriors on horseback dueling. 32s, Urn, decorative pattern. 42s, Pitcher (not gilded), winged horses.

1987, Mar. 31

3239 A1262 5s multicolored .20 .20
3240 A1262 8s multicolored .20 .20
3241 A1262 20s multicolored .45 .30
3242 A1262 30s multicolored .70 .45
3243 A1262 32s multicolored .75 .50
3244 A1262 42s multicolored .90 .60
Nos. 3239-3244 (6) 3.20 2.25

Miniature Sheet

Modern Architecture — A1263

Designs: a, Ludmila Zhivkova conf. center, Varna. b, Ministry of Foreign Affairs, Sofia. c, Interpred Building, Sofia. d, Hotel, Sandanski.

1987, Apr. 7 *Perf. 13½x13*

3245 Sheet of 4 3.25 1.90
a.-d. A1263 30s any single .75 .45

Exists imperf. with black control number.

European Freestyle Wrestling Championships A1264

1987, Apr. 22 *Perf. 13*

3246 A1264 5s multicolored .20 .20
3247 A1264 13s multi, diff. .40 .20

CAPEX '87, Toronto A1265

1987, Apr. 24

3248 A1265 42s multicolored 1.00 .40

10th Congress of the Natl. Front — A1266

1987, May 11

3249 A1266 5s multicolored .20 .20

15th Communist Youth Congress — A1267

1987, May 13

3250 A1267 5s George Dimitrov .20 .20

8th Intl. Humor and Satire Biennial, Gabrovo — A1268

1987, May 15 *Perf. 13x13½*

3251 A1268 13s multicolored .35 .20

13th World Rhythmic Gymnastics Championships, Varna — A1269

Gymnasts.

1987, Aug. 5 Photo. *Perf. 13*

3252 A1269 5s Maria Gigova .20 .20
3252A A1269 8s Iliana Raeva .20 .20
3252B A1269 13s Anelia Ralenkova .30 .20
3252C A1269 25s Pilyana Georgieva .55 .30
3252D A1269 30s Lilia Ignatova .65 .40
3252E A1269 42s Bianca Panova .90 .50
Nos. 3252-3252E (6) 2.80 1.80

Souvenir Sheet

Perf. 13x13½

3252F A1269 1 l Neshka Robeva, coach 2.50 1.50

Exists imperf. with black control number.

Vassil Kolarov — A1270

1987, June 3 *Perf. 13*

3253 A1270 5s dk red, yel & dk bl .20 .20

Stela Blagoeva (b. 1887) — A1271

1987, June 4

3254 A1271 5s pink & sepia .20 .20

Rabotnichesko Delo Newspaper, 60th Anniv. — A1272

1987, May 28

3255 A1272 5s black & lake .20 .20

Deer A1273

1987, June 23 Litho.

3256 A1273 5s Capreolus capreolus, vert. .20 .20
3257 A1273 10s Alces alces .25 .20
3258 A1273 32s Dama dama, vert. .75 .25
3259 A1273 40s Cervus nippon, vert. 1.10 .30
3260 A1273 42s Cervus elaphus 1.10 .30
3261 A1273 60s Rangifer tarandus, vert. 1.40 .45
a. Min. sheet, #3256-3261, imperf 6.25 2.75
Nos. 3256-3261 (6) 4.80 1.70

Vassil Levski (1837-73) A1274

Various portraits.

1987, June 19 Photo.

3262 A1274 5s red brn & dark grn .20 .20
3263 A1274 13s dark grn & red brn .35 .20

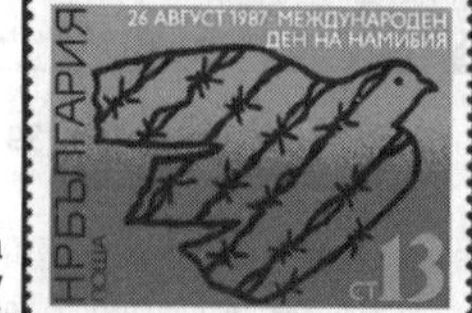

Namibia Day A1275

1987, July 8

3264 A1275 13s org, blk & dark red .30 .20

Georgi Kirkov (1867-1919), Revolutionary A1276

1987, July 17 *Perf. 13x13½*

3265 A1276 5s claret & dp claret .20 .20

Bees and Plants — A1277

1987, July 29 Litho. *Perf. 13*

3266 A1277 5s Phacelia tanacetifolia .20 .20
3267 A1277 10s Helianthus annuus .20 .20
3268 A1277 30s Robinia pseudoacacia .60 .35
3269 A1277 32s Lavandula vera .65 .40
3270 A1277 42s Tilia parvifolia .90 .50
3271 A1277 60s Onobrychis sativa 1.10 .70
a. Min. sheet of 6, #3266-3271 4.75 2.75
Nos. 3266-3271 (6) 3.65 2.35

BULGARIA '89 — A1278

1987, Sept. 3 *Perf. 13½x13*
3272 A1278 13s No. 1 .45 .20

HAFNIA '87 — A1279

1987, Sept. 8 *Perf. 13*
3273 A1279 42s multicolored 1.00 .60

No. 3273 issued in sheets of 3 plus 2 labels picturing emblems of the HAFNIA '87 and BULGARIA '89 exhibitions, and 1 label with background similar to Denmark Type A32 with castle instead of denomination.

Portrait of a Girl, by Stefan Ivanov — A1280

Paintings in the Sofia City Art Galler: 8s, Grape-gatherer, by Bencho Obreshkov. 20s, Portrait of a Lady with a Hat, by David Perets. 25s, Listeners of Marimba, by Kiril Tsonev. 32s, Boy with an Harmonica, by Nenko Balkanski. 60s, Rumyana, by Vasil Stoilov.

1987, Sept. 15 **Litho.** *Perf. 14*
3274 A1280 5s shown .20 .20
3275 A1280 8s multicolored .20 .20
3276 A1280 20s multicolored .50 .30
3277 A1280 25s multicolored .60 .35
3278 A1280 32s multicolored .75 .45
3279 A1280 60s multicolored 1.25 .80
Nos. 3274-3279 (6) 3.50 2.30

Intl. Atomic Energy Agency, 30th Anniv. A1281

1987, Sept. 15 **Photo.** *Perf. 13½x13*
3280 A1281 13s red, lt blue & emer .35 .20

Songbirds A1282

1987, Oct. 12 **Litho.** *Perf. 12½x12*
3281 A1282 5s Troglodytes troglodytes .20 .20
3282 A1282 13s Emberiza cirinella .20 .20
3283 A1282 20s Sitta europaea .30 .20
3284 A1282 30s Turdus merula .45 .30
3285 A1282 42s Coccothraustes coccothraustes .70 .35
3286 A1282 60s Cinclus cinclus 1.00 .45
a. Min. sheet of 6, #3281-3286 2.75 2.25
Nos. 3281-3286 (6) 2.85 1.70

Balkan War, 75th Anniv. A1283

1987, Sept. 15 **Photo.** *Perf. 13½*
3287 A1283 5s buff, blk & brt org .20 .20

Newspaper Anniversaries — A1283a

1987, Sept. 24 **Photo.** *Perf. 13*
3287A A1283a 5s multicolored .20 .20

Rabotnik, 95th anniv., *Rabotnicheski Vstnik*, 90th anniv. and *Rabotnichesko Delo*, 60th anniv.

October Revolution, Russia, 70th Anniv. — A1284

Lenin and: 5s, Revolutionary. 13s, Cosmonaut.

1987, Oct. 27 **Photo.** *Perf. 13*
3288 A1284 5s rose brn & red org .20 .20
3289 A1284 13s brt ultra & red org .20 .20

1988 Winter Olympics, Calgary A1285

1987, Oct. 27 **Litho.** *Perf. 13x13½*
3290 A1285 5s Biathlon .20 .20
3291 A1285 13s Slalom .40 .20
3292 A1285 30s Women's figure skating .85 .45
3293 A1285 42s 4-Man bobsled 1.10 .60
Nos. 3290-3293 (4) 2.55 1.45

Souvenir Sheet

3294 A1285 1 l Ice hockey 2.75 1.50

No. 3294 exists imperf. Same value.

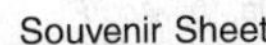
Souvenir Sheet

Soviet Space Achievements, 1937-87 — A1286

Designs: No. 3295a, Vega probe. No. 3295b, Mir-Soyuz Space Station.

1987, Dec. 24 **Photo.** *Perf. 13½x13*
3295 A1286 Sheet of 2 3.00 1.50
a.-b. 50s any single 1.25 .75

Exists imperf.

New Year 1988 A1287

Sofia stamp exhibition emblem within folklore patterns.

1987, Dec. 25 *Perf. 13*
3296 A1287 5s multicolored .20 .20
3297 A1287 13s multi, diff. .35 .20

Souvenir Sheet

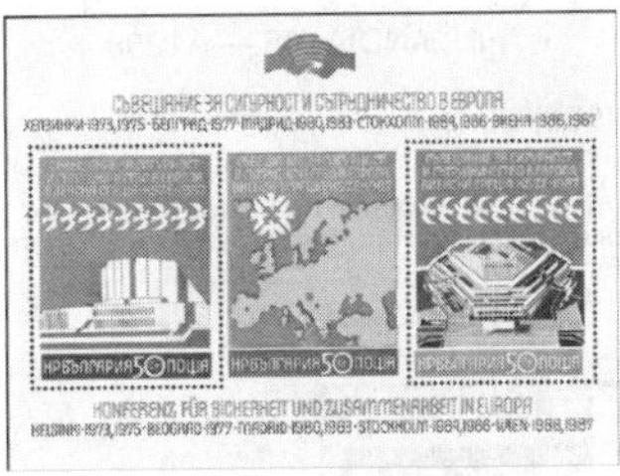
European Security Conferences — A1288

Conferences held in Helsinki, 1973, and Vienna, 1987: a, Helsinki Conf. Center. b, Map of Europe. c, Vienna Conf. Center.

Perf. 13x13½ on 2 or 4 Sides

1987, Dec. 30
3298 Sheet of 3 4.25 3.00
a.-c. A1288 50s any single 1.50 .75

Exists imperf.

A1289

НР БЪЛГАРИЯ
ПОЩА 5cm
A1290

1988, Jan. 20
3299 A1289 5s multicolored .20 .20

Christo Kabaktchiev (b. 1878), party leader.

1988, Jan. 25 **Litho.** *Perf. 12*

Marine flowers.

3300 A1290 5s Scilla bythynica .20 .20
3301 A1290 10s Geum rhodopaeum .20 .20
3302 A1290 13s Caltha polypetala .20 .20
3303 A1290 25s Nymphoides peltata .30 .20
3304 A1290 30s Cortusa matthioli .40 .20
3305 A1290 42s Stratiotes aloides .60 .45
a. Min. sheet of 6, #3300-3305 1.75 1.50
Nos. 3300-3305 (6) 1.90 1.45

Liberation of Bulgaria, 110th Anniv. A1291

1988, Feb. 15 **Photo.** *Perf. 13*
3306 A1291 5s Officer, horse .20 .20
3307 A1291 13s Soldiers .35 .20

8th Intl. Civil Servants Congress, Sofia — A1292

1988, Mar. 22 **Photo.** *Perf. 13*
3308 A1292 13s multicolored .30 .20

State Railways, Cent. — A1293

Locomotives: 5s, Jantra, 1888. 13s, Christo Botev, 1905. 25s, 0-10-1, 1918. 32s, 4-12-1 heavy duty, 1943. 42s, Diesel, 1964. 60s, Electric, 1979.

1988, Mar. 25 **Litho.** *Perf. 11*
3309 A1293 5s multicolored .20 .20
3310 A1293 13s multicolored .25 .20
3311 A1293 25s multicolored .50 .30
3312 A1293 32s multicolored .65 .35
3313 A1293 42s multicolored .80 .45
3314 A1293 60s multicolored 1.00 .60
a. Min. sheet of 6, #3309-3314 3.50 2.00
Nos. 3309-3314 (6) 3.40 2.10

Ivan Nedyalkov (1880-1925) A1294

Postal workers, heroes of socialism: 8s, Delcho Spasov (1918-43). 10s, Nikola

Ganchev (1915-43). 13s, Ganka Stoyanova Rasheva (1921-44).

1988, Mar. 31 Photo. *Perf. 13½x13*

3315 A1294 5s buff & dark rose brn .20 .20
3316 A1294 8s pale ultra & violet blue .20 .20
3317 A1294 10s pale olive grn & olive grn .25 .20
3318 A1294 13s pale pink & lake .25 .20
Nos. 3315-3318 (4) .90 .80

Georgi Traikov (b. 1898), Statesman A1295

Intl. Red Cross and Red Crescent Organizations, 125th Annivs. — A1296

1988, Apr. 8 Litho. *Perf. 13x13½*

3319 A1295 5s orange & brn .20 .20

1988, Apr. 26 Photo. *Perf. 13*

3320 A1296 13s multicolored .25 .20

Children's Drawings Type of 1982

Designs: 5s, Girl wearing a folk costume, vert. 8s, Painter at easel, vert. 13s, Children playing. 20s, Ringing bells for peace. 32s, Accordion player, vert. 42s, Cosmonaut, vert. 50s, Assembly emblem.

1988, Apr. 28 Litho. *Perf. 14*

3321 A1093 5s multicolored .20 .20
3322 A1093 8s multicolored .20 .20
3323 A1093 13s multicolored .30 .20
3324 A1093 20s multicolored .40 .25
3325 A1093 32s multicolored .65 .40
3326 A1093 42s multicolored .90 .50
Nos. 3321-3326 (6) 2.65 1.75

Souvenir Sheet

3327 A1093 50s multicolored 1.10 .60

4th Intl. Children's Assembly, Sofia. No. 3327 exists imperf.

Karl Marx A1297

1988, May 5 *Perf. 13*

3328 A1297 13s multicolored .30 .20

Birds — A1297a

1988, May 6 Litho. *Perf. 13x13½*

3328A A1297a 5s *Ciconia ciconia* .25 .20
3328B A1297a 5s *Larus argentatus* .25 .20
3328C A1297a 8s *Ardea cinerea* .25 .20
3328D A1297a 8s *Corvus corone cornix* .25 .20
3328E A1297a 10s *Accipiter gentillis* .30 .20
3328F A1297a 42s *Bubo bubo* 1.00 .50
Nos. 3328A-3328F (6) 2.30 1.50

Dated 1987.

Sofia Zoo A1298

1988, May 20

3329 A1298 5s Loxodonta africana .20 .20
3330 A1298 13s Ceratotherium simum .25 .20
3331 A1298 25s Lycaon pictus .50 .30
3332 A1298 30s Pelecanus onocrotalus .65 .35
3333 A1298 32s Bucorvus abyssinicus .70 .40
3334 A1298 42s Nyctea scandiaca .90 .55
a. Min. sheet of 6, #3329-3334 3.75 1.75
Nos. 3329-3334 (6) 3.20 2.00

FINLANDIA '88 — A1299

1988, June 7

3335 A1299 30s Finland No. 1 .70 .35

No. 3335 printed in miniature sheets of 3 plus 3 labels picturing skyline, SOFIA '89 and FINLANDIA '88 exhibition emblems. Exists imperf.

2nd Joint USSR-Bulgaria Space Flight — A1300

1988, June 7

3336 A1300 5s shown .20 .20
3337 A1300 13s Rocket, globe .30 .20

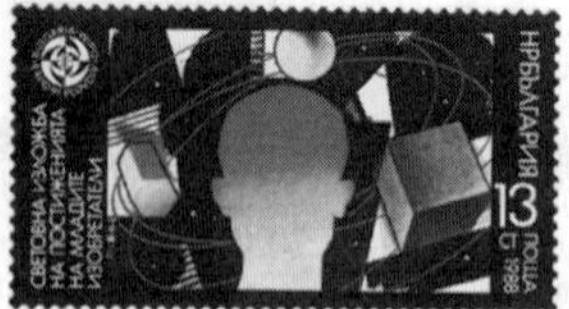

EXPO '91, Plovdiv — A1301

1988, June 7 *Perf. 13½x13*

3338 A1301 13s multicolored .30 .20

1988 European Soccer Championships — A1302

1988, June 10 *Perf. 13*

3339 A1302 5s Corner kick .20 .20
3340 A1302 13s Heading the ball .25 .20
3341 A1302 30s Referee, player .55 .35
3342 A1302 42s Player holding trophy .85 .55
Nos. 3339-3342 (4) 1.85 1.30

Souvenir Sheet

3343 A1302 1 l Stadium 2.25 1.25

Paintings by Dechko Usunov (1899-1986) A1303

Designs: 5s, *Portrait of a Young Girl.* 13s, *Portrait of Maria Wassilewa.* 30s, *Self-portrait.*

1988, June 14 *Perf. 13x13½*

3344 A1303 5s multicolored .20 .20
3345 A1303 13s multicolored .30 .20
3346 A1303 30s multicolored .70 .35
Nos. 3344-3346 (3) 1.20 .75

Souvenir Sheet

1st Woman in Space, 25th Anniv. — A1304

1988, June 16 *Perf. 13½x13*

3347 A1304 1 l multicolored 2.75 1.50

Valentina Tereshkova's flight, June 16-19, 1963.

Kurdzhali Region Religious Art — A1305

Designs: 5s, *St. John the Baptist,* 1592. 8s, *St. George Slaying the Dragon,* 1841.

1988, June 27 *Perf. 13x13½*

3348 A1305 5s multicolored .20 .20
3349 A1305 8s multicolored .20 .20

1988 Summer Olympics, Seoul — A1306

1988, July 25 Litho. *Perf. 13*

3350 A1306 5s High jump .20 .20
3351 A1306 13s Weight lifting .30 .20
3352 A1306 30s Greco-Roman wrestling .60 .40
3353 A1306 42s Rhythmic gymnastics .90 .50
Nos. 3350-3353 (4) 2.00 1.30

Souvenir Sheet

3354 A1306 1 l Volleyball 2.75 1.25

No. 3354 exists imperf.

Dimitr and Karaja A1307

1988, July 25 Litho. *Perf. 13*

3355 A1307 5s blk, dark olive bister & grn .20 .20

120th anniv. of the deaths of Haji Dimitr and Stefan Karaja, patriots killed during the Balkan Wars.

Problems of Peace and Socialism, 30th Anniv. — A1308

1988, July 26 Photo.

3356 A1308 13s multicolored .20 .20

Paintings in the Ludmila Zhivkova Art Gallery A1309

Paintings: No. 3357, *Harbor, Algiers,* by Albermarke (1875-1947). No. 3358, *Portrait of Ermin David in the Studio,* by Jul Pasken (1885-1930). No. 3359, *Madonna with Child and Sts. Sebastian and Roko,* by Giovanni Rosso (1494-1540). No. 3360, *The Barren Tree,* by Roland Udo (1879-1982).

1988, July 27 Litho. *Perf. 14*

3357 A1309 30s multicolored .65 .40
3358 A1309 30s multicolored .65 .40
3359 A1309 30s multicolored .65 .40
3360 A1309 30s multicolored .65 .40
Nos. 3357-3360 (4) 2.60 1.60

St. Clement of Ohrid University, Sofia, 100th Anniv. — A1310

1988, Aug. 22 *Perf. 13*
3361 A1310 5s blk & pale yel .20 .20

PRAGA '88 A1311

1988, Aug. 22
3362 A1311 25s Czechoslovakia #2 in vermilion .60 .30

Printed in miniature sheets of 3 plus 3 labels picturing skyline, PRAGA '88 and SOFIA '89 exhibition emblems.
Exists imperf.

OLYMPHILEX '88 — A1312

1988, Sept. 1
3363 A1312 62s Korea No. 1 1.25 .75

Printed in miniature sheets of 3 plus 3 labels picturing skyline, OLYMPHILEX '88 and SOFIA '89 exhibition emblems.
Exists imperf.

A1313

A1314

1988, Sept. 15
3364 A1313 5s dp bl, lt bl & red .20 .20

Kremikovtsi steel mill, 25th anniv.

1988, Sept. 16 *Perf. 13½x13*
3365 A1314 13s dark red & ultra .25 .20

80th Interparliamentary Conference.

Transportation Commission 80th Congress — A1315

1988, Oct. 17
3366 A1315 13s deep lil rose & blk .25 .20

Kurdzhali Region Artifacts A1316

5s, Earthenware bowl, 13th-14th cent. 8s, Medieval fortification, Gorna Krepost Village, vert.

1988, Sept. 20 *Perf. 13*
3367 A1316 5s multicolored .20 .20
3368 A1316 8s multicolored .20 .20

Chiprovo Uprising, 300th Anniv. — A1317

1988, Sept. 23
3369 A1317 5s multicolored .20 .20

Bears A1318

1988, Sept. 26 *Perf. 12½*
3370 A1318 5s *Ursus arctos* .20 .20
3371 A1318 8s *Thalassarctos maritimus* .20 .20
3372 A1318 13s *Melursus ursinus* .30 .20
3373 A1318 20s *Helarctos malayanus* .45 .25
3374 A1318 32s *Selenarctos thibetanus* .70 .40
3375 A1318 42s *Tremarctos ornatus* .95 .50
a. Min. sheet of 6, #3370-3375 3.25 1.50
Nos. 3370-3375 (6) 2.80 1.75

ECOFORUM for Peace — A1319

1988, Oct. 29 *Perf. 13*
3376 A1319 20s multicolored .50 .25

PLOVDIV '88 — A1320

Design: Amphitheater ruins, PRAGA '88 and PLOVDIV '88 emblems.

1988, Nov. 2
3377 A1320 5s multicolored .20 .20

Exists in imperf. sheet of six.

Radio & Television Authority, 25th Anniv. — A1321

1988, Nov. 17 **Litho.** *Perf. 13*
3378 A1321 5s multicolored .20 .20

BULGARIA '89 — A1321a

1988, Nov. 22 **Litho.** *Perf. 13*
3379 A1321a 42s No. 1 1.10 .60

Printed in miniature sheets of 3+3 labels picturing exhib. emblem and conf. center.
Exists imperf.

Souvenir Sheet

Danube Cruise Excursion Industry, 40th Anniv. — A1321b

1988, Nov. 25 *Perf. 13½x13*
3380 Sheet of 2 5.00 2.75
a. A1321b 1 l *Russia* 2.50 1.40
b. A1321b 1 l *Aleksandr Stamboliski* 2.50 1.40

Traffic Safety A1321c

1988, Nov. 28
3381 A1321c 5s multicolored .20 .20

New Year 1989 — A1321d

1988, Dec. 20 *Perf. 13*
3382 A1321d 5s shown .20 .20
3383 A1321d 13s multi, diff. .35 .25

Hotels in Winter A1322

1988, Dec. 19 **Litho.** *Perf. 13½x13*
3384 A1322 5s shown .20 .20
3385 A1322 8s multi, diff. .20 .20
3386 A1322 13s multi, diff. .30 .20
3387 A1322 30s multi, diff. .70 .40
Nos. 3384-3387 (4) 1.40 1.00

Souvenir Sheet

Soviet Space Shuttle *Energija-Buran* — A1322a

1988, Dec. 28 *Perf. 13½x13*
3387A A1322a 1 l dark blue 3.00 1.50

BULGARIA '89 — A1322b

Traditional modes of postal conveyance.

1988, Dec. 29 *Perf. 13½x13*
3387B A1322b 25s Mail coach .50 .30
3387C A1322b 25s Biplane .50 .30
3387D A1322b 25s Truck .50 .30
3387E A1322b 25s Steam packet .50 .30
Nos. 3387B-3387E (4) 2.00 1.20

Philatelic Exhibitions — A1323

1989 **Litho.** *Perf. 13*
3388 A1323 42s France No. 1 1.00 .50
3389 A1323 62s India No. 200 1.50 .80

BULGARIA '89 and PHILEXFRANCE '89 (42s) or INDIA '89 (62s).
Nos. 3388-3389 each printed in sheets of 3 + 3 labels picturing skylines, BULGARIA '89

and PHILEXFRANCE or INDIA exhibition labels. Exist in sheets of 4 also. Exist imperf.

Issue dates: 42s, Feb. 23; 62s, Jan. 14.

Souvenir Sheet

Universiade Winter Games, Sofia — A1324

Designs: a, Downhill skiing. b, Ice hockey. c, Cross-country skiing. d, Speed skating.

1989, Jan. 30 Litho. *Imperf.*
Simulated Perforations

3390	Sheet of 4	2.40	1.25
a.-d.	A1324 25s multicolored	.55	.30

No. 3390 exists imperf. without simulated perforations and containing black control number.

Humor and Satire Festival, Gabrovo A1325

1989, Feb. 7 *Perf. 13½x13*

3391	A1325	13s Don Quixote	.30	.20

Endangered Plant Species — A1326

1989, Feb. 22 *Perf. 13x13½*

3392	A1326	5s *Ramonda serbica*	.20	.20
3393	A1326	10s *Paeonia maskula*	.20	.20
3394	A1326	25s *Viola perinensis*	.50	.30
3395	A1326	30s *Dracunculus vulgaris*	.60	.35
3396	A1326	42s *Tulipa splendens*	.85	.50
3397	A1326	60s *Rindera umbellata*	1.25	.70
a.		Min. sheet of 6, #3392-3397	4.25	2.50
		Nos. 3392-3397 (6)	3.60	2.25

World Wildlife Fund A1327

Bats.

1989, Feb. 27 *Perf. 13*

3398	A1327	5s *Nyctalus noctula*	.25	.20
3399	A1327	13s *Rhinolophus ferrumequinum*	.35	.20
3400	A1327	30s *Myotis myotis*	.75	.35
3401	A1327	42s *Vespertilio murinus*	1.10	.50
a.		Min. sheet of 4, #3398-3401	2.50	1.25
		Nos. 3398-3401 (4)	2.45	1.25

Aleksandr Stamboliski (1879-1923), Premier — A1328

1989, Mar. 1 *Perf. 13½x13*

3402	A1328	5s brt org & blk	.20	.20

Souvenir Sheet

Soviet-Bulgarian Joint Space Flight, 10th Anniv. — A1329

Designs: a, Liftoff. b, Crew.

1989, Apr. 10 *Perf. 13*

3403	A1329	Sheet of 2	2.40	1.25
a.-b.		50s any single	1.10	.60

Exists imperf.

EXPO '91 Young Inventors Exhibition, Plovdiv — A1330

1989, Apr. 20 *Perf. 13½x13*

3404	A1330	5s multicolored	.20	.20

Petko Enev (b. 1889) A1331

Stanke Dimitrov Marek (b. 1889) — A1332

1989, Apr. 28 *Perf. 13½x13, 13x13½*

3405	A1331	5s scarlet & black	.20	.20
3406	A1332	5s scarlet & black	.20	.20

Icons — A1333

Photocopier A1334

Paintings by Bulgarian artists: No. 3407, Archangel Michael, by Dimiter Molerov. No. 3408, Mother and Child, by Toma Vishanov. No. 3409, St. John, by Vishanov. No. 3410, St. Dimitri, by Ivan Terziev.

1989, Apr. 28 *Perf. 13x13½*

3407	A1333	30s multicolored	.65	.35
3408	A1333	30s multicolored	.65	.35
3409	A1333	30s multicolored	.65	.35
3410	A1333	30s multicolored	.65	.35
		Nos. 3407-3410 (4)	2.60	1.40

Nos. 3408, 3410 exist in sheets of four. Nos. 3407-3410 exist in souvenir sheets of four and together in one sheet of four, imperf.

1989, May 5

3411	A1334	5s shown	.20	.20
3412	A1334	8s Computer	.20	.20
3413	A1334	35s Telephone	.80	.45
3414	A1334	42s Dish receiver	.90	.50
		Nos. 3411-3414 (4)	2.10	1.35

Bulgarian Communications, 110th anniv. Nos. 3411-3413 exist in imperf. sheets of six.

Souvenir Sheet

58th FIP Congress — A1335

1989, May 22

3415	A1335	1 l Charioteer	2.25	1.00

Exists imperf.

1st Communist Party Congress in Bulgaria, 70th Anniv. — A1336

Famous Men — A1337

1989, June 15

3416	A1336	5s mar, blk & dk red	.20	.20

1989

#3417, Ilya Blaskov. #3418, Sofronii, Bishop of Vratza. #3419, Vassil Aprilov (b. 1789), educator, historian. #3420, Christo Jassenov (1889-1925). 10s, Stoyan Zagorchinov (1889-1969).

3417	A1337	5s black & gray ol	.20	.20
3418	A1337	5s blk, brn blk & pale green	.20	.20
3419	A1337	8s lt blue, blk & vio blk	.30	.20
3420	A1337	8s tan, blk & dark red brown	.25	.20
3421	A1337	10s blk, pale pink & gray blue	.30	.20
		Nos. 3417-3421 (5)	1.25	1.00

Issued: #3417-3418, June 15; #3419, Aug. 1; #3420, Sept. 25; 10s, Aug. 5.

French Revolution, Bicent. — A1338

1989, June 26 *Perf. 13½x13*

3422	A1338	13s Anniv. emblem	.25	.20
3423	A1338	30s Jean-Paul Marat	.60	.35
3424	A1338	42s Robespierre	.85	.50
		Nos. 3422-3424 (3)	1.70	1.05

7th Army Games — A1339

1989, June 30 *Perf. 13*

3425	A1339	5s Gymnast	.20	.20
3426	A1339	13s Equestrian	.30	.20
3427	A1339	30s Running	.65	.40
3428	A1339	42s Shooting	.95	.50
		Nos. 3425-3428 (4)	2.10	1.30

22nd World Canoe and Kayak Championships, Plovdiv — A1340

1989, Aug. 11 Litho. *Perf. 13*

3429	A1340	13s Woman paddling	.30	.20
3430	A1340	30s Man rowing	.60	.25

Photography, 150th Anniv. — A1341

1989, Aug. 29 *Perf. 13½x13*

3431	A1341	42s blk, buff & yel	.95	.45

September 9 Revolution, 45th Anniv. — A1342

1989, Aug. 30 *Perf. 13*

3432	A1342	5s Revolutionaries	.20	.20
3433	A1342	8s Couple embracing	.20	.20
3434	A1342	13s Faces in a crowd	.20	.20
		Nos. 3432-3434 (3)	.60	.60

Natural History Museum, Cent. A1343

1989, Aug. 31

3435	A1343	13s multicolored	.30	.20

Postal Workers Killed in World War II — A1343a

Designs: 5s, L.D. Dardjikov. 8s, I.B. Dobrev. 10s, N.P. Antonov.

1989, Sept. 22 **Litho.** *Perf. 13*

3436	A1343a	5s multicolored	.20	.20
3437	A1343a	8s multicolored	.20	.20
3438	A1343a	13s multicolored	.30	.20
		Nos. 3436-3438 (3)	.70	.60

12th Shipping Unions Congress (FIATA) — A1344

1989, Sept. 25 **Litho.** *Perf. 13½x13*

3439	A1344	42s light bl & dark bl	.85	.45

Jawaharlal Nehru, 1st Prime Minister of Independent India — A1346

1989, Oct. 10

3440	A1346	13s blk, pale yel & brn	.30	.20

Souvenir Sheet

European Ecology Congress — A1347

1989, Oct. 12 *Perf. 13*

3441	A1347	Sheet of 2	3.75	1.75
a.		50s multicolored	1.25	.60
b.		1 l multicolored	2.25	1.10

Snakes A1368

1989, Oct. 20 **Litho.** *Perf. 13*

3491	A1368	5s *Eryx jaculus turcicus*	.20	.20
3492	A1368	10s *Elaphe longissima*	.25	.20
3493	A1368	25s *Elaphe situla*	.55	.30
3494	A1368	30s *Elaphe quatuorlineata*	.65	.35
3495	A1368	42s *Telescopus fallax*	.90	.50
3496	A1368	60s *Coluber rubriceps*	1.25	.70
a.		Min. sheet of 6, #3491-3496	4.25	2.00
		Nos. 3491-3496 (6)	3.80	2.25

Intl. Youth Science Fair, Plovdiv, 1989 — A1369

1989, Nov. 4

3497	A1369	13s multicolored	.25	.20

1990 World Soccer Championships, Italy — A1370

Various athletes: No. 3502a, Athletes facing right. No. 3502b, Athletes facing left.

1989, Dec. 1

3498	A1370	5s shown	.20	.20
3499	A1370	13s multi, diff.	.30	.20
3500	A1370	30s multi, diff.	.70	.35
3501	A1370	42s multi, diff.	1.00	.50
		Nos. 3498-3501 (4)	2.20	1.25

Souvenir Sheet

3502		Sheet of 2	2.40	1.10
a.-b.		A1370 50s any single	1.10	.55

Air Sports A1371

1989, Dec. 8

3503	A1371	5s Glider planes	.20	.20
3504	A1371	13s Hang glider	.30	.20
3505	A1371	30s Sky diving	.70	.35
3506	A1371	42s Three sky divers	1.00	.50
		Nos. 3503-3506 (4)	2.20	1.25

82nd General conference of the FAI, Varna.

Traffic Safety A1372

1989, Dec. 12

3507	A1372	5s multicolored	.20	.20

New Year 1990 — A1373

1989, Dec. 25 **Litho.** *Perf. 13*

3508	A1373	5s Santa's sleigh	.20	.20
3509	A1373	13s Snowman	.30	.20

Cats A1374

#3510, Persian. #3511, Tiger. 8s, Tabby. #3513, Himalayan. #3514, Persian, diff. 13s, Siamese. #3511, 3514-3515 vert.

Perf. 13½x13, 13x13½

1989, Dec. 26 **Background Color**

3510	A1374	5s gray	.20	.20
3511	A1374	5s yellow	.20	.20
3512	A1374	8s orange	.20	.20
3513	A1374	10s blue	.25	.20
3514	A1374	10s brown orange	.25	.20
3515	A1374	13s red	.30	.20
		Nos. 3510-3515 (6)	1.40	1.20

Explorers and Their Ships — A1375

1990, Jan. 17 *Perf. 13*

3516	A1375	5s Columbus	.20	.20
3517	A1375	8s da Gama	.20	.20
3518	A1375	13s Magellan	.25	.20
3519	A1375	32s Drake	.60	.35
3520	A1375	42s Hudson	.75	.50
3521	A1375	60s Cook	1.00	.70
a.		Min. sheet of 6, #3516-3521	3.75	1.75
		Nos. 3516-3521 (6)	3.00	2.15

Natl. Esperanto Movement, Cent. — A1376

1990, Feb. 23 **Litho.** *Perf. 13*

3522	A1376	10s multicolored	.30	.20

Paintings by Foreign Artists in the Natl. Museum A1377

Artists: No. 3523, Suzanna Valadon (1867-1938). No. 3524, Maurice Brianchon (1899-1978). No. 3525, Moise Kisling (1891-1953). No. 3526, Giovanni Beltraffio (1467-1516).

1990, Mar. 23 *Perf. 14*

3523	A1377	30s multicolored	.65	.40
3524	A1377	30s multicolored	.65	.40
3525	A1377	30s multicolored	.65	.40
3526	A1377	30s multicolored	.65	.40
		Nos. 3523-3526 (4)	2.60	1.60

1990 World Soccer Championships, Italy — A1378

Various athletes.

1990, Mar. 26 *Perf. 13*

3527	A1378	5s multicolored	.20	.20
3528	A1378	13s multi, diff.	.30	.20
3529	A1378	30s multi, diff.	.70	.40
3530	A1378	42s multi, diff.	.95	.50
		Nos. 3527-3530 (4)	2.15	1.30

Souvenir Sheet

3531		Sheet of 2	2.40	1.25
a.	A1378	50s Three players	1.10	.60
b.	A1378	50s Two players	1.10	.60

Bavaria No. 1 A1379

1990, Apr. 6 **Litho.** *Perf. 13*

3532	A1379	42s vermilion & blk	1.00	.50

ESSEN '90, Germany, Apr. 12-22. No. 3532 printed in sheets of 3 + 3 labels.

Souvenir Sheet

Penny Black, 150th Anniv. A1380

1990, Apr. 10

3533		Sheet of 2	2.25	1.25
a.	A1380	50s Great Britain #1	1.10	.60
b.	A1380	50s Sir Rowland Hill	1.10	.60

Cooperative Farming in Bulgaria, Cent. — A1381

1990, Apr. 17

3534	A1381	5s multicolored	.20	.20

Dimitar Chorbadjiski-Chudomir (1890-1967) — A1382

1990, Apr. 24
3535 A1382 5s multicolored .20 .20

Labor Day, Cent. — A1383

1990, May 1 *Perf. 13x13½*
3536 A1383 10s multicolored .25 .20

ITU, 125th Anniv. — A1384

1990, May 13 Litho. *Perf. 13½x13*
3537 A1384 20s bl, red & blk .50 .25

Belgium No. 1 A1385

1990, May 23 *Perf. 13*
3538 A1385 30s multicolored .75 .40

Belgica '90. No. 3538 printed in sheets of 3 + 3 labels.

Lamartine (1790-1869), French Poet — A1386

1990, June 15 *Perf. 13½x13*
3539 A1386 20s multicolored .45 .25

Dinosaurs — A1387

1990, June 19 *Perf. 12½*
3540 A1387 5s Brontosaurus .20 .20
3541 A1387 8s Stegosaurus .20 .20
3542 A1387 13s Edaphosaurus .30 .20
3543 A1387 25s Rhamphorhynchus .60 .30
3544 A1387 32s Protoceratops .80 .40
3545 A1387 42s Triceratops 1.10 .55
a. Min. sheet of 6, #3540-3545 3.50 1.60
Nos. 3540-3545 (6) 3.20 1.85

1992 Summer Olympic Games, Barcelona — A1388

1990, July 13 *Perf. 13½x13*
3546 A1388 5s Swimming .20 .20
3547 A1388 13s Handball .30 .20
3548 A1388 30s Hurdling .75 .40
3549 A1388 42s Cycling 1.10 .55
Nos. 3546-3549 (4) 2.35 1.35

Souvenir Sheet

3550 Sheet of 2 2.75 1.25
a. A1388 50s Tennis, forehand 1.25 .60
b. A1388 50s Tennis, backhand 1.25 .60

Butterflies A1389

1990, Aug. 8 Litho. *Perf. 13*
3551 A1389 5s Zerynthia Polyxena .20 .20
3552 A1389 10s Panaxia quadripunctaria .20 .20
3553 A1389 20s Proserpinus proserpina .20 .20
3554 A1389 30s Hyles lineata .25 .20
3555 A1389 42s Thecla betulae .30 .20
3556 A1389 60s Euphydryas cynthia 1.75 .60
a. Min. sheet of 6, #3551-3556 3.00 1.75
Nos. 3551-3556 (6) 2.90 1.60

Airplanes — A1390

1990, Aug. 30 Litho. *Perf. 13½x13*
3557 A1390 5s Airbus A-300 .20 .20
3558 A1390 10s Tu-204 .20 .20
3559 A1390 25s Concorde .30 .25
3560 A1390 30s DC-9 .40 .30
3561 A1390 42s Il-86 .55 .40
3562 A1390 60s Boeing 747 .75 .55
a. Min. sheet of 6, #3557-3562 3.25 2.00
Nos. 3557-3562 (6) 2.40 1.90

Exarch Joseph I (1840-1915), Religious Leader — A1391

1990, Sept. 27 *Perf. 13*
3563 A1391 5s blk, pur & grn .20 .20

Intl. Traffic Safety Year A1392

1990, Oct. 9 Litho. *Perf. 13*
3564 A1392 5s multicolored .20 .20

Olymphilex '90, Varna — A1393

1990, Oct. 16 *Perf. 13x13½*
3565 A1393 5s Shot put .20 .20
3566 A1393 13s Discus .25 .20
3567 A1393 42s Hammer throw .90 .55
3568 A1393 60s Javelin 1.25 .70
a. Souv. sheet of 4, #3565-3568, imperf. 13.00 7.50
Nos. 3565-3568 (4) 2.60 1.65

Space Exploration — A1394

Designs: 5s, Sputnik, 1957, USSR. 8s, Vostok, 1961, USSR. 10s, Voshkod 2, 1965, USSR. 20s, Apollo-Soyuz, 1975, US-USSR. 42s, Space Shuttle Columbia, 1981, US. 60s, Galileo, 1989-1996, US. 1 l, Apollo 11 Moon landing, 1969, US.

1990, Oct. 22 *Perf. 13½x13*
3569 A1394 5s multicolored .20 .20
3570 A1394 8s multicolored .20 .20
3571 A1394 10s multicolored .20 .20
3572 A1394 20s multicolored .40 .25
3573 A1394 42s multicolored .90 .55
3574 A1394 60s multicolored 1.25 .70
Nos. 3569-3574 (6) 3.15 2.10

Souvenir Sheet

3575 A1394 1 l multicolored 2.75 1.50

St. Clement of Ohrid — A1395

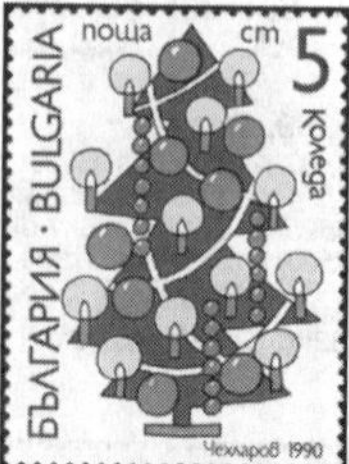
Christmas A1396

1990, Nov. 29 Litho. *Perf. 13*
3576 A1395 5s multicolored .20 .20

1990, Dec. 25 Litho. *Perf. 13*
3577 A1396 5s Christmas tree .20 .20
3578 A1396 20s Santa Claus .40 .25

European Figure Skating Championships, Sofia — A1397

1991, Jan. 18 *Perf. 13½x13*
3579 A1397 15s multicolored .35 .20

Farm Animals A1398

1991-92 *Perf. 14x13½*
3581 A1398 20s Sheep .20 .20
3582 A1398 25s Goose .20 .20
3583 A1398 30s Hen, chicks .35 .20
3584 A1398 40s Horse .35 .25
3585 A1398 62s Goat .55 .30
3586 A1398 86s Sow .80 .50
3587 A1398 95s Goat .55 .30
3588 A1398 1 l Donkey 1.00 .40
3589 A1398 2 l Bull 2.00 .50
3590 A1398 5 l Turkey 3.25 1.25
3591 A1398 10 l Cow 5.75 1.75
Nos. 3581-3591 (11) 15.00 5.85

Issued: 20s, 25s, 40s, 86s, 1 l, 8/21; 10 l, 2/22; 95s, 5/5/92; others, 2/11/91.

Mushrooms A1399

1991, Mar. 19 *Perf. 12½x13*
3597 A1399 5s Amanita phalloides .20 .20
3598 A1399 10s Amanita verna .20 .20
3599 A1399 20s Amanita pantherina .20 .20
3600 A1399 32s Amanita muscaria .40 .30
3601 A1399 42s Gyromitra esculenta .45 .35
3602 A1399 60s Boletus satanas .70 .50
a. Min. sheet of 6, #3597-3602 3.25 1.50
Nos. 3597-3602 (6) 2.15 1.75

French Impressionists A1400

Designs: 20s, Good Morning, by Gauguin. 43s, Madame Dobini, by Degas. 62s, Peasant Woman, by Pissarro. 67s, Woman with Black Hair, by Manet. 80s, Blue Vase, by Cezanne. 2 l, Jeanny Samari, by Renoir. 3 l, Self portrait, by Van Gogh.

1991, Apr. 1 *Perf. 13*
3603 A1400 20s multicolored .25 .20
3604 A1400 43s multicolored .50 .40
3605 A1400 62s multicolored .70 .55
3606 A1400 67s multicolored .80 .60
3607 A1400 80s multicolored 1.00 .75
3608 A1400 2 l multicolored 2.25 1.75
Nos. 3603-3608 (6) 5.50 4.25

Miniature Sheet

3609 A1400 3 l multicolored 4.75 2.75

Swiss Confederation, 700th Anniv. — A1401

1991, Apr. 11
3610 A1401 62s multicolored .90 .55

Philatelic Review, Cent. — A1402

1991, May 7 Litho. *Perf. 13*
3611 A1402 30s multicolored .45 .25

Europa — A1403

1991, May 10 *Perf. 13x13½*
3612 A1403 43s Meteosat .70 .40
3613 A1403 62s Ariane rocket 1.00 .55

Horses — A1404

1991, May 21 *Perf. 13x12½*
3614 A1404 5s Przewalski's horse .20 .20
3615 A1404 10s Tarpan .20 .20
3616 A1404 25s Arabian .35 .20
3617 A1404 35s Arabian .45 .30
3618 A1404 42s Shetland pony .55 .35
3619 A1404 60s Draft horse .80 .50
a. Min. sheet of 6, #3614-3619 3.25 1.50
Nos. 3614-3619 (6) 2.55 1.75

EXPO 91, Plovdiv — A1405

1991, June 6 Litho. *Perf. 13½x13*
3620 A1405 30s multicolored .45 .30

Wolfgang Amadeus Mozart A1406

1991, July 2 *Perf. 13*
3621 A1406 62s multicolored 1.00 .55

Space Shuttle Missions, 10th Anniv. A1407

1991, July 23 Litho. *Perf. 13*
3622 A1407 12s Columbia .20 .20
3623 A1407 32s Challenger .30 .20
3624 A1407 50s Discovery .40 .20
3625 A1407 86s Atlantis, vert. .75 .40
3626 A1407 1.50 l Buran, vert. 1.25 .60
3627 A1407 2 l Atlantis, diff., vert. 1.50 .75
Nos. 3622-3627 (6) 4.40 2.35

Souvenir Sheet

3628 A1407 3 l US shuttle, earth 4.25 2.00

1992 Winter Olympics, Albertville A1408

1991, Aug. 7 Litho. *Perf. 13x13½*
3629 A1408 30s Luge .40 .30
3630 A1408 43s Slalom skiing .50 .40
3631 A1408 67s Ski jumping .85 .60
3632 A1408 2 l Biathlon 2.50 1.75
Nos. 3629-3632 (4) 4.25 3.05

Souvenir Sheet

3633 A1408 3 l Two-man bobsled 4.75 2.75

Sheraton Sofia Hotel Balkan A1409

1991, Sept. 6 Litho. *Perf. 13*
3634 A1409 62s multicolored 1.25 .55

Printed in sheets of 3 + 3 labels.

Dogs — A1410

1991, Oct. 11 *Perf. 13x13½*
3635 A1410 30s Japanese .25 .20
3636 A1410 43s Chihuahua .40 .20
3637 A1410 62s Pinscher .55 .30
3638 A1410 80s Yorkshire terrier .70 .35
3639 A1410 1 l Chinese .90 .45
3640 A1410 3 l Pug 2.50 1.25
a. Min. sheet of 6, #3635-3640 5.75 2.75
Nos. 3635-3640 (6) 5.30 2.75

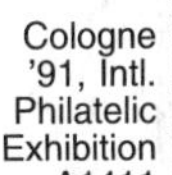

Cologne '91, Intl. Philatelic Exhibition A1411

1991, Oct. 21 *Perf. 13*
3641 A1411 86s multicolored 1.60 .75

Printed in sheets of 3 + 3 labels.

Souvenir Sheet

Brandenburg Gate, Bicent. — A1412

1991, Oct. 23
3642 A1412 4 l multicolored 7.50 3.50

Exists imperf.

Phila Nippon '91 A1413

1991, Nov. 11
3643 A1413 62s Japan #1 1.10 .55

Printed in sheets of 3 + 3 labels.

Bulgarian Railroad, 125th Anniv. — A1414

1991, Nov. 30
3644 A1414 30s Locomotive .55 .30
3645 A1414 30s Passenger car .55 .30

Medicinal Plants — A1415

Designs: 30s, Pulsatilla vernalis. 40s, Pulsatilla pratensis. 55s, Pulsatilla halleri. 60s, Aquilegia nigricans. 1 l, Hippophae rhamnoides. 2 l, Ribes nigrum.

1991, Nov. 20 Litho. *Perf. 13*
3646 A1415 30s +15s label .40 .20
3647 A1415 40s multicolored .35 .20
3648 A1415 55s multicolored .50 .25
3649 A1415 60s multicolored .55 .30
3650 A1415 1 l multicolored .90 .45
3651 A1415 2 l multicolored 1.75 .90
a. Min. sheet of 6, #3646-3651 4.75 2.50
Nos. 3646-3651 (6) 4.45 2.30

No. 3646 printed se-tenant with label. No. 3651a sold for 5 l, but does not contain the 15s label printed with No. 3646.

Basketball, Cent. A1416

1991, Dec. 6 *Perf. 13½x13*
3652 A1416 43s Ball below rim .50 .25
3653 A1416 62s Ball at rim .75 .40
3654 A1416 90s Ball in cylinder 1.10 .55
3655 A1416 1 l Ball in basket 1.25 .65
Nos. 3652-3655 (4) 3.60 1.85

El Greco, 450th Birth Anniv. — A1417

Paintings: 43s, Christ Carrying the Cross. 50s, Holy Family with St. Anne. 60s, St. John the Evangelist and St. John the Baptist. 62s, St. Andrew and St. Francis. 1 l, Holy Family with St. Mary Magdalene. 2 l, Cardinal Nino de Guevara. 3 l, Holy Family with St. Anne (detail).

1991, Dec. 13 *Perf. 13*
3656 A1417 43s multicolored .45 .25
3657 A1417 50s multicolored .55 .30
3658 A1417 60s multicolored .65 .35
3659 A1417 62s multicolored .70 .40
3660 A1417 1 l multicolored 1.10 .55
3661 A1417 2 l multicolored 2.00 1.00
Nos. 3656-3661 (6) 5.45 2.85

Souvenir Sheet

3662 A1417 3 l multicolored 4.25 2.00

No. 3662 contains one 43x53mm stamp.

Christmas — A1418

1991, Dec. 18
3663 A1418 30s Snowman, candle, bell, heart .55 .30
3664 A1418 62s Star, angel, flower, house, tree 1.10 .55

Marine Mammals — A1419

Designs: 30s, Phogophoca graenlandica. 43s, Orcinus orca. 62s, Odobenus rosmarus. 68s, Tursiops truncatus. 1 l, Monachus monachus. 2 l, Phocaena phocaena.

1991, Dec. 24
3665 A1419 30s multicolored .35 .20
3666 A1419 43s multicolored .50 .25
3667 A1419 62s multicolored .75 .40
3668 A1419 68s multicolored .80 .40
3669 A1419 1 l multicolored 1.25 .65
3670 A1419 2 l multicolored 2.50 1.25
a. Min. sheet of #3665-3670 6.50 3.25
Nos. 3665-3670 (6) 6.15 3.15

Settlement of Jews in Bulgaria, 500th Anniv. — A1420

1992, Mar. 5 **Litho.** ***Perf. 13***

3671 A1420 1 l multicolored 1.75 .90

Gioacchino Rossini (1792-1868), Composer — A1421

1992, Mar. 11

3672 A1421 50s multicolored .90 .45

Plovdiv Fair, Cent. A1422

1992, Mar. 25

3673 A1422 1 l buff & black 1.75 .90

Fiat Croma — A1423

Automobiles.

1992, Mar. 26 ***Perf. 13½x13***

3674 A1423 30s Volvo 740 .25 .20
3675 A1423 45s Ford Escort .45 .30
3676 A1423 50s shown .50 .30
3677 A1423 50s Mercedes 600 .50 .30
3678 A1423 1 l Peugeot 605 1.00 .55
3679 A1423 2 l BMW 316 1.50 .90
Nos. 3674-3679 (6) 4.20 2.55

Francisco de Orellana A1424

Explorers: No. 3681, Vespucci. No. 3682, Magellan. No. 3683, Gonzalo Jimenez de Quesada (1500-1579). 2 l, Drake. 3 l, Pedro de Valdivia (1500-1553). 4 l, Columbus.

1992, Apr. 22 **Litho.** ***Perf. 13***

3680 A1424 50s multicolored .45 .25
3681 A1424 50s multicolored .45 .25
3682 A1424 1 l multicolored .90 .45
3683 A1424 1 l multicolored .90 .45
3684 A1424 2 l multicolored 1.75 .90
3685 A1424 3 l multicolored 2.70 1.40
Nos. 3680-3685 (6) 7.15 3.70

Souvenir Sheet

3686 A1424 4 l multicolored 3.75 1.75

Granada '92 A1425

1992, Apr. 23

3687 A1425 62s multicolored .55 .30

No. 3687 printed in sheets of 3 + 3 labels.

Discovery of America, 500th Anniv. — A1426

1992, Apr. 24

3688 1 l Ships, map .75 .45
3689 2 l Columbus, ship 1.50 .90
a. A1426 Pair, #3688-3689 2.25 1.40

Europa.

SOS Children's Village A1427

1992, June 15 **Litho.** ***Perf. 13***

3690 A1427 1 l multicolored .90 .45

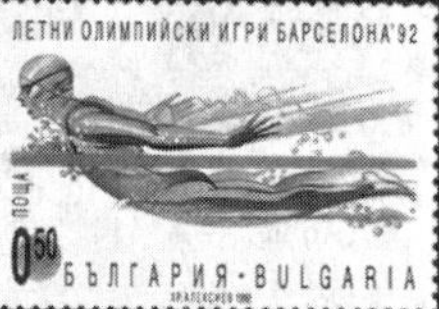

1992 Summer Olympics, Barcelona — A1428

1992, July 15 ***Perf. 13½x13***

3691 A1428 50s Swimming .45 .25
3692 A1428 50s Long jump .45 .25
3693 A1428 1 l High jump .90 .45
3694 A1428 3 l Gymnastics 2.70 1.40
Nos. 3691-3694 (4) 4.50 2.35

Souvenir Sheet

Perf. 13x13½

3695 A1428 4 l Torch, vert. 4.00 1.75

Motorcycles — A1429

Designs: 30s, 1902 Laurin & Klement. No. 3697, 1928 Puch 200 Luxus. No. 3698, 1931 Norton CS1. 70s, 1950 Harley Davidson. 1 l, 1986 Gilera SP 01. 2 l, 1990 BMW K1.

1992, July 30 ***Perf. 13***

3696 A1429 30s multicolored .20 .20
3697 A1429 50s multicolored .30 .20
3698 A1429 50s multicolored .30 .20
3699 A1429 70s multicolored .40 .20
3700 A1429 1 l multicolored .60 .30
3701 A1429 2 l multicolored 1.25 .65
Nos. 3696-3701 (6) 3.05 1.75

Genoa '92 Intl. Philatelic Exhibition A1430

1992, Sept. 18 ***Perf. 13***

3702 A1430 1 l multicolored .90 .45

This is a developing set. Numbers may change.

Insects A1431

1992 **Litho.** ***Perf. 14x13½***

3710 A1431 1 l Dragonfly *.20*
3711 A1431 2 l Mayfly *.25*
3712 A1431 3 l Locust *.30*
3713 A1431 4 l Stag beetle *.45*
3714 A1431 5 l Carrion beetle *.55*
3715 A1431 7 l Ant *.75*
3716 A1431 20 l Bee *2.25*
3717 A1431 50 l Praying mantis *5.75*
Nos. 3710-3717 (8) *10.50*

Issued: 7, 20 l, 9/25; 3, 50 l, 11/30; 1, 2, 4, 5 l, 12/15/93.

A1432

A1433

1992, Sept. 30 ***Perf. 13***

3719 A1432 1 l blk, pink & rose .90 .45

Higher Institute of Architecture and Building, 50th anniv.

1992, Oct. 16 **Litho.** ***Perf. 13***

Trees: No. 3720, Quercus mestensis. No. 3721, Aesculus hippocastanum. No. 3722, Quercus thracica. No. 3723, Pinus peuce. 2 l, Acer heldreichii. 3 l, Pyrus bulgarica.

3720 A1433 50s multicolored .30 .20
3721 A1433 50s multicolored .30 .20
3722 A1433 1 l multicolored .60 .30
3723 A1433 1 l multicolored .60 .30
3724 A1433 2 l multicolored 1.25 .65
3725 A1433 3 l multicolored 2.00 1.00
Nos. 3720-3725 (6) 5.05 2.65

Ethnographical Museum, Cent. — A1434

1992, Oct. 23

3726 A1434 1 l multicolored .90 .45

Tanker Bulgaria — A1435

1992, Oct. 30 **Litho.** ***Perf. 13***

3727 A1435 30s Freighter Bulgaria .20 .20
3728 A1435 50s Castor .30 .20
3729 A1435 1 l Hero of Sevastopol .60 .30
3730 A1435 2 l shown 1.25 .65
3731 A1435 2 l Aleko Constantinov 1.25 .65
3732 A1435 3 l Varna 2.00 1.00
Nos. 3727-3732 (6) 5.60 3.00

Bulgarian Merchant Fleet, Cent.

Bulgaria, Member of the Council of Europe — A1436

1992, Nov. 6 **Litho.** ***Perf. 13***

3733 A1436 7 l multicolored 6.25 3.00

Souvenir Sheet

4th World Congress of Popular Sports, Varna — A1437

1992, Nov. 17 **Litho.** ***Perf. 13***

3734 A1437 4 l multicolored *3.50*

Christmas A1438

1992, Dec. 1 ***Perf. 13½x13***

3735 A1438 1 l Santa Claus *.75*
3736 A1438 7 l Madonna & Child *5.25*

Wild Cats — A1439

1992, Dec. 18 **Litho.** ***Perf. 13***

3737 A1439 50s Panthera pardus *.25*
3738 A1439 50s Acinonyx jubatus *.25*
3739 A1439 1 l Panthera onca *.50*

3740 A1439 2 l Panthera tigris *1.00*
3741 A1439 2 l Felis concolor *1.00*
3742 A1439 3 l Panthera leo *1.50*
Nos. 3737-3742 (6) *4.50*

Sports A1440

1992, Dec. 18
3743 A1440 50s Baseball *.35*
3744 A1440 50s Cricket *.35*
3745 A1440 1 l Polo *.75*
3746 A1440 1 l Harness racing *.75*
3747 A1440 2 l Field hockey *1.50*
3748 A1440 3 l Football *2.25*
Nos. 3743-3748 (6) *5.95*

Owls A1441

1992, Dec. 23
3749 A1441 30s Aegolius funereus *.20*
3750 A1441 50s Strix aluco *.25*
3751 A1441 1 l Asio otus *.50*
3752 A1441 2 l Otus scops *1.00*
3753 A1441 2 l Asio flammeus *1.00*
3754 A1441 3 l Tyto alba *1.50*
Nos. 3749-3754 (6) *4.45*

Nos. 3749, 3751, 3753-3754 are vert.

Paintings Depicting History of Bulgaria A1442

Artists: 50s, Dimiter Gyudzhenov. 1 l, 3 l, Nikolai Pavlovich. 2 l, Dimiter Panchev. 4 l, Mito Ganovski.

1992, Dec. 28
3755 A1442 50s multicolored *.40*
3756 A1442 1 l multicolored *.75*
3757 A1442 2 l multicolored *1.50*
3758 A1442 3 l multicolored *2.25*
Nos. 3755-3758 (4) *4.90*

Souvenir Sheet

3759 A1442 4 l multicolored, vert. *3.25*

Archeological Museum, Cent. — A1443

1993 World Biathlon Championships, Borovetz — A1444

1993, Jan. 1 Litho. *Perf. 13x13½*
3760 A1443 1 l multicolored *.75*

1993, Feb. 5
3761 A1444 1 l Woman aiming rifle *.75*
3762 A1444 7 l Skiing *5.25*

Neophit Rilski, Birth Bicent. A1445

1993, Apr. 22 Litho. *Perf. 13½x13*
3763 A1445 1 l henna brn & ol bis *.75*

Contemporary Art — A1446

Europa: 3 l, Sculpture of centaur, by Georgi Chapkinov. 8 l, Painting of geometric forms, by D. Bujukliski.

1993, Apr. 29 *Perf. 13x13½*
3764 A1446 3 l multicolored *1.10*
3765 A1446 8 l multicolored *2.40*

Fish A1447

1993, June 29 Litho. *Perf. 13*
3766 A1447 1 l C.a.j. bicaudatus *.75*
3767 A1447 2 l Mollienesia velifera *1.50*
3768 A1447 3 l Aphyosemion bivittatum *2.25*
3769 A1447 3 l Pterophyllum eimekei *2.25*
3770 A1447 4 l Symphysodon discus *3.00*
3771 A1447 8 l Trichogaster leeri *6.00*
Nos. 3766-3771 (6) *15.75*

Fruit — A1448

1993, July 8 *Perf. 13x13½*
3772 A1448 1 l Malus domestica *.20*
3773 A1448 2 l Pyrus sativa *.30*
3774 A1448 2 l Persica vulgaris *.30*
3775 A1448 3 l Cydonia oblonga *.45*
3776 A1448 5 l Punica granatum *.90*
3777 A1448 7 l Ficus carica *1.40*
Nos. 3772-3777 (6) *3.55*

Claudio Monteverdi (1567-1643), Composer — A1449

1993, July 20 Litho. *Perf. 13½x13*
3778 A1449 1 l multicolored *.75*

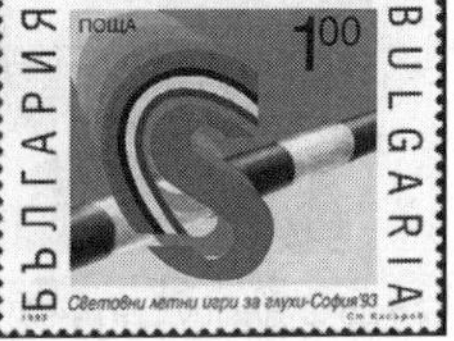
17th World Summer Games for the Deaf A1450

1993, July 20 *Perf. 13*
3779 A1450 1 l shown *.75*
3780 A1450 2 l Swimming *1.50*
3781 A1450 3 l Cycling *2.25*
3782 A1450 4 l Tennis *3.00*
Nos. 3779-3782 (4) *7.50*

Souvenir Sheet

3783 A1450 5 l Soccer

Miniature Sheet

A1451

Council of Preslav, Cyrillic Alphabet in Bulgaria, 1100th Anniv.: a, Baptism of Christian convert. b, Tsar Boris I (852-889). c, Tsar Simeon (893-927). d, Battle between Bulgarians and Byzantines.

1993, Sept. 16 Litho. *Perf. 13½x13*
3784 A1451 5 l Sheet of 4, #a.-d. *3.75*

Alexander of Battenberg (1857-93), Prince of Bulgaria — A1452

1993, Sept. 23 *Perf. 13x13½*
3785 A1452 3 l multicolored *.50*

Peter I. Tchaikovsky (1840-93) A1453

1993, Sept. 30 *Perf. 13½x13*
3786 A1453 3 l multicolored *.50*

Small Arms — A1454

Isaac Newton (1643-1725) A1455

1993, Oct. 22 Litho. *Perf. 13½x14*
3787 A1454 1 l Crossbow, 16th cent. *.20*
3788 A1454 2 l Pistol, 18th cent. *.35*
3789 A1454 3 l Luger, 1908 *.50*
3790 A1454 3 l Pistol, 1873 *.50*
3791 A1454 5 l Rifle, 1938 *.85*
3792 A1454 7 l Kalashnikov, 1947 *1.25*
Nos. 3787-3792 (6) *3.65*

1993, Oct. 29 *Perf. 13½x13*
3793 A1455 1 l multicolored *.20*

Organized Philately in Bulgaria, Cent. A1456

1993, Nov. 16
3794 A1456 1 l multicolored *.20*

Ecology A1457

1993, Nov. 17
3795 A1457 1 l shown *.20*
3796 A1457 7 l Ecology *1.25*

Game Animals A1458

1993, Nov. 25
3797 A1458 1 l Anas platrhynchos *.20*
3798 A1458 1 l Phasianus colchicus *.20*
3799 A1458 2 l Vulpes vulpes *.35*
3800 A1458 3 l Capreolus capreolus *.50*
3801 A1458 6 l Lepus europaeus *1.00*
3802 A1458 8 l Sus scrofa *1.40*
Nos. 3797-3802 (6) *3.65*

Christmas A1459

Signs of Zodiac on sundial: No. 3803a, Taurus, Gemini, Cancer. b, Libra, Virgo, Leo. No. 3804a, Aquarius, Pisces, Aries. b, Capricorn, Sagittarius, Scorpio.

1993, Dec. 1
3803 A1459 1 l Pair, #a.-b. *.35*
3804 A1459 7 l Pair, #a.-b. *2.50*

When placed together, Nos. 3803-3804 form a complete sundial.

Regional Folk Costumes for Men
A1460 A1461

1993, Dec. 16 Litho. *Perf. 13½x14*
3805 A1460 1 l Sofia *.20*
3806 A1461 1 l Plovdiv *.20*
3807 A1460 2 l Belogradchik *.25*
3808 A1460 3 l Shumen *.30*
3809 A1461 3 l Oryakhovitsa *.30*
3810 A1461 8 l Kurdzhali *.90*
Nos. 3805-3810 (6) *2.15*

1994 Winter Olympics, Lillehammer A1462

1994, Feb. 8 ***Perf. 13***

3811 A1462 1 l Freestlye skiing .20
3812 A1462 2 l Speed skating .25
3813 A1462 3 l 2-Man luge .30
3814 A1462 4 l Hockey .45
Nos. 3811-3814 (4) 1.20

Souvenir Sheet

3815 A1462 5 l Downhill skiing .60

Nikolai Pavlovich (1835-94) A1463

1994, Feb. 16 ***Perf. 13½x13***

3816 A1463 3 l multicolored .30

Dinosaurs — A1464

1994, Apr. 27 **Litho.** ***Perf. 13***

3817 A1464 2 l Plesiosaurus .20
3818 A1464 3 l Iguanodon .20
3819 A1464 3 l Archaeopteryx .20
3820 A1464 4 l Edmontonia .20
3821 A1464 5 l Styracosaurus .20
3822 A1464 7 l Tyrannosaurus Rex .30
Nos. 3817-3822 (6) 1.30

1994 World Cup Soccer Championships, US — A1465

Players in championships of : 3 l, Chile, 1962. 6 l, England, 1966. 7 l, Mexico, 1970. 9 l, West Germany, 1974. No. 3827a, Mexico, 1986, vert. b, US, 1994.

1994, Apr. 28

3823 A1465 3 l multicolored .20
3824 A1465 6 l multicolored .25
3825 A1465 7 l multicolored .30
3826 A1465 9 l multicolored .35
Nos. 3823-3826 (4) 1.10

Souvenir Sheet

3827 A1465 5 l Sheet of 2, #a.-b. .50

For No. 3827 with inscription reading up along the left margin, see No. 3851.

Europa A1466

European Discoveries: 3 l, Axis of symmetry. 15 l, Electrocardiogram.

1994, Apr. 29 **Litho.** ***Perf. 13½***

3828 A1466 3 l multicolored .60
3829 A1466 15 l multicolored 2.40

Boris Hristov (1914-93) — A1467

1994, May 18 **Litho.** ***Perf. 13***

3830 A1467 3 l brown & bister .20

Cricetus Cricetus A1468

Designs: 3 l, In nest. 7 l, Emerging from burrow. 10 l, Standing on hind legs. 15 l, Finding berry.

1994, Sept. 23 **Litho.** ***Perf. 13***

3831 A1468 3 l multicolored .25
3832 A1468 7 l multicolored .35
3833 A1468 10 l multicolored .45
3834 A1468 15 l multicolored .65
Nos. 3831-3834 (4) 1.70

World Wildlife Fund.

Space Program — A1469

Intl. Olympic Committee, Cent. — A1470

1994, Nov. 4 **Litho.** ***Perf. 13***

3835 A1469 3 l multicolored .20

1994, Nov. 7

3836 A1470 3 l multicolored .20

Icons — A1471

Christmas A1472

1994, Nov. 24 **Litho.** ***Perf. 13x13½***

3837 A1471 2 l Christ .20
3838 A1471 3 l Christ, the healer .20
3839 A1471 5 l Crucifixion .20
3840 A1471 7 l Archangel Michael .25
3841 A1471 8 l Sts. Cyril, Methodius .25
3842 A1471 15 l Madonna & Child .45
Nos. 3837-3842 (6) 1.55

1994, Dec. 1

3843 A1472 3 l Ancient coin .20
3844 A1472 15 l Coin, diff. 1.00

Roses A1473

1994, Dec. 12 ***Perf. 13***

Color of Rose

3845 A1473 2 l yellow .20
3846 A1473 3 l rose red .20
3847 A1473 5 l white .20
3848 A1473 7 l salmon .20
3849 A1473 10 l carmine .30
3850 A1473 15 l orange & yellow .40
Nos. 3845-3850 (6) 1.50

Souvenir Sheet

No. 3827 with Additional Inscription in Left Sheet Margin

1994, Dec. 15 **Litho.** ***Perf. 13***

3851 A1465 5 l Sheet of 2, #a.-b. .55

Trams — A1474

1994, Dec. 29

3852 A1474 1 l Model 1912 .20
3853 A1474 2 l Model 1928 .20
3854 A1474 3 l Model 1931 .20
3855 A1474 5 l Model 1942 .20
3856 A1474 8 l Model 1951 .25
3857 A1474 10 l Model 1961 .30
Nos. 3852-3857 (6) 1.35

Vassil Petleshkov (1845-76), Revolutionary — A1475

1995, Feb. 27 **Litho.** ***Perf. 13½x13***

3858 A1475 3 l multicolored .20

End of World War II, 50th Anniv. — A1476

Europa: 15 l, Dove holding olive branch standing on gun barrel.

1995, May 3 **Litho.** ***Perf. 13***

3859 A1476 3 l multicolored 1.00
3860 A1476 15 l multicolored 2.50

Souvenir Sheet

Men's World Volleyball League, Cent. A1477

Designs: a, 10 l, Player digging ball. b, 15 l, Player spiking ball, vert.

1995, May 25 **Litho.** ***Perf. 13***

3861 A1477 Sheet of 2, #a.-b. .80

Souvenir Sheet

European Nature Conservation Year — A1478

Designs: a, 10 l, Pancratium maritimum. b, 15 l, Aquila heliaca. Illustration reduced.

1995, June 23 **Litho.** ***Perf. 13***

3862 A1478 Sheet of 2, #a.-b. 2.00

Antarctic Wildlife — A1479

1 l, Euphausia superba. 2 l, Chaenocephalus. 3 l, Physeter catodon. 5 l, Leptonychotes weddelli. 8 l, Stercorarius skua. 10 l, Aptenodytes forsteri, vert.

1995, June 29

3863 A1479 1 l multicolored .20
3864 A1479 2 l multicolored .20
3865 A1479 3 l multicolored .20
3866 A1479 5 l multicolored .20
3867 A1479 8 l multicolored .25
3868 A1479 10 l multicolored .30
Nos. 3863-3868 (6) 1.35

Stephan Stambolov (1854-95), Revolutionary Leader, Politician — A1480

1995, July 6 **Litho.** ***Perf. 13***

3869 A1480 3 l multicolored .20

1996 Summer Olympics, Atlanta A1481

Designs: 3 l, Pole vault. 7 l, High jump. 10 l, Women's long jump. 15 l, Track.

1995, July 17

3870 A1481 3 l multicolored .20
3871 A1481 7 l multicolored .20
3872 A1481 10 l multicolored .30
3873 A1481 15 l multicolored .45
Nos. 3870-3873 (4) 1.15

Legumes — A1482

1995, July 31

3874 A1482 2 l Pisum sativum .20
3875 A1482 3 l Glicine .20
3876 A1482 3 l Cicer arietinum .20
3877 A1482 4 l Spinacia oleracea .20
3878 A1482 5 l Arachis hypogaea .20
3879 A1482 15 l Lens esculenta .45
Nos. 3874-3879 (6) 1.45

Organized Tourism in Bulgaria, Cent. — A1483

1995, Aug. 21 Litho. *Perf. 13*

3880 A1483 3 l multicolored .20

Vassil Zahariev (1895-1971), Graphic Artist — A1484

Designs: 2 l, Woodcut of a man. 3 l, Woodcut of building in valley. 5 l, Self-portrait. 10 l, Carving of two women.

1995, Sept. 4 Litho. *Perf. 13*

3881 A1484 2 l multicolored .20
3882 A1484 3 l multicolored .20
3883 A1484 5 l multicolored .20
3884 A1484 10 l multicolored .30
Nos. 3881-3884 (4) .90

UN, 50th Anniv. A1485

1995, Sept. 12

3885 A1485 3 l multicolored .20

Airplanes — A1486

1995, Sept. 26 Litho. *Perf. 13*

3886 A1486 3 l PO-2 .20
3887 A1486 5 l Li-2 .20
3888 A1486 7 l JU52-3M .20
3889 A1486 10 l FV-58 .30
Nos. 3886-3889 (4) .90

Motion Pictures, Cent. — A1487

Designs: 2 l, Charlie Chaplin, Mickey Mouse. 3 l, Marilyn Monroe, Marlene Dietrich. 5 l, Humphrey Bogart. 8 l, Sophia Loren, Liza Minnelli. 10 l, Toshiro Mifune. 15 l, Katya Paskaleva.

1995, Oct. 16

3890 A1487 2 l multicolored .20
3891 A1487 3 l multicolored .20
3892 A1487 5 l multicolored .20
3893 A1487 8 l multicolored .25
3894 A1487 10 l multicolored .30
3895 A1487 15 l multicolored .45
Nos. 3890-3895 (6) 1.60

Minerals A1488

1995, Nov. 20 Litho. *Perf. 13*

3896 A1488 1 l Agate .20
3897 A1488 2 l Sphalerite .20
3898 A1488 5 l Calcite .20
3899 A1488 7 l Quartz .20
3900 A1488 8 l Pyromorphite .25
3901 A1488 10 l Almandine .30
Nos. 3896-3901 (6) 1.35

Christmas A1489

1995, Dec. 8 Litho. *Perf. 13*

3902 A1489 3 l shown .20
3903 A1489 15 l Magi .45

Southern Fruit, by Cyril Tsonev (1896-1961) — A1490

1996, Jan. 25 Litho. *Perf. 13*

3904 A1490 3 l multicolored .20

Martin Luther (1483-1546) — A1491

1996, Feb. 5

3905 A1491 3 l multicolored .20

Historic Buildings A1492

Monasteries: 3 l, Preobragenie. 5 l, Arapovsky. 10 1, Drianovo. 20 l, Bachkovo. 25 l, Troyan. 40 l, Zografski.

1996, Feb. 28 *Perf. 14x13½*

3906 A1492 3 l green .20
3907 A1492 5 l red .20
3908 A1492 10 l blue .30
3909 A1492 20 l yellow orange .60
3910 A1492 25 l brown .75
3911 A1492 40 l purple 1.25
Nos. 3906-3911 (6) 3.30

5th Meeting of European Bank for Reconstruction and Development A1493

1996, Apr. 15 Litho. *Perf. 13*

3912 A1493 7 l shown .20
3913 A1493 30 l Building, diff. .50

Conifers A1494

Designs: 5 l, Taxus baccata. 8 l, Abies alba. 10 l, Picea abies. 20 l, Pinus silvestris. 25 l, Pinus heldreichii. 40 l, Juniperus excelsa.

1996, Apr. 23 *Perf. 13½x13*

3914 A1494 5 l multicolored .20
3915 A1494 8 l multicolored .20
3916 A1494 10 l multicolored .20
3917 A1494 20 l multicolored .30
3918 A1494 25 l multicolored .45
3919 A1494 40 l multicolored .65
Nos. 3914-3919 (6) 2.00

A1495

A1496

10 l, People in distress. 40 l, Khristo Botev (1848-1876), poet, patriot, horiz.

1996, May 1 *Perf. 13*

3920 A1495 10 l multicolored .20
3921 A1495 40 l multicolored .65

April Uprising, death of Khristo Botev, 120th anniv.

1996, May 6

Uniforms: 5 l, Light brown dress uniform. 8 l, Brown combat, helmet. 10 l, Brown uniform, holding gun with fixed bayonet. 20 l, Early red, blue dress uniform. 25 l, Officer's early green dress uniform. 40 l, Soldier's green uniform.

1996, May 6

3922 A1496 5 l multicolored .20
3923 A1496 8 l multicolored .20
3924 A1496 10 l multicolored .20
3925 A1496 20 l multicolored .30
3926 A1496 25 l multicolored .45
3927 A1496 40 l multicolored .65
Nos. 3922-3927 (6) 2.00

Republic of Bulgaria, 50th Anniv. — A1497

1996, May 13 Litho. *Perf. 13½*

3928 A1497 10 l multicolored .20

Famous Women A1498

Europa: 10 l, Elisaveta Bagriana (1893-1990), poet. 40 l, Katia Popova (1924-66), opera singer.

1996, May 29 Litho. *Perf. 13*

3929 A1498 10 l multicolored 1.00
Complete booklet, 5 #3929 5.50
3930 A1498 40 l multicolored 1.75
Complete booklet, 5 #3930 10.00

A1499

A1500

10 l, Soccer player. 15 l, Soccer player, diff.

1996, June 4

Souvenir Sheet

3931 A1499 Sheet of 2, #a.-b. .60

Euro '96, European Soccer Championships, Great Britain.

1996, July 4

3932 A1500 5 l Wrestling .20
3933 A1500 8 l Boxing .20
3934 A1500 10 l Women's shot put .25
3935 A1500 25 l Women sculling .60
Nos. 3932-3935 (4) 1.25

Souvenir Sheet

3936 A1500 15 l Pierre de Coubertin .40

1996 Summer Olympic Games, Atlanta. Olymphilex '96 (#3936).

Crabs A1501

Designs: 5 l, Gammarus arduus. 10 l, Asellus aquaticus. 12 l, Astacus astacus. 25 l, Palaemon serratus. 30 l, Cumella limicola. 40 l, Carcinus mediterraneus.

1996, July 30

3937 A1501 5 l multicolored .20
3938 A1501 10 l multicolored .25
3939 A1501 12 l multicolored .30
3940 A1501 25 l multicolored .60
3941 A1501 30 l multicolored .70
3942 A1501 40 l multicolored .95
Nos. 3937-3942 (6) 3.00

Francisco Goya (1746-1828) A1502

Entire paintings or details: 8 l, Young Woman with a Letter. 26 l, The Second of May, 1808. 40 l, Neighboring Women on a Balcony.

No. 3947: a, 10 l, The Clothed Maja. b, 15 l, The Naked Maja.

1996, July 9 Litho. *Perf. 13*

3943 A1502 5 l multicolored .20
3944 A1502 8 l multicolored .20
3945 A1502 26 l multicolored .60
3946 A1502 40 l multicolored 1.00
Nos. 3943-3946 (4) 2.00

Souvenir Sheet

Perf. 13½x13

3947 A1502 Sheet of 2, #a.-b. .65

No. 3947 contains two 54x29mm stamps.

Souvenir Sheet

St. John of Rila (876-946), Founder of Rila Monastery — A1503

1996, Sept. 3

3948 A1503 10 l multicolored .25

Bulgarian Renaissance Houses A1504

Various multi-level houses.

1996, Sept. 12 Litho. *Perf. 14x13½*

Background Color

3949 A1504 10 l buff .20
3950 A1504 15 l orange yellow .20
3951 A1504 30 l yellow green .30
3952 A1504 50 l red lilac .45
3953 A1504 60 l apple green .55
3954 A1504 100 l green blue .95
Nos. 3949-3954 (6) 2.65

Steam Locomotives — A1505

1996, Sept. 24 *Perf. 13*

3955 A1505 5 l 1836 .20
3956 A1505 10 l 1847 .20
3957 A1505 12 l 1848 .20
3958 A1505 26 l 1876 .25
Nos. 3955-3958 (4) .85

Natl. Gallery of Art, Cent. A1506

1996, Oct. 14 Litho. *Perf. 13*

3959 A1506 15 l multicolored .20

Defeat of Byzantine Army by Tsar Simeon, 1100th Anniv. — A1507

10 l, Sword hilt, soldiers on horseback. 40 l, Sword blade, dagger, fallen soldiers.

1996, Oct. 21

3960 A1507 10 l multicolored .20
3961 A1507 40 l multicolored .35
a. Pair, #3960-3961 .55

No. 3961 is a continuous design.

UNICEF, 50th Anniv. — A1508

Children's drawings: 7 l, Diver, fish. 15 l, Circus performers. 20 l, Boy, artist's pallete. 60 l, Women seated at table.

1996, Nov. 18 Litho. *Perf. 13*

3962 A1508 7 l multicolored .20
3963 A1508 15 l multicolored .30
3964 A1508 20 l multicolored .40
3965 A1508 60 l multicolored 1.25
Nos. 3962-3965 (4) 2.15

A1509

A1510

1996, Nov. 26

3966 A1509 15 l Candles on tree .30
3967 A1509 60 l Church 1.25

Christmas.

1996, Dec. 11 Litho. *Perf. 13*

Painting of Old Bulgarian Town, by Tsanko Lavrenov (1896-1978).

3968 A1510 15 l multicolored .30

Puppies A1511

1997, Feb. 25 Litho. *Perf. 13*

3969 A1511 5 l Pointer .20
3970 A1511 7 l Chow chow .20
3971 A1511 25 l Carakachan dog .30
3972 A1511 50 l Basset hound .60
Nos. 3969-3972 (4) 1.30

Alexander Graham Bell (1847-1922) — A1512

1997, Mar. 10

3973 A1512 30 l multicolored .40

Ivan Milev (1897-1927), Painter — A1513

Stories and Legends — A1514

Paintings: 5 l, Boy drinking from jar. 15 l, Person with head bowed holding up hand. 30 l, Woman. 60 l, Woman carrying child.

1997, Mar. 20

3974 A1513 5 l multicolored .20
3975 A1513 15 l multicolored .20
3976 A1513 30 l multicolored .50
3977 A1513 60 l multicolored 1.00
Nos. 3974-3977 (4) 1.90

1997, Apr. 14

Europa: 120 l, "March" lady in folk costume, symbol of spring. 600 l, St. George.

3978 A1514 120 l multicolored 1.25
3979 A1514 600 l multicolored 1.50

Konstantin Kissimov (1897-1965), Actor — A1515

1997, Apr. 16

3980 A1515 120 l multicolored .20

A1516

A1517

1997, Apr. 21

3981 A1516 60 l multicolored .20

Heinrich von Stephan (1831-97).

1997, May 2 *Perf. 13½*

Historical Landmarks: 80 l, Nessebar. 200 l, Ivanovo Rock Churches. 300 l, Boyana Church. 500 l, Madara horseman. 600 l, Tomb of Sveshtari. 1000 l, Tomb of Kazanlak.

3982 A1517 80 l brn & multi .20
3983 A1517 200 l pur & multi .20
3984 A1517 300 l bis & multi .30
3985 A1517 500 l grn & multi .45
3986 A1517 600 l yel & multi .55
3987 A1517 1000 l org & multi 1.00
Nos. 3982-3987 (6) 2.70

Composers A1518

Designs: a, Gaetano Donizetti (1797-1848). b, Franz Schubert (1797-1828). c, Felix Mendelssohn (1809-1847). d, Johannes Brahms (1833-1897).

1997, May 29 Litho. *Perf. 13½x13*

3988 A1518 120 l Sheet of 4, #a.-d. 1.10

Plants in Bulgaria's Red Book — A1519

Designs: 80 l, Trifolium rubens. 100 l, Tulipa hageri. 120 l, Inula spiraeifolia. 200 l, Paeonia tenuifolia.

1997, June 24 *Perf. 13*

3989 A1519 80 l multicolored .20
3990 A1519 100 l multicolored .20
3991 A1519 120 l multicolored .20
3992 A1519 200 l multicolored .25
Nos. 3989-3992 (4) .85

A1520

A1521

1997, June 29 Litho. *Perf. 13*
3993 A1520 120 l multicolored .20

Civil aviation in Bulgaria, 50th anniv.

1997, July 3
3994 A1521 120 l multicolored .20

Evlogy Georgiev (1819-97), banker, philanthopist.

Sofia '97, Modern Pentathlon World Championship — A1522

60 l, Equestrian cross-country, running. 80 l, Fencing, swimming. 100 l, Running, women's fencing. 120 l, Men's shooting, diving. 200 l, Equestrian jumping, women's shooting.

1997, July 25
3995 A1522 60 l multicolored .20
3996 A1522 80 l multicolored .20
3997 A1522 100 l multicolored .20
3998 A1522 120 l multicolored .20
3999 A1522 200 l multicolored .20
Nos. 3995-3999 (5) 1.00

City of Moscow, 850th Anniv. — A1523

1997, July 30
4000 A1523 120 l multicolored .20

No. 4000 is printed se-tenant with label for Moscow '97 Intl. Philatelic Exhibition.

Diesel Engine, Cent. A1524

1997, Sept. 8 Litho. *Perf. 13½x13*
4001 A1524 80 l Boat .20
4002 A1524 100 l Tractor .20
4003 A1524 120 l Truck .20
4004 A1524 200 l Forklift .30
Nos. 4001-4004 (4) .90

43rd General Assembly of Atlantic Club of Bulgaria — A1525

Designs: a, Goddess Tyche. b, Eagle on sphere. c, Building, lion statue, denomination UL. d, Building, denomination UR.

1997, Oct. 2 *Perf. 13*
4005 A1525 120 l Sheet of 4, #a.-d. .55

Miguel de Cervantes (1547-1616) — A1526

1997, Oct. 15
4006 A1526 120 l multicolored .20

Asen Raztsvetnikov (1897-1951), Poet, Writer — A1527

1997, Nov. 5
4007 A1527 120 l multicolored .20

Tsar Samuel (d. 1014), Ascension to Throne, 1000th Anniv. A1528

1997, Nov. 18 *Perf. 13½x13*
4008 A1528 120 l Inscription .20
4009 A1528 600 l Tsar, soldiers .85
a. Pair, #4008-4009 1.00

Christmas A1529

Designs: 120 l, Snow-covered houses, stars inside shape of Christmas tree, animals. 600 l, Nativity scene.

1997, Dec. 8 *Perf. 13x13½*
4010 A1529 120 l multicolored .20
4011 A1529 600 l multicolored .85

1998 Winter Olympic Games, Nagano A1530

Designs: 60 l, Speed skating. 80 l, Skiing. 120 l, Biathlon. 600 l, Pairs figure skating.

1997, Dec. 17 *Perf. 13½x13*
4012 A1530 60 l multicolored .20
4013 A1530 80 l multicolored .20
4014 A1530 120 l multicolored .20
4015 A1530 600 l multicolored .85
Nos. 4012-4015 (4) 1.45

For overprint see No. 4029.

Coat of Arms of Bulgaria A1531

1997, Dec. 22 Litho. *Perf. 13½x13*
4016 A1531 120 l multicolored .35

Souvenir Sheet

Bulgarian Space Program, 25th Anniv. — A1532

Illustration reduced.

1997, Dec. 22 *Perf. 13*
4017 A1532 120 l multicolored .35

Christo Botev (1848-76), Revolutionary, Poet — A1533

Bertolt Brecht (1898-1956), Playwright A1534

1998, Jan. 6 Litho. *Perf. 13*
4018 A1533 120 l multicolored .20

1998, Feb. 10
4019 A1534 120 l multicolored .20

Bulgarian Telegraph Agency, Cent. A1535

1998, Feb. 13
4020 A1535 120 l multicolored .20

Illustrations by Alexander Bozhinov (1878-1968) A1536

Designs: a, Bird wearing bonnet. b, Black bird wearing hat. c, Grandfather Frost, children. d, Girl among flowers looking upward at rain.

1998, Feb. 24 *Perf. 13½x13*
4021 A1536 120 l Sheet of 4, #a.-d. .60

A1537

Easter — A1538

1998, Feb. 27 *Perf. 13*
4022 A1537 120 l Prince Alexander .20
4023 A1537 600 l Monument .65
a. Pair, #4022-4023 .80

Bulgarian independence from Turkey, 120th anniv.

1998, Mar. 27 Litho. *Perf. 13*
4024 A1538 120 l multicolored .20

Bulgarian Olympic Committee, 75th Anniv. — A1539

1998, Mar. 30
4025 A1539 120 l multicolored .20

PHARE (Intl. Post and Telecommunications Program) — A1540

1998, Apr. 24 Litho. *Perf. 13*
4026 A1540 120 l multicolored .35

National Days and Festivals — A1541

Europa: 120 l, Girls with flowers, "Enyovden." 600 l, Masked men with bells, "Kukery."

1998, Apr. 27
4027 A1541 120 l multicolored .25
4028 A1541 600 l multicolored 1.75

No. 4014 Overprinted

1998, Apr. 29 *Perf. 13½x13*

4029 A1530 120 l multicolored 2.50

Dante and Virgil in Hell, by Eugene Delacroix (1798-1863) A1542

1998, Apr. 30

4030 A1542 120 l multicolored .35

A1543

A1544

1998, May 15 *Perf. 13*

4031 A1543 120 l multicolored .20

Soccer Team of Central Sports Club of the Army, 50th anniv.

1998, May 25

Cats: 60 l, European tabby. 80 l, Siamese. 120 l, Exotic shorthair. 600 l, Birman.

4032 A1544 60 l multicolored .20
4033 A1544 80 l multicolored .20
4034 A1544 120 l multicolored .20
4035 A1544 600 l multicolored 1.10
Nos. 4032-4035 (4) 1.70

Are You Jealous?, by Paul Gauguin (1848-1903) — A1545

1998, June 4

4036 A1545 120 l multicolored .30

Neophit Hylendarsky-Bozvely (1745-1848), Priest, Author — A1546

1998, June 4

4037 A1546 120 l multicolored .35

1998 World Cup Soccer Championships, France — A1547

Lion mascot with soccer ball, various stylized soccer plays.

1998, June 10

4038 A1547 60 l multicolored .20
4039 A1547 80 l multicolored .20
4040 A1547 120 l multicolored .35
4041 A1547 600 l multicolored 1.60
Nos. 4038-4041 (4) 2.35

Souvenir Sheet

4042 A1547 120 l Mascot, Eiffel Tower .35

A. Aleksandrov's Flight on Mir, 10th Anniv. — A1548

1998, June 17 **Litho.** *Perf. 13*

4043 A1548 120 l multicolored .20

Lisbon '98 — A1549

Designs: a, Map showing route around Cape of Good Hope, Vasco da Gama (1460-1524). b, Sailing ship, map of Africa.

1998, June 23

4044 A1549 600 l Sheet of 2, #a.-b. + 2 labels 1.40

Helicopters — A1550

80 l, Focke Wulf FW61, 1937. 100 l, Sikorsky R-4, 1943. 120 l, Mil Mi-12 (V-12), 1970. 200 l, McDonnell-Douglas MD-900, 1995.

1998, July 7 **Litho.** *Perf. 13*

4045 A1550 80 l multicolored .20 .20
4046 A1550 100 l multicolored .25 .25
4047 A1550 120 l multicolored .30 .30
4048 A1550 200 l multicolored .45 .45
Nos. 4045-4048 (4) 1.20 1.20

Souvenir Sheet

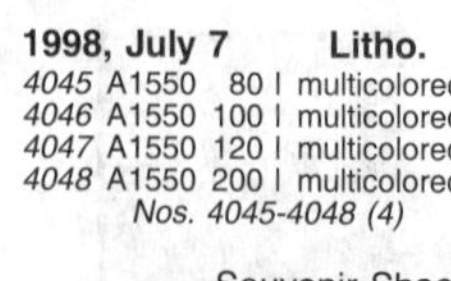

Intl. Year of the Ocean — A1551

Monachus monachus. Illustration reduced.

1998, July 14 **Litho.** *Perf. 13*

4049 A1551 120 l multicolored .35 .30

Dimitr Talev (1898-1966), Writer — A1552

1998, Sept. 14

4050 A1552 180 l multicolored .20 .20

A1553

A1554

1998, Sept. 22

4051 A1553 180 l multicolored .20 .20

Declaration of Bulgarian Independence, 90th anniv.

1998, Sept. 24

Butterflies, flowers: 60 l, Limenitis redukta, ligularia sibirica. 180 l, Vanessa cardui, anthemis macrantha. 200 l, Vanessa atalanta, trachelium jacquinii. 600 l, Anthocharis gruneri, geranium tuberosum.

4052 A1554 60 l multicolored .20 .20
4053 A1554 180 l multicolored .20 .20
4054 A1554 200 l multicolored .25 .25
4055 A1554 600 l multicolored .75 .75
Nos. 4052-4055 (4) 1.40 1.40

Christo Smirnenski (1898-1923), Poet — A1555

1998, Sept. 29

4056 A1555 180 l multicolored .20 .20

Universal Declaration of Human Rights, 50th Anniv. — A1556

1998, Oct. 26 **Litho.** *Perf. 13*

4057 A1556 180 l multicolored .20 .20

Giordano Bruno (1548-1600), Philosopher — A1557

1998, Oct. 26

4058 A1557 180 l multicolored .20 .20

Greetings Stamps A1558

#4059, Man diving through flaming heart, "I Love You." #4060, Baby emerging from chalice, "Happy Birthday." #4061, Grape vine, bird, wine coming from vat, "Happy Holiday." #4062, Waiter carrying tray with glass & ttle of wine, "Happy Name Day."

1998, Nov. 11

4059 A1558 180 l multi .20 .20
4060 A1558 180 l multi, vert. .20 .20
4061 A1558 180 l multi, vert. .20 .20
4062 A1558 180 l multi, vert. .20 .20
Nos. 4059-4062 (4) .80 .80

Christmas A1559

1998, Dec. 2 **Litho.** *Perf. 13½x13*

4063 A1559 180 l multicolored .20 .20

Ivan Geshov (1849-1924), Finance Minister — A1560

1999, Feb. 8 **Litho.** *Perf. 13*

4064 A1560 180 l multicolored .20 .20

Third Bulgarian State, 120th Anniv. — A1561

Designs: a, Reflection of National Assembly. b, Men, paper, Council of Ministers. c, Scales of Justice, Supreme Court of Appeal. d, Coins, Bulgarian Natl. Bank. e, Soldiers, Bulgarian Army. f, Lion, lightpost, Sofia, capital of Bulgaria.

1999, Feb. 10

4065 A1561 180 l Sheet of 6, #a.-f. 1.25 1.25

Bulgarian Culture and Art — A1562

180 l, Georgy Karakashev (1899-1970), set designer. 200 l, Bencho Obreshkov (1899-1970), artist. 300 l, Assen Naydenov (1899-1995), conductor. 600 l, Pancho Vladiguerov (1899-1978), composer.

1999, Mar. 12 Litho. *Perf. 13*

4066	A1562	180 l multicolored	.20	.20
4067	A1562	200 l multicolored	.20	.20
4068	A1562	300 l multicolored	.30	.30
4069	A1562	600 l multicolored	.50	.35
		Nos. 4066-4069 (4)	1.20	1.05

Bulgaria '99—A1562a

Parrots: a, Trichoglossus haematodus. b, Platycercus eximius. c, Melopsittacus undulatus. d, Ara chloroptera.

1999, Mar. 15 Litho. *Perf. 13x13¼*
Sheet of 4

4069A A1562a 600 l #a.-d. *20.00 16.00*

NATO, 50th Anniv. — A1563

1999, Mar. 29 Litho. *Perf. 13*

4070 A1563 180 l multicolored .20 .20

Easter A1564

1999, Apr. 1

4071 A1564 180 l multicolored .20 .20

National Parks and Nature Preserves — A1565

Europa: 180 l, Duck, pond, Ropotamo Preserve. 600 l, Ibex, waterfall, Central Balkan Natl. Park.

1999, Apr. 13 Litho. *Perf. 13*

4072	A1565	180 l multicolored	.40	.20
4073	A1565	600 l multicolored	1.10	.65

IBRA '99, Intl. Philatelic Exhibition, Nuremberg — A1566

1999, Apr. 15

4074 A1566 600 l multicolored .65 .65

No. 4074 is divided in half by vert. simulated perfs. and was issued in sheets of 3 + 3 labels.

Council of Europe, 50th Anniv. — A1567

1999, May 5 Litho. *Perf. 13*

4075 A1567 180 l multicolored .20 .20

Foreign Culture and Art — A1567a

Designs: 180 l, Honoré de Balzac (1799-1850), novelist. 200 l, Johann Wolfgang von Goethe (1749-1832), poet. 250 l, Aleksandr Pushkin (1799-1837), poet. 600 l, Diego Velázquez (1599-1660), painter.

1999, May 18

4076	A1567a	180 l multi	.20	.20
4077	A1567a	200 l multi	.20	.20
4078	A1567a	300 l multi	.30	.30
4078A	A1567a	600 l multi	.65	.65
		Nos. 4076-4078A (4)	1.35	1.35

Bicycles — A1568

Designs: 180 l, Large front-wheeled bicycle, 1867. 200 l, Multi-gear bicycle. 300 l, BMX racing bike. 600 l, Mountain racing bike.

1999, June 1 Litho. *Perf. 13¼*

4079	A1568	180 l multicolored	.20	.20
4080	A1568	200 l multicolored	.20	.20
4081	A1568	300 l multicolored	.35	.35
4082	A1568	600 l multicolored	.65	.65
		Nos. 4079-4082 (4)	1.40	1.40

Sts. Cyril and Methodius — A1569

Various paintings of Sts. Cyril and Methodius standing side by side with denomination at: a, UL. b, UR. c, LL. d, LR.

1999, June 15 Litho. *Perf. 13¼*

4083 A1569 600 l Sheet of 4, #a.-d. 12.50 10.00

Bulgaria '99, European Philatelic Exhibition.

Flowers A1570

a, Oxytropis urumovii. b, Campanula transsilvanica. c, Iris reichenbachii. d, Gentiana punctata.

1999, July 20

4084 A1570 60s Sheet of 4, #a.-d. 10.00 10.00

Bulgaria '99, European Philatelic Exhibition.

Mushrooms — A1571

Designs: a, 10s, Russula virescens. b, 18s, Agaricus campestris. c, 20s, Hygrophorus russula. d, 60s, Lepista nuda.

1999, July 27

4085 A1571 Sheet of 4, #a.-d. 2.75 2.75

Souvenir Sheet

Total Solar Eclipse, Aug. 11, 1999 — A1572

Illustration reduced.

1999, Aug. 10 *Perf. 13*

4086 A1572 20s multicolored .50 .50

A1573

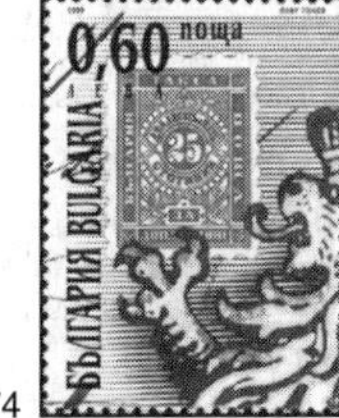

A1574

1999, Sept. 23 Litho. *Perf. 13*

4087 A1573 18s multicolored .20 .20

Organized agrarian movement in Bulgaria, 100th anniv.

Souvenir Sheet of 4

1999, Oct. 5 *Perf. 13x13½*

Lion (portion) and: a, No. J2. b, Dove and letter. c, Eastern hemisphere. d, Western hemisphere.

4088 A1574 60s #a.-d. 8.00 7.00

Bulgaria '99, UPU 125th anniv.

Birds, Eggs and Nests — A1575

8s, Lanius minor. 18s, Turdus viscivorus. 20s, Prunella modularis. 60s, Emberiza hortulana.

1999, Oct. 6 *Perf. 13*

4089	A1575	8s multicolored	.20	.20
4090	A1575	18s multicolored	.20	.20
4091	A1575	20s multicolored	.20	.20
4092	A1575	60s multicolored	.70	.70
		Nos. 4089-4092 (4)	1.30	1.30

Endangered Turtles — A1576

10s, Testudo graeca. 18s, Emys orbicularis. 30s, Testudo hermanni. 60s, Mauremys caspica.

1999, Oct. 8 *Perf. 13*

4093	A1576	10s multicolored	.20	.20
4094	A1576	18s multicolored	.20	.20
4095	A1576	30s multicolored	.40	.40
4096	A1576	60s multicolored	.75	.75
		Nos. 4093-4096 (4)	1.55	1.55

Olympic Sports A1577

1999, Oct. 10

4097 A1577	10s Boxing	.20	.20
4098 A1577	20s High jump	.20	.20
4099 A1577	30s Weight lifting	.35	.35
4100 A1577	60s Wrestling	.65	.65
	Nos. 4097-4100 (4)	1.40	1.40

Fountains — A1578

Fountains from: 1s, Sopotski Monastery. 8s, Karlovo. 10s, Koprivshchitsa. 18s, Sandanski. 20s, Karlovo. 60s, Sokolski Monastery.

1999 Litho. *Perf. 13½x14*

Fountain Color

4101 A1578	1s bister	.20	.20
4102 A1578	8s green	.20	.20
4103 A1578	10s brown	.20	.20
4104 A1578	18s light blue	.30	.30
4105 A1578	20s dark blue	.35	.35
4109 A1578	60s brown	1.00	1.00
	Nos. 4101-4109 (6)	2.25	2.25

Issued: 8s, 60s, 11/22/99; others, 1999.

This is an expanding set. Numbers may change.

Police Trade Unions' European Council, 10th Anniv. — A1579

1999, Nov. 8 Litho. *Perf. 13*

4113 A1579 18s multi .30 .30

A1580

A1581

Various gold artifacts from Panagyurishte.

1999, Nov. 15 *Perf. 13½x14*

4114 A1580	2s multi	.20	.20
4115 A1580	3s multi	.20	.20
4116 A1580	5s multi	.20	.20
4117 A1580	30s multi	.50	.50
4118 A1580	1 l multi	1.60	1.60
	Nos. 4114-4118 (5)	2.70	2.70

1999, Nov. 22 *Perf. 13*

4119 A1581	18s Icon, 1600	.30	.30
4120 A1581	60s Icon, 1607	1.00	1.00

Scouting A1582

10s, Scout, campfire. 18s, Scout assisting another. 30s, Salute. 60s, Scouts, cross.

1999, Dec. 6

4121 A1582	10s multi	.20	.20
4122 A1582	18s multi	.30	.30
4123 A1582	30s multi	.50	.50
4124 A1582	60s multi	1.00	1.00
	Nos. 4121-4124 (4)	2.00	2.00

Expo 2005, Japan — A1583

1999, Dec. 21 *Perf. 13*

4125 A1583 18s multi .30 .30

Start of Negotiations for Bulgaria's Entry into European Community — A1584

2000, Feb. 15 Litho. *Perf. 13*

4126 A1584 18s multi .30 .30

Souvenir Sheet

Ciconia Ciconia — A1585

Illustration reduced.

2000, Mar. 22

4127 A1585 60s multi 2.75 1.75

Petar Beron (1800-71), Scientist — A1586

Zakhari Stoyanov (1850-89), Writer — A1586a

Kolyo Ficheto (1800-81), Architect — A1586b

2000, Mar. 30 Litho. *Perf. 13¼*

4128 A1586	10s multi	.20	.20
4129 A1586a	20s multi	.30	.30
4130 A1586b	50s multi	.75	.75
	Nos. 4128-4130 (3)	1.25	1.25

Europa A1587

2000, Apr. 26 Litho. *Perf. 13*

4131 A1587	18s shown	.30	.30
4132 A1587	60s Madonna and child at R	1.00	1.00

2000 Summer Olympics, Sydney — A1588

2000, Apr. 28 *Perf. 13¼x13*

4133 A1588	10s Judo	.20	.20
4134 A1588	18s Tennis	.30	.30
4135 A1588	20s Shooting	.35	.35
4136 A1588	60s Long jump	1.00	1.00
	Nos. 4133-4136 (4)	1.85	1.85

Bulgarian Art A1589

Designs: No. 4137, Friends, by Assen Vassilev (1900-81). No. 4138, Landscape from Veliko Turnovo, by Ivan Hristov (1900-87). No. 4139, At the Fountain, sculpture by Ivan Funev (1900-83). No. 4140, All Souls' Day, by Pencho Georgiev (1900-40).

2000, May 23 *Perf. 13*

4137 A1589	18s multi	.30	.30
4138 A1589	18s multi	.30	.30
4139 A1589	18s multi	.30	.30
4140 A1589	18s multi	.30	.30
	Nos. 4137-4140 (4)	1.20	1.20

Souvenir Sheet

Fairy Tales — A1590

Designs: a, Puss in Boots, by Charles Perrault. b, Little Red Riding Hood, by the Brothers Grimm. c, Thumbelina, by Hans Christian Andersen.

Illustration reduced.

2000, May 23 *Perf. 13¼x13*

4141 A1590 18s Sheet of 3, #a-c + 3 labels .90 .90

Expo 2000, Hanover — A1591

Illustration reduced.

2000, May 31 *Perf. 13*

4142 A1591 60s multi + label 1.00 1.00

Birth and Death Anniversaries — A1592

Designs: 10s, Johann Gutenberg, inventor of movable type (c. 1400-68). 18s, Johann Sebastian Bach, composer (1685-1750). 20s, Guy de Maupassant, writer (1850-93). 60s, Antoine de Saint-Exupéry, writer (1900-44).

2000, June 20

4143 A1592	10s multi	.20	.20
4144 A1592	18s multi	.30	.30
4145 A1592	20s multi	.35	.35
4146 A1592	60s multi	1.00	1.00
	Nos. 4143-4146 (4)	1.85	1.85

Airships — A1593

Designs: 10s, Le Jaune over Paris. 18s, LZ-13 Hansa over Cologne. 20s, N-1 Norge over Rome. 60s, Graf Zeppelin over Sofia.

2000, July 3 Litho. *Perf. 13¼*

4147 A1593	10s multi	.20	.20
4148 A1593	18s multi	.25	.25
4149 A1593	20s multi	.30	.30
4150 A1593	60s multi	.85	.85
	Nos. 4147-4150 (4)	1.60	1.60

Ivan Vazov (1850-1921), Writer — A1594

2000, July 9

4151 A1594 18s multi .25 .25

Souvenir Sheet

European Security and Cooperation Conference, Helsinki, 25th Anniv. — A1595

No. 4152: a, Hands. b, Three "e's."

Illustration reduced.

2000, July 19 Litho. *Perf. 13*

4152 A1595 20s Sheet of 2, #a-b .60 .60

Churches
A1596

Panel colors: 22s, Blue. 24s, Red violet. 50s, Bister. 65s, Bright green. 3 l, Brown. 5 l, Red.

2000, Sept. 1 ***Perf. 14x13¾***
4153-4158 A1596 Set of 6 8.75 8.75

Animals
A1597

Designs: 10s, Capra ibex. 22s, Ovis ammon. 30s, Bison bonasus. 65s, Bos grunniens.

2000, Sept. 25 ***Perf. 13***
4159-4162 A1597 Set of 4 1.10 .75

Flowers — A1598

Designs: 10s, Gladiolus segetum. 22s, Hepatica nobilis. 30s, Adonis vernalis. 65s, Anemone pavonina.

2000, Oct. 17 ***Perf. 13x13¼***
4163-4166 A1598 Set of 4 1.10 .75

European Convention on Human Rights, 50th Anniv. A1599

2000, Nov. 3 **Litho.** ***Perf. 13¼x13***
4167 A1599 65s multi .65 .65

Bulgarian Orders — A1600

Designs: 12s, Bravery. 22s, St. Alexander. 30s, Citizen's merit. 65s, Sts. Cyril and Methodius.

2000, Nov. 28 ***Perf. 13***
4168-4171 A1600 Set of 4 1.25 1.25

Souvenir Sheet

Christianity, 2000th Anniv. — A1601

No. 4172: a, 22s, St. Boris Michael (2000 at UL). b, 22s, St. Sofroni Vrachanski (2000 at LL). c, 65s, Madonna and Child (2000 at UL). d, 65s, Exarch Antim I (2000 at LL).

2000, Nov. 28 ***Perf. 13¼x13***
4172 A1601 Sheet of 4, #a-d 1.75 1.75

First Bulgarian Law, 120th Anniv. — A1602

2000, Dec. 8 ***Perf. 13x13¼***
4173 A1602 22s multi .20 .20

Advent of New Millennium — A1603

2001, Jan. 8 ***Perf. 13x12¾***
4174 A1603 22s multi .20 .20

Souvenir Sheet

Electrified City Transport in Bulgaria, Cent. — A1604

No. 4175: a, 22s, Streetcar. b, 65s, Two streetcars.

2001, Jan. 12 ***Perf. 13***
4175 A1604 Sheet, 2 each #4175a-4175b 1.75 1.75

Viticulture
A1605

Wine glass, wine grapes and buildings: 12s, Muscat, Evxinograd Palace. 22s, Gumza, Baba Vida Fortress. 30s, Wide Melnik, houses in Melnik. 65s, Mavroud, Assenova Fortress.

2001, Feb. 7
4176-4179 A1605 Set of 4 1.25 1.25

Souvenir Sheet

Bulgaria and the Information Society — A1606

No. 4180: a, 22s, Circuits, "@" character. b, 65s, Letters, Dr. John Atanasov (1903-95), computer pioneer.

2001, Mar. 1 ***Perf. 13¼x13***
4180 A1606 Sheet, #a-b .85 .85

Souvenir Sheet

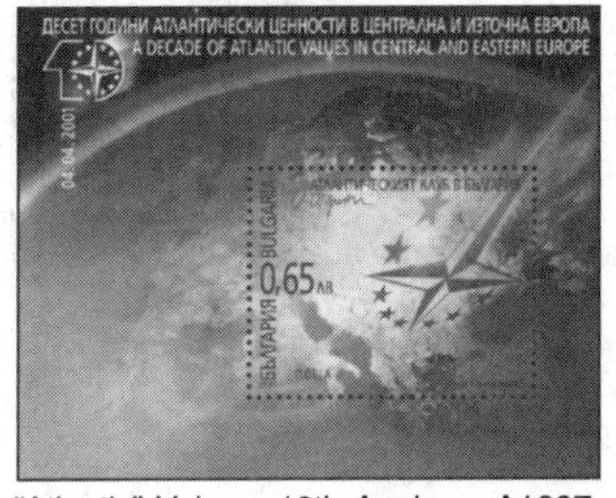
"Atlantic" Values, 10th Anniv. — A1607

2001, Apr. 4 ***Perf. 13x12¾***
4181 A1607 65s multi .60 .60

Europa
A1608

Designs: 22s, Aerial view of Rila Lakes. 65s, Rock bridges, Rhodope Mountains.

2001, Apr. 18 ***Perf. 12¾x13***
4182-4183 A1608 Set of 2 .80 .80

Todor Kableshkov (1851-1876), Organizer of 1876 April Uprising — A1609

2001, May 1 ***Perf. 13***
4184 A1609 22s multi .20 .20

Protected Species Neophron Percnopterus — A1610

Designs: 12s, Juvenile in flight. 22s, Juvenile with mouth open. 30s, Adult and chick. 65s, Adult and eggs.

2001, May 21 **Litho.** ***Perf. 13***
4185-4188 A1610 Set of 4 1.50 1.50

Souvenir Sheet

Athletes — A1611

No. 4189: a, 22s, Georgi Asparuchov (1943-71), soccer player. b, 30s, Dan Kolov (1892-1940), wrestler. c, 65s, Krum Lekarski (1898-1981), equestrian.

2001, June 29
4189 A1611 Sheet of 3, #a-c, + 3 labels 1.25 1.25

UN High Commissioner for Refugees, 50th Anniv. — A1612

2001, July 11
4190 A1612 65s multi .60 .60

Writers
A1613

Designs: 22s, Aleksandr Zhendov (1901-53). 65s, Ilya Beshkov (1901-58).

2001, July 24
4191-4192 A1613 Set of 2 .85 .85

Constitutional Court, 10th Anniv. — A1614

2001, Oct. 3
4193 A1614 25s multi .25 .25

Souvenir Sheet

Sofia Summit 2001 — A1615

Flags of various countries: a, 12s. b, 24s. c, 25s. d, 65s.

2001, Oct. 5 ***Perf. 13¼x13***
4194 A1615 Sheet of 4, #a-d 1.25 1.25

Year of Dialogue Among Civilizations A1616

2001, Oct. 9 ***Perf. 13***
4195 A1616 65s multi .60 .60

Souvenir Sheet

Intl. Black Sea Preservation Day — A1617

2001, Oct. 31
4196 A1617 65s multi .60 .60

Christmas A1618

2001, Nov. 19
4197 A1618 25s multi .25 .25

Lighthouses A1619

Designs: 25s, Shabla. 32s, Kaliakra.

2001, Nov. 19 ***Perf. 14x13½***
4198-4199 A1619 Set of 2 .55 .55

Souvenir Sheet

Zograf Monastery, Mount Athos, Greece — A1620

No. 4200: a, 25s, Monastery. b, 65s, Icon of St, George.

2001, Nov. 27
4200 A1620 Sheet of 2, #a-b .85 .85

Cartoons — A1621

Illustration reduced.

2001, Dec. 12 Litho. ***Perf. 13¼x13***
4201 A1621 25s multi + label .25 .25

Printed in sheets of 3 stamps and labels.

Vincenzo Bellini (1801-35), Italian Composer — A1622

2001, Dec. 17 ***Perf. 13***
4202 A1622 25s multi .25 .25

Builders of the Bulgarian State A1623

Designs: 10s, Ancient Bulgarian calendar. 25s, Khans Kubrat (632-51) and Asparukh (681-700). 30s, Khans Krum (803-14) and Omurtag (814-31). 65s, King Boris I (852-89) and Tsar Simeon I (893-927).

2001, Dec. 21
4203-4206 A1623 Set of 4 1.25 1.25

Introduction of Euro Currency in 12 European Nations — A1624

2002, Jan. 3
4207 A1624 65s multi .60 .60

UN Disarmament Committee, 50th Anniv. — A1625

2002, Jan. 23
4208 A1625 25s multi .25 .25

Souvenir Sheet

Balkanmax 2002 — A1626

No. 4209: a, 25s, Natural bridge. b, 65s, Buteo rufinus.

2002, Jan. 29
4209 A1626 Sheet of 2, #a-b .80 .80

2002 Winter Olympics, Salt Lake City A1627

Designs: 25s, Figure skater. 65s, Speed skater.

2002, Feb. 5 ***Perf. 13¼x13***
4210-4211 A1627 Set of 2 .80 .80

10th Natl. Antarctic Expedition — A1628

Illustration reduced.

2002, Mar. 20
4212 A1628 25s multi + label .25 .25

Issued in sheets of 3 stamps and 3 different labels.

Europa A1629

Circus performers: 25s, Elephant trainer. 65s, Clown.

2002, Mar. 22 ***Perf. 13***
4213-4214 A1629 Set of 2 .80 .80

Famous Bulgarians — A1630

Designs: 25s, Veselin Stoyanov (1902-69), composer. 34s, Angel Karaliichev (1902-72), writer.

2002, Mar. 27 ***Perf. 13¼x13***
4215-4216 A1630 Set of 2 .55 .55

Paintings — A1631

Designs: 10s, Industrial Landscape, by Vasil Barakov, vert. 25s, Illustration for book *Under the Yoke*, by Boris Angelushev. 65s, The Balcony and the Canary, by Ivan Nenov, vert.

2002, Apr. 17 ***Perf. 13***
4217-4219 A1631 Set of 3 .95 .95

Stamp Designers A1632

Designs: 25s, Stefan Kanchev (1915-2001). 65s, Alexander Popilov (1916-2001).

2002, Apr. 26 ***Perf. 13¼x13***
4220-4221 A1632 Set of 2 .85 .85

Fruits and Vegetables A1633

Designs: 10s, Cucumis melo. 25s, Citrullus lanatus. 27s, Cucurbita pepo. 65s, Lagenaria siceraria.

2002, May 8 Litho. *Perf. 13¼x13*
4222-4225 A1633 Set of 4 1.25 1.25

Roosters A1634

Designs: 10s, Bankivski, vert. 20s, Leghorn. 25s, Bergich Crower. 65s, Plymouth Rock, vert.

2002, May 10 *Perf. 13x13¼, 13¼x13*
4226-4229 A1634 Set of 4 1.10 1.10

Visit of Pope John Paul II to Bulgaria A1635

2002, May 24 Litho. *Perf. 13*
4230 A1635 65s multi .65 .65

Souvenir Sheet

Chess — A1636

No. 4231: a, 25s, Chess pieces. b, 65s, Hand moving piece.

2002, May 27
4231 A1636 Sheet of 2, #a-b .90 .90

Admission to Council of Europe, 10th Anniv. A1637

2002, May 29
4232 A1637 25s multi .25 .25

Carvings by Peter Kushlev A1638

Designs: 6s, Rabbit and fawn. 12s, Deer. 36s, Bird. 44s, Boar.

Perf. 13¾x13½
2002, Aug. 12 Litho.
4233-4236 A1638 Set of 4 1.00 1.00

Ships A1639

Designs: 12s, Maria Luisa. 36c, Percenk. 49c, Kaliakra. 65c, Sofia.

2002, Oct. 18 *Perf. 13¼x13*
4237-4240 A1639 Set of 4 1.60 1.60

Christmas A1640

2002, Nov. 20
4241 A1640 36s multi .40 .40

Souvenir Sheet

Invitation to Join NATO — A1641

2002, Nov. 21 *Perf. 13*
4242 A1641 65s multi .65 .65

Souvenir Sheet

Start of European Security and Cooperation Negotiations, 30th Anniv. — A1642

2002, Nov. 22 *Perf. 13¼x13*
4243 A1642 65s multi .65 .65

Tsars A1643

Designs: 18s, Samuel (d. 1014). 36s, Peter II (d. 1197), Assen (d. 1196). 49s, Kaloyan (d. 1207). 65s, Ivan Assen II (d. 1241).

2002, Dec. 6 Litho. *Perf. 13¼x13*
4244-4247 A1643 Set of 4 1.75 1.75

SEMI-POSTAL STAMPS

Catalogue values for unused stamps in this section are for Never Hinged items.

Regular Issues of 1911-20 Surcharged:

a

b

c

Perf. 11½x12, 12x11½
1920, June 20 Unwmk.
B1 A43 (a) 2s + 1s ol grn .20 .20
B2 A44 (b) 5s + 2½s grn .20 .20
B3 A44 (b) 10s + 5s rose .20 .20
B4 A44 (b) 15s + 7½s vio .20 .20
B5 A44 (b) 25s + 12½s dp bl .20 .20
B6 A44 (b) 30s + 15s choc .20 .20
B7 A44 (b) 50s + 25s yel brn .20 .20
B8 A29 (c) 1 l + 50s dk brn .20 .20
B9 A37a (a) 2 l + 1 l brn org .25 .25
B10 A38 (a) 3 l + 1½ l claret .55 .45
Nos. B1-B10 (10) 2.40 2.30

Surtax aided ex-prisoners of war. Value, Nos. B1-B7 imperf., $7.75.

Tsar Boris Type of 1937
Souvenir Sheet

1937, Nov. 22 Photo. *Imperf.*
B11 A140 2 l + 18 l ultra 6.00 4.00

19th anniv. of the accession of Tsar Boris III to the throne.

Stamps of 1917-21 Surcharged in Black

1939, Oct. 22 *Perf. 12½, 12*
B12 A34 1 l + 1 l on 15s slate .20 .20
B13 A69 2 l + 1 l on 1½ l ol grn .20 .20
B14 A69 4 l + 2 l on 2 l dp grn .20 .20
B15 A69 7 l + 4 l on 3 l Prus bl .50 .30
B16 A69 14 l + 7 l on 5 l red brn .85 .50
Nos. B12-B16 (5) 1.95 1.40

Surtax aided victims of the Sevlievo flood. The surcharge on #B13-B16 omits "leva."

Map of Bulgaria SP2

1947, June 6 Typo. *Perf. 11½*
B17 SP2 20 l + 10 l dk brn red & grn .45 .30

30th Jubilee Esperanto Cong., Sofia, 1947.

Postman — SP3

Radio Towers — SP6

#B19, Lineman. #B20, Telephone operators.

1947, Nov. 5
B18 SP3 4 l + 2 l ol brn .20 .20
B19 SP3 10 l + 5 l brt red .20 .20
B20 SP3 20 l + 10 l dp ultra .20 .20
B21 SP6 40 l + 20 l choc .70 .55
Nos. B18-B21 (4) 1.30 1.15

Christo Ganchev — SP7

Actors' Portraits: 10 l+6 l, Adriana Budevska. 15 l+7 l, Vasil Kirkov. 20 l+15 l, Sava Ognianov. 30 l+20 l, Krostyu Sarafov.

1947, Dec. 8 Litho. *Perf. 10½*
B22 SP7 9 l + 5 l Prus grn .20 .20
B23 SP7 10 l + 6 l car lake .20 .20
B24 SP7 15 l + 7 l rose vio .20 .20
B25 SP7 20 l + 15 l ultra .20 .20
B26 SP7 30 l + 20 l vio brn .50 .30
Nos. B22-B26 (5) 1.30 1.10

National Theater, 50th anniversary.

Souvenir Sheet

Olympic Emblem — SP8

1964, Oct. 10 Litho. *Imperf.*
B27 SP8 40s + 20s bis, red & bl 2.50 1.40

18th Olympic Games, Tokyo, Oct. 10-25.

Horsemanship Type of 1965
Miniature Sheet

1965, Sept. 30 Photo. *Imperf.*
B28 A630 40s + 20s Hurdle race 2.00 1.00

Space Exploration Type of 1966

Designs: 20s+10s, Yuri A. Gagarin, Alexei Leonov and Valentina Tereshkova. 30s+10s, Rocket and globe.

1966, Sept. 29 Photo. *Perf. 11½x11*
B29 A652 20s + 10s pur & gray 1.00 .35

Miniature Sheet
B30 A652 30s + 10s gray, fawn & blk 2.00 .95

Winter Olympic Games Type of 1967

Sports and Emblem: 20s+10s, Slalom. 40s+10s, Figure skating couple.

1967, Sept. Photo. *Perf. 11*
B31 A687 20s + 10s multi 1.10 .30

Souvenir Sheet
Imperf
B32 A687 40s + 10s multi 2.25 .85

Type of Olympic Games Issue, 1968

Designs: 20s+10s, Rowing. 50s+10s, Stadium, Mexico City, and communications satellite.

1968, June 24 Photo. *Perf. 10½*
B33 A702 20s + 10s vio bl, gray & pink 1.00 .30

Miniature Sheet
Imperf
B34 A702 50s + 10s gray, blk & Prus bl 2.25 1.50

Sports Type of Regular Issue, 1969

Designs: 13s+5s, Woman with ball. 20s+10s, Acrobatic jump.

1969, Oct. Photo. *Perf. 11*
Gymnasts in Light Gray
B35 A732 13s + 5s brt rose & vio .40 .20
B36 A732 20s + 10s citron & bl grn .70 .30

Miniature Sheet

Soccer Ball — SP9

1970, Mar. 4 Photo. *Imperf.*

B37	SP9	80s + 20s multi	2.25	1.40

9th World Soccer Championships for the Jules Rimet Cup, Mexico City, May 30-June 21, 1970.

Souvenir Sheet

Yuri A. Gagarin — SP10

1971, Apr. 12 Photo. *Imperf.*

B38	SP10	40s + 20s multi	2.25	1.10

10th anniversary of the first man in space.

SP11

SP12

Bulgarian lion, magnifying glass, stamp tongs

1971, July 10 Photo. *Perf. 12½*

B39	SP11	20s + 10s brn org, blk & gold	.90	.40

11th Congress of Bulgarian Philatelists, Sofia, July, 1971.

1989, Nov. 10 Litho. *Perf. 13x13½*

Toys: a, Skateboarding. b, Doll, ball. c, Rope. d, Train set.

Souvenir Sheet

B40	Sheet of 4	3.00	1.40
a.-d.	SP12 30s +15s any single	.65	.35

For the benefit of the Children's Foundation.

AIR POST STAMPS

Regular Issues of 1925-26 Overprinted in Various Colors

1927-28 Unwmk. *Perf. 11½*

C1	A76	2 l ol (R) ('28)	1.10	.70
C2	A74	4 l lake & yel (Bl)	1.10	.70
C3	A77	10 l brn blk & brn org (G) ('28)	17.00	13.00

Overprinted Vertically and Surcharged with New Value

C4	A77	1 l on 6 l dp bl & pale lem (C)	1.10	.70
a.		Inverted surcharge	*340.00*	*275.00*
b.		Pair, one without surcharge	*440.00*	
		Nos. C1-C4 (4)	20.30	15.10

Nos. C2-C4 overprinted in changed colors were not issued, value set $10.50.

Dove Delivering Message AP1

Junkers Plane, Rila Monastery AP2

1931, Oct. 28 Typo.

C5	AP1	1 l dk green	.20	.20
C6	AP1	2 l maroon	.20	.20
C7	AP1	6 l dp blue	.30	.20
C8	AP1	12 l carmine	.30	.30
C9	AP1	20 l dk violet	.65	.55
C10	AP1	30 l dp orange	1.00	1.25
C11	AP1	50 l orange brn	2.25	1.40
		Nos. C5-C11 (7)	4.90	4.10

Counterfeits exist. See Nos. C15-C18.

1932, May 9

C12	AP2	18 l blue grn	14.00	11.00
C13	AP2	24 l dp red	14.00	11.00
C14	AP2	28 l ultra	14.00	11.00
		Nos. C12-C14 (3)	42.00	33.00

Catalogue values for unused stamps in this section, from this point to the end of the section, are for Never Hinged items.

1938, Dec. 27

C15	AP1	1 l violet brown	.25	.20
C16	AP1	2 l green	.20	.20
C17	AP1	6 l deep rose	.70	.30
C18	AP1	12 l peacock blue	.85	.30
		Nos. C15-C18 (4)	2.00	1.00

Counterfeits exist.

Mail Plane — AP3

Plane over Tsar Assen's Tower — AP4

Designs: 4 l, Plane over Bachkovski Monastery. 6 l, Bojurishte Airport, Sofia. 10 l, Plane, train and motorcycle. 12 l, Planes over Sofia Palace. 16 l, Plane over Pirin Valley. 19 l, Plane over Rila Monastery. 30 l, Plane and Swallow. 45 l, Plane over Sofia Cathedral. 70 l, Plane over Shipka Monument. 100 l, Plane and Royal Cipher.

1940, Jan. 15 Photo. *Perf. 13*

C19	AP3	1 l dk green	.20	.20
C20	AP4	2 l crimson	1.10	.20
C21	AP4	4 l red orange	.20	.20
C22	AP3	6 l dp blue	.20	.20
C23	AP4	10 l dk brown	.30	.20
C24	AP3	12 l dull brown	.50	.20
C25	AP3	16 l brt bl vio	.55	.25
C26	AP3	19 l sapphire	.75	.30
C27	AP4	30 l rose lake	1.10	.50
C28	AP4	45 l gray violet	2.75	.95
C29	AP4	70 l rose pink	2.75	1.25
C30	AP4	100 l dp slate bl	9.00	3.75
		Nos. C19-C30 (12)	19.40	8.20

Nos. 368 and 370 Overprinted in Black

1945, Jan. 26

C31	A181	1 l bright green	.20	.20
C32	A181	4 l red orange	.20	.20

A similar overprint on Nos. O4, O5, O7 and O8 was privately applied.

Type of Parcel Post Stamps of 1944 Surcharged or Overprinted in Various Colors

Imperf

C37	PP5	10 l on 100 l dl yel (Bl)	.20	.20
C38	PP5	45 l on 100 l dl yel (C)	.30	.20
C39	PP5	75 l on 100 l dl yel (G)	.40	.25
C40	PP5	100 l dl yel (V)	.70	.35
		Nos. C37-C40 (4)	1.60	1.00

Plane and Sun — AP16

Pigeon with Letter — AP17

Plane, Letter AP18

Wings, Posthorn AP19

Winged Letter — AP20

Plane, Sun — AP21

Pigeon, Posthorn AP22

Mail Plane AP23

Conventionalized Figure Holding Pigeon — AP24

1946, July 15 Litho. *Perf. 13*

C41	AP16	1 l dull lilac	.20	.20
C42	AP16	2 l slate gray	.20	.20
C43	AP17	4 l violet blk	.20	.20
C44	AP18	6 l blue	.20	.20
C45	AP19	10 l turq green	.20	.20
C46	AP19	12 l yellow brn	.20	.20
C47	AP20	16 l rose violet	.20	.20
C48	AP19	19 l carmine	.20	.20
C49	AP21	30 l orange	.20	.20
C50	AP22	45 l lt ol grn	.20	.20
C51	AP22	75 l red brown	.25	.20
C52	AP23	100 l slate blk	.65	.25
C53	AP24	100 l red	.65	.25
		Nos. C41-C53 (13)	3.55	2.70

No. C47 exists imperf. Value $90.

People's Republic

Plane over Plovdiv AP25

1947, Aug. 31 Photo. *Imperf.*

C54	AP25	40 l dull olive grn	.60	.50

Plovdiv International Fair, 1947.

Baldwin's Tower — AP26

1948, May 23 Litho. *Perf. 11½*

C55	AP26	50 l ol brn, *cr*	.75	.60

Stamp Day and the 10th Congress of Bulgarian Philatelic Societies, June 1948.

Romanian and Bulgarian Parliament Buildings AP27

Romanian and Bulgarian Flags, Bridge over Danube AP28

1948, Nov. 3 Photo.

C56	AP27	40 l ol gray, *cr*	.25	.20
C57	AP28	100 l red vio, *cr*	.50	.30

Romanian-Bulgarian friendship.

Mausoleum of Pleven — AP29

1949, June 26

C58	AP29	50 l brown	2.00	1.25

7th Congress of Bulgarian Philatelic Associations, June 26-27, 1949.

Symbols of the UPU — AP30

Frontier Guard and Dog — AP31

1949, Oct. 10 *Perf. 11½*
C59 AP30 50 l violet blue 1.75 .75

75th anniv. of the UPU.

1949, Oct. 31
C60 AP31 60 l olive black 1.25 .90

Dimitrov Mausoleum AP32

1950, July 3 *Perf. 10½*
C61 AP32 40 l olive brown 3.00 1.50

1st anniv. of the death of George Dimitrov.

Belogradchic Rocks — AP33

Air View of Plovdiv Fair — AP34

Designs: 16s, Beach, Varna. 20s, Harvesting grain. 28s, Rila monastery. 44s, Studena dam. 60s, View of Dimitrovgrad. 80s, View of Trnovo. 1 l, University building, Sofia. 4 l, Partisans' Monument.

1954, Apr. 1 **Unwmk.** *Perf. 13*
C62 AP33 8s olive black .20 .20
C63 AP34 12s rose brown .20 .20
C64 AP33 16s brown .20 .20
C65 AP33 20s brn red, *cream* .20 .20
C66 AP33 28s dp bl, *cream* .20 .20
C67 AP33 44s vio brn, *cream* .20 .20
C68 AP33 60s red brn, *cream* .25 .20
C69 AP34 80s dk grn, *cream* .30 .20
C70 AP33 1 l dk bl grn, *cream* 1.25 .35
C71 AP34 4 l deep blue 3.00 .80
Nos. C62-C71 (10) 6.00 2.75

Glider on Mountainside AP35

60s, Glider over airport. 80s, Three gliders.

1956, Oct. 15 **Photo.**
C72 AP35 44s brt blue .20 .20
C73 AP35 60s purple .30 .20
C74 AP35 80s dk blue grn .50 .20
Nos. C72-C74 (3) 1.00 .60

30th anniv. of glider flights in Bulgaria.

Passenger Plane — AP36

1957, May 21 **Unwmk.** *Perf. 13*
C75 AP36 80s deep blue .65 .30

10th anniv. of civil aviation in Bulgaria.

Sputnik 3 over Earth AP37

1958, Nov. 28 *Perf. 11*
C76 AP37 80s brt grnsh blue 3.00 2.25

International Geophysical Year, 1957-58. Value, imperf. $7.50.

Lunik 1 Leaving Earth for Moon — AP38

1959, Feb. 28 *Perf. 10½*
C77 AP38 2 l brt blue & ocher 3.00 2.75

Launching of 1st man-made satellite to orbit moon. Value, imperf. in slightly different colors, $7.50 unused, $5.25 canceled.

Statue of Liberty and Tu-110 Airliner AP39

Perf. 10½
1959, Nov. 11 **Photo.** **Unwmk.**
C78 AP39 1 l violet bl & pink 1.75 1.50

Visit of Khrushchev to US. Value, imperf. $5.

Lunik 2 and Moon — AP40

1960, June 23 **Litho.** *Perf. 11*
C79 AP40 1.25 l blue, blk & yel 3.50 1.60

Russian rocket to the Moon, Sept. 12, 1959.

Sputnik 5 and Dogs Belka and Strelka — AP41

1961, Jan. 14 **Photo.** *Perf. 11*
C80 AP41 1.25 l brt grnsh bl & org 4.00 2.50

Russian rocket flight of Aug. 19, 1970.

Maj. Yuri A. Gagarin and Vostok 1 AP42

1961, Apr. 26 **Unwmk.**
C81 AP42 4 l grnsh bl, blk & red 2.50 1.50

First manned space flight, Apr. 12, 1961.

Soviet Space Dogs AP43

1961, June 28 *Perf. 11*
C82 AP43 2 l slate & dk car 2.00 1.00

Venus-bound Rocket — AP44

1961, June 28
C83 AP44 2 l brt bl, yel & org 4.00 2.50

Soviet launching of the Venus space probe, 2/12/61.

Maj. Gherman Titov AP45

Design: 1.25 l, Spaceship Vostok 2.

1961, Nov. 20 **Photo.** *Perf. 11x10½*
C84 AP45 75s dk ol grn & gray grn 1.75 1.00
C85 AP45 1.25 l vio bl, lt bl & pink 2.25 1.00

1st manned space flight around the world, Maj. Gherman Titov of Russia, 8/6-7/61.

Iskar River Narrows AP46

Designs: 2s, Varna and sailboat. 3s, Melnik. 10s, Trnovo. 40s, Pirin mountains.

1962, Feb. 3 **Unwmk.** *Perf. 13*
C86 AP46 1s bl grn & gray bl .20 .20
C87 AP46 2s blue & pink .20 .20
C88 AP46 3s brown & ocher .25 .20
C89 AP46 10s black & lemon .45 .20
C90 AP46 40s dk green & green 1.10 .30
Nos. C86-C90 (5) 2.20 1.10

Ilyushin Turboprop Airliner AP47

1962, Aug. 18 *Perf. 11*
C91 AP47 13s blue & black .60 .25

15th anniversary of TABSO airline.

Konstantin E. Tsiolkovsky and Rocket Launching — AP48

Design: 13s, Earth, moon and rocket on future flight to the moon.

1962, Sept. 24 *Perf. 11*
C92 AP48 5s dp green & gray 1.90 .85
C93 AP48 13s ultra & yellow 1.10 .35

13th meeting of the International Astronautical Federation.

Maj. Andrian G. Nikolayev — AP49

Designs: 2s, Lt. Col. Pavel R. Popovich. 40s, Vostoks 3 and 4 in orbit.

1962, Dec. 9 **Photo.** **Unwmk.**
C94 AP49 1s bl, sl grn & blk .20 .20
C95 AP49 2s bl grn, grn & blk .25 .20
C96 AP49 40s dk bl grn, pink & blk 1.60 .85
Nos. C94-C96 (3) 2.05 1.25

First Russian group space flight of Vostoks 3 and 4, Aug. 12-15, 1962.

Spacecraft "Mars 1" Approaching Mars — AP50

Design: 13s, Rocket launching spacecraft, Earth, Moon and Mars.

1963, Feb. 25 **Unwmk.** *Perf. 11*
C97 AP50 5s multicolored .50 .30
C98 AP50 13s multicolored 1.00 .45

Launching of the Russian spacecraft "Mars 1," Nov. 1, 1962.

Lt. Col. Valeri F. Bykovski AP51

Designs: 2s, Lt. Valentina Tereshkova. 5s, Globe and trajectories.

1963, Aug. 26 **Unwmk.** *Perf. 11½*
C99 AP51 1s pale vio & Prus bl .20 .20
C100 AP51 2s citron & red brn .20 .20
C101 AP51 5s rose & dk red .20 .20
Nos. C99-C101 (3) .60 .60

The space flights of Valeri Bykovski, June 14-19, and Valentina Tereshkova, first woman cosmonaut, June 16-19, 1963. An imperf. souvenir sheet contains one 50s stamp showing Spasski tower and globe in lilac and red brown. Light blue border with red brown inscription. Size: 77x67mm. Value $2.50. See No. CB3.

Nos. C99-C100 Surcharged in Magenta or Green

1964, Aug. 22

C102	AP51	10s on 1s (M)	.30	.20
C103	AP51	20s on 2s	.65	.25

International Space Exhibition in Riccione, Italy. Overprint in Italian on No. C103.

St. John's Monastery, Rila — AP52

13s, Notre Dame, Paris; French inscription.

1964, Dec. 22 Photo. *Perf. 11½*

C104	AP52	5s pale brn & blk	.20	.20
C105	AP52	13s lt ultra & sl bl	.65	.20

The philatelic exhibition at St. Ouen (Seine) organized by the Franco-Russian Philatelic Circle and philatelic organizations in various People's Democracies.

Paper Mill, Bukijovtz AP53

10s, Metal works, Plovdiv. 13s, Metal works, Kremikovtsi. 20s, Oil refinery, Stara-Zagora. 40s, Fertilizer plant, Stara-Zagora. 1 l, Rest home, Meded.

1964-68 Unwmk. *Perf. 13*

C106	AP53	8s grnsh blue	.20	.20
C107	AP53	10s red lilac	.20	.20
C108	AP53	13s brt violet	.25	.20
C109	AP53	20s slate blue	.75	.20
C110	AP53	40s dk olive grn	1.10	.20
C111	AP53	1 l red ('68)	1.90	.30
		Nos. C106-C111 (6)	4.40	1.30

Issue dates: 1 l, May 6. Others, Dec. 7.

Three-master AP54

Veliko Turnovo — AP55

Means of Communication: 2s, Postal coach. 3s, Old steam locomotive. 5s, Early cars. 10s, Montgolfier balloon. 13s, Early plane. 20s, Jet planes. 40s, Rocket and satellites. 1 l, Postrider.

1969, Mar. 31 Photo. *Perf. 13x12½*

C112	AP54	1s gray & multi	.20	.20
C113	AP54	2s gray & multi	.20	.20
C114	AP54	3s gray & multi	.20	.20
C115	AP54	5s gray & multi	.20	.20
C116	AP54	10s gray & multi	.20	.20
C117	AP54	13s gray & multi	.25	.20
C118	AP54	20s gray & multi	.50	.25
C119	AP54	40s gray & multi	.90	.40
		Nos. C112-C119 (8)	2.65	1.85

Miniature Sheet

Imperf

C120	AP54	1 l gold & org	2.25	1.50

SOFIA 1969 Philatelic Exhibition, Sofia, May 31-June 8.

1973, July 30 Photo. *Perf. 13*

Designs: Historic buildings in various cities.

C121	AP55	2s shown	.20	.20
C122	AP55	13s Roussalka	.25	.20
C123	AP55	20s Plovdiv	1.50	.80
C124	AP55	28s Sofia	.65	.20
		Nos. C121-C124 (4)	2.60	1.40

Aleksei A. Leonov and Soyuz AP56

Designs: 18s, Thomas P. Stafford and Apollo. 28s, Apollo and Soyuz over earth. 1 l, Apollo Soyuz link-up.

1975, July 15

C125	AP56	13s blue & multi	.30	.20
C126	AP56	18s purple & multi	.40	.20
C127	AP56	28s multicolored	1.00	.30
		Nos. C125-C127 (3)	1.70	.70

Souvenir Sheet

C128	AP56	1 l violet & multi	2.00	1.25

Apollo Soyuz space test project (Russo-American cooperation), launching July 15; link-up July 17.

Balloon Over Plovdiv — AP57

1977, Sept. 3

C129	AP57	25s yellow, brn & red	.50	.20

Alexei Leonov Floating in Space — AP58

Designs: 25s, Mariner 6, US spacecraft. 35s, Venera 4, USSR Venus probe.

1977, Oct. 14 Photo. *Perf. 13½*

C130	AP58	12s multicolored	.20	.20
C131	AP58	25s multicolored	.40	.20
C132	AP58	35s multicolored	.60	.25
		Nos. C130-C132 (3)	1.20	.65

Space era, 20 years.

TU-154, Balkanair Emblem AP59

1977 *Perf. 13*

C133	AP59	35s ultra & multi	.75	.35

30th anniv. of Bulgarian airline, Balkanair. Issued in sheets of 6 stamps + 3 labels (in lilac) with inscription and Balkanair emblem.

Baba Vida Fortress AP60

Design: 35s, Peace Bridge, connecting Rousse, Bulgaria, with Giurgiu, Romania.

1978 Photo. *Perf. 13*

C134	AP60	25s multicolored	.40	.40
C135	AP60	35s multicolored	.55	.55

The Danube, European Intercontinental Waterway. Issued in sheets containing 5 each of Nos. C134-C135 and 2 labels, one showing course of Danube, the other hydrofoil and fish.

Red Cross AP61

1978, Mar. Photo. *Perf. 13*

C136	AP61	25s multicolored	.50	.20

Centenary of Bulgarian Red Cross.

AP62

AP63

Clock towers.

1979, June 5 Litho. *Perf. 12x12½*

C137	AP62	13s Byalla Cherkva	.20	.20
C138	AP62	23s Botevgrad	.30	.20
C139	AP62	25s Pazardgick	.30	.20
C140	AP62	35s Grabovo	.40	.20
C141	AP62	53s Tryavna	.75	.30
		Nos. C137-C141 (5)	1.95	1.10

1980, Oct. 22 Photo. *Perf. 12x12½*

C142	AP62	13s Bjala	.20	.20
C143	AP62	23s Rasgrad	.35	.25
C144	AP62	25s Karnabat	.40	.20
C145	AP62	35s Serlievo	.50	.25
C146	AP62	53s Berkovitza	.80	.35
		Nos. C142-C146 (5)	2.25	1.25

1980

C147	AP63	13s shown	.20	.20
C148	AP63	25s Parachutist	.40	.20

15th World Parachute Championships, Kazanluk.

DWVY-1 Aircraft — AP64

1981, June 27 Litho. *Perf. 12½*

C149	AP64	5s shown	.20	.20
C150	AP64	12s LAS-7	.20	.20
C151	AP64	25s LAS-8	.40	.20
C152	AP64	35s DAR-1	.50	.20
C153	AP64	45s DAR-3	.70	.25
C154	AP64	55s DAR-9	.90	.30
		Nos. C149-C154 (6)	2.90	1.35

AP65

AP66

1983, June 28

C155		Sheet of 2	1.50	1.00
a.		AP65 50s Valentina Tereshkova	.75	.50
b.		AP65 50s Svetlana Savitskaya	.75	.50

Women in space, 20th anniv.

1983, July 20 Photo. *Perf. 13*

C156	AP66	5s TV tower, Tolbukhin	.20	.20
C157	AP66	13s Postwoman	.25	.20
C158	AP66	30s TV tower, Mt. Botev	.60	.30
a.		Strip of 3, #C156-C158	.95	.50

World Communications Year. Emblems of World Communications Year, Bulgarian Post, UPU and ITU on attached margins.

Souvenir Sheet

Geophysical Map of the Moon, Russia's Luna I, II and III Satellites — AP67

1984, Oct. 24 Photo. *Perf. 13*

C159	AP67	1 l multicolored	1.50	.75

Conquest of Space.

Intl. Civil Aviation Org., 40th Anniv. — AP68

1984, Dec. 21 Photo. Perf. 13
C160 AP68 42s Balkan Airlines jet .85 .40

Balkan Airlines — AP69

Design: Helicopter MU-8, passenger jet TU-154 and AN-21 transport plane.

1987, Aug. 25 Photo.
C161 AP69 25s multicolored .75 .35

2nd Joint Soviet-Bulgarian Space Flight — AP70

Cosmonauts: A. Aleksandrov, A. Solovov and V. Savinich.

1989, June 7 Litho. Perf. 13½x13
C162 AP70 13s multicolored .35 .20

AIR POST SEMI-POSTAL STAMPS

Catalogue values for unused stamps in this section are for Never Hinged items.

Statue of Liberty, Plane and Bridge SPAP1

Perf. 11½.
1947, May 24 Unwmk. Litho.
CB1 SPAP1 70 l + 30 l red brn .95 .95

5th Philatelic Congress, Trnovo, and CIPEX, NYC, May, 1947.

Bulgarian Worker SPAP2

1948, Feb. 28 Photo. Perf. 12x11½.
CB2 SPAP2 60 l henna brn, *crean* .45 .35

2nd Bulgarian Workers' Congress, and sold by subscription only, at a premium of 16 l over face value.

Type of Air Post Stamps, 1963

Valeri Bykovski & Valentina Tereshkova.

1963, Aug. 26 Unwmk. Perf. 11½
CB3 AP51 20s + 10s pale bluish grn & dk grn 1.25 .45

See note after No. C101.

SPECIAL DELIVERY STAMPS

Catalogue values for unused stamps in this section are for Never Hinged items.

Postman on Bicycle — SD1

Mail Car — SD2

Postman on Motorcycle — SD3

1939 Unwmk. Photo. Perf. 13
E1 SD1 5 l deep blue .60 .20
E2 SD2 6 l copper brn .25 .20
E3 SD3 7 l golden brn .35 .20
E4 SD2 8 l red orange .65 .20
E5 SD1 20 l bright rose 1.25 .40
Nos. E1-E5 (5) 3.10 1.20

POSTAGE DUE STAMPS

D1

D2

Large Lozenge Perf. 5½ to 6½
1884 Typo. Unwmk.
J1 D1 5s orange 160.00 15.00
J2 D1 25s lake 77.50 10.00
J3 D1 50s blue 13.00 5.00
Nos. J1-J3 (3) 250.50 30.00

1886 Imperf.
J4 D1 5s orange 75.00 2.50
J5 D1 25s lake 125.00 2.50
J6 D1 50s blue 5.00 2.75
Nos. J4-J6 (3) 205.00 7.75

1887 Perf. 11½
J7 D1 5s orange 9.50 1.00
J8 D1 25s lake 9.50 1.00
J9 D1 50s blue 3.50 1.00
Nos. J7-J9 (3) 22.50 3.00

Same, Redrawn

24 horizontal lines of shading in upper part instead of 30 lines

1892 Perf. 10½, 11½
J10 D1 5s orange 7.50 1.25
J11 D1 25s lake 7.50 1.25

1893
Pelure Paper
J12 D2 5s orange 10.00 3.50

D3

D4

1895 Imperf.
J13 D3 30s on 50s blue 7.00 2.00

Perf. 10½, 11½
J14 D3 30s on 50s blue 7.00 2.00

Wmk. Coat of Arms in the Sheet
1896 Perf. 13
J15 D4 5s orange 3.00 .75
J16 D4 10s purple 2.00 .75
J17 D4 30s green 1.40 .45
Nos. J15-J17 (3) 6.40 1.95

Nos. J15-J17 are also known on unwatermarked paper from the edges of sheets.

In 1901 a cancellation, "T" in circle, was applied to Nos. 60-65 and used provisionally as postage dues.

D5

D6

1901-04 Unwmk. Perf. 11½
J19 D5 5s dl rose .20 .20
J20 D5 10s yel grn .40 .20
J21 D5 20s dl bl ('04) 3.25 .20
J22 D5 30s vio brn .35 .20
J23 D5 50s org ('02) 5.50 4.00
Nos. J19-J23 (5) 9.70 4.80

Nos. J19-J23 exist imperf. and in pairs imperf. between. Value, imperf., $250.

1915 Unwmk. Perf. 11½
Thin Semi-Transparent Paper
J24 D6 5s green .20 .20
J25 D6 10s purple .20 .20
J26 D6 20s dl rose .20 .20
J27 D6 30s dp org 1.10 .20
J28 D6 50s dp bl .35 .20
Nos. J24-J28 (5) 2.05 1.00

1919-21 Perf. 11½, 12x11½
J29 D6 5s emerald .20 .20
a. 5s gray green ('21) .30 .20
J30 D6 10s violet .20 .20
J31 D6 20s salmon .20 .20
a. 20s yellow .20 .20
J32 D6 30s orange .20 .20
a. 30s red orange ('21) .65 .65
J33 D6 50s blue .20 .20
J34 D6 1 l emerald ('21) .20 .20
J35 D6 2 l rose ('21) .20 .20
J36 D6 3 l brown org ('21) .35 .20
Nos. J29-J36 (8) 1.75 1.60

Stotinki values of the above series surcharged 10s or 20s were used as ordinary postage stamps. See Nos. 182-185.

The 1919 printings are on thicker white paper with clean-cut perforations, the 1921 printings on thicker grayish paper with rough perforations.

Most of this series exist imperforate and in pairs imperforate between.

Heraldic Lion — D7

1932, Aug. 15
Thin Paper
J37 D7 1 l olive bister .25 .20
J38 D7 2 l rose brown .25 .20
J39 D7 6 l brown violet .75 .35
Nos. J37-J39 (3) 1.25 .75

Lion of Trnovo — D8

National Arms — D9

1933, Apr. 10
J40 D8 20s dk brn .20 .20
J41 D8 40s dp bl .20 .20
J42 D8 80s car rose .20 .20
J43 D9 1 l org brn .25 .20
J44 D9 2 l olive .30 .25
J45 D9 6 l dl vio .20 .20
J46 D9 14 l ultra .25 .20
Nos. J40-J46 (7) 1.60 1.45

Catalogue values for unused stamps in this section, from this point to the end of the section, are for Never Hinged items.

National Arms — D10

1947, June Typo. Perf. 10½
J47 D10 1 l chocolate .20 .20
J48 D10 2 l deep claret .20 .20
J49 D10 8 l deep orange .20 .20
J50 D10 20 l blue .25 .20
Nos. J47-J50 (4) .85 .80

Arms of the People's Republic — D11

1951 Perf. 11½x10½
J51 D11 1 l chocolate .20 .20
J52 D11 2 l claret .20 .20
J53 D11 8 l red orange .25 .20
J54 D11 20 l deep blue .60 .30
Nos. J51-J54 (4) 1.25 .90

OFFICIAL STAMPS

Catalogue values for unused stamps in this section are for Never Hinged items.

Bulgarian Coat of Arms
O1 O2

1942 Unwmk. Typo. Perf. 13
O1 O1 10s yel grn .20 .20
O2 O1 30s red .20 .20
O3 O1 50s bister .20 .20
O4 O2 1 l vio bl .20 .20
O5 O2 2 l dk grn .20 .20
O6 O2 3 l lilac .20 .20
O7 O2 4 l rose .20 .20
O8 O2 5 l carmine .20 .20
Nos. O1-O8 (8) 1.60 1.60

1944 Perf. 10½x11½
O9 O2 1 l blue .20 .20
O10 O2 2 l brt red .20 .20

Lion Rampant
O3 O4

O5

1945 Imperf.
O11 O5 1 l pink .20 .20

Perf. 10½x11½, Imperf.

O12	O3	2 l blue green	.20	.20
O13	O4	3 l bister brown	.20	.20
O14	O4	4 l light ultra	.20	.20
O15	O5	5 l brown lake	.20	.20
		Nos. O11-O15 (5)	1.00	1.00

In 1950, four stamps prepared for official use were issued as regular postage stamps. See Nos. 724-727.

PARCEL POST STAMPS

Catalogue values for unused stamps in this section are for Never Hinged items.

Weighing Packages — PP1

Parcel Post — PP2

Designs: 3 l, 8 l, 20 l, Parcel post truck. 4 l, 6 l, 10 l, Motorcycle.

Perf. 12½x13½, 13½x12½

1941-42 Photo. Unwmk.

Q1	PP1	1 l slate grn	.20	.20
Q2	PP2	2 l crimson	.20	.20
Q3	PP2	3 l dull brn	.20	.20
Q4	PP2	4 l red org	.20	.20
Q5	PP1	5 l deep blue	.20	.20
Q6	PP1	5 l slate grn ('42)	.20	.20
Q7	PP2	6 l red vio	.20	.20
Q8	PP2	6 l henna brn ('42)	.20	.20
Q9	PP1	7 l dark blue	.20	.20
Q10	PP1	7 l dk brn ('42)	.20	.20
Q11	PP2	8 l brt bl grn	.20	.20
Q12	PP2	8 l green ('42)	.25	.20
Q13	PP2	9 l olive gray	.20	.20
Q14	PP2	9 l dp olive ('42)	.20	.20
Q15	PP2	10 l orange	.20	.20
Q16	PP2	20 l gray vio	.40	.20
Q17	PP2	30 l dull blk	.55	.20
Q18	PP2	30 l sepia ('42)	.50	.20
		Nos. Q1-Q18 (18)	4.50	3.60

Arms of Bulgaria — PP5

1944 Litho. *Imperf.*

Q21	PP5	1 l dk carmine	.20	.20
Q22	PP5	3 l blue grn	.20	.20
Q23	PP5	5 l dull bl grn	.20	.20
Q24	PP5	7 l rose lilac	.20	.20
Q25	PP5	10 l deep blue	.20	.20
Q26	PP5	20 l orange brn	.20	.20
Q27	PP5	30 l dk brn car	.20	.20
Q28	PP5	50 l red orange	.30	.20
Q29	PP5	100 l blue	.50	.25
		Nos. Q21-Q29 (9)	2.20	1.85

For overprints and surcharges see Nos. 448-454, C37-C40.

POSTAL TAX STAMPS

The use of stamps Nos. RA1 to RA18 was compulsory on letters, etc., to be delivered on Sundays and holidays. The money received from their sale was used toward maintaining a sanatorium for employees of the post, telegraph and telephone services.

View of Sanatorium PT1

Sanatorium, Peshtera PT2

1925-29 Unwmk. Typo. *Perf. 11½*

RA1	PT1	1 l blk, *grnsh bl*	2.75	.20
RA2	PT1	1 l chocolate ('26)	2.75	.20
RA3	PT1	1 l orange ('27)	3.00	.20
RA4	PT1	1 l pink ('28)	4.50	.20
RA5	PT1	1 l vio, *pnksh* ('29)	4.25	.20
RA6	PT2	2 l blue green	.35	.20
RA7	PT2	2 l violet ('27)	.35	.20
RA8	PT2	5 l deep blue	3.00	.80
RA9	PT2	5 l rose ('27)	3.75	.40
		Nos. RA1-RA9 (9)	24.70	2.60

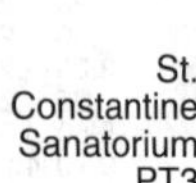

St. Constantine Sanatorium PT3

1930-33

RA10	PT3	1 l red brn & ol grn	4.00	.20
RA11	PT3	1 l ol grn & yel ('31)	.50	.20
RA12	PT3	1 l red vio & ol brn ('33)	.50	.20
		Nos. RA10-RA12 (3)	5.00	.60

Trojan Rest Home — PT4

Sanatorium PT5

1935 Wmk. 145 *Perf. 11, 11½*

RA13	PT4	1 l choc & red org	.30	.20
RA14	PT4	1 l emer & indigo	.30	.20
RA15	PT5	5 l red brn & indigo	1.40	.35
		Nos. RA13-RA15 (3)	2.00	.75

St. Constantine Sanatorium PT6

2 l, Children at seashore. 5 l, Rest home.

1941 Unwmk. Photo. *Perf. 13*

RA16	PT6	1 l dark olive green	.20	.20
RA17	PT6	2 l red orange	.20	.20
RA18	PT6	5 l deep blue	.30	.20
		Nos. RA16-RA18 (3)	.70	.60

See Nos. 702-705 for same designs in smaller size issued as regular postage.

BURKINA FASO

bur-'kē-nə-'fä-sō

Upper Volta

LOCATION — Northwestern Africa, north of Ghana
GOVT. — Republic
AREA — 105,869 sq. mi.
POP. — 11,575,898 (1999 est.)
CAPITAL — Ouagadougou

In 1919 the French territory of Upper Volta was detached from the southern section of Upper Senegal and Niger and made a separate colony. In 1933 the colony was divided among its neighbors: French Sudan, Ivory Coast, and Niger Territory. The Republic of Upper Volta was proclaimed December 11, 1958; the name was changed to Burkina Faso on August 4, 1984.

100 Centimes = 1 Franc

Catalogue values for unused stamps in this country are for Never Hinged items, beginning with Scott 70 in the regular postage section, Scott B1 in the semi-postal section, Scott C1 in the air-post section, Scott J21 in the postage due section, and Scott O1 in the official section.

See French West Africa Nos. 67, 84 for additional stamps inscribed "Haute Volta" and "Afrique Occidentale Francaise."

Stamps and Types of Upper Senegal and Niger, 1914-17, Overprinted in Black or Red

1920-28 Unwmk. *Perf. 13½x14*

No.	Type	Description	Unused	Used
1	A4	1c brn vio & vio	.20	.20
2	A4	2c gray & brn vio (R)	.20	.20
3	A4	4c blk & bl	.20	.20
4	A4	5c yel grn & bl grn	.60	.25
5	A4	5c ol brn & dk brn ('22)	.20	.20
6	A4	10c red org & rose	1.00	.50
7	A4	10c yel grn & bl grn ('22)	.20	.20
8	A4	10c claret & bl ('25)	.25	.25
a.		Overprint omitted	80.00	
9	A4	15c choc & org	.40	.30
10	A4	20c brn vio & blk (R)	.65	.55
11	A4	25c ultra & bl	.80	.50
12	A4	25c blk & bl grn ('22)	.45	.40
a.		Overprint omitted	65.00	
13	A4	30c ol brn & brn (R)	1.50	1.25
14	A4	30c red org & rose ('22)	.40	.35
15	A4	30c vio & brn red ('25)	.40	.35
16	A4	30c dl grn & bl grn ('27)	.70	.60
17	A4	35c car rose & vio	.45	.30
18	A4	40c gray & car rose	.45	.35
19	A4	45c bl & brn (R)	.35	.20
20	A4	50c blk & grn	1.75	1.25
21	A4	50c ultra & bl ('22)	.50	.50
22	A4	50c red org & bl ('25)	.60	.60
23	A4	60c org red ('26)	.20	.20
24	A4	65c bis & pale bl ('28)	.80	.60
25	A4	75c org & brn	.30	.30
26	A4	1fr brn & brn vio	.80	.70
27	A4	2fr grn & bl	1.25	.80
28	A4	5fr vio & blk (R)	2.50	2.25
		Nos. 1-28 (28)	18.10	14.35

No. 9 Surcharged in Various Colors

1922

No.	Type	Description	Unused	Used
29	A4	0,01c on 15c (Bk)	.40	.40
a.		Double surcharge	65.00	65.00
30	A4	0,02c on 15c (Bl)	.40	.40
31	A4	0,05c on 15c (R)	.40	.40
		Nos. 29-31 (3)	1.20	1.20

Type of 1920 Surcharged

1922

No.	Type	Description	Unused	Used
32	A4	60c on 75c vio, *pnksh*	.35	.35

Stamps and Types of 1920 Surcharged with New Value and Bars

1924-27

No.	Type	Description	Unused	Used
33	A4	25c on 2fr grn & bl	.45	.45
34	A4	25c on 5fr vio & blk	.45	.45
35	A4	65c on 45c bl & brn ('25)	.50	.50
36	A4	85c on 75c org & brn ('25)	.70	.70
37	A4	90c on 75c brn red & sal pink ('27)	.70	.70
38	A4	1.25fr on 1fr dp bl & lt bl (R) ('26)	.45	.45
39	A4	1.50fr on 1fr dp bl & ultra ('27)	1.25	1.25
40	A4	3fr on 5fr dl red & brn org ('27)	1.60	1.60
41	A4	10fr on 5fr ol grn & lil rose ('27)	7.25	7.25
42	A4	20fr on 5fr org brn & vio ('27)	10.00	10.00
		Nos. 33-42 (10)	23.35	23.35

Hausa Chief — A5

Hausa Woman — A6

Hausa Warrior A7

1928 Typo. *Perf. 13½x14*

No.	Type	Description	Unused	Used
43	A5	1c indigo & grn	.20	.20
44	A5	2c brn & lil	.20	.20
45	A5	4c blk & yel	.20	.20
46	A5	5c indigo & gray bl	.20	.20
47	A5	10c indigo & pink	.55	.55
48	A5	15c brn & bl	1.00	1.00
49	A5	20c brn & grn	1.00	1.00
50	A6	25c brn & yel	1.50	1.50
51	A6	30c dp grn & grn	1.40	1.40
52	A6	40c blk & pink	1.40	1.40
53	A6	45c brn & blue	2.00	2.00
54	A6	50c blk & grn	1.60	1.60
55	A6	65c indigo & bl	2.00	2.00
56	A6	75c blk & lil	1.75	1.75
57	A6	90c brn red & lil	1.75	1.75

Perf. 14x13½

No.	Type	Description	Unused	Used
58	A7	1fr brn & grn	1.50	1.50
59	A7	1.10fr indigo & lil	1.50	1.50
60	A7	1.50fr ultra & grysh	2.50	2.50
61	A7	2fr blk & bl	2.25	2.25
62	A7	3fr brn & yel	2.50	2.50
63	A7	5fr brn & lil	2.50	2.50
64	A7	10fr blk & grn	13.00	13.00
65	A7	20fr blk & pink	17.50	17.50
		Nos. 43-65 (23)	60.00	60.00

Common Design Types pictured following the introduction.

Colonial Exposition Issue
Common Design Types

1931 Engr. *Perf. 12½*
Country Name Typo. in Black

No.	Type	Description	Unused	Used
66	CD70	40c dp grn	2.00	2.00
67	CD71	50c violet	2.25	2.25
68	CD72	90c red org	2.25	2.25
69	CD73	1.50fr dull blue	2.75	2.75
		Nos. 66-69 (4)	9.25	9.25

Catalogue values for unused stamps in this section, from this point to the end of the section, are for Never Hinged items.

Republic

President Ouezzin Coulibaly — A8

Deer Mask and Deer — A9

1959 Unwmk. Engr. *Perf. 13*

No.	Type	Description	Unused	Used
70	A8	25fr black & magenta	.45	.40

1st anniv. of the proclamation of the Republic; Ouezzin Coulibaly, Council President, who died in December, 1958.

Imperforates
Most Upper Volta stamps from 1959 onward exist imperforate in issued and trial colors, and also in small presentation sheets in issued colors.

1960

Animal Masks: 1fr, 2fr, 4fr, Wart hog. 5fr, 6fr, 8fr, Monkey. 10fr, 15fr, 20fr, Buffalo. 25fr, Coba (antelope). 30fr, 40fr, 50fr, Elephant. 60fr, 85fr, Secretary bird.

No.	Type	Description	Unused	Used
71	A9	30c rose & violet	.20	.20
72	A9	40c buff & dp claret	.20	.20
73	A9	50c bl grn & gray ol	.20	.20
74	A9	1fr red, blk & red brn	.20	.20
75	A9	2fr emer, yel grn & dk grn	.20	.20
76	A9	4fr bl, vio & ind	.20	.20
77	A9	5fr ol bis, red & brn	.20	.20
78	A9	6fr grnsh bl & vio brn	.20	.20
79	A9	8fr org & red brn	.20	.20
80	A9	10fr lt yel grn & plum	.20	.20
81	A9	15fr org, ultra & brn	.20	.20
82	A9	20fr green & ultra	.25	.20
83	A9	25fr bl, emer & dp claret	.25	.20
84	A9	30fr dk bl grn, blk & brn	.30	.20
85	A9	40fr ultra, ind & dk car	.40	.20
86	A9	50fr brt pink, brn & grn	.45	.20
87	A9	60fr org brn & bl	.55	.25
88	A9	85fr gray ol & dk bl	.80	.30
		Nos. 71-88 (18)	5.20	3.75

C.C.T.A. Issue
Common Design Type

1960 Engr. *Perf. 13*

No.	Type	Description	Unused	Used
89	CD106	25fr vio bl & slate	.40	.25

Emblem of the Entente — A9a

Pres. Maurice Yameogo — A10

1960 Photo. *Perf. 13x13½*

No.	Type	Description	Unused	Used
90	A9a	25fr multicolored	.40	.30

Council of the Entente.

1960, May 1 Engr. *Perf. 13*

No.	Type	Description	Unused	Used
91	A10	25fr dk vio brn & slate	.25	.20

Flag, Village and Couple — A11

1960, Aug. 5 Unwmk. *Perf. 13*

No.	Type	Description	Unused	Used
92	A11	25fr red brn, blk & red	.40	.25

Proclamation of independence, Aug. 5, 1960.

World Meteorological Organization Emblem — A12

1961, May 4

No.	Type	Description	Unused	Used
93	A12	25fr blk, bl & red	.30	.25

First World Meteorological Day.

Arms of Republic — A13

1961, Dec. 8 Photo. *Perf. 12x12½*

No.	Type	Description	Unused	Used
94	A13	25fr multicolored	.25	.20

The 1961 independence celebrations.

WMO Emblem, Weather Station and Sorghum Grain — A14

1962, Mar. 23 Unwmk. *Perf. 13*

No.	Type	Description	Unused	Used
95	A14	25fr dk bl, emer & brn	.40	.35

UN 2nd World Meteorological Day, Mar. 23.

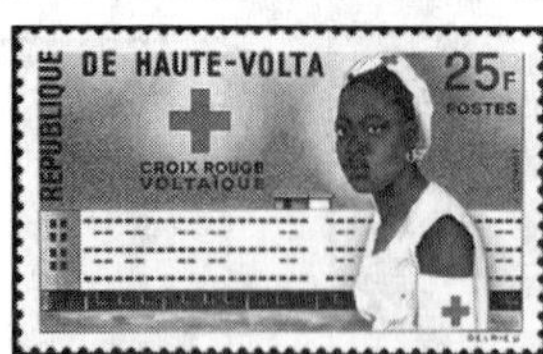

Hospital and Nurse — A15

1962, June 23 *Perf. 13x12*
96 A15 25fr multicolored .45 .35

Founding of Upper Volta Red Cross.

Buffalos at Water Hole — A16

Designs: 10fr, Lions, horiz. 15fr, Defassa waterbuck. 25fr, Arly reservation, horiz. 50fr, Diapaga reservation, horiz. 85fr, Buffon's kob.

Perf. 12½x12, 12x12½

1962, June 30 **Engr.**
97 A16 5fr sepia, bl & grn .20 .20
98 A16 10fr red brn, grn & yel .25 .20
99 A16 15fr sepia, grn & yel .60 .30
100 A16 25fr vio brn, bl & grn .60 .35
101 A16 50fr vio brn, bl & grn .85 .70
102 A16 85fr red brn, bl & grn 2.00 1.25
Nos. 97-102 (6) 4.50 3.00

Abidjan Games Issue
Common Design Type

Designs: 20fr, Soccer. 25fr, Bicycling. 85fr, Boxing. All horiz.

1962, July 21 **Photo.** ***Perf. 12½x12***
103 CD109 20fr multicolored .30 .20
104 CD109 25fr multicolored .50 .25
105 CD109 85fr multicolored .95 .40
Nos. 103-105 (3) 1.75 .85

African-Malgache Union Issue
Common Design Type

1962, Sept. 8 **Unwmk.**
106 CD110 30fr red, bluish grn & gold .70 .50

Weather Map and UN Emblem A17

1963, Mar. 23 ***Perf. 12x12½***
107 A17 70fr multicolored .85 .45

3rd World Meteorological Day, Mar. 23.

Friendship Games, Dakar, Apr. 11-21 — A18

1963, Apr. 11 **Engr.** ***Perf. 13***
108 A18 20fr Basketball .30 .20
109 A18 25fr Discus .30 .20
110 A18 50fr Judo .65 .25
Nos. 108-110 (3) 1.25 .65

Amaryllis A19

Flowers: 50c, Hibiscus. 1fr, Oldenlandia grandiflora. 1.50fr, Rose moss (portulaca). 2fr, Tobacco. 4fr, Morning glory. 5fr, Striga senegalensis. 6fr, Cowpea. 8fr, Lepidagathis heudelotiana. 10fr, Spurge. 25fr, Argyreia nervosa. 30fr, Rangoon creeper. 40fr, Water lily. 50fr, White plumeria. 60fr, Crotalaria retusa. 85fr, Hibiscus.

1963 **Photo.**
111 A19 50c multi, vert. .20 .20
112 A19 1fr multi, vert. .20 .20
113 A19 1.50fr multi, vert. .20 .20
114 A19 2fr multi, vert. .20 .20
115 A19 4fr multi, vert. .20 .20
116 A19 5fr multi, vert. .20 .20
117 A19 6fr multi, vert. .20 .20
118 A19 8fr multi, vert. .20 .20
119 A19 10fr multi, vert. .20 .20
120 A19 15fr multi .20 .20
121 A19 25fr multi .30 .20
122 A19 30fr multi .35 .20
123 A19 40fr multi .40 .30
124 A19 50fr multi .55 .40
125 A19 60fr multi .65 .45
126 A19 85fr multi .90 .55
Nos. 111-126 (16) 5.15 4.10

Centenary Emblem and Globe — A20

Scroll — A21

1963, Oct. 21 **Unwmk.** ***Perf. 12***
127 A20 25fr multicolored .60 .40

Centenary of International Red Cross.

1963, Dec. 10 **Photo.** ***Perf. 13x12½***
128 A21 25fr dp claret, gold & bl .45 .25

15th anniv. of the Universal Declaration of Human Rights.

Sound Wave Patterns A22

1964, Jan. 16 ***Perf. 12½x13***
129 A22 25fr multicolored .25 .20

Upper Volta's admission to the ITU.

Recording Rain Gauge and WMO Emblem A23

1964, Mar. 23 **Engr.** ***Perf. 13***
130 A23 50fr dk car rose, grn & bl .55 .40

4th World Meteorological Day, Mar. 23.

World Connected by Letters and Carrier Pigeon — A24

60fr, World connected by letters and jet plane.

1964, Mar. 29 **Photo.** ***Perf. 13x12***
131 A24 25fr gray brn & ultra .25 .20
132 A24 60fr gray brn & org .60 .40

Upper Volta's admission to the UPU.

IQSY Emblem and Seasonal Allegories — A25

1964, Aug. 17 **Engr.** ***Perf. 13***
133 A25 30fr grn, ocher & car .50 .25

International Quiet Sun Year.

Cooperation Issue
Common Design Type

1964, Nov. 7 **Unwmk.** ***Perf. 13***
134 CD119 70fr dl bl grn, dk brn & car .65 .40

Hotel Independance, Ouagadougou — A26

1964, Dec. 11 **Litho.** ***Perf. 12½x13***
135 A26 25fr multicolored 1.10 .45

Pigmy Long-tailed Sunbird — A27

Comoe Waterfall — A28

1965, Mar. 1 **Photo.** ***Perf. 13x12½***
Size: 22x36mm
136 A27 10fr shown .35 .20
137 A27 15fr Olive-bellied Sunbird .50 .25
138 A27 20fr Splendid Sunbird .80 .45
Nos. 136-138,C20 (4) 10.65 4.40

1965 **Engr.** ***Perf. 13***

25fr, Great Waterfall of Banfora, horiz.

139 A28 5fr yel grn, bl & red brn .30 .20
140 A28 25fr dk red, brt bl & grn .40 .20
Nos. 139-140 (2) .70 .40

Soccer — A29

Abraham Lincoln — A30

Designs: 25fr, Boxing gloves and ring. 70fr, Tennis rackets, ball and net.

1965, July 15 **Unwmk.** ***Perf. 13***
141 A29 15fr brn, red & dk grn .20 .20
142 A29 25fr pale org, bl & brn .30 .20
143 A29 70fr dk car & brt grn .60 .30
Nos. 141-143 (3) 1.10 .70

1st African Games, Brazzaville, July 18-25.

1965, Nov. 3 **Photo.** ***Perf. 13x12½***
144 A30 50fr green & multi .50 .40

Centenary of death of Abraham Lincoln.

Pres. Maurice Yameogo — A31

1965, Dec. 11 **Photo.** ***Perf. 13x12½***
145 A31 25fr multicolored .25 .20

Mantis A32

Wart Hog A33

Headdress A34

1966 ***Perf. 13x12½, 12½x13***
146 A33 1fr Nemopistha imperatrix .20 .20
147 A33 2fr Ball python .20 .20
148 A32 3fr shown .20 .20
149 A32 4fr Grasshopper .20 .20
150 A33 5fr shown .20 .20
151 A32 6fr Scorpion .20 .20
152 A33 8fr Green monkey .20 .20
153 A32 10fr Dromedary .40 .20
154 A33 15fr Leopard .40 .20
155 A32 20fr Cape buffalo .55 .20
156 A33 25fr Hippopotamus .60 .20
157 A32 30fr Agama lizard .45 .20
158 A33 45fr Common puff adder .90 .25
159 A33 50fr Chameleon 1.10 .35
160 A33 60fr Ugada limbata 1.40 .40
161 A33 85fr Elephant 1.50 .50
Nos. 146-161 (16) 8.50 3.90

1966, Apr. 9 **Photo.** ***Perf. 13x12½***

25fr, Plumed headdress. 60fr, Male dancer.

162 A34 20fr yel grn, choc & red .35 .20
163 A34 25fr multicolored .40 .20
164 A34 60fr org, dk brn & red 1.00 .35
Nos. 162-164 (3) 1.75 .75

Intl. Negro Arts Festival, Dakar, Senegal, 4/1-24.

Pô Church A35

Design: No. 166, Bobo-Dioulasso Mosque.

1966, Apr. 15 ***Perf. 12½x13***
165 A35 25fr multicolored .45 .20
166 A35 25fr bl, cream & red brn .45 .20

The Red Cross Helping the World — A36

1966, June **Photo.** ***Perf. 13x12½***
167 A36 25fr lemon, blk & car .40 .20

Issued to honor the Red Cross.

Boy Scouts in Camp A37

15fr, Two Scouts on a cliff exploring the country.

1966, June 15 ***Perf. 12½x13***
168 A37 10fr multicolored .20 .20
169 A37 15fr blk, bis brn, & dl yel .20 .20

Issued to honor the Boy Scouts.

Cow Receiving Injection A38

1966, Aug. 16 Photo. ***Perf. 12½x13***
170 A38 25fr yel, blk & blue .85 .35

Campaign against cattle plague.

Plowing with Donkey A39

Design: 30fr, Crop rotation, Kamboince Experimental Station.

1966, Sept. 15 Photo. ***Perf. 12½x13***
171 A39 25fr multicolored .45 .20
172 A39 30fr multicolored .45 .20

Natl. and rural education; 3rd anniv. of the Kamboince Experimental Station (No. 172).

UNESCO Emblem and Map of Africa A40

UNICEF Emblem and Children A41

1966, Dec. 10 Engr. ***Perf. 13***
173 A40 50fr brt bl, blk & red .50 .25
174 A41 50fr dk vio, dp lil & dk red .50 .25

20th anniv. of UNESCO and of UNICEF.

Arms of Upper Volta — A42

Symbols of Agriculture, Industry, Men and Women — A43

1967, Jan. 2 Photo. ***Perf. 12½x13***
175 A42 30fr multicolored .45 .20

Europafrica Issue

1967, Feb. 4 Photo. ***Perf. 12½***
176 A43 60fr multicolored .75 .30

Scout Handclasp and Jamboree Emblem A44

5fr, Jamboree emblem, Scout holding hat.

1967, June 8 Photo. ***Perf. 12½x13***
177 A44 5fr multicolored .25 .20
178 A44 20fr multicolored .65 .40

12th Boy Scout World Jamboree, Farragut State Park, Idaho, Aug. 1-9. See No. C41.

Bank Book and Hands with Coins A45

1967, Aug. 22 Engr. ***Perf. 13***
179 A45 30fr slate grn, ocher & olive .40 .20

National Savings Bank.

Mailman on Bicycle — A46

1967, Oct. 15 Engr. ***Perf. 13***
180 A46 30fr dk bl, emer & brn .55 .30

Stamp Day.

Monetary Union Issue
Common Design Type

1967, Nov. 4 Engr. ***Perf. 13***
181 CD125 30fr dk vio & dl bl .40 .20

View of Nizier A47

Olympic Emblem and: 50fr, Les Deux-Alps, vert. 100fr, Ski lift and view of Villard-de-Lans.

1967, Nov. 28
182 A47 15fr brt bl, grn & brn .30 .20
183 A47 50fr brt bl & slate grn .65 .40
184 A47 100fr brt bl, grn & red 1.40 .60
Nos. 182-184 (3) 2.35 1.20

10th Winter Olympic Games, Grenoble, France, Feb. 6-18, 1968.

White and Black Men Holding Human Rights Emblem A48

1968, Jan. 2 Photo. ***Perf. 12½x13***
185 A48 20fr brt bl, gold & dp car .40 .20
186 A48 30fr grn, gold & dp car .50 .20

International Human Rights Year.

Administration School and Student — A49

1968, Feb. 2 Engr. ***Perf. 13***
187 A49 30fr ol bis, Prus bl & brt grn .40 .30

National School of Administration.

WHO Emblem and Sick People A50

1968, Apr. 7 Engr. ***Perf. 13***
188 A50 30fr ind, brt bl & car rose .40 .20
189 A50 50fr brt bl, sl grn & lt brn .60 .25

WHO, 20th anniversary.

Telephone Office, Bobo-Dioulasso — A51

1968, Sept. 30 Photo. ***Perf. 12½x12***
190 A51 30fr multicolored .50 .35

Opening of the automatic telephone office in Bobo-Dioulasso.

Weaver A52

1968, Oct. 30 Engr. ***Perf. 13***
Size: 36x22mm
191 A52 30fr magenta, brn & ocher .45 .30

See No. C58.

Grain Pouring over World, Plower and FAO Emblem — A53

1969, Jan. 7 Engr. ***Perf. 13***
192 A53 30fr slate, vio bl & maroon .35 .30

UNFAO world food program.

Automatic Looms and ILO Emblem A54

1969, Mar. 15 Engr. ***Perf. 13***
193 A54 30fr brt grn, mar & indigo .40 .25

ILO, 50th anniversary.

Smith A55

1969, Apr. 3 Engr. ***Perf. 13***
Size: 36x22mm
194 A55 5fr magenta & blk .20 .20

See No. C64.

Blood Donor — A56

1969, May 15 Engr. ***Perf. 13***
195 A56 30fr blk, bl & car .55 .35

League of Red Cross Societies, 50th anniv.

Nile Pike — A57

Fish: 20fr, Nannocharax gobioides. 25fr, Hemigrammocharax polli. 55fr, Alestes luteus. 85fr, Micralestes voltae.

1969 Engr. ***Perf. 13***
Size: 36x22mm
196 A57 20fr brt bl, brn & yel .50 .20
197 A57 25fr slate, brn & dk brn .50 .20
198 A57 30fr dk olive & blk .75 .35
199 A57 55fr dk grn, yel & ol 1.00 .40
200 A57 85fr slate brn & pink 1.75 1.00
Nos. 196-200,C66-C67 (7) 7.50 3.60

Development Bank Issue
Common Design Type

1969, Sept. 10 Engr. ***Perf. 13***
201 CD130 30fr sl grn, grn & ocher .45 .30

Millet A58

Design: 30fr, Cotton.

1969, Oct. 30 Photo. ***Perf. 12½x13***
202 A58 15fr dk brn, grn & yel .20 .20
203 A58 30fr dp claret & brt bl .30 .20
Nos. 202-203,C73-C74 (4) 2.85 1.20

ASECNA Issue
Common Design Type

1969, Dec. 12 Engr. ***Perf. 13***
204 CD132 100fr brown .80 .50

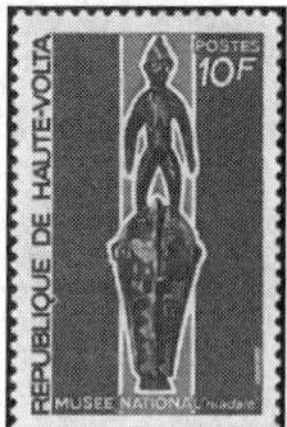

Niadale Mask — A59

Carvings from National Museum: 30fr, Niaga. 45fr, Man and woman, Iliu Bara. 80fr, Karan Weeba figurine.

1970, Mar. 5 Engr. ***Perf. 13***
207 A59 10fr dk car rose, org & dk brn .20 .20
209 A59 30fr dk brn, brt vio & grnsh bl .30 .20
211 A59 45fr yel grn, brn & bl .55 .30
212 A59 80fr pur, rose lil & brn .95 .50
Nos. 207-212 (4) 2.00 1.20

African Huts and European City — A60

1970, Apr. 25 Engr. ***Perf. 13***
213 A60 30fr dk brn, red & bl .45 .30

Issued for Linked Cities' Day.

Mask for Nebwa Gnomo Dance A61

Designs: 8fr, Cauris dancers, vert. 20fr, Gourmantchés dancers, vert. 30fr, Larllé dancers.

1970, May 7 Photo. *Perf. 13*

214 A61 5fr lt brn, vio bl & blk .25 .20
215 A61 8fr org brn, car & blk .25 .20
216 A61 20fr dk brn, sl grn & ocher .40 .20
217 A61 30fr dp car, dk gray & brn .50 .20
Nos. 214-217 (4) 1.40 .80

Education Year Emblem, Open Book and Pupils A62

Design: 90fr, Education Year emblem, telecommunication and education symbols.

1970, May 14 *Perf. 12½x12*

218 A62 40fr black & multi .35 .20
219 A62 90fr olive & multi .65 .35

International Education Year.

UPU Headquarters Issue

Abraham Lincoln, UPU Headquarters and Emblem — A63

1970, May 20 Engr. *Perf. 13*

220 A63 30fr dk car rose, ind & red brn .50 .20
221 A63 60fr dk bl grn, vio & red brn .75 .25

See note after CD133, Common Design section.

Ship-building Industry — A64

45fr, Chemical industry. 80fr, Electrical industry.

1970, June 15

222 A64 15fr brt pink, red brn & blk .55 .25
223 A64 45fr emerald, dp bl & blk .55 .25
224 A64 80fr red brn, claret & blk 1.10 .35
Nos. 222-224 (3) 2.20 .85

Hanover Fair.

Cattle Vaccination A65

1970, June 30 Photo. *Perf. 13*

225 A65 30fr Prus bl, yel & sepia .50 .20

National Veterinary College.

Vaccination and Red Cross — A66

1970, Aug. 28 Engr. *Perf. 12½x13*

226 A66 30fr chocolate & car .55 .30

Issued for the Upper Volta Red Cross. For surcharge see No. 252.

Europafrica Issue

Nurse with Child, by Frans Hals — A67

Paintings: 30fr, Courtyard of a House in Delft, by Pieter de Hooch. 150fr, Christina of Denmark, by Hans Holbein. 250fr, Courtyard of the Royal Palace at Innsbruck, Austria, by Albrecht Dürer.

1970, Sept. 25 Litho. *Perf. 13x14*

227 A67 25fr multicolored .25 .20
228 A67 30fr multicolored .35 .20
229 A67 150fr multicolored 1.40 .60
230 A67 250fr multicolored 2.00 1.00
Nos. 227-230 (4) 4.00 2.00

Citroen A68

Design: 40fr, Old and new Citroen cars.

1970, Oct. 16 Engr. *Perf. 13*

231 A68 25fr ol brn, mar & sl grn .80 .30
232 A68 40fr brt grn, plum & sl .95 .50

57th Paris Automobile Salon.

Professional Training Center A69

1970, Dec. 10 Engr. *Perf. 13*

233 A69 50fr grn, bis & brn .40 .20

Opening of Professional Training Center under joint sponsorship of Austria and Upper Volta.

Upper Volta Arms and Soaring Bird — A70

1970, Dec. 10 Photo.

234 A70 30fr lt blue & multi .35 .20

Tenth anniversary of independence, Dec. 11.

Political Maps of Africa — A71

1970, Dec. 14 Litho. *Perf. 13½*

235 A71 50fr multicolored .50 .25

10th anniv. of the declaration granting independence to colonial territories and countries.

Beingolo Hunting Horn — A72

Musical Instruments: 15fr, Mossi guitar, vert. 20fr, Gourounsi flutes, vert. 25fr, Lunga drums.

1971, Mar. 1 Engr. *Perf. 13*

236 A72 5fr blue, brn & car .20 .20
237 A72 15fr grn, crim rose & brn .40 .20
238 A72 20fr car rose, bl & gray .70 .20
239 A72 25fr brt grn, red brn & ol gray .70 .20
Nos. 236-239 (4) 2.00 .80

Voltaphilex I, National Phil. Exhibition.

Four Races — A73

1971, Mar. 21 Engr. *Perf. 13*

240 A73 50fr rose cl, lt grn & dk brn .50 .25

Intl. year against racial discrimination.

Telephone and Globes A74

1971, May 17 Engr. *Perf. 13*

241 A74 50fr brn, gray & dk pur .50 .25

3rd World Telecommunications Day.

Cane Field Worker, Banfora Sugar Mill — A75

Cotton and Voltex Mill Emblem — A76

1971, June 24 Photo. *Perf. 13*

242 A75 10fr multicolored .20 .20
243 A76 35fr multicolored .25 .20

Industrial development.

Gonimbrasia Hecate — A77

Butterflies and Moths: 2fr, Hamanumida daedalus. 3fr, Ophideres materna. 5fr, Danaus chrysippus. 40fr, Hypolimnas misippus. 45fr, Danaus petiverana.

1971, June 30

244 A77 1fr blue & multi .20 .20
245 A77 2fr lt lilac & multi .20 .20
246 A77 3fr multicolored .20 .20
247 A77 5fr gray & multi .40 .20
248 A77 40fr ocher & multi 1.75 .35
249 A77 45fr multicolored 2.25 1.00
Nos. 244-249 (6) 5.00 2.15

Kabuki Actor — A78

40fr, African mask and Kabuki actor.

1971, Aug. 12 Photo. *Perf. 13*

250 A78 25fr multicolored .25 .20
251 A78 40fr multicolored .40 .20

Philatokyo 71, Philatelic Exposition, Tokyo, Apr. 19-29.

No. 226 Surcharged

1971 Engr. *Perf. 12½x13*

252 A66 100fr on 30fr choc & car 1.00 .40

10th anniversary of Upper Volta Red Cross.

Seed Preparation A79

Designs: 75fr, Old farmer with seed packet, vert. 100fr, Farmer in rice field.

1971, Sept. 30 Photo. *Perf. 13*

253 A79 35fr ocher & multi .25 .20
254 A79 75fr lt blue & multi .50 .20
255 A79 100fr brown & multi .65 .35
Nos. 253-255 (3) 1.40 .75

National campaign for seed protection.

Outdoor Classroom A80

Design: 50fr, Mother learning to read.

1971, Oct. 14

256 A80 35fr multicolored .30 .20
257 A80 50fr multicolored .50 .20

Women's education.

Joseph Dakiri, Soldiers Driving Tractors — A81

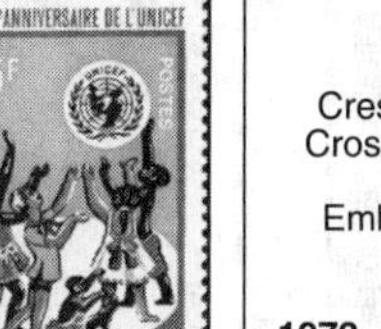
Children and UNICEF Emblem — A84

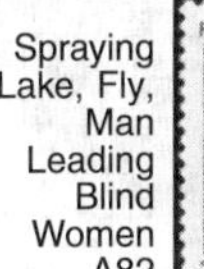

Spraying Lake, Fly, Man Leading Blind Women A82

40fr, Dakiri & soldiers gathering harvest.

1971, Oct. 13 ***Perf. 12x12½***

258 A81 15fr blk, yel & red brn .30 .20
259 A81 40fr blue & multi .45 .20

Joseph Dakiri (1938-1971), inaugurator of the Army-Aid-to-Agriculture Program.

1971, Nov. 26 **Photo.** ***Perf. 13***

260 A82 40fr dk brn, yel & bl .45 .25

Drive against onchocerciasis, roundworm infestation.
For surcharge see No. 295.

1971, Dec. 11 ***Perf. 13***

262 A84 45fr red, bister & blk .45 .25

UNICEF, 25th anniv.

Peulh House A85

Upper Volta Houses: 20fr, Gourounsi house. 35fr, Mossi houses. 45fr, Bobo house, vert. 50fr, Dagari house, vert. 90fr, Bango house, interior.

Perf. 13x13½, 13½x13

1971-72 **Photo.**

263 A85 10fr ver & multi .20 .20
264 A85 20fr multicolored .30 .20
265 A85 35fr brt grn & multi .35 .30
266 A85 45fr multi ('72) .50 .20
267 A85 50fr multi ('72) .55 .25
268 A85 90fr multi ('72) 1.10 .40
Nos. 263-268 (6) 3.00 1.55

Town Halls of Bobo-Dioulasso and Chalons-sur-Marne — A86

1971, Dec. 23 ***Perf. 13x12½***

269 A86 40fr yellow & multi .45 .25

Kinship between the cities of Bobo-Dioulasso, Upper Volta, and Chalons-sur-Marne, France.

Louis Armstrong — A87

1972, May 17 ***Perf. 14x13***

270 A87 45fr multicolored 1.25 .65

Black musician. See No. C104.

Red Crescent, Cross and Lion Emblems A88

1972, June 23 ***Perf. 13x14***

271 A88 40fr yellow & multi .50 .35

World Red Cross Day. See No. C105.

Coiffure of Peulh Woman — A89

Designs: Various hair styles.

1972, July 23 **Litho.** ***Perf. 13***

272 A89 25fr blue & multi .20 .20
273 A89 35fr emerald & multi .25 .20
274 A89 75fr yellow & multi .45 .20
Nos. 272-274 (3) .90 .60

Classroom A90

15fr, Clinic. 20fr, Factory. 35fr, Cattle. 40fr, Plowers. 85fr, Road building machinery.

1972, Oct. 30 **Engr.** ***Perf. 13***

275 A90 10fr sl grn, lt grn & choc .20 .20
276 A90 15fr brt grn, brn org & brn .20 .20
277 A90 20fr bl, lt brn & grn .35 .20
278 A90 35fr grn, brn & brt bl .60 .20
279 A90 40fr choc, pink & sl grn .60 .35
Nos. 275-279,C106 (6) 2.85 1.65

2nd Five-Year Plan.

West African Monetary Union Issue

Common Design Type

1972, Nov. 2

280 CD136 40fr brn, bl & gray .25 .20

Lottery Office and Emblem A91

1972, Nov. 6 **Litho.**

281 A91 35fr multicolored .35 .20

5th anniversary of National Lottery.

Domestic Animals — A92

1972, Dec. 4 **Litho.** ***Perf. 13½x12½***

282 A92 5fr Donkeys .20 .20
283 A92 10fr Geese .20 .20
284 A92 30fr Goats .35 .20
285 A92 50fr Cow .45 .20
286 A92 65fr Dromedaries .70 .35
Nos. 282-286 (5) 1.90 1.15

Mossi Woman's Hair Style, and Village — A93

1973, Jan. 24 **Engr.** ***Perf. 13***

287 A93 5fr slate grn, org & choc .30 .20
288 A93 40fr bl, org & chocolate .40 .20

Eugene A. Cernan and Lunar Module A94

65fr, Ronald E. Evans & splashdown. 100fr, Capsule, in orbit & interior, horiz. 150fr, Harrison H. Schmitt & lift-off. 200fr, Conference & moon-buggy. 500fr, Moon-buggy & capsule, horiz.

Perf. 12½x13½, 13½x12½

1973, Mar. 29 **Litho.**

289 A94 50fr multi .30 .20
290 A94 65fr multi .40 .20
291 A94 100fr multi .60 .30
292 A94 150fr multi .90 .45
293 A94 200fr multi 1.25 .60
Nos. 289-293 (5) 3.45 1.75

Souvenir Sheet

294 A94 500fr multi 3.50 1.60

Apollo 17 moon mission.

No. 260 Surcharged in Red

1973, Apr. 7 **Photo.** ***Perf. 13***

295 A82 45fr on 40fr multi .50 .25

WHO, 25th anniversary.

Scout Bugler A95

1973, July 18 **Litho.** ***Perf. 12½x13***

296 A95 20fr multicolored .20 .20
Nos. 296,C160-C163 (5) 3.35 1.80

African Postal Union Issue

Common Design Type

1973, Sept. 12 **Engr.** ***Perf. 13***

297 CD137 100fr brt red, mag & dl yel .65 .25

Pres. Kennedy, Saturn 5 on Assembly Trailer A96

Pres. John F. Kennedy (1917-1963) and: 10fr, Atlas rocket carrying John H. Glenn. 30fr, Titan 2 rocket and Gemini 3 capsule.

1973, Sept. 12 **Litho.** ***Perf. 12½x13***

298 A96 5fr multicolored .20 .20
299 A96 10fr multicolored .20 .20
300 A96 30fr multicolored .20 .20
Nos. 298-300,C167-C168 (5) 4.00 2.25

Cross-examination — A97

Designs: 65fr, "Diamond Ede." 70fr, Forensic Institute. 150fr, Robbery scene.

1973, Sept. 15 ***Perf. 13x12½***

301 A97 50fr multicolored .30 .20
302 A97 65fr multicolored .40 .20
303 A97 70fr multicolored .40 .20
304 A97 150fr multicolored .90 .40
Nos. 301-304 (4) 2.00 1.00

Interpol, 50th anniversary. See No. C170.

Market Place, Ouagadougou — A98

40fr, Swimming pool, Hotel Independence.

1973, Sept. 30

305 A98 35fr multicolored .30 .20
306 A98 40fr multicolored .40 .30
Nos. 305-306,C171 (3) 1.70 1.00

Tourism. See No. C172.

Protestant Church — A99

Design: 40fr, Ouahigouya Mosque.

1973, Sept. 28 ***Perf. 13x12½***

307 A99 35fr multicolored .25 .20
308 A99 40fr multicolored .25 .20
Nos. 307-308,C173 (3) 1.90 1.00

Houses of worship.

Kiembara Dancers A100

Folklore: 40fr, Dancers.

1973, Nov. 30 Litho. ***Perf. 12½x13***

309 A100 35fr multicolored .25 .20
310 A100 40fr multicolored .25 .20
Nos. 309-310,C174-C175 (4) 2.65 1.45

Yuri Gagarin and Aries — A101

Famous Men and their Zodiac Signs: 10fr, Lenin and Taurus. 20fr, John F. Kennedy, rocket and Gemini. 25fr, John H. Glenn, orbiting capsule and Cancer. 30fr, Napoleon and Leo. 50fr, Goethe and Virgo. 60fr, Pelé and Libra. 75fr, Charles de Gaulle and Scorpio. 100fr, Beethoven and Sagittarius. 175fr, Conrad Adenauer and Capricorn. 200fr, Edwin E. Aldrin, Jr. (Apollo XI) and Aquarius. 250fr, Lord Baden-Powell and Pisces.

1973, Dec. 15 Litho. ***Perf. 13x14***

311 A101 5fr multicolored .20 .20
312 A101 10fr multicolored .20 .20
313 A101 20fr multicolored .20 .20
314 A101 25fr multicolored .20 .20
315 A101 30fr multicolored .20 .20
316 A101 50fr multicolored .30 .20
317 A101 60fr multicolored .40 .20
318 A101 75fr multicolored .45 .20
319 A101 100fr multicolored .60 .30
320 A101 175fr multicolored 1.10 .55
321 A101 200fr multicolored 1.25 .55
322 A101 250fr multicolored 1.50 .70
Nos. 311-322 (12) 6.60 3.70

See Nos. C176-C178.

Rivera with Italian Flag and Championship '74 Emblem — A102

40fr, World Cup, soccer ball, World Championship '74 emblem & Pelé with Brazilian flag.

1974, Jan. 15 ***Perf. 13x12½***

323 A102 5fr multicolored .20 .20
324 A102 40fr multicolored .25 .20
Nos. 323-324,C179-C181 (5) 2.60 1.45

10th World Cup Soccer Championship, Munich, June 13-July 7.

Charles de Gaulle A103

40fr, De Gaulle memorial. 60fr, Pres. de Gaulle.

1974, Feb. 4 Litho. ***Perf. 12½x13***

325 A103 35fr multicolored .20 .20
326 A103 40fr multicolored .20 .20
327 A103 60fr multicolored .35 .20
a. Strip of 3, Nos. 325-327 .75 .45
Nos. 325-327,C183 (4) 2.75 1.60

Gen. Charles de Gaulle (1890-1970), president of France. See #C184.

N'Dongo and Cameroun Flag A104

World Cup, Emblems and: 20fr, Kolev and Bulgarian flag. 50fr, Keita and Mali flag.

1974, Mar. 19

328 A104 10fr multicolored .20 .20
329 A104 20fr multicolored .20 .20
330 A104 50fr multicolored .35 .20
Nos. 328-330,C185-C186 (5) 3.00 1.75

10th World Cup Soccer Championship, Munich, June 13-July 7.

Map and Flags of Members A105

1974, May 29 Photo. ***Perf. 13x12½***

331 A105 40fr blue & multi .25 .20

15th anniversary of the Council of Accord.

UPU Emblem and Mail Coach — A106

1974, July 23 Litho. ***Perf. 13½***

332 A106 35fr shown .25 .20
333 A106 40fr Steamship .25 .20
334 A106 85fr Mailman .50 .30
Nos. 332-334,C189-C191 (6) 4.00 2.20

Universal Postal Union centenary.
For overprints see #339-341, C197-C200.

Soccer Game, Winner Italy, in France, 1938 — A107

World Cup, Game and Flags: 25fr, Uruguay, in Brazil, 1950. 50fr, East Germany, in Switzerland, 1954.

1974, Sept. 2 Litho. ***Perf. 13½***

335 A107 10fr multicolored .20 .20
336 A107 25fr multicolored .20 .20
337 A107 50fr multicolored .35 .20
Nos. 335-337,C193-C195 (6) 4.75 2.60

World Cup Soccer winners.

Map and Farm Woman — A108

1974, Oct. 2 Litho. ***Perf. 13x12½***

338 A108 35fr yellow & multi .20 .20

Kou Valley Development.

Nos. 332-334 Overprinted in Red "100e ANNIVERSAIRE DE L'UNION POSTALE UNIVERSELLE / 9 OCTOBRE 1974"

1974, Oct. 9

339 A106 35fr multicolored .25 .20
340 A106 40fr multicolored .25 .20
341 A106 85fr multicolored .50 .30
Nos. 339-341,C197-C199 (6) 5.00 2.70

Universal Postal Union centenary.

Flowers, by Pierre Bonnard A109

Flower Paintings by: 10fr, Jan Brueghel. 30fr, Jean van Os. 50fr, Van Brussel.

1974, Oct. 31 Litho. ***Perf. 12½x13***

342 A109 5fr multicolored .20 .20
343 A109 10fr multicolored .20 .20
344 A109 30fr multicolored .20 .20
345 A109 50fr multicolored .25 .20
Nos. 342-345,C201 (5) 2.85 1.80

Churchill as Officer of India Hussars — A110

Churchill: 75fr, As Secretary of State for Interior. 100fr, As pilot. 125fr, meeting with Roosevelt, 1941. 300fr, As painter. 450fr, and "HMS Resolution."

1975, Jan. 11 ***Perf. 13½***

346 A110 50fr multicolored .30 .20
347 A110 75fr multicolored .45 .20
348 A110 100fr multicolored .55 .30
349 A110 125fr multicolored .70 .40
350 A110 300fr multicolored 1.60 .80
Nos. 346-350 (5) 3.60 1.90

Souvenir Sheet

351 A110 450fr multicolored 2.50 1.25

Sir Winston Churchill, birth centenary.

US No. 619 and Minutemen — A111

US Stamps: 40fr, #118 and Proclamation of Independence. 75fr, #798 and Signing the Constitution. 100fr, #703 and Surrender at Yorktown. 200fr, #1003 and George Washington. 300fr, #644 and Surrender of Burgoyne at Saratoga. 500fr, #63, 68, 73, 157, 179, 228 and 1483a.

1975, Feb. 17 Litho. ***Perf. 11***

352 A111 35fr multicolored .20 .20
353 A111 40fr multicolored .25 .20
354 A111 75fr multicolored .40 .20
355 A111 100fr multicolored .55 .30
356 A111 200fr multicolored 1.25 .55
357 A111 300fr multicolored 1.60 .80
Nos. 352-357 (6) 4.25 2.25

Souvenir Sheet

Imperf

358 A111 500fr multicolored 3.00 1.50

American Bicentennial.

"Atlantic" No. 2670, 1904-12 — A112

Locomotives from Mulhouse, France, Railroad Museum: 25fr, No. 2029, 1882. 50fr, No. 2129, 1882.

1975, Feb. 28 Litho. ***Perf. 13x12½***

359 A112 15fr multicolored .20 .20
360 A112 25fr multicolored .20 .20
361 A112 50fr multicolored .35 .20
Nos. 359-361,C203-C204 (5) 2.80 1.60

French Flag and Renault Petit Duc, 1910 — A113

Flags and Old Cars: 30fr, US and Ford Model T, 1909. 35fr, Italy and Alfa Romeo "Le Mans," 1931.

1975, Apr. 6 ***Perf. 14x13½***

362 A113 10fr multicolored .20 .20
363 A113 30fr multicolored .20 .20
364 A113 35fr multicolored .20 .20
Nos. 362-364,C206-C207 (5) 3.00 1.75

Washington and Lafayette — A114

American Bicentennial: 40fr, Washington reviewing troops at Valley Forge. 50fr, Washington taking oath of office.

1975, May 6 Litho. *Perf. 14*

365 A114 30fr multicolored .20 .20
366 A114 40fr multicolored .25 .20
367 A114 50fr multicolored .35 .20
Nos. 365-367,C209-C210 (5) 4.20 2.25

Souvenir Sheet

367A A114 500fr multicolored 3.50 1.60

Schweitzer and Pelicans — A115

15fr, Albert Schweitzer and bateleur eagle.

1975, May 25 Litho. *Perf. 13½*

368 A115 5fr multicolored .20 .20
369 A115 15fr multicolored .20 .20
Nos. 368-369,C212-C214 (5) 4.00 2.10

Albert Schweitzer, birth centenary.

Apollo and Soyuz Orbiting Earth — A116

Design: 50fr, Apollo and Soyuz near link-up.

1975, July 18

370 A116 40fr multicolored .25 .20
371 A116 50fr multicolored .35 .20
Nos. 370-371,C216-C218 (5) 4.60 2.40

Apollo-Soyuz space test project, Russo-American cooperation, launched July 15, link-up July 17.

Maria Picasso Lopez, Artist's Mother A117

Paintings by Pablo Picasso (1881-1973): 60fr, Self-portrait. 90fr, First Communion.

1975, Aug. 7

372 A117 50fr multicolored .35 .20
373 A117 60fr multicolored .40 .20
374 A117 90fr multicolored .60 .30
Nos. 372-374,C220-C221 (5) 4.60 2.45

Expo '75 Emblem and Tanker, Idemitsu Maru — A118

Oceanographic Exposition, Okinawa: 25fr, Training ship, Kaio Maru. 45fr, Firefighting ship, Hiryu. 50fr, Battleship, Yamato. 60fr, Container ship, Kamakura Maru.

1975, Sept. 26 Litho. *Perf. 11*

375 A118 15fr multicolored .20 .20
376 A118 25fr multicolored .20 .20
377 A118 45fr multicolored .30 .20
377A A118 50fr multicolored .35 .20
378 A118 60fr multicolored .40 .20
Nos. 375-378,C223 (6) 2.20 1.40

Woman, Globe and IWY Emblem — A119

1975, Nov. 20 Photo. *Perf. 13*

379 A119 65fr multicolored .40 .25

International Women's Year.

Msgr. Joanny Thevenoud and Cathedral — A120

65fr, Father Guillaume Templier & Cathedral.

1975, Nov. 20 Engr. *Perf. 13x12½*

380 A120 55fr grn, blk & dl red .20 .20
381 A120 65fr blk, org & dl red .25 .20

75th anniv. of the Evangelization of Upper Volta.

Farmer's Hat, Hoe and Emblem A121

1975, Dec. 10 Photo. *Perf. 13x13½*

382 A121 15fr buff & multi .20 .20
383 A121 50fr lt green & multi .20 .20

Development of the Volta valleys.

Sledding and Olympic Emblem — A122

Innsbruck Background, Olympic Emblem and: 45fr, Figure skating. 85fr, Skiing.

1975, Dec. 16 Litho. *Perf. 13½*

384 A122 35fr multicolored .20 .20
385 A122 45fr multicolored .25 .20
386 A122 85fr multicolored .50 .25
Nos. 384-386,C225-C226 (5) 3.00 1.65

12th Winter Olympic Games, Innsbruck, Austria, Feb. 4-15, 1976.

Gymnast and Olympic Emblem — A123

1976, Mar. 17

387 A123 40fr shown .20 .20
388 A123 50fr Sailing .25 .20
389 A123 100fr Soccer .55 .30
Nos. 387-389,C228-C229 (5) 2.40 1.40

21st Olympic Games, Montreal, Canada, July 17-Aug. 1.

Olympic Emblem and Sprinters A124

Olympic Emblem and: 55fr, Equestrian. 75fr, Hurdles.

1976, Mar. 25 Litho. *Perf. 11*

390 A124 30fr multicolored .20 .20
391 A124 55fr multicolored .30 .20
392 A124 75fr multicolored .40 .20
Nos. 390-392,C231-C232 (5) 2.65 1.50

21st Olympic Games, Montreal.
For overprints see #420-422, C245-C247.

Blind Woman and Man — A125

1976, Apr. 7 Engr. *Perf. 13*

393 A125 75fr dk brn, grn & org .40 .25
394 A125 250fr dk brn, ocher & org 1.40 .80

Drive against onchocerciasis, roundworm infestation.

"Deutschland" over Friedrichshafen — A126

Airships: 40fr, "Victoria Louise" over sailing ships. 50fr, "Sachsen" over German countryside.

1976, May 11 Litho. *Perf. 11*

395 A126 10fr multicolored .70 .20
396 A126 40fr multicolored .25 .20
397 A126 50fr multicolored .35 .20
Nos. 395-397,C234-C236 (6) 5.30 2.60

75th anniversary of the Zeppelin.

Viking Lander and Probe on Mars — A127

Viking Mars project: 55fr, Viking orbiter in flight. 75fr, Titan rocket start for Mars, vert.

1976, June 24 *Perf. 13½*

398 A127 30fr multicolored .20 .20
399 A127 55fr multicolored .25 .20
400 A127 75fr multicolored .30 .20
Nos. 398-400,C238-C239 (5) 3.25 1.85

World Map, Arms of Upper Volta A128

Design: 100fr, World map, arms and dove.

1976, Aug. 19 Litho. *Perf. 12½*

401 A128 55fr brown & multi .25 .20
402 A128 100fr blue & multi .40 .30

5th Summit Conference of Non-aligned Countries, Colombo, Sri Lanka, Aug. 9-19.

Bicentennial, Interphil 76 Emblems and Washington at Battle of Trenton — A129

90fr, Bicentennial, Interphil 76 emblems, Seat of Government, Pennsylvania.

1976, Sept. 30 *Perf. 13½*

403 A129 60fr multicolored .40 .20
404 A129 90fr multicolored .60 .25
Nos. 403-404,C241-C243 (5) 5.00 2.45

American Bicentennial, Interphil 76, Philadelphia, Pa., May 29-June 6.

UPU and UN Emblems — A130

1976, Dec. 8 Engr. *Perf. 13*

405 A130 200fr red, olive & blue 1.00 .60

UN Postal Administration, 25th anniv.

Arms of Tenkodogo A131

Bronze Statuette A132

Coats of Arms: 20fr, 100fr, Ouagadougou.

1977, May 2 Litho. *Perf. 13*

406 A131 10fr multicolored .20 .20
407 A131 20fr multicolored .20 .20
408 A131 65fr multicolored .35 .25
409 A131 100fr multicolored .55 .35
Nos. 406-409 (4) 1.30 1.00

1977, June 13 Photo. *Perf. 13*

Design: 65fr, Woman with bowl, bronze.

410 A132 55fr multicolored .30 .20
411 A132 65fr multicolored .35 .20

#410-411 issued in sheets and coils with black control number on every 5th stamp.

Granaries
A133

Handbags
A134

1977, June 20 Photo. *Perf. 13½x13*

412 A133 5fr Samo .20 .20
413 A133 35fr Boromo .20 .20
414 A133 45fr Banfora .25 .20
415 A133 55fr Mossi .30 .20
Nos. 412-415 (4) .95 .80

1977, June 20

416 A134 30fr Gouin .20 .20
417 A134 40fr Bissa .20 .20
418 A134 60fr Lobi .35 .20
419 A134 70fr Mossi .40 .25
Nos. 416-419 (4) 1.15 .85

Nos. 390-392 Overprinted in Gold:
a. VAINQUEUR 1976 / LASSE VIREN / FINLANDE
b. VAINQUEUR 1976 / ALWIN SCHOCKEMOHLE / R.F.A.
c. VAINQUEUR 1976 / JOHANNA SCHALLER / R.D.A.

1977, July 4 Litho. *Perf. 11*

420 A124 (a) 30fr multicolored .20 .20
421 A124 (b) 55fr multicolored .30 .20
422 A124 (c) 75fr multicolored .40 .20
Nos. 420-422,C245-C246 (5) 3.30 1.75

Winners, 21st Olympic Games.

Crinum Ornatum — A135

Haemanthus Multiflorus
A136

Hannoa Undulata
A137

Designs: Flowers, flowering branches and wild fruits. 175fr, 300fr, horiz.

1977 Litho. *Perf. 12½*

423 A137 2fr Cordia myxa .20 .20
424 A137 3fr Opilia celtidifolia .20 .20
425 A135 15fr shown .20 .20
426 A136 25fr shown .20 .20
427 A137 50fr shown .25 .20
428 A135 90fr Cochlospermum planchonii .45 .35
429 A135 125fr Clitoria ternatea .65 .50
430 A136 150fr Cassia alata .80 .60
431 A136 175fr Nauclea latifolia .90 .70
432 A136 300fr Bombax costatum 1.60 1.25
433 A135 400fr Eulophia cucullata 2.00 1.60
Nos. 423-433 (11) 7.45 6.00

Issued: 25fr, 150fr, 175fr, 300fr, 8/1; 2fr, 3fr, 50fr, 8/8; 15fr, 90fr, 125fr, 400fr, 8/23.

De Gaulle and Cross of Lorraine
A138

Designs: 200fr, King Baudouin of Belgium.

1977, Aug. 16 *Perf. 13½x14*

434 A138 100fr multicolored .55 .25
435 A138 200fr multicolored 1.10 .40

Elizabeth II
A139

Designs: 300fr, Elizabeth II taking salute. 500fr, Elizabeth II after Coronation.

1977, Aug. 16

436 A139 200fr multicolored .80 .30
437 A139 300fr multicolored 1.25 .50

Souvenir Sheet

438 A139 500fr multicolored 2.00 .90

25th anniv. of reign of Queen Elizabeth II.
For overprints see Nos. 478-480.

Lottery Tickets, Cars and Map of Upper Volta in Flag Colors — A140

1977, Sept. 16 Photo. *Perf. 13*

439 A140 55fr multicolored .30 .25

10th anniversary of National Lottery.

Selma Lagerlof, Literature — A141

Nobel Prize Winners: 65fr, Guglielmo Marconi, physics. 125fr, Bertrand Russell, literature. 200fr, Linus C. Pauling, chemistry. 300fr, Robert Koch, medicine. 500fr, Albert Schweitzer, peace.

1977, Sept. 22 Litho. *Perf. 13½*

440 A141 55fr multicolored .30 .20
441 A141 65fr multicolored .40 .20
442 A141 125fr multicolored .60 .25
443 A141 200fr multicolored 1.10 .40
444 A141 300fr multicolored 1.60 .65
Nos. 440-444 (5) 4.00 1.70

Souvenir Sheet

445 A141 500fr multicolored 2.50 1.20

The Three Graces, by Rubens
A142

Paintings by Peter Paul Rubens (1577-1640): 55fr, Heads of Black Men, horiz. 85fr, Bathsheba at the Fountain. 150fr, The Drunken Silenus. 200fr, 300fr, Life of Maria de Medicis, diff.

1977, Oct. 19 Litho. *Perf. 14*

446 A142 55fr multicolored .30 .20
447 A142 65fr multicolored .40 .20
448 A142 85fr multicolored .45 .25
449 A142 150fr multicolored .80 .40
450 A142 200fr multicolored 1.10 .45
451 A142 300fr multicolored 1.60 .60
Nos. 446-451 (6) 4.65 2.10

Lenin in His Office
A143

85fr, Lenin Monument, Kremlin. 200fr, Lenin with youth. 500fr, Lenin & Leonid Brezhnev.

1977, Oct. 28 Litho. *Perf. 12*

452 A143 10fr multicolored .20 .20
453 A143 85fr multicolored .45 .25
454 A143 200fr multicolored 1.10 .65
455 A143 500fr multicolored 2.50 1.60
Nos. 452-455 (4) 4.25 2.70

Russian October Revolution, 60th anniv.

Stadium and Brazil No. C79 — A144

Stadium and: 65fr, Brazil #1144. 125fr, Gt. Britain #458. 200fr, Chile #340. 300fr, Switzerland #350. 500fr, Germany #1147.

1977, Dec. 30 Litho. *Perf. 13½*

456 A144 55fr multicolored .30 .20
457 A144 65fr multicolored .40 .20
458 A144 125fr multicolored .60 .25
459 A144 200fr multicolored 1.10 .40
460 A144 300fr multicolored 1.60 .65
Nos. 456-460 (5) 4.00 1.70

Souvenir Sheet

461 A144 500fr multicolored 2.50 1.25

11th World Cup Soccer Championship, Argentina.
For overprints see Nos. 486-491.

Jean Mermoz and Seaplane — A145

History of Aviation: 75fr, Anthony H. G. Fokker. 85fr, Wiley Post. 90fr, Otto Lilienthal, vert. 100fr, Concorde. 500fr, Charles Lindbergh and "Spirit of St. Louis."

1978, Jan. 2 Litho. *Perf. 13½*

462 A145 65fr multicolored .35 .20
463 A145 75fr multicolored .40 .20
464 A145 85fr multicolored .45 .20
465 A145 90fr multicolored .50 .20
466 A145 100fr multicolored .55 .20
Nos. 462-466 (5) 2.25 1.00

Souvenir Sheet

467 A145 500fr multicolored 2.50 1.25

Crataeva Religiosa — A146

1978, Feb. 28 Litho. *Perf. 12½*

468 A146 55fr shown .30 .25
469 A146 75fr Fig tree .40 .30

Souvenir Sheet

Virgin and Child, by Rubens — A147

1978, May 24 Litho. *Perf. 13½x14*

470 A147 500fr multicolored 2.50 1.25

Peter Paul Rubens (1577-1640).

Antenna and ITU Emblem
A148

1978, May 30 *Perf. 13*

471 A148 65fr silver & multi .40 .20

10th World Telecommunications Day.

Fetish Gate of Bobo — A149

1978, July 10 Litho. *Perf. 13½*

472 A149 55fr shown .30 .20
473 A149 65fr Mossi fetish .40 .20

Capt. Cook and "Endeavour" — A150

Capt. James Cook (1728-1779) and: 85fr, Death on Hawaiian beach. 250fr, Navigational instruments. 350fr, "Resolution."

1978, Sept. 1 Litho. *Perf. 14½*

474 A150 65fr multicolored .40 .20
475 A150 85fr multicolored .45 .20
476 A150 250fr multicolored 1.40 .65
477 A150 350fr multicolored 1.90 .80
Nos. 474-477 (4) 4.15 1.85

Nos. 436-438 Overprinted Vertically in Silver: "ANNIVERSAIRE DU COURONNEMENT 1953-1978"

1978, Oct. 24 Litho. *Perf. 13½x14*

478 A139 200fr multicolored 1.10 .40
479 A139 300fr multicolored 1.60 .65

Souvenir Sheet

480 A139 500fr multicolored 2.50 1.25

25th anniversary of Coronation of Queen Elizabeth II. Overprint in 3 lines on 200fr, in 2 lines on 300fr and 500fr.

#478-480 exist with overprint in metallic red.

Trent Castle, by Dürer — A151

Paintings by Albrecht Durer (1471-1528): 150fr, Virgin and Child with St. Anne, vert. 250fr, Sts. George and Eustachius, vert. 350fr, Hans Holzschuher, vert.

Perf. 14x13½, 13½x14

1978, Nov. 20 Litho.

481 A151 65fr multicolored .40 .20
482 A151 150fr multicolored .80 .40
483 A151 250fr multicolored 1.40 .65
484 A151 350fr multicolored 1.90 .65
Nos. 481-484 (4) 4.50 1.90

Human Rights Emblem A152

1978, Dec. 10 Litho. *Perf. 12½*

485 A152 55fr multicolored .30 .20

Universal Declaration of Human Rights, 30th anniv.

Nos. 456-461 Overprinted in Silver

a, VAINQUEURS 1950 URUGUAY / 1978 / ARGENTINE
b, VAINQUEURS 1970 BRESIL / 1978 ARGENTINE
c, VAINQUEURS 1966 GRANDE BRETAGNE / 1978 ARGENTINE
d, VAINQUEURS / 1962 BRESIL / 1978 ARGENTINE
e, VAINQUEURS 1954 ALLEMAGNE (RFA) / 1978 ARGENTINE
f, VAINQUEURS 1974 ALLEMAGNE (RFA) / 1978 ARGENTINE

1979, Jan. 4 Litho. *Perf. 13½*

486 A144(a) 55fr multicolored .30 .20
487 A144(b) 65fr multicolored .40 .20
488 A144(c) 125fr multicolored .60 .25
489 A144(d) 200fr multicolored 1.10 .40
490 A144(e) 300fr multicolored 1.60 .65
Nos. 486-490 (5) 4.00 1.70

Souvenir Sheet

491 A144(f) 500fr multicolored 2.50 1.25

Winners, World Soccer Cup Championships 1950-1978.

Radio Station A153

Design: 65fr, Mail plane at airport.

1979, Mar. 30 Litho. *Perf. 12½*

492 A153 55fr multicolored .30 .20
493 A153 65fr multicolored .40 .20

Post and Telecommunications Org., 10th anniv.

Teacher and Pupils, IYC Emblem — A154

1979, Apr. 9 *Perf. 13½*

494 A154 75fr multicolored .40 .20

International Year of the Child.

Telecommunications — A155

1979, May 17 Litho. *Perf. 13*

495 A155 70fr multicolored .45 .20

11th Telecommunications Day.

Basketmaker and Upper Volta No. 111 — A156

Design: No. 497, May of Upper Volta, Concorde, truck and UPU emblem.

1979, June 8 Photo.

496 A156 100fr multicolored .65 .35
497 A156 100fr multicolored .65 .35

Philexafrique II, Libreville, Gabon, June 8-17. Nos. 496, 497 each printed in sheets of 10 and 5 labels showing exhibition emblem.

Synodontis Voltae A157

Fresh-water Fish: 50fr, Micralestes comoensis. 85fr, Silurus.

1979, June 10 Litho. *Perf. 12½*

498 A157 20fr multicolored .20 .20
499 A157 50fr multicolored .35 .20
500 A157 85fr multicolored .55 .30
Nos. 498-500 (3) 1.10 .70

Rowland Hill, Train and Upper Volta No. 60 — A158

Sir Rowland Hill (1795-1879), originator of penny postage, Trains and Upper Volta Stamps: 165fr, #59. 200fr, #57. 300fr, #56. 500fr, #55.

1979, June Litho. *Perf. 13½*

501 A158 65fr multicolored .40 .20
502 A158 165fr multicolored 1.10 .55
503 A158 200fr multicolored 1.40 .65
504 A158 300fr multicolored 2.00 1.00
Nos. 501-504 (4) 4.90 2.40

Souvenir Sheet

505 A158 500fr multicolored 3.50 1.60

Wildlife Fund Emblem and Protected Animals — A159

1979, Aug. 30 Litho. *Perf. 14½*

506 A159 30fr Waterbuck .75 .20
507 A159 40fr Roan antelope 1.25 .20
508 A159 60fr Caracal 2.00 .20
509 A159 100fr African bush elephant 3.00 .75
510 A159 175fr Hartebeest 5.00 1.00
511 A159 250fr Leopard 10.50 1.00
Nos. 506-511 (6) 22.50 3.35

Adult Students and Teacher — A160

Design: 55fr, Man reading book, vert.

1979, Sept. 8 *Perf. 12½x13, 13x12½*

512 A160 55fr multicolored .40 .20
513 A160 250fr multicolored 1.60 .85

World Literacy Day.

Map of Upper Volta, Telephone Receiver and Lines, Telecom Emblem — A161

1979, Sept. 20 *Perf. 13x12½*

514 A161 200fr multicolored 1.40 .65

3rd World Telecommunications Exhibition, Geneva, Sept. 20-26.

King Vulture — A162

1979, Oct. 26 Litho. *Perf. 13*

515 A162 5fr shown .20 .20
516 A162 10fr Hoopoe .20 .20
517 A162 15fr Bald vulture .20 .20
518 A162 25fr Egrets .20 .20
519 A162 35fr Ostrich .25 .20
520 A162 45fr Crowned crane .30 .20
521 A162 125fr Eagle .80 .40
Nos. 515-521 (7) 2.15 1.60

Control Tower, Emblem, Jet — A163

1979, Dec. 12 Photo. *Perf. 13x12½*

522 A163 65fr multicolored .45 .20

ASECNA (Air Safety Board), 20th anniv.

Central Bank of West African States — A164

1979, Dec. 28 Litho. *Perf. 12½*

523 A164 55fr multicolored .40 .20

Eugene Jamot, Map of Upper Volta, Tsetse Fly — A165

1979, Dec. 28 *Perf. 13x13½*

524 A165 55fr multicolored .40 .20

Eugene Jamot (1879-1937), discoverer of sleeping sickness cure.

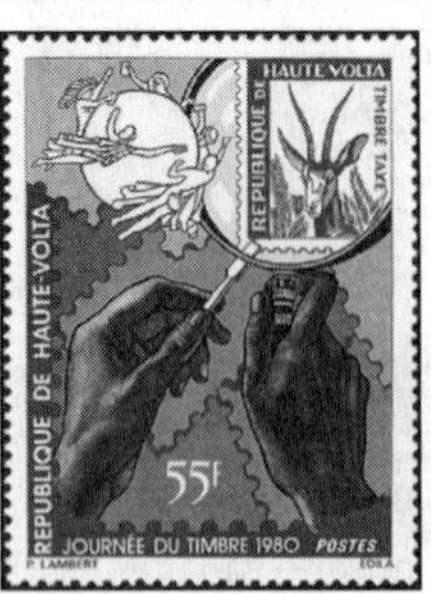

UPU Emblem, Upper Volta Type D4 under Magnifier
A166

1980, Feb. 26 Litho. *Perf. 12½x13*

525 A166 55fr multicolored .40 .20

Stamp Day.

World Locomotive Speed Record, 25th Anniversary
A167

1980, Mar. 30 Litho. *Perf. 12½*

526 A167 75fr multicolored .50 .25
527 A167 100fr multicolored .65 .35

Pres. Sangoule Lamizana, Pope John Paul II, Cardinal Pau Zoungrana, Map of Upper Volta — A168

1980, May 10 Litho. *Perf. 12½*

528 A168 65fr shown .45 .20

Size: 21x36mm

529 A168 100fr Pope John Paul II .65 .35

Visit of Pope John Paul II to Upper Volta.

A169

A170

1980, May 17 *Perf. 13x12½*

530 A169 50fr multicolored .35 .20

12th World Telecommunications Day.

1980, June 12 Litho. *Perf. 13*

531 A170 65fr Sun and earth .45 .20
532 A170 100fr Solar energy .65 .35

Downhill Skiing, Lake Placid '80 Emblem — A171

1980, June 26 *Perf. 14½*

533 A171 65fr shown .35 .20
534 A171 100fr Women's down-hill .50 .30

535 A171 200fr Figure skating 1.25 .50
536 A171 350fr Slalom, vert. 1.90 1.00
Nos. 533-536 (4) 4.00 2.00

Souvenir Sheet

537 A171 500fr Speed skating 3.50 1.60

12th Winter Olympic Game Winners, Lake Placid, NY, Feb. 12-24.

Map of Europe and Africa, Jet — A172

Hand Holding Back Sand Dune — A173

Europafrica Issue

1980, July 14 Litho. *Perf. 13*

538 A172 100fr multicolored .65 .35

1980, July 18

Operation Green Sahel: 55fr, Hands holding seedlings.

539 A173 50fr multicolored .35 .20
540 A173 55fr multicolored .40 .20

Gourmantche Chief Initiation — A174

1980, Sept. 12 Litho. *Perf. 14*

541 A174 30fr shown .20 .20
542 A174 55fr Moro Naba, Mossi Emperor .35 .20
543 A174 65fr Princess Guimbe Quattara, vert. .45 .20
Nos. 541-543 (3) 1.00 .60

A175

A176

Gourounsi mask, conference emblem.

1980, Oct. 6 *Perf. 13½x13*

544 A175 65fr multicolored .45 .20

World Tourism Conf., Manila, Sept. 27.

1980, Nov. 5 Litho. *Perf. 12½*

545 A176 55fr Agriculture .40 .20
546 A176 65fr Transportation .45 .20
547 A176 75fr Dam, highway .50 .25
548 A176 100fr Industry .65 .35
Nos. 545-548 (4) 2.00 1.00

West African Economic Council, 5th anniv.

20th Anniv. of Independence — A177

1980, Dec. 11 *Perf. 13*

549 A177 500fr multicolored 3.50 1.60

Madonna and Child, by Raphael — A178

West African Postal Union, 5th Anniv. — A179

Christmas: Paintings of Madonna and Child, by Raphael.

1980, Dec. 22 *Perf. 12½*

550 A178 60fr multicolored .40 .20
551 A178 150fr multicolored 1.00 .50
552 A178 250fr multicolored 1.60 .80
Nos. 550-552 (3) 3.00 1.50

1980, Dec. 24 Photo. *Perf. 13½*

553 A179 55fr multicolored .40 .20

Dung Beetle
A180

Perf. 13x13½, 13½x13

1981, Mar. 10 Litho.

554 A180 5fr shown .20 .20
555 A180 10fr Crickets .20 .20
556 A180 15fr Termites .20 .20
557 A180 20fr Praying mantis, vert. .20 .20
558 A180 55fr Emperor moth .40 .25
559 A180 65fr Locust, vert. .45 .25
Nos. 554-559 (6) 1.65 1.30

Antelope Mask, Kouroumba
A181

Designs: Various ceremonial masks.

1981, Mar. 20 Litho. *Perf. 13*

560 A181 45fr multicolored .25 .20
561 A181 55fr multicolored .30 .20
562 A181 85fr multicolored .50 .25
563 A181 105fr multicolored .60 .35
Nos. 560-563 (4) 1.65 1.00

Notre Dame of Kologh' Naba College, 25th Anniv.
A182

1981, Mar. 30

564 A182 55fr multicolored .30 .20

Heinrich von Stephan, UPU Founder, Birth Sesquicentennial — A183

1981, May 4 Litho. *Perf. 13*

565 A183 65fr multicolored .35 .20

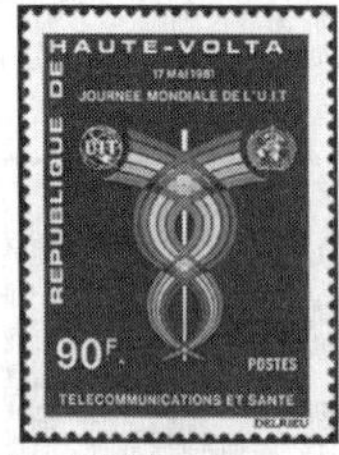

13th World Telecommunications Day — A184

1981, May 17 *Perf. 13½x13*

566 A184 90fr multicolored .50 .25

Diesel Train, Abidjan-Niger Railroad — A185

Designs: Trains.

1981, July 6 Litho. *Perf. 13*

567 A185 25fr shown .20 .20
568 A185 30fr Gazelle .20 .20
569 A185 40fr Belier .25 .20
Nos. 567-569 (3) .65 .60

Tree Planting Month
A186

1981, July 15

570 A186 70fr multicolored .45 .25

Natl. Red Cross, 20th Anniv.
A187

1981, July 31 *Perf. 12½x13*

571 A187 70fr multicolored .45 .25

Intl. Year of the Disabled — A188

1981, Aug. 20 Litho. *Perf. 13x12½*

572 A188 70fr multicolored .45 .25

View of Koudougou A189

1981, Sept. 3 Litho. *Perf. 12½*

573 A189 35fr shown .25 .20
574 A189 45fr Toma .30 .20
575 A189 85fr Volta Noire .55 .30
Nos. 573-575 (3) 1.10 .70

World Food Day — A190

1981, Oct. 16 *Perf. 13*

576 A190 90fr multicolored .60 .30

Elephant A191

Designs: Various protected species.

1981, Oct. 21 Photo. *Perf. 14*

577 A191 5fr multicolored .20 .20
578 A191 15fr multicolored .20 .20
579 A191 40fr multicolored .25 .20
580 A191 60fr multicolored .40 .20
581 A191 70fr multicolored .45 .20
Nos. 577-581 (5) 1.50 1.00

Fight Against Apartheid — A192

Mangoes — A193

1981, Dec. 9 Litho. *Perf. 12½*

582 A192 90fr red orange .60 .30

1981, Dec. 15 *Perf. 13x13½, 13½x13*

583 A193 20fr Papayas, horiz. .20 .20
584 A193 35fr Fruits, vegetables, horiz. .25 .20
585 A193 75fr shown .50 .25
586 A193 90fr Melons, horiz. .60 .35
Nos. 583-586 (4) 1.55 1.00

Guinea Hen — A194

West African Rice Development Assoc., 10th Anniv. — A195

Designs: Breeding animals. 10fr, 25fr, 70fr, 250fr, 300fr horiz.

1981, Dec. 22 *Perf. 13*

587 A194 10fr Donkey .20 .20
588 A194 25fr Pig .20 .20
589 A194 70fr Cow .45 .25
590 A194 90fr shown .55 .30
591 A194 250fr Rabbit 1.60 .80
Nos. 587-591 (5) 3.00 1.75

Souvenir Sheet

592 A194 300fr Sheep 2.00 1.00

1981, Dec. 29

593 A195 90fr multicolored .60 .30

20th Anniv. of World Food Program — A196

1982, Jan. 18

594 A196 50fr multicolored .35 .20

Traditional Houses — A197

1982, Apr. 23 Litho. *Perf. 12½*

595 A197 30fr Morhonaba Palace, vert. .20 .20
596 A197 70fr Bobo .45 .25
597 A197 100fr Gourounsi .65 .35
598 A197 200fr Peulh 1.40 .65
599 A197 250fr Dagari 1.60 .80
Nos. 595-599 (5) 4.30 2.25

14th World Telecommunications Day — A198

1982, May 17

600 A198 125fr multicolored .85 .40

Water Lily — A199

25th Anniv. of Cultural Aid Fund — A201

African Postal Union A200

1982, Sept. 22 *Perf. 13x12½*

601 A199 25fr shown .20 .20
602 A199 40fr Kapoks .20 .20
603 A199 70fr Frangipani .35 .20
604 A199 90fr Cochlospermum planchonii .60 .25
605 A199 100fr Cotton .50 .25
Nos. 601-605 (5) 1.85 1.10

1982, Oct. 7

606 A200 70fr multicolored .45 .25
607 A200 90fr multicolored .60 .30

1982, Nov. 10 *Perf. 12½x13*

608 A201 70fr multicolored .45 .25

Map, Hand Holding Grain, Steer Head A202

1982 *Perf. 12½*

609 A202 90fr multicolored .60 .30

Traditional Hairstyle A203

1983, Jan. Litho. *Perf. 12½*

610 A203 90fr lt green & multi .50 .25
611 A203 120fr lt blue & multi .70 .35
612 A203 170fr pink & multi .95 .50
Nos. 610-612 (3) 2.15 1.10

For overprints see Nos. 884-886.

8th Film Festival, Ouagadougou — A204

1983, Feb. 10 Litho. *Perf. 13x12½*

613 A204 90fr Scene .60 .30
614 A204 500fr Filmmaker Dumarou Ganda 3.50 1.60

UN Intl. Drinking Water and Sanitation Decade, 1981-90 — A205

1983, Apr. 21 Litho. *Perf. 13½x13*

615 A205 60fr Water drops .40 .20
616 A205 70fr Carrying water .45 .25

Manned Flight Bicentenary A206

Portraits and Balloons: 15fr, J.M. Montgolfier, 1783. 25fr, Etienne Montgolfier's balloon, 1783, Pilatre de Rozier. 70fr, Charles & Roberts flight, 1783, Jacques Charles. 90fr, Flight over English Channel, John Jeffries. 100fr, Testu-Brissy's horseback flight, Wilhemine Reichardt. 250fr, Andree's Spitzbergen flight, 1897, S.A. Andree. 300fr, Piccard's stratosphere flight, 1931, August Piccard.

1983, Apr. 15 Litho. *Perf. 13½*

617 A206 15fr multicolored .20 .20
618 A206 25fr multicolored .20 .20
619 A206 70fr multicolored .45 .25
620 A206 90fr multicolored .60 .30
621 A206 100fr multicolored .65 .35
622 A206 250fr multicolored 1.60 .80
Nos. 617-622 (6) 3.70 2.10

Souvenir Sheet

623 A206 300fr multicolored 2.00 1.00

No. 623 contains one stamp 38x47mm. Nos. 621-623 airmail.

World Communications Year — A207

1983, May 26 Litho. *Perf. 12½*

624 A207 30fr Man reading letter .20 .20
625 A207 35fr Like No. 624 .20 .20
626 A207 45fr Aircraft over stream .25 .20
627 A207 90fr Girl on telephone .50 .25
Nos. 624-627 (4) 1.15 .85

Fishing Resources A208

1983, July 28 Litho. *Perf. 13*

628 A208 20fr Synadontis gambiensis .20 .20
629 A208 30fr Palmotochromis .20 .20
630 A208 40fr Boy fishing, vert. .20 .20
631 A208 50fr Fishing with net .20 .20
632 A208 75fr Fishing with basket .20 .20
Nos. 628-632 (5) 1.00 1.00

Anti-deforestation — A209

1983, Sept. 13 Litho. *Perf. 13*

633 A209 10fr Planting saplings .20 .20
634 A209 50fr Tree nursery .20 .20
635 A209 100fr Prevent forest fires .35 .20
636 A209 150fr Woman cooking .50 .25
637 A209 200fr Prevent felling, vert. .65 .35
Nos. 633-637 (5) 1.90 1.20

Fresco Detail, by Raphael — A210

Paintings: 120fr, Self-portrait, by Pablo Picasso, 1901, vert. 185fr, Self-portrait at the palette, by Manet, 1878, vert. 350fr, Fresco Detail, diff., by Raphael. 500fr, Goethe, by George Oswald May, 1779, vert.

1983, Nov. Litho. *Perf. 13*

638 A210 120fr multicolored .40 .20
639 A210 185fr multicolored .60 .30
640 A210 300fr multicolored 1.00 .50
641 A210 350fr multicolored 1.25 .60
642 A210 500fr multicolored 1.60 .80
Nos. 638-642 (5) 4.85 2.40

25th Anniv. of the Republic A211

1983, Dec. 9 Litho. *Perf. 14*

643 A211 90fr Arms .30 .20
644 A211 500fr Family, flag 1.60 .80

A212

Scouting — A213

1984, May 29 Litho. *Perf. 12½*

645 A212 90fr multicolored .30 .20
646 A212 100fr multicolored .35 .20

Council of Unity, 25th anniv.

1984, June 15 Litho. *Perf. 13½*

647 A213 25fr Polystictus leoninus .20 .20
648 A213 185fr Pterocarpus Lucens .85 .45
649 A213 200fr Phlebopus colossus sudanicus 1.10 .50
650 A213 250fr Cosmos sulphureus 1.25 .60
651 A213 300fr Trametes versicolor 1.50 .80
652 A213 400fr Ganoderma lucidum 2.00 1.10
Nos. 647-652 (6) 6.90 3.65

Souvenir Sheet

653 A213 600fr Leucocoprinus cepaestipes 3.25 1.60

Nos. 651-653 are airmail. For overprints see Nos. 669-674.

Wildlife A214

Wildlife — A215

1984, July 19

654 A214 15fr Cheetah, four cubs .45 .20
655 A214 35fr Two adults .90 .40
656 A214 90fr One adult 2.25 .50
657 A214 120fr Cheetah, two cubs 2.40 1.00
658 A214 300fr Baboons 1.25 .55
659 A214 400fr Vultures 1.50 .80
Nos. 654-659 (6) 8.75 3.45

Souvenir Sheet

660 A215 1000fr Antelopes 4.00 1.90

World Wildlife Fund (Nos. 654-567); Rotary Intl. (Nos. 658, 660); Natl. Boy Scouts (No. 659). Nos. 658-660 are airmail.

Sailing Ships and Locomotives — A216

1984, Aug. 14 *Perf. 12½*

661 A216 20fr Maiden Queen .20 .20
662 A216 40fr CC 2400 ch .20 .20
663 A216 60fr Scawfell .25 .20
664 A216 100fr PO 1806 .40 .20
665 A216 120fr Harbinger .45 .25
666 A216 145fr Livingstone .55 .30
667 A216 400fr True Briton 1.50 .80
668 A216 450fr Pacific C51 1.60 .85
Nos. 661-668 (8) 5.15 3.00

Burkina Faso

Natl. Defense — A216a

Design: 120fr, Capt. Sankara, crowd, horiz.

1984, Nov. 21 Litho. *Perf. 13½*

668A A216a 90fr multicolored
668B A216a 120fr multicolored

Nos. 647-652 Ovptd. with Two Bars and "BURKINA FASO"

1985, Mar. 5 Litho. *Perf. 13½*

669 A213 25fr multicolored .20 .20
670 A213 185fr multicolored .55 .25
671 A213 200fr multicolored .60 .30
672 A213 250fr multicolored .75 .40
673 A213 300fr multicolored .90 .45
674 A213 400fr multicolored 1.25 .60
Nos. 669-674 (6) 4.25 2.20

A217

Designs: 5fr, 120fr, Flag. 15fr, 150fr, Natl. Arms, vert. 90fr, 185fr, Map.

1985, Mar. 8 Litho. *Perf. 12½*

675 A217 5fr multicolored
676 A217 15fr multicolored
677 A217 90fr multicolored
678 A217 120fr multicolored
679 A217 150fr multicolored
680 A217 185fr multicolored

Nos. 678-680 are airmail.

1986 World Cup Soccer Championships, Mexico — A218

Various soccer plays and Aztec artifacts.

1985, Apr. 20 Litho. *Perf. 13*

681 A218 25fr multicolored .20 .20
682 A218 45fr multicolored .20 .20
683 A218 90fr multicolored .35 .20
684 A218 100fr multicolored .40 .20
685 A218 150fr multicolored .55 .25
686 A218 200fr multicolored .70 .40
687 A218 250fr multicolored .90 .45
Nos. 681-687 (7) 3.30 1.90

Souvenir Sheet

688 A218 500fr multicolored 1.90 1.25

Nos. 681-685 vert. No. 684-688 are airmail. No. 688 contains one 40x32mm stamp.

Motorcycle, Cent. — A220

1985, May 26

689 A220 50fr Steam tricycle, G.A. Long .20 .20
690 A220 75fr Pope .25 .20
691 A220 80fr Manet-90 .30 .20
692 A220 100fr Ducati .40 .20
693 A220 150fr Jawa .55 .30
694 A220 200fr Honda .70 .40
695 A220 250fr B.M.W. .90 .50
Nos. 689-695 (7) 3.30 2.00

Nos. 692-695 are airmail.

Reptiles A221

1985, June 20

696 A221 5fr Chamaeleon dilepis .20 .20
697 A221 15fr Agama stellio .20 .20
698 A221 35fr Lacerta Lepida .20 .20
699 A221 85fr Hiperolius marmoratus .30 .20
700 A221 100fr Echis leucogaster .40 .20
701 A221 150fr Kinixys erosa .55 .30
702 A221 250fr Python regius .90 .45
Nos. 696-702 (7) 2.75 1.75

#696-697 vert. #700-702 are airmail.

A222

Queen Mother, 85th Birthday A222a

75fr, On pony bobs. 85fr, Wedding, 1923. 500fr, Holding infant Elizabeth, 1926. 600fr, Coronation of King George VI, 1937. 1000fr, Christening of Prince William, 1982. #707A, Christening of Prince Harry, 1985.

1985, June 21 *Perf. 13½*

703 A222 75fr multicolored .25 .20
704 A222 85fr multicolored .25 .20
705 A222 500fr multicolored 1.60 .80
706 A222 600fr multicolored 1.90 .90
Nos. 703-706 (4) 4.00 2.10

Litho. & Embossed

Perf. 13¼

706A A222a 1500fr gold & multi

Souvenir Sheets

Litho.

707 A222 1000fr multicolored 3.25 1.60

Litho. & Embossed

707A A222a 1500fr gold & multi

Nos. 705-707A are airmail.

Vintage Autos and Aircraft — A223

1985, June 21

708 A223 5fr Benz Victoria, 1893 .20 .20
709 A223 25fr Peugeot 174, 1927 .20 .20
710 A223 45fr Louis Bleriot .20 .20
711 A223 50fr Breguet 14 .20 .20
712 A223 500fr Bugatti Coupe Napoleon T41 Royale 1.90 .90
713 A223 500fr Airbus A300-P4 1.90 .90
714 A223 600fr Mercedes-Benz 540K, 1938 2.25 1.25
715 A223 600fr Airbus A300B 2.25 1.25
Nos. 708-715 (8) 9.10 5.10

Souvenir Sheet

716 A223 1000fr Louis Bleriot, Karl Benz 4.00 1.90

Automobile, cent. Nos. 712-716 are airmail.

Audubon Birth Bicent. A224

Illustrations of No. American bird species by Audubon and scouting trefoil.

1985, June 21

717 A224 60fr Aix sponsa .25 .20
718 A224 100fr Mimus polyglotos .40 .20
719 A224 300fr Icterus galbula 1.25 .60
720 A224 400fr Sitta carolinensis 1.50 .80
721 A224 500fr Asyndesmus lewis 1.50 .90
722 A224 600fr Buteo cagopus 2.25 1.10
Nos. 717-722 (6) 7.15 3.80

Souvenir Sheet

723 A224 1000fr Columba leucocephala 4.00 1.90

Nos. 721-723 are airmail.

ARGENTINA '85, Buenos Aires — A225

Various equestrians.

1985, July 5 ***Perf. 13***

724 A225 25fr Gaucho, piebald .20 .20
725 A225 45fr Horse and rider, Andes Mountains .20 .20
726 A225 90fr Rodeo .30 .20
727 A225 100fr Hunting gazelle .40 .20
728 A225 150fr Gauchos, 3 horses .55 .25
729 A225 200fr Rider beside mount .70 .35
730 A225 250fr Contest .90 .40
Nos. 724-730 (7) 3.25 1.80

Souvenir Sheet

731 A225 500fr Foal 1.90 .70

Nos. 727-731 are airmail.

Locomotives — A226

1985, July 23

732 A226 50fr 105-30 electric, tank wagon .20 .20
733 A226 75fr Diesel shunting locomotive .25 .20
734 A226 80fr Diesel locomotive .25 .20
735 A226 100fr Diesel railcar .35 .20
736 A226 150fr No. 6093 .50 .25
737 A226 200fr No. 105 diesel railcar .60 .35
738 A226 250fr Diesel, passenger car .75 .40
Nos. 732-738 (7) 2.90 1.80

Nos. 735-738 are airmail.

Artifacts — A227

Fungi — A228

10fr, 4-legged jar, Tikare. 40fr, Lidded pot with bird handles, P. Bazega. 90fr, Mother and child, bronze statue, Ouagadougou. 120fr, Drummer, bronze statue, Ouagadougou.

1985, July 27 ***Perf. 13x12½***

739-742 A227 1.10 .55

No. 742 is airmail.

1985, Aug. 8 ***Perf. 13***

743 A228 15fr Philiota mutabilis .20 .20
744 A228 20fr Hypholoma (nematoloma) fasciculare .20 .20
745 A228 30fr Ixocomus granulatus .20 .20
746 A228 60fr Agaricus campestris .20 .20
747 A228 80fr Trachypus scaber .30 .20
748 A228 150fr Armillaria mellea .50 .25
749 A228 250fr Marasmius scorodonius .75 .40
Nos. 743-749 (7) 2.35 1.65

Nos. 748 is airmail.

ITALIA '85 A228a

Paintings by Botticelli: 25fr, Virgin and Child. 45fr, Portrait of a Man. 90fr, Mars and Venus. 100fr, Birth of Venus. 150fr, Allegory of the Calumny. 200fr, Pallas and the Centaur. 250fr, Allegory of Spring. 500fr, The Virgin of Melagrana.

1985, Oct. 25 Litho. ***Perf. 12½x13***

749A A228a 25fr multicolored .20 .20
749B A228a 45fr multicolored .25 .20
749C A228a 90fr multicolored .45 .25
749D A228a 100fr multicolored .50 .25
749E A228a 150fr multicolored .70 .40
749F A228a 200fr multicolored 1.00 .50
749G A228a 250fr multicolored 1.25 .60
Nos. 749A-749G (7) 4.35 2.40

Souvenir Sheet

749H A228a 500fr multicolored 2.50 1.25

No. 749D-749H are airmail.

Intl. Red Cross in Burkina Faso, 75th Anniv. A229

1985, Nov. 10

750 A229 40f Helicopter .20 .20
751 A229 85fr Ambulance .30 .20
752 A229 150fr Henri Dunant .60 .25
753 A229 250fr Physician, patient .90 .35
Nos. 750-753 (4) 2.00 1.00

Nos. 752-753 are vert. and airmail.

Child Survival A230

1986, Jan. 6

754 A230 90fr Breast-feeding .50 .25

Dated 1985.

Dodo Carnival — A231

1986, Jan. 6 ***Perf. 12½***

755 A231 20fr Three children, drummer .20 .20
756 A231 25fr Lion, 4 dancers .20 .20
757 A231 40fr Two dancers, two drummers .25 .20
758 A231 45fr Three dancers .25 .20
759 A231 90fr Zebra, ostrich, dancers .50 .25
760 A231 90fr Elephant, dancer .50 .25
Nos. 755-760 (6) 1.90 1.30

Dated 1985.

Christopher Columbus (1451-1506) — A232

Columbus: 250fr, At Court of King of Portugal, the Nina. 300fr, Using astrolable, the Santa Maria. 400fr, Imprisonment at Hispanola, 1500, the Santa Maria. 450fr, At San Salvador, 1492, the Pinta. 1000fr, Fleet departing Palos harbor, 1492.

1986, Feb. 10 ***Perf. 13½***

761 A232 250fr multicolored 1.40 .70
762 A232 300fr multicolored 1.60 .80
763 A232 400fr multicolored 2.25 1.10
764 A232 450fr multicolored 2.50 1.25
Nos. 761-764 (4) 7.75 3.85

Souvenir Sheet

765 A232 1000fr multicolored 5.50 2.75

Nos. 764-765 are airmail. Dated 1985.

Railroad Construction — A233

1986, Feb. 10

766 A233 90fr Man, woman carrying rail .50 .25
767 A233 120fr Laying rails .65 .30
768 A233 185fr Diesel train on new tracks 1.00 .50
769 A233 500fr Adler locomotive, 1835 2.75 1.40
Nos. 766-769 (4) 4.90 2.45

Souvenir Sheet

770 A233 1000fr Electric train, Series 290 diesel 5.00 2.75

German Railways, sesquicentennial. Nos. 769-770 are airmail. Dated 1985.

Intl. Peace Year — A234

World Health by the Year 2000 — A235

1986, Oct. 10 Photo. ***Perf. 12½x13***

771 A234 90fr blue 1.10 .55

1986, Aug. 8 Litho. ***Perf. 13***

Designs: 100fr, Primary care medicine. 150fr, Mass inoculations.

772 A235 90fr multicolored .65 .30

Size: 26x30mm

Perf. 12½x13

773 A235 100fr multicolored .70 .30
774 A235 120fr multicolored .85 .40
Nos. 772-774 (3) 2.20 1.00

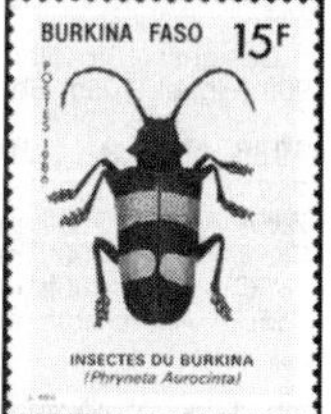

Insects — A236

World Post Day — A237

1986, Sept. 10 Litho. ***Perf. 12½x13***

775 A236 15fr Phryneta aurocinta .20 .20
776 A236 20fr Sternocera interrupta .20 .20
777 A236 40fr Prosoprocera lactator .35 .20
778 A236 45fr Gonimbrasia hecate .40 .20
778A A236 85fr Charaxes epijasius .85 .35
Nos. 775-778A (5) 2.00 1.15

1986, Oct. 9 ***Perf. 13***

779 A237 120fr multicolored .70 .35

UN Child Survival Campaign — A238

Designs: 30fr, Mother feeding child. 60fr, Adding medicines to food. 90fr, Nurse vaccinating child. 120fr, Nurse weighing child.

1986, Oct. 8 Litho. ***Perf. 11½x12***

780 A238 30fr multicolored
781 A238 60fr multicolored
782 A238 90fr multicolored
783 A238 120frmulti — —
Nos. 780-783 (0) .00 .00

Mammals A239

Designs: 50fr, Warthog. 65fr, Hyena. 90fr, Antelope. 100fr, Gazelle. 120fr, Bushbuck. 145fr, Kudu. 500fr, Gazelle, diff.

1986, Nov. 3 Litho. ***Perf. 13x12½***

784 A239 50fr multicolored
784A A239 65fr multicolored
784B A239 90fr multicolored
784C A239 100fr multicolored
784D A239 120fr multicolored
784E A239 145fr multicolored
784F A239 500fr multicolored

Traditional Dances — A240

Designs: 10fr, Namende. 25fr, Mouhoun. 90fr, Houet. 105fr, Seno. 120fr, Ganzourgou.

1986, Nov. 3 Litho. *Perf. 12½x13*

785 A240 10fr multicolored
785A A240 25fr multicolored
785B A240 90fr multicolored
785C A240 105fr multicolored
785D A240 120fr multicolored

Hairstyles A241

1986, Nov. 4 Litho. *Perf. 12½x13*

788 A241 35fr Peul .30 .20
789 A241 75fr Dafing .55 .30
790 A241 90fr Peul, diff. .70 .35
791 A241 120fr Mossi .95 .50
792 A241 185fr Peul, diff. 1.50 .75
Nos. 788-792 (5) 4.00 2.10

10th African Film Festival — A242

Intl Women's Day — A243

1987, Feb. 21 Litho. *Perf. 12x12½*

793 A242 90fr Maps, cameras
794 A242 120fr Jolson, cameramen
795 A242 185fr Charlie Chaplin

60th Anniv. of the film *The Jazz Singer* (120fr); 10th anniv. of the death of Charlie Chaplin (185fr).

1987, Mar. 8 *Perf. 13½*

796 A243 90fr multicolored

Flora — A244

Fight Against Leprosy — A245

1987, June 6 Litho. *Perf. 12½x13*

797 A244 70fr Calotropis procera .50 .25
798 A244 75fr Acacia seyal .55 .25
799 A244 85fr Parkia biglobosa .60 .30
800 A244 90fr Sterospernum kunthianum .65 .30
801 A244 100fr Dichrostachys cinerea .70 .35
802 A244 300fr Combretum paniculatum 2.10 1.00
Nos. 797-802 (6) 5.10 2.45

1987, Aug. 6 *Perf. 13*

Raoul Follereau (1903-1977) and: 90fr, Doctors examining African youth. 100fr, Laboratory research. 120fr, Gerhard Hansen (1841-1912), microscope, bacillus under magnification. 300fr, Follereau embracing cured leper.

803 A245 90fr multicolored .60 .25
804 A245 100fr multicolored .70 .35
805 A245 120fr multicolored .85 .40
806 A245 300fr multicolored 2.10 1.00
Nos. 803-806 (4) 4.25 2.00

World Environment Day — A246

1987, Aug. 18 Litho. *Perf. 13x12½*

807 A246 90fr shown .70 .35
808 A246 145fr Emblem, huts 1.10 .55

Pre-Olympic Year — A247

1987, Aug. 31 *Perf. 12½*

809 A247 75fr High jump .55 .30
810 A247 85fr Tennis, vert. .60 .30
811 A247 90fr Ski jumping .70 .35
812 A247 100fr Soccer .75 .40
813 A247 145fr Running 1.10 .55
814 A247 350fr Pierre de Coubertin, tennis, vert. 2.60 1.25
Nos. 809-814 (6) 6.30 3.15

Pierre de Coubertin (1863-1937).

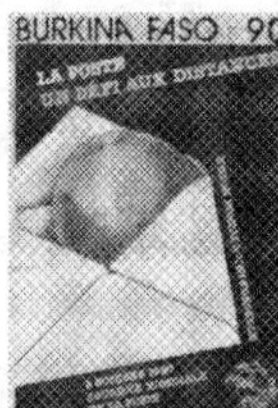

World Post Day — A248

1987, Oct. 5 Litho. *Perf. 12½x13*

815 A248 90fr multicolored

Fight Against Apartheid — A249

1987, Nov. 11 Litho. *Perf. 13*

816 A249 90fr shown 1.00 .50
817 A249 100fr Luthuli, book, 1962 1.10 .55

Albert John Luthuli (1898-1967), South African reformer, author and 1960 Nobel Peace Prize winner. No. 817 incorrectly inscribed "1899-1967."

Traditional Costumes — A250

1987, Dec. 4 Litho. *Perf. 11½x12*

818 A250 10fr Dagari
819 A250 30fr Peul
820 A250 90fr Mossi
821 A250 200fr Senoufo

No. 822 has been reserved for a 500fr stamp.

Traditional Musical Instruments A251

Perf. 12x11½, 11½x12

1987, Dec. 4 Litho.

823 A251 20fr Xylophone .20 .20
824 A251 25fr 3-Stringed lute, vert. .25 .20
825 A251 35fr Zither .30 .20
826 A251 90fr Conical drum .75 .40
827 A251 1000fr Calabash drum, vert. 7.50 3.75
Nos. 823-827 (5) 9.00 4.75

Intl. Year of Shelter for the Homeless — A252

1987, Dec. 4 Litho. *Perf. 13*

828 A252 90fr multicolored .65 .30

Five-year Natl. Development Plan — A253

1987, Dec. 15 *Perf. 13½*

829 A253 40fr Small businesses .30 .20
830 A253 55fr Agriculture .40 .20
831 A253 60fr Constructing schools .45 .25
832 A253 90fr Transportation and communications .65 .30
833 A253 100fr Literacy .75 .35
834 A253 120fr Animal husbandry .90 .45
Nos. 829-834 (6) 3.45 1.75

World Health Organization, 40th Anniv. — A254

1988, Mar. 31 Litho. *Perf. 12½x13*

835 A254 120fr multicolored .80 .40

1988 Summer Olympics, Seoul A255

1988, May 5 *Perf. 13x12½*

836 A255 30fr shown .25 .20
837 A255 160fr Torch, vert. 1.10 .50
838 A255 175fr Soccer 1.25 .60
839 A255 235fr Volleyball, vert. 1.50 .75
840 A255 450fr Basketball, vert. 2.90 1.50
Nos. 836-840 (5) 7.00 3.55

Souvenir Sheet

Perf. 12½x13

841 A255 500fr Runners 3.25 1.60

No. 841 contains one stamp, size: 40x52mm plus two labels.

Ritual Masks A256

1988, May 30 Litho. *Perf. 13*

842 A256 10fr Epervier, Houet .20 .20
843 A256 20fr Jeunes Filles, Oullo .20 .20
844 A256 30fr Bubale, Houet .20 .20
845 A256 40fr Forgeron, Mouhoun .35 .20
846 A256 120fr Nounouma, Ouri .80 .40
847 A256 175fr Chauve-souris, Ouri 1.25 .60
Nos. 842-847 (6) 3.00 1.80

Nos. 842-846 vert.

Handicrafts A257

1988, Aug. 22 Litho. *Perf. 13½*

848 A257 5fr Kieriebe ceramic pitcher, vert. .20 .20
849 A257 15fr Mossi basket .20 .20
850 A257 25fr Gurunsi chair .20 .20
851 A257 30fr Bissa basket .20 .20
852 A257 45fr Ougadougou leather box .35 .20
853 A257 85fr Ougadougou bronze statue, vert. .70 .35
854 A257 120fr Ougadougou leather valise .80 .40
Nos. 848-854 (7) 2.65 1.75

World Post Day — A258

1988, Oct. 9 Litho. *Perf. 13*

855 A258 120fr multicolored .80 .40

Aquatic Fauna A259

1988, Oct. 31 *Perf. 12*

856 A259 70fr Angler martin .50 .25
857 A259 100fr Mormyrus rume .70 .35
858 A259 120fr Frog .80 .40
859 A259 160fr Duck 1.10 .55
Nos. 856-859 (4) 3.10 1.55

Civil Rights and Political Activists A260

Designs: 80fr, Mohammed Ali Jinnah (1876-1948), 1st Governor General of Pakistan. 120fr, Mahatma Gandhi (1869-1948), India. 160fr, John F. Kennedy. 235fr, Martin Luther King, Jr.

1988, Nov. 22 Litho. *Perf. 14*

860 A260 80fr multicolored .50 .25
861 A260 120fr multicolored .80 .40
862 A260 160fr multicolored 1.00 .50
863 A260 235fr multicolored 1.50 .75
Nos. 860-863 (4) 3.80 1.90

A261

A262

Christmas: Stained-glass windows.

1988, Dec. 2 *Perf. 12*

864 A261 120fr Adoration of the shepherds .85 .40
865 A261 160fr Adoration of the Magi 1.00 .50
866 A261 450fr Madonna and child 2.90 1.50
867 A261 1000fr Flight into Egypt 6.25 3.25
Nos. 864-867 (4) 11.00 5.65

1989, Feb. 25 Litho. *Perf. 14*

868 A262 75fr shown .20 .20
869 A262 500fr Ababacar Makharam 1.60 .80
870 A262 500fr Jean Tchissoukou 1.60 .80
871 A262 500fr Paulin Vieyra 1.60 .80
Nos. 868-871 (4) 5.00 2.60

Souvenir Sheet

872 Sheet of 3 9.00 4.50
a.-c. A262 500fr like #869-871, inscribed in gold 3.00 1.50

Panafrican Film Festival (FESPACO), 20th anniv. Nos. 869-872 are airmail.

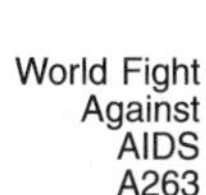

World Fight Against AIDS A263

1989, Apr. 7 Litho. *Perf. 13*

873 A263 120fr multicolored .80 .40

Council for Rural Development, 30th Anniv. — A264

1989, May 3 Litho. *Perf. 15x14*

874 A264 75fr multicolored .50 .25

Parasitic Plants — A265

Legumes and cereals.

1989, Oct. 9 Litho. *Perf. 11½*

Granite Paper

875 A265 20fr *Striga generiodes* .20 .20
876 A265 50fr *Striga hermonthica* .30 .20
877 A265 235fr *Striga aspera* 1.50 .80
878 A265 450fr *Alectra vogelii* 3.00 1.50
Nos. 875-878 (4) 5.00 2.70

Dogs A266

1989, Oct. 9 *Perf. 15x14½*

879 A266 35fr Sahel .25 .20
880 A266 50fr Puppy .35 .20
881 A266 60fr Hunting dog .40 .20
882 A266 350fr Guard dog 2.25 1.10
Nos. 879-882 (4) 3.25 1.70

Solidarity with the Palestinian People — A267

1989, Nov. 15 *Perf. 13*

883 A267 120fr Monument, Place de la Palestine .80 .40

Nos. 610-612 Overprinted

1988, Dec. 21 Litho. *Perf. 12½*

884 A203 90fr multicolored .60 .30
885 A203 120fr multicolored .85 .40
886 A203 170fr multicolored 1.25 .60
Nos. 884-886 (3) 2.70 1.30

Visit of Pope John Paul II A268

1990, Jan. 1 Litho. *Perf. 15x14*

887 A268 120fr Our Lady of Yagma .85 .40
888 A269 160fr Pope, crowd 1.25 .60

150th Anniv. of the Postage Stamp A269

1990, Mar. 20 Litho. *Perf. 15x14*

889 A269 120fr multicolored 1.00 .50

Souvenir Sheet

Perf. 14x15

890 A269 500fr Penny Black, ship 4.00 2.00

Stamp World London '90.

World Cup Soccer Championships, Italy — A270

1990, Apr. 26 Litho. *Perf. 11½*

891 A270 30fr multicolored .25 .20
892 A270 150fr multi, diff. 1.10 .55

Souvenir Sheet

893 A270 1000fr multi, horiz. 7.25 3.75

Intl. Literacy Year A271

1990, July 10 Litho. *Perf. 13*

894 A271 40fr multicolored .30 .20
895 A271 130fr multicolored .90 .45

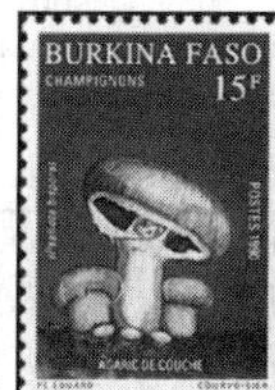

Mushrooms — A272

1990, May 17 Litho. *Perf. 11½*

896 A272 10fr Cantharellus cibarius .20 .20
897 A272 15fr Psalliota bispora .20 .20
898 A272 60fr Amanita caesarea .50 .25
899 A272 190fr Boletus badius 1.50 .75
a. Souv. sheet of 4, #896-899 2.25 1.10
Nos. 896-899 (4) 2.40 1.40

Intl. Exposition of Handicrafts — A273

1990, Sept. 25 Litho. *Perf. 13*

900 A273 35fr Masks, fans, vert. .30 .20
901 A273 45fr shown .40 .20
902 A273 270fr Rattan chair, vert. 2.50 1.25
Nos. 900-902 (3) 3.20 1.65

Gen. Charles de Gaulle (1890-1970) A274

1990, Nov. 22 Litho. *Perf. 13*

903 A274 200fr multicolored 1.75 .90

Minerals A275

1991, Feb. 4 Litho. *Perf. 15x14*

904 A275 20fr Quartz .20 .20
905 A275 50fr Granite .40 .20
906 A275 280fr Amphibolite 2.25 1.10
Nos. 904-906 (3) 2.85 1.50

African Film Festival — A276

Fight Against Drugs — A277

1991, Feb. 20 *Perf. 11½*

907 A276 150fr multicolored 1.25 .60

Souvenir Sheet

908 A276 1000fr Award 8.00 4.00

1991, Feb. 20

909 A277 130fr multicolored 1.00 .55

Samuel F.B. Morse (1791-1872), Inventor — A278

1991, May 17 Litho. *Perf. 13*

910 A278 200fr multicolored 1.60 .80

Native Girl — A279

Flowers A280

1991-93 Litho. *Perf. 14½x15*

911 A279 5fr gray & multi .20 .20
912 A279 10fr yellow & multi .20 .20
913 A279 25fr lilac rose & multi .20 .20
914 A279 50fr red lilac & multi .30 .20
915 A279 130fr blue & multi 1.10 .55
916 A279 150fr multicolored 1.25 .60

920 A279 200fr multicolored 1.60 .80
922 A279 330fr orange & multi 2.75 1.40
Nos. 911-922 (8) 7.60 4.15

Issued: 150fr, 200fr, 6/20/91; 130fr, 330fr, 1/15/93; 5-50fr, 5/3/94.
This is an expanding set. Numbers may change.

1991, July 31 Litho. *Perf. 11½*
926 A280 5fr Grewia tenax .20 .20
927 A280 15fr Hymenocardia acide .20 .20
928 A280 60fr Cassia sieberiana, vert. .50 .25
929 A280 100fr Adenium obesum .80 .40
930 A280 300fr Mitragyna inermis 2.40 1.25
Nos. 926-930 (5) 4.10 2.30

Traditional Dance Costumes A281

World Post Day — A282

1991, Aug. 20 *Perf. 12½*
931 A281 75fr Warba .60 .30
932 A281 130fr Wiskamba 1.00 .50
933 A281 280fr Pa-zenin 2.25 1.10
Nos. 931-933 (3) 3.85 1.90

1991, Oct. 9 *Perf. 13½*
934 A282 130fr multicolored 1.00 .50

Cooking Utensils A283

1992, Jan. 8 Litho. *Perf. 11½*
935 A283 45fr Pancake fryer .35 .20
936 A283 130fr Cooking pot, vert. 1.00 .55
937 A283 310fr Mortar & pestle, vert. 2.40 1.25
938 A283 500fr Ladle, calabash 4.00 2.00
Nos. 935-938 (4) 7.75 4.00

1992 African Soccer Championships, Senegal — A284

1992, Jan. 17 *Perf. 13½*
939 A284 50fr Yousouf Fofana .40 .20
940 A284 100fr Francois-Jules Bocande .80 .40

Souvenir Sheet
Perf. 13x12½
941 A284 500fr Trophy 4.00 2.00

UN Decade For the Handicapped — A285

1992, Mar. 31 Litho. *Perf. 12½*
942 A285 100fr multicolored .85 .40

World Health Day — A286

1992, Apr. 7 *Perf. 13*
943 A286 330fr multicolored 2.75 1.40

Discovery of America, 500th Anniv. A287

1992, Aug. 12 Litho. *Perf. 12½*
944 A287 50fr Columbus, Santa Maria .40 .25
945 A287 150fr Ships, natives 1.25 .65

Souvenir Sheet
946 A287 350fr Map 3.00 1.50

Genoa '92. No. 946 contains one 52x31mm stamp.

A288

A289

Insects.

1992, Aug. 17 *Perf. 15x14*
947 A288 20fr Dysdercus voelkeri .20 .20
948 A288 40fr Rhizopertha dominica .35 .20
949 A288 85fr Orthetrum microstigma .75 .35
950 A288 500fr Apis mellifera 4.25 2.25
Nos. 947-950 (4) 5.55 3.00

1992, Dec. 21 Litho. *Perf. 11½*
Christmas: 10fr, Boy, creche. 130fr, Children decorating creche. 1000fr, Boy holding painting of Madonna and Child.

951 A289 10fr multicolored .20 .20
952 A289 130fr multicolored 1.00 .50
953 A289 1000fr multicolored 8.00 4.00
Nos. 951-953 (3) 9.20 4.70

Invention of the Diesel Engine, Cent. A290

1993, Jan. 25 Litho. *Perf. 11½*
954 A290 1000fr multicolored 8.00 4.00

The date of issue is in question.

Paris '94, Philatelic Exhibition A291

1993, July 15
955 A291 400fr multicolored 3.50 1.75
956 A291 650fr multi, diff. 5.50 2.75

African Film Festival — A292

Birds — A293

Designs: 250fr, Monument to the cinema. 750fr, M. Douta (1919-1991), comedian, horiz.

Perf. 11½x12, 12x11½
1993, Feb. 16 Litho.
957 A292 250fr multicolored 2.00 1.00
958 A292 750fr multicolored 6.00 3.00

1993, Mar. 31 *Perf. 11½x12*
100fr, Mycteria ibis. 200fr, Leptoptilos crumeniferus. 500fr, Ephippiorhynchus senegalensis.

959 A293 100fr multicolored .80 .40
960 A293 200fr multicolored 1.60 .80
961 A293 500fr multicolored 4.00 2.00
a. Souvenir sheet of 3, #959-961 9.50 4.75
Nos. 959-961 (3) 6.40 3.20

No. 961a sold for 1200fr.

1994 World Cup Soccer Championships, US — A294

1993, Apr. 8 *Perf. 15*
962 A294 500fr shown 4.00 2.00
963 A294 1000fr Players, US flag 8.00 4.00

Fruit Trees — A295

150fr, Saba senegalensis, vert. 300fr, Butyrospermum parkii. 600fr, Adansonia digitata, vert.

1993, June 2 Litho. *Perf. 11½*
964 A295 150fr multicolored 1.25 .65
965 A295 300fr multicolored 2.50 1.25
966 A295 600fr multicolored 5.00 2.50
Nos. 964-966 (3) 8.75 4.40

Traditional Jewelry A296

1993, Sept. 25 Litho. *Perf. 11½*
967 A296 200fr Ring for hair 1.60 .85
968 A296 250fr Agate necklace, vert. 2.00 1.00
969 A296 500fr Bracelet 4.00 2.00
Nos. 967-969 (3) 7.60 3.85

Gazella Rufifrons A297

1993, Dec. 10 Litho. *Perf. 14½*
970 A297 30fr shown 1.00 .50
971 A297 40fr Two facing left 1.00 .50
972 A297 60fr Two standing 2.25 1.50
973 A297 100fr Young gazelle 4.75 2.50
a. Souvenir sheet, #970-973 6.00 6.00
Nos. 970-973 (4) 9.00 5.00

World Wildlife Fund (#970-973). No. 973a sold for 400fr.

Kingfishers — A298

1994, Mar. 8 Litho. *Perf. 11½*
974 A298 600fr Halcyon senegalensis 2.00 1.00
975 A298 1200fr Halcyon chelicuti 4.25 2.25

Souvenir Sheet
976 A298 2000fr Ceyx picta 7.00 3.50

1994 World Cup Soccer Championships, US — A299

1994, Mar. 28
977 A299 1000fr Players, US map 3.50 1.75
978 A299 1800fr Soccer ball, players 6.50 3.25
a. Souvenir sheet of 1 7.00 3.50

No. 978a sold for 2000fr.

First Manned Moon Landing, 25th Anniv. — A300

1994, July 15 Litho. *Perf. 11½*
979 A300 750fr Astronaut, flag 3.75 1.90
980 A300 750fr Lunar module, earth 3.75 1.90
a. Pair, #979-980 7.50 3.75

No. 980a is a continuous design.

First Stamp Exhibition, Paris, 1994
A301

1994, Apr. 28

981 A301 1500fr Dogs 7.75 3.75
a. Souvenir sheet of 1 7.75 3.75

Legumes — A302

40fr, Hibiscus sabdariffa. 45fr, Solanum aethiopicum. 75fr, Solanum melongena. 100fr, Hibiscus esculentus.

1994 Litho. *Perf. 11½*

982 A302 40fr multicolored .20 .20
983 A302 45fr multicolored .25 .20
984 A302 75fr multicolored .40 .20
985 A302 100fr multicolored .50 .25
Nos. 982-985 (4) 1.35 .85

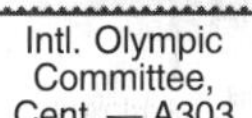

Intl. Olympic Committee, Cent. — A303

Domestic Animals — A304

1994, Oct. 10 *Perf. 15*

986 A303 320fr multicolored 1.60 .80

1994, Oct. 10 *Perf. 11½*

987 A304 150fr Pig, horiz. .75 .35
988 A304 1000fr Capra hircus 4.75 2.50
989 A304 1500fr Ovis aries, horiz. 7.25 3.75
Nos. 987-989 (3) 12.75 6.60

Elvis Presley (1935-77)
A305

A305a

Portraits in feature films: 300fr, Loving You. 500fr, Jailhouse Rock. 1000fr, Blue Hawaii. 1500fr, Marilyn Monroe, Presley.

1995 Litho. *Perf. 13½*

990-992 A305 Set of 3 7.50 3.75

Souvenir Sheets

993 A305 1500fr multicolored 6.00 3.00

Litho. & Embossed

993A A305a 3000fr gold & multi

Nos. 990-992 exist in souvenir sheets of one. No. 993 contains one 51x42mm stamp with continuous design. No. 993A, exists in souvenir sheets of silver & multi with different designs in sheet margin.

Issued: No. 993A, 2/24/95.

See Nos. 1012-1015A.

Crocodile — A306

1995, Feb. 6 Litho. *Perf. 15x14½*

994 A306 10fr brown & multi .20 .20
995 A306 20fr lilac & multi .20 .20
996 A306 25fr olive brn & multi .20 .20
997 A306 30fr green & multi .20 .20
998 A306 40fr red brn & multi .20 .20
999 A306 50fr gray & multi .25 .20
1000 A306 75fr gray vio & multi .35 .20
1001 A306 100fr gray brn & multi .50 .25
1002 A306 150fr olive & multi .75 .40
1003 A306 175fr gray bl & multi .90 .45
1004 A306 250fr brn lake & multi 1.25 .65
1005 A306 400fr bl grn & multi 2.00 1.00
Nos. 994-1005 (12) 7.00 4.15

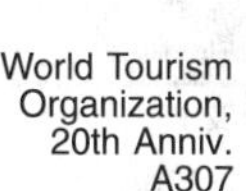

World Tourism Organization, 20th Anniv.
A307

Designs: 150fr, Man riding donkey, vert. 350fr, Bobo-Dioulasso railroad station. 450fr, Grand Mosque, Bani. 650fr, Gazelle, map.

1995, Jan. 26 Litho. *Perf. 11½*

1006 A307 150fr multicolored .75 .40
1007 A307 350fr multicolored 1.75 .90
1008 A307 450fr multicolored 2.25 1.10
1009 A307 650fr multicolored 3.25 1.60
Nos. 1006-1009 (4) 8.00 4.00

FESPACO '95 — 1010

Motion pictures: 150fr, "Rabi," Gaston Kabore. 250fr, "Tilai," Idrissa Ouedraogo.

1995 *Perf. 13½*

1010 A308 150fr multicolored .80 .40
1011 A308 250fr multicolored 1.40 .70

Nos. 1010-1011 exist in souvenir sheets of one. Motion pictures, cent.

Traditional Houses
A308a

1995 Litho. *Perf. 13½*

1011A A308a 70fr Mossi
1011B A308a 100fr Kassena
1011C A308a 200fr Bobo

An additional stamp was issued in this set. The editors would like to examine it.

Stars of Motion Pictures Type of 1995

Marilyn Monroe in feature films: 400fr, The Joyful Parade. 650fr, The Village Tramp. 750fr, Niagara.

1500fr, The Seven Year Itch. 3000fr, Marilyn Monroe (1926-62).

1995 Litho. *Perf. 13½*

1012-1014 A305 Set of 3 7.50 3.75

Souvenir Sheets

1015 A305 1500fr multicolored 6.00 3.00

Litho. & Embossed

1015A A305a 3000fr gold & multi

#1012-1014 exist in souvenir sheets of 1. #1015 contains one 42x51mm stamp with continuous design. #1015A exists in souvenir sheets of silver & multi with different designs in sheet margin.

Birds — A309

Designs: 450fr, Laniarius barbarus. 600fr, Estrilda bengala. 750fr, Euplectes afer.

1995, Apr. 5 Litho. *Perf. 11½*

1016 A309 450fr multicolored 2.00 1.00
1017 A309 600fr multicolored 2.75 1.40
1018 A309 750fr multicolored 3.50 1.75
a. Souv. sheet, #1016-1018 9.00 4.50
Nos. 1016-1018 (3) 8.25 4.15

No. 1018a sold for 2000fr.

Reptiles
A310

Designs: 450fr, Psammophis sibilans. 500fr, Eryx muelleri. 1500fr, Turtle.

1995, Dec. 31

1019 A310 450fr multicolored 2.00 1.00
1020 A310 500fr multicolored 2.25 1.10
1021 A310 1500fr multicolored 6.75 3.50
Nos. 1019-1021 (3) 11.00 5.60

1996 Summer Olympics, Atlanta
A311

Design: 3000fr, Tennis, diff.

1995, Sept. 20 Litho. *Perf. 13½*

1022 A311 150fr Basketball .70 .35
1023 A311 250fr Baseball 1.25 .60
1024 A311 650fr Tennis 3.00 1.50
1025 A311 750fr Table tennis 3.50 1.75
a. Souv. sheet, #1022-1025 8.50 4.25
Nos. 1022-1025 (4) 8.45 4.20

Souvenir Sheets

1026 A311 1500fr Equestrian event 7.00 7.00

Litho. & Embossed

1026A A311 3000fr gold & multi

No. 1026A also exists as a silver & multi souvenir sheet with different design in sheet margin. Both the gold & silver stamps also exist together in a souvenir sheet of 2.

Sports Figures
A312

Ayrton Senna (1960-94), World Driving Champion — A313

Designs: 300fr, Juan Manuel Fangio, race car driver, 1955 Mercedes W 196. 400fr, Andre Agassi, US tennis player. 500fr, Ayrton Senna (1960-94), race car driver, McLaren MP 4/6 Honda. 1000fr, Michael Schumacher, race car driver, 1995 Benetton B 195.

1500fr, Enzo Ferrari, 412 TR, F40.

1995, Sept. 20

1027 A312 300fr multi 2.25 1.10
1028 A312 400fr multi 3.25 1.60
1029 A312 500fr multi 4.00 2.00
1030 A312 1000fr multi 8.00 4.00
a. Souvenir sheet of 3, #1027, 1029-1030 14.50 7.25
Nos. 1027-1030 (4) 17.50 8.70

Souvenir Sheets

1031 A312 1500fr multicolored *7.00 3.50*

Litho. & Embossed

1032 A313 3000fr gold & multi

#1027-1030 exist in souvenir sheets of 1. #1031 contains one 55x48mm stamp.

No. 1032 also exists as a silver & multi souvenir sheet with different design in sheet margin. Both the gold and silver stamps also exist together in a souvenir sheet of 2.

For surcharge see No. 1078.

Souvenir Sheets

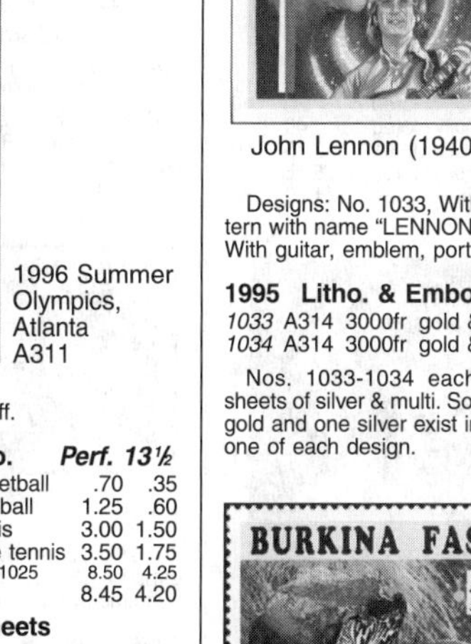

John Lennon (1940-1980) — A314

Designs: No. 1033, With guitar, circular pattern with name "LENNON," portrait. No. 1034, With guitar, emblem, portrait.

1995 Litho. & Embossed *Perf. 13½*

1033 A314 3000fr gold & multi
1034 A314 3000fr gold & multi

Nos. 1033-1034 each exist in souvenir sheets of silver & multi. Souvenir sheets of one gold and one silver exist in same designs and one of each design.

1995 Boy Scout Jamboree, Holland
A315

Mushrooms: 150fr, Russula nigricans. 250fr, Lepiota rhacodes. 300fr, Xerocomus subtomentos. 400fr, Boletus erythropus. 500fr, Russula sanguinea. 650fr, Amanita rubescens. 750fr, Amanita vaginata. 1000fr, Geastrum sessil.

No. 1043, Amanita muscaria. No. 1044, Morchella esculenta.

1996, Feb. 20 Litho. *Perf. 13½*

1035-1042 A315 Set of 8 16.00 8.00
1041a Sheet of 4, #1035, 1037, 1040-1041 7.50 3.75
1042a Sheet of 4, #1036, 1038-1039, 1042 8.50 4.25

Souvenir Sheets

1043-1044 A315 1500fr each 6.00 3.00

Mushrooms — A316

Designs: 175fr, Hygrophore perroquet. 250fr, Pleurote en huitre. 300fr, Pezize (oreille d'ane). 450fr, Clavaire jolie.

1996, Jan. 24

1045-1048 A316 Set of 4 4.50 2.25
1048a Souv. sheet, #1045-1048 4.50 2.25

#1045-1048 each exist in souv. sheets of 1.

UN, 50th Anniv. A317

Designs: 500fr, UN headquarters, New York. 1000fr, UN emblem, people, vert.

1995, Dec. 20 *Perf. 11½*

1049 A317 500fr multicolored 2.75 1.25
1050 A317 1000fr multicolored 5.25 2.75

Christmas A318

Designs: 150fr, Christmas tree, children pointing to picture of nativity scene. 450fr, Yagma Grotto. 500fr, Flight into Egypt. 1000fr, Adoration of the Magi.

1995, Dec. 18

1051 A318 150fr multicolored .80 .40
1052 A318 450fr multicolored 2.40 1.25
1053 A318 500fr multicolored 2.75 1.40
1054 A318 1000fr multicolored 5.25 2.75
Nos. 1051-1054 (4) 11.20 5.80

Entertainers — A319

Portraits: No. 1062, Elvis Presley, smiling. No. 1063, Presley, hand under chin. No. 1064, Stevie Wonder.

1996, May 14 Litho. *Perf. 13½*

Souvenir Sheets

1062-1064 A319 1500fr each 5.25 2.50

Numbers have been reserved for a set of 8 individual stamps released with these souvenir sheets.

Dated 1995.

Butterflies and Insects A320

100fr, Epiphora bauhiniae. 150fr, Kraussella amabile. 175fr, Charaxes epijasius. 250fr, Locusta migratoria.

1996 Litho. *Perf. 13½*

1065 A320 100fr multi, vert. .40 .20
1066 A320 150fr multi, vert. .70 .35
1067 A320 175fr multi, vert. .80 .40
1068 A320 250fr multi 1.10 .60
Nos. 1065-1068 (4) 3.00 1.55

Two souvenir sheets containing Nos. 1065, 1067 and Nos. 1066, 1068, respectively, exist.

Butterflies A321

Designs: 150fr, Morpho rega. 250fr, Hypolymnas misippus. 450fr, Pseudacraea boisduvali. 600fr, Charaxes castor. 1500fr, Antanartia delius.

1996, June 28 Litho. *Perf. 13½*

1069 A321 150fr multicolored .70 .35
1070 A321 250fr multicolored 1.10 .55
1071 A321 450fr multicolored 2.00 1.00
1072 A321 600fr multicolored 2.75 2.75
Nos. 1069-1072 (4) 6.55 4.65

Souvenir Sheet

1073 A321 1500fr multicolored 6.75 6.75
a. Ovptd. in sheet margin 6.25 6.25

Overprint in silver in sheet margin of No. 1073a contains Hong Kong '97 Exhibition emblem and two line inscription in Chinese. Issued in 1997.

Insects — A321a

c, 25fr, Sauterelle. d, 75fr, Schistocerca gregaria. e, 300fr, Pardolata haasi. f, 400fr, Psammomys obesus.

1996, June 28 Litho. *Perf. 13½*

1073B A321a Strip of 4, #c.-f. 2.75 1.40

1998 World Cup Soccer Championships, France — A322

Various soccer plays.

1996 Litho. *Perf. 13*

1074 A322 50fr multi .20 .20
1075 A322 150fr multi, vert. .65 .25
1076 A322 250fr multi, vert. 1.10 .55
1077 A322 450fr multi, vert. 1.90 1.00
Nos. 1074-1077 (4) 3.85 2.00

No. 1028 Ovptd. in Metallic Red

1996 Litho. *Perf. 13½*

1078 A312 400fr multicolored 1.60 .80

No. 1078 exists in souvenir sheet of 1.

Wild Cats — A323

Designs: 100fr, Panthera leo. 150fr, Acinonyx jubatus. 175fr, Lynx caracal. 250fr, Panthera pardus.

Illustration reduced.

1996 *Perf. 12½x12*

1079 A323 100fr multicolored .40 .20
1080 A323 150fr multicolored .55 .30
1081 A323 175fr multicolored .65 .35
1082 A323 250fr multicolored .95 .45
Nos. 1079-1082 (4) 2.55 1.30

Orchids — A324

Various orchids.

1996, Aug. 30 Litho. *Perf. 12½x13*

1083 A324 100fr blue & multi 1.10 .55
1084 A324 175fr lilac & multi 1.90 .95
1085 A324 250fr orange & multi 2.75 1.25
1086 A324 300fr olive & multi 3.25 1.60
Nos. 1083-1086 (4) 9.00 4.35

UNICEF, 50th Anniv. — A324a

Design: 250fr, Vaccination of child.

1996 (?) Litho. *Perf. 11¾*

1086A A324a 250fr multi

The editors suspect that more stamps were issued in this set, and would like to examine any examples.

Birds — A325

Designs: 500fr, Falco peregrinus. 750fr, Crossoptilon mantchuricum. 1000fr, Branta canadensis. 1500fr, Pelecanus crispus.

1996, June 25 *Perf. 12½x12*

1087 A325 500fr multicolored 2.00 1.00
1088 A325 750fr multicolored 2.50 1.25
1089 A325 1000fr multicolored 3.75 1.90
1090 A325 1500fr multicolored 5.75 2.75
Nos. 1087-1090 (4) 14.00 6.90

#1087-1090 each printed se-tenant with labels.

Diana, Princess of Wales (1961-97) A325a

Various portraits, color of sheet margin: #1090A, blue. #1090K, deep pink.

#1090U, In yellow. #1090V, Wearing tiara.

1997 Litho. *Perf. 13½*

Sheets of 9

1090A A325a 150fr #Ab-Aj 4.75 2.40
1090K A325a 180fr #Kl-Kti 5.75 3.00

Souvenir Sheets

1090U-1090V A325a 2000fr each 7.25 3.50

#1090U-1090V each contain one 41x46mm stamp.

See Nos. 1126-1128.

Flowers A325b

Design: 175fr, Costus pectabilis. 400fr, Crotalaria retusa.

1997 (?) Litho. *Perf. 13¼x13½*

1090X A325b 175fr multi
1097Z A325b 400fr multi — —

Issued: 400fr, 12/22.

Three additional stamps were issued in this set. The editors would like to examine them.

A326

A327

Various portraits, color of sheet margin: No. 1091, Pale pink. No. 1092, Pale blue. No. 1093, Pale yellow.

No. 1094, In white dress, serving food to child (in sheet margin). No. 1095, Wearing wide-brimmed hat.

1998 Litho. *Perf. 14*

Sheets of 6

1091 A326 425fr #a.-f. 8.75 4.50
1092 A326 530fr #a.-f. 11.00 5.50
1093 A326 590fr #a.-f. 12.00 6.00

Souvenir Sheets

1094-1095 A326 1500fr each 5.00 2.50

Diana, Princess of Wales (1961-97).

1998 Litho. *Perf. 14*

1096 A327 260fr shown .60 .30

Souvenir Sheet

1097 A327 1500fr Portrait, diff. 5.00 2.50

Mother Teresa (1910-97). No. 1096 was issued in sheets of 6. Nos. 1096-1097 have birth date inscribed "1907."

Birds — A328

5fr, White-winged triller. 10fr, Golden sparrow. 100fr, American goldfinch. 170fr, Red-legged thrush. 260fr, Willow warbler. 425fr, Blue grosbeak.

No. 1104: a, Bank swallow. b, Kirtland's warbler. c, Long-tailed minivet. d, Blue-gray gnatcatcher. e, Reed-bunting. f, Black-collared apalis. g, American robin. h, Cape long-claw. i, Wood thrush.

No. 1105: a, Song sparrow. b, Dartford warbler. c, Eastern bluebird. d, Rock thrush. e, Northern mockingbird. f, Northern cardinal. g, Eurasian goldfinch. h, Varied thrush. i, Northern oriole.

No. 1106, Golden whistler. No. 1107, Barn swallow, horiz.

1998, Oct. 1 Litho. *Perf. 13½*

1098-1103 A328 Set of 6 3.50 1.75

Sheets of 9

1104 A328 260fr #a.-i. 8.25 4.00
1105 A328 425fr #a.-i. 14.00 7.00

Souvenir Sheets

1106-1107 A328 1500fr each 5.50 2.75

Butterflies and Moths A329

No. 1108: a, Arctia caja. b, Nymphalis antiopa. c, Brahmaea wallichii. d, Issoria lathonia. e, Speyeria cybele. f, Vanessa virginiensis. g, Rothchildia orizaba. h, Cethosia hypsea. i, Marpesia petreus.

No. 1109: a, Agraulis vanillae. b, Junonia coenia. c, Danaus gilippus. d, Polygonia comma. e, Anthocharis cardamines. f, Heliconius aoede. g, Atlides halesus. h, Mesosemia croseus. i, Automeris io.

No. 1110, Papilio xuthus. No. 1111, Pterourus multicaudatus. No. 1112, Pterourus troilus. No. 1113, Papilio machaon.

1998, Oct. 25

Sheets of 9

1108 A329 170fr #a.-i. 5.25 2.75
1109 A329 530fr #a.-i. 16.00 8.00

Souvenir Sheets

1110-1113 A329 1500fr each 5.50 2.75

#1110-1113 contain one 56x42mm stamp.

Christmas 1114

Fauna, flora with Christmas items: 100fr, Tersina viridis, holly, vert. 170fr, Citherias menander, present, vert. 260fr, Chrysanthemum, reindeer, sleigh, vert. 425fr, Swallowtail butterfly, greeting card. 530fr, European bee eater, Santa Claus, snowman.

No. 1119, Anthemis tinctoria, sleigh. No. 1120, Papilio ulysses, greeting card.

1998, Dec. 1 Litho. *Perf. 14*

1114-1118 A330 Set of 5 5.50 2.75

Souvenir Sheets

1119-1120 A330 1500fr each 5.50 2.75

Handicrafts A330a

Design: 25f, Stool with carved heads. 100fr, Dagari stool. 150fr, Basket. 170f, Wooden statue, Wooden statue, Pasoré region, vert.

1996-98 (?) Litho. *Perf. 11¾*

1120B A330a 25fr multi
1120G A330a 100fr multi
1120H A330a 150fr multi
1120I A330a 170fr multi
1120J A330a 260fr multi

Issued: No. 1120B, 170fr, 260f, 6/20/98. Six additional stamps were issued in this set. The editors would like to examine them.

34th Organization for African Unity Summit, Ouagadougou — A330b

Design: 170fr, OAU emblem, horses.

1998, May 20 Litho. *Perf. 13x13¼*

1120K A330b 170fr multi

An additional stamp was issued in this set. The editors would like to examine it.

Protected Wildlife — A330c

Designs: 170fr, Leptoptilos crumeniferus. 200fr, Acionyx jubatus. 260fr, Orycteropus afer. 530fr, Struthio camulus. 590fr, Hippopotamus amphibus, horiz.

Perf. 13¼x13, 13x13¼

1998, May 20 Litho.

1120M A330c 170fr multi
1120N A330c 200fr multi
1120O A330c 260fr multi
1120P A330c 530fr multi
1120Q A330c 590fr multi

15th FESPACO Film Festival — A330d

Film: 150fr, Enfance et Jeunesse. 250fr, Etalon de Yennega.

1997, Feb. 5 Litho. *Perf. 11½x11¾*

1120R A330d 150fr multi
1120S A330d 250fr multi — —

Wild Animals — A330e

Design: 150fr, Bubale.

Perf. 11½x11¾

1997, Mar. 20 Litho.

1120V A330e 150fr multi

Three additional stamps were issued in this set. The editors would like to examine them.

Trains - A331

No. 1121: a, CDR No. 19, Ireland. b, EMD "F" Series Bo-Bo, US. c, Class 72000, France. d, Class AE 4/4 Bo-Bo, Switzerland. e, Class 277, Spain. f, ET 403 four car train, West Germany. g, Class EM2 Co-Co, UK. h, Europe Dutch Swiss Tee.

No. 1122: a, DF 4 East Wind IV Co-Co, China. b, Union Pacific Railroad, US. c, No. 3.641, Norway. d, Class GE 4/4 Bo-bo, Switzerland. e, Class GE Bo-Bo, South Africa. f, WDM-2 Co-Co, India. g, Kraus Mafeei Co-Co, US. h, RTG Four-car transit, France.

No. 1123, ETR 401 Pendolino, Italy. No. 1124, No. 12 Sarah Siddons, UK.

1998, Nov. 10

Sheets of 8

1121 A331 170fr #a.-h. 5.00 2.50
1122 A331 425fr #a.-h. 12.50 6.25

Souvenir Sheets

1123-1124 A331 1500fr each 5.50 2.75

Intl. Fund for Agricultural Development Type of 1998

150fr, Restoration of degraded soils.

1998, Mar. 20 Litho. *Perf. 13½*

1124A A331a 150fr multi

Intl. Fund for Agricultural Development, 20th Anniv. — A331a

Design: 400fr, "20," wheat stalk.

1998 (?) Litho. *Perf. 13½x13¼*

1125 A331a 400fr multi

The editors suspect that more stamps were issued in this set, and would like to examine any examples.

Ceramics — A331b

Design: 450fr, Vase.

Perf. 11½x11¾

1997, Sept. 11 Litho.

1125H A331b 450fr multi

Three additional stamps were released in this set. The editors would like to examine them.

Fish A331c

Design: 100fr, Aplocheiolichthys pfaffi.

1997, Nov. 20 Litho. *Perf. 13¼*

1125I A331c 100fr multi

Three additional stamps were issued in this set. The editors would like to examine them.

African Soccer Championships — A331d

Design: 175fr, Goalie making save. 150fr, Four players.

1998, Jan. 20 Litho. *Perf. 13x13¼*

1125M A331d 150fr multi — —
1125N A331d 175fr multi

Two additional stamps were issued in this set. The editors would like to examine them.

Traditional Costumes A331e

Design: 150fr, Peulh (Togore). 250fr, Peulh (Boodi). 450fr, Bissa (Gangadruku).

1998, Feb. 20 Litho. *Perf. 13½x13*

1125Q A331e 150fr multi — —
1125S A331e 250fr multi
1125T A331e 450fr multi

An additional stamps were released in this set. The editors would like to examine them.

Diana, Princess of Wales Type

425fr, Diana in white blouse. 590fr, Diana with Pope John Paul II. #1127A: various portraits, color of sheet margin is violet.

1500fr, Diana speaking, American Red Cross emblem in sheet margin. 2000fr, Diana wearing Japanese kimono.

1997 Litho. *Perf. 13½*

1126 A325a 425fr multi 1.60 1.60
1127 A325a 590fr multi 2.25 1.10

Sheet of 9

1127A A325a 180fr #b-j 6.00 3.00

Souvenir Sheets

1127K A325a 1500fr multi 5.50 2.75
1128 A325a 2000fr multi 7.50 3.75

No. 1127 was issued in sheets of 9. #1127K contains one 41x46mm stamp.

Airplanes A332

No. 1129: a, Sukhoi Su-24. b, Yakovlev Yak-38. c, Tupolev Blackjack. d, Antonov An-26. e, Antonov An-22 Anteus. f, Antonov An-124.

1000fr, Ilyushin Il-76T.

1999, Sept. 8 Litho. *Perf. 14*

1129 A332 425fr Sheet of 6, #a.-f. 8.50 8.50

Souvenir Sheet

1130 A332 1000fr multicolored 3.25 3.25

No. 1130 contains one 57x43mm stamp.

Ships A333

No. 1131: a, Portland. b, Goethe. c, Fulton.

No. 1132: a, CSS Nashville. b, Cutty Sark. c, Brilliant. d, Eagle. e, Red Jacket. f, USS Columbia. g, HMS Rose. h, Resolution. i, 1000-ton paquebot. j, Mayflower.

No. 1133: a, USS Tennessee. b, HMS Alacrity. c, Bismarck. d, Yamoto. e, Aurora. f, Iowa class battleship. g, Liberty Ship. h, F209. i, Star. j, Big Eagle.

No. 1134, Batavia. No. 1135, Grand Voilier.

1999, Sept. 8

Sheets of 3 and 10

1131 A333 170fr #a.-c. 1.75 1.75
1132 A333 100fr #a.-j. 3.25 3.25
1133 A333 200fr #a.-j. 6.50 6.50

Souvenir Sheets

1134-1135 A333 1000fr each 3.25 3.25

Domesticated Animals — A334

5fr, Tabby cat, vert. 10fr, Chinchilla. 20fr, Yorkshire terriers. 25fr, Cocker spaniels.

No. 1140, vert.: a, Afghan hound. b, Fox terrier. c, Pug. d, Dalmatian. e, Boston terrier. f, Cocker spaniel.

No. 1141: a, American wirehaired. b, Tabby. c, Blue Burmese. d, Abyssinian. e, Lilac Burmese. f, Siamese.

No. 1142, Persian. No. 1143, Japanese bobtail, vert. No. 1144, Labrador retriever, vert. No. 1145, Labrador retrievers, vert.

1999, Oct. 4

1136-1139 A334 Set of 4 .20 .20

Sheets of 6

1140 A334 260fr #a.-f. 5.25 5.25
1141 A334 530fr #a.-f. 10.50 10.50

Souvenir Sheets

1142-1145 A334 1000fr each 3.25 3.25

Domesticated Animals — A335

No. 1146 - Horses: a, Gelderlander. b, Trait lourd. c, Vladimir. d, Percheron. e, Sumba. f, Dartmoor.

No. 1147 - Dogs: a, French bulldog. b, Bernese. c, Griffon. d, King Charles spaniel. e, Spitz. f, Yorkshire terrier.

No. 1148 - Cats: a, American wirehaired. b, Japanese bobtail. c, Himalayan. d, LaPerm. e, Lilac Siamese colorpoint. f, Norwegian forest cat.

No. 1149, Shetland pony, vert. No. 1150, Basset hound, vert. No. 1151, Japanese bobtail, diff., vert.

1999, Oct. 4 **Sheets of 6**

1146 A335 170fr #a.-f. 3.50 3.50
1147 A335 425fr #a.-f. 8.50 8.50
1148 A335 590fr #a.-f. 11.50 11.50

Souvenir Sheets

1149-1151 A335 1000fr each 3.25 3.25

Fight Against Hunger — A337

1999, Dec. **Litho.** ***Perf. 14***

1157 A337 350fr multi 1.00 1.00

Issued in sheets of 5.

FESPACO '99 Film Festival - A338

Award winning film: 170fr, Tilai, by Idrissa Ouédraogo. 260fr, Map of Africa, camera, clapper board, vert.

1999 **Litho.** ***Perf. 13x13¼, 13¼x13***

1158 A338 170fr multi
1159 A338 260fr multi
1159A A338 425fr multi

Issued: 1159A, 2/22/99. The editors suspect other stamps with this theme may have been issued, and would like to examine examples. Numbers have been reserved for these possible additions.

Council of the Entente, 40th Anniv. A338a

Denomination color: 170fr, Black. 260fr, Green.

1999, May 5 **Litho.** ***Perf. 13x13¼***

1160-1161 A338a Set of 2

Lions A338b

1999, May 26 **Litho.** ***Perf. 13x13¼***

Panel Colors

1161A A338b 170fr blue
1161B A338b 260fr red — —
1161C A338b 425fr green — —
1161D A338b 530fr orange
1161E A338b 590fr purple
1161A-1161E, Set of 5 7.50

Philex France 99.

Orchids — A339

No. 1162: a, Angraecum orchid cape. b, Disa kirstenbosck pride. c, Disa blackii. d, Angraecum long icalear. e, Bulbophyllum falcatum. f, Phragmipedium schlimii (two flowers). g, Polystachya affinis. h, Jumellea sagittata (with leaves).

No. 1163: a, Angraecum sesquipedale. b, Oeceoclades maculata. c, Ancistrochilus childianus. d, Polystachyabella. e, Bulbophyllum lepidum. f, Vanilla imperialis. g, Tridactyle tridactylites. h, Eulophia guineensis.

No. 1164: a, Ansellia africana. b, Aerangis luteo-alba. c, Disa uniflora. d, Angraecum distichum. e, Bulbophyllum falcatum. f, Phragmepedium schlimii (pink flower). g, Polystachya affinis. h, Jumellea sagittata (without leaves).

No. 1165, Disa tripetaloides, horiz. No. 1166, Liparis guineensis, horiz. No. 1167, Bolusiella talbotii, horiz.

2000, Jan. 10 **Litho.** ***Perf. 14***

Sheets of 8, #a.-h.

1162-1164 A339 260fr each 7.25 7.25

Souvenir Sheets

1165-1167 A339 1500fr each 5.25 5.25

Space Exploration A340

No. 1168: a, Robert H. Goddard and 1926 rocket. b, Sputnik 1. c, X-15. d, Chinese, inventors of rockets. e, V-2. f, Explorer 1.

No. 1169: a, Vostok 1. b, Friendship 7. c, Soyuz 1. d, Freedom 7. e, Gemini 4. f, Apollo 7.

No. 1170, horiz.: a, Gemini 8. b, Agena target vehicle. c, Soyuz 11. d, Salyut 1. e, Apollo 18. f, Soyuz 19.

No. 1171, Tacsat satellite. No. 1172, Hubble Space Telescope. No. 1173, Viking Lander, horiz.

2000, Jan. 10

Sheets of 6

1168 A340 350fr #a.-f. 7.50 7.50
1169 A340 425fr #a.-f. 9.00 9.00
1170 A340 530fr #a.-f. 11.00 11.00

Souvenir Sheets

1171-1173 A340 1500fr each 5.50 5.50

No. 1173 contains one 57x42mm stamp.

Peter Pan — A341

Designs: a, 75fr, Fairy, red flowers. b, 75fr, Parrot. c, 75fr, Moon, Wendy, Michael, John. d, 75fr, White flower. e, 80fr, Fairy, pink flower. f, 80fr, Butterflies. g, 80fr, Peter Pan. h, 80fr, Fairy. i, 90fr, Red flower. j, 90fr, Butterflies. k, 90fr, Egret. l, 90fr, White flower. m, 100fr, Mermaid. n, 100fr, Pirate ship, crocodile's tail. o, 100fr, Crocodile's head. p, 100fr, Captain Hook.

2000, Jan. 10 ***Perf. 12¼***

1174 A341 Sheet of 16, #a.-p. 4.25 4.25

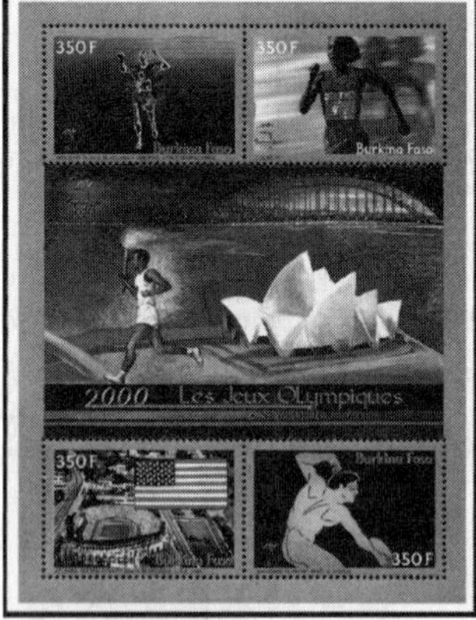

2000 Summer Olympics, Sydney — A343

No. 1191: a, Hannes Kohlemainen. b, Runner. c, US flag, Fulton County Stadium, Atlanta. d, Discus thrower.

Illustration reduced.

2000, Nov. 12 **Litho.** ***Perf. 14***

1191 A343 350fr Sheet of 4, #a-d 3.75 3.75

First Zeppelin Flight, Cent. — A344

No. 1192, 350fr: a, LZ-1, b, LZ-2 (dark gray at left). c, LZ-2 (white at left) d, LZ-5. e, LZ-8. f, LZ-7.

No. 1193, 350fr: a, LZ-9. b, LZ-10. c, LZ-11. d, LZ-127. e, LZ-129. f, LZ-130.

No. 1194, 1500fr, LZ-1. No. 1195, 1500fr, LZ-4.

Illustration reduced.

2000, Nov. 12

Sheets of 6, #a-f

1192-1193 A344 Set of 2 11.00 11.00

Souvenir Sheets

1194-1195 A344 Set of 2 8.00 8.00

Berlin Film Festival, 50th Anniv. — A345

No. 1196: a, Le Grand Blond Avec Une Chaussure Noire. b Ruy Guerra. c, Mario Monicelli. d, Mudhur Jaffrey. e, Orökbefogadás. f, Palermo Oder Wolfsburg.

Illustration reduced.

2000, Nov. 12 **Litho.** ***Perf. 14***

Sheet of 6

1196 A345 420fr #a-f 7.25 7.25

Souvenir Sheet

1197 A345 1500fr Platoon 4.50 4.50

Souvenir Sheets

Public Railways, 175th Anniv. — A346

No. 1198: a, George Stephenson, Locomotion No. 1. b, Stourbridge Lion.

No. 1199: a, George Stephenson, Brusselton inclined plane. b, Robert Stephenson, turnpike crossing near Darlington. c, Locomotive built by George Stephenson. d, Experiment passenger coach built by Robert Stephenson.

Illustration reduced.

2000, Nov. 12

Sheets of 2 and 4

1198 A346 550fr #a-b 3.25 3.25
1199 A346 800fr #a-d 9.25 9.25

Fruits — A347

2000 Litho. *Perf. 14¾*

1200 A347 100fr Baobab

The editors suspect that other stamps of this type were issued and would like to examine any examples.

Fruit Type of 2000

2000, Feb. 23 Litho. *Perf. 14¾*

1201 A347 170fr Tamarind, horiz.

Two additional stamps were released in this set. The editors would like to examine them.

Elephants A348

2000, Mar. 22 Litho. *Perf. 14¾*

1204 A348 200fr Facing left

Two additional stamps were released in this set. The editors would like to examine them.

National Culture Week Type of 2000

2000 Litho. *Perf. 13x13½*

1209 A349 530fr Musicians — —

The editors suspect that additional stamps were released in this set and would like to examine any examples.

National Culture Week A349

2000 Litho. *Perf. 13x13½*

1210 A349 590fr Dancers

The editors suspect that additional stamps were issued in this set and would like to examine any examples.

Molluscs A350

Designs: 30fr, Limnaea natalensis. 250fr, Achatina achatina. 260fr, Biomphalaria pfeifferi.

2002, Apr. 28 Litho. *Perf. 13x13¼*

1213 A350 30fr multi — —
1215 A350 250fr multi — —
1216 A350 260fr multi — —

Two additional stamps were released in this set. The editors would like to examine any examples.

Belem-Yegre Museum — A351

Designs: 260fr, Main entrance. 530fr, Tombstone, vert.

2000 Litho. *Perf. 15x14¾, 14¾x15*

1220 A351 260fr multi — —
1221 A351 530fr multi — —

The editors suspect that additional stamps were issued in this set and would like to examine any examples.

Statuettes in National Museum — A352

Designs: 170fr, Kurumba. 260fr, Mossi. 590fr, San.

2001 Litho. *Perf. 13¼x13*

1223 A352 170fr multi — —
1224 A352 260fr multi — —
1225 A352 590fr multi — —

The editors suspect that additional stamps were issued in this set and would like to examine any examples.

Birds A353

Designs: 25fr, Anaplectes rubriceps. 50fr, Dendrocygna viduata. 590fr, Francolinus bicalcaratus, vert.

2001 Litho. *Perf. 13x13¼, 13¼x13*

1226 A353 25fr multi — —
1227 A353 50fr multi — —
1229 A353 590fr multi — —

The editors suspect that additional stamps were issued in this set and would like to examine any examples.

Tourism A354

Designs: 590fr, Sindou Peaks.

2001 Litho. *Perf. 13x13¼*

1233 A354 590fr multi — —

The editors suspect that additional stamps were issued in this set and would like to examine any examples.

SEMI-POSTAL STAMPS

Catalogue values for unused stamps in this section are for Never Hinged items.

Anti-Malaria Issue

Common Design Type

Perf. 12½x12

1962, Apr. 7 Engr. Unwmk.

B1 CD108 25fr + 5fr red org .50 .50

Freedom from Hunger Issue

Common Design Type

1963, Mar. 21 *Perf. 13*

B2 CD112 25fr + 5fr dk grn, bl & brn .50 .50

CAN '96 (African Nations) Soccer Championships — SP1

Designs: 150fr+25fr, Stallions, soccer ball. 250fr+25fr, Map of Africa, soccer player.

1996, Jan. 2 Litho. *Perf. 11½*

B3 SP1 150fr +25fr multi .95 .45
  a. Souvenir sheet of 1 2.75 1.40
B4 SP1 250fr +25fr multi 1.50 .75

No. B3a sold for 500fr.

AIR POST STAMPS

Catalogue values for unused stamps in this section are for Never Hinged items.

Plane over Map Showing Air Routes — AP1

200fr, Plane at airport, Ouagadougou. 500fr, Champs Elysees, Ouagadougou.

Unwmk.

1961, Mar. 4 Engr. *Perf. 13*

C1 AP1 100fr multicolored .90 .40
C2 AP1 200fr multicolored 2.25 .70
C3 AP1 500fr multicolored 5.25 2.40
  Nos. C1-C3 (3) 8.40 3.50

Air Afrique Issue

Common Design Type

1962, Feb. 17

C4 CD107 25fr brt pink, dk pur & lt grn .30 .20

UN Emblem and Upper Volta Flag — AP2

Perf. 13½x12½

1962, Sept. 22 Photo.

C5 AP2 50fr multicolored .50 .25
C6 AP2 100fr multicolored 1.00 .50

Admission to UN, second anniversary.

Post Office, Ouagadougou — AP3

1962, Dec. 11 *Perf. 13x12*

C7 AP3 100fr multicolored 1.00 .40

Jet Over Map AP4

1963, June 24

C8 AP4 200fr multicolored 3.50 1.50

First jet flight, Ouagadougou to Paris.

For surcharge see No. C10.

African Postal Union Issue

Common Design Type

1963, Sept. 8 Unwmk. *Perf. 12½*

C9 CD114 85fr dp vio, ocher & red .90 .50

No. C8 Surcharged in Red

1963, Nov. 19 *Perf. 13x12*

C10 AP4 50fr on 200fr multi .90 .40

See note after Mauritania No. C26.

Europafrica Issue

Common Design Type

50fr, Sunburst & Europe linked with Africa.

1964, Jan. 6 *Perf. 12x13*

C11 CD116 50fr multicolored .85 .50

Ramses II, Abu Simbel — AP5

Greek Sculptures AP6

1964, Mar. 8 Engr. *Perf. 13*

C12 AP5 25fr dp green & choc .35 .30
C13 AP5 100fr brt bl & brn 1.40 1.25

UNESCO world campaign to save historic monuments of Nubia.

1964, July 1 Unwmk. *Perf. 13*

C14 AP6 15fr Greek Portrait Head .35 .20
C15 AP6 25fr Seated boxer .45 .20
C16 AP6 85fr Victorious athlete .95 .60
C17 AP6 100fr Venus of Milo 1.50 .70
  a. Min. sheet of 4, #C14-C17 6.00 6.00
  Nos. C14-C17 (4) 3.25 1.70

18th Olympic Games, Tokyo, Oct. 10-25.

West African Gray Woodpecker AP7

President John F. Kennedy (1917-1963) AP8

1964, Oct. 1 Engr. *Perf. 13*

C18 AP7 250fr multicolored 6.00 2.25

1964, Nov. 25 Photo. *Perf. 12½*

C19 AP8 100fr orange, brn & lil 1.50 .80
a. Souvenir sheet of 4 4.50 4.50

Bird Type of Regular Issue, 1965

1965, Mar. 1 Photo. *Perf. 13*

Size: 27x48mm

C20 A27 500fr Abyssinian roller 9.00 3.50

Earth and Sun — AP9

1965, Mar. 23 Engr.

C21 AP9 50fr multicolored .45 .20

5th World Meteorological Day.

Hughes Telegraph, ITU Emblem and Dial Telephone — AP10

1965, May 17 Unwmk. *Perf. 13*

C22 AP10 100fr red, sl grn & bl grn .80 .40

ITU, centenary.

Intl. Cooperation Year — AP10a

1965, June 21 Photo. *Perf. 13*

C23 AP10a 25fr multicolored .20 .20
C24 AP10a 100fr multicolored .55 .25
a. Min. sheet, 2 each #C23-C24 1.90 1.90

Sacred Sabou Crocodile — AP11

1965, Aug. 9 Engr. *Perf. 13*

C25 AP11 60fr shown .60 .30
C26 AP11 85fr Lion, vert. .80 .40

Early Bird Satellite over Globe — AP12

Tiros Satellite and Weather Map — AP13

1965, Sept. 15 Unwmk. *Perf. 13*

C27 AP12 30fr brt bl, brn & brn red .30 .20

Space communications.

1966, Mar. 23 Engr. *Perf. 13*

C28 AP13 50fr dk car, brt bl & blk .40 .30

6th World Meteorological Day.

FR-1 Satellite over Ouagadougou Space Tracking Station — AP14

1966, Apr. 28 *Perf. 13*

C29 AP14 250fr mag, ind & org brn 2.00 .90

Inauguration of WHO Headquarters, Geneva — AP15

1966, May 3 Photo.

C30 AP15 100fr yel, blk & bl .80 .45

Air Afrique Issue

Common Design Type

1966, Aug. 31 Photo. *Perf. 13*

C31 CD123 25fr tan, blk & yel grn .30 .20

Sir Winston Churchill, British Lion and "V" Sign — AP16

1966, Nov. 5 Engr. *Perf. 13*

C32 AP16 100fr slate grn & car rose 1.00 .55

Sir Winston Spencer Churchill (1874-1965), statesman and WWII leader.

Pope Paul VI, Peace Dove, UN General Assembly and Emblem — AP17

1966, Nov. 5

C33 AP17 100fr dk blue & pur 1.00 .55

Pope Paul's appeal for peace before the UN General Assembly, Oct. 4, 1965.

Blind Man and Lions Emblem — AP18

1967, Feb. 28 Engr. *Perf. 13*

C34 AP18 100fr dk vio bl, brt bl & dk brn 1.40 .55

50th anniversary of Lions Intl.

UN Emblem and Rain over Landscape AP19

Diamant Rocket — AP20

1967, Mar. 23 Engr. *Perf. 13*

C35 AP19 50fr ultra, dk grn & bl grn .50 .25

7th World Meteorological Day.

1967, Apr. 18 Engr. *Perf. 13*

French Spacecraft: 20fr, FR-1 satellite, horiz. 30fr, D1-C satellite. 100fr, D1-D satellite, horiz.

C36 AP20 5fr brt bl, sl grn & org .20 .20
C37 AP20 20fr lilac & slate blue .20 .20
C38 AP20 30fr red brn, brt bl & emer .30 .20
C39 AP20 100fr emer & dp claret .90 .40
Nos. C36-C39 (4) 1.60 1.00

For overprint see No. C69.

Albert Schweitzer (1875-1965), Medical Missionary and Organ Pipes — AP21

1967, May 12 Engr. *Perf. 13*

C40 AP21 250fr claret & blk 1.75 .95

World Map and 1967 Jamboree Emblem — AP22

1967, June 8 Photo.

C41 AP22 100fr multicolored 1.00 .55

12th Boy Scout World Jamboree, Farragut State Park, Idaho, Aug. 1-9.

Madonna and Child, 15th Century AP23

Paintings: 20fr, Still life by Paul Gauguin. 50fr, Pietà, by Dick Bouts. 60fr, Anne of Cleves, by Hans Holbein the Younger. 90fr, The Money Lender and his Wife, by Quentin Massys (38x40mm). 100fr, Blessing of the Risen Christ, by Giovanni Bellini. 200fr, The Handcart, by Louis Le Nain, horiz. 250fr, The Four Evangelists, by Jacob Jordaens.

Perf. 12½x12, 12x12½, 13½ (90fr)

1967-68 Photo.

C42 AP23 20fr multi ('68) .25 .20
C43 AP23 30fr multi .30 .20
C44 AP23 50fr multi .50 .25
C45 AP23 60fr multi ('68) .60 .25
C46 AP23 90fr multi ('68) .85 .40
C47 AP23 100fr multi 1.00 .40
C48 AP23 200fr multi ('68) 2.00 .70
C49 AP23 250fr multi 2.75 1.00
Nos. C42-C49 (8) 8.25 3.40

See Nos. C70-C72.

African Postal Union Issue, 1967

Common Design Type

1967, Sept. 9 Engr. *Perf. 13*

C50 CD124 100fr multicolored .80 .35

Caravelle "Ouagadougou" — AP24

1968, Feb. 29 Engr. *Perf. 13*
C51 AP24 500fr bl, dp cl & blk 3.75 1.40

WMO Emblem, Sun, Rain, Wheat — AP25

1968, Mar. 23 Engr. *Perf. 13*
C52 AP25 50fr dk red, ultra & gray grn .45 .25

8th World Meteorological Day.

Europafrica Issue

Clove Hitch — AP25a

1968, July 20 Photo. *Perf. 13*
C53 AP25a 50fr yel bis, blk & dk red .40 .20

See note after Niger No. C89.

Vessel in Form of Acrobat with Bells, Colima Culture — AP26

Mexican Sculptures: 30fr, Ballplayer, Veracruz, vert. 60fr, Javelin thrower, Colima, vert. 100fr, Seated athlete with cape, Jalisco.

1968, Oct. 14 Engr. *Perf. 13*
C54 AP26 10fr dk red, ocher & choc .20 .20
C55 AP26 30fr bl grn, brt grn & dk brn .25 .20
C56 AP26 60fr ultra, ol & mar .45 .25
C57 AP26 100fr brt grn, bl & mar .65 .35
Nos. C54-C57 (4) 1.55 1.00

19th Olympic Games, Mexico City, 10/12-27.

Artisan Type of Regular Issue

1968, Oct. 30 Engr. *Perf. 13*
Size: 48x27mm
C58 A52 100fr Potter .70 .30

PHILEXAFRIQUE Issue

Too Late or The Letter, by Armand Cambon AP27

1968, Nov. 22 Photo. *Perf. 12½*
C59 AP27 100fr multicolored 1.00 .75

PHILEXAFRIQUE, Phil. Exhib., Abidjan, Feb. 14-23, 1969. Printed with alternating rose claret label.

Albert John Luthuli — AP28

Design: No. C61, Mahatma Gandhi.

1968, Dec. 16 Photo. *Perf. 12½*
C60 AP28 100fr dk grn, yel grn & blk .75 .40
C61 AP28 100fr dk grn, yel & blk .75 .40
a. Min. sheet, 2 each #C60-C61 3.00 3.00

Exponents of non-violence.

2nd PHILEXAFRIQUE Issue
Common Design Type

50fr, Upper Volta #59, dancers & musicians.

1969, Feb. 14 Engr. *Perf. 13*
C62 CD128 50fr pur, bl car & brn .55 .55

Weather Sonde, WMO Emblem, Mule and Cattle in Irrigated Field — AP29

1969, Mar. 24 Engr. *Perf. 13*
C63 AP29 100fr dk brn, brt bl & grn .90 .50

9th World Meteorological Day.

Artisan Type of Regular Issue

Design: 150fr, Basket weaver.

1969, Apr. 3 Engr. *Perf. 13*
Size: 48x27mm
C64 A55 150fr brn, bl & blk 1.25 .60

Lions Emblem, Eye and Blind Man — AP30

1969, Apr. 30 Photo.
C65 AP30 250fr red & multi 2.50 1.00

12th Congress of District 403 of Lions Intl., Ouagadougou, May 2-3.

Fish Type of Regular Issue

Designs: 100fr, Phenacogrammus pabrensis. 150fr, Upside-down catfish.

1969 Engr. *Perf. 13*
Size: 48x27mm
C66 A57 100fr slate, pur & yel 1.10 .55
C67 A57 150fr org brn, gray & slate 1.90 .90

Earth and Astronaut — AP31

Embossed on Gold Foil

1969 *Die-cut Perf. 10½x10*
C68 AP31 1000fr gold 8.25 8.25

Apollo 8 mission, which put the first man into orbit around the moon, Dec. 21-27, 1968.

No. C39 Overprinted in red with Lunar Landing Module and: "L'HOMME SUR LA LUNE / JUILLET 1969 / APOLLO 11"

1969, July 25 Engr. *Perf. 13*
C69 AP20 100fr emer & dp claret 2.25 1.90

See note after Mali No. C80.

Painting Type of 1967-68

Paintings: 50fr, Napoleon Crossing Great St. Bernard Pass, by Jacques Louis David. 150fr, Napoleon Awarding the First Cross of the Legion of Honor, by Jean-Baptiste Debret. 250fr, Napoleon Before Madrid, by Carle Vernet.

1969, Aug. 18 Photo. *Perf. 12½x12*
C70 AP23 50fr carmine & multi .45 .35
C71 AP23 150fr violet & multi 1.10 .80
C72 AP23 250fr green & multi 2.25 1.40
Nos. C70-C72 (3) 3.80 2.55

Napoleon Bonaparte (1769-1821).

Agriculture Type of Regular Issue

1969, Oct. 30 Photo. *Perf. 12½x13*
Size: 47½x27mm
C73 A58 100fr Peanuts .75 .25
C74 A58 200fr Rice 1.60 .55

AP32

AP33

Tree of Life, symbols of science, agriculture and industry.

1969, Nov. 21 Photo. *Perf. 12x13*
C75 AP32 100fr multicolored .65 .35

See note after Mauritania No. C28.

1970, Apr. 22 Photo. *Perf. 12½*

Designs: 20fr, Lenin. 100fr, Lenin Addressing Revolutionaries in Petrograd, by V. A. Serov, horiz.

C76 AP33 20fr ocher & brn .20 .20
C77 AP33 100fr blk, lt grn & red .65 .40

Lenin (1870-1924), Russian communist leader.

Pres. Roosevelt with Stamp Collection — AP34

10fr, Franklin Delano Roosevelt, vert.

1970, June 4 Photo. *Perf. 12½*
C78 AP34 10fr dk brn, emer & red brn .20 .20
C79 AP34 200fr vio bl, gray & dk car 1.40 .45

Soccer Game and Jules Rimet Cup — AP35

100fr, Goalkeeper catching ball, globe.

1970, June 4 Engr. *Perf. 13*
C80 AP35 40fr olive, brt grn & brn .40 .20
C81 AP35 100fr blk, lil, brn & grn .90 .40

9th World Soccer Championships for the Jules Rimet Cup, Mexico City, 5/30-6/21/70.

EXPO Emblem, Monorail and "Cranes at the Seashore" AP36

UN Emblem, Dove and Star — AP37

Design: 150fr, EXPO emblem, rocket, satellites and "Geisha."

1970, Aug. 7 Photo. *Perf. 12½*
C82 AP36 50fr multicolored .35 .20
C83 AP36 150fr green & multi 1.00 .60

Issued to publicize EXPO '70 International Exhibition, Osaka, Japan, Mar. 15-Sept. 13.

1970, Oct. 2 Engr. *Perf. 13*

250fr, UN emblem and doves, horiz.

C84 AP37 60fr dk bl, bl & grn .40 .20
C85 AP37 250fr dk red brn, vio bl & ol 1.60 .65

25th anniversary of the United Nations.

Holy Family — AP38

Silver Embossed

1970, Nov. 27 ***Die-Cut Perf. 10***
C86 AP38 300fr silver 2.50 2.50

Gold Embossed

C87 AP38 1000fr gold 9.00 9.00

Christmas.

Family and Upper Volta Flag — AP39

Gamal Abdel Nasser — AP41

UN "Key to a Free World" — AP40

Litho.; Gold Embossed

1970, Dec. 10 ***Perf. 12½***
C88 AP39 500fr gold, blk & red 2.50 1.50

10th anniversary of independence, Dec. 11.

1970, Dec. 14 Engr. ***Perf. 13***
C89 AP40 40fr red, bister & blue .35 .20

UN Declaration of Independence for Colonial Peoples, 10th anniv.

1971, Jan. 30 Photo. ***Perf. 12½***
C90 AP41 100fr green & multi .65 .30

Nasser (1918-1970), president of Egypt.

Herons, Egyptian Art, 1354 — AP42

250fr, Page from Koran, Egypt, 1368-1388.

1971, May 13 Photo. ***Perf. 13***
C91 AP42 100fr multi .55 .25
C92 AP42 250fr multi, vert. 1.40 .70

Olympic Rings and Various Sports — AP43

1971, June 10 Engr. ***Perf. 13***
C93 AP43 150fr vio bl & red 1.00 .60

Pre-Olympic Year.

Boy Scout and Buildings — AP44

1971, Aug. 12 Photo. ***Perf. 12½***
C94 AP44 45fr multicolored .35 .20

13th Boy Scout World Jamboree, Asagiri Plain, Japan, Aug. 2-10.

De Gaulle, Map of Upper Volta, Cross of Lorraine — AP45

Charles de Gaulle — AP46

1971, Nov. 9 Photo. ***Perf. 13x12***
C95 AP45 40fr lt brn, grn & blk .40 .35

Lithographed; Gold Embossed
Perf. 12½

C96 AP46 500fr gold & grn 4.00 3.75

Gen. Charles de Gaulle (1890-1970), president of France.

African Postal Union Issue, 1971
Common Design Type

Design: 100fr, Mossi dancer and UAMPT building, Brazzaville, Congo.

1971, Nov. 13 Photo. ***Perf. 13x13½***
C97 CD135 100fr bl & multi .65 .35

Gen. Sangoule Lamizana AP47

Kabuki Actor and Ice Hockey AP48

1971, Dec. 11 ***Perf. 12½***
C98 AP47 35fr sep, blk, gold & ultra .25 .20

Inauguration of 2nd Republic of Upper Volta.

1972, Feb. 15 Engr. ***Perf. 13***
C99 AP48 150fr red, bl & pur 1.00 .60

11th Winter Olympic Games, Sapporo, Japan, Feb. 3-13.

Music, by Pietro Longhi AP49

Design: 150fr, Gondolas and general view, by Ippolito Caffi, horiz.

1972, Feb. 28 Photo. ***Perf. 13***
C100 AP49 100fr gold & multi .65 .35
C101 AP49 150fr gold & multi 1.10 .40

UNESCO campaign to save Venice.

Running and Olympic Rings — AP50

Design: 200fr, Discus and Olympic rings.

1972, May 5 Engr. ***Perf. 13***
C102 AP50 65fr dp bl, brn & grn .35 .20
C103 AP50 200fr dp bl & brn 1.10 .35
a. Min. sheet of 2, #C102-C103 1.60 1.60

20th Olympic Games, Munich, 8/26-9/10.

Musician Type of Regular Issue

Design: 500fr, Jimmy Smith and keyboard.

1972, May 17 Photo. ***Perf. 14x13***
C104 A87 500fr green & multi 4.00 1.90

Red Crescent Type of Regular Issue

1972, June 23 ***Perf. 13x14***
C105 A88 100fr yellow & multi .65 .25

2nd Plan Type of Regular Issue

Design: 85fr, Road building machinery.

1972, Oct. 30 Engr. ***Perf. 13***
C106 A90 85fr brick red, bl & blk .90 .50

Presidents Pompidou and Lamizana — AP51

Design: 250fr, Presidents Pompidou and Lamizana, different design.

1972, Nov. 20 Photo. ***Perf. 13***
Size: 48x37mm

C107 AP51 40fr gold & multi .45 .35

Photogravure; Gold Embossed
Size: 56x36mm

C108 AP51 250fr yel grn, dk grn & gold 2.50 2.50

Visit of Pres. Georges Pompidou of France, Nov. 1972.

Skeet-shooting, Scalzone, Italy — AP52

Gold-medal Winners: 40fr, Pentathlon, Peters, Great Britain. 45fr, Dressage, Meade, Great Britain. 50fr, Weight lifting, Talts, USSR. 60fr, Boxing, light-weight, Seales, US. 65fr, Fencing, Ragno-Lonzi, Italy. 75fr, Gymnastics, rings, Nakayama, Japan. 85fr, Gymnastics, Touritcheva, USSR. 90fr, 110m high hurdles, Milburn, US. 150fr, Judo, Kawaguchi, Japan. 200fr, Sailing, Finn class, Maury, France. 250fr, Swimming, Spitz, US (7 gold). 300fr, Women's high jump, Meyfarth, West Germany. 350fr, Field Hockey, West Germany. 400fr, Javelin, Wolfermann, West Germany. No. C124, Women's diving, King, US. No. C125, Cycling, Morelon, France. No. C126, Individual dressage, Linsenhoff, West Germany.

1972-73 Litho. ***Perf. 12½***
C109 AP52 35fr multi ('73) .20 .20
C110 AP52 40fr multi .20 .20
C111 AP52 45fr multi ('73) .25 .20
C112 AP52 50fr multi ('73) .25 .20
C113 AP52 60fr multi ('73) .30 .20
C114 AP52 65fr multi .35 .20
C115 AP52 75fr multi ('73) .40 .20
C116 AP52 85fr multi .40 .20
C117 AP52 90fr multi ('73) .45 .25
C118 AP52 150fr multi ('73) .80 .40
C119 AP52 200fr multi 1.10 .50
C120 AP52 250fr multi ('73) 1.40 .65
C121 AP52 300fr multi 1.60 .80
C122 AP52 350fr multi ('73) 1.90 .90
C123 AP52 400fr multi ('73) 2.00 1.10
Nos. C109-C123 (15) 11.60 6.20

Souvenir Sheets

C124 AP52 500fr multi 2.25 1.60
C125 AP52 500fr multi ('73) 2.25 1.60
C126 AP52 500fr multi ('73) 2.25 1.60

20th Olympic Games, Munich.

Nativity, by Della Notte — AP53

Christmas: 200fr, Adoration of the Kings, by Albrecht Dürer.

1972, Dec. 23 Photo. *Perf. 13*
C127 AP53 100fr gold & multi .50 .25
C128 AP53 200fr gold & multi 1.10 .65

Madonna and Child, by Albrecht Dürer AP54

Christmas: 75fr, Virgin Mary, Child and St. John, by Joseph von Führich. 100fr, The Virgin of Grand Duc, by Raphael. 125fr, Holy Family, by David. 150fr, Madonna and Child, artist unknown. 400fr, Flight into Egypt, by Gentile da Fabriano, horiz.

1973, Mar. 22 Litho. *Perf. 12½x13*
C129 AP54 50fr multi .35 .20
C130 AP54 75fr multi .50 .25
C131 AP54 100fr multi .65 .35
C132 AP54 125fr multi .80 .40
C133 AP54 150fr multi 1.00 .50
Nos. C129-C133 (5) 3.30 1.70

Souvenir Sheet

C134 AP54 400fr multi 2.50 1.40

Manned Lunar Buggy on Moon — AP55

Moon Exploration: 65fr, Lunakhod, Russian unmanned vehicle on moon. 100fr, Lunar module returning to orbiting Apollo capsule. 150fr, Apollo capsule in moon orbit. 200fr, Space walk. 250fr, Walk in Sea of Tranquillity.

1973, Apr. 30 Litho. *Perf. 13x12½*
C135 AP55 50fr multi .35 .20
C136 AP55 65fr multi .40 .20
C137 AP55 100fr multi .65 .35
C138 AP55 150fr multi 1.00 .50
C139 AP55 200fr multi 1.40 .65
Nos. C135-C139 (5) 3.80 1.90

Souvenir Sheet

C140 AP55 250fr multi 1.60 .80

Giraffes AP56

African Wild Animals: 150fr, Elephants. 200fr, Leopard, horiz. 250fr, Lion, horiz. 300fr, Rhinoceros, horiz. 500fr, Crocodile, horiz.

Perf. 12½x13, 13x12½
1973, May 3 Litho.
C141 AP56 100fr multi 65 .35
C142 AP56 150fr multi 1.00 .50
C143 AP56 200fr multi 1.40 .65
C144 AP56 250fr multi 1.60 .80
C145 AP56 500fr multi 3.50 1.60
Nos. C141-C145 (5) 8.15 3.90

Souvenir Sheet

C146 AP56 300fr multi 2.00 1.00

Europafrica Issue

Girl Reading Letter, by Jan Vermeer AP57

Paintings: 65fr, Portrait of a Lady, by Roger van der Weyden. 100fr, Young Lady at her Toilette, by Titian. 150fr, Jane Seymour, by Hans Holbein. 200fr, Mrs. Williams, by John Hoppner. 250fr, Milkmaid, by Jean-Baptiste Greuze.

1973, June 7 Litho. *Perf. 12½x13*
C147 AP57 50fr multi .35 .20
C148 AP57 65fr multi .40 .20
C149 AP57 100fr multi .65 .35
C150 AP57 150fr multi 1.00 .50
C151 AP57 200fr multi 1.40 .65
Nos. C147-C151 (5) 3.80 1.90

Souvenir Sheet

C152 AP57 250fr multi 1.60 .80

For overprint see No. C165-C166.

Africa Encircled by OAU Flags AP58

1973, June 7
C153 AP58 45fr multi .30 .20

10th anniv. of Org. for African Unity.

Locomotive "Pacific" 4546, 1908 — AP59

Locomotives from Railroad Museum, Mulhouse, France: 40fr, No. 242, 1927. 50fr, No. 2029, 1882. 150fr, No. 701, 1885-92. 250fr, "Coupe-Vent" No. C145, 1900. 350fr, Buddicomb No. 33, Paris to Rouen, 1884.

1973, June 30 *Perf. 13x12½*
C154 AP59 10fr multi .20 .20
C155 AP59 40fr multi .25 .20
C156 AP59 50fr multi .35 .20
C157 AP59 150fr multi 1.00 .50
C158 AP59 250fr multi 1.60 .80
Nos. C154-C158 (5) 3.40 1.90

Souvenir Sheet

C159 AP59 350fr multi 2.25 1.25

Boy Scout Type of 1973

40fr, Flag signaling. 75fr, Skiing. 150fr, Cooking. 200fr, Hiking. 250fr, Studying stars.

1973, July 18 Litho. *Perf. 12½x13*
C160 A95 40fr multi .25 .20
C161 A95 75fr multi .50 .25
C162 A95 150fr multi 1.00 .50
C163 A95 200fr multi 1.40 .65
Nos. C160-C163 (4) 3.15 1.60

Souvenir Sheet

C164 A95 250fr multi 1.60 .80

Nos. C148 and C150 Surcharged in Silver New Value and "SECHERESSE / SOLIDARITE AFRICAINE / ET INTERNATIONALE"

1973, Aug. 16
C165 AP57 100fr on 65fr multi .65 .35
C166 AP57 200fr on 150fr multi 1.40 .65

Drought relief.

Kennedy Type, 1973

John F. Kennedy and: 200fr, Firing Saturn 1 rocket, Apollo program. 300fr, First NASA manned space capsule. 400fr, Saturn 5 countdown.

1973, Sept. 12 Litho. *Perf. 12½x13*
C167 A96 200fr multi 1.40 .65
C168 A96 300fr multi 2.00 1.00

Souvenir Sheet

C169 A96 400fr multi 2.50 1.40

10th death anniv. of Pres John F. Kennedy.

Interpol Type of 1973

Souvenir Sheet

Design: Victim in city street.

1973, Sept. 15 *Perf. 13x12½*
C170 A97 300fr multi 2.00 1.00

Tourism Type of 1973

1973, Sept. 30
C171 A98 100fr Waterfalls 1.00 .50

Souvenir Sheet

C172 A98 275fr Elephant 1.90 .90

House of Worship Type of 1973

Cathedral of the Immaculate Conception.

1973, Sept. 28
C173 A99 200fr multi 1.40 .60

Folklore Type of 1973

100fr, 225fr, Bobo masked dancers, diff.

1973, Nov. 30 Litho. *Perf. 12½x13*
C174 A100 100fr multi .65 .35
C175 A100 225fr multi 1.50 .70

Zodiac Type of 1973

Souvenir Sheets

Zodiacal Light and: #C176, 1st 4 signs of Zodiac. #C177, 2nd 4 signs. #C178, Last 4 signs.

1973, Dec. 15 *Perf. 13x14*
C176 A101 250fr multi 1.60 .80
C177 A101 250fr multi 1.60 .80
C178 A101 250fr multi 1.60 .80

Nos. C176-C178 have multicolored margin showing night sky and portraits: No. C176, Louis Armstrong; No. C177, Mahatma Gandhi; No. C178, Martin Luther King.

Soccer Championship Type, 1974

Championship '74 emblem and: 75fr, Gento, Spanish flag. 100fr, Bereta, French flag. 250fr, Best, British flag. 400fr, Beckenbauer, West German flag.

1974, Jan. 15 Litho. *Perf. 13x12½*
C179 A102 75fr multi .30 .20
C180 A102 100fr multi .60 .35
C181 A102 250fr multi 1.25 .50
Nos. C179-C181 (3) 2.15 1.05

Souvenir Sheet

C182 A102 400fr multi 2.50 1.40

De Gaulle Type, 1974

300fr, De Gaulle, Concorde, horiz. 400fr, De Gaulle, French space shot.

Perf. 13x12½, 12½x13
1974, Feb. 4 Litho.
C183 A103 300fr multi 2.00 1.00

Souvenir Sheet

C184 A103 400fr multi 2.50 1.40

Soccer Cup Championship Type, 1974

World Cup, Emblems and: 150fr, Brindisis, Argentinian flag. No. C186, Kenko, Zaire flag. No. C187, Streich, East German flag. 400fr, Cruyff, Netherlands flag.

1974, Mar. 19 *Perf. 12½x13*
C185 A104 150fr multi .75 .40
C186 A104 300fr multi 1.50 .75

Souvenir Sheets

C187 A104 300fr multi 1.50 .75
C188 A104 400fr multi 2.00 1.00

UPU Type, 1974

UPU Emblem and: 100fr, Dove carrying mail. 200fr, Air Afrique 707. 300fr, Dish antenna. 500fr, Telstar satellite.

1974, July 23 *Perf. 13½*
C189 A106 100fr multi .50 .25
C190 A106 200fr multi 1.00 .50
C191 A106 300fr multi 1.50 .75
Nos. C189-C191 (3) 3.00 1.50

Souvenir Sheet

C192 A106 500fr multi 2.50 1.25

For overprint see No. C197-C200.

Soccer Cup Winners Type, 1974

World Cup, Game and Flags: 150fr, Brazil, in Sweden, 1958. 200fr, Brazil, in Chile, 1962. 250fr, Brazil, in Mexico, 1970. 450fr, England, in England, 1966.

1974, Sept. 2
C193 A107 150fr multi 1.00 .50
C194 A107 200fr multi 1.40 .70
C195 A107 250fr multi 1.60 .80
Nos. C193-C195 (3) 4.00 2.00

Souvenir Sheet

C196 A107 450fr multi 3.00 1.50

Nos. C189-C192 Overprinted in Red "100e ANNIVERSAIRE DE L'UNION POSTALE UNIVERSELLE / 9 OCTOBRE 1974"

1974, Oct. 9
C197 A106 100fr multi .60 .35
C198 A106 200fr multi 1.40 .65
C199 A106 300fr multi 2.00 1.00
Nos. C197-C199 (3) 4.00 2.00

Souvenir Sheet

C200 A106 500fr multi 3.00 1.40

Universal Postal Union, centenary.

Flower Type of 1974

Flower Paintings by: 300fr, Auguste Renoir. 400fr, Carl Brendt.

1974, Oct. 31 Litho. *Perf. 12½x13*
C201 A109 300fr multi 2.00 1.00

Souvenir Sheet

C202 A109 400fr multi 2.50 1.40

Locomotive Type of 1975

Locomotives from Railroad Museum, Mulhouse, France: 100fr, Crampton No. 80, 1852. 200fr, No. 701, 1885-92. 300fr, "Forquenot," 1882.

1975, Feb. 28 Litho. *Perf. 13x12½*
C203 A112 100fr multi .65 .35
C204 A112 200fr multi 1.40 .65

Souvenir Sheet

C205 A112 300fr multi 2.00 1.00

Old Cars Type, 1975

Flags and Old Cars: 150fr, Germany and Mercedes-Benz, 1929. 200fr, Germany and Maybach, 1936. 400fr, Great Britain and Rolls Royce Silver Ghost, 1910.

1975, Apr. 6 *Perf. 14x13½*
C206 A113 150fr multi 1.00 .50
C207 A113 200fr multi 1.40 .65

Souvenir Sheet

C208 A113 400fr multi 2.50 1.40

American Bicentennial Type

200fr, Washington crossing Delaware. 300fr, Hessians Captured at Trenton.

1975, May 6 Litho. *Perf. 14*
C209 A114 200fr multi 1.40 .65
C210 A114 300fr multi 2.00 1.00

Schweitzer Type of 1975

Albert Schweitzer and: 150fr, Toucan. 175fr, Vulturine guinea fowl. 200fr, King vulture. 450fr, Crested corythornis.

1975, May 25 Litho. *Perf. 13½*
C212 A115 150fr multi .95 .50
C213 A115 175fr multi 1.25 .55
C214 A115 200fr multi 1.40 .65
Nos. C212-C214 (3) 3.60 1.70

Souvenir Sheet

C215 A115 450fr multi 3.00 1.50

Apollo Soyuz Type of 1975

100fr, Apollo, Soyuz near link-up. 200fr, Cosmonauts Alexei Leonov, Valeri Kubasov. 300fr, Astronauts Donald K. Slayton, Vance Brand, Thomas P. Stafford. 500fr, Apollo Soyuz emblem, US, USSR flags.

1975, July 18 Litho. *Perf. 13½*

C216 A116 100fr multi .60 .35
C217 A116 200fr multi 1.40 .65
C218 A116 300fr multi 2.00 1.00
Nos. C216-C218 (3) 4.00 2.00

Souvenir Sheet

C219 A116 500fr multi 3.50 1.60

Picasso Type of 1975

Picasso Paintings: 150fr, El Prado, horiz. 350fr, Couple in Patio. 400fr, Science and Charity.

1975, Aug. 7

C220 A117 150fr multi 1.00 .50
C221 A117 350fr multi 2.25 1.25

Souvenir Sheet

C222 A117 400fr multi 2.50 1.40

EXPO '75 Type of 1975

Expo '75 emblem and: 150fr, Passenger liner Asama Maru. 300fr, Future floating city Aquapolis.

1975, Sept. 26 Litho. *Perf. 11*

C223 A118 150fr multi .75 .40

Souvenir Sheet

Perf. 13½

C224 A118 300fr multi 1.50 .75

Winter Olympic Games Type of 1975

Innsbruck Background, Olympic Emblem and: 100fr, Ice hockey. 200fr, Ski jump. 300fr, Speed skating.

1975, Dec. 15 *Perf. 13½*

C225 A122 100fr multi .65 .35
C226 A122 200fr multi 1.40 .65

Souvenir Sheet

C227 A122 300fr multi 2.00 1.00

Olympic Games Type of 1976

Olympic Emblem and: 125fr, Heavyweight judo. 150fr, Weight lifting. 500fr, Sprint.

1976, Mar. 17 Litho. *Perf. 13½*

C228 A123 125fr multi .65 .30
C229 A123 150fr multi .75 .40

Souvenir Sheet

C230 A123 500fr multi 2.50 1.25

Summer Olympic Games Type of 1976

Olympic emblem and: 150fr, Pole vault. 200fr, Gymnast on balance beam. 500fr, Two-man sculls.

1976, Mar. 25 *Perf. 11*

C231 A124 150fr multi .75 .40
C232 A124 200fr multi 1.00 .50

Souvenir Sheet

C233 A124 500fr multi 2.50 1.25

For overprint see No. C245-C247.

Zeppelin Type of 1976

Airships: 100fr, Graf Zeppelin over Swiss Alps. 200fr, LZ-129 over city. 300fr, Graf Zeppelin. 500fr, Zeppelin over Bodensee.

1976, May 11

C234 A126 100fr multi .60 .35
C235 A126 200fr multi 1.40 .65
C236 A126 300fr multi 2.00 1.00
Nos. C234-C236 (3) 4.00 2.00

Souvenir Sheet

C237 A126 500fr multi 3.50 1.60

Viking Mars Type of 1976

Designs: 200fr, Viking lander assembly. 300fr, Viking orbiter in descent on Mars. 450fr, Viking in Mars orbit.

1976, June 24 Litho. *Perf. 13½*

C238 A127 200fr multi 1.00 .50
C239 A127 300fr multi 1.50 .75

Souvenir Sheet

C240 A127 450fr multi 2.25 1.10

American Bicentennial Type

Bicentennial and Interphil '76 Emblems and: 100fr, Siege of Yorktown. 200fr, Battle of Cape St. Vincent. 300fr, Peter Francisco's bravery. 500fr, Surrender of the Hessians.

1976, Sept. 30 Litho. *Perf. 13½*

C241 A129 100fr multi .60 .35
C242 A129 200fr multi 1.40 .65
C243 A129 300fr multi 2.00 1.00
Nos. C241-C243 (3) 4.00 2.00

Souvenir Sheet

C244 A129 500fr multi 3.50 1.60

Nos. C231-C233 Overprinted in Gold:
a. VAINQUEUR 1976 / TADEUSZ SLUSARSKI / POLOGNE
b. VAINQUEUR 1976 / NADIA COMANECI / ROUMANIE
c. VAINQUEUR 1976 / FRANK ET ALF HANSEN / NORVEGE

1976, July 4 Litho. *Perf. 11*

C245 A124(a) 150fr multi 1.00 .50
C246 A124(b) 200fr multi 1.40 .65

Souvenir Sheet

C247 A124(c) 500fr multi 3.50 1.60

Winners, 21st Olympic Games.

UPU Emblem over Globe — AP60

1978, Aug. 8 Litho. *Perf. 13*

C248 AP60 350fr multi 2.25 1.50

Congress of Paris, establishing UPU, cent.

Jules Verne, Apollo 11 Emblem, Footprint on Moon, Neil Armstrong — AP61

Space Conquest: 50fr, Yuri Gagarin and moon landing. 100fr, Montgolfier hot air balloon and memorial medal, 1783; Bleriot's monoplane, 1909.

1978, Sept. 27 Litho. *Perf. 13x12½*

C249 AP61 50fr multi .35 .20
C250 AP61 60fr multi .40 .20
C251 AP61 100fr multi .65 .35
Nos. C249-C251 (3) 1.40 .75

Anti-Apartheid Year — AP62

1978, Oct. 12 Litho. *Perf. 13*

C252 AP62 100fr blue & multi .65 .35

Philexafrique II-Essen Issue

Common Design Types

#C253, Hippopotamus, Upper Volta #C18. #C254, Hummingbird, Hanover #1.

1978, Nov. 1 Litho. *Perf. 12½*

C253 CD138 100fr multi .65 .35
C254 CD139 100fr multi .65 .35

Nos. C253-C254 printed se-tenant.

Sun God Horus with Sun — AP63

Jules Verne and Balloon — AP64

300fr, Falcon with cartouches, UNESCO emblem.

1978, Dec. 4

C255 AP63 200fr multi 1.40 .65
C256 AP63 300fr multi 2.00 1.00

UNESCO Campaign to safeguard monuments at Philae.

1978, Dec. 10 Engr. *Perf. 13*

C257 AP64 200fr multi 1.40 .65

Verne (1828-1905), science fiction writer.

Bicycling, Olympic Rings — AP65

Designs: Bicycling scenes.

1980 *Perf. 14½*

C258 AP65 65fr multi .65 .30
C259 AP65 150fr multi, vert. 1.00 .50
C260 AP65 250fr multi 1.60 .80
C261 AP65 350fr multi 2.25 1.25
Nos. C258-C261 (4) 5.50 2.85

Souvenir Sheet

C262 AP65 500fr multi 3.50 1.60

22nd Summer Olympic Games, Moscow, July 19-Aug. 3.

Nos. C258-C262 Overprinted with Name of Winner and Country

1980, Nov. 22 Litho. *Perf. 14½*

C263 AP65 65fr multi .40 .20
C264 AP65 150fr multi 1.00 .50
C265 AP65 250fr multi 1.60 .80
C266 AP65 350fr multi 2.25 1.25
Nos. C263-C266 (4) 5.25 2.75

Souvenir Sheet

C267 AP65 500fr multi 3.50 1.60

1982 World Cup — AP66

Designs: Various soccer players.

1982, June 22 Litho. *Perf. 13½*

C268 AP66 70fr multi .45 .25
C269 AP66 90fr multi .60 .30
C270 AP66 150fr multi 1.00 .45
C271 AP66 300fr multi 2.00 1.00
Nos. C268-C271 (4) 4.05 2.00

Souvenir Sheet

C272 AP66 500fr multi 3.50 1.60

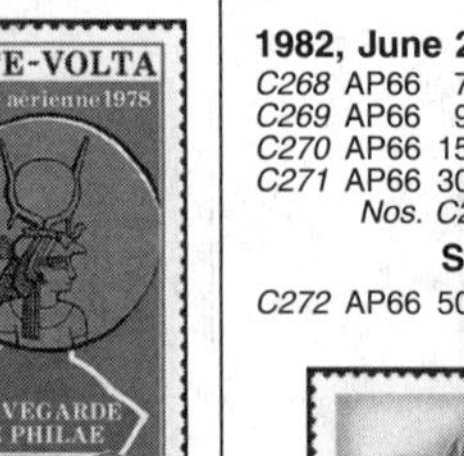

Anniversaries and Events — AP67

1983, June Litho. *Perf. 13½*

C273 AP67 90fr Space Shuttle .30 .20
C274 AP67 120fr World Soccer Cup .40 .20
C275 AP67 300fr Cup, diff. 1.00 .50
C276 AP67 450fr Royal Wedding 1.50 .70
Nos. C273-C276 (4) 3.20 1.60

Souvenir Sheet

C277 AP67 500fr Prince Charles, Lady Diana 1.60 1.60

Pre-Olympics, 1984 Los Angeles — AP68

1983, Aug. 1 Litho. *Perf. 13*

C278 AP68 90fr Sailing .30 .20
C279 AP68 120fr Type 470 .40 .20
C280 AP68 300fr Wind surfing 1.00 .50
C281 AP68 400fr Wind surfing, diff. 1.40 .65
Nos. C278-C281 (4) 3.10 1.55

Souvenir Sheet

C282 AP68 500fr Soling Class, Wind surfing 1.60 1.60

Christmas AP69

Rubens Paintings.

1983 Litho. *Perf. 13*

C283 AP69 120fr Adoration of the Shepherds .40 .20
C284 AP69 350fr Virgin of the Garland 1.25 .60
C285 AP69 500fr Adoration of the Kings 1.60 .80
Nos. C283-C285 (3) 3.25 1.60

1984 Summer Olympics — AP70

1984, Mar. 26 Litho. *Perf. 12½*

C286	AP70	90fr Handball, vert.	.30	.20
C287	AP70	120fr Volleyball, vert.	.40	.20
C288	AP70	150fr Handball, diff.	.50	.25
C289	AP70	250fr Basketball	.80	.40
C290	AP70	300fr Soccer	1.00	.50
		Nos. C286-C290 (5)	3.00	1.55

Souvenir Sheet

C291	AP70	500fr Volleyball, diff.	1.60	.80

Local Birds — AP71

1984, May 14 Litho. *Perf. 12½*

C292	AP71	90fr Phoenicopterus roseus	.30	.20
C293	AP71	185fr Choriotis kori, vert.	.60	.30
C294	AP71	200fr Buphagus erythrorhynchus, vert.	.65	.35
C295	AP71	300fr Bucorvus leadbeateri	1.00	.50
		Nos. C292-C295 (4)	2.55	1.35

AP72

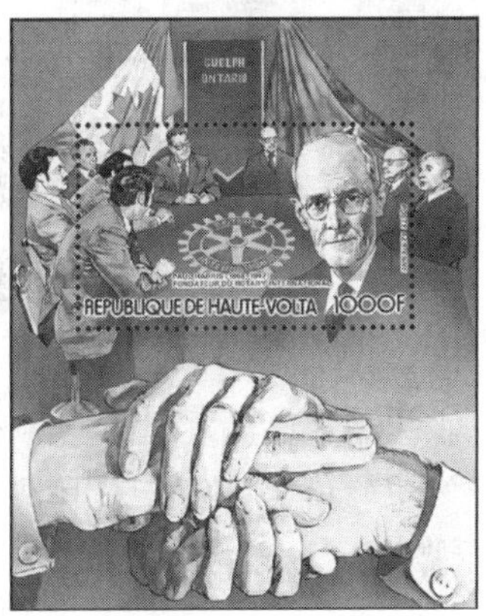

Famous Men — AP73

Designs: 5fr, Houari Boumediene (1927-1978), president of Algeria 1965-78. 125fr, Gottlieb Daimler (1834-1900), German automotive pioneer, and 1886 Daimler. 250fr, Louis Bleriot (1872-1936), French aviator, first to fly the English Channel in a heavier-than-air craft. 300fr, Abraham Lincoln. 400fr, Henri Dunant (1828-1910), founder of the Red Cross. 450fr, Auguste Piccard (1884-1962), Swiss physicist, inventor of the bathyscaphe Trieste, 1948. 500fr, Robert Baden-Powell (1856-1941), founder of Boy Scouts. 600fr, Anatoli Karpov, Russian chess champion. 1000fr, Paul Harris (1868-1947), founder of Rotary Intl.

1984, May 21 Litho. *Perf. 13½*

C296	AP72	5fr multi	.20	.20
C297	AP72	125fr multi	.50	.25
C298	AP72	250fr multi	1.00	.50
C299	AP72	300fr multi	1.25	.60
C300	AP72	400fr multi	1.60	.80
C301	AP72	450fr multi	1.90	.90
C302	AP72	500fr multi	2.00	1.00
C303	AP72	600fr multi	2.25	1.25
		Nos. C296-C303 (8)	10.70	5.50

Souvenir Sheet

C304	AP73	1000fr multi	4.00	2.00

No. C304 contains one 51x30mm stamp.

Burkina Faso

Butterflies — AP73a

1984, May 23 *Perf. 13½*

C305	AP73a	10fr Graphium pylades	.20	.20
C306	AP73a	120fr Hypolimnas misippus	.50	.25
C307	AP73a	400fr Danaus chrysippus	1.60	.80
C308	AP73a	450fr Papilio demodocus	1.90	.90
		Nos. C305-C308 (4)	4.20	2.15

Philexafrica '85, Lome — AP74

1985, May 20 Litho. *Perf. 13*

C309	AP74	200fr Solar & wind energy	.55	.25
C310	AP74	200fr Children	.55	.25
a.		Pair, #C309-C310 + label	1.10	.75

PHILEXAFRICA '85, Lome — AP75

National development: No. C311, Youth. No. C312, Communications and transportation.

1985, Nov. 16 Litho. *Perf. 13*

C311	AP75	250fr multi	.90	.45
C312	AP75	250fr multi	.90	.45
a.		Pair, #C311-C312 + label	1.80	1.25

Intl. Youth Year (No. C311).

French Revolution, Bicent. — AP76

Designs: 150fr, *Oath of the Tennis Court,* by David. 200fr, *Storming of the Bastille,* by Thevenin. 600fr, *Rouget de Lisle Singing La Marseillaise,* by Pils.
Illustration reduced.

1989, May 3 Litho. *Perf. 13*

C313	AP76	150fr multi	.90	.45
C314	AP76	200fr multi	1.25	.60
C315	AP76	600fr multi	3.50	1.75
		Nos. C313-C315 (3)	5.65	2.80

PHILEXFRANCE '89.

POSTAGE DUE STAMPS

Postage Due Stamps of Upper Senegal and Niger, 1914, Overprinted in Black or Red

1920 Unwmk. *Perf. 14x13½*

J1	D2	5c green	.30	.30
J2	D2	10c rose	.30	.30
J3	D2	15c gray	.30	.30
J4	D2	20c brown (R)	.40	.40
J5	D2	30c blue	.45	.45
J6	D2	50c black (R)	.65	.65
J7	D2	60c orange	.65	.65
J8	D2	1fr violet	.95	.95
		Nos. J1-J8 (8)	4.00	4.00

Type of 1914 Issue Surcharged

1927

J9	D2	2fr on 1fr lilac rose	2.25	2.25
J10	D2	3fr on 1fr orange brn	2.50	2.50

Red-fronted Gazelle
D3 D4

1928 Typo.

J11	D3	5c green	.30	.30
J12	D3	10c rose	.30	.30
J13	D3	15c dark gray	.40	.40
J14	D3	20c dark brown	.40	.40
J15	D3	30c dark blue	.50	.50
J16	D3	50c black	1.75	1.75
J17	D3	60c orange	2.00	2.00
J18	D3	1fr dull violet	3.50	3.50
J19	D3	2fr lilac rose	6.00	6.00
J20	D3	3fr orange brn	6.50	6.50
		Nos. J11-J20 (10)	21.65	21.65

Catalogue values for unused stamps in this section, from this point to the end of the section, are for Never Hinged items.

Republic

1962, Jan. 31 *Perf. 14x13½*

Denomination in Black

J21	D4	1fr bright blue	.20	.20
J22	D4	2fr orange	.20	.20
J23	D4	5fr brt vio blue	.20	.20
J24	D4	10fr red lilac	.20	.20
J25	D4	20fr emerald	.45	.45
J26	D4	50fr rose red	1.10	1.10
		Nos. J21-J26 (6)	2.35	2.35

OFFICIAL STAMPS

Catalogue values for unused stamps in this section are for Never Hinged items.

Elephant — O1

Perf. 12½

1963, Feb. 1 Unwmk. Photo.

Center in Sepia

O1	O1	1fr red brown	.20	.20
O2	O1	5fr yel green	.20	.20
O3	O1	10fr deep vio	.20	.20
O4	O1	15fr red org	.25	.25
O5	O1	25fr brt rose lilac	.35	.35
O6	O1	50fr brt green	.55	.55
O7	O1	60fr brt red	.70	.70
O8	O1	85fr dk slate grn	1.10	1.10
O9	O1	100fr brt blue	1.75	1.75
O10	O1	200fr bright rose	3.00	3.00
		Nos. O1-O10 (10)	8.30	8.30

BURMA

'bər-mə

Myanmar

LOCATION — Bounded on the north by China; east by China, Laos and Thailand; south and west by the Bay of Bengal, Bangladesh and India.
GOVT. — Republic
AREA — 261,228 sq. mi.
POP. — 48,081,302 (1999 est.)
CAPITAL — Yangon (Rangoon)

Burma was part of India from 1826 until April 1, 1937, when it became a self-governing unit of the British Commonwealth and received a constitution. On January 4, 1948, Burma became an independent nation. In 1990 they became the Union of Myanmar.

12 Pies = 1 Anna
16 Annas = 1 Rupee
100 Pyas = 1 Kyat (1953)

Catalogue values for unused stamps in this country are for Never Hinged items, beginning with Scott 35 in the regular postage section and Scott O28 in the official section.

Watermarks

Wmk. 254-Elephant Heads

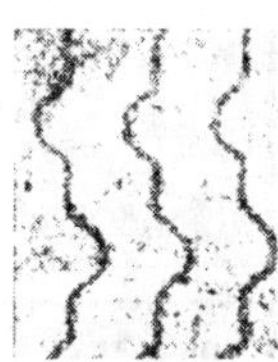
Wmk. 257-Curved Wavy Lines

Stamps of India 1926-36 Overprinted

1937, Apr. 1 Wmk. 196 *Perf. 14*

1	A46	3p slate	.20	.20
2	A71	½a green	.20	.20
3	A68	9p dark green	.25	.20
4	A72	1a dark brown	.20	.20
5	A49	2a ver (small die)	.20	.20
6	A57	2a6p buff	.20	.20
7	A51	3a carmine rose	.40	.30
8	A70	3a6p deep blue	.40	.20
9	A52	4a olive green	.45	.20
10	A53	6a bister	.40	.35
11	A54	8a red violet	.90	.20
12	A55	12a claret	1.50	.85

Overprinted

13	A56	1r green & brown	5.00	2.00
14	A56	2r brn org & car rose	7.50	7.50
15	A56	5r dk violet & ultra	10.00	*13.50*
16	A56	10r car & green	27.50	*45.00*
17	A56	15r ol green & ultra	125.00	80.00
18	A56	25r blue & ocher	250.00	175.00
		Nos. 1-18 (18)	430.30	326.30

For overprints see #1N1-1N3, 1N25-1N26, 1N47.

King George VI
A1 A2

Royal Barge — A3

Elephant Moving Teak Log — A4

Farmer Plowing Rice Field — A5

Sailboat on Irrawaddy River — A6

Peacock — A7

George VI — A8

Perf. 13½x14

1938-40		Litho.	Wmk. 254	
18A	A1	1p red org ('40)	1.40	.75
19	A1	3p violet	.20	*.30*
20	A1	6p ultramarine	.20	.20
21	A1	9p yel green	.55	*.75*
22	A2	1a brown violet	.20	.20
23	A2	1½a turquoise grn	.20	*.55*
24	A2	2a carmine	.30	.20

Perf. 13

25	A3	2a6p rose lake	6.00	*8.50*
26	A4	3a dk violet	6.00	1.40
27	A5	3a6p dp bl & brt bl	1.00	*3.50*
28	A2	4a slate blue, perf. 13½x14	.25	.20
29	A6	8a slate green	2.25	.30

Perf. 13½

30	A7	1r brt ultra & dk violet	3.25	.25
31	A7	2r dk vio & red brown	6.00	1.60
32	A8	5r car & dull vio	22.50	18.00
33	A8	10r gray grn & brn	40.00	40.00
		Nos. 18A-33 (16)	90.30	76.70
		Set, never hinged	110.00	

See Nos. 51-65. For overprints and surcharges see Nos. 34-50, O15-O27, 1N4-1N11, 1N28-1N30, 1N37-1N46, 1N48-1N49.

No. 25 Surcharged in Black

1940, May 6			*Perf. 13*	
34	A3	1a on 2a6p rose lake	3.00	1.50
		Never hinged	4.25	

Centenary of first postage stamp.

Catalogue values for unused stamps in this section, from this point to the end of the section, are for Never Hinged items.

Nos. 18A to 33 Overprinted in Black:

a 

b

1945				
35	A1(a)	1p red orange	.20	.20
36	A1(a)	3p violet	.20	*.40*
37	A1(a)	6p ultramarine	.20	*.30*
38	A1(a)	9p yel green	.20	*.50*
39	A2(a)	1a brown violet	.20	.20
40	A2(a)	1½a turq green	.20	.20
41	A2(a)	2a carmine	.20	.20
42	A3(b)	2a6p rose lake	.45	*.60*
43	A4(b)	3a dk violet	.75	.20
44	A5(b)	3a6p dp bl & brt bl	.20	*.70*
45	A2(a)	4a slate blue	.20	*.25*
46	A6(b)	8a slate green	.20	*.50*
47	A7(b)	1r brt ultra & dk vio	.30	*.50*
48	A7(b)	2r dk vio & red brn	.30	*1.00*
49	A8(b)	5r car & dull vio	.70	*1.00*
50	A8(b)	10r gray grn & brn	1.50	1.00
		Nos. 35-50 (16)	6.00	7.75

Types of 1938

Perf. 13½x14

1946, Jan. 1		Litho.	Wmk. 254	
51	A1	3p brown	.20	*1.10*
52	A1	6p violet	.20	.20
53	A1	9p dull green	.20	*1.40*
54	A2	1a deep blue	.20	.20
55	A2	1½a salmon	.20	.20
56	A2	2a rose lake	.20	*.30*

Perf. 13

57	A3	2a6p greenish blue	1.75	*2.75*
58	A4	3a blue violet	6.75	2.50
59	A5	3a6p ultra & gray blk	.20	*1.40*
60	A2	4a rose lil, perf. 13½x14	.20	.20
61	A6	8a deep magenta	2.25	*1.75*

Perf. 13½

62	A7	1r dp mag & dk vio	1.25	.25
63	A7	2r sal & red brn	7.50	1.75
64	A8	5r red brn & dk grn	7.50	*11.00*
65	A8	10r dk vio & car	7.50	*15.00*
		Nos. 51-65 (15)	36.10	40.00

For overprints see Nos. 70-84, O28-O42.

Burmese Man — A9

Burmese Woman — A10

Mythological Chinze — A11

Elephant Hauling Teak — A12

1946, May 2			*Perf. 13*	
66	A9	9p peacock green	.20	.20
67	A10	1½a brt violet	.20	.20
68	A11	2a carmine	.20	.20
69	A12	3a6p ultramarine	.40	.20
		Nos. 66-69 (4)	1.00	.80

Victory of the Allied Nations in WWII.

Nos. 51-65 Overprinted in Black

1947, Oct. 1		*Perf. 13½x14, 13, 13½*		
70	A1	3p brown	.45	.45
71	A1	6p violet	.20	*.25*
72	A1	9p dull green	.20	*.25*
	a.	Inverted overprint	12.50	12.50
73	A2	1a deep blue	.20	*.25*
74	A2	1½a salmon	1.25	.20
75	A2	2a rose lake	.35	.20
76	A3	2a6p greenish bl	1.40	.75
77	A4	3a blue violet	2.50	1.25
78	A5	3a6p ultra & gray blk	.50	*.75*
79	A2	4a rose lilac	1.60	.25
80	A6	8a dp magenta	1.60	.70
81	A7	1r dp mag & dk vio	2.25	.30
82	A7	2r sal & red brn	2.50	2.50
83	A8	5r red brn & dk grn	3.50	*3.75*
84	A8	10r dk vio & car	3.50	*3.75*
		Nos. 70-84 (15)	22.00	*15.60*

The overprint is slightly larger on #76-78, 80-84. The Burmese characters read "Interim Government."

Other denominations are known with the overprint inverted or double.

Issues of the Republic

U Aung San Map and Chinze — A13

Martyrs' Memorial — A14

Perf. 12½x12

1948, Jan. 6		Litho.	Unwmk.	
85	A13	½a emerald	.20	.20
86	A13	1a deep rose	.20	.20
87	A13	2a carmine	.20	.20
88	A13	3½a blue	.20	.20
89	A13	8a lt chocolate	.20	.20
		Nos. 85-89 (5)	1.00	1.00

Attainment of independence, Jan. 4, 1948.

1948, July 19		Engr.	*Perf. 14x13½*	
90	A14	3p ultramarine	.20	.20
91	A14	6p green	.20	.20
92	A14	9p dp carmine	.20	.20
93	A14	1a purple	.20	.20
94	A14	2a lilac rose	.20	.20
95	A14	3½a dk slate green	.20	.20
96	A14	4a yel brown	.20	.20
97	A14	8a orange red	.20	.20
98	A14	12a claret	.20	.20
99	A14	1r blue green	.20	.20
100	A14	2r deep blue	.50	.35
101	A14	5r chocolate	1.25	.80
		Nos. 90-101 (12)	3.75	3.15

1st anniv. of the assassination of Burma's leaders in the fight for independence.

Ball Game (Chinlon) A15

Bell A16

Mythical Bird — A17

Rice Planting A18

Throne — A19

Designs: 6p, Dancer. 9p, Musician. 3a, Spinning. 3a6p, Royal Palace. 4a, Cutting teak. 8a, Plowing rice field.

Perf. 12½ (A15-A17), 12x12½ (A18), 13 (A19)

1949, Jan. 4				
102	A15	3p ultramarine	.20	.20
103	A15	6p green	.20	.20
104	A15	9p carmine	.20	.20
105	A16	1a red orange	.20	.20
106	A17	2a orange	.20	.20
107	A18	2a6p lilac rose	.20	.20
108	A18	3a purple	.20	.20
109	A18	3a6p dk slate grn	.20	.20
110	A16	4a chocolate	.20	.20
111	A18	8a carmine	.25	.20
112	A19	1r blue green	.40	.20
	a.	Perf. 14		2.50
113	A19	2r deep blue	.90	.30
114	A19	5r chocolate	1.75	.70
115	A19	10r orange red	4.00	1.00
		Nos. 102-115 (14)	9.10	4.20

See Nos. 122-135, 139-152, O56-O67.

UPU Monument, Bern — A20

1949, Oct. 9		Unwmk.	*Perf. 13*	
116	A20	2a orange	.20	.20
117	A20	3½a olive grn	.20	.20
118	A20	6a lilac	.30	.20
119	A20	8a crimson	.40	.20
120	A20	12½a ultra	.50	.20
121	A20	1r blue green	.75	.50
		Nos. 116-121 (6)	2.35	1.50

75th anniv. of the UPU.

Types of 1949

Designs as before.

Perf. 13½x14, 14x13½, 13

1952-53 Litho. Wmk. 254

122 A15 3p brown orange .20 .20
123 A15 6p deep plum .20 .20
124 A15 9p blue .20 .20
125 A16 1a violet bl .20 .20
126 A17 2a green ('52) .20 .20
127 A18 2a6p green .20 .20
128 A18 3a sal pink ('52) .20 .20
129 A18 3a6p brown orange .20 .20
130 A16 4a vermilion .20 .20
131 A18 8a lt blue ('52) .20 .20
132 A19 1r rose violet .25 .20
133 A19 2r yel green .55 .25
134 A19 5r ultramarine 1.75 .85
135 A19 10r aquamarine 3.25 1.60
Nos. 122-135 (14) 7.80 4.90

Map of Burma and Monument — A21

1953, Jan. 4 ***Perf. 14***

136 A21 14p green .20 .20

Perf. 13

Size: 36½x26mm

137 A21 20p salmon pink .20 .20
138 A21 25p ultramarine .20 .20

Fifth anniversary of independence.
For surcharge see No. 166.

Types of 1949

Designs: 2p, Dancer. 3p, Musician. 20p, Spinning. 25p, Royal Palace. 30p, Cutting teak. 50p, Plowing rice field.

1954, Jan. 4 ***Perf. 14x13½, 13, 14***

139 A15 1p brown orange .20 .20
140 A15 2p plum .20 .20
141 A15 3p blue .20 .20
142 A16 5p ultramarine .20 .20
143 A18 10p yel green .20 .20
144 A17 15p green .20 .20
145 A18 20p vermilion .20 .20
146 A18 25p lt red org .20 .20
147 A16 30p vermilion .20 .20
148 A18 50p blue .25 .20
149 A19 1k rose violet .50 .20
150 A19 2k green 1.00 .20
151 A19 5k ultramarine 2.75 .20
152 A19 10k light blue 5.00 .25
Nos. 139-152 (14) 11.30 2.85

For overprints and surcharges see Nos. 163-165, 173-175, O68-O79, O80-O81, O83, O85, O87.

Peace Pagoda, Monks' Hostels and Meeting-cave — A22

Designs: 10p, Sangha (community) of Cambodia. 15p, Council meeting. 50p, Sangha of Thailand. 1k, Sangha of Ceylon. 2k, Sangha of Laos.

1954 Typo. ***Perf. 13***

153 A22 10p deep blue .20 .20
154 A22 15p deep claret .20 .20
155 A22 35p dark brown .20 .20
156 A22 50p green .20 .20
157 A22 1k carmine .30 .20
158 A22 2k violet .60 .40
Nos. 153-158 (6) 1.70 1.40

6th Buddhist Council, Rangoon, 1954-56.

Marble Markers of 5th Buddhist Council A23

Designs: 40p, Thatbyinnyu Pagoda. 60p, Shwedagon Pagoda, Rangoon. 1.25k, Aerial View of 6th Buddhist Council, Yegu.

Perf. 11x11½

1956, May 24 Litho. Unwmk.

159 A23 20p blue & gray olive .20 .20
160 A23 40p blue & brt yel grn .20 .20
161 A23 60p green & lemon .20 .20
162 A23 1.25k gray blue & yel .30 .20
Nos. 159-162 (4) .90 .80

2500th anniv. of the Buddhist Era.

Nos. 146, 149-150 Surcharged or Overprinted

1959, Nov. 9 Wmk. 254 ***Perf. 13, 14***

163 A18 15p on 25p lt red org .20 .20
164 A19 1k rose violet .25 .20
165 A19 2k green .55 .45
Nos. 163-165 (3) 1.00 .85

Centenary of Mandalay, former capital.
The two lines of overprint are 4mm apart on No. 163; 7mm on Nos. 164-165.

No. 136 Surcharged:

1961, June ***Perf. 14***

166 A21 15p on 14p green .30 .20

Children A24

Unwmk.

1961, Dec. 11 Litho. ***Perf. 13***

167 A24 15p claret & rose claret .20 .20

15th anniversary of UNICEF.

Runner with Torch — A25

Soccer, Pole Vault and Shot Put — A26

Designs: 50p, Women runners. 1k, Hurdling, weight lifting, boxing, bicycling and swimming.

1961, Dec. 11 Photo. ***Perf. 14x13***

168 A25 15p red & ultra .20 .20
169 A26 25p dk green & ocher .20 .20
170 A26 50p vio blue & pink .20 .20
171 A25 1k brt green & yel .40 .25
Nos. 168-171 (4) 1.00 .85

2nd South East Asia Peninsular Games, Rangoon.

Map and Flag of Burma — A27

Wmk. 254

1963, Mar. 2 Engr. ***Perf. 13***

172 A27 15p red .20 .20

First anniversary of new government.

Nos. 143 and 148 Overprinted in Violet or Red: "FREEDOM FROM HUNGER"

1963, Mar. 21 Litho.

173 A18 10p yel green (V) .20 .20
174 A18 50p blue (R) .20 .20

FAO "Freedom from Hunger" campaign.

No. 145 Overprinted

1963, May 1

175 A18 20p vermilion .20 .20

Issued for May Day.

White-browed Fantail — A28

Indian Roller — A29

Birds: 20p, Red-whiskered bulbul. 25p, Crested serpent eagle. 50p, Sarus crane. 1k, Malabar pied hornbill. 2k, Lineated kalij pheasant. 5k, Green peafowl.

Perf. 13½

1964, Apr. 16 Unwmk. Photo.

Size: 25x21mm

176 A28 1p gray .20 .20
177 A28 2p carmine rose .20 .20
178 A28 3p blue green .20 .20

Size: 22x26½mm

179 A29 5p violet blue .20 .20
180 A29 10p orange brn .20 .20
181 A29 15p olive .20 .20

Size: 35x25mm

182 A28 20p rose & brn .20 .20

Size: 27x36½mm, 36½x27mm

183 A29 25p yel & brown .20 .20
184 A29 50p red, blk & gray .50 .20
185 A29 1k gray, ind & yel 1.00 .20
186 A28 2k pale ol, ind & red 2.00 .30
187 A29 5k citron, dk bl & red 4.75 .70
Nos. 176-187 (12) 9.85 3.00

See Nos. 197-208. For overprints see Nos. O82, O84, O86, O88-O93, O94-O115.

ITU Emblem, Old and New Communication Equipment — A30

1965, May 17 Litho. ***Perf. 15***

Size: 32x22mm

188 A30 20p bright pink .20 .20

Perf. 13

Size: 34x24½mm

189 A30 50p dull green .25 .25

Centenary of the ITU.

ICY Emblem A31

1965, July 1 Unwmk. ***Perf. 13***

190 A31 5p violet blue .20 .20
191 A31 10p brown orange .20 .20
192 A31 15p olive .20 .20
Nos. 190-192 (3) .60 .60

International Cooperation Year.

Rice Farmer — A32

Cogwheel and Hammer — A33

1966, Mar. 2

193 A32 15p multicolored .20 .20

Issued for Farmers' Day.

1967, May 1 Litho. Unwmk.

194 A33 15p lt blue, yel & black .20 .20

Issued for Labor Day, May 1.

Aung San, Tractor and Farmers A34

1968, Jan. 4 Unwmk. ***Perf. 13***

195 A34 15p sky bl, blk & ocher .20 .20

20th anniversary of independence.

Largest Burmese Pearl — A35

1968, Mar. 4 Litho. ***Perf. 13½x13***

196 A35 15p blue, ultra, gray & yel .20 .20

Burmese pearl industry.

Bird Types of 1964 in Changed Sizes; Designs as Before

Unwmk.

1968, July 1 Photo. ***Perf. 14***

Size: 21x17mm

197 A28 1p gray .20 .20
198 A28 2p carmine rose .20 .20
199 A28 3p blue green .20 .20

Size: 23½x28mm

200 A29 5p violet blue .20 .20
201 A29 10p orange brown .20 .20
202 A29 15p olive .20 .20

Size: 38½x21, 21x38½mm

203 A28 20p rose & brown .20 .20
204 A29 25p yel & brown .20 .20
205 A29 50p ver, blk, & gray .30 .20
206 A29 1k gray, ind & yel .65 .20
207 A28 2k dull cit, ind & red 1.40 .25
208 A29 5k yel, dk blue & red 3.25 .55
Nos. 197-208 (12) 7.20 2.80

For overprints see Nos. O92-O102.

Wheat — A36

1969, Mar. 2 Litho. *Perf. 13*

209 A36 15p blue, emerald & yel	.20	.20

Issued for Peasant's Day.

ILO Emblem A37

1969, Oct. 29 Photo. Wmk. 254

210 A37 15p dk blue grn & gold	.20	.20
211 A37 50p dp carmine & gold	.20	.20

50th anniv. of the ILO.

Soccer — A38

Designs: 25p, Runner, horiz. 50p, Weight lifter. 1k, Women's volleyball.

Perf. 12½x13, 13x12½

1969, Dec. 1 Litho. Wmk. 254

212 A38 15p brt olive & multi	.20	.20
213 A38 25p brown & multi	.20	.20
214 A38 50p brt green & multi	.25	.20
215 A38 1k blue, yel grn & blk	.45	.30
Nos. 212-215 (4)	1.10	.90

5th South East Asia Peninsular Games, Rangoon.

Burmese Flags and Marching Soldiers — A39

1970, Mar. 27 *Perf. 13*

216 A39 15p multicolored	.20	.20

Issued for Armed Forces Day.

Solar System and UN Emblem A40

1970, June 26 Photo. Unwmk.

217 A40 15p lt ultra & multi	.20	.20

25th anniversary of the United Nations.

Scroll, Marchers, Peacock Emblem — A41

Designs: 25p, Students' boycott demonstration. 50p, Banner and marchers at Shwedagon Camp.

1970, Nov. 23 Litho. *Perf. 13x13½*

218 A41 15p ultra & multi	.20	.20
219 A41 25p multicolored	.20	.20
220 A41 50p lt blue & multi	.25	.20
Nos. 218-220 (3)	.65	.60

50th National Day (Students' 1920 uprising).

Workers, Farmers, Technicians — A42

15p, Burmese of various races, & flags. 25p, Hands holding document. 50p, Red party flag.

1971, June 28 Litho. *Perf. 13½*

221 A42 5p blue & multi	.20	.20
222 A42 15p blue & multi	.20	.20
223 A42 25p blue & multi	.20	.20
224 A42 50p blue & multi	.25	.20
a. Souvenir sheet of 4, #221-224	.45	.45
Nos. 221-224 (4)	.85	.80

1st Congress of Burmese Socialist Program Party.

Child Drinking Milk — A43

UNICEF, 25th Anniv.: 50p, Marionettes.

1971, Dec. 11 *Perf. 14½*

225 A43 15p lt ultra & multi	.20	.20
226 A43 50p emerald & multi	.30	.20

Aung San, Independence Monument, Pinlon — A44

Union Day, 25th Anniv.: 50p, Bogyoke Aung San and people in front of Independence Monument. 1k, Map of Burma with flag pointing to Pinlon, vert.

1972, Feb. 12 *Perf. 14*

227 A44 15p ocher & multi	.20	.20
228 A44 50p blue & multi	.25	.20
229 A44 1k green, ultra & red	.40	.20
Nos. 227-229 (3)	.85	.60

Burmese and Double Star A45

1972 Litho. *Perf. 14*

230 A45 15p bister & multi	.20	.20

Revolutionary Council, 10th anniversary.

"Your Heart is your Health" — A46

1972, Apr. 7 *Perf. 14x14½*

231 A46 15p yellow, red & black	.20	.20

World Health Day.

Burmese of Various Ethnic Groups A47

1973, Feb. 12 Litho. *Perf. 14*

232 A47 15p multicolored	.20	.20

1973 census.

Casting Vote — A48

Natl. Referendum: 10p, Voters holding map of Burma. 15p, Farmer & soldier holding ballots.

Perf. 14x14½, 14½x14

1973, Dec. 15 Litho.

233 A48 5p deep org & black	.20	.20
234 A48 10p blue & multi	.20	.20
235 A48 15p blue & multi, vert.	.20	.20
Nos. 233-235 (3)	.60	.60

Open-air Meeting A49

Designs: 15p, Regional flags. 1k, Scales of justice and Burmese emblem.

1974, Mar. 2 Photo. *Perf. 13*

Size: 80x26mm

236 A49 15p blue & multi	.20	.20

Size: 37x25mm

237 A49 50p blue & multi	.20	.20
238 A49 1k lt blue, bis & blk	.40	.25
Nos. 236-238 (3)	.80	.65

First meeting of People's Parliament.

Messenger Bird and UPU Emblem — A50

UPU Cent.: 20p, Mother reading letter to child, vert. 50p, Simulated block of stamps, vert. 1k, Burmese doll, vert. 2k, Mailman delivering letter to family.

1974, May 22

239 A50 15p grn, lt grn & org	.20	.20
240 A50 20p multicolored	.20	.20
241 A50 50p green & multi	.25	.20
242 A50 1k ultra & multi	.50	.25
243 A50 2k blue & multi	.95	.50
Nos. 239-243 (5)	2.10	1.35

Children A51 Man and Woman A52

Designs: 3p, Girl. 5p, 15p, Man and woman. 10p, Children (like 1p). 50p, Woman with fan. 1k, Seated woman. 5k, Drummer.

Perf. 13, 13x13½ (#248-251)

1974-78 Photo.

244 A51 1p rose & lilac rose	.20	.20
245 A51 3p dk brown & pink	.20	.20
246 A51 5p pink & violet	.20	.20
246A A51 10p Prus blue ('76)	.20	.20
247 A51 15p lt grn & ol ('75)	.20	.20
248 A52 20p lt blue & multi	.20	.20
249 A52 50p ocher & multi	.25	.20
250 A52 1k brt rose & multi	.55	.30
251 A52 5k ol green & multi	2.00	1.40
Nos. 244-251 (9)	4.00	3.10

For different country names see Nos. 298-303.

IWY Emblem, Woman and Globe A53

IWY: 2k, Symbolic flower, globe and IWY emblem, vert.

1975, Dec. 15 Photo. *Perf. 13½*

252 A53 50p green & black	.20	.20
253 A53 2k black & blue	.70	.50

Burmese with Raised Fists A54

Constitution Day: 50p, Demonstrators with banners and emblem. 1k, People and map of Burma, emblem.

1976, Jan. 3 *Perf. 14*

254 A54 20p blue & black	.20	.20
255 A54 50p blue, blk & brn	.25	.20

Size: 56x20mm

256 A54 1k blue & multi	.45	.20
Nos. 254-256 (3)	.90	.60

Students, Campaign Emblem — A55

Abacus A56

Intl. Literacy Year: 50p, Campaign emblem. 1k, Emblem, book and globe.

1976, Sept. 8 Photo. *Perf. 14*

257 A55 10p salmon & black	.20	.20
258 A56 15p blue grn & multi	.20	.20
259 A56 50p ultra, org & blk	.25	.20
260 A55 1k multicolored	.60	.30
Nos. 257-260 (4)	1.25	.90

Steam Locomotive A57

Diesel Train Emerging from Tunnel — A58

Cent. of Burma's Railroad: 20p, Early train and oxcart. 25p, Old and new trains approaching station. 50p, Railroad bridge.

1977, May 1 ***Perf. 13½***

261 A57 15p multicolored .20 .20

Size: 38x26, 26x38mm

262 A57 20p multicolored .20 .20
263 A57 25p multicolored .20 .20
264 A57 50p multicolored .25 .20
265 A58 1k multicolored .50 .20
Nos. 261-265 (5) 1.35 1.00

Karaweik Pagoda A59

Design: 1k, Karaweik Pagoda, front view.

1977

266 A59 50p light brown .20 .20

Size: 78x25mm

267 A59 1k multicolored .35 .25

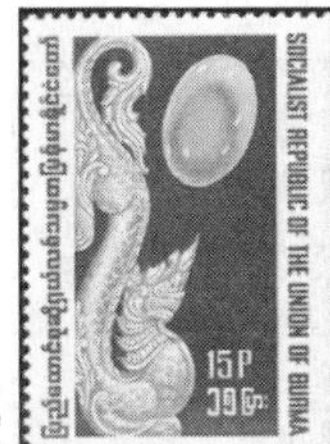
Jade Dragon — A60

Precious Jewelry: 20p, Gold bird with large pearl. 50p, Hand holding pearl necklace with pendant. 1k, Gold dragon, horiz.

1978 Photo. ***Perf. 13***

268 A60 15p green & yel grn .20 .20
269 A60 20p multicolored .20 .20
270 A60 50p multicolored .30 .20

Size: 55x20mm

Perf. 14

271 A60 1k multicolored .50 .30
Nos. 268-271 (4) 1.20 .90

Satellite over Map of Asia A61

1979, Feb., 12 Photo. ***Perf. 13***

272 A61 25p multicolored .20 .20

IYC Emblem in Map of Burma — A62

Weather Balloon, WMO Emblem — A63

1979, Dec. Photo. ***Perf. 13½***

273 A62 25p multicolored .20 .20
274 A62 50p multicolored .30 .20

International Year of the Child.

1980, Mar. 23 Photo. ***Perf. 13½***

275 A63 25p shown .20 .20
276 A63 50p Weather satellite, cloud .30 .20

World Meteorological Day.

Weight Lifting, Olympic Rings A64

1980, Dec. Litho. ***Perf. 14***

277 A64 20p shown .20 .20
278 A64 50p Boxing .20 .20
279 A64 1k Soccer .40 .25
Nos. 277-279 (3) .80 .65

22nd Summer Olympic Games, Moscow, July 19-Aug. 3.

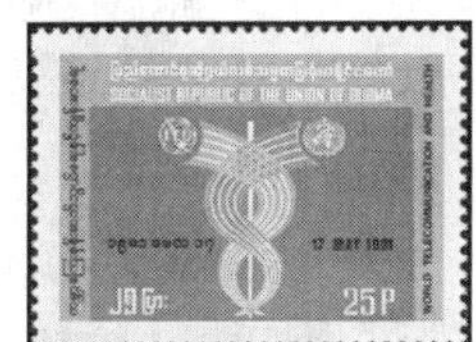
13th World Telecommunications Day — A65

1981, May 17 Photo. ***Perf. 13½***

280 A65 25p orange & black .20 .20

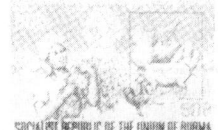
World Food Day — A66

1981, Oct. 16 Photo. ***Perf. 13½***

281 A66 25p Livestock, produce .20 .20
282 A66 50p Farmer, rice, produce .20 .20
283 A66 1k Emblems .40 .25
Nos. 281-283 (3) .80 .65

Intl. Year of the Disabled A67

1981, Dec. 12

284 A67 25p multicolored .20 .20

World Communications Year — A68

1983, Sept. 15 Litho. ***Perf. 14½x14***

285 A68 15p pale blue & black .20 .20
286 A68 25p dull lake & black .20 .20
287 A68 50p pale brn, blk & lake .30 .20
288 A68 1k buff, blk, beige & yel grn .60 .40
Nos. 285-288 (4) 1.30 1.00

Fish, Ship, Globe, FAO Emblem — A69

1983, Oct. 16 Photo. ***Perf. 14x14½***

289 A69 15p brt blue, bister & blk .20 .20
290 A69 25p yel grn, pale org & blk .20 .20
291 A69 50p org, pale grn & blk .30 .20
292 A69 1k yel, ultra & black .60 .40
Nos. 289-292 (4) 1.30 1.00

World Food Day.

Stylized Trees, Hemispheres and Log — A70

1984, Oct. 16 ***Perf. 14½x14***

293 A70 15p org, black & blue .20 .20
294 A70 25p pale yel, blk & lt vio .20 .20
295 A70 50p pale pink, blk & lt grn .30 .20
296 A70 1k yel, blk & lt rose vio .60 .40
Nos. 293-296 (4) 1.30 1.00

World Food Day.

Intl. Youth Year — A71

1985, Oct. 15 ***Perf. 14x14½***

297 A71 15p multicolored .20 .20

Types of 1974
Inscribed: Union of Burma

1989 Photo. ***Perf. 13½***

298 A51 15p olive & lt green .20 .20
299 A52 50p violet & brown .25 .25
300 A52 1k multicolored .55 .55
Nos. 298-300 (3) 1.00 1.00

Issued: 15p, 6/26; 50p, 6/12; 1k, 9/6.

UNION OF MYANMAR

Inscribed: Union of Myanmar

1990-91 Photo. ***Perf. 13½***

301 A51 15p olive & lt green .20 .20
301A A51 20p brown, greenish blue & black ('91) — —
302 A52 50p violet & brown .25 .25
303 A52 1k multicolored .50 .50

Issued: 15p, May 26; 50p, May 12.

Fountain, Natl. Assembly Park — A74

Illustration reduced.

1990, May 27 Litho. ***Perf. 14½x14***

304 A74 1k multicolored 1.00 .50

State Law and Order Restoration Council.

A75

A76

1990, Dec. 20 Litho. ***Perf. 14x14½***

305 A75 2k multicolored 1.75 1.10

UN Development Program, 40th anniv.

1991, Jan. 26

306 A76 50p Nawata ruby 1.00 .65

Painting of Freedom Fighters — A77

Bronze Statue — A78

1992, Jan. 4 Litho. ***Perf. 14x14½***

307 A77 50p multicolored .40 .40
308 A78 2k multicolored 1.60 1.60

A79

A80

1992, Apr. 10 Litho. ***Perf. 14x14½***
309 A79 50p multicolored .50 .50

National Sports Festival.

1992, Dec. 1 Litho. ***Perf. 14x14½***
310 A80 50p red .60 .35

World Campaign Against AIDS.

A81

Artifacts — A82

1992, Dec. 5 Litho. ***Perf. 14x14½***
Background Color
311 A81 50p pink .20 .20
312 A81 1k yellow .40 .40
313 A81 3k orange 1.25 1.25
314 A81 5k green 2.00 2.00
Nos. 311-314 (4) 3.85 3.85

Intl. Conference on Nutrition, Rome.

1993, Sept. 1 Litho. ***Perf. 14x14½***
315 A82 5k Bird 1.60 1.60
316 A82 10k shown 3.25 3.25

Natl. Assembly — A83

1993, Jan. 1 Litho. ***Perf. 14x14½***
317 A83 50p multicolored .25 .25
318 A83 3k multicolored 1.25 1.25

Equestrian Festival — A84

1993, Oct. 23 Litho. ***Perf. 14½x14***
319 A84 3k multicolored 1.50 1.00

A85

A86

1994, June 5 Litho. ***Perf. 14***
320 A85 4k multicolored 1.75 1.50

Environment day.

1994, Sept. 15 Litho. ***Perf. 14***
321 A86 3k multicolored 1.25 1.25

Union of Solidarity & Development, 1st anniv.

Armed Forces, 50th Anniv. A87

1995, Mar. 27 Litho. ***Perf. 14½x14***
322 A87 50p multicolored .25 .25

A88

A89

1995, June 26 Litho. ***Perf. 14***
323 A88 2k multicolored .80 .80

Prevent drug abuse.

1995, Oct. 17 Litho. ***Perf. 14x14½***
324 A89 50p multicolored .40 .40

Myanmar motion pictures, 60th anniv.

A90

A91

1995, Oct. 24
325 A90 4k UN, 50th Anniv. 2.00 2.00

1995, Nov. 1
326 A91 50p pink & multi .25 .25
327 A91 2k green & multi 1.00 1.00

University of Yangon (Rangoon), 75th anniv.

Visit Myanmar Year A92

Designs: 50p, Couple in boat on Inlay Lake with food bowl for Buddha, Buddhist monks. 4k, Decorated royal barge on Kandawgyi (Royal Lake), Yangoon. 5k, Royal moat, entrance of Yadanabon (Mandalay), vert.

Perf. 14½x14, 14x14½
1996, Mar. 1 Litho.
328 A92 50p multicolored .20 .20
329 A92 4k multicolored 1.75 1.75
330 A92 5k multicolored 2.25 2.25
Nos. 328-330 (3) 4.20 4.20

UNICEF, 50th Anniv. — A93

Stylized designs: 1k, Mother breastfeeding. 2k, Vaccinating child. 4k, Girls going to school.

1996, Dec. 11 Litho. ***Perf. 14x14½***
331 A93 1k multicolored .40 .40
332 A93 2k multicolored .85 .85
333 A93 4k multicolored 1.75 1.75
Nos. 331-333 (3) 3.00 3.00

Intl. Letter Writing Week A94

Designs: 2k, Men in canoe. 5k, Stylized figures forming pyramid, flag, map, vert.

1996, Oct. 7 ***Perf. 14½x14, 14x14½***
334 A94 2k multicolored .85 .85
335 A94 5k multicolored 2.00 2.00

A95

A96

1997, July 24 Litho. ***Perf. 14x14½***
336 A95 1k blue & multi .40 .40
337 A95 2k yellow & multi .85 .85

Assoc. of Southeast Asian Nations (ASEAN), 30th anniv.

1998, Jan. 4 Litho. ***Perf. 14x14½***
338 A96 2k multicolored .90 .90

Independence, 50th anniv.

Musical Instruments A97

1998 Photo. ***Perf. 13¼***
339 A97 5k Xylophone 2.00 2.00
340 A97 10k Mon brass gongs 3.75 3.75
341 A97 20k Rakhine (drum) 7.75 7.75
342 A97 30k Harp 11.50 11.50
343 A97 50k Shan pot drum 18.00 18.00
344 A97 100k Kachin brass gong 37.50 37.50
Nos. 339-344 (6) 80.50 80.50

Issued: 5k, 8/28/98.

Decade of Disabled Persons (1993-2002) A98

1998 Litho. ***Perf. 14***
345 A98 2k yellow & multi .75 .75
346 A98 5k apple green & multi 1.90 1.90

UPU, 125th Anniv. — A99

1999 Litho. ***Perf. 14x14¼***
347 A99 2k blue & multi .75 .75
348 A99 5k purple & multi 1.90 1.90

Independence, 52nd Anniv. — A100

2000
349 A100 2k multi .70 .70

World Meteorological Day — A101

2000 Photo. Perf. 14x14¼, 14¼x14

350 A101 2k Anemometer, vert. .65 .65
351 A101 5k shown 1.75 1.75
352 A101 10k Cloud, sun 3.25 3.25
Nos. 350-352 (3) 5.65 5.65

Diplomatic Relations with People's Republic of China, 50th Anniv. — A102

2000 Litho. Perf. 14¼x14

353 A102 5k multi 1.90 1.90

Myanmar postal officials have declared as "illegal" the following items inscribed "Union of Myanmar."

Sheets of nine stamps of various denominations depicting:

Personalities of the 20th Century, Musical stars, Orchids with Rotary emblems, Mushrooms with Rotary emblems, Cats and dogs with Scout emblems, Chess, Fish, Owls, and Trains (two different).

Sheets of six stamps of various denominations depicting:

Bruce Lee, Horror movie scenes, and Marilyn Monroe (two different).

Souvenir sheets of two stamps of various denominations depicting:

Formula 1 race cars (two different), Golfers (six different), and Classic cars (eight different).

Souvenir sheets of one depicting:

Dutch royal wedding, Bruce Lee (three different), Tiger Woods (three different), Impressionist paintings (six different), Elvis Presley (six different), and Chess (twelve different).

OFFICIAL STAMPS

Stamps of India, 1926-34, Overprinted in Black

1937 Wmk. 196 Perf. 14

O1 A46 3p gray .40 .20
O2 A71 ½a green 2.25 .20
O3 A68 9p dark green 1.50 .40
O4 A72 1a dark brown 1.50 .25
O5 A49 2a vermilion 2.25 .55
O6 A57 2a6p buff 2.25 .90
O7 A52 4a olive grn 1.50 .90
O8 A53 6a bister 2.25 *3.50*
O9 A54 8a red violet 1.40 1.00
O10 A55 12a claret 1.40 *1.75*

Overprinted

O11 A56 1r green & brown 11.00 3.25
O12 A56 2r buff & car rose 20.00 17.50
O13 A56 5r dk vio & ultra 47.50 32.50
O14 A56 10r car & green 140.00 *85.00*
Nos. O1-O14 (14) 235.20 *147.90*

For overprint see No. 1N27.

Regular Issue of 1938 Overprinted in Black

Perf. 13½x14, 13, 13½

1939 Wmk. 254

O15 A1 3p violet .20 .20
O16 A1 6p ultramarine .20 .20
O17 A1 9p yel green 3.25 .20
O18 A2 1a brown violet .20 .20
O19 A2 1½a turquoise green 3.00 .20
O20 A2 2a carmine .80 .20
O21 A2 4a slate blue 3.50 .40

Overprinted

O22 A3 2a6p rose lake 16.00 2.40
O23 A6 8a slate green 16.00 3.00
O24 A7 1r brt ultra & dk vio 25.00 3.00
O25 A7 2r dk vio & red brn 30.00 5.00
O26 A8 5r car & dull vio 27.50 *32.50*
O27 A8 10r gray grn & brn 80.00 42.50
Nos. O15-O27 (13) 205.65 90.00

For overprints see Nos. 1N12-1N16, 1N31-1N36, 1NO1.

Catalogue values for unused stamps in this section, from this point to the end of the section, are for Never Hinged items.

Nos. 51-56, 60 Overprinted Like Nos. O15-O21

1946 Perf. 13½x14

O28 A1 3p brown 1.40 *2.25*
O29 A1 6p violet 1.40 *1.75*
O30 A1 9p dull green .20 *2.40*
O31 A2 1a deep blue .20 *1.60*
O32 A2 1½a salmon .20 .20
O33 A2 2a rose lake .20 *1.75*
O34 A2 4a rose lilac 1.50 .55

Nos. 57, 61-65 Ovptd. Like Nos. O22-O27

Perf. 13, 13½

O35 A3 2a6p greenish blue .20 *4.00*
O38 A6 8a deep magenta 2.00 *2.75*
O39 A7 1r dp mag & dk vio .70 *2.75*
O40 A7 2r salmon & red brn 8.00 *30.00*
O41 A8 5r red brn & dk grn 10.00 *35.00*
O42 A8 10r dk violet & car 19.00 *40.00*
Nos. O28-O42 (13) 45.00 *125.00*

Nos. O28 to O42 Overprinted in Black

1947

O43 A1 3p brown .20 *.35*
O44 A1 6p violet .70 .10
O45 A1 9p dull green 1.10 .75
O46 A2 1a deep blue 1.50 .70
O47 A2 1½a salmon 3.00 .25
O48 A2 2a rose lake 1.50 .20
O49 A3 2a6p greenish bl 21.00 7.75
O50 A2 4a rose lilac 7.00 .35
O51 A6 8a dp magenta 6.00 3.50
O52 A7 1r dp mag & dk vio 12.00 1.90
O53 A7 2r sal & red brn *12.00* *16.00*
O54 A8 5r red brn & dk grn *12.00* *17.50*
O55 A8 10r dk vio & car *12.00* *26.00*
Nos. O43-O55 (13) *90.00* *75.35*

The overprint is slightly larger on Nos. O49 and O51 to O55. The Burmese characters read "Interim Government."

Issues of the Republic

Nos. 102-106, 109-115 Overprinted in Carmine or Black

a. Overprint 13mm long.
b. Overprint 15mm long.

1949 Unwmk. Perf. 12½, 13

O56 A15(a) 3p ultra (C) .20 .20
O57 A15(a) 6p green (C) .20 .20
O58 A15(a) 9p carmine .20 .20
O59 A16(a) 1a red orange .20 .20
O60 A17(a) 2a orange .20 .20
O61 A18(b) 3a6p dk sl grn (C) .20 .20
O62 A16(a) 4a chocolate .20 .20
O63 A18(b) 8a carmine .20 .20
O64 A19(b) 1r blue green (C) .35 .25
O65 A19(b) 2r dp blue (C) .65 .40
O66 A19(b) 5r chocolate 1.60 1.25
O67 A19(b) 10r orange red 3.25 2.50
Nos. O56-O67 (12) 7.45 6.00

Same Overprint in Black on Nos. 139-142, 144-152

Perf. 14x13½, 13, 14

1954-57 Wmk. 254

O68 A15(a) 1p brown org .20 .20
O69 A15(a) 2p plum .20 .20
O70 A15(a) 3p blue .20 .20
O71 A16(a) 5p ultra .20 .20
O72 A17(a) 15p green .20 .20
O72A A18(b) 20p ver ('57) .20 .20
O73 A18(b) 25p lt red org .20 .20
O74 A16(a) 30p vermilion .20 .20
O75 A18(b) 50p blue .20 .20
O76 A19(b) 1k rose violet .50 .20
O77 A19(b) 2k green .85 .20
O78 A19(b) 5k ultra 1.60 .35
O79 A19(b) 10k light blue 3.25 .45
Nos. O68-O79 (13) 8.00 3.00

No. 141 Ovptd. Service

1964 Litho. Perf. 14

O80 A15 3p blue *10.00* *7.00*

Nos. 139, 141-142, 144, 177-179, 181, 183 Ovptd.

1964-65

Overprint: 11½mm

O81 A15 1p brown orange *3.00* *.75*
O82 A28 2p carmine rose ('65) *2.50* *.60*
O83 A15 3p blue *3.00* *.75*
O84 A28 3p blue green ('65) *2.50* *.60*
O85 A16 5p ultramarine *3.00* *.75*
O86 A28 5p violet blue ('65) *2.50* *.60*
O87 A17 15p green *3.00* *.75*
O88 A28 15p olive ('65) *2.50* *.60*
O89 A29 25p yel & brn ('65) *2.60* *.60*
Nos. O81-O89 (9) *24.60* *6.00*

#176-178 Ovptd. #181 Ovptd.

1966

Overprint: 15mm

O90 A28 1p black
O91 A28 2p carmine rose
O92 A28 3p blue green

Overprint: 12mm

O93 A28 15p olive

Nos. 176-179, 181-187 Overprinted in Black or Red

1967 Unwmk. Photo. Perf. 13½

Overprint: 15mm

Size: 25x21mm

O94 A28 1p gray .20 .20
O95 A28 2p carmine rose .20 .20
O96 A28 3p blue green .20 .20

Size: 22x26½mm

O97 A29 5p violet blue .20 .20
O98 A29 15p olive .20 .20

Size: 35x25mm

O99 A28 20p rose & brown .20 .20

Size: 27x36½mm, 36½x27mm

O100 A29 25p yel & brown (R) .20 .20
O101 A29 50p red, blk & gray .25 .20
O102 A29 1k gray, ind & yel (R) .50 .20
O103 A28 2k pale ol, ind & red (R) 1.10 .30
O104 A29 5k cit, dk bl & red (R) 2.75 .65
Nos. O94-O104 (11) 6.00 2.75

Similar Overprint on Nos. 197-200, 202-208 in Black or Red

1968 Unwmk. Perf. 14

Size: 21x17mm

Overprint: 13mm

O105 A28 1p gray .20 .20
O106 A28 2p carmine rose .20 .20
O107 A28 3p blue green .20 .20

Size: 23½x28mm

Overprint: 15mm

O108 A29 5p violet blue .20 .20
O109 A29 15p olive .20 .20

Size: 38½x21mm, 21x38½mm

Overprint: 14mm

O110 A28 20p rose & brn .20 .20
O111 A29 25p yel & brown (R) .20 .20
O112 A29 50p ver, blk & gray .25 .20
O113 A29 1k gray, ind & yel (R) .50 .20
O114 A28 2k dl cit, ind & red (R) 1.10 .25
O115 A29 5k yel, dk bl & red (R) 2.75 .55
Nos. O105-O115 (11) 6.00 2.60

OCCUPATION STAMPS

Issued by Burma Independence Army (in conjunction with Japanese occupation officials)

Stamps of Burma, 1937-40, Overprinted in Blue, Black Blue, Black or Red

Henzada Issue

#1, 3, 5 Overprinted in Blue or Black

Henzada Type I

1942, May Wmk. 196 Perf. 14

1N1 A46 3p slate 5.00 *15.00*
1N2 A68 9p dark green 25.00 *50.00*
1N3 A49 2a vermilion 125.00 *175.00*

On 1938-40 George VI Issue

Perf. 13½x14

Wmk. 254

1N4 A1 1p red orange 200.00 *250.00*
1N5 A1 3p violet 30.00 *45.00*
1N6 A1 6p ultra 25.00 *45.00*
1N7 A1 9p yel green 400.00
1N8 A2 1a brown violet 9.00 *35.00*
1N9 A2 1½a turq green 25.00 *55.00*
1N10 A2 2a carmine 25.00 *55.00*
1N11 A2 4a slate blue 50.00 *85.00*

On Official Stamps of 1939

1N12 A1 3p violet 75.00 *200.00*
1N13 A1 6p ultra 100.00 *200.00*
1N14 A2 1½a turq green 100.00 *250.00*
1N15 A2 2a carmine 275.00 400.00
1N16 A2 4a slate blue 1,350.

Authorities believe this overprint was officially applied only to postal stationery and that the adhesive stamps existing with it were not regularly issued. It has been called "Henzada Type II."

Myaungmya Issue

1937 George V Issue Overprinted in Black

Myaungmya Type I

1942, May Wmk. 196 *Perf. 14*

1N25 A68	9p dk green	110.00	
1N26 A70	3a6p deep blue	50.00	

On Official Stamp of 1937, No. O8

1N27 A53	6a bister	75.00	

On 1938-40 George VI Issue

Perf. 13½x14

Wmk. 254

1N28 A1	9p yel green	100.00	
1N29 A2	1a brown vio	400.00	
1N30 A2	4a sl blue (blk ovpt. over red)	175.00	

On Official Stamps of 1939

1N31 A1	3p violet	27.50	50.00
1N32 A1	6p ultra	17.50	*40.00*
1N33 A2	1a brown vio	17.50	*40.00*
1N34 A2	1½a turq green	400.00	
1N35 A2	2a carmine	27.50	*75.00*
1N36 A2	4a slate blue	15.00	*55.00*

1938-40 George VI Issue Overprinted

Myaungmya Type II

1942, May

1N37 A1	3p violet	20.00	*50.00*
1N38 A1	6p ultra	60.00	*85.00*
1N39 A1	9p yel green	24.00	*50.00*
1N40 A2	1a brown vio	17.50	*42.50*
1N41 A2	2a carmine	24.00	*60.00*
1N42 A2	4a slate blue	40.00	*80.00*

Nos. 30-31 Overprinted

Myaungmya Type III

1N43 A7	1r brt ultra & dk vio	200.00	
1N44 A7	2r dk vio & red brn	175.00	

Pyapon Issue

No. 5 and 1938-40 George VI Issue Overprinted

1942, May

1N45 A1	6p ultra	75.00	
1N46 A2	1a brown vio	75.00	*200.00*
1N47 A49	2a vermilion	75.00	
1N48 A2	2a carmine	150.00	*250.00*
1N49 A2	4a slate blue	400.00	400.00
	Nos. 1N45-1N49 (5)	775.00	

Counterfeits of the peacock overprints exist.

OCCUPATION OFFICIAL STAMP

Myaungmya Issue

Burma No. O23 Overprinted in Black

1942, May Wmk. 254 *Perf. 13*

1NO1 A6	8a slate green	100.00	

Overprint characters translate: "Office use." Two types of overprint differ mainly in base of peacock which is either 5mm or 8mm.

ISSUED UNDER JAPANESE OCCUPATION

Yano Seal — OS1

Wmk. ABSORBO DUPLICATOR and Outline of Elephant in Center of Sheet

Handstamped

1942, June 1 *Perf. 12x11*

Without Gum

2N1 OS1	1(a) vermilion	35.00	*40.00*

This stamp is the handstamped impression of the personal chop or seal of Shizuo Yano, chairman of the committee appointed to re-establish the Burmese postal system. It was prepared in Rangoon on paper captured from the Burma Government Offices. Not every stamp shows a portion of the watermark.

Farmer Plowing — OS2

Vertically Laid Paper

Without Gum

Wmk. ELEPHANT BRAND and Outline of Trumpeting Elephant Covering Several Stamps

1942, June 15 Litho. *Perf. 11x12*

2N2 OS2	1a scarlet	12.50	*17.50*

See illustration OS4.

Same, Surcharged with New Value

1942, Oct. 15

2N3 OS2	5c on 1a scarlet	11.50	*17.00*

Rice Harvest - A83

General Nogi - A84

Power Plant - A85

Admiral Togo - A86

Diamond Mountains, Korea - A89

Meiji Shrine, Tokyo - A90

Yomei Gate, Nikko - A91

Mount Fuji and Cherry Blossoms - A94

Torii of Miyajima Shrine - A96

Stamps of Japan, 1937-42, Handstamp Surcharged with New Value in Black

1942, Sept. Wmk. 257 *Perf. 13*

2N4	A83	¼a on 1s fawn	24.00	*27.50*
2N5	A84	½a on 2s crim	26.00	*30.00*
2N6	A85	¾a on 3s green	50.00	*55.00*
2N7	A86	1a on 5s brn lake	45.00	35.00
2N8	A89	3a on 7s dp green	90.00	*95.00*
2N9	A86	4a on 4s dk green	40.00	40.00
a.		4a on 4s + 2s dk green (#B5)	100.00	*125.00*
2N10	A90	8a on 8s dk pur & pale vio	150.00	150.00
a.		Red surcharge	225.00	*250.00*
2N11	A91	1r on 10s lake	18.00	*22.50*
2N12	A94	2r on 20s ultra	50.00	*55.00*
a.		Red surcharge	37.50	37.50
2N13	A96	5r on 30s pck bl	12.00	*22.50*
a.		Red surcharge	22.50	*27.50*
		Nos. 2N4-2N13 (10)	505.00	*532.50*

Numerous double, inverted, etc., surcharges exist.

Re-surcharged in Black

1942, Oct. 15

2N14	A83	1c on ¼a on 1s	40.00	40.00
2N15	A84	2c on ½a on 2s	45.00	45.00
2N16	A85	3c on ¾a on 3s	50.00	50.00
a.		"3C." in blue	175.00	
2N17	A86	5c on 1a on 5s	50.00	50.00
a.		"3C." in blue	125.00	
2N18	A89	10c on 3a on 7s	100.00	100.00
2N19	A86	15c on 4a on 4s	25.00	*30.00*
2N20	A90	20c on 8a on 8s (#2N10)	350.00	300.00
a.		On #2N10a	250.00	175.00
		Nos. 2N14-2N20 (7)	660.00	615.00

No. 2N16a was issued in the Shan States.

Done locally, numerous different handstamps of each denomination can exist.

Stamps of Japan, 1937-42, Handstamp Surcharged with New Value in Black

1942, Oct. 15

2N21	A83	1c on 1s fawn	17.50	17.50
2N22	A84	2c on 2s crim	37.50	30.00
2N23	A85	3c on 3s green	37.50	37.50
a.		"3C." in blue	85.00	*100.00*
2N24	A86	5c on 5s brn lake	40.00	*42.50*
a.		"5C." in violet	125.00	*175.00*
2N25	A89	10c on 7s dp grn	50.00	50.00
2N26	A86	15c on 4s dk grn	15.00	20.00
2N27	A90	20c on 8s dk pur & pale vio	100.00	75.00
		Nos. 2N21-2N27 (7)	297.50	*272.50*

Nos. 2N23a and 2N24a were issued in the Shan States.

Burma State Government Crest — OS3

Unwmk.

1943, Feb. 15 Litho. *Perf. 12*

Without Gum

2N29 OS3	5c carmine	10.00	*12.50*
a.	Imperf.	12.50	*15.00*

This stamp was intended to be used to cover the embossed George VI envelope stamp and generally was sold affixed to such envelopes. It is also known used on private envelopes.

Farmer Plowing — OS4

1943, Mar. Typo.

Without Gum

2N30 OS4	1c deep orange	1.00	1.00
2N31 OS4	2c yel green	1.00	*1.50*
2N32 OS4	3c blue	1.00	1.00
a.	Laid paper	10.00	10.00
2N33 OS4	5c carmine	.50	*.65*
a.	Small "5c"	3.00	*4.00*
b.	Imperf.		
2N34 OS4	10c violet brown	.75	*.90*
2N35 OS4	15c red violet	.25	.25
a.	Laid paper	10.00	
2N36 OS4	20c dull purple	.25	*.75*
2N37 OS4	30c blue green	.25	*.75*
	Nos. 2N30-2N37 (8)	5.00	*6.80*

Small "c" in Nos. 2N34 to 2N37.

Burmese Soldier Carving "Independence" OS5

Farmer Rejoicing OS6

Boy with Burmese Flag — OS7

Hyphen-hole Perf., Pin-Perf. x Hyphen-hole Perf.

1943, Aug. 1 Typo.

2N38 OS5	1c orange	1.00	*2.00*
a.	Perf. 11	3.50	*4.00*
2N39 OS6	3c blue	1.00	*2.00*
a.	Perf. 11	3.50	*4.00*
2N40 OS7	5c rose	1.00	*2.00*
a.	Perf. 11	3.50	*4.00*
	Nos. 2N38-2N40 (3)	3.00	*6.00*

Declaration of the independence of Burma by the Ba Maw government, Aug. 1, 1943.

Burmese Girl Carrying Water Jar — OS8

Elephant Carrying Teak Log — OS9

Watch Tower of Mandalay Palace — OS10

1943, Oct. 1 Litho. *Perf. 12½*

2N41 OS8	1c dp salmon	17.00	*10.00*
2N42 OS8	2c yel green	.60	*1.25*
2N43 OS8	3c violet	.60	*1.00*
2N44 OS9	5c rose	.65	*1.00*
2N45 OS9	10c blue	.80	.60
2N46 OS9	15c vermilion	.80	*1.00*
2N47 OS9	20c yel green	.80	*1.25*
2N48 OS9	30c brown	.80	*1.25*
2N49 OS10	1r vermilion	.35	*3.00*
2N50 OS10	2r violet	.35	*5.00*
	Nos. 2N41-2N50 (10)	22.75	*25.35*

No. 2N49 exists imperforate. Canceled to order copies of Nos. 2N42-2N50 same values as unused.

Bullock Cart
OS11

Shan Woman
OS12

1943, Oct. 1 *Perf. 12½*

2N51	OS11	1c brown	22.50	*35.00*
2N52	OS11	2c yel green	22.50	*35.00*
2N53	OS11	3c violet	20.00	*30.00*
2N54	OS11	5c ultra	4.50	*12.00*
2N55	OS12	10c blue	20.00	*35.00*
2N56	OS12	20c rose	22.50	*35.00*
2N57	OS12	30c brown	22.50	*35.00*
		Nos. 2N51-2N57 (7)	134.50	*217.00*

For use only in the Shan States. Perak No. N34 also used in Shan States. CTO's ½ used value.

Surcharged in Black

1944, Nov. 1

2N58	OS11	1c brown	4.00	*5.00*
2N59	OS11	2c yel green	.20	*1.25*
a.		Inverted surcharge	150.00	*200.00*
2N60	OS11	3c violet	2.50	*4.00*
2N61	OS11	5c ultra	1.25	1.50
2N62	OS12	10c blue	2.50	*3.50*
2N63	OS12	20c rose	.60	*1.50*
2N64	OS12	30c brown	.75	*1.50*
		Nos. 2N58-2N64 (7)	11.80	*18.25*

Top line of surcharge reads: "Bama naing ngan daw" (Burma State). Bottom line repeats denomination in Burmese. Surcharge applied when the Shan States came under Burmese government administration, Dec. 24, 1943. CTO's same value as unused.

BURUNDI

bu-'rün-dē

LOCATION — Central Africa, adjoining the ex-Belgian Congo Republic, Rwanda and Tanzania
GOVT. — Republic
AREA — 10,759 sq. mi.
POP. — 5,735,937 (1999 est.)
CAPITAL — Bujumbura

Burundi was established as an independent country on July 1, 1962. With Rwanda, it had been a UN trusteeship territory (Ruanda-Urundi) administered by Belgium. A military coup overthrew the monarchy November 28, 1966.

100 Centimes = 1 Franc

Catalogue values for all unused stamps in this country are for Never Hinged items.

Flower Issue of Ruanda-Urundi, 1953 Overprinted:

Perf. 11½

1962, July 1 Unwmk. Photo.

Flowers in Natural Colors

1	A27	25c dk grn & dull org	.20	.20
2	A27	40c grn & salmon	.20	.20
3	A27	60c blue grn & pink	.20	.20
4	A27	1.25fr dk grn & blue	9.75	9.75
5	A27	1.50fr vio & apple grn	.30	.25
6	A27	5fr dp plum & lt bl grn	.40	.30
7	A27	7fr dk grn & fawn	.85	.55
8	A27	10fr dp plum & pale ol	1.25	.80
		Nos. 1-8 (8)	13.15	12.25

Animal Issue of Ruanda-Urundi, 1959-61 with Similar Overprint or Surcharge in Black or Violet Blue

Size: 23x33mm, 33x23mm

9	A29	10c multicolored	.20	.20
10	A30	20c multicolored	.20	.20
11	A29	40c multicolored	.20	.20
12	A30	50c multicolored	.20	.20
a.		Larger overprint and bar	.20	.20
13	A29	1fr multicolored	.20	.20
14	A30	1.50fr multi (VB)	.20	.20
15	A29	2fr multicolored	.20	.20
16	A30	3fr multicolored	.20	.20
17	A30	3.50fr on 3fr multi	.20	.20
18	A30	4fr on 10fr multi ("XX" 6mm wide)	.20	.20
a.		"XX" 4mm wide	.45	.45
19	A30	5fr multicolored	.20	.20
20	A30	6.50fr multicolored	.25	.20
21	A30	8fr multicolored	.30	.25
a.		Violet blue overprint	.65	.65
22	A30	10fr multicolored	.35	.30

Size: 45x26½mm

23	A30	20fr multicolored	.65	.65
24	A30	50fr multi (ovpt. bars 2mm wide)	1.25	1.10
a.		Overprint bars 4mm wide	1.90	1.10
		Nos. 9-24 (16)	5.00	4.70

On #12a, "Burundi" is 13mm long; bar is continuous line across sheet. On #12, "Burundi" is 10mm; bar is 29mm. #12a was issued in 1963.

Two types of overprint exist on 10c, 40c, 1fr and 2fr: I, "du" is below "me"; bar 22½mm. II, "du" below "oy"; bar 20mm.

The 50c and 3fr exist in two types, besides the larger 50c overprint listed as No. 12: I, "du" is closer to "Royaume" than to "Burundi"; bar is less than 29mm; wording is centered above bar. II, "du" is closer to "Burundi"; bar is more than 30mm; wording is off-center leftward.

King Mwami Mwambutsa IV and Royal Drummers — A1

Flag and Arms of Burundi — A2

2fr, 8fr, 50fr, Map of Burundi and King.

Unwmk.

1962, Sept. 27 Photo. *Perf. 14*

25	A1	50c dull rose car & dk brn	.20	.20
26	A2	1fr dk grn, red & emer	.20	.20
27	A1	2fr brown ol & dk brn	.20	.20
28	A1	3fr vermilion & dk brn	.20	.20
29	A2	4fr Prus bl, red & emer	.20	.20
30	A1	8fr violet & dk brn	.20	.20
31	A1	10fr brt green & dk brn	.20	.20
32	A2	20fr brown, red & emer	.35	.20
33	A1	50fr brt pink & dk brn	1.00	.40
		Nos. 25-33 (9)	2.75	2.00

Burundi's independence, July 1, 1962.

See #47-50. For overprints see #45-46, 51-52.

Ruanda-Urundi Nos. 151-152 Surcharged:

Photogravure, Surcharge Engraved

1962, Oct. 31 ***Perf. 11½***

Inscription in French

34	A31	3.50fr on 3fr ultra & red	.20	.20
35	A31	6.50fr on 3fr ultra & red	.20	.20
36	A31	10fr on 3fr ultra & red	.30	.25

Inscription in Flemish

37	A31	3.50fr on 3fr ultra & red	.20	.20
38	A31	6.50fr on 3fr ultra & red	.20	.20
39	A31	10fr on 3fr ultra & red	.30	.25
		Nos. 34-39 (6)	1.40	1.30

Dag Hammarskjold, Secretary General of the United Nations, 1953-61.

King Mwami Mwambutsa IV, Map of Burundi and Emblem — A3

1962, Dec. 10 Photo. *Perf. 14*

40	A3	8fr yel, bl grn & blk brn	.30	.20
41	A3	50fr gray grn, bl grn & blk brn	1.10	.30

WHO drive to eradicate malaria.

Stamps of type A3 without anti-malaria emblem are listed as Nos. 27, 30 and 33.

Sowing Seed over Africa — A4

1963, Mar. 21 ***Perf. 14x13***

42	A4	4fr olive & dull pur	.20	.20
43	A4	8fr dp org & dull pur	.20	.20
44	A4	15fr emerald & dull pur	.20	.20
		Nos. 42-44 (3)	.60	.60

FAO "Freedom from Hunger" campaign.

Nos. 27 and 33 Overprinted in Dark Green

1963, June 19 Unwmk. *Perf. 14*

45	A1	2fr brn olive & dk brn	1.60	1.25
46	A1	50fr brt pink & dk brn	1.90	1.25

Conquest and peaceful use of outer space.

Types of 1962 Inscribed: "Premier Anniversaire" in Red or Magenta

1963, July 1 Photo.

47	A2	4fr olive, red & emer (R)	.20	.20
48	A1	8fr orange & dk brn (M)	.20	.20
49	A1	10fr lilac & dk brn (M)	.20	.20
50	A2	20fr gray, red & emer (R)	.40	.25
		Nos. 47-50 (4)	1.00	.85

First anniversary of independence.

Nos. 26 and 32 Surcharged in Brown

1963, Sept. 24 Unwmk. *Perf. 14*

51	A2	6.50fr on 1fr multi	.30	.20
52	A2	15fr on 20fr multi	.55	.25

Red Cross Flag over Globe with Map of Africa — A5

1963, Sept. 26 ***Perf. 14x13***

53	A5	4fr emer, car & gray	.20	.20
54	A5	8fr brn ol, car & gray	.25	.20
55	A5	10fr blue, car & gray	.35	.20
56	A5	20fr lilac, car & gray	.70	.30
		Nos. 53-56 (4)	1.50	.90

Centenary of International Red Cross. See No. B7.

"1962", Arms of Burundi, UN and UNESCO Emblems — A6

UN Agency Emblems: 8fr, ITU. 10fr, World Meteorological Organization. 20fr, UPU. 50fr, FAO.

1963, Nov. 4 Unwmk. *Perf. 14*

57	A6	4fr yel, ol grn & blk	.20	.20
58	A6	8fr pale lil, Prus bl & blk	.20	.20
59	A6	10fr blue, lil & blk	.20	.20
60	A6	20fr yel grn, grn & blk	.35	.20
61	A6	50fr yel, red brn & blk	.90	.30
a.		Souvenir sheet of 2	3.00	3.00
		Nos. 57-61 (5)	1.85	1.10

1st anniv. of Burundi's admission to the UN. No. 61a contains two imperf. stamps with simulated perforations similar to Nos. 60-61. The 20fr stamp shows the FAO and the 50fr the WMO emblems.

UNESCO Emblem, Scales and Map — A7

Designs: 3.50fr, 6.50fr, Scroll, scales and "UNESCO." 10fr, 20fr, Abraham Lincoln, broken chain and scales.

1963, Dec. 10 Litho. *Perf. 14x13½*

62	A7	50c pink, lt bl & blk	.20	.20
63	A7	1.50fr org, lt bl & blk	.20	.20
64	A7	3.50fr fawn, lt grn & blk	.20	.20
65	A7	6.50fr lt vio, lt grn & blk	.20	.20
66	A7	10fr blue, bis & blk	.25	.20
67	A7	20fr pale brn, ocher, bl & blk	.45	.20
		Nos. 62-67 (6)	1.50	1.20

15th anniv. of the Universal Declaration of Human Rights and the cent. of the American Emancipation Proclamation (Nos. 66-67).

Ice Hockey — A8

Impala — A9

3.50fr, Women's figure skating. 6.50fr, Torch. 10fr, Men's speed skating. 20fr, Slalom.

Unwmk.

1964, Jan. 25 Photo. *Perf. 14*

68	A8	50c	olive, blk & gold	.20	.20
69	A8	3.50fr	lt brown, blk & gold	.20	.20
70	A8	6.50fr	pale gray, blk & gold	.40	.20
71	A8	10fr	gray, blk & gold	.50	.20
72	A8	20fr	tan, blk & gold	1.00	.30
			Nos. 68-72 (5)	2.30	1.10

Issued to publicize the 9th Winter Olympic Games, Innsbruck, Jan. 29-Feb. 9, 1964.

A souvenir sheet contains two stamps (10fr+5fr and 20fr+5fr) in tan, black and gold.

Canceled to Order

Starting about 1964, values in the used column are for "canceled to order" stamps. Postally used copies sell for much more.

Perf. 14x13, 13x14

1964, Feb. 10 Litho.

Animals: 1fr, 5fr, Hippopotamus, horiz. 1.50fr, 10fr, Giraffe. 2fr, 8fr, Cape buffalo, horiz. 3fr, 6.50fr, Zebra, horiz. 3.50fr, 15fr, Defassa waterbuck. 20fr, Cheetah. 50fr, Elephant. 100fr, Lion.

Size: 21½x35mm, 35x21½mm

73	A9	50c	multi	.20	.20
74	A9	1fr	multi	.20	.20
75	A9	1.50fr	multi	.20	.20
76	A9	2fr	multi	.20	.20
77	A9	3fr	multi	.20	.20
78	A9	3.50fr	multi	.20	.20

Size: 26x42mm, 42x26mm

79	A9	4fr	multi	.25	.20
80	A9	5fr	multi	.30	.20
81	A9	6.50fr	multi	.35	.20
82	A9	8fr	multi	.40	.20
83	A9	10fr	multi	.50	.20
84	A9	15fr	multi	.65	.20

Perf. 14

Size: 53x33mm

85	A9	20fr	multi	.85	.20
86	A9	50fr	multi	2.25	.30
87	A9	100fr	multi	4.00	.65
			Nos. 73-87,C1-C7 (22)	14.50	5.15

Burundi Dancer — A10

Designs: Various Dancers and Drummers.

Unwmk.

1964, Aug. 21 Litho. *Perf. 14*

Dancers Multicolored

88	A10	50c	gold & emerald	.20	.20
89	A10	1fr	gold & vio blue	.20	.20
90	A10	4fr	gold & brt blue	.20	.20
91	A10	6.50fr	gold & red	.20	.20
92	A10	10fr	gold & brt blue	.30	.20
93	A10	15fr	gold & emerald	.45	.20
94	A10	20fr	gold & red	.65	.25
a.			Souvenir sheet of 3, #92-94	2.75	2.75
			Nos. 88-94 (7)	2.20	1.45

1965, Sept. 10

Dancers Multicolored

88a	A10	50c	silver & emerald	.20	.20
89a	A10	1fr	silver & violet blue	.20	.20
90a	A10	4fr	silver & bright blue	.20	.20
91a	A10	6.50fr	silver & red	.20	.20
92a	A10	10fr	silver & bright blue	.20	.20
93a	A10	15fr	silver & emerald	.20	.20
94b	A10	20fr	silver & red	.30	.30
c.			Souvenir sheet of 3, #92a-94b	2.00	2.00
			Nos. 88a-94b (7)	1.50	1.50

New York World's Fair, 1964-65.

Pope Paul VI and King Mwami Mwambutsa IV — A11

22 Sainted Martyrs — A12

4fr, 14fr, Pope John XXIII and King Mwami.

1964, Nov. 12 Photo. *Perf. 12*

95	A11	50c	brt bl, gold & red brn	.20	.20
96	A12	1fr	mag, gold & slate	.20	.20
97	A11	4fr	pale rose lil, gold & brn	.20	.20
98	A12	8fr	red, gold & brn	.20	.20
99	A11	14fr	lt grn, gold & brn	.40	.20
100	A11	20fr	red brn, gold & grn	.65	.30
			Nos. 95-100 (6)	1.85	1.30

Canonization of 22 African martyrs, 10/18/64.

Shot Put — A13

African Purple Gallinule — A14

Sports: 1fr, Discus. 3fr, Swimming. 4fr, Running. 6.50fr, Javelin, woman. 8fr, Hurdling. 10fr, Broad jump. 14fr, Diving, woman. 18fr, High jump. 20fr, Vaulting.

3fr, 8fr, 10fr, 18fr, 20fr are horiz.

1964, Nov. 18 Litho. *Perf. 14*

101	A13	50c	olive & multi	.20	.20
102	A13	1fr	brt pink & multi	.20	.20
103	A13	3fr	multi	.20	.20
104	A13	4fr	multi	.20	.20
105	A13	6.50fr	multi	.20	.20
106	A13	8fr	lt bl & multi	.20	.20
107	A13	10fr	multi	.20	.20
108	A13	14fr	multi	.25	.20
109	A13	18fr	bister & multi	.30	.20
110	A13	20fr	gray & multi	.35	.20
			Nos. 101-110 (10)	2.30	2.00

18th Olympic Games, Tokyo, Oct. 10-25, 1964. See No. B8.

1965 Unwmk. *Perf. 14*

Birds: 1fr, 5fr, Little bee eater. 1.50fr, 6.50fr, Secretary bird. 2fr, 8fr, Yellow-billed stork. 3fr, 10fr, Congo peacock. 3.50fr, 15fr, African anhinga. 20fr, Saddle-billed stork. 50fr, Abyssinian ground hornbill. 100fr, Crowned crane.

Birds in Natural Colors

Size: 21x35mm

111	A14	50c	tan, grn & blk	.20	.20
112	A14	1fr	pink, mag & blk	.20	.20
113	A14	1.50fr	blue & blk	.20	.20
114	A14	2fr	yel grn, dk grn & blk	.20	.20
115	A14	3fr	yellow, brn & blk	.20	.20
116	A14	3.50fr	yel grn, dk grn & blk	.20	.20

Size: 26x43mm

117	A14	4fr	tan, grn & blk	.20	.20
118	A14	5fr	pink, mag & blk	.20	.20
119	A14	6.50fr	blue & blk	.20	.20
120	A14	8fr	yel grn, dk grn & blk	.20	.20
121	A14	10fr	yel, brn & blk	.20	.20
122	A14	15fr	yel grn, dk grn & blk	.35	.20

Size: 33x53mm

123	A14	20fr	rose lilac & blk	.45	.30
124	A14	50fr	yellow, brn & blk	1.25	.20
125	A14	100fr	green, yel & blk	2.75	.40
			Nos. 111-125 (15)	7.00	3.30

Issue dates: Nos. 111-116, Mar. 31. Nos. 117-122, Apr. 16. Nos. 123-125, Apr. 30.

For overprints see #174-184, C35A-C35I.

Relay Satellite and Morse Key — A15

3fr, Telstar & old telephone handpiece. 4fr, Relay satellite & old wall telephone. 6.50fr, Orbiting Geophysical Observatory & radar screen. 8fr, Telstar II & headphones. 10fr, Sputnik II & radar aerial. 14fr, Syncom & transmission aerial. 20fr, Interplanetary Explorer & tracking aerial.

1965, July 3 Litho. *Perf. 13*

126	A15	1fr	multi	.20	.20
127	A15	3fr	multi	.20	.20
128	A15	4fr	multi	.20	.20
129	A15	6.50fr	multi	.20	.20
130	A15	8fr	multi	.20	.20
131	A15	10fr	multi	.20	.20
132	A15	14fr	multi	.25	.20
133	A15	20fr	multi	.30	.20
			Nos. 126-133 (8)	1.75	1.60

Cent. of the ITU. Perf. and imperf. souv. sheets of 2 contain Nos. 131, 133. Size: 120x86mm. Value, both sheets, $7.50.

Globe and ICY Emblem — A16

Designs: 4fr, Map of Africa and UN development emblem. 8fr, Map of Asia and Colombo Plan emblem. 10fr, Globe and UN emblem. 18fr, Map of the Americas and Alliance for Progress emblem. 25fr, Map of Europe and EUROPA emblems. 40fr, Map of Outer Space and satellite with UN wreath.

1965, Oct. 1 Litho. *Perf. 13*

134	A16	1fr	ol green & multi	.20	.20
135	A16	4fr	dull blue & multi	.20	.20
136	A16	8fr	pale yellow & multi	.20	.20
137	A16	10fr	lilac & multi	.20	.20
138	A16	18fr	salmon & multi	.25	.20
139	A16	25fr	gray & multi	.35	.20
140	A16	40fr	blue & multi	.60	.20
a.			Souvenir sheet of 3, #138-140	2.25	2.25
			Nos. 134-140 (7)	2.00	1.40

International Cooperation Year.

Protea A17

Flowers: 1fr, 5fr, Crossandra. 1.50fr, 6.50fr, Ansellia. 2fr, 8fr, Thunbergia. 3fr, 10fr, Schizoglossum. 3.50fr, 15fr, Dissotis. 4fr, 20fr, Protea. 50fr, Gazania. 100fr, Hibiscus. 150fr, Markhamia.

1966 Unwmk. *Perf. 13½*

Size: 26x26mm

141	A17	50c	multi	.20	.20
142	A17	1fr	multi	.20	.20
143	A17	1.50fr	multi	.20	.20
144	A17	2fr	multi	.20	.20
145	A17	3fr	multi	.20	.20
146	A17	3.50fr	multi	.20	.20

Size: 31x31mm

147	A17	4fr	multi	.20	.20
148	A17	5fr	multi	.20	.20
149	A17	6.50fr	multi	.20	.20
150	A17	8fr	multi	.20	.20
151	A17	10fr	multi	.20	.20
152	A17	15fr	multi	.30	.20

Size: 39x39mm

153	A17	20fr	multi	.40	.20
154	A17	50fr	multi	1.00	.25
155	A17	100fr	multi	1.90	.40
156	A17	150fr	multi	2.75	.55
			Nos. 141-156,C17-C25 (25)	15.55	5.75

Issue dates: Nos. 141-147, Feb. 28; Nos. 148-153, May 18; Nos. 154-156, June 15.

For overprints see Nos. 159-173, C27-C35.

Souvenir Sheets

Allegory of Prosperity and Equality Tapestry by Peter Colfs — A18

1966, Nov. 4 Litho. *Perf. 13½*

157	A18	Sheet of 7 (1.50fr)	.65	.25
158	A18	Sheet of 7 (4fr)	1.10	.50

20th anniv. of UNESCO. Each sheet contains 6 stamps showing a reproduction of the Colfs tapestry from the lobby of the General Assembly Building, NYC, and one stamp with the UNESCO emblem plus a label. The labels on Nos. 157-158 and C26 are inscribed in French or English. The 3 sheets with French inscription have light blue marginal border. The 3 sheets with English inscription have pink border. See No. C26.

Republic

Nos. 141-152, 154-156 Overprinted

1967 Litho. *Perf. 13½*

Size: 26x26mm

159 A17 50c multi .20 .20
160 A17 1fr multi .20 .20
161 A17 1.50fr multi .20 .20
162 A17 2fr multi .20 .20
163 A17 3fr multi .20 .20
164 A17 3.50fr multi .20 .20

Size: 31x31mm

165 A17 4fr multi .80 .30
166 A17 5fr multi .20 .20
167 A17 6.50fr multi .20 .20
168 A17 8fr multi .25 .20
169 A17 10fr multi .30 .20
170 A17 15fr multi .40 .20

Size: 39x39mm

171 A17 50fr multi 3.75 1.25
172 A17 100fr multi 6.25 2.50
173 A17 150fr multi 5.00 2.25
Nos. 159-173,C27-C35 (24) 29.65 11.80

Nos. 111, 113, 116, 118-125 Overprinted "REPUBLIQUE DU BURUNDI" and Horizontal Bar

1967 Litho. *Perf. 14*

Birds in Natural Colors

Size: 21x35mm

174 A14 50c multi 1.25 .65
175 A14 1.50fr blue & black .20 .20
176 A14 3.50fr multi .20 .20

Size: 26x43mm

177 A14 5fr multi .20 .20
178 A14 6.50fr blue & black .20 .20
179 A14 8fr multi .20 .20
180 A14 10fr yel, brn & blk .30 .20
181 A14 15fr multi .65 .20

Size: 33x53mm

182 A14 20fr multi 2.00 .40
183 A14 50fr multi 4.00 1.40
184 A14 100fr multi 6.00 2.75
Nos. 174-184 (11) 15.20 6.60

Haplochromis Multicolor — A19

Various Tropical Fish.

1967 Photo. *Perf. 13½*

Size: 42x19mm

186 A19 50c multi .20 .20
187 A19 1fr multi .20 .20
188 A19 1.50fr multi .20 .20
189 A19 2fr multi .20 .20
190 A19 3fr multi .20 .20
191 A19 3.50fr multi .20 .20

Size: 50x25mm

192 A19 4fr multi .25 .20
193 A19 5fr multi .30 .20
194 A19 6.50fr multi .40 .20
195 A19 8fr multi .50 .20
196 A19 10fr multi .70 .20
197 A19 15fr multi 1.00 .20

Size: 59x30mm

198 A19 20fr multi 1.40 .20
199 A19 50fr multi 2.50 .20
200 A19 100fr multi 4.00 .30
201 A19 150fr multi 5.25 .45
Nos. 186-201,C46-C54 (25) 26.00 5.40

Issue Dates: Nos. 186-191, Apr. 4; Nos. 192-197, Apr. 28; Nos. 198-201, May 18.

Ancestor Figures, Ivory Coast — A20

African Art: 1fr, Seat of Honor, Southeast Congo. 1.50fr, Antelope head, Aribinda Region. 2fr, Buffalo mask, Upper Volta. 4fr, Funeral figures, Southwest Ethiopia.

1967, June 5 Photo. *Perf. 13½*

202 A20 50c silver & multi .20 .20
203 A20 1fr silver & multi .20 .20
204 A20 1.50fr silver & multi .20 .20
205 A20 2fr silver & multi .20 .20
206 A20 4fr silver & multi .20 .20
Nos. 202-206,C36-C40 (10) 2.25 2.00

Scouts on Hiking Trip — A21

Designs: 1fr, Cooking at campfire. 1.50fr, Lord Baden-Powell. 2fr, Boy Scout and Cub Scout giving Scout sign. 4fr, First aid.

1967, Aug. 9 Photo. *Perf. 13½*

207 A21 50c silver & multi .20 .20
208 A21 1fr silver & multi .20 .20
209 A21 1.50fr silver & multi .20 .20
210 A21 2fr silver & multi .25 .20
211 A21 4fr silver & multi .30 .20
Nos. 207-211,C41-C45 (10) 3.00 2.00

60th anniv. of the Boy Scouts and the 12th Boy Scout World Jamboree, Farragut State Park, Idaho, Aug. 1-9.

The Gleaners, by Francois Millet A22

Paintings Exhibited at EXPO '67: 8fr, The Water Carrier of Seville, by Velazquez. 14fr, The Triumph of Neptune and Amphitrite, by Nicolas Poussin. 18fr, Acrobat Standing on a Ball, by Picasso. 25fr, Marguerite van Eyck, by Jan van Eyck. 40fr, St. Peter Denying Christ, by Rembrandt.

1967, Oct. 12 Photo. *Perf. 13½*

212 A22 4fr multi .20 .20
213 A22 8fr multi .20 .20
214 A22 14fr multi .25 .20
215 A22 18fr multi .30 .20
216 A22 25fr multi .50 .20
217 A22 40fr multi .75 .25
a. Souvenir sheet of 2, #216-217 1.75 1.50
Nos. 212-217 (6) 2.20 1.25

EXPO '67 International Exhibition, Montreal, Apr. 28-Oct. 27. Printed in sheets of 10 stamps and 2 labels inscribed in French or English. No. 217a exists imperf.

Place de la Revolution and Pres. Michel Micombero — A23

Designs: 5fr, President Michel Micombero and flag. 14fr, Formal garden and coat of arms. 20fr, Modern building and coat of arms.

1967, Nov. 23 *Perf. 13½*

218 A23 5fr multi .20 .20
219 A23 14fr multi .25 .20
220 A23 20fr multi .40 .20
221 A23 30fr multi .55 .25
Nos. 218-221 (4) 1.40 .85

First anniversary of the Republic.

Madonna by Carlo Crivelli — A24

Designs: 1fr, Adoration of the Shepherds by Juan Bautista Mayno. 4fr, Holy Family by Anthony Van Dyck. 14fr, Nativity by Maitre de Moulins.

1967, Dec. 7 Photo. *Perf. 13½*

222 A24 1fr multi .20 .20
223 A24 4fr multi .20 .20
224 A24 14fr multi .25 .20
225 A24 26fr multi .60 .25
Nos. 222-225 (4) 1.25 .85

Christmas 1967. Printed in sheets of 25 and one corner label inscribed "Noel 1967" and giving name of painting and painter.

Slalom — A25

10fr, Ice hockey. 14fr, Women's skating. 17fr, Bobsled. 26fr, Ski jump. 40fr, Speed skating. 60fr, Hand holding torch, and Winter Olympics emblem.

1968, Feb. 16 Photo. *Perf. 13½*

226 A25 5fr silver & multi .20 .20
227 A25 10fr silver & multi .20 .20
228 A25 14fr silver & multi .25 .20
229 A25 17fr silver & multi .30 .20
230 A25 26fr silver & multi .50 .20
231 A25 40fr silver & multi .75 .20
232 A25 60fr silver & multi 1.25 .20
Nos. 226-232 (7) 3.45 1.40

Issued to publicize the 10th Winter Olympic Games, Grenoble, France, Feb. 6-18. Issued in sheets of 10 stamps and label.

The Lacemaker, by Vermeer A26

Paintings: 1.50fr, Portrait of a Young Man, by Botticelli. 2fr, Maja Vestida, by Goya, horiz.

1968, Mar. 29 Photo. *Perf. 13½*

233 A26 1.50fr gold & multi .20 .20
234 A26 2fr gold & multi .20 .20
235 A26 4fr gold & multi .20 .20
Nos. 233-235,C59-C61 (6) 2.00 1.20

Issued in sheets of 6.

Moon Probe A27

Designs: 6fr, Russian astronaut walking in space. 8fr, Weather satellite. 10fr, American astronaut walking in space.

1968, May 15 Photo. *Perf. 13½*

Size: 35x35mm

236 A27 4fr silver & multi .20 .20
237 A27 6fr silver & multi .20 .20
238 A27 8fr silver & multi .20 .20
239 A27 10fr silver & multi .25 .20
Nos. 236-239,C62-C65 (8) 2.55 1.60

Issued to publicize peaceful space explorations.

A souvenir sheet contains one 25fr stamp in Moon Probe design and one 40fr in Weather Satellite design. Stamp size: 41x41mm. Value $2. Sheet exists imperf. Price $3.

Salamis Aethiops A28

Butterflies: 1fr, 5fr, Graphium ridleyanus. 1.50fr, 6.50fr, Cymothoe. 2fr, 8fr, Charaxes eupale. 3fr, 10fr, Papilio bromius. 3.50fr, 15fr, Teracolus annae. 20fr, Salamis aethiops. 50fr, Papilio zonobia. 100fr, Danais chrysippus. 150fr, Salamis temora.

1968

Size: 30x33½mm

240 A28 50c gold & multi .20 .20
241 A28 1fr gold & multi .20 .20
242 A28 1.50fr gold & multi .20 .20
243 A28 2fr gold & multi .20 .20
244 A28 3fr gold & multi .20 .20
245 A28 3.50fr gold & multi .30 .20

Size: 33½x37½mm

246 A28 4fr gold & multi .35 .20
247 A28 5fr gold & multi .40 .20
248 A28 6.50fr gold & multi .65 .20
249 A28 8fr gold & multi .80 .20
250 A28 10fr gold & multi .95 .20
251 A28 15fr gold & multi 1.25 .20

Size: 41x46mm

252 A28 20fr gold & multi 1.60 .20
253 A28 50fr gold & multi 3.25 .20
254 A28 100fr gold & multi 6.25 .30
255 A28 150fr gold & multi 8.25 .50
Nos. 240-255,C66-C74 (25) 35.05 5.40

Issue dates: Nos. 240-245, June 7; Nos. 246-251, June 28; Nos. 252-255, July 19.

Women, Along the Manzanares, by Goya — A29

Paintings: 7fr, The Letter, by Pieter de Hooch. 11fr, Woman Reading a Letter, by Gerard Terborch. 14fr, Man Writing a Letter, by Gabriel Metsu.

1968, Sept. 30 Photo. *Perf. 13½*

256 A29	4fr multi	.20	.20
257 A29	7fr multi	.20	.20
258 A29	11fr multi	.20	.20
259 A29	14fr multi	.30	.20
	Nos. 256-259,C84-C87 (8)	2.90	1.60

International Letter Writing Week.

Soccer — A30

1968, Oct. 24

260 A30	4fr shown	.20	.20
261 A30	7fr Basketball	.20	.20
262 A30	13fr High jump	.20	.20
263 A30	24fr Relay race	.35	.20
264 A30	40fr Javelin	.60	.30
	Nos. 260-264,C88-C92 (10)	4.20	2.20

19th Olympic Games, Mexico City, Oct. 12-27. Printed in sheets of 8.

Virgin and Child, by Fra Filippo Lippi — A31

Paintings: 5fr, The Magnificat, by Sandro Botticelli. 6fr, Virgin and Child, by Albrecht Durer. 11fr, Madonna del Gran Duca, by Raphael.

1968, Nov. 26 Photo. *Perf. 13½*

265 A31	3fr multi	.20	.20
266 A31	5fr multi	.20	.20
267 A31	6fr multi	.20	.20
268 A31	11fr multi	.25	.20
a.	Souvenir sheet of 4, #265-268	1.00	1.00
	Nos. 265-268,C93-C96 (8)	2.00	1.60

Christmas 1968. For overprints see Nos. 272-275, C100-C103.

WHO Emblem and Map of Africa — A32

1969, Jan. 22

269 A32	5fr gold, dk grn & yel	.20	.20
270 A32	6fr gold, vio & ver	.20	.20
271 A32	11fr gold, pur & red lil	.25	.20
	Nos. 269-271 (3)	.65	.60

20th anniv. of WHO in Africa.

Nos. 265-268 Overprinted in Silver

1969, Feb. 17 Photo. *Perf. 13½*

272 A31	3fr multi	.20	.20
273 A31	5fr multi	.20	.20
274 A31	6fr multi	.20	.20
275 A31	11fr multi	.25	.20
	Nos. 272-275,C100-C103 (8)	2.20	1.65

Man's 1st flight around the moon by the US spacecraft Apollo 8, Dec. 21-27, 1968.

Map of Africa, and CEPT Emblem A33

Designs: 14fr, Plowing with tractor. 17fr, Teacher and pupil. 26fr, Maps of Europe and Africa and CEPT (Conference of European Postal and Telecommunications Administrations) emblem, horiz.

1969, Mar. 12 Photo. *Perf. 13*

276 A33	5fr multi	.20	.20
277 A33	14fr multi	.20	.20
278 A33	17fr multi	.25	.20
279 A33	26fr multi	.35	.20
	Nos. 276-279 (4)	1.00	.80

5th anniv. of the Yaounde (Cameroun) Agreement, creating the European and African-Malgache Economic Community.

Resurrection, by Gaspard Isenmann — A34

Paintings: 14fr, Resurrection by Antoine Caron. 17fr, Noli me Tangere, by Martin Schongauer. 26fr, Resurrection, by El Greco.

1969, Mar. 24

280 A34	11fr gold & multi	.20	.20
281 A34	14fr gold & multi	.20	.20
282 A34	17fr gold & multi	.25	.20
283 A34	26fr gold & multi	.35	.20
a.	Souvenir sheet of 4, #280-283	1.50	1.50
	Nos. 280-283 (4)	1.00	.80

Easter 1969.

Potter — A35

ITU Emblem and: 5fr, Farm workers. 7fr, Foundry worker. 10fr, Woman testing corn crop.

1969, May 17 Photo. *Perf. 13½*

284 A35	3fr multicolored	.20	.20
285 A35	5fr multicolored	.20	.20
286 A35	7fr multicolored	.20	.20
287 A35	10fr multicolored	.20	.20
	Nos. 284-287 (4)	.80	.80

50th anniv. of the ILO.

Industry and Bank's Emblem A36

African Development Bank Emblem and: 17fr, Communications. 30fr, Education. 50fr, Agriculture.

1969, July 29 Photo. *Perf. 13½*

288 A36	10fr gold & multi	.20	.20
289 A36	17fr gold & multi	.30	.20
290 A36	30fr gold & multi	.50	.20
291 A36	50fr gold & multi	.80	.25
a.	Souvenir sheet of 4, #288-291	1.90	1.90
	Nos. 288-291 (4)	1.80	.85

African Development Bank, 5th anniv.

Girl Reading Letter, by Vermeer A37

Paintings: 7fr, Graziella (young woman), by Auguste Renoir. 14fr, Woman writing a letter, by Gerard Terborch. 26fr, Galileo Galilei, painter unknown. 40fr, Ludwig van Beethoven, painter unknown.

1969, Oct. 24 Photo. *Perf. 13½*

292 A37	4fr multicolored	.20	.20
293 A37	7fr multicolored	.20	.20
294 A37	14fr multicolored	.30	.20
295 A37	26fr multicolored	.55	.20
296 A37	40fr multicolored	.75	.20
a.	Souvenir sheet of 2, #295-296	1.75	1.75
	Nos. 292-296 (5)	2.00	1.00

Intl. Letter Writing Week, Oct. 7-13.

Rocket Launching A38

Moon Landing: 6.50fr, Rocket in space. 7fr, Separation of landing module from capsule. 14fr, 26fr, Landing module landing on moon. 17fr, Capsule in space. 40fr, Neil A. Armstrong leaving landing module. 50fr, Astronaut on moon.

1969, Nov. 6 Photo. *Perf. 13½*

297 A38	4fr blue & multi	.20	.20
298 A38	6.50fr vio blue & multi	.25	.20
299 A38	7fr vio blue & multi	.25	.20
300 A38	14fr black & multi	.35	.20
301 A38	17fr vio blue & multi	.55	.25
	Nos. 297-301,C104-C106 (8)	3.75	2.15

Souvenir Sheet

302	Sheet of 3	3.00	3.00
a.	A38 26fr multicolored	.50	.50
b.	A38 40fr multicolored	.75	.75
c.	A38 50fr multicolored	1.00	1.00

See note after Algeria No. 427.

Madonna and Child, by Rubens — A39

Paintings: 6fr, Madonna and Child with St. John, by Giulio Romano. 10fr, Magnificat Madonna, by Botticelli.

1969, Dec. 2 Photo.

303 A39	5fr gold & multi	.20	.20
304 A39	6fr gold & multi	.20	.20
305 A39	10fr gold & multi	.25	.20
a.	Souvenir sheet of 3, #303-305	.75	.75
	Nos. 303-305,C107-C109 (6)	2.45	1.30

Christmas 1969.

Sternotomis Bohemani — A40

Designs: Various Beetles and Weevils.

1970 *Perf. 13½*

Size: 39x28mm

306 A40	50c multicolored	.20	.20
307 A40	1fr multicolored	.20	.20
308 A40	1.50fr multicolored	.20	.20
309 A40	2fr multicolored	.20	.20
310 A40	3fr multicolored	.20	.20
311 A40	3.50fr multicolored	.20	.20

Size: 46x32mm

312 A40	4fr multicolored	.25	.20
313 A40	5fr multicolored	.25	.20
314 A40	6.50fr multicolored	.30	.20
315 A40	8fr multicolored	.35	.20
316 A40	10fr multicolored	.70	.20
317 A40	15fr multicolored	.90	.20

Size: 52x36mm

318 A40	20fr multicolored	1.25	.20
319 A40	50fr multicolored	2.50	.20
320 A40	100fr multicolored	4.75	.35
321 A40	150fr multicolored	7.00	.50
	Nos. 306-321,C110-C118 (25)	30.45	5.75

Issue dates: Nos. 306-313, Jan. 20; Nos. 314-318, Feb. 17; Nos. 319-321, Apr. 3.

Jesus Condemned to Death — A41

Stations of the Cross, by Juan de Aranoa y Carredano: 1.50fr, Jesus carries His Cross. 2fr, Jesus falls the first time. 3fr, Jesus meets His mother. 3.50fr, Simon of Cyrene helps carry the cross. 4fr, Veronica wipes the face of Jesus. 5fr, Jesus falls the second time.

1970, Mar. 16 Photo. *Perf. 13½*

322 A41	1fr gold & multi	.20	.20
323 A41	1.50fr gold & multi	.20	.20
324 A41	2fr gold & multi	.20	.20
325 A41	3fr gold & multi	.20	.20
326 A41	3.50fr gold & multi	.20	.20
327 A41	4fr gold & multi	.20	.20
328 A41	5fr gold & multi	.20	.20
a.	Souv. sheet, #322-328 + label	.75	.75
	Nos. 322-328,C119-C125 (14)	3.60	2.90

Easter 1970.

Parade and EXPO '70 Emblem — A42

Designs (EXPO '70 Emblem and): 6.50fr, Aerial view. 7fr, African pavilions. 14fr, Pagoda, vert. 26fr, Recording pavilion and pool. 40fr, Tower of the Sun, vert. 50fr, Flags of participating nations.

1970, May 5 Photo. Perf. 13½

329 A42	4fr gold & multi	.20	.20
330 A42	6.50fr gold & multi	.20	.20
331 A42	7fr gold & multi	.20	.20
332 A42	14fr gold & multi	.25	.20
333 A42	26fr gold & multi	.40	.20
334 A42	40fr gold & multi	.55	.20
335 A42	50fr gold & multi	.80	.20
	Nos. 329-335 (7)	2.60	1.40

EXPO '70 Intl. Exhibition, Osaka, Japan, Mar. 15-Sept. 13, 1970. See No. C126.

White Rhinoceros — A43

Fauna: a, i, Camel. c, d, Dromedary. g, r, Okapi. f, m, Addax. j, o, Rhinoceros. l, p, Burundi cow (each animal in 2 different poses).

Map of the Nile: b, Delta and pyramids. e, dhow. h, Falls. k, Blue Nile and crowned crane. n, Victoria Nile and secretary bird. q, Lake Victoria and source of Nile on Mt. Gikizi. Continuous design.

1970, July 8 Photo. Perf. 13½

336	Sheet of 18	12.50	4.00
a.-r.	A43 7fr any single	.75	.20

Publicizing the southernmost source of the Nile on Mt. Gikizi in Burundi. See No. C127.

Winter Wren, Firecrest, Skylark and Crested Lark — A44

Birds: 2fr, 3.50fr, 5fr, vert.; others horiz.

1970, Sept. 30 Photo. Perf. 13½
Stamp Size: 44x33mm

337 A44	Block of 4	1.60	.20
a.	2fr Northern shrike	.40	
b.	2fr European starling	.40	
c.	2fr Yellow wagtail	.40	
d.	2fr Bank swallow	.40	
338 A44	Block of 4	1.60	.20
a.	3fr Winter wren	.40	
b.	3fr Firecrest	.40	
c.	3fr Skylark	.40	
d.	3fr Crested lark	.40	
339 A44	Block of 4	2.40	.20
a.	3.50fr Woodchat shrike	.60	
b.	3.50fr Common rock thrush	.60	
c.	3.50fr Black redstart	.60	
d.	3.50fr Ring ouzel	.60	
340 A44	Block of 4	3.00	.20
a.	4fr European Redstart	.75	
b.	4fr Hedge sparrow	.75	
c.	4fr Gray wagtail	.75	
d.	4fr Meadow pipit	.75	
341 A44	Block of 4	4.00	.20
a.	5fr Eurasian hoopoe	.85	
b.	5fr Pied flycatcher	.85	
c.	5fr Great reed warbler	.85	
d.	5fr Eurasian kingfisher	.85	
342 A44	Block of 4	5.00	.20
a.	6.50fr House martin	1.10	
b.	6.50fr Sedge warbler	1.10	
c.	6.50fr Fieldfare	1.10	
d.	6.50fr European Golden oriole	1.10	
	Nos. 337-342,C132-C137 (12)	48.10	3.65

Nos. 337-342 are printed in sheets of16.

Library, UN Emblem — A45

Designs: 5fr, Students taking test, and emblem of University of Bujumbura. 7fr, Students in laboratory and emblem of Ecole Normale Superieure of Burundi. 10fr, Students with electron-microscope and Education Year emblem.

1970, Oct. 23

343 A45	3fr gold & multi	.20	.20
344 A45	5fr gold & multi	.20	.20
345 A45	7fr gold & multi	.25	.20
346 A45	10fr gold & multi	.30	.20
	Nos. 343-346 (4)	.95	.80

Issued for International Education Year.

Pres. and Mrs. Michel Micombero — A46

Designs: 7fr, Pres. Michel Micombero and Burundi flag. 11fr, Pres. Micombero and Revolution Memorial.

1970, Nov. 28 Photo. Perf. 13½

347 A46	4fr gold & multi	.20	.20
348 A46	7fr gold & multi	.20	.20
349 A46	11fr gold & multi	.25	.20
a.	Souvenir sheet of 3	.75	.50
	Nos. 347-349 (3)	.65	.60

4th anniv. of independence. No. 349a contains 3 stamps similar to Nos. 347-349, but inscribed "Poste Aerienne." Exists imperf.

See Nos. C140-C142.

Lenin with Delegates A47

Designs (Lenin, Paintings): 5fr, addressing crowd. 6.50fr, with soldier and sailor. 15fr, speaking from balcony. 50fr, Portrait.

1970, Dec. 31 Photo. Perf. 13½
Gold Frame

350 A47	3.50fr dk red brown	.20	.20
351 A47	5fr dk red brown	.20	.20
352 A47	6.50fr dk red brown	.20	.20
353 A47	15fr dk red brown	.30	.20
354 A47	50fr dk red brown	1.10	.20
	Nos. 350-354 (5)	2.00	1.00

Lenin's birth centenary (1870-1924).

Lion — A48

1971, Mar. 19 Photo. Perf. 13½
Size: 38x38mm

355	Strip of 4	1.40	.20
a.	A48 1fr Lion	.35	
b.	A48 1fr Cape buffalo	.35	
c.	A48 1fr Hippopotamus	.35	
d.	A48 1fr Giraffe	.35	
356	Strip of 4	1.75	.20
a.	A48 2fr Hartebeest	.40	
b.	A48 2fr Black rhinoceros	.40	
c.	A48 2fr Zebra	.40	
d.	A48 2fr Leopard	.40	
357	Strip of 4	2.10	.20
a.	A48 3fr Grant's gazelles	.50	
b.	A48 3fr Cheetah	.50	
c.	A48 3fr African white-backed vultures	.50	
d.	A48 3fr Johnston's okapi	.50	
358	Strip of 4	2.50	.20
a.	A48 5fr Chimpanzee	.60	
b.	A48 5fr Elephant	.60	
c.	A48 5fr Spotted hyenas	.60	
d.	A48 5fr Beisa	.60	
359	Strip of 4	3.75	.40
a.	A48 6fr Gorilla	.80	
b.	A48 6fr Gnu	.80	
c.	A48 6fr Wart hog	.80	
d.	A48 6fr Cape hunting dog	.80	
360	Strip of 4	4.25	.45
a.	A48 11fr Sable antelope	1.00	
b.	A48 11fr Caracal lynx	1.00	
c.	A48 11fr Ostriches	1.00	
d.	A48 11fr Bongo	1.00	
	Nos. 355-360,C146-C151 (12)	35.00	3.65

For overprints and surcharges see Nos. C152, CB15-CB18.

The Resurrection, by Il Sodoma — A49

Paintings: 6fr, Resurrection, by Andrea del Castagno. 11fr, Noli me Tangere, by Correggio.

1971, Apr. 2

361 A49	3fr gold & multi	.20	.20
362 A49	6fr gold & multi	.20	.20
363 A49	11fr gold & multi	.30	.20
a.	Souvenir sheet of 3, #361-363	.60	.60
	Nos. 361-363,C143-C145 (6)	1.45	1.20

Easter 1971. No. 363a exists imperf.

Young Venetian Woman, by Dürer — A50

Dürer Paintings: 11fr, Hieronymus Holzschuher. 14fr, Emperor Maximilian I. 17fr, Holy Family, from Paumgartner Altar. 26fr, Haller Madonna. 31fr, Self-portrait, 1498.

1971, Sept. 20

364 A50	6fr multicolored	.20	.20
365 A50	11fr multicolored	.25	.20
366 A50	14fr multicolored	.40	.20
367 A50	17fr multicolored	.45	.25
368 A50	26fr multicolored	.65	.35
369 A50	31fr multicolored	.80	.40
a.	Souvenir sheet of 2, #368-369	1.60	1.60
	Nos. 364-369 (6)	2.75	1.60

International Letter Writing Week. Albrecht Dürer (1471-1528), German painter and engraver. No. 369a exists imperf.

Nos. 364-369, 369a Overprinted in Black and Gold: "VIème CONGRES / DE L'INSTITUT INTERNATIONAL / DE DROIT D'EXPRESSION FRANCAISE"

1971, Oct. 8

370 A50	6fr multicolored	.20	.20
371 A50	11fr multicolored	.25	.20
372 A50	14fr multicolored	.30	.20
373 A50	17fr multicolored	.35	.20
374 A50	26fr multicolored	.50	.20
375 A50	31fr multicolored	.65	.20
a.	Souvenir sheet of 2	1.25	1.25
	Nos. 370-375 (6)	2.25	1.20

6th Cong. of the Intl. Legal Institute of the French-speaking Area, Bujumbura, 8/10-19.

Madonna and Child, by Il Perugino — A51

Paintings of the Madonna and Child by: 5fr, Andrea del Sarto. 6fr, Luis de Morales.

1971, Nov. 2 Photo. Perf. 13½

376 A51	3fr dk green & multi	.20	.20
377 A51	5fr dk green & multi	.20	.20
378 A51	6fr dk green & multi	.20	.20
a.	Souvenir sheet of 3, #376-378	.40	.40
	Nos. 376-378,C153-C155 (6)	1.75	1.20

Christmas 1971. No. 378a exists imperf.
For surcharges see #B49-B51, CB19-CB21.

Lunar Orbiter A52

Designs: 11fr, Vostok. 14fr, Luna 1. 17fr, Apollo 11 astronaut on moon. 26fr, Soyuz 11. 40fr, Lunar Rover (Apollo 15).

1972, Jan. 15

379 A52	6fr gold & multi	.20	.20
380 A52	11fr gold & multi	.25	.20
381 A52	14fr gold & multi	.30	.20
382 A52	17fr gold & multi	.40	.20
383 A52	26fr gold & multi	.40	.30
384 A52	40fr gold & multi	.60	.30
a.	Souvenir sheet of 6	2.25	2.25
	Nos. 379-384 (6)	2.15	1.40

Conquest of space. See No. C156.
No. 384a contains one each of Nos. 379-384 inscribed "APOLLO 16."

Slalom and Sapporo '72 Emblem — A53

Sapporo '72 Emblem and: 6fr, Figure skating, pairs. 11fr, Figure skating, women's. 14fr, Ski jump. 17fr, Ice hockey. 24fr, Speed skating, men's. 26fr, Snow scooter. 31fr, Downhill skiing. 50fr, Bobsledding.

1972, Feb. 3

385 A53	5fr silver & multi	.20	.20
386 A53	6fr silver & multi	.20	.20
387 A53	11fr silver & multi	.20	.20
388 A53	14fr silver & multi	.25	.20
389 A53	17fr silver & multi	.30	.20
390 A53	24fr silver & multi	.35	.20
391 A53	26fr silver & multi	.40	.20
392 A53	31fr silver & multi	.50	.20
393 A53	50fr silver & multi	.80	.20
	Nos. 385-393 (9)	3.20	1.80

11th Winter Olympic Games, Sapporo, Japan, Feb. 3-13. Printed in sheets of 12. See No. C157.

Issued: #385-390, 2/1; #391-393, 2/21.

Ecce Homo, by Quentin Massys — A54

Paintings: 6.50fr, Crucifixion, by Rubens. 10fr, Descent from the Cross, by Jacopo da Pontormo. 18fr, Pieta, by Ferdinand Gallegos. 27fr, Trinity, by El Greco.

1972, Mar. 20 Photo. *Perf. 13½*

394 A54 3.50fr gold & multi .20 .20
395 A54 6.50fr gold & multi .20 .20
396 A54 10fr gold & multi .25 .20
397 A54 18fr gold & multi .35 .20
398 A54 27fr gold & multi .75 .20
a. Souv. sheet, #394-398 + label 3.00 2.75
Nos. 394-398 (5) 1.75 1.00

Easter 1972. Printed in sheets of 8 with label. No. 398a exists imperf.

Gymnastics, Olympic Rings and "Motion" A55

1972, May 19

399 A55 5fr shown .20 .20
400 A55 6fr Javelin .20 .20
401 A55 11fr Fencing .25 .20
402 A55 14fr Bicycling .25 .20
403 A55 17fr Pole vault .30 .20
Nos. 399-403,C158-C161 (9) 3.05 1.80

Souvenir Sheet

404 Sheet of 2 1.75 1.25
a. A55 31fr Discus .45 .45
b. A55 40fr Soccer .60 .60

20th Olympic Games, Munich, 8/26-9/11.

Prince Rwagasore, Pres. Micombero, Burundi Flag, Drummers A56

7fr, Rwagasore, Micombero, flag, map of Africa, globe. 13fr, Micombero, flag, globe.

1972, Aug. 24 Photo. *Perf. 13½*

405 A56 5fr silver & multi .20 .20
406 A56 7fr silver & multi .20 .20
407 A56 13fr silver & multi .25 .20
a. Souvenir sheet of 3, #405-407 .50
Nos. 405-407,C162-C164 (6) 1.65 1.20

10th anniversary of independence.

Madonna and Child, by Andrea Solario — A57

Paintings of the Madonna and Child by: 10fr, Raphael. 15fr, Botticelli.

1972, Nov. 2

408 A57 5fr lt blue & multi .20 .20
409 A57 10fr lt blue & multi .20 .20
410 A57 15fr lt blue & multi .25 .20
a. Souvenir sheet of 3, #408-410 .50
Nos. 408-410,C165-C167 (6) 1.95 1.20

Christmas 1972. Sheets of 20 stamps + label.

For surcharges see #B56-B58, CB26-CB28.

Platycoryne Crocea — A58

1972

Size: 33x33mm

411 A58 50c *shown* .20 .20
412 A58 1fr *Cattleya trianaei* .20 .20
413 A58 2fr *Eulophia cucullata* .20 .20
414 A58 3fr *Cymbidium hamsey* .20 .20
415 A58 4fr *Thelymitra pauciflora* .20 .20
416 A58 5fr *Miltassia* .20 .20
417 A58 6fr *Miltonia* .20 .20

Size: 38x38mm

418 A58 7fr Like 50c .20 .20
419 A58 8fr Like 1fr .20 .20
420 A58 9fr Like 2fr .20 .20
421 A58 10fr Like 3fr .25 .20
Nos. 411-421,C168-C174 (18) 11.00 3.60

Orchids. Issued: #411-417, 11/6; #418-421, 11/29.

Henry Morton Stanley — A59

Designs: 7fr, Porters, Stanley's expedition. 13fr, Stanley entering Ujiji.

1973, Mar. 19 Photo. *Perf. 13½*

422 A59 5fr gold & multi .20 .20
423 A59 7fr gold & multi .20 .20
424 A59 13fr gold & multi .20 .20
Nos. 422-424,C175-C177 (6) 1.60 1.20

Exploration of Africa by David Livingstone (1813-1873) and Henry Morton Stanley (John Rowlands; 1841-1904).

Crucifixion, by Roger van der Weyden — A60

Easter (Paintings): 5fr, Flagellation of Christ, by Caravaggio. 13fr, The Burial of Christ, by Raphael.

1973, Apr. 10

425 A60 5fr gold & multi .20 .20
426 A60 7fr gold & multi .20 .20
427 A60 13fr gold & multi .20 .20
a. Souvenir sheet of 3, #425-427 .60 .60
Nos. 425-427,C178-C180 (6) 1.75 1.20

INTERPOL Emblem, Flag — A61

Design: 10fr, INTERPOL flag and emblem. 18fr, INTERPOL Headquarters and emblem.

1973, May 19 Photo. *Perf. 13½*

428 A61 5fr silver & multi .20 .20
429 A61 10fr silver & multi .20 .20
430 A61 18fr silver & multi .30 .20
Nos. 428-430,C181-C182 (5) 1.60 1.00

Intl. Criminal Police Organization, 50th anniv.

Signs of the Zodiac, Babylon — A62

Designs: 5fr, Greek and Roman gods representing planets. 7fr, Ptolemy (No. 433a) and Ptolemaic solar system. 13fr, Copernicus (No. 434a) and heliocentric system.

a, UL. b, UR. c, LL. d, LR.

1973, July 27 Photo. *Perf. 13½*

431 A62 3fr Block of 4, #a.-d. .20 .20
432 A62 5fr Block of 4, #a.-d. .25 .20
433 A62 7fr Block of 4, #a.-d. .30 .20
434 A62 13fr Block of 4, #a.-d. .75 .20
e. Souvenir sheet of 4, #431-434 2.75 1.40
Nos. 431-434,C183-C186 (8) 9.25 2.65

500th anniversary of the birth of Nicolaus Copernicus (1473-1543), Polish astronomer.

Flowers and Butterflies — A63

Block of 4 containing 2 flower & 2 butterfly designs. The 1fr, 2fr, 5fr and 11fr have flower designs listed as "a" and "d" numbers, butterflies as "b" and "c" numbers; the arrangement is reversed for the 3fr and 6fr.

1973, Sept. 3 Photo. *Perf. 13*

Stamp Size: 34x41½mm

435 A63 Block of 4 .35 .20
a. 1fr *Protea cynaroides* .20 .20
b. 1fr *Precis octavia* .20 .20
c. 1fr *Epiphora bauhiniae* .20 .20
d. 1fr *Gazania longiscapa* .20 .20
436 A63 Block of 4 .35 .20
a. 2fr *Kniphofia* .20 .20
b. 2fr *Cymothoe coccinata* .20 .20
c. 2fr *Nudaurelia zambesina* .20 .20
d. 2fr *Freesia refracta* .20 .20
437 A63 Block of 4 .40 .20
a. 3fr *Calotis eupompe* .20 .20
b. 3fr *Narcissus* .20 .20
c. 3fr *Cineraria hybrida* .20 .20
d. 3fr *Cyrestis camillus* .20 .20
438 A63 Block of 4 .65 .20
a. 5fr *Iris tingitana* .20 .20
b. 5fr *Pappilio demodocus* .20 .20
c. 5fr *Catopsilia avelaneda* .20 .20
d. 5fr *Nerine sarniensis* .20 .20
439 A63 Block of 4 .80 .20
a. 6fr *Hypolimnas dexithea* .20 .20
b. 6fr *Zantedeschia tropicalis* .20 .20
c. 6fr *Sandersonia aurantiaca* .20 .20
d. 6fr *Drurya antimachus* .20 .20
440 A63 Block of 4 1.75 .25
a. 11fr *Nymphaea capensis* .40 .20
b. 11fr *Pandoriana pandora* .40 .20
c. 11fr *Precis orythia* .40 .20
d. 11fr *Pelargonium domestica* .40 .20
Nos. 435-440,C187-C192 (12) 34.80 4.45

Virgin and Child, by Giovanni Bellini — A64

Virgin and Child by: 10fr, Jan van Eyck. 15fr, Giovanni Boltraffio.

1973, Nov. 13 Photo. *Perf. 13*

441 A64 5fr gold & multi .20 .20
442 A64 10fr gold & multi .20 .20
443 A64 15fr gold & multi .20 .20
a. Souvenir sheet of 3, #441-443 .50 .50
Nos. 441-443,C193-C195 (6) 1.90 1.20

Christmas 1973.

For surcharges see #B59-B61, CB29-CB31.

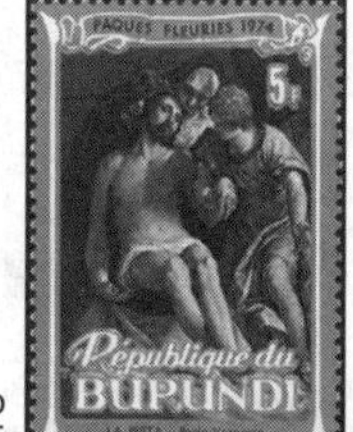

Pietá, by Paolo Veronese — A65

Paintings: 10fr, Virgin and St. John, by van der Weyden. 18fr, Crucifixion, by van der Weyden. 27fr, Burial of Christ, by Titian. 40fr, Pietá, by El Greco.

1974, Apr. 19 Photo. *Perf. 14x13½*

444 A65 5fr gold & multi .20 .20
445 A65 10fr gold & multi .20 .20
446 A65 18fr gold & multi .30 .20
447 A65 27fr gold & multi .40 .20
448 A65 40fr gold & multi .65 .20
a. Souvenir sheet of 5, #444-448 1.60 1.60
Nos. 444-448 (5) 1.75 1.00

Easter 1974.

Fish — A66

1974, May 30 Photo. *Perf. 13*
Stamp Size: 35x35mm

449 A66 Block of 4 .30 .20
a. 1fr *Haplochromis multicolor* .20 .20
b. 1fr *Pantodon buchholzi* .20 .20
c. 1fr *Tropheus duboisi* .20 .20
d. 1fr *Distichodus sexfasciatus* .20 .20
450 A66 Block of 4 .30 .20
a. 2fr *Pelmatochromis kribensis* .20 .20
b. 2fr *Nannaethiops tritaeniatus* .20 .20
c. 2fr *Polycentropsis abbreviata* .20 .20
d. 2fr *Hemichromis bimaculatus* .20 .20
451 A66 Block of 4 .30 .20
a. 3fr *Ctenopoma acutirostre* .20 .20
b. 3fr *Synodontis angelicus* .20 .20
c. 3fr *Tilapia melanopleura* .20 .20
d. 3fr *Aphyosemion bivittatum* .20 .20
452 A66 Block of 4 .50 .20
a. 5fr *Monodactylus argenteus* .20 .20
b. 5fr *Zanclus canescens* .20 .20
c. 5fr *Pygoplites diacanthus* .20 .20
d. 5fr *Cephalopholis argus* .20 .20
453 A66 Block of 4 .60 .20
a. 6fr *Priacanthus arenatus* .20 .20
b. 6fr *Pomacanthus arcuatus* .20 .20
c. 6fr *Scarus guacamaia* .20 .20
d. 6fr *Zeus faber* .20 .20
454 A66 Block of 4 1.00 .20
a. 11fr *Lactophrys quadricornis* .20 .20
b. 11fr *Balistes vetula* .20 .20
c. 11fr *Acanthurus bahianus* .20 .20
d. 11fr *Holocanthus ciliaris* .20 .20
Nos. 449-454,C207-C212 (12) 18.75 2.85

Soccer and Cup A67

Designs: Various soccer scenes and cup.

1974, July 4 Photo. *Perf. 13*
455 A67 5fr gold & multi .20
456 A67 6fr gold & multi .20
457 A67 11fr gold & multi .20
458 A67 14fr gold & multi .25
459 A67 17fr gold & multi .25
a. Souvenir sheet of 3 1.40
Nos. 455-459,C196-C198 (8) 2.40

World Soccer Championship, Munich, June 13-July 7. No. 459a contains 3 stamps similar to Nos. C196-C198 without "Poste Aerienne."

Nos. 455-459 and 459a exist imperf.

Flags over UPU Headquarters, Bern — A68

#460b, G.P.O., Bujumbura. #461a, Mailmen ("11F" in UR). #461b, Mailmen ("11F" in UL). #462a, UPU emblem. #462b, Means of transportation. #463a, Pigeon over globe showing Burundi. #463b, Swiss flag, pigeon over map showing Bern. Pairs are continuous designs.

1974, July 23
460 A68 6fr Pair, #a.-b. .35
461 A68 11fr Pair, #a.-b. .60
462 A68 14fr Pair, #a.-b. .80
463 A68 17fr Pair, #a.-b. .90
c. Souvenir sheet of 8, #460-463 2.75
Nos. 460-463,C199-C202 (8) 9.90
Set, used 1.00

Cent. of UPU.

St. Ildefonso Writing Letter, by El Greco A69

Paintings: 11fr, Lady Sealing Letter, by Chardin. 14fr, Titus at Desk, by Rembrandt. 17fr, The Love Letter, by Vermeer. 26fr, The Merchant G. Gisze, by Holbein. 31fr, Portrait of Alexandre Lenoir, by David.

1974, Oct. 1 Photo. *Perf. 13*
468 A69 6fr gold & multi .20
469 A69 11fr gold & multi .20
470 A69 14fr gold & multi .25
471 A69 17fr gold & multi .25
472 A69 26fr gold & multi .40
473 A69 31fr gold & multi .45
a. Souvenir sheet of 2, #472-473 1.10
Nos. 468-473 (6) 1.75

International Letter Writing Week, Oct. 6-12. No. 473a exists imperf.

Virgin and Child, by Bernaert van Orley — A70

Paintings of the Virgin and Child: 10fr, by Hans Memling. 15fr, by Botticelli.

1974, Nov. 7 Photo. *Perf. 13*
474 A70 5fr gold & multi .20
475 A70 10fr gold & multi .20
476 A70 15fr gold & multi .25
a. Souvenir sheet of 3, #474-476 .50
Nos. 474-476,C213-C215 (6) 1.95

Christmas 1974. Sheets of 20 stamps and one label. No. 476a exists imperf.

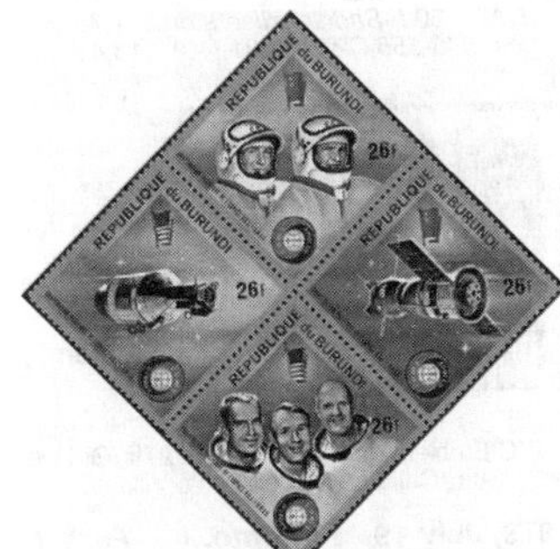

Apollo-Soyuz Space Mission and Emblem — A71

1975, July 10 Photo. *Perf. 13*
477 A71 Block of 4 .80
a. 26fr A.A. Leonov, V.N. Kubasov, Soviet flag .20
b. 26fr Soyuz and Soviet flag .20
c. 26fr Apollo and American flag .20
d. 26fr D.K. Slayton, V.D. Brand, T.P. Stafford, American flag .20
478 A71 Block of 4 1.25
a. 31fr Apollo-Soyuz link-up .30
b. 31fr Apollo, blast-off .30
c. 31fr Soyuz, blast-off .30
d. 31fr Kubasov, Leonov, Slayton, Brand, Stafford .30
Nos. 477-478,C216-C217 (4) 4.30

Apollo Soyuz space test project (Russo-American cooperation), launching July 15; link-up, July 17.

Addax — A72

1975, July 31 Photo. *Perf. 13½*
479 Strip of 4 .20
a. A72 1fr shown .20
b. A72 1fr Roan antelope .20
c. A72 1fr Nyala .20
d. A72 1fr White rhinoceros .20
480 Strip of 4 .20
a. A72 2fr Mandrill .20
b. A72 2fr Eland .20
c. A72 2fr Salt's dik-dik .20
d. A72 2fr Thomson's gazelles .20
481 Strip of 4 .20
a. A72 3fr African small-clawed otter .20
b. A72 3fr Reed buck .20
c. A72 3fr Indian civet .20
d. A72 3fr Cape buffalo .20
482 Strip of 4 .35
a. A72 5fr White-tailed gnu .20
b. A72 5fr African wild asses .20
c. A72 5fr Black-and-white colobus monkey .20
d. A72 5fr Gerenuk .20
483 Strip of 4 .35
a. A72 6fr Dama gazelle .20
b. A72 6fr Black-backed jackal .20
c. A72 6fr Sitatungas .20
d. A72 6fr Zebra antelope .20
484 Strip of 4 .65
a. A72 11fr Fennec .20
b. A72 11fr Lesser kudus .20
c. A72 11fr Blesbok .20
d. A72 11fr Serval .20
Nos. 479-484,C218-C223 (12) 12.70

For overprints see Nos. C224-C227.

Jonah, by Michelangelo — A73

Paintings from Sistine Chapel: #485b, Libyan Sybil. #486a, Prophet Isaiah. #486b, Delphic Sybil. #487a, Daniel. #487b, Cumaean Sybil.

1975, Dec. 3 Photo. *Perf. 13*
485 A73 5fr Pair, #a.-b. .20
486 A73 13fr Pair, #a.-b. .40
487 A73 27fr Pair, #a.-b. .75
c. Souvenir sheet of 6, #485-487 2.00
Nos. 485-487,C228-C230 (6) 4.90

Michelangelo Buonarotti (1475-1564), Italian sculptor, painter and architect. Printed in sheets of 18 stamps + 2 labels.

For surcharges see Nos. B65-B67, CB35-CB37.

Speed Skating — A74

Basketball — A75

Designs (Innsbruck Games Emblem and): 24fr, Figure skating, women's. 26fr, Two-man bobsled. 31fr, Cross-country skiing.

1976, Jan. 23 Photo. *Perf. 14x13½*
491 A74 17fr dp bl & multi .30
492 A74 24fr multi .45
493 A74 26fr multi .50
494 A74 31fr plum & multi .55
a. Souvenir sheet of 3, perf. 13½ 2.25
Nos. 491-494,C234-C236 (7) 3.70

12th Winter Olympic Games, Innsbruck, Austria, Feb. 4-15.

No. 494a contains stamps similar to #C234-C236, without "POSTE AERIENNE."

1976, May 3 Litho. *Perf. 13½*

Montreal Games Emblem and: #495b, 497a, 499b, Pole vault. #496a, 497b, 499d, Running. #496b, 498a, 499a, Soccer. #498b, 499c, Basketball.

495 A75 14fr Pair, #a.-b. .50
496 A75 17fr Pair, #a.-b. .60
497 A75 28fr Pair, #a.-b. 1.00
498 A75 40fr Pair, #a.-b. 1.40
Nos. 495-498,C237-C239 (7) 7.15

Souvenir Sheet

499 Sheet of 4 1.60
a. A75 14fr red & multi .25
b. A75 17fr olive & multi .25
c. A75 28fr blue & multi .40
d. A75 40fr magenta & multi .60

21st Olympic Games, Montreal, Canada, July 17-Aug. 1.

Virgin and Child, by Dirk Bouts — A76

Virgin and Child by: 13fr, Giovanni Bellini. 27fr, Carlo Crivelli.

1976, Oct. 18 Photo. *Perf. 13½*
504 A76 5fr gold & multi .20
505 A76 13fr gold & multi .20
506 A76 27fr gold & multi .40
a. Souvenir sheet of 3, #504-506 .75
Nos. 504-506,C250-C252 (6) 2.10

Christmas 1976. Sheets of 20 stamps and descriptive label.

For surcharges see #B71-B73, CB41-CB43.

St. Veronica, by Rubens A77

Paintings by Rubens: 21fr, Christ on the Cross. 27fr, Descent from the Cross. 35fr, The Deposition.

1977, Apr. 5 Photo. *Perf. 13*
507 A77 10fr gold & multi .20
508 A77 21fr gold & multi .30
509 A77 27fr gold & multi .40
510 A77 35fr gold & multi .55
a. Souvenir sheet of 4 1.50
Nos. 507-510 (4) 1.45

Easter 1977. Sheets of 30 stamps and descriptive label. No. 510a contains 4 stamps similar to Nos. 507-510 inscribed "POSTE AERIENNE."

A78

#511a, Alexander Graham Bell. #511b, Intelsat Satellite, Modern & Old Telephones. #512a, Switchboard operator, c. 1910, wall telephone. #512b, Intelsat, radar. #513a, A.G. Bell, 1st telephone. #513b, Satellites around globe, videophone.

1977, May 17 Photo. *Perf. 13*
511 A78 10fr Pair, #a.-b. .20
512 A78 17fr Pair, #a.-b. .30
513 A78 26fr Pair, #a.-b. .50
Nos. 511-513,C253-C254 (5) 1.75

Centenary of first telephone call by Alexander Graham Bell, Mar. 10, 1876.

Buffon's Kob — A80

1977, Aug. 22 Photo. *Perf. 14x14½*

517 Strip of 4 .40
a. A80 2fr shown .20
b. A80 2fr Marabous .20
c. A80 2fr Brindled gnu .20
d. A80 2fr River hog .20
518 Strip of 4 .60
a. A80 5fr Zebras .20
b. A80 5fr Shoebill .20
c. A80 5fr Striped hyenas .20
d. A80 5fr Chimpanzee .20
519 Strip of 4 1.00
a. A80 8fr Flamingos .25
b. A80 8fr Nile crocodiles .25
c. A80 8fr Green mamba .25
d. A80 8fr Greater kudus .25
520 Strip of 4 1.25
a. A80 11fr Hyrax .30
b. A80 11fr Cobra .30
c. A80 11fr Jackals .30
d. A80 11fr Verreaux's eagles .30
521 Strip of 4 2.50
a. A80 21fr Honey badger .60
b. A80 21fr Harnessed antelopes .60
c. A80 21fr Secretary bird .60
d. A80 21fr Klipspringer .60
522 Strip of 4 2.50
a. A80 27fr African big-eared fox .60
b. A80 27fr Elephants .60
c. A80 27fr Vulturine guineafowl .60
d. A80 27fr Impalas .60
Nos. 517-522,C258-C263 (12) 28.25

The Goose Girl, by Grimm — A81

Fairy Tales: 5fr, by Grimm Brothers. 11fr, by Aesop. 14fr, by Hans Christian Andersen. 17fr, by Jean de La Fontaine. 26fr, English fairy tales.

1977, Sept. 14 *Perf. 14*

523 Block of 4 .40
a. A81 5fr shown .20
b. A81 5fr The Two Wanderers .20
c. A81 5fr The Man of Iron .20
d. A81 5fr Snow White and Rose Red .20
524 Block of 4 .85
a. A81 11fr The Quarreling Cats .20
b. A81 11fr The Blind and the Lame .20
c. A81 11fr The Hermit and the Bear .20
d. A81 11fr The Fox and the Stork .20
525 Block of 4 1.00
a. A81 14fr The Princess and the Pea .25
b. A81 14fr The Old Tree Mother .25
c. A81 14fr The Ice Maiden .25
d. A81 14fr The Old House .25
526 Block of 4 1.25
a. A81 17fr The Oyster and the Suitors .30
b. A81 17fr The Wolf and the Lamb .30
c. A81 17fr Hen with the Golden Egg .30
d. A81 17fr The Wolf as Shepherd .30
527 Block of 4 2.00
a. A81 26fr Three Heads in the Well .50
b. A81 26fr Mother Goose .50
c. A81 26fr Jack and the Beanstalk .50
d. A81 26fr Alice in Wonderland .50
Nos. 523-527 (5) 5.50

Security Council Chamber, UN Nos. 28, 46, 37, C7 — A82

UN Stamps and: 8fr, UN General Assembly, interior. 21fr, UN Meeting Hall.

1977, Oct. 10 Photo. *Perf. 13½*

528 A82 Block of 4 .65
a. 8fr No. 25 .20
b. 8fr No. C5 .20
c. 8fr No. 23 .20
d. 8fr No. 2 .20
529 A82 Block of 4 .75
a. 10fr No. 28 .20
b. 10fr No. 46 .20
c. 10fr No. 37 .20
d. 10fr No. C7 .20
530 A82 Block of 4 1.50
a. 21fr No. 45 .35
b. 21fr No. 42 .35
c. 21fr No. 17 .35
d. 21fr No. 13 .35
e. Souvenir sheet of 3 .65
Nos. 528-530,C264-C266 (6) 10.05

25th anniv. (in 1976) of the UN Postal Administration. No. 530e contains 8fr in design of No. 529d, 10fr in design of No. 530b, 21fr in design of No. 528c.

Virgin and Child — A83

Designs: Paintings of the Virgin and Child.

1977, Oct. 31 Photo. *Perf. 14x13*

531 A83 5fr By Meliore Toscano .20
532 A83 13fr By J. Lombardos .20
533 A83 27fr By Emmanuel Tzanes, 1610-1680 .40
a. Souvenir sheet of 3, #531-533 .75
Nos. 531-533,C267-C269 (6) 2.20

Christmas 1977. Sheets of 24 stamps with descriptive label.
For surcharges see #B74-B76, CB44-CB46.

Cruiser Aurora, Russia Nos. 211, 303, 1252, 187 — A84

Russian Stamps and: 8fr, Kremlin, Moscow. 11fr, Pokrovski Cathedral, Moscow. 13fr, Labor Day parade, 1977 and 1980 Olympic Games emblem.

1977, Nov. 14 Photo. *Perf. 13*

534 A84 Block of 4 .40
a. 5fr No. 211 .20
b. 5fr No. 303 .20
c. 5fr No. 1252 .20
d. 5fr No. 187 .20
535 A84 Block of 4 .65
a. 8fr No. 856 .20
b. 8fr No. 1986 .20
c. 8fr No. 908 .20
d. 8fr No. 2551 .20
536 A84 Block of 4 .85
a. 11fr No. 3844b .20
b. 11fr No. 3452 .20
c. 11fr No. 3382 .20
d. 11fr No. 3837 .20
537 A84 Block of 4 1.00
a. 13fr No. 4446 .25
b. 13fr No. 3497 .25
c. 13fr No. 2926 .25
d. 13fr No. 2365 .25
Nos. 534-537 (4) 2.90

60th anniv. of Russian October Revolution.

Ship at Dock, Arms and Flag — A85

Burundi Arms and Flag and: 5fr, Men at lathes. 11fr, Male leopard dance. 14fr, Coffee harvest. 17fr, Government Palace.

1977, Nov. 25 Photo. *Perf. 13½*

538 A85 1fr sil & multi .20
539 A85 5fr sil & multi .20
540 A85 11fr sil & multi .20
541 A85 14fr sil & multi .20
542 A85 17fr sil & multi .20
Nos. 538-542 (5) 1.00

15th anniversary of independence.

A86

A87

Paintings of the Virgin and Child by: 13fr, Rubens. 17fr, Solario. 27fr, Tiepolo. 31fr, Gerard David. 40fr, Bellini.

1979, Feb. Photo. *Perf. 14x13*

543 A86 13fr multi .20
544 A86 17fr multi .25
545 A86 27fr multi .40
546 A86 31fr multi .50
547 A86 40fr multi .65
Nos. 543-547 (5) 2.00

Christmas 1978. See No. C270.

1979 Photo. *Perf. 13½x13*

548 A87 1fr *Abyssinian hornbill* .20
549 A87 2fr *Snakebird* .20
550 A87 3fr *Melittophagus pusillus* .20
551 A87 5fr *Flamingo* .20
552 A87 8fr *Afropavo congenis* .20
553 A87 10fr *Gallinule* .35
554 A87 20fr *Martial eagle* .65
555 A87 27fr *Ibis* .85
556 A87 50fr *Saddle-billed stork* 1.75
Nos. 548-556,C273-C281 (18) 13.45

Mother and Infant, IYC Emblem A88

IYC Emblem and: 20fr, Infant. 27fr, Girl with doll. 50fr, Children in Children's Village.

1979, July 19 Photo. *Perf. 14*

557 A88 10fr multi .20
558 A88 20fr multi .25
559 A88 27fr multi .30
560 A88 50fr multi .55
Nos. 557-560 (4) 1.30

Intl. Year of the Child. See No. B82.

A89

A90

Virgin and Child by: 20fr, del Garbo. 27fr, Giovanni Penni. 31fr, G. Romano. 50fr, Jacopo Bassano.

1979, Oct. 12

561 A89 20fr multi .30
562 A89 27fr multi .40
563 A89 31fr multi .55
564 A89 50fr multi .75
Nos. 561-564,B83-B86 (8) 4.00

Christmas 1979. See Nos. C271, CB48.

1979, Nov. 6

Designs: 20fr, Rowland Hill, Penny Black. Stamps of Burundi: 27fr, German East Africa Nos. 17, N17. 31fr, Nos. 4, 24. 40fr, Nos. 29, 294. 60fr, Heinrich von Stephan, Nos. 464-465.

565 A90 20fr multi .30
566 A90 27fr multi .40
567 A90 31fr multi .50
568 A90 40fr multi .60
569 A90 60fr multi .90
Nos. 565-569 (5) 2.70

Sir Rowland Hill (1795-1879), originator of penny postage. See No. C272.

A91

#570a, 110-meter hurdles. #570b, Hurdles, Thomas Munkelt. A#570c, Hurdles, R.D.A. #571a, Discus. #571b, Discus, V. Rasshchupkin. #571c, Discus, U.R.S.S. #572a, shown. #572b, "Football." #572c, Soccer, Tchecoslovaquie.

1980, Oct. 24 Photo. *Perf. 13x13½*

570 A91 20fr Strip of 3, #a.-c. 1.25
571 A91 30fr Strip of 3, #a.-c. 1.60
572 A91 40fr Strip of 3, #a.-c. 2.25
Nos. 570-572 (3) 5.10

22nd Summer Olympic Games, Moscow, July 19-Aug. 3.
See No. C282.

Virgin and Child, by Mainardi A92

Christmas 1980 (Paintings): 30fr, Holy Family, by Michelangelo. 40fr, Virgin and Child, by di Cosimo. 45fr, Holy Family, by Fra Bartolomeo.

1980, Dec. 12 Photo. *Perf. 13½x13*

579 A92 10fr multi .20
580 A92 30fr multi .30
581 A92 40fr multi .40
582 A92 45fr multi .45
Nos. 579-582,B87-B90 (8) 2.75

UPRONA Party National Congress, 1979 — A93

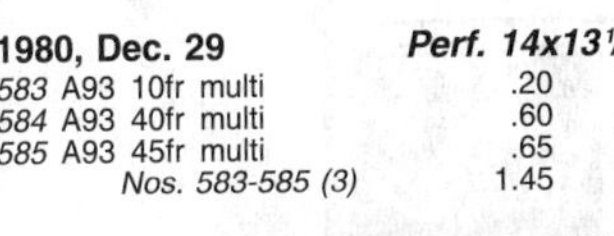

1980, Dec. 29 *Perf. 14x13½*

583 A93 10fr multi .20
584 A93 40fr multi .60
585 A93 45fr multi .65
Nos. 583-585 (3) 1.45

Johannes Kepler, Dish Antenna A94

1981, Feb. 12 *Perf. 14*

586 A94 10fr shown .20
587 A94 40fr Satellite .60
588 A94 45fr Satellite, diff. .65
a. Souvenir sheet of 3, #586-588 1.50
Nos. 586-588 (3) 1.45

350th death anniv. of Johannes Kepler and 1st earth satellite station in Burundi.

Lion A95

1983, Apr. 22 **Photo.** *Perf. 13*

589 A95 2fr shown
590 A95 3fr Giraffes
591 A95 5fr Rhinoceros
592 A95 10fr Cape buffalo
593 A95 20fr Elephant
594 A95 25fr Hippopotamus
595 A95 30fr Zebra
596 A95 50fr Warthog
597 A95 60fr Oryx
598 A95 65fr Wild dog
599 A95 70fr Cheetah
600 A95 75fr Wildebeest
601 A95 85fr Hyena
Nos. 589-601 (13) *450.00* 350.00

Nos. 589-601 Overprinted in Silver with World Wildlife Fund Emblem

1983 **Photo.** *Perf. 13*

589a A95 2fr multi
590a A95 3fr multi
591a A95 5fr multi
592a A95 10fr multi
593a A95 20fr multi
594a A95 25fr multi
595a A95 30fr multi
596a A95 50fr multi
597a A95 60fr multi
598a A95 65fr multi
599a A95 70fr multi
600a A95 75fr multi
601a A95 85fr multi
Nos. 589a-601a (13) *750.00* 400.00

Apparently there is speculation in these two sets.

20th Anniv. of Independence, July 1, 1982 — A96

Flags, various arms, map or portrait.

1983 *Perf. 14*

602 A96 10fr multi .20
603 A96 25fr multi .40
604 A96 30fr multi .45
605 A96 50fr multi .75
606 A96 65fr multi 1.00
Nos. 602-606 (5) 2.80

Christmas 1983 — A97

Virgin and Child paintings: 10fr, by Luca Signorelli (1450-1523). 25fr, by Esteban Murillo (1617-1682). 30fr, by Carlo Crivelli (1430-1495). 50fr, by Nicolas Poussin (1594-1665).

1983, Oct. 3 **Litho.** *Perf. 14½x13½*

607 A97 10fr multi .20
608 A97 25fr multi .40
609 A97 30fr multi .45
610 A97 50fr multi .75
Nos. 607-610,B91-B94 (8) 3.65

See Nos. C285, CB50.

Butterflies — A98

#611a, Cymothoe coccinata. #611b, Papilio zalmoxis. #612a, Asterope pechueli. #612b, Papilio antimachus. #613a, Papilio hesperus. #613b, Bebearia mardania. #614a, Euphaedra neophron. #614b, Euphaedra perseis. #615a, Euphaedra imperialis. #615b, Pseudocraea striata.

1984, June 29 **Photo.** *Perf. 13*

611 A98 5fr Pair, #a.-b. 3.00 1.00
612 A98 10fr Pair, #a.-b. 4.50 2.75
613 A98 30fr Pair, #a.-b. 12.50 6.50
614 A98 35fr Pair, #a.-b. 15.00 8.75
615 A98 65fr Pair, #a.-b. 30.00 16.00
Nos. 611-615 (5) 65.00

For surcharges see No. 654D.

19th UPU Congress, Hamburg A99

UPU emblem and: 10fr, German East Africa, #17, N17. 30fr, #4, 24. 35fr, #294, 595. 65fr, Dr. Heinrich von Stephan, #464-465.

1984, July 14 **Litho.** *Perf. 13x13½*

621 A99 10fr multi .20
622 A99 30fr multi .45
623 A99 35fr multi .50
624 A99 65fr multi 1.00
Nos. 621-624 (4) 2.15

See No. C286.

1984 Summer Olympics — A100

Gold medalists: 10fr, Jesse Owens, US, track and field, Berlin, 1936. 30fr, Rafer Johnson, US, decathlon, 1960. 35fr, Bob Beamon, US, long jump, 1968. 65fr, Kipchoge Keino, Kenya, 3000-meter steeplechase, 1972.

1984, Aug. 6 *Perf. 13½x13*

625 A100 10fr multi .25
626 A100 30fr multi .70
627 A100 35fr multi .85
628 A100 65fr multi 1.50
Nos. 625-628 (4) 3.30

See No. C287.

Christmas 1984 — A101

Paintings: 10fr, Rest During the Flight into Egypt, by Murillo (1617-1682). 25fr, Virgin and Child, by R. del Garbo. 30fr, Virgin and Child, by Botticelli (1445-1510). 50fr, The Adoration of the Shepherds, by Giacomo da Bassano (1517-1592).

1984, Dec. 15 *Perf. 13½*

629 A101 10fr multi .20
630 A101 25fr multi .40
631 A101 30fr multi .45
632 A101 50fr multi .75
Nos. 629-632,B95-B98 (8) 3.65

See Nos. C288, CB51.

Flowers — A102

1986, July 31 **Photo.** *Perf. 13x13½*

633 A102 2fr Thunbergia .20
634 A102 3fr Saintpaulia .20
635 A102 5fr Clivia .20
636 A102 10fr Cassia .20
637 A102 20fr Strelitzia .25
638 A102 35fr Gloriosa .55
Nos. 633-638,C289-C294 (12) 8.40

Intl. Peace Year — A103

1986, May 1 **Litho.** *Perf. 14*

639 A103 10fr Rockets as housing .20
640 A103 20fr Atom as flower .20
641 A103 30fr Handshake .25
642 A103 40fr Globe, chicks .35
a. Souvenir sheet of 4, #639-642 .90
Nos. 639-642 (4) 1.00

No. 642a exists imperf.

Great Lake Nations Economic Community (CEPGI), 10th Anniv. — A104

Outline maps of Lake Tanganyika, CEPGI emblem and: 5fr, Aviation. 10fr, Agriculture. 15fr, Industry. 25fr, Electrification. 35fr, Flags of Burundi, Rwanda and Zaire.

1986, May 1 **Photo.** *Perf. 13½x14½*

643 A104 5fr multi .20
644 A104 10fr multi .20
645 A104 15fr multi .20
646 A104 25fr multi .30
647 A104 35fr multi .45
a. Souv. sheet, #643-647 + label 1.25
Nos. 643-647 (5) 1.35

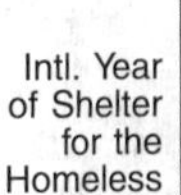

Intl. Year of Shelter for the Homeless A105

1987, June **Litho.** *Perf. 14*

648 A105 10fr Hovel .30
649 A105 20fr Drain pipe shelter .55
650 A105 80fr Shoveling sand 2.15
651 A105 150fr Children, house model 4.00
a. Souvenir sheet of 4, #648-651 7.00
Nos. 648-651 (4) 7.00

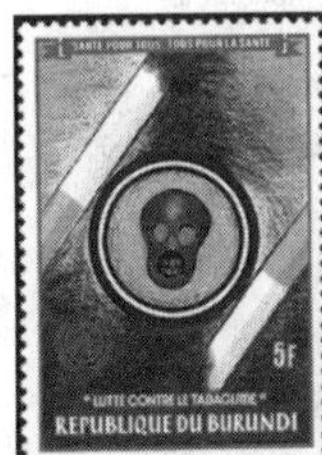

A106

A107

1987(?) **Litho.** *Perf. 14*

652 A106 5fr shown .20
653 A106 20fr Skull, lungs .30
654 A106 80fr Cigarette, face 1.25
Nos. 652-654 (3) 1.75

WHO Anti-smoking campaign.

No. 613 Surcharged

1989 **Photo.** *Perf. 13*

654D A98 80fr on 30fr, pair #e.-f.

Numbers have been reserved for additional values in this set.

1990 **Litho.** *Perf. 14*

655 A107 5fr red lil & multi .20
656 A107 10fr blue & multi .25
657 A107 20fr gray & multi .50
658 A107 30fr ol grn & multi .70
659 A107 50fr brt blue & multi 1.25
660 A107 80fr grn bl & multi 2.00
a. Souv. sheet of 6, #655-660, perf. 13½ 4.75
Nos. 655-660 (6) 4.90

Visit of Pope John Paul II.

Animals A108

1991, Oct. 4 **Litho.** *Perf. 14*

661 A108 5fr Hippopotamus .20
662 A108 10fr Chickens .20
663 A108 20fr Lion .30
664 A108 30fr Elephant .50
665 A108 50fr Guinea fowl .80
666 A108 80fr Crocodile 1.25
a. Souv. sheet of 6, #661-666, perf. 13½ 3.25
Nos. 661-666 (6) 3.25

No. 666a exists imperf.

Flowers — A108a

1992, June 2 Litho. *Perf. 14*

666B A108a 15fr Impatiens petersiana .40
666C A108a 20fr Lachenalia aloides .50
666D A108a 30fr Nymphaea lotus .85
666E A108a 50fr Clivia miniata 1.25
f. Souvenir sheet of 4, #666B-666E, perf. 13½ 3.00
Nos. 666B-666E (4) 3.00

A109

Native Music and Dancing A110

15fr, Native drummer. 30fr, Two dancers. 115fr, Drummers. 200fr, Five dancers.

1992, Apr. 2 Litho. *Perf. 14*

667 A109 15fr multicolored .25
668 A109 30fr multicolored .50
669 A110 115fr multicolored 1.75
670 A110 200fr multicolored 3.00
a. Souvenir sheet 5.75
Nos. 667-670 (4) 5.50

No. 670a contains one each of Nos. 667-668, perf. 13x13½, and Nos. 669-670, perf. 13½x13.

Independence, 30th Anniv. — A111

30fr, 140fr, People with flag. 85fr, 115fr, Natl. flag. 110fr, 200fr, Monument. 120fr, 250fr, Map.

1992, June 30 Litho. *Perf. 15*

671 A111 30fr multi .35
672 A111 85fr multi 1.00
673 A111 110fr multi, vert. 1.25
674 A111 115fr multi 1.25
675 A111 120fr multi, vert. 1.40
676 A111 140fr multi 1.60
677 A111 200fr multi, vert. 2.25
678 A111 250fr multi, vert. 3.00
Nos. 671-678 (8) 12.10

Discovery of America, 500th Anniv. A112

Columbus' fleet, globe and: 200fr, Pre-Columbian artifacts. 400fr, Fruits and vegetables.

1992, Oct. 12 Litho. *Perf. 15*

679 A112 200fr multicolored 3.00
680 A112 400fr multicolored 6.25

Felis Serval A113

1992, Oct. 16

681 A113 30fr shown .40
682 A113 130fr Two seated 1.60
683 A113 200fr One standing, one lying 2.50
684 A113 220fr Two faces 3.00
Nos. 681-684 (4) 7.50

World Wildlife Fund.

Mushrooms A114

1992 Summer Olympics, Barcelona A115

Designs: 10fr, Russula ingens. 15fr, Russula brunneorigida. 20fr, Amanita zambiana. 30fr, Russula subfistulosa. 75fr, 85fr, Russula meleagris. 100fr, Russula immaculata. 110fr, like #685. 115fr, like #686. 120fr, 130fr, Russula sejuncta. 250fr, Afroboletus luteolus.

1992-93 *Perf. 11½x12*

Granite Paper

685 A114 10fr multicolored .20
686 A114 15fr multicolored .25
687 A114 20fr multicolored .30
688 A114 30fr multicolored .50
689 A114 75fr multicolored 1.10
690 A114 85fr multicolored 1.40
691 A114 100fr multicolored 1.50
691A A114 110fr multicolored 1.60
691B A114 115fr multicolored 1.75
692 A114 120fr multicolored 1.90
693 A114 130fr multicolored 2.00
694 A114 250fr multicolored 3.75
Nos. 685-694 (12) 16.25

Issued: 110fr, 115fr, 1993; others, 9/30/92.

1992, Nov. 6 *Perf. 15*

695 A115 130fr Runners 2.00
696 A115 500fr Hurdler 7.75

A116

A116a

Christmas (Details of Adoration of the Kings, by Gentile da Fabriano): a, 100fr, Crowd, horses. b, 130fr, Kings. c, 250fr, Nativity scene.

1992, Dec. 7 Litho. *Perf. 11½*

697 A116 Strip of 3, #a.-c. 5.25
d. Souvenir sheet of 3, #697a-697c 6.50

Nos. 697a-697c have white border. No. 697d has continuous design and sold for 580fr.

1992, Dec. 5 Litho. *Perf. 15*

Designs: 200fr, Emblems. 220fr, Profile of person made from fruits and vegetables.

697E A116a 200fr multicolored 5.25
697F A116a 220fr multicolored 5.75

Intl. Conference on Nutrition, Rome.

European Common Market A117

Designs: 130fr, Flags, stars. 500fr, Europe, Africa, clasped hands, stars.

1993, Mar. 29 Litho. *Perf. 15*

698 A117 130fr multicolored 1.50
699 A117 500fr multicolored 5.75

1994 World Cup Soccer Championships, US — A118

Players, stadium, US flag and: 130fr, Statue of Liberty. 200fr, Golden Gate Bridge.

1993, July 5 Litho. *Perf. 15*

700 A118 130fr multicolored 1.50
701 A118 200fr multicolored 2.25

Traditional Musical Instruments — A119

1993, Apr. 30 Litho. *Perf. 15*

702 A119 200fr Indonongo 2.25
703 A119 220fr Ingoma 2.50
704 A119 250fr Ikembe 2.75
705 A119 300fr Umuduri 3.50
Nos. 702-705 (4) 11.00

A120

A121

1993, June 4 Litho. *Perf. 11½*

706 A120 130fr Papilio bromius 1.50
707 A120 200fr Charaxes eupale 2.25
708 A120 250fr Cymothoe caenis 2.75
709 A120 300fr Graphium ridleyanus 3.50
a. Souvenir sheet of 4, #706-709 11.50
Nos. 706-709 (4) 10.00

No. 709a sold for 980fr.

1993, Dec. 9 *Perf. 14*

710 A121 100fr Cattle 1.10
711 A121 120fr Sheep 1.40
712 A121 130fr Pigs 1.50
713 A121 250fr Goats 2.75
Nos. 710-713 (4) 6.75

Christmas — A122

Rock Stars — A123

Natives adoring Christ Child: a, 100fr, Woman carrying baby, two people kneeling. b, 130fr, With Christ Child. 250fr, c, Woman carrying baby, three other people.

1993, Dec. 10 *Perf. 11½*

714 A122 Strip of 3, #a.-c. 5.00
d. Souvenir sheet of 3, #714a-714c 6.00

#714a-714c have white border. #714d has continuous design and sold for 580fr.

1994 Litho. *Perf. 15*

715 A123 60fr Elvis Presley .65
716 A123 115fr Mick Jagger 1.25
717 A123 120fr John Lennon 1.25
718 A123 200fr Michael Jackson 2.25
a. Souvenir sheet, #715-718 6.50
Nos. 715-718 (4) 5.40

No. 718a sold for 600fr.

A124

A125

1994, Oct. 10 Litho. *Perf. 15*

719 A124 150fr multicolored 1.10

Intl. Olympic Committee, cent.

1994, Dec. 14 Photo. *Perf. 15*

Christmas (Madonna and Child): a, 115fr, Chinese. b, 120fr, Japanese. c, 250fr, Polish.

720 A125 Strip of 3, #a.-c. 5.00
d. Souvenir sheet of 1, #720c 2.75

A126

A127

115fr, FAO, 50th anniv. 120fr, UN, 50th anniv.

1995, Feb. 21 Litho. *Perf. 11½*

721 A126 115fr multicolored 1.25
722 A126 120fr multicolored 1.25

1995 Litho. *Perf. 11½*

Flowers: 15fr, Cassia didymobotrya. 20fr, Mitragyna rubrostipulosa. 30fr, Phytolacca dodecandra. 85fr, Acanthus pubescens. 100fr, Bulbophyllum comatum. 110fr, Angraecum evradianum. 115fr, Eulophia burundiensis. 120fr, Habenaria adolphii.

Granite Paper

723 A127	15fr multicolored	.20	
724 A127	20fr multicolored	.20	
725 A127	30fr multicolored	.30	
726 A127	85fr multicolored	.80	
727 A127	100fr multicolored	.90	
728 A127	110fr multicolored	1.00	
729 A127	115fr multicolored	1.00	
730 A127	120fr multicolored	1.10	
	Nos. 723-730 (8)	5.50	

Transportation Methods — A128

30fr, Otraco bus. 115fr, Transintra semi truck. 120fr, Arnolac tugboat. 250fr, Air Burundi airplane.

1995, Nov. 16 Litho. *Perf. 11½*

731 A128	30fr multicolored	.45	
732 A128	115fr multicolored	1.75	
733 A128	120fr multicolored	1.75	
734 A128	250fr multicolored	3.50	
	Nos. 731-734 (4)	7.45	

A129

A130

Christmas (African sculpture): a, 100fr, Boy with panga, basket on head. b, 130fr, Boy carrying sheaf of wheat. c, 250fr, Mother, children.

1995, Dec. 26 Litho. *Perf. 11½x12*

735 A129	Strip of 3, #a.-c.	2.25	
d.	Souvenir sheet of 3, #735a-735c	2.25	

1996, June 28 Litho. *Perf. 14*

Athlete, national flag: 130fr, Venuste Niyongabo. 500fr, Arthemon Hatungimana.

736 A130	130fr multicolored	.65	
737 A130	500fr multicolored	2.50	

1996 Summer Olympic Games, Atlanta.

Birds A131

Designs: 15fr, Hagedashia hagedash. 20fr, Alopochen aegyptiacus. 30fr, Haliaeetus vocifer. 120fr, Ardea goliath. 165fr, Balearica regulorum. 220fr, Actophilornis africana.

1996 Litho. *Perf. 14*

740 A131	15fr multicolored	.20	
741 A131	20fr multicolored	.20	
742 A131	30fr multicolored	.30	
743 A131	120fr multicolored	1.10	
744 A131	165fr multicolored	1.60	
745 A131	220fr multicolored	2.00	
	Nos. 740-745 (6)	5.40	

Fish of Lake Tanganyika A132

Designs: 30fr, Julidochromis malieri. 115fr, Cyphotilapia frontosa. 120fr, Lamprologus brichardi. 250fr, Synodonis petricola.

1996, June 4 Litho. *Perf. 11¾x11½*

746 A132	30fr multicolored	.20	.20
747 A132	115fr multicolored	.40	.40
748 A132	120fr multicolored	.40	.40
749 A132	250fr multicolored	.85	.85
a.	Souv. sheet, #746-749, perf 11¾	2.10	2.10
	Nos. 746-749 (4)	1.85	1.85

No. 749a sold for 615fr.

Although ostensibly issued in 1996, this set was not available in the philatelic marketplace until 1999.

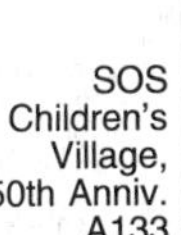

SOS Children's Village, 50th Anniv. A133

100fr, Children in Village. 250fr, Children, flags. 270fr, Children around flagpole.

1998, Dec. 26 Litho. *Perf. 14*

750 A133	100fr multicolored	.35	.35
751 A133	250fr multicolored	.85	.85
752 A133	270fr multicolored	.90	.90
	Nos. 750-752 (3)	2.10	2.10

Christmas — A134

Various paintings of Madonna and Child.

1999, Jan. 19 *Perf. 11¾*

Frame color

753 A134	100fr green	.35	.35
754 A134	130fr yellow brown	.45	.45
755 A134	250fr rose	.85	.85
a.	Souvenir sheet of 3, #753-755	2.00	2.00
	Nos. 753-755 (3)	1.65	1.65

Nos. 753-755 are dated "1996," "1997," and "1998," respectively.

No. 755a sold for 580fr.

Diana, Princess of Wales (1961-97) A135

Denominations: a, 100fr. b, 250fr. c, 300fr.

1999, Sept. 30 *Perf. 13¾*

756 A135	Sheet of 6, 2 each #a.-c.	4.50	4.50

Fight Against Hunger — A136

2000, Feb. 28 Litho. *Perf. 14*

757 A136	350fr Danny Kaye	1.10	1.10

Issued in sheets of 5.

Space — A137

No. 758, horiz.: a, Space plane (2003). b, Reuseable space plane. c, Future space ship. d, Galileo. e, Space telescope. f, Space platform. g, Satellite launched Feb. 17, 1996. h, Cassini. i, Solar probe. j, Vehicle without fenders. k, Vehicle with fenders. l, Spacecraft for Mars.

Illustration reduced.

2000, July 24 Litho. *Perf. 14*

758 A137	165fr Sheet of 12, #a-l	5.25	5.25

Souvenir Sheet

759 A137	1500fr Newton's telescope	4.00	4.00

SEMI-POSTAL STAMPS

Prince Louis Rwagasore — SP1

Prince and Stadium SP2

#B3, B6, Prince, memorial monument.

Perf. 14x13, 13x14

1963, Feb. 15 Photo. Unwmk.

B1 SP1	50c + 25c brt vio	.20	.20
B2 SP2	1fr + 50c red org & dk bl	.20	.20
B3 SP2	1.50fr + 75c lem & dk vio	.20	.20
B4 SP1	3.50fr + 1.50fr lil rose	.20	.20
B5 SP2	5fr + 2fr rose pink & dk bl	.20	.20
B6 SP2	6.50fr + 3fr gray ol & dk vio	.20	.20
	Nos. B1-B6 (6)	1.20	1.20

Issued in memory of Prince Louis Rwagasore (1932-61), son of King Mwami Mwambutsa IV and Prime Minister. The surtax was for the stadium and monument in his honor.

Red Cross Type of Regular Issue

Souvenir Sheet

1963, Sept. 26 Litho. *Imperf.*

B7	Sheet of 4	2.00	2.00
a.	A5 4fr + 2fr fawn, red & black	.30	.30
b.	A5 8fr + 2fr green, red & black	.40	.40
c.	A5 10fr + 2fr gray, red & black	.45	.45
d.	A5 20fr + 2fr ultra, red & black	.65	.65

Surtax for Red Cross work in Burundi.

Olympic Type of Regular Issue

Souvenir Sheet

Designs: 18fr+2fr, Hurdling, horiz. 20fr+5fr, Vaulting, horiz.

1964, Nov. 18 *Perf. 13½*

B8	Sheet of 2	3.00	2.75
a.	A13 18fr + 2fr yel grn & multi	1.25	1.00
b.	A13 20fr + 5fr brt pink & multi	1.25	1.00

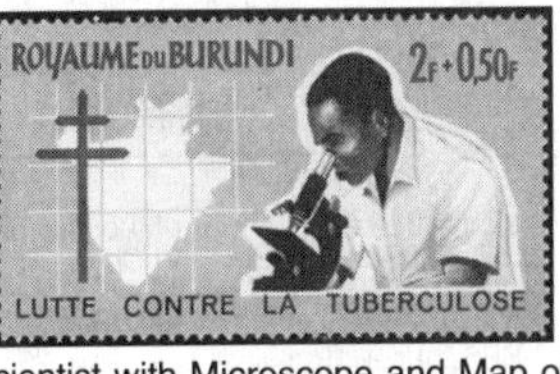

Scientist with Microscope and Map of Burundi — SP3

Lithographed and Photogravure

1965, Jan. 28 Unwmk. *Perf. 14½*

B9 SP3	2fr + 50c multi	.20	.20
B10 SP3	4fr + 1.50fr multi	.20	.20
B11 SP3	5fr + 2.50fr multi	.20	.20
B12 SP3	8fr + 3fr multi	.25	.20
B13 SP3	10fr + 5fr multi	.40	.20
	Nos. B9-B13 (5)	1.25	1.00

Souvenir Sheet

Perf. 13x13½

B14 SP3	10fr + 10fr multi	.85	.85

Issued for the fight against tuberculosis.

Coat of Arms, 10fr Coin, Reverse SP4

Designs (Coins of Various Denominations): 4fr+50c, 8fr+50c, 15fr+50c, 40fr+50c, King Mwambutsa IV, obverse.

Lithographed; Embossed on Gilt Foil

1965, Aug. 9 *Imperf.*

Diameter: 39mm

B15 SP4	2fr + 50c crim & org	.20	.20
B16 SP4	4fr + 50c ultra & ver	.20	.20

Diameter: 45mm

B17 SP4	6fr + 50c org & gray	.20	.20
B18 SP4	8fr + 50c bl & mag	.20	.20

Diameter: 56mm

B19 SP4	12fr + 50c lt grn & red lil	.25	.25
B20 SP4	15fr + 50c yel grn & lt lil	.30	.30

Diameter: 67mm

B21 SP4	25fr + 50c vio bl & buff	.50	.50
B22 SP4	40fr + 50c brt pink & red brn	.75	.75
	Nos. B15-B22 (8)	2.60	2.60

Stamps are backed with patterned paper in blue, orange and pink engine-turned design.

Prince Louis Rwagasore and Pres. John F. Kennedy SP5

4fr+1fr, 20fr+5fr, Prince Louis, memorial. 20fr+2fr, 40fr+5fr, Pres. John F. Kennedy, library shelves. 40fr+2fr, King Mwambutsa IV at Kennedy grave, Arlington, vert.

1966, Jan. 21 Photo. Perf. 13½

B23 SP5 4fr + 1fr gray bl & dk brn .20 .20
B24 SP5 10fr + 1fr pale grn, ind & brn .20 .20
B25 SP5 20fr + 2fr lil & dp grn .40 .20
B26 SP5 40fr + 2fr gray grn & dk brn .65 .20
Nos. B23-B26 (4) 1.45 .80

Souvenir Sheet

B27 Sheet of 2 1.50 1.00
a. SP5 20fr + 5fr gray bl & dk brn .50 .45
b. SP5 40fr + 5fr lilac & dp grn .75 .50

Issued in memory of Prince Louis Rwagasore and President John F. Kennedy.

Republic

Winston Churchill and St. Paul's, London SP6

Designs: 15fr+2fr, Tower of London and Churchill. 20fr+3fr, Big Ben and Churchill.

1967, Mar. 23 Photo. Perf. 13½

B28 SP6 4fr + 1fr multi .20 .20
B29 SP6 15fr + 2fr multi .35 .20
B30 SP6 20fr + 3fr multi .45 .20
Nos. B28-B30 (3) 1.00 .60

Issued in memory of Sir Winston Churchill (1874-1965), statesman and World War II leader.

A souvenir sheet contains one airmail stamp, 50fr+5fr, with Churchill portrait centered. Size: 80x80mm. Exists perf. and imperf. Value, each sheet, $3.50.

Nos. B28-B30 Overprinted

1967, July 14 Photo. Perf. 13½

B31 SP6 4fr + 1fr multi .20 .20
B32 SP6 15fr + 2fr multi .40 .20
B33 SP6 20fr + 3fr multi .65 .30
Nos. B31-B33 (3) 1.25 .70

50th anniversary of Lions International. Exist with dates transposed.

The souvenir sheets described below No. B30 also received this Lions overprint. Value, each $3.50.

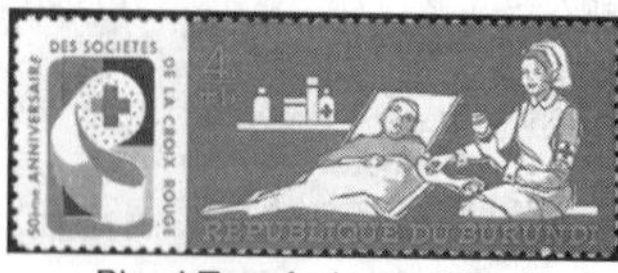

Blood Transfusion and Red Cross — SP7

Designs: 7fr+1fr, Stretcher bearers and wounded man. 11fr+1fr, Surgical team. 17fr+1fr, Nurses tending blood bank.

1969, June 26 Photo. Perf. 13½

B34 SP7 4fr + 1fr multi .20 .20
B35 SP7 7fr + 1fr multi .20 .20
B36 SP7 11fr + 1fr multi .30 .20
B37 SP7 17fr + 1fr multi .30 .20
Nos. B34-B37,CB9-CB11 (7) 2.60 1.40

League of Red Cross Societies, 50th anniv.

Pope Paul VI and Map of Africa — SP8

3fr+2fr, 17fr+2fr, Pope Paul VI. 10fr+2fr, Flag made of flags of African Nations. 14fr+2fr, View of St. Peter's, Rome. 40fr+2fr, 40fr+5fr, Martyrs of Uganda. 50fr+2fr, 50fr+5fr, Pope on Throne.

1969, Sept. 12 Photo. Perf. 13½

B38 SP8 3fr + 2fr multi, vert. .20 .20
B39 SP8 5fr + 2fr multi .20 .20
B40 SP8 10fr + 2fr multi .30 .20
B41 SP8 14fr + 2fr multi .40 .20
B42 SP8 17fr + 2fr multi, vert. .50 .20
B43 SP8 40fr + 2fr multi 1.00 .20
B44 SP8 50fr + 2fr multi 1.10 .20
Nos. B38-B44 (7) 3.70 1.40

Souvenir Sheet

B45 Sheet of 2 2.00 1.75
a. SP8 40fr + 5fr multi .90 .75
b. SP8 50fr + 5fr multi 1.00 .90

Visit of Pope Paul VI to Uganda, 7/31-8/2.

Virgin and Child, by Albrecht Dürer — SP9

Christmas (Paintings): 11fr+1fr, Madonna of the Eucharist, by Sandro Botticelli. 20fr+1fr, Holy Family, by El Greco.

1970, Dec. 14 Photo. Perf. 13½
Gold Frame

B46 SP9 6.50fr + 1fr multi .20 .20
B47 SP9 11fr + 1fr multi .25 .20
B48 SP9 20fr + 1fr multi .40 .20
a. Souv. sheet of 3, #B46-B48 .90 .90
Nos. B46-B48,CB12-CB14 (6) 2.20 1.20

Nos. 376-378 Surcharged in Gold and Black

1971, Nov. 27

B49 A51 3fr + 1fr multi .20 .20
B50 A51 5fr + 1fr multi .20 .20
B51 A51 6fr + 1fr multi .20 .20
a. Souvenir sheet of 3 .55 .55
Nos. B49-B51,CB19-CB21 (6) 1.90 1.20

UNICEF, 25th anniv. #B51a contains 3 stamps similar to #B49-B51 with 2fr surtax each.

"La Polenta," by Pietro Longhi SP10

Designs: 3fr+1fr, Archangel Michael, Byzantine icon from St. Mark's 6fr+1fr, "Gossip," by Pietro Longhi. 11fr+1fr, "Diana's Bath," by Giovanni Batista Pittoni. All stamps inscribed UNESCO.

1971, Dec. 27

B52 SP10 3fr + 1fr gold & multi .20 .20
B53 SP10 5fr + 1fr gold & multi .20 .20
B54 SP10 6fr + 1fr gold & multi .20 .20
B55 SP10 11fr + 1fr gold & multi .30 .20
a. Souvenir sheet of 4 .75 .50
Nos. B52-B55,CB22-CB25 (8) 2.40 1.60

The surtax was for the UNESCO campaign to save the treasures of Venice. No. B55a contains 4 stamps similar to Nos. B52-B55, but with 2fr surtax. Sheet exists imperf.

Nos. 408-410 Surcharged "+1F" in Silver

1972, Dec. 12 Photo. Perf. 13½

B56 A57 5fr + 1fr multi .20 .20
B57 A57 10fr + 1fr multi .25 .20
B58 A57 15fr + 1fr multi .30 .20
a. Souvenir sheet of 3 .75 .70
Nos. B56-B58,CB26-CB28 (6) 2.10 1.20

Christmas 1972. No. B58a contains 3 stamps similar to Nos. B56-B58, but with 2fr surtax.

Nos. 441-443 Surcharged "+1F" in Silver

1973, Dec. 14 Photo. Perf. 13

B59 A64 5fr + 1fr multi .20 .20
B60 A64 10fr + 1fr multi .20 .20
B61 A64 15fr + 1fr multi .30 .20
a. Souvenir sheet of 3 .65 .65
Nos. B59-B61,CB29-CB31 (6) 2.00 1.20

Christmas 1973. No. B61a contains 3 stamps similar to Nos. B59-B61 with 2fr surtax each.

Christmas Type of 1974

1974, Dec. 2 Photo. Perf. 13

B62 A70 5fr + 1fr multi .20 .20
B63 A70 10fr + 1fr multi .20 .20
B64 A70 15fr + 1fr multi .30 .20
a. Souvenir sheet of 3 .75 .75
Nos. B62-B64,CB32-CB34 (6) 2.20 1.50

No. B64a contains 3 stamps similar to Nos. B62-B64 with 2fr surtax each.

Nos. 485-487 Surcharged "+ 1F" in Silver and Black

1975, Dec. 22 Photo. Perf. 13
Pairs, #a.-b.

B65 A73 5fr + 1fr #485 .25
B66 A73 13fr + 1fr #486 .60
B67 A73 27fr + 1fr #487 1.00
c. Souvenir sheet of 6 2.50
Nos. B65-B67,CB35-CB37 (6) 5.15

Michelangelo Buonarroti (1475-1564), 500th birth anniversary. No. B67c contains 6 stamps similar to Nos. B65a-B67b with 2fr surcharge each.

Nos. 504-506 Surcharged "+1f" in Silver and Black

1976, Nov. 25 Photo. Perf. 13½

B71 A76 5fr + 1fr multi .20
B72 A76 13fr + 1fr multi .25
B73 A76 27fr + 1fr multi .40
a. Souvenir sheet of 3 .85
Nos. B71-B73,CB41-CB43 (6) 2.25

Christmas 1976. No. B73a contains 3 stamps similar to Nos. B71-B73 with 2fr surtax each.

Nos. 531-533 Surcharged "+1fr" in Silver and Black

1977 Photo. Perf. 14x13

B74 A83 5fr + 1fr multi .20
B75 A83 13fr + 1fr multi .25
B76 A83 27fr + 1fr multi .40
a. Souvenir sheet of 3 .85
Nos. B74-B76,CB44-CB46 (6) 2.25

Christmas 1977. No. B76a contains 3 stamps similar to Nos. B74-B76 with 2fr surtax each.

Christmas Type of 1979

1979, Feb. Photo. Perf. 14x13

B77 A86 13fr + 1fr multi .25
B78 A86 17fr + 1fr multi .30
B79 A86 27fr + 1fr multi .40
B80 A86 31fr + 1fr multi .50
B81 A86 40fr + 1fr multi .60
Nos. B77-B81 (5) 2.05

IYC Type of 1979

1979, July 19 Photo. Perf. 14

B82 Sheet of 4 1.25 1.00
a. A88 10fr + 2fr like #557 .20 .20
b. A88 20fr + 2fr like #558 .25 .20
c. A88 27fr + 2fr like #559 .30 .20
d. A88 50fr + 2fr like #560 .55 .30

Christmas Type of 1979

1979, Dec. 10 Photo. Perf. 13½

B83 A89 20fr + 1fr like #561 .30
B84 A89 27fr + 1fr like #562 .40
B85 A89 31fr + 1fr like #563 .50
B86 A89 50fr + 2fr like #564 .80
Nos. B83-B86 (4) 2.00

Christmas Type of 1980

1981, Jan. 16 Photo. Perf. 13½x13

B87 A92 10fr + 1fr like #579 .20
B88 A92 30fr + 1fr like #580 .30
B89 A92 40fr + 1fr like #581 .40
B90 A92 50fr + 1fr like #582 .50
Nos. B87-B90 (4) 1.40

Christmas Type of 1983

1983, Nov. 2 Litho. Perf. 14½x13½

B91 A97 10fr + 1fr like #607 .20
B92 A97 25fr + 1fr like #608 .40
B93 A97 30fr + 1fr like #609 .50
B94 A97 50fr + 1fr like #610 .75
Nos. B91-B94 (4) 1.85

Christmas Type of 1984

1984, Dec. 15 Perf. 13½

B95 A101 10fr + 1fr like #629 .20
B96 A101 25fr + 1fr like #630 .40
B97 A101 30fr + 1fr like #631 .50
B98 A101 50fr + 1fr like #632 .75
Nos. B95-B98 (4) 1.85

Multi-party Elections, 1st Anniv.
SP11 SP12

30fr+10fr, Pres. Buyoya handing Baton of Power to Pres. Ndadaye. 110fr+10fr, Pres. Ndadaye giving inauguration speech. 115fr+10fr, Arms, map of Burundi. 120fr+10fr, Warrior, flag of Burundi, trees, map of Burundi.

1994, Oct. 20 Litho. Perf. 15

B99 SP11 30fr +10fr multi .30
B100 SP11 110fr +10fr multi .90
B101 SP12 115fr +10fr multi .95
B102 SP12 120fr +10fr multi 1.00
Nos. B99-B102 (4) 3.15

AIR POST STAMPS

Animal Type of Regular Issue

6fr, Zebra. 8fr, Cape buffalo (bubalis). 10fr, Impala. 14fr, Hippopotamus. 15fr, Defassa waterbuck. 20fr, Cheetah. 50fr, Elephant.

Unwmk.

1964, July 2 Litho. Perf. 14
Size: 42x21mm, 21x42mm

C1 A9 6fr multi .20 .20
C2 A9 8fr multi .20 .20
C3 A9 10fr multi, vert. .25 .20
C4 A9 14fr multi .35 .20

C5 A9 15fr multi, vert. .40 .20

Size: 53x32½mm

C6 A9 20fr multi .60 .20
C7 A9 50fr multi 1.75 .40
Nos. C1-C7 (7) 3.75 1.60

Bird Type of Regular Issue

Birds: 6fr, Secretary bird. 8fr, African anhinga. 10fr, African peacock. 14fr, Bee eater. 15fr, Yellow-billed stork. 20fr, Saddle-billed stork. 50fr, Abyssinian ground hornbill. 75fr, Martial eagle. 130fr, Lesser flamingo.

1965, June 10 Litho. *Perf. 14*

Size: 26x43mm

C8 A14 6fr multi .20 .20
C9 A14 8fr multi .20 .20
C10 A14 10fr multi .30 .20
C11 A14 14fr multi .30 .20
C12 A14 15fr multi .40 .20

Size: 33x53mm

C13 A14 20fr multi .60 .20
C14 A14 50fr multi 1.25 .20
C15 A14 75fr multi 1.75 .25
C16 A14 130fr multi 3.00 .35
Nos. C8-C16 (9) 8.00 2.00

For overprints see Nos. C35A-C35I.

Flower Type of Regular Issue

Flowers: 6fr, Dissotis. 8fr, Crossandra. 10fr, Ansellia. 14fr, Thunbergia. 15fr, Schizoglossum. 20fr, Gazania. 50fr, Protea. 75fr, Hibiscus. 130fr, Markhamia.

1966, Oct. 10 Unwmk. *Perf. 13½*

Size: 31x31mm

C17 A17 6fr multi .20 .20
C18 A17 8fr multi .20 .20
C19 A17 10fr multi .25 .20
C20 A17 14fr multi .30 .20
C21 A17 15fr multi .40 .20

Size: 39x39mm

C22 A17 20fr multi .45 .20
C23 A17 50fr multi 1.10 .20
C24 A17 75fr multi 1.60 .25
C25 A17 130fr multi 2.50 .30
Nos. C17-C25 (9) 7.00 1.95

For overprints see Nos. C27-C35.

Tapestry Type of Regular Issue

Souvenir Sheet

1966, Nov. 4 Unwmk. *Perf. 13½*

C26 A18 Sheet of 7 (14fr) 1.50 1.00

See note after No. 158.

REPUBLIC

Nos. C17-C25 Overprinted

1967 Litho. *Perf. 13½*

Size: 31x31mm

C27 A17 6fr multi .20 .20
C28 A17 8fr multi .25 .20
C29 A17 10fr multi .25 .20
C30 A17 14fr multi .50 .20
C31 A17 15fr multi .50 .20

Size: 39x39mm

C32 A17 20fr multi .70 .20
C33 A17 50fr multi 1.90 .50
C34 A17 75fr multi 3.00 .50
C35 A17 130fr multi 4.00 1.10
Nos. C27-C35 (9) 11.30 3.30

Nos. C8-C16 Overprinted "REPUBLIQUE / DU / BURUNDI" and Horizontal Bar

1967 Litho. *Perf. 14*

Size: 26x43mm

C35A A14 6fr multi *.20*
C35B A14 8fr multi *.20*
C35C A14 10fr multi *.20*
C35D A14 14fr multi *.30*
C35E A14 15fr multi *.50*

Size: 33x53mm

C35F A14 20fr multi *.75*
C35G A14 50fr multi *1.90*
C35H A14 75fr multi *3.00*
C35I A14 130fr multi *3.50*
Nos. C35A-C35I (9) *10.55*

African Art Type of Regular Issue

10fr, Spirit of Bakutu figurine, Equatorial Africa. 14fr, Pearl throne of Sultan of the Bamum, Cameroun. 17fr, Bronze head of Mother Queen of Benin, Nigeria. 24fr, Statue of 109th Bakouba king, Kata-Mbula, Central Congo. 26fr, Baskets and lances, Burundi.

1967, June 5 Photo. *Perf. 13½*

C36 A20 10fr gold & multi .20 .20
C37 A20 14fr gold & multi .20 .20
C38 A20 17fr gold & multi .20 .20
C39 A20 24fr gold & multi .25 .20
C40 A20 26fr gold & multi .40 .20
Nos. C36-C40 (5) 1.25 1.00

Boy Scout Type of Regular Issue

10fr, Scouts on hiking trip. 14fr, Cooking at campfire. 17fr, Lord Baden-Powell. 24fr, Boy Scout & Cub Scout giving Scout sign. 26fr, First aid.

1967, Aug. 9 *Perf. 13½*

C41 A21 10fr gold & multi .20 .20
C42 A21 14fr gold & multi .25 .20
C43 A21 17fr gold & multi .30 .20
C44 A21 24fr gold & multi .40 .20
C45 A21 26fr gold & multi .70 .20
Nos. C41-C45 (5) 1.85 1.00

A souvenir sheet of 2 contains one each of #C44-C45 and 2 labels in the designs of #208-209 with commemorative inscriptions was issued 1/8/68. Size: 100x100mm

Fish Type of Regular Issue

Designs: Various Tropical Fish

1967, Sept. 8 Photo. *Perf. 13½*

Size: 50x23mm

C46 A19 6fr multi .20 .20
C47 A19 8fr multi .20 .20
C48 A19 10fr multi .30 .20
C49 A19 14fr multi .40 .20
C50 A19 15fr multi .40 .20

Size: 58x27mm

C51 A19 20fr multi .50 .20
C52 A19 50fr multi 1.25 .20
C53 A19 75fr multi 2.00 .20
C54 A19 130fr multi 3.25 .25
Nos. C46-C54 (9) 8.50 1.85

Boeing 707 of Air Congo and ITY Emblem — AP1

Designs: 14fr, Boeing 727 of Sabena over lake. 17fr, Vickers VC10 of East African Airways over lake. 26fr, Boeing 727 of Sabena over airport.

1967, Nov. 3 Photo. *Perf. 13*

C55 AP1 10fr blk, yel brn & sil .20 .20
C56 AP1 14fr blk, org & sil .20 .20
C57 AP1 17fr blk, brt bl & sil .25 .20
C58 AP1 26fr blk, brt rose lil & sil .35 .20
Nos. C55-C58 (4) 1.00 .80

Opening of the jet airport at Bujumbura and for International Tourist Year, 1967.

Paintings Type of Regular Issue

Paintings: 17fr, Woman with Cat, by Renoir. 24fr, The Jewish Bride, by Rembrandt, horiz. 26fr, Pope Innocent X, by Velazquez.

1968, Mar. 29 Photo. *Perf. 13½*

C59 A26 17fr multi .35 .20
C60 A26 24fr multi .45 .20
C61 A26 26fr multi .60 .20
Nos. C59-C61 (3) 1.40 .60

Issued in sheets of 6.

Space Type of Regular Issue

14fr, Moon Probe. 18fr, Russian astronaut walking in space. 25fr, Weather satellite. 40fr, American astronaut walking in space.

1968, May 15 Photo. *Perf. 13½*

Size: 41x41mm

C62 A27 14fr sil & multi .25 .20
C63 A27 18fr sil & multi .30 .20
C64 A27 25fr sil & multi .45 .20
C65 A27 40fr sil & multi .70 .20
Nos. C62-C65 (4) 1.70 .80

Butterfly Type of Regular Issue

Butterflies: 6fr, Teracolus annae. 8fr, Graphium ridleyanus. 10fr, Cymothoe. 14fr, Charaxes eupale. 15fr, Papilio bromius. 20fr, Papilio zenobia. 50fr, Salamis aethiops. 75fr, Danais chrysippus. 130fr, Salamis temora.

1968, Sept. 9 Photo. *Perf. 13½*

Size: 38x42mm

C66 A28 6fr gold & multi .20 .20
C67 A28 8fr gold & multi .20 .20
C68 A28 10fr gold & multi .35 .20
C69 A28 14fr gold & multi .40 .20
C70 A28 15fr gold & multi .50 .20

Size: 44x49mm

C71 A28 20fr gold & multi .60 .20
C72 A28 50fr gold & multi 1.25 .20
C73 A28 75fr gold & multi 2.50 .20
C74 A28 130fr gold & multi 4.00 .20
Nos. C66-C74 (9) 10.00 1.80

Painting Type of Regular Issue

Paintings: 17fr, The Letter, by Jean H. Fragonard. 26fr, Young Woman Reading Letter, by Jan Vermeer. 40fr, Lady Folding Letter, by Elisabeth Vigée-Lebrun. 50fr, Mademoiselle Lavergne, by Jean Etienne Liotard.

1968, Sept. 30 Photo. *Perf. 13½*

C84 A29 17fr multi .25 .20
C85 A29 26fr multi .45 .20
C86 A29 40fr multi .60 .20
C87 A29 50fr multi .70 .20
Nos. C84-C87 (4) 2.00 .80

Olympic Games Type

1968, Oct. 24

C88 A30 10fr Shot put .20 .20
C89 A30 17fr Running .25 .20
C90 A30 26fr Hammer throw .40 .20
C91 A30 50fr Hurdling .70 .20
C92 A30 75fr Broad jump 1.10 .30
Nos. C88-C92 (5) 2.65 1.10

Christmas Type of 1968

Paintings: 10fr, Virgin and Child, by Correggio. 14fr, Nativity, by Federigo Baroccio. 17fr, Holy Family, by El Greco. 26fr, Adoration of the Magi, by Maino.

1968, Nov. 26 Photo. *Perf. 13½*

C93 A31 10fr multi .20 .20
C94 A31 14fr multi .25 .20
C95 A31 17fr multi .30 .20
C96 A31 26fr multi .40 .20
a. Souv. sheet of 4, #C93-C96 1.10
Nos. C93-C96 (4) 1.15 .80

For overprints see Nos. C100-C103.

Human Rights Flame, Hand and Globe — AP2

1969, Jan. 22

C97 AP2 10fr multi .20 .20
C98 AP2 14fr multi .25 .20
C99 AP2 26fr lil & multi .40 .20
Nos. C97-C99 (3) .85 .60

International Human Rights Year, 1968.

Nos. C93-C96 Overprinted in Silver

1969, Feb. 17 Photo. *Perf. 13½*

C100 A31 10fr multi .20 .20
C101 A31 14fr multi .30 .20
C102 A31 17fr multi .35 .20
C103 A31 26fr multi .50 .25
Nos. C100-C103 (4) 1.35 .85

Man's 1st flight around the moon by the US spacecraft Apollo 8, Dec. 21-27, 1968.

Moon Landing Type of 1969

Designs: 26fr, Neil A. Armstrong leaving landing module. 40fr, Astronaut on moon. 50fr, Splashdown in the Pacific.

1969, Nov. 6 Photo. *Perf. 13½*

C104 A38 26fr gold & multi .50 .25
C105 A38 40fr gold & multi .75 .40
C106 A38 50fr gold & multi .90 .45
Nos. C104-C106 (3) 2.15 1.10

Christmas Type of 1969

Paintings: 17fr, Madonna and Child, by Benvenuto da Garofalo. 26fr, Madonna and Child, by Jacopo Negretti. 50fr, Madonna and Child, by Il Giorgione. All horizontal.

1969, Dec. 2 Photo.

C107 A39 17fr gold & multi .40 .20
C108 A39 26fr gold & multi .50 .20
C109 A39 50fr gold & multi .90 .30
a. Souv. sheet of 3, #C107-C109 1.90 1.50
Nos. C107-C109 (3) 1.80 .70

Insect Type of Regular Issue

Designs: Various Beetles and Weevils.

1970 *Perf. 13½*

Size: 46x32mm

C110 A40 6fr gold & multi .20 .20
C111 A40 8fr gold & multi .20 .20
C112 A40 10fr gold & multi .20 .20
C113 A40 14fr gold & multi .30 .20
C114 A40 15fr gold & multi .35 .20

Size: 52x36mm

C115 A40 20fr gold & multi 1.00 .20
C116 A40 50fr gold & multi 2.00 .25
C117 A40 75fr gold & multi 3.00 .25
C118 A40 130fr gold & multi 3.75 .40
Nos. C110-C118 (9) 11.00 2.10

Issued: #C110-C115, 1/20; $C116-C118, 2/27.

Easter Type of 1970

Stations of the Cross, by Juan de Aranoa y Carredano: 8fr, Jesus meets the women of Jerusalem. 10fr, Jesus falls a third time. 14fr, Jesus stripped. 15fr, Jesus nailed to the cross. 18fr, Jesus dies on the cross. 20fr, Descent from the cross. 50fr, Jesus laid in the tomb.

1970, Mar. 16 Photo. *Perf. 13½*

C119 A41 8fr gold & multi .20 .20
C120 A41 10fr gold & multi .20 .20
C121 A41 14fr gold & multi .25 .20
C122 A41 15fr gold & multi .25 .20
C123 A41 18fr gold & multi .30 .20
C124 A41 20fr gold & multi .30 .20
C125 A41 50fr gold & multi .70 .30
a. Souv. sheet of 7, #C119-C125 + label 2.25 1.75
Nos. C119-C125 (7) 2.20 1.50

EXPO '70 Type of Regular Issue

Souvenir Sheet

Designs: 40fr, Tower of the Sun, vert. 50fr, Flags of participating nations, vert.

1970, May 5 Photo. *Perf. 13½*

C126 Sheet of 2 1.40 1.40
a. A42 40fr multi .50 .50
b. A42 50fr multi .60 .60

Rhinoceros Type of Regular Issue

Fauna: a, i, Camel. c, d, Dromedary. g, r, Okapi. f, m, Addax. j, o, Rhinoceros. l, p, Burundi cow (each animal in 2 different poses).

Map of the Nile: b, Delta and pyramids. e, dhow. h, Falls. k, Blue Nile and crowned crane. n, Victoria Nile and secretary bird. q, Lake Victoria and source of Nile on Mt. Gikizi. Continuous design.

1970, July 8 Photo. *Perf. 13½*

C127 Sheet of 18 5.25
a.-r. A43 14fr any single .30 .20

Publicizing the southernmost source of the Nile on Mt. Gikizi in Burundi.

UN Emblem and Headquarters, NYC — AP3

25th Anniv. of the UN (UN Emblem and): 11fr, Security Council and mural by Per Krohg. 26fr, Pope Paul VI and U Thant. 40fr, Flags in front of UN Headquarters, NYC.

1970, Oct. 23 Photo. Perf. 13½

C128 AP3 7fr gold & multi .20 .20
C129 AP3 11fr gold & multi .20 .20
C130 AP3 26fr gold & multi .40 .20
C131 AP3 40fr gold & multi .60 .20
a. Souvenir sheet of 2 1.10 .90
Nos. C128-C131 (4) 1.40 .80

No. C131a contains 2 stamps similar to Nos. C130-C131 but without "Poste Aerienne." Exists imperf.

Bird Type of Regular Issue

8fr, 14fr, 30fr, vert.; 10fr, 20fr, 50fr, horiz.

1970 Photo. Perf. 13½
Stamp size: 52x44mm

C132 A44 Block of 4 2.00 .20
a. 8fr Northern shrike .50 .20
b. 8fr European starling .50 .20
c. 8fr Yellow wagtail .50 .20
d. 8fr Bank swallow .50 .20
C133 A44 Block of 4 2.50 .20
a. 10fr Winter wren .60 .20
b. 10fr Firecrest .60 .20
c. 10fr Skylark .60 .20
d. 10fr Crested lark .60 .20
C134 A44 Block of 4 3.00 .25
a. 14fr Woodchat shrike .75 .20
b. 14fr Common rock thrush .75 .20
c. 14fr Black redstart .75 .20
d. 14fr Ring ouzel .75 .20
C135 A44 Block of 4 5.00 .35
a. 20fr European redstart 1.25 .20
b. 20fr Hedge sparrow 1.25 .20
c. 20fr Gray wagtail 1.25 .20
d. 20fr Meadow pipit 1.25 .20
C136 A44 Block of 4 7.00 .55
a. 30fr Eurasian hoopoe 1.75 .20
b. 30fr Pied flycatcher 1.75 .20
c. 30fr Great reed warbler 1.75 .20
d. 30fr Eurasian kingfisher 1.75 .20
C137 A44 Block of 4 11.00 .90
a. 50fr House martin 2.75 .20
b. 50fr Sedge warbler 2.75 .20
c. 50fr Fieldfare 2.75 .20
d. 50fr European Golden oriole 2.75 .20
Nos. C132-C137 (6) 30.50 2.45

Queen Fabiola and King Baudouin of Belgium AP4

Designs: 20fr, Pres. Michel Micombero and King Baudouin. 40fr, Pres. Micombero and coats of arms of Burundi and Belgium.

1970, Nov. 28 Photo. Perf. 13½

C140 AP4 6fr multicolored .20 .20
C141 AP4 20fr multicolored .45 .20
C142 AP4 40fr multicolored .90 .30
a. Souvenir sheet of 3 1.50 1.50
Nos. C140-C142 (3) 1.55 .70

Visit of the King and Queen of Belgium. No. C142a contains 3 stamps similar to Nos. C140-C142, but without "Poste Aerienne." No. C142a exists imperf.

Easter Type of Regular Issue

Paintings of the Resurrection: 14fr, by Louis Borrassá. 17fr, Piero della Francesca. 26fr, Michel Wohlgemuth.

1971, Apr. 2 Photo. Perf. 13½

C143 A49 14fr gold & multi .20 .20
C144 A49 17fr gold & multi .25 .20
C145 A49 26fr gold & multi .30 .20
a. Souv. sheet of 3, #C143-C145 1.00 .75
Nos. C143-C145 (3) .75 .60

Easter 1971. No. C145a sheet exists imperf.

Animal Type of Regular Issue

1971 Photo. Perf. 13½
Size: 44x44mm

C146 Strip of 4 1.50 .20
a. A48 10fr Lion .35 .20
b. A48 10fr Cape buffalo .35 .20
c. A48 10fr Hippopotamus .35 .20
d. A48 10fr Giraffe .35 .20
C147 Strip of 4 2.25 .25
a. A48 14fr Hartebeest .55 .20
b. A48 14fr Black rhinoceros .55 .20
c. A48 14fr Zebra .55 .20
d. A48 14fr Leopard .55 .20
C148 Strip of 4 3.00 .25
a. A48 17fr Grant's gazelles .75 .20
b. A48 17fr Cheetah .75 .20
c. A48 17fr African white-backed vultures .75 .20
d. A48 17fr Johnston's okapi .75 .20
C149 Strip of 4 3.50 .35
a. A48 24fr Chimpanzee .85 .20
b. A48 24fr Elephant .85 .20
c. A48 24fr Spotted Hyenas .85 .20
d. A48 24fr Beisa .85 .20
C150 Strip of 4 4.00 .40
a. A48 26fr Gorilla 1.00 .20
b. A48 26fr Gnu 1.00 .20
c. A48 26fr Warthog 1.00 .20
d. A48 26fr Cape hunting dog 1.00 .20
C151 Strip of 4 5.00 .55
a. A48 31fr Sable antelope 1.25 .20
b. A48 31fr Caracal lynx 1.25 .20
c. A48 31fr Ostriches 1.25 .20
d. A48 31fr Bongo 1.25 .20
Nos. C146-C151 (6) 19.25 2.00

For overprint and surcharges see Nos. C152, CB15-C18.

No. C146 Overprinted in Gold and Black

1971, July 20 Photo. Perf. 13½

C152 Strip of 4 .60 .20
a. A48 10fr Lion .20 .20
b. A48 10fr Cape buffalo .20 .20
c. A48 10fr Hippopotamus .20 .20
d. A48 10fr Giraffe .20 .20

Intl. Year Against Racial Discrimination.

Christmas Type of Regular Issue

Paintings of the Madonna and Child by: 14fr, Cima de Conegliano. 17fr, Fra Filippo Lippi. 31fr, Leonardo da Vinci.

1971, Nov. 2 Photo. Perf. 13½

C153 A51 14fr red & multi .30 .20
C154 A51 17fr red & multi .35 .20
C155 A51 31fr red & multi .50 .20
a. Souv. sheet of 3, #C153-C155 1.10 1.10
Nos. C153-C155 (3) 1.15 .60

Christmas 1971. No. C155a exists imperf.

For surcharges see Nos. CB19-CB21.

Spacecraft Type of Regular Issue

Souvenir Sheet

1972, Jan. 15 Photo. Perf. 13½

C156 Sheet of 6 2.50 2.00
a. A52 6fr Lunar Orbiter .20 .20
b. A52 11fr Vostok .20 .20
c. A52 14fr Luna I .25 .20
d. A52 17fr Apollo 11 astronaut on moon .35 .20
e. A52 26fr Soyuz 11 .50 .20
f. A52 40fr Lunar rover (Apollo 15) .70 .25

Sapporo '72 Type of Regular Issue

Souvenir Sheet

Emblem and: 26fr, Snow scooter. 31fr, Downhill skiing. 50fr, Bobsledding.

1972, Feb. 3

C157 Sheet of 3 1.50 1.25
a. A53 26fr silver & multi .35 .25
b. A53 31fr silver & multi .40 .30
c. A53 50fr silver & multi .65 .40

Olympic Games Type of 1972

1972, July 24 Photo. Perf. 13½

C158 A55 24fr Weight lifting .35 .20
C159 A55 26fr Hurdles .40 .20
C160 A55 31fr Discus .50 .20
C161 A55 40fr Soccer .60 .20
Nos. C158-C161 (4) 1.85 .80

Independence Type of 1972

Designs: 15fr, Prince Rwagasore, Pres. Micombero, Burundi flag, drummers. 18fr, Rwagasore, Micombero, flag, map of Africa, globe. 27fr, Micombero, flag, globe.

1972, Aug. 24 Photo. Perf. 13½

C162 A56 15fr gold & multi .25 .20
C163 A56 18fr gold & multi .30 .20
C164 A56 27fr gold & multi .45 .20
a. Souv. sheet of 3, #C162-C164 1.10 1.10
Nos. C162-C164 (3) 1.00 .60

Christmas Type of 1972

Paintings of the Madonna and Child by: 18fr, Sebastiano Mainardi. 27fr, Hans Memling. 40fr, Lorenzo Lotto.

1972, Nov. 2 Photo. Perf. 13½

C165 A57 18fr dk car & multi .30 .20
C166 A57 27fr dk car & multi .40 .20
C167 A57 40fr dk car & multi .60 .20
a. Souv. sheet of 3, #C165-C167 1.40 1.40
Nos. C165-C167 (3) 1.30 .60

For surcharges see Nos. CB26-CB28.

Orchid Type of Regular Issue

1973, Jan. 18 Photo. Perf. 13½
Size: 38x38mm

C168 A58 13fr *Thelymitra pauciflora* .80 .20
C169 A58 14fr *Miltassia* .80 .20
C170 A58 15fr *Miltonia* .90 .20
C171 A58 18fr *Platycoryne crocea* 1.00 .20
C172 A58 20fr *Cattleya trianei* 1.25 .20
C173 A58 27fr *Eulophia cucullata* 1.75 .20
C174 A58 36fr *Cymbidium hamsey* 2.25 .20
Nos. C168-C174 (7) 8.75 1.40

African Exploration Type of 1973

Designs: 15fr, Livingstone writing his diary. 18fr, "Dr. Livingstone, I presume." 27fr, Livingstone and Stanley discussing expedition.

1973, Mar. 19 Photo. Perf. 13½

C175 A59 15fr gold & multi .25 .20
C176 A59 18fr gold & multi .30 .20
C177 A59 27fr gold & multi .45 .20
a. Souv. sheet of 3 1.10 1.10
Nos. C175-C177 (3) 1.00 .60

#C177a contains 3 stamps similar to #C175-C177, but without "Poste Aerienne."

Easter Type of 1973

Paintings: 15fr, Christ at the Pillar, by Guido Reni. 18fr, Crucifixion, by Mathias Grunewald. 27fr, Descent from the Cross, by Caravaggio.

1973, Apr. 10

C178 A60 15fr gold & multi .30 .20
C179 A60 18fr gold & multi .35 .20
C180 A60 27fr gold & multi .50 .20
a. Souv. sheet of 3, #C178-C180 1.25 1.25
Nos. C178-C180 (3) 1.15 .60

INTERPOL Type of Regular Issue

Designs: 27fr, INTERPOL emblem and flag. 40fr, INTERPOL flag and emblem.

1973, May 19 Photo. Perf. 13½

C181 A61 27fr gold & multi .40 .20
C182 A61 40fr gold & multi .50 .20

Copernicus Type of Regular Issue

Designs: 15fr, Copernicus (C183a), Earth, Pluto, and Jupiter. 18fr, Copernicus (No. C184a), Venus, Saturn, Mars. 27fr, Copernicus (No. C185a), Uranus, Neptune, Mercury. 36fr, Earth and various spacecrafts.

a, UL. b, UR. c, LL. d, LR.

1973, July 27 Photo. Perf. 13½

C183 A62 15fr Block of 4, #a.-d. 1.40 .30
C184 A62 18fr Block of 4, #a.-d. 1.60 .35
C185 A62 27fr Block of 4, #a.-d. 2.00 .50
C186 A62 36fr Block of 4, #a.-d. 2.75 .70
e. Souv. sheet, #C183-C186 7.00 7.00
Nos. C183-C186 (4) 7.75 1.85

Flower-Butterfly Type of 1973

Designs: Each block of 4 contains 2 flower and 2 butterfly designs. The 10fr, 14fr, 24fr and 31fr have flower designs listed as "a" and "d" numbers, butterflies as "b" and "c" numbers; the arrangement is reversed for the 17fr and 26fr.

1973, Sept. 28 Photo. Perf. 13
Stamp Size: 35x45mm

C187 A63 Block of 4 3.00 .40
a. 10fr *Protea cynaroides* .75 .20
b. 10fr *Precis octavia* .75 .20
c. 10fr *Epiphora bauhiniae* .75 .20
d. 10fr *Gazania longiscapa* .75 .20
C188 A63 Block of 4 4.00 .50
a. 14fr *Kniphofia* 1.00 .20
b. 14fr *Cymothoe coccinata* 1.00 .20
c. 14fr *Nudaurelia zambesina* 1.00 .20
d. 14fr *Freesia refracta* 1.00 .20
C189 A63 Block of 4 5.00 .60
a. 17fr *Calotis eupompe* 1.25 .20
b. 17fr *Narcissus* 1.25 .20
c. 17fr *Cineraria hybrida* 1.25 .20
d. 17fr *Cyrestis camillus* 1.25 .20
C190 A63 Block of 4 5.50 .50
a. 24fr *Iris tingitana* 1.25 .20
b. 24fr *Papilio demodocus* 1.25 .20
c. 24fr *Catopsilia avelaneda* 1.25 .20
d. 24fr *Nerine sarniensis* 1.25 .20
C191 A63 Block of 4 6.00 .55
a. 26fr *Hypolimnas dexithea* 1.50 .20
b. 26fr *Zantedeschia tropicalis* 1.50 .20
c. 26fr *Sandersonia aurantiaca* 1.50 .20
d. 26fr *Drurya antimachus* 1.50 .20
C192 A63 Block of 4 7.00 .65
a. 31fr *Nymphaea capensis* 1.75 .20
b. 31fr *Pandoriana pandora* 1.75 .20
c. 31fr *Precis orythia* 1.75 .20
d. 31fr *Pelargonium domestica* 1.75 .20
Nos. C187-C192 (6) 30.50 3.20

Christmas Type of 1973

Virgin and Child by: 18fr, Raphael. 27fr, Pietro Perugino. 40fr, Titian.

1973, Nov. 19

C193 A64 18fr gold & multi .30 .20
C194 A64 27fr gold & multi .40 .20
C195 A64 40fr gold & multi .60 .20
a. Souv. sheet of 3, #C193-C195 1.40 1.40
Nos. C193-C195 (3) 1.30 .60

For surcharges see Nos. CB239-CB31.

Soccer Type of Regular Issue

Designs: Various soccer scenes and cup.

1974, July 4 Photo. Perf. 13

C196 A67 20fr gold & multi .30
C197 A67 26fr gold & multi .40
C198 A67 40fr gold & multi .60
Nos. C196-C198 (3) 1.30

For souvenir sheet see No. 459a.

UPU Type of 1974

#C199a, Flags over UPU Headquarters, Bern. #C199b, G.P.O., Usumbura. #C200a, Mailmen ("26F" in UR). #C200b, Mailmen ("26F" in UL). #C201a, UPU emblem. #C201b, Means of transportation. #C202a, Pigeon over globe showing Burundi. #C202b, Swiss flag, pigeon over map showing Bern.

1974, July 23

C199 A68 24fr Pair, #a.-b. 1.25
C200 A68 26fr Pair, #a.-b. 1.50
C201 A68 31fr Pair, #a.-b. 2.00
C202 A68 40fr Pair, #a.-b. 2.50
c. Souv. sheet, #C199-C202 7.50
Nos. C199-C202 (4) 7.25

Fish Type of 1974

1974, Sept. 9 Photo. Perf. 13
Size: 35x35mm

C207 A66 Block of 4 1.50 .20
a. 10fr *Haplochromis multicolor* .35 .20
b. 10fr *Pantodon buchholzi* .35 .20
c. 10fr *Tropheus duboisi* .35 .20
d. 10fr *Distichodus sexfasciatus* .35 .20
C208 A66 Block of 4 1.75 .20
a. 14fr *Pelmatochromis kribensis* .40 .20
b. 14fr *Nannaethiops tritaeniatus* .40 .20
c. 14fr *Polycentropsis abbreviata* .40 .20
d. 14fr *Hemichromis bimaculatus* .40 .20
C209 A66 Block of 4 2.50 .20
a. 17fr *Ctenopoma acutirostre* .60 .20
b. 17fr *Synodontis angelicus* .60 .20
c. 17fr *Tilapia melanopleura* .60 .20
d. 17fr *Aphyosemion bivittatum* .60 .20
C210 A66 Block of 4 3.00 .30
a. 24fr *Monodactylus argenteus* .75 .20
b. 24fr *Zanclus canescens* .75 .20
c. 24fr *Pygoplites diacanthus* .75 .20
d. 24fr *Cephalopholis argus* .75 .20
C211 A66 Block of 4 3.00 .35
a. 26fr *Priacanthus arenatus* .75 .20
b. 26fr *Pomacanthus arcutus* .75 .20
c. 26fr *Scarus guacamaia* .75 .20
d. 26fr *Zeus faber* .75 .20
C212 A66 Block of 4 4.00 .40
a. 31fr *Lactophrys quadricornis* 1.00 .20
b. 31fr *Balistes vetula* 1.00 .20
c. 31fr *Acanthurus bahianus* 1.00 .20
d. 31fr *Holocanthus ciliaris* 1.00 .20
Nos. C207-C212 (6) 15.75 1.65

Christmas Type of 1974

Paintings of the Virgin and Child: 18fr, by Hans Memling. 27fr, by Filippino Lippi. 40fr, by Lorenzo di Gredi.

1974, Nov. 7 Photo. *Perf. 13*

C213 A70 18fr gold & multi .30 .25
C214 A70 27fr gold & multi .40 .30
C215 A70 40fr gold & multi .60 .45
a. Souv. sheet of 3, #C213-C215 1.50 1.50
Nos. C213-C215 (3) 1.30 1.00

Christmas 1974. Sheets of 20 stamps and one label. No. C215a exists imperf.

Apollo-Soyuz Type of 1975

1975, July 10 Photo. *Perf. 13*

C216 A71 Block of 4 1.00
a. 27fr A.A. Leonov, V.N. Kubasov, Soviet flag .25
b. 27fr Soyuz and Soviet flag .25
c. 27fr Apollo and American flag .25
d. 27fr Slayton, Brand, Stafford, American flag .25
C217 A71 Block of 4 1.25
a. 40fr Apollo-Soyuz link-up .30
b. 40fr Apollo, blast-off .30
c. 40fr Soyuz, blast-off .30
d. 40fr Kubasov, Leonov, Slayton, Brand, Stafford .30

Nos. C216-C217 are printed in sheets of 32 containing 8 blocks of 4.

Animal Type of 1975

1975, Sept. 17 Photo. *Perf. 13½*

C218 Strip of 4 1.00
a. A72 10fr Addax .25
b. A72 10fr Roan antelope .25
c. A72 10fr Nyala .25
d. A72 10fr White rhinoceros .25
C219 Strip of 4 1.25
a. A72 14fr Mandrill .30
b. A72 14fr Eland .30
c. A72 14fr Salt's dik-dik .30
d. A72 14fr Thomson's gazelles .30
C220 Strip of 4 1.50
a. A72 17fr African small-clawed otter .35
b. A72 17fr Reed buck .35
c. A72 17fr Indian civet .35
d. A72 17fr Cape buffalo .35
C221 Strip of 4 2.00
a. A72 24fr White-tailed gnu .50
b. A72 24fr African wild asses .50
c. A72 24fr Black-and-white colobus monkey .50
d. A72 24fr Gerenuk .50
C222 Strip of 4 2.25
a. A72 26fr Dama gazelle .55
b. A72 26fr Black-backed jackal .55
c. A72 26fr Sitatungas .55
d. A72 26fr Zebra antelope .55
C223 Strip of 4 2.75
a. A72 31fr Fennec .65
b. A72 31fr Lesser kudus .65
c. A72 31fr Blesbok .65
d. A72 31fr Serval .65
Nos. C218-C223 (6) 10.75

Nos. C218-C219 Overprinted in Black and Silver with IWY Emblem and: "ANNEE INTERNATIONALE / DE LA FEMME"

1975, Nov. 19 Photo. *Perf. 13½*

C224 Strip of 4 .60 .20
a. A72 10fr Addax .20 .20
b. A72 10fr Roan antelope .20 .20
c. A72 10fr Nyala .20 .20
d. A72 10fr White rhinoceros .20 .20
C225 Strip of 4 .80 .20
a. A72 14fr Mandrill .20 .20
b. A72 14fr Oryx .20 .20
c. A72 14fr Dik-dik .20 .20
d. A72 14fr Thomson's gazelles .20 .20

International Women's Year 1975.

Nos. C222-C223 Overprinted in Black and Silver with UN Emblem and:"30ème ANNIVERSAIRE DES/ NATIONS UNIES"

1975, Nov. 19

C226 Strip of 4 1.60 .30
a. A72 26fr Dama gazelle .40 .20
b. A72 26fr Wild dog .40 .20
c. A72 26fr Sitatungas .40 .20
d. A72 26fr Striped duiker .40 .20
C227 Strip of 4 1.90 .30
a. A72 31fr Fennec .45 .20
b. A72 31fr Lesser kudus .45 .20
c. A72 31fr Blesbok .45 .20
d. A72 31fr Serval .45 .20

United Nations, 30th anniversary.

Michelangelo Type of 1975

Paintings from Sistine Chapel: #C228a, Zachariah. #C228b, Joel. #C229a, Erythrean Sybil. #C229b, Prophet Ezekiel. #C230a, Persian Sybil. #C230b, Prophet Jeremiah.

1975, Dec. 3 Photo. *Perf. 13*

C228 A73 18fr Pair, #a.-b. .70
C229 A73 31fr Pair, #a.-b. 1.25
C230 A73 40fr Pair, #a.-b. 1.60
c. Souv. sheet of 6, #C228-C230 3.75
Nos. C228-C230 (3) 3.55

Printed in sheets of 18 stamps + 2 labels. For surcharges see Nos. CB35-CB37.

Olympic Games Type, 1976

Designs (Olympic Games Emblem and): 18fr, Ski jump. 36fr, Slalom. 50fr, Ice hockey.

1976, Jan. 23 Photo. *Perf. 14x13½*

C234 A74 18fr ol brn & multi .30
C235 A74 36fr grn & multi .70
C236 A74 50fr pur & multi .90
a. Souvenir sheet of 4 2.00
Nos. C234-C236 (3) 1.90

No. C236a contains 4 stamps similar to Nos. 491-494, perf. 13½, inscribed "POSTE AERIENNE."

21st Olympic Games, Montreal, Canada, July 17-Aug. 1 — AP5

Montreal Games Emblem and: #C237b, C239a, C240b, High jump. #C238a, C239b, C240a, Athlete on rings. #C237a, C238b, C240c, Hurdles.

1976, May 3 Litho. *Perf. 13½*

C237 AP5 27fr Pair, #a.-b. .80
C238 AP5 31fr Pair, #a.-b. 1.10
C239 AP5 50fr Pair, #a.-b. 1.75
Nos. C237-C239 (3) 3.65

Souvenir Sheet

C240 AP5 Sheet of 3, #a.-c. 1.75

Battle of Bunker Hill, by John Trumbull — AP6

Paintings: 26fr, Franklin, Jefferson and John Adams. 36fr, Declaration of Independence, by John Trumbull.

1976, July 16 Photo. *Perf. 13*

C244 AP6 18fr Pair, #a.-b. .70
C245 AP6 26fr Pair, #a.-b. .90
C246 AP6 36fr Pair, #a.-b. 1.50
c. Souv. sheet of 6, #C244-C246 3.25
Nos. C244-C246 (3) 3.10

American Bicentennial.

Christmas Type of 1976

Paintings: 18fr, Virgin and Child with St. Anne, by Leonardo da Vinci. 31fr, Holy Family with Lamb, by Raphael. 40fr, Madonna of the Basket, by Correggio.

1976, Oct. 18 Photo. *Perf. 13½*

C250 A76 18fr gold & multi .25
C251 A76 31fr gold & multi .45
C252 A76 40fr gold & multi .60
a. Souv. sheet of 3, #C250-C252 1.40
Nos. C250-C252 (3) 1.30

Christmas 1976. Sheets of 20 stamps and descriptive label.
For surcharges see Nos. CB41-CB43.

A.G. Bell Type of 1977

10fr, A.G. Bell and 1st telephone. #C253a, 17fr, A.G. Bell speaking into microphone. #C253a, C255e, Satellites around globe, videophone. #C254a, Switchboard operator, c.1910, wall telephone. #C254b, 26fr, Intelsat satellite, modern & old telephones. #C255c, Intelsat, radar.

1977, May 17 Photo. *Perf. 13*

C253 A78 18fr Pair, #a.-b. .25
C254 A78 36fr Pair, #a.-b. .50
C255 Sheet of 5 1.75 1.00
a. A78 10fr multi .20 .20
b. A78 17fr multi .25 .20
c. A79 18fr multi .25 .20
d. A79 26fr multi .40 .25
e. A79 36fr multi .50 .25

#C255c, C255e are air post stamps.

Animal Type of 1977

1977, Aug. 22 Photo. *Perf. 14x14½*

C258 Strip of 4 1.00
a. A80 9fr Buffon's kob .25
b. A80 9fr Marabous .25
c. A80 9fr Brindled gnu .25
d. A80 9fr River hog .25
C259 Strip of 4 1.25
a. A80 13fr Zebras .30
b. A80 13fr Shoebill .30
c. A80 13fr Striped hyenas .30
d. A80 13fr Chimpanzee .30
C260 Strip of 4 2.75
a. A80 30fr Flamingos .70
b. A80 30fr Nile Crocodiles .70
c. A80 30fr Green mamba .70
d. A80 30fr Greater kudus .70
C261 Strip of 4 3.50
a. A80 35fr Hyrax .85
b. A80 35fr Cobra .85
c. A80 35fr Jackals .85
d. A80 35fr Verreaux's eagles .85
C262 Strip of 4 5.25
a. A80 54fr Honey badger 1.25
b. A80 54fr Harnessed antelopes 1.25
c. A80 54fr Secretary bird 1.25
d. A80 54fr Klipspringer 1.25
C263 Strip of 4 6.25
a. A80 70fr African big-eared fox 1.50
b. A80 70fr Elephants 1.50
c. A80 70fr Vulturine guineafowl 1.50
d. A80 70fr Impalas 1.50
Nos. C258-C263 (6) 20.00

UN Type of 1977

Designs (UN Stamps and): 24fr, UN buildings by night. 27fr, UN buildings and view of Manhattan. 35fr, UN buildings by day.

1977, Oct. 10 Photo. *Perf. 13½*

C264 A82 Block of 4 1.90
a. 24fr No. 77 .45
b. 24fr No. 78 .45
c. 24fr No. 40 .45
d. 24fr No. 32 .45
C265 A82 Block of 4 2.00
a. 27fr No. 50 .50
b. 27fr No. 21 .50
c. 27fr No. 30 .50
d. 27fr No. 44 .50
C266 A82 Block of 4 3.25
a. 35fr No. C6 .75
b. 35fr No. 105 .75
c. 35fr No. 4 .75
d. 35fr No. 1 .75
e. Souvenir sheet of 3 1.40
Nos. C264-C266 (3) 7.15

No. C266e contains 24fr in design of No. C265b, 27fr in design of No. C266a, 35fr in design of No. C264c.

Christmas Type of 1977

Designs: Paintings of the Virgin and Child.

1977, Oct. 31 Photo. *Perf. 14x13*

C267 A83 18fr Master of Moulins .30
C268 A83 31fr Workshop of Lorenzo de Credi .50
C269 A83 40fr Palma Vecchio .60
a. Souv. sheet of 3, #C267-C269 1.50
Nos. C267-C269 (3) 1.40

Sheets of 24 stamps and descriptive label.
For surcharges see Nos. CB44-CB46.

Christmas 1978 Type of 1979

Souvenir Sheet

1979, Feb. Photo. *Perf. 14x13½*

C270 Sheet of 5 2.00
a. A86 13fr like #543 .20
b. A86 17fr like #544 .25
c. A86 27fr like #545 .40
d. A86 31fr like #546 .50
e. A86 40fr like #547 .60

Christmas Type of 1979

Souvenir Sheet

1979, Oct. 12 *Perf. 13½*

C271 Sheet of 4 2.00 1.25
a. A89 20fr like #561 .30 .20
b. A89 27fr like #562 .40 .25
c. A89 31fr like #563 .50 .30
d. A89 50fr like #564 .75 .40

Hill Type of 1979

Souvenir Sheet

1979, Nov. 6

C272 Sheet of 5 3.50 1.75
a. A90 20fr like #565 .40 .20
b. A90 27fr like #566 .55 .25
c. A90 31fr like #567 .60 .30
d. A90 40fr like #568 .80 .35
e. A90 50fr like #569 1.00 .50

Bird Type of 1979

1979 Photo. *Perf. 13½x3*

C273 A87 6fr like #548 .20
C274 A87 13fr like #549 .40
C275 A87 18fr like #550 .55
C276 A87 26fr like #551 .75
C277 A87 31fr like #552 1.00
C278 A87 36fr like #553 1.10
C279 A87 40fr like #554 1.25
C280 A87 54fr like #555 1.60
C281 A87 70fr like #556 2.00
Nos. C273-C281 (9) 8.85

Olympic Type of 1980

Souvenir Sheet

1980, Oct. 24 Photo. *Perf. 13½*

C282 Sheet of 9 4.25
a. A91 20fr like #570 .30
b. A91 20fr like #571 .30
c. A91 20fr like #572 .30
d. A91 30fr like #573 .45
e. A91 30fr like #574 .45
f. A91 30fr like #575 .45
g. A91 40fr like #576 .60
h. A91 40fr like #577 .60
i. A91 40fr like #578 .60

Christmas Type of 1980

Souvenir Sheet

1980, Dec. 12 Photo. *Perf. 13½x13*

C283 Sheet of 4 1.90 1.40
a. A92 10fr like #579 .20 .20
b. A92 30fr like #580 .45 .30
c. A92 40fr like #581 .60 .40
d. A92 45fr like #582 .65 .45

UPRONA Type of 1980

Souvenir Sheet

1980, Dec. 29 *Perf. 14½x13½*

C284 Sheet of 3 1.50
a. A93 10fr like #583 .20
b. A93 40fr like #584 .60
c. A93 45fr like #585 .65

Christmas Type of 1983

Souvenir Sheet

1983, Oct. 3 Litho. *Perf. 14½x13½*

C285 Sheet of 4 1.75
a. A97 10fr like #607 .20
b. A97 25fr like #608 .40
c. A97 30fr like #609 .45
d. A97 50fr like #610 .75

UPU Congress Type of 1984

Souvenir Sheet

1984, July 14 *Perf. 13x13½*

C286 Sheet of 4 2.25
a. A99 10fr like #621 .20
b. A99 30fr like #622 .45
c. A99 35fr like #623 .50
d. A99 65fr like #624 1.00

Summer Olympics Type of 1984

Souvenir Sheet

1984, Aug. 6 *Perf. 13½x13*

C287 Sheet of 4 2.25
a. A100 10fr like #625 .20
b. A100 30fr like #626 .45
c. A100 35fr like #627 .50
d. A100 65fr like #628 1.00

Christmas Type of 1984

Souvenir Sheet

1984, Dec. 15 *Perf. 13½*

C288 Sheet of 4 1.75
a. A101 10fr like #629 .20
b. A101 25fr like #630 .40
c. A101 30fr like #631 .45
d. A101 50fr like #632 .75

Flower Type of 1986 with Dull Lilac Border

1986, July 31 Photo. *Perf. 13x13½*

C289 A102 70fr like #633 .80
C290 A102 75fr like #634 .90
C291 A102 80fr like #635 1.00
C292 A102 85fr like #636 1.10
C293 A102 100fr like #637 1.25
C294 A102 150fr like #638 1.75
Nos. C289-C294 (6) 6.80

Animals AP8

1992, June 2 Litho. *Perf. 14*

C298 AP8 100fr M. nemestrina 1.50
C299 AP8 115fr Equus grevyi 1.75
C300 AP8 200fr Long horn cattle 3.00
C301 AP8 220fr Pelecanus onocrotalus 3.50
a. Souvenir sheet of 4, #C298-C301, perf. 13½ 10.00
Nos. C298-C301 (4) 9.75

AIR POST SEMI-POSTAL STAMPS

Coin Type of Semi-Postal Issue

Designs (Coins of Various Denominations): 3fr+1fr, 11fr+1fr, 20fr+1fr, 50fr+1fr, Coat of Arms, reverse. 5fr+1fr, 14fr+1fr, 30fr+1fr, 100fr+1fr, King Mwambutsa IV, obverse.

Lithographed; Embossed on Gilt Foil

1965, Nov. 15 *Imperf.*

Diameter: 39mm

CB1 SP4 3fr + 1fr lt & dk vio .20 .20
CB2 SP4 5fr + 1fr pale grn & red .20 .20

Diameter: 45mm

CB3 SP4 11fr + 1fr org & lilac .25 .25
CB4 SP4 14fr + 1fr red & emer .30 .30

Diameter: 56mm

CB5 SP4 20fr + 1fr ultra & blk .40 .40
CB6 SP4 30fr + 1fr dp org & mar .60 .60

Diameter: 67mm

CB7 SP4 50fr + 1fr bl & vio bl 1.00 1.00
CB8 SP4 100fr + 1fr rose & dp cl 2.25 2.25
Nos. CB1-CB8 (8) 5.20 5.20

Stamps are backed with patterned paper in blue, orange, and pink engine-turned design.

Red Cross Type of Semi-Postal Issue

Designs: 26fr+3fr, Laboratory. 40fr+3fr, Ambulance and thatched huts. 50fr+3fr, Red Cross nurse with patient.

1969, June 26 Photo. *Perf. 13½*

CB9 SP7 26fr + 3fr multi .40 .20
CB10 SP7 40fr + 3fr multi .55 .20
CB11 SP7 50fr + 3fr multi .65 .20
Nos. CB9-CB11 (3) 1.60 .60

Perf. and imperf. souvenir sheets exist containing 3 stamps similar to Nos. CB9-CB11, but without "Poste Aerienne." Size: 90½x97mm

Christmas Type of Semi-Postal Issue

Paintings: 14fr+3fr, Virgin and Child, by Velázquez. 26fr+3fr, Holy Family, by Joos van Cleve. 40fr+3fr, Virgin and Child, by Rogier van der Weyden.

1970, Dec. 14 Photo. *Perf. 13½*

CB12 SP9 14fr + 3fr multi .25 .20
CB13 SP9 26fr + 3fr multi .45 .20
CB14 SP9 40fr + 3fr multi .65 .20
a. Souv. sheet of 3, #CB12-CB14 1.50 1.50
Nos. CB12-CB14 (3) 1.35 .60

No. C147 Surcharged in Gold and Black

1971, Aug. 9 Photo. *Perf. 13½*

CB15 Strip of 4 .80 .20
a. A48 14fr+2fr Hartebeest .20 .20
b. A48 14fr+2fr Black rhinoceros .20 .20
c. A48 14fr+2fr Zebra .20 .20
d. A48 14fr+2fr Leopard .20 .20

UNESCO campaign against illiteracy.

No. C148 Surcharged in Gold and Black

1971, Aug. 9

CB16 Strip of 4 1.00 .20
a. A48 17fr+1fr Grant's gazelles .25 .20
b. A48 17fr+1fr Cheetah .25 .20
c. A48 17fr+1fr African white-backed vultures .25 .20
d. A48 17fr+1fr Johnston's okapi .25 .20

International help for refugees.

Nos. C150-C151 Surcharged in Black and Gold

a

b

1971, Aug. 16

CB17 Strip of 4 2.25 .45
a. A48(a) 26fr+1fr Gorilla .55 .20
b. A48(a) 26fr+1fr Gnu .55 .20
c. A48(a) 26fr+1fr Warthog .55 .20
d. A48(a) 26fr+1fr Cape hunting dog .55 .20
CB18 Strip of 4 3.00 .60
a. A48(b) 31fr+1fr Sable antelope .75 .20
b. A48(b) 31fr+1fr Caracal lynx .75 .20
c. A48(b) 31fr+1fr Ostriches .75 .20
d. A48(b) 31fr+1fr Bongo .75 .20

75th anniv. of modern Olympic Games (#CB17); Olympic Games, Munich, 1972 (#CB18).

Nos. C153-C155 Surcharged

1971, Nov. 27 Photo. *Perf. 13½*

CB19 A51 14fr + 1fr multi .30 .20
CB20 A51 17fr + 1fr multi .40 .20
CB21 A51 31fr + 1fr multi .60 .20
Nos. CB19-CB21 (3) 1.30 .60

25th anniv. of UNICEF.

Casa D'Oro, Venice SPAP1

Views in Venice: 17fr+1fr, Doge's Palace. 24fr+1fr, Church of Sts. John and Paul. 31fr+1fr, Doge's Palace and Piazzetta at Feast of Ascension, by Canaletto.

1971, Dec. 27

CB22 SPAP1 10fr + 1fr multi .20 .20
CB23 SPAP1 17fr + 1fr multi .30 .20
CB24 SPAP1 24fr + 1fr multi .45 .20
CB25 SPAP1 31fr + 1fr multi .55 .20
a. Souvenir sheet of 4 1.50 1.50
Nos. CB22-CB25 (4) 1.50 .80

Surtax for the UNESCO campaign to save the treasures of Venice. No. CB25a contains 4 stamps similar to Nos. CB22-CB25, but with 2fr surtax.

Nos. C165-C167, C193-C195 Surcharged "+1F" in Silver

1972, Dec. 12 Photo. *Perf. 13½*

CB26 A57 18fr + 1fr multi .30 .20
CB27 A57 27fr + 1fr multi .45 .20
CB28 A57 40fr + 1fr multi .60 .20
a. Souvenir sheet of 3 1.50 1.50
Nos. CB26-CB28 (3) 1.35 .60

Christmas 1972. No. CB28a contains 3 stamps similar to Nos. CB26-CB28 but with 2fr surtax.

1973, Dec. 14 Photo. *Perf. 13*

CB29 A64 18fr + 1fr multi .30 .20
CB30 A64 27fr + 1fr multi .40 .20
CB31 A64 40fr + 1fr multi .60 .20
a. Souvenir sheet of 3 1.50 1.50
Nos. CB29-CB31 (3) 1.30 .60

Christmas 1973. No. CB31 contains 3 stamps similar to Nos. CB29-CB31 with 2fr surtax each.

Christmas Type of 1974

1974, Dec. 2 Photo. *Perf. 13*

CB32 A70 18fr + 1fr multi .30 .20
CB33 A70 27fr + 1fr multi .50 .30
CB34 A70 40fr + 1fr multi .70 .40
a. Souvenir sheet of 3 1.75 1.75
Nos. CB32-CB34 (3) 1.50 .90

Christmas 1974. No. CB34a contains 3 stamps similar to Nos. CB32-CB34 with 2fr surtax.

Nos. C228-C230 Surcharged "+ 1F" in Silver and Black

1975, Dec. 22 Photo. *Perf. 13*

CB35 A73 18fr +1fr Pair, #a-b .70
CB36 A73 31fr +1fr Pair, #a-b 1.10
CB37 A73 40fr +1fr Pair, #a-b 1.50
c. Souvenir sheet of 6 4.25
Nos. CB35-CB37 (3) 3.30

Michelangelo Buonarroti (1475-1564). No. CB37c contains 6 stamps similar to Nos. CB35-CB37 with 2fr surtax each.

Nos. C250-C252 Surcharged "+1f" in Silver and Black

1976, Nov. 25 Photo. *Perf. 13½*

CB41 A76 18fr + 1fr multi .30
CB42 A76 31fr + 1fr multi .50
CB43 A76 40fr + 1fr multi .60
a. Souvenir sheet of 3 1.50
Nos. CB41-CB43 (3) 1.40

Christmas 1976. No. CB43a contains 3 stamps similar to Nos. CB41-CB43 with 2fr surtax each.

Nos. C267-C269 Surcharged "+1fr" in Silver and Black

1977 Photo. *Perf. 14x13*

CB44 A83 18fr + 1fr multi .30
CB45 A83 31fr + 1fr multi .50
CB46 A83 40fr + 1fr multi .60
a. Souvenir sheet of 3 1.50
Nos. CB44-CB46 (3) 1.40

Christmas 1977. No. CB46a contains 3 stamps similar to Nos. CB44-CB46 with 2fr surtax each.

Christmas 1978 Type

Souvenir Sheet

1979, Feb. Photo. *Perf. 14x13*

CB47 Sheet of 5 3.00
a. A86 13fr + 2fr multi .30
b. A86 17fr + 2fr multi .35
c. A86 27fr + 2fr multi .55
d. A86 31fr + 2fr multi .70
e. A86 40fr + 2fr multi .85

Christmas Type of 1979

Souvenir Sheet

1979, Dec. 10 Photo. *Perf. 13½*

CB48 Sheet of 4 2.75
a. A89 20fr + 2fr like #561 .45
b. A89 27fr + 2fr like #562 .55
c. A89 31fr + 2fr like #563 .70
d. A89 50fr + 2fr like #564 1.00

Christmas Type of 1980

Souvenir Sheet

1981, Jan. 16 Photo. *Perf. 13½x13*

CB49 Sheet of 4 2.50
a. A92 10fr + 2fr like #579 .20
b. A92 30fr + 2fr like #580 .55
c. A92 40fr + 2fr like #581 .75
d. A92 50fr + 2fr like #582 .90

Christmas Type of 1983

Souvenir Sheet

1983, Nov. 2 Litho. *Perf. 14½x13½*

CB50 Sheet of 4 1.90
a. A97 10fr + 2fr like #607 .20
b. A97 25fr + 2fr like #608 .40
c. A97 30fr + 2fr like #609 .50
d. A97 50fr + 2fr like #610 .75

Christmas Type of 1984

Souvenir Sheet

1984, Dec. 15 *Perf. 13½*

CB51 Sheet of 4 1.90
a. A101 10fr + 2fr like #629 .20
b. A101 25fr + 2fr like #630 .40
c. A101 30fr + 2fr like #631 .50
d. A101 50fr + 2fr like #632 .75

BUSHIRE

bü-'shir

LOCATION — On Persian Gulf

Bushire is a Persian port which British troops occupied Aug. 8, 1915.

20 Chahis (or Shahis) = 1 Kran
10 Krans = 1 Toman

Watermark

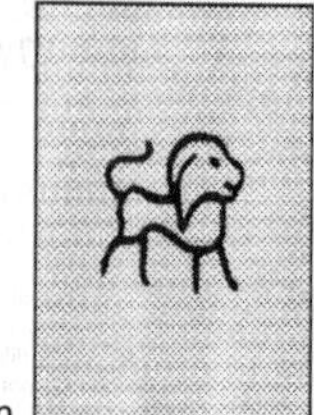

Wmk. 161 - Lion

ISSUED UNDER BRITISH OCCUPATION

Basic Iranian Designs

Shah Ahmed — A32

Imperial Crown — A33

King Darius, Ahura-Mazda Overhead — A34

Ruins of Persepolis — A35

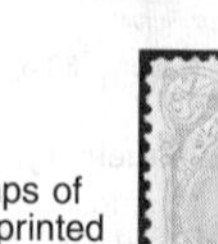

Iranian Stamps of 1911-13 Overprinted in Black

Perf. 11½, 11½x11

Typo. & Engr.

1915, Aug. 15 Unwmk.

N1 A32 1c green & org 27.50 30.00
N2 A32 2c red & sepia 27.50 27.50
N3 A32 3c gray brn & grn 32.50 40.00
N4 A32 5c brown & car 300.00 300.00
N5 A32 6c green & red brn 26.00 22.50
N6 A32 9c yel brn & vio 27.50 *30.00*
a. Double overprint

N7	A32	10c	red & org brn	30.00	*32.50*
N8	A32	12c	grn & ultra	37.50	*40.00*
N9	A32	1k	ultra & car	52.50	27.50
a.			Double overprint	5,250.	
N10	A32	24c	vio & grn	52.50	40.00
N11	A32	2k	grn & red vio	175.00	140.00
N12	A32	3k	vio & blk	150.00	*160.00*
N13	A32	5k	red & ultra	82.50	75.00
N14	A32	10k	ol bis & cl	75.00	75.00
			Nos. N1-N14 (14)	1,096.	1,040.

Nos. N1-N14, except No. N4, exist without period after "Occupation." This variety sells for more.

Forged overprints exist of Nos. N1-N29.

The Bushire overprint exists on Iran No. 537 but is considered a forgery.

On Iranian Stamps of 1915

Perf. 11, 11½

1915, Sept. **Wmk. 161**

N15	A33	1c	car & indigo	350.	350.
N16	A33	2c	blue & car	5,250.	*8,500.*
N17	A33	3c	dk grn	375.	*400.*
N18	A33	5c	red	5,250.	*4,750.*
N19	A33	6c	ol grn & car	4,000.	*4,000.*
N20	A33	9c	yel brn & vio	500.	*525.*
N21	A33	10c	bl grn & yel brn	800.	*900.*
N22	A33	12c	ultra	950.	*1,250.*
N23	A34	1k	sil, yel brn & gray	350.	*375.*
N24	A33	24c	yel brn & dk brn	450.	400.
N25	A34	2k	sil, bl & rose	300.	350.
N26	A34	3k	sil, vio & brn	450.	*475.*
N27	A34	5k	sil, brn & grn	425.	*450.*
a.			Inverted overprint		10,000.
N28	A35	1t	gold, pur & blk	350.	*400.*
N29	A35	3t	gold, cl & red brn	2,500.	*2,750.*

Persia resumed administration of Bushire post office Oct. 16, 1915.

Vol. 1 Number Additions, Deletions & Changes

Number in 2003 Catalogue	Number in 2004 Catalogue
United States	
new	248a
250c	deleted
new	498g
new	502e
new	506a
new	507a
new	508a
new	509a
new	511a
new	512b
new	514a
new	515d
new	516a
new	517c
530c	deleted
new	554d
new	556b
new	557c
new	562c
new	568c
new	1252b
new	1373b
new	1383b
new	1384h
new	1418f
new	1424c
new	1427b
new	1454b
1455b	deleted
new	1542f
new	1557d
new	1632c
new	1683b
new	1683c
new	1688n
new	1689v
new	1736c
new	1757l
new	1822a
new	1823b
1869f	deleted
new	2001b
new	2015c
new	2041b
2147a	deleted
new	2175f
new	2457b
2514a	2514b
new	2515b
new	2630b
new	2872e
new	2949d
new	3030d
3051a	3051A
3051b	2051Ab
3051c	3051Ac
3058a	deleted
3271b	3271a
new	3410g
new	3420a
new	3472a
new	3485e
new	3492d
new	3557a
new	3611k
new	3613a
new	3622a
new	1LB3b
new	U311a
new	U312b
new	U313a
new	U314a
new	U315a
new	U317a
new	W428A
new	U429m
new	U466C

Number in 2003 Catalogue	Number in 2004 Catalogue
United States	
new	U548Ab
new	U616a
new	U638a
new	U646a
new	UC8a
new	UC8b
new	UC8c
UC8a	UC8d
UC8b	UC8e
UC8c	UC8f
UC8d	UC8g
new	UC61a
new	UO86a
new	R15ca
R285c	deleted
RB2d	deleted
new	57XU1a
new	57XU4a
Canal Zone	
new	20e
new	22h
new	J11C
new	J11Cd
Ryukyu Islands	
new	8b
new	16e
new	16e
new	16f
16a	16A
new	16Ab
16b	16B
new	122b
new	122c
new	123a
new	C14b
Albania	
new	1327A-1327E
Andorra (Spanish)	
22b	deleted
Angola	
13	13a
13a	13
Ascension	
54	41D
55	42Cd
55a	42C
55b	42Ce
56	43C
Australia – New South Wales	
51a	footnote
108B	108c
108c	108B
108d	108e
Australia – Tasmania	
new	13d
new	23c
48a	48e
48d	48c
48e	48d
new	48a
Australia – Western Australia	
53	53a
53a	53
Australia	
O10a	deleted

Number in 2003 Catalogue	Number in 2004 Catalogue
Austria	
89	deleted
new	89b
97	deleted
new	97b
98	deleted
new	98b
99	deleted
new	99b
100	deleted
new	100b
110	deleted
new	110a
111	deleted
114	deleted
new	114a
114b	deleted
115	deleted
new	116a
118a	deleted
196b	196c
new	196b
new	219b
new	221a
new	222b
new	223b
new	323b
1603	1600
1606	1601
1606A	1602
1607	1603
1608	1604
1609	1605
1613	1606
1613A	1607
1614	1608
new	J1b
new	J2b
new	J3a
new	J5a
new	J7a
new	J48a
Bechuanaland	
6b	6a
new	6b
Belgium	
123	123b
new	123
1759	1758
1760	1759
1761	1760
1762	1761
Q487	1848A
Benin	
1183-1189	deleted
1211-1217	deleted
Bolivia	
new	36c
Bulgaria	
new	1436a

Pronunciation Symbols

ə .... banana, collide, abut

ˈə, ˌə .... humdrum, abut

ᵊ .... immediately preceding \l\, \n\, \m\, \ŋ\, as in battle, mitten, eaten, and sometimes open \ˈō-pᵊm\, lock and key \-ᵊŋ-\; immediately following \l\, \m\, \r\, as often in French table, prisme, titre

ər .... further, merger, bird

ˈər-, ˈə-r .... as in two different pronunciations of hurry \ˈhər-ē, ˈhə-rē\

a .... mat, map, mad, gag, snap, patch

ā .... day, fade, date, aorta, drape, cape

ä .... bother, cot, and, with most American speakers, father, cart

ȧ .... father as pronounced by speakers who do not rhyme it with *bother*; French patte

au̇ .... now, loud, out

b .... baby, rib

ch .... chin, nature \ˈnā-chər\

d .... did, adder

e .... bet, bed, peck

ˈē, ˌē .... beat, nosebleed, evenly, easy

ē .... easy, mealy

f .... fifty, cuff

g .... go, big, gift

h .... hat, ahead

hw .... whale as pronounced by those who do not have the same pronunciation for both *whale* and *wail*

i .... tip, banish, active

ī .... site, side, buy, tripe

j .... job, gem, edge, join, judge

k .... kin, cook, ache

k̲ .... German ich, Buch; one pronunciation of loch

l .... lily, pool

m .... murmur, dim, nymph

n .... no, own

ⁿ .... indicates that a preceding vowel or diphthong is pronounced with the nasal passages open, as in French *un bon vin blanc* \œⁿ -bōⁿ -vaⁿ -bläⁿ\

ŋ .... sing \ˈsiŋ\, singer \ˈsiŋ-ər\, finger \ˈfiŋ-gər\, ink \ˈiŋk \

ō .... bone, know, beau

ȯ .... saw, all, gnaw, caught

œ .... French boeuf, German Hölle

œ̄ .... French feu, German Höhle

ȯi .... coin, destroy

p .... pepper, lip

r .... red, car, rarity

s .... source, less

sh .... as in shy, mission, machine, special (actually, this is a single sound, not two); with a hyphen between, two sounds as in *grasshopper* \ˈgras-ˌhä-pər\

t .... tie, attack, late, later, latter

th .... as in thin, ether (actually, this is a single sound, not two); with a hyphen between, two sounds as in *knighthood* \ˈnīt-ˌhu̇d\

t̲h̲ .... then, either, this (actually, this is a single sound, not two)

ü .... rule, youth, union \ˈyün-yən\, few \ˈfyü\

u̇ .... pull, wood, book, curable \ˈkyu̇r-ə-bəl\, fury \ˈfyu̇r-ē\

ue .... German füllen, hübsch

ue̅ .... French rue, German fühlen

v .... vivid, give

w .... we, away

y .... yard, young, cue \ˈkyü\, mute \ˈmyüt\, union \ˈyün-yən\

ʸ .... indicates that during the articulation of the sound represented by the preceding character the front of the tongue has substantially the position it has for the articulation of the first sound of *yard,* as in French *digne* \dēnʸ\

z .... zone, raise

zh .... as in vision, azure \ˈa-zhər\ (actually, this is a single sound, not two); with a hyphen between, two sounds as in *hogshead* \ˈhȯgz-ˌhed, ˈhägz-\

\ .... slant line used in pairs to mark the beginning and end of a transcription: \ˈpen\

ˈ .... mark preceding a syllable with primary (strongest) stress: \ˈpen-mən-ˌship\

ˌ .... mark preceding a syllable with secondary (medium) stress: \ˈpen-mən-ˌship\

\- .... mark of syllable division

( ) .... indicate that what is symbolized between is present in some utterances but not in others: *factory* \ˈfak-t(ə-)rē\

÷ .... indicates that many regard as unacceptable the pronunciation variant immediately following: *cupola* \ˈkyü-pə-lə, ÷-ˌlō\

Illustrated Identifier

This section pictures stamps or parts of stamp designs that will help identify postage stamps that do not have English words on them.

Many of the symbols that identify stamps of countries are shown here as well as typical examples of their stamps.

See the Index and Identifier on the previous pages for stamps with inscriptions such as "sen," "posta," "Baja Porto," "Helvetia," "K.S.A.", etc.

Linn's Stamp Identifier is now available. The 144 pages include more 2,000 inscriptions and over 500 large stamp illustrations. Available from Linn's Stamp News, P.O. Box 29, Sidney, OH 45365-0029.

1. HEADS, PICTURES AND NUMERALS

GREAT BRITAIN

Great Britain stamps never show the country name, but, except for postage dues, show a picture of the reigning monarch.

Victoria

Edward VII

George V

Edward VIII

George VI

Elizabeth II

Some George VI and Elizabeth II stamps are surcharged in annas, new paisa or rupees. These are listed under Oman.

Silhouette (sometimes facing right, generally at the top of stamp)

The silhouette indicates this is a British stamp. It is not a U.S. stamp.

VICTORIA

Queen Victoria

INDIA

Other stamps of India show this portrait of Queen Victoria and the words "Service" and "Annas."

AUSTRIA

YUGOSLAVIA

(Also BOSNIA & HERZEGOVINA if imperf.)

BOSNIA & HERZEGOVINA

Denominations also appear in top corners instead of bottom corners.

HUNGARY

Another stamp has posthorn facing left

BRAZIL

AUSTRALIA

Kangaroo and Emu

GERMANY

Mecklenburg-Vorpommern

SWITZERLAND

2. ORIENTAL INSCRIPTIONS

CHINA

Any stamp with this one character is from China (Imperial, Republic or People's Republic). This character appears in a four-character overprint on stamps of Manchukuo. These stamps are local provisionals, which are unlisted. Other overprinted Manchukuo stamps show this character, but have more than four characters in the overprints. These are listed in People's Republic of China.

Some Chinese stamps show the Sun.

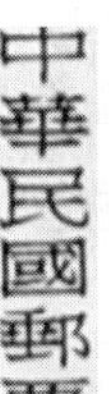

Most stamps of Republic of China show this series of characters.

Stamps with the China character and this character are from People's Republic of China. 人

中国人民邮政

Calligraphic form of People's Republic of China

Chinese stamps without China character

REPUBLIC OF CHINA

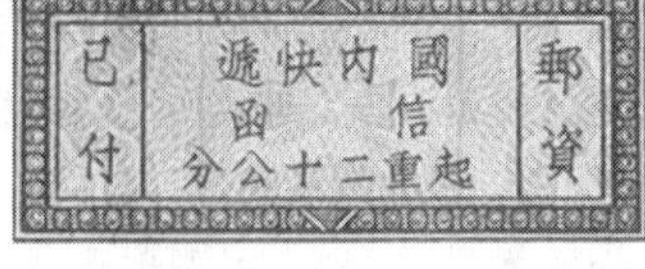

PEOPLE'S REPUBLIC OF CHINA

Mao Tse-tung

MANCHUKUO

Temple

Emperor Pu-Yi

The first 3 characters are common to many Manchukuo stamps.

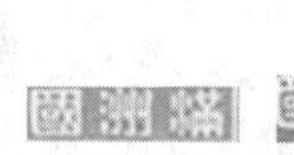
The last 3 characters are common to other Manchukuo stamps.

Orchid Crest 

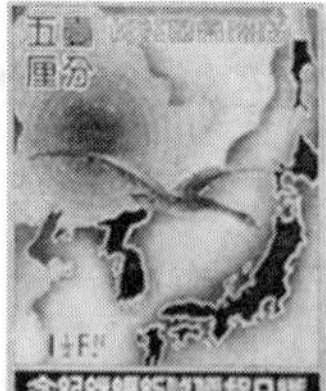
Manchukuo stamp without these elements

JAPAN

Chrysanthemum Crest

Country Name

Japanese stamps without these elements

The number of characters in the center and the design of dragons on the sides will vary.

RYUKYU ISLANDS

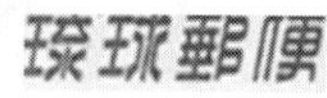
Country Name

PHILIPPINES (Japanese Occupation)

Country Name

NORTH BORNEO (Japanese Occupation)

Indicates Japanese Occupation Country Name

MALAYA (Japanese Occupation)

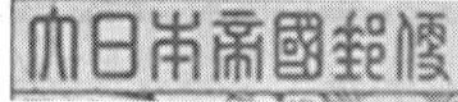
Indicates Japanese Occupation

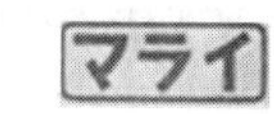
Country Name

BURMA (Japanese Occupation)

Indicates Japanese Occupation

Country Name

Other Burma Japanese Occupation stamps without these elements

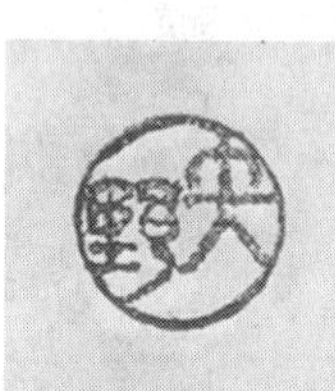

Burmese Script

KOREA

These two characters, in any order, are common to stamps from the Republic of Korea (South Korea) or the unlisted stamps of the People's Democratic Republic of Korea (North Korea).

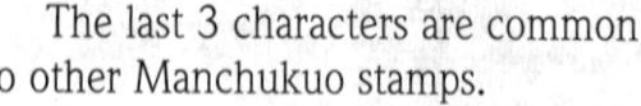

This series of four characters can be found on the stamps of both Koreas.

Yin Yang appears on some stamps.

대한민국우표

Indicates Republic of Korea (South Korea)

South Korean postage stamps issed after 1952 do not show currency expressed in Latin letters. Stamps wiith "HW," "HWAN," "WON," "WN," "W" or "W" with two lines through it, if not illustrated in listings of stamps before this date, are revenues. North Korean postage stamps do not have currency expressed in Latin letters.

THAILAND

Country Name

King Chulalongkorn

King Prajadhipok and Chao P'ya Chakri

3. CENTRAL AND EASTERN ASIAN INSCRIPTIONS

INDIA - FEUDATORY STATES

Alwar

Bhor

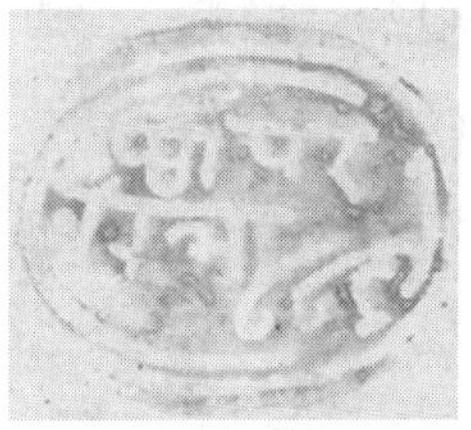

Bundi

Similar stamps come with different designs in corners and differently drawn daggers (at center of circle).

Dhar

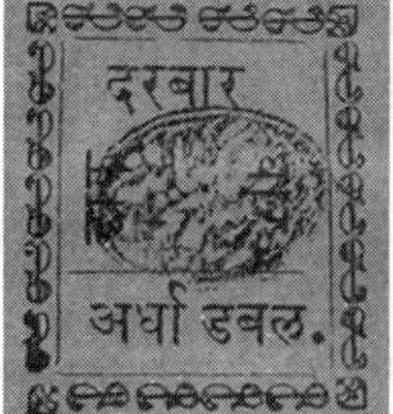

Faridkot

Hyderabad

Similar stamps exist with straight line frame around stamp, and also with different central design which is inscribed "Postage" or "Post & Receipt."

Indore

Jhalawar

A similar stamp has the central figure in an oval.

Nandgaon

Nowanuggur

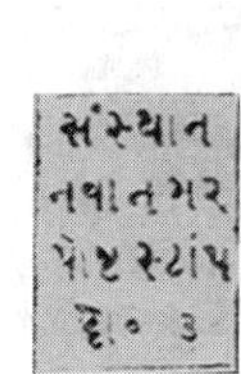

Poonch

Similar stamps exist in various sizes

Rajpeepla

Soruth

BANGLADESH

বাংলাদেশ

Country Name

NEPAL

Similar stamps are smaller, have squares in upper corners and have five or nine characters in central bottom panel.

TANNU TUVA

ISRAEL

GEORGIA

This inscription is found on other pictorial stamps.

საქართველო

Country Name

ARMENIA

The four characters are found somewhere on pictorial stamps. On some stamps only the middle two are found.

4. AFRICAN INSCRIPTIONS

ETHIOPIA

5. ARABIC INSCRIPTIONS

AFGHANISTAN

Many early Afghanistan stamps show Tiger's head, many of these have ornaments protruding from outer ring, others show inscriptions in black.

Arabic Script

Mosque Gate & Crossed Cannons
The four characters are found somewhere on pictorial stamps. On some stamps only the middle two are found.

BAHRAIN

EGYPT

Postage

INDIA - FEUDATORY STATES

Jammu & Kashmir

Text and thickness of ovals vary. Some stamps have flower devices in corners.

India-Hyderabad

IRAN

Country Name

Royal Crown

Lion with Sword

Symbol

IRAQ

JORDAN

LEBANON

Similar types have denominations at top and slightly different design.

LIBYA

Country Name in various styles

Other Libya stamps show Eagle and Shield (head facing either direction) or Red, White and Black Shield (with or without eagle in center).

SAUDI ARABIA

Tughra (Central design)

Palm Tree and Swords

SYRIA

THRACE

YEMEN

PAKISTAN

PAKISTAN - BAHAWALPUR

Country Name in top panel, star and crescent

TURKEY

Star & Crescent is a device found on many Turkish stamps, but is also found on stamps from other Arabic areas (see Pakistan-Bahawalpur)

Tughra (similar tughras can be found on stamps of Turkey in Asia, Afghanistan and Saudi Arabia)

Mohammed V

Mustafa Kemal

Plane, Star and Crescent

TURKEY IN ASIA

Other Turkey in Asia pictorials show star & crescent.
Other stamps show tughra shown under Turkey.

6. GREEK INSCRIPTIONS

GREECE

Country Name in various styles

(Some Crete stamps overprinted with the Greece country name are listed in Crete.)

Lepta

Drachma Drachmas Lepton

Abbreviated Country Name 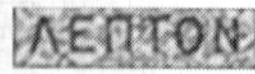

Other forms of Country Name

No country name

CRETE

Country Name

These words are on other stamps

Grosion

Crete stamps with a surcharge that have the year "1922" are listed under Greece.

EPIRUS **IONIAN IS.**

Country Name

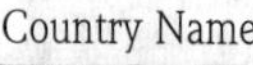

7. CYRILLIC INSCRIPTIONS

RUSSIA

Postage Stamp

Imperial Eagle

Postage in various styles

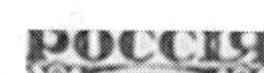

Abbreviation for Kopeck Abbreviation for Ruble Russia

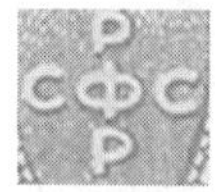

Abbreviation for Russian Soviet Federated Socialist Republic

RSFSR stamps were overprinted (see below)

Abbreviation for Union of Soviet Socialist Republics

This item is footnoted in Latvia

RUSSIA - Army of the North

"OKCA"

RUSSIA - Wenden

RUSSIAN OFFICES IN THE TURKISH EMPIRE

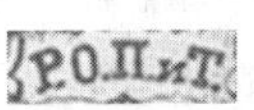

These letters appear on other stamps of the Russian offices.

The unoverprinted version of this stamp and a similar stamp were overprinted by various countries (see below).

ARMENIA

BELARUS

FAR EASTERN REPUBLIC

Country Name

SOUTH RUSSIA

Country Name

FINLAND

Circles and Dots on stamps similar to Imperial Russia issues

BATUM

Forms of Country Name

TRANSCAUCASIAN FEDERATED REPUBLICS

Abbreviation for Country Name

KAZAKHSTAN

КАЗАКСТАН

Country Name

KYRGYZSTAN

КЫРГЫЗСТАН

КЫРГЫЗСТАН Country Name

ROMANIA

TADJIKISTAN

Country Name & Abbreviation

UKRAINE

Україні

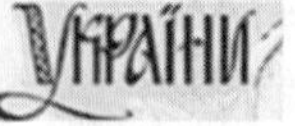

Україну

Country Name in various forms

УС РР

The trident appears on many stamps, usually as an overprint.

Abbreviation for Ukrainian Soviet Socialist Republic

WESTERN UKRAINE

Abbreviation for Country Name

AZERBAIJAN

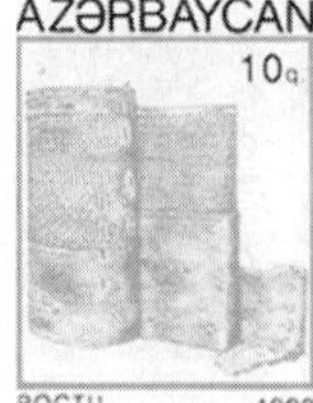

AZƏRBAYCAN

Country Name

А.С.С.Р.

Abbreviation for Azerbaijan Soviet Socialist Republic

MONTENEGRO

ЦРНЕГОРЕ

ЦРНА ГОРА

Country Name in various forms

Abbreviation for country name

No country name (A similar Montenegro stamp without country name has same vignette.)

SERBIA

СРПСКА СРБИЈА

Country Name in various forms

К.С.

Abbreviation for country name

No country name

YUGOSLAVIA

Showing country name

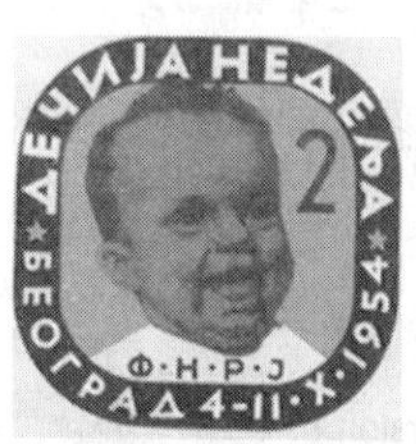

No Country Name

MACEDONIA

МАКЕДОНИЈА

МАКЕДОНИЈА

Country Name

МАКЕДОНСКИ

Different form of Country Name

BULGARIA

Country Name Postage

Stotinka

STOTINKI СТОТ.

Stotinki (plural) Abbreviation for Stotinki

Country Name in various forms and styles

Б✱ЛГАРИЯ

Н Р България

НРБЪЛГАРИЯ

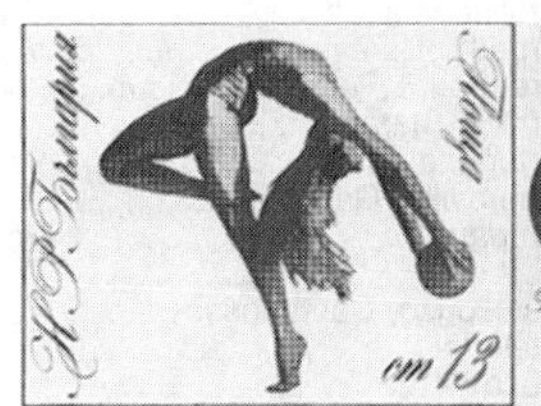

No country name

Abbreviation for Lev, leva

MONGOLIA

ШУУДАН ТӨГРӨГ

Country name in one word Tugrik in Cyrillic

МОНГОЛ ШУУДАН МӨНГӨ

Country name in two words Mung in Cyrillic

Mung in Mongolian

Tugrik in Mongolian

Arms

No Country Name

INDEX AND IDENTIFIER

All page numbers shown are those in this Volume 1.

Postage stamps that do not have English words on them are shown in the Identifier which begins on page 1092.

D ....Vol. 3

E.A.F. overprinted on stamps of Great Britain ....Vol. 3

F surcharged on French stamps ....Vol. 2

Oakway, S.C. 151

P on Straits Settlements .... Vol. 4

Qatar .... Vol. 5

R (Armenia)..456

2004
VOLUME 1
DEALER DIRECTORY
YELLOW PAGE LISTINGS

This section of your Scott Catalogue contains advertisements to help you conveniently find what you need, when you need it...!

Accessories

BROOKLYN GALLERY COIN & STAMP
8725 4th Avenue
Brooklyn, NY 11209
718-745-5701
718-745-2775 Fax
Email: info@brooklyngallery.com
Web: www.brooklyngallery.com

Appraisals

CONNEXUS
P.O. Box 819
Snow Camp, NC 27349
336-376-8207
Email: Connexus1@world.att.net

RANDY SCHOLL STAMP CO.
Southhampton Square
7460 Jager Court
Cincinnati, OH 45230-4344
Email: randyscholl@fuse.net

Approvals-Personalized WW & U.S.

THE KEEPING ROOM
P.O. Box 257
Trumbull, CT 06611
203-372-8436

Asia

HENRY GITNER PHILATELISTS, INC.
P.O. Box 3077-S
Middletown, NY 10940
845-343-5151 or 800-947-8267
845-343-0068 Fax
Email: hgitner@hgitner.com
Web: www.hgitner.com

MICHAEL ROGERS, INC.
199 E. Welbourne Ave.
Suite 3
Winter Park, FL 32789
407-644-2290 or 800-843-3751
407-645-4434 Fax
Email: mrogersinc@aol.com
Web: www.michaelrogersinc.com

Auctions

DANIEL F. KELLEHER CO., INC.
24 Farnsworth Street
Suite 605
Boston, MA 02210
617-443-0033
617-443-0789 Fax

JACQUES C. SCHIFF, JR., INC.
195 Main Street
Ridgefield Park, NJ 07660
201-641-5566
From NYC: 662-2777
201-641-5705 Fax

SAM HOUSTON PHILATELICS
13310 Westheimer #150
Houston, TX 77077
281-493-6386 or 800-231-5926
281-496-1445 Fax
Email: shduck@aol.com
Web: www.shduck.com

STAMP CENTER/DUTCH COUNTRY AUCTIONS
4115 Concord Pike
Wilmington, DE 19803
302-478-8740
302-478-8779 Fax
Email: scdca@dol.net
Web: www.thestampcenter.com

Auctions - Mail Bid

DALE ENTERPRISES, INC.
P.O. Box 539-C
Emmaus, PA 18049
610-433-3303
610-965-6089 Fax
Email: daleent@fast.net
Web: www.dalestamps.com

Auctions-Public

ALAN BLAIR STAMPS/AUCTIONS
5407 Lakeside Avenue
Suite 4
Richmond, VA 23228
800-689-5602 Phone/Fax
Email: alanblair@prodigy.net

Australia

COLONIAL STAMP COMPANY
5757 Wilshire Blvd. PH #8
Los Angeles, CA 90036
323-933-9435
323-939-9930 Fax
Email: gwh225@aol.com
Web: www.colonialstamps.com

Austria

AMEEN STAMPS
8831 Long Point Road
Suite 204
Houston, TX 77055
713-468-0644
713-468-2420 Fax
Email: rameen@ev1.net

HENRY GITNER PHILATELISTS, INC.
P.O. Box 3077-S
Middletown, NY 10940
845-343-5151 or 800-947-8267
845-343-0068 Fax
Email: hgitner@hgitner.com
Web: www.hgitner.com

JOSEPH EDER
P.O. Box 185529
Hamden, CT 06518
203-281-0742
203-230-2410 Fax
Email: j.eder@worldnet.att.net
Web: www.ederstamps.com

Bahamas

COLONIAL STAMP COMPANY
5757 Wilshire Blvd. PH #8
Los Angeles, CA 90036
323-933-9435
323-939-9930 Fax
Email: gwh225@aol.com
Web: www.colonialstamps.com

Bangkok

COLONIAL STAMP COMPANY
5757 Wilshire Blvd. PH #8
Los Angeles, CA 90036
323-933-9435
323-939-9930 Fax
Email: gwh225@aol.com
Web: www.colonialstamps.com

Barbados

COLONIAL STAMP COMPANY
5757 Wilshire Blvd. PH #8
Los Angeles, CA 90036
323-933-9435
323-939-9930 Fax
Email: gwh225@aol.com
Web: www.colonialstamps.com

Bermuda

COLONIAL STAMP COMPANY
5757 Wilshire Blvd. PH #8
Los Angeles, CA 90036
323-933-9435
323-939-9930 Fax
Email: gwh225@aol.com
Web: www.colonialstamps.com

British Asia

THE STAMP ACT
P.O. Box 1136
Belmont, CA 94002
650-592-3315
650-508-8104 Fax
Email: bchang@ix.netcom.com or bob @thestampact.com
Web: thestampact.com

Auctions

British Commonwealth

EMPIRE STAMP CO.
P.O. Box 8337
Calabasa, CA 91372-8337
800-616-7278 or 818-225-1181
818-225-1182 Fax
Email: info@empirestamps.com
Web: www.empirestamps.com

JAY'S STAMP CO.
Box 28484
Dept. S
Philadelphia, PA 19149-0184
215-743-0207 Phone/Fax
Email: jasc@comcast.net
Web: www.jaysco.com

British Commonwealth

METROPOLITAN STAMP CO., INC.
P.O. Box 1133
Chicago, IL 60690-1133
815-439-0142
815-439-0143 Fax
Email: metrostamp@aol.com

VICTORIA STAMP CO.
P.O. Box 745
Ridgewood, NJ 07451
201-652-7283
201-612-0024
Email: VictoriaStampCo@aol.com
Web: www.VictoriaStampCo.com

British Commonwealth

THE BRITISH COMMONWEALTH
O·F N·A·T·I·O·N·S

We are active buyers and sellers of stamps and postal history of all areas of pre-1960 British Commonwealth, including individual items, collections or estates. Want lists from all reigns are accepted with references.

L. W. Martin, Jr.

"VISIT OUR BOOTH AT MOST MAJOR SHOWS"

CROWN COLONY STAMPS
P.O. Box 1198
BELLAIRE, TEXAS 77402
PH. (713) 781-6563 • FAX (713) 789-9998
E-mail: crowncolony@compuserve.com

British E. Africa

COLONIAL STAMP COMPANY
5757 Wilshire Blvd. PH #8
Los Angeles, CA 90036
323-933-9435
323-939-9930 Fax
Email: gwh225@aol.com
Web: www.colonialstamps.com

British Guiana

COLONIAL STAMP COMPANY
5757 Wilshire Blvd. PH #8
Los Angeles, CA 90036
323-933-9435
323-939-9930 Fax
Email: gwh225@aol.com
Web: www.colonialstamps.com

Brunei

COLONIAL STAMP COMPANY
5757 Wilshire Blvd. PH #8
Los Angeles, CA 90036
323-933-9435
323-939-9930 Fax
Email: gwh225@aol.com
Web: www.colonialstamps.com

Burma

COLONIAL STAMP COMPANY
5757 Wilshire Blvd. PH #8
Los Angeles, CA 90036
323-933-9435
323-939-9930 Fax
Email: gwh225@aol.com
Web: www.colonialstamps.com

Bushire

COLONIAL STAMP COMPANY
5757 Wilshire Blvd. PH #8
Los Angeles, CA 90036
323-933-9435
323-939-9930 Fax
Email: gwh225@aol.com
Web: www.colonialstamps.com

Central America

GUY SHAW
P.O. Box 10025
Bakersfield, CA 93389
661-834-7135 Phone/Fax
Email: guyshaw@guyshaw.com
Web: www.guyshaw.com

China

MICHAEL ROGERS, INC.
199 E. Welbourne Ave.
Suite 3
Winter Park, FL 32789
407-644-2290 or 800-843-3751
407-645-4434 Fax
Email: mrogersinc@aol.com
Web: www.michaelrogersinc.com

Classics

GARY POSNER, INC.
1407 Avenue Z
PMB #535
Brooklyn, NY 11235
800-323-4279
718-241-2801
Email: garyposnerinc@aol.com
Web: www.garyposnerinc.com
www.gemstamps.com

British Commonwealth

Aron R. Halberstam Philatelists, Ltd.

POB 150168, Van Brunt Station
Brooklyn, NY 11215-0168, USA
Tel: 718-788-3978 Fax: 718-965-3099
Toll Free: 800-343-1303
E-mail:arh@aronrhalberstam.com

British Commonwealth
Pre-1960

Call or write to request our free Price List, or send us your Want Lists. We are also eager buyers of better Commonwealth singles or sets and collections. Let us know what you have to offer.

Accepted on all orders. Member

Visit our Website: www.aronrhalberstam.com

BRITISH EMPIRE EXCLUSIVELY

Request a catalogue for our next Public Auction. Please specify your interests.

Want lists invited from serious collectors of the BRITISH EMPIRE. References please.

Selling? Ask us about consigning *your* collection to a future sale.

Victoria Stamp Co.

PHOEBE A. MacGILLIVARY
P.O. BOX 745, RIDGEWOOD, NJ 07451
PHONE 201-652-7283 • FAX 201-612-0024
www.VictoriaStampCo.com
Email: VictoriaStampCo@aol.com

Conservation Stamps

SAM HOUSTON DUCK CO.
P.O. Box 820087
Houston, TX 77282
281-493-6386 or 800-231-5926
281-496-1445 Fax
Email: shduck@aol.com
Web: www.shduck.com

Ducks

MICHAEL JAFFE
P.O. Box 61484
Vancouver, WA 98666
360-695-6161 or 800-782-6770
360-695-1616 Fax
Email: mjaffe@brookmanstamps.com
Web: www.brookmanstamps.com

SAM HOUSTON DUCK CO.
P.O. Box 820087
Houston, TX 77282
281-493-6386 or 800-231-5926
281-496-1445 Fax
Email: shduck@aol.com
Web: www.shduck.com

Ducks - Foreign

METROPOLITAN STAMP CO., INC.
P.O. Box 1133
Chicago, IL 60690-1133
815-439-0142
815-439-0143 Fax
Email: metrostamp@aol.com

Errors, Freaks & Oddities

SAM HOUSTON PHILATELICS
13310 Westheimer #150
Houston, TX 77077
281-493-6386 or 800-231-5926
281-496-1445 Fax
Email: shduck@aol.com
Web: www.shduck.com

Fiji

COLONIAL STAMP COMPANY
5757 Wilshire Blvd. PH #8
Los Angeles, CA 90036
323-933-9435
323-939-9930 Fax
Email: gwh225@aol.com
Web: www.colonialstamps.com

France

JOSEPH EDER
P.O. Box 185529
Hamden, CT 06518
203-281-0742
203-230-2410 Fax
Email: j.eder@worldnet.att.net
Web: www.ederstamps.com

German Colonies

COLONIAL STAMP COMPANY
$1 million photo price list, $5.00 (refundable against purchase)
5757 Wilshire Blvd. PH #8
Los Angeles, CA 90036
323-933-9435
323-939-9930 Fax
Email: gwh225@aol.com
Web: www.colonialstamps.com

German Colonies

JOSEPH EDER
P.O. Box 185529
Hamden, CT 06518
203-281-0742
203-230-2410 Fax
Email: j.eder@worldnet.att.net
Web: www.ederstamps.com

German Occupation

JOSEPH EDER
P.O. Box 185529
Hamden, CT 06518
203-281-0742
203-230-2410 Fax
Email: j.eder@worldnet.att.net
Web: www.ederstamps.com

Germany

JOSEPH EDER
P.O. Box 185529
Hamden, CT 06518
203-281-0742
203-230-2410 Fax
Email: j.eder@worldnet.att.net
Web: www.ederstamps.com

Germany- Third Reich

JOSEPH EDER
P.O. Box 185529
Hamden, CT 06518
203-281-0742
203-230-2410 Fax
Email: j.eder@worldnet.att.net
Web: www.ederstamps.com

New Issues

Great Britain

COLONIAL STAMP COMPANY
5757 Wilshire Blvd. PH #8
Los Angeles, CA 90036
323-933-9435
323-939-9930 Fax
Email: gwh225@aol.com
Web: www.colonialstamps.com

Insurance

COLLECTIBLES INSURANCE AGENCY
P.O. Box 1200 SSC
Westminster, MD 21158
888-837-9537
410-876-9233 Fax
Email: info@insurecollectibles.com
Web: www.collectinsure.com

Japan

MICHAEL ROGERS, INC.
199 E. Welbourne Ave.
Suite 3
Winter Park, FL 32789
407-644-2290 or 800-843-3751
407-645-4434 Fax
Email: mrogersinc@aol.com
Web: www.michaelrogersinc.com

Korea

MICHAEL ROGERS, INC.
199 E. Welbourne Ave.
Suite 3
Winter Park, FL 32789
407-644-2290 or 800-843-3751
407-645-4434 Fax
Email: mrogersinc@aol.com
Web: www.michaelrogersinc.com

Latin America

GUY SHAW
P.O. Box 10025
Bakersfield, CA 93389
661-834-7135 Phone/Fax
Email: guyshaw@guyshaw.com
Web: www.guyshaw.com

Manchukuo

MICHAEL ROGERS, INC.
199 E. Welbourne Ave.
Suite 3
Winter Park, FL 32789
407-644-2290 or 800-843-3751
407-645-4434 Fax
Email: mrogersinc@aol.com
Web: www.michaelrogersinc.com

New Issues

DALE ENTERPRISES, INC.
P.O. Box 539-C
Emmaus, PA 18049
610-433-3303
610-965-6089 Fax
Email: daleent@fast.net
Web: www.dalestamps.com

DAVIDSON'S STAMP SERVICE
P.O. Box 36355
Indianapolis, IN 46236-0355
317-826-2620
Email: davidson@in.net
Web: www.newstampissues.com

New Issues- Retail

BOMBAY PHILATELIC INC.
P.O. Box 540819
Lake Worth, FL 33454
561-791-9557
561-791-9024 Fax
Email: sales@bombaystamps.com
Web: www.bombaystamps.com

New Issues- Wholesale

BOMBAY PHILATELIC INC.
P.O. Box 540819
Lake Worth, FL 33454
561-791-9557
561-791-9024 Fax
Email: sales@bombaystamps.com
Web: www.bombaystamps.com

One of a Kinds

DALE ENTERPRISES, INC.
P.O. Box 539-C
Emmaus, PA 18049
610-433-3303
610-965-6089 Fax
Email: daleent@fast.net
Web: www.dalestamps.com

Philatelic Literature

LEWIS KAUFMAN
P.O. Box 255
Kiamesha Lake, NY 12751
845-794-8013 Phone/Fax
800-491-5453 Phone/Fax
Email: mamet1@aol.com

Publications - Collector

AMERICAN PHILATELIC SOCIETY
Dept. TZ
P.O. Box 8000
State College, PA 16803
814-237-3803
814-237-6128 Fax
Email: flsente@stamps.org
Web: www.stamps.org

South America

GUY SHAW
P.O. Box 10025
Bakersfield, CA 93389
661-834-7135 Phone/Fax
Email: guyshaw@guyshaw.com
Web: www.guyshaw.com

Stamp Shows

ATLANTIC COAST EXHIBITIONS
Division of Beach Philatelics
42 Baltimore Lane
Palm Coast, FL 32137-8850
386-445-4550
386-447-0811 Fax
Email: mrstamp2@aol.com
Web: www.beachphilatelics.com

STAMP STORES

Arizona

B.J.'S STAMPS
Barbara J. Johnson
6342 W. Bell Road
Glendale, AZ 85308
623-878-2080
623-412-3456 Fax
Email: info@bjstamps.com
Web: www.bjstamps.com

California

ASHTREE STAMP & COIN
2410 N. Blackstone
Fresno, CA 93703-1747
559-227-7167

BROSIUS STAMP & COIN
2105 Main Street
Santa Monica, CA 90405
310-396-7480
310-396-7455 Fax

COLONIAL STAMP CO./BRITISH EMPIRE SPECIALIST
5757 Wilshire Blvd. PH #8
(by appt.)
Los Angeles, CA 90036
323-933-9435
323-939-9930 Fax
Email: gwh225@aol.com
Web: www.colonialstamps.com

FISCHER-WOLK PHILATELICS
24771 "G" Alicia Parkway
Laguna Hills, CA 92653
949-837-2932
Email: fischerwolk@earthlink.net

NATICK STAMPS & HOBBIES
405 S. Myrtle Avenue
Monrovia, CA 91016
626-305-7333
626-305-7335 Fax
Email: natickco@earthlink.net
Web: www.natickco.com

STANLEY M. PILLER & ASSOCIATES
3351 Grand Avenue
Oakland, CA 94610
510-465-8290
510-465-7121 Fax
Email: stmpdlr@aol.com
Web: www.smpiller.com

Colorado

ACKLEY'S STAMPS
3230 N. Stone Avenue
Colorado Springs, CO 80907
719-633-1153
Email: ackl9@aol.com

SHOWCASE STAMPS
3865 Wadsworth
Wheat Ridge, CO 80033
303-425-9252
Email: kbeiner@colbi.net
Web: www.showcasestamps.com

Connecticut

MILLER'S STAMP SHOP
41 New London Turnpike
Uncasville, CT 06382
860-848-0468 or 800-67-STAMP
860-848-1926 Fax
Email: millstamps@aol.com
Web: www.millerstamps.com

Connecticut

SILVER CITY COIN & STAMP
41 Colony Street
Meriden, CT 06451
203-235-7634
203-237-4915 Fax

Florida

BEACH PHILATELICS
Daytona Flea Market (Fri.-Sun.)
I 95 Exit 87 (Tamoka Farms Rd.)
Corner Shoppes Bldg.
Booths 70-72
Daytona Beach, FL 32119
386-503-6598

CORBIN STAMP & COIN, INC.
108 West Robertson Street
Brandon, FL 33511
813-651-3266

R.D.C. STAMPS
7381 SW 24th Street
Miami, FL 33155-1402
305-264-4213
305-262-2919 Fax
Email: rdcstamps@aol.com

SUN COAST STAMP CO.
3231 Gulf Gate Drive
Suite 102
Sarasota, FL 34231
941-921-9761 or 800-927-3351
941-921-1762 Fax
Email: email@suncoaststamp.com
Web: www.stampfinder.com

WINTER PARK STAMP SHOP
Ranch Mall (17-92)
325 S. Orlando Ave.
Suite 1-2
Winter Park, FL 32789-3608
407-628-1120 or 800-845-1819
407-628-0091 Fax
Email:
jim@winterparkstampshop.com
Web:
www.winterparkstampshop.com

Georgia

STAMPS UNLIMITED OF GEORGIA
133 Carnegie Way
Room 250
Atlanta, GA 30303
404-688-9161

Illinois

DON CLARK'S STAMPS & COINS
937 1/2 W. Galena Blvd.
Aurora, IL 60506
630-896-4606

DR. ROBERT FRIEDMAN & SONS
2029 West 75th Street
Woodridge, IL 60517
630-985-1515
630-985-1588 Fax

Indiana

KNIGHT STAMP & COIN CO.
237 Main Street
Hobart, IN 46342
219-942-4341 or 800-634-2646
Email: knight@knightcoin.com
Web: www.knightcoin.com

Kentucky

COLLECTORS STAMPS LTD.
4012 Dupont Circle #313
Louisville, KY 40207
502-897-9045
Email: csl@aye.net

Maryland

BALTIMORE COIN & STAMP EXCHANGE
10194 Baltimore National Pike
Unit 104
Ellicott City, MD 21042
410-418-8282
410-418-4813 Fax

BULLDOG STAMP COMPANY
4641 Montgomery Avenue
Bethesda, MD 20814
301-654-1138

Massachusetts

KAPPY'S COINS & STAMPS
534 Washington Street
Norwood, MA 02062
781-762-5552
781-762-3292 Fax
Email: kappyscoins@aol.com

Michigan

THE MOUSE AND SUCH
696 N. Mill Street
Plymouth, MI 48170
734-454-1515
734-454-9812 Fax
Email:
weluvstamps@hotmail.com

New Jersey

AALLSTAMPS
38 N. Main Street
P.O. Box 249
Milltown, NJ 08850
732-247-1093
732-247-1094 Fax
Email: mail@aallstamps.com
Web: www.aallstamps.com

BERGEN STAMPS & COLLECTIBLES
717 American Legion Drive
Teaneck, NJ 07666
201-836-8987

New Jersey

RON RITZER STAMPS INC.
Millburn Mall
2933 Vauxhall Road
Vauxhall, NJ 07088
908-687-0007
908-687-0795 Fax
Email: ritzerstamps@earthlink.net

TRENTON STAMP & COIN CO.
Thomas DeLuca
Store: Forest Glen Plaza
1804 Route 33
Hamilton Square, NJ 08690
Mail: P.O. Box 8574
Trenton, NJ 08650
800-446-8664
609-587-8664 Fax
Email: TOMD4TSC@aol.com

New York

CHAMPION STAMP CO., INC.
432 West 54th Street
New York, NY 10019
212-489-8130
212-581-8130 Fax
Email: championstamp@aol.com
Web: www.championstamp.com

Ohio

FEDERAL COIN & STAMP EXCHANGE
P.O. Box 14579
401 Euclid Ave.
Suite 45
Cleveland, OH 44114
216-861-1160
216-861-5960 Fax

HILLTOP STAMP SERVICE
Richard A. Peterson
P.O. Box 626
Wooster, OH 44691
330-262-8907 or 330-262-5378
Email: hilltop@bright.net

THE LINK STAMP CO.
3461 E. Livingston Ave.
Columbus, OH 43227
614-237-4125 Phone/Fax
800-546-5726 Phone/Fax

Florida

STAMP STORES

Pennsylvania

PHILLY STAMP & COIN CO., INC.
1804 Chestnut Street
Philadelphia, PA 19103
215-563-7341
215-563-7382 Fax
Email: phillysc@netreach.net
Web: www.phillystampandcoin.com

Tennessee

HERRON HILL, INC.
5007 Black Road
Suite 140
Memphis, TN 38117
901-683-9644

Topicals

United States

Texas

SAM HOUSTON PHILATELICS
13310 Westheimer #150
Houston, TX 77077
281-493-6386 or 800-231-5926
281-496-1445 Fax
Email: shduck@aol.com
Web: www.shduck.com

Virginia

KENNEDY'S STAMPS & COINS
7059 Brookfield Plaza
Springfield, VA 22150
703-569-7300
703-569-7644 Fax
Email: kennedy@patriot.net

LATHEROW & CO., INC.
5054 Lee Hwy.
Arlington, VA 22207
703-538-2727 or 800-647-4624
703-538-5210 Fax

Washington

TACOMA MALL BLVD. COIN & STAMP
5225 Tacoma Mall Blvd. E101
Tacoma, WA 98409
253-472-9632
253-472-8948 Fax
Email: kfeldman01@sprynet.com

Wisconsin

JIM LUKES' STAMP & COIN
815 Jay Street
P.O. Box 1780
Manitowoc, WI 54221
920-682-2324 Phone/Fax

Topicals - Columbus

MR. COLUMBUS
Box 1492
Fennville, MI 49408
616-543-4755
Email: columbus@accn.org

Topicals - Miscellaneous

BOMBAY PHILATELIC INC.
540819
Lake Worth, FL 33454
561-791-9557
561-791-9024 Fax
Email: sales@bombaystamps.com
Web: www.bombaystamps.com

United States

BOB & MARTHA FRIEDMAN
624 Homestead Place
Joliet, IL 60435
815-725-6666
815-725-4134 Fax

BROOKMAN STAMP CO.
P.O. Box 90
Vancouver, WA 98666
360-695-1391 or 800-545-4871
360-695-1616 Fax
Email: dave@brookmanstamps.com
Web: www.brookmanstamps.com

United States

DALE ENTERPRISES, INC.
P.O. Box 539-C
Emmaus, PA 18049
610-433-3303
610-965-6089 Fax
Email: daleent@fast.net
Web: www.dalestamps.com

DR. ROBERT FRIEDMAN & SONS
2029 West 75th Street
Woodridge, IL 60517
630-985-1515
630-985-1588 Fax

GARY POSNER, INC.
1407 Avenue Z
PMB #535
Brooklyn, NY 11235
800-323-4279
718-241-2801
Email: garyposnerinc@aol.com
Web: www.garyposnerinc.com
www.gemstamps.com

HENRY GITNER PHILATELISTS, INC.
P.O. Box 3077-S
Middletown, NY 10940
845-343-5151 or 800-947-8267
845-343-0068 Fax
Email: hgitner@hgitner.com
Web: www.hgitner.com

WULFF'S STAMPS
P.O. Box 661746
Sacramento, CA 95866
800-884-0656 Phone/Fax
916-489-0656 Phone/Fax
Email: service@wulffstamps.com
Web: www.wulffstamps.com

U.S. - Booklets

DALE ENTERPRISES, INC.
P.O. Box 539-C
Emmaus, PA 18049
610-433-3303
610-965-6089 Fax
Email: daleent@fast.net
Web: www.dalestamps.com

LEWIS KAUFMAN
P.O. Box 255
Kiamesha Lake, NY 12751
845-794-8013 Phone/Fax
800-491-5453 Phone/Fax
Email: mamet1@aol.com

U.S. - Classics

DALE ENTERPRISES, INC.
P.O. Box 539-C
Emmaus, PA 18049
610-433-3303
610-965-6089 Fax
Email: daleent@fast.net
Web: www.dalestamps.com

U.S. - Collections Wanted

BOB & MARTHA FRIEDMAN
624 Homestead Place
Joliet, IL 60435
815-725-6666
815-725-4134 Fax

U.S. - Collections Wanted

DR. ROBERT FRIEDMAN & SONS
2029 West 75th Street
Woodridge, IL 60517
630-985-1515
630-985-1588 Fax

U.S. - Errors, Freaks & Oddities

GARY POSNER, INC.
1407 Avenue Z
PMB #535
Brooklyn, NY 11235
800-323-4279
718-241-2801
Email: garyposnerinc@aol.com
Web: www.garyposnerinc.com
www.gemstamps.com

U.S. - Federal Ducks Stamps

METROPOLITAN STAMP CO., INC.
P.O. Box 1133
Chicago, IL 60690-1133
815-439-0142
815-439-0143 Fax
Email: metrostamp@aol.com

SAM HOUSTON DUCK CO.
P.O. Box 820087
Houston, TX 77282
281-493-6386 or 800-231-5926
281-496-1445 Fax
Email: shduck@aol.com
Web: www.shduck.com

U.S. - Mint Sheets

METROPOLITAN STAMP CO., INC.
P.O. Box 1133
Chicago, IL 60690-1133
815-439-0142
815-439-0143 Fax
Email: metrostamp@aol.com

U.S. - Plate Blocks

GARY POSNER, INC.
1407 Avenue Z
PMB #535
Brooklyn, NY 11235
800-323-4279
718-241-2801
Email: garyposnerinc@aol.com
Web: www.garyposnerinc.com
www.gemstamps.com

LEWIS KAUFMAN
P.O. Box 255
Kiamesha Lake, NY 12751
845-794-8013 Phone/Fax
800-491-5453 Phone/Fax
Email: mamet1@aol.com

U.S. - Price Lists

DALE ENTERPRISES, INC.
P.O. Box 539-C
Emmaus, PA 18049
610-433-3303
610-965-6089 Fax
Email: daleent@fast.net
Web: www.dalestamps.com

U.S. - Price Lists

ROBERT E. BARKER
P.O. Box 1100
Warren, ME 04864
207-273-6200 or 800-833-0217
207-273-4254 or 888-325-5158 Fax
Email: rebarker@rebarker.com
Web: www.rebarker.com

U.S. - Proofs & Essays

LEWIS KAUFMAN
P.O. Box 255
Kiamesha Lake, NY 12751
845-794-8013 Phone/Fax
800-491-5453 Phone/Fax
Email: mamet1@aol.com

U.S. - Rare Stamps

GARY POSNER, INC.
@Address:1407 Avenue Z
PMB #535
Brooklyn, NY 11235
800-323-4279
718-241-2801
Email: garyposnerinc@aol.com
Web: www.garyposnerinc.com
www.gemstamps.com

U.S. - Souvenir Pages/Panels

LEWIS KAUFMAN
P.O. Box 255
Kiamesha Lake, NY 12751
845-794-8013 Phone/Fax
800-491-5453 Phone/Fax
Email: mamet1@aol.com

U.S. - State Duck Stamps

SAM HOUSTON DUCK CO.
P.O. Box 820087
Houston, TX 77282
281-493-6386 or 800-231-5926
281-496-1445 Fax
Email: shduck@aol.com
Web: www.shduck.com

Want Lists

BROOKMAN INTERNATIONAL
P.O. Box 450
Vancouver, WA 98666
360-695-1391 or 800-545-4871
360-695-1616 Fax
Email: dave@brookmanstamps.com

CHARLES P. SCHWARTZ
P.O. Box 165
Mora, MN 55051
320-679-4705
Email: charlesp@ecenet.com

Want Lists- British Empire 1840-1935 German Colonies/Offices

COLONIAL STAMP COMPANY
5757 Wilshire Blvd. PH #8
Los Angeles, CA 90036
323-933-9435
323-939-9930 Fax
Email: gwh225@aol.com
Web: www.colonialstamps.com

Want Lists - U.S.

GARY POSNER, INC.
1407 Avenue Z
PMB #535
Brooklyn, NY 11235
800-323-4279
718-241-2801
Email: garyposnerinc@aol.com
Web: www.garyposnerinc.com
www.gemstamps.com

Wanted - Estates

DALE ENTERPRISES, INC.
P.O. Box 539-C
Emmaus, PA 18049
610-433-3303
610-965-6089 Fax
Email: daleent@fast.net
Web: www.dalestamps.com

United States

Wanted - U.S.

GARY POSNER, INC.
1407 Avenue Z
PMB #535
Brooklyn, NY 11235
800-323-4279
718-241-2801
Email: garyposnerinc@aol.com
Web: www.garyposnerinc.com
www.gemstamps.com

Wanted - Worldwide Collections

BOB & MARTHA FRIEDMAN
624 Homestead Place
Joliet, IL 60435
815-725-6666
815-725-4134 Fax

DR. ROBERT FRIEDMAN & SONS
2029 West 75th Street
Woodridge, IL 60517
630-985-1515
630-985-1588 Fax

Wholesale Dealers

GARY POSNER, INC.
1407 Avenue Z
PMB #535
Brooklyn, NY 11235
800-323-4279
718-241-2801
Email: garyposnerinc@aol.com
Web: www.garyposnerinc.com
www.gemstamps.com

Wholesale -U.S.

GARY POSNER, INC.
1407 Avenue Z
PMB #535
Brooklyn, NY 11235
800-323-4279
718-241-2801
Email: garyposnerinc@aol.com
Web: www.garyposnerinc.com
www.gemstamps.com

Worldwide-Collections

BOB & MARTHA FRIEDMAN
624 Homestead Place
Joliet, IL 60435
815-725-6666
815-725-4134 Fax

DR. ROBERT FRIEDMAN & SONS
2029 West 75th Street
Woodridge, IL 60517
630-985-1515
630-985-1588 Fax

Worldwide-Year Sets

BOMBAY PHILATELIC INC.
P.O. Box 540819
Lake Worth, FL 33454
561-791-9557
561-791-9024 Fax
Email: sales@bombaystamps.com
Web: www.bombaystamps.com

WALLACE STAMPS
Box 82
Port Washington, NY 11050
516-883-557

INDEX TO ADVERTISERS 2004 VOLUME 1

ADVERTISER **PAGE**